THE AMERICAN HERITAGE DICTIONARY OF THE ENGLISH LANGUAGE

THIRD EDITION

HOUGHTON MIFFLIN COMPANY

Boston · New York · London

Words are included in this Dictionary on the basis of their usage. Words that are known to have current trademark registrations are shown with an initial capital and are also identified as trademarks. No investigation has been made of common-law trademark rights in any word, because such investigation is impracticable. The inclusion of any word in this Dictionary is not, however, an expression of the Publisher's opinion as to whether or not it is subject to proprietary rights. Indeed, no definition in this Dictionary is to be regarded as affecting the validity of any trademark.

Houghton Mifflin Company gratefully acknowledges Mead Data Central, Inc., providers of the LEXIS®/NEXIS® services, for its assistance in the preparation of this edition of *The American Heritage Dictionary.*

Library of Congress Cataloging-in-Publication Data

The American heritage dictionary of the English language.
—3rd ed.

p. cm.

ISBN 0-395-44895-6

1. English language—Dictionaries.

PE1628.A623 1992 92-851
423—dc20 CIP

Manufactured in the United States of America

TABLE OF CONTENTS

INTRODUCTION

Almost a quarter of a century ago a new dictionary bearing the name *American Heritage* appeared. That book was notable because it did four things and it did them well. It faithfully recorded the language in easily understood definitions. It provided guidance toward accuracy, precision, and grace in the use of English that intelligent people need and seek in a dictionary. It traced, whenever possible, the development of English words to their origins and keyed many to an Appendix of Indo-European Roots. And it presented complex lexical data in a typographically attractive design accented by thousands of photographs and line drawings in spacious margins. *The American Heritage Dictionary of the English Language, Third Edition*, builds upon this distinguished, innovative foundation.

The pages of the Third Edition, a lexicon of more than 200,000 boldface forms, hundreds of thousands of meanings, and nearly 4,000 pieces of art, reflect the rich and varied texture of American English as it has been used over time by a broad group of educated speakers. This Dictionary is the product of four years of work by 175 contributors. In preparing the Dictionary, our editors have had access to a database containing hundreds of millions of lines of text that could be searched for any word in context.

The A–Z vocabulary, containing more than 16,000 words and meanings new to this Edition, is a comprehensive, detailed record of the language. Use of citations allowed the editors to identify new words and new meanings, identify levels of usage, and select more than 4,000 quoted illustrations from nearly 2,000 sources for use in exemplifying entry words in printed context. The quoted illustrations range from the works of Shakespeare, Pope, and Ruskin to the works of contemporary writers such as Joyce Carol Oates, Joan Didion, John Updike, and Tom Wicker. More than 30,000 nonquoted illustrative examples were also derived from study of the citations. Finally, the citations were used to determine the status of variants. For example, 4,000 electronic citations were accrued for the spelling *ambiance* and about 2,000 were found for the variant *ambience*. On the basis of this 2:1 ratio the Dictionary gives *ambience* as an "unequal," or less frequently occurring, variant of the entry word *ambiance*.

If language is a reflection of the ethos of the generation speaking it, then the new entries and meanings in this Edition have much to say about us and our time. The great majority of the new words relate to social and life patterns; to the life sciences with an emphasis on health, medicine, genetics, and ecology; and to the physical sciences with an emphasis on computer technology and electronics, physics, and astronomy.

The goal of the Third Edition is to provide the user with comprehension and appreciation of the language in a readable manner. Keeping the needs of the contemporary user in mind, we have presented the central and often the most frequently sought meaning of a word first. The definitions are worded in concise, lucid prose without the specialized terms and abbreviations that make most dictionaries forbidding and confusing.

The Third Edition contains more than 500 notes and comments on matters of grammar, diction, pronunciation, and levels and nuances of usage. Citations were used in identifying new and evolving usage problems, attesting and evaluating the currency of certain usages, studying various levels of usage, and evaluating their sociolinguistic implications. The 173-member Usage Panel, with 75 new members and chaired by Geoffrey Nunberg, a linguist associated with Stanford University, has made an important contribution to the content and direction of the Usage Notes through responses to periodic surveys developed by the Chair and the editors. The Usage Panel of the Third Edition consists chiefly of writers, editors, and scholars, 22 of whom are professors of linguistics or English. Other Panelists occupy distinguished positions in law, diplomacy, government, business, science and technology, medicine, and the arts. Eighteen are recipients of the Pulitzer Prize and one is a Nobel Laureate. These men and women, who reside in 28 states and in Canada and England, are a cross section of today's critical, literary, and scholarly community.

A list of usage issues–old and new–was prepared by the Chair and the editors, and from it the usage program for the Third Edition was developed. Some of the usage issues are entirely new. An example is the Note at *world-class*. Other issues discussed in previous editions were resurveyed. An example is the use of *contact* as a verb. In some instances the Panel's views are more conservative than in the past: only 27 percent of the current Panel accepts *hopefully* as a sentence adverb, a usage that in 1969 was acceptable to 44 percent of the Panel. Other Notes, such as the one that discusses the use of *above* as a noun, present guidance and linguistic analysis without Panel opinions. The Usage Notes are not confined solely to matters of stylistic excellence. Our concern with usage extends to issues of gender, ethnicity, and sexual preference.

Considerable attention is devoted in this Edition to the history of words. The etymologies have been thoroughly revised and expanded by a group of 25 specialists whose work reflects original scholarly research in many fields, including African, Persian, Turkish, and Native American languages. Special symbols, abbreviations, and complex technical vocabulary have been avoided in the etymologies. More than 400 word history paragraphs, most of which contain dates of first occurrence of the words in English, appear at entries with especially interesting etymologies. These word histories, such as the one at *nerd*, provide a social, historical, and cultural context for the evolution of words and explain the various linguistic processes that contribute to the development of language.

A great many Modern English words can be traced to the reconstructed ancestral language called Proto-Indo-European. The etymologies in the Third Edition, like those in the First, trace many words to their earliest ascertainable origins, usually in Proto-Indo-European, by means of cross-references to a new and thoroughly revised Appendix of Indo-European Roots. The Appendix, in a major departure from previous style, gives the root followed by a brief gloss and a list of some of the Modern English words derived from it. The individual roots entry then follows. For example, the Modern English words *fierce* and *treacle*, at first glance strange semantic companions, both derive from the root **ghwer-*, "wild."

The Third Edition contains hundreds of labeled words and meanings whose occurrence is restricted to certain areas of the United States. An important new feature unique to the Third Edition is the inclusion of more than 100 Regional Notes that explore the various linguistic and historical processes contributing to the development of these terms. These processes are apparent in the Regional Notes at entries such as *absquatulate*.

In an effort to assist the reader in using the language with color, vitality, and freshness, the Third Edition devotes more attention than ever before to synonymy by including more than 900 synonym paragraphs. The fully cross-referenced synonym paragraphs are of two kinds. The first, liberally illustrated with quotations, discriminates shades of meaning. The second kind lists exact synonyms, that is, words sharing a common irreducible element of meaning, and provides antonyms when applicable.

The American Heritage Dictionary of the English Language, Third Edition, like the First, is the product of significant advances in the use of computer technology. The Third Edition is derived from a complex, highly versatile structured database. Every element in the Dictionary was parsed, examined, and coded to reflect its lexical function and position within the base. In combination, these elements form dictionary entries, and on a broader scale they reflect a multitude of relationships across the lexicon. Use of the database in connection with electronically generated citations places the Third Edition a generation ahead of other dictionaries.

It is no longer possible for a few general editors working strictly within a publishing house to compile a true and accurate record of the language as it is used today. Semantic, etymological, linguistic, and technical complexities inherent in the language require the counsel of specialists from many disciplines. These specialists' names are listed under Special Contributors and Consultants. We wish to thank all of them for helping us in our pursuit of accuracy and truth. Special thanks go to John Simpson, Co-Editor of the *New Oxford English Dictionary*, for valuable comments made during the early stages of the project. And to all members of our Editorial Staff who gave unstintingly of their time and expended great effort in the development of the Third Edition, we express our deepest gratitude.

Anne H. Soukhanov

EDITORIAL AND PRODUCTION STAFF

EDITORIAL STAFF

Executive Editor
Anne H. Soukhanov

Senior Lexicographer
David A. Jost

Senior Coordinating Editor
Kaethe Ellis

Managing Editor
Marion Severynse

Vice President and Director of Editorial, Art, Production, and Manufacturing Services
Margery S. Berube

Publisher
Jonathan P. Latimer

Senior Editors
Joseph P. Pickett, David R. Pritchard, David M. Weeks

Editor
Joseph M. Patwell

Associate Editors
Jim A. Craig, Donna Cremans, Paul G. Evenson, Susan M. Innes, Nina Judith Katz, James P. Marciano, Martha Fairman Phelps, Rosemary E. Previte, Hanna Schonthal

Assistant Editors
Michael H. Choi, Ann-Marie Imbornoni, Daniel G. Prior

Editorial Assistant
Laura P. Chesterton

Administrative Assistance
Kenneth C. Carpenter, Jennifer L. Crawford, Beth Jaffe, Craig LaPine, Margaret M. May, Laurie A. McCrohon, Cara Murray, Rebecca A. Parker, Heidi Stahl, Alisa Stepanian

Contributing Editor, Synonymy
Anne D. Steinhardt

Contributing Editor, Pronunciation
Rima Elkin McKinzey

Coordinating Editor, Dictionaries
Pamela Burton DeVinne

Contributing Editors
Ihsan A. Al-Shehbaz, Elizabeth J.W. Baer, Ethan Balk, John K. Bollard, Carol J. Botteron, Guy J. Buckle, Karen Ann Cenci, Mary Lynn Czymbor, Ronald E. Doel, Leon A. Feldman, Nancy Fliesler, Ian A. Grable, David S. Greenes, Michael K. Hahn, Kristin Hanson, W.M. Havighurst, Paul G.K. Jodka, Elizabeth A. Jordan, Victoria M. McClellan, Ramona R. Michaelis, Sonja N. Nelson, Trudy Nelson, Barry John Perlman, Richard E. Plotkin, Lois J. Principe, David C. Roberts, Paul R. Schwankl, James E. Shea, Jeffrey E. Topal, Monica L. Zangwill

Citations Clerk
Shari Lynn Wheeler

Copyediting
Frances Barna, Alice P. Carman, Maria A. Morelli

Proofreading
Kathryn Blatt, Becky Cheston, Jennifer L. Dougherty, Judith L. Drummond, Valerie A. English, Bruce E. Frost II, Stella Gelboin, Rhonda L. Holmes, Katherine M. Isaacs, Eric C. Meyer, Maria Rodriguez Montenegro, Denis Moynihan, James F. Mulhern, Jill R. Norton, Lori Ohliger, Thelma Prince, Carole A. Ricciardi, Ann M. Rossi, A. Nancy Rourke

PRODUCTION STAFF

Production and Manufacturing Manager
Christopher Leonesio

Production Supervisor
Patricia McTiernan

Senior Art and Production Coordinator
Margaret Anne Miles

Database Keyboarding
Miriam E. Palmerola, *Supervisor*

Lawrence Annucci, Edward Coleman, Cary Hawkins Doran, Kathleen R. Klingenberg, Sean Brosnahan Meehan, Donna Whiting

Manufacturing Supervisor
Greg Mroczek

Senior Manufacturing Assistant
Jill M. Lazer

Administrative Assistance
Christina M. Granados, Lauren B. Hunnewell

Database Development and Composition Services

Auto-Graphics, Inc.
Paul Cope, *Vice President, Publishing Operations*
Robert Eiferd, *Manager of Programming*
Kathi Pittman & Laura Stein, *Project Managers*

Structured Database Design
Joseph V. Gangemi, *Consultant*

In Remembrance
Jim A. Craig
1961–1991
Friend, Colleague,
and Editor

SPECIAL CONTRIBUTORS AND CONSULTANTS

Usage
Geoffrey Nunberg, Ph.D.
Stanford University

Dialect
Sr. Mary Dominic Pitts, O.P, Ph.D.
Aquinas Junior College

Indo-European Roots Appendix
Calvert Watkins, Ph.D.
Harvard University

Language and Etymology Consultants

Patrick S. Diehl, Ph.D., University of California, Berkeley

Deborah W. Anderson, Ph.D., University of California, Los Angeles

Martin E. Huld, Ph.D., Department of English, University of California, Los Angeles

Brian D. Joseph, Ph.D., Department of Linguistics, Ohio State University

Reuven Merkin, Ph.D., Professor, Academy of the Hebrew Language, Jerusalem, Israel

African Languages

George N. Clements, Ph.D., Department of Modern Languages and Linguistics, Cornell University

Austronesian Languages

R. David Zorc, Ph.D., Senior Linguist, MRM Language Research Center

Caribbean Languages

Richard Allsopp, Ph.D., Caribbean Lexicography Project, University of the West Indies at Cave Hill, Barbados

Celtic Languages

Lionel S. Joseph, Ph.D., Harvard University

Central and South American Languages

Richard F. Townsend, Ph.D., Department of Africa, Oceania, and the Americas, Art Institute of Chicago

Hipólito Rafael Chacón, M.A., Department of Art History, University of Chicago

Dialect

Craig M. Carver, Ph.D., *Dictionary of American Regional English*

East Asian Languages

Stephen A. Bladey

Thomas Creamer, M.A.

English Language and Linguistics

G.W. Abernethy, *Middle English Dictionary*

Sara E. Kimball, Ph.D., Department of English, University of Texas at Austin

Henry Kučera, Ph.D., Department of Linguistics, Brown University

Marilyn S. Miller, M.S.L., *Middle English Dictionary*

Robert N. Mory, Ph.D., *Middle English Dictionary*

Lee Pederson, Ph.D., Department of English, Emory University

David W. Ruddy, M.A., University of Michigan

David M. Yerkes, Ph.D., Professor of English, Department of English, Columbia University

Greek and Latin

Vincent P. McCarren, Ph.D., *Middle English Dictionary*

Rex E. Wallace, Ph.D., Classics Department, University of Massachusetts, Amherst

Roger D. Woodard, Ph.D., Classics Department, University of Southern, California

North American Indian Languages

Ives Goddard, Ph.D., Department of Anthropology, Smithsonian Institution

Russian, Persian, and Ural-Altaic Languages

Alexander Lehrman, Ph.D., Department of Foreign Languages and Literatures, University of Delaware

Science Etymology

Sharon L. Marshall, Ph.D., M.D., Harvard and Tufts Universities

Yiddish

Marvin I. Herzog, Ph.D., Department of Linguistics, Columbia University

Special Consultants

Architecture

Edward F. Ford, M.Arch.
Associate Professor of Architecture, School of Architecture, University of Virginia

Art

H. Kristina Haugland, M.A.
Assistant Curator, Costume and Textiles, Philadelphia Museum of Art

Cinema

P. Adams Sitney, Ph.D.
Continuing Lecturer, Department of Visual Arts and Council of the Humanities, Princeton University

Dance

Mara Peets, M.A.
Teaching Fellow, Expository Writing Program, Columbia University; Writer/Researcher and Assistant Director, *Video Dictionary of Classical Ballet*

Economics, Business, and Finance

David L. Scott, Ph.D.
Professor of Accounting and Finance, Department of Accounting and Finance, Valdosta State College, Georgia

History and Government

John A. Garraty, Ph.D.
Gouverneur Morris Professor Emeritus, Department of History, Columbia University

Law

Robert M. Landis, J.D.
Partner and formerly Chair, Dechert Price & Rhoads

Meteorology

David B. Johnson, Ph.D.
National Center for Atmospheric Research, Boulder, Colorado

Military Science and Weapons

Daniel P. Bolger, Ph.D.
U.S. Army Infantry Officer

Music

Mary Davenport
Professor of Music, School for the Arts, Boston University

Mythology

William S. Bonds, Ph.D.
Associate Professor and Chair, Department of Classical Languages, University of the South

Philosophy

Hilary Kornblith, Ph.D.
Associate Professor, Department of Philosophy, University of Vermont

Religion

William A. Graham, Ph.D.
Professor of the History of Religion and Islamic Studies, Department of Near Eastern Languages and Civilizations, Harvard University

Van A. Harvey, Ph.D.
George Edwin Barnell Professor of Religious Studies, Department of Religious Studies, Stanford University

Martin E. Marty, Ph.D.
Fairfax M. Cone Distinguished Professor of the History of Modern Christianity, Divinity School, University of Chicago

Richard P. McBrien, S.T.D.
Crowley-O'Brien-Walter Professor of Theology, Department of Theology, University of Notre Dame

Paul Mendes-Flohr, Ph.D.
Professor, Department of Jewish Thought, Hebrew University, Jerusalem, Israel

Frank E. Reynolds, Ph.D.
Professor of the History of Religions and Buddhist Studies, Divinity School and Department of South Asian Languages and Civilizations, University of Chicago

Jack D. Van Horn, Ph.D.
Associate Professor, Department of Religion, College of William and Mary

Science and Technology

Donald C.S. Allison, Ph.D.
Professor and Head, Department of Computer Science, Virginia Polytechnic Institute and State University

William Ira Bennett, M.D.
Editor, *Harvard Health Letter,* Harvard Medical School

Sheila Ewing Browne, Ph.D.
Professor of Chemistry and Chair, Department of Chemistry, Mount Holyoke College

Neal D. Buffaloe, Ph.D.
Professor Emeritus of Biology, University of Central Arkansas

F.J. Collier
Collections Manager, Department of Paleobiology, National Museum of Natural History, Smithsonian Institution

Brooks B. Ellwood, Ph.D.
Professor and Acting Chair, Department of Geology, University of Texas at Arlington

R.J. Emry, Ph.D.
Curator, Division of Vertebrate Paleontology, Department of Paleobiology, National Museum of Natural History, Smithsonian Institution

Frank Espey, M.D.
Neurological Surgery (retired), Greenville, S.C.

William S. Haubrich, M.D.
Head, Division of Gastroenterology, Scripps Clinical Research Foundation

Nicholas Hotton III, Ph.D.
Curator, Division of Vertebrate Paleontology, Department of Paleobiology, National Museum of Natural History, Smithsonian Institution

Lynn Margulis, Ph.D.
Department of Botany, University of Massachusetts at Amherst

J.W. Pierce, Ph.D.
Chair, Department of Paleobiology, National Museum of Natural History, Smithsonian Institution

C.E. Ray, Jr.
Curator, Division of Vertebrate Paleontology, Department of Paleobiology, National Museum of Natural History, Smithsonian Institution

Richard Evans Schultes, Ph.D.
Jeffrey Professor of Biology and Director, Harvard Botanical Museum (Emeritus)

James Trefil, Ph.D.
Clarence J. Robinson Professor of Physics, George Mason University

Sociology

Mary Waters, Ph.D.
John L. Loeb Associate Professor of the Social Sciences, Harvard University

Sports

Robert W. Creamer
Formerly Senior Editor, *Sports Illustrated*

Trademarks

Ted J. Murphy
International and Information Services Manager, U.S. Trademark Association

THE USAGE PANEL

Geoffrey Nunberg, Ph.D. *Chair*
Department of Linguistics, Stanford University
Edwin Newman *Chair Emeritus*
Journalist; lecturer; author

Elie Abel Educator; writer; Professor Emeritus, Stanford University
Shana Alexander Writer; formerly columnist, *Life* and *Newsweek*
Cleveland Amory Humorist; humanitarian; President, The Fund for Animals
Roger Angell Writer and Fiction Editor, *New Yorker*
Isaac Asimov* Writer; Professor of Biochemistry, Boston University School of Medicine
James Atlas Writer; Editor, *New York Times Magazine*
Margaret Atwood Writer
Kathryn H. Au Educational psychologist, Kamehameha (Hawaii) Schools
Louis Auchincloss Writer
Ralph Backlund Senior Contributing Editor, *Smithsonian*; formerly Producer and Executive Producer for news and public affairs, CBS; formerly Associate Editor and Managing Editor, *Horizon*
John Bainbridge Staff writer, *New Yorker*; columnist, *Gourmet*
Sheridan Baker Professor Emeritus of English, University of Michigan
Letitia Baldrige Author; lecturer on manners
Jacques Barzun Writer; literary consultant; educator
Carolyn Wilkerson Bell Professor of English, Randolph-Macon Woman's College
Daniel Bell Henry Ford II Professor of Social Sciences Emeritus, Harvard University; Scholar in Residence, American Academy of Arts and Sciences
Pierre Berton Canadian writer and broadcaster
Alton Blakeslee Science Editor (retired), Associated Press
Harold Bloom Writer; Sterling Professor of Humanities, Yale University; Berg Professor of English, New York University; MacArthur Fellow
Roy Blount, Jr. Writer; Contributing Editor, *Atlantic*
Kallia H. Bokser Coordinator, Office for the Aging, New York City Housing Authority; proposal writer
Dwight Bolinger* Professor Emeritus of Romance Languages and Literatures, Harvard University; Visiting Professor Emeritus of Linguistics, Stanford University
The Hon. Julian Bond Formerly Georgia state legislator; Professor, American University and Harvard University; lecturer; host, public affairs television program
The Hon. Daniel J. Boorstin Librarian of Congress Emeritus; recipient, Pulitzer Prize and National Book Award Medal for Distinguished Contribution to American Letters
Charles P. Boren Associate Editor (retired), *Lewiston* (Idaho) *Morning Tribune*
Barbara Taylor Bradford Writer
The Hon. William W. Bradley U.S. Senator from New Jersey; formerly professional basketball player
Leo Braudy Bing Professor of English, University of Southern California
Paul Brooks Writer; formerly Editor in Chief, Houghton Mifflin Company
Heywood Hale Broun Writer; actor; television newsperson
Rachel M. Brownstein Professor of English, Brooklyn College and the Graduate Center, City University of New York
William F. Buckley, Jr. President, National Review Inc.
Gabrielle Burton Writer
Gerald Carson* Social historian; writer; advertising agency executive
Claudia Cassidy Writer; formerly music and drama critic, *Chicago Tribune*; formerly critic at large, *Chicago* magazine
Walter C. Clemens, Jr. Writer; Professor of Political Science, Boston University; Adjunct Research Fellow, Harvard University Center for Science and International Affairs
Pat Conroy Novelist
Claire Kehrwald Cook Editorial Director, Modern Language Association of America; author, *Line by Line: How to Edit Your Own Writing*
Robin Cook, M.D. Physician; writer
Alistair Cooke Journalist and broadcaster
Roy H. Copperud* Professor Emeritus of Journalism, University of Southern California; columnist, *Editor & Publisher*; author of works on English usage; recipient, Humanities Award, Association of American Publishers
Norman Cousins* Adjunct Professor, School of Medicine, University of California, Los Angeles; writer; formerly Editor, *Saturday Review*; formerly Chair, Pulitzer Prize jury in literature
Malcolm Cowley* Writer; literary adviser, Viking Press, Inc.; formerly Associate Editor, *New Republic*
Robert W. Creamer Writer; biographer; formerly Senior Editor, *Sports Illustrated*
Gene D. Dahmen Attorney; past President, Boston Bar Association
Marshall B. Davidson* Writer; Senior Editor, *Horizon*; formerly Editor of Publications, Metropolitan Museum of Art, New York
Robertson Davies Writer; founding Master, Massey College, University of Toronto; Professor of English and Drama
Lois DeBakey Writer, lecturer, and consultant; Professor of Scientific Communication, Baylor College of Medicine; Adjunct Professor of Scientific Communication, Tulane University School of Medicine
Vine Deloria, Jr. Standing Rock Sioux Tribe Professor of Law, Religious Studies, Political Science, and History, University of Colorado
Annie Dillard Writer; recipient, Pulitzer Prize
William K. Durr Professor of Education Emeritus, Michigan State University; past President, International Reading Association
Andrea Dworkin Writer
Freeman J. Dyson Writer; Professor of Physics, Institute for Advanced Study, Princeton, New Jersey
Anne Edwards Biographer and novelist; past President, Authors Guild
Gretel Ehrlich Writer; Guggenheim Fellow from Wyoming
Ralph Ellison Writer; educator

Carolly Erickson Historian; writer
Howard Fast Writer
Frances FitzGerald Writer; contributor, *New Yorker*; recipient, Pulitzer Prize
Elizabeth Frank Writer; Joseph E. Harry Professor of Modern Languages and Literature, Bard College; recipient, Pulitzer Prize
Reuven Frank Formerly President, NBC News; formerly Executive Producer, *Huntley-Brinkley Report*
John Kenneth Galbraith Economist; writer; formerly U.S. Ambassador to India; formerly Paul M. Warburg Professor of Economics, Harvard University
Sara Garnes Linguist; Associate Professor of English, Ohio State University
Michael G. Gartner President, NBC News; language columnist; past President, American Society of Newspaper Editors; member, Pulitzer Prize Board
J. Edward Gates Lexicographer; editor; Professor Emeritus of English, Indiana State University
A. Bartlett Giamatti* Sports executive; educator; Commissioner of Baseball; formerly President, National Baseball League; formerly President, Yale University
Francine duPlessix Gray Writer
Linda Gregerson Assistant Professor of English, University of Michigan
Patricia Hampl Writer; Professor of English, University of Minnesota
The Hon. Mark O. Hatfield U.S. Senator from Oregon
The Hon. S.I. Hayakawa* Writer; educator; President Emeritus, San Francisco State University; formerly U.S. Senator from California
Mark Helprin Writer; Contributing Editor, *Wall Street Journal*; Senior Fellow, Hudson Institute
Douglas R. Hofstadter Professor of Cognitive Science and Computer Science, Indiana University, Bloomington; recipient, Pulitzer Prize
Gloria Hom Educator and consultant; Chair, Economics Department, Mission College; member, California State University Board of Trustees; member, Board of Trustees, Dominican College of San Rafael
Paul Horgan Novelist, biographer, and historian; Professor Emeritus and Author in Residence, Wesleyan University; recipient, Pulitzer Prize
The Hon. Shirley M. Hufstedler Attorney; formerly U.S. Secretary of Education; formerly Judge, U.S. Court of Appeals for the Ninth Circuit
John K. Hutchens Retired member, Editorial Board, Book-of-the-Month Club; retired literary and drama reviewer, *New York Times*, *New York Herald Tribune*, and *Boston Evening Transcript*
Jennifer James Cultural anthropologist; writer
Joyce Johnson Writer; recipient, National Book Critics Circle Award
William F. Johnston* Associate Professor and Newspaper Internship Coordinator, School of Communications, University of Washington
Erica Jong Poet and novelist; President, Authors Guild
The Hon. Barbara Jordan Educator, attorney, and writer; Lyndon B. Johnson Centennial Professor in National Policy, Lyndon B. Johnson School of Public Affairs, University of Texas at Austin; formerly U.S. Representative from Texas
June M. Jordan Poet; Professor of African American Studies and Women's Studies, University of California, Berkeley
Alfred E. Kahn Professor of Economics Emeritus, Cornell University; formerly Economic Adviser to the President of the United States
Roger Kahn Author; journalist
Justin Kaplan Writer; recipient, Pulitzer Prize and National Book Award
Stanley Kauffmann Film critic, *New Republic*; Professor of Drama, the Graduate Center, City University of New York
Alfred Kazin Writer; Distinguished Professor of English Emeritus, the Graduate Center, City University of New York
Trudy Kehret-Ward Educator; writer
Garrison Keillor Author and host of *American Radio Company*
Elizabeth T. Kennan President, Mount Holyoke College
Walter Kerr Drama critic (retired), *New York Times*; formerly drama critic, *New York Herald Tribune*; past President, New York Drama Critics' Circle; recipient, Pulitzer Prize
Florence King Writer; critic
Maxine Hong Kingston Writer; recipient, National Book Award, National Book Critics Circle Award, and Anisfield-Wolf Race Relations Award
Galway Kinnell Poet; Samuel F.B. Morse Professor of Arts and Science, New York University; recipient, Pulitzer Prize
The Hon. Jeremy K.B. Kinsman Sous-ministre adjoint, Affaires politiques et de la sécurité internationale, Affaires exterieures, Ottawa, Canada
The Hon. Jeane J. Kirkpatrick Diplomat; writer; educator; formerly U.S. Ambassador to the United Nations
Maxine Kumin Writer; formerly Consultant in Poetry, Library of Congress; recipient, Pulitzer Prize
Charles Kuralt News correspondent, CBS
J.J. Lamberts Professor Emeritus of English, Arizona State University; author of works on English usage
Milton I. Levine, M.D. Formerly Professor of Clinical Pediatrics, New York Hospital – Cornell Medical Center; radio commentator, CBS; formerly syndicated columnist
Flora Lewis Senior Columnist, *New York Times*
Robert E. Lewis Lexicographer; Editor in Chief, *Middle English Dictionary*; Professor of English, University of Michigan
Sara Lawrence Lightfoot Professor of Education, Harvard University; writer; recipient, MacArthur Prize
J. Anthony Lukas Author; journalist; recipient, Pulitzer Prize
Russell Lynes Writer; formerly Managing Editor, *Harper's*
Claudine B. Malone Management consultant; formerly Associate Professor, Harvard Business School
William Manchester Writer in Residence and Adjunct Professor of History, Wesleyan University; Fellow, Pierson College, Yale University
Robert Manning Writer; editor; formerly Editor in Chief, *Atlantic*
Richard Curry Marius Novelist and biographer; Director of Expository Writing, Harvard University
Suzanne R. Massie Writer; lecturer on Russian history and culture; Fellow, Harvard Russian Research Center
Alice E. Mayhew Editorial Director, Trade Division, Simon & Schuster
The Hon. Eugene McCarthy Writer, poet, and lecturer; formerly U.S. Senator from Minnesota
David McCord Poet; essayist; Honorary Curator of the Poetry and Farnsworth Rooms, Harvard University Library
Kenneth McCormick Senior Consulting Editor, Bantam Doubleday Dell; formerly Editor in Chief, Doubleday & Company, Inc.
Mary McGrory Journalist; columnist, *Washington Post* and Universal Press Syndicate; recipient, Pulitzer Prize
Leonard Michaels Professor of English, University of California, Berkeley
James A. Michener Writer; recipient, Pulitzer Prize and Presidential Medal of Freedom
Hassan Minor, Jr. Special Assistant to the President, Howard University
Richard Scott Mitchell* Mineralogist; educator; writer; Professor of Environmental Science, University of Virginia; Executive Editor, *Rocks and Minerals*
Jessica Mitford Writer
Lance Morrow Essayist and Senior Writer, *Time*; recipient, National Magazine Award
The Hon. Daniel Patrick Moynihan U.S. Senator from New York; formerly Professor of Political Science, Harvard University
Cullen Murphy Managing Editor, *Atlantic*
The Hon. Maurine Neuberger Formerly U.S. Senator from Oregon; formerly Oregon state legislator
His Excellency Thomas M.T. Niles U.S. Representative to the European Community; formerly U.S. Ambassador to Canada
David Ogilvy, O.B.E. Advertising copywriter; Officer of the Order

of Arts and Letters (France); past Chair, United Negro College Fund

Cynthia Ozick Novelist; essayist; member, American Institute of Arts and Letters

Robert S Pirie President and Chief Executive Officer, Rothschild Inc.

Alvin F. Poussaint, M.D. Associate Professor of Psychiatry, Harvard Medical School

Ellen F. Prince Professor of Linguistics, University of Pennsylvania

Jane Bryant Quinn Journalist; syndicated financial columnist, *Newsweek* and *Woman's Day*

Tony Randall Actor

William James Raspberry Syndicated urban affairs columnist and broadcast commentator; formerly member, Pulitzer Prize Board

Edward W. Rosenheim* Editor; writer; Professor of English, University of Chicago

Judith Rossner Novelist

Leo Rosten Writer; social scientist; editor

Berton Roueché Writer

Vermont Royster Writer; educator; William Rand Kenan, Jr., Professor of Journalism and Mass Communication, University of North Carolina at Chapel Hill; Editor Emeritus, *Wall Street Journal*; recipient, Pulitzer Prize

Carl Sagan David Duncan Professor of Astronomy and Space Sciences and Director, Laboratory for Planetary Studies, Cornell University; writer; recipient, Pulitzer Prize

Robert Saudek Division Chief, Library of Congress; television producer; Lecturer on Visual Studies, Harvard University; founding President, Museum of Broadcasting

Arthur M. Schlesinger, Jr. Writer; historian; educator; formerly Special Assistant to the President of the United States; recipient, Pulitzer Prize

Glenn T. Seaborg University Professor of Chemistry, University of California, Berkeley; formerly Chair, U.S. Atomic Energy Commission; recipient, Nobel Prize

Art Seidenbaum* Journalist; Editor, Opinion Section, *Los Angeles Times*

Harvey Shapiro Poet; editor

Elaine Showalter Professor of English, Princeton University

John Simon Drama critic, *New York*; film critic, *National Review*

Carlota S. Smith Professor of Linguistics and Director, Center for Cognitive Science, University of Texas

Jack Smith Columnist, *Los Angeles Times*

Susan Sontag Writer

Theodore C. Sorensen Attorney; writer; formerly Special Counsel to the President of the United States

Susan Stamberg Special Correspondent, National Public Radio

Wallace Stegner Writer; founder and formerly Director, Stanford University Writing Program; recipient, Pulitzer Prize and National Book Award

Shane Templeton Foundation Professor of Curriculum and Instruction, University of Nevada, Reno

Paul Theroux Novelist; travel writer

Elizabeth Marshall Thomas Writer

Nina Totenberg Legal Affairs Correspondent, National Public Radio and *MacNeil/Lehrer NewsHour*

Elizabeth C. Traugott Professor of Linguistics and English, Stanford University

Calvin Trillin Staff writer, *New Yorker*; syndicated columnist

Anne Tyler Novelist; recipient, Pulitzer Prize

The Hon. Stewart L. Udall Writer; Chairman of the Board, The Archaeological Conservancy, Santa Fe, New Mexico; formerly U.S. Secretary of the Interior and U.S. Representative from Arizona

Helen H. Vendler A. Kingsley Porter University Professor of English, Harvard University

Douglas Turner Ward Actor; playwright; recipient, Vernon Rice Award and Obie Award

Calvert Watkins Victor S. Thomas Professor of Linguistics and the Classics, Harvard University; past President, Linguistic Society of America

Fay Weldon Writer

Eudora Welty Writer

Jacqueline Grennan Wexler Writer; formerly President, Hunter College, City University of New York

Tom Wicker Author; journalist; Editor, *New York Times*

Alden S. Wood Lecturer on Editorial Procedures, Simmons College; national columnist on language and English usage

Richard A. Young Writer, editor, lecturer, and engineer; Publisher, *Pollution Engineering*; Executive Director, National Registry of Environmental Professionals

William Zinsser Writer, editor, and educator; author of *On Writing Well* and *Writing to Learn*

* We regret that these members of the Usage Panel died during the course of the project.

A NATURAL HISTORY OF ENGLISH: LANGUAGE, CULTURE, AND THE AMERICAN HERITAGE

LEE PEDERSON

American speech and writing record the transactions of nearly 400 years of social history. Dialects embody patterns of sound, syntax, and meaning; literature documents those spoken forms in poetry and prose. Through the process of communication, a native language becomes the social inheritance of its speakers. In describing the linguistic resources of American English this Dictionary becomes a cultural property book for all the American people.

A century before Noah Webster organized his first American dictionary (1806), Jonathan Edwards defined the materials of inquiry in remarkably modern terms:

> By *conversation*, I mean intelligent beings expressing their minds one to another in words, or other signs intentionally directed to us for our notice, whose immediate and main design is to be signification of the mind of him who gives it.

Defining conversation as one might characterize language today, Edwards recognized the conceptual, symbolic, and functional aspects of human communication: the engagement of thought, the use of signs, and the transmission of ideas from one mind to another.

Today the English language makes conversation possible among 350 million native speakers who share its system of symbolic behavior. This number includes speakers of American, Australian, British, Canadian, Irish, New Zealand, and Scots English as members of the most influential speech community in the history of civilization. Their common cultural heritage makes possible the use of a single language by the members of these different groups, but each national variety with all its regional and social dialects reflects unique social experience. In a natural history of a national language, the richest gatherings of such material endure in folk speech – the unaffected, conservative expression of common people, as preserved in their oral traditions. National folk usage forms a subset of social dialects within regional dialects that comprise the larger divisions, the national varieties of a language.

Such experience makes a national vocabulary the most accessible and productive source of cultural information. Words are the complex linguistic structures that transmit the native lexicon through the systems of sound, grammar, and meaning. Words are also cultural emblems, symbols with social meaning that preserve the experience of human activity. Ralph Waldo Emerson said that words are signs of natural facts and wrote: "The etymologist finds the deadest word to have been once a brilliant picture. Language is fossil poetry." He demonstrated by his own example, moreover, that words are also signs of sociohistorical facts by giving the American meaning to *transcendentalism.* George Washington furnished the earliest citations for *Democrat* and *Republican* and was the first to receive the designation *favorite son.* Noah Webster made the earliest use of the phrase *American English* with characteristic impatience but ultimate accuracy: "In fifty years from this time [1806], the American English will be spoken by more people than all other dialects of the language." Such thought, conversation, and social interaction shaped the national character and gave substance to the lexicon. Contributions came from every sector of the American culture.

As the central component of American English culture, the national language transmits the essential messages of all other cultural systems. All of these are inseparable from language: *family* (kinship and marriage), *training* (education and economics), *values* (morality, ethics, and religious rites), *government* (political and social control), *technology* (artifacts of survival), and *fine arts* (artifacts of the creative imagination and of spiritual expression). From the earliest days on its first frontiers, American English carried forward the messages of the culture and the experience of the past. As it did its work, the national language established an identity and expressed native ideas in an American voice. This Dictionary records that American voice and gives substance to its underlying systems, *language* and *culture.*

Henry David Thoreau recognized a national dictionary as "a very concentrated and trustworthy natural history of the people":

> What they have a word for, they have a thing for. A traveller may tell us that he *thinks* they used a pavement or built their cabins in a certain form, or soaked their seed corn in water . . . ; but when one gives us the word for these things, the question is settled, – that is a clincher. Let us know what words they had and how they used them, and we can infer almost all the rest. The lexicographer not only *says* that a certain people have or do a certain thing, but, being evidently a disinterested party, it may be allowed that he brings sufficient evidence to prove it. He does not so much assert as exhibit. He has no transient or private purposes to serve.

THE HISTORICAL BACKGROUND OF AMERICAN ENGLISH

This natural history of the American people is the essential gift of the mother tongue. With all speakers of the English language Americans share the results of 1,500 years of linguistic development, and English had itself evolved for a full millennium before the first American words were spoken in Virginia. Furthermore, as a member of the Germanic language group of the Indo-European language family, English shares an ultimate heritage with most of the modern languages of Europe and Asia and with the official languages of every government in North and South America.

The essential features of the Germanic languages are these: (1) a thoroughgoing modification of the consonant system, especially the so-called First Germanic Consonant Shift, which distinguishes the system from all other Indo-European consonant patterns. It is captured in Grimm's Law and accounts for the differences between initial sounds in such cognate pairs as Latin/English *pater/father*, *tu/thou*, and *hortus/garden*; (2) mutation of vowels by neighboring sounds (umlaut) and the adaptation of the vowel system to express grammatical functions; (3) regular word stress on the first syllable; (4) seven classes of strong (irregular) verbs, such as *sing*, *sang*, *sung*; (5) three classes of weak (regular) verbs, such as *love*, *loved*, *loved*; (6) strong and weak adjectives that disappeared in Medieval English but endure elsewhere, as in Modern German and Norwegian definite and indefinite articles; and (7) a core vocabulary of common words. These shared characteristics define the 13 modern Germanic languages: Danish, Faroese, Icelandic, Norwegian, Swedish, German, Yiddish, Low German, Dutch, Afrikaans, Flemish, Frisian, and English.

The history of the English language begins with the arrival of Germanic invaders from the continent, said to be in A.D. 449 according to the Anglo-Saxon Chronicle. In the eighth century the Venerable Bede identified these Germanic peoples as Angles, Saxons, and Jutes. In Britain they encountered their Indo-European relatives, the British Celts, who had settled in Britain centuries before. Like the Native Americans, the Celts left their greatest linguistic legacy in place names, such as *Avon*, *Brynmawr* (Welsh for "great hill"), *Dover*, *Thames*, and *London*. The Celts and Germans, however, were never separated by a distance greater than the narrow English Channel and shared a common Indo-European ancestry. Conversely, in North America, native inhabitants and newcomers emerged from different environments thousands of miles apart, from homelands distinguished by their native forms of vegetation, animal life, and social behavior.

As the dialects of the invaders merged in England they gave rise to the Northumbrian, Mercian, and Saxon varieties of the language that is called Old English today. Three tenth-century texts show the close similarities of those dialects in their respective translations of the Medieval Latin (Matthew 6:9) "pater noster, qui est in caelis, sanctificetur nomen tuum":

> NORTHUMBRIAN
> *Fader urer thu arth in heofnas, sie gehalgad noma thin*
> Father our thou art in heaven, be hallowed name thy
>
> MERCIAN
> *Fæder ure thu the in heofunum earth, beo gehalgad thin noma*
> Father our thou which in heaven art, be hallowed thy name
>
> WEST SAXON
> *Fæder ure thu the eart on heofonum, si thin nama gehalgod*
> Father our thou which art in heaven, be thy name hallowed

Despite differences in pronunciation, word formation, and syntax, simple and effective conversation was surely possible among speakers of these different regional dialects of English. Conversation was also possible between the English and their Viking conquerors, the Norwegians and the Danes, many of whom settled primarily in what are now the northeast counties and took up peaceful ways with English wives. The fact that cultural interaction extended through most of the Old English period (449–1066) is evidenced in the greatest literary monument of the Anglo-Saxons, their epic poem *Beowulf*, which has a thoroughly Scandinavian setting and cast.

Words shared by Anglo-Saxons and Vikings include *bring*, *can*, *come*, *father*, *folk*, *house*, *life*, *man*, *mine*, *mother*, *see*, *sit*, *smile*, *sorrow*, *summer*, *thine*, *wife*, *will*, *winter*, and *wise*. In addition to hundreds of such intimate correspondences, the Scandinavians gave English many other familiar words through cultural interaction: *anger*, *fellow*, *happy*, *husband*, *meek*, *root*, *rotten*, *skill*, *skin*, *skull*, *sky*, and *ugly*. A second and much greater influence was brought to bear on the language and culture after the Battle of Hastings in 1066, when the Normans, French-speaking descendants of the Vikings, arrived from Normandy.

FRENCH INFLUENCES

The Norman-French presence marked the beginning of great changes in English social behavior, reflecting a gradual evolution of institutional and conversational forms. The chronicles and other writings show that Old English was in transition before the coming of the Normans, and later poetry and prose record unmodified Germanic forms deep into the Middle English period. In England, French became the official language of the dominant culture and spread its influence into every social system. Earlier, on the continent, the Normans had adopted Frankish laws, developed a system of knightly conduct, and perfected the skills of cavalry warfare. Through force and friendship they gave the English a chivalric code, a parliamentary system of government, and one of the most distinctive architectural styles in all of European civilization. During the period of Norman dominion, English vernaculars evolved without a native standard dialect. The cultural influence of the Vikings emerged most clearly in Scandinavian loan words that marked regional speech in those northern counties where they had settled earlier, as the regional dialects of England were broadly reorganized. In the process, Middlesex became the preeminent focal area, and from its center arose the London Standard, the most influential social variety the English language has ever known.

Several dialects of 14th-century England were the immediate ancestors of the London Standard, but it drew most from the speech of the Southeast Midland region. The recorded usage of that era illustrates great linguistic change, a process that began more than 200 years earlier through the mingling of English and French. Causal relations for the change are hard to establish because phonological, grammatical, lexical, and cultural modifications were under way before the Battle of Hastings.

Romance language words, such as *cheese*, *copper*, and *dish*, entered Germanic dialects from Latin before the invasion of England in A.D. 449; from the same source came *cleric*, *psalm*, and *temple* with the Christianization of England in the seventh century. Later Romance loans in Old English include *pride* (French), *capon* and *castle* (French or Latin), and *apostle*, *epistle*, *lily*, and *peony* (Latin). Old English texts of the tenth century – the Vercelli Book, Exeter Book, Junius Manuscript, and *Beowulf* Manuscript – show the early simplification of weakly stressed vowels and inflectional patterns. During the reign of Edward the Confessor (1042–1066) a Norman association was firmly established between the king and his cousin, William the Conqueror, underscored by the installation of Robert of Jumièges as archbishop of Canterbury in 1051.

During the next 300 years the French presence altered the development of English through direct contributions and reinforcement of linguistic trends already under way. Four voiced fricative consonants emerged as distinctive elements of the sound system during this period, the initial sounds of *veal*, *zeal*, and *thee*, as well as the medial sound of *leisure*. None of these were distinctive in Old English, which had only the fricatives of *feel*, *seal*, *thing*, and *pressure*, respectively. The single outright contribution of Norman French to the English sound system was the diphthong of *joy*. French usage did accelerate the leveling of weakly stressed vowels, the simplification of noun, pronoun, and adjective inflections, and the transfer of many strong (irregular) verbs to weak (regular) conjugations. For example, Old English forms of modern *doom* included *domes* (genitive singular), *domas* (nominative plural), and *domum* (dative plural); all became *doomes* in Middle English. Strong verbs such as *creopan*, *helpan*, and *slœpan* became the weak verbs *creep*, *help*, and *sleep*, although a residue of the old patterns endures in the past forms *crept* and *slept*, as well as *holp* (pronounced like *hope*) in several current American dialects.

More French loan words entered English during the 14th century than during any comparable period before or since. As the French language fell into disuse in England, many of its culturally useful words were borrowed. Here the relationship between speech and writing is an important consideration. The documented evidence of the written forms is conservative and lags behind current usage. After King John lost the province of Normandy in 1204, French influence on English society began to decline. Before the Hundred Years' War (1337–1453) began, English speech had already returned as the native tongue of the nobility, and before the century closed, it had replaced French in the courts, Parliament, schools, and finally the highly formal documents of title, deeds, and wills.

Chaucer composed *The Canterbury Tales* in his native Southeast Midland dialect and so demonstrated the appropriateness of London speech as a literary medium, but *The Canterbury Tales* did not mark the triumph of a standard language within the culture at large. Just two years before he began his masterwork, Chaucer worried about the diversity of current speech in his envoy for *Troilus and Criseyde* (c. 1385):

> And for ther is so gret diversite
> In Englissh and in writyng of oure tonge,
> So prey I God that non myswrite the[e],
> Ne the[e] mysmetre for defaute of tonge;
> And red wherso thow be, or elles songe,
> That thow be understonde, God I biseche!
> But yet to purpos of my rather speche.

He prayed that none miswrite, mismeter (wrongly scan the measures), or misunderstand the purpose of his earlier (*rather*) speech, his spoken words that became this "litel bok."

THE EMERGENCE OF MODERN ENGLISH

Chaucer had good reason for concern. The Great Vowel Shift was beginning a modification in quality of all long vowels and diphthongs, and the inconsistent treatment of weakly stressed vowels placed many syllables in jeopardy. The shift raised [a] to [æ] (and later to [e]), [e] to [i], [ɔ] to [o], and [o] to [u]. The vowels formerly pronounced [i] and [u] became, respectively, [əi] (later [ai]) and [əu] (later [au]).* Thus Chaucer's final vowels in *diversite* and *the[e]* rhyme with modern *they*; his verb *write* rhymes with modern *feet*; *biseche* and *speche* rhyme with modern *aitch*; and the vowel in *oure* rhymes with the vowel in *boot*. Although metrical evidence is difficult to interpret, Chaucer quite possibly pronounced the weakly stressed *e* in *myswrite* and *elles* but ignored it in *tonge*, *understonde*, *speche*, and other words in the same stanza that comprise those seven iambic pentameter lines of rhyme royal.

At the outset of the Early Modern English period (1500–1700) fewer than 5 million people in the world spoke English, as compared to 12 million speakers of French, 10 million of German, and 8 million of Spanish. During the next two centuries those "intelligent beings expressing their minds" in English included More, Tyndale, Milton, Newton, Locke, and Dryden. At its center was Elizabethan English, the language of Shakespeare, Marlowe, Bacon, Donne, Raleigh, Spenser, and the queen herself. From this stage of linguistic development came the earliest varieties of American English. By 1700 the number of English speakers had nearly doubled, while German, Italian, and Spanish had scarcely maintained their numbers of two centuries earlier, and only French surpassed the growth rate of English among the western European nations.

As an emergent world language, English advanced with the spread of the London Standard and general education, with the loosening of class distinctions, and through the influence of what would today be called the mass media. By the year 1500 printed books in all of Europe included 35 thousand titles, most of which were in Latin. During the next 140 years 20 thousand English titles appeared in print, and scribal composition of manuscripts became virtually a lost art. England regained its cultural self-reliance with those new sources of influence and the spread of empire. In 1579 E.K., the anonymous editor of Spenser's *The Shepheardes Calender*, commended his author and reflected the spirit of the age:

> For in my opinion it is one special prayse, of many whych are dew to this Poete, that he hath laboured to restore, as to theyr rightfull heritage such good and naturall English words, as haue ben long time out of vse and almost cleane disherited. Which is the onely cause, that our Mother tonge, which truely of it self is both ful enough for prose and stately enough for verse, hath long time ben counted most bare and barrein of both.

The English recognized the legitimacy of their native tongue for all modes of communication, including those technical fields formerly dominated by Latin and Greek. In

*All pronunciations in this article are in the notation of the International Phonetic Alphabet. The Pronunciation Key lists these symbols and their equivalents in the pronunciation system employed for this Dictionary.

his *Elementary* (1582) Richard Mulcaster defended the use of English and explained the implications of his work:

> For the account of our tongue, both in pen and speech, no man will doubt therof who is able to judge what those things be which make any tongue to be of account; which things I take to be three: the autority of the people which speak it, the matter and argument wherein the speech dealeth, the manifold use for which the speech serveth. For all which three our tongue needeth not to give place to any of her peers.

Mulcaster and others wrote rules for pronunciation and grammar and tried to enrich the national word store. Earlier the Italians, Spanish, French, and Germans had done the same things for their own varieties of speech, as the transformation of local vernaculars into national languages characterized the Renaissance in every European country that it touched.

During the reign of Elizabeth I (1558–1603) a language pattern developed that was to become the base form of early American English. London usage reflected the linguistic patriotism of the English Renaissance and accepted forms from a variety of regional and social dialects in the development of a spoken standard. Roger Ascham, Elizabeth's Latin tutor, was a Yorkshireman; Raleigh preserved his distinctive Devonshire speech throughout his life; Essex was from Hertfordshire; Sidney, from Kent; Shakespeare, from Warwickshire; Donne, although of Welsh ancestry, emerged from the London merchant class. The language habits of all those speakers contributed to the shaping of the urban pattern and to the development of vigorous conversational speech.

THE BEGINNINGS OF AMERICAN ENGLISH

The fluid structure of Early Modern English underlies the formation of American English. Although the Great Vowel Shift had assigned new values to the long vowels, many British, Scots, and Irish social dialects were slow to accept all of these emergent features. Morphology and syntax showed inventiveness and flexibility in word formation and adaptations, as with the free use of affixes in word building (*re–*, *de–*, *–ish*, *–ize*), functional shift of parts of speech (nouns used as verbs, verbs as nouns, and both as adjectival or adverbial modifiers), frequent parenthetical expression, and phrase structures of predication, complementation, and coordination that reflect the intonational contours of the spoken language.

Drawn from that rapidly flowing stream, American English shows a much greater uniformity than its origins might suggest. Einar Haugen has called this evolution of the national language in America "Babel in reverse." The concept of the American melting pot can be found in the writing of Michel Guillaume Jean de Crèvecoeur (J. Hector St. John), a Norman-French immigrant and the eponym of St. Johnsbury, Vermont. In *Letters from an American Farmer* (1782) he provided the logic for a unified American language and culture:

> What, then, is the American, this new man? He is either a European or the descendant of a European; hence that strange mixture of blood, which you will find in no other country. . . . *He* is an American, who, leaving behind him all his ancient prejudices and manners, receives new ones from the new mode of life he has embraced, the new government he obeys, and the new rank he holds. He becomes an American by being received in the broad lap of our great Alma Mater [Dear Mother]. Here individuals of all nations are melted into a new race of men, whose labors and posterity will one day cause great changes in the world. Americans are the western pilgrims who are carrying along with them that great mass of arts, sciences, vigor, and industry which began long since in the East; they will finish the great circle. The Americans were once scattered all over Europe; here they are incorporated into one of the finest systems of population which has ever appeared, and which will hereafter become distinct by the power of the different climates they inhabit. The American ought therefore to love this country better than that wherein either he or his forefathers were born.

The first substantial collection of immigrant literature appeared in New England, where writers worked with Elizabethan patterns and recorded a variety of occasional spellings and distinctive forms. In *The History of Plimoth Plantation, 1620–1647*, William Bradford wrote *burthen*, *fadom*, *furder*, *gifen* (*given*), *gusle* (*guzzle*), *trible* (*triple*), and *vacabund* (*vagabond*). Roger Williams rhymed *abode/God*, *blood/good*, and *America/away* in *A Key into the Language of America* (1643). Anne Bradstreet paired *conceit/great*, *stood/flood*, and *satisfy/reality* in *The Tenth Muse Lately Sprung Up in America* (1650). Two generations later Edward Taylor alternated *spoil* and *spile*, as well as *soot* and *sut*, and rhymed *is/kiss*, *far/cur*, and *vile/soil*.

Early American grammar also showed a great variety of forms. In 1630, while sailing westward aboard the *Arbella*, John Winthrop preached "A Modell of Christian Charity" with the line "We must love brotherly without dissimulation; we must love one another with a pure heart fervently." Bradford used *rid*, *runned* (and *ranne*), *drunk*, *writ*, and *shrunk* as past forms of *ride*, *run*, *drink*, *write*, and *shrink*, respectively. Williams declared, "My disease is I know not what" and offered the interrogative form "Sleep you?" Mary Rowlandson wrote, "It is not my tongue or pen can express the sorrow of my heart" in her captive narrative of 1676.

During these same years cultural activity all along the Atlantic seaboard produced the first Americanisms. The following native words, among hundreds of others, originated, gained special meaning, or entered the English language through American speech in the 17th century: *creek* (stream), *fat pine*, *green corn*, and *papoose* from Massachusetts; *catfish*, *corn* (maize), *mock[ing]bird*, *polecat* (skunk), and *raccoon* from Virginia; *Chippewa*, *groundhog*, *Manhattan*, and *Podunk* from New York; *gang* [of birds], *hominy*, *snakeroot*, and *Virginian* from Maryland; *frontier people*, *oyster rake*, *samp*, and *wampum* from Rhode Island; *grocery* (store), *hotcakes* (corn cakes), *peavine* (a climbing plant similar to the pea), and *sunfish* from Pennsylvania; *settlement* and *swampland* from Connecticut; *Dutch grass* (any one of various grasses) and *hickory nut* from South Carolina; *frontier* from New Jersey. Beyond the frontiers *pilot* (a guide over a land route) appeared in what is now Colorado, and *Miami* from what is now Illinois.

NATIVE AMERICAN INFLUENCES

These words suggest the importance of Native American loans, especially for artifacts and places. From the Algonquian dialects alone English and French in the New World borrowed more than a hundred terms that remain current today. In addition to *Chippewa*, *hominy*, *Manhattan*, *papoose*, *Podunk*, *samp*, *squash*, and *wampum*, the eastern tribes provided *caribou, mackinaw, pone, Tammany, terrapin,* and *toboggan*. Such terms often suggest multiple language contacts; as *caribou* and *toboggan* entered through Canadian French in the north, *barbecue, canoe,* and *cushaw* came out of the West Indies through Spanish. Spanish later transmitted *coyote* and *peyote* from the Nahuatl language of Mexico. From Quechua, probably through the cooperative efforts of French and Spanish, the New Orleans term *lagniappe* appeared somewhat later. American place names are the greatest Native American contribution. From *Appalachia* and the *Alleghenies*, across all five of the Great Lakes (*Erie, Ontario, Huron, Michigan,* and *Superior* [Ojibwa *Gitchi* via French *Supérieur*]); from *Chicago* to *Sitka*, native words cover the continent. Emblematic of American language and culture are the blends, such as *Bayou La Batre*, Alabama (Choctaw *bayuk*, "creek" + French *de la Batre*, "of the [artillery] battery"), and *Minneapolis*, Minnesota (Dakota *minne*, "water" + Greek/English *(a)polis*, "city"), or the loan translations *Spearfish*, South Dakota, *Ten Sleep*, Wyoming, *Warroad*, Minnesota, and *Yellow Dirt Creek*, Georgia, besides the native loans of the state names *Alabama* (people), *Dakota* (people), and *Minnesota* (Dakota *minne*, "water" + *sota*, "white").

LOANS FROM THE EUROPEAN LANGUAGES

Early loans from European languages correspond with Dutch, French, and German settlements in the coastal colonies and along the first interior frontiers. During their New Amsterdam experience the Dutch added to American English the words *boss, Bowery, coleslaw, cookie, sleigh, stoop,* and *waffle*. Later they gave more place names, such as *Catskill, Kinderhook,* and *Schuyler*. Although Thoreau spoke of "*Yankee* ingenuity" in 1843, the durable nickname probably had its origin in *Jan* (*Janke*), the Dutch diminutive for *John* (*Johnny*); Saint Nicholas, clipped to *Sinterklaas* in a Dutch dialect, became *Santa Claus* before the Revolutionary War.

French loans contrast sharply with the Dutch and later German contributions. Although they also gave English such ordinary household words as *chowder, pumpkin, sashay, shanty,* and *shivaree*, the enterprising French illustrate their experience in a distinctive set of loans. Explorers, missionaries, and frontier warriors made American words of *bateau, crevasse, levee, portage, prairie,* and *voyageur*. As the English, Dutch, and Swedes struggled to control the seaboard, the French ranged across the interior and left their mark with the names of places at *Bienville, Cape Girardeau, Prairie du Chien,* and *Sault Sainte Marie*.

Early German loans on the frontier are difficult to ascertain. Like the Scandinavians and Anglo-Saxons in England, the Germans and English spoke languages with a common word stock that still endures in the basic vocabularies of both cultures. For the same reason it is impossible to determine whether *nosh* (snack) and *schlemiel* are of Yiddish or German origin and whether *spook* and *dumb* (stupid) are of Dutch or German origin, because in each case the words occur in both languages. Only when the Germans established discrete territories, as the Dutch had in New York, did the loans begin to appear in significant numbers from Pennsylvania, Cincinnati, Chicago, Milwaukee, St. Louis, and east-central Texas. From early Pennsylvania, American English probably received *smearcase, ponhaws* (*pannhass*, "pan" + "hare," or "scrapple"), *rainworm* (earthworm), and possibly George Washington's most familiar title, *The Father of His Country*, which first appeared as *Der Landes Vater* on a *Nord Amerikanische Kalender* for 1779.

THE AMERICAN FRONTIER

The frontier contributions of the Swedes and folk speakers of British, Irish, and Scots dialects are virtually impossible to identify because these Northern Europeans were soon united in a common culture. As Crèvecoeur described the people at the outbreak of the Revolution:

> They are a mixture of English, Scotch, Irish, French, Dutch, Germans, and Swedes. From this promiscuous breed, that race now called Americans have arisen. The eastern provinces [i.e., the coastal colonies] must indeed be excepted as being the unmixed descendants of Englishmen.

Early frontier speech probably included the pronouns *hit* (for *it*), *hisn, ourn, theirn,* and *yourn*, the inflected verb forms *clumb, drug, holp,* and *riz*, the auxiliary construction *mought could* (or *might could*), and a large number of folk pronunciations and lexical items, forms transmitted through the oral tradition of the common people. Scots forms, also appearing in the poetry of Burns, include *duds* (clothes), *gumption, hunkers, mountain billy* (hillbilly), *tow* (hemp fiber), and the distinctive pronunciations reflected in *chimla* (*chimney*), *het* (*heated*), and *southron* (*southern*), as well as the simplification of consonant clusters, as in *kin'* (*kind*) and *sin'* (*since*), and the total assimilation of *l* after back vowels, as in *ca'* (*call*), *fu'* (*full*), and *howe* (*hollow*). From Irish sources probably came *mammy, moonshine,* and *mountain dew*. General English folk forms also included *clean, flat,* and *plumb* (all meaning "completely"), *passel* (from *parcel*), and *sass* (from *sauce*). Many of these forms appear in Middle English, and all survive in current American Midland and Southern dialects.

THE EVOLUTION OF DIALECTS IN AMERICAN ENGLISH

During the 18th century the principal regions of American English developed. These are the historic cultural areas. Every major regional dialect area, past and present, corresponds almost perfectly with a cultural area delimited by other social systems. The presbyteries of Appalachia mark the pattern of Scottish settlement, the Dutch and German barns show a Germanic presence in the eastern and east-central states, the methods of cooking cornmeal in *pones, dodgers,* and *hushpuppies* reflect the settlement patterns of various groups, and the superstitions connected with chicken clavicles (*wishbone, pulley bone,* or *lucky bone*) identify social groups, as do the Southern greetings *hey* and *Christmas Gift!* The styles of folk, blues, jazz, and rock music also correspond with cultural areas, contrasting the perfected forms of the Carter Family in southern Appalachia, Huddie Ledbetter in the Red River Delta, and Robert Johnson in the Yazoo Delta, the rural blues of Richard Amerson and the urban blues of Bill Broonzy, the Kansas City jazz of Count Basie and the Chicago jazz of Bud Freeman, or the middle Georgia rock of the Allman Brothers and the southern California rock of the Beach Boys. All of these are as regionally distinctive as are the voices of the musicians. Wherever clear-cut boundaries of culture can be reconstructed on the basis of historical information from archaeology, music, graphic arts, or the social sciences, dialect differences can be predicted, based on the most persuasive kind of circumstantial evidence: the recorded experience of the forebears of a speech community.

Because language changes, many of the following historical dialect features – such as *bucket*, *firefly*, *hushpuppy*, and *lariat* – may no longer reflect current usage, especially among the young and better educated. Elsewhere, general currency forms – such as *harmonica*, *headcheese*, *mantelpiece*, and *wishbone* – serve as useful internal, subregional dialect features, contrasting with folk forms in systematic dialect study, as, for example, *French harp*, *souse*, *fireboard*, and *pulley bone*, respectively. Finally, the diachronic perspective of essay and the synchronic perspective of the Dictionary itself make it impossible to integrate such examples in their historical settings in terms wholly consistent with usage today or with ultimate etymologies. For those reasons, the designation of some forms listed below will not conform with either the current regional labels or the ultimate etymological sources identified in the text of the Dictionary. The social evolution of such words, however, provides historical context and cultural foundations for the contemporary usage the Dictionary describes.

Modern American seaboard dialects preserve the early system from Maine to the Florida Keys and along the Gulf shores to Brownsville, Texas. The coastal communities shared the evolution of urban British pronunciation, grammar, and vocabulary, but very different speech forms developed throughout the interior along the old frontier. Neither of these regions is a uniform cultural area, but remarkable concordances of speech endure. Early centers at Boston, New York, and Philadelphia were quite different from their southern counterparts at Richmond, Charleston, and New Orleans. Along the Atlantic and Gulf coasts, however, the dialects shared important features: the loss of constricted *r* after vowels (making *popper* homophonous with *Papa*); a contrast of stressed vowels in *Mary*, *merry*, and *marry*; a most distinctive diphthong in *dues*, *news*, and *shoes* that approaches that in *few*, *music*, and *pupil*; the loss of *h* in *whip*, *white*, *wheelbarrow*, and similar words; and even a "broad *a*" in *hammer*, *pasture*, and *Saturday*. Besides the familiar British past form *et* (of *eat*), the coastal dialects also shared lexical features, such as *hog's head cheese*, *haslets* (or *harslets*), and *piazza* (porch).

The coastal pattern divides near the Potomac River. To the north the language and culture drifted away from British influence more quickly than they did in the South, where the early planters of Jefferson's agrarian democracy required close association with British commerce, education, and industry. Southern coastal dialects preserved several other British features: the "clear *l*" of *lean* in *Billy* and *Nelly*, as opposed to the "dark *l*" of *look* and *law*, a flapped *r* in *three* and *thresh*, as heard in some British pronunciations of *very*, and even an occasional back vowel in *pot* and *crop*. Along the Gulf Coast these forms had mixed currency, largely because of the powerful influence of New Orleans, a cultural center that dominated the entire interior South until the Civil War. Basic Northern and Southern contrasts persist from the Potomac to the mouth of the Rio Grande: the Southern drawls (patterns of diphthongs, lengthening, and intonation), the vowel of *ride* [a] (which Northerners confuse with *rod* [ɑ]), the vowel of *bird* [ɜɪ] (which Northerners confuse with Brooklynese), a positional variant [əʊ] in *house* and *mouse* but not in *rouse* and *cows*, the plural pronoun *you-all* (or *y'all*), the past form *drug* (of *drag*), and a large set of vocabulary forms, such as *mosquito hawk* (dragonfly), *crocus sack* (burlap bag), *snap beans* (string beans), and *tote* (carry).

The New Orleans focal area interrupts this pattern, extending its influence from Mobile Bay to beyond the Sabine River. A Coastal and New Orleans contrast is marked by *serenade*, *bateau*, *clabber cheese*, and *mush* along the Southern coast, except in the area of New Orleans dominion, where *shivaree* (*charivari*), *pirogue*, *cream cheese*, and *cush-cush* (mush) prevail. Although *cush* has currency throughout the South, nowhere else is there a double form to match the New Orleans usage. Other distinctive terms are *flambeau* (makeshift torch), *(h)armonica* (instead of Southern *harp*), *lagniappe* (something extra, instead of South Carolina *brawtus*, Texas-Spanish *pilon*, and Florida-Minorcan *countra*), *wishbone* (instead of South Midland and Southern *pulley bone*), and *creole tomatoes* (instead of Northern *cherry tomatoes* and Southern *tommytoes*).

Unlike coastal speech, the Midland dialects of that transition area between the North and South grew up in the interior. From Pennsylvania to Georgia the eastern boundary of the Midland dialect area coincides with the geography of the old frontier. Settlers took the land in the great migrations out of Pennsylvania, Maryland, and Virginia during the half century (1725–1775) that preceded the Revolutionary War. Thomas Walker's discovery of the Cumberland Gap in 1750 provided a southern gateway to the Midwest, that passage into Kentucky for the ancestors of both Jefferson Davis and Abraham Lincoln. Before the War of 1812 the frontier extended in the north out of Pittsburgh and down the Ohio River and in the south out of the Yadkin Valley of North Carolina, across Tennessee and Kentucky along the Wilderness Trail of Pennsylvania's Daniel Boone.

Like other American dialects, the Midland varieties rose from a British-English base in Pennsylvania, but the social composition on the frontier was different. Six of the seven ethnic groups mentioned by Crèvecoeur did not speak British English before they arrived in North America. Later those residents of the interior Midland dialect areas were without ports of entry to receive the influence of English culture and to share in the development of the prestigious London forms. More important, the frontier people occupied themselves mainly with survival in a hostile region. Those factors influenced the disparate groups in a uniform way: Midland dialects resisted the phonological changes under way in England and in the coastal colonies to the north and south; English, Irish, and Scots folk speech reinforced the regional grammar and vocabulary, giving these American dialects identities of their own.

The Midland pattern contrasts most sharply with the interior varieties of Northern and Southern speech. With a domain that in modern times extends from western New England and upstate New York, along the southern shores of the Great Lakes and then northwestward into the upper Midwest, the Inland Northern dialect spread from its eastern source after the War of 1812. The construction of the Erie Canal from Albany to Buffalo gave upstate New York and New England access to the Great Lakes, as had the wagon roads that preceded the watercourse and the railroads that followed it. As Northern speech extended out of upper New Jersey and northern Pennsylvania, a major dialect boundary was established with the southern limit of *darning needle* (dragonfly), *pail*, and *whiffletree*, contrasting with North Midland *snake feeder*, *bucket*, and *single-*

tree. From upstate New York and across Ohio, Indiana, Illinois, and Iowa westward, the division of Northern and North Midland remains apparent in the pronunciation of *fog* and *hog*, which are pronounced with the vowel of *father* in the North and the vowel of *dog* in the North Midland; in the pronunciation of the diphthong of *cow*, *house*, and *towel*, which is [ɑʊ] in the North, beginning with a lower vowel that is closer to that of *father*, and [æʊ] in the North Midland, beginning with a vowel that is closer to that of *lather*; and in the existence of an excrescent *r* in "*warsh*" and "*Warshington*" in some Midland speech. Formerly distinctive are the Northern terms *stone wall*, *pail*, *swill*, *teeter-totter*, *faucet*, *pit* (of a cherry or peach), and *firefly*, contrasting with the Midland terms *stone fence*, *bucket*, *slops*, *seesaw*, *spicket* (spigot), *seed*, and *lightning bug*. In the West the Northern/Midland distinction is most clearly heard in the pronunciation of *car*, *yard*, and similar words: the Northern pronunciation is marked by a vowel closer to that of *father*; the Midland pronunciation, by one closer to the vowel of *saw*.

Prior to the Civil War other interior forms spread from south of the Great Lakes to the fringes of the plantation cultures from Virginia to Texas and gave rise to the principal Midland varieties, North Midland and South Midland. Between those contrasting cultures the Midland area is perhaps best divided by a phonological Mason-Dixon Line established by the pronunciation of the medial consonant of *greasy*, with [s] to the north and [z] to the south. On the Atlantic Coast the boundary replicates the historic Mason-Dixon Line, the common border of Pennsylvania and Maryland. Philadelphia, with the pronunciation [s], must be considered a Northern territory. Westward, however, the difference in pronunciation marks the division within the Midland territory, from Ohio to Missouri. Heading south, a traveler encounters the line at approximately the same place where grits replace hash browns on the breakfast menu, and where the words *nice*, *white*, and *rice* are all pronounced with a vowel Northerners confuse with the vowel common to *cat*, *hat*, and *sat*, whether the side dish is served with Indiana- or Kentucky-fried chicken. With this feature comes the first suggestion of the drawl, indigenous bluegrass music, and stock car instead of Indy-type or midget automobile racing. Along the same line the northern extent of Southern cultural penetration appears in these contrasts: North Midland *bunk*, *wishbone*, *husks*, *headcheese*, *fritters*, *bag*, and *turtle*, versus South Midland *pallet*, *pulley bone*, *shucks*, *souse* (or *pressed meat*), *flitters*, *sack*, and *terrapin*.

South Midland speech is a Southern dialect, formerly called Hill Southern in contrast with the Upcountry and Lower Southern patterns (Plantation Southern) to the south and east. The principal South Midland/Southern boundary follows the Blue Ridge across Virginia, the Carolinas, and Georgia. In South Carolina and Georgia the boundary coincides with the 180-day growing season for cotton, the waterways, the soil types, and the cultural organizations inseparable from the plantation systems devoted to the cultivation of indigo, rice, and cane, as well as cotton.

Those geographic features and cultural factors underlie the Midland enclaves, as far south as the Florida Panhandle, and their Southern counterparts as far north as the St. Francis Basin of Arkansas and the bootheel of Missouri, the cotton country around New Madrid. South Midland is marked by the presence of a constricted *r* after a vowel in *bird*, *car*, and *horse* and monophthongs in *right* and *ride*, whereas Southern preserves a diphthong in *right* and similar words. Lexical contrasts include South Midland *green beans*, *red worm*, *fireboard*, *French harp* (for *harmonica*), and *tow sack* (for *burlap bag*), versus Southern *snap beans*, *earthworm*, *mantelpiece*, *harp*, and *crocus sack*. In the east, South Midland contrasts with Virginia Piedmont Southern: *snake feeder*, *peanuts*, and *terrapin*, versus *snake doctor*, *goobers*, and *cooter*. In the Mississippi Valley the South Midland dialect occupies the territory bypassed by the plantation cultures as unsuitable for the production of cotton, cane, and rice.

Where the planters extended their operations north and west, as in upper Louisiana, western Tennessee, Arkansas, and eastern Texas, Lower Southern features outline the area. The Coastal and Gulf plains were settled from the east, but the deltas of the Mississippi, Atchafalaya, Red, Yazoo, and St. Francis rivers received their populations from the south. As a result, interior Southern areas do not show the predictable gradations of uniformity from east to west that are found in the North and North Midland regions.

Instead, the pattern extends from north to south, from the Piedmont at the southern fringe of eastern Appalachia, through the Coastal Plains and Piney Woods, to the Atlantic and Gulf coastal regions. In the Piney Woods dialects of the interior lower plains of Georgia, Florida, Alabama, Mississippi, and Louisiana, as well as the dialects of upper East Texas, below the plains and above the coastal strip, a striking configuration emerges. Piney Woods pronunciation includes three systematic features: (1) constricted postvocalic *r*, as in *beard*, *bird*, and *butter*; (2) excrescent constriction, yielding "*Chicargo*" (Chicago), *croker sack* (crocus sack), *skeeter hawk* (mosquito hawk), and "*tomaters*" (tomatoes); and (3) vocalized *l* in *hotel*, *hospital*, and *bulge*. These forms mark the regional vocabulary: *piney-woods rooter* (range hog), *smut* (soot), *mantelboard* (mantelpiece), *corndodger* (cornmeal dumpling), *pinders* (peanuts), *press peach* (cling peach), and *fat lighterd* (resinous kindling).

Lower Southern dialects are distinguished by coastal forms and by the distinctive contributions of the New Orleans focal area. Coastal Southern pronunciation includes the loss of constricted *r* after vowels, the contrast between the stressed vowels of *Mary*, *merry*, and *marry*, a "clear *l*" in *Billy* and *Nelly*, and vocabulary items such as *mosquito hawk*, *crocus sack*, *hoghead cheese* (or *hog's head cheese*), and *red bug* (instead of *chigger*). Besides *locker* (for *closet*) and *flambeau* (for *makeshift lamp*), the domain of New Orleans is marked by the pervasiveness of *gallery* (for *porch*), *lagniappe*, *pirogue* (dugout canoe), *cream cheese* (cottage cheese), *wishbone* (instead of South Midland and Southern *pulley bone*), and *(h)armonica* (instead of South Midland *French harp* or Southern *harp*). Such forms appear as far north as Lake Providence and Monroe, Louisiana; Yazoo City, Mississippi; and along the Gulf Coast beyond the Sabine River into Texas and eastward to Mobile Bay.

Western dialects begin beyond the 98th meridian, 40 miles west of the Red River in North Dakota and 50 miles west of Fort Worth in Texas, where annual rainfall usually fails to exceed the 22 inches required for traditional Midwestern farming. Thus, modern agricultural methods, such as dry farming and irrigation through reservoirs, and tools, such as the Oliver moldboard plow and the springtooth harrow, opened the West for general settlement only after the Civil War. Before that, pioneers followed the Oregon and

Mormon trails into the Upper Rockies and the Pacific Northwest, and the Santa Fe and Old Spanish trails into the Lower Rockies and California. Today, Western dialects divide primarily south to north, marked by the extent of the Spanish influence through Texas, New Mexico, and southern California, at least as far north as lower Colorado or even Montana among ranchers.

History complicates the speech of the West, by the blending of Northern, Midland, and Southern forms as well as by a heavy Spanish influence from Texas to California. The North Midland boundary extends over Iowa and cuts across South Dakota in a northwesterly direction. In Montana and Idaho the presence of North and South Midland features reflects the history of the frontier and the enterprises of cattle, agriculture, and mining. Throughout the Rocky Mountains and the urban West Coast the dialects of early settlers determined the pattern. Seattle and San Francisco speech grew from an Inland Northern base quite similar to old-fashioned Chicago speech. Denver and Los Angeles also developed from the same source, although the Hispanic influence in both places and the successive waves of newcomers from the East, especially in Los Angeles, have obscured the regional pattern that endures with greater stability in Seattle and San Francisco. The Midland influence is strongest west of the Rockies, from Idaho to Arizona, and especially in the conservative speech of Boise, Salt Lake City, and Phoenix. American English in Wyoming, Colorado, and Utah, for example, includes old-fashioned Inland Northern features, such as [ɪ] in *creek*, fully constricted postvocalic *r*, [hw] in *wheel*, *whip*, and similar words, and homophony in *marry*, *Mary*, and *merry*, and *teeter-totter* (seesaw); Midlands *green beans*, *gunnysack*, and *anymore* (meaning "nowadays" in positive statements); and Southern *roasting ears* (corn on the cob), *slop bucket*, and *clabber*. Beside these are the distinctive Interior Western pronunciations [æ] instead of [a] in *Colorado* and *Nevada*, [i] instead of [e] in *rodeo*, and widespread replacement of [a] for [ɔ] in *automobile*, *log*, and *Utah*.

THE INFLUENCE OF BILINGUALISM

The national idiom grew through contacts between various languages and dialects. Spanish, French, and German bilingualism marks the regional patterns of Florida, Louisiana, Pennsylvania, and south Texas. Gullah, an English-based pidgin, developed in the Sea Islands of South Carolina and Georgia. From that source many varieties of American Black folk speech are derived, reflecting various stages of creolization as the dialects merge with the dominant patterns. Social dialects grew through urban and rural experiences throughout the country, many of these related to the Americanization of European bilinguals in the urban North and the integration of Black people in all sectors of society. These dialects are further conditioned and refined by formal and situational styles, including slang, ethnic variation, and patterns of usage reflecting socioeconomic class.

Before urban American Spanish gained prominence in San Antonio, Los Angeles, and Miami, that language had already made large contributions to American English in the West. Besides place names, extending from the *Rio Grande* to *Montana*, the Spanish vocabulary marks the cattle country with Western words: *arroyo*, *bronc(o)*, *canyon*, *chaparral*, *cinch*, *corral*, *frijol*, *hoosegow*, *lariat*, *lasso*, *mesa*, *mustang*, *patio*, *pronto*, *ranch*, *remuda*, *rodeo*, *sombrero*, and *tortilla*.

In bilingual communities Spanish speakers of English tend to avoid regional dialect forms in favor of terms from the general vocabulary, despite the distinctive accent and syntax carried over from the parent language. The same tendency appears among the French in Louisiana, who freely use their native loans, such as *banquette* (sidewalk), *boudin* (blood sausage), *fais-dodo* (country dance), and *jambalaya*, as well as loan translations and adaptations, such as *coffee black*, *cream cheese* (cottage cheese), *green beans*, *(h)armonica*, and *wishbone*, resisting the Southern regionalisms *clabber cheese*, *snap beans*, and *pulley bone*. German, Italian, Scandinavian, Slavic, Spanish, and Yiddish speakers reflect the same trend in the urban North, perhaps through learning from books rather than by simple oral acquisition and perhaps through efforts to translate from their native tongues. In becoming Americans all of these people enriched the national language and culture. If examples are limited to food alone, Germans provided *bock beer* and *pretzels*, Italians brought *antipasto* and *pizza*, Scandinavians added *lingonberries* and *smorgasbord*; Slavs contributed *kolacky* and *kielbasa*, Yiddish-speaking Germans and Slavs gave *bagels* and *gefilte fish*; and Mexican Spanish provided the base for an endless variety of *enchiladas*, *burritos*, and *tacos*, as its cooking entered the fast-food industry.

CONTRIBUTIONS FROM AFRICAN LANGUAGES

The full impact of African languages through Gullah and Plantation Creole remains to be assessed properly, but evidence suggests the influence is significant. Among certain and probable African loans, these have gained currency in the national language: *banana*, *cola* (kola), *goober*, *gumbo*, *juke* (*-box*, *-joint*, and *-step*), *okra*, *voodoo*, and *yam*, as well as, perhaps, *boogie-woogie*, *chigger*, *gorilla*, and *tote*. Some are regionally restricted to the South: *cooter* (turtle), *cush* and *cush-cush*, and *pinder* (peanut). Others seem limited to the South Carolina and Georgia Low Country: *buckra* (white man), *det* (heavy), as in *det rain* and *det shower*, and *pinto* (coffin). In addition to the loan words from Gullah, the creolization of that auxiliary language may also have left its mark on American English phonology and grammar. As a contact vernacular, a language of business (and a possible source of the word *pidgin*), Gullah provided a medium of communication for African slaves and their American overseers. Thus, the pidgin was a language variety native to neither group. In the development of Plantation Creole the language acquired highly complex phonological and grammatical rules, as well as a complete vocabulary, necessary in a self-reliant, independent language. General Southern features today include many correspondences with Plantation Creole, the creolized English Black folk speech of the plantation cultures of cane, cotton, indigo, and rice. Southern vowel nasality often replaces nasal consonants in *am*, *been*, and *bacon*, but this feature occurs in Parisian and Louisiana French as well as in Plantation Creole and West African languages. The simplification of consonant clusters, as in *des* (for *desk* and *desks*) or *tase* (for *taste* and *tastes*), is commonplace in all of those languages, as well as in the Scots dialect of Robert Burns, who like American Southerners, Black and white, often assimilated *l* after back vowels, as in *fa'* (*fall*) and *saut* (*salt*). Similarly, the pervasive deletion of articles, copulas, prepositions, and other function words, so characteristic of Gullah and its creolized extensions, is a feature regularly associated with the speech of French, German, and Spanish bilinguals. Nevertheless, this fact remains: large numbers of Black and white speakers share those features across the lower South, especially in those areas dominated by the plantation cultures.

THE INFLUENCE OF SOCIAL DIALECTS

As creolization reflects the blending of languages and cultures, so slang, argot, and social dialects mark the activities of subcultures within the basic social structure. Although nothing as widespread as Cockney and Australian rhyming slang has developed in America, inventive usage here has steadily modified native speech. Most slang originates in the specialized conversations of particular groups, in which usage reinforces group identity and develops into private codes that may later gain widespread acceptance. These include such now-familiar terms as *clout* and *gerrymander* from politics, *blues* and *jazz* from music, *headline* and *editorial* from journalism, and *by a nose*, *inside track*, *front-runner*, *shoo-in*, and *sure thing* from the vocabulary of horse racing. The distinctive words of other groups – pickpockets, CB operators, and computer specialists – suggest the ways in which the subcultures function and illustrate the ways in which language develops.

Social dialects also underlie the regional patterns of speech, reflecting absolute factors, such as sex, age, and ethnic origin, and relative factors, such as education, experience, and social position. Since a healthy language is always changing, the age and experience of its speakers are recorded by incipient, dominant, and recessive forms, as demonstrated in the vocabulary of automobiles: the emergent *gas-guzzler* and *pimpmobile*, the durable *sedan* and *limousine*, and the relic *tin lizzie* and *roadster*. Ethnic terms are the cultural birthrights of individual speakers and great linguistic resources for society at large. Yiddish *schlock*, *chutzpah*, *macher* (fixer, operator, clever fellow), and *schmaltz* have moved from the Jewish communities to the national language, as have the specialized Sicilian terms *capo*, *Cosa Nostra*, and *Mafia* in urban American subcultures. Education reinforces language trends with the spread of generalized patterns of pronunciation, grammar, and vocabulary, but these are challenged by migrant accents in Chicago today just as they were in London 400 years ago. As Latinos made *macho* an American word, Black people have put many Southern regionalisms, such as *funky*, *uptight*, and *right on*, into common usage. The language reflects cultural patterns, refined and strengthened through association and social status.

Social dialects also mark the evolution of a language. In America the middle classes have generated great changes. These include the absorption of immigrant cultures at the lower level and influence upon the dominant culture at the higher level. As the linguistic and cultural forms are traditionally conservative in both aristocratic and folk groups, however different their social styles, middle-class society and speech alter those conventional patterns from below and from above. Just as members of the secular and regular clergy, educators, lawyers, politicians, and physicians helped shape the London Standard from the early Middle Ages through the English Renaissance because they were conversant with both the ruling class and the common people, so new patterns of American usage grow today through the influence of upper-middle-class dialects. Even stronger influences appear from the speech of the lower middle class, especially in urban centers, where large numbers of workers come in contact with the entire community in their daily work.

Of these, ethnic dialects preserve the most complicated social varieties of language and reflect the essential spirit of American culture. As frontier societies developed distinctive regional patterns, Spanish, French, Dutch, Scandinavian, and German settlers used their native languages before adopting the dominant English dialect. English, Irish, and Scots folk speech constituted probably the most influential ethnic varieties on the frontier, but these were modified by the language habits of their neighbors. In the process of Americanization, Europeans, Africans, and Asians gave the language some of its most familiar words: *chop suey*, *hamburger*, *hillbilly*, *jukebox*, *pizza*, *prairie*, *rodeo*, *Santa Claus*, *smorgasbord*, and *tycoon*.

The national vocabulary reflects the intimacy of conversation and the evolution of democratic social forms. John Adams proposed that Congress establish an American Academy "for refining, correcting, improving, and ascertaining the English language." Later, when asked to preside over such activities, Thomas Jefferson responded:

> There are so many differences between us and England, of soil, climate, culture, productions, laws, religion, and government, that we must be left far behind the march of circumstances, were we to hold ourselves rigorously to their standard. If, like the French Academicians, it were proposed *to fix* our language, it would be fortunate, that the step was not taken in the days of our Saxon ancestors whose vocabulary would illy express the science of this day. Judicious neology can alone give strength and copiousness to language, and enable it to be the vehicle of new ideas.

Instead of rules from a National Academy of English, Americans accepted the common-law customs of intelligent conversation with all its modifications through time and circumstance. Current usage may reject "illy express" and "judicious neology," but history shows the correctness of Jefferson's message. He recognized the certainty of change, the function of language as a cultural tool, and the importance of thoughtful selection of vocabulary. Through common-law customs of speech and writing the national language develops words and documents social facts. This Dictionary orders those materials of discourse, records the natural history of a people, and transmits the substance of the American heritage.

THE INDO-EUROPEAN ORIGIN OF ENGLISH

CALVERT WATKINS

The name *Indo-European* is given for geographic reasons to the large and well-defined linguistic family that includes most of the languages of Europe, past and present, as well as those found in a vast area extending across Iran and Afghanistan to the northern half of the Indian subcontinent. In modern times the family has spread by colonization throughout the Western Hemisphere.

A curious byproduct of the age of colonialism and mercantilism was the introduction of Sanskrit in the 18th century to European intellectuals and scholars long familiar with Latin and Greek and with the European languages of culture – Romance, Germanic, and Slavic. The comparison of this ancient tongue with the two classical languages revolutionized the perception of linguistic relationships.

Speaking to the Asiatick Society in Calcutta on February 2, 1786, the English Orientalist and jurist Sir William Jones (1746–1794) uttered his now famous pronouncement:

> The Sanskrit language, whatever be its antiquity, is of a wonderful structure; more perfect than the Greek, more copious than the Latin, and more exquisitely refined than either, yet bearing to both of them a stronger affinity, both in the roots of verbs and in the forms of grammar, than could possibly have been produced by accident; so strong, indeed, that no philologer could examine them all three, without believing them to have sprung from some common source, which, perhaps, no longer exists.

Jones was content with the assertion of a common original language, without exploring the details. Others took up the cause, but it remained for the German philologist Franz Bopp (1791–1867) to found the new science of comparative grammar, with the publication in 1816 of his work *On the Conjugational System of the Sanskrit Language, in Comparison with that of the Greek, Latin, Persian, and Germanic Languages*. He was 25 years old when it appeared.

It has been rightly said that the comparatist has one fact and one hypothesis. The one fact is that certain languages present similarities among themselves which are so numerous and so precise that they cannot be attributed to chance and which are such that they cannot be explained as borrowings or as universal features. The one hypothesis is that these languages must then be the result of descent from a common original. Certain similarities may be accidental: the Greek verb "to breathe," "blow," has a root *pneu-*, and in the language of the Klamath of Oregon the verb "to blow" is *pniw-*. Other similarities may reflect universal or near-universal features of human language: in the languages of most countries where the bird is known, the *cuckoo* has a name derived from the noise it makes. A vast number of languages around the globe have "baby talk" words like *mama* and *papa*. Finally, languages commonly borrow words and other features from each other, in a whole gamut of ways ranging from casual or chance contact to learned coinages of the kind that English systematically makes from Latin and Greek.

But where all of these possibilities must be excluded, the comparatist assumes genetic filiation: descent from a common ancestor, which in the case of Indo-European, as Sir William Jones surmised almost two centuries ago, no longer exists.

In the early part of the 19th century scholars set about systematically exploring the similarities observable among the principal languages spoken now or formerly in the regions from Iceland and Ireland in the west to India in the east and from Scandinavia in the north to Italy and Greece in the south. They were able to group these languages into a *family* that they called *Indo-European* (the term first occurs in English in 1813, though in a sense slightly different from today's). The similarities among the different Indo-European languages require us to assume that they are the continuation of a single prehistoric language (called *Indo-European* or *Proto-Indo-European*). In the words of the greatest Indo-Europeanist of his age, the French scholar Antoine Meillet (1866–1936), "We will term *Indo-European language* every language which at any time whatever, in any place whatever, and however altered, is a form taken by this ancestor language, and which thus continues by an uninterrupted tradition the use of Indo-European."

Those dialects or branches of Indo-European still represented today by one or more languages are Indic and Iranian, Greek, Armenian, Slavic, Baltic, Albanian, Celtic, Italic, and Germanic. The present century has seen the addition of two branches to the family, neither of which has left any living trace: Hittite and other Anatolian languages, the earliest attested in the Indo-European family, spoken in what is now Turkey in the second millennium B.C.; and the two Tocharian languages, the easternmost of Indo-European dialects, spoken in Chinese Turkestan (modern Xinjiang Uygur) in the first millennium A.D.

It should be pointed out that the Indo-European family is only one of many language families that have been identified around the world, comprising several thousand different languages. We have good reason, however, to be especially interested in the history of the Indo-European family. Our own language, English, is the most prevalent member of that family, being spoken as a native language by nearly 350 million people and being the most important second language in the world. The total number of speakers of all Indo-European languages amounts to approximately half the population of the earth.

English is thus one of many direct descendants of Indo-European: one of the dialects of the parent language became prehistoric Common Germanic, which subdivided into dialects of which one was West Germanic; this in turn broke up into further dialects, one of which emerged into documentary attestation as Old English. From Old English we can follow the development of the language directly, in texts, down to the present day. This history is our linguistic heritage; our ancestors, in a real cultural sense, are our linguistic ancestors. Only a small proportion of people in the United States can trace their biological ancestry back more than a century or two, and certainly a large segment of the population had languages other than English in their backgrounds only a few generations ago. But every individual is part of a culture, with language its external expression. That language, our language, has an ancestry, a history. Indeed, languages have perhaps the longest uninterrupted histories of all the cultural phenomena that we can study.

But it must be stressed that linguistic heritage, while it may well tend to correspond with cultural continuity, does not imply genetic or biological descent. The transmission of language by conquest, assimilation, migration, or any other ethnic movement is a complex and enigmatic process that this discussion does not propose to examine – beyond the general proposition that in the case of Indo-European no genetic conclusions can or should be drawn.

The comparative method – what we have called the comparatist's "one fact and one hypothesis" – remains today the most powerful device for elucidating linguistic history. When it is carried to a successful conclusion, the comparative method leads not merely to the assumption of the previous existence of an antecedent common language but to a reconstruction of all the salient features of that language. In the best circumstances, as with Indo-European, we can reconstruct the sounds, forms, words, even the structure of sentences – in short, both grammar and lexicon – of a language spoken before the human race had invented the art of writing. It is worth reflecting on this accomplishment. A reconstructed grammar and dictionary cannot claim any sort of completeness, to be sure, and the reconstruction may always be changed because of new data or better analysis. But it remains true, as one distinguished scholar has put it, that a reconstructed protolanguage is "a glorious artifact, one which is far more precious than anything an archaeologist can ever hope to unearth."

English, genetically a member of the Germanic branch of Indo-European and retaining much of the basic structure of its origin, has an exceptionally mixed lexicon. During the millennium of its documented history, it has borrowed extensively from its Germanic and Romance neighbors and from Latin and Greek. At the same time, it has lost the great bulk of its original Old English vocabulary. However, the inherited vocabulary, though now numerically a small proportion of the total, remains the genuine core of the language; all of the 100 words shown to be the most frequent in the Corpus of Present-Day American English, also known as the Brown Corpus, are native, inherited words; and of the second 100, eighty-three are native. Precisely because of its propensity to borrow from ancient and modern Indo-European languages, especially those mentioned above but including nearly every other member of the family, English has in a way replaced much of the Indo-European lexicon it lost. Thus, while the distinction between native and borrowed vocabulary remains fundamentally important, more than 50 percent of the basic roots of Indo-European as represented in Julius Pokorny's *Indogermanisches Etymologisches Wörterbuch* (Bern, 1959) are represented in modern English by one means or the other. Indo-European therefore looms doubly large in the background of our language.

NOTE: *At the end of the Dictionary is an Appendix listing many Indo-European roots ancestral to at least one English word, with descriptions of the details of their descent, cross-referred throughout to the individual etymologies in the body of the Dictionary. A preface to the Appendix is a longer article by Professor Watkins, entitled "Indo-European and the Indo-Europeans," containing a description of the reconstructed language and a series of observations of the cultural inferences that can be drawn from it.*

USAGE IN THE AMERICAN HERITAGE DICTIONARY: THE PLACE OF CRITICISM

GEOFFREY NUNBERG

Ever since the conception of "correctness" first emerged in the 18th century, there has never been a time when standards of usage were not controversial. Swift's proposals for improving English were derided by Whig pamphleteers. Noah Webster remonstrated with the influential Dr. Robert Lowth for defending a construction like *the King of England's hat,* and was in turn excoriated by later grammarians for countenancing the double negative. And so on, to the present day.

This litigious history may be disconcerting to those who would like to think of the English rules of correctness as long-settled standards from which we have lately fallen away. But a healthy tradition of language criticism requires controversy. This Dictionary contains over 500 Usage Notes and comments, which deal with several thousand words and usages altogether. That is a good deal more than what is found in most dictionaries. But at the most conservative estimate, an educated speaker of English knows around 100,000 words and constructions. And these can be combined in an infinite number of ways, most of them infelicitous – for there are many more ways to get a word wrong than to get it right. The number of possible mistakes in English is inexhaustibly vast, and no one could hope to catalog them all.

So traditional usage criticism has had to provide critical methods rather than lists. As a matter of convenience, of course, these methods are usually demonstrated in disputations over a body of canonical rules and dicta. When readers with an interest in these matters pick up a new usage book or a dictionary containing usage guidance, they invariably turn first to the entries dealing with the modification of *unique,* the proper use of *disinterested,* the distinction between *shall* and *will,* and the like. These, however, are merely the traditional occasions for discussions of usage and scarcely exhaust the scope of the subject.

Modern controversies about usage are different from their predecessors. The earlier disputes were waged intramurally, with everyone tacitly agreed about the stakes and the ground rules. Between Webster and Lowth there was no disagreement about the central premise of language criticism: that some forms of expression are preferable to others. Now that assumption itself has become controversial.

Modern discussions of usage often take the form of engagements in a battle between irreconcilable camps. On one side of the field is ranged the party of science, the "descriptivists," who hold that all standards are ultimately based on the facts of use and that the business of dictionaries and usage books is simply to record those facts in a neutral way. On the other side stand the "prescriptivists," who insist that language is subject to a higher morality and that people who care about the state of the language have an obligation to defend traditional values in the face of growing laxity and permissiveness.

Certainly language criticism was not originally conceived as an apology for traditional values. The 18th-century founders of the tradition were champions of a new class of writers, freed by an expanded reading public from a direct dependence on aristocratic patronage. The object of their criticism, whether of language, literature, or life, was to usurp the authority of the court and the aristocracy as a source of social values. Hence their insistence that the spoken language must defer to the written and that custom must sometimes defer to criticism – for in that era "custom" was simply another name for the practices of the privileged. Serious language criticism since then has been more often than not an arm of traditional liberalism, which reserved its sternest admonitions for the transgressions of the educated and the powerful. Matthew Arnold could berate the *London Times* for its "orthographical antics." Edmund Wilson taxed Walter Lippmann, Lionel Trilling, and John F. Kennedy for their stylistic lapses.

Usage doctrines must change with the times, of course. The fundamental linguistic virtues – order, clarity, and conciseness – are unassailable, yet they must be constantly reinterpreted against an evolving social background. It is no longer permissible to pretend that the English language is a club for gentlemen who have "their" Latin authors at their fingertips. The language is too important to be left to nostalgic reveries. Nevertheless, it is also too important to be excused from responsible critical review.

USAGE IN THIS DICTIONARY

In the treatment of usage the editors of *The American Heritage Dictionary of the English Language, Third Edition,* have tried to construct each Usage Note as a miniature critical exercise and to provide, within the limits of space, the kinds of information that readers will require to resolve the question to their own satisfaction.

Naturally the Notes vary greatly in content and length according to the point at issue. Some provide no more than brief comments on relatively technical points. (What is the difference between *flotsam* and *jetsam?*) At the other end of the spectrum, several Notes run close to a thousand words – far longer than the discussions of usage in any other dictionary. The longer Notes deal primarily with complex grammatical questions or with questions of particular social or critical interest (*I, man, he, hopefully,* and *unique,* for example). In these cases we have begun the Note with a brief summary for the reader who has only a cursory interest in the issue.

The material provided in the Notes falls into three broad categories: information about use, summaries and analyses of critical arguments, and observations about the opinions of writers and critics. Speaking very broadly, all questions of usage involve a weighing of one or more of these three considerations.

USE The doctrine that correctness rests on use is hardly an invention of modern linguistics. Horace insisted that the laws of speech are fixed by custom, "whose arbitrary sway/ Words and the forms of language must obey," a dictum quoted with approval by the grammarians of every succeeding era. Of course, the rules of the language are determined by use, but whose? Where use is uniform, the question does not arise. It is a curious fact of English that the phrase *more than one* takes a singular verb, despite its sense, as in *More than one student* has *left.* Doubtless it would be more logical to say *More than one student* have *left,* but it would not be English.

Still, usage is often divided, sometimes unaccountably but more often according to social or geographic differences. And in these cases Horace's dictum offers little by way of helpful advice, as Noah Webster observed with some impatience:

> But what kind of custom did Horace design to lay down as the standard of speaking? Was it a local custom? . . . Is it the practice of a court, or a few eminent scholars, that he designed to constitute a standard?

Webster's questions have no general answer. It depends on the word. Sometimes local custom is the only determinant, and we find as many standards as there are speech communities.

In other cases people do insist that there must be some one general standard, usually as determined by the practice of educated middle-class speakers. The Dictionary records facts about the use of items like these either in usage labels such as *Non-Standard* (see the Guide to the Dictionary) or, in particularly complicated cases, in the Usage Notes. Take the past tense form *snuck.* It originated as a nonstandard regional variant for *sneaked,* and many people still have a lingering prejudice against it: 67 percent of the Usage Panel disapproves of it. In recent years, however, *snuck* has become increasingly frequent in reputable writing (the *American Heritage Dictionary* files contain citations for it from the *New Republic* and the *San Francisco Chronicle,* as well as from the works of writers like Anne Tyler and Garrison Keillor). And while the files show that *sneaked* is by far more prevalent in edited prose by a factor of about 7 to 2, it is no longer possible to label *snuck* as nonstandard, even though many educated users of English continue to consider it informal.

While the practice of the educated middle class often determines what counts as "Standard English," it does not have the last word in all matters of divided usage. Not even the most assiduously "descriptivist" dictionary would think of basing its definitions of *annuity* or *zabaglione* simply on the way the words are used by educated speakers in general. Here readers do not expect to find a mirror of their own practice; they want to know how the words are used by experts in finance or Italian cooking. Of course, those are specialists' terms, but the point applies to many words in the general vocabulary as well. A great many educated speakers use *ironic* to mean simply "coincidental," as in *It's ironic that he was also using a borrowed bat when he hit a grand slam last week against the Dodgers.* The use, then, is unquestionably Standard English, and it is certainly the responsibility of a dictionary to record it. But the meaning of *ironic* is not at the disposition of the general public in quite the way the past tense of *sneak* is. *Ironic* is still a literary sort of word, and it is likely that a good many of the people who have used it to mean "coincidental" were reaching for a literary effect at the time. As long as literary folk continue to use *ironic* in a narrower sense – and what is no less important, as long as a large proportion of the general public continues to think of the word as literary – a dictionary has the responsibility to note that in this case the general use is sometimes at odds with the use of the writers and critics who have particular authority about the notion in question.

It is never easy to say which group has authority over any given usage, of course. Who owns *disinterested?* Is the word *kudos* by now a common or garden-variety English plural like *peas,* or is it still an elegant borrowing that should be held responsible to its origin as a Greek singular? We will want to take the facts of use into consideration when we approach these questions, but it is the height of scientistic self-deception to suppose that use provides an objective criterion for resolving them. Lexicographers invariably have to make critical evaluations of the raw facts of use. And where the verdict of use is equivocal, a dictionary should give readers the wherewithal to make up their own minds.

CRITICISM Custom fixes the rules of language but does not justify them. Even complete uniformity of use doesn't make a practice exempt from critical review. After all, custom is partly determined by our beliefs about the world and society, and in these we might all be wrong. At one time everybody used *fish* to refer to whales, but the practice was abandoned in the light of new zoological evidence. And until quite recently, everybody used the words *man* and *men* to mean simply "human beings," but now many people have abandoned that practice in the light of new conceptions of social justice.

The prescriptive tradition had its origins in the Age of Criticism as a method no different in kind from the criticism of artistic works or of civil society in general. The 18th-century writers established the battery of principles to which usage might be held accountable – the familiar arguments from analogy, logic, etymology, meaning, and the rest. Granted, they often applied these principles with the overzealous love of rules and systems that they brought to all their critical enterprises, so that we may sometimes feel, as Leslie Stephen put it, that they "sanctioned the attempt to do by rule and compasses what ought to be done by the eye." And much of the "logic" they invoked was derived either from speculative philosophy or from inappropriate parallels to Latin grammar, with the result that it often turns out to be of dubious relevance to the facts of English. It is fair to criticize the double negative in a sentence like *I never got nothing* on the grounds that it is associated with nonstandard varieties of English. But one cannot fault the construction on logical grounds without also being willing to assert the illogicality of standard French and Italian.

Linguists of a generation or so ago were fond of citing

examples such as these in an effort to undermine the entire prescriptive program, and some of them went on to argue that the rules of language are simply immune from criticism, since they answer to natural laws inaccessible to cursory reflection. But the fact that particular prescriptive arguments are sometimes unsound does not vitiate the case for criticism in general. If modern linguistics teaches us that the logic of language structure is a good deal more subtle and elusive than traditional grammarians supposed, it does not follow that the grammar of every variety has achieved complete consistency or functional perfection – particularly with regard to the relatively "unnatural" requirements of written public communication.

In fact there is no reason that the methods of scientific linguistics and of traditional criticism should be regarded as incompatible. Modern syntax and semantics have developed an impressive array of analytical tools, which often make it possible to capture distinctions and subtleties that elude the sometimes coarse apparatus of traditional, Latin-based school grammar. These techniques can be as useful in analyzing prescriptive rules as in describing the facts of actual speech, and we have turned to them here in the course of analyzing a number of traditional questions, as well as some of the grammatical complications raised by the new concerns about matters of gender (see, for example, the entries at *dare, different, each other, plus,* and *than,* and at *man* and *he*). We have avoided the use of unfamiliar technical terminology, since we are interested in providing a critical method, not in communicating a body of scientific results. We believe, along with an increasing number of linguists, that there is an important place for a "critical linguistics" in the study of usage.

OPINION: THE ROLE OF THE USAGE PANEL Custom can provide precedents and criticism can provide principles, but each has to be evaluated at the bar of opinion. Of course, dictionaries register received opinion at every turn (what else could justify labeling a usage as "offensive"?). But it is often useful to have a more explicit way of gauging the opinions of people who have a critical interest in the language. This, then, is the role of the Dictionary's Usage Panel, a group of 173 well-known writers, critics, and scholars. Panel members are regularly surveyed on a broad range of usage questions, from the distinction between *each other* and *one another* to the status of words such as the noun *lifestyle* and the verb *impact.* The results of these surveys are included in many of the Usage Notes.

The Usage Panel should not be thought of as an Academy, charged with ruling on all questions of disputed usage. Indeed, the opinions of the Panel are often divided, even though at times the Panelists seem to speak with a single voice. In earlier surveys, for example, 99 percent of the Panelists rejected *between you and I* and *ain't I* in formal writing. But the Panel's judgment on questions like these merely reflects the hegemony of Standard English. The results of the surveys are far more interesting when they involve questions that are matters of dispute among educated speakers. In the most recent survey, for example, 49 percent of the Panel accepted the use of *alternative* to refer to one of three or more choices, as in *Of the three alternatives, the first is the least distasteful.*

One might think that faced with this sort of disagreement readers interested merely in knowing which usage is "correct" would be perplexed: if there is no agreement among so august a group as this, what hope is there of fixing standards? But this misses the point. In the first place, the variation may itself be instructive. In the most recent survey, for example, we included several questions about words of uncertain pronunciation, such as *banal, err, harass,* and *hegemony.* We were not surprised to find a lack of consensus – the Usage Panel was split exactly 50–50 on which syllable takes the emphasis in *harass,* for example – but the results did serve to make the no less useful point that on these matters, at least, there *is* no agreed-upon standard.

More important, the Panel's diverging opinions underscore the point that usage questions are always controversial – *must* be controversial, if discussions of usage are to be instructive. The Usage Panel surveys are most interesting in providing a rough indication of just how controversial an issue is, that is, how seriously the views of individual critics have been taken by people with a critical interest in the language. This fact becomes clear when we compare the Panel's reactions on different items. For instance, if you read what some critics have had to say about new forms like the use of *parent* as a verb, or the word *lifestyle,* you may be led to believe that they are all egregious New Age jargon. But collectively, the Panel was more discriminating. Fully 98 percent of the Panel rejected the sentence *Critics have charged that the department was remiss in not trying to dialogue with representatives of the community.* By contrast, *lifestyle* is acceptable to a large majority of the Panel, 70 percent, in the sentence *Salaries in the Bay Area may be higher, but it may cost employees as much as 30 percent more to maintain their lifestyles.* Readers, of course, will want to make up their own minds about each of these usages, but the opinions of the Panel may carry some weight, especially when taken together with the critical discussions in the Usage Notes.

CHANGING ATTITUDES In preparing this edition of the Dictionary, we were able for the first time to use the results of the Usage Panel surveys to draw another kind of comparison, one that shows the shifts in critical attitudes over time. The Usage Panel was first polled in 1964, nearly a generation ago. That is not a long time on the linguistic scale of things, for language as a whole changes much more slowly than other social institutions. But it is time enough for usages to change significantly in their status, particularly when they involve the sorts of innovations and neologisms that criticism often focuses on.

One notable trend, for example, is that a number of words and constructions that were questionable a generation ago have become more acceptable. The verb *contact* was problematic to many language critics of the 1950's and 1960's, but resistance seems to have abated: between 1969 and the most recent survey the Panel's acceptance of *contact* rose from 34 to 65 percent. The pattern of increasing acceptability was repeated with the use of the verb *intrigue* to mean "arouse interest" (up from 52 to 78 percent) and with various senses of the words *host, identify,* and many others. The tendency is not surprising. Innovations rarely remain for long on the linguistic littoral; most either make their way onto dry land or are carried off with the receding tide.

But other shifts in the Panel's opinions may have less to do with changing patterns of usage than with changes in critical standards. In evaluating the most recent survey, for example, we were struck by the Panelists' increased indifference to traditional injunctions against using certain words in ways that appear to be inconsistent with their Latin origins. Fully 68 percent of the Panel now accepts the use of *aggravate* to mean "irritate," up from 43 percent in 1969. The same shift is evident with the use of *anxious* to mean "eager" (up from 23 to 52 percent), *transpire* to mean "happen" (up from 38 to 58 percent), *cohort* to refer to a single person (up from 31 to 71 percent), and several other words of this type.

Does this mean that the Panel has become generally more liberal or permissive? It is true that its composition has changed over the years. The membership of the current Panel is more numerous and younger than it was in 1969, and it includes a greater proportion of women and members of minority groups than before. Yet on many other canonical usage issues the current Panelists have proved to be no less conservative than their predecessors. For example, 89 percent rejects the use of *disinterested* to mean "uninterested," a figure not significantly different from the 93 percent who rejected this usage in 1969. And on a few issues, such as the use of *hopefully* as a sentence adverb, the Panel is actually more conservative now than it was a generation ago. Why then the shift in the Panelists' opinions on *aggravate* and the rest? Perhaps they have come to believe that it is no longer possible to expect adherence to general usage standards that presuppose a familiarity with classical languages, even if many of them note that they still observe the traditional strictures in their own writing. (See also the Usage Notes at *data, dilemma, celibate, minimal,* and *nauseous.*)

THE SCOPE OF COVERAGE

THE TRADITIONAL CANON These changes in critical attitudes should not obscure the fact that most of the traditional canon of usage questions has emerged largely intact from the controversies of recent years. When people think about "usage questions," they still have in mind the same points of grammar and diction that occupied critics a century ago: the differences between *who* and *whom, between* and *among, enormity* and *enormousness*; the qualification of absolute terms such as *unique, equal,* and *parallel*; and so forth. These questions exemplify the consideration of usage in its most general form; they are ostensibly motivated by very broad critical principles that apply to writing of all sorts and about all subjects: criteria of logic, coherence, clarity, and concision. Over the years, to be sure, the traditional canon has accumulated a good deal of unexamined grammatical lore that does not hold up well under scrutiny; see, for example, the Notes at *and* and *preposition.* But we believe that canonical issues like these give language criticism its historical continuity; thus they still constitute the largest single category among the Usage Notes in the Dictionary. In some cases we have added Notes dealing with questions that, though not historically part of the canon, have much the quality of traditional issues: the use of *periodic* to mean "occasional," the use of *specious* to mean "false," the modification of *infinite,* and the potential ambiguity of *deceptively.* The traditional canon has always been surrounded by a penumbra of items like these, introduced by individual writers or reference books in the interest of making particular points. What makes the canon central, after all, is not so much the particular words included, but the broader linguistic questions raised.

NEW WORDS, NEW ISSUES The Dictionary's treatment of usage has been extended to cover a variety of new issues. Notes are included for a host of new words that have attracted commentary. Some of these are drawn from the language of particular domains: new social movements (*caring, parent, wellness, lifestyle,* and *father,* for example); postmodernism (*about*); publicity (*world-class, legend,* and *showcase*); technology (*parameter, input,* and *access*). Others have a more general provenance: the use of *go* to mean "say" or the use of *holocaust* to mean simply "disaster" or "misfortune." Of course the Dictionary's coverage of such items cannot be "comprehensive" – the class is far too fluid for that – but we have tried to cover items of particular critical interest.

In other cases, we have included Usage Notes for items not often touched on by criticism, which exemplify problems that might be considered appropriate elements in a revised usage canon. For example, there are Notes on several terms, such as *black English, nonstandard,* and *literacy,* that figure in recent public discussions of language questions. In including items like these, of course, we may be open to a charge of special pleading. But such words are only examples of a kind of scientific and technical terminology that has become increasingly important in public discussion. So we have also included Usage Notes on questions such as the difference between *methodology* and *method,* whether a *cross section* is necessarily "representative," and whether one can speak of a quantity as having been "reduced by 150 percent." Obviously the brief of usage criticism cannot be extended to cover all of the specialized discourse of the sciences. But the program of criticism can make at least a token effort to acknowledge the role that scientific and quantitative argumentation has come to play in general discourse.

USAGE AND SOCIAL JUSTICE Over the past 30 years the most radical change in the scope of language criticism has been its extension to a wide range of usages involving the relation between language and questions of social diversity and social justice. Discussion of these issues constitutes the most important and extensive additions to the treatment of usage in this Edition. One category includes the names of various social groups defined along lines of ethnicity, religion, race, physical capacity, and sexual preference, as discussed in the Notes at *Asian, black, Chicano, color, gay, handicapped, Hispanic, Jew, Jewess, Kanaka, Moslem, Native American,* and *Negress.* In one sense, of course, these questions are not genuinely "new." But in the past they were not taken up as part of the public discussion of language standards. Only recently have these issues emerged as critical questions, whether as a result of the rise of official pluralism or of a more general tendency to emphasize the political and ideological aspects of usage.

In matters like these, of course, a dictionary has no authority to lay down standards of "correct" usage (at least not in the linguistic sense of the term). Most of these words are subject to a great deal of variation, even among members of the groups they apply to, and their connotations and use can change very rapidly. The Dictionary can help by providing information on the social and linguistic backgrounds of the questions. Thus the Note at *Hispanic* explains how that term is different in meaning from *Latino.* At the least, this information may spare some readers from resorting to unnecessary circumlocution or from giving inadvertent offense.

USAGE AND GENDER With a few exceptions (as with *black* and *gay*), the usage questions raised by the names of ethnic categories and the like are socially complex but linguistically simple. Replacement of one such word by another rarely causes grammatical difficulties or creates ancillary linguistic problems. But gender differences are so extensively and intricately woven into the fabric of the language that efforts to change usage often require a great deal of attentiveness and linguistic ingenuity. So it is not surprising that feminism has had more extensive consequences for questions of usage than any other recent social movement or that the debate over these issues has been particularly energetic. In this Edition we have greatly expanded coverage of these issues, which are discussed in the Usage Notes at *blond, brunette, –ess, –ette, feminist, gender, he, heroine, lady, man,* and *Ms.*

With these items, as with the names of ethnic and social categories, we have tried to present the linguistic and social background that readers will require to make informed decisions about the issues. Because the linguistic program of feminism has called for such extensive and varied changes in usage, we have also made an effort to gauge its overall effects on the attitudes and practice of writers, both in general and with regard to particular words and constructions. To this end, we included a number of questions about these issues in recent Usage Panel surveys. Generally speaking, we found that a great majority of the Panelists of both sexes have adopted at least a few of the recommendations of feminists. But virtually all the Panelists were discriminating in their revisions; they found some usages more objectionable than others. (In reporting the results on these items, we have sometimes broken down the Panelists' responses on the basis of gender. Not surprisingly, women were consistently more likely than men to reject usages that might be labeled sexist. But men and women showed roughly the same patterns in differentiating one item from the next. Thus both groups found *hostess* more acceptable than *sculptress,* and so forth.)

Fewer than 40 percent of the Panelists say they would use the masculine pronoun *his* to complete the sentence *A child who wants to become a doctor should be encouraged by_____ parents and teachers,* against 81 percent (including 58 percent of the women members) who accepted the generic use of *man* in *If early man suffered from a lack of information, modern man is tyrannized by an excess of it.*

Like most critical users of the language, the Panelists seem to have revised their usage on a case-by-case basis, evaluating each item in the light of the sometimes conflicting claims of syntax, established use, and social justice. In a sense, one can say that the feminist linguistic program has already succeeded, in requiring most literate people to reflect carefully on the ways in which usage might imply or reinforce gender stereotypes. Of course, the Panel's divisions reflect controversies about these usages that are not likely to be resolved in the near future. But these are precisely the kinds of controversies about particular words and principles that ensured the vitality of traditional language criticism in the 18th and 19th centuries. Here as elsewhere, what matters is not that we should expect to achieve uniformity but that we should find in our differences the occasion for lively critical discussion.

THE MATHEMATICS OF LANGUAGE

HENRY KUČERA

Language is such a characteristically human activity and such a potentially exquisite transmitter of literary imagination that many of us find it difficult to view it as having prosaic, predictable, or even mathematical properties. And yet, over the past few decades, we have seen much of our language communication recorded, processed, and transmitted by computers that are capable of reducing our written words to electronic signals, allowing us to search through them and organize them, and then, if need be, transmit them electronically and almost instantaneously over long distances. *Word processing* and *information retrieval*, as we have rather unimaginatively named these computer manipulations of our language records, is not only a billion-dollar industry but a new information medium that is revolutionizing communication as much as the invention of movable print type did more than 500 years ago.

It still takes people to formulate ideas and to write the novels and the poems. But now the drudgery of having to retype entire pages of a manuscript in order to make corrections is gone. We have the opportunity to look up synonyms and definitions in an electronic dictionary, and even the possibility of relying on the machine to find and correct our misspellings or check our grammar and style.

Computers – machines that some of us still think of as fast number crunchers – can encode, manipulate, process, and in a limited way understand language only because of the remarkable properties of natural language systems as they have evolved through a long history. In its essence, language is a hierarchically organized structure of symbols, which allows us to express a potentially infinite number of ideas through finite means. The basic building blocks of this system are very few: a set of contrastive sounds – the phonemes of the language – that we can represent by letters and letter combinations in our alphabetical writing systems. These elementary building blocks are combined in highly restricted ways into the basic meaningful units, the words of the language. These words, again in accordance with systematic combinatory principles, form meaningful sequences of syntactically well-formed sentences. The entire system thus consists of combining a finite inventory of discrete units into a potentially infinite set of discourses, just as the ten numerals of our number system can be combined into an infinite set of different mathematical values and expressions.

This analogous organization of language and numeric systems makes it easily possible to represent linguistic units by numbers and to manipulate them as if they were mathematical objects. Having a computer find a misspelled word is not magic: if the machine has a lexicon available, with words coded as numbers, it can compare the numeric code of the word we write with the numerical value of the word in its word list through a simple arithmetical operation. If no match is found, our word is not in the computer's lexicon, and we have a good candidate for a misspelling.

EFFICIENCY AND REDUNDANCY

But languages – as they have evolved spontaneously in communities over the ages – possess much more complex mathematical properties than those resulting from a hierarchical structure of discrete units. Languages exhibit both efficiency and redundancy, two contradictory characteristics balanced against each other to achieve both a communicational usefulness and reliability.

Consider redundancy first: of the 33 or so phonemes of English, only a small subset of their possible permutations can form actual words. Adult English speakers know, for example, that *trip* is an English word. But they also know that *tlip* is not an English word and do not have to go to a dictionary to discover that fact. Intuition tells them that no English word can begin with *tl–*. But when faced with *trin*, English speakers – though not recognizing the word – may have to seek help in a dictionary. The form *trin* is at least theoretically a possible English word because it does not violate any of the general constraints on permissible sequences of English sounds.

Even on this elementary phonological level, we find a substantial redundancy, the imposition of constraints on possible sequences and, consequently, the introduction of some information waste into the system. This waste is needed to enable us to communicate without overwhelming numbers of errors and misunderstandings. If every possible permutation of sounds were an actual English word, our communication system would be very efficient indeed, and all our words could be very short. There would be no need for any word of more than four sounds: mathematically we could have over a million of those. But communicating in such a system would be extremely difficult. Our physiological limitations in producing and perceiving sounds and sound sequences, and the properties of human memory, would make the learning and use of such a system practically impossible. Even if one could learn this distressingly efficient language, every noise, every imperfection or error that would distort our perception of even a single sound, would disrupt our understanding, because the lack of redundancy in the system would not allow us to guess what we might have missed. Worse still, if we heard one sound where another was intended, we would have heard a legitimate, albeit unintended word. Thus redundancy, a universal property of all languages, is one of our great communicational friends.

Of course, the constraints on the permissible sequences of sounds that are used to achieve this redundancy may differ substantially from language to language; there are many languages, for example, in which a word can begin with the initial *tl–* cluster prohibited in English. The same is true on higher levels. English – a configurational language that relies on word order to signal many grammatical functions – imposes severe restrictions on possible sequences of words within a sentence. Languages with a "free" word order, such as Latin or Russian, allow seemingly endless permutations of words. These permutations are possible because these languages have an elaborate system of inflected forms and paradigms in which a small set of endings is combined in highly restricted ways with the stems of the word to signal the syntactic relations that are achieved through word order in English.

A branch of mathematics known as *information theory* provides a formal means of measuring the redundancy of a communication system. For natural languages these measurements are complex and difficult, but some overall estimates are possible. On the phonological level we have calculated for several languages (English, German, Russian, and Czech) that – taking only the constraints on sound sequences within syllables into account – redundancy reaches about 50 percent. All languages, of course, also have restrictions on which syllables may follow one another; the overall redundancy estimate thus must be put at least at the 80 percent level.

The other side of the coin in language design is efficiency. It has been known for a long time that very frequently occurring words tend to be short. We even clip or abbreviate words as they become more common: *telephone* to *phone*, *airplane* to *plane*, and so on. Computer analysis of large samples of language texts provides accurate data to support this general conclusion. In the one-million-word Corpus of Present-Day American English, also known as the Brown Corpus, compiled from samples taken from 500 different sources of 15 different genres and styles of writing, words accounting for 57 percent of the running texts (i.e., 57 percent of the one million word tokens) have 4 letters or fewer. Examples of these are *the, and, but, of, that,* and *have*. But an entirely different situation comes to view if we construct a "dictionary" from the Corpus, that is, a collection of different words, known in formal linguistics as *types*, with each word appearing only once in the list regardless of the number of times it may be repeated in the text. Here, words of 4 or fewer characters account for less than 9 percent of the lexicon.

The discrepancy between the two suggests the communication efficiency of language: the system is designed so that the short words are repeated often in an average text and thus accumulate high frequency figures. Longer words are used sparingly, and the repeat rate of the truly long words is negligible. For every occurrence of a 10-letter word, there are 8 occurrences of a 3-letter word, and for every instance of a 20-letter word, there are 3,524 occurrences of a 3-letter word.

This principle in human languages is similar to the design of artificial communication systems. In International Morse code, the most frequently used English letter, namely *e*, has the shortest symbol, one short signal requiring minimum transmission time. Conversely, the infrequently used letters, such as *j, q,* and *y*, have the longest codes, various sequences of three long signals and one short. Samuel F.B. Morse did by planning what languages have achieved in their natural evolution.

HOW MANY WORDS?

On occasion, every linguist with an interest in the quantitative properties of language will be faced with some form of the ultimate numerical question: "How many words did Shakespeare use?" "How many words does a person know?" "How many words should a dictionary have?"

The first question, at least, has a definite, though not simple answer: Shakespeare's complete works consist of a total of 884,647 words of text containing a total of 29,066 different words, including proper names. In order to understand the significance of these numbers, we have to be quite certain of what we mean by a word. What is it that we are counting? Even if we focus only on written language and define a word simply as a string of letters bounded by space on each side, our problem does not entirely go away. We still have to decide whether to consider inflected forms, such as those formed from the verb *play* (*plays, playing, played*), to be words in their own right or simply members of a single class represented by the stem form PLAY. If we take the first approach, we have four distinct words. If we take the second, we have only one, comprising a set of grammatical forms, differing only in inflection, that linguists call a *lemma*. Even in English, where the inflectional system is quite limited, we have to exercise great terminological care when making any statistical statements about the size of the vocabulary used by a writer or found in a work. In a highly inflected language like Russian, where many nouns have ten different case and number forms, the difference between the number of word forms and the number of lemmas is dramatic indeed.

Conventional dictionaries are, by and large, collections of lemmas represented by their stem forms, which appear as boldface entries in an alphabetical order. Their inflected forms are given when the formation involves irregularity or a spelling change, but the inflections are generally not listed when regular. The concept of a word, as we have become used to it from the dictionary structure, is thus closer to that of a lemma than that of a word form.

In frequency and vocabulary studies of an author or a collection of texts, however, word forms, not lemmas, are usually counted. There are several reasons for this: computers can detect as different words strings of letters that are not identical, but they cannot easily recognize and put together items belonging to a single lemma. Lemmatization involves a number of methodological linguistic decisions, some of them quite difficult. The figure of 29,066 different words used by Shakespeare thus refers to word forms, not lemmas. Assuming that the research results on Modern English also hold, at least approximately, for Shakespeare's works, we can conclude that the total vocabulary of lemmas in the poet's work is about 18,000.

Given these rules of the game, how does the richness of Shakespeare's vocabulary compare to present-day English usage? In the analysis of the Brown Corpus, word forms have been assigned to their lemma groups on the basis of well-defined principles, but the statistics for individual word forms have also been compiled. The two sets of results indicate that this one-million-word database contains 61,805 word forms, which belong to 37,851 lemmas. The number of different words in the Brown Corpus is thus more than twice that of the complete works of Shakespeare, though the size of the two databases is comparable. Does this mean that Shakespeare's vocabulary was modest or that over the last few hundred years English has evolved into a much richer language lexically? Not necessarily. Many words have undoubtedly been added to our lexical store, but the main reason for the discrepancy is almost certainly the fact that the corpus of Shakespeare's writings is quite homogeneous in content and style, while the Brown Corpus is intentionally heterogeneous in order to make it representative of contemporary usage. The content of the Corpus was therefore selected from 500 different sources ranging from newspapers to scientific writing to general fiction.

If all words were statistically equal, then each word form would occur about 16 times in the one-million-word text, and each lemma about 26 times. In actuality, the rate of repetition of individual words, and thus their frequency, is extremely uneven. The overall statistics are quite striking: the use rate of the first 100 most frequent words is so high that they account for a full 47.4 percent of all the text. Of all the running words (tokens) contained in the one million, the 100 most frequent lemmas constitute 49.6 percent of all the text. To account for 80 percent of the entire one-million-word text takes only 2,854 different word forms belonging to 2,124 distinct lemmas.

The fact that one needs to know fewer than 3,000 words in order to understand 80 percent of a reasonably representative modern English text does not mean that this kind of vocabulary could guarantee any of us cultural survival in a modern society. It must be realized, first of all, that many of the most frequently occurring words in English are function words: articles, prepositions, and auxiliary verb forms, such as those of *be*, *have*, or *do*. The definite article *the* is by far the most frequently used word in English, occurring 69,975 times in the one-million-word corpus. Although in the overall text the dominant parts of speech are nouns and verbs, accounting for about 26 percent and 18 percent, respectively, of all the word tokens, the part-of-speech representation in the highest frequency category strongly favors function words. The lemmas occupying the frequency ranks 1 through 32 are all function words or pronouns; the first content word, the verb *say*, appears only at rank 33, and the first noun, *man*, at rank 44.

These function words, essential as they may be for signaling the exact role of content words and their syntactic relation in a sentence, are also precisely the ones that, because of their high predictability, can be most easily guessed if they happen to be omitted from a text. Such omissions are just what characterizes the style of newspaper headlines. The headline *Actor Found in Critical Condition after Explosion* has been deprived of all articles and auxiliaries; in a full text the sentence would read something like *An actor has been found in a critical condition after an explosion*. Thus, a 12-word sentence has been reduced to a 7-word headline without any loss of information. Conversely, the less predictable a word is in a given context, the more its presence contributes to the "surprise value" of the sentence, to its informational role. In this sense, the less frequent the word, the more important it will be – statistically speaking, at least – for an understanding of the communication.

If understanding 80 percent of any text were sufficient for us to function as literate people, we could manage with a vocabulary of fewer than 3,000 words and could dispense with dictionaries. Since it is not, dictionaries, which offer us the spelling, the pronunciation, and the definitions of both the frequent and the rare, become our indispensable companions.

COMPUTERS AND GRAMMAR

In the last few years we have developed computers with an even more impressive degree of linguistic ability: we now have programs that can find and correct at least some errors in grammar. At first glance, this kind of machine ability may seem astonishing. As difficult as it may be to master the subtleties of English spelling, an explanation of how a spelling checker works is not difficult to understand. But grammar does not deal with specific lists of sentences, as a spelling lexicon does with words. It deals with a potentially infinite variety of human expressions. The sentences that we encounter are often quite new to us, yet we can understand them even though we have never seen or heard them before. Learning one's native language surely does not consist of memorizing sentences. Instead, it consists of internalizing an abstract knowledge of the acceptable structures that can then be applied to the creation and understanding of new strings of words.

All native speakers of English, even those who have never studied "grammar," possess a basic, reliable intuition of what is and what is not a possible English sentence, just as they know what is a possible English word. This grammatical intuition, however, is much more abstract and sophisticated than the speaker's phonological intuition. Consider a simple example: a native speaker of English knows that the sentence *She told him to behave himself* is well-formed but that *She told him to behave him* and *She told himself to behave himself* are totally unacceptable. If one considers the details of the mental process allowing us to make these seemingly simple decisions, their true complexity becomes immediately apparent. We know that *himself* rather than *him* is required as the last word of the first example because the person told to be on good behavior is both the underlying actor and the object of the verb *behave*: linguists call this a "reflexive construction." The pronoun *him*, the third word of the same example, on the other hand, is the object of the verb *told*, obviously different from the subject, identified by *she*, and hence impossible to be expressed by a reflexive pronoun.

Programming a computer to detect and correct errors in sentence structure is a very difficult process, but if one is willing to live with less than absolute perfection, it is certainly possible. In essence, the process involves teaching the machine how to parse a sentence, that is, how to break it into its component parts of speech, reveal their syntactic relationships, find important constituents such as individual phrases, subjects, and objects, decide whether the subject and the verb agree, and so on.

What needs to be borne in mind is that grammar analysis is possible only because we can formalize the rules of linguistic structures: computers can do wonderful things only if we tell them, in very explicit and formally precise ways, how to do them. Describing the abstract rules of grammar – the mathematical properties of language in the broadest sense of the term – makes this task possible. We can thus remain quite confident about who controls the human-machine interaction: it is still the human being who must discover the linguistic principles and instruct the machine how to apply them, no matter how impressive the ultimate performance of the machines may be.

GUIDE TO THE DICTIONARY

The American Heritage Dictionary of the English Language, Third Edition, is a record of the language as it is used by a broad and diverse group of educated speakers and writers over the long term. Its word list reflects the many complex elements that constitute our language. This Guide, which explains the conventions used in presenting the great array of information contained in the Dictionary, is intended to enable you to find and understand that information quickly and easily.

GUIDEWORDS

A pair of boldface guidewords, together with the page number, is printed at the top of each page. The word on the left represents the first boldface entry on that page of the Dictionary. The word on the right represents the last boldface entry on that page. Thus, **biodegradable** and **biomedicine** and all the entries that fall alphabetically between them are entered and defined on page 189.

THE ENTRY WORDS: ALPHABETICAL ORDER

Each entry word, printed in boldface type, is set slightly to the left of the text column. All entries – including biographical and geographic names, abbreviations, symbols, and compounds of two or more words – are listed in strict alphabetical order:

abs.
Absaroka Range
Absaroke
abscess
abscise
abscisic acid
abscissa
abscission
abcission zone

For the sake of convenience, proper names are listed according to their most important element, such as a surname shared by a number of important people. In these cases, the alphabetical sequence applies only to those letters preceding the first comma:

George
George, Saint
George I[1]
George I[2]
. . . . . .
George VI
George, Henry
George, Lake
George River

SUPERSCRIPT NUMBERS. Words with identical spellings but different etymologies are entered separately and have superscript, or raised, numbers. In most cases, these numbers reflect the frequency of use:

tick[1] (tĭk) *n.* **1.** A light, sharp, clicking sound made repeatedly by a machine, such as a clock. . . . [Middle English *tek,* light tap.]

tick[2] (tĭk) *n.* **1.** Any of numerous small bloodsucking parasitic arachnids of the family Ixodidae, many of which transmit febrile diseases, such as Rocky Mountain spotted fever and Lyme disease. . . . [Middle English *teke, tik,* perhaps from Old English **ticca.*]

tick[3] (tĭk) *n.* **1.a.** A cloth case for a mattress or pillow. . . . [Middle English *tikke,* probably from Middle Dutch *tīke,* ultimately from Latin *thēca,* receptacle, from Greek *thēkē.* See **dhē-** in Appendix.]

tick[4] (tĭk) *n. Chiefly British.* Credit or an amount of credit. [Short for TICKET.]

SYLLABICATION

An entry word and its inflected and derived forms are divided into syllables by means of centered dots:

ac·e·tate (ăs′ĭ-tāt′) *n.*

In entries, such as *ethyl acetate,* that consist of two or more words separated by spaces, the words without centered dots are divided into syllables at their own places in the Dictionary.

Pronunciations are syllabicated for the sake of clarity. The syllabication of the pronunciation may not match the syllabication of the entry word because the division of the pronunciation follows phonological rules, while the division of the entry word reflects the long-established practices of printers and editors in breaking words at the end of a line of text.

PRONUNCIATION

The pronunciation is enclosed in parentheses and appears after the boldface entry word. If an entry word and a variant to that entry word have the same pronunciation, the pronunciation is given immediately after the variant. If the variant or variants do not have the same pronunciation as the entry word, pronunciations follow the forms to which they apply. Differing or variant pronunciations are given wherever necessary. If an entry or a variant requires more than one pronunciation, subsequent pronunciations show only those syllables that are different in sound quality or stress from the first pronunciation or that are necessary for clarity.

The key to the pronunciation symbols appears in a block in the margin of every other page. A fuller key appears at the end of this Guide to the Dictionary.

PRONUNCIATION SYMBOLS. The symbols used in this Dictionary enable you to produce a satisfactory pronunciation with no more than a quick reference to the key. All pronunciations given here are acceptable in all circumstances. When more than one pronunciation is given, the first is assumed to be the most common, but the difference in frequency may be insignificant.

For most words a single set of symbols can represent the pronunciation found in each regional variety of American English. You will supply those features of your own regional speech that are called forth by the pronunciation key in this Dictionary. The pronunciations are exclusively those of educated speech.

EXPLANATION OF THE SCHWA. Most symbols in the pronunciation key are self-explanatory, but one requires brief discussion. The nonalphabetical symbol (ə) is called a *schwa.* It is used in this Dictionary to represent a reduced vowel, a vowel that receives the weakest level of stress within a word. The schwa sound varies, sometimes according to the vowel it is representing and often according to the sounds surrounding it:

sis•ter (sĭs′tər)

a•bun•dant (ə-bŭn′dənt)

STRESS. The relative emphasis with which the syllables of a word or phrase are spoken, called *stress*, is indicated in three different ways. The strongest, or primary, stress is marked with a bold mark (′). An intermediate, or secondary, level of stress is marked with a similar but lighter mark (ʹ). The weakest stress is unmarked. Words of one syllable show no stress mark.

VARIANTS

Though standardization of English in the United States is more extensive than at any earlier time, many variant spellings and stylings remain in common use. All variants shown in this Dictionary are acceptable in any context unless indicated otherwise by a restrictive label, such as a dialect label. Variants, set in boldface type, are of two kinds: equal and unequal.

EQUAL VARIANTS. The word *or* joining an entry word and its variant form or forms indicates that these forms occur with virtually equal frequency in edited sources, based on our electronic and printed citational evidence:

ar•chae•ol•o•gy or **ar•che•ol•o•gy** (är′kē-ŏl′ə-jē) *n.*

UNEQUAL VARIANTS. The word *also* joining an entry word and its variant form or forms indicates that the variant form occurs less frequently:

am•bi•ance also **am•bi•ence** (ăm′bē-əns, äɴ-byäɴs′) *n.*

Variants that are not adjacent to their entry words in alphabetical order are entered as separate cross-references at the appropriate places in the alphabetical word list:

me•di•e•val also **me•di•ae•val** (mē′dē-ē′vəl, mĕd′ē-) *adj.*

me•di•ae•val (mē′dē-ē′vəl, mĕd′ē-) *adj.* Variant of **medieval.**

BRITISH VARIANTS. A number of variants consist of spellings preferred in British English. These variants, such as *defence* and *colour*, are labeled *Chiefly British.* They are entered at their own alphabetical places but are not given at the entries to which they relate:

de•fence (dĭ-fĕns′) *n. & v. Chiefly British.* Variant of **defense.**

One exception to this general rule has to do with words, such as *realize*, that end with the suffix *–ize.* The British spelling ending in *–ise* is not entered in this Dictionary unless it also commonly occurs in the United States. When a word that has a chiefly British variant occurs in compounds, the variant is not repeated at the compound. For example, the chiefly British variant *colour* is given for *color* but not for *colorblind*, *color guard*, and other such compounds.

PART-OF-SPEECH LABELS

The following italicized labels indicate parts of speech:

adj.	adjective
adv.	adverb
conj.	conjunction
def.art.	definite article
indef.art.	indefinite article
interj.	interjection
n.	noun
prep.	preposition
pron.	pronoun
v.	verb

These italicized labels indicate inflected forms:

pl.	plural
sing.	singular

Words such as *cattle* that occur only in the plural are labeled *pl.n.*

These italicized labels are used for the traditional classification of verbs:

tr.	transitive
intr.	intransitive
aux.	auxiliary

The labels for word elements are:

pref.	prefix
suff.	suffix

Entries that are abbreviations, such as *A.M.* and *blvd.*, are labeled *abbr.* Nouns that are often used to modify other nouns are labeled *attributive.*

Certain entries do not carry labels. They include contractions, symbols, trademarks, and the word elements *–i–* and *–o–*, which never occur in initial or final position in a word:

I'll (īl). **1.** I will. **2.** I shall.

I[2] **1.** The symbol for the element **iodine** (sense 1).

Walk•man (wôk′măn′, -mən). A trademark used for a pocket-sized audiocassette player, radio, or combined unit with lightweight earphones.

Sometimes an entry word fulfills more than one grammatical function. For example, *current* can be an adjective (*current pricing*; *current negotiations*) and a noun (*a current of air*; *the swift current of a river*; *electric current*). In such cases the different parts of speech are defined within a single entry called a *combined entry*. The shift in grammatical function is indicated by a boldface dash followed by the boldface entry word and the appropriate part-of-speech label. If the syllabication or pronunciation differs, it is also included. Inflected forms are given if necessary and are followed by definitions:

> **re·bel** (rĭ-bĕl′) *intr.v.* **-belled, -bel·ling, -bels. 1.** To refuse allegiance to and oppose by force an established government or ruling authority. **2.** To resist or defy an authority or a generally accepted convention. **3.** To feel or express strong unwillingness or repugnance: *She rebelled at the unwelcome suggestion.* **— reb·el** (rĕb′əl) *n.* One who rebels or is in rebellion: *"He is the perfect recruit for fascist movements: a rebel not a revolutionary, contemptuous yet envious of the rich and involved with them"* (Stanley Hoffman). *—attributive.* Often used to modify another noun: *rebel troops; a rebel army.*

INFLECTED FORMS

An inflected form of a word differs from the main entry form by the addition of a suffix or by a change in its base form to indicate grammatical features such as number, person, mood, or tense. In this Dictionary the following inflected forms appear with entry words:

1. Principal parts of all verbs, whether regular or irregular
2. All degrees of comparison of adjectives and adverbs formed by inflection
3. Irregular plurals of nouns and plurals whose formation might cause a spelling problem

Inflected forms follow the part-of-speech label. They are set in boldface type, divided into syllables, and given pronunciations as necessary. Inflected forms are usually shortened to the last syllable of the entry word plus the inflectional ending. Irregular inflected forms are spelled out to the extent required for clarity. When inflected forms are shortened, each shortened inflected form is preceded by a boldface hyphen:

> **cap·i·tal·ize** (kăp′ĭ-tl-īz′) *v.* **-ized, -iz·ing, -iz·es.**

A syllable consisting of a single letter at the beginning or end of an entry word never stands alone, nor is it dropped in inflected forms:

> **a·ble** (ā′bəl) *adj.* **a·bler, a·blest.**

> **ra·di·us** (rā′dē-əs) *n., pl.* **-di·i** (-dē-ī′) or **-di·us·es.**

PRINCIPAL PARTS OF VERBS. The principal parts of verbs are entered in this order: *past tense, past participle, present participle,* and *third person singular present tense.* When the past tense and the past participle are identical, one form represents both:

> **fly**[1] (flī) *v.* **flew** (flo͞o), **flown** (flōn), **fly·ing, flies** (flīz).

> **walk** (wôk) *v.* **walked, walk·ing, walks.**

COMPARISON OF ADJECTIVES AND ADVERBS. Adjectives and adverbs whose comparative and superlative degrees are formed by adding *-er* and *-est* to the unchanged word show these comparative and superlative suffixes immediately after the part-of-speech label:

> **high** (hī) *adj.* **high·er, high·est.**

Irregular comparative and superlative forms are given in full, as in *bad, worse, worst.*

The existence of *-er* and *-est* forms does not preclude the use of *more* and *most* with a simple adjective or adverb to express the comparative and superlative degrees. Often the comparative and superlative can be expressed either way, as in *cloudier* or *more cloudy, cloudiest* or *most cloudy.*

PLURALS OF NOUNS. Plurals of nouns other than those formed regularly by adding the suffixes *-s* or *-es* are shown and labeled *pl.*:

> **mouse** (mous) *n., pl.* **mice** (mīs).

When a noun has a regular and an irregular plural form, both forms appear, with the most common shown first:

> **a·quar·i·um** (ə-kwâr′ē-əm) *n., pl.* **-i·ums** or **-i·a** (-ē-ə).

Regular plurals are also shown when spelling might be a problem:

> **ra·di·o** (rā′dē-ō) *n., pl.* **-os.**

> **hon·ey** (hŭn′ē) *n., pl.* **-eys.**

A noun that is chiefly or exclusively plural in both form and meaning is labeled *pl.n.*:

> **cat·tle** (kăt′l) *pl.n.* **1.** Any of various mammals of the genus *Bos,* including cows, steers, bulls, and oxen, often raised for meat and dairy products.

A noun that is always plural in form but is not necessarily used with a plural verb is labeled like this:

> **aer·o·bics** (â-rō′bĭks) *n. (used with a sing. or pl. verb).* **1.** A system of physical conditioning designed to enhance circulatory and respiratory efficiency that involves vigorous, sustained exercise, such as jogging, swimming, or cycling, thereby improving the body's utilization of oxygen. **2.** A program of physical fitness that involves such exercise. [From AEROBIC.]

> **pol·i·tics** (pŏl′ĭ-tĭks) *n. Abbr.* **pol., polit. 1.** *(used with a sing. verb).* **a.** The art or science of government or governing, especially the governing of a political entity, such as a nation, and the administration and control of its internal and external affairs. **b.** Political science. **2.** *(used with a sing. or pl. verb).* **a.** The activities or affairs engaged in by a government, politician, or political party: *"All politics is local"* (Thomas P. O'Neill, Jr.). *"Politics have appealed to me since I was at Oxford because they are exciting morning, noon, and night"* (Jeffrey Archer).

SEPARATE ENTRIES FOR INFLECTED FORMS. Irregular inflected forms are entered separately in the Dictionary when they occur more than one entry away from the main entry word:

> **men** (mĕn) *n.* Plural of **man.**
> **went** (wĕnt) *v.* **1.** Past tense of **go**[1]**.**

Such entries carry a part-of-speech label and are given pronunciations as necessary.

Inflected forms are not shown at variant spellings that are cross-references to main entries:

> **par·a·lyse** (păr′ə-līz′) *v. Chiefly British.* Variant of **paralyze.**

Some verbs, such as *do, be,* and *have,* have archaic inflected forms, such as *dost, art,* and *hadst,* that occur frequently enough to justify their inclusion in this Dictionary. These forms are also entered separately:

> **dost** (dŭst) *v. Archaic.* A second person singular present tense of **do**[1]**.**

LABELS

This Dictionary uses various labels to indicate entries related to particular subject areas, to provide guidance regarding various levels of usage, and to indicate words indigenous to specific geographic areas.

SUBJECT LABELS. A subject label identifies the special area of knowledge to which an entry word or a definition applies:

> **e·qui·mo·lar** (ē′kwə-mō′lər, ĕk′wə-) *adj. Chemistry.* Having an equal number of moles.
>
> **tri·mor·phic** (trī-môr′fĭk) also **tri·mor·phous** (-fəs) *adj.* **1.** *Biology.* Having or occurring in three differing forms. **2.** *Chemistry.* Crystallizing in three distinct forms.

STATUS LABELS. Status labels indicate that an entry word or a definition is limited to a particular level or style of usage. All words and definitions not restricted by such a label should be regarded as appropriate for use in all contexts.

Non-Standard. This, the most restrictive label in the Dictionary, is applied to forms and usages that educated speakers and writers consider unacceptable:

> **an·y·ways** (ĕn′ē-wāz′) *adv. Non-Standard.* In any case.

Usage Problem. The label *Usage Problem* warns of possible difficulties involving grammar, diction, and writing style. A word or definition so labeled is discussed in a Usage Note:

> **snuck** (snŭk) *v. Usage Problem.* A past tense and a past participle of **sneak.** See Usage Note at **sneak.**
>
> **well·ness** (wĕl′nĭs) *n. Usage Problem.* Good physical and mental health, especially when maintained by proper diet, exercise, and habits. —*attributive. Usage Problem.* Often used to modify another noun: *wellness programs; a wellness clinic.*
>
> ***USAGE NOTE:*** It can be argued that *wellness* serves a useful function as a means of describing a state that includes not just physical health but fitness and emotional well-being. The word is first recorded in 1654 but has never been given the acceptance of its antonym *illness.* In the most recent survey 68 percent of the Usage Panel found the word unacceptable in the sentence *A number of corporations have implemented employee wellness programs, aimed at enhancing spiritual values, emotional stability, fitness, and nutrition.*

Offensive. This label is reserved for words and expressions such as racial, ethnic, or gender slurs that are not only derogatory and insulting to the person to whom they are directed but also a discredit to the one using them. This label may occur alone or in combination as *Offensive Slang.*

Vulgar. This label warns of social taboos attached to a word; it may appear alone or in combination as *Vulgar Slang.*

Obscene. A word that violates accepted standards of decency carries the label *Obscene.*

Slang. This label indicates a style of language that is distinguished by a striving for rhetorical effect through the use of extravagant, often facetious figures of speech. Slang either dies out or is eventually incorporated into the standard language as its rhetorical effect is lost. Some forms of slang occur in most cultivated speech but not in formal discourse. An example of a word labeled *Slang* is:

> **white-knuck·le** (hwīt′nŭk′əl, wīt′-) *adj. Slang.* Characterized by tense nervousness or apprehension: *a white-knuckle emergency landing; white-knuckle time in the hospital waiting room.*

Informal. Those whose speech is standard use not only the language of formal discourse but also the language of conversation. The great majority of words are acceptable at both levels, though many words that are acceptable in conversation with friends and colleagues would be unsuitable in the formal prose of an article written for publication in the journal of a learned society, for example. An example of an entry labeled *Informal* is:

> **wish list** *n. Informal.* An often mental list of things wanted.

TEMPORAL LABELS. Temporal labels signal words or senses whose use in modern English is uncommon.

Archaic. This label is applied to words and senses that once were common but are now rare, though they may be familiar because of their occurrence in certain contexts, such as the literature of an earlier time. Specifically, this label is attached to entry words and senses for which there is only sporadic evidence in print after 1755:

> **en·ter·tain·ment** (ĕn′tər-tān′mənt) *n.* . . . **5.** *Archaic.* Maintenance; support. **6.** *Obsolete.* **Employment.**

Obsolete. The label *Obsolete* is used with entry words and senses no longer in active use, except, for example, in literary quotations. Specifically, this label is attached to entry words and senses for which there is little or no printed evidence since 1755. Sense 6 of *entertainment* is an example.

ENGLISH-LANGUAGE LABELS. This Dictionary contains a number of labels noting the restriction of particular entry words and senses to specific areas of the English-speaking world. Among them is *Chiefly British,* which acknowledges that words are seldom restricted exclusively to the British or American vocabulary and in fact are often in use elsewhere in the world, as in New Zealand. Here is a typical example of a word labeled *Chiefly British*:

> **win·kle²** (wĭng′kəl) *tr.v.* **-kled, -kling, -kles.** *Chiefly British.* To pry, extract, or force from a place or position. Often used with *out.*

Other English-language labels are:

Australian	*Irish*
Canadian	*Scots*
Caribbean	*South African*

DIALECT LABELS. When a word or sense is commonly used in a specific area of the United States and little used – even if known – in other areas, it has been given a dialect label. Any entry or definition so labeled carries the symbol ♦ in the left margin next to the entry word:

> ♦ **bo·da·cious** also **bow·da·cious** (bō-dā′shəs) or **bar·da·cious** (bär-) *Southern & South Midland U.S.*

This Dictionary uses dialect labels singly and in various combinations ranging from the very general (*Regional*) to the very specific (*Cincinnati*). The very specific labels, which are self-explanatory, serve as descriptors of geographic regions such as cities, states, and interstate areas.

Major areas of distribution. Major, generalized areas of dialect distribution are labeled as follows and can occur in any number of combinations:

Northern U.S. – from New Jersey and Pennsylvania north to New England and west to Washington and Oregon

Southern U.S. – from southern Maryland along the coastal plains of Virginia, North and South Carolina, Georgia, Florida, Alabama, Mississippi, and Louisiana to eastern Texas and also including the "Upper South" as defined in the section "Midwestern and Midland"

Eastern U.S. – the Atlantic states from Maine to Florida, also including Vermont, New Hampshire, and upstate New York

Western U.S. – west of the 100th parallel, which extends southward from the Dakotas to western Oklahoma and Texas.

Subcategories of distribution. Within the major areas are these subcategories, the labels for which also can occur in various combinations:

For the north:

New England – Maine, New Hampshire, Vermont, Massachusetts, Connecticut, and Rhode Island

Northeastern U.S. – New England, New York State, Pennsylvania, and New Jersey

Upper Northern or *Inland Northern U.S.* – western upstate New York; northwest Pennsylvania; northern Ohio, Indiana, and Illinois; Michigan; Wisconsin; and Minnesota

Lower Northern or *North Midland U.S.* – southern New Jersey and Pennsylvania; northern Delaware, Maryland, and West Virginia; Ohio; Indiana; Illinois; Iowa; and Nebraska

Upper Midwest – Minnesota, Iowa, North and South Dakota, and Nebraska

Northwestern U.S. or *Pacific Northwest* – Washington, Oregon, Idaho, Montana, and Wyoming

For the south:

Southeastern U.S. – North and South Carolina, Georgia, Florida, Tennessee, Alabama, and Mississippi

Upper Southern or *South Midland U.S.* – southern Delaware, Maryland, West Virginia, Ohio, Indiana, and Illinois; western Virginia and North Carolina; northern Georgia, Alabama, Mississippi, and Louisiana; Tennessee; Kentucky; Arkansas; and eastern Oklahoma

Lower Southern U.S. – Florida, Georgia, Alabama, Mississippi, Louisiana, and eastern Texas

Eastern Lower Southern or *South Atlantic U.S.* – North and South Carolina, Georgia, and Florida

For the east:

Central Atlantic U.S. – Delaware; Washington, D.C.; eastern Virginia, Maryland, and Pennsylvania; and southern New Jersey

North Atlantic Coast – Maine, Massachusetts, Rhode Island, Connecticut, southeast New York State, and northern New Jersey

For the west:

Southwestern U.S. – Oklahoma, Texas, New Mexico, Arizona, and southern California

Midwestern and Midland. In addition to the labels just described, two labels are used that overlap with but lie outside the overall scheme. *Midwestern U.S.* designates regional terms that occur throughout the area from Michigan westward to the Dakotas and from Ohio westward to Kansas, an area that includes parts of several dialect areas. *Midland U.S.*, a term previously used in American dialect geography, includes the *Lower North* and the *Upper South.* The collective label *Midland* is distinguished from *Midwestern*, which does not include the South. Two *Midland* words are *Indian turnip* for *jack-in-the-pulpit* and *Italian* for *submarine.*

Gullah. The label *Gullah* refers not to a region but to the distinctive dialect of English spoken by American Black people who live on the coast and coastal islands of Georgia, South Carolina, and northern Florida.

CROSS-REFERENCES

A cross-reference signals that additional information about one entry can be found at another entry. Cross-references have two main functions: to avoid needless duplication of information and to indicate where further discussion of a word occurs.

The entry referred to is printed in boldface type preceded by a brief descriptive or instructional phrase:

> **bade** (băd, bād) *v.* A past tense of **bid.**

The cross-reference indicates that *bade* is a past tense at the entry *bid*, where further information about the entry can be found.

The word *See* is also used to introduce certain cross-references:

> **feath·er·edge** (fĕth′ər-ĕj′) *n.* . . . **2.** See **deckle edge.**

A full definition is given at the entry referred to, in this case *deckle edge.* At the end of the definition of *deckle edge* the phrase *Also called* appears followed by one or more words, here, *featheredge*, that have the same meaning:

> **deckle edge** *n.* The rough edge of handmade paper formed in a deckle. Also called *featheredge.*

A cross-reference referring to only one definition in an entry having two or more definitions contains that definition number:

> **tsar** (zär, tsär) *n.* Variant of **czar** (sense 1).

Some cross-references refer to tables. The boldface term in the cross-reference is the entry at which the table can be found:

> **kro·na²** (krō′nə) *n., pl.* **-nor** (-nôr′, -nər). *Abbr.* **kr., k., K.** See table at **currency.**

> **lep·ton²** (lĕp′tŏn′) *n.* Any of a family of elementary particles that participate in the weak interaction, including the electron, the muon, and their associated neutrinos. See table at **subatomic particle.**

ORDER OF SENSES

Entries containing more than one sense are arranged for the convenience of contemporary dictionary users with the central and often the most commonly sought meanings first. Senses and subsenses are grouped to show their relationships with each other. For example, in the entry for *fatal* shown below, the commonly sought meaning "Causing or capable of causing death" appears first and the now obsolete sense "Having been destined; fated" comes last in the series of five:

> **fa·tal** (fāt′l) *adj.* **1.** Causing or capable of causing death. **2.** Causing ruin or destruction; disastrous: *"Such doctrines, if true, would be absolutely fatal to my theory"* (Charles Darwin). **3.** Of decisive importance; fateful. **4.** Determining destiny; controlled by fate. **5.** *Obsolete.* Having been destined; fated.

Electronic and printed citations have been used to determine how all words should be defined.

DIVISION OF SENSES. Boldface letters before senses indicate that two or more subsenses are closely related:

> **phe·nom·e·non** (fĭ-nŏm′ə-nŏn′, -nən) *n., pl.* **-na** (-nə). **1.** . . . **2.** *pl.* **-nons. a.** An unusual, significant, or unaccountable fact or occurrence; a marvel. **b.** A remarkable or outstanding person; a paragon. See Synonyms at **wonder. 3.** *Philosophy.* **a.** That which appears real to the mind, regardless of whether its underlying existence is proved or its nature understood. **b.** In Kantian philosophy, the appearance of an object to the mind as opposed to its existence in and of itself, independent of the mind.

In a combined entry the senses are numbered in separate sequences after each part of speech:

> **ber·ry** (bĕr′ē) *n., pl.* **-ries. 1.a.** *Botany.* An indehiscent fruit derived from a single ovary and having the whole wall fleshy, such as the grape or tomato. **b.** A small, juicy, fleshy fruit, such as a blackberry or raspberry, regardless of its botanical structure. **2.** The small, dark egg of certain crustaceans or fishes. **—berry** *intr.v.* **-ried, -ry·ing, -ries. 1.** To hunt for or gather berries: *went berrying in July.* **2.** To bear or produce berries.

Information applicable only to a particular sense or subsense is shown after the number or letter of that sense or subsense:

> **ra·dix** (rā′dĭks) *n.* . . . **1.** *Biology.* A root or point of origin. **2.** *Abbr.* **rad.** *Mathematics.* The base of a system of numbers, such as 2 in the binary system and 10 in the decimal system.

In this entry the subject label *Biology* applies only to the first sense. The subject label *Mathematics* and the abbreviation *rad.* apply only to the second sense.

The same principles hold with respect to information about capitalization and plural use:

> **lam·en·ta·tion** (lăm′ən-tā′shən) *n.* **1.** The act of lamenting. **2.** A lament. **3. Lamentations** *(used with a sing. verb). Abbr.* **Lam., Lm** *Bible.* See table at **Bible.**

In this entry the form *Lamentations* at sense 3 indicates that only the capitalized plural form is used to refer to the biblical book. The usage label *used with a sing. verb* means that this form, with this meaning, is used only with a singular verb. The abbreviations *Lam.* and *Lm* and the subject label *Bible* apply only to sense 3.

Labels and other information applicable to all senses in an entry with more than one part of speech appear before the first part of speech in that entry:

> **kedge** (kĕj) *Nautical. n.* A light anchor used for warping a vessel. **—kedge** *v.* **kedged, kedg·ing, kedg·es.** *—tr.* To warp (a vessel) by means of a light anchor. *—intr.* To move by means of a light anchor.

The positioning of the label *Nautical* before the noun part-of-speech label, the first such label in the entry, indicates that *Nautical* applies to the entire combined entry – in this case, the noun and the verb.

SPECIAL WORDING OF SOME DEFINITIONS

Information that is essential to the accurate presentation of a meaning of a word is included in a phrasal definition. In certain instances, however, the defining language varies.

FULL-SENTENCE EXPANDERS. Supplementary information is sometimes included in a full sentence after the phrasal definition if, on the basis of citational and other evidence, it is considered to be of special import:

> **me·ter²** (mē′tər) *n. Abbr.* **m** The international standard unit of length, approximately equivalent to 39.37 inches. It was redefined in 1983 as the distance traveled by light in a vacuum in 1/299,792,458 of a second.

EXPLANATORY NOTES. Words whose meanings do not permit standard definitions have explanatory notes, beginning with *Used* or *Often used.* Words requiring notes of this kind include function words, interjections, intensives, some auxiliary verbs, and words labeled *Offensive* and *Offensive Slang.* An example is the explanatory note at the interjection *ugh*:

> Used to express horror, disgust, or repugnance.

ATTRIBUTIVES

It has long been a characteristic feature of English that nouns, like adjectives, can be used to modify other nouns. Nouns used in this way are labeled *attributives* in this Dictionary. An attributive is a word that freely occurs as a modifier of a broad group of other nouns, does not undergo comparison in the manner of true adjectives, cannot be modified by *very,* and does not regularly occur in the predicate after *be.*

Attributives are included as subsections of some noun entries. Verbal illustrations exemplify typical contexts of their usage:

> **gas** (găs) *n., pl.* **gas·es** or **gas·ses. 1.a.** The state of matter distinguished from the solid and liquid states by relatively low density and viscosity, relatively great expansion and contraction with changes in pressure and temperature, the ability to diffuse readily, and the spontaneous tendency to become distributed uniformly throughout any container. **b.** A substance in the gaseous state. **2.** A gaseous fuel, such as natural gas. **3.** Gasoline. **4.** The speed control of a gasoline engine: *Step on the gas.* **5.** A gaseous asphyxiant, irritant, or poison. **6.** A gaseous anesthetic, such as nitrous oxide. **7.a.** Flatulence. **b.** Flatus. **8.** *Slang.* Idle or boastful talk. **9.** *Slang.* Someone or something exceptionally exciting or entertaining: *The party was a gas. —attributive.* Often used to modify another noun: *gas tanks; gas stoves.*

ILLUSTRATIVE EXAMPLES

In this Dictionary there are tens of thousands of illustrative examples, of which more than 4,000 are quoted from over 2,000 separate sources. These illustrative examples, which follow the definitions and are set in italic type, show the entry words in typical contexts. The examples are taken from our files of electronic and printed citations showing patterns of word usage by a broad group of educated speakers in a wide array of publications. Such examples are especially helpful in showing changing usage, attesting to the existence of new words and meanings, illustrating transitive and intransitive verbs, revealing figurative uses of words, and exemplifying levels and styles of usage. Here are some instances of the use of quoted illustrations:

self-con·fi·dence (sĕlf′kŏn′fĭ-dəns) *n.* Confidence in oneself or one's own abilities: *"Without self-confidence we are as babes in the cradle"* (Virginia Woolf).

wis·dom (wĭz′dəm) *n.* **1.** Understanding of what is true, right, or lasting; insight: *"One cannot have wisdom without living life"* (Dorothy McCall). **2.** Common sense; good judgment: *"It is a characteristic of wisdom not to do desperate things"* (Henry David Thoreau).

Illustrative examples that are not direct quotations appear in entries such as the verb *speak*:

speak (spēk) *v.* **spoke** (spōk), **spo·ken** (spō′kən), **speak·ing, speaks.** —*intr.* . . . **4.a.** To make a statement in writing: *The biography speaks of great loneliness.* **b.** To act as spokesperson: *spoke for the entire staff.* **5.a.** To convey a message by nonverbal means: *Actions speak louder than words.* **b.** To be expressive: *spoke with her eyes.* **c.** To be appealing: *His poetry speaks to one's heart.*

PHRASAL VERBS

A phrasal verb is an expression consisting of a verb and an adverb or a preposition with a unitary meaning that cannot be deduced from the sum total of the meanings of its constituent parts. Phrasal verbs, set in boldface type and introduced by the heading ***phrasal verbs,*** follow the main definitions and precede the idioms, if any are present. Phrasal verbs are listed in alphabetical order:

set[1] (sĕt) *v.* **set, set·ting, sets.** —*tr.* **1.** To put in a specified position; place: *set a book on a table.* . . . —***phrasal verbs.*** **set about.** To begin or start: *set about solving the problem.* **set apart. 1.** To reserve for a specific use. **2.** To make noticeable: *character traits that set her apart.* **set aside. 1.** To separate and reserve for a special purpose. **2.** To discard or reject. **3.** To declare invalid; annul or overrule: *The court has set aside the conviction.* **set at.** To attack or assail: *The dogs set at the fox.* **set back. 1.** To slow down the progress of; hinder. **2.** *Informal.* To cost: *That coat set me back $1,000.* **set by.** To reserve for future use: *It is wise to set food and money by in case of a future emergency.*

IDIOMS

An idiom is an expression consisting of two or more words having a meaning that cannot be deduced from the sum total of the meanings of its constituent parts. Idioms, set in boldface type and introduced by the heading ***idioms,*** are fully defined in the last part of an entry. Idioms are listed in alphabetical order:

♦ **take** (tāk) *v.* **took** (to͝ok), **tak·en** (tā′kən), **tak·ing, takes.** —*tr.* **1.** To get into one's possession by force, skill, or artifice . . . —***idioms.*** **on the take.** *Informal.* Taking or seeking to take bribes or illegal income: *"There were policemen on the take"* (Scott Turow). **take a bath.** *Informal.* To experience serious financial loss: *"Small investors who latched on to hot new issues took a bath in Wall Street"* (Paul A. Samuelson). **take account of.** To take into consideration. **take away from.** To detract: *Her stringy hair takes away from her lovely face.* **take care.** To be careful: *Take care or you will slip on the ice.* **take care of.** To assume responsibility for the maintenance, support, or treatment of. **take charge.** To assume control or command.

ETYMOLOGIES

Etymologies appear in square brackets following the definitions. An etymology traces the history of a word from one language to another as far back in time as can be determined with reasonable certainty. The most recent stage before Modern English is given first, with each earlier stage following in sequence:

cab·in (kăb′ĭn) *n.* **1.** A small, roughly built house; a cottage. . . . [Middle English *caban,* from Old French *cabane,* from Old Provençal *cabana,* from Late Latin *capanna.*]

A language name, linguistic form, and brief definition, or gloss, of that form are given for each stage of the derivation. In order to avoid redundancy, however, a language, form, or gloss is not repeated if it is identical to the corresponding item in the immediately preceding stage. In the example shown for *cabin,* the different Middle English, Old French, and Late Latin forms have the same gloss, which is the same as the first definition of the Modern English word *cabin*: "small, roughly built house."

CONTENT OF ETYMOLOGIES. The etymologies in this Dictionary are designed to be as readable as possible. They rarely use abbreviations, symbols, or highly technical terms. The traditional language of descriptive grammar is used to identify parts of speech and various grammatical and morphological forms and processes, such as *diminutive, frequentative, variant, stem, past participle,* and *metathesis.* All of these terms are fully defined entries in the Dictionary. Likewise, every language that is cited in an etymology is either a Dictionary entry or is glossed in the etymology itself.

Sometimes a stage in the history of the word is not attested, yet there is reasonable certainty from comparative evidence about what the missing linguistic form looked like and what language it belonged to. These unattested forms are preceded by an asterisk indicating their hypothetical nature:

cer·tain (sûr′tn) *adj.* **1.** Definite; fixed: *set aside a certain sum each week.* **2.** Sure to come or happen; inevitable: *certain success.* **3.** Established beyond doubt or question; indisputable: *What is certain is that every effect must have a cause.* . . . [Middle English, from Old French, from Vulgar Latin **certānus,* from Latin *certus,* past participle of *cernere,* to determine. See **krei-** in Appendix.]

If a word is taken from the name of a person or place, such names are identified with pertinent information as to time or place. The etymology usually stops there, although a further etymology of the name itself is occasionally given.

Some words are not given etymologies. These include interjections, trademarks, and ethnic names that are Anglicizations of the group's name for itself. A large and important group of words not given explicit etymologies consists of compounds and derivatives, such as *sodium chloride, emergence,* and *euploid,* formed in English from words or word elements that are themselves entries in the Dictionary. If only a portion of an entry is used in an etymology, the unused portion of the entry is enclosed within parentheses:

bal·lis·to·car·di·o·gram (bə-lĭs′tō-kär′dē-ə-grăm′) *n.* A recording made by a ballistocardiograph. [BALLIST(IC) + CARDIOGRAM.]

Derivatives such as *emergence,* from *emerge,* in which only the final vowel of one constituent has been deleted, are assumed to be sufficiently understandable not to need etymologies.

INDO-EUROPEAN ROOTS. It is remarkable that the great bulk of the now vast vocabulary of English can be traced back to the reconstructed ancestral language called Proto-Indo-European. English words can be so traced either through their native origins in Old English and Proto-Germanic or through borrowings from nearly every other Indo-European language, but chiefly from Germanic, Romance, Latin, and Greek. The etymologies in this Dictionary take many such words back to their earliest ascertainable origins either in Proto-Indo-European or in the prehistoric stage of one of its chief branches, such as Germanic or Celtic. Each word is traced back to its earliest documentary attestation in its own etymology, then cross-referred to the Appendix of Indo-European Roots found at the end of the Dictionary. An introductory essay by Professor Calvert Watkins discusses some of the cultural inferences that may be drawn from this material (see pages 2081–2089). Also included are an explanatory Guide to the Appendix (pages 2090–2091), a table of the principal sound correspondences, and a diagram of the Indo-European languages on the endpapers.

STYLE OF ETYMOLOGIES. The etymologies present a great deal of complex information in a small space, and for this reason certain typographic and stylistic conventions are used. The word *from* indicates origin of any kind – by inheritance, borrowing, derivation, or composition. When a compound word is split into its component elements, a colon introduces them. Each element is traced in turn to its further origins. Parentheses enclose the further history of a part of a compound:

> **pseud·e·pig·ra·pha** (sōō′dĭ-pĭg′rə-fə) *pl.n.* **1.** Spurious writings, especially writings falsely attributed to biblical characters or times. **2.** A body of texts written between 200 B.C. and A.D. 200 and spuriously ascribed to various prophets and kings of Hebrew Scriptures. [Greek, from neuter pl. of *pseudepigraphos,* falsely ascribed : *pseudēs,* false; see PSEUDO– + *epigraphein,* to inscribe (*epi-,* epi- + *graphein,* to write; see **gerbh-** in Appendix).]

At times it is necessary to cross-refer from one etymology to another, either to avoid repeating part of a lengthy and complex derivation or to indicate the close relationship between two different Modern English words:

> **bat³** (băt) *tr.v.* **bat·ted, bat·ting, bats.** To wink or flutter: *bat one's eyelashes.* [Probably a variant of BATE².]

A word or word element in an etymology printed in small capitals is an entry in the Dictionary and should be referred to for more etymological information. Linguistic forms that are not Modern English words appear in italics, and glosses and language names appear in roman type.

The transliterations of Greek, Russian, Arabic, and Hebrew are as shown in the table at **alphabet.** Old English thorn (þ) and edh (ð) are both given as *th,* whereas Old Norse thorn is spelled as *th* and the phonemically distinct edh as *dh.* In Latin all long vowels are marked with macrons. Mandarin Chinese forms are given in the Pinyin system. The transcription of African and Native American languages occasionally requires the use of symbols – usually drawn from the International Phonetic Alphabet – whose values will be apparent to specialists but are not discussed here.

UNDEFINED FORMS

At the end of many entries additional boldface words appear without definitions – words either formed from the entry words by the addition of suffixes or otherwise closely and clearly related to the entry words. These *run-on entries* are related in basic meaning to the entry word but have different grammatical functions, as indicated by their part-of-speech labels. Multisyllabic run-ons are divided into syllables and show primary and secondary stresses as needed. Pronunciations are included as required:

> **ex·cuse** (ĭk-skyōōz′) *tr.v.* . . . [Middle English *excusen,* from Old French *excuser,* from Latin *excūsāre* : *ex-,* ex- + *causa,* accusation; see CAUSE.] **—ex·cus′a·ble** *adj.* **—ex·cus′a·ble·ness** *n.* **—ex·cus′a·bly** *adv.* **—ex·cus′er** *n.*

Undefined run-ons are usually entered in alphabetical order. However, when different run-ons have the same grammatical function and the same meaning, they are separated by a comma and share a single part-of-speech label. For instance, at the entry *lampoon* the variants *lampooner* and *lampoonist* have the same meaning and function and are therefore run on together:

> **lam·poon** (lăm-pōōn′) *n.* . . . [French *lampon,* perhaps from *lampons,* let us drink (from a common refrain in drinking songs), first person pl. imperative of *lamper,* to gulp down, of Germanic origin.] **—lam·poon′er, lam·poon′ist** *n.* **—lam·poon′er·y** *n.*

In other instances, undefined run-ons have the same grammatical function but different meanings. These appear separately, as is the case with *excusableness* and *excuser* at the entry *excuse.*

In some cases an entry word appears unchanged as a run-on at the end of that entry with a different part-of-speech label. This indicates that the word is related in basic meaning to the entry word but has a different grammatical function.

SYNONYM PARAGRAPHS

Synonyms of special interest are listed after the entry for the central word in the group. Synonym paragraphs are introduced by the heading ***SYNONYMS.*** There are two kinds of synonym paragraphs. The first consists of a group of undiscriminated, alphabetically ordered words sharing a single, irreducible meaning. Antonyms, if applicable, appear at the end of the paragraph, as seen at the entry for the adjective *plentiful*:

> ***SYNONYMS:*** *plentiful, abundant, ample, copious, plenteous.* The central meaning shared by these adjectives is "being fully as much as one needs or desires": *a plentiful supply of stationery; her abundant talent; ample space; copious provisions; a plenteous crop of wheat.*
> ***ANTONYM:*** *scant.*

The second kind, exemplified at the adjective entry *real¹*, consists of fully discriminated synonyms ordered in a way that reflects their interrelationship. A brief sentence explaining the initial point of comparison of the words is given, followed by explanations of connotations and varying shades of meaning:

> ***SYNONYMS:*** *real, actual, true, existent.* These adjectives are compared as they mean not imaginary but having verifiable existence. *Real* implies that something is genuine or authentic or that what it seems or purports to be tallies with fact: *Don't lose the bracelet; it's made of real gold. My mother showed real sympathy for my predicament. "The general, in a well-feigned or real ecstasy, embraced him"* (William Hickling Prescott). *Actual* means existing and not merely potential or possible: *"rocks, trees . . . the* actual *world"* (Henry David Thoreau); *"what the actual things were which produced the emotion that you experienced"* (Ernest Hemingway). *True* implies that something is consistent with fact, reality, or the actual state of things: *"It is undesirable to believe a proposition when there is no ground whatever for supposing it true"* (Bertrand Russell). *Existent* applies to what has life or being: *Much of the beluga caviar existent in the world is found in the Soviet Union and Iran.* See also Synonyms at **authentic.**

In both kinds of paragraphs the synonyms are set in lightface italic type. Illustrative examples, many of them quoted, exemplify the use of the synonyms in context.

SYNONYM CROSS-REFERENCES. Every synonym in a synonym paragraph is itself cross-referenced to that synonym paragraph. For instance, the word *true* is discussed in the synonym paragraph at the entry *real*. Therefore, definition 1a of the entry *true* – the definition directly tied in with the synonym paragraph at *real* – contains a cross-reference to the synonym paragraph at *real*:

> **true** (tro͞o) *adj.* **tru·er, tru·est. 1.a.** Consistent with fact or reality; not false or erroneous. See Synonyms at **real[1]**.

Sometimes a word is discussed in more than one synonym paragraph. Cross-references are given to all the synonym paragraphs that include this word. An example is *unaffected*, which appears in synonym paragraphs at both *naive* and *sincere*:

> **un·af·fect·ed** (ŭn′ə-fĕk′tĭd) *adj.* **1.** Not changed, modified, or affected. **2.** Marked by lack of affectation; genuine. See Synonyms at **naive, sincere.**

At times the entry word central to one synonym group is a synonym in a group of synonyms at another entry. Such is the case with the entry *real*. At the end of the synonym paragraph at *real*, a cross-reference directs you to another synonym paragraph at the entry *authentic*.

USAGE NOTES

Usage Notes following many entries present important information and guidance on matters of grammar, diction, pronunciation, and registers and nuances of usage. For detailed discussion of usage and our Usage Panel, see Geoffrey Nunberg's essay on pages xxvi–xxx.

Some Notes, such as the one at *world-class*, contain opinions of the Usage Panel:

> **world-class** (wûrld′klăs′) *adj.* **1.** Ranking among the foremost in the world; of an international standard of excellence; of the highest order: *a world-class figure skater.* **2.** *Usage Problem.* Great, as in importance, concern, or notoriety.
>
> ***USAGE NOTE:*** The adjective *world-class* became current as a result of its original use to describe athletes capable of performing at an international level of competition, as in *A ten-second time would put him in the first rank of world-class sprinters.* In recent years it has been extended to mean "of an international standard of excellence" and has been applied to a wide variety of categories. When used of things that naturally admit such comparison, the extended use of the word is generally acceptable to the Usage Panel. In the most recent survey 65 percent accepted the description *world-class restaurant,* and 53 percent accepted *world-class sports car.* But the expression is not generally accepted as a vague way of emphasizing magnitude or degree. The sentence *Johann Sebastian Bach's 300th birthday will rank as a world-class anniversary* was acceptable to only 7 percent, and only 4 percent accepted a description of AIDS as *a world-class tragedy.*

An example of a Usage Note without an opinion of the Usage Panel is found at the entry *criterion*:

> ***USAGE NOTE:*** Like the analogous etymological plurals *agenda* and *data, criteria* is widely used as a singular form. Unlike them, however, it is not yet acceptable in that use.

USAGE NOTE CROSS-REFERENCES. A Note containing information related to the content of another Note ends with a cross-reference:

> **well[2]** (wĕl) *adv.* **bet·ter** (bĕt′ər), **best** (bĕst).
>
> ***USAGE NOTE:*** Used as an adjective applied to people, *well* usually refers to a state of health, whereas *good* has a much wider range of senses. It has always been a first principle of grammatical criticism that there should be no difference without a distinction, and perhaps for this reason, some critics have insisted that the expression *feel good* cannot be used in reference to health. It is true that there is a distinction between *feel well* and *feel good,* but both can be applied to a state of health. Thus a patient suffering from a chronic disease might appropriately say to a doctor *I feel good today,* which implies a relative lack of physical discomfort. By contrast, *I feel well today* would be appropriate if the patient believes that the ailment has disappeared. See Usage Note at **good.**

The Note at *well[2]* concludes with a cross-reference to related information in the Note at the entry *good.* Similarly, the Note at *good* concludes with a cross-reference to the Note at *well[2]*:

> **good** (go͝od). *Abbr.* **gd., G, G.** *adj.* **bet·ter** (bĕt′ər), **best** (bĕst).
>
> ***USAGE NOTE:*** *Good* is properly used as an adjective with linking verbs such as *be, seem,* or *appear*: *The future looks good. The soup tastes good.* It should not be used as an adverb with other verbs: *The car runs well* (not *good*). Thus, *The dress fits well and looks good.* See Usage Note at **well[2].**

If an entry without a Note is discussed in a Note elsewhere, that entry contains a cross-reference to the Note where a full discussion is to be found. For example, the entry *–ess* contains a Usage Note. The content of this Note has direct bearing on the use of the word *stewardess.* Consequently, the entry *stewardess* has a cross-reference directing the reader to the Note at *–ess*:

> **stew·ard·ess** (sto͞o′ər-dĭs, styo͞o′-) *n.* A woman flight attendant. See Usage Note at **–ess.**

REGIONAL NOTES

This Dictionary contains hundreds of words and meanings whose occurrence is restricted to certain areas of the United States. The symbol ♦ signals that an entry word, a definition, or another word under discussion in an entry involves a matter of dialect. Many entries contain Regional Notes explaining in detail a point of dialect. For example, the word *dragonfly* is widespread in American English, but dialect terms for the insect abound. These dialect terms, listed at the entry for *dragonfly*, are discussed in the Regional Note at the end of the entry:

> ♦ **drag·on·fly** (drăg′ən-flī′) *n., pl.* **-flies.** Any of various large insects of the order Odonata or suborder Anisoptera, having a long slender body and two pairs of narrow, net-veined wings that are usually held outstretched while the insect is at rest. Also called ♦*darning needle,* ♦*devil's darning needle,* ♦*ear sewer,* ♦*mosquito hawk,* ♦*skeeter hawk,* ♦*snake doctor,* ♦*snake feeder,* ♦*spindle.*
>
> ♦ ***REGIONAL NOTE:*** Regional terms for the dragonfly are numerous, providing good evidence for dialect boundaries in the United States. The greatest variety of terms is to be found in the South, where the most widespread term is *snake doctor* (a name based on a folk belief that dragonflies take care of snakes). The Midland equivalent is *snake feeder.* Speakers from the Lower South, on the other hand, are more likely to refer to the same insect as a *mosquito hawk* or, in the South Atlantic states, a *skeeter hawk.* The imagery outside the South alludes more to the insect's shape than to its behavior or diet: Upper Northern speakers call it a *darning needle* or a *devil's darning needle*; those in Coastal New Jersey, a *spindle*; and Northern Californians, an *ear sewer.*

REGIONAL NOTE CROSS-REFERENCES. Regional Notes are fully cross-referenced. In the case of *snake doctor*, a term appropriately labeled to reflect its use in the South, the entry contains two cross-references – a "See" cross-reference directing the reader to the main entry at *dragonfly*, where the full definition and a list of synonymous terms are found, and a "Regional Note" cross-reference directing the reader to the Regional Note at *dragonfly* for full discussion of the distribution of these terms:

> **snake doctor** *n.* **1.** *Chiefly Southern U.S.* See **dragonfly.** See Regional Note at **dragonfly. 2.** See **hellgrammite.**

WORD HISTORIES

In addition to etymologies, which necessarily contain information in a compressed form, this Dictionary provides word history paragraphs at entries whose etymologies are of particular interest. In these paragraphs the bare facts of the etymology are expanded to give a fuller understanding of how important linguistic processes operate, how words move from one language to another, and how the history of an individual word can be related to historical and cultural developments. For example, the history of the word *alligator* involves borrowing from Spanish into English, as its etymology reveals, but the word history also describes the role of taboo deformation in the history of the word *alligator* and in that of *crocodile* as well. Usually the word history also contains the date at which the word was first recorded in English:

al·li·ga·tor (ăl′ĭ-gā′tər) *n.* **1.** Either of two large reptiles, *Alligator mississipiensis* of the southeast United States or *A. sinensis* of China, having sharp teeth and powerful jaws. They differ from crocodiles in having a broader, shorter snout. **2.** Leather made from the hide of one of these reptiles. **3.** A tool or fastener having strong, adjustable, often toothed jaws. —*attributive.* Often used to modify another noun: *an alligator pond; an alligator handbag.* [Alteration of Spanish *el lagarto,* the lizard : *el,* the (from Latin *ille,* that; see **al-**[1] in Appendix) + *lagarto,* lizard (from Latin *lacertus*).]

WORD HISTORY: In *The Travailes of an Englishman,* published in 1568, Job Hortop says that "in this river we killed a monstrous Lagarto or Crocodile." This killing gives rise to the first recorded instance of *alligator* in English, obviously in a different form from the one familiar to modern speakers. *Alligator,* which comes to us from Spanish *el lagarto,* "the lizard," was modified in pronunciation and form in several ways before taking on the form *alligator.* Such changes, referred to by linguists as taboo deformation, are not uncommon in a name for something that is feared and include, for example, the change in sequence of the *r* and *t* that occurred between *el lagarto* and *alligator.* An interesting parallel case is *crocodile,* which appears in Spanish, for example, as *cocodrilo,* with a similar difference in the sequence of the *r.* The earliest recorded form of *alligator* that is similar to ours appears in Shakespeare's *Romeo and Juliet* (First Folio, 1623): "In his needie shop a tortoyrs hung,/An Allegater stuft."

Yet another example showing how the facts of etymology are expanded in a word history paragraph to give the reader a better understanding of the historical and social forces shaping word and sense development is found at the entry *holocaust,* where meaning, usage, and history are clearly delineated by the definitions, the Usage Note, and the word history paragraph:

hol·o·caust (hŏl′ə-kôst′, hō′lə-) *n.* **1.** Great or total destruction, especially by fire. **2. a.** Widespread destruction. **b.** A great disaster. **3. a. Holocaust.** The genocide of European Jews and others by the Nazis during World War II: *"Israel emerged from the Holocaust and is defined in relation to that catastrophe"* (Emanuel Litvinoff). **b.** A massive slaughter: *"an important document in the so-far sketchy annals of the Cambodian holocaust"* (Rod Nordland). **4.** A sacrificial offering that is consumed entirely by flames. [Middle English, burnt offering, from Old French *holocauste,* from Latin *holocaustum,* from Greek *holokauston,* from neuter of *holokaustos,* burnt whole : *holo-,* holo- + *kaustos,* burnt (from *kaiein,* to burn).] **—hol′o·caus′tal, hol′o·caus′tic** *adj.*

USAGE NOTE: When referring to the massive destruction of human beings by other human beings, *holocaust* has a secure place in the language. Fully 99 percent of the Usage Panel accepts the use of *holocaust* in the phrase *nuclear holocaust.* Sixty percent accepts the sentence *As many as two million people may have died in the holocaust that followed the Khmer Rouge takeover in Cambodia.* But because of its associations with genocide, extended applications of *holocaust* may not always be received with equanimity. When the word is used to refer to death brought about by natural causes, the percentage of the Panel's acceptance drops sharply. Only 31 percent of the Panel accepts the sentence *In East Africa five years of drought have brought about a holocaust in which millions have died.* Just 11 percent approved the use of *holocaust* to summarize the effects of the AIDS epidemic. This suggests that other figurative usages such as *the huge losses in the Savings and Loan holocaust* may be viewed as overblown or in poor taste.

WORD HISTORY: Totality of destruction has been central to the meaning of *holocaust* since it first appeared in Middle English in the 14th century and referred to the biblical sacrifice in which a male animal was wholly burnt on the altar in worship of God. *Holocaust* comes from Greek *holokauston* ("that which is completely burnt"), which was a translation of Hebrew *ôlâ* (literally "that which goes up," that is, in smoke). In this sense of "burnt sacrifice," *holocaust* is still used in some versions of the Bible. In the 17th century the meaning of *holocaust* broadened to "something totally consumed by fire," and the word eventually was applied to fires of extreme destructiveness. In the 20th century *holocaust* has taken on a variety of figurative meanings, summarizing the effects of war, rioting, storms, epidemic diseases, and even economic failures. Most of these usages arose after World War II, but it is unclear whether they permitted or resulted from the use of *holocaust* in reference to the mass murder of European Jews and others by the Nazis. This application of the word occurred as early as 1942, but the phrase *the Holocaust* did not become established until the late 1950's. Here it parallels and may have been influenced by another Hebrew word, *sho'ah* ("catastrophe"). In the Bible *sho'ah* has a range of meanings including "personal ruin or devastation" and "a wasteland or desert." *Sho'ah* was first used to refer to the Nazi slaughter of Jews in 1939, but its phrase *ha-sho'ah* ("the catastrophe") only became established after World War II. *Holocaust* has also been used to translate *hurban* ("destruction"), another Hebrew word used to summarize the genocide of Jews by the Nazis. This sense of *holocaust* has since broadened to include the mass slaughter of other peoples, but when capitalized it refers specifically to the destruction of Jews and other Europeans by the Nazis and may also encompass the Nazi persecution of Jews that preceded the outbreak of the war.

PRONUNCIATION KEY

A list of the pronunciation symbols used in this Dictionary is given below in the column headed **AHD.** The column headed **EXAMPLES** contains words chosen to illustrate how the **AHD** symbols are pronounced. The letters that correspond in sound to the **AHD** symbols are shown in boldface. The third column, headed **IPA** (International Phonetic Alphabet), gives the equivalent transcription symbols most often used by scholars. Although similar, the **AHD** and **IPA** symbols are not precisely the same because they were conceived for different purposes. Additional information on pronunciation is given in the "Guide to the Dictionary" in the section headed "Pronunciation."

EXAMPLES	**AHD**	**IPA**
p**a**t	ă	æ
p**ay**	ā	e
c**ar**e	âr	ɛr, er
f**a**ther	ä	ɑ:, ɑ
bi**b**	b	b
chur**ch**	ch	tʃ
dee**d**, mill**ed**	d	d
p**e**t	ĕ	ɛ
b**ee**	ē	i
fi**f**e, **ph**ase, rou**gh**	f	f
ga**g**	g	g
hat	h	h
which	hw	hw (also ʍ)
p**i**t	ĭ	ɪ
p**ie**, b**y**	ī	aɪ
p**ier**	îr	ɪr, ir
ju**dg**e	j	dʒ
ki**ck**, **c**at, pi**que**	k	k
lid, need**le***	l (nēd′l)	l, l̩ ['nidl̩]
mu**m**	m	m
no, sudd**en***	n (sŭd′n)	n, n̩ ['sʌdn̩]
thi**ng**	ng	ŋ
p**o**t	ŏ	ɑ
t**oe**	ō	o
c**augh**t, p**aw**, f**o**r, h**o**rrid, h**oa**rse**	ô	ɔ
n**oi**se	oi	ɔɪ
t**oo**k	o͝o	ʊ
b**oo**t	o͞o	u
out	ou	aʊ
po**p**	p	p
roa**r**	r	ɹ
sau**c**e	s	s
ship, di**sh**	sh	ʃ
tigh**t**, stopp**ed**	t	t
thin	th	θ
this	*th*	ð
c**u**t	ŭ	ʌ
urge, t**er**m, f**ir**m, w**or**d, h**ear**d	ûr	ɝ, ɜr
val**v**e	v	v
with	w	w
yes	y	j
zebra, **x**ylem	z	z
vi**s**ion, plea**s**ure, gara**g**e	zh	ʒ
about, it**e**m, ed**i**ble, gall**o**p, circ**u**s	ə	ə
butt**er**	ər	ɚ

FOREIGN	**AHD**	**IPA**
French f**eu**, *German* sch**ö**n	œ	œ
French t**u**, *German* **ü**ber	ü	y
German i**ch**, *Scottish* lo**ch**	KH	ç, x
French bo**n*****	N	õ, æ̃, ã, œ̃

*In English the consonants *l* and *n* often constitute complete syllables by themselves.

Regional pronunciations of *–or–* vary. In pairs such as **for, four; horse, hoarse; and **morning, mourning,** the vowel varies between (ô) and (ō). In this Dictionary these vowels are represented as follows: **for** (fôr), **four** (fôr, fōr); **horse** (hôrs), **hoarse** (hôrs, hōrs); and **morning** (môr′ning), **mourning** (môr′ning, mōr′-). Other words for which both forms are shown include **more, glory,** and **borne.** A similar variant occurs in words such as **coral, forest,** and **horrid,** where the pronunciation of *o* before *r* varies between (ô) and (ŏ). In these words the (ôr) pronunciation is given first: **forest** (fôr′ist, fŏr′-).

***The IPA symbols show nasality with a diacritic mark over the vowel, whereas the Dictionary uses N to reflect that the preceding vowel is nasalized.

a[1] or **A** (ā) *n., pl.* **a's** or **A's. 1.** The first letter of the modern English alphabet. **2.** Any of the speech sounds represented by the letter *a*. **3.** The first in a series. **4.** The best or highest in quality or rank: *grade A milk*. **5.** Something shaped like the letter A. **6.** *Music.* **a.** The sixth tone in the scale of C major or the first tone in the relative minor scale. **b.** A key or scale in which A is the tonic. **c.** A written or printed note representing this tone. **d.** A string, key, or pipe tuned to the pitch of this tone. **7. A.** One of four types of blood in the ABO system.

a[2] (ə; ā *when stressed*) *indef.art.* **1.** Used before nouns and noun phrases that denote a single but unspecified person or thing: *a region; a person*. **2.** Used before terms, such as *few* or *many*, that denote number, amount, quantity, or degree: *only a few of the voters; a bit more rest; a little excited*. **3. a.** Used before a proper name to denote a type or a member of a class: *the wisdom of a Socrates*. **b.** Used before a mass noun to indicate a single type or example: *a dry wine*. **4.** The same: *birds of a feather*. **5.** Any: *not a drop to drink*. [Middle English, variant of *an*, an. See AN[1].]

USAGE NOTE: In modern written English, the form *a* is used before a word beginning with a consonant sound, however it may be spelled (*a frog, a university, a euphemism*). The form *an* is used before a word beginning with a vowel sound (*an orange, an hour*). At one time, *an* was an acceptable alternative before words beginning with a consonant sound but spelled with a vowel (*an one, an united appeal*), but this usage is now entirely obsolete. • *An* was also once a common variant before words beginning with *h* in which the first syllable was unstressed; thus 18th-century authors wrote either *a historical* or *an historical* but *a history*, not *an history*. This usage had a phonetic justification inasmuch as the initial *h* in words such as *historical* and *heroic* was often dropped, a practice that was largely abandoned by the late 19th century in educated speech. By 1926 H.W. Fowler could regard the continued use of *an* before such words as pedantic. Nowadays it survives primarily before the word *historical;* one rarely encounters a reference to *an hysterectomy* or *an hereditary trait*. The use of a phrase like *an historic opportunity* is a harmless adornment in formal writing.

a[3] (ə) *prep.* In every; to each; per: *once a month; one dollar a pound*. [Middle English, from Old English *an*, in. See ON.]

a[4] (ə) *aux.v. Informal.* Have: *He'd a come if he could*. [Middle English, alteration of *haven*, to have. See HAVE.]

a[5] *abbr.* **1.** Also **a.** Absent. **2.** *Physics.* Acceleration. **3.** Also **a.** Are (measurement).

A or **A.** *abbr.* **1.** Also **a.** or **A.** Acre. **2.** Ammeter. **3.** Ampere. **4.** Or **Å.** Angstrom. **5.** Also **a.** or **A.** Area.

a. *abbr.* **1.** About. **2.** Acreage. **3.** Acting. **4.** Adjective. **5.** Afternoon. **6.** Also **A.** Amateur. **7.** *Latin.* Anno (in the year). **8.** *Latin.* Annus (year). **9.** Anode. **10.** Anonymous. **11.** Also **A.** Answer. **12.** *Latin.* Ante (before). **13.** Anterior.

A. *abbr.* **1.** Academician; academy. **2.** *Music.* Alto. **3.** America; American.

a–[1] or **an–** *pref.* Without; not: *amoral*. [Greek. See **ne** in Appendix.]

a–[2] *pref.* **1.** On; in: *abed*. **2.** In the act of: *aborning*. **3.** In the direction of: *astern*. **4.** In a specified state or condition: *abuzz*. [Middle English, from Old English, from *an*, on. See ON.]

A1C *abbr.* Airman first class.

AA *abbr.* **1.** Alcoholics Anonymous. **2.** Antiaircraft.

A.A. *abbr.* Associate in Arts.

AAA *abbr.* **1.** Agricultural Adjustment Administration. **2.** American Automobile Association. **3.** Antiaircraft artillery.

AAAL *abbr.* American Academy of Arts and Letters.

AAAS *abbr.* American Association for the Advancement of Science.

Aa·chen (ä′kən, ä′KHən) also **Aix-la-Cha·pelle** (āks′lä-shə-pĕl′, ĕks′-). A city of western Germany near the Belgian and Dutch borders. Charlemagne may have been born here in 742; he later made the city his northern capital. Population, 239,801.

AAF *abbr.* Army Air Forces.

aah (ä) *interj.* Used to express pleasure, satisfaction, surprise, or great joy. **—aah** *intr.v.* **aahed, aah·ing, aahs.** To exclaim in pleasure, satisfaction, surprise, or great joy: *The crowd was oohing and aahing beside the panda's enclosure.* **—aah** *n.*

Aa·land Islands (ä′lənd, ō′länd′). See **Ahvenanmaa.**

Aal·borg (ôl′bôrg′). See **Ålborg.**

Aalst (älst) also **A·lost** (ä-lôst′). A city of west-central Belgium west-northwest of Brussels. It was the capital of Austrian Flanders in the 18th century. Population, 78,068.

Aal·to (äl′tô), **Alvar.** 1898–1976. Finnish architect and furniture designer noted for his use of contrasting materials.

A and R *abbr.* Artists and repertory.

AAPSS *abbr.* American Academy of Political and Social Sciences.

Aar (är). See **Aare.**

AAR *abbr.* Against all risks.

aard·vark (ärd′värk′) *n.* A burrowing mammal *(Orycteropus afer)* of southern Africa, having a stocky, hairy body, large ears, a long tubular snout, and powerful digging claws. [Obsolete Afrikaans : *aarde*, earth (from Middle Dutch *aerde;* see **er-**[2] in Appendix) + *vark*, pig (from Middle Dutch *varken;* see **porko-** in Appendix).]

aard·wolf (ärd′wo͝olf′) *n.* A mammal *(Proteles cristatus)* native to southern and eastern Africa that resembles the hyena, has gray fur with black stripes, and feeds mainly on termites and insect larvae. [Afrikaans : *aarde*, earth (from Middle Dutch *aerde;* see **er-**[2] in Appendix) + *wolf*, wolf (from Middle Dutch; see **wlk^{w}o-** in Appendix).]

Aa·re (är′ə) or **Aar** (är). A river of central and northern Switzerland rising in the Bernese Alps and flowing about 295 km (183 mi) to join the Rhine River at the Swiss–German border.

Aar·hus (ôr′ho͞os′). See **Århus.**

Aar·on (âr′ən, ăr′-). In the Old Testament, the elder brother of Moses who helped lead the Hebrews out of Egypt.

Aaron, Henry Louis. Known as "Hank." Born 1934. American baseball player who surpassed (1974) Babe Ruth's lifetime record of 714 home runs and retired (1976) with a total of 755 home runs.

Aa·ron·ic (â-rŏn′ĭk, ă-rŏn′-) also **Aa·ron·i·cal** (-ĭ-kəl) *adj.* **1.** Of, having to do with, or characteristic of Aaron. **2.** *Mormon Church.* Of or having to do with the lower order of priests.

Aar·on's beard (âr′ənz, ăr′-) *n.* See **rose of Sharon** (sense 2).

Aaron's rod *n. Architecture.* A rod-shaped molding decorated with a design of leaves, scrolls, or a twined serpent.

A.A.S. *abbr.* Associate in Applied Sciences.

AAU *abbr.* Amateur Athletic Union.

AAUP *abbr.* American Association of University Professors.

AAUW *abbr.* American Association of University Women.

ab (ăb) *n. Slang.* An abscess caused by injecting an illegal drug, usually heroin.

Ab (äb, äv, ôv) *n.* Variant of **Av.**

AB[1] (ā′bē′) *n.* One of four types of blood in the ABO system.

AB[2] *abbr.* **1.** Airman basic. **2.** Alberta.

ab. *abbr.* About.

A.B. *abbr.* **1.** Also **a.b.** Able-bodied seaman. **2.** *Latin.* Artium Baccalaureus (Bachelor of Arts).

ab–[1] *pref.* Away from: *aboral*. [Latin. See **apo-** in Appendix.]

ab–[2] *pref.* Used to indicate an electromagnetic unit in the centimeter-gram-second system: *abcoulomb*. [From ABSOLUTE.]

a·ba (ə-bä′, ä′bə) *n.* **1.** A fabric woven of the hair of camels or goats. **2.** A loose-fitting sleeveless garment made of this fabric, traditionally worn by Arabs. [Arabic *'abā'*.]

A·ba (ä′bə). A city of southeast Nigeria northeast of Port Harcourt. It is an important market and transportation center. Population, 210,700.

ABA *abbr.* **1.** Abscisic acid. **2.** American Bankers Association. **3.** Also **A.B.A.** American Bar Association. **4.** American Booksellers Association.

ab·a·ca also **ab·a·cá** (ăb′ə-kä′) *n.* **1.** A bananalike plant

Phoenician

The first letter of the alphabet originally represented the sound of the Semitic glottal stop at the beginning of the word *'aleph*, "ox."

Early Greek

Because their language had no glottal stop, the Greeks reassigned the letter to the vowel *a*.

Roman

The classical Roman capital form is still used today.

aardwolf

Proteles cristatus

(Musa textilis) native to the Philippines and having broad leaves with long stalks. **2.** The fibers obtained from the stalks of this plant, used to make cordage, fabric, and paper. In this sense, also called *manila, Manila hemp.* [Spanish *abacá,* from Tagalog *abaká.*]

ab•a•ci (ăb′ə-sī′, ə-băk′ī′) *n.* A plural of **abacus.**

♦ **a•back** (ə-băk′) *adv.* **1.** By surprise: *He was taken aback by her caustic remarks.* **2.** *New England & Southern U.S.* Behind: *aback of the house.* **3.** *Upper Southern U.S.* Ago: *several years aback.* **4.** *Nautical.* In such a way that the wind pushes against the forward side of a sail or sails. **5.** *Archaic.* Back; backward. **—aback** *adj. New England.* Being at a standstill; unable to move: *"You run your business that way and first thing you know you're all aback"* (Dialect Notes).

A•ba•co and Cays (ăb′ə-kō′; kēz, kāz). An island group, the northernmost of the Bahamas, in the Atlantic Ocean east of southern Florida.

ab•a•cus (ăb′ə-kəs, ə-băk′əs) *n., pl.* **ab•a•cus•es** or **ab•a•ci** (ăb′ə-sī′, ə-băk′ī′). **1.** A manual computing device consisting of a frame holding parallel rods strung with movable counters. **2.** *Architecture.* A slab on the top of the capital of a column. [Middle English, from Latin, from Greek *abax, abak-,* counting board, probably from Hebrew *'ābāq,* dust.]

abacus

WORD HISTORY: The adjective *dusty,* with its connotations of disuse and age, might seem to be an appropriate word to describe the abacus, since this counting device was used for solving arithmetical problems in the days before the advent of calculators and computers. Originally the abacus was, in fact, dusty. The source of our word *abacus,* the Greek word *abax,* probably comes from Hebrew *'ābāq,* "dust," although the details of transmission are obscure. In postbiblical usage *'ābāq* meant "sand used as a writing surface." The Greek word *abax* has as one of its senses "a board sprinkled with sand or dust for drawing geometric diagrams." This board is a relative of the abacus with movable counters strung on rods that is familiar to us. The first use of the word *abacus,* recorded in Middle English in a work written before 1387, refers to a sand-board abacus, in this case, one used by the Arabs. The difference in form between the Middle English word *abacus* and its Greek source *abax* is explained by the fact that Middle English actually borrowed Latin *abacus,* which came from the Greek genitive form *(abakos)* of *abax.*

Ab•a•dan (ä′bə-dän′, ăb′ə-dăn′). A city of southwest Iran on **Abadan Island** in the delta of the Shatt al Arab at the head of the Persian Gulf. The city's oil installations were heavily damaged in 1980 during the war with Iraq. Population, 296,081.

a•baft (ə-băft′) *Nautical. adv.* Toward the stern. **—abaft** *prep.* Toward the stern from. [Middle English *on baft* : *on,* at; see ON + *baft,* to the rear (from Old English *beæftan,* behind : *be,* by, at; see **ambhi** in Appendix + *æftan,* behind; see **apo-** in Appendix).]

A•ba•kan (ä′bə-kän′). A city of south-central Russia east-southeast of Novosibirsk. It is a commercial and industrial center on the Yenisei River and the Siberian Railroad. Population, 147,000.

ab•a•lo•ne (ăb′ə-lō′nē, ăb′ə-lō′-) *n.* Any of various large, edible marine gastropods of the genus *Haliotis,* having an ear-shaped shell with a row of holes along the outer edge. The colorful, pearly interior of the shell is often used for making ornaments. Also called *ear shell.* [American Spanish *abulón.*]

ab•am•pere (ăb-ăm′pîr′) *n.* The centimeter-gram-second electromagnetic unit of current equal to ten amperes.

a•ban•don (ə-băn′dən) *tr.v.* **-doned, -don•ing, -dons. 1.** To withdraw one's support or help from, especially in spite of duty, allegiance, or responsibility; desert: *abandon a friend in trouble.* **2.** To give up by leaving or ceasing to operate or inhabit, especially as a result of danger or other impending threat: *abandoned the ship.* **3.** To surrender one's claim to, right to, or interest in; give up entirely. See Synonyms at **relinquish. 4.** To cease trying to continue; desist from: *abandoned the search for the missing hiker.* **5.** To yield (oneself) completely, as to emotion. **—abandon** *n.* **1.** Unbounded enthusiasm; exuberance. **2.** A complete surrender of inhibitions. [Middle English *abandounen,* from Old French *abandoner,* from *a bandon* : *a,* at (from Latin *ad;* see AD–) + *bandon,* control; see **bhā-²** in Appendix.] **—a•ban′don•ment** *n.*

a•ban•doned (ə-băn′dənd) *adj.* **1.** Deserted; forsaken. **2.** Exuberantly enthusiastic. **3.** Recklessly unrestrained.

ab•ap•i•cal (ăb-ăp′ĭ-kəl, -ā′pĭ-) *adj.* Being opposite to or directed away from the apex.

a•base (ə-bās′) *tr.v.* **a•based, a•bas•ing, a•bas•es.** To lower in rank, prestige, or esteem. See Synonyms at **degrade.** [Middle English *abassen,* from Old French *abaissier* : Latin *ad-,* ad– + Vulgar Latin **bassiāre* (from Medieval Latin *bassus,* low).] **—a•base′ment** *n.*

a•bash (ə-băsh′) *tr.v.* **a•bashed, a•bash•ing, a•bash•es.** To make ashamed or uneasy; disconcert. See Synonyms at **embarrass.** [Middle English *abaishen,* to lose one's composure, from Old French *esbahir, esbahiss-* : *es-,* intensive pref. (from Latin *ex-;* see EX–) + *baer,* to gape; see BAY².] **—a•bash′ment** *n.*

a•ba•sia (ə-bā′zhə) *n.* Impaired muscular coordination in walking. [A–¹ + Greek *basis,* step; see **gʷā-** in Appendix + –IA¹.]

a•bate (ə-bāt′) *v.* **a•bat•ed, a•bat•ing, a•bates.** —*tr.* **1.** To reduce in amount, degree, or intensity; lessen. See Synonyms at **decrease. 2.** To deduct from an amount; subtract. **3.** *Law.* **a.** To put an end to. **b.** To make void. —*intr.* **1.** To fall off in degree or intensity; subside. **2.** *Law.* To become void. [Middle English *abaten,* from Old French *abattre,* to beat down : *a-,* to (from Latin *ad-;* see AD–) + *batre,* to beat; see BATTER¹.]

a•bate•ment (ə-bāt′mənt) *n.* **1.** Diminution in degree or intensity; moderation. **2.** The amount lowered; a reduction. **3.** *Law.* The act of eliminating or annulling.

ab•at•toir (ăb′ə-twär′) *n.* **1.** A slaughterhouse. **2.** Something likened to a slaughterhouse: *"The hand of God and mankind's self-inflicted blows seem equally heavy. . . . giving a strong cumulative impression of the world as an abattoir"* (Manchester Guardian Weekly). [French, from *abattre,* to strike down, from Old French. See ABATE.]

ab•ax•i•al (ăb-ăk′sē-əl) *adj. Biology.* Located away from or on the opposite side of the axis, as of an organ or organism.

abb. *abbr.* **1.** Abbess. **2.** Abbey. **3.** Abbot.

Ab•ba (ăb′ə, ä′bə) *n.* **1.** *Bible.* In the New Testament, God. **2. abba.** Used as a title of honor for bishops and patriarchs in some Christian churches of Egypt, Syria, and Ethiopia. [Middle English, from Late Latin *abbā,* from Greek *abba.* See ABBOT.]

ab•ba•cy (ăb′ə-sē) *n., pl.* **-cies.** The office, term, or jurisdiction of an abbot. [Middle English *abbatie,* from Late Latin *abbātia,* from *abbās, abbāt-,* abbot. See ABBOT.]

Ab•bas•side also **Ab•bas•sid** (ăb′ə-sīd′, ə-băs′ĭd′). An Arabic dynasty (750–1258) that expanded the Moslem empire. It was named for al-Abbas (566?–652), paternal uncle of the prophet Mohammed.

ab•ba•tial (ə-bā′shəl) *adj.* Of or having to do with an abbey, abbot, or abbess. [Middle English *abbacyal,* from Late Latin *abbātiālis,* from *abbās, abbāt-,* abbot. See ABBOT.]

ab•bé (ăb′ā′, ă-bā′) *n. Roman Catholic Church.* **1.** Used as a title for the Superior of a monastery in a French-speaking area. **2.** Used as a title for a cleric in major or minor orders in a French-speaking area. [French, from Old French *abbe,* from Late Latin *abbātem,* accusative of *abbās,* abbot. See ABBOT.]

ab•bess (ăb′ĭs) *n. Abbr.* **abb. 1.** The superior of a convent. **2.** Used as a title for such a person. [Middle English *abesse,* from Old French, from Late Latin *abbātissa,* from *abbās, abbāt-,* abbot. See ABBOT.]

Ab•be•vil•li•an (ăb′ə-vĭl′ē-ən) *adj.* Of or relating to the earliest Paleolithic archaeological sites in Europe, characterized by bifacial stone hand axes. [After *Abbeville,* a city of northern France.]

ab•bey (ăb′ē) *n., pl.* **-beys.** *Abbr.* **abb. 1.** A monastery supervised by an abbot. **2.** A convent supervised by an abbess. **3.** A church that is or once was part of a monastery or convent. [Middle English, from Old French *abaie,* from Late Latin *abbātia.* See ABBACY.]

Ab•bey (ăb′ē), **Edwin Austin.** 1852–1911. American artist who illustrated editions of Herrick and Shakespeare and painted the mural *Quest of the Holy Grail* (1890–1902).

ab•bot (ăb′ət) *n. Abbr.* **abb. 1.** The superior of a monastery. **2.** Used as a title for such a person. [Middle English *abbod,* from Old English, from Late Latin *abbās, abbāt-,* from Greek *abbā,* from Aramaic *abbā,* father.]

Ab•bot (ăb′ət), **Charles Greeley.** 1872–1973. American astrophysicist noted for his pioneering study of solar radiation.

Ab•bott (ăb′ət), **Berenice.** 1898–1991. American photographer known especially for her series of black-and-white portraits of New York City.

Abbott, Grace. 1878–1939. American social reformer noted for her opposition to child labor and her promotion of maternal and infant health care programs.

Abbott, Sir **John Joseph Caldwell.** 1821–1893. Canadian politician who served as Conservative prime minister (1891–1892).

Abbott, Lyman. 1835–1922. American Congregational cleric, writer, and editor who sought progressive Christian solutions to social problems.

Abbott, Robert Sengstacke. 1868–1940. American newspaper publisher who founded and edited (1905–1940) the *Chicago Defender,* which was an early advocate of Black civil rights.

Abbott, William. Known as "Bud." 1898–1974. American comedian noted for his partnership with Lou Costello. Abbott and Costello appeared in numerous motion pictures, including *The Naughty Nineties* (1945), which features their famous "Who's on First" routine.

abbr. or **abbrev.** *abbr.* Abbreviation.

ab•bre•vi•ate (ə-brē′vē-āt′) *tr.v.* **-at•ed, -at•ing, -ates. 1.** To make shorter. See Synonyms at **shorten. 2.** To reduce (a word or phrase) to a shorter form intended to represent the full form. [Middle English *abbreviaten,* from Late Latin *abbreviāre, abbreviāt-* : *ab-* (variant of *ad-,* ad-) + *breviāre,* to shorten (from *brevis,* short; see **mregh-u-** in Appendix).] **—ab•bre′vi•a′tor** *n.*

ab•bre•vi•a•tion (ə-brē′vē-ā′shən) *n. Abbr.* **abbr., abbrev. 1.** The act or product of shortening. **2.** A shortened form of a word or phrase used chiefly in writing to represent the complete form, such as *Mass.* for *Massachusetts* or *USMC* for *United States Marine Corps.* **3.** *Music.* Any of various symbols used in notation to indicate that a series of notes is to be repeated.

ă pat	oi boy
ā pay	ou out
âr care	ŏŏ took
ä father	ōō boot
ĕ pet	ŭ cut
ē be	ûr urge
ĭ pit	th thin
ī pie	*th* this
îr pier	hw which
ŏ pot	zh vision
ō toe	ə about, item
ô paw	♦ regionalism

Stress marks: ′ (primary); ′ (secondary), as in **dictionary** (dĭk′shə-nĕr′ē)

ABC (ā′bē-sē′) *n., pl.* **ABC's.** **1.** Often **ABC's.** The alphabet. **2.** **ABC's.** The rudiments of reading and writing.

ABC art *n.* See **minimalism** (sense 1).

ab·cou·lomb (ăb-ko͞o′lŏm′, -lōm′) *n.* The centimeter-gram-second electromagnetic unit of charge, equal to ten coulombs.

ABC soil *n.* Soil in which three distinct layers can be seen in vertical section.

ABD (ā′bē-dē′) *n.* A candidate for a doctorate who has completed all the requirements for the degree, such as courses and examinations, with the exception of the dissertation. [*a(ll) b(ut) d(issertation).*]

Ab·di·as (ăb-dī′əs). See **Obadiah** (sense 1).

ab·di·cate (ăb′dĭ-kāt′) *v.* **-cat·ed, -cat·ing, -cates.** —*tr.* To relinquish (power or responsibility) formally. —*intr.* To relinquish formally a high office or responsibility. [Latin *abdīcāre, abdīcāt-*, to disclaim : *ab-*, away; see AB–[1] + *dīcāre*, to proclaim; see **deik-** in Appendix.] —**ab′di·ca·ble** (-kə-bəl) *adj.* —**ab′di·ca′tion** *n.* —**ab′di·ca′tor** *n.*

ab·do·men (ăb′də-mən, ăb-dō′mən) *n.* **1.** The part of the body that lies between the thorax and the pelvis and encloses the stomach, intestines, liver, spleen, and pancreas. Also called *belly.* **2.** The posterior segment of the body in arthropods. [Latin, belly.] —**ab·dom′i·nal** (ăb-dŏm′ə-nəl) *adj.* —**ab·dom′i·nal·ly** *adv.*

ab·dom·i·nous (ăb-dŏm′ə-nəs) *adj.* Potbellied.

ab·du·cens (ăb-do͞o′sənz, -dyo͞o′-) *n., pl.* **ab·du·cen·tes** (ăb′do͞o-sĕn′tēz′, -dyo͞o-). Either of the sixth pair of cranial nerves that convey motor impulses to the rectus muscle on the lateral side of each eye. [Latin *abdūcēns*, present participle of *abdūcere*, to take away. See ABDUCT.]

ab·duct (ăb-dŭkt′) *tr.v.* **-duct·ed, -duct·ing, -ducts.** **1.** To carry off by force; kidnap. **2.** *Physiology.* To draw away from the midline of the body or from an adjacent part or limb. [Latin *abdūcere, abduct-* : *ab-*, away; see AB–[1] + *dūcere*, to lead; see **deuk-** in Appendix.] —**ab·duc′tion** *n.*

ab·duc·tor (ăb-dŭk′tər) *n.* **1.** One, such as a kidnapper, that abducts. **2.** *Anatomy.* A muscle that draws a body part, such as a finger, arm, or toe, away from the midline of the body or of an extremity.

Ab·dul-A·ziz (ăb′do͝ol-ä-zēz′). 1830–1876. Turkish sultan (1861–1876) whose reforms of educational and legal systems were offset by his increasingly absolutist rule, which led to uprisings and his deposition.

Ab·dul Ha·mid II (ăb′do͝ol hä-mēd′, -mĭt′). 1842–1918. Turkish sultan (1876–1909) whose autocratic rule led to revolts by the Young Turks.

Ab·dul-Jab·bar (ăb-do͞ol′jə-bär′), **Kareem.** Originally Lew Alcindor. Born 1947. American basketball player. As a center for the Los Angeles Lakers (1975–1989) he became the all-time leading scorer in National Basketball Association history in 1984.

Ab·dul·lah ibn-Hu·sein (ăb′do͞o-lä′ ĭb′n-ho͞o-sān′). 1882–1951. Transjordanian emir (1921–1946) and first king of independent Jordan (1946–1951). He annexed the West Bank of the Jordan River in 1950 and was assassinated a year later by a Palestinian nationalist.

Ab·dul-Me·djid I also **Ab·dul-Me·jid I** (ăb′do͞ol-mĕ-jēd′, -jĭt′). 1823–1861. Turkish sultan (1839–1861) whose social reforms were overshadowed by extravagances that contributed to the financial ruin of Turkey in the late 1800's.

a·beam (ə-bēm′) *adv. Nautical.* At right angles to the keel of a ship.

a·be·ce·dar·i·an (ā′bē-sē-dâr′ē-ən) *n.* **1.** One who teaches or studies the alphabet. **2.** One who is just learning; a beginner. —**abecedarian** *adj.* **1.** Having to do with the alphabet. **2.** Being arranged alphabetically. **3.** Elementary or rudimentary. [Middle English, from Medieval Latin *abecedārium*, alphabet, from Late Latin *abecedārius*, alphabetical : from the names of the letters A B C D + *-ārius*, -ary.]

a·bed (ə-bĕd′) *adv.* In bed.

A·bed·ne·go (ə-bĕd′nĭ-gō′). In the Old Testament, a young man who with Meshach and Shadrach emerged unharmed from the fiery furnace of Babylon.

A·bel (ā′bəl). In the Old Testament, the son of Adam and Eve who was slain by his elder brother, Cain.

Abel, Sir **Frederick Augustus.** 1827–1902. British chemist noted for his research and writings concerning explosives. He invented cordite (1889) with Sir James Dewar.

Ab·e·lard (ăb′ə-lärd′) also **A·bé·lard** (ä-bā-lär′), **Peter** or **Pierre.** 1079–1142. French theologian and philosopher whose application of the principles of ancient Greek logic to the doctrines of the medieval Catholic Church led to charges of heresy. He secretly married his pupil Héloise after she bore him a child, thus angering her family, who arranged to have him attacked and castrated. He became a monk and continued in his work. Héloise became a nun.

a·bele (ə-bēl′) *n.* See **white poplar.** [Dutch *abeel*, from Old French *aubel*, from Medieval Latin *albellus*, diminutive of Latin *albus*, white. See **albho-** in Appendix.]

a·be·li·a (ə-bē′lē-ə, ə-bēl′yə) *n.* Any of various deciduous or evergreen ornamental shrubs of the genus *Abelia*, native to Asia and Mexico and having opposite simple leaves and small white, pink, or purple flowers. [New Latin, after Clarke *Abel* (1780–1826), British botanist.]

A·be·lian group (ə-bēl′yən, ə-bē′lē-ən) *n.* See **commutative group.** [After Niels Henrik *Abel* (1802–1829), Norwegian mathematician.]

a·bel·mosk (ā′bəl-mŏsk′) *n.* A hairy annual or biennial plant *(Abelmoschus moschatus)* native to tropical Asia and having yellow flowers with crimson centers. It is cultivated for its seed. Also called *ambrette, musk mallow.* [New Latin *abelmoschus*, from Arabic *ḥabbalmusk*, grain of musk : *ḥabb*, grain + *musk*, musk (from Persian *mušk;* see MUSK).]

Ab·e·na·ki (ä′bə-nä′kē, ăb′ə-năk′ē) or **Ab·na·ki** (ăb-nä′kē, ăb-) *n., pl.* **Abenaki** or **-kis** or **Abnaki** or **-kis.** **1.a.** Any of various Native American peoples formerly inhabiting northern New England and southeast Canada, with present-day populations in Maine and southern Quebec. **b.** A member of any of these peoples. **2.a.** A confederacy of Abenaki and other peoples formed in the mid-18th century in opposition to the Iroquois confederacy and the English colonists. **b.** A member of this confederacy. **3.** Either or both of the two Eastern Algonquian languages of the Abenaki peoples. Also called *Wabanaki.*

ABEND *abbr. Computer Science.* Abnormal end of task.

A·be·o·ku·ta (ăb′ē-ō-ko͞o′tə). A city of southwest Nigeria north of Lagos. It is a trade center in an agricultural region. Population, 301,000.

Ab·er·deen (ăb′ər-dēn′). **1.** (*also* ăb′ər-dēn′). A city of northeast Scotland on the North Sea at the mouth of the Dee River. It is known as "the Granite City" because stone from local quarries is used in many of its buildings. Population, 212,542. **2.** A town of northeast Maryland east-northeast of Baltimore. Aberdeen Proving Ground, a major research, development, and testing installation, is nearby. Population, 11,533. **3.** A city of northeast South Dakota northeast of Pierre. It is a trade center in a wheat and livestock region. Population, 25,851. **4.** A city of western Washington west-southwest of Tacoma. Located on Grays Harbor, it has lumbering, fishing, and shipping industries. Population, 18,739.

Aberdeen An·gus (ăng′gəs) *n.* A breed of black, hornless beef cattle that originated in Scotland. Also called *Black Angus.* [After *Aberdeen* and *Angus*, former counties of Scotland.]

Ab·er·nath·y (ăb′ər-năth′ē), **Ralph David.** 1926–1990. American civil rights leader who was a founder and president (1968–1977) of the Southern Christian Leadership Conference.

ab·er·rant (ă-bĕr′ənt) *adj.* **1.** Deviating from the proper or expected course. **2.** Deviating from what is normal; untrue to type. [Latin *aberrāns, aberrant-*, present participle of *aberrāre*, to go astray. See ABERRATION.] —**ab·er′rance, ab·er′ran·cy** *n.* —**ab·er′rant·ly** *adv.*

ab·er·rat·ed (ăb′ə-rā′tĭd) *adj.* Characterized by defects, abnormality, or deviation from the usual, typical, or expected course.

ab·er·ra·tion (ăb′ə-rā′shən) *n.* **1.** A deviation from the proper or expected course. See Synonyms at **deviation.** **2.** A departure from the normal or typical: *events that were aberrations from the norm.* **3.** *Psychology.* A disorder or abnormal alteration in one's mental state. **4.a.** A defect of focus, such as blurring in an image. **b.** An imperfect image caused by a physical defect in an optical element, as in a lens. **5.** *Astronomy.* The apparent displacement of the position of a celestial body in the direction of motion of an observer on Earth, caused by the motion of Earth and the finite velocity of light. **6.** *Genetics.* A deviation in the normal structure or number of chromosomes in an organism. [Latin *aberrātiō, aberrātiōn-*, diversion, from *aberrātus*, past participle of *aberrāre*, to go astray : *ab-*, away from; see AB–[1] + *errāre*, to stray; see **ers-** in Appendix.]

a·bet (ə-bĕt′) *tr.v.* **a·bet·ted, a·bet·ting, a·bets.** **1.** To approve, encourage, and support (an action or a plan of action); urge and help on. See Synonyms at **incite.** **2.** To urge, encourage, or help (a person): *abetted the thief in robbing the bank.* [Middle English *abetten*, from Old French *abeter*, to entice : *a-*, to (from Latin *ad-;* see AD–) + *beter*, to bait; see **bheid-** in Appendix.] —**a·bet′ment** *n.* —**a·bet′tor, a·bet′ter** *n.*

ab ex·tra (ăb ĕk′strə) *adv.* From without. [Latin *ab extrā* : *ab*, from + *extrā*, outside.]

a·bey·ance (ə-bā′əns) *n.* **1.** The condition of being temporarily set aside; suspension. **2.** *Law.* A condition of undetermined ownership, as of an estate that has not yet been assigned. [Anglo-Norman, variant of Old French *abeance*, desire, from *abaer*, to gape at : *a-*, at (from Latin *ad-;* see AD–) + *baer*, to gape; see BAY[2].] —**a·bey′ant** *adj.*

ab·far·ad (ăb-făr′ăd′, -əd) *n.* The centimeter-gram-second electromagnetic unit of capacitance, equal to one billion farads.

ab·hen·ry (ăb-hĕn′rē) *n., pl.* **-ries.** The centimeter-gram-second electromagnetic unit of inductance, equal to one billionth of a henry.

ab·hor (ăb-hôr′) *tr.v.* **-horred, -hor·ring, -hors.** **1.** To regard with horror or loathing. **2.** To reject vehemently; shun: *"The problem with Establishment Republicans is they abhor the unseemliness of a political brawl"* (Patrick J. Buchanan). [Middle English *abhorren*, from Latin *abhorrēre*, to shrink from : *ab-*, from; see AB–[1] + *horrēre*, to shudder.] —**ab·hor′rer** *n.*

ab·hor·rence (ăb-hôr′əns, -hŏr′-) *n.* **1.** One that is disgusting, loathsome, or repellent. **2.** A feeling of repugnance or loathing.

ab·hor·rent (ăb-hôr′ənt, -hŏr′-) *adj.* **1.** Disgusting, loath-

Kareem Abdul-Jabbar

abelmosk
Abelmoschus moschatus

Aberdeen Angus

some, or repellent. **2.** Feeling repugnance or loathing. **3.** *Archaic.* Being strongly opposed. **—ab·hor′rent·ly** *adv.*

A·bib (ä-vēv′) *n.* The seventh month of the year in the Hebrew calendar, corresponding to Nisan. [Hebrew *'ābîb,* spring.]

a·bid·ance (ə-bīd′ns) *n.* **1.** The act or condition of abiding; continuance. **2.** Adherence; compliance: *abidance by parliamentary procedure.*

a·bide (ə-bīd′) *v.* **a·bode** (ə-bōd′), or **a·bid·ed, a·bid·ing, a·bides.** *—tr.* **1.** To put up with; tolerate: *can't abide such incompetence.* See Synonyms at **bear**[1]. **2.** To wait patiently for. **3.** To be in store for; await: *"I will abide the coming of my lord"* (Tennyson). **4.** To withstand: *a thermoplastic that will abide rough use and great heat.* *—intr.* **1.** To remain in a place. **2.** To continue to be sure or firm; endure. See Synonyms at **stay**[1]. **3.** To dwell or sojourn. ***—idiom.*** **abide by.** To conform to; comply with: *abide by the rules; had to abide by the judge's decision.* [Middle English *abiden,* from Old English *ābīdan* : *ā-,* intensive + *bīdan,* to remain; see **bheidh-** in Appendix.] **—a·bid′er** *n.*

a·bid·ing (ə-bī′dĭng) *adj.* Lasting for a long time; enduring: *an abiding love of music.* **—a·bid′ing·ly** *adv.*

Ab·i·djan (ăb′ĭ-jän′). The capital and largest city of Ivory Coast, in the southern part of the country on an enclosed lagoon of the Gulf of Guinea. In 1983 Yamoussoukro was designated as the future capital. Abidjan's population is 1,500,000.

ab·i·et·ic acid (ăb′ē-ĕt′ĭk) *n.* A yellowish resinous powder, $C_{19}H_{29}COOH$, isolated from rosin and used in lacquers, varnishes, and soaps. [From Latin *abiēs, abiet-,* silver fir.]

Ab·i·gail (ăb′ĭ-găl′). In the Old Testament, the wife of David.

Ab·i·lene (ăb′ə-lēn′). **1.** A city of central Kansas west of Topeka. Dwight D. Eisenhower lived in Abilene during his youth; the Eisenhower Center includes his family homestead, a museum and library, and his grave. Population, 6,572. **2.** A city of west-central Texas west-southwest of Fort Worth. Founded in 1881 with the coming of the railroad, the city first prospered as a shipping center for cattle. Population, 98,315.

a·bil·i·ty (ə-bĭl′ĭ-tē) *n., pl.* **-ties. 1.** The quality of being able to do something; the physical, mental, financial, or legal power to perform. **2.** A natural or acquired skill or talent. [Middle English *abilite,* from Old French *habilite,* from Latin *habilitās,* from *habilis,* handy. See ABLE.]

SYNONYMS: *ability, capacity, faculty, talent, skill, competence, aptitude.* These nouns denote the qualities in a person that permit or facilitate achievement or accomplishment. *Ability* is the power, mental or physical, to do something: *"To make a fortune some assistance from fate is essential. Ability alone is insufficient"* (Ihara Saikaku). *Capacity* refers to an innate potential for growth, development, or accomplishment: *"Not by age but by capacity is wisdom acquired"* (Plautus). *Faculty* denotes an inherent power or ability: *An unerring faculty for detecting hypocrisy is one of her most useful attributes. Talent* emphasizes inborn ability, especially in the arts: *"There is no substitute for talent. Industry and all the virtues are of no avail"* (Aldous Huxley). *Skill* stresses ability that is acquired or developed through experience: *"The intellect, character and skill possessed by any man are the product of certain original tendencies and the training which they have received"* (Edward L. Thorndike). *Competence* suggests the ability to do something satisfactorily but not necessarily outstandingly well: *The concerto was performed by a violinist of unquestioned competence but limited imagination. Aptitude* implies inherent capacity for learning, understanding, or performing: *Even as a child he showed an unusual aptitude for mathematics.*

–ability or **–ibility** *suff.* Ability, inclination, or suitability for a specified action or condition: *teachability.* [Middle English *-abilitie,* from Old French *-abilite,* from Latin *-ābilitās,* from *-ābilis,* -able.]

ab in·i·ti·o (ăb′ ĭ-nĭsh′ē-ō′) *adv. Abbr.* **ab init.** From the beginning. [Latin *ab initiō* : *ab,* from + *initiō,* ablative of *initium,* beginning.]

ab in·tra (ăb ĭn′trə) *adv.* From within. [Latin *ab intrā* : *ab,* from + *intrā,* within.]

a·bi·o·gen·e·sis (ā′bī-ō-jĕn′ĭ-sĭs) *n.* The supposed development of living organisms from nonliving matter. Also called *autogenesis, spontaneous generation.* **—a′bi·o·ge·net′ic** (-jə-nĕt′ĭk), **a′bi·o·ge·net′i·cal** *adj.* **—a′bi·og′e·nist** (-ŏj′ə-nĭst) *n.*

a·bi·o·gen·ic (ā′bī-ō-jĕn′ĭk) *adj.* Not produced by living organisms. **—a′bi·o·gen′i·cal·ly** *adv.*

a·bi·o·log·i·cal (ā′bī-ə-lŏj′ĭ-kəl) *adj.* Not associated with or derived from living organisms. **—a′bi·o·log′i·cal·ly** *adv.*

a·bi·ot·ic (ā′bī-ŏt′ĭk) *adj.* Nonliving: *The abiotic factors of the environment include light, temperature, and atmospheric gases.* **—a·bi·o′sis** (-ō′sĭs) *n.* **—a·bi·ot′ic·al·ly** *adv.*

Ab·i·tib·i Lake (ăb′ĭ-tĭb′ē). An irregularly shaped lake of eastern Ontario and southwest Quebec, Canada. It is the source of the **Abitibi River,** which flows about 370 km (230 mi) west and north to an arm of James Bay.

ab·ject (ăb′jĕkt′, ăb-jĕkt′) *adj.* **1.** Brought low in condition or status. See Synonyms at **mean**[2]. **2.** Being of the most contemptible kind: *abject cowardice.* **3.** Being of the most miserable kind; wretched: *abject poverty.* [Middle English, outcast, from Latin *abiectus,* past participle of *abicere,* to cast away : *ab-,* from; see AB–[1] + *iacere,* to throw; see **yē-** in Appendix.] **—ab′ject′ly** *adv.* **—ab·ject′ness, ab·jec′tion** *n.*

ab·jure (ăb-jo͝or′) *tr.v.* **-jured, -jur·ing, -jures. 1.** To renounce under oath; forswear. **2.** To recant solemnly; repudiate: *abjure one's beliefs.* **3.** To give up (an action or practice, for example); abstain from: *"For nearly 21 years after his resignation as Prime Minister in 1963, he abjured all titles, preferring to remain just plain 'Mr.'"* (Time). [Middle English *abjuren,* from Old French *abjurer,* from Latin *abiūrāre* : *ab-,* away; see AB–[1] + *iūrāre,* to swear; see **yewes-** in Appendix.] **—ab′ju·ra′tion** *n.* **—ab·jur′er** *n.*

abl. *abbr.* Ablative (grammar).

ab·late (ă-blāt′) *v.* **-lat·ed, -lat·ing, -lates.** *—tr.* To remove by erosion, melting, evaporation, or vaporization. *—intr.* To become ablated; undergo ablation. [Back-formation from ABLATION.]

ab·la·tion (ă-blā′shən) *n.* **1.** Surgical excision or amputation of a body part or tissue. **2.** The erosive processes by which a glacier is reduced. **3.** *Aerospace.* The dissipation of heat generated by atmospheric friction, especially in the atmospheric reentry of a spacecraft or missile, by means of a melting heat shield. [Late Latin *ablātiō, ablātiōn-,* from Latin *ablātus,* past participle of *auferre,* to carry away : *ab-,* away; see AB–[1] + *lātus,* carried; see **tele-** in Appendix.]

ab·la·tive[1] (ăb′lə-tĭv) *adj. Abbr.* **abl.** Of, relating to, or being a grammatical case indicating separation, direction away from, sometimes manner or agency, and the object of certain verbs. It is found in Latin and other Indo-European languages. **—ablative** *n. Abbr.* **abl. 1.** The ablative case. **2.** A word in this case. [Middle English, from Latin *ablātīvus,* from *ablātus,* carried away. See ABLATION.]

ab·la·tive[2] (ă-blā′tĭv) *adj.* **1.** Of, relating to, or capable of ablation. **2.** Tending to ablate. [From ABLATION.]

ab·la·tive absolute (ăb′lə-tĭv) *n.* In Latin grammar, an adverbial phrase syntactically independent from the rest of the sentence and containing a noun plus a participle, an adjective, or a noun, both in the ablative case.

ab·laut (ăb′lout′, äp′-) *n.* A vowel change, characteristic of Indo-European languages, that accompanies a change in grammatical function; for example, *i, a, u* in *sing, sang, sung.* Also called *gradation.* [German : *ab,* off (from Old High German *aba;* see **apo-** in Appendix) + *Laut,* sound (from Middle High German *lūt,* from Old High German *hlūt;* see **kleu-** in Appendix).]

a·blaze (ə-blāz′) *adj.* **1.** Being on fire: *The house is ablaze.* **2.** Radiant with bright color: *a maple tree ablaze in autumn.* **—a·blaze′** *adv.*

a·ble (ā′bəl) *adj.* **a·bler, a·blest. 1.** Having sufficient ability or resources. **2.** Especially capable or talented. [Middle English, from Old French, from Latin *habilis,* from *habēre,* to handle. See **ghabh-** in Appendix.] **—a′bly** (ā′blē) *adv.*

USAGE NOTE: The construction *able to* ascribes to its subject the ability to accomplish the action expressed in its complement: *The troupe was able to get a grant for the project from a large corporation. The new submarine is able to dive twice as fast as the older model.* It should be avoided when such an ascription is unwarranted, as with passive constructions involving forms of the verb *be;* thus it is inconsistent to say *The problem was able to be solved through the method she had learned about in business school,* since this sentence ascribes no capacity or ability to the problem itself. In such cases, *can* or *could* can usually be substituted: *The problem could be solved . . .* By contrast, passives with *get* ascribe a more active role to their subjects, and here the *able to* construction can be used: *He was able to get himself accepted by a top law school.*

–able or **–ible** *suff.* **1.** Susceptible, capable, or worthy of a specified action: *debatable.* **2.** Inclined or given to a specified state or action: *changeable.* [Middle English, from Old French, from Latin *-ābilis* : *-ā-* and *-i-,* thematic vowels + *-bilis,* adj. suff.]

a·ble-bod·ied (ā′bəl-bŏd′ēd) *adj.* Physically strong and healthy: *"It required an immediate end to welfare for the able-bodied poor"* (David A. Stockman).

able-bodied seaman *n. Abbr.* **A.B., a.b.** A merchant seaman certified for all seaman's duties. Also called *able seaman.*

a·bloom (ə-blo͞om′) *adj.* Being in bloom; flowering.

ab·lu·tion (ə-blo͞o′shən, ă-blo͞o′-) *n.* **1.** A washing or cleansing of the body, especially as part of a religious rite. **2.** The liquid so used. [Middle English *ablucioun,* from Latin *ablūtiō, ablūtiōn-,* from *ablūtus,* past participle of *abluere,* to wash away : *ab-,* away; see AB–[1] + *-luere,* to wash; see **leu(ə)-** in Appendix.] **—ab·lu′tion·ar′y** (-shə-nĕr′ē) *adj.*

ABM (ā′bē-ĕm′) *n.* See **antiballistic missile.**

abn *abbr.* Airborne.

Ab·na·ki (ăb-nä′kē, ăb-) *n.* Variant of **Abenaki.**

ab·ne·gate (ăb′nĭ-găt′) *tr.v.* **-gat·ed, -gat·ing, -gates. 1.** To give up (rights or a claim, for example); renounce. **2.** To deny (something) to oneself. [Latin *abnegāre, abnegāt-,* to refuse : *ab-,* away; see AB–[1] + *negāre,* to deny; see **ne** in Appendix.] **—ab′ne·ga′tor** *n.*

ab·ne·ga·tion (ăb′nĭ-gā′shən) *n.* Self-denial.

ab·nor·mal (ăb-nôr′məl) *adj.* Not typical, usual, or regular; not normal; deviant. [Alteration (influenced by AB–[1]) of obsolete *anormal,* from Medieval Latin *anormālis,* blend of Late Latin *abnormis* (Latin *ab-,* away from; see AB–[1] + Latin *norma,* rule; see **gnō-** in Appendix) and *anōmalus;* see ANOMALOUS.] **—ab·nor′mal·ly** *adv.*

ab·nor·mal·i·ty (ăb′nôr-măl′ĭ-tē) *n., pl.* **-ties. 1.** The condition of not being normal. **2.** A phenomenon or occurrence that is not normal.

abnormal psychology *n.* Psychopathology.

Ab·o or **ab·o** (ăb′ō) *n., pl.* **-os.** *Offensive Slang.* Used as a disparaging term for an Australian aborigine: *"A group of Australian words such as abo (aborigine) or tyke (Catholic) display a degree of intolerance"* (Leonard Santorelli).

a·board (ə-bôrd′, ə-bōrd′) *adv.* **1.** On board a ship, train, aircraft, or other passenger vehicle. **2.** In or into a group, organization, or business: *"By bringing aboard a number of blacks as department heads, lawyers, and accountants, the Mayor has also broadened the racial mix in top city jobs"* (Christian Science Monitor). **3.** *Baseball.* On base. **—aboard** *prep.* On board of; on; in. [Middle English *abord* : *a-,* on; see A–[2] + *bord,* ship (from Old English *bord*).]

a·bode (ə-bōd′) *v.* A past tense and a past participle of **abide.** **—abode** *n.* **1.** A dwelling place; a home. **2.** The act of abiding; a sojourn. [Middle English *abod,* home, from *abiden,* to wait. See ABIDE.]

ab·ohm (ă-bōm′) *n.* The centimeter-gram-second electromagnetic unit of resistance, equal to one billionth of an ohm.

a·bol·ish (ə-bŏl′ĭsh) *tr.v.* **-ished, -ish·ing, -ish·es. 1.** To do away with; annul. **2.** To destroy completely. [Middle English *abolisshen,* from Old French *abolir, aboliss-,* from Latin *abolēre.* See **al-**[2] in Appendix.] **—a·bol′ish·a·ble** *adj.* **—a·bol′ish·er** *n.* **—a·bol′ish·ment** *n.*

SYNONYMS: *abolish, exterminate, extinguish, extirpate, eradicate, obliterate.* These verbs mean to get rid of. *Abolish* applies only to doing away with conditions, practices, or regulations, not material things or persons: *The legislature passed a law to abolish the surtax. Exterminate* suggests total destruction, as of living things, by a deliberate, selective method: *Entire peoples were exterminated in the concentration camps. Extinguish* means to put out a flame or something likened to a flame: *Repeated rebuffs couldn't extinguish my enthusiasm. Extirpate* suggests effective destruction by removing roots or entrenched causes: *The police arrested dealers in an attempt to extirpate drug abuse. Eradicate* shares the connotations of *extirpate* but stresses the resistance to dislodgment offered by the object: *Scientists are working to find a serum to eradicate the disease. Obliterate* means to destroy so as to leave no trace: *Amnesia mercifully obliterated his memory of the accident.*

ab·o·li·tion (ăb′ə-lĭsh′ən) *n.* **1.** The act of doing away with or the state of being done away with; annulment. **2.** Abolishment of slavery. [Latin *abolitiō, abolitiōn-,* from *abolitus,* past participle of *abolēre,* to abolish. See ABOLISH.] **—ab′o·li′tion·ar′y** (-lĭsh′ə-nĕr′ē) *adj.*

ab·o·li·tion·ism (ăb′ə-lĭsh′ə-nĭz′əm) *n.* Advocacy of the abolition of slavery. **—ab′o·li′tion·ist** *n.*

ab·o·ma·sum (ăb′ō-mā′səm) *n., pl.* **-sa** (-sə). The fourth division of the stomach in ruminant animals, such as cows, sheep, and deer, in which digestion takes place. **—ab′o·ma′sal** (-səl) *adj.*

A-bomb (ā′bŏm′) *n.* See **atom bomb** (sense 1).

a·bom·i·na·ble (ə-bŏm′ə-nə-bəl) *adj.* **1.** Unequivocally detestable; loathsome: *abominable treatment of prisoners.* **2.** Thoroughly unpleasant or disagreeable: *abominable weather.* [Middle English *abhominable,* from Old French, from Latin *abōminābilis,* from *abōminārī,* to abhor. See ABOMINATE.] **—a·bom′i·na·bly** *adv.*

abominable snowman *n.* A hairy humanlike animal reportedly inhabiting the snows of the high Himalaya Mountains. Also called *yeti.*

a·bom·i·nate (ə-bŏm′ə-nāt′) *tr.v.* **-nat·ed, -nat·ing, -nates.** To detest thoroughly; abhor. [Latin *abōminārī, abōmināt-,* to deprecate as a bad omen : *ab-,* away; see AB–[1] + *ōmen,* omen.] **—a·bom′i·na′tor** *n.*

a·bom·i·na·tion (ə-bŏm′ə-nā′shən) *n.* **1.** Abhorrence; disgust. **2.** A cause of abhorrence or disgust.

ab·o·ral (ă-bôr′əl, ăbōr′-) *adj.* Located opposite to or away from the mouth.

ab·o·rig·i·nal (ăb′ə-rĭj′ə-nəl) *adj.* **1.** Having existed in a region from the beginning: *aboriginal forests.* See Synonyms at **native. 2.** Of or relating to aborigines. **—aboriginal** *n.* An aborigine. **—ab′o·rig′i·nal·ly** *adv.*

ab·o·rig·i·ne (ăb′ə-rĭj′ə-nē) *n.* **1.** A member of the indigenous or earliest known population of a region. **2. aborigines.** The flora and fauna native to a geographic area. [From Latin *aborīgines,* original inhabitants (folk etymology of a pre-Roman tribal name) : *ab-,* from; see AB–[1] + *orīgine,* ablative of *orīgo,* beginning; see ORIGIN.]

a·born·ing (ə-bôr′nĭng) *adv.* While coming into being or getting under way: *"Our own revolutionary war almost died aborning through lack of popular support"* (William Randolph Hearst, Jr.).

a·bort (ə-bôrt′) *v.* **a·bort·ed, a·bort·ing, a·borts.** *—intr.* **1.** To give birth before the embryo or fetus is capable of surviving on its own; miscarry. **2.** To cease growth before full development or maturation. **3.** To terminate an operation or procedure, as with a project, a missile, an airplane, or a space vehicle, before completion. *—tr.* **1. a.** To cause to terminate pregnancy prematurely, before the embryo or fetus is viable. **b.** To cause the expulsion of (an embryo or fetus) before it is viable. **2.** To interfere with the development of; conclude prematurely: *abort plans for a corporate takeover.* **3.** To terminate before completion: *abort a trip because of illness; abort a spaceflight; abort a takeoff.* **4.** To stop the progress of (a disease, for example). **—abort** *n.* **1.** The act of terminating an operation or procedure, as with a project, a missile, an airplane, or a space vehicle, before completion. **2.** *Computer Science.* A procedure to terminate execution of a program when an unrecoverable error or malfunction occurs. [Latin *abortāre,* frequentative of *aborīrī, abort-,* to disappear, miscarry : *ab-,* away; see AB–[1] + *orīrī,* to appear; see **er-**[1] in Appendix.]

a·bor·ti·fa·cient (ə-bôr′tə-fā′shənt) *adj.* Causing abortion. **—abortifacient** *n.* A substance or device used to induce abortion.

a·bor·tion (ə-bôr′shən) *n.* **1.** Induced termination of pregnancy and expulsion of an embryo or fetus that is incapable of survival. **2.** A miscarriage. **3.** Cessation of normal growth, especially of an organ or other body part, prior to full development or maturation. **4.** An aborted organism. **5.** Something malformed or incompletely developed; a monstrosity.

a·bor·tion·ist (ə-bôr′shə-nĭst) *n.* One who performs abortions.

a·bor·tive (ə-bôr′tĭv) *adj.* **1.** Failing to accomplish an intended objective; fruitless: *an abortive attempt to conclude the negotiations.* **2.** *Biology.* Partially or imperfectly developed: *an abortive organ.* **—a·bor′tive·ly** *adv.* **—a·bor′tive·ness** *n.*

ABO system *n.* A classification system for human blood that identifies four major blood types based on the presence or absence of two antigens, A and B, on red blood cells. The four blood types (A, B, AB, and O, in which O designates blood that lacks both antigens) are important in determining the compatability of blood for transfusion.

a·bou·li·a (ə-bo͞o′lē-ə, ə-byo͞o′-) *n.* Variant of **abulia.**

a·bound (ə-bound′) *intr.v.* **a·bound·ed, a·bound·ing, a·bounds. 1.** To be great in number or amount. **2.** To be fully supplied or filled; teem. See Synonyms at **teem**[1]. [Middle English *abounden,* from Old French *abonder,* from Latin *abundāre,* to overflow : *ab-,* away; see AB–[1] + *undāre,* to flow (from *unda,* wave; see **wed-**[1] in Appendix).]

a·bout (ə-bout′) *adv. Abbr.* **a., ab., abt. 1.** Approximately; nearly: *The interview lasted about an hour.* **2.** Almost: *The job is about done.* **3.** To a reversed position or direction: *Turn about and walk away slowly.* **4.** In no particular direction: *wandering about with no place to go.* **5.** All around; on every side: *Let's look about for help.* **6.** In the area or vicinity; near: *spoke to a few spectators standing about.* **7.** In succession; one after another: *Turn about is fair play.* **—about** *prep.* **1.** On all sides of; surrounding: *I found an English garden all about me.* **2.** In the vicinity of; around: *explored the rivers and streams about the estate.* **3.** Almost the same as; close to; near. **4. a.** In reference to; relating to; concerned with: *a book about snakes; objectivity—a part of what biography is about.* **b.** In the act or process of: *While you're about it, please clean your room.* **5.** In the possession or innate character of: *Keep your wits about you.* **6. a.** Ready or prepared to do something: *The chorus is about to sing.* **b.** *Usage Problem.* Used with a negative to indicate strong intention: *I am not about to concede the point.* **—about** *adj.* **1.** Moving here and there; astir: *The patient is up and about.* **2.** Being in evidence or existence: *Rumors are about concerning his resignation.* [Middle English, from Old English *onbūtan* : *on,* in; see ON + *būtan,* outside; see **ud-** in Appendix.]

USAGE NOTE: The construction *not about to* is often used to express determination: *We are not about to negotiate with terrorists.* A majority of the Usage Panel considers this usage acceptable in speech but not in formal writing. • *About* is traditionally used to refer to the relation between a narrative and its subject: *a book about Cézanne, a movie about the Boston Massacre.* This use has lately been extended to refer to the relation between various nonlinguistic entities and the things they make manifest, as in *The party was mostly about showing off their new offices* or *His designs are about the use of rough-textured materials.* This practice probably originates with the expression *That's what it's all about* and may partly reflect implicit deference to the postmodern doctrine that every social artifact and activity can be regarded as a text subject to interpretation. But the usage is still too voguish to have won general acceptance; it is rejected by 59 percent of the Usage Panel in the example *A designer teapot isn't about making tea; it is about letting people know that you have a hundred dollars to spend on a teapot.*

a·bout-face (ə-bout′fās′) *n.* **1. a.** The act of pivoting to face in the opposite direction from the original, especially in a military formation. **b.** A military command to turn clockwise 180°. **2.** A total change of attitude or viewpoint. **—about-face** *intr.v.* **-faced, -fac·ing, -fac·es.** To reverse direction.

a·bove (ə-bŭv′) *adv.* **1.** On high; overhead: *the clouds above.* **2.** In heaven; heavenward. **3. a.** Upstairs: *a table in the dining room above.* **b.** To a degree that is over zero: *15° above.* **4.** In or

ă pat	oi boy
ā pay	ou out
âr care	o͝o took
ä father	o͞o boot
ĕ pet	ŭ cut
ē be	ûr urge
ĭ pit	th thin
ī pie	*th* this
îr pier	hw which
ŏ pot	zh vision
ō toe	ə about, item
ô paw	♦ regionalism

Stress marks: ′ (primary); ′ (secondary), as in **dictionary** (dĭk′shə-nĕr′ē)

to a higher place. **5.** In an earlier part of a given text: *"The problems cited above have led to a number of suggestions for reform"* (Wharton Magazine). **6.** In or to a higher rank or position: *the ranks of major and above.* **—above** *prep.* **1.** Over or higher than: *a cool spring above the timberline.* **2.** Superior to in rank, position, or number; greater than: *put principles above expediency.* **3.** Beyond the level or reach of: *a shot that was heard above the music.* **4.** In preference to. **5.** Too honorable to bend to: *I am above petty intrigue.* **6.** More than: *somewhat above normal temperature.* **—above** *n. Usage Problem.* An earlier part of a given text: *Refer to the above for that information.* **—above** *adj.* Appearing earlier in the same text: *flaws in the above interpretation.* [Middle English *aboven,* from Old English *abufan* : *a-,* on; see A–[2] + *būfan,* above; see **upo** in Appendix.]

USAGE NOTE: The use of *above* as an adjective or noun in referring to a preceding text is most common in business and legal writing. In general writing its use as an adjective (*the above figures*) was accepted by a majority of the Usage Panel in an earlier survey, but its use as a noun (*read the above*) was accepted by only a minority.

above all *adv.* Over and above all other factors or considerations.

a•bove•board (ə-bŭv′bôrd′, -bōrd′) *adv. & adj.* Without deceit or trickery; straightforward in manner. [Originally a gambling term referring to the fact that when a gambler's hands were above the board or gaming table, he could not engage in trickery, such as changing cards, below the table.]

A B R A C A D A B R A
A B R A C A D A B R
A B R A C A D A B
A B R A C A D A
A B R A C A D
A B R A C A
A B R A C
A B R A
A B R
A B
A

abracadabra

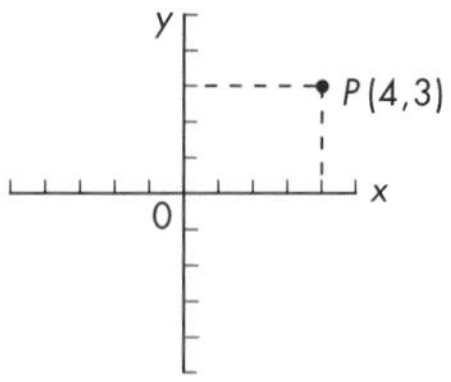

a•bove•ground (ə-bŭv′ground′) *adj.* **1.** Situated or taking place on or above the surface of the ground: *aboveground nuclear testing.* **2.** Operating or existing within the establishment or in accordance with conventional standards: *journalistic practices unacceptable to the aboveground press; an aboveground corps of 20,000 priests in Poland.* **—a•bove′ground′** *adv.*

abp. or **Abp.** *abbr.* Archbishop.

abr. *abbr.* **1.** Abridged. **2.** Abridgment.

ab•ra•ca•dab•ra (ăb′rə-kə-dăb′rə) *n.* **1.** A magical charm or incantation having the power to ward off disease or disaster. **2.** Foolish or unintelligible talk. [Late Latin, magical formula.]

WORD HISTORY: "Abracadabra," says the magician, unaware that at one time the thing to do with the word was wear it, not say it. *Abracadabra* was a magic word, the letters of which were arranged in an inverted pyramid and worn as an amulet around the neck to protect the wearer against disease or trouble. One fewer letter appeared in each line of the pyramid, until only *a* remained to form the vertex of the triangle. As the letters disappeared, so supposedly did the disease or trouble. While magicians still use *abracadabra* in their performances, the word itself has acquired another sense, "foolish or unintelligible talk."

a•bra•chi•a (ə-brā′kē-ə) *n.* Congenital absence of the arms. [A–[1] + Greek *brakhiōn,* arm; see BRACE + –IA[1].]

a•brad•ant (ə-brād′nt) *n.* An abrasive. **—abradant** *adj.* Abrasive.

a•brade (ə-brād′) *tr.v.* **a•brad•ed, a•brad•ing, a•brades.** **1.** To wear down or rub away by friction; erode. See Synonyms at **chafe. 2.** To make weary through constant irritation; wear down spiritually. [Latin *abrādere,* to scrape off : *ab-,* away; see AB–[1] + *rādere,* to scrape; see **rēd-** in Appendix.]

y, P(4,3), 0, x

abscissa
P, abscissa 4; ordinate 3

A•bra•ham (ā′brə-hăm′). In the Old Testament, the first patriarch and progenitor of the Hebrew people. He was the father of Isaac.

Abraham, Plains of. A field adjoining the upper part of Quebec City, Canada. In 1759 the British under Gen. James Wolfe defeated the French under Gen. Louis Montcalm in a decisive battle of the French and Indian Wars. The victory led to British supremacy in Canada.

a•bran•chi•ate (ā-brăng′kē-ĭt, -āt′) *n.* An animal that has no gills. **—abranchiate** also **a•bran•chi•al** (-kē-əl) *adj.* Having no gills.

a•brash (ä-brăsh′, ə-bräzh′) *n.* The natural and variable change in color that occurs in an Oriental rug over time when different dyes are used. [Arabic, mottled, possibly of Persian origin.]

ab•ra•sion (ə-brā′zhən) *n.* **1.** The process of wearing down or rubbing away by means of friction. **2. a.** A scraped or worn area. **b.** A scraped area on the skin or on a mucous membrane, resulting from injury or irritation. [Medieval Latin *abrāsiō, abrāsiōn-,* from Latin *abrāsus,* past participle of *abrādere,* to scrape off. See ABRADE.]

ab•ra•sive (ə-brā′sĭv, -zĭv) *adj.* **1.** Causing abrasion. **2.** Harsh and rough in manner. **—abrasive** *n.* A substance that abrades.

ab•re•act (ăb′rē-ăkt′) *tr.v.* **-act•ed, -act•ing, -acts.** To release (repressed emotions) by acting out, as in words, behavior, or the imagination, the situation causing the conflict. [Translation of German *abreagieren* : *ab-,* away + *reagieren,* to react.] **—ab′re•ac′tion** *n.*

a•breast (ə-brĕst′) *adv.* **1.** Side by side: *ships docked two abreast.* **2.** Up to date with: *keeping abreast of the latest developments.*

a•bridge (ə-brĭj′) *tr.v.* **a•bridged, a•bridg•ing, a•bridg•es.** **1.** To reduce the length of (a written text); condense. **2.** To cut short; curtail. See Synonyms at **shorten.** [Middle English *abregen,* from Old French *abregier,* from Late Latin *abbreviāre,* to shorten. See ABBREVIATE.] **—a•bridg′er** *n.*

a•bridg•ment also **a•bridge•ment** (ə-brĭj′mənt) *n. Abbr.* **abr. 1.** The act of abridging or the state of being abridged. **2.** A written text that has been abridged.

a•brin (ā′brĭn) *n.* A poisonous protein found in the seeds of the rosary pea. [New Latin *Abrus precatorius,* Indian licorice (from *Abrus,* genus name, from Greek *habros,* graceful, delicate) + –IN.]

a•broach (ə-brōch′) *adj.* **1.** Opened or positioned so that a liquid, such as wine, can be let out. **2.** In a state of action; astir. [Middle English *abroche* : *a-,* on, in; see A–[2] + *broche,* a pointed object, spigot; see BROACH[1].]

a•broad (ə-brôd′) *adv. & adj.* **1.** Out of one's own country. **2.** In a foreign country or countries. **3.** Away from one's home. **4.** In circulation; at large. **5.** Covering a large area; widely: *"An epidemic is abroad in America"* (Richard M. Smith). **6.** Not on target; in error. **—abroad** *n.* A foreign country or countries in which to live or travel: *"Do you like abroad or hate it?"* (John le Carré). [Middle English *abrod* : *a-,* in, on; see A–[2] + *brod,* broad; see BROAD.]

ab•ro•gate (ăb′rə-gāt′) *tr.v.* **-gat•ed, -gat•ing, -gates.** To abolish, do away with, or annul, especially by authority. [Latin *abrogāre, abrogāt-* : *ab-,* away; see AB–[1] + *rogāre,* to ask; see **reg-** in Appendix.] **—ab′ro•ga′tion** *n.*

a•brupt (ə-brŭpt′) *adj.* **1.** Unexpectedly sudden: *an abrupt change in the weather.* **2.** Surprisingly and unceremoniously curt; brusque. **3.** Touching on one subject after another with sudden transitions: *abrupt prose.* **4.** Steeply inclined. See Synonyms at **steep[1]. 5.** *Botany.* Terminating suddenly rather than gradually; truncate: *an abrupt leaf.* [Latin *abruptus,* past participle of *abrumpere,* to break off : *ab-,* away; see AB–[1] + *rumpere,* to break; see **reup-** in Appendix.] **—a•brupt′ly** *adv.* **—a•brupt′ness** *n.*

a•brup•tion (ə-brŭp′shən) *n.* An instance of suddenly breaking away or off.

A•bruz•zi (ä-bro͞ot′sē, ə-bro͞ot′-) also **A•bruz•zi e Mo•li•se** (ā mô-lē′zĕ). A region of central Italy bordering on the Adriatic Sea. Mostly mountainous, it includes Mount Corno, the highest peak of the Apennines.

abs *abbr.* Absolute temperature.

abs. *abbr.* **1.** Absence; absent. **2.** Absolute; absolutely. **3.** Abstract.

Ab•sa•ro•ka Range (ăb-săr′ə-kə). A section of the Rocky Mountains in northwest Wyoming and southern Montana. It rises to 4,007.7 m (13,140 ft) at Franks Peak.

Ab•sa•ro•ke (ăb-săr′ə-kə) *n., pl.* **Absaroke** or **-kes.** See **Crow[1].**

ab•scess (ăb′sĕs′) *n.* A localized collection of pus in part of the body, formed by tissue disintegration and surrounded by an inflamed area. **—abscess** *intr.v.* **-scessed, -scess•ing, -scess•es.** To form an abscess. [Latin *abscessus,* from past participle of *abscēdere,* to go away : *ab-,* away; see AB–[1] + *cēdere,* to go; see **ked-** in Appendix.]

ab•scise (ăb-sīz′) *v.* **-scised, -scis•ing, -scis•es.** *—tr.* To cut off; remove. *—intr.* To shed by abscission. [Latin *abscindere, absciss-* : *ab-,* away; see AB–[1] + *caedere,* to cut; see **kae-id-** in Appendix.]

ab•scis•ic acid (ăb-sĭz′ĭk) *n. Abbr.* **ABA** A plant hormone, $C_{15}H_{20}O_4$, involved in the abscission of leaves, flowers, and fruits and the dormancy of buds and seeds.

ab•scis•sa (ăb-sĭs′ə) *n., pl.* **-scis•sas** or **-scis•sae** (-sĭs′ē). *Symbol* **x** The coordinate representing the position of a point along a line perpendicular to the *y*-axis in a plane Cartesian coordinate system. [New Latin *(linea) abscissa,* (line) cut off, from Latin *abscissus,* past participle of *abscindere,* to abscise. See ABSCISE.]

ab•scis•sion (ăb-sĭzh′ən) *n.* **1.** The act of cutting off. **2.** *Botany.* The shedding of leaves, flowers, or fruits following the formation of the abscission zone.

abscission zone *n.* The region at the base of a leaf, flower, fruit, or other plant part, where the formation of a cork layer results in the separation of that part from the plant body.

ab•scond (ăb-skŏnd′) *intr.v.* **-scond•ed, -scond•ing, -sconds.** To leave quickly and secretly and hide oneself, often to avoid arrest or prosecution. [Latin *abscondere,* to hide : *abs-, ab-,* away; see AB–[1] + *condere,* to put; see **dhē-** in Appendix.] **—ab•scond′er** *n.*

ab•sence (ăb′səns) *n. Abbr.* **abs. 1.** The state of being away. **2.** The time during which one is away. **3.** Lack; want: *an absence of leadership.*

ab•sent (ăb′sənt) *adj. Abbr.* **abs., a, a. 1.** Not present; missing: *absent friends; absent parents.* **2.** Not existent; lacking: *a country in which morality is absent.* **3.** Exhibiting or feeling inattentiveness: *an absent nod.* **—absent** (ăb-sĕnt′) *tr.v.* **-sent•ed, -sent•ing, -sents.** To keep (oneself) away: *They absented themselves from the debate.* **—absent** *prep.* Without: *"Absent a legislative fix, this is an invitation for years of litigation"* (Brian E. O'Neill). [Middle English, from Old French, from Latin *absēns, absent-,* present participle of *abesse,* to be away : *abs-, ab-,* away; see AB–[1] + *esse,* to be; see **es-** in Appendix.] **—ab′sent•ly** *adv.*

ab•sen•tee (ăb′sən-tē′) *n.* One that is absent. **—absentee**

adj. **1.** Of or relating to one that is absent. **2.** Not in residence: *absentee landlords.* See Usage Note at **–ee**[1].

absentee ballot *n.* A ballot marked and mailed in advance by a voter away from the place where he or she is registered.

ab·sen·tee·ism (ăb′sən-tē′ĭz′əm) *n.* **1.** Habitual failure to appear, especially for work or other regular duty. **2.** The rate of occurrence of habitual absence from work or duty.

ab·sent-mind·ed (ăb′sənt-mīn′dĭd) *adj.* Deep in thought and heedless of present circumstances or activities; preoccupied. See Synonyms at **abstracted.** **—ab′sent-mind′ed·ly** *adv.* **—ab′sent-mind′ed·ness** *n.*

absent without leave *adj.* Absent from one's assigned military post or duties without official permission; AWOL.

ab·sinthe also **ab·sinth** (ăb′sĭnth) *n.* **1.** A perennial aromatic European herb *(Artemisia absinthium),* naturalized in eastern North America and having pinnatifid, silvery silky leaves and numerous nodding flower heads. Also called *common wormwood.* **2.** A green liqueur having a bitter anise or licorice flavor and a high alcohol content, prepared from absinthe and other herbs. Production of absinthe is now prohibited in many countries because of its toxicity. [Middle English, wormwood, from Old French, from Latin *absinthium,* from Greek *apsinthion.*]

ab·so·lute (ăb′sə-lo͞ot′, ăb′sə-lo͞ot′) *adj. Abbr.* **abs. 1.** Perfect in quality or nature; complete. **2.** Not mixed; pure. See Synonyms at **pure. 3.a.** Not limited by restrictions or exceptions; unconditional: *absolute trust.* **b.** Unqualified in extent or degree; total: *absolute silence.* See Usage Note at **infinite. 4.** Unconstrained by constitutional or other provisions: *an absolute ruler.* **5.** Not to be doubted or questioned; positive: *absolute proof.* **6.** *Grammar.* **a.** Of, relating to, or being a word, phrase, or construction that is isolated syntactically from the rest of a sentence, as *the referee having finally arrived* in *The referee having finally arrived, the game began.* **b.** Of, relating to, or being a transitive verb when its object is implied but not stated. For example, *inspires* in *We have a teacher who inspires* is an absolute verb. **c.** Of, relating to, or being an adjective or a pronoun that stands alone when the noun it modifies is being implied but not stated. For example, in *Theirs were the best, theirs* is an absolute pronoun and *best* is an absolute adjective. **7.** *Physics.* **a.** Relating to measurements or units of measurement derived from fundamental units of length, mass, and time. **b.** Relating to absolute temperature. **8.** *Law.* Complete and unconditional; final. **—absolute** *n.* **1.** Something that is absolute. **2. Absolute.** *Philosophy.* **a.** Something regarded as the ultimate basis of all thought and being. Used with *the.* **b.** Something regarded as independent of and unrelated to anything else. [Middle English *absolut,* from Latin *absolūtus,* unrestricted, past participle of *absolvere,* to absolve : *ab-,* away; see AB–[1] + *solvere,* to loosen; see **leu-** in Appendix.] **—ab′so·lute′ness** *n.*

absolute alcohol *n.* Ethyl alcohol containing no more than one percent water.

absolute ceiling *n.* The maximum altitude above sea level at which an aircraft or missile can maintain horizontal flight under standard atmospheric conditions.

ab·so·lute·ly (ăb′sə-lo͞ot′lē, ăb′sə-lo͞ot′lē) *adv. Abbr.* **abs. 1.** Definitely and completely; unquestionably. **2.** *Grammar.* In a manner that does not take an object.

USAGE NOTE: For some time, *absolutely* has been used informally as a vague intensive, as in *an absolutely magnificent painting.* In an earlier survey, a majority of the Usage Panel disapproved of this usage in formal writing.

absolute magnitude *n.* The intrinsic magnitude of a celestial body computed as if viewed from a distance of 10 parsecs, or 32.6 light-years.

absolute music *n.* Instrumental music that depends solely on its rhythmic, melodic, and contrapuntal structures.

absolute pitch *n.* **1.** The precise pitch of an isolated tone, as established by its rate of vibration measured on a standard scale. **2.** *Music.* The ability to identify or sing any tone heard. In this sense, also called *perfect pitch.*

absolute scale *n.* **1.** A scale of temperature with absolute zero as the minimum. **2.** The Kelvin scale.

absolute temperature *n. Abbr.* **abs** Temperature measured or calculated on an absolute scale.

absolute value *n.* **1.** The numerical value of a real number without regard to its sign. For example, the absolute value of −4 is 4. Also called *numerical value.* **2.** The modulus of a complex number, equal to the square root of the sum of the squares of the real and imaginary parts of the number.

absolute zero *n. Physics.* The temperature at which substances possess no thermal energy, equal to −273.15°C, or −459.67°F.

ab·so·lu·tion (ăb′sə-lo͞o′shən) *n.* The formal remission of sin imparted by a priest, as in the sacrament of penance. [Middle English, from Old French, from Latin *absolūtiō,* acquittal, from *absolūtus,* past participle of *absolvere,* to absolve. See ABSOLUTE.]

ab·so·lut·ism (ăb′sə-lo͞o′tĭz′əm) *n.* **1.a.** A political theory holding that all power should be vested in one ruler or other authority. **b.** A form of government in which all power is vested in a single ruler or other authority. **2.** An absolute doctrine, principle, or standard. **—ab′so·lut′ist** *n.* **—ab′so·lu·tis′tic** (-lo͞o-tĭs′tĭk) *adj.*

ab·solve (əb-zŏlv′, -sŏlv′) *tr.v.* **-solved, -solv·ing, -solves. 1.** To pronounce clear of guilt or blame. **2.** To relieve of a requirement or an obligation. **3.a.** To grant a remission of sin to. **b.** To pardon or remit (a sin). [Middle English *absolven,* from Latin *absolvere.* See ABSOLUTE.] **—ab·solv′a·ble** *adj.* **—ab·solv′er** *n.*

ab·sorb (əb-sôrb′, -zôrb′) *tr.v.* **-sorbed, -sorb·ing, -sorbs. 1.** To take (something) in through or as through pores or interstices. **2.** To occupy the full attention, interest, or time of; engross. See Synonyms at **monopolize. 3.** *Physics.* To retain (radiation or sound, for example) wholly, without reflection or transmission. **4.** To take in; assimilate: *immigrants who were absorbed into the social mainstream.* **5.** To receive (an impulse) without echo or recoil: *a fabric that absorbs sound; a bumper that absorbs impact.* **6.** To take over (a cost or costs). **7.** To endure; accommodate: *couldn't absorb the additional hardships.* [Middle English, to swallow up, from Old French *absorber,* from Latin *absorbēre* : *ab-,* away; see AB–[1] + *sorbēre,* to suck.] **—ab·sorb′a·bil′i·ty** *n.* **—ab·sorb′a·ble** *adj.* **—ab·sorb′er** *n.* **—ab·sorb′ing·ly** *adv.*

ab·sorbed (əb-sôrbd′, -zôrbd′) *adj.* Wholly involved or occupied; engrossed. See Synonyms at **abstracted. —ab·sorb′ed·ly** (əb-sôr′bĭd-lē, -zôr′-) *adv.* **—ab·sorb′ed·ness** *n.*

ab·sor·be·fa·cient (əb-sôr′bə-fā′shənt, -zôr′-) *adj.* Inducing or causing absorption. **—absorbefacient** *n.* A medicine or an agent that induces absorption. [ABSORBE(NT) + –FACIENT.]

ab·sorb·ent (əb-sôr′bənt, -zôr′-) *adj.* Capable of absorbing: *absorbent cotton.* **—absorbent** *n.* A substance that is capable of absorbing. **—ab·sorb′en·cy** *n.*

ab·sorp·tance (əb-sôrp′təns, -zôrp′-) *n.* The ratio of absorbed to incident radiation. [ABSORPT(ION) + –ANCE.]

ab·sorp·tion (əb-sôrp′shən, -zôrp′-) *n.* **1.** The act or process of absorbing or the condition of being absorbed. **2.** A state of mental concentration. [Latin *absorptiō, absorptiōn-,* from *absorptus,* past participle of *absorbēre,* to absorb. See ABSORB.] **—ab·sorp′tive** (-tĭv) *adj.* **—ab′sorp·tiv′i·ty** *n.*

absorption spectrum *n. Physics.* The electromagnetic spectrum, broken by a specific pattern of dark lines or bands, observed when radiation traverses an absorbing medium.

◆ **ab·squat·u·late** (ăb-skwŏch′ə-lāt′) *intr.v.* **-lat·ed, -lat·ing, -lates.** *Midland U.S.* **1.a.** To depart in a hurry; abscond: *"Your horse has absquatulated!"* (Robert M. Bird). **b.** To die. **2.** To argue. [Mock-Latinate formation, purporting to mean "to go off and squat elsewhere."]

◆ REGIONAL NOTE: The vibrant energy of American English sometimes appears in the use of Latin affixes to create jocular pseudo-Latin "learned" words. There is a precedent for this in the language of Shakespeare, whose plays contain scores of made-up Latinate words. Midland *absquatulate* has a prefix *ab–,* "away from," and a suffix *–ate,* "to act upon in a specified manner," affixed to a nonexistent base form *–squatul–,* probably suggested by *squat.* Hence the whimsical *absquatulate,* "to squat away from." Another such coinage is Northern *busticate,* which joins *bust* with *–icate* by analogy with verbs like *medicate.* Southern *argufy* joins *argue* to a redundant *–fy,* "to make; cause to become." These creations are largely confined to regions of the United States where change is slow, and where the 19th-century love for Latinate words and expressions is still manifest. For example, Appalachian speech is characterized by the frequent use of *recollect, aggravate, oblige,* and other such words.

ab·stain (ăb-stān′, əb-) *intr.v.* **-stained, -stain·ing, -stains.** To refrain from something by one's own choice: *abstain from traditional political rhetoric.* See Synonyms at **refrain**[1]. [Middle English *absteinen,* to avoid, from Old French *abstenir,* from Latin *abstinēre,* to hold back : *abs-, ab-,* away; see AB–[1] + *tenēre,* to hold; see **ten-** in Appendix.] **—ab·stain′er** *n.*

ab·ste·mi·ous (ăb-stē′mē-əs, əb-) *adj.* **1.** Eating and drinking in moderation: *an abstemious person.* **2.a.** Sparingly used or consumed: *abstemious meals.* **b.** Restricted to bare necessities: *an abstemious way of life.* [From Latin *abstēmius* : *abs-, ab-,* away; see AB–[1] + **tēmum,* liquor, variant of *tēmētum.*] **—ab·ste′mi·ous·ly** *adv.* **—ab·ste′mi·ous·ness** *n.*

ab·sten·tion (ăb-stĕn′shən, əb-) *n.* The act or habit of deliberate self-denial. [Late Latin *abstentiō, abstentiōn-,* from *abstentus,* past participle of Latin *abstinēre,* to hold back. See ABSTAIN.]

ab·sti·nence (ăb′stə-nəns) *n.* **1.** The act or practice of refraining from indulging an appetite, as for food. **2.** Abstention from alcoholic beverages. [Middle English, from Old French *abstenance,* from Latin *abstinentia,* from *abstinēns, abstinent-,* present participle of *abstinēre,* to hold back. See ABSTAIN.] **—ab′sti·nent** *adj.* **—ab′sti·nent·ly** *adv.*

SYNONYMS: *abstinence, self-denial, temperance, sobriety, continence.* These nouns refer to restraint of one's appetites or desires. *Abstinence* implies the willful avoidance of pleasures, especially of food and drink, thought to be harmful or self-indulgent: *"To many, total abstinence is easier than total moderation"* (Saint Augustine). *Self-denial* suggests resisting one's own desires for the achievement of a higher goal, such as the good of another person: *She practiced self-denial in order to provide for her family's needs. Temperance* in its general sense refers to moderation and self-restraint (*negotiations marked by the temperance of the partici-*

absinthe
Artemisia absinthium

ă pat	oi boy
ā pay	ou out
âr care	o͝o took
ä father	o͞o boot
ĕ pet	ŭ cut
ē be	ûr urge
ĭ pit	th thin
ī pie	*th* this
îr pier	hw which
ŏ pot	zh vision
ō toe	ə about, item
ô paw	◆ regionalism

Stress marks: ′ (primary); ′ (secondary), as in **dictionary** (dĭk′shə-nĕr′ē)

abstract expressionism
Asheville, 1948
by Willem de Kooning

Abu Simbel
Great Temple of
Rameses II

pants), *sobriety* to gravity in bearing, manner, or treatment (*sobriety of décor*); both nouns denote moderation in or abstinence from the consumption of alcoholic liquor: *Teetotalers preach temperance for everyone. "Something can (has) been* [sic] *said for sobriety/but very little"* (John Berryman). *Continence* specifically refers to abstention from sexual activity.

---

ab·stract (ăb-străkt′, ăb′străkt′) *adj. Abbr.* **abs. 1.** Considered apart from concrete existence: *an abstract concept.* **2.** Not applied or practical; theoretical: See Synonyms at **theoretical. 3.** Difficult to understand; abstruse: *abstract philosophical problems.* **4.** Thought of or stated without reference to a specific instance: *abstract words like* truth *and* justice. **5.** Impersonal, as in attitude or views. **6.** Having an intellectual and affective artistic content that depends solely on intrinsic form rather than on narrative content or pictorial representation: *abstract painting and sculpture.* **—abstract** (ăb′străkt′) *n.* **1.** A statement summarizing the important points of a text. **2.** Something abstract. **—abstract** (ăb-străkt′) *tr.v.* **-stract·ed, -stract·ing, -stracts. 1.** To take away; remove. **2.** To remove without permission; filch. **3.** To consider (a quality, for example) without reference to a particular example or object. **4.** (ăb′străkt′). To summarize; epitomize. **5.** To create artistic abstractions of (something else, such as a concrete object or another style): *"The Bauhaus Functionalists were . . . busy unornamenting and abstracting modern architecture, painting and design"* (John Barth). [Middle English, from Latin *abstractus,* past participle of *abstrahere,* to draw away : *abs-, ab-,* away; see AB–[1] + *trahere,* to draw.] **—ab·stract′er** *n.* **—ab·stract′ly** *adv.* **—ab·stract′ness** *n.*

ab·stract·ed (ăb-străk′tĭd, ăb′străk′-) *adj.* **1.** Removed or separated from something else; apart. **2.** Lost or deep in thought; preoccupied. **—ab·stract′ed·ly** *adv.* **—ab·stract′ed·ness** *n.*

SYNONYMS: *abstracted, absorbed, distraught, absent-minded.* These adjectives apply to lack of heed to or lack of awareness of matters requiring one's immediate attention. *Abstracted* implies being so deep in thought as to be mentally elsewhere: *"He walked on, sucking his cigar, and apparently in as abstracted a mood as Mr. Cargill himself"* (Sir Walter Scott). *Absorbed* suggests complete and often pleasurable mental involvement in the object of thought: *"He eyed the coming tide with an absorbed attention"* (Charles Dickens). *Distraught* emphasizes mental agitation that makes concentration difficult or impossible: *Distraught with grief, I signed away my rights to the property. Absent-minded* implies that the mind is straying from the matter at hand: *Some professors are absent-minded.*

---

abstract expressionism *n.* A school of painting that flourished after World War II until the early 1960's, characterized by the view that art is nonrepresentational and chiefly improvisational.

ab·strac·tion (ăb-străk′shən, əb-) *n.* **1.a.** The act or process of abstracting or the state of having been abstracted. **b.** An abstract concept, idea, or term. **c.** An abstract quality. **2.** Preoccupation; absent-mindedness. **3.** An abstract work of art.

ab·strac·tion·ism (ăb-străk′shə-nĭz′əm) *n.* The theory and practice of abstract art. **—ab·strac′tion·ist** *n.*

ab·strac·tive (ăb-străk′tĭv, əb-) *adj.* Of or derived by abstraction.

abstract of title *n. Law.* A brief history of the transfers of a piece of land, including all claims that could be made against it.

ab·struse (ăb-stro͞os′, əb-) *adj.* Difficult to understand; recondite. See Synonyms at **ambiguous.** [Latin *abstrūsus,* past participle of *abstrūdere,* to hide : *abs-, ab-,* away; see AB–[1] + *trūdere,* to push; see **treud-** in Appendix.] **—ab·struse′ly** *adv.* **—ab·struse′ness** *n.*

ab·surd (əb-sûrd′, -zûrd′) *adj.* **1.** Ridiculously incongruous or unreasonable. See Synonyms at **foolish. 2.** Of, relating to, or manifesting the view that there is no order or value in human life or in the universe. **3.** Of or relating to absurdism or the absurd. **—absurd** *n.* The condition or state in which human beings exist in a meaningless, irrational universe wherein people's lives have no purpose or meaning. Used chiefly with *the.* [Latin *absurdus.*] **—ab·surd′i·ty** (-sûr′dĭ-tē, -zûr′-), **ab·surd′ness** *n.* **—ab·surd′ly** *adv.*

ab·surd·ism (əb-sûr′dĭz-əm, -zûr′-) *n.* **1.** A philosophy, often translated into art forms, holding that human beings exist in a meaningless, irrational universe and that any search for order by them will bring them into direct conflict with this universe: *"True absurdism is not less but more real than reality"* (John Simon). **2.** An act or an instance of the ridiculous: *"This strained conceit never quite locates screen equivalents for the stage absurdisms"* (Village Voice). **—ab·surd′ist** *adj.* & *n.*

abt. *abbr.* About.

A·bu-Bakr (ä′bo͞o-bä′kər) also **A·bu Bekr** (ä′bo͞o bĕk′ər). 573–634. First caliph of the Moslem empire (632–634). Ascending to power after the death of his son-in-law Mohammed, he made Islam a political and military force throughout Arabia.

A·bu Dha·bi (ä′bo͞o dä′bē). A sheikdom and city of eastern Arabia on the Persian Gulf. The city is the capital of the federated United Arab Emirates. With enormous oil revenues, the sheikdom has one of the highest per capita incomes in the world. Population, 242,975.

a·build·ing (ə-bĭl′dĭng) *adj.* In the process of being built or of building: *"He sees motels and restaurants abuilding"* (Wall Street Journal).

A·bu·ja (ä-bo͞o′jä). A city of central Nigeria northeast of Lagos. It was designated the capital in 1982 in an attempt to relieve the racial and ethnic divisions of the country, but the first government ministries did not move to the site until 1987 and the city remains largely undeveloped. Population, 15,000.

A·bu·kir or **A·bu Qir** (ä′bo͞o-kîr′, ăb′o͞o-). A village of northern Egypt in the Nile River delta on the **Bay of Abukir.** Adm. Horatio Nelson's victory over a French fleet off Abukir in 1798 restored British prestige in the Mediterranean and ended French hopes of establishing a stronghold in the Middle East.

a·bu·li·a also **a·bou·li·a** (ə-bo͞o′lē-ə, ə-byo͞o′-) *n.* Loss or impairment of the ability to make decisions or act independently. [New Latin, from Greek *aboulia,* indecision : *a-,* without; see A–[1] + *boulē,* will; see **g^welə-** in Appendix.] **—a·bu′lic** (-lĭk) *adj.*

a·bun·dance (ə-bŭn′dəns) *n.* **1.** A great or plentiful amount. **2.** Fullness to overflowing: *"My thoughts . . . are from the abundance of my heart"* (Thomas De Quincey). **3.** Affluence; wealth.

a·bun·dant (ə-bŭn′dənt) *adj.* **1.** Occurring in or marked by abundance; plentiful. See Synonyms at **plentiful. 2.** Abounding with; rich: *a region abundant in wildlife.* [Middle English *aboundant,* from Old French *abondant,* from Latin *abundāns, abundant-,* present participle of *abundāre,* to overflow. See ABOUND.] **—a·bun′dant·ly** *adv.*

A·bu Qir (ä′bo͞o kîr′, ăb′o͞o). See **Abukir.**

a·buse (ə-byo͞oz′) *tr.v.* **a·bused, a·bus·ing, a·bus·es. 1.** To use wrongly or improperly; misuse. **2.** To hurt or injure by maltreatment; ill-use. **3.** To assail with contemptuous, coarse, or insulting words; revile. **4.** *Obsolete.* To deceive or trick. **—abuse** (ə-byo͞os′) *n.* **1.** Improper use or handling; misuse: *drug abuse.* **2.** Physical maltreatment: *spousal abuse.* **3.** A corrupt practice or custom: *abuse of power.* **4.** Insulting or coarse language: *verbal abuse.* [Middle English *abusen,* from Old French *abuser,* from *abus,* improper use, from Latin *abūsus,* past participle of *abūtī,* to misuse : *ab-,* away; see AB–[1] + *ūtī,* to use.] **—a·bus′er** *n.*

SYNONYMS: *abuse, misuse, mistreat, ill-treat, maltreat.* These verbs mean to treat a person or thing wrongfully, incorrectly, or harmfully. *Abuse* applies to injurious, improper, or unreasonable treatment: *"We abuse land because we regard it as a commodity belonging to us"* (Aldo Leopold). *Misuse* stresses incorrect or unknowledgeable handling: *"How often misused words generate misleading thoughts"* (Herbert Spencer). *Mistreat, ill-treat,* and *maltreat* all share the sense of inflicting injury, often intentionally, as through malice: *"I had seen many more patients die from being mistreated for consumption than from consumption itself"* (Earl of Lytton). *The army of occupation had orders not to ill-treat the local citizenry. "When we misuse [a language other than our native language], we are in fact trying to reduce its element of foreignness. We let ourselves maltreat it as though it naturally belonged to us"* (Manchester Guardian Weekly).

A·bu Sim·bel (ä′bo͞o sĭm′bəl, -bĕl). A village of southern Egypt on the Nile River. It is the site of massive rock temples dating from c. 1250 B.C. that were raised (1964–1966) to avoid flooding from the Aswan High Dam.

a·bu·sive (ə-byo͞o′sĭv, -zĭv) *adj.* **1.** Of or relating to abuse. **2.a.** Characterized by abuse: *abusive police tactics.* **b.** Serving to abuse: *"argued . . . that homes are abusive, that foster homes are abusive"* (National Review). **3.** Physically injurious to another: *abusive punishment.* **—a·bu′sive·ly** *adv.*

a·but (ə-bŭt′) *v.* **a·but·ted, a·but·ting, a·buts.** —*intr.* To touch at one end or side; lie adjacent. —*tr.* To border upon; be next to. [Middle English *abutten,* from Old French *abouter,* to border on (*a-,* to, from Latin *ad-;* see AD– + *bouter,* to strike; see **bhau-** in Appendix) and from Old French *abuter,* to end at (from *but,* end; see BUTT[4]).] **—a·but′ter** *n.*

a·bu·ti·lon (ə-byo͞ot′l-ŏn′) *n.* See **flowering maple.** [New Latin *Abutilon,* genus name.]

a·but·ment (ə-bŭt′mənt) *n.* **1.** The act or process of abutting. **2.a.** Something that abuts. **b.** The point of contact of two abutting objects or parts. **3.a.** The part of a structure that bears the weight or pressure of an arch. **b.** A structure that supports the end of a bridge. **c.** A structure that anchors the cables of a suspension bridge.

a·buzz (ə-bŭz′) *adj.* Filled with or as if with a buzzing sound: *a field abuzz with snowmobiles; a room abuzz with talk.*

ab·volt (ăb′vōlt′) *n.* The centimeter-gram-second electromagnetic unit of potential difference, equal to one hundred-millionth of a volt.

A·by·dos (ə-bī′dŏs). **1.** An ancient town of Asia Minor on the Asiatic coast of the Hellespont in modern-day Turkey. It was the scene of the legendary tale of Hero and Leander. **2.** An ancient city of southern Egypt on the Nile River northwest of Thebes. One of the oldest Egyptian cities, it was a religious center for the worship of Osiris and a burial site for the kings of the earliest dynasties.

a·bysm (ə-bĭz′əm) *n.* An abyss. [Middle English *abime,* from Old French *abisme,* from Vulgar Latin **abissimus,* alteration of Late Latin *abyssus.* See ABYSS.]

a·bys·mal (ə-bĭz′məl) *adj.* **1.** Resembling an abyss in depth; unfathomable. **2.** Very profound; limitless: *abysmal misery.* See

Synonyms at **deep.** **3.** Very bad: *an abysmal performance.* **—a·bys′mal·ly** *adv.*

a·byss (ə-bĭs′) *n.* **1.** An unfathomable chasm; a yawning gulf. **2.** An immeasurably profound depth or void: *"lost in the vast abysses of space and time"* (Loren Eiseley). **3. a.** The primeval chaos out of which it was believed that the earth and sky were formed. **b.** The abode of evil spirits; hell. [Middle English *abissus,* from Late Latin *abyssus,* from Greek *abussos,* bottomless : *a-,* without; see A–¹ + *bussos,* bottom.]

a·bys·sal (ə-bĭs′əl) *adj.* **1.** Abysmal; unfathomable. **2.** Of or relating to the great depths of the oceans.

Ab·ys·sin·i·a (ăb′ĭ-sĭn′ē-ə). See **Ethiopia.** **—Ab′ys·sin′i·an** *adj. & n.*

Abyssinian cat *n.* A slender, short-haired cat of a breed developed from Near Eastern stocks, having a reddish-brown coat tipped with small black markings.

Ab·zug (ăb′zo͝og′, -zŭg′), **Bella.** Born 1920. American politician who was a U.S. representative from New York State (1971–1976) and is noted for her support of the peace movement and feminism.

ac or **AC** *abbr.* Alternating current.

Ac¹ The symbol for the element **actinium.**

Ac² *abbr. Bible.* Acts of the Apostles.

ac. *abbr.* **1.** Acre. **2.** Air-cool.

a.c. *abbr. Latin.* Ante cibum (before meals).

a/c *abbr.* **1.** Account. **2.** Account current. **3.** Or **a.c.** Air conditioning.

ac– *pref.* Variant of **ad–** (sense 1).

–ac *suff.* Used to form adjectives from nouns: *ammoniac.* [New Latin *-acus,* from Greek *-akos.*]

a·ca·cia (ə-kā′shə) *n.* **1.** Any of various often spiny trees or shrubs of the genus *Acacia* in the pea family, having alternate, bipinnately compound leaves or leaves represented by flattened leafstalks and heads or spikes of small flowers. **2.** Any of several other leguminous plants, such as the rose acacia. **3.** See **gum arabic.** [Middle English, from Latin, from Greek *akakia.*]

acad. *abbr.* Academic; academy.

ac·a·deme (ăk′ə-dēm′) *n.* **1. a.** The academic environment, community, or world. **b.** Academic life. **2.** A place in which instruction is given to students. **3.** A scholar, especially a pedant. [From Latin *Acadēmīa,* the Academy. See ACADEMY.]

ac·a·de·mi·a (ăk′ə-dē′mē-ə) *n.* The academic community; academe. [New Latin *acadēmīa,* from Latin, the Academy. See ACADEMY.]

ac·a·dem·ic (ăk′ə-dĕm′ĭk) *adj. Abbr.* **acad. 1.** Of, relating to, or characteristic of a school, especially one of higher learning. **2. a.** Relating to studies that are liberal or classical rather than technical or vocational. **b.** Relating to scholarly performance: *a student's academic average.* **3.** Relating or belonging to a scholarly organization. **4.** Scholarly to the point of being unaware of the outside world. See Synonyms at **pedantic. 5.** Based on formal education. **6.** Formalistic or conventional. **7.** Theoretical or speculative without a practical purpose or intention. See Synonyms at **theoretical. 8.** Having no practical purpose or use. **—academic** *n.* **1.** One who is a member of an institution of higher learning. **2.** A person who has an academic viewpoint or a scholarly background. **—ac′a·dem′i·cal·ly** *adv.*

academic freedom *n.* Liberty to teach and pursue knowledge and to discuss it openly without restriction or interference by school or public officials or other authorities.

ac·a·de·mi·cian (ăk′ə-də-mĭsh′ən, ə-kăd′ə-) *n. Abbr.* **A. 1.** An academic. **2.** A member of an art, literary, or scientific academy or society.

ac·a·dem·i·cism (ăk′ə-dĕm′ĭ-sĭz′əm) also **a·cad·e·mism** (ə-kăd′ə-mĭz′əm) *n.* Traditional formalism, especially when reflected in art.

ac·a·dem·ics (ăk′ə-dĕm′ĭks) *n. (used with a pl. verb).* College or university courses and studies: *"Academics are a much more important priority to him than athletics"* (Gerald McIntosh).

a·cad·e·mism (ə-kăd′ə-mĭz′əm) *n.* Variant of **academicism.**

a·cad·e·my (ə-kăd′ə-mē) *n., pl.* **-mies.** *Abbr.* **A., acad. 1.** A school for special instruction. **2.** A secondary or college-preparatory school, especially a private one. **3. a.** The academic community; academe: *"When there's moral leadership from the White House and from the academy, people tend to adjust"* (Jesse Jackson). **b.** Higher education in general. Used with *the.* **c.** A society of scholars, scientists, or artists. **4. Academy. a.** Plato's school for advanced education. **b.** Platonism. **c.** The disciples of Plato. [Latin *Acadēmīa,* the school where Plato taught, from Greek *Akadēmīa.*]

A·ca·di·a (ə-kā′dē-ə). A region and former French colony of eastern Canada, chiefly in Nova Scotia but also including New Brunswick, Prince Edward Island, Cape Breton Island, and the coastal area from the St. Lawrence River south into Maine. During the French and Indian War (1755–1763) many Acadians migrated or were deported by the British to southern territories, including Louisiana, where their descendants came to be known as Cajuns.

A·ca·di·an (ə-kā′dē-ən) *adj.* Of or relating to Acadia or its people, language, or culture. **—Acadian** *n.* **1. a.** One of the early French settlers of Acadia. **b.** A descendant of these settlers, especially a Cajun. **2.** A dialect of French spoken by the Acadians.

a·can·tha (ə-kăn′thə) *n., pl.* **-thae** (-thē). A sharp spiny part or structure, such as the spinous process of a vertebra. [Greek, thorn.]

a·can·thi (ə-kăn′thī′) *n.* A plural of **acanthus.**

acantho– or **acanth–** *pref.* Thorn: *acanthocephalan.* [From Greek *akanthos,* thorn plant. See ACANTHUS.]

a·can·tho·ceph·a·lan (ə-kăn′thə-sĕf′ə-lən) also **a·can·tho·ceph·a·lid** (-lĭd) *n.* See **spiny-headed worm.** [From New Latin *Acanthocephala,* phylum name : ACANTHO– + Greek *kephalē,* head; see –CEPHALOUS.] **—a·can′tho·ceph′a·lan** *adj.*

a·can·thoid (ə-kăn′thoid′) *adj.* Shaped like a thorn or spine.

ac·an·thop·ter·yg·i·an (ăk′ən-thŏp′tə-rĭj′ē-ən) *n.* Any of a large group of fishes of the superorder Acanthopterygii, having bony skeletons and spiny rays in the dorsal and anal fins and including the bass, perch, mackerel, and swordfish. [From New Latin *Acanthopterygii* : ACANTHO– + Greek *pterugion,* diminutive of *pterux,* wing; see **pet-** in Appendix.] **—ac′an·thop′ter·yg′i·an** *adj.*

a·can·thus (ə-kăn′thəs) *n., pl.* **-thus·es** or **-thi** (-thī′). **1.** Any of various perennial herbs or small shrubs of the genus *Acanthus,* native to the Mediterranean and having pinnately lobed basal leaves with spiny margins and showy spikes of white or purplish flowers. Also called *bear's breech.* **2.** *Architecture.* A design patterned after the leaves of one of these plants, used especially on the capitals of Corinthian columns. [New Latin *Acanthus,* genus name, from Greek *akanthos,* thorn plant, from *akantha,* thorn.]

acanthus

a·cap·ni·a (ā-kăp′nē-ə) *n.* A condition marked by the presence of less than the normal amount of carbon dioxide in the blood and tissues. [New Latin, from Latin *acapnos,* without smoke (which contains carbon dioxide), from Greek *akapnos* : *a-,* not; see A–¹ + *kapnos,* smoke.]

a cap·pel·la (ä′ kə-pĕl′ə) *adv. Music.* Without instrumental accompaniment. [Italian : *a,* in the manner of + *cappella,* chapel, choir.]

Ac·a·pul·co (ăk′ə-po͞ol′kō, ä′kä-po͞ol′kô) also **Ac·a·pul·co de Juá·rez** (də hwär′ĕs, -ĕz, wär′-). A city of southern Mexico on the Pacific Ocean. It is a popular resort with a fine natural harbor surrounded by cliffs and promontories. Population, 301,902.

Acapulco gold *n. Slang.* Mexican-grown marijuana that is considered to be very strong.

ac·a·ri (ăk′ə-rī′) *n.* Plural of **acarus.**

ac·a·ri·a·sis (ăk′ə-rī′ə-sĭs) *n.* Infestation with or disease caused by mites. [ACAR(ID) + –IASIS.]

ac·a·rid (ăk′ə-rĭd) *n.* An arachnid of the order Acarina, which includes the mites and ticks. [From New Latin *Acaridae,* family name, from *Acarus,* type genus, from Greek *akari,* a kind of mite.] **—ac′a·rid** *adj.*

ac·a·roid resin also **ac·ca·roid resin** (ăk′ə-roid′) *n.* A yellow or reddish resin obtained from various Australian grass trees and used in varnishes, lacquers, and paper manufacture. Also called *accroides gum, gum accroides.* [From New Latin *acaroides,* from Greek *akari,* a kind of mite.]

ac·a·rol·o·gy (ăk′ə-rŏl′ə-jē) *n.* The study of mites and ticks. [ACAR(ID) + –LOGY.] **—ac′a·rol′o·gist** *n.*

ac·a·ro·pho·bi·a (ăk′ə-rə-fō′bē-ə) *n.* An abnormal fear of mites, other small insects, or worms. [ACAR(ID) + –PHOBIA.]

a·car·pous (ā-kär′pəs) *adj. Botany.* **1.** Producing no fruit; sterile. **2.** Having no fruit.

ac·a·rus (ăk′ər-əs) *n., pl.* **-ri** (-rī′). A mite, especially one of the genus *Acarus.* [New Latin *Acarus.* See ACARID.]

a·cat·a·lec·tic (ā-kăt′l-ĕk′tĭk) *adj.* Having a metrically complete pattern, especially having the full number of syllables in the final foot. Used of verse. [Late Latin *acatalēcticus,* from Greek *akatalēktikos* : *a-,* not; see A–¹ + *katalēktikos,* incomplete; see CATALECTIC.]

a·cau·date (ā-kô′dāt′) also **a·cau·dal** (ā-kôd′l) *adj.* Having no tail.

a·cau·les·cent (ā′kô-lĕs′ənt) *adj. Botany.* Stemless or apparently so.

acc. or **acc** *abbr.* Accusative.

Ac·cad (ăk′ăd′, ä′käd′). See **Akkad.**

ac·ca·roid resin (ăk′ə-roid′) *n.* Variant of **acaroid resin.**

ac·cede (ăk-sēd′) *intr.v.* **-ced·ed, -ced·ing, -cedes. 1.** To give one's consent, often at the insistence of another; concede. See Synonyms at **assent. 2.** To arrive at or come into an office or dignity: *accede to the throne.* **3.** To become a party to an agreement or treaty. [Middle English *acceden,* to come near, from Latin *accēdere,* to go near : *ad-,* ad- + *cēdere,* to go; see **ked-** in Appendix.] **—ac·ced′ence** (-sēd′ns) *n.* **—ac·ced′er** *n.*

ac·cel·er·an·do (ä-chĕl′ə-rän′dō) *adv. & adj. Music.* Gradually accelerating or quickening in time. Used chiefly as a direction. [Italian, present participle of *accelerare,* to hasten, from Latin *accelerāre.* See ACCELERATE.]

ac·cel·er·ant (ăk-sĕl′ər-ənt) *n.* A substance, such as a petroleum distillate, that is used as a catalyst, as in the spreading of an intentionally set fire.

ac·cel·er·ate (ăk-sĕl′ə-rāt′) *v.* **-at·ed, -at·ing, -ates.** —*tr.* **1.** To increase the speed of. **2.** To cause to occur sooner than expected. **3.** To cause to develop or progress more quickly: *a substance used to accelerate a fire.* **4. a.** To speed up (an academic course, for example). **b.** To make it possible for (a student)

ă pat	oi boy
ā pay	ou out
âr care	o͝o took
ä father	o͞o boot
ĕ pet	ŭ cut
ē be	ûr urge
ĭ pit	th thin
ī pie	*th* this
îr pier	hw which
ŏ pot	zh vision
ō toe	ə about, item
ô paw	♦ regionalism

Stress marks: ′ (primary); ′ (secondary), as in **dictionary** (dĭk′shə-nĕr′ē)

to finish an academic course faster than usual. **5.** *Physics.* To cause a change of velocity. —*intr.* **1.** To move or act faster. See Synonyms at **speed.** **2.** To engage in an academic program that progresses faster than usual. [Latin *accelerāre, accelerāt-* : *ad-,* intensive pref.; see AD– + *celerāre,* to quicken (from *celer,* swift).] **—ac·cel′er·a′tive** *adj.*

ac·cel·er·a·tion (ăk-sĕl′ə-rā′shən) *n.* **1.a.** The act of accelerating. **b.** The process of being accelerated. **2.** *Abbr.* **a** *Physics.* The rate of change of velocity with respect to time.

acceleration of gravity *n. Abbr.* **g** The acceleration of freely falling bodies under the influence of terrestrial gravity, equal to approximately 9.81 meters (32 feet) per second per second.

ac·cel·er·a·tor (ăk-sĕl′ə-rā′tər) *n.* **1.** A device, especially the gas pedal of a motor vehicle, for increasing speed. **2.** *Chemistry.* A substance that increases the speed of a reaction. **3.** *Physics.* A device, such as a cyclotron or linear accelerator, that accelerates charged subatomic particles or nuclei to high energies. In this sense, also called *atom smasher.*

ac·cel·er·o·graph (ăk-sĕl′ər-ə-grăf′) *n.* An accelerometer equipped to measure and record ground motion during an earthquake.

ac·cel·er·om·e·ter (ăk-sĕl′ə-rŏm′ĭ-tər) *n.* An instrument used to measure acceleration. [ACCELER(ATION) + –METER.]

ac·cent (ăk′sĕnt′) *n.* **1.** The relative prominence of a particular syllable of a word by greater intensity or by variation or modulation of pitch or tone. **2.** Vocal prominence or emphasis given to a particular syllable, word, or phrase. **3.** A characteristic pronunciation, especially: **a.** One determined by the regional or social background of the speaker. **b.** One determined by the phonetic habits of the speaker's native language carried over to his or her use of another language. **4.** A mark or symbol used in the printing and writing of certain languages to indicate the vocal quality to be given to a particular letter: *an acute accent.* **5.** A mark or symbol used in printing and writing to indicate the stressed syllables of a spoken word. **6.** Rhythmically significant stress in a line of verse. **7.** *Music.* **a.** Special stress given to a note within a phrase. **b.** A mark representing this stress. **8.** *Mathematics.* **a.** A mark used as a superscript to distinguish among variables represented by the same symbol. **b.** A mark used as a superscript to indicate the first derivative of a variable. **9.** A mark or one of several marks used as a superscript to indicate a unit, such as feet (′) and inches (″) in linear measurement. **10.** A distinctive feature or quality, such as a feature that accentuates or complements a decorative style. **11.** Particular importance or interest; emphasis: *The accent is on comfort.* See Synonyms at **emphasis. —accent** (ăk′sĕnt′, ăk-sĕnt′) *tr.v.* **-cent·ed, -cent·ing, -cents. 1.** To stress or emphasize the pronunciation of. **2.** To mark with a printed accent. **3.** To focus attention on; accentuate: *a program that accents the development of leadership.* [Middle English, from Old French, from Latin *accentus,* accentuation : *ad-,* ad- + *cantus,* song (from *canere,* to sing; see **kan-** in Appendix).]

ac·cen·tu·al (ăk-sĕn′cho͞o-əl) *adj.* **1.** Of or relating to accent. **2.** Based on stress accents: *accentual rhythm; accentual verse.* [From Latin *accentus,* accent. See ACCENT.] **—ac·cen′tu·al·ly** *adv.*

ac·cen·tu·ate (ăk-sĕn′cho͞o-āt′) *tr.v.* **-at·ed, -at·ing, -ates. 1.** To stress or emphasize; intensify: *"enacted sweeping land-reform plans that accentuated the already chaotic pattern of landholding"* (James Fallows). **2.** To pronounce with a stress or an accent. **3.** To mark with an accent. [Medieval Latin *accentuāre, accentuāt-,* from Latin *accentus,* accent. See ACCENT.] **—ac·cen′tu·a′tion** *n.*

ac·cept (ăk-sĕpt′) *v.* **-cept·ed, -cept·ing, -cepts.** —*tr.* **1.** To receive (something offered), especially with gladness. **2.** To admit to a group, an organization, or a place: *accepted me as a new member of the club.* **3.a.** To regard as proper, usual, or right: *Such customs are widely accepted.* **b.** To regard as true; believe in: *Scientists have accepted the new theory.* **c.** To understand as having a specific meaning. **4.** To endure resignedly or patiently: *accept one's fate.* **5.a.** To answer affirmatively: *accept an invitation.* **b.** To agree to take (a duty or responsibility). **6.** To be able to hold (something applied or inserted): *This wood will not accept oil paints.* **7.** To receive officially: *accept the committee's report.* **8.** To consent to pay, as by a signed agreement. —*intr.* To receive something, especially with favor. Often used with *of.* [Middle English *accepten,* from Latin *acceptāre,* frequentative of *accipere,* to receive : *ad-,* ad- + *capere,* to take; see **kap-** in Appendix.]

ac·cept·a·ble (ăk-sĕp′tə-bəl) *adj.* **1.** Worthy of being accepted. **2.** Adequate to satisfy a need, requirement, or standard; satisfactory. **—ac·cept′a·bil′i·ty, ac·cept′a·ble·ness** *n.* **—ac·cept′a·bly** *adv.*

ac·cep·tance (ăk-sĕp′təns) *n. Abbr.* **acpt. 1.** The act or process of accepting. **2.** The state of being accepted or acceptable. **3.** Favorable reception; approval. **4.** Belief in something; agreement. **5.a.** A formal indication by a debtor of willingness to pay a time draft or bill of exchange. **b.** A written instrument so accepted. **6.** *Law.* Compliance by one party with the terms and conditions of another's offer so that a contract becomes legally binding between them.

ac·cep·tant (ăk-sĕp′tənt) *adj.* Accepting willingly.

ac·cep·ta·tion (ăk′sĕp-tā′shən) *n.* **1.** The usual or accepted meaning, as of a word or expression. See Synonyms at **meaning. 2.** Favorable reception; approval.

ac·cept·ed (ăk-sĕp′tĭd) *adj.* Widely encountered, used, or recognized: *"an aura of dismal monotony, an accepted tedium of both journey and season"* (John Fowles).

ac·cept·er (ăk-sĕp′tər) *n.* **1.** One that accepts: *an accepter of fate.* **2.** Variant of **acceptor** (sense 1).

ac·cep·tor (ăk-sĕp′tər) *n.* **1.** Also **ac·cept·er.** One who signs a time draft or bill of exchange. **2.** *Chemistry.* **a.** The reactant in an induced reaction that has an increased rate of reaction in the presence of the inductor. **b.** The atom that contributes no electrons to a covalent bond.

ac·cess (ăk′sĕs) *n.* **1.** A means of approaching, entering, exiting, or making use of; passage. **2.** The act of approaching. **3.** The right to approach, enter, exit, or make use of: *has access to the restricted area; has access to classified material.* **4.** Increase by addition. **5.** An outburst or onset: *an access of rage.* **—access** *tr.v.* **-cessed, -cess·ing, -cess·es. 1.** To obtain access to (data or processes). **2.** *Usage Problem.* To obtain access to (goods or information), usually by technological means. [Middle English *acces,* a coming to, from Old French, from Latin *accessus,* past participle of *accēdere,* to arrive : *ad-,* ad- + *cēdere,* to come; see **ked-** in Appendix.]

USAGE NOTE: The verb *access* is well established in its computational sense "to obtain access to (data or processes)," as in *This program makes it considerably easier to access files on another disk.* In recent years it has come to be used in nontechnical contexts with the more general sense of "to obtain access to (goods or information), usually by technological means," as in *You can access your cash at any of 300 automatic tellers throughout the area.* This example was judged unacceptable by 82 percent of the Usage Panel.

access broker *n.* A former high-level political figure with close ties to an incumbent political administration who parlays those ties and other personal connections into a lucrative public relations or lobbying venture, often involving foreign clients.

access code *n.* An alphanumeric sequence that permits access to an electronic network, such as a telephone network or an automated teller machine.

ac·ces·si·ble (ăk-sĕs′ə-bəl) *adj.* **1.** Easily approached or entered. **2.** Easily obtained: *accessible money.* **3.** Easy to talk to or get along with: *an accessible manager.* **4.** Easily swayed or influenced: *accessible to flattery.* **—ac·ces′si·bil′i·ty, ac·ces′si·ble·ness** *n.* **—ac·ces′si·bly** *adv.*

ac·ces·sion (ăk-sĕsh′ən) *n.* **1.** The attainment of a dignity or rank: *the queen's accession to the throne.* **2.a.** Something that has been acquired or added; an acquisition. **b.** An increase by means of something added. **3.** *Law.* **a.** The addition to or increase in value of property by means of improvements or natural growth. **b.** The right of a proprietor to ownership of such addition or increase. **4.** Agreement or assent. **5.** Access; admittance. **6.** A sudden outburst. **—accession** *tr.v.* **-sioned, -sion·ing, -sions.** To record in the order of acquisition: *a curator accessioning newly acquired paintings.* **—ac·ces′sion·al** *adj.*

ac·ces·sor·ize (ăk-sĕs′ə-rīz′) *tr.v.* **-ized, -iz·ing, -iz·es.** *Usage Problem.* To furnish with accessories: *"She was the first to take . . . glamour . . . and apply it to clothes* [by] *accessorizing them at whim"* (Atlantic). See Usage Note at **–ize.**

ac·ces·so·ry (ăk-sĕs′ə-rē) *n., pl.* **-ries. 1.a.** A subordinate or supplementary item; an adjunct. **b.** Something nonessential but desirable that contributes to an effect or result. See Synonyms at **appendage. 2.** *Law.* **a.** One who incites, aids, or abets a lawbreaker in the commission of a crime but is not present at the time of the crime. Also called *accessory before the fact.* **b.** One who aids a criminal after the commission of a crime, but was not present at the time of the crime. Also called *accessory after the fact.* **—accessory** *adj.* **1.** Having a secondary, supplementary, or subordinate function. **2.** *Law.* Serving to aid or abet a lawbreaker, either before or after the commission of the crime, without being present at the time the crime was committed. [Middle English *accessorie,* from Medieval Latin *accessōrius,* from *accessor,* helper, from Latin *accessus,* approach. See ACCESS.] **—ac′ces·so′ri·al** (-sə-sôr′ē-əl, -sōr-) *adj.* **—ac·ces′so·ri·ly** *adv.* **—ac·ces′so·ri·ness** *n.*

accessory after the fact *n., pl.* **accessories after the fact.** *Law.* See **accessory** (sense 2b).

accessory apartment *n.* A rental apartment within a single-family dwelling. Also called *granny flat, in-law rental.*

accessory before the fact *n., pl.* **accessories before the fact.** *Law.* See **accessory** (sense 2a).

accessory cell *n.* See **subsidiary cell.**

accessory fruit *n.* A fruit, such as the pear or strawberry, that develops from a ripened ovary or ovaries but includes a significant portion derived from nonovarian tissue. Also called *false fruit, pseudocarp.*

accessory nerve *n.* Either of the 11th pair of cranial nerves, which convey motor impulses to the pharynx and muscles of the upper thorax, back, and shoulders.

accessory pigment *n. Botany.* A pigment that absorbs light energy and transfers it to chlorophyll A.

access road *n.* A road that affords access into and out of an area.

access time *n. Computer Science.* The time lag between a request for information stored in a computer and its delivery.

ac·ciac·ca·tu·ra (ä-chä′kə-to͝or′ə) *n. Music.* A short grace note one half step below a principal note, sounded immediately before or at the same time as the principal note to add sustained dissonance. [Italian, from *acciaccare,* to crush.]

ac·ci·dence (ăk′sĭ-dəns, -dĕns′) *n. Grammar.* The section of morphology that deals with the inflections of words. [Middle English, from Late Latin *accidentia,* from Latin *accidēns, accident-,* accident. See ACCIDENT.]

ac·ci·dent (ăk′sĭ-dənt, -dĕnt′) *n.* **1.a.** An unexpected, undesirable event: *car accidents on icy roads.* **b.** An unforeseen incident: *went to college in England by happy accident.* **2.** Lack of intention; chance: *ran into an old friend by accident.* **3.** *Logic.* A circumstance or an attribute that is not essential to the nature of something. [Middle English, chance event, from Old French, from Latin *accidēns, accident-,* present participle of *accidere,* to happen : *ad-,* ad- + *cadere,* to fall; see **kad-** in Appendix.]

ac·ci·den·tal (ăk′sĭ-dĕn′tl) *adj.* **1.** Occurring unexpectedly, unintentionally, or by chance. **2.** *Music.* Of or relating to a sharp, flat, or natural not indicated in the key signature. **—accidental** *n.* **1.** A property, a factor, or an attribute that is not essential. **2.** *Music.* A chromatically altered note not belonging to the key signature. **—ac′ci·den′tal·ly** *adv.*

SYNONYMS: *accidental, fortuitous, contingent, incidental, adventitious.* These adjectives apply to what comes about without design or intent. *Accidental* primarily refers to what occurs by chance: *Their accidental meeting led to a renewal of their acquaintance.* It can also mean subordinate or nonessential: *"Poetry is something to which words are the accidental, not by any means the essential form"* (Frederick W. Robertson). *Fortuitous* stresses chance or accident even more strongly and inferentially minimizes relation or cause: *"the happy combination of fortuitous circumstances"* (Sir Walter Scott). *Contingent* in this context describes what is possible but uncertain because of chance or unforeseen or uncontrollable factors: *"The results of confession were not contingent, they were certain"* (George Eliot). *Incidental* refers to what is an adjunct to something else and does not necessarily imply the operation of chance: *"There is scarcely any practice which is so corrupt as not to produce some incidental good"* (Enoch Mellor). *Adventitious* applies to what is not inherent in something but is added extrinsically, sometimes by accident or chance: *"The court tries to understand 'whether the young man's misconduct was adventitious or the result of some serious flaw in his character'"* (Harry F. Rosenthal).

accident insurance *n.* Insurance against injury or death because of accident.

ac·ci·dent-prone (ăk′sĭ-dənt-prōn′) *adj.* Having or susceptible to having a greater than average number of accidents or mishaps.

ac·cip·i·ter (ăk-sĭp′ĭ-tər) *n.* A hawk of the genus *Accipiter,* characterized by short wings and a long tail. [Latin, hawk. See **ōku-** in Appendix.] **—ac·cip′i·trine′** (-trīn′, -trĭn) *adj.*

ac·claim (ə-klām′) *v.* **-claimed, -claim·ing, -claims.** *—tr.* To praise enthusiastically and often publicly; applaud. See Synonyms at **praise.** *—intr.* To shout approval. **—acclaim** *n.* Enthusiastic applause; acclamation. [From Latin *acclāmāre* : *ad-,* ad- + *clāmāre,* to shout; see **kelə-²** in Appendix.] **—ac·claim′er** *n.*

ac·cla·ma·tion (ăk′lə-mā′shən) *n.* **1.** A shout or salute of enthusiastic approval. **2.** An oral vote, especially an enthusiastic vote of approval taken without formal ballot: *a motion passed by acclamation.* [Latin *acclāmātiō, acclāmātiōn-,* from *acclāmātus,* past participle of *acclāmāre,* to shout at. See ACCLAIM.] **—ac·clam′a·to′ry** (ə-klăm′ə-tôr′ē, -tōr′ē) *adj.*

ac·cli·mate (ə-klī′mĭt, ăk′lə-māt′) *tr. & intr.v.* **-mat·ed, -mat·ing, -mates.** To accustom or become accustomed to a new environment or situation; adapt. See Synonyms at **harden.** [French *acclimater* : *a-,* to (from Latin *ad-;* see AD–) + *climat,* climate (from Old French; see CLIMATE).]

ac·cli·ma·tion (ăk′lə-mā′shən) *n.* **1.** The process of acclimating or of becoming acclimated. **2.** Acclimatization.

ac·cli·ma·ti·za·tion (ə-klī′mə-tĭ-zā′shən) *n.* The physiological adaptation of an animal or a plant to changes in climate or environment, such as light, temperature, or altitude.

ac·cli·ma·tize (ə-klī′mə-tīz′) *v.* **-tized, -tiz·ing, -tiz·es.** *—tr.* **1.** To acclimate. See Synonyms at **harden. 2.** To adapt (oneself), especially to environmental or climatic changes. *—intr.* To become acclimated or adapted. **—ac·cli′ma·tiz′er** *n.*

ac·cliv·i·ty (ə-klĭv′ĭ-tē) *n., pl.* **-ties.** An upward slope, as of a hill. [Latin *acclīvitās,* from *acclīvis,* uphill : *ad-,* ad- + *clīvus,* slope; see **klei-** in Appendix.]

ac·co·lade (ăk′ə-lād′, -läd′) *n.* **1.a.** An expression of approval; praise. **b.** A special acknowledgment; an award. **2.** A ceremonial embrace, as of greeting or salutation. **3.** Ceremonial bestowal of knighthood. **—accolade** *tr.v.* **-lad·ed, -lad·ing, -lades.** To praise or honor: *"His works are invariably accoladed as definitive even as they sparkle and spark"* (Malcolm S. Forbes). [French, an embrace, accolade, from *accoler,* to embrace, from Old French *acoler,* from Vulgar Latin **accolāre* : Latin *ad-;* see AD– + Latin *collum,* neck; see **kʷel-¹** in Appendix.]

WORD HISTORY: Those who have received so many accolades that they have no fear of getting it in the neck may have to reconsider their situation. In tracing *accolade* back to its Latin origins, we find that it was formed from the prefix *ad–,* "to, on," and the noun *collum,* "neck," which may bring the word *collar* to mind. From these elements came the Vulgar Latin word **accollāre,* which, in turn, was the source of French *accolade,* "an embrace." An embrace was originally given to a knight when dubbing him, a fact that accounts for *accolade* having the technical sense "ceremonial bestowal of knighthood," the sense in which the word is first recorded in English in 1623.

ac·com·mo·date (ə-kŏm′ə-dāt′) *v.* **-dat·ed, -dat·ing, -dates.** *—tr.* **1.** To do a favor or service for; oblige. See Synonyms at **oblige. 2.** To provide for; supply with. **3.** To hold comfortably without crowding. See Synonyms at **contain. 4.** To make suitable; adapt. See Synonyms at **adapt. 5.** To allow for; consider: *an economic proposal that accommodates the special needs and interests of the elderly.* **6.** To settle; reconcile. *—intr. Physiology.* To become adjusted, as the eye to focusing on objects at a distance. [Latin *accomodāre, accomodāt-,* to fit : *ad-,* ad- + *commodus,* suitable; see COMMODIOUS.] **—ac·com′mo·da′tive** *adj.* **—ac·com′mo·da′tive·ness** *n.* **—ac·com′mo·da′tor** *n.*

ac·com·mo·dat·ing (ə-kŏm′ə-dā′tĭng) *adj.* Helpful and obliging. **—ac·com′mo·dat′ing·ly** *adv.*

ac·com·mo·da·tion (ə-kŏm′ə-dā′shən) *n.* **1.** The act of accommodating or the state of being accommodated; adjustment. **2.** Something that meets a need; a convenience. **3. accommodations. a.** Room and board; lodgings. **b.** A seat, compartment, or room on a public vehicle. **4.** Reconciliation or settlement of opposing views. **5.** *Physiology.* The automatic adjustment in the focal length of the lens of the eye to permit retinal focus of images of objects at varying distances. **6.** A financial favor, such as a loan.

ac·com·mo·da·tion·ist (ə-kŏm′ə-dā′shə-nĭst) *n.* One that compromises with or adapts to the viewpoint of the opposition: *"The episode revealed . . . the conceptual fissure within the . . . Administration. The split is between the realists and the accommodationists"* (National Review). **—ac·com′mo·da′tion·ist** *adj.*

accommodation ladder *n. Nautical.* A portable ladder hung from the side of a ship.

ac·com·pa·ni·ment (ə-kŭm′pə-nē-mənt, ə-kŭmp′nē-) *n.* **1.** *Music.* A vocal or instrumental part that supports another, often solo, part. **2.** Something, such as a situation, that accompanies something else; a concomitant. **3.** Something added for embellishment, completeness, or symmetry; complement.

ac·com·pa·nist (ə-kŭm′pə-nĭst, ə-kŭmp′nĭst) *n. Music.* A performer, such as a pianist, who plays an accompaniment.

ac·com·pa·ny (ə-kŭm′pə-nē, ə-kŭmp′nē) *v.* **-nied, -ny·ing, -nies.** *—tr.* **1.** To be or go with as a companion. **2.** To add to; supplement: *Wine accompanies the meal.* **3.** To coexist or occur with. **4.** *Music.* To perform an accompaniment to. *—intr. Music.* To play an accompaniment. [Middle English *accompanien,* from Old French *acompagnier* : *a-,* to (from Latin *ad-;* see AD–) + *compaignon,* companion; see COMPANION¹.]

SYNONYMS: *accompany, conduct, escort, chaperon.* These verbs are compared when they mean to be with or to go with another or others. *Accompany* suggests going with another on an equal basis: *She went to Europe accompanied by her colleague. Conduct* implies guidance of others: *The usher conducted us to our seats. Escort* stresses protective guidance: *The picture shows the party chairperson escorting the candidate through the crowd. Chaperon* specifies adult supervision of young persons: *Teachers often chaperon their classes on field trips.*

USAGE NOTE: It is traditionally claimed that the preposition to use with *accompany* in the passive should be *by* in the case of persons and *with* otherwise: *The candidate was accompanied by six burly bodyguards. The salmon was accompanied with a delicious watercress salad.* However, *by* is quite commonly used in sentences of the second type, and the usage is grammatically defensible. The phrase introduced with *by* normally represents the subject of a related active sentence; thus, the sentence *The salmon was accompanied by a delicious watercress salad* is the unexceptional passive of the sentence *A delicious watercress salad accompanied the salmon.* By the same token, *with* can be used with persons when they are the instruments of an act of accompanying performed by someone else. We can say *The Secret Service accompanied the candidate with six burly bodyguards,* or we can use the passive *The candidate was accompanied with six burly bodyguards (by the Secret Service).* The choice between the two prepositions really depends on the intended sense. Although the traditional rule may serve as a guide to which sense is likely to feel the most natural, it should not be taken as a categorical stricture.

ac·com·plice (ə-kŏm′plĭs) *n.* One who aids or abets a lawbreaker in a criminal act, either as a principal or an accessory. [Alteration of COMPLICE.]

ac·com·plish (ə-kŏm′plĭsh). *tr.v.* **-plished, -plish·ing, -plish·es. 1.** To succeed in doing; bring to pass. See Synonyms at **perform. 2.** To reach the end of; complete. [Middle English *accomplisshen,* from Old French *acomplir, accompliss-,* to complete : *a-, to* (from Latin *ad-;* see AD–) + *complir,* to complete

acciaccatura
A. Grace note
B. Principal note

ă pat	oi boy
ā pay	ou out
âr care	o͝o took
ä father	o͞o boot
ĕ pet	ŭ cut
ē be	ûr urge
ĭ pit	th thin
ī pie	*th* this
îr pier	hw which
ŏ pot	zh vision
ō toe	ə about, item
ô paw	♦ regionalism

Stress marks: **′** (primary); **′** (secondary), as in **dictionary** (dĭk′shə-nĕr′ē)

(from Latin *complēre,* to fill out; see COMPLETE).] **—ac·com′plish·a·ble** *adj.* **—ac·com′plish·er** *n.*

ac·com·plished (ə-kŏm′plĭsht) *adj.* **1.** Skilled; expert: *an accomplished pianist.* **2.** Unquestionable; indubitable: *That smoking causes health problems is an accomplished fact.*

ac·com·plish·ment (ə-kŏm′plĭsh-mənt) *n.* **1.** The act of accomplishing or the state of being accomplished; completion. **2.** Something completed successfully; an achievement. **3.** Social poise and grace.

ac·cord (ə-kôrd′) *v.* **-cord·ed, -cord·ing, -cords.** *—tr.* **1.** To cause to conform or agree; bring into harmony. **2.** To grant, especially as being due or appropriate: *accorded the President the proper deference.* See Synonyms at **grant. 3.** To bestow upon: *I accord you my blessing.* *—intr.* To be in agreement, unity, or harmony. See Synonyms at **agree. —accord** *n.* **1.** Agreement; harmony: *act in accord with university policies.* **2.** A settlement or compromise of conflicting opinions. **3.** A settlement of points at issue between nations. **4.** Spontaneous or voluntary desire to take a certain action: *The children returned on their own accord.* [Middle English *accorden,* from Old French *acorder,* from Vulgar Latin **accordāre* : Latin *ad-,* ad- + Latin *cor,* heart; see **kerd-** in Appendix.]

ac·cor·dance (ə-kôr′dns) *n.* **1.** Agreement; conformity: *in accordance with your instructions.* **2.** The act of granting.

ac·cor·dant (ə-kôr′dnt) *adj.* Being in agreement or harmony; consonant. **—ac·cor′dant·ly** *adv.*

ac·cord·ing as (ə-kôr′dĭng) *conj.* **1.** Corresponding to the way in which; precisely as. **2.** Depending on whether; if.

ac·cord·ing·ly (ə-kôr′dĭng-lē) *adv.* **1.** In accordance; correspondingly. **2.** So; consequently.

according to *prep.* **1.** As stated or indicated by; on the authority of: *according to historians.* **2.** In keeping with; in agreement with: *according to instructions.* **3.** As determined by: *a list arranged according to the alphabet.*

accordion

ac·cor·di·on (ə-kôr′dē-ən) *n. Music.* A portable instrument with a small keyboard and free metal reeds that sound when air is forced past them by pleated bellows operated by the player. **—accordion** *adj.* Having folds or bends like the bellows of an accordion: *accordion pleats; accordion blinds.* [German *Akkordion,* from *Akkord,* chord, from French *accord,* harmony, from Old French *acorder,* from Medieval Latin *accordāre,* to accord. See ACCORD.] **—ac·cor′di·on·ist** *n.*

ac·cost (ə-kôst′, ə-kŏst′) *tr.v.* **-cost·ed, -cost·ing, -costs.** To approach and speak to in an aggressive, hostile, or sexually suggestive manner. [French *accoster,* from Old French, from Medieval Latin *accostāre,* to adjoin : Latin *ad-,* ad- + Latin *costa,* side; see **kost-** in Appendix.]

ac·couche·ment (ä′ko͞osh-mäN′) *n.* A confinement during childbirth; lying-in. [French, from *accoucher,* to assist in childbirth, from Old French : *a-,* to (from Latin *ad-;* see AD–) + *coucher,* to lay down; see COUCH.]

♦**ac·count** (ə-kount′) *n.* **1.a.** A narrative or record of events. **b.** A reason given for a particular action. **2.** *Abbr.* **a/c, acct. a.** A formal banking, brokerage, or business relationship established to provide for regular services, dealings, and other financial transactions. **b.** A precise list or enumeration of financial transactions. **c.** Money deposited for checking, savings, or brokerage use. **d.** A customer having a business or credit relationship with a firm: *salespeople visiting their accounts.* **3.** Worth, standing, or importance: *a landowner of some account.* **4.** Profit or advantage: *turned her writing skills to good account.* **—account** *tr.v.* **-count·ed, -count·ing, -counts.** To consider as being; deem. See Synonyms at **consider.** See Usage Note at **as**[1]. ***—phrasal verb.* account for. 1.** To constitute the governing or primary factor: *Bad weather accounted for the long delay.* **2.** To provide an explanation or justification: *The suspect couldn't account for his time that night.* ***—idioms.* call to account. 1.** To challenge or contest. **2.** To hold answerable for. **on account.** On credit. **on account of. 1.** Because of; for the sake of: *"We got married on account of the baby"* (Anne Tyler). **2.** *Chiefly Southern U.S.* Because: *"He got picked up by the cops on account of he was walking with his shopping bag and they said there was numbers in it"* (Jimmy Breslin). **on no account.** Under no circumstances. **on (one's) own account. 1.** For oneself. **2.** On one's own; by oneself: *He wants to work on his own account.* **take into account.** To take into consideration; allow for. [Middle English, from Old French *acont,* from *aconter,* to reckon : *a-,* to (from Latin *ad-;* see AD–) + *cunter,* to count (ultimately from Latin *computāre,* to sum up; see COMPUTE).]

ac·count·a·ble (ə-koun′tə-bəl) *adj.* **1.** Liable to being called to account; answerable. See Synonyms at **responsible. 2.** That can be explained: *an accountable phenomenon.* **—ac·count′a·bil′i·ty, ac·count′a·ble·ness** *n.* **—ac·count′a·bly** *adv.*

ac·count·ant (ə-koun′tənt) *n. Abbr.* **acct.** One that keeps, audits, and inspects the financial records of individuals or business concerns and prepares financial and tax reports. **—ac·count′an·cy** (-tən-sē) *n.*

account executive *n.* A person, as in an advertising or a public relations firm, who manages clients' accounts.

ac·count·ing (ə-koun′tĭng) *n.* The bookkeeping methods involved in making a financial record of business transactions and in the preparation of statements concerning the assets, liabilities, and operating results of a business.

ac·cou·ter or **ac·cou·tre** (ə-ko͞o′tər) *tr.v.* **-tered, -ter·ing, -ters** or **-tred, -tre·ing, -tres.** To outfit and equip, as for military duty. See Synonyms at **furnish.** [French *accoutrer,* from Old French *acoustrer,* arrange, equip : *a-,* to (from Latin *ad-;* see AD–) + *coustrer,* sew; see COUTURE.]

ac·cou·ter·ment or **ac·cou·tre·ment** (ə-ko͞o′tər-mənt, -trə-) *n.* **1.** Often **accouterments** or **accoutrements. a.** Ancillary items of equipment or dress. **b.** Military equipment other than uniforms and weapons. **2. accouterments** or **accoutrements.** Outward forms of recognition; trappings: *the standard accouterments of the historical novel; cathedral ceilings, heated swimming pools, and other accoutrements signaling great wealth.* **3.** *Archaic.* The act of accoutering.

Ac·cra (ăk′rə, ə-krä′). The capital and largest city of Ghana, in the southeast part of the country on the Gulf of Guinea. Originally the capital of an ancient Ga kingdom, it became an important economic center after the completion in 1923 of a railroad to the mining and agricultural hinterland. Population, 859,640.

ac·cred·it (ə-krĕd′ĭt) *tr.v.* **-it·ed, -it·ing, -its. 1.** To ascribe or attribute to; credit with. **2.a.** To supply with credentials or authority; authorize. See Synonyms at **authorize. b.** To appoint as an ambassador to a foreign government. **3.a.** To attest to and approve as meeting a prescribed standard. See Synonyms at **approve. b.** To recognize (an institution of learning) as maintaining those standards requisite for its graduates to gain admission to other reputable institutions of higher learning or to achieve credentials for professional practice. **4.** To believe. [French *accréditer* : *a-,* to (from Latin *ad-;* see AD–) + *crédit,* credit (from Old French; see CREDIT).]

ac·cred·i·ta·tion (ə-krĕd′ĭ-tā′shən) *n.* The act of accrediting or the state of being accredited, especially the granting of approval to an institution of learning by an official review board after the school has met specific requirements.

ac·cres·cent (ə-krĕs′ənt) *adj. Botany.* Increasing in size after flowering, as the calyx of the ground cherry. [Latin *accrēscēns, accrēscent-,* present participle of *accrēscere,* to grow. See ACCRUE.]

ac·crete (ə-krēt′) *v.* **-cret·ed, -cret·ing, -cretes.** *—tr.* To make larger or greater, as by increased growth. *—intr.* **1.** To grow together; fuse. **2.** To grow or increase gradually, as by addition. [Back-formation from ACCRETION.]

ac·cre·tion (ə-krē′shən) *n.* **1.a.** Growth or increase in size by gradual external addition, fusion, or inclusion. **b.** Something added externally to promote such growth or increase. **2.** *Biology.* The growing together or adherence of parts that are normally separate. **3.** *Geology.* **a.** Slow addition to land by deposition of water-borne sediment. **b.** An increase of land along the shores of a body of water, as by alluvial deposit. **4.** *Astronomy.* An increase in the mass of a celestial object by the collection of surrounding interstellar gases and objects by gravity. [Latin *accrētiō, accrētiōn-,* from *accrētus,* past participle of *accrēscere,* to grow. See ACCRUE.] **—ac·cre′tion·ar′y** (-shə-nĕr′ē), **ac·cre′tive** *adj.*

accretion disk *n.* A disk of interstellar material surrounding a celestial object with an intense gravitational field, such as a black hole.

Ac·cring·ton (ăk′rĭng-tən). A borough of northwest England north of Manchester. It is the center of a textile-processing area. Population, 79,200.

ac·croi·des gum (ə-kroi′dēz, ă-kroi′-) *n.* See **acaroid resin.** [Alteration of New Latin *acaroides;* see ACAROID RESIN + GUM[1].]

ac·cru·al (ə-kro͞o′əl) *n.* **1.** The act or process of accumulating; an increase. **2.** Something that accumulates or increases.

ac·crue (ə-kro͞o′) *v.* **-crued, -cru·ing, -crues.** *—intr.* **1.** To come to one as a gain, an addition, or an increment: *interest accruing in my savings account.* **2.** To increase, accumulate, or come about as a result of growth: *common sense that accrues with experience.* **3.** To come into existence as a claim that is legally enforceable. *—tr.* To accumulate over time: *I have accrued 15 days of sick leave.* [Middle English *acreuen,* ultimately from Latin *accrēscere,* to grow : *ad-,* ad- + *crēscere,* to arise; see **ker-**[2] in Appendix.] **—ac·crue′ment** *n.*

acct. *abbr.* **1.** Account. **2.** Accountant.

ac·cul·tur·ate (ə-kŭl′chə-rāt′) *v.* **-at·ed, -at·ing, -ates.** *—tr.* To cause (a society, for example) to change by the process of acculturation. *—intr.* To change or be modified by acculturation.

ac·cul·tur·a·tion (ə-kŭl′chə-rā′shən) *n.* **1.** The modification of the culture of a group or an individual as a result of contact with a different culture. **2.** The process by which the culture of a particular society is instilled in a human being from infancy onward. **—ac·cul′tur·a′tion·al** *adj.* **—ac·cul′tur·a′tive** *adj.*

ac·cum·bent (ə-kŭm′bənt) *adj.* Lying down; reclining. [Latin *accumbēns, accumbent-,* present participle of *accumbere,* to recline at table : *ad-,* ad- + *cumbere,* to recline.]

ac·cu·mu·late (ə-kyo͞om′yə-lāt′) *v.* **-lat·ed, -lat·ing, -lates.** *—tr.* To gather or pile up; amass. See Synonyms at **gather.** *—intr.* To mount up; increase. [Latin *accumulāre, accumulāt-* : *ad-,* ad- + *cumulāre,* to pile up (from *cumulus,* heap; see **keuə-** in Appendix).] **—ac·cu′mu·la·ble** (-lə-bəl) *adj.*

ac·cu·mu·la·tion (ə-kyo͞om′yə-lā′shən) *n.* **1.** The act of gathering or amassing, as into a heap or pile: *"Little things grew by continual accumulation"* (Samuel Johnson). **2.** The process of growing into a large amount or heap. **3.** A mass heaped up or collected: *an accumulation of rubbish.*

ac·cu·mu·la·tive (ə-kyōōm′yə-lā′tĭv, -lə-tĭv) *adj.* **1.** Characterized by or showing the effects of accumulation; cumulative. **2.** Tending to accumulate. **—ac·cu′mu·la·tive·ly** *adv.* **—ac·cu′mu·la·tive·ness** *n.*

ac·cu·mu·la·tor (ə-kyōōm′yə-lā′tər) *n.* **1.** One that accumulates: *an accumulator of old magazines.* **2.** A register or electric circuit in a calculator or computer, in which the results of arithmetical and logical operations are formed. **3.** *Chiefly British.* An automobile storage battery.

ac·cu·ra·cy (ăk′yər-ə-sē) *n.* **1.** Conformity to fact. **2.** Precision; exactness.

ac·cu·rate (ăk′yər-ĭt) *adj.* **1.** Conforming exactly to fact; errorless. **2.** Deviating only slightly or within acceptable limits from a standard. **3.** Capable of providing a correct reading or measurement: *an accurate scale.* [Latin *accūrātus,* done with care, past participle of *accūrāre,* to do with care : *ad-,* ad- + *cūrāre,* to care for (from *cūra,* care; see CURE).] **—ac′cu·rate·ly** *adv.* **—ac′cu·rate·ness** *n.*

ac·curs·ed (ə-kûr′sĭd, ə-kûrst′) **ac·curst** (ə-kûrst′) *adj.* **1.** Abominable; hateful: *this accursed mud.* **2.** Being under a curse; doomed. [Middle English *acursed,* past participle of *acursen,* to put a curse on : *a-,* intensive pref. (from Old English *ā-*) + Old English *cursian,* to curse (from *curs,* curse).] **—ac·curs′ed·ly** *adv.* **—ac·curs′ed·ness** *n.*

accus *abbr.* Accusative.

ac·cu·sa·tion (ăk′yōō-zā′shən) *n.* **1.** An act of accusing or the state of being accused. **2.** A charge of wrongdoing that is made against a person or other party.

ac·cu·sa·tive (ə-kyōō′zə-tĭv) *adj.* *Abbr.* **acc., acc, accus** Of, relating to, or being the case of a noun, pronoun, adjective, or participle that is the direct object of a verb or the object of certain prepositions. **—accusative** *n.* The accusative case. [Middle English *acusatif,* from Old French, from Latin *(casus) accūsātīvus,* (case) of accusation, from *accūsātus,* past participle of *accūsāre,* to accuse. See ACCUSE.] **—ac·cu′sa·tive·ly** *adv.*

ac·cu·sa·to·ri·al (ə-kyōō′zə-tôr′ē-əl, -tōr′-) **ac·cu·sa·to·ry** (-tôr′ē, -tōr′ē) *adj.* Containing or implying accusation: *an accusatorial glare.* **—ac·cu′sa·to′ri·al·ly** *adv.*

ac·cuse (ə-kyōōz′) *v.* **-cused, -cus·ing, -cus·es.** *—tr.* **1.** To charge with a shortcoming or an error. **2.** To charge formally with a wrongdoing. *—intr.* To make a charge of wrongdoing against another. [Middle English *acusen,* from Latin *accūsāre* : *ad-,* ad- + *causa,* lawsuit.] **—ac·cus′er** *n.* **—ac·cus′ing·ly** *adv.*

ac·cused (ə-kyōōzd′) *n.* *Law.* The defendant or defendants in a criminal case.

ac·cus·tom (ə-kŭs′təm) *tr.v.* **-tomed, -tom·ing, -toms.** To familiarize, as by constant practice, use, or habit: *I have accustomed myself to working long hours.* [Middle English *accustomen,* from Old French *acostumer* : *a-,* to (from Latin *ad-;* see AD–) + *costume,* custom; see CUSTOM.]

ac·cus·tomed (ə-kŭs′təmd) *adj.* **1.** Frequently practiced, used, or experienced; customary: *spoke with her accustomed modesty.* See Synonyms at **usual. 2.** Being in the habit of: *I am accustomed to sleeping late.* **3.** Having been adapted to the existing environment and conditions: *eyes not accustomed to desert sun.*

AC/DC (ā′sē-dē′sē) *adj.* *Offensive Slang.* Engaging in or practicing bisexuality. [From the likening of a bisexual person to an appliance that works on either alternating or direct current.]

ace (ās) *n.* **1.** *Games.* **a.** A single spot or pip on a playing card, die, or domino. **b.** A playing card, die, or domino having one spot or pip. **2.** *Sports.* In racket games: **a.** A serve that one's opponent fails to return. **b.** A point scored by such a serve. **3.** *Sports.* The act of hitting a golf ball in the hole with one's first shot. **4.** A military aircraft pilot who has destroyed five or more enemy aircraft. **5.** An expert in a given field. **—ace** *adj.* Topnotch; first-rate. **—ace** *tr.v.* **aced, ac·ing, ac·es. 1.** *Sports.* To serve an ace against. **2.** *Sports.* To hit an ace in golf. **3.** *Slang.* To get the better of (someone): *a candidate who aced his opponents in the primaries.* **4.** *Slang.* To receive a grade of A on: *She aced the exam.* ***—idioms.*** **ace in the hole.** A hidden advantage or resource kept in reserve until needed. **within an ace of.** On the verge of; very near to: *came within an ace of losing the election.* [Middle English *as,* from Old French, from Latin, unit.]

–acean *suff.* **1.** Variant of **–aceous. 2.** An organism belonging to a taxonomic group: *cetacean.* [From New Latin *-ācea,* neuter pl. of *-āceus,* -aceous.]

a·ce·di·a (ə-sē′dē-ə) *n.* Spiritual torpor and apathy; ennui: *"There is a name for the generic shoulder shrug—the buzzing indifference, as if it's always 90 degrees in the shade after a large lunch. The word is acedia. It is the weariness of effort that extends to the heart and becomes a weariness of caring"* (Melvin Maddocks). [Late Latin, from Greek *akēdeia,* indifference : *a-,* a-; see A–[1] + *kēdos,* care.]

A·cel·da·ma[1] (ə-sĕl′də-mə). In the New Testament, a potter's field near Jerusalem purchased by the priests as a burial ground for strangers with the reward that Judas had received for betraying Jesus and had later returned to them.

A·cel·da·ma[2] (ə-sĕl′də-mə) *n.* A place with dreadful associations. [After ACELDAMA[1].]

a·cel·lu·lar (ā-sĕl′yə-lər) *adj.* Containing no cells; not made of cells.

–aceous or **–acean** *suff.* **1.a.** Of or relating to: *amylaceous.* **b.** Resembling or having the nature of: *amentaceous.* **2.** Belonging to a taxonomic group: *orchidaceous.* [New Latin *-āceus,* from Latin *-āceus.*]

a·ceph·a·lous (ā-sĕf′ə-ləs) *adj.* **1.** *Biology.* Headless or lacking a clearly defined head: *acephalous worms.* **2.** Having no leader. [From Medieval Latin *acephalus,* from Greek *akephalos* : *a-,* without; see A–[1] + *kephalē,* head; see –CEPHALOUS.]

♦ **a·ce·qui·a** (ə-sā′kē-ə, ä-sä′-) *n.* *Southwestern U.S.* An irrigation canal. [Spanish, from Arabic *as-sāqīyah.*]

ac·er·ate (ăs′ə-rāt′) **ac·er·at·ed** (-rā′tĭd) *adj.* Acerose. [From Latin *ācer,* sharp. See **ak-** in Appendix.]

a·cerb (ə-sûrb′) *adj.* Variant of **acerbic.**

ac·er·bate (ăs′ər-bāt′) *tr.v.* **-bat·ed, -bat·ing, -bates.** To vex or annoy. [Latin *acerbāre, acerbāt-,* to make harsh, from *acerbus,* harsh. See ACERBIC.]

a·cer·bic (ə-sûr′bĭk) also **a·cerb** (ə-sûrb′) *adj.* Sour or bitter, as in taste, character, or tone: *"At times, the playwright allows an acerbic tone to pierce through otherwise arid or flowery prose"* (Alvin Klein). See Synonyms at **bitter.** [From Latin *acerbus.* See **ak-** in Appendix.] **—a·cer′bi·cal·ly** *adv.*

a·cer·bi·ty (ə-sûr′bĭ-tē) *n., pl.* **-ties.** Sourness of taste, character, or tone.

ac·er·ose (ăs′ə-rōs′) *adj.* Needlelike, as the leaves of pine; acerate. [New Latin *acerōsus,* incorrect use (as if from Latin *acus,* needle, or *ācer,* sharp) of Latin *acerōsus,* full of chaff, from Latin *acus, acer-,* chaff. See **ak-** in Appendix.]

a·cer·vu·lus (ə-sûr′vyə-ləs) *n., pl.* **-li.** A tiny cushionlike or blisterlike structure produced by certain fungi on a plant host and consisting of a mass of hyphae-bearing asexually produced spores. [New Latin, diminutive of Latin *acervus,* heap.]

acet. *abbr.* Acetone.

acet– *pref.* Variant of **aceto–.**

ac·e·tab·u·lum (ăs′ĭ-tăb′yə-ləm) *n., pl.* **-la** (-lə). **1.** *Anatomy.* The cup-shaped cavity at the base of the hipbone into which the ball-shaped head of the femur fits. **2.** *Zoology.* The cavity in the body of an insect into which the leg fits. **3.** *Zoology.* A cup-shaped structure, such as the sucker of a tapeworm or leech. [Latin, vinegar cup, from *acētum,* vinegar. See ACETUM.] **—ac′e·tab′u·lar** (-lər) *adj.*

ac·e·tal (ăs′ĭ-tăl′) *n.* **1.** A colorless, flammable, volatile liquid, $CH_3CH(OC_2H_5)_2$, used in cosmetics and as a solvent. **2.** Any of the class of compounds formed from aldehydes combined with alcohol. [ACET(O)– + AL(COHOL).]

ac·et·al·de·hyde (ăs′ĭ-tăl′də-hīd′) *n.* A colorless, flammable liquid, C_2H_4O, used to manufacture acetic acid, perfumes, and drugs. Also called *aldehyde.*

a·cet·a·mide (ə-sĕt′ə-mīd′, ăs′ĭt-ăm′īd′) *n.* The crystalline amide of acetic acid, CH_3CONH_2, used as a solvent and wetting agent and in lacquers and explosives.

a·cet·a·min·o·phen (ə-sē′tə-mĭn′ə-fən, ăs′ə-) *n.* A crystalline compound, $C_8H_9NO_2$, used in chemical synthesis and in medicine to relieve pain and reduce fever. [ACET(O)– + AMIN(O)– + PHEN(OL).]

ac·et·an·i·lide (ăs′ĭt-ăn′l-īd′) also **ac·et·an·i·lid** (-ăn′-lĭd) *n.* A white crystalline compound, $C_6H_5NH(COCH_3)$, used in medicine to relieve pain and reduce fever. [ACET(O)– + ANIL(INE) + –IDE.]

ac·e·tate (ăs′ĭ-tāt′) *n.* **1.** A salt or ester of acetic acid. **2.** Cellulose acetate or any of various products, especially fibers, derived from it.

a·ce·tic (ə-sē′tĭk) *adj.* Of, relating to, or containing acetic acid or vinegar. [From Latin *acētum,* vinegar. See ACETUM.]

acetic acid *n.* A clear, colorless organic acid, CH_3COOH, with a distinctive pungent odor, used as a solvent and in the manufacture of rubber, plastics, acetate fibers, pharmaceuticals, and photographic chemicals. It is the chief acid of vinegar.

a·ce·ti·fy (ə-sē′tə-fī′, ə-sĕt′ə-) *tr. & intr.v.* **-fied, -fy·ing, -fies.** To convert or become converted to acetic acid or vinegar. **—a·ce′ti·fi·ca′tion** (-fĭ-kā′shən) *n.* **—a·ce′ti·fi·er** *n.*

aceto– or **acet–** *pref.* **1.** Acetic acid: *acetify.* **2.** Acetyl: *acetanilide.* [From Latin *acētum,* vinegar. See ACETUM.]

ac·e·to·a·ce·tic acid (ăs′ĭ-tō-ə-sē′tĭk, ə-sē′tō-) *n.* A ketone body, CH_3COCH_2COOH, excreted in the urine in certain diabetic conditions.

ac·e·tone (ăs′ĭ-tōn′) *n.* *Abbr.* **acet.** A colorless, volatile, extremely flammable liquid ketone, CH_3COCH_3, widely used as an organic solvent. **—ac′e·ton′ic** (-tŏn′ĭk) *adj.*

acetone body *n.* See **ketone body.**

ac·e·to·phe·net·i·din (ăs′ĭ-tō-fə-nĕt′ĭ-dĭn, ə-sē′tō-) *n.* A white powder or crystalline solid, $CH_3CONHC_6H_4OC_2H_5$, derived from coal tar and used in medicine to reduce fever and relieve pain. Also called *phenacetin.* [ACETO– + PHEN(O)– + E(THYL) + –ID(E) + –IN.]

a·ce·tous (ə-sē′təs, ăs′ĭ-təs) *adj.* **1.** Of, relating to, or producing acetic acid or vinegar. **2.** Having an acetic taste; sour-tasting. [Middle English, sour, from Medieval Latin *acētōsus,* vinegary, from Latin *acētum,* vinegar. See ACETUM.]

a·ce·tum (ə-sē′təm) *n.* **1.** Vinegar. **2.** An acetic acid solution of a drug. [Latin *acētum.* See **ak-** in Appendix.]

a·ce·tyl (ə-sēt′l, ăs′ĭ-tl) *n.* The acetic acid radical CH_3CO. **—ac′e·tyl′ic** (ăs′ĭ-tĭl′ĭk) *adj.*

ace
Playing card

acerose
Needles of the whitebark pine
Pinus albicaulis

ă pat	oi boy
ā pay	ou out
âr care	ŏŏ took
ä father	ōō boot
ĕ pet	ŭ cut
ē be	ûr urge
ĭ pit	th thin
ī pie	*th* this
îr pier	hw which
ŏ pot	zh vision
ō toe	ə about, item
ô paw	♦ regionalism

Stress marks: ′ (primary); ′ (secondary), as in **dictionary** (dĭk′shə-nĕr′ē)

achene
Left to right: Buttercup, dandelion, and swamp-beggar ticks

Achilles

acid rain
Detail of statue corroded by acid rain

a·cet·y·late (ə-sĕt′l-āt′) *tr.v.* **-lat·ed, -lat·ing, -lates.** To bring an acetyl group into (an organic molecule). **—a·cet′y·la′tion** *n.*

a·ce·tyl·cho·line (ə-sēt′l-kō′lēn′) *n.* A white crystalline derivative of choline, $C_7H_{17}NO_3$, that is released at the ends of nerve fibers in the somatic and parasympathetic nervous systems and is involved in the transmission of nerve impulses in the body.

a·ce·tyl·cho·lin·es·ter·ase (ə-sēt′l-kō′lə-nĕs′tə-rās′, -rāz′) *n.* An enzyme found in nerve synapses that cleaves acetylcholine into acetate and choline.

a·ce·tyl-co·A (ə-sēt′l- kō′ā′, ăs′ĭ-tl-) *n.* See **acetyl coenzyme A.**

acetyl coenzyme A *n.* A compound, $C_{25}H_{38}N_7O_{17}P_3S$, that functions as a coenzyme in many biological acetylation reactions and is formed as an intermediate in the oxidation of carbohydrates, fats, and proteins. Also called *acetyl-coA.*

a·cet·y·lene (ə-sĕt′l-ēn′, -ən) *n.* A colorless, highly flammable or explosive gas, C_2H_2, used for metal welding and cutting and as an illuminant. **—a·cet′y·len′ic** (ə-sĕt′l-ĕn′ĭk) *adj.*

acetylene series *n.* A series of unsaturated aliphatic hydrocarbons, each containing at least one triple carbon bond, having chemical properties resembling acetylene and having the general formula C_nH_{2n-2}, with acetylene being the simplest member.

a·ce·tyl·sal·i·cyl·ic acid (ə-sēt′l-săl′ĭ-sĭl′ĭk) *n.* See **aspirin** (sense 1).

ace·y-deuc·y (ā′sē-do͞o′sē, -dyo͞o′-) *n.* *Games.* A variation of backgammon. [ACE + DEUCE[1].]

A·chae·a (ə-kē′ə) also **A·cha·ia** (ə-kī′ə, ə-kā′ə). An ancient region of southern Greece occupying the northern part of the Peloponnesus on the Gulf of Corinth. The cities of the region banded together in the early third century B.C. to form the Achaean League, which defeated Sparta but was eventually beaten by the Romans, who annexed Achaea in 146 B.C. and later gave the name to a province that included all of Greece south of Thessaly.

A·chae·an (ə-kē′ən) also **A·cha·ian** (ə-kā′ən, ə-kī′-) *n.* **1.** A native or inhabitant of Achaea. **2.** One of a Hellenic people believed to have inhabited the Peloponnesus and to have created the Mycenaean civilization. **3.** A Greek, especially of the Mycenaean era. **—A·chae′an** *adj.*

ach·a·la·sia (ăk′ə-lā′zhə) *n.* The failure of a ring of muscle fibers, such as a sphincter of the esophagus, to relax. [New Latin : A–[1] + Greek *khalasis,* relaxation (from *khalan,* to loosen).]

A·cha·tes (ə-kā′tēz) *n.* **1.** *Mythology.* The faithful companion of Aeneas in Virgil's *Aeneid.* **2.** A loyal friend.

ache (āk) *intr.v.* **ached, ach·ing, aches. 1.** To suffer a dull, sustained pain. **2.** To feel sympathy or compassion. **3.** To yearn painfully: *refugees who ached for their homeland.* **—ache** *n.* **1.** A dull, steady pain. See Synonyms at **pain. 2.** A longing or desire; a yen. [Middle English *aken,* from Old English *acan.*]

A·che·be (ä-chā′bā), **Chinua.** Born 1930. Nigerian writer whose works, including the novel *Things Fall Apart* (1958), describe traditional African life in conflict with colonial rule and westernization.

a·chene also **a·kene** (ā-kēn′) *n.* A small, dry, indehiscent one-seeded fruit with a thin wall, as in the sunflower. [New Latin *achenium* : Greek *a-,* a-; see A–[1] + Greek *khainein,* to yawn.] **—a·che′ni·al** (-nē-əl) *adj.*

A·cher·nar (ā′kər-när′) *n.* A star in the constellation Eridanus that is one of the brightest stars in the sky and is 114 light-years from Earth. [From Arabic *'āḫir an-nahr,* the end of the river (referring to the star's position in the constellation Eridanus).]

Ach·er·on (ăk′ə-rŏn′, -rən) *n.* *Greek Mythology.* The river of woe, one of the five rivers of Hades.

Ach·e·son (ăch′ĭ-sən), **Dean Gooderham.** 1893–1971. American statesman who promoted the Marshall Plan and helped establish NATO.

A·cheu·li·an also **A·cheu·le·an** (ə-sho͞o′lē-ən) *adj.* Of or relating to a stage of tool culture of the European Lower Paleolithic Age between the second and third interglacial periods, characterized by symmetrical stone hand axes. [French *acheuléen,* after St. *Acheul,* a hamlet in northern France.]

a·chieve (ə-chēv′) *v.* **a·chieved, a·chiev·ing, a·chieves.** *—tr.* **1.** To perform or carry out with success; accomplish. See Synonyms at **perform. 2.** To attain with effort or despite difficulty. See Synonyms at **reach.** *—intr.* To accomplish something successfully. [Middle English *acheven,* from Old French *achever,* from *a chief (venir),* (to come) to a head. See CHIEF.] **—a·chiev′a·ble** *adj.* **—a·chiev′er** *n.*

a·chieved (ə-chēvd′) *adj.* Highly successful because of great skill and ability: *"The author . . . is not merely lucky, but an achieved and deserving fiction writer"* (Wright Morris).

a·chieve·ment (ə-chēv′mənt) *n.* **1.** The act of accomplishing or finishing. **2.** Something accomplished successfully, especially by means of exertion, skill, practice, or perseverance. See Synonyms at **feat[1].**

Ach·ill (ăk′ĭl). A mountainous and barren island off the northwest coast of Ireland. At its western end is **Achill Head.**

ach·il·le·a (ăk′ə-lē′ə, ə-kĭl′ē-ə) *n.* See **yarrow.** [New Latin *achillēa,* from Latin, a plant that healed wounds, from Greek *achilleios,* of Achilles, from *Achilleus,* Achilles.]

A·chil·les (ə-kĭl′ēz) *n.* *Greek Mythology.* The hero of Homer's *Iliad,* the son of Peleus and Thetis and slayer of Hector.

A·chil·les' heel (ə-kĭl′ēz) *n.* A seemingly small but actually mortal weakness. [From Achilles' being vulnerable only in the heel.]

Achilles jerk *n.* *Physiology.* A reflex bending of the foot resulting from the contraction of lower leg muscles.

Achilles tendon *n.* The large tendon connecting the heel bone to the calf muscle of the leg.

a·chir·a (ə-chîr′ə) *n.* See **edible canna** (sense 1). [New Latin, A–[1] + Greek *kheir,* hand.]

ach·la·myd·e·ous (ăk′lə-mĭd′ē-əs, ā′klə-) *adj.* Having no perianth, as the flowers of a willow.

a·chlor·hy·dri·a (ā′klôr-hī′drē-ə, ā′klōr-) *n.* Absence of hydrochloric acid in the gastric secretions of the stomach. [A–[1] + CHLOR(O)– + HYDR(O)– + –IA[1].] **—a·chlor·hy′dric** *adj.*

a·chlo·ro·phyl·lous (ā-klôr′ə-fĭl′əs, ā-klōr′-) *adj.* *Botany.* Having no chlorophyll.

a·cho·li·a (ā-kō′lē-ə) *n.* A decrease in or an absence of bile secretion. [New Latin : A–[1] + Greek *kholē,* bile; see **ghel-[2]** in Appendix.]

A·cho·ma·wi (ə-chō′mə-wē′) *n., pl.* **Achomawi** or **-wis. 1.a.** A Native American people inhabiting northeast California. **b.** A member of this people. Also called *Pit River.* **2.** The Hokan language of the Achomawi.

a·chon·drite (ā-kŏn′drīt′) *n.* A stony meteorite that contains no chondrules. **—a′chon·drit′ic** (-drĭt′ĭk) *adj.*

a·chon·dro·pla·sia (ā-kŏn′drō-plā′zhə, -zhē-ə) *n.* Improper development of cartilage at the ends of the long bones, resulting in a form of congenital dwarfism. **—a·chon′dro·plas′tic** (-plăs′tĭk) *adj.*

ach·ro·mat·ic (ăk′rə-măt′ĭk) *adj.* **1.** Designating color perceived to have zero saturation and therefore no hue, such as neutral grays, white, or black. **2.** Refracting light without spectral color separation. **3.** *Biology.* Difficult to stain with standard dyes. Used in reference to cells or tissues. **4.** *Music.* Having only the diatonic tones of the scale. [From Greek *akhrōmatos* : *a-;* see A–[1] + *khrōma,* color.] **—ach′ro·mat′i·cal·ly** *adv.* **—a·chro′ma·tism** (ā-krō′mə-tĭz′əm), **ach′ro·ma·tic′i·ty** (ăk′rō-mə-tĭs′ĭ-tē) *n.*

achromatic lens *n.* A combination of lenses made of different glass, used to produce images free of chromatic aberrations.

a·chro·ma·tin (ā-krō′mə-tĭn) *n.* The part of a cell nucleus that remains less colored than the rest of the nucleus when stained or dyed. [ACHROMAT(IC) + –IN.] **—a·chro′ma·tin′ic** *adj.*

a·chro·ma·tize (ā-krō′mə-tīz′) *tr.v.* **-tized, -tiz·ing, -tiz·es.** To rid of color; render achromatic.

a·chro·mic (ā-krō′mĭk) *adj.* Having no color; colorless. [A–[1] + CHROM(O)– + –IC.]

ach·y (ā′kē) *adj.* **-i·er, -i·est.** Experiencing aches. **—ach′i·ness** *n.*

a·cic·u·la (ə-sĭk′yə-lə) *n., pl.* **-lae** (-lē′). A slender, needlelike part or structure, such as the spines or bristles of some plants and animals and the crystals of certain minerals. [Latin, hairpin, diminutive of *acus,* needle. See **ak-** in Appendix.] **—a·cic′u·late** (-lĭt, -lāt′), **a·cic′u·lat′ed** (-lā′tĭd) *adj.*

a·cic·u·lar (ə-sĭk′yə-lər) *adj.* Having the shape of a needle: *acicular crystals.*

ac·id (ăs′ĭd) *n.* **1.** *Chemistry.* **a.** Any of a large class of sour-tasting substances whose aqueous solutions are capable of turning blue litmus indicators red, of reacting with and dissolving certain metals to form salts, and of reacting with bases or alkalis to form salts. **b.** A substance that ionizes in solution to give the positive ion of the solvent. **c.** A substance capable of yielding hydrogen ions. **d.** A proton donor. **e.** An electron acceptor. **f.** A molecule or ion that can combine with another by forming a covalent bond with two electrons of the other. **2.** A substance having a sour taste. **3.** The quality of being sarcastic, bitter, or scornful. **4.** *Slang.* See **LSD[1]. —acid** *adj.* **1.** *Chemistry.* **a.** Of or relating to an acid. **b.** Having a high concentration of acid. **2.** Having a sour taste. See Synonyms at **sour. 3.** Biting, sarcastic, or scornful: *an acid wit; an acid tone of voice.* [From Latin *acidus,* sour, from *acēre,* to be sour. See **ak-** in Appendix.] **—ac′id·ly** *adv.* **—ac′id·ness** *n.*

ac·i·dan·the·ra (ăs′ĭ-dăn′thər-ə) *n.* Any of several ornamental African plants of the genus *Acidanthera,* having fibrous corms, swordlike leaves, and large, fragrant flowers with straight tubes. Also called *peacock orchid.* [New Latin : Greek *akis, akid-,* needle; see **ak-** in Appendix + New Latin *anthera;* see ANTHER.]

ac·id-base equilibrium (ăs′ĭd-bās′) *n.* The state that exists when acidic and basic ions in solution exactly neutralize each other.

acid-base indicator *n.* A substance that indicates the degree of acidity or basicity of a solution through characteristic color changes.

ac·i·de·mi·a (ăs′ĭ-dē′mē-ə) *n.* Abnormal acidity of the blood.

ac·id-fast (ăs′ĭd-făst′) *adj.* Not decolorized by acid after staining, as bacteria that retain dye after an acid rinse. **—ac′id-fast′ness** *n.*

ac·id·head (ăs′ĭd-hĕd′) *n.* *Slang.* A person who uses LSD.

a·cid·ic (ə-sĭd′ĭk) *adj.* **1.** Acid. **2.** Tending to form an acid.

a·cid·i·fy (ə-sĭd′ə-fī′) *tr. & intr.v.* **-fied, -fy·ing, -fies.** To make or become acid. **—a·cid′i·fi′a·ble** *adj.* **—a·cid′i·fi·ca′tion** (-fĭ-kā′shən) *n.* **—a·cid′i·fi′er** *n.*

ac·i·dim·e·ter (ăs′ĭ-dĭm′ĭ-tər) *n.* A hydrometer used to determine the specific gravity of acid solutions. **—a·cid′i·met′ric** (ə-sĭd′ə-mĕt′rĭk) *adj.* **—ac′i·dim′e·try** *n.*

a·cid·i·ty (ə-sĭd′ĭ-tē) *n.* **1.** The state, quality, or degree of being acid. **2.** Hyperacidity.

ac·i·do·phil·ic (ăs′ĭ-dō-fĭl′ĭk) also **ac·i·doph·i·lus** (-dŏf′ə-ləs) *adj. Microbiology.* **1.** Growing well in an acid medium: *acidophilic bacteria.* **2.** Easily stained with acid dyes: *an acidophilic cell.* **—a·cid′o·phil′** (ə-sĭd′ə-fĭl′), **a·cid′o·phile′** (-fīl′) *n.*

acidophilus milk *n.* Milk fermented by bacterial cultures that thrive in dilute acid, often used to alter the bacterial flora of the gastrointestinal tract in the treatment of certain digestive disorders. [New Latin *acidophilus,* specific epithet of several species of bacteria : ACID + *-philus,* -philous.]

ac·i·do·sis (ăs′ĭ-dō′sĭs) *n.* An abnormal increase in the acidity of the body's fluids, caused either by accumulation of acids or by depletion of bicarbonates. **—ac′i·dot′ic** (-dŏt′ĭk) *adj.*

acid precipitation *n.* Precipitation abnormally high in sulfuric and nitric acid content that is caused by atmospheric pollutants.

acid rain *n.* Acid precipitation falling as rain.

acid rock *n. Music.* Rock music having a prominent repetitive beat and lyrics that suggest psychedelic experiences.

acid test *n.* A decisive or critical test, as of worth or quality. [From the testing of gold in nitric acid.]

a·cid·u·late (ə-sĭj′ə-lāt′) *tr. & intr.v.* **-lat·ed, -lat·ing, -lates.** To make or become slightly acid. [ACIDUL(OUS) + -ATE[1].] **—a·cid′u·la′tion** *n.*

a·cid·u·lous (ə-sĭj′ə-ləs) *adj.* Slightly sour in taste or in manner. See Synonyms at **sour.** [From Latin *acidulus,* diminutive of *acidus,* sour. See ACID.]

ac·i·dur·i·a (ăs′ĭ-dŏŏr′ē-ə, -dyŏŏr′-) *n.* A condition marked by the presence of acid in the urine.

acid washing *n.* A washing process in which stones soaked in chlorine acid are used to soften and bleach fabric, especially denim garments. **—ac′id-washed′** (ăs′ĭd-wŏsht′, -wôsht′) *adj.*

ac·i·nar (ăs′ĭ-nər, -när′) *adj.* Of or relating to an acinus.

ac·i·nus (ăs′ə-nəs) *n., pl.* **-ni** (-nī′). *Anatomy.* One of the small saclike dilations composing a compound gland. [Latin, berry.] **—a·cin′ic** (ə-sĭn′ĭk), **ac′i·nous** *adj.*

ack. *abbr.* Acknowledge; acknowledgment.

ack-ack (ăk′ăk′) *n. Slang.* **1.** An antiaircraft gun. **2.** Antiaircraft fire. [British telephone code for AA, abbreviation for ANTIAIRCRAFT.]

ack·ee (ăk′ē, ə-kē′) *n.* Variant of **akee.**

ac·knowl·edge (ăk-nŏl′ĭj) *tr.v.* **-edged, -edg·ing, -edg·es.** *Abbr.* **ack. 1.a.** To admit the existence, reality, or truth of. **b.** To recognize as being valid or having force or power. **2.a.** To express recognition of: *acknowledge a friend's smile.* **b.** To express thanks or gratitude for. **3.** To report the receipt of. **4.** *Law.* To accept or certify as legally binding: *acknowledge a deed.* [Probably blend of Middle English *knowlechen,* to acknowledge (from *knowen,* to know; see KNOW) and Middle English *aknouen,* to recognize (from Old English *oncnāwan,* to know : *on-,* on; see ON + *cnāwan,* to know; see KNOW).] **—ac·knowl′edge·a·ble** *adj.*

SYNONYMS: *acknowledge, admit, own, avow, confess, concede.* These verbs mean to make a disclosure, usually with reluctance or under pressure. To *acknowledge* is to accept responsibility for something one makes known: *He acknowledged that the purchase had been a mistake. Admit* usually implies marked reluctance in acknowledging one's acts or accepting a different point of view: *"There are some faults which men readily admit, but others not so readily"* (Epictetus). *Own* stresses personal acceptance of and responsibility for one's thoughts or deeds: *She owned that she had fears for the child's safety. Avow,* a strong term, means to assert openly and boldly: *"Many a man thinks, what he is ashamed to avow"* (Samuel Johnson). *Confess* usually emphasizes disclosure of something damaging or inconvenient to oneself: *I have to confess that I lied to you.* To *concede* is to admit something, such as the validity of an argument, often against one's will: *The lawyer refused to concede that the two cases were at all similar.*

ac·knowl·edged (ăk-nŏl′ĭjd) *adj.* Commonly accepted or recognized.

ac·knowl·edg·ment or **ac·knowl·edge·ment** (ăk-nŏl′ĭj-mənt) *n. Abbr.* **ack. 1.** The act of admitting or owning to something. **2.** Recognition of another's existence, validity, authority, or right. **3.** An answer or response in return for something done. **4.** An expression of thanks or a token of appreciation. **5.** A formal declaration made to authoritative witnesses to ensure legal validity.

a·clin·ic line (ā-klĭn′ĭk) *n.* See **magnetic equator.** [From Greek *aklinēs,* not inclining to either side : *a-,* a-; see A-[1] + *klinein,* to lean; see **klei-** in Appendix.]

ACLU *abbr.* American Civil Liberties Union.

ac·me (ăk′mē) *n.* The highest point, as of perfection. See Synonyms at **summit.** [Greek *akmē.* See **ak-** in Appendix.]

ac·ne (ăk′nē) *n.* An inflammatory disease of the sebaceous glands and hair follicles of the skin that is marked by the eruption of pimples or pustules, especially on the face. [New Latin, probably from misreading of Greek *akmē,* facial eruption, point. See ACME.] **—ac′ned** *adj.*

acne rosacea *n.* See **rosacea.**

a·cock (ə-kŏk′) *adv. & adj.* In a cocked position.

a·coe·lo·mate (ə-sē′lə-māt′) *n.* An animal that lacks a coelom. Acoelomates, which include the flatworm, fluke, tapeworm, and ribbonworm, exhibit bilateral symmetry and possess one internal space, the digestive cavity. **—a·coe′lo·mate** (-lə-mĭt) *adj.*

a·coe·lous (ā-sē′ləs) *adj.* Lacking a true body cavity or digestive tract. [A-[1] + COEL(OM) + -OUS.]

ac·o·lyte (ăk′ə-līt′) *n.* **1.** One who assists the celebrant in the performance of liturgical rites. **2.** A devoted follower or attendant. [Middle English *acolit,* from Old French, from Medieval Latin *acolytus,* from Greek *akolouthos,* attendant. See ANACOLUTHON.]

A·co·ma[1] (ăk′ə-mə, -mô′, ä′kə-) *n., pl.* **Acoma** or **-mas. 1.a.** A Pueblo people, the founders and inhabitants of Acoma. **b.** A member of this people. **2.** The Keresan language of the Acoma.

A·co·ma[2] (ăk′ə-mə, -mô′, ä′kə-). A pueblo of west-central New Mexico west of Albuquerque. Founded c. 1100–1250, it is regarded as the oldest continuously inhabited community in the United States. Population, 500.

A·con·ca·gua (ăk′ən-kä′gwə, ä′kən-). A mountain, 7,025.4 m (23,034 ft) high, in the Andes of western Argentina near the Chilean border. The highest peak of the Western Hemisphere, it was first scaled in 1897.

ac·o·nite (ăk′ə-nīt′) *n.* **1.** Any of various, usually poisonous perennial herbs of the genus *Aconitum,* having tuberous roots, palmately lobed leaves, blue or white flowers with large hoodlike upper sepals, and an aggregate of follicles. **2.** The dried poisonous roots of these plants, used as a source of drugs. Also called *monkshood.* [French *aconit,* from Latin *aconītum,* from Greek *akoniton.*]

A·ço·res (ä-sôr′ĕsh). See **Azores.**

a·corn (ā′kôrn′, ā′kərn) *n.* The fruit of an oak, consisting of a single-seeded, thick-walled nut set in a woody, cuplike base. [Middle English *akorn,* from Old English *æcern.*]

WORD HISTORY: A thoughtful glance at the word *acorn* might produce the surmise that it is made up of *oak* and *corn,* especially if we think of *corn* in its sense of "a kernel or seed of a plant," as in *peppercorn.* The fact that others thought the word was so constituted partly accounts for the present form *acorn.* Here we see the workings of the process of linguistic change known as folk etymology, an alteration in form of a word or phrase so that it resembles a more familiar term mistakenly regarded as analogous. *Acorn* actually goes back to Old English *æcern,* "acorn," which in turn goes back to the Indo-European root *ōg-,* meaning "fruit, berry."

acorn squash *n.* A type of winter squash shaped somewhat like an acorn and having longitudinal ridges, a variously colored rind, and yellow to orange flesh.

acorn worm *n.* Any of a class (Enteropneusta) of hemichordate, wormlike animals that inhabit shallow burrows in mud or sand flats of intertidal zones and are equipped with an acornlike proboscis used for digging and collecting food.

a·cous·tic (ə-kōō′stĭk) also **a·cous·ti·cal** (-stĭ-kəl) *adj.* **1.** Of or relating to sound, the sense of hearing, or the science of sound. **2.** Designed to carry sound or to aid in hearing. **3.** *Music.* **a.** Of, relating to, or being an instrument that does not feature electronically modified sound: *an acoustic guitar; an acoustic bass.* **b.** Being a performance that features such instruments: *opened the show with an acoustic set.* **—acoustic** *n. Music.* An acoustic instrument. [Greek *akoustikos,* pertaining to hearing, from *akouein,* to hear. See **keu-** in Appendix.] **—a·cous′ti·cal·ly** *adv.*

ac·ous·ti·cian (ăk′ōō-stĭsh′ən) *n.* A specialist in acoustics.

acoustic nerve *n.* Either of the eighth pair of cranial nerves that divides to form the cochlear nerve and the vestibular nerve. Also called *auditory nerve.*

a·cous·tics (ə-kōō′stĭks) *n.* **1.** *(used with a sing. verb).* The scientific study of sound, especially of its generation, transmission, and reception. **2.** *(used with a pl. verb).* The total effect of sound, especially as produced in an enclosed space.

a·cous·to·e·lec·tric (ə-kōō′stō-ĭ-lĕk′trĭk) *adj.* Of or relating to electroacoustics. [ACOUST(IC) + ELECTRIC.] **—a·cous′to·e·lec′tri·cal·ly** *adv.*

a·cous·to·op·tics (ə-kōō′stō-ŏp′tĭks) *n.* *(used with a sing. verb).* The science of the interaction of acoustic and optical phenomena. [ACOUST(IC) + OPTICS.] **—a·cous′to·op′ti·cal** *adj.* **—a·cous′to·op′ti·cal·ly** *adv.*

ACP *abbr.* American College of Physicians.

acpt. *abbr.* Acceptance.

ac·quaint (ə-kwānt′) *tr.v.* **-quaint·ed, -quaint·ing, -quaints. 1.a.** To cause to come to know personally: *Let me acquaint you with my family.* **b.** To make familiar: *acquainted myself with the controls.* **2.** To inform: *Please acquaint us with your plans.* [Middle English *aqueinten,* from Old French *acointier,* from Medieval Latin *adcognitāre,* from Latin *accognitus,* past

aconite

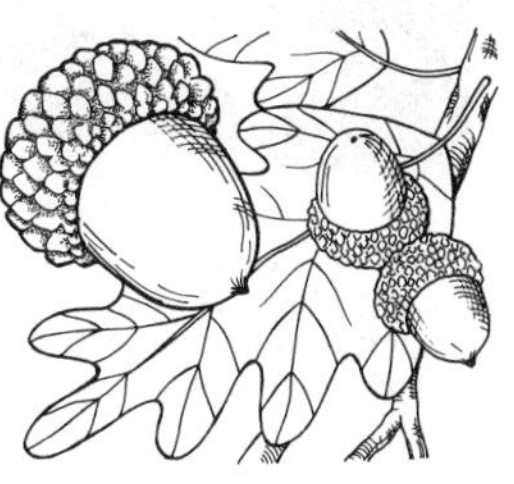

acorn

acorn squash

ă pat	oi boy
ā pay	ou out
âr care	ŏŏ took
ä father	ōō boot
ĕ pet	ŭ cut
ē be	ûr urge
ĭ pit	th thin
ī pie	*th* this
îr pier	hw which
ŏ pot	zh vision
ō toe	ə about, item
ô paw	♦ regionalism

Stress marks: ′ (primary); ′ (secondary), as in **dictionary** (dĭk′shə-nĕr′ē)

participle of *accognoscere,* to know perfectly : *ad-,* intensive pref.; see AD– + *cognoscere,* to know; see COGNITION.]

ac·quain·tance (ə-kwān′təns) *n.* **1.** Knowledge of a person acquired by a relationship less intimate than friendship. **2.** A person whom one knows. **3.** Knowledge or information about something or someone. **—ac·quain′tance·ship′** *n.*

ac·quaint·ed (ə-kwān′tĭd) *adj.* **1.** Known by or familiar with another. **2.** Informed or familiar: *Are you fully acquainted with the facts?*

ac·qui·esce (ăk′wē-ĕs′) *intr.v.* **-esced, -esc·ing, -esc·es.** To consent or comply passively or without protest. See Synonyms at **assent.** [Latin *acquiēscere* : *ad-,* ad- + *quiēscere,* to rest (from *quiēs,* rest; see **kʷeiə-** in Appendix).]

USAGE NOTE: When *acquiesce* takes a preposition, it is usually used with *in* (*acquiesced in the ruling*) but sometimes with *to* (*acquiesced to her parents' wishes*). *Acquiesced with* is obsolete.

ac·qui·es·cence (ăk′wē-ĕs′əns) *n.* **1.** Passive assent or agreement without protest. **2.** The state of being acquiescent.

ac·qui·es·cent (ăk′wē-ĕs′ənt) *adj.* Disposed or willing to acquiesce. See Synonyms at **obedient.** **—ac′qui·es′cent·ly** *adv.*

ac·quire (ə-kwīr′) *tr.v.* **-quired, -quir·ing, -quires. 1.** To gain possession of: *acquire 100 shares of stock.* **2.** To get by one's own efforts: *acquire proficiency in math.* **3.** *Aerospace.* To locate (a satellite, for example) with a detector, especially radar. [Middle English *acqueren,* from Old French *aquerre,* from Latin *acquīrere,* to add to : *ad-,* ad- + *quaerere,* to seek, get.] **—ac·quir′a·ble** *adj.* **—ac·quir′er** *n.*

ac·quired antibody (ə-kwīrd′) *n.* An antibody produced by an immune response, in contrast to one occurring naturally in an individual.

acquired character *n.* A nonhereditary change of function or structure in a plant or animal made in response to the environment. Also called *acquired characteristic.*

acquired immune deficiency syndrome *n.* AIDS.

acquired immunity *n.* Immunity obtained either from the development of antibodies in response to exposure to an antigen, as from vaccination or an attack of an infectious disease, or from the transmission of antibodies, as from mother to fetus through the placenta or the injection of antiserum.

acrobat
Members of the National China Acrobats performing on unicycles

ac·quire·ment (ə-kwīr′mənt) *n.* **1.** The act of acquiring. **2.** An attainment, such as a skill or social accomplishment.

ac·qui·si·tion (ăk′wĭ-zĭsh′ən) *n.* **1.** The act of acquiring. **2.** Something acquired, especially an addition to an established category or group. **3.** *Aerospace.* The process of locating a satellite, guided missile, or moving target so that its track or orbit can be determined. [Middle English *adquisicioun,* attainment, from Latin *acquisitiō, acquisitiōn-,* from *acquisitus,* past participle of *acquīrere,* to acquire. See ACQUIRE.]

ac·quis·i·tive (ə-kwĭz′ĭ-tĭv) *adj.* **1.** Characterized by a strong desire to gain and possess. **2.** Tending to acquire and retain ideas or information: *an acquisitive mind.* **—ac·quis′i·tive·ly** *adv.* **—ac·quis′i·tive·ness** *n.* **—ac·quis′i·tor** (-tər) *n.*

ac·quit (ə-kwĭt′) *tr.v.* **-quit·ted, -quit·ting, -quits. 1.** *Law.* To free or clear from a charge or accusation. **2.** To release or discharge from a duty. **3.** To conduct (oneself) in a specified manner. **4.** *Obsolete.* To repay. [Middle English *aquiten,* from Old French *aquiter* : *a-,* to (from Latin *ad-;* see AD–) + *quite,* free, clear (from Medieval Latin *quittus,* variant of Latin *quiētus,* past participle of *quiēscere,* to rest; see QUIET).] **—ac·quit′ter** *n.*

ac·quit·tal (ə-kwĭt′l) *n. Law.* **1.** Judgment, as by a jury or judge, that a defendant is not guilty of a crime as charged. **2.** The state of being found or proved not guilty.

ac·quit·tance (ə-kwĭt′ns) *n.* A written release from an obligation, specifically a receipt indicating payment in full.

acr– *pref.* Variant of **acro–.**

acropolis
As reconstructed by Friedrich Ritter von Thiersch (1852–1921)

a·cre (ā′kər) *n. Abbr.* **A, a., A., ac. 1.** A unit of area in the U.S. Customary System, used in land and sea floor measurement and equal to 160 square rods, 4,840 square yards, or 43,560 square feet. See table at **measurement. 2. acres.** Property in the form of land; estate. **3.** Often **acres.** A wide expanse, as of land or other matter: *"Everything was streaky pink marble and acres of textureless carpeting"* (Anne Tyler). **4.** *Archaic.* A field or plot of arable land. [Middle English *aker,* field, acre, from Old English *æcer.* See **agro-** in Appendix.]

A·cre (ä′krə, ā′kər) also **Ak·ko** (ä-kō′, ä′kō). A port of northern Israel on the Bay of Haifa. During the Crusades it changed hands many times between Christians and Moslems. Acre was ceded to the Arabs in the United Nations partition of Palestine in 1948 but was captured by Israel shortly thereafter. Population, 37,700.

a·cre·age (ā′kər-ĭj, ā′krĭj) *n. Abbr.* **a.** Area of land measured in acres.

a·cre-foot (ā′kər-fo͝ot′) *n.* The volume of water, 43,560 cubic feet, that will cover an area of one acre to a depth of one foot.

a·cre-inch (ā′kər-ĭnch′) *n.* One twelfth of an acre-foot, equal to 3,630 cubic feet.

ac·rid (ăk′rĭd) *adj.* **1.** Unpleasantly sharp, pungent, or bitter to the taste or smell. See Synonyms at **bitter. 2.** Caustic in language or tone. [From Latin *ācer,* sharp (probably modeled on ACID). See **ak-** in Appendix.] **—a·crid′i·ty** (ə-krĭd′ĭ-tē), **ac′rid·ness** *n.* **—ac′rid·ly** *adv.*

ac·ri·dine (ăk′rĭ-dēn′) *n.* A coal tar derivative, $C_{13}H_9N$, that has a strongly irritating odor and is used in the manufacture of dyes and synthetics.

ac·ri·fla·vine (ăk′rə-flā′vēn′, -vĭn) *n.* A brown or orange powder, $C_{14}H_{14}N_3Cl$, derived from acridine and used as a topical antiseptic. [ACRI(DINE) + FLAVIN.]

ac·ri·mo·ni·ous (ăk′rə-mō′nē-əs) *adj.* Bitter and sharp in language or tone; rancorous: *an acrimonious on-air exchange between the candidate and the anchorperson.* **—ac′ri·mo′ni·ous·ly** *adv.* **—ac′ri·mo′ni·ous·ness** *n.*

ac·ri·mo·ny (ăk′rə-mō′nē) *n.* Bitter, sharp, ill-natured animosity, especially as it is exhibited in speech or behavior. [Latin *ācrimōnia,* sharpness, from *ācer,* sharp. See **ak-** in Appendix.]

A·cris·i·us (ə-krĭz′ē-əs) *n. Greek Mythology.* A king of Argos and father of Danaë who was killed by his grandson Perseus.

acro– or **acr–** *pref.* **1.a.** Top; summit: *acropetal.* **b.** Height: *acrophobia.* **2.a.** Tip; beginning: *acronym.* **b.** Extremity of the body: *acromegaly.* [From Greek *akros,* extreme. See **ak-** in Appendix.]

ac·ro·bat (ăk′rə-băt′) *n.* **1.** One who is skilled in feats of balance and agility in gymnastics. **2.** One who is facile at changing one's viewpoint or position on short notice in response to the circumstances. [French *acrobate,* from Greek *akrobatēs,* from *akrobatein,* to walk on tiptoe : *akros,* high; see ACRO– + *bainein, bat-,* to walk; see **gʷā-** in Appendix.] **—ac′ro·bat′ic** *adj.* **—ac′ro·bat′i·cal·ly** *adv.*

ac·ro·bat·ics (ăk′rə-băt′ĭks) *n. (used with a sing. or pl. verb).* **1.a.** The gymnastic moves of an acrobat. **b.** The art, skill, or performance of an acrobat. **2.** A display of spectacular virtuosic skill and agility: *vocal acrobatics.*

ac·ro·cen·tric (ăk′rō-sĕn′trĭk) *adj.* Having the centromere located near one end of the chromosome so that one chromosomal arm is long and the other is short. **—ac′ro·cen′tric** *n.*

ac·ro·ceph·a·ly (ăk′rə-sĕf′ə-lē) *n.* See **oxycephaly.** **—ac′ro·ce·phal′ic** (-sə-făl′ĭk) *adj.*

ac·ro·dont (ăk′rə-dŏnt′) *adj.* Having teeth attached to the edge of the jawbone without sockets. [ACR(O)– + –ODONT.] **—ac′ro·dont′** *n.*

ac·ro·lect (ăk′rə-lĕct′) *n. Linguistics.* The variety of language in an area undergoing decreolization that is closest to the standard variety of a major international language, such as standard Jamaican English. [ACRO– + (DIA)LECT.]

a·cro·le·in (ə-krō′lē-ĭn) *n.* A colorless, flammable, poisonous liquid aldehyde, CH_2CHCHO, having an acrid odor and vapors irritating to the eyes. [ACR(ID) + OLEIN.]

ac·ro·meg·a·ly (ăk′rō-mĕg′ə-lē) *n.* A chronic disease of adults marked by enlargement of the bones of the extremities, face, and jaw that is caused by overactivity of the pituitary gland. [French *acromégalie* : Greek *akron,* extremity; see ACRO– + Greek *megas, megal-,* big; see **meg-** in Appendix.] **—ac′ro·me·gal′ic** (-mĭ-găl′ĭk) *adj. & n.*

ac·ro·mel·ic (ăk′rō-mĕl′ĭk) *adj.* Of or relating to the end of the extremities. [ACRO– + Greek *melos,* limb.]

a·cro·mi·on (ə-krō′mē-ən) *n.* The outer end of the scapula to which the collarbone is attached. [New Latin *acrōmion,* from Greek *akrōmion* : *akros,* extreme; see **ak-** in Appendix + *ōmion,* diminutive of *ōmos,* shoulder.]

ac·ro·nym (ăk′rə-nĭm′) *n.* A word formed from the initial letters of a name, such as *WAC* for *W*omen's *A*rmy *C*orps, or by combining initial letters or parts of a series of words, such as *radar* for *ra*dio *d*etecting *a*nd *r*anging. [ACR(O)– + –ONYM.] **—ac′ro·nym′ic, a·cron′y·mous** (ə-krŏn′ə-məs) *adj.*

a·crop·e·tal (ə-krŏp′ĭ-tl) *adj.* Developing or maturing from the base toward the apex, as in those plant organs in which the younger tissues are nearer the apex. **—a·crop′e·tal·ly** *adv.*

ac·ro·pho·bi·a (ăk′rə-fō′bē-ə) *n.* An abnormal fear of high places.

a·crop·o·lis (ə-krŏp′ə-lĭs) *n.* The fortified height or citadel of an ancient Greek city. [Greek *akropolis* : *akron,* top; see ACRO– + *polis,* city; see **pelə-**[3] in Appendix.]

ac·ro·some (ăk′rə-sōm′) *n.* A caplike structure at the anterior end of a spermatozoon that produces enzymes aiding in egg penetration. [ACRO– + –SOME[3].] **—ac′ro·so′mal** (-sō′məl) *adj.*

a·cross (ə-krôs′, ə-krŏs′) *prep.* **1.** On, at, or from the other side of: *across the street.* **2.** So as to cross; through: *drew lines across the paper.* **3.** From one side of to the other: *a bridge across a river.* **4.** Into contact with: *came across my old roommate.* **—across** *adv.* **1.** From one side to the other: *The footbridge swayed when I ran across.* **2.** On or to the opposite side: *We came across by ferry.* **3.** Crosswise; crossed. **4.** In such a manner as to be comprehensible, acceptable, or successful: *put our idea across; get a message across.* **—across** *adj.* Being in a crossed position: *seated with arms across.* [Middle English *acrois,* from Anglo-Norman *an croiz* : *an,* in (from Latin *in;* see IN–[2]) + *croiz,* cross (from Latin *crux;* see CROSS).]

a·cross-the-board (ə-krôs′thə-bôrd′, -bōrd′, ə-krŏs′-) *adj.* **1.** Including all categories or members, especially in an occupation or industry: *an across-the-board pay hike; an across-the-board policy decision.* **2.** *Sports & Games.* Of, relating to, or being a racing wager whereby equal amounts are bet on the same contestant to win, place, or show.

a·cros·tic (ə-krôʹstĭk, ə-krŏsʹtĭk) *n.* **1.** A poem or series of lines in which certain letters, usually the first in each line, form a name, motto, or message when read in sequence. **2.** See **word square.** [French *acrostiche,* from Old French, from Greek *akrostikhis* : *akron,* head, end; see ACRO– + *stikhos,* line; see **steigh-** in Appendix.] —**a·crosʹtic** *adj.* —**a·crosʹti·cal·ly** *adv.*

WORD HISTORY: An acrostic gives the reader two for one, and the etymology of the word emphasizes one of these two. Our word goes back to the Greek word *akrostikhis,* "acrostic," which is a combination of Greek *akron,* "head," and *stikhos,* "row, line of verse." Literally *akrostikhis* means "the line at the head," emphasizing the fact that an acrostic has in addition to horizontal rows a vertical row formed of the letters at the "head" or start of each line. In ancient manuscripts, in which a line of verse did not necessarily correspond to a line of text, an acrostic would have looked particularly striking, with each of its lines standing by itself and beginning with a capital letter. Our word for this type of composition is first found in English in the 16th century.

ACRR *abbr.* American Council on Race Relations.

ac·ry·late resin (ăkʹrə-lātʹ) *n.* Any of a class of acrylic resins used in emulsion paints, adhesives, plastics, and textile and paper finishes. Also called *acrylate.*

a·cryl·ic (ə-krĭlʹĭk) *n.* **1.** An acrylic resin. **2.** A paint containing acrylic resin. **3.** A painting done in acrylic resin. **4.** An acrylic fiber. [ACR(OLEIN) + –YL + –IC.] —**a·crylʹic** *adj.*

acrylic acid *n.* An easily polymerized, colorless, corrosive liquid, $H_2C{:}CHCOOH$, used as a monomer for acrylate resins.

acrylic fiber *n.* Any of numerous synthetic fibers polymerized from acrylonitrile.

acrylic resin *n.* Any of numerous thermoplastic or thermosetting polymers or copolymers of acrylic acid, methacrylic acid, esters of these acids, or acrylonitrile, used to produce paints, synthetic rubbers, and lightweight plastics.

ac·ry·lo·ni·trile (ăkʹrə-lō-nīʹtrəl, -trēl, -trīl) *n.* A colorless, liquid organic compound, $H_2C{:}CHCN$, used in the manufacture of acrylic rubber and fibers. [ACRYL(IC RESIN) + NITRILE.]

ACS *abbr.* **1.** American Chemical Society. **2.** American College of Surgeons.

act (ăkt) *n.* **1.** The process of doing or performing something: *the act of thinking.* **2.** Something done or performed; a deed: *a charitable act.* **3.** A decisional product, such as a statute, decree, or enactment, delivered by a legislative or a judicial body. **4.** A formal written record of proceedings or transactions. **5. a.** One of the major divisions of a play or an opera. **b.** A theatrical performance that forms part of a longer presentation: *a juggling act.* **6.** A manifestation of intentional or unintentional insincerity; a pose: *put on an act.* —**act** *v.* **act·ed, act·ing, acts.** —*tr.* **1.** To play the part of; assume the dramatic role of: *She plans to act Lady Macbeth in summer stock.* **2.** To perform (a role) on the stage: *act the part of the villain.* **3. a.** To behave like or pose as; impersonate: *Don't act the fool.* **b.** To behave in a manner suitable for: *Act your age.* —*intr.* **1.** To behave or comport oneself: *She acts like a born leader.* **2.** To perform in a dramatic role or roles. **3.** To be suitable for theatrical performance: *This scene acts well.* **4.** To behave affectedly or unnaturally; pretend. **5.** To appear or seem to be: *The dog acted ferocious.* **6.** To carry out an action: *We acted immediately. The governor has not yet acted on the bill.* **7.** To operate or function in a specific way: *His mind acts quickly.* **8.** To serve or function as a substitute for another: *A coin can act as a screwdriver.* **9.** To produce an effect: *waited five minutes for the anesthetic to act.* —***phrasal verbs.*** **act out. 1. a.** To perform in or as if in a play; dramatize: *act out a story.* **b.** To realize in action: *wanted to act out his theory.* **2.** To express (unconscious impulses, for example) in an overt manner without awareness or understanding. **act up. 1.** To misbehave. **2.** To malfunction. **3.** *Informal.* To become active or troublesome after a period of quiescence: *My left knee acts up in damp weather. Her arthritis is acting up again.* —***idioms.*** **be in on the act.** To be included in an activity. **clean up (one's) act.** *Slang.* To improve one's behavior or performance. **get into the act.** To insert oneself into an ongoing activity, project, or situation. **get (one's) act together.** *Slang.* To get organized. [Middle English, from Old French *acte,* from Latin *āctus,* a doing, and *āctum,* a thing done, both from *agere, āct-,* to drive, do. See **ag-** in Appendix.] —**acʹta·bilʹi·ty** *n.* —**actʹa·ble** *adj.*

USAGE NOTE: The words *act* and *action* both mean "a deed" and "the process of doing." However, other senses of *act,* such as "a decision made by a legislative body" and of *action,* such as "habitual or vigorous activity" show that *act* tends to refer to a deed while *action* tends to refer to the process of doing. The demands of meaning or idiom will often require one word or the other: *class act* and *class action,* for example, are not interchangeable. In cases where either can be used, either is acceptable: my *act* (or *action*) was premature.

ACT *abbr.* American College Test.

A.C.T. *abbr.* Australian Capital Territory.

Ac·tae·on (ăk-tēʹən) *n. Greek Mythology.* A young hunter who, having inadvertently observed Artemis while she was bathing, was turned by her into a stag and killed by his own dogs.

actg. *abbr.* Acting.

ACTH (āʹsēʹtē-āchʹ) *n.* A hormone produced by the anterior lobe of the pituitary gland that stimulates the secretion of cortisone and other hormones by the adrenal cortex. Also called *adrenocorticotropin, corticotropin.* [A(DRENO)C(ORTICO)T(ROPIC) H(ORMONE).]

ac·tin (ăkʹtĭn) *n.* A protein found in muscle that together with myosin functions in muscle contraction. [Latin *āctus,* motion (from *agere, āct-,* to drive, do; see ACT) + –IN.]

actin– *pref.* Variant of **actino–.**

ac·ti·nal (ăkʹtĭ-nəl, ăk-tīʹ-) *adj.* Of, relating to, or located on the part of a radially symmetric animal from which the tentacles radiate or the side where the oral area is found. —**acʹti·nal·ly** *adv.*

act·ing (ăkʹtĭng) *adj.* **1.** *Abbr.* **a., actg.** Temporarily assuming the duties or authority of another. See Synonyms at **temporary. 2. a.** That contains directions for use in a dramatic performance: *the play's acting text.* **b.** That is appropriate for dramatic performance: *an acting comedy.* —**acting** *n.* **1.** The occupation of an actor or actress. **2.** Performance as an actor or actress. **3.** False behavior; pretense.

ac·tin·i·a (ăk-tĭnʹē-ə) also **ac·tin·i·an** (-ən) *n., pl.* **-i·ae** (-ē-ēʹ) also **-i·ans.** A sea anemone or a related animal. [New Latin *Actinia,* type genus, from Greek *aktis, aktin-,* ray. See ACTINO–.]

ac·tin·ic (ăk-tĭnʹĭk) *adj.* Of, relating to, or exhibiting actinism. —**ac·tinʹi·cal·ly** *adv.*

actinic ray *n.* Photochemically active radiation, as of the sun.

ac·ti·nide (ăkʹtə-nīdʹ) *n.* Any of a series of chemically similar, radioactive elements with atomic numbers ranging from 89 (actinium) through 103 (lawrencium).

ac·ti·nism (ăkʹtə-nĭzʹəm) *n.* The intrinsic property in radiation that produces photochemical activity.

ac·tin·i·um (ăk-tĭnʹē-əm) *n. Symbol* **Ac** A radioactive element found in uranium ores, used in equilibrium with its decay products as a source of alpha rays. Its longest lived isotope is Ac 227 with a half-life of 21.7 years. Atomic number 89; melting point 1,050°C; boiling point (estimated) 3,200°C; specific gravity (calculated) 10.07; valence 3. See table at **element.**

actino– or **actin–** *pref.* **1.** Radial in form: *actinoid.* **2.** Actinic radiation: *actinometer.* [From Greek *aktis, aktin-,* ray.]

ac·ti·noid (ăkʹtə-noidʹ) *adj.* Having a radial form, as a starfish.

ac·tin·o·lite (ăk-tĭnʹə-lītʹ) *n.* A greenish variety of amphibole.

ac·ti·no·mere (ăk-tĭnʹə-mîrʹ) *n.* One of the segments forming the body of a radially symmetric animal.

ac·ti·nom·e·ter (ăkʹtə-nŏmʹĭ-tər) *n.* Any of several radiometric instruments, such as a pyrheliometer, used chiefly for meteorological measurements of terrestrial and solar radiation. —**acʹti·no·metʹric** (-nō-mĕtʹrĭk), **acʹti·no·metʹri·cal** *adj.* —**acʹti·nomʹe·try** *n.*

ac·ti·no·mor·phic (ăkʹtə-nō-môrʹfĭk) also **ac·ti·no·mor·phous** (-fəs) *adj.* Of or relating to a flower that can be divided into equal halves along any diameter, such as the flowers of the rose or tulip. —**acʹti·no·morʹphy** *n.*

ac·ti·no·my·ces (ăkʹtə-nō-mīʹsēzʹ) *n., pl.* **actinomyces.** Any of various filamentous, mostly anaerobic microorganisms of the genus *Actinomyces,* which includes the causative agents of actinomycosis. [New Latin, genus name : ACTINO– + Greek *mukēs,* fungus.] —**acʹti·no·my·ceʹtal** (-mī-sētʹl) *adj.*

ac·ti·no·my·cete (ăkʹtə-nō-mīʹsētʹ, -mī-sētʹ) *n.* Any of various filamentous or rod-shaped, often pathogenic microorganisms of the order Actinomycetales that are found in soil and resemble bacteria and fungi. —**acʹti·no·my·ceʹtous** *adj.*

ac·ti·no·my·cin (ăkʹtə-nō-mīʹsĭn) *n.* Any of various red, often toxic, polypeptide antibiotics obtained from soil bacteria.

actinomycin D *n.* See **dactinomycin.**

ac·ti·no·my·co·sis (ăkʹtə-nō-mī-kōʹsĭs) *n.* An inflammatory disease of cattle, hogs, and sometimes human beings, caused by microorganisms of the genus *Actinomyces* and characterized by lumpy tumors of the mouth, neck, chest, and abdomen. Also called *lumpy jaw.* —**acʹti·no·my·cotʹic** (-kŏtʹĭk) *adj.*

ac·ti·non (ăkʹtə-nŏnʹ) *n.* A radioactive, inert, gaseous isotope of radon, with a half-life of 3.92 seconds. [ACTIN(IUM) + –ON[2].]

ac·ti·no·u·ra·ni·um (ăkʹtə-nō-yŏŏ-rāʹnē-əm) *n.* The isotope of uranium with mass number 235, fissionable with slow neutrons. [ACTIN(IUM) + URANIUM.]

ac·tion (ăkʹshən) *n.* **1.** The state or process of acting or doing. **2.** A deed. See Usage Note at **act. 3.** A movement or a series of movements. **4.** Manner of movement: *a horse with good action; a gearshift with smooth action.* **5.** Habitual or vigorous activity; energy: *a woman of action.* **6.** Often **actions.** Behavior or conduct. **7. a.** The operating parts of a mechanism. **b.** The manner in which such parts operate. **8.** A change that occurs in the body or in a bodily organ as a result of its functioning. **9.** A physical change, as in position, mass, or energy, that an object or a system undergoes. **10.** The series of events and episodes that form the plot of a story or play. **11.** The appearance of animation of a figure in painting or sculpture. **12.** *Law.* A judicial proceeding whose purpose is to obtain relief at the hands of a court. **13.** Armed encounter; combat: *killed in action.* **14.** The most important or exciting work or activity in a specific field or area: *always*

actinia
Sea anemone

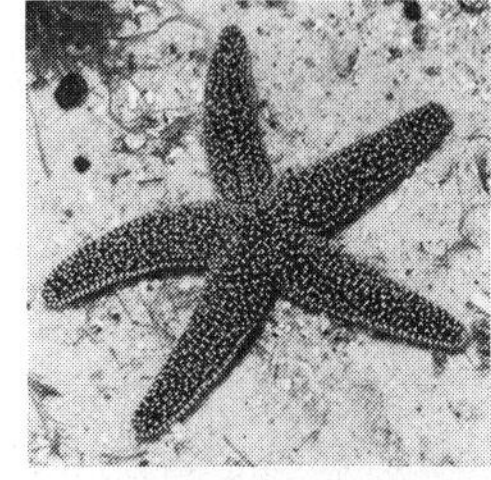

actinoid
A starfish
Asterias forbesii

ă **pat**	oi **boy**
ā **pay**	ou **out**
âr **care**	ŏŏ **took**
ä **father**	ōō **boot**
ĕ **pet**	ŭ **cut**
ē **be**	ûr **urge**
ĭ **pit**	th **thin**
ī **pie**	*th* **this**
îr **pier**	hw **which**
ŏ **pot**	zh **vision**
ō **toe**	ə **about, item**
ô **paw**	♦ **regionalism**

Stress marks: **ʹ** (primary); ʹ (secondary), as in **dictionary** (dĭkʹshə-nĕrʹē)

heads for where the action is. —*attributive.* Often used to modify another noun: *an action film; action stories.*

ac·tion·a·ble (ăk′shə-nə-bəl) *adj. Law.* Giving cause for legal action: *an actionable statement.* —**ac′tion·a·bly** *adv.*

action painting *n.* A style of abstract painting that uses techniques such as the dribbling or splashing of paint to achieve a spontaneous effect. —**action painter** *n.*

action potential *n.* A momentary change in electrical potential on the surface of a nerve or muscle cell that takes place when it is stimulated, especially by the transmission of a nerve impulse: *Stimulating a nerve fiber causes an action potential to spread across the nerve cell, making it contract.*

Ac·ti·um (ăk′shē-əm, -tē-). A promontory and ancient town of western Greece. In 31 B.C. it was the site of Octavian's victory over Mark Antony and Cleopatra. The battle established Octavian (later Augustus) as the ruler of Rome.

ac·ti·vate (ăk′tə-vāt′) *v.* **-vat·ed, -vat·ing, -vates.** —**activate** *tr.v.* **1.** To set in motion; make active or more active. **2.** To organize or create (a military unit, for example): *activate the National Guard.* **3.** To treat (sewage) with aeration and bacteria to aid decomposition. **4.** *Chemistry.* To accelerate a reaction in, as by heat. **5.** *Physics.* To make (a substance) radioactive. **6.** *Biology.* To convert (certain biological compounds) into biologically active derivatives. —**ac′ti·va′tion** *n.* —**ac′ti·va′tor** *n.*

action painting
Untitled ink on paper by Jackson Pollock, c. 1950
India ink, 17½" x 22¼" (irregular). The Museum of Modern Art, New York, Gift of Mr. and Mrs. Ronald Lauder in honor of Eliza Parkinson Cobb.

ac·ti·vat·ed charcoal (ăk′tə-vā′tĭd) *n.* Highly absorbent carbon obtained by heating granulated charcoal to exhaust contained gases, resulting in a highly porous form with a very large surface area. It is used primarily for purifying gases by adsorption, solvent recovery, or deodorization and as an antidote to certain poisons. Also called *activated carbon.*

ac·ti·va·tion analysis (ăk′tə-vā′shən) *n.* A method for analyzing a material for its component chemical elements by bombarding it with nuclear particles or gamma rays and identifying the resultant radiations.

ac·tive (ăk′tĭv) *adj.* **1.** Being in physical motion: *active fish in the aquarium.* **2.** Functioning or capable of functioning. **3.** Disposed to take action or effectuate change: *a director who takes active interest in corporate operations.* **4. a.** Engaged in activity; participating: *an active member of a club.* **b.** Busy: *active stock and bond markets.* **c.** Being in continuous use or operation: *an active brokerage account.* **5.** Being in a state of action; not passive or quiescent: *an active volcano.* **6. a.** Characterized by energetic action or activity; lively. **b.** Requiring physical exertion and energy: *Tennis is an active sport.* **7.** *Grammar.* **a.** Indicating that the subject of the sentence is performing or causing the action expressed by the verb. Used of a verb form or voice. **b.** Expressing action rather than a state of being. Used of verbs such as *run, speak,* and *move.* **8.** Producing profit, interest, or dividends: *active accounts; active stocks.* **9.** Being on full military duty and receiving full pay. **10.** *Music.* Suggesting that something follows: *active tones.* —**active** *n.* **1.** *Grammar.* **a.** The active voice. **b.** A construction or form in the active voice. **2.** A participating member of an organization: *union actives.* [Middle English *actif,* from Old French, from Latin *āctīvus,* from *agere, āct-,* to drive, do. See ACT.] —**ac′tive·ly** *adv.* —**ac′tive·ness** *n.*

SYNONYMS: *active, energetic, dynamic, vigorous, lively.* These adjectives are compared as they mean engaged in activity. *Active,* the most neutral, merely means being in a state of action as opposed to being passive or quiescent: *an active toddler; an active imagination; saw active service in the army. Energetic* suggests sustained enthusiastic action with unflagging vitality: *an energetic fund raiser for the college. Dynamic* connotes energy and forcefulness that is often inspiring to others: *A dynamic speaker, the senator often persuades her colleagues to change their votes. Vigorous* implies healthy strength and robustness: *"a vigorous crusader against apartheid and government press restrictions"* (Christian Science Monitor). *Lively* suggests brisk alertness, animation, and energy: *I take a lively interest in politics.*

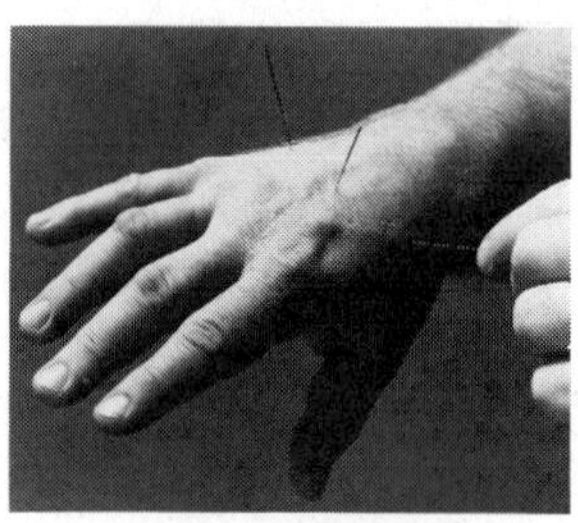

acupuncture

active immunity *n.* Immunity resulting from the development of antibodies in response to the presence of an antigen, as from vaccination or exposure to an infectious disease.

active site *n.* The part of an enzyme at which catalysis of the substrate occurs.

active transport *n.* The movement of a chemical substance through a gradient of concentration or electrical potential in the direction opposite to normal diffusion, requiring the expenditure of energy: *active transport across a cell membrane.*

ac·tiv·ism (ăk′tə-vĭz′əm) *n.* The theory, doctrine, or practice of assertive, often militant action, such as mass demonstrations or strikes, used as a means of opposing or supporting a controversial issue, entity, or person. —**ac·tiv·ist′ic** *adj.*

ac·tiv·ist (ăk′tə-vĭst) *n.* A proponent or practitioner of activism: *political activists.* —**activist** *adj.* **1.** Of, relating to, or engaged in activism. **2.** Of, relating to, or being an activist.

ac·tiv·i·ty (ăk-tĭv′ĭ-tē) *n., pl.* **-ties.** **1.** The state of being active. **2.** Energetic action or movement; liveliness. **3. a.** A specified pursuit in which a person partakes. **b.** An educational process or procedure intended to stimulate learning through actual experience. **4.** The intensity of a radioactive source. **5.** The ability to take part in a chemical reaction. **6.** A physiological process: *respiratory activity.*

act of God *n., pl.* **acts of God.** An unusual, extraordinary, or unforeseeable manifestation of the forces of nature beyond the powers of human intervention, such as a tornado or a bolt of lightning.

ac·to·my·o·sin (ăk′tə-mī′ə-sĭn) *n.* The system of actin and myosin that, with other substances, constitutes muscle fiber and is responsible for muscular contraction. [ACT(IN) + MYOSIN.]

Ac·ton (ăk′tən). A town of northeast Massachusetts, a residential and manufacturing suburb of Boston. Population, 17,544.

Acton, First Baron. Title of John Emerich Edward Dalberg Acton. 1834–1902. British historian who led English Roman Catholics in their opposition to the doctrine of papal infallibility.

ac·tor (ăk′tər) *n.* **1.** A theatrical performer. **2.** One who takes part; a participant: *"France, Britain . . . and any other external actors now involved . . . in the affairs of the continent"* (Helen Kitchen). **3.** *Law.* One, such as the manager of a business, who acts for another. [Middle English *actour,* doer, probably from Latin *āctor,* doer, from *agere, āct-,* to drive, do. See ACT.]

ac·tress (ăk′trĭs) *n.* A woman who is an actor. See Usage Note at **-ess.**

Acts of the Apostles (ăkts) *pl.n.* *(used with a sing. verb). Abbr.* **Ac** *Bible.* See table at **Bible.**

ac·tu·al (ăk′cho͞o-əl) *adj.* **1.** Existing and not merely potential or possible. See Synonyms at **real**[1]. **2.** Being, existing, or acting at the present moment; current. **3.** Based on fact: *an actual account of the accident.* [Middle English, from Old French, active, from Late Latin *āctuālis,* from *agere, āct-,* to drive, do. See ACT.] —**ac′tu·al·ly** *adv.*

ac·tu·al·i·ty (ăk′cho͞o-ăl′ĭ-tē) *n., pl.* **-ties.** **1.** The state or fact of being actual; reality. See Synonyms at **existence.** **2.** Often **actualities.** Actual conditions or facts.

ac·tu·al·ize (ăk′cho͞o-ə-līz′) *v.* **-ized, -iz·ing, -iz·es.** —*tr.* **1.** To realize in action or make real: *"More flexible life patterns could . . . nurture and renew our spirits through opportunities to actualize personal dreams"* (Fred Best). **2.** To describe or portray realistically. —*intr.* To become actual. —**ac′tu·al·i·za′tion** (-ə-lĭ-zā′shən) *n.*

ac·tu·ar·y (ăk′cho͞o-ĕr′ē) *n., pl.* **-ies.** A statistician who computes insurance risks and premiums. [Latin *āctuārius,* secretary of accounts, from *ācta,* records, from *agere, āct-,* to drive, do. See ACT.] —**ac′tu·ar′i·al** (-âr′ē-əl) *adj.* —**ac′tu·ar′i·al·ly** *adv.*

ac·tu·ate (ăk′cho͞o-āt′) *tr.v.* **-at·ed, -at·ing, -ates.** **1.** To put into motion or action: *electrical relays that actuate the elevator's movements.* **2.** To move to action: *a speech that actuated dissent.* [Medieval Latin *āctuāre, āctuāt-,* from Latin *āctus,* act, from *agere, āct-,* to drive, do. See ACT.] —**ac′tu·a′tion** *n.*

ac·tu·a·tor (ăk′cho͞o-ā′tər) *n.* One that activates, especially a device responsible for actuating a mechanical device, such as one connected to a computer by a sensor link.

a·cu·i·ty (ə-kyo͞o′ĭ-tē) *n.* Acuteness of vision or perception; keenness. [Middle English *acuite,* from Old French, ultimately from Latin *acūtus,* sharp. See ACUTE.]

a·cu·le·ate (ə-kyo͞o′lē-ĭt, -āt′) *adj.* **1.** *Biology.* Having a stinger, as a bee or wasp. **2.** *Botany.* Having sharp prickles. [Latin *acūleātus,* from *acūleus,* sting, diminutive of *acus,* needle. See ACUMEN.]

a·cu·men (ə-kyo͞o′mən, ăk′yə-) *n.* Quickness, accuracy, and keenness of judgment or insight. [Latin *acūmen,* from *acuere,* to sharpen, from *acus,* needle. See **ak-** in Appendix.]

a·cu·mi·nate (ə-kyo͞o′mə-nĭt, -nāt′) *adj.* Tapering gradually to a sharp point, as the tips of certain leaves. —**acuminate** (ə-kyo͞o′mə-nāt′) *tr.v.* **-nat·ed, -nat·ing, -nates.** To sharpen or taper. [Latin *acūminātus,* past participle of *acūmināre,* to sharpen, from *acūmen,* acuteness. See ACUMEN.] —**a·cu′mi·na′tion** *n.*

ac·u·pres·sure (ak′yə-prĕsh′ər) *n.* See **shiatsu.** [ACU(PUNCTURE) + PRESSURE.]

ac·u·punc·ture (ăk′yo͞o-pŭngk′chər) *n.* A technique, as for relieving pain or inducing regional anesthesia, in which thin needles are inserted into the body at specific points. —**acupuncture** *tr.v.* **-tured, -tur·ing, -tures.** To subject to acupuncture. [Latin *acus,* needle; see ACUMEN + PUNCTURE.] —**ac′u·punc′tur·ist** *n.*

a·cute (ə-kyo͞ot′) *adj.* **1.** Having a sharp point or tip. **2.** Keenly perceptive or discerning; penetrating: *"a raw, chilling and psychologically acute novel of human passions reduced to their deadliest essence"* (Literary Guild Magazine). See Synonyms at **sharp.** **3.** Reacting readily to impressions; sensitive: *acute observers of the human comedy.* **4.** Of great importance or consequence; crucial: *an acute lack of research funds.* **5.** Extremely sharp or severe; intense: *acute pain; acute relief.* **6.** *Medicine.* **a.** Having a rapid onset and following a short but severe course: *acute disease.* **b.** Afflicted by a disease exhibiting a rapid onset followed by a short, severe course: *acute patients.* **7.** *Music.* High in pitch; shrill. **8.** *Geometry.* Designating angles less than 90°. [Latin *acūtus,* past participle of *acuere,* to sharpen, from *acus,* needle. See **ak-** in Appendix.] —**a·cute′ly** *adv.* —**a·cute′ness** *n.*

acute accent *n.* A mark (′) indicating: **a.** A raised pitch in certain languages such as Chinese and Ancient Greek. **b.** Stress of a spoken sound or syllable. **c.** Metrical stress in poetry. **d.** Sound quality or vowel length.

acv *abbr.* Actual cash value.

ACV *abbr.* Air-cushion vehicle.

a·cy·clic (ā-sī′klĭk, ā-sĭk′lĭk) *adj.* **1.** *Botany.* Not cyclic. Used especially of flowers whose parts are arranged in spirals rather than in whorls, as in magnolias. **2.** *Chemistry.* Having an open-chain molecular structure rather than a ring-shaped structure.

a·cy·clo·vir (ā-sī′klō-vîr, -klə-) *n.* A synthetic purine nucleoside analog, $C_8H_{10}N_5O_3$, derived from guanine and used topically in the treatment of herpes simplex infections, especially such infections of the genitals. [A–[1] + CYCLO– + VIR(AL) or VIR(US).]

ac·yl (ăs′əl) *n.* *Chemistry.* A radical having the general formula RCO-, derived from an organic acid. [AC(ID) + –YL.]

ad[1] (ăd) *n.* An advertisement.

ad[2] (ăd) *n.* *Sports.* An advantage in tennis.

AD *abbr.* **1.** Active duty. **2.** Air-dried.

ad. *abbr.* Adapter.

A.D. *abbr.* Often **A.D.** Anno Domini.

ad– *pref.* **1. ac–** or **af–** or **ag–** or **al–** or **ap–** or **as–** or **at–.** Toward; to. Before *c, f, g, k, l, p, q, s,* and *t, ad-* is usually assimilated to *ac-, af-, ag-, ac-, al-, ap-, ac-, as-,* and *at-,* respectively. **2.** Near; at: *adrenal.* [Latin, from *ad,* to. See **ad-** in Appendix.]

–ad *suff.* In the direction of; toward: *cephalad.* [From Latin *ad,* to. See **ad-** in Appendix.]

A·da[1] (ā′də). A city of south-central Oklahoma southeast of Oklahoma City. It is the center of a horse-breeding area. Population, 15,902.

A·da[2] (ā′də) *n.* *Computer Science.* A programming language, based on Pascal and developed for the U.S. Department of Defense. [After Augusta *Ada* Byron, Countess of Lovelace (1815–1852).]

ADA *abbr.* **1.** American Dental Association. **2.** American Diabetes Association. **3.** Americans for Democratic Action.

ad·age (ăd′ĭj) *n.* A saying that sets forth a general truth and that has gained credit through long use. See Synonyms at **saying.** [French, from Old French, from Latin *adagium.*]

USAGE NOTE: It is sometimes claimed that the expression *old adage* is redundant, inasmuch as a saying must have a certain tradition behind it to count as an *adage* in the first place. But the word *adage* is first recorded by the *OED* in the phrase *old adage,* showing that this redundancy itself is very old. Such idiomatic redundancy is paralleled by similar phrases such as *young whelp.*

a·da·gio (ə-dä′jō, -jē-ō′, -zhō, -zhē-ō) *adv. & adj.* *Music.* In a slow tempo, usually considered to be slower than andante but faster than larghetto. Used chiefly as a direction. **—adagio** *n., pl.* **-gios. 1.** *Music.* A slow passage, movement, or work, especially one using adagio as the direction. **2.** A section of a pas de deux in which the ballerina and her partner perform steps requiring lyricism and great skill in lifting, balancing, and turning. [Italian : *ad-,* at (from Latin; see AD–) + *agio,* ease (from Old Provençal *aize*) from Vulgar Latin **adiacēs,* from Latin *adiacēns,* convenient. See ADJACENT.]

A·dak (ā′dăk′). An island of western Alaska in the central Aleutian Islands. It was an important military base during World War II.

Ad·am[1] (ăd′əm). In the Old Testament, the first man and the husband of Eve.

Ad·am[2] (ăd′əm) *adj.* Of, relating to, or characteristic of the neoclassic style of furniture and architecture originated by Robert and James Adam.

Adam, Robert. 1728–1792. British architect who led the neoclassical movement in England and is noted for his elegant interior designs and for collaborations with his brother **James** (1730–1794).

Ad·am-and-Eve (ăd′əm-ənd-ēv′) *n.* See **puttyroot.**

ad·a·mant (ăd′ə-mənt, -mănt′) *adj.* Impervious to pleas, appeals, or reason; stubbornly unyielding. See Synonyms at **inflexible. —adamant** *n.* **1.** A stone once believed to be impenetrable in its hardness. **2.** An extremely hard substance. [From Middle English, a hard precious stone, from Old French *adamaunt,* from Latin *adamās, adamant-,* hard steel, diamond, anything inflexible, from Greek *adamas, adamant-,* hard steel, diamond, anything fixed or unalterable, unconquerable. See **demə-** in Appendix.]

ad·a·man·tine (ăd′ə-măn′tēn′, -tīn′, -tĭn) *adj.* **1.** Made of or resembling adamant. **2.** Having the hardness or luster of a diamond. **3.** Unyielding; inflexible: *"If there is one dominant trait that emerges from this account, it is adamantine willpower"* (Eugene Linden).

Ad·ams (ăd′əmz), **Abigail Smith.** 1744–1818. First Lady of the United States (1797–1801) as the wife of President John Adams. Her letters to her husband provide a vivid picture of life in colonial Massachusetts.

Adams, Ansel. 1902–1984. American photographer noted for his magnificent black-and-white photographs of the American wilderness.

Adams, Brooks. 1848–1927. American historian who theorized that civilizations rise and fall according to a pattern of economic growth and decline.

Adams, Charles Francis. 1807–1886. American public official who as an ambassador during the Civil War helped dissuade Great Britain from officially recognizing the Confederacy.

Adams, Franklin Pierce. Known as "F.P.A." 1881–1960. American humorist whose column "The Conning Tower" appeared in New York newspapers for more than 20 years.

Adams, Henry Brooks. 1838–1918. American historian noted for his nine-volume *History of the United States during the Administrations of Jefferson and Madison* (1889–1891). He also wrote a famous autobiography, *The Education of Henry Adams* (1918).

Adams, John. 1735–1826. The first Vice President (1789–1797) and second President (1797–1801) of the United States. He was a major figure during the American Revolution, the drafting of the Declaration of Independence, and the shaping of the Constitution.

Adams, John Quincy. 1767–1848. The sixth President of the United States (1825–1829). As secretary of state (1817–1825) he helped formulate the Monroe Doctrine. After his presidency he served in the House of Representatives (1831–1848), where he advocated antislavery measures.

Adams, Maude Kiskadden. 1872–1953. American actress whose successes included more than 1,500 performances as the lead in *Peter Pan.*

Adams, Mount. A peak, 3,753.6 m (12,307 ft) high, in the Cascade Range of southwest Washington.

Adams, Samuel. 1722–1803. American Revolutionary leader whose agitations spurred Bostonians toward rebellion against British occupation and rule. He was a member of the First and Second Continental Congresses, signed the Declaration of Independence, and served as governor of Massachusetts (1794–1797).

Ad·am's apple (ăd′əmz) *n.* The slight projection at the front of the throat formed by the largest cartilage of the larynx, usually more prominent in men than in women.

Adam's Bridge also **Ra·ma's Bridge** (rä′məz). A chain of shoals extending about 29 km (18 mi) between India and Sri Lanka. According to Hindu legend, the bridge was built to transport Rama, hero of the *Ramayana,* to the island to rescue his wife from the demon king Ravana.

Ad·am's-nee·dle (ăd′əmz-nēd′l) *n.* Any of several closely related, stemless plants of the genus *Yucca,* especially *Y. filamentosa* and *Y. smalliana* of the southeast United States. [From the spines on its leaves.]

Adam's Peak. A mountain, 2,244.8 m (7,360 ft) high, in south-central Sri Lanka. It is a sacred place of pilgrimage for Buddhists, Hindus, and Moslems.

A·da·na (ä′də-nə, ə-dä′nə). A city of southern Turkey on the Seyhan River near the Mediterranean Sea. Probably founded by the Hittites, it was colonized by the Romans in 66 B.C. Population, 574,515.

a·dapt (ə-dăpt′) *v.* **a·dapt·ed, a·dapt·ing, a·dapts.** *—tr.* To make suitable to or fit for a specific use or situation. *—intr.* To become adapted: *a species that has adapted well to winter climes.* [Middle English *adapten,* from Latin *adaptāre* : *ad-,* ad- + *aptāre,* to fit (from *aptus,* fitting; see APT).]

SYNONYMS: *adapt, accommodate, adjust, conform, fit, reconcile.* The central meaning shared by these verbs is "to make suitable to or consistent with a particular situation or use": *adapted themselves to city life; can't accommodate myself to the new requirements; adjusting their behavior to the rules; conforming her life to accord with her principles; made the punishment fit the crime; couldn't reconcile his reassuring words with his hostile actions.*
ANTONYM: *unfit.*

a·dapt·a·ble (ə-dăp′tə-bəl) *adj.* Capable of adapting or of being adapted. **—a·dapt′a·bil′i·ty, a·dapt′a·ble·ness** *n.*

ad·ap·ta·tion (ăd′ăp-tā′shən) *n.* **1.a.** The act or process of adapting. **b.** The state of being adapted. **2.a.** Something, such as a device or mechanism, that is changed or changes so as to become suitable to a new or special application or situation. **b.** A composition that has been recast into a new form: *The play is an adaptation of a short novel.* **3.** *Biology.* An alteration or adjustment in structure or habits, often hereditary, by which a species or individual improves its condition in relationship to its environment. **4.** *Physiology.* The responsive adjustment of a sense organ, such as the eye, to varying conditions, such as light intensity. **5.** Change in behavior of a person or group in response or adjustment to new or modified surroundings. **—ad′ap·ta′tion·al** *adj.* **—ad′ap·ta′tion·al·ly** *adv.*

a·dapt·er also **a·dap·tor** (ə-dăp′tər) *n.* *Abbr.* **ad.** One that adapts, such as a device used to effect operative compatibility between different parts of one or more pieces of apparatus.

a·dap·tion (ə-dăp′shən) *n.* Adaptation.

a·dap·tive (ə-dăp′tĭv) *adj.* Tending to, designed for, suitable for, or having a capacity for adaptation: *created adaptive clothing for children and young adults with special needs.* **—a·dap′tive·ly** *adv.* **—a·dap′tive·ness** *n.*

adaptive radiation *n.* Diversification of a species or single ancestral type into several forms that are each adaptively specialized to a specific environmental niche.

a·dap·tor (ə-dăp′tər) *n.* Variant of **adapter.**

A·dar (ä-där′, ä′där) *n.* The sixth month of the year in the Jewish calendar. See table at **calendar.** [Hebrew *'ădār,* from Akkadian *adaru,* a month of the Akkadian calendar corresponding to parts of February and March.]

Adar She·ni (shā-nē′) *n.* An extra month of the Hebrew year, having 29 days, added in leap years after the regular month of

Abigail Adams
Detail of portrait by Gilbert Stuart

John Adams
Detail of portrait by Gilbert Stuart

John Quincy Adams
Detail of 1864 portrait by George Peter Alexander Healy (1813–1894)

ă pat	oi boy
ā pay	ou out
âr care	ŏŏ took
ä father	ōō boot
ĕ pet	ŭ cut
ē be	ûr urge
ĭ pit	th thin
ī pie	*th* this
îr pier	hw which
ŏ pot	zh vision
ō toe	ə about, item
ô paw	♦ regionalism

Stress marks: ′ (primary); ′ (secondary), as in **dictionary** (dĭk′shə-nĕr′ē)

Adar. See table at **calendar.** [Hebrew *'ădār šēnî,* second Adar.]

ad·ax·i·al (ăd-ăk′sē-əl) *adj.* **1.** Located on the side nearest to the axis of an organ or organism. **2.** Of or relating to the side or surface facing or nearest to the axis of an organ, such as the upper surface of a leaf; ventral.

ADC *abbr.* **1.** Also **a.d.c.** Aide-de-camp. **2.** Aid to Dependent Children. **3.** Air Defense Command.

add (ăd) *v.* **add·ed, add·ing, adds.** —*tr.* **1.** To combine (a column of figures, for example) to form a sum. **2.** To join or unite so as to increase in size, quantity, quality, or scope: *added 12 inches to the deck; flowers that added beauty to the dinner table.* **3.** To say or write further. —*intr.* **1.** To find a sum in arithmetic. **2.a.** To constitute an addition: *an exploit that will add to her reputation.* **b.** To create or make an addition: *gradually added to my meager savings.* —***phrasal verb.* add up. 1.** To be reasonable, plausible, or consistent; make sense: *The witness's testimony simply did not add up.* **2.** To amount to an expected total: *a bill that didn't add up.* **3.** To formulate an opinion of: *added up the other competitors in one glance.* —***idiom.* add up to.** To constitute; amount: *This movie adds up to a lot of tears.* [Middle English *adden,* from Latin *addere* : *ad-,* ad- + *dare,* to give; see **dō-** in Appendix.] —**add′a·ble, add′i·ble** *adj.*

ADD *abbr.* Attention deficit disorder.

add. *abbr.* **1.** Addendum. **2.** Addition.

Ad·dams (ăd′əmz), **Charles Samuel.** 1912–1988. American cartoonist known for the macabre humor and Gothic settings of his cartoons, many of which first appeared in the *New Yorker.*

Addams, Jane. 1860–1935. American social reformer and pacifist who founded Hull House (1889), a care and education center for the poor of Chicago, and worked for peace and many social reforms. She shared the 1931 Nobel Peace Prize.

ad·dax (ăd′ăks′) *n.* An antelope *(Addax nasomaculatus)* of northern Africa having long, spirally twisted horns. [Latin, of African origin.]

addax
Addax nasomaculatus

ad·ded value (ăd′ĭd) *n.* The intangible, subjective, perceived difference setting one brand apart from another in the mind of a consumer.

ad·dend (ăd′ĕnd′, ə-dĕnd′) *n.* Any of a set of numbers to be added. [Short for ADDENDUM.]

ad·den·dum (ə-dĕn′dəm) *n., pl.* **-da** (-də). *Abbr.* **add.** Something added or to be added, especially a supplement to a book. [Latin, neuter of *addendus,* gerundive of *addere,* to add. See ADD.]

add·er¹ (ăd′ər) *n.* One that adds, especially a computational device that performs arithmetic addition.

ad·der² (ăd′ər) *n.* **1.** See **viper** (sense 1). **2.** Any of several nonvenomous snakes, such as the milk snake of North America, popularly believed to be harmful. [Middle English, from *an addre,* alteration of *a naddre* : *a,* a; see A² + *naddre,* snake (from Old English *nǣdre*).]

WORD HISTORY: The biblical injunction to be wise as serpents and innocent as doves looks somewhat alien in the Middle English guise "Loke ye be prudent as neddris and symple as dowves." *Neddris,* which is perhaps the strangest-looking word in this Middle English passage, would be *adders* in Modern English, with a different meaning and form. *Adder,* an example of specialization in meaning, no longer refers to just any serpent or snake, as it once did, but now denotes only specific kinds of snakes. *Adder* also illustrates a process known as false splitting, or juncture loss: the word came from Old English *nǣdre* and kept its *n* into the Middle English period, but later during that stage of the language people started analyzing the phrase *a naddre* as *an addre*—the false splitting that has given us adder.

ad·der's-mouth (ăd′ərz-mouth′) *n.* Any of various chiefly terrestrial orchids of the genus *Malaxis,* having terminal clusters of small, often greenish flowers. [From the resemblance of its flowers to the open mouths of snakes.]

ad·der's-tongue (ăd′ərz-tŭng′) *n.* **1.** See **adder's-tongue fern. 2.** See **dogtooth violet.**

adder's-tongue fern *n.* Any of various ferns in the genus *Ophioglossum,* having leaves divided into a simple, sterile blade and a slender, spikelike spore-bearing segment. Also called *adder's-tongue.* [From the resemblance of the spike at the base of the frond to a snake's tongue.]

ad·dict (ə-dĭkt′) *tr.v.* **-dict·ed, -dict·ing, -dicts. 1.** To devote or give (oneself) habitually or compulsively: *She was addicted to rock music.* **2.** To cause to become compulsively and physiologically dependent on a habit-forming substance: *He was addicted to cocaine.* —**addict** (ăd′ĭkt) *n.* **1.** One who is addicted, as to narcotics. **2.** A devoted believer or follower: *"We are all . . . addicts of change"* (Christopher Lasch). [Latin *addīcere, addict-,* to sentence : *ad-,* ad- + *dīcere,* to adjudge; see **deik-** in Appendix.] —**ad·dic′tive** *adj.*

ad·dic·tion (ə-dĭk′shən) *n.* **1.** The quality or condition of being addicted: *had an addiction for fast cars.* **2.** Compulsive physiological need for a habit-forming substance: *"the international traffickers who sell addiction and the users struggling to fight free of it"* (Richard M. Smith).

Ad·dis Ab·a·ba (ăd′ĭs ăb′ə-bə, ä′dĭs ä′bə-bä′). The capital and largest city of Ethiopia, in the center of the country on a plateau more than 2,440 m (8,000 ft) above sea level. Captured by the Italians in 1936 and made the capital of Italian East Africa, it was retaken by the Allies in 1941 and returned to Ethiopian sovereignty. Population, 1,408,068.

Ad·di·son (ăd′ĭ-sən). A village of northeast Illinois, a residential and industrial suburb of Chicago. Population 29,826.

Addison, Joseph. 1672–1719. English essayist whose witty and elegant works appeared in *The Tatler,* founded by Richard Steele in 1709, and *The Spectator,* founded by Addison and Steele in 1711. —**Ad′di·so′ni·an** (-sō′nē-ən) *adj.*

Ad·di·son's disease (ăd′ĭ-sənz) *n.* A disease caused by partial or total failure of adrenocortical function, which is characterized by a bronzelike pigmentation of the skin and mucous membranes, anemia, weakness, and low blood pressure. [After Thomas *Addison* (1793–1860), British physician.]

ad·di·tion (ə-dĭsh′ən) *n. Abbr.* **add., addn. 1.** The act or process of adding, especially the process of computing with sets of numbers so as to find their sum. **2.** Something added, such as a room or section appended to a building. —***idioms.* in addition.** Also; as well as. **in addition to.** Over and above; besides. [Middle English, from Old French, from Latin *additiō, additiōn-,* from *additus,* past participle of *addere,* to add. See ADD.] —**ad·di′tion·al** *adj.* —**ad·di′tion·al·ly** *adv.*

ad·di·tive (ăd′ĭ-tĭv) *n.* A substance added in small amounts to something else to improve, strengthen, or otherwise alter it. —**additive** *adj.* **1.** Marked by, produced by, or involving addition. **2.** *Color.* Of or being any of certain primary colors of wavelengths that may be mixed with one another to produce other colors.

additive identity *n. Mathematics.* An identity element that in a given mathematical system leaves unchanged any element to which it is added.

additive inverse *n. Mathematics.* See **inverse** (sense 2b).

ad·dle (ăd′l) *v.* **-dled, -dling, -dles.** —*tr.* To muddle; confuse: *"My brain is a bit addled by whiskey"* (Eugene O'Neill). See Synonyms at **confuse.** —*intr.* **1.** To become confused. **2.** To become rotten; spoil. [From Middle English *adel,* rotten, from Old English *adel,* pool of excrement.]

ad·dle·pat·ed (ăd′l-pā′tĭd) *adj.* **1.** Eccentric: *"seeking sympathy from her addlepated old dad"* (Rita Kempley). **2.** Mixed up and confused: *"shackled with dime-a-dance disco, bland ballads and addlepated fluff"* (People).

addn. *abbr.* Addition.

addnl. *abbr.* Additional.

add-on (ăd′ŏn′, -ôn′) *n.* One thing added as a supplement to another, especially a component that increases the capability of the system to which it is added.

ad·dress (ə-drĕs′) *tr.v.* **-dressed, -dress·ing, -dress·es. 1.** To speak to: *addressed me in low tones.* **2.** To make a formal speech to. **3.** To direct (a spoken or written message) to the attention of: *address a protest to the faculty senate.* **4.** To mark with a destination: *address a letter.* **5.a.** To direct the efforts or attention of (oneself): *address oneself to a task.* **b.** To deal with: *addressed the issue of absenteeism.* **6.** To dispatch or consign (a ship, for example) to an agent or factor. **7.** *Sports.* To adjust and aim the club at (a golf ball) in preparing for a stroke. —**address** *n.* **1.** A formal spoken or written communication: *used the proper address for a priest.* **2.** A formal speech. **3.** (*also* ăd′rĕs′). The written or printed directions on mail or other deliverable items indicating destination. **4.** (*also* ăd′rĕs′). The location at which a particular organization or person may be found or reached. **5.** Often **addresses.** Courteous attentions. **6.** The manner or bearing of a person, especially in conversation. **7.** Skill, deftness, and grace in dealing with people or situations. See Synonyms at **tact. 8.** The act of dispatching or consigning a ship, as to an agent or a factor. **9.** *Computer Science.* A number used in information storage or retrieval that is assigned to a specific memory location. [Middle English *adressen,* to direct, from Old French *adresser,* from Vulgar Latin **addīrēctiāre* : Latin *ad-,* ad- + Vulgar Latin **dīrēctiāre,* to straighten (from Latin *dīrēctus,* past participle of *dīrigere,* to direct; see DIRECT).]

ad·dress·a·ble (ə-drĕs′ə-bəl) *adj.* Accessible through an address, as in computer memory.

ad·dress·ee (ăd′rĕ-sē′, ə-drĕs′ē′) *n.* The one to whom something is addressed.

ad·dress·er also **ad·dres·sor** (ə-drĕs′ər) *n.* One, such as a person or a machine, that addresses.

ad·duce (ə-do͞os′, ə-dyo͞os′) *tr.v.* **-duced, -duc·ing, -duc·es.** To cite as an example or means of proof in an argument. [Latin *addūcere,* to bring to : *ad-,* ad- + *dūcere,* to lead; see **deuk-** in Appendix.] —**ad·duce′a·ble, ad·duc′i·ble** *adj.*

ad·duct (ə-dŭkt′, ă-dŭkt′) *tr.v.* **-duct·ed, -duct·ing, -ducts.** *Physiology.* To draw inward toward the median axis of the body or toward an adjacent part or limb. [Back-formation from ADDUCTOR.] —**ad·duc′tion** *n.* —**ad·duc′tive** *adj.*

ad·duc·tor (ə-dŭk′tər) *n.* A muscle that draws a body part, such as a finger, an arm, or a toe, inward toward the median axis of the body or of an extremity. [From Latin *addūcere,* to bring to. See ADDUCE.]

Ade (ād), **George.** 1866–1944. American humorist whose newspaper columns, plays, and books, such as *Fables in Slang* (1899), reflect the humor and common sense of ordinary people.

-ade *suff.* A sweetened beverage of: *limeade.* [Middle English, from Old French, ultimately from Latin *-āta,* feminine of *-ātus,* -ate. See -ATE¹.]

ă pat	oi boy
ā pay	ou out
âr care	o͝o took
ä father	o͞o boot
ĕ pet	ŭ cut
ē be	ûr urge
ĭ pit	th thin
ī pie	*th* this
îr pier	hw which
ŏ pot	zh vision
ō toe	ə about, item
ô paw	♦ regionalism

Stress marks: ′ (primary); ′ (secondary), as in **dictionary** (dĭk′shə-nĕr′ē)

Ad·e·laide (ăd′l-ād′). A city of southern Australia northwest of Melbourne. A port of entry at the mouth of the Torrens River, it was founded in 1836. Metropolitan area population, 983,200.

A·dé·lie Coast also **A·dé·lie Land** (ə-dā′lē). A region of Antarctica near George V Coast, under French sovereignty since 1938.

Adélie penguin *n.* A common Antarctic penguin *(Pygoscelis adeliae)* that has white underparts and a black back and head and lives and breeds in large exposed rookeries.

a·demp·tion (ə-dĕmp′shən) *n. Law.* The disposal by a testator of specific property bequeathed in his or her will so as to invalidate the bequest. [Latin *ademptiō, ademptiōn-,* a taking away, from *ademptus,* past participle of *adimere,* to take away : *ad-,* ad- + *emere,* to buy, take; see **em-** in Appendix.]

A·den (äd′n, ād′n). **1.** A former British colony and protectorate of southern Arabia, part of Southern Yemen (now Yemen) since 1967. **2.** The largest city of Yemen, in the southern part of the country on the Gulf of Aden. It has been one of the chief ports of southern Arabia since ancient times and became a major trading and refueling station after the opening of the Suez Canal in 1869. Aden was the capital of Southern Yemen from 1967 until 1990. Population, 271,600.

Aden, Gulf of. An arm of the Arabian Sea lying between Yemen on the Arabian Peninsula and Somalia in eastern Africa. It is connected with the Red Sea by the Bab el Mandeb.

aden– *pref.* Variant of **adeno–.**

Ad·en·au·er (ăd′n-ou′ər, äd′-), **Konrad.** 1876–1967. First chancellor of West Germany (1949–1963), under whom the country began economic reconstruction and became a member of NATO and the Common Market.

ad·e·nec·to·my (ăd′n-ĕk′tə-mē) *n.* Surgical excision of a gland.

ad·e·nine (ăd′n-ēn′, -ĭn) *n.* A purine base, $C_5H_5N_5$, that is a constituent of DNA and RNA.

ad·e·ni·tis (ăd′n-ī′tĭs) *n.* Inflammation of a lymph node or gland.

adeno– or **aden–** *pref.* Gland: *adenectomy.* [From Greek *adēn, aden-.*]

ad·e·no·car·ci·no·ma (ăd′n-ō-kär′sə-nō′mə) *n.* A malignant tumor originating in glandular tissue. **—ad′e·no·car′ci·nom′a·tous** (-nŏm′ə-təs, -nō′mə-təs) *adj.*

ad·e·no·hy·poph·y·sis (ăd′n-ō-hī-pŏf′ĭ-sĭs) *n.* The anterior glandular lobe of the pituitary gland that secretes many hormones, including ACTH, prolactin, and somatotropin. **—ad′e·no·hy·poph′y·se′al, ad′e·no·hy·poph′y·si′al** (-pŏf′ĭ-sē′əl) *adj.*

ad·e·noid (ăd′n-oid′) *n.* A lymphoid tissue growth located at the back of the nose in the upper part of the throat that when swollen may obstruct normal breathing and make speech difficult. Often used in the plural. **—adenoid** *adj.* Of, relating to, or resembling lymphatic glands or lymphoid tissue.

ad·e·noi·dal (ăd′n-oid′l) *adj.* **1.** Of or relating to the adenoids. **2.** Suggestive of the vocal sound caused by abnormally enlarged adenoids: *a singer with an adenoidal voice.*

ad·e·no·ma (ăd′n-ō′mə) *n., pl.* **-mas** or **-ma·ta** (-mə-tə). A benign epithelial tumor having a glandular origin and structure. **—ad′e·nom′a·toid′** (ăd′n-ŏm′ə-toid′) *adj.* **—ad′e·nom′a·tous** (-ŏm′ə-təs) *adj.*

a·den·o·sine (ə-dĕn′ə-sēn′) *n.* A nucleoside, $C_{10}H_{13}N_5O_4$, that is a structural component of nucleic acids and the major molecular component of ADP, AMP, and ATP. [Blend of ADENINE and RIBOSE.]

adenosine diphosphate *n.* ADP.

adenosine mon·o·phos·phate (mŏn′ō-fŏs′fāt′) *n.* **1.** AMP. **2.** Cyclic AMP.

adenosine tri·phos·pha·tase (trī-fŏs′fə-tās′, -tāz′) *n.* ATPase.

adenosine triphosphate *n.* ATP.

ad·e·no·sis (ăd′n-ō′sĭs) *n.* A disease of a gland, especially one marked by the abnormal formation or enlargement of glandular tissue.

ad·e·no·vi·rus (ăd′n-ō-vī′rəs) *n.* Any of a group of DNA-containing viruses that cause conjunctivitis and upper respiratory tract infections in humans. **—ad′e·no·vi′ral** *adj.*

a·den·yl·ate cy·clase (ə-dĕn′l-ĭt sī′klās, -klāz, ăd′n-ĭl′ĭt) *n.* An enzyme that catalyzes the formation of cylic AMP from ATP. Also called *adenyl cyclase.* [ADEN(INE) + –YL + –ATE[2] + CYCL– + –ASE.]

ad·e·nyl·ic acid (ăd′n-ĭl′ĭk) *n.* See **AMP.** [ADEN(INE) + –YL + –IC + ACID.]

a·dept (ə-dĕpt′) *adj.* Very skilled. See Synonyms at **proficient.** **—adept** (ăd′ĕpt′) *n.* A highly skilled person; an expert: *"The adepts in Washington mean to give rather than to take"* (Lewis H. Lapham). [Latin *adeptus,* past participle of *adipīscī,* to attain : *ad-,* ad- + *apīscī,* to grasp.] **—a·dept′ly** *adv.* **—a·dept′ness** *n.*

ad·e·quate (ăd′ĭ-kwĭt) *adj.* **1.** Sufficient to satisfy a requirement or meet a need. See Synonyms at **sufficient.** **2.** Barely satisfactory or sufficient: *The skater's technique was only adequate.* [Latin *adaequātus,* past participle of *adaequāre,* to equalize : *ad-,* ad- + *aequāre,* to make equal, from *aequus,* equal.] **—ad′e·qua·cy** (-kwə-sē), **ad′e·quate·ness** *n.* **—ad′e·quate·ly** *adv.*

à deux (ä′ dœ′) *adj.* Of or involving two individuals, especially when of a private or intimate nature. **—à deux** *adv.* Privately with only two individuals involved: *dining à deux.* [French.]

ad fem·i·nam (ăd fĕm′ĭ-năm′, -nəm) *adj.* Appealing to irrelevant personal considerations concerning women, especially prejudices against them: *"Its treatment of* [him] *and its ad feminam attack on his wife . . . often border on character assassination"* (Simon Karlinsky). [Latin *ad,* to + *fēminam,* accusative of *fēmina,* woman.] **—ad fem′i·nam′** *adv.*

ADH *abbr.* Antidiuretic hormone.

ad·here (ăd-hîr′) *intr.v.* **-hered, -her·ing, -heres. 1.** To stick fast by or as if by suction or glue. **2.** To be a devoted follower or supporter. **3.** To carry out a plan, a scheme, or an operation without deviation: *We will adhere to our plan.* [French *adhérer,* from Latin *adhaerēre,* to stick to : *ad-,* ad- + *haerēre,* to stick.]

ad·her·ence (ăd-hîr′əns, -hĕr′-) *n.* **1.** The process or condition of adhering. **2.** Faithful attachment; devotion: *"Adherence to the rule of law . . . is a very important principle"* (William H. Webster).

ad·her·ent (ăd-hîr′ənt, -hĕr′-) *n.* A supporter, as of a cause or an individual. **—adherent** *adj.* **1.** Sticking or holding fast. **2.** *Botany.* Joined but not united. Used of dissimilar parts or organs. **—ad·her′ent·ly** *adv.*

ad·he·sion (ăd-hē′zhən) *n.* **1.** The act or state of adhering. **2.** Attachment or devotion; loyalty. **3.** Assent or agreement to join. **4.** *Medicine.* A condition in which bodily tissues that are normally separate grow together. **5.** *Physics.* The physical attraction or joining of two substances, especially the macroscopically observable attraction of dissimilar substances. **6.** *Medicine.* A fibrous band of scar tissue that binds together normally separate anatomical structures. [French *adhésion,* from Latin *adhaesiō, adhaesiōn-,* from *adhaesus,* past participle of *adhaerēre,* to adhere. See ADHERE.]

ad·he·si·o·to·my (ăd-hē′zē-ŏt′ə-mē) *n., pl.* **-mies.** Surgical division or separation of adhesions.

ad·he·sive (ăd-hē′sĭv, -zĭv) *adj.* **1.** Tending to adhere; sticky. **2.** Gummed so as to adhere. **3.** Tending to persist; difficult if not impossible to shake off: *"He feels an adhesive dread, a sudden acquaintance with the . . . darker side of mankind"* (George F. Will). **—adhesive** *n.* A substance, such as paste or cement, that provides or promotes adhesion. **—ad·he′sive·ly** *adv.* **—ad·he′sive·ness** *n.*

adhesive tape *n.* A tape lined on one side with an adhesive.

ad hoc (ăd hŏk′, hōk′) *adv.* For the specific purpose, case, or situation at hand and for no other: *a committee formed ad hoc to address the issue of salaries.* **—ad hoc** *adj.* **1.** Formed for or concerned with one specific purpose: *an ad hoc compensation committee.* **2.** Improvised and often impromptu: *"On an ad hoc basis, Congress has . . . placed . . . ceilings on military aid to specific countries"* (New York Times). [Latin *ad,* to + *hoc,* this.]

ad hoc·ism also **ad hoc-ism** or **ad-hoc·ism** (ăd hŏk′ĭz-əm, hō′kĭz-) *n.* The tendency to establish temporary, chiefly improvisational policies and procedures to deal with specific problems and tasks: *"In the absence of specific policies carefully tended by specialists, ad hocism took root"* (U.S. News & World Report).

ad hom·i·nem (hŏm′ə-nĕm′, -nəm) *adj.* Appealing to personal considerations rather than to logic or reason: *Debaters should avoid ad hominem arguments that question their opponents' motives.* [Latin *ad,* to + *hominem,* accusative of *homō,* man.] **—ad hom′i·nem′** *adv.*

ad·i·a·bat·ic (ăd′ē-ə-băt′ĭk, ā′dī-ə-) *adj.* Of, relating to, or denoting a reversible thermodynamic process executed at constant entropy and occurring without gain or loss of heat. [From Greek *adiabatos,* impassable : *a-,* a-; see A–[1] + *diabatos,* passable (*dia,* dia- + *batos,* passable, from *bainein,* to go; see **gʷā-** in Appendix).] **—ad′i·a·bat′i·cal·ly** *adv.*

a·dieu (ə-dyo͞o′, ə-do͞o′) *interj.* Used to express farewell. **—adieu** *n., pl.* **a·dieus** or **a·dieux** (ə-dyo͞oz′, ə-do͞oz′). A farewell. [Middle English, from Old French *a dieu,* (I commend you) to God : *a,* to (from Latin *ad;* see AD–) + *Dieu,* God (from Latin *deus;* see **deiw-** in Appendix).]

A·di·ge (ä′dĭ-jā′, ä′dē-jĕ′). A river of northeast Italy rising in the Alps and flowing about 410 km (255 mi) generally south then east to the Adriatic Sea at the Gulf of Venice.

ad in·fi·ni·tum (ăd ĭn′fə-nī′təm) *adv. & adj.* To infinity; having no end. [Latin *ad,* to + *īnfīnītum,* accusative of *īnfīnītus,* infinite.]

ad in·ter·im (ĭn′tər-əm) *adv. Abbr.* **ad int.** In or for the meantime; temporarily. **—ad interim** *adj.* Acting or done ad interim; temporary. See Synonyms at **temporary.** [Latin *ad,* to, for + *interim,* the meantime.]

ad·i·os (ăd′ē-ōs′, ä′dē-) *interj.* Used to express farewell. [Spanish *adiós,* probably translated from French *à dieu.* See ADIEU.]

ad·i·po·cere (ăd′ə-pō-sîr′) *n.* A brown, fatty, waxlike substance that forms on dead animal tissues in response to moisture. [ADIPO(SE) + Latin *cēra,* wax.]

ad·i·po·cyte (ăd′ə-pō-sīt′) *n.* See **fat cell.**

ad·i·pose (ăd′ə-pōs′) *adj.* Of, relating to, or composed of animal fat; fatty. **—adipose** *n.* The fat found in adipose tissue. [New Latin *adipōsus,* from Latin *adeps, adip-,* fat.] **—ad′i·pose′ness, ad′i·pos′i·ty** (-pŏs′ĭ-tē) *n.*

adder's-tongue fern
Ophioglossum vulgatum

Adélie penguin
Pygoscelis adeliae

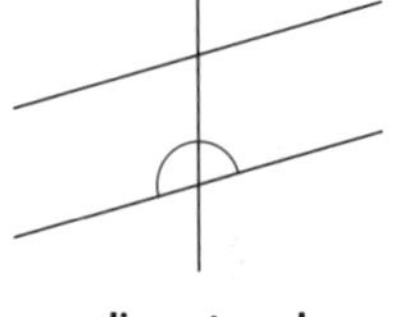
adjacent angle

adipose tissue *n.* A type of connective tissue that contains stored cellular fat.

Ad·i·ron·dack Mountains (ăd′ə-rŏn′dăk′). A group of mountains in northeast New York between the St. Lawrence River valley in the north and the Mohawk River valley in the south. The range is part of the Appalachian system and rises to 1,629.9 m (5,344 ft). Lakes, forests, and numerous winter sports resorts, including Lake Placid, site of the 1932 and 1984 Winter Olympics, attract many tourists.

ad·it (ăd′ĭt) *n.* An almost horizontal entrance to a mine. [Latin *aditus,* access, from past participle of *adīre,* to approach : *ad-,* ad- + *īre,* to go; see **ei-** in Appendix.]

adj. *abbr.* **1.** *Grammar.* Adjective. **2.** Adjunct. **3.** Adjustment. **4.** Also **Adj.** Adjutant.

ad·ja·cen·cy (ə-jā′sən-sē) *n., pl.* **-cies. 1.** The state of being adjacent; contiguity. **2.** A thing that is adjacent.

ad·ja·cent (ə-jā′sənt) *adj.* **1.** Close to; lying near: *adjacent cities.* **2.** Next to; adjoining: *adjacent garden plots.* [Middle English, from Latin *adiacēns, adiacent-,* present participle of *adiacēre,* to lie near : *ad-,* ad- + *iacēre,* to lie; see **yē-** in Appendix.] **—ad·ja′cent·ly** *adv.*

adjacent angle *n. Mathematics.* Either of two angles having a common side and a common vertex.

ad·jec·ti·val (ăj′ĭk-tī′vəl) *adj. Grammar.* Of, relating to, or functioning as an adjective. **—ad′jec·ti′val·ly** *adv.*

ad·jec·tive (ăj′ĭk-tĭv) *n. Abbr.* **adj., a.** *Grammar.* Any of a class of words used to modify a noun or other substantive by limiting, qualifying, or specifying and distinguished in English morphologically by one of several suffixes, such as *-able, -ous, -er,* and *-est,* or syntactically by position directly preceding a noun or nominal phrase, such as *white* in *a white house.* **—adjective** *adj.* **1.** *Grammar.* Adjectival: *an adjective clause.* **2.** *Law.* Prescriptive; remedial: *adjective law.* **3.** Not standing alone; derivative or dependent. [Middle English, from Old French *adjectif,* from Late Latin *adiectīvus,* from *adiectus,* past participle of *adiicere,* to add to : *ad-,* ad- + *iacere,* to throw; see **yē-** in Appendix.] **—ad′jec·tive·ly** *adv.*

adjective pronoun *n. Grammar.* A pronoun acting as an adjective, such as *which* in *which dictionaries?*

ad·join (ə-join′) *v.* **-joined, -join·ing, -joins.** *—tr.* **1.** To be next to; be contiguous to: *property that adjoins ours.* **2.** To attach: *"I do adjoin a copy of the letter that I have received"* (John Fowles). *—intr.* To be contiguous. [Middle English *ajoinen,* from Old French *ajoindre, ajoin-,* from Latin *adiungere,* to join to : *ad-,* ad- + *iungere,* to join; see **yeug-** in Appendix.]

ad·join·ing (ə-joi′nĭng) *adj.* Neighboring; contiguous.

ad·journ (ə-jûrn′) *v.* **-journed, -journ·ing, -journs.** *—tr.* To suspend until a later stated time. *—intr.* **1.** To suspend proceedings to another time or place. **2.** To move from one place to another: *After the meal we adjourned to the living room.* [Middle English *ajournen,* from Old French *ajourner* : *a-,* to (from Latin *ad-;* see AD–) + *jour,* day (from Late Latin *diurnum,* from Latin *diurnus,* daily, from *diēs,* day; see **deiw-** in Appendix).] **—ad·journ′ment** *n.*

adjt. also **Adjt.** *abbr.* Adjutant.

ad·judge (ə-jŭj′) *tr.v.* **-judged, -judg·ing, -judg·es. 1.** *Law.* **a.** To determine or decide by judicial procedure; adjudicate. **b.** To order judicially; rule. **c.** To award (damages, for example) by law. **2.** To regard, consider, or deem: *was adjudged incompetent.* [Middle English *ajugen,* from Old French *ajuger,* from Latin *adiūdicāre.* See ADJUDICATE.]

ad·ju·di·cate (ə-jo͞o′dĭ-kāt′) *tr.v.* **-cat·ed, -cat·ing, -cates. 1.** *Law.* To hear and settle (a case) by judicial procedure. **2.** To study and settle (a dispute or controversy): *had to ask the school principal to adjudicate the quarrel.* [Latin *adiūdicāre, adiūdicāt-,* to award to (judicially) : *ad-,* ad- + *iūdicāre,* to judge (from *iūdex,* judge; see JUDGE).] **—ad·ju′di·ca′tion** *n.* **—ad·ju′di·ca′tive** *adj.* **—ad·ju′di·ca′tor** *n.*

ad·junct (ăj′ŭngkt′) *n. Abbr.* **adj. 1.** Something attached to another in a dependent or subordinate position. See Synonyms at **appendage. 2.** A person associated with another in a subordinate or auxiliary capacity. **3.** *Grammar.* A clause or phrase added to a sentence that, while not essential to the sentence's structure, amplifies its meaning, such as *for several hours* in *We waited for several hours.* **4.** *Logic.* A nonessential attribute of a thing. **—adjunct** *adj.* **1.** Added or connected in a subordinate or auxiliary capacity: *an adjunct clause.* **2.** Attached to a faculty or staff in a temporary or auxiliary capacity: *an adjunct professor of history.* [From Latin *adiūnctus,* past participle of *adiungere,* to join to. See ADJOIN.] **—ad·junc′tion** (ə-jŭngk′shən) *n.* **—ad·junc′tive** *adj.*

ad·ju·ra·tion (ăj′ə-rā′shən) *n.* An earnest, solemn appeal. **—ad·jur′a·to′ry** (ə-jo͝or′ə-tôr′ē, -tōr′ē) *adj.*

ad·jure (ə-jo͝or′) *tr.v.* **-jured, -jur·ing, -jures. 1.** To command or enjoin solemnly, as under oath: *"adjuring her in the name of God to declare the truth"* (Increase Mather). **2.** To appeal to or entreat earnestly. [Middle English *adjuren,* from Latin *adiūrāre,* to swear to : *ad-,* ad- + *iūrāre,* to swear; see **yewes-** in Appendix.] **—ad·jur′er, ad·ju′ror** *n.*

ad·just (ə-jŭst′) *v.* **-just·ed, -just·ing, -justs.** *—tr.* **1.** To change so as to match or fit; cause to correspond. **2.** To bring into proper relationship. **3.** To adapt or conform, as to new conditions: *"unable to adjust themselves to their environment"* (Karl A. Menninger). See Synonyms at **adapt. 4.** To bring the components of into a more effective or efficient calibration or state: *adjust the timing of a car's engine.* **5.** To treat disorders of (the spine) by correcting slight dislocations between vertebrae using chiropractic techniques. **6.** To decide how much is to be paid on (an insurance claim). *—intr.* **1.** To adapt oneself; conform. **2.** To achieve a psychological balance in one's life with regard to one's own needs and the needs of others. [Obsolete French *adjuster,* from Old French *ajoster,* from Vulgar Latin **adiuxtāre,* to put close to : Latin *ad-,* ad- + Latin *iuxtā,* near; see **yeug-** in Appendix.] **—ad·just′a·ble** *adj.* **—ad·just′a·bly** *adv.* **—ad·just′er, ad·jus′tor** *n.*

ad·just·ment (ə-jŭst′mənt) *n. Abbr.* **adj. 1.** The act of adjusting or the state of being adjusted. **2.** A means of adjusting. **3.** Settlement of a debt or claim. **4.** A modification, fluctuation, or correction: *made an adjustment on the telephone bill; an adjustment in the consumer price index.*

ad·ju·tant (ăj′ə-tənt) *n.* **1.** *Abbr.* **adj., Adj., adjt., Adjt.** A staff officer who helps a commanding officer with administrative affairs. **2.** An assistant. **3.** See **marabou** (sense 1). [From Latin *adiūtāns, adiūtant-,* present participle of *adiūtāre,* to help. See AID.] **—ad′ju·tan·cy** *n.*

adjutant general *n., pl.* **adjutants general.** *Abbr.* **A.G., AG 1.** An adjutant of a unit having a general staff. **2.** An officer in charge of the National Guard in one of the U.S. states. **3. Adjutant General.** The chief administrative officer, a major general, of the U.S. Army.

adjutant stork *n.* See **marabou** (sense 1).

ad·ju·vant (ăj′ə-vənt) *n.* **1.** A pharmacological agent added to a drug to increase or aid its effect. **2.** An immunological agent that increases the antigenic response. [From Latin *adiuvāns, adiuvant-,* present participle of *adiuvāre,* to help. See AID.]

Ad·ler (ăd′lər, ăd′-), **Alfred.** 1870–1937. Austrian psychiatrist who rejected Sigmund Freud's emphasis on sexuality and theorized that neurotic behavior is an overcompensation for feelings of inferiority.

Ad·ler (ăd′lər), **Cyrus.** 1863–1940. American religious leader and educator who was president of the Jewish Theological Seminary of America (1924–1940) and edited scholarly works concerning Judaism.

Ad·ler (ăd′lər, ăd′-), **Felix.** 1851–1933. German-born American educator and reformer who founded the Society for Ethical Culture (1876), an organization dedicated to the teaching and application of ethical ideals.

Adler, Mortimer Jerome. Born 1902. American philosopher and educator whose numerous published works include *How to Read a Book* (1940) and *The Conditions of Philosophy* (1965).

Ad·le·ri·an (ăd-lîr′ē-ən) *adj.* Of, relating to, or being a psychological school based on the belief that behavior arises in subconscious efforts to compensate for inferiority or deficiency and that neurosis results from overcompensation. [After Alfred ADLER.]

ad lib (ăd lĭb′) *adv.* In an unrestrained manner; spontaneously. [Short for AD LIBITUM.]

ad-lib (ăd-lĭb′) *v.* **-libbed, -lib·bing, -libs.** *—tr.* To improvise and deliver extemporaneously. *—intr.* To engage in improvisation, as during delivery of a speech. **—ad-lib** (ăd′lĭb′) *n.* Words, music, or actions uttered, performed, or carried out in an extemporaneous manner. **—ad-lib** *adj.* Uttered, performed, or carried out spontaneously. See Synonyms at **extemporaneous. —ad-lib′ber** *n.*

ad lib·i·tum (ăd lĭb′ĭ-təm) *adj. Music.* At the discretion of the performer. Used chiefly as a direction giving license to alter or omit a part. [Latin *ad,* according to + *libitum,* past participle of *libēre,* to please.]

ad loc. *abbr. Latin.* Ad locum (to, or at, the place).

adm. *abbr.* **1.** Administration. **2.** Administrative. **3.** Administrator.

ad·meas·ure (ăd-mĕzh′ər) *tr.v.* **-ured, -ur·ing, -ures.** To divide and distribute proportionally; apportion. [Middle English *amesuren,* from Old French *amesurer* : *a-,* to (from Latin *ad-;* see AD–) + *mesurer,* to measure (from Late Latin *mēnsūrāre,* to measure, from Latin *mēnsūra,* measure; see MEASURE).] **—ad·meas′ure·ment** *n.* **—ad·meas′ur·er** *n.*

Ad·me·tus (ăd-mē′təs) *n. Greek Mythology.* A king of Thessaly and husband of Alcestis.

admin. *abbr.* **1.** Administration. **2.** Administrative. **3.** Administrator.

ad·min·is·ter (ăd-mĭn′ĭ-stər) *v.* **-tered, -ter·ing, -ters.** *—tr.* **1.** To have charge of; manage. **2. a.** To give or apply in a formal way: *administer the last rites.* **b.** To apply as a remedy: *administer a sedative.* **3.** To mete out; dispense: *administer justice.* **4.** To manage or dispose of (a trust or an estate) under a will or an official appointment. **5.** To impose, offer, or tender (an oath, for example). *—intr.* **1.** To manage as an administrator. **2.** To minister: *administering to their every whim.* [Middle English *administren,* from Old French *administrer,* from Latin *administrāre* : *ad,* ad- + *ministrāre,* to manage; see MINISTER.] **—ad·min′is·tra·ble** (-ĭ-strə-bəl) *adj.* **—ad·min′is·trant** *adj. & n.*

ad·min·is·trate (ăd-mĭn′ĭ-strāt′) *tr.v.* **-trat·ed, -trat·ing, -trates.** To administer.

ad·min·is·tra·tion (ăd-mĭn′ĭ-strā′shən) *n. Abbr.* **admin., adm. 1.** Management, especially of business affairs. **2.** The activity of a sovereign state in the exercise of its powers or duties. **3.** Often **Administration.** Those who constitute the executive branch of a government. **4.** Management of an institution, public or private. **5.** The term of office of an executive officer or a body. **6.** *Law.* Management and disposal of a trust or an estate. **7.** The dispensing, applying, or tendering of something, such as an oath, a sacrament, or medicine. **—ad·min′is·tra′tive** (-strā′tĭv, -strə-) *adj.* **—ad·min′is·tra′tive·ly** *adv.*

administrative segregation *n.* Solitary confinement.

ad·min·is·tra·tor (ăd-mĭn′ĭ-strā′tər) *n. Abbr.* **admin., adm. 1.** One who administers, especially business or public affairs; an executive. **2.** One appointed to administer an estate.

ad·mi·ra·ble (ăd′mər-ə-bəl) *adj.* Deserving admiration. **—ad′mi·ra·ble·ness** *n.* **—ad′mi·ra·bly** *adv.*

ad·mi·ral (ăd′mər-əl) *n.* **1.** The commander in chief of a fleet. **2.** A flag officer. **3.a.** A commissioned rank in the U.S. Navy or Coast Guard that is above vice-admiral and below Admiral of the Fleet. **b.** One who holds the rank of admiral, Admiral of the Fleet, rear admiral, or vice-admiral. **4.** Any of various brightly colored butterflies of the genera *Limenitis* and *Vanessa.* **5.** *Archaic.* The ship carrying an admiral; flagship. [Middle English *amiral, admiral,* from Old French and from Medieval Latin *amīrālis, admīrālis,* both from Arabic *'amīr a 'ālī,* high commander.]

Ad·mi·ral of the Fleet (ăd′mər-əl) *n.* **1.** The highest rank in the U.S. Navy, equivalent to General of the Army. **2.** One who holds this rank. Also called *Fleet Admiral.*

ad·mi·ral·ty (ăd′mər-əl-tē) *n., pl.* **-ties. 1.a.** A court exercising jurisdiction over all maritime cases. **b.** Maritime law. **2. Admiralty.** The department of the British government that once had control over all naval affairs.

Ad·mi·ral·ty Inlet (ăd′mər-əl-tē). An arm of the Pacific Ocean in northwest Washington. It is the northernmost part of Puget Sound and lies between Whidbey Island and the mainland.

Admiralty Islands. A group of volcanic islands of the southwest Pacific Ocean in the Bismarck Archipelago. Discovered by the Dutch in 1616, the islands are now part of Papua New Guinea.

Admiralty Range. A mountain group of Antarctica on the northern coast of Victoria Land northwest of Ross Sea. The range was discovered by Sir James Ross on his 1841 expedition.

ad·mi·ra·tion (ăd′mə-rā′shən) *n.* **1.** A feeling of pleasure, wonder, and approval. See Synonyms at **regard. 2.** An object of wonder and esteem; a marvel. **3.** *Archaic.* Wonder.

♦ **ad·mire** (ăd-mīr′) *v.* **-mired, -mir·ing, -mires.** —*tr.* **1.** To regard with pleasure, wonder, and approval. **2.** To have a high opinion of; esteem or respect. **3.** *Chiefly New England & Upper Southern U.S.* To enjoy (something): *"I just admire to get letters, but I don't admire to answer them"* (Dialect Notes). **4.** *Archaic.* To marvel or wonder at. —*intr. New England & Upper Southern U.S.* To marvel at something. [French *admirer,* from Old French *amirer,* from Latin *admīrārī,* to wonder at : *ad-,* ad- + *mīrārī,* to wonder (from *mīrus,* wonderful; see **smei-** in Appendix).] **—ad·mir′er** *n.* **—ad·mir′ing·ly** *adv.*

ad·mis·si·ble (ăd-mĭs′ə-bəl) *adj.* **1.** That can be accepted; allowable: *admissible evidence.* **2.** Worthy of admission. **—ad·mis′si·bil′i·ty, ad·mis′si·ble·ness** *n.* **—ad·mis′si·bly** *adv.*

ad·mis·sion (ăd-mĭsh′ən) *n.* **1.a.** The act of admitting or allowing to enter. **b.** The state of being allowed to enter. **2.** Right to enter; access. **3.** The price required or paid for entering; an entrance fee. **4.** A confession, as of having committed a crime. **5.** A voluntary acknowledgment of truth. **6.** A fact or statement granted or admitted; a concession. [Middle English, from Latin *admissiō, admissiōn-,* from *admissus,* past participle of *admittere,* to admit. See ADMIT.] **—ad·mis′sive** (-mĭs′ĭv) *adj.*

USAGE NOTE: It is often maintained that *admittance* should be used only to refer to achieving physical access to a place (*He was denied admittance to the courtroom*), and that *admission* should be used for the wider sense of achieving entry to a group or institution (*her admission to the club; China's admission to the United Nations*). This distinction is often ignored, though many writers continue to observe it. But *admission* is much more common in the sense "a fee paid for the right of entry": *The admission to the movie was five dollars.*

ad·mit (ăd-mĭt′) *v.* **-mit·ted, -mit·ting, -mits.** —*tr.* **1.** To permit to enter. **2.** To serve as a means of entrance: *A ticket that admits the whole group.* **3.** To permit to exercise the rights, functions, or privileges of: *was admitted to the bar association.* **4.** To have room for; accommodate. **5.** To afford opportunity for; permit. **6.** To grant to be real, valid, or true; acknowledge: *admit the truth.* See Synonyms at **acknowledge. 7.** To grant as true or valid, as for the sake of argument; concede. —*intr.* **1.** To afford possibility: *a problem that admits of no solution.* **2.** To allow entrance; afford access: *a door admitting to the hall.* **3.** To make acknowledgment. [Middle English *amitten, admitten,* from Old French *amettre, admettre,* from Latin *admittere* : *ad-,* ad- + *mittere,* to send.]

ad·mit·tance (ăd-mĭt′ns) *n.* **1.** The act of admitting or entering. **2.a.** Permission to enter. **b.** Right of entry. See Usage Note at **admission. 3.** *Symbol* **Y** *Electricity.* The reciprocal of impedance.

ad·mit·ted·ly (ăd-mĭt′ĭd-lē) *adv.* By general admission; confessedly.

ad·mix (ăd-mĭks′) *tr. & intr.v.* **-mixed, -mix·ing, -mix·es.** To mix; blend. [Back-formation from obsolete *admixt,* mixed into, from Middle English, from Latin *admixtus,* past participle of *admiscēre,* to mix into : *ad-,* ad- + *miscēre,* to mix; see **meik-** in Appendix.]

ad·mix·ture (ăd-mĭks′chər) *n.* **1.a.** The act of mixing or mingling. **b.** The state of being mingled or mixed. **2.** Something that is produced by mixing; a mixture. **3.** Something added in mixing. See Synonyms at **mixture.**

ad·mon·ish (ăd-mŏn′ĭsh) *tr.v.* **-ished, -ish·ing, -ish·es. 1.** To reprove gently but earnestly. **2.** To counsel (another) against something to be avoided; caution. **3.** To remind of something forgotten or disregarded, as an obligation or a responsibility. [Middle English *amonishen, admonishen,* alteration of *amonesten,* from Old French *amonester, admonester,* from Vulgar Latin **admonestāre,* from Latin *admonēre* : *ad-,* ad- + *monēre,* to warn; see **men-**[1] in Appendix.] **—ad·mon′ish·er** *n.* **—ad·mon′ish·ing·ly** *adv.* **—ad·mon′ish·ment** *n.*

SYNONYMS: *admonish, reprove, rebuke, reprimand, reproach.* These verbs refer to adverse criticism intended as a corrective or caution. *Admonish* implies the giving of advice or a warning so that a fault can be rectified or a danger avoided: *"A gallows erected on an eminence admonished the offenders of the fate that awaited them"* (William Hickling Prescott). *Reprove* usually suggests gentle criticism and constructive intent: *With a quick look the teacher reproved the child for whispering in class. Rebuke* and *reprimand* both refer to sharp, often angry criticism; of the two *reprimand* more frequently implies formal or official censure: *"Some of the most heated criticism . . . has come from the Justice Department, which rarely rebukes other agencies in public"* (Howard Kurtz). *"A committee at* [the university] *asked its president to reprimand a scientist who tested gene-altered bacteria on trees"* (New York Times). *Reproach* usually refers to regretful or unhappy criticism arising from a sense of disappointment: *"Even if I had done wrong you should not have reproached me in public—people wash their dirty linen at home"* (Napoleon Bonaparte).

admiral
Red admiral
Vanessa atalanta

ad·mo·ni·tion (ăd′mə-nĭsh′ən) *n.* **1.** Mild, kind, yet earnest reproof. **2.** Cautionary advice or warning. [Middle English *amonicioun,* from Old French *amonition,* from Latin *admonitiō, admonitiōn-,* from *admonitus,* past participle of *admonēre,* to admonish. See ADMONISH.]

ad·mon·i·to·ry (ăd-mŏn′ĭ-tôr′ē, -tōr′ē) *adj.* Expressing admonition.

ad·nate (ăd′nāt′) *adj. Biology.* United to a part or organ of a different kind, as stamens attached to petals. [Latin *adnātus,* variant of *agnātus,* past participle of *agnāscī,* to grow upon. See AGNATE.] **—ad·na′tion** *n.*

ad nau·se·am (ăd nô′zē-əm) *adv.* To a disgusting or ridiculous degree; to the point of nausea. [Latin *ad,* to + *nauseam,* accusative of *nausea,* sickness.]

ad·nex·a (ăd-nĕk′sə) *pl.n.* Accessory or adjoining anatomical parts, as ovaries and oviducts in relation to the uterus. [Latin, neuter pl. of *adnexus,* past participle of *adnectere,* to bind to. See ANNEX.] **—ad·nex′al** *adj.*

ad·noun (ăd′noun′) *n. Grammar.* An adjective used as a noun, such as *merciful* in *Blessed are the merciful.* [Latin *ad,* to; see AD– + NOUN.] **—ad·nom′i·nal** (ăd-nŏm′ə-nəl) *adj.*

a·do (ə-do͞o′) *n.* Bustle; fuss; trouble; bother. [Middle English, from the phrase *at do* : *at,* to (used with infinitive) (from Old Norse *at;* see **ad-** in Appendix) + *do,* do; see DO[1].]

A·do (ä′dō). A city of southwest Nigeria northeast of Lagos. It was once the capital of a Yoruba state that was probably founded in the 15th century. Population, 253,300.

a·do·be (ə-dō′bē) *n.* **1.a.** A sun-dried, unburned brick of clay and straw. **b.** The clay or soil from which this brick is made. **2.** A structure built with this type of brick. —*attributive.* Often used to modify another noun: *an adobe house; adobe walls.* [Spanish, from Arabic *aṭ-ṭūbah,* the brick : *al,* the + *ṭūbah,* brick.]

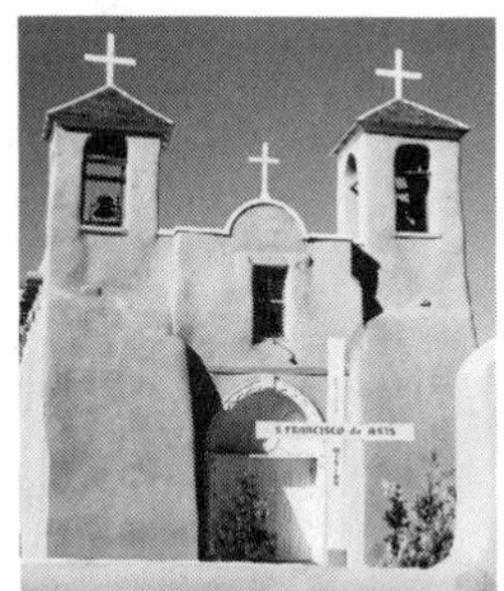

adobe
Saint Francis Mission
in Ranchos de Taos,
New Mexico

a·do·bo (ä-dō′bō) *n., pl.* **-bos.** A Philippine dish of marinated vegetables and meat or fish seasoned with garlic, soy sauce, and spices and served with rice. [Spanish, from Old Spanish *adobar,* to stew, from Old French *adouber,* to dub, arm, prepare, of Germanic origin.]

ad·o·les·cence (ăd′l-ĕs′əns) *n.* **1.** The period of physical and psychological development from the onset of puberty to maturity. **2.** A transitional period of development between youth and maturity: *the adolescence of a nation.*

ad·o·les·cent (ăd′l-ĕs′ənt) *adj.* Of, relating to, or undergoing adolescence. See Synonyms at **young. —adolescent** *n.* A young person who has undergone puberty but who has not reached full maturity; a teenager. [Middle English, from Old French, from Latin *adolēscēns, adolēscent-,* present participle of *adolēscere,* to grow up : *ad-,* ad- + *alēscere,* to grow, inchoative of *alere,* to nourish; see **al-**[2] in Appendix.]

WORD HISTORY: The adolescent grows up to become the adult. The words *adolescent* and *adult* that refer to these two stages in the human life cycle ultimately come from forms of the same Latin word, *adolēscere,* meaning "to grow up." The present participle of *adolēscere, adolēscēns,* from which *adolescent* derives, means "growing up," while the past participle *adultus,* the source of *adult,* means "grown up." Appropriately enough, *adolescent,* first

ă **pat**	oi **boy**
ā **pay**	ou **out**
âr **care**	o͝o **took**
ä **father**	o͞o **boot**
ĕ **pet**	ŭ **cut**
ē **be**	ûr **urge**
ĭ **pit**	th **thin**
ī **pie**	*th* **this**
îr **pier**	hw **which**
ŏ **pot**	zh **vision**
ō **toe**	ə **about, item**
ô **paw**	♦ **regionalism**

Stress marks: **′** (primary); ′ (secondary), as in **dictionary** (dĭk′shə-nĕr′ē)

recorded in English in a work written perhaps in 1440, seems to have come into the language before *adult,* first recorded in a work published in 1531.

Ad·o·nai (ä′dō-nī′, -noi′) *n.* Lord. Used in Judaism as a spoken substitute for the ineffable name of God. [Hebrew *'ădōnāy,* my lord, from Hebrew *'ādôn,* lord.]

A·don·is (ə-dŏn′ĭs, ə-dō′nĭs) *n.* **1.** *Greek Mythology.* A strikingly beautiful youth loved by Aphrodite. **2.** Often **adonis.** A very handsome young man. [Greek *Adōnis,* from Phoenician *adōn,* lord.]

a·dopt (ə-dŏpt′) *tr.v.* **a·dopt·ed, a·dopt·ing, a·dopts. 1.** To take into one's family through legal means and raise as one's own child. **2. a.** To take and follow (a course of action, for example) by choice or assent: *adopt a new technique.* **b.** To take up and make one's own: *adopt a new idea.* **3.** To take on or assume: *adopted an air of importance.* **4.** To vote to accept: *adopt a resolution.* **5.** To choose as standard or required in a course: *adopt a new line of English textbooks.* [Middle English *adopten,* from Old French *adopter,* from Latin *adoptāre* : *ad-,* ad- + *optāre,* to choose.] **—a·dopt′a·ble** *adj.* **—a·dopt′er** *n.* **—a·dop′tion** *n.*

USAGE NOTE: One refers to an *adopted* child but to *adoptive* parents.

a·dop·tee (ə-dŏp′tē, ə-dŏp-tē′) *n.* One, such as a child, that is or has been adopted.

a·dop·tive (ə-dŏp′tĭv) *adj.* **1. a.** Of or having to do with adoption. **b.** Characteristic of adoption. **2.** Related by adoption: *"increased honesty and sharing between birth families, adoptive families and adoptees"* (Robyn S. Quinter). See Usage Note at **adopt. —a·dop′tive·ly** *adv.*

adoptive immunotherapy *n.* A form of immunotherapy used in the treatment of cancer in which an individual's own white blood cells are coupled with a naturally produced growth factor to enhance their cancer-fighting capacity.

a·dor·a·ble (ə-dôr′ə-bəl, ə-dōr′-) *adj.* **1.** Delightful, lovable, and charming: *an adorable set of twins.* **2.** Worthy of adoration. **—a·dor′a·bil′i·ty, a·dor′a·ble·ness** *n.* **—a·dor′a·bly** *adv.*

ad·o·ral (ăd-ôr′əl, -ōr′-) *adj.* Situated toward or near the mouth.

ad·o·ra·tion (ăd′ə-rā′shən) *n.* **1.** The act of worship. **2.** Profound love or regard.

a·dore (ə-dôr′, ə-dōr′) *v.* **a·dored, a·dor·ing, a·dores.** *—tr.* **1.** To worship as God or a god. **2.** To regard with deep, often rapturous love. See Synonyms at **revere**[1]. **3.** To like very much: *adores mink coats.* *—intr.* To worship. [Middle English *adouren,* from Old French *adourer,* from Latin *adōrāre,* to pray to : *ad-,* ad- + *ōrāre,* to pray.] **—a·dor′er** *n.* **—a·dor′ing·ly** *adv.*

a·dorn (ə-dôrn′) *tr.v.* **a·dorned, a·dorn·ing, a·dorns. 1.** To lend beauty to; decorate: *"the pale mimosas that adorned the favorite promenade"* (Ronald Firbank). **2.** To fit out with or as if with ornaments: *"The sugar plantations were adorned with windmills"* (Alec Waugh). **3.** To enhance the distinction, beauty, splendor, or glory of; add luster to: *"Virtue adorned his mind"* (John Ford). [Middle English *adornen,* from Old French *adourner,* from Latin *adōrnāre* : *ad-,* ad- + *ōrnāre,* to decorate; see **ar-** in Appendix.] **—a·dorn′er** *n.*

a·dorn·ment (ə-dôrn′mənt) *n.* **1.** The act of adorning. **2.** Something that beautifies or adorns; an ornament. *"Japanese food is on the whole superb, one of the adornments of the culture"* (James Fallows).

A·dour (ə-do͝or′). A river of southwest France rising in the Pyrenees and flowing about 338 km (210 mi) north then west to the Bay of Biscay near Biarritz.

ADP[1] (ā′dē′pē′) *n.* An ester of adenosine, $C_{10}H_{15}N_5O_{10}P_2$, that is converted to ATP for the storage of energy. [A(DENOSINE) D(I)P(HOSPHATE).]

ADP[2] *abbr.* *Computer Science.* Automatic data processing.

A·dras·te·a (ə-drăs′tē-ə) *n.* The satellite of Jupiter that is third in distance from the planet. [Latin *Adrastēa,* daughter of Jupiter and distributor of rewards and punishments, from Greek *Adrasteia,* so called from an altar erected to her by Adrastos, king of Argos.]

ad·re·nal (ə-drē′nəl) *adj.* **1.** At, near, or on the kidneys. **2.** Of or relating to the adrenal glands or their secretions. **—adrenal** *n.* The adrenal gland. [AD– + RENAL.] **—ad·re′nal·ly** *adv.*

adrenal cortex *n.* The outer portion of the adrenal glands that produces several steroid hormones, including cortisol and aldosterone.

ad·re·nal·ec·to·my (ə-drē′nə-lĕk′tə-mē) *n.* The surgical excision of one or both of the adrenal glands.

adrenal gland *n.* Either of two small, dissimilarly shaped endocrine glands, one located above each kidney, consisting of the cortex, which secretes several steroid hormones, and the medulla, which secretes epinephrine. Also called *suprarenal gland.*

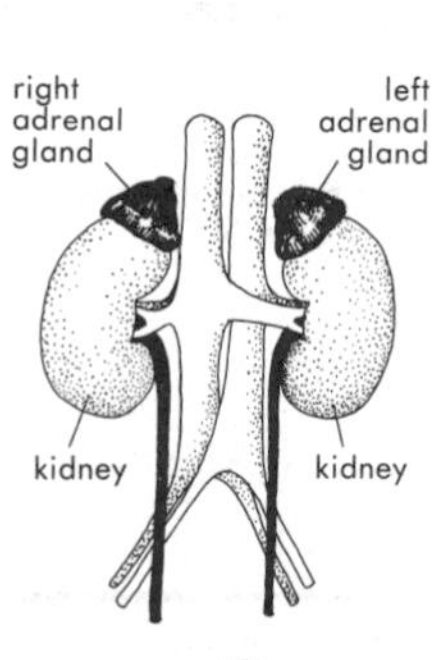

adrenal gland

A·dren·a·lin (ə-drĕn′ə-lĭn). A trademark used for a medicinal preparation of adrenaline.

a·dren·a·line (ə-drĕn′ə-lĭn) *n.* See **epinephrine** (sense 1).

ad·re·nal·ize (ə-drē′nə-līz′, ə-drĕn′ə-) *tr.v.* **-ized, -iz·ing, -izes.** To stir up and spur to action.

adrenal medulla *n.* The inner, reddish-brown portion of the adrenal glands that synthesizes, stores, and releases epinephrine and norepinephrine.

ad·re·ner·gic (ăd′rə-nûr′jĭk) *adj.* Producing or activated by epinephrine or an epinephrinelike substance: *an adrenergic nerve fiber.* [ADREN(ALINE) + Greek *ergon,* work; see **werg-** in Appendix.] **—ad′re·ner′gi·cal·ly** *adv.*

a·dre·no·chrome (ə-drē′nō-krōm′, -nə-) *n.* A naturally occurring chemical formed during the oxidation of epinephrine. [ADREN(ALINE) + CHROME.]

a·dre·no·cor·ti·cal (ə-drē′nō-kôr′tĭ-kəl) *adj.* Of, relating to, or derived from the adrenal cortex. [ADREN(AL) + CORTICAL.]

ad·re·no·cor·ti·co·ster·oid (ə-drē′nō-kôr′tĭ-kō-stîr′oid, -stĕr′-) *n.* A steroid derived from the adrenal cortex or one that produces physiological effects similar to those of the adrenal cortex. [ADREN(AL) + CORTICOSTEROID.]

ad·re·no·cor·ti·co·trop·ic (ə-drē′nō-kôr′tĭ-kō-trŏp′ĭk, -trō′pĭk) also **ad·re·no·cor·ti·co·troph·ic** (-trŏf′ĭk, -trō′fĭk) *adj.* Stimulating or otherwise acting on the adrenal cortex. [ADREN(AL) + CORTICO– + –TROPIC.]

adrenocorticotropic hormone also **adrenocorticotrophic hormone** *n.* ACTH.

ad·re·no·cor·ti·co·trop·in (ə-drē′nō-kôr′tĭ-kō-trŏp′ĭn, -trō′pĭn) also **ad·re·no·cor·ti·co·troph·in** (-trŏf′ĭn, trō′fĭn) *n.* See **ACTH.** [ADREN(AL) + CORTICOTROPIN.]

ad·re·no·lyt·ic (ə-drē′nə-lĭt′ĭk) *adj.* Inhibiting or preventing the action of adrenergic nerves or the effects of epinephrine: *an adrenolytic drug.* [ADREN(AL) + –LYTIC.] **—ad·re′no·lyt′ic** *n.*

A·dri·a·my·cin (ā′drē-ə-mī′sən). A trademark used for an antibiotic containing doxorubicin and used as an antineoplastic agent.

A·dri·an (ā′drē-ən). A city of southeast Michigan southwest of Detroit. It is a trade center in a fertile farming region. Population, 21,186.

Adrian IV. Originally Nicholas Breakspear. 1100?–1159. English-born pope (1154–1159) whose papacy was marked by disputes with Emperor Frederick I. He is reputed to have bestowed sovereignty over Ireland on Henry II of England (c. 1155).

Adrian, Edgar Douglas. First Baron Adrian. 1889–1977. British physiologist. He shared a 1932 Nobel Prize for major advances in the understanding of the nervous and muscular systems.

A·dri·a·no·ple (ā′drē-ə-nō′pəl). See **Edirne.**

A·dri·at·ic Sea (ā′drē-ăt′ĭk). An arm of the Mediterranean Sea between Italy and the Balkan Peninsula. It extends from the Gulf of Venice southward to the Strait of Otranto, which links it to the Ionian Sea.

a·drift (ə-drĭft′) *adv. & adj.* **1.** Drifting or floating freely; not anchored. **2.** Without direction or purpose.

a·droit (ə-droit′) *adj.* **1.** Dexterous; deft. **2.** Skillful and adept under pressing conditions. See Synonyms at **dexterous.** [French, from *à droit* : *à,* to (from Latin *ad;* see AD–) + *droit,* right (from Latin *dīrēctus;* see DIRECT).] **—a·droit′ly** *adv.* **—a·droit′ness** *n.*

ad·sci·ti·tious (ăd′sĭ-tĭsh′əs) *adj.* Not inherent or essential; derived from something outside. [From Latin *adscītus,* past participle of *adscīscere,* to adopt : *ad-,* ad- + *scīscere,* to accept, inchoative of *scīre,* to know; see **skei-** in Appendix.]

ad seg (ăd′ sĕg′) *n.* *Informal.* Administrative segregation.

ad·sorb (ăd-sôrb′, -zôrb′) *tr.v.* **-sorbed, -sorb·ing, -sorbs.** To take up by adsorption. [AD– + Latin *sorbēre,* to suck.] **—ad·sorb′a·ble** *adj.*

ad·sor·bate (-sôr′bĭt, -bāt′, ăd-zôr′-) *n.* An adsorbed substance.

ad·sor·bent (ăd-sôr′bənt, -zôr′-) *adj.* Capable of adsorption. **—adsorbent** *n.* An adsorptive material, such as activated charcoal.

ad·sorp·tion (ăd-sôrp′shən, -zôrp′-) *n.* The accumulation of gases, liquids, or solutes on the surface of a solid or liquid. [From ADSORB.] **—ad·sorp′tive** (-tĭv) *adj.*

ad·su·ki bean (ăd-so͞o′kē, -zo͞o′-) *n.* Variant of **adzuki bean.**

ad·u·lar·i·a (ăj′ə-lâr′ē-ə, -lăr′-) *n.* A variety of transparent or translucent orthoclase. [Italian, from French *adulaire,* after *Adula,* a mountain group of southeast Switzerland.]

ad·u·late (ăj′ə-lāt′) *tr.v.* **-lat·ed, -lat·ing, -lates.** To praise or admire excessively; fawn on. [Back-formation from ADULATION.] **—ad′u·la′tor** *n.* **—ad′u·la·to′ry** (-lə-tôr′ē, -tōr′ē) *adj.*

ad·u·la·tion (ăj′ə-lā′shən) *n.* Excessive flattery or admiration. [Middle English *adulacioun,* from Old French, from Latin *adūlātiō, adūlātiōn-,* from *adūlātus,* past participle of *adūlārī,* to flatter.]

a·dult (ə-dŭlt′, ăd′ŭlt) *n.* **1.** One who has attained maturity or legal age. **2.** *Biology.* A fully grown, mature organism. **—adult** *adj.* **1.** Fully developed and mature. **2.** Intended for or befitting adults: *adult education.* **3.** Containing or dealing in explicitly sexual material; pornographic: *adult movies; adult bookstores.* [From Latin *adultus,* past participle of *adolēscere,* to grow up. See ADOLESCENT.] **—a·dult′hood′** *n.* **—a·dult′ness** *n.*

a·dul·ter·ant (ə-dŭl′tər-ənt) *n.* A substance that adulterates. **—adulterant** *adj.* Serving to adulterate.

a·dul·ter·ate (ə-dŭl′tə-rāt′) *tr.v.* **-at·ed, -at·ing, -ates.**

To make impure by adding extraneous, improper, or inferior ingredients. **—adulterate** (-tər-ĭt) *adj.* **1.** Spurious; adulterated. **2.** Adulterous. [Latin *adulterāre, adulterāt-,* to pollute. See **al-**[1] in Appendix.] **—a·dul′ter·a′tion** *n.* **—a·dul′ter·a′tor** *n.*

SYNONYMS: *adulterate, debase, doctor, load, sophisticate.* The central meaning shared by these verbs is "to make impure or inferior by adding foreign substances, especially by way of fraudulently increasing weight or quantity": *adulterate coffee with ground acorns; silver debased with copper; doctored the wine with water; rag paper loaded with wood fiber; alcohol sophisticated with ether.*

a·dul·ter·er (ə-dŭl′tər-ər) *n.* One who commits adultery.

a·dul·ter·ess (ə-dŭl′trĭs, -tər-ĭs) *n.* A woman who commits adultery.

a·dul·ter·ine (ə-dŭl′tə-rīn′, -rēn′) *adj.* **1.** Characterized by adulteration; spurious. **2.** Unauthorized by law; illegal. **3.** Born of adultery: *adulterine offspring.* [Latin *adulterīnus,* from *adulter,* adulterer, perhaps back-formation from *adulterāre,* to pollute. See ADULTERATE.]

a·dul·ter·ous (ə-dŭl′tər-əs, -trəs) *adj.* Relating to, inclined to, or marked by adultery. **—a·dul′ter·ous·ly** *adv.*

a·dul·ter·y (ə-dŭl′tə-rē, -trē) *n., pl.* **-ies.** Voluntary sexual intercourse between a married person and a partner other than the lawful spouse. [Middle English, from Old French *adultere,* from Latin *adulterium,* from *adulter,* adulterer. See ADULTERATE.]

a·dult-on·set diabetes (ə-dŭlt′ŏn′sĕt, -ôn′-) *n.* Non-insulin-dependent diabetes mellitus.

ad·um·brate (ăd′əm-brāt′, ə-dŭm′-) *tr.v.* **-brat·ed, -brat·ing, -brates. 1.** To give a sketchy outline of. **2.** To prefigure indistinctly; foreshadow. **3.** To disclose partially or guardedly. [Latin *adumbrāre, adumbrāt-,* to represent in outline : *ad-,* ad- + *umbra,* shadow.] **—ad′um·bra′tion** *n.* **—ad·um′bra·tive** (ə-dŭm′brə-tĭv) *adj.* **—ad·um′bra·tive·ly** *adv.*

a·dust (ə-dŭst′) *adj.* **1.** Burned; scorched. **2.** *Archaic.* Browned by the sun; sunburned. **3.** *Archaic.* Melancholy in appearance; gloomy. [Middle English, from Latin *adūstus,* past participle of *adūrere,* to set fire to : *ad-,* ad- + *ūrere,* to burn.]

adv. *abbr.* **1.** *Grammar.* Adverb; adverbial. **2.** *Latin.* Adversus (against). **3.** Advertisement. **4.** Advisory.

ad va·lo·rem (ăd′ və-lôr′əm, -lōr′-) *adj. Abbr.* **a.v., a/v, ad val.** In proportion to the value: *ad valorem duties on imported goods.* [Latin *ad,* to + *valorem,* value.]

ad·vance (ăd-văns′) *v.* **-vanced, -vanc·ing, -vanc·es.** *—tr.* **1.** To move or cause to move forward. **2.** To put forward; propose or suggest: *advanced a novel theory during the seminar.* **3.** To aid the growth or progress of. **4.** To raise in rank; promote. **5.** To cause to occur sooner: *advance a deadline by one week.* **6.** To raise in amount or rate; increase. **7.** To pay (money or interest) before due. **8.** To supply or lend, especially on credit. **9.** To serve as an advance person for (a trip to be made by a politician or a dignitary): *"advanced the China trip during which the first trade agreements . . . were signed"* (Suzanne Perney). **10.** *Archaic.* To lift. *—intr.* **1.a.** To go or move forward or onward. **b.** To move against another, as when attacking: *advance on the enemy's position.* **2.** To make progress; improve. **3.** To rise in rank, position, or value. **4.** To serve as an advance person for a trip to be made by a politician or a dignitary. **—advance** *n.* **1.** The act or process of moving or going forward. **2.** A forward move, as toward an objective; progress: *an advance in genetic engineering.* **3.** An increase of price or value. **4. advances.** Opening approaches made to secure acquaintance, favor, or an agreement; overtures. **5.a.** The furnishing of funds or goods on credit. **b.** The funds or goods so furnished; a loan. **6.** Payment of money before due: *an advance on next week's salary.* **—advance** *adj.* **1.** Made or given ahead of time: *an advance payment.* **2.** Going before, in front, or forward. **—*idioms.* in advance.** Ahead of time; beforehand. **in advance of.** In front of; ahead of. [Middle English *avauncen,* from Old French *avauncer,* from Vulgar Latin *abantiāre, from Latin *abante,* from before : *ab-,* ab- + *ante,* before; see **ant-** in Appendix.] **—ad·vanc′er** *n.*

SYNONYMS: *advance, forward, foster, further, promote.* The central meaning shared by these verbs is "to cause to move ahead, as toward a goal": *advance a worthy cause; forwarding their own interests; fostered friendly relations; furthering your career; efforts to promote sales.*
ANTONYM: *retard.*
USAGE NOTE: *Advance,* as a noun, is used for forward movement (*the advance of the army*) or for progress or improvement in a figurative sense. *Advancement* is used mainly in the figurative sense: *career advancement.* In the figurative sense, moreover, there is a distinction between the two terms deriving from the transitive and intransitive forms of the verb *advance.* The noun *advancement* (unlike *advance*) often implies the existence of an agent or outside force. Thus, *the advance of science* means simply the progress of science, whereas *the advancement of science* implies progress resulting from the action of an agent or force: *The purpose of the legislation was the advancement of science.*

ad·vanced (ăd-vănst′) *adj.* **1.** Highly developed or complex. **2.** Being at a higher level than others: *an advanced text in physics.* **3.** Ahead of the times; progressive: *advanced teaching methods.* **4.** Far along in course or time: *an advanced stage of illness; a person of advanced age.*

advanced degree *n.* A university degree, such as a master's or doctorate, that is higher than a bachelor's.

Ad·vanced level (ăd-vănst′) *n. Chiefly British.* A level.

advanced standing *n.* The status of a college student granted credit, usually after passing a qualifying test, for courses omitted or taken elsewhere.

advance guard *n.* A detachment of troops sent ahead of a main force to reconnoiter and provide protection.

advance man or **ad·vance·man** (ăd-văns′măn′) *n.* A man who travels ahead to arrange the details of scheduling, publicity, security, and other matters connected with a trip or a public appearance, especially one to be made by a politician or a dignitary: *"'Spontaneous' crowds are painstakingly built through days of effort by political advancemen"* (Timothy G. Smith).

ad·vance·ment (ăd-văns′mənt) *n.* **1.** A forward step; an improvement. **2.** Development; progress: *the advancement of knowledge.* **3.** A promotion, as in rank. **4.** The act of moving forward. See Usage Note at **advance.**

advance person *n.* A person who travels ahead to arrange the details of a trip or a public appearance, especially one to be made by a politician or a dignitary.

ad·van·tage (ăd-văn′tĭj) *n.* **1.** A beneficial factor or combination of factors. **2.** Benefit or profit; gain: *It is to your advantage to invest wisely.* **3.** A relatively favorable position; superiority of means: *A better education gave us the advantage.* **4.** *Sports.* **a.** The first point scored in tennis after deuce. **b.** The resulting score. **—advantage** *tr.v.* **-taged, -tag·ing, -tag·es.** To afford profit or gain to; benefit. **—*idioms.* take advantage of. 1.** To put to good use; avail oneself of: *take advantage of all educational opportunities.* **2.** To profit selfishly by; exploit: *took advantage of the customer.* **to advantage.** To good effect; favorably: *The roses were displayed to advantage in a blue vase.* [Middle English *avauntage,* from Old French, from *avant,* before, from Latin *abante,* from before. See ADVANCE.]

SYNONYMS: *advantage, edge, handicap, odds.* The central meaning shared by these nouns is "a factor or combination of factors conducive to superiority and success": *has the advantage of a superior education; a manufacturing edge given by sophisticated technology; a golfing champion with a handicap of 2; odds overwhelmingly in our favor.*
ANTONYM: *disadvantage.*

ad·van·ta·geous (ăd′văn-tā′jəs, -vən-) *adj.* Affording advantage; beneficial. See Synonyms at **beneficial. —ad′van·ta′geous·ly** *adv.* **—ad′van·ta′geous·ness** *n.*

ad·vect (ăd-vĕkt′) *tr.v.* **-vect·ed, -vect·ing, -vects. 1.** To convey horizontally by advection. **2.** To transport (a substance) by advection. [Back-formation from ADVECTION.]

ad·vec·tion (ăd-vĕk′shən) *n.* A local change in the properties, such as temperature, of an air mass caused by the horizontal movement of the air mass. [Latin *advectiō, advectiōn-,* act of conveying, from *advectus,* past participle of *advehere,* to carry to : *ad-,* ad- + *vehere,* to carry; see **wegh-** in Appendix.]

ad·vent (ăd′vĕnt′) *n.* **1.** The coming or arrival, especially of something extremely important: *the advent of the computer.* **2.** Also **Advent. a.** The period beginning on the fourth Sunday before Christmas, observed by many Christians as a season of prayer, fasting, and penitence in preparation for Christmas. **b.** *Theology.* The coming of Jesus at the Incarnation. **c.** *Theology.* See **Second Coming.** [Middle English, the Advent season, from Old French, from Latin *adventus,* arrival, from past participle of *advenīre,* to come to : *ad-,* ad- + *venīre,* to come; see **gʷā-** in Appendix.]

Ad·vent·ist (ăd′vĕn′tĭst, ăd-vĕn′-) *n.* A member of any of several Christian denominations that believe Jesus's Second Coming and the end of the world are near. **—Ad′vent′·ism** *n.*

ad·ven·ti·tia (ăd′vĕn-tĭsh′ə, -vən-) *n.* The membranous outer covering of an organ or a blood vessel. [New Latin, from Latin *adventīcius,* foreign. See ADVENTITIOUS.] **—ad′ven·ti′tial** *adj.*

ad·ven·ti·tious (ăd′vĕn-tĭsh′əs, -vən-) *adj.* **1.** Not inherent but added extrinsically. See Synonyms at **accidental. 2.** *Biology.* Of or belonging to a structure that develops in an unusual place: *adventitious roots.* [From Latin *adventīcius,* foreign, from *adventus,* arrival. See ADVENT.] **—ad′ven·ti′tious·ly** *adv.* **—ad′ven·ti′tious·ness** *n.*

ad·ven·tive (ăd-vĕn′tĭv) *Biology. adj.* Not native to and not fully established in a new habitat or environment; locally or temporarily naturalized: *an adventive weed.* **—adventive** *n.* An adventive organism. [From Latin *adventus,* arrival. See ADVENT.] **—ad·ven′tive·ly** *adv.*

Advent Sunday *n.* The first Sunday of Advent.

ad·ven·ture (ăd-vĕn′chər) *n.* **1.a.** An undertaking or enterprise of a hazardous nature. **b.** An undertaking of a questionable nature, especially one involving intervention in another state's affairs. **2.** An unusual or exciting experience: *an adventure in dining.* **3.** Participation in hazardous or exciting experiences: *the love of adventure.* **4.** A financial speculation or business venture. **—adventure** *v.* **-tured, -tur·ing, -tures.** *—tr.* To hazard or risk. *—intr.* To engage in hazardous activities; take risks. [Middle English *aventure,* from Old French, from Latin *adventūrus,* future participle of *advenīre,* to arrive. See ADVENT.]

ă **pat**	oi **boy**
ā **pay**	ou **out**
âr **care**	o͝o **took**
ä **father**	o͞o **boot**
ĕ **pet**	ŭ **cut**
ē **be**	ûr **urge**
ĭ **pit**	th **thin**
ī **pie**	*th* **this**
îr **pier**	hw **which**
ŏ **pot**	zh **vision**
ō **toe**	ə **about, item**
ô **paw**	♦ **regionalism**

Stress marks: **′** (primary); ′ (secondary), as in **dictionary** (dĭk′shə-nĕr′ē)

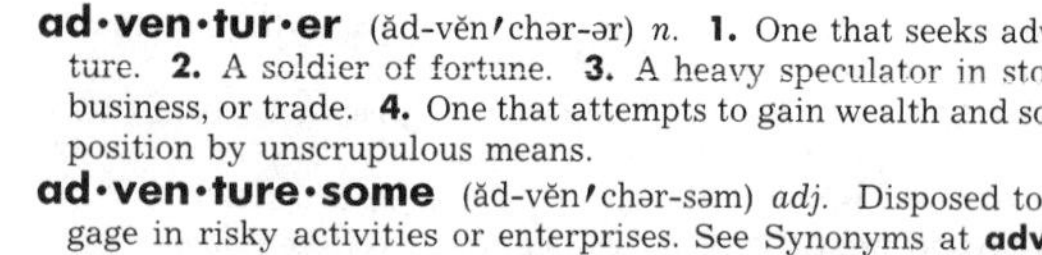

ad•ven•tur•er (ăd-vĕn′chər-ər) *n.* **1.** One that seeks adventure. **2.** A soldier of fortune. **3.** A heavy speculator in stocks, business, or trade. **4.** One that attempts to gain wealth and social position by unscrupulous means.

ad•ven•ture•some (ăd-vĕn′chər-səm) *adj.* Disposed to engage in risky activities or enterprises. See Synonyms at **adventurous.** —**ad•ven′ture•some•ly** *adv.* —**ad•ven′ture•some•ness** *n.*

ad•ven•tur•ess (ăd-vĕn′chər-ĭs) *n.* A woman who seeks social and financial advancement by unscrupulous means.

adventure travel *n.* Nontraditional, strenuous outdoor vacation travel, typically to remote places renowned for their natural beauty and involving activities such as camping, trekking, mountain and rock climbing, white-water rafting, sailing, diving, or viewing big game. —**adventure traveler** *n.*

ad•ven•tur•ism (ăd-vĕn′chə-rĭz′əm) *n.* Involvement in risky enterprises without regard to proper procedures and possible consequences, especially the reckless intervention by a nation in the affairs of another nation or region: *"American strategic interests would . . . be even more jeopardized by Soviet adventurism in the Middle East"* (Christopher T. Rand). —**ad•ven′tur•ist** *adj. & n.*

ad•ven•tur•ous (ăd-vĕn′chər-əs) *adj.* **1.** Inclined to undertake new and daring enterprises. **2.** Hazardous; risky. —**ad•ven′tur•ous•ly** *adv.* —**ad•ven′tur•ous•ness** *n.*

SYNONYMS: *adventurous, adventuresome, audacious, daredevil, daring, venturesome.* The central meaning shared by these adjectives is "taking, willing to take, or seeking out risks": *adventurous pioneers; an adventuresome prospector; an audacious explorer; a daredevil test pilot; daring acrobats; a venturesome investor.*

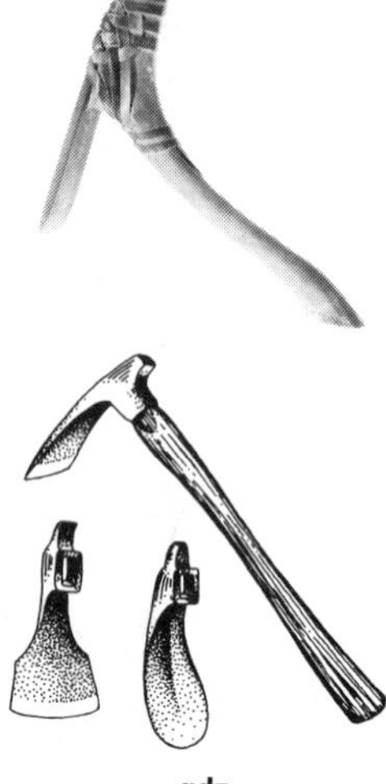

adz
Top: XVIII Dynasty Egyptian adz with bronze blade, wood handle, and leather binding
Bottom: Carpenter's adz (*top*), shipbuilder's adz (*bottom left*), and curved-blade adz (*bottom right*)

ad•verb (ăd′vûrb) *n. Abbr.* **adv.** *Grammar.* **1.** A part of speech comprising a class of words that modify a verb, an adjective, or another adverb. **2.** A word belonging to this class, such as *rapidly* in *The dog runs rapidly.* [Middle English *adverbe,* from Old French, from Latin *adverbium* : *ad-,* in relation to; see AD– + *verbum,* word; see **wer-**[5] in Appendix.]

ad•ver•bi•al (ăd-vûr′bē-əl) *adj. Abbr.* **adv.** *Grammar.* Of, relating to, or being an adverb. —**ad•ver′bi•al•ly** *adv.*

ad ver•bum (ăd vûr′bəm) *adv.* Word for word; verbatim. [Latin : *ad,* in accordance with + *verbum,* word.]

ad•ver•sar•i•al (ăd′vər-sâr′ē-əl) *adj.* Relating to or characteristic of an adversary; involving antagonistic elements: *"the chasm between management and labor in this country, an often needlessly adversarial . . . atmosphere"* (Steve Lohr).

ad•ver•sar•y (ăd′vər-sĕr′ē) *n., pl.* **-ies. 1.** An opponent; an enemy. See Synonyms at **opponent. 2. Adversary.** *Theology.* The Devil; Satan. Often used with *the.* [Middle English *adversarie,* from Latin *adversārius,* enemy, from *adversus,* against. See ADVERSE.]

ad•ver•sa•tive (ăd-vûr′sə-tĭv) *adj.* Expressing antithesis or opposition: *the adversative conjunction* but. —**adversative** *n.* A word that expresses antithesis or opposition. [Latin *adversātīvus,* from *adversātus,* past participle of *adversārī,* to oppose, from *adversus,* against. See ADVERSE.] —**ad•ver′sa•tive•ly** *adv.*

ad•verse (ăd-vûrs′, ăd′vûrs′) *adj.* **1.** Acting or serving to oppose; antagonistic: *adverse criticism.* **2.** Contrary to one's interests or welfare; harmful or unfavorable: *adverse circumstances.* **3.** Moving in an opposite or opposing direction: *adverse currents.* **4.** *Archaic.* Placed opposite. [Middle English, from Old French *advers,* from Latin *adversus,* past participle of *advertere,* to turn toward : *ad-,* ad- + *vertere,* to turn; see **wer-**[2] in Appendix.] —**ad•verse′ly** *adv.* —**ad•verse′ness** *n.*

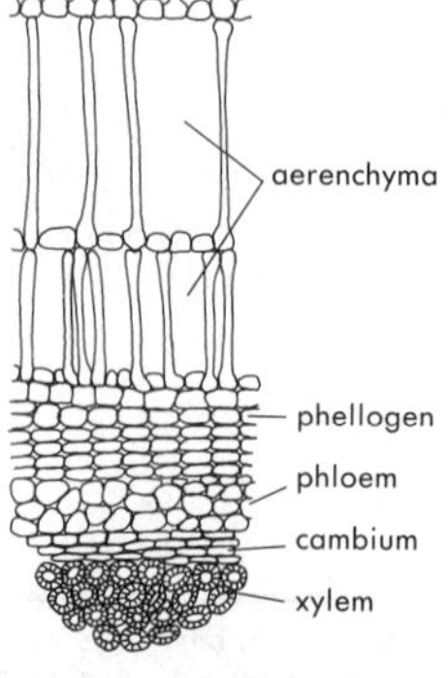

aerenchyma

ad•ver•si•ty (ăd-vûr′sĭ-tē) *n., pl.* **-ties. 1.** A state of hardship or affliction; misfortune. **2.** A calamitous event. See Synonyms at **misfortune.**

ad•vert[1] (ăd-vûrt′) *intr.v.* **-vert•ed, -vert•ing, -verts.** To call attention; refer: *advert to a problem.* See Synonyms at **refer.** [Middle English *adverten,* from Old French *advertir,* to notice, from Latin *advertere,* to turn toward. See ADVERSE.]

ad•vert[2] (ăd′vûrt) *n. Chiefly British.* An advertisement.

ad•ver•tise (ăd′vər-tīz′) *v.* **-tised, -tis•ing, -tis•es.** —*tr.* **1.** To make public announcement of, especially to proclaim the qualities or advantages of (a product or business) so as to increase sales. See Synonyms at **announce. 2.** To make known; call attention to: *advertised my intention to resign.* **3.** To warn or notify: *"This event advertises me that there is such a fact as death"* (Henry David Thoreau). —*intr.* **1.** To call the attention of the public to a product or business. **2.** To inquire or seek in a public notice, as in a newspaper: *advertise for an apartment.* [Middle English *advertisen,* to notify, from Old French *advertir, advertiss-,* to notice. See ADVERT[1].] —**ad′ver•tis′er** *n.*

ad•ver•tise•ment (ăd′vər-tīz′mənt, ăd-vûr′tĭs-, -tĭz-) *n. Abbr.* **adv., advt. 1.** The act of advertising. **2.** A notice, such as a poster, newspaper display, or paid announcement in the electronic media, designed to attract public attention or patronage.

ad•ver•tis•ing (ăd′vər-tī′zĭng) *n.* **1.** The activity of attracting public attention to a product or business, as by paid announcements in print or on the air. **2.** The business of designing and writing advertisements for publication or broadcast. **3.** Advertisements considered as a group: *This paper takes no advertising.*

ad•vice (ăd-vīs′) *n.* **1.** Opinion about what could or should be done about a situation or problem; counsel. **2.** Often **advices.** Information communicated; news: *advices from an ambassador.* [Middle English *avis, advice,* from Old French *avis,* from *(ester) a vis,* to seem : *a,* to (from Latin *ad;* see AD–) + *vis,* seen (from Latin *vīsum,* what seems (good), from neuter past participle of *vidēre,* to see; see **weid-** in Appendix).]

SYNONYMS: *advice, counsel, recommendation.* The central meaning shared by these nouns is "an opinion as to a decision or course of action": *sound advice for those looking for work; accepted the counsel of her attorney; refused to follow his recommendation.* See also Synonyms at **news.**

ad•vis•a•ble (ăd-vī′zə-bəl) *adj.* Worthy of being recommended or suggested; prudent. —**ad•vis′a•bil′i•ty, ad•vis′a•ble•ness** *n.* —**ad•vis′a•bly** *adv.*

ad•vise (ăd-vīz′) *v.* **-vised, -vis•ing, -vis•es.** —*tr.* **1.** To offer advice to; counsel. **2.** To recommend; suggest: *advised patience.* **3.** *Usage Problem.* To inform; notify. —*intr.* **1.** To take counsel; consult: *She advised with her associates.* **2.** To offer advice. [Middle English *avisen, advisen,* from Old French *aviser,* from *avis,* advice. See ADVICE.]

SYNONYMS: *advise, counsel, recommend.* The central meaning shared by these verbs is "to give recommendations to someone about a decision or course of action": *advised him to take advantage of the opportunity; will counsel her to be prudent; recommended that we wait.* See also Synonyms at **confer.**

USAGE NOTE: The use of *advise* in the sense of "inform, notify," was found acceptable by a majority of the Usage Panel in an earlier survey, but many members would prefer that this usage be restricted to business correspondence and legal contexts. Thus one may say *The suspects were advised of their rights,* but it would be considered pretentious to say *You'd better advise your friends that the date of the picnic has been changed.*

ad•vised (ăd-vīzd′) *adj.* **1.** Thought out; considered. Often used in combination: *well-advised; ill-advised.* **2.** Informed: *Keep me advised of further developments.*

ad•vis•ed•ly (ăd-vī′zĭd-lē) *adv.* With careful consideration; deliberately.

ad•vi•see (ăd-vī-zē′) *n.* One that is advised.

ad•vise•ment (ăd-vīz′mənt) *n.* Careful consideration: *Your request will be taken under advisement.*

ad•vis•er or **ad•vi•sor** (ăd-vī′zər) *n.* **1.** One that advises, such as a person or firm that offers official or professional advice to clients. **2.** An educator who advises students in academic and personal matters.

ad•vi•so•ry (ăd-vī′zə-rē) *adj. Abbr.* **adv. 1.** Empowered to advise: *an advisory committee.* **2.** Relating to or containing advice, especially a warning: *an advisory memorandum regarding airworthiness.* —**advisory** *n., pl.* **-ries.** A report giving information, especially a warning: *a weather advisory.*

ad•vo•ca•cy (ăd′və-kə-sē) *n.* The act of pleading or arguing in favor of something, such as a cause, an idea, or a policy; active support.

advocacy journalism *n.* Journalism in which the writer or the publication expresses a subjective view or promotes a certain cause. —**advocacy journalist** *n.*

advocacy tank *n.* A research and problem-solving institution functioning essentially as a lobby in that it attempts, through seminars and studies, to persuade legislators to adopt the views held by its staff, as on matters of foreign policy, economics, defense, or human rights.

ad•vo•cate (ăd′və-kāt′) *tr.v.* **-cat•ed, -cat•ing, -cates.** To speak, plead, or argue in favor of. See Synonyms at **support.** —**advocate** (-kĭt, -kāt′) *n.* **1.** One that argues for a cause; a supporter or defender: *an advocate of civil rights.* **2.** One that pleads in another's behalf; an intercessor: *advocates for abused children and spouses.* **3.** A lawyer. [From Middle English *advocat,* lawyer, from Old French *advocat,* from Latin *advocātus,* past participle of *advocāre,* to summon for counsel : *ad-,* ad- + *vocāre,* to call; see **wek^{w}-** in Appendix.] —**ad′vo•ca′tor** *n.* —**ad•voc′a•to′ry** (ăd-vŏk′ə-tôr′ē, -tōr′ē, ăd′və-kə-) *adj.*

ad•vow•son (ăd-vou′zən) *n.* The right in English ecclesiastical law of presentation to a vacant benefice. [Middle English *avouson,* from Old French *avoeson,* from Medieval Latin *advocātia,* from Latin *advocātiō,* a summoning, from *advocāre,* to summon. See ADVOCATE.]

advt. *abbr.* Advertisement.

ad•y•na•mi•a (ăd′ə-nā′mē-ə) *n.* Loss of strength or vigor, usually because of disease. [A–[1] + DYNAM(ISM) + –IA[1].] —**ad′y•nam′ic** (-năm′ĭk) *adj.*

ad•y•tum (ăd′ĭ-təm) *n., pl.* **-ta** (-tə). The sanctum in an ancient temple. [Latin, from Greek *aduton,* from *adutos,* not to be entered : *a-,* not; see A–[1] + *duein,* to enter.]

adz or **adze** (ădz) *n.* An axlike tool with a curved blade at right angles to the handle, used for dressing wood. [Middle English *adese,* from Old English *adesa.*]

Ad•zhar•i•a (ə-jär′ē-ə) or **Ad•zhar•i•stan** (ə-jär′ĭ-stăn′, ŭj′ə-ryĭ-stän′). A region of southwest Georgia bordering on the Black Sea and Turkey. Colonized by the Greeks in the fourth and fifth centuries B.C., it was ruled by the Romans and the

Turks before its acquisition by Russia in 1878. **—Ad·zhar′** (ə-jär′) *n.* **—Ad·zhar′i·an** *adj. & n.*

ad·zu·ki bean (ăd-zo͞o′kē) also **ad·su·ki bean** (-so͞o′-, -zo͞o′-) or **a·zu·ki bean** (ə-zo͞o′-) *n.* **1.** An erect or twining East Asian herb *(Vigna angularis)* of the pea family, having edible sprouts and reddish seeds used to make flour. **2.** A seed of this plant. [Japanese *azuki,* from Chinese *xiăo dòu* : *xiăo,* small + *dòu,* bean.]

aech·me·a (ĕk-mē′ə, ĕk′mē-ə) *n.* Any of various tropical American bromeliads of the genus *Aechmea,* grown indoors for their attractive, often patterned leaves and showy bracts. [New Latin, from Greek *aikhmē,* point of a spear.]

ae·ci·o·spore (ē′sē-ə-spôr′, -spōr′, -shē-) *n.* A binucleate spore of a rust fungus, formed in a chainlike series in an aecium. [AECI(UM) + SPORE.]

ae·ci·um (ē′sē-əm, ē′shē-) *n., pl.* **-ci·a** (-sē-ə, -shē-ə). A cup-like structure of some rust fungi that contains chains of aeciospores. [New Latin, from Greek *aikia,* injury, from *aeikēs,* unseemly, injurious.] **—ae′ci·al** (ē′sē-əl, -shē-) *adj.*

a·e·des (ā-ē′dēz) *n., pl.* **aedes.** A mosquito of the genus *Aëdes,* including *A. aegypti,* which transmits diseases such as yellow fever and dengue. Also called *yellow-fever mosquito.* [New Latin *Aēdēs,* genus name, from Greek *aēdēs,* unpleasant : *a-,* not; see A–[1] + *ēdos,* pleasure; see **swād-** in Appendix.] **—a·e′dine** (-dīn, -dēn) *adj.*

ae·dile (ē′dīl′) *n.* An elected official of ancient Rome who was responsible for public works and games and who supervised markets, the grain supply, and the water supply. [Latin *aedīlis,* from *aedēs,* house.]

Ae·ga·de·an Isles (ē-gā′dē′ən) also **Ae·ga·tes** (-tēz). See **Egadi Islands.**

Ae·ge·an (ĭ-jē′ən) *adj.* Of or relating to the Bronze Age civilization that flourished in the Aegean area, as at Crete.

Aegean Sea. An arm of the Mediterranean Sea off southeast Europe between Greece and Turkey. The numerous **Aegean Islands** dotting the sea include the Cyclades, the Dodecanese, and the Sporades. Most of the islands belong to Greece.

Ae·geus (ē′jo͞os, ē′jē-əs) *n. Greek Mythology.* A king of Athens and the father of Theseus.

Ae·gi·na (ĭ-jī′nə). An island off southeast Greece in the Saronic Gulf of the Aegean Sea near Athens. It was a prosperous maritime city-state in the fifth century B.C. but declined after its defeat by Athens and the expulsion of its population. The first Greek coins were struck here.

Aeg·ir (ăg′ər, ĕj′ĭr) *n. Mythology.* The Norse god of the sea.

ae·gis also **e·gis** (ē′jĭs) *n.* **1.** Protection: *a child whose welfare is now under the aegis of the courts.* **2.** Sponsorship; patronage: *a concert held under the aegis of the parents' association.* **3.** *Greek Mythology.* The shield or breastplate of Zeus, later an attribute of Athena, carrying at its center the head of Medusa. [Latin, from Greek *aigis.*]

Ae·gis·thus (ĭ-jĭs′thəs) *n. Greek Mythology.* The son of Thyestes and lover of Clytemnestra. He helped Clytemnestra kill her husband Agamemnon upon Agamemnon's return from the Trojan War.

Ae·gos·pot·a·mi (ē′gəs-pŏt′ə-mī′) or **Ae·gos·pot·a·mos** (-mŏs′). A small river and ancient town of southern Thrace in present-day western Turkey. The culminating battle of the Peloponnesian War, in which Lysander and the Spartans destroyed the Athenian fleet, took place at the mouth of the river in 405 B.C.

Ael·fric (ăl′frĭk). Also called "Grammaticus." 955?–1020? Anglo-Saxon abbot who is considered the greatest Old English prose writer. His works include *Catholic Homilies, Lives of the Saints,* and a Latin grammar.

–aemia *suff.* Variant of **–emia.**

Ae·ne·as (ĭ-nē′əs) *n. Greek & Roman Mythology.* The Trojan hero of Virgil's epic poem, the *Aeneid,* and son of Anchises and Aphrodite. He escaped the sack of Troy and wandered for seven years before settling in Italy.

a·e·ne·ous or **a·e·ne·us** (ā-ē′nē-əs) *adj.* Brassy or golden green in color. [From Latin *aēneus,* of bronze, from *aes,* bronze. See **ayes-** in Appendix.]

Ae·o·li·a (ē-ō′lē-ə). See **Aeolis.**

Ae·o·li·an (ē-ō′lē-ən) *adj.* **1.** Of or relating to Aeolis or its people or culture. **2.** *Greek Mythology.* Of or relating to Aeolus. **3. aeolian.** Variant of **eolian.** **—Aeolian** *n.* **1.** One of a Hellenic people of central Greece that occupied Aeolis and Lesbos around 1100 B.C. **2.** See **Aeolic** (sense 1).

Aeolian harp *n. Music.* An instrument consisting of an open box over which are stretched strings that sound when the wind passes over them. Also called *wind harp.* [From AEOLIAN, relating to Aeolus, god of the winds.]

Aeolian Islands. See **Lipari Islands.**

Ae·ol·ic (ē-ŏl′ĭk) *n.* **1.** A group of dialects of ancient Greek spoken by the Aeolians. Also called *Aeolian.* **2.** Any of several verse forms built around a central choriamb, used especially by Sappho, Alcaeus, and their imitators.

Ae·o·lis (ē′ə-lĭs) or **Ae·o·li·a** (ē-ō′lē-ə). An ancient region of the western coast of Asia Minor in present-day Turkey. It was made up of a group of cities founded by the Aeolians c. 1100 B.C.

Ae·o·lus (ē′ə-ləs) *n.* **1.** *Greek Mythology.* The god of the winds. **2.** A king of Thessaly and ancestor of the Aeolians.

ae·on (ē′ŏn′, ē′ən) *n.* Variant of **eon.**

ae·o·ni·an (ē-ō′nē-ən) *adj.* Variant of **eonian.**

ae·py·or·nis (ē′pē-ôr′nĭs) *n.* A genus of extinct, large, flightless birds native to Madagascar. [New Latin *Aepyornis,* genus name : Greek *aipus,* high + Greek *ornis,* bird; see **or-** in Appendix.]

ae·quor·in (ē-kwôr′ĭn, ē-kwŏr′-) *n.* A protein secreted by certain jellyfish that interacts with seawater to produce bioluminescent light. [New Latin *Aequorea,* jellyfish genus (from Latin *aequoreus,* of the sea, from *aequor,* smooth surface, from *aequus,* smooth) + –IN.]

aer– *pref.* Variant of **aero–.**

aer·ate (âr′āt) *tr.v.* **-at·ed, -at·ing, -ates. 1.** To supply or charge (liquid) with a gas, especially to charge with carbon dioxide. **2.** To expose to the circulation of air for purification. **3.** To expose (a tissue) to oxygen, as in the oxygenation of the blood by respiration. **—aer·a′tion** *n.*

aer·a·tor (âr′ā′tər) *n.* One that aerates, as a machine for aerating turf or a device for aerating liquids.

aer·en·chy·ma (â-rĕng′kə-mə) *n.* A spongy tissue with large air spaces found between the cells of the stems and leaves of aquatic plants, providing buoyancy and allowing the circulation of gases. [New Latin : AER(O)– + Greek *enkhuma,* filling (from *enkhein,* to pour in : *en-,* in; see EN–[2] + *khein,* to pour; see CHYME).]

aer·i·al (âr′ē-əl, ā-ĭr′ē-əl) *adj.* **1.** Of, in, or caused by the air. **2.** Living in the air. **3.** Reaching high into the air; lofty. **4.** Suggestive of air, as in lightness; airy. **5.** Unsubstantial; imaginary. **6.** Of, for, or by means of aircraft: *aerial photography.* **7.** *Botany.* Growing or borne above the ground or water: *aerial roots.* **—aerial** (âr′ē-əl) *n.* See **antenna** (sense 2). [From Latin *āerius,* from Greek *aerios,* from *aēr,* air. See **wer-**[1] in Appendix.]

aer·i·al·ist (âr′ē-ə-lĭst) *n.* An acrobat who performs in the air, as on a trapeze or tightrope.

aerial ladder *n.* A ladder that can be extended to reach high places, especially one mounted on a fire engine.

aerial yam *n.* See **air potato.**

aer·ie or **aer·y** also **ey·rie** or **eyr·y** (âr′ē, ĭr′ē) *n., pl.* **-ies. 1.** The nest of a bird, such as an eagle, built on a cliff or other high place. **2.** A house or stronghold perched on a height. [Medieval Latin *aeria,* from Old French *aire,* from Latin *ārea,* open space, threshing-floor.]

aer·o (âr′ō) *adj.* Aerodynamic in styling. Used especially of an automobile or a van.

aero– or **aer–** *pref.* **1.a.** Air; atmosphere: *aeroballistics.* **b.** Gas: *aerosol.* **2.** Aviation: *aeronautics.* [Greek, from *aēr,* air. See **wer-**[1] in Appendix.]

aer·o·al·ler·gen (âr′ō-ăl′ər-jən) *n.* Any of various airborne substances, such as pollen or spores, that can cause an allergic response.

aer·o·bal·lis·tics (âr′ō-bə-lĭs′tĭks) *n. (used with a sing. verb).* Ballistics, especially of missiles, in the atmosphere. **—aer′o·bal·lis′tic** *adj.*

aer·o·bat·ics (âr′ə-băt′ĭks) *n. (used with a sing. or pl. verb).* Spectacular stunts, such as rolls and loops, performed in an airplane or glider. [AERO– + (ACRO)BATICS.] **—aer′o·bat′** *n.* **—aer′o·bat′ic** *adj.*

aer·obe (âr′ōb′) *n.* An organism, such as a bacterium, requiring oxygen to live. Also called *aerobium.* [French *aérobie* : Greek *aēr,* air; see AERO– + Greek *bios,* life; see **gʷei-** in Appendix.]

aer·o·bic (â-rō′bĭk) *adj.* **1.** *Biology.* **a.** Living or occurring only in the presence of oxygen: *aerobic bacteria.* **b.** Of or relating to aerobes. **2.** Involving or improving oxygen consumption by the body: *aerobic exercise.* **3.** Relating to or used in aerobics: *aerobic shoes.* **—aer·o′bi·cal·ly** *adv.*

aer·o·bi·cize (â-rō′bĭ-sīz′) *intr.v.* **-cized, -ciz·ing, -ciz·es.** To perform vigorous exercise as part of a program to improve physical fitness.

aer·o·bics (â-rō′bĭks) *n. (used with a sing. or pl. verb).* **1.** A system of physical conditioning designed to enhance circulatory and respiratory efficiency that involves vigorous, sustained exercise, such as jogging, swimming, or cycling, thereby improving the body's utilization of oxygen. **2.** A program of physical fitness that involves such exercise. [From AEROBIC.]

aer·o·bi·ol·o·gy (âr′ō-bī-ŏl′ə-jē) *n.* The study of the sources, dispersion, and effects of airborne biological materials, such as pollen, spores, and microorganisms. **—aer′o·bi·o·log′i·cal** (-ə-lŏj′ĭ-kəl) *adj.* **—aer′o·bi·o·log′i·cal·ly** *adv.*

aer·o·bi·o·sis (âr′ō-bī-ō′sĭs) *n.* Life sustained by an organism in the presence of air or oxygen. **—aer′o·bi·ot′ic** (-ŏt′ĭk) *adj.*

aer·o·bi·um (â-rō′bē-əm) *n.* See **aerobe.** [New Latin, from AEROBE.]

aer·o·cul·ture (âr′ə-kŭl′chər) *n.* See **aeroponics.** [AERO– + (AGRI)CULTURE.]

aer·o·drome (âr′ə-drōm′) *n. Chiefly British.* An airdrome.

aer·o·dy·nam·ic (âr′ō-dī-năm′ĭk) also **aer·o·dy·nam·i·cal** (-ĭ-kəl) *adj.* **1.** Of or relating to aerodynamics. **2.** Styled with distinctively rounded edges so as to reduce wind drag and thereby increase fuel efficiency. Used especially of automobiles and vans. **—aer′o·dy·nam′i·cal·ly** *adv.*

aer·o·dy·nam·ics (âr′ō-dī-năm′ĭks) *n. (used with a sing.*

aerialist

aerial ladder
Attached to a firefighting vehicle

aerie
Bald eagle's nest

ă pat	oi boy
ā pay	ou out
âr care	o͝o took
ä father	o͞o boot
ĕ pet	ŭ cut
ē be	ûr urge
ĭ pit	th thin
ī pie	*th* this
îr pier	hw which
ŏ pot	zh vision
ō toe	ə about, item
ô paw	♦ regionalism

Stress marks: **′** (primary); ′ (secondary), as in **dictionary** (dĭk′shə-nĕr′ē)

verb). The dynamics of bodies moving relative to gases, especially the interaction of moving objects with the atmosphere. **—aer′o·dy·nam′i·cist** (-ĭ-sĭst) *n.*

aer·o·dyne (âr′ə-dīn′) *n.* A heavier-than-air aircraft deriving lift from motion. [AERO– + Greek *dunamis,* power, from *dunasthai,* to be able. See **deu-²** in Appendix.]

aer·o·em·bo·lism (âr′ō-ĕm′bə-lĭz′əm) *n.* Embolism that occurs as a result of the entrance of air bubbles into a blood vessel after surgical procedures or trauma.

aer·o·foil (âr′ə-foil′) *n. Chiefly British.* Variant of **airfoil.**

aer·o·gram also **aer·o·gramme** (âr′ə-grăm′) *n.* An airmail letter in the form of a lightweight sheet of stationery that folds into its own envelope for mailing at a relatively low postage rate. Also called *air letter.*

aer·o·lite (âr′ə-līt′) also **aer·o·lith** (-lĭth′) *n.* A chiefly siliceous meteorite. **—aer′o·lit′ic** (-lĭt′ĭk) *adj.*

aer·ol·o·gy (â-rŏl′ə-jē) *n.* Meteorology of the total vertical extent of the atmosphere as opposed to the study of the atmosphere near Earth's surface. **—aer′o·log′ic** (âr′ə-lŏj′ĭk), **aer′o·log′i·cal** *adj.* **—aer·ol′o·gist** *n.*

aer·o·mag·net·ics (âr′ō-măg-nĕt′ĭks) *n. (used with a sing. verb).* The science of magnetic characteristics associated with atmospheric conditions. **—aer′o·mag·net′ic** *adj.* **—aer′o·mag·net′i·cal·ly** *adv.*

aer·o·me·chan·ics (âr′ō-mĭ-kăn′ĭks) *n. (used with a sing. verb).* The science of the motion and equilibrium of air and other gases, comprising aerodynamics and aerostatics. **—aer′o·me·chan′i·cal** *adj.* **—aer′o·me·chan′i·cal·ly** *adv.*

aer·o·med·i·cine (âr′ō-mĕd′ĭ-sĭn) *n.* The medical study and treatment of physiological and psychological disorders associated with atmospheric or space flight. Also called *aerospace medicine, aviation medicine.* **—aer′o·med′i·cal** (-kəl) *adj.*

aer·o·me·te·or·o·graph (âr′ō-mē′tē-ôr′ə-grăf′, -ŏr′-) *n.* An aircraft instrument for simultaneously recording temperature, atmospheric pressure, and humidity.

aer·om·e·ter (â-rŏm′ĭ-tər) *n.* An instrument for determining the weight and density of air or another gas.

aer·o·naut (âr′ə-nôt′) *n.* A pilot or navigator of a lighter-than-air craft, such as a balloon. [AERO– + Greek *nautēs,* sailor; see **nāu-** in Appendix.]

aer·o·nau·tic (âr′ə-nô′tĭk) also **aer·o·nau·ti·cal** (-tĭ-kəl) *adj.* Of or relating to aeronautics. **—aer′o·nau′ti·cal·ly** *adv.*

aer·o·nau·tics (âr′ə-nô′tĭks) *n. (used with a sing. verb).* **1.** The design and construction of aircraft. **2.** The theory and practice of aircraft navigation.

aer·o·neu·ro·sis (âr′ō-no͝o-rō′sĭs, -nyo͝o-) *n.* Nervous exhaustion from prolonged piloting of aircraft.

aer·on·o·my (â-rŏn′ə-mē) *n.* The study of the upper atmosphere, especially of regions of ionized gas. **—aer·on′o·mer** *n.* **—aer′o·nom′ic, aer′o·nom′i·cal** *adj.* **—aer·on′o·mist** *n.*

aer·o·pause (âr′ō-pôz′) *n.* The region of the atmosphere above which aircraft cannot fly.

aer·o·pha·gia (âr′ə-fā′jə) *n.* The abnormal, spasmodic swallowing of air, especially as a symptom of hysteria.

aer·o·pho·bi·a (âr′ə-fō′bē-ə) *n.* An abnormal fear of air, especially drafts.

aer·o·phore (âr′ə-fôr′, -fōr′-) *n.* A device to supply air to a nonbreathing infant or to a person in an environment where there is no oxygen, such as a closed mine or an underwater area.

aer·o·phyte (âr′ə-fīt′) *n.* See **epiphyte.**

aer·o·plane (âr′ə-plān′) *n. Chiefly British.* Variant of **airplane.**

aer·o·pon·ics (âr′ə-pŏn′ĭks) *n. (used with a sing. verb).* A technique for growing plants without soil or hydroponic media. The plants are held above a system that constantly mists the roots with nutrient-laden water. Also called *aeroculture.* [AERO– + (HYDRO)PONICS.]

aer·o·sol (âr′ə-sôl′, -sŏl′) *n.* **1.** A gaseous suspension of fine solid or liquid particles. **2. a.** A substance, such as paint, a detergent, or an insecticide, packaged under pressure with a gaseous propellant for release as a spray of fine particles. **b.** An aerosol bomb. [AERO– + SOL(UTION).]

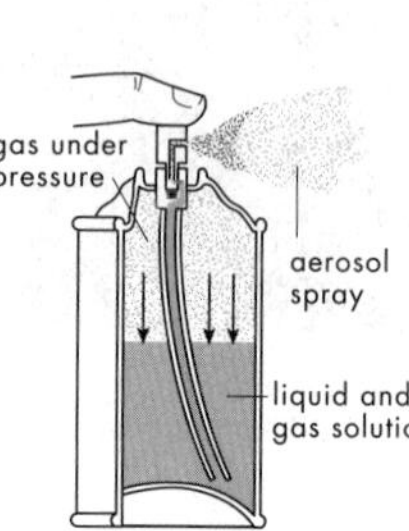

aerosol bomb

aerosol bomb *n.* A usually hand-held container or dispenser from which an aerosol is released.

aer·o·space (âr′ō-spās′) *adj.* **1.** Of or relating to Earth's atmosphere and the space beyond. **2.** Of or relating to the science or technology of flight. **—aer′o·space′** *n.*

aerospace engineering *n.* Engineering related to aircraft and space vehicles.

aerospace medicine *n.* See **aeromedicine.**

aer·o·sphere (âr′ō-sfîr′) *n.* The lower portion of the atmosphere in which both uncrewed and crewed flight is possible.

aer·o·stat (âr′ō-stăt′) *n.* An aircraft, especially a balloon or dirigible, deriving its lift from the buoyancy of surrounding air rather than from aerodynamic motion. [French *aérostat* : Greek *aēr,* air; see AERO– + Greek *statos,* standing; see STATO–.] **—aer′o·stat′ic, aer′o·stat′i·cal** *adj.*

aer·o·stat·ics (âr′ō-stăt′ĭks) *n. (used with a sing. verb).* The science of gases in equilibrium and of the equilibrium of balloons or aircraft under changing atmospheric flight conditions.

aer·o·tax·is (âr′ə-tăk′sĭs) *n.* Movement of an organism, especially a bacterium, toward or away from air or oxygen. **—aer′o·tac′tic** *adj.*

aer·o·ther·mo·dy·nam·ics (âr′ō-thûr′mō-dī-năm′ĭks) *n.* **1.** *(used with a sing. verb).* The study of the thermodynamics of gases, especially at high relative velocities. **2.** *(used with a pl. verb).* The thermodynamics of such gases.

aer·y¹ (âr′ē, ā′ə-rē) *adj.* **-i·er, -i·est.** Ethereal. [Latin *āerius,* of the air. See AERIAL.]

aer·y² (âr′ē, îr′ē) *n.* Variant of **aerie.**

Aes·chy·lus (ĕs′kə-ləs, ē′skə-). 525–456 B.C. Greek tragic dramatist whose plays were the first to include two actors in addition to the chorus. Only 7 of his 90 dramas survive, including the *Oresteia* trilogy (458). **—Aes′chy·le′an** (-lē′ən) *adj.*

Aes·cu·la·pi·an (ĕs′kyə-lā′pē-ən) *adj.* Relating to the healing arts; medical.

Aes·cu·la·pi·us (ĕs′kyə-lā′pē-əs) *n. Roman Mythology.* The god of medicine and healing. [Latin, Greek *Asklēpios.*]

Ae·sir (ā′sîr′, ā′zîr′) *pl.n. Mythology.* The Norse gods. [Old Norse, plural of *āss,* god. See **ansu-** in Appendix.]

Ae·sop (ē′səp, -sŏp′). Sixth century B.C. Greek fabulist traditionally considered the author of *Aesop's Fables,* including "The Tortoise and the Hare" and "The Fox and the Grapes."

Ae·so·pi·an (ē-sō′pē-ən) also **Ae·sop·ic** (ē-sŏp′ĭk) *adj.* **1.** Relating to or characteristic of the animal fables of Aesop. **2.** So veiled in allegorical suggestions and hidden meanings as to elude political censorship: *"They could express their views only in a diluted form, resorting to Aesopian hints and allusions"* (Isaac Deutscher).

aes·the·sia or **es·the·sia** (ĕs-thē′zhə) *n.* The ability to feel or perceive. [Back-formation from ANESTHESIA.]

aes·thete or **es·thete** (ĕs′thēt) *n.* **1.** One who cultivates an unusually high sensitivity to beauty, as in art or nature. **2.** One whose pursuit and admiration of beauty is regarded as excessive or affected. [Back-formation from AESTHETIC.]

aes·thet·ic or **es·thet·ic** (ĕs-thĕt′ĭk) *—adj.* **1.** Relating to the philosophy or theories of aesthetics. **2.** Of or concerning the appreciation of beauty or good taste: *the aesthetic faculties.* **3.** Characterized by a heightened sensitivity to beauty. **4.** Artistic: *The play was an aesthetic success.* **5.** *Informal.* Conforming to accepted notions of good taste. *—n.* **1.** A guiding principle in matters of artistic beauty and taste; artistic sensibility: *"a generous Age of Aquarius aesthetic that said that everything was art"* (William Wilson). **2.** An underlying principle, a set of principles, or a view often manifested by outward appearances or style of behavior: *"What troubled him was the squalor of* [the colonel's] *aesthetic"* (Lewis H. Lapham). [German *ästhetisch,* from New Latin *aesthēticus,* from Greek *aisthētikos,* of sense perception, from *aisthēta,* perceptible things, from *aisthanesthai,* to perceive. See **au-** in Appendix.] **—aes·thet′i·cal·ly** *adv.*

aes·the·ti·cian or **es·the·ti·cian** (ĕs′thĭ-tĭsh′ən) *n.* **1.** One versed in the theory of beauty and artistic expression. **2.** One skilled in giving facials, massages, depilations, manicures, pedicures, and other beauty treatments.

aes·thet·i·cism or **es·thet·i·cism** (ĕs-thĕt′ĭ-sĭz′əm) *n.* **1.** Devotion to and pursuit of the beautiful; sensitivity to artistic beauty and refined taste. **2.** The doctrine that beauty is the basic principle from which all other principles, especially moral ones, are derived. **3.** The belief that art and artists have no obligation other than to strive for beauty.

aes·thet·i·cize also **es·thet·i·cize** (ĕs-thĕt′ə-sīz′) *tr.v.* **-cized, -ciz·ing, -ciz·es.** To depict in an idealized or artistic manner: *"When they range too far from experience, aestheticize life too much, the pictures are disappointing"* (Village Voice).

aes·thet·ics or **es·thet·ics** (ĕs-thĕt′ĭks) *n.* **1.** *(used with a sing. verb).* **a.** The branch of philosophy that deals with the nature and expression of beauty, as in the fine arts. **b.** In Kantian philosophy, the branch of metaphysics concerned with the laws of perception. **2.** *(used with a sing. verb).* The study of the psychological responses to beauty and artistic experiences. **3.** *(used with a sing. or pl. verb).* A conception of what is artistically valid or beautiful: *minimalist aesthetics.* **4.** *(used with a sing. or pl. verb).* An artistically beautiful or pleasing appearance: *"They're looking for quality construction, not aesthetics"* (Ron Schram).

aes·ti·val (ĕs′tə-vəl) *adj.* Variant of **estival.**

aes·ti·vate (ĕs′tə-vāt′) *v.* Variant of **estivate.**

aes·ti·va·tion (ĕs′tə-vā′shən) *n.* Variant of **estivation.**

Aeth·el·red II (ĕth′əl-rĕd′). See **Ethelred II.**

Ae·ther (ē′thər) *n. Greek Mythology.* The poetic personification of the clear upper air breathed by the Olympians. [Latin, from Greek *aithēr,* upper air.]

ae·ti·ol·o·gy (ē′tē-ŏl′ə-jē) *n.* Variant of **etiology.**

Aet·na (ĕt′nə), **Mount.** See Mount **Etna.**

Ae·to·li·a (ē-tō′lē-ə, -tōl′yə). An ancient region of central Greece north of the Gulfs of Corinth and Calydon (Patras). Aetolia was briefly significant in Greek history after the formation in 290 B.C. of the Aetolian League, a military confederation that was defeated by the Achaeans later in the third century. **—Ae·to′li·an** *adj. & n.*

AF *abbr.* **1.** Air force. **2.** Audio frequency.

af– *pref.* Variant of **ad–** (sense 1).

a·far (ə-fär′) *adv.* From, at, or to a great distance: *saw it afar off; traveled afar.* **—afar** *n.* A long distance: *Tales from afar.*

[Middle English *afer*, from *on fer*, far and from *of fer*, from afar, from Old English *feor*, far. See FAR.]

A·fars and Is·sas (ə-färs′; ī′səs). See **Djibouti** (sense 1).

AFB *abbr.* Air force base.

AFDC *abbr.* Aid to Families with Dependent Children.

♦**a·feard** also **a·feared** (ə-fîrd′) *adj.* *New England, Upper Southern U.S. & Ozarks.* Afraid. [Middle English *afered*, from Old English *āfǣred*, past participle of *āfǣran*, to frighten : *ā-*, intensive pref. + *fǣran*, to frighten (from *fǣr*, danger; see FEAR).]

a·feb·rile (ā-fĕb′rəl, ā-fē′brəl) *adj.* Having no fever.

af·fa·ble (ăf′ə-bəl) *adj.* **1.** Easy and pleasant to speak to; approachable. See Synonyms at **amiable. 2.** Gentle and gracious: *an affable smile.* [Middle English *affabil*, from Old French *affable*, from Latin *affābilis*, from *affārī*, to speak to : *ad-*, ad- + *fārī*, to speak; see **bhā-**[2] in Appendix.] **—af′fa·bil′i·ty** *n.* **—af′fa·bly** *adv.*

af·fair (ə-fâr′) *n.* **1.** Something done or to be done; business. **2. affairs.** Transactions and other matters of professional or public business: *affairs of state.* **3.a.** An occurrence, an event, or a matter: *The senator's death was a tragic affair.* **b.** A social function. **4.** An object or a contrivance: *Their first car was a ramshackle affair.* **5.** A matter of personal concern. **6. affairs.** Personal business: *get one's affairs in order.* **7.** A matter causing public scandal and controversy: *the Dreyfus affair.* **8.** A romantic and sexual relationship, sometimes one of brief duration, between two people who are not married to each other. [Middle English *affaire*, from Old French *afaire*, from *a faire*, to do : *a*, to (from Latin *ad*; see AD–) + *faire*, to do (from *facere*; see **dhē-** in Appendix).]

SYNONYMS: *affair, business, concern, lookout.* The central meaning shared by these nouns is "something that involves one personally": *I won't comment on that; it's not my affair. That's none of your business. Mind your own concerns. It's your lookout to see that your application is filed on time.*

af·faire d'a·mour (ä-fâr′ dä-mo͝or′) *n., pl.* **af·faires d'a·mour** (ä-fâr′ dä-mo͝or′). A love affair. [French : *affaire*, affair + *de*, of + *amour*, love.]

af·faire de coeur (ä-fâr′ də kœr′) *n., pl.* **af·faires de coeur** (ä-fâr′ də kœr′). A love affair. [French : *affaire*, affair + *de*, of + *cœur*, heart.]

af·faire d'hon·neur (ä-fâr′ dô-nœr′) *n., pl.* **af·faires d'hon·neur** (ä-fâr′ dô-nœr′). An affair of honor; a duel. [French : *affaire*, affair + *de*, of + *honneur*, honor.]

af·fect[1] (ə-fĕkt′) *tr.v.* **-fect·ed, -fect·ing, -fects. 1.** To have an influence on or effect a change in: *Inflation affects the buying power of the dollar.* **2.** To act on the emotions of; touch or move. **3.** To attack or infect, as a disease: *Rheumatic fever can affect the heart.* **—affect** (ăf′ĕkt′) *n.* **1.** *Psychology.* **a.** A feeling or emotion as distinguished from cognition, thought, or action. **b.** A strong feeling having active consequences. **2.** *Obsolete.* A disposition, feeling, or tendency. [Latin *afficere*, *affect-* : *ad-*, ad- + *facere*, to do; see **dhē-** in Appendix.]

SYNONYMS: *affect, influence, impress, touch, move, strike.* These verbs are compared as they mean to produce a mental or emotional effect. To *affect* is to act upon a person's emotions: *The adverse criticism the book received didn't affect the author one way or another. Influence* implies a degree of control or sway over the thinking and actions, as well as the emotions, of another: *"Humanity is profoundly influenced by what you do"* (John Paul II). To *impress* is to produce a marked, deep, often enduring effect: *"The Tibetan landscape particularly impressed him"* (Doris Kerns Quinn). *Touch* usually means to arouse a tender response, such as love, gratitude, or compassion: *"The tributes* [to the two deceased musicians] *were fitting and touching"* (Daniel Cariaga). *Move* suggests profound emotional effect that sometimes leads to action or has a further consequence: *The account of her experiences as a refugee moved us to tears. Strike* implies keenness or force of mental response to a stimulus: *I was struck by the sudden change in his behavior.*

USAGE NOTE: *Affect*[1] and *effect* have no senses in common. As a verb *affect*[1] is most commonly used in the sense of "to influence" (*how smoking affects health*). *Effect* means "to bring about or execute": *layoffs designed to effect savings.* Thus the sentence *These measures may affect savings* could imply that the measures may reduce savings that have already been realized, whereas *These measures may effect savings* implies that the measures will cause new savings to come about.

af·fect[2] (ə-fĕkt′) *tr.v.* **-fect·ed, -fect·ing, -fects. 1.** To put on a false show of; simulate: *affected a British accent.* See Synonyms at **pretend. 2.a.** To have or show a liking for: *affects dramatic clothes.* **b.** *Archaic.* To fancy; love. **3.** To tend to by nature; tend to assume: *a substance that affects crystalline form.* **4.** To imitate; copy: *"Spenser, in affecting the ancients, writ no language"* (Ben Jonson). [Middle English *affecten*, from Latin *affectāre*, to strive after, frequentative of *afficere*, *affect-*, to affect, influence. See AFFECT[1].] **—af·fect′er** *n.*

af·fec·ta·tion (ăf′ĕk-tā′shən) *n.* **1.** A show, pretense, or display. **2.a.** Behavior that is assumed rather than natural; artificiality. **b.** A particular habit, as of speech or dress, adopted to give a false impression. [Latin *affectātiō*, *affectātiōn-*, from *affectātus*, past participle of *affectāre*, to strive after. See AFFECT[2].]

SYNONYMS: *affectation, pose, air, mannerism.* These nouns refer to personal behavior assumed for effect. An *affectation* is an artificial habit, as of speech or dress, that is often adopted in imitation of an admired person and that can be identified by others as being unnatural: *"His* [Arthur Rubinstein's] *playing stripped away . . . the affectations and exaggerations that characterized Chopin interpretation before his arrival"* (Michael Kimmelman). *Pose* denotes an attitude adopted with the aim of calling favorable attention to oneself or making an impression on other people: *His humility is only a pose. Air,* meaning a distinctive but intangible quality, does not always imply sham: *an air of authority.* In the plural, however, it suggests affectation and especially a wish to seem more important than is actually the case: *Don't put on airs. Mannerism* denotes an idiosyncratic trait, manner, or quirk, often one that others find obtrusive and distracting: *He had a mannerism of closing his eyes as he talked, as if he were deep in thought.*

af·fect·ed[1] (ə-fĕk′tĭd) *adj.* **1.** Acted upon, influenced, or changed. **2.** Emotionally stirred or moved. **3.** Infected or attacked, as by disease. [From AFFECT[1].]

af·fect·ed[2] (ə-fĕk′tĭd) *adj.* **1.** Assumed or simulated to impress others: *an affected accent.* **2.** Speaking or behaving in an artificial way to make an impression. **3.** Disposed or inclined. [From AFFECT[2].] **—af·fect′ed·ly** *adv.* **—af·fect′ed·ness** *n.*

af·fect·ing (ə-fĕk′tĭng) *adj.* Inspiring or capable of inspiring strong emotion; moving. See Synonyms at **moving.** [From AFFECT[1].] **—af·fect′ing·ly** *adv.*

af·fec·tion (ə-fĕk′shən) *n.* **1.** A tender feeling toward another; fondness. See Synonyms at **love. 2.** Often **affections.** Feeling or emotion: *an unbalanced state of affections.* **3.** A disposition to feel, do, or say; a propensity. **4.** *Obsolete.* Prejudice; partiality. [Middle English *affeccioun*, from Old French *affection*, from Latin *affectiō*, *affectiōn-*, from *affectus*, past participle of *afficere*, to affect, influence. See AFFECT[1].] **—af·fec′tion·al** *adj.* **—af·fec′tion·al·ly** *adv.*

af·fec·tion·ate (ə-fĕk′shə-nĭt) *adj.* **1.** Having or showing fond feelings or affection; loving and tender. **2.** *Obsolete.* Inclined or disposed. **—af·fec′tion·ate·ly** *adv.* **—af·fec′tion·ate·ness** *n.*

af·fec·tive (ə-fĕk′tĭv) *adj.* **1.** *Psychology.* Influenced by or resulting from the emotions: *affective disorders.* **2.** Concerned with or arousing feelings or emotions; emotional. **—af·fec′tive·ly** *adv.* **—af′fec·tiv′i·ty** (ăf′ĕk-tĭv′ĭ-tē) *n.*

af·fect·less (ăf′fĕkt′lĭs) *adj.* Having or showing no emotion; unfeeling: *"Mass-culture banality is killing our souls and making everybody affectless"* (New Yorker). **—af′fect′less·ness** *n.*

af·fen·pin·scher (ăf′ən-pĭn′shər) *n.* A breed of small dogs of European origin, having wiry, shaggy hair and a tufted muzzle. [German : *Affe*, ape (from Middle High German, from Old High German *affo*) + *Pinscher*, a type of dog with ears operated on or "pinched" to make them stand up (from English PINCH).]

af·fer·ent (ăf′ər-ənt) *adj.* Carrying inward to a central organ or section, as nerves that conduct impulses from the periphery of the body to the brain or spinal cord. [Latin *afferēns*, *afferent-*, present participle of *afferre*, to bring toward : *ad-*, ad- + *ferre*, to bring; see **bher-**[1] in Appendix.] **—af′fer·ent·ly** *adv.*

af·fi·ance (ə-fī′əns) *tr.v.* **-anced, -anc·ing, -anc·es.** To bind in a pledge of marriage; betroth. [From Middle English *affiaunce*, assurance, from Old French, from *affier*, to trust to, from Medieval Latin *affīdāre* : Latin *ad-*, ad- + Latin *fīdus*, faithful; see **bheidh-** in Appendix.]

af·fi·ant (ə-fī′ənt) *n.* *Law.* One who makes an affidavit. [From *affy*, to make affidavit, from Middle English *affien*, to trust, from Old French *affier*, to promise. See AFFIANCE.]

af·fi·da·vit (ăf′ĭ-dā′vĭt) *n.* *Law.* A written declaration made under oath before a notary public or other authorized officer. [Medieval Latin *affīdāvit*, from third person sing. past tense of Latin *affīdāre*, to pledge. See AFFIANCE.]

af·fil·i·ate (ə-fĭl′ē-āt′) *v.* **-at·ed, -at·ing, -ates.** *—tr.* **1.** To adopt or accept as a member, subordinate associate, or branch. **2.** To associate (oneself) as a subordinate, subsidiary, employee, or member: *affiliated herself with a new law firm.* **3.** To assign the origin of. *—intr.* To become closely connected or associated: *The two unions voted to affiliate.* **—affiliate** (-ē-ĭt, -āt′) *n.* A person, an organization, or an establishment associated with another as a subordinate, subsidiary, or member: *network affiliates.* [Medieval Latin *affīliāre*, to adopt : Latin *ad-*, ad- + Latin *fīlius*, son; see **dhē(i)-** in Appendix.] **—af·fil′i·a′tion** *n.*

af·fine (ə-fīn′) *adj.* *Mathematics.* **1.** Of or relating to a transformation of coordinates that is equivalent to a translation, contraction, or expansion with respect to a fixed origin and fixed coordinate system. **2.** Of or relating to the geometry of affine transformations. [French *affin*, closely related, from Old French. See AFFINED.]

af·fined (ə-fīnd′) *adj.* **1.** Linked by a very close relationship. **2.** Beholden to another; bound. [French *affiné*, from Old French *affin*, closely related, from Latin *affīnis*, related by marriage : *ad-*, ad- + *fīnis*, boundary.]

af·fin·i·ty (ə-fĭn′ĭ-tē) *n., pl.* **-ties. 1.** A natural attraction or feeling of kinship. **2.** Relationship by marriage. **3.** An inherent similarity between persons or things. See Synonyms at **likeness. 4.** *Biology.* A relationship or resemblance in structure between species that suggests a common origin. **5.** *Immunology.* The at-

ă pat	oi boy
ā pay	ou out
âr care	o͝o took
ä father	o͞o boot
ĕ pet	ŭ cut
ē be	ûr urge
ĭ pit	th thin
ī pie	*th* this
îr pier	hw which
ŏ pot	zh vision
ō toe	ə about, item
ô paw	♦ regionalism

Stress marks: ′ (primary); ′ (secondary), as in **dictionary** (dĭk′shə-nĕr′ē)

traction between an antigen and an antibody. **6.** *Chemistry.* An attraction or force between particles that causes them to combine. [Middle English *affinite,* from Old French *afinite,* from Latin *affīnitās,* from *affīnis,* related by marriage. See AFFINED.]

USAGE NOTE: In the sense of "attraction," *affinity* may be followed by *of, between,* or *with.* Thus one may speak of *the close affinity of James and Samuel,* or of *the affinity between James and Samuel,* or of *James's affinity with Samuel.* In its chemical use *affinity* is generally followed by *for: a dye with an affinity for synthetic fabrics.* In general usage *affinity* should not be used as a simple synonym for *liking.* In an earlier survey, a majority of the Usage Panel rejected the example *Her affinity for living in California led her to reject a chance to return to New York.*

affinity group *n.* A group of people who share a common interest, background, or goal.

af·firm (ə-fûrm′) *v.* **-firmed, -firm·ing, -firms.** —*tr.* **1.** To declare positively or firmly; maintain to be true. See Synonyms at **assert. 2.** To support or uphold the validity of; confirm. —*intr. Law.* To declare solemnly and formally but not under oath. [Middle English *affermen,* from Old French *afermer,* from Latin *affirmāre* : *ad-,* ad- + *firmāre,* to strengthen (from *firmus,* strong; see **dher-** in Appendix).] —**af·firm′a·ble** *adj.* —**af·firm′a·bly** *adv.* —**af·fir′mant** *adj. & n.* —**af·firm′er** *n.*

Afghan hound

af·fir·ma·tion (ăf′ər-mā′shən) *n.* **1.** The act of affirming or the state of being affirmed; assertion. **2.** Something declared to be true; a positive statement or judgment. **3.** *Law.* A solemn declaration given in place of a sworn statement by a person who conscientiously objects to taking an oath.

af·fir·ma·tive (ə-fûr′mə-tĭv) *adj.* **1.** Asserting that something is true or correct, as with the answer "yes": *an affirmative reply.* **2.** Giving assent or approval; confirming: *an affirmative vote.* **3.** Positive; optimistic: *an affirmative outlook.* **4.** *Logic.* Of, relating to, or being a proposition in which the predicate affirms something about the subject, such as the statement *apples have seeds.* —**affirmative** *n.* **1.** A word or statement of agreement or assent, such as the word *yes.* **2.** The side in a debate that upholds the proposition: *Her team will speak for the affirmative.* —**affirmative** *adv. Informal.* Used in place of the response "yes" to express confirmation or consent. —**af·fir′ma·tive·ly** *adv.*

USAGE NOTE: The expressions *in the affirmative* and *in the negative,* as in *She answered in the affirmative,* are generally regarded as pompous. *She answered yes* would be more acceptable even at the most formal levels of style.

affirmative action *n.* A policy or a program that seeks to redress past discrimination through active measures to ensure equal opportunity, as in education and employment.

af·fix (ə-fĭks′) *tr.v.* **-fixed, -fix·ing, -fix·es. 1.** To secure to something; attach: *affix a label to a package.* **2.** To impute; attribute: *affix blame to him.* **3.** To place at the end; append: *affix a postscript to a letter.* **4.** *Grammar.* To add as an affix. —**affix** (ăf′ĭks′) *n.* **1.** Something that is attached, joined, or added; an appendage or addition. **2.** *Linguistics.* A word element, such as a prefix or suffix, that can only occur attached to a base, stem, or root. [Medieval Latin *affixāre,* frequentative of Latin *affīgere, affix-* : *ad-,* ad- + *fīgere,* to fasten; see **dhīgʷ-** in Appendix.] —**af·fix′a·ble** *adj.* —**af·fix′er** *n.*

Afghanistan

af·fla·tus (ə-flā′təs) *n.* A strong creative impulse; divine inspiration. [Latin *afflātus,* from past participle of *afflāre,* to breathe on : *ad-,* ad- + *flāre,* to blow; see **bhlē-** in Appendix.]

af·flict (ə-flĭkt′) *tr.v.* **-flict·ed, -flict·ing, -flicts.** To inflict grievous physical or mental suffering on. [Middle English *afflighten,* from *afflight,* disturbed, frightened, from Latin *afflictum,* past participle of *afflīgere,* to cast down : *ad-,* ad- + *flīgere,* to strike.] —**af·flict′er** *n.* —**af·flic′tive** *adj.* —**af·flic′tive·ly** *adv.*

SYNONYMS: *afflict, agonize, excruciate, rack, torment, torture.* The central meaning shared by these verbs is "to bring great harm or suffering to someone": *afflicted with arthritis; agonizing pain; excruciating spasms of neuralgia; racked with cancer; tormented by migraine headaches; tortured by painful emotions.*

af·flic·tion (ə-flĭk′shən) *n.* **1.** A condition of pain, suffering, or distress. See Synonyms at **trial. 2.** A cause of pain, suffering, or distress. See Synonyms at **burden¹.**

af·flu·ence (ăf′lo͞o-əns, ə-flo͞o′-) *n.* **1.** A plentiful supply of material goods; wealth. **2.** A great quantity; an abundance. **3.** A flowing to or toward a point; afflux.

af·flu·en·cy (ăf′lo͞o′ən-sē, ə-flo͞o′-) *n.* Affluence.

af·flu·ent (ăf′lo͞o-ənt, ə-flo͞o′-) *adj.* **1.** Generously supplied with money, property, or possessions; prosperous or rich. See Synonyms at **rich. 2.** Plentiful; abundant. **3.** Flowing freely; copious. —**affluent** *n.* **1.** A stream or river that flows into a larger one; a tributary. **2.** A person who is well-off financially: *"the so-called emerging affluents"* (Leslie Tweeton). [Middle English, abundant, flowing, from Old French, from Latin *affluēns, affluent-,* present participle of *affluere,* to abound in : *ad-,* ad- + *fluere,* to flow; see **bhleu-** in Appendix.] —**af′flu·ent·ly** *adv.*

af·flux (ăf′lŭks′) *n.* A flow to or toward an area, especially of blood or other fluid toward a body part: *an afflux of blood to the head.* [Medieval Latin *affluxus,* from Latin, past participle of *affluere,* to flow to. See AFFLUENT.]

af·ford (ə-fôrd′, ə-fōrd′) *tr.v.* **-ford·ed, -ford·ing, -fords. 1.** To have the financial means for; be able to meet the cost of: *not able to afford a new car.* **2.** To be able to spare or give up: *can't afford an hour for lunch.* **3.** To be able to do or bear without disadvantage or risk to oneself: *can afford to be tolerant.* **4.** To make available; provide: *a sport affording good exercise; a tree that affords ample shade.* [Middle English *aforthen,* from Old English *geforthian,* to carry out : *ge-,* perfective pref.; see YCLEPT + *forthian,* to further (from *forth,* forth, forward; see **per¹** in Appendix).]

af·ford·a·ble (ə-fôr′də-bəl, ə-fōr′-) *adj.* That can be afforded: *affordable housing; an affordable risk.* —**af·ford′a·bil′i·ty** *n.* —**af·ford′a·bly** *adv.*

af·for·est (ə-fôr′ĭst, ə-fŏr′-) *tr.v.* **-est·ed, -est·ing, -ests.** To convert (open land) into a forest by planting trees or their seeds. [Medieval Latin *afforēstāre* : Latin *ad-,* ad- + Medieval Latin *forēstāre* (from *forēsta,* forest; see FOREST).] —**af·for′es·ta′tion** *n.*

af·fray (ə-frā′) *n.* A noisy quarrel or brawl. See Synonyms at **conflict.** —**affray** *tr.v.* **-frayed, -fray·ing, -frays.** *Archaic.* To frighten. [Middle English, from Old French *effrei, esfrei,* from *esfraier, esfreer,* to disturb. See **prī-** in Appendix.]

af·fri·cate (ăf′rĭ-kĭt) *n. Linguistics.* A complex speech sound consisting of a stop consonant followed by a fricative; for example, the initial sounds of *child* and *joy.* Also called *affricative.* [Latin *affricātus,* past participle of *affricāre,* to rub against : *ad-,* ad- + *fricāre,* to rub.]

af·fric·a·tive (ə-frĭk′ə-tĭv) *Linguistics. adj.* Of, relating to, or forming an affricate. —**affricative** *n.* See **affricate.**

af·fright (ə-frīt′) *tr.v.* **-fright·ed, -fright·ing, -frights.** To arouse fear in; terrify: *"Many of nature's greatest oddities, that would affright dwellers up here, are accepted down there"* (David Mazel). —**affright** *n.* **1.** Great fear; terror. **2.** A cause of terror. [Middle English *afrighten,* from Old English *āfyrhtan* : *ā-,* intensive pref. + *fyrhtan,* to frighten (from *fyrhto,* fright).] —**af·fright′ment** *n.*

af·front (ə-frŭnt′) *tr.v.* **-front·ed, -front·ing, -fronts. 1.** To insult intentionally, especially openly. See Synonyms at **offend. 2.a.** To meet defiantly; confront. **b.** *Obsolete.* To meet or encounter face to face. —**affront** *n.* **1.** An open or intentional offense, slight, or insult: *Such behavior is an affront to society.* **2.** *Obsolete.* A hostile encounter or meeting. [Middle English *afrounten,* from Old French *afronter* : Latin *ad-,* ad- + Latin *frōns, front-,* face; see FRONT.]

Aff·ton (ăf′tən). A city of eastern Missouri, a suburb of St. Louis. Population, 23,181.

af·fu·sion (ə-fyo͞o′zhən) *n.* A pouring on of liquid, as in baptism. [Late Latin *affūsiō, affūsiōn-,* from Latin *affūsus,* past participle of *affundere,* to pour on : *ad-,* ad- + *fundere,* to pour; see **gheu-** in Appendix.]

Afg. *abbr.* Afghanistan.

Af·ghan (ăf′găn′, -gən) *adj.* Of or relating to Afghanistan or its people, language, or culture. —**Afghan** *n.* **1.** A native or inhabitant of Afghanistan. **2.** See **Pashto. 3. afghan. a.** A coverlet or shawl of wool, knitted or crocheted in colorful geometric designs. **b.** A carpet of similar design. **4.** An Afghan hound. [Persian *afghān,* an Afghan.]

Afghan hound *n.* A large, slender hunting dog having long, thick hair, a pointed muzzle, and drooping ears.

af·ghan·i (ăf-găn′ē, -gä′nē) *n.* See table at **currency.** [Pashto.]

Af·ghan·i·stan (ăf-găn′ĭ-stăn′). *Abbr.* **Afg.** A landlocked country of southwest-central Asia. Mostly arid and mountainous, the country depends on agriculture; its mineral wealth is largely undeveloped. Since ancient times Afghanistan has been crisscrossed by invasion routes. Kabul is the capital and the largest city. Population, 13,051,358.

a·fi·cio·na·do (ə-fĭsh′ē-ə-nä′dō, ə-fĭs′ē-, ə-fē′sē-) *n., pl.* **-dos.** An enthusiastic admirer or follower; a devotee or a fan: *"West Coast aficionados of postwar coffee-shop architecture"* (Karal Ann Marling). [Spanish, past participle of *aficionar,* to induce a liking for, from *afición,* liking, from Latin *affectiō, affectiōn-.* See AFFECTION.]

a·field (ə-fēld′) *adv.* **1.** Off the usual or desired track. See Synonyms at **amiss. 2.** Away from one's home or usual environment. **3.** To or on a field.

a·fire (ə-fīr′) *adv. & adj.* **1.** On fire. **2.** Intensely interested.

AFL *abbr.* **1.** American Federation of Labor. **2.** American Football League.

a·flame (ə-flām′) *adv. & adj.* **1.** On or as if on fire. **2.** Keenly excited and interested.

af·la·tox·i·co·sis (ăf′lə-tŏk′sĭ-kō′sĭs) *n.* Poisoning caused by the consumption of substances or foods contaminated with aflatoxin. [AFLA(TOXIN) + TOXICOSIS.]

af·la·tox·in (ăf′lə-tŏk′sĭn) *n.* Any of a group of toxic compounds produced by certain molds, especially *Aspergillus flavus,* that contaminate stored food supplies such as animal feed and peanuts. [New Latin *A(spergillus) fla(vus),* species name (ASPERGILLUS + Latin *flavus,* yellow; see FLAVO–) + TOXIN.]

AFL-CIO *abbr.* American Federation of Labor and Congress of Industrial Organizations.

a·float (ə-flōt′) *adv. & adj.* **1.** In a floating position or condition. **2.** On a boat or ship away from the shore; at sea. **3.** In circulation; prevailing: *Rumors are afloat.* **4.** Awash; flooded. **5.** Drifting about; moving without guidance. **6.** Free or out of difficulty, especially financial difficulty: *couldn't keep the business afloat.*

a·flut·ter (ə-flŭt′ər) *adj.* **1.** Being in a flutter; fluttering: *with flags aflutter.* **2.** Nervous and excited.

A.F. of L. *abbr.* American Federation of Labor.

a·foot (ə-fo͝ot′) *adv. & adj.* **1.** On foot; walking. **2.** In the process of being carried out; astir: *plans afoot to resign.*

♦**a·fore** (ə-fôr′, ə-fōr′) *adv., prep. & conj. Chiefly Southern & Midland U.S.* Before. [Middle English, from Old English *onforan* : *on,* at; see ON + *fōran,* before, from *fore.* See FORE.]

a·fore·men·tioned (ə-fôr′mĕn′shənd, ə-fōr′-) *adj.* Mentioned previously.

a·fore·said (ə-fôr′sĕd′, ə-fōr′-) *adj.* Spoken of earlier.

a·fore·thought (ə-fôr′thôt′, ə-fōr′-) *adj.* Planned or intended beforehand; premeditated: *malice aforethought.*

a·fore·time (ə-fôr′tīm′, ə-fōr′-) *Archaic. adv.* At a former or past time; previously. **—aforetime** *adj.* Earlier; former.

a for·ti·o·ri (ä fôr′tē-ôr′ē, ā fôr′tē-ō′rī′) *adv.* For a still stronger reason; all the more. Used of a conclusion that is logically more certain than another. [Latin : *ā, ab,* from + *fortiōrī,* ablative of *fortior,* stronger.]

a·foul of (ə-foul′) *prep.* **1.** In or into collision, entanglement, or conflict with. **2.** Up against; in trouble with: *ran afoul of the law.* **3.** Entangled with: *The anchor fell afoul of the wreckage.*

AFP *abbr.* Alpha-fetoprotein.

Afr. *abbr.* Africa; African.

a·fraid (ə-frād′) *adj.* **1.** Filled with fear: *afraid of ghosts; afraid to die; afraid for his life.* **2.** Having feelings of aversion or unwillingness in regard to something: *not afraid of hard work; afraid to show emotion.* **3.** Filled with regret or concern. Used especially to soften an unpleasant statement: *I'm afraid you're wrong.* [Middle English *affraied,* past participle of *affraien,* to frighten, from Old French *esfraier, esfreer,* to disturb, of Germanic origin. See **prī-** in Appendix.]

SYNONYMS: *afraid, apprehensive, fearful.* The central meaning shared by these adjectives is "filled with fear": *afraid of snakes; feeling apprehensive before surgery; fearful of criticism.*
ANTONYM: *unafraid.*
WORD HISTORY: The notion of removal from a state of peace happens to be the basis for constructing **exfredāre,* literally "to remove from peace," the Vulgar Latin ancestor of our word *afraid.* This Vulgar Latin word is made up of the Latin prefix *ex–,* "out of," and a Vulgar Latin verb of the form **fridāre* or **fretāre,* which came from Germanic **frithuz,* "peace." The Old French word *esfraier,* "to disturb," which subsequently developed from **exfredāre,* came into Middle English as *affraien,* a verb whose earliest recorded sense, found in a text composed possibly around 1300, is "to frighten, disturb." *Affray,* the descendant of *affraien,* is little used in contemporary writing and speech, but the same cannot be said of the descendant of the past participle of *affraien,* our adjective *afraid.*

A-frame (ā′frām′) *n.* A structure, such as a house, with steeply angled sides that meet at the top in the shape of the letter A.

af·reet also **af·rit** (ăf′rēt′, ə-frēt′) *n. Mythology.* A powerful evil spirit or gigantic and monstrous demon in Arabic mythology. [Arabic *'ifrīt.*]

a·fresh (ə-frĕsh′) *adv.* Once more; anew; again: *start afresh.*

Af·ri·ca (ăf′rĭ-kə). *Abbr.* **Afr.** The second-largest continent, lying south of Europe between the Atlantic and Indian oceans. The hottest continent, Africa has vast mineral resources, many of which are still undeveloped.

Af·ri·can (ăf′rĭ-kən) *adj. Abbr.* **Afr.** Of or relating to Africa or its peoples, languages, or cultures. **—African** *n.* **1.** A native or inhabitant of Africa. **2.** A person of African descent.

Af·ri·can-A·mer·i·can or **African American** (ăf′rĭ-kən-ə-mĕr′ĭkən) *—adj.* Of or relating to Americans of African ancestry; Afro-American. *—n.* An American of African ancestry; an Afro-American: *"The words . . . are stinging reminders of the unresolved tension among African-Americans"* (Derrick Z. Jackson). See Usage Note at **black.**

African daisy *n.* Any of several African plants in the composite family, especially those in the genera *Arctotis, Gerbera,* and *Lonas,* that have showy flower heads.

Af·ri·can·ism (ăf′rĭ-kə-nĭz′əm) *n.* **1.** A characteristically African cultural feature, such as a belief or custom. **2.** A linguistic feature of an African language occurring in a non-African language.

Af·ri·can·ist (ăf′rĭ-kə-nĭst) *n.* A specialist in African affairs, cultures, or languages.

Af·ri·can·ize (ăf′rĭ-kə-nīz′) *v.* **-ized, -iz·ing, -iz·es.** *—tr.* **1.** To make African, as in culture. **2.** To transfer to African control: *"the Government's plan to Africanize the service"* (BBC Summary of World Broadcasts). *—intr.* To become African.

Af·ri·can·ized bee (ăf′rĭ-kə-nīzd′) *n.* A hybrid strain of honeybee introduced into Brazil in the mid-1950's and distinguished by aggressive traits such as the tendency to mass swarm and sting with great frequency. The bee was developed by a geneticist attempting to produce a commercial honeybee better adapted to the tropics. Also called *Africanized honeybee, killer bee.*

African lily *n.* A South African rhizomatous plant *(Agapanthus africanus)* having violet funnel-shaped flowers grouped in umbels. Also called *agapanthus, lily of the Nile.*

African mahogany *n.* **1.a.** Any of several African trees of the genus *Khaya,* having wood similar to that of the New World mahogany. **b.** The wood of any of these trees, used to make furniture, cabinets, and boat interiors. **2.** Any of various other African woods similar to mahogany.

African marigold *n.* An aromatic annual Mexican plant *(Tagetes erecta)* in the composite family, having pinnately lobed leaves and showy, solitary, yellow to orange flower heads.

African millet *n.* See **pearl millet.**

African oil palm *n.* See **oil palm** (sense 1).

African sleeping sickness *n.* See **sleeping sickness** (sense 1).

African swine fever *n.* See **hog cholera.**

African tulip tree *n.* A tropical African evergreen tree *(Spathodea campaulata)* having compound leaves and showy orange-scarlet or yellow flowers. Also called *tulip tree.*

African violet *n.* Any of various East African herbs of the genus *Saintpaulia,* having a basal leaf rosette and a showy cluster of violet or sometimes pink or white flowers. African violets are grown as indoor ornamentals.

Af·ri·kaans (ăf′rĭ-käns′, -känz′) *n.* A language that developed from 17th-century Dutch and is an official language of South Africa. Also called *Taal.* **—Afrikaans** *adj.* Of or relating to Afrikaans or Afrikaners. [*Afrikaans,* from Dutch *Afrikaansch,* African, from Latin *Āfricānus.* See AFRIKANER.]

Af·ri·ka·ner (ăf′rĭ-kä′nər) *n.* An Afrikaans-speaking South African of European ancestry, especially one descended from 17th-century Dutch settlers. [Afrikaans, an African, from Dutch, from Latin *Āfricānus,* from *Āfrica,* Africa, from *Āfer, Āfr-,* an African.]

af·rit (ăf′rēt′, ə-frēt′) *n. Mythology.* Variant of **afreet.**

Af·ro (ăf′rō) *n., pl.* **-ros.** A rounded, very thick, tightly curled hair style. **—Afro** *adj.* African in style or origin. [Probably short for AFRO-AMERICAN.]

Afro– *pref.* African: *Afro-Asiatic.* [From Latin *Āfer, Āfr-,* an African.]

Af·ro-A·mer·i·can (ăf′rō-ə-mĕr′ĭ-kən) *adj.* Of or relating to Americans of African ancestry or to their history or culture. **—Afro-American** *n.* An American of African ancestry. See Usage Note at **black.**

Af·ro-A·si·at·ic (ăf′rō-ā′zhē-ăt′ĭk, -shē-, -zē-) *n.* A large family of languages spoken in northern Africa and southwest Asia, comprising the Semitic, Chadic, Cushitic, Berber, and ancient Egyptian languages; formerly known as Hamito-Semitic. **—Af′ro-A′si·at′ic** *adj.*

aft (ăft) *adv. & adj. Nautical.* At, in, toward, or close to the stern of a vessel or the rear of an aircraft or a spacecraft. [Middle English *afte,* back, from Old English *æftan,* behind. See **apo-** in Appendix.]

AFT *abbr.* American Federation of Teachers.

aft. *abbr.* Afternoon.

af·ter (ăf′tər) *prep.* **1.a.** Behind in place or order: *Z comes after Y.* **b.** Next to or lower than in order or importance. **2.** In quest or pursuit of: *seek after fame; go after big money.* **3.** Concerning: *asked after you.* **4.** Subsequent in time to; at a later time than: *come after dinner.* **5.** Subsequent to and because of or regardless of: *They are still friends after all their differences.* **6.** Following continually: *year after year.* **7.** In the style of or in imitation of: *satires after Horace.* **8.** With the same or close to the same name as; in honor or commemoration of: *named after her mother.* **9.** According to the nature or desires of; in conformity to: *a tenor after my own heart.* **10.** Past the hour of: *five minutes after three.* **—after** *adv.* **1.** Behind; in the rear. **2.** At a later or subsequent time; afterward: *three hours after; departed shortly after.* **—after** *adj.* **1.** Subsequent in time or place; later; following: *in after years.* **2.** *Nautical.* Nearer the stern of a vessel. **—after** *conj.* Following or subsequent to the time that: *I saw them after I arrived.* **—after** *n.* Afternoon. [Middle English, from Old English *æfter.* See **apo-** in Appendix.]

af·ter-ac·tion (ăf′tər-ăk′shən) *adj.* Relating to or being a retrospective view or analysis of a battle: *an after-action report; after-action surveys of the sector.*

after all also **af·ter·all** (ăf′tər-ôl′) *adv.* **1.** In spite of everything to the contrary; nevertheless: *We chose to take a plane after all.* **2.** Everything else having been considered; ultimately: *"How will that affect the Nicaraguan situation, which afterall must still be the main target of any regional plan?"* (Martin Cohen).

af·ter·birth (ăf′tər-bûrth′) *n.* The placenta and fetal membranes expelled from the uterus following childbirth.

af·ter·burn·er (ăf′tər-bûr′nər) *n.* **1.** A device for augmenting the thrust of a jet engine by burning additional fuel with the uncombined oxygen in the hot exhaust gases. **2.** A device for burning or chemically altering unburned or partially burned carbon compounds in exhaust gases.

af·ter·care (ăf′tər-kâr′) *n.* Treatment or care given to convalescent patients after release from a hospital.

af·ter·clap (ăf′tər-klăp′) *n.* An unexpected, often unpleasant sequel to a matter that had been considered closed.

A-frame

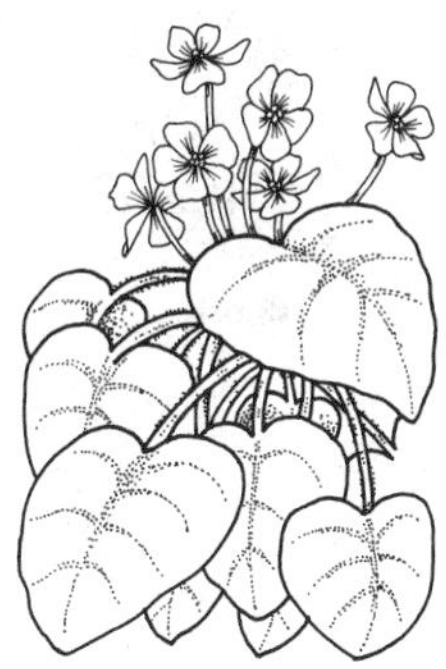

African violet

Afro

ă pat	oi boy
ā pay	ou out
âr care	o͝o took
ä father	o͞o boot
ĕ pet	ŭ cut
ē be	ûr urge
ĭ pit	th thin
ī pie	*th* this
îr pier	hw which
ŏ pot	zh vision
ō toe	ə about, item
ô paw	♦ regionalism

Stress marks: **′** (primary); ′ (secondary), as in **dictionary** (dĭk′shə-nĕr′ē)

af·ter·damp (ăf′tər-dămp′) *n.* An asphyxiating mixture of gases, primarily nitrogen and carbon dioxide, left in a mine after a fire or an explosion. [AFTER + DAMP, gas.]

af·ter·deck (ăf′tər-dĕk′) *n. Nautical.* The part of a ship's deck past amidships toward the stern.

af·ter·ef·fect (ăf′tər-ĭ-fĕkt′) *n.* An effect following its cause after some delay, especially a delayed or prolonged physiological or psychological response to a stimulus.

af·ter·glow (ăf′tər-glō′) *n.* **1.** The atmospheric glow that remains for a short time after sunset. **2.** The light emitted after removal of a source of energy, especially: **a.** The glow of an incandescent metal as it cools. **b.** The emission of light from a phosphor after removal of excitation. **3.** The comfortable feeling following a pleasant experience. **4.** A lingering impression of past glory or success.

af·ter-hours (ăf′tər-ourz′) *adj.* **1.** Occurring after closing time: *after-hours socializing.* **2.** Open after a legal or established closing time: *an after-hours club.*

agaric

af·ter·im·age (ăf′tər-ĭm′ĭj) *n.* A visual image that persists after the visual stimulus causing it has ceased to act: *"the red afterimage of the . . . flame pulsing before my eyes"* (Anthony Hyde). Also called *photogene.*

af·ter·life (ăf′tər-līf′) *n.* **1.** A life believed to follow death. **2.** The part of one's life that follows a particular event.

af·ter·mar·ket (ăf′tər-mär′kĭt) *n.* The demand for goods and services, such as parts and repairs, associated with the upkeep of a previous purchase.

af·ter·math (ăf′tər-măth′) *n.* **1.** A consequence, especially of a disaster or misfortune: *famine as an aftermath of drought.* **2.** A period of time following a disastrous event: *in the aftermath of war.* **3.** A second growth or crop in the same season, as of grass after mowing. [AFTER + obsolete *math,* mowing (from Old English *mǣth;* see **mē-**[4] in Appendix).]

af·ter·most (ăf′tər-mōst′) *adj.* **1.** *Nautical.* Nearest the stern; farthest aft. **2.** Nearest the end or rear; hindmost or last.

af·ter·noon (ăf′tər-no͞on′) *n.* **1.** *Abbr.* **aft., a.** The part of day from noon until sunset. **2.** The latter part: *in the afternoon of life.*

af·ter·pains (ăf′tər-pānz′) *pl.n.* Cramps or pains following childbirth, caused by contractions of the uterus.

af·ter·piece (ăf′tər-pēs′) *n.* A short comic piece performed after a play.

agave

af·ter-ri·pen·ing (ăf′tər-rī′pə-nĭng) *n.* A period during which certain changes must occur in some dormant but fully developed seeds before germination.

af·ter·sen·sa·tion (ăf′tər-sĕn-sā′shən) *n.* A sensory impression, such as an afterimage or aftertaste, that persists after the stimulus has ceased to act.

af·ter-shave (ăf′tər-shāv′) *n.* A usually fragrant lotion for use on the face after shaving.

af·ter·shock (ăf′tər-shŏk′) *n.* **1.** A quake of lesser magnitude, usually one of a series, following a large earthquake in the same area. **2.** A further reaction following the shock of a deeply disturbing occurrence or revelation: *"The industry continued to reel from aftershocks of a disastrous* [year]*"* (David Lake).

af·ter·taste (ăf′tər-tāst′) *n.* **1.** A taste persisting in the mouth after the substance that caused it is no longer present. **2.** A feeling that remains after an event or experience, especially one that was unpleasant.

af·ter-tax also **af·ter·tax** (ăf′tər-tăks) *adj.* Relating to or being that which remains after payment, especially of income taxes: *after-tax profits.*

af·ter·thought (ăf′tər-thôt′) *n.* An idea, a response, or an explanation that occurs to one after an event or a decision.

af·ter·time (ăf′tər-tīm′) *n.* The time to come; the future.

af·ter·ward (ăf′tər-wərd) also **af·ter·wards** (-wərdz) *adv.* At a later time; subsequently.

af·ter·word (ăf′tər-wûrd′) *n.* See **epilogue** (sense 2).

af·ter·work (ăf′tər-wûrk′) *adj.* Relating to, taken during, engaged in, occurring in, or intended for the hours after one's work has been finished: *the afterwork hours; an afterwork beer; afterwork lifestyle.*

af·ter·world (ăf′tər-wûrld′) *n.* A world thought to exist after death.

aft·most (ăft′mōst′) *adj. Nautical.* Farthest aft; aftermost.

Ag The symbol for the element **silver** (sense 1). [From Latin *argentum,* silver. See ARGENT.]

A.G. also **AG** *abbr.* **1.** Adjutant general. **2.** *Law.* Attorney general.

ag– *pref.* Variant of **ad–** (sense 1).

a·ga also **a·gha** (ä′gə, ăg′ə) *n.* Used as a title for a civil or military leader, especially in Turkey. [Turkish *ağa,* from Old Turkic *aqa,* older brother.]

A·ga·de (ə-gä′də). See **Akkad** (sense 2).

a·gain (ə-gĕn′) *adv.* **1.** Once more; anew: *try again.* **2.** To a previous place, position, or state: *left home but went back again.* **3.** Furthermore; moreover. **4.** On the other hand: *She might go, and again she might not.* **5.** In return; in response; back. [Middle English (influenced by Old Norse *i gegn,* again), from Old English *ongeagn,* against.]

again and again *adv.* Repeatedly; frequently.

a·gainst (ə-gĕnst′) *prep.* **1.** In a direction or course opposite to: *row against the current.* **2.** So as to come into forcible contact with: *waves dashing against the shore.* **3.** In contact with so as to rest or press on: *leaned against the tree.* **4.** In hostile opposition or resistance to: *struggle against fate.* **5.** Contrary to; opposed to: *against my better judgment.* **6.** In contrast or comparison with the setting or background of: *dark colors against a fair skin.* **7.** In preparation for; in anticipation of: *food stored against winter.* **8.** As a defense or safeguard from: *protection against the cold.* **9.** To the account or debt of: *drew a check against my bank balance.* **10.** Directly opposite to; facing. [Middle English, alteration of *againes,* from Old English *ongeagn.*]

A·ga Khan III (ä′gə kän′). Originally Aga Sultan Sir Mohammed Shah. 1877–1957. Indian leader of the Ismaili Moslem sect. He appointed his grandson Prince Karim (born 1936) to succeed him as **Aga Khan IV.**

a·ga·lac·ti·a (ā-gə-lăk′tē-ə, -shē-ə, ăg′ə-) *n.* Absence of or faulty secretion of milk following childbirth. [New Latin, from Greek *agalaktia,* lack of milk : *a-,* without; see A–[1] + *gala, galakt-,* milk; see **melg-** in Appendix.]

a·ga·ma (ə-gä′mə, ăg′ə-) *n.* Any of various small, long-tailed, insect-eating lizards of the family Agamidae, found in the Old World tropics. [American Spanish, of Cariban origin.]

Ag·a·mem·non (ăg′ə-mĕm′nŏn′, -nən) *n. Greek Mythology.* The king of Mycenae and leader of the Greeks in the Trojan War, who was the son of Atreus and the father of Orestes, Electra, and Iphigenia. He was killed by his wife Clytemnestra upon his return from Troy.

a·gam·ete (ā-găm′ēt′, ā′gə-mēt′) *n.* An asexual reproductive cell, such as a spore. [From Greek *agametos,* unmarried, variant of *agamos.* See AGAMIC.]

a·gam·ic (ā-găm′ĭk) also **ag·a·mous** (ăg′ə-məs) *adj. Biology.* Occurring or reproducing without the union of male and female cells; asexual or parthenogenetic. [From Late Latin *agamus,* unmarried, from Greek *agamos* : *a-,* not; see A–[1] + *gamos,* marriage; see –GAMY.] —**a·gam′i·cal·ly** *adv.*

a·gam·o·gen·e·sis (ā-găm′ə-jĕn′ĭ-sĭs, ăg′ə-mō-) *n.* Asexual reproduction, as by budding, cell division, or parthenogenesis. [Greek *agamos,* unmarried; see AGAMIC + –GENESIS.]

a·gam·o·sperm·y (ə-găm′ə-spûr′mē, ăg′ə-mō-) *n. Botany.* The asexual formation of embryos and seeds without the occurrence of fertilization. [From Greek *agamos,* unmarried; see AGAMIC + Greek *sperma,* seed; see SPERM[1].]

ag·a·mous (ăg′ə-məs) *adj. Biology.* Variant of **agamic.**

A·ga·ña (ə-gä′nyə, ä-gä′nyä). The capital of Guam, on the western coast of the island. It was almost completely destroyed in World War II. Population, 896.

ag·a·pan·thus (ăg′ə-păn′thəs) *n.* See **African lily.** [New Latin *Agapanthus,* genus name : Greek *agapē,* love + Greek *anthos,* flower.]

a·gape[1] (ə-gāp′, ə-găp′) *adv. & adj.* **1.** In a state of wonder or amazement, as with the mouth wide open. **2.** Wide open.

a·ga·pe[2] (ä-gä′pā, ä′gə-pā′) *n.* **1.** Christian love. **2.** Love that is spiritual, not sexual, in its nature. **3.** In the early Christian Church, the love feast accompanied by Eucharistic celebration. [Greek *agapē,* love.]

a·gar (ä′gär′, ä′gär′) also **a·gar-a·gar** (ä′gär-ä′gär′, ä′gär-ä′-) *n.* **1.** A gelatinous material derived from certain marine algae. It is used as a base for bacterial culture media and as a stabilizer and thickener in many food products. **2.** A culture medium containing this material. [Short for Malay *agar-agar.*]

ag·a·ric (ăg′-ər-ĭk, ə-găr′ĭk) *n.* **1.** Any of various mushrooms of the genera *Agaricus, Fomes,* or related genera, having large umbrellalike caps with numerous gills beneath. **2.** The dried fruiting body of certain fungal species in the genus *Fomes,* formerly used in medicine, especially to inhibit the production of sweat. [Middle English *agarik,* a kind of fungus, from Latin *agaricum,* from Greek *agarikon,* from *Agaria,* a town in Sarmatia.]

Ag·as·siz (ăg′ə-sē), **Elizabeth Cabot Cary.** 1822–1907. American educator who helped organize the predecessor of Radcliffe College (1879) and served as Radcliffe's first president (1894–1899).

Agassiz, (Jean) Louis (Rodolphe). 1807–1873. Swiss-born American naturalist noted for his study of fossil fish and for recognizing from geologic evidence that ice ages had occurred in the Northern Hemisphere.

Agassiz, Lake. A glacial lake of the Pleistocene epoch extending over present-day northwest Minnesota, northeast North Dakota, southern Manitoba, and southwest Ontario.

ag·ate (ăg′ĭt) *n.* **1.** A fine-grained, fibrous variety of chalcedony with colored bands or irregular clouding. **2.** *Games.* A playing marble made of agate or a glass imitation of it. **3.** A tool with agate parts, such as a burnisher tipped with agate. **4.** *Printing.* A type size, approximately 5½ points. [Middle English *achate, agaten,* from Old French *acate, agate,* alteration (influenced by Greek *agathē,* good) of Latin *achātēs,* from Greek *akhatēs.*]

agate line *n. Printing.* A measure of space, usually one column wide and $\frac{1}{14}$ of an inch deep, used especially for classified advertisements.

a·ga·ve (ə-gä′vē, ə-gä′-) *n.* Any of numerous plants of the genus *Agave,* native to hot, dry regions of the New World and having basal rosettes of tough, sword-shaped, often spiny-margined leaves. Agaves are grown for ornament, fiber, and food.

Also called *century plant.* [New Latin *Agave,* genus name, from Greek *agauē,* feminine of *agauos,* noble.]

Ag·a·wam (ăg′ə-wŏm′). A town of southwest Massachusetts on the Connecticut River near Springfield. It was settled in 1635. Population, 26,271.

agcy. *abbr.* Agency.

age (āj) *n.* **1.** The length of time that one has existed; duration of life: *23 years of age.* **2.** The time of life when a person becomes qualified to assume certain civil and personal rights and responsibilities, usually at 18 or 21 years; legal age: *under age; of age.* **3.** One of the stages of life: *the age of adolescence; at an awkward age.* **4.** The state of being old; old age: *hair white with age.* **5.** Often **Age. a.** A period in the history of humankind marked by a distinctive characteristic or achievement: *the Stone Age; the computer age.* **b.** A period in the history of the earth, usually shorter than an epoch: *the Ice Age.* **c.** A period of time marked by the presence or influence of a dominant figure: *the Elizabethan Age.* See Synonyms at **period. 6. a.** The period of history during which a person lives: *a product of his age.* **b.** A generation: *ages yet unborn.* **7. ages.** *Informal.* An extended period of time: *left ages ago.* **—age** *v.* **aged, ag·ing, ag·es.** *—tr.* **1.** To cause to become old. **2.** To cause to mature or ripen under controlled conditions: *aging wine.* **3.** To change (the characteristics of a device) through use, especially to stabilize (an electronic device). *—intr.* **1.** To become old. **2.** To manifest traits associated with old age. **3.** To develop a certain quality of ripeness; become mature: *cheese aging at room temperature.* See Synonyms at **mature.** ***—phrasal verb.* age out.** *Informal.* To reach an age, 18 or 21 years, for example, at which one is no longer eligible for certain special services, such as education or protection, from the state. [Middle English, from Old French *aage,* from Vulgar Latin **aetāticum,* from Latin *aetās, aetāt-,* age. See **aiw-** in Appendix.] **—ag′er** *n.*

-age *suff.* **1.** Collection; mass: *sewerage.* **2.** Relationship; connection: *parentage.* **3.** Condition; state: *vagabondage.* **4. a.** An action: *blockage.* **b.** Result of an action: *breakage.* **5.** Residence or place of: *vicarage.* **6.** Charge or fee: *cartage.* [Middle English, from Old French, from Vulgar Latin *-*āticum,* abstract n. suff., from Latin *-āticum,* n. and adj. suff.]

ag·ed (ā′jĭd) *adj.* **1.** Being of advanced age; old. See Synonyms at **elderly. 2.** Characteristic of old age. **3.** (ājd). Having reached the age of: *aged three.* **4.** (ājd). Brought to a desired ripeness or maturity: *aged cheese.* **5.** *Geology.* Approaching the base level of erosion. **—aged** *n.* Elderly people considered as a group. Used with *the.* **—ag′ed·ly** *adv.* **—ag′ed·ness** *n.*

A·gee (ā′jē), **James.** 1909–1955. American writer and critic who won a 1957 Pulitzer Prize for his novel *A Death in the Family.*

age group *n.* All the people of a particular age or range of ages.

age·ing (ā′jĭng) *n. Chiefly British.* Variant of **aging.**

age·ism also **ag·ism** (ā′jĭz′əm) *n.* Discrimination based on age, especially prejudice against the elderly. **—age′ist** *adj. & n.*

age·less (āj′lĭs) *adj.* **1.** Seeming never to grow old. **2.** Existing forever; eternal. **—age′less·ly** *adv.* **—age′less·ness** *n.*

SYNONYMS: *ageless, eternal, timeless.* The central meaning shared by these adjectives is "existing unchanged forever": *the ageless themes of love and revenge; eternal truths; timeless beauty.*

Ag·e·nais (ä′zhə-nā′) or **Ag·e·nois** (-nwä′). A historical region of southwest France. Ruled by England at various times during the Hundred Years' War, it finally passed to France after 1444.

a·gen·cy (ā′jən-sē) *n., pl.* **-cies.** *Abbr.* **agcy. 1.** The condition of being in action; operation. **2.** The means or mode of acting; instrumentality. **3.** A business or service authorized to act for others: *an employment agency.* **4.** An administrative division of a government or international body. [Medieval Latin *agentia,* from Latin *agēns, agent-,* present participle of *agere,* to do. See AGENT.]

agency shop *n.* An establishment in which a union represents all employees regardless of union membership but requires that nonmembers pay union dues or fees.

a·gen·da (ə-jĕn′də) *n., pl.* **-das. 1.** A list or program of things to be done or considered: *"They share with them an agenda beyond the immediate goal of democratization of the electoral process"* (Daniel Sneider). **2.** A plural of **agendum.** [Latin, pl. of *agendum,* agendum. See AGENDUM.]

USAGE NOTE: It is true that Cicero would have used *agendum* to refer to a single item of business before the Roman Senate, with *agenda* as its plural. But in Modern English a phrase such as *item on the agenda* expresses the sense of *agendum,* and *agenda* is used as a singular noun to denote the set or list of such items, as in *The agenda for the meeting has not yet been set.* If a plural of *agenda* is required, the form should be *agendas: The agendas of both meetings are exceptionally varied.*

a·gen·dum (ə-jĕn′dəm) *n., pl.* **-da** (-də) also **-dums.** Something to be done, especially an item on a program or list. [Latin, neuter gerundive of *agere,* to do. See **ag-** in Appendix.]

a·gen·e·sis (ā-jĕn′ĭ-sĭs) *n.* Absence or incomplete development of an organ or body part.

A·ge·nois (ä′zhə-nwä′). See **Agenais.**

a·gent (ā′jənt) *n. Abbr.* **agt. 1.** One that acts or has the power or authority to act. **2.** One empowered to act for or represent another: *an author's agent; an insurance agent.* **3.** A means by which something is done or caused; instrument. **4.** A force or substance that causes a change: *a chemical agent.* **5.** A representative or official of a government or administrative department of a government: *an FBI agent.* **6.** A spy. [Middle English, from Latin *agēns, agent-,* present participle of *agere,* to do. See **ag-** in Appendix.]

a·gen·tial (ā-jĕn′shəl) *adj.* Of, relating to, or acting as an agent or agency.

A·gent Orange (ā′jənt) *n.* A herbicide containing trace amounts of the toxic contaminant dioxin that was used in the Vietnam War to defoliate areas of forest. [From the orange identifying strip on drums in which it was stored.]

a·gent pro·vo·ca·teur (ä-zhäɴ′ prô-vô′kä-tœr′) *n., pl.* **a·gents pro·vo·ca·teurs** (ä-zhäɴ′ prô-vô′kä-tœr′). A person employed to associate with suspected individuals or groups with the purpose of inciting them to commit acts that will make them liable to punishment. [French : *agent,* agent + *provocateur,* instigator.]

a·gent·ry (ā′jən-trē) *n., pl.* **-ries.** The office or functions of an agent.

Age of Aquarius *n.* An astrological era held to have brought to the world increased spirituality and harmony among people.

age of consent *n. Law.* The age at which a person is legally considered competent to give consent, as to sexual intercourse.

age of reason *n.* **1.** An era in which rationalism prevails, especially the period of the Enlightenment in England, France, and the United States. **2.** An age at which a person is considered capable of making reasoned judgments.

age-old (āj′ōld′) *adj.* Very old or of long standing.

ag·er·a·tum (ăj′ə-rā′təm) *n.* **1.** Any of various New World plants of the genus *Ageratum* in the composite family, especially *A. houstonianum,* having showy, colorful flower heads. **2.** Any of several other plants having flower clusters similar to the ageratum. [New Latin *Agēratum,* genus name, from Greek *agēratos,* ageless : *a-,* not; see A–[1] + *gēras,* old age; see **gerə-**[1] in Appendix.]

A·ges·i·la·us II (ə-jĕs′ə-lā′əs). 444?–360? B.C. Spartan king (399?–360?). Considered one of the most brilliant military leaders of antiquity, he successfully defended Sparta during the Corinthian War (394–387).

ag·gie[1] (ăg′ē) *n. Games.* A playing marble. [AG(ATE) + –IE.]

ag·gie[2] (ăg′ē) *n. Informal.* **1.** An agricultural school or college. **2.** A student enrolled at such a school or college. [AG(RICULTURAL) + –IE.]

ag·gior·na·men·to (ə-jôr′nə-mĕn′tō) *n., pl.* **-tos.** The process of bringing an institution or organization up to date; modernization. [Italian, from *aggiornare,* to update : *a-,* to (from Latin *ad-;* see AD–) + *giorno,* day (from Latin *diurnus,* daily; see DIURNAL).]

ag·glom·er·ate (ə-glŏm′ə-rāt′) *tr. & intr.v.* **-at·ed, -at·ing, -ates.** To form or collect into a rounded mass. **—agglomerate** (-ər-ĭt) *adj.* Gathered into a rounded mass. **—agglomerate** (-ər-ĭt) *n.* **1.** A confused or jumbled mass; a heap. **2.** A volcanic rock consisting of rounded and angular fragments fused together. [Latin *agglomerāre, agglomerāt-,* to mass together : *ad-,* ad- + *glomerāre,* to form into a ball (from *glomus,* ball).] **—ag·glom′er·a′tive** (-ə-rā′tĭv, -ər-ə-tĭv) *adj.* **—ag·glom′er·a′tor** *n.*

ag·glom·er·a·tion (ə-glŏm′ə-rā′shən) *n.* **1.** The act or process of gathering into a mass. **2.** A confused or jumbled mass: *"To avoid the problems of large urban agglomerations, the state decentralized the university system"* (Bickley Townsend).

ag·glu·tin·a·ble (ə-glo͞ot′n-ə-bəl) *adj.* Capable of agglutinating. **—ag·glu′tin·a·bil′i·ty** *n.*

ag·glu·ti·nate (ə-glo͞ot′n-āt′) *v.* **-nat·ed, -nat·ing, -nates.** *—tr.* **1.** To cause to adhere, as with glue. **2.** *Linguistics.* To form (words) by combining words or words and word elements. **3.** *Physiology.* To cause (red blood cells or bacteria) to clump together. *—intr.* **1.** To join together into a group or mass. **2.** *Linguistics.* To form words by agglutination. **3.** *Physiology.* To clump together; undergo agglutination. **—agglutinate** *n.* See **agglutination** (sense 2). [Latin *agglūtināre, agglūtināt-* : *ad-,* ad- + *glūtināre,* to glue (from *glūten,* glue).] **—ag·glu′ti·nant** *adj. & n.*

ag·glu·ti·na·tion (ə-glo͞ot′n-ā′shən) *n.* **1.** The act or process of agglutinating; adhesion of distinct parts. **2.** A clumped mass of material formed by agglutination. Also called *agglutinate.* **3.** *Linguistics.* The formation of words from morphemes that retain their original forms and meanings with little change during the combination process. **4.** The clumping together of red blood cells or bacteria, usually in response to a particular antibody.

ag·glu·ti·na·tive (ə-glo͞ot′n-ā′tĭv, -ə-tĭv) *adj.* **1.** Tending toward, concerning, or characteristic of agglutination. **2.** *Linguistics.* Of, relating to, or being a language in which words are formed primarily by means of agglutination.

ag·glu·ti·nin (ə-glo͞ot′n-ĭn) *n. Physiology.* A substance, such as an antibody, that is capable of causing agglutination of a particular antigen, especially red blood cells or bacteria. [AG-GLUTIN(ATION) + –IN.]

James Agee

ă pat	oi boy
ā pay	ou out
âr care	o͝o took
ä father	o͞o boot
ĕ pet	ŭ cut
ē be	ûr urge
ĭ pit	th thin
ī pie	*th* this
îr pier	hw which
ŏ pot	zh vision
ō toe	ə about, item
ô paw	♦ regionalism

Stress marks: **′** (primary); ′ (secondary), as in **dictionary** (dĭk′shə-nĕr′ē)

ag·glu·tin·o·gen (ăg′lo͞o-tĭn′ə-jən, ə-glo͞o′tn-) *n. Physiology.* An antigen that stimulates the production of a particular agglutinin, such as an antibody. [AGGLUTIN(IN) + –GEN.] **—ag′glu·tin′o·gen′ic** (ăg′lo͞o-tĭn′ə-jĕn′ĭk, ə-glo͞o′tn-) *adj.*

ag·grade (ə-grād′) *tr.v.* **-grad·ed, -grad·ing, -grades.** To fill and raise the level of (the bed of a stream) by deposition of sediment. **—ag′gra·da′tion** (ăg′rə-dā′shən) *n.* **—ag′gra·da′tion·al** *adj.*

ag·gran·dize (ə-grăn′dīz′, ăg′rən-) *tr.v.* **-dized, -diz·ing, -diz·es. 1.** To increase the scope of; extend. **2.** To make greater in power, influence, stature, or reputation. **3.** To make appear greater; exaggerate: *aggrandize one argument while belittling another.* [French *agrandir, agrandiss-,* from Old French : *a-,* to (from Latin *ad-;* see AD–) + *grandir,* to grow larger (from Latin *grandīre,* from *grandis,* large).] **—ag·gran′dize·ment** (ə-grăn′dĭz-mənt, -dīz′-) *n.* **—ag·gran′diz′er** *n.*

ag·gra·vate (ăg′rə-vāt′) *tr.v.* **-vat·ed, -vat·ing, -vates. 1.** To make worse or more troublesome. **2.** To rouse to exasperation or anger; provoke. See Synonyms at **annoy.** [Latin *aggravāre, aggravāt-* : *ad-,* ad- + *gravāre,* to burden (from *gravis,* heavy; see **gʷere-**[1] in Appendix).] **—ag′gra·vat′ing·ly** *adv.* **—ag′gra·va′tive** *adj.* **—ag′gra·va′tor** *n.*

USAGE NOTE: It is sometimes claimed that *aggravate* should be used only to mean "to make worse" and not "to irritate." Based on this view it would be appropriate to say *The endless wait for luggage aggravates the misery of modern air travel,* but not *It's the endless wait for luggage that aggravates me the most.* But the latter use dates back as far as the 17th century and is accepted by 68 percent of the Usage Panel. As H.W. Fowler wrote, "the extension from aggravating a person's temper to aggravating the person himself is slight and natural, and when we are told that Wackford Squeers [in Dickens's *Nicholas Nickleby*] pinched the boys in aggravating places we may reasonably infer that his choice of places aggravated both the pinches and the boys."

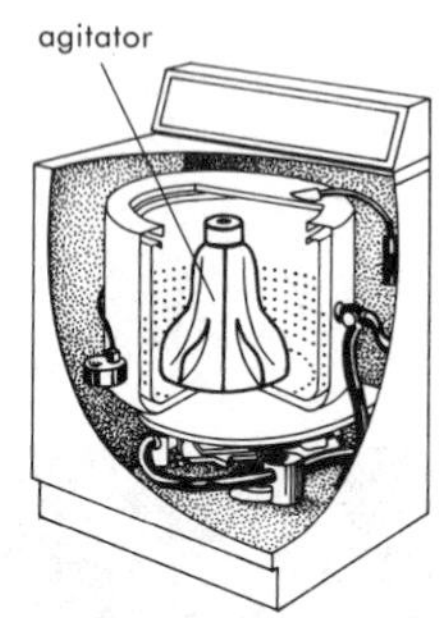

agitator
Cutaway view of a washing machine

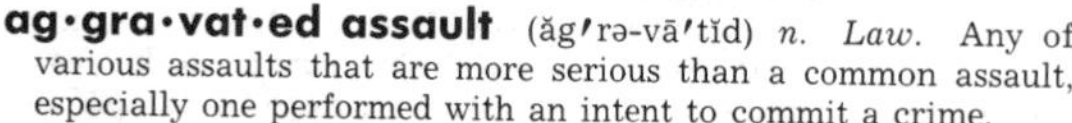

ag·gra·vat·ed assault (ăg′rə-vā′tĭd) *n. Law.* Any of various assaults that are more serious than a common assault, especially one performed with an intent to commit a crime.

ag·gra·va·tion (ăg′rə-vā′shən) *n.* **1.** The act of aggravating or the state of being aggravated. **2.** A source of continuing, increasing irritation or trouble. **3.** Exasperation.

ag·gre·gate (ăg′rĭ-gĭt) *adj.* **1.** Constituting or amounting to a whole; total: *aggregate sales in that market.* **2.** *Botany.* Crowded or massed into a dense cluster. **3.** Composed of a mixture of minerals separable by mechanical means. **—aggregate** *n.* **1.** A total considered with reference to its constituent parts; a gross amount: *"An empire is the aggregate of many states under one common head"* (Edmund Burke). **2.** The mineral materials, such as sand or stone, used in making concrete. **—aggregate** (-gāt′) *tr.v.* **-gat·ed, -gat·ing, -gates. 1.** To gather into a mass, sum, or whole. **2.** To amount to; total. ***—idiom.* in the aggregate.** Taken into account as a whole: *Unit sales for December amounted in the aggregate to 100,000.* [Middle English *aggregat,* from Latin *aggregātus,* past participle of *aggregāre,* to add to : *ad-,* ad- + *gregāre,* to collect (from *grex, greg-,* flock; see **ger-** in Appendix).] **—ag′gre·gate·ly** *adv.* **—ag′gre·ga′tion** *n.* **—ag′gre·ga′tive** *adj.* **—ag′gre·ga′tor** *n.*

aggregate fruit *n.* A fruit, such as the raspberry, consisting of many individual small fruits derived from separate ovaries within a single flower, borne together on a common receptacle.

ag·gress (ə-grĕs′) *intr.v.* **-gressed, -gress·ing, -gress·es.** To initiate an attack, a war, a quarrel, or a fight: *"America and the European countries should press back when the Soviets overstep and aggress, as in Afghanistan"* (Washington Post). [French *agresser,* from Latin *aggredī, aggress-,* to attack : *ad-,* ad- + *gradī,* to go; see **ghredh-** in Appendix.]

USAGE NOTE: *Aggress* has occasionally been unjustly maligned as an upstart back-formation, that is, as having been created by people who incorrectly thought that *aggression* was formed from the verb *aggress.* As used in the field of psychology *aggress* may be a back-formation from *aggression,* but *aggress* has been in general use since the 16th century and in fact antedates *aggression.*

ag·gres·sion (ə-grĕsh′ən) *n.* **1.** The act of initiating hostilities or invasion. **2.** The practice or habit of launching attacks. **3.** *Psychology.* Hostile or destructive behavior or actions.

ag·gres·sive (ə-grĕs′ĭv) *adj.* **1.** Inclined to behave in a hostile fashion. **2.** Assertive, bold, and enterprising: *an aggressive young executive.* **3.** Intense or harsh, as in color. **4.** Fast growing; tending to spread quickly: *an aggressive tumor.* **—ag·gres′sive·ly** *adv.* **—ag·gres′sive·ness** *n.*

ag·gres·sor (ə-grĕs′ər) *n.* One that engages in aggression.

ag·grieve (ə-grēv′) *tr.v.* **-grieved, -griev·ing, -grieves. 1.** To distress; afflict. **2.** To inflict an injury or injuries on. [Middle English *agreven,* from Old French *agrever,* from Latin *aggravāre,* to make worse. See AGGRAVATE.]

ag·grieved (ə-grēvd′) *adj.* **1.** Feeling distress or affliction. **2.** Treated wrongly; offended. **3.** *Law.* Treated unjustly, as by denial of or infringement upon one's legal rights. **—ag·griev′ed·ly** (ə-grē′vĭd-lē) *adv.* **—ag·griev′ed·ness** *n.*

ag·gro (ăg′rō) *n., pl.* **-gros.** *Chiefly British.* **1.a.** Irritation and exasperation: *"Postponing new hospitals and roads causes far less aggro than sacking town hall or Whitehall workers"* (Economist). **b.** A raucous rivalry or grievance, characterized by angry public confrontations or violence: *"The Commons met in apprehensive mood yesterday following the ructions in the Chamber last week. Were we in for more aggro or were the lads on the Westminster terraces going to return to more civilized conduct?"* (Financial Times). **c.** A fistfight. **2.** Aggressive nature. **—aggro** *adj. Slang.* Very aggressive, fearless, and stylish, as in surfing or skateboarding: *"Nat was aggro . . . Not content to ride in a straight line across the wave's face, Nat was a pioneer of the vertical move"* (Kem Nunn). [Short for AGGRAVATION and AGGRESSION.]

a·gha (ä′gə, ăg′ə) *n.* Variant of **aga.**

a·ghast (ə-găst′) *adj.* Struck by shock, terror, or amazement. [Middle English *agast,* past participle of *agasten,* to frighten : *a-,* intensive pref. (from Old English *ā-*) + *gasten,* to frighten (from Old English *gǣstan,* from *gāst,* ghost).]

ag·ile (ăj′əl, -īl′) *adj.* **1.** Characterized by quickness, lightness, and ease of movement; nimble. See Synonyms at **nimble. 2.** Mentally alert: *an agile mind.* [French, from Latin *agilis,* from *agere,* to drive, do. See **ag-** in Appendix.] **—ag′ile·ly** *adv.* **—ag′ile·ness** *n.*

a·gil·i·ty (ə-jĭl′ĭ-tē) *n.* The state or quality of being agile; nimbleness. [Middle English *agilite,* from Old French, from Medieval Latin *agilitās,* from Latin *agilis.* See AGILE.]

♦ **a·gin** (ə-gĭn′) *Chiefly Upper Southern U.S. prep.* **1.** Against. **2.** Opposed to: *I'm agin him.* **3.** Next to; beside; near. **4.** By or before (a specified time). **—agin** *conj.* By the time that. [Regional variant of AGAINST.]

♦ ***REGIONAL NOTE:*** The spelling of *agin* reflects both the raised vowel before a nasal consonant, typical of Southern dialects, and a reduced final consonant cluster, typical of several regional varieties. *Agin* has a wide spectrum of senses in the regional speech of those who pronounce it this way. Indeed, these regional senses are tied to the pronunciation, for standard English *against* does not quite capture the full implication of the assertion *"I'm agin him"*—that is, "opposed to him and all that he stands for." Another regional sense recalls the original literal Old English sense of "facing; next to" (see the first four senses of *against* in the Oxford English Dictionary), where standard English would have *by: Their house is agin the mountain. Agin* may be used figuratively with regard to time chiefly in South Midland dialects, meaning "by or before (a specified time)": *"I'll be there agin daylight"* (North Carolina informant in DARE).

A·gin·court (ăj′ĭn-kôrt′, -kōrt′). A village of northern France west-northwest of Arras. On October 25, 1415, Henry V of England decisively defeated a much larger French army here. The victory demonstrated the effectiveness of longbow-equipped troops over heavily armored feudal knights.

ag·ing (ā′jĭng) *n.* **1.** The process of growing old or maturing. **2.** An artificial process for imparting the characteristics and properties of age.

ag·ism (ā′jĭz′əm) *n.* Variant of **ageism.**

ag·i·ta (ăj′ĭ-tə) *n.* Acid indigestion: *"Agita . . . can afflict those who indulge in too much good . . . food"* (New York Times). [Italian, from *agitare,* to agitate, from Latin *agitāre.* See AGITATE.]

ag·i·tate (ăj′ĭ-tāt′) *v.* **-tat·ed, -tat·ing, -tates.** *—tr.* **1.** To cause to move with violence or sudden force. **2.** To upset; disturb: *was agitated by the alarming news.* **3.** To arouse interest in (a cause, for example) by use of the written or spoken word; debate. *—intr.* To stir up public interest in a cause: *agitate for a tax reduction.* [Latin *agitāre, agitāt-,* frequentative of *agere,* to drive, do. See **ag-** in Appendix.] **—ag′i·tat′ed·ly** (-tā′tĭd-lē) *adv.* **—ag′i·ta′tive** *adj.*

SYNONYMS: *agitate, churn, convulse, rock, shake.* The central meaning shared by these verbs is "to cause to move to and fro violently": *land agitated by tremors; a storm churning the waves; buildings and streets convulsed by the detonation of a bomb; a tornado rocking trees and houses; an explosion that shook the ground.*

ag·i·ta·tion (ăj′ĭ-tā′shən) *n.* **1.** The act of agitating or the state of being agitated. **2.** Extreme emotional disturbance; perturbation. **3.** The stirring up of public interest in a matter of controversy, such as a political or social issue. **—ag′i·ta′tion·al** *adj.*

ag·i·ta·to (ăj′ĭ-tä′tō) *adv. & adj. Music.* In a restless, agitated style. Used chiefly as a direction. [Italian, past participle of *agitare,* from Latin *agitāre,* to agitate. See AGITATE.]

ag·i·ta·tor (ăj′ĭ-tā′tər) *n.* **1.** One who agitates, especially one who engages in political agitation. **2.** An apparatus that shakes or stirs, as in a washing machine.

ag·it·prop (ăj′ĭt-prŏp′) *n.* **1.** Communist-oriented political propaganda disseminated especially through literature, drama, art, or music. **2.** The means or vehicle, such as a government department or a state-controlled press, by which such propaganda is disseminated. **3.** Something, such as a film, that is designed to impress a certain political or social perspective on its audience, with little or no consideration given to accuracy: *"It also is a conspiracy movie, agitprop against today's targets, big government and big business"* (George F. Will). *—attributive.* Often used to

ă pat	oi boy
ā pay	ou out
âr care	o͝o took
ä father	o͞o boot
ĕ pet	ŭ cut
ē be	ûr urge
ĭ pit	th thin
ī pie	*th* this
îr pier	hw which
ŏ pot	zh vision
ō toe	ə about, item
ô paw	♦ regionalism

Stress marks: **′** (primary); ′ (secondary), as in **dictionary** (dĭk′shə-nĕr′ē)

modify another noun: *a massive agitprop campaign; agitprop filmmaking.* [Russian, short for *otdel agitatsii i propagandy,* incitement and propaganda section (of the central and local committees of the Russian Communist party); name changed in 1934.]

A·gla·ia (ə-glā′ə, ə-glī′ə) *n. Greek Mythology.* One of the three Graces.

a·gleam (ə-glēm′) *adv. & adj.* Brightly shining.

ag·let (ăg′lĭt) *n.* **1.** A tag or metal sheath on the end of a lace, cord, or ribbon to facilitate its passing through eyelet holes. **2.** A similar device used for an ornament. [Middle English, from Old French *aguillette,* diminutive of *aguille,* needle, from Vulgar Latin **acūcula,* from Late Latin *acucula,* diminutive of Latin *acus,* needle. See **ak-** in Appendix.]

a·gley (ə-glī′, ə-glā′, ə-glē′) *adv. Scots.* Off to one side; awry. [A–[2] + Scots *gley,* to squint (from Middle English *glien,* possibly of Scandinavian origin).]

a·glit·ter (ə-glĭt′ər) *adv. & adj.* Glittering; sparkling.

a·glow (ə-glō′) *adv. & adj.* In a glow; glowing.

a·gly·cone (ə-glī′kōn′) or **a·gly·con** (-kŏn) *n.* The nonsugar component of a glycoside molecule that results from hydrolysis of the molecule. [*a-,* together (from Greek *ha-;* see HAPLOID) + GLYC(O)– + –ONE.]

ag·nail (ăg′nāl′) *n.* **1.** A hangnail. **2.** A painful sore or swelling around a fingernail or toenail. [Middle English *angnail,* corn, from Old English *angnægl* : *ang-,* painful; see **angh-** in Appendix + *nægel,* peg, nail; see NAIL.]

ag·nate (ăg′nāt′) *adj.* **1.** Related on or descended from the father's or male side. **2.** Coming from a common source; akin. **—agnate** *n.* A relative on the father's or male side only. [Latin *agnātus,* past participle of *agnāscī,* to become an agnate : *ad-,* ad- + *nāscī,* to be born; see **genə-** in Appendix.] **—ag·nat′ic** (ăg-năt′ĭk) *adj.* **—ag·nat′i·cal·ly** *adv.* **—ag·na′tion** *n.*

ag·na·than (ăg′nə-thən) *adj.* Lacking a lower jaw: *agnathan fish.* [A–[1] + Greek *gnathos,* jaw + –AN[1].]

Ag·nes (ăg′nĭs), Saint. Died c. A.D. 304. Roman Christian who, according to tradition, was martyred as a virgin at the age of 13. She is the patron saint of young girls.

Ag·new (ăg′no͞o′, -nyo͞o′), **Spiro Theodore.** Born 1918. Vice President of the United States (1969–1973) under Richard M. Nixon. Agnew resigned amid charges of illegal financial dealings during his governorship of Maryland (1966–1968).

Ag·ni (ŭg′nē) *n. Hinduism.* The Vedic god of fire and guardian of humanity.

ag·no·men (ăg-nō′mən) *n., pl.* **-nom·i·na** (-nŏm′ə-nə). An additional cognomen given to a Roman citizen, often in honor of military victories. [Latin : *ad-,* ad- (influenced by *agnōscere,* to recognize) + *nōmen,* name; see **nō-men-** in Appendix.]

Ag·non (ăg′nôn′), **Shmuel Yosef.** 1888–1970. Polish-born Israeli writer. His dramatic novels, written in Hebrew, include *A Guest for the Night* (1939). He shared the 1966 Nobel Prize for literature.

ag·no·sia (ăg-nō′zhə) *n.* Loss of the ability to interpret sensory stimuli, such as sounds or images. [Greek *agnōsia,* ignorance : *a-,* not; see A–[1] + *gnōsis,* knowledge (from *gignōskein,* to know; see **gnō-** in Appendix).]

ag·nos·tic (ăg-nŏs′tĭk) *n.* One who believes that there can be no proof of the existence of God but does not deny the possibility that God exists. **—agnostic** *adj.* **1.** Relating to or being an agnostic. **2.** Noncommittal: *"I favored European unity, but I was agnostic about the form it should take"* (Henry A. Kissinger). [A–[1] + GNOSTIC.] **—ag·nos′ti·cal·ly** *adv.*

WORD HISTORY: An agnostic does not deny the existence of God and heaven, for example, but rather holds that one cannot know for certain if they exist or not. The term *agnostic* was fittingly coined by the 19th-century British scientist Thomas H. Huxley, who believed that only material phenomena were objects of exact knowledge. He made up the word from the prefix *a–,* meaning "without, not," as in *amoral,* and the noun *Gnostic. Gnostic* is related to the Greek word *gnōsis,* "knowledge," which was used by early Christian writers to mean "higher, esoteric knowledge of spiritual things"; hence, *Gnostic* referred to those with such knowledge. In coining the term *agnostic,* Huxley was considering as "Gnostics" a group of his fellow intellectuals—"ists," as he called them—who had eagerly embraced various doctrines or theories that explained the world to their satisfaction. Because he was a "man without a rag of a label to cover himself with," Huxley coined the term *agnostic* for himself, its first published use being in 1870.

ag·nos·ti·cism (ăg-nŏs′tĭ-sĭz′əm) *n.* **1.** The doctrine that certainty about first principles or absolute truth is unattainable and that only perceptual phenomena are objects of exact knowledge. **2.** The belief that there can be no proof either that God exists or that God does not exist.

Ag·nus De·i (ăg′nəs dē′ī′, än′yo͞os dā′ē, ăg′no͞os′) *n.* **1.** Lamb of God; Jesus. Also called *Paschal Lamb.* **2.a.** A liturgical prayer to Jesus. **b.** A musical setting for this prayer. [Late Latin : Latin *agnus,* lamb + Latin *dei,* genitive of *deus,* god.]

a·go (ə-gō′) *adv. & adj.* **1.** Gone by; past: *two years ago.* **2.** In the past: *It happened ages ago.* [Middle English, past participle of *agon,* to go away, from Old English *āgān* : *ā-,* intensive pref. + *gān,* to go; see **ghē-** in Appendix.]

a·gog (ə-gŏg′) *adv. & adj.* Full of keen anticipation or excitement; eager. See Synonyms at **eager**[1]. [Middle English *agogge,* from Old French *en gogue,* in merriment : *en,* in (from Latin *in;* see IN–[2]) + *gogue,* merriment.]

–agog *suff.* Variant of **–agogue.**

à go·go or **à·go-go** (ə-gō′gō′) *—adv.* In a fast and lively manner; freely: *dancing à gogo.* *—n.* A nightclub for fast, lively dancing, drinking, and socializing. [French *à gogo,* galore, from Old French *a gogo* : *a,* to (from Latin *ad;* see AD–) + *gogo* (probably reduplicated form of *gogue,* merriment).]

–agogue or **–agog** *suff.* A substance that stimulates the flow of: *emmenagogue.* [French, from Late Latin *-agōgus,* from Greek *-agōgos,* from *agōgos,* drawing off, from *agein,* to lead, drive. See **ag-** in Appendix.]

ag·on (ăg′ŏn, -ōn, ä-gōn′) *n., pl.* **a·gon·es** (ə-gō′nēz). **1.** A conflict, especially between the protagonist and antagonist in a work of literature or drama. **2.** The part of an ancient Greek drama, especially a comedy, in which two characters engage in verbal dispute. **3.** A test of will; a conflict: *"Freud's originality stemmed from his aggression and ambition in his agon with biology"* (Harold Bloom). [Greek *agōn.* See AGONY.]

ag·o·nal (ăg′ə-nəl) *adj.* Associated with or relating to great pain, especially the agony of death.

a·gone (ə-gôn′, ə-gŏn′) *adv. & adj. Archaic.* Gone by; past. [Middle English *agon,* past participle of *agon,* to go away. See AGO.]

a·gon·es (ə-gō′nēz) *n.* Plural of **agon.**

a·gon·ic (ā-gŏn′ĭk, ə-gŏn′-) *adj.* Having no angle. [From Greek *agōnos* : *a-,* without; see A–[1] + *gōnia,* angle; see DIAGONAL.]

agonic line *n.* An imaginary line on the earth's surface connecting points where the magnetic declination is zero.

ag·o·nist (ăg′ə-nĭst) *n.* **1.** One involved in a struggle or competition. **2.** *Physiology.* A contracting muscle that is resisted or counteracted by another muscle, the antagonist. **3.** *Biochemistry.* A substance that can combine with a nerve receptor to produce a reaction typical for that substance. [Late Latin *agōnista,* contender, from Greek *agōnistēs,* from *agōn,* contest. See AGONY.]

ag·o·nis·tic (ăg′ə-nĭs′tĭk) also **ag·o·nis·ti·cal** (-tĭ-kəl) *adj.* **1.** Striving to overcome in argument; combative. **2.** Struggling to achieve effect; strained and contrived. **3.** Of or relating to contests, originally those of the ancient Greeks. **—ag′o·nis′ti·cal·ly** *adv.*

ag·o·nize (ăg′ə-nīz′) *v.* **-nized, -niz·ing, -niz·es.** *—intr.* **1.** To suffer extreme pain or great anguish. **2.** To make a great effort; struggle. See Synonyms at **writhe.** *—tr.* To cause great pain or anguish to. See Synonyms at **afflict.** [Medieval Latin *agōnizāre,* from Greek *agōnizesthai,* to struggle, from *agōn,* contest. See AGONY.] **—ag′o·niz′ing·ly** *adv.*

ag·o·ny (ăg′ə-nē) *n., pl.* **-nies. 1.** The suffering of intense physical or mental pain. **2.** The struggle that precedes death. **3.** A sudden or intense emotion: *an agony of doubt.* **4.** A violent, intense struggle. [Middle English *agonie,* from Old French, from Late Latin *agōnia,* from Greek, from *agōn,* struggle, from *agein,* to drive. See **ag-** in Appendix.]

agony column *n.* A newspaper column containing advertisements chiefly about missing relatives or friends.

ag·o·ra[1] (ăg′ər-ə) *n., pl.* **-o·rae** (ə-rē′) or **-o·ras.** A place of congregation, especially an ancient Greek marketplace. [Greek. See **ger-** in Appendix.]

a·go·ra[2] (ä′gə-rä′) *n., pl.* **-rot** or **-roth** (-rōt′). See table at **currency.** [Hebrew *'ăgôrâ,* from *'āgar,* to hire.]

ag·o·ra·pho·bi·a (ăg′ər-ə-fō′bē-ə) *n.* An abnormal fear of open or public places. [Greek *agora,* market place; see **ger-** in Appendix + –PHOBIA.] **—ag·o·ra·pho′bi·ac′** (-ăk′) *n.* **—ag′o·ra·pho′bic** (-fō′bĭk, -fŏb′ĭk) *adj. & n.*

a·gou·ti (ə-go͞o′tē) *n., pl.* **-tis** or **-ties. 1.** A burrowing rodent of the genus *Dasyprocta,* native to tropical America and usually having brown fur streaked with gray. **2.** The alternation of light and dark bands of color in the fur of various animals, producing a grizzled appearance. [French, from American Spanish *agutí,* from Guarani *acutí.*]

agouti

agr– *pref.* Variant of **agro–.**

A·gra (ä′grə). A city of north-central India on the Jumna River southeast of New Delhi. It was a Mogul capital in the 16th and 17th centuries and is the site of the Taj Mahal, built by the emperor Shah Jahan after the death of his favorite wife in 1629. Population, 694,191.

a·graffe also **a·grafe** (ə-grăf′) *n.* **1.** A hook-and-loop arrangement used for a clasp on armor and clothing. **2.** A cramp iron for holding stones together in building. [French *agrafe,* from *agrafer,* to hook onto : *a-,* to (from Latin *ad-;* see AD–) + *grafer,* to hook (from *grafe,* hook, from Old High German *krāpfo*).]

a·gran·u·lo·cy·to·sis (ā-grăn′yə-lō-sī-tō′sĭs) *n.* An acute disease marked by high fever and a sharp drop in circulating granular white blood cells. It may be drug-induced or the result of exposure to radiation.

ag·ra·pha also **Ag·ra·pha** (ăg′rə-fə) *pl.n.* The sayings of Jesus not in the Bible. [Greek, from neuter pl. of *agraphos,* unwritten : *a-,* not; see A–[1] + *graphein,* to write; see **gerbh-** in Appendix.]

a·graph·i·a (ā-grăf′ē-ə) *n.* A disorder marked by loss of the ability to write. [A-[1] + Greek *graphein,* to write; see **gerbh-** in Appendix + -IA[1].] **—a·graph′ic** *adj.*

a·grar·i·an (ə-grâr′ē-ən) *adj.* **1.** Relating to or concerning the land and its ownership, cultivation, and tenure. **2.a.** Relating to agricultural or rural matters. **b.** Intended to further agricultural interests: *agrarian lobbyists.* **—agrarian** *n.* A person who favors equitable distribution of land. [From Latin *agrārius,* from *ager, agr-,* field. See **agro-** in Appendix.] **—a·grar′i·an·ly** *adv.*

a·grar·i·an·ism (ə-grâr′ē-ə-nĭz′əm) *n.* A movement for equitable distribution of land and for agrarian reform.

a·gree (ə-grē′) *v.* **a·greed, a·gree·ing, a·grees.** —*intr.* **1.** To grant consent; accede. **2.** To come into or be in accord, as of opinion. **3.** To be of one opinion; concur. **4.** To come to an understanding or to terms. **5.** To be compatible or in correspondence: *The copy agrees with the original.* **6.** To be suitable, appropriate, pleasing, or healthful: *Spicy food does not agree with me.* **7.** *Grammar.* To correspond in gender, number, case, or person. —*tr.* To grant or concede: *My parents agreed that we should go.* [Middle English *agreen,* from Old French *agreer,* from Vulgar Latin **aggrātāre* : Latin *ad-,* ad- + Latin *grātus,* pleasing; see **g^wer-[2]** in Appendix.]

SYNONYMS: *agree, conform, harmonize, accord, correspond, coincide.* These verbs all indicate a compatible relationship between people or things. *Agree* may indicate mere lack of incongruity or discord: *The testimony of all the witnesses agrees on that point.* Often, however, it suggests acceptance of ideas or actions and thus accommodation: *We finally agreed on a price for the house. Conform* stresses correspondence in essence or basic characteristics, sometimes as a result of accommodation to established standards: *The kinds of books in her library conform to her level of education. Students are required to conform to the rules. Harmonize* implies a relationship of unlike elements combined or arranged to make a pleasing whole: *Beige harmonizes with black. Accord* implies harmonious relationship, unity, or consistency, as in feeling or essential nature: *"The creed* [upon which America was founded] *was widely seen as both progressive and universalistic: It accorded with the future, and it was open to all"* (Everett Carll Ladd). *Correspond* refers either to actual similarity in form or nature (*The dots on the pattern correspond with the seam allowance on the cut fabric*) or to similarity in function, character, or structure: *The Diet in Japan corresponds to the American Congress. Coincide* stresses exact agreement in space, time, or thought: *"His interest happily coincided with his duty"* (Edward A. Freeman). See also Synonyms at **assent.**
ANTONYM: *disagree.*

Agrippina the Younger

a·gree·a·ble (ə-grē′ə-bəl) *adj.* **1.** To one's liking; pleasing. See Synonyms at **amiable. 2.** Suitable; conformable. **3.** Ready to consent or submit. **—a·gree′a·bil′i·ty, a·gree′a·ble·ness** *n.* **—a·gree′a·bly** *adv.*

a·gree·ment (ə-grē′mənt) *n. Abbr.* **agt. 1.** The act of agreeing. **2.** Harmony of opinion; accord. **3.** An arrangement between parties regarding a method of action; a covenant. **4.** *Law.* **a.** A properly executed and legally binding compact. **b.** The writing or document embodying this compact. **5.** *Grammar.* Correspondence in gender, number, case, or person between words.

agri. *abbr.* **1.** Agricultural. **2.** Agriculture.

agri– *pref.* Variant of **agro–.**

ag·ri·a (ăg′rē-ə) *n.* An extensive pustular eruption. [From Greek *agrios,* wild. See **agro-** in Appendix.]

ag·ri·busi·ness (ăg′rə-bĭz′nĭs) *n.* Farming engaged in as a large-scale business operation embracing the production, processing, and distribution of agricultural products and the manufacture of farm machinery, equipment, and supplies.

agric. *abbr.* **1.** Agriculture. **2.** Agriculturist.

ag·ri·chem·i·cal (ăg′rĭ-kĕm′ĭ-kəl) *n.* Variant of **agrochemical.**

ag·ri·cide (ăg′rĭ-sīd′) *n.* The abuse of agricultural land through improper farming methods, which renders it unfit to support plant or animal life.

A·gric·o·la (ə-grĭk′ə-lə), **Gnaeus Julius.** A.D. 37–93. Roman soldier and politician who as governor of Britain (77–84) brought most of its inhabitants under Roman control. He also circumnavigated Britain, thereby discovering it to be an island.

ag·ri·cul·ture (ăg′rĭ-kŭl′chər) *n. Abbr.* **agri., agric.** The science, art, and business of cultivating the soil, producing crops, and raising livestock; farming. [Middle English, from Latin *agrīcultūra* : *agrī,* genitive of *ager,* field; see **agro-** in Appendix + *cultūra,* cultivation; see CULTURE.] **—ag′ri·cul′tur·al** *adj.* **—ag′ri·cul′tur·al·ly** *adv.* **—ag′ri·cul′tur·ist, ag′ri·cul′tur·al·ist** *n.*

A·gri·gen·to (ä′grĭ-jĕn′tō, ăg′rĭ-). A city of southwest Sicily, Italy, overlooking the Mediterranean Sea. It was founded c. 580 B.C. by Greek colonists. Population, 51,931.

ag·ri·ma·tion (ăg′rə-mā′shən) *n.* Automated farming, especially the use of robots to perform heretofore manual operations that require acute vision, dexterity, and the ability to make choices. [AGRI(CULTURE) + (AUTO)MATION.]

ag·ri·mo·ny (ăg′rə-mō′nē) *n., pl.* **-nies. 1.** Any of various perennial herbaceous plants of the genus *Agrimonia,* having pinnately compound leaves and spikelike clusters of small yellow flowers. **2.** Any of several similar or related plants, such as the hemp agrimony. [Middle English, from Old French *aigremoine,* from Latin *agrimōnia* (influenced by Old French *aigre,* sour), alteration of *argemōnia,* from Greek *argemōnē,* poppy, possibly from *argos,* white. See **arg-** in Appendix.]

A·grip·pa (ə-grĭp′ə), **Marcus Vipsanius.** 63–12 B.C. Roman soldier and statesman who commanded the fleet that defeated the forces of Mark Antony and Cleopatra at Actium (31).

Ag·rip·pi·na[1] (ăg′rə-pī′nə, -pē′-). Known as "the Elder." 13 B.C.?–A.D. 33. Roman matron and mother of Caligula. She was influential in the struggle for power during the reign of Tiberius.

Ag·rip·pi·na[2] (ăg′rə-pī′nə, -pē′-). Known as "the Younger." A.D. 15?–59. Roman empress. She murdered her husband, the emperor Claudius, so that her son by a previous marriage, Nero, would become emperor. Nero, distrusting his mother, had her murdered.

agro– or **agri–** or **agr–** *pref.* **1.** Field; soil: *agrology.* **2.** Agriculture: *agroindustrial.* [From Greek *agros,* field. See **agro-** in Appendix.]

ag·ro·bi·ol·o·gy (ăg′rō-bī-ŏl′ə-jē) *n.* The study of plant nutrition and growth as related to soil condition, especially to determine ways to increase crop yield. **—ag′ro·bi′o·log′ic** (-ə-lŏj′ĭk), **ag′ro·bi′o·log′i·cal** *adj.* **—ag′ro·bi′o·log′i·cal·ly** *adv.* **—ag′ro·bi·ol′o·gist** *n.*

ag·ro·chem·i·cal (ăg′rə-kĕm′ĭ-kəl) also **ag·ri·chem·i·cal** (ăg′rĭ-) *n.* **1.** A chemical, such as a hormone, a fungicide, or an insecticide, that improves the production of crops. **2.** A chemical or product, such as cellulose, derived from plants.

ag·ro·in·dus·tri·al (ăg′rō-ĭn-dŭs′trē-əl) *n.* Of or relating to the production or supply of various needs, such as water or power, for agriculture and industry.

a·grol·o·gy (ə-grŏl′ə-jē) *n.* The applied science of soils in relation to crops. **—ag′ro·log′ic** (ăg′rə-lŏj′ĭk), **ag′ro·log′i·cal** *adj.* **—ag′ro·log′i·cal·ly** *adv.* **—a·grol′o·gist** *n.*

a·gron·o·my (ə-grŏn′ə-mē) *n.* Application of the various soil and plant sciences to soil management and crop production; scientific agriculture. **—ag′ro·nom′ic** (ăg′rə-nŏm′ĭk), **ag′ro·nom′i·cal** *adj.* **—a·gron′o·mist** *n.*

ag·ros·tol·o·gy (ăg′rə-stŏl′ə-jē) *n.* The study of grasses. [Greek *agrōstis,* a kind of wild grass (from *agros,* field; see AGRO–) + –LOGY.] **—ag′ros·tol′o·gist** *n.*

a·ground (ə-ground′) *adv. & adj.* **1.** Onto or on a shore, reef, or the bottom of a body of water: *a ship that ran aground; a ship aground offshore.* **2.** On the ground: *combat aircraft aloft and aground.*

agt. *abbr.* **1.** Agent. **2.** Agreement.

a·gua·ca·te (ä′gwə-kä′tē) *n.* The avocado. [American Spanish, from Nahuatl *ahuacatl.*]

A·gua·dil·la (ä′gwə-dē′ə, ä′gwä-*thē*′ä). A town of northwest Puerto Rico on Mona Passage. Christopher Columbus reputedly landed at the site of Aguadilla in 1493. Population, 22,039.

A·guas·ca·lien·tes (ä′gwäs-kä-lyĕn′tĕs). A city of central Mexico northeast of Guadalajara. It was built over an intricate system of tunnels constructed by ancient, still unidentified inhabitants. Population, 293,152.

a·gue (ā′gyo͞o) *n.* **1.** A febrile condition in which there are alternating periods of chills, fever, and sweating. Used chiefly in reference to the fevers associated with malaria. **2.** A chill or fit of shivering. [Middle English, from Old French *(fievre) ague,* sharp (fever), from Medieval Latin *(febris) acūta,* from Latin, feminine of *acūtus.* See ACUTE.] **—a′gu·ish** (ā′gyo͞o-ĭsh) *adj.* **—a′gu·ish·ly** *adv.* **—a′gu·ish·ness** *n.*

A·gui·nal·do (ä′gē-näl′dō), **Emilio.** 1869–1964. Philippine leader of a rebellion against Spanish rule (1896–1898) and an uprising against American authority (1899–1901) that ended with his capture and subsequent oath of allegiance to the United States.

A·gul·has (ə-gŭl′əs), **Cape.** A rugged headland of South Africa, the southernmost point of Africa. Its meridian, longitude 20° east, marks the division between the Atlantic and Indian oceans.

ah (ä) *interj.* Used to express various emotions, such as satisfaction, surprise, delight, dislike, or pain.

A.h. *abbr.* Ampere-hour.

A.H. *abbr.* **1.** *Latin.* Anno Hebraico (in the Hebrew year). **2.** *Latin.* Anno Hegirae (in the year of the Hegira).

a·ha (ä-hä′) *interj.* Used to express surprise, pleasure, or triumph.

AHA *abbr.* **1.** American Heart Association. **2.** American Hospital Association.

A·hab (ā′hăb′). Ninth century B.C. Pagan king of Israel and husband of Jezebel who, according to the Old Testament, was overthrown by Jehu.

a·head (ə-hĕd′) *adv.* **1.** At or to the front or head. **2.a.** In advance; before: *Pay ahead, and you'll receive a discount.* **b.** In or into the future; for the future: *planned ahead.* **3.a.** In an advanced position or a configuration registering the future: *Set the clock ahead.* **b.** At or to a different time; earlier or later: *moved the appointment ahead, from Tuesday to Monday.* **4.a.** In a forward direction; onward: *The train moved ahead slowly.* **b.** In the prescribed direction or sequence for normal use: *You won't hear anything unless you roll the tape ahead.* **5.** In or into a more advantageous position: *wanted to get ahead in life.* **—*idiom.* be ahead.** To be winning or in a superior position: *The home team*

ă pat	oi boy
ā pay	ou out
âr care	o͝o took
ä father	o͞o boot
ĕ pet	ŭ cut
ē be	ûr urge
ĭ pit	th thin
ī pie	*th* this
îr pier	hw which
ŏ pot	zh vision
ō toe	ə about, item
ô paw	♦ regionalism

Stress marks: ′ (primary); ′ (secondary), as in **dictionary** (dĭk′shə-nĕr′ē)

was ahead in the second period. Your company is ahead in developing the new technology.

ahead of *prep.* **1.** In front of. **2.** In advance of; at an earlier time than: *arrived ahead of the others.* **3.** In a superior or advanced position to; more successful than: *We are way ahead of you in that field.*

a·hem (ə-hĕm′) *interj.* Used to attract attention or to express doubt or warning.

AHF *abbr.* Antihemophilic factor.

a·him·sa (ə-hĭm′sä′) *n.* A Buddhist and Hindu doctrine of nonviolence expressing belief in the sacredness of all living creatures. [Sanskrit *ahiṁsā* : *a-*, not; see **ne** in Appendix + *hiṁsā*, injury (from *hiṁsati*, he injures).]

a·his·tor·i·cal (ā′hĭ-stôr′ĭ-kəl, -stŏr′-) *adj.* Unconcerned with or unrelated to history, historical development, or tradition: *"All of this is totally ahistorical. There is virtually no evidence in the historical record to support any of it"* (Heritage Foundation Reports).

Ah·ma·da·bad or **Ah·me·da·bad** (ä′mə-də-bäd′). A city of northwest India north of Bombay. Founded in 1412 as the capital of a former Gujarat kingdom, it is a commercial and cultural center with many outstanding mosques, temples, and tombs. Population, 2,059,725.

a·hold (ə-hōld′) *n.* Hold; grip: *"I knew I could make it all right if I got . . . back to the hotel and got ahold of that bottle of brandy"* (Jimmy Breslin). *"Can you tell me how to get ahold of them?"* (Margaret Truman).

–aholic *suff.* One that is addicted to or compulsively in need of: *workaholic.* [From (ALC)OHOLIC.]

A-ho·ri·zon (ā′hə-rī′zən) *n.* In ABC soil, the uppermost zone of soil, containing humus; topsoil. Also called *zone of leaching.*

a·hoy (ə-hoi′) *interj. Nautical.* Used to hail a ship or person or to attract attention.

Ah·ri·man (ä′rĭ-mən) *n.* The spirit of evil in Zoroastrianism, understood by some as the arch rival of Ormazd. [Persian *ahriman*, from Middle Persian *ahraman*, from Avestan *angrō mainiiuš*, the evil spirit : *angrō*, evil + *mainiiuš*, spirit; see **men-**[1] in Appendix.]

A·hu·ra Maz·da (ä-ho͝or′ə măz′də) *n.* Ormazd. [Avestan *ahurō mazdå*, the Wise Lord : *ahura-*, lord; see **ansu-** in Appendix + *mazdā-*, wise; see **men-**[1] in Appendix.]

Ah·vaz or **Ah·waz** (ä-wäz′). A city of southwest Iran north-northeast of Basra, Iraq. Modern Ahvaz was built on extensive ruins of an ancient Persian city. Population, 471,000.

Ah·ven·an·maa (ä′və-nän-mä′) also **Å·land Islands** or **Aa·land Islands** (ä′lənd, ō′länd′). An archipelago in the Baltic Sea at the entrance to the Gulf of Bothnia between Sweden and Finland. Colonized in the 12th century by Swedes, the islands were ceded to Russia in 1809 and became part of Finland after World War I.

Ah·waz (ä-wäz′). See **Ahvaz.**

ai[1] (ī) *n.* See **sloth** (sense 2a). [Portuguese, of Tupian origin.]

ai[2] *abbr.* Airborne intercept.

AI *abbr.* **1.** Artificial insemination. **2.** *Computer Science.* Artificial intelligence.

a.i. *abbr. Latin.* Ad interim (in the meantime).

aid (ād) *intr. & tr.v.* **aid·ed, aid·ing, aids.** To furnish with help, support, or relief. See Synonyms at **help.** **—aid** *n.* **1.** The act or result of helping; assistance. **2.a.** An assistant or a helper. **b.** A device that assists: *visual aids such as slides.* **c.** A hearing aid. **3.** An aide or an aide-de-camp. **4.** A monetary payment to a feudal lord by a vassal in medieval England. [Middle English *aiden*, from Old French *aider*, from Latin *adiūtāre*, frequentative of *adiuvāre, adiūt-*, to help : *ad-*, to; see **ad-** in Appendix + *iuvāre*, to help.] **—aid′er** *n.*

aide (ād) *n.* **1.** An aide-de-camp. **2.** An assistant; a helper: *a nurse's aide.* See Synonyms at **assistant.** [French, from *aider*, to aid. See AID.]

aide-de-camp (ād′dĭ-kămp′) *n., pl.* **aides-de-camp.** *Abbr.* **ADC** A military officer acting as secretary and confidential assistant to a superior officer of general or flag rank. [French : *aide*, assistant + *de*, of + *camp*, camp.]

aide-mé·moire (ād′măm-wär′, ĕd-) *n., pl.* **aide-mémoire** or **aide-mémoires.** **1.** A memorandum setting forth the major points of a proposed discussion or agreement, used especially in diplomatic communications. Also called *position paper.* **2.** Something, such as a mnemonic device, that serves as an aid to memory. [French : *aide*, aid + *memoire*, memory.]

AIDS (ādz) *n.* A severe immunological disorder caused by the retrovirus HIV, resulting in a defect in cell-mediated immune response that is manifested by increased susceptibility to opportunistic infections and to certain rare cancers, especially Kaposi's sarcoma. It is transmitted primarily by venereal routes or exposure to contaminated blood or blood products. [A(CQUIRED) I(MMUNE) D(EFICIENCY) S(YNDROME).]

AIDS-re·lat·ed complex (ādz′rĭ-lā′-tĭd) *n.* ARC.

Ai·e·a (ī-ā′ə, ī-ā′ä). A city of south-central Oahu, Hawaii, a residential suburb of Honolulu. Population, 32,879.

ai·grette or **ai·gret** (ā-grĕt′, ā′grĕt′) *n.* **1.** An ornamental tuft of upright plumes, especially the tail feathers of an egret. **2.** An ornament, such as a spray of gems, resembling a tuft of plumes. [French, egret, from Old French. See EGRET.]

ai·guille (ā-gwēl′) *n.* **1.** A sharp, pointed mountain peak. **2.** A needle-shaped drill for boring holes in rock or masonry. [French, needle, from Old French. See AGLET.]

ai·guil·lette (ā′gwə-lĕt′) *n.* An ornamental cord worn on the shoulder of a military uniform. [French. See AGLET.]

Ai·ken (ā′kən), **Conrad Potter.** 1889–1973. American writer noted primarily for his poetry. He won a 1930 Pulitzer Prize for *Selected Poems.*

ai·ki·do (ī′kē-dō′, ī-kē′dō) *n. Sports.* A Japanese art of self-defense that employs holds and locks and that uses the principles of nonresistance in order to debilitate the strength of the opponent. [Japanese *aikidō* : *ai*, mutual + *ki*, spirit + *dō*, art.]

ail (āl) *v.* **ailed, ail·ing, ails.** *—intr.* To feel ill or have pain. *—tr.* To cause physical or mental pain or uneasiness to; trouble. See Synonyms at **trouble.** [Middle English *eilen*, from Old English *eglian*, from *egle*, troublesome.]

ai·lan·thus (ā-lăn′thəs) *n.* Any of several deciduous, Asian trees of the genus *Ailanthus*, especially the tree-of-heaven. [New Latin *Ailanthus*, genus name, alteration (influenced by Greek *anthos*, flower) of Ambonese *ai lanto.*]

ai·le·ron (ā′lə-rŏn′) *n.* Either of two movable flaps on the wings of an airplane that can be used to control the plane's rolling and banking movements. [French, diminutive of *aile*, wing, from Old French, from Latin *āla.*]

Ai·ley (ā′lē, ī′lē), **Alvin, Jr.** 1931–1989. American choreographer whose works combine the styles of modern dance, ballet, jazz, and African ethnic dance.

ail·ment (āl′mənt) *n.* A physical or mental disorder, especially a mild illness.

ai·lu·ro·phile (ī-lo͝or′ə-fīl′, ā-lo͝or′-) *n.* One who loves cats. [Greek *ailouros*, cat + –PHILE.]

ai·lu·ro·phobe (ī-lo͝or′ə-fōb′, ā-lo͝or′-) *n.* One who hates or fears cats. [Greek *ailouros*, cat + –PHOBE.] **—ai·lu′ro·pho′bi·a** *n.*

aim (ām) *v.* **aimed, aim·ing, aims.** *—tr.* To direct (a weapon or remark, for example) toward an intended goal or mark. *—intr.* **1.** To direct a weapon: *a gunner aiming carefully.* **2.** To determine a course: *aim for a better education.* **3.** To propose to do something; intend. **—aim** *n.* **1.a.** The act of aiming. **b.** Skill at hitting a target: *The shooter's aim was perfect.* **2.a.** The line of fire of an aimed weapon. **b.** The degree of accuracy of a weapon. **3.** A purpose or intention toward which one's efforts are directed. **4.** *Obsolete.* A target; a mark. **5.** *Obsolete.* A conjecture; a guess. [Middle English *aimen*, from Old French *esmer*, to estimate (from Latin *aestimāre*) and from Old French *aesmer* (from Vulgar Latin **ad estimāre* : Latin *ad-*, ad- + Latin *aestimāre*, to estimate).]

SYNONYMS: *aim, direct, level, point, train.* The central meaning shared by these verbs is "to turn something in the direction of an intended goal or target": *aimed the camera at the guests; directing her eyes on the book; leveled criticism at the administration; pointing a finger at the suspect; trained the gun on the intruder.* See also Synonyms at **intention.**

aim·less (ām′lĭs) *adj.* Devoid of direction or purpose. **—aim′less·ly** *adv.* **—aim′less·ness** *n.*

ain (ān) *adj. Scots.* Own.

ain't (ānt). *Non-Standard.* **1.** Am not. **2.** Used also as a contraction for *are not, is not, has not,* and *have not.*

USAGE NOTE: The use of *ain't* as a contraction of *am not, are not, is not, has not,* and *have not* has a long history, but *ain't* has come to be regarded as a mark of illiteracy and has by now acquired such a stigma that it is beyond any possibility of rehabilitation. However, it is used by educated speakers, for example, when they want to strike a jocular or demotic note, as in fixed expressions like *Say it ain't so* or *You ain't just whistling Dixie.* • The stigmatization of *ain't* leaves us with no happy alternative for use in first-person questions. The widely used *aren't I?*, though illogical, was found acceptable for use in speech by a majority of the Usage Panel in an earlier survey, but in writing there is no acceptable substitute for the admittedly stilted *am I not?*

Ain·tab (īn-tăb′). See **Gaziantep.**

Ai·nu (ī′no͞o) *n., pl.* **Ainu** or **-nus.** **1.** A member of an indigenous people of Japan, now inhabiting parts of Hokkaido, Sakhalin, and the Kuril Islands. **2.** The language of the Ainu.

ai·o·li (ī-ō′lē, ā-ō′-) *n.* A rich sauce of crushed garlic, egg yolks, lemon juice, and olive oil used especially to garnish fish and vegetables. [Provençal : *ai*, garlic (from Latin *allium*) + *oli*, oil (from Latin *oleum*; see OIL).]

air (âr) *n.* **1.a.** A colorless, odorless, tasteless, gaseous mixture, mainly nitrogen (approximately 78 percent) and oxygen (approximately 21 percent) with lesser amounts of argon, carbon dioxide, hydrogen, neon, helium, and other gases. **b.** This mixture with varying amounts of moisture and particulate matter, enveloping Earth; the atmosphere. **c.** The atmosphere in an enclosure. **2.a.** The sky; the firmament. **b.** A giant void; nothingness: *The money vanished into thin air.* **3.** An atmospheric movement; a breeze or wind. **4.** Aircraft: *send troops to Europe by air.* **5.a.** Public utterance; vent: *gave air to their grievances.* **b.** The electronic broadcast media: *"often ridiculed . . . extremist groups on air"* (Christian Science Monitor). **6.** A peculiar or characteristic impression; an aura. **7.** Personal bearing, appearance, or manner;

aigrette
Detail from the late 15th-century tapestry *The Start of the Hunt,* from *The Hunt of the Unicorn* series

aiguille
The Matterhorn, near Zermatt, Switzerland

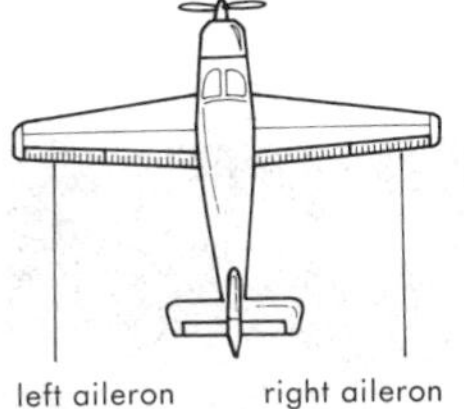

aileron

mien. **8. airs.** An affected, often haughty pose; affectation. See Synonyms at **affectation. 9.** *Music.* A melody or tune, especially: **a.** The soprano or treble part in a harmonized composition. **b.** A solo with or without accompaniment. **10.** Air conditioning. **11.** *Archaic.* Breath. —*attributive.* Often used to modify another noun: *air movements; air safety.* —**air** *v.* **aired, air·ing, airs.** —*tr.* **1.** To expose so that air can dry, cool, or freshen; ventilate. **2.** To give vent to publicly: *airing my pet peeves.* See Synonyms at **vent[1]. 3.** To broadcast on television or radio: *"The ad was submitted to CBS . . . which accepted and aired it"* (New York). —*intr.* To be broadcast on television or radio: *"tidbits that will air on tonight's 6 o'clock news"* (Terry Ann Knopf). —***idioms.* in the air.** Abroad; prevalent: *Excitement was in the air.* **up in the air.** Not yet decided; uncertain. [Partly from Middle English *air,* gas, atmosphere (from Old French, from Latin *āēr,* from Greek *aēr;* see **wer-[1]** in Appendix) and partly from French *air,* nature, quality, place of origin (from Latin *ager,* place, field; see AGRICULTURE, and Latin *ārea,* open space, threshing floor; see AREA). N., sense 9, from French *air,* tune, from Italian *aria.* See ARIA.]

air bag *n.* **1.** An automotive passive restraint consisting of a bag that is designed to inflate upon collision and prevent passengers from pitching forward. **2.** A large inflatable bag made of strong rubber, used by rescue workers to lift a vehicle or heavy machinery or debris that has fallen upon or otherwise trapped a victim.

air ball *n. Basketball.* A shot that misses the backboard, rim, and net.

air base *n.* A base for military aircraft.

air bladder *n. Biology.* **1.** An air-filled structure in many fishes that functions to maintain buoyancy or, in some species, to aid in respiration. Also called *swim bladder.* **2.** See **float** (sense 2).

airbrush

air·boat (âr′bōt′) *n. Nautical.* See **swamp boat.**

air·borne (âr′bôrn′, -bōrn′) *adj. Abbr.* **abn 1.** Carried by or through the air: *airborne pollen.* **2.** Transported in aircraft: *airborne troops.* **3.** In flight; flying: *The plane is airborne.*

air brake *n.* **1.** A brake, especially on a motor vehicle, that is operated by compressed air. **2.** A surface, such as an aileron, that can be projected into the airstream in order to decrease the air speed of an airplane by increasing drag; a spoiler.

air·brush (âr′brŭsh′) *n.* An atomizer using compressed air to spray a liquid, such as paint, on a surface. —**airbrush** *tr.v.* **-brushed, -brush·ing, -brush·es.** To spray with an airbrush.

air·burst (âr′bûrst′) *n.* Explosion of a bomb or shell in the atmosphere.

air chamber *n.* **1.** An enclosure filled with air for a special purpose. **2.** A chamber, especially in a hydraulic system, in which air elastically compresses and expands to regulate the flow of a fluid.

air-con·di·tion (âr′kən-dĭsh′ən) *tr.v.* **-tioned, -tion·ing, -tions.** To provide with or ventilate by air conditioning.

air conditioner *n.* An apparatus for controlling, especially lowering, the temperature and humidity of an enclosed space.

air conditioning *n. Abbr.* **a.c., a/c 1.** The state of temperature and humidity produced by an air conditioner. **2.** A system of air conditioners.

air-cool (âr′ko͞ol′) *tr.v.* **-cooled, -cool·ing, -cools.** *Abbr.* **ac. 1.** To cool (an engine, for example) by a flow of air. **2.** To air-condition.

air cover *n.* **1.** Protective use of military aircraft during ground operations. **2.** The aircraft used to protect and otherwise support ground troops.

air·craft (âr′krăft′) *n., pl.* **aircraft.** A machine or device, such as an airplane, a helicopter, a glider, or a dirigible, that is capable of atmospheric flight.

aircraft carrier *n.* A large naval vessel designed as a mobile air base, having a long flat deck on which aircraft can take off and land at sea.

Airedale

air·crew (âr′kro͞o) *n.* The crew operating an aircraft.

air cushion *n.* **1.** Trapped air that supports a vehicle a short distance above the surface of land or water. **2.** A device that uses trapped air to absorb the shock of motion, especially in vehicles. Also called *air spring.* —**air′-cush′ion** (âr′ko͝osh′ən), **air′-cush′ioned** (-ənd) *adj.*

air-cush·ion vehicle (âr′ko͝osh′ən) *n.* A usually propeller-driven vehicle designed for traveling over land or water on a supportive cushion of slowly moving, low-pressure air. Also called *ground-effect machine, hovercraft.*

air dam *n.* A strip of metal or plastic, running the width of a car and fitted beneath the front bumper, intended to enhance aerodynamics by blocking the flow of turbulent air under the vehicle.

air·date (âr′dāt′) *n.* The date on which a program is scheduled to be broadcast.

air door *n.* A strong, temperature-controlled current of air, usually directed upward, that is used instead of a door.

air·drome (âr′drōm′) *n.* An airport.

air·drop (âr′drŏp′) *n.* A delivery, as of supplies or troops, by parachute from aircraft. —**airdrop** *tr. & intr.v.* **-dropped, -drop·ping, -drops.** To drop or be dropped from an aircraft.

air-dry (âr′drī′) *tr.v.* **-dried, -dry·ing, -dries.** To dry by exposure to the air. —**air-dry** *adj.* Sufficiently dry so that further exposure to air does not yield more moisture to be evaporated.

Aire·dale (âr′dāl′) *n.* A large terrier of a breed having long legs and a wiry tan coat marked with black. [After *Airedale,* a valley of north-central England.]

air·fare (âr′fâr′) *n.* Fare for travel by aircraft.

air·field (âr′fēld′) *n.* **1.** The area of fields and runways where aircraft can take off and land. **2.** An airport.

air·flow (âr′flō′) *n.* **1.** A flow of air. **2.** The air currents caused by the motion of an object such as an airplane or automobile.

air·foil (âr′foil′) *n.* A part or surface, such as a wing, propeller blade, or rudder, whose shape and orientation control stability, direction, lift, thrust, or propulsion.

air force *n. Abbr.* **AF 1.** The aviation branch of a country's armed forces, such as the U.S. Air Force. **2.** A unit of the U.S. Air Force larger than a division and smaller than a command.

air·frame (âr′frām′) *n.* The structure of an aircraft, such as an airplane, a helicopter, or a rocket, exclusive of its power plant.

air·freight (âr′frāt′) *n.* **1.** A system of transporting freight by air. **2.** The amount charged for transporting freight by air. —**air′freight′** *v.*

air gas *n.* See **producer gas.**

air·glow (âr′glō′) *n.* A low- or middle-latitude, more or less steady, faint photochemical luminescence in the upper atmosphere.

air gun *n.* A gun discharged by compressed air.

air·head[1] (âr′hĕd′) *n. Slang.* A silly, rather unintelligent person.

air·head[2] (âr′hĕd′) *n.* An area of hostile or enemy-controlled territory secured by paratroops. [AIR + (BEACH)HEAD.]

air hole *n.* **1.** A hole or opening through which gas or air may pass. **2.** An opening in the frozen surface of a body of water. **3.** See **air pocket.**

air hunger *n.* See **dyspnea.**

air·ing (âr′ĭng) *n.* **1.** Exposure to air for freshening or drying. **2.** Exposure to open air for exercise or health-promoting activity. **3.** Exposure to public attention. **4.** A radio or television broadcast.

air lane *n.* A regular route of travel for aircraft. Also called *airway.*

air layering *n.* A method of propagating plants by wounding a stem or branch, applying a hormone to the wound, wrapping the stem or branch with damp sphagnum moss and polyethylene plastic to encourage root formation, and finally removing the rooted stem or branch as an independent plant.

air·less (âr′lĭs) *adj.* **1.** Having no air. **2.** Lacking fresh air; stuffy. **3.** Lacking movement of air; still. —**air′less·ness** *n.*

air letter *n.* See **aerogram.**

air·lift (âr′lĭft′) *n.* **1.** A system of transporting troops, civilian passengers, or supplies by air, as when surface routes are blocked. **2.** A flight transporting troops, civilian passengers, or supplies, as when surface routes are blocked. —**airlift** *v.* **-lift·ed, -lift·ing, -lifts.** —*tr.* To transport by air, as when ground routes are blocked. —*intr.* To transport troops, civilian passengers, or supplies by air.

air·line (âr′līn′) *n.* **1.** A system for scheduled air transport of passengers and freight. **2.** A business providing a system of scheduled air transport. In this sense, also called *airway.*

air·lin·er (âr′lī′nər) *n.* An airplane operated by an airline and adapted for carrying passengers.

air lock *n.* **1.** An airtight chamber, usually located between two regions of unequal pressure, in which air pressure can be regulated. **2.** A bubble or pocket of air or vapor, as in a pipe, that stops the normal flow of fluid through the conducting part.

air·mail (âr′māl′) *tr.v.* **-mailed, -mail·ing, -mails.** *Abbr.* **A.M.** To send (a letter, for example) by air. —**airmail** *adj.* Of, relating to, or for use with air mail. —**air mail** also **airmail** *n.* **1.** The system of conveying mail by aircraft. **2.** Mail conveyed or to be conveyed by aircraft.

air·man (âr′mən) *n. Abbr.* **Amn 1.a.** An enlisted rank in the U.S. Air Force that is above airman basic and below airman first class. **b.** A person who holds this rank. **2.** An enlisted person in the U.S. Navy working with aircraft. **3.** An aviator.

airman basic *n. Abbr.* **AB 1.** An enlisted rank in the U.S. Air Force that is below airman and is used for recruits. **2.** A person who holds this rank.

airman first class *n. Abbr.* **A1C 1.** An enlisted rank in the U.S. Air Force that is above airman and below sergeant. **2.** A person who holds this rank.

air mass *n.* A large body of air with only small horizontal variations of temperature, pressure, and moisture.

air mattress *n.* An inflatable airtight sack on which to sleep or float in water.

Air Medal (âr) *n.* A decoration awarded by the U.S. Army, Air Force, or Navy for meritorious airborne conduct.

air mile *n.* A unit of distance in air travel, equal to one international nautical mile (6,076.115 feet).

air·mo·bile also **air-mo·bile** (âr′mō′bəl, -bēl, -bīl) *adj.* Capable of being transported and deployed, usually by helicopter, to a combat zone or from one site to another within a theater of operations: *an airmobile infantry regiment.*

air·park (âr′pärk′) *n.* A small airport typically located near a business area or an industrial park.

air piracy *n.* Any seizure or exercise of control, by force or violence or by threat of force or violence and with wrongful intent, of an aircraft in flight in air commerce. **—air pirate** *n.*

air·plane (âr′plān′) *n. Abbr.* **AP** Any of various winged vehicles capable of flight, generally heavier than air and driven by jet engines or propellers.

air plant *n.* See **epiphyte.**

air·play (âr′plā′) *n.* The broadcasting of a phonograph record, tape, or compact disc on the air by a radio station.

air pocket *n.* A downward air current that causes an aircraft to lose altitude abruptly. Also called *air hole.*

air police *n. Abbr.* **AP** The military police branch of an air force.

air·port (âr′pôrt′, -pōrt′) *n.* **1.** A tract of leveled land where aircraft can take off and land, usually equipped with hard-surfaced landing strips, a control tower, hangars, aircraft maintenance and refueling facilities, and accommodations for passengers and cargo. **2.** Such an installation in which the landing area is on water.

air potato or **air-po·ta·to** (âr′pə-tā′tō) *n.* A tropical Old World yam *(Dioscorea bulbifera)* having axillary potatolike tubers, some of which are edible after cooking. It is a weed in the tropics and Florida. Also called *aerial yam, potato yam.*

air·pow·er or **air power** (âr′pou′ər) *n.* The tactical and strategic strength of a country's air force.

air pump *n.* Equipment for compressing, removing, or forcing a flow of air.

air raid *n.* An attack by military aircraft, especially when armed with bombs and rockets.

air rifle *n.* A low-powered rifle, such as a BB gun, that uses manually compressed air to fire small pellets.

air rights *pl.n.* The rights to develop further the heretofore unused space above a building or other structure, such as a turnpike.

air sac *n.* **1.** An air-filled space in the body of a bird that forms a connection between the lungs and bone cavities and aids in breathing and temperature regulation. **2.** See **alveolus** (sense 3). **3.** A saclike, thin-walled enlargement in the trachea of an insect.

air·screw (âr′skrōō′) *n. Chiefly British.* The propeller of an airplane.

air shed *n.* **1.** The air supply of a given region. **2.** The geographic region that shares an air supply. [AIR + (WATER)SHED.]

air·ship (âr′shĭp′) *n.* A self-propelled lighter-than-air craft with directional control surfaces. Also called *dirigible.*

air shower *n.* **1.** A cleansing process during which jets of air blow tiny pieces of lint and dust off the clothing of employees who work in clean rooms. **2.** The equipment for this process.

air·sick (âr′sĭk′) *adj.* Suffering from airsickness.

air·sick·ness (âr′sĭk′nĭs) *n.* Nausea, vomiting, or dizziness induced by the motion that occurs during air flight.

air·side (âr′sīd′) *n.* The part of an airport directly involved in the arrival and departure of aircraft. *—attributive.* Often used to modify another noun: *airside operations; airside security devices.*

air sock *n.* See **windsock.**

air·space or **air space** (âr′spās′) *n.* **1.** The portion of the atmosphere above a particular land area, especially that of a political subdivision such as a nation. **2. a.** The space occupied by an aircraft. **b.** A designated sector of space, such as that in the vicinity of an airport. **3. a.** *Chiefly British.* Space available for broadcasting within a particular frequency: *"Mobile radio has to compete for air space with other services such as broadcast radio, television, and even military services"* (Financial Times). **b.** See **airtime** (sense 1).

air speed *n. Abbr.* **AS, a/s** The speed, especially of an aircraft, relative to the air.

air splint *n.* An inflatable cylinder used to immobilize fractured or injured limbs to promote healing.

air spring *n.* See **air cushion** (sense 2).

air strike *n.* An air attack on a ground or naval target.

air·strip (âr′strĭp′) *n.* See **landing strip.**

airt (ârt) *n. Scots.* A cardinal point on the compass; a direction. [Middle English *art,* from Scottish Gaelic *aird,* from Old Irish *aird,* point of the compass.]

air taxi *n.* A small aircraft that makes short local flights to areas not serviced by regular airlines.

air terrorism *n.* The systematic use of air piracy, including acts of skyjacking, hostage-taking, bombing, and sabotage, as a means of coercion or of gaining international attention. Also called *air terror.*

air·tight (âr′tīt′) *adj.* **1.** *Abbr.* **at.** Impermeable by air. **2.** Having no weak points; sound: *an airtight excuse.*

air·time (âr′tīm′) *n.* **1.** The time that a radio or television station is broadcasting. Also called *airspace.* **2.** The time at which a radio or television program is broadcast.

air-to-air (âr′tə-âr′) *adj.* Operating between, launched from, or involving rockets or aircraft in flight: *air-to-air missiles; air-to-air communications.*

air-to-sur·face (âr′tə-sûr′fĭs) *adj.* Operating from or designed to be fired from aircraft at targets on the ground: *air-to-surface missiles.*

air vesicle *n. Biology.* See **float** (sense 2).

air walk *n.* A passageway enclosed with glass or plastic that connects one building with another at a level well above ground.

air·wave (âr′wāv′) *n.* The medium used for the transmission of radio and television signals. Often used in the plural.

air·way (âr′wā′) *n.* **1. a.** A passageway or shaft in which air circulates, as in ventilating a mine. **b.** A covered, self-propelled passageway used for airline passenger and crew embarkation and debarkation at airport terminal gates. **2. a.** See **air lane. b.** See **airline** (sense 2).

air·wor·thy (âr′wûr′thē) *adj.* **-thi·er, -thi·est.** Being in fit condition to fly: *an airworthy helicopter; airworthy avionics.* **—air′wor′thi·ness** *n.*

air·y (âr′ē) *adj.* **-i·er, -i·est. 1.** Of, relating to, or having the constitution of air. **2.** High in the air; lofty. **3.** Open to the air: *airy chambers.* **4.** Performed in the air; aerial. **5.** Immaterial; illusory; unreal: *an airy apparition.* **6.** Speculative, visionary, and often impractical: *airy theories about socioeconomic improvement.* **7.** Being as light as air; delicate. **8.** Displaying lofty nonchalance: *dismissed us with an airy wave of the hand.* **9.** Lighthearted; gay: *an airy mood.* **—air′i·ly** *adv.* **—air′i·ness** *n.*

SYNONYMS: *airy, diaphanous, ethereal, filmy, gauzy, gossamer, sheer, transparent, vaporous.* The central meaning shared by these adjectives is "so light and insubstantial as to resemble air or a thin film": *an airy organdy blouse; a hat with a diaphanous veil; ethereal mist; the filmy wings of a moth; gauzy clouds of dandelion down; gossamer cobwebs; sheer silk stockings; transparent chiffon; vaporous muslin.*

air·y-fair·y (âr′ē-fâr′ē) *Chiefly British. n., pl.* **-ies.** An intellectual: *"They'd wanted him for Ambassador in Paris but he'd turned it down; he'd no patience with the airy-fairies"* (John le Carré). **—airy-fairy** *adj.* So speculative, visionary, and flimsy as to lack all substance, purpose, and practicality: *"The issue . . . is largely obscured by an increasingly unreal debate about airy-fairy constitutional modalities"* (Manchester Guardian Weekly).

A·i·sha also **A·ye·sha** (ä′ē-shä′). 611–678. The favorite wife of Mohammed. She led an unsuccessful revolt against Mohammed's successor, Ali.

aisle (īl) *n.* **1.** A part of a church divided laterally from the nave by a row of pillars or columns. **2.** A passageway between rows of seats, as in an auditorium or an airplane. **3.** A passageway for inside traffic, as in a department store, warehouse, or supermarket. [Alteration (influenced by ISLE, and more recently by French *aile,* wing, from Latin *āla*) of Middle English *ele,* from Old French, wing of a building, from Latin *āla.*]

Aisne (ān). A river of northern France rising in the Argonne Forest and flowing about 266 km (165 mi) northwest and west to the Oise River. Four major World War I battles were fought along its banks, including the final defeat of the Germans by French and American troops in September–October 1918.

ait (āt) *n. Chiefly British.* A small island. [Middle English *eit,* from Old English *īgeth,* diminutive of *īg, ieg,* island. See ISLAND.]

aitch (āch) *n.* The letter *h.* [French *hache.*]

aitch·bone (āch′bōn′) *n.* **1.** The rump bone, especially of cattle. **2.** The cut of beef containing the rump bone. [Middle English *hach-boon,* from the phrase **an hach-boon,* an aitchbone, alteration of **a nachebon* : *nache,* buttock (from Old French, from Late Latin *naticas,* accusative pl. of *natica,* buttock, from Latin *natis*) + *bōn,* bone (from Old English *bān*).]

Aix-en-Pro·vence (āk′sän-prō-väns′, ĕk′-). A city of southeast France north of Marseilles. Founded in 123 B.C. by the Romans as a military colony near the site of mineral springs, the city has long been a popular spa and an important cultural center. Population, 121,327.

air rifle

Aix-la-Cha·pelle (āks′lä-shä-pĕl′, ĕks′-). See **Aachen.**

A·jac·cio (ä-yä′chō). A city of western Corsica, France, on the **Gulf of Ajaccio,** an inlet of the Mediterranean Sea. Ajaccio was the birthplace of Napoleon Bonaparte. Population, 54,089.

A·jan·ta (ə-jŭn′tə). A village of west-central India southwest of Amravati. Nearby caves dating from c. 200 B.C. to A.D. 650 contain remarkable examples of Buddhist art.

a·jar (ə-jär′) *adv. & adj.* Partially opened: *left the door ajar.* [Middle English *on char* : *on,* in; see ON + *char,* turn, from Old English *cierr.*]

A·jax¹ (ā′jăks′) *n. Greek Mythology.* **1.** The son of Telamon of Salamis and a warrior of great stature and prowess who fought against Troy. **2.** The son of Ileus of Locris and a warrior of small stature and arrogant character who fought against Troy.

A·jax² (ā′jăks′). A town of southeast Ontario, Canada, on Lake Erie northeast of Toronto. It is a manufacturing center. Population, 25,475.

Aj·man (ăj-män′). A sheikdom of eastern Arabia, part of the federation of United Arab Emirates on the Persian Gulf. Population, 3,725.

Aj·mer (ŭj-mîr′). A city of northwest India southwest of Delhi. Founded c. A.D. 145, it is a trade and manufacturing center. Population, 375,593.

A·jodh·ya (ə-yōd′yə). A village of northern India on the Ghaghara River near Faizabad. Long associated with Hindu legend, it

ă **pat**	oi **boy**
ā **pay**	ou **out**
âr **care**	ŏŏ **took**
ä **father**	ōō **boot**
ĕ **pet**	ŭ **cut**
ē **be**	ûr **urge**
ĭ **pit**	th **thin**
ī **pie**	*th* **this**
îr **pier**	hw **which**
ŏ **pot**	zh **vision**
ō **toe**	ə **about, item**
ô **paw**	♦ **regionalism**

Stress marks: ′ (primary); ′ (secondary), as in **dictionary** (dĭk′shə-nĕr′ē)

is a pilgrimage center and one of the seven sites sacred to Hindus.

AK *abbr.* Alaska.

a.k.a. or **aka** *abbr.* Also known as.

A·kan (ä′kän′) *n., pl.* **Akan** or **A·kans. 1.** A South Central Niger-Congo language spoken in parts of Ghana and the Ivory Coast whose two main varieties are Fante and Twi, including Ashanti. **2.** A member of a people of Ghana and the Ivory Coast, including the Fante and the Twi. **—A′kan′** *adj.*

a·kar·y·o·cyte (ā-kăr′ē-ō-sīt′) *n.* A cell having no nucleus.

A·ka·shi (ä-kä′shē). A city of southwest Honshu, Japan, west of Kobe on **Akashi Strait,** the eastern end of the Inland Sea. Akashi is a manufacturing center. Population, 263,365.

Akbar the Great
Detail from *The Emperor Akbar Hunting,* c. 1600–1610

Ak·bar (ăk′bär). Known as "the Great." 1542–1605. Mongol emperor of India (1556–1605) who conquered most of northern India and exercised religious tolerance.

AKC *abbr.* American Kennel Club.

ak·ee also **ac·kee** (ăk′ē, ə-kē′) *n.* **1.** A tropical western African evergreen tree *(Blighia sapida)* having leathery red and yellow fruits. It is naturalized and cultivated in the tropics and in Florida. **2.** The edible, fleshy, ripe aril of this tree, especially popular as a food in Jamaica. The seeds and unripe arils are poisonous. [Possibly Kru *akee* or Akan (Twi) *aŋkyē,* wild cashew.]

a·kene (ā-kēn′) *n.* Variant of **achene.**

A·khe·na·ton or **A·khe·na·ten** (ä′kə-nät′n, äk-nät′n) also **Ikh·na·ton** (ĭk-nät′n). Originally **A·men·ho·tep IV** (ä′-mən-hō′tĕp, ăm′ən-). Died c. 1358 B.C. King of Egypt (1375?–1358?) who rejected the old gods and initiated a new form of sun worship.

A·ki·ba ben Jo·seph (ä-kē′bä bĕn jō′zəf, -səf, ə-kē′və). A.D. 50?–132. Jewish religious leader whose scholarship, particularly a reinterpretation of the Halakah, profoundly influenced Judaism.

A·ki·hi·to (ä′kē-hē′tō). Born 1933. Emperor of Japan (since 1989). He succeeded his father, Hirohito.

a·kim·bo (ə-kĭm′bō) *adv.* In or into a position in which the hands are on the hips and the elbows are bowed outward: *children standing akimbo by the fence.* **—akimbo** *adj.* **1.** Placed in such a way as to have the hands on the hips and the elbows bowed outward: *children standing with arms akimbo.* **2.** Being in a bent, bowed, or arched position: *"There he remained, dead to the world, limbs akimbo, until we left"* (Alex Shoumatoff). *"[She] often skips into a veritable ballet of akimbo limbs"* (Jack Kroll). [Middle English *in kenebowe.*]

Akhenaton

a·kin (ə-kĭn′) *adj.* **1.** Of the same kin; related by blood. **2.** Having a similar quality or character; analogous. **3.** *Linguistics.* Sharing a common origin or ancestral forms.

a·ki·ne·sia (ā′kĭ-nē′zhə, -kī-) *n.* Loss of normal motor function, resulting in impaired muscle movement. [Greek *akinēsia* : *a-,* not; see A–¹ + *-kinēsia,* motion (from *kinēsis;* see –KINESIS).] **—a′ki·net′ic** (-nĕt′ĭk) *adj.*

A·ki·ta (ä-kē′tə, ä′kĭ-tä′). A city of northwest Honshu, Japan, on the Sea of Japan. It is a major port. Population, 296,381.

Ak·kad also **Ac·cad** (ăk′ăd′, ä′käd′). **1.** An ancient region of Mesopotamia occupying the northern part of Babylonia. It reached the height of its power in the third millennium B.C. **2.** Also **A·ga·de** (ə-gä′də). An ancient city of Mesopotamia and capital of the Akkadian empire.

Ak·ka·di·an (ə-kā′dē-ən) *n.* **1.** A native or inhabitant of ancient Akkad. **2.** The Semitic language of Mesopotamia. In this sense, also called *Assyrian.* **—Ak·ka′di·an** *adj.*

Ak·ko (ä-kō′, ä′kō). See **Acre.**

Ak·ron (ăk′rən). A city of northeast Ohio south-southeast of Cleveland. Its first rubber factory was established in 1869 by B.F. Goodrich (1841–1888). In the early 20th century Akron was known as "the rubber capital of the world." Population, 237,177.

Ak·sum or **Ax·um** (äk′so͞om′). A town of northern Ethiopia. From the first to the eighth century A.D. it was the capital of an empire that controlled much of northern Ethiopia. According to tradition, the Ark of the Covenant was brought here from Jerusalem and placed in the Church of Saint Mary of Zion, where the rulers of Ethiopia were crowned.

Ak·tyu·binsk (äk-tyo͞o′bĭnsk). A city of western Kazakhstan northwest of Astrakhan. Founded in 1869, it is a metallurgical center. Population, 231,000.

Al The symbol for the element **aluminum.**

AL *abbr.* **1.** Alabama. **2.** American League.

al. *abbr.* Alcohol; alcoholic.

al– *pref.* Variant of **ad–** (sense 1).

–al¹ *suff.* Of, relating to, or characterized by: *parental.* [Middle English, from Old French, from Latin *-ālis,* adj. suff.]

–al² *suff.* Action; process: *retrieval.* [Middle English *-aille,* from Old French, from Latin *-ālia,* from neuter pl. of *-ālis.*]

–al³ *suff.* Aldehyde: *citronellal.* [From AL(DEHYDE).]

a·la (ā′lə) *n., pl.* **a·lae** (ā′lē). A winglike structure or part, such as the external ear, the flattened border of some stems, fruits, and seeds, or either one of the two side petals of certain flowers in the pea family. [Latin *āla,* wing.]

Ala. *abbr.* Alabama.

à la also **a la** (ä′ lä, ä′ lə, ăl′ə) *prep.* In the style or manner of: *a poem à la Ogden Nash.* [French, short for *à la mode de,* in the manner of.]

Al·a·bam·a¹ (ăl′ə-băm′ə) *n., pl.* **Alabama** or **-as. 1.a.** A tribe of the Creek confederacy formerly inhabiting southern Alabama and now located in eastern Texas. **b.** A member of this tribe. **2.** The Muskogean language of the Alabama.

Al·a·bam·a² (ăl′ə-băm′ə). *Abbr.* **AL, Ala.** A state of the southeast United States. It was admitted as the 22nd state in 1819. Alabama was first explored by the Spanish, and the southern section was claimed by the United States as part of the Louisiana Purchase (1803). Montgomery is the capital and Birmingham the largest city. Population, 3,893,978. **—Al′a·ba′mi·an** (-bā′mē-ən), **Al′a·bam′an** *adj. & n.*

Alabama River. A river formed in central Alabama north of Montgomery by the confluence of the Coosa and Tallapoosa rivers and flowing about 507 km (315 mi) southwest to join the Tombigbee River north of Mobile.

al·a·bas·ter (ăl′ə-băs′tər) *n.* **1.** A dense translucent, white or tinted fine-grained gypsum. **2.** A variety of hard calcite, translucent and sometimes banded. **3.** *Color.* A pale yellowish pink to yellowish gray. [Middle English *alabastre,* from Old French, from Latin *alabaster,* from Greek *alabastros, alabastos,* possibly of Egyptian origin.]

à la carte also **a la carte** (ä′lə kärt′, ăl′ə) *adv. & adj.* With a separate price for each item on the menu. [French : *à,* by + *la,* the + *carte,* menu.]

a·lack (ə-lăk′) *interj.* Used to express sorrow, regret, or alarm: *" 'Las and fearful alack—nobody can make such high claims for the people then living in Maine"* (John Gould). [On the model of ALAS. See LACK.]

a·lac·ri·ty (ə-lăk′rĭ-tē) *n.* **1.** Cheerful willingness; eagerness. **2.** Speed or quickness; celerity. [Latin *alacritās,* from *alacer,* lively.] **—a·lac′ri·tous** (-təs) *adj.*

A·lad·din (ə-lăd′n) *n.* In the *Arabian Nights,* a boy who acquires a magic lamp and a magic ring with which he can summon two jinn to fulfill any desire.

a·lae (ā′lē) *n.* Plural of **ala.**

A·lai or **A·lay** (ä′lī′). A mountain range of southwest Kirghiz. A western branch of the Tien Shan, it extends about 322 km (200 mi) west from the Chinese border and rises to 5,880.4 m (19,280 ft).

à la king (ä′lə kĭng′, ăl′ə) *adj.* Cooked in a cream sauce with green pepper or pimiento and mushrooms.

Al Al·a·mayn (ăl ăl′ə-mān′, ä′lə-). See **El Alamein.**

♦**al·a·me·da** (ăl′ə-mē′də, -mā′-) *n.* *Southwestern U.S.* A tree-shaded promenade or public park. See Regional Note at **ramada.** [Spanish, from *álamo,* poplar, alamo.]

Al·a·me·da (ăl′ə-mē′də). A city of west-central California on an island in San Francisco Bay near Oakland. It is the site of a naval air base. Population, 63,852.

Al·a·mein (ăl′ə-mān′), **El.** See **El Alamein.**

♦**al·a·mo** (ăl′ə-mō′) *n., pl.* **-mos.** *Southwestern U.S.* A poplar tree, especially a cottonwood. [Spanish *álamo.*]

Al·a·mo (ăl′ə-mō′). A chapel built after 1744 as part of a mission in San Antonio, Texas. During the Texas Revolution against Mexican rule some 182 people were besieged here from February 24 to March 6, 1836. All the insurgents, including Davy Crockett and Jim Bowie, were killed.

a·la·mode (ä′lə-mōd′, ăl′ə-) *n.* A lustrous plain-weave silk fabric for head coverings and scarfs. [From À LA MODE.]

à la mode (ä′lə mōd′, ăl′ə) *adj.* **1.** According to the prevailing style or fashion. **2.** Served with ice cream: *apple pie à la mode.* [French : *à,* in + *la,* the + *mode,* fashion.]

Al·a·mo·gor·do (ăl′ə-mə-gôr′dō). A city of south-central New Mexico northeast of Las Cruces. The first atomic bomb was exploded in a test on June 16, 1945, at the White Sands Missile Range northwest of the city. Population, 24,024.

Å·land Islands (ä′lənd, ō′länd′). See **Ahvenanmaa.**

al·a·nine (ăl′ə-nēn′) *n.* A crystalline amino acid, $C_3H_7NO_2$, that is a constituent of many proteins. [German *Alanin,* ultimately from *Aldehyd,* aldehyde. See ALDEHYDE.]

a·lar (ā′lər) or **a·la·ry** (ā′lə-rē) *adj.* **1.** Resembling, containing, or composed of wings or alae. **2.** *Anatomy.* Concerned with the armpit; axillary. [Latin *ālāris,* from *āla,* wing.]

A·lar (ăl′är). A trademark used for daminozide.

A·lar·cón (ä′lär-kôn′), **Pedro Antonio de.** 1833–1891. Spanish writer noted particularly for his shorter novels, such as *The Three-Cornered Hat* (1874).

Al·ar·ic (ăl′ər-ĭk). A.D. 370?–410. King of the Visigoths (395–410) who plundered Greece in 395 and attacked Italy, conquering Rome in 410.

a·larm (ə-lärm′) *n.* **1.** A sudden fear caused by the realization of danger. **2.** A warning of existing or approaching danger. **3.** *Abbr.* **alm** An electrical, electronic, or mechanical device that serves to warn of danger by means of a sound or signal. **4.** The sounding mechanism of an alarm clock. **5.** A call to arms. **—alarm** *tr.v.* **a·larmed, a·larm·ing, a·larms. 1.** To fill with alarm; frighten. **2.** To give warning to. [Middle English, from Old French *alarme,* from Old Italian *allarme,* from *all'arme,* to arms : *alla,* to the (from Latin *ad illa* : *ad-,* ad- + *illa,* pl. of *illud,* the; see **al-¹** in Appendix) + *arme,* arms (from Latin *arma;* see **ar-** in Appendix).] **—a·larm′ing·ly** *adv.*

SYNONYMS: *alarm, alert, tocsin, warning.* The central meaning shared by these nouns is "a signal that warns of imminent danger": *a burglar alarm; sirens signaling a bomb alert; a tocsin ring-*

ing from church steeples; factory whistles sounding a forest-fire warning.. See also Synonyms at **fear, frighten.**

alarm clock *n.* A clock that can be set to sound a bell or buzzer at a desired hour.

a·larm·ist (ə-lär′mĭst) *n.* A person who needlessly alarms or attempts to alarm others, as by inventing or spreading false or exaggerated rumors of impending danger or catastrophe. **—a·larm′ism** *n.*

alarm reaction *n.* The initial stage in the body's response to stressful stimuli, characterized by adaptive physiological changes, such as increased hormonal activity and increased heart rate.

a·la·rum (ə-lär′əm, ə-lăr′-) *n.* A warning or an alarm, especially a call to arms: *"This instrument called television can teach and illuminate, cautioned Edward R. Murrow, but only to the extent that its operators choose to use it. . . . an era later . . . Murrow's alarum remains as up to date as tonight's news"* (Harry F. Waters). [Middle English *alarom,* variant of *alarm,* alarm. See ALARM.]

a·la·ry (ā′lə-rē) *adj.* Variant of **alar.**

a·las (ə-lăs′) *interj.* Used to express sorrow, regret, grief, compassion, or apprehension of danger or evil. [Middle English, from Old French *a las, helas,* ah (I am) miserable, from Latin *lassus,* weary. See **lē-** in Appendix.]

A·las·ka (ə-lăs′kə). *Abbr.* **AK, Alas.** A state of the United States in extreme northwest North America, separated from the other mainland states by British Columbia, Canada. It was admitted as the 49th state in 1959 and is the largest state of the Union. The territory was purchased from Russia in 1867 for $7,200,000 and was known as Seward's Folly (after Secretary of State William H. Seward, who negotiated the purchase) until gold was discovered in the late 1800's. Juneau is the capital and Anchorage the largest city. There are plans to move the capital to Willow, near Anchorage. Population, 401,851. **—A·las′kan** *adj. & n.*

Alaska, Gulf of. An inlet of the Pacific Ocean between the Alaska Peninsula and Alexander Archipelago.

Alaska cedar *n.* **1.** An evergreen tree *(Chamaecyparis nootkatensis)* of northwest North America. Also called *Nootka cypress.* **2.** The decay-resistant wood of this tree, used for boats, construction materials, and furniture.

Alaska Highway. Formerly **Al·can Highway** (ăl′kăn′). A road extending 2,450.5 km (1,523 mi) northwest from Dawson Creek, British Columbia, to Fairbanks, Alaska. Originally built by U.S. troops in 1942 as a supply route for military installations, it was opened to unrestricted traffic in 1947.

Alaskan king crab *n.* See **king crab** (sense 1).

Alaskan malamute *n.* Malamute.

Alaska Peninsula. A peninsula of south-central to southwest Alaska. It is a continuation of the Aleutian Range between the Bering Sea and the Pacific Ocean.

Alaska Range. A mountain range of south-central Alaska rising to 6,197.6 m (20,320 ft) at Mount McKinley, the highest mountain of North America.

Alaska Standard Time *n.* Standard time in the ninth time zone west of Greenwich, England, reckoned at 135°W and used throughout Alaska except for the western Aleutian Islands. Also called *Alaska Time.*

a·las·tor also **A·las·tor** (ə-lăs′tər, -tôr′) *n.* An avenging deity or spirit, the masculine personification of Nemesis, frequently evoked in Greek tragedy. [Greek *alastōr,* from *alastos,* unforgettable : *a-,* not; see A–[1] + *lanthanein, lath-,* to escape notice.]

A·la-Tau (ăl′ə-tou′, ä′lə-). Several mountain ranges of the Tien Shan in central Asia, eastern Kirghiz, and southern Russia. The highest elevation is about 5,490 m (18,000 ft).

a·late (ā′lāt′) also **a·lat·ed** (ā′lā′tĭd) *adj.* Having winglike extensions or parts; winged: *alate leaves.* [Latin *ālātus,* from *āla,* wing.]

Al·a·va (ăl′ə-və), **Cape.** A cape of northwest Washington State just south of Cape Flattery. It is the westernmost point of the coterminous United States.

A·lay (ä′lī′). See **Alai.**

alb (ălb) *n.* A long, white linen robe with tapered sleeves worn by a priest at Mass. [Middle English *albe,* from Old English, from Medieval Latin *alba,* from *(vestis) alba,* white (garment), feminine of Latin *albus,* white. See **albho-** in Appendix.]

Alb. *abbr.* Albania; Albanian.

Al·ba (ăl′bə), Duke of. See Duke of **Alva.**

Al·ba·ce·te (ăl′bə-sā′tē, äl′vä-thĕ′tĕ). A city of southeast Spain west-southwest of Valencia. It was the site of battles between Moors and Christians in 1145 and 1146. Population, 121,909.

al·ba·core (ăl′bə-kôr′, -kōr′) *n., pl.* **albacore** or **-cores.** A large marine fish *(Thunnus alalunga)* of warm seas, having edible flesh that is a major source of canned tuna. [Portuguese *albacor,* from Arabic *al-bakrah* : *al,* the + *bakrah,* young camel.]

Al·ba Lon·ga (ăl′bə lông′gə, lŏng′-). A city of ancient Latium in central Italy southeast of Rome. It was founded before 1100 B.C. and according to legend was the birthplace of Romulus and Remus.

Al·ba·ni·a (ăl-bā′nē-ə, -bān′yə, ôl-). *Abbr.* **Alb.** A country of southeast Europe on the Adriatic Sea. Long a warring ground for rulers and peoples ranging from the Romans and Turks to the Serbs and Bulgarians, Albania became a republic in 1925, then a satellite of the U.S.S.R. in 1944. In 1961 the country's leaders broke with the Soviets and developed close economic ties with China, a relationship that deteriorated after the death of Mao Zedong in 1976. Tiranë is the capital and the largest city. Population, 2,841,300.

Al·ba·ni·an (ăl-bā′nē-ən, -bān′yən, ôl-) *adj. Abbr.* **Alb.** Of or relating to Albania or its people, language, or culture. **—Albanian** *n.* **1.** A native or an inhabitant of Albania. **2.** The Indo-European language of the Albanians.

Al·ba·no (äl-bä′nō). A lake of central Italy southeast of Rome in an extinct volcanic crater.

Al·ba·ny (ôl′bə-nē). **1.** A city of southwest Georgia on the Flint River southeast of Columbus. It is an industrial and processing center in a pecan- and peanut-growing area. Population, 74,550. **2.** The capital (since 1797) of New York, in the eastern part of the state on the west bank of the Hudson River at the head of deep-water navigation. The early 17th-century Dutch settlement Fort Orange was renamed Albany when the English took control in 1664. Population, 101,727. **3.** A city of northwest Oregon on the Willamette River south of Salem. It is a lumbering and metallurgical center. Population, 26,678.

Albania

Albany River. A river rising in western Ontario, Canada, and flowing about 982 km (610 mi) east and northeast to James Bay. It was an important fur-trading route.

al·ba·tross (ăl′bə-trôs′, -trŏs′) *n., pl.* **albatross** or **-tross·es. 1.** Any of several large, web-footed birds constituting the family Diomedeidae, chiefly of the oceans of the Southern Hemisphere, and having a hooked beak and long, narrow wings. **2. a.** A constant, worrisome burden. **b.** An obstacle to success. [Probably alteration (influenced by Latin *albus,* white) of *alcatras,* pelican, from Portuguese or Spanish *alcatraz,* from Arabic *al-ġaṭṭās* : *al,* the + *ġaṭṭās,* white-tailed sea eagle. Sense 2, after the *albatross* in *The Rime of the Ancient Mariner* by Samuel Taylor Coleridge, which the mariner killed and had to wear around his neck as a penance.]

al·be·do (ăl-bē′dō) *n., pl.* **-dos.** The fraction of incident electromagnetic radiation reflected by a surface, especially of a celestial body. [Late Latin, whiteness, from Latin *albus,* white. See **albho-** in Appendix.]

Al·bee (ôl′bē, ŏl′-, ăl′-), **Edward Franklin.** Born 1928. American playwright. Best known for *Who's Afraid of Virginia Woolf?* (1962), he won a Pulitzer Prize in 1967 for *A Delicate Balance* and in 1975 for *Seascape.*

al·be·it (ôl-bē′ĭt, ăl-) *conj.* Even though; although; notwithstanding: *clear albeit cold weather.* [Middle English *al be it* : *al,* even if; see ALL + *be,* subjunctive of *ben,* to be; see BE + *it,* it; see IT.]

Al·be·marle (ăl′bə-märl′). A city of central North Carolina in the Piedmont east-northeast of Charlotte. It is a trade and processing center. Population, 15,110.

Albemarle Sound. A large body of shallow, generally fresh water in northeast North Carolina. It is separated from the Atlantic Ocean by a narrow barrier island.

albatross
Top: Wandering albatross
Diomedea exulans
Bottom: Laysan albatross
Diomedea immutabilis

Al·bé·niz (ăl-bā′nēs′, äl-), **Isaac.** 1860–1909. Spanish composer and pianist. A student of Franz Liszt, he composed piano works based on Spanish folk music.

Al·bers (ăl′bərz, ŏl′-), **Josef.** 1888–1976. German-born American painter whose works, such as the series *Homage to the Square* (1950–1959), are characterized by simple geometric patterns of various colors.

Al·bert (ăl′bərt), Prince. 1819–1861. German-born consort (1840–1861) of Victoria who strongly influenced the queen and was a patron of the arts, sciences, and industry.

Albert I. 1875–1934. King of the Belgians (1909–1934) who during World War I led the forces that reconquered Belgium (1918).

Albert, Lake. Also **Mo·bu·to Lake** (mō-bo͞o′tō) or **Albert Nyan·za** (nī-ăn′zə, nyän′-). A shallow lake of east-central Africa in the Great Rift Valley on the border between Uganda and Zaire. It was discovered in 1864 by Sir Samuel Baker and named for Victoria's consort.

Al·ber·ta (ăl-bûr′tə). *Abbr.* **AB, Alta.** A province of western Canada between British Columbia and Saskatchewan. It joined the confederation in 1905. Wheat and cattle farming were the basis of the province's economy until the discovery of oil and natural gas in the early 1960's. Edmonton is the capital and the largest city. Population, 2,237,724. **—Al·ber′tan** *adj. & n.*

Albert Lea (lē). A city of southern Minnesota near the Iowa border south of Minneapolis. It is a trade center in a farming area. Population, 19,200.

Albert Nile (nīl). Part of the upper Nile River in northwest Uganda.

Albert Nyan·za (nī-ăn′zə, nyän′-). See Lake **Albert.**

Al·ber·tus Mag·nus (ăl-bûr′təs măg′nəs), Saint. Originally Albert, Count von Bollstadt. 1206?–1280. German religious philosopher noted as the teacher of Thomas Aquinas.

al·bes·cent (ăl-bĕs′ənt) *adj.* Becoming white or moderately white; whitish. [Latin *albēscēns, albēscent-,* present participle of *albēscere,* to become white, from *albus,* white. See **albho-** in Appendix.]

Al·bi·gen·ses (ăl′bə-jĕn′sēz′) *pl.n.* The members of a Cath-

ă pat	oi boy
ā pay	ou out
âr care	o͝o took
ä father	o͞o boot
ĕ pet	ŭ cut
ē be	ûr urge
ĭ pit	th thin
ī pie	*th* this
îr pier	hw which
ŏ pot	zh vision
ō toe	ə about, item
ô paw	♦ regionalism

Stress marks: ′ (primary); ′ (secondary), as in **dictionary** (dĭk′shə-nĕr′ē)

albino
Albino deer

arist religious sect of southern France in the 12th and 13th centuries, exterminated for heresy during the Inquisition. [Medieval Latin, pl. of *Albigēnsis,* inhabitant of *Albiga,* Albi, a town of southern France where the sect was dominant.] **—Al′bi·gen′sian** (-shən, -sē-ən) *adj.* **—Al′bi·gen′sian·ism** *n.*

al·bi·nism (ăl′bə-nĭz′əm) *n.* **1.** Congenital absence of normal pigmentation or coloration in a person, an animal, or a plant. **2.** The condition of being an albino. [French *albinisme,* from German *Albinismus,* from *Albino,* albino, from Portuguese. See ALBINO.] **—al′bi·nis′tic** *adj.*

al·bi·no (ăl-bī′nō) *n., pl.* **-nos. 1.** A person or an animal lacking normal pigmentation, with the result being that the skin and hair are abnormally white or milky and the eyes have a pink or blue iris and a deep-red pupil. **2.** A plant that lacks chlorophyll. [Portuguese, from *albo,* white, from Latin *albus.* See **albho-** in Appendix.]

Al·bi·nus (ăl-bī′nəs). See **Alcuin.**

Al·bi·on (ăl′bē-ən). England or Great Britain. Often used poetically.

al·bite (ăl′bīt) *n.* A widely distributed white feldspar, $NaAlSi_3O_8$, that is one of the common rock-forming plagioclase group. [Latin *albus,* white; see **albho-** in Appendix + -ITE[1].] **—al·bit′ic** (-bĭt′ĭk), **al·bit′i·cal** (-ĭ-kəl) *adj.*

Al·boin (ăl′boin, -bō-ĭn). Died 572. King of the Lombards (565?–572) who led the Germanic invasion of present-day Italy, where he established the Lombard kingdom.

Ål·borg also **Aal·borg** (ôl′bôrg′). A city of northern Denmark north-northeast of Århus. Chartered in 1342, it is a major port. Population, 154,840.

Al·bright (ôl′brīt, ŏl′-), **Horace Marden.** 1890–1987. American conservationist and cofounder of the National Park Service.

alcazar
Segovia, Spain

al·bum (ăl′bəm) *n.* **1.** A book with blank pages for the insertion and preservation of collections, as of stamps, photographs, or autographs. **2.a.** A set of phonograph records stored together in jackets under one binding. **b.** The holder for such records. **c.** One or more 12-inch long-playing records in a slipcase. **d.** A phonograph record. **e.** A recording of different musical pieces. **3.** A printed collection of musical compositions, pictures, or literary selections. **4.** A tall, handsomely printed book, popular especially in the 19th century, often having profuse illustrations and short, sentimental texts. [Latin, blank tablet, from neuter of *albus,* white. See **albho-** in Appendix.]

al·bu·men (ăl-byōō′mən) *n.* **1.** The white of an egg, which consists mainly of albumin dissolved in water. **2.** See **albumin.** [Latin *albūmen,* from *albus,* white. See **albho-** in Appendix.]

al·bu·min (ăl-byōō′mĭn) *n.* A class of simple, water-soluble proteins that can be coagulated by heat and are found in egg white, blood serum, milk, and many other animal and plant juices and tissues. Also called *albumen.* [ALBUM(EN) + -IN.] **—al·bu′mi·nous** *adj.*

al·bu·mi·noid (ăl-byōō′mə-noid′) *n.* See **scleroprotein. —albuminoid** also **al·bu·mi·noi·dal** (-byōō′mə-noid′l) *adj.* Composed of or resembling albumin.

al·bu·mi·nu·ri·a (ăl-byōō′mə-nŏŏr′ē-ə, -nyŏŏr-) *n.* The presence of albumin in the urine, sometimes indicating kidney disease. **—al·bu′mi·nu′ric** (-nŏŏr′ĭk, -nyŏŏr′-) *adj.*

al·bu·mose (ăl′byə-mōs′, -mōz′) *n.* A class of substances derived from albumins and formed by the enzymatic breakdown of proteins during digestion. [French : *albumine,* albumin; see ALBUMIN + *-ose,* -ose; see -OSE[2].]

Al·bu·quer·que (ăl′bə-kûr′kē). A city of central New Mexico on the upper Rio Grande southwest of Santa Fe. Founded in 1706, it is a noted health resort. Population, 331,767.

Al·bu·quer·que (ăl′bə-kûr′kē, ăl′bə-kûr′-), **Affonso de.** Known as "Affonso the Great." 1453–1515. Portuguese colonial administrator considered the founder of the Portuguese empire in the East.

Louisa May Alcott

alc. *abbr.* Alcohol; alcoholic.

Al·cae·us (ăl-sē′əs). fl. 611?–580 B.C. Greek poet who reputedly invented Alcaic verse.

Al·ca·ic (ăl-kā′ĭk) *adj.* Of, relating to, or being a verse form used in Greek and Latin poetry, consisting of strophes having four tetrametric lines. **—Alcaic** *n.* Verse composed in strophes of four tetrametric lines. [Late Latin *Alcaicus,* of Alcaeus, from Greek *Alkaïkos,* from *Alkaios,* Alcaeus.]

al·cai·de also **al·cay·de** (ăl-kī′dē) *n.* The commander or governor of a fortress in Spain or Portugal. [Spanish, from Arabic *al-qā'id,* the commander : *al,* the + *qā'id,* commander (from *qāda,* to command).]

Al·ca·lá de He·na·res (ăl′kə-lä′ dā hĕ-när′əs, äl′kä-lä′ *thĕ* ĕ-nä′rĕs). A town of central Spain east-northeast of Madrid. Cervantes and Catherine of Aragon were born here. Population, 146,994.

al·cal·de (ăl-kăl′dē, äl-) *n.* The mayor or chief judicial official of a Spanish town. [Spanish, from Arabic *al-qāḍī* : *al,* the + *qāḍī,* judge (from *qaḍā,* to judge).]

Al·can Highway (ăl′kăn′). See **Alaska Highway.**

Al·ca·traz (ăl′kə-trăz′). A rocky island of western California in San Francisco Bay. It was a military prison from 1859 to 1933 and a federal prison until 1963. It is now a tourist attraction. The island has long been known as "the Rock."

al·cay·de (ăl-kī′dē) *n.* Variant of **alcaide.**

al·caz·ar (ăl-kăz′ər, -kä′zər, ăl′kə-zär′) *n.* A Spanish palace or fortress, originally one built by the Moors. [Spanish *alcázar,* from Arabic *alqaṣr* : *al,* the + *qaṣr,* castle (from Latin *castra,* fort, pl. of *castrum,* camp; see **kes-** in Appendix).]

Al·ces·tis (ăl-sĕs′tĭs) *n.* *Greek Mythology.* The wife of King Admetus of Thessaly, who agreed to die in place of her husband and was later rescued from Hades by Hercules.

al·che·mist (ăl′kə-mĭst) *n.* A practitioner of alchemy. **—al′che·mis′tic, al′che·mis′ti·cal** *adj.*

al·che·mize (ăl′kə-mīz′) *tr.v.* **-mized, -miz·ing, -miz·es.** To transform by or as if by alchemy.

al·che·my (ăl′kə-mē) *n.* **1.** A medieval chemical philosophy having as its asserted aims the transmutation of base metals into gold, the discovery of the panacea, and the preparation of the elixir of longevity. **2.** A seemingly magical power or process of transmuting: *"He wondered by what alchemy it was changed, so that what sickened him one hour, maddened him with hunger the next"* (Marjorie K. Rawlings). [Middle English *alkamie,* from Old French *alquemie,* from Medieval Latin *alchymia,* from Arabic *al-kīmiyā'* : *al,* the + *kīmiyā',* chemistry (from Late Greek *khēmeia, khumeia,* perhaps from Greek *Khēmia,* Egypt).] **—al·chem′i·cal** (ăl-kĕm′ĭ-kəl), **al·chem′ic** *adj.*

Al·ci·bi·a·des (ăl′sə-bī′ə-dēz′). 450?–404 B.C. Athenian politician and general whose brilliant military career foundered during the Peloponnesian War (431–404), during which he changed allegiance three times.

Al·cin·dor (ăl-sĭn′dər), **Lew.** See Kareem **Abdul-Jabbar.**

Al·cin·o·us (ăl-sĭn′ō-əs) *n.* *Greek Mythology.* A king of Phaeacia, father of Nausicaa, who entertained Odysseus.

Alc·me·ne (ălk-mē′nē) *n.* *Greek Mythology.* Amphitryon's wife, who gave birth to Hercules after being seduced by Zeus.

al·co·hol (ăl′kə-hôl′, -hŏl′) *n.* **1.** *Abbr.* **al., alc.** A colorless, volatile, flammable liquid, C_2H_5OH, synthesized or obtained by fermentation of sugars and starches and widely used, either pure or denatured, as a solvent and in drugs, cleaning solutions, explosives, and intoxicating beverages. Also called *ethanol, ethyl alcohol, grain alcohol.* **2.** Intoxicating liquor containing alcohol. **3.** Any of a series of hydroxyl compounds, the simplest of which are derived from saturated hydrocarbons, have the general formula $C_nH_{2n+1}OH$, and include ethanol and methanol. [Medieval Latin, fine metallic powder, especially of antimony, from Arabic *al-kuḥl* : *al,* the + *kuḥl,* powder of antimony.]

WORD HISTORY: The *al-* in *alcohol* may alert some readers to the fact that this is a word of Arabic descent, as is the case with *algebra* and *alkali*—*al* being the Arabic definite article corresponding to *the* in English. The origin of *-cohol* is less obvious, however. Its Arabic ancestor was *kuḥl,* a fine powder most often made from antimony and used by women to darken their eyelids; in fact, *kuḥl* has given us the word *kohl* for such a preparation. Arabic chemists came to use *al-kuḥl* to mean "any fine powder produced in a number of ways, including the process of heating a substance to a gaseous state and then recooling it." The English word *alcohol,* derived through Medieval Latin from Arabic, is first recorded in 1543 in this sense. Arabic chemists also used *al-kuḥl* to refer to other substances such as essences that were obtained by distillation, a sense first found for English *alcohol* in 1672. One of these distilled essences, known as "alcohol of wine," is the constituent of fermented liquors that causes intoxication. This essence took over the term *alcohol* for itself, whence it has come to refer to the liquor that contains this essence as well as to a class of chemical compounds such as methanol.

al·co·hol·ic (ăl′kə-hô′lĭk, -hŏl′ĭk) *adj.* *Abbr.* **al., alc. 1.** Related to or resulting from alcohol. **2.** Containing or preserved in alcohol. **3.** Suffering from alcoholism. **—alcoholic** *n.* A person who drinks alcoholic substances habitually and to excess or who suffers from alcoholism.

al·co·hol·ic·i·ty (ăl′kə-hô-lĭs′ĭ-tē) *n.* Alcoholic content.

al·co·hol·ism (ăl′kə-hô-lĭz′əm, -hŏ-) *n.* **1.** The compulsive consumption of and psychophysiological dependence on alcoholic beverages. **2.** A chronic, progressive pathological condition, mainly affecting the nervous and digestive systems, caused by the excessive and habitual consumption of alcohol. **3.** Temporary mental disturbance and muscular incoordination caused by excessive consumption of alcohol.

al·co·hol·om·e·ter (ăl′kə-hô-lŏm′ĭ-tər) also **al·co·hol·me·ter** (ăl′kə-hôl-mē′tər, -hŏl-) *n.* An instrument, such as a hydrometer, used to determine the amount of alcohol in a liquid. **—al′co·hol·om′e·try** *n.*

Al·co·ran (ăl′kə-răn′) *n.* See **Koran.** [Middle English, from Medieval Latin *alcorānum,* from Arabic *al qur'ān* : *al,* the + *qur'ān,* reading; see KORAN.]

Al·cott (ôl′kət, -kŏt, ŏl′-), **Amos Bronson.** 1799–1888. American educator and transcendentalist philosopher who maintained that learning should be based on pleasure and imagination instead of discipline.

Alcott, Louisa May. 1832–1888. American writer and reformer best known for her largely autobiographical novel *Little Women* (1868–1869).

al·cove (ăl′kōv′) *n.* **1.** A recess or partly enclosed extension connected to or forming part of a room. **2.** A secluded structure, such as a bower, in a garden. [French *alcôve,* from Spanish *alcoba,* from Arabic *al-qubbah,* the vault : *al,* the + *qubbah,* vault.]

Al·cuin (ăl′kwĭn) also **Al·bi·nus** (ăl-bī′nəs). 735?–804.

Anglo-Saxon prelate and scholar who was a leader in the revival of learning in medieval Europe.

Al·cy·o·ne (ăl-sī′ə-nē) *n.* **1.** *Greek Mythology.* The daughter of Aeolus who, in grief over the death of her husband Ceyx, threw herself into the sea and was changed into a kingfisher. **2.** *Greek Mythology.* A nymph, one of the Pleiades. **3.** *Astronomy.* The brightest star in the Pleiades, in the constellation Taurus. [Latin, from Greek *Alkuonē,* from *alkuōn,* kingfisher.]

Ald. *abbr.* Alderman.

Al·dab·ra Islands (ăl-dăb′rə). A group of four coral islands in the Indian Ocean north of Madagascar. Part of Seychelles since 1976, the islands are known for their giant tortoises and other unusual flora and fauna.

Al·dan (ăl-dän′). A river of southeast Russia rising in the Stanovoy Range and flowing about 2,253 km (1,400 mi) north and east around the **Aldan Plateau** then generally northwest to the Lena River north of Yakutsk.

Al·deb·a·ran (ăl-dĕb′ər-ən) *n.* A double star in the constellation Taurus, 68 light-years from Earth, and one of the brightest stars in the sky. [Middle English *Aldeboran,* from Medieval Latin *Aldebaran,* from Arabic *ad-dabarān* : *al,* the + *dabarān,* following (the Pleiades) (from *dabara,* to follow).]

al·de·hyde (ăl′də-hīd′) *n.* **1.** Any of a class of highly reactive organic chemical compounds obtained by oxidation of primary alcohols, characterized by the common group CHO, and used in the manufacture of resins, dyes, and organic acids. **2.** See **acetaldehyde.** [German *Aldehyd,* from New Latin, short for *alcohol dehydrogenātum,* dehydrogenized alcohol.]

Al·den (ôl′dən), **John.** 1599?–1687. Pilgrim colonist and political figure whose courtship of Priscilla Mullins (born c. 1602) is the subject of a popular legend.

al den·te (ăl dĕn′tē, äl dĕn′tā) *adj.* Cooked enough to be firm but not soft: *pasta al dente.* [Italian : *al,* to the + *dente,* tooth.] **—al den′te** *adv.*

al·der (ôl′dər) *n.* **1.** Any of various deciduous shrubs or trees of the genus *Alnus,* native chiefly to northern temperate regions and having alternate, simple, toothed leaves and tiny fruits in woody, conelike catkins. **2.** The wood of these plants, used in carvings and for making furniture and cabinets. [Middle English, from Old English *alor.*]

Al·der (äl′dər), **Kurt.** 1902–1958. German chemist. He shared a 1950 Nobel Prize for discoveries concerning the structure of organic matter.

al·der·man (ôl′dər-mən) *n.* **1.** *Abbr.* **Ald.** A member of the municipal legislative body in a town or city in many jurisdictions. **2.** A member of the higher branch of the municipal or borough council in England and Ireland before 1974. **3. a.** A noble of high rank or authority in Anglo-Saxon England. **b.** The chief officer of a shire in Anglo-Saxon England. [Middle English, a person of high rank, from Old English *ealdorman* : *ealdor,* elder, chief (from *eald,* old; see **al-**[2] in Appendix) + *man,* man; see MAN.] **—al′der·man·cy** (-sē) *n.* **—al′der·man′ic** (-măn′ĭk) *adj.*

Al·der·ney[1] (ôl′dər-nē). A British island in the English Channel. The northernmost of the larger Channel Islands, it is separated from the French coast by a swift channel, the **Race of Alderney.**

Al·der·ney[2] (ôl′dər-nē) *n., pl.* **-neys.** One of a breed of small dairy cattle originally raised in the Channel Islands.

Al·der·shot (ôl′dər-shŏt′). A municipal borough of south-central England southwest of London. It is the site of a large military training center. Population, 80,800.

al·di·carb (ăl′dĭ-kärb′) *n.* A crystalline compound, $C_7H_{14}N_2O_2S$, used in agriculture as a pesticide on crops such as cotton, potatoes, and sugar beets. [(PROPION)ALD(EHYDE) + *(methyl)carb(amoyloxime),* $C_2H_{14}N_2O_2S$.]

al·dol (ăl′dôl′, -dōl′, -dŏl′) *n.* **1.** A thick, colorless to pale yellow liquid, $C_4H_8O_2$, obtained from acetaldehyde and used in perfumery and as a solvent. **2.** A similar aldehyde. [ALD(EHYDE) + -OL[1].]

al·dol·ase (ăl′də-lās′) *n.* An enzyme present in certain living tissues, including skeletal and heart muscle tissues, that catalyzes the breakdown of a fructose ester into triose sugars.

al·dose (ăl′dōs′, -dōz′) *n.* *Chemistry.* Any of a class of monosaccharide sugars containing an aldehyde group. [ALD(EHYDE) + -OSE[1].]

al·dos·ter·one (ăl-dŏs′tə-rōn′) *n.* A steroid hormone secreted by the adrenal cortex that regulates the salt and water balance in the body. [ALD(EHYDE) + STER(OL) + -ONE.]

al·dos·ter·on·ism (ăl-dŏs′tə-rō-nĭz′əm, ăl′dō-stĕr′ə-) *n.* A disorder marked by excessive secretion of the hormone aldosterone, which can cause weakness, cardiac irregularities, and abnormally high blood pressure.

Al·drich (ôl′drĭch, ŏl′-), **Thomas Bailey.** 1836–1907. American writer and editor best known for his editorship of the *Atlantic Monthly* (1881–1890) and his novel *The Story of a Bad Boy* (1870).

Al·dridge (ôl′drĭj, ŏl′-), **Ira Frederick.** 1804?–1867. American-born actor whose tragic leading roles, most notably in *Othello,* were acclaimed in Europe.

al·drin (ôl′drĭn) *n.* An insecticide containing a naphthalene-derived compound, $C_{12}H_8Cl_6$. [After Kurt ALDER.]

Al·drin (ôl′drĭn, ŏl′-), **Edwin Eugene, Jr.** Known as "Buzz." Born 1930. American astronaut who as a crew member of Apollo 11 became the second human being to walk on the moon (July 20, 1969).

Al·dus Ma·nu·tius (ôl′dəs mə-no͞o′shəs, -shē-əs, -nyo͞o′-, ŏl′-). See Aldus **Manutius.**

ale (āl) *n.* A fermented alcoholic beverage containing malt and hops, similar to but heavier than beer. [Middle English, from Old English *ealu, alu.* See **alu-** in Appendix.]

a·le·a·to·ry (ā′lē-ə-tôr′ē, -tōr′ē) *adj.* **1.** Dependent on chance, luck, or an uncertain outcome: *an aleatory contract between an oil prospector and a landowner.* **2.** Of or characterized by gambling: *aleatory contests.* **3.** Also **a·le·a·to·ric** (ā′lē-ə-tôr′ĭk, -tōr′-). *Music.* Using or consisting of sounds to be chosen by the performer or left to chance; indeterminate: *An object placed inside the piano added an aleatory element to the piece.* [Latin *āleātōrius,* from *āleātor,* gambler, from *ālea,* dice.]

a·lec·i·thal (ā-lĕs′ə-thəl) *adj.* Having little or no yolk: *an alecithal egg.* [A-[1] + LECITH(IN) + -AL[1].]

A·lec·to (ə-lĕk′tō) *n.* *Greek and Roman Mythology.* One of the Furies.

a·lee (ə-lē′) *adv.* *Nautical.* At, on, or to the leeward side.

al·e·gar (ăl′ĭ-gər, ā′lĭ-) *n.* Vinegar produced by the fermentation of ale. [Middle English, blend of *ale,* ale; see ALE, and *vinegar,* vinegar; see VINEGAR.]

ale·house (āl′hous′) *n.* A place where ale is sold and served.

A·lei·chem (ä-lā′kĕm, -KHĕm,), **Shalom** or **Sholem.** Originally Solomon Rabinowitz. 1859–1916. Russian-born Jewish humorist whose stories and plays, originally written in Yiddish, were the basis for the musical *Fiddler on the Roof.*

A·leix·an·dre (ä′lĕk-sän′drə), **Vicente.** 1898–1984. Spanish poet. He won the 1977 Nobel Prize for literature.

A·lek·san·drovsk (ăl′ĭk-săn′drəfsk, ə-lĭk-sän′-). See **Zaporozhe.**

A·le·mán (ä′lā-män′), **Mateo.** 1547–1610? Spanish-born Mexican writer whose greatest work is the picaresque novel *Guzmán de Alfarache* (1599).

Al·e·man·ni (ăl′ə-măn′ī) *pl.n.* A group of Germanic tribes that settled in Alsace and nearby areas during the fourth century A.D. and were defeated by the Franks in 496. [Latin, of Germanic origin. See **man-**[1] in Appendix.]

Al·e·man·nic (ăl′ə-măn′ĭk) *n.* **1.** A group of High German dialects spoken in Alsace, Switzerland, and parts of southern Germany. **2.** The Germanic dialect of the Alemanni. **—Alemannic** *adj.* **1.** Of or relating to the Alemannic dialects of High German. **2.** Of or relating to the Alemanni or their language.

A·lem·bert (ăl′əm-bâr′, ä-läN-bĕr′), **Jean Le Rond d′.** 1717–1783. French mathematician and philosopher who defined the laws of dynamics governing equilibrium and centrifugal force. He also contributed to Diderot's *Encyclopédie.*

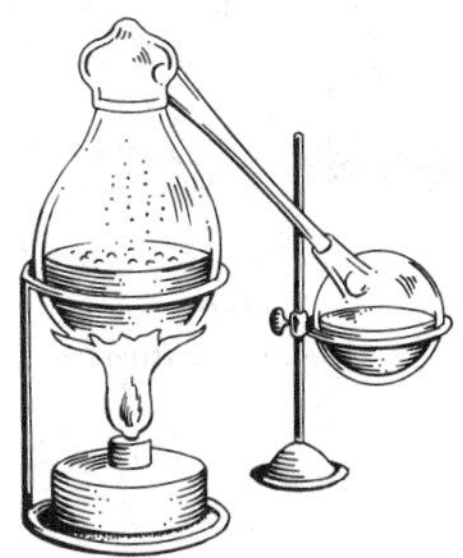

alembic

a·lem·bic (ə-lĕm′bĭk) *n.* **1.** An apparatus consisting of two vessels connected by a tube, formerly used for distilling liquids. **2.** A device that purifies or alters by a process comparable to distillation. [Middle English *alambic,* from Old French, from Medieval Latin *alembicus,* from Arabic *al-'anbīq* : *al,* the + *'anbīq,* still (from Greek *ambix,* cup).]

Al·en·çon (ăl-äN-sôN′). A town of northwest France on the Sarthe River west-southwest of Paris. Its lacework industry dates to the 17th century. Population, 31,608.

A·lep (ə-lĕp′). See **Aleppo.**

a·leph (ā′lĕf, -ləf) *n.* The first letter of the Hebrew alphabet. See table at **alphabet.** [Hebrew *'alep,* from *'elep,* ox, from Canaanite *'alp.*]

a·leph-null (ā′lĕf-nŭl′, -ləf-) *n.* *Mathematics.* The first transfinite number.

A·lep·po (ə-lĕp′ō) also **A·lep** (ə-lĕp′). A city of northwest Syria near the Turkish border. Inhabited perhaps as early as the sixth millennium B.C., Aleppo was a key point on the caravan route across Syria to Baghdad and later a major center of Christianity in the Middle East. Population, 985,413.

a·lert (ə-lûrt′) *adj.* **1.** Vigilantly attentive; watchful: *alert to danger; an alert bank guard.* See Synonyms at **aware. 2.** Mentally responsive and perceptive; quick. **3.** Brisk or lively in action: *the bird's alert hopping from branch to branch.* **—alert** *n.* **1.** A signal that warns of attack or danger: *Sirens sounded the alert for an air raid.* See Synonyms at **alarm. 2.** A condition or period of heightened watchfulness or preparation for action: *Nuclear-armed bombers were put on alert during the crisis.* **—alert** *tr.v.* **a·lert·ed, a·lert·ing, a·lerts.** To notify of approaching danger or action; warn: *a flashing red light that alerted motorists to trouble ahead.* **—*idiom.* on the alert.** Watchful and prepared for danger, emergency, or opportunity: *bird watchers on the alert for a rare species.* [French *alerte,* from Italian *all' erta,* on the lookout : *alla,* to the, on the (from Latin *ad illam,* to that : *ad-,* ad- + *illam,* accusative of *illa,* that; see **al-**[1] in Appendix) + *erta,* lookout, from past participle of *ergere,* to raise (from Latin *ērigere;* see ERECT).]

Al·es·san·dri·a (ăl′ĭ-săn′drē-ə, ä′lĕs-sän′-). A city of northwest Italy east-southeast of Turin. It was founded c. 1168 as a stronghold of the Lombard League. Population, 100,518.

al·eu·rone (ăl′yə-rōn′) also **a·leu·ron** (-rŏn′) *n.* A granular protein found in the endosperm of many seeds or forming the outermost layer in cereal grains. [From Greek *aleuron,* meal.] **—al′eu·ron′ic** (-rŏn′ĭk) *adj.*

A·leut (ə-lo͞ot′, ăl′ē-o͞ot′) *n., pl.* **Aleut** or **A·leuts. 1. a.** A

ă pat	oi boy
ā pay	ou out
âr care	o͝o took
ä father	o͞o boot
ĕ pet	ŭ cut
ē be	ûr urge
ĭ pit	th thin
ī pie	*th* this
îr pier	hw which
ŏ pot	zh vision
ō toe	ə about, item
ô paw	♦ regionalism

Stress marks: ′ (primary); ′ (secondary), as in **dictionary** (dĭk′shə-nĕr′ē)

Alexander the Great
As depicted on
an ancient coin

alfalfa
Medicago sativa

Alfonso XIII

Native American people inhabiting the Aleutian Islands and coastal areas of southwest Alaska. The Aleut are related culturally and linguistically to the Eskimo. **b.** A member of this people. **2.** Either or both of the two languages of the Aleut. See Usage Note at **Native American.** [Russian.]

A·leu·tian (ə-lo͞o′shən) *adj.* Of or relating to the Aleut, their language, or their culture. **—Aleutian** *n.* A native or inhabitant of the Aleutian Islands, especially an Aleut.

Aleutian Islands. A chain of rugged, volcanic islands of southwest Alaska curving about 1,931 km (1,200 mi) west from the Alaska Peninsula and separating the Bering Sea from the Pacific Ocean. The islands were discovered in 1741 by Vitus Bering, a Danish explorer employed by Russia, and remained under Russian control until Alaska was purchased by the United States in 1867. Military bases on the islands are of vital strategic importance because of their proximity to Russia.

Aleutian Range. A volcanic mountain chain of southwest Alaska extending about 965 km (600 mi) west from Anchorage along the Alaska Peninsula and continuing, partly submerged as the Aleutian Islands, to Attu Island.

A level *n. Chiefly British.* **1.** The later of two standardized tests in a secondary school subject, used as a qualification for entrance into a university. **2.** The educational background and skills required to pass this test. [A(DVANCED) LEVEL.]

ale·wife[1] (āl′wīf′) *n.* A fish *(Alosa pseudoharengus)* closely related to the herrings and native to North American Atlantic waters and some inland lakes. [Perhaps from ALEWIFE[2].]

ale·wife[2] (āl′wīf′) *n.* A woman who keeps an alehouse.

al·ex·an·der also **Al·ex·an·der** (ăl′ĭg-zăn′dər) *n.* A cocktail made with crème de cacao, sweet cream, and brandy or gin. [From the name *Alexander.*]

Alexander I[1] (ăl′ĭg-zăn′dər). 1777–1825. Czar of Russia (1801–1825) whose plans to liberalize his country's government were forestalled by wars with Napoleon I.

Alexander I[2]**.** Originally **Alexander O·bre·no·vić** (ō-brĕn′ə-vĭch′). 1876–1903. King of Serbia (1889–1903) whose efforts to increase his power at the expense of the national assembly led to his assassination.

Alexander I[3]**.** 1888–1934. King of Yugoslavia (1921–1934) who unified the peoples of Serbia, Croatia, and Slovenia (1929) and was assassinated by Croatian separatists.

Alexander I Island. An island of British Antarctic Territory in Bellingshausen Sea off the coast of the Antarctic Peninsula. Originally thought to be part of the Antarctic landmass, it was proved to be an island by a U.S. exploratory team in 1940.

Alexander II. 1818–1881. Czar of Russia (1855–1881) who emancipated the serfs in 1861.

Alexander III[1]**.** Known as "Alexander the Great." 356–323 B.C. King of Macedonia (336–323) and conquerer of Asia Minor, Syria, Egypt, Babylonia, and Persia. His reign marked the beginning of the Hellenistic Age.

Alexander III[2]**.** Originally Orlando Bandinelli. Died 1181. Pope (1159–1181) who excommunicated Frederick I (1165) and established papal supremacy.

Alexander VI. Originally Rodrigo Borgia. 1431–1503. Pope (1492–1503) noted as a patron of the arts and for his corrupt papacy.

Alexander Archipelago. A group of more than 1,000 islands off southeast Alaska. The rugged, heavily forested islands are the exposed tops of submerged coastal mountains that rise steeply from the Pacific Ocean.

Alexander Nev·ski (nĕv′skē, nĕf′-). 1220?–1263. Russian saint and national hero named after the Neva River, where he defeated the Swedes in 1240.

Alexander of Tu·nis (to͞o′nĭs, tyo͞o′-), First Earl. Title of Harold Rupert Leofric George Alexander. 1891–1969. British field marshal who during World War II led maneuvers at Dunkirk and in Burma, North Africa, and Italy.

Alexander Se·ve·rus (sə-vîr′əs), **Marcus Aurelius.** A.D. 208?–235. Emperor of Rome (222–235) who succeeded his cousin and adoptive father, Heliogabalus.

Al·ex·an·der·son (ăl′ĭg-zăn′dər-sən), **Ernst Frederick Werner.** 1878–1975. Swedish-born American electrical engineer and inventor who demonstrated the first practical television system (1930).

Alexander the Great. See **Alexander III**[1]**.**

Al·ex·an·dra (ăl′ĭg-zăn′drə, -zän′-). 1872–1918. Last czarina of Russia (1894–1917). The wife of Nicholas II, she was influenced by Rasputin and meddled in politics. After the Bolshevik revolution, she and her family were imprisoned and executed.

Al·ex·an·dret·ta (ăl′ĭg-zăn-drĕt′ə). See **Iskenderun.**

Al·ex·an·dri·a (ăl′ĭg-zăn′drē-ə). **1.** A city of northern Egypt on the Mediterranean Sea at the western tip of the Nile Delta. It was founded by Alexander the Great in 332 B.C. and became a repository of Jewish, Arab, and Hellenistic culture famous for its extensive libraries. Its pharos (lighthouse) was one of the Seven Wonders of the World. Population, 2,821,000. **2.** A city of central Louisiana on the Red River northwest of Baton Rouge. The original city was destroyed by Union troops in May 1864 during the Civil War. Population, 51,565. **3.** An independent city of northern Virginia on the Potomac River opposite Washington, D.C. Primarily a residential suburb of the capital, the city has many historic buildings, including Gadsby's Tavern, built in 1752. George Washington helped lay out the streets in 1749. Population, 103,217.

Al·ex·an·dri·an (ăl′ĭg-zăn′drē-ən) *adj.* **1.** Of or relating to Alexander the Great: *the Alexandrian conquests.* **2.** Of or relating to Alexandria, Egypt. **3.** Of, characteristic of, or belonging to a learned school of Hellenistic literature, science, and philosophy located at Alexandria in the last three centuries B.C.: *Alexandrian scholars; an Alexandrian preference for the explication of earlier works.*

al·ex·an·drine also **Al·ex·an·drine** (ăl′ĭg-zăn′drĭn) *—n.* **1.** A line of English verse composed in iambic hexameter, usually with a caesura after the third foot. **2.** A line of French verse consisting of 12 syllables with a caesura usually falling after the sixth syllable. *—adj.* Characterized by or composed in either of these meters. [French *alexandrin,* from Old French, from *Alexandre,* title of a romance about Alexander the Great that was written in this meter.]

al·ex·an·drite (ăl′ĭg-zăn′drīt′) *n.* A greenish chrysoberyl that appears red in artificial light, used as a gemstone. [German *Alexandrit,* after ALEXANDER I[1].]

a·lex·i·a (ə-lĕk′sē-ə) *n.* Loss of the ability to read, usually caused by brain lesions. Also called *word blindness.* [A–[1] + Greek *lexis,* speech (from *legein,* to speak; see **leg-** in Appendix) + –IA[1].]

a·lex·in (ə-lĕk′sĭn) *n.* See **complement** (sense 6). [Greek *alexein,* to ward off + –IN.]

A·lex·is I Mi·khai·lo·vich (ä-lĕk′sĭs; mĭ-kī′lə-vĭch, mə-KHĪ′-). 1629–1676. Czar of Russia (1645–1676) who approved church reforms and implemented a new code of law that established serfdom (1649).

A·lex·i·us I Com·ne·nus (ə-lĕk′sē-əs; kŏm-nē′nəs). 1048–1118. Emperor of Byzantium (1081–1118) whose reign was marked by the First Crusade (1096–1099).

al·fal·fa (ăl-făl′fə) *n.* A southwest Asian perennial herb *(Medicago sativa)* having compound leaves with three leaflets and clusters of usually blue-violet flowers. It is widely cultivated as a pasture and hay crop. [Spanish, from Arabic *al-fasfaṣah.*]

Al Fay·yam (ăl′ fā-o͞om′, fī-, ĕl′). A city of northern Egypt on the Nile River south-southwest of Cairo. The surrounding area is rich in archaeological remains. Population, 218,500.

Al·fie·ri (ăl-fē-âr′ē, äl-fyâr′ē), Conte **Vittorio.** 1749–1803. Italian playwright whose works, including 19 tragedies, influenced Italian nationalism.

al·fil·a·ri·a or **al·fil·e·ri·a** (ăl-fĭl′ə-rē′ə) *n.* An annual Mediterranean plant *(Erodium cicutarium)* having pinnately dissected leaves and small pink or purple flowers. It is a widespread weed and is used for spring forage in the western United States. Also called *filaree, pin clover.* [American Spanish *alfilerillo,* any of various cacti whose leaves end in sharp points, from Spanish, diminutive of *alfiler,* pin, from Arabic *al-ḫilal,* the thorn : *al,* the + *ḫilal,* thorn.]

Al·föld (ôl′føld) also **Great Alföld.** An extensive plain of central Hungary extending into northern Yugoslavia and western Romania. The **Little Alföld** lies in northwest Hungary and southern Czechoslovakia.

Al·fon·so I (ăl-fŏn′sō, -zō). 1110?–1185. King of Portugal (1139–1185) who won Portuguese independence from Castile (1139) and established a monarchy.

Alfonso V. 1432–1481. King of Portugal (1438–1481) noted for his victories over the Moors in Africa (1458 and 1471).

Alfonso XIII. 1886–1941. King of Spain (1886–1931) who abdicated on the establishment of a republican government and died in exile.

Al·fred (ăl′frĭd). Known as "the Great." 849–899. King of the West Saxons (871–899), scholar, and lawmaker who repelled the Danes and helped consolidate England into a unified kingdom.

al·fres·co (ăl-frĕs′kō) *adv.* In the fresh air; outdoors: *dining alfresco.* **—alfresco** *adj.* Taking place outdoors; outdoor: *an alfresco conference.* [Italian *al fresco,* in the fresh (air) : *a il,* in the + *fresco,* fresh.]

Alf·vén (äl-vän′), **Hannes Olof Gösta.** Born 1908. Swedish physicist. He won a 1970 Nobel Prize for his theories on plasma physics.

alg. *abbr. Mathematics.* Algebra.

Alg. *abbr.* Algeria.

al·ga (ăl′gə) *n., pl.* **-gae** (-jē). Any of various chiefly aquatic, eukaryotic, photosynthetic organisms, ranging in size from single-celled forms to the giant kelp. Algae were once considered to be plants but are now classified separately because they lack true roots, stems, leaves, and embryos. [Latin, seaweed.] **—al′gal** (ăl′gəl) *adj.*

al·gar·ro·ba or **al·ga·ro·ba** (ăl′gə-rō′bə) *n.* **1.** See **mesquite** (sense b). **2.** See **carob** (sense 2). **3.** The edible pod of either the mesquite or the carob tree. [Spanish, from Arabic *al-ḫarrūbah* : *al,* the + *ḫarrūbah,* carob.]

Al·gar·ve (äl-gär′və). A medieval Moorish kingdom in present-day southern Portugal. It was conquered in 1253 by Alfonso III (1210–1279).

al·ge·bra (ăl′jə-brə) *n. Abbr.* **alg.** *Mathematics.* **1.** A generalization of arithmetic in which symbols, usually letters of the alphabet, represent numbers or members of a specified set of numbers and are related by operations that hold for all numbers in the set. **2.** A set together with operations defined in the set that obey specified laws. [Middle English, bone-setting, and Italian, algebra, both from Medieval Latin, from Arabic *al-jabr,* the (science of) reuniting : *al,* the + *jabr,* reunification, bone-setting.] —**al′ge·bra′ist** (-brā′ĭst) *n.*

al·ge·bra·ic (ăl′jə-brā′ĭk) *adj. Mathematics.* **1.** Of, relating to, or designating algebra. **2.** Designating an expression, an equation, or a function in which only numbers, letters, and arithmetic operations are contained or used. **3.** Indicating or restricted to a finite number of operations involving algebra. —**al′ge·bra′i·cal·ly** *adv.*

algebraic language *n.* **1.** *Mathematics.* The conventional method of writing expressions and formulas. **2.** *Computer Science.* A computer language whose statements are designed to resemble algebraic expressions.

algebraic number *n. Mathematics.* A number that is a root of a polynomial equation with rational coefficients.

Al·ge·ci·ras (ăl′jĭ-sîr′əs, äl′hĕ-thĕ′räs). A city of southern Spain on the **Bay of Algeciras** opposite Gibraltar. It is a port and tourist center. Population, 92,474.

Al·ger (ăl′jər), **Horatio.** 1832–1899. American writer of inspirational adventure books, such as *Ragged Dick* (1867), featuring impoverished boys who through hard work and virtue achieve great wealth and respect.

Al·ge·ri·a (ăl-jîr′ē-ə). *Abbr.* **Alg.** A country of northwest Africa bordering on the Mediterranean Sea. Algeria gained its independence from France in 1962 after a long terrorist and guerrilla campaign. Algiers is the capital and the largest city. Population, 16,948,000. —**Al·ge′ri·an** *adj. & n.*

–algia *suff.* Pain: *neuralgia.* [Greek, from *algos,* pain.]

al·gi·cide (ăl′jĭ-sīd′) *n.* A substance used to kill or inhibit the growth of algae. [ALG(A) + –CIDE.]

al·gid (ăl′jĭd) *adj.* Cold; chilly. [Latin *algidus,* from *algēre,* to be cold.] —**al·gid′i·ty** (-jĭd′ĭ-tē) *n.*

Al·giers (ăl-jîrz′). The capital and largest city of Algeria, in the north on the **Bay of Algiers,** an arm of the Mediterranean Sea. An ancient North African port, Algiers was captured by French forces in 1830 and was later a pivotal center of the struggle for Algerian independence. Population, 1,523,000.

al·gin (ăl′jĭn) *n.* Any of several derivatives, such as sodium alginate or alginic acid, of a gelatinous substance extracted from certain brown algae and widely used as a thickening, stabilizing, emulsifying, or suspending agent in industrial, pharmaceutical, and food products, such as ice cream. [ALG(A) + –IN.]

al·gi·nate (ăl′jə-nāt′) *n.* A salt of alginic acid, such as sodium alginate.

al·gin·ic acid (ăl-jĭn′ĭk) *n.* An insoluble colloidal acid in the form of a carboxylated polysaccharide that is abundant in the cell walls of brown algae.

algo– *pref.* Pain: *algophobia.* [From Greek *algos,* pain.]

al·goid (ăl′goid′) *adj.* Of or resembling algae.

Al·gol (ăl′gŏl′, -gôl′) *n.* A double, eclipsing variable star in the constellation Perseus, almost as bright as Polaris. [Arabic *al-ġūl* : *al,* the + *ġūl,* ghoul; see GHOUL.]

AL·GOL also **Algol** (ăl′gŏl′, -gôl′) *n. Computer Science.* An algebraic computer language for solving primarily mathematical and scientific problems using algorithms. [*alg(orithmic) o(riented) l(anguage).*]

al·go·lag·ni·a (ăl′gō-lăg′nē-ə) *n.* Sexual gratification derived from inflicting or experiencing pain. [New Latin : ALGO– + Greek *lagneia,* lust (from *lagnos,* lustful; see **slēg-** in Appendix).] —**al′go·lag′nic** *adj.* —**al′go·lag′nist** *n.*

al·gol·o·gy (ăl-gŏl′ə-jē) *n.* See **phycology.** [ALG(A) + –LOGY.] —**al′go·log′i·cal** (ăl′gə-lŏj′ĭ-kəl) *adj.* —**al′go·log′i·cal·ly** *adv.* —**al·gol′o·gist** *n.*

Al·gon·ki·an (ăl-gŏng′kē-ən) *n., pl.* **Algonkian** or **-ans. 1.** *Geology.* Late Proterozoic. **2.** Variant of **Algonquian.** [After the *Algonkin* Indians. See ALGONQUIN.]

Al·gon·kin (ăl-gŏng′kĭn) *n., pl.* **Algonkin** or **-kins.** Variant of **Algonquin.**

Al·gon·qui·an (ăl-gŏng′kwē-ən, -kē-ən) also **Al·gon·ki·an** (-kē-ən) *n., pl.* **Algonquian** or **-ans** also **Algonkian** or **-ans. 1.** A family of North American Indian languages spoken or formerly spoken in an area from Labrador to the Carolinas between the Atlantic coast and the Rocky Mountains. **2.** A member of a people traditionally speaking an Algonquian language. [From ALGONQUIN.] —**Al·gon′qui·an** *adj.*

Al·gon·quin (ăl-gŏng′kwĭn, -kĭn) also **Al·gon·kin** (-kĭn) *n., pl.* **Algonquin** or **-quins** also **Algonkin** or **-kins. 1.a.** Any of various Native American peoples inhabiting the Ottawa River valley of Quebec and Ontario. **b.** A member of one of these peoples. **2.** Any of the varieties of the Ojibwa language spoken by the peoples called Algonquin. [Canadian French.]

al·go·pho·bi·a (ăl′gə-fō′bē-ə) *n.* An abnormal fear of pain.

al·go·rism (ăl′gə-rĭz′əm) *n.* **1.** The Arabic system of numeration; the decimal system. **2.** Computation with Arabic figures. [Middle English *algorisme,* from Old French, from Medieval Latin *algorismus,* after Muhammad ibn-Musa al- KHWARIZMI.]

al·go·rithm (ăl′gə-rĭth′əm) *n. Mathematics.* A step-by-step problem-solving procedure, especially an established, recursive computational procedure for solving a problem in a finite number of steps. [Variant (probably influenced by ARITHMETIC) of ALGORISM.] —**al′go·rith′mic** (-rĭth′mĭk) *adj.*

algorithmic language *n. Computer Science.* A programming language in which an algorithmic procedure can be expressed accurately.

al·gor mor·tis (ăl′gər môr′tĭs) *n.* The cooling of the body that follows death. [Latin *algor,* coolness + *mortis,* genitive of *mors,* death.]

Al·gren (ôl′grĭn), **Nelson.** 1909–1981. American writer noted for his novels about the pride and longings of impoverished people, including *The Man with the Golden Arm* (1949).

Al·ham·bra[1] (ăl-hăm′brə). A citadel and palace on a hill overlooking Granada, Spain. Built by Moorish kings in the 12th and 13th centuries, the Alhambra is the finest example of Moorish architecture in Spain.

Al·ham·bra[2] (ăl-hăm′brə). A city of southern California, a residential suburb of Los Angeles. Population, 64,615.

Al Hil·lah (ăl hĭl′ə, ĕl). A city of central Iraq on a branch of the Euphrates River south of Baghdad. It was built c. 1100, largely of material salvaged from the nearby ruins of Babylon. Population, 215,249.

A·li (ä-lē′). 600?–661. Moslem caliph (656–661) after whose assassination Islam was divided into Sunnite and Shiite sects.

Ali, Muhammad. Originally Cassius Marcellus Clay. Born 1942. American prizefighter who won the world heavyweight title in 1964, 1974, and 1978.

A·li·ák·mon (äl-yäk′môn, ä′lē-äk′-). A river, about 322 km (200 mi) long, of northern Greece. It is the longest river in the country.

a·li·as (ā′lē-əs, āl′yəs) *n.* **1.** An assumed name: *The swindler worked under various aliases.* **2.** *Electronics.* A false signal in telecommunication links from beats between signal frequency and sampling frequency. —**alias** *adv.* Also known as; otherwise: *Johnson, alias Johns.* [Latin, otherwise, from *alius,* other. See **al-**[1] in Appendix.]

A·li Ba·ba (ä′lē bä′bə, ăl′ē) *n.* A poor woodcutter in the *Arabian Nights* who gains entrance to the treasure cave of the 40 thieves by saying the magic words "Open, Sesame!"

al·i·bi (ăl′ə-bī′) *n., pl.* **-bis. 1.** *Law.* **a.** A form of defense whereby a defendant attempts to prove that he or she was elsewhere when the crime in question was committed. **b.** The fact of having been elsewhere when a crime in question was committed. **2.** *Usage Problem.* An explanation offered to avoid blame or justify action; an excuse. —**alibi** *intr.v.* **-bied, -bi·ing, -bis.** *Usage Problem.* To make an excuse for oneself. [Latin, elsewhere : *alius,* other; see **al-**[1] in Appendix + *ubi,* where; see **kʷo-** in Appendix.]

USAGE NOTE: *Alibi* (noun) in its nonlegal sense of "an excuse" is acceptable in written usage to almost half of the Usage Panel. As an intransitive verb (*they never alibi*), it is unacceptable in written usage to a large majority of the Panel.

al·i·ble (ăl′ə-bəl) *adj.* Having nutrients; nourishing. [Latin *alibilis,* from *alere,* to nourish. See **al-**[2] in Appendix.]

Al·i·can·te (ăl′ĭ-kăn′tē, ä′lē-kän′tě). A city of southeast Spain on the Mediterranean Sea south of Valencia. It is a port and tourist center. Population, 253,722.

Al·ice (ăl′ĭs). A city of southern Texas west of Corpus Christi. It is in a cattle-raising area that includes the enormous King Ranch. Population, 20,961.

Alice Springs. A town of Australia located near the center of the country. Tourism and mining are important to its economy. Population, 22,000.

al·i·cy·clic (ăl′ĭ-sī′klĭk, -sĭk′lĭk) *adj.* Of or relating to organic compounds having both aliphatic and cyclic characteristics or structures. [ALI(PHATIC) + CYCLIC.]

al·i·dade (ăl′ĭ-dād′) also **al·i·dad** (-dăd′) *n.* **1.** An indicator or a sighting apparatus on a plane table, used in angular measurement. **2.** A topographic surveying and mapping instrument used for determining directions, consisting of a telescope and attached parts. [French, from Medieval Latin *alidada,* sighting rod, from Arabic *al-ʿiḍādah,* the revolving radius of a circle, from *ʿaḍud,* humerus.]

a·li·en (ā′lē-ən, āl′yən) *adj.* **1.** Owing political allegiance to another country or government; foreign: *alien residents.* **2.** Belonging to, characteristic of, or constituting another and very different place, society, or person; strange. See Synonyms at **foreign. 3.** Dissimilar, inconsistent, or opposed, as in nature: *emotions alien to her temperament.* See Synonyms at **extrinsic.** —**alien** *n.* **1.** An unnaturalized foreign resident of a country. Also called *noncitizen.* **2.** A person from another and very different family, people, or place. **3.** A person who is not included in a group; an outsider. **4.** A creature from outer space: *science fiction about an invasion of aliens.* **5.** *Ecology.* A plant or an animal that occurs in or is naturalized in a region to which it is not native. —**alien** *tr.v.* **-ened, -en·ing, -ens.** *Law.* To transfer (property) to another; alienate. [Middle English, from Old French, from Latin *aliēnus,* from *alius,* other. See **al-**[1] in Appendix.]

al·ien·a·ble (āl′yə-nə-bəl, ā′lē-ə-) *adj. Law.* Transferrable to the ownership of another. —**al′ien·a·bil′i·ty** *n.*

al·ien·ate (āl′yə-nāt′, ā′lē-ə-) *tr.v.* **-at·ed, -at·ing, -ates. 1.** To cause to become unfriendly or hostile; estrange: *alienate a friend; alienate potential supporters by taking extreme positions.* See Synonyms at **estrange. 2.** To cause to become withdrawn or

alga
Irish moss
Chondrus crispus

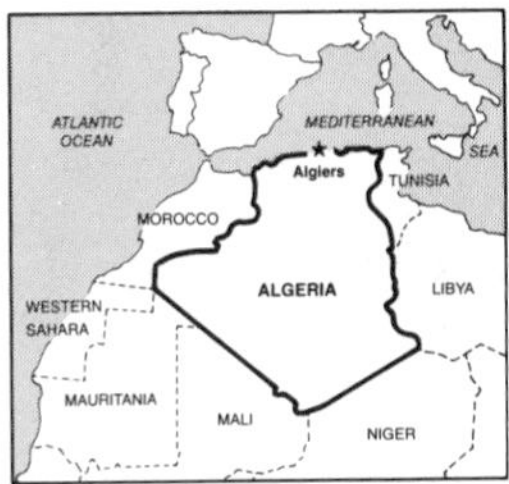

Algeria

Muhammad Ali

ă pat	oi boy
ā pay	ou out
âr care	ŏŏ took
ä father	ōō boot
ĕ pet	ŭ cut
ē be	ûr urge
ĭ pit	th thin
ī pie	*th* this
îr pier	hw which
ŏ pot	zh vision
ō toe	ə about, item
ô paw	♦ regionalism

Stress marks: ′ (primary); ′ (secondary), as in **dictionary** (dĭk′shə-nĕr′ē)

unresponsive; isolate or dissociate emotionally: *The numbing labor tended to alienate workers.* **3.** To cause to be transferred; turn away: *"He succeeded . . . in alienating the affections of my only ward"* (Oscar Wilde). **4.** *Law.* To transfer (property or a right) to the ownership of another, especially by an act of the owner rather than by inheritance. [Latin *aliēnāre, aliēnāt-,* from Latin *aliēnus,* alien. See ALIEN.] **—al'ien·a'tor** *n.*

al·ien·a·tion (āl'yə-nā'shən, ā'lē-ə-) *n.* **1.** The act of alienating or the condition of being alienated; estrangement: *Alcoholism often leads to the alienation of family and friends.* **2.** Emotional isolation or dissociation. **3.** *Psychology.* A state of estrangement between the self and the objective world or between different parts of the personality. **4.** *Law.* The act of transferring property or title to it to another.

al·ien·ee (āl'yə-nē', ā'lē-ə-) *n.* *Law.* One to whom or to which ownership of property is transferred.

al·ien·ist (āl'yə-nĭst, ā'lē-ə-) *n.* *Law.* A physician who has been accepted by a court of law as an expert on the mental competence of principals or witnesses appearing before it. [French *aliéniste,* from *aliéné,* insane, from Latin *aliēnātus,* past participle of *aliēnāre,* to deprive of reason. See ALIENATE.]

al·ien·or (āl'yə-nôr', ā'lē-ə-) *n.* *Law.* One that transfers ownership of property to another.

al·i·es·ter·ase (ăl'ē-ĕs'tə-rās', -rāz') *n.* *Chemistry.* An enzyme contributing to ester-link hydrolysis, particularly in aliphatic esters. [ALI(PHATIC) + ESTERASE.]

a·li·form (ā'lə-fôrm', ăl'ə-) *adj.* *Biology.* Shaped like a wing; alar. [Latin *āla,* wing + -FORM.]

A·li·garh (ăl'ĭ-gär', ä'lē-gŭr'). A city of north-central India southeast of Delhi. It is noted for its university, established in 1875 as Anglo-Oriental College. Population, 320,861.

a·light¹ (ə-līt') *intr.v.* **a·light·ed** or **a·lit** (ə-lĭt'), **a·light·ing, a·lights. 1.** To come down and settle, as after flight: *a sparrow alighting on a branch.* **2.** To set down, as from a vehicle; dismount: *The queen alighted from the carriage.* **3.** To come by chance: *alight on a happy solution.* [Middle English *alighten,* from Old English *ālīhtan* : *ā-,* intensive pref. + *līhtan,* to relieve of a burden (from *līht,* light; see LIGHT²).]

a·light² (ə-līt') *adj.* **1.** Burning; lighted: *The discarded match was still alight.* **2.** Illuminated: *The sky was alight with millions of stars.* [Middle English, past participle of *alighten,* to set on fire, from Old English *ālīhtan,* to illuminate : *ā-,* intensive pref. + *līhtan,* to shine (from *lēoht,* a light; see LIGHT¹).] **—a·light'** *adv.*

a·lign also **a·line** (ə-līn') *—v.* **a·ligned, a·lign·ing, a·ligns** also **a·lined, a·lin·ing, a·lines.** *—tr.* **1.** To arrange in a line or so as to be parallel: *align the tops of a row of pictures; aligned the car with the curb.* **2.** To adjust (parts of a mechanism, for example) to produce a proper relationship or orientation: *aligning the wheels of a truck.* **3.** To ally (oneself, for example) with one side of an argument or cause: *aligned themselves with the free traders.* *—intr.* To fall into line. [French *aligner,* from Old French : *a-,* to (from Latin *ad-;* see AD-) + *ligne,* line (from Latin *līnea;* see LINE¹).] **—a·lign'er** *n.*

a·lign·ment also **a·line·ment** (ə-līn'mənt) *n.* **1.** Arrangement or position in a straight line or in parallel lines. **2. a.** The process of adjusting parts so that they are in proper relative position: *A set of gears needs periodic alignment.* **b.** The condition of having parts so adjusted: *Binocular lenses that are out of alignment will yield a double image.* **3.** A ground plan: *Blueprints for the building included an alignment and a profile.* **4.** The act of aligning or the condition of being aligned.

a·like (ə-līk') *adj.* Having close resemblance; similar: *The twins are as alike as two peas in a pod. Friends are generally alike in background and tastes.* **—alike** *adv.* In the same manner or to the same degree: *They dress and walk alike.* [Middle English *alich* (influenced by Old Norse *ālīkr*), blend of *ilich* (from Old English *gelīc*) and *anlich* (from Old English *onlīc;* see **līk-** in Appendix).] **—a·like'ness** *n.*

al·i·ment (ăl'ə-mənt) *n.* **1.** Something that nourishes; food. **2.** Something that supports or sustains. **—aliment** (-mĕnt') *tr.v.* **-ment·ed, -ment·ing, -ments.** To supply with sustenance, such as food: *required by court order to aliment the abandoned family.* [Middle English, from Latin *alimentum,* from *alere,* to nourish. See **al-²** in Appendix.] **—al'i·men'tal** (-mĕn'tl) *adj.* **—al'i·men'tal·ly** *adv.*

al·i·men·ta·ry (ăl'ə-mĕn'tə-rē, -trē) *adj.* **1.** Concerned with food, nutrition, or digestion. **2.** Providing nourishment.

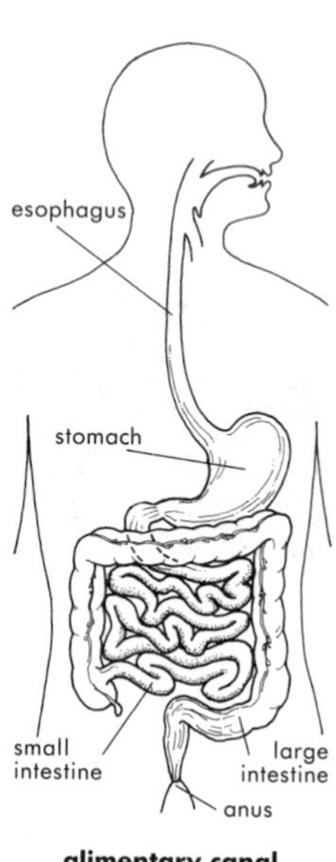

alimentary canal

alimentary canal *n.* The mucous membrane-lined tube of the digestive system through which food passes, in which digestion takes place, and from which wastes are eliminated. It extends from the mouth to the anus and includes the pharynx, esophagus, stomach, and intestines. Also called *digestive tract.*

al·i·men·ta·tion (ăl'ə-mĕn-tā'shən) *n.* **1.** The act or process of giving or receiving nourishment. **2.** Support; sustenance. **—al'i·men'ta·tive** (-tə-tĭv) *adj.*

al·i·mo·ny (ăl'ə-mō'nē) *n., pl.* **-nies. 1.** *Law.* An allowance for support made under court order to a divorced person by the former spouse, usually the chief provider during the marriage. Alimony may also be granted without a divorce, as between legally separated persons. **2.** A means of livelihood; maintenance. [Latin *alimōnia,* sustenance, from *alere,* to nourish. See **al-²** in Appendix.]

a·line (ə-līn') *v.* Variant of **align.**

A-line (ā'līn') *adj.* Having a fitted top and a flared bottom: *an A-line dress.* [From garments being shaped like a capital *A.*]

a·line·ment (ə-līn'mənt) *n.* Variant of **alignment.**

al·i·phat·ic (ăl'ə-făt'ĭk) *adj.* Of, relating to, or designating a group of organic chemical compounds in which the carbon atoms are linked in open chains. [From Greek *aleiphar, aleiphat-,* oil, from *aleiphein,* to anoint with oil. See **leip-** in Appendix.]

Al·i·quip·pa (ăl'ĭ-kwĭp'ə). A borough of western Pennsylvania on the Ohio River northwest of Pittsburgh. It is in a highly industrialized area. Population, 17,094.

al·i·quot (ăl'ĭ-kwŏt', -kwət) *Mathematics. adj.* Of, relating to, or denoting an exact divisor or factor of a quantity, especially of an integer. **—aliquot** *n.* An aliquot part. [Latin *aliquot,* some number : *alius,* some; see **al-¹** in Appendix + *quot,* how many; see **kʷo-** in Appendix.]

A list *n.* *Informal.* The most desirable guests for exclusive parties; the fashionable elite: *Hollywood's A list gathered at a private party.*

a·lit (ə-lĭt') *v.* A past tense and a past participle of **alight¹.**

a·live (ə-līv') *adj.* **1.** Having life; living. See Synonyms at **living. 2.** In existence or operation; active: *keep your hopes alive.* **3.** Full of living or moving things; abounding: *a pool alive with trout.* **4.** Full of activity or animation; lively: *a face alive with mischief.* **—*idiom.* alive to.** Aware of; sensitive to: *alive to the moods of others.* [Middle English : *a-,* in a specified state; see A-² + *live,* life (from Old English *līf;* see LIFE).] **—a·live'ness** *n.*

a·li·yah (ä'lē-ä') *n.* Immigration of Jews into Israel. [Hebrew *'alīyâ,* ascent.]

a·liz·a·rin (ə-lĭz'ər-ĭn) also **a·liz·a·rine** (-ĭn, -ə-rēn') *n.* An orange-red crystalline compound, $C_{14}H_6O_2(OH)_2$, used in making dyes. [French *alizarine,* from French *alizari,* madder root, from Spanish, probably from Arabic *al-'aṣārah,* the juice : *al,* the + *'aṣārah,* juice (from *'aṣara,* to squeeze).]

al·ka·hest (ăl'kə-hĕst') *n.* The hypothetical universal solvent once sought by alchemists. [Medieval Latin *alchahest,* first used by Paracelsus (1493–1541), and said to have been coined by him in imitation of Arabic words.] **—al'ka·hes'tic, al'ka·hes'ti·cal** *adj.*

al·ka·les·cent (ăl'kə-lĕs'ənt) *adj.* Becoming alkaline; slightly alkaline. [ALKAL(I) + -ESCENT.] **—al'ka·les'cence, al'ka·les'cen·cy** *n.*

al·ka·li (ăl'kə-lī') *n., pl.* **-lis** or **-lies.** *Chemistry.* **1.** A carbonate or hydroxide of an alkali metal, the aqueous solution of which is bitter, slippery, caustic, and characteristically basic in reactions. **2.** Any of various soluble mineral salts found in natural water and arid soils. **3.** Alkali metal. [Middle English, alkaline substance from calcined plant ashes, from Medieval Latin, from Arabic *al-qalīy,* the ashes of saltwort : *al,* the + *qalīy,* ashes (from *qalā,* to fry).]

alkali metal *n.* Any of a group of soft, white, low-density, low-melting, highly reactive metallic elements, including lithium, sodium, potassium, rubidium, cesium, and francium.

al·ka·lim·e·ter (ăl'kə-lĭm'ĭ-tər) *n.* An apparatus for measuring alkalinity. **—al'ka·lim'e·try** *n.*

al·ka·line (ăl'kə-lĭn, -līn') *adj.* **1.** Of, relating to, or containing an alkali. **2.** Having a pH greater than 7.

al·ka·line-earth metal (ăl'kə-lĭn-ûrth', -līn'-) *n.* Any of a group of metallic elements, especially calcium, strontium, magnesium, and barium, but generally including beryllium and radium. Also called *alkaline earth.*

al·ka·lin·i·ty (ăl'kə-lĭn'ĭ-tē) *n.* *Abbr.* **alky.** The alkali concentration or alkaline quality of an alkali-containing substance.

al·ka·lize (ăl'kə-līz') also **al·ka·lin·ize** (-lə-nīz') *—v.* **-lized, -liz·ing, -liz·es** also **-ized, -iz·ing, -iz·es.** *—tr.* To make alkaline. *—intr.* To become an alkali. **—al'ka·li·za'tion** (-lĭ-zā'shən) *n.*

al·ka·loid (ăl'kə-loid') *n.* Any of various organic compounds normally with basic chemical properties and usually containing at least one nitrogen atom in a heterocyclic ring, occurring chiefly in many vascular plants and some fungi. Many alkaloids, such as nicotine, quinine, cocaine, and morphine, are known for their poisonous or medicinal attributes. [ALKAL(I) + -OID.] **—al'ka·loid'al** (-loid'l) *adj.*

al·ka·lo·sis (ăl'kə-lō'sĭs) *n.* Abnormally high alkalinity of the blood and body fluids. [ALKAL(I) + -OSIS.] **—al'ka·lot'ic** (-lŏt'ĭk) *adj.*

al·kane (ăl'kān') *n.* Any member of the alkane series. [ALK(YL) + (METH)ANE.]

alkane series *n.* *Chemistry.* A group of saturated open-chain hydrocarbons having the general formula C_nH_{2n+2}, the most abundant of which is methane. Also called *methane series, paraffin series.*

al·ka·net (ăl'kə-nĕt') *n.* **1. a.** A European perennial herb *(Alkanna tinctoria)* having cymes of blue flowers and red roots. **b.** The root of this plant or the red dye extracted from the root. **2.** Any of various hairy plants of the Eurasian genus *Anchusa,* having blue or violet flowers grouped on elongated cymes. [Middle English, from Old Spanish *alcaneta,* diminutive of *alcana,* henna, from Medieval Latin *alchanna,* from Arabic *al-ḥinnā',* the henna : *al,* the + *ḥinnā',* henna.]

al·kene (ăl'kēn') *n.* Any of a series of unsaturated, open-chain hydrocarbons with one or more carbon-carbon double bonds, having the general formula C_nH_{2n}. [ALK(YL) + -ENE.]

al·kine (ăl′kīn′) *n.* Variant of **alkyne.**

Alk·maar (älk′mär′). A town of northern Netherlands north-northwest of Amsterdam. Chartered in 1254, it has a famous cheese market. Population, 83,892.

al·ky (ăl′kē) *n., pl.* **-kies.** *Slang.* An alcoholic: *"Nobody ever admitted we were alkies"* (Dwight Espe). [Shortening and alteration of ALCOHOLIC + –Y[3].]

alky. *abbr.* Alkalinity.

al·kyd (ăl′kĭd) *n.* A widely used durable synthetic resin derived from glycerol and phthalic anhydride. Also called *alkyd resin.* [ALKY(L) + (ACI)D.]

al·kyl (ăl′kəl) *n. Chemistry.* A monovalent radical, such as ethyl or propyl, having the general formula C_nH_{2n+1}. [German *Alkohol,* alcohol (from Medieval Latin *alcohol,* antimony; see ALCOHOL) + –YL.]

al·kyl·ate (ăl′kə-lāt′) *tr.v.* **-at·ed, -at·ing, -ates.** *Chemistry.* To add one or more alkyl groups to (a compound).

al·kyl·a·tion (ăl′kə-lā′shən) *n. Chemistry.* A process in which an alkyl group is added to or substituted in a compound, as in the reaction of alkenes with alkanes to make high-octane fuels.

al·kyne also **al·kine** (ăl′kīn′) *n.* Any of a series of open-chain hydrocarbons with a carbon-carbon triple bond and the general formula C_nH_{2n-2}. [ALKY(L) + –(I)NE[2].]

♦**all** (ôl) *adj.* **1.** Being or representing the entire or total number, amount, or quantity: *All the windows are open. Deal all the cards.* See Synonyms at **whole. 2.** Constituting, being, or representing the total extent or the whole: *all Christendom.* **3.** Being the utmost possible of: *argued the case in all seriousness.* **4.** Every: *got into all manner of trouble.* **5.** Any whatsoever: *beyond all doubt.* **6.** *Pennsylvania.* Finished; used up: *The apples are all.* See Regional Note at **gum band. 7.** *Informal.* Being more than one: *Who all came to the party?* See Regional Note at **you-all.** —**all** *n.* The whole of one's fortune, resources, or energy; everything one has: *The brave defenders gave their all.* —**all** *pron.* **1.** The entire or total number, amount, or quantity; totality: *All of us are sick. All that I have is yours.* **2.** Everyone; everything: *justice for all.* —**all** *adv.* **1.** Wholly; completely: *a room painted all white; directions that were all wrong.* **2.** Each; apiece: *a score of five all.* **3.** So much: *I am all the better for that experience.* —***idioms.* all along.** From the beginning; throughout: *saw through the disguise all along.* **all but.** Nearly; almost: *all but crying with relief.* **all in.** Tired; exhausted. **all in all.** Everything being taken into account: *All in all, the criticism seemed fair.* **all of.** *Informal.* Not more than: *a conversation that took all of five minutes.* **all that.** *Informal.* To the degree expected. **at all. 1.** In any way: *unable to walk at all.* **2.** To any extent; whatever: *not at all sorry.* [Middle English *al,* from Old English *eall.* See **al-**[3] in Appendix.]

USAGE NOTE: The construction *all that* is used informally in questions and negative sentences to mean "to the degree expected," as in *I know it won an Oscar, but the film is not all that exciting.* In an earlier survey, the Usage Panel rejected the use of this construction in formal writing. • Sentences of the form *All X's are not Y* may be ambiguous. *All of the departments did not file a report* may mean that some departments did not file, or that none did. If the first meaning is intended, it can be unambiguously expressed by the sentence *Not all of the departments filed a report.* If the second meaning is intended, a paraphrase such as *None of the departments filed a report* or *All of the departments failed to file a report* can be used. Note that the same problem can arise with other universal terms like *every* in negated sentences, as in the ambiguous *Every department did not file a report.* See Usage Note at **every.**

all– *pref.* Variant of **allo–.**

al·la breve (ăl′ə brĕv′, ä′lə brĕv′ā) *adv. & adj. Music.* In duple or quadruple meter with the half note being the unit of time. [Italian : *alla,* according to the + *breve,* breve.]

Al·lah (ăl′ə, ä′lə) *n.* God, especially in Islam. [Arabic *Allāh.*]

Al·la·ha·bad (ăl′ə-hə-băd′, ä′lə-hə-bäd′). A city of north-central India at the junction of the Jumna and Ganges rivers east of Varanasi. It was built on the site of an ancient Indo-Aryan holy city and is still a pilgrimage site for Hindus. Population, 616,051.

Al·lais (ä-lā′), **Maurice.** Born 1911. French economist. He won a 1988 Nobel Prize for his theories of market behavior and the efficient use of resources.

al·la·man·da (ăl′ə-măn′də) *n.* Any of several tropical American evergreen shrubs of the genus *Allamanda,* widely cultivated in warm regions for their showy yellow or purple trumpet-shaped flowers. [New Latin *Allamanda,* genus name, after Jean Nicholas Sébastian *Allamand* (1713–1787), Swiss scientist.]

all-A·mer·i·can (ôl′ə-mĕr′ĭ-kən) *adj.* **1.** Representative of the people of the United States or their ideals; typically American: *an all-American family; their all-American generosity.* **2.** *Sports.* Chosen as the best amateur in the United States at a particular position or event: *an all-American fullback.* **3.** Composed entirely of Americans or American materials: *an all-American negotiating team; cars of all-American manufacture.* **4.** Of all the American nations: *an all-American conference.* —**all-American** *n.* Often **All-American.** An all-American athlete.

al·lan·toid (ə-lăn′toid′) also **al·lan·toid·al** (ăl′ən-toid′l) —*adj.* **1.** Of or having an allantois. **2.** Shaped like a sausage. —*n.* See **allantois.** [New Latin *allantoīdes.* See ALLANTOIS.]

al·lan·to·in (ə-lăn′tō-ĭn) *n.* A white, crystalline oxidation product, $C_4H_6N_4O_3$, of uric acid that is the metabolic end product of vertebrate purine oxidation and is used medicinally to promote tissue growth. [ALLANTO(IS) + –IN.]

al·lan·to·is (ə-lăn′tō-ĭs) *n., pl.* **al·lan·to·i·des** (ăl′ən-tō′ĭ-dēz′). A membranous sac that develops from the posterior part of the alimentary canal in the embryos of mammals, birds, and reptiles. It is important in the formation of the umbilical cord and placenta in mammals. Also called *allantoid.* [New Latin, from *allantoīdes,* from Greek *allantoeidēs,* sausage-shaped : *allas, allant-,* sausage + *-oeidēs,* -oid.] —**al′lan·to′ic** (ăl′ən-tō′ĭk) *adj.*

al·lar·gan·do (ä′lär-gän′dō) *adv. & adj. Music.* In a gradually broadening style and slowing tempo. Used chiefly as a direction. [Italian, present participle of *allargare,* to broaden : *al-,* to (from Latin *ad-;* see AD–) + *largare,* to broaden (from *largo,* broad, from Latin *largus*).]

all-a·round (ôl′ə-round′) also **all-round** (ôl′round′) *adj.* **1.** Comprehensive in extent or depth: *a good all-around education.* **2.** Able to do many things well; versatile: *an all-around athlete.* See Synonyms at **versatile.**

al·lay (ə-lā′) *tr.v.* **-layed, -lay·ing, -lays. 1.** To reduce the intensity of; relieve. See Synonyms at **relieve. 2.** To calm or pacify; set to rest: *allayed the fears of the worried citizens.* [Middle English *aleien,* from Old English *ālecgan,* to lay down : *ā-,* intensive pref. + *lecgan,* to lay; see LAY[1].] —**al·lay′er** *n.*

all clear *n.* A signal, usually by siren, that an air raid is over or a danger has passed.

al·le·ga·tion (ăl′ĭ-gā′shən) *n.* **1.** Something alleged; an assertion: *allegations of disloyalty.* **2.** The act of alleging. **3.** A statement asserting something without proof: *The newspaper's charges of official wrongdoing were mere allegations.* **4.** *Law.* An assertion made by a party that must be proved or supported with evidence. [French *allégation,* from Latin *allēgātiō, allēgātiōn-,* from *allēgātus,* past participle of *allēgāre,* to dispatch, adduce : *ad-,* ad- + *lēgāre,* to depute; see LEGATE.]

al·lege (ə-lĕj′) *tr.v.* **-leged, -leg·ing, -leg·es. 1.** To assert to be true; affirm: *alleging his innocence of the charge.* **2.** To assert without or before proof: *The indictment alleges that the commissioner took bribes.* **3.** To state (a plea or excuse, for example) in support or denial of a claim or accusation: *The defendant alleges temporary insanity.* **4.** *Archaic.* To bring forward as an authority. [Middle English *alleggen,* from Old French *alegier,* to vindicate, justify (influenced by *aleguer,* to give a reason), from *esligier,* to pay a fine, justify oneself, from Late Latin **exlītigāre,* to clear at law : Latin *ex-,* out; see EX– + Latin *lītigāre,* to sue; see LITIGATE.] —**al·lege′a·ble** *adj.* —**al·leg′er** *n.*

al·leged (ə-lĕjd′, ə-lĕj′ĭd) *adj.* Represented as existing or as being as described but not so proved; supposed. —**al·leg′ed·ly** (ə-lĕj′ĭd-lē) *adv.*

USAGE NOTE: An *alleged* burglar is someone who has been accused of being a burglar but against whom no charges have been proved. An *alleged* incident is an event that is said to have taken place but has not yet been verified. In their zeal to protect the rights of the accused, newspapers and law enforcement officials sometimes misuse *alleged.* A man arrested for murder may be only an *alleged* murderer, for example, but he is a real, not an *alleged,* suspect in that his status as a suspect is not in doubt. Similarly, if the money from a safe is known to have been stolen and not merely mislaid, then we may safely speak of a theft without having to qualify our description with *alleged.*

Al·le·ghe·ny Mountains (ăl′ĭ-gā′nē) also **Al·le·ghe·nies** (-nēz). A mountain range forming the western part of the Appalachian Mountains. The range extends about 805 km (500 mi) from northern Pennsylvania to southwest Virginia and rises to approximately 1,483 m (4,862 ft) in northeast West Virginia.

Allegheny River. A river rising in north-central Pennsylvania and flowing about 523 km (325 mi) northwest into New York then southwest into Pennsylvania again, where it joins the Monongahela River at Pittsburgh to form the Ohio River.

Allegheny spurge *n.* A perennial herb *(Pachysandra procumbens),* native to the southeast United States and sometimes grown as an ornamental or ground cover for its usually mottled leaves. [After the ALLEGHENY (MOUNTAINS).]

al·le·giance (ə-lē′jəns) *n.* **1.** Loyalty or the obligation of loyalty, as to a nation, sovereign, or cause. See Synonyms at **fidelity. 2.** The obligations of a vassal to a lord. [Middle English *alligeaunce,* alteration of *ligeaunce,* from Old French *ligeance,* from *lige,* liege. See LIEGE.] —**al·le′giant** *adj.*

al·le·gor·i·cal (ăl′ĭ-gôr′ĭkəl, -gŏr′-) also **al·le·gor·ic** (-ĭk) *adj.* Of, characteristic of, or containing allegory: *an allegorical painting of Victory leading an army.* —**al′le·gor′i·cal·ly** *adv.*

al·le·go·rize (ăl′ĭ-gô-rīz′, -gō-, -gə-) *v.* **-rized, -riz·ing, -riz·es.** —*tr.* **1.** To express as or in the form of an allegory: *a story of barnyard animals that allegorizes the fate of Soviet socialism.* **2.** To interpret allegorically: *allegorize the quest for the Holy Grail as an inner spiritual search.* —*intr.* To use or make allegory: *sculptors who rendered the moral world by allegorizing.* —**al′le·go′ri·za′tion** (-gôr′ĭ-zā′shən, -gōr′, -gŏr′) *n.* —**al′le·go·riz′er** *n.*

al·le·go·ry (ăl′ĭ-gôr′ē, -gōr′ē) *n., pl.* **-ries. 1.a.** A literary, dramatic, or pictorial device in which characters and events stand for abstract ideas, principles, or forces, so that the literal sense

ă pat	oi boy
ā pay	ou out
âr care	ŏŏ took
ä father	ōō boot
ĕ pet	ŭ cut
ē be	ûr urge
ĭ pit	th thin
ī pie	*th* this
îr pier	hw which
ŏ pot	zh vision
ō toe	ə about, item
ô paw	♦ regionalism

Stress marks: ′ (primary); ′ (secondary), as in **dictionary** (dĭk′shə-nĕr′ē)

has or suggests a parallel, deeper symbolic sense. **b.** A story, picture, or play in which this device is used. John Bunyan's *Pilgrim's Progress* and Herman Melville's *Moby Dick* are allegories. **2.** A symbolic representation: *The blindfolded figure with scales is an allegory of justice.* [Middle English *allegorie,* from Latin *allēgoria,* from Greek, from *allēgorein,* to interpret allegorically : *allos,* other; see **al-**[1] in Appendix + *agoreuein,* to speak publicly (from *agora,* marketplace; see **ger-** in Appendix).] **—al′le·go′rist** *n.*

Gracie Allen

al·le·gret·to (ăl′ĭ-grĕt′ō, ä′lĭ-) *Music. adv. & adj.* In a moderately quick tempo, usually considered to be slightly slower than allegro but faster than andante. Used chiefly as a direction. **—allegretto** *n., pl.* **-tos.** An allegretto passage or movement. [Italian, diminutive of *allegro,* allegro. See ALLEGRO.]

al·le·gro (ə-lĕg′rō, ə-lā′grō) *Music. adv. & adj. Abbr.* **allo** In a quick, lively tempo, usually considered to be faster than allegretto but slower than presto. Used chiefly as a direction. **—allegro** *n., pl.* **-gros.** *Abbr.* **allo** An allegro passage or movement. [Italian, from Latin *alacer,* lively.]

al·lele (ə-lēl′) *n.* One member of a pair or series of genes that occupy a specific position on a specific chromosome. [German *Allel,* short for *Allelomorph,* allelomorph. See ALLELOMORPH.] **—al·le′lic** (ə-lē′lĭk, ə-lĕl′ĭk) *adj.* **—al·le′lism** *n.*

al·le·lo·morph (ə-lē′lə-môrf′, ə-lĕl′ə-) *n.* An allele. [Greek *allēlōn,* mutually (from *allos,* other; see **al-**[1] in Appendix) + -MORPH.] **—al·le′lo·mor′phic** *adj.* **—al·le′lo·mor′phism′** *n.*

al·le·lop·a·thy (ə-lē-lŏp′ə-thē, ăl′ə-) *n.* The inhibition of growth in one species of plants by chemicals produced by another species. [Greek *allēlōn,* reciprocally (from *allos,* another; see **al-**[1] in Appendix) + -PATHY.] **—al·le′lo·path′ic** (ə-lē′lə-păth′ĭk, ə-lĕl′ə-) *adj.*

al·le·lu·ia (ăl′ə-lo͞o′yə) *interj.* Hallelujah. [Middle English, from Medieval Latin *alleluia,* from Late Greek *allelouia,* from Hebrew *hallĕlûyāh,* praise the Lord. See HALLELUJAH.]

al·le·mande (ăl′ə-mănd′, -mänd′, ăl′ə-mănd′, -mänd′) *n.* **1.a.** A stately 16th-century dance in 2/2 time. **b.** *Music.* A composition written to or as if to accompany this dance, often used as the first movement of a suite. **2.** A lively, late 18th-century dance in 3/4 time. [French, feminine of *allemand,* German, from Latin *Alemanni,* an ancient Germanic tribe. See ALEMANNI.]

Woody Allen
Photographed in 1987

Al·len (ăl′ən), **Ethan.** 1738–1789. American Revolutionary soldier whose troops, the Green Mountain Boys, helped capture Fort Ticonderoga from the British (1775).

Allen, Fred. 1894–1956. American humorist famous for his dry, satirical work in vaudeville, radio, and early television.

Allen, Frederick Lewis. 1890–1954. American editor and historian noted for his editorship of *Harper's* (1941–1953) and his books of social history, including *The Big Change* (1952).

Allen, Grace Ethel Cecile Rosalie. Known as "Gracie." 1906–1964. American comedienne best remembered as the confused but unflappable foil to her husband and stage partner, George Burns.

Allen, Richard. 1760–1831. American religious leader and the first bishop of the African Methodist Episcopal Church (1816–1831).

Allen, William. 1532–1594. English Roman Catholic cardinal who directed the work on the Douay Bible.

Allen, Woody. Born 1935. American comic actor, writer, and filmmaker whose films include *Annie Hall* (1977), which won two Academy Awards.

Al·len·by (ăl′ən-bē), First Viscount. Title of Edmund Henry Hynman. 1861–1936. British field marshal noted for his military successes in the Middle East during World War I.

Al·len·de Gos·sens (ä-yĕn′dā gô′sĕns), **Salvador.** 1908–1973. Chilean politician who as president (1970–1973) was considered the first democratically elected Marxist head of government. He was killed in a coup d'état.

alligator
American alligator
Alligator mississipiensis

Allen Park. A city of southeast Michigan, a suburb of Detroit. Population, 34,196.

Al·len·ti·ac (ə-lĕn′tē-ăk′) *n., pl.* **Allentiac** or **-acs. 1.** A member of a South American Indian people inhabiting west-central Argentina. **2.** The extinct language of the Allentiac. [Spanish *alentiaco.*] **—Al·len′ti·ac′** *adj.*

Al·len·town (ăl′ən-toun′). A city of eastern Pennsylvania north-northwest of Philadelphia. Founded in 1762, the city is an industrial and commercial center. Population, 103,758.

al·ler·gen (ăl′ər-jən) *n.* A substance, such as pollen, that causes an allergy. [German *Allergen* : *Allergie,* allergy; see ALLERGY + *-gen,* -gen.] **—al′ler·gen′ic** (-jĕn′ĭk) *adj.*

al·ler·gic (ə-lûr′jĭk) *adj.* **1.** Of, characterized by, or caused by an allergy: *an allergic reaction to airborne pollen.* **2.** Having an allergy: *allergic children; highly allergic to penicillin.* **3.** *Informal.* Having a dislike; averse: *allergic to work.*

al·ler·gist (ăl′ər-jĭst) *n.* A physician specializing in the diagnosis and treatment of allergies.

al·ler·gy (ăl′ər-jē) *n., pl.* **-gies. 1.** An abnormally high sensitivity to certain substances, such as pollens, foods, or microorganisms. Common indications of allergy may include sneezing, itching, and skin rashes. **2.** *Informal.* An adverse sentiment; antipathy: *an allergy to cocktail parties.* [German *Allergie* : Greek *allos,* other; see ALLO- + Greek *ergon,* action; see **werg-** in Appendix.]

al·le·thrin (ăl′ə-thrĭn′) *n.* A synthetic clear or amber-colored viscous insecticide, $C_{19}H_{26}O_3$, similar to pyrethrin. [ALL(YL) + (PYR)ETHRIN.]

al·le·vi·ate (ə-lē′vē-āt′) *tr.v.* **-at·ed, -at·ing, -ates.** To make (pain, for example) more bearable: *a drug that alleviates cold symptoms.* See Synonyms at **relieve.** [Late Latin *alleviāre, alleviāt-,* to lighten : Latin *ad-,* ad- + *levis,* light; see **legʷh-** in Appendix.] **—al·le′vi·a′tion** *n.* **—al·le′vi·a′tor** *n.*

al·le·vi·a·tive (ə-lē′vē-ā′tĭv) also **al·le·vi·a·to·ry** (-ə-tôr′ē, -tōr′ē) *adj.* Reducing pain or severity; palliative: *alleviative treatment for an incurable disease.*

al·ley[1] (ăl′ē) *n., pl.* **-leys. 1.** A narrow street or passageway between or behind city buildings. **2.** A path between flower beds or trees in a garden or park. **3.** A straight, narrow course or track; a lane: *an alley for lawn bowling.* **4.** *Sports.* Either of the parallel lanes at the sides of a tennis court, which widen the inbounds area for doubles play. **—*idiom.* up (one's) alley.** *Informal.* Compatible with one's interests or qualifications: *an assignment that is right up your alley.* [Middle English *alei,* from Old French *alee,* from *aller,* to walk, from Latin *ambulāre.* See AMBULATE.]

al·ley[2] (ăl′ē) *n., pl.* **-leys.** *Games.* A large playing marble, often used as the shooter. [Short for ALABASTER.]

alley cat *n.* A homeless or stray cat.

alley crop·ping (krŏp′ĭng) *n.* A method of planting in which rows of a crop are sown between rows or hedges of nitrogen-fixing plants, the roots of which enrich the soil.

alley light *n.* A searchlight mounted on the side or top of a police patrol car or other such motor vehicle, used for sideways illumination.

al·ley·way (ăl′ē-wā′) *n.* A narrow passage between buildings.

all-fired (ôl′fīrd′) *adv. Informal.* Used as an intensive: *Don't be so all-fired aggressive.* [Alteration of *hell-fired.*]

All Fools' Day (fo͞olz) *n.* See **April Fools' Day.**

all fours *pl.n. (used with a sing. verb). Games.* Any of several card games resembling whist and in which points are scored in four ways: for the high trump, the low trump, the jack of trumps, and the game.

all get-out also **all get out** (gĕt′out′) *n. Informal.* The utmost degree that is possible or even imaginable: *"It's snowing like all get-out up here"* (Hans Thorner).

all hail *interj.* Used to express acclamation, a welcome, or a greeting.

All·hal·low·mas (ôl′hăl′ō-məs) *n. Archaic.* **1.** All Saints' Day. **2.** The feast observed on All Saints' Day. [Middle English *Alhalwemesse,* from Old English *ealra hālgena mæsse* : *ealra,* genitive pl. of *eall,* all; see ALL + *hālgena,* genitive pl. of *hālga,* saint (from *hālig,* holy; see HOLY) + *mæsse,* Mass; see MASS.]

All·hal·lows (ôl′hăl′ōz) *n.* See **All Saints' Day.** [Middle English *al halwes* : *al,* all; see ALL + *halwes,* pl. of *halwe,* saint; see ALLHALLOWMAS.]

all-heal or **all·heal** (ôl′hēl′) *n.* Any of several plants, such as the self-heal or the valerian, once thought to have broad healing powers.

al·li·a·ceous (ăl′ē-ā′shəs) *adj.* Of or resembling onion, garlic, or similar plants of the genus *Allium,* particularly in taste and smell. [Latin *allium,* garlic + -ACEOUS.]

al·li·ance (ə-lī′əns) *n.* **1.a.** A close association of nations or other groups, formed to advance common interests or causes: *an alliance of labor unions opposing the bill.* **b.** A formal agreement establishing such an association, especially an international treaty of friendship. **2.** A connection based on kinship, marriage, or common interest; a bond or tie: *the shifting alliances within a large family.* **3.** Close similarity in nature or type; affinity: *the ancient alliance between mathematics and music.* **4.** The act of becoming allied or the condition of being allied: *the church, acting in alliance with community groups.* [Middle English, from Old French *aliance,* from *alier,* to ally. See ALLY.]

Al·li·ance (ə-lī′əns). A city of northeast Ohio southwest of Youngstown. It was settled by Quakers in 1805. Population, 24,315.

al·lied (ə-līd′, ăl′īd′) *adj.* **1.** Joined or united in a close relationship: *allied tribes.* **2.** Of a similar nature; related: *city planning and allied studies.* **3. Allied.** Of or relating to the Allies: *the Allied invasion of southern Italy.*

Al·lier (ä-lyā′). A river rising in south-central France and flowing about 410 km (255 mi) northward past Vichy to the Loire River.

al·li·ga·tor (ăl′ĭ-gā′tər) *n.* **1.** Either of two large reptiles, *Alligator mississipiensis* of the southeast United States or *A. sinensis* of China, having sharp teeth and powerful jaws. They differ from crocodiles in having a broader, shorter snout. **2.** Leather made from the hide of one of these reptiles. **3.** A tool or fastener having strong, adjustable, often toothed jaws. **—*attributive.*** Often used to modify another noun: *an alligator pond; an alligator handbag.* [Alteration of Spanish *el lagarto,* the lizard : *el,* the (from Latin *ille,* that; see **al-**[1] in Appendix) + *lagarto,* lizard (from Latin *lacertus*).]

WORD HISTORY: In *The Travailes of an Englishman,* published in 1568, Job Hortop says that "in this river we killed a monstrous Lagarto or Crocodile." This killing gives rise to the first recorded instance of *alligator* in English, obviously in a different form from the one familiar to modern speakers. *Alligator,* which comes to us from Spanish *el lagarto,* "the lizard," was modified in pronunciation and form in several ways before taking on the form *alligator.* Such changes, referred to by linguists as taboo deformation, are not uncommon in a name for something that is feared and include, for example, the change in sequence of the *r* and *t* that occurred between *el lagarto* and *alligator.* An interesting parallel case is *crocodile,* which appears in Spanish, for example, as *cocodrilo,* with a similar difference in the sequence of the *r.* The earliest recorded form of *alligator* that is similar to ours appears in Shakespeare's *Romeo and Juliet* (First Folio, 1623): "In his needie shop a tortoyrs hung,/An Allegater stuft."

al·li·ga·tor·ing (ăl′ĭ-gā′tər-ĭng) *n.* The formation of cracks on the surface of paint layers. [From the resemblance of the cracks to the pattern of an alligator's scales.]

alligator pear *n.* See **avocado** (sense 1). [By folk etymology from American Spanish *aguacate,* avocado (the trees are said to grow in areas infested by alligators). See AGUACATE.]

alligator snapping turtle *n.* A large freshwater snapping turtle *(Macrochelys temmincki)* of the south-central United States, having a rough carapace and powerful hooked jaws. Also called *alligator snapper.*

alligator weed *n.* An aquatic South American perennial plant *(Alternanthera philoxeroides)* having opposite, lance-shaped leaves and tight clusters of small whitish flowers. It is a mat-forming weed in warm, freshwater habitats, such as the southeast United States.

all-im·por·tant (ôl′ĭm-pôr′tnt) *adj.* Of the greatest importance; crucial. **—all′-im·por′tance** *n.*

all-in·clu·sive (ôl′in-klo͞o′sĭv) *adj.* Including everything; comprehensive.

al·lit·er·ate (ə-lĭt′ə-rāt′) *v.* **-at·ed, -at·ing, -ates.** *—intr.* **1.** To use alliteration in speech or writing. **2.** To have or contain alliteration. *—tr.* To form or arrange with alliteration. [Back-formation from ALLITERATION.]

al·lit·er·a·tion (ə-lĭt′ə-rā′shən) *n.* The repetition of the same consonant sounds or of different vowel sounds at the beginning of words or in stressed syllables, as in *"on scrolls of silver snowy sentences"* (Hart Crane). [From AD– + Latin *littera,* letter.]

al·lit·er·a·tive (ə-lĭt′ə-rā′tĭv, -ər-ə-) *adj.* Of, showing, or characterized by alliteration. **—al·lit′er·a′tive·ly** *adv.* **—al·lit′er·a′tive·ness** *n.*

al·li·um (ăl′ē-əm) *n.* Any of numerous, usually bulbous plants of the genus *Allium* in the lily family, having long stalks bearing clusters of variously colored flowers and including many ornamental and food plants, such as onions, leeks, chives, garlic, and shallots. [Latin *allium,* garlic.]

all-night (ôl′nīt′) *adj.* **1.** Continuing all through the night: *an all-night party.* **2.** Open all during the night: *an all-night diner.*

all night·er or **all-night·er** (ôl′nī′tər) *n. Informal.* A project or event lasting all through the night.

allo *abbr.* Allegro.

allo– or **all–** *pref.* **1.** Other; different: *allopatric.* **2.** Isomeric: *allocholesterol.* [Greek, from *allos,* other. See **al-**[1] in Appendix.]

al·lo·an·ti·bod·y (ăl′ō-ăn′tĭ-bŏd′ē) *n.* See **isoantibody.**

al·lo·an·ti·gen (ăl′ō-ăn′tĭ-jən) *n.* See **isoantigen.**

al·lo·cate (ăl′ə-kāt′) *tr.v.* **-cat·ed, -cat·ing, -cates. 1.** To set apart for a special purpose; designate: *allocate a room to be used for storage.* **2.** To distribute according to a plan; allot: *allocate rations for a week-long camping trip.* [Medieval Latin *allocāre, allocāt-* : Latin *ad-,* ad- + Latin *locāre,* to place (from *locus,* place).] **—al′lo·ca·ble** (-kə-bəl) *adj.* **—al′lo·ca′tion** *n.*

SYNONYMS: *allocate, appropriate, designate, earmark.* The central meaning shared by these verbs is "to set aside for a specified purpose": *allocated time for recreation; appropriated funds for public education; designated a location for the new hospital; money earmarked for a vacation.* See also Synonyms at **assign.**

al·lo·cu·tion (ăl′ə-kyo͞o′shən) *n.* A formal and authoritative speech; an address. [Latin *allocūtiō, allocūtiōn-,* from *allocūtus,* past participle of *alloquī,* to speak to : *ad-,* ad- + *loquī,* to speak; see **tolkʷ-** in Appendix.]

al·log·a·my (ə-lŏg′ə-mē) *n. Biology.* See **cross-fertilization** (sense 1).

al·lo·ge·ne·ic (ăl′ə-jə-nē′ĭk) also **al·lo·gen·ic** (-jĕn′ĭk) *adj.* Being genetically different although belonging to or obtained from the same species: *allogeneic tissue grafts.* [ALLO– + Greek *genea,* race; see **gene-** in Appendix + –IC.]

al·lo·graft (ăl′ə-grăft′) *n.* A graft of tissue obtained from a donor genetically different from, though of the same species as the recipient. Also called *homograft.*

al·lo·graph (ăl′ə-grăf′) *n.* **1.** A variant shape of a letter. **2.** A letter or combination of letters that can represent one phoneme, as *f* and *gh* can represent the phoneme /f/. **3.** Writing, especially a signature, made by one person for another.

al·lom·er·ism (ə-lŏm′ə-rĭz′əm) *n.* Consistency in crystalline form with variation in chemical composition. **—al·lom′er·ous** *adj.*

al·lom·e·try (ə-lŏm′ĭ-trē) *n.* The study of the change in proportion of various parts of an organism as a consequence of growth. **—al′lo·met′ric** (ăl′ə-mĕt′rĭk) *adj.*

al·lo·morph[1] (ăl′ə-môrf′) *n.* See **paramorph. —al′lo·mor′phic** *adj.* **—al′lo·mor′phism** *n.*

al·lo·morph[2] (ăl′ə-môrf′) *n.* Any of the variant forms of a morpheme. For example, the phonetic *s* of *cats, z* of *dogs,* and *ĭz* of *horses* and the *en* of *oxen* are allomorphs of the English plural morpheme. [ALLO– + MORPH(EME).] **—al′lo·mor′phic** *adj.* **—al′lo·mor′phism** *n.*

al·lo·nym (ăl′ə-nĭm′) *n.* The name of a person, usually a historical person, assumed by a writer. [French *allonyme* : Greek *allos,* other; see ALLO– + Greek *onoma,* name; see ONOMATOPOEIA.] **—al·lon′y·mous** (ə-lŏn′ə-məs) *adj.* **—al·lon′y·mous·ly** *adv.*

al·lo·path (ăl′ə-păth′) also **al·lop·a·thist** (ə-lŏp′ə-thĭst) *n.* One who practices or advocates allopathy.

al·lop·a·thy (ə-lŏp′ə-thē) *n.* A method of treating disease with remedies that produce effects different from those caused by the disease itself. [German *Allopathie* : Greek *allos,* other; see ALLO– + Greek *patheia,* suffering; see –PATHY.] **—al′lo·path′ic** (ăl′ə-păth′ĭk) *adj.* **—al′lo·path′i·cal·ly** *adv.*

al·lo·pat·ric (ăl′ə-păt′rĭk) *adj. Ecology.* Occurring in separate, nonoverlapping geographic areas. Often used of populations of related organisms unable to crossbreed because of geographic separation. [ALLO– + Greek *patra,* fatherland (from *patēr,* father; see **pəter-** in Appendix) + –IC.] **—al′lo·pat′ri·cal·ly** *adv.* **—al·lop′a·try** (ə-lŏp′ə-trē) *n.*

al·lo·phane (ăl′ə-fān′) *n.* An amorphous, translucent, variously colored mineral, essentially hydrous aluminum silicate. [From Greek *allophanēs,* appearing otherwise : *allos,* other; see ALLO– + *phainesthai,* to appear, passive of *phainein,* to show; see FANTASY.]

al·lo·phone (ăl′ə-fōn′) *n. Linguistics.* A predictable phonetic variant of a phoneme. For example, the aspirated *t* of *top,* the unaspirated *t* of *stop,* and the *tt* (pronounced *d*) of *batter* are allophones of the English phoneme *t.* [ALLO– + PHONE(ME).] **—al′lo·phon′ic** (-fŏn′ĭk) *adj.*

al·lo·pol·y·ploid (ăl′ə-pŏl′ē-ploid′) *adj.* Having three or more complete sets of chromosomes derived from different species. **—allopolyploid** *n.* An organism with three or more complete sets of chromosomes derived from different species. **—al′lo·pol′y·ploi′dy** *n.*

al·lo·pu·ri·nol (ăl′ō-pyo͝or′ə-nôl′, -nōl′, -nŏl′) *n.* A drug, $C_5H_4N_4O$, used to treat gout because it promotes the excretion of uric acid. [ALLO– + PURIN(E) + –OL[2].]

all-or-none (ôl′ər-nŭn′) *adj.* Characterized by either a complete response or by a total lack of response or effect, as in neurological action above a threshold: *"Nerve impulses follow the All or None Law—that is, a nerve impulse generated by a weak stimulus is just as strong as one generated by a strong stimulus"* (Fundamentals of Biology).

all-or-noth·ing (ôl′ər-nŭth′ĭng) *adj.* **1.** Involving either complete success or failure, with no intermediate result: *"Downhill races are all-or-nothing events, decided on the basis of one run"* (Neil Amdur). **2.** Refusing to accept less than all demands; uncompromising: *an all-or-nothing negotiating position.*

al·lo·ster·ic (ăl′ə-stĕr′ĭk) *adj.* Of or involving molecular binding to an enzyme at a site other than the enzymatically active one. **—al′lo·ster′i·cal·ly** *adv.* **—al·los′ter·y** (ə-lŏs′tə-rē) *n.*

al·lot (ə-lŏt′) *tr.v.* **-lot·ted, -lot·ting, -lots. 1.** To parcel out; distribute or apportion: *allotting land to homesteaders; allot blame.* **2.** To assign as a portion; allocate: *allotted 20 minutes to each speaker.* See Synonyms at **assign.** [Middle English *alotten,* from Old French *aloter* : *a-,* to (from Latin *ad-;* see AD–) + *lot,* portion (of Germanic origin).] **—al·lot′ter** *n.*

al·lot·ment (ə-lŏt′mənt) *n.* **1.** The act of allotting: *the allotment of ration coupons.* **2.** Something allotted: *The sailors drank their daily allotment of rum.* **3.** A portion of military pay that is regularly deducted and set aside, as for the payee's dependents or for insurance.

al·lo·trans·plant (ăl′ō-trăns′plănt′) *tr.v.* **-plant·ed, -plant·ing, -plants.** To transfer (an organ or body tissue) between two genetically different individuals belonging to the same species. **—allotransplant** *n.* An organ or tissue transferred between genetically different individuals of the same species. **—al′lo·trans′plan·ta′tion** *n.*

al·lo·trope (ăl′ə-trōp′) *n.* A structurally differentiated form of an element that exhibits allotropy. [Back-formation from ALLOTROPY.]

al·lot·ro·py (ə-lŏt′rə-pē) *n.* The existence, especially in the solid state, of two or more crystalline or molecular structural forms of an element. **—al′lo·trop′ic** (ăl′ə-trŏp′ĭk, -trō′pĭk), **al′lo·trop′i·cal** *adj.* **—al′lo·trop′i·cal·ly** *adv.*

all′ ot·ta·va (äl′ə-tä′və, äl′ō-) *adv. & adj. Music.* Ottava. [Italian : *all',* at the + *ottava,* octave.]

al·lot·tee (ə-lŏt′ē′) *n.* One to whom something is allotted.

all out *adv.* With every possible effort: *worked all out to make the deadline.*

all-out (ôl′out′) *adj.* Using all available means or resources: *an all-out sprint; an all-out conservation program.*

all over *adv.* **1.** Over the whole area or extent: *a cloth embroidered all over with roses.* **2.** Everywhere: *searched all over for*

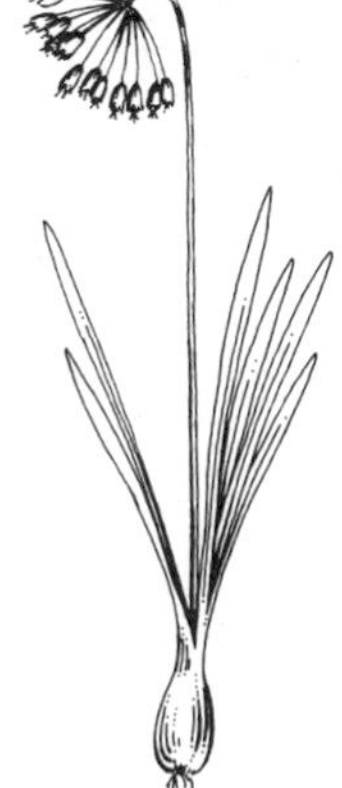

allium
Nodding wild onion
Allium cernuum

ă pat	oi boy
ā pay	ou out
âr care	o͝o took
ä father	o͞o boot
ĕ pet	ŭ cut
ē be	ûr urge
ĭ pit	th thin
ī pie	*th* this
îr pier	hw which
ŏ pot	zh vision
ō toe	ə about, item
ô paw	♦ regionalism

Stress marks: ′ (primary); ′ (secondary), as in **dictionary** (dĭk′shə-nĕr′ē)

her missing key. **3.** In all respects: *Carefree and fun-loving—that's him all over.*

all-o•ver also **all•o•ver** (ôl′ō′vər) *adj.* Covering an entire surface: *wallpaper with an all-over pattern; an allover tan.*

all-o•vers (ôl′ō′vərz) *pl.n. Informal.* A feeling of great unease or extreme nervousness.

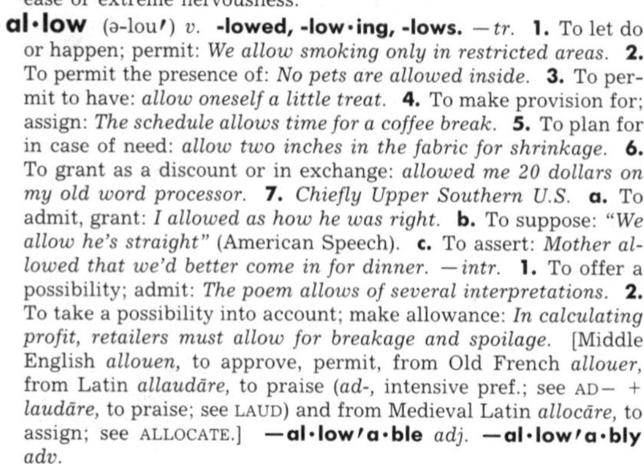

♦ **al•low** (ə-lou′) *v.* **-lowed, -low•ing, -lows.** —*tr.* **1.** To let do or happen; permit: *We allow smoking only in restricted areas.* **2.** To permit the presence of: *No pets are allowed inside.* **3.** To permit to have: *allow oneself a little treat.* **4.** To make provision for; assign: *The schedule allows time for a coffee break.* **5.** To plan for in case of need: *allow two inches in the fabric for shrinkage.* **6.** To grant as a discount or in exchange: *allowed me 20 dollars on my old word processor.* **7.** *Chiefly Upper Southern U.S.* **a.** To admit, grant: *I allowed as how he was right.* **b.** To suppose: *"We allow he's straight"* (American Speech). **c.** To assert: *Mother allowed that we'd better come in for dinner.* —*intr.* **1.** To offer a possibility; admit: *The poem allows of several interpretations.* **2.** To take a possibility into account; make allowance: *In calculating profit, retailers must allow for breakage and spoilage.* [Middle English *allouen,* to approve, permit, from Old French *allouer,* from Latin *allaudāre,* to praise (*ad-,* intensive pref.; see AD– + *laudāre,* to praise; see LAUD) and from Medieval Latin *allocāre,* to assign; see ALLOCATE.] **—al•low′a•ble** *adj.* **—al•low′a•bly** *adv.*

allspice
Pimenta dioica

al•low•ance (ə-lou′əns) *n.* **1.** The act of allowing. **2.** An amount that is allowed or granted: *finished my weekly allowance of two eggs.* **3.** Something, such as money, given at regular intervals or for a specific purpose: *a travel allowance that covers hotel and restaurant bills.* **4.** A price reduction, especially one granted in exchange for used merchandise: *The dealer gave us an allowance on our old car.* **5.** A consideration for possibilities or modifying circumstances: *an allowance for breakage; made allowances for rush-hour traffic in estimating travel time.* **6.** An allowed difference in dimension of closely mating machine parts. **—allowance** *tr.v.* **-anced, -anc•ing, -anc•es. 1.** To put on a fixed allowance: *cut expenses by strictly allowancing the sales representatives.* **2.** To dispense in fixed quantities; ration.

al•low•ed•ly (ə-lou′ĭd-lē) *adv.* By general admission; admittedly.

al•loy (ăl′oi′, ə-loi′) *n.* **1.** A homogeneous mixture or solid solution of two or more metals, the atoms of one replacing or occupying interstitial positions between the atoms of the other: *Brass is an alloy of copper and zinc.* **2.** A mixture; an amalgam: *"Television news has . . . always been an alloy of journalism and show business"* (Bill Moyers). **3.** The relative degree of mixture with a base metal; fineness. **4.** Something added that lowers value or purity. **—alloy** (ə-loi′, ăl′oi′) *tr.v.* **-loyed, -loy•ing, -loys. 1.** To combine (metals) to form an alloy. **2.** To combine; mix: *idealism that was alloyed with political skill.* **3.** To debase by the addition of an inferior element. [Alteration (influenced by French *aloi*) of obsolete *allay,* from Middle English *alay,* from Old North French *allai,* from *allayer,* to alloy, from Latin *alligāre,* to bind : *ad-,* ad- + *ligāre,* to bind; see **leig-** in Appendix.]

alluvial fan

all-pur•pose (ôl′pûr′pəs) *adj.* Having many purposes or uses.

all right *adj.* **1. a.** In proper or satisfactory operational or working order: *checked to see if the tires were all right.* **b. all-right** (ôl′rīt′). *Informal.* Satisfactory; good: *an all-right fellow; an all-right movie.* **2.** Correct: *Your answers are all right.* **3.** Average; mediocre: *The performance was just all right, not remarkable.* **4.** Uninjured; safe: *The passengers were shaken up but are all right.* **5.** Fairly healthy; well: *I am feeling all right again.* **—all right** *adv.* **1.** In a satisfactory way; adequately: *I held up all right under pressure.* **2.** Very well; yes. Used as a reply to a question or to introduce a declaration: *Will you join us? All right. All right, here's the plan.* **3.** Without a doubt: *It's cold, all right.*

USAGE NOTE: *All right,* usually pronounced as if it were a single word, probably should have followed the same orthographic development as *already* and *altogether.* But despite its use by a number of reputable authors, the spelling *alright* has never been accepted as a standard variant, and the writer who chooses to risk that spelling had best be confident that readers will acknowledge it as a token of willful unconventionality rather than as a mark of ignorance.

all-round (ôl′round′) *adj.* Variant of **all-around.**

All Saints' Day (sānts) *n.* November 1, the day on which a Christian feast honoring all the saints is observed. Also called *Allhallows.*

all•seed (ôl′sēd′) *n.* Any of several plants, such as knotgrass, producing numerous seeds.

All Souls' Day (sōlz) *n. Roman Catholic Church.* November 2, the day on which special prayers are offered for the souls in purgatory.

all•spice (ôl′spīs′) *n.* **1.** A tropical American evergreen tree *(Pimenta dioica)* having opposite, simple leaves and small white flowers clustered in cymes. **2.** The dried, nearly ripe berries of this plant used as a spice, especially in baking. Also called *pimento.*

all-star (ôl′stär′) *adj.* Made up wholly of star performers: *an all-star cast.* **—all-star** *n. Sports.* One chosen for a team of star players.

All•ston (ôl′stən), **Washington.** 1779–1843. American painter whose romantic works, such as *Elijah in the Desert,* often depict religious subjects.

all-ter•rain vehicle (ôl′tə-rān′) *n. Abbr.* **ATV** A small, open motor vehicle having one seat and three or more wheels fitted with large tires. It is designed chiefly for recreational use over roadless, rugged terrain.

all the same *adv.* Nevertheless: *I was ill, but I finished the job all the same.*

all-time (ôl′tīm′) *adj.* Exceeding all others up to the present time: *an all-time speed skating record.*

all told *adv.* With everything considered; in all: *All told, we won 100 games.*

al•lude (ə-lo͞od′) *intr.v.* **-lud•ed, -lud•ing, -ludes.** To make an indirect reference: *The candidate alluded to the recent war by saying, "We've all made sacrifices."* [Latin *allūdere,* to play with : *ad-,* ad- + *lūdere,* to play (from *lūdus,* game; see **leid-** in Appendix).]

USAGE NOTE: *Allude* and *allusion* are often used where the more general terms *refer* and *reference* would be preferable. *Allude* and *allusion* apply to indirect references in which the source is not specifically identified: *"Well, we'll always have Paris," he told the travel agent, in an allusion to* Casablanca. *Refer* and *reference,* unless qualified, usually imply specific mention of a source: *I will refer to* Hamlet *for my conclusion: As Polonius says, "Though this be madness, yet there is method in't."* See Usage Note at **refer.**

al•lure (ə-lo͝or′) *v.* **-lured, -lur•ing, -lures.** —*tr.* To attract with something desirable; entice: *Promises of quick profits allure the unwary investor.* —*intr.* To be highly, often subtly attractive: *charms that still allure.* **—allure** *n.* The power to attract; enticement. [Middle English *aluren,* from Old French *alurer* : *a-,* to (from Latin *ad-;* see AD–) + *loirre,* bait (of Germanic origin).] **—al•lure′ment** *n.* **—al•lur′er** *n.* **—al•lur′ing•ly** *adv.*

al•lu•sion (ə-lo͞o′zhən) *n.* **1.** The act of alluding; indirect reference: *Without naming names, the candidate criticized the national leaders by allusion.* **2.** An instance of indirect reference: *an allusion to classical mythology in a poem.* See Usage Note at **allude.** [Late Latin *allūsiō, allūsiōn-,* a playing with, from Latin *allūsus,* past participle of *allūdere,* to play with. See ALLUDE.]

al•lu•sive (ə-lo͞o′sĭv) *adj.* Containing or characterized by indirect references: *an allusive speech.* **—al•lu′sive•ly** *adv.* **—al•lu′sive•ness** *n.*

al•lu•vi•a (ə-lo͞o′vē-ə) *n.* A plural of **alluvium.**

al•lu•vi•al (ə-lo͞o′vē-əl) *adj.* Of, relating to, or found in alluvium: *alluvial soil; alluvial gold.*

alluvial fan *n.* A fan-shaped accumulation of alluvium deposited at the mouth of a ravine or at the juncture of a tributary stream with the main stream.

al•lu•vi•on (ə-lo͞o′vē-ən) *n.* **1.** See **alluvium. 2.** The flow of water against a shore or bank. **3.** Inundation by water; flood. **4.** *Law.* The increasing of land area along a shore by deposited alluvium or by the recession of water. [Latin *alluviō, alluviōn-,* from *alluere,* to wash against : *ad-,* ad- + *-luere,* to wash; see **leu(ə)-** in Appendix.]

al•lu•vi•um (ə-lo͞o′vē-əm) *n., pl.* **-vi•ums** or **-vi•a** (-vē-ə). Sediment deposited by flowing water, as in a river bed, flood plain, or delta. Also called *alluvion.* [Medieval Latin, flood, from neuter of Latin *alluvius,* alluvial, from *alluere,* to wash against. See ALLUVION.]

al•ly (ə-lī′, ăl′ī) *v.* **-lied, -ly•ing, -lies.** —*tr.* **1.** To place in a friendly association, as by treaty: *Italy allied itself with Germany during World War II.* **2.** To unite or connect in a personal relationship, as in friendship or marriage. —*intr.* To enter into an alliance: *Several tribes allied to fend off the invaders.* **—ally** *n., pl.* **-lies. 1.** One that is allied with another, especially by treaty: *entered the war as an ally of France.* **2.** One in helpful association with another: *legislators who are allies on most issues.* See Synonyms at **partner. 3. Allies. a.** The nations allied against the Central Powers of Europe during World War I. They were Russia, France, Great Britain, and later many others, including the United States. **b.** The nations, primarily Great Britain, France, the Soviet Union, and the United States, allied against the Axis during World War II. [Middle English *allien,* from Old French *alier,* from Latin *alligāre,* to bind to. See ALLOY.]

al•lyl (ăl′əl) *n.* The univalent, unsaturated organic radical C_3H_5. [Latin *allium,* garlic + –YL (so called because it was first obtained from garlic).] **—al•lyl′ic** (ə-lĭl′ĭk) *adj.*

alm *abbr.* Alarm.

Al•ma (ăl′mə). A city of south-central Quebec, Canada, on the Saguenay River. There are granite quarries in the area. Population, 26,322.

Al•ma-A•ta (ăl′mə-ä′tə, əl-mä′ə-tä′). A city of southeast Kazakhstan near the Chinese border south of Lake Balkash. The city was founded in the 1850's as a fort and trading center and is the capital of the republic. Population, 1,068,000.

Al•ma•gest (ăl′mə-jĕst′) *n.* **1.** A comprehensive treatise on astronomy, geography, and mathematics compiled by Ptolemy about A.D. 150. **2. almagest.** Any of several medieval treatises concerned with astronomy or alchemy. [Middle English *almageste,* from Old French, from Arabic *al-majisti* : *al,* the + Greek *megistē (suntaxis),* greatest (composition), feminine of *megistos,* greatest, superlative of *megas,* great; see **meg-** in Appendix.]

al·ma ma·ter or **Al·ma Ma·ter** (ăl′mə mä′tər, ăl′mə) *n.* **1.** The school, college, or university that one has attended. **2.** The anthem of an institution of higher learning. [Latin *alma,* nourishing + *mater,* mother.]

al·ma·nac (ôl′mə-năk′, ăl′-) *n.* **1.** An annual publication including calendars with weather forecasts, astronomical information, tide tables, and other related tabular information. **2.** An annual publication composed of various lists, charts, and tables of information in one field or many unrelated fields. [Middle English *almenak,* from Medieval Latin *almanach,* perhaps from Late Greek *almenikhiaka,* ephemeris.]

Al Ma·nam·ah (ăl′ mə-năm′ə, mă-). See **Manama.**

al·man·dine (ăl′mən-dēn′) also **al·man·dite** (-dīt′) *n.* A deep violet-red garnet, $FeAl_2Si_3O_{12}$, found in metamorphic rocks and used as a gemstone. [Alteration of obsolete *alabandyne,* from Middle English *alabandine,* from Late Latin *(gemma) alabandina,* (gem) of Alabanda, from *Alabanda,* a town of ancient Asia Minor.]

Al·ma-Tad·e·ma (ăl′mə-tăd′ə-mə), Sir **Lawrence.** 1836–1912. Dutch-born British painter noted for his romantic works of classical Greek and Roman and ancient Egyptian scenes.

Al·me·lo (äl′mə-lō′). A city of eastern Netherlands near the German border. It is a manufacturing center. Population, 62,941.

al·me·mar (ăl-mē′mär) *n. Judaism.* See **bema** (sense 1). [Hebrew *'almēmār,* from Arabic *al-minbar,* the pulpit.]

Al·me·rí·a (ăl′mə-rē′ə, äl′mĕ-). A city of southeast Spain on the **Gulf of Almería,** an arm of the Mediterranean Sea. Probably founded by Phoenicians, the city is a thriving port. Population, 149,310.

al·might·y (ôl-mī′tē) *adj.* **1.** Having absolute power; all-powerful: *almighty God.* **2.** *Informal.* Great; extreme: *an almighty din.* **—almighty** *adv. Informal.* Used as an intensive: *almighty scared.* **—Almighty** *n.* God. Used with *the.* [Middle English *almighti,* from Old English *ealmihtig* : *eall,* all; see ALL + *mihtig,* mighty (from *miht,* might; see MIGHT[1]).] **—al·might′i·ly** *adv.*

al·mond (ä′mənd, ăm′ənd) *n.* **1.a.** A deciduous tree *(Prunus dulcis),* native to Asia and northern Africa and having alternate, simple leaves, pink flowers, and leathery fruits. **b.** The ellipsoidal kernel of this tree, either eaten as a nut or used for extraction of an oil for flavoring. **2.** Any of several other plants, such as the Indian almond, especially those with fruits or seeds suggestive of the almond. **3.** Something having the oval form of an almond. **4.** *Color.* A pale tan. [Middle English *almande,* from Old French, from Late Latin *amandula,* alteration of Latin *amygdala,* from Greek *amugdalē.*]

al·mo·ner (ăl′mə-nər, ä′mə-) *n.* **1.** One who distributes alms. **2.** *Chiefly British.* A hospital social worker. [Middle English *aumoner,* from Old French *aumonier,* from *amosne,* alms, from Late Latin *eleēmosyna,* alms. See ALMS.]

al·most (ôl′mōst′, ôl-mōst′) *adv.* Slightly short of; not quite; nearly: *almost time to go; almost asleep; almost finished.* See Usage Note at **none.** [Middle English, from Old English *ealmǣst* : *eall,* all; see ALL + *mǣst,* most; see MOST.]

alms (ämz) *pl.n.* Money or goods given as charity to the poor. [Middle English *almes,* from Old English *ælmesse,* from Late Latin *eleēmosyna,* from Greek *eleēmosunē,* from *eleēmōn,* pitiful, from *eleos,* pity.]

alms·house (ämz′hous′) *n.* A poorhouse.

alms·man (ämz′mən) *n.* One dependent on alms for support.

al·ni·co (ăl′nĭ-kō′) *n.* Any of several hard, strong alloys of iron, aluminum, nickel, cobalt and sometimes copper, niobium, or tantalum, used to make strong permanent magnets. [AL(UMINUM) + NI(CKEL) + CO(BALT).]

al·o·ca·sia (ăl′ə-kā′zhə, -zhē-ə) *n.* Any of various tropical Asian aroids of the genus *Alocasia,* grown as ornamentals for their large heart-shaped or arrowhead-shaped leaves. [New Latin, probably alteration of *Colocasia,* from Greek *kolokasia,* lotus root.]

al·oe (ăl′ō) *n.* **1.** Any of various chiefly African plants of the genus *Aloe,* having rosettes of succulent, often spiny-margined leaves and long stalks bearing yellow, orange, or red tubular flowers. **2.** See **aloe vera. 3. aloes.** *(used with a sing. verb).* A laxative drug obtained from the processed juice of a certain species of aloe. In this sense, also called *bitter aloes.* [Middle English, from Old English *aluwe,* from Latin *aloē,* from Greek.] **—al′o·et′ic** (ăl′ō-ĕt′ĭk) *adj.*

aloe ver·a (vĕr′ə, vîr′ə) *n.* **1.** A species of aloe *(Aloe vera)* native to the Mediterranean region. **2.** The mucilaginous juice or gel obtained from the leaves of this plant, widely employed in cosmetic and pharmaceutical preparations for its soothing and healing properties. Also called *aloe.* [Latin *aloē,* aloe plant + *vera,* true.]

a·loft (ə-lôft′, ə-lŏft′) *adv.* **1.** In or into a high place; high or higher up. **2.** *Nautical.* At or toward the upper rigging. **—aloft** *prep.* On or above: *birds perching aloft telephone wires.* [Middle English, from Old Norse *ā lopt* : *ā,* in; see **an-** in Appendix + *lopt,* air.]

a·log·i·cal (ā-lŏj′ĭ-kəl) *adj.* Beyond or outside the bounds of logic. **—a·log′i·cal·ly** *adv.* **—a·log′i·cal·ness** *n.*

♦**a·lo·ha** (ə-lō′ə, -hä, ä-lō′ä′, -hä′) *interj. Chiefly Hawaii.* Used as a traditional greeting or farewell. [Hawaiian.]

al·o·in (ăl′ō-ĭn) *n.* A bitter, yellow crystalline compound obtained from the aloe and used as a laxative. [ALO(E) + -IN.]

a·lone (ə-lōn′) *adj.* **1.** Being apart from others; solitary. **2.** Being without anyone or anything else; only. **3.** Considered separately from all others of the same class. **4.** Being without equal; unique. **—alone** *adv.* **1.** Without others: *sang alone while the choir listened.* **2.** Without help: *carried the suitcases alone.* **3.** Exclusively; only: *The burden of proof rests on the prosecution alone.* [Middle English : *al,* all; see ALL + *one,* one; see ONE.] **—a·lone′ness** *n.*

SYNONYMS: *alone, lonely, lonesome, solitary.* These adjectives are compared as they describe lack of companionship. *Alone* emphasizes being apart from others but does not necessarily imply unhappiness: *"I am never less alone, than when I am alone"* (James Howell). *Lonely* often connotes painful awareness of being alone: *" 'No doubt they are dead,' she thought, and felt . . . sadder and . . . lonelier for the thought"* (Ouida). *Lonesome* emphasizes a plaintive desire for companionship: *"You must keep up your spirits, mother, and not be lonesome because I'm not at home"* (Charles Dickens). *Solitary* often shares the connotations of *lonely* and *lonesome: "Only solitary men know the full joys of friendship"* (Willa Cather). Frequently, however, it stresses physical isolation that is self-imposed: *She thoroughly enjoyed her solitary dinner.*

a·long (ə-lông′, ə-lŏng′) *prep.* **1.** Over the length of: *walked along the path.* **2.** On a line or course parallel and close to; continuously beside: *rowed along the shore; the trees along the avenue.* **3.** In accordance with: *The committee split along party lines over the issue.* **—along** *adv.* **1.** Forward; onward: *We drove along, admiring the view. Farther along, we passed a hitchhiker.* **2.** As a companion: *Bring your friend along.* **3.** In accompaniment or association; together: *packed an atlas along with other books.* See Usage Note at **together. 4.** With one; at hand: *Luckily, I had my camera along. Our guests should be along soon.* **5.** *Informal.* Advanced to some degree: *getting along in years.* [Middle English, from Old English *andlang,* extending opposite : *and-,* facing; see **ant-** in Appendix + *lang,* long; see LONG[1].]

a·long·shore (ə-lông′shôr′, -shōr′, ə-lŏng′-) *adv.* Along, near, or by the shore.

a·long·side (ə-lông′sīd′, ə-lŏng′-) *adv.* Along, near, at, or to the side: *stood with a bodyguard alongside; honked and drove up alongside.* **—alongside** *prep.* By the side of; side by side with.

USAGE NOTE: In its prepositional use *alongside* may optionally be accompanied by *of: The barge lay alongside,* or *alongside of, the pier.*

A·lon·so (ə-lŏn′zō, ä-lôn′sō), **Alicia.** Born c. 1921. Cuban ballerina and choreographer best known for her performances in *Giselle* and Agnes De Mille's *Fall River Legend.*

a·loof (ə-lo͞of′) *adj.* Distant physically or emotionally; reserved and remote: *stood apart with aloof dignity.* **—aloof** *adv.* At a distance but within view; apart. [A-[2] + LUFF, windward part of a ship (obsolete).] **—a·loof′ly** *adv.* **—a·loof′ness** *n.*

al·o·pe·cia (ăl′ə-pē′shə, -shē-ə) *n.* Loss of hair; baldness. [Latin *alōpecia,* fox-mange, from Greek *alōpekia,* from *alōpēx,* fox. See **wl̥p-ē-** in Appendix.] **—al′o·pe′cic** (-pē′sĭk) *adj.*

A·lost (ä-lôst′). See **Aalst.**

a·loud (ə-loud′) *adv.* **1.** With use of the voice; orally: *Read this passage aloud.* **2.** In a loud tone; loudly: *crying aloud for help.*

alp (ălp) *n.* **1.** A high mountain. **2.** A very large mound or mass. [Back-formation from the ALPS.]

ALPA *abbr.* Air Line Pilots Association.

al·pac·a (ăl-păk′ə) *n., pl.* **alpaca** or **-as. 1.** A domesticated South American mammal *(Lama pacos),* related to the llama and having fine, long wool. **2.a.** The silky wool of this mammal. **b.** Cloth made from alpaca. **c.** A coat made of this cloth. **3.** A glossy cotton or rayon and wool fabric. [American Spanish, from Aymara *allpaca.*]

al·pen·glow (ăl′pən-glō′) *n.* A rosy glow that suffuses snow-covered mountain peaks at dawn or dusk on a clear day. [Partial translation of German *Alpenglühen* : *Alpen,* Alps + *glühen,* to glow.]

al·pen·horn (ăl′pən-hôrn′) *n.* A curved wooden horn, sometimes as long as 6 meters (approximately 20 feet), used by herders in the Alps to call cows to pasture. [German : *Alpen,* Alps + *Horn,* horn, from Middle High German, from Old High German. See **ker-[1]** in Appendix.]

al·pen·stock (ăl′pən-stŏk′) *n.* A long staff with an iron point, used by mountain climbers. [German *Alpenstock* : *Alpen,* Alps + *Stock,* staff (from Middle High German *stoc,* from Old High German).]

al·pes·trine (ăl-pĕs′trĭn) *adj.* Growing at high altitudes; alpine or subalpine. [From Medieval Latin *alpestris,* from Latin *Alpēs,* the Alps.]

al·pha (ăl′fə) *n.* **1.** The first letter of the Greek alphabet. See table at **alphabet. 2.** The first one; the beginning. **3.** *Chemistry.* The first position from a designated carbon atom in an organic molecule at which an atom or radical may be substituted. **4.** *Astronomy.* The brightest or main star in a constellation. **5.** The mathematical estimate of the return on a security when the return on the market as a whole is zero. Alpha is derived from *a* in the

almond
Prunus dulcis

alpaca
Lama pacos

alpenhorn

ă pat	oi boy
ā pay	ou out
âr care	o͝o took
ä father	o͞o boot
ĕ pet	ŭ cut
ē be	ûr urge
ĭ pit	th thin
ī pie	*th* this
îr pier	hw which
ŏ pot	zh vision
ō toe	ə about, item
ô paw	♦ regionalism

Stress marks: **′** (primary); ′ (secondary), as in **dictionary** (dĭk′shə-nĕr′ē)

formula $R_i = a + bR_m$, which measures the return on a security (R_i) for a given return on the market (R_m) where b is beta. **—alpha** *adj.* **1.** First in order of importance. **2.** *Chemistry.* Closest to the functional group of atoms in an organic molecule. **3.** Alphabetical. [Greek, from Canaanite *'alp,* ox.]

al·pha-ad·re·ner·gic (ăl′fə-ăd′rə-nûr′jĭk) *adj.* Of, relating to, or being an alpha-receptor.

alpha-adrenergic block·ing agent (blŏk′ĭng) *n.* See **alpha-blocker.**

alpha-adrenergic receptor *n.* See **alpha-receptor.**

alpha and omega *n.* **1.** The first and the last: *"I am Alpha and Omega, the beginning and the ending, saith the Lord"* (Revelation 1:8). **2.** The most important part.

al·pha·bet (ăl′fə-bĕt′, -bĭt) *n.* **1.** The letters of a language, arranged in the order fixed by custom. **2.** A system of characters or symbols representing sounds or things. **3.** The basic or elementary principles; rudiments. [Middle English *alphabete,* from Latin *alphabētum,* from Greek *alphabētos* : *alpha,* alpha; see ALPHA + *bēta,* beta; see BETA.]

al·pha·bet·i·cal (ăl′fə-bĕt′ĭ-kəl) also **al·pha·bet·ic** (-bĕt′ĭk) *adj.* **1.** Arranged in the customary order of the letters of a language. **2.** Of, relating to, or expressed by an alphabet. **—al′pha·bet′i·cal·ly** *adv.*

al·pha·bet·ize (ăl′fə-bĭ-tīz′) *tr.v.* **-ized, -iz·ing, -iz·es. 1.** To arrange in alphabetical order. **2.** To supply with an alphabet. **—al′pha·bet′i·za′tion** (-bĕt′ĭ-zā′shən) *n.* **—al′pha·bet′iz′er** *n.*

TABLE OF ALPHABETS

Because it is more convenient to use a single system of spelling to represent the speech sounds of many different languages, words from languages that use other writing systems are usually transliterated into Roman characters. The transliterations shown here are those used in the etymologies in this Dictionary for four of the most important non-Roman alphabets. The names of the Hebrew and Greek letters are also entered and defined in the Dictionary as English nouns. (In some cases the English spelling differs from the transliterated letter name shown here, chiefly in the absence of diacritical marks—for example English **omega** versus Greek **ōmega**.) The Cyrillic letters shown are those used in modern Russian. For the history of the English alphabet, see "Development of the Alphabet" on the facing page.

HEBREW

FORMS	NAME	SOUND
א	'aleph	'
ב	bēth	b
ג	gimel	g
ד	dāleth	d
ה	hē	h
ו	vāv, wāw	w
ז	zayin	z
ח	ḥeth	ḥ
ט	ṭeth	ṭ
י	yodh	y
כ ך	kāph	k
ל	lāmedh	l
מ ם	mēm	m
נ ן	nūn	n
ס	samekh	s
ע	'ayin	'
פ ף	pē	p
צ ץ	ṣadhe	ṣ
ק	qōph	q
ר	rēsh	r
שׂ	sin	ś
שׁ	shin	š
ת	tāv, tāw	t

Vowels are not represented in normal Hebrew writing, but for certain purposes they are indicated by a system of subscript and superscript dots. The transliterations with subscript dots are pharyngeal consonants as in Arabic. The second forms shown are used when the letter falls at the end of a word.

ARABIC

FORMS 1	2	3	4	NAME	SOUND
ا	ـا			'alif	'
ب	ـب	ـبـ	بـ	bā	b
ت	ـت	ـتـ	تـ	tā	t
ث	ـث	ـثـ	ثـ	thā	t
ج	ـج	ـجـ	جـ	jīm	j
ح	ـح	ـحـ	حـ	ḥā	ḥ
خ	ـخ	ـخـ	خـ	khā	ḫ
د	ـد			dāl	d
ذ	ـذ			dhāl	d̲
ر	ـر			rā	r
ز	ـز			zāy	z
س	ـس	ـسـ	سـ	sīn	s
ش	ـش	ـشـ	شـ	shīn	š
ص	ـص	ـصـ	صـ	ṣād	ṣ
ض	ـض	ـضـ	ضـ	ḍād	ḍ
ط	ـط	ـطـ	طـ	ṭā	ṭ
ظ	ـظ	ـظـ	ظـ	ẓā	ẓ
ع	ـع	ـعـ	عـ	'ayn	'
غ	ـغ	ـغـ	غـ	ghayn	ğ
ف	ـف	ـفـ	فـ	fā	f
ق	ـق	ـقـ	قـ	qāf	q
ك	ـك	ـكـ	كـ	kāf	k
ل	ـل	ـلـ	لـ	lām	l
م	ـم	ـمـ	مـ	mīm	m
ن	ـن	ـنـ	نـ	nūn	n
ه	ـه	ـهـ	هـ	hā	h
و	ـو			wāw	w
ى	ـى	ـيـ	يـ	yā	y

The different forms in the four numbered columns are used when the letters are in: 1. isolation; 2. juncture with a previous letter; 3. juncture with letters on both sides; 4. juncture with a following letter.

Long vowels are represented by the consonants *'alif* (for *ā*), *wāw* (for *ū*), and *yā* (for *ī*). Short vowels are not usually written; they can, however, be indicated by the following signs: *′fatha* (for *a*), *, kesra* (for *i*), and *' damma* (for *u*).

Transliterations with subscript dots represent "emphatic" or pharyngeal consonants, which are pronounced in the usual way except that the pharynx is tightly narrowed during articulation. When two dots are placed over the *hā*, the new letter thus formed is called *tā marbūta,* and is pronounced (t).

There are several other diacritical marks indicating such situations as the doubling of a consonant or the elision of a vowel.

GREEK

FORMS	NAME	SOUND
Α α	alpha	a
Β β	beta	b
Γ γ	gamma	g (n)
Δ δ	delta	d
Ε ε	epsilon	e
Ζ ζ	zēta	z
Η η	ēta	ē
Θ θ	thēta	th
Ι ι	iota	i
Κ κ	kappa	k
Λ λ	lambda	l
Μ μ	mu	m
Ν ν	nu	n
Ξ ξ	xi	x
Ο ο	omicron	o
Π π	pi	p
Ρ ρ	rhō	r (rh)
Σ σ	sigma	s
Τ τ	tau	t
Υ υ	upsilon	u
Φ φ	phi	ph
Χ χ	chi, khi	kh
Ψ ψ	psi	ps
Ω ω	ōmega	ō

The superscript ' on an initial vowel or *rhō* represents aspiration or "rough breathing," and is transliterated by h. Lack of aspiration on an initial vowel is indicated by the superscript ', called the smooth breathing. When *gamma* precedes *kappa, xi, khi,* or another *gamma,* it has the value *n* and is so transliterated. The second lowercase form of *sigma* is used only in final position.

CYRILLIC

FORMS	SOUND
А а	a
Б б	b
В в	v
Г г	g
Д д	d
Е е Ё ё	e, ë[1]
Ж ж	zh
З з	z
И и Й й	i, ĭ
К к	k
Л л	l
М м	m
Н н	n
О о	o
П п	p
Р р	r
С с	s
Т т	t
У у	u
Ф ф	f
Х х	kh
Ц ц	ts
Ч ч	ch
Ш ш	sh
Щ щ	shch
Ъ ъ	"[2]
Ы ы	y
Ь ь	'[3]
Э э	e
Ю ю	yu
Я я	ya

[1]The variant *ë* occurs only in stressed position, and is pronounced as a very short (ô) or (yô).

[2]This letter, called the "hard sign," is very rare in modern Russian. It indicates that the previous consonant remains hard even when followed by a front vowel.

[3]This letter, called the "soft sign," indicates that the previous consonant is palatalized even when a front vowel does not follow.

DEVELOPMENT OF THE ALPHABET

In early forms of writing such as hieroglyphics, pictorial signs represented whole words or syllables. By around 1500 B.C. the Canaanites, a Semitic-speaking people living in ancient Palestine and Syria, began to use such signs to stand for individual speech sounds, writing them from right to left. A version of this alphabet was adopted by their successors the Phoenicians, who simplified the forms and added several new ones. Trade with the Phoenicians brought the alphabet to the early Greeks, who reassigned some of the semitic consonant symbols to vowel sounds such as a, e, ē, and o. The Greeks also split the Semitic *wāw* into two letters, *wau* (later called *digamma*, "double gamma," whose sound [w] was lost in classical Greek but whose form survives in modern F) and *u* (later *u psilon*, "simple u"), the ancestor of modern U, V, W, and Y.

In Italy, a western variant of the Greek alphabet was adopted by the Etruscans. Our modern letters derive from the Romans, who adapted the Etruscan script for monumental inscriptions and wrote from left to right. Because Etruscan writing did not distinguish between the sounds of *c* and *g*, the Romans created the new letter G by adding a stroke to C. The classical Greek Y and Z were added to represent the sounds ü and z in words borrowed from Greek. The English alphabet reached its total of 26 letters only after medieval scribes added *w* (originally written *uu*) and Renaissance printers separated the variant pairs *i/j* and *u/v*.

During the Middle Ages, the Roman capitals evolved into uncials and then to Carolingian minuscules and Italic cursive script, which are the prototypes of many modern printed and handwritten letters.

PROTO-CANAANITE	SEMITIC NAMES	SEMITIC SOUNDS	PHOENICIAN	EARLY GREEK	GREEK NAMES	GREEK SOUNDS	ETRUSCAN	CLASSICAL ROMAN	UNCIAL	CAROLINGIAN MINUSCULE	ITALIC CURSIVE	MODERN PRINTED	MODERN SCRIPT
c. 1500 B.C.			c. 1000 B.C.	c. 800 B.C.			c. 500 B.C.		300-700	800	1400		
	'aleph 'ox'	[']			alpha	[a]		A	A	a	a	A a	Aa
	bēth 'house'	[b]			bēta	[b]		B	B	b	b	B b	Bb
	gaml, gīmel 'camel'	[g]			gamma	[g]		C	C	c	c	C c	Cc
	dag 'fish' dāleth 'door'	[d]			delta	[d]		D	D	d	d	D d	Dd
	hē	[h]			e (psilon)	[ĕ]		E	E	e	e	E e	Ee
	wāw	[w]			wau, digamma	[w]		F	F	f	f	F f	Ff
	zayin	[z]			zēta	[z]		G	G	g	g	G g	Gg
	hēth	[ḥ]			ēta	[h, ē]		H	h	h	h	H h	Hh
	yōdh 'arm'	[y]			iōta	[i,y]		I	ı	ı	i	I i	Ii
									J	j	j	J j	Jj
	kaph 'hand'	[k]			kappa	[k]		K	K	k	k	K k	Kk
	lāmedh	[l]			lambda	[l]		L	L	l	l	L l	Ll
	mēm 'water'	[m]			mu	[m]		M	m	m	m	M m	Mm
	nahš 'snake' nūn 'fish'	[n]			nu	[n]		N	N	n	n	N n	Nn
	samekh	[s]			xi	[ks]							
	'ayin 'eye'	[']			o (micron)	[ŏ]		O	O	o	o	O o	Oo
	pē	[p]			pi	[p]		P	P	p	p	P p	Pp
	qōph	[q]			koppa	[q]		Q	q	q	q	Q q	Qq
	rōsh, rēsh 'head'	[r]			rhō	[r]		R	R	r	r	R r	Rr
	thann 'bow' shin 'tooth'	[th, š]			sigma	[s]		S	S	ſ	s	S s	Ss
	tāw 'mark'	[t]			tau	[t]		T	T	t	t	T t	Tt
											u	U u	Uu
				Y	u (psilon)	[ü, w]	Y	V	U	u	v	V v	Vv
											w	W w	Ww
								X	X	x	x	X x	Xx
								Y	Y	Y	y	Y y	Yy
								Z	Z	z	z	Z z	Zz

altar
Saint Joseph's Church, Winsted, Connecticut

al·pha-block·er (ăl′fə-blŏk′ər) *n. Physiology.* A drug that opposes the excitatory effects of norepinephrine released from sympathetic nerve endings at alpha receptors and that causes vasodilation and a decrease in blood pressure. Also called *alpha-adrenergic blocking agent.*

Al·pha Cen·tau·ri (ăl′fə sĕn-tôr′ē) *n.* A multiple star in Centaurus whose three components represent the brightest object in the constellation, 4.4 light-years from Earth.

Alpha Cru·cis (kro͞o′sĭs) *n.* A double star in the constellation Southern Cross.

alpha decay *n.* The radioactive decay of an atomic nucleus by emission of an alpha particle.

al·pha-fe·to·pro·tein (ăl′fə-fē′tō-prō′tēn, -tē-ĭn) *n. Abbr.* **AFP** An antigen produced in the liver of a fetus that can appear in certain diseases of adults, such as liver cancer. Its level in amniotic fluid can be used in the detection of certain fetal abnormalities, including Down syndrome and spina bifida.

alpha globulin *n.* A type of globulin in blood plasma that exhibits great colloidal mobility in electrically charged neutral or alkaline solutions.

alpha helix *n.* A common structure of proteins, characterized by a single, spiral chain of amino acids stabilized by hydrogen bonds. **—al′pha-hel′i·cal** (ăl′fə-hĕl′ĭ-kəl, hē′lĭ-) *adj.*

al·pha·mer·ic (ăl′fə-mĕr′ĭk) *adj.* Variant of **alphanumeric.**

al·pha-naph·thol (ăl′fə-năf′thôl, -thōl, -năp′-) *n.* An isomeric form of naphthol, $C_{10}H_7OH$, occurring as colorless or yellow prisms or powder, used in making dyes and perfumes and in organic synthesis.

al·pha·nu·mer·ic (ăl′fə-no͞o-mĕr′ĭk, -nyo͞o-) also **al·pha·mer·ic** (-fə-mĕr′ĭk) *adj.* **1.** Consisting of both letters and numbers. **2.** Consisting of or utilizing alphabetic and numerical symbols and punctuation marks, mathematical symbols, and other conventional symbols: *an alphanumeric code.* [ALPHA(BETIC) + NUMERIC(AL).] **—al′pha·nu·mer′i·cal** *adj.* **—al′pha·nu·mer′i·cal·ly** *adv.*

alpha particle *n.* A positively charged particle, indistinguishable from a helium atom nucleus and consisting of two protons and two neutrons.

alpha privative *n.* The prefix *a-* or *an-* before vowels, used in Greek and in English words borrowed from Greek to express absence or negation.

alpha ray *n.* A stream of alpha particles or a single high-speed alpha particle.

al·pha-re·cep·tor (ăl′fə-rĭ-sĕp′tər) *n.* A site in the autonomic nervous system in which excitatory responses occur when adrenergic agents, such as norepinephrine and epinephrine, are released. Activation of alpha-receptors causes various physiological reactions, including the stimulation of associated muscles and the constriction of blood vessels. Also called *alpha-adrenergic receptor.*

alpha rhythm *n.* A pattern of smooth, regular electrical oscillations in the human brain that occur when a person is awake and relaxed. As recorded by the electroencephalograph, alpha rhythms have a frequency of 8 to 13 hertz. Also called *alpha wave.*

Al·phe·us (ăl-fē′əs). A river of the Peloponnesus in southern Greece flowing about 113 km (70 mi) to the Ionian Sea.

al·pine (ăl′pīn′) *adj.* **1. Alpine.** Of, relating to, or characteristic of the Alps or their inhabitants. **2.** Of or relating to high mountains. **3.** *Biology.* Living or growing on mountains above the timberline: *alpine plants.* **4.** *Sports.* **a.** Intended for or concerned with mountaineering. **b. Alpine.** Of or relating to competitive downhill racing and slalom skiing events. [Middle English, from Latin *Alpīnus,* from *Alpēs,* the Alps.]

al·pin·ist also **Al·pin·ist** (ăl′pə-nĭst) *n. Sports.* A mountain climber. **—al′pin·ism** *n.*

Alps (ălps). A mountain system of south-central Europe, about 805 km (500 mi) long and 161 km (100 mi) wide, curving in an arc from the Riviera on the Mediterranean Sea through northern Italy and southeast France, Switzerland, southern Germany, and Austria and into northwest Yugoslavia. The highest peak is Mont Blanc, 4,810.2 m (15,771 ft), on the French-Italian border.

al·read·y (ôl-rĕd′ē) *adv.* **1.** By this or a specified time; before: *The children were already asleep when we got home.* **2.** So soon: *Are you quitting already?* **3.** *Non-Standard.* Used as an intensive: *Be quiet already. Enough already.* [Middle English *alredi* : *al,* all; see ALL + *redi,* ready; see READY.]

al·right (ôl-rīt′) *adv. Non-Standard.* All right: *"Alright, it might be fun to hunt tigers"* (Carl Icahn). See Usage Note at **all right.**

ALS *abbr.* Amyotrophic lateral sclerosis.

a.l.s. or **A.L.S.** *abbr.* Autograph letters, signed.

Al·sace (ăl-săs′, -sās′). A region and former province of eastern France between the Rhine River and the Vosges Mountains. Along with neighboring Lorraine, it was annexed by Germany in 1871 after the Franco-Prussian War and returned to France by the Treaty of Versailles (1919).

Al·sa·tian (ăl-sā′shən) *adj.* Of or relating to Alsace or to its inhabitants or culture. **—Alsatian** *n.* **1.** A native or inhabitant of Alsace. **2.** *Chiefly British.* A German shepherd.

Al·sek (ăl′sĕk′). A river of northwest Canada and southeast Alaska flowing about 418 km (260 mi) to the Pacific Ocean.

al·sike clover (ăl′sīk′) *n.* A perennial European clover *(Trifolium hybridum)* with whitish or pink flowers, naturalized over much of North America and grown as a pasture and hay plant. [After *Alsike,* near Uppsala in eastern Sweden.]

Al·sip (ôl′sĭp). A village of northeast Illinois, a suburb of Chicago. Population, 17,134.

al·so (ôl′sō) *adv.* **1.** In addition; besides. **2.** Likewise; too: *If you will stay, I will also.* **—also** *conj.* And in addition: *It's a pretty cat, also friendly.* [Middle English, from Old English *ealswā* : *eall,* all; see **al-**[3] in Appendix + *swā,* so; see SO[1].]

SYNONYMS: *also, too, likewise, besides, moreover, furthermore.* These adverbs indicate the presence of or introduce something additional. The first three generally imply that the additional element or consideration is equal in weight to what precedes it. *Also* is more formal in tone than *too: He is gentle, but he is also capable of fierce intellectual combat. If you buy a car, you'll need a parking place, too. Likewise* is even more formal than *also* and may imply similarity between elements as well as equality: *You forgot to mention that her parents were likewise going to attend the ceremony. Besides* often introduces an element that reinforces what has gone before: *I don't feel like cooking; besides, there's no food in the house. Moreover* and *furthermore* frequently stress the importance of what is to come: *The cellar was dark and forbidding; moreover, I knew a family of mice had nested there. I don't want you to go; furthermore, I forbid it.*

USAGE NOTE: *Also* is sometimes held to be inappropriate when used to begin a sentence, as in *The warranty covers all powertrain components. Also, participating dealers back their work with a free lifetime service guarantee.* This example was acceptable to 63 percent of the Usage Panel, however.

Al·sop (ôl′səp, ŏl′-), **Joseph Wright, Jr.** 1910–1989. American journalist who with his brother **Stewart** (1914–1974) wrote the syndicated column "Matter of Fact" (1945–1958).

al·so-ran (ôl′sō-răn′) *n.* **1.** A horse that does not win, place, or show in a race. **2.** A loser in a competition, as in an election: *"had enough support to place him in the middle of the also-rans"* (George F. Will). **3.** One that has little talent or success: *just an also-ran in the art world.*

al·stroe·me·ri·a (ăl′strə-mîr′ē-ə) *n.* Any of several South American perennial herbs of the genus *Alstroemeria,* popular as cut flowers for their showy, variously colored blooms. [New Latin, genus name, after Baron Clas *Alstroemer* (1736–1794), Swedish naturalist.]

alt (ălt) *Music. adj.* Pitched in the first octave above the treble staff; high. **—alt** *n.* **1.** The first octave above the treble staff. **2.** A note or tone in the alt octave. [Latin *altus,* high. See **al-**[2] in Appendix.]

alt. *abbr.* **1.** Alteration. **2.** Alternate. **3.** Altitude.

Alta. *abbr.* Alberta.

Al·ta Cal·i·for·nia (ăl′tə kăl′ĭ-fôr′nyə, -fôr′nē-ə) Also **Up·per California** (ŭp′ər). The Spanish possessions along the Pacific coast north of the peninsula of Baja California. Early maps of the area often depicted California as an island. When this misconception was corrected in the 18th century, the peninsula came to be called Baja California and the rest of the mainland, Alta California.

Al·ta·de·na (ăl′tə-dē′nə). An unincorporated community of southern California at the foot of the San Gabriel Mountains near Pasadena. It is mainly residential. Population, 40,983.

Al·ta·ic (ăl-tā′ĭk) *n.* A language family of Europe and Asia that includes the Turkic, Tungusic, and Mongolian subfamilies. **—Altaic** *adj.* **1.** Of or relating to the Altai Mountains. **2.** Of or relating to Altaic.

Al·tai Mountains or **Al·tay Mountains** (ăl′tī′). A mountain system of central Asia, mostly in eastern Kazakhstan and south-central Russia but also extending into western Mongolia and northern China. It rises to 4,508.8 m (14,783 ft).

Al·tair (ăl-tīr′, -târ′, ăl′tīr′, -târ′) *n.* A very bright, variable, double star in the constellation Aquila, approximately 15.7 light-years from Earth. [Arabic *an-nasr aṭ-ṭā'ir* : *an-nasr,* the eagle (*al,* the + *nasr,* eagle) + *aṭ-ṭā'ir* (*al,* the + *ṭā'ir,* flying).]

Al·ta·ma·ha (ôl′tə-mə-hô′). A river of southeast Georgia formed by the confluence of the Oconee and Ocmulgee rivers and flowing about 220 km (137 mi) generally east-southeast to **Altamaha Sound,** an inlet of the Atlantic Ocean.

Al·ta·mi·ra (ăl′tə-mîr′ə, ăl′tä-mē′rä). A group of caverns of northern Spain west-southwest of Santander. The caves contain magnificent specimens of Paleolithic art discovered in 1879.

Al·ta·mont (ăl′tə-mŏnt′). An unincorporated community of southern Oregon, a suburb of Klamath Falls. Population, 19,805.

Al·ta·monte Springs (ăl′tə-mŏnt′). A city of east-central Florida, a residential suburb of Orlando. Population, 22,028.

al·tar (ôl′tər) *n.* **1.** An elevated place or structure before which religious ceremonies may be enacted or upon which sacrifices may be offered. **2.** A structure, typically a table, before which the divine offices are recited and upon which the Eucharist is celebrated in Christian churches. [Middle English *altar* and Old French *auter,* both from Latin *altāre.*]

altar boy *n.* An attendant to an officiating cleric in the performance of a liturgical service; an acolyte.

♦ **altar call** *n.* A specified time at the end of a Protestant service when worshipers may come forward to make or renew a profession of faith. Also called ♦ *invitation.*

al·tar·piece (ôl′tər-pēs′) *n.* A piece of artwork, such as a painting or carving, that is placed above and behind an altar.

altar rail *n.* A railing in front of the altar that separates the chancel from the rest of a church.

Al·tay Mountains (äl′tī′). See **Altai Mountains.**

alt·az·i·muth (ăl-tăz′ə-məth) *n.* **1.** A mounting for astronomical telescopes that permits both horizontal and vertical rotation. **2.** A telescope having such a mounting. [ALT(ITUDE) + AZIMUTH.]

Alt·dorf (ält′dôrf). A town of central Switzerland near the southeast tip of the Lake of Lucerne. A statue commemorates the legendary exploits of William Tell, marking the spot where he supposedly shot an apple off his son's head. Population, 8,200.

Al·ten·burg (äl′tən-bûrg′, -bo͝ork′). A city of east-central Germany south of Leipzig. It was built on the site of early ninth-century Slavic fortifications. Population, 54,999.

al·ter (ôl′tər) *v.* **-tered, -ter·ing, -ters.** —*tr.* **1.** To change or make different; modify: *altered my will.* **2.** To adjust (a garment) for a better fit. **3.** To castrate or spay (an animal, such as a cat or a dog). —*intr.* To change or become different. [Middle English *alteren,* from Old French *alterer,* from Medieval Latin *alterāre,* from Latin *alter,* other. See **al-**[1] in Appendix.]

al·ter·a·ble (ôl′tər-ə-bəl) *adj.* That can be altered: *alterable clothing; alterable conditions of employment.* **—al′ter·a·bil′i·ty, al′ter·a·ble·ness** *n.* **—al′ter·a·bly** *adv.*

al·ter·a·tion (ôl′tə-rā′shən) *n. Abbr.* **alt. 1.** The act or procedure of altering. **2.** The condition resulting from altering; modification.

al·ter·a·tive (ôl′tə-rā′tĭv, -tər-ə-tĭv) *adj.* **1.** Tending to alter or produce alteration. **2.** *Medicine.* Tending to restore to normal health. **—alterative** *n. Medicine.* A treatment or medication that restores health.

al·ter·cate (ôl′tər-kāt′) *intr.v.* **-cat·ed, -cat·ing, -cates.** To argue or dispute vehemently; wrangle. [Latin *altercārī, altercāt-,* to quarrel, from *alter,* other. See **al-**[1] in Appendix.]

al·ter·ca·tion (ôl′tər-kā′shən) *n.* A vehement quarrel.

alter ego *n.* **1.** Another side of oneself; a second self. **2.** An intimate friend or a constant companion. [Latin : *alter,* other + *ego,* I, self.]

al·ter·nar·i·a (ôl′tər-nâr′ē-ə, ăl′-) *n.* Any of various fungi in the genus *Alternaria,* many of which cause plant diseases, chiefly blights and leaf spots. [New Latin, genus name, from Latin *alternus,* alternate. See ALTERNATE.]

al·ter·nate (ôl′tər-nāt′, ăl′-) *v.* **-nat·ed, -nat·ing, -nates.** —*intr.* **1.** To occur in successive turns: *showers alternating with sunshine.* **2.** To pass back and forth from one state, action, or place to another: *alternated between happiness and depression.* —*tr.* **1.** To do or execute by turns. **2.** To cause to follow in turns; interchange regularly. **—alternate** (-nĭt) *adj.* **1.** Happening or following in turns; succeeding each other continuously: *alternate seasons of the year.* See Usage Note at **alternative. 2.** Designating or relating to every other one of a series: *alternate lines.* **3.** Serving or used in place of another; substitute: *an alternate plan.* **4.** *Botany.* **a.** Arranged singly at each node, as leaves or buds on a stem. **b.** Arranged regularly between other parts, as stamens between petals. **—alternate** (-nĭt) *n. Abbr.* **alt. 1.** A person acting in the place of another; a substitute. **2.** An alternative. [Latin *alternāre, alternāt-,* from *alternus,* by turns, from *alter,* other. See **al-**[1] in Appendix.] **—al′ter·nate·ly** *adv.* **—al′ter·nate·ness** *n.*

al·ter·nate angle (ôl′tər-nĭt, ăl′-) *n. Mathematics.* One of a pair of nonadjacent angles on opposite sides of a transversal that cuts two lines. The angles are both exterior or both interior to the two lines.

alternate host *n.* **1.** One of two species of host on which some pathogens, such as certain rust fungi, must develop to complete their life cycles. **2.** A species of host other than the principal host on which a parasite can survive.

al·ter·nat·ing current (ôl′tər-nā′tĭng, ăl′-) *n. Abbr.* **ac, AC** An electric current that reverses direction in a circuit at regular intervals.

al·ter·na·tion (ôl′tər-nā′shən, ăl′-) *n.* Successive change from one thing or state to another and back again.

alternation of generations *n.* The regular alternation of forms or of mode of reproduction in the life cycle of an organism, such as the alternation between diploid and haploid phases, or between sexual and asexual reproductive cycles. Also called *metagenesis, xenogenesis.*

al·ter·na·tive (ôl-tûr′nə-tĭv, ăl-) *n.* **1.a.** The choice between two mutually exclusive possibilities. **b.** A situation presenting such a choice. **c.** Either of these possibilities. See Synonyms at **choice. 2.** *Usage Problem.* One of a number of things from which one must be chosen. **—alternative** *adj.* **1.** Allowing or necessitating a choice between two or more things. **2.a.** Existing outside traditional or established institutions or systems: *an alternative lifestyle.* **b.** Espousing or reflecting values that are different from those of the establishment: *an alternative newspaper; alternative greeting cards.* **—al·ter′na·tive·ly** *adv.*

USAGE NOTE: Some traditionalists hold that *alternative* should be used only in situations where the number of choices involved is exactly two, because of the word's historical relation to Latin *alter,* "the other of two." H.W. Fowler, among others, has considered this restriction a fetish. The Usage Panel is evenly divided on the issue, with 49 percent accepting the sentence *Of the three alternatives, the first is the least distasteful.* • *Alternative* is also sometimes used to refer to a variant or substitute in cases where there is no element of choice involved, as in *We will do our best to secure alternative employment for employees displaced by the closing of the factory.* This sentence is unacceptable to 60 percent of the Usage Panel. • *Alternative* should not be confused with *alternate.* Correct usage requires *The class will meet on alternate* (not *alternative*) *Tuesdays.*

alternative school *n.* A school that is nontraditional, especially in educational ideals, methods of teaching, or curriculum.

al·ter·na·tor (ôl′tər-nā′tər, ăl′-) *n.* An electric generator that produces alternating current.

al·the·a also **al·thae·a** (ăl-thē′ə) *n.* **1.** See **rose of Sharon** (sense 1). **2.** See **hollyhock.** [Latin, mallows, from Greek *althaia,* from *althainein,* to heal. See **al-**[2] in Appendix.]

alt·horn (ălt′hôrn′) or **Alt·horn** *n. Music.* Any of several upright, valved brass wind instruments used especially in bands. [German : *alt,* alto (from Italian *alto;* see ALTO) + *Horn,* horn, from Middle High German, from Old High German. See **ker-**[1] in Appendix.]

al·though also **al·tho** (ôl-thō′) *conj.* Regardless of the fact that; even though. [Middle English : *al,* all; see ALL + *though,* though; see THOUGH.]

USAGE NOTE: As conjunctions, *although* and *though* are generally interchangeable: *Although* (or *though*) *she smiled, she was angry. Although* is usually placed at the beginning of its clause (as in the preceding example), whereas *though* may occur elsewhere and is the more common term when used to link words or phrases, as in *wiser though poorer,* or in constructions such as *Fond though* (not *although*) *I am of opera, I'd rather not sit through the* Ring *cycle this weekend.*

al·tim·e·ter (ăl-tĭm′ĭ-tər) *n.* An instrument for determining elevation, especially an aneroid barometer used in aircraft that senses pressure changes accompanying changes in altitude. [Latin *altus,* high; see **al-**[2] in Appendix + -METER.] **—al′ti·met′ric** (ăl′tə-mĕt′rĭk) *adj.* **—al·tim′e·try** *n.*

al·ti·pla·no (äl′tĭ-plä′nō) *n., pl.* **-nos.** A high plateau, as in the Andean regions of Bolivia, Peru, and Argentina. [American Spanish : Latin *altus,* high; see **al-**[2] in Appendix + Latin *planum,* plain; see PLANE[1].]

al·ti·tude (ăl′tĭ-to͞od′, -tyo͞od′) *n. Abbr.* **alt. 1.** The height of a thing above a reference level, especially above sea level or above the earth's surface. See Synonyms at **elevation. 2.** A high location or area. **3.** *Astronomy.* The angular distance of a celestial object above the horizon. **4.** The perpendicular distance from the base of a geometric figure to the opposite vertex, parallel side, or parallel surface. **5.** High position or rank. [Middle English, from Latin *altitūdō,* from *altus,* high. See **al-**[2] in Appendix.] **—al′ti·tu′di·nal** (-to͞od′n-əl, -tyo͞od′-) *adj.*

altitude sickness *n.* A collection of symptoms, including shortness of breath, headache, and nosebleed, brought on by decreased oxygen in the atmosphere, such as that encountered at high altitudes.

al·to (ăl′tō) *n., pl.* **al·tos.** *Abbr.* **A.** *Music.* **1.** A low, female singing voice; a contralto. **2.** A countertenor. **3.** The range between soprano and tenor. **4.** A singer whose voice lies within this range. **5.** An instrument that sounds within this range. **6.** A vocal or instrumental part written for a voice or an instrument within this range. —*attributive.* Often used to modify another noun: *an alto flute; an alto balalaika.* [Italian, from Latin *altus,* high. See **al-**[2] in Appendix.]

alto clef *n. Music.* The C clef positioned to indicate that the third line from the bottom of a staff represents the pitch of middle C.

al·to·cu·mu·lus (ăl′tō-kyo͞o′myə-ləs) *n.* A cloud formation of rounded, fleecy, white or gray masses. [Latin *altus,* high; see **al-**[2] in Appendix + CUMULUS.]

al·to·geth·er (ôl′tə-gĕth′ər) *adv.* **1.** Entirely; completely; utterly: *lost the TV picture altogether; an altogether new approach.* **2.** With all included or counted; all told: *There were altogether 20 people at the dinner.* **3.** On the whole; with everything considered: *Altogether, I'm sorry it happened.* **—altogether** *n.* A state of nudity. Often used with *the: in the altogether.* [Middle English *al togeder* : *al,* all; see ALL + *togeder,* together; see TOGETHER.]

USAGE NOTE: *Altogether* should be distinguished from *all together. All together* is used of a group to indicate that its members performed or underwent an action collectively: *The nations stood all together. The prisoners were herded all together. All together* can be used only if it is possible to rephrase the sentence so that *all* and *together* may be separated by other words: *The books lay all together in a heap. All the books lay together in a heap. Altogether* should be used only when the sense could be expressed by *entirely* or *completely.*

Al·ton (ôl′tən). A city of southwest Illinois on bluffs of the Mississippi River north of St. Louis, Missouri. Lewis and Clark spent the winter of 1803–1804 just south of the site. Population, 34,171.

altazimuth
Mid 18th-century Russian telescope built by Mikhail V. Lomonosov (1711–1765)

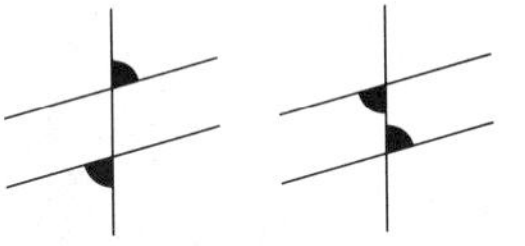

alternate angle

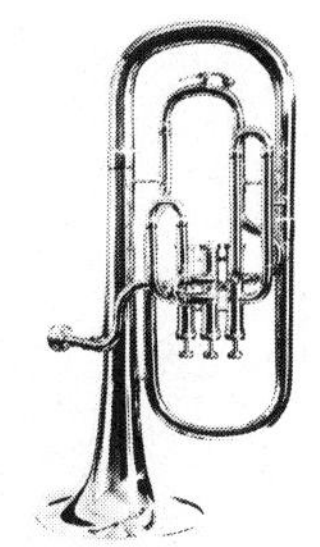

althorn

ă **pat**	oi **boy**
ā **pay**	ou **out**
âr **care**	o͝o **took**
ä **father**	o͞o **boot**
ĕ **pet**	ŭ **cut**
ē **be**	ûr **urge**
ĭ **pit**	th **thin**
ī **pie**	*th* **this**
îr **pier**	hw **which**
ŏ **pot**	zh **vision**
ō **toe**	ə **about, item**
ô **paw**	♦ regionalism

Stress marks: ′ (primary); ′ (secondary), as in **dictionary** (dĭk′shə-nĕr′ē)

Al·too·na (ăl-to͞o′nə). A city of central Pennsylvania on the eastern slopes of the Allegheny Mountains east of Pittsburgh. It was laid out in 1849 by the Pennsylvania Railroad as a switching point for locomotives used to cross the mountains. Population, 57,078.

al·to-re·lie·vo also **al·to-ri·lie·vo** (ăl′tō-rĭ-lē′vō, äl′tō-rēl-yä′vō) *n., pl.* **al·to-re·lie·vos** also **al·to-ri·lie·vi** (äl′tō-rēl-yä′vē). See **high relief.** [Italian *altorilievo* : *alto,* high; see ALTO + *rilievo,* relief; see BAS-RELIEF.]

al·to·stra·tus (ăl′tō-strā′təs, -străt′əs) *n.* An extended cloud formation of bluish or gray sheets or layers. [Latin *altus,* high; see **al-**[2] in Appendix + STRATUS.]

al·tri·cial (ăl-trĭsh′əl) *adj.* Helpless, naked, and blind when hatched: *altricial birds.* [From Latin *altrīx, altrīc-,* feminine of *altōr,* nourisher, from *alere,* to nourish. See **al-**[2] in Appendix.]

al·tru·ism (ăl′tro͞o-ĭz′əm) *n.* Unselfish concern for the welfare of others; selflessness. [French *altruisme,* probably from Italian *altrui,* someone else, from Latin *alter,* other. See **al-**[1] in Appendix.] **—al′tru·ist** *n.* **—al′tru·is′tic** *adj.* **—al′tru·is′ti·cal·ly** *adv.*

Al·tus (ăl′təs). A city of southwest Oklahoma near the Texas border southwest of Oklahoma City. It is a trade center in a farming region. Population, 23,101.

Al U·bay·yid (äl′ o͞o-bā′ĭd) also **El O·beid** (ĕl′ ō-bād′). A city of central Sudan southwest of Khartoum. Founded in the 1820's, it is an important transshipment center. Population, 140,000.

al·u·la (ăl′yə-lə) *n., pl.* **-lae** (-lē′). A small joint in the middle of a bird's wing, homologous with the thumb and bearing three or four quill-like feathers. Also called *bastard wing, spurious wing.* [New Latin, diminutive of Latin *āla,* wing.] **—al′u·lar** (-lər) *adj.*

al·um (ăl′əm) *n.* Any of various double sulfates of a trivalent metal such as aluminum, chromium, or iron and a univalent metal such as potassium or sodium, especially aluminum potassium sulfate, $AlK(SO_4)_2 \cdot 12H_2O$, widely used in industry as clarifiers, hardeners, and purifiers and medicinally as topical astringents and styptics. [Middle English, from Old French, from Latin *alūmen.*]

a·lu·mi·na (ə-lo͞o′mə-nə) *n.* Any of several forms of aluminum oxide, Al_2O_3, occurring naturally as corundum, in a hydrated form in bauxite, and with various impurities as ruby, sapphire, and emery, used in aluminum production and in abrasives, refractories, ceramics, and electrical insulation. Also called *aluminum oxide.* [New Latin *alūmina,* from Latin *alūmen, alūmin-,* alum.]

a·lu·mi·nate (ə-lo͞o′mə-nāt′, -nĭt) *n.* A chemical compound containing aluminum as part of a negative ion.

a·lu·mi·nif·er·ous (ə-lo͞o′mə-nĭf′ər-əs) *adj.* Containing or yielding aluminum, alumina, or alum. [Latin *alūmen, alūmin-,* alum + -FEROUS.]

al·u·min·i·um (ăl′yə-mĭn′ē-əm) *n. Chiefly British.* Variant of **aluminum.**

a·lu·mi·nize (ə-lo͞o′mə-nīz′) *tr.v.* **-nized, -niz·ing, -niz·es.** To coat or cover with aluminum or aluminum paint.

a·lu·mi·nous (ə-lo͞o′mə-nəs) *adj.* Of, relating to, or containing aluminum or alum.

a·lu·mi·num (ə-lo͞o′mə-nəm) *n. Symbol* **Al** A silvery-white, ductile metallic element, the most abundant in the earth's crust but found only in combination, chiefly in bauxite. Having good conductive and thermal properties, it is used to form many hard, light, corrosion-resistant alloys. Atomic number 13; atomic weight 26.98; melting point 660.2°C; boiling point 2,467°C; specific gravity 2.69; valence 3. See table at **element.** [ALUMIN(A) + -(I)UM.]

aluminum oxide *n.* See **alumina.**

aluminum plant *n.* A succulent herb *(Pilea cadierei)* often grown as a houseplant for its silver-colored leaves.

aluminum sulfate *n.* A white crystalline compound, $Al_2(SO_4)_3$, used chiefly in papermaking, water purification, sanitation, and tanning.

a·lum·na (ə-lŭm′nə) *n., pl.* **-nae** (-nē′). A woman graduate or former student of a school, college, or university. See Usage Note at **alumnus.** [Latin, feminine of *alumnus,* pupil. See ALUMNUS.]

a·lum·nus (ə-lŭm′nəs) *n., pl.* **-ni** (-nī′). A male graduate or former student of a school, college, or university. [Latin, pupil, from *alere,* to nourish. See **al-**[2] in Appendix.]

USAGE NOTE: The fact that the plural *alumni* of the masculine *alumnus* differs from the plural *alumnae* of the feminine *alumna* has created a certain amount of awkwardness with the advent of coeducational institutions. Most commonly, *alumni* is used for graduates of both sexes. But those who object to the choice of masculine forms in such cases may prefer the phrase *alumni and alumnae* or the form *alumnae/i;* this is the choice, for example, of many women's colleges that have begun to admit men.

Al·um Rock (ăl′əm). An unincorporated community of west-central California, a planned residential suburb of San Jose. Population, 17,471.

al·um·root (ăl′əm-ro͞ot′, -ro͝ot′) *n.* Any of various North American perennials of the genus *Heuchera* having palmately lobed basal leaves and leafless stalks bearing numerous small greenish, white, or reddish flowers.

al·u·nite (ăl′yə-nīt′) *n.* A gray mineral, chiefly $K_2Al_3(OH)_6(SO_4)_3$, used in making alum and fertilizer. [French, from *alun,* alum, from Latin *alūmen.*]

Al·va (ăl′və, äl′vä) also **Al·ba** (ăl′bə), Duke of. Title of Fernando Álvarez de Toledo. 1508–1582. Spanish general and colonial administrator of the Netherlands (1567–1573).

Al·va·ra·do (ăl′və-rä′dō, äl′vä-rä′thô), **Pedro de.** 1485–1541. Spanish general and colonial administrator who took part in the conquest of Mexico and became governor of Guatemala (1530).

Al·va·rez (ăl′və-rĕz′), **Luis Walter.** 1911–1988. American physicist. He won a 1968 Nobel Prize for his study of subatomic particles.

Ál·va·rez Quin·te·ro (äl′vä-rĕth′ kēn-tĕ′rō), **Serafín.** 1871–1938. Spanish dramatist who collaborated with his brother **Joaquín** (1873–1944) on nearly 200 plays, which helped revitalize Spanish theater in the 20th century.

al·ve·o·lar (ăl-vē′ə-lər) *adj.* **1.** Of or relating to an alveolus. **2.** *Anatomy.* **a.** Relating to the jaw section containing the tooth sockets: *the alveolar ridge.* **b.** Relating to the alveoli of the lungs. **3.** *Linguistics.* Formed with the tip of the tongue touching or near the inner ridge of the gums of the upper front teeth, as the English *t, d,* and *s.* **—alveolar** *n. Linguistics.* An alveolar sound. **—al·ve′o·lar·ly** *adv.*

al·ve·o·late (ăl-vē′ə-lĭt) *adj.* Having a honeycombed surface. **—al·ve′o·la′tion** (-lā′shən) *n.*

al·ve·o·lus (ăl-vē′ə-ləs) *n., pl.* **-li** (-lī′). **1.** A small angular cavity or pit, such as a honeycomb cell. **2.** A tooth socket in the jawbone. **3.** A tiny, thin-walled, capillary-rich sac in the lungs where the exchange of oxygen and carbon dioxide takes place. In this sense, also called *air sac.* [Latin, small hollow, diminutive of *alveus,* a hollow, from *alvus,* belly.]

Al·vin (ăl′vĭn). A city of southeast Texas south of Houston. It is chiefly residential. Population, 16,515.

al·ways (ôl′wāz, -wĭz, -wēz) *adv.* **1.** At all times; invariably: *always late.* **2.** For all time; forever: *They will always be friends.* **3.** At any time; in any event: *You can always resign if you're unhappy.* [Middle English *alweis* : *alwei,* always (from Old English *ealne weg* : *ealne,* accusative of *eall,* all; see ALL + *weg,* way; see **wegh-** in Appendix) + *-es,* adv. suff.; see -S[3].]

Al·yce clover or **al·yce clover** (ăl′ĭs) *n.* A tropical Asiatic herb *(Alysicarpus vaginalis)* with alternate, simple leaves and reddish flowers, grown as a pasture and hay crop and naturalized in Florida and the West Indies. [Probably by folk etymology from New Latin *Alysicarpus (vaginalis),* genus name : Greek *halusis,* chain; see **wel-**[2] in Appendix + Greek *karpos,* fruit; see -CARP.]

a·lys·sum (ə-lĭs′əm) *n.* **1.** See **sweet alyssum. 2.** Any of various chiefly Mediterranean weeds or ornamentals of the genus *Alyssum* in the mustard family, having racemes of white or yellow flowers. Also called *madwort.* **3.** See **hoary alyssum.** [New Latin *Alyssum,* genus name, from Latin *alysson,* kind of madder, from Greek *alusson,* a plant believed to cure rabies : *a-,* not; see A-[1] + *lussa,* rabies; see **wḷkʷo-** in Appendix.]

Alz·heim·er's disease (älts′hī-mərz, ălts′-, ôlts′-, ôlz′hī-mərs) *n.* A disease marked by progressive loss of mental capacity resulting from degeneration of the brain cells. [After Alois *Alzheimer* (1864–1915), German neurologist.]

am[1] (ăm) *v.* First person singular present indicative of **be.** [Middle English, from Old English *eom.* See **es-** in Appendix.]

am[2] or **AM** *abbr.* Amplitude modulation.

Am[1] The symbol for the element **americium.**

Am[2] *abbr. Bible.* Amos.

Am. *abbr.* America; American.

A.M. *abbr.* **1.** Airmail. **2.** Or **A.M.** *Latin.* Anno mundi (in the year of the world). **3.** Also **a.m.** or **A.M.** Ante meridiem. See Usage Note at **ante meridiem. 4.** *Latin.* Artium magister (Master of Arts).

AMA also **A.M.A.** *abbr.* American Medical Association.

A·ma·do (ə-mä′do͞o), **Jorge.** Born 1912. Brazilian writer whose novels concern social injustice.

A·ma·ga·sa·ki (ä′mə-gə-sä′kē). A city of southern Honshu, Japan, on Osaka Bay. It is a port, an industrial center, and a suburb of Osaka. Population, 509,115.

a·mah also **a·ma** (ä′mə, ä′mä) *n.* A housemaid, especially a wet nurse, in India and the Far East. [Portuguese *ama,* nurse, from Medieval Latin *amma,* mother.]

Am·a·lek·ite (ăm′ə-lĕk′-īt′, ə-măl′ĭ-kīt′) *n.* A member of an ancient nomadic people of Canaan said in the Old Testament to be descendants of Esau's grandson Amalek. [Hebrew *'ămālēqî,* from *'ămālēq,* Amalek.]

a·mal·gam (ə-măl′gəm) *n.* **1.** Any of various alloys of mercury with other metals, as with tin or silver. **2.** A combination of diverse elements; a mixture: *an amalgam of strength, reputation, and commitment to ethical principles.* See Synonyms at **mixture.** [Middle English, from Old French *amalgame,* from Medieval Latin *amalgama,* probably ultimately from Greek *malagma,* soft mass.]

a·mal·ga·mate (ə-măl′gə-māt′) *v.* **-mat·ed, -mat·ing, -mates.** *—tr.* **1.** To combine into a unified or integrated whole; unite. See Synonyms at **mix. 2.** To mix or alloy (a metal) with mercury. *—intr.* **1.** To become combined; unite. **2.** To unite or blend with another metal. **—a·mal′ga·ma′tive** *adj.* **—a·mal′ga·ma′tor** *n.*

a·mal·ga·ma·tion (ə-măl′gə-mā′shən) *n.* **1.** The act of amalgamating or the condition resulting from this act. **2.** A consolidation or merger, as of several corporations. **3.** The production of a metal alloy of mercury.

Am·al·the·a (ăm′əl-thē′ə) *n.* The satellite of Jupiter that is fourth in distance from the planet. [Latin *Amalthēa,* nymph who nursed the infant Jupiter with goat's milk, from Greek *Amaltheia.*]

a·man·dine (ä′mən-dēn′, ăm′ən-) *adj.* Prepared or garnished with almonds: *swordfish amandine.* [French, from *amande,* almond, from Old French *almande.* See ALMOND.]

am·a·ni·ta (ăm′ə-nī′tə, -nē′-) *n.* Any of various mushrooms in the genus *Amanita,* many of which are extremely poisonous. [New Latin *Amanīta,* genus name, from Greek *amanitai,* a fungus.]

a·man·ta·dine (ə-măn′tə-dēn′) *n.* An antiviral drug, $C_{10}H_{17}N*HCl$, also used in the treatment of Parkinson's disease. [Alteration of *adamantane,* a hydrocarbon + –INE[2].]

a·man·u·en·sis (ə-măn′yo͞o-ĕn′sĭs) *n., pl.* **-ses** (-sēz). One who is employed to take dictation or to copy manuscript. [Latin *āmanuēnsis,* from the phrase *(servus) ā manū,* (slave) at handwriting : *ā, ab,* by; see AB–[1] + *manū,* ablative of *manus,* hand; see **man-**[2] in Appendix.]

am·a·ranth (ăm′ə-rănth′) *n.* **1.** Any of various annuals of the genus *Amaranthus* having dense green or reddish clusters of tiny flowers and including several weeds, ornamentals, and food plants. **2.** An imaginary flower that never fades. **3.** *Color.* A deep reddish purple to dark or grayish, purplish red. **4.** A dark red to purple azo dye. [New Latin *amaranthus,* genus name, alteration of Latin *amarantus,* from Greek *amarantos,* unfading : *a-,* not; see A–[1] + *marainein,* to wither; see **mer-** in Appendix.]

am·a·ran·thine (ăm′ə-răn′thĭn, -thīn′) *adj.* **1.** Of, relating to, or resembling the amaranth. **2.** Eternally beautiful and unfading; everlasting. **3.** *Color.* Deep purple-red.

am·a·relle (ăm′ə-rĕl′) *n.* A type of sour cherry having pale red fruit and colorless or nearly colorless juice. [German, from Medieval Latin *amarellum,* from Latin *amārus,* bitter.]

am·a·ret·to (ăm′ə-rĕt′ō) *n., pl.* **-tos.** An Italian liqueur flavored with almond. [Italian, diminutive of *amaro,* bitter, from Latin *amārus.*]

Am·a·ril·lo (ăm′ə-rĭl′ō, -rĭl′ə). A city of northern Texas in the Panhandle north of Lubbock. The city grew after the coming of the railroad in 1887 and the discovery of gas (1918) and oil (1921). Population, 149,230.

am·a·ryl·lis (ăm′ə-rĭl′ĭs) *n.* **1.** Any of several chiefly tropical American bulbous plants of the genus *Hippeastrum* grown as ornamentals for their large, showy, funnel-shaped, variously colored flowers that are grouped in umbels. **2.** See **belladonna lily. 3.** Any of several similar or related plants. **4. Amaryllis.** Used in classical pastoral poetry as a conventional name for a shepherdess. [New Latin *Amaryllis,* genus name, from Latin, name of a shepherdess, from Greek *Amarullis.*]

a·mass (ə-măs′) *tr.v.* **a·massed, a·mass·ing, a·mass·es.** To gather together for oneself, as for one's pleasure or profit; accumulate: *amassed a fortune.* See Synonyms at **gather.** [Middle English, to accumulate, from Old French *amasser,* to assemble : *a-,* to (from Latin *ad-;* see AD–) + *masser,* to gather together (from Latin *massa,* lump, mass; see MASS).] **—a·mass′a·ble** *adj.* **—a·mass′er** *n.* **—a·mass′ment** *n.*

am·a·teur (ăm′ə-tûr′, -tər, -ə-cho͝or′, -chər, -tyo͝or′) *n.* **1.** *Abbr.* **a., A.** A person who engages in an art, a science, a study, or an athletic activity as a pastime rather than as a profession. **2.** *Abbr.* **a., A.** *Sports.* An athlete who has never participated in competition for money. **3.** One lacking the skill of a professional, as in an art. **—amateur** *adj.* **1.** *Abbr.* **a., A.** Of, relating to, or performed by an amateur. **2.** *Abbr.* **a., A.** Made up of amateurs. **3.** Not professional; unskillful. [French, from Latin *amātor,* lover, from *amāre,* to love.] **—am′a·teur·ism** *n.*

SYNONYMS: *amateur, dabbler, dilettante, tyro.* The central meaning shared by these nouns is "one engaging in a pursuit but lacking professional skill": *a musician who is a gifted amateur, not a professional; a dabbler in the graphic arts; a sculptor but a mere dilettante; a tyro in the art of writing poetry.*

ANTONYM: *professional.*

WORD HISTORY: When Mrs. T.W. Atkinson remarked in her 1863 *Recollections of the Tartar Steppes and their Inhabitants,* "I am no amateur of these melons," she used *amateur* in a sense unfamiliar to us. That sense, "a lover, an admirer," is, however, clearly descended from the senses of the word's ultimate Latin source, *amātor,* "lover, devoted friend, devotee, enthusiastic pursuer of an objective," and from its immediate Latin-derived French source, *amateur,* with a similar range of meanings. First recorded in English in 1784 with the sense in which Mrs. Atkinson used it, *amateur* is found in 1786 with a meaning more familiar to us, "a person who engages in an art, for example, as a pastime rather than as a profession," a sense that had already developed in French. Given the limitations of doing something as an amateur, it is not surprising that the word is soon after recorded in the disparaging sense we still use to refer to someone who lacks professional skill or ease in performance.

am·a·teur·ish (ăm′ə-tûr′ĭsh, -cho͝or′-, -tyo͝or′-) *adj.* Characteristic of an amateur; not professional. **—am′a·teur′ish·ly** *adv.* **—am′a·teur′ish·ness** *n.*

A·ma·ti (ä-mä′tē) *n., pl.* **-tis.** *Music.* A violin made by Nicolò Amati or the members of his family.

Amati, Nicolò or **Nicola.** 1596–1684. Italian violin maker who taught his craft to Stradivari and Guarneri.

am·a·tive (ăm′ə-tĭv) *adj.* Inclined toward love; amorous. [Medieval Latin *amātīvus,* capable of love, from *amātus,* past participle of Latin *amāre,* to love.] **—am′a·tive′·ly** *adv.* **—am′a·tive′·ness** *n.*

am·a·tol (ăm′ə-tôl′, -tŏl′) *n.* A highly explosive mixture of ammonium nitrate and trinitrotoluene. [From AM(MONIUM) + (TRINITRO)TOL(UENE).]

am·a·to·ry (ăm′ə-tôr′ē, -tōr′ē) *adj.* Of, relating to, or expressive of love, especially sexual love. [Latin *amātōrius,* from *amātor,* lover. See AMATEUR.]

am·au·ro·sis (ăm′ô-rō′sĭs) *n.* Total loss of vision, especially when occurring without pathological changes to the eye. [Greek *amaurōsis,* from *amauros,* dark.] **—am′au·rot′ic** (-rŏt′ĭk) *adj.*

♦**a·maze** (ə-māz′) *tr.v.* **a·mazed, a·maz·ing, a·maz·es. 1.** To affect with great wonder; astonish. See Synonyms at **surprise.** See Regional Note at **possum. 2.** *Obsolete.* To bewilder; perplex. **—amaze** *n.* Amazement; wonder. [From Middle English *masen,* to bewilder, and from *amased,* bewildered (from Old English *āmasod*), both from Old English *āmasian,* to bewilder : *ā-,* intensive pref. + **masian,* to confuse.] **—a·maz′ed·ly** (ə-mā′zĭd-lē) *adv.* **—a·maz′ed·ness** *n.*

a·maze·ment (ə-māz′mənt) *n.* **1.** A state of extreme surprise or wonder; astonishment. **2.** *Obsolete.* Bewilderment; perplexity.

Am·a·zon (ăm′ə-zŏn′, -zən) *n.* **1.** *Greek Mythology.* A member of a nation of women warriors reputed to have lived in Scythia. **2.** Often **amazon.** A tall, aggressive, strong-willed woman. [Middle English, from Latin *Amāzōn,* from Greek, probably of Iranian origin.]

Am·a·zo·ni·a (ăm′ə-zō′nē-ə). The vast basin of the Amazon River in northern South America. It remains largely unpopulated and undeveloped, especially in the interior.

Am·a·zo·ni·an (ăm′ə-zō′nē-ən) *adj.* **1.** Of or relating to the Amazon River or to Amazonia. **2.** Characteristic of or resembling an Amazon. **3.** Often **amazonian.** Strong and aggressive. Used of women.

am·a·zon·ite (ăm′ə-zə-nīt′) *n.* A green variety of microcline, often used as a semiprecious stone. Also called *amazon stone.* [After the AMAZON (RIVER).]

Amazon River. The second-longest river in the world, flowing about 6,275 km (3,900 mi) from northern Peru across northern Brazil to a wide delta on the Atlantic Ocean. It was probably first explored by the Spanish navigator Vicente Yáñez Pinzón in 1500.

amazon stone *n.* See **amazonite.**

am·bage (ăm′bĭj) *n. Archaic.* **1.** Often **ambages.** Ambiguity. **2. ambages.** Winding ways or indirect proceedings. [Back-formation from Middle English *ambages,* equivocation, from Latin *ambāges* : *ambi-,* around; see AMBI– + *agere,* to drive; see **ag-** in Appendix.] **—am·ba′gious** (ăm-bā′jəs) *adj.*

am·ba·rel·la (ăm′bə-rĕl′ə) *n.* **1.** A tree *(Spondias cytherea)* native to the Pacific islands and grown in tropical and subtropical regions for its edible fruits. **2.** The orange-yellow, egg-shaped fruit of this tree, eaten fresh or pickled, or used to make preserves. Also called *Otaheite apple.* [Sinhalese *æmbarælla,* from Sanskrit *āmravāṭakaḥ,* a kind of tree : *āmraḥ,* mango tree (from *amlaḥ,* tart) + *vāṭakaḥ,* diminutive of *vāṭaḥ,* enclosure, garden; see **wer-**[4] in Appendix.]

am·bas·sa·dor (ăm-băs′ə-dər, -dôr′) *n.* **1.** A diplomatic official of the highest rank appointed and accredited as representative in residence by one government or sovereign to another, usually for a specific length of time. **2.** A diplomatic official heading his or her country's permanent mission to certain international organizations, such as the United Nations. **3.** An authorized messenger or representative. **4.** An unofficial representative: *ambassadors of good will.* [Middle English *ambassadour,* from Old French *ambassadeur,* from Medieval Latin *ambactia,* mission, from Latin *ambactus,* servant, ultimately of Celtic origin. See **ag-** in Appendix.] **—am·bas′sa·do′ri·al** (-dôr′ē-əl, -dōr′-) *adj.* **—am·bas′sa·dor·ship′** *n.*

ambassador at large *n., pl.* **ambassadors at large.** An ambassador who is not assigned to a specific country.

am·bas·sa·dress (ăm-băs′ə-drĭs) *n. Usage Problem.* A woman ambassador. See Usage Note at **–ess.**

Am·ba·to (äm-bä′tō). A city of central Ecuador in a high Andean valley south of Quito. It is a commercial center and popular tourist site. Population, 100,454.

am·beer (ăm′bîr) *n. Chiefly Southern U.S.* Saliva colored by tobacco chewed or held in the mouth; tobacco juice. [Alteration (influenced by *beer* with reference to color and foam of the spittle) of *amber* with reference to color.]

am·ber (ăm′bər) *n.* **1.** A hard, translucent, yellow, orange, or brownish-yellow fossil resin, used for making jewelry and other ornamental objects. **2.** *Color.* A brownish yellow. **—amber** *adj.* **1.** *Color.* Having the color of amber; brownish-yellow. **2.** Made of or resembling amber: *an amber necklace.* [Middle English *ambre,* from Old French, from Medieval Latin *ambra, ambar,* from Arabic *'anbar,* ambergris, amber.]

am·ber·gris (ăm′bər-grĭs′, -grēs′) *n.* A waxy, grayish sub-

amanita

amaryllis

Amazon
Detail from a Greek vase

ă pat	oi boy
ā pay	ou out
âr care	o͝o took
ä father	o͞o boot
ĕ pet	ŭ cut
ē be	ûr urge
ĭ pit	th thin
ī pie	*th* this
îr pier	hw which
ŏ pot	zh vision
ō toe	ə about, item
ô paw	♦ regionalism

Stress marks: ′ (primary); ′ (secondary), as in **dictionary** (dĭk′shə-nĕr′ē)

stance formed in the intestines of sperm whales and found floating at sea or washed ashore. It is added to perfumes to slow down the rate of evaporation. [Middle English, from Old French *ambre gris* : *ambre*, amber; see AMBER + *gris*, gray; see GRIZZLE.]

am·ber·jack (ăm′bər-jăk′) *n., pl.* **amberjack** or **-jacks.** A food and game fish of the genus *Seriola*, native to temperate and tropical marine waters. [AMBER + JACK, a fish.]

ambi– *pref.* Both: *ambiversion.* [Latin, around. See **ambhi** in Appendix.]

am·bi·ance also **am·bi·ence** (ăm′bē-əns, äN-byäNs′) *n.* The special atmosphere or mood created by a particular environment: *"The curriculum and intellectual ambiance are virtually identical"* (Robert Kanigel). [French, from *ambiant*, surrounding, from Latin *ambiēns, ambient-*. See AMBIENT.]

am·bi·dex·ter·i·ty (ăm′bĭ-dĕk-stĕr′ĭ-tē) *n.* **1.** The state or quality of being ambidextrous. **2.** Deceit or hypocrisy.

am·bi·dex·trous (ăm′bĭ-dĕk′strəs) *adj.* **1.** Able to use both hands with equal facility. **2.** Unusually skillful; adroit. **3.** Deceptive or hypocritical. [From *ambidexter*, ambidextrous (archaic), from Middle English, double dealer, from Medieval Latin : Latin *ambi-*, on both sides; see AMBI– + Latin *dexter*, right-handed.] **—am′bi·dex′trous·ly** *adv.*

am·bi·ence (ăm′bē-əns, äN-byäNs′) *n.* Variant of **ambiance.**

am·bi·ent (ăm′bē-ənt) *adj.* Surrounding; encircling: *ambient sound; ambient air.* [Latin *ambiēns, ambient-*, present participle of *ambīre*, to surround : *ambi-*, around; see AMBI– + *īre*, to go; see **ei-** in Appendix.]

am·bi·gu·i·ty (ăm′bĭ-gyo͞o′ĭ-tē) *n., pl.* **-ties. 1.** Doubtfulness or uncertainty as regards interpretation: *"leading a life of alleged moral ambiguity"* (Anatole Broyard). **2.** Something of doubtful meaning: *a poem full of ambiguities.*

ambiguity error *n.* A gross error, usually transient, in the readout of an electronic device that is caused by imprecise synchronism, as in analog-to-digital conversion.

am·big·u·ous (ăm-bĭg′yo͞o-əs) *adj.* **1.** Open to more than one interpretation: *an ambiguous reply.* **2.** Doubtful or uncertain: *"The theatrical status of her frequently derided but constantly revived plays remained ambiguous"* (Frank Rich). [From Latin *ambiguus*, uncertain, from *ambigere*, to go about : *ambi-*, around; see AMBI– + *agere*, to drive; see **ag-** in Appendix.]

SYNONYMS: *ambiguous, equivocal, obscure, recondite, abstruse, vague, cryptic, enigmatic.* These adjectives mean lacking clarity of meaning. *Ambiguous* indicates the presence of two or more possible meanings: *Frustrated by ambiguous instructions, the parents were never able to assemble the new toy.* Something *equivocal* is unclear or misleading, sometimes as a result of a deliberate effort to avoid exposure of one's position: *"The polling had a complex and equivocal message for potential female candidates at all levels"* (David S. Broder). *Obscure* implies that meaning is hidden, either from lack of clarity of expression or from inherent difficulty of comprehension: *Those who do not appreciate Kafka's work say his style is obscure and too complex. Recondite* and *abstruse* connote the erudite obscurity of the scholar: *"some recondite problem in historiography"* (Walter Laqueur). *The professor's lectures were so abstruse that students tended to avoid them.* What is *vague* is unclear because it is expressed in indefinite form or because it reflects imprecision of thought: *"Vague . . . forms of speech . . . have so long passed for mysteries of science"* (John Locke). *Cryptic* suggests a puzzling terseness that is often intended to discourage understanding: *The new insurance policy is written without cryptic or mysterious terms.* Something *enigmatic* is mysterious, puzzling, and often challenging: *I didn't grasp the meaning of that enigmatic comment until much later.*

am·bi·po·lar (ăm′bĭ-pō′lər) *adj.* **1.** Applying equally to both positive and negative ions. **2.** Operating in two directions simultaneously.

am·bi·sex·u·al (ăm′bĭ-sĕk′sho͞o-əl) *adj.* **1.** Sexually attracted to either sex indiscriminately. **2.** Suited to either sex: *"The patterns also are available for men because* [the designer] *believes in ambisexual fashion"* (Women's Wear Daily). **—ambisexual** *n.* An ambisexual person or thing. **—am′bi·sex′u·al′i·ty** (-ăl′ĭ-tē) *n.*

am·bit (ăm′bĭt) *n.* **1.** An external boundary; a circuit. **2.** Sphere or scope. See Synonyms at **range.** [Latin *ambitus*, from past participle of *ambīre*, to go around. See AMBIENT.]

am·bi·tion (ăm-bĭsh′ən) *n.* **1. a.** An eager or strong desire to achieve something, such as fame or power. **b.** The object or goal desired: *Her ambition is the presidency.* **2.** Desire for exertion or activity; energy: *had no ambition to go dancing.* [Middle English *ambicioun*, excessive desire for honor, power, or wealth, from Old French *ambition*, from Latin *ambitiō, ambitiōn-*, from *ambitus*, past participle of *ambīre*, to go around (for votes). See AMBIENT.]

am·bi·tious (ăm-bĭsh′əs) *adj.* **1.** Full of, characterized by, or motivated by ambition. **2.** Greatly desirous; eager: *"I am not ambitious of ridicule"* (Edmund Burke). **3.** Requiring or showing much effort; challenging: *an ambitious schedule.* **—am·bi′tious·ly** *adv.* **—am·bi′tious·ness** *n.*

am·biv·a·lence (ăm-bĭv′ə-ləns) *n.* **1.** The coexistence of opposing attitudes or feelings, such as love and hate, toward a person, an object, or an idea. **2.** Uncertainty or indecisiveness as to which course to follow. [German *Ambivalenz* : Latin *ambi-*, ambi- + Latin *valentia*, vigor (from *valēns, valent-*, present participle of *valēre*, to be strong; see **wal-** in Appendix).]

am·biv·a·lent (ăm-bĭv′ə-lənt) *adj.* Exhibiting or feeling ambivalence.

am·bi·ver·sion (ăm′bĭ-vûr′zhən, -shən) *n.* A personality trait including the qualities of both introversion and extroversion. [AMBI– + (INTRO)VERSION or (EXTRO)VERSION.] **—am′bi·vert′** (-vûrt′) *n.*

am·ble (ăm′bəl) *intr.v.* **-bled, -bling, -bles. 1.** To walk slowly or leisurely; stroll. **2.** To move along at an easy gait by using both legs on one side alternately with both on the other. Used of a horse. **—amble** *n.* **1.** An unhurried or leisurely walk. **2.** An easy gait, especially that of a horse. [Middle English *amblen*, from Old French *ambler*, from Latin *ambulāre*, to walk.] **—am′bler** *n.*

Am·bler (ăm′blər), **Eric.** Born 1909. British writer noted for his suspense novels, including *A Passage of Arms* (1959).

am·blyg·o·nite (ăm-blĭg′ə-nīt′) *n.* A white or greenish mineral, (Li,Na)Al(PO_4)(F,OH), that is an important source of lithium. [German *Amblygonit*, from Greek *amblugōnios*, obtuse-angled : *amblus*, blunt; see **mel-**[1] in Appendix + *gōnia*, angle; see **genu-**[1] in Appendix.]

am·bly·o·pi·a (ăm′blē-ō′pē-ə) *n.* Dimness of vision, especially when occurring in one eye without apparent physical defect or disease. Also called *lazy eye.* [New Latin, from Greek *ambluōpia*, from *ambluōpos*, dim-sighted : *amblus*, dim; see **mel-**[1] in Appendix + *ōps*, eye; see MYOPIA.] **—am′bly·o′pic** (-ō′pĭk, -ŏp′ĭk) *adj.*

am·bo (ăm′bō′) *n., pl.* **am·bos** or **am·bo·nes** (ăm-bō′nēz). One of the two pulpits or raised stands in early Christian churches from which parts of the service were chanted or read. [Medieval Latin, from Greek *ambōn*, raised edge.]

am·boi·na (ăm-boi′nə) *n.* Variant of **amboyna.**

Am·boi·na (ăm-boi′nə). See **Ambon.**

Am·boi·nese (ăm′boi-nēz′, -nēs′, -ăm′-) *n.* Variant of **Ambonese.**

Am·bon (ăm′bôn) also **Am·boi·na** (ăm-boi′nə). An island of eastern Indonesia in the Moluccas near Ceram.

am·bo·nes (ăm-bō′nēz) *n.* A plural of **ambo.**

Am·bo·nese (ăm′bə-nēz′, -nēs′, ăm′-) or **Am·boi·nese** (-boi-) *n., pl.* **Ambonese** or **Amboinese. 1.** A native or inhabitant of Ambon. **2.** The Austronesian language of Ambon.

am·boy·na also **am·boi·na** (ăm-boi′nə) *n.* See **padauk.** [After *Amboyna*, (Ambon).]

am·brette (ăm-brĕt′) *n.* See **abelmosk.** [French, from Old French, diminutive of *ambre*, amber. See AMBER.]

Am·brose (ăm′brōz′), Saint. A.D. 340?–397. Writer, composer, and bishop of Milan (374–397) who imposed orthodoxy on the early Christian Church. **—Am·bro′sian** (ăm-brō′zhən) *adj.*

am·bro·sia (ăm-brō′zhə, -zhē-ə) *n.* **1.** *Greek & Roman Mythology.* The food of the gods, thought to confer immortality. **2.** Something with an especially delicious flavor or fragrance. **3.** A dessert containing primarily oranges and flaked coconut. [Latin, from Greek, from *ambrotos*, immortal, immortalizing : *a-*, not; see A–[1] + *-mbrotos*, mortal; see **mer-** in Appendix.]

am·bro·sial (ăm-brō′zhəl, -zhē-əl) also **am·bro·sian** (-zhən, -zhē-ən) *adj.* **1.** Suggestive of ambrosia; fragrant or delicious. See Synonyms at **delicious. 2.** Of or worthy of the gods; divine. **—am·bro′sial·ly** *adv.*

am·bro·type (ăm′brō-tīp′) *n.* An early type of photograph made by imaging a negative on glass backed by a dark surface. [Greek *ambrotos*, immortal; see AMBROSIA + TYPE.]

am·bry (ăm′brē) *n., pl.* **-bries. 1.** *Chiefly British.* A pantry. **2.** A niche near the altar of a church for keeping sacred vessels and vestments. [Middle English *almerie*, place for safekeeping, from Old French *almarie*, from Medieval Latin *almārium*, from Latin *armārium*, closet, from *arma*, tools. See ARM[2].]

ambs·ace (ām′zās′) *n.* **1.** *Games.* Double aces. **2.** Bad luck; misfortune. **3.** The smallest amount possible or the most worthless thing. [Middle English *ambes as*, from Old French, from Latin *ambās ās* : *ambō*, both + *ās*, unit.]

am·bu·lac·rum (ăm′byə-lăk′rəm, -lā′krəm) *n., pl.* **-lac·ra** (-lăk′rə, -lā′krə). One of the five radial areas on the undersurface of the starfish and similar echinoderms, from which the tube feet are protruded and withdrawn. [Latin, walk planted with trees, from *ambulāre*, to walk.] **—am′bu·lac′ral** *adj.*

am·bu·lance (ăm′byə-ləns) *n.* A specially equipped vehicle used to transport the sick or injured. [French, from *(hôpital) ambulant*, mobile (hospital), from Latin *ambulāns, ambulant-*, present participle of *ambulāre*, to walk.]

ambulance chaser *n. Slang.* **1.** A lawyer who obtains clients by persuading accident victims to sue for damages. **2.** A lawyer avid for clients.

am·bu·lant (ăm′byə-lənt) *adj.* Moving or walking about. [French, from Latin *ambulāns, ambulant-*, present participle of *ambulāre*, to walk.]

am·bu·late (ăm′byə-lāt′) *intr.v.* **-lat·ed, -lat·ing, -lates.** To walk from place to place; move about. [Latin *ambulāre, ambulāt-*, to walk. See **ambhi** in Appendix.]

am·bu·la·to·ry (ăm′byə-lə-tôr′ē, -tōr′ē) *adj.* **1.** Of, relating to, or adapted for walking. **2.** Capable of walking; not bedridden: *an ambulatory patient.* **3.** Moving about. **4.** *Law.* That can be changed or revoked, as a will during the life of the testator. **—ambulatory** *n., pl.* **-ries.** A covered place for walking, as in a cloister. **—am′bu·la·to′ri·ly** *adv.*

am·bus·cade (ăm′bə-skād′, ăm′bə-skād′) *n.* An ambush. **—ambuscade** *tr.v.* **-cad·ed, -cad·ing, -cades.** To attack suddenly and without warning from a concealed place; ambush. See Synonyms at **ambush.** [French *embuscade* (from Old French *embuschier,* to ambush) and Old Italian *imboscata,* from feminine past participle of *imboscare,* to ambush, both from Old Frankish **boscu,* bush, woods.] **—am′bus·cad′er** *n.*

am·bush (ăm′bo͝osh) *n.* **1.** The act of lying in wait to attack by surprise. **2.** A sudden attack made from a concealed position. **3. a.** Those hiding in order to attack by surprise. **b.** The hiding place used for this. **4.** A hidden peril or trap. **—ambush** *tr.v.* **-bushed, -bush·ing, -bush·es.** To attack from a concealed position. [Middle English *embush,* from Old French *embusche,* from *embuschier,* to ambush, from Old Frankish **boscu,* bush, woods.] **—am′bush′er** *n.*

SYNONYMS: *ambush, ambuscade, bushwhack, waylay.* The central meaning shared by these verbs is "to attack suddenly and without warning from a place of concealment": *guerrillas ambushing a platoon of regulars; highwaymen ambuscading a stagecoach; tax collectors bushwhacked by moonshiners; a truck waylaid and its driver robbed.*

Am·chit·ka (ăm-chĭt′kə). An island off western Alaska in the Rat Islands of the western Aleutians.

a·me·ba (ə-mē′bə) *n.* Variant of **amoeba.**

am·e·bi·a·sis also **am·oe·bi·a·sis** (ăm′ə-bī′ə-sĭs) *n.* An infection or a disease caused by amoebas, especially *Entamoeba histolytica.*

a·me·bic dysentery or **a·moe·bic dysentery** (ə-mē′bĭk) *n.* An acute disease caused by ingesting substances contaminated with the amoeba *Entamoeba histolytica* and characterized by severe diarrhea, nausea, and inflammation of the intestines.

a·me·bo·cyte (ə-mē′bə-sīt′) *n.* Variant of **amoebocyte.**

a·me·lio·rate (ə-mēl′yə-rāt′) *tr. & intr.v.* **-rat·ed, -rat·ing, -rates.** To make or become better; improve. See Synonyms at **improve.** [Alteration of MELIORATE.]

a·me·lio·ra·tion (ə-mēl′yə-rā′shən) *n.* **1.** The act or an instance of ameliorating. **2.** The state of being ameliorated; improvement.

a·men (ā-mĕn′, ä-mĕn′) *interj.* Used at the end of a prayer or a statement to express assent or approval. [Middle English, from Old English, from Late Latin *āmēn,* from Greek *amēn,* from Hebrew *'āmēn,* certainly, verily.]

A·men also **A·mon** (ä′mən) *n. Mythology.* The Egyptian god of life and reproduction, represented as a man with a ram's head.

a·me·na·ble (ə-mē′nə-bəl, ə-mĕn′ə-) *adj.* **1.** Responsive to advice, authority, or suggestion; tractable. See Synonyms at **obedient. 2.** Responsible to higher authority; accountable. See Synonyms at **responsible. 3.** Open to testing, criticism, or judgment. [Probably alteration of Middle English *menable,* from Old French, from *mener,* to lead, from Latin *mināre,* to drive, from *minārī,* to threaten, from *minae,* threats. See **men-²** in Appendix.] **—a·me′na·bil′i·ty, a·me′na·ble·ness** *n.* **—a·me′na·bly** *adv.*

amen corner *n.* **1.** A place in a church reserved for persons leading congregational responses. **2.** A group of ardent worshipers in a church.

a·mend (ə-mĕnd′) *v.* **a·mend·ed, a·mend·ing, a·mends.** *—tr.* **1.** To change for the better; improve: *amended the earlier proposal so as to make it more comprehensive.* **2.** To remove the faults or errors in; correct. See Synonyms at **correct. 3.** To alter (a legislative measure, for example) formally by adding, deleting, or rephrasing. *—intr.* To better one's conduct; reform. [Middle English *amenden,* from Old French *amender,* from Latin *ēmendāre* : *ex-,* ex- + *mendum,* fault.]

a·men·da·to·ry (ə-mĕn′də-tôr′ē, -tōr′ē) *adj.* Serving or tending to amend; corrective.

a·mend·ment (ə-mĕnd′mənt) *n.* **1.** The act of changing for the better; improvement: *"Society may sometimes show signs of repentance and amendment"* (George G. Coulton). **2.** A correction or an alteration, as in a manuscript. **3. a.** Formal revision of, addition to, or change, as in a bill or a constitution. **b.** A statement of such a change: *The 19th Amendment to the Constitution gave women the right to vote.*

a·mends (ə-mĕndz′) *pl.n. (used with a sing. or pl. verb).* Recompense for grievance or injury: *The new law offers no amends to victims of crime. I assured them that no amends are necessary. You must make amends to them for the insult.* See Synonyms at **reparation.** [Middle English *amendes,* from Old French, pl. of *amende,* reparation, from *amender,* to amend. See AMEND.]

A·men·ho·tep III (ä′mən-hō′tĕp, ăm′ən-) also **Am·e·no·phis III** (ăm′ə-nō′fĭs). King of Egypt (1411?–1375 B.C.) who sponsored the building of many monuments.

Amenhotep IV. See **Akhenaton.**

a·men·i·ty (ə-mĕn′ĭ-tē, ə-mē′nĭ-) *n., pl.* **-ties. 1.** The quality of being pleasant or attractive; agreeableness. **2.** Something that contributes to physical or material comfort. **3.** A feature that increases attractiveness or value, especially of a piece of real estate or a geographic location. **4. amenities.** Social courtesies; pleasantries. [Middle English *amenite,* from Old French, from Latin *amoenitās,* from *amoenus,* pleasant.]

SYNONYMS: *amenity, comfort, convenience, facility.* The central meaning shared by these nouns is "something that increases physical ease or facilitates work": *a sunny apartment with amenities including air conditioning; a suite with comforts such as a whirlpool bath; a kitchen with every convenience; a school with excellent facilities for students.*

Am·e·no·phis III (ăm′ə-nō′fəs). See **Amenhotep III.**

a·men·or·rhe·a or **a·men·or·rhoe·a** (ā-mĕn′ə-rē′ə) *n.* Abnormal suppression or absence of menstruation. [A–¹ + Greek *mēn,* month; see **mē-²** in Appendix + –RRHEA.] **—a·men′or·rhe′ic** *adj.*

a·men·sa·lism (ā-mĕn′sə-lĭz′əm) *n.* A symbiotic relationship between organisms in which one species is harmed or inhibited and the other species is unaffected. [Probably A–¹ + (COM)-MENSALISM.]

am·ent¹ (ăm′ənt, ā′mənt) *n.* See **catkin.** [Latin *āmentum,* strap.]

a·ment² (ā′mĕnt′, ā′mənt) *n.* A person whose intellectual capacity remains undeveloped. [From Latin *āmēns, āment-,* insane : *ā-, ab-,* out of; see AB–¹ + *mēns,* mind; see **men-¹** in Appendix.]

am·en·ta·ceous (ăm′ən-tā′shəs, ā′mən-) *adj. Botany.* **1.** Resembling or consisting of a catkin. **2.** Bearing catkins.

a·men·tia (ā-mĕn′shə, -shē-ə) *n.* Insufficient mental development. [Latin *āmentia,* madness, senselessness, from *āmēns, āment-,* insane. See AMENT².]

am·en·tif·er·ous (ăm′ən-tĭf′ər-əs, ā′mən-) *adj. Botany.* Bearing catkins.

Amer. *abbr.* America; American.

Am·er·a·sian (ăm′ə-rā′zhən, -shən) *n.* A person of American and Asian descent, especially one whose mother is Asian and whose father is American. [AMER(ICAN) + ASIAN.] **—Am′er·a′sian** *adj.*

a·merce (ə-mûrs′) *tr.v.* **a·merced, a·merc·ing, a·merc·es. 1.** *Law.* To punish by a fine imposed arbitrarily at the discretion of the court. **2.** To punish by imposing an arbitrary penalty. [Middle English *amercen,* from Anglo-Norman *amercier,* from *à merci,* at the mercy of : *à,* to (from Latin *ad;* see AD–) + *merci,* mercy (from Latin *mercēs,* wages).] **—a·merce′a·ble** *adj.* **—a·merce′ment** *n.*

A·mer·i·ca (ə-mĕr′ĭ-kə). *Abbr.* **A., Am., Amer. 1.** The United States. **2..** Also the **A·mer·i·cas** (-kəz) The landmasses and islands of North America, South America, Mexico, and Central America included in the Western Hemisphere.

A·mer·i·can (ə-mĕr′ĭ-kən) *adj. Abbr.* **A., Amer. 1.** Of or relating to the United States of America or its people, language, or culture. **2.** Of or relating to North or South America, the West Indies, or the Western Hemisphere. **3.** Of or relating to any of the Native American peoples. **4.** Indigenous to North or South America. Used of plants and animals. **—American** *n. Abbr.* **A., Amer. 1.** A native or inhabitant of America. **2.** A citizen of the United States. **—A·mer′i·can·ness** *n.*

A·mer·i·ca·na¹ (ä-mĕ′rē-kä′nä). A city of southeast Brazil, a suburb of São Paulo. Population, 121,743.

A·mer·i·ca·na² (ə-mĕr′ə-kä′nə, -kăn′ə, -kā′nə) *n.* **1.** *(used with a pl. verb).* Materials relating to American history, folklore, or geography or considered to be typical of American culture: *Americana are featured in the exhibit.* **2.** *(used with a sing. verb).* The culture of America: *Americana reflects the influence of many immigrations.*

American Beauty *n.* A type of rose bearing large, long-stemmed purplish-red flowers.

American cheese *n.* A smooth, mild, white to yellow cheddar.

American chestnut *n.* An eastern North American deciduous tree *(Castanea dentata),* once valuable for its timber and nuts but now found mostly as sprouts from old stumps, the aboveground parts having died from chestnut blight.

American dream also **American Dream** *n.* An American ideal of a happy and successful life to which all may aspire: *"In the deepening gloom of the Depression, the American Dream represented a reaffirmation of traditional American hopes"* (Anthony Brandt).

American eagle *n.* See **bald eagle.**

American elk *n.* See **wapiti.**

American elm *n.* A North American deciduous tree *(Ulmus americana)* having double serrate leaves and winged fruits. It is grown chiefly as an ornamental shade tree but often dies from Dutch elm disease.

American English *n.* The English language as used in the United States.

American Falls. A section, 50.9 m (167 ft) high, of Niagara Falls in western New York north of Buffalo.

American foxhound *n.* Any of an American breed of foxhounds having drooping ears and a smooth, glossy coat that is usually black, tan, and white.

American gothic also **American Gothic** *adj.* Exceptionally conservative, hard-working, and self-disciplined: *"She's tight-lipped, pinched as an American gothic farmwoman's bun"* (Rita Kempley). [After the painting *American Gothic* by Grant Wood

American Falls

ă pat	oi boy
ā pay	ou out
âr care	o͝o took
ä father	o͞o boot
ĕ pet	ŭ cut
ē be	ûr urge
ĭ pit	th thin
ī pie	*th* this
îr pier	hw which
ŏ pot	zh vision
ō toe	ə about, item
ô paw	♦ regionalism

Stress marks: **′** (primary); ′ (secondary), as in **dictionary** (dĭk′shə-nĕr′ē)

(1892–1942), which portrays an Iowa farmer-preacher and his daughter standing in front of a house with a Gothic window.] **—American gothic, American Gothic** *n.*

American Indian *n.* See **Native American.** See Usage Note at **Native American.**

A·mer·i·can·ism (ə-mĕr′ĭ-kə-nĭz′əm) *n.* **1.** A custom, trait, or tradition originating in the United States. **2.** A word, phrase, or idiom characteristic of English as it is spoken in the United States. **3.** Allegiance to the United States and its customs and institutions.

A·mer·i·can·ist (ə-mĕr′ĭ-kə-nĭst) *n.* **1.** One who studies a facet of America, such as its history or geology. **2.** A specialist in the study of American aboriginal cultures or languages. **3.** One that is sympathetic to the United States and its policies.

A·mer·i·can·ize (ə-mĕr′ĭ-kə-nīz′) *v.* **-ized, -iz·ing, -iz·es.** *—tr.* To assimilate into American culture. *—intr.* To become American, as in spirit. **—A·mer′i·can·i·za′tion** (-kə-nĭ-zā′shən) *n.*

American kestrel *n.* See **sparrow hawk** (sense 2).

American plan *n. Abbr.* **AP** A system of hotel management in which a guest pays a fixed daily rate for room and meals.

American Revolution *n.* The war between the American colonies and Great Britain (1775–1783), leading to the formation of the independent United States.

American saddle horse *n.* A three- or five-gaited high-stepping saddle horse of a breed originating in Kentucky.

American Sa·mo·a (sə-mō′ə). *Abbr.* **AS.** An unincorporated territory of the United States in the southern Pacific Ocean northeast of Fiji comprising the eastern islands of the Samoan archipelago. American Samoa has been administered by the United States since 1899. Pago Pago, on Tutuila, the largest island of the group, is the capital. Population, 32,279.

American Sign Language *n. Abbr.* **ASL** An American system of communication for the hearing-impaired that employs manual signs. Also called *Ameslan.*

American Spanish *n.* The Spanish language as used in the Western Hemisphere.

American Staf·ford·shire terrier (stăf′ərd-shîr′, -shər) *n.* A strong, muscular terrier of an American breed with powerful jaws, a broad skull, and short hair, originally developed for dog-fighting. Also called *pit bull, pit bull terrier, Staffordshire terrier.*

American Standard Version *n. Abbr.* **ASV** *Bible.* A revised version of the King James Bible published in the United States in 1901.

A·mer·i·cas (ə-mĕr′ĭ-kəz), **the.** See **America** (sense 2).

am·er·i·ci·um (ăm′ə-rĭsh′ē-əm) *n. Symbol* **Am** A white metallic transuranic element of the actinide series, having isotopes with mass numbers from 237 to 246 and half-lives from 25 minutes to 7,950 years. Its longest-lived isotopes, Am 241 and Am 243, are alpha-ray emitters used as radiation sources in research. Atomic number 95; specific gravity 11.7; valence 3, 4, 5, 6. See table at **element.** [After AMERICA.]

A·mer·i·cus (ə-mĕr′ĭ-kəs). A city of southwest-central Georgia southeast of Columbus. It is a processing center for the varied resources of the region. Population, 16,120.

Am·er·in·di·an (ăm′ə-rĭn′dē-ən) also **Am·er·ind** (ăm′ə-rĭnd′) *n.* See **Native American.** See Usage Note at **Native American.** [AMER(ICAN) + IND(IAN).] **—Am′er·in′di·an, Am′er·ind′** *adj.* **—Am′er·in′dic** *adj.*

A·mers·foort (ä′mərz-fôrt′, -fōrt′, ä′mərs-). A city of central Netherlands northeast of Utrecht. The old section of the city has medieval houses. Population, 86,896.

Ames (āmz). A city of central Iowa north of Des Moines. Iowa State University of Science and Technology (founded 1858) is here. Population, 45,775.

Am·es·lan (ăm′ĭ-slăn′) *n.* See **American Sign Language.**

Ames test *n.* A test used to determine the mutagenic potential of a substance based on the mutation rate of bacteria that are exposed to the substance. [After *Bruce Ames* (born 1928), American biochemist.]

am·e·thop·ter·in (ăm′ə-thŏp′tə-rĭn′) *n.* Methotrexate. [A(MINO)– + METH– + *pter(oyl),* a chemical radical + –IN.]

am·e·thyst (ăm′ə-thĭst) *n.* **1.** A purple or violet form of transparent quartz used as a gemstone. **2.** A purple variety of corundum used as a gemstone. **3.** *Color.* A moderate purple to grayish reddish purple. [Middle English *amatist,* from Old French, from Latin *amethystus,* from Greek *amethustos* : *a-,* not; see A–[1] + **methustos,* intoxicated (from *methuskein,* to intoxicate, from *methuein,* to be drunk (from the belief that it was a remedy for drunkenness) from *methu,* wine; see **medhu-** in Appendix).] **—am′e·thys′tine** (-thĭs′tĭn, -tīn′) *adj.*

am·e·tro·pi·a (ăm′ĭ-trō′pē-ə) *n.* An eye abnormality, such as nearsightedness, farsightedness, or astigmatism, resulting from faulty refractive ability of the eye. [Greek *ametros,* without measure (*a-,* without; see A–[1] + *metron,* measure; see METER[1]) + –OPIA.] **—am′e·trop′ic** (-trŏp′ĭk, -trō′pĭk) *adj.*

Amex *abbr.* American Stock Exchange.

Am·ga (äm-gä′). A river rising in eastern Russia and flowing about 1,287 km (800 mi) generally northeast to the Aldan River east of Yakutsk.

Am·gun (äm-go͞on′). A river of southeast Russia flowing about 788 km (490 mi) northeast to the Amur River.

Am·har·ic (ăm-hăr′ĭk) *n.* A Semitic language that is the official language of Ethiopia. [After *Amhara,* a former kingdom of northwest Ethiopia.] **—Am·har′ic** *adj.*

Am·herst (ăm′ərst, -hərst). **1.** A town of western Massachusetts northeast of Northampton. Amherst College (established 1821) and a branch of the University of Massachusetts (1863) are here. Emily Dickinson was born in Amherst and lived in the town her entire life. Population, 33,229. **2.** A city of western New York, a suburb of Buffalo. Population, 66,100.

Am·herst (ăm′ərst), **Jeffrey** also **Jeffery** Baron Amherst. 1717–1797. British general active in North America during the French and Indian War. He seized Forts Ticonderoga and Crown Point in 1759 and captured Montreal in 1760.

a·mi·a·ble (ā′mē-ə-bəl) *adj.* **1.** Friendly and agreeable in disposition; good-natured and likable. **2.** Cordial; sociable; congenial: *an amiable gathering.* [Middle English, from Old French, from Late Latin *amīcābilis.* See AMICABLE.] **—a′mi·a·bil′i·ty, a′mi·a·ble·ness** *n.* **—a′mi·a·bly** *adv.*

SYNONYMS: *amiable, affable, good-natured, obliging, agreeable, pleasant.* These adjectives mean willing or showing a willingness to please. *Amiable* implies friendliness: *"an amiable villain with a cocky, sidelong grin"* (Hal Hinson). *Affable* especially fits a person who is easy to approach, responsive in conversation, and slow to anger: *She is affable enough when she is not preoccupied with business problems. Good-natured* suggests a tolerant, easygoing disposition; sometimes it also implies a docile nature: *You are too good-natured to resent a little criticism. Obliging* specifies willingness or eagerness to be of help to others or indulge their wishes: *The obliging waiter was in no hurry for us to pay the bill and leave. Agreeable* suggests being in accord with one's own feelings, nature, or tastes: *"My idea of an agreeable person . . . is a person who agrees with me"* (Benjamin Disraeli). *Pleasant* applies broadly to agreeable manner, behavior, or appearance: *"I couldn't handle it, I didn't enjoy it and it probably didn't make me a pleasant person to be around"* (James Caan).

am·i·an·thus (ăm′ē-ăn′thəs) also **am·i·an·tus** (-təs) *n.* An asbestos with fine, silky fibers. [Latin *amiantus,* from Greek *amiantos,* undefiled : *a-,* not; see A–[1] + *miantos,* defiled (from *miainein,* to defile).]

am·i·ca·ble (ăm′ĭ-kə-bəl) *adj.* Characterized by or exhibiting friendliness or good will; friendly. [Middle English, from Late Latin *amīcābilis,* from Latin *amīcus,* friend.] **—am′i·ca·bil′i·ty, am′i·ca·ble·ness** *n.* **—am′i·ca·bly** *adv.*

am·ice (ăm′ĭs) *n.* A liturgical vestment consisting of an oblong piece of white linen worn around the neck and shoulders and partly under the alb. [Middle English, probably from Old French *amis,* pl. of *amit,* from Latin *amictus,* mantle, from past participle of *amicīre,* to wrap around : *ambi-,* around; see AMBI– + *iacere,* to throw; see **yē-** in Appendix.]

a·mi·cus cu·ri·ae (ə-mē′kəs kyo͝or′ē-ī′) *n., pl.* **a·mi·ci cu·riae** (ə-mē′kē). *Law.* A party that is not involved in a particular litigation but that is allowed by the court to advise it on a matter of law directly affecting the litigation. [Latin *amīcus,* friend + *curiae,* genitive of *curia,* court.]

a·mid (ə-mĭd′) also **a·midst** (ə-mĭdst′) *prep.* Surrounded by; in the middle of. [Middle English : *a-,* in; see A–[2] + *mid,* middle (from Old English *midde,* middle; see **medhyo-** in Appendix).]

am·ide (ăm′īd′, -ĭd) *n.* **1.** An organic compound, such as acetamide, containing the $CONH_2$ radical. **2.** A compound with a metal replacing hydrogen in ammonia, such as sodium amide, $NaNH_2$. [AM(MONIA) + –IDE.] **—a·mid′ic** (ə-mĭd′ĭk, ă-mĭd′-) *adj.*

am·i·dol (ăm′ĭ-dôl′, -dōl′, -dŏl′) *n.* A colorless crystalline compound, $C_6H_3(NH_2)_2OH{\cdot}2HCl$, used as a photographic developer. [German *Amidol,* a trademark.]

a·mid·ships (ə-mĭd′shĭps′) also **a·mid·ship** (-shĭp′) *adv. Nautical.* Midway between the bow and the stern.

a·midst (ə-mĭdst′) *prep.* Variant of **amid.** [Middle English *amiddes* : *amidde;* see AMID + *-es,* adverbial suffix; see –S[3].]

Am·i·ens (ăm′ē-ənz, ä-myăN′). A city of northern France on the Somme River north of Paris. Settled in pre-Roman times, it has been a textile center since the Middle Ages. The city's Gothic cathedral is the largest church in France. Population, 131,332.

a·mi·go (ə-mē′gō) *n., pl.* **-gos.** A friend. [Spanish, from Latin *amīcus,* friend.]

A·min Da·da (ä-mēn′ dä-dä′, dä′dä), **Idi.** Born c. 1925. Ugandan dictator (1971–1979) whose brutal and repressive regime ended when he fled the country after being deposed in a coup d'état.

A·min·di·vi Islands (ä′mĭn-dē′vē). A group of islands in the Arabian Sea off the southwest coast of India, part of the region of Lakshadweep.

a·mine (ə-mēn′, ăm′ēn) *n.* Any of a group of organic compounds of nitrogen, such as ethylamine, $C_2H_5NH_2$, that may be considered ammonia derivatives in which one or more hydrogen atoms have been replaced by a hydrocarbon radical. [AM(MONIUM) + –INE[2].]

–amine *suff.* Amine: *diamine.* [From AMINE.]

a·mi·no (ə-mē′nō, ăm′ə-nō′) *adj.* Relating to an amine or other chemical compound containing an NH_2 group combined with a nonacid organic radical. [From AMINO–.]

amino– *pref.* Containing NH_2 combined with a nonacid organic radical: *aminopyrine.* [From AMINE.]

amino acid *n.* An organic compound containing both an amino group (NH_2) and a carboxylic acid group (COOH), especially any of the 20 compounds that have the basic formula $NH_2CHRCOOH$, and that link together by peptide bonds to form proteins.

a·mi·no·ac·i·de·mi·a (ə-mē′nō-ăs′ĭ-dē′mē-ə, ăm′ə-nō-) *n.* A condition in which excessive amounts of amino acids are present in the blood.

a·mi·no·ac·i·du·ri·a (ə-mē′nō-ăs′ĭ-do͝or′ē-ə, -dyo͝or′-, ăm′ə-nō-) *n.* A disorder of protein metabolism in which excessive amounts of amino acids are excreted in the urine.

a·mi·no·ben·zo·ic acid (ə-mē′nō-bĕn-zō′ĭk, ăm′ə-nō-) *n.* Any of three benzoic acid derivatives, $C_7H_7NO_2$, especially the yellowish para form, which is part of the vitamin B complex.

a·mi·no·phe·nol (ə-mē′nō-fē′nôl, -nŏl, ăm′ə-nō-) *n.* One of three organic compounds with composition $C_6H_4NH_2OH$, used as photographic developers and dye intermediates.

a·mi·no·py·rine (ə-mē′nō-pī′rēn′, ăm′ə-nō-) *n.* A colorless crystalline compound, $C_{13}H_{17}N_3O$, used to reduce fever and relieve pain. [AMINO– + (ANTI)PYRINE.]

a·mir (ə-mîr′, ā-mîr′) *n.* Variant of **emir.**

A·mis (ā′mĭs), **Kingsley.** Born 1922. British writer best known for his novels, including *Lucky Jim* (1954) and *Jake's Thing* (1978).

A·mish (ä′mĭsh, ăm′ĭsh) *n.* An orthodox Anabaptist sect that separated from the Mennonites in the late 17th century and exists today primarily in southeast Pennsylvania. **—Amish** *adj.* Of or relating to this sect or its members. [German *amisch,* after Jacob *Amman,* 17th-century Swiss Mennonite bishop.]

a·miss (ə-mĭs′) *adj.* **1.** Out of proper order: *What is amiss?* **2.** Not in perfect shape; faulty. **—amiss** *adv.* In an improper, defective, unfortunate, or mistaken way. [Middle English *amis,* probably from Old Norse *ā mis,* so as to miss : *ā,* on; see **an-** in Appendix + *mis,* act of missing; see **mei-**[1] in Appendix.]

SYNONYMS: *amiss, afield, astray, awry, wrong.* The central meaning shared by these adverbs is "not in the right way or on the proper course": *spoke amiss; straying far afield; afraid the letter would go astray; thinking awry; plans that went wrong.* ***ANTONYM:*** *aright.*

am·i·trip·tyl·ine (ăm′ĭ-trĭp′tə-lēn′) *n.* An antidepressant drug, $C_{20}H_{23}N$. [Perhaps AMI(NO)– + *tript-* (alteration and shortening of TRYPTOPHAN) + –YL + –INE[2].]

am·i·ty (ăm′ĭ-tē) *n., pl.* **-ties.** Peaceful relations, as between nations; friendship. [Middle English *amite,* from Old French, from Vulgar Latin **amīcitās,* from Latin *amīcus,* friend.]

Am·man (ä-män′, ä′män). The capital and largest city of Jordan, in the north-central part of the country. Occupying a site inhabited since prehistoric times, the city was known as Philadelphia while the Romans and Byzantines controlled it. Population, 777,500.

am·me·ter (ăm′mē′tər) *n. Abbr.* **A** An instrument that measures electric current. [AM(PERE) + –METER.]

am·mine (ăm′ēn′, ă-mēn′) *n.* Any of a class of inorganic coordination compounds of ammonia and a metallic salt. [AMM(ONIA) + –INE[2].] **—am′mi·no′** (ăm′ə-nō′, ə-mē′nō) *adj.*

am·mo (ăm′ō) *n. Informal.* Ammunition.

am·mo·nia (ə-mōn′yə) *n.* **1.** A colorless, pungent gas, NH_3, extensively used to manufacture fertilizers and a wide variety of nitrogen-containing organic and inorganic chemicals. **2.** See **ammonium hydroxide.** [New Latin, from Latin *(sāl) ammōniacus,* (salt) of Amen, from Greek *Ammōniakos,* from *Ammōn,* Amen (from its having been obtained from a region near the temple of Amen, in Libya).]

am·mo·ni·ac[1] (ə-mō′nē-ăk′) also **am·mo·ni·a·cal** (ăm′ə-nī′ə-kəl) *adj.* Of, containing, or similar to ammonia.

am·mo·ni·ac[2] (ə-mō′nē-ăk′) *n.* A strong-smelling gum resin from the stems of a plant *(Dorema ammoniacum)* of western Asia, formerly used in perfumery and in medicine as an expectorant and a stimulant. Also called *gum ammoniac.* [Middle English *ammoniak,* from Latin *ammōniacum,* from *Ammōniacus,* of Amen, from Greek *Ammōniakos.* See AMMONIA.]

am·mo·ni·ate (ə-mō′nē-āt′) *tr.v.* **-at·ed, -at·ing, -ates.** To treat or combine with ammonia. **—ammoniate** *n.* A compound that contains ammonia. **—am·mo′ni·a′tion** *n.*

ammonia water *n.* See **ammonium hydroxide.**

am·mon·i·fi·ca·tion (ə-mŏn′ə-fĭ-kā′shən, ə-mō′nə-) *n.* **1.** Impregnation with ammonia or an ammonium compound. **2.** Production of ammonia or ammonium compounds in the decomposition of organic matter, especially through the action of bacteria.

am·mon·i·fy (ə-mŏn′ə-fī′, ə-mō′nə-) *tr. & intr.v.* **-fied, -fy·ing, -fies.** To subject or be subjected to ammonification. **—am·mon′i·fi′er** *n.*

am·mo·nite (ăm′ə-nīt′) also **am·mo·noid** (-noid′) *n.* The coiled, flat, chambered fossil shell of an extinct mollusk belonging to the class Cephalopoda, which was abundant in the Cretaceous period. [New Latin *Ammōnītēs,* from Latin *(cornū) Ammōnis,* (horn) of Amen, ammonite, genitive of *Ammōn,* Amen, from Greek.] **—am′mo·nit′ic** (-nĭt′ĭk) *adj.*

Am·mon·ite (ăm′ə-nīt′) *n.* **1.** A member of an ancient Semitic people living east of the Jordan River, mentioned frequently in the Old Testament. **2.** The Semitic language of the Ammonites. [From Late Latin *Ammōnītēs,* the Ammonites, from Hebrew *'ammônî,* Ammonite, from *'ammôn,* Ammon, from Canaanite *'amm,* people, kinsman.] **—Am′mon·ite′** *adj.*

am·mo·ni·um (ə-mō′nē-əm) *n.* The univalent chemical ion NH_4+, derived from ammonia, whose compounds chemically resemble the alkali metals. [AMMON(IA) + –IUM.]

ammonium bicarbonate *n.* A white crystalline salt, bicarbonate of ammonium, NH_4HCO_3, used in fire-extinguishing compounds and in baking powder.

ammonium carbamate *n.* A salt, a carbonate of ammonium, $NH_4NH_2CO_2$, which is an intermediate in the manufacture of urea and a component of smelling salts.

ammonium carbonate *n.* **1.** A carbonate of ammonium, $(NH_4)_2CO_3$. **2.** The double salt of ammonium bicarbonate and ammonium carbamate, which is produced commercially and is a white powder with the composition $NH_4HCO_3 \cdot NH_2COONH_4$, used in smelling salts.

ammonium chloride *n.* A slightly hygroscopic, white crystalline compound, NH_4Cl, used in dry cells, as a soldering flux, and as an expectorant. Also called *sal ammoniac.*

ammonium hydroxide *n.* A colorless, basic, aqueous solution of ammonia, NH_4OH, used as a household cleanser and in the manufacture of a wide variety of products, including textiles, rayon, rubber, fertilizer, and plastic. Also called *ammonia, ammonia water.*

ammonium nitrate *n.* A colorless crystalline salt, NH_4NO_3, used in fertilizers, explosives, and solid rocket propellants.

ammonium sulfate *n.* A brownish-gray to white crystalline salt, $(NH_4)_2SO_4$, used in fertilizers and water purification.

ammonium thiocyanate *n.* A colorless, crystalline compound, NH_4SCN, used in dyeing fabric, electroplating, and in making melamine.

am·mo·noid (ăm′ə-noid′) *n.* Variant of **ammonite.**

am·mu·ni·tion (ăm′yə-nĭsh′ən) *n.* **1.** All projectiles, such as bullets and shot, together with their fuses and primers, that can be fired from guns or otherwise propelled. **2.** Nuclear, biological, chemical, or explosive materiel, such as rockets or grenades, that are used as weapons. **3.** An object used as a missile in offense or defense: *Rocks were my only ammunition against the bear.* **4.** A means of attacking or defending an argument, thesis, or point of view. [Obsolete French *amunition,* from *l'amunition,* the provisioning, alteration of *la munition,* from Old French, from Latin *mūnītiō, mūnītiōn-,* fortification. See MUNITION.]

Amn *abbr.* Airman.

Am·ne Ma·chin Shan (ăm′nē mə-jĭn′ shän). A range of mountains of west-central China. The highest peak is **Amne Machin** at 7,164.5 m (23,490 ft).

am·ne·sia (ăm-nē′zhə) *n.* Partial or total loss of memory, usually resulting from shock, psychological disturbance, brain injury, or illness. [Greek *amnēsia,* forgetfulness, probably from *amnēstia* : *a-,* not; see A–[1] + *mimnēskein,* to remember; see **men-**[1] in Appendix.] **—am·ne′si·ac′** (-nē′zē-ăk′, -zhē-ăk′), **am·ne′sic** (-zĭk, -sĭk) *n. & adj.* **—am·nes′tic** (-nĕs′tĭk) *adj.*

am·nes·ty (ăm′nĭ-stē) *n., pl.* **-ties.** A general pardon granted by a government, especially for political offenses. **—amnesty** *tr.v.* **-tied, -ty·ing, -ties.** To grant a general pardon to. [Latin *amnestia,* from Greek, from *amnēstos,* not remembered : *a-,* not; see A–[1] + *mimnēskein,* to remember; see **men-**[1] in Appendix.]

am·ni·a (ăm′nē-ə) *n.* A plural of **amnion.**

am·ni·o·cen·te·sis (ăm′nē-ō-sĕn-tē′sĭs) *n., pl.* **-ses** (-sēz). A procedure in which a small sample of amniotic fluid is drawn out of the uterus through a needle inserted in the abdomen. The fluid is then analyzed to detect genetic abnormalities in the fetus or to determine the sex of the fetus. [New Latin *amniocentēsis* : AMNION + Greek *kentēsis,* act of pricking (from *kentein,* to prick; see **kent-** in Appendix).]

am·ni·og·ra·phy (ăm′nē-ŏg′rə-fē) *n., pl.* **-phies.** Radiographic examination of the uterine cavity and fetus following injection of a radiopaque substance into the amnion. [AMNIO(N) + –GRAPHY.]

am·ni·on (ăm′nē-ən, -ŏn′) *n., pl.* **-ni·ons** or **-ni·a** (-nē-ə). A thin, tough, membranous sac that encloses the embryo or fetus of a mammal, bird, or reptile. It is filled with a serous fluid in which the embryo is suspended. [Greek *amniōn.*] **—am′ni·ot′ic** (-ŏt′ĭk), **am′ni·on′ic** (-ŏn′ĭk) *adj.*

am·ni·os·co·py (ăm′nē-ŏs′kə-pē) *n., pl.* **-pies.** Examination of the amniotic cavity and fetus using an optical instrument that is inserted directly into the amniotic cavity. [AMNIO(N) + –SCOPY.] **—am′ni·o·scope′** (-ə-skōp′) *n.*

am·o·bar·bi·tal (ăm′ō-bär′bĭ-tăl′, -tôl′) *n.* A barbiturate, $C_{11}H_{18}N_2O_3$, used as a sedative and a hypnotic. [AM(YL) + BARBITAL.]

a·moe·ba also **a·me·ba** (ə-mē′bə) *n., pl.* **-bas** or **-bae** (-bē). A protozoan of the genus *Amoeba* or related genera, occurring in water and soil and as a parasite in other animals. An amoeba has no definite form and consists essentially of a mass of protoplasm containing one nucleus or more surrounded by a delicate, flexible outer membrane. It moves by means of pseudopods. [New Latin, genus name, from Greek *amoibē,* change, from *ameibein,* to change. See **mei-**[1] in Appendix.] **—a·moe′bic** (-bĭk) *adj.*

am·oe·bae·an or **am·oe·be·an** (ăm′ə-bē′ən) *adj.* Answering alternately in prosody. [From Late Latin *amoebaeus,*

ammonite
Cross section of a Jurassic ammonite

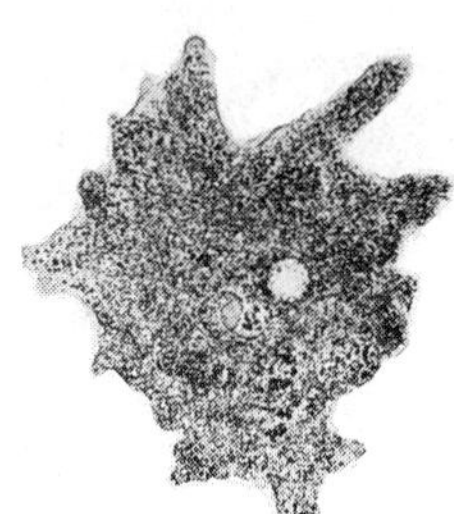

amoeba

ă pat	oi boy
ā pay	ou out
âr care	o͝o took
ä father	o͞o boot
ĕ pet	ŭ cut
ē be	ûr urge
ĭ pit	th thin
ī pie	*th* this
îr pier	hw which
ŏ pot	zh vision
ō toe	ə about, item
ô paw	♦ regionalism

Stress marks: **′** (primary); ′ (secondary), as in **dictionary** (dĭk′shə-nĕr′ē)

from Greek *amoibaios,* from *amoibē,* change. See AMOEBA.]

am·oe·bi·a·sis (ăm′ə-bī′ə-sĭs) *n.* Variant of **amebiasis.**

amoebic dysentery *n.* Variant of **amebic dysentery.**

a·moe·bo·cyte also **a·me·bo·cyte** (ə-mē′bə-sīt′) *n.* A cell, such as a leukocyte, having amoeboid form or motion. [AMOEB(A) + –CYTE.]

a·moe·boid (ə-mē′boid′) *adj.* **1.** Of or resembling an amoeba, especially in changeability of form and means of locomotion. **2.** Having an irregular or asymmetric shape: *an amoeboid coffee table.*

a·mok (ə-mŭk′, ə-mŏk′) *adv. & adj.* Variant of **amuck.**

a·mo·le (ə-mō′lē) *n.* **1.** The root, bulb, or another plant part of several chiefly western North American plants, such as certain species of *Agave, Chlorogalum,* and *Yucca,* used as a substitute for soap. **2.** A plant so used. [American Spanish, from Nahuatl *amolli.*]

A·mon (ä′mən) *n. Mythology.* Variant of **Amen.**

a·mong (ə-mŭng′) also **a·mongst** (ə-mŭngst′) *prep.* **1.** In the midst of; surrounded by: *a pine tree among cedars.* **2.** In the group, number, or class of: *She is among the wealthy.* **3.** In the company of; in association with: *traveling among a group of tourists.* **4.** By many or the entire number of; with many: *a custom popular among the Greeks.* **5.** By the joint action of: *Among us, we will finish the job.* **6.** With portions to each of: *Distribute this among you.* **7.** Each with the other: *Don't fight among yourselves.* See Usage Note at **between.** [Middle English, from Old English *āmang* : *ā,* in; see A–[2] + *gemang,* throng; see **mag-** in Appendix.]

a·mon·til·la·do (ə-mŏn′tl-ä′dō, -tē-ä′-) *n., pl.* **-dos.** A pale dry sherry. [Spanish : *a-,* to (from Latin *ad-;* see AD–) + *Montilla,* a town of southern Spain.]

a·mor·al (ā-môr′əl, ā-mŏr′-) *adj.* **1.** Not admitting of moral distinctions or judgments; neither moral nor immoral. **2.** Lacking moral sensibility; not caring about right and wrong. **—a·mor′al·ism** *n.* **—a′mo·ral′i·ty** (ā′mô-răl′ĭ-tē, -mə-) *n.* **—a·mor′al·ly** *adv.*

am·o·ret·to (ăm′ə-rĕt′ō, ä′mə-) *n., pl.* **-ti** (-tē) or **-tos.** A cupid. [Italian, diminutive of *Amore,* Cupid, from Latin *Amor,* from *amor,* love. See AMOROUS.]

am·o·rist (ăm′ər-ĭst) *n.* **1.** One dedicated to love, especially sexual love. **2.** One who writes about love. [Latin *amor,* love; see AMOROUS + –IST.]

Am·o·rite (ăm′ə-rīt′) *n.* A member of one of several ancient Semitic peoples primarily inhabiting Canaan, where they preceded the Israelites, and Babylonia. [From Hebrew *'ĕmōrî,* Amorite, from Akkadian *amurru,* westerner, Amorite.] **—Am′o·rite′** *adj.*

amphibian
Amphibian aircraft

am·o·rous (ăm′ər-əs) *adj.* **1.** Strongly attracted or disposed to love, especially sexual love. **2.** Indicative of love or sexual desire: *an amorous glance.* **3.** Of or associated with love: *an amorous poem.* **4.** Being in love; enamored: *amorous of you since the day we met.* [Middle English, from Old French *amoureus,* from Medieval Latin *amōrōsus,* from Latin *amor,* love, from *amāre,* to love.] **—am′or·ous·ly** *adv.* **—am′or·ous·ness** *n.*

a·mor·phism (ə-môr′fĭz′əm) *n.* The state or quality of being amorphous.

a·mor·phous (ə-môr′fəs) *adj.* **1.** Lacking definite form; shapeless. See Synonyms at **shapeless.** **2.** Of no particular type; anomalous. **3.** Lacking organization; formless. **4.** Lacking distinct crystalline structure. [From Greek *amorphos* : *a-,* without; see A–[1] + *morphē,* shape.] **—a·mor′phous·ly** *adv.* **—a·mor′phous·ness** *n.*

am·or·ti·za·tion (ăm′ər-tĭ-zā′shən, ə-môr′tĭ-) *n.* **1.a.** The act or process of amortizing. **b.** The money set aside for this purpose. **2.** In reckoning the yield of a bond bought at a premium, the periodic subtraction from its current yield of a proportionate share of the premium between the purchase date and the maturity date.

am·or·tize (ăm′ər-tīz′, ə-môr′-) *tr.v.* **-tized, -tiz·ing, -tiz·es.** **1.** To liquidate (a debt, such as a mortgage) by installment payments or payment into a sinking fund. **2.** To write off an expenditure for (office equipment, for example) by prorating over a certain period. [Middle English *amortisen,* to alienate in mortmain, from Old French *amortir, amortiss-,* from Vulgar Latin **admortīre,* to deaden : Latin *ad-,* ad- + Latin *mors, mort-,* death; see **mer-** in Appendix.] **—am′or·tiz′a·ble** *adj.*

A·mos (ā′məs) *n. Bible.* **1.** A Hebrew prophet of the eighth century B.C. He was the earliest prophet to have a book of the Bible named for him. **2.** *Abbr.* **Am.** See table at **Bible.**

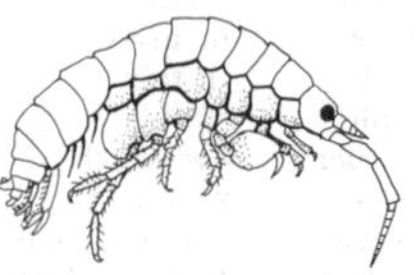

amphipod

a·mount (ə-mount′) *n. Abbr.* **amt.** **1.** The total of two or more quantities; the aggregate. **2.** A number; a sum. **3.** A principal plus its interest, as in a loan. **4.** The full effect or meaning; import. **5.** Quantity: *a great amount of intelligence.* **—amount** *intr.v.* **a·mount·ed, a·mount·ing, a·mounts.** **1.** To add up in number or quantity: *The purchases amounted to 50 dollars.* **2.** To add up in import or effect: *That plan will never amount to anything.* **3.** To be equivalent or tantamount: *accusations that amount to an indictment.* [From Middle English *amounten,* to ascend, from Old French *amonter,* from *amont,* upward, from Latin *ad montem,* to the hill : *ad,* to; see **ad-** in Appendix + *mōns, mont-,* hill; see **men-**[2] in Appendix.]

a·mour (ə-mo͝or′) *n.* A love affair, especially an illicit one. [Middle English, from Old French, from Old Provençal, from Latin *amor,* love. See AMOROUS.]

a·mour-pro·pre (ä-mo͝or-prôp′rə) *n.* Respect for oneself; self-esteem. See Synonyms at **conceit.** [French : *amour,* love + *propre,* own.]

A·moy[1] (ä-moi′). See **Xiamen.**

A·moy[2] (ä-moi′, ə-moi′) *n.* The dialect of Chinese spoken in and around the city of Xiamen in Fujian province in southeast China. [After *Amoy* (Xiamen).]

amp (ămp) *n. Informal.* **1.** An ampere. **2.** An amplifier, especially one used to amplify music.

AMP (ā′em-pē′) *n.* A mononucleotide, $C_{10}H_{14}N_5O_7P$, found in animal cells and reversibly convertible to ADP and ATP; adenosine monophosphate. Also called *adenylic acid.* [A(DENOSINE) M(ONO)P(HOSPHATE).]

am·per·age (ăm′pər-ĭj, ăm′pîr′-) *n.* The strength of an electric current expressed in amperes.

am·pere (ăm′pîr′) *n. Abbr.* **A** **1.** A unit of electric current in the meter-kilogram-second system. It is the steady current that when flowing in straight parallel wires of infinite length and negligible cross section, separated by a distance of one meter in free space, produces a force between the wires of 2×10^{-7} newtons per meter of length. **2.** A unit in the International System specified as one International coulomb per second and equal to 0.999835 ampere. See table at **measurement.** [After André Marie AMPÈRE.]

Am·père (ăm′pîr, äN-pĕr′), **André Marie.** 1775–1836. French physicist and mathematician who formulated Ampère's law, a mathematical description of the magnetic field produced by a current-carrying conductor.

am·pere-hour (ăm′pîr-our′) *n. Abbr.* **amp hr, A.h.** The electric charge transferred past a specified circuit point by a current of one ampere in one hour.

am·pere-turn (ăm′pîr-tûrn′) *n. Abbr.* **At** A unit of magnetomotive force in the meter-kilogram-second system equal to the magnetomotive force around a path linking one turn of a conducting loop carrying a current of one ampere.

am·per·sand (ăm′pər-sănd′) *n.* The character or sign (&) representing the word *and.* [Alteration of *and per se and,* & (the sign) by itself (is the word) and.]

am·phet·a·mine (ăm-fĕt′ə-mēn′, -mĭn) *n.* **1.** A colorless, volatile liquid, $C_9H_{13}N$, used primarily as a central nervous system stimulant. **2.** A derivative of amphetamine, such as dextroamphetamine or a phosphate or sulfate of amphetamine, used as a central nervous system stimulant in the treatment of certain conditions, such as narcolepsy and depression. [A(LPHA) + M(ETHYL) + PH(ENYL) + ET(HYL) + AMINE.]

amphi– *pref.* **1.** Both: *amphibiotic.* **2.** On both sides: *amphistylar.* **3.** Around: *amphithecium.* [Latin, from Greek, from *amphi,* on both sides, around. See **ambhi** in Appendix.]

am·phi·ar·thro·sis (ăm′fē-är-thrō′sĭs) *n., pl.* **-ses** (-sēz). A type of articulation between bony surfaces that permits limited motion and is connected by ligaments or elastic cartilage, such as that between the vertebrae.

am·phib·i·an (ăm-fĭb′ē-ən) *n.* **1.** A cold-blooded, smooth-skinned vertebrate of the class Amphibia, such as a frog or salamander, that characteristically hatches as an aquatic larva with gills. The larva then transforms into an adult having air-breathing lungs. **2.** An animal capable of living both on land and in water. **3.** An aircraft that can take off and land on either land or water. **4.** A tracked or wheeled vehicle that can operate both on land and in water. [From New Latin *Amphibia,* class name, from Greek, neuter pl. of *amphibios,* amphibious : *amphi-,* amphi- + *bios,* life; see **gʷei-** in Appendix.]

am·phi·bi·ot·ic (ăm′fə-bī-ŏt′ĭk) *adj.* Living in water during an early stage of development and on land during the adult stage.

am·phib·i·ous (ăm-fĭb′ē-əs) *adj.* **1.** *Biology.* Living or able to live both on land and in water. **2.** Able to operate both on land and in water: *amphibious tanks.* **3.** Relating to or organized for a military landing by means of combined naval and land forces. **4.** Of a mixed or twofold nature. [From Latin *amphibius,* from Greek *amphibios.* See AMPHIBIAN.] **—am·phib′i·ous·ly** *adv.* **—am·phib′i·ous·ness** *n.*

am·phi·bole (ăm′fə-bōl′) *n.* Any of a large group of structurally similar hydrated double silicate minerals, such as hornblende, containing various combinations of sodium, calcium, magnesium, iron, and aluminum. [French, from Late Latin *amphibolus,* ambiguous, from Greek *amphibolos,* doubtful, from *amphiballein,* to throw on either side : *amphi-,* amphi- + *ballein,* to throw; see **gʷele-** in Appendix.] **—am′phi·bol′ic** (-bŏl′ĭk) *adj.*

am·phib·o·lite (ăm-fĭb′ə-līt′) *n.* A chiefly amphibole rock with minor plagioclase and little quartz. **—am·phib′o·lit′ic** (-lĭt′ĭk).

am·phib·o·lous (ăm-fĭb′ə-ləs) *adj.* Having a grammatical structure that allows of two interpretations; equivocal. [From Late Latin *amphibolus.* See AMPHIBOLE.]

am·phi·brach (ăm′fə-brăk′) *n.* A trisyllabic metrical foot having one accented or long syllable between two unaccented or short syllables, as in the word *remember.* [Latin *amphibrachys,* from Greek *amphibrakhus* : *amphi-,* amphi- + *brakhus,* short; see **mregh-u-** in Appendix.]

am·phic·ty·o·ny (ăm-fĭk′tē-ə-nē) *n., pl.* **-nies.** A league of neighboring ancient Greek states sharing a common religious center or shrine, especially the one at Delphi. [Greek *Amphi-*

ktuonia, from *amphiktuones,* variant of *amphiktiones,* neighbors : *amphi-,* on the periphery; see AMPHI– + *ktizein,* to settle; see **tkei-** in Appendix.] **—am·phic′ty·on′ic** (-ŏn′ĭk) *adj.*

am·phi·dip·loid (ăm′fĭ-dĭp′loid) *adj. Genetics.* Having a diploid set of chromosomes derived from each parent. **—amphidiploid** *n.* An organism or individual having a diploid set of chromosomes derived from each parent. **—am′phi·dip′loid·y** *n.*

am·phim·a·cer (ăm-fĭm′ə-sər) *n.* A trisyllabic metrical foot having an unaccented or short syllable between two accented or long syllables, as in *Peter Pan.* Also called *cretic.* [Latin *amphimacrus,* from Greek *amphimakros* : *amphi-,* amphi- + *makros,* long; see **māk-** in Appendix.]

am·phi·mix·is (ăm′fə-mĭk′sĭs) *n., pl.* **-mix·es** (-mĭk′sēz′). The union of the sperm and egg in sexual reproduction. [AMPHI– + Greek *mixis,* a mingling (from *mignunai, mik-,* to mingle; see **meik-** in Appendix).] **—am′phi·mic′tic** (-mĭk′tĭk) *adj.*

Am·phi·on (ăm-fī′ən) *n. Greek Mythology.* The son of Zeus and the twin brother of Zethus, with whom he built a wall around Thebes by charming the stones into place with the music of his magical lyre.

am·phi·ox·us (ăm′fē-ŏk′səs) *n.* See **lancelet.** [AMPHI– + Greek *oxus,* sharp; see **ak-** in Appendix.]

am·phi·pod (ăm′fə-pŏd′) *n.* A small crustacean of the order Amphipoda, such as the beach flea, having a laterally compressed body with no carapace. [From New Latin *Amphipoda,* order name : AMPHI– + New Latin *-poda,* -pod.]

am·phip·ro·style (ăm-fĭp′rō-stīl′, ăm′fĭ-prō′stīl′) *adj. Architecture.* Having a prostyle or set of columns at each end but none along the sides. [Latin *amphiprostȳlos,* from Greek *amphiprostulos* : *amphi-,* amphi- + *prostulos,* with pillars in front; see PROSTYLE.] **—am·phip′ro·style′** *n.*

am·phis·bae·na (ăm′fĭs-bē′nə) *n. Mythology.* A serpent having a head at each end of its body. [Middle English *amphibena,* from Latin *amphisbaena,* from Greek *amphisbaina* : *amphis,* both ways (from *amphi-,* on both sides; see AMPHI–) + *bainein,* to go; see **gʷā-** in Appendix.] **—am′phis·bae′nic** *adj.*

am·phi·sty·lar (ăm′fĭ-stī′lər) *adj. Architecture.* Having columns at both front and back or on each side. [From AMPHI– + Greek *stulos,* pillar; see **stā-** in Appendix.]

am·phi·the·a·ter (ăm′fə-thē′ə-tər) *n.* **1.** An oval or a round structure having tiers of seats rising gradually outward from an open space or arena at the center. **2.** An arena where contests and spectacles are held. **3.** A level area surrounded by upward sloping ground. **4.** An upper, sloping gallery with seats for spectators, as in a theater or an operating room. [Middle English *amphitheatre,* from Latin *amphitheātrum,* from Greek *amphitheatron* : *amphi-,* amphi- + *theatron,* theater; see THEATER.] **—am′phi·the·at′ric** (-ăt′rĭk), **am′phi·the·at′ri·cal** *adj.* **—am′phi·the·at′ri·cal·ly** *adv.*

am·phi·the·ci·um (ăm′fə-thē′shē-əm, -sē-əm) *n., pl.* **-ci·a** (-shē-ə, -sē-ə). The outer layer of cells of the spore-containing capsule of a moss. [New Latin : AMPHI– + Greek *thēkion,* diminutive of *thēkē,* receptacle; see **dhē-** in Appendix.]

Am·phi·tri·te (ăm′fĭ-trī′tē) *n. Greek Mythology.* A Nereid, goddess of the sea and the wife of Poseidon.

am·phit·ro·pous (ăm-fĭt′rə-pəs) *adj. Botany.* Partly inverted and attached near the center to the funiculus: *an amphitropous ovule.*

Am·phit·ry·on (ăm-fĭt′rē-ən) *n. Greek Mythology.* A king of Thebes and the husband of Alcmene.

am·pho·ra (ăm′fər-ə) *n., pl.* **-pho·rae** (-fə-rē′) or **-pho·ras.** A two-handled jar with a narrow neck used by the ancient Greeks and Romans to carry wine or oil. [Middle English, from Latin, from Greek *amphoreus,* short for *amphiphoreus* : *amphi-,* amphi- + *phoreus,* bearer (from *pherein,* to bear; see **bher-**[1] in Appendix).] **—am′pho·ral** *adj.*

am·pho·ter·ic (ăm′fə-tĕr′ĭk) *adj.* Having the characteristics of an acid and a base and capable of reacting chemically either as an acid or a base. [From Greek *amphoteros,* each of two, from *amphō,* both.]

am·pho·ter·i·cin B (ăm′fə-tĕr′ĭ-sĭn) *n.* An antibiotic derived from strains of the actinomycete *Streptomyces nodosus* and used specifically in treating systemic fungal infections. [AMPHOTERIC + –IN.]

amp hr *abbr.* Ampere-hour.

am·pi·cil·lin (ăm′pĭ-sĭl′ĭn) *n.* A type of penicillin that is effective against gram-negative and gram-positive bacteria. It is used in treating gonorrhea and infections of the intestinal, urinary, and respiratory tracts. [Blend of AMINO– and PENICILLIN.]

am·ple (ăm′pəl) *adj.* **-pler, -plest.** **1.** Of large or great size, amount, extent, or capacity: *an ample living room.* See Synonyms at **spacious.** **2.a.** Large in degree, kind, or quantity: *an ample reward.* **b.** More than enough: *ample evidence.* **3.** Fully sufficient to meet a need or purpose: *had ample food for the party.* See Synonyms at **plentiful.** [Middle English, from Old French, from Latin *amplus.*] **—am′ple·ness** *n.* **—am′ply** (-plē) *adv.*

am·plex·i·caul (ăm-plĕk′sĭ-kôl′) *adj. Botany.* Clasping the stem, as the bases of certain leaves do. [Latin *amplexus,* an embracing, from past participle of *amplectī,* to embrace (*ambi-,* amphi- + *plectere,* to twine; see **plek-** in Appendix) + Latin *caulis,* stem.]

am·pli·fi·ca·tion (ăm′plə-fĭ-kā′shən) *n.* **1.** The act or result of amplifying, enlarging, or extending. **2.a.** An addition to or expansion of a statement or idea. **b.** A statement with such an addition. **3.** *Physics.* **a.** The process of increasing the magnitude of a variable quantity, especially the magnitude of voltage, power, or current, without altering any other quality. **b.** The result of such a process. **4.** *Electronics.* See **gain**[1] (sense 4).

am·pli·fi·er (ăm′plə-fī′ər) *n.* **1.** One that amplifies, enlarges, or extends. **2.** *Electronics.* A device, especially one using transistors or electron tubes, that produces amplification of an electrical signal.

am·pli·fy (ăm′plə-fī′) *v.* **-fied, -fy·ing, -fies.** *—tr.* **1.** To make larger or more powerful; increase. **2.** To add to, as by illustrations; make complete. **3.** To exaggerate. **4.** To produce amplification of: *amplify an electrical signal.* *—intr.* To write or discourse at length; expatiate: *Let me amplify so that you will understand the overall problem.* [Middle English *amplifien,* from Old French *amplifier,* from Latin *amplificāre* : *amplus,* large + *-ficāre,* -fy.]

am·pli·tude (ăm′plĭ-to͞od′, -tyo͞od′) *n.* **1.** Greatness of size; magnitude. **2.** Fullness; copiousness. **3.** Breadth or range, as of intelligence. **4.** *Astronomy.* The angular distance along the horizon from true east or west to the intersection of the vertical circle of a celestial body with the horizon. **5.** *Physics.* The maximum absolute value of a periodically varying quantity. **6.** *Mathematics.* **a.** The maximum absolute value of a periodic curve measured along its vertical axis. **b.** The angle made with the positive horizontal axis by the vector representation of a complex number. **7.** *Electronics.* The maximum absolute value reached by a voltage or current waveform. [Latin *amplitūdō,* from *amplus,* large.]

amphitheater
Théâtre Antique,
Orange, France

amplitude modulation *n. Abbr.* **am, AM** *Electronics.* **1.** The encoding of a carrier wave by variation of its amplitude in accordance with an input signal. **2.** A broadcast system that uses amplitude modulation.

am·poule also **am·pule** or **am·pul** (ăm′po͞ol, -pyo͞ol) *n.* A small glass vial that is sealed after filling and used chiefly as a container for a hypodermic injection solution. [French, from Old French, from Latin *ampulla.* See AMPULLA.]

am·pul·la (ăm-po͝ol′ə, -pŭl′ə) *n., pl.* **-pul·lae** (-po͝ol′ē, -pŭl′ē). **1.** A nearly round bottle with two handles used by the ancient Romans for wine, oil, or perfume. **2.** *Ecclesiastical.* A vessel for consecrated wine or holy oil. **3.** *Anatomy.* A small dilatation in a canal or duct, especially one in the semicircular canal of the ear. [Middle English, from Old English, from Latin, diminutive of *amphora.* See AMPHORA.] **—am·pul′lar** *adj.*

am·pu·tate (ăm′pyo͞o-tāt′) *tr.v.* **-tat·ed, -tat·ing, -tates.** To cut off (a part of the body), especially by surgery. [Latin *amputāre, amputāt-,* to cut around : *ambi-,* around; see AMBI– + *putāre,* to cut; see **peu-** in Appendix.] **—am′pu·ta′tion** *n.* **—am′pu·ta′tor** *n.*

am·pu·tee (ăm′pyo͞o-tē′) *n.* A person who has had one or more limbs removed by amputation.

Am·ra·va·ti (əm-rä′və-tē, ăm-). A town of central India west of Nagpur. It is the site of a stupa dating from the second century A.D. Population, 261,404.

am·ri·ta also **am·ree·ta** (ŭm-rē′tə) *n. Mythology.* **1.** The ambrosia, prepared by the Hindu gods, that bestows immortality. **2.** The immortality that is achieved by drinking this substance. [Sanskrit *amṛtam* : *a-,* without; see **ne** in Appendix + *mṛtam,* death; see **mer-** in Appendix.]

amphora
c. 540 B.C.
neck amphora
painted by Exekias

Am·rit·sar (əm-rĭt′sər). A city of northwest India near the Pakistan border. Founded in 1577 by the fourth guru of the Sikhs, Ram Das (1534–1581), it has remained the center of the Sikh faith. In the Amritsar massacre of April 13, 1919, hundreds of Indian nationalists were killed by British-led troops. Population, 594,844.

AMS *abbr.* **1.** Agricultural Marketing Service. **2.** Auditory memory span.

Am·ster·dam (ăm′stər-dăm′). **1.** The constitutional capital and largest city of the Netherlands, in the western part of the country on the Ij, an inlet of the Ijsselmeer. Linked to the North Sea by a ship canal, the city has an important stock exchange and is a major center of the diamond-cutting industry. Population, 676,439. **2.** A city of east-central New York on the Mohawk River northwest of Albany. Settled in 1783, it was named Amsterdam because many of its early inhabitants were from the Netherlands. Population, 21,872.

amt. *abbr.* Amount.

am·trac also **am·track** (ăm′trăk′) *n.* A small, flat-bottomed amphibious vehicle that moves by means of finned tracks and is used to carry troops from ship to shore. [AM(PHIBIOUS) + TRAC(TOR).]

amu *abbr. Physics.* Atomic mass unit.

a·muck (ə-mŭk′) also **a·mok** (ə-mŭk′, ə-mŏk′) *—adv.* **1.** In a frenzy to do violence or kill: *rioters running amuck in the streets.* **2.** In or into a jumbled or confused state: *The plans went amuck.* *—adj.* Crazed with murderous frenzy: *amuck troops.* [Malay *amok.*]

A·mu Dar·ya (ä′mo͞o där′yə, ə-mo͞o′ dŭr-yä′). Formerly **Ox·us** (ŏk′səs). A river of central Asia flowing about 2,574 km (1,600 mi) generally northwest from the Pamir Mountains to the southern Aral Sea. In ancient times it figured significantly in the history of Persia and in the campaigns of Alexander the Great.

ă pat	oi boy
ā pay	ou out
âr care	o͝o took
ä father	o͞o boot
ĕ pet	ŭ cut
ē be	ûr urge
ĭ pit	th thin
ī pie	*th* this
îr pier	hw which
ŏ pot	zh vision
ō toe	ə about, item
ô paw	♦ regionalism

Stress marks: **′** (primary); ′ (secondary), as in **dictionary** (dĭk′shə-nĕr′ē)

amulet
Top: Tlingit bear with protruding tongue
Bottom: Late 19th-century Tunisian amulets suspended from a belt clip

am·u·let (ăm′yə-lĭt) *n.* An object worn, especially around the neck, as a charm against evil or injury. [Latin *amulētum.*]

A·mund·sen (ä′mənd-sən, ä′mo͝on-), **Roald.** 1872–1928. Norwegian explorer who in 1911 became the first person to reach the South Pole.

Amundsen Gulf. An inlet of the Arctic Ocean in Northwest Territories, Canada, opening on the Beaufort Sea. It was first navigated completely by Roald Amundsen during his 1903–1905 expedition to the region.

Amundsen Sea. An arm of the southern Pacific Ocean off the coast of Marie Byrd Land, Antarctica. It was explored and named by a Norwegian, Nils Larsen, in the late 1920's.

A·mur River (ä-mo͝or′) also **Hei·long Jiang** (hā′lông′ jyäng′). A river of northeast Asia flowing about 2,896 km (1,800 mi) mainly along the border between China and Russia. One of the chief waterways of Asia, it drains into Tatar Strait opposite Sakhalin Island.

a·muse (ə-myo͞oz′) *tr.v.* **a·mused, a·mus·ing, a·mus·es. 1.** To occupy in an agreeable, pleasing, or entertaining fashion. **2.** To cause to laugh or smile by giving pleasure. **3.** *Archaic.* To delude or deceive. [Middle English, from Old French *amuser,* to stupefy : *a-,* to (from Latin *ad-;* see AD–) + *muser,* to stare stupidly; see MUSE.] **—a·mus′a·ble** *adj.* **—a·mus′er** *n.*

SYNONYMS: *amuse, entertain, divert, regale.* These verbs refer to actions that provide pleasure, especially as a means of passing time. *Amuse,* the least specific, implies directing the attention away from serious matters: *I amused myself with a game of solitaire. Entertain* suggests acts undertaken to furnish amusement: *"They* [timetables and catalogs] *are much more entertaining than half the novels that are written"* (W. Somerset Maugham). *Divert* implies distraction from worrisome thought or care: *"I had neither Friends or Books to divert me"* (Richard Steele). To *regale* is to entertain with something enormously enjoyable: *"He loved to regale his friends with tales about the many memorable characters he had known as a newspaperman"* (David Rosenzweig).

a·muse·ment (ə-myo͞oz′mənt) *n.* **1.** The state of being amused, entertained, or pleased. **2.** Something that amuses, entertains, or pleases.

amusement park *n.* A commercially operated enterprise that offers rides, games, and other forms of entertainment.

a·mus·ing (ə-myo͞o′zĭng) *adj.* **1.** Entertaining or pleasing. **2.** Arousing laughter. **—a·mus′ing·ly** *adv.* **—a·mus′ing·ness** *n.*

a·mu·sive (ə-myo͞o′zĭv, -sĭv) *adj.* Providing or arousing amusement.

AMVETS *abbr.* American Veterans.

a·myg·da·la (ə-mĭg′də-lə) *n., pl.* **-lae** (-lē). *Anatomy.* An almond-shaped mass of gray matter in the anterior portion of the temporal lobe. Also called *amygdaloid nucleus.* [Latin, almond, from Greek *amugdalē.*]

a·myg·dale (ə-mĭg′dāl) *n.* An amygdule. [From Latin *amygdala,* almond. See AMYGDALA.]

a·myg·da·lin (ə-mĭg′də-lĭn) *n.* A glycoside, $C_{20}H_{27}NO_{11}$, commonly found in seeds and other plant parts of many members of the rose family, such as kernels of the apricot, peach, and bitter almond, which breaks down into hydrocyanic acid, benzaldehyde, and glucose. [From Late Latin *amygdalus,* almond tree, from Greek *amygdalos.*]

a·myg·da·line (ə-mĭg′də-lĭn, -līn′) *adj.* Of, relating to, or resembling an almond. [Latin *amygdalīnus,* from Greek *amugdalinos,* from *amugdalē,* almond.]

a·myg·da·loid (ə-mĭg′də-loid′) *n.* A volcanic rock containing many amygdules. **—amygdaloid** also **a·myg·da·loi·dal** (ə-mĭg′də-loi′dl) *adj.* **1.** Shaped like an almond. **2.** *Anatomy.* Of or relating to the amygdala. **3.** Resembling a volcanic rock that contains many amygdules. [Latin *amygdala,* almond; see AMYGDALA + –OID.]

amygdaloid nucleus *n.* See **amygdala.**

a·myg·dule (ə-mĭg′dyo͞ol) *n.* A small gas bubble in igneous, especially volcanic, rock filled with secondary minerals such as zeolite, calcite, or quartz. [Latin *amygdala,* almond (from its shape); see AMYGDALA + (NOD)ULE.]

am·yl (ăm′əl) *n.* The univalent organic radical, C_5H_{11}, occurring in many organic compounds in eight isomeric forms. Also called *pentyl.* [Blend of AMYL– and –YL.]

amyl– *pref.* Variant of **amylo–.**

am·y·la·ceous (ăm′ə-lā′shəs) *adj.* Of, relating to, or resembling starch; starchy.

amyl acetate *n.* An organic compound, $CH_3COOC_5H_{11}$, occurring in isomeric mixtures and used as a flavoring agent, as a paint and lacquer solvent, and in the preparation of penicillin. Also called *banana oil.*

amyl alcohol *n.* Any of eight isomers of the alcohol composition $C_5H_{11}OH$, one of which is the principal constituent of fusel oil.

am·y·lase (ăm′ə-lās′, -lāz′) *n.* A group of enzymes that are present in saliva, pancreatic juice, and parts of plants and help convert starch to sugar.

amyl nitrite *n.* A volatile yellow liquid, $C_5H_{11}NO_2$, used in medicine as a vasodilator.

amylo– or **amyl–** *pref.* Starch: *amylose.* [From Latin *amylum,* starch. See AMYLUM.]

Roald Amundsen

amusement park

am·y·loid (ăm′ə-loid′) *n.* **1.** A starchlike substance. **2.** *Pathology.* A hard, waxy deposit consisting of protein and polysaccharides that results from the degeneration of tissue. **—amyloid** *adj.* Starchlike.

am·y·loid·o·sis (ăm′ə-loi-dō′sĭs) *n.* A disorder marked by the deposition of amyloid in various organs and tissues of the body. It may be associated with a chronic disease such as rheumatoid arthritis, tuberculosis, or multiple myeloma.

am·y·lol·y·sis (ăm′ə-lŏl′ĭ-sĭs) *n.* Conversion of starch to sugars by the action of enzymes or acids. **—am′y·lo·lyt′ic** (-lō-lĭt′ĭk) *adj.*

am·y·lop·sin (ăm′ə-lŏp′sĭn) *n.* The starch-digesting amylase produced by the pancreas and present in pancreatic juice. [AMYLO– + (TRY)PSIN.]

am·y·lose (ăm′ə-lōs′, -lōz′) *n.* **1.** The inner portion of a starch granule, consisting of relatively soluble polysaccharides having an unbranched, linear, or spiral structure. **2.** A polysaccharide, such as starch or cellulose.

am·y·lum (ăm′ə-ləm) *n.* Starch. [Latin, from Greek *amulon,* starch, from neuter of *amulos,* not ground at a mill : *a-,* not; see A–[1] + *mulē,* mill; see **melə-** in Appendix.]

a·my·o·to·ni·a (ā′mī-ə-tō′nē-ə) *n.* Lack of muscle tone.

a·my·o·tro·phic lateral sclerosis (ā′mī-ə-trō′fĭk, -trŏf′ĭk, ā-mī′-) *n. Abbr.* **ALS** A chronic, progressive disease marked by gradual degeneration of the nerve cells in the central nervous system that control voluntary muscle movement. The disorder causes muscle weakness and atrophy and usually results in death. Also called *Lou Gehrig's disease.*

an[1] (ən; ăn *when stressed*) *indef.art.* The form of *a* used before words beginning with a vowel or with an unpronounced *h*: *an elephant; an hour.* See Usage Note at **a**[2]**, every.** [Middle English, from Old English *ān,* one. See **oi-no-** in Appendix.]

an[2] also **an′** (ən, ăn *when stressed*) *conj. Archaic.* And if; if. [Middle English, short for *and,* and, from Old English. See AND.]

AN *abbr.* Airman, Navy.

an. *abbr. Latin.* **1.** Anno (in the year). **2.** Ante (before).

an– *pref.* Variant of **a–**[1]**.**

–an[1] *suff.* **1.** Of, relating to, or resembling: *brachyuran.* **2.** One relating to, belonging to, or resembling: *librarian.* [Middle English, from Old French, from Latin *-ānus,* adj. and n. suff.]

–an[2] *suff.* **1.** Unsaturated carbon compound: *urethan.* **2.** Anhydride of a carbohydrate: *dextran.* [Alteration of –ANE.]

an·a[1] (ăn′ə, ä′nə) *n., pl.* **ana** or **-as. 1.** A collection of various materials that reflect the character of a person or place: *definitive ana of the early American West.* **2.** An item in such a collection. [From New Latin *-āna,* as in titles of such collections. See –ANA.]

an·a[2] (ăn′ə) *adv.* Both in the same quantity; of each. Used to refer to ingredients in prescriptions. [Middle English, from Medieval Latin, from Greek, at the rate of. See **an-** in Appendix.]

ANA *abbr.* **1.** American Newspaper Association. **2.** American Nurses Association. **3.** Association of National Advertisers.

ana– *pref.* **1.** Upward; up: *anabolism.* **2.** Backward; back: *anaplasia.* **3.** Again; anew: *anaphylaxis.* [Greek, from *ana,* up. See **an-** in Appendix.]

–ana or **–iana** *suff.* A collection of items relating to a specified person or place: *Americana.* [New Latin *-āna,* from Latin *-āna,* neuter pl. of *-ānus,* adj. and n. suff. See –AN[1].]

an·a·bae·na (ăn′ə-bē′nə) *n.* Any of various freshwater algae of the genus *Anabaena* that sometimes occur in drinking water and cause a bad taste and odor. [New Latin *Anabaena,* genus name, from Greek *anabainein,* to go up : *ana-,* ana- + *bainein,* to go; see **gʷā-** in Appendix.]

An·a·bap·tist (ăn′ə-băp′tĭst) *n.* A member of a radical movement of the 16th-century Reformation which believed in the primacy of the Bible, in baptism as an external witness of the believer's personal covenant of inner faith, and in separation of church from state and of believers from nonbelievers. [From Late Greek *anabaptizein,* to baptize again : Greek *ana-,* ana- + Greek *baptizein,* to baptize (from *baptein,* to dip).] **—An′a·bap′tism** *n.*

an·a·bas (ăn′ə-băs′) *n.* A freshwater fish of the family Anabantidae, native to Africa and southeast Asia and including the gourami and climbing perch. [Greek *anabas,* climbing, aorist participle of *anabainein,* to go up. See ANABAENA.]

a·nab·a·sis (ə-năb′ə-sĭs) *n., pl.* **-ses** (-sēz′). **1.** An advance; an expedition. **2.** A large-scale military advance, specifically the Greek mercenary expedition across Asia Minor in 401 B.C. led by Cyrus the Younger of Persia, as described by Xenophon. It was unsuccessful, and the Greeks, led by Xenophon, retreated to the Black Sea. [Greek, from *anabainein,* to go up. See ANABAENA.]

an·a·bat·ic (ăn′ə-băt′ĭk) *adj.* Of or relating to rising wind currents. [Greek *anabatikos,* skilled in mounting, from *anabainein,* to rise. See ANABAENA.]

an·a·bi·o·sis (ăn′ə-bī-ō′sĭs) *n.* **1.** A restoring to life from a deathlike condition; resuscitation. **2.** A state of suspended animation, especially one in which certain aquatic invertebrates are able to survive long periods of drought. [Greek *anabiōsis,* from *anabioun,* to return to life : *ana-,* ana- + *bioun,* to live (from *bios,* life; see **gʷei-** in Appendix).] **—an′a·bi·ot′ic** (-ŏt′ĭk) *adj.*

anabolic steroid *n.* A group of synthetic hormones that promote the storage of protein and the growth of tissue, sometimes used by athletes to increase muscle size and strength.

a•nab•o•lism (ə-năb′ə-lĭz′əm) *n.* The phase of metabolism in which simple substances are synthesized into the complex materials of living tissue. [ANA– + (META)BOLISM.] **—an′a•bol′ic** (ăn′ə-bŏl′ĭk) *adj.*

a•nach•ro•nism (ə-năk′rə-nĭz′əm) *n.* **1.** Representation of someone as existing or something as happening in other than the chronological, proper, or historical order. **2.** One that is out of its proper or chronological order: *"He is interested in the spirit of the play, and he is not averse to throwing in an anachronism or two if he thinks it will help underscore a point"* (Skylines). [French *anachronisme,* from New Latin *anachronismus,* from Late Greek *anakhronismos,* from *anakronizesthai,* to be an anachronism : Greek *ana-,* ana- + Greek *khronizein,* to take time (from *khronos,* time).] **—a•nach′ro•nis′tic, a•nach′ro•nous** (-nəs) *adj.* **—a•nach′ro•nis′ti•cal•ly, a•nach′ro•nous•ly** *adv.*

an•a•cli•sis (ăn′ə-klī′sĭs, ə-năk′lĭ-) *n.* Psychological dependence on others. [Greek *anaklisis,* a leaning back, from *anaklinein,* to lean on : *ana-,* on-; see ANA– + *klinein,* to lean; see **klei-** in Appendix.] **—an′a•clit′ic** (-klĭt′ĭk) *adj.*

an•a•co•lu•thon (ăn′ə-kə-lo͞o′thŏn′) *n., pl.* **-thons** or **-tha** (-thə). *Grammar.* An abrupt change within a sentence to a second construction inconsistent with the first, sometimes used for rhetorical effect; for example, *I warned him that if he continues to drink, what will become of him?* [Late Latin, from Late Greek *anakolouthon,* inconsistency in logic, from Greek, neuter of *anakolouthos,* inconsistent : *an-,* not; see A–[1] + *akolouthos,* following (*a-,* together; see **sem-**[1] in Appendix + *keleuthos,* path).] **—an′a•co•lu′thic** *adj.*

an•a•con•da (ăn′ə-kŏn′də) *n.* **1.** A large nonvenomous arboreal snake *(Eunectes murinus)* of tropical South America that kills its prey by suffocating it in its coils. **2.** A similar or related snake. [Perhaps alteration of Singhalese *henakandayā,* whip snake.]

A•nac•re•on (ə-năk′rē-ən). 563?–478? B.C. Greek poet noted for his songs praising love and wine.

A•nac•re•on•tic (ə-năk′rē-ŏn′tĭk) *adj.* Of or in the manner of the poems of Anacreon, especially being convivial or amatory in subject. **—Anacreontic** *n.* A poem written in the style of Anacreon.

an•a•cru•sis (ăn′ə-kro͞o′sĭs) *n.* **1.** One or more unstressed syllables at the beginning of a line of verse, before the reckoning of the normal meter begins. **2.** *Music.* An upbeat. [New Latin, from Greek *anakrousis,* beginning of a tune, from *anakrouein,* to strike up a song : *ana-,* ana- + *krouein,* to push.]

♦ **an•a•dam•a bread** (ăn′ə-dăm′ə) *n. New England.* A loaf of bread made of white flour, cornmeal, and molasses. [Origin unknown.]

an•a•dem (ăn′ə-dĕm′) *n. Archaic.* A wreath or garland for the head. [Latin *anadēma,* from Greek, from *anadein,* to bind up : *ana-,* ana- + *dein,* to bind.]

an•a•di•plo•sis (ăn′ə-də-plō′sĭs) *n., pl.* **-ses** (-sēz). Rhetorical repetition at the beginning of a phrase of the word or words with which the previous phrase ended; for example, *He is a man of loyalty—loyalty always firm.* [Late Latin *anadiplōsis,* from Greek *anadiplōsis,* from *anadiploun,* to redouble : *ana-,* ana- + *diploun,* to double (from *diplous,* double; see **dwo-** in Appendix).]

a•nad•ro•mous (ə-năd′rə-məs) *adj.* Migrating up rivers from the sea to breed in fresh water. Used of fish. [From Greek *anadromos,* running up, from *anadromē,* a running back : *ana-,* ana- + *dromos,* a running.]

A•na•dyr (ä′nə-dîr′). A river of northeast Russia rising in the **Anadyr Plateau** and flowing about 1,118 km (695 mi) south and then east to **Anadyr Bay,** an inlet of the Bering Sea. There are coal and gold deposits near the river's mouth.

a•nae•mi•a (ə-nē′mē-ə) *n.* Variant of **anemia.**

a•nae•mic (ə-nē′mĭk) *adj.* Variant of **anemic.**

an•aer•obe (ăn′ə-rōb′, ăn-âr′ōb′) *n.* An organism, such as a bacterium, that can live in the absence of atmospheric oxygen. **—an′aer•o′bic** (ăn′ə-rō′bĭk, -âr-ō′bĭk) *adj.* **—an′aer•o′bic•al•ly** *adv.*

an•aer•o•bi•o•sis (ăn′ə-rō′bī-ō′sĭs, ăn′â-rō′-) *n.* Life sustained by an organism in the absence of oxygen. **—an′aer•o′bi•ot′ic** (-ŏt′ĭk) *adj.*

an•aes•the•sia (ăn′ĭs-thē′zhə) *n.* Variant of **anesthesia.**

an•aes•the•si•ol•o•gist (ăn′ĭs-thē′zē-ŏl′ə-jĭst) *n.* Variant of **anesthesiologist.**

an•aes•the•si•ol•o•gy (ăn′ĭs-thē′zē-ŏl′ə-jē) *n.* Variant of **anesthesiology.**

an•aes•thet•ic (ăn′ĭs-thĕt′ĭk) *adj. & n.* Variant of **anesthetic.**

a•naes•the•tist (ə-nĕs′thĭ-tĭst) *n.* Variant of **anesthetist.**

a•naes•the•tize (ənĕs′thĭ-tīz′) *v.* Variant of **anesthetize.**

an•a•gen•e•sis (ăn′ə-jĕn′ĭ-sĭs) *n.* A pattern of evolution that results in linear descent with no branching or splitting of the population.

an•a•glyph (ăn′ə-glĭf′) *n.* **1.** An ornament carved in low relief. **2.** A moving or still picture consisting of two slightly different perspectives of the same subject in contrasting colors that are superimposed on each other, producing a three-dimensional effect when viewed through two correspondingly colored filters. [From Late Latin *anaglyphus,* carved in low relief, from Greek *anagluphos* : *ana-,* ana- + *gluphein,* to carve; see **gleubh-** in Appendix.] **—an′a•glyph′ic, an′a•glyp′tic** (-glĭp′tĭk) *adj.*

an•a•go•ge also **an•a•go•gy** (ăn′ə-gō′jē) *n., pl.* **-ges** also **-gies.** A mystical interpretation of a word, passage, or text, especially scriptural exegesis that detects allusions to heaven or the afterlife. [Late Latin *anagōgē,* from Late Greek, spiritual uplift, from *anagein,* to lift up : *ana-,* ana- + *agein,* to lead; see **ag-** in Appendix.] **—an′a•gog′ic** (-gŏj′ĭk), **an′a•gog′i•cal** *adj.* **—an′a•gog′i•cal•ly** *adv.*

an•a•gram (ăn′ə-grăm′) *n.* **1.** A word or phrase formed by reordering the letters of another word or phrase, such as *satin* to *stain.* **2. anagrams.** *(used with a sing. verb). Games.* A game whose object is to form words from a group of randomly picked letters. [New Latin *anagramma,* from Greek *anagrammatismos,* from *anagrammatizein,* to rearrange letters in a word : *ana-,* from bottom to top; see ANA– + *gramma, grammat-,* letter; see **gerbh-** in Appendix.] **—an′a•gram•mat′ic** (-grə-măt′ĭk) *adj.* **—an′a•gram•mat′i•cal•ly** *adv.*

an•a•gram•ma•tize (ăn′ə-grăm′ə-tīz′) *tr.v.* **-tized, -tiz•ing, -tiz•es.** To make an anagram of. [Late Greek *anagrammatizein,* to rearrange letters in a word. See ANAGRAM.]

An•a•heim (ăn′ə-hīm′). A city of southern California southeast of Los Angeles. It is the site of Disneyland, opened in 1955. Population, 219,494.

A•ná•huac (ə-nä′wäk′). An extensive plateau of central Mexico. A heavily populated and highly industrial area that includes Mexico City, it was the center of a pre-Columbian Aztec civilization.

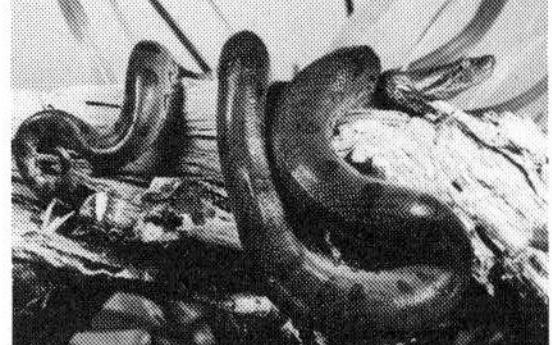

anaconda
Giant anaconda
Eunectes murinus

a•nal (ā′nəl) *adj.* **1.** Of, relating to, or near the anus. **2.** *Psychology.* **a.** Of or relating to the second stage of psychosexual development in psychoanalytic theory, during which gratification is derived from sensations associated with the anus. **b.** Indicating personality traits that originated during toilet training and are distinguished as anal-expulsive or anal-retentive. [From Latin *ānus,* anus.] **—a′nal•ly** *adv.*

anal. *abbr.* **1.** Analogous; analogy. **2.** Analysis; analytic.

a•nal•cime (ə-năl′sēm′) also **a•nal•cite** (-sīt′) *n.* A white or light-colored zeolite, $NaAlSi_2O_6 \cdot H_2O$, found in certain basalts. [French, from Greek *analkimos,* weak (from its weak electric power) : *an-,* not; see A–[1] + *alkimos,* brave (from *alkē,* strength).] **—a•nal•cim′ic** *adj.*

an•a•lects (ăn′ə-lĕkts′) also **an•a•lec•ta** (ăn′ə-lĕk′tə) *pl.n.* Selections from or parts of a literary work or group of works. Often used as a title. [Greek *analekta,* selected things, from neuter pl. of *analektos,* gathered together, from *analegein,* to gather : *ana-,* ana- + *legein,* to gather; see **leg-** in Appendix.] **—an′a•lec′tic** *adj.*

an•a•lem•ma (ăn′ə-lĕm′ə) *n.* A graduated scale in the shape of a figure eight, indicating the sun's declination and the equation of time for every day of the year and usually found on sundials and globes. [Latin, sundial, from Greek *analēmma,* from *analambanein,* to take up. See ANALEPTIC.]

an•a•lep•tic (ăn′ə-lĕp′tĭk) *adj.* Restorative or stimulating, as a drug or medication. **—analeptic** *n.* A medication used as a central nervous system stimulant. [Greek *analēptikos,* from *analambanein,* to take up : *ana-,* ana- + *lambanein, lēp-,* to take.]

a•nal-ex•pul•sive (ā′nəl-ĭk-spŭl′sĭv) *adj. Psychology.* Indicating personality traits, such as conceit, suspicion, ambition, and generosity, originating in habits, attitudes, or values associated with infantile pleasure in the expulsion of feces.

an•al•ge•si•a (ăn′əl-jē′zē-ə, -zhə) *n. Pathology.* A deadening or absence of the sense of pain without loss of consciousness. [Greek *analgēsia* : *an-,* without; see A–[1] + *algēsia,* pain (from *algein,* to feel pain, from *algos,* pain).] **—an′al•get′ic** (-jĕt′ĭk) *adj.*

an•al•ge•sic (ăn′əl-jē′zĭk, -sĭk) *n.* A medication that reduces or eliminates pain. **—analgesic** *adj.* Of or causing analgesia.

an•a•log (ăn′ə-lôg′, -lŏg′) *n. & adj.* Variant of **analogue.**

analog computer also **analogue computer** *n. Computer Science.* A computer in which numerical data are represented by measurable physical variables, such as electrical signals.

an•a•log•i•cal (ăn′ə-lŏj′ĭ-kəl) *adj.* Of, expressing, composed of, or based on an analogy: *the analogical use of a metaphor.* **—an′a•log′i•cal•ly** *adv.*

a•nal•o•gist (ə-năl′ə-jĭst) *n.* One who looks for or reasons from analogies: *"Learning more from books than from life, he was an analogist"* (Times Literary Supplement).

a•nal•o•gize (ə-năl′ə-jīz′) *v.* **-gized, -giz•ing, -giz•es.** *—tr.* To make an analogy to. *—intr.* To look for or reason by analogy.

a•nal•o•gous (ə-năl′ə-gəs) *adj. Abbr.* **anal. 1.** Similar or alike in such a way as to permit the drawing of an analogy. **2.** *Biology.* Similar in function but not in structure and evolutionary origin. [From Latin *analogus,* from Greek *analogos,* proportionate : *ana-,* according to; see ANA– + *logos,* proportion; see **leg-** in Appendix.] **—a•nal′o•gous•ly** *adv.* **—a•nal′o•gous•ness** *n.*

an•a•logue also **an•a•log** (ăn′ə-lôg′, -lŏg′) *—n.* **1.** Something that bears an analogy to something else: *Surimi is marketed as an analogue of crabmeat.* **2.** *Biology.* An organ or structure that is similar in function to one in another kind of organism but is of dissimilar evolutionary origin. **3.** *Chemistry.* A structural derivative of a parent compound that often differs from it by a

ă pat	oi boy
ā pay	ou out
âr care	o͝o took
ä father	o͞o boot
ĕ pet	ŭ cut
ē be	ûr urge
ĭ pit	th thin
ī pie	*th* this
îr pier	hw which
ŏ pot	zh vision
ō toe	ə about, item
ô paw	♦ regionalism

Stress marks: ′ (primary); ′ (secondary), as in **dictionary** (dĭk′shə-nĕr′ē)

single element. —*adj.* **1.** Often **analog.** Of, relating to, or being a device in which data are represented by variable measurable physical quantities. **2.** Often **analog.** *Computer Science.* Of or relating to an analog computer. [French, analogous, analogue, from Medieval Latin *analogus,* from Greek *analogos,* proportionate. See ANALOGOUS.]

analogue computer *n. Computer Science.* Variant of **analog computer.**

a·nal·o·gy (ə-năl′ə-jē) *n., pl.* **-gies.** *Abbr.* **anal. 1.a.** Similarity in some respects between things that are otherwise dissimilar. **b.** A comparison based on such similarity. See Synonyms at **likeness. 2.** *Biology.* Correspondence in function or position between organs of dissimilar evolutionary origin or structure. **3.** A form of logical inference or an instance of it, based on the assumption that if two things are known to be alike in some respects, then they must be alike in other respects. **4.** *Linguistics.* **a.** The process by which words and morphemes are re-formed or created on the model of existing grammatical patterns in a language, as Modern English *name : names* for Old English *nama : naman* on the model of nouns like *stone : stones.* **b.** The process by which inflectional paradigms are made more regular by the replacement of an uncommon or irregular stem or affix by one that is common or regular, as *bit* in Modern English *bit, bitten* for Old English *bāt, biten.* [Middle English *analogie,* from Old French, from Latin *analogia,* from Greek, from *analogos,* proportionate. See ANALOGOUS.]

an·al·pha·bet·ic (ăn-ăl′fə-bĕt′ĭk) *adj.* **1.** Not alphabetical. **2.** Unable to read; illiterate. **—analphabetic** *n.* One who is unable to read; an illiterate. [From Greek *analphabētos,* not knowing the alphabet : *an-,* not; see A–[1] + *alphabētos,* alphabet; see ALPHABET.]

a·nal-re·ten·tive (ā′nəl-rĭ-tĕn′tĭv) *adj. Psychology.* Indicating personality traits, such as meticulousness, avarice, and obstinacy, originating in habits, attitudes, or values associated with infantile pleasure in retention of feces.

a·nal·y·sand (ə-năl′ĭ-sănd′) *n.* A person who is being psychoanalyzed. [From ANALYZE, on the model of MULTIPLICAND.]

a·nal·y·sis (ə-năl′ĭ-sĭs) *n., pl.* **-ses** (-sēz′). *Abbr.* **anal. 1.** The separation of an intellectual or substantial whole into its constituent parts for individual study. **2.** *Chemistry.* **a.** The separation of a substance into its constituent elements to determine either their nature (qualitative analysis) or their proportions (quantitative analysis). **b.** The stated findings of such a separation or determination. **3.** *Mathematics.* **a.** A branch of mathematics principally involving differential and integral calculus, sequences, and series and concerned with limits and convergence. **b.** The method of proof in which a known truth is sought as a consequence of a series of deductions from that which is the thing to be proved. **4.** *Linguistics.* The use of function words such as prepositions, pronouns, or auxiliary verbs instead of inflectional endings to express a grammatical relationship; for example, *the cover of the dictionary* instead of *the dictionary's cover.* **5.** Psychoanalysis. **6.** Systems analysis. [Medieval Latin, from Greek *analusis,* a dissolving, from *analuein,* to undo : *ana-,* throughout; see ANA– + *luein,* to loosen; see **leu-** in Appendix.]

analysis of variance *n.* An analysis of the variation in the outcomes of an experiment to assess the contribution of each variable to the variation.

an·a·lyst (ăn′ə-lĭst) *n.* **1.** One that analyzes. **2.** A licensed practitioner of psychoanalysis. **3.** A systems analyst.

an·a·lyt·ic (ăn′ə-lĭt′ĭk) or **an·a·lyt·i·cal** (-ĭ-kəl) *adj. Abbr.* **anal. 1.** Of or relating to analysis or analytics. **2.** Dividing into elemental parts or basic principles. **3.** Reasoning or acting from a perception of the parts and interrelations of a subject: *"Many of the most serious pianists have turned toward more analytic playing, with a renewed focus on the architecture and ideas of music"* (Annalyn Swan). **4.** Expert in or using analysis, especially in thinking: *an analytic mind; an analytic approach.* See Synonyms at **logical. 5.** *Logic.* Following necessarily; tautologous: *an analytic truth.* **6.** *Mathematics.* **a.** Using, subjected to, or capable of being subjected to a methodology involving algebra and calculus. **b.** Proving a known truth by reasoning from that which is to be proved. **7.** *Linguistics.* Expressing a grammatical category by using two or more words instead of an inflected form. **8.** Psychoanalytic. [Medieval Latin *analyticus,* from Greek *analutikos,* from *analuein,* to resolve. See ANALYSIS.] **—an′a·lyt′i·cal·ly** *adv.*

analytical balance *n.* A balance for chemical analysis.

analytic geometry *n. Mathematics.* The analysis of geometric structures and properties principally by algebraic operations on variables defined in terms of position coordinates.

an·a·lyt·ics (ăn′ə-lĭt′ĭks) *n. (used with a sing. or pl. verb).* The branch of logic dealing with analysis.

an·a·lyze (ăn′ə-līz′) *tr.v.* **-lyzed, -lyz·ing, -lyz·es. 1.** To separate into parts or basic principles so as to determine the nature of the whole; examine methodically. **2.** *Chemistry.* To make a chemical analysis of. **3.** *Mathematics.* To make a mathematical analysis of. **4.** To psychoanalyze. [Perhaps from French *analyser,* from *analyse,* analysis, from Greek *analusis.* See ANALYSIS.] **—an′a·lyz′a·ble** *adj.* **—an′a·ly·za′tion** (-lĭ-zā′shən) *n.* **—an′a·lyz′er** *n.*

SYNONYMS: *analyze, anatomize, dissect, resolve.* The central meaning shared by these verbs is "to separate into constituent parts for study": *analyze an ore to see if it contains iron; anatomizing the doctrine of free enterprise; medical students dissecting cadavers; vapor condensing and being resolved into water.*

an·am·ne·sis (ăn′ăm-nē′sĭs) *n., pl.* **-ses** (-sēz). **1.** *Psychology.* A recalling to memory; recollection. **2.** *Medicine.* The complete case history of a patient. [Greek *anamnēsis,* from *anamimnēskein,* to remind : *ana-,* ana- + *mimnēskein,* to recall; see **men-**[1] in Appendix.] **—an′am·nes′tic** (-nĕs′tĭk) *adj.* **—an′am·nes′ti·cal·ly** *adv.*

an·a·mor·phic (ăn′ə-môr′fĭk) *adj.* Having, producing, or designating different optical magnification along mutually perpendicular radii: *an anamorphic lens.*

an·a·mor·pho·sis (ăn′ə-môr′fə-sĭs) *n., pl.* **-ses** (-sēz′). **1.a.** An image that appears distorted unless it is viewed from a special angle or with a special instrument. **b.** The production of such an image. **2.** Evolutionary increase in complexity of form and function. [New Latin, from Late Greek *anamorphoun,* to transform : Greek *ana-,* ana- + Greek *morphē,* shape.]

An·a·ni·as (ăn′ə-nī′əs). In the New Testament, a liar who dropped dead when Peter rebuked him.

An·an·ke (ə-năng′kē, ə-năn′-) *n.* The satellite of Jupiter that is 14th in distance from the planet. [Greek *Anankē,* mother of Adrasteia, distributor of rewards and punishments, by Jupiter, from *anankē,* necessity.]

an·a·pest also **an·a·paest** (ăn′ə-pĕst′) *n.* **1.** A metrical foot composed of two short syllables followed by one long one, as in the word *seventeen.* **2.** A line of verse using this meter; for example, *"'Twas the night before Christmas, when all through the house"* (Clement Clarke Moore). [Latin *anapestus,* from Greek *anapaistos* : *ana-,* ana- + *paiein, pais-,* to strike (so called because an anapest is a reversed dactyl); see **peu-** in Appendix.] **—an′a·pes′tic** *adj.*

an·a·phase (ăn′ə-fāz′) *n. Biology.* The stage of mitosis and meiosis in which the chromosomes move to opposite ends of the nuclear spindle.

a·naph·o·ra (ə-năf′ər-ə) *n.* The deliberate repetition of a word or phrase at the beginning of several successive verses, clauses, or paragraphs; for example, *"We shall fight on the beaches, we shall fight on the landing grounds, we shall fight in the fields and in the streets, we shall fight in the hills"* (Winston S. Churchill). [Late Latin, from Greek, from *anapherein,* to bring back : *ana-,* ana- + *pherein,* to carry; see **bher-**[1] in Appendix.]

an·aph·ro·dis·i·a (ăn-ăf′rə-dĭz′ē-ə, -dĭzh′ə) *n.* Decline or absence of sexual desire. [Greek, want of power to inspire love : *an-,* without; see A–[1] + *aphrodisia,* sexual pleasures; see APHRODISIAC.] **—an·aph′ro·dis′i·ac** (ăn-ăf′rə-dĭz′ē-ăk′) *adj. & n.*

anaphylactic shock *n.* A sudden, severe allergic reaction characterized by a sharp drop in blood pressure, urticaria, and breathing difficulties that is caused by the injection of a foreign substance, such as a drug or bee venom, into the body after a preliminary or sensitizing injection. The reaction may be fatal if emergency treatment, including the administration of epinephrine injections, is not given immediately. Also called *anaphylaxis.*

an·a·phy·lax·is (ăn′ə-fə-lăk′sĭs) *n.* **1.** Hypersensitivity especially in animals to a substance, such as foreign protein or a drug, that is induced by a small preliminary or sensitizing injection of or exposure to the substance. **2.** See **anaphylactic shock.** [ANA– + (PRO)PHYLAXIS.] **—an′a·phy·lac′tic** (-lăk′tĭk), **an′a·phy·lac′toid** (-toid) *adj.* **—an′a·phy·lac′ti·cal·ly** *adv.*

an·a·pla·sia (ăn′ə-plā′zhə) *n.* Reversion of cells to an immature or a less differentiated form, as occurs in most malignant tumors.

an·a·plas·tic (ăn′ə-plăs′tĭk) *adj.* **1.** *Medicine.* Relating to the surgical restoration of a lost or absent part. **2.** Of or characterized by cells that have become less differentiated.

A·ná·po·lis (ä-nä′po͞o-lĭs). A city of central Brazil southeast of Brasília. It is a transportation hub. Population, 160,571.

an·arch (ăn′ärk′) *n.* An adherent of anarchy or a leader practicing it. [Back-formation from ANARCHY.]

an·ar·chic (ăn-är′kĭk) or **an·ar·chi·cal** (-kĭ-kəl) *adj.* **1.a.** Of, like, or supporting anarchy: *anarchic oratory.* **b.** Likely to produce or result in anarchy. **2.** Lacking order or control: *an anarchic state of affairs in the office; an anarchic mobile sculpture.* **—an·ar′chi·cal·ly** *adv.*

an·ar·chism (ăn′ər-kĭz′əm) *n.* **1.** The theory or doctrine that all forms of government are oppressive and undesirable and should be abolished. **2.** Active resistance and terrorism against the state, as used by some anarchists. **3.** Rejection of all forms of coercive control and authority: *"He was inclined to anarchism; he hated system and organization and uniformity"* (Bertrand Russell). **—an′ar·chis′tic** (-kĭs′tĭk) *adj.*

an·ar·chist (ăn′ər-kĭst) *n.* An advocate or a participant in anarchism.

an·ar·cho·syn·di·cal·ism (ăn-är′kō-sĭn′dĭ-kə-lĭz′əm) *n.* Syndicalism. [ANARCH(Y) + SYNDICALISM.]

an·ar·chy (ăn′ər-kē) *n., pl.* **-chies. 1.** Absence of any form of political authority. **2.** Political disorder and confusion. **3.** Absence of any cohesive principle, such as a common standard or purpose. [New Latin *anarchia,* from Greek *anarkhia,* from *anarkhos,* without a ruler : *an-,* without; see A–[1] + *arkhos,* ruler; see –ARCH.]

an·ar·thri·a (ăn-är′thrē-ə) *n.* Loss of the motor ability that enables speech. [New Latin, from Greek *anarthros,* not articulated. See ANARTHROUS.] —**an·ar′thric** (-thrĭk) *adj.*

an·ar·throus (ăn-är′thrəs) *adj.* **1.** *Linguistics.* Occurring without an article. Used especially of Greek nouns. **2.** *Zoology.* Lacking joints. [From Greek *anarthros,* not articulated : *an-,* without; see A–[1] + *arthron,* joint; see **ar-** in Appendix.]

an·a·sar·ca (ăn′ə-sär′kə) *n.* A general accumulation of serous fluid in various tissues and body cavities. [Middle English, from Medieval Latin : Greek *ana,* throughout; see ANA– + Greek *sarx, sark-,* flesh.] —**an′a·sar′cous** (-sär′kəs) *adj.*

A·na·sa·zi (ä′nə-sä′zē) *n., pl.* **Anasazi. 1.** A Native American people inhabiting southern Colorado and Utah and northern New Mexico and Arizona from about A.D. 100 and whose descendants are the present-day Pueblo peoples. Anasazi culture includes an early Basket Maker phase and a later Pueblo phase marked by the construction of cliff dwellings and by expert craftsmanship in weaving and pottery. **2.** A member of this people. [Navajo *'anaasází,* inhabitants of the now ruined Pueblos.]

an·as·tig·mat (ăn-ăs′tĭg-măt′) *n.* An anastigmatic lens.

an·as·tig·mat·ic (ăn-ăs′tĭg-măt′ĭk) *adj.* Free from astigmatism. Used of a compound lens in which the separate components compensate for the astigmatic effects of each lens.

a·nas·to·mose (ə-năs′tə-mōz′, -mōs′) *v.* **-mosed, -mos·ing, -mos·es.** —*tr.* To join by anastomosis. —*intr.* To be connected by anastomosis, as blood vessels. [Probably back-formation from ANASTOMOSIS.]

a·nas·to·mo·sis (ə-năs′tə-mō′sĭs) *n., pl.* **-ses** (-sēz). **1.** The connection of separate parts of a branching system to form a network, as of leaf veins, blood vessels, or a river and its branches. **2.** *Medicine.* The surgical connection of separate or severed tubular hollow organs to form a continuous channel, as between two parts of the intestine. [Late Latin *anastomōsis,* from Greek, outlet, from *anastomoun,* to furnish with a mouth : *ana-,* ana- + *stoma,* mouth.] —**a·nas′to·mot′ic** (-mŏt′ĭk) *adj.*

a·nas·tro·phe (ə-năs′trə-fē) *n. Grammar.* Inversion of the normal syntactic order of words; for example, *"Matter too soft a lasting mark to bear"* (Alexander Pope). [Late Latin *anastrophē,* from Greek, from *anastrephein,* to turn upside-down : *ana-,* ana- + *strephein,* to turn; see **streb(h)-** in Appendix.]

anat. *abbr.* Anatomical; anatomist; anatomy.

an·a·tase (ăn′ə-tās′, -tāz′) *n.* A rare blue or light yellow to brown crystalline mineral, the rarest of three forms of titanium dioxide, TiO_2, used as a pigment, especially in paint. [French, from Greek *anatasis,* extension (from its long crystals), from *anateinein,* to extend : *ana-,* ana- + *teinein,* to stretch; see **ten-** in Appendix.]

a·nath·e·ma (ə-năth′ə-mə) *n., pl.* **-mas. 1.** A formal ecclesiastical ban, curse, or excommunication. **2.** A vehement denunciation; a curse: *"the sound of a witch's anathemas in some unknown tongue"* (Nathaniel Hawthorne). **3.** One that is cursed or damned. **4.** One that is greatly reviled, loathed, or shunned. [Late Latin, an accursed thing, from Greek *anathēma,* from *anatithenai,* to dedicate : *ana-,* ana- + *tithenai,* to put; see **dhē-** in Appendix.]

a·nath·e·ma·tize (ə-năth′ə-mə-tīz′) *tr.v.* **-tized, -tiz·ing, -tiz·es.** To proclaim an anathema on; curse. [Late Latin *anathematīzāre,* from Greek *anathematizein,* from *anathema, anathemat-,* anathema. See ANATHEMA.] —**a·nath′e·ma·ti·za′tion** (-tĭ-zā′shən) *n.*

An·a·to·li·a (ăn′ə-tō′lē-ə, -tōl′yə). The Asian part of Turkey. It is usually considered synonymous with Asia Minor.

An·a·to·li·an (ăn′ə-tō′lē-ən) *adj.* **1.** Of or relating to Anatolia or its people, language, or culture. **2.** Of or relating to a branch of the Indo-European language family that includes Hittite and other extinct languages of ancient Anatolia. —**Anatolian** *n.* **1.** A native or inhabitant of Anatolia. **2.** The Anatolian languages.

an·a·tom·i·cal (ăn′ə-tŏm′ĭ-kəl) also **an·a·tom·ic** (-tŏm′ĭk) *adj. Abbr.* **anat. 1.** Concerned with anatomy. **2.** Concerned with dissection. **3.** Related to the structure of an organism. —**an′a·tom′i·cal·ly** *adv.*

a·nat·o·mist (ə-năt′ə-mĭst) *n. Abbr.* **anat.** An expert in or a student of anatomy.

a·nat·o·mize (ə-năt′ə-mīz′) *tr.v.* **-mized, -miz·ing, -miz·es. 1.** To dissect (an organism) to study the structure and relation of the parts. **2.** To analyze in minute detail: *"Pynchon is the devil who went beyond the grave to anatomize the remains of the modern soul"* (Josephine Hendin). See Synonyms at **analyze.** —**a·nat′o·mi·za′tion** (-mĭ-zā′shən) *n.*

a·nat·o·my (ə-năt′ə-mē) *n., pl.* **-mies.** *Abbr.* **anat. 1.** The bodily structure of a plant or an animal or of any of its parts. **2.** The science of the shape and structure of organisms and their parts. **3.** A treatise on anatomic science. **4.** Dissection of a plant or animal to study the structure, position, and interrelation of its various parts. **5.** A skeleton. **6.** The human body. **7.** A detailed examination or analysis: *the anatomy of a crime.* [Middle English *anatomie,* from Late Latin *anatomia,* from Greek *anatomē,* dissection : *ana-,* ana- + *tomē,* a cutting (from *temnein,* to cut; see **tem-** in Appendix).]

a·nat·ro·pous (ə-năt′rə-pəs) *adj. Botany.* Completely inverted so that the micropyle is facing downward and situated near the base of the funiculus: *an anatropous ovule.*

a·nat·to (ə-nä′tō) *n.* Variant of **annatto.**

An·ax·ag·o·ras (ăn′ăk-săg′ər-əs). 500?–428 B.C. Greek philosopher who correctly explained solar eclipses and believed matter to be composed of atoms.

A·nax·i·man·der (ə-năk′sə-măn′dər). 611–547 B.C. Greek philosopher and astronomer who speculated that the universe arose out of the separation of opposite qualities from one primordial substance.

anc. *abbr.* Ancient.

–ance *suff.* **1.** State or condition: *absorptance.* **2.** Action: *continuance.* [Middle English, from Old French, from Latin *-antia,* n. suff. (*-ant,* -ant + *-ia,* n. suff.) and from Latin *-entia* (*-ent,* -ent + *-ia,* n. suff.).]

an·ces·tor (ăn′sĕs′tər) *n.* **1.** A person from whom one is descended, especially if more remote than a grandparent; a forebear. **2.** A forerunner or predecessor. **3.** *Law.* The person from whom an estate has been inherited. **4.** *Biology.* The actual or hypothetical organism or stock from which later kinds evolved. [Middle English *auncestre,* from Old French, from Latin *antecessor,* predecessor, from *antecessus,* past participle of *antecēdere,* to precede : *ante-,* ante- + *cēdere,* to go; see **ked-** in Appendix.]

SYNONYMS: *ancestor, forebear, forefather, progenitor.* The central meaning shared by these nouns is "a person from whom one is descended": *ancestors who were farmers; an island once owned by his forebears; methods as old as our forefathers; the wisdom of our progenitors.*
ANTONYM: *descendant.*

an·ces·tral (ăn-sĕs′trəl) *adj.* Of, relating to, or evolved from an ancestor or ancestors. —**an·ces′tral·ly** *adv.*

an·ces·try (ăn′sĕs′trē) *n., pl.* **-tries. 1.** Ancestral descent or lineage. **2.** Ancestors considered as a group. [Middle English *auncestrie,* alteration (influenced by *auncestre*) of Old French *ancesserie,* from *ancessour,* ancestor, from Latin *antecessor.* See ANCESTOR.]

An·chi·ses (ăn-kī′sēz′) *n. Greek & Roman Mythology.* The father of Aeneas who was rescued by his son during the sack of Troy.

an·chor (ăng′kər) *n.* **1.** *Nautical.* A heavy object attached to a vessel by a cable or rope and cast overboard to keep the vessel in place either by its weight or by its flukes, which grip the bottom. **2.** A rigid point of support, as for securing a rope. **3.** A source of security or stability. **4.** *Sports.* **a.** An athlete, usually the strongest member of a team, who performs the last stage of a relay race or other competition. **b.** The end of a tug-of-war team. Also called *anchorman.* **5.** An anchorperson. —**anchor** *v.* **-chored, -chor·ing, -chors.** —*tr.* **1.** To hold fast by or as if by an anchor. See Synonyms at **fasten. 2.** *Sports.* To serve as an anchor for (a team or competition). **3.** To narrate or coordinate (a newscast). **4.** To provide or form an anchor store for: *Two major stores anchor each end of the shopping mall.* —*intr. Nautical.* To drop anchor or lie at anchor. [Middle English *anker, ancher,* from Old English *ancor,* from Latin *ancora, anchora,* from Greek *ankura.*]

WORD HISTORY: The history of the word *anchor* can be said to be a case study in various levels of sophistication. To begin with, the early history of the word illustrates the kind of borrowing done by the various Germanic peoples from the more advanced culture of the Roman Empire. *Ancora,* the Latin source of our word *anchor,* was borrowed into several Germanic languages, including Old English and Old High German, an indication that this appropriation occurred during the period of initial contact between Germanic peoples and the Roman Empire. If the early history of *anchor* illustrates borrowing from a more advanced culture by a less advanced one, a later stage in the word's history may illustrate a misplaced sophistication. The Latin word *ancora* itself came from Greek *ankura* but was sometimes spelled *anchora* in Latin because of a false analogy with other Greek words, in which the sound (k) was spelled *ch.* As far back as the 14th century English writers who were familiar with this Latin spelling inserted the *ch* in the word, otherwise spelled with a *k* or *c,* thus causing difficulty for many a beginning speller of later times.

an·chor·age (ăng′kər-ĭj) *n.* **1.** A place for anchoring. **2.** A fee charged for the privilege of anchoring. **3.** The act of anchoring or the condition of being at anchor. **4.** A means of securing or stabilizing: *The Bank of England is often regarded as the anchorage of the European financial community.*

An·chor·age (ăng′kər-ĭj). A city of southern Alaska on Cook Inlet south-southwest of Fairbanks. Founded in 1915 as construction headquarters for the Alaska Railroad, it is the largest city in the state. Population, 174,431.

an·cho·ress (ăng′kər-ĭs) *n.* A woman who has retired into seclusion for religious reasons. [Middle English *anchoryse, ankres,* from *ancre,* anchorite, from Old English *ancra,* from Old Irish *anchara,* from Late Latin *anachōrēta.* See ANCHORITE.]

an·cho·rite (ăng′kə-rīt′) also **an·cho·ret** (-rĕt′) *n.* A person who has retired into seclusion for religious reasons. [Middle English, from Medieval Latin *anchōrīta,* from Late Latin *anachōrēta,* from Late Greek *anakhōrētēs,* from *anakhōrein,* to retire : *ana-,* ana- + *khōrein,* to withdraw; see **ghē-** in Appendix.] —**an′cho·rit′ic** (-rĭt′ĭk) *adj.*

an·chor·man (ăng′kər-măn′) *n.* **1.** A man who narrates or

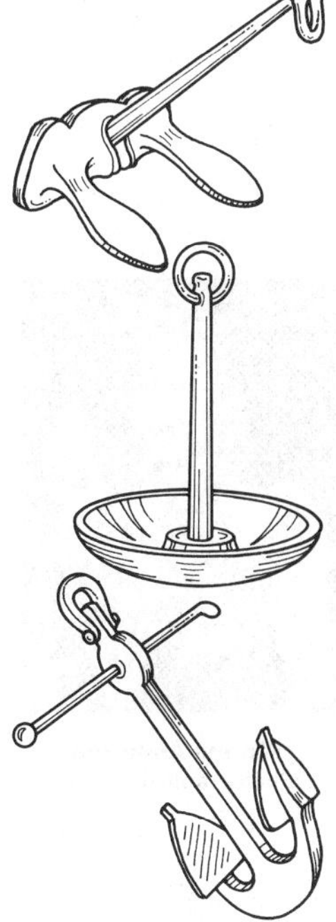

anchor
Top: Stockless
Center: Mushroom
Bottom: Admiralty

ă **pat** oi b**oy**
ā **pay** ou **out**
âr **care** ŏŏ t**oo**k
ä f**a**ther ōō b**oo**t
ĕ p**e**t ŭ c**u**t
ē b**e** ûr **ur**ge
ĭ p**i**t th **th**in
ī p**ie** *th* **th**is
îr p**ier** hw **wh**ich
ŏ p**o**t zh vi**s**ion
ō t**oe** ə **a**bout, ...m
ô p**aw** ♦ reg... ...mary);
Stress marks... ...n
′ (seconda... ...′shə-nĕr′ē)
dictiona...

coordinates a newscast in which several correspondents give reports. **2.** *Sports.* See **anchor** (sense 4).

an·chor·per·son (ăng′kər-pûr′sən) *n.* An anchorman or an anchorwoman.

anchor store *n.* A large business establishment, such as a department store or a supermarket, that is prominently located in a shopping mall, usually at one end. The anchor store attracts customers who are then expected to patronize the other shops in the mall.

an·chor·wom·an (ăng′kər-wo͝om′ən) *n.* A woman who narrates or coordinates a newscast in which several correspondents give reports.

an·cho·vy (ăn′chō′vē, ăn-chō′vē) *n., pl.* **anchovy** or **-vies.** A small, herringlike marine fish of the family Engraulidae, especially the European fish *(Engraulis encrasicholus),* widely used in appetizers and various dishes. [Spanish *anchova,* possibly from Vulgar Latin **apiuva,* variant of Latin **aphyē,* from Greek *aphuē.*]

Marian Anderson
Photographed in 1943

an·chy·lose (ăng′kə-lōs′, -lōz′) *v.* Variant of **ankylose.**

an·chy·lo·sis (ăng′kə-lō′sĭs) *n.* Variant of **ankylosis.**

an·cien ré·gime (äɴ-syăɴ′ rā-zhēm′) *n.* **1.** The political and social system that existed in France before the Revolution of 1789. **2.** A sociopolitical or other system that no longer exists. [French : *ancien,* old + *régime,* regime.]

an·cient¹ (ān′shənt) *adj. Abbr.* **anc. 1.** Of great age; very old. **2.** Of or relating to times long past, especially those of the historical period before the fall of the Western Roman Empire (A.D. 476). See Synonyms at **old. 3.** Old-fashioned; antiquated. **4.** Having the qualities associated with age, wisdom, or long use; venerable. **—ancient** *n.* **1.** A very old person. **2.** A person who lived in times long past. **3. ancients. a.** The peoples of the classical nations of antiquity. **b.** The ancient Greek and Roman authors. [Middle English *auncien,* from Old French, from Vulgar Latin **anteānus* : Latin *ante,* before; see **ant-** in Appendix + *-ānus,* adj. and n. suff.] **—an′cient·ly** *adv.* **—an′cient·ness** *n.*

an·cient² (ān′shənt) *n.* **1.** *Archaic.* An ensign; a flag. **2.** *Obsolete.* A flag-bearer or lieutenant. [Alteration of ENSIGN.]

ancient history *n.* **1.** The history of times long past. **2.** *Informal.* Common knowledge, especially of a recent event that has lost its original impact or importance.

an·cil·lar·y (ăn′sə-lĕr′ē) *adj.* **1.** Subordinate: *"For Degas, sculpture was never more than ancillary to his painting"* (Herbert Read). **2.** Auxiliary; helping: *an ancillary pump.* **—ancillary** *n., pl.* **-ies. 1.** Something, such as a workbook, that is subordinate to something else, such as a textbook. **2.** *Archaic.* A servant. [From Latin *ancilla,* maidservant, feminine diminutive of *anculus,* servant. See **kʷel-¹** in Appendix.]

An·co·hu·ma (ăng′kə-ho͞o′mə, äng′kō-o͞o′mä). A mountain, about 6,554 m (21,490 ft) high, of western Bolivia near the eastern shore of Lake Titicaca.

andiron
Pair of andirons

an·con (ăng′kŏn′) *n., pl.* **-con·es** (-kō′nēz). A projecting bracket that is used in classical architecture to carry the upper elements of a cornice; a console. [Latin *ancōn,* from Greek *ankōn,* elbow.]

An·co·na (ăng-kō′nə, ăn-, än-). A city of central Italy on the Adriatic Sea. It is a leading port and an industrial and commercial center. Population, 106,421.

-ancy *suff.* Condition or quality: *buoyancy.* [Latin *-antia* and *-entia;* see -ANCE.]

an·cy·lo·sto·mi·a·sis (ăn′sə-lō-stō-mī′ə-sĭs, ăng′kə-lō-) *n.* A disease caused by hookworm infestation and marked by progressive anemia. Also called *hookworm disease, tunnel disease.* [New Latin *Ancylostoma,* hookworm genus (Greek *ankulos,* curved + Greek *stoma,* mouth) + -IASIS.]

An·cy·ra (ăn-sī′rə). See **Ankara.**

and (ənd, ən; ănd *when stressed*) *conj.* **1.** Together with or along with; in addition to; as well as. Used to connect words, phrases, or clauses that have the same grammatical function in a construction. **2.** Added to; plus: *Two and two makes four.* **3.** Used to indicate result. **4.** *Usage Problem.* To. Used between finite verbs, such as *go, come, try, write,* or *see: try and find it; come and see.* **5.** *Archaic.* If: *and it pleases you.* [Middle English, from Old English. See **en** in Appendix.]

USAGE NOTE: It is frequently asserted that sentences beginning with *and* or *but* express "incomplete thoughts" and are therefore incorrect. But this rule was ridiculed by grammarians like Wilson Follett (who ascribed it to "schoolmarmish rhetoric") and H.W. Fowler (who called it a "superstition"), and the stricture has been ignored by writers from Shakespeare to Virginia Woolf. Members of the Usage Panel were asked whether they paid attention to the rule in their own writing: 24 percent answered "always or usually," 36 percent answered "sometimes," and 40 percent answered "rarely or never." See Usage Notes at **both, but, try, with.**

AND (ănd) *n. Computer Science.* A logic operator equivalent to the sentential connective "and." [From AND.]

and. *abbr. Music.* Andante.

And. *abbr.* Andorra.

An·da·lu·sia (ăn′də-lo͞o′zhə, -zhē-ə, -shē-ə). A region of southern Spain on the Mediterranean Sea, the Strait of Gibraltar, and the Atlantic Ocean. The area contains magnificent Moorish architecture, including the historic towns of Seville, Granada, and Córdoba. **—An′da·lu′sian** (-zhən, -shən) *adj. & n.*

an·da·lu·site (ăn′də-lo͞o′sīt′) *n.* A mineral aluminum silicate, Al_2SiO_5, usually found in prisms of various colors. [After ANDALUSIA.]

An·da·man·ese (ăn′də-mə-nēz′, -nēs′) *n., pl.* **Andamanese. 1.** Also **An·da·man** (ăn′də-mən). A member of an indigenous people of the Andaman Islands. **2.** The language of the Andamanese, of no known linguistic affiliation. **—An′da·man·ese′** *adj.*

An·da·man Islands (ăn′də-mən). A group of Indian islands in the eastern part of the Bay of Bengal south of Burma. They are separated from the Malay Peninsula by the **Andaman Sea,** an arm of the Bay of Bengal.

an·dan·te (än-dän′tā, ăn-dăn′tē) *Music. adv. & adj. Abbr.* **and.** In a moderately slow tempo, usually considered to be slower than allegretto but faster than adagio. Used chiefly as a direction. **—andante** *n.* An andante passage or movement. [Italian, from present participle of *andare,* to walk, ultimately perhaps from Latin *ambulāre.*]

an·dan·ti·no (än′dän-tē′nō, ăn′dăn) *Music. adv. & adj.* In a tempo variously construed as slightly faster or slower than andante. Used chiefly as a direction. **—andantino** *n., pl.* **-nos.** An andantino passage or movement. [Italian, diminutive of *andante,* andante. See ANDANTE.]

An·der·lecht (än′dər-lĕkt′, -lĕᴋʜt′). A commune of central Belgium, an industrial and residential suburb of Brussels. Erasmus lived here from 1517 to 1521. Population, 92,912.

An·der·sen (ăn′dər-sən), **Hans Christian.** 1805–1875. Danish writer known for his fairy tales, including "The Princess and the Pea" and "The Ugly Duckling."

An·der·son (ăn′dər-sən). **1.** A city of east-central Indiana northeast of Indianapolis. There are numerous prehistoric mounds nearby. Population, 64,695. **2.** A city of northwest South Carolina southwest of Greenville near the Georgia border. It is a trade and shipping center in an agricultural region. Population, 27,965.

Anderson, Carl David. Born 1905. American physicist. He won a 1936 Nobel Prize for his discovery of the positron.

Anderson, Dame **Judith.** 1898–1992. Australian-born actress noted for her roles in the plays of Shakespeare and Eugene O'Neill and for her chilling portrayal of Mrs. Danvers in the 1940 film *Rebecca.*

Anderson, Margaret Caroline. 1893?–1973. American editor who founded and edited *The Little Review* (1914–1929), an influential literary magazine.

Anderson, Marian. Born 1902. American contralto. Acclaimed for her renditions of spirituals, she was the first Black singer to perform at New York City's Metropolitan Opera (1955).

Anderson, Maxwell. 1888–1959. American playwright whose works, some of which are in blank verse, include *Both Your Houses,* which won a 1933 Pulitzer Prize, and *Winterset* (1935).

Anderson, Philip Warren. Born 1923. American physicist. He shared a 1977 Nobel Prize for developments in computer memory systems.

Anderson, Sherwood. 1876–1941. American writer whose often autobiographical works include *Winesburg, Ohio* (1919).

Anderson River. A river of northwestern Northwest Territories, Canada, meandering about 748 km (465 mi) north, west, and north again to Liverpool Bay, an arm of the Arctic Ocean.

An·der·son·ville (ăn′dər-sən-vĭl′). A village of southwest-central Georgia north-northeast of Americus. Its notorious Confederate prison, where more than 12,000 soldiers died during the Civil War, is now a national historic site.

An·des (ăn′dēz). A mountain system of western South America extending more than 8,045 km (5,000 mi) along the Pacific coast from Venezuela to Tierra del Fuego. The Andes rise at many points to more than 6,710 m (22,000 ft). **—An′de·an** (ăn′dē-ən, ăn-dē′ən) *adj. & n.*

an·de·site (ăn′dĭ-zīt′) *n.* A gray, fine-grained volcanic rock, chiefly plagioclase and feldspar. [After ANDES.]

AND gate *n. Computer Science.* A logic circuit with two or more input wires that emits a signal only if all input wires receive coincident signals.

♦**and·i·ron** (ănd′ī′ərn) *n.* One of a pair of metal supports used for holding up logs in a fireplace. Also called *dog,* ♦*dog iron,* ♦*firedog.* [Middle English *aundiren,* alteration (influenced by Middle English *īren,* iron) of Old French *andier,* of Celtic origin.]

An·di·zhan (ăn′dĭ-zhăn′, än-dĭ-zhän′). A city of eastern Uzbekistan east-southeast of Tashkent. It is an industrial center in a cotton-raising area. Population, 275,000.

AND NOT gate *n. Computer Science.* A logic circuit that acts as the logical operator AND NOT. A signal is transmitted only if A is true and B is not.

and/or (ăn′dôr′) *conj.* Used to indicate that either or both of the items connected by it are involved.

USAGE NOTE: *And/or* is widely used in legal and business writing. Its use in general writing to mean "one or the other or both" is acceptable but can appear stilted. See Usage Note at **or¹.**

AND-OR circuit (ănd′ôr′) *n. Computer Science.* A gating circuit that produces an output signal only if one of several possible combined input signals is received.

ă **pat**	oi **boy**
ā **pay**	ou **out**
âr **care**	o͝o **took**
ä **father**	o͞o **boot**
ĕ **pet**	ŭ **cut**
ē **be**	ûr **urge**
ĭ **pit**	th **thin**
ī **pie**	*th* **this**
	hw **which**
	vision
	bout, item
	egionalism
	′ (primary);
	as in
	shə-nĕr′ē)

An·dor·ra (ăn-dôr′ə, -dŏr-ə). *Abbr.* **And.** A tiny country of southwest Europe between France and Spain in the eastern Pyrenees. Although it pays nominal yearly homage to its suzerains in France and Spain, it is an independent republic. Andorra la Vella (population, 14,928) is the capital. The country's population is 38,051. **—An·dor′ran** *adj. & n.*

an·dou·ille (ăn-do͞o′ē) *n.* A spicy smoked sausage made with pork and garlic, used especially in Cajun cooking. [French, from Old French *andoille,* from Medieval Latin **indūctilia,* things to be introduced, from *indūctilis, indūct-,* introduceable, from Latin *indūcere,* to introduce into a casing. See INDUCE.]

An·do·ver (ăn′dō′vər, -də-). A town of northeast Massachusetts south of Lawrence. Phillips Andover Academy (founded 1778) is here. Population, 26,370.

andr– *pref.* Variant of **andro–.**

An·dra·da e Sil·va (äɴ-drä′də ĕ sēl′və), **José Bonifácio de.** 1763?–1838. Brazilian politician, scientist, and poet who led the movement for Brazilian independence from Portugal.

an·dra·dite (ăn-drä′dīt) *n.* A green to brown or black calcium-iron garnet, $Ca_3Fe_2(SiO_4)_3$. [After José Bonifácio de ANDRADA E SILVA.]

An·dré (än′drā, ăn′drē), **John.** 1751–1780. British army officer hanged as a spy in the American Revolution for conspiring with Benedict Arnold.

An·dre·a del Sar·to (än-drā′ə dĕl sär′tō). Originally Andrea d'Agnolo di Francesco. 1486–1531. Italian painter whose works, including a fresco cycle of the life of John the Baptist, epitomize Florentine classicism.

An·dre·a·nof Islands (ăn′drē-ăn′əf, -ôf, än′drē-ä′nəf). A group of islands of southwest Alaska in the central Aleutian Islands.

An·dre·ev or **An·dre·yev** (än-drā′əf, -yəf), **Leonid Nikolaevich.** 1871–1919. Russian writer noted for his realistic and pessimistic stories, novels, and plays.

An·drew (ăn′dro͞o), Saint. One of the 12 Apostles. According to legend, he was martyred at Patrai (c. A.D. 60).

Andrews, Roy Chapman. 1884–1960. American naturalist noted for his contributions to paleontology and geology.

An·dre·yev (än-drā′əf, -yəf), **Leonid Nikolaevich.** See Leonid Nikolaevich **Andreev.**

An·dri·a (än′drē-ə). A city of southern Italy west-northwest of Bari. The imposing Castel del Monte, built in the 13th century, is nearby. Population, 83,319.

An·drić (än′drĭch), **Ivo.** 1892–1975. Yugoslavian writer. He won the 1961 Nobel Prize for literature.

andro– or **andr–** *pref.* **1.** Male; masculine: *androgen.* **2.** Stamen or anther: *androecium.* [Greek, from *anēr, andr-,* man. See **ner-²** in Appendix.]

An·dro·cles (ăn′drə-klēz′) also **An·dro·clus** (-kləs) *n.* A legendary Roman slave held to have been spared in the arena by a lion that remembered him as the man who had once removed a thorn from its paw.

an·droe·ci·um (ăn-drē′shē-əm, -shəm) *n., pl.* **-ci·a** (-shē-ə, -shə). The stamens of a flower considered as a group. [New Latin : ANDR(O)– + Greek *oikion,* diminutive of *oikos,* house; see **weik-¹** in Appendix.] **—an·droe′cial** (-shəl) *adj.*

an·dro·gen (ăn′drə-jən) *n.* A steroid hormone, such as testosterone or androsterone, that controls the development and maintenance of masculine characteristics. **—an′dro·gen′ic** (-jĕn′ĭk) *adj.*

an·drog·e·nize (ăn-drŏj′ə-nīz′) *tr.v.* **-nized, -niz·ing, -niz·es.** To treat with male hormones, usually in large doses. **—an·drog′e·ni·za′tion** (-nĭ-zā′shən) *n.*

an·dro·gyne (ăn′drə-jīn′) *n.* An androgynous individual. [French, from Old French, from Latin *androgynus.* See ANDROGYNOUS.]

an·drog·y·nous (ăn-drŏj′ə-nəs) *adj.* **1.** *Biology.* Having both female and male characteristics; hermaphroditic. **2.** Being neither distinguishably masculine nor feminine, as in dress, appearance, or behavior; unisex: *"The diet and exercise cult was born of a desire to develop androgynous bodies that are more muscular than softly curved"* (New York Times). [From Latin *androgynus,* hermaphrodite, from Greek *androgunos* : *andro-,* andro- + *gunē,* woman; see –GYNOUS.] **—an·drog′y·nous·ly** *adv.* **—an·drog′y·ny** (-ə-nē) *n.*

an·droid (ăn′droid′) *adj.* Possessing human features. **—android** *n.* An automaton that is created from biological materials and resembles a human being. Also called *humanoid.*

An·drom·a·che (ăn-drŏm′ə-kē) *n. Greek Mythology.* The faithful wife of Hector, captured by the Greeks at the fall of Troy.

an·drom·e·da (ăn-drŏm′ĭ-də) *n.* Any of several shrubs of the genera *Pieris* or *Andromeda* or their relatives. [From ANDROMEDA.]

An·drom·e·da (ăn-drŏm′ĭ-də) *n.* **1.** *Greek Mythology.* The daughter of Cepheus and Cassiopeia and wife of Perseus, who had rescued her from a sea monster. **2.** A constellation in the Northern Hemisphere between Lacerta and Perseus and south of Cassiopeia. It contains a large spiral galaxy visible to the naked eye. The spiral is 1.84 × 10^5 light-years from Earth. [Latin, from Greek *Andromedē.*]

An·dro·pov (ăn-drŏp′ôf, -ŏv), **Yuri.** 1914–1984. Soviet politician who was general secretary of the Communist Party from 1982 to 1984.

An·dros (ăn′drəs). **1.** The largest island of the Bahamas, in the western part of the archipelago. **2.** (*also* än′drôs′). An island of southeast Greece in the Aegean Sea. The northernmost of the Cyclades, it was colonized by Athens in the fifth century B.C.

An·dros (ăn′drŏs, -drəs), Sir **Edmund.** 1637–1714. English colonial administrator in America whose attempt to unify the New England colonies under his governorship (1686–1689) was met by revolt.

An·dros·cog·gin (ăn′drə-skŏg′ĭn). A river of northeast New Hampshire and southwest Maine flowing about 253 km (157 mi) to the Kennebec River near the Maine coast.

an·dros·ter·one (ăn-drŏs′tə-rōn′) *n.* A steroid hormone excreted in urine that reinforces masculine characteristics. [ANDRO– + STER(OL) + –ONE.]

–androus *suff.* Having a specified number or kind of stamens: *monandrous.* [From New Latin *-andrus,* from Greek *-andros,* having men, from *anēr, andr-,* man. See **ner-²** in Appendix.]

–andry *suff.* **1.** The condition of having a specified kind or number of husbands: *monandry.* **2.** The condition of having a specified kind or number of stamens: *polyandry.* [Greek *-andria,* from *anēr, andr-,* man. See **ner-²** in Appendix.]

–ane *suff.* A saturated hydrocarbon: *hexane.* [Variant of –ENE, –INE² and –ONE.]

an·ec·dot·age (ăn′ĭk-dō′tĭj) *n.* Anecdotes considered as a group.

an·ec·dot·al (ăn′ĭk-dōt′l) or **an·ec·dot·ic** (-dŏt′ĭk) also **an·ec·dot·i·cal** (-ĭ-kəl) *adj.* Of, characterized by, or full of anecdotes. **—an′ec·dot′al·ist** *n.* **—an′ec·dot′al·ly** *adv.*

an·ec·dote (ăn′ĭk-dōt′) *n.* **1.** A short account of an interesting or humorous incident. **2.** *pl.* **-dotes** or **-do·ta** (-dō′tə) Secret or hitherto undivulged particulars of history or biography. [French, from Greek *anekdota,* unpublished items : *an-,* not; see A–¹ + *ekdota,* neuter pl. of *ekdotos,* published (from *ekdidonai,* to publish : *ek-,* out; see ECTO– + *didonai,* to give; see **dō-** in Appendix).]

an·ec·dot·ic (ăn′ĭk-dŏt′ĭk) also **an·ec·dot·i·cal** (-ĭ-kəl) *adj.* **1.** Given to telling anecdotes. **2.** Variant of **anecdotal.** **—an′ec·dot′i·cal·ly** *adv.*

an·ec·dot·ist (ăn′ĭk-dō′tĭst) *n.* One who tells, collects, or publishes anecdotes.

an·e·cho·ic (ăn′ĕ-kō′ĭk) *adj.* Neither having nor producing echoes: *an anechoic chamber.*

a·ne·mi·a also **a·nae·mi·a** (ə-nē′mē-ə) *n.* A pathological deficiency in the oxygen-carrying component of the blood, measured in unit volume concentrations of hemoglobin, red blood cell volume, or red blood cell number. [New Latin, from Greek *anaimia* : *an-,* without; see A–¹ + *haima,* blood.]

a·ne·mic also **a·nae·mic** (ə-nē′mĭk) *adj.* **1.** Of, relating to, or suffering from anemia. **2.** Lacking vitality; listless and weak: *an anemic attempt to hit the baseball; an anemic economic recovery.* **—a·ne′mi·cal·ly** *adv.*

anemo– *pref.* Wind: *anemometer.* [From Greek *anemos,* wind. See **anə-** in Appendix.]

a·nem·o·cho·ry (ə-nĕm′ə-kôr′ē, -kōr′ē) *n.* Dispersal of seeds, fruits, or other plant parts by wind.

a·nem·o·graph (ə-nĕm′ə-grăf′) *n.* A recording anemometer.

an·e·mog·ra·phy (ăn′ə-mŏg′rə-fē) *n.* The science of recording anemometrical measurements.

an·e·mom·e·ter (ăn′ə-mŏm′ĭ-tər) *n.* An instrument for indicating and measuring wind force and velocity.

an·e·mom·e·try (ăn′ə-mŏm′ĭ-trē) *n.* Measurement of wind force and velocity. **—an′e·mo·met′ri·cal** *adj.*

a·nem·o·ne (ə-nĕm′ə-nē) *n.* **1.** Any of various perennial herbs of the genus *Anemone,* native chiefly to northern temperate regions and having palmately lobed leaves and large flowers with showy sepals. Also called *windflower.* **2.** A sea anemone. [Latin *anemōnē,* from Greek.]

anemone fish *n.* A small, brightly colored marine fish of the genus *Amphiprion,* found near sea anemones. Also called *clown anemone, clown fish.*

an·e·moph·i·lous (ăn′ə-mŏf′ə-ləs) *adj.* Pollinated by wind-dispersed pollen.

an·en·ceph·a·ly (ăn′ən-sĕf′ə-lē) *n., pl.* **-lies.** Congenital absence of most of the brain and spinal cord. **—an′en·ce·phal′ic** (-sə-făl′ĭk) *adj.*

a·nent (ə-nĕnt′) *prep.* Regarding; concerning: *"This question remains a vital consideration anent the debate over the possibility of limiting nuclear war to military objectives"* (New York Times). [Middle English, from Old English *onefn,* near : *on,* on; see ON + *efn,* even.]

an·er·oid (ăn′ə-roid′) *adj.* Not using liquid. [French *anéroïde* : Greek *a-,* without; see A–¹ + Late Greek *nēron,* water; see **newo-** in Appendix.]

aneroid barometer *n.* A barometer in which variations of atmospheric pressure are indicated by the relative bulges of a thin elastic metal disk covering a partially evacuated chamber.

an·es·the·sia also **an·aes·the·sia** (ăn′ĭs-thē′zhə) *n.* **1.** Total or partial loss of sensation, especially tactile sensibility, induced by disease, injury, acupuncture, or an anesthetic, such as

Andorra

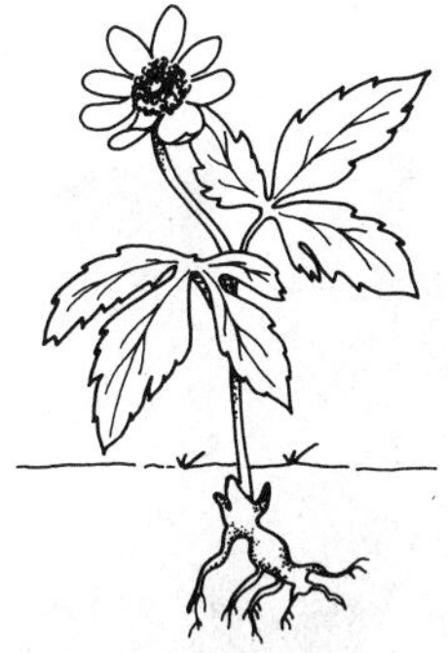

anemone
Top: Wood anemone
Anemone quinquefolia
Bottom: American warty sea anemone
Bunodosoma cavernata

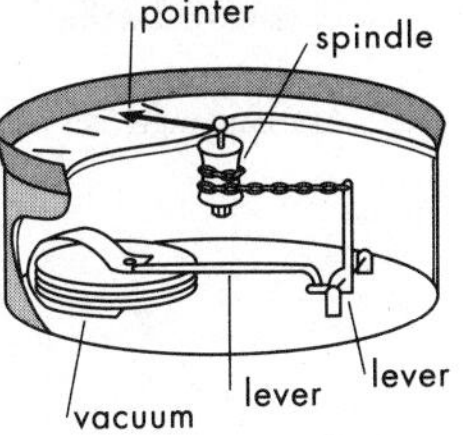

aneroid barometer

chloroform or nitrous oxide. **2.** Local or general insensibility to pain with or without the loss of consciousness, induced by an anesthetic. [New Latin *anaesthesia,* from Greek *anaisthēsia,* insensibility : *an-,* without; see A-[1] + *aisthēsis,* feeling (from *aisthanesthai,* to feel; see **au-** in Appendix).]

angel
Bronze angel, 1475, by Jean Barbet

WORD HISTORY: The following passage, written on November 21, 1846, by Oliver Wendell Holmes, a physician-poet and the father of the Supreme Court justice of the same name, allows us to pinpoint the entry of *anesthesia* and *anesthetic* into English: "Every body wants to have a hand in a great discovery. All I will do is to give you a hint or two as to names—or the name—to be applied to the state produced and the agent. The state should, I think, be called 'Anaesthesia' [from the Greek word *anaisthēsia,* "lack of sensation"]. This signifies insensibility . . . The adjective will be 'Anaesthetic.' Thus we might say the state of Anaesthesia, or the anaesthetic state." This citation is taken from a letter to William Thomas Green Morton, who in October of that year had successfully demonstrated the use of ether at Massachusetts General Hospital in Boston. Although *anaesthesia* is recorded in Nathan Bailey's *Universal Etymological English Dictionary* in 1721, it is clear that Holmes really was responsible for its entry into the language. The *Oxford English Dictionary* has several citations for *anesthesia* and *anesthetic* in 1847 and 1848, indicating that the words gained rapid acceptance.

an·es·the·si·ol·o·gist also **an·aes·the·si·ol·o·gist** (ăn′ĭs-thē′zē-ol′ə-jĭst) *n.* A physician specializing in anesthesiology.

an·es·the·si·ol·o·gy also **an·aes·the·si·ol·o·gy** (ăn′ĭs-thē′zē-ŏl′ə-jē) *n.* The medical study and application of anesthetics.

an·es·thet·ic also **an·aes·thet·ic** (ăn′ĭs-thĕt′ĭk) —*adj.* **1.** Relating to or resembling anesthesia. **2.** Causing anesthesia. **3.** Insensitive. —*n.* **1.** An agent that causes loss of sensation with or without the loss of consciousness. **2.** Something likened to this in effect: *Some people feel that television becomes an anesthetic for the mind after too many hours of steady viewing.* [From Greek *anaisthētos,* without feeling : *an-,* without; see A-[1] + *aisthētos,* perceptible (from *aisthanesthai,* to feel; see ANESTHESIA).] **—an′es·thet′i·cal·ly** *adv.*

Angel Fall

a·nes·the·tist also **a·naes·the·tist** (ə-nĕs′thĭ-tĭst) *n.* A person specially trained to administer anesthetics.

a·nes·the·tize also **a·naes·the·tize** (ə-nĕs′thĭ-tīz′) *tr.v.* **-tized, -tiz·ing, -tiz·es.** To induce anesthesia in. **—an·es′the·ti·za′tion** (-tĭ-zā′shən) *n.*

an·es·trus (ăn-ĕs′trəs) *n.* An interval of sexual inactivity between two periods of estrus in mammals that breed cyclically.

A·ne·to (ə-nā′tō, ä-nĕ′-), **Pico de.** A peak, 3,406.2 m (11,168 ft) high, in northeast Spain near the French border. It is the highest elevation in the Pyrenees.

an·eu·ploid (ăn′yo͞o-ploid′) *adj.* Having a chromosome number that is not a multiple of the haploid number for the species. **—aneuploid** *n.* A cell or an organism characterized by an aneuploid chromosome number.

an·eu·ploi·dy (ăn′yə-ploid′ē) *n.* The state or condition of being aneuploid.

an·eu·rysm also **an·eu·rism** (ăn′yə-rĭz′əm) *n.* A localized, pathological, blood-filled dilatation of a blood vessel caused by a disease or weakening of the vessel's wall. [Middle English *aneurisme,* ultimately from Greek *aneurusma,* from *aneurein,* to dilate : *ana-,* throughout; see ANA- + *eurus,* wide.] **—an′eu·rys′mal** (-məl) *adj.*

a·new (ə-no͞o′, ə-nyo͞o′) *adv.* **1.** Once more; again. **2.** In a new and different way, form, or manner. [Middle English : *a,* of (from Old English *of;* see OF) + *new,* new thing (from Old English *nīwe;* see NEW), or : *a-,* on; see A-[2] + *new.*]

ANF *abbr.* Atrial natriuretic factor.

an·frac·tu·os·i·ty (ăn-frăk′cho͞o-ŏs′ĭ-tē) *n., pl.* **-ties. 1.** The condition or quality of having many twists and turns. **2.** A winding channel, passage, or crevice. **3.** A complicated or involved process.

angelfish
Arabian angelfish

an·frac·tu·ous (ăn-frăk′cho͞o-əs) *adj.* Full of twists and turns; tortuous. [From Late Latin *anfrāctuōsus,* from Latin *anfrāctus,* winding : *an-* (from *ambi-,* around; see AMBI-) + *frāctus,* past participle of *frangere,* to break; see **bhreg-** in Appendix.]

Ang. *abbr.* Angola.

An·ga·ra (än′gə-rä′). A river of central Russia flowing about 1,850 km (1,150 mi) north and west from Lake Baikal to the Yenisei River.

An·garsk (än-gärsk′). A city of south-central Russia on the Angara River near Irkutsk. It is a manufacturing center. Population, 256,000.

an·ga·ry (ăng′gə-rē) also **an·gar·i·a** (ăng-gâr′ē-ə) *n.* The legal right of a belligerent to seize, use, or destroy the property of a neutral, provided that full compensation is made. [Late Latin *angaria,* service to a lord, from Greek *angareia,* impressment for public service, from *angaros,* conscript courier.]

an·gel (ān′jəl) *n.* **1.a.** *Theology.* An immortal, spiritual being attendant upon God. In medieval angelology, there are nine orders of spiritual beings. From the highest to the lowest in rank, they are: seraphim, cherubim, thrones, dominations or diminions, virtues, powers, principalities, archangels, and angels. **b.** The conventional representation of such a being in the image of a human figure with a halo and wings. **2.** A guardian spirit or guiding influence. **3.a.** A kind and lovable person. **b.** One who manifests goodness, purity, and selflessness. **4.** *Christian Science.* God's thoughts passing to man. **5.** *Informal.* A financial backer of an enterprise, especially a dramatic production or a political campaign. [Middle English, from Old English *engel* or Old French *angele,* both from Late Latin *angelus,* from Late Greek *angelos,* from Greek, messenger.] **—an·gel′ic** (ăn-jĕl′ĭk), **an·gel′i·cal** *adj.* **—an·gel′i·cal·ly** *adv.*

angel cake *n.* Angel food cake.

angel dust *n. Slang.* Phencyclidine.

An·ge·le·no (ăn′jə-lē′nō) *n., pl.* **-nos.** A native or inhabitant of Los Angeles. [American Spanish *Angeleño,* after LOS ANGELES.]

An·gel Fall or **Falls** (ān′jəl). A waterfall, about 980 m (3,212 ft) high, in southeast Venezuela. It is the highest uninterrupted waterfall in the world.

an·gel·fish (ān′jəl-fĭsh′) *n., pl.* **angelfish** or **-fish·es. 1.** A brightly colored fish of the family Pomacanthidae of warm seas, having a laterally compressed body. **2.** A freshwater fish *(Pterophyllum scalare),* native to rivers of tropical South America and having a laterally compressed, usually striped body. It is popular in aquariums. In this sense, also called *scalare.*

angel food cake *n.* An almond-flavored sponge cake made of egg whites, sugar, and flour.

an·gel·i·ca (ăn-jĕl′ĭ-kə) *n.* **1.a.** Any of various herbs of the genus *Angelica* in the parsley family, having pinnately compound leaves and small white or greenish flowers in compound umbels, especially *A. archangelica,* whose roots and fruits are used in flavoring liqueurs and whose stems are candied and eaten. **b.** The edible stem, leaf, or root of *Angelica archangelica.* **2.** Often **Angelica.** A sweet white wine or liqueur. [Medieval Latin *(herba) angelica,* angelic (herb), angelica, from Late Latin, feminine of *angelicus,* angelic, from Late Greek *angelikos,* from Greek, of a messenger, from *angelos,* messenger.]

angelica tree *n.* See **Hercules' club** (sense 1).

An·gel·i·co (ăn-jĕl′ĭ-kō′), Fra. Also known as **Giovanni da Fie·so·le** (fyĕ′zō-lā, -zô-lĕ). 1400?–1455. Italian Dominican friar and painter of the Florentine school.

An·gell (ān′jəl), Sir **Norman.** 1872–1967. British economist and pacifist. He won the 1933 Nobel Peace Prize.

an·gel·ol·o·gy (ān′jəl-ŏl′ə-jē) *n.* The branch of theology having to do with angels.

angel shark *n.* Any of several raylike sharks of the genus *Squatina,* having a broad, flat head and body.

an·gel's trumpet (ān′jəlz) *n.* Any of several New World plants of the genera *Brugmansia* or *Datura,* having large, variously colored trumpet-shaped flowers. All parts of the plants contain the poisonous belladonna alkaloids.

An·ge·lus also **an·ge·lus** (ăn′jə-ləs) *n. Roman Catholic Church.* **1.** A devotional prayer at morning, noon, and night to commemorate the Annunciation. **2.** A bell rung as a call to recite this prayer. [Medieval Latin, from Late Latin, angel, first word of the devotion. See ANGEL.]

an·ger (ăng′gər) *n.* A strong feeling of displeasure or hostility. **—anger** *v.* **-gered, -ger·ing, -gers.** —*tr.* To make angry; enrage or provoke. —*intr.* To become angry: *She angers too quickly.* [Middle English, from Old Norse *angr,* sorrow. See **angh-** in Appendix.]

SYNONYMS: *anger, rage, fury, ire, wrath, resentment, indignation.* These nouns denote varying degrees of marked displeasure. *Anger,* the most general, is strong displeasure: *suppressed her anger; threw a book in a fit of anger. Rage* and *fury* are closely related in the sense of intense, explosive, often destructive emotion: *"Heaven has no rage like love to hatred turned"* (William Congreve). *"Beware the fury of a patient man"* (John Dryden). *Ire* is a term for anger that is frequently encountered in literature: *"The best way to escape His ire/Is, not to seem too happy"* (Robert Browning). *Wrath* applies especially to fervid anger that seeks vengeance or punishment, often on an epic scale: *rebellious words sure to kindle a parent's wrath; the wrath of God. Resentment* refers to ill will and smoldering anger generated by a sense of grievance: *The strike can be traced to the personal resentment of the foreman against the factory owner. Indignation* is righteous anger at something regarded as being wrongful, unjust, or evil: *"public indignation about takeovers causing people to lose their jobs"* (Allan Sloan).

an·ger·ly (ăng′gər-lē) *adv. Archaic.* Angrily: *"Again thou blushest angerly"* (Tennyson).

An·gers (ăn′jərz, äN-zhā′). A city of western France east-northeast of Nantes. Of pre-Roman origin, Angers was the historical capital of Anjou. Population, 136,038.

An·ge·vin (ăn′jə-vĭn) *adj.* **1.** Of or relating to the historical region and former province of Anjou, France. **2.** Of or relating to the House of Anjou, especially as represented by the Plantagenet kings of England descended from Geoffrey, Count of Anjou (died 1151). [French, from Old French, from Medieval Latin *Andegavinus,* from *Andegavia,* Anjou, France.]

an·gi·na (ăn-jī′nə, ăn′jə-) *n.* **1.** Angina pectoris. **2.** A condition, such as severe sore throat, in which spasmodic attacks of suffocating pain occur. [Latin, quinsy, from Greek *ankhonē,* a strangling. See **angh-** in Appendix.] **—an·gi′nal** *adj.* **—an′-gi·nose′** (-jə-nōs′) *adj.*

angina pec·to·ris (pĕk′tər-ĭs) *n.* Severe paroxysmal pain in the chest associated with an insufficient supply of blood to the heart. [New Latin : Latin *angina,* quinsy + *pectoris,* genitive of *pectus,* chest.]

angio– *pref.* **1.** Blood and lymph vessel: *angiogram.* **2.** Pericarp: *angiosperm.* [New Latin, from Greek *angeio-,* from *angeion,* vessel, blood vessel, diminutive of *angos,* vessel.]

an·gi·o·car·di·og·ra·phy (ăn′jē-ō-kär′dē-ŏg′rə-fē) *n.* Examination of the heart and associated blood vessels using x-rays following the injection of a radiopaque substance. **—an′-gi·o·car′di·o·graph′ic** (-ə-grăf′ĭk) *adj.*

an·gi·o·gram (ăn′jē-ə-grăm′) *n.* An x-ray of one or more blood vessels produced by angiography and used in diagnosing pathological conditions of the cardiovascular system.

an·gi·og·raph·y (ăn′jē-ŏg′rə-fē) *n.* Examination of the blood vessels using x-rays following the injection of a radiopaque substance. **—an′gi·o·graph′ic** (-grăf′ĭk) *adj.*

an·gi·ol·o·gy (ăn′jē-ŏl′ə-jē) *n.* The study of blood and lymph vessels.

an·gi·o·ma (ăn′jē-ō′mə) *n., pl.* **-mas** or **-ma·ta** (-mə-tə). A tumor composed chiefly of lymph and blood vessels. **—an′-gi·o′ma·tous** (-ō′mə-təs, -ŏm′ə-) *adj.*

an·gi·op·a·thy (ăn′jē-op′ə-thē) *n., pl.* **-thies.** Any of several diseases of the blood or lymph vessels.

an·gi·o·plas·ty (ăn′jē-ə-plăs′tē) *n., pl.* **-ties.** A procedure in which a catheter equipped with a tiny balloon at the tip is inserted into an artery that has been narrowed by the accumulation of fatty deposits. The balloon is then inflated to clear the blockage and widen the artery.

an·gi·o·sar·co·ma (ăn′jē-ō-sär-kō′mə) *n.* A malignant tumor arising from vascular tissue.

an·gi·o·sperm (ăn′jē-ə-spûrm′) *n.* A plant whose ovules are enclosed in an ovary; a flowering plant.

an·gi·o·ten·sin (ăn′jē-ō-tĕn′sĭn) *n.* Either of two polypeptide hormones, one of which is a powerful vasoconstrictor, that function in the body in controlling arterial pressure. [ANGIO– + TENS(ION) + –IN.]

Ang·kor (ăng′kôr, -kōr). A major archaeological site in northwest Cambodia and the capital of the Khmer empire from the 9th to the 15th century. The ruins include two important Hindu temple complexes, Angkor Wat (12th century) and Angkor Thom (13th century). The site has been extensively damaged by warfare.

Angl. *abbr.* Anglican.

an·gle[1] (ăng′gəl) *intr.v.* **-gled, -gling, -gles. 1.** To fish with a hook and line. **2.** To try to get something by using schemes, tricks, or other artful means: *angle for a promotion.* **—angle** *n. Obsolete.* A fishhook or fishing tackle. [Middle English *anglen,* from *angel,* fishhook, from Old English.]

an·gle[2] (ăng′gəl) *n.* **1.** *Mathematics.* **a.** The figure formed by two lines diverging from a common point. **b.** The figure formed by two planes diverging from a common line. **c.** The rotation required to superimpose either of two such lines or planes on the other. **d.** The space between such lines or surfaces. **e.** A solid angle. **2.** A sharp or projecting corner, as of a building. **3. a.** The place, position, or direction from which an object is presented to view: *a handsome building looked at from any angle.* **b.** An aspect, as of a problem, seen from a specific point of view. See Synonyms at **phase. 4.** *Slang.* A devious method; a scheme. **—angle** *v.* **-gled, -gling, -gles.** *—tr.* **1.** To move or turn (something) at an angle: *angled the chair toward the window.* **2.** *Sports.* To hit (a ball or puck, for example) at an angle. **3.** *Informal.* To impart a biased aspect or point of view to: *angled the story in such a way as to criticize the candidate.* *—intr.* To continue along or turn at an angle or by angles: *The road angles sharply to the left. The path angled through the woods.* [Middle English, from Old French, from Latin *angulus.*]

An·gle (ăng′gəl) *n.* A member of a Germanic people that migrated to England from southern Jutland in the 5th century A.D., founded the kingdoms of Northumbria, East Anglia, and Mercia, and together with the Jutes and Saxons formed the Anglo-Saxon peoples. [From Latin *Anglī,* the Angles, of Germanic origin.]

angle bracket *n.* **1.** Either of a pair of symbols, < >, used to enclose written or printed material. **2.** *Mathematics.* Either of these symbols, used especially together to indicate the average of a contained quantity. Also called *bracket.*

angle iron *n.* A length of steel or iron bent at a right angle along its long dimension, used as a support or structural framework.

angle of attack *n.* The acute angle between the chord of an airfoil and a line representing the undisturbed relative airflow.

angle of incidence *n. Physics.* The angle formed by a ray incident on a surface and a perpendicular to the surface at the point of incidence.

angle of reflection *n. Physics.* The angle formed by a reflected ray and a perpendicular to the surface at the point of reflection.

angle of refraction *n. Physics.* The angle formed by a refracted ray and a perpendicular to the refracting surface at the point of refraction.

angle of yaw *n.* The angle between an aircraft's longitudinal axis and its line of travel, as seen from above.

angle plate *n.* A right-angled metal bracket that is used on the faceplate of a lathe to hold the pieces that are being worked.

an·gler (ăng′glər) *n.* **1.** One who fishes with a hook. **2.** A scheming person. **3.** An anglerfish.

an·gler·fish (ăng′glər-fĭsh′) *n., pl.* **anglerfish** or **-fish·es.** A marine fish of the order Lophiiformes or Pediculati, having a long dorsal fin ray that is suspended over the mouth and that serves as a lure to attract prey.

An·gle·sey or **An·gle·sea** (ăng′gəl-sē). An island of northwest Wales in the Irish Sea. It has druidic ruins, especially dolmens, and is said to have been the last refuge of the druids from the invading Romans.

an·gle·site (ăng′glĭ-sīt′) *n.* A lead sulfate mineral, $PbSO_4$, occurring in colorless or tinted crystals and formed by the weathering of lead ore. [After ANGLESEY.]

an·gle·worm (ăng′gəl-wûrm′) *n.* A worm, such as an earthworm, that is used as bait in fishing.

An·gli·a (ăng′glē-ə). **1.** The Medieval and Late Latin name for England. **2.** See **East Anglia.**

An·gli·an (ăng′glē-ən) *adj.* Of or relating to East Anglia or to the Angles. **—Anglian** *n.* **1.** An Angle. **2.** The Old English dialects of Mercia and Northumbria.

An·gli·can (ăng′glĭ-kən) *adj. Abbr.* **Angl. 1.** Of, having to do with, or characteristic of the Church of England or any of the churches related to it in origin and communion, such as the Protestant Episcopal Church. **2.** Of or relating to England or the English. **—Anglican** *n.* A member of the Church of England or of any of the churches related to it. [Medieval Latin *Anglicānus,* English, from *Anglicus,* from Late Latin *Anglī,* the Angles. See ANGLE.]

Anglican Church *n.* The Church of England and the churches in other nations that are in complete agreement with it as to doctrine and discipline and are in communion with the Archbishop of Canterbury. Also called *Anglican Communion.*

An·gli·can·ism (ăng′glĭ-kə-nĭz′əm) *n.* The faith, doctrine, system, and practice of the Anglican Church.

An·gli·ce (ăng′glĭ-sē′) *adv.* In the English form: *Firenze,* Anglice *Florence.* [Medieval Latin *Anglicē,* from *Anglicus,* English. See ANGLICAN.]

An·gli·cism also **an·gli·cism** (ăng′glĭ-sĭz′əm) *n.* **1.** A word, a phrase, or an idiom peculiar to the English language, especially as spoken in England; a Briticism. **2.** A typically English quality. [From Medieval Latin *Anglicus,* English. See ANGLICAN.]

An·gli·cist (ăng′glĭ-sĭst) *n.* A specialist in English linguistics.

An·gli·cize also **an·gli·cize** (ăng′glĭ-sīz′) *—v.* **-cized, -ciz·ing, -ciz·es.** *—tr.* To make English or similar to English in form, idiom, style, or character. *—intr.* To become English in form or character. **—An′gli·ci·za′tion** (-sĭ-zā′shən) *n.*

an·gling (ăng′glĭng) *n.* The act, process, or art of fishing with a hook and line and usually a rod.

An·glo also **an·glo** (ăng′glō) *n., pl.* **-glos. 1.** *Informal.* An Anglo-American. **2.** An English-speaking person, especially a white North American who is not of Hispanic or French descent. [Short for ANGLO-AMERICAN.] **—An′glo** *adj.*

Anglo– *pref.* England; English: *Anglo-Saxon.* [New Latin, from Medieval Latin *Anglī,* the English people, from Late Latin, the Angles. See ANGLE.]

An·glo-A·mer·i·can (ăng′glō-ə-mĕr′ĭ-kən) *n.* An American, especially an inhabitant of the United States, whose language and ancestry are English. **—Anglo-American** *adj.* **1.** Of, relating to, or between England and America, especially the United States. **2.** Of or relating to Anglo-Americans.

An·glo-Cath·o·lic (ăng′glō-kăth′lĭk, -kăth′ə-lĭk) *n.* A member of the Anglican Church whose religious convictions emphasize sacramental worship. **—An′glo-Cath′o·lic** *adj.*

An·glo-French (ăng′glō-frĕnch′) *adj.* Of, relating to, or between England and France or their peoples; English and French. **—Anglo-French** *n.* See **Anglo-Norman** (sense 2).

An·glo-In·di·an (ăng′glō-ĭn′dē-ən) *adj.* Of, relating to, or between England and India. **—Anglo-Indian** *n.* **1.** A person of English and Indian descent. **2.** A person of English birth or ancestry living in India. **3.** The variety of English used in India.

An·glo-I·rish (ăng′glō-ī′rĭsh) *n.* **1.** A native of England living in Ireland. **2.** A native of Ireland living in England. **3.** A person of mixed Irish and English ancestry. **4.** See **Irish English. —An′glo-I′rish** *adj.*

An·glo-Nor·man (ăng′glō-nôr′mən) *n.* **1.** One of the Normans who lived in England after the Norman Conquest of England in 1066 or a descendant of these settlers. **2. a.** The dialect of Old French, derived chiefly from Norman French, that was used by the Anglo-Normans. **b.** The form of this dialect used in English law until the 17th century. In this sense, also called *Anglo-French.* **—An′glo-Nor′man** *adj.*

An·glo·phile (ăng′glə-fīl′) also **An·glo·phil** (-fĭl) *n.* One who admires England, its people, and its culture. **—An′glo·phile, An′glo·phil′ic** (ăng′glə-fĭl′ĭk) *adj.* **—An′glo·phil′i·a** (-fĭl′ē-ə) *n.*

An·glo·phobe (ăng′glə-fōb′) *n.* One who dislikes or fears England, its people, or its culture. **—An′glo·pho′bi·a** *n.* **—An′glo·pho′bic** (-fō′bĭk) *adj.*

An·glo·phone also **an·glo·phone** (ăn′glə-fōn′) *n.* An English-speaking person, especially one in a country where two or

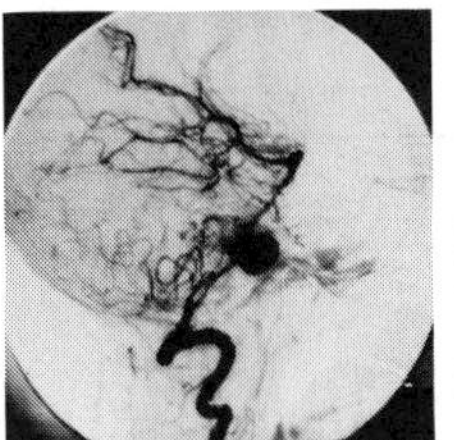

angiogram
Showing an aneurysm and hemorrhaging in the basal artery

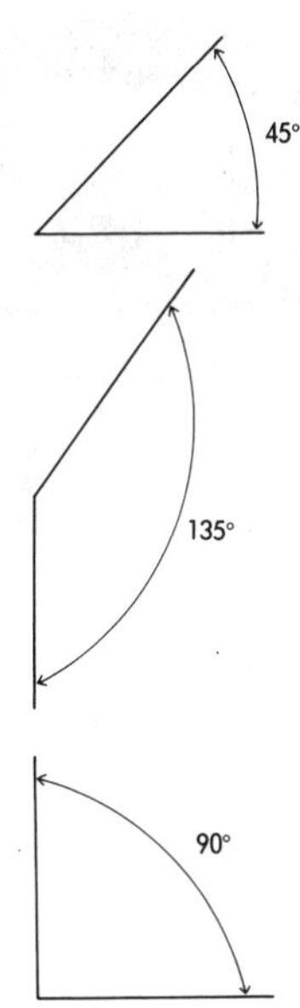

angle[2]
Top: Acute angle
Center: Obtuse angle
Bottom: Right angle

ă pat	oi boy
ā pay	ou out
âr care	ŏŏ took
ä father	ōō boot
ĕ pet	ŭ cut
ē be	ûr urge
ĭ pit	th thin
ī pie	*th* this
îr pier	hw which
ŏ pot	zh vision
ō toe	ə about, item
ô paw	♦ regionalism

Stress marks: ′ (primary); ′ (secondary), as in **dictionary** (dĭk′shə-nĕr′ē)

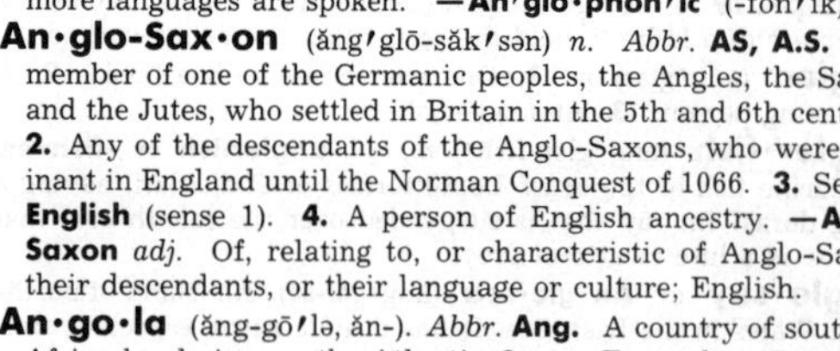
more languages are spoken. —**An′glo·phon′ic** (-fŏn′ĭk) *adj.*

An·glo-Sax·on (ăng′glō-săk′sən) *n. Abbr.* **AS, A.S. 1.** A member of one of the Germanic peoples, the Angles, the Saxons, and the Jutes, who settled in Britain in the 5th and 6th centuries. **2.** Any of the descendants of the Anglo-Saxons, who were dominant in England until the Norman Conquest of 1066. **3.** See **Old English** (sense 1). **4.** A person of English ancestry. —**Anglo-Saxon** *adj.* Of, relating to, or characteristic of Anglo-Saxons, their descendants, or their language or culture; English.

Angola

An·go·la (ăng-gō′lə, ăn-). *Abbr.* **Ang.** A country of southwest Africa bordering on the Atlantic Ocean. Formerly a Portuguese colony, the country became independent in 1975 after a long guerrilla war and has been torn by civil strife ever since. Luanda is the capital and the largest city. Population, 8,140,000. —**An·go′lan** *adj. & n.*

An·go·ra[1] (ăng-gôr′ə, -gōr′ə, ăng′gər-ə). See **Ankara.**

An·go·ra[2] (ăng-gôr′ə, -gōr′ə) *n.* **1.** Often **angora. a.** The long, silky hair of the Angora goat. **b.** The fine, long hair of the Angora rabbit, sometimes blended with wool in fabrics. **c.** A yarn or fabric made from either of these fibers. **2.** An Angora cat. **3.** An Angora goat. **4.** An Angora rabbit. [After *Angora* (Ankara), Turkey.]

Angora cat *n.* A domestic cat having long, silky hair. It is now rare as a pure breed in the United States.

Angora goat *n.* Any of a breed of domestic goats having long, silky hair.

Angora rabbit *n.* Any of a breed of domestic rabbits having long, soft, usually white hair.

an·gos·tu·ra bark (ăng′gə-stŏŏr′ə, -styŏŏr′ə) *n.* The bitter, aromatic bark of either of two South American trees *(Galipea officinalis* or *Cusparia trifoliata),* used as a flavoring in bitters and as a tonic. [After *Angostura* (Ciudad Bolívar), Venezuela.]

An·gou·lême (äɴ-gōō-lām′, -lĕm′). A city of western France north-northeast of Bordeaux. It was ceded to England in 1360 but was retaken by France in 1373. Population, 46,197.

An·gou·mois (äɴ′gōō-mwä′). A historical region and former province of western France in the Charente River valley. Occupied by Gallic peoples in pre-Roman times, it later was part of Aquitaine, was briefly ceded to England (1360–1373), and became a French duchy in 1515.

Angora goat

an·gry (ăng′grē) *adj.* **-gri·er, -gri·est. 1.** Feeling or showing anger; incensed or enraged: *an angry customer.* **2.** Indicative of or resulting from anger: *an angry silence.* **3.** Having a menacing aspect; threatening: *angry clouds on the horizon.* **4.** Inflamed and painful: *an angry sore.* [Middle English *angri,* from *anger,* anger. See ANGER.]

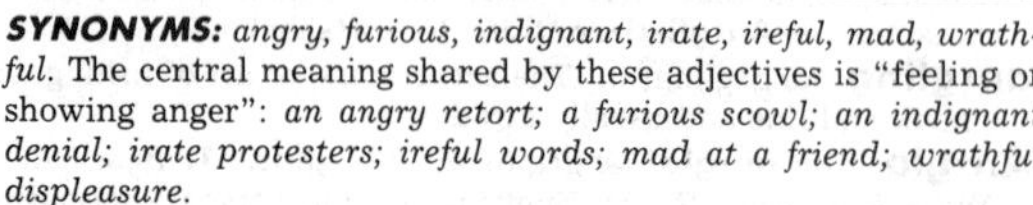
SYNONYMS: *angry, furious, indignant, irate, ireful, mad, wrathful.* The central meaning shared by these adjectives is "feeling or showing anger": *an angry retort; a furious scowl; an indignant denial; irate protesters; ireful words; mad at a friend; wrathful displeasure.*

angry young man also **Angry Young Man** *n.* **1.** One of a group of English writers of the 1950's whose works are characterized by vigorous social protest. **2.** A vigorous critic of economic or social injustice.

angst[1] (ängkst) *n.* A feeling of anxiety or apprehension often accompanied by depression. [German, from Middle High German *angest,* from Old High German *angust.* See **angh-** in Appendix.]

angst[2] *abbr.* Angstrom.

ang·strom or **ång·strom** (ăng′strəm) *n. Abbr.* **angst, Å, A** A unit of length equal to one hundred-millionth (10^{-8}) of a centimeter, used especially to specify radiation wavelengths. Also called *angstrom unit.* See table at **measurement.** [After Anders Jonas ÅNGSTRÖM.]

Ång·ström (ăng′strəm, ông′strœm), **Anders Jonas.** 1814–1874. Swedish physicist and astronomer who founded the science of spectroscopy and discovered by studying the solar spectrum that there is hydrogen in the sun's atmosphere.

angstrom unit *n. Abbr.* **a.u., A.u.** See **angstrom.**

An·guil·la (ăng-gwĭl′ə, ăn-). An island of the British West Indies in the northern Leeward Islands. Settled by the British in the 17th century, it was part of the self-governing colony of St. Kitts-Nevis-Anguilla until 1967, when it seceded unilaterally. A bid for full independence led to the landing of British troops in 1969.

an·guish (ăng′gwĭsh) *n.* Agonizing physical or mental pain; torment. See Synonyms at **regret.** —**anguish** *v.* **-guished, -guish·ing, -guish·es.** —*tr.* To cause to feel or suffer anguish. —*intr.* To feel or suffer anguish. [Middle English *angwisshe,* from Old French *anguisse,* from Latin *angustiae,* distress, from *angustus,* narrow. See **angh-** in Appendix.]

anhinga

an·guished (ăng′gwĭsht) *adj.* Feeling, expressing, or caused by anguish: *anguished victims of the earthquake; anguished screams for help.*

an·gu·lar (ăng′gyə-lər) *adj.* **1.** Having, forming, or consisting of an angle or angles. **2.** Measured by an angle or by degrees of an arc. **3.** Bony and lean; gaunt: *an angular face.* **4.** Lacking grace or smoothness; awkward: *an angular gait.* **5.** Rigid, stiff, and unyielding in character or disposition: *"the cold, angular brand of materialism"* (David K. Willis). [Latin *angulāris,* from *angulus,* angle.] —**an′gu·lar·ly** *adv.* —**an′gu·lar·ness** *n.*

angular acceleration *n.* The rate of change of angular velocity with respect to time.

an·gu·lar·i·ty (ăng′gyə-lăr′ĭ-tē) *n., pl.* **-ties. 1.** The quality or condition of being angular. **2. angularities.** Angular forms, outlines, or corners.

angular momentum *n.* **1.** The vector product of the position vector (from a reference point) and the linear momentum of a particle. **2.** The vector sum of the angular momentums of each component particle of an extended body.

angular velocity *n.* The rate of change of angular displacement with respect to time.

an·gu·late (ăng′gyə-lĭt, -lāt′) *adj.* Having angles or an angular shape. —**angulate** (-lāt′) *tr. & intr.v.* **-lat·ed, -lat·ing, -lates.** To make or become angular. —**an′gu·late·ly** *adv.*

an·gu·la·tion (ăng′gyə-lā′shən) *n.* **1.** The formation of angles. **2.** An angular part, position, or formation.

an·hin·ga (ăn-hĭng′gə) *n.* Any of a genus *(Anhinga)* of long-necked birds having a sharp, pointed bill and inhabiting swampy regions of tropical and subtropical America. Also called *darter, snakebird, water turkey.* [Portuguese, from Tupi *ayingá.*]

An·hui (än′hwē′) also **An·hwei** (-hwā′, -wā′). A province of east-central China. It was made a separate province in the 17th century under the Manchu dynasty. Hefei is the capital. Population, 51,560,000.

anhydr. *abbr.* Anhydrous.

an·hy·dride (ăn-hī′drīd′) *n.* A chemical compound formed from another, often an acid, by the removal of water. [ANHYDR(OUS) + –IDE.]

an·hy·drite (ăn-hī′drīt) *n.* A colorless, white, gray, blue, or lilac mineral of anhydrous calcium sulfate, $CaSO_4$, occurring as layers in gypsum deposits. [ANHYDR(OUS) + –ITE[1].]

an·hy·drous (ăn-hī′drəs) *adj. Abbr.* **anhydr.** Without water, especially water of crystallization. [From Greek *anudros* : *an-,* without; see A–[1] + *hudōr,* water; see **wed-[1]** in Appendix.]

a·ni (ä-nē′) *n.* Any of several chiefly tropical American birds of the genus *Crotophaga,* related to the cuckoo and having black plumage and a long tail. [American Spanish *ani* or Portuguese *ani,* both from Tupi *ani.*]

an·il (ăn′ĭl) *n.* The indigo plant or the blue dye obtained from it. [French, from Portuguese, from Arabic *an-nīl,* the indigo plant, from Persian *nīl,* from Sanskrit *nīlī,* from *nīla-,* dark blue.]

an·ile (ăn′īl′, ā′nīl′) *adj.* **1.** Of or like an old woman. **2.** Senile. [Latin *anīlis,* from *anus,* old woman.] —**a·nil′i·ty** (ə-nĭl′ĭ-tē) *n.*

an·i·line also **an·i·lin** (ăn′ə-lĭn) —*n.* A colorless, oily, poisonous benzene derivative, $C_6H_5NH_2$, used in the manufacture of rubber, dyes, resins, pharmaceuticals, and varnishes. —*adj.* Derived from aniline. [ANIL + –INE[2].]

a·ni·lin·gus (ā′nə-lĭng′gəs) *n.* Oral stimulation of the anus for sexual excitement. [New Latin : Latin *ānus,* anus + Latin *lingere,* to lick; see **leigh-** in Appendix.]

anim. *abbr. Music.* Animato.

an·i·ma (ăn′ə-mə) *n.* **1.** The inner self of an individual; the soul. **2.** In Jungian psychology: **a.** The unconscious or true inner self of an individual, as opposed to the persona, or outer aspect of the personality. **b.** The feminine inner personality, as present in the unconscious of the male. It is in contrast to the animus, which represents masculine characteristics. [Latin *anima.* See **ane-** in Appendix.]

an·i·mad·ver·sion (ăn′ə-măd-vûr′zhən, -shən) *n.* **1.** Strong criticism. **2.** A critical or censorious remark: *"Witness* [the] *animadversions on the bleeding hearts who worried about the hostages"* (Benjamin DeMott). [Latin *animadversiō, animadversiōn-,* from *animadversus,* past participle of *animadvertere,* to turn the mind toward. See ANIMADVERT.]

an·i·mad·vert (ăn′ə-măd-vûrt′) *intr.v.* **-vert·ed, -vert·ing, -verts.** To remark or comment critically, usually with strong disapproval or censure: *"a man . . . who animadverts on miserly patients, egocentric doctors, psychoanalysis and Lucky Luciano with evenhanded fervor"* (Irwin Faust). [Middle English *animadverten,* to notice, from Latin *animadvertere* : *animus,* mind; see **ane-** in Appendix + *advertere,* to turn toward; see ADVERSE.]

an·i·mal (ăn′ə-məl) *n.* **1.** A multicellular organism of the kingdom Animalia, differing from plants in certain typical characteristics such as capacity for locomotion, nonphotosynthetic metabolism, pronounced response to stimuli, restricted growth, and fixed bodily structure. **2.** An animal organism other than a human being, especially a mammal. **3.** A person who behaves in a bestial or brutish manner. **4.** A human being considered with respect to his or her physical, as opposed to spiritual, nature. **5.** A person having a specified aptitude or set of interests: *"that rarest of musical animals, an instrumentalist who is as comfortable on a podium with a stick as he is playing his instrument"* (Lon Tuck). —**animal** *adj.* **1.** Relating to, characteristic of, or derived from an animal or animals: *animal fat.* **2.** Relating to the physical as distinct from the spiritual nature of people: *animal instincts and desires.* See Synonyms at **brute.** [Middle English, from Latin, from *animāle,* neuter of *animālis,* living, from *anima,* soul. See **ane-** in Appendix.]

animal cracker *n.* A small cookie baked in the shape of an animal.

an·i·mal·cule (ăn′ə-măl′kyōōl) also **an·i·mal·cu·lum** (-kyə-ləm) *n., pl.* **-cules** also **-cu·la** (-kyə-lə). **1.** A microscopic or minute organism, such as an amoeba or a paramecium, usually considered to be an animal. **2.** *Archaic.* A tiny animal, such as a mosquito. [New Latin *animalculum,* diminutive of Latin *animal,* animal, from *anima,* soul. See ANIMA.]

animal heat *n.* The heat generated in the body of a warm-blooded vertebrate as the result of its physiological and metabolic processes.

animal husbandry *n.* The branch of agriculture concerned with the care and breeding of domestic animals such as cattle, hogs, sheep, and horses.

an·i·mal·ism (ăn′ə-mə-lĭz′əm) *n.* **1.** Enjoyment of vigorous health and physical drives. **2.** Indifference to all but the physical appetites. **3.** The doctrine that the human being is purely animal with no spiritual nature. **—an′i·mal·ist** *n.* **—an′i·mal·is′tic** (-lĭs′tĭk) *adj.*

an·i·mal·i·ty (ăn′ə-măl′ĭ-tē) *n.* **1.** The characteristics or nature of an animal. **2.** Animals considered as a group; the animal kingdom. **3.** The animal instincts of human beings as distinct from their spiritual nature.

an·i·mal·ize (ăn′ə-mə-līz′) *tr.v.* **-ized, -iz·ing, -iz·es. 1.** To cause (another) to behave like an animal. **2.** To depict or represent in the form of an animal. **—an′i·mal·i·za′tion** (-mə-lĭ-zā′shən) *n.*

animal kingdom *n.* A main classification of living organisms that includes all animals.

animal magnetism *n.* **1.** A special personal power or presence held to facilitate the hypnotism of others. **2.** Magnetic personal charm. **3.** Sex appeal.

animal pole *n. Embryology.* The portion of an egg opposite the vegetal pole that contains the nucleus and most of the cytoplasm.

animal spirits *pl.n.* The vitality of good health.

animal starch *n.* See **glycogen.**

an·i·mate (ăn′ə-māt′) *tr.v.* **-mat·ed, -mat·ing, -mates. 1.** To give life to; fill with life. **2.** To impart interest or zest to; enliven: *"The party was animated by all kinds of men and women"* (René Dubos). **3.** To fill with spirit, courage, or resolution; encourage. See Synonyms at **encourage. 4.** To inspire to action; prompt. **5.** To impart motion or activity to. **6.** To make, design, or produce (a cartoon, for example) so as to create the illusion of motion. **—animate** (ăn′ə-mĭt) *adj.* **1.** Possessing life; living. See Synonyms at **living. 2.** Of or relating to animal life as distinct from plant life. **3.** Belonging to the class of nouns that stand for living things: *The word* dog *is animate; the word* car *is inanimate.* [Latin *animāre, animāt-,* from *anima,* soul. See **ane-** in Appendix.]

an·i·mat·ed (ăn′ə-mā′tĭd) *adj.* **1.** Having life; alive. See Synonyms at **living. 2.** Filled with activity, vigor, or spirit; lively. **3.** Designed or constructed in the form of an animated cartoon. **—an′i·mat′ed·ly** *adv.*

animated cartoon *n.* A motion picture or television film consisting of a photographed series of drawings that simulates motion by means of very slight, continuous changes in the shapes of the drawings.

an·i·mat·ic (ăn′ə-măt′ĭk) *n.* A rough-draft, television test commercial with a sound track, developed by an advertising agency for its client, in which animated cutout figures replace live participants and real objects. Animatics are used in testing the effectiveness of planned, finished commercials. **—an·i·mat′ic** *adj.*

an·i·ma·tion (ăn′ə-mā′shən) *n.* **1.** The act, process, or result of imparting life, interest, spirit, motion, or activity. **2.** The quality or condition of being alive, active, spirited, or vigorous. **3. a.** The art or process of preparing animated cartoons. **b.** An animated cartoon.

a·ni·ma·to (ä′nē-mä′tō) *adv. & adj. Abbr.* **anim.** *Music.* In an animated or lively manner. Used chiefly as a direction. [Italian, from *animare,* to animate, from Latin *animāre.* See ANIMATE.]

an·i·ma·tor (ăn′ə-mā′tər) *n.* **1.** One that provides or imparts life, interest, spirit, or vitality. **2.** One, such as an artist or a technician, who designs, develops, or produces an animated cartoon.

an·i·mism (ăn′ə-mĭz′əm) *n.* **1.** The attribution of conscious life to natural objects or to nature itself. **2.** The belief in the existence of spiritual beings that are separable or separate from bodies. **3.** The hypothesis holding that an immaterial force animates the universe. [From Latin *anima,* soul. See **ane-** in Appendix.] **—an′i·mist** *n.* **—an′i·mis′tic** *adj.*

an·i·mos·i·ty (ăn′ə-mŏs′ĭ-tē) *n., pl.* **-ties.** Bitter hostility or open enmity; active hatred. See Synonyms at **enmity.** [Middle English *animosite,* from Old French, from Late Latin *animōsitās,* courage, from Latin *animōsus,* bold, from *animus,* soul, spirit. See **ane-** in Appendix.]

an·i·mus (ăn′ə-məs) *n.* **1.** An attitude that informs one's actions; disposition. **2.** A feeling of animosity; ill will. See Synonyms at **enmity. 3.** In Jungian psychology, the masculine inner personality as present in women. [Latin. See **ane-** in Appendix.]

an·i·on (ăn′ī′ən) *n.* A negatively charged ion, especially the ion that migrates to an anode in electrolysis. [From Greek, neuter present participle of *anienai,* to go up : *ana-,* ana- + *ienai,* to go; see **ei-** in Appendix.] **—an′i·on′ic** (-ŏn′ĭk) *adj.* **—an′i·on′i·cal·ly** *adv.*

anis- *pref.* Variant of **aniso-.**

an·ise (ăn′ĭs) *n.* **1.** An annual, aromatic Mediterranean herb *(Pimpinella anisum)* in the parsley family, cultivated for its seedlike fruits and the oil obtained from them and used to flavor foods, liqueurs, and candies. **2.** Anise seed. [Middle English *anis,* from Old French, from Latin *anīsum,* from Greek *anison.*]

anise hyssop *n.* A North American perennial herb *(Agastache foeniculum)* in the mint family, having spikelike clusters of violet-blue flowers and aromatic leaves sometimes used for tea. [Probably so called from the fragrance of its seeds.]

an·i·sei·ko·ni·a (ăn-ī′sī-kō′nē-ə) *n.* A condition in which the shape and size of the ocular image differ in each eye. [From ANIS(O)- + Greek *eikōn,* image.] **—an·i′sei·kon′ic** (-kŏn′ĭk) *adj.*

anise seed or **an·i·seed** (ăn′ĭ-sēd′) *n.* The seedlike fruit of the anise.

an·i·sette (ăn′ĭ-sĕt′, -zĕt′) *n.* A liqueur flavored with anise. [French, diminutive of *anis,* anise, from Old French. See ANISE.]

aniso- or **anis-** *pref.* Unequal; dissimilar: *anisogamy.* [From Greek *anisos* : *an-,* without; see A-[1] + *isos,* equal.]

an·i·so·gam·ete (ăn-ī′sō-găm′ēt, gə-mēt′, ăn′ī-) *n.* See **heterogamete.**

an·i·sog·a·my (ăn′ī-sŏg′ə-mē) *n.* A union between two gametes that differ in size or form. **—an′i·so·gam′ic** (-sə-găm′ĭk) *adj.*

an·i·so·met·ric (ăn-ī′sə-mĕt′rĭk, ăn′ī-) *adj.* Not isometric.

an·i·so·me·tro·pi·a (ăn-ī′sə-mĭ-trō′pē-ə) *n.* A condition in which the refractive power of one eye differs from that of the other. [ANISO- + Greek *metron,* measure; see METER[1] + -OPIA.] **—an·i′so·me·trop′ic** (-trŏp′ĭk, -trō′pĭk) *adj.*

an·i·so·trop·ic (ăn-ī′sə-trŏp′ĭk, -trō′pĭk) *adj.* **1.** Not isotropic. **2.** *Physics.* Having properties that differ according to the direction of measurement. **—an·i′so·trop′i·cal·ly** *adv.* **—an′i·sot′ro·pism** (-sŏt′rə-pĭz′əm), **an′i·sot′ro·py** (-sŏt′rə-pē) *n.*

ani
Smooth-billed ani
Crotophaga ani

An·jou[1] (ăn′jōō′, äɴ-zhōō′). **1.** A historical region and former province of northwest France in the Loire River valley. Ruled by the powerful counts of Anjou in the early Middle Ages, it was annexed to the French crown lands by Louis XI in the 1480's. **2.** A town of southern Quebec, Canada, a suburb of Montreal. Population, 37,346.

An·jou[2] (ăn′zhōō, -jōō) *n.* A variety of pear with green skin and firm, smooth flesh.

An·ka·ra (ăng′kər-ə, äng′-). Formerly **An·cy·ra** (ăn-sī′rə) and **An·go·ra** (ăng-gôr′ə, -gōr′ə, ăng′gər-ə). The capital of Turkey, in the west-central part of the country at an elevation of about 915 m (3,000 ft). An important commercial center from ancient times until the late 19th century, the city declined until it replaced Istanbul as the capital in 1923. Population, 1,877,755.

an·ker·ite (ăng′kə-rīt′) *n.* A white, gray, or red iron-rich dolomitic or carbonate mineral, $Ca(Fe,Mg,Mn)(CO_3)_2$. [After M.J. *Anker* (1771–1843), Austrian mineralogist.]

ankh (ăngk) *n.* An ansate cross. [Egyptian *'nḫ,* life.]

an·kle (ăng′kəl) *n.* **1.** The joint formed by the articulation of the lower leg bones with the talus. The ankle connects the foot with the leg. **2.** The slender section of the leg immediately above the foot. [Middle English *ancle, ankel,* partly from Old English *anclēow* and partly of Scandinavian origin.]

an·kle·bone (ăng′kəl-bōn′) *n.* See **talus[1]** (sense 1).

an·klet (ăng′klĭt) *n.* **1.** An ornament worn around the ankle. **2.** A sock that reaches just above the ankle.

an·ky·lose also **an·chy·lose** (ăng′kə-lōs′, -lōz′) *—v.* **-losed, -los·ing, -los·es.** *—tr.* To join or consolidate by ankylosis. *—intr.* To become joined or consolidated by ankylosis. [Back-formation from ANKYLOSIS.]

an·ky·lo·sis also **an·chy·lo·sis** (ăng′kə-lō′sĭs) *n.* **1.** *Anatomy.* The consolidation of bones or their parts to form a single unit. **2.** *Pathology.* The stiffening and immobility of a joint as the result of disease, trauma, surgery, or abnormal bone fusion. [New Latin, from Greek *ankulōsis,* stiffening of the joints, from *ankuloun,* to crook, bend, from *ankulos,* crooked, bent.] **—an′ky·lot′ic** (-lŏt′ĭk) *adj.*

an·lace (ăn′lĭs) *n.* A two-edged medieval dagger. [Middle English *anelas,* possibly from *alesnes,* awl, of Germanic origin.]

an·la·ge also **An·la·ge** (än′lä′gə) *n., pl.* **-ges** or **-gen** (-gən). **1.** *Biology.* The initial clustering of embryonic cells from which a part or an organ develops; primordium. **2.** A fundamental principle; the foundation for a future development. [German, fundamental principle, from Middle High German *anlāge,* request : *ane-,* on (from Old High German *ana-;* see **an-** in Appendix) + *lāge,* act of laying (from Old High German *lāga;* see **legh-** in Appendix).]

Ann (ăn), **Cape.** A peninsula of northeast Massachusetts projecting into the Atlantic Ocean northeast of Gloucester.

ann. *abbr.* **1.** Annals. **2.** Annual. **3.** Annuity.

an·na (ä′nə) *n.* A copper coin formerly used in India and Pakistan. [Hindi *ānā,* from Sanskrit *aṇu-,* small.]

An·na·ba (ə-nä′bə, ă-nä′). A city of northeast Algeria on the Mediterranean Sea near the Tunisian border. Founded by the Carthaginians, it was an early center of Christianity. Population, 222,607.

An·na I·va·nov·na (ä′nə ē-vä′nəv-nə). 1693–1740. Empress of Russia (1730–1740) who intervened in the War of the

ă pat	oi boy
ā pay	ou out
âr care	ŏŏ took
ä father	ōō boot
ĕ pet	ŭ cut
ē be	ûr urge
ĭ pit	th thin
ī pie	*th* this
îr pier	hw which
ŏ pot	zh vision
ō toe	ə about, item
ô paw	♦ regionalism

Stress marks: ′ (primary); ′ (secondary), as in **dictionary** (dĭk′shə-nĕr′ē)

Polish Succession (1733–1735) and attacked Turkey (1736).

An Na·jaf (ăn năj′ăf′). A city of south-central Iraq on a lake near the Euphrates River. It is a starting point for the pilgrimage to Mecca. Population, 242,603.

an·nal·ist (ăn′ə-lĭst) *n.* One who writes annals; a chronicler.

an·nals (ăn′əlz) *pl.n. Abbr.* **ann. 1.** A chronological record of the events of successive years. **2.** A descriptive account or record; a history: *"the short and simple annals of the poor"* (Thomas Gray). **3.** A periodical journal in which the records and reports of a learned field are compiled. [Latin *(librī) annālēs,* yearly (books), annals, pl. of *annālis,* yearly, from *annus,* year. See **at-** in Appendix.]

An·nam (ə-năm′, ăn′ăm′). A region and former kingdom of central Vietnam on the South China Sea between Tonkin and Cochin China. It was ruled by China from 111 B.C. until A.D. 939 and came under French control in the 19th century. —**An′na·mese′** (ăn′ə-mēz′, -mēs′), **An′nam·ite′** *adj. & n.*

An·nan·dale (ăn′ən-dāl′). A city of northeast Virginia, a suburb of Alexandria and Washington, D.C. Population, 35,300.

An·nap·o·lis (ə-năp′ə-lĭs). The capital of Maryland, in the central part of the state on an inlet of Chesapeake Bay south-southeast of Baltimore. Settled in 1649, it was the site of the Annapolis Convention in 1786, which led to the federal Constitutional Convention of 1787. The U.S. Naval Academy, founded in 1845, is in Annapolis. Population, 31,740.

Anne of Cleves

Annapolis Roy·al (roi′əl). A town of western Nova Scotia, Canada, on an arm of the Bay of Fundy. One of the oldest settlements in Canada, it was founded as **Port Royal** by the French in 1605 and renamed by the British after 1710 in honor of Queen Anne.

An·na·pur·na (ăn′ə-po͝or′nə, -pûr′-). A massif of the Himalaya Mountains in north-central Nepal. It rises to 8,083.7 m (26,504 ft) at **Annapurna I** in the west. **Annapurna II,** in the east, is 7,942.5 m (26,041 ft) high.

Ann Ar·bor (är′bər). A city of southeast Michigan west of Detroit. A research and educational center, it is the seat of the University of Michigan (founded 1817). Population, 107,966.

an·nat·to also **a·nat·to** (ə-nä′tō), **ar·nat·to** (är-nä′tō) *n., pl.* **-tos. 1.** A tropical American evergreen shrub or small tree *(Bixa orellana),* having heart-shaped leaves and showy, rose-pink or sometimes white flowers. Also called *lipstick tree.* **2.** The seed of this plant, used as a coloring and sometimes as a flavoring, especially in Latin American cuisine. **3.** A yellowish-red dyestuff obtained from the seed aril of this plant, used especially to dye fabric and to color food products such as margarine and cheese. [Of Cariban origin.]

Anne (ăn). 1665–1714. Queen of Great Britain and Ireland (1702–1714). The last monarch of the Stuart line, she was also the last English ruler to exercise the royal veto over Parliament (1707).

an·neal (ə-nēl′) *v.* **-nealed, -neal·ing, -neals.** —*tr.* **1.** To subject (glass or metal) to a process of heating and slow cooling in order to toughen and reduce brittleness. **2.** To strengthen or harden. —*intr.* To become strengthened or hardened: *"the time she needed for opinion to anneal around her policy"* (Alexander M. Haig, Jr.). [Middle English *anelen,* from Old English *onǣlan,* to set fire to : *on,* on; see ON + *ǣlan,* to kindle.]

An·ne·cy (ăn′ə-sē′, än-sē′). A city of southern France in the Alps on **Lake Annecy** east-northeast of Lyon. It is a popular resort and tourist center. Population, 49,965.

annual ring
Cross section from the trunk of a white pine (*Pinus strobus*)

an·ne·lid (ăn′ə-lĭd) also **an·nel·i·dan** (ə-nĕl′ĭ-dən) —*n.* Any of various worms or wormlike animals of the phylum Annelida, characterized by an elongated, cylindrical, segmented body and including the earthworm and leech. —*adj.* Of or belonging to the phylum Annelida. [From New Latin *Annelida,* phylum name, from French *annelés,* pl. past participle of *anneler,* to ring, from Old French *anel,* ring, from Latin *ānellus,* diminutive of *ānus,* ring.]

Anne of Aus·tri·a (ô′strē-ə). 1601–1666. Wife of Louis XIII of France and regent (1643–1661) for her son Louis XIV.

Anne of Cleves (klēvz). 1515–1557. Queen of England (January–July 1540) as the fourth wife of Henry VIII.

an·nex (ə-nĕks′, ăn′ĕks′) *tr.v.* **-nexed, -nex·ing, -nex·es. 1.** To append or attach, especially to a larger or more significant thing. **2.** To incorporate (territory) into an existing political unit such as a country, state, county, or city. **3.** To add or attach, as an attribute, a condition, or a consequence. —**annex** (ăn′ĕks′, ăn′ĭks) *n.* **1.** A building added on to a larger one or an auxiliary building situated near a main one. **2.** An addition, such as an appendix, that is made to a record or other document. [Middle English *annexen,* from Old French *annexer,* from Latin *annectere, annex-,* to connect : *ad-,* ad- + *nectere,* to bind; see **ned-** in Appendix.] —**an′nex·a′tion** (ăn′ĭk-sā′shən) *n.* —**an′nex·a′tion·al** *adj.* —**an′nex·a′tion·ism** *n.* —**an′nex·a′tion·ist** *n.*

an·nexe (ăn′ĭks) *n. Chiefly British.* Variant of **annex.**

An·nie Oak·ley (ăn′ē ōk′lē) *n.* A free ticket or pass. [After Annie OAKLEY (from the association of the punched ticket with one of her bullet-riddled targets).]

an·ni·hi·late (ə-nī′ə-lāt′) *v.* **-lat·ed, -lat·ing, -lates.** —*tr.* **1.a.** To destroy completely: *The naval force was annihilated during the attack.* **b.** To reduce to nonexistence. **c.** To defeat decisively; vanquish. **2.** To nullify or render void; abolish. —*intr. Physics.* To participate in annihilation, as do an electron and a positron. [Late Latin *annihilāre, annihilāt-* : Latin *ad-,* ad- + Latin *nihil,* nothing; see **ne** in Appendix.] —**an·ni′hi·la·bil′i·ty** (-lə-bĭl′ĭ-tē) *n.* —**an·ni′hi·la·ble** (-lə-bəl) *adj.* —**an·ni′hi·la′tor** *n.*

ă pat	oi boy
ā pay	ou out
âr care	o͝o took
ä father	o͞o boot
ĕ pet	ŭ cut
ē be	ûr urge
ĭ pit	th thin
ī pie	*th* this
îr pier	hw which
ŏ pot	zh vision
ō toe	ə about, item
ô paw	♦ regionalism

Stress marks: ′ (primary); ′ (secondary), as in **dictionary** (dĭk′shə-nĕr′ē)

an·ni·hi·la·tion (ə-nī′ə-lā′shən) *n.* **1.a.** The act or process of annihilating. **b.** The condition or result of having been annihilated; utter destruction. **2.** *Physics.* The phenomenon in which a particle and an antiparticle, such as an electron and a positron, meet and are converted completely to energy approximately equivalent to the sum of their masses.

an·ni·hi·la·tive (ə-nī′ə-lā′tĭv, -ə-lə-) *adj.* Capable of causing utter destruction or serving to destroy utterly: *"The possession of annihilative power has not slowed down the drive toward even more fiendish modes of inflicting wholesale death"* (Saturday Review).

An·nis·ton (ăn′ĭ-stən). A city of northeast Alabama in the foothills of the Appalachian Mountains east-northeast of Birmingham. It was founded in 1872 as an iron-manufacturing company town and opened to noncompany settlers in 1883. Population, 29,523.

an·ni·ver·sa·ry (ăn′ə-vûr′sə-rē) *n., pl.* **-ries. 1.** The annually recurring date of a past event, especially one of historical, national, or personal importance: *a wedding anniversary; the anniversary of the founding of Rome.* **2.** A celebration commemorating such a date. —*attributive.* Often used to modify another noun: *an anniversary party; an anniversary ring.* [Middle English *anniversarie,* from Medieval Latin *(diēs) anniversāria,* anniversary (day), from Latin, feminine of *anniversārius,* returning yearly : *annus,* year; see **at-** in Appendix + *versus,* past participle of *vertere,* to turn; see **wer-**[2] in Appendix.]

an·no Dom·i·ni (ăn′ō dŏm′ə-nī′, dŏm′ə-nē) *adv. Abbr.* **A.D., A.D.** In a specified year of the Christian era. [Medieval Latin : *annō,* in the year + *Dominī,* genitive of *Dominus,* Lord.]

an·no·tate (ăn′ō-tāt′) *v.* **-tat·ed, -tat·ing, -tates.** —*tr.* To furnish (a literary work) with critical commentary or explanatory notes; gloss. —*intr.* To gloss a text. [Latin *annotāre, annotāt-,* to note down : *ad-,* ad- + *notāre,* to write (from *nota,* note; see **gnō-** in Appendix).] —**an′no·ta′tive** *adj.* —**an′no·ta′tor** *n.*

an·no·ta·tion (ăn′ō-tā′shən) *n.* **1.** The act or process of furnishing critical commentary or explanatory notes. **2.** A critical or explanatory note; a commentary.

an·nounce (ə-nouns′) *v.* **-nounced, -nounc·ing, -nounc·es.** —*tr.* **1.** To make known publicly. **2.** To proclaim the presence or arrival of: *announce a caller.* **3.** To provide an indication of beforehand; foretell: *The invention of the microchip announced a new generation of computers.* **4.** To serve as an announcer for: *announce a football game on TV.* —*intr.* **1.** To declare one's candidacy: *Presidential candidates announce two years in advance of the elections.* **2.** To serve as an announcer. [Middle English *announcen,* from Old French *anoncier,* from Latin *annūntiāre* : *ad-,* ad- + *nūntiāre,* to report (from *nūntius,* message; see **neu-** in Appendix).]

SYNONYMS: *announce, advertise, broadcast, declare, proclaim, promulgate, publish.* The central meaning shared by these verbs is "to bring to public notice": *announced a cease-fire; advertise a forthcoming concert; broadcasting their beliefs; declared her intention to run for office; proclaiming his opinions; promulgated a policy of nonresistance; publishing the marriage banns.*

WORD HISTORY: The injunction not to shoot the messenger could as well be not to shoot the announcer, given the etymology of the word *announce.* First recorded in English before 1500 in the sense "to proclaim, make known," *announce* came into English via Old French from Latin. The Latin source *annūntiāre* is made up of the directional prefix *ad–* and the verb *nūntiāre,* "to bring word of a fact or occurrence." This verb is in turn derived from the noun *nūntium,* "a message," which also yielded *nūntius,* "a messenger."

an·nounce·ment (ə-nouns′mənt) *n.* **1.a.** The act of making known publicly. **b.** Something announced. **2.** An engraved or printed formal statement or notice, as of a wedding.

an·nounc·er (ə-noun′sər) *n.* One that announces, especially a radio or television employee who provides program continuity, delivers announcements, or gives running comments on sports events.

an·noy (ə-noi′) *v.* **-noyed, -noy·ing, -noys.** —*tr.* **1.** To cause slight irritation to (another) by troublesome, often repeated acts. **2.** To harass or disturb by repeated attacks. —*intr.* To be annoying. [Middle English *anoien,* from Old French *anoier, ennuyer,* from Vulgar Latin **inodiāre,* to make odious, from Latin *in odiō,* odious : *in,* in; see IN–[2] + *odiō,* ablative of *odium,* hatred; see **od-** in Appendix.]

SYNONYMS: *annoy, irritate, bother, irk, vex, provoke, aggravate, peeve, rile.* These verbs mean to disturb or disquiet a person so as to evoke moderate anger. *Annoy* refers to mild disturbance caused by an act that tries one's patience: *The sound of footsteps on the bare floor annoyed the downstairs neighbors. Irritate* is closely related but somewhat stronger: *Your interruptions only serve to irritate the entire staff. Bother* implies troublesome imposition: *Hasn't he bothered them enough with his phone calls? Irk* connotes a wearisome quality: *The city council's failure to take action on the legislation irked the community. Vex* applies to an act capable of arousing anger or perplexity: *Hecklers in the crowd asked irrelevant questions for the sole purpose of vexing the* *speaker. Provoke* implies strong and often deliberate incitement to anger: *Her behavior was enough to provoke an angel. Aggravate* is an approximate equivalent: *"Threats only served to aggravate people in such cases"* (Thackeray). *Peeve,* somewhat informal in tone, suggests rather minor disturbance that produces a querulous, resentful response: *The flippancy of your answer peeved me.* To *rile* is to upset one's equanimity and stir one up: *It riled me no end to listen to such lies.*

---

an·noy·ance (ə-noi′əns) *n.* **1.** The act of annoying or the state of being annoyed. **2.** A cause of irritation or vexation; a nuisance.

an·noy·ing (ə-noi′ĭng) *adj.* Causing vexation or irritation; troublesome: *an annoying cough.* **—an·noy′ing·ly** *adv.*

an·nu·al (ăn′yo͞o-əl) *adj. Abbr.* **ann. 1.** Recurring, done, or performed every year; yearly: *an annual trip to Paris.* **2.** Of, relating to, or determined by a year: *an annual income.* **3.** *Botany.* Living or growing for only one year or season. **—annual** *n.* **1.** A periodical published yearly; a yearbook. **2.** *Botany.* A plant that completes its entire life cycle in a single growing season. [Middle English *annuel,* from Old French, from Late Latin *annuālis,* ultimately from Latin *annus,* year. See **at-** in Appendix.] **—an′nu·al·ly** *adv.*

an·nu·al·ize (ăn′yo͞o-ə-līz′) *tr.v.* **-ized, -iz·ing, -iz·es.** To adjust or calculate so as to reflect a rate that is based on a full year: *Brokers annualize a yield on an investment by multiplying weekly dividends by 52 and dividing the answer by the net asset value per share.*

annual ring *n. Botany.* The layer of wood formed in a plant during a single year. Annual rings appear concentric when viewed in cross section.

an·nu·i·tant (ə-no͞o′ĭ-tənt, ə-nyo͞o′-) *n.* **1.** One that receives or is qualified to receive an annuity. **2.** An officially retired U.S. intelligence officer who is actually still on the government's payroll and is available for assignments.

an·nu·i·ty (ə-no͞o′ĭ-tē, ə-nyo͞o′-) *n., pl.* **-ties.** *Abbr.* **ann. 1.a.** The annual payment of an allowance or income. **b.** The right to receive this payment or the obligation to make this payment. **2.** An investment on which one receives fixed payments for a lifetime or for a specified number of years. [Middle English *annuite,* from Anglo-Norman, from Medieval Latin *annuitās,* from Latin *annuus,* yearly, from *annus,* year. See **at-** in Appendix.]

an·nul (ə-nŭl′) *tr.v.* **-nulled, -nul·ling, -nuls. 1.** To make or declare void or invalid, as a marriage or a law; nullify. **2.** To obliterate the effect or existence of: *"The significance of the past . . . is annulled in idle gusts of electronic massacre"* (Alexander Cockburn). [Middle English *annullen,* from Old French *annuller,* from Late Latin *annullāre* : Latin *ad-,* ad- + Latin *nullus,* none; see **ne** in Appendix.]

an·nu·lar (ăn′yə-lər) *adj.* Shaped like or forming a ring. [Latin *ānulāris,* from *ānulus,* ring. See ANNULUS.]

annular eclipse *n.* A solar eclipse in which the moon covers all but a bright ring around the circumference of the sun.

annular ligament *n.* The fibrous band of tissue that surrounds the ankle joint or the wrist joint.

an·nu·late (ăn′yə-lĭt, -lāt′) also **an·nu·lat·ed** (-lā′tĭd) *adj.* Having or consisting of rings or ringlike segments. [Latin *ānulātus,* from *ānulus,* ring. See ANNULUS.]

an·nu·la·tion (ăn′yə-lā′shən) *n.* **1.** The act or process of forming rings. **2.** A ringlike structure, segment, or part.

an·nu·let (ăn′yə-lĭt) *n. Architecture.* A ringlike molding around the capital of a pillar. [Latin *ānulus,* ring; see ANNULUS + -ET.]

an·nu·li (ăn′yə-lī′) *n.* A plural of **annulus.**

an·nul·ment (ə-nŭl′mənt) *n.* **1.** An act of making or declaring void. **2.** The retrospective as well as prospective invalidation of a marriage, as for nonconsummation, effected by means of a declaration stating that the marriage was never valid.

an·nu·lus (ăn′yə-ləs) *n., pl.* **-lus·es** or **-li** (-lī′). **1.** A ringlike figure, part, structure, or marking, such as a growth ring on the scale of a fish. **2.a.** A ring or group of thick-walled cells around the sporangia of many ferns that functions in spore release. **b.** The ringlike remains of a broken partial veil, found around the stipes of certain mushrooms. **3.** *Mathematics.* The figure bounded by and containing the area between two concentric circles. [Latin *ānulus,* ring, diminutive of *ānus.*]

an·nun·ci·ate (ə-nŭn′sē-āt′) *tr.v.* **-at·ed, -at·ing, -ates.** To announce; proclaim: *"They do not so properly affirm, as annunciate it"* (Charles Lamb). [Latin *annūntiāre, annūntiāt-.* See ANNOUNCE.]

an·nun·ci·a·tion (ə-nŭn′sē-ā′shən) *n.* **1.** The act of announcing. **2.** An announcement; a proclamation. **3. Annunciation. a.** The angel Gabriel's announcement to the Virgin Mary of the Incarnation. **b.** The Christian feast celebrating this event. **c.** March 25, the day on which this feast is observed.

an·nun·ci·a·tor (ə-nŭn′sē-ā′tər) *n.* One that announces, especially an electrical signaling device used in hotels or offices to indicate the sources of calls on a switchboard.

an·nus mi·rab·i·lis (ăn′əs mĭ-răb′ə-lĭs) *n., pl.* **an·ni mi·ra·bi·les** (ăn′ī mĭ-răb′ə-lēz, ăn′ē). A year notable for disasters or wonders; a fateful year: *"Hungary's blood bath was the saddest event in that annus mirabilis"* (C.L. Sulzberger). [New Latin : Latin *annus,* year + Latin *mīrābilis,* wondrous.]

a·no·a (ə-nō′ə) *n.* A small buffalo *(Bubalus* or *Anoa depressicornis)* of Celebes and the Philippines, having short, pointed horns. [Native word in Celebes.]

an·ode (ăn′ōd′) *n. Abbr.* **a. 1.** A positively charged electrode, as of an electrolytic cell, a storage battery, or an electron tube. **2.** The negatively charged terminal of a primary cell or of a storage battery that is supplying current. [Greek *anodos,* a way up : *ana-,* ana- + *hodos,* way.]

an·o·dize (ăn′ə-dīz′) *tr.v.* **-dized, -diz·ing, -diz·es.** To coat (a metallic surface) electrolytically with a protective or decorative oxide. [ANOD(E) + -IZE.] **—an′o·di·za′tion** (-dĭ-zā′shən) *n.*

an·o·dyne (ăn′ə-dīn′) *adj.* **1.** Capable of soothing or eliminating pain. **2.** Relaxing: *anodyne novels about country life.* **3.** Watered-down; insipid: *"At the time, I thought that passage was pretty anodyne"* (Conor Cruise O'Brien). **—anodyne** *n.* **1.** A medicine, such as aspirin, that relieves pain. **2.** A source of soothing comfort. [Latin *anōdynus,* from Greek *anōdunos,* free from pain : *an-,* without; see A–[1] + *odunē,* pain; see **ed-** in Appendix.]

a·noint (ə-noint′) *tr.v.* **a·noint·ed, a·noint·ing, a·noints. 1.** To apply oil, ointment, or a similar substance to. **2.** To put oil on during a religious ceremony as a sign of sanctification or consecration. **3.** To choose by or as if by divine intervention. [Middle English *enointen,* from Old French *enoint,* past participle of *enoindre,* from Latin *inunguere, inūnct-* : *in-,* on; see IN–[2] + *unguere,* to smear.] **—a·noint′ment** *n.*

a·noint·ing of the sick (ə-noin′tĭng) *n. Roman Catholic Church.* The sacrament of anointing a critically ill or weak person, with prayers for recovery and an act of penance or confession.

a·no·le (ə-nō′lē) *n.* Any of various chiefly tropical New World lizards of the genus *Anolis,* characterized by a distensible throat flap and the ability to change color. Also called *chameleon.* [French *anolis,* of Cariban origin.]

a·nom·a·lous (ə-nŏm′ə-ləs) *adj.* **1.** Deviating from the normal or common order, form, or rule. **2.** Equivocal, as in classification or nature. [From Late Latin *anōmalos,* from Greek, uneven : probably from *an-,* not; see A–[1] + *homalos,* even (from *homos,* same; see **sem-**[1] in Appendix).]

a·nom·a·ly (ə-nŏm′ə-lē) *n., pl.* **-lies. 1.** Deviation or departure from the normal or common order, form, or rule: *"NASA's system for tracking anomalies for flight readiness reviews failed"* (Presidential Commission Report on the Challenger Disaster). **2.** One that is peculiar, irregular, abnormal, or difficult to classify: *"Both men are anomalies: they have . . . likable personalities but each has made his reputation as a heavy"* (David Pauly). **3.** *Astronomy.* The angular deviation, as observed from the sun, of a planet from its perihelion. **—a·nom′a·lis′tic** (-lĭs′tĭk), **a·nom′a·lis′ti·cal** *adj.* **—a·nom′a·lis′ti·cal·ly** *adv.*

an·o·mic (ə-nŏm′ĭk, ə-nō′mĭk) *adj.* Socially unstable, alienated, and disorganized: *"anomic loners musing over their fate"* (Francine du Plessix Gray). **—anomic** *n.* A socially unstable, alienated person: *"The picture* [is] *about two anomics who inch their way to spiritual rebirth"* (Pauline Kael).

an·o·mie or **an·o·my** (ăn′ə-mē) *n.* **1.** Social instability caused by steady erosion of standards and values. **2.** Alienation and purposelessness experienced by a person or a class as a result of a lack of standards and values. **3.** Personal disorganization resulting in unsocial behavior. [French, from Greek *anomia,* lawlessness, from *anomos,* lawless : *a-,* without; see A–[1] + *nomos,* law; see **nem-** in Appendix.]

a·non (ə-nŏn′) *adv.* **1.** At another time; later. **2.** In a short time; soon. **3.** *Archaic.* At once; forthwith. ***—idiom.* ever** (or **now) and anon.** Time after time; now and then. [Middle English, at once, from Old English *on ān* : *on,* in; see ON + *ān,* one; see **oi-no-** in Appendix.]

anon. *abbr.* Anonymous.

an·o·nym (ăn′ə-nĭm′) *n.* **1.** An anonymous person. **2.** A pseudonym. [French *anonyme,* from Late Latin *anōnymus,* anonymous. See ANONYMOUS.]

an·o·nym·i·ty (ăn′ə-nĭm′ĭ-tē) *n., pl.* **-ties. 1.** The quality or state of being unknown or unacknowledged. **2.** One that is unknown or unacknowledged.

a·non·y·mous (ə-nŏn′ə-məs) *adj. Abbr.* **anon., a. 1.** Having an unknown or unacknowledged name: *an anonymous author.* **2.** Having an unknown or withheld authorship or agency: *an anonymous letter; an anonymous phone call.* **3.** Having no distinctive character or recognition factor: *"a very great, almost anonymous center of people who just want peace"* (Alan Paton). [From Late Latin *anōnymus,* from Greek *anōnumos,* nameless : *an-,* without; see A–[1] + *onuma,* name; see **nō-men-** in Appendix.]

a·noph·e·les (ə-nŏf′ə-lēz′) *n.* Any of various mosquitoes of the genus *Anopheles,* which can carry the malaria parasite and transmit the disease to human beings. [From Greek *anōphelēs,* useless : *an-,* without; see A–[1] + *ophelos,* advantage.] **—a·noph′e·line′** (-līn′, -lĭn) *adj.*

an·o·rak (ăn′ə-răk′) *n.* A heavy jacket with a hood; a parka. [Greenlandic Eskimo *annoraaq,* formerly spelled *ánoráK.*]

an·o·rec·tic (ăn′ə-rĕk′tĭk) also **an·o·ret·ic** (-rĕt′ĭk) *—adj.* **1.** Marked by loss of appetite. **2.** Suppressing or causing loss of appetite. **3.** Of or affected with anorexia nervosa. *—n.* **1.** One who is affected with anorexia nervosa. **2.** An anorectic drug.

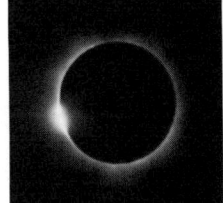

annular eclipse
Solar eclipse, March 7, 1970

Annunciation
Early 16th-century painting, *The Annunciation,* by Juan de Flandes

anorak

[From Greek *anorektos* : *an-*, without; see A–[1] + *orektos*, from *oregein*, to reach out for. See **reg-** in Appendix.]

an·o·rex·i·a (ăn′ə-rĕk′sē-ə) *n.* Loss of appetite, especially as a result of disease. [Greek : *an-*, without; see A–[1] + *orexis*, appetite (from *oregein*, to reach out for; see **reg-** in Appendix).]

anorexia nerv·o·sa (nûr-vō′sə) *n.* A psychophysiological disorder usually occurring in teenage women that is characterized by an abnormal fear of becoming obese, a distorted self-image, a persistent aversion to food, and severe weight loss. It is often accompanied by self-induced vomiting, amenorrhea, and other physiological changes. [New Latin : *anorexia*, anorexia + *nervosa*, nervous.]

an·o·rex·ic (ăn′ə-rĕk′sĭk) *adj.* **1.** Suffering from or afflicted with anorexia nervosa. **2.** Anorectic. **3.** Characterized by severe economy of style and expression: *"The book consists of nineteen rather anorexic stories, stripped of all but vestigial traces of emotion and often of plot"* (Madison Bell). **—an′o·rex′ic** *n.*

an·or·thite (ăn-ôr′thīt) *n.* A rare plagioclase feldspar with high calcium oxide content occurring in igneous rocks. [From Greek *an-*, not; see A–[1] + *orthos*, straight (from its oblique crystals).]

ansate cross
Held in right hand

an·or·tho·site (ăn-ôr′thə-sīt′) *n.* A variety of diorite consisting chiefly of feldspar. [French *anorthose*, a kind of feldspar (Greek *an-*, not; see A–[1] + Greek *orthos*, straight) + –ITE[1].]

an·os·mi·a (ăn-ŏz′mē-ə) *n.* Loss of the sense of smell. [New Latin : Greek *an-*, without; see A–[1] + Greek *osmē*, odor.] **—an·os′mic** *adj.*

an·oth·er (ə-nŭth′ər) *adj.* **1.** One more; an additional: *had another cup of coffee.* **2.** Distinctly different from the first: *took another route to town.* **3.** Some other: *put it off to another day.* **—another** *pron.* **1.** An additional one: *one encore followed by another.* **2.** A different one: *This shirt is too big; I'll try another.* **3.** One of an undetermined number or group: *for one reason or another.* See Usage Note at **each other.** [Middle English *on other* : *on*, one; see ONE + *other*, other; see OTHER.]

A·nou·ilh (ä-no͞o′ē), **Jean.** 1910–1987. French playwright whose works, such as *Antigone* (1944), juxtapose harsh reality and fantasy.

ant

an·ov·u·lant (ăn′ŏv′yə-lənt) *n.* A drug that suppresses ovulation. [AN– + OVUL(ATION) + –ANT.] **—an·ov′u·lant** *adj.*

an·o·vu·la·tion (ăn-ō′vyə-lā′shən, -ŏv′yə-) *n.* The failure, cessation, or suppression of ovulation.

an·o·vu·la·to·ry (ăn-ō′vyə-lə-tôr′ē, -tōr′ē, -ŏv′yə-) *adj.* **1.** Relating to or causing the suppression of ovulation: *an anovulatory drug.* **2.** Not associated with or influenced by ovulation.

an·ox·e·mi·a (ăn′ŏk-sē′mē-ə) *n.* An abnormal reduction in the oxygen content of the blood. [AN– + OX(O)– + –EMIA.] **—an′ox·e′mic** *adj.*

an·ox·i·a (ăn-ŏk′sē-ə) *n.* **1.** Absence of oxygen. **2.** A pathological deficiency of oxygen, especially hypoxia. [AN– + OX(O)– + –IA[1].] **—an·ox′ic** (-ŏk′sĭk) *adj.*

ans. *abbr.* Answer.

an·sate (ăn′sāt′) *adj.* Having a handle or a part resembling a handle. [Latin *ānsātus*, from *ānsa*, handle.]

ansate cross *n.* A cross shaped like a T with a loop at the top; an ankh.

An·schluss (än′shlo͝os′) *n.* A political union, especially the one unifying Nazi Germany and Austria in 1938. [German, annexation, from *anschliessen*, to enclose, annex : *an*, on (from Middle High German *ane*, from Old High German *ana*; see **an-** in Appendix) + *schliessen*, to close (from Middle High German *sliezen*, from Old High German *sliozan*).]

antae

anta
Representative plan of a Greek temple

An·selm (ăn′sĕlm), Saint. 1033–1109. Italian-born English prelate, philosopher, and theologian who founded Scholasticism and is best known for his ontological argument for the existence of God.

an·ser·ine (ăn′sə-rīn′, -rĭn) *adj.* **1.** Of or belonging to the subfamily Anserinae, which comprises the geese. **2.** Of or resembling a goose; gooselike. [Latin *ānserīnus*, pertaining to geese, from *ānser*, goose. See **ghans-** in Appendix.]

An·shan (än′shän′). A city of northeast China south-southwest of Shenyang. It has an enormous integrated iron and steel complex. Population, 1,280,000.

An·so·ni·a (ăn-sō′nē-ə, -sōn′yə). A city of southwest Connecticut west-northwest of New Haven. It was first settled in 1651. Population, 19,039.

an·swer (ăn′sər) *n. Abbr.* **ans., a., A. 1.a.** A spoken or written reply, as to a question. **b.** A correct reply. **2.a.** A solution, as to a problem. **b.** A correct solution. **3.** An act in retaliation or response: *Our only possible answer was to sue.* **4.** Something markedly similar to another of the same class: *cable TV's answer to the commercial networks' sportscasts.* **5.** *Law.* A defendant's defense against charges. **—answer** *v.* **-swered, -swer·ing, -swers.** *—intr.* **1.** To speak, write, or act as a return, as to a question. **2.** To be liable or accountable: *You must answer for your actions.* **3.** To serve the purpose; suffice: *"Often I do use three words where one would answer"* (Mark Twain). **4.** To correspond; match: *I found a dog answering to that description.* *—tr.* **1.** To speak, write, or act as a return to; respond to. **2.** To respond correctly to. **3.** To fulfill the demands or needs of; serve: *"My fortune has answered my desires"* (Isaak Walton). **4.** To conform or correspond to: *The suspect answers the description given by the police.* [Middle English *answere*, from Old English *andswaru*. See **swer-** in Appendix.]

SYNONYMS: *answer, respond, reply, retort.* These verbs relate to action taken in return to a stimulus. *Answer, respond,* and *reply,* the most general, all mean to speak, write, or act in response: *"the attempt to answer questions, without first discovering precisely what question it is which you desire to answer"* (G.E. Moore). *You didn't really expect the President to respond personally to your letter, did you? The opposing team scored three runs; the home team replied with two of their own. Respond* also denotes a reaction to something that stimulates one to a course of action, often voluntary (*A bystander responded immediately to the victim's obvious need for help*), or to an involuntary emotional response (*She responded in spite of herself to the antics of the puppy*). To *retort* is to answer verbally in a quick, caustic, or witty manner: *"You don't need to worry about appearing too intelligent," retorted his opponent.* See also Synonyms at **satisfy.**

an·swer·a·ble (ăn′sər-ə-bəl) *adj.* **1.** Subject to being called to answer; accountable. See Synonyms at **responsible. 2.** That can be answered or refuted: *an answerable charge.* **3.** *Archaic.* **a.** Suitable. **b.** Corresponding. **—an′swer·a·bil′i·ty, an′swer·a·ble·ness** *n.* **—an′swer·a·bly** *adv.*

an·swer·back (ăn′sər-băk′) *n.* A response to a transmission made over a two-way radio.

an·swer·ing machine (ăn′sər-ĭng) *n.* An electrical or electronic device for answering one's telephone and recording callers' messages.

answering service *n.* A business service that answers its clients' telephones and conveys messages to the clients.

ant (ănt) *n.* Any of various social insects of the family Formicidae, characteristically having wings only in the males and fertile females and living in colonies that have a complex social organization. **—*idiom.* ants in (one's) pants.** *Slang.* A state of restless impatience: *"She's got ants in her pants"* (Bobbie Ann Mason). [Middle English *amte*, from Old English *ǣmete*.]

ant. *abbr.* **1.** Antenna. **2.** Antiquarian; antiquary; antiquity. **3.** Antonym.

Ant. *abbr.* Antarctica.

ant– *pref.* Variant of **anti–.**

–ant *suff.* **1.a.** Performing, promoting, or causing a specified action: *acceptant.* **b.** Being in a specified state or condition: *flippant.* **2.a.** One that performs, promotes, or causes a specified action: *deodorant.* **b.** One that undergoes a specified action: *inhalant.* [Middle English, from Old French, from Latin *-āns, -ant-*, present participle suff. of verbs in *-āre*.]

an·ta (ăn′tə) *n., pl.* **-tae** (-tē). *Architecture.* **1.** A thickening of the projecting end of the lateral wall of a Greek temple. **2.** A pier that constitutes one boundary of the porch. [From Latin *antae*, pilasters.]

ant·ac·id (ănt-ăs′ĭd) *adj.* Counteracting or neutralizing acidity, especially of the stomach. **—antacid** *n.* A substance, such as magnesia or sodium bicarbonate, that neutralizes acid.

an·tae (ăn′tē) *n. Architecture.* Plural of **anta.**

an·tag·o·nism (ăn-tăg′ə-nĭz′əm) *n.* **1.** Hostility that results in active resistance, opposition, or contentiousness. See Synonyms at **enmity. 2.** The condition of being an opposing principle, force, or factor: *the inherent antagonism of capitalism and social-ism.* **3.** *Biochemistry.* Interference in the physiological action of a chemical substance by another having a similar structure.

an·tag·o·nist (ăn-tăg′ə-nĭst) *n.* **1.** One who opposes and contends against another; an adversary. See Synonyms at **opponent. 2.** The principal character in opposition to the protagonist or hero of a narrative or drama. **3.** *Physiology.* A muscle that counteracts the action of another muscle, the agonist. **4.** *Biochemistry.* A chemical substance that interferes with the physiological action of another, especially by combining with and blocking its nerve receptor. **—an·tag′o·nis′tic** *adj.* **—an·tag′o·nis′ti·cal·ly** *adv.*

an·tag·o·nize (ăn-tăg′ə-nīz′) *tr.v.* **-nized, -niz·ing, -niz·es. 1.** To incur the dislike of. **2.** To counteract. [Greek *antagōnizesthai*, to struggle against : *anti-*, anti- + *agōnizesthai*, to struggle (from *agōn*, contest; see AGONY).]

An·ta·kya (än-täk′yä). See **Antioch** (sense 2).

An·tal·ya (än-täl′-yä). A city of southwest Turkey on the **Gulf of Antalya,** an inlet of the Mediterranean Sea. The city is situated on a steep cliff and surrounded by an old wall. Population, 173,501.

An·ta·na·na·ri·vo (ăn′tə-năn′ə-rē′vō, än′tə-nä′nə-). Formerly **Ta·nan·a·rive** (tə-năn′ə-rēv′, tä-nä-nä-rēv′). The capital and largest city of Madagascar, in the east-central part of the country. It was founded in the 17th century as a walled citadel. Population, 700,000.

Ant·arc·ti·ca (ănt-ärk′tĭ-kə, -är′tĭ-). *Abbr.* **Ant.** A continent lying chiefly within the Antarctic Circle and asymmetrically centered on the South Pole. Some 95 percent of Antarctica is covered by an icecap averaging 1.6 km (1 mi) in thickness. The region was first explored in the early 1800's, and although there are no permanent settlements, many countries have made territorial claims. The Antarctic Treaty of 1959, signed by 12 nations, prohibited military operations on the continent and provided for the interchange of scientific data. **—Ant·arc′tic** *adj. & n.*

ă pat	oi boy
ā pay	ou out
âr care	o͝o took
ä father	o͞o boot
ĕ pet	ŭ cut
ē be	ûr urge
ĭ pit	th thin
ī pie	*th* this
îr pier	hw which
ŏ pot	zh vision
ō toe	ə about, item
ô paw	♦ regionalism

Stress marks: ′ (primary); ′ (secondary), as in **dictionary** (dĭk′shə-nĕr′ē)

Antarctic Archipelago. See **Palmer Archipelago.**

Antarctic Circle. The parallel of latitude approximately 66°33′ south. It forms the boundary between the South Temperate and South Frigid zones.

Antarctic Ocean. The waters surrounding Antarctica, actually the southern extensions of the Atlantic, Pacific, and Indian oceans.

Antarctic Peninsula also **Palm•er Peninsula** (pä′mər). A region of Antarctica extending about 1,931 km (1,200 mi) north toward South America.

An•tar•es (ăn-târ′ēz, -tăr′-) *n.* A giant, red, double and variable star, the brightest in the constellation Scorpio, about 424 light-years from Earth. [Greek *antarēs* : *anti,* instead of; see ANTI– + *Arēs,* Mars.]

ant bear *n.* A large anteater *(Myrmecophaga jubata),* native to South America and characterized by white stripes that run along both sides of its body.

ant cow *n.* An aphid that yields a honeylike substance on which ants feed.

an•te (ăn′tē) *n.* **1.** *Games.* The stake that each poker player must put into the pool before receiving a hand or before receiving new cards. See Synonyms at **bet. 2.** A price to be paid, especially as one's share; cost: *"Whether they could actually turn back Soviet policy depended on many factors that Moscow might yet choose to test by upping the ante"* (Foreign Affairs). **—ante** *v.* **-ted** or **-teed, -te•ing, -tes.** *—tr.* **1.** *Games.* To put (one's stake) into the pool in poker. **2.** To pay: *Let's ante up the bill. —intr.* To pay up. [From Latin, before. See **ant-** in Appendix.]

ante– *pref.* **1.** Prior to; earlier: *antenatal.* **2.** In front of; before: *anteroom.* [Latin, from *ante,* before. See **ant-** in Appendix.]

ant•eat•er (ănt′ē′tər) *n.* **1.** Any of several tropical American mammals of the family Myrmecophagidae, which lack teeth and feed on ants and termites, especially *Myrmecophaga tridactyla,* having an elongated, narrow snout, a long, sticky tongue, and an extended, shaggy-haired tail. **2.** Any of several other animals, including the echidna, aardvark, and pangolin, that feed on ants.

an•te•bel•lum (ăn′tē-bĕl′əm) *adj.* Belonging to the period before a war, especially the American Civil War. [Latin *ante bellum* : *ante,* before + *bellum,* war.]

an•te•cede (ăn′tĭ-sēd′) *tr.v.* **-ced•ed, -ced•ing, -cedes.** To precede. [Latin *antecēdere* : *ante-,* ante- + *cēdere,* to go; see **ked-** in Appendix.]

an•te•ce•dence (ăn′tĭ-sēd′ns) *n.* Precedence.

an•te•ce•dent (ăn′tĭ-sēd′nt) *adj.* Going before; preceding. **—antecedent** *n.* **1.** One that precedes another. **2. a.** A preceding occurrence, cause, or event. See Synonyms at **cause. b. antecedents.** The important events and occurrences in one's early life. **3. antecedents.** One's ancestors. **4.** *Grammar.* The word, phrase, or clause to which a pronoun refers. **5.** *Mathematics.* The first term of a ratio. **6.** *Logic.* The conditional member of a hypothetical proposition. **—an′te•ce′dent•ly** *adv.*

an•te•cham•ber (ăn′tē-chām′bər) *n.* A smaller room serving as an entryway into a larger room. [French *antichambre* : *anti,* before (from Latin *ante-,* ante-) + *chambre,* chamber (from Old French *chaumbre;* see CHAMBER).]

an•te•choir (ăn′tĭ-kwīr′) *n.* A place in front of the choir reserved for the clergy and choir members.

an•te•date (ăn′tĭ-dāt′) *tr.v.* **-dat•ed, -dat•ing, -dates. 1.** To be of an earlier date than; precede in time. **2. a.** To assign to a date earlier than that of the actual occurrence. **b.** To date as of a time before that of actual execution: *antedate a contract; antedate a check.* **—antedate** *n.* A date given to an event or a document that is earlier than the actual date.

an•te•di•lu•vi•an (ăn′tĭ-də-lo͞o′vē-ən) *adj.* **1.** Extremely old and antiquated. See Synonyms at **old. 2.** Occurring or belonging to the era before the Flood written about in the Bible. [From ANTE– + *dīluvium,* flood; see DILUVIAL.] **—an′te•di•lu′vi•an** *n.*

an•te•fix (ăn′tē-fĭks′) *n., pl.* **-fix•es** or **-fix•a** (-fĭk′sə). *Architecture.* An upright ornament along the eaves of a tiled roof designed to conceal the joints between the rows of tiles. [From Latin *antefīxa,* pl. of *antefīxum,* something fastened in front, from *antefīxus,* fastened in front : *ante-,* ante- + *fīxus,* fastened, past participle of *fīgere,* to fasten; see **dhīgʷ-** in Appendix.] **—an′te•fix′al** *adj.*

an•te•lope (ăn′tl-ōp′) *n., pl.* **antelope** or **-lopes. 1. a.** Any of various swift-running ruminant mammals of the family Bovidae, native to Africa and Asia and having long horns and a slender build. **b.** An animal, such as the pronghorn, that resembles a true antelope. **2.** Leather made from the hide of the African and Asian ruminant. [Middle English, heraldic beast, probably from Old French *antelop,* savage beast with sawlike horns, from Medieval Latin *anthalopus,* from Late Greek *anthalops.*]

an•te•me•rid•i•an (ăn′tē-mə-rĭd′ē-ən) *adj.* Of, relating to, or taking place in the morning. [Latin *antemerīdiānus* : *ante-,* ante- + *merīdiānus,* of noon; see MERIDIAN.]

an•te me•rid•i•em (ăn′tē mə-rĭd′ē-əm) *adv. & adj. Abbr.* **A.M., a.m., A.M.** Before noon. Used chiefly in the abbreviated form to specify the hour: *10:30 A.M.; an A.M. appointment.* [Latin *ante,* before + *merīdiem,* accusative of *merīdiēs,* noon.]

USAGE NOTE: Strictly speaking, *12 A.M.* denotes midnight, and *12 P.M.* denotes noon, but there is sufficient confusion over these uses to make it advisable to use *12 noon* and *12 midnight* where clarity is required.

an•te•mor•tem (ăn′tē-môr′təm) *adj.* Preceding death. [Latin *ante,* before; see ANTE– + *mortem,* accusative of *mors, mort-,* death. See MORTAL.]

an•te•na•tal (ăn′tē-nāt′l) *adj.* Occurring before birth; prenatal: *antenatal diagnostic procedures.* **—an′te•na′tal•ly** *adv.*

anteater

an•ten•na (ăn-tĕn′ə) *n., pl.* **-ten•nae** (-tĕn′ē). *Abbr.* **ant. 1. a.** *Zoology.* One of the paired, flexible, segmented sensory appendages on the head of an insect, a myriapod, or a crustacean functioning primarily as an organ of touch. **b.** Something likened to this sensory appendage, as in function or form: *sensitive public relations antennae.* **2.** *pl.* **-nas.** A metallic apparatus for sending or receiving electromagnetic waves. In this sense, also called *aerial.* [Medieval Latin, from Latin, sail yard, translation of Greek *keraia,* insect feeler, yardarm.] **—an•ten′nal** *adj.*

an•ten•nule (ăn-tĕn′yo͞ol) *n. Zoology.* A small antenna or similar organ, especially one of the first pair of small antennae on the head of a crustacean. [French, diminutive of *antenne,* antenna, from Medieval Latin *antenna,* sail yard. See ANTENNA.]

an•te•pen•di•um (ăn′tē-pĕn′dē-əm) *n., pl.* **-di•a** (-dē-ə). A decorative hanging for the front of an altar, a lectern, or a pulpit. [Medieval Latin : Latin *ante-,* ante- + *pendēre,* to hang; see **(s)pen-** in Appendix.]

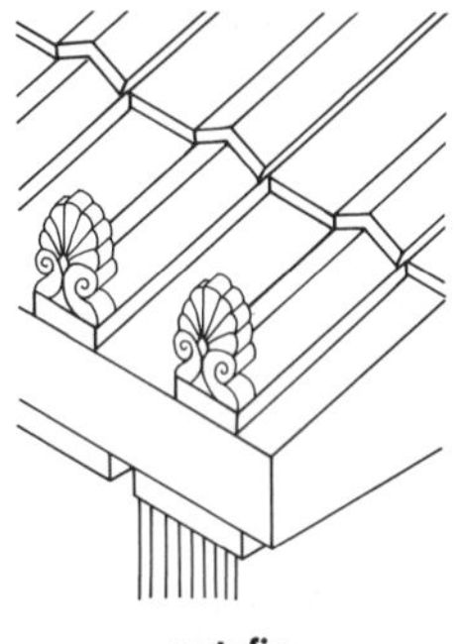

antefix

an•te•pe•nult (ăn′tē-pē′nŭlt′, -pĭ-nŭlt′) *n.* The third syllable from the end in a word, such as *te* in *antepenult.* [Short for Late Latin *antepaenultima,* from feminine of *antepaenultimus,* antepenultimate. See ANTEPENULTIMATE.]

an•te•pe•nul•ti•mate (ăn′tē-pĭ-nŭl′tə-mĭt) *adj.* Coming before the next to the last in a series. **—antepenultimate** *n.* An antepenult. [From Late Latin *antepaenultimus* : Latin *ante-,* ante- + Latin *paenultimus,* next to last; see PENULT.]

an•te•ri•or (ăn-tîr′ē-ər) *adj. Abbr.* **a. 1.** Placed before or in front. **2.** Occurring before in time; earlier. **3.** *Anatomy.* **a.** Located near or toward the head in lower animals. **b.** Located on or near the front of the body in higher animals. **c.** Located on or near the front of an organ or on the ventral surface of the body in human beings. **4.** *Botany.* In front of and facing away from the axis or stem. [Latin, comparative of *ante,* before. See **ant-** in Appendix.] **—an•te′ri•or•ly** *adv.*

An•te•ro (ăn-târ′ō), **Mount.** A peak, 4,352 m (14,269 ft) high, in the Sawatch Mountains of central Colorado.

an•te•room (ăn′tē-ro͞om′, -ro͝om′) *n.* An outer room that opens into another room, often used as a waiting room.

ant•he•li•on (ănt-hē′lē-ən, ăn-thē′-) *n., pl.* **-li•a** (-lē-ə) or **-ons.** A luminous, white, halolike area occasionally seen in the sky opposite the sun on the parhelic circle. [Greek *anthēlion,* from neuter of *anthēlios,* opposite the sun : *anti-,* anti- + *hēlios,* sun; see **sāwel-** in Appendix.]

ant•hel•min•tic (ănt′hĕl-mĭn′tĭk, ăn′thĕl-) also **ant•hel•min•thic** (-thĭk) *—adj.* Acting to expel or destroy parasitic intestinal worms. *—n.* An agent that destroys or causes the expulsion of parasitic intestinal worms. [ANT(I)– + Greek *helmins, helminth-,* worm; see **wel-²** in Appendix.]

anthemion
Detail from the frieze of the Erechtheum in Athens, Greece, showing two anthemions and one palmette

an•them (ăn′thəm) *n.* **1.** A hymn of praise or loyalty. **2.** A sacred composition set to words from the Bible. **3.** A modern ballad accompanied by rock music instrumentation. [Middle English *anteme,* from Old English *antefn,* from Late Latin *antiphōna,* from Late Greek, from neuter pl. of *antiphōnos,* sounding in answer : *anti-,* in return; see ANTI– + *phōnē,* voice; see **bhā-²** in Appendix.]

an•the•mi•on (ăn-thē′mē-ən) *n., pl.* **-mi•a** (-mē-ə). A pattern of honeysuckle or palm leaves in a radiating cluster, used as a motif in Greek art. [Greek, diminutive of *anthemon,* flower, from *anthos.*]

an•ther (ăn′thər) *n. Botany.* The pollen-bearing part of the stamen. [Medieval Latin *anthēra,* pollen, from Latin, a medicine extracted from flowers, from Greek, from feminine of *anthēros,* flowery, from *anthos,* flower.]

an•ther•id•i•um (ăn′thə-rĭd′ē-əm) *n., pl.* **-i•a** (-ē-ə). *Botany.* A sperm-producing organ occurring in seedless plants, fungi, and algae. [New Latin : *anthēra,* anther; see ANTHER + *-idium,* diminutive suff. (from Greek *-idion*).]

an•ther•o•zoid (ăn′thər-ə-zō′ĭd) *n. Botany.* A male gamete produced by an antheridium.

an•the•sis (ăn-thē′sĭs) *n. Botany.* The period during which a flower is fully open and functional. [Greek *anthēsis,* flowering, from *anthein,* to bloom, from *anthos,* flower.]

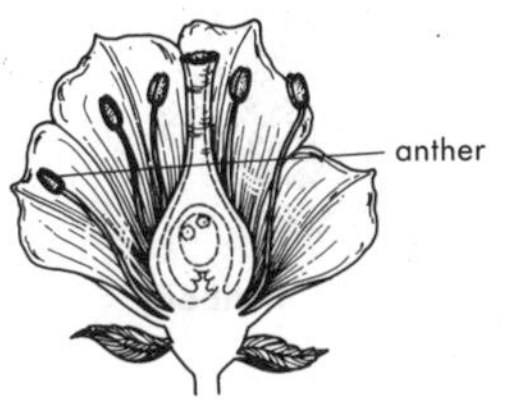

anther

ant•hill (ănt′hĭl′) *n.* A mound of soil, sand, or dirt formed by ants or termites in digging or building a nest.

antho– *pref.* Flower: *anthocyanin.* [Greek, from *anthos,* flower.]

an•tho•cy•a•nin (ăn′thō-sī′ə-nĭn) also **an•tho•cy•an** (-sī′ən, -ăn′) *n.* Any of various water-soluble pigments that impart to flowers and other plant parts colors ranging from violet and blue to most shades of red. [ANTHO– + CYANIN(E).]

an•thol•o•gize (ăn-thŏl′ə-jīz′) *v.* **-gized, -giz•ing, -giz•es.** *—intr.* To compile or publish an anthology. *—tr.* To include (material) in an anthology. **—an•thol′o•gist** *n.*

an•thol•o•gy (ăn-thŏl′ə-jē) *n., pl.* **-gies. 1.** A collection of literary pieces, such as poems, short stories, or plays. **2.** A miscellany, an assortment, or a catalog, as of complaints, comments,

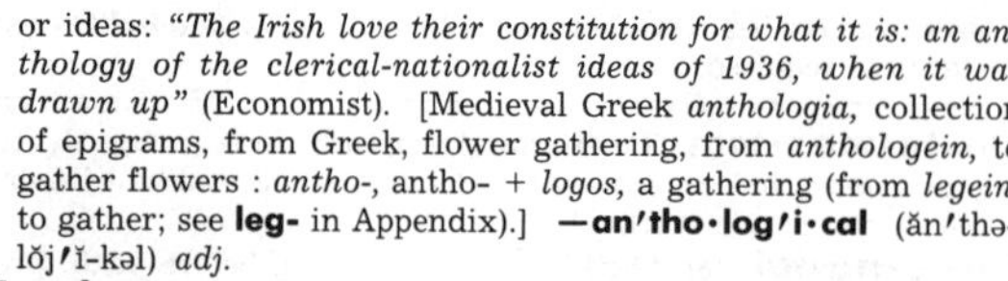
or ideas: *"The Irish love their constitution for what it is: an anthology of the clerical-nationalist ideas of 1936, when it was drawn up"* (Economist). [Medieval Greek *anthologia,* collection of epigrams, from Greek, flower gathering, from *anthologein,* to gather flowers : *antho-,* antho- + *logos,* a gathering (from *legein,* to gather; see **leg-** in Appendix).] **—an′tho·log′i·cal** (ăn′thə-lŏj′ĭ-kəl) *adj.*

Susan B. Anthony
Photographed in 1896 by Theodore C. Marceau (1868?–1922)

An·tho·ny (ăn′thə-nē), Saint. A.D.250?–350? Egyptian ascetic monk considered to be the founder of Christian monasticism.

Anthony, Susan Brownell. 1820–1906. American feminist leader and suffragist who was instrumental in the passage of legislation that gave married women legal rights over their children, property, and wages. In 1869 she cofounded the National Woman Suffrage Association.

Anthony of Pad·u·a (păj′o͞o-ə, păd′yo͞o-ə), Saint. 1195–1231. Portuguese-born Franciscan monk who, according to legend, once preached to an attentive school of fish.

an·tho·zo·an (ăn′thə-zō′ən) *n.* Any of a class (Anthozoa) of marine organisms, such as the corals and sea anemones, that have radial segments and grow singly or in colonies. **—an′tho·zo′an, an′tho·zo′ic** (-zō′ĭk) *adj.*

an·thra·cene (ăn′thrə-sēn′) *n.* A crystalline hydrocarbon, $C_{14}H_{10}$, extracted from coal tar and used in the manufacture of dyes and organic chemicals. [Greek *anthrax, anthrak-,* charcoal + –ENE.]

an·thra·ces (ăn′thrə-sēz′) *n.* Plural of **anthrax** (sense 2).

an·thra·cite (ăn′thrə-sīt′) *n.* A dense, shiny coal that has a high carbon content and little volatile matter and burns with a clean flame. Also called *hard coal.* [Probably ultimately from Greek *anthrakitis,* a kind of coal, from *anthrax, anthrak-,* charcoal.] **—an′thra·cit′ic** (-sĭt′ik) *adj.*

an·thrac·nose (ăn-thrăk′nōs) *n.* Any of several diseases of plants caused by certain fungi and characterized by dead spots on the leaves, twigs, or fruits. [French : Greek *anthrax, anthrak-,* carbuncle + Greek *nosos,* disease.]

an·thra·co·sis (ăn′thrə-kō′sĭs) *n.* See **black lung.** [New Latin : Greek *anthrax, anthrak-,* charcoal + –OSIS.]

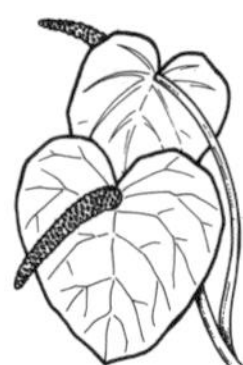

anthurium

an·thrax (ăn′thrăks′) *n.* **1.** An infectious, usually fatal disease of warm-blooded animals, especially of cattle and sheep, caused by the bacterium *Bacillus anthracis.* The disease can be transmitted to human beings through contact with contaminated animal substances, such as hair, feces, or hides, and is characterized by ulcerative skin lesions. **2.** *pl.* **-thra·ces** (-thrə-sēz′) A lesion caused by anthrax. [Middle English *antrax,* malignant boil, from Latin *anthrax,* carbuncle, from Greek.]

anthrop. *abbr.* **1.** Anthropological. **2.** Anthropology.

an·throp·ic (ăn-thrŏp′ĭk) also **an·throp·i·cal** (-ĭ-kəl) *adj.* Of or relating to human beings or the era of human life. [Greek *anthrōpikos,* from *anthrōpos,* human being.]

anthropo– *pref.* Human being: *anthropometry.* [Greek, from *anthrōpos,* human being.]

an·thro·po·cen·tric (ăn′thrə-pə-sĕn′trĭk) *adj.* **1.** Regarding human beings as the central element of the universe. **2.** Interpreting reality exclusively in terms of human values and experience. **—an′thro·po·cen′tri·cal·ly** *adv.* **—an′thro·po·cen′trism** *n.*

an·thro·po·gen·e·sis (ăn′thrə-pə-jĕn′ĭ-sĭs) *n.* The scientific study of the origin and development of human beings. **—an′thro·po·gen′ic** (-jĕn′ĭk) *adj.*

an·thro·poid (ăn′thrə-poid′) *adj.* **1.** Resembling a human being, especially in shape or outward appearance. **2.** Of or belonging to the group of great apes of the family Pongidae, which includes the gorilla, chimpanzee, and orangutan. **3.** Resembling or characteristic of an ape; apelike. **—anthropoid** *n.* An ape of the family Pongidae. Also called *anthropoid ape.* **—an′thro·poid′al** (-poid′l) *adj.*

an·thro·pol·o·gy (ăn′thrə-pŏl′ə-jē) *n. Abbr.* **anthrop. 1.** The scientific study of the origin, the behavior, and the physical, social, and cultural development of human beings. **2.** That part of Christian teaching concerning the genesis, nature, and future of human beings: *"changing the church's anthropology to include more positive images of women"* (Priscilla Hart). **—an′thro·po·log′i·cal** (-pə-lŏj′ĭ-kəl), **an′thro·po·log′ic** (-ĭk) *adj.* **—an′thro·po·log′i·cal·ly** *adv.* **—an′thro·pol′o·gist** *n.*

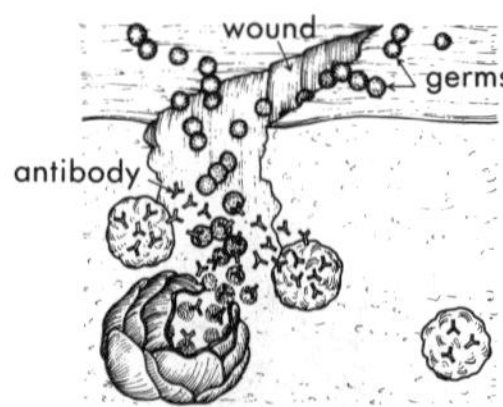

antibody

an·thro·pom·e·try (ăn′thrə-pŏm′ĭ-trē) *n.* The study of human body measurement for use in anthropological classification and comparison. **—an′thro·po·met′ric** (-pə-mĕt′rĭk), **an′thro·po·met′ri·cal** (-rĭ-kəl) *adj.* **—an′thro·po·met′ri·cal·ly** *adv.* **—an′thro·pom′e·trist** *n.*

an·thro·po·mor·phism (ăn′thrə-pə-môr′fĭz′əm) *n.* Attribution of human motivation, characteristics, or behavior to inanimate objects, animals, or natural phenomena. **—an′thro·po·mor′phic** *adj.* **—an′thro·po·mor′phi·cal·ly** *adv.*

an·thro·po·mor·phize (ăn′thrə-pə-môr′fīz′) *v.* **-phized, -phiz·ing, -phiz·es.** *—tr.* To ascribe human characteristics to. *—intr.* To ascribe human characteristics to things not human.

an·thro·po·mor·phous (ăn′thrə-pə-môr′fəs) *adj.* **1.** Having or suggesting human form and appearance. **2.** Ascribing human motivation, characteristics, or behavior to things not human, such as inanimate objects, animals, or natural phenomena.

an·thro·pop·a·thism (ăn′thrə-pŏp′ə-thĭz′əm) *n.* Attribution of human feelings to things not human, such as inanimate objects, animals, or natural phenomena. [Late Greek *anthrōpopathēs,* involved in human suffering (from Greek, having human feelings, from *anthrōpopathein,* to have human feelings : *anthrōpo-,* anthropo- + *pathos,* feeling; see PATHOS) + –ISM.]

an·thro·poph·a·gus (ăn′thrə-pŏf′ə-gəs′) *n., pl.* **-gi** (-jī′). An eater of human flesh; a cannibal. [Latin *anthrōpophagus,* from Greek *anthrōpophagos,* man-eating : *anthrōpo-,* anthropo- + *-phagos,* -phagous.] **—an′thro·po·phag′ic** (-pə-făj′ĭk), **an′thro·poph′a·gous** (-pŏf′ə-gəs) *adj.* **—an′thro·poph′a·gy** (-jē) *n.*

an·thro·pos·o·phy (ăn′thrə-pŏs′ə-fē) *n.* The doctrines and beliefs of a modern religious sect derived from theosophy and claiming to develop knowledge and realization of spiritual reality. [ANTHROPO– + (THEO)SOPHY.] **—an′thro·po·soph′i·cal** (-pə-sŏf′ĭ-kəl) *adj.* **—an′thro·pos′o·phist** *n.*

an·thur·i·um (ăn-tho͝or′ē-əm) *n.* Any of various evergreen tropical American plants of the genus *Anthurium,* grown as ornamentals for their attractive leaves and their showy, often red spathes. [New Latin *Anthurium,* genus name : ANTH(O)– + Greek *oura,* tail; see **ors-** in Appendix.]

an·ti (ăn′tī, -tē) *n., pl.* **-tis.** A person who is opposed to something, such as a group, policy, proposal, or practice. **—anti** *adj.* Opposed: *"Douglas MacArthur had a coterie of worshipers, balanced off by an equal number . . . who were vehemently anti"* (Joseph C. Harsch). **—anti** *prep.* Opposed to; against. [From ANTI–.]

anti– or **ant–** *pref.* **1.a.** Opposite: *antimere.* **b.** Opposing; against: *antiapartheid.* **c.** Counteracting; neutralizing: *antibody.* **2.** Inverse: *antilogarithm.* [Greek, from *anti,* opposite. See **ant-** in Appendix.]

an·ti·a·bor·tion (ăn′tē-ə-bôr′shən, ăn′tī-) *adj.* Opposed to abortion: *the antiabortion movement.* **—an′ti·a·bor′tion·ist** *n.*

an·ti·air·craft (ăn′tē-âr′krăft′, ăn′tī-) *adj. Abbr.* **AA, A.A.** Designed for defense, especially from a surface position, against aircraft or missile attack. **—antiaircraft** *n.* An antiaircraft weapon.

an·ti·al·ler·gic (ăn′tē-ə-lûr′jĭk, ăn′tī-) *adj.* Preventing or relieving allergies.

an·ti-A·mer·i·can (ăn′tē-ə-mĕr′ĭ-kən, ăn′tī-) *adj.* Opposed or hostile to the government, official policies, or people of the United States. **—an′ti-A·mer′i·can·ism** *n.*

an·ti-an·ti·bod·y (ăn′tē-ăn′tĭ-bŏd′ē, ăn′tī-) *n.* An antibody that attacks other antibodies, especially one produced in response to the injection of another antibody.

an·ti·an·xi·e·ty (ăn′tē-ăng-zī′ĭ-tē, ăn′tī-) *adj.* Preventing or reducing anxiety: *an antianxiety drug.*

an·ti·a·part·heid (ăn′tē-ə-pärt′hīt′, -hāt′, ăn′tī-) *adj.* Opposing the system of official racial segregation in South Africa: *antiapartheid activism.*

an·ti·ar·rhyth·mic (ăn′tē-ə-rĭth′mĭk, ăn′tī-) *adj.* Preventing or alleviating irregularities in the force or rhythm of the heart. **—antiarrhythmic** *n.* An antiarrhythmic substance, such as lidocaine.

an·ti-art (ăn′tē-ärt′, ăn′tī-) *n.* Art, specifically Dada, that rejects traditional art forms and theories.

an·ti·at·om (ăn′tē-ăt′əm, ăn′tī-) *n.* An atom composed of antiparticles.

an·ti·bac·ter·i·al (ăn′tē-băk-tîr′ē-əl, ăn′tī-) *adj.* Destroying or inhibiting the growth of bacteria. **—an′ti·bac·ter′i·al** *n.*

an·ti·bal·lis·tic missile (ăn′tĭ-bə-lĭs′tĭk, ăn′tī-) *n.* A defensive missile designed to intercept and destroy a ballistic missile in flight. Also called *ABM.*

an·ti·bar·y·on (ăn′tē-băr′ē-ŏn′, ăn′tī-) *n.* The antiparticle of a baryon.

An·tibes (äɴ-tēb′). A city of southeast France on the Riviera between Nice and Cannes. A seaport and fashionable resort, it is the center of one of Europe's largest flower-growing regions. Population, 62,859.

an·ti·bi·o·sis (ăn′tē-bī-ō′sĭs, ăn′tī-) *n.* **1.** An association between two or more organisms that is detrimental to at least one of them. **2.** The antagonistic association between an organism and the metabolic substances produced by another.

an·ti·bi·ot·ic (ăn′tĭ-bī-ŏt′ĭk, ăn′tī-) *n.* A substance, such as penicillin or streptomycin, produced by or derived from certain fungi, bacteria, and other organisms, that can destroy or inhibit the growth of other microorganisms. Antibiotics are widely used in the prevention and treatment of infectious diseases. **—antibiotic** *adj.* **1.** Of or relating to antibiotics. **2.** Of or relating to antibiosis. **3.** Destroying life or preventing the inception or continuance of life. **—an′ti·bi·ot′i·cal·ly** *adv.*

an·ti-Black or **an·ti-black** (ăn′tē-blăk′, ăn′tī-) *adj.* Hostile or opposed to Black people: *"Many . . . are . . . trying to mitigate their . . . anti-black attitudes . . . by forming a renewed identification with 'blackness' and the ghetto"* (Alvin F. Poussaint).

an·ti·bod·y (ăn′tĭ-bŏd′ē, ăn′tī-) *n.* **1.** A protein substance produced in the blood or tissues in response to a specific antigen, such as a bacterium or a toxin. Antibodies destroy or weaken bacteria and neutralize organic poisons, thus forming the basis of immunity. **2.** An object composed of antimatter.

an·ti·busi·ness (ăn′tē-bĭz′nĭs, ăn′tī-) *adj.* Hostile to business, especially to big corporations.

an·ti·bus·ing (ăn′tē-bŭs′ĭng, ăn′tī-) *adj.* Opposed to the busing of students as a means of achieving racial balance in public schools.

an·tic (ăn′tĭk) *n.* **1.** A ludicrous or extravagant act or gesture; a caper. **2.** *Archaic.* A buffoon, especially a performing clown. —**antic** *adj.* Ludicrously odd; fantastic. [From Italian *antico,* ancient (used of grotesque designs on some ancient Roman artifacts), from Latin *antīquus,* former, old. See **ant-** in Appendix.] —**an′ti·cal·ly** *adv.*

an·ti·can·cer (ăn′tī-kăn′sər, ăn′tī-) also **an·ti·can·cer·ous** (-sər-əs) *adj.* Effective in treating cancer: *anticancer drugs.*

an·ti·cat·a·lyst (ăn′tē-kăt′l-ĭst, ăn′tī-) *n.* **1.** A substance that retards or arrests a chemical reaction. **2.** A substance that reduces or destroys the effectiveness of a catalyst.

an·ti·cath·ode (ăn′tē-kăth′ōd′, ăn′tī-) *n.* An electrode that is the target in a cathode-ray tube, especially in an x-ray tube.

an·ti·chlor (ăn′tĭ-klôr′, -klōr′, ăn′tī-) *n.* A substance, such as sodium thiosulfate, used to neutralize the excess chlorine or hypochlorite left after bleaching textiles, fiber, or paper pulp. [ANTI– + CHLOR(INE).] —**an′ti·chlo·ris′tic** (-klə-rĭs′tĭk) *adj.*

an·ti-choice (ăn′tē-chois′, ăn′tī-) *adj.* Opposed to the right of women to choose or reject abortion.

an·ti·cho·lin·er·gic (ăn′tē-kō′lə-nûr′jĭk, ăn′tī-) *adj.* Inhibiting or blocking the physiological action of acetylcholine at a receptor site: *anticholinergic drugs.* —**an′ti·cho′lin·er′gic** *n.*

an·ti·cho·lin·es·ter·ase (ăn′tē-kō′lə-nĕs′tə-rās′, -rāz′, ăn′tī-) *n.* A substance that inhibits the activity of cholinesterase.

an·ti·christ (ăn′tĭ-krīst′, ăn′tī-) *n.* **1.** An enemy of Christ. **2.** **Antichrist.** The epithet of the great antagonist who was expected by the early Church to set himself up against Christ in the last days before the Second Coming. **3.** A false Christ. [Middle English *Antecrist,* from Old French and from Old English, both from Late Latin *Antichrīstus,* from Late Greek *Antikhristos* : Greek *anti-,* anti- + Greek *Khristos,* Christ; see CHRIST.]

an·tic·i·pant (ăn-tĭs′ə-pənt) *adj.* **1.** Coming or acting in advance: *clouds anticipant of a storm.* **2.** Expectant; anticipating: *a team anticipant of victory.* —**anticipant** *n.* One who anticipates.

an·tic·i·pate (ăn-tĭs′ə-pāt′) *tr.v.* **-pat·ed, -pat·ing, -pates.** **1.** To feel or realize beforehand; foresee. **2.** To look forward to, especially with pleasure; expect. **3.** To act in advance so as to prevent; forestall. **4.** To foresee and fulfill in advance. See Synonyms at **expect.** **5.** To cause to happen in advance; accelerate. **6.** To use in advance, as income not yet available. **7.** To pay (a debt) before it is due. [Latin *anticipāre, anticipāt-,* to take before : *ante-,* ante- + *capere,* to take; see **kap-** in Appendix.] —**an·tic′i·pat′a·ble** *adj.* —**an·tic′i·pa′tor** *n.* —**an·tic′i·pa·to′ry** (-pə-tôr′ē, -tōr′ē) *adj.*

USAGE NOTE: Some people hold that *anticipate* is improperly used as a simple synonym for *expect;* they would restrict its use to situations in which advance action is taken either to forestall (*anticipate her opponent's next move*) or to fulfill (*anticipate my desires*). In earlier surveys, however, a majority of the Usage Panel accepted the use of *anticipate* to mean "to feel or to realize beforehand" and "to look forward to." The word *unanticipated,* however, is not established as a synonym for *unexpected.* Thus 77 percent of the Usage Panel rejected the sentence *They always set aside a little extra food for unanticipated guests,* inasmuch as guests for whom advance provision has been made cannot be said to be unanticipated, though they may very well be unexpected.

an·tic·i·pa·tion (ăn-tĭs′ə-pā′shən) *n.* **1.** The act of anticipating. **2.** An expectation. **3.** Foreknowledge, intuition, and presentiment. **4.** The use or assignment of funds, especially from a trust fund, before they are legitimately available for use. **5.** *Music.* Introduction of one note of a new chord before the previous chord is resolved.

an·tic·i·pa·tive (ăn-tĭs′ə-pā′tĭv, -pə-tĭv) *adj.* Expectant. —**an·tic′i·pa′tive·ly** *adv.*

an·ti·cit·y (ăn′tē-sĭt′ē, ăn′tī-) *adj.* Hostile to cities and urban environments: *anticity development trends.*

an·ti·cler·i·cal (ăn′tē-klĕr′ĭ-kəl, ăn′tī-) *adj.* Opposed to the influence of the church or the clergy in political affairs. —**an′ti·cler′i·cal·ism** *n.*

an·ti·cli·max (ăn′tē-klī′măks′, ăn′tī-) *n.* **1.** A decline viewed in disappointing contrast with a previous rise: *the anticlimax of a brilliant career.* **2.** Something trivial or commonplace that concludes a series of significant events: *After a week of dramatic negotiations, all that followed was anticlimax.* **3.** A sudden descent in speaking or writing from the impressive or significant to the ludicrous or inconsequential, or an instance of it: *"Waggish non-Yale men never seem weary of calling 'for God, for Country and for Yale' the outstanding single anticlimax in the English language"* (Time). —**an′ti·cli·mac′tic** (-klī-măk′tĭk) *adj.* —**an′ti·cli·mac′ti·cal·ly** *adv.*

an·ti·cli·nal (ăn′tē-klī′nəl, ăn′tī-) *adj.* **1.** Sloping downward in opposite directions, as in an anticline. **2.** *Botany.* Of or relating to the plane of a cell division perpendicular to the surface of a plant organ.

an·ti·cline (ăn′tĭ-klīn′) *n. Geology.* A fold with strata sloping downward on both sides from a common crest.

an·ti·clock·wise (ăn′tē-klŏk′wīz, ăn′tī-) *adv. & adj.* Counterclockwise.

an·ti·co·ag·u·lant (ăn′tē-kō-ăg′yə-lənt, ăn′tī-) *n.* A substance that prevents the clotting of blood. —**anticoagulant** *adj.* Acting as an anticoagulant.

an·ti·co·don (ăn′tē-kō′dŏn, ăn′tī-) *n.* A sequence of three adjacent nucleotides in transfer RNA designating a specific amino acid that binds to a corresponding codon in messenger RNA during protein synthesis.

an·ti·col·li·sion also **an·ti·col·li·sion** (ăn′tē-kə-lĭzh′ən, ăn′tī-) *adj.* Serving to prevent midair collisions: *aircraft anticollision devices.*

an·ti·com·pet·i·tive (ăn′tē-kəm-pĕt′ĭ-tĭv, ăn′tī-) *adj.* That discourages competition among businesses: *anticompetitive foreign trade restrictions.*

an·ti·con·vul·sant (ăn′tē-kən-vŭl′sənt, ăn′tī-) *n.* A drug that prevents or relieves convulsions. —**an′ti·con·vul′sive** (-sĭv) *adj.*

An·ti·cos·ti (ăn′tĭ-kô′stē, -kŏs′tē). An island of eastern Quebec, Canada, at the head of the Gulf of St. Lawrence. It was discovered by Jacques Cartier in 1534.

an·ti·crime (ăn′tē-krīm′, ăn′tī-) *adj.* Intended to curb or eradicate criminal activity: *an anticrime bill; anticrime efforts in the neighborhoods.*

an·ti·cy·clone (ăn′tē-sī′klōn′, ăn′tī-) *n.* An extensive system of winds spiraling outward from a high-pressure center, circling clockwise in the Northern Hemisphere and counterclockwise in the Southern Hemisphere. —**an′ti·cy·clon′ic** (-klŏn′ĭk) *adj.*

an·ti·de·pres·sant (ăn′tē-dĭ-prĕs′ənt, ăn′tī-) *n.* A drug used to prevent or relieve mental depression. —**an′ti·de·pres′sive** (-prĕs′ĭv) *adj.*

an·ti·deu·ter·on (ăn′tē-do͞o′tə-rŏn′, -dyo͞o′-, ăn′tī-) *n.* The antimatter equivalent of deuteron.

an·ti·di·ar·rhe·al (ăn′tē-dī′ə-rē′əl, an′tī-) *n.* A substance used to prevent or treat diarrhea. —**an′ti·di′ar·rhe′al** *adj.*

an·ti·di·u·ret·ic hormone (ăn′tē-dī′ə-rĕt′ĭk, ăn′tī-) *n. Abbr.* **ADH** See **vasopressin.**

an·ti·dote (ăn′tĭ-dōt′) *n.* **1.** A remedy or other agent used to neutralize or counteract the effects of a poison. **2.** An agent that relieves or counteracts: *jogging as an antidote to nervous tension.* [Middle English, from Latin *antidotum,* from Greek *antidoton,* from *antididonai,* to give as a remedy against : *anti-,* anti- + *didonai, do-,* to give; see **dō-** in Appendix.] —**an′ti·dot′al** (ăn′tĭ-dōt′l) *adj.* —**an′ti·dot′al·ly** *adv.*

USAGE NOTE: *Antidote* may be followed by *to, for,* or *against: an antidote to boredom; an antidote for snakebite; an antidote against inflation.*

an·ti·dump·ing (ăn′tē-dŭm′pĭng, ăn′tī-) *adj.* Intended to discourage importation and sale of foreign-made goods at prices substantially below domestic prices for the same items.

an·ti·e·lec·tron (ăn′tē-ĭ-lĕk′trŏn′, ăn′tī-) *n.* See **positron.**

an·ti·en·zyme (ăn′tē-ĕn′zīm′, ăn′tī-) *n.* A substance that neutralizes or counteracts the actions of an enzyme. —**an′ti·en′zy·mat′ic** (-zī-măt′ĭk, -zĭ-), **an′ti·en·zy′mic** (-zī′mĭk) *adj.*

an·ti·es·tab·lish·ment (ăn′tē-ĭ-stăb′lĭsh-mənt, ăn′tī-) *adj.* Marked by opposition or hostility to conventional social, political, or economic values or principles.

An·tie·tam (ăn-tē′təm). A creek of north-central Maryland emptying into the Potomac River. The bloody and inconclusive Civil War Battle of Antietam (or Sharpsburg, as it is often called in the South) was fought along its banks on September 17, 1862.

an·ti·feb·rile (ăn′tē-fĕb′rəl, -fē′brəl, -brĭl′, ăn′tī-) *adj.* Capable of reducing fever; antipyretic. —**antifebrile** *n.* An agent that reduces fever.

an·ti·fed·er·al·ist also **An·ti·fed·er·al·ist** (ăn′tē-fĕd′ər-ə-lĭst, -fĕd′rə-lĭst, ăn′tī-) *n.* An opponent of the ratification of the U.S. Constitution. —**an′ti·fed′er·al·ist** *adj.* —**an′ti·fed′er·al·ism** *n.*

an·ti·fem·i·nist (ăn′tē-fĕm′ə-nĭst, ăn′tī-) *adj.* Characterized by ideas or behavior reflecting a disbelief in the economic, political, and social equality of the sexes. —**an′ti·fem′i·nism** *n.* —**an′ti·fem′i·nist** *n.*

an·ti·fer·til·i·ty (ăn′tē-fər-tĭl′ĭ-tē, ăn′tī-) *adj.* Capable of reducing or eliminating fertility; contraceptive.

an·ti·fluor·i·da·tion·ist (ăn′tē-flo͝or′ĭ-dā′shə-nĭst, -flôr′-, -flōr′-, ăn′tī-) *n.* One who is strongly opposed to the fluoridation of public water supplies.

an·ti·foul·ing paint (ăn′tē-fou′lĭng, ăn′tī-) *n.* Paint that counteracts or prevents the fouling of underwater surfaces, such as the undersides of boats.

an·ti·freeze (ăn′tĭ-frēz′) *n.* A substance, often a liquid such as ethylene glycol or alcohol, mixed with another liquid to lower its freezing point.

an·ti·fun·gal (ăn′tē-fŭng′gəl, ăn′tī-) *adj.* Destroying or inhibiting the growth of fungi. —**an′ti·fun′gal** *n.*

an·ti·gal·ax·y (ăn′tē-găl′ək-sē, ăn′tī-) *n.* A galaxy that is made up of antimatter.

an·ti·gen (ăn′tĭ-jən) also **an·ti·gene** (-jēn′) *n.* A substance that when introduced into the body stimulates the production of an antibody. Antigens include toxins, bacteria, foreign blood cells, and the cells of transplanted organs. —**an′ti·gen′ic** (-jĕn′ĭk) *adj.* —**an′ti·gen′i·cal·ly** *adv.* —**an′ti·ge·nic′i·ty** (-jə-nĭs′ĭ-tē) *n.*

anticipation
Harmonic anticipation

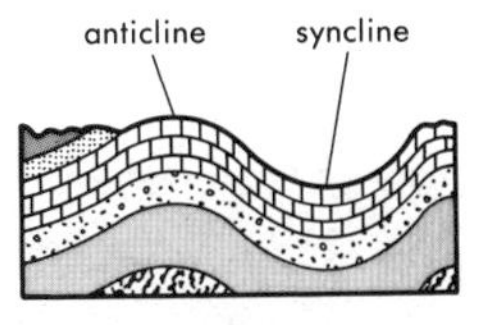

anticline

ă pat	oi boy
ā pay	ou out
âr care	o͝o took
ä father	o͞o boot
ĕ pet	ŭ cut
ē be	ûr urge
ĭ pit	th thin
ī pie	*th* this
îr pier	hw which
ŏ pot	zh vision
ō toe	ə about, item
ô paw	♦ regionalism

Stress marks: ′ (primary); ′ (secondary), as in **dictionary** (dĭk′shə-nĕr′ē)

An·tig·o·ne (ăn-tĭg′ə-nē) *n. Greek Mythology.* The daughter of Oedipus and Jocasta. She performed funeral rites over her brother's body in defiance of her uncle Creon.

An·tig·o·nus I (ăn-tĭg′ə-nəs). 382–301 B.C. King of Macedonia (306–301). One of Alexander III's generals, he tried to gain sole control of Asia after Alexander's death but was killed in battle.

an·ti·grav·i·ty (ăn′tē-grăv′ĭ-tē, ăn′tī-) *n.* The hypothetical effect of reducing or canceling a gravitational field. **—an′ti·grav′i·ty** *adj.*

an·ti·green·mail (ăn′tē-grēn′māl′, ăn′tī-) *adj.* Intended to counteract greenmail: *antigreenmail strategies; antigreenmail legislation.*

An·ti·gua and Bar·bu·da (ăn-tē′gə; bär-bo͞o′də). A country in the northern Leeward Islands of the Caribbean Sea, comprising the island of Antigua and the smaller islands of Barbuda and Redonda. The country became independent in 1981. St. John's is the capital. Population, 72,000. **—An·ti′guan** *adj. & n.*

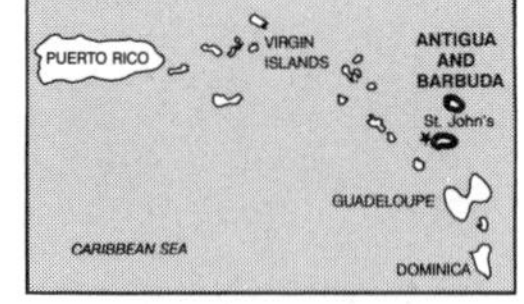

Antigua and Barbuda

an·ti·he·li·um (ăn′tē-hē′lē-əm, ăn′tī-) *n.* The antimatter equivalent of helium.

an·ti·he·mo·phil·ic factor (ăn′tē-hē′mə-fĭl′ĭk, ăn′tī-) *n. Abbr.* **AHF** A protein substance in blood plasma that participates in and is essential for the blood-clotting process. Most cases of hemophilia are caused by a deficiency of this factor. Also called *antihemophilic globulin, factor VIII.*

an·ti·he·ro also **an·ti-he·ro** (ăn′tē-hîr′ō, ăn′tī-) *n., pl.* **-roes.** A main character in a dramatic or narrative work who is characterized by a lack of traditional heroic qualities, such as idealism or courage. **—an′ti·her·o′ic** (-hĭ-rō′ĭk) *adj.* **—an′ti·her′o·ism** (-hĕr′ō-ĭz′əm) *n.*

an·ti·her·o·ine or **an·ti-her·o·ine** (ăn′tē-hĕr′ō-ĭn, ăn′tī-) *n.* **1.** A woman protagonist, as in a play or book, characterized by a lack of traditional heroic qualities. **2.** A woman protagonist whose character and behavior are contrary to those of the traditional heroine.

an·ti·his·ta·mine (ăn′tē-hĭs′tə-mēn′, -mĭn) *n.* A drug used to counteract the physiological effects of histamine production in allergic reactions and colds. **—an′ti·his′ta·min′ic** (-mĭn′ĭk) *adj.*

an·ti·hy·dro·gen (ăn′tē-hī′drə-jən, ăn′tī-) *n.* The antimatter equivalent of hydrogen.

an·ti·hy·per·ten·sive (ăn′tē-hī′pər-tĕn′sĭv, an′tī-) *adj.* Reducing or controlling high blood pressure. **—an′ti·hy′per·ten′sive** *n.*

an·ti-in·fec·tive (ăn′tē-ĭn-fĕk′tĭv, ăn′tī-) *adj.* Capable of preventing or counteracting infection: *an anti-infective agent.* **—an′ti-in·fec′tive** *n.*

an·ti-in·flam·ma·to·ry (ăn′tē-ĭn-flăm′ə-tôr′ē, -tōr′ē, ăn′tī-) *adj.* Preventing or reducing inflammation. **—an′ti-in·flam′ma·to′ry** *n.*

an·ti-in·tel·lec·tu·al (ăn′tē-ĭn′tl-ĕk′cho͞o-əl, ăn′tī-) *adj.* Opposed or hostile to intellectuals or intellectual views. **—an′-ti-in′tel·lec′tu·al** *n.* **—an′ti-in′tel·lec′tu·al·ism** *n.*

an·ti·knock (ăn′tī-nŏk′) *n.* A substance, such as tetraethyl lead, added to gasoline to reduce engine knock.

An·ti-Leb·a·non Range (ăn′tē-lĕb′ə-nən). A mountain range on the Syria-Lebanon border, rising to 2,815.8 m (9,232 ft) at Mount Hermon.

an·ti·lep·ton (ăn′tē-lĕp′tŏn, ăn′tī-) *n.* The antiparticle of a lepton.

An·til·les (ăn-tĭl′ēz). The islands of the West Indies except for the Bahamas, separating the Caribbean Sea from the Atlantic Ocean and divided into the **Greater Antilles** to the north and the **Lesser Antilles** to the east.

an·ti·log (ăn′tē-lôg′, -lŏg′, ăn′tī-) *n.* An antilogarithm.

an·ti·log·a·rithm (ăn′tē-lô′gə-rĭth′əm, -lŏg′ə-, ăn′tī-) *n.* The number for which a given logarithm stands; for example, where log x equals y, the x is the antilogarithm of y. **—an′ti·log′a·rith′mic** *adj.*

an·ti·ma·cas·sar (ăn′tē-mə-kăs′ər) *n.* A protective covering for the backs of chairs and sofas. [ANTI– + *Macassar,* a brand of hair oil.]

an·ti·mag·net·ic (ăn′tē-măg-nĕt′ĭk, ăn′tī-) *adj.* Impervious to the effect of a magnetic field; resistant to magnetization.

an·ti·ma·lar·i·al (ăn′tē-mə-lâr′ē-əl, ăn′tī-) *adj.* Preventing or relieving the symptoms of malaria. **—antimalarial** *n.* A drug used to treat malaria.

antimissile missile
U.S. Hawk missiles

an·ti·mat·ter (ăn′tī-măt′ər, ăn′tī-) *n.* A hypothetical form of matter that is identical to physical matter except that its atoms are composed of antielectrons, antiprotons, and antineutrons.

an·ti·mere (ăn′tĭ-mîr′) *n. Zoology.* A part or division in the body of a bilaterally or radially symmetric animal that corresponds to an opposite or similar part. **—an′ti·mer′ic** (-mĕr′ĭk) *adj.*

an·ti·me·tab·o·lite (ăn′tē-mĭ-tăb′ə-līt′, ăn′tī-) *n.* A substance that closely resembles an essential metabolite and therefore interferes with physiological reactions involving it.

an·ti·mi·cro·bi·al (ăn′tē-mī-krō′bē-əl, ăn′tī-) also **an·ti·mi·cro·bic** (-bĭk) *adj.* Capable of destroying or inhibiting the growth of microorganisms: *antimicrobial drugs.* **—an′ti·mi·cro′bial** *n.*

an·ti·mis·sile missile (ăn′tē-mĭs′əl, ăn′tī-) *n.* A missile designed to intercept and destroy another missile in flight.

an·ti·mi·tot·ic (ăn′tē-mī-tŏt′ĭk, ăn′tī-) *adj.* Preventing or interfering with mitosis: *an antimitotic drug.* **—an′ti·mi·tot′ic** *n.*

an·ti·mo·ni·al (ăn′tə-mō′nē-əl) *adj.* Of or containing antimony. **—antimonial** *n.* A medicine containing antimony.

an·ti·mo·ny (ăn′tə-mō′nē) *n. Symbol* **Sb** A metallic element having four allotropic forms, the most common of which is a hard, extremely brittle, lustrous, silver-white, crystalline material. It is used in a wide variety of alloys, especially with lead in battery plates, and in the manufacture of flame-proofing compounds, paint, semiconductor devices, and ceramic products. Atomic number 51; atomic weight 121.75; melting point 630.5°C; boiling point 1,380°C; specific gravity 6.691; valence 3, 5. See table at **element.** [Middle English *antimonie,* from Medieval Latin *antimōnium,* perhaps from Arabic *al-'iṯmid,* perhaps from Greek *stimmi.*]

an·ti·ne·o·plas·tic (ăn′tē-nē′ə-plăs′tĭk, ăn′tī-) *adj.* Inhibiting or preventing the growth or development of malignant cells. **—an′ti·ne′o·plas′tic** *n.*

an·ti·neu·tri·no (ăn′tē-no͞o-trē′nō, -nyo͞o-, ăn′tī-) *n., pl.* **-nos.** The antiparticle of the neutrino.

an·ti·neu·tron (ăn′tē-no͞o′trŏn′, -nyo͞o′-, ăn′tī-) *n.* The antiparticle of the neutron.

an·ti·node (ăn′tĭ-nōd′) *n.* For a standing wave, the region or point of maximum amplitude between adjacent nodes.

an·ti·noise (ăn′tē-noiz′, ăn′tī-) *adj.* Designed to reduce environmental noise, as in a community: *an antinoise ordinance.*

an·ti·nome (ăn′tə-nōm′) *n.* One that is contradictory or contrary to another; an opposite. [ANTI– + Greek *nomos,* law; see ANTINOMY.]

an·ti·no·mi·an (ăn′tĭ-nō′mē-ən) *n.* An adherent of antinomianism. **—antinomian** *adj.* **1.** Of or relating to the doctrine of antinomianism. **2.** Opposed to or denying the fixed meaning or universal applicability of moral law: *"By raising segregation and racial persecution to the ethical level of law, it puts into practice the antinomian rules of Orwell's world. Evil becomes good, inhumanity is interpreted as charity, egoism as compassion"* (Elie Wiesel). [From Medieval Latin *Antinomī,* antinomians, pl. of *antinomus,* opposed to the moral law : Greek *anti-,* anti- + Greek *nomos,* law; see **nem-** in Appendix.]

an·ti·no·mi·an·ism (ăn′tĭ-nō′mē-ə-nĭz′əm) *n.* **1.** *Theology.* The doctrine or belief that the Gospel frees Christians from required obedience to any law, whether scriptural, civil, or moral, and that salvation is attained solely through faith and the gift of divine grace. **2.** The belief that moral laws are relative in meaning and application as opposed to fixed or universal.

an·tin·o·my (ăn-tĭn′ə-mē) *n., pl.* **-mies. 1.** Contradiction or opposition, especially between two laws or rules. **2.** A contradiction between principles or conclusions that seem equally necessary and reasonable; a paradox. [Latin *antinomia,* from Greek : *anti-,* anti- + *nomos,* law; see **nem-** in Appendix.] **—an′ti·nom′ic** (ăn′tĭ-nŏm′ĭk) *adj.*

an·ti·nov·el also **an·ti-nov·el** (ăn′tē-nŏv′əl, ăn′tī-) *n.* A fictional work characterized by the absence of traditional elements of the novel, such as coherent plot structure, consistent point of view, and realistic character portrayal. **—an′ti·nov′el·ist** *n.*

an·ti·nu·cle·ar (ăn′tē-no͞o′klē-ər, -nyo͞o′-, ăn′tī-) *adj.* **1.** Opposing the production or use of nuclear power or nuclear weaponry; anti-nuke. **2.** Reacting with the components of a cell nucleus: *antinuclear antibodies.*

an·ti·nu·cle·on (ăn′tē-no͞o′klē-ŏn′, -nyo͞o′-, ăn′tī-) *n.* The antiparticle of a nucleon.

an·ti-nuke or **an·ti·nuke** (ăn′tē-no͞ok′, -nyo͞ok′, ăn′tī-) *adj.* Antinuclear. **—an′ti-nuk′er** *n.*

An·ti·och (ăn′tē-ŏk′). **1.** An ancient town of Phrygia north of present-day Antalya, Turkey. It was a center of Hellenistic influence and was visited by Saint Paul in biblical times. **2.** Also **An·ta·kya** (än-täk′yä). A city of southern Turkey on the Orontes River near the Mediterranean Sea. Founded c. 300 B.C. by Seleucus I, it was an important military and commercial center in the Roman era and an early center of Christianity. Population, 94,942. **3.** A city of western California northeast of Oakland on the San Joaquin River near the mouth of the Sacramento River. It is a processing and shipping center. Population, 42,683.

An·ti·o·chus (ăn-tī′ə-kəs). A Seleucid dynasty ruling in Syria (280–64 B.C.). Its most important member was **Antiochus III,** known as "the Great" (242–187, ruled 223–187), who conquered much of Asia Minor but was defeated by the Romans in 190.

an·ti·ox·i·dant (ăn′tē-ŏk′sĭ-dənt, ăn′tī-) *n.* A chemical compound or substance that inhibits oxidation.

an·ti·par·a·sit·ic (ăn′tē-păr′ə-sĭt′ĭk, ăn′tī-) *adj.* Destroying or inhibiting the growth and reproduction of human or animal parasites. **—an′ti·par′a·sit′ic** *n.*

an·ti·par·ti·cle (ăn′tē-pär′tĭ-kəl, ăn′tī-) *n.* A subatomic particle, such as a positron, an antiproton, or an antineutron, having the same mass, average lifetime, spin, magnitude of magnetic moment, and magnitude of electric charge as the particle to which it corresponds but having the opposite sign of electric charge, opposite intrinsic parity, and opposite direction of magnetic moment. See table at **subatomic particle.**

an·ti·pas·to (än′tē-päs′tō) *n., pl.* **-tos** or **-ti** (-tē). An appetizer usually consisting of an assortment of ingredients, such as smoked meats, cheese, fish, and vegetables. [Italian : *anti-*, before (from Latin *ante-*; see ANTE–) + *pasto*, food (from Latin *pastus*, past participle of *pāscere*, to feed; see **pā-** in Appendix).]

An·tip·a·ter (ăn-tĭp′ə-tər). 398?–319 B.C. Macedonian general and regent (334–323) who governed the empire during Alexander III's military campaigns. He served again as regent in 321 to 319.

an·tip·a·thet·ic (ăn-tĭp′ə-thĕt′ĭk) also **an·tip·a·thet·i·cal** (-ĭ-kəl) *adj.* **1.a.** Having or showing a strong aversion or repugnance: *antipathetic to new ideas.* **b.** Opposed in nature or character; antagonistic: *antipathetic factions within the party.* **2.** Causing a feeling of antipathy; repugnant: *"The whole place and everything about it was antipathetic to her"* (Anthony Trollope). —**an·tip′a·thet′i·cal·ly** *adv.*

an·tip·a·thy (ăn-tĭp′ə-thē) *n., pl.* **-thies. 1.** A strong feeling of aversion or repugnance. See Synonyms at **enmity. 2.** An object of aversion. [Latin *antipathīa*, from Greek *antipatheia*, from *antipathēs*, of opposite feelings : *anti-*, anti- + *pathos*, feeling; see PATHOS.]

an·ti·pe·ri·od·ic (ăn′tē-pîr′ē-ŏd′ĭk, ăn′tī-) *adj.* Preventing regular recurrence of the symptoms of a disease, as in malaria. —**an′ti·pe′ri·od′ic** *n.*

an·ti·per·son·nel (ăn′tē-pûr′sə-nĕl′, ăn′tī-) *adj. Abbr.* **AP** Designed to inflict death or bodily injury rather than material destruction: *antipersonnel grenades.*

an·ti·per·spi·rant (ăn′tē-pûr′spər-ənt, ăn′tī-) *n.* An astringent preparation applied to the skin to decrease perspiration. —**an′ti·per′spi·rant** *adj.*

an·ti·phlo·gis·tic (ăn′tē-flə-jĭs′tĭk, ăn′tī-) *adj.* Reducing inflammation or fever. —**an′ti·phlo·gis′tic** *n.*

an·ti·phon (ăn′tə-fŏn′) *n.* **1.** A devotional composition sung responsively as part of a liturgy. **2.a.** A short liturgical text chanted or sung responsively preceding or following a psalm, psalm verse, or canticle. **b.** Such a text formerly used as a response but now rendered independently. **3.** A response; a reply: *"It would be truer . . . to see* [conservation] *as an antiphon to the modernization of the 1950s and 1960s"* (Raphael Samuel). [Late Latin *antiphōna*, sung responses. See ANTHEM.]

an·tiph·o·nal (ăn-tĭf′ə-nəl) *adj.* **1.** Relating to or resembling an antiphon. **2.** Answering responsively, as in antiphony. **3.** Occurring or responding in turns; alternating: *"this curious antiphonal relationship between the two men"* (Henry A. Kissinger). —**antiphonal** *n.* An antiphonary. —**an·tiph′o·nal·ly** *adv.*

an·tiph·o·nar·y (ăn-tĭf′ə-nĕr′ē) *n., pl.* **-ies.** A bound collection of antiphons, especially of the responsive choral parts of the Divine Office.

an·tiph·o·ny (ăn-tĭf′ə-nē) *n., pl.* **-nies. 1.** Responsive or antiphonal singing or chanting. **2.** A composition that is sung responsively; an antiphon. **3.** A responsive or reciprocal interchange, as of ideas or opinions: *"Sheridan's play shows both sides of the coin. He establishes an antiphony of cynicism and sentimentality"* (Jonathan Miller).

an·tiph·ra·sis (ăn-tĭf′rə-sĭs) *n.* The use of a word or phrase in a sense contrary to its normal meaning for ironic or humorous effect, as in *a mere babe of 40 years.* [Late Latin, from Greek, from *antiphrazein*, to express by the opposite : *anti-*, anti- + *phrazein*, to speak; see PHRASE.]

an·tip·o·dal (ăn-tĭp′ə-dəl) *adj.* **1.** Of, relating to, or situated on the opposite side or sides of the earth: *Australia and Great Britain occupy antipodal regions.* **2.** Diametrically opposed; exactly opposite.

an·ti·pode (ăn′tĭ-pōd′) *n.* A direct or diametrical opposite: *"We just sit and listen to the fullness of the quiet, as an antipode to focused busyness"* (Kathryn A. Knox). [Back-formation from ANTIPODES.]

an·tip·o·des (ăn-tĭp′ə-dēz′) *pl.n.* **1.** Any two places or regions that are on diametrically opposite sides of the earth. **2.** *(used with a sing. or pl. verb).* Something that is the exact opposite or contrary of another; an antipode. [Middle English, people with feet opposite ours, from Latin, from Greek, from pl. of *antipous*, with the feet opposite : *anti-*, anti- + *pous, pod-*, foot; see **ped-** in Appendix.] —**an·tip′o·de′an** *adj.*

An·tip·o·des (ăn-tĭp′ə-dēz′). **1.** Australia and New Zealand. Usually used informally. **2.** A group of rocky islands of the southern Pacific Ocean southeast of New Zealand, to which they belong. They were discovered by British seamen in 1800 and are so named because they are diametrically opposite Greenwich, England.

an·ti·pol·lu·tion (ăn′tē-pə-lo͞o′shən, ăn′tī-) *adj.* Intended to counteract or eliminate environmental pollution: *antipollution filters; antipollution laws.* —**an′ti·pol·lu′tion·ist** *n.*

an·ti·pope (ăn′tĭ-pōp′) *n.* A person claiming to be or elected pope in opposition to the one chosen by church law, as during a schism. [Middle English, from Old French *antipape*, from Medieval Latin *antipāpa* : Latin *anti-*, anti- + *pāpa*, pope; see POPE.]

an·ti·pov·er·ty (ăn′tē-pŏv′ər-tē, ăn′tī-) *adj.* Created or intended to alleviate poverty: *antipoverty programs.*

an·ti·pro·ton (ăn′tē-prō′tŏn′, ăn′tī-) *n.* The antiparticle of the proton.

an·ti·pru·rit·ic (ăn′tē-pro͞o-rĭt′ĭk, ăn′tī-) *adj.* Preventing or relieving itching: *an antipruritic agent.* —**an′ti·pru·rit′ic** *n.*

an·ti·psy·chot·ic (ăn′tē-sī-kŏt′ĭk, ăn′tī-) *adj.* Counteracting or diminishing the symptoms of psychotic disorders, such as schizophrenia, paranoia, and manic-depressive psychosis. —**an′ti·psy·chot′ic** *n.*

an·ti·py·ret·ic (ăn′tē-pī-rĕt′ĭk, ăn′tī-) *adj.* Reducing or tending to reduce fever. —**antipyretic** *n.* A medication that reduces fever. —**an′ti·py·re′sis** (-rē′sĭs) *n.*

an·ti·py·rine (ăn′tē-pī′rēn) *n.* A toxic white powder, $C_{11}H_{12}N_2O$, formerly used to reduce fever and relieve pain. [Originally a trademark.]

antiq. *abbr.* **1.** Antiquarian; antiquary. **2.** Antiquities. **3.** Antiquity.

an·ti·quar·i·an (ăn′tĭ-kwâr′ē-ən) *adj. Abbr.* **antiq., ant. 1.** Of or relating to antiquaries or to the study or collecting of antiquities. **2.** Dealing in or having to do with old or rare books. —**antiquarian** *n.* One who studies, collects, or deals in antiquities. —**an′ti·quar′i·an·ism** *n.*

an·ti·quark (ăn′tē-kwôrk′, ăn′tī-) *n.* The antiparticle of a quark.

an·ti·quar·y (ăn′tĭ-kwĕr′ē) *n., pl.* **-ies.** *Abbr.* **antiq., ant.** An antiquarian. [Latin *antīquārius*, from *antīquus*, old. See ANTIQUE.]

an·ti·quate (ăn′tĭ-kwāt′) *tr.v.* **-quat·ed, -quat·ing, -quates. 1.** To make obsolete or old-fashioned. **2.** To antique. [Late Latin *antīquāre, antīquāt-*, to make old, from Latin, to leave in an old state, from *antīquus*, old. See ANTIQUE.] —**an′ti·qua′tion** *n.*

an·ti·quat·ed (ăn′tĭ-kwā′tĭd) *adj.* **1.** Too old to be fashionable, suitable, or useful; outmoded. See Synonyms at **old. 2.** Very old; aged: *"The antiquated Earth, as one might say,/Beat like the heart of Man"* (William Wordsworth). —**an′ti·quat′ed·ness** *n.*

an·tique (ăn-tēk′) *adj.* **1.** Belonging to, made in, or typical of an earlier period. See Synonyms at **old. 2.** Of or belonging to ancient times, especially of, from, or characteristic of ancient Greece or Rome. **3.** Of or dealing in antiques. **4.** Old-fashioned: *wore a suit of rather antique appearance.* —**antique** *n.* **1.** An object having special value because of its age, especially a domestic item or piece of furniture or handicraft esteemed for its artistry, beauty, or period of origin. **2.** The style or manner of ancient times, especially that of ancient Greek or Roman art: *an admirer of the antique.* —**antique** *v.* **-tiqued, -tiqu·ing, -tiques.** —*tr.* To give the appearance of an antique to: *antiqued an oak chest.* —*intr.* To hunt or shop for antiques. [French, from Latin *antīquus*. See **ant-** in Appendix.] —**an·tique′ly** *adv.* —**an·tique′ness** *n.*

an·tiqu·er (ăn-tē′kər) *n.* One who treats or finishes new furniture so as to make it appear old or antique.

an·tiq·ui·ty (ăn-tĭk′wĭ-tē) *n., pl.* **-ties.** *Abbr.* **antiq., ant. 1.** Ancient times, especially the times preceding the Middle Ages. **2.** The people, especially the writers and artisans, of ancient times: *inventions unknown to antiquity.* **3.** The quality of being old or ancient; considerable age: *a carving of great antiquity.* **4.** Often **antiquities.** Something, such as an object or a relic, belonging to or dating from ancient times.

an·ti·ra·chit·ic (ăn′tē-rə-kĭt′ĭk, ăn′tī-) *adj.* Curing or preventing rickets: *antirachitic drugs.* —**an′ti·ra·chit′ic** *n.*

an·ti-roll bar (ăn′tē-rōl′, ăn′tī-) *n.* See **anti-sway bar.**

An·ti·sa·na (ăn′tĭ-sä′nə). An active volcano, about 5,760 m (18,885 ft) high, of north-central Ecuador in the Andes southeast of Quito.

an·ti-sat·el·lite or **an·ti·sat·el·lite** (ăn′tē-săt′l-īt, ăn′tī-) *adj. Abbr.* **ASAT, Asat.** Directed against enemy satellites: *antisatellite weapons.*

an·ti·scor·bu·tic (ăn′tē-skôr-byo͞o′tĭk, ăn′tī-) *adj.* Curing or preventing scurvy: *an antiscorbutic vitamin.* —**an′ti·scor·bu′tic** *n.*

an·ti·se·cre·to·ry (ăn′tē-sĭ-krē′tə-rē, ăn′tī-) *adj.* Inhibiting or decreasing secretion, especially gastric secretions. —**an′ti·se·cre′to·ry** *n.*

an·ti-Sem·ite (ăn′tē-sĕm′īt′, ăn′tī-) *n.* One who discriminates against or who is hostile toward or prejudiced against Jews. —**an′ti-Se·mit′ic** (-sə-mĭt′ĭk) *adj.*

an·ti-Sem·i·tism (ăn′tē-sĕm′ĭ-tĭz′əm, ăn′tī-) *n.* **1.** Hostility toward or prejudice against Jews or Judaism. **2.** Discrimination against Jews.

an·ti·sep·sis (ăn′tĭ-sĕp′sĭs) *n.* Destruction of disease-causing microorganisms to prevent infection.

an·ti·sep·tic (ăn′tĭ-sĕp′tĭk) *adj.* **1.** Of, relating to, or producing antisepsis. **2.** Capable of preventing infection by inhibiting the growth of microorganisms. **3.** Thoroughly clean; aseptic. See Synonyms at **clean. 4.** Of or associated with the use of antiseptics. **5.a.** Devoid of enlivening or enriching qualities: *"This is . . . not at all lighthearted or amiable music. In fact, the tone is unremittingly sober and antiseptic"* (Donal Henahan). **b.** Free of disturbing or unpleasant features; sanitized: *an antiseptic version of history.* —**antiseptic** *n.* A substance that inhibits the growth and reproduction of disease-causing microorganisms. —**an′ti·sep′ti·cal·ly** *adv.*

an·ti·se·rum (ăn′tĭ-sîr′əm) *n., pl.* **-se·rums** or **-se·ra** (-sîr′ə). Human or animal serum containing antibodies that are specific for one or more antigens.

an·ti·slav·er·y (ăn′tē-slā′və-rē, -slāv′rē, ăn′tī-) *adj.* Opposed to the practice or institution of slavery. —**an′ti·slav′er·y** *n.*

an·ti·smog (ăn′tē-smŏg′, -smôg′, ăn′tī-) *adj.* Intended to re-

ă pat	oi boy
ā pay	ou out
âr care	o͝o took
ä father	o͞o boot
ĕ pet	ŭ cut
ē be	ûr urge
ĭ pit	th thin
ī pie	*th* this
îr pier	hw which
ŏ pot	zh vision
ō toe	ə about, item
ô paw	♦ regionalism

Stress marks: ′ (primary); ′ (secondary), as in **dictionary** (dĭk′shə-nĕr′ē)

duce pollutants that cause smog: *antismog devices for cars and power plants.*

an·ti·smok·ing (ăn′tē-smō′kĭng, ăn′tī-) *adj.* Opposed to or prohibiting the smoking of tobacco, especially in public: *an antismoking campaign; an antismoking ordinance.*

an·ti·so·cial (ăn′tē-sō′shəl, ăn′tī-) *adj.* **1.** Shunning the society of others; not sociable. **2.** Hostile to or disruptive of the established social order; marked by or engaging in behavior that violates accepted mores: *Criminal behavior or conduct that violates the rights of other individuals is antisocial.* **3.** Disrespectful of others; rude. **—an′ti·so′cial·ly** *adv.*

an·ti·spas·mod·ic (ăn′tē-spăz-mŏd′ĭk, ăn′tī-) *adj.* Relieving or preventing spasms, especially of smooth muscle. **—antispasmodic** *n.* An antispasmodic agent. Also called *spasmolytic.*

an·ti·stat·ic (ăn′tē-stăt′ĭk, ăn′tī-) also **an·ti·stat** (-tē-stăt′, -tī-) *adj.* Preventing or inhibiting the buildup of static electricity. **—an′ti·stat′ic** *n.*

An·tis·the·nes (ăn-tĭs′thə-nēz′). 444?–371? B.C. Greek philosopher who founded the Cynic school.

an·tis·tro·phe (ăn-tĭs′trə-fē) *n.* **1.** The second stanza, and those like it, in a poem consisting of alternating stanzas in contrasting metric form. **2.** The second division of the triad of a Pindaric ode, having the same stanza form as the strophe. **3.a.** The choral movement in classical Greek drama following and in the same meter as the strophe, sung while the chorus moves in the opposite direction from that of the strophe. **b.** The part of a choral ode sung while this movement is executed. [Late Latin *antistrophē,* antistrophe of Greek tragedy, from Greek, strophic correspondence, from *antistrephein,* to turn back : *anti-,* back; see ANTI– + *strephein,* to turn; see STROPHE.] **—an′ti·stroph′ic** (ăn′tĭ-strŏf′ĭk) *adj.* **—an′ti·stroph′i·cal·ly** *adv.*

antler
Top: Moose
Alces alces
Center: Reindeer
Rangifer tarandus
Bottom: White-tailed deer
Odocoileus virginianus

an·ti·sub·ma·rine (ăn′tē-sŭb′mə-rēn′, -sŭb′mə-rēn′, ăn′-tī-) *adj. Abbr.* **AS** Directed against enemy submarines.

an·ti-sway bar (ăn′tē-swā′, ăn′tī-) *n.* A metal bar connecting the left and right suspension systems at the front or rear of an automobile or a truck, used to stabilize the chassis against sway. Also called *anti-roll bar, stabilizer bar, sway bar.*

an·ti·take·o·ver (ăn′tē-tāk′ō′vər, ăn′tī-) *adj.* Of, relating to, or constituting measures or statutes intended to prevent acquisition of a target company by another company hostile to the target's management.

an·ti·tank (ăn′tē-tăngk′, ăn′tī-) *adj. Abbr.* **AT, a/t** Designed for combat or defense against armored vehicles, especially tanks.

an·ti·ter·ror·ist (ăn′tē-tĕr′ər-ist, ăn′tī-) *adj.* Intended to prevent or counteract terrorism; counterterror: *antiterrorist measures.* **—an′ti·ter′ror·ism** *n.*

an·ti·theft (ăn′tē-thĕft′, ăn′tī-) *adj.* Designed to prevent theft: *an antitheft automotive device.*

an·tith·e·sis (ăn-tĭth′ĭ-sĭs) *n., pl.* **-ses** (-sēz′). **1.** Direct contrast; opposition. **2.** The direct or exact opposite: *Hope is the antithesis of despair.* **3.a.** A figure of speech in which sharply contrasting ideas are juxtaposed in a balanced or parallel phrase or grammatical structure, as in *"Hee for God only, shee for God in him"* (John Milton). **b.** The second and contrasting part of such a juxtaposition. **4.** The second stage of the Hegelian dialectic process, representing the opposite of the thesis. [Late Latin, from Greek, from *antitithenai,* to oppose : *anti-,* anti- + *tithenai, the-,* to set; see **dhē-** in Appendix.]

an·ti·thet·i·cal (ăn′tĭ-thĕt′ĭ-kəl) also **an·ti·thet·ic** (-ĭk) *adj.* **1.** Of, relating to, or marked by antithesis. **2.** Being in diametrical opposition. See Synonyms at **opposite.** [From Medieval Latin *antitheticus,* from Greek *antithetikos,* from *antitithenai,* to oppose. See ANTITHESIS.] **—an′ti·thet′i·cal·ly** *adv.*

an·ti·tox·ic (ăn′tē-tŏk′sĭk) *adj.* **1.** Counteracting a toxin or poison. **2.** Of, relating to, or containing an antitoxin: *an antitoxic serum.*

an·ti·tox·in (ăn′tē-tŏk′sĭn) *n.* **1.** An antibody formed in response to and capable of neutralizing a specific toxin of biological origin. **2.** An animal or human serum containing antitoxins. It is used in medicine to prevent or treat diseases caused by the action of biological toxins, such as tetanus, botulism, and diphtheria.

an·ti·trade (ăn′tĭ-trād′) *n.* The westerly winds above the surface trade winds of the tropics, which become the prevailing westerly winds of the middle latitudes. Often used in the plural.

Anubis
From XXI Dynasty
funerary papyrus

an·ti·trust (ăn′tē-trŭst′, ăn′tī-) *adj.* Opposing or intended to regulate business monopolies, such as trusts or cartels: *antitrust legislation.*

an·ti·tu·mor (ăn′tĭ-to͞o′mər, -tyo͞o′-) also **an·ti·tu·mor·al** (-mər-əl) *adj.* Counteracting or preventing the formation of malignant tumors; anticancer.

an·ti·tus·sive (ăn′tē-tŭs′ĭv, ăn′tī-) *adj.* Capable of relieving or suppressing coughing. **—an′ti·tus′sive** *n.*

an·ti·type (ăn′tĭ-tīp′) *n.* **1.** One that is foreshadowed by or identified with an earlier symbol or type, such as a figure in the New Testament who has a counterpart in the Old Testament. **2.** An opposite or contrasting type. [Medieval Latin *antitypus,* from Late Greek *antitupos,* copy, antitype, from Greek, corresponding, representing : *anti-,* equal to, like; see ANTI– + *tupos,* print, impression.] **—an′ti·typ′i·cal** (-tĭp′ĭ-kəl) *adj.*

an·ti-u·to·pi·a (ăn′tē-yo͞o-tō′pē-ə, ăn′tī-) *n.* **1.** An imaginary place or society characterized by human misery and oppression; a dystopia. **2.** A work describing such a place or society. **—an′ti-u·to′pi·an** *adj. & n.*

an·ti·ven·in (ăn′tē-vĕn′ĭn, ăn′tī-) *n.* **1.** An antitoxin active against the venom of a snake, spider, or other venomous animal or insect. **2.** An animal serum containing antivenins. It is used in medicine to treat poisoning caused by animal or insect venom. [ANTI– + VEN(OM) + –IN.]

an·ti·vi·ral (ăn′tē-vī′rəl, ăn′tī-) *adj.* Destroying or inhibiting the growth and reproduction of viruses: *an antiviral drug.* **—an′ti·vi′ral** *n.*

an·ti·vi·ta·min (ăn′tē-vī′tə-mĭn, ăn′tī-) *n.* A substance that destroys or inhibits the metabolic action of a vitamin.

an·ti·war (ăn′tē-wôr′, ăn′tī-) *adj.* Opposed to war: *an antiwar protest.*

an·ti-white (ăn′tē-hwīt′, wīt′, ăn′tī-) *adj.* Hostile or opposed to white people: *"To talk about black does not mean we are anti-white"* (Ron Clark).

ant·ler (ănt′lər) *n.* One of a pair of hornlike, bony, deciduous growths, usually elongated and branched, on the head of a deer, moose, elk, caribou, or other member of the deer family. [Middle English *aunteler,* from Old French *antoillier,* from Vulgar Latin **antoculāre, anteoculāre* : Latin *ante-,* ante- + Latin *oculāris,* of the eye; see OCULAR.] **—ant′lered** *adj.*

Ant·li·a (ănt′lē-ə) *n.* A constellation in the Southern Hemisphere near Hydra and Vela. [Latin *antlia,* pump, from Greek, ship's hold, bilge-water, from *antlos.*]

ant lion *n.* **1.** Any of various insects of the family Myrmeleontidae, the adults of which resemble dragonflies. **2.** The large-jawed larva of the ant lion, which digs a conical crater in the sand designed to trap ants and other insects for food. In this sense, also called *doodlebug.*

An·to·fa·gas·ta (än′tō-fə-gä′stə). A city of northern Chile on the Pacific Ocean. It is a shipping center for minerals found in the area. Population, 185,486.

An·to·ni·nus Pi·us (ăn′tə-nī′nəs pī′əs). A.D. 86–161. Emperor of Rome (138–161) who was the adopted son and successor of Hadrian.

An·to·ni·on·i (ăn-tō′nē-ō′nē), **Michelangelo.** Born 1912. Italian filmmaker whose works, notably *L'Avventura* (1959), are rich character studies.

An·to·ni·us (ăn-tō′nē-əs), **Marcus.** See **Mark Antony.**

an·to·no·ma·sia (ăn′tə-nə-mā′zhə) *n.* **1.** The substitution of a title or epithet for a proper name, as in calling a sovereign "Your Majesty." **2.** The substitution of a personal name for a common noun to designate a member of a group or class, as in calling a traitor a "Benedict Arnold." [Latin, from Greek *antonomazein,* to name instead : *anti-,* instead of; see ANTI– + *onomazein,* to name (from *onoma,* name; see **nō-men-** in Appendix).]

an·to·nym (ăn′tə-nĭm′) *n. Abbr.* **ant.** A word having a meaning opposite to that of another word: *The word* wet *is an antonym of the word* dry. [ANT(I)– + –ONYM.] **—an′to·nym′ic** *adj.* **—an·ton′y·mous** (ăn-tŏn′ə-məs) *adj.* **—an·ton′y·my** *n.*

an·tra (ăn′trə) *n.* Plural of **antrum.**

an·tre (ăn′tər) *n.* A cavern; a cave. [French, from Latin *antrum.* See ANTRUM.]

an·trorse (ăn′trôrs′) *adj. Biology.* Directed forward and upward, as the hairs on certain plant stems. [New Latin *antrōrsum,* from Latin *anterior,* before (perhaps after *intrōrsum,* inwards, from *interior,* inside). See ANTERIOR.] **—an′trorse′ly** *adv.*

an·trum (ăn′trəm) *n., pl.* **-tra** (-trə). **1.** A cavity or chamber, especially one in a bone. **2.** Either of the sinuses in the bones of the upper jaw, opening into the nasal cavity. [Late Latin, cavity in the body, from Latin, cave, from Greek *antron.*] **—an′tral** *adj.*

ant·sy (ănt′sē) *adj.* **-si·er, -si·est.** *Slang.* **1.** Restless or impatient; fidgety: *The long wait made the children antsy.* **2.** Nervous; apprehensive: *"Camps got shot up all the time, but if there wasn't a shoot-up, they'd get antsy"* (Harper's). [Perhaps from the incessant motions of ants.]

An·tung (än′to͝ong′). See **Dandong.**

Ant·werp (ănt′wərp) also **An·vers** (äN-vâr′). A city of northern Belgium on the Scheldt River north of Brussels. One of Europe's busiest ports, it has been a center of the diamond industry since the 15th century. The first stock exchange was founded here in 1460. Population, 490,524.

a·ñu also **an·yu** (ä′nyo͞o) *n.* **1.** A twining Andean herb *(Tropaeolum tuberosum)* having large flowers with yellow petals and long red spurs. **2.** The edible tubers of this plant. [American Spanish *añú,* from Quechua *áñu.*]

A·nu·bis (ə-no͞o′bĭs, ə-nyo͞o′-) *n. Mythology.* A jackal-headed Egyptian god and the son of Osiris. He conducted the dead to judgment.

A·nu·ra·dha·pur·a (ŭn′ə-rä′də-po͝or′ə, ə-no͝or′ə-). A town of north-central Sri Lanka north-northeast of Colombo. The ancient capital of Singhalese kings of Ceylon, it has extensive ruins and is a Buddhist pilgrimage center. Population, 36,000.

a·nu·ran (ə-no͝or′ən, ə-nyo͝or′-) *n.* See **salientian.** [From New Latin *Anura,* order of frogs and toads : A–[1] + Greek *oura,* tail; see **ors-** in Appendix.]

an·u·re·sis (ăn′yə-rē′sĭs) *n.* **1.** Inability to urinate. **2.** See **anuria.** [A–[1] + Greek *ourēsis,* urination, from *ourein,* to urinate, from *ouron,* urine.] **—an′u·ret′ic** (-rĕt′ĭk) *adj.*

a·nu·ri·a (ə-no͝or′ē-ə, ə-nyo͝or′-) *n.* The absence of urine formation. Also called *anuresis.* **—a·nu′ric** (ə-no͝or′ĭk, ə-nyo͝or′-) *adj.*

a·nu·rous (ə-no͝or′əs, ə-nyo͝or′-) *adj.* Having no tail; tailless.

a·nus (ā′nəs) *n., pl.* **a·nus·es.** The opening at the lower end of the alimentary canal through which solid waste is eliminated from the body. [Middle English, from Latin.]

An·vers (äɴ-vâr′). See **Antwerp.**

an·vil (ăn′vĭl) *n.* **1.** A heavy block of iron or steel with a smooth, flat top on which metals are shaped by hammering. **2.** The fixed jaw in a set of calipers against which an object to be measured is placed. **3.** *Anatomy.* See **incus** (sense 1). [Middle English *anfilt,* from Old English. See **pel-**[5] in Appendix.]

anx·i·e·ty (ăng-zī′ĭ-tē) *n., pl.* **-ties. 1.a.** A state of uneasiness and apprehension, as about future uncertainties. **b.** A cause of anxiety: *For some people, air travel is a real anxiety.* **2.** *Psychiatry.* A state of intense apprehension, uncertainty, and fear resulting from the anticipation of a threatening event or situation, often to a degree that the normal physical and psychological functioning of the affected individual is disrupted. **3.** Eager, often agitated desire: *my anxiety to make a good impression.* [Latin *ānxietās,* from *ānxius,* anxious. See ANXIOUS.]

SYNONYMS: *anxiety, worry, care, concern, solicitude.* These nouns are compared as they refer to troubled states of mind. *Anxiety* suggests feelings of fear and apprehension, especially when these emotions seem unrelated to objective sources: *"Feelings of resentment and rage over this devious form of manipulation cannot surface in the child . . . because he does not see through the subterfuge. At the most, he will experience feelings of anxiety, shame, insecurity, and helplessness"* (Alice Miller). *Worry* implies persistent doubt or fear that disturbs one's peace of mind: *"Rich people have about as many worries as poor ones, I think"* (Louisa May Alcott). *Care* denotes a burdened state of mind arising from heavy responsibilities: *"To be happy one must be . . . well fed, unhounded by sordid cares"* (H.L. Mencken). *Concern* stresses involvement in the source of mental unrest; it combines serious thought with emotion: *"Concern for man himself and his fate must always form the chief interest of all technical endeavors"* (Albert Einstein). *Solicitude* is active and sometimes excessive concern for the well-being of another or others: *"Animosity had given way first to grudging concessions of admiration and then to worried solicitude for Lindbergh's safety"* (Warren Trabant).

anx·ious (ăngk′shəs, ăng′shəs) *adj.* **1.** Uneasy and apprehensive about an uncertain event or matter; worried. **2.** Attended with, showing, or causing anxiety: *spent an anxious night waiting for the test results.* **3.** *Usage Problem.* Eagerly or earnestly desirous. [From Latin *ānxius,* from *angere,* to torment. See **angh-** in Appendix.] **—anx′ious·ly** *adv.* **—anx′ious·ness** *n.*

USAGE NOTE: *Anxious* has a long history of use roughly as a synonym for *eager,* but many would prefer that the distinction between the two words be maintained and that *anxious* be used only when its subject is worried or uneasy about the anticipated event. In the traditional view, one may say *We are anxious to see the strike settled soon* but not *We are anxious to see the new show of British sculpture at the museum.* Fifty-two percent of the Usage Panel rejects *anxious* in the latter sentence. But general adoption of *anxious* to mean "eager" is understandable, at least in colloquial discourse, since it provides a means of adding emotional urgency to an assertion, in its implication that the subject's desire for a certain outcome is so strong that frustration of that desire will lead to unhappiness. Note, in this connection, the analogous use of sentences such as *I'm dying to see your new baby* in informal style.

an·y (ĕn′ē) *adj.* **1.** One, some, every, or all without specification: *Take any book you want. Are there any messages for me? Any child would love that. Give me any food you don't want.* **2.** Exceeding normal limits, as in size or duration: *The patient cannot endure chemotherapy for any length of time.* **—any** *pron.* *(used with a sing. or pl. verb).* Any one or more persons, things, or quantities. **—any** *adv.* To any degree or extent; at all: *didn't feel any better.* [Middle English *ani,* from Old English *ǣnig.* See **oi-no-** in Appendix.]

USAGE NOTE: Used as a pronoun, *any* can take either a singular or plural verb, depending on how it is construed: *Any of these books is suitable* (that is, *any one*). *But are any* (that is, *some*) *of them available?* • The construction of *any* is often used in informal contexts to mean "of all," as in *He is the best known of any living playwright.* In an earlier survey this example was unacceptable in writing to 67 percent of the Usage Panel. • *Any* is also used to mean "at all" before a comparative adjective or adverb in questions and negative sentences: *Is she any better? Is he doing any better? He is not any friendlier than before.* This usage is entirely acceptable. The related use of *any* to modify a verb is considered informal. In writing, one should avoid sentences like *It didn't hurt any* or *If the child cries any, give her the bottle.* See Usage Notes at **every, he**[1].

An·yang (än′yäng′). A city of eastern China north-northeast of Zhengzhou. It was a capital of the Shang dynasty and one of the earliest centers of Chinese civilization. Population, 250,000.

an·y·bod·y (ĕn′ē-bŏd′ē, -bŭd′ē) *pron.* Any person; anyone. See Usage Note at **anyone. —anybody** *n.* A person of consequence: *Everybody who is anybody was at the reception.* See Usage Note at **every, he**[1].

an·y·how (ĕn′ē-hou′) *adv.* **1.** In whatever way or manner; however: *I'll cook it anyhow you like. They came anyhow they could—by boat, train, or plane.* **2.** In a careless way; haphazardly: *clothes stuffed anyhow into the suitcase.* **3.a.** In any case; at least: *I think they're asleep; anyhow, they're quiet.* **b.** Nevertheless: *It sounds crazy, but I believe it anyhow.*

♦**an·y·more** (ĕn′ē-môr′, -mōr′) *adv.* **1.a.** Any longer; at the present: *Do they make this model anymore?* **b.** From now on: *We promised not to quarrel anymore.* **2.** *Regional.* Nowadays.

♦***REGIONAL NOTE:*** In standard American English the word *anymore* is often found in negative sentences: *They don't live here anymore.* But *anymore* is widely used in regional American English in positive sentences with the meaning "nowadays": *"We use a gas stove anymore"* (Oklahoma informant in DARE). Its use, which appears to be spreading, is centered in the South Midland and Midwestern states—Tennessee, Kentucky, Indiana, Oklahoma, and Iowa—and the Western states that received settlers from those areas. The earliest recorded examples are from Northern Ireland, where the positive use of *anymore* still occurs.

an·y·one (ĕn′ē-wŭn′, -wən) *pron.* Any person.

USAGE NOTE: The one-word form *anyone* is used to mean "any person." The two-word form *any one* is used to mean "whatever one (person or thing) of a group." *Anyone may join* means that admission is open to everybody. *Any one may join* means that admission is open to one person only. When followed by *of,* only *any one* can be used: *Any one* (not *anyone*) *of the boys could carry it by himself.* • *Anyone* is often used in place of *everyone* in sentences like *She is the most thrifty person of anyone I know.* In an earlier survey 64 percent of the Usage Panel found this sentence unacceptable in writing. • *Anyone* and *anybody* are singular terms and always take a singular verb. See Usage Note at **he**[1].

an·y·place (ĕn′ē-plās′) *adv.* To, in, or at any place; anywhere. See Usage Note at **everyplace.**

an·y·thing (ĕn′ē-thĭng′) *pron.* Any object, occurrence, or matter whatever. **—anything** *adv.* To any degree or extent; at all: *They aren't anything like last year's team.* **—anything** *n.* Something or someone of importance: *"You had to be something to start with, and Jeremy never was anything"* (Anne Tyler). ***—idiom.* anything but.** By no means; not at all: *I was anything but happy about going.*

an·y·time (ĕn′ē-tīm′) *adv.* At any time.

an·yu (ä′nyo͞o) *n.* Variant of **añu.**

an·y·way (ĕn′ē-wā′) *adv.* **1.** In any way or manner whatever: *Get the job done anyway you can.* **2.** In any case; at least: *I don't know if it was lost or stolen; anyway, it's gone.* **3.** Nevertheless; regardless: *It was raining but they played the game anyway.*

an·y·ways (ĕn′ē-wāz′) *adv. Non-Standard.* In any case.

an·y·where (ĕn′ē-hwâr′, -wâr′) *adv.* **1.** To, in, or at any place. **2.** To any extent or degree; at all: *The project isn't anywhere near completion.* **3.** Used to indicate limits of variation: *Anywhere from 300 to 400 patients suffered secondary infections.* **—anywhere** *n.* Any place whatsoever.

an·y·wise (ĕn′ē-wīz′) *adv. Non-Standard.* In any case.

An·zac (ăn′zăk′) *n.* A soldier from New Zealand or Australia. [*A(ustralian and) N(ew) Z(ealand) A(rmy) C(orps).*] **—An′zac′** *adj.*

An·zi·o (ăn′zē-ō, än′tsyô). A town of central Italy on the Tyrrhenian Sea south-southeast of Rome. In World War II Allied troops landed at Anzio on January 22, 1944. Population, 27,094.

a/o *abbr.* Account of.

ao dai (ou′ dī, ô′) *n., pl.* **ao dais.** The traditional dress of Vietnamese women, consisting of a long tunic that is slit on the sides and worn over loose trousers. [Vietnamese *ào dài* : *ào,* tunic (of Chinese origin) + *dài,* long.]

AOH *abbr.* Ancient Order of Hibernians.

A-OK also **A-O·kay** (ā′ō-kā′) *adj. Informal.* Being in perfect condition or order. **—A-OK** *adv. & n.*

Ao·mo·ri (ou′mə-rē, ä′ô-môr′ē). A city of extreme northern Honshu, Japan, on **Aomori Bay.** Opened to foreign trade in 1906, it is now the chief port of northern Honshu. Population, 294,050.

A-one also **A-1** (ā′wŭn′) *adj. Informal.* First-class; excellent. [From classification for ships in The Lloyd's Register of Shipping.]

aor. *abbr. Grammar.* Aorist.

A·o·rang·i (ä′ō-räng′gē). See Mount **Cook** (sense 1).

a·o·rist (ā′ər-ĭst) *Grammar. n. Abbr.* **aor. 1.** A form of a verb in some languages, such as Classical Greek, that expresses action without indicating its completion or continuation. **2.** A form of a verb in some languages, such as Classical Greek or Sanskrit, that in the indicative mood expresses past action. [From Greek *aoristos,* indefinite, aorist tense : *a-,* not; see A-[1] + *horistos,* definable (from *horizein,* to define; see HORIZON).] **—a′o·ris′tic** *adj.* **—a′o·ris′ti·cal·ly** *adv.*

a·or·ta (ā-ôr′tə) *n., pl.* **-tas** or **-tae** (-tē). *Anatomy.* The main trunk of the systemic arteries, carrying blood from the left side of the heart to the arteries of all limbs and organs except the

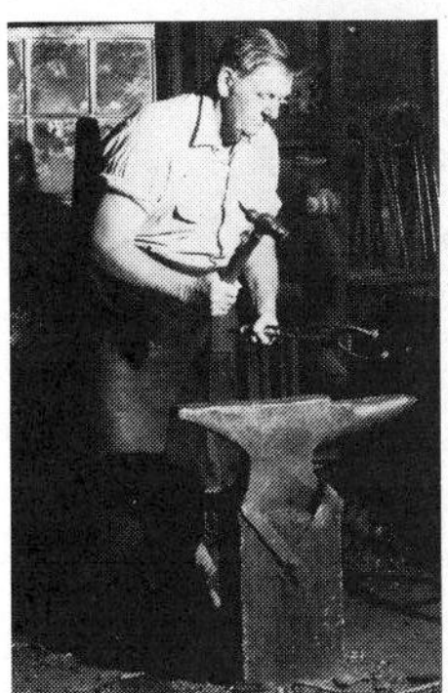

anvil

ao dai

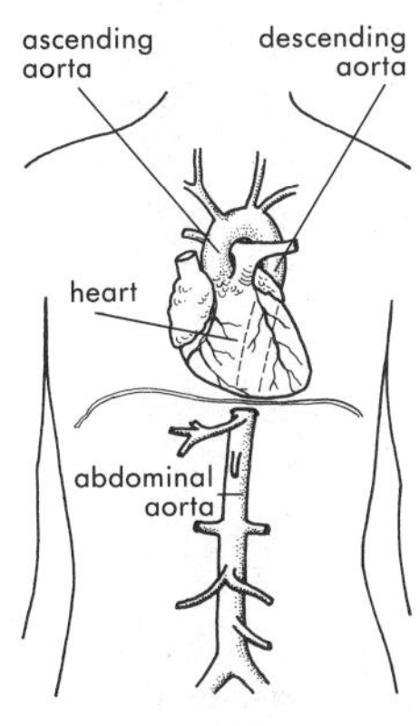

aorta

ă pat	oi boy
ā pay	ou out
âr care	o͝o took
ä father	o͞o boot
ĕ pet	ŭ cut
ē be	ûr urge
ĭ pit	th thin
ī pie	*th* this
îr pier	hw which
ŏ pot	zh vision
ō toe	ə about, item
ô paw	♦ regionalism

Stress marks: ′ (primary); ′ (secondary), as in **dictionary** (dĭk′shə-nĕr′ē)

lungs. [New Latin, from Greek *aortē,* from *aeirein,* to lift. See **wer-**[1] in Appendix.] **—a·or′tal, a·or′tic** *adj.*

aortic arch *n. Anatomy.* One of a series of paired arteries in a vertebrate embryo that connects the ventral arterial system to the dorsal arterial system.

a·or·tog·ra·phy (ā′ôr-tŏg′rə-fē) *n.* Examination of the aorta using x-rays following the injection of a radiopaque substance. **—a·or′to·graph′ic** (-tə-grăf′ĭk) *adj.*

a·ou·dad (ä′o͞o-dăd′, ou′dăd′) *n.* A wild sheep *(Ammotragus lervia)* of northern Africa, having long, curved horns and a beardlike growth of hair on the neck and chest. Also called *Barbary sheep.* [French, from Berber, audad.]

AP *abbr.* **1.** Advanced placement. **2.** Airplane. **3.** Air police. **4.** American plan. **5.** Antipersonnel. **6.** Also **A.P.** Associated Press.

ap. *abbr.* Apothecary.

a.p. *abbr.* **1.** Additional premium. **2.** Author's proof.

ap–[1] *pref.* Variant of **ad–** (sense 1).

ap–[2] *pref.* Variant of **apo–.**

APA *abbr.* **1.** American Philological Association. **2.** American Philosophical Association. **3.** American Psychiatric Association. **4.** American Psychological Association.

a·pace (ə-pās′) *adv.* **1.** At a rapid pace; swiftly. **2.** In such a way or at such a speed as to keep up the requisite momentum; abreast. [Middle English *a pas,* from Old French : *a,* to (from Latin *ad;* see AD–) + *pas,* step; see PACE[1].]

a·pache (ə-păsh′, ä-păsh′) *n., pl.* **a·paches** (ə-păsh′, ä-păsh′). **1.** A member of the Parisian underworld. **2.** A thug; a ruffian. [French, from *Apache,* Apache Indian. See APACHE.]

A·pach·e (ə-păch′ē) *n., pl.* **Apache** or **-es. 1.a.** A Native American people inhabiting the southwest United States and northern Mexico. Various Apache tribes offered strong resistance to encroachment on their territory in the latter half of the 19th century. Present-day Apache populations are located in Arizona, New Mexico, and Oklahoma. **b.** A member of this people. **2.** Any of the Apachean languages of the Apache. [American Spanish.]

A·pach·e·an (ə-păch′ē-ən) *n.* **1.** The subgroup of Athabaskan comprising the languages of the Apache and Navajo. **2.** A speaker of any of these languages.

Ap·a·lach·i·co·la (ăp′ə-lăch′ĭ-kō′lə). A river of northwest Florida flowing about 180 km (112 mi) southward from the Georgia border to **Apalachicola Bay,** an inlet of the Gulf of Mexico.

ap·a·nage (ăp′ə-nĭj) *n.* Variant of **appanage.**

Ap·a·po·ris (ä′pə-pōr′ēs, -pôr′-). A river rising in south-central Colombia and flowing about 805 km (500 mi) southeast to the Japurá River on the Brazilian border.

♦ **ap·a·re·jo** (ăp′ə-rā′hō, -rā′ō) *n., pl.* **-jos.** *Southwestern U.S.* A packsaddle made of a stuffed leather pad. [American Spanish, from Spanish, equipment, from *aparejar,* to prepare, from Vulgar Latin **appariculāre.* See APPAREL.]

a·part (ə-pärt′) *adv.* **1.a.** At a distance in place, position, or time: *railings spaced two feet apart; born three years apart.* **b.** Away from another or others: *grew apart over the years; decided to live apart.* **2.** In or into parts or pieces: *split apart.* **3.** One from another: *I can't tell the twins apart.* **4.** Aside or in reserve, as for a separate use or purpose: *funds set apart for the project.* **5.** As a distinct item or entity: *Quality sets it apart.* **6.** So as to except or exclude from consideration; aside: *All joking apart, I think you're crazy.* **—apart** *adj.* Set apart; isolated. Used after a noun or in the predicate: *a people who have existed over the centuries as a world apart.* [Middle English, from Old French *a part* : *a,* to (from Latin *ad-;* see AD–) + *part,* side (from Latin *pars, part-;* see PART).] **—a·part′ness** *n.*

apart from *prep.* With the exception of; besides: *Apart from a few scratches, the car was undamaged.*

a·part·heid (ə-pärt′hīt′, -hāt′) *n.* **1.** An official policy of racial segregation practiced in the Republic of South Africa, involving political, legal, and economic discrimination against nonwhites. **2.** Any policy or practice of separating or segregating groups. **3.** The condition of being separated from others; segregation. [Afrikaans : Dutch *apart,* separate (from French *à part,* apart; see APART) + *-heid,* -hood.]

WORD HISTORY: Although South Africa has not furnished a great number of words that have achieved general currency in British and American English, one in particular, *apartheid,* has gained wide circulation. The first recorded use of *apartheid* as an English term, in the *Cape Times* on October 24, 1947, is an ironic commentary on much of the word's use since then: "Mr. Hofmeyr said apartheid could not be reconciled with a policy of progress and prosperity for South Africa." According to the March 15, 1961, issue of the *London Times,* the word *self-development* was supposed to replace *apartheid* as the official term used by the South African Broadcasting Corporation for "the Government's race policies." And in *Move Your Shadow,* published in 1985, Joseph Lelyveld says that the "word is [now] shunned, even resented by the [National Party's] high priests as if it were an epithet fashioned by the country's enemies." But *apartheid* as a word and as a reality has been slow to disappear. The history of *apartheid,* however, offers a possible model for change in this policy, for the word is an example of a mixture and combination of resources, in this case linguistic. *Apartheid* is an English word that came into South African English from Afrikaans, the language of the Dutch settlers of South Africa. They in turn had made up the word from the Dutch word *apart,* "separate," and the suffix *-heid,* which corresponds to our suffix *-hood.* Thus *apartheid* literally means "separateness." The Dutch had earlier borrowed the word *apart,* as did we, from the French phrase *à part,* meaning "to one side."

a·part·ment (ə-pärt′mənt) *n. Abbr.* **apt. 1.** A room or suite of rooms designed as a residence and generally located in a building occupied by more than one household. **2.** An apartment house: *a row of high-rise apartments.* **3.** A room. **4. apartments.** *Chiefly British.* A suite of rooms within a larger building set aside for a particular purpose or person. [French *appartement,* from Italian *appartamento,* from *appartare,* to separate, from *a parte,* apart : *a,* to (from Latin *ad-;* see AD–) + *parte,* side (from Latin *pars, part-;* see PART).]

apartment house *n.* A building divided into apartments. Also called *apartment building.*

ap·a·tet·ic (ăp′ə-tĕt′ĭk) *adj. Zoology.* Relating to or characterized by coloration serving as natural camouflage. [Greek *apatētikos,* deceptive, from *apatētēs,* deceiver, from *apateuein,* to cheat, from *apatē,* deceit.]

ap·a·thet·ic (ăp′ə-thĕt′ĭk) also **ap·a·thet·i·cal** (-ĭ-kəl) *adj.* **1.** Feeling or showing a lack of interest or concern; indifferent. **2.** Feeling or showing little or no emotion; unresponsive. [From APATHY, on the model of PATHETIC.] **—ap′a·thet′i·cal·ly** *adv.*

ap·a·thy (ăp′ə-thē) *n.* **1.** Lack of interest or concern, especially regarding matters of general importance or appeal; indifference. **2.** Lack of emotion or feeling; impassiveness. [Latin *apathīa,* from Greek *apatheia,* from *apathēs,* without feeling : *a-,* without; see A–[1] + *pathos,* feeling; see **kʷent(h)-** in Appendix.]

ap·a·tite (ăp′ə-tīt′) *n.* A natural, variously colored calcium fluoride phosphate, $Ca_5F(PO_4)_3$, with chlorine, hydroxyl, or carbonate sometimes replacing the fluoride. It is a source of phosphorus for plants and is used in the manufacture of fertilizers. [From Greek *apatē,* deceit (from its often being mistaken for other minerals).]

APB *abbr.* All points bulletin.

ape (āp) *n.* **1.a.** Any of various large, tailless Old World primates of the family Pongidae, including the chimpanzee, gorilla, gibbon, and orangutan. **b.** A monkey. **2.** A mimic or an imitator. **3.** *Informal.* A clumsy or boorish person. **—ape** *tr.v.* **aped, ap·ing, apes.** To mimic slavishly but often with an absurd result. See Synonyms at **imitate. —ape** *adj. Informal.* Completely unrestrained, especially with enthusiasm: *The fans at the concert were really ape.* ***—idiom.* go ape.** *Informal.* To become wildly excited or enthusiastic. [Middle English, from Old English *apa.*] **—ap′er** *n.*

a·peak (ə-pēk′) *adv. & adj. Nautical.* In a vertical or almost vertical position or direction: *rowers holding their oars apeak.* [Alteration of *apike,* probably from French *à pic* : *à,* to (from Latin *ad-;* see AD–) + *pic,* peak (from Old French).]

A·pel·doorn (ăp′əl-dôrn′, -dōrn′, -ä′pəl-). A city of east-central Netherlands north of Arnhem. It is a popular tourist center. Population, 144,108.

A·pel·les (ə-pĕl′ēz). fl. fourth century B.C. Greek painter whose works, none of which survives, are described in ancient writings.

ape-man (āp′măn′) *n.* **1.** Any of various extinct primates, such as pithecanthropus, sometimes considered intermediate in evolution between the anthropoid apes and modern human beings. **2.** A person or creature held to combine characteristics of apes and humans, as: **a.** A brawny or brutish man. **b.** An archetype of the primitive or instinctual aspect of human nature: *"The superman has created the airplane and the radio, the ape-man has got hold of them"* (Los Angeles Times).

Ap·en·nines (ăp′ə-nīnz′). A mountain system extending about 1,352 km (840 mi) from northwest Italy south to the Strait of Messina. The highest peak is Mount Corno, rising to 2,915.8 m (9,560 ft).

a·per·çu (ä′pĕr-sü′) *n., pl.* **-çus** (-sü′). **1.** A discerning perception; an insight. **2.** A short outline or summary; a synopsis. [French, from past participle of *apercevoir,* to perceive : *a-,* to (from Latin *ad-;* see AD–) + *perceivre,* to perceive; see PERCEIVE.]

a·pe·ri·ent (ə-pîr′ē-ənt) *adj.* Gently stimulating evacuation of the bowels; laxative. **—aperient** *n.* A mild laxative. [Latin *aperiēns, aperient-,* present participle of *aperīre,* to open. See **wer-**[4] in Appendix.]

a·pe·ri·od·ic (ā′pîr-ē-ŏd′ĭk) *adj.* **1.** Occurring without periodicity. **2.** *Physics.* Without periodic vibrations. **—a′pe·ri·od′i·cal·ly** *adv.* **—a·pe′ri·o·dic′i·ty** (-ə-dĭs′ĭ-tē) *n.*

a·pé·ri·tif (ä-pĕr′ĭ-tēf′) *n.* An alcoholic drink taken as an appetizer before a meal. [French, from Old French *aperitif,* purgative, from Medieval Latin *aperitīvus,* from Late Latin *apertīvus,* from Latin *apertus,* past participle of *aperīre,* to open. See **wer-**[4] in Appendix.]

ap·er·ture (ăp′ər-chər) *n.* **1.** An opening, such as a hole, gap, or slit. **2.a.** A usually adjustable opening in an optical instrument, such as a camera or a telescope, that limits the amount of light passing through a lens or onto a mirror. **b.** The diameter of such an opening, often expressed as an f-number. **c.** The diameter of the objective of a telescope. [Middle English, from Latin *apertūra,* from *apertus,* past participle of *aperīre,* to open. See **wer-**[4] in Appendix.] **—ap′er·tur′al** *adj.*

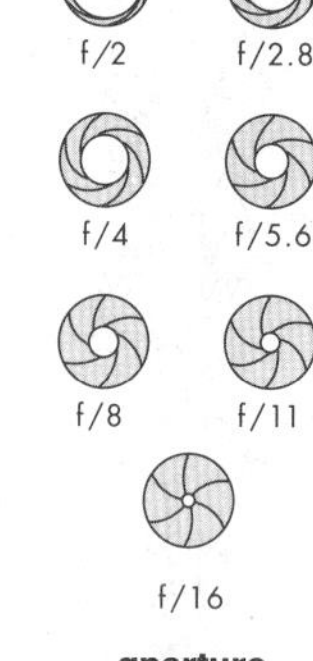

aperture

ă pat	oi boy
ā pay	ou out
âr care	o͝o took
ä father	o͞o boot
ĕ pet	ŭ cut
ē be	ûr urge
ĭ pit	th thin
ī pie	*th* this
îr pier	hw which
ŏ pot	zh vision
ō toe	ə about, item
ô paw	♦ regionalism

Stress marks: **′** (primary); ′ (secondary), as in **dictionary** (dĭk′shə-nĕr′ē)

aperture card *n.* A punched card on which frames of a microfilmed document are mounted.

a·pet·al·ous (ā-pĕt′l-əs) *adj. Botany.* Having no petals. **—a·pet′al·y** (ā-pĕt′l-ē) *n.*

a·pex (ā′pĕks) *n., pl.* **a·pex·es** or **a·pi·ces** (ā′pĭ-sēz′, ăp′ĭ-). **1.** The highest point; the vertex: *the apex of a triangle; the apex of a hill.* **2.** The point of culmination. See Synonyms at **summit. 3.** The usually pointed end of an object; the tip: *the apex of a leaf.* [Latin.]

Ap·gar score (ăp′gär) *n.* A system of assessing the general physical condition of a newborn infant based on a rating of 0, 1, or 2 for five criteria: heart rate, respiration, muscle tone, skin color, and response to stimuli. The five scores are added together, with a perfect score being 10. [After Virginia *Apgar* (1909–1974), American physician.]

a·phaer·e·sis or **a·pher·e·sis** (ə-fĕr′ĭ-sĭs) *n., pl.* **-ses** (-sēz′). *Linguistics.* The loss of one or more sounds from the beginning of a word, as in *till* for *until.* [Late Latin, from Greek *aphairesis,* from *aphairein,* to take away : *apo-,* apo- + *hairein,* to take.] **—aph′ae·ret′ic** (ăf′ə-rĕt′ĭk) *adj.*

a·pha·gi·a (ə-fā′jē-ə, -jə) *n.* Loss of the ability to swallow.

aph·a·nite (ăf′ə-nīt′) *n.* A dense, homogeneous rock with constituents so fine that they cannot be seen by the naked eye. [From Greek *aphanēs,* unseen : *a-,* not; see A–[1] + *phainesthai, phan-,* to appear (from *phainein,* to show; see PHENOMENON).] **—aph′a·nit′ic** (-nĭt′ĭk) *adj.*

a·pha·sia (ə-fā′zhə) *n.* Partial or total loss of the ability to articulate ideas or comprehend spoken or written language, resulting from damage to the brain caused by injury or disease. [Greek, from *aphatos,* speechless : *a-,* not; see A–[1] + *phatos,* spoken, speakable (from *phanai,* to speak; see –PHASIA).] **—a·pha′si·ac′** (-zē-ăk′) *n.* **—a·pha′sic** (-zĭk, -sĭk) *adj. & n.*

a·phe·li·on (ə-fē′lē-ən, ə-fēl′yən) *n., pl.* **-li·a** (-lē-ə). The point on the orbit of a celestial body that is farthest from the sun. [From New Latin *aphēlium* : Greek *apo-,* apo- + Greek *hēlios,* sun; see **sāwel-** in Appendix.]

a·pher·e·sis (ə-fĕr′ĭ-sĭs) *n.* **1.** *Linguistics.* Variant of **aphaeresis. 2.** *Medicine.* A procedure in which blood is drawn from a donor and separated into its components, some of which are retained, such as plasma or platelets, and the remainder returned by transfusion to the donor. Also called *hemapheresis.*

aph·e·sis (ăf′ĭ-sĭs) *n., pl.* **-ses** (-sēz′). *Linguistics.* The loss of an initial, usually unstressed vowel, as in *cute* from *acute.* [Greek, a release, from *aphienai,* to let go : *apo-,* apo- + *hienai, he-,* to send; see DIESIS.] **—a·phet′ic** (ə-fĕt′ĭk) *adj.* **—a·phet′i·cal·ly** *adv.*

a·phid (ā′fĭd, ăf′ĭd) *n.* Any of various small, soft-bodied insects of the family Aphididae that have mouthparts specially adapted for piercing and feed by sucking sap from plants. Also called *plant louse.* [New Latin *Aphis, Aphid-,* type genus. See APHIS.] **—a·phid′i·an** (ə-fĭd′ē-ən) *adj. & n.*

a·phi·des (ā′fĭ-dēz′, ăf′ĭ-) *n.* Plural of **aphis.**

aphid lion *n.* The larva of any of several insects of the family Chrysopidae, such as the lacewing, that feed on aphids.

a·phis (ā′fĭs, ăf′ĭs) *n., pl.* **a·phi·des** (ā′fĭ-dēz′, ăf′ĭ-). An aphid, especially one of the genus *Aphis.* [New Latin *Aphis,* genus name.]

a·pho·ni·a (ā-fō′nē-ə) *n.* Loss of the voice resulting from disease, injury to the vocal cords, or various psychological causes, such as hysteria. [New Latin, from Greek *aphōnia,* speechlessness, from *aphōnos,* voiceless : *a-,* without; see A–[1] + *phōnē,* voice; see **bhā-**[2] in Appendix.] **—a·phon′ic** (ā-fŏn′ĭk, ā-fō′nĭk) *adj.*

aph·o·rism (ăf′ə-rĭz′əm) *n.* **1.** A tersely phrased statement of a truth or opinion; an adage. See Synonyms at **saying. 2.** A brief statement of a principle. [French *aphorisme,* from Old French, from Late Latin *aphorismus,* from Greek *aphorismos,* from *aphorizein,* to delimit, define : *apo-,* apo- + *horizein,* to delimit, define; see HORIZON.] **—aph′o·rist** *n.* **—aph′o·ris′tic** (-rĭs′tĭk) *adj.* **—aph′o·ris′ti·cal·ly** *adv.*

aph·o·rize (ăf′ə-rīz′) *intr.v.* **-rized, -riz·ing, -riz·es.** To express oneself in or as if in aphorisms.

a·pho·tic (ā-fō′tĭk) *adj.* **1.** Having no light. **2.** Of or relating to the region of a body of water that is not reached by sunlight and in which photosynthesis is unable to occur.

aph·ro·dis·i·ac (ăf′rə-dĭz′ē-ăk′, -dē′zē-) *adj.* Arousing or intensifying sexual desire. **—aphrodisiac** *n.* Something, such as a drug or food, having such an effect. [Greek *aphrodisiakos,* from *aphrodisia,* sexual pleasures, from *Aphroditē,* Aphrodite.] **—aph′ro·di·si′a·cal** (-dĭ-zī′ĭ-kəl) *adj.*

aph·ro·di·te (ăf′rə-dī′tē) *n.* A brightly colored butterfly *(Argynnis aphrodite)* of North America. [From APHRODITE.]

Aph·ro·di·te (ăf′rə-dī′tē) *n. Greek Mythology.* The goddess of love and beauty. Also called *Cytherea.* [Greek *Aphroditē.*]

a·phyl·lous (ā-fĭl′əs) *adj. Botany.* Bearing no leaves; leafless. [From New Latin *aphyllus,* from Greek *aphullos* : *a-,* without; see A–[1] + *phullon,* leaf; see –PHYLLOUS.] **—a′phyl′ly** (ā′fĭl′ē) *n.*

A·pi·a (ə-pē′ə, ä′pē-ä′). The capital of Western Samoa, on the northern coast of Upolo island in the southern Pacific Ocean. Population, 33,170.

a·pi·an (ā′pē-ən) *adj.* Of, relating to, or having the characteristics of bees. [From Latin *apis,* bee.]

a·pi·ar·i·an (ā′pē-âr′ē-ən) *adj.* Relating to bees or to the keeping and care of bees.

a·pi·a·rist (ā′pē-ə-rĭst, -ĕr′ĭst) *n.* One who keeps bees, specifically one who cares for and raises bees for commercial or agricultural purposes. Also called *beekeeper.*

a·pi·ar·y (ā′pē-ĕr′ē) *n., pl.* **-ies.** A place where bees and beehives are kept, especially a place where bees are raised for their honey. [Latin *apiārium,* beehive, from *apis,* bee.]

a·pi·cal (ā′pĭ-kəl, ăp′ĭ-) *adj.* **1.** Of, relating to, located at, or constituting an apex. **2.** *Linguistics.* Of, relating to, or articulated with the tip of the tongue, as *t, d,* and *s.* [From Latin *apex, apic-,* top.] **—ap′i·cal·ly** *adv.*

apical dominance *n. Botany.* The inhibitory influence on the growth of lateral buds exerted by the terminal bud of a growing plant shoot.

apical meristem *n. Botany.* A meristem located at the tip of a plant shoot or root.

a·pi·ces (ā′pĭ-sēz′, ăp′ĭ-) *n.* A plural of **apex.**

a·pic·u·late (ə-pĭk′yə-lĭt) *adj.* Ending abruptly with a sharp, flexible tip: *an apiculate leaf.* [From New Latin *apiculus,* sharp point, diminutive of Latin *apex, apic-,* point.]

a·pi·cul·ture (ā′pĭ-kŭl′chər) *n.* The raising and care of bees for commercial or agricultural purposes. [Latin *apis,* bee + CULTURE.] **—a′pi·cul′tur·al** *adj.* **—a′pi·cul′tur·ist** *n.*

a·piece (ə-pēs′) *adv.* To or for each one; each: *There is enough bread for everyone to have two slices apiece.* [Middle English *a pece* : *a,* a; see A[2] + *pece,* piece; see PIECE.]

a·pi·o (ä′pē-ō) *n., pl.* **-os.** See **arracacha.** [American Spanish, from Spanish, celery, from Latin *apium,* perhaps from *apis,* bee.]

A·pis (ā′pĭs) *n.* A sacred bull of the ancient Egyptians.

ap·ish (ā′pĭsh) *adj.* **1.** Resembling an ape. **2.** Slavishly or foolishly imitative: *"My own performances were apish imitations of Olivier's stirring cadences"* (Robert Brustein). **3.** Silly; outlandish. **—ap′ish·ly** *adv.* **—ap′ish·ness** *n.*

a·piv·o·rous (ā-pĭv′ər-əs) *adj. Zoology.* Feeding on bees. [Latin *apis,* bee + –VOROUS.]

APL (ā′pē-ĕl′) *n. Computer Science.* A programming language designed for use at remote terminals. It has specific capabilities for handling arrays. [*A P(rogramming) L(anguage).*]

a·pla·cen·tal (ā′plə-sĕn′tl) *adj.* Having no placenta, as marsupials and monotremes.

ap·la·nat·ic (ăp′lə-năt′ĭk) *adj.* Of or relating to optical systems that correct for spherical aberration. [From A–[1] + Greek *planasthai,* to wander; see **pelə-**[2] in Appendix.]

a·pla·sia (ə-plā′zhə, -zhē-ə) *n.* Defective development resulting in the absence of all or part of an organ or tissue.

a·plas·tic (ā-plăs′tĭk) *adj.* **1.** Lacking form. **2.** *Pathology.* **a.** Unable to form or regenerate tissue. **b.** Of, relating to, or characterized by aplasia.

aplastic anemia *n.* A form of anemia in which the capacity of the bone marrow to generate red blood cells is defective. This anemia may be caused by bone marrow disease or exposure to toxic agents, such as radiation, chemicals, or drugs. Also called *pancytopenia.*

a·plen·ty (ə-plĕn′tē) *adj.* In plentiful supply; abundant: *"There were warning signs aplenty for their candidates as well"* (Michael Gelb). **—a·plen′ty** *adv.*

ap·lite (ăp′līt′) also **hap·lite** (hăp′līt′) *n.* A fine-grained, light-colored granitic rock consisting primarily of orthoclase and quartz. [German *Aplit,* from Greek *haplous,* single. See HAPLOID.] **—ap·lit′ic** (ă-plĭt′ĭk) *adj.*

a·plomb (ə-plŏm′, ə-plŭm′) *n.* Self-confident assurance; poise. See Synonyms at **confidence.** [French, from Old French *a plomb,* perpendicularly : *a,* according to (from Latin *ad-*; see AD–) + *plomb,* lead weight (from Latin *plumbum,* lead).]

ap·ne·a also **ap·noe·a** (ăp′nē-ə, ăp-nē′ə) *n.* Temporary absence or cessation of breathing. [New Latin, from Greek *apnoia* : *a-,* without; see A–[1] + *pnoia,* breathing, from *pnein,* to breathe. See **pneu-** in Appendix.] **—ap·ne′ic** *adj. & n.*

A·po (ä′pō). The highest mountain, 2,956.1 m (9,692 ft), of the Philippines, an active volcano on southeast Mindanao.

APO or **A.P.O.** *abbr.* Army Post Office.

apo– or **ap–** *pref.* **1.a.** Away from; off: *aphelion.* **b.** Separate: *apocarpous.* **2.** Without; not: *apogamy.* **3.** Related to; derived from: *apomorphine.* **4.** Metasomatic: *apophyllite.* [Greek, from *apo,* away from. See **apo-** in Appendix.]

Apoc. *abbr. Bible.* **1.** Apocalypse. **2.** Apocrypha; Apocryphal.

a·poc·a·lypse (ə-pŏk′ə-lĭps′) *n.* **1.a. Apocalypse.** *Abbr.* **Apoc.** *Bible.* The Book of Revelation. **b.** Any of a number of anonymous Jewish or Christian texts from around the second century B.C. to the second century A.D. containing prophetic or symbolic visions, especially of the imminent destruction of the world and the salvation of the righteous. **2.** Great or total devastation; doom: *the apocalypse of nuclear war.* **3.** A prophetic disclosure; a revelation. [Middle English *Apocalipse,* from Late Latin *Apocalypsis,* from Greek *apokalupsis,* revelation, Apocalypse, from *apokaluptein,* to uncover : *apo-,* apo- + *kaluptein,* to cover; see **kel-**[1] in Appendix.]

a·poc·a·lyp·tic (ə-pŏk′ə-lĭp′tĭk) also **a·poc·a·lyp·ti·cal** (-tĭ-kəl) *adj.* **1.** Of or relating to an apocalypse. **2.** Involving or portending widespread devastation or ultimate doom: *"now*

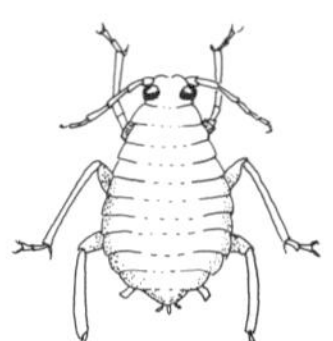
aphid

Aphrodite
Aphrodite Victorious

apiarist
Extracting frames from a hive

Apis

speaks in apocalyptic terms about the probable conflict ahead" (Financial Times). **3.** Characterized by usually exaggerated predictions of or allusions to a disastrous outcome: *"Stripped of its apocalyptic tone, what this amounts to is an advocacy of teaching names, dates and places by rote"* (Stefan Kanfer). **4.** Of a revelatory or prophetic nature. **—a·poc′a·lyp′ti·cal·ly** *adv.*

a·poc·a·lyp·ti·cism (ə-pŏk′ə-lĭp′tĭ-sĭz′əm) *n.* Belief in apocalyptic prophecies, especially regarding the imminent destruction of the world and the foundation of a new world order as a result of the triumph of good over evil.

ap·o·car·pous (ăp′ə-kär′pəs) *adj.* Having carpels that are free from one another. Used of a single flower with two or more separate pistils, as in roses. **—ap′o·car′py** (ăp′ə-kär′pē) *n.*

ap·o·chro·mat·ic (ăp′ə-krō-măt′ĭk) *adj.* Corrected for both chromatic and spherical aberration, as a lens.

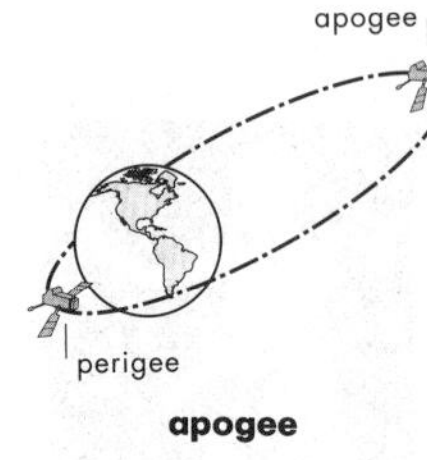

apogee

a·poc·o·pe (ə-pŏk′ə-pē) *n. Linguistics.* The loss of one or more sounds from the end of a word, as in Modern English *sing* from Middle English *singen.* [Late Latin, from Greek *apokopē,* from *apokoptein,* to cut off : *apo-,* apo- + *koptein,* to cut.]

ap·o·crine (ăp′ə-krĭn, -krīn′, -krēn′) *adj.* Of or relating to a type of glandular secretion in which the apical portion of the secreting cell is released along with the secretory products. [Probably from Greek *apokrinein,* to set apart : *apo-,* apo- + *krinein,* to separate; see **krei-** in Appendix.]

A·poc·ry·pha (ə-pŏk′rə-fə) *n. (used with a sing. or pl. verb).* **1.** *Abbr.* **Apoc.** *Bible.* The 14 books of the Septuagint included in the Vulgate but considered uncanonical by Protestants because they are not part of the Hebrew Scriptures. The Roman Catholic canon accepts 11 of these books and includes them in the Douay Bible. See table at **Bible. 2.** *Abbr.* **Apoc.** Various early Christian writings proposed as additions to the New Testament but rejected by the major canons. **3. apocrypha.** Writings or statements of questionable authorship or authenticity. [Middle English *apocripha,* not authentic, from Late Latin *Apocrypha,* the Apocrypha, from Greek *Apokrupha,* neuter pl. of *apokruphos,* secret, hidden, from *apokruptein,* to hide away : *apo-,* apo- + *kruptein, kruph-,* to hide.]

a·poc·ry·phal (ə-pŏk′rə-fəl) *adj.* **1.** Of questionable authorship or authenticity. **2.** Erroneous; fictitious: *"Wildly apocryphal rumors about starvation in Petrograd . . . raced through Russia's trenches"* (W. Bruce Lincoln). **3. Apocryphal.** *Abbr.* **Apoc.** *Bible.* Of or having to do with the Apocrypha. **—a·poc′ry·phal·ly** *adv.*

ap·o·dal (ăp′ə-dl) also **ap·o·dous** (-dəs) *adj.* Having no limbs, feet, or footlike appendages. [From Greek *apous : a-,* without; see A-¹ + *pous, pod-,* foot; see **ped-** in Appendix.]

ap·o·dic·tic (ăp′ə-dĭk′tĭk) *adj.* Necessarily or demonstrably true; incontrovertible. [Latin *apodīcticus,* from Greek *apodeiktikos,* from *apodeiktos,* demonstrable, from *apodeiknunai,* to demonstrate : *apo-,* apo- + *deiknunai,* to show; see **deik-** in Appendix.] **—ap′o·dic′ti·cal·ly** *adv.*

a·pod·o·sis (ə-pŏd′ə-sĭs) *n., pl.* **-ses** (-sēz′). The main clause of a conditional sentence, as *The game will be canceled* in *The game will be canceled if it rains.* [Late Latin, from Greek, from *apodidonai,* to give back : *apo-,* apo- + *didonai,* to give; see **dō-** in Appendix.]

ap·o·dous (ăp′ə-dəs) *adj.* Variant of **apodal.**

ap·o·en·zyme (ăp′ō-ĕn′zīm) *n.* The protein component of an enzyme, to which the coenzyme attaches to form an active enzyme.

a·pog·a·my (ə-pŏg′ə-mē) *n. Botany.* The development of an embryo without the occurrence of fertilization. **—ap′o·gam′ic** (ăp′ə-găm′ĭk), **a·pog′a·mous** *adj.*

ap·o·gee (ăp′ə-jē) *n.* **1.a.** The point in the orbit of the moon or of an artificial satellite most distant from the center of the earth. **b.** The point in an orbit most distant from the body being orbited. **2.** The farthest or highest point; the apex: *"The golden age of American sail, which began with the fast clipper ships in 1848, reached its apogee in the Gold Rush years"* (Los Angeles Times). [French *apogée,* from New Latin *apogaeum,* from Greek *apogaion,* from neuter of *apogaios,* far from the earth : *apo-,* apo- + *gaia,* earth.] **—ap′o·ge′an** (-jē′ən) *adj.*

Apollo
Apollo Belvedere

a·po·lit·i·cal (ā′pə-lĭt′ĭ-kəl) *adj.* **1.** Having no interest in or association with politics. **2.** Having no political importance: *an apolitical event.* **—a′po·lit′i·cal·ly** *adv.*

A·pol·li·naire (ə-pŏl′ə-nâr′), **Guillaume.** Originally Wilhelm Apollinaris de Kostrowitzky. 1880–1918. French poet and leading figure in avant-garde literary and artistic circles.

A·pol·lo (ə-pŏl′ō) *n.* **1.** *Greek Mythology.* The god of prophecy, music, medicine, and poetry, sometimes identified with the sun. **2. apollo** *pl.* **-los.** A young man of great physical beauty. [Latin, from Greek *Apollōn.*]

Ap·ol·lo·ni·an (ăp′ə-lō′nē-ən) *adj.* **1.** *Greek Mythology.* Of or relating to Apollo or his cult. **2.** Often **apollonian. a.** Characterized by clarity, harmony, and restraint. **b.** In the philosophy of Friedrich Nietzsche, of or embodying the power of critical reason as opposed to the creative-intuitive. **3.** Often **apollonian.** Serenely high-minded; noble.

a·pol·o·get·ic (ə-pŏl′ə-jĕt′ĭk) also **a·pol·o·get·i·cal** (-ĭ-kəl) *—adj.* **1.** Offering or expressing an apology or excuse: *an apologetic note; an apologetic smile.* **2.** Self-deprecating; humble: *an apologetic manner.* **3.** Justifying or defending in speech or writing. *—n.* A formal defense or apology. See Synonyms at **apology.** [Middle English, formal defense, from Latin *apologēticus,* from Greek *apologētikos,* suitable for defense, from *apologeisthai,* to defend oneself verbally, from *apologos,* apology, story. See APOLOGUE.] **—a·pol′o·get′i·cal·ly** *adv.*

a·pol·o·get·ics (ə-pŏl′ə-jĕt′ĭks) *n. (used with a sing. verb).* **1.** The branch of theology that is concerned with defending or proving the truth of Christian doctrines. **2.** Formal argumentation in defense of something, such as a position or system.

ap·o·lo·gi·a (ăp′ə-lō′jē-ə, -jə) *n.* A formal defense or justification. See Synonyms at **apology.** [Latin, apology, from Greek *apologia.* See APOLOGY.]

a·pol·o·gist (ə-pŏl′ə-jĭst) *n.* A person who argues in defense or justification of something, such as a doctrine, a policy, or an institution.

a·pol·o·gize (ə-pŏl′ə-jīz′) *intr.v.* **-gized, -giz·ing, -giz·es. 1.** To make excuse for or regretful acknowledgment of a fault or offense. **2.** To make a formal defense or justification in speech or writing. **—a·pol′o·giz′er** *n.*

ap·o·logue (ăp′ə-lôg′, -lŏg′) *n.* A moral fable, especially one having animals or inanimate objects as characters. [French, from Latin *apologus,* from Greek *apologos : apo-,* apo- + *logos,* speech; see **leg-** in Appendix.]

a·pol·o·gy (ə-pŏl′ə-jē) *n., pl.* **-gies. 1.** An acknowledgment expressing regret or asking pardon for a fault or offense. **2.a.** A formal justification or defense. **b.** An explanation or excuse: *"The consequence of those measures will be the best apology for my conduct"* (Daniel Defoe). **3.** An inferior substitute: *The sagging cot was a poor apology for a bed.* [Latin *apologia,* from Greek : *apo-,* apo- + *logos,* speech; see **leg-** in Appendix.]

SYNONYMS: *apology, apologetic, apologia, defense, justification.* The central meaning shared by these nouns is "a statement that justifies or defends something, such as a past action or a policy": *a report that is an apology for capital punishment; an apologetic for fascism; a version of the story that is an apologia for malfeasance; offered a defense based on ignorance of the circumstances; an intellectually untenable justification for police brutality.*

a·po·lune (ăp′ə-lo͞on′) *n.* The point of an orbit around the moon farthest from the moon's center. [APO– + Latin *luna,* moon; see LUNE.]

ap·o·mict (ăp′ə-mĭkt′) *n.* A plant that reproduces by or is reproduced by apomixis. [Back-formation from *apomictic,* produced by apomixis : APO– + Greek *miktos,* mixed (from *mignunai,* to mix; see APOMIXIS).] **—ap′o·mic′tic** *adj.* **—ap′o·mic′ti·cal·ly** *adv.*

ap·o·mix·is (ăp′ə-mĭk′sĭs) *n.* Reproduction without meiosis or formation of gametes. [APO– + Greek *mixis,* a mingling (from *mignunai,* to mingle; see **meik-** in Appendix).]

ap·o·mor·phine (ăp′ə-môr′fēn′) *n.* A poisonous white crystalline alkaloid, $C_{17}H_{17}NO_2$, derived from morphine and used medicinally to induce vomiting.

ap·o·neu·ro·sis (ăp′ə-no͝o-rō′sĭs, -nyo͝o-) *n., pl.* **-ses** (-sēz′). A sheetlike fibrous membrane, resembling a flattened tendon, that serves as a fascia to bind muscles together or as a means of connecting muscle to bone. [Greek *aponeurōsis,* from *aponeurousthai,* to become tendinous : *apo-,* apo- + *neuron,* sinew; see **(s)neəu-** in Appendix.] **—ap′o·neu·rot′ic** (-rŏt′ĭk) *adj.*

a·poph·a·sis (ə-pŏf′ə-sĭs) *n.* Allusion to something by denying that it will be mentioned, as in *I will not bring up my opponent's questionable financial dealings.* [Late Latin, from Greek, from *apophanai,* to say no : *apo-,* apo- + *phanai,* to say; see **bhā-²** in Appendix.]

ap·o·phthegm (ăp′ə-thĕm′) *n.* Variant of **apothegm.**

a·poph·y·ge (ə-pŏf′ə-jē) *n. Architecture.* The outward curve at the top and bottom of a column where the shaft joins the capital or base. [Greek *apophugē,* from *apopheugein,* to flee : *apo-,* apo- + *pheugein, phug-,* to flee.]

a·poph·yl·lite (ə-pŏf′ə-līt′, ăp′ə-fĭl′īt′) *n.* A white, pale pink, or pale green crystalline mineral, essentially $KCa_4Si_8O_{20}(F,OH)\cdot 8H_2O$.

a·poph·y·sis (ə-pŏf′ĭ-sĭs) *n., pl.* **-ses** (-sēz′). **1.** *Anatomy.* A natural swelling, projection, or outgrowth of an organ or part, such as the process of a vertebra. **2.** *Geology.* A branch from a dike or vein. [New Latin, from Greek *apophusis,* from *apophuein,* to send out branches : *apo-,* apo- + *phuein,* to grow; see **bheuə-** in Appendix.] **—a·poph′y·sate′** (-sāt′), **a·poph′y·se′al** (-sē′əl) *adj.*

ap·o·plec·tic (ăp′ə-plĕk′tĭk) *adj.* **1.** Of, resembling, or produced by apoplexy: *an apoplectic fit.* **2.a.** Having or inclined to have apoplexy. **b.** Exhibiting symptoms associated with apoplexy. **3.** Extremely angry; furious: *"members of Congress who otherwise become apoplectic about wasteful government spending"* (Dan Morgan). **—ap′o·plec′ti·cal·ly** *adv.*

ap·o·plex·y (ăp′ə-plĕk′sē) *n.* **1.** Sudden impairment of neurological function, especially that resulting from a cerebral hemorrhage; a stroke. **2.** A sudden effusion of blood into an organ or tissue. **3.** A fit of extreme anger; rage: *"The proud . . . members suffered collective apoplexy, and this year they are out for blood"* (David Finch). [Middle English *apoplexie,* from Old French, from Late Latin *apoplēxia,* from Greek, from *apoplēssein,* to cripple by a stroke : *apo-,* intensive prefix; see APO– + *plēssein, plēk-,* to strike; see **plāk-²** in Appendix.]

ă pat	oi boy
ā pay	ou out
âr care	o͝o took
ä father	o͞o boot
ĕ pet	ŭ cut
ē be	ûr urge
ĭ pit	th thin
ī pie	*th* this
îr pier	hw which
ŏ pot	zh vision
ō toe	ə about, item
ô paw	♦ regionalism

Stress marks: ′ (primary); ′ (secondary), as in **dictionary** (dĭk′shə-nĕr′ē)

a·port (ə-pôrt′, ə-pōrt′) *adv. Nautical.* On or toward the port or left side of a ship.

ap·o·se·mat·ic coloration (ăp′ə-sə-măt′ĭk) *n.* See **warning coloration.**

ap·o·si·o·pe·sis (ăp′ə-sī′ə-pē′sĭs) *n., pl.* **-ses** (-sēz). A sudden breaking off of a thought in the middle of a sentence, as though the speaker were unwilling or unable to continue. [Late Latin *aposiōpēsis,* from Greek, from *aposiōpan,* to become silent : *apo-,* intensive pref.; see APO– + *siōpan,* to be silent (from *siōpē,* silence).] **—ap′o·si′o·pet′ic** (-pĕt′ĭk) *adj.*

ap·o·spor·y (ăp′ə-spôr′ē, -spōr′ē, ə-pŏs′pə-rē) *n.* The development of a gametophyte directly from a sporophyte without the occurrence of meiosis or spore formation. **—a·pos′por·ous** (ə-pŏs′pər-əs) *adj.*

a·pos·ta·sy (ə-pŏs′tə-sē) *n., pl.* **-sies.** Abandonment of one's religious faith, a political party, one's principles, or a cause. [Middle English *apostasie,* from Old French, from Late Latin *apostasia,* defection, from Late Greek, from Greek *apostasis,* revolt, from *aphistanai,* to revolt : *apo-,* apo- + *histanai,* to stand, place; see **stā-** in Appendix.]

a·pos·tate (ə-pŏs′tāt′, -tĭt) *n.* One who practices apostasy. [Middle English, from Old French, from Late Latin *apostata,* from Greek *apostatēs,* from *aphistanai,* to revolt. See APOSTASY.] **—a·pos′tate′** *adj.*

a·pos·ta·tize (ə-pŏs′tə-tīz′) *intr.v.* **-tized, -tiz·ing, -tiz·es.** To abandon one's religious faith, a political party, one's principles, or a cause.

a pos·te·ri·o·ri (ä′ pŏ-stîr′ē-ôr′ē, -ôr′ī, -ōr′ē, -ōr′ī, ā′) *adj.* Derived by or designating the process of reasoning from facts or particulars to general principles or from effects to causes; inductive; empirical. [Medieval Latin : Latin *a,* from + Latin *posteriōrī,* ablative of *posterior,* later.]

a·pos·tle (ə-pŏs′əl) *n.* **1.a. Apostle.** One of a group made up especially of the 12 disciples chosen by Jesus to preach the gospel. **b.** A missionary of the early Christian Church. **c.** A leader of the first Christian mission to a country or region. **2.** *Mormon Church.* One of the 12 members of the administrative council. **3.a.** One who pioneers an important reform movement, cause, or belief: *an apostle of conservation.* **b.** A passionate adherent; a strong supporter. [Middle English, from Old English *apostol* and from Old French *apostle,* both from Late Latin *apostolus,* from Greek *apostolos,* messenger, from *apostellein,* to send off : *apo-,* apo- + *stellein,* to send; see **stel-** in Appendix.] **—a·pos′tle·hood′** *n.* **—a·pos′tle·ship′** *n.*

A·pos·tles' Creed (ə-pŏs′əlz) *n.* A Christian creed traditionally ascribed to the 12 Apostles and used typically in public worship services.

a·pos·to·late (ə-pŏs′tə-lāt′, -lĭt) *n.* **1.** The office, duties, or mission of an apostle. **2.** An association of individuals for the dissemination of a religion or a doctrine. [Late Latin *apostolātus,* from *apostolus,* apostle. See APOSTLE.]

ap·os·tol·ic (ăp′ə-stŏl′ĭk) *adj.* **1.** Of, relating to, or contemporary with the 12 Apostles. **2.** Of or relating to the faith, teaching, or practice of the 12 Apostles. **3.a.** Of or relating to a succession of spiritual authority from the 12 Apostles, regarded by Anglicans, Roman Catholics, Eastern Orthodox, and some others to have been perpetuated by successive ordinations of bishops and to be requisite for valid orders and administration of sacraments. **b.** *Roman Catholic Church.* Of or relating to the pope as the successor of Saint Peter; papal.

apostolic delegate *n. Roman Catholic Church.* An ecclesiastical representative of the Vatican to a country having no formal diplomatic relations with it.

Ap·os·tol·ic Father (ăp′ə-stŏl′ĭk) *n.* A church father of the first or second century A.D. who was believed to have received personal instruction from the 12 Apostles or from their disciples.

a·pos·tro·phe¹ (ə-pŏs′trə-fē) *n.* The superscript sign (') used to indicate the omission of a letter or letters from a word, the possessive case, and the plurals of numbers, letters, and abbreviations. [French, from Late Latin *apostrophus,* from Greek *apostrophos,* from *apostrephein,* to turn away : *apo-,* apo- + *strephein,* to turn; see **streb(h)-** in Appendix.] **—ap′os·troph′ic** (ăp′ə-strŏf′ĭk) *adj.*

a·pos·tro·phe² (ə-pŏs′trə-fē) *n.* The direct address of an absent or imaginary person or of a personified abstraction, especially as a digression in the course of a speech or composition. [Late Latin *apostrophē,* from Greek, from *apostrephein,* to turn away. See APOSTROPHE¹.] **—ap′os·troph′ic** (ăp′ə-strŏf′ĭk) *adj.*

a·pos·tro·phize (ə-pŏs′trə-fīz′) *tr. & intr.v.* **-phized, -phiz·ing, -phiz·es.** To address by or speak or write in apostrophe.

a·poth·e·car·ies' measure (ə-pŏth′ĭ-kĕr′ēz) *n.* A system of liquid volume measure used in pharmacy.

apothecaries' weight *n.* A system of weights used in pharmacy and based on an ounce equal to 480 grains and a pound equal to 12 ounces.

a·poth·e·car·y (ə-pŏth′ĭ-kĕr′ē) *n., pl.* **-ies.** *Abbr.* **ap. 1.** One that prepares and sells drugs and other medicines; a pharmacist. **2.** See **pharmacy** (sense 2). [Middle English *apotecarie,* from Old French *apotecaire* and from Medieval Latin *apothēcārius,* both from Late Latin, clerk, from Latin *apothēca,* storehouse, from Greek *apothēkē* : *apo-,* away; see APO– + *thēkē,* receptacle; see **dhē-** in Appendix.]

ap·o·the·ci·um (ăp′ə-thē′sē-əm, -shē-) *n., pl.* **-ci·a** (-sē-ə, -shē-ə). A disk-shaped or cup-shaped ascocarp of some lichens and the fungi Ascomycetes. [From Latin *apothēca,* storehouse. See APOTHECARY.] **—ap′o·the′cial** (-shəl) *adj.*

ap·o·thegm also **ap·o·phthegm** (ăp′ə-thĕm′) *n.* A terse, witty, instructive saying; a maxim. [Greek *apophthegma,* from *apophthengesthai,* to speak plainly : *apo-,* intensive pref.; see APO– + *phthengesthai, phtheg-,* to speak.] **—ap′o·theg·mat′ic** (-thĕg-măt′ĭk), **ap′o·theg·mat′i·cal** (-ĭ-kəl) *adj.* **—ap′o·theg·mat′i·cal·ly** *adv.*

ap·o·them (ăp′ə-thĕm′) *n. Mathematics.* The perpendicular distance from the center of a regular polygon to any of its sides. [APO– + Greek *thema,* something laid down; see THEME.]

Apostle
Detail of Leonardo da Vinci's fresco *The Last Supper*; *left to right*: Judas, Saint Peter, and Saint John

a·poth·e·o·sis (ə-pŏth′ē-ō′sĭs, ăp′ə-thē′ə-sĭs) *n., pl.* **-ses** (-sēz′). **1.** Exaltation to divine rank or stature; deification. **2.** An exalted or glorified example: *Their leader was the apotheosis of courage.* [Late Latin *apotheōsis,* from Greek, from *apotheoun,* to deify : *apo-,* change; see APO– + *theos,* god; see **dhēs-** in Appendix.]

ap·o·the·o·size (ăp′ə-thē′ə-sīz′, ə-pŏth′ē-ə-sīz′) *tr.v.* **-sized, -siz·ing, -siz·es.** To glorify; exalt.

ap·o·tro·pa·ic (ăp′ə-trō-pā′ĭk) *adj.* Intended to ward off evil: *an apotropaic symbol.* [From Greek *apotropaios,* from *apotrepein,* to ward off : *apo-,* apo- + *trepein,* to turn; see **trep-** in Appendix.] **—ap′o·tro·pa′i·cal·ly** *adv.*

app. *abbr.* **1.** Apparatus. **2.** Appendix. **3.** Applied. **4.a.** Appoint. **b.** Appointed. **5.** Apprentice.

Ap·pa·la·chi·a (ăp′ə-lā′chē-ə, -chə, -lăch′ē-ə, -lăch′ə). A region of the eastern United States including the Appalachian Mountains.

Ap·pa·la·chi·an Mountains (ăp′ə-lā′chē-ən, -chən, -lăch′ē-ən, -lăch′ən). A mountain system of eastern North America extending about 2,574 km (1,600 mi) southwest from Newfoundland, New Brunswick, and southern Quebec, Canada, to central Alabama. The range includes the Allegheny, Blue Ridge, and Cumberland mountains. Mount Mitchell in western North Carolina is the highest peak, rising to 2,038.6 m (6,684 ft).

Appalachian tea *n.* See **withe rod.**

Appalachian Trail. A hiking path of the eastern United States extending about 3,298 km (2,050 mi) from Mount Katahdin in central Maine to Springer Mountain in northern Georgia. It is the world's longest continuous mountain trail.

ap·pall (ə-pôl′) *tr.v.* **-palled, -pall·ing, -palls.** To fill with consternation or dismay. See Synonyms at **dismay.** [Middle English *apallen,* to grow faint, from Old French *apalir* : *a-,* to (from Latin *ad-*; see AD–) + *palir,* to grow pale (from *pale,* pale, from Latin *pallidus,* from *pallēre,* to grow pale; see **pel-¹** in Appendix).]

appaloosa
Dreamfinder, National Grand Champion

ap·pall·ing (ə-pô′lĭng) *adj.* Causing consternation or dismay; frightful: *appalling working conditions; appalling violence.* **—ap·pall′ing·ly** *adv.*

ap·pa·loo·sa (ăp′ə-lo͞o′sə) *n.* A breed of saddle horse developed in northwest North America, characteristically having a spotted rump. [Origin unknown.]

ap·pa·nage also **ap·a·nage** (ăp′ə-nĭj) *n.* **1.** A source of revenue, such as land, given by a sovereign for the maintenance of a member of the ruling family. **2.** Something extra offered to or claimed by a party as due; a perquisite: *The leaders of the opposition party agreed to accept another government's appanages, and in doing so became an officially paid agency of a foreign power.* **3.** A rightful or customary accompaniment or adjunct. [French *apanage,* from Old French, from *apaner,* to make provisions for, possibly from Medieval Latin *appānāre* : Latin *ad-,* ad- + Latin *pānis,* bread; see **pā-** in Appendix.]

ap·pa·rat (ăp′ə-răt′, ä′pə-rät′) *n.* See **apparatus** (sense 1). [Russian, the government organization or staff, from German *Apparat,* a political organization, from Latin *apparātus,* preparation. See APPARATUS.]

ap·pa·ra·tchik (ä′pə-rä′chĭk) *n., pl.* **-tchiks** or **-tchi·ki** (-chĭ-kē). **1.** A member of a Communist apparat. **2.** An unquestioningly loyal subordinate, especially of a political leader or organization. [Russian, from *apparat,* apparat. See APPARAT.]

ap·pa·ra·tus (ăp′ə-rā′təs, -răt′əs) *n., pl.* **apparatus** or **-tus·es.** *Abbr.* **app. 1.a.** The totality of means by which a designated function is performed or a specific task executed, as in a system of government. **b.** A political organization or an underground political movement. Also called *apparat.* **2.a.** An appliance or device for a particular purpose: *an x-ray apparatus.* **b.** An integrated group of materials or devices used for a particular purpose: *dental apparatus.* See Synonyms at **equipment. 3.** *Physiology.* A group or system of organs that collectively perform a specific function or process: *the respiratory apparatus; the digestive apparatus.* [Latin *apparātus,* preparation, from past participle of *apparāre,* to prepare : *ad-,* ad- + *parāre,* to prepare; see **perə-¹** in Appendix.]

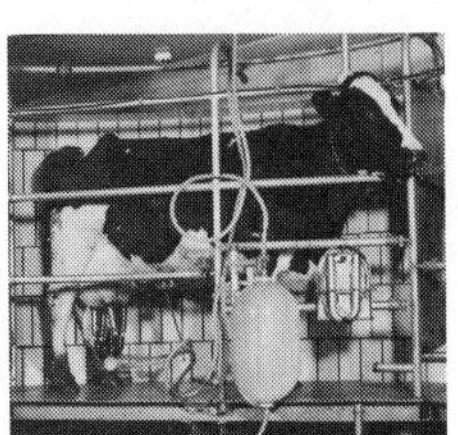

apparatus
Milking machine

ap·par·el (ə-păr′əl) *n.* **1.** Clothing, especially outer garments; attire. **2.** A covering or an adornment: *trees with their apparel of foliage.* **—apparel** *tr.v.* **-eled, -el·ing, -els** or **-elled, -el·ling, -els. 1.** To clothe or dress. **2.** To adorn or embellish. [Middle English *appareil,* from Old French *apareil,* preparation, from *apa-*

reillier, to prepare, possibly from Vulgar Latin **appariculāre,* from Latin *apparāre.* See APPARATUS.]

ap·par·ent (ə-păr′ənt, ə-pâr′-) *adj.* **1.** Readily seen; visible. **2.** Readily understood; clear or obvious. **3.** Appearing as such but not necessarily so; seeming: *an apparent advantage.* [Middle English, from Old French *aparant,* present participle of *aparoir,* to appear. See APPEAR.] **—ap·par′ent·ly** *adv.* **—ap·par′ent·ness** *n.*

SYNONYMS: *apparent, clear, clear-cut, distinct, evident, manifest, obvious, patent, plain.* The central meaning shared by these adjectives is "readily seen, perceived, or understood": *Angry for no apparent reason; a clear danger; clear-cut evidence of tampering; distinct fingerprints; evident hostility; manifest pleasure; obvious errors; patent advantages; making my meaning plain.*

USAGE NOTE: Used before a noun, *apparent* means "seeming": *For all his apparent wealth, Pat had no money to pay the rent.* Used after a form of the verb *be,* however, *apparent* can mean either "seeming" (as in *His virtues are only apparent*) or "obvious" (as in *The effects of the drought are apparent to anyone who sees the parched fields*). Writers should take care that the intended meaning is clear from the context.

apparent horizon *n.* See **horizon** (sense 1).

apparent magnitude *n. Astronomy.* See **magnitude** (sense 2).

ap·pa·ri·tion (ăp′ə-rĭsh′ən) *n.* **1.** A ghostly figure; a specter. **2.** A sudden or unusual sight. **3.** The act of appearing; appearance. [Middle English *apparicioun,* from Old French *apparition,* from Late Latin *appāritiō, appāritiōn-,* an appearance, from Latin *appāritus,* past participle of *appārēre,* to appear. See APPEAR.] **—ap′pa·ri′tion·al** *adj.*

ap·par·i·tor (ə-păr′ĭ-tər) *n.* An official who was formerly sent to carry out the orders of a civil or ecclesiastical court. [Middle English, from Latin *appāritor,* from *appārēre,* to appear. See APPEAR.]

ap·peal (ə-pēl′) *n.* **1.** An earnest or urgent request, entreaty, or supplication. **2.** A resort or application to a higher authority, as for sanction, corroboration, or a decision: *an appeal to reason.* **3.** *Law.* **a.** The transfer of a case from a lower to a higher court for a new hearing. **b.** A case so transferred. **c.** A request for a new hearing. **4.** The power of attracting or of arousing interest: *a city with appeal for tourists.* **—appeal** *v.* **-pealed, -peal·ing, -peals.** —*intr.* **1.** To make an earnest or urgent request, as for help. **2.** To have recourse, as for corroboration; resort: *I appeal to your sense of justice.* **3.** *Law.* To make or apply for an appeal. **4.** To be attractive or interesting. —*tr. Law.* To transfer or apply to transfer (a case) to a higher court for rehearing. [Middle English *apel,* from Old French, from *apeler,* to appeal, from Latin *appellāre,* to entreat. See **pel-**[5] in Appendix.] **—ap·peal′a·bil′i·ty** *n.* **—ap·peal′a·ble** *adj.* **—ap·peal′er** *n.*

ap·pear (ə-pîr′) *intr.v.* **-peared, -pear·ing, -pears. 1.** To become visible: *a plane appearing in the sky.* **2.** To come into existence: *New strains of viruses appear periodically.* **3.** To seem or look to be: *appeared unhappy.* **4.** To seem likely: *They will be late, as it appears.* **5.** To come before the public: *has appeared in two plays; appears on the nightly news.* **6.** *Law.* To present oneself formally before a court as defendant, plaintiff, or counsel. [Middle English *aperen,* from Old French *aparoir, aper-,* from Latin *appārēre* : *ad-,* ad- + *pārēre,* to show.]

SYNONYMS: *appear, emerge, issue, loom, materialize, show.* The central meaning shared by these verbs is "to come into view": *a ship appearing on the horizon; a star that emerged from behind a cloud; a diver issuing from the water; a peak that loomed through the mist; a flash of lightning that seemed to materialize from nowhere; a ruffle showing at the edge of the sleeve.* See also Synonyms at **seem.**

ap·pear·ance (ə-pîr′əns) *n.* **1.** The act or an instance of coming into sight. **2.** The act or an instance of coming into public view: *The author made a rare personal appearance.* **3.** Outward aspect: *an untidy appearance.* **4.** Something that appears; a phenomenon. **5.** A superficial aspect; a semblance: *keeping up an appearance of wealth.* **6. appearances.** Outward indications; circumstances: *a cheerful person, to all appearances.*

ap·pease (ə-pēz′) *tr.v.* **-peased, -peas·ing, -peas·es. 1.** To bring peace, quiet, or calm to; soothe. **2.** To satisfy or relieve: *appease thirst.* **3.** To pacify or attempt to pacify (an enemy) by granting concessions, often at the expense of principle. See Synonyms at **pacify.** [Middle English *appesen,* from Old French *apesier* : *a-,* to (from Latin *ad-;* see AD–) + *pais,* peace (from Latin *pāx;* see **pag-** in Appendix).] **—ap·peas′a·ble** *adj.* **—ap·peas′a·bly** *adv.* **—ap·peas′er** *n.*

ap·pease·ment (ə-pēz′mənt) *n.* **1.a.** An act of appeasing. **b.** The condition of being appeased. **2.** The policy of granting concessions to potential enemies to maintain peace.

ap·pel (ə-pĕl′) *n. Sports.* A quick stamp of the foot used in fencing as a feint to produce an opening. [French, from *appeler,* to call, from Old French *apeler,* to appeal. See APPEAL.]

ap·pel·lant (ə-pĕl′ənt) *Law. adj.* Of or relating to an appeal; appellate. **—appellant** *n.* One that appeals a court decision. [Middle English, from Old French *apelant,* from present participle of *apeler,* to appeal. See APPEAL.]

ap·pel·late (ə-pĕl′ĭt) *adj. Law.* Having the power to hear appeals and to review court decisions. [Latin *appellātus,* past participle of *appellāre,* to entreat. See APPEAL.]

ap·pel·la·tion (ăp′ə-lā′shən) *n.* **1.** A name, title, or designation. See Synonyms at **name. 2.** The act of naming. [Middle English *appelacion,* from Old French *appelation,* from Latin *appellātiō, appellātiōn-,* from *appellātus,* past participle of *appellāre,* to entreat. See APPEAL.]

ap·pel·la·tive (ə-pĕl′ə-tĭv) *adj.* **1.** Of or relating to the assignment of names. **2.** *Grammar.* Of or relating to a common noun. **—appellative** *n.* A name or descriptive epithet. [Middle English, common (noun), from Old French *appelatif,* from Late Latin *appellātīvus,* from Latin *appellātus,* past participle of *appellāre,* to call upon, entreat. See APPEAL.] **—ap·pel′la·tive·ly** *adv.*

ap·pel·lee (ăp′ə-lē′) *n. Law.* One against whom an appeal is taken. [French *appelé,* from Old French *apele,* from past participle of *apeler,* to appeal. See APPEAL.]

ap·pend (ə-pĕnd′) *tr.v.* **-pend·ed, -pend·ing, -pends. 1.** To add as a supplement or an appendix: *appended a list of errors to the report.* **2.** To fix to; attach: *append a charm to the bracelet.* [Latin *appendere,* to hang upon : *ad-,* ad- + *pendere,* to hang; see **(s)pen-** in Appendix.]

ap·pend·age (ə-pĕn′dĭj) *n.* **1.** Something added or attached to an entity of greater importance or size; an adjunct. **2.** *Biology.* A part or an organ, such as an arm, a leg, a tail, or a fin, that is joined to the axis or trunk of a body.

SYNONYMS: *appendage, appurtenance, adjunct, accessory, attachment.* These nouns denote subordinate elements that are added to another entity. An *appendage* supplements without being essential: *"Water jets can be angled to either side, making rudders unnecessary, and the complete absence of appendages at the stern decreases hull resistance"* (R.J.L. Dicker). An *appurtenance* belongs naturally as a subsidiary attribute, part, or member to that with which it is associated: *"an internationally known first-class hotel . . . equipped with such appurtenances as computers, word processors, copiers and telex"* (Oscar Millard). An *adjunct* is added as an auxiliary to something else but is often self-sustaining: *"Intelligence analysts say they believe that of all the countries of the Middle East, none use terrorism more effectively as an adjunct to diplomacy than Syria"* (Elaine Sciolino). An *accessory* is usually nonessential but desirable and adds to the effect of something already complete in itself: *We bought a car with such accessories as air conditioning, stereo, and a sunroof.* An *attachment* contributes a supplementary function to the principal thing, to which it can be physically linked: *The food processor has an attachment for making pasta.*

ap·pen·dant (ə-pĕn′dənt) *adj.* **1.** Affixed as an appendage. **2.** Accompanying; attendant: *faith and its appendant hope.* **3.** Belonging to a land grant as a subsidiary right in English law. **—ap·pen′dant** *n.*

ap·pen·dec·to·my (ăp′ən-dĕk′tə-mē) *n., pl.* **-mies.** Surgical removal of the vermiform appendix. [APPEND(IX) + -ECTOMY.]

ap·pen·di·ces (ə-pĕn′dĭ-sēz′) *n.* A plural of **appendix.**

ap·pen·di·ci·tis (ə-pĕn′dĭ-sī′tĭs) *n.* Inflammation of the vermiform appendix. [New Latin, from Latin *appendix, appendic-,* appendage. See APPENDIX.]

WORD HISTORY: Even though the word *appendicitis* was in use in 1885, the year in which the *Oxford English Dictionary* published the section "Anta–Battening" that would have contained the word, the editor, James Murray, omitted this "crack-jaw medical and surgical word" on the advice of Oxford's Regius Professor of Medicine, Sir Henry Wentworth Acland. As K.M. Elisabeth Murray, the granddaughter and biographer of James Murray, points out, "The problem of what scientific words to include was a continuing one, and James Murray was always under pressure—from his advisers . . . who thought the emphasis should be on words from good literature and from those in the [Oxford University] Press who wanted to save cost and time—not to include scientific words of recent origin." In 1902 no less a person than Edward VII had his appendix removed, and his coronation was postponed because of the operation. *Appendicitis* hence came into widespread use and has remained so, thereby pointing up the lexicographer's difficult task of selecting the new words that people will look for in their dictionaries.

ap·pen·dic·u·lar (ăp′ən-dĭk′yə-lər) *adj.* Of, relating to, or consisting of an appendage or appendages, especially the limbs: *the appendicular skeleton.* [From Latin *appendicula,* diminutive of *appendix, appendic-,* appendix. See APPENDIX.]

ap·pen·dix (ə-pĕn′dĭks) *n., pl.* **-dix·es** or **-di·ces** (-dĭ-sēz′). *Abbr.* **app. 1.a.** An appendage. **b.** A collection of supplementary material, usually at the end of a book. **2.** The vermiform appendix. **3.** *Anatomy.* A supplementary or accessory part of a bodily organ or structure. [Latin, from *appendere,* to hang upon. See APPEND.]

ap·per·ceive (ăp′ər-sēv′) *tr.v.* **-ceived, -ceiv·ing, -ceives.** *Psychology.* To perceive in terms of past experiences. [From APPERCEPTION.]

ap·per·cep·tion (ăp′ər-sĕp′shən) *n. Psychology.* **1.** Conscious perception with full awareness. **2.** The process of understanding by which newly observed qualities of an object are related to past experience. [New Latin *apperceptiō, apperceptiōn-* : Latin *ad-*, ad- + Latin *perceptiō*, perception; see PERCEPTION.] **—ap′per·cep′tive** (-sĕp′tĭv) *adj.*

ap·per·tain (ăp′ər-tān′) *intr.v.* **-tained, -tain·ing, -tains.** To belong as a proper function or part; pertain: *problems appertaining to social reform.* [Middle English *appertenen,* from Old French *apartenir,* from Vulgar Latin **appartenēre,* from Late Latin *appertinēre* : *ad-*, ad- + *pertinēre,* to belong; see PERTAIN.]

ap·pe·stat (ăp′ĭ-stăt′) *n.* The area in the brain that is believed to regulate appetite and food intake. [APPE(TITE) + —STAT.]

ap·pe·tence (ăp′ĭ-təns) *n.* **1.** A strong craving or desire. **2.** A tendency or propensity. **3.** A natural attraction or affinity. [Probably French *appétence,* from Latin *appetentia,* from *appetēns, appetent-,* present participle of *appetere,* to strive after. See APPETITE.]

ap·pe·ten·cy (ăp′ĭ-tən-sē) *n., pl.* **-cies.** Appetence. [Latin *appetentia.* See APPETENCE.]

ap·pe·tite (ăp′ĭ-tīt′) *n.* **1.** An instinctive physical desire, especially one for food or drink. **2.** A strong wish or urge: *an appetite for learning.* [Middle English *apetit,* from Old French, from Latin *appetītus,* strong desire, from past participle of *appetere,* to strive after : *ad-*, ad- + *petere,* to seek; see **pet-** in Appendix.] **—ap′pe·ti′tive** (ăp′ĭ-tī′tĭv, ə-pĕt′ĭ-tĭv) *adj.*

ap·pe·tiz·er (ăp′ĭ-tī′zər) *n.* A food or drink served usually before a meal to stimulate the appetite.

ap·pe·tiz·ing (ăp′ĭ-tī′zĭng) *adj.* Appealing to or stimulating the appetite. **—ap′pe·tiz′ing·ly** *adv.*

Ap·pi·an Way (ăp′ē-ən). An ancient Roman road between Rome and Capua, begun in A.D. 312 and later extended to Brindisi, with a total length of more than 563 km (350 mi).

appl. *abbr.* Applied.

ap·plaud (ə-plôd′) *v.* **-plaud·ed, -plaud·ing, -plauds.** —*intr.* To express approval, especially by clapping the hands. —*tr.* **1.** To express approval of (someone or something) especially by such clapping. **2.** To commend highly; praise: *applauded her decision to complete her degree.* [Middle English *applauden,* from Latin *applaudere* : *ad-*, ad- + *plaudere,* to clap.] **—ap·plaud′a·ble** *adj.* **—ap·plaud′a·bly** *adv.* **—ap·plaud′er** *n.*

SYNONYMS: *applaud, cheer, root.* The central meaning shared by these verbs is "to express approval or encouragement in audible form, especially by clapping": *applauded at the end of the concert; cheered when the home team scored; rooting for the underdog in the tennis championship.*

ap·plause (ə-plôz′) *n.* **1.** Approval expressed especially by the clapping of hands. **2.** Praise; commendation: *a scientific discovery that won critical applause.* [Medieval Latin *applausus,* from past participle of Latin *applaudere,* to applaud. See APPLAUD.]

ap·ple (ăp′əl) *n.* **1.a.** A deciduous Eurasian tree *(Malus pumila)* having alternate simple leaves and white or pink flowers. **b.** The firm, edible, usually rounded fruit of this tree. **2.a.** Any of several other plants, especially those with fruits suggestive of the apple, such as the crab apple or custard apple. **b.** The fruit of any of these plants. ***—idiom.* apple of (one's) eye.** One that is treasured: *Her grandson is the apple of her eye.* [Middle English *appel,* from Old English *æppel.*]

apple green *n. Color.* A moderate or vivid yellow green to light or strong yellowish green. **—ap′ple-green′** (ăp′əl-grēn′) *adj.*

ap·ple·jack (ăp′əl-jăk′) *n.* **1.** Brandy distilled from hard cider. **2.** An alcoholic drink made from hard cider that has been frozen.

apple of Peru *n.* An annual Peruvian plant *(Nicandra physalodes),* grown as an ornamental for its pale violet-blue, bell-shaped flowers and fruits enclosed in papery, inflated calyxes. Also called *shoo-fly plant.*

ap·ple-pie (ăp′əl-pī′) *adj. Informal.* **1.** Nearly perfect: *put the room in apple-pie order.* **2.** Often **apple pie.** Of, relating to, or marked by values regarded as distinctively American: *"Family, neighborhood, community are apple pie virtues, unassailable and unavoidable in political rhetoric"* (Ronald Brownstein).

ap·ple-pol·ish (ăp′əl-pŏl′ĭsh) *v.* **-ished, -ish·ing, -ish·es.** *Informal.* —*intr.* To seek favor by toadying. —*tr.* To seek favor with; flatter. See Synonyms at **fawn**[1]. **—apple polisher, ap′ple-pol′ish·er** *n.*

ap·ple·sauce (ăp′əl-sôs′) *n.* **1.** Apples stewed to a pulp, sweetened, and sometimes spiced. **2.** *Slang.* Nonsense.

Ap·ple·seed (ăp′əl-sēd′), **Johnny.** See John **Chapman.**

Ap·ple·ton (ăp′əl-tən). A city of eastern Wisconsin on the Fox River southwest of Green Bay. The first hydroelectric plant in the United States was built here in 1882. Population, 58,913.

Appleton, Sir **Edward Victor.** 1892–1965. British physicist. He won a 1947 Nobel Prize for his discovery of the F layer of the ionosphere.

Ap·ple Valley (ăp′əl). A city of southeast Minnesota, a residential suburb of Minneapolis–St. Paul. Population, 21,818.

ap·pli·ance (ə-plī′əns) *n.* **1.** A device or instrument designed to perform a specific function, especially an electrical device, such as a toaster, for household use. See Synonyms at **tool.** **2.** A dental or surgical device designed to perform a therapeutic or corrective function. [From APPLY.]

ap·pli·ca·ble (ăp′lĭ-kə-bəl, ə-plĭk′ə-) *adj.* That can be applied; appropriate: *gave applicable examples to support her argument.* **—ap′pli·ca·bil′i·ty** *n.* **—ap′pli·ca·bly** *adv.*

ap·pli·cant (ăp′lĭ-kənt) *n.* One that applies, as for a job. [Middle English, from Latin *applicāns,* present participle of *applicāre,* to affix. See APPLY.]

ap·pli·ca·tion (ăp′lĭ-kā′shən) *n.* **1.** The act of applying. **2.** Something applied, such as a cosmetic or curative agent. **3.a.** The act of putting something to a special use or purpose: *an application of a new method.* **b.** A specific use to which something is put: *the application of science to industry.* **4.** The capacity of being usable; relevance: *Geometry has practical application in aviation and navigation.* **5.** Close attention; diligence: *shows application to her work.* See Synonyms at **effort.** **6.a.** A request, as for assistance, employment, or admission to a school. **b.** The form or document on which such a request is made. **—application** also **applications** *adj. Computer Science.* Of or being a computer program designed for a specific task or use: *applications software for a missile guidance system.* [Middle English *applicacion,* from Old French, from Latin *applicātiō, applicātiōn-,* from *applicātus,* past participle of *applicāre,* to affix. See APPLY.]

ap·pli·ca·tive (ăp′lĭ-kā′tĭv, ə-plĭk′ə-) *adj.* **1.** Characterized by actual application; applied. **2.** Practical; applicatory. **—ap′pli·ca′tive·ly** *adv.*

ap·pli·ca·tor (ăp′lĭ-kā′tər) *n.* An instrument for applying something, such as medicine or glue.

ap·pli·ca·to·ry (ăp′lĭ-kə-tôr′ē, -tōr′ē, ə-plĭk′ə-) *adj.* Readily applicable; practical.

ap·plied (ə-plīd′) *adj. Abbr.* **app., appl.** Put into practice or a particular use: *applied physics.*

ap·pli·qué (ăp′lĭ-kā′) *n.* A decoration or ornament, as in needlework, made by cutting pieces of one material and applying them to the surface of another. **—appliqué** *tr.v.* **-quéd, -qué·ing, -qués.** To decorate by cutting pieces of one material and applying them to the surface of another. [French, past participle of *appliquer,* to apply, from Latin *applicāre,* to affix. See APPLY.]

appliqué
Stitching a piece of fabric on a quilt

ap·ply (ə-plī′) *v.* **-plied, -ply·ing, -plies.** —*tr.* **1.** To bring into nearness or contact with something; put on, upon, or to: *applied glue sparingly to the paper.* **2.** To put to or adapt for a special use: *applies all her money to her mortgage.* **3.** To put into action: *applied the brakes.* **4.** To devote (oneself or one's efforts) to something: *applied myself to my studies.* —*intr.* **1.** To be pertinent or relevant: *a rule that applies to everyone.* **2.** To request or seek assistance, employment, or admission: *will apply to college.* See Synonyms at **resort.** [Middle English *applien,* from Old French *aplier,* from Latin *applicāre,* to affix : *ad-*, ad- + *plicāre,* to fold together; see **plek-** in Appendix.]

ap·pog·gia·tu·ra (ə-pŏj′ə-to͝or′ə) *n. Music.* An embellishing note, usually one step above or below the note it precedes and indicated by a small note or special sign. [Italian, from *appoggiato,* past participle of *appoggiare,* to lean on, from Vulgar Latin **appodiāre* : Latin *ad-*, ad- + *podium,* support (from Greek *podion,* base, from *pous, pod-,* foot; see **ped-** in Appendix).]

ap·point (ə-point′) *tr.v.* **-point·ed, -point·ing, -points.** *Abbr.* **app., appt.** **1.** To select or designate to fill an office or position: *appointed her the chief operating officer of the company.* **2.** To fix or set by authority or by mutual agreement: *will appoint a date for the examination.* **3.** To furnish; equip: *a house that is comfortably appointed.* **4.** *Law.* To direct the disposition of (property) to a person or persons in exercise of a power granted for this purpose by a preceding deed. [Middle English *appointen,* from Old French *apointier,* to arrange, from *a point,* to the point : *a,* to (from Latin *ad;* see AD—) + *point,* point; see POINT.]

SYNONYMS: *appoint, designate, name, nominate, tap.* The central meaning shared by these verbs is "to select for an office or position": *was appointed chairperson of the committee; expects to be designated leader of the opposition; a new commissioner of public safety named by the mayor; wants to be nominated as her party's candidate; was tapped for fraternity membership.* See also Synonyms at **furnish.**

ap·point·ee (ə-poin′tē′, ăp′oin-) *n.* **1.** One who is appointed to an office or position. **2.** *Law.* One to whom a power of appointment of property is granted.

ap·point·ive (ə-poin′tĭv) *adj.* Relating to or filled by appointment: *an appointive office.*

ap·point·ment (ə-point′mənt) *n. Abbr.* **appt.** **1.a.** The act of appointing or designating for an office or position. **b.** The office or position to which one has been appointed. **2.** An arrangement to do something or meet someone at a particular time and place. See Synonyms at **engagement.** **3. appointments.** Furnishings, fittings, or equipment. **4.** *Law.* The act of directing the disposition of property by virtue of a power granted for this purpose.

ap·poin·tor (ə-poin′tər, ə-poin′tôr′) *n. Law.* One that executes a power of appointment of property.

Ap·po·mat·tox (ăp′ə-măt′əks). A town of south-central Virginia east of Lynchburg. Confederate general Robert E. Lee surrendered to Union general Ulysses S. Grant at Appomattox Courthouse on April 9, 1865, ending the Civil War. The site is now a national historical park. Population, 1,345.

ap·por·tion (ə-pôr′shən, ə-pōr′-) *tr.v.* **-tioned, -tion·ing, -tions.** To divide and assign according to a plan; allot. See Syn-

ă pat	oi boy
ā pay	ou out
âr care	o͝o took
ä father	o͞o boot
ĕ pet	ŭ cut
ē be	ûr urge
ĭ pit	th thin
ī pie	*th* this
îr pier	hw which
ŏ pot	zh vision
ō toe	ə about, item
ô paw	♦ regionalism

Stress marks: ′ (primary); ′ (secondary), as in **dictionary** (dĭk′shə-nĕr′ē)

onyms at **assign.** [French *apportioner,* from Old French : *a-,* to (from Latin *ad-,* ad-) + *portionner,* to divide into portions (from *portion,* portion; see PORTION).]

ap·por·tion·ment (ə-pôr′shən-mənt, ə-pōr′-) *n.* **1.a.** The act of apportioning. **b.** The condition of having been apportioned. **2.a.** The proportional distribution of the number of members of the U.S. House of Representatives on the basis of the population of each state. **b.** Allotment of direct taxes on the basis of state population.

ap·pose (ă-pōz′) *tr.v.* **-posed, -pos·ing, -pos·es.** To place in proximity; juxtapose. [Probably AD– + *-pose* (as in COMPOSE).]

ap·po·site (ăp′ə-zĭt) *adj.* Strikingly appropriate and relevant. See Synonyms at **relevant.** [Latin *appositus,* past participle of *appōnere,* to put near : *ad-,* ad- + *pōnere,* to put; see **apo-** in Appendix.] **—ap′po·site·ly** *adv.* **—ap′po·site·ness** *n.*

ap·po·si·tion (ăp′ə-zĭsh′ən) *n.* **1.** *Grammar.* **a.** A construction in which a noun or noun phrase is placed with another as an explanatory equivalent, both having the same syntactic relation to the other elements in the sentence; for example, *Copley* and *the painter* in *The painter Copley was born in Boston.* **b.** The relationship between such nouns or noun phrases. **2.** A placing side by side or next to each other. **3.** *Biology.* The growth of successive layers of a cell wall. [Middle English *apposicioun,* from Latin *appositiō, appositiōn-,* from *appositus,* past participle of *appōnere,* to put near. See APPOSITE.] **—ap′po·si′tion·al** *adj.* **—ap′po·si′tion·al·ly** *adv.*

ap·pos·i·tive (ə-pŏz′ĭ-tĭv) *adj.* Of, relating to, or being in apposition. **—appositive** *n. Grammar.* A word or phrase that is in apposition. **—ap·pos′i·tive·ly** *adv.*

ap·prais·al (ə-prā′zəl) *n.* **1.** The act or an instance of appraising. **2.** An expert or official valuation, as for taxation.

ap·praise (ə-prāz′) *tr.v.* **-praised, -prais·ing, -prais·es. 1.** To evaluate, especially in an official capacity. **2.** To estimate the quality, amount, size, and other features of; judge. See Synonyms at **estimate.** [Middle English *appreisen,* possibly from Old French *aprisier,* from Late Latin *appretiāre* : Latin *ad-,* ad- + Latin *pretium,* price; see **per-**[5] in Appendix.] **—ap·prais′a·ble** *adj.* **—ap·praise′ment** *n.* **—ap·prais′er** *n.*

ap·pre·cia·ble (ə-prē′shə-bəl) *adj.* Possible to estimate, measure, or perceive: *appreciable changes in temperature.* See Synonyms at **perceptible.** **—ap·pre′cia·bly** *adv.*

ap·pre·ci·ate (ə-prē′shē-āt′) *v.* **-at·ed, -at·ing, -ates.** *—tr.* **1.** To recognize the quality, significance, or magnitude of: *appreciated their freedom.* **2.** To be fully aware of or sensitive to; realize: *I appreciate your problems.* **3.** To be thankful for or show gratitude for: *I really appreciate your help.* **4.** To admire greatly; value. **5.** To raise in value or price, especially over time. *—intr.* To increase in value or price, especially over time. [Late Latin *appretiāre, appretiāt-,* to appraise. See APPRAISE.] **—ap·pre′ci·a′tor** *n.* **—ap·pre′cia·to′ry** (-shə-tôr′ē, -tōr′ē) *adj.*

SYNONYMS: *appreciate, value, prize, esteem, treasure, cherish.* These verbs mean to have a favorable opinion of someone or something. *Appreciate* applies especially when high regard is based on critical assessment, comparison, and judgment: *"As students so far from home, we have learned to appreciate those of life's pleasures that are not readily available in the People's Republic of China"* (Sports Illustrated). *Value* implies high regard for the importance or worth of the object: *"In principle, the modern university values nothing more than the free exchange of ideas necessary for the pursuit of knowledge"* (Eloise Salholz). *Prize* often suggests pride of possession: *"the nonchalance prized by teen-agers"* (Elaine Louie). *Esteem* implies respect of a formal sort: *"If he had never esteemed my opinion before, he would have thought highly of me then"* (Jane Austen). *Treasure* and *cherish* stress solicitous care for what is considered precious and often suggest affectionate regard: *We treasure our freedom. "They seek out the Salish Indian woman for the wisdom of her 86 years, and to learn the traditions she cherishes"* (Tamara Jones).

ap·pre·ci·a·tion (ə-prē′shē-ā′shən) *n.* **1.** Recognition of the quality, value, significance, or magnitude of people and things. **2.** A judgment or opinion, especially a favorable one. **3.** An expression of gratitude. **4.** Awareness or delicate perception, especially of aesthetic qualities or values. **5.** A rise in value or price, especially over time.

ap·pre·cia·tive (ə-prē′shə-tĭv, -shē-ā′tĭv) *adj.* Capable of or showing appreciation. **—ap·pre′cia·tive·ly** *adv.*

ap·pre·hend (ăp′rĭ-hĕnd′) *v.* **-hend·ed, -hend·ing, -hends.** *—tr.* **1.** To take into custody; arrest: *apprehended the murderer.* **2.** To grasp mentally; understand: *a candidate who apprehends the significance of geopolitical issues.* **3.** To become conscious of, as through the emotions or senses; perceive. *—intr.* To understand something. [Middle English *apprehenden,* from Old French *apprehender,* from Latin *apprehendere,* to seize : *ad-,* ad- + *prehendere,* to grasp; see **ghend-** in Appendix.]

SYNONYMS: *apprehend, comprehend, understand, grasp.* These verbs are compared as they denote perception of the nature and significance of something. *Apprehend* can imply awareness or consciousness that comes through the emotions or senses: *"We should not pretend to understand the world only by the intellect; we apprehend it just as much by feeling"* (Carl Jung). *Apprehend* also denotes taking in with the mind: *"Intelligence is quickness to apprehend"* (Alfred North Whitehead). Both *comprehend* and *understand* stress complete realization and knowledge: *"To comprehend is to know a thing as well as that thing can be known"* (John Donne). *"No one who has not had the responsibility can really understand what it is like to be President"* (Harry S. Truman). To *grasp* is to seize and hold an idea firmly: *"We have grasped the mystery of the atom and rejected the Sermon on the Mount"* (Omar N. Bradley).

ap·pre·hen·si·ble (ăp′rĭ-hĕn′sə-bəl) *adj.* Capable of being understood: *apprehensible truths.* **—ap′pre·hen′si·bly** *adv.*

ap·pre·hen·sion (ăp′rĭ-hĕn′shən) *n.* **1.** Fearful or uneasy anticipation of the future; dread. **2.** The act of seizing or capturing; arrest. **3.** The ability to apprehend or understand; understanding. [Middle English *apprehencioun,* perception, from Old French *apprehension,* from Late Latin *apprehēnsiō, apprehēnsiōn-,* from Latin *apprehēnsus,* past participle of *apprehendere,* to seize. See APPREHEND.]

SYNONYMS: *apprehension, foreboding, presentiment, misgiving.* These nouns denote consternation that something untoward may be impending. *Apprehension* is fearful anticipation that something adverse is going to happen: *The student looked around the examination room with apprehension. Foreboding* is a sense of coming misfortune that is less clearly based on a definite reason: *"The second half of the book builds a steadily escalating sense of foreboding"* (Sven Birkerts). *Presentiment* denotes a somewhat nonspecific feeling that something, but not necessarily something unpleasant, is imminent: *The lawyer had a presentiment that the judge would dismiss the case against her client. Misgiving* suggests mistrust or uncertainty, as from loss of confidence in a decision made or from fearful doubts about a course of action undertaken: *"A prudent mind can see room for misgiving, lest he who prospers should one day suffer reverse"* (Sophocles).

ap·pre·hen·sive (ăp′rĭ-hĕn′sĭv) *adj.* **1.** Anxious or fearful about the future; uneasy. See Synonyms at **afraid. 2.** Capable of understanding and quick to apprehend. **—ap′pre·hen′sive·ly** *adv.* **—ap′pre·hen′sive·ness** *n.*

ap·pren·tice (ə-prĕn′tĭs) *n. Abbr.* **app. 1.** One bound by legal agreement to work for another for a specific amount of time in return for instruction in a trade, an art, or a business. **2.** One who is learning a trade or occupation, especially as a member of a labor union. **3.** A beginner; a learner. *—attributive.* Often used to modify another noun: *an apprentice electrician; an apprentice sailor.* **—apprentice** *tr.v.* **-ticed, -tic·ing, -tic·es.** To place or take on as a beginner or learner. [Middle English *apprentis,* from Old French *aprentis,* from Vulgar Latin **apprenditīcius,* from **apprenditus,* alteration of Latin *apprehēnsus,* past participle of *apprehendere,* to seize. See APPREHEND.] **—ap·pren′tice·ship′** *n.*

ap·pressed (ə-prĕst′) *adj.* Lying flat or pressed closely against something, as hairs on certain plant stems. [From Latin *appressus,* past participle of *apprimere,* to press down : *ad-,* ad- + *premere,* to press; see **per-**[4] in Appendix.]

ap·prise (ə-prīz′) *tr.v.* **-prised, -pris·ing, -pris·es.** To give notice to; inform: *apprised us of our rights.* [French *apprendre, appris-,* from Old French *aprendre,* to learn, from Vulgar Latin *apprendere,* from Latin *apprehendere.* See APPRENTICE.]

ap·prize (ə-prīz′) *tr.v.* **-prized, -priz·ing, -priz·es.** To appreciate; value.

ap·proach (ə-prōch′) *v.* **-proached, -proach·ing, -proach·es.** *—intr.* **1.** To come near or nearer, as in space or time: *Spring approaches.* **2.** *Sports.* To make an approach in golf. *—tr.* **1.** To come or go near or nearer to: *approached the tunnel.* **2.** To come close to, as in appearance, quality, or condition; approximate: *The performance approaches perfection.* **3.** To make a proposal or overtures to with a specific end in view: *approached the administration for a raise.* **4.** To begin to deal with or work on: *approached the task with dread.* **—approach** *n.* **1.** The act of approaching: *the approach of night.* **2.** A fairly close resemblance; an approximation. **3.** A way or means of reaching something; an access: *an approach to the bridge.* **4.** The method used in dealing with or accomplishing: *a logical approach to the problem.* **5.** An advance or overture made by one person to another. **6.** *Sports.* **a.** The golf stroke following the drive from the tee with which a player tries to get the ball onto the putting green. **b.** The steps taken by a bowler before delivering the ball. **c.** The part of the area behind the foul line in a bowling alley used by a bowler in delivering the ball. [Middle English *approchen,* from Old French *aprochier,* from Late Latin *appropiāre* : Latin *ad-,* ad- + Latin *propius,* nearer, comparative of *prope,* near; see **per**[1] in Appendix.]

ap·proach·a·ble (ə-prō′chə-bəl) *adj.* **1.** Possible to approach; accessible: *a retreat in the mountains approachable in winter only by helicopter.* **2.** Easy to talk to or deal with; friendly. **—ap·proach′a·bil′i·ty** *n.*

ap·pro·bate (ăp′rə-bāt′) *tr.v.* **-bat·ed, -bat·ing, -bates.** To sanction officially; authorize. [Middle English *approbaten,* from Latin *approbāre, approbāt-,* to approve. See APPROVE.] **—ap′pro·ba′tive, ap·pro′ba·to′ry** (ə-prō′bə-tôr′ē, -tōr′ē) *adj.*

ap·pro·ba·tion (ăp′rə-bā′shən) *n.* **1.** An expression of warm approval; praise. **2.** Official approval.

ap·pro·pri·a·ble (ə-prō′prē-ə-bəl) *adj.* That can be appropriated: *appropriable funds.*

ă pat	oi boy
ā pay	ou out
âr care	o͝o took
ä father	o͞o boot
ĕ pet	ŭ cut
ē be	ûr urge
ĭ pit	th thin
ī pie	*th* this
îr pier	hw which
ŏ pot	zh vision
ō toe	ə about, item
ô paw	♦ regionalism

Stress marks: ′ (primary); ′ (secondary), as in **dictionary** (dĭk′shə-nĕr′ē)

ap·pro·pri·ate (ə-prō′prē-ĭt) *adj.* Suitable for a particular person, condition, occasion, or place; fitting. **—appropriate** (-āt′) *tr.v.* **-at·ed, -at·ing, -ates. 1.** To set apart for a specific use: *appropriating funds for education.* **2.** To take possession of or make use of exclusively for oneself, often without permission: *Lee appropriated my unread newspaper and never returned it.* [Middle English *appropriat,* from Late Latin *appropriātus,* past participle of *appropriāre,* to make one's own : Latin *ad-,* ad- + Latin *proprius,* own; see **per**[1] in Appendix.] **—ap·pro′pri·ate·ly** *adv.* **—ap·pro′pri·ate·ness** *n.* **—ap·pro′pri·a′tive** (-ā′tĭv) *adj.* **—ap·pro′pri·a′tor** *n.*

SYNONYMS: *appropriate, arrogate, commandeer, confiscate, preempt, usurp.* The central meaning shared by these verbs is "to seize for oneself or as one's right": *appropriated the family car; arrogating to himself the most interesting tasks; commandeered a plane for the escape; confiscating alien property; preempted the glory for herself; usurped the throne.* See also Synonyms at **allocate, fit**[1].

ap·pro·pri·a·tion (ə-prō′prē-ā′shən) *n.* **1.** The act of appropriating. **2.a.** Something appropriated, especially public funds set aside for a specific purpose. **b.** A legislative act authorizing the expenditure of a designated amount of public funds for a specific purpose.

ap·prov·al (ə-prōō′vəl) *n.* **1.** The act of approving. **2.** An official approbation; sanction. **3.** Favorable regard; commendation. ***—idiom.* on approval.** For examination or trial by a customer without the obligation to buy: *took the dress on approval.*

ap·prove (ə-prōōv′) *v.* **-proved, -prov·ing, -proves.** *—tr.* **1.** To consider right or good; think or speak favorably of. **2.** To consent to officially or formally; confirm or sanction. **3.** *Obsolete.* To prove or attest. *—intr.* To show, feel, or express approval: *didn't approve of the decision.* [Middle English *approven,* from Old French *aprover,* from Latin *approbāre* : *ad-,* ad- + *probāre,* to test (from *probus,* good; see **per**[1] in Appendix).] **—ap·prov′a·ble** *adj.* **—ap·prov′ing·ly** *adv.*

SYNONYMS: *approve, endorse, sanction, certify, accredit, ratify.* These verbs mean to express a favorable opinion or to signify satisfaction or acceptance. Though *approve,* the most widely applicable, often means simply to consider right or good (*knew my parents wouldn't approve of what I had done*), it can also denote official consent: *"The colonel or commanding officer approves the sentence of a regimental court-martial"* (Charles James). *Endorse* implies the expression of support, often by public statement: *The senator will give a speech endorsing her party's gubernatorial candidate. Sanction* usually implies not only approval (*Public opinion ought not to sanction the use of force*) but also official authorization (*The privilege of voting is a right sanctioned by law*). *Certify* and *accredit* imply official approval based on compliance with requirements or standards: *"The proper officers, comparing every article with its voucher, certified them to be right"* (Benjamin Franklin). *The board of higher education will accredit only those institutions offering a sufficiently rigorous curriculum.* To *ratify* is to invest with legal authority by giving official sanction: *"Amendments . . . shall be valid . . . when ratified by the Legislatures of three fourths of the several States"* (U.S. Constitution, Article V).

ap·proved school (ə-prōōvd′) *n. Chiefly British.* A school for young offenders; a reform school.

approx. *abbr.* **1.** Approximate. **2.** Approximately.

ap·prox·i·mate (ə-prŏk′sə-mĭt) *adj. Abbr.* **approx. 1.** Almost exact or correct: *the approximate time of the accident.* **2.** Very similar; closely resembling: *sketched an approximate likeness of the suspect.* **3.** *Botany.* Close together but not united. **—approximate** (-māt′) *v.* **-mat·ed, -mat·ing, -mates.** *—tr.* **1.** To come close to; be nearly the same as: *This meat substitute approximates the real thing.* **2.** To bring near. **3.** To bring together, as cut edges of tissue. *—intr.* To come near or close, as in degree, nature, or quality. [Middle English, from Late Latin *approximātus,* past participle of *approximāre,* to approach : Latin *ad-,* ad- + *proximāre,* to come near (from *proximus,* nearest; see **per**[1] in Appendix).] **—ap·prox′i·mate·ly** *adv.*

ap·prox·i·ma·tion (ə-prŏk′sə-mā′shən) *n.* **1.** The act, process, or result of approximating. **2.** *Mathematics.* An inexact result adequate for a given purpose. **—ap·prox′i·ma′tive** (-mā′tĭv) *adj.* **—ap·prox′i·ma′tive·ly** *adv.*

appt. *abbr.* Appoint; appointment.

apptd. *abbr.* Appointed.

ap·pur·te·nance (ə-pûr′tn-əns) *n.* **1.** Something added to another, more important thing; an appendage. See Synonyms at **appendage. 2. appurtenances.** Equipment, such as clothing, tools, or instruments, used for a specific purpose or task; gear. **3.** *Law.* A right, privilege, or property considered incident to the principal property for passage of title, conveyance, or inheritance. [Middle English *appurtenaunce,* from Anglo-Norman *apurtenance,* from Vulgar Latin **appertinentia,* from Late Latin *appertinēns, appertinent-,* present participle of *appertinēre,* to appertain. See APPERTAIN.] **—ap·pur′te·nant** *adj.*

APR *abbr.* Annual percentage rate.

Apr. or **Apr** *abbr.* April.

a·prax·i·a (ā-prăk′sē-ə) *n.* Total or partial loss of the ability to perform coordinated movements or manipulate objects in the absence of motor or sensory impairment. [Greek, inaction : *a-,* without; see A–[1] + *praxis,* action; see PRAXIS.] **—a·prac′tic** (ā-prăk′tĭk), **a·prax′ic** (ā-prăk′sĭk) *adj.*

a·près (ä′prā, ăp′rā) *prep.* After. Often used in combination: *an après-dinner entertainment; a concert après dinner.* [French, from Old French, from Late Latin *ad pressum* : *ad,* to; see AD– + *pressum,* nearby (from neuter of Latin *pressus,* past participle of *premere,* to press closely; see PRESS[1]).]

a·près-ski (ä′prā-skē′, ăp′rā-) *n.* Social events or activities that take place after skiing. **—après-ski** *adj.* Concerned with or designed for use after skiing: *après-ski wear.* [French : *après,* after + *ski,* skiing.]

a·pri·cot (ăp′rĭ-kŏt′, ā′prĭ-) *n.* **1.a.** A deciduous Asian tree *(Prunus armeniaca)* having alternate leaves and clusters of usually white flowers. **b.** The edible, yellow-orange fruit of this tree. **2.** *Color.* A moderate, light, or strong orange to strong orange yellow. [Alteration of earlier *abrecock,* ultimately from Arabic *al-barqūq,* the plum : *al,* the + Greek *praikokion,* apricot (from Latin *praecoquus,* ripe early : *prae-,* pre- + *coquere,* to cook, ripen; see **pek**^{w}**-** in Appendix).]

apricot
Prunus armeniaca

A·pril (ā′prəl) *n. Abbr.* **Apr., Apr** The fourth month of the year in the Gregorian calendar. See table at **calendar.** [Middle English, from Latin *aprīlis.*]

April fool *n.* **1.** The victim of a joke or trick played on April Fools' Day. **2.** The joke or trick so played.

April Fools' Day (fōōlz) *n.* April 1, celebrated in various countries, such as the United States and Great Britain, and marked by the playing of practical jokes. Also called *All Fools' Day.*

a pri·o·ri (ä′ prē-ôr′ē, -ōr′ē, ā′ prī-ôr′ī, -ōr′ī′) *adj.* **1.** Proceeding from a known or assumed cause to a necessarily related effect; deductive. **2.** Based on a hypothesis or theory rather than on experiment or experience. **3.** Made before or without examination; not supported by factual study. [Medieval Latin *ā priōrī* : *ā,* from + *priōrī,* former.] **—a′ pri·o′ri** *adv.* **—a′ pri·or′i·ty** (-ôr′ĭ-tē, -ŏr′-) *n.*

a·pron (ā′prən) *n.* **1.a.** A garment, usually fastened in the back, worn over all or part of the front of the body to protect clothing. **b.** Something, such as a protective shield for a machine, that resembles this garment in appearance or function. **2.** The paved strip in front of and around airport hangars and terminal buildings. **3.** The part of a stage in a theater extending in front of the curtain. **4.** A platform, as of planking, at the entrance to a dock. **5.a.** A covering or structure along a shoreline for protection against erosion. **b.** A platform serving a similar purpose below a dam or in a sluiceway. **6.** A continuous conveyor belt. **7.** An area covered by sand and gravel deposited at the front of a glacial moraine. **—apron** *tr.v.* **a·proned, a·pron·ing, a·prons.** To cover, protect, or provide with an apron. [Middle English, from *an apron,* alteration of *a napron,* from Old French *naperon,* diminutive of *nape,* tablecloth, from Latin *mappa,* napkin. See MAP.]

apron
Loading dock

apron string *n.* The string of an apron. Usually used in the plural with *tied* to indicate complete control or dominance: *a grown man still tied to his mother's apron strings.*

ap·ro·pos (ăp′rə-pō′) *adj.* Being at once opportune and to the point. See Synonyms at **relevant. —apropos** *adv.* **1.** At an appropriate time; opportunely. **2.** By the way; incidentally: *Apropos, where were you yesterday?* **—apropos** *prep.* With regard to; concerning: *Apropos our date for lunch, I can't go.* [French *à propos* : *à,* to (from Latin *ad-;* see AD–) + *propos,* purpose (from Latin *prōpositum,* from *prōponere, prōposit-,* to intend; see PROPOSE).]

apropos of *prep.* With reference to; speaking of: *a funny story apropos of politics.*

apse (ăps) *n.* **1.** *Architecture.* A semicircular or polygonal, usually domed projection of a building, especially the altar or east end of a church. **2.** *Astronomy.* Apsis. [Variant of APSIS.] **—ap′si·dal** (ăp′sĭ-dəl) *adj.*

ap·sis (ăp′sĭs) *n., pl.* **-si·des** (-sĭ-dēz′). **1.** *Architecture.* An apse. **2.** *Astronomy.* The point of greatest or least distance of the orbit of a celestial body from a center of attraction. [Late Latin *apsis,* from Latin, arch, vault, from Greek *hapsis,* from *haptein,* to fasten.]

apse

apt (ăpt) *adj.* **1.** Exactly suitable; appropriate: *an apt reply.* See Synonyms at **fit**[1]. **2.** Having a natural tendency; inclined: *She is apt to take offense easily.* See Usage Notes at **liable, likely. 3.** Quick to learn or understand: *an apt student.* [Middle English, from Old French *apte,* from Latin *aptus,* past participle of *apere,* to fasten.] **—apt′ly** *adv.* **—apt′ness** *n.*

APT (ā′pē-tē′) *n. Computer Science.* A language designed for programming numerically controlled machine tools. [*A(utomatically) P(rogrammed) T(ool).*]

apt. *abbr.* Apartment.

ap·ter·al (ăp′tər-əl) *adj. Architecture.* Having no columns along the sides. Used especially of a classical temple. [From Greek *apteros,* wingless : *a-,* without; see A–[1] + *pteron,* wing; see –PTER.]

ap·ter·ous (ăp′tər-əs) *adj. Biology.* Having no wings or winglike extensions: *an apterous insect.*

ap·ter·yx (ăp′tə-rĭks′) *n.* See **kiwi** (sense 1). [New Latin : A–[1] + Greek *pterux,* wing; see **pet-** in Appendix.]

ap·ti·tude (ăp′tĭ-tōōd′, -tyōōd′) *n.* **1.** An inherent ability, as for learning; a talent. See Synonyms at **ability.** **2.** Quickness in learning and understanding; intelligence. **3.** The condition or quality of being suitable; appropriateness. [Middle English, tendency, from Late Latin *aptitūdō,* aptitude, from Latin *aptus,* apt. See APT.]

aptitude test *n.* A standardized test designed to measure the ability of a person to develop skills or acquire knowledge.

Ap·u·lei·us (ăp′yə-lē′əs), **Lucius.** fl. second century A.D. Roman philosopher and satirist whose best-known work is *The Golden Ass.*

A·pu·lia (ə-po͝ol′yə) also **Pu·glia** (po͞o′lyä). A region of southeast Italy bordering on the Adriatic Sea, Strait of Otranto, and Gulf of Taranto. Its southern portion forms the heel of the Italian "boot."

A·pu·re (ə-po͝or′ā). A river of west-central Venezuela originating in the Andes of Colombia and flowing about 805 km (500 mi) eastward to the Orinoco River.

A·pu·rí·mac (ä′pə-rē′mäk). A river of southern Peru rising in the Andes and flowing about 885 km (550 mi) generally northwest to join the Urubamba River and form the Ucayali River.

A·pus (ā′pəs) *n.* A constellation in the Southern Hemisphere near Musca and Pavo. [Latin *apus,* a kind of swallow, from Greek *apous,* without feet, sand martin : *a-,* without; see A-[1] + *pous,* foot; see **ped-** in Appendix.]

ap·y·rase (ăp′ə-rās′, -rāz′) *n.* Any of various enzymes that catalyze the hydrolysis of ATP, causing the release of phosphate and energy. [A(DENOSINE) + PYR(O)- + (PHOSPHAT)ASE.]

aq. *abbr.* **1.** Aqua. **2.** Aqueous.

A·qa·ba (ä′kə-bə, ăk′ə-), **Gulf of.** An arm of the Red Sea between the Sinai Peninsula and northwest Saudi Arabia. It has long been of strategic importance in the Middle East.

aq·ua (ăk′wə, ä′kwə) *n., pl.* **aq·uae** (ăk′wē, ä′kwī′) or **aq·uas.** *Abbr.* **aq. 1.** Water. **2.** An aqueous solution. **3.** *Color.* A light bluish green to light greenish blue. [Middle English, from Latin. See **akʷ-ā-** in Appendix.] **—aq′ua** *adj.*

aqua- *pref.* Water: *aquacade.* [From Latin *aqua,* water. See AQUA.]

aq·ua·cade (ăk′wə-kād′, ä′kwə-) *n.* An entertainment spectacle of swimmers and divers, often performing in unison to the accompaniment of music. [AQUA- + (CAVAL)CADE.]

aq·ua·cul·ture (ăk′wə-kŭl′chər, ä′kwə-) also **aq·ui·cul·ture** (ăk′wĭ-kŭl′chər, ä′kwĭ-) *n.* **1.** The science, art, and business of cultivating marine or freshwater food fish or shellfish, such as oysters, clams, salmon, and trout, under controlled conditions. **2.** *Botany.* Hydroponics. **—aq′ua·cul′tur·al** *adj.* **—aq′ua·cul′tur·ist** *n.*

aq·uae (ăk′wē, ä′kwī′) *n.* A plural of **aqua.**

aqua for·tis also **aq·ua·for·tis** (ăk′wə-fôr′tĭs, ä′kwə-) *n.* See **nitric acid.** [New Latin : Latin *aqua,* water + Latin *fortis,* strong.]

Aq·ua-Lung (ăk′wə-lŭng′, ä′kwə-). A trademark used for an underwater breathing apparatus.

aq·ua·ma·rine (ăk′wə-mə-rēn′, ä′kwə-) *n.* **1.** A transparent blue-green variety of beryl, used as a gemstone. **2.** *Color.* A pale blue to light greenish blue. [Latin *aqua marīna,* sea water : *aqua,* water; see AQUA + *marīna,* of the sea; see MARINE.]

aq·ua·naut (ăk′wə-nôt′, ä′kwə-) *n.* A person trained to live in underwater installations and conduct, assist in, or be a subject of scientific research. Also called *oceanaut.* [AQUA- + Greek *nautēs,* sailor; see **nāu-** in Appendix.]

aq·ua·plane (ăk′wə-plān′, ä′kwə-) *n.* A board pulled over the water by a motorboat and ridden by a person standing up. **—aquaplane** *intr.v.* **-planed, -plan·ing, -planes.** To ride on such a board. [AQUA- + PLANE[1].]

aqua re·gi·a (rē′jē-ə, rē′jə) *n.* A corrosive, fuming, volatile mixture of hydrochloric and nitric acids, used for testing metals and dissolving platinum and gold. Also called *nitrohydrochloric acid.* [New Latin : Latin *aqua,* water + Latin *rēgia,* royal (because it dissolves gold, the "royal metal").]

aq·ua·relle (ăk′wə-rĕl′, ä′kwə-) *n.* A drawing done in transparent watercolors. [French, from obsolete Italian *acquarella,* water color, diminutive of *acqua,* water, from Latin *aqua.* See **akʷ-ā-** in Appendix.] **—aq′ua·rel′list** *n.*

a·quar·i·a (ə-kwâr′ē-ə) *n.* A plural of **aquarium.**

A·quar·i·an (ə-kwâr′ē-ən) *n.* One who is born under the sign of Aquarius. **—A·quar′i·an** *adj.*

a·quar·ist (ə-kwâr′ĭst) *n.* One who maintains an aquarium.

a·quar·i·um (ə-kwâr′ē-əm) *n., pl.* **-i·ums** or **-i·a** (-ē-ə). **1.** A tank, bowl, or other water-filled enclosure in which living fish or other aquatic animals and plants are kept. **2.** A place for the public exhibition of live aquatic animals and plants. [Latin *aquārium,* source of water, from neuter of *aquārius,* of water, from *aqua,* water. See **akʷ-ā-** in Appendix.]

A·quar·i·us (ə-kwâr′ē-əs) *n.* **1.** A constellation in the equatorial region of the Southern Hemisphere near Pisces and Aquila. Also called *Water Bearer.* **2.a.** The 11th sign of the zodiac in astrology. Also called *Water Bearer.* **b.** One who is born under this sign. [Middle English, from Latin, water carrier, the constellation Aquarius, from *aqua,* water. See AQUA.]

a·quat·ic (ə-kwăt′ĭk, ə-kwŏt′-) *adj.* **1.** Consisting of, relating to, or being in water: *an aquatic environment.* **2.** Living or growing in, on, or near the water: *aquatic animals and plants.* **3.** Taking place in or on the water: *an aquatic sport.* **—aquatic** *n.* **1.** An organism that lives in, on, or near the water. **2. aquatics.** *Sports.* Athletic activities performed in or on the water. [Middle English *aquatique,* from Old French, from Latin *aquāticus,* from *aqua,* water. See **akʷ-ā-** in Appendix.] **—a·quat′i·cal·ly** *adv.*

aq·ua·tint (ăk′wə-tĭnt′, ä′kwə-) *n.* **1.** A process of etching capable of producing several tones by varying the etching time of different areas of a copper plate so that the resulting print resembles the flat tints of an ink or wash drawing. **2.** An etching made by this process. [French *aquatinte,* from Italian *acquatinta* : *acqua,* water (from Latin *aqua;* see AQUA) + *tinta,* dyed (from Latin *tincta,* feminine past participle of *tingere,* to dye).] **—aq′ua·tint′** *v.* **—aq′ua·tint′er, aq′ua·tint′ist** *n.*

a·qua·vit (ä′kwə-vēt′) *n.* A strong, clear Scandinavian liquor distilled from potato or grain mash and flavored with caraway seed. [Swedish, Danish and Norwegian *akvavit,* from Medieval Latin *aqua vītae,* highly distilled spirits : Latin *aqua,* water; see AQUA + Latin *vītae,* genitive of *vīta,* life; see VITAL.]

aqua vi·tae (vī′tē) *n.* Strong distilled alcohol, especially a strong liquor such as whiskey or brandy. [Middle English *aqua vite,* from Medieval Latin *aqua vītae.* See AQUAVIT.]

aq·ue·duct (ăk′wĭ-dŭkt′) *n.* **1.a.** A pipe or channel designed to transport water from a remote source, usually by gravity. **b.** A bridgelike structure supporting a conduit or canal passing over a river or low ground. **2.** *Anatomy.* A channel or passage in an organ or a body part, especially such a channel for conveying fluid. [Latin *aquaeductus* : *aquae,* genitive of *aqua,* water; see AQUA + *ductus,* a leading; see DUCT.]

a·que·ous (ā′kwē-əs, ăk′wē-) *adj. Abbr.* **aq. 1.** Relating to, similar to, containing, or dissolved in water; watery. **2.** *Geology.* Formed from matter deposited by water, as certain sedimentary rocks. [From Medieval Latin *aqueus,* from Latin *aqua,* water. See AQUA.]

aqueous humor *n. Anatomy.* The clear, watery fluid circulating in the chamber of the eye between the cornea and the lens.

aqui- *pref.* Water: *aquifer.* [Latin, from *aqua,* water. See **akʷ-ā-** in Appendix.]

aq·ui·cul·ture (ăk′wĭ-kŭl′chər, ä′kwĭ-) *n.* Variant of **aquaculture. —aq′ui·cul′tur·al** *adj.* **—aq′ui·cul′tur·ist** *n.*

A·quid·neck Island (ə-kwĭd′nĕk). See **Rhode Island[1].**

aq·ui·fer (ăk′wə-fər, ä′kwə-) *n.* An underground bed or layer of earth, gravel, or porous stone that yields water. **—a·quif′er·ous** (ə-kwĭf′ər-əs) *adj.*

A·qui·la[1] (ăk′wə-lə, ä′kwē-lä). See **L'Aquila.**

Aq·ui·la[2] (ăk′wə-lə) *n.* A constellation in the Northern Hemisphere near Aquarius and Serpens Cauda. [Middle English, from Latin *aquila,* eagle, the constellation Aquila.]

aq·ui·le·gi·a (ăk′wə-lē′jē-ə, -lē′jə) *n.* See **columbine.** [Medieval Latin *aquilēgia.*]

aq·ui·line (ăk′wə-līn′, -lĭn) *adj.* **1.** Of, relating to, or having the characteristics of an eagle. **2.** Curved or hooked like an eagle's beak: *an aquiline nose.* [Latin *aquilīnus,* from *aquila,* eagle.] **—aq′ui·lin′i·ty** (-lĭn′ĭ-tē) *n.*

A·qui·nas (ə-kwī′nəs), Saint **Thomas.** 1225–1274. Italian Dominican monk, theologian, and philosopher. The outstanding representative of Scholasticism, he applied Aristotelian methods to Christian theology. His masterwork is *Summa Theologica* (1266–1273).

A·qui·no (ä-kē′nō), **Corazón Cojuangco.** Born 1933. Philippine political leader. After the assassination of her husband, **Benigno S. Aquino, Jr.** (1932–1983), on his return to the Philippines from political exile, she ran for president (1986) against 20-year incumbent Ferdinand Marcos. Following the apparently fraudulent election, Marcos fled the country and Aquino became president.

Aq·ui·taine (ăk′wĭ-tān′). A historical region of southwest France between the Pyrenees and the Garonne River. The duchy of Aquitaine was joined with France after the marriage of Eleanor of Aquitaine to King Louis VII in 1137, but its possession was disputed after her subsequent marriage to Henry II of England.

Aq·ui·ta·ni·a (ăk′wĭ-tā′nē-ə). A Roman division of southwest Gaul extending from the Pyrenees to the Garonne River and roughly coextensive with the historical region of Aquitaine. Its Iberian peoples were conquered by Julius Caesar in 56 B.C. The region passed to the Franks in A.D. 507.

a·quiv·er (ə-kwĭv′ər) *adj.* Marked by quivering: *The children were aquiver with anticipation before the circus parade.*

ar[1] (är) *n.* Variant of **are[2].**

ar[2] (är) *n.* The letter *r.* [Middle English *arre,* from Late Latin *er.*]

Ar The symbol for the element **argon.**

AR *abbr.* **1.** Also **A/R.** Account receivable. **2.** Arkansas.

ar. *abbr.* Arrival; arrive.

Ar. *abbr.* **1.** Arabia; Arabian. **2.** Arabic. **3.** Arabist.

A.R. *abbr.* Army regulation.

-ar *suff.* Of, relating to, or resembling: *polar.* [Middle English, from Old French *-er,* from Latin *-āris,* alteration of *-ālis,* -al.]

A·ra (âr′ə) *n.* A constellation in the Southern Hemisphere near the constellations Norma and Telescopium. [Latin *āra,* altar, the constellation Ara. See **as-** in Appendix.]

Ar·ab (ăr′əb) *n.* **1.** A member of a Semitic people inhabiting Arabia, whose language and Islamic religion spread widely

aquarium

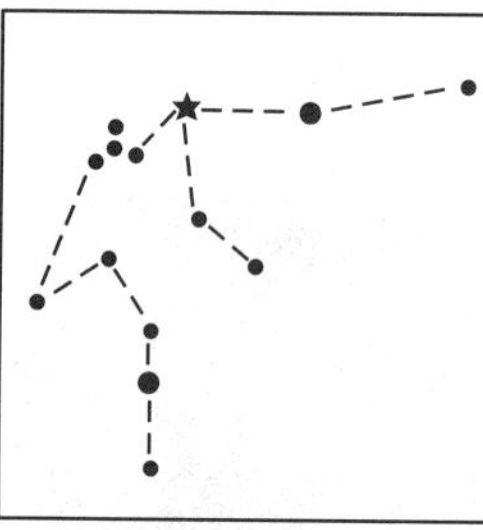

Aquarius

aqueduct
Pont du Gard
near Nîmes, France

Corazón Aquino

throughout the Middle East and northern Africa from the seventh century. **2.** A member of an Arabic-speaking people. **3.** An Arabian horse. **4.** *Offensive Slang.* A waif. [French *Arabe,* from Latin *Arabs,* from Greek *Araps, Arab-,* from Arabic *'arab.*] **—Ar'ab** *adj.*

Arab. *abbr.* **1.** Arabian. **2.** Arabic. **3.** Arabist.

ar·a·besque (ăr'ə-bĕsk') *n.* **1.** A ballet position in which the dancer stands on one leg with the other extended to the back. **2.** A complex, ornate design of intertwined floral, foliate, and geometric figures. **3.** *Music.* A usually short, whimsical composition especially for the piano that features many embellished passages. **4.** An intricate or elaborate pattern or design: *"the fluctuating shapes of a cloudscape, the complex arabesque of a camera movement, the blink of a character's eye"* (Nigel Andrews). **—arabesque** *adj.* In the fashion of or formed as an arabesque. [French, from Italian *arabesco,* in Arabian fashion, from *Arabo,* an Arab, from Latin *Arabus,* from *Arabs.* See ARAB.]

A·ra·bi·a (ə-rā'bē-ə) also **A·ra·bi·an Peninsula** (-bē-ən). *Abbr.* **Ar.** A peninsula of southwest Asia between the Red Sea and the Persian Gulf. Politically, it includes Saudi Arabia, Yemen, Oman, the United Arab Emirates, Qatar, Bahrain, and Kuwait. Arabia has an estimated one third of the world's oil reserves.

A·ra·bi·an (ə-rā'bē-ən) *adj. Abbr.* **Ar., Arab.** Of or concerning Arabia or the Arabs; Arab. **—Arabian** *n. Abbr.* **Ar., Arab. 1.** A native or inhabitant of Arabia. **2.** An Arabian horse.

Arabian camel *n.* See **dromedary.**

Arabian Desert. A desert of eastern Egypt between the Nile Valley and the Red Sea. Porphyry, granite, and sandstone found here have been used as building materials since ancient times.

Arabian Gulf. See **Persian Gulf.**

Arabian horse *n.* Any of a breed of swift, intelligent, graceful horses native to Arabia.

Arabian Peninsula. See **Arabia.**

Arabian Sea. The northwest part of the Indian Ocean between Arabia and western India. It has long been an important trade route between India and the West.

Ar·a·bic (ăr'ə-bĭk) *adj.* Of or relating to Arabia, the Arabs, their language, or their culture. **—Arabic** *n. Abbr.* **Ar., Arab.** A Semitic language consisting of numerous dialects that is the principal language of Arabia, Jordan, Syria, Iraq, Lebanon, Egypt, and parts of northern Africa.

Arabic numeral *n.* One of the numerical symbols 1, 2, 3, 4, 5, 6, 7, 8, 9, or 0.

a·rab·i·nose (ə-răb'ə-nōs', ăr'ə-bə-) *n.* A crystalline pentose sugar, $C_5H_{10}O_5$, obtained from plant polysaccharides such as gums and hemicelluloses. [(GUM) ARAB(IC) + -IN + -OSE[2].]

Ar·ab·ist (ăr'ə-bĭst) *n.* **1.** *Abbr.* **Ar., Arab.** A specialist in the Arabic language or culture. **2.** One who is favorably disposed toward Arab concerns and policies.

ar·a·ble (ăr'ə-bəl) *adj.* Fit for cultivation, as by plowing. **—arable** *n.* Land fit to be cultivated. [Middle English, from Old French, from Latin *arābilis,* from *arāre,* to plow.] **—ar'a·bil'i·ty** *n.*

A·ra·ca·ju (ä-rä'kä-zho͞o'). A city of east-central Brazil near the Atlantic Ocean south-southeast of Recife. It is a commercial center in a cotton- and sugar-producing region. Population, 287,934.

ar·a·chi·don·ic acid (ăr'ə-kĭ-dŏn'ĭk) *n.* An unsaturated fatty acid, $C_{20}H_{32}O_2$, found in animal fats, that is essential in human nutrition and is a precursor in the biosynthesis of some prostaglandins. [From *arachidic,* of the groundnut, from New Latin *Arachis,* groundnut genus, from Greek *arakis, arakid-,* diminutive of *arakos,* a leguminous plant.]

A·rach·ne (ə-răk'nē) *n. Greek Mythology.* A maiden who was transformed into a spider by Athena for challenging her to a weaving contest.

a·rach·nid (ə-răk'nĭd) *n.* Any of various arthropods of the class Arachnida, such as spiders, scorpions, mites, and ticks, characterized by four pairs of segmented legs and a body that is divided into two regions, the cephalothorax and the abdomen. Also called *arachnoid.* [From New Latin *Arachnida,* class name, from Greek *arakhnē,* spider.] **—a·rach'ni·dan** (-nĭ-dən) *adj.* & *n.*

a·rach·noid (ə-răk'noid') *adj.* **1.** *Anatomy.* Of or relating to a delicate membrane enclosing the spinal cord and brain. **2.** Of, relating to, or resembling arachnids. **3.** Covered with or consisting of thin, soft, entangled hairs or fibers resembling those of a cobweb or spider's web. **—arachnoid** *n.* **1.** See **arachnid. 2.** *Anatomy.* A delicate membrane that encloses the spinal cord and brain, and lies between the pia mater and dura mater. [New Latin *arachnoidēs,* from Greek *arakhnoeidēs,* cobweblike : *arakhnē,* spider + *-oeidēs,* -oid.]

a·rach·no·pho·bi·a (ə-răk'nə-fō'bē-ə, -nō-) *n.* An abnormal fear of spiders. [ARACHN(ID) + -PHOBIA.]

A·rad (ä-räd'). A city of western Romania on the Mureşul River near the Hungarian border. Ruled by Turkey and later by Hungary, it became part of Romania in 1920. Population, 183,774.

Ar·a·fat (ăr'ə-făt', ăr'ə-făt'), **Yasir.** Born 1929. Leader of Al Fatah, an Arab guerrilla group, and the Palestine Liberation Organization, both of which advocate the establishment of an independent Palestinian state.

A·ra·fu·ra Sea (ä'rə-fo͞o'rə). A shallow part of the western Pacific Ocean between the Timor and Coral seas, separating New Guinea from Australia.

Ar·a·gon (ăr'ə-gŏn'). A region and former kingdom of northeast Spain. It was united with Castile in 1479. **—Ar'a·go·nese'** (ăr'ə-gə-nēz', -nēs') *adj.* & *n.*

A·ra·gon (ăr-ä-gôN'), **Louis.** 1897–1982. French writer who was a founder of literary surrealism.

a·rag·o·nite (ə-răg'ə-nīt', ăr'ə-gə-) *n.* An orthorhombic mineral form of crystalline calcium carbonate, dimorphous with calcite. [After ARAGON.]

A·ra·guaí·a or **A·ra·gua·ya** (är'ə-gwī'ə). A river rising in central Brazil and flowing about 2,092 km (1,300 mi) generally northward to the Tocantins River. There are numerous falls on the river.

a·ra·li·a (ə-rā'lē-ə, ə-rāl'yə) *n.* Any of several plants in the genera *Aralia* and *Polyscias,* cultivated as ornamentals. [Of unknown origin.]

Ar·al Sea (ăr'əl). An inland sea lying between southern Kazakhstan and northwest Uzbekistan. Once the fourth-largest inland body of water in the world, it is fast disappearing because of diversion of its two sources, the Amu Darya and the Syr Darya.

Ar·am (âr'əm, ăr'-, ā'răm). In the Old Testament, an ancient country of southwest Asia, roughly coextensive with present-day Syria.

Ar·a·mae·an (ăr'ə-mē'ən) *adj.* & *n.* Variant of **Aramean.**

Ar·a·ma·ic (ăr'ə-mā'ĭk) *n.* A Semitic language, comprising several dialects, originally of the ancient Arameans but widely used by non-Aramean peoples throughout southwest Asia from the seventh century B.C. to the seventh century A.D. Also called *Aramean, Chaldean.* **—Ar'a·ma'ic** *adj.*

ar·a·me (ăr'ə-mā, ə-rä'-) *n.* An edible, mild-flavored seaweed. [Japanese.]

Ar·a·me·an or **Ar·a·mae·an** (ăr'ə-mē'ən) *—adj.* Of or relating to Aram, its inhabitants, their language, or their culture. *—n.* **1.** One of a group of Semitic peoples inhabiting Aram and parts of Mesopotamia from the 11th to the 8th century B.C. **2.** See **Aramaic.**

Ar·an Islands (ăr'ən). Three small islands of western Ireland at the entrance to Galway Bay. The barren, primitive islands have many prehistoric and early Christian remains.

A·rap·a·ho also **A·rap·a·hoe** (ə-răp'ə-hō') *n., pl.* **Arapaho** or **-hos** also **Arapahoe** or **-hoes. 1.a.** A Native American people formerly inhabiting eastern Colorado and southeast Wyoming, with present-day populations in Oklahoma and central Wyoming. Traditional Arapaho life was based on the buffalo-hunting culture of the Great Plains. **b.** A member of this people. **2.** The Algonquian language of the Arapaho. [Crow *aaraxpéahu,* those with lots of tattoos.]

ar·a·pai·ma (ăr'ə-pī'mə) *n.* A large South American freshwater food fish *(Arapaima gigas)* that typically attains a length of 3 meters (10 feet). Also called *pirarucu.* [American Spanish or Portuguese, both probably of Tupian origin.]

Ar·a·rat (ăr'ə-răt'), **Mount.** A massif of extreme eastern Turkey near the Iranian border rising to about 5,168 m (16,945 ft). It is the traditional resting place of Noah's ark.

A·ras (ə-räs'). Formerly **A·rax·es** (ə-răk'sēz). A river rising in northeast Turkey and flowing about 965 km (600 mi) generally eastward.

A·rau·ca (ə-rou'kə). A river rising in northern Colombia and flowing about 805 km (500 mi) eastward to the Orinoco River in central Venezuela.

Ar·au·ca·ni·an (ăr'ô-kā'nē-ən) also **A·rau·can** (ə-rô'kən) *n.* **1.** A member of a widespread group of South American Indian peoples of south-central Chile and the western pampas of Argentina. **2.** The language of the Araucanians, which constitutes an independent language family. [Spanish *araucano,* from *Arauco,* a former region of southern Chile.] **—Ar'au·ca'ni·an** *adj.*

ar·au·car·i·a (ăr'ô-kâr'ē-ə) *n.* Any of several evergreen coniferous trees of the genus *Araucaria* native to South America and Australia, having awl-shaped leaves and whorled branches and including the monkey puzzle and Norfolk Island pine. [From Spanish *Araucaria,* (tree) of Arauco, a former province of south-central Chile.]

Ar·a·wak (ăr'ə-wäk') *n., pl.* **Arawak** or **-waks. 1.** A member of a South American Indian people formerly inhabiting much of the Greater Antilles and now living chiefly in certain regions of Guiana. **2.** The Arawakan language of the Arawak.

Ar·a·wa·kan (ăr'ə-wä'kən) *n., pl.* **Arawakan** or **-kans. 1.** A member of a widespread group of Indian peoples living in an area of South America that includes parts of Colombia, Venezuela, Guiana, the Amazon basin of Brazil, Paraguay, Bolivia, Peru, and formerly most of the Greater Antilles. **2.** The largest and most important Indian linguistic family in South America, consisting of the languages spoken by the Arawakan peoples. **—Ar'a·wa'kan** *adj.*

A·rax·es (ə-răk'sēz). See **Aras.**

arb (ärb) *n. Informal.* An arbitrageur. [Short for ARBITRAGEUR.]

ar·ba·lest also **ar·ba·list** (är'bə-lĭst) *n.* A medieval missile launcher designed on the principle of the crossbow. [Middle English *arblast,* from Old English, from Old French *arbaleste,* from Late Latin *arcuballista* : Latin *arcus,* bow + Latin *ballista,* ballista; see BALLISTA.] **—ar'ba·lest'er** (-lĕs'tər) *n.*

Ar·be·la (är-bē'lə). An ancient town of Assyria in present-day

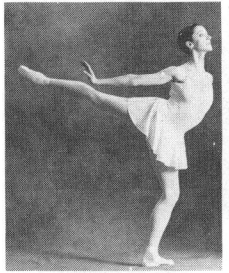

arabesque
Top: Carla Stallings in *Concerto Barocco*
Bottom: Design on an early 17th-century Turkish ivory dagger grip

Arabian horse
Arabian stallion

Yasir Arafat

ă pat	oi boy
ā pay	ou out
âr care	o͝o took
ä father	o͞o boot
ĕ pet	ŭ cut
ē be	ûr urge
ĭ pit	th thin
ī pie	*th* this
îr pier	hw which
ŏ pot	zh vision
ō toe	ə about, item
ô paw	♦ regionalism

Stress marks: **'** (primary); ' (secondary), as in **dictionary** (dĭk'shə-nĕr'ē)

northern Iraq. Its name is sometimes given to the battle fought at Gaugamela, about 97 km (60 mi) away, in which Alexander the Great defeated Darius III in 331 B.C.

ar·bi·ter (är′bĭ-tər) *n.* **1.** One chosen or appointed to judge or decide a disputed issue; an arbitrator. **2.** One who has the power to judge or ordain at will: *an arbiter of fashion.* See Synonyms at **judge.** [Middle English *arbitre,* from Old French, from Latin *arbiter.*]

arbor¹

ar·bi·tra·ble (är′bĭ-trə-bəl) *adj.* **1.** Subject to arbitration: *an arbitrable wage and health benefits policy.* **2.** Appropriate for referral to an arbitrator: *an arbitrable dispute.*

ar·bi·trage (är′bĭ-träzh′) *n.* The purchase of securities on one market for immediate resale on another market in order to profit from a price discrepancy. **—arbitrage** *intr.v.* **-traged, -trag·ing, -trag·es.** To be involved in arbitrage. [Middle English, arbitration, from Old French, from *arbitrer,* to judge, from Latin *arbitrārī,* to give judgment. See ARBITRATE.]

ar·bi·tra·geur (är′bĭ-trä-zhûr′) *n.* One that engages in arbitrage. [French, from *arbitrage,* arbitration. See ARBITRAGE.]

ar·bit·ra·ment (är-bĭt′rə-mənt) *n.* **1.** The act of arbitrating; arbitration. **2.** The judgment of an arbitrator or arbiter. [Middle English *arbitrement,* from Old French, from *arbitrer,* to judge. See ARBITRAGE.]

arcade
The Arcade,
Cleveland, Ohio

ar·bi·trar·y (är′bĭ-trĕr′ē) *adj.* **1.** Determined by chance, whim, or impulse, and not by necessity, reason, or principle: *stopped at the first motel we passed, an arbitrary choice; arbitrary division of the group into halves.* **2.** Based on or subject to individual judgment or preference: *The diet imposes overall calorie limits, but daily menus are arbitrary.* **3.** Established by a court or judge rather than by a specific law or statute: *an arbitrary penalty.* **4.** Not limited by law; despotic: *the arbitrary rule of a dictator.* [Middle English *arbitrarie,* from Latin *arbitrārius,* from *arbiter, arbitr-,* arbiter.] **—ar′bi·trar′i·ly** (-trâr′ə-lē) *adv.* **—ar′bi·trar′i·ness** *n.*

SYNONYMS: *arbitrary, capricious, whimsical.* The central meaning shared by these adjectives is "determined by or arising from whim or caprice rather than judgment or reason": *an arbitrary decision; a capricious refusal; the butt of whimsical persecution.*

ar·bi·trate (är′bĭ-trāt′) *v.* **-trat·ed, -trat·ing, -trates.** *—tr.* **1.** To judge or decide in or as in the manner of an arbitrator: *arbitrate a dispute.* **2.** To submit to settlement or judgment by arbitration: *Management and labor agreed to arbitrate their remaining differences.* *—intr.* **1.** To serve as an arbitrator or arbiter. **2.** To submit a dispute to arbitration. [Latin *arbitrārī, arbitrāt-,* to give judgment, from *arbiter, arbitr-,* arbiter.]

ar·bi·tra·tion (är′bĭ-trā′shən) *n.* The process by which the parties to a dispute submit their differences to the judgment of an impartial person or group appointed by mutual consent or statutory provision.

ar·bi·tra·tor (är′bĭ-trā′tər) *n.* **1.** A person chosen to settle the issue between parties engaged in a dispute. See Synonyms at **judge.** **2.** One having the ability or power to make authoritative decisions; an arbiter.

ar·bor¹ (är′bər) *n.* A shady resting place in a garden or park, often made of rustic work or latticework on which plants, such as climbing shrubs or vines, are grown. [Middle English *erber,* from Old French *erbier,* garden, from *erbe,* herb. See HERB.]

ar·bor² (är′bər) *n.* **1.** An axis or shaft supporting a rotating part on a lathe. **2.** A bar for supporting cutting tools. **3.** A spindle of a wheel, as in watches and clocks. **4.** *pl.* **ar·bo·res** (är′bə-rēz′). A tree, as opposed to a shrub. [French *arbre,* from Latin *arbor,* tree.]

Ar·bor Day (är′bər) *n.* An unofficial holiday observed in all 50 states of the United States, most often on the last Friday in April, for the public planting of trees.

ar·bo·re·al (är-bôr′ē-əl, -bōr′-) *adj.* **1.** Relating to or resembling a tree. **2.** Living in trees; arboreous: *arboreal apes.* [From Latin *arboreus,* from *arbor,* tree.] **—ar·bo′re·al·ly** *adv.*

ar·bo·re·ous (är-bôr′ē-əs, -bōr′-) *adj.* **1.** Having many trees; wooded. **2.** Resembling or characteristic of a tree; treelike. **3.** Arboreal.

ar·bo·res (är′bə-rēz′) *n.* Plural of **arbor²** (sense 4).

ar·bo·res·cent (är′bə-rĕs′ənt) *adj.* Having the size, form, or characteristics of a tree; treelike. [Latin *arborēscēns, arborēscent-,* present participle of *arborēscere,* to grow to be a tree, from *arbor,* tree.] **—ar′bo·res′cence** *n.*

arch¹
Top: Arc de Triomphe,
Paris, France
Center: Gateway Arch,
St. Louis, Missouri
Bottom: Natural Bridge,
near Lexington, Virginia

ar·bo·re·tum (är′bə-rē′təm) *n., pl.* **-tums** or **-ta** (-tə). A place where an extensive variety of woody plants are cultivated for scientific, educational, and ornamental purposes. [Latin *arborētum,* a place grown with trees, from *arbor,* tree.]

ar·bo·ri·cul·ture (är′bər-ĭ-kŭl′chər, är-bôr′ĭ-, -bōr′-) *n.* The planting and care of woody plants, especially trees.

ar·bor·ist (är′bər-ĭst) *n.* A specialist in the care of woody plants, especially trees. [From Latin *arbor,* tree.]

ar·bo·ri·za·tion (är′bər-ĭ-zā′shən) *n.* **1.** A branching, treelike shape or arrangement, as that of the dendrite of a nerve cell. **2.** The formation of a treelike shape or arrangement.

ar·bo·rize (är′bə-rīz′) *intr.v.* **-rized, -riz·ing, -riz·es.** To have or produce branching formations, as the bronchial tubes of the lungs.

ar·bor·vi·tae also **ar·bor vi·tae** (är′bər-vī′tē) *n.* **1.a.** Any of several North American or eastern Asian evergreen trees or shrubs of the genus *Thuja,* having flattened branchlets with opposite, scalelike leaves and small cones. They are grown as ornamentals and for timber. **b.** Any similar plant of the genus *Platycladus* or *Thujopsis.* Also called *thuja.* **2.** *Anatomy.* The white nerve tissue of the cerebellum, which has a treelike outline in a median section. [Latin *arbor,* tree + *vītae,* genitive of *vīta,* life; see VITAL.]

ar·bour (är′bər) *n. Chiefly British.* Variant of **arbor¹.**

ar·bo·vi·rus (är′bə-vī′rəs) *n.* Any of a large group of viruses transmitted by arthropods, such as mosquitoes and ticks, that include the causative agents of encephalitis, yellow fever, and dengue. [*ar(thropod-)bo(rne) virus.*] **—ar′bo·vi′ral** *adj.* **—ar′bo·vi·rol′o·gy** (är′bō-vī-rŏl′ə-jē) *n.*

Ar·buth·not (är-bŭth′nət, är′bəth-nŏt′), **John.** 1667–1735. Scottish physician and writer noted for his satirical anti-Whig pamphlets published as *Law Is a Bottomless Pit* (1712) and later retitled *The History of John Bull.*

ar·bu·tus (är-byo͞o′təs) *n.* **1.** Any of various broad-leaved evergreen trees or shrubs of the genus *Arbutus,* including the madroña and strawberry tree, that are native chiefly to warm regions in the Americas and Europe. **2.** The trailing arbutus. [Latin *arbutus,* arbutus.]

arc (ärk) *n.* **1.** Something shaped like a curve or an arch: *the vivid arc of a rainbow.* **2.** *Mathematics.* A segment of a circle. **3.** *Electricity.* A luminous discharge of current that is formed when a strong current jumps a gap in a circuit or between two electrodes. **4.** *Astronomy.* The apparent path of a celestial body as it rises above and falls below the horizon. **—arc** *intr.v.* **arced** or **arcked** (ärkt), **arc·ing** or **arck·ing** (är′kĭng), **arcs. 1.** To form an arc. **2.** To move or seem to move in a curved path: *the stars that arc across the sky.* [Middle English *ark,* from Old French *arc,* from Latin *arcus.*]

ARC¹ (ärk) *n.* A combination of symptoms, including fever, lymphadenopathy, blood abnormalities, and susceptibility to opportunistic infections. The complex was first considered to be a precursor to AIDS, but it is now thought of as a milder form of the disease. [A(IDS)-R(ELATED) C(OMPLEX).]

ARC² *abbr.* American Red Cross.

ar·cade (är-kād′) *n.* **1.** An arched, roofed building or part of a building. **2.** A series of arches supported by columns, piers, or pillars. **3.** A roofed passageway or lane, especially one with shops on either side. **4.** A commercial establishment featuring rows of coin-operated games. **—arcade** *tr.v.* **-cad·ed, -cad·ing, -cades.** To provide with or form into an arcade: *closed off and arcaded the narrow street.* [French, from Italian *arcata,* from *arco,* arch, from Latin *arcus.*]

Ar·cade (är-kād′). A community of north-central California, a suburb of Sacramento. Population, 37,600.

Ar·ca·di·a¹ (är-kā′dē-ə). **1.** Also **Ar·ca·dy** (är′kə-dē). A region of ancient Greece in the Peloponnesus. Its inhabitants, relatively isolated from the rest of the known civilized world, proverbially lived a simple, pastoral life. **2.** A city of southern California, a residential suburb of Los Angeles at the foot of the San Gabriel Mountains. Population, 45,994.

Ar·ca·di·a² also **ar·ca·di·a** (är-kā′dē-ə) *n.* A region offering rural simplicity and contentment.

Ar·ca·di·an (är-kā′dē-ən) *adj.* **1.** Of or relating to the ancient Greek region of Arcadia or its people, language, or culture. **2.** Often **arcadian.** Rustic, peaceful, and simple; pastoral: *a country life of arcadian contentment.* **—Arcadian** *n.* **1.** A native or inhabitant of the ancient Greek region of Arcadia. **2.** Often **arcadian.** One who leads or prefers a simple, rural life. **3.** The dialect of ancient Greek used in Arcadia.

Ar·ca·dy (är′kə-dē). See **Arcadia¹** (sense 1).

ar·ca·na (är-kā′nə) *n.* A plural of **arcanum.**

ar·cane (är-kān′) *adj.* Known or understood by only a few: *arcane economic theories.* See Synonyms at **mysterious.** [Latin *arcānus,* secret, from *arca,* chest.]

ar·ca·num (är-kā′nəm) *n., pl.* **-na** (-nə) or **-nums. 1.** A deep secret; a mystery. **2.** Often **arcana.** Specialized knowledge or detail that is mysterious to the average person: *"knows the arcana of police procedure and the intricacies of litigation"* (George F. Will). **3.** A secret essence or remedy; an elixir. [Latin, from neuter of *arcānus,* secret. See ARCANE.]

arc-bou·tant (är′bo͞o-täɴ′) *n., pl.* **arcs-bou·tants** (är′bo͞o-täɴ′). *Architecture.* See **flying buttress.** [French : *arc,* arch (from Old French; see ARC) + *boutant,* present participle of *bouter,* to thrust (from Old French; see BUTT¹).]

arc cosecant *n. Mathematics.* The inverse function of the cosecant of an angle.

arc cosine *n. Mathematics.* The inverse function of the cosine of an angle.

arc cotangent *n. Mathematics.* The inverse function of the cotangent of an angle.

arch¹ (ärch) *n.* **1.** A structure, especially one of masonry, forming the curved, pointed, or flat upper edge of an open space and supporting the weight above it, as in a bridge or doorway. **2.** A structure, such as a freestanding monument, shaped like an inverted U. **3.** A curve with the ends down and the middle up: *the arch of a raised eyebrow.* **4.** *Anatomy.* An organ or structure having a curved or bowlike appearance, especially either of two arched sections of the bony structure of the foot. **—arch** *v.*

arched, arch·ing, arch·es. —*tr.* **1.** To provide with an arch: *arch a passageway.* **2.** To cause to form an arch or similar curve. **3.** To bend backward: *The dancers alternately arched and hunched their backs.* **4.** To span: *"the rude bridge that arched the flood"* (Ralph Waldo Emerson). —*intr.* To form an arch or archlike curve: *The high fly ball arched toward the stands.* [Middle English, from Old French *arche,* from Vulgar Latin **arca,* from Latin *arcus.*]

arch² (ärch) *adj.* **1.** Chief; principal: *their arch foe.* **2.** Mischievous; roguish: *an arch glance.* [From ARCH–¹.] **—arch′ly** *adv.* **—arch′ness** *n.*

arch. *abbr.* **1.** Archaic; archaism. **2.** Archery. **3.** Archipelago. **4.a.** Architect; architecture. **b.** Architectural.

Arch. *abbr.* Archbishop.

arch–¹ *pref.* **1.** Chief; highest; most important: *archenemy.* **2.** Extreme or most characteristic of its kind: *archconservative.* [Middle English *arche-,* from Old English *ærce-* and from Old French *arche-,* both from Latin *archi-,* from Greek *arkhi-,* archi-.]

arch–² *pref.* Variant of **archi–.**

–arch *suff.* Ruler; leader: *matriarch.* [Middle English *-arche,* from Old French, from Late Latin *-archa,* from Latin *-archēs,* from Greek *-arkhēs,* from *arkhos,* ruler, from *arkhein,* to rule.]

Ar·chae·an (är-kē′ən) *adj.* Variant of **Archean.**

archaeo– or **archeo–** *pref.* Ancient; earlier; primitive: *archaeopteryx.* [New Latin, from Greek *arkhaio-,* from *arkhaios,* ancient. See ARCHAIC.]

ar·chae·ol·o·gy or **ar·che·ol·o·gy** (är′kē-ŏl′ə-jē) *n.* *Abbr.* **archaeol.** The systematic recovery and study of material evidence, such as graves, buildings, tools, and pottery, remaining from past human life and culture. [French *archéologie,* from New Latin *archaeologia,* from Greek *arkhaiologia,* antiquarian lore : *arkhaio-,* archaeo- + *-logia,* -logy.] **—ar′chae·o·log′i·cal** (-ə-lŏj′ĭ-kəl), **ar′chae·o·log′ic** *adj.* **—ar′chae·ol′o·gist** *n.*

ar·chae·op·ter·yx (är′kē-ŏp′tər-ĭks) *n.* An extinct primitive bird (genus *Archaeopteryx*) of the Jurassic period, having lizardlike characteristics, such as teeth and a long, bony tail. It may represent a transitional form between reptiles and birds. [New Latin : ARCHAEO– + Greek *pterux,* bird, wing; see **pet-** in Appendix.]

Ar·chae·o·zo·ic (är′kē-ə-zō′ĭk) *adj. & n.* Variant of **Archeozoic.**

ar·cha·ic (är-kā′ĭk) also **ar·cha·i·cal** (-ĭ-kəl) *adj. Abbr.* **arch.** **1.** Of, relating to, or characteristic of a much earlier, often more primitive period: *an archaic bronze statuette.* **2.** No longer current or applicable; antiquated: *archaic laws.* See Synonyms at **old.** **3.** Of, relating to, or characteristic of words and language that were once common but are now used chiefly to suggest an earlier style or period. [Greek *arkhaikos,* old-fashioned, from *arkhaios,* ancient, from *arkhē,* beginning, from *arkhein,* to begin.] **—ar·cha′i·cal·ly** *adv.*

archaic smile *n.* A representation of the human mouth with slightly upturned corners, characteristic of early Greek sculpture produced before the fifth century B.C.

ar·cha·ism (är′kē-ĭz′əm, -kā-) *n. Abbr.* **arch.** **1.** An archaic word, phrase, idiom, or other expression. **2.** An archaic style, quality, or usage. [New Latin *archaeismus,* from Greek *arkhaismos,* from *arkhaios,* ancient. See ARCHAIC.] **—ar′cha·ist** *n.* **—ar′cha·is′tic** (-ĭs′tĭk) *adj.*

ar·cha·ize (är′kē-īz′, -kā-) *v.* **-ized, -iz·ing, -iz·es.** —*tr.* To give an archaic quality or character to; make archaic. —*intr.* To use archaisms, as in prose, to suggest the past. **—ar′cha·iz′er** *n.*

arch·an·gel (ärk′ān′jəl) *n.* **1.** A high-ranking angel. **2. archangels.** The eighth of the nine orders of spiritual beings in medieval angelology. [Middle English, from Old French *archangele,* from Late Latin *archangelus,* from Late Greek *arkhangelos* : Greek *arkh-,* archi- + Greek *angelos,* angel.] **—arch′an·gel′ic** (-ăn-jĕl′ĭk) *adj.*

Arch·an·gel (ärk′ān′jəl). See **Arkhangelsk.**

arch·bish·op (ärch-bĭsh′əp) *n. Abbr.* **abp., Abp., Arch., Archbp.** A bishop of the highest rank, heading an archdiocese or a province. [Middle English *archebishop,* from Old English *arcebisceop,* from Late Latin *archiepiscopus,* from Late Greek *arkhiepiskopos* : Greek *arkhi-,* archi- + *episkopos,* bishop; see BISHOP.]

arch·bish·op·ric (ärch-bĭsh′əp-rĭk) *n.* **1.** The rank, office, or term of an archbishop. **2.** The area under an archbishop's jurisdiction; an archdiocese.

Archbp. *abbr.* Archbishop.

arch·con·ser·va·tive (ärch′kən-sûr′və-tĭv) *adj.* Highly conservative, especially in political viewpoint. **—arch′con·ser′va·tive** *n.*

arch·dea·con (ärch-dē′kən) *n.* A church official, as in the Anglican Church, who is in charge of temporal and other affairs in a diocese, with powers delegated from the bishop. [Middle English *archedeken,* from Old English *arcediakon,* from Late Latin *archidiāconus,* from Late Greek *arkhidiakonos* : Greek *arkhi-,* archi- + *diakonos,* deacon.] **—arch·dea′con·ate** (-kə-nĭt) *n.* **—arch·dea′con·ship′** *n.*

arch·dea·con·ry (ärch-dē′kən-rē) *n., pl.* **-ries.** **1.** The rank or office of an archdeacon. **2.** The district or residence of an archdeacon.

arch·di·o·cese (ärch-dī′ə-sĭs, -sēs′, -sēz′) *n.* The district under an archbishop's jurisdiction. **—arch′di·oc′e·san** (-ŏs′ĭ-sən) *adj.*

arch·du·cal (ärch-dōō′kəl, -dyōō′-) *adj.* Of or having to do with an archduke or an archduchy. [French *archiducal,* from *archiduc,* archduke. See ARCHDUKE.]

arch·duch·ess (ärch-dŭch′ĭs) *n.* **1.** The wife or widow of an archduke. **2.** A woman, especially an Austrian princess, holding an archduchy in her own right. **3.** Used as a title for such a noblewoman. [French *archiduchesse,* feminine of *archiduc,* archduke. See ARCHDUKE.]

arch·duch·y (ärch-dŭch′ē) *n., pl.* **-ies.** The territory over which an archduke or an archduchess has authority. [French *archiduché,* from obsolete French *archeduché* : *arche-,* arch- + *duché,* duchy; see DUCHY.]

arch·duke (ärch-dōōk′, -dyōōk′) *n.* **1.** In certain royal families, especially that of imperial Austria, a nobleman having a rank equivalent to that of a sovereign prince. **2.** Used as a title for such a nobleman. [Obsolete French *archeduc* : *arche-,* arch- + *duc,* duke; see DUKE.]

Ar·che·an also **Ar·chae·an** (är-kē′ən) *adj.* Of or relating to the oldest known rocks, those of the Precambrian era, that are predominantly igneous in composition. [From Greek *arkhaios,* ancient. See ARCHAIC.]

arched (ärcht) *adj.* **1.** Forming an arch or a curve like that of an arch. **2.** Provided, made, or covered with an arch.

ar·che·go·ni·um (är′kĭ-gō′nē-əm) *n., pl.* **-ni·a** (-nē-ə). A multicellular, often flask-shaped, egg-producing organ occurring in mosses, ferns, and most gymnosperms. [New Latin, from Greek *arkhegonos,* original : *arkhe-, arkhi-,* archi- + *gonos,* offspring; see **gene-** in Appendix.] **—ar′che·go′ni·al** *adj.* **—ar′che·go′ni·ate** (-ĭt) *adj.*

arch·en·ceph·a·lon (är′kĕn-sĕf′ə-lŏn′) *n.* The part of the primitive embryonic brain from which the forebrain and midbrain develop.

arch·en·e·my (ärch-ĕn′ə-mē) *n.* **1.** A principal enemy. **2.** Often **Archenemy.** *Theology.* The Devil; Satan. Used with *the.*

ar·chen·ter·on (är-kĕn′tə-rŏn′, -tər-ən) *n.* The central cavity of the gastrula, which ultimately becomes the intestinal or digestive cavity. **—ar′chen·ter′ic** (är′kĕn-tĕr′ĭk) *adj.*

archeo– *pref.* Variant of **archaeo–.**

ar·che·ol·o·gy (är′kē-ŏl′ə-jē) *n.* Variant of **archaeology.**

Ar·che·o·zo·ic also **Ar·chae·o·zo·ic** (är′kē-ə-zō′ĭk) —*adj.* Of, belonging to, or designating the earlier of two divisions of the Precambrian era. —*n.* The Archeozoic era.

arch·er (är′chər) *n.* One that shoots with a bow and arrow. [Middle English, from Old French *archier,* from Late Latin *arcārius,* alteration of *arcuārius,* maker of bows, from Latin *arcus,* bow.]

Arch·er (är′chər) *n.* See **Sagittarius.**

arch·er·fish (är′chər-fĭsh′) *n., pl.* **archerfish** or **-fish·es.** Any of various freshwater fishes of the family Toxotidae that spit drops of water at insects and prey on those knocked to the surface of the water.

arch·er·y (är′chə-rē) *n.* **1.** *Abbr.* **arch.** The art, sport, or skill of shooting with a bow and arrow. **2.** The equipment of an archer. **3.** A group of archers.

ar·che·type (är′kĭ-tīp′) *n.* **1.** An original model or type after which other similar things are patterned; a prototype: *" 'Frankenstein' . . . 'Dracula' . . . 'Dr. Jekyll and Mr. Hyde' . . . the archetypes that have influenced all subsequent horror stories"* (New York Times). **2.** An ideal example of a type; quintessence: *an archetype of the successful entrepreneur.* [Latin *archetypum,* from Greek *arkhetupon,* from neuter of *arkhetupos,* original : *arkhe-, arkhi-,* archi- + *tupos,* model, stamp.] **—ar′che·typ′al** (-tī′pəl), **ar′che·typ′ic** (-tĭp′ĭk), **ar′che·typ′i·cal** *adj.* **—ar′che·typ′i·cal·ly** *adv.*

arch·fiend (ärch-fēnd′) *n.* **1.** A principal fiend. **2. Archfiend.** *Theology.* The Devil; Satan. Used with *the.*

archi– or **arch–** *pref.* **1.** Chief; highest; most important: *archiepiscopal.* **2.** Earlier; primitive: *archenteron.* [French *archi-* and Italian *arci-,* both from Latin *archi-,* from Greek *arkhi-, arkh-,* from *arkhein,* to begin, rule.]

ar·chi·di·ac·o·nal (är′kĭ-dī-ăk′ə-nəl) *adj.* Of or having to do with an archdeacon or an archdeacon's office. [Middle English, from Late Latin *archidiāconus,* archdeacon. See ARCHDEACON.]

ar·chi·di·ac·o·nate (är′kĭ-dī-ăk′ə-nĭt) *n.* The office or position of an archdeacon. [Medieval Latin *archidiāconātus,* from Late Latin *archidiāconus,* archdeacon. See ARCHDEACON.]

ar·chi·e·pis·co·pal (är′kē-ĭ-pĭs′kə-pəl) *adj.* Of or having to do with an archbishop or an archbishopric. [Medieval Latin *archiepiscopālis,* from Late Latin *archiepiscopus,* archbishop. See ARCHBISHOP.] **—ar′chi·e·pis′co·pal′i·ty** (-păl′ĭ-tē) *n.* **—ar′chi·e·pis′co·pal·ly** *adv.* **—ar′chi·e·pis′co·pate** *n.*

ar·chil (är′kĭl, -chĭl) *n.* Variant of **orchil.**

ar·chi·man·drite (är′kə-măn′drīt′) *n.* *Eastern Orthodox Church.* **1.** A cleric ranking below a bishop. **2.** The head of a monastery or a group of monasteries. [Late Latin *archimandrīta,* from Late Greek *arkhimandritēs* : Greek *arkhi-,* archi- + *mandra,* monastery (from Greek, cattle pen).]

Archimedean screw *n.* An ancient apparatus for raising water, consisting of either a spiral tube around an inclined axis or an

archaeopteryx

archangel
Detail from late 15th-century *Annunciation* by Botticelli

archery

ă pat	oi boy
ā pay	ou out
âr care	ŏŏ took
ä father	ōō boot
ĕ pet	ŭ cut
ē be	ûr urge
ĭ pit	th thin
ī pie	*th* this
îr pier	hw which
ŏ pot	zh vision
ō toe	ə about, item
ô paw	♦ regionalism

Stress marks: ′ (primary); ′ (secondary), as in **dictionary** (dĭk′shə-nĕr′ē)

inclined tube containing a tight-fitting, broad-threaded screw. Also called *Archimedes' screw.*

Ar·chi·me·des (är′kə-mē′dēz). 287?–212 B.C. Greek mathematician, engineer, and physicist. Among the most important intellectual figures of antiquity, he discovered formulas for the area and volume of various geometric figures, applied geometry to hydrostatics and mechanics, devised numerous ingenious mechanisms, such as the Archimedean screw, and discovered the principle of buoyancy. **—Ar′chi·me′de·an** (-mē′dē-ən, -mĭ-dē′-) *adj.*

Ar·chi·me·des′ screw (är′kə-mē′dēz) *n.* See **Archimedean screw.**

ar·chine also **ar·shin** (är-shēn′) *n.* A unit of length formerly used in Russia and Turkey, equal to about 71 centimeters (28 inches). [Russian *arshin,* from Tatar *arshyn,* an ell; akin to Turkish *arşin,* of Persian origin.]

architrave

ar·chi·pel·a·go (är′kə-pĕl′ə-gō′) *n., pl.* **-goes** or **-gos. 1.** *Abbr.* **arch.** A large group of islands: *the Philippine archipelago.* **2.** A sea, such as the Aegean, containing a large number of scattered islands. [Italian *Arcipelago,* the Aegean Sea : *arci-* (from Greek *arkhi-,* archi-) + Italian *pelago,* sea (from Latin *pelagus,* from Greek *pelagos,* sea; see **plāk-**[1] in Appendix).] **—ar′chi·pe·lag′ic** (-pə-lăj′ĭk) *adj.*

Ar·chi·pen·ko (är′kə-pĕng′kō), **Alexander Porfirievich.** 1887–1964. Russian-born American sculptor noted for his cubist and purely abstract works, such as *Dual* (1955).

archit. *abbr.* Architecture.

ar·chi·tect (är′kĭ-tĕkt′) *n.* **1.** *Abbr.* **arch., archt.** One who designs and supervises the construction of buildings or other large structures. **2.** One that plans or devises: *a country considered to be the chief architect of war in the Middle East.* [Latin *architectus,* from Greek *arkhitektōn* : *arkhi-,* archi- + *tektōn,* builder; see **teks-** in Appendix.]

ar·chi·tec·ton·ic (är′kĭ-tĕk-tŏn′ĭk) also **ar·chi·tec·ton·i·cal** (-ĭ-kəl) *adj.* **1.** Of or relating to architecture or design. **2.** Having qualities, such as design and structure, that are characteristic of architecture: *a work of art forming an architectonic whole.* **3.** *Philosophy.* Of or relating to the scientific systematization of knowledge. [Latin *architectonicus,* architectural, from Greek *arkhitektonikos,* from *arkhitektōn,* architect. See ARCHITECT.] **—ar′chi·tec·ton′i·cal·ly** *adv.*

ar·chi·tec·ton·ics (är′kĭ-tĕk-tŏn′ĭks) *n.* *(used with a sing. verb).* **1.** The science of architecture. **2.** Structural design: *the architectonics of an elaborate fugue.* **3.** *Philosophy.* The scientific systematization of knowledge.

ar·chi·tec·ture (är′kĭ-tĕk′chər) *n.* *Abbr.* **archit., arch. 1.** The art and science of designing and erecting buildings. **2.** Buildings and other large structures: *the low, brick-and-adobe architecture of the Southwest.* **3.** A style and method of design and construction: *Byzantine architecture.* **4.** Orderly arrangement of parts; structure: *the architecture of the federal bureaucracy; the broad architecture of a massive novel; computer architecture.* [Latin *architectūra,* from *architectus,* architect. See ARCHITECT.] **—ar′chi·tec′tur·al** *adj.* **—ar′chi·tec′tur·al·ly** *adv.*

ar·chi·trave (är′kĭ-trāv′) *n.* **1.** The lowermost part of an entablature in classical architecture that rests directly on top of a column. Also called *epistyle.* **2.** The molding around a door or window. [French, from Old French, from Old Italian : *archi-,* archi- + *trave,* beam (from Latin *trabs, trab-;* see **treb-** in Appendix).]

ar·chi·val (är-kī′vəl) *adj.* Of, relating to, kept in, or suitable for archives: *"An archival material should have a neutral or slightly alkaline pH; it should also . . . have good aging properties"* (Artist's Magazine).

arctic fox
Alopex lagopus

ar·chive (är′kīv′) *n.* **1.** Often **archives.** A place or collection containing records, documents, or other materials of historical interest: *old land deeds in the municipal archives; the studio archives, a vast repository of silent-film prints and outtakes.* **2.** A repository for stored memories or information: *the archive of the mind.* [From French *archives,* from Latin *archīva,* from Greek *arkheia,* pl. of *arkheion,* town hall, from *arkhē,* government, from *arkhein,* to rule.] **—ar′chive′** *v.*

ar·chi·vist (är′kə-vĭst, -kī′-) *n.* One who is in charge of archives.

ar·chi·volt (är′kə-vōlt′) *n.* *Architecture.* A decorative molding carried around an arched wall opening. [French *archivolte* or Italian *archivolto* (French, from Italian) : *arco,* arch (from Latin *arcus*) + *volta,* vault (from Latin *volūta;* see VAULT[1]).]

arch·lib·er·al (ärch′lĭb′ər-əl, -lĭb′rəl) *adj.* Highly liberal, especially in political viewpoint. **—arch′lib′er·al** *n.*

ar·chon (är′kŏn′, -kən) *n.* **1.** A high official; a ruler. **2.** One of the nine principal magistrates of ancient Athens. **3.** An authoritative figure; a leader: *archons of cultural modernism.* [Latin *archōn,* from Greek *arkhōn,* from present participle of *arkhein,* to rule.] **—ar′chon·ship′** *n.*

arch·priest (ärch′prēst′) *n.* *Roman Catholic Church.* **1.a.** Used formerly as a title for a priest holding first rank among the members of a cathedral chapter, acting as chief assistant to a bishop. **b.** An honorific title applied to a priest, which may be accompanied by a specific function. **2.** *Eastern Orthodox Church.* The highest rank a married priest can hold. [Middle English *archeprest,* from Old French *archeprestre,* from Late Latin *archipresbyter,* from Late Greek *arkhipresbuteros* : Greek *arkhi-,* archi- + *presbuteros,* priest; see PRESBYTER.]

arch·ri·val (ärch′rī′vəl) *n.* A principal rival.

archt. *abbr.* Architect.

arch·way (ärch′wā′) *n.* **1.** A passageway under an arch. **2.** An arch over an entrance or passageway.

-archy *suff.* Rule; government: *oligarchy.* [From words such as (MON)ARCHY.]

ar·ci·form (är′sə-fôrm′) *adj.* Formed in the shape of an arc. [Latin *arci-* (from *arcus,* bow) + -FORM.]

arc-jet engine (ärk′jĕt′) *n.* A rocket engine that operates by heating the propellant gas with an electric arc.

arcked (ärkt) *v.* A past tense and a past participle of **arc.**

arck·ing (är′kĭng) *v.* A present participle of **arc.**

arc lamp *n.* An electric light in which a current traverses a gas between two incandescent electrodes and generates an arc that produces light. Also called *arc light.*

arc secant *n.* *Mathematics.* The inverse function of the secant of an angle.

arc sine *n.* *Mathematics.* The inverse function of the sine of an angle.

arc tangent *n.* *Mathematics.* The inverse function of the tangent of an angle.

arc·tic (ärk′tĭk, är′tĭk) *adj.* Extremely cold; frigid. See Synonyms at **cold. —arctic** *n.* A warm, waterproof overshoe. [Alteration (influenced by Latin *arcticus*) of Middle English *artic,* northern, from Medieval Latin *articus,* from Latin *arcticus,* from Greek *arktikos,* from *arktos,* bear, the northern constellation Ursa Major. See **r̥tko-** in Appendix.]

Arc·tic (ärk′tĭk, är′tĭk). A region between the North Pole and the northern timberlines of North America and Eurasia. **—Arc′tic** *adj.*

Arctic Archipelago. A group of more than 50 large islands of Northwest Territories, Canada, in the Arctic Ocean between North America and Greenland.

arctic char *n.* A char *(Salvelinus alpinus)* native to the fresh waters of Alaska and northern Canada.

Arctic Circle. The parallel of latitude approximately 66°33′ north. It forms the boundary between the North Temperate and North Frigid zones.

arctic fox *n.* A fox *(Alopex lagopus)* of Arctic regions, having fur that is white or light gray in winter and brown or blue-gray in summer.

Arctic Ocean. The waters surrounding the North Pole between North America and Eurasia. The smallest ocean in the world, it is covered by pack ice throughout the year.

Arctic Red River (rĕd). A river rising in the Mackenzie Mountains of western Northwest Territories, Canada, and flowing about 499 km (310 mi) generally north-northwest to the Mackenzie River.

arctic tern *n.* A tern *(Sterna paradisaea)* that is noted for its extremely long migrations, typically from the Arctic to the Antarctic and back each year.

Arc·tu·rus (ärk-to͝or′əs, -tyo͝or′-) *n.* The fourth brightest star in the sky and the brightest star in the constellation Boötes, approximately 36 light-years from Earth. [Middle English, from Latin *Arctūrus,* from Greek *Arktouros* : *arktos,* bear; see **r̥tko-** in Appendix + *ouros,* guard, from its position behind Ursa Major; see **wer-**[3] in Appendix.]

ar·cu·ate (är′kyo͞o-ĭt, -āt′) also **ar·cu·at·ed** (-ā′tĭd) *adj.* Having the form of a bow; curved. [Latin *arcuātus,* past participle of *arcuāre,* to bend like a bow, from *arcus,* bow.] **—ar′cu·ate·ly** *adv.*

arcuate nucleus *n.* Any of various specialized groups of nerve cells in the medulla oblongata, thalamus, or hypothalamus of the brain.

ar·cu·a·tion (är′kyo͞o-ā′shən) *n.* **1.** The process of curving or the condition of being curved. **2.** The use of arches or vaults in building.

-ard or **-art** *suff.* One that habitually or excessively is in a specified condition or performs a specified action: *drunkard.* [Middle English, from Old French, of Germanic origin. See **kar-** in Appendix.]

ar·deb (är′dĕb′) *n.* A unit of dry measure in several countries of the Middle East, standardized in Egypt to equal 198 liters (5.62 U.S. bushels) but varying widely elsewhere. [Arabic dialectal *'ardabb,* from Aramaic *'rdb* or from Coptic *artab* or from Greek *artabē,* all probably of Old Persian origin.]

Ar·den (är′dn). An unincorporated city of north-central California, a residential suburb of Sacramento. Population, 49,130.

Arden, Elizabeth. 1884?–1966. Canadian-born American businesswoman whose original beauty salon, founded in 1910, grew into an international cosmetics corporation.

Arden, Forest of. A wooded area, formerly very extensive, of central England west of Stratford-upon-Avon. It provided the setting for Shakespeare's *As You Like It.*

Ar·dennes (är-dĕn′). A plateau region of northern France, southeast Belgium, and northern Luxembourg east and south of the Meuse River. It was the scene of heavy fighting in World War I and World War II, notably during the Battle of the Bulge in December 1944 and January 1945.

ar·dent (är′dnt) *adj.* **1.** Expressing or characterized by warmth of feeling; passionate: *an ardent lover.* **2.** Displaying or characterized by strong enthusiasm or devotion; fervent: *"an im-*

passioned age, so ardent and serious in its pursuit of art" (Walter Pater). **3.a.** Burning; fiery. **b.** Glowing; shining: *ardent eyes.* [Middle English *ardaunt,* from Old French *ardant,* from Latin *ārdēns, ārdent-,* present participle of *ārdēre,* to burn. See **as-** in Appendix.] **—ar′den·cy** (-dn-sē) *n.* **—ar′dent·ly** *adv.*

ardent spirits *pl.n.* Strong alcoholic liquors, such as whiskey or gin.

Ard·more (ärd′môr, -mōr). A city of southern Oklahoma near the Texas border south-southeast of Oklahoma City. It is a commercial and industrial center. Population, 23,689.

ar·dor (är′dər) *n.* **1.** Fiery intensity of feeling. See Synonyms at **passion.** **2.** Strong enthusiasm or devotion; zeal: *"The dazzling conquest of Mexico gave a new impulse to the ardor of discovery"* (William Hickling Prescott). **3.** Intense heat or glow, as of fire. [Middle English *ardour,* from Old French, from Latin *ārdor,* from *ārdēre,* to burn. See **as-** in Appendix.]

ar·dour (är′dər) *n. Chiefly British.* Variant of **ardor.**

ar·du·ous (är′jo͞o-əs) *adj.* **1.** Demanding great effort or labor; difficult: *"the arduous work of preparing a Dictionary of the English Language"* (Macaulay). **2.** Testing severely the powers of endurance; strenuous: *a long, arduous, and exhausting war.* **3.** Hard to traverse, climb, or surmount. See Synonyms at **burdensome, hard.** [From Latin *arduus,* high, steep.] **—ar′du·ous·ly** *adv.* **—ar′du·ous·ness** *n.*

are[1] (är) *v.* Second person singular and plural and first and third person plural present indicative of **be.** [Middle English *aren,* from Old English *aron.* See **er-[1]** in Appendix.]

are[2] (âr, är) also **ar** (är) *n. Abbr.* **a, a.** A metric unit of area equal to 100 square meters (119.6 square yards). [French, from Latin *ārea,* open space. See AREA.]

ar·e·a (âr′ē-ə) *n. Abbr.* **A, A., a.** **1.** A roughly bounded part of the space on a surface; a region: *a farming area; the New York area.* **2.** A surface, especially an open, unoccupied piece of ground: *a landing area; a playing area.* **3.** A distinct part or section, as of a building, set aside for a specific function: *a storage area in the basement.* **4.** A division of experience, activity, or knowledge; a field: *studies in the area of finance; a job in the health-care area.* **5.** An open, sunken space next to a building; an areaway. **6.** *Abbr.* **A** The extent of a planar region or of the surface of a solid measured in square units. **7.** *Computer Science.* A section of storage set aside for a particular purpose. [Latin *ārea,* open space; possibly akin to *ārēre,* to be dry. See ARID.]

SYNONYMS: *area, region, belt, zone, district, locality.* These nouns all denote extents of space, especially on a surface, that can be differentiated from others by particular qualities or characteristics. *Area* and *region* are the most inclusive: *a dialect spoken over a large area; a blighted urban area; a recreation area; tropical regions of South America; polar regions; pain in the abdominal region.* A *belt* is a tract, frequently but not always longer than it is wide, that is distinguished from others in a single stated respect: *the Corn Belt; a snow belt.* A *zone* may be an area that encircles, as on a map (*the Torrid Zone*); it may also be an area with strictly defined, often arbitrarily set boundaries (*a residential zone; a demilitarized zone; a nuclear-free zone*). If the area is a subdivision for administrative purposes, it is called a *district: a congressional district. District* can also refer to a less specific area with respect to such features as its use: *the financial district.* A *locality* is an area with vague or undefined limits: *The turnout of voters was low in many localities.*

Ar·e·a Code (âr′ē-ə) also **area code** *n.* A number, often with three digits, assigned to a telephone area, as in the United States and Canada, and used when placing a call to that area.

area rug *n.* A rug that covers a limited area of floor space in a room.

ar·e·a·way (âr′ē-ə-wā′) *n.* **1.** A small, sunken area allowing access or light and air to basement doors or windows. **2.** An often narrow passageway between buildings.

a·re·ca (ə-rē′kə, ăr′ĭ-kə) *n.* Any of certain tropical Old World palms, such as those in the genera *Areca* and *Chrysalidocarpus.* [Portuguese, from Malayalam *aṭekka,* areca nut, from Tamil *aṭaikkāy.*]

areca nut *n.* See **betel nut.**

A·re·ci·bo (ä′rə-sē′bō). A city of northern Puerto Rico on the Atlantic Ocean. It is a commercial and industrial center. Population, 48,779.

a·re·na (ə-rē′nə) *n.* **1.** A large modern building for the presentation of sports events and spectacles. **2.** A place or scene where forces contend or events unfold: *withdrew from the political arena; the world as an arena of moral conflict.* **3.** The area in the center of an ancient Roman amphitheater where contests and other spectacles were held. [Latin *harēna, arēna,* sand, a sand-strewn place of combat in an amphitheater, perhaps of Etruscan origin.]

WORD HISTORY: Fans watching contact sports such as boxing, hockey, or football in modern arenas might be struck by the connection between the word *arena* and the notion of gladiatorial combat. This word is from Latin *harēna* (also spelled *arēna*), "sand." *Harēna* then came to mean the part of a Roman amphitheater that was covered with sand to absorb the blood spilled by the combatants. *Arena* is first recorded in English during the 17th century, denoting this area of a Roman amphitheater.

ar·e·na·ceous (ăr′ə-nā′shəs) *adj.* **1.** Resembling, derived from, or containing sand. **2.** Growing in sandy areas. [From Latin *harēnāceus, arēnāceus* : *harēna, arēna,* sand; see ARENA + *-āceus,* -aceous.]

arena theater *n.* A theater without a proscenium, in which the stage is at the center of the auditorium and is surrounded by seats. Also called *theater-in-the-round.*

A·rendt (âr′ənt, är′-), **Hannah.** 1906–1975. German-born American historian whose major published works include *The Origins of Totalitarianism* (1951) and *On Revolution* (1963).

ar·e·nic·o·lous (ăr′ə-nĭk′ə-ləs) *adj.* Growing, living, or burrowing in sand: *arenicolous worms.* [Latin *harēna, arēna,* sand; see ARENA + -COLOUS.]

aren't (ärnt, är′ənt). Are not. See Usage Note at **ain't.**

a·re·o·la (ə-rē′ə-lə) also **ar·e·ole** (âr′ē-ōl′) *n., pl.* **-lae** (-lē′) or **-las** also **-oles** (-ōlz′). **1. areole. a.** *Biology.* A small space or interstice in a tissue or part, such as the area bounded by small veins in a leaf or the wing of an insect. **b.** A small, specialized, cushionlike area on a cactus from which hairs, glochids, spines, branches, or flowers may arise. **2.** *Anatomy.* A small ring of color around a center portion, as about the nipple of the breast. [Latin *āreola,* small open space, diminutive of *ārea,* open place. See AREA.] **—a·re′o·lar, a·re′o·late** (-lĭt) *adj.* **—a·re′o·la′tion** *n.*

Ar·e·op·a·gite (ăr′ē-ŏp′ə-jīt′, -gīt′) *n.* A member of the council of the Areopagus. **—Ar′e·op·a·git′ic** (-jĭt′ĭk, gĭt′-) *adj.*

Ar·e·op·a·gus (ăr′ē-ŏp′ə-gəs) *n.* The highest judicial and legislative council of ancient Athens. [Latin, from Greek *Areios pagos,* Areopagus, hill of Ares (where the tribunal met) : *Areios,* of Ares (from *Arēs,* Ares) + *pagos,* stiff mass, hill (from *pēgnunai, pag-,* to stick, stiffen; see **pag-** in Appendix).]

A·re·qui·pa (ăr′ə-kē′pə, ä′rĕ-kē′pä). A city of southern Peru at the foot of El Misti. Founded in 1540 on the site of an Incan village, it is the commercial center of southern Peru and northern Bolivia. Population, 108,023.

Ar·es (âr′ēz) *n. Greek Mythology.* The god of war.

a·rête (ə-rāt′) *n.* A sharp, narrow mountain ridge or spur. [French, from Old French *areste,* fishbone, spine, from Late Latin *arista,* awn, fishbone, from Latin, awn.]

ar·e·thu·sa (ăr′ə-tho͞o-zə, -sə) *n.* See **swamp pink.** [From ARETHUSA.]

Ar·e·thu·sa (ăr′ə-tho͞o-zə, -sə) *n. Greek Mythology.* A wood nymph who was changed into a fountain by Artemis. [Latin, from Greek *Arethousa.*]

A·re·ti·no (ăr′ə-tē′nō, är′-), **Pietro.** 1492–1556. Italian writer and satirist best known for his literary attacks on his wealthy and powerful contemporaries and for six volumes of letters.

A·rez·zo (ä-rĕt′sō). A city of central Italy on the Arno River southeast of Florence. It was originally an Etruscan settlement and later a Roman military station and colony. Population, 91,535.

arg. *abbr. Heraldry.* Argent.

Arg. *abbr.* **1.** Argentina. **2.** Argentine.

ar·gal (är′gəl) *n.* Variant of **argol.**

ar·ga·li (är′gə-lē) *n., pl.* **argali** or **-lis.** A large wild sheep *(Ovis ammon)* of the mountains of central and northern Asia, having large, spirally curved horns. [Mongolian, mountain ewe.]

ar·gent (är′jənt) *n.* **1.** *Abbr.* **arg.** *Heraldry.* The metal silver, represented by the color white. **2.** *Archaic.* Silver or something resembling it. [Middle English, from Old French, from Latin *argentum,* silver. See **arg-** in Appendix.]

Ar·gen·teuil (är-zhäɴ-tœ′yə). A city of northern France, a residential and industrial suburb of Paris on the Seine River. It grew around a convent founded by Charlemagne in the seventh century. Population, 95,347.

ar·gen·tic (är-jĕn′tĭk) *adj.* Of or containing silver.

ar·gen·tif·er·ous (är′jən-tĭf′ər-əs) *adj.* Bearing or producing silver.

Ar·gen·ti·na (är′jən-tē′nə). *Abbr.* **Arg.** A country of southeast South America stretching about 3,701 km (2,300 mi) from its border with Bolivia to southern Tierra del Fuego, an island it shares with Chile. Argentina is one of the most highly developed Latin American countries, with an economy based both on agriculture and on diversified industry. It proclaimed its independence from Spain in 1816. Buenos Aires is the capital and the largest city. Population, 27,947,446. **—Ar′gen·tine′** (-tēn′, -tīn′), **Ar′gen·tin′e·an** (-tĭn′ē-ən) *adj. & n.*

ar·gen·tine (är′jən-tīn′, -tēn′) *adj.* Relating to or resembling silver; silvery. **—argentine** *n.* **1.** Silver. **2.** Any of various silvery metals. [Middle English, from Old French *argentin,* from Latin *argentīnus,* from *argentum,* silver. See **arg-** in Appendix.]

ar·gen·tite (är′jən-tīt′) *n.* A valuable silver ore, Ag_2S, with a lead-gray color and metallic luster that is often tarnished a dull black.

ar·gil (är′jĭl) *n.* Clay, especially a white clay used by potters. [Middle English *argilla,* from Latin, from Greek *argillos.* See **arg-** in Appendix.]

ar·gil·la·ceous (är′jə-lā′shəs) *adj.* Containing, made of, or

arena
Boston Garden

Argentina

ă pat	oi boy
ā pay	ou out
âr care	o͝o took
ä father	o͞o boot
ĕ pet	ŭ cut
ē be	ûr urge
ĭ pit	th thin
ī pie	*th* this
îr pier	hw which
ŏ pot	zh vision
ō toe	ə about, item
ô paw	♦ regionalism

Stress marks: ′ (primary); ′ (secondary), as in **dictionary** (dĭk′shə-nĕr′ē)

resembling clay; clayey. [From Latin *argillāceus* : *argilla,* argil; see ARGIL + *-āceus,* -aceous.]

ar·gil·lite (är′jə-līt′) *n.* A metamorphic rock, intermediate between shale and slate, that does not possess true slaty cleavage. [Latin *argilla,* argil; see ARGIL + –ITE[1].]

ar·gi·nase (är′jə-nās′, -nāz) *n.* An enzyme found primarily in the liver that catalyzes the hydrolysis of arginine to form urea and ornithine. [From German *Arginin,* arginine. See ARGININE.]

ar·gi·nine (är′jə-nēn′) *n.* An amino acid, $C_6H_{14}N_4O_2$, obtained from the hydrolysis or digestion of plant and animal protein. [German *Arginin,* possibly from Greek *arginoeis,* bright. See **arg-** in Appendix.]

Ar·give (är′jīv′, -gīv′) *adj.* **1.** Of or relating to Argos or the ancient region of Argolis. **2.** Of or relating to Greece or the Greeks. **—Argive** *n.* A Greek, especially an inhabitant of Argos or Argolis. [Latin *Argīvus,* from Greek *Argeios,* from ARGOS.]

Ar·go (är′gō′) *n.* **1.** *Greek Mythology.* The ship in which Jason sailed in search of the Golden Fleece. **2.** Formerly, a constellation in the Southern Hemisphere, lying between Canis Major and the Southern Cross, now divided into four smaller constellations, Carina, Puppis, Pyxis, and Vela. [Latin *Argō,* from Greek.]

ar·gol (är′gôl′) also **ar·gal** (-gəl) *n.* Crude potassium bitartrate, a by-product of winemaking. [Middle English *argoile,* from Anglo-Norman *argoil,* ultimately from Latin *argilla,* clay. See ARGIL.]

Ar·go·lis (är′gə-lĭs). An ancient region of southern Greece in the northeast Peloponnesus, dominated by the city of Argos.

Argolis, Gulf of. An inlet of the Aegean Sea on the eastern coast of the Peloponnesus in southern Greece.

argosy

ar·gon (är′gŏn′) *n.* *Symbol* **Ar** A colorless, odorless, inert gaseous element constituting approximately one percent of Earth's atmosphere, from which it is commercially obtained by fractionation for use in electric light bulbs, fluorescent tubes, and radio vacuum tubes and as an inert gas shield in arc welding. Atomic number 18; atomic weight 39.94; melting point −189.2°C; boiling point −185.7°C. See table at **element.** [Greek, neuter of *argos,* idle, inert : *a-,* without; see A–[1] + *ergon,* work; see **werg-** in Appendix.]

ar·go·naut (är′gə-nôt′) *n.* See **paper nautilus.** [Latin, Argonaut. See ARGONAUT.]

Ar·go·naut (är′gə-nôt′) *n.* **1.** *Greek Mythology.* One who sailed with Jason on the *Argo* in search of the Golden Fleece. **2.** Also **argonaut.** A person who is engaged in a dangerous but rewarding quest; an adventurer. [Latin *Argonauta,* from Greek *Argonautēs* : *Argō,* the ship Argo + *nautēs,* sailor (from *naus,* ship; see **nāu-** in Appendix).]

Ar·gonne (är-gŏn′, är′gŏn). A wooded and hilly region of northeast France between the Meuse and Aisne rivers. The area was a major battleground during World War I.

Ar·gos (är′gŏs, -gəs). A city of ancient Greece in the northeast Peloponnesus near the head of the Gulf of Argolis. Inhabited from the early Bronze Age, it was one of the most powerful cities of ancient Greece until the rise of Sparta.

ar·go·sy (är′gə-sē) *n., pl.* **-sies. 1.** *Nautical.* **a.** A large merchant ship. **b.** A fleet of ships. **2.** A rich source or supply: *an argosy of adventure lore.* [Alteration of obsolete *ragusye,* from Italian *ragusea,* vessel of Ragusa (Dubrovnik).]

ar·got (är′gō, -gət) *n.* A specialized vocabulary or set of idioms used by a particular group: *thieves' argot.* See Synonyms at **dialect.** [French.]

argyle

ar·gu·a·ble (är′gyo͞o-ə-bəl) *adj.* **1.** Open to argument: *an arguable question, still unresolved.* **2.** That can be argued plausibly; defensible in argument: *three arguable points of law.* **—ar′gu·a·bly** *adv.*

ar·gue (är′gyo͞o) *v.* **-gued, -gu·ing, -gues.** *—tr.* **1.** To put forth reasons for or against; debate: *"It is time to stop arguing tax-rate reductions and to enact them"* (Paul Craig Roberts). **2.** To attempt to prove by reasoning; maintain or contend: *The speaker argued that more immigrants should be admitted to the country.* **3.** To give evidence of; indicate: *"Similarities cannot always be used to argue descent"* (Isaac Asimov). **4.** To persuade or influence (another), as by presenting reasons: *argued the clerk into lowering the price.* *—intr.* **1.** To put forth reasons for or against something: *argued for dismissal of the case; argued against an immediate counterattack.* **2.** To engage in a quarrel; dispute. [Middle English *arguen,* from Old French *arguer,* from Latin *argūtāre,* to babble, chatter, frequentative of *arguere,* to make clear. See **arg-** in Appendix.] **—ar′gu·er** *n.*

SYNONYMS: *argue, quarrel, wrangle, squabble, bicker.* These verbs denote verbal exchange expressing conflict of positions or opinions. To *argue* is to present reasons or facts in an attempt to persuade an adversary in debate or to induce another to espouse a cause or point of view one advocates: *"I am not arguing with you—I am telling you"* (James McNeill Whistler). *Quarrel* stresses animosity and often a suspension of amicable relations: *There's no point in quarreling about the past. Wrangle* refers to loud, contentious argument: *"audiences . . . who can be overheard wrangling about film facts in restaurants and coffee houses"* (Sheila Benson). *Squabble* suggests disagreeable argument, usually over a petty or trivial matter: *"The one absolutely certain way of bringing this nation to ruin . . . would be to permit it to become a tangle of squabbling nationalities"* (Theodore Roosevelt). *Bicker* connotes sharp, persistent, bad-tempered exchange: *"The same reason that*

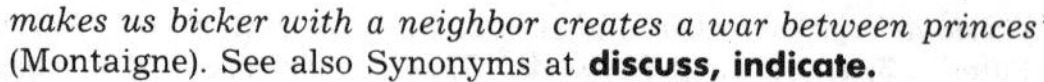

makes us bicker with a neighbor creates a war between princes" (Montaigne). See also Synonyms at **discuss, indicate.**

◆ **ar·gu·fy** (är′gyə-fī′) *v.* **-fied, -fy·ing, -fies.** *Chiefly Southern U.S.* *—tr.* To dispute (a point). *—intr.* To argue aimlessly; wrangle. See Regional Note at **absquatulate.** **—ar′gu·fi′er** *n.*

ar·gu·ment (är′gyə-mənt) *n.* **1.a.** A discussion in which disagreement is expressed; a debate. **b.** A quarrel; a dispute. **c.** *Archaic.* A reason or matter for dispute or contention: *"sheath'd their swords for lack of argument"* (Shakespeare). **2.a.** A course of reasoning aimed at demonstrating truth or falsehood: *presented a careful argument for extraterrestrial life.* **b.** A fact or statement put forth as proof or evidence; a reason: *The current low mortgage rates are an argument for buying a house now.* **3.a.** A summary or short statement of the plot or subject of a literary work. **b.** A topic; a subject: *"You and love are still my argument"* (Shakespeare). **4.** *Logic.* The minor premise in a syllogism. **5.** *Mathematics.* **a.** The independent variable of a function. **b.** The amplitude of a complex number. **6.** *Computer Science.* A value used to evaluate a procedure or subroutine. [Middle English, from Old French, from Latin *argūmentum,* from *arguere,* to make clear. See ARGUE.]

SYNONYMS: *argument, dispute, controversy.* These nouns denote discussion involving conflicting points of view. *Argument* stresses the advancement by each side of facts and reasons buttressing its contention and intended to persuade the other side: *Emotions are seldom swayed by argument. Dispute* stresses division of opinion by its implication of contradictory points of view and often implies animosity: *A dispute arose among union members about the terms of the new contract. Controversy* is especially applicable to major differences of opinion involving large groups of people rather than individuals: *The use of nuclear power is the subject of widespread controversy.*

ar·gu·men·ta (är′gyə-mĕn′tə) *n.* Plural of **argumentum.**

ar·gu·men·ta·tion (är′gyə-mĕn-tā′shən) *n.* **1.** The presentation and elaboration of an argument or arguments. **2.** Deductive reasoning in debate. **3.** A debate.

ar·gu·men·ta·tive (är′gyə-mĕn′tə-tĭv) *adj.* **1.** Given to arguing; disputatious. **2.** Of or characterized by argument: *an argumentative discourse.* **—ar′gu·men′ta·tive·ly** *adv.* **—ar′gu·men′ta·tive·ness** *n.*

SYNONYMS: *argumentative, combative, contentious, disputatious, quarrelsome, scrappy.* The central meaning shared by these adjectives is "given to or fond of arguing": *an intelligent but argumentative child; combative impulses; a contentious mood; a disputatious lawyer; is quarrelsome when drinking; a scrappy litigator.*

ar·gu·men·tum (är′gyə-mĕn′təm) *n., pl.* **-ta** (-tə). *Logic.* An argument, demonstration, or appeal to reason. [Latin. See ARGUMENT.]

Ar·gun River (är-go͞on′) also **Er·gun He** (ĕr′go͞on′ hĕ′, œr′gün′ hə′). A river of east-central Asia rising in northeast China and flowing about 1,529 km (950 mi) west then generally northeast along the Russia-China border.

Ar·gus (är′gəs) *n.* **1.** *Greek Mythology.* A giant with 100 eyes who was made guardian of Io and was later slain by Hermes. **2.** An alert person; a guardian. [Latin, from Greek *Argos.*]

Ar·gus-eyed (är′gəs-īd′) *adj.* Extremely observant; vigilant.

ar·gus pheasant (är′gəs) *n.* A large bird *(Argusianus argus)* of southern Asia and the East Indies, having long tail feathers marked with brilliantly colored, eyelike spots. [After *Argus,* whose hundred eyes were given to a peacock's tail.]

ar·gy-bar·gy (är′gē-bär′gē) *n., pl.* **-gies.** *Chiefly British.* A lively or disputatious discussion. [Scots, reduplication of *argie,* argument, from ARGUE.]

ar·gyle also **ar·gyll** (är′gīl′) *n.* **1.** A knitting pattern of varicolored, diamond-shaped areas on a solid background. **2.** A sock knit in this pattern. [After Clan Campbell of *Argyle, Argyll,* a former county of western Scotland, originally from the pattern of their tartan.]

Ar·gy·rol (är′jə-rôl′, -rōl′, -rŏl′). A trademark used for a silver-protein compound employed as a local antiseptic.

ar·hat (är′hət) *n.* *Buddhism.* One who has attained enlightenment. [Sanskrit, from present participle of *arhati,* he deserves.] **—ar′hat·ship′** *n.*

År·hus also **Aar·hus** (ôr′ho͞os′). A city of central Denmark, a commercial and industrial center on **Århus Bay,** an arm of the Kattegat. First mentioned in the mid-tenth century, Århus is one of the country's oldest cities. Population, 250,404.

a·ri·a (är′ē-ə) *n.* *Music.* **1.** A solo vocal piece with instrumental accompaniment, as in an opera. **2.** An air; a melody. [Italian, from Latin *āera,* accusative of *āēr,* air, from Greek *aēr.* See **wer-**[1] in Appendix.]

Ar·i·ad·ne (ăr′ē-ăd′nē) *n.* *Greek Mythology.* The daughter of Minos and Pasiphaë who gave Theseus the thread with which he found his way out of the Minotaur's labyrinth.

Ar·i·an[1] (âr′ē-ən, ăr′-) *adj.* **1.** Of or relating to Arianism: *the Arian heresy.* **2.** Of or relating to Arius. **—Arian** *n.* A believer in Arianism.

Ar•i•an² (ăr′ē-ən, âr′-) *n.* One who is born under the sign of Aries. **—Ar′i•an** *adj.*

-arian *suff.* Believer in; advocate of: *utilitarian.* [Latin *-ārius,* -ary + -AN¹.]

Ar•i•an•ism (âr′ē-ə-nĭz′əm, ăr′-) *n. Theology.* The doctrines of Arius, denying that Jesus was of the same substance as God and holding instead that he was only the highest of created beings.

A•ri•as Sán•chez (ä′rē-äs sän′chĕs), **Oscar.** Born 1941. Costa Rican politician who as president (since 1986) proposed an accord to bring peace to Central America. He won the 1987 Nobel Peace Prize.

a•ri•bo•fla•vi•no•sis (ā-rī′bō-flā′və-nō′sĭs, -bə-) *n.* A condition caused by the dietary deficiency of riboflavin that is characterized by mouth lesions, seborrhea, and vascularization of the cornea.

A•ri•ca (ə-rē′kə, ä-rē′kä). A city of northern Chile on the Pacific Ocean near the Peruvian border. Claimed by both Peru and Chile until 1929, it is a free port and popular resort. Population, 139,320.

ar•id (ăr′ĭd) *adj.* **1.** Lacking moisture, especially having insufficient rainfall to support trees or woody plants: *an arid climate.* **2.** Lacking interest or feeling; lifeless and dull: *a technically perfect but arid musical performance.* [Latin *āridus,* from *ārēre,* to be dry. See **as-** in Appendix.] **—a•rid′i•ty** (ə-rĭd′ĭ-tē), **ar′id•ness** *n.*

Ar•i•el (âr′ē-əl) *n.* **1.** A mischievous spirit in Shakespeare's *The Tempest.* **2.** The satellite of Uranus that is second in distance from the planet.

Ar•ies (âr′ēz, âr′ē-ēz′) *n.* **1.** A constellation in the Northern Hemisphere near Taurus and Pisces. **2.a.** The first sign of the zodiac in astrology. **b.** One who is born under this sign. Also called *Ram.* [Middle English, zodiacal sign Aries, from Latin *ariēs,* ram, zodiacal sign Aries.]

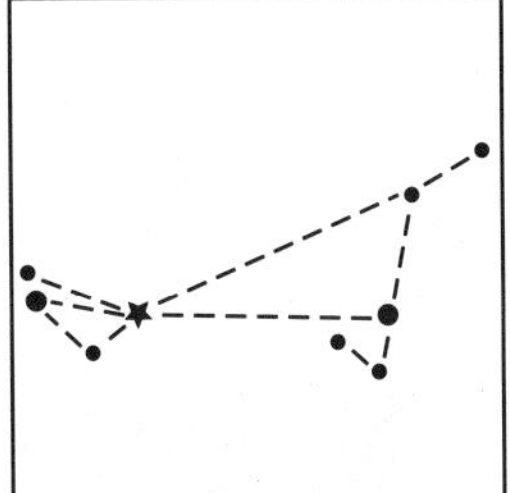

Aries

a•ri•et•ta (ä′rē-ĕt′ə) also **a•ri•ette** (-ĕt′) *n. Music.* A short aria. [Italian, diminutive of *aria,* aria. See ARIA.]

a•right (ə-rīt′) *adv.* In a proper manner; correctly. [Middle English, from Old English *ariht* : *a-,* on; see A-² + *riht,* right; see RIGHT.]

A•rik•a•ra (ə-rĭk′ər-ə) *n., pl.* **Arikara** or **-ras. 1.a.** A Native American people formerly inhabiting the Missouri River valley from Kansas into the Dakotas and now located in western North Dakota. Traditional Arikara life was based on agriculture and trade with the Plains Indians to the west. **b.** A member of this people. **2.** The Caddoan language of the Arikara.

ar•il (ăr′əl) *n.* A fleshy, usually brightly colored cover of a seed, arising from the hilum or funiculus. [Medieval Latin *arillus,* grape seed.] **—ar′iled** *adj.* **—ar′il•late′** (-lāt′, -lĭt) *adj.*

a•ri•o•so (ä′rē-ō′sō, -zō) *Music. n., pl.* **-sos. 1.a.** A declamatory style used in opera and oratorio, similar to recitative but having greater melodic variation. **b.** A passage rendered in this style. **2.** A short vocal solo having the melodic style but not the form of an aria. **—arioso** *adv. & adj.* In a melodic style like that of an aria. Used chiefly as a direction. [Italian, from *aria,* aria. See ARIA.]

A•ri•os•to (är′ē-ŏs′tō, -ō′stō, ăr′-), **Ludovico** or **Lodovico.** 1474–1533. Italian writer primarily known for his epic comic poem *Orlando Furioso* (1532).

a•rise (ə-rīz′) *intr.v.* **a•rose** (ə-rōz′), **a•ris•en** (ə-rĭz′ən), **a•ris•ing, a•ris•es. 1.** To get up, as from a sitting or prone position; rise. **2.** To move upward; ascend. **3.** To come into being; originate: *hoped that a new spirit of freedom was arising.* **4.** To result, issue, or proceed: *mistakes that arise from a basic misunderstanding.* See Synonyms at **stem¹.** [Middle English *arisen,* from Old English *ārīsan* : *ā-,* intensive pref. + *rīsan,* to rise.]

a•ris•ta (ə-rĭs′tə) *n., pl.* **-tae** (-tē) or **-tas.** A bristlelike part or appendage, such as the awn of grains and grasses or the process near the tip of the antenna of certain flies. [Latin, beard of grain, spike.] **—a•ris′tate** (-tāt) *adj.*

Ar•is•tar•chus (ăr′ĭ-stär′kəs). 217?–145? B.C. Greek grammarian and critic noted for his arrangement of and commentary on the *Iliad* and the *Odyssey.*

Aristarchus of Sa•mos (sā′mŏs′, săm′ŏs′, sä′môs). fl. 270 B.C. Greek astronomer who was among the first to propose that the sun is the center of the universe and that the earth moves around the sun.

Ar•is•ti•des also **Ar•is•tei•des** (ăr′ĭ-stī′dēz). Known as "the Just." 530?–468? B.C. Athenian statesman and general who fought in the Battle of Marathon (490) and in the victory over the Persians at Salamis (480). He was a central figure in the confederation of Greek states known as the Delian League (478).

Ar•is•tip•pus of Cy•re•ne (ăr′ĭ-stĭp′əs; sī-rē′nē). 435?–366? B.C. Greek philosopher who founded the Cyrenaic school, based on the pursuit of pleasure tempered by prudence to avoid discomfort.

ar•is•toc•ra•cy (ăr′ĭ-stŏk′rə-sē) *n., pl.* **-cies. 1.** A hereditary ruling class; nobility. **2.a.** Government by a ruling class. **b.** A state or country having this form of government. **3.a.** Government by the citizens deemed to be best qualified to lead. **b.** A state having such a government. **4.** A group or class considered superior to others. [Late Latin *aristocratia,* government by the best, from Greek *aristokratia* : *aristos,* best; see **ar-** in Appendix + *kratos,* power; see -CRACY.]

a•ris•to•crat (ə-rĭs′tə-krăt′, ăr′ĭs-) *n.* **1.** A member of a ruling class or of the nobility. **2.** A person having the tastes, manners, or other characteristics of the aristocracy: *a natural aristocrat who insists on the best accommodations.* **3.** A person who advocates government by an aristocracy. **4.** One considered the best of its kind: *the aristocrat of cars.* [French *aristocrate,* from *aristocratie,* aristocracy, from Old French, from Late Latin *aristocratia.* See ARISTOCRACY.] **—a•ris′to•crat′ic, a•ris′to•crat′i•cal** *adj.* **—a•ris′to•crat′i•cal•ly** *adv.*

Ar•is•toph•a•nes (ăr′ĭ-stŏf′ə-nēz). 448?–388? B.C. Athenian playwright considered to be the greatest ancient writer of satirical comedy. Among his surviving plays are *The Clouds* (423) and *Lysistrata* (411).

Aristophanes of By•zan•ti•um (bĭ-zăn′shē-əm, -tē-əm). 257?–180? B.C. Greek philologist who systematized the punctuation, pronunciation, and accentuation of Greek.

Ar•is•to•te•li•an also **Ar•is•to•te•le•an** (ăr′ĭ-stə-tē′lē-ən, -tēl′yən, ə-rĭs′tə-) *adj.* Of or relating to Aristotle or to his philosophy. *—n.* **1.** A follower of Aristotle or his teachings. **2.** A person whose thinking and methods tend to be empirical, scientific, or commonsensical. **—Ar′is•to•te′li•an•ism** *n.*

Aristotelian logic *n.* **1.** Aristotle's deductive method of logic, especially the theory of the syllogism. **2.** The formal logic based on Aristotle's and dealing with the relations between propositions in terms of their form instead of their content.

Ar•is•tot•le (ăr′ĭ-stŏt′l). 384–322 B.C. Greek philosopher. A pupil of Plato, the tutor of Alexander the Great, and the author of works on logic, metaphysics, ethics, natural sciences, politics, and poetics, he profoundly influenced Western thought. In his philosophical system theory follows empirical observation and logic, based on the syllogism, is the essential method of rational inquiry.

a•rith•me•tic (ə-rĭth′mĭ-tĭk) *n. Mathematics.* **1.** The mathematics of integers, rational numbers, real numbers, or complex numbers under addition, subtraction, multiplication, and division. **2.** A book on this kind of mathematics. [Middle English *arsmetike, arithmetic,* from Old French *arismetique,* from Late Latin *arismetica,* alteration of Latin *arithmētica,* from Greek *arithmētikē (tekhnē),* (the art) of counting, from *arithmein,* to count, from *arithmos,* number. See **ar-** in Appendix.] **—ar′ith•met′ic** (ăr′ĭth-mĕt′ĭk), **ar′ith•met′i•cal** (-ĭ-kəl) *adj.* **—ar′ith•met′i•cal•ly** *adv.* **—a•rith′me•ti′cian** (-tĭsh′ən) *n.*

arithmetic mean *n. Mathematics.* The value obtained by dividing the sum of a set of quantities by the number of quantities in the set. Also called *average.*

arithmetic progression *n. Mathematics.* A sequence, such as the odd integers 1, 3, 5, 7, . . . , in which each term after the first is formed by adding a constant to the preceding term.

-arium *suff.* A place or device containing or associated with: *planetarium.* [Latin, neuter of *-ārius,* -ary.]

A•ri•us (ə-rī′əs, ăr′ē-, âr′-). A.D. 256?–336. Greek Christian theologian and founder of Arianism, a doctrine that led to his condemnation as a heretic.

Ar•i•zo•na (ăr′ĭ-zō′nə). *Abbr.* **AZ, Ariz.** A state of the southwest United States on the Mexican border. It was admitted as the 48th state in 1912. First explored by the Spanish in 1539, the area was acquired by the United States in 1848 through the Treaty of Guadalupe Hidalgo. Phoenix is the capital and the largest city. Population, 2,718,425. **—Ar′i•zo′nan, Ar′i•zo′ni•an** *adj. & n.*

Ar•ju•na (är′jə-nə, -jo͝o-) *n. Hinduism.* The prince in the *Bhagavad-Gita* to whom Krishna expounds the nature of being, the nature of God, and the way human beings can come to know God.

ark (ärk) *n.* **1.** Often **Ark.** *Bible.* In the Old Testament, the chest containing the Ten Commandments written on stone tablets, carried by the Hebrews during their desert wanderings. Also called *Ark of the Covenant.* **2.** Often **Ark.** *Judaism.* The Holy Ark. **3.** *Bible.* In the Old Testament, the boat built by Noah for survival during the Flood. **4.** *Nautical.* A large, commodious boat. **5.** A shelter or refuge. [Middle English, from Old English *arc,* from Germanic **arca,* from Latin *arca,* chest.]

Ar•kan•sas (är′kən-sô′). *Abbr.* **AR, Ark.** A state of the south-central United States bordered on the east by the Mississippi River. It was admitted as the 25th state in 1836. The region was first explored by members of Hernando de Soto's expedition in 1541 and passed to the United States in 1803 as part of the Louisiana Purchase. Little Rock is the capital and the largest city. Population, 2,286,435. **—Ar•kan′san** (är-kăn′zən) *adj. & n.*

Ar•kan•sas River (är′kən-sô′, är-kăn′zəs). A river of the south-central United States rising in the Rocky Mountains in central Colorado and flowing about 2,333 km (1,450 mi) generally southeastward to the Mississippi River in southeast Arkansas. It was an important trade and travel route in the 19th century.

Ar•kan•sas stone (är′kən-sô′) *n.* A stone used for sharpening and grinding metals, especially the metal blades of knives.

Ark•han•gelsk (är-kăn′gĕlsk, -KHän′-) or **Arch•an•gel** (ärk′ān′jəl). A city of northwest Russia on the Northern Dvina River near its mouth on the White Sea. Although icebound much of the year, it is a leading port and can generally be opened to navigation by icebreakers. Population, 408,000.

Ark of the Covenant *n. Bible.* See **ark** (sense 1).

Ark•wright (ärk′rīt′), Sir **Richard.** 1732–1792. British inventor and manufacturer who patented a machine for spinning cotton

ă pat	oi boy
ā pay	ou out
âr care	o͝o took
ä father	o͞o boot
ĕ pet	ŭ cut
ē be	ûr urge
ĭ pit	th thin
ī pie	*th* this
îr pier	hw which
ŏ pot	zh vision
ō toe	ə about, item
ô paw	♦ regionalism

Stress marks: ′ (primary); ′ (secondary), as in **dictionary** (dĭk′shə-nĕr′ē)

armadillo
Nine-banded armadillo
Dasypus novemcinctus

thread (1769) and established cotton mills that were among the first to use machinery on a large scale.

Arl·berg (ärl′bûrg, -běrk). An Alpine pass, 1,813.5 m (5,946 ft) high, in western Austria. The rail tunnel crossing the pass was built in 1880–1884 and is 10 km (6.2 mi) long.

Ar·len (är′lən), **Harold.** 1905–1986. American composer of more than 500 songs, including the 1939 Oscar winner "Over the Rainbow."

Arlen, Michael. 1895–1956. Armenian-born British writer noted for his novels about London society, including *The Green Hat* (1924).

Arles (ärlz, ärl). **1.** A medieval kingdom of eastern and southeast France. It was formed in 933 and gradually split up after 1246. **2.** A city of south-central France on the Rhone River delta. A flourishing city in Roman times, it has an arena built in the second century A.D. that is now used for bullfights. Population, 37,571.

Ar·ling·ton (är′lĭng-tən). **1.** A town of eastern Massachusetts, a residential suburb of Boston. Population, 48,219. **2.** A city of northern Texas midway between Dallas and Fort Worth. It has a huge industrial park and is the site of the Pecan Bowl. Population, 160,123. **3.** A county and unincorporated city of northern Virginia across the Potomac River from Washington, D.C. Mainly residential, it is the site of **Arlington National Cemetery,** where American war dead and other notables, including William Howard Taft and John F. Kennedy, are buried. The Tomb of the Unknown Soldier commemorates members of the Armed Forces who were killed in World War I, World War II, the Korean War, and the Vietnam War. Population, 152,700.

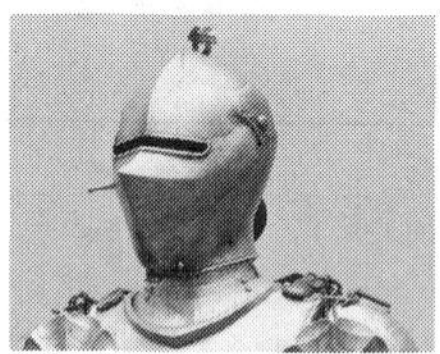
armet
Late 15th-century Spanish

Arlington Heights. A village of northeast Illinois, a manufacturing and residential suburb of Chicago. Population, 66,116.

arm[1] (ärm) *n.* **1.** An upper limb of the human body, connecting the hand and wrist to the shoulder. **2.** A part similar to a human arm, such as the forelimb of an animal or a long part projecting from a central support in a machine. **3.** Something, such as a sleeve on a garment or a support on a chair, that is designed to cover or support the human arm. **4.** A relatively narrow extension jutting out from a large mass: *an arm of the sea.* See Synonyms at **branch. 5.** An administrative or functional branch, as of an organization. **6.** Power or authority: *the long arm of the law.* —***idioms.*** **an arm and a leg.** *Slang.* An excessively high price: *a cruise that cost an arm and a leg.* **at arm's length.** At such a distance that physical or social contact is discouraged: *kept the newcomer at arm's length at first.* **with open arms.** With great cordiality and hospitality. [Middle English, from Old English *earm.* See **ar-** in Appendix.]

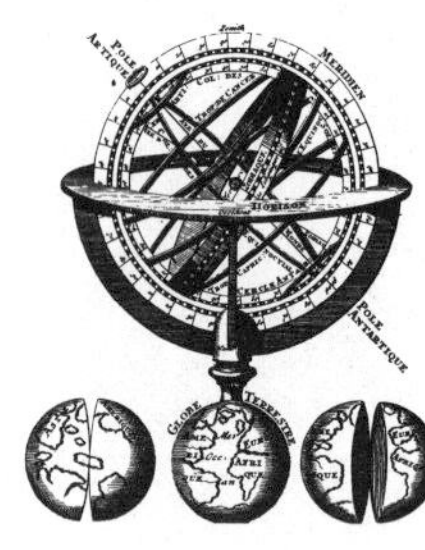
armillary sphere

arm[2] (ärm) *n.* **1.** A weapon, especially a firearm: *troops bearing arms; ICBMs, bombs, and other nuclear arms.* **2.** A branch of a military force: *infantry, armor, and other combat arms.* **3. arms. a.** Warfare: *a call to arms against the invaders.* **b.** Military service: *several million volunteers under arms; the profession of arms.* **4. arms. a.** *Heraldry.* Bearings. **b.** Insignia, as of a state, an official, a family, or an organization. —**arm** *v.* **armed, arm·ing, arms.** —*intr.* **1.** To supply or equip oneself with weaponry. **2.** To prepare oneself for warfare or conflict. —*tr.* **1.** To equip with weapons: *armed themselves with loaded pistols; arm a missile with a warhead; arm a nation for war.* **2.** To equip with what is needed for effective action: *tax advisers who were armed with the latest forms.* **3.** To provide with something that strengthens or protects: *a space reentry vehicle that was armed with a ceramic shield.* **4.** To prepare (a weapon) for use or operation, as by releasing a safety device. —***idiom.*** **up in arms.** Extremely upset; indignant. [Middle English *armes,* weapons, from Old French, from Latin *arma.* V., from Middle English *armen,* from Old French *armer,* from Latin *armāre,* from *arma,* arms. See **ar-** in Appendix.] —**arm′er** *n.*

Arm. *abbr.* Armenia; Armenian.

ar·ma·da (är-mä′də, -mā′-) *n.* **1.** A fleet of warships. **2.** A large group of moving things: *an armada of ants crossing the lawn.* [Spanish, from Medieval Latin *armāta.* See ARMY.]

ar·ma·dil·lo (är′mə-dĭl′ō) *n., pl.* **-los.** Any of several omnivorous, burrowing, edentate mammals (family Dasypodidae), native to southern North America and South America and characterized by an armorlike covering consisting of jointed, bony plates. [Spanish, diminutive of *armado,* armored, past participle of *armar,* to arm, from Latin *armāre,* from *arma,* arms. See **ar-** in Appendix.]

Ar·ma·ged·don (är′mə-gĕd′n) *n.* **1.** *Bible.* The scene of a final battle between the forces of good and evil, prophesied to occur at the end of the world. **2.** A decisive or catastrophic conflict. [Late Latin *Armagedōn,* from Greek, from Hebrew *har měgiddô, měgiddōn,* the mountain region of Megiddo.]

armoire
Early 18th-century French

Ar·magh (är-mä′, är′mä′). An urban district of southern Northern Ireland. Reputedly founded by Saint Patrick, it is the seat of both the Roman Catholic and Protestant primates of Ireland. Population, 12,700.

Ar·ma·gnac[1] (är′mən-yăk′). A historical region and former countship of southwest France in Gascony. Added to the French royal domain in 1607, the area is now noted for its viniculture.

Ar·ma·gnac[2] (är′mən-yăk′) *n.* A dry brandy.

ar·ma·ment (är′mə-mənt) *n.* **1.** The weapons and supplies of war with which a military unit is equipped. **2.** Often **armaments.** All the military forces and war equipment of a country. **3.** A military force equipped for war. **4.** The process of arming for war. [Latin *armāmenta,* tools, from *arma,* arms. See ARM[2].]

ar·ma·men·tar·i·um (är′mə-mĕn-târ′ē-əm) *n., pl.* **-i·ums** or **-i·a** (-ē-ə). The complete equipment of a physician or medical institution, including books, supplies, and instruments. [Latin, arsenal, from *armāmenta,* tools. See ARMAMENT.]

ar·ma·ture (är′mə-cho͝or′, -chər) *n.* **1.** *Electricity.* **a.** The rotating part of a dynamo, consisting essentially of copper wire wound around an iron core. **b.** The moving part of an electromagnetic device such as a relay, buzzer, or loudspeaker. **c.** A piece of soft iron connecting the poles of a magnet. **2.** *Biology.* A protective covering, structure, or organ of an animal or a plant, such as teeth, claws, thorns, or the shell of a turtle. **3.** A framework serving as a supporting core for clay sculpture. [Middle English, armor, from Old French, from Latin *armātūra,* equipment, from *armātus,* past participle of *armāre,* to arm, from *arma,* arms. See **ar-** in Appendix.]

arm·chair (ärm′châr′) *n.* A chair with side structures to support the arms or elbows. —**armchair** *adj.* Remote from active involvement: *armchair warriors in the Pentagon; an armchair traveler.*

armed forces (ärmd) *pl.n.* The military forces of a country. Also called *armed services.*

Ar·me·ni·a[1] (är-mē′nē-ə, -mēn′yə). *Abbr.* **Arm.** A region of Asia Minor south of Georgia. Formerly a kingdom that extended into northeast Turkey and northwest Iran, it was probably the first state to adopt Christianity as a national religion (c. A.D. 303). The area was acquired by Russia from Persia in 1828 and became a Soviet republic in 1921 and a constituent republic in 1936. Yerevan is the capital. Population, 3,317,000.

Ar·me·nia[2] (är-mē′nē-ə, -nyə, -nyä). A city of west-central Colombia west of Bogotá. It is an industrial center and transportation hub. Population, 179,727.

Ar·me·ni·an (är-mē′nē-ən, -mēn′yən) *adj. Abbr.* **Arm.** Of or relating to Armenia or its people, language, or culture. —**Armenian** *n. Abbr.* **Arm. 1. a.** A native or inhabitant of Armenia. **b.** A person of Armenian ancestry. **2.** The Indo-European language of the Armenians.

Armenian Church *n.* An autonomous Christian church established in Armenia in the fourth century A.D. It differs from other Eastern churches in professing a form of Monophysitism.

Ar·men·tières (är′mən-tîrz′, -mäN-tyĕr′). A city of northern France west-northwest of Lille. It became known through the World War I song "Mademoiselle from Armentières." Population, 24,834.

ar·met (är′mĕt′) *n.* A medieval light helmet with a neck guard and movable visor. [Old French, alteration (influenced by Old Italian *elmetto,* helmet) of *arme,* weapon. See ARM[2].]

arm·ful (ärm′fo͝ol′) *n.* The amount that an arm or arms can hold.

arm·hole (ärm′hōl′) *n.* An opening in a garment for an arm.

ar·mi·ger (är′mə-jər) *n.* **1.** A bearer of armor for a knight; a squire. **2.** A person entitled to bear heraldic arms. [Medieval Latin, from Latin, arms-bearing : *arma,* arms; see ARM[2] + *gerere,* to carry.]

Ar·mi·jo (är-mē′hō). A community of central New Mexico, a suburb of Albuquerque. Population, 18,900.

ar·mil·lar·y sphere (är′mə-lĕr′ē, är-mĭl′ə-rē) *n.* An old astronomical model with solid rings, all circles of a single sphere, used to display relationships among the principal celestial circles. [Translation of French *sphère armillaire,* from Latin *armilla,* bracelet, from *armus,* shoulder. See **ar-** in Appendix.]

Ar·min (är-mēn′). See **Arminius.**

Ar·min·i·an (är-mĭn′ē-ən) *adj.* Of or relating to the theology of Jacobus Arminius and his followers, who believed that predestination was conditioned by God's foreknowledge of human free choices. —**Ar·min′i·an** *n.* —**Ar·min′i·an·ism** *n.*

Ar·min·i·us (är-mĭn′ē-əs) also **Ar·min** (-mēn′). 17? B.C.–A.D. 21. German hero who led the defeat of three legions of Romans in the Teutoburger Wald (A.D. 9), thereby liberating the Germans from Roman rule.

Arminius, Jacobus. 1560–1609. Dutch theologian and founder of Arminianism, which opposed the absolute predestinarianism of John Calvin and was influential throughout Europe.

ar·mi·stice (är′mĭ-stĭs) *n.* A temporary cessation of fighting by mutual consent; a truce. [French, from New Latin *armistitium* : Latin *arma,* arms; see ARM[2] + Latin *-stitium,* a stopping; see **stā-** in Appendix.]

Ar·mi·stice Day (är′mĭ-stĭs) *n.* November 11, formerly observed in the United States in commemoration of the signing of the armistice ending World War I in 1918. Since 1954 it has been incorporated into the observances of Veterans Day.

arm·let (ärm′lĭt) *n.* **1.** A band worn on the arm for ornament or identification. **2.** A small arm, as of the sea.

arm·load (ärm′lōd′) *n.* The amount that can be carried in one arm or both arms: *an armload of laundry.*

ar·moire (ärm-wär′, ärm′wär) *n.* A large, often ornate cabinet or wardrobe. [French *armoire,* from Old French *armaire,* from Latin *armārium,* chest, from *arma,* tools. See **ar-** in Appendix.]

ar·mor (är′mər) *n.* **1.** A defensive covering, such as chain mail, worn to protect the body against weapons. **2.** A tough, protective covering, such as the bony scales covering certain animals or the metallic plates on tanks or warships. **3.** A safeguard or protection: *faith, the missionary's armor.* **4.a.** The combat arm that deploys armored vehicles, such as tanks. **b.** The armored vehicles of an army. **—armor** *tr.v.* **-mored, -mor·ing, -mors.** To cover with armor. [Middle English *armure,* from Old French *armeure,* from Latin *armātūra,* equipment. See ARMATURE.]

ar·mor-clad (är′mər-klăd′) *adj.* Covered with or wearing armor: *armor-clad warships.*

ar·mor·er (är′mər-ər) *n.* **1.** A manufacturer of weapons, especially firearms. **2.** An enlisted person in charge of maintenance and repair of the small arms of a military unit. **3.** One that makes or repairs armor.

ar·mo·ri·al (är-môr′ē-əl, -mōr′-) *adj. Heraldry.* Of or relating to heraldry or heraldic arms. **—armorial** *n.* A book or treatise on heraldry. [From Middle English *armorie,* arms, from Old French *armeurerie,* from *armeure,* armor. See ARMOR.]

Ar·mor·ic (är-môr′ĭk, -mŏr′-) also **Ar·mor·i·can** (-ĭ-kən) *—adj.* Of or relating to Armorica or its people, language, or culture. *—n.* **1.** A native or inhabitant of Armorica. **2.** See **Breton** (sense 2).

Ar·mor·i·ca (är-môr′ĭ-kə, -mŏr′-). An ancient and literary name for the northwest part of France, especially Brittany.

armor plate *n.* Specially formulated hard steel plate used to cover warships, vehicles, and fortifications. **—ar′mor-plat′ed** (är′mər-plā′tĭd) *adj.*

ar·mor·y (är′mə-rē) *n., pl.* **-ies. 1.a.** A storehouse for arms; an arsenal. **b.** A building for storing arms and military equipment, especially one serving as headquarters for military reserve personnel. **2.** An arms factory.

ar·mour (är′mər) *n. & v. Chiefly British.* Variant of **armor.**

arm·pit (ärm′pĭt′) *n.* **1.** The hollow under the upper part of the arm at the shoulder. **2.** *Slang.* A thoroughly disreputable or disgusting thing, place, or situation: *"I think of PCP as the armpit of drugs. It is dirty, explosive, poisonous"* (Ray Brett).

arm·rest (ärm′rĕst′) *n.* A support for the arm, as on a piece of furniture or within a motor vehicle.

Arm·strong (ärm′strông′), **Edwin Howard.** 1890–1954. American engineer and inventor whose improvements to radio communication included the development of frequency modulation (1933).

Armstrong, Louis. Known as "Satchmo." 1900–1971. American jazz trumpeter. A virtuoso musician and popular, gravelly voiced singer, he greatly influenced the development of jazz.

Armstrong, Neil Alden. Born 1930. American astronaut who as commander of Apollo 11 became the first human being to walk on the moon (July 20, 1969).

arm-twist (ärm′twĭst′) *v.* **-twist·ed, -twist·ing, -twists.** *Informal. —intr.* To engage in the use of personal or political pressure to persuade or to gain support: *"headed off to Capitol Hill to cajole and arm-twist"* (Evan Thomas). *—tr.* To subject to or induce by the use of personal or political pressure: *The government arm-twisted the manufacturers into accepting new antipollution standards.* **—arm twister, arm′-twist′er** *n.*

arm-twist·ing (ärm′twĭs′tĭng) *n. Informal.* The use of personal or political pressure in an effort to persuade or to gain support.

arm-wres·tle (ärm′rĕs′əl) *intr. & tr.v.* **-tled, -tling, -tles.** *Sports.* To engage in or subject (another) to arm wrestling. **—arm wrestler, arm′-wres′tler** *n.*

arm wrestling *n. Sports.* A form of wrestling in which two opponents sit facing each other with usually right hands interlocked and elbows firmly planted, as on a table surface, and attempt to force each other's arm down. Also called *Indian wrestling.*

ar·my (är′mē) *n., pl.* **-mies. 1.a.** A large body of people organized and trained for land warfare. **b.** *Often* **Army.** The entire military land forces of a country. **c.** A tactical and administrative military unit consisting of a headquarters, two or more corps, and auxiliary forces. **2.** A large group of people organized for a specific cause: *the construction army that built the Panama Canal.* **3.** A multitude; a host: *An army of waiters served at the banquet.* See Synonyms at **multitude.** [Middle English *armee,* from Old French, from Medieval Latin *armāta,* from Latin *armāta,* feminine past participle of *armāre,* to arm, from *arma,* arms. See **ar-** in Appendix.]

army ant *n.* Any of various rapacious tropical ants of the family Formicidae that move in swarms and that subsist on other insects. Also called *driver ant, legionary ant.*

army brat *n.* The child of a member, typically a career officer, of the U.S. Army.

ar·my·worm (är′mē-wûrm′) *n.* A caterpillar belonging to either of two genera of moth, *Pseudaletia* or *Spodoptera,* large groups of which destroy crops and other vegetation.

ar·nat·to (är-nä′tō) *n.* Variant of **annatto.**

Arne (ärn), **Thomas Augustine.** 1710–1778. British composer noted for his songs, oratorios, and operas, including *Alfred* (1740), which introduced the song "Rule, Britannia."

Arn·hem (ärn′hĕm′, är′nəm). A city of eastern Netherlands on the lower Rhine River east-southeast of Utrecht. In World War II British airborne troops suffered a major defeat here in September 1944. Population, 128,598.

Arn·hem Land (är′nəm). A region of northern Australia west of the Gulf of Carpentaria. The country's largest aboriginal reservation is here.

ar·ni·ca (är′nĭ-kə) *n.* **1.** Any of various perennial herbs of the genus *Arnica* in the composite family, having opposite, simple leaves and mostly radiate heads of yellow flowers. **2.** A tincture of the dried flower heads of the European species *A. montana,* applied externally to reduce the pain and inflammation of bruises and sprains. [New Latin *Arnica,* genus name.]

Ar·no (är′nō). A river of central Italy rising in the northern Apennines and flowing about 241 km (150 mi) to the Ligurian Sea. Flooding of the Arno has caused severe damage to art treasures in Florence.

Arno, Peter. 1904–1968. American cartoonist whose satirical drawings of high society regularly appeared in the *New Yorker.*

Ar·nold (är′nəld). A city of eastern Missouri, a suburb of St. Louis. Population, 19,141.

Arnold, Benedict. 1741–1801. American Revolutionary general and traitor whose plan to surrender West Point to the British for 20,000 pounds was foiled when his accomplice John André was captured (1780).

Arnold, Matthew. 1822–1888. British poet and critic whose poems, such as "Dover Beach" (1867), express moral and religious doubts. His classic study *Culture and Anarchy* (1869) is a polemic against Victorian materialism.

Arnold, Thomas. 1795–1842. British educator and historian who as headmaster of Rugby School (1827–1842) introduced classes in mathematics, modern languages, and modern history into the classical curriculum.

Ar·nold·son (är′nəld-sən), **Klas Pontus.** 1844–1916. Swedish politician and pacifist. He shared the 1908 Nobel Peace Prize for efforts to keep peace between Sweden and Norway.

Arns·berg (ärnz′bərg, ärns′bĕrk). A city of west-central Germany south-southeast of Münster. It was founded in 1077 and received a municipal charter in 1237. Population, 75,135.

A·roe Islands (ä′ro͞o). See **Aru Islands.**

ar·oid (ăr′oid′, âr′-) *n.* Any of various perennial herbs in the arum family, including houseplants such as the anthurium, dieffenbachia, and philodendron and having tiny flowers crowded in a spadix that is subtended by a spathe. [AR(UM) + –OID.] **—ar′oid′** *adj.*

a·roint (ə-roint′) *tr.v.* **a·roint·ed, a·roint·ing, a·roints.** *Archaic.* Begone; avaunt: *"Aroint thee, witch!"* (Shakespeare). [Origin unknown.]

a·ro·ma (ə-rō′mə) *n.* **1.a.** A quality that can be perceived by the olfactory sense: *the aroma of garlic and onions.* See Synonyms at **smell. b.** A pleasant characteristic odor, as of a plant, spice, or food: *the aroma of roses.* See Synonyms at **fragrance. 2.** A distinctive, intangible quality; an aura: *the aroma of success.* [Alteration (influenced by Latin *arōma,* spice) of Middle English *aromat,* aromatic substance, from Old French, from Latin *arōmata,* pl. of *arōma,* from Greek, aromatic herb.]

a·ro·ma·ther·a·py (ə-rō′mə-thĕr′ə-pē) *n., pl.* **-pies.** The use of selected fragrant substances in lotions and inhalants in an effort to affect mood and promote health.

ar·o·mat·ic (ăr′ə-măt′ĭk) *adj.* **1.** Having an aroma; fragrant or sweet-smelling: *aromatic herbs.* **2.** *Chemistry.* Of, relating to, or containing one or more six-carbon rings characteristic of the benzene series and related organic groups. **—aromatic** *n.* An aromatic plant or substance, such as a medication. **—ar′o·mat′i·cal·ly** *adv.* **—ar′o·mat′ic·ness** *n.*

ar·o·ma·tic·i·ty (ăr′ə-mə-tĭs′ĭ-tē, ə-rō′mə-) *n.* Aromatic quality or character, especially the distinctive structure or properties of the aromatic chemical compounds.

a·ro·ma·tize (ə-rō′mə-tīz′) *tr.v.* **-tized, -tiz·ing, -tiz·es. 1.** To make aromatic or fragrant: *swirled the wine to aromatize it.* **2.** *Chemistry.* To subject to a reaction that converts a substance into an aromatic compound. **—a·ro′ma·ti·za′tion** (-tĭ-zā′shən) *n.*

A·roos·took (ə-ro͞os′tək, -ro͝os′-). A river rising in northern Maine and flowing about 225 km (140 mi) generally eastward to the St. John River in New Brunswick, Canada.

a·rose (ə-rōz′) *v.* Past tense of **arise.**

a·round (ə-round′) *adv.* **1.a.** On all sides: *dirty clothes lying around.* **b.** In close to all sides from all directions: *a field bordered around with tall trees.* **2.** In a circle or with a circular motion: *spun around twice.* **3.** In circumference or perimeter: *a pond two miles around.* **4.** In succession or rotation. **5.** In or toward the opposite direction or position: *wheeled around.* **6.a.** To or among various places; here and there: *wander around.* **b.** To a specific place: *Come around again sometime.* **7.** In or near one's current location: *waited around for the next flight.* **8.** From the beginning to the end: *frigid weather the year around.* **9.** Approximately; about: *weighed around 30 pounds; around $1.3 billion in debt.* **—around** *prep.* **1.** On all sides of: *trees around the field.* **2.** In such a position as to encircle or surround: *a sash around the waist.* **3.a.** Here and there within; throughout: *on the political stump around the country.* **b.** In the immediate vicinity of; near: *She lives around Norfolk.* **4.** On or to the farther side of: *the house around the corner.* **5.** So as to pass, bypass, or avoid: *a way around an obstacle; got around the difficulty somehow.* **6.** Approximately at: *woke up around seven.* **7.** In such a way as to have a basis or center in: *an economy focused around farming and light industry.* **—around** *adj.* **1.** Being in existence: *Our old dog*

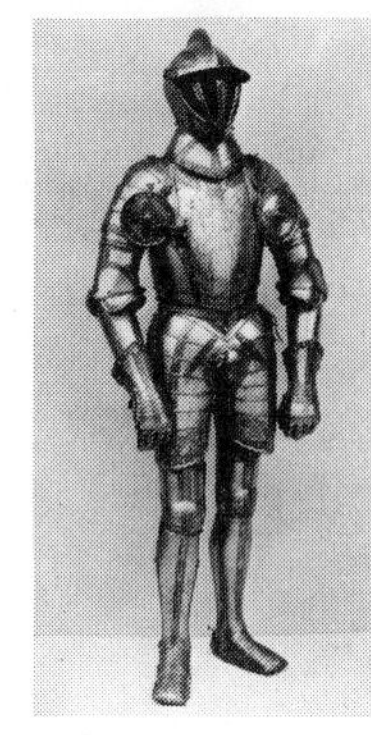

armor
Top: 16th-century Japanese
Bottom: 16th-century German

Louis Armstrong

Neil Armstrong

ă pat	oi boy
ā pay	ou out
âr care	o͝o took
ä father	o͞o boot
ĕ pet	ŭ cut
ē be	ûr urge
ĭ pit	th thin
ī pie	*th* this
îr pier	hw which
ŏ pot	zh vision
ō toe	ə about, item
ô paw	♦ regionalism

Stress marks: ′ (primary); ′ (secondary), as in **dictionary** (dĭk′shə-nĕr′ē)

is no longer around. **2.** Being in evidence; present: *asked if the store manager was around.* **—*idiom.* been around.** *Informal.* Having had many and varied experiences: *a young executive who has been around.* [Middle English : probably *a-*, in; see A–[2] + *round,* circle; see ROUND[1].]

a·round-the-clock (ə-round′thə-klŏk′) *adj.* Variant of **round-the-clock.**

a·rouse (ə-rouz′) *v.* **a·roused, a·rous·ing, a·rous·es.** *—tr.* **1.** To awaken from or as if from sleep. **2.** To stir up; excite: *The odd sight aroused our curiosity.* See Synonyms at **provoke.** *—intr.* To be or become aroused; stir. [From ROUSE, on the model of such pairs as *rise, arise.*] **—a·rous′al** *n.*

Arp (ärp), **Jean** or **Hans.** 1887–1966. French artist and a founder of Dada. He is particularly noted for his abstract reliefs and three-dimensional sculptures.

Ar·pád (är′päd). Died 907. Hungarian national hero who founded the first Hungarian dynasty (c. 884).

ar·peg·gi·o (är-pĕj′ē-ō′, -pĕj′ō) *n., pl.* **-os.** *Music.* **1.** The playing of the tones of a chord in rapid succession rather than simultaneously. **2.** A chord played or sung in this manner. [Italian, from *arpeggiare,* to play the harp, from *arpa,* harp, of Germanic origin. See HARP.]

ar·pent (är-päN′) *n.* Any of various French units of land measurement, especially one used in parts of Canada and the southern United States and equal to about 0.4 hectare (0.85 acre). [French, from Old French, from Latin *arepennis,* half acre. See **per**[1] in Appendix.]

ar·que·bus (är′kə-bəs, -kwə-) *n.* Variant of **harquebus.**

arr. *abbr.* **1.** Arranged. **2. a.** Arrival; arrive. **b.** Arrived.

ar·ra·ca·cha (ä′rä-kä′chä) *n.* A perennial Andean herb *(Arracacia xanthorrhiza)* in the parsley family, grown for its large, fleshy, edible roots. Also called *apio.* [Spanish, from Quechua *aracacha.*]

ar·rack (ăr′ək, ə-răk′) *n.* A strong alcoholic drink of the Middle East and the Far East, usually distilled from fermented palm sap, rice, or molasses. [Arabic *'araq,* sweet juice, as in *'araq at-tamr,* fermented juice of the date.]

ar·raign (ə-rān′) *tr.v.* **-raigned, -raign·ing, -raigns. 1.** *Law.* To call (an accused person) before a court to answer the charge made against him or her by indictment, information, or complaint. **2.** To call to account; accuse: *"Johnson arraigned the modern politics of this country as entirely devoid of all principle"* (James Boswell). [Middle English *arreinen,* from Old French *araisnier,* from Vulgar Latin **adratiōnāre,* to call to account : Latin *ad-,* ad- + Latin *ratiō, ratiōn-,* account; see REASON.] **—ar·raign′er** *n.* **—ar·raign′ment** *n.*

Ar·ran (ăr′ən). A granite island of western Scotland in the Firth of Clyde. It is a resort area noted for its scenery and its hunting and fishing.

ar·range (ə-rānj′) *v.* **-ranged, -rang·ing, -rang·es.** *—tr.* **1.** To put into a specific order or relation; dispose: *arrange shoes in a neat row.* **2.** To plan or prepare for: *arrange a picnic.* **3.** To bring about an agreement concerning; settle: *"It has been arranged for him by his family to marry a girl of his own class"* (Edmund Wilson). **4.** *Music.* To reset (a composition) for other instruments or voices or for another style of performance. *—intr.* **1.** To come to an agreement. **2.** To make preparations; plan: *arrange for a big wedding.* [Middle English *arengen,* from Old French *arengier* : *a-,* to (from Latin *ad-;* see AD–) + *rengier,* to put in a line (from *reng,* line; see **sker-**[2] in Appendix).] **—ar·rang′er** *n.*

SYNONYMS: *arrange, marshal, order, organize, sort, systematize.* The central meaning shared by these verbs is "to distribute or dispose persons or things properly or methodically": *arranging figures in numerical sequence; marshal all the relevant facts for the presentation; tried to order my chaotic life; organizing and coordinating fund-raising efforts; sorted the sweaters according to color; systematizing a vast assortment of rules into a cohesive whole.*

ANTONYM: *disarrange.*

ar·range·ment (ə-rānj′mənt) *n.* **1.** The act or process of arranging: *the arrangement of a time and place for the meeting.* **2.** The condition, manner, or result of being arranged; disposal: *provided flowers and saw to their arrangement.* **3.** A collection of things that have been arranged: *the circular arrangement of megaliths called Stonehenge.* **4.** Often **arrangements.** A provision or plan made in preparation for an undertaking: *made arrangements for surgery.* **5.** An agreement or settlement; a disposition: *Our dog will be looked after by arrangement with a neighbor.* **6.** *Music.* **a.** An adaptation of a composition for other instruments or voices or for another style of performance. **b.** A composition so arranged.

ar·rant (ăr′ənt) *adj.* Completely such; thoroughgoing: *an arrant fool; the arrant luxury of the ocean liner.* [Variant of ERRANT.] **—ar′rant·ly** *adv.*

ar·ras (ăr′əs) *n.* **1.** A wall hanging; a tapestry. **2.** A curtain or a wall hanging, especially one of Flemish origin. [Middle English, after ARRAS.]

Ar·ras (ăr′əs, ə-räs′). A city of northern France south-southwest of Lille. It was a famous woolen and tapestry center in the Middle Ages. Population, 41,736.

Ar·rau (ä-rou′), **Claudio.** 1903–1991. Chilean-born American pianist particularly noted for his interpretation of Beethoven's piano works.

ar·ray (ə-rā′) *tr.v.* **-rayed, -ray·ing, -rays. 1.** To set out for display or use; place in an orderly arrangement: *arrayed the whole regiment on the parade ground.* **2.** To dress in finery; adorn. **—array** *n.* **1.** An orderly, often imposing arrangement: *an array of royal jewels.* **2.** An impressively large number, as of persons or objects: *an array of heavily armed troops; an array of spare parts.* See Synonyms at **display. 3.** Splendid attire; finery. **4.** *Mathematics.* **a.** A rectangular arrangement of quantities in rows and columns, as in a matrix. **b.** Numerical data linearly ordered by magnitude. **5.** *Computer Science.* An arrangement of memory elements in one or several planes. [Middle English *arraien,* from Anglo-Norman *arraier,* from Vulgar Latin **arrēdāre.* See **reidh-** in Appendix.]

ar·ray·al (ə-rā′əl) *n.* **1.** The act or process of arranging in an orderly or imposing manner. **2.** Something so arranged; an array.

ar·rear·age (ə-rîr′ĭj) *n.* **1.** The state of being behind in the fulfillment of obligations or of being overdue in payment. **2.** A payment owed.

ar·rears (ə-rîrz′) *pl.n.* **1.** An unpaid, overdue debt or an unfulfilled obligation. **2.** The state of being behind in fulfilling obligations: *an account in arrears.* [Middle English *arrers,* from *arrere,* behind, from Old French *arere,* from Vulgar Latin **ad retrō,* backward : Latin *ad,* to; see AD– + Latin *retrō,* behind; see **re-** in Appendix.]

ar·rest (ə-rĕst′) *v.* **-rest·ed, -rest·ing, -rests.** *—tr.* **1.** To stop; check: *a brake that automatically arrests motion; arrested the growth of the tumor.* **2.** To seize and hold under the authority of law. **3.** To capture and hold briefly (the attention, for example); engage. *—intr.* **1.** To undergo cardiac arrest: *The patient arrested en route to the hospital.* **2.** To behave in a certain manner when taken into legal detention: *a suspect who did not arrest well.* **—arrest** *n.* **1. a.** The act of detaining in legal custody: *the arrest of a criminal suspect.* **b.** The state of being so detained: *a criminal under arrest.* **2.** A device for stopping motion, especially of a moving part. [Middle English *aresten,* from Old French *arester,* from Vulgar Latin **arrestāre* : Latin *ad-,* ad- + Latin *restāre,* to stand still (*re-,* re- + *stāre,* to stand; see **stā-** in Appendix).] **—ar·rest′er, ar·res′tor** *n.* **—ar·rest′ment** *n.*

ar·rest·ee (ə-rĕs-tē′) *n.* One who is under arrest.

ar·rest·ing (ə-rĕs′tĭng) *adj.* Attracting and holding the attention. See Synonyms at **noticeable. —ar·rest′ing·ly** *adv.*

Ar·rhe·ni·us (ə-rē′nē-əs, ə-rā′-), **Svante August.** 1859–1927. Swedish physicist and chemist. He won a 1903 Nobel Prize for his electrolytic theory of dissociation.

ar·rhyth·mi·a (ə-rĭth′mē-ə) *n.* An irregularity in the force or rhythm of the heartbeat. [New Latin, from Greek *arruthmia,* lack of rhythm, from *arruthmos,* unrhythmical : *a-,* without; see A–[1] + *rhuthmos,* rhythm; see RHYTHM.]

ar·rhyth·mic (ə-rĭth′mĭk) *adj.* Lacking rhythm or regularity of rhythm: *"a slight arrhythmic imperfection when the car idles"* (Garrison Keillor). **—ar·rhyth′mi·cal·ly** *adv.*

ar·ri·ba (ə-rē′bə) *interj.* Used as an exclamation of pleasure, approval, or elation. [Spanish, from Latin *ad rīpam,* on the shore : *ad,* to; see AD– + *rīpa,* shore.]

ar·ri·ère-ban (ăr′ē-âr-bän′, -băn′) *n.* **1.** A medieval royal proclamation by which vassals were summoned to military service. **2.** The vassals summoned. [French, from Old French *ariereban,* alteration (influenced by *arere,* behind) of *herban.* See **koro-** in Appendix.]

ar·ri·ère-pen·sée (ăr′ē-âr′päN-sā′) *n.* A mental reservation, as about the validity of something. [French : *arrière,* in back (from Old French *arere;* see ARREARS) + *pensée,* thought (from *penser,* to think; see PENSIVE).]

ar·ris (ăr′ĭs) *n., pl.* **arris** or **-ris·es.** The sharp edge or ridge formed by two surfaces meeting at an angle, as in a molding. [Alteration of Old French *areste,* fishbone, spine. See ARÊTE.]

ar·ri·val (ə-rī′vəl) *n. Abbr.* **ar., arr. 1.** The act of arriving. **2.** One that arrives or has arrived. **3.** The reaching of a goal or an objective as a result of effort or a process: *our ultimate arrival at a compromise.*

ar·rive (ə-rīv′) *intr.v.* **-rived, -riv·ing, -rives.** *Abbr.* **ar., arr. 1.** To reach a destination. **2.** To come at length; take place: *The day of reckoning has arrived.* **3.** To achieve success or recognition: *He had finally arrived as a designer.* **—*phrasal verb.* arrive at.** To reach through effort or a process: *arrive at a decision after much thought.* [Middle English *ariven,* from Old French *ariver,* from Vulgar Latin **arrīpāre,* to reach the shore : Latin *ad-,* ad- + Latin *rīpa,* shore.] **—ar·riv′er** *n.*

ar·ri·viste (ă-rē-vēst′) *n.* **1.** A person who has recently attained high position or great power without due effort or merit; an upstart. **2.** An unscrupulous, vulgar social climber; a bounder. [French, from *arriver,* to arrive, from Old French *ariver.* See ARRIVE.]

ar·ro·ba (ə-rō′bə) *n.* **1.** A unit of weight formerly used in Spanish-speaking countries, equal to about 11.3 kilograms (25 pounds). **2.** A unit of weight formerly used in Portuguese-speaking countries, equal to about 14.4 kilograms (32 pounds). **3.** A liquid measure formerly used in Spanish-speaking countries, having varying value but equal to about 16.2 liters (17 quarts) when used to measure wine. [Spanish and Portuguese, both from Arabic *ar-rub',* the quarter (of a quintal) : *al,* the + *rub',* quarter.]

ă pat	oi boy
ā pay	ou out
âr care	o͝o took
ä father	o͞o boot
ĕ pet	ŭ cut
ē be	ûr urge
ĭ pit	th thin
ī pie	*th* this
îr pier	hw which
ŏ pot	zh vision
ō toe	ə about, item
ô paw	♦ regionalism

Stress marks: ′ (primary); ′ (secondary), as in **dictionary** (dĭk′shə-nĕr′ē)

Ar·roe Islands (ä′ro͞o). See **Aru Islands.**

ar·ro·gance (ăr′ə-gəns) *n.* The state or quality of being arrogant; overbearing pride.

ar·ro·gant (ăr′ə-gənt) *adj.* **1.** Making or disposed to make claims to unwarranted importance or consideration out of overbearing pride. **2.** Marked by or arising from arrogance: *an arrogant contempt for the weak.* See Synonyms at **proud.** [Middle English *arrogaunt,* from Old French, from Latin *arrogāns, arrogant-,* present participle of *arrogāre,* to arrogate. See ARROGATE.] **—ar′ro·gant·ly** *adv.*

ar·ro·gate (ăr′ə-gāt′) *tr.v.* **-gat·ed, -gat·ing, -gates. 1.** To take or claim for oneself without right; appropriate: *Presidents who have arrogated the power of Congress to declare war.* See Synonyms at **appropriate. 2.** To ascribe on behalf of another in an unwarranted manner. [Latin *arrogāre, arrogāt-* : *ad-,* ad- + *rogāre,* to ask; see **reg-** in Appendix.] **—ar′ro·ga′tion** *n.* **—ar′ro·ga′tive** *adj.* **—ar′ro·ga′tor** *n.*

ar·ron·disse·ment (ä-rôɴ′dēs-mäɴ′) *n.* **1.** The chief administrative subdivision of a department in France. **2.** A municipal subdivision in some large French cities. [French, from Old French, rounded projection on a wall, from *arrondir, arrondiss-,* to round out : *a,* to (from Latin *ad-;* see AD–) + *rondir,* to make round (from *rond,* round; see ROUND[1]).]

ar·row (ăr′ō) *n.* **1.** A straight, thin shaft with a pointed head at one end and often flight-stabilizing vanes at the other, meant to be shot from a bow. **2.** Something, such as a directional symbol, that is similar to an arrow in form or function. [Middle English *arwe,* from Old English.]

Ar·row (ăr′ō), **Kenneth Joseph.** Born 1921. American economist. He shared a 1972 Nobel Prize for theories that help assess business risks and governmental economic policies.

arrow arum *n.* An emergent perennial herb *(Peltandra virginica)* of eastern North America, having arrowhead-shaped leaves and an elongate, pointed spathe. Also called *tuckahoe.*

ar·row·head (ăr′ō-hĕd′) *n.* **1.** The pointed, removable striking tip of an arrow. **2.** Something, such as a mark indicating a limit on a drawing, that is shaped like the head of an arrow. **3.a.** Any of various aquatic or wetland perennial plants of the genus *Sagittaria,* having arrowhead-shaped leaves and panicles of white, unisexual flowers. **b.** The edible tubers of the Eurasian species *S. sagittifolia* or of the North American species *S. latifolia.*

ar·row·root (ăr′ō-ro͞ot′, -ro͝ot′) *n.* **1.a.** A starch obtained from the rhizomes of a tropical American perennial herb *(Maranta arundinacea).* It is used especially in cooking as a thickener. **b.** The rhizome of this plant, cooked and eaten as a vegetable or used for starch extraction. **c.** The plant itself. **2.a.** The edible starch obtained from the rhizomes or tubers of plants in the genera *Canna* and *Tacca.* **b.** Any of these plants. [By folk etymology from Arawak *aru-aru,* meal of meals (because it was used to draw poison from arrow wounds).]

WORD HISTORY: The arrowroot is just one of many plants that the European settlers and explorers discovered in the New World. The Arawak, a people who formerly lived on the Caribbean Islands and continue to inhabit certain regions of Guiana, named this plant *aru-aru,* meaning "meal of meals," so called because they thought very highly of the starchy, nutritious meal made from the arrowroot. The plant also had medicinal value because its tubers could be used to draw poison from wounds inflicted by poison arrows. The medicinal application of the roots provided the impetus for English speakers to remake *aru-aru* into *arrowroot,* first recorded in English in 1696. Folk etymology—the process by which an unfamiliar element in a word is changed to resemble a more familiar word, often one that is semantically associated with the word being refashioned—has triumphed once again, thus denying us the direct borrowing of *aru-aru* and giving us *arrowroot* instead.

ar·row-wood (ăr′ō-wo͝od′) *n.* Any of several North American species of viburnum, such as *Viburnum dentatum,* having straight, tough stems formerly used by certain Native American peoples to make arrows.

arrow worm *n.* Any of various small, slender marine worms of the phylum Chaetognatha having a narrow, almost transparent body and sickle-shaped bristles on each side of the mouth.

ar·roy·o (ə-roi′ō) *n., pl.* **-os. 1.** A deep gully cut by an intermittent stream; a dry gulch. **2.** A brook; a creek. [Spanish, from Vulgar Latin **arrugiu,* gold mine, underground passage, masculine variant of Latin *arrugia,* a galleried mine.]

ARS *abbr.* Agricultural Research Service.

arse (ärs) *n. Chiefly British.* Variant of **ass[2].**

ar·se·nal (är′sə-nəl) *n.* **1.** A governmental establishment for the storing, development, manufacturing, testing, or repairing of arms, ammunition, and other war materiel. **2.** A stock of weapons. **3.** A store or supply: *an arsenal of retorts.* [Italian *arsenale,* from obsolete Italian *arzanale,* from Arabic *dār-aṣ-ṣināʿah* : *dār,* house + *aṣ-,* the + *ṣināʿah,* manufacture (from *ṣanaʿa,* to make).]

ar·se·nate (är′sə-nĭt, -nāt′) *n.* A salt or ester of arsenic acid.

ar·se·nic (är′sə-nĭk) *n.* **1.** *Symbol* **As** A highly poisonous metallic element having three allotropic forms, yellow, black, and gray, of which the brittle, crystalline gray is the most common. Arsenic and its compounds are used in insecticides, weed killers, solid-state doping agents, and various alloys. Atomic number 33; atomic weight 74.922; valence 3, 5. Gray arsenic melts at 817°C (at 28 atm pressure), sublimes at 613°C, and has a specific gravity of 5.73. See table at **element. 2.** Arsenic trioxide. **—ar·sen·ic** (är-sĕn′ĭk) *adj.* Of or containing arsenic, especially with valence 5. [Middle English *arsenik,* from Old French, from Latin *arsenicum,* from Greek *arsenikon,* yellow orpiment, alteration of Syriac *zarnīkā,* from Middle Persian **zarnīk,* from Old Iranian **zarna-,* golden. See **ghel-[2]** in Appendix.]

ar·sen·ic acid (är-sĕn′ĭk) *n.* A poisonous, white, translucent crystalline compound, H_3AsO_4, used to manufacture arsenates.

ar·sen·i·cal (är-sĕn′ĭ-kəl) *adj.* Of or containing arsenic. **—arsenical** *n.* A drug or preparation containing arsenic.

ar·se·nic trioxide (är′sə-nĭk) *n.* A poisonous, white amorphous powder, As_2O_3, used in insecticides, rat poisons, and weed killers.

ar·se·nide (är′sə-nīd′) *n.* A compound of arsenic with a more electropositive element.

ar·se·ni·ous (är-sē′nē-əs) *adj.* Of or containing arsenic, especially with valence 3.

ar·se·no·py·rite (är′sə-nō-pī′rīt) *n.* A silver-white to gray arsenic ore, essentially FeAsS. Also called *mispickel.*

ar·shin (är-shēn′) *n.* Variant of **archine.**

ar·sine (är-sēn′, är′sēn′) *n.* A colorless, flammable, very poisonous gas, H_3As, having an odor like garlic and used in chemical warfare, as a solid-state doping agent, and in organic synthesis. [ARS(ENIC) + –INE[2].]

ar·sis (är′sĭs) *n., pl.* **-ses** (-sēz′). **1.a.** The short or unaccented part of a metrical foot, especially in quantitative verse. **b.** The accented or long part of a metrical foot, especially in accentual verse. **2.** *Music.* The upbeat or unaccented part of a measure. [Middle English, raising of the voice, from Late Latin, raising of the voice, accented part of a metrical foot, from Greek, raising of the foot, marking the upbeat, the unaccented part of a metrical foot, from *aeirein,* to lift. See **wer-[1]** in Appendix.]

ar·son (är′sən) *n.* The crime of maliciously, voluntarily, and willfully setting fire to the building, buildings, or other property of another or of burning one's own property for an improper purpose, as to collect insurance. [Anglo-Norman, from Late Latin *ārsiō, ārsiōn-,* from Latin *ārsus,* past participle of *ārdēre,* to burn. See **as-** in Appendix.] **—ar′son·ist** *n.*

ars·phen·a·mine (ärs-fĕn′ə-mēn′) *n.* A yellow hygroscopic powder, $C_{12}H_{12}As_2N_2O_2 \cdot 2HCl \cdot 2H_2O$, formerly used to treat syphilis. [ARS(ENIC) + PHEN(YL) + AMINE.]

art[1] (ärt) *n.* **1.** Human effort to imitate, supplement, alter, or counteract the work of nature. **2.a.** The conscious production or arrangement of sounds, colors, forms, movements, or other elements in a manner that affects the sense of beauty, specifically the production of the beautiful in a graphic or plastic medium. **b.** The study of these activities. **c.** The product of these activities; human works of beauty considered as a group. **3.** High quality of conception or execution, as found in works of beauty; aesthetic value. **4.** A field or category of art, such as music, ballet, or literature. **5.** A nonscientific branch of learning; one of the liberal arts. **6.a.** A system of principles and methods employed in the performance of a set of activities: *the art of building.* **b.** A trade or craft that applies such a system of principles and methods: *the art of the lexicographer.* **7.a.** Skill that is attained by study, practice, or observation: *the art of the baker; the blacksmith's art.* **b.** Skill arising from the exercise of intuitive faculties: *"Self-criticism is an art not many are qualified to practice"* (Joyce Carol Oates). **8.a. arts.** Artful devices, stratagems, and tricks. **b.** Artful contrivance; cunning. **9.** *Printing.* Illustrative material. [Middle English, from Old French, from Latin *ars, art-.* See **ar-** in Appendix.]

SYNONYMS: *art, craft, expertise, knack, know-how, technique.* The central meaning shared by these nouns is "skill in doing or performing that is attained by study, practice, or observation": *the art of expressing oneself clearly; pottery that reveals craft and fine workmanship; political expertise; a knack for teaching; the know-how to sew one's own clothes; an outstanding keyboard technique.*

art[2] (ərt; ärt *when stressed*) *v. Archaic.* A second person singular present indicative of **be.** [Middle English, from Old English *eart.* See **er-[1]** in Appendix.]

art. *abbr.* **1.** Article. **2.** Artificial. **3.** Artillery. **4.** Artist.

–art *suff.* Variant of **–ard.**

Ar·ta·xer·xes I (är′tə-zûrk′sēz′). Died 424 B.C. King of Persia (465–425) who sanctioned the practice of Judaism in Jerusalem.

Artaxerxes II. Died 359 B.C. King of Persia (404–359) whose reign was marked by many rebellions and by a peace agreement with Sparta (386).

art dec·o also **Art Dec·o** (dĕk′ō) *n.* A decorative and architectural style of the period 1925–1940, characterized by geometric designs, bold colors, and the use of plastic and glass. *—attributive.* Often used to modify another noun: *art deco furnishings; art deco jewelry.* [French *Art Déco,* from *Exposition Internationale des Arts Décoratifs et Industriels Modernes,* a 1925 exposition in Paris, France.]

ar·te·fact (är′tə-făkt′) *n.* Variant of **artifact.**

Ar·te·mis (är′tə-mĭs) *n. Greek Mythology.* The virgin goddess of the hunt and the moon and twin sister of Apollo. [Greek.]

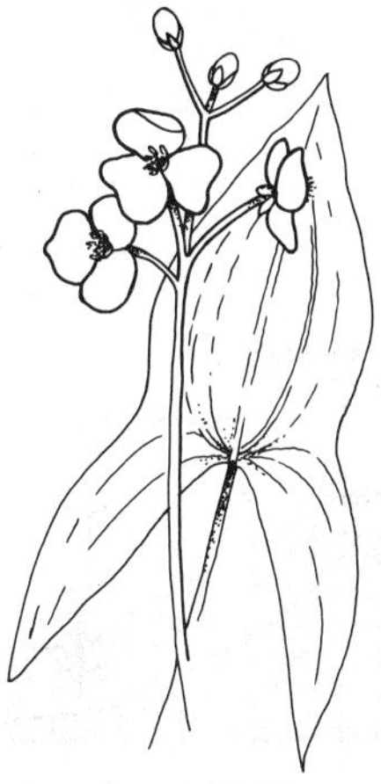

arrowhead
Top: From 8000 to 10,000 B.C.
Bottom: Broad-leaved arrowhead *Sagittaria latifolia*

Artemis

ar·te·mis·i·a (är′tə-mĭzh′ē-ə, -mĭzh′ə, -mĭz′ē-ə) *n.* Any of various aromatic plants of the genus *Artemisia* in the composite family, having green or grayish foliage and usually numerous small discoid flower heads and including the mugwort, sagebrush, tarragon, and wormweed. [Middle English *artemesie,* mugwort, from Old French, from Latin *artemisia,* from Greek, wormwood, after ARTEMIS (to whom it was sacred).]

ar·te·ri·al (är-tîr′ē-əl) *adj.* **1.** Of, like, or in an artery or arteries. **2.** Of, relating to, or being the blood in the arteries that has absorbed oxygen in the lungs and is bright red. **3.** Being a main road or channel with many branches: *an arterial highway; an arterial route.* —**arterial** *n.* A through road or street. —**ar·te′ri·al·ly** *adv.*

ar·te·ri·al·ize (är-tîr′ē-ə-līz′) *tr.v.* **-ized, -iz·ing, -iz·es.** To convert (venous blood) into bright red arterial blood by absorption of oxygen in the lungs. —**ar·te′ri·al·i·za′tion** (-ĭ-zā′shən) *n.*

arterio– *pref.* Artery: *arteriovenous.* [Greek *artērio-,* from *artēria,* artery. See **wer-**[1] in Appendix.]

ar·te·ri·og·ra·phy (är-tîr′ē-ŏg′rə-fē) *n.* Examination of the arteries using x-rays following injection of a radiopaque substance. —**ar·te′ri·o·gram′** (-ə-grăm′) *n.* —**ar·te′ri·o·graph′ic** (-ə-grăf′ĭk) *adj.*

ar·te·ri·ole (är-tîr′ē-ōl′) *n.* One of the small terminal branches of an artery, especially one that connects with a capillary. [New Latin *arteriola,* diminutive of Latin *artēria,* artery, from Greek. See **wer-**[1] in Appendix.] —**ar·te′ri·o′lar** (-ō′lər, -ə-lər) *adj.*

ar·te·ri·o·scle·ro·sis (är-tîr′ē-ō-sklə-rō′sĭs) *n.* A chronic disease in which thickening, hardening, and loss of elasticity of the arterial walls result in impaired blood circulation. —**ar·te′ri·o·scle·rot′ic** (-rŏt′ĭk) *adj.*

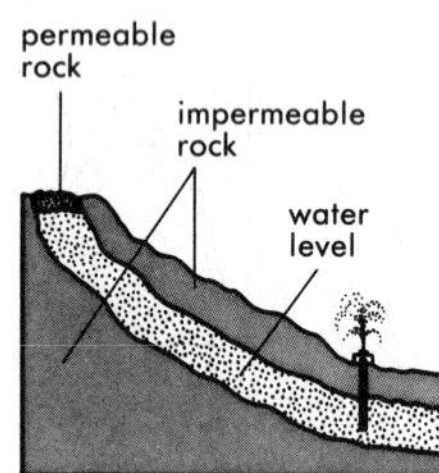

artesian well

ar·te·ri·o·ve·nous (är-tîr′ē-ō-vē′nəs) *adj.* Of, relating to, or connecting both arteries and veins.

ar·te·ri·tis (är′tə-rī′tĭs) *n.* Inflammation of an artery.

ar·ter·y (är′tə-rē) *n., pl.* **-ies. 1.** *Anatomy.* Any of a branching system of muscular, elastic tubes that carry blood away from the heart to the cells, tissues, and organs of the body. **2.** A major route of transportation into which local routes flow. See Synonyms at **way.** [Middle English *arterie,* from Latin *artēria,* from Greek. See **wer-**[1] in Appendix.]

ar·te·sian well (är-tē′zhən) *n.* A well drilled through impermeable strata to reach water capable of rising to the surface by internal hydrostatic pressure. [French *artésien,* from Old French, of Artois, from *Arteis,* Artois, France.]

Ar·te·vel·de (är′tə-vĕl′də), **Jacob van.** Called "the Brewer of Ghent." 1290?–1345. Flemish political leader who maintained the neutrality of Flanders during hostilities between England and France and encouraged Edward III to claim the French throne.

art film *n.* A film intended to be a serious artistic work, often experimental and not designed for mass appeal.

art form *n.* An activity or a piece of artistic work that can be regarded as a medium of artistic expression.

Chester A. Arthur

art·ful (ärt′fəl) *adj.* **1.** Exhibiting art or skill: *"The furniture is an artful blend of antiques and reproductions"* (Michael W. Robbins). **2.** Skillful in accomplishing a purpose, especially by the use of cunning or craft. See Synonyms at **sly. 3.** Artificial. —**art′ful·ly** *adv.* —**art′ful·ness** *n.*

arthr– *pref.* Variant of **arthro–.**

ar·thral·gia (är-thrăl′jə, -jē-ə) *n.* Neuralgic pain in a joint or joints. —**ar·thral′gic** (-jĭk) *adj.*

ar·thri·tis (är-thrī′tĭs) *n.* Inflammation of a joint or joints resulting in pain and swelling. —**ar·thrit′ic** (-thrĭt′ĭk) *adj. & n.* —**ar·thrit′i·cal·ly** *adv.*

arthro– or **arthr–** *pref.* Joint: *arthropathy.* [Greek, from *arthron,* joint. See **ar-** in Appendix.]

ar·throd·e·sis (är-thrŏd′ĭ-sĭs) *n.* The surgical fixation of a joint, ultimately resulting in bone fusion. Basically, the procedure is artificially induced ankylosis performed to relieve pain or provide support in a diseased or injured joint. [ARTHRO– + Greek *desis,* binding together (from *dein,* to bind).]

ar·throg·ra·phy (är-thrŏg′rə-fē) *n.* Examination of the interior of a joint using x-rays following the injection of a radiopaque substance. —**ar′thro·gram′** (är′thrə-grăm′) *n.*

artichoke
Cynara scolymus

ar·thro·gry·po·sis (är′thrə-grə-pō′sĭs) *n.* **1.** The permanent fixation of a joint in a contracted position. **2.** A congenital disorder marked by generalized stiffness of the joints, often accompanied by muscle and nerve degeneration, which results in severely impaired mobility of the limbs. Also called *arthrogryposis multiplex congenita.* [ARTHRO– + Late Latin *grypōsis,* hooking (from Late Greek, from Greek *grupousthai,* to become hooked, from *grupos,* hook-nosed).]

ar·thro·mere (är′thrə-mîr′) *n.* One of the segments or divisions in the body of a jointed animal, such as an arthropod. —**ar′thro·mer′ic** (är′thrə-mĕr′ĭk, -mîr′ĭk) *adj.*

ar·throp·a·thy (är-thrŏp′ə-thē) *n.* A disease or an abnormality of a joint.

ar·thro·pod (är′thrə-pŏd′) *n.* Any of numerous invertebrate animals of the phylum Arthropoda, including the insects, crustaceans, arachnids, and myriapods, that are characterized by a chitinous exoskeleton and a segmented body to which jointed appendages are articulated in pairs. [From New Latin *Arthropoda,* phylum name : ARTHRO– + New Latin *-poda,* -pod.] —**ar′thro·pod** *adj.* —**ar·throp′o·dous** (är-thrŏp′ə-dəs), **ar·throp′o·dal** (-dəl) *adj.*

ar·thros·co·py (är-thrŏs′kə-pē) *n., pl.* **-pies.** Examination of the interior of a joint, such as the knee, using a type of endoscope that is inserted into the joint through a small incision. —**ar′thro·scope′** (är′thrə-skōp′) *n.* —**ar′thro·scop′ic** (-skŏp′ĭk) *adj.* —**ar′thro·scop′ic·al·ly** *adv.*

ar·thro·sis (är-thrō′sĭs) *n., pl.* **-ses** (-sēz). **1.** *Anatomy.* An articulation or a joint between bones. **2.** A degenerative disease of a joint. [Greek *arthrōsis,* from *arthroun,* from *arthron,* joint. See ARTHRO–.]

ar·throt·o·my (är-thrŏt′ə-mē) *n.* Surgical incision into a joint.

Ar·thur (är′thər) *n.* A legendary British hero, said to have been king of the Britons in the sixth century A.D. and to have held court at Camelot.

Arthur, Chester Alan. 1829–1886. The 21st President of the United States (1881–1885) who became President after the assassination of James A. Garfield. He supported the 1883 Pendleton Act, which created the Civil Service Commission to regulate federal appointments.

Ar·thu·ri·an (är-thoo͝r′ē-ən) *adj.* Of or relating to King Arthur and his Knights of the Round Table.

ar·ti·choke (är′tĭ-chōk′) *n.* **1.a.** A Mediterranean thistlelike plant *(Cynara scolymus)* in the composite family, having pinnately divided leaves and large discoid heads of bluish flowers. **b.** The edible, immature flower head of this plant. Also called *globe artichoke.* **2.** The Jerusalem artichoke. [Ultimately from Old Spanish *alcarchofa,* from Arabic *al-ḫaršūf.*]

WORD HISTORY: Those who have been warned to watch out for the sharp-tipped bracts toward the innermost part of an artichoke may have wondered whether the name of this vegetable has anything to do with choking. Originally it did not. Our word goes back to an Arabic word for the same plant, *al-ḫaršūf.* The Arabic word passed into Spanish, a not uncommon occurrence given the fact that Moslems ruled much of Spain for several centuries during the Middle Ages. The Old Spanish word *alcarchofa* was variously modified as it passed through Italian, a Northern dialect form being *articiocco,* which looks more like *artichoke* than *al-ḫaršūf.* In English, where the word is first recorded in the early 16th century, a potpourri of spellings and explanations of it are found. For example, people who did not know the long history of the word explained it by the notion that the flower had a "choke," that is, something that chokes, in its "heart."

ar·ti·cle (är′tĭ-kəl) *n. Abbr.* **art. 1.** An individual thing or element of a class; a particular object or item: *an article of clothing; articles of food.* **2.** A particular section or item of a series in a written document, as in a contract, constitution, or treaty. **3.** A nonfictional literary composition that forms an independent part of a publication, as of a newspaper or magazine. **4.** *Grammar.* Any of a class of words used to signal nouns and to specify their application. In English, the indefinite articles are *a* and *an* and the definite article is *the.* **5.** A particular part or subject; a specific matter or point. —**article** *tr.v.* **-cled, -cling, -cles.** To bind by articles set forth in a contract, such as one of apprenticeship. [Middle English, from Old French, from Latin *articulus,* part, diminutive of *artus,* joint. See **ar-** in Appendix.]

article of faith *n., pl.* **articles of faith.** A very basic belief not to be doubted.

ar·tic·u·la·ble (är-tĭk′yə-lə-bəl) *adj.* That can be articulated: *articulable doubts.*

ar·tic·u·lar (är-tĭk′yə-lər) *adj.* Of or relating to a joint or joints: *the articular surfaces of bones.* [Middle English *articuler,* from Latin *articulāris,* from *articulus,* small joint. See ARTICLE.] —**ar·tic′u·lar·ly** *adv.*

ar·tic·u·late (är-tĭk′yə-lĭt) *adj.* **1.** Endowed with the power of speech. **2.** Composed of distinct, meaningful syllables or words, as human speech. **3.** Expressing oneself easily in clear and effective language: *an articulate speaker.* **4.** Characterized by the use of clear, expressive language: *an articulate essay.* **5.** *Anatomy.* Consisting of sections united by joints; jointed. —**articulate** (är-tĭk′yə-lāt′) *v.* **-lat·ed, -lat·ing, -lates.** —*tr.* **1.** To pronounce distinctly and carefully; enunciate. **2.** To utter (a speech sound) by making the necessary movements of the speech organs. **3.** To express in coherent verbal form; give words to: *couldn't articulate my fears.* **4.** To fit together into a coherent whole; unify: *articulate statewide nursing programs.* **5.** *Anatomy.* To unite by forming a joint or joints. —*intr.* **1.** To speak clearly and distinctly. **2.** To utter a speech sound. **3.** *Anatomy.* To form a joint; be jointed: *The thighbone articulates with the bones of the hip.* [Latin *articulātus,* past participle of *articulāre,* to divide into joints, utter distinctly, from *articulus,* small joint. See ARTICLE.] —**ar·tic′u·late·ly** *adv.* —**ar·tic′u·late·ness, ar·tic′u·la·cy** *n.*

ar·tic·u·la·tion (är-tĭk′yə-lā′shən) *n.* **1.** The act of vocal expression; utterance or enunciation: *an articulation of the group's sentiments.* **2.a.** The act or manner of producing a speech sound. **b.** A speech sound, especially a consonant. **3.a.** A jointing together or being jointed together. **b.** The method or manner of jointing. **4.** *Anatomy.* **a.** A fixed or movable joint between bones. **b.** A movable joint between inflexible parts of the body of an animal, as the divisions of an appendage in arthropods. **5.** *Botany.* **a.** A joint between two separable parts, as a leaf and a stem. **b.** A node or a space on a stem between two nodes. **—ar·tic′u·la·to′ry** (-lə-tôr′ē, -tōr′ē), **ar·tic′u·la′·tive** (-lā′tĭv, -lə-tĭv) *adj.*

ar·tic·u·la·tor (är-tĭk′yə-lā′tər) *n.* **1.** One that articulates: *an articulator of the students' concerns.* **2.** One of the organs of speech, such as the lips or tongue.

ar·ti·fact also **ar·te·fact** (är′tə-făkt′) *n.* **1.** An object produced or shaped by human craft, especially a tool, a weapon, or an ornament of archaeological or historical interest. **2.** A typical product or result: *"The very act of looking at a naked model was an artifact of male supremacy"* (Philip Weiss). **3.** *Biology.* A structure or substance not normally present but produced by an external agent or action, such as a structure seen in a microscopic specimen after fixation that is not present in the living tissue. [Latin *arte,* ablative of *ars,* art; see ART^1 + *factum,* something made, from neuter past participle of *facere,* to make; see **dhē-** in Appendix.] **—ar′ti·fac′tu·al** (-făk′cho͞o-əl) *adj.*

ar·ti·fice (är′tə-fĭs) *n.* **1.** An artful or crafty expedient; a stratagem. **2.** Subtle but base deception; trickery. **3.** Cleverness or skill; ingenuity. [French, from Old French, craftsmanship, from Latin *artificium,* from *artifex, artific-,* craftsman : *ars, art-,* art; see ART^1 + *-fex,* maker; see **dhē-** in Appendix.]

SYNONYMS: *artifice, trick, ruse, wile, feint, stratagem, maneuver, dodge.* These nouns are compared as they denote means for achieving an end by indirection. *Artifice* refers to something especially contrived to lead to a desired result or create a desired effect: *"His sincerity, although often aided by the actor's artifice, seems genuine"* (Richard Cohen). *Trick* in this sense implies willful deception and often less than honorable motivation: *"The . . . boys . . . had all sorts of tricks to prevent us from winning"* (W.H. Hudson). *Ruse* stresses the creation of a false impression: *Her pretended deafness was a ruse to enable her to learn their plans. Wile* suggests deceiving and entrapping a victim by playing on his or her weak points: *"He did not fail to see/His uncle's cunning wiles and treachery"* (William Morris). *Feint* denotes a deceptive act calculated to distract attention from one's real purpose: *One person bumped into me as a feint while the other stole my wallet. Stratagem* implies careful planning for achieving an objective or obtaining an advantage: *That you have used every ruthless stratagem to win the much-coveted promotion hasn't endeared you to your rivals. Maneuver* applies to calculated and skillful tactics and often to a single strategic move: *"To this day they always speak of that Reform Bill as if it had been a dishonest maneuver"* (Standard). *Dodge* stresses shifty and ingenious deception: *" 'It was all false, of course?' 'All, sir,' replied Mr. Weller, ' . . . artful dodge' "* (Charles Dickens).

ar·tif·i·cer (är-tĭf′ĭ-sər) *n.* **1.** A skilled worker; a craftsperson. **2.** One that contrives, devises, or constructs something: *"The labyrinth . . . was built by Daedalus, a most skillful artificer"* (Thomas Bulfinch).

ar·ti·fi·cial (är′tə-fĭsh′əl) *adj. Abbr.* **art. 1.a.** Made by human beings; produced rather than natural. **b.** Brought about or caused by sociopolitical or other human-generated forces or influences: *set up artificial barriers against women and minorities; an artificial economic boom.* **2.** Made in imitation of something natural; simulated. **3.** Not genuine or natural: *an artificial smile.* [Middle English, from Old French, from Latin *artificiālis,* belonging to art, from *artificium,* craftsmanship. See ARTIFICE.] **—ar′·ti·fi′ci·al′i·ty** (-fĭsh′ē-ăl′ĭ-tē) *n.* **—ar′ti·fi′cial·ly** *adv.*

SYNONYMS: *artificial, synthetic, ersatz, simulated.* These adjectives are compared as they refer to what is made by human beings rather than natural in origin. Of these terms *artificial* is broadest in meaning and connotation: *an artificial sweetener; artificial flowers. Synthetic* often implies the use of a chemical process to produce a substance that will look or function like the original, often with certain advantages, such as enhanced durability or convenience of use or care: *synthetic rubber; a synthetic fabric.* An *ersatz* product is a transparently inferior imitation: *ersatz coffee; ersatz mink. Simulated* refers to what is made to resemble or substitute for another often costlier substance: *a purse of simulated alligator hide; simulated mahogany paneling.*

artificial horizon *n.* An instrument displaying a line on a flight indicator that lies within the horizontal plane and about which the pitching and banking movements of an aircraft are shown.

artificial insemination *n. Abbr.* **AI** Introduction of semen into the vagina or uterus without sexual contact.

artificial intelligence *n. Abbr.* **AI** *Computer Science.* **1.** The ability of a machine to perform those activities that are normally thought to require intelligence. **2.** The branch of computer science concerned with the development of machines having this ability.

artificial language *n.* **1.** A language invented for a specific purpose and based on a set of prescribed rules. **2.** *Computer Science.* A language designed for use in a specific field.

artificial respiration *n.* A procedure used to restore or maintain respiration in a person who has stopped breathing. The method uses mechanical or manual means to force air into and out of the lungs in a rhythmic fashion.

artificial selection *n.* Human intervention in animal or plant reproduction to ensure that certain desirable traits are represented in successive generations.

ar·til·ler·ist (är-tĭl′ər-ĭst) *n.* A soldier in the artillery.

ar·til·ler·y (är-tĭl′ə-rē) *n. Abbr.* **arty., art. 1.** Large-caliber weapons, such as cannon, howitzers, and missile launchers, that are operated by crews. **2.** The combat arm that specializes in the use of such weapons. **3.** The science of the use of guns; gunnery. **4.** Weapons, such as catapults, arbalests, and other early devices, used for discharging missiles. [Middle English *artillerie,* from Old French, from *artillier,* to equip, perhaps alteration of *atiller,* from Vulgar Latin **apticulāre,* from Latin *aptāre,* to fit, adapt, from *aptus,* apt. See APT.]

ar·til·ler·y·man (är-tĭl′ə-rē-mən) *n.* A soldier in the artillery.

artillery plant *n.* A tropical American plant *(Pilea microphylla)* having fleshy leaves and an explosive discharge of pollen.

ar·ti·o·dac·tyl (är′tē-ō-dăk′təl) *n.* Any of various hoofed mammals of the order Artiodactyla, which includes cattle, deer, camels, hippopotamuses, sheep, and goats, that have an even number of toes, usually two or sometimes four, on each foot. [From New Latin *Artiodactyla,* order name : Greek *artios,* even; see **ar-** in Appendix + Greek *daktulos,* toe.] **—ar′ti·o·dac′tyl, ar′ti·o·dac′ty·lous** (-tə-ləs) *adj.*

ar·ti·san (är′tĭ-zən, -sən) *n.* A skilled manual worker; a craftsperson. [Probably French, from Italian *artigiano,* from Vulgar Latin **artitiānus,* from Latin *artītus,* skilled in the arts, past participle of *artīre,* to instruct in the arts, from *ars, art-,* art. See **ar-** in Appendix.] **—ar′ti·san·ship′** *n.*

art·ist (är′tĭst) *n. Abbr.* **art. 1.** One, such as a painter or sculptor, who is able by virtue of imagination and talent to create works of aesthetic value, especially in the fine arts. **2.** A person whose work shows exceptional creative ability or skill: *You are an artist in the kitchen.* **3.** One who works in the performing arts. **4.** One who is adept at an activity, especially one involving trickery or deceit: *a con artist.* [French *artiste,* from Old French, lettered person, from Medieval Latin *artista,* from Latin *ars, art-.* See **ar-** in Appendix.]

ar·tiste (är-tēst′) *n.* **1.** A public performer or entertainer, especially a singer or dancer. **2.** A person with artistic pretensions. [French. See ARTIST.]

ar·tis·tic (är-tĭs′tĭk) *adj.* **1.** Of or relating to art or artists: *the artistic community.* **2.** Sensitive to or appreciative of art or beauty: *an artistic temperament.* **3.** Showing imagination and skill: *an artistic design.* **—ar·tis′ti·cal·ly** *adv.*

art·ist·ry (är′tĭ-strē) *n.* **1.** Artistic ability: *a sculptor of great artistry.* **2.** Artistic quality or craft: *the artistry of a poem.*

art·ist's video or **art·ists' video** (är′tĭsts) *n.* A videotape that concentrates on an artist's life, method, and works, with the main goals being rejection of the commercial qualities of network television and a deep exploration into the subject matter through the use of new techniques in imagery and sound. Also called *video art.*

art·less (ärt′lĭs) *adj.* **1.** Having or displaying no guile, cunning, or deceit. See Synonyms at **naive. 2.** Free of artificiality; natural: *artless charm.* **3.** Lacking art, knowledge, or skill; uncultured and ignorant. **4.** Poorly made or done; crude. **—art′less·ly** *adv.* **—art′less·ness** *n.*

art nou·veau also **Art Nou·veau** (är′ no͞o-vō′, ärt′) *n.* A style of decoration and architecture of the late 19th and early 20th centuries, characterized particularly by the depiction of leaves and flowers in flowing, sinuous lines. [French : *art,* art + *nouveau,* new.]

art nouveau
Late 19th- to early 20th-century American vase made by the Alvin Manufacturing Company

Ar·tois (är-twä′). A historical region and former province of northern France near the English Channel between Picardy and Flanders. It was ruled at various times by Flanders, Burgundy, Austria, and Spain.

art runner *n.* A private art dealer who functions as a broker in sales transactions by linking prospective buyers and sellers of works of art. After an exhibition or an auction, the art runner moves unsold works from one gallery to another to stimulate sales.

arts medicine (ärts) *n.* A branch of medicine dealing with the special health needs of performers, such as the injuries and disorders suffered by musicians that result from playing a musical instrument.

art song *n. Music.* A lyric song intended to be sung in recital, usually accompanied by a piano.

art·sy-craft·sy (ärt′sē-krăft′sē) *adj. Informal.* **1.** Decorative rather than functional: *artsy-craftsy furniture.* **2.** Pretentiously or self-consciously artistic.

art·work (ärt′wûrk′) *n.* **1.** Work in the graphic or plastic arts, especially small handmade decorative or artistic objects. **2.** An illustrative and decorative element, such as a line drawing or a photograph, used in a printed work, such as a book.

art·y (är′tē) *adj.* **-i·er, -i·est.** *Informal.* Showily or affectedly artistic. **—art′i·ly** *adv.* **—art′i·ness** *n.*

arty. *abbr.* Artillery.

A·ru·ba (ə-ro͞o′bə). An island of the Netherlands in the Leeward Islands north of the Venezuela coast. It is a popular Caribbean resort area.

a·ru·gu·la (ə-ro͞o′gə-lə) *n.* See **rocket^2** (sense 1). [Probably Italian dialectal, from Latin *ērūca,* colewort.]

A·ru Islands also **A·roe Islands** or **Ar·roe Islands** (ä′ro͞o). An island group of eastern Indonesia, part of the Moluccas in the

ă pat	oi boy
ā pay	ou out
âr care	o͝o took
ä father	o͞o boot
ĕ pet	ŭ cut
ē be	ûr urge
ĭ pit	th thin
ī pie	*th* this
îr pier	hw which
ŏ pot	zh vision
ō toe	ə about, item
ô paw	♦ regionalism

Stress marks: ′ (primary); ′ (secondary), as in **dictionary** (dĭk′shə-nĕr′ē)

Arafura Sea southwest of New Guinea. The islands were discovered by the Dutch and colonized by them after 1623.

ar·um (ăr′əm, âr′-) *n.* **1.** Any of several Old World plants, such as the cuckoopint, of the genus *Arum,* having basal, arrowhead-shaped leaves. **2.** Any of several related plants, such as the arrow arum and water arum. [Latin, wake-robin, from Greek *aron.*]

arum lily *n. Chiefly British.* The calla lily.

a·rus·pex (ə-rŭs′pĕks′) *n.* Variant of **haruspex.**

A·ru·wi·mi (är′ə-wē′mē, ăr′-). A river of central Africa rising in northeast Zaire near Lake Albert and flowing about 1,287 km (800 mi) generally westward to the Congo River.

ARV *abbr. Bible.* American Revised Version.

Ar·vad·a (är-văd′ə). A city of north-central Colorado, a residential suburb of Denver. Population, 84,576.

ARVIN *abbr.* Army of the Republic of Vietnam.

–ary *suff.* **1.** Of or relating to: *bacillary.* **2.** One that relates to or is connected with: *boundary.* [Middle English *-arie,* from Old French, from Latin *-ārius,* adj. and n. suff.]

Ar·y·an (âr′ē-ən, ăr′-) *n.* **1.** See **Indo-Iranian. 2.** A member of the people who spoke the parent language of the Indo-European languages. **3.** A member of any people speaking an Indo-European language. **4.** In Nazism, a Caucasian Gentile, especially of Nordic type. **—Aryan** *adj.* **1.** Of or relating to Indo-Iranian. **2.** Of or relating to the Indo-European languages or the hypothetical language from which they are derived. **3.** Of or relating to a speaker of an Indo-European language. **4.** In Nazism, of or relating to a Caucasian Gentile. [From Sanskrit *ārya-,* noble, Aryan.]

ar·y·te·noid (ăr′ĭ-tē′noid′, ə-rĭt′n-oid′) *Anatomy. n.* **1.** Either of two small pitcher-shaped cartilages at the back of the larynx to which the vocal cords are attached. **2.** A muscle connected to either of these cartilages. **3.** Any of several small mucous glands located in front of these cartilages. **—arytenoid** *adj.* Of or relating to these cartilages or an associated muscle or gland. [New Latin *arytaenoīdēs,* from Greek *arutainoeidēs,* shaped like a ladle : *arutaina,* ladle (from *aruein,* to draw water) + *-oeidēs,* -oid.] **—ar′y·te·noid′al** *adj.*

♦**as**[1] (ăz; əz *when unstressed*) *adv.* **1.** To the same extent or degree; equally: *The child sang as sweetly as a nightingale.* **2.** For instance: *large carnivores, as the bear or lion.* **3.** When taken into consideration in a specified relation or form: *this definition as distinguished from the second one.* **—as** *conj.* **1.** To the same degree or quantity that. Often used as a correlative after *so* or *as: You are as sweet as sugar. The situation is not so bad as you suggest.* **2.** In the same manner or way that: *Think as I think.* **3.** At the same time that; while: *slipped on the ice as I ran home.* **4.** For the reason that; because: *went to bed early, as I was exhausted.* **5.** With the result that: *He was so foolish as to lie.* **6.** Though: *Great as the author was, he proved a bad model. Ridiculous as it seems, the tale is true.* **7.** In accordance with which or with the way in which: *The hotel is quite comfortable as such establishments go. The sun is hot, as everyone knows.* **8.** *Informal.* That: *I don't know as I can answer your question.* **—as** *pron.* **1.** That; which; who. Used after *same* or *such: I received the same grade as you did.* **2.** *Chiefly Upper Southern U.S.* Who, whom, which, or that: *Those as want to can come with me.* **—as** *prep.* **1.** In the role, capacity, or function of: *acting as a mediator.* **2.** In a manner similar to; the same as: *On this issue they thought as one.* **—*idioms.* as is.** *Informal.* Just the way it is, with no changes or modifications: *bought the samovar as is from an antique dealer.* **as it were.** In a manner of speaking; as if such were so. [Middle English, from Old English *ealswā.* See ALSO.]

USAGE NOTE: Traditionally, a distinction has been drawn between comparisons using *as . . . as* and comparisons using *so . . . as.* The *so . . . as* construction is traditionally required in negative sentences (as in Shakespeare's *" 'tis not so deep as a well"*), in questions (as in *Is it so bad as she says?*), and in certain *if* clauses (as in *If it is so bad as you say, you ought to leave*). But this *so . . . as* construction is becoming increasingly rare in American English, and the use of *as . . . as* is now entirely acceptable in all contexts. • In a comparison involving both *as . . . as* and *than,* the second *as* should be retained in written style. One writes *He is as smart as, or smarter than, his brother,* not *He is as smart or smarter than his brother,* which is considered unacceptable in formal style. • In many dialects, *as* is used in place of *that* in sentences like *We are not sure as we want to go* or *It's not certain as he left.* This construction is not sufficiently well established to be used in writing. • *As* should be preceded by a comma when it expresses a causal relation, as in *She won't be coming, as we didn't invite her.* When used to express a time relation, *as* is not preceded by a comma: *She was finishing the painting as I walked into the room.* When a clause introduced by *as* begins a sentence, care should be taken that it is clear whether *as* is used to mean "because" or "at the same time as." The sentence *As they were leaving, I walked to the door* may mean either that I walked to the door because they left or at the same time that they were leaving. • *As* is sometimes used superfluously to introduce the complements of verbs like *consider, deem,* and *account,* as in *They considered it as one of the landmark decisions of the civil rights movement. The measure was deemed as unnecessary.* This usage may have arisen by analogy to *regard* and *esteem,* where *as* is standardly used in this way: *We regarded her as the best writer among us.* But the use of *as* with verbs like *consider* is not sufficiently well established to be acceptable in writing. See Usage Notes at **because, equal, like**[2], **so**[1], **than.**

♦***REGIONAL NOTE:*** American dialects often vary from Standard English in the form and usage of relative pronouns. Where Standard English has three relative pronouns—*who, which,* and *that*—regional dialects, particularly those of the South and Midlands, allow *as* and *what* as relative pronouns: *"Them as thinks they can whup me jest come ahead"* (Publication of the American Dialect Society). *The car what hit him never stopped.*

as[2] (ăs) *n., pl.* **as·ses** (ăs′ēz′, ăs′ĭz). **1.** An ancient Roman coin of copper or copper alloy. **2.** An ancient Roman unit of weight equal to about one troy pound. [Latin *ās.*]

As The symbol for the element **arsenic** (sense 1).

AS *abbr.* **1.** Also **a/s.** Air speed. **2.** American Samoa **3.** Also **A.S.** Anglo-Saxon. **4.** Antisubmarine. **5.** Associate in Science.

As. *abbr.* Asia; Asian.

as– *pref.* Variant of **ad–** (sense 1).

as·a·fet·i·da or **as·a·foet·i·da** (ăs′ə-fĕt′ĭ-də) *n.* A brownish, bitter, foul-smelling resinous material obtained from the roots of several plants of the genus *Ferula* in the parsley family and formerly used in medicine. [Middle English, from Medieval Latin : *asa,* gum (from Persian *azā,* mastic) + Latin *fetida,* feminine of *fetidus,* stinking; see FETID.]

A·sa·hi·ka·wa (ä′sə-hē-kä′wə, ä′sä-hē′kä-wä) also **A·sa·hi·ga·wa** (ä′sə-hē-gä′wə, ä′sä-hē′gä-wä). A city of west-central Hokkaido, Japan. It is the commercial, industrial, and transportation center of a fertile agricultural area. Population, 363,630.

A·sa·ma (ə-sä′mə), **Mount.** A volcano, 2,543.7 m (8,340 ft) high, of central Honshu, Japan, near Nagano. One of the largest and most active volcanoes in Japan, it erupted violently in 1783.

A·san·te (ə-săn′tē) *n.* Variant of **Ashanti**[1].

ASAP or **asap** *abbr.* As soon as possible.

ASAT also **Asat.** *abbr.* Anti-satellite.

as·bes·tos also **as·bes·tus** (ăs-bĕs′təs, ăz-) *—n. Abbr.* **asb.** Either of two incombustible, chemical-resistant, fibrous mineral forms of impure magnesium silicate, used for fireproofing, electrical insulation, building materials, brake linings, and chemical filters. *—adj.* Of, made of, or containing one or the other of these two mineral forms. [Middle English *asbestus,* from Latin *asbestos,* mineral or gem, from Greek, mineral or gem, unslaked lime, from *asbestos,* unquenchable : *a-,* not; see A–[1] + *sbennunai, sbes-,* to quench.] **—as·bes′tine** (-tĭn), **as·bes′tic** (-tĭk) *adj.*

as·bes·to·sis (ăs′bĕs-tō′sĭs, ăz′-) *n.* A chronic, progressive lung disease caused by prolonged inhalation of asbestos particles. [ASBEST(OS) + –OSIS.] **—as′bes·tot′ic** (-tŏt′ĭk) *adj.*

as·bes·tus (ăs-bĕs′təs, ăz-) *n. & adj.* Variant of **asbestos.**

As·bur·y (ăz′bə-rē), **Francis.** 1745–1816. British-born American religious leader and first Methodist Episcopal cleric to become a bishop in the colonies (1784).

As·bur·y Park (ăz′bĕr′ē, -bə-rē). A city of eastern New Jersey on the Atlantic Ocean. It is a popular resort. Population, 17,015.

ASCAP *abbr.* American Society of Composers, Authors, and Publishers.

♦**a·scared** (ə-skârd′) *adj. Chiefly Upper Southern U.S.* Afraid. [Probably *a-* (variant of *y-,* past participle pref.; see YCLEPT) + *scared,* past participle of SCARE.]

as·ca·ri·a·sis (ăs′kə-rī′ə-sĭs) *n.* Infestation with or disease caused by a parasitic roundworm *Ascaris lumbricoides.* [ASCAR(ID) + –IASIS.]

as·ca·rid (ăs′kə-rĭd) *n.* Any of various nematode worms of the family Ascaridae, which includes the common intestinal parasite *Ascaris lumbricoides.* [Sing. of *ascarides,* intestinal worms, from Late Latin, from Greek *askarides,* pl. of *askaris,* intestinal worm.]

ASCE *abbr.* American Society of Civil Engineers.

as·cend (ə-sĕnd′) *v.* **-cend·ed, -cend·ing, -cends.** *—intr.* **1.** To go or move upward; rise. See Synonyms at **rise. 2.** To slope upward. *—tr.* **1.** To move upward upon or along; climb: *ascended the mountain.* **2.** To succeed to; occupy: *ascended the throne upon the death of her father.* [Middle English *ascenden,* from Old French *ascendre,* from Latin *ascendere* : *ad-,* ad- + *scandere,* to climb; see **skand-** in Appendix.] **—as·cend′a·ble, as·cend′i·ble** *adj.*

as·cen·dance also **as·cen·dence** (ə-sĕn′dəns) *n.* Ascendancy.

as·cen·dan·cy also **as·cen·den·cy** (ə-sĕn′dən-sē) *n.* Superiority or decisive advantage; domination: *"Germany only awaits trade revival to gain an immense mercantile ascendancy"* (Winston S. Churchill).

as·cen·dant also **as·cen·dent** (ə-sĕn′dənt) *—adj.* **1.** Inclining or moving upward; ascending or rising. **2.** Dominant in position or influence; superior. *—n.* **1.** The position or state of being dominant or in control: *a conservative policy currently in the ascendant.* **2.** The point of the ecliptic or the sign of the zodiac that rises in the east at the time of a person's birth or other event. **3.** An ancestor.

as·cend·er (ə-sĕn′dər) *n.* **1.** *Printing.* The part of the tall lowercase letters, such as *b, d,* and *h,* that extends above the other lowercase letters. **2.** A letter with such a part.

as·cend·ing (ə-sĕn′dĭng) *adj.* **1.** Moving, going, or growing

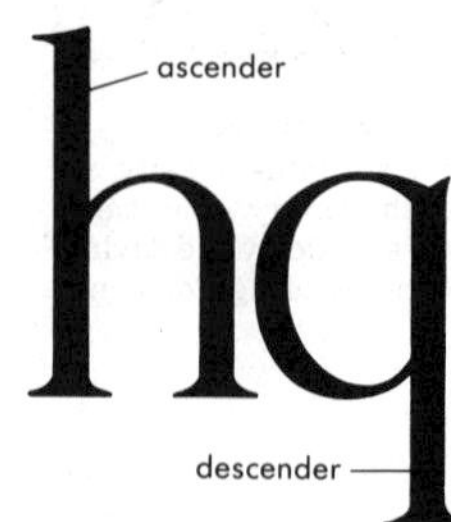

ascender

ă pat	oi boy
ā pay	ou out
âr care	o͝o took
ä father	o͞o boot
ĕ pet	ŭ cut
ē be	ûr urge
ĭ pit	th thin
ī pie	*th* this
îr pier	hw which
ŏ pot	zh vision
ō toe	ə about, item
ô paw	♦ regionalism

Stress marks: ′ (primary); ′ (secondary), as in **dictionary** (dĭk′shə-nĕr′ē)

upward: *an ascending minor scale.* **2.** *Botany.* Growing or directing upward from a curved or slanted base, as certain plant stems. **—as·cend′ing·ly** *adv.*

ascending rhythm *n.* See **rising rhythm.**

as·cen·sion (ə-sĕn′shən) *n.* **1.** The act or process of ascending; ascent. **2.** *Astronomy.* The rising of a star above the horizon. **3. Ascension.** *Theology.* The bodily rising of Jesus into heaven on the 40th day after his Resurrection. [Middle English *ascensioun,* from Old French *ascention,* from Latin *ascēnsiō, ascēnsiōn-,* from *ascēnsus,* past participle of *ascendere,* to ascend. See ASCEND.] **—as·cen′sion·al** *adj.*

Ascension Day *n.* The 40th day after Easter, on which the Christian feast of the Ascension is observed. Also called *Holy Thursday.*

Ascension Island. An island in the southern Atlantic northwest of St. Helena. Discovered by the Portuguese on Ascension Day in 1501, it was taken by the British in 1815 and has been administered by St. Helena since 1922.

as·cent (ə-sĕnt′) *n.* **1.** The act or process of rising or going upward. **2.** An advancement, especially in social status. **3.** An upward slope or incline. **4.** A going back in time or upward in genealogical succession. [From ASCEND, on the model of DESCENT.]

as·cer·tain (ăs′ər-tān′) *v.* *—tr.* **-tained, -tain·ing, -tains. 1.** To discover with certainty, as through examination or experimentation. See Synonyms at **discover. 2.** *Archaic.* To make certain, definite, and precise. [Middle English *acertainen,* to inform, from Old French *acertener, ascertain-* : *a-,* to (from Latin *ad-;* see AD–) + *certain,* certain; see CERTAIN.] **—as′cer·tain′a·ble** *adj.* **—as′cer·tain′a·ble·ness** *n.* **—as′cer·tain′a·bly** *adv.* **—as′cer·tain′ment** *n.*

as·cet·ic (ə-sĕt′ĭk) *n.* A person who renounces material comforts and leads a life of austere self-discipline, especially as an act of religious devotion. **—ascetic** *adj.* **1.** Leading a life of self-discipline and self-denial, especially for spiritual improvement. See Synonyms at **severe. 2.** Pertaining to or characteristic of an ascetic; self-denying and austere: *an ascetic existence.* [Late Greek *askētikos,* from Greek *askētēs,* practitioner, hermit, monk, from *askein,* to work.] **—as·cet′i·cal·ly** *adv.*

as·cet·i·cism (ə-sĕt′ĭ-sĭz′əm) *n.* **1.** The principles and practices of an ascetic; extreme self-denial and austerity. **2.** The doctrine that the ascetic life releases the soul from bondage to the body and permits union with the divine.

Asch (ăsh), **Sholem** or **Shalom.** 1880–1957. Polish-born American Yiddish writer who sought to reconcile Judaism and Christianity in his controversial novels, such as *The Nazarene* (1939).

As·cham (ăs′kəm), **Roger.** 1515–1568. English scholar who as Latin secretary to Edward VI, Mary I, and Elizabeth I advocated the use of the vernacular in literature.

as·ci (ăs′ī′, -kī′) *n.* *Botany.* Plural of **ascus.**

as·cid·i·an (ə-sĭd′ē-ən) *n.* See **sea squirt.** [From New Latin *Ascidia,* genus name, from Greek *askidion,* diminutive of *askos,* wineskin.]

as·cid·i·um (ə-sĭd′ē-əm) *n., pl.* **-i·a** (ə-sĭd′ē-ə). *Botany.* A pitcher-shaped or bottle-shaped part or organ, such as the hollow tubular leaf of a pitcher plant. [New Latin, from Greek *askidion,* diminutive of *askos,* wineskin.] **—as·cid′i·ate′** *adj.* **—as·cid′i·form′** (-ə-fôrm′) *adj.*

ASCII (ăs′kē) *n.* *Computer Science.* **1.** A standard for defining codes for information exchange between equipment produced by different manufacturers. **2.** A code that follows this standard. [*A(merican) S(tandard) C(ode for) I(nformation) I(nterchange).*]

as·ci·tes (ə-sī′tēz) *n., pl.* **ascites.** An abnormal accumulation of serous fluid in the abdominal cavity. [Middle English *aschites,* from Late Latin *ascītes,* from Greek *askitēs,* from *askos,* belly, wineskin.] **—as·cit′ic** (-sĭt′ĭk) *adj.*

As·cle·pi·us (ə-sklē′pē-əs) *n.* *Greek Mythology.* Apollo's son, the god of medicine.

asco– *pref.* Ascus: *ascospore.* [New Latin, from Greek *askos,* bag, wineskin.]

as·co·carp (ăs′kə-kärp′) *n.* *Botany.* An ascus-bearing structure found in ascomycetous fungi.

as·co·go·ni·um (ăs′kə-gō′nē-əm) *n., pl.* **-ni·a** (-nē-ə). *Botany.* The female reproductive organ of ascomycetous fungi.

as·co·my·cete (ăs′kō-mī′sēt′, -mī-sēt′) *n.* *Botany.* Any of various members of a large group of fungi characterized by the presence of sexually produced spores formed within an ascus. Also called *sac fungus.* **—as′co·my·ce′tous** (-sē′təs) *adj.*

a·scor·bate (ə-skôr′bāt, -bĭt) *n.* A salt of ascorbic acid. [ASCORB(IC ACID) + –ATE[2].]

a·scor·bic acid (ə-skôr′bĭk) *n.* A white, crystalline vitamin, $C_6H_8O_6$, found in citrus fruits, tomatoes, potatoes, and leafy green vegetables and used to prevent scurvy. Also called *vitamin C.* [A–[1] + SCORB(UT)IC.]

as·co·spore (ăs′kə-spôr′, -spōr′) *n.* A sexually produced fungal spore formed within an ascus. **—as′co·spo′rous** (-spôr′əs, -spōr′-, ăs-kŏs′pər-əs), **as′co·spor′ic** (-spôr′ĭk, -spŏr′-) *adj.*

as·cot (ăs′kət, -kŏt′) *n.* A broad neck scarf knotted so that its ends are laid flat with one end upon the other. [After the racetrack near ASCOT.]

As·cot (ăs′kət). A village of south-central England southwest of London. The Royal Ascot horse races, initiated by Queen Anne in 1711, are held annually in June on Ascot Heath.

as·cribe (ə-skrīb′) *v.* *—tr.* **-cribed, -crib·ing, -cribes. 1.** To attribute to a specified cause, source, or origin: *ascribed the poor harvest to drought.* See Synonyms at **attribute. 2.** To assign as a quality or characteristic: *ascribed jealousy to the critics.* [Middle English *ascriben,* from Old French *ascrivre,* from Latin *ascrībere* : *ad-,* ad- + *scrībere,* to write; see **skrībh-** in Appendix.]

as·crip·tion (ə-skrĭp′shən) *n.* **1.** The act of ascribing. **2.** A statement that ascribes. [Latin *ascrīptiō, ascrīptiōn-,* addendum, from *ascrīptus,* past participle of *ascrībere,* to ascribe. See ASCRIBE.] **—as·crip′tive** *adj.*

ASCU *abbr.* Association of State Colleges and Universities.

As·cu·lum (ăs′kyə-ləm). An ancient Roman town of southeast Italy south of present-day Foggia. Pyrrhus of Epirus defeated a Roman force here in 279 B.C. but suffered a heavy loss of troops.

as·cus (ăs′kəs) *n., pl.* **as·ci** (ăs′ī′, -kī′). *Botany.* A membranous, often club-shaped structure in which typically eight ascospores are formed through sexual reproduction of ascomycetes. [New Latin, from Greek *askos,* bag.]

ASE *abbr.* American Stock Exchange.

–ase *suff.* Enzyme: *amylase.* [From DIASTASE.]

a·sep·a·lous (ā-sĕp′ə-ləs) *adj.* *Botany.* Having no sepals.

a·sep·sis (ə-sĕp′sĭs, ā-) *n.* **1.** The state of being free of pathogenic microorganisms. **2.** The process of removing pathogenic microorganisms or protecting against infection by such organisms.

a·sep·tic (ə-sĕp′tĭk, ā-) *adj.* **1.a.** Free of pathogenic microorganisms: *aseptic surgical instruments.* **b.** Using methods to protect against infection by pathogenic microorganisms: *aseptic surgical techniques.* **2.** Lacking animation or emotion: *an aseptic smile.* **—a·sep′ti·cal·ly** *adv.* **—a·sep′ti·cism** *n.*

a·sex·u·al (ā-sĕk′shōō-əl) *adj.* **1.** Having no evident sex or sex organs; sexless. **2.** Relating to, produced by, or involving reproduction that occurs without the union of male and female gametes, as in binary fission or budding. **3.** Lacking interest in or desire for sex. **—a·sex′u·al′i·ty** (-ăl′ĭ-tē) *n.* **—a·sex′u·al·ly** *adv.*

as far as *conj.* To the degree or extent that: *They returned at nine, as far as we know.*

as for *prep.* With regard to.

asg. *abbr.* **1.** Assigned. **2.** Assignment.

As·gard (ăs′gärd′, äz′-) *n.* *Mythology.* The heavenly residence of the Norse gods and slain heroes of war.

asgd. *abbr.* Assigned.

asgmt. *abbr.* Assignment.

ash[1] (ăsh) *n.* **1.** The grayish-white to black powdery residue left when something is burned. **2.** *Geology.* Pulverized particulate matter ejected by volcanic eruption. **3. ashes.** Ruins: *the ashes of a lost culture.* **4. ashes.** Human remains, especially after cremation or decay. [Middle English *asshe,* from Old English *æsce.* See **as-** in Appendix.]

ash[2] (ăsh) *n.* **1.** Any of various chiefly deciduous ornamental or timber trees of the genus *Fraxinus,* having opposite, pinnately compound leaves, clusters of small flowers, and one-seeded winged fruits. **2.** The strong, elastic wood of this tree, used for furniture, tool handles, and sporting goods such as baseball bats. **3.** *Linguistics.* The letter *æ* in Old English and some modern phonetic alphabets, representing the vowel sound of Modern English *ash.* [Middle English *asshe,* from Old English *æsc.*]

a·shamed (ə-shāmd′) *adj.* **1.** Feeling shame or guilt: *Are you ashamed for having lied?* **2.** Feeling inferior, inadequate, or embarrassed: *ashamed of my torn coat.* **3.** Reluctant through fear of humiliation or shame: *ashamed to ask for help.* [Middle English, from Old English *āsceamod,* past participle of *āsceamian,* to feel shame : *ā-,* intensive pref. + *sceamian,* to feel shame.]

A·shan·ti[1] (ə-shăn′tē, ə-shän′-) also **A·san·te** (-sän′tē) *n., pl.* **Ashanti** or **-tis** also **Asante** or **-tes. 1.** A member of an Akan people of Ghana, formerly united in the Ashanti kingdom. **2.** The Twi language of the Ashanti.

A·shan·ti[2] (ə-shăn′tē, -shän′-). A region and former kingdom of western Africa in present-day central Ghana. The powerful Ashanti confederation of states, formed in the late 17th century, was defeated by the British in 1896 and annexed to the British Gold Coast colony in 1901.

♦ **ash·cake** (ăsh′kāk′) *n.* *Chiefly Southern U.S.* See **johnnycake.** See Regional Note at **johnnycake.** [From its being baked in hot ashes.]

ash·can or **ash can** (ăsh′kăn′) *n.* **1.** A large, usually metal receptacle for trash. **2.** *Slang.* A depth change.

Ash·can school (ăsh′kăn′) *n.* A group of U.S. painters of the early 20th century who painted realistic scenes of everyday urban life.

Ash·croft (ăsh′krôft′, -krŏft′), Dame **Peggy.** Originally Edith Margaret Emily Ashcroft. 1907–1991. British actress who won an Academy Award for *A Passage to India* (1984).

Ash·dod (ăsh′dŏd′, äsh-dōd′). A city of southwest Israel on the Mediterranean Sea west of Jerusalem near the site of ancient **Ashdod,** an important Philistine city-state that was settled as early as the Bronze Age. Population, 68,900.

Ashe (ăsh), **Arthur Robert, Jr.** Born 1943. American tennis player who was the first Black player to win the U.S. Open singles championship (1968) and the Wimbledon singles title (1975).

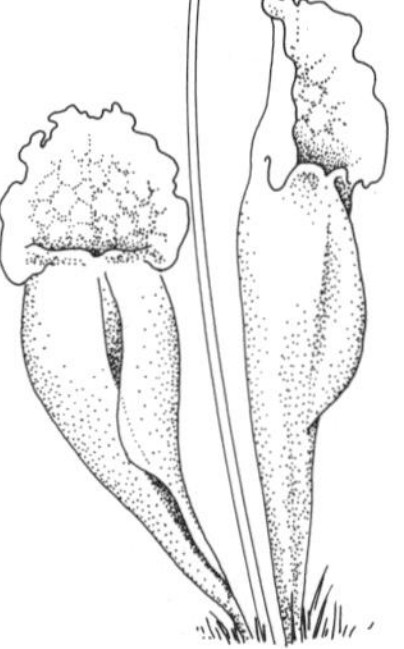

ascidium
Pitcher plant
Sarracenia purpurea

ash[2]
White ash
Fraxinus americana

ash·en¹ (ăsh′ən) *adj.* **1.** Consisting of ashes. **2.** Resembling ashes, especially in color; very pale: *A face ashen with grief.*

ash·en² (ăsh′ən) *adj.* Of, relating to, or made from the wood of the ash tree.

Ash·er (ăsh′ər). In the Old Testament, a son of Jacob and the forebear of one of the tribes of Israel.

Ashe·ville (ăsh′vĭl′). A city of western North Carolina in the Blue Ridge west-northwest of Charlotte. A popular tourist center, it is the site of Thomas Wolfe's home and of Biltmore, a magnificent mansion with extensive parks and gardens built by George Washington Vanderbilt. Population, 53,583.

Ash·ke·lon (ăsh′kə-lŏn′, äsh′kĕ-lôn′). See **Ashqelon.**

Ash·ke·naz·i (äsh′kə-nä′zē) *n., pl.* **-naz·im** (-năz′ĭm, -nä′zĭm). A member of the branch of European Jews, historically Yiddish-speaking, who settled in central and northern Europe. [From Medieval Hebrew *Ashkenaz,* Germany, from Hebrew *Ashkĕnāz,* one of Noah's grandsons, name of a neighboring but unidentified nation.] **—Ash′ke·naz′ic** (-nä′zĭk) *adj.*

Ash·ke·na·zy (äsh′kə-nä′zē), **Vladimir Davidovitch.** Born 1937. Soviet pianist noted for his intellectual interpretation of classical, romantic, and modern music.

Ash·kha·bad (äsh′kä-băd′, -KHä-bät′). The capital of Turkmenistan, in the south-central part of the republic. It was founded as a fortress in 1881. A major earthquake in 1948 virtually destroyed the old city. Population, 356,000.

Ash·land (ăsh′lənd). **1.** A city of northeast Kentucky on the Ohio–West Virginia border. Settled in 1786, it is a shipping point with varied industries. Population, 27,064. **2.** A city of north-central Ohio southeast of Cleveland. It is a manufacturing center in an agricultural region. Population, 20,326.

ash·lar (ăsh′lər) *n.* **1.a.** A squared block of building stone. **b.** Masonry of such stones. **2.** A thin, dressed rectangle of stone for facing walls. [Middle English *assheler,* from Old French *aisselier,* board, from *aissele,* from Medieval Latin *axicellus,* from Latin *assis.*]

ash-leaved maple (ăsh′lēvd′) or **ash-leaf maple** (-lēf′) *n.* See **box elder.**

a·shore (ə-shôr′, ə-shōr′) *adv.* **1.** To or onto the shore: *driven ashore by the wind.* **2.** On land: *spent the day ashore.*

as how *conj. Informal.* That: *The child allowed as how he had already done his homework.*

Ash·qe·lon or **Ash·ke·lon** (ăsh′kə-lŏn′, äsh′kĕ-lôn′). An ancient city of southwest Palestine on the Mediterranean Sea. Inhabited as early as the third millennium B.C., it was a seat of worship for the goddess Astarte.

ash·ram (äsh′rəm) *n. Hinduism.* A usually secluded residence of a religious community and its guru. [Sanskrit *āśramaḥ* : *ā-,* to + *śramaḥ,* toil, penance, austerity (from *śramati,* he toils, practices austerity).]

Ash·ta·bu·la (ăsh′tə-byo͞o′lə). A city of northeast Ohio on Lake Erie northeast of Cleveland. It is an industrial center in an agricultural region. Population, 23,449.

Ash·ton (ăsh′tən), Sir **Frederick.** 1906–1988. British choreographer whose ballets include *The Dream* (1964) and *A Month in the Country* (1976).

Ash·ton-un·der-Lyne (ăsh′tən-ŭn-dər-līn′). A borough of northwest England, an industrial suburb of Manchester. Population, 218,800.

Ash·to·reth (ăsh′tə-rĕth′) *n. Mythology.* The ancient Syrian and Phoenician goddess of sexual love and fertility.

ash·tray (ăsh′trā′) *n.* A receptacle for tobacco ashes and cigarette butts.

A·shur (ä′sho͝or′) also **As·sur** (ä′so͝or′, ä′sho͝or′) *n.* The principal Assyrian deity.

A·shur·ba·ni·pal (ä′sho͝or-bä′nə-päl′) also **As·sur·ba·ni·pal** (ä′so͝or-). fl. seventh century B.C. King of Assyria (669–626) who was a noted patron of literature and the arts.

Ash Wednesday (ăsh) *n.* The seventh Wednesday before Easter and the first day of Lent, on which many Christians receive a mark of ashes on the forehead as a token of penitence and mortality.

ash·y (ăsh′ē) *adj.* **-i·er, -i·est. 1.** Of, relating to, or covered with ashes. **2.** Having the color of ashes; pale. **—ash′i·ness** *n.*

ASI *abbr.* Air speed indicator.

A·sia (ā′zhə, ā′shə). *Abbr.* **As.** The world's largest continent. It occupies the eastern part of the Eurasian landmass and its adjacent islands and is separated from Europe by the Ural Mountains.

Asia Minor. A peninsula of western Asia between the Black Sea and the Mediterranean Sea. It is generally coterminous with Asian Turkey and is usually considered synonymous with Anatolia.

A·sian (ā′zhən, ā′shən) *adj. Abbr.* **As.** Of or relating to Asia or its peoples, languages, or cultures. **—Asian** *n.* **1.** A native or inhabitant of Asia. **2.** A person of Asian descent.

USAGE NOTE: The term *Asian* is now preferred for persons of South and East Asian ancestry (Indians, Southeast Asians, Chinese, Koreans, Japanese, Indonesians, Filipinos, and others) in place of the term *Oriental,* an older usage that denotes some of these groups. *Oriental* has been objected to on two grounds: because it suggests racial, rather than cultural identity, and because it identifies the place of origin in terms of its location relative to the West (i.e., "from the East"), rather than in absolute terms.

Asian American *n.* A U.S. citizen or resident of Asian descent.

Asian influenza *n.* Influenza caused by a strain of the most common influenza virus (type A), which was first isolated in China during the 1957 epidemic. Also called *Asian flu.*

A·sian·i·za·tion (ā′zhə-nĭ-zā′shən) *n.* **1.** The act or process of making or becoming Asian in character, culture, or outlook. **2.** Development of more complex, integral relations among Asian nations, apart from external involvements.

Asian pear *n.* See **sand pear.**

Asian tiger mosquito *n.* A mosquito *(Aeder albopictus),* once confined to Asia but now present in parts of tropical and subtropical America, that transmits dengue and yellow fever.

A·si·at·ic (ā′zhē-ăt′ĭk, -shē-, -zē-) *adj.* Asian: *the Asiatic reaches of the Soviet Union; a tropical Asiatic plant.*

Asiatic cholera *n.* See **cholera** (sense 1).

a·side (ə-sīd′) *adv.* **1.** To or toward the side: *step aside.* **2.** Out of one's thoughts or mind: *put my doubts aside.* **3.** Apart: *a day set aside for relaxing.* **4.** In reserve; away: *put a little money aside.* **5.** Set out of the way; dispensed with: *All joking aside, can you swim 15 miles?* **—aside** *n.* **1.** A piece of dialogue intended for the audience and supposedly not heard by the other actors on stage. **2.** A remark made in an undertone so as to be inaudible to others nearby. **3.** A parenthetical departure; a digression.

aside from *prep.* Excluding; except for: *Aside from a mild fever, the patient feels fine.*

as if *conj.* **1.** In the same way that it would be if: *looked as if she were made of ice.* **2.** That: *It seemed as if the meeting would never end.*

As·i·mov (ăz′ĭ-môf′, -mŏf′), **Isaac.** 1920–1992. Russian-born American scientist and prolific writer whose works include popular explanations of scientific principles and volumes of science fiction, including *The Foundation Trilogy.*

as·i·nine (ăs′ə-nīn′) *adj.* **1.** Utterly stupid or silly: *asinine behavior.* **2.** Of, relating to, or resembling an ass. [Latin *asinīnus,* of an ass, from *asinus,* ass.]

ask (ăsk) *v.* **asked, ask·ing, asks.** *—tr.* **1.** To put a question to. **2.** To seek an answer to: *ask a question.* **3.** To seek information about: *asked directions.* **4.** To make a request of or for: *asked me for money; asking a favor.* **5.** To require or call for as a price or condition: *asked ten dollars for the book.* **6.** To expect or demand: *ask too much of a child.* **7.** To invite: *asked them to dinner.* **8.** *Archaic.* To publish, as marriage banns. *—intr.* **1.** To make inquiry; seek information. **2.** To make a request: *asked for help.* ***—idiom.*** **ask for it** (or **trouble).** *Informal.* To persist in an action despite the likelihood that it will result in difficulty or punishment. [Middle English *asken,* from Old English *āscian.* See **ais-** in Appendix.]

SYNONYMS: *ask, question, inquire, query, interrogate, examine, quiz.* These verbs mean to seek information from a person. *Ask* is the most neutral term: *asked her what was wrong; asked the way to the library; ask too many questions. Question* often implies the asking of a series of questions, as in determining the scope of a problem: *The prosecutor questioned the witness in great detail. Inquire,* which often implies a comprehensive search for knowledge or truth, in this sense refers to a simple request for information: *inquired where the books were kept; will inquire how we can be of help; inquired about her health. Query* usually suggests questioning to settle a doubt: *The proofreader queried the spelling of the word. Interrogate,* a more formal word, applies especially to official questioning: *The suspects were called in and interrogated by detectives. Examine* refers particularly to close and detailed questioning to ascertain the extent of a person's knowledge or the adequacy of his or her qualifications: *At the end of the semester students are examined in every subject. Only lawyers who have been examined and certified by the bar association are admitted to practice. Quiz* is used most frequently to denote the informal examination of students to verify their comprehension of classwork or reading: *The teacher quizzed the pupils on the multiplication tables.*

a·skance (ə-skăns′) also **a·skant** (ə-skănt′) *adv.* **1.** With disapproval, suspicion, or distrust. **2.** With a sideways glance; obliquely. [Origin unknown.]

a·skew (ə-skyo͞o′) *adv. & adj.* To one side; awry: *rugs lying askew.* [Probably A-² + SKEW.]

ask·ing price (ăs′kĭng) *n.* The price at which an item is offered for sale.

ASL *abbr.* American Sign Language.

a·slant (ə-slănt′) *adv. & adj.* At a slant; obliquely. **—aslant** *prep.* Obliquely over or across.

a·sleep (ə-slēp′) *adj.* **1.** In a state of sleep; sleeping. **2.a.** Inactive; dormant. **b.** Indifferent: *politicians who are asleep to the needs of their constituents.* **3.** Numb: *My leg is asleep.* **4.** Dead. **—asleep** *adv.* **1.** In or into a state of sleep. **2.** In or into a state of apathy or indifference. **3.** Into the sleep of the dead.

as long as *conj.* **1.** Since: *As long as you've offered, I accept.* **2.** On the condition that: *I will cooperate as long as I am notified on time.*

a·slope (ə-slōp′) *adv. & adj.* At a slope or slant.

a·slosh (ə-slŏsh′) *adv. & adj.* Awash.

As·ma·ra (ăz-mä′rə). A city of northern Ethiopia near the Red Sea at an altitude of about 2,227 m (7,300 ft). It was used as a base for the Italian invasion of Ethiopia (1935–1936). Population, 474,241.

ASME *abbr.* American Society of Mechanical Engineers.

As·mo·de·us (ăz′mə-dē′əs, ăs′-) *n.* The king of the demons in Jewish demonology.

As·nières-sur-Seine (ä-nyĕr′sür-sān′, -sĕn′). A city of north-central France, a residential suburb of Paris. Population, 71,077.

A·so (ä′sō′), **Mount.** Also **A·so-san** (ä′sō-sän′). A volcanic mountain of central Kyushu, Japan. It is topped by one of the world's largest calderas, containing five volcanic cones, one of which is active. The highest cone rises to 1,593 m (5,223 ft).

a·so·cial (ā-sō′shəl) *adj.* **1.** Not social: *"Bears are asocial, secretive animals"* (David Graber). **2.** Avoiding or averse to the society of others; not sociable: *"It's not that you're so asocial, but a man who likes people doesn't wind up in the Antarctic"* (Saul Bellow). **3.** Unable or unwilling to conform to normal standards of social behavior; antisocial: *"crime, riots, drug use and other asocial behavior"* (Derek Shearer). **4.** Inconsiderate of others; self-centered. **—asocial** *n.* One that exhibits behavior and characteristics deemed asocial: *"the other, and usually neglected, victims . . . the asocials . . . those who violated the Nazi work ethic and social norms"* (Mary Nolan).

as of *prep.* On; at: *The project was terminated as of January 1.*

A·so·ka (ə-sō′kə). Known as "the Great." Died 232 B.C. King of Magadha (273–232) who was converted to Buddhism and adopted it as the state religion.

A·so-san (ä′sō-sän′). See Mount **Aso.**

asp (ăsp) *n.* Any of several venomous snakes of Africa, Asia, and Europe, such as the small cobra *(Naja haje)* or the horned viper *(Cerastes cornutus).* [Middle English *aspis,* from Latin, from Greek.]

as·par·a·gin·ase (ə-spăr′ə-jə-nās′, -nāz′) *n.* An enzyme isolated from bacteria that catalyzes the hydrolysis of asparagine and is used in the chemotherapeutic treatment of leukemia.

as·par·a·gine (ə-spăr′ə-jēn′) *n.* A crystalline amino acid, $C_4H_8N_2O_3$, found in many plants, that is easily hydrolyzed to aspartic acid. [ASPARAG(US) + –INE[2].]

as·par·a·gus (ə-spăr′ə-gəs) *n.* **1.** The tender young shoots of a Eurasian plant *(Asparagus officinalis),* eaten as a vegetable. **2.** Any of various perennial plants of the Old World genus *Asparagus* having leaflike stems, scalelike leaves, and small flowers. [Latin, from Greek *asparagos.*]

asparagus bean *n.* See **yard-long bean.**

asparagus beetle *n.* A small, spotted beetle *(Crioceris asparagi)* that infests and damages asparagus plants.

asparagus fern *n.* A fernlike, evergreen, southern African plant *(Asparagus setaceus)* having small whitish flowers and red or purple-black berries.

asparagus pea *n.* An Asiatic twining herb *(Psophocarpus tetragonolobus)* having tuberous roots and long, four-angled pods. Also called *winged bean.*

as·par·tame (ăs′pər-tām′, ə-spär′-) *n.* An artificial sweetener, $C_{14}H_{18}N_2O_5$, formed from aspartic acid. [ASPART(IC ACID) + (PHENYL)A(LANINE) + M(ETHYL) + E(STER).]

a·spar·tate (ə-spär′tāt) *n.* A salt or ester of aspartic acid. [ASPART(IC ACID) + –ATE[2].]

as·par·tic acid (ə-spär′tĭk) *n.* A nonessential amino acid, $C_4H_7NO_4$, found especially in young sugar cane and sugar-beet molasses. [From ASPARAGUS (from its being obtained from an amino acid found in asparagus).]

as·par·to·kin·ase (ə-spär′tō-kī′nās) *n.* An enzyme that catalyzes aspartic acid phosphorylation by ATP. [ASPART(IC ACID) + KINASE.]

As·pa·sia (ă-spā′zhə). fl. c. 440 B.C. Greek courtesan and lover of Pericles who was noted for her wisdom, wit, and beauty.

A.S.P.C.A. *abbr.* American Society for the Prevention of Cruelty to Animals.

as·pect (ăs′pĕkt) *n.* **1.** A particular look or facial expression; mien: *"He was serious of aspect but wholly undistinguished"* (Louis Auchincloss). **2.** Appearance to the eye, especially from a specific vantage point. **3.** A way in which something can be viewed by the mind: *looked at all aspects of the situation.* See Synonyms at **phase. 4.** A position facing or commanding a given direction; exposure. **5.** A side or surface facing in a particular direction: *the ventral aspect of the body.* **6. a.** The configuration of the stars or planets in relation to one another. **b.** This configuration, thought by astrologers to influence human affairs. **7.** *Grammar.* A category of the verb designating primarily the relation of the action to the passage of time, especially in reference to completion, duration, or repetition. **8.** *Archaic.* An act of looking or gazing. [Middle English, from Latin *aspectus,* a view, from past participle of *aspicere,* to look at : *ad-,* ad- + *specere,* to look; see **spek-** in Appendix.]

aspect ratio *n.* **1.** The width-to-height ratio of a television image. **2.** The span-to-mean-chord ratio of an airfoil.

as·pen (ăs′pən) *n.* Any of several trees of the genus *Populus* having leaves attached by flattened leafstalks so that they flutter readily in the wind. **—aspen** *adj.* **1.** Of or relating to one of these trees. **2.** Shivering or trembling like the leaves of one of these trees. [Middle English *aspe,* from Old English *æspe.*]

As·pen (ăs′pən). A city of west-central Colorado in the Sawatch Range of the Rocky Mountains. Founded c. 1879 by silver prospectors, it is now a fashionable ski resort. Population, 3,678.

as·per·ate (ăs′pə-rāt′) *tr.v.* **-at·ed, -at·ing, -ates.** To make uneven; roughen. [Latin *asperāre, asperāt-,* from *asper,* rough.]

as·per·ges (ə-spûr′jēz) *n. Roman Catholic Church.* The ceremony of sprinkling the altar, clergy, and congregation with holy water. [From Latin *asperges (me),* you will sprinkle (me), the first words of the rite, from *aspergere,* to sprinkle. See ASPERSE.]

as·per·gill (ăs′pər-jĭl) *n. Roman Catholic Church.* Variant of **aspergillum.**

as·per·gil·lo·sis (ăs′pər-jə-lō′sĭs) *n.* An infection or a disease caused by fungi of the genus *Aspergillus.* [ASPERGILL(US) + –OSIS.]

as·per·gil·lum (ăs′pər-jĭl′əm) or **as·per·gill** (-jĭl) *n., pl.* **-gil·la** (-jĭl′ə) or **-gil·lums.** *Roman Catholic Church.* An instrument, such as a brush or a perforated container, used for sprinkling holy water. [New Latin from Latin *aspergere,* to sprinkle. See ASPERSE.]

as·per·gil·lus (ăs′pər-jĭl′əs) *n., pl.* **-gil·li** (-jĭl′ī′). Any of various fungi of the genus *Aspergillus,* which includes many common molds. [New Latin, from *aspergillum,* aspergill (from its resemblance to an aspergillum brush). See ASPERGILLUM.]

as·per·i·ty (ă-spĕr′ĭ-tē) *n.* **1. a.** Roughness or harshness, as of surface, sound, or climate: *the asperity of northern winters.* **b.** Severity; rigor. **2.** Harshness of manner; ill temper or irritability. [Middle English *asperite,* from Old French *asprete,* from Latin *asperitās,* from *asper,* rough.]

as·perse (ə-spûrs′) *tr.v.* **-persed, -pers·ing, -pers·es. 1.** To spread false or damaging charges or insinuations against. See Synonyms at **malign. 2.** To sprinkle, especially with holy water. [Middle English, to besprinkle, from Latin *aspergere, aspers-* : *ad-,* ad- + *spargere,* to strew.]

as·per·sion (ə-spûr′zhən, -shən) *n.* **1. a.** An unfavorable or damaging remark; slander: *Don't cast aspersions on my honesty.* **b.** The act of defaming or slandering. **2.** A sprinkling, especially with holy water.

as·phalt (ăs′fôlt′) *n.* **1.** A brownish-black solid or semisolid mixture of bitumens obtained from native deposits or as a petroleum byproduct, used in paving, roofing, and waterproofing. **2.** Mixed asphalt and crushed stone gravel or sand, used for paving or roofing. **—asphalt** *tr.v.* **-phalted, -phalt·ing, -phalts.** To pave or coat with this mixture. [Middle English *aspalt,* from Medieval Latin *asphaltus,* from Greek *asphaltos.*] **—as·phal′tic** *adj.*

as·phal·tite (ăs′fôl-tīt′) *n.* A solid, dark-colored complex of hydrocarbons found in natural veins and deposits.

asphalt jungle *n.* A huge city or a specified urban area, typically congested and crime-ridden.

a·spher·ic (ā-sfîr′ĭk, ā-sfĕr′-) also **a·spher·i·cal** (-ĭ-kəl) *adj.* Varying slightly from sphericity and having only slight aberration, as a lens.

as·pho·del (ăs′fə-dĕl′) *n.* **1. a.** Any of several chiefly Mediterranean plants of the genera *Asphodeline* and *Asphodelus* in the lily family, having linear leaves and elongate clusters of white, pink, or yellow flowers. **b.** Any of several other plants, such as the bog asphodel. **2.** In Greek poetry and mythology, the flowers of Hades and the dead, sacred to Persephone. **3.** In early English and French poetry, the daffodil. [Latin *asphodelus,* from Greek *asphodelos.*]

as·phyx·i·a (ăs-fĭk′sē-ə) *n.* A condition in which an extreme decrease in the amount of oxygen in the body accompanied by an increase of carbon dioxide leads to loss of consciousness or death. Asphyxia can be induced by choking, drowning, electric shock, injury, or the inhalation of toxic gases. [New Latin, from Greek *asphuxia,* stopping of the pulse : *a-,* not; see A–[1] + *sphuxis,* heartbeat (from *sphuzein, sphug-,* to throb).]

as·phyx·i·ant (ăs-fĭk′sē-ənt) *adj.* Inducing or tending to induce asphyxia. **—asphyxiant** *n.* A substance, such as a toxic gas, or an event, such as drowning, that induces asphyxia.

as·phyx·i·ate (ăs-fĭk′sē-āt′) *v.* **-at·ed, -at·ing, -ates.** —*tr.* To cause asphyxia in; smother. —*intr.* To undergo asphyxia; suffocate. **—as·phyx′i·a′tion** *n.* **—as·phyx′i·a′tor** *n.*

as·pic[1] (ăs′pĭk) *n.* A clear jelly typically made of stock and gelatin and used as a glaze or garnish or to make a mold of meat, fish, or vegetables. [French, from *aspic,* asp (from the resemblance of the jelly's coloration to an asp's). See ASPIC[2].]

as·pic[2] (ăs′pĭk) *n. Archaic.* An asp. [French, from Old French, alteration of *aspe,* from Latin *aspis.* See ASP.]

as·pi·dis·tra (ăs′pĭ-dĭs′trə) *n.* Any of several eastern Asian plants of the genus *Aspidistra* in the lily family, especially *A. elatior,* which has large evergreen basal leaves and small, brownish bell-shaped flowers and is widely cultivated as a houseplant. Also called *cast-iron plant.* [New Latin *Aspidistra,* genus name, from Greek *aspis, aspid-,* shield.]

as·pi·rant (ăs′pər-ənt, ə-spīr′-) *n.* One who aspires, as to advancement, honors, or a high position. **—aspirant** *adj.* Seeking recognition, distinction, or advancement.

as·pi·rate (ăs′pə-rāt′) *tr.v.* **-rat·ed, -rat·ing, -rates. 1.** *Linguistics.* **a.** To pronounce (a vowel or word) with the initial

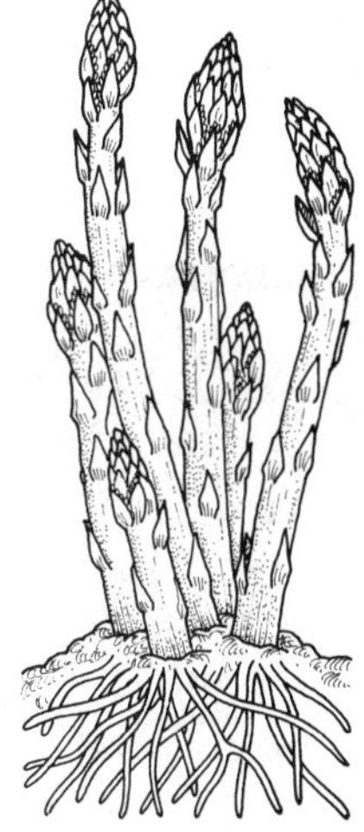

asparagus
Asparagus officinalis

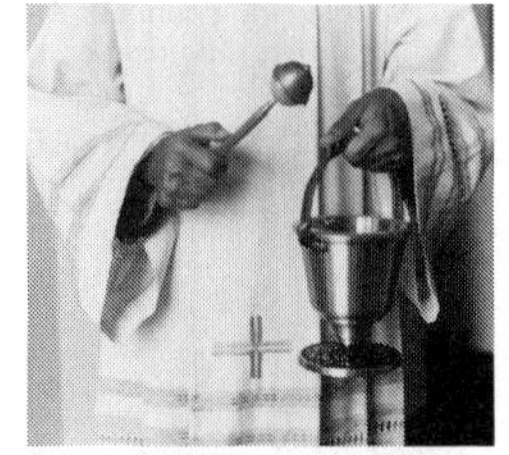

aspergillum
Priest with aspergillum in right hand

ă pat	oi boy
ā pay	ou out
âr care	ŏŏ took
ä father	ōō boot
ĕ pet	ŭ cut
ē be	ûr urge
ĭ pit	th thin
ī pie	*th* this
îr pier	hw which
ŏ pot	zh vision
ō toe	ə about, item
ô paw	♦ regionalism

Stress marks: ′ (primary); ′ (secondary), as in **dictionary** (dĭk′shə-nĕr′ē)

release of breath associated with English *h,* as in *hurry.* **b.** To follow (a consonant, especially a stop consonant) with a puff of breath that is clearly audible before the next sound begins, as in English *pit* or *kit.* **2.** To draw (something) into the lungs; inhale. **3.** *Medicine.* To remove (liquids or gases) by means of a suction device. **—aspirate** (-pər-ĭt) *n.* **1.** *Linguistics.* **a.** The speech sound represented by English *h.* **b.** The puff of air accompanying the release of a stop consonant. **c.** A speech sound followed by a puff of breath. **2.** *Medicine.* Matter removed by aspiration. [Latin *aspirāre, aspirāt-,* to breath on : *ad-,* ad- + *spirāre,* to breathe.]

as·pi·ra·tion (ăs′pə-rā′shən) *n.* **1.** Expulsion of breath in speech. **2.** *Linguistics.* **a.** The pronunciation of a consonant with an aspirate. **b.** A speech sound produced with an aspirate. **3.** The act of breathing in; inhalation. **4.** *Medicine.* The process of removing fluids or gases from the body with a suction device. **5.a.** A strong desire for high achievement. **b.** An object of such desire; an ambition.

ass[1]
Somali ass
Equus africanus somalicus

as·pi·ra·tor (ăs′pə-rā′tər) *n.* **1.** A device for removing liquids or gases by suction, especially an instrument that uses suction to remove substances, such as mucus or serum, from a body cavity. **2.** A suction pump used to create a partial vacuum.

as·pir·a·to·ry (ə-spīr′ə-tôr′ē, -tōr′ē) *adj.* Of, relating to, or suited for breathing or suction.

as·pire (ə-spīr′) *intr.v.* **-pired, -pir·ing, -pires.** **1.** To have a great ambition; desire strongly: *aspired to stardom.* **2.** To strive toward an end: *aspiring to great knowledge.* **3.** To soar. [Middle English *aspiren,* from *aspirer,* from Latin *aspīrāre,* to desire. See ASPIRATE.] **—as·pir′er** *n.* **—as·pir′ing·ly** *adv.*

as·pi·rin (ăs′pər-ĭn, -prĭn) *n.* **1.** A white, crystalline compound, $CH_3COOC_6H_4COOH$, derived from salicylic acid and commonly used in tablet form to relieve pain and reduce fever and inflammation. Also called *acetylsalicylic acid.* **2.** A tablet of aspirin. [Originally a trademark.]

a·squint (ə-skwĭnt′) *adv. & adj.* With a sidelong glance. [Middle English : *a-,* on; see A–[2] + *-squint;* akin to *-skwyn,* in Middle English *of skwyn,* obliquely.]

As·quith (ăs′kwĭth), **Herbert Henry.** First Earl of Oxford and Asquith. 1852–1928. British Liberal politician and prime minister (1908–1916) who introduced unemployment insurance and old-age pensions and supported the Parliament Act of 1911, which established salaries for elected members and restricted the power of veto in the House of Lords.

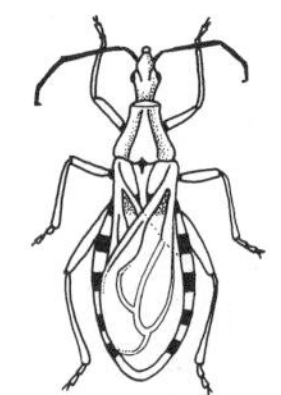

assassin bug
Bloodsucking conenose
Triatoma sanguisuga

ASR *abbr.* Air-sea rescue.

as regards *prep.* In regard to.

ass[1] (ăs) *n., pl.* **ass·es** (ăs′ĭz). **1.** Any of several hoofed mammals of the genus *Equus,* resembling and closely related to the horses but having a smaller build and longer ears, and including the domesticated donkey. **2.** A vain, self-important, silly, or aggressively stupid person. [Middle English *asse,* from Old English *assa,* perhaps of Celtic origin, ultimately from Latin *asinus.*]

ass[2] (ăs) *n., pl.* **ass·es** (ăs′ĭz). *Vulgar Slang.* **1.a.** The buttocks. **b.** The anus. **2.** Sexual intercourse. [Middle English *ars,* from Old English *ears.* See **ors-** in Appendix.]

As·sad (ä-säd′), **Hafez al-.** Born c. 1928. Syrian political leader who seized control of the government in 1970 and was elected president in 1971.

as·sa·gai (ăs′ə-gī′) *n.* Variant of **assegai.**

as·sai[1] (ä-sī′) *n.* **1.** Any of several feather-leaved South American palms, especially *Euterpe edulis* and *E. oleracea,* which are important sources of heart of palm. **2.** A beverage made from the fleshy purple fruit of one of these palms. [Portuguese *assaí,* from Tupi *assahi.*]

as·sai[2] (ä-sī′) *adv. Music.* Very. Used in tempo directions: *allegro assai.* [Italian, from Vulgar Latin **ad satis,* to sufficiency. See ASSET.]

assembly line
In a flashlight factory

as·sail (ə-sāl′) *tr.v.* **-sailed, -sail·ing, -sails.** **1.** To attack with or as if with violent blows; assault. **2.** To attack verbally, as with ridicule or censure. See Synonyms at **attack.** **3.** To trouble; beset: *was assailed by doubts.* [Middle English *assailen,* from Old French *asalir, asaill-,* from Vulgar Latin **assalīre,* variant of Latin *assilīre,* to jump on : *ad-,* onto; see AD– + *salīre,* to jump; see **sel-** in Appendix.] **—as·sail′a·ble** *adj.* **—as·sail′a·ble·ness** *n.* **—as·sail′er** *n.* **—as·sail′ment** *n.*

as·sail·ant (ə-sā′lənt) *n.* A person who attacks another.

As·sam (ă-săm′). A former kingdom of extreme northeast India, now a state separated from the rest of the country by Bangladesh. The kingdom was founded by invaders from Burma and China in the 13th century.

As·sam·ese (ăs′ə-mēz′, -mēs′) *adj.* Of or relating to Assam or its people, language, or culture. **—Assamese** *n., pl.* **Assamese.** **1.** A native or inhabitant of Assam. **2.** The Indic language of the Assamese.

as·sas·sin (ə-săs′ĭn) *n.* **1.** One who murders by surprise attack, especially one who carries out a plot to kill a prominent person. **2. Assassin.** A member of a secret order of Moslem fanatics who terrorized and killed Christian Crusaders and others. [French, from Medieval Latin *assassīnus,* from Arabic *ḥaššāšīn,* pl. of *ḥaššāš,* hashish user, from *ḥašīš,* hashish.]

WORD HISTORY: At first glance, one would be hard-pressed to find a link between pleasure and the acts of assassins. Such was not the case, however, with those who gave us the word *assassin.* They were members of a secret Islamic order originating in the 11th century who believed it was a religious duty to harass and murder their enemies. The most important members of the order were those who actually did the killing. Having been promised paradise in return for dying in action, the killers, it is said, were made to yearn for paradise by being given a life of pleasure that included the use of hashish. Hence, the name for the secret order as a whole, *ḥaššāšīn,* "hashish users." After passing through French or Italian, the word came into English and is recorded in 1603 with reference to the Moslem assassins.

as·sas·si·nate (ə-săs′ə-nāt′) *tr.v.* **-nat·ed, -nat·ing, -nates.** **1.** To murder (a prominent person) by surprise attack, as for political reasons. **2.** To destroy or injure treacherously: *assassinate a rival's character.* **—as·sas′si·na′tion** *n.* **—as·sas′si·na′tive** *adj.* **—as·sas′si·na′tor** *n.*

assassin bug *n.* Any of various predatory bugs of the family Reduviidae, which have short, curved, powerful beaks used to prey on other insects or, in certain genera, modified to suck blood from mammals. Also called *reduviid.*

As·sa·teague Island (ăs′ə-tēg′). A long narrow island along the coast of Maryland and Virginia separating Chincoteague Bay from the Atlantic Ocean. It is a popular resort area.

as·sault (ə-sôlt′) *n.* **1.** A violent physical or verbal attack. **2.a.** A military attack, such as one launched against a fortified area or place. **b.** The concluding stage of an attack in which close combat occurs with the enemy. **3.** *Law.* **a.** An unlawful threat or attempt to do bodily injury to another. **b.** The act or an instance of unlawfully threatening or attempting to injure another. **4.a.** *Law.* Sexual assault. **b.** The crime of rape. **—assault** *v.* **-sault·ed, -sault·ing, -saults.** *—tr.* **1.** To make an assault upon; attack. See Synonyms at **attack.** **2.** To rape. *—intr.* To make an assault. [Middle English *assaut,* from Old French, from Vulgar Latin **assaltus,* variant of Latin *assultus,* from past participle of *assilīre,* to jump on. See ASSAIL.] **—as·sault′er** *n.*

assault and battery *n. Law.* An assault upon a victim that is carried out by striking the victim, knocking the victim down, or otherwise doing violence to the victim.

as·saul·tive (ə-sôl′tĭv) *adj.* Inclined to or suggestive of violent attack.

as·say (ăs′ā′, ă-sā′) *n.* **1.a.** Qualitative or quantitative analysis of a substance, especially of an ore or drug, to determine its components. **b.** A substance to be so analyzed. **c.** The result of such an analysis. **2.** An analysis or examination. **3.** *Archaic.* An attempt; an essay. **—assay** (ă-sā′, ăs′ā′) *v.* **-sayed, -say·ing, -says.** *—tr.* **1.** To subject to chemical analysis. **2.** To examine by trial or experiment; put to a test: *assay one's ability to speak Chinese.* **3.** To evaluate; assess: *assayed the situation before taking action.* See Synonyms at **estimate.** **4.** To attempt; try. *—intr.* To be shown by analysis to contain a certain proportion of usually precious metal. [Middle English, from Old French *essai, assai.* See ESSAY.] **—as·say′a·ble** *adj.* **—as·say′er** *n.*

as·se·gai or **as·sa·gai** (ăs′ə-gī′) *n.* **1.** A light spear or lance, especially one with a short shaft and long blade for close combat, used by southern African tribesmen. **2.** A southern African tree *(Curtisia dentata)* having wood used for making spears or lances. [Obsolete French *azagaie,* probably from Old Spanish *azagayah,* from Arabic *az-zaġāyah* : *al,* the + Berber *zaghāyah,* spear.]

as·sem·blage (ə-sĕm′blĭj) *n.* **1.a.** The act of assembling. **b.** The state of being assembled. **2.** A collection of people or things; a gathering. **3.** A fitting together of parts, as those in a machine. **4.** A sculptural composition consisting of an arrangement of miscellaneous objects, such as pieces of metal, cloth, and string. **—as·sem′blag·ist** *n.*

as·sem·ble (ə-sĕm′bəl) *v.* **-bled, -bling, -bles.** *—tr.* **1.** To bring or call together into a group or whole: *assembled the jury.* **2.** To fit together the parts or pieces of: *assemble a machine; assemble data.* *—intr.* To gather together; congregate. See Synonyms at **gather.** [Middle English *assemblen,* from Old French *assembler,* from Vulgar Latin **assimulāre* : Latin *ad-,* ad- + Latin *simul,* together; see **sem-**[1] in Appendix.]

as·sem·bler (ə-sĕm′blər) *n.* **1.** One that assembles, as a worker who puts together components of an item being manufactured. **2.** *Computer Science.* A program operating on symbolic input data to produce the equivalent executable machine code. **3.** *Computer Science.* See **assembly language.**

as·sem·bly (ə-sĕm′blē) *n., pl.* **-blies.** *Abbr.* **assy.** **1.a.** The act of assembling. **b.** The state of being assembled. **2.** A group of persons gathered together for a common reason, as for a legislative, religious, educational, or social purpose. **3. Assembly.** The lower house of the legislature in certain U.S. states. **4.a.** The putting together of manufactured parts to make a completed product, such as a machine or an electronic circuit. **b.** A set of parts so assembled. **5.** A signal by bugle or drum for troops to come together in formation. **6.** *Computer Science.* The automatic translation of symbolic code into machine code.

assembly language *n. Computer Science.* A programming language that is a close approximation of the binary machine code. Also called *assembler.*

assembly line *n.* **1.** An arrangement of workers, machines, and equipment in which the product being assembled passes consecutively from operation to operation until completed. Also called *production line.* **2.** A process in which finished products are turned out in a mechanically efficient, though impersonal, manner: *a university that functions as a sports assembly line.*

as•sem•bly•man (ə-sĕm′blē-mən) *n.* A man who is a member of a legislative assembly.

Assembly of God *n.* A Pentecostal congregation founded in the United States in 1914.

assembly time *n. Computer Science.* The time required for an assembler to translate symbolic language into machine instructions.

as•sem•bly•wom•an (ə-sĕm′blē-wo͝om′ən) *n.* A woman who is a member of a legislative assembly.

as•sent (ə-sĕnt′) *intr.v.* **-sent•ed, -sent•ing, -sents.** To agree, as to a proposal; concur. **—assent** *n.* **1.** Agreement; concurrence: *reached assent on a course of action.* **2.** Acquiescence; consent: *gave my assent.* [Middle English *assenten,* from Old French *assentir,* from Latin *assentārī* : *ad-,* ad- + *sentīre,* to feel; see **sent-** in Appendix.] **—as•sent′er, as•sen′tor** *n.* **—as•sent′ing•ly** *adv.* **—as•sen′tive** *adj.* **—as•sen′tive•ness** *n.*

SYNONYMS: *assent, agree, accede, acquiesce, consent, concur, subscribe.* These verbs denote concurrence with another's views, proposals, or actions. *Assent* implies agreement, as with a statement or a proposal, especially when it results from deliberation: *They readily assented to our suggestion. Agree* and *accede* are related in the sense that assent has been reached after discussion or efforts at persuasion, but *accede* implies that one person or group has yielded, as to the insistence of the other: *"It was not possible to agree to a proposal so extraordinary and unexpected"* (William Robertson). *"In an evil hour this proposal was acceded to"* (Mary E. Herbert). *Acquiesce* suggests passive assent, often despite reservations, because of inability or unwillingness to oppose: *I had to acquiesce in her decision despite my private opinion. Consent* implies voluntary acquiescence to the desire or proposal of another: *Her parents refused to consent to her marriage. Concur* refers to agreement with another's position and may suggest that one has reached the same conclusion independently: *"I concurred with our incumbent in getting up a petition against the Reform Bill"* (George Eliot). *Subscribe* indicates hearty consent or approval: *"I am contented to subscribe to the opinion of the best-qualified judge of our time"* (Sir Walter Scott).

---

as•sen•ta•tion (ăs′ĕn-tā′shən) *n.* Hasty, typically servile agreement with another's opinions.

As•ser (ä′sər), **Tobias Michael Carel.** 1838–1913. Dutch statesman and jurist. He shared the 1911 Nobel Peace Prize.

as•sert (ə-sûrt′) *tr.v.* **-sert•ed, -sert•ing, -serts. 1.** To state or express positively; affirm: *asserted his innocence.* **2.** To defend or maintain (one's rights, for example). **3.** To put (oneself) forward boldly or forcefully in an effort to make an opinion known, for example: *I had to assert myself in the meeting in order to ensure acquisition of the new book.* [Latin *asserere, assert-* : *ad-,* ad- + *serere,* to join; see **ser-[2]** in Appendix.] **—as•sert′a•ble, as•sert′i•ble** *adj.* **—as•sert′er, as•ser′tor** *n.*

SYNONYMS: *assert, asseverate, declare, affirm, aver, avow.* These verbs all mean to make a positive statement. To *assert* is to state one's opinion confidently but often without proof to support it: *"I have endeavored to assert nothing but what I had good authority for"* (William Sewel). *Asseverate* connotes sober sincerity of assertion: *"The taxpayer also asseverates that his return from Greece proves conclusively that his intentions were and are honorable"* (Daily Report for Executives). *Declare* has the approximate force of *assert* but may suggest formality of statement and authority in the speaker: *Congress declared that it would reduce the budget deficit. Affirm* and *aver* stress the speaker's confidence in the validity of the statement: *Scientists cannot affirm the existence of life on other planets. She averred that solitude was necessary for creative work. Avow* implies frank and open acknowledgment or admission: *"thinks the book succeeds in achieving its avowed purpose: to explain how the Court's current role evolved through history"* (Tony Mauro).

---

as•sert•ed (ə-sûr′tĭd) *adj.* Confidently stated to be so but without proof; alleged: *the asserted value of a painting.* **—as•sert′ed•ly** *adv.*

as•ser•tion (ə-sûr′shən) *n.* **1.** The act of asserting. **2.** Something declared or stated positively, often with no support or attempt at proof. **—as•ser′tion•al** *adj.*

as•ser•tive (ə-sûr′tĭv) *adj.* Inclined to bold or confident assertion; aggressively self-assured. **—as•ser′tive•ly** *adv.* **—as•ser′tive•ness** *n.*

assertiveness training *n.* A method of training a person to become more self-confident and boldly affirmative in his or her interpersonal relationships.

as•ses[1] (ăs′ēz′, ăs′ĭz) *n.* Plural of **as[2]**.

ass•es[2] (ăs′ĭz) *n.* Plural of **ass[1]**.

ass•es[3] (ăs′ĭz) *n. Vulgar Slang.* Plural of **ass[2]**.

as•sess (ə-sĕs′) *tr.v.* **-sessed, -sess•ing, -sess•es. 1.** To estimate the value of (property) for taxation. **2.** To set or determine the amount of (a payment, such as a tax or fine). **3.** To charge (a person or property) with a special payment, such as a tax or fine. **4.** To determine the value, significance, or extent of; appraise. See Synonyms at **estimate.** [Middle English *assessen,* from Old French *assesser,* from Latin *assidēre, assess-,* to sit by as an assistant judge : *ad-,* ad- + *sedēre,* to sit; see **sed-** in Appendix.] **—as•sess′a•ble** *adj.*

as•sess•ment (ə-sĕs′mənt) *n.* **1.** The act of assessing; appraisal. **2.** An amount assessed, as for taxation.

as•ses•sor (ə-sĕs′ər) *n.* **1.** An official who evaluates property for taxation. **2.** An assistant to a judge or magistrate, usually selected for special knowledge in a particular area. **—as′ses•so′ri•al** (ăs′ə-sôr′ē-əl, -sōr′-) *adj.*

as•set (ăs′ĕt′) *n.* **1.** A useful or valuable quality, person, or thing; an advantage or a resource: *An agreeable personality is a great asset; proved herself an asset to the company.* **2.** A valuable item that is owned. **3.** A spy working in his or her own country and controlled by the enemy: *"One of our assets working out of Leningrad managed to take a drive out of town"* (Frederick Forsyth). **4. assets. a.** *Accounting.* The entries on a balance sheet showing all properties, tangible and intangible, and claims against others that may be applied, directly or indirectly, to cover the liabilities of a person or business, such as cash, stock, and goodwill. **b.** The entire property owned by a person, especially a bankrupt, that can be used to settle debts. [Back-formation from English *assets,* sufficient goods to settle a testator's debts and legacies, from Anglo-Norman *asetz,* from *asez,* enough, from Vulgar Latin **ad satis,* to sufficiency : Latin *ad-,* ad- + *satis,* enough; see **sā-** in Appendix.]

as•sev•er•ate (ə-sĕv′ə-rāt′) *tr.v.* **-at•ed, -at•ing, -ates.** To declare seriously or positively; affirm. See Synonyms at **assert.** [Latin *asseverāre, asseverāt-* : *ad-,* ad- + *sevērus,* serious; see **wēro-** in Appendix.] **—as•sev′er•a′tion** *n.*

ass•hole (ăs′hōl′) *n. Vulgar Slang.* **1.** The anus. **2.** A thoroughly contemptible, detestable person. [ASS[2] + HOLE.]

as•sib•i•late (ə-sĭb′ə-lāt′) *tr.v.* **-lat•ed, -lat•ing, -lates.** To pronounce with a hissing sound; make sibilant. [AD– + SIBILATE.] **—as•sib′i•la′tion** *n.*

as•si•du•i•ty (ăs′ĭ-do͞o′ĭ-tē, -dyo͞o′-) *n., pl.* **-ties. 1.** Persistent application or diligence; unflagging effort. **2.** Often **assiduities.** Constant personal attention and often obsequious solicitude.

as•sid•u•ous (ə-sĭj′o͞o-əs) *adj.* **1.** Constant in application or attention; diligent: *an assiduous worker who strove for perfection.* See Synonyms at **busy. 2.** Unceasing; persistent: *assiduous research.* [From Latin *assiduus,* from *assidēre,* to attend to : *ad-,* ad- + *sedēre,* to sit; see **sed-** in Appendix.] **—as•sid′u•ous•ly** *adv.* **—as•sid′u•ous•ness** *n.*

as•sign (ə-sīn′) *tr.v.* **-signed, -sign•ing, -signs. 1.** To set apart for a particular purpose; designate. **2.** To select for a duty or office; appoint. **3.** To give out as a task; allot. **4.** To ascribe; attribute. **5.** *Law.* To transfer (property, rights, or interests) from one to another. **6.** To place (a person or a military unit) under a specific command. **—assign** *n. Law.* An assignee. [Middle English *assignen,* from Old French *assigner,* from Latin *assignāre* : *ad-,* ad- + *signāre,* to mark (from *signum,* sign; see **sekʷ-[1]** in Appendix).] **—as•sign′a•bil′i•ty** *n.* **—as•sign′a•ble** *adj.* **—as•sign′a•bly** *adv.* **—as•sign′er** *n.*

SYNONYMS: *assign, allot, apportion, allocate.* These verbs mean to set aside or give out in portions or shares. Both *assign,* which applies to an authoritative act, and *allot* refer to arbitrary distribution, but neither implies equality or fairness of division: *The hardest work was assigned to the strongest laborers. We allot a half hour a day for recreation.* To *apportion* is to divide according to prescribed rules and implies fair distribution: *"The first duty of a legislator is to apportion penalties"* (Walter Savage Landor). *Allocate* usually means to set something apart from a larger quantity, as of money, for a specific purpose or for a particular person or group: *A portion of the budget was allocated for the education of each student.* See also Synonyms at **attribute.**

---

as•sig•nat (ăs′ĭg-năt′, ăs′ēn-yä′) *n.* Any of the notes issued as paper currency in France (1789–1796) by the revolutionary government and secured by confiscated lands. [French, from Latin *assignātus,* past participle of *assignāre,* to assign. See ASSIGN.]

as•sig•na•tion (ăs′ĭg-nā′shən) *n.* **1.** The act of assigning. **2.** Something assigned, especially an allotment. **3.** An appointment for a meeting between lovers; a tryst. See Synonyms at **engagement. —as′sig•na′tion•al** *adj.*

as•signed risk (ə-sīnd′) *n.* A poor risk that an insurance company is compelled to cover under state laws.

as•sign•ee (ə-sī′nē′, ăs′ĭ-nē′) *n. Law.* **1.** A party to which a transfer of property, rights, or interest is made. **2.** One appointed to act for another; a deputy or an agent.

as•sign•ment (ə-sīn′mənt) *n. Abbr.* **asg., asgmt. 1.** The act of assigning. **2.** Something, such as a task, that is assigned. See Synonyms at **task. 3.** A position or post of duty to which one is assigned. **4.** *Law.* **a.** The transfer of a claim, right, interest, or property from one to another. **b.** The instrument by which this transfer is effected.

as•sign•or (ə-sī′nôr′, ə-sī′nər, ăs′ə-nôr′) *n. Law.* One that makes an assignment.

as•sim•i•la•ble (ə-sĭm′ə-lə-bəl) *adj.* That can be assimilated: *assimilable nutrients; assimilable information.* **—as•sim′i•la•bil′i•ty** *n.*

as•sim•i•late (ə-sĭm′ə-lāt′) *v.* **-lat•ed, -lat•ing, -lates.** —*tr.* **1.** *Physiology.* **a.** To consume and incorporate nutrients into the body after digestion. **b.** To transform (food) into living tissue by

ă pat	oi boy
ā pay	ou out
âr care	o͝o took
ä father	o͞o boot
ĕ pet	ŭ cut
ē be	ûr urge
ĭ pit	th thin
ī pie	*th* this
îr pier	hw which
ŏ pot	zh vision
ō toe	ə about, item
ô paw	♦ regionalism

Stress marks: **′** (primary); ′ (secondary), as in **dictionary** (dĭk′shə-nĕr′ē)

the process of anabolism; metabolize constructively. **2.** To incorporate and absorb into the mind: *assimilate knowledge.* **3.** To make similar; cause to resemble. **4.** *Linguistics.* To alter (a sound) by assimilation. **5.** To absorb (immigrants or a culturally distinct group) into the prevailing culture. —*intr.* To become assimilated. [Middle English *assimilaten,* from Latin *assimilāre, assimilāt-,* to make similar to : *ad-,* ad- + *similis,* like; see **sem-**[1] in Appendix.] **—as·sim′i·la′tor** *n.*

as·sim·i·la·tion (ə-sĭm′ə-lā′shən) *n.* **1.a.** The act or process of assimilating. **b.** The state of being assimilated. **2.** *Physiology.* The conversion of nutriments into living tissue; constructive metabolism. **3.** *Linguistics.* The process by which a sound is modified so that it becomes similar or identical to an adjacent or nearby sound. For example, the prefix *in-* becomes *im-* in *impossible* by assimilation to the labial *p* of *possible.* **4.** The process whereby a minority group gradually adopts the customs and attitudes of the prevailing culture.

as·sim·i·la·tion·ism (ə-sĭm′ə-lā′shə-nĭz′əm) *n.* A policy of furthering cultural or racial assimilation. **—as·sim′i·la′tion·ist** *adj. & n.*

as·sim·i·la·tive (ə-sĭm′ə-lā′tĭv) also **as·sim·i·la·to·ry** (-lə-tôr′ē, -tōr′ē) *adj.* Marked by or causing assimilation.

As·sin·i·boin also **As·sin·i·boine** (ə-sĭn′ə-boin′) *n., pl.* **Assiniboin** or **-boins** also **Assiniboine** or **-boines. 1.a.** A Native American people formerly inhabiting southern Manitoba, now located in Montana, Alberta, and Saskatchewan. The Assiniboin became nomadic buffalo hunters after migrating to the northern Great Plains in the 18th century. **b.** A member of this people. **2.** The Siouan language of the Assiniboin. [French *Assiniboine,* of Ojibwa origin.] **—As·sin′i·boin′** *adj.*

As·sin·i·boine (ə-sĭn′ə-boin′). A river of south-central Canada rising in southern Saskatchewan and flowing about 949 km (590 mi) generally eastward to the Red River at Winnipeg, Manitoba. Its valley is one of Canada's leading wheat-growing areas.

As·si·si (ə-sē′zē, -sē, ə-sĭs′ē). A town of central Italy east-southeast of Perugia. Saint Francis of Assisi was born here in 1182 and died here in 1226. The town is a religious and tourist center. Population, 19,000.

as·sist (ə-sĭst′) *v.* **-sist·ed, -sist·ing, -sists.** —*tr.* To give help or support to, especially as a subordinate or supplement; aid: *The clerk assisted the judge by looking up related precedents. Her breathing was assisted by a respirator.* —*intr.* **1.** To give aid or support. See Synonyms at **help. 2.** To be present, as at a conference. **—assist** *n.* **1.** An act of giving aid; help. **2.** *Sports.* **a.** A fielding and throwing of a baseball in such a way that enables a teammate to put out a runner. **b.** A pass of a basketball or an ice hockey puck that enables a teammate to score a goal. **c.** The action of a soccer player who enables a teammate to score by presenting the ball for a goal. **d.** Official credit that is given for such an act. **3.** A mechanical device providing aid. [Middle English *assisten,* from Old French *assister,* from Latin *assistere* : *ad-,* ad- + *sistere,* to stand; see **stā-** in Appendix.] **—as·sist′er** *n.*

as·sis·tance (ə-sĭs′təns) *n.* **1.** The act of assisting. **2.** Aid; help: *financial assistance.*

as·sis·tant (ə-sĭs′tənt) *n. Abbr.* **asst.** One that assists; a helper. **—assistant** *adj.* **1.** Holding an auxiliary position; subordinate. **2.** Giving aid; auxiliary.

SYNONYMS: *assistant, aide, coadjutant, coadjutor, helper, lieutenant, second.* The central meaning shared by these nouns is "a person who holds a position auxiliary to another and assumes some of his or her responsibilities": *an editorial assistant; a senator's aide; the general's coadjutant; a bishop's coadjutor; a teacher's helper; a politician's lieutenant; a prizefighter's second.*

assistant professor *n.* A college or university teacher who ranks above an instructor and below an associate professor.

as·sis·tant·ship (ə-sĭs′tənt-shĭp′) *n.* An academic position that carries a stipend and usually involves part-time teaching or research, given to a qualified graduate student.

as·size (ə-sīz′) *n.* **1.a.** A session of a court. **b.** A decree or edict rendered at such a session. **2.a.** An ordinance regulating weights and measures and the weights and prices of articles of consumption. **b.** The standards so established. **3.** *Law.* A judicial inquest, the writ by which it is instituted, or the verdict of the jurors. **4. assizes. a.** One of the periodic court sessions formerly held in each of the counties of England and Wales for the trial of civil or criminal cases. **b.** The time or place of such sessions. [Middle English *assise,* from Old French, from past participle of *asseoir,* to seat, from Latin *assidēre,* to sit beside : *ad-,* ad- + *sedēre,* to sit; see ASSIDUOUS.]

assn. *abbr.* Association.

assoc. *abbr.* **1.** Associate. **2.** Association.

as·so·ci·a·ble (ə-sō′shē-ə-bəl, -shə-bəl) *adj.* That can be associated: *words associable with politics.* **—as·so′ci·a·bil′i·ty, as·so′ci·a·ble·ness** *n.*

as·so·ci·ate (ə-sō′shē-āt′, -sē-) *v.* **-at·ed, -at·ing, -ates.** —*tr.* **1.** To join as a partner, ally, or friend. **2.** To connect or join together; combine. **3.** To connect in the mind or imagination: *"I always somehow associate Chatterton with autumn"* (John Keats). —*intr.* **1.** To join in or form a league, union, or association. See Synonyms at **join. 2.** To keep company. **—associate** (-ĭt, -āt′) *n. Abbr.* **assoc. 1.** A person united with another or others in an act, an enterprise, or a business; a partner or colleague. **2.** A companion; a comrade. **3.** One that habitually accompanies or is associated with another; an attendant circumstance. **4.** A member of an institution or society who is granted only partial status or privileges. **5.** Often **Associate.** A degree conferred by a two-year college after the prescribed course of study has been successfully completed: *an Associate in Arts.* **—associate** (-ĭt, -āt′) *adj.* **1.** Joined with another or others and having equal or nearly equal status: *an associate editor.* **2.** Having partial status or privileges: *an associate member of the club.* **3.** Following or accompanying; concomitant. [Middle English *associaten,* from Latin *associāre, associāt-* : *ad-,* ad- + *socius,* companion; see **sekʷ-**[1] in Appendix.]

Assumption
The Assumption
by Titian

ă pat, ā pay, âr care, ä father, ĕ pet, ē be, ĭ pit, ī pie, îr pier, ŏ pot, ō toe, ô paw, oi boy, ou out, o͝o took, o͞o boot, ŭ cut, ûr urge, th thin, *th* this, hw which, zh vision, ə about, item, ♦ regionalism

Stress marks: ′ (primary); ′ (secondary), as in **dictionary** (dĭk′shə-nĕr′ē)

associate professor *n.* A college or university professor who ranks above an assistant professor and below a professor.

as·so·ci·a·tion (ə-sō′sē-ā′shən, -shē-) *n.* **1.** The act of associating or the state of being associated. **2.** *Abbr.* **assn., assoc.** An organized body of people who have an interest, an activity, or a purpose in common; a society. **3.a.** A mental connection or relation between thoughts, feelings, ideas, or sensations. **b.** A remembered or imagined feeling, emotion, idea, or sensation linked to a person, object, or idea. **4.** *Chemistry.* Any of various processes of combination, such as hydration, solvation, or complex-ion formation, depending on relatively weak chemical bonding. **5.** *Ecology.* A large number of organisms in a specific geographic area constituting a community with one or two dominant species. **—as·so′ci·a′tion·al** *adj.*

association area *n.* An area of the cerebral cortex where motor and sensory functions are integrated.

association football *n. Chiefly British.* Soccer.

as·so·ci·a·tion·ism (ə-sō′sē-ā′shə-nĭz′əm, ə-sō′shē-) *n.* The psychological theory that association is the basic principle of all mental activity. **—as·so′ci·a′tion·ist** *adj. & n.* **—as·so′ci·a′tion·is′tic** *adj.*

as·so·ci·a·tive (ə-sō′shē-ā′tĭv, -sē-, -shə-tĭv) *adj.* **1.** Of, characterized by, resulting from, or causing association. **2.** *Mathematics.* Independent of the grouping of elements. For example, if $a + (b + c) = (a + b) + c$, the operation indicated by + is associative. **—as·so′ci·a′tive·ly** *adv.*

associative learning *n.* A learning principle based on the belief that ideas and experiences reinforce one another and can be mentally linked to enhance the learning process.

associative neuron *n.* A nerve cell found within the central nervous system that links sensory and motor neurons.

as·soil (ə-soil′) *tr.v.* **-soiled, -soil·ing, -soils.** *Archaic.* **1.** To absolve; pardon. **2.** To atone for. [Middle English *assoilen,* from Old French *assoldre, assoil-,* from Latin *absolvere,* to set free : *ab-,* away; see AB–[1] + *solvere,* to loosen; see **leu-** in Appendix.]

as·so·nance (ăs′ə-nəns) *n.* **1.** Resemblance of sound, especially of the vowel sounds in words, as in: *"that dolphin-torn, that gong-tormented sea"* (William Butler Yeats). **2.** The repetition of identical or similar vowel sounds, especially in stressed syllables, with changes in the intervening consonants, as in the phrase *tilting at windmills.* **3.** Rough similarity; approximate agreement. [French, from Latin *assonāre,* to respond to : *ad-,* ad- + *sonāre,* to sound; see **swen-** in Appendix.] **—as′so·nant** *adj. & n.* **—as′so·nan′tal** (-năn′tl) *adj.*

as·sort (ə-sôrt′) *v.* **-sort·ed, -sort·ing, -sorts.** —*tr.* **1.** To separate into groups according to kind; classify. **2.** To supply with (an appropriate variety or assortment, as of goods). —*intr.* **1.** To agree in kind; fall into the same class. **2.** To associate with others; keep company. [Middle English *assorte,* from Old French *assorter* : *a-,* to (from Latin *ad-;* see AD–) + *sorte,* kind (from Latin *sors, sort-,* chance, lot; see **ser-**[2] in Appendix).] **—as·sort′a·tive** (ə-sôr′tə-tĭv) *adj.* **—as·sort′er** *n.*

as·sort·ed (ə-sôr′tĭd) *adj. Abbr.* **asstd. 1.** Consisting of a number of different kinds: *assorted sizes.* See Synonyms at **miscellaneous. 2.** Separated according to kind or class. **3.** Suited or matched. Often used in combination: *well-assorted accessories; an ill-assorted set of ski equipment.*

as·sort·ment (ə-sôrt′mənt) *n.* **1.** The act of assorting; separation into classes. **2.** A collection of various kinds; a variety.

A.S.S.R. or **ASSR** *abbr.* Autonomous Soviet Socialist Republic.

asst. *abbr.* Assistant.

asstd. *abbr.* **1.** Assisted. **2.** Assorted.

as·suage (ə-swāj′) *tr.v.* **-suaged, -suag·ing, -suag·es. 1.** To make (something burdensome or painful) less intense or severe: *assuage her grief.* See Synonyms at **relieve. 2.** To satisfy or appease (hunger or thirst, for example). **3.** To pacify or calm: *assuage their insecurity.* [Middle English *asswagen,* from Old French *assuagier,* from Vulgar Latin **assuāviāre* : Latin *ad-,* ad- + *suāvis,* sweet; see **swād-** in Appendix.] **—as·suage′ment** *n.*

as·sua·sive (ə-swā′sĭv, -zĭv) *adj.* Soothing; calming. [AD– + SUASIVE (sense influenced by ASSUAGE).]

as·sume (ə-so͞om′) *tr.v.* **-sumed, -sum·ing, -sumes. 1.** To take upon oneself: *assume responsibility; assume another's debts.* **2.** To undertake the duties of (an office): *assumed the presidency.* **3.** To take on; adopt: *"The god assumes a human form"* (John Ruskin). **4.** To put on; don: *The queen assumed a velvet robe.* **5.** To affect the appearance or possession of; feign. See Synonyms at **pretend. 6.** To take for granted; suppose: *assumed that prices would rise.* See Synonyms at **presume. 7.** To take over without justification; seize: *assume control.* **8.** *Theology.* To take up or receive into heaven. [Middle English *assumen,* from Latin *assūmere* : *ad-*, ad- + *sūmere,* to take; see **em-** in Appendix.] **—as·sum′a·ble** *adj.* **—as·sum′a·bly** *adv.* **—as·sum′er** *n.*

as·sumed (ə-so͞omd′) *adj.* **1.** Taken up or used so as to deceive; pretended: *an assumed name.* **2.** Taken for granted; supposed: *an assumed increase in population.* **—as·sum′ed·ly** (ə-so͞o′mĭd-lē) *adv.*

as·sum·ing (ə-so͞o′mĭng) *adj.* Presumptuous; arrogant. **—assuming** *conj.* On the assumption that; supposing: *Assuming the house is for sale, would you buy it?* **—as·sum′ing·ly** *adv.*

as·sump·sit (ə-sŭmp′sĭt) *n. Law.* **1.** An agreement or promise made orally or in writing not under seal; a contract. **2.** A legal action to enforce or recover damages for a breach of such an agreement. [New Latin, from third person sing. past tense of Latin *assūmere,* to undertake. See ASSUME.]

as·sump·tion (ə-sŭmp′shən) *n.* **1.** The act of taking to or upon oneself: *assumption of an obligation.* **2.** The act of taking over: *assumption of command.* **3.** The act of taking for granted: *assumption of a false theory.* **4.** Something taken for granted or accepted as true without proof; a supposition: *a valid assumption.* **5.** Presumption; arrogance. **6.** *Logic.* A minor premise. **7. Assumption. a.** *Theology.* The bodily taking up of the Virgin Mary into heaven after her death. **b.** A Christian feast celebrating this event. **c.** August 15, the day on which this feast is observed. [Middle English *assumpcion,* from Latin *assumptiō, assumptiōn-*, adoption, from *assumptus,* past participle of *assūmere,* to adopt. See ASSUME.]

as·sump·tive (ə-sŭmp′tĭv) *adj.* **1.** Characterized by assumption. **2.** Taken for granted; assumed. **3.** Presumptuous; assuming. **—as·sump′tive·ly** *adv.*

As·sur (ä′so͝or′, ä′sho͝or′) *n.* Variant of **Ashur.**

as·sur·ance (ə-sho͝or′əns) *n.* **1.** The act of assuring. **2.** A statement or indication that inspires confidence; a guarantee or pledge: *gave her assurance that the plan would succeed.* **3.** Freedom from doubt; certainty: *set sail in the assurance of favorable winds.* See Synonyms at **certainty. 4.** Self-confidence. See Synonyms at **confidence. 5.** Excessive self-confidence; presumption. **6.** *Chiefly British.* Insurance, especially life insurance.

As·sur·ba·ni·pal (ä′so͝or-bä′nə-päl′). See **Ashurbanipal.**

as·sure (ə-sho͝or′) *tr.v.* **-sured, -sur·ing, -sures. 1.** To inform positively, as to remove doubt: *assured us that the train would be on time.* **2.** To cause to feel sure: *assured her of his devotion.* **3.** To give confidence to; reassure. **4.** To make certain; ensure: *"Nothing in history assures the success of our civilization"* (Herbert J. Muller). **5.** To make safe or secure. **6.** *Chiefly British.* To insure, as against loss. [Middle English *assuren,* from Old French *assurer,* from Vulgar Latin **assēcūrāre,* to make sure : Latin *ad-*, ad- + *sēcūrus,* secure; see SECURE.] **—as·sur′a·ble** *adj.* **—as·sur′er** *n.*

USAGE NOTE: *Assure, ensure,* and *insure* all mean "to make secure or certain." Only *assure* is used with reference to a person in the sense of "to set the mind at rest": *assured the leader of his loyalty.* Although *ensure* and *insure* are generally interchangeable, only *insure* is now widely used in American English in the commercial sense of "to guarantee persons or property against risk."

as·sured (ə-sho͝ord′) *adj.* **1.** Made certain; guaranteed: *an assured income.* **2.** Exhibiting confidence or authority: *paints with an assured hand.* **3.** *Chiefly British.* Insured. **—assured** *n., pl.* **assured** or **assureds.** See **insured. —as·sur′ed·ly** (-ĭd-lē) *adv.* **—as·sur′ed·ness** *n.*

as·sur·gent (ə-sûr′jənt) *adj.* **1.** Rising or tending to rise. **2.** *Botany.* Slanting or curving upward; ascending. [Latin *assurgēns, assurgent-*, present participle of *assurgere,* to rise up to : *ad-*, ad- + *surgere,* to rise; see SURGE.] **—as·sur′gen·cy** *n.*

assy. *abbr.* Assembly.

As·syr·i·a (ə-sîr′ē-ə). An ancient empire and civilization of western Asia in the upper valley of the Tigris River. In its zenith between the ninth and seventh centuries B.C. the empire extended from the Mediterranean Sea across Arabia and Armenia.

As·syr·i·an (ə-sîr′ē-ən) *adj. Abbr.* **Assyr.** Of or relating to Assyria or its people, language, or culture. **—Assyrian** *n.* **1.** A native or inhabitant of Assyria. **2.** See **Akkadian** (sense 2). **3.** The Assyrian dialects of Akkadian.

As·syr·i·ol·o·gy (ə-sîr′ē-ŏl′ə-jē) *n.* The study of the civilization and language of Assyria. **—As·syr′i·ol′o·gist** *n.*

-ast *suff.* One associated with: *ecdysiast.* [From Latin *-astēs,* from Greek *-astēs,* n. suff.]

A·staire (ə-stâr′), **Fred.** 1899–1987. American dancer and actor noted for his elegant style and his partnership with Ginger Rogers in several motion pictures, including *Top Hat* (1935).

As·tar·te (ə-stär′tē) *n. Mythology.* A Near Eastern goddess traditionally associated with love and fertility.

a·sta·sia (ə-stā′zhə) *n.* Inability to stand because of motor incoordination. [Greek, unsteadiness, from *astatos,* unsteady : *a-*, not; see A-[1] + *statos,* standing; see **stā-** in Appendix.]

a·stat·ic (ā-stăt′ĭk) *adj.* **1.** Unsteady; unstable. **2.** *Physics.* Having no particular directional characteristics. **—a·stat′i·cal·ly** *adv.* **—a·stat′i·cism** *n.*

as·ta·tine (ăs′tə-tēn′, -tĭn) *n. Symbol* **At** A highly unstable radioactive element, the heaviest of the halogen series, that resembles iodine in solution. Its longest lived isotope has a mass number of 210 and has a half-life of 8.3 hours. Atomic number 85; melting point 302°C; boiling point 337°C; valence probably 1, 3, 5, 7. See table at **element.** [Greek *astatos,* unstable; see ASTASIA + -INE[2].]

Fred Astaire

as·ter (ăs′tər) *n.* **1.** Any of various plants of the genus *Aster* in the composite family, having radiate flower heads with white, pink, or violet rays and a usually yellow disk. **2.** The China aster. **3.** *Biology.* A star-shaped structure formed in the cytoplasm of a cell and having raylike fibers that surround the centrosome during mitosis. [Latin *astēr,* a plant, star, from Greek *astēr.* See **ster-**[3] in Appendix.]

as·te·ri·at·ed (ă-stîr′ē-ā′tĭd) *adj. Mineralogy.* Exhibiting asterism. [From Greek *asterios,* starry, from *astēr,* star. See **ster-**[3] in Appendix.]

as·ter·isk (ăs′tə-rĭsk′) *n.* **1.** A star-shaped figure (*) used in printing to indicate an omission or a reference to a footnote. **2.** *Linguistics.* An asterisk used to indicate an unattested sound, affix, or word. **—asterisk** *tr.v.* **-isked, -isk·ing, -isks.** To mark with an asterisk. [Middle English, from Late Latin *asteriscus,* from Greek *asteriskos,* diminutive of *astēr,* star. See **ster-**[3] in Appendix.]

as·ter·ism (ăs′tə-rĭz′əm) *n.* **1.** *Printing.* Three asterisks in triangular form used to call attention to a following passage. **2.** *Astronomy.* A cluster of stars smaller than a constellation. **3.** *Mineralogy.* A six-rayed starlike figure optically produced in some crystal structures by reflected or transmitted light. [Greek *asterismos,* constellation, from *astēr,* star. See **ster-**[3] in Appendix.] **—as′ter·is′mal** *adj.*

a·stern (ə-stûrn′) *adv. & adj. Nautical.* **1.** Behind a vessel. **2.** At or to the stern of a vessel. **3.** With or having the stern foremost; backward.

a·ster·nal (ā-stûr′nəl) *adj. Anatomy.* **1.** Not connected to the sternum. **2.** Lacking a sternum.

as·ter·oid (ăs′tə-roid′) *n.* **1.** *Astronomy.* Any of numerous small celestial bodies that revolve around the sun, with orbits lying chiefly between Mars and Jupiter and characteristic diameters between a few and several hundred kilometers. Also called *minor planet, planetoid.* **2.** *Zoology.* See **starfish. —asteroid** also **as·ter·oi·dal** (ăs′tə-roid′l) *adj.* Star-shaped. [Greek *asteroeidēs,* starlike : *astēr,* star; see **ster-**[3] in Appendix + *-oeidēs,* -oid.]

As·ter·o·pe (ă-stĕr′ə-pē′) *n.* Variant of **Sterope.**

aster yel·lows (yĕl′ōz) *pl.n.* *(used with a sing. verb).* A widespread disease of plants caused by a mycoplasma, usually resulting in stunted growth and yellowing of infected individuals.

as·the·ni·a (ăs-thē′nē-ə) *n.* Loss or lack of bodily strength; weakness; debility. [New Latin, from Greek *astheneia,* from *asthenēs,* weak : *a-*, without; see A-[1] + *sthenos,* strength.]

as·then·ic (ăs-thĕn′ĭk) *adj.* **1.** Relating to or exhibiting asthenia; weak. **2.** Having a slender, lightly muscled physique. **—asthenic** *n.* A person having such a physique.

as·the·no·pi·a (ăs′thə-nō′pē-ə) *n.* Weakness or fatigue of the eyes, usually accompanied by headache and dimming of vision. [ASTHEN(IA) + -OPIA.] **—as′the·nop′ic** (-nŏp′ĭk) *adj.*

as·then·o·sphere (ăs-thĕn′ə-sfîr′) *n.* A zone of the earth's mantle that lies beneath the lithosphere and consists of several hundred kilometers of deformable rock. [Greek *asthenēs,* weak; see ASTHENIA + SPHERE.]

asth·ma (ăz′mə, ăs′-) *n.* A chronic respiratory disease, often arising from allergies, that is characterized by sudden recurring attacks of labored breathing, chest constriction, and coughing. [Middle English *asma,* from Medieval Latin, from Greek *asthma.*] **—asth·mat′ic** (-măt′ĭk) *adj. & n.* **—asth·mat′i·cal·ly** *adv.*

as though *conj.* As if: *looked as though they had quarreled.*

As·ti (ä′stē). A city of northwest Italy southeast of Turin. It is noted for its sparkling wines. Population, 76,950.

a·stig·ma·tism (ə-stĭg′mə-tĭz′əm) *n.* **1.** A refractive defect of a lens or other optical system that prevents light rays from converging at a single point, resulting in a blurred or imperfect image. **2.** A visual defect in which the unequal curvature of one or more refractive surfaces of the eye, usually the cornea, prevents light rays from focusing clearly at one point on the retina, resulting in blurred vision. [A-[1] + Greek *stigma, stigmat-*, point (from *stizein, stig-*, to tattoo; see **steig-** in Appendix).] **—as′tig·mat′ic** (ăs′tĭg-măt′ĭk) *adj. & n.* **—as′tig·mat′i·cal·ly** *adv.*

a·stil·be (ə-stĭl′bē) *n.* Any of various chiefly eastern Asian perennial herbs of the genus *Astilbe,* having compound basal leaves and showy panicles of tiny colorful flowers. Also called *spirea.* [New Latin *astilbē* : A-[1] + Greek *stilbos,* glittering.]

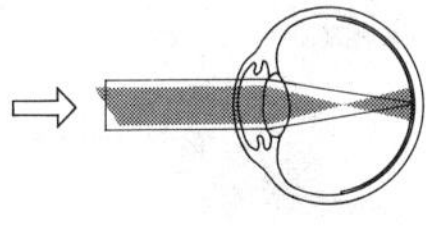

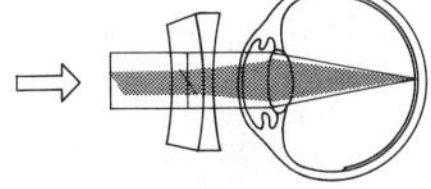
astigmatism

a·stir (ə-stûr′) *adj.* **1.** Moving about; being in motion. **2.** Having gotten out of bed.

ASTM *abbr.* American Society for Testing and Materials.

as to *prep.* **1.** With regard to: *We are puzzled as to how it happened.* **2.** According to: *candidates who were chosen as to ability.*

As·to·lat (ăs′tə-lŏt′, -lăt′) *n.* In Arthurian legend, an English town, possibly located in present-day Surrey.

as-told-to (ăz-tōld′to͞o) *adj. Informal.* Written by a professional author based on conversations with the subject: *one of those quickie, as-told-to autobiographies.*

a·stom·a·tous (ā-stŏm′ə-təs, ā-stō′mə-) also **as·tom·ous** (ăs′tə-məs) or **a·stom·a·tal** (ā-stŏm′ə-təl, ā-stō′mə-) *adj.* Having no mouth or oral opening.

As·ton (ăs′tən), **Francis William.** 1877–1945. British chemist and physicist. He won a 1922 Nobel Prize for developments that led to the discovery of isotopes in nonradioactive elements.

a·ston·ied (ə-stŏn′ēd) *adj. Archaic.* Being in a bewildered state; dazed. [Middle English *astonied,* past participle of *astonien,* to amaze. See ASTONISH.]

a·ston·ish (ə-stŏn′ĭsh) *tr.v.* **-ished, -ish·ing, -ish·es.** To fill with sudden wonder or amazement. See Synonyms at **surprise.** [Probably alteration of Middle English *astonien,* from Old French *estoner,* from Vulgar Latin **extonāre* : Latin *ex-,* ex- + Latin *tonāre,* to thunder; see **(s)tenə-** in Appendix.] **—a·ston′ish·ing·ly** *adv.*

a·ston·ish·ment (ə-stŏn′ĭsh-mənt) *n.* **1.** Great surprise or amazement. **2.** A cause of amazement; a marvel.

As·tor (ăs′tər), **John Jacob.** 1763–1848. German-born American fur trader and capitalist who became the wealthiest man of his time in the United States.

Astor, Nancy Witcher Langhorne. Viscountess Astor. 1879–1964. American-born British politician. In 1919 she became the first woman to sit in the House of Commons, serving there until 1945.

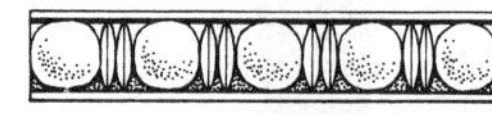
astragal

As·to·ri·a (ă-stôr′ē-ə, -stōr′-). A city of northwest Oregon near the mouth of the Columbia River. Fort Astoria, a fur-trading post established in 1811 by John Jacob Astor's Pacific Fur Company, was the first permanent American settlement along the Pacific coast. Population, 9,998.

a·stound (ə-stound′) *tr.v.* **a·stound·ed, a·stound·ing, a·stounds.** To astonish and bewilder. See Synonyms at **surprise.** [From Middle English *astoned,* past participle of *astonen,* to amaze. See ASTONISH.] **—a·stound′ing·ly** *adv.*

astr– *pref.* Variant of **astro–.**

as·tra·chan (ăs′trə-kăn′, -kən) *n.* Variant of **astrakhan.**

a·strad·dle (ə-străd′l) *adv.* **1.** In a straddling position; astride. **2.** Across or over both sides. **—astraddle** *prep.* So as to straddle or bridge; astride.

astrolabe
17th-century astrolabe engraved by Abd al-A'imma (1668–1720)

As·trae·a (ă-strē′ə) *n. Greek Mythology.* The goddess of justice.

as·tra·gal (ăs′trə-gəl) *n. Architecture.* A narrow convex molding often having the form of beading. [Latin *astragalus,* from Greek *astragalos.* See **ost-** in Appendix.]

as·trag·a·lus (ə-străg′ə-ləs) *n., pl.* **-li** (-lī′). See **talus**[1] (sense 1). [New Latin, from Greek *astragalos,* vertebra. See **ost-** in Appendix.] **—as·trag′a·lar** *adj.*

as·tra·khan also **as·tra·chan** (ăs′trə-kăn′, -kən) *n.* **1.** The curly, wavy fur made of the skins of young lambs from Astrakhan. **2.** A fabric with a curly, looped pile, made to resemble this fur.

As·tra·khan (ăs′trə-kăn′, ä-strä-KHän′). A city of southwest Russia on the Volga River delta. The Tartar city was conquered by Ivan the Terrible in 1556. Population, 493,000.

as·tral (ăs′trəl) *adj.* **1.** Of, relating to, emanating from, or resembling the stars. **2.** *Biology.* Of, relating to, or shaped like the mitotic aster; star-shaped. [Late Latin *astrālis,* from Latin *astrum,* star, from Greek *astron.* See **ster-**[3] in Appendix.] **—as′tral·ly** *adv.*

astral body *n.* A supersensible body believed by theosophists to coexist with and survive the death of the human physical body.

as·tra·pho·bi·a (ăs′trə-fō′bē-ə) *n.* An abnormal fear of lightning and thunder. [Greek *astrapē,* lightning; see **ster-**[3] in Appendix + –PHOBIA.]

a·stray (ə-strā′) *adv.* **1.** Away from the correct path or direction. See Synonyms at **amiss. 2.** Away from the right or good, as in thought or behavior; straying to or into wrong or evil ways. [Middle English, from Old French *estraie,* past participle of *estraier,* to stray. See STRAY.] **—a·stray′** *adj.*

a·stride (ə-strīd′) *adv.* **1.** With a leg on each side: *riding astride.* **2.** With the legs wide apart. **—astride** *prep.* **1.** On or over and with a leg on each side of. **2.** Situated on both sides of. **3.** Lying across or over; spanning.

astronaut
Edwin E. Aldrin, Jr., on the moon

as·trin·gent (ə-strĭn′jənt) *adj.* **1.** *Medicine.* Tending to draw together or constrict tissues; styptic. **2.** Sharp and penetrating; severe: *astringent remarks.* **—astringent** *n.* A substance or preparation that draws together or constricts body tissues and is effective in stopping the flow of blood or other secretions. [Latin *astringēns, astringent-,* present participle of *astringere,* to bind fast : *ad-,* ad- + *stringere,* to bind; see **streig-** in Appendix.] **—as·trin′gen·cy** *n.* **—as·trin′gent·ly** *adv.*

as·tri·on·ics (ăs′trē-ŏn′ĭks) *n. (used with a sing. verb).* **1.** Electronics used in astronautics. **2.** The adaptation of electronics for astronautics. [ASTR(ONAUTIC) + (AV)IONICS.]

astro– or **astr–** *pref.* **1.a.** Star: *astrophysics.* **b.** Celestial body: *astrometry.* **c.** Outer space: *astronaut.* **2.** The aster of a cell: *astrosphere.* [Greek, from *astron,* star. See **ster-**[3] in Appendix.]

as·tro·bi·ol·o·gy (ăs′trō-bī-ŏl′ə-jē) *n.* See **exobiology. —as′tro·bi′o·log′i·cal** (-ə-lŏj′ĭ-kəl) *adj.* **—as′tro·bi·ol′o·gist** *n.*

as·tro·bleme (ăs′trə-blĕm′, -blēm′) *n.* A scar on the earth's surface left from the impact of a meteorite. [ASTRO– + Greek *blēma,* missile, wound (from *ballein,* to throw; see **gʷelə-** in Appendix).]

as·tro·chem·is·try (ăs′trō-kĕm′ĭ-strē) *n.* The chemistry of stars and interstellar space. **—as′tro·chem′ist** *n.*

as·tro·cyte (ăs′trə-sīt′) *n.* A star-shaped cell, especially a neuroglial cell of nervous tissue. **—as′tro·cyt′ic** (-sĭt′ĭk) *adj.*

as·tro·cy·to·ma (ăs′trō-sī-tō′mə) *n., pl.* **-mas** or **-ma·ta** (-mə-tə). A malignant tumor of nervous tissue composed of astrocytes.

as·tro·dome (ăs′trə-dōm′) *n.* A transparent dome on the top of an aircraft, through which celestial observations are made for navigation.

as·tro·dy·nam·ics (ăs′trō-dī-năm′ĭks) *n. (used with a sing. verb).* The dynamics of natural and human-made bodies in outer space. **—as′tro·dy·nam′ic** *adj.*

as·tro·gate (ăs′trə-gāt′) *intr.v.* **-gat·ed, -gat·ing, -gates.** To navigate a spacecraft, as in celestial flight. [ASTRO– + (NAVI)GATE.] **—as′tro·ga′tion** *n.* **—as′tro·ga′tor** *n.*

as·tro·ge·ol·o·gy (ăs′trō-jē-ŏl′ə-jē) *n.* The geology of celestial bodies. **—as′tro·ge·ol′o·gist** *n.*

astrol. *abbr.* **1.** Astrologer; astrological. **2.** Astrology.

as·tro·labe (ăs′trə-lāb′) *n.* A medieval instrument, now replaced by the sextant, that was once used to determine the altitude of the sun or other celestial bodies. [Middle English *astrelabie,* from Old French *astrelabe,* from Medieval Latin *astrolabium,* from Greek *astrolabon,* planisphere : *astro-,* astro- + *lambanein, lab-,* to take.]

as·trol·o·gy (ə-strŏl′ə-jē) *n. Abbr.* **astrol. 1.** The study of the positions and aspects of celestial bodies in the belief that they have an influence on the course of natural earthly occurrences and human affairs. **2.** *Obsolete.* Astronomy. [Middle English *astrologie,* from Old French, from Latin *astrologia,* from Greek : *astro-,* astro- + *-logia,* -logy.] **—as·trol′o·ger** *n.* **—as′tro·log′i·cal** (ăs′trə-lŏj′ĭ-kəl), **as′tro·log′ic** *adj.* **—as′tro·log′i·cal·ly** *adv.*

as·trom·e·try (ə-strŏm′ĭ-trē) *n.* The scientific measurement of the positions and motions of celestial bodies. **—as′tro·met′ric** (ăs′trō-mĕt′rĭk), **as′tro·met′ri·cal** *adj.*

astron. *abbr.* Astronomer; astronomical; astronomy.

as·tro·naut (ăs′trə-nôt′) *n.* A person trained to pilot, navigate, or otherwise participate in the flight of a spacecraft. [ASTRO– + Greek *nautēs,* sailor (from *naus,* ship; see **nāu-** in Appendix).]

as·tro·nau·tics (ăs′trə-nô′tĭks) *n. (used with a sing. or pl. verb).* The science and technology of space flight. **—as′tro·nau′tic, as′tro·nau′ti·cal** *adj.* **—as′tro·nau′ti·cal·ly** *adv.*

as·tro·nav·i·ga·tion (ăs′trō-năv′ĭ-gā′shən) *n.* See **celestial navigation. —as′tro·nav′i·ga′tor** *n.*

as·tron·o·mer (ə-strŏn′ə-mər) *n. Abbr.* **astron.** One that specializes in astronomy.

as·tro·nom·i·cal (ăs′trə-nŏm′ĭ-kəl) also **as·tro·nom·ic** (-nŏm′ĭk) *adj.* **1.** *Abbr.* **astron.** Of or relating to astronomy. **2.** Of enormous magnitude; immense: *an astronomical increase in the deficit.* **—as′tro·nom′i·cal·ly** *adv.*

astronomical distance *n.* The distance from one celestial body to another, measured in light-years, parsecs, or astronomical units.

astronomical unit *n. Abbr.* **A.U.** A unit of length used in measuring astronomical distances within the solar system equal to the mean distance from Earth to the sun, approximately 150 million kilometers (93 million miles).

astronomical year *n.* See **solar year.**

as·tron·o·my (ə-strŏn′ə-mē) *n. Abbr.* **astron.** The scientific study of matter in outer space, especially the positions, dimensions, distribution, motion, composition, energy, and evolution of celestial bodies and phenomena. [Middle English *astronomie,* from Old French, from Latin *astronomia,* from Greek : *astro-,* astro- + *-nomia,* -nomy.]

as·tro·pho·tog·ra·phy (ăs′trō-fə-tŏg′rə-fē) *n.* Astronomical photography. **—as′tro·pho′to·graph′ic** (-fō′tə-grăf′ĭk) *adj.*

as·tro·phys·ics (ăs′trō-fĭz′ĭks) *n. (used with a sing. verb).* The branch of astronomy that deals with the physics of stellar phenomena. **—as′tro·phys′i·cal** *adj.* **—as′tro·phys′i·cist** (-fĭz′ĭ-sĭst) *n.*

as·tro·sphere (ăs′trō-sfîr′) *n.* **1.** The central portion of a cell aster exclusive of the rays. **2.** The entire cell aster with the exception of the centrosome.

As·tro·Turf (ăs′trō-tûrf′). A trademark used for an artificial grasslike ground covering.

As·tu·ri·as (ăs-tŏŏr′ē-əs, -tyŏŏr′-, äs-tōō′ryäs). A region and former kingdom of northwest Spain south of the Bay of Biscay. The original Iberian inhabitants were conquered by Rome in the second century B.C. **—As·tu′ri·an** *adj. & n.*

As·tu·ri·as (ə-stŏŏr′ē-əs, ä-stōō′ryäs), **Miguel Angel.** 1899–1974. Guatemalan writer whose *El Señor Presidente* (1946) is often considered his greatest novel. He won the 1966 Nobel Prize for literature.

as·tute (ə-stōōt′, ə-styōōt′) *adj.* Having or showing shrewdness and discernment, especially with respect to one's own concerns. See Synonyms at **shrewd.** [Latin *astūtus,* from *astus,* craft. See **wes-**[1] in Appendix.] **—as·tute′ly** *adv.* **—as·tute′ness** *n.*

As·ty·a·nax (ə-stī′ə-năks′) *n. Greek Mythology.* The young son of Hector and Andromache, killed when the Greeks conquered Troy.

a·sty·lar (ā-stī′lər) *adj. Architecture.* Not having columns or pilasters. [A-[1] + Greek *stulos,* pillar; see **stā-** in Appendix + -AR.]

A·sun·ción (ä-so͞on'syôn'). The capital and largest city of Paraguay, in the southern part of the country on the Paraguay River. It is Paraguay's chief port and industrial center. Population, 455,517.

a·sun·der (ə-sŭn'dər) *adv.* **1.** Into separate parts or pieces: *broken asunder.* **2.** Apart from each other either in position or in direction: *The curtains had been drawn asunder.* [Middle English, from Old English *on sundran* : *on,* on; see ON + *sundran,* separately (from *sunder,* apart).] **—a·sun'der** *adj.*

ASV *abbr. Bible.* American Standard Version.

As·wan (ăs'wän, ăs-wän', äs-). A city of southern Egypt at the First Cataract of the Nile River near the **Aswan High Dam.** Construction of the dam, dedicated in 1971, required the relocation of some 90,000 people and numerous archaeological treasures. The city's population is 182,700.

a·swarm (ə-swôrm') *adj.* Filled or overrun, as with moving objects or beings: *The playground was aswarm with children.*

as well as *conj.* And in addition: *courageous as well as strong.* **—as well as** *prep.* In addition to: *The editors as well as the proofreaders are working overtime.*

a·swirl (ə-swûrl') *adj.* Moving with a swirling or whirling motion: *couples aswirl on the dance floor.*

a·swoon (ə-swo͞on') *adv. & adj.* In a faint or swoon: *fairly aswoon with delight.* [Middle English *aswowne,* ultimately from Old English *geswōgen,* fainted, past participle of **swōgan,* to lose consciousness.]

a·sy·lum (ə-sī'ləm) *n.* **1.** An institution for the care of people, especially those with physical or mental impairments, who require organized supervision or assistance. **2.** A place offering protection and safety; a shelter. **3.** A place, such as a church, formerly constituting an inviolable refuge for criminals or debtors. **4.** The protection afforded by a sanctuary. See Synonyms at **shelter. 5.** Protection and immunity from extradition granted by a government to a political refugee from another country. [Middle English *asilum,* refuge, from Latin *asȳlum,* from Greek *asulon,* sanctuary, from neuter of *asulos,* inviolable : *a-,* without; see A-[1] + *sulon,* right of seizure.]

a·sym·met·ri·cal (ā'sĭ-mĕt'rĭkəl) also **a·sym·met·ric** (-rĭk) *adj.* Having no balance or symmetry. **—a'sym·met'ri·cal·ly** *adv.*

a·sym·me·try (ā-sĭm'ĭ-trē) *n.* Lack of balance or symmetry.

a·symp·to·mat·ic (ā'sĭmp-tə-măt'ĭk) *adj.* Neither causing nor exhibiting symptoms of disease. **—a'symp·to·mat'i·cal·ly** *adv.*

as·ymp·tote (ăs'ĭm-tōt', -ĭmp-) *n. Mathematics.* A line considered a limit to a curve in the sense that the perpendicular distance from a moving point on the curve to the line approaches zero as the point moves an infinite distance from the origin. [Ultimately from Greek *asumptōtos,* not intersecting : *a-,* not; see A-[1] + *sumptōtos,* intersecting (from *sumpiptein,* to converge : *sun-,* syn- + *piptein, ptō-,* to fall; see **pet-** in Appendix).] **—as'ymp·tot'ic** (-tŏt'ĭk), **as'ymp·tot'i·cal** *adj.* **—as'ymp·tot'i·cal·ly** *adv.*

a·syn·ap·sis (ā'sĭ-năp'sĭs) *n.* The failure of homologous chromosomes to pair during meiosis.

a·syn·chro·nism (ā-sĭng'krə-nĭz'əm) or **a·syn·chron·y** (-krə-nē) *n.* Lack of temporal concurrence or synchronism. **—a·syn'chro·nous** (-nəs) *adj.* **—a·syn'chro·nous·ly** *adv.*

a·syn·de·ton (ə-sĭn'dĭ-tŏn') *n.* The omission of conjunctions from constructions in which they would normally be used, as in *"Are all thy conquests, glories, triumphs, spoils,/Shrunk to this little measure?"* (Shakespeare). [Late Latin, from Greek *asundeton,* from neuter of *asundetos,* without conjunctions : *a-,* not; see A-[1] + *sundetos,* bound together (from *sundein,* to bind together : *sun-,* syn- + *dein,* to bind).] **—as'yn·det'ic** (ăs'ĭn-dĕt'ĭk) *adj.* **—as'yn·det'i·cal·ly** *adv.*

a·syn·tac·tic (ā'sĭn-tăk'tĭk) *adj.* Not conforming to accepted patterns of syntax.

As·yut (ä-syo͞ot'). A city of east-central Egypt on the Nile River. It is an industrial and trade center. Population, 274,400.

at[1] (ăt; ət *when unstressed*) *prep.* **1.a.** In or near the area occupied by; in or near the location of: *at the market; at our destination.* **b.** In or near the position of: *always at my side; at the center of the page.* **2.** To or toward the direction or location of, especially for a specific purpose: *Questions came at us from all sides.* **3.** Present during; attending: *at the dance.* **4.** Within the interval or span of: *at the dinner hour; at a glance.* **5.** In the state or condition of: *at peace with one's conscience.* **6.** In the activity or field of: *skilled at playing chess; good at math.* **7.** To or using the rate, extent, or amount of; to the point of: *at 30 cents a pound; at high speed; at 20 paces; at 350°F.* **8.** On, near, or by the time or age of: *at three o'clock; at 72 years of age.* **9.** On account of; because of: *rejoice at a victory.* **10.** By way of; through: *exited at the rear gate.* **11.** In accord with; following: *at my request.* **12.** Dependent upon: *at the mercy of the court.* **13.** Occupied with: *at work.* **—*idiom.* at it.** *Informal.* Engaged in verbal or physical conflict; arguing or fighting: *The neighbors are at it again.* [Middle English, from Old English *æt.* See **ad-** in Appendix.]

at[2] (ät) *n., pl.* **at.** See table at **currency.** [Thai.]

aT *abbr.* Attotesla.

At[1] The symbol for the element **astatine.**

At[2] *abbr.* Ampere-turn.

AT *abbr.* **1.** Air temperature. **2.** Also **a/t.** Antitank. **3.** Automatic transmission.

at. *abbr.* **1.** Airtight. **2.** Atomic.

at- *pref.* Variant of **ad-** (sense 1).

A·ta·ba·li·pa (ä'tə-bä'lĭ-pä'). See **Atahualpa.**

At·a·brine (ăt'ə-brĭn, -brēn'). A trademark used for an antimalarial preparation of quinacrine hydrochloride.

At·a·ca·ma Desert (ăt'ə-kăm'ə, ä'tä-kä'mä). An arid region of northwest Chile. One of the driest areas in the world, it has yielded great nitrate and copper wealth.

at·a·ghan (ăt'ə-găn', -gən) *n.* Variant of **yataghan.**

A·ta·hual·pa (ä'tə-wäl'pə) also **A·ta·ba·li·pa** (-bä'lĭ-pä'). 1502?-1533. Last Incan emperor of Peru (1525-1533). He was captured by the Spaniards, convicted of plotting against Pizarro, and executed by garrote despite his agreement to a vast ransom.

At·a·lan·ta (ăt'ə-lăn'tə) *n. Greek Mythology.* A maiden hunter who agreed to marry any man who could defeat her in a footrace. She was outrun by Hippomenes, who won by dropping along the course three golden apples, which she paused to pick up.

at·a·man (ăt'ə-măn') *n., pl.* **-mans.** A Cossack chief. Also called *hetman.* [Russian, from South Turkic, leader of an armed band : *ata,* father + *-man,* augmentative suff.]

at·a·mas·co lily (ăt'ə-măs'kō) *n.* A bulbous plant *(Zephyranthes atamasco)* of the southeast United States, having a showy, solitary, white to pinkish flower on a long stalk. [Virginia Algonquian *attamusco.*]

at·a·rac·tic (ăt'ə-răk'tĭk) also **at·a·rax·ic** (-răk'sĭk) *—adj.* Relating to or producing calmness and peace of mind. *—n.* A drug that reduces nervous tension; a tranquilizer. [From Greek *ataraktos,* undisturbed : *a-,* not; see A-[1] + *taraktos,* disturbed (from *tarassein, tarak-,* to disturb).]

at·a·rax·i·a (ăt'ə-răk'sē-ə) *n.* Peace of mind or emotional tranquillity; calmness. [Greek, from *ataraktos,* undisturbed. See ATARACTIC.]

at·a·rax·ic (ăt'ə-răk'sĭk) *adj. & n.* Variant of **ataractic.**

A·tas·ca·de·ro (ə-tăs'kə-dâr'ō, ə-tăs'-). An unincorporated community of southwest California north of San Luis Obispo. It was founded in 1913 as a model community. Population, 16,232.

At·a·türk (ăt'ə-tûrk', ä-tä-tûrk'), **Kemal.** See **Kemal Atatürk.**

at·a·vism (ăt'ə-vĭz'əm) *n.* **1.** The reappearance of a characteristic in an organism after several generations of absence, usually caused by the chance recombination of genes. **2.** An individual or a part that exhibits atavism. Also called *throwback.* **3.** The return of a trait or recurrence of previous behavior after a period of absence. [French *atavisme,* from Latin *atavus,* ancestor : *atta,* father + *avus,* grandfather; see **awo-** in Appendix.] **—at'a·vist** *n.* **—at'a·vis'tic** *adj.* **—at'a·vis'ti·cal·ly** *adv.*

a·tax·i·a (ə-tăk'sē-ə) also **a·tax·y** (ə-tăk'sē) *n.* Loss of the ability to coordinate muscular movement. [Greek, disorder : *a-,* not; see A-[1] + *taxis,* order.] **—a·tax'ic** *adj. & n.*

At·ba·ra (ăt'bər-ə, ăt'-). A river of northeast Africa rising in northwest Ethiopia and flowing about 805 km (500 mi) to the Nile River in eastern Sudan.

at bat or **at-bat** (ăt-băt') *n. Baseball.* A player's official turn to bat, counted in figuring a batting average unless there is interference from the catcher or unless the player is hit by the ball, makes a sacrifice hit, or is walked.

At·chi·son (ăch'ĭ-sən). A city of northeast Kansas northwest of Kansas City. The city was an important outfitting point for westward travelers, especially after the foundation of the Atchison, Topeka, and Santa Fe Railroad in 1859. Population, 11,407.

ate (āt) *v.* Past tense of **eat.**

A·te (ā'tē, ä'tē, ä'tā) *n. Greek Mythology.* The goddess of criminal rashness and consequent punishment.

-ate[1] *suff.* **1.a.** Having: *nervate.* **b.** Characterized by: *Latinate.* **c.** Resembling: *lyrate.* **2.a.** One that is characterized by: *laminate.* **b.** Rank; office: *rabbinate.* **3.** To act upon in a specified manner: *acidulate.* [Ultimately from Latin *-ātus,* past participle suff. of verbs in *-āre.*]

-ate[2] *suff.* **1.** A derivative of a specified chemical compound or element: *aluminate.* **2.** A salt or ester of a specified acid whose name ends in *-ic: acetate.* [New Latin *-ātum,* from Latin, neuter of *-ātus,* past participle suff. of verbs in *-āre.*]

A-team (ā'tēm') *n.* **1.** A detachment of 12 soldiers in the Special Forces. **2.** *Informal.* A group having a special mission, especially in a leadership role: *"America is the A-team among nations, bursting with energy, courage and determination"* (Ronald Reagan). [Informal name for *A-detachment* : A[1], first in a series + DETACHMENT.]

at·e·lec·ta·sis (ăt'l-ĕk'tə-sĭs) *n.* **1.** Total or partial collapse of the lung. **2.** A congenital condition characterized by the incomplete expansion of the lungs at birth. [New Latin : Greek *atelēs,* incomplete (*a-,* not; see A-[1] + *telos,* end; see TELO-) + Greek *ektasis,* stretching out (from *ekteinein,* to stretch out : *ek-,* out; see ECTO- + *teinein,* to stretch; see EPITASIS).]

at·el·ier (ăt'l-yā') *n.* A workshop or studio, especially for an artist or a designer. [French, from Old French *astelier,* carpenter's shop, from *astele,* splinter, from Late Latin *astella,* alteration of Latin *astula,* diminutive of *assis,* board.]

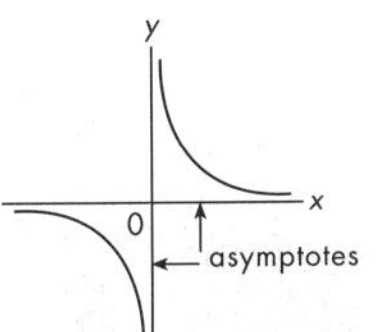

asymptote
Asymptotes of a hyperbola; $xy = 1$

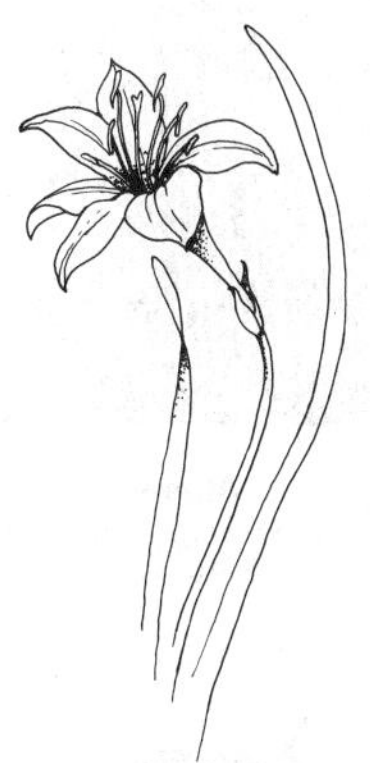
atamasco lily
Zephyranthes atamasco

atelier

ă pat	oi boy
ā pay	ou out
âr care	o͝o took
ä father	o͞o boot
ĕ pet	ŭ cut
ē be	ûr urge
ĭ pit	th thin
ī pie	*th* this
îr pier	hw which
ŏ pot	zh vision
ō toe	ə about, item
ô paw	♦ regionalism

Stress marks: **'** (primary); ' (secondary), as in **dictionary** (dĭk'shə-nĕr'ē)

Athena
Mourning Athena, c. 460 B.C.

Atlas
Atlas, 1937, by Lee Lawrie (1877–1963), in forecourt of the International Building, Rockefeller Center, New York City

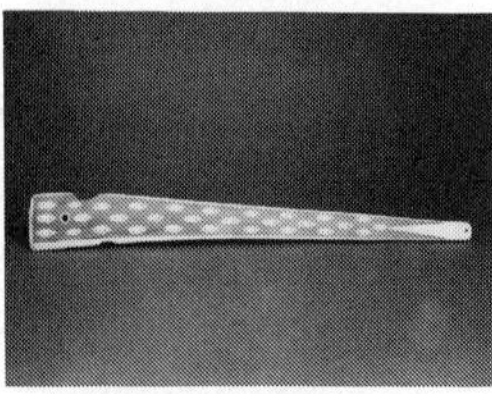

atlatl
Decorated Eskimo atlatl

a·te·moy·a (ä′tə-moi′ə, ăt′ə-) *n.* **1.** A conical or heart-shaped green fruit with edible, sweet, white flesh. **2.** The tree producing this fruit, a hybrid between the cherimoya and the sweetsop. [Philippine English *ates,* sweetsop (from Tagalog *átis*) + (CHERI)MOYA.]

a tem·po (ä tĕm′pō) *adv. & adj. Music.* In the time originally designated; resuming the initial tempo of a section or movement after a specified deviation from it. Used chiefly as a direction. [Italian : *a,* in + *tempo,* time.]

a·tem·po·ral (ā-tĕm′pər-əl) *adj.* Independent of time; timeless.

A·ten (ät′n) *n. Mythology.* Variant of **Aton.**

A·te·ri·an (ə-tîr′ē-ən) *adj.* Of or relating to a northern African Paleolithic culture, largely Mousterian but using tanged points and leaf-shaped spearheads. [French *atérien,* after Bir el Ater (Constantine), a city of northeast Algeria.]

Ath·a·bas·ca or **Ath·a·bas·ka** (ăth′ə-băs′kə). A river rising in the Rocky Mountains of southwest Alberta, Canada, and flowing about 1,231 km (765 mi) east and north to **Lake Athabasca** on the border of northern Alberta and Saskatchewan. The river and lake are important constituents of the Mackenzie River system.

Ath·a·bas·kan or **Ath·a·bas·can** (ăth′ə-băs′kən) also **Ath·a·pas·can** (-păs′-) *n.* **1.** A group of related North American Indian languages including the Apachean languages and languages of Alaska, northwest Canada, and coastal Oregon and California. **2.** A member of an Athabaskan-speaking people. [After Lake ATHABASCA, from Cree *athapaskaaw,* there is scattered grass.] **—Ath′a·bas′kan** *adj.*

Ath·a·na·sian (ăth′ə-nā′zhən) *adj.* Of or relating to Athanasius. **—Athanasian** *n.* A follower of Athanasius, especially in opposition to Arianism.

Athanasian Creed *n.* A Christian creed of the early fifth century, originally attributed to Athanasius but now considered to be of unknown origin.

Ath·a·na·sius (ăth′ə-nā′shəs), Saint. Known as "the Great." A.D.293?–373. Greek patriarch of Alexandria and leading defender of Christian orthodoxy against Arianism.

Ath·a·pas·can (ăth′ə-păs′kən) *n.* Variant of **Athabaskan.**

a·the·ism (ā′thē-ĭz′əm) *n.* **1.a.** Disbelief in or denial of the existence of God or gods. **b.** The doctrine that there is no God or gods. **2.** Godlessness; immorality. [French *athéisme,* from *athée,* atheist, from Greek *atheos,* godless : *a-,* without; see A–[1] + *theos,* god; see **dhēs-** in Appendix.]

a·the·ist (ā′thē-ĭst) *n.* One that disbelieves or denies the existence of God or gods.

a·the·is·tic (ā′thē-ĭs′tĭk) also **a·the·is·ti·cal** (-tĭ-kəl) *adj.* **1.** Relating to or characteristic of atheism or atheists. **2.** Inclined to atheism. **—a′the·is′ti·cal·ly** *adv.*

ath·e·ling (ăth′ə-lĭng, ăth′-) *n.* An Anglo-Saxon nobleman or prince, especially the heir to a throne. [Middle English, from Old English *ætheling.*]

Ath·el·stan (ăth′əl-stăn′). 895?–939. King of Mercia and Wessex (924?–939) who was the first Saxon ruler to establish his authority over all of England.

A·the·na (ə-thē′nə) also **A·the·ne** (-nē) *n. Greek Mythology.* The goddess of wisdom, the practical arts, and warfare.

ath·e·nae·um also **ath·e·ne·um** (ăth′ə-nē′əm) *n.* **1.** An institution, such as a literary club or scientific academy, for the promotion of learning. **2.** A place, such as a library, where printed materials are available for reading. [Late Latin *Athēnaeum,* a Roman school, after Greek *Athēnaion,* the temple of Athena, from *Athēna,* Athena.]

Ath·ens (ăth′ənz). **1.** The capital and largest city of Greece, in the eastern part of the country near the Saronic Gulf. It was at the height of its cultural achievements and imperial power in the fifth century B.C. during the time of Pericles. Athens became the capital of modern Greece in 1834, two years after the country achieved its independence from Turkey. Population, 885,737. **2.** A city of northeast Georgia east-northeast of Atlanta. It was founded in 1785 as the site of the University of Georgia (established 1801). Population, 42,549. **3.** A city of southeast Ohio in the foothills of the Appalachian Mountains west of Marietta. Settled c. 1797, it is a processing and manufacturing center. Population, 19,743.

a·the·o·ret·i·cal (ā′thē-ə-rĕt′ĭ-kəl) *adj.* Unrelated to or lacking a theoretical basis.

ath·er·o·gen·e·sis (ăth′ər-ō-jĕn′ĭ-sĭs) *n.* Formation of atheromatous deposits, especially on the innermost layer of arterial walls. [ATHERO(MA) + –GENESIS.] **—ath′er·o·gen′ic** (-jĕn′ĭk) *adj.* **—ath′er·o·gen·i′ci·ty** (-jə-nĭs′ĭtē) *n.*

ath·er·o·ma (ăth′ə-rō′mə) *n., pl.* **-mas** or **-ma·ta** (-mə-tə). A deposit or degenerative accumulation of lipid-containing plaques on the innermost layer of the wall of an artery, especially on one of the larger arteries. [Latin *atherōma,* tumor full of pus that is like gruel, from Greek, from *athēra,* gruel.] **—ath′er·o·ma·to′sis** (-tō′sĭs) *n.* **—ath′er·om′a·tous** (-rŏm′ə-təs, -rō′mə-) *adj.*

ath·er·o·scle·ro·sis (ăth′ə-rō-sklə-rō′sĭs) *n.* A form of arteriosclerosis characterized by the deposition of atheromatous plaques containing cholesterol and lipids on the innermost layer of the walls of large and medium-sized arteries. [ATHERO(MA) + SCLEROSIS.] **—ath′er·o·scle·rot′ic** (-rŏt′ĭk) *adj.* **—ath′er·o·scle·rot′i·cal·ly** *adv.*

a·thirst (ə-thûrst′) *adj.* **1.** Strongly desirous; eager: *athirst for freedom.* **2.** *Archaic.* Thirsty.

athl. *abbr.* Athlete; athletic; athletics.

ath·lete (ăth′lēt′) *n. Abbr.* **athl.** A person possessing the natural or acquired traits, such as strength, agility, and endurance, that are necessary for physical exercise or sports, especially those performed in competitive contexts. [Middle English, from Latin *athlēta,* from Greek *athlētēs,* contestant, from *athlein,* to contend, possibly from *athlos,* contest.]

WORD HISTORY: Athletes who believe that winning is the most important aspect of athletics have etymological support for their view, even if the way one plays the game is more important than winning a prize. The word *athlete* may ultimately go back to the Greek word *athlos,* "contest, especially a contest for a prize." Two other possible sources are *athlon,* "prize won in a contest," and **athleus,* "one who competes." The Greek word *athlētēs,* derived from at least one of these sources, meant "combatant, champion," and was used especially for competitors in games. Our word *athlete,* borrowed from Greek by way of Latin, is first recorded in Middle English (possibly before 1425) with reference to wrestlers.

ath·lete's foot (ăth′lēts) *n.* A contagious fungal infection of the skin usually affecting the feet and sometimes the hands, characterized by itching, blisters, cracking, and scaling.

ath·let·ic (ăth-lĕt′ĭk) *adj.* **1.** *Abbr.* **athl.** Of, relating to, or befitting athletics or athletes. **2.** Physically strong; muscular. See Synonyms at **muscular. 3.** *Anthropology.* Having a large skeletal structure and well-developed muscles; mesomorphic. **—ath·let′i·cal·ly** *adv.* **—ath·let′i·cism** (-lĕt′ĭ-sĭz′əm) *n.*

ath·let·ics (ăth-lĕt′ĭks) *n. (used with a sing. or pl. verb). Abbr.* **athl. 1.** Activities, such as sports, exercises, and games, that require physical skill and stamina. **2.** The principles or system of training and practice for such activities.

athletic supporter *n.* An elastic support for the male genitals, worn especially in athletic or other strenuous activity.

ath·o·dyd (ăth′ə-dĭd′) *n.* A simple, essentially tubular jet engine, such as a ramjet. [A(ERO)– + TH(ERM)ODY(NAMIC) + D(UCT).]

at-home or **at home** (ət-hōm′, ăt-) **—***n.* An informal reception in one's home. **—***adj.* **1.** Being, occurring, or functioning in one's home: *at-home workers; at-home care.* **2.** Designed for or appropriate for one's home: *at-home fashions.*

Ath·os (ăth′ŏs, ā′thŏs, ä′thôs), **Mount.** A peak, about 2,034 m (6,670 ft) high, of northeast Greece. It is the site of the virtually independent monastic community of **Mount Athos,** originally founded in the tenth century.

a·thwart (ə-thwôrt′) *adv.* **1.** From side to side; crosswise or transversely. **2.** So as to thwart, obstruct, or oppose; perversely. **—athwart** *prep.* **1.** From one side to the other of; across: *"the Stars that shoot athwart the Night"* (Alexander Pope). **2.** Contrary to; against. **3.** *Nautical.* Across the course, line, or length of. [Middle English : *a-,* on; see A–[2] + *thwert,* across; see THWART.]

a·tilt (ə-tĭlt′) *adv. & adj.* **1.** In a tilted position; inclined upward. **2.** Tilting or as if tilting with a lance.

a·tin·gle (ə-tĭng′gəl) *adj.* Experiencing a prickling sensation, as from excitement; being in a state of tingling.

–ation *suff.* **1.a.** Action or process: *strangulation.* **b.** The result of an action or process: *acculturation.* **2.** State, condition, or quality of: *eburnation.* [Middle English *-acioun,* from Old French *-ation,* from Latin *-ātiō, -ātiōn-,* n. suff : *-ā-,* stem vowel of verbs in *-āre* + *-tiō, -tiōn-,* abstract n. suff.]

A·ti·tlán (ä′tē-tlän′). A volcanic lake of southwest Guatemala. Among the lofty mountains nearby are three inactive volcanoes, including **Atitlán,** rising to 3,539.2 m (11,604 ft).

–ative *suff.* Of, relating to, or associated with: *talkative.* [Middle English, from Old French *-atif, -ative,* from Latin *-ātīvus,* from *-ātus,* past participle suff. See –ATE[1].]

At·ka Island (ăt′kə, ät′-). An island of southwest Alaska in the Andreanof group of the central Aleutian Islands. It was the site of a major U.S. military base during World War II.

Atka mackerel *n.* A food fish *(Pleurogrammus monopterygius)* native to northern Pacific waters.

Atl. *abbr.* Atlantic.

At·lan·ta (ăt-lăn′tə). The capital and largest city of Georgia, in the northwest part of the state. It was founded in 1837 at the end of the railroad line as Terminus and renamed Atlanta in 1845. Almost entirely burned on November 15, 1864, before the start of Union general William Tecumseh Sherman's march to the sea, the city was rapidly rebuilt and became the permanent state capital in 1877. Population, 425,022. **—At·lan′tan** *n.*

At·lan·te·an[1] (ăt′lăn-tē′ən, ăt-lăn′tē-) *adj.* Of, relating to, or like Atlas, especially in having a fundamental role or great strength. [From Greek *Atlas, Atlant-,* Atlas. See ATLAS.]

At·lan·te·an[2] (ăt′lăn-tē′ən, ăt-lăn′tē-) *adj.* Of or relating to Atlantis.

at·lan·tes (ăt-lăn′tēz) *n. Architecture.* Plural of **atlas[2]** (sense 1).

At·lan·tic (ăt-lăn′tĭk) *adj.* **1.** *Abbr.* **Atl.** Of, in, near, upon, or relating to the Atlantic Ocean. **2.** Of, on, near, or relating to the eastern coast of the United States. **3.** Of or concerning countries bordering the Atlantic Ocean, especially those of Europe and North America. [Middle English *Atlantik,* from Latin *(mare) At-*

lanticum, Atlantic (sea), from Greek *(pelagos) Atlantikos,* from *Atlas, Atlant-,* Atlas. See **tela-** in Appendix.]

Atlantic City. A city of southeast New Jersey on the Atlantic Ocean. It is a popular resort and convention center with a famous boardwalk. Legalized gambling was introduced in 1978. Population, 40,199.

Atlantic croaker *n.* A small, silvery food fish *(Micropogonias undulatus)* common in Atlantic waters south of Massachusetts.

Atlantic In·tra·coast·al Waterway (ĭn′trə-kō′stəl). A system of inland waterways including rivers, bays, and canals along the Atlantic coast of the United States. It extends from Cape Cod to southern Florida and forms part of the Intracoastal Waterway that affords protected passage from Massachusetts to southern Texas.

At·lan·ti·cism (ăt-lăn′tĭ-sĭz′əm) *n.* A doctrine assuming the mutuality of western European and North American interests and advocating cooperative political and economic action, especially on defense issues. **—At·lan′ti·cist** *n.*

Atlantic Ocean. The world's second-largest ocean, divided into the **North Atlantic** and the **South Atlantic.** It extends from the Arctic in the north to the Antarctic in the south between the eastern Americas and western Europe and Africa.

Atlantic Provinces. The Canadian provinces of New Brunswick, Prince Edward Island, Nova Scotia, and Newfoundland.

Atlantic salmon *n.* A species of salmon *(Salmo salar)* native to northern Atlantic waters and valued as a food fish.

Atlantic Standard Time *n.* Standard time in the fourth time zone west of Greenwich, England, reckoned at 60° west and used, for example, in Puerto Rico and the Canadian Maritime Provinces. Also called *Atlantic Time.*

At·lan·tis (ăt-lăn′tĭs) *n. Mythology.* A legendary island in the Atlantic Ocean west of Gibraltar, said by Plato to have sunk beneath the sea during an earthquake.

at·las¹ (ăt′ləs) *n., pl.* **-las·es. 1.** A book or bound collection of maps, sometimes with supplementary illustrations and graphic analyses. **2.** A volume of tables, charts, or plates that systematically illustrates a particular subject: *an anatomical atlas.* **3.** A large size of drawing paper, measuring 26 × 33 or 26 × 34 inches. [After *Atlas,* legendary king of northern Africa, sometimes identified with, or considered descended from, the Titan Atlas.]

at·las² (ăt′ləs) *n., pl.* **-es. 1.** *pl.* **at·lan·tes** (ăt-lăn′tēz) *Architecture.* A standing or kneeling figure of a man used as a supporting column for an entablature. **2.** *Anatomy.* The top or first cervical vertebra of the neck, which supports the skull. [From ATLAS.]

At·las (ăt′ləs) *n.* **1.** *Greek Mythology.* A Titan condemned by Zeus to support the heavens upon his shoulders. **2.** The satellite of Saturn that is closest to the planet. **3. atlas.** A person who supports a great burden. [Greek. See **tela-** in Appendix.]

Atlas cedar *n.* A northern African evergreen tree *(Cedrus atlantica),* having green to silvery-blue foliage and widely grown as an ornamental. [After the ATLAS MOUNTAINS.]

Atlas Mountains. A system of ranges and plateaus of northwest Africa extending from southwest Morocco to northern Tunisia between the Sahara Desert and the Mediterranean Sea and rising to 4,167.8 m (13,665 ft).

at·la·tl (ät-lät′l) *n.* A spear-throwing device usually consisting of a stick fitted with a thong or socket to steady the butt of the spear during the throw. [Nahuatl, from *atla,* to throw.]

At·li (ät′lē) *n.* A legendary king corresponding to the historical figure of Attila. In the *Volsunga Saga* he is the second husband of Gudrun.

atm or **atm.** *abbr. Physics.* Atmosphere; atmospheric.

ATM *abbr.* Automated teller machine; automatic teller machine.

at·man (ät′mən) *n. Hinduism.* **1.** The individual soul or essence. **2. Atman.** The essence that is eternal, unchanging, and indistinguishable from the essence of the universe. [Sanskrit *ātman,* breath, spirit.]

at·mom·e·ter (ăt-mŏm′ĭ-tər) *n.* An instrument that measures the rate of water evaporation. [Greek *atmos,* vapor; see ATMOSPHERE + -METER.] **—at′mo·met′ric** (-mō-mĕt′rĭk) *adj.* **—at·mom′e·try** *n.*

atmos. *abbr. Physics.* Atmosphere; atmospheric.

at·mos·phere (ăt′mə-sfîr′) *n.* **1.** *Abbr.* **atm, atm., atmos.** The gaseous mass or envelope surrounding a celestial body, especially the one surrounding Earth, and retained by the celestial body's gravitational field. **2.** The air or climate in a specific place. **3.** *Abbr.* **atm, atm.** *Physics.* A unit of pressure equal to the air pressure at sea level, approximately equal to 1.01325 × 10^5 newtons per square meter. See table at **measurement. 4.** A dominant intellectual or emotional tone or attitude, especially one related to a specific environment or state of affairs: *a prevailing atmosphere of distrust.* **5.** The dominant tone or mood of a work of art. **6.** An aesthetic quality or effect, especially a distinctive and pleasing one, associated with a particular place: *a restaurant with an Old World atmosphere.* [New Latin *atmosphaera* : Greek *atmos,* vapor; see **wet-¹** in Appendix + Latin *sphaera,* sphere; see SPHERE.]

at·mos·pher·ic (ăt′mə-sfĕr′ĭk, -sfîr′-) also **at·mos·pher·i·cal** (-ĭ-kəl) *adj. Abbr.* **atm, atm., atmos. 1.** Of, relating to, or existing in the atmosphere. **2.** Produced by, dependent on, or coming from the atmosphere. **3.** Resembling or representing the atmosphere; having or giving the effect of translucence: *a painting suffused with a hazy, atmospheric glow.* **4.** Intended to evoke a particular emotional tone or aesthetic quality: *lush atmospheric touches in every room.* **—at′mos·pher′i·cal·ly** *adv.*

atmospheric pressure *n.* Pressure caused by the weight of the atmosphere. At sea level it has a mean value of one atmosphere but reduces with increasing altitude.

at·mos·pher·ics (ăt′mə-sfĕr′ĭks, -sfîr′-) *n.* **1.** *(used with a sing. verb).* **a.** Electromagnetic radiation produced by natural phenomena such as lightning. **b.** Radio interference produced by electromagnetic radiation. Also called *sferics.* **2.** *(used with a pl. verb).* **a.** Features, events, or statements intended to create a particular mood or attitude. **b.** A consciously created mood or attitude, often without substantive basis: *"Soviet sensitivities are not so tender; their calculations are based on an assessment of their interests, not on atmospherics"* (Henry A. Kissinger).

at·mo·sphe·ri·um (ăt′mə-sfîr′ē-əm) *n.* An optical device designed to project images of atmospheric phenomena, such as clouds, on the inside of a dome. [ATMOSPHER(E) + (PLANETAR)IUM.]

at. no. also **at no** *abbr.* Atomic number.

a·toll (ăt′ôl′, -ŏl′, ā′tôl′, ā′tŏl′) *n.* A ringlike coral island and reef that nearly or entirely encloses a lagoon. [Perhaps ultimately from Tamil *aṭar,* to be close together, thick, crowded.]

at·om (ăt′əm) *n.* **1.a.** A part or particle considered to be an irreducible constituent of a specified system. **b.** The irreducible, indestructible material unit postulated by ancient atomism. **2.** An extremely small part, quantity, or amount. **3.** *Physics & Chemistry.* **a.** A unit of matter, the smallest unit of an element, having all the characteristics of that element and consisting of a dense, central, positively charged nucleus surrounded by a system of electrons. The entire structure has an approximate diameter of 10^{-8} centimeter and characteristically remains undivided in chemical reactions except for limited removal, transfer, or exchange of certain electrons. **b.** This unit regarded as a source of nuclear energy. See table at **subatomic particle.** [Middle English *attome,* from Latin *atomus,* from Greek *atomos,* indivisible, atom : *a-,* not; see A-¹ + *tomos,* cutting (from *temnein,* to cut; see **tem-** in Appendix).]

atom bomb *n.* **1.** An explosive weapon of great destructive power derived from the rapid release of energy in the fission of heavy atomic nuclei, as of uranium 235. Also called *A-bomb, atomic bomb, fission bomb.* **2.** A bomb deriving its destructive power from the release of nuclear energy.

a·tom·ic (ə-tŏm′ĭk) *adj.* **1.** *Abbr.* **at.** Of or relating to an atom or atoms. **2.** Of or employing nuclear energy: *an atomic submarine; atomic weapons.* **3.** Very small; infinitesimal. **—a·tom′i·cal·ly** *adv.*

atomic age also **Atomic Age** *n.* The current era as characterized by the discovery, technological applications, and sociopolitical consequences of nuclear energy.

atomic bomb *n.* See **atom bomb** (sense 1).

atomic clock *n.* An extremely precise timekeeping device regulated in correspondence with a characteristic invariant frequency of an atomic or molecular system.

atomic energy *n.* See **nuclear energy.**

at·o·mic·i·ty (ăt′ə-mĭs′ĭ-tē) *n.* **1.** The state of being composed of atoms. **2.** *Chemistry.* **a.** The number of atoms in a molecule. **b.** Valence.

atomic mass *n.* The mass of an atom, usually expressed in atomic mass units.

atomic mass unit *n. Abbr.* **amu** A unit of mass equal to 1⁄12 the mass of the most abundant isotope of carbon, carbon 12, which is assigned a mass of 12. Also called *dalton.*

atomic number *n. Symbol* **Z** *Abbr.* **at. no., at no** The number of protons in an atomic nucleus.

atomic theory *n.* The physical theory of the structure, properties, and behavior of the atom.

atomic veteran *n.* A former member of the armed forces who was exposed to radioactivity during the testing or use of atom bombs in or after World War II.

atomic weight *n. Abbr.* **at wt** The average mass of an atom of an element, usually expressed relative to the mass of carbon 12, which is assigned 12 atomic mass units.

at·om·ism (ăt′ə-mĭz′əm) *n.* **1.** *Philosophy.* The ancient theory of Democritus, Epicurus, and Lucretius, according to which simple, minute, indivisible, and indestructible particles are the basic components of the entire universe. **2.** *Philosophy.* A theory according to which social institutions, values, and processes arise solely from the acts and interests of individuals, who thus constitute the only true subject of analysis. **3.a.** The division of or tendency to divide a society into subclasses, groups, or units. **b.** The understanding of society as a set of independent wills, based on a belief in the priority of individual over cooperative values: *"the kind of atomism and individualism that is implicit in what might be called the John Wayne conception of society and the individual"* (Saturday Review). **—at′om·ist** *n.*

at·om·is·tic (ăt′ə-mĭs′tĭk) also **at·om·is·ti·cal** (-tĭ-kəl) *adj.* **1.** Of or having to do with atoms or atomism. **2.** Consisting of many separate, often disparate elements: *an atomistic culture.* **—at′om·is′ti·cal·ly** *adv.*

at·om·ize (ăt′ə-mīz′) *tr.v.* **-ized, -iz·ing, -iz·es. 1.** To reduce to or separate into atoms. **2.** To reduce to tiny particles or a fine spray. **3.** To break into small fragments. **4.** To subject to

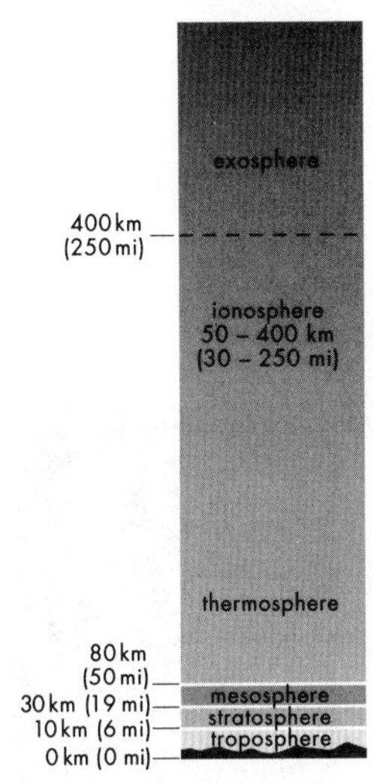

atmosphere

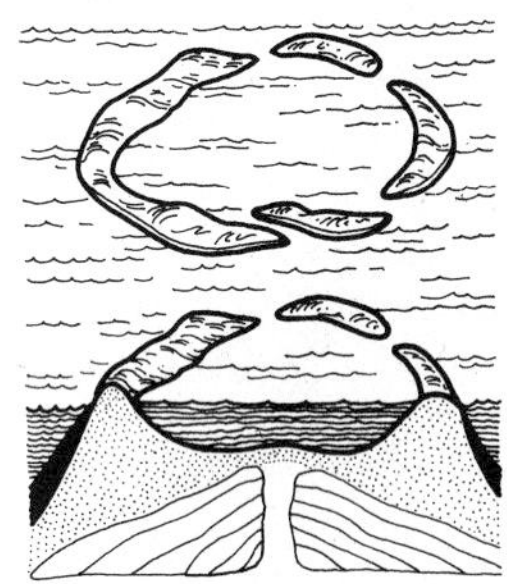
atoll
Top: Aerial view
Bottom: Cutaway drawing

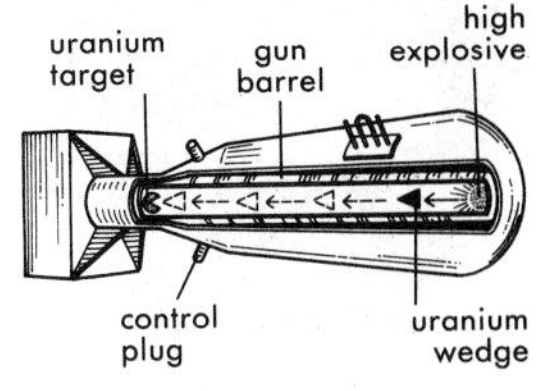

atom bomb

ă pat	oi boy
ā pay	ou out
âr care	ŏŏ took
ä father	ōō boot
ĕ pet	ŭ cut
ē be	ûr urge
ĭ pit	th thin
ī pie	*th* this
îr pier	hw which
ŏ pot	zh vision
ō toe	ə about, item
ô paw	♦ regionalism

Stress marks: ′ (primary); ′ (secondary), as in **dictionary** (dĭk′shə-nĕr′ē)

bombardment with atomic weapons. **—at′om·i·za′tion** (-ĭ-zā′shən) *n.*

at·om·iz·er (ăt′ə-mī′zər) *n.* A device for converting a substance, especially a perfume or medicine, to a fine spray.

atom smasher *n.* See **accelerator** (sense 3).

at·o·my[1] (ăt′ə-mē) *n., pl.* **-mies.** *Archaic.* **1.** A tiny particle; a mote. **2.** A tiny being. [From Latin *atomī,* pl. of *atomus,* atom. See ATOM.]

at·o·my[2] (ăt′ə-mē) *n., pl.* **-mies.** *Archaic.* A gaunt person; a skeleton. [From *an atomy,* respelling of ANATOMY.]

A·ton also **A·ten** (ät′n) *n. Mythology.* An Egyptian god of the sun, regarded during the reign of Akhenaton as the only god.

atrium
Isabella Stewart Gardner Museum, Boston

a·to·nal (ā-tō′nəl) *adj. Music.* Lacking a tonal center or key; characterized by atonality. **—a·to′nal·ly** *adv.*

a·to·nal·ism (ā-tō′nə-lĭz′əm) *n. Music.* Atonal composition or the theory of atonal composition. **—a·to′nal·ist** *adj. & n.* **—a·to′nal·is′tic** *adj.*

a·to·nal·i·ty (ā′tō-năl′ĭ-tē) *n., pl.* **-ties.** *Music.* The absence of a tonal center and of harmonies derived from a diatonic scale corresponding to such a center; lack of tonality.

a·tone (ə-tōn′) *v.* **a·toned, a·ton·ing, a·tones.** *—intr.* **1.** To make amends, as for a sin or fault: *These crimes must be atoned for.* **2.** *Archaic.* To agree. *—tr.* **1.** To expiate. **2.** *Archaic.* To conciliate; appease: *"So heaven, atoned, shall dying Greece restore"* (Alexander Pope). **3.** *Obsolete.* To reconcile or harmonize. [Middle English *atonen,* to be reconciled, from *at one,* in agreement : *at,* at; see AT[1] + *one,* one; see ONE.] **—a·ton′a·ble, a·tone′a·ble** *adj.* **—a·ton′er** *n.*

a·tone·ment (ə-tōn′mənt) *n.* **1.** Amends or reparation made for an injury or wrong; expiation. **2.a.** *Theology.* Reconciliation or an instance of reconciliation between God and human beings. **b. Atonement.** The redemptive life and death of Jesus. **c. Atonement.** The reconciliation of God and human beings brought about by Jesus. **3.** *Christian Science.* The radical obedience and purification, exemplified in the life of Jesus, by which humanity finds oneness with God. **4.** *Obsolete.* Reconciliation; concord.

a·ton·ic (ā-tŏn′ĭk) *adj.* **1.** Not accented: *an atonic syllable.* **2.** *Pathology.* Relating to, caused by, or exhibiting lack of muscle tone. **—atonic** *n.* A word, syllable, or sound that is unaccented. [From Greek *atonos.* See ATONY.] **—at′o·nic′i·ty** (ăt′ə-nĭs′ĭ-tē, ăt′n-ĭs-) *n.*

at·o·ny (ăt′ə-nē, ăt′n-ē) *n.* **1.** Lack of normal muscle tone. **2.** Lack of accent or stress. [Late Latin *atonia,* from Greek, from *atonos,* slack : *a-,* without; see A–[1] + *tonos,* stretching, tone; see TONE.]

a·top (ə-tŏp′) *adv.* To, on, or at the top. **—atop** *prep.* On top of. **—a·top′** *adj.*

a·top·ic (ā-tŏp′ĭk) *adj.* Of, relating to, or caused by a hereditary predisposition toward the development of certain hypersensitivity reactions, such as hay fever, asthma, or chronic urticaria, upon exposure to specific antigens: *atopic dermatitis.* [From Greek *atopia,* unusualness, from *atopos,* out of the way : *a-,* not; see A–[1] + *topos,* place.] **—at′o·py** (ăt′ə-pē) *n.*

-ator *suff.* One that acts in a specified manner: *radiator.* [Latin *-ātor* : *-ā-,* stem vowel of verbs in *-āre* + *-tor,* agent n. suff. (later reanalyzed as *-ātus,* -ate + *-or,* -or).]

attaché case

-atory *suff.* **1.a.** Of or relating to: *perspiratory.* **b.** Tending to: *amendatory.* **2.** One that is connected with: *reformatory.* [From Latin *-ātōrius* and *-ātōrium,* both from *-ātor,* -ator.]

a·tox·ic (ā-tŏk′sĭk) *adj.* Not poisonous or toxic.

ATP (ā′tē′pē′) *n.* An adenosine-derived nucleotide, $C_{10}H_{16}N_5O_{13}P_3$, that supplies large amounts of energy to cells for various biochemical processes, including muscle contraction and sugar metabolism, through its hydrolysis to ADP. [A(DENOSINE) T(RI)P(HOSPHATE).]

ATP·ase (ā′tē-pē′ās, -āz) *n.* An enzyme that catalyzes the hydrolysis of ATP; adenosine triphosphatase.

at·ra·bil·ious (ăt′rə-bĭl′yəs) also **at·ra·bil·i·ar** (-bĭl′ē-ər) *adj.* **1.** Inclined to melancholy. **2.** Having a peevish disposition; surly. [From Latin *ātra bīlis,* black bile (translation of Greek *melankholia;* see MELANCHOLY) : *ātra,* black; see **āter-** in Appendix + *bīlis,* bile.] **—at′ra·bil′ious·ness** *n.*

a·trem·ble (ə-trĕm′bəl) *adj.* Being in a state of shaking or trembling, as from fear or excitement.

a·tre·sia (ə-trē′zhə, -zhē-ə) *n.* **1.** The absence or closure of a normal body orifice or tubular passage such as the anus, intestine, or external ear canal. **2.** The degeneration and resorption of one or more ovarian follicles before a state of maturity has been reached. [New Latin : Greek *a-,* not, without; see A–[1] + *trēsis,* perforation, orifice; see **terə-**[1] in Appendix.] **—a·tre·sic** (-zĭk, -sĭk) *adj.*

A·treus (ā′trōōs′, ā′trē-əs) *n. Greek Mythology.* A king of Mycenae, brother of Thyestes and father of Agamemnon and Menelaus.

a·tri·a (ā′trē-ə) *n.* A plural of **atrium.**

atrial na·tri·u·ret·ic factor (nā′trē-yōō-rĕt′ĭk) *n. Abbr.* **ANF** A hormonal substance produced by the right atrium of the heart that stimulates the excretion of sodium and water by the kidneys and helps regulate blood pressure. [ATRIAL + *natrium,* sodium (from NATRON) + URETIC + FACTOR.]

a·tri·o·ven·tric·u·lar (ā′trē-ō-vĕn-trĭk′yə-lər) *adj.* Of, relating to, or involving the atria and the ventricles of the heart.

atrioventricular node *n.* A small mass of specialized cardiac muscle fibers, located in the wall of the right atrium of the heart, that receives heartbeat impulses from the sinoatrial node and directs them to the walls of the ventricles. Also called *AV node.*

a·trip (ə-trĭp′) *adj. Nautical.* Just clear of the bottom. Used of an anchor.

a·tri·um (ā′trē-əm) *n., pl.* **a·tri·a** (ā′trē-ə) or **-ums. 1.** *Architecture.* A rectangular court, as: **a.** A usually skylighted central area, often containing plants, in some modern buildings, especially of a public or commercial nature. **b.** The open area in the center of an ancient Roman house. **c.** The forecourt of a building, such as an early Christian church, enclosed on three or four sides with porticoes. **2.** *Anatomy.* A bodily cavity or chamber, especially either of the upper chambers of the heart that receives blood from the veins and forces it into a ventricle. In this sense, also called *auricle.* [Latin *ātrium.* See **āter-** in Appendix.] **—a′tri·al** *adj.*

a·tro·cious (ə-trō′shəs) *adj.* **1.** Extremely evil or cruel; monstrous: *an atrocious crime.* See Synonyms at **outrageous. 2.** Exceptionally bad; abominable: *atrocious decor; atrocious behavior.* [From Latin *atrōx, atrōc-,* frightful, cruel. See **āter-** in Appendix.] **—a·tro′cious·ly** *adv.* **—a·tro′cious·ness** *n.*

a·troc·i·ty (ə-trŏs′ĭ-tē) *n., pl.* **-ties. 1.** Appalling or atrocious condition, quality, or behavior; monstrousness. **2.a.** An appalling or atrocious action, situation, or object. **b.** An act of cruelty and violence inflicted by an enemy armed force on civilians or prisoners: *wartime atrocities.*

at·ro·phy (ăt′rə-fē) *n., pl.* **-phies. 1.** *Pathology.* A wasting or decrease in size of a bodily organ, tissue, or part owing to disease, injury, or lack of use: *muscular atrophy of a person affected with paralysis.* **2.** A wasting away, deterioration, or diminution: *intellectual atrophy.* **—atrophy** *v.* **-phied, -phy·ing, -phies.** *—tr.* To cause to wither or deteriorate; affect with atrophy. *—intr.* To waste away; wither or deteriorate. [Late Latin *atrophia,* from Greek, from *atrophos,* ill-nourished : *a-,* without; see A–[1] + *trophē,* food.] **—a·troph′ic** (ā-trŏf′ĭk) *adj.*

at·ro·pine (ăt′rə-pēn′, -pĭn) also **at·ro·pin** (-pĭn) *n.* A poisonous, bitter, crystalline alkaloid, $C_{17}H_{23}NO_3$, obtained from belladonna and other related plants. It is used to dilate the pupils of the eyes and as an antispasmodic. [From New Latin *Atropa,* genus name of belladonna, from Greek *atropos,* unchangeable. See ATROPOS.]

At·ro·pos (ăt′rə-pŏs′, -pəs) *n. Greek Mythology.* One of the three Fates, the cutter of the thread of destiny. [Greek, from *atropos,* inexorable : *a-,* not; see A–[1] + *tropos,* changeable; see –TROPOUS.]

At·si·na (ăt-sē′nə) *n., pl.* **Atsina** or **-nas. 1.a.** A Native American people formerly inhabiting the plains of northern Montana and southern Saskatchewan, with a present-day population in north central Montana. **b.** A member of this people. **2.** The Algonquian language of the Atsina, dialectally related to Arapaho. Also called *Gros Ventre.*

att. *abbr.* **1.** Attached. **2.** Attention. **3.** *Law.* Attorney.

at·tach (ə-tăch′) *v.* **-tached, -tach·ing, -tach·es.** *—tr.* **1.** To fasten, secure, or join. **2.** To connect as an adjunct or associated condition or part: *Many major issues are attached to this legislation. They gained influence by attaching themselves to prominent city institutions.* **3.** To affix or append; add: *We attached several riders to the document.* **4.** To ascribe or assign: *attached no significance to the threat.* **5.** To bind by emotional ties, as of affection or loyalty: *I am attached to my family.* **6.** To assign (personnel) to a military unit on a temporary basis. **7.** *Law.* To seize (persons or property) by legal writ. *—intr.* To adhere, belong, or relate: *Very little prestige attaches to this position.* [Middle English *attachen,* from Old French *attachier,* alteration of *estachier,* from *estache,* stake, of Germanic origin.] **—at·tach′a·ble** *adj.* **—at·tach′er** *n.*

at·ta·ché (ăt′ə-shā′, ă-tă-) *n.* **1.** A person officially assigned to the staff of a diplomatic mission to serve in a particular capacity: *a cultural attaché; a military attaché.* **2.** An attaché case. [French, from past participle of *attacher,* to attach. See ATTACH.]

attaché case *n.* A slim briefcase with flat, rigid sides, hinges, and usually a lock.

at·tached (ə-tăcht′) *adj.* **1.** *Abbr.* **att.** *Architecture.* Joined to or by a wall, especially by sharing a wall with another building; not freestanding: *a block of attached houses.* **2.** *Biology.* Living in a permanently fixed state in the adult stage, as the barnacle.

at·tach·ment (ə-tăch′mənt) *n.* **1.** The act of attaching or the condition of being attached. **2.** Something, such as a tie, band, or fastener, that attaches one thing to another. **3.** A bond, as of affection or loyalty; fond regard. **4.** A supplementary part; an accessory. See Synonyms at **appendage. 5.** *Law.* **a.** Legal seizure of property or a person. **b.** The writ ordering such a seizure.

at·tack (ə-tăk′) *v.* **-tacked, -tack·ing, -tacks.** *—tr.* **1.** To set upon with violent force. **2.** To criticize strongly or in a hostile manner. **3.** To start work on with purpose and vigor: *attack a problem.* **4.** To begin to affect harmfully: *The disease had already attacked the central nervous system.* *—intr.* To make an attack; launch an assault: *The enemy attacked during the night.* **—attack** *n.* **1.** The act or an instance of attacking; an assault. **2.** An expression of strong criticism; hostile comment: *vicious attacks in all the newspapers.* **3.** *Sports.* **a.** An offensive action in a sport or game. **b.** The players executing such an action. **4.** The initial movement in a task or undertaking: *made an optimistic attack on the pile of paperwork.* **5.** An episode or onset of a disease, especially an occurrence of a chronic disease: *an asthma attack.* **6.** The experience or beginning of a feeling, need, or desire: *an attack of hunger; an attack of melancholy.* **7.a.** *Music.* The beginning or manner of beginning a piece, passage, or tone. **b.** Decisiveness and clarity in artistic expression: *a careful performance, but one lacking the rigorous attack the work demands.* [French *attaquer,* from Old French, from Old Italian **estaccare,* of Germanic origin.] **—at·tack′er** *n.*

SYNONYMS: *attack, bombard, assail, storm, assault, beset.* These verbs mean to set upon, physically or figuratively. *Attack* applies to offensive action, physical or verbal, and especially to the onset of planned aggression: *The commandos attacked the outpost at dawn. The governor was attacked by the press for failing to keep a campaign promise. Bombard* suggests showering with bombs or shells (*The fleet anchored in the bay and bombarded the town*) or figuratively with words (*The television star was bombarded with invitations*). *Assail* implies repeated attacks: *an area assailed by enemy forces from both directions; a novel assailed by critics; a member of the jury assailed by doubts. Storm* refers to a sudden, sweeping attempt to achieve a victory: *Some of the rebels were killed in the act of storming the citadel. "Yet, only a few months after triumphantly storming the country,* [the President] *is obliged to storm Capitol Hill, with greater difficulty and with less than complete success"* (Economist). *Assault* usually implies sudden, intense violence: *Muggers often assault their victims on dark streets. Strobe lights assaulted my eyes. Beset* suggests beleaguerment from all sides by an enemy force or by adversity: *The fox was beset by hunters and hounds. The city council is beset by problems.*

at·tain (ə-tān′) *v.* **-tained, -tain·ing, -tains.** —*tr.* **1.** To gain as an objective; achieve. **2.** To arrive at, as by virtue of persistence or the passage of time. See Synonyms at **reach.** —*intr.* To succeed in a directed effort, process, or progression: *attained to high office; eventually attained to wisdom.* [Middle English *atteignen,* from Old French *ataindre, ataign-,* to reach to, from Vulgar Latin **attangere,* from Latin *attingere* : *ad-,* ad- + *tangere,* to touch; see **tag-** in Appendix.] **—at·tain′a·bil′i·ty, at·tain′a·ble·ness** *n.* **—at·tain′a·ble** *adj.*

at·tain·der (ə-tān′dər) *n.* **1.** In the ancient common law, the state into which an offender was placed when a sentence against him for a capital offense was handed down. **2.** *Obsolete.* Dishonor. [Middle English *atteindre,* act of attainting, from Old French *ataindre,* to convict, affect, attainder. See ATTAIN.]

at·tain·ment (ə-tān′mənt) *n.* **1.** The act of attaining or the condition of being attained. **2.** Something, such as an accomplishment or achievement, that is attained.

at·taint (ə-tānt′) *tr.v.* **-taint·ed, -taint·ing, -taints. 1.** To impart stigma to; disgrace: *"No breath of calumny ever attainted the personal purity of Savonarola"* (Henry Hart Milman). **2.** To pass a sentence of attainder against. **3.** *Archaic.* To infect or corrupt, as with illness or vice. **4.** *Archaic.* To accuse. **—attaint** *n.* **1.** *Obsolete.* Attainder. **2.** *Archaic.* A disgrace; a stigma. [Middle English *attainten,* from Old French *ataint,* past participle of *ataindre,* to affect. See ATTAIN.]

at·tar (ăt′ər) also **ot·tar** (ŏt′ər) or **ot·to** (ŏt′ō) *n.* A fragrant essential oil or perfume obtained from flowers: *attar of roses.* [Persian *'aṭir,* perfumed, from Arabic *'iṭr,* perfume.]

At·tar (ăt′ər, ə-tär′). Died c. 1229. Persian poet and mystic whose masterpiece, *Conference of the Birds,* is an allegorical survey of Sufism.

At·ta·wa·pis·kat (ăt′ə-wə-pĭs′kət). A river, about 748 km (465 mi) long, of northern Ontario, Canada, flowing from **Attawapiskat Lake** east and northeast into James Bay.

at·te·let (ăt′l-ā′) *n.* A slender skewer, usually ornamented at the top, used decoratively, especially in serving garnishes. [French, variant of *hâtelet,* from Old French *hastelet.* See HASLET.]

at·tempt (ə-tĕmpt′) *tr.v.* **-tempt·ed, -tempt·ing, -tempts. 1.a.** To make an effort; endeavor: *I attempted to read the entire novel in one sitting.* **b.** To try to perform, make, or achieve: *We attempted the difficult maneuver without assistance.* **2.** *Archaic.* To tempt. **3.** *Archaic.* To attack with the intention of subduing. **—attempt** *n.* **1.** An effort or a try. **2.** An attack; an assault: *an attempt on someone's life.* [Middle English *attempten,* from Old French *attempter,* from Latin *attemptāre* : *ad-,* ad- + *temptāre,* to test.] **—at·tempt′a·ble** *adj.* **—at·tempt′er** *n.*

at·tend (ə-tĕnd′) *v.* **-tend·ed, -tend·ing, -tends.** —*tr.* **1.** To be present at: *attended class.* **2.** To accompany as a circumstance or follow as a result: *The speech was attended by wild applause.* **3.a.** To accompany or wait upon as a companion or servant. **b.** To take care of (a sick person, for example). See Synonyms at **tend**[2]. **4.** To take charge of: *They attended our affairs during our absence.* **5.** To listen to; heed: *attended my every word.* **6.** *Archaic.* To wait for; expect. —*intr.* **1.** To be present. **2.** To take care; give attention: *We'll attend to that problem later.* **3.** To apply or direct oneself: *attended to their business.* **4.** To pay attention: *attended disinterestedly to the debate.* **5.** To remain ready to serve; wait. **6.** *Obsolete.* To delay or wait. [Middle English *attenden,* from Old French *atendre,* from Latin *attendere,* to heed : *ad-,* ad- + *tendere,* to stretch; see **ten-** in Appendix.] **—at·tend′er** *n.*

at·ten·dance (ə-tĕn′dəns) *n.* **1.** The act of attending. **2.** The persons or number of persons that are present. **3.** The frequency with which a person is present.

at·ten·dant (ə-tĕn′dənt) *n.* **1.** One who attends or waits on another. **2.** One who is present. **3.** An accompanying thing or circumstance; a concomitant. **—attendant** *adj.* **1.** Being present: *ships and attendant sailors.* **2.** Accompanying or following as a result: *attendant circumstances.* **—at·tend′ant·ly** *adv.*

at·tend·ee (ə-tĕn′dē′, ăt′ĕn-) *n.* One who is present at or attends a function. See Usage Note at **-ee**[1].

at·tend·ing (ə-tĕn′dĭng) *adj.* **1.** Being the principal physician supervising a patient's care. **2.** Being a physician on the regular medical staff of a hospital. **—attending** *n.* **1.** The principal physician supervising a patient's care. **2.** A staff physician.

at·ten·tion (ə-tĕn′shən) *n. Abbr.* **att., attn. 1.** Concentration of the mental powers upon an object; a close or careful observing or listening. **2.** The ability or power to concentrate mentally. **3.** Observant consideration; notice: *Your suggestion has come to our attention.* **4.** Consideration or courtesy: *attention to others' feelings.* **5. attentions.** Acts of courtesy, consideration, or gallantry, especially by a suitor. **6.** A military posture, with the body erect, eyes to the front, arms at the sides, and heels together. **—attention** *interj.* Used as a command to assume an erect military posture. [Middle English *attencioun,* from Latin *attentiō, attentiōn-,* from *attentus,* past participle of *attendere,* to heed. See ATTEND.] **—at·ten′tion·al** *adj.*

attention deficit disorder *n. Abbr.* **ADD** A childhood syndrome characterized by impulsiveness, hyperactivity, and short attention span, which often leads to learning disabilities and various behavioral problems.

attention span *n.* The length of time during which a person can concentrate or focus attention on a particular object or idea without diversion.

at·ten·tive (ə-tĕn′tĭv) *adj.* **1.** Giving care or attention; watchful: *attentive to detail.* **2.** Marked by or offering devoted and assiduous attention to the pleasure or comfort of others. See Synonyms at **thoughtful. 3.** Expressing affectionate interest through close observation and gallant gestures: *He played the attentive suitor, complete with roses and bonbons.* **—at·ten′tive·ly** *adv.* **—at·ten′tive·ness** *n.*

at·ten·u·ate (ə-tĕn′yo͞o-āt′) *v.* **-at·ed, -at·ing, -ates.** —*tr.* **1.** To make slender, fine, or small. **2.** To reduce in force, value, amount, or degree; weaken. **3.** To lessen the density of; rarefy. **4.** *Biology.* To make (bacteria or viruses) less virulent. **5.** *Electronics.* To reduce (the amplitude of an electrical signal) with little or no distortion. —*intr.* To become thin, weak, or fine. **—attenuate** (-yo͞o-ĭt) *adj.* **1.** Reduced or weakened, as in strength, value, or virulence. **2.** *Botany.* Gradually tapering to a slender point. [Latin *attenuāre, attenuāt-* : *ad-,* ad- + *tenuāre,* to make thin (from *tenuis,* thin; see **ten-** in Appendix).] **—at·ten′u·a′tion** *n.*

at·ten·u·a·tor (ə-tĕn′yo͞o-ā′tər) *n.* A device that attenuates an electrical signal.

at·test (ə-tĕst′) *v.* **-test·ed, -test·ing, -tests.** —*tr.* **1.** To affirm to be correct, true, or genuine. **2.a.** To certify by signature or oath. **b.** To certify in an official capacity. **3.** To supply or be evidence of: *splendid tombs that attested their power.* See Synonyms at **indicate. 4.** To put under oath. —*intr.* To bear witness; give testimony: *attested to their good faith.* **—attest** *n. Archaic.* Attestation. [Latin *attestārī* : *ad-,* ad- + *testārī,* to be witness (from *testis,* witness; see **trei-** in Appendix).] **—at·test′ant** *n.* **—at′tes·ta′tion** (ăt′ĕs-tā′shən, ăt′ə-stā′-) *n.* **—at·test′er, at·tes′tor** *n.*

Att. Gen. *abbr. Law.* Attorney general.

at·tic (ăt′ĭk) *n.* **1.** A story or room directly below the roof of a building, especially a house. **2.** A low wall or story above the cornice of a classical façade. [From *Attic story,* story of a building enclosed by one decorative structure placed above another, much taller decorative structure, usually involving the Attic order, an architectural order having square columns of any of the basic five orders, from French *attique,* from *attique,* Attic, from Latin *Atticus.* See ATTIC.]

At·tic (ăt′ĭk) *adj.* **1.** Of, relating to, or characteristic of ancient Attica, Athens, or the Athenians. **2.** Characterized by purity, simplicity, and elegant wit: *Attic prose.* **—Attic** *n.* The ancient Greek dialect of Attica, in which the bulk of classical Greek literature is written. [Latin *Atticus,* from Greek *Attikos,* from *Attikē,* Attica.]

At·ti·ca (ăt′ĭ-kə). An ancient region of east-central Greece around Athens. According to Greek legend, the four Attic tribes were unified into a single state by the Athenian king Theseus.

At·ti·cism (ăt′ĭ-sĭz′əm) *n.* **1.** A characteristic feature of Attic Greek. **2. atticism.** An expression characterized by conciseness and elegance.

At·ti·la (ăt′l-ə, ə-tĭl′ə). Called "the Scourge of the Gods." A.D. 406?–453. King of the Huns (433?–453) and the most successful of the barbarian invaders of the Roman Empire.

at·tire (ə-tīr′) *tr.v.* **-tired, -tir·ing, -tires.** To dress or clothe, especially in elaborate or splendid garments. **—attire** *n.* **1.** Clothing or array; apparel. **2.** The antlers of a deer. [Middle English *atiren,* from Old French *atirier* : *a-,* to (from Latin *ad-;* see AD–) + *tire,* order, rank; see TIER[1].]

at·ti·tude (ăt′ĭ-to͞od′, -tyo͞od′) *n.* **1.** A position of the body or manner of carrying oneself: *stood in a graceful attitude.* See Synonyms at **posture. 2.** A state of mind or a feeling; disposition: *an*

ă pat	oi boy
ā pay	ou out
âr care	o͝o took
ä father	o͞o boot
ĕ pet	ŭ cut
ē be	ûr urge
ĭ pit	th thin
ī pie	*th* this
îr pier	hw which
ŏ pot	zh vision
ō toe	ə about, item
ô paw	♦ regionalism

Stress marks: ′ (primary); ′ (secondary), as in **dictionary** (dĭk′shə-nĕr′ē)

attitude of open hostility. **3.** The orientation of an aircraft's axes relative to a reference line or plane, such as the horizon. **4.** The orientation of a spacecraft relative to its direction of motion. **5.** A position similar to an arabesque in which a ballet dancer stands on one leg with the other raised either in front or in back and bent at the knee. [French, from Italian *attitudine,* from Late Latin *aptitūdō, aptitūdin-,* faculty, from Latin *aptus,* fit. See APTITUDE.] **—at'ti·tu'di·nal** (ăt'ĭ-to͞od'n-əl, -tyo͞od'-) *adj.*

at·ti·tu·di·nize (ăt'ĭ-to͞od'n-īz', -tyo͞od'-) *intr.v.* **-nized, -niz·ing, -niz·es.** To assume an affected attitude; posture.

At·tle·bor·o (ăt'l-bûr'ō, -bŭr'ō). A city of southeast Massachusetts northeast of Providence, Rhode Island. Its jewelry industry began in 1780. Population, 34,196.

Att·lee (ăt'lē), **Clement Richard.** 1883–1967. British politician who as prime minister (1945–1951) formed the Labor government that established the National Health Service, expanded public ownership of industry, and granted independence to India (1947) and Burma (1948).

attn. *abbr.* Attention.

atto– *pref.* One quintillionth (10^{-18}): *attotesla.* [From Danish or Norwegian *atten,* eighteen, from Old Norse *āttjān.* See **oktō(u)** in Appendix.]

at·torn (ə-tûrn') *intr.v.* **-torned, -torn·ing, -torns.** *Law.* To agree to remain as a tenant of property after its ownership has been transferred. [Middle English *attournen,* from Old French *atorner,* to assign to : *a-,* to (from Latin *ad-;* see AD–) + *torner,* to turn; see TURN.] **—at·torn'ment** *n.*

at·tor·ney (ə-tûr'nē) *n., pl.* **-neys.** *Abbr.* **att., atty.** *Law.* A person legally appointed by another to act as his or her agent in the transaction of business, specifically one qualified and licensed to act for plaintiffs and defendants in legal proceedings. See Synonyms at **lawyer.** [Middle English *attourney,* from Old French *atorne,* from past participle of *atorner,* to appoint. See ATTORN.] **—at·tor'ney·ship'** *n.*

attorney at law or **at·tor·ney-at-law** (ə-tûr'nē-ət-lô') *n., pl.* **attorneys at law** or **at·tor·neys-at-law** (-nēz-). *Law.* An attorney.

attorney general *n., pl.* **attorneys general** or **attorney generals.** *Abbr.* **A.G., AG, Att. Gen., Atty. Gen.** *Law.* **1.** The chief law officer and legal counsel of the government of a state or nation. **2. Attorney General.** The head of the U.S. Department of Justice and a member of the President's cabinet.

at·to·tes·la (ăt'ō-tĕs'lə) *n.* *Abbr.* **aT** One-quintillionth (10^{-18}) of a tesla.

at·tract (ə-trăkt') *v.* **-tract·ed, -tract·ing, -tracts.** *—tr.* **1.** To cause to draw near or adhere; direct to or toward itself or oneself: *Magnetic poles are attracted to their opposites. The fire attracted significant coverage from the media.* **2.** To arouse or compel the interest, admiration, or attention of: *We were attracted by the display of lights.* *—intr.* To possess or use the power of attraction. [Middle English *attracten,* from Latin *attrahere, attract-* : *ad-,* ad- + *trahere,* pull.] **—at·tract'a·ble** *adj.* **—at·tract'er, at·trac'tor** *n.*

at·trac·tion (ə-trăk'shən) *n.* **1.** The act or capability of attracting. **2.** The quality of attracting; charm. **3. a.** A feature or characteristic that attracts. **b.** A person, place, thing, or event that is intended to attract: *The main attraction was a Charlie Chaplin film.*

at·trac·tive (ə-trăk'tĭv) *adj.* **1.** Having the power to attract. **2.** Pleasing to the eye or mind; charming. **—at·trac'tive·ly** *adv.* **—at·trac'tive·ness** *n.*

attrib. *abbr.* *Grammar.* Attribute; attributive.

at·trib·ute (ə-trĭb'yo͞ot) *tr.v.* **-ut·ed, -ut·ing, -utes.** **1.** To relate to a particular cause or source; ascribe. **2.** To regard as the work of a specified agent or creator: *attributed the painting to Titian.* **—attribute** (ăt'rə-byo͞ot') *n.* **1.** A quality or characteristic inherent in or ascribed to someone or something. **2.** An object associated with and serving to identify a character, a personage, or an office: *Lightning bolts are an attribute of Zeus.* **3.** *Abbr.* **attrib.** *Grammar.* A word or phrase syntactically subordinate to another word or phrase that it modifies; for example, *my sister's* and *brown* in *my sister's brown dog.* [Latin *attribuere, attribūt-* : *ad-,* ad- + *tribuere,* to allot; see TRIBUTE.] **—at·trib'ut·a·ble** *adj.* **—at·trib'ut·er, at·trib'u·tor** *n.*

SYNONYMS: *attribute, ascribe, impute, credit, assign, refer.* These verbs mean to consider as resulting from, proper to, or belonging to a person or thing. *Attribute* and *ascribe,* often interchangeable, have the widest application: *a symphony attributed to Mozart; an invention ascribed to the 15th century. Impute* is often used in laying guilt or fault to another: *"We usually* ascribe *good; but* impute *evil"* (Samuel Johnson). *Credit* frequently applies to an accomplishment or virtue: *"Some excellent remarks were made on immortality, but mainly borrowed from and credited to Plato"* (Oliver Wendell Holmes, Sr.). *Assign* and *refer* are often used to classify or categorize according to character or chronology: *Program music as a genre is usually assigned to the Romantic period. "A person thus prepared will be able to refer any particular history he takes up to its proper place in universal history"* (Joseph Priestley). See also Synonyms at **quality, symbol.**

at·tri·bu·tion (ăt'rə-byo͞o'shən) *n.* **1.** The act of attributing, especially of establishing a particular person, place, or time as the creator, provenance, or era of a work of art. **2.** Something, such as a quality or characteristic, that is related to a particular possessor; an attribute. **—at'tri·bu'tion·al** *adj.*

at·trib·u·tive (ə-trĭb'yə-tĭv) *n.* *Abbr.* **attrib.** *Grammar.* A word or word group, such as an adjective, that is placed adjacent to the noun it modifies without a linking verb; for example, *pale* in *the pale girl.* **—attributive** *adj.* **1.** *Abbr.* **attrib.** *Grammar.* Of, relating to, or being an attributive, as an adjective. **2.** Of or having the nature of an attribution or attribute. **—at·trib'u·tive·ly** *adv.* **—at·trib'u·tive·ness** *n.*

at·trit (ə-trĭt') also **at·trite** (ə-trīt') *tr.v.* **-trit·ted, -trit·ting, -trits** also **-trit·ed, -trit·ing, -trites.** **1.** To lose (personnel, for example) by attrition. **2.** To destroy or kill (troops, for example) by use of firepower: *"Pro-active counterattacks are a useful way to attrit the enemy"* (John H. Cushman, Jr.). [Back-formation from ATTRITION.]

at·tri·tion (ə-trĭsh'ən) *n.* **1.** A rubbing away or wearing down by friction. **2.** A gradual diminution in number or strength because of constant stress. **3.** A gradual, natural reduction in membership or personnel, as through retirement, resignation, or death. **4.** *Theology.* Repentance for sin motivated by fear of punishment rather than by love of God. [Middle English *attricioun,* regret, breaking, from Old French *attrition,* abrasion, from Late Latin *attritiō, attritiōn-,* act of rubbing against, from Latin *attrītus,* past participle of *atterere,* to rub against : *ad-,* against; see AD– + *terere,* to rub; see **terə-**[1] in Appendix.]

At·tu (ăt'to͞o'). An island of southwest Alaska, the westernmost of the Aleutians. In World War II it was occupied by the Japanese from June 1942 until June 1943.

At·tucks (ăt'əks), **Crispus.** 1723?–1770. American patriot who was among the five persons killed in the Boston Massacre.

at·tune (ə-to͞on', ə-tyo͞on') *tr.v.* **-tuned, -tun·ing, -tunes.** **1.** To bring into a harmonious or responsive relationship: *an industry that is not attuned to the demands of the market.* **2.** *Music.* To put (an instrument) into correct tune.

atty. *abbr.* *Law.* Attorney.

Atty. Gen. *abbr.* *Law.* Attorney General.

ATV *abbr.* All-terrain vehicle.

At·wa·ter (ăt'wô'tər, -wŏt'ər). A city of central California west-northwest of Merced. It is a commercial center in an irrigated farming area. Population, 17,530.

a·twit·ter (ə-twĭt'ər) *adj.* Being in a state of nervous excitement; twittering: *a crowd atwitter with expectation.*

at wt *abbr.* Atomic weight.

a·typ·i·cal (ā-tĭp'ĭ-kəl) also **a·typ·ic** (-ĭk) *adj.* Not conforming to type; unusual or irregular. **—a'typ·i·cal'i·ty** (-kăl'ĭ-tē) *n.* **—a·typ'i·cal·ly** *adv.*

au *n.* Author.

Au The symbol for the element **gold** (sense a). [From Latin *aurum,* gold.]

a.u. or **A.u.** *abbr.* Angstrom unit.

A.U. *abbr.* Astronomical unit.

au·bade (ō-bäd') *n.* **1.** *Music.* A song or instrumental composition concerning, accompanying, or evoking daybreak. **2.** A poem or song of or about lovers separating at dawn. [French, from Old French *albade,* from Old Provençal *albada,* from *alba,* dawn, aubade, from Latin *alba,* feminine of *albus,* white. See **albho-** in Appendix.]

Aube (ōb). A river of northeast France flowing about 225 km (140 mi) to the Seine River north-northwest of Troyes.

Au·ber (ō-bĕr'), **Daniel François Esprit.** 1782–1871. French operatic composer whose works include *La Muette de Portici* (1828) and *Fra Diavolo* (1829).

au·ber·gine (ō'bĕr-zhēn', ō'bər-jēn) *n.* See **eggplant** (sense 1). [French, from Catalan *albergina,* from Arabic *al-bāḏinjān,* the eggplant, from Persian *bādingān.*]

Au·ber·vil·liers (ō'bər-vēl-yā'). A town of north-central France northeast of Paris. It is an important industrial center. Population, 67,719.

Au·brey (ô'brē), **John.** 1626–1697. English antiquarian and writer whose *Brief Lives,* published posthumously, contains character sketches of his notable friends, including Thomas Hobbes, John Milton, and Francis Bacon.

au·burn (ô'bərn) *n.* *Color.* A moderate reddish brown to brown. [Middle English, from Old French *auborne,* blond, from Latin *alburnus,* whitish, from *albus,* white. See **albho-** in Appendix.] **—au'burn** *adj.*

Au·burn (ô'bərn). **1.** A city of eastern Alabama north-northeast of Tuskegee. It is the seat of Auburn University (founded 1856). Population, 28,471. **2.** A city of southern Maine on the Androscoggin River opposite Lewiston. It was settled in 1765. Population, 23,128. **3.** A city of west-central New York in the Finger Lakes region west-southwest of Syracuse. Founded in 1793, it is a manufacturing center. Population, 32,548. **4.** A city of western Washington east-northeast of Tacoma. It is a center of the state's aircraft industry. Population, 26,417.

Au·bus·son (ō'bə-sən, -sôN') *n.* A tapestry or usually pileless, densely patterned carpet woven in Aubusson, a city of central France, or similar to the ones made there.

A.U.C. *abbr.* *Latin.* **1.** Ab urbe condita (from the founding of the city [of Rome in 753? B.C.]). **2.** Anno urbis conditae (in the year from the founding of the city [of Rome in 753? B.C.]).

Auck·land (ôk'lənd). The largest city of New Zealand, on an isthmus of northwest North Island. It is a major port and an industrial center. Metropolitan area population, 860,000.

au cou·rant (ō′ ko͞o-räɴ′) *adj.* **1.** Informed on current affairs; up-to-date. **2.** Fully familiar; knowledgeable. [French : *au*, in the + *courant*, current.]

auc·tion (ôk′shən) *n.* **1.** A public sale in which property or items of merchandise are sold to the highest bidder. **2.** *Games.* **a.** The bidding in bridge. **b.** Auction bridge. —**auction** *tr.v.* **-tioned, -tion·ing, -tions.** To sell at or by an auction: *auctioned off the remaining inventory.* [Latin *auctiō, auctiōn-*, from *auctus*, past participle of *augēre*, to increase. See **aug-** in Appendix.]

auction bridge *n. Games.* A variety of bridge in which tricks made in excess of the contract are scored toward game.

auc·tion·eer (ôk′shə-nîr′) *n.* One that conducts an auction. —**auctioneer** *tr.v.* **-eered, -eer·ing, -eers.** To sell at auction.

auc·to·ri·al (ôk-tôr′ē-əl, -tōr′-) *adj.* Of or relating to an author. [From Latin *auctor*, author. See AUTHOR.]

au·cu·ba (ô′kyə-bə) *n.* Any of several eastern Asian evergreen shrubs of the genus *Aucuba*, especially *A. japonica*, grown as an ornamental chiefly for its glossy, leathery leaves. [New Latin : possibly from Japanese *auku*, green + Japanese *ba*, leaved.]

aud. *abbr.* **1.** Audit; auditor. **2.** Audition.

au·da·cious (ô-dā′shəs) *adj.* **1.** Fearlessly, often recklessly daring; bold. See Synonyms at **adventurous, brave. 2.** Unrestrained by convention or propriety; insolent. **3.** Spirited and original: *an audacious interpretation of two Jacobean dramas.* [French *audacieux*, from Old French *audace*, boldness, from Latin *audācia*, from *audāx, audāc-*, bold, from *audēre*, to dare, from *avidus*, avid. See AVID.] —**au·da′cious·ly** *adv.* —**au·da′cious·ness** *n.*

au·dac·i·ty (ô-dăs′ĭ-tē) *n., pl.* **-ties. 1.** Fearless daring; intrepidity. **2.** Bold or insolent heedlessness of restraints, as of those imposed by prudence, propriety, or convention. See Synonyms at **temerity. 3.** An act or instance of intrepidity or insolent heedlessness.

Au·den (ôd′n), **W(ystan) H(ugh).** 1907–1973. British-born American writer and critic whose poems, published in collections such as *The Dance of Death* (1933) and *The Double Man* (1941), established his importance in 20th-century literature.

au·di·al (ô′dē-əl) *adj.* Of or relating to the sense of hearing; aural. [AUDI(O)– + –AL[1].]

au·di·ble (ô′də-bəl) *adj.* That is heard or that can be heard. —**audible** *n. Football.* A new or substitute offensive play called by the quarterback or a defensive formation called by a linebacker at the line of scrimmage as an adjustment to the opposing side's formation. Also called *automatic.* [Late Latin *audībilis*, from Latin *audīre*, to hear. See **au-** in Appendix.] —**au′di·bil′i·ty** *n.* —**au′di·ble·ness** *n.* —**au′di·bly** *adv.*

au·di·ence (ô′dē-əns) *n.* **1. a.** The spectators or listeners assembled at a performance, for example, or attracted by a radio or television program. **b.** The readership for printed matter, as for a book. **2.** A body of adherents; a following: *The tenor expanded his audience by recording popular songs as well as opera.* **3.** A formal hearing, as with a religious or state dignitary. **4.** An opportunity to be heard or to express one's views. **5.** The act of hearing or attending. [Middle English, from Old French, from Latin *audientia*, from *audiēns*, present participle of *audīre*, to hear. See **au-** in Appendix.]

au·dile (ô′dīl′) *adj.* **1.** Capable of learning chiefly from auditory, rather than tactile or visual, stimuli. **2.** Auditory. —**audile** *n.* An audile person. [From Latin *audīre*, to hear. See **au-** in Appendix.]

au·di·o (ô′dē-ō′) *adj.* **1.** Of or relating to humanly audible sound. **2. a.** Of or relating to the broadcasting or reception of sound. **b.** Of or relating to high-fidelity sound reproduction. —**audio** *n., pl.* **-di·os. 1.** The part of television or motion-picture equipment that has to do with sound. **2.** The broadcasting, reception, or reproduction of sound. **3.** Audible sound. **4.** A sound signal. [From AUDIO–.]

audio– *pref.* **1.** Hearing: *audio-lingual.* **2.** Sound: *audiophile.* [From Latin *audīre*, to hear. See **au-** in Appendix.]

audio book *n.* A taped reading of a book or book condensation reproduced in cassette form.

au·di·o·cas·sette (ô′dē-ō-kə-sĕt′, -kă-) *n.* **1.** A cassette containing blank or prerecorded audiotape. **2.** A tape recording reproduced in cassette form.

audio frequency *n. Abbr.* **AF** A range of frequencies, usually from 15 hertz to 20,000 hertz, characteristic of signals audible to the normal human ear.

au·di·o·gram (ô′dē-ə-grăm′) *n.* A graphic record of hearing ability for various sound frequencies that is used to measure hearing loss.

au·di·o-lin·gual (ô′dē-ō-lĭng′gwəl) *adj.* Relating to or involving a system of language acquisition that focuses intensively on listening and speaking.

au·di·ol·o·gy (ô′dē-ŏl′ə-jē) *n.* The study of hearing, especially hearing defects and their treatment. —**au′di·o·log′i·cal** (-ə-lŏj′ĭ-kəl) *adj.* —**au′di·ol′o·gist** *n.*

au·di·om·e·ter (ô′dē-ŏm′ĭ-tər) *n.* An instrument for measuring hearing activity for pure tones of normally audible frequencies. Also called *sonometer.* —**au′di·o·met′ric** (-ō-mĕt′rĭk) *adj.* —**au′di·om′e·try** *n.*

au·di·o·phile (ô′dē-ə-fīl′) *n.* A person having an ardent interest in stereo or high-fidelity sound reproduction.

au·di·o·tape (ô′dē-ō-tāp′) *n.* **1.** A relatively narrow magnetic tape used to record sound for subsequent playback. **2.** A tape recording of sound. —**audiotape** *tr. v.* **-taped, -tap·ing, -tapes.** To record (sound) on magnetic tape: *audiotaped the interview for replay on radio.*

au·di·o·typ·ing (ô′dē-ō-tī′pĭng) *n.* Typing done directly from an audiotape. —**au′di·o·typ′ist** *n.*

au·di·o-vis·u·al also **au·di·o·vis·u·al** (ô′dē-ō-vĭzh′-o͞o-əl) —*adj. Abbr.* **AV, A.V. 1.** Both audible and visible. **2.** Of or relating to materials, such as films and tape recordings, that present information in audible and pictorial form: *a corporation's audio-visual department.* —*n.* An aid, other than printed matter, that uses sight or sound to present information: *language tapes, videocassettes, and other audio-visuals.*

au·dit (ô′dĭt) *n. Abbr.* **aud. 1.** An examination of records or financial accounts to check their accuracy. **2.** An adjustment or correction of accounts. **3.** An examined and verified account. —**audit** *v.* **-dit·ed, -dit·ing, -dits.** —*tr.* **1.** To examine, verify, or correct the financial accounts of: *Independent accountants audit the company annually. The IRS audits questionable income tax returns.* **2.** To attend (a course) without requesting or receiving academic credit. —*intr.* To examine financial accounts. [Middle English (influenced by *auditor*, auditor), from Latin *audītus*, a hearing, from past participle of *audīre*, to hear. See **au-** in Appendix.]

au·di·tion (ô-dĭsh′ən) *n.* **1.** The sense or power of hearing. **2.** The act of hearing. **3.** *Abbr.* **aud.** A trial performance, as by an actor, dancer, or musician, to demonstrate suitability or skill. —**audition** *v.* **-tioned, -tion·ing, -tions.** —*intr.* To take part in a trial performance: *auditioned for the role and got it.* —*tr.* To evaluate (a person) in a trial performance. [Latin *audītiō, audītiōn-*, from *audītus*, past participle of *audīre*, to hear. See **au-** in Appendix.]

au·di·tive (ô′dĭ-tĭv) *adj.* Of or relating to hearing; auditory.

au·di·tor (ô′dĭ-tər) *n. Abbr.* **aud. 1.** One that audits accounts. **2.** One who audits a course. **3.** One who hears; a listener. [Middle English, from Anglo-Norman *auditour*, from Latin *audītor*, listener, from *audīre*, to hear. See **au-** in Appendix.]

au·di·to·ri·um (ô′dĭ-tôr′ē-əm, -tōr′-) *n., pl.* **-ri·ums** or **-ri·a** (-tôr′ē-ə, -tōr′-). **1.** A large room to accommodate an audience in a building such as a school or theater. **2.** A large building for public meetings or performances. [Latin, from *audīre*, to hear. See **au-** in Appendix.]

au·di·to·ry (ô′dĭ-tôr′ē, -tōr′ē) *adj.* Of or relating to hearing, the organs of hearing, or the sense of hearing. [Late Latin *audītōrius*, from Latin *audīre*, to hear. See **au-** in Appendix.]

auditory nerve *n. Anatomy.* See **acoustic nerve.**

Au·du·bon (ô′də-bŏn′, -bən), **John James.** 1785–1851. Haitian-born American ornithologist and artist whose extensive observations of eastern North American avifauna led to the publication of *The Birds of America* (1827–1838), a collection of his engravings that is considered a classic work in ornithology and American art.

Auf·klä·rung (ouf′klā′ro͝ong) *n.* The Enlightenment. [German : *auf*, up (from Middle High German *ūf*, from Old High German; see **upo** in Appendix) + *Klärung*, a making clear (from *klären*, to make clear, from Middle High German *klæren*, from *klār*, clear, from Latin *clārus*; see CLEAR).]

auf Wie·der·seh·en (ouf vē′dər-zā′ən) *interj.* Used to express farewell. [German : *auf*, until + *Wiedersehen*, seeing again.]

aug. *abbr. Grammar.* Augmentative.

Aug. *abbr.* August.

Au·ge·an (ô-jē′ən) *adj.* **1.** Exceedingly filthy from long neglect. **2.** Requiring heroic efforts of cleaning or correction: *the Augean task of reforming the bureaucracy.* [After *Augeas*, legendary Greek king who did not clean his stable for thirty years.]

au·gend (ô′jĕnd′) *n. Mathematics.* A quantity to which the addend is added. [Latin *augendum*, a thing to be increased, from neuter gerundive of *augēre*, to increase. See **aug-** in Appendix.]

au·ger (ô′gər) *n.* **1.** A tool for boring holes in wood or ice. **2.** A large tool for boring into the earth. [Middle English, from *an auger*, alteration of *a nauger*, from Old English *nafogār*, auger. See **nobh-** in Appendix.]

aught[1] also **ought** (ôt) —*pron.* Anything whatever: *"Neither of his parents had aught but praise for him"* (Louis Auchincloss). —*adv. Archaic.* In any respect; at all. [Middle English, from Old English *āuht.* See **aiw-** in Appendix.]

aught[2] also **ought** (ôt) *n.* **1.** A cipher; zero. **2.** *Archaic.* Nothing. [From *an aught*, alteration of *a naught.* See NAUGHT.]

au·gite (ô′jīt′) *n.* A dark-green to black pyroxene mineral, $(Ca,Na)(Mg,Fe,Al)(Si,Al)_2O_6$, that contains large amounts of aluminum, iron, and magnesium. [Latin *augītis*, a precious stone, from Greek *augītēs*, from *augē*, brightness.]

aug·ment (ôg-mĕnt′) *v.* **-ment·ed, -ment·ing, -ments.** —*tr.* **1.** To make (something already developed or well under way) greater, as in size, extent, or quantity: *Continuing rains augmented the flood waters.* **2.** To add an augment to. —*intr.* To become augmented. See Synonyms at **increase.** —**augment** (ôg′mĕnt′) *n.* **1.** An enlargement or increase. **2.** The prefixation of a vowel accompanying a past tense, especially of Greek and Sanskrit verbs. [Middle English *augmenten*, from Old French *augmenter*,

John James Audubon
Self-portrait, c. 1822

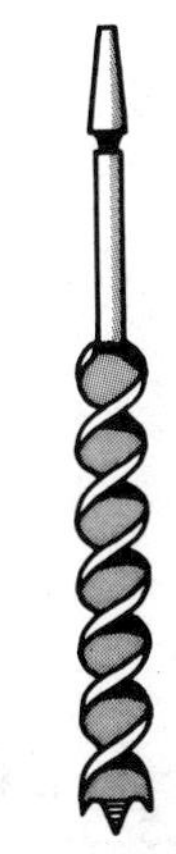
auger
Double twist auger bit

ă pat	oi boy
ā pay	ou out
âr care	o͝o took
ä father	o͞o boot
ĕ pet	ŭ cut
ē be	ûr urge
ĭ pit	th thin
ī pie	*th* this
îr pier	hw which
ŏ pot	zh vision
ō toe	ə about, item
ô paw	♦ regionalism

Stress marks: ′ (primary); ′ (secondary), as in **dictionary** (dĭk′shə-nĕr′ē)

from Late Latin *augmentāre*, from Latin *augmentum*, an increase, from *augēre*, to increase. See **aug-** in Appendix.] **—aug·ment′a·ble** *adj.* **—aug·ment′er** *n.*

aug·men·ta·tion (ôg′mĕn-tā′shən) *n.* **1.** The act or process of augmenting. **2.** The condition of being augmented. **3.** Something that augments. **4.** *Music.* The repetition of a theme in notes of usually double time value.

aug·men·ta·tive (ôg-mĕn′tə-tĭv) *adj.* **1.** Having the ability or tendency to augment. **2.** *Grammar.* Indicating an increase in the size, force, or intensity of the meaning of an adjacent word, as *up* does in *eat up.* **—augmentative** *n. Abbr.* **aug.** *Grammar.* An augmentative word.

aug·ment·ed (ôg-mĕn′tĭd) *adj. Music.* Larger by a semitone than the corresponding major or perfect interval.

au gra·tin (ō grät′n, grăt′n, grä-tăN′) *adj.* Covered with bread crumbs and sometimes butter and grated cheese, and then browned in an oven: *potatoes au gratin.* [French : *au,* with the + *gratin,* scraping from the pan.]

Augs·burg (ôgz′bûrg′, ouks′bo͝ork′). A city of southern Germany west-northwest of Munich. Founded by Augustus as a Roman garrison c. 14 B.C., it was a major commercial and banking center in the 15th and 16th centuries. Population, 244,400.

auk
Razor-billed auk
Alca torda

au·gur (ô′gər) *n.* **1.** One of a group of ancient Roman religious officials who foretold events by observing and interpreting signs and omens. **2.** A seer or prophet; a soothsayer. **—augur** *v.* **-gured, -gur·ing, -gurs.** *—tr.* **1.** To predict, especially from signs or omens; foretell. See Synonyms at **foretell. 2.** To serve as an omen of; betoken: *trends that augur change in society.* *—intr.* **1.** To make predictions from signs or omens. **2.** To be a sign or omen: *A smooth dress rehearsal augured well for the play.* [Middle English, from Latin. See **aug-** in Appendix.] **—au′gu·ral** (ô′gyə-rəl) *adj.*

au·gu·ry (ô′gyə-rē) *n., pl.* **-ries. 1.** The art, ability, or practice of auguring; divination. **2.** A sign of something coming; an omen. [Middle English *augurie,* from Old French, from Latin *augurium,* from *augur,* augur. See AUGUR.]

au·gust (ô-gŭst′) *adj.* **1.** Inspiring awe or admiration; majestic: *the august presence of the monarch.* See Synonyms at **grand. 2.** Venerable for reasons of age or high rank. [Latin *augustus.* See **aug-** in Appendix.] **—au·gust′ly** *adv.* **—au·gust′ness** *n.*

Au·gust (ô′gəst) *n. Abbr.* **Aug.** The eighth month of the year in the Gregorian calendar. See table at **calendar.** [Middle English, from Old English, from Latin *(mēnsis) Augustus,* (month) of Augustus, after AUGUSTUS.]

Au·gus·ta (ô-gŭs′tə, ə-gŭs′-). **1.** A city of eastern Georgia on the South Carolina border north-northwest of Savannah. It is a popular resort known especially for its golf tournaments. Population, 47,532. **2.** The capital of Maine, in the southwest part of the state on the Kennebec River north-northeast of Portland. A trading post was established here in 1628. Population, 21,819.

Au·gus·tan (ô-gŭs′tən) *adj.* **1.** Of or characteristic of Augustus or his reign or times. **2.** Of or characteristic of English literature during the early 18th century. **—Au·gus′tan** *n.*

Au·gus·tine[1] (ô′gə-stēn′, ô-gŭs′tĭn), Saint. A.D. 354–430. Early Christian church father and philosopher who served (396–430) as the bishop of Hippo (in present-day Algeria).

Au·gus·tine[2] (ô′gə-stēn′, ô-gŭs′tĭn) also **Aus·tin** (ô′stən), Saint. Called "Apostle of the English." Died c. 604. Italian-born missionary and prelate who introduced Christianity to southern Britain.

Au·gus·tin·i·an (ô′gə-stĭn′ē-ən) *adj.* **1.** Of or relating to Saint Augustine of Hippo or his doctrines. **2.** Being or belonging to any of several religious orders following or influenced by the rule of Saint Augustine. **—Augustinian** *n.* **1.** A follower of the principles and doctrines of Saint Augustine. **2.** A monk or friar belonging to any of the Augustinian orders. **—Au′gus·tin′i·an·ism, Au·gus′tin·ism** (ô-gŭs′tĭ-nĭz′əm) *n.*

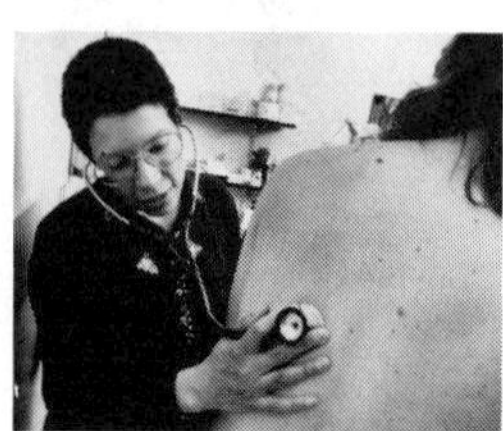

auscultation

Au·gus·tus (ô-gŭs′təs). Originally **Oc·ta·vi·an** (ŏk-tā′vē-ən). 63 B.C.–A.D. 14. First emperor of Rome (27 B.C.–A.D. 14) and grand-nephew of Julius Caesar. He defeated Mark Antony and Cleopatra in 31 and subsequently gained control over the empire. In 29 he was named emperor, and in 27 he was given the honorary title Augustus.

au jus (ō zho͞os′, zhü′) *adj.* Served with the natural juices or gravy: *roast beef au jus.* [French : *au,* with the + *jus,* juice.]

auk (ôk) *n.* Any of several diving sea birds (family Alcidae) of northern regions, such as the razor-billed auk, having a chunky body, short wings, and webbed feet. [Norwegian *alk,* from Old Norse *ālka.*]

auk·let (ôk′lĭt) *n.* Any of various small auks (genus *Aethia* and related genera) of northern Pacific coasts and waters.

auld (ôld) *adj. Scots.* Old.

auld lang syne (ôld′ lăng zīn′, sīn′) *n.* The good old days. [Scots : *auld,* old + *lang,* long + *syne,* since.]

Aum (ōm) *n. Hinduism & Buddhism.* Variant of **Om[2].**

au na·tu·rel (ō′ năch′ə-rĕl′, ō′ nä-tü-rĕl′) *adj.* **1.a.** Nude. **b.** In a natural state: *an au naturel hairstyle.* **2.** Cooked simply. [French : *au,* in the + *naturel,* natural (state).]

Aung San Suu Kyi (oung′ sän′ so͞o′ chē′). Born 1945. Burmese political leader who won the 1991 Nobel Peace Prize for her work promoting democracy in her country.

Au·nis (ō-nēs′). A historical region and former province of western France on the Atlantic Ocean. A part of Aquitaine, it was recovered from England in 1373 and incorporated into the French crown lands.

aunt (ănt, änt) *n.* **1.** The sister of one's father or mother. **2.** The wife of one's uncle. [Middle English *aunte,* from Anglo-Norman, from Latin *amita,* paternal aunt.] **—aunt′hood** *n.*

aunt·ie also **aunt·y** (ăn′tē, än′-) *n., pl.* **-ies.** *Informal.* Aunt.

au pair (ô pâr′) *n.* A young foreigner who does domestic work for a family in exchange for room and board and a chance to learn the family's language. [French : *au,* at the + *pair,* equal.]

au·ra (ôr′ə) *n., pl.* **au·ras** or **au·rae** (ôr′ē). **1.** An invisible breath, emanation, or radiation. **2.** A distinctive but intangible quality that seems to surround a person or thing; atmosphere: *An aura of defeat pervaded the candidate's headquarters.* **3.** *Pathology.* A sensation, as of a cold breeze or a bright light, that precedes the onset of certain disorders, such as an epileptic seizure or an attack of migraine. [Middle English, gentle breeze, from Latin, from Greek, breath. See **wer-[1]** in Appendix.]

au·ral[1] (ôr′əl) *adj.* Of, relating to, or perceived by the ear. [From Latin *auris,* ear. See **ous-** in Appendix.] **—au′ral·ly** *adv.*

au·ral[2] (ôr′əl) *adj.* Characterized by or relating to an aura.

Au·rang·a·bad (ou-rŭng′gə-bäd′, -ə-bäd′). A town of western India east-northeast of Bombay. Founded in 1610, it is near the site of a mausoleum erected by Aurangzeb in honor of his empress. Population, 284,607.

Au·rang·zeb also **Au·rung·zeb** or **Au·rung·zebe** (ôr′əng-zĕb′). 1618–1707. Hindustani emperor (1658–1707) who imposed Moslem orthodoxy and expanded the empire.

au·rar (ou′rär′, œ′rär′) *n.* Plural of **eyrir.**

au·re·ate (ôr′ē-ĭt) *adj.* **1.** Of a golden color; gilded. **2.** Inflated and pompous in style. [Middle English *aureat,* from Late Latin *aureātus,* from *aureus,* golden, from *aurum,* gold.] **—au′re·ate·ly** *adv.* **—au′re·ate·ness** *n.*

Au·re·lian (ô-rēl′yən, ô-rē′lē-ən). A.D. 212?–275. Emperor of Rome (A.D. 270–275) who held the barbarians in check beyond the Rhine River and regained Britain, Gaul, Spain, Syria, and Egypt for the empire.

au·re·ole (ôr′ē-ōl′) also **au·re·o·la** (ô-rē′ə-lə) *n.* **1.** A circle of light or radiance surrounding the head or body of a representation of a deity or holy person; a halo. **2.** *Astronomy.* See **corona** (sense a). [Middle English, from Late Latin *(corōna) aureola,* golden (crown), feminine of Latin *aureolus,* golden, from *aureus,* from *aurum,* gold.]

Au·re·o·my·cin (ôr′ē-ō-mī′sĭn). A trademark used for chlortetracycline.

au re·voir (ō′ rə-vwär′) *interj.* Used to express farewell. [French : *au,* till the + *revoir,* seeing again.]

au·ric (ôr′ĭk) *adj.* Of, relating to, derived from, or containing gold, especially with valence 3. [From Latin *aurum,* gold.]

au·ri·cle (ôr′ĭ-kəl) *n.* **1.** *Anatomy.* **a.** The outer projecting portion of the ear. Also called *pinna.* **b.** See **atrium** (sense 2). **2.** *Biology.* An earlobe-shaped part, process, or appendage, especially at the base of an organ. [Middle English, auricle of the heart, from Old French, little ear, from Latin *auricula,* ear, from diminutive of *auris.* See **ous-** in Appendix.] **—au′ri·cled** (-kəld) *adj.*

au·ric·u·la (ô-rĭk′yə-lə) *n., pl.* **-las** or **-lae** (-lē′). **1.** A central European primrose *(Primula auricula)* having large yellow flowers grouped in umbels. Also called *bear's ear.* **2.** Any of numerous hybrids of this species with other primroses. [Latin auricle. See AURICLE.]

au·ric·u·lar (ô-rĭk′yə-lər) *adj.* **1.** Of or relating to the sense of hearing or the organs of hearing. **2.** Perceived by or spoken into the ear: *an auricular confession.* **3.** Shaped like an ear or an earlobe; having earlike parts or extensions. **4.** Of or relating to an auricle of the heart: *auricular fibrillation.* [Middle English *auriculer,* spoken into the ear, from Late Latin *auriculāris,* from Latin *auricula,* ear. See AURICLE.] **—au·ric′u·lar·ly** *adv.*

au·ric·u·late (ô-rĭk′yə-lĭt, -lāt′) also **au·ric·u·lat·ed** (-lāt′ĭd) *adj.* **1.** Having ears, auricles, or earlobe-shaped parts or extensions. **2.** Shaped like an earlobe. [From Latin *auricula,* auricle. See AURICLE.] **—au·ric′u·late·ly** *adv.*

au·rif·er·ous (ô-rĭf′ər-əs) *adj.* Containing gold; gold-bearing. [From Latin *aurifer,* gold-bearing : *aurum,* gold + *-fer,* -fer.]

au·ri·form (ôr′ə-fôrm′) *adj.* Shaped like an ear. [Latin *auris,* ear; see **ous-** in Appendix + –FORM.]

Au·ri·ga (ô-rī′gə) *n.* A constellation in the Northern Hemisphere near Lynx and Perseus that contains the bright star Capella, which is 42 light-years from Earth. Also called *Charioteer.* [Latin *aurīga,* charioteer, Auriga. See **ōs-** in Appendix.]

Au·ri·gnac (ô′rēn-yăk′). A village of southern France at the foot of the Pyrenees. It is the site of caves containing prehistoric relics.

Au·rig·na·cian (ôr′ĭg-nā′shən, ôr′ēn-yā′-) *adj.* Of or relating to the Old World Upper Paleolithic culture between Mousterian and Solutrean, associated with early *Homo sapiens* and characterized by artifacts such as figures of stone and bone, graphic artwork, the use of dress and adornment, and a type of tool culture. [After AURIGNAC.]

au·rochs (ou′rŏks′, ôr′ŏks′) *n., pl.* **aurochs. 1.** See **urus. 2.** See **wisent.** [Obsolete German, variant of German *Auerochs,* from Middle High German *ūrohse,* from Old High German *ūrohso* : *ūro,* aurochs + *ohso,* ox.]

au·ro·ra (ô-rôr′ə, ô-rōr′ə, ə-rôr′ə, ə-rōr′ə) *n.* **1.** Aurora borealis. **2.** Aurora australis. **3.** The dawn. [Middle English, dawn, from Latin *aurōra.* See **aus-** in Appendix.] —**au·ro′ral, au·ro′re·an** (-ē-ən) *adj.* —**au·ro′ral·ly** *adv.*

Au·ro·ra¹ (ô-rôr′ə, ô-rōr′ə, ə-rôr′ə, ə-rōr′ə) *n. Roman Mythology.* The goddess of the dawn. [Latin *Aurōra.* See AURORA.]

Au·ro·ra² (ô-rôr′ə, ô-rōr′ə, ə-rôr′ə, ə-rōr′ə). **1.** A town of southern Ontario, Canada, north of Toronto. It is a manufacturing center. Population, 16,267. **2.** A city of north-central Colorado, a residential suburb of Denver. Population, 158,588. **3.** A city of northeast Illinois on the Fox River west of Chicago. It is an industrial center and was one of the first U.S. cities to use electricity for street lighting. Population, 81,293.

aurora aus·tra·lis (ô-strā′lĭs) *n.* A luminous phenomenon of southern regions that corresponds to the aurora borealis of northern regions. Also called *southern lights.* [New Latin *aurōra austrālis* : Latin *aurōra,* dawn + Latin *austrālis,* southern.]

aurora bo·re·al·is (bôr′ē-ăl′ĭs, bōr′-) *n.* Luminous bands or streamers of light that are sometimes visible in the night skies of northern regions and are thought to be caused by the ejection of charged particles into the magnetic field of the earth. Also called *northern lights.* [New Latin *aurōra boreālis* : Latin *aurōra,* dawn + Latin *boreālis,* northern.]

au·rous (ôr′əs) *adj.* Of or relating to gold, especially with valence 1. [Latin *aurum,* gold + –OUS.]

Au·rung·zeb or **Au·rung·zebe** (ôr′əng-zĕb′). See **Aurangzeb.**

AUS *abbr.* Army of the United States.

Aus. *abbr.* **1.a.** Australia. **b.** Australian. **2.a.** Austria. **b.** Austrian.

Ausch·witz (oush′vĭts′). See **Oświęcim.**

aus·cul·tate (ô′skəl-tāt′) *tr.v.* **-tat·ed, -tat·ing, -tates.** *Medicine.* To examine by auscultation. [Back-formation from AUSCULTATION.] —**aus′cul·ta′tive** *adj.* —**aus·cul′ta·to′ry** (ô-skŭl′tə-tôr′ē, -tōr′ē) *adj.*

aus·cul·ta·tion (ô′skəl-tā′shən) *n.* **1.** The act of listening. **2.** *Medicine.* The act of listening for sounds made by internal organs, as the heart and lungs, to aid in the diagnosis of certain disorders. [Latin *auscultātiō, auscultātiōn-,* from *auscultātus,* past participle of *auscultāre,* to listen to. See **ous-** in Appendix.]

aus·form (ôs′fôrm′) *tr.v.* **-formed, -form·ing, -forms.** To subject (especially steel) to deformation, quenching, and tempering to improve its wear properties. [AUS(TENITIC) + (DE)FORM.]

aus·land·er (ou′slĕn′dər, -slăn′-) *n.* A foreigner. [German *Ausländer,* from *Ausland,* outland : *aus,* out (from Middle High German *ūz,* from Old High German; see **ud-** in Appendix) + *Land,* land (from Middle High German *lant,* from Old High German; see **lendh-** in Appendix).]

aus·pex (ô′spĕks′) *n., pl.* **aus·pi·ces** (ô′spĭ-sēz′). An augur of ancient Rome, especially one who interpreted omens derived from the observation of birds. [Latin. See AUSPICE.]

aus·pi·cate (ô′spĭ-kāt′) *tr.v.* **-cat·ed, -cat·ing, -cates.** To begin or inaugurate with a ceremony intended to bring good luck. [Latin *auspicārī, auspicāt-,* from *auspex, auspic-,* bird augur. See AUSPICE.]

aus·pice (ô′spĭs) *n., pl.* **aus·pi·ces** (ô′spĭ-sĭz, -sēz′). **1.** Also **auspices.** Protection or support; patronage. **2.** A sign indicative of future prospects; an omen: *Auspices for the venture seemed favorable.* **3.** Observation of and divination from the actions of birds. [Latin *auspicium,* bird divination, auspices, from *auspex, auspic-,* bird augur. See **awi-** in Appendix.]

aus·pi·ces¹ (ô′spĭ-sēz′) *n.* Plural of **auspex.**

aus·pi·ces² (ô′spĭ-sĭz, -sēz′) *n.* Plural of **auspice.**

aus·pi·cious (ô-spĭsh′əs) *adj.* **1.** Attended by favorable circumstances; propitious: *an auspicious time to ask for a raise in salary.* See Synonyms at **favorable. 2.** Marked by success; prosperous. —**aus·pi′cious·ly** *adv.* —**aus·pi′cious·ness** *n.*

Aus·sie (ô′sē, ô′zē) *n. Informal.* A native or inhabitant of Australia. [From AUS(TRALIAN).] —**Aus′sie** *adj.*

Aust. *abbr.* **1.a.** Australia. **b.** Australian. **2.a.** Austria. **b.** Austrian.

Aus·ten (ô′stən), **Jane.** 1775–1817. British writer who is noted for her penetrating observation of middle-class manners and morality and her irony, wit, and meticulous style. Her novels include *Pride and Prejudice* (1813) and *Emma* (1816).

aus·ten·ite (ô′stə-nīt′) *n.* A nonmagnetic solid solution of ferric carbide or carbon in iron, used in making corrosion-resistant steel. [After Sir William Chandler Roberts-*Austen* (1843–1902), British metallurgist.] —**aus′ten·it′ic** (-ĭt′ĭk) *adj.*

aus·tere (ô-stîr′) *adj.* **-ter·er, -ter·est. 1.** Severe or stern in disposition or appearance; somber and grave: *the austere figure of a Puritan minister.* **2.** Strict or severe in discipline; ascetic: *a desert nomad's austere life.* **3.** Having no adornment or ornamentation; bare: *an austere style.* See Synonyms at **severe.** [Middle English, from Old French, from Latin *austērus,* from Greek *austēros.*] —**aus·tere′ly** *adv.* —**aus·tere′ness** *n.*

aus·ter·i·ty (ô-stĕr′ĭ-tē) *n., pl.* **-ties. 1.** The quality of being austere. **2.** Severe and rigid economy: *wartime austerity.* **3.** An austere habit or practice.

Aus·ter·litz (ô′stər-lĭts′, ous′tər-). A town of southern Czechoslovakia. Nearby, on December 2, 1805, Napoleon decisively defeated the Russian and Austrian armies of Czar Alexander I and Emperor Francis II.

Aus·tin¹ (ô′stən). See Saint **Augustine².**

Aus·tin² (ô′stən, ŏs′tən). **1.** A city of southeast Minnesota near the Iowa border southwest of Rochester. It is a processing and manufacturing center. Population, 23,020. **2.** The capital of Texas, in the south-central part of the state. Austin was selected as the capital of the Republic of Texas in 1839 and became the permanent capital of the state of Texas in 1870. The main campus of the University of Texas (established 1881) is here. Population, 345,496.

Austin, Alfred. 1835–1913. British writer who became poet laureate in 1896 and wrote several volumes of poetry, including *The Season* (1861).

Austin, John. 1790–1859. British legal theorist who maintained that law is a form of command determined by power relationships and is therefore distinct from moral principles.

Austin, Mary Hunter. 1868–1934. American writer known for her literary interest in the peoples and cultures of the Mojave Desert and for her ardent support of women's rights.

Austin, Stephen Fuller. 1793–1836. American colonizer and political leader who worked to make Texas a state of Mexico but later helped Texas settlers gain their independence (1836).

Aus·tin·town (ô′stən-toun′). A community of northeast Ohio, a suburb of Youngstown. Population, 33,636.

Austl. *abbr.* Australia; Australian.

aus·tral¹ (ô′strəl) *adj.* Of, relating to, or coming from the south. [Latin *austrālis,* from *auster, austr-,* south.]

aus·tral² (ous-träl′) *n., pl.* **-tral·es** (-trä′lĕs). See table at **currency.** [American Spanish, from Spanish, from the south, from Latin *austrālis.* See AUSTRAL¹.]

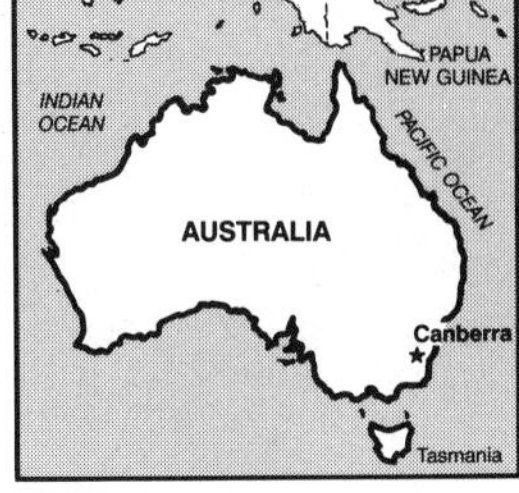

Australia

Aus·tral·a·sia (ô′strə-lā′zhə, -shə). **1.** The islands of the southern Pacific Ocean, including Australia, New Zealand, and New Guinea. **2.** Broadly, all of Oceania. —**Aus′tral·a′sian** *adj. & n.*

Aus·tra·lia (ô-strāl′yə). *Abbr.* **Aus., Aust., Austl. 1.** The world's smallest continent, southeast of Asia between the Pacific and Indian oceans. **2.** A commonwealth comprising the continent of Australia, the island state of Tasmania, two external territories, and several dependencies. The first British settlement, a penal colony at Fort Jackson (now part of Sydney), was established in 1788. The present-day states grew as separate colonies; six of them formed a federation in 1901. In 1911 Northern Territory joined the commonwealth and the Capital Territory, site of Canberra, was created. Canberra is the capital and Sydney is the largest city. Population, 15,544,500.

Aus·tra·lian (ô-strāl′yən) *adj. Abbr.* **Aus., Aust., Austl. 1.** Of or relating to Australia or its peoples, languages, or cultures. **2.** *Ecology.* Of, relating to, or being the zoogeographic region that includes Australia and the islands adjacent to it, including New Guinea, New Zealand, Polynesia, and Tasmania. —**Australian** *n. Abbr.* **Aus., Aust., Austl. 1.** A native or inhabitant of Australia. **2.** A member of any of the aboriginal peoples of Australia. **3.** Any of the languages of the aboriginal peoples of Australia.

Australian Alps. A chain of mountain ranges of southeast Australia in the southern part of the Great Dividing Range. Mount Kosciusko, rising to 2,231.4 m (7,316 ft), is the highest elevation and the tallest peak in Australia.

Austria

Australian ballot *n.* A printed ballot that bears the names of all candidates and the texts of propositions and is distributed to the voter at the polls and marked in secret. Also called *secret ballot.*

Australian crawl *n. Sports.* A crawl stroke in swimming that is executed with a flutter kick to each arm stroke.

Australian pine *n.* See **beefwood.**

Australian terrier *n.* A small dog of a breed originally bred in Australia, having a coarse, blackish coat with tan markings.

Aus·tra·loid (ô′strə-loid′) *adj. Anthropology.* Of, relating to, or being a human racial classification traditionally distinguished by physical characteristics such as dark skin and dark curly hair, and including the aboriginal peoples of Australia along with various peoples of southeast Asia, especially the Malay Archipelago. No longer in scientific use. [AUSTRAL(IAN) + –OID.] —**Aus′tra·loid′** *n.*

aus·tra·lo·pith·e·cine (ô-strā′lō-pĭth′ĭ-sīn′, -sēn′) *n.* Any of several extinct humanlike primates of the genus *Australopithecus,* known chiefly from Pleistocene fossil remains found in southern and eastern Africa. —**australopithecine** *adj.* Of, relating to, or characteristic of these extinct humanlike primates. [From New Latin *Australopithēcus* : Latin *austrālis,* southern; see AUSTRAL¹ + *pithēcus,* ape (from Greek *pithēkos*).]

Aus·tra·sia (ô-strā′zhə, -shə). The eastern portion of the kingdom of the Franks from the sixth to the eighth century, including parts of eastern France, western Germany, and the Netherlands. It eventually became part of the Carolingian empire. —**Aus·tra′sian** *adj. & n.*

Aus·tri·a (ô′strē-ə). *Abbr.* **Aus., Aust.** A landlocked country of central Europe. A Roman and Carolingian territory, it was later a powerful empire ruled by the Hapsburgs. The empire was broken up in 1918, and the republic of Austria was annexed by Adolf Hitler in 1938. Full sovereignty was restored in 1955. Vienna is the capital and the largest city. Population, 7,555,338. —**Aus′tri·an** *adj. & n.*

ă pat	oi boy
ā pay	ou out
âr care	ŏŏ took
ä father	ōō boot
ĕ pet	ŭ cut
ē be	ûr urge
ĭ pit	th thin
ī pie	*th* this
îr pier	hw which
ŏ pot	zh vision
ō toe	ə about, item
ô paw	♦ regionalism

Stress marks: ′ (primary); ′ (secondary), as in **dictionary** (dĭk′shə-nĕr′ē)

Aus·tri·a-Hun·ga·ry (ô′strē-ə-hŭng′gə-rē). A former dual monarchy of central Europe consisting of Austria, Hungary, Bohemia, and parts of Poland, Romania, Yugoslavia, and Italy. It was formed in 1867 after agitation by Hungarian nationalists within the Austrian empire and lasted until 1918. **—Aus′tro-Hun·gar′i·an** (ô′strō-hŭng-gâr′ē-ən) *adj. & n.*

Austro–¹ *pref.* Southern: *Austro-Asiatic.* [From Latin *auster, austr-,* south. See **aus-** in Appendix.]

Austro–² *pref.* Austria; Austrian: *Austro-Hungarian.*

Aus·tro-A·si·at·ic (ô′strō-ā′zhē-ăt′ĭk, -shē-, -zē-) *n.* A family of languages of southeast Asia once dominant in northeast India and Indochina, including Mon-Khmer and Munda. **—Aus′tro-A′si·at′ic** *adj.*

Aus·tro·ne·sia (ô′strō-nē′zhə, -shə). The islands of the Pacific Ocean, including Indonesia, Melanesia, Micronesia, and Polynesia.

Aus·tro·ne·sian (ô′strō-nē′zhən, -shən) *adj.* Of or relating to Austronesia or its peoples, languages, or cultures. **—Austronesian** *n.* A family of languages that includes the Formosan, Indonesian, Malay, Melanesian, Micronesian, and Polynesian subfamilies.

aut– *pref.* Variant of **auto–.**

au·ta·coid also **au·to·coid** (ô′tə-koid′) *n.* An organic substance, such as a hormone, produced in one part of an organism and transported by the blood, lymph, or sap to another part of the organism where it exerts a physiologic effect on that part. [AUT(O)– + Greek *akos,* cure + –OID.] **—au′ta·coid′al** (-koid′l) *adj.*

au·tarch (ô′tärk) *n.* An absolute ruler; a despot. [Greek *autarkhos,* self-governing, autarch. See AUTARCHY¹.]

au·tar·chy¹ (ô′tär′kē) *n., pl.* **-chies. 1.** Absolute rule or power; autocracy. **2.** A country under such rule. [From Greek *autarkhos,* self-governing, autarch : *aut-, auto-,* auto- + *arkhos,* ruler (from *arkhein,* to rule).] **—au·tar′chic, au·tar′chi·cal** *adj.*

au·tar·chy² (ô′tär′kē) *n.* Variant of **autarky.**

au·tar·ky or **au·tar·chy** (ô′tär′kē) *n., pl.* **-kies** or **-chies. 1.** A policy of national self-sufficiency and nonreliance on imports or economic aid. **2.** A self-sufficient region or country. [Greek *autarkeia,* self-sufficiency, from *autarkēs,* self-sufficient : *aut-, auto-,* auto- + *arkein,* to suffice.] **—au·tar′kic, au·tar′ki·cal** *adj.*

au·te·col·o·gy (ô′tĭ-kŏl′ə-jē) *n.* The branch of ecology that deals with the biological relationship between an individual organism or an individual species and its environment. **—au′te·co·log′i·cal** (-kə-lŏj′ĭ-kəl) *adj.*

Au·teuil (ō-toi′, ō-tœ′yə). A former town between the Seine River and the Bois de Boulogne, now part of Paris. It was a favorite gathering place for French literary figures, including Molière and La Fontaine.

au·teur (ō-tûr′, ō-tœr′) *n.* A filmmaker, usually a director, who exercises creative control over his or her works and has a strong personal style. [French, from Old French *autor,* author. See AUTHOR.]

au·teur·ism (ō-tûr′ĭz′əm) *n.* Belief in the primary creative importance of the director in filmmaking, often combined with a critical advocacy of the works of certain strong, distinctive directors. Also called *auteur theory.* **—au·teur′ist** *adj. & n.*

auth. *abbr.* **1.** Authentic. **2.** Author. **3.** Authority. **4.** Authorized.

au·then·tic (ô-thĕn′tĭk) *adj. Abbr.* **auth. 1.** Conforming to fact and therefore worthy of trust, reliance, or belief: *an authentic account by an eyewitness.* **2.** Having a claimed and verifiable origin or authorship; not counterfeit or copied: *an authentic medieval sword.* **3.** *Law.* Executed with due process: *an authentic deed.* **4.** *Music.* **a.** Of, relating to, or being a medieval mode having a range from its final tone to the octave above it. **b.** Of, relating to, or being a cadence with the dominant chord immediately preceding the tonic chord. **5.** *Obsolete.* Authoritative. [Middle English *autentik,* from Old French *autentique,* from Late Latin *authenticus,* from Greek *authentikos,* from *authentēs,* author.] **—au·then′ti·cal·ly** *adv.*

SYNONYMS: *authentic, bona fide, genuine, real, true, undoubted, unquestionable.* The central meaning shared by these adjectives is "not counterfeit or copied": *an authentic painting by Corot; a bona fide transfer of property; genuine crabmeat; a real diamond; true courage; undoubted evidence; an unquestionable antique.* ***ANTONYM:*** *counterfeit.*

au·then·ti·cate (ô-thĕn′tĭ-kāt′) *tr.v.* **-cat·ed, -cat·ing, -cates.** To establish the authenticity of; prove genuine: *a specialist who authenticated the antique samovar.* See Synonyms at **confirm. —au·then′ti·ca′tion** *n.* **—au·then′ti·ca′tor** *n.*

au·then·tic·i·ty (ô′thĕn-tĭs′ĭ-tē) *n.* The quality or condition of being authentic, trustworthy, or genuine.

au·thor (ô′thər) *n.* **1.** *Abbr.* **auth., au a.** The original writer of a literary work. **b.** One who practices writing as a profession. **2.** An originator or creator: *the author of a new theory.* **3. Author.** God. **—author** *tr.v.* **-thored, -thor·ing, -thors.** *Usage Problem.* To assume responsibility for the content of (a published or an unpublished text). [Middle English *auctour,* from Old French *autor,* from Latin *auctor,* creator, from *auctus,* past participle of *augēre,* to create. See **aug-** in Appendix.] **—au·thor′i·al** (ô-thôr′ē-əl, ô-thŏr′-) *adj.*

USAGE NOTE: The verb *author,* which had been out of use for a long period, has been rejuvenated in recent years with the sense "to assume responsibility for the content of a published text." As such it is not quite synonymous with the verb *write;* one can write, but not author, a love letter or an unpublished manuscript, and the writer who ghostwrites a book for a celebrity cannot be said to have "authored" the creation. The sentence *He has authored a dozen books on the subject* was unacceptable to 74 percent of the Usage Panel, probably because it implies that the fact of having a book published is worthy of special lexical distinction, a notion that sits poorly with conventional literary sensibilities, and which seems to smack of press agentry. The sentence *The Senator authored a bill limiting uses of desert lands in California* was similarly rejected by 64 percent of the Panel, though here the usage is common journalistic practice, and is perhaps justified by the observation that we do not expect that legislators will actually write the bills to which they attach their names. · The verb *coauthor* is well established in reference to scientific and scholarly publications, where it serves a useful purpose, since the people listed as authors routinely include research collaborators who have played no part in the actual writing of the text but are nonetheless entitled to credit for the published results.

au·thor·i·tar·i·an (ə-thôr′ĭ-târ′ē-ən, ə-thŏr′-, ô-thôr′-, ô-thŏr′-) *adj.* **1.** Characterized by or favoring absolute obedience to authority, as against individual freedom: *an authoritarian regime.* **2.** Of, relating to, or expecting unquestioning obedience. See Synonyms at **dictatorial. —au·thor′i·tar′i·an** *n.* **—au·thor′i·tar′i·an·ism** *n.*

au·thor·i·ta·tive (ə-thôr′ĭ-tā′tĭv, ə-thŏr′-, ô-thôr′-, ô-thŏr′-) *adj.* **1.** Having or arising from authority; official: *an authoritative decree; authoritative sources.* **2.** Of acknowledged accuracy or excellence; highly reliable: *an authoritative account of the revolution.* **3.** Wielding authority; commanding: *the captain's authoritative manner.* **—au·thor′i·ta′tive·ly** *adv.* **—au·thor′i·ta′tive·ness** *n.*

au·thor·i·ty (ə-thôr′ĭ-tē, ə-thŏr′-, ô-thôr′-, ô-thŏr′-) *n., pl.* **-ties.** *Abbr.* **auth. 1. a.** The power to enforce laws, exact obedience, command, determine, or judge. **b.** One that is invested with this power, especially a government or government officials: *land titles issued by the civil authority.* **2.** Power assigned to another; authorization: *Deputies were given authority to make arrests.* **3.** A public agency or corporation with administrative powers in a specified field: *a city transit authority.* **4. a.** An accepted source of expert information or advice: *a noted authority on birds; a reference book often cited as an authority.* **b.** A quotation or citation from such a source: *biblical authorities for a moral argument.* **5.** Justification; grounds: *On what authority do you make such a claim?* **6.** A conclusive statement or decision that may be taken as a guide or precedent. **7.** Power to influence or persuade resulting from knowledge or experience: *political observers who acquire authority with age.* **8.** Confidence derived from experience or practice; firm self-assurance: *played the sonata with authority.* [Middle English *auctorite,* from Old French *autorite,* from Latin *auctōritās, auctōritāt-,* from *auctor,* creator. See AUTHOR.]

au·thor·i·za·tion (ô′thər-ĭ-zā′shən) *n.* **1.** The act of authorizing. See Synonyms at **permission. 2.** Something that authorizes; sanction.

au·thor·ize (ô′thə-rīz′) *tr.v.* **-ized, -iz·ing, -iz·es. 1.** To grant authority or power to. **2.** To give permission for; sanction: *the city agency that authorizes construction projects.* **3.** To be sufficient grounds for; justify. [Middle English *auctorisen,* from Old French *autoriser,* from Medieval Latin *auctōrizāre,* from Latin *auctor,* author. See AUTHOR.] **—au′thor·iz′er** *n.*

SYNONYMS: *authorize, accredit, commission, empower, license.* The central meaning shared by these verbs is "to give someone the authority to act": *authorized her partner to negotiate in her behalf; a representative who was accredited by his government; commissioned the real-estate agent to purchase the house for us; was empowered to make decisions during the president's absence; a pharmacist licensed to practice in two states.*

Au·thor·ized Version (ô′thə-rīzd′) *n. Abbr.* **AV, A.V.** *Bible.* See **King James Bible.**

au·thor·ship (ô′thər-shĭp′) *n.* **1.** The act, fact, or occupation of writing. **2.** Source or origin, as of a book or idea: *a poem of disputed authorship.*

au·tism (ô′tĭz′əm) *n.* **1.** Abnormal introversion and egocentricity; acceptance of fantasy rather than reality. **2.** *Psychology.* Infantile autism. **—au′tist** *n.* **—au·tis′tic** (-tĭk) *adj. & n.* **—au·tis′ti·cal·ly** *adv.*

au·to (ô′tō) *n., pl.* **-tos.** An automobile. **—auto** *intr.v.* **-toed, -to·ing, -tos.** To go by or ride in an automobile. [Short for AUTOMOBILE.]

auto. *abbr.* **1.** Automatic. **2.** Automotive.

auto– or **aut–** *pref.* **1.** Self; same: *autogamy.* **2.** Automatic: *autopilot.* [Greek, from *autos,* self.]

au·to·an·ti·bod·y (ô′tō-ăn′tĭ-bŏd′ē) *n.* An antibody that attacks the cells and tissues of the organism in which it is formed.

au·to·bahn (ô′tə-bän′, ou′tō-) *n.* An expressway in Germany and German-speaking countries. [German : *Auto,* automobile; see AUTO + *Bahn,* road, from Middle High German *ban.* See **gʷhen-** in Appendix.]

au·to·bi·og·ra·phy (ô′tō-bī-ŏg′rə-fē, -bē-) *n., pl.* **-phies.** The biography of a person written by that person. **—au′to·bi·og′ra·pher** *n.* **—au′to·bi′o·graph′ic** (-bī′ə-grăf′ĭk), **au′to·bi′o·graph′i·cal** *adj.* **—au′to·bi′o·graph′i·cal·ly** *adv.*

au·to·bus (ô′tō-bŭs′) *n., pl.* **-bus·es** or **-bus·ses.** A motor coach; a bus.

au·to·ca·tal·y·sis (ô′tō-kə-tăl′ĭ-sĭs) *n., pl.* **-ses** (-sēz′). Catalysis of a chemical reaction by one of the products of the reaction. **—au′to·cat′a·lyt′ic** (-kăt′l-ĭt′ĭk) *adj.* **—au′to·cat′a·lyt′i·cal·ly** *adv.*

au·toch·thon (ô-tŏk′thən) *n., pl.* **-thons** or **-tho·nes** (-thə-nēz′). **1.** One of the earliest known inhabitants of a place; an aborigine. **2.** *Ecology.* An indigenous plant or animal. [Greek *autokhthōn* : *auto-,* auto- + *khthōn,* earth; see **dhghem-** in Appendix.]

au·toch·tho·nous (ô-tŏk′thə-nəs) also **au·toch·tho·nal** (-thə-nəl) or **au·toch·thon·ic** (ô′tŏk-thŏn′ĭk) *adj.* **1.** Originating where found; indigenous: *autochthonous rocks; an autochthonous people; autochthonous folktales.* See Synonyms at **native. 2.** *Biology.* Originating or formed in the place where found: *an autochthonous blood clot.* **—au·toch′thon·ism, au·toch′tho·ny** *n.* **—au·toch′tho·nous·ly** *adv.*

au·to·clave (ô′tō-klāv′) *n.* A strong, pressurized, steam-heated vessel, as for laboratory experiments, sterilization, or cooking. [French : Greek *auto-,* auto- + Latin *clāvis,* key.]

au·to·coid (ô′tə-koid′) *n.* Variant of **autacoid.**

au·toc·ra·cy (ô-tŏk′rə-sē) *n., pl.* **-cies. 1.** Government by a single person having unlimited power; despotism. **2.** A country or state that is governed by a single person with unlimited power.

au·to·crat (ô′tə-krăt′) *n.* **1.** A ruler having unlimited power; a despot. **2.** A person with unlimited power or authority: *a corporate autocrat.* [French *autocrate,* from Greek *autokratēs,* ruling by oneself : *auto-,* auto- + *-kratēs,* -crat.] **—au′to·crat′ic, au′to·crat′i·cal** *adj.* **—au′to·crat′i·cal·ly** *adv.*

au·to·cross (ô′tō-krôs′, -krŏs′) *n. Sports.* A competition for automobiles that tests driving skill and speed. [AUTO(MOBILE) + (MOTO)CROSS.]

au·to-da-fé (ô′tō-də-fā′, ou′tō-) *n., pl* **au·tos-da-fé** (ô′tōz-, ou′tōz-). **1.** Public announcement of the sentences imposed on persons tried by the Inquisition and the public execution of those sentences by the secular authorities. **2.** The burning of a heretic at the stake. [Portuguese *auto da fé* : *auto,* act + *da,* of the + *fé,* faith.]

au·to-de·struct (ô′tō-dĭ-strŭkt′) *intr.v.* **-struct·ed, -struct·ing, -structs.** To destroy itself or oneself; self-destruct. [AUTO– + (SELF-)DESTRUCT.]

au·to·di·dact (ô′tō-dī′dăkt′) *n.* A self-taught person. [From Greek *autodidaktos,* self-taught : *auto-,* auto- + *didaktos,* taught; see DIDACTIC.] **—au′to·di·dac′tic** *adj.*

au·to·dyne (ô′tə-dīn′) *n.* A heterodyne radio device in which one tube serves simultaneously as oscillator and detector. [AUTO– + (HETERO)DYNE.] **—au′to·dyne′** *adj.*

au·toe·cious (ô-tē′shəs) *adj. Biology.* Having all stages of a life cycle occurring on the same host. [From AUTO– + Greek *oikos,* house; see **weik-**[1] in Appendix.] **—au·toe′cism** (-sĭz′əm) *n.*

au·to·er·o·tism (ô′tō-ĕr′ə-tĭz′əm) or **au·to·e·rot·i·cism** (-ĭ-rŏt′ĭ-sĭz′əm) *n.* **1.** Self-satisfaction of sexual desire, as by masturbation. **2.** The arousal of sexual feeling without an external stimulus. **—au′to·e·rot′ic** (-ĭ-rŏt′ĭk) *adj.*

au·tog·a·my (ô-tŏg′ə-mē) *n.* **1.** *Botany.* Self-fertilization in plants. **2.** *Biology.* The union of nuclei within and arising from a single cell, as in certain protozoans and fungi. **—au′to·gam′ic** (ô′tō-găm′ĭk), **au·tog′a·mous** *adj.*

au·to·gen·e·sis (ô′tō-jĕn′ĭ-sĭs) also **au·tog·e·ny** (ô-tŏj′ə-nē) *n.* See **abiogenesis. —au′to·ge·ne′tic** (-jə-nĕt′ĭk) *adj.* **—au′to·ge·net′i·cal·ly** *adv.*

au·tog·e·nous (ô-tŏj′ə-nəs) also **au·to·gen·ic** (ô′tə-jĕn′ĭk) *adj.* **1.** Produced from within; self-generating. **2.** *Medicine.* Originating with the individual to which applied: *an autogenous graft; an autogenous vaccine.* **—au·tog′e·nous·ly** *adv.*

au·tog·e·ny (ô-tŏj′ə-nē) *n.* Variant of **autogenesis.**

au·to·gi·ro also **au·to·gy·ro** (ô′tō-jī′rō) *n., pl.* **-ros.** An aircraft powered by a conventional propeller and supported in flight by a freewheeling, horizontal rotor that provides lift. [A former trademark.]

au·to·graph (ô′tə-grăf′) *n.* **1.** A person's own signature or handwriting. **2.** A manuscript in the author's handwriting. **—autograph** *tr.v.* **-graphed, -graph·ing, -graphs. 1.** To write one's name or signature on or in; sign. **2.** To write in one's own handwriting. **—autograph** *adj.* Written in the writer's own handwriting: *an autograph letter.* [Late Latin *autographum,* from neuter of Latin *autographus,* written with one's own hand, from Greek *autographos* : *auto-,* auto- + *graphein,* to write; see –GRAPH.] **—au′to·graph′ic, au′to·graph′i·cal** *adj.* **—au′to·graph′i·cal·ly** *adv.*

au·tog·ra·phy (ô-tŏg′rə-fē) *n.* **1.** The writing of something in one's own handwriting. **2.** Autographs considered as a group.

au·to·gy·ro (ô′tō-jī′rō) *n.* Variant of **autogiro.**

Au·to·harp (ô′tō-härp′). A trademark used for a musical instrument similar to a zither.

au·to·hyp·no·sis (ô′tō-hĭp-nō′sĭs) *n.* **1.** The act or process of hypnotizing oneself. **2.** A self-induced hypnotic state. Also called *self-hypnosis.* **—au′to·hyp·not′ic** (-nŏt′ĭk) *adj.*

au·to·im·mune (ô′tō-ĭ-myo͞on′) *adj.* Of or relating to an immune response by the body against one of its own tissues or types of cells. **—au′to·im·mu′ni·ty** *n.* **—au′to·im′mu·ni·za′tion** (-ĭm′yə-nə-zā′shən) *n.*

au·to·in·fec·tion (ô′tō-ĭn-fĕk′shən) *n.* Infection, such as recurrent boils, caused by bacteria, viruses, or parasites that persist on or in the body.

au·to·in·oc·u·la·tion (ô′tō-ĭ-nŏk′yə-lā′shən) *n.* **1.** Inoculation with a vaccine made from microorganisms obtained from the recipient's own body. **2.** An infection caused by a disease that has spread from a different part of the body. **—au′to·in·oc′u·la·ble** *adj.*

au·to·in·tox·i·ca·tion (ô′tō-ĭn-tŏk′sĭ-kā′shən) *n.* Self-poisoning caused by endogenous microorganisms, metabolic wastes, or other toxins produced within the body. Also called *autotoxemia.*

au·to·load·ing (ô′tō-lō′dĭng) *adj.* Semiautomatic.

au·tol·o·gous (ô-tŏl′ə-gəs) *adj.* Derived or transferred from the same individual's body: *autologous blood donation.* [AUTO– + *-logous,* as in HOMOLOGOUS.]

au·tol·y·sate (ô-tŏl′ĭ-sāt′, -zāt′) *n. Biochemistry.* An end product of autolysis.

au·tol·y·sin (ô-tŏl′ĭ-sĭn, ô′tə-lī′sĭn) *n. Biochemistry.* A substance, such as an enzyme, that is capable of destroying the cells or tissues of an organism within which it is produced.

au·tol·y·sis (ô-tŏl′ĭ-sĭs) *n. Biochemistry.* The destruction of tissues or cells of an organism by the action of substances, such as enzymes, that are produced within the organism. Also called *self-digestion.* **—au′to·lyt′ic** (ô′tə-lĭt′ĭk) *adj.*

au·to·mak·er (ô′tō-mā′kər) *n.* A manufacturer of automotive vehicles; a carmaker.

Au·to·mat (ô′tə-măt′). A trademark used for automated restaurant services in which food is dispensed from vending machines.

au·tom·a·ta (ô-tŏm′ə-tə) *n.* A plural of **automaton.**

au·to·mate (ô′tə-māt′) *v.* **-mat·ed, -mat·ing, -mates.** *—tr.* **1.** To convert to automatic operation: *automate a factory.* **2.** To control or operate by automation. *—intr.* To convert to or make use of automation. [Back-formation from AUTOMATION.]

automated teller machine

au·to·mat·ed teller machine (ô′tə-mā′tĭd) *n. Abbr.* **ATM** An unattended electronic machine in a public place, connected to a data system and related equipment and activated by a bank customer to obtain cash withdrawals and other banking services. Also called *automated bank teller, automated teller, automatic teller, automatic teller machine, cash machine.*

au·to·mat·ic (ô′tə-măt′ĭk) *adj. Abbr.* **auto. 1.a.** Acting or operating in a manner essentially independent of external influence or control: *an automatic light switch; a budget deficit that caused automatic spending cuts.* **b.** Self-regulating: *an automatic washing machine.* **2.a.** Acting or done without volition or conscious control; involuntary: *automatic shrinking of the pupils of the eyes in strong light.* See Synonyms at **spontaneous. b.** Acting or done as if by machine; mechanical: *an automatic reply to a familiar question.* **3.a.** Capable of firing continuously until ammunition is exhausted or the trigger is released: *an automatic rifle.* **b.** Semiautomatic: *an automatic pistol.* **—automatic** *n.* **1.** An automatic machine or device. **2.a.** An automatic firearm. **b.** A semiautomatic firearm. **3.** A transmission or a motor vehicle with an automatic gear-shifting mechanism. **4.** *Football.* See **audible.** [From Greek *automatos* : *auto-,* auto- + *-matos,* willing; see **men-**[1] in Appendix.] **—au′to·mat′i·cal·ly** *adv.* **—au′to·ma·tic′i·ty** (-mə-tĭs′ĭ-tē) *n.*

WORD HISTORY: The words *automatic pilot* or *automatic transmission* bring to mind mechanical devices that operate with minimal human intervention. Yet the word *automatic,* which goes back to the Greek word *automatos,* "acting of one's own will, self-acting, of itself," made up of two parts, *auto–,* "self," and *–matos,* "willing," is first recorded in English in 1748 with reference to motions of the body, such as the peristaltic action of the intestines: "The Motions are called automatic from their Resemblance to the Motions of Automata, or Machines, whose Principle of Motion is within themselves." Although the writer had machines in mind, *automatic* could be used of living things, a use we still have, although not the primary one. The association of *automatic* chiefly with machinery may represent one instance of many in which we have come to see the world in mechanical terms.

automatic pilot *n.* A navigation mechanism, as on an aircraft, that automatically maintains a preset course. Also called *robot pilot.*

automatic teller *n.* See **automated teller machine.**

automatic teller machine *n. Abbr.* **ATM** See **automated teller machine.**

au·to·ma·tion (ô′tə-mā′shən) *n.* **1.** The automatic operation or control of equipment, a process, or a system. **2.** The techniques and equipment used to achieve automatic operation or control. **3.**

ă pat	oi boy
ā pay	ou out
âr care	o͝o took
ä father	o͞o boot
ĕ pet	ŭ cut
ē be	ûr urge
ĭ pit	th thin
ī pie	*th* this
îr pier	hw which
ŏ pot	zh vision
ō toe	ə about, item
ô paw	♦ regionalism

Stress marks: **′** (primary); ′ (secondary), as in **dictionary** (dĭk′shə-nĕr′ē)

The condition of being automatically controlled or operated. [From AUTOMATIC.] **—au′to·ma′tive** *adj.*

au·tom·a·tism (ô-tŏm′ə-tĭz′əm) *n.* **1. a.** The state or quality of being automatic. **b.** Automatic mechanical action. **2.** *Philosophy.* The theory that the body is a machine whose functions are accompanied but not controlled by consciousness. **3.** *Physiology.* **a.** The involuntary functioning of an organ or other body structure that is not under conscious control, such as the beating of the heart or the dilation of the pupil of the eye. **b.** The reflexive action of a body part. **4.** *Psychology.* **a.** Suspension of consciousness in order to express subconscious ideas and feelings. **b.** Mechanical, seemingly aimless behavior characteristic of various mental disorders. [From Latin *automaton,* automaton. See AUTOMATON.] **—au·tom′a·tist** *n.*

au·tom·a·ti·za·tion (ô-tŏm′ə-tĭ-zā′shən) *n.* Automation.

au·tom·a·tize (ô-tŏm′ə-tīz′) *tr.v.* **-tized, -tiz·ing, -tiz·es. 1.** To make automatic. **2.** To turn into an automaton. [From AUTOMATIC.]

au·tom·a·ton (ô-tŏm′ə-tən, -tŏn′) *n., pl.* **-tons** or **-ta** (-tə). **1.** A self-operating machine or mechanism, especially a robot. **2.** One that behaves or responds in a mechanical way. [Latin, self-operating machine, from Greek, from neuter of *automatos,* self-acting. See AUTOMATIC.] **—au·tom′a·tous** *adj.*

au·to·mo·bile (ô′tə-mō-bēl′, -mō′bēl′) *n.* A self-propelled passenger vehicle that usually has four wheels and an internal-combustion engine, used for land transport. Also called *motorcar.* **—automobile** *adj.* Of or relating to automobiles; automotive. [French : Greek *auto-,* auto- + French *mobile,* mobile (from Old French; see MOBILE).] **—au′to·mo·bil′ist** *n.*

au·to·mo·tive (ô′tə-mō′tĭv) *adj. Abbr.* **auto. 1.** Moving by itself; self-propelling or self-propelled. **2.** Of or relating to self-propelled vehicles.

au·to·nom·ic (ô′tə-nŏm′ĭk) *adj.* **1.** *Physiology.* **a.** Of, relating to, or controlled by the autonomic nervous system. **b.** Occurring involuntarily: *an autonomic reflex.* **2.** Resulting from internal stimuli; spontaneous. **—au′to·nom′i·cal·ly** *adv.*

autonomic nervous system *n.* The part of the vertebrate nervous system that regulates involuntary action, as of the intestines, heart, and glands, and that is divided into the sympathetic nervous system and the parasympathetic nervous system.

au·ton·o·mous (ô-tŏn′ə-məs) *adj.* **1.** Not controlled by others or by outside forces; independent: *an autonomous judiciary; an autonomous division of a corporate conglomerate.* **2.** Independent in mind or judgment; self-directed. **3. a.** Independent of the laws of another state or government; self-governing. **b.** Of or relating to a self-governing entity: *an autonomous legislature.* **c.** Self-governing with respect to local or internal affairs: *an autonomous region of a country.* **4.** Autonomic. [From Greek *autonomos* : *auto-,* auto- + *nomos,* law; see **nem-** in Appendix.] **—au·ton′o·mous·ly** *adv.*

au·ton·o·my (ô-tŏn′ə-mē) *n., pl.* **-mies. 1.** The condition or quality of being autonomous; independence. **2. a.** Self-government or the right of self-government; self-determination. **b.** Self-government with respect to local or internal affairs: *granted autonomy to a national minority.* **3.** A self-governing state, community, or group. [Greek *autonomia,* from *autonomos,* self-ruling. See AUTONOMOUS.] **—au·ton′o·mist** *n.*

au·to·pen (ô′tō-pĕn′) *n.* A mechanical device used for writing imitations of a personal signature.

au·toph·a·gy (ô-tŏf′ə-jē) *n.* The process of self-digestion by a cell through the action of enzymes originating within the same cell.

au·to·pil·er (ô′tō-pī′lər) *n. Computer Science.* A specific automatic compiler. [AUTO– + (COM)PILER.]

au·to·pi·lot (ô′tō-pī′lət) *n.* Automatic pilot.

au·to·plas·ty (ô′tō-plăs′tē) *n.* Surgical repair or reconstruction of a body part using tissue taken from another part of the body. **—au′to·plas′tic** *adj.* **—au′to·plas′ti·cal·ly** *adv.*

au·to·pol·y·ploid (ô′tō-pŏl′ə-ploid′) *adj.* Having more than two sets of chromosomes all derived from the same species. **—autopolyploid** *n.* An organism having more than two sets of chromosomes, all of which were derived from the same species. **—au′to·pol′y·ploid′y** *n.*

au·top·sy (ô′tŏp′sē, ô′təp-) *n., pl.* **-sies. 1.** Examination of a cadaver to determine or confirm the cause of death. Also called *necropsy, postmortem, postmortem examination.* **2.** A critical assessment or examination after the fact: *a post-election campaign autopsy.* [Greek *autopsia,* a seeing for oneself : *auto-,* auto- + *opsis,* sight; see **okʷ-** in Appendix.] **—au·top′sic, au·top′si·cal** *adj.* **—au′top′sist** *n.*

au·to·ra·di·o·gram (ô′tō-rā′dē-ō-grăm′) *n.* See **autoradiograph.**

au·to·ra·di·o·graph (ô′tō-rā′dē-ō-grăf′) *n.* An image recorded on a photographic film or plate produced by the radiation emitted from a specimen, such as a section of tissue, that has been treated or injected with a radioactively labeled isotope or that has absorbed or ingested such an isotope. Also called *autoradiogram.* **—au′to·ra′di·o·graph′ic** *adj.* **—au′to·ra′di·og′ra·phy** (-ŏg′rə-fē) *n.*

au·to·route (ô′tō-ro͞ot′) *n.* An expressway in France and French-speaking countries. [French : *auto,* automobile; see AUTO + *route,* road (from Old French; see ROUTE).]

au·to·some (ô′tə-sōm′) *n.* A chromosome that is not a sex chromosome. **—au′to·so′mal** (-sō′məl) *adj.* **—au′to·so′mal·ly** *adv.*

au·to·stra·da (ô′tō-strä′də, ou′tō-) *n.* An expressway in Italy. [Italian : *auto,* automobile; see AUTO + *strada,* street (from Late Latin *strāta,* paved road; see STREET).]

au·to·sug·ges·tion (ô′tō-səg-jĕs′chən) *n. Psychology.* The process by which a person induces self-acceptance of an opinion, belief, or plan of action. **—au′to·sug·gest′** *v.* **—au′to·sug·gest′i·bil′i·ty** (-ə-bĭl′ĭ-tē) *n.* **—au′to·sug·gest′i·ble** *adj.* **—au′to·sug·ges′tive** (-tĭv) *adj.*

au·tot·o·mize (ô-tŏt′ə-mīz′) *v.* **-mized, -miz·ing, -miz·es.** *—tr.* To cause the autotomy of. *—intr.* To undergo autotomy.

au·tot·o·my (ô-tŏt′ə-mē) *n.* The spontaneous casting off of a limb or other body part, such as the tail of certain lizards or the claw of a lobster, especially when the organism is injured or under attack. **—au′to·tom′ic** (ô′tə-tŏm′ĭk) *adj.*

au·to·tox·e·mi·a also **au·to·tox·ae·mi·a** (ô′tō-tŏk-sē′mē-ə) *n.* See **autointoxication.**

au·to·tox·in (ô′tō-tŏk′sĭn) *n.* A poison that acts on the organism in which it is generated. **—au′to·tox′ic** *adj.*

au·to·trans·form·er (ô′tō-trăns-fôr′mər) *n.* An electrical transformer in which the primary and secondary coils have some or all windings in common.

au·to·troph (ô′tə-trŏf′, -trōf′) *n.* An organism capable of synthesizing its own food from inorganic substances, using light or chemical energy. Green plants, algae, and certain bacteria are autotrophs. **—au′to·troph′ic** (-trŏf′ĭk, -trō′fĭk) *adj.* **—au′to·troph′i·cal·ly** *adv.* **—au·tot′ro·phy** (ô-tŏt′rə-fē) *n.*

au·to·work·er (ô′tō-wûr′kər) *n.* A worker in the automobile industry.

au·tumn (ô′təm) *n.* **1.** The season of the year between summer and winter, lasting from the autumnal equinox to the winter solstice and from September to December in the Northern Hemisphere; fall. **2.** A period of maturity verging on decline. **—autumn** *adj.* **1.** Of, having to do with, occurring in, or appropriate to the season of autumn: *autumn foliage.* **2.** Grown during the season of autumn: *autumn crops.* [Middle English *autumpne,* from Old French *automne,* from Latin *autumnus.*] **—au·tum′nal** (-tŭm′nəl) *adj.* **—au·tum′nal·ly** *adv.*

autumnal equinox *n.* **1.** The point at which the ecliptic intersects the celestial equator, the sun having a southerly motion. **2.** The moment at which the sun passes through the autumnal equinox, about September 23, marking the beginning of autumn.

autumn crocus *n.* A corm-producing European and North African plant *(Colchicum autumnale)* having showy colorful flowers that appear in the fall. Also called *meadow saffron.*

au·tun·ite (ō-tŭn′īt′, ô′tə-nīt′) *n.* A yellowish, fluorescent mineral of uranium with the composition $Ca(UO_2)_2(PO_4)_2 \cdot 10-12H_2O$. [After *Autun,* a city of east-central France.]

Au·vergne (ō-vûrn′, ō-vĕrn′). A historical region and former province of central France traversed north to south by the **Auvergne Mountains,** a chain of extinct volcanoes. Auvergne became part of the French royal domain in 1615.

aux. *abbr.* **1.** Auxiliary. **2.** *Grammar.* Auxiliary verb.

aux·e·sis (ôg-zē′sĭs, ôk-sē′-) *n.* Growth resulting from increase in cell size without cell division. [Greek *auxēsis,* growth, from *auxanein, auxē-,* to grow. See **aug-** in Appendix.] **—aux·et′ic** (ôg-zĕt′ĭk) *adj.* **—aux·et′i·cal·ly** *adv.*

aux·il·ia·ry (ôg-zĭl′yə-rē, -zĭl′ə-rē) *adj. Abbr.* **aux., auxil. 1.** Giving assistance or support; helping. **2.** Acting as a subsidiary; supplementary: *the main library and its auxiliary branches.* **3.** Held in or used as a reserve: *auxiliary troops; an auxiliary power generator.* **4.** *Nautical.* Equipped with a motor as well as sails. **5.** *Grammar.* Of, relating to, or being an auxiliary verb. **—auxiliary** *n., pl.* **-ries.** *Abbr.* **aux., auxil. 1.** An individual or a group that assists or functions in a supporting capacity: *a volunteers' auxiliary at a hospital.* **2.** A member of a foreign body of troops serving a country in war. **3.** *Grammar.* An auxiliary verb. **4.** *Nautical.* **a.** A sailing vessel equipped with a motor. **b.** A vessel, such as a supply ship or a tug, that is designed for and used in instances and services other than combat. [Middle English, from Latin *auxiliārius,* from *auxilium,* help. See **aug-** in Appendix.]

auxiliary verb *n. Abbr.* **aux. v., aux.** *Grammar.* A verb, such as *have, can,* or *will,* that accompanies the main verb in a clause and helps to make distinctions in mood, voice, aspect, and tense.

aux·in (ôk′sĭn) *n.* Any of several plant hormones that regulate various functions, including cell elongation. [From Greek *auxein,* to grow. See **aug-** in Appendix.] **—aux·in′ic** *adj.* **—aux·in′i·cal·ly** *adv.*

aux·o·troph (ôk′sə-trŏf, -trōf′) *n.* An organism, such as a strain of bacteria, that has lost the ability to synthesize certain substances required for its growth and metabolism as the result of mutational changes. [Back-formation from AUXOTROPHIC.]

aux·o·troph·ic (ôk′sə-trŏf′ĭk, -trō′fĭk) *adj.* Requiring one or more specific substances for growth and metabolism that the parental organism was able to synthesize on its own. Used with respect to organisms, such as strains of bacteria, algae, or fungi, that can no longer synthesize certain growth factors because of mutational changes. [Greek *auxein,* to increase; see AUXIN + –TROPHIC.]

aux. v. *abbr. Grammar.* Auxiliary verb.

Av (äv, ôv) also **Ab** (äb, äv, ôv) *n.* The 11th month of the year in the Jewish calendar. See table at **calendar.** [Hebrew *'āb,* from Canaanite *'ab.*]

AV or **A.V.** *abbr.* **1.** Audio-visual. **2.** *Bible.* Authorized Version.

av. *abbr.* **1.** Also **Av.** Avenue. **2.** Average. **3.** Avoirdupois.

a.v. or **a/v** *abbr.* Ad valorem.

a·vail (ə-vāl′) *v.* **a·vailed, a·vail·ing, a·vails.** —*tr.* To be of use or advantage to; help: *Nothing could avail the dying patient.* —*intr.* To be of use, value, or advantage; serve: *Halfway measures will no longer avail.* **—avail** *n.* Use, benefit, or advantage: *labored to no avail.* **—*idiom.* avail (oneself) of.** To make use of. [Middle English *availen* : *a-,* intensive pref. (from Latin *ad-;* see AD–) + Old French *valoir, vail-,* to be worth (from Latin *valēre;* see **wal-** in Appendix).] **—a·vail′ing·ly** *adv.*

a·vail·a·ble (ə-vā′lə-bəl) *adj.* **1.** Present and ready for use; at hand; accessible: *kept a fire extinguisher available at all times.* **2.** Capable of being gotten; obtainable: *a bedspread available in three colors.* **3.** Qualified and willing to serve: *a list of available candidates.* **4.** *Archaic.* **a.** Capable of bringing about a beneficial result or effect. **b.** *Law.* Valid. Used especially of a plea. **—a·vail′a·bil′i·ty, a·vail′a·ble·ness** *n.* **—a·vail′a·bly** *adv.*

av·a·lanche (ăv′ə-lănch′) *n.* **1.** A fall or slide of a large mass, as of snow or rock, down a mountainside. **2.** A massive or overwhelming amount; a flood: *received an avalanche of mail.* **—avalanche** *v.* **-lanched, -lanch·ing, -lanch·es.** —*intr.* To fall or slide in a massive or overwhelming amount. —*tr.* To overwhelm; inundate. [French; akin to Provençal *lavanca,* ravine, perhaps akin to Latin *lābī,* to slip.]

avalanche lily *n.* A western North American corm-producing plant *(Erythronium grandiflorum)* in the lily family, having white or golden-yellow flowers with red anthers. [So called because it grows near the snow line and blooms when the snow begins to melt.]

Av·a·lon (ăv′ə-lŏn′) *n.* In Arthurian legend, an island paradise in the western seas to which King Arthur went at his death.

Avalon Peninsula. A large, irregularly shaped peninsula of southeast Newfoundland, Canada. Most of the province's population resides here.

a·vant-garde (ä′vänt-gärd′, ăv′änt-) *n.* A group active in the invention and application of new techniques in a given field, especially in the arts. **—avant-garde** *adj.* Of, relating to, or being part of an innovative group, especially one in the arts: *avant-garde painters; an avant-garde theater piece.* [French, from Old French, vanguard. See VANGUARD.] **—a′vant-gard′ism** *n.* **—a′vant-gard′ist** *n.*

av·a·rice (ăv′ə-rĭs) *n.* Immoderate desire for wealth; cupidity. [Middle English, from Old French, from Latin *avāritia,* from *avārus,* greedy, from *avēre,* to desire.]

av·a·ri·cious (ăv′ə-rĭsh′əs) *adj.* Immoderately desirous of wealth or gain; greedy. **—av′a·ri′cious·ly** *adv.* **—av′a·ri′cious·ness** *n.*

a·vas·cu·lar (ā-văs′kyə-lər) *adj.* Not associated with or supplied by blood vessels. **—a·vas′cu·lar′i·ty** (-lăr′ĭ-tē) *n.*

a·vast (ə-văst′) *interj. Nautical.* Used as a command to stop or desist. [From Middle Dutch *hou vast,* hold fast : *hou, houd,* imperative of *houden,* to hold + *vast,* fast; see **past-** in Appendix.]

av·a·tar (ăv′ə-tär′) *n.* **1.** The incarnation of a Hindu deity, especially Vishnu, in human or animal form. **2.** An embodiment, as of a quality or concept; an archetype: *the very avatar of cunning.* **3.** A temporary manifestation or aspect of a continuing entity: *occultism in its present avatar.* [Sanskrit *avatāraḥ* : *ava,* down + *tarati,* he crosses; see **tere-**[2] in Appendix.]

a·vaunt (ə-vônt′, ə-vänt′) *adv.* Hence; away. [Middle English, forward, from Old French *avant,* from Latin *abante* : *ab-,* from; see AB–[1] + *ante,* before; see ANTE–.]

AVC *abbr.* **1.** American Veterans Committee. **2.** Automatic volume control.

avdp. *abbr.* Avoirdupois.

a·ve (ä′vā) *n.* **1.** An expression of hail or farewell. **2. Ave.** *Roman Catholic Church.* Hail Mary. [Middle English, from Latin.]

ave. or **Ave.** or **AVE** *abbr.* Avenue.

A·vel·la·ne·da (ä-vĕl′yä-nĕ′dä, ä-vĕ′yä-, ä-vĕ′zhä-nĕ′thä). A city of eastern Argentina near Buenos Aires. It is an important commercial and industrial center. Population, 330,654.

A·ve Ma·ri·a (ä′vā mə-rē′ə) *n. Roman Catholic Church.* Hail Mary. [Middle English, from Medieval Latin.]

a·venge (ə-vĕnj′) *tr.v.* **a·venged, a·veng·ing, a·veng·es. 1.** To inflict a punishment or penalty in return for; revenge: *avenge a murder.* **2.** To take vengeance on behalf of: *avenged their wronged parents.* [Middle English *avengen,* from Old French *avengier* : *a-,* to (from Latin *ad-;* see AD–) + *vengier,* to vindicate (from Latin *vindicāre,* to claim; see VINDICATE).] **—a·veng′er** *n.* **—a·veng′ing·ly** *adv.*

av·ens (ăv′ənz) *n., pl.* **avens. 1.** Any of various perennial herbs of the genus *Geum* in the rose family, having often pinnate basal leaves and variously colored flowers with many pistils. **2.** The mountain avens. [Middle English *avence,* from Old French, from Medieval Latin *avencia.*]

Av·en·tine (ăv′ən-tīn′, -tēn′). One of the seven hills of ancient Rome. It was turned over to the plebes for settlement in 456 B.C. **—Av′en·tine′** *adj.*

a·ven·tu·rine (ə-vĕn′chə-rēn′, -rĭn) also **a·ven·tu·rin** (-rĭn) *n.* **1.** An opaque or semitranslucent brown glass flecked with small metallic particles, often of copper or chromic oxide. **2.** Any of several varieties of quartz or feldspar flecked with particles of mica, hematite, or other materials. In this sense, also called *sunstone.* [French, from *aventure,* accident (so called because of its accidental discovery or the randomness of inclusions in it). See ADVENTURE.] **—a·ven′tu·rine′** *adj.*

av·e·nue (ăv′ə-no͞o′, -nyo͞o′) *n.* **1.** *Abbr.* **Ave., AVE, Av., ave., av.** A wide street or thoroughfare. **2. a.** A broad roadway lined with trees. **b.** *Chiefly British.* The drive leading from the main road up to a country house. **3.** A means of access or approach: *new avenues of trade.* [French, from Old French, arrival, from feminine past participle of *avenir,* to approach, from Latin *advenīre,* to come to. See ADVENT.]

Av·en·zo·ar (ăv′ən-zō′ər). 1090?–1162. Spanish-Arab physician and writer whose *Practical Manual of Treatments and Diet* showed an advanced understanding of the human body based on science rather than speculation.

a·ver (ə-vûr′) *tr.v.* **a·verred, a·verr·ing, a·vers. 1.** To affirm positively; declare. See Synonyms at **assert. 2.** *Law.* **a.** To assert formally as a fact. **b.** To justify or prove. [Middle English *averren,* from Old French *averer,* from Vulgar Latin **adverāre* : Latin *ad-,* ad- + Latin *vērus,* true; see **wēro-** in Appendix.] **—a·ver′ment** *n.* **—a·ver′ra·ble** *adj.*

av·er·age (ăv′ər-ĭj, ăv′rĭj) *n. Abbr.* **av., avg. 1.** *Mathematics.* **a.** A number that typifies a set of numbers of which it is a function. **b.** See **arithmetic mean. 2. a.** An intermediate level or degree: *near the average in size.* **b.** The usual or ordinary kind or quality: *Although the wines vary, the average is quite good.* **3.** *Sports.* The ratio of a team's or player's successful performances such as wins, hits, or goals, divided by total opportunities for successful performance, such as games, times at bat, or shots: *finished the season with a .500 average; a batting average of .274.* **4.** *Law.* **a.** The loss of a ship or cargo, caused by damage at sea. **b.** The incurrence of damage or loss of a ship or a cargo at sea. **c.** The equitable distribution of such a loss among concerned parties. **d.** A charge incurred through such a loss. **5.** *Nautical.* Small expenses or charges that are usually paid by the master of a ship. **—average** *adj.* **1.** *Mathematics.* Of, relating to, or constituting an average. **2.** Being intermediate between extremes, as on a scale: *a player of average ability.* **3.** Usual or ordinary in kind or character: *a poll of average people; average eyesight.* **4.** Assessed in accordance with the laws of average. **—average** *v.* **-aged, -ag·ing, -ag·es.** —*tr.* **1.** *Mathematics.* To calculate the average of: *average a set of numbers.* **2.** To do or have an average of: *averaged three hours of work a day.* **3.** To distribute proportionately: *average one's income over four years so as to minimize the tax rate.* —*intr.* **1.** To be or amount to an average: *Some sparrows are six inches long, but they average smaller. Our expenses averaged out to 45 dollars per day.* **2.** To buy or sell more goods or shares to obtain more than an average price. [From Middle English *averay,* charge above the cost of freight, from Old French *avarie,* from Old Italian *avaria,* duty, from Arabic *'awārīyah,* damaged goods, from *'awar,* blemish.] **—av′er·age·ly** *adv.* **—av′er·age·ness** *n.*

SYNONYMS: *average, medium, mediocre, fair, middling, indifferent, tolerable.* These adjectives indicate rank or position around the middle of a scale of evaluation. *Average* and *medium* apply to what is midway between extremes on such a scale; usually they imply both sufficiency and lack of distinction: *a novel of average merit; an orange of medium size. Mediocre* stresses the undistinguished aspect of what is average: *"The caliber of the students . . . has gone from mediocre to above average"* (Judy Pasternak). What is *fair* is passable but substantially below excellent: *a fair student; in fair health; have a fair idea of what's going on. Middling* refers to middle position between best and worst: *gave a middling performance at best. Indifferent* applies to what is of less than striking character, being neither very good nor very bad: *"One and the same thing can at the same time be good, bad, and indifferent, e.g., music is good to the melancholy, bad to those who mourn, and neither good nor bad to the deaf"* (Spinoza). Something that is *tolerable* is merely acceptable: *prepared a tolerable dinner.*

A·ver·no (ä-vĕr′nō). Ancient name **A·ver·nus** (ə-vûr′nəs). A small crater lake of southern Italy near the Tyrrhenian Sea west of Naples. Because of its gloomy aspect and intense sulfuric vapors, now extinguished, the ancient Romans regarded it as the entrance to the underworld.

A·ver·ro·ës or **A·ver·rho·ës** (ə-vĕr′ō-ēz′, ăv′ə-rō′ēz). 1126–1198. Spanish-Arab physician and philosopher best known for his commentaries on Aristotle. Although he was a Moslem, his work was most influential among medieval Christian theologians.

a·verse (ə-vûrs′) *adj.* Having a feeling of opposition, distaste, or aversion; strongly disinclined: *was averse to sharing a table with them; investors who are averse to risk-taking.* [Latin *āversus,* past participle of *āvertere,* to turn away. See AVERT.] **—a·verse′ly** *adv.* **—a·verse′ness** *n.*

a·ver·sion (ə-vûr′zhən, -shən) *n.* **1.** A fixed, intense dislike; repugnance: *formed an aversion to crowds.* **2.** One that is intensely disliked and avoided. **3.** A feeling of extreme repugnance accompanied by avoidance or rejection: *Her aversion to alcohol consumption caused her to shun all social gatherings where such*

ă pat	oi boy
ā pay	ou out
âr care	o͝o took
ä father	o͞o boot
ĕ pet	ŭ cut
ē be	ûr urge
ĭ pit	th thin
ī pie	*th* this
îr pier	hw which
ŏ pot	zh vision
ō toe	ə about, item
ô paw	♦ regionalism

Stress marks: **′** (primary); ′ (secondary), as in **dictionary** (dĭk′shə-nĕr′ē)

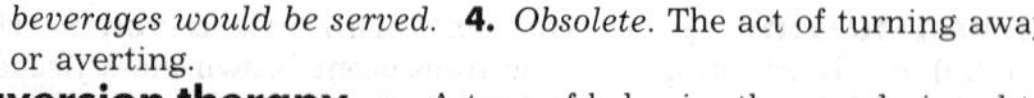

beverages would be served. **4.** *Obsolete.* The act of turning away or averting.

aversion therapy *n.* A type of behavior therapy designed to modify antisocial habits or addictions by creating a strong association with a disagreeable or painful stimulus.

a·ver·sive (ə-vûr′sĭv, -zĭv) *adj.* Causing avoidance of an unpleasant or punishing stimulus, as in techniques of behavior modification. **—a·ver′sive·ly** *adv.* **—a·ver′sive·ness** *n.*

a·vert (ə-vûrt′) *tr.v.* **a·vert·ed, a·vert·ing, a·verts. 1.** To turn away: *avert one's eyes.* **2.** To ward off (something about to happen); prevent: *averted an accident by turning sharply.* See Synonyms at **prevent.** [Middle English *averten,* from Old French *avertir,* from Latin *āvertere* : *ā-, ab-,* away from; see AB–^{1} + *vertere,* to turn; see **wer-^{2}** in Appendix.] **—a·vert′i·ble, a·vert′a·ble** *adj.*

aviator glasses

A·ver·y (ā′və-rē), **Milton Clark.** 1893–1965. American artist. Influenced by the works of Henri Matisse, his style of subtle colors and flat patterns influenced abstract expressionism.

A·ves·ta (ə-vĕs′tə) *n.* A body of ancient Persian writings, a sacred text of Zoroastrianism. [Middle Persian *apastāk,* the basic (text) and *apastāk,* the (hymns of) praise.]

A·ves·tan (ə-vĕs′tən) *n.* The eastern dialect of Old Iranian, in which the Avesta is written. **—Avestan** *adj.* Of or relating to the Avesta or Avestan.

avg. *abbr.* Average.

a·vi·an (ā′vē-ən) *adj.* Of, relating to, or characteristic of birds. [From Latin *avis,* bird. See **awi-** in Appendix.]

a·vi·ar·y (ā′vē-ĕr′ē) *n., pl.* **-ies.** A large enclosure for holding birds in confinement. [Latin *aviārium,* from *avis,* bird. See **awi-** in Appendix.] **—a′vi·a·rist** (-ə-rĭst, -ĕr′ĭst) *n.*

a·vi·ate (ā′vē-āt′, ăv′ē-) *intr.v.* **-at·ed, -at·ing, -ates.** To operate an aircraft; fly. [Back-formation from AVIATION.]

a·vi·a·tion (ā′vē-ā′shən, ăv′ē-) *n. Abbr.* **avn. 1.** The operation of aircraft. **2.** The design, development, and production of aircraft. **3.** Military aircraft. [French, from Latin *avis,* bird. See **awi-** in Appendix.]

aviation medicine *n.* See **aeromedicine.**

a·vi·a·tor (ā′vē-ā′tər, ăv′ē-) *n.* One who operates an aircraft; a pilot. [French *aviateur,* from *aviation,* aviation. See AVIATION.]

aviator glasses *pl.n.* Eyeglasses having a lightweight metal frame and oval lenses that narrow toward the bridge of the nose.

a·vi·a·trix (ā′vē-ā′trĭks, ăv′ē-) *n.* A woman who operates an aircraft; a woman pilot.

Av·i·cen·na (ăv′ĭ-sĕn′ə). 980–1037. Persian physician and philosopher noted for his *Canon of Medicine,* a standard medical textbook used in Europe until the 17th century.

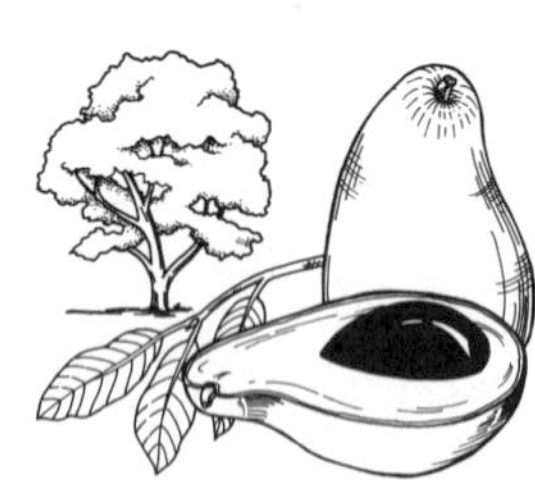

avocado
Persea americana

a·vi·cul·ture (ā′vĭ-kŭl′chər, ăv′ĭ-) *n.* The raising, keeping, and care of birds. [Latin *avis,* bird; see **awi-** in Appendix + CULTURE.] **—a′vi·cul′tur·ist** *n.*

av·id (ăv′ĭd) *adj.* **1.** Having an ardent desire or unbounded craving; greedy: *avid for adventure.* **2.** Marked by keen interest and enthusiasm: *an avid sports fan.* See Synonyms at **eager^1.** [Latin *avidus,* from *avēre,* to desire.] **—av′id·ly** *adv.*

av·i·din (ăv′ĭ-dĭn) *n.* A protein found in uncooked egg white that binds to and inactivates biotin. An abundance of avidin in the duct can result in a deficiency of biotin. [AVID + (BIOT)IN, from its affinity for biotin.]

a·vid·i·ty (ə-vĭd′ĭ-tē) *n.* **1.** Ardent desire or craving; eagerness. **2.** Keen interest or enthusiasm: *followed the tournament with avidity.* **3.** *Chemistry.* **a.** The dissociation-dependent strength of an acid or base. **b.** Degree of affinity.

a·vi·fau·na (ā′və-fô′nə, ăv′ə-) *n.* The birds of a specific region or period. [Latin *avis,* bird; see **awi-** in Appendix + FAUNA.] **—a′vi·fau′nal** *adj.*

A·vi·gnon (ä-vē-nyôN′). A city of southeast France on the Rhone River. It was the seat of the papacy from 1309 to 1378 and the residence of several antipopes from 1378 to 1417. Population, 89,132.

Á·vi·la (ä′və-lə, ä′vē-lä). A town of central Spain west-northwest of Madrid. It is a religious and tourist center. Population, 42,165.

Á·vi·la Ca·ma·cho (ä′vē-lä′ kə-mä′chō), **Manuel.** 1897–1955. Mexican general and politician whose presidency (1940–1946) was a period of stability.

avocet
American avocet
Recurvirostra americana

A·vi·lés (ä′-və-lās′, ä′vē-lĕs′). A town of northwest Spain on an inlet of the Bay of Biscay. It is a port and an industrial center. Population, 89,992.

a·vi·on·ics (ā′vē-ŏn′ĭks, ăv′ē-) *n.* **1.** *(used with a sing. verb).* The science and technology of electronics and the development of electronic devices as applied to aeronautics and astronautics: *Avionics has become even more important with the development of the space program.* **2.** *(used with a pl. verb).* The electronic systems, equipment, and other devices so developed: *The avionics on this spacecraft represent a new generation of sophistication.* [AVI(ATION) + (ELECTR)ONICS.] **—a′vi·on′ic** *adj.*

a·vir·u·lent (ā-vîr′yə-lənt, ā-vîr′ə-) *adj.* Not virulent. **—a·vir′u·lence** *n.*

a·vi·ta·min·o·sis (ā-vī′tə-mĭ-nō′sĭs) *n.* A disease, such as scurvy, beriberi, or pellagra, caused by deficiency of one or more essential vitamins. **—a·vi′ta·min·ot′ic** (-nŏt′ĭk) *adj.*

avn. *abbr.* Aviation.

AV node (ā′vē′) *n.* See **atrioventricular node.** [A(TRIO)V(ENTRICULAR) NODE.]

a·vo (ä′vōō) *n., pl.* **a·vos.** See table at **currency.** [Portuguese, shortened from *oitavo,* eighth, from Latin *octāvus.* See OCTAVE.]

av·o·ca·do (ăv′ə-kä′dō, ä′və-) *n., pl.* **-dos. 1.** A tropical American tree *(Persea americana)* having oval or pear-shaped fruit with leathery skin, yellowish-green flesh, and a large seed. Also called *alligator pear.* **2.** The edible fruit of this tree. **3.** *Color.* A dull green. [American Spanish, alteration (influenced by Spanish *avocado,* earlier form of *abogado,* lawyer) of Nahuatl *ahuacatl.*]

WORD HISTORY: The history of *avocado* takes us back to the Nahuatl (the language of the Aztecs) word *ahuacatl,* "fruit of the avocado tree" or "testicle." The word *ahuacatl* was compounded with others, as in *ahuacamolli,* meaning "avocado soup or sauce," from which the Spanish-Mexican word *guacamole* derives. In trying to pronounce *ahuacatl,* the Spanish who found the fruit and its Nahuatl name in Mexico came up with *aguacate,* but other Spanish speakers substituted the form *avocado* for the Nahuatl word because *ahuacatl* sounded like the early Spanish word *avocado* (now *abogado*), meaning "lawyer." In borrowing the Spanish *avocado,* first recorded in English in 1697 in the compound *avogato pear* (with a spelling that probably reflects Spanish pronunciation), we have lost many of the traces of the more interesting Nahuatl word.

av·o·ca·tion (ăv′ō-kā′shən) *n.* **1.** An activity taken up in addition to one's regular work or profession, usually for enjoyment; a hobby. **2.** One's regular work or profession. **3.** *Archaic.* A distraction or diversion. [Latin *āvocātiō, āvocātiōn-,* diversion, from *āvocātus,* past participle of *āvocāre,* to call away : *ā-, ab-,* away; see AB–^{1} + *vocāre,* to call; see **wek^w-** in Appendix.] **—av′o·ca′tion·al** *adj.* **—av′o·ca′tion·al·ly** *adv.*

av·o·cet (ăv′ə-sĕt′) *n.* Any of several long-legged shore birds of the genus *Recurvirostra,* characterized by a long slender, upturned beak. [French *avocette,* from Italian *avocetta.*]

A·vo·ga·dro (ä′və-gä′drō, ä′vō-), **Amedeo.** 1776–1856. Italian chemist and physicist who advanced the hypothesis that has come to be called Avogadro's law. From this hypothesis other physicists were able to calculate Avogadro's number.

A·vo·ga·dro's law (ä′və-gä′drōz, ä′vō-) *n.* The principle that equal volumes of all gases under identical conditions of pressure and temperature contain the same number of molecules.

Avogadro's number also **Avogadro number** *n. Symbol* **N** The number of molecules in a mole of a substance, approximately 6.0225 × 10^{23}.

a·void (ə-void′) *tr.v.* **a·void·ed, a·void·ing, a·voids. 1.** To stay clear of; shun. See Synonyms at **escape. 2.** To keep from happening: *avoid illness with rest and a balanced diet.* **3.** *Law.* To annul or make void; invalidate. **4.** *Obsolete.* To void or expel. [Middle English *avoiden,* from Anglo-Norman *avoider,* to empty out, variant of Old French *esvuidier* : *es-,* out (from Latin *ex-;* see EX–) + *vuidier,* to empty (from *voide,* empty; see VOID).] **—a·void′a·ble** *adj.* **—a·void′a·bly** *adv.* **—a·void′er** *n.*

a·void·ance (ə-void′ns) *n.* **1.** The act of shunning or avoiding. **2.** *Law.* An annulment.

av·oir·du·pois (ăv′ər-də-poiz′) *n.* **1.** *Abbr.* **avdp., av.** Avoirdupois weight. **2.** *Informal.* Weight or heaviness, especially of a person. [Middle English *avoir de pois,* commodities sold by weight, alteration of Old French *aveir de peis,* goods of weight : *aveir, avoir,* to have (from Latin *habēre;* see ABLE) + *de,* of (from Latin *dē-,* from; see DE–) + *peis, pois,* weight (from Vulgar Latin **pēsum,* from Latin *pēnsum,* past participle of *pendere,* to hang; see **(s)pen-** in Appendix).]

avoirdupois weight *n.* A system of weights and measures based on a pound containing 16 ounces or 7,000 grains and equal to 453.59 grams.

A·von (ā′vŏn, ā′vən, ăv′ən) also **Up·per Avon** (ŭp′ər). A river of south-central England flowing 154.5 km (96 mi) to the Severn. It is known for its associations with Shakespeare.

a·vouch (ə-vouch′) *tr.v.* **a·vouched, a·vouch·ing, a·vouch·es. 1.** To declare the provable truth or validity of; affirm: *She avouched that she herself was innocent.* **2.** To vouch for. **3.** To accept responsibility for (an action, for example); acknowledge. **4.** To avow; confess. [Middle English *avouchen,* to cite as a warrant, from Old French *avochier,* from Latin *advocāre,* to summon. See ADVOCATE.]

a·vow (ə-vou′) *tr.v.* **a·vowed, a·vow·ing, a·vows. 1.** To acknowledge openly, boldly, and unashamedly; confess: *avow guilt.* See Synonyms at **acknowledge. 2.** To state positively. See Synonyms at **assert.** [Middle English *avowen,* from Old French *avouer,* from Latin *advocāre,* to call upon. See ADVOCATE.] **—a·vow′a·ble** *adj.* **—a·vow′a·bly** *adv.* **—a·vow′ed·ly** (-ĭd-lē) *adv.* **—a·vow′er** *n.*

a·vow·al (ə-vou′əl) *n.* A frank admission or acknowledgment.

a·vulse (ə-vŭls′) *tr.v.* **a·vulsed, a·vuls·ing, a·vuls·es.** To separate, cut, or tear off by avulsion. [Latin *āvellere, āvuls-,* to tear off : *ā-, ab-,* away; see AB–^{1} + *vellere,* to pull.]

a·vul·sion (ə-vŭl′shən) *n.* **1.** *Medicine.* The forcible tearing away of a body part by trauma or surgery. **2.** The sudden movement of soil from one property to another as a result of a flood or a shift in the course of a boundary stream.

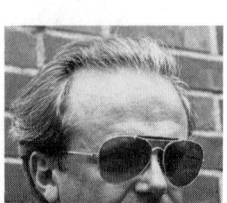

a·vun·cu·lar (ə-vŭng′kyə-lər) *adj.* **1.** Of or having to do with an uncle. **2.** Regarded as being similar to an uncle, especially in benevolence. [From Latin *avunculus,* maternal uncle. See **awo-** in Appendix.]

aw (ô) *interj.* Used to express sympathy, disgust, or disbelief.

AW *abbr.* **1.** Aircraft warning. **2.** Articles of War. **3.** Automatic weapon.

a.w. *abbr.* **1.** Also **A/W.** Actual weight. **2.** All water.

AWACS (ā′wăks) *n., pl.* **AWACS.** A military surveillance system, carried by aircraft, that is capable of tracking a large number of other aircraft from a great distance. —*attributive.* Often used to modify another noun: *AWACS surveillance; AWACS operations.* [*A(irborne) W(arning) A(nd) C(ontrol) S(ystem).*]

a·wait (ə-wāt′) *v.* **a·wait·ed, a·wait·ing, a·waits.** —*tr.* **1.a.** To wait for. See Synonyms at **expect. b.** To be in a state of abeyance until: *a contract awaiting signature.* **2.** To be in store for: *Death awaits us all.* **3.** *Obsolete.* To lie in ambush for. —*intr.* **1.** To wait. **2.** To be in store: *A busy day awaits.* [Middle English *awaiten,* from Old North French *awaitier* : *a-,* on (from Latin *ad-;* see AD–) + *waitier,* to watch; see WAIT.]

a·wake (ə-wāk′) *v.* **a·woke** (ə-wōk′) or **a·waked, a·waked** or **a·wok·en** (ə-wō′kən), **a·wak·ing, a·wakes.** —*tr.* **1.** To rouse from sleep; waken. **2.** To stir the interest of; excite. **3.** To stir up (memories, for example). —*intr.* **1.** To wake up. **2.** To become alert. **3.** To become aware or cognizant: *awoke to reality.* See Usage Note at **wake[1]. —awake** *adj.* **1.** Completely conscious; not in a state of sleep. **2.** Vigilant; watchful. See Synonyms at **aware.** [Middle English *awaken,* from Old English *āwacan* : *ā-,* intensive pref. + *wacan,* wake; see WAKE[1].]

a·wak·en (ə-wā′kən) *v.* **-ened, -en·ing, -ens.** —*tr.* To cause to wake. —*intr.* To wake up. See Usage Note at **wake[1].** [Middle English *awakenen,* from Old English *āwæcnian* : *ā-,* on, up; see A–[2] + *wæcnian,* to waken; see WAKEN.] **—a·wak′en·er** *n.*

a·ward (ə-wôrd′) *tr.v.* **a·ward·ed, a·ward·ing, a·wards. 1.** To grant as merited or due: *awarded prizes to the winners.* **2.** To give as legally due: *awarded damages to the plaintiff.* See Synonyms at **grant. —award** *n.* **1.** Something awarded or granted, as for merit. **2.** A decision, such as one made by a judge or arbitrator. [Middle English *awarden,* from Anglo-Norman *awarder,* to decide (a legal case), variant of Old North French *eswarder* : *es-,* out (from Latin *ex;* see EX–) + *warder,* to judge, guard; see **wer-[3]** in Appendix.] **—a·ward′a·ble** *adj.* **—a·ward′er** *n.*

a·ward·ee (ə-wôr-dē′) *n.* The recipient of an award.

a·ware (ə-wâr′) *adj.* **1.** Having knowledge or cognizance: *aware of their limitations.* **2.** *Archaic.* Vigilant; watchful. [Middle English, variant of *iwar,* from Old English *gewær.* See **wer-[3]** in Appendix.] **—a·ware′ness** *n.*

SYNONYMS: *aware, cognizant, conscious, sensible, awake, alert, watchful, vigilant.* These adjectives mean mindful or heedful of something. *Aware* implies knowledge gained through one's own perceptions, as of the attitudes of others, or by means of information: *Are you aware of your opponent's hostility? I am aware that Congress has passed the legislation. Cognizant* is a rather formal equivalent of *aware: "Our research indicates that the nation's youth are cognizant of the law"* (Jerry D. Jennings). *Conscious* emphasizes the recognition of something sensed or felt: *"an importance . . . of which even Americans are barely conscious"* (William Stanley Jevons). *Sensible* implies knowledge gained through intellectual perception or through intuition: *"I am sensible that the mention of such a circumstance may appear trifling"* (Henry Hallam). To be *awake* is to have full consciousness of something: *"as much awake to the novelty of attention in that quarter as Elizabeth herself"* (Jane Austen). *Alert* stresses quickness to recognize and respond: *alert enough to spot the opportunity when it came. Watchful* and *vigilant* imply being on the lookout for what is dangerous or potentially so: *a watchful parent with a toddler in tow; keeping a vigilant eye on every building where a fire might start.*

a·wash (ə-wŏsh′, ə-wôsh′) *adv.* **1.a.** Washed by the sea. **b.** Washing about. **2.** In such a position or way as to be covered with or as if with water. **—awash** *adj.* **1.** Level with or washed by waves. **2.** Overflowing with or as if with water: *"Some of America's big cities are awash in vacant office space"* (Ross K. Baker). **3.** Floating on or as if on waves.

A·wash River (ä′wäsh′) also **Ha·wash River** (hä′-). A river of eastern Ethiopia flowing about 805 km (500 mi) northeast to the Danakil Desert.

a·way (ə-wā′) *adv.* **1.** From a particular thing or place: *ran away from the lion; sent the children away to boarding school.* **2.a.** At or to a distance in space or time: *We live a block away from the park.* **b.** At or by a considerable interval: *away back in the 17th century; away off on the horizon.* **3.a.** In a different direction; aside: *glanced away.* **b.** On the way: *We want to get away early in the day.* **4.** In or into storage or safekeeping: *put the toys away; jewels locked away in a safe.* **5.** Out of existence or notice: *The music faded away.* **6.** So as to remove, separate, or eliminate: *chipped the paint away; cleared away the debris.* **7.** From one's possession: *gave the tickets away.* **8.** Continuously; steadily: *toiled away at the project for more than a year.* **9.** Freely; at will: *Fire away!* **—away** *adj.* **1.** Absent: *The neighbors are away.* **2.** Distant, as in space or time: *The city is miles away. The game was still a week away.* **3.** Played on an opponent's field or grounds: *an away game.* **4.** *Baseball.* Out: *bases loaded, with two away.* [Middle English, from Old English *aweg* : *a-,* on; see A–[1] + *weg,* way; see **wegh-** in Appendix.]

awe (ô) *n.* **1.** A mixed emotion of reverence, respect, dread, and wonder inspired by authority, genius, great beauty, sublimity, or might: *We felt awe when contemplating the works of Bach. The imprisoned soldiers were in awe of their captors.* **2.** *Archaic.* **a.** The power to inspire dread. **b.** Dread. **—awe** *tr.v.* **awed, aw·ing, awes.** To inspire with awe. [Middle English, from Old Norse *agi.*]

a·wea·ry (ə-wîr′ē) *adj. Archaic.* Tired; weary.

a·weath·er (ə-wĕ*th*′ər) *adv. Nautical.* To the windward side.

a·weigh (ə-wā′) *adj. Nautical.* Hanging clear of the bottom. Used of an anchor.

awe·some (ô′səm) *adj.* **1.** Inspiring awe: *an awesome thunderstorm.* **2.** Expressing awe: *stood in awesome silence before the ancient ruins.* **3.** *Slang.* Remarkable; outstanding: *"a totally awesome arcade game"* (Los Angeles Times). **—awe′some·ly** *adv.* **—awe′some·ness** *n.*

awe·struck (ô′strŭk′) also **awe·strick·en** (-strĭk′ən) *adj.* Full of awe.

aw·ful (ô′fəl) *adj.* **1.** Extremely bad or unpleasant; terrible: *had an awful day at the office.* **2.** Commanding awe: *"this sea, whose gently awful stirrings seem to speak of some hidden soul beneath"* (Herman Melville). **3.** Filled with awe, especially: **a.** Filled with or displaying great reverence. **b.** *Obsolete.* Afraid. **4.** Formidable in nature or extent: *an awful burden; an awful risk.* **—awful** *adv. Informal.* Extremely; very: *was awful sick.* [Middle English *aweful,* awe-inspiring, blend of *awe,* awe; see AWE, and **ayfull,* awful (from Old English *egefull* : *ege,* dread + *-full,* -ful).] **—aw′ful·ly** *adv.* **—aw′ful·ness** *n.*

a·while (ə-hwīl′, ə-wīl′) *adv.* For a short time.

USAGE NOTE: *Awhile,* an adverb, is never preceded by a preposition such as *for,* but the two-word form *a while* may be preceded by a preposition. In writing, each of the following is acceptable: *stay awhile; stay for a while; stay a while* (but not *stay for awhile*).

a·whirl (ə-hwûrl′, ə-wûrl′) *adj.* **1.** Having a whirling motion; spinning: *leaves awhirl in the wind.* **2.** Being in a condition suggestive of a whirl, such as a state of excited activity or confusion: *"All we could do was just stand there, our minds awhirl with the fluky wonder of it all"* (David Mazel). **—a·whirl′** *adv.*

awk·ward (ôk′wərd) *adj.* **1.** Not graceful; ungainly. **2.a.** Not dexterous; clumsy. **b.** Clumsily or unskillfully performed: *The opera was marred by an awkward aria.* **3.a.** Difficult to handle or manage: *an awkward bundle to carry.* **b.** Difficult to effect; uncomfortable: *an awkward pose.* **4.a.** Marked by or causing embarrassment or discomfort: *an awkward remark; an awkward silence.* **b.** Requiring great tact, ingenuity, skill, and discretion: *An awkward situation arose during the peace talks.* [Middle English *awkeward,* in the wrong way : *awke,* wrong (from Old Norse *öfugr,* backward; see **apo-** in Appendix) + *-ward,* -ward.] **—awk′ward·ly** *adv.* **—awk′ward·ness** *n.*

SYNONYMS: *awkward, clumsy, maladroit, inept, gauche, ungainly.* These adjectives mean lacking grace or skill in movement, manner, or performance. *Awkward* and *clumsy,* the least specific, are often interchangeable. Both emphasize lack of physical dexterity (*an awkward dancer; clumsy fingers*); both can also suggest embarrassment or lack of ease (*several awkward moments in the discussion; offered a clumsy apology*). *Maladroit* implies tactlessness or lack of skill in social relations: *a maladroit comment. Inept* applies to inappropriate actions and speech: *If the rumor is true, can anything be more inept than to repeat it now? Gauche* suggests a lack of social polish: *too gauche to leave the room when the conversation became intimate. Ungainly* implies a lack of grace in form or movement: *long, ungainly legs; an ungainly gesture.*

awl (ôl) *n.* A pointed tool for making holes, as in wood or leather. [Middle English *aul,* probably blend of Old English *æl* and Old English *awel,* fleshhook.]

awn (ôn) *n.* A slender, bristlelike appendage found on the spikelets of many grasses. [Middle English *awne,* from Old Norse *ögn* or from Old English *agen;* see **ak-** in Appendix.] **—awned** *adj.* **—awn′less** *adj.*

awn·ing (ô′nĭng) *n.* A rooflike structure, often made of canvas or plastic, that serves as a shelter, as over a storefront, window, door, or deck. [Origin unknown.]

a·woke (ə-wōk′) *v.* A past tense of **awake.**

a·wok·en (ə-wō′kən) *v.* A past participle of **awake.**

AWOL or **awol** (ā′wôl′) —*adj.* Absent without leave. —*n.* One who is absent without leave.

a·wry (ə-rī′) *adv.* **1.** In a position that is turned or twisted toward one side; askew. **2.** Away from the correct course; amiss. See Synonyms at **amiss. —a·wry′** *adj.*

aw-shucks (ô′shŭks′) *adj. Informal.* Characterized by a shy, self-effacing, often unsophisticated manner: *"He grinned his aw-shucks grin, passed a hand over his face and said, 'Hi ya, guys!'"* (William Manchester).

ax or **axe** (ăks) —*n., pl.* **ax·es** (ăk′sĭz). **1.** A tool with a bladed, usually heavy head mounted crosswise on a handle, used

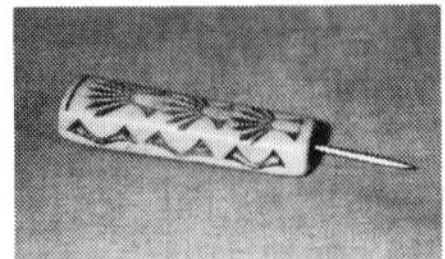

awl
Carved bone handle on a Native American awl

awning

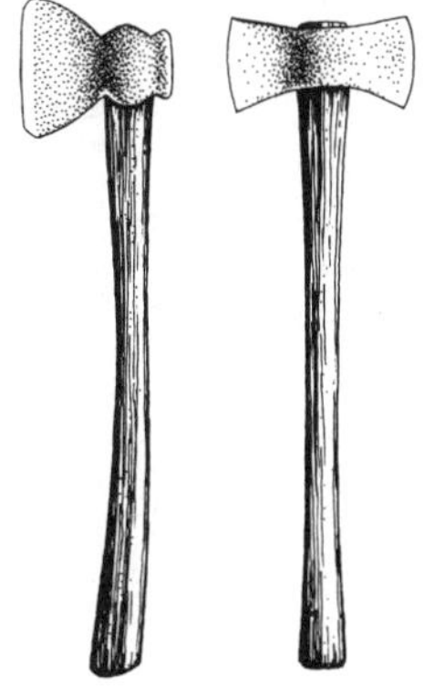

ax
Left: Broadax
Right: Full double-bitted ax

ă pat	oi boy
ā pay	ou out
âr care	ŏŏ took
ä father	ōō boot
ĕ pet	ŭ cut
ē be	ûr urge
ĭ pit	th thin
ī pie	*th* this
îr pier	hw which
ŏ pot	zh vision
ō toe	ə about, item
ô paw	♦ regionalism

Stress marks: **′** (primary); ′ (secondary), as in **dictionary** (dĭk′shə-nĕr′ē)

for felling trees or chopping wood. **2.** Any of various bladed, hand-held implements used as a cutting tool or weapon. **3.** *Informal.* A sudden termination of employment: *My colleague got the ax yesterday.* **4.** *Slang.* A musical instrument, especially a guitar. —*tr.v.* **axed, ax•ing, ax•es. 1.** To use a heavy, bladed cutting implement in order to chop or fell (something). **2.** *Informal.* To remove ruthlessly or suddenly: *a social program that was axed to effectuate budget cuts.* —*idiom.* **ax to grind.** A selfish or subjective aim: *He claimed to be disinterested, but I knew he had an ax to grind.* [Middle English, from Old English *æx.*]

WORD HISTORY: To understand the origin of the idiom *ax to grind,* we need to know that *grind* means "to sharpen." This phrase is said to have come from a story by the 19th-century journalist Charles Miner (alias Poor Robert) about a seemingly friendly man who was able by flattery to persuade a young boy to turn a grindstone for him. The tale first appeared in the Luzerne, Pennsylvania, *Federalist* on September 7, 1810, under the title "Who'll Turn Grindstones?" and later in an 1815 book entitled *Essays from the Desk of Poor Robert the Scribe.* Because "Poor Robert" was confused with "Poor Richard," the story has often been erroneously attributed to Benjamin Franklin. The idiom itself is an Americanism—a word or expression originating in the United States. It was at first restricted to political contexts, but quotations from James Joyce ("Skin-the-Goat . . . evidently with an axe to grind, was airing his grievances") and George Bernard Shaw ("distinguished statesmen of different nations . . . each with a national axe to grind") attest that the phrase has traveled abroad and, as we know only too well, is no longer found only in political contexts.

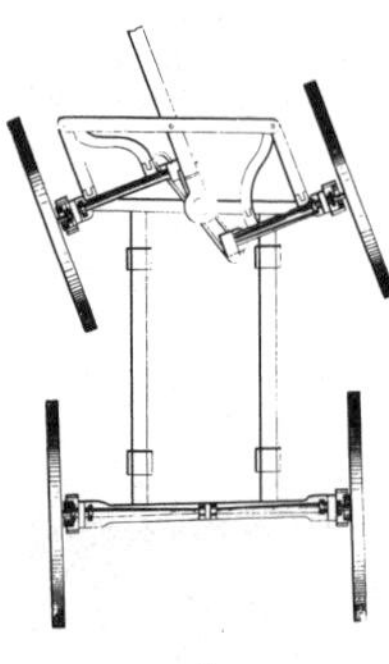

axle

ax. *abbr.* **1.** *Mathematics & Logic.* Axiom. **2.** Axis.

axe (ăks) *n. & v.* Variant of **ax.**

ax•el (ăk′səl) *n. Sports.* A jump in figure skating that is initiated from the outer forward edge of one skate, followed by one and one half midair turns and a return to the outer backward edge of the other skate. [After *Axel* Paulsen, 19th-century Norwegian figure skater.]

Ax•el Hei•berg (ăk′səl hī′bûrg′). An island of northern Northwest Territories, Canada, in the Arctic Ocean west of Ellesmere Island.

Ax•el•rod (ăk′səl-räd′), **Julius.** Born 1912. American biochemist. He shared a 1970 Nobel Prize for studies of how nerve impulses are transmitted.

a•xen•ic (ā-zĕn′ĭk, ā-zē′nĭk) *adj.* Not contaminated by or associated with any other living organisms. Usually used in reference to pure cultures of microorganisms that are completely free of the presence of other organisms. —**a•xen′i•cal•ly** *adv.*

ax•es¹ (ăk′sēz′) *n.* Plural of **axis.**

ax•es² (ăk′sĭz) *n.* Plural of **ax.**

ax•i•al (ăk′sē-əl) *adj.* **1.** Relating to, characterized by, or forming an axis. **2.** Located on, around, or in the direction of an axis. —**ax′i•al′i•ty** (-ăl′ĭ-tē) *n.* —**ax′i•al•ly** *adv.*

axial skeleton *n.* The bones constituting the head and trunk of a vertebrate body.

ax•il (ăk′sĭl) *n.* The upper angle between a lateral organ, such as a leafstalk, and the stem that bears it. [Latin *axilla,* armpit.]

ax•ile (ăk′sīl) *adj.* Situated along the central axis of an ovary having two or more locules: *axile placentation.* [AX(IS) + -ILE¹.]

ax•il•la (ăk-sĭl′ə) *n., pl.* **-il•lae** (-sĭl′ē). *Anatomy.* **1.** The armpit. **2.** A body part analogous to the armpit, such as the hollow under a bird's wing. [Latin.]

ax•il•lar (ăk-sĭl′ər, ăk′sə-lər) or **ax•il•lar•y** (ăk′sə-lĕr′ē) *n., pl.* **axillars** or **-ies.** One of the feathers in the axilla of a bird's wing.

ax•il•lar•y (ăk′sə-lĕr′ē) *adj.* **1.** *Anatomy.* Of, relating to, or located near the axilla. **2.** *Botany.* Of, relating to, or located in an axil. —**axillary** *n.* Variant of **axillar.**

axillary bud *n.* A lateral bud.

ax•i•ol•o•gy (ăk′sē-ŏl′ə-jē) *n. Philosophy.* The study of the nature of values and value judgments. [Greek *axios,* worth; see **ag-** in Appendix + -LOGY.] —**ax′i•o•log′i•cal** (-ə-lŏj′ĭ-kəl) *adj.* —**ax′i•o•log′i•cal•ly** *adv.* —**ax′i•ol′o•gist** *n.*

ax•i•om (ăk′sē-əm) *n.* **1.** A self-evident or universally recognized truth; a maxim: *"It is an economic axiom as old as the hills that goods and services can be paid for only with goods and services"* (Albert Jay Nock). **2.** An established rule, principle, or law. **3.** *Abbr.* **ax.** A self-evident principle or one that is accepted as true without proof as the basis for argument; a postulate. [Middle English, from Old French *axiome,* from Latin *axiōma, axiōmat-,* from Greek, from *axios,* worthy. See **ag-** in Appendix.]

ax•i•o•mat•ic (ăk′sē-ə-măt′ĭk) also **ax•i•o•mat•i•cal** (-ĭ-kəl) *adj.* Of, relating to, or resembling an axiom; self-evident: *"the axiomatic pillars of a new code of the law of nations"* (William Taylor). —**ax′i•o•mat′i•cal•ly** *adv.*

ax•is (ăk′sĭs) *n., pl.* **ax•es** (ăk′sēz′). *Abbr.* **ax. 1.** A straight line about which a body or geometric object rotates or may be conceived to rotate. **2.** *Mathematics.* **a.** An unlimited line, half-line, or line segment serving to orient a space or a geometric object, especially a line about which the object is symmetric. **b.** A reference line from which distances or angles are measured in a coordinate system. **3.** A center line to which parts of a structure or body may be referred. **4.** An imaginary line to which elements of a work of art, such as a picture, are referred for measurement or symmetry. **5.** *Anatomy.* **a.** The second cervical vertebra on which the head turns. **b.** Any of various central structures, such as the spinal column, or standard abstract lines used as a positional referent. **6.** *Botany.* The main stem or central part about which organs or plant parts such as branches are arranged. **7.** One of three mutually perpendicular lines that define the orientation of an aircraft, with one being along its direction of travel and the other two being perpendicular to the direction of travel. **8.** A line through the optical center of a lens that is perpendicular to both its surfaces. **9.** One of three or four imaginary lines used to define the faces of a crystal and the position of its atoms. **10. a.** An alliance of powers, such as nations, to promote mutual interests and policies. **b. Axis.** The alliance of Germany and Italy in 1936, later including Japan and other nations, that opposed the Allies in World War II. [Middle English, from Latin.]

axis deer *n.* A deer *(Axis axis)* of central Asia, having a brown coat with white spots. [Latin *axis,* a spotted Indian quadruped.]

ax•i•sym•met•ric (ăk′sē-sĭ-mĕt′rĭk) also **ax•i•sym•met•ri•cal** (-rĭ-kəl) *adj.* Having symmetry around an axis: *an axisymmetric cone.* —**ax′i•sym•met′ri•cal•ly** *adv.*

ax•le (ăk′səl) *n.* **1.** A supporting shaft or member on or with which a wheel or a set of wheels revolves. **2. a.** The spindle of an axletree. **b.** Either end of an axletree. [Middle English *axel,* from Old Norse *öxull.*]

ax•le•tree (ăk′səl-trē′) *n.* A crossbar or rod supporting a vehicle, such as a cart, that has terminal spindles on which the wheels revolve. [Blend of Middle English *axel,* axle; see AXLE, and Middle English *axtre,* axletree (*ax,* from Old English *eax* + *tre,* tree; see TREE).]

ax•man (ăks′mən) *n.* A man who wields an ax.

Ax•min•ster (ăks′mĭn′stər) *n.* A carpet with stiff backing and a soft, colorful cut pile usually arranged in a complex pattern. [After *Axminster,* a town of southwest England.]

ax•o•lotl (ăk′sə-lŏt′l) *n.* Any of several salamanders (genus *Ambystoma*) native to Mexico and the western United States that, unlike most amphibians, often retain their external gills and become sexually mature without undergoing metamorphosis. [Nahuatl.]

ax•on (ăk′sŏn′) also **ax•one** (-sōn′) *n.* The usually long process of a nerve fiber that generally conducts impulses away from the body of the nerve cell. [Greek *axōn,* axis.] —**ax′on•al** (ăk′sə-nəl, ăk-sŏn′əl) *adj.*

ax•o•neme (ăk′sə-nēm′) *n.* **1.** The bundle of fibrils that constitutes the central core of a cilium or flagellum. **2.** The axial thread of a chromosome. [Greek *axōn,* axis + *nēma,* thread; see **(s)nē-** in Appendix.] —**ax′o•ne′mal** *adj.*

ax•o•no•met•ric (ăk′sə-nō-mĕt′rĭk) *adj.* Of or relating to a method of projection in which an object is drawn with its horizontal and vertical axes to scale but with its curved lines and diagonals distorted. [From *axonometry* : Greek *axōn,* axis + -METRY.]

ax•o•plasm (ăk′sə-plăz′əm) *n.* The cytoplasm of an axon. [Greek *axōn* + -PLASM.] —**ax′o•plas′mic** (-plăz′mĭk) *adj.*

Ax•um (äk′so͞om′). See **Aksum.**

ay¹ (ī) *interj.* Used before *me* to express distress or regret.

ay² (ī) *n. & adv.* Variant of **aye¹.**

ay³ (ā) *adv.* Variant of **aye².**

a•yah (ä′yə, ā′ə, ī′ə) *n.* A maid or nurse native to India. [Hindi *āyā,* from Portuguese *aia,* nursemaid, from Latin *avia,* grandmother. See **awo-** in Appendix.]

a•ya•tol•lah (ī′ə-tō′lə, -tō-lä′) *n. Islam.* **1.** A high-ranking male Shiite religious authority, generally assuming a political role and regarded as worthy of imitation. **2.** Used as a title for such a leader. [Persian *ayātollah,* from Arabic *'āyatullāh* : *'āyah,* Koranic verse, miracle + *allāh,* Allah.]

AYC *abbr.* American Youth Congress.

aye¹ also **ay** (ī) —*n.* An affirmative vote or voter. —*adv.* Yes; yea: *"between the Scylla and Charybdis of Aye and No"* (John Henry Newman). [Perhaps from Middle English **ayye* : *ay,* always; see AYE² + *ye,* yes; see YEA.]

aye² also **ay** (ā) *adv.* Always; ever. [Middle English *ai,* from Old Norse *ei.* See **aiw-** in Appendix.]

aye-aye (ī′ī′) *n.* A nocturnal lemur *(Daubentonia madagascariensis)* native to northern Madagascar, having prominent ears, a long, bushy tail, and rodentlike teeth. [French, from Malagasy *aiay,* probably imitative of its cry.]

A•ye•sha (ä′ē-shä′). See **Aisha.**

AYH *abbr.* American Youth Hostels.

a•yin (ī′ĭn) *n.* The 16th letter of the Hebrew alphabet. See table at **alphabet.** [Hebrew *'ayin.*]

Ayl•mer (āl′mər). A town of southwest Quebec, Canada, on the Ottawa River west of Hull. It is a resort community. Population, 26,695.

Ay•ma•ra (ī′mä-rä′, ī′mə-) *n., pl.* **Aymara** or **-ras. 1.** A member of a South American Indian people inhabiting parts of highland Bolivia and Peru. **2.** The Aymaran language of the Aymara.

Ay•ma•ran (ī′mä-rän′) *n.* A subgroup of the Quechumaran languages, the most important language being Aymara. —**Aymaran** *adj.* Of or relating to the Aymara or their language or culture.

ă pat	oi boy
ā pay	ou out
âr care	o͝o took
ä father	o͞o boot
ĕ pet	ŭ cut
ē be	ûr urge
ĭ pit	th thin
ī pie	*th* this
îr pier	hw which
ŏ pot	zh vision
ō toe	ə about, item
ô paw	♦ regionalism

Stress marks: ′ (primary); ′ (secondary), as in **dictionary** (dĭk′shə-nĕr′ē)

Ayr (âr). A burgh of southwest Scotland at the mouth of the **Ayr River** on the Firth of Clyde. It is a resort and a fishing port. Population, 48,600.

Ayr·shire (âr′shîr, -shər) *n.* Any of various brown and white dairy cattle of a breed that originated in Ayr, Scotland.

♦ **a-yuh** (ā′yə, ī′yə, ā-yŭ′) *interj. New England.* Used to express agreement.

A·yut·thay·a (ä-yo͞o′tə-yä′). A city of south-central Thailand on an island in the Chao Phraya River north of Bangkok. It was founded c. 1350 and was the capital of a Siamese kingdom until 1767, when it was destroyed by the Burmese. Ayutthaya is the center of a rich agricultural region. Population, 55,319.

AZ *abbr.* Arizona.

az. *abbr.* **1.** Azimuth. **2.** Azure.

az– *pref.* Variant of **azo–.**

a·zal·ea (ə-zāl′yə) *n.* Any of various shrubs of the genus *Rhododendron* having showy, variously colored flowers. [Greek, from feminine of *azaleos,* dry (so called because it grows in dry soil or from the texture of its wood). See **as-** in Appendix.]

a·zan (ä-zän′) *n. Islam.* The Moslem summons to prayer, called by the muezzin from a minaret of a mosque five times a day. [Arabic *'aḏān,* from *'aḏḏana,* to call to prayer, from *'uḏn,* ear.]

A·za·ni·a (ə-zā′nē-ə, ə-zān′yə). South Africa. The term is often used by Black African nationalists. **—A·za′ni·an** *adj. & n.*

az·a·thi·o·prine (ăz′ə-thī′ə-prēn′) *n.* An immunosuppressive agent used especially to prevent organ rejection in kidney transplant recipients. [Probably from AZ(O)– + THIO– + P(U)-RINE.]

A·za·zel (ə-zā′zəl, ăz′ə-zĕl′) *n.* **1.** *Bible.* In the Old Testament, the evil spirit in the wilderness to whom a scapegoat was sent on the Day of Atonement. **2.** *Islam.* One of the jinn. [Hebrew *'ăzā'zēl,* removal, scapegoat (ritually sent into the wilderness), perhaps originally a divine name.]

a·ze·o·trope (ə-zē′ə-trōp′, ā′zé-) *n.* A liquid mixture of two or more substances that retains the same composition in the vapor state as in the liquid state when distilled or partially evaporated under a certain pressure. [A–[1] + Greek *zein,* to boil; see ZEOLITE + Greek *-tropos,* turning; see –TROPOUS.] **—a′ze·o·trop′ic** (a′zē-ə-trŏp′ĭk, -trō′pĭk) *adj.* **—a′ze·ot′ro·py** (-ŏt′rə-pē) *n.*

A·zer·bai·jan (ăz′ər-bī-jän′, ä′zər-). A region of Transcaucasia north of Iran. It was settled by the Medes before the eighth century B.C. and was a separate kingdom after the death of Alexander the Great. The territory was ceded to Russia by Persia in 1813 and 1828 and became a constituent republic in 1936. Baku is the capital. Population, 6,614,000.

A·zer·bai·ja·ni (ăz′ər-bī-jä′nē, äz′ər-) *adj.* Of or relating to Azerbaijan or its people, language, or culture. **—Azerbaijani** *n., pl.* **Azerbaijani** or **-nis. 1.** A native or inhabitant of Azerbaijan. **2.** The Turkic language of Azerbaijan.

az·ide (ăz′īd, ā′zīd) *n.* A chemical compound that contains the group N_3. **—az·i·do** (az′ĭ-dō′) *adj.*

a·z·i·do·thy·mi·dine (ə-zī′dō-thī′mĭ-dēn′, ə-zē′-, ăz′ĭ-) *n.* An antiviral drug that inhibits replication of the retrovirus that causes AIDS; AZT. Also called *zidovudine.*

A·zil·ian (ə-zĭl′yən) *adj. Archaeology.* Of or relating to a Mesolithic western European culture. [After le Mas d'*Azil,* a village of southern France.]

az·i·muth (ăz′ə-məth) *n. Abbr.* **az. 1.** The horizontal angular distance from a reference direction, usually the northern point of the horizon, to the point where a vertical circle through a celestial body intersects the horizon, usually measured clockwise. Sometimes the southern point is used as the reference direction, and the measurement is made clockwise through 360°. **2.** The horizontal angle of the observer's bearing in surveying, measured clockwise from a referent direction, as from the north, or from a referent celestial body, usually Polaris. **3.** The lateral deviation of a projectile or bomb. [Middle English *azimut,* from Old French, from Arabic *as-sumūt,* pl. of *as-samt,* the way, compass bearing, from Latin *sēmita,* path.] **—az′i·muth′al** (-mŭth′əl) *adj.* **—az′i·muth′al·ly** *adv.*

azimuthal equidistant projection *n.* A map projection of the earth designed so that a straight line from the central point on the map to any other point gives the shortest distance between the two points.

az·ine (ăz′ēn′, ā′zēn′) *n.* A six-membered heterocyclic compound, such as pyridine, that contains one or more atoms of nitrogen with a ring structure resembling that of benzene.

azine dye *n.* Any of various dyes derived from phenazine.

az·o (ăz′ō, ā′zō) *adj.* Containing a nitrogen group, especially N=N. [From AZO–.]

azo– or **az–** *pref.* Containing a nitrogen group, especially one attached at both ends in a covalent bond to other groups: *azole.* [From French *azote,* nitrogen : Greek *a-,* not; see A–[1] + Greek *zōē,* life (from the fact that nitrogen does not support respiration); see **g^w^ei-** in Appendix.]

azo dye *n.* Any of various red, brown, or yellow acidic or basic dyes derived from amino compounds.

a·zo·ic (ā-zō′ĭk) *adj.* Of or relating to geologic periods that precede the appearance of life.

az·ole (ăz′ōl′, ā′zōl′) *n.* A class of organic compounds having a five-membered heterocyclic ring with two double bonds.

a·zon·al (ā-zō′nəl) *adj.* Not divided into zones.

a·zon·ic (ā-zŏn′ĭk, ā-zō′nĭk) *adj.* Not restricted to a particular zone or region; not local.

A·zores (ā′zôrz, ā′zōrz, ə-zôrz′, ə-zōrz′) also **A·ço·res** (ä-sôr′ĕsh). A group of volcanic islands in the northern Atlantic Ocean about 1,448 km (900 mi) west of mainland Portugal, of which they are administrative districts. Fishing, farming, and tourism are important to their economy. **—A·zor′e·an, A·zor′i·an** *adj. & n.*

az·ote (ăz′ōt, ā′zōt, ə-zōt′) *n.* Used formerly as a name for nitrogen. [French. See AZO–.]

az·o·te·mi·a (ăz′ə-tē′mē-ə, ā′zə-) *n.* See **uremia.** [French *azote,* nitrogen; see AZO– + –EMIA.] **—az′o·te′mic** (-mĭk) *adj.*

az·oth (ăz′ŏth, -ôth) *n.* Mercury considered in alchemy to be the primary source of all metals. [Middle English *azoc,* from Old French, from Arabic *az-zā'uq,* the mercury, from Syriac *zīwag,* from Middle Persian **zhīwak,* from Old Iranian **jīvaka-,* lively; akin to Sanskrit *jīvaka-,* lively, from *jīva-,* alive. See **g^w^ei-** in Appendix.]

a·zo·to·bac·ter (ā-zō′tə-băk′tər) *n.* Any of various rod-shaped, nonpathogenic, nitrogen-fixing bacteria of the genus *Azotobacter,* found in soil and water. [French *azote,* nitrogen; see AZO– + BACTER(IA).]

az·o·tu·ri·a (ăz′ə-to͝or′ē-ə, -tyo͝or′-) *n.* Increase of nitrogenous substances, especially urea, in the urine. [French *azote,* nitrogen; see AZO– + –URIA.]

A·zov (ăz′ôf, ā′zôf, ə-zôf′), **Sea of.** The northern arm of the Black Sea between Russia and the Ukraine. The shallow sea has important fisheries.

AZT (ā′zē-tē′) *n.* Azidothymidine. [AZ(IDO)T(HYMIDINE).]

Az·tec (ăz′tĕk′) *n.* **1.** A member of a people of central Mexico whose civilization was at its height at the time of the Spanish conquest in the early 16th century. **2.** The Nahuatl language of the Aztecs. **—Aztec** also **Az·tec·an** (-tĕk′ən) *adj.* Of or relating to the Aztecs or their language, culture, or empire. [Spanish *Azteca,* from Nahuatl *Aztecatl* : *aztatl-,* cranes + *lan-,* near + *ztecatl,* place.]

a·zu·ki bean (ə-zo͞o′kē) *n.* Variant of **adzuki bean.**

az·ure (ăzh′ər) *n.* **1.** *Abbr.* **az. a.** *Color.* A light purplish blue. **b.** *Heraldry.* The color blue. **2.** The blue sky. [Middle English, from Old French *azur,* from Medieval Latin *azura,* from Arabic *al-lāzaward,* from Persian *lājvard,* lapis lazuli.]

az·ur·ite (ăzh′ə-rīt′) *n.* An azure blue vitreous mineral of basic copper carbonate, $Cu_3(CO_3)_2(OH)_2$, used as a copper ore and as a gemstone. Also called *chessylite.*

A·zu·sa (ə-zo͞o′sə). A city of southern California east of Pasadena. It is a residential and industrial center in a citrus-growing region. Population, 29,380.

a·zy·gous (ā-zī′gəs) *adj. Anatomy.* Occurring singly; not one of a pair, as a vein or muscle.

azalea
Flame azalea
Rhododendron calendulaceum

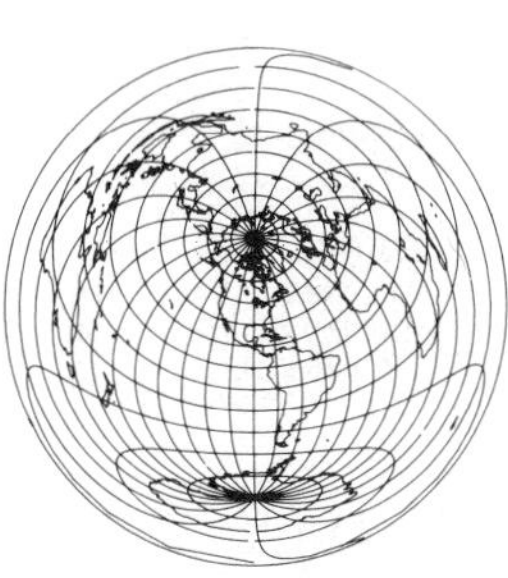

azimuthal equidistant projection

Bb

Phoenician
The second letter of the Phoenician alphabet stood for the sound of *b* in *bēth,* "house."

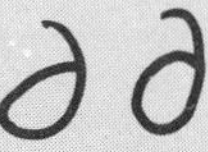

Early Greek
The Greeks altered its shape slightly and called it *bēta.*

B

Roman
Eventually the upper loop was closed as *bēta* evolved into the Roman capital B still used today.

b[1] (bē) or **B** (bē) *n., pl.* **b's** or **B's.** **1.** The second letter of the modern English alphabet. **2.** Any of the speech sounds represented by the letter *b.* **3.** The second in a series. **4.** *Music.* **a.** The seventh tone in the scale of C major or the second tone in the relative minor scale. **b.** A key or scale in which B is the tonic. **c.** A written or printed note representing this tone. **d.** A string, key, or pipe tuned to the pitch of this tone. **5.** A human blood type of the ABO system. **6.** The second best or second highest in quality or rank: *a mark of B on an English theme.*

b[2] *abbr. Physics.* **1.** Barn. **2.** Or **B.** Bel. **3.** Bottom quark.

B[1] **1.** The symbol for the element **boron. 2.** The symbol for **magnetic flux density.**

B[2] or **b** *abbr.* **1.** Baryon number. **2.** *Games.* Bishop.

b. or **B.** *abbr.* **1.** Base. **2.** *Music.* Basso. **3.** Bay. **4.** Billion. **5.** Bolivar. **6.** Book. **7.** Born. **8.** Breadth. **9.** Brother.

B. *abbr.* **1.** Bachelor. **2.** Bacillus. **3.** Baumé scale. **4.** Bible. **5.** Brotherhood.

Ba The symbol for the element **barium.**

B.A. *abbr.* **1.** Bachelor of Arts. **2.** British Academy.

baa (bă, bä) *intr.v.* **baaed, baa·ing, baas.** To make a bleating sound, as a sheep or goat. **—baa** *n.* The bleat of a sheep or goat. [Imitative.]

Ba·al (bā′əl) *n., pl.* **-als** or **-al·im** (-ə-lĭm). **1.** Any of various local fertility and nature gods of the ancient Semitic peoples considered to be false idols by the Hebrews. **2.** Often **baal.** A false god or idol. [Hebrew *ba'al,* lord, Baal.]

Baal·bek (bäl′bĕk′, bā′əl-). Formerly **He·li·op·o·lis** (hē′lē-ŏp′ə-lĭs). A town of eastern Lebanon northeast of Beirut. It is the site of an ancient Phoenician city probably devoted to the worship of Baal and is now noted for its extensive Roman ruins. Population, 24,000.

Baal Shem Tov also **Baal Shem Tob** (bäl′ shĕm′ tôv′). Originally Israel ben Eliezer. 1700?–1760. Polish-born Jewish religious leader and mystic who founded Hasidism.

Bab (bäb, băb), **the.** Title of Ali Mohammad of Shiraz. 1819?–1850. Persian founder of Babism, a 19th-century religion that forbade polygamy, begging, trading in slaves, and the use of alcohol or drugs.

Bab. *abbr.* Babylonian.

ba·ba (bä′bə) *n.* A leavened rum cake, usually made with raisins. [French, from Polish *baba,* old woman.]

baba au rhum (bä′bä ō rŭm′) *n.* Baba. [French : *baba,* baba + *au,* with the + *rhum,* rum.]

Ba·bar (bä′bər). See **Baber.**

ba·bas·su (bä′bə-so͞o′) *n.* A Brazilian feather-leaved palm *(Orbignya barbosiana)* having hard-shelled fruits whose seeds yield an edible vegetable oil. [Portuguese *babaçú,* from Tupi *babassú, oauaussu.*]

Bab·bage (băb′ĭj), **Charles.** 1792–1871. British mathematician and inventor of an analytical machine based on principles similar to those used in modern digital computers.

Bab·bitt (băb′ĭt) *n.* A member of the middle class whose attachment to its business and social ideals is such as to make that person a model of narrow-mindedness and self-satisfaction. [After George F. *Babbitt,* the main character in the novel *Babbitt* by Sinclair Lewis.] **—Bab′bitt·ry** *n.*

Babbitt, Irving. 1865–1933. American humanist and scholar whose New Humanism movement sought to revive interest in classical virtues in literary criticism.

Babbitt, Isaac. 1799–1862. American inventor who patented (1839) a bearing housing lined with an alloy of tin, antimony, and copper now known as babbitt metal.

Babbitt, Milton Byron. Born 1916. American composer whose works, including *Vision and Prayer* (1961), for soprano and synthesizer, combine serial music and electronic effects.

bab·bitt metal (băb′ĭt) *n.* Any of several soft, silvery antifriction alloys composed of tin usually with small amounts of copper and antimony. [After Isaac BABBITT.]

bab·ble (băb′əl) *v.* **-bled, -bling, -bles.** *—intr.* **1.** To utter a meaningless confusion of words or sounds. **2.** To talk foolishly or idly; chatter: *"In 1977* [he] *was thought of as crazy because he was babbling about supply side"* (Newt Gingrich). **3.** To make a continuous low, murmuring sound, as flowing water. *—tr.* **1.** To utter rapidly and indistinctly. **2.** To blurt out impulsively; disclose without careful consideration. **—babble** *n.* **1.** Inarticulate or meaningless talk or sounds. **2.** Idle talk; prattle. **3.** A continuous low, murmuring sound. [Middle English *babelen.*]

bab·bler (băb′lər) *n.* **1.** One that babbles: *a babbler of half-truths.* **2.** A tape recording of several dozen voices talking at the same time, used as an antibugging device to make private or secret conversations inaudible to eavesdroppers.

babe (bāb) *n.* **1.** A baby; an infant. **2.** An innocent or naive person. **3.** *Slang.* A young woman. [Middle English.]

ba·bel also **Ba·bel** (băb′əl, bā′bəl) *n.* **1.** A confusion of sounds or voices. See Synonyms at **noise. 2.** A scene of noise and confusion. [After BABEL.]

Ba·bel (bā′bəl, băb′əl). In the Old Testament, a city (now thought to be Babylon) in Shinar where construction of a heaven-reaching tower was interrupted when the builders became unable to understand one another's language.

Bab el Man·deb (băb′ ĕl măn′dĕb). A strategically important strait, 27.4 km (17 mi) wide, between the Arabian Peninsula and eastern Africa. It links the Red Sea with the Gulf of Aden.

Ba·ber also **Ba·bar** or **Ba·bur** (bä′bər). Originally Zahir ud-Din Mohammed. 1483–1530. Mongol conqueror of India who made periodic raids into India (1519–1524), captured Delhi and Agra (1526), and founded the Mogul dynasty.

ba·be·sia (bə-bē′zhə) *n.* A genus of parasitic sporozoans of the family Babesiidae that infect the red blood cells of human beings and of animals such as dogs, cattle, and sheep. Also called *piroplasm.* [New Latin *Babesia,* genus name, after Victor *Babeş* (1854–1926), Romanian bacteriologist.]

ba·be·si·o·sis (bə-bē′zē-ō′sĭs) also **bab·e·si·a·sis** (băb′ĭ-zī′ə-sĭs) *n.* **1.** A tick-borne protozoan infection of animals, such as Texas fever of cattle, that is caused by species of *Babesia.* **2.** A human protozoan disease of red blood cells caused by *Babesia* species that is transmitted by the northern deer tick, characterized by fever, malaise, and hemolytic anemia, and prevalent on the coastal islands of the northeast United States. Also called *piroplasmosis.*

Ba·bi·a Gó·ra (bä′bē-ə go͝or′ə). A peak, 1,726 m (5,659 ft) high, of the Beskids in the West Beskids on the border between Poland and Czechoslovakia. It is the highest elevation in the range.

Ba·bian Jiang (bä′byän′ jyäng′). See **Black River** (sense 1).

Ba·bin·ski reflex (bə-bĭn′skē) also **Ba·bin·ski's reflex** (-skēz) *n.* An extension of the great toe, sometimes with fanning of the other toes, in response to stroking of the sole of the foot. It is a normal reflex in infants, but it is usually associated with a disturbance of the pyramidal tract in children and adults. Also called *Babinski sign, Babinski's sign.* [After Joseph François Felix *Babinski* (1857–1932), French neurologist.]

bab·i·ru·sa also **bab·i·rus·sa** or **bab·i·rous·sa** (băb′ə-ro͞o′sə, bä′bə-) *n.* A nocturnal, forest-dwelling wild pig *(Babyrousa babyrussa)* of the East Indies, having long, upward-curving tusks in the male. [Malay *bābīrūsa* : *bābī,* hog + *rūsa,* deer.]

babirusa
Babyrousa babyrussa

Ba·bi Yar (bä′bē yär′, bä′byē). A ravine outside Kiev in north-central Ukraine where the Jews of the city were killed by German troops in 1941. The massacre is commemorated in Yevgeny Yevtushenko's 1961 poem "Babi Yar."

bab·ka (bäb′kə) *n.* A coffee cake flavored with orange rind, almonds, and raisins. [Polish, diminutive of *baba,* old woman.]

ba·boo (bä′bo͞o) *n.* Variant of **babu.**

ba·boon (bă-bo͞on′) *n.* **1.** Any of several large, terrestrial African and Asian monkeys of the family Cercopithecidae, especially of the genus *Papio* or *Chaeropithecus* and related genera, characterized by an elongated, doglike muzzle, a short tail, and bare calluses on the buttocks. **2.** *Slang.* A brutish person; a boor. [Middle English *babewin,* from Old French *babuin,* gaping figure, gargoyle, baboon, perhaps blend of Old French *babine,* muzzle, and *babau,* grimace.] **—ba·boon′er·y** *n.* **—ba·boon′ish** *adj.*

ba·bu also **ba·boo** (bä′bo͞o) *n.* **1.** Used as a Hindi courtesy title for a man, equivalent to *Mr.* **2.a.** A Hindu clerk who is literate in English. **b.** *Offensive.* A native of India who has acquired some superficial education in English. [Hindi *bābū,* father.]

ba·bul (bə-bo͞ol′) *n.* A tropical African tree *(Acacia nilotica)* that yields a gum similar to gum arabic and has a bark used in tanning. [Persian *bābul.*]

Ba·bur (bä′bər). See **Baber.**

ba·bush·ka (bə-bo͝osh′kə) *n.* A woman's head scarf, folded triangularly and worn tied under the chin. [Russian, grandmother, diminutive of *baba,* old woman.]

Ba·bu·yan Islands (bä′bo͞o-yän′). An island group of the Philippines separated from the northern coast of Luzon by the narrow **Babuyan Channel.** The group comprises 24 islands, including **Babuyan Island** in the northeast.

ba·by (bā′bē) *n., pl.* **-bies. 1.a.** A very young child; an infant. **b.** The youngest member of a family or group. **c.** A very young animal. **2.** An adult or a young person who behaves in an infantile way. **3.** *Slang.* A girl or young woman. **4.** *Slang.* An object of personal concern or interest: *Keeping the boat in good repair is your baby.* **—baby** *adj.* **-i·er, -iest. 1.** Of or having to do with a baby. **2.** Infantile or childish. **3.** Small in comparison with others of the same kind: *baby vegetables.* *—tr.* **-bied, -by·ing, -bies.** To treat with often inordinate indulgence and solicitude. See Synonyms at **pamper.** [Middle English.] **—ba′by·hood′** *n.* **—ba′by·ish** *adj.*

baby blue *n. Color.* A very light to very pale greenish or purplish blue.

ba·by-blue-eyes (bā′bē-blo͞o′īz′) *pl.n. (used with a sing. or pl. verb).* An annual plant *(Nemophila menziesii),* native to California and having showy flowers that typically are bright blue with white centers.

baby bond *n.* A bond issued in an amount less than $1,000.

baby boom *n.* A sudden, large increase in the birthrate, especially the one in the United States after World War II from 1947 through 1961. **—ba′by-boom′** (bā′bē-bo͞om′) *adj.*

ba·by boom·er also **ba·by-boom·er** (bā′bē-bo͞o′mər) *n.* A member of a baby-boom generation.

baby bust *n.* A sudden decline in the birthrate.

baby carriage *n.* A four-wheeled carriage, often with a hood that folds back and having a handle for pushing, used for wheeling an infant about.

baby grand *n. Music.* A small grand piano about 1.5 meters (5 feet) long.

Bab·y·lon¹ (băb′ə-lən, -lŏn′). The capital of ancient Babylonia in Mesopotamia on the Euphrates River. Established as capital c. 1750 B.C. and rebuilt in regal splendor by Nebuchadnezzar II after its destruction (c. 689 B.C.) by the Assyrians, Babylon was the site of the Hanging Gardens, one of the Seven Wonders of the World.

Bab·y·lon² (băb′ə-lən, -lŏn′) *n.* **1.** A city or place of great luxury, sensuality, and often vice and corruption. **2.** A place of captivity or exile.

Bab·y·lo·ni·a (băb′ə-lō′nē-ə, -lōn′yə). An ancient empire of Mesopotamia in the Euphrates River valley. It flourished under Hammurabi and Nebuchadnezzar II but declined after 562 B.C. and fell to the Persians in 539.

Bab·y·lo·ni·an (băb′ə-lō′nē-ən) *adj. Abbr.* **Bab. 1.** Of or relating to Babylonia or Babylon or their people, culture, or language. **2.** Characterized by a luxurious, pleasure-seeking, and often immoral way of life. **—Babylonian** *n. Abbr.* **Bab. 1.** A native or inhabitant of Babylon or Babylonia. **2.** The form of Akkadian used in Babylonia.

ba·by's breath (bā′bēz) *n.* Any of several Eurasian plants of the genus *Gypsophila,* such as *G. paniculata,* having numerous small, white flowers in profusely branched panicles. It is especially popular in flower arrangements and bouquets.

ba·by-sit (bā′bē-sĭt′) *v.* **-sat** (-săt′), **-sit·ting, -sits.** *—intr.* To take care of someone or something needing attention or guidance. *—tr.* To take care of: *baby-sat the children; baby-sat the Soviet defector; baby-sit a breaking news story.*

WORD HISTORY: The verb *baby-sit* is of interest to parents, children, and linguists. It is interesting to the last group because it illustrates one of two types of the linguistic process called back-formation. The first type is based on misunderstanding, as in the case of our word *pea.* In Middle English the ancestor of *pea* had plural forms, such as *pese* and *pease,* that were identical with singular forms. In other words, the *s* was part of the word, not a plural ending. But around the beginning of the 17th century people began to interpret the sound represented by *s* as a plural ending, and a new singular, spelled *pea* in Modern English, was developed. On the other hand, in the case of *baby-sit,* first recorded in 1947, and *baby sitter,* first recorded in 1937, no misunderstanding is involved. The agent noun *baby sitter* with its *-er* suffix could have been derived from the verb *baby-sit,* as *diver* was from *dive,* but the evidence seems to show that the pattern was reversed, and the agent noun preceded the verb from which it would normally have been derived.

baby sitter *n.* **1.** A person engaged to care for one or more children when the parents or guardians are not at home. **2.** A person who cares for or watches someone or something that needs constant attention and guidance.

baby's tears also **ba·by-tears** (bā′bē-tîrz′) *pl.n. (used with a sing. or pl. verb).* An evergreen, mat-forming perennial *(Soleirolia soleirolii)* native to Corsica and Sardinia, grown as an ornamental for its numerous tiny, roundish leaves.

baby tooth *n.* See **milk tooth.**

BAC *abbr.* Blood alcohol concentration.

Ba·cău (bə-kou′). A city of eastern Romania north-northeast of Bucharest. It is an industrial center in an oil-producing region. Population, 165,655.

bac·ca·lau·re·ate (băk′ə-lôr′ē-ĭt) *n.* **1.** See **bachelor's degree. 2.** A farewell address in the form of a sermon delivered to a graduating class. [Medieval Latin *baccalaureātus* (influenced by *bacca,* berry + *laureātus,* crowned with laurel), from *baccalārius,* bachelor. See BACHELOR.]

bac·ca·rat (bä′kə-rä′, băk′ə-) *n. Games.* A card game in which the winner is the player who holds two or three cards totaling closest to nine. [French *baccara,* from Provençal.]

bac·cate (băk′āt′) *adj.* **1.** Resembling a berry in texture or form; berrylike. **2.** Bearing berries. [From Latin *bacca,* berry.]

Bac·chae (băk′ē) *pl.n. Greek & Roman Mythology.* The priestesses and women followers of Bacchus. [Latin, from Greek *Bakkhai,* pl. of *Bakkhē,* female worshiper of Bacchus, from *Bakkhos,* Bacchus.]

bac·cha·nal (băk′ə-năl′, -näl′, băk′ə-nəl) *n.* **1.** A participant in the Bacchanalia. **2.** Often **bacchanals.** The Bacchanalia. **3.** A drunken or riotous celebration. **4.** A reveler. **—bacchanal** *adj.* Of, relating to, or typical of the worship of Bacchus. [Latin *bacchānālis,* of Bacchus, probably from *Bacchānālia,* Bacchanalia, from *Bacchus,* Bacchus, from Greek *Bakkhos.*]

Bac·cha·na·lia (băk′ə-nāl′yə, -nā′lē-ə) *n., pl.* **Bacchanalia. 1.** The ancient Roman festival in honor of Bacchus. **2. bacchanalia.** A riotous, boisterous, or drunken festivity; a revel. [Latin, from *Bacchus,* Bacchus, from Greek *Bakkhos.*] **—Bac′cha·na′lian** *adj. & n.*

bac·chant (bə-kănt′, -känt′, băk′ənt) *n., pl.* **bac·chants** or **bac·chan·tes** (bə-kăn′tēz, -kän′-, -kănts′, -känts′). **1.** *Greek & Roman Mythology.* A priest or votary of Bacchus. **2.** A boisterous reveler. [Latin *bacchāns, bacchant-,* present participle of *bacchārī,* to celebrate the festival of Bacchus, from *Bacchus,* Bacchus, from Greek *Bakkhos.*] **—bac·chan·tic** (-kăn′tĭk) *adj.*

bac·chan·te (bə-kăn′tē, -kän′-, -kănt′, -känt′) *n. Greek & Roman Mythology.* A priestess or female votary of Bacchus. [French, from Latin *bacchāns, bacchant-.* See BACCHANT.]

bac·chan·tes (bə-kăn′tēz, -kän′-, -kănts′, -känts′) *n.* A plural of **bacchant.**

Bac·chic (băk′ĭk) *adj.* **1.** *Greek & Roman Mythology.* Of or relating to Bacchus. **2. bacchic.** Drunken and carousing.

Bac·chus (băk′əs) *n. Greek & Roman Mythology.* See **Dionysus.**

bach also **batch** (băch) *intr.v.* **bached, bach·ing, bach·es** also **batched, batch·ing, batch·es.** *Informal.* To live alone and keep house as a bachelor. [Short for BACHELOR.] **—bach** *n.*

Bach (bäKH, bäk), **Johann Sebastian.** 1685–1750. German composer and organist of the late baroque period. Among the greatest composers in history, he wrote more than 200 cantatas, the *Saint Matthew Passion* (1729), the Mass in B minor (1733–1738), orchestral works such as the the six *Brandenburg Concertos,* and numerous works for organ, harpsichord, other solo instruments, and chamber ensembles. Four of his children became noted musicians: **Wilhelm Friedemann Bach** (1710–1784); **Carl Philipp Emanuel Bach** (1714–1788), an important figure in the development of the symphony; **Johann Christoph Friedrich Bach** (1732–1795); and **Johann Christian Bach** (1735–1782).

bach·e·lor (băch′ə-lər, băch′lər) *n. Abbr.* **B. 1.** An unmarried man. **2.** A person who has completed the undergraduate curriculum of a college or university and holds a bachelor's degree. **3.** A male animal that does not mate during the breeding season, especially a young male fur seal kept from the breeding territory by older males. **4.** A young knight in the service of another knight in feudal times. [Middle English *bacheler,* squire, youth, bachelor, from Old French, from Medieval Latin *baccalārius,* tenant farmer, perhaps of Celtic origin.] **—bach′e·lor·dom, bach′e·lor·hood′, bach′e·lor·ship′** *n.*

bach·e·lor's (băch′ə-lərz, băch′lərz) *n.* A bachelor's degree.

bachelor's button *n., pl.* **bachelor's buttons. 1.** See **cornflower. 2.** Any of several plants that have buttonlike flowers or flower heads.

bachelor's degree *n.* An academic degree conferred by a college or university upon those who complete the undergraduate curriculum. Also called *baccalaureate.*

bac·il·lar·y (băs′ə-lĕr′ē, bə-sĭl′ə-rē) also **ba·cil·lar** (bə-sĭl′ər, băs′ə-lər) *adj.* **1.** Shaped like a rod or rods. **2.a.** Consisting of small rods or rodlike structures. **b.** Caused by, relating to, or resembling bacilli: *bacillary dysentery.* [From BACILLUS.]

ba·cil·lus (bə-sĭl′əs) *n., pl.* **-cil·li** (-sĭl′ī′). *Abbr.* **B. 1.** Any of various rod-shaped, spore-forming, aerobic bacteria of the genus *Bacillus* that often occur in chains and include *Bacillus anthracis,* the causative agent of anthrax. **2.** Any of various bacteria, especially a rod-shaped bacterium. [Late Latin, diminutive of Latin *baculum,* rod. See **bak-** in Appendix.]

Ba·cil·lus Cal·mette-Gué·rin vaccine (bə-sĭl′əs kăl-

baboon

babushka

Johann Sebastian Bach

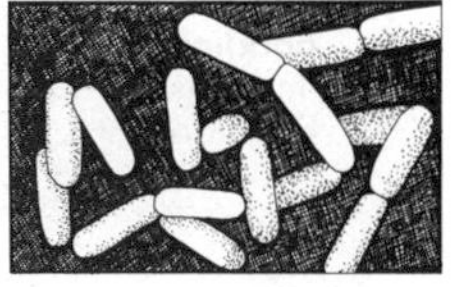

bacillus

ă pat	oi boy
ā pay	ou out
âr care	o͝o took
ä father	o͞o boot
ĕ pet	ŭ cut
ē be	ûr urge
ĭ pit	th thin
ī pie	*th* this
îr pier	hw which
ŏ pot	zh vision
ō toe	ə about, item
ô paw	♦ regionalism

Stress marks: ′ (primary); ′ (secondary), as in **dictionary** (dĭk′shə-nĕr′ē)

backboard

backgammon
Detail of a late 15th-century Austrian illuminated page from *Der Renner* by Hugo von Trimberg

backhand
German tennis player Steffi Graf

backhoe

mĕt′gä-răn′) *n. Abbr.* **BCG** A preparation consisting of attenuated human tubercle bacilli that is used for immunization against tuberculosis. [After Albert L.C. *Calmette* (1863–1933) and Camille *Guérin* (1872–1961), French bacteriologists.]

bacillus thu·rin·gi·en·sis (tho͞o-rĭn′jē-ĕn′sĭs) *n.* BT. [After THURINGIA.]

bac·i·tra·cin (băs′ĭ-trā′sĭn) *n.* A polypeptide antibiotic obtained from a strain of a bacterium *(Bacillus subtilis)* and used as a topical ointment in the treatment of certain bacterial infections, especially those caused by cocci. [BACI(LLUS) + Margaret *Tracy*, an American child in whose blood it was first isolated + –IN.]

back¹ (băk) *n.* **1.a.** The posterior portion of the trunk of the human body between the neck and the pelvis; the dorsum. **b.** The analogous dorsal region in other animals. **2.** The backbone or spine. **3.** The part or area farthest from the front. **4.** The part opposite to or behind that adapted for view or use: *the back of the hand; wrote on the back of the photograph.* **5.** The reverse side, as of a coin. **6.** A part that supports or strengthens from the rear: *the back of a couch.* **7.a.** The part of a book where the pages are stitched or glued together into the binding. **b.** The binding itself. **8.** *Sports.* **a.** A player who takes a position behind the front line of other players in certain games, such as football. **b.** This playing position. **—back** *v.* **backed, back·ing, backs.** *—tr.* **1.** To cause to move backward or in a reverse direction: *Back the car up ten feet and then make the turn.* **2.** To furnish or strengthen with a back or backing. **3.** To provide with financial or spiritual help; support or sustain: *backed our candidate with a $1,000-a-plate dinner.* See Synonyms at **support. 4.** To bet or wager on. **5.** To adduce evidence in support of; substantiate: *backed the argument with facts.* **6.** To form the back or background of: *Snowcapped mountains back the village.* *—intr.* **1.** To move backward. **2.** To shift to a counterclockwise direction. Used of the wind. **—back** *adj.* **1.** Located or placed in the rear: *Deliveries should be made at the back entrance.* **2.** Distant from a center of activity; remote. **3.** Of a past date; not current: *a back issue of a periodical.* **4.** Being owed or due from an earlier time; in arrears: *back pay.* **5.** Being in a backward direction. **6.** *Linguistics.* Pronounced with the back of the tongue, as *oo* in *cool.* Used of vowels. **—back** *adv.* **1.** At, to, or toward the rear or back; backward. **2.** In, to, or toward a former location: *went back for the class reunion.* **3.** In, to, or toward a former condition. **4.** In, to, or toward a past time. **5.** In reserve or concealment. **6.** In check or under restraint: *Barriers held the crowd back.* **7.** In reply or return. ***—phrasal verbs.* back away.** To withdraw from a position; retreat. **back down.** To withdraw from a position, opinion, or commitment. **back off.** To retreat or draw away. **back out. 1.** To withdraw from (an enterprise or a plan) before completion. **2.** To fail to keep a commitment or promise. **back up. 1.** To cause to accumulate or undergo accumulation: *The accident backed the traffic up for blocks. Traffic backed up in the tunnel.* **2.** *Computer Science.* To make a backup of (a program or file). ***—idiom.* back and fill. 1.** *Nautical.* To maneuver a vessel in a narrow channel by adjusting the sails so as to let the wind in and out of them in alteration. **2.** To vacillate in one's actions or decisions. [Middle English *bak,* from Old English *bæc.*] **—back′less** *adj.*

USAGE NOTE: The expression *back of* is an informal variant of *in back of* and is best avoided in writing: *There was a small stable in back of* (not simply *back of*) *the house.*

back² (băk) *n.* A shallow vat or tub used chiefly by brewers. [Dutch *bak,* from French *bac,* from Old French, boat, from Vulgar Latin **baccus,* vessel, probably of Celtic origin.]

back·ache (băk′āk′) *n.* Discomfort or a pain in the region of the back or spine.

back and forth *adv.* **1.** Backward and forward; to and fro. **2.** From side to side. **—back′-and-forth′** (băk′ăn-fôrth′, -fōrth′) *n. & adj.*

Back Bay (băk). An area of Boston, Massachusetts, largely consisting of filled-in land reclaimed from mud flats after the 1850's.

back·beat (băk′bēt′) *n. Music.* A loud, steady, rhythmic beat characteristic of rock music. [BACK(GROUND) + BEAT.]

back·bench (băk′bĕnch′) *n.* **1.** *Chiefly British.* The rear benches in the House of Commons where junior members of Parliament sit behind government officeholders and their counterparts in the opposition party. **2.** New members of Congress considered as a group: *"a revolt of the backbench fueled by a powerful lobbying campaign"* (Washington Post). **—back·bench′er** *n.*

back·bite (băk′bīt′) *v.* **-bit** (-bĭt′), **-bit·ten** (-bĭt′n), **-bit·ing, -bites.** *—tr.* To speak spitefully or slanderously about (another). *—intr.* To speak spitefully or slanderously about a person. **—back′bit′er** *n.*

back·board (băk′bôrd′, -bōrd′) *n.* **1.a.** A board placed under or behind something to provide firmness or support. **b.** A board placed beneath the body of a person with an injury to the neck or back, used especially in transporting the person in such a way as to avoid further injury. **2.** *Basketball.* The elevated vertical board from which the basket projects.

back·bone (băk′bōn′) *n.* **1.** The vertebrate spine or spinal column. **2.** Something, such as the keel of a ship, that resembles a backbone in appearance or position. **3.** A main support or major sustaining factor: *the backbone of a thesis.* **4.** Strength of character; determination: *displayed grit and backbone in facing adversity.* **—back′boned′** *adj.*

back·break·ing (băk′brā′kĭng) *adj.* Demanding great exertion, especially physical exertion; arduous and exhausting. **—back′break′er** *n.*

back burner *n. Informal.* A position of relatively little importance: *put the issue on the back burner.*

back channel *n.* A means by which actions, especially in government and diplomacy, are carried out secretly rather than through regular avenues of communication. **—back′-chan′nel** (băk′chăn′əl) *adj. & v.*

back·cloth (băk′klôth, -klŏth) *n.* See **backdrop** (sense 1).

back·coun·try (băk′kŭn′trē) *n.* A sparsely inhabited rural region.

back·court (băk′kôrt′, -kōrt′) *n.* **1.** *Sports.* **a.** The part of a court between the service line and the base line in tennis and other net games. **b.** The part of the playing area farthest from the goal or target wall in certain court games, such as handball. **2.** *Basketball.* **a.** The half of the court that a team defends. **b.** The part of a team that forms the two guard positions. **c.** The players in these positions.

back·cross (băk′krôs′, -krŏs′) *tr.v.* **-crossed, -cross·ing, -cross·es.** To cross (a hybrid) with one of its parents, or with an individual genetically identical to one of its parents. **—backcross** *n.* **1.** The act of making such a cross. **2.** An individual resulting from such a cross.

back dive *n. Sports.* A dive performed from a board or platform with the diver's back to the water.

back·door (băk′dôr′, -dōr′) *adj.* Secret or surreptitious; clandestine: *a backdoor romance.* **—back′door′** *adv.*

back·drop (băk′drŏp′) *n.* **1.** A painted curtain hung at the back of a stage set. Also called *backcloth.* **2.** The setting, as of a historical event; the background.

backed (băkt) *adj.* Having or furnished with a back or backing. Often used in combination: *a low-backed chair; a high-backed sofa.*

back·er (băk′ər) *n.* **1.** One that backs a person, a group, or an enterprise: *financial backers of a ballet company.* **2.** A person who bets on a contestant. **3.** A worker who provides or works with backs or backing.

back·field (băk′fēld′) *n.* **1.** *Football.* **a.** The players stationed behind the line of scrimmage. **b.** The positions filled by these players. **c.** The area in which these players line up. **2.** *Sports.* The primarily defensive players in soccer, field hockey, and rugby.

back·fire (băk′fīr′) *n.* **1.** An explosion of prematurely ignited fuel or of unburned exhaust gases in an internal-combustion engine. **2.** The backward escape of gases or cartridge fragments when a gun is fired. **3.** Another fire started to extinguish or control an oncoming fire, as in a forest, by burning an area in the path of the oncoming flames. **—backfire** *intr.v.* **-fired, -fir·ing, -fires. 1.** To explode in the manner of or make the sound of a backfire. **2.** To start or use a backfire in extinguishing or controlling a forest fire. **3.** To produce an unexpected, undesired result.

back-for·ma·tion or **back formation** (băk′fôr-mā′shən) *n.* **1.** A new word created by removing an affix from an already existing word, as *vacuum clean* from *vacuum cleaner,* or by removing what is mistakenly thought to be an affix, as *pea* from the earlier English plural *pease.* **2.** The process of forming words in this way.

back·gam·mon (băk′găm′ən) *n. Games.* A board game for two persons, played with pieces whose moves are determined by throws of dice. [BACK¹ + GAMMON¹.]

back·ground (băk′ground′) *n. Abbr.* **bg., bkgd. 1.** The ground or scenery located behind something. **2.a.** The part of a pictorial representation that appears as if it were in the distance and that provides relief for the principal objects in the foreground. **b.** The general scene or surface against which designs, patterns, or figures are represented or viewed. **3.** A position or an area of relative inconspicuousness or unimportance. **4.** The circumstances and events surrounding or leading up to an event or occurrence. **5.** A person's experience, training, and education: *Her background in the arts is impressive.* **6.** Subdued music played especially as an accompaniment to dialogue in a dramatic performance. **7.** Sound or radiation present at a relatively constant low level at a specific location. **—back′ground′** *v.*

back·ground·er (băk′groun′dər) *n.* An informal meeting at which an official provides background information, as to news reporters, about a governmental issue: *"In a White House backgrounder on July 18 I had sketched the Administration's philosophy for post-Vietnam Asia"* (Henry A. Kissinger).

back·hand (băk′hănd′) *n.* **1.** *Sports.* A stroke or motion, as of a racket, made with the back of the hand facing outward and the arm moving forward. **2.** Handwriting characterized by letters that slant to the left. **—backhand** *adj.* Backhanded. **—backhand** *adv.* With a backhanded stroke or motion. **—backhand** *tr.v.* **-hand·ed, -hand·ing, -hands.** *Sports.* To perform, catch, or hit with a backhand: *She backhanded the ball crosscourt.*

back·hand·ed (băk′hăn′dĭd) *adj.* **1.** *Sports.* Made with or using a backhand: *a backhanded shot into the opponent's court.* **2.** Oblique or roundabout: *a backhanded compliment.* **—back′hand′ed·ly** *adv.* **—back′hand′ed·ness** *n.*

back·hoe (băk′hō′) *n.* An excavator whose bucket is rigidly attached to a hinged pole on the boom and is drawn backward to the machine when in operation. **—back′hoe′** *v.*

back•ing (băk′ĭng) *n.* **1.** Something forming a back: *the backing of a carpet.* **2.a.** Support or aid: *financial backing.* **b.** Approval or endorsement: *The President has backing from the farm belt.*

back•lash (băk′lăsh′) *n.* **1.** A sudden or violent backward whipping motion. **2.** An antagonistic reaction to an earlier action: *"White backlash increases as the pressure for change in South Africa mounts"* (Masipula Sithole). **3.** A snarl formed in the part of a fishing line that is wound around the reel. **4.** The play resulting from loose connections between gears or other mechanical elements. **—back′lash′** *v.*

back•light (băk′līt′) *n.* A type of spotlight, used in photography, that illuminates a subject from behind. **—backlight** *tr.v.* **-light•ed** or **-lit** (-lĭt′), **-light•ing, -lights.** To light (a subject, for example), from behind: *"Desert sunshine backlights her chestnut curls and moon-white skin with an otherworldly halo"* (Los Angeles Times).

back•list (băk′lĭst′) *n.* A publisher's list of older titles kept in print. **—back′list′** *v.*

back•lit (băk′lĭt′) *v.* A past tense and a past participle of **backlight.**

back•log (băk′lŏg′, -lôg′) *n.* **1.** A reserve supply or source. **2.** An accumulation, especially of unfinished work or unfilled orders. **3.** A large log at the back of a fire in a fireplace. **—backlog** *v.* **-logged, -log•ging, -logs.** *—tr.* To acquire (something) as a backlog. *—intr.* To become a backlog.

back matter *n.* Material, such as an index or appendix, that follows the main body of a book. Also called *end matter.*

back mutation *n.* A reversal process whereby a gene that has undergone mutation returns to its previous state.

back•pack (băk′păk′) *n.* **1.** A knapsack, often mounted on a lightweight frame, that is worn on a person's back, as to carry camping supplies. **2.** A piece of equipment, often containing life-support devices, designed to be used while being carried on the back: *a parachute in a backpack; an astronaut's backpack.* **—backpack** *v.* **-packed, -pack•ing, -packs.** *—intr.* To hike while carrying a backpack. *—tr.* To carry in a backpack. **—back′pack′er** *n.* **—back′pack′ing** *n.*

back•ped•al (băk′pĕd′l) *v.* **-aled, -al•ing, -als** or **-alled, -al•ling, -als.** *—intr.* **1.** *Sports.* To move backward, especially in boxing or football. **2.** To retreat or withdraw: *The senator later backpedaled on the issue.* *—tr.* To pedal (a bicycle or other such vehicle) backward, in order to brake it.

back•pres•sure (băk′prĕsh′ər) *n.* Residual pressure opposing the free flow of a gas or liquid, as in a pipe or an exhaust system.

back•rest (băk′rĕst′) *n.* A rest or support for the back.

Back River. A river, about 965 km (600 mi) long, of central Northwest Territories, Canada. It rises in several lakes and flows northeast and north to an inlet south of Boothia Peninsula.

back•room or **back room** (băk′ro͞om′, -ro͝om′) *—n.* **1.** A room located at the rear. **2.** The meeting place used by an inconspicuous controlling group. *—adj.* **1.** Of, relating to, or taking place in a backroom: *backroom card games.* **2.** Marked by the exercise of inconspicuous control and maneuvering: *backroom politics.*

back•rush (băk′rŭsh′) *n.* The seaward return of water after the landward motion of a wave. Also called *backwash.*

back•saw (băk′sô′) *n.* A saw that is reinforced by a metal band along its back edge.

back•scat•ter (băk′skăt′ər) *n.* The deflection of waves or particles by electromagnetic or nuclear forces through angles greater than 90° to the initial direction of travel. **—back′scat′ter** *v.*

back seat *n.* **1.** A seat in the back, especially of a vehicle. **2.** A subordinate position, as in a group or hierarchy.

back-seat driver (băk′sēt′) *n.* **1.** A passenger who constantly advises, corrects, or nags the driver of a motor vehicle. **2.** A person who persists in giving unsolicited advice.

back•set (băk′sĕt′) *n.* **1.** A setback or reversal. **2.** An eddy or countercurrent in water.

back•shore (băk′shôr′, -shōr′) *n.* The part of a shore between the foreshore and the landward edge that is above high water except in the most severe storms.

back•side (băk′sīd′) *n.* *Informal.* The buttocks; the rump.

back•slap (băk′slăp′) *v.* **-slapped, -slap•ping, -slaps.** *—intr.* To demonstrate effusive good will. *—tr.* To demonstrate effusive good will to (another or others). **—back′slap′per** *n.*

back•slide (băk′slīd′) *intr.v.* **-slid** (-slĭd′), **-slid•ing, -slides.** To revert to sin or wrongdoing, especially in religious practice. **—back′slid′er** *n.*

back•space (băk′spās′) *v.* *—intr.* **-spaced, -spac•ing, -spac•es.** To move the carriage of a typewriter or the cursor of a computer back one or more spaces by striking the key used for this purpose. **—backspace** *n.* The key on a typewriter or computer keyboard used for backspacing.

back•spin (băk′spĭn′) *n.* A spin that tends to retard, arrest, or reverse the linear motion of an object, especially of a ball.

back•stab (băk′stăb′) *v.* *—tr.* **-stabbed, -stab•bing, -stabs.** To attack (someone) unfairly, especially in an underhanded, deceitful manner: *"Some backstab each other and threaten to settle their differences with a punch"* (Thomas Boswell). **—back′stab′ber** *n.*

back•stage (băk′stāj′) *adv.* **1.** In or toward the area behind the performing space in a theater, especially the area comprising the dressing rooms. **2.** In secret; privately. **—backstage** (băk′stāj′) *adj.* **1.** Of, relating to, occurring in, or situated behind the performing area of a theater. **2.** Concealed from the public; private.

back•stairs (băk′stârz′) also **back•stair** (-stâr′) *adj.* Furtively carried on; clandestine: *backstairs gossip.*

back•stay (băk′stā′) *n.* **1.** *Nautical.* A rope or shroud extending from the top of a mast aft to a ship's side or stern to help support the mast. **2.** A supporting device at or for the back of something else.

back•stitch (băk′stĭch′) *n.* A stitch made by inserting the needle at the midpoint of a preceding stitch so that the stitches overlap by half lengths. **—back′stitch′** *v.*

back•stop (băk′stŏp′) *n.* **1.** *Sports.* A screen or fence used to prevent a ball from being thrown or hit far out of a playing area, as in baseball. **2.** *Baseball.* A catcher. **3.** Something that supports or bolsters. **—backstop** *tr.v.* **-stopped, -stop•ping, -stops.** **1.** To serve as a backstop for. **2.a.** To support or bolster: *"The firm lacks a topflight strategic-consulting arm to backstop its technology gurus"* (Alex Beam). **b.** To substitute for (another) in an emergency.

back•sto•ry (bak′stôr′ē, -stōr′ē) *n.* A prequel.

back•stretch (băk′strĕch′) *n.* *Sports.* The part of an oval racecourse farthest from the spectators and opposite the homestretch.

back•stroke (băk′strōk′) *n.* **1.** *Sports.* A swimming stroke executed with the swimmer lying on his or her back. **2.** A backhanded stroke or motion: *a saw that cuts on the backstroke.* **—back′stroke′** *v.* **—back′strok′er** *n.*

back•swept (băk′swĕpt′) *adj.* Swept, angled, or slanting backward: *a backswept hairstyle.*

back•swim•mer (băk′swĭm′ər) *n.* Any of various aquatic bugs of the family Notonectidae that swim on their backs by means of broadened, oarlike hind legs.

back•sword (băk′sôrd′, -sōrd′) *n.* **1.** A sword with only one cutting edge. **2.** A one-handed fencing stick; a singlestick.

back talk *n.* Insolent or impudent retorts.

back-to-back (băk′tə-băk′) *adj.* Consecutive: *back-to-back performances; back-to-back home runs.*

back•track (băk′trăk′) *intr.v.* **-tracked, -track•ing, -tracks.** **1.** To go back over the course by which one has come. **2.** To reverse one's position or policy.

back•up (băk′ŭp′) *n.* **1.a.** A reserve or substitute. **b.** *Computer Science.* A copy of a program or file that is stored separately from the original. **2.a.** Support or backing. **b.** *Music.* A background accompaniment, as for a performer. **3.** An overflow or accumulation caused by clogging or by a stoppage: *a backup in the sink; a backup of traffic at the drawbridge.* **—backup** *adj.* Extra; standby: *a backup pilot.*

back•ward (băk′wərd) *adj.* **1.** Directed or facing toward the back or rear. **2.** Done or arranged in a manner or an order that is opposite to previous occurrence or normal use. **3.** Unwilling to act; reluctant; shy. **4.** Behind others in progress or development: *The technology was backward, but the system worked.* **—backward** or **back•wards** (-wərdz) *adv.* **1.** To or toward the back or rear. **2.** With the back leading. **3.** In a reverse manner or order. **4.** To, toward, or into the past. **5.** Toward a worse or less advanced condition. **—*idiom.* bend** (or **lean**) **over backward.** To make an effort greater than is required. **—back′ward•ly** *adv.* **—back′ward•ness** *n.*

USAGE NOTE: The adverb may be spelled *backward* or *backwards,* and the forms are interchangeable: *stepped backward; a mirror facing backwards.* Only *backward* is an adjective: *a backward view.*

back•wash (băk′wŏsh′, -wôsh′) *n.* **1.a.** A backward flow of water, as from the action of oars. **b.** See **backrush. 2.** A backward flow of air, as from the propeller of an aircraft. **3.** A result of an event; an aftermath.

back•wa•ter (băk′wô′tər, -wŏt′ər) *n.* **1.a.** Water held or pushed back by or as if by a dam or current. **b.** A body of water thus formed. **2.** A place or situation regarded as isolated, stagnant, or backward: *"The running of family fortunes has always been a backwater—albeit a lucrative one—of the investment management business"* (Business Week). **3.** A rowing or paddling stroke in which the oar or paddle is pushed forward, used to check a boat's forward motion or move it backward.

back•woods (băk′wo͝odz′) *pl.n.* *(used with a sing. or pl. verb).* **1.** Heavily wooded, uncultivated, thinly settled areas. **2.** An area that is far from population centers or that is held to be culturally backward. **—back′woods′man** *n.*

back yard also **back•yard** (băk′yärd′) *—n.* A yard at the rear of a house. *—attributive.* Often used to modify another noun: *backyard barbecues; backyard gossip.*

Ba•co•lod (bä-kō′lôd′). A city of northwest Negros Island in the south-central Philippines. It is a major port and processing center in a sugar-cane region. Population, 262,415.

backpack

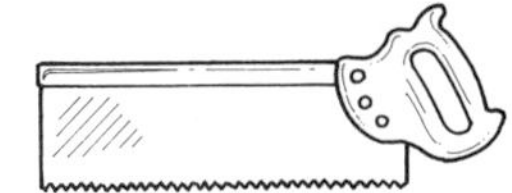

backsaw

ă pat	oi boy
ā pay	ou out
âr care	o͝o took
ä father	o͞o boot
ĕ pet	ŭ cut
ē be	ûr urge
ĭ pit	th thin
ī pie	*th* this
îr pier	hw which
ŏ pot	zh vision
ō toe	ə about, item
ô paw	♦ regionalism

Stress marks: **′** (primary); ′ (secondary), as in **dictionary** (dĭk′shə-nĕr′ē)

CLOSTRIDIUM TETANI

TREPONEMA PALLIDUM

STREPTOCOCCUS

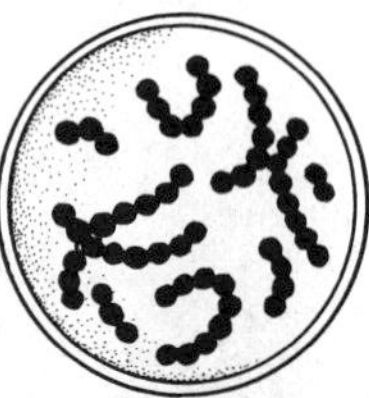

bacterium

Robert Baden-Powell

ba·con (bā′kən) *n.* The salted and smoked meat from the back and sides of a pig. [Middle English, from Old French, of Germanic origin.]

Ba·con (bā′kən), **Francis**[1]. First Baron Verulam and Viscount Saint Albans. 1561–1626. English philosopher, essayist, courtier, jurist, and statesman. His writings include *The Advancement of Learning* (1605) and the *Novum Organum* (1620), in which he proposed a theory of scientific knowledge based on observation and experiment that came to be known as the inductive method.

Bacon, Francis[2]. Born 1909. Irish-born British painter best known for his portraits in which subjects are distorted and invested with feelings of terror.

Bacon, Nathaniel. 1647–1676. English-born American colonist who led Bacon's Rebellion (1676), in which a group of frontiersmen captured and burned Jamestown in an attempt to gain reforms and greater participation in the government of Virginia.

Bacon, Roger. Known as "the Admirable Doctor." 1214?–1292. English friar, scientist, and philosopher whose *Opus Majus* (1267) argued that Christian studies should encompass the sciences.

Ba·co·ni·an (bā-kō′nē-ən) *adj.* Of, relating to, or characteristic of the works or thought of the philosopher Francis Bacon. —**Baconian** *n.* **1.** A follower of the doctrines of Francis Bacon. **2.** One who believes in the Baconian theory.

Baconian theory *n.* The theory that Francis Bacon was the author of the plays attributed to Shakespeare.

bact. *abbr.* Bacteria; bacterial.

bacter– *pref.* Variant of **bacterio–.**

bac·te·re·mi·a (băk′tə-rē′mē-ə) *n.* The presence of bacteria in the blood. —**bac′te·re′mic** (-mĭk) *adj.* —**bac′te·re′mi·cal·ly** *adv.*

bacteri– *pref.* Variant of **bacterio–.**

bac·te·ri·a (băk-tîr′ē-ə) *n. Abbr.* **bact.** Plural of **bacterium.**

bac·te·ri·al (băk-tîr′ē-əl) *adj. Abbr.* **bact.** Relating to or caused by bacteria: *a bacterial enzyme; bacterial diseases.* —**bac·te′ri·al** *n.* —**bac·te′ri·al·ly** *adv.*

bac·te·ri·cide (băk-tîr′ĭ-sīd′) *n.* An agent that destroys bacteria. —**bac·te′ri·cid′al** (-sīd′l) *adj.*

bac·ter·in (băk′tər-ĭn) *n.* A suspension of killed or weakened bacteria used as a vaccine.

bacterio– or **bacteri–** or **bacter–** *pref.* Bacteria; bacterial: *bacteriology.* [New Latin *bacterium,* bacterium. See BACTERIUM.]

bac·te·ri·o·cin (băk-tîr′ē-ə-sĭn′) *n.* An antibacterial substance, such as colicin, produced by a strain of certain bacteria and harmful to another strain within the same family. [BACTERIO– + (COLI)CIN.]

bac·te·ri·o·gen·ic (băk-tîr′ē-ə-jĕn′ĭk) also **bac·te·ri·og·e·nous** (-ŏj′ə-nəs) *adj.* Caused by bacteria.

bac·te·ri·ol·o·gy (băk-tîr′ē-ŏl′ə-jē) *n. Abbr.* **bacteriol.** The study of bacteria, especially in relation to medicine and agriculture. —**bac·te′ri·o·log′ic** (-ə-lŏj′ĭk), **bac·te′ri·o·log′i·cal** *adj.* —**bac·te′ri·o·log′i·cal·ly** *adv.* —**bac·te′ri·ol′o·gist** *n.*

bac·te·ri·ol·y·sis (băk-tîr′ē-ŏl′ĭ-sĭs) *n., pl.* **-ses** (-sēz′). Dissolution or destruction of bacteria. —**bac·te′ri·o·lyt′ic** (-ə-lĭt′ĭk) *adj.*

bac·te·ri·o·phage (băk-tîr′ē-ə-fāj′) *n.* A virus that infects and lyses certain bacteria. —**bac·te′ri·o·phag′ic** (-fāj′ĭk) *adj.* —**bac·te′ri·oph′a·gy** (-ŏf′ə-jē) *n.*

bac·te·ri·o·rho·dop·sin (băk-tîr′ē-ō-rō-dŏp′sĭn) *n. Microbiology.* A purple pigment similar to rhodopsin occurring in the cell membranes of bacteria of the genus *Halobacterium* that converts sunlight directly into chemical energy.

bac·te·ri·os·co·py (băk-tîr′ē-ŏs′kə-pē) *n.* Microscopic examination of bacteria.

bac·te·ri·o·sta·sis (băk-tîr′ē-ō-stā′sĭs) *n., pl.* **-ses** (-sēz). The inhibition of growth, but not the killing, of bacteria.

bac·te·ri·o·stat (băk-tîr′ē-ə-stăt′) *n.* An agent, such as a chemical or biological material, that inhibits bacterial growth. —**bac·te′ri·o·stat′ic** *adj.*

bac·te·ri·um (băk-tîr′ē-əm) *n., pl.* **-te·ri·a** (-tîr′ē-ə). Any of the unicellular, prokaryotic microorganisms of the class Schizomycetes, which vary in terms of morphology, oxygen and nutritional requirements, and motility, and may be free-living, saprophytic, or pathogenic, the latter causing disease in plants or animals. [New Latin, from Greek *baktērion,* diminutive of *baktron,* rod. See **bak-** in Appendix.]

bac·te·ri·u·ri·a (băk-tîr′ē-yo͝or′ē-ə) *n.* The presence of bacteria in urine.

bac·te·rize (băk′tə-rīz′) *tr.v.* **-rized, -riz·ing, -riz·es.** To change the composition of (something) by means of bacterial action. —**bac′te·ri·za′tion** (-rĭ-zā′shən) *n.*

bac·te·roid (băk′tə-roid′) *adj.* Resembling bacteria in appearance or action. —**bacteroid** *n.* Any of various structurally modified bacteria, such as those occurring on the root nodules of leguminous plants.

Bac·tra (băk′trə). See **Balkh.**

Bac·tri·a (băk′trē-ə). An ancient country of southwest Asia. It was an eastern province of the Persian Empire before its conquest by the Greeks in 328 B.C.. The kingdom was destroyed c. 130 B.C. by nomadic tribes. —**Bac′tri·an** *adj. & n.*

Bactrian camel *n.* A two-humped camel *(Camelus bactrianus)* native to central and southwest Asia.

bac·u·li·form (băk′yə-lə-fôrm′, bə-kyo͞o′lə-) *adj.* Rod-shaped. [Latin *baculum,* stick; see **bak-** in Appendix + –FORM.]

bad[1] (băd) *adj.* **worse** (wûrs), **worst** (wûrst). **1.** Not achieving an adequate standard; poor: *a bad recital.* **2.** Evil; sinful. **3.** Disobedient or naughty: *bad children.* **4.** Disagreeable, unpleasant, or disturbing: *a bad piece of news.* **5.** Unfavorable: *bad reviews for the play.* **6.** Not fresh; rotten or spoiled: *bad meat.* **7.** Injurious in effect; detrimental: *bad habits.* **8.** Not working properly; defective: *a bad telephone connection.* **9.** Full of or exhibiting faults or errors: *bad grammar.* **10.** Having no validity; void: *passed bad checks.* **11.** Severe; intense: *a bad cold.* **12.a.** Being in poor health or in pain: *I feel bad today.* **b.** Being in poor condition; diseased: *bad lungs.* **13.** Sorry; regretful: *She feels bad about how she treated you.* **14. bad·der, bad·dest.** *Slang.* Very good; great. —**bad** *n.* Something that is below standard or expectations, as of ethics or decency: *weighing the good against the bad.* —**bad** *adv. Usage Problem.* Badly. —***idioms.* in bad.** *Informal.* In trouble or disfavor. **not half** (or **so**) **bad.** *Informal.* Reasonably good. [Middle English *badde.*] —**bad′ness** *n.*

SYNONYMS: bad, evil, wicked. These adjectives are compared as they mean departing from moral or ethical standards. *Bad* is the most inclusive; it applies to what is regarded as being unpleasant, offensive, or blameworthy: *bad weather; a bad temper. "A bad book is as much of a labor to write as a good one"* (Aldous Huxley). *Evil,* a stronger term, adds to *bad* connotations of depravity and corruptive influence: *"The unconscious is not just evil by nature, it is also the source of the highest good"* (Carl Jung). *Wicked* suggests conscious or premeditated moral transgression: *"this wicked man Hitler, the repository and embodiment of many forms of soul-destroying hatred, this monstrous product of former wrongs and shame"* (Winston S. Churchill).

USAGE NOTE: *Bad* is often used as an adverb in sentences such as *The house was shaken up pretty bad* or *We need water bad.* This usage is common in informal speech but is widely regarded as unacceptable in formal writing. In an earlier survey, the sentence *His tooth ached so bad he could not sleep* was unacceptable to 92 percent of the Usage Panel. • The use of *badly* with *want,* once considered incorrect, is now entirely acceptable: *We wanted badly to be at the wedding.* • The adverb *badly* is often used as the complement of verbs such as *feel,* as in *I felt badly about the whole affair,* where the choice of *badly* as opposed to *bad* may convey an implication that the distress is emotional, rather than physical. Although the origin of this usage is a matter of dispute, the usage is now widespread and is supported by analogy to the use of other adverbs with *feel* (as in *We feel strongly about this issue*). In an earlier survey, a majority of the Usage Panel accepted this use of *badly* in speech, though *bad* is less likely to occasion objections. • *Badly* is also used in some regions to mean "unwell," as in *He was looking badly after the accident* (compare *poorly,* which is also used in this way). In an earlier survey, however, the usage was found unacceptable in formal writing by 75 percent of the Usage Panel.

bad[2] (băd) *v. Archaic.* A past tense of **bid.**

bad actor *n.* One that consistently behaves or reacts poorly: *"Perhaps . . . they will not be able to keep out the criminals and the bad actors who could end up harming the honest operators"* (Economist). *"Phosphorus is not the only bad actor in lake eutrophication"* (Chemical Week).

Ba·da·joz (bä′də-hōz′, *-thä-*hôth′). A city of southwest Spain on the Guadiana River near the Portugal border. An ancient fortress city, it rose to prominence under the Moors as the seat (1022–1094) of a vast independent emirate. Population, 92,800.

Ba·da·lo·na (bä′də-lō′nə, *-thä-*lô′nä). A city of northeast Spain, an industrial suburb of Barcelona on the Mediterranean Sea. Population, 229,281.

bad·ass (băd′ăs′) *Vulgar Slang. n.* A mean-tempered or belligerent person. —**badass** *adj.* Mean; belligerent.

bad blood *n.* Enmity or bitterness among individuals or groups of people.

bade (băd, bād) *v.* A past tense of **bid.**

Ba·den (bäd′n). A historical region of southwest Germany. In the 1840's it was a center of the German liberal movement.

Ba·den-Ba·den (bäd′n-bäd′n). A city of southwest Germany in the Black Forest near the French border. Founded as a Roman garrison in the third century A.D., it has long been one of Europe's most fashionable spas. Population, 48,622.

Ba·den-Pow·ell (băd′n-pō′əl), Sir **Robert Stephenson Smyth.** 1857–1941. British soldier who founded the Boy Scouts (1908) and with his sister **Agnes** (1858–1945) the Girl Guides (1910).

badge (băj) *n.* **1.a.** A device or emblem worn as an insignia of rank, office, or membership in an organization. **b.** An emblem given as an award or honor. **2.** A characteristic mark. See Synonyms at **sign.** [Middle English *bagge,* from Norman French *bage.*] —**badge** *v.*

badg·er (băj′ər) *n.* **1.a.** Any of several carnivorous, burrowing mammals of the family Mustelidae, such as *Meles meles* of Eurasia or *Taxidea taxus* of North America, having short legs, long claws on the front feet, and a heavy, grizzled coat. **b.** The fur or hair of this mammal. **c.** Any of several similar mammals, such as the ratel. **2. Badger.** *Slang.* A native or inhabitant of Wisconsin. **—badger** *tr.v.* **-ered, -er·ing, -ers.** To harry or pester persistently. See Synonyms at **harass.** [Perhaps from BADGE.]

WORD HISTORY: Our name for the Eurasian species of this mammal, which is noted for championing its burrow just like a knight of old, may come from the badger's knightly emblem. The creature's white head with a broad black stripe on each side of the snout may have brought to mind a badge, hence the name *badger.* One good piece of supporting evidence for this theory is that an earlier name for the animal was *bauson,* which comes from the Old French word *baucenc,* usually referring to a white patch on a horse and also meaning "badger." *Bauson* is first recorded before 1375, *badger* in 1523.

Bad Hom·burg (bät′ hŏm′bûrg′, -bo͝ork′). A city of west-central Germany at the foot of the Taunus Mountains near Frankfurt. It is a famous spa and resort. Population, 50,647.

bad·i·nage (băd′n-äzh′) *n.* Light, playful banter. [French, from *badin,* joker, from Provençal *badar,* to gape, from Latin **batāre.*]

bad·lands (băd′lăndz′) *pl.n.* Barren land characterized by roughly eroded ridges, peaks, and mesas.

Bad·lands also **Bad Lands** (băd′lăndz′). A heavily eroded arid region of southwest South Dakota and northwest Nebraska. The Badlands National Monument in South Dakota was established in 1939 to protect the area's colorful rock formations and prehistoric fossils.

bad·ly (băd′lē) *adv.* *Usage Problem.* **1.** In a bad manner. **2.** Very much; greatly. See Usage Note at **bad**[1].

bad·min·ton (băd′mĭn′tən) *n.* *Sports.* A sport played by volleying a shuttlecock back and forth over a high, narrow net by means of a light, long-handled racket. [After *Badminton,* the Duke of Beaufort's country seat in western England.]

bad·mouth or **bad-mouth** (băd′mouth′, -mouth′) *tr.v.* **-mouthed, -mouth·ing, -mouths.** *Slang.* To criticize or disparage, often spitefully or unfairly; run down: *"those cross-Atlantic aficionados who persistently idolize the British theater and bad-mouth Broadway"* (Benedict Nightingale).

bad news *pl.n. (used with a sing. verb). Slang.* One that is unpleasant or undesirable: *A troublemaker within a group is always bad news.*

B.A.E. *abbr.* **1.** Bachelor of Aeronautical Engineering. **2.** Bachelor of Agricultural Engineering. **3.** Bachelor of Architectural Engineering. **4.** Bachelor of Art Education. **5.** Bachelor of Arts in Education.

Bae·da (bē′də). See **Bede.**

bae·de·ker (bā′dĭ-kər) *n.* A guidebook to countries or a country. [After Karl BAEDEKER.]

Bae·de·ker (bā′dĭ-kər), **Karl.** 1801–1859. German publisher who established a series of guidebooks in 1829.

B.A.Ed. *abbr.* Bachelor of Arts in Education.

B.Ae.E. *abbr.* Bachelor of Aeronautical Engineering.

bael (bĕl, bāl, bīl) *n.* The round to pear-shaped, yellowish, edible fruit of a chiefly Indian tree *(Aegle marmelos),* used in southern Asia as a food and as a medicine to treat dysentery. [Hindi *bēl;* akin to Sanskrit *bilvaḥ,* Tamil *viḷā, viḷavu.*]

Ba·ez (bī-ĕz′, bī′ĕz′), **Joan.** Born 1941. American folk singer and political activist.

Baf·fin (băf′ĭn). A region of northeast Northwest Territories, Canada, including Baffin Island, the Queen Elizabeth and Parry islands, and Melville Peninsula.

Baffin, William. 1584?–1622. English explorer who led several expeditions (1612–1616) in search of the Northwest Passage.

Baffin Bay. An ice-clogged body of water between northeast Canada and Greenland. It connects with the Arctic Ocean to the north and west and with the Atlantic Ocean to the south by way of Davis Strait.

Baffin Island. An island of northeast Northwest Territories, Canada, west of Greenland.

baf·fle (băf′əl) *tr.v.* **-fled, -fling, -fles. 1.** To frustrate or check (a person) as by confusing or perplexing; stymie. **2.** To impede the force or movement of. **—baffle** *n.* **1.** A usually static device that regulates the flow of a fluid or light. **2.** A partition that prevents interference between sound waves in a loudspeaker. [Perhaps blend of Scottish Gaelic *bauchle,* to denounce, revile publicly, and French *bafouer,* to ridicule.] **—baf′fle·ment** *n.* **—baf′fler** *n.*

baf·fle·gab (băf′əl-găb′) *n.* *Slang.* Gobbledegook. [BAFFLE + GAB.]

bag (băg) *n.* *Abbr.* **bg. 1.a.** A container of flexible material, such as paper, plastic, or leather, that is used for carrying or storing items. **b.** A handbag; a purse. **c.** A piece of hand luggage, such as a suitcase or a satchel. **d.** An organic sac or pouch, such as the udder of a cow. **2.** An object that resembles a pouch. **3.** *Nautical.* The bulging part of a sail. **4.** The amount that a bag can hold. **5.** An amount of game taken or legally permitted to be taken. **6.** *Baseball.* A base. **7.** *Slang.* An area of interest or skill: *Cooking is not my bag.* **8.** *Slang.* A woman considered ugly or unkempt. **—bag** *v.* **bagged, bag·ging, bags.** *—tr.* **1.** To put into or as if into a bag. **2.** To cause to bulge like a pouch. **3.** To capture or kill as game: *bagged six grouse.* **4.** *Informal.* To gain possession of; capture. *—intr.* **1.** To hang loosely. **2.** To swell out; bulge. ***—idioms.*** **bag it.** *Slang.* **1.** To be a truant. **2.** To cease discussion of an issue: *Finally in disgust I told my debating opponent to bag it.* **in the bag.** Assured of a successful outcome; virtually accomplished or won. [Middle English *bagge,* from Old Norse *baggi.*] **—bag′ful** *n.* **—bag′ger** *n.*

bag and baggage *adv.* **1.** With all one's belongings. **2.** To a complete degree; entirely.

ba·gasse (bə-găs′) *n.* The dry, fibrous residue remaining after the extraction of juice from the crushed stalks of sugar cane, used as a source of cellulose for some paper products. [French, from Spanish *bagazo,* dregs, from Latin *bāca,* berry.]

bag·a·telle (băg′ə-tĕl′) *n.* **1.** An unimportant or insignificant thing; a trifle. **2.** A short piece of verse or music. **3.** *Games.* A game played on an oblong table with a cue and balls. [French, from Italian *bagatella,* diminutive of dialectal *bagata,* little property, possibly from Latin *bāca,* berry.]

Bag·dad (băg′dăd′). See **Baghdad.**

Bage·hot (băj′ət), **Walter.** 1826–1877. British economist, social scientist, and journalist who wrote *The English Constitution* (1867), an analysis of the comparative powers of the branches of British government.

ba·gel (bā′gəl) *n.* A glazed, ring-shaped roll with a tough, chewy texture, made from plain yeast dough that is dropped briefly into nearly boiling water and then baked. [Yiddish *beygl,* from Middle High German **bougel,* diminutive of *bouc,* ring, from Old High German *boug.* See **bheug-** in Appendix.]

bag·gage (băg′ĭj) *n.* **1.** The trunks, bags, parcels, and suitcases in which one carries one's belongings while traveling; luggage. **2.** The movable equipment and supplies of an army. **3.** Superfluous or burdensome practices, regulations, ideas, or traits. **4.a.** A wanton or immoral woman. **b.** An impudent or saucy girl or woman. *—attributive.* Often used to modify another noun: *a baggage handler; baggage claim.* [Middle English *bagage,* from Old French *bague,* bundle, perhaps of Germanic origin.]

Bag·gies (băg′ēz). A trademark used for a variety of plastic storage bags. This trademark, often styled without a final *s* and in lowercase, sometimes occurs in print with the meaning "a small plastic bag": "[He] *pulls out a Baggie full of parsley"* (Washington Post). *"Police found marijuana in a baggie he had dropped into a truck"* (National Law Journal).

bag·ging (băg′ĭng) *n.* Material used for making bags.

bag·gy (băg′ē) *adj.* **-gi·er, -gi·est.** Bulging or hanging loosely: *baggy trousers.* **—bag′gi·ly** *adv.* **—bag′gi·ness** *n.*

Bagh·dad or **Bag·dad** (băg′dăd′). The capital and largest city of Iraq, in the center of the country on the Tigris River. Founded in the eighth century, it became a large and powerful city whose greatness is reflected in the *Arabian Nights.* Population, 2,200,000.

bag job *n.* *Slang.* A black bag job.

bag lady *n.* *Slang.* A homeless woman, especially one in a big city, who carries her possessions in a shopping bag.

bag·man (băg′mən) *n.* **1.** *Slang.* A person who collects money, as for racketeers. **2.** *Chiefly British.* A traveling salesman.

ba·gnio (băn′yō, bän′-) *n., pl.* **-gnios. 1.** A brothel. **2.** *Obsolete.* A prison for slaves in Asian countries. **3.** *Obsolete.* A public bathhouse in Italy or Turkey. [Italian *bagno,* bath, from Latin *balneum,* from Greek *balaneion.*]

bag of waters *n.* See **water bag.**

bag people *pl.n.* *Slang.* Homeless people considered as a group.

bag·pipe (băg′pīp′) *n.* *Music.* An instrument having a flexible bag inflated either by a tube with valves or by bellows, a double-reed melody pipe, and from one to four drone pipes. Often used in the plural. **—bag′pipe′** *v.* **—bag′pip′er** *n.*

ba·guette (bă-gĕt′) *n.* **1.a.** A gem cut in the form of a narrow rectangle. **b.** The form of such a gem. **2.** *Architecture.* A narrow, convex molding. **3.** A small, narrow loaf of French bread often used for sandwiches. [French, rod, from Italian *bacchetta,* diminutive of *bacchio,* rod, from Latin *baculum,* stick. See **bak-** in Appendix.]

Ba·gui·o (bä′gē-ō′). A city of northwest Luzon, Philippines. It is a mountain resort and the summer capital of the country. Population, 119,009.

bag·wig (băg′wĭg′) *n.* A wig with the back hair encased in a small silk sack, worn in the 18th century.

bag·worm (băg′wûrm′) *n.* Any of several moths of the family Psychidae, which construct fibrous cases of silk spun together with leaves, twigs, or grass. The plant-feeding larvae and wingless adult females live in these cases.

bah (bä, bă) *interj.* Used to express impatient rejection or contempt.

Ba·ha'i (bä-hä′ē, bə-hī′) *adj.* Of or relating to a religion founded in 1863 in Iran and emphasizing the spiritual unity of all humankind. **—Baha'i** *n.* A teacher of or a believer in this faith. [Persian *bahā'ī,* a follower of *Bahā'ullāh* (see BAHAULLAH), "the Splendor of God". *bahā'ī,* from *bahā',* splendor, from Arabic.] **—Ba·ha'ism** (bə-hä′ĭz′əm, -hī′-) *n.* **—Ba·ha'ist** *n.*

Ba·ha·mas (bə-hä′məz, -hā′-) also **Ba·ha·ma Islands** (-mə). An island country in the Atlantic Ocean east of Florida and Cuba comprising some 700 islands and islets and numerous cays. The country gained its independence from Great Britain in 1973. Nassau, on New Providence Island, is the capital and the largest

Joan Baez
At a 1977 Kent State University rally

bagpipe

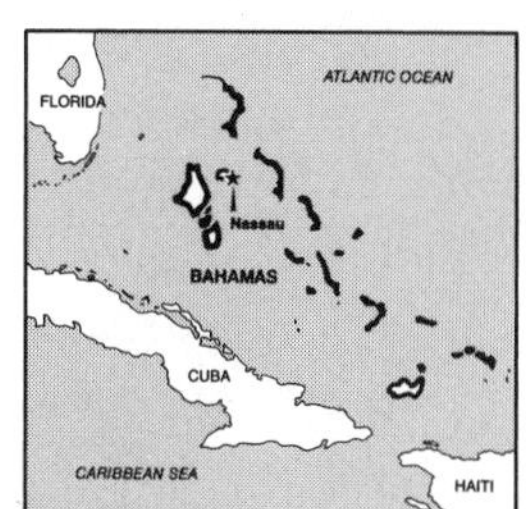

Bahamas

ă pat	oi boy
ā pay	ou out
âr care	o͝o took
ä father	o͞o boot
ĕ pet	ŭ cut
ē be	ûr urge
ĭ pit	th thin
ī pie	*th* this
îr pier	hw which
ŏ pot	zh vision
ō toe	ə about, item
ô paw	♦ regionalism

Stress marks: **′** (primary); ′ (secondary), as in **dictionary** (dĭk′shə-nĕr′ē)

city. Population, 218,000. —**Ba·ha′mi·an** (-hā′mē-ən, -hä′-), **Ba·ha′man** (-hā′mən, -hā′-) *adj. & n.*

Ba·ha·sa Indonesia (bä-hä′sə) *n.* See **Indonesian** (sense 4). [Indonesian, Indonesian language, from Sanskrit *bhāṣā,* speech, language.]

Bahasa Ma·lay (mə-lā′, mā′lā) also **Bahasa Me·la·yo** (mə-lä′yo͞o) *n.* See **Malay** (sense 2). [Malay, Malay language, from Sanskrit *bhāṣā,* speech, language.]

Ba·ha·ul·lah (bä-hä′o͞o-lä′). Originally Mirza Huseyn Ali. 1817–1892. Persian religious leader who was a follower of the Bab and founded the Baha'i sect (1863).

Ba·ha·wal·pur (bə-hä′wəl-po͝or′, -hä′wəl-po͝or′). A region and former princely state of east-central Pakistan between the Sutlej River and the Indian border.

Ba·hi·a (bə-hē′ə, bä-ē′ə). See **Salvador.** —**Ba·hi′an** *adj. & n.*

Ba·hí·a Blan·ca (bə-hē′ə blăng′kə, bä-ē′ä vläng′kä). A city of eastern Argentina on the **Bahía Blanca,** an inlet of the Atlantic Ocean southwest of Buenos Aires. It is a major shipping and commercial center. Population, 223,818.

Ba·hi·a grass (bə-hē′ə) *n.* A perennial, sod-forming tropical American grass *(Paspalum notatum)* grown in warm regions, such as the southern United States, for forage, soil binding, and turf. [After *Bahia* (Salvador), Brazil.]

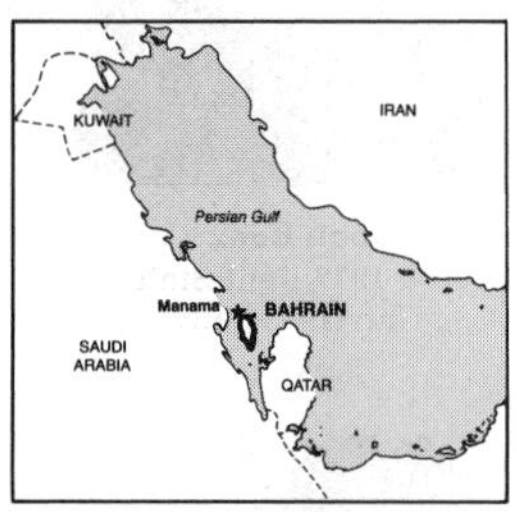

Bahrain

Bah·rain or **Bah·rein** (bä-rān′). A country comprising an archipelago of low, sandy islands in the Persian Gulf between Qatar and Saudi Arabia. It was the first Arabian country to strike oil (1932). A British protectorate after 1861, Bahrain became independent in 1971. Manama, on **Bahrain Island,** the largest in the archipelago, is the capital. Population, 350,798. —**Bah·rain′i** *adj. & n.*

Bahr el Gha·zal (bâr′ ĕl′ gə-zăl′, bär′ ĕl′ gä-zĭl′). A river of southwest Sudan flowing about 805 km (500 mi) east to Lake No, where it joins the Bahr el Jebel.

Bahr el Jeb·el (jĕb′əl). A river, about 956 km (594 mi) long, of southern Sudan. It is a section of the White Nile.

baht (bät) *n., pl.* **bahts** or **baht.** See table at **currency.** [Thai *bāt.*]

♦ **bai·gnet** (bĕn-yā′) *n. Southern Louisiana.* Variant of **beignet.**

Bai·kal or **Bay·kal** (bī-kôl′, -kŏl′). **Lake.** A lake of south-central Russia. It is the largest freshwater lake in Eurasia and the world's deepest lake, with a maximum depth of 1,742.2 m (5,712 ft).

bail[1] (bāl) *n.* **1.** Security, usually a sum of money, exchanged for the release of an arrested person as a guarantee of that person's appearance for trial. **2.** Release from imprisonment provided by the payment of such money. **3.** A person who provides this security. —**bail** *tr.v.* **bailed, bail·ing, bails. 1.** To secure the release of by providing security. **2.** To release (a person) for whom security has been paid. **3.** *Informal.* To extricate from a difficult situation: *always bailing you out of trouble.* **4.** To transfer (property) to another for a special purpose but without permanent transference of ownership. [Middle English, custody, from Old French, from *baillier,* to take charge of, from Latin *bāiulāre,* to carry a load, from *bāiulus,* carrier of a burden.] —**bail′er** *n.*

bail[2] (bāl) *v.* **bailed, bail·ing, bails.** —*tr.* **1.** To remove (water) from a boat by repeatedly filling a container and emptying it over the side. **2.** To empty (a boat) of water by bailing. —*intr.* To empty a boat of water by bailing. —**bail** *n.* A container used for emptying water from a boat. —***phrasal verb.* bail out. 1.** To parachute from an aircraft; eject. **2.** To abandon a project or enterprise. [From Middle English *baille,* bucket, from Old French, from Vulgar Latin **bāiulā,* water container, from Latin *bāiulāre,* to carry a load.] —**bail′er** *n.*

bail[3] (bāl) *n.* **1.** The arched, hooplike handle of a container, such as a pail. **2.** An arch or hoop, such as one of those used to support the top of a covered wagon. **3.** A hinged bar on a typewriter that holds the paper against the platen. [Middle English *beil,* perhaps from Old English **bēgel* or of Scandinavian origin; see **bheug-** in Appendix.]

bail[4] (bāl) *n.* **1.** *Chiefly British.* A pole or bar used to confine or separate animals. **2.** *Sports.* One of the two crossbars that form the top of a wicket used in the game of cricket. [Old French dialectal, probably from Latin *baculum,* stick. See BACILLUS.]

bail·a·ble (bā′lə-bəl) *adj.* **1.** Eligible for bail: *a bailable defendant.* **2.** Allowing or admitting of bail: *a bailable offense.*

bail·ee (bā-lē′) *n.* A person to whom property is bailed.

bai·ley (bā′lē) *n.* **-leys. 1.** The outer wall of a castle. **2.** The space enclosed by this outer wall. [Middle English *bailli,* from Old French *baille,* probably from Latin *bacula,* pl. of *baculum,* log, stick. See BACILLUS.]

Bai·ley (bā′lē), **Gamaliel.** 1807–1859. American journalist who edited antislavery periodicals, such as the *Cincinnati Philanthropist* (1836–1843) and the *National Era* (1847–1859), in which Harriet Beecher Stowe's novel *Uncle Tom's Cabin* was published serially (1851–1852).

Bailey, Nathan or **Nathaniel.** Died 1742. British lexicographer whose *Universal Etymological English Dictionary,* first published in 1721, was used as a reference by Samuel Johnson and was the first English dictionary to treat etymology consistently.

Bailey bridge *n.* A steel bridge designed to be shipped in parts and assembled rapidly. [After Sir Donald *Bailey* (1901–1985), British engineer.]

bail·ie (bā′lē) *n.* **1.** A Scottish municipal officer corresponding to an English alderman. **2.** *Obsolete.* A bailiff. [Middle English *baillie,* town official, from Old French *bailiff,* from Medieval Latin **bāiulīvus.* See BAILIFF.]

bail·iff (bā′lĭf) *n.* **1.** A court attendant entrusted with duties such as the maintenance of order in a courtroom during a trial. **2.** An official who assists a British sheriff and who has the power to execute writs, processes, and arrests. **3.** *Chiefly British.* An overseer of an estate; a steward. [Middle English *baillif,* from Old French *baillis, baillif-,* overseer of an estate, steward, from Medieval Latin **bāiulīvus,* from Latin *bāiulus,* carrier.]

bail·i·wick (bā′lə-wĭk′) *n.* **1.** A person's specific area of interest, skill, or authority. See Synonyms at **field. 2.** The office or district of a bailiff. [Middle English *bailliwik* : *baillif,* bailiff; see BAILIFF + *wik,* town (from Old English *wīc,* from Latin *vīcus;* see VICINITY).]

bail·ment (bāl′mənt) *n.* **1.** The process of providing bail for an accused person. **2.** The act of delivering goods or personal property to another in trust.

bail·or (bā′lər, bā-lôr′) *n.* One who bails property to another.

bail·out (bāl′out′) *n.* A rescue from financial difficulties: *corporate bailouts.*

bails·man (bālz′mən) *n.* One who provides bail or security for another.

bain-ma·rie (băn′mə-rē′) *n., pl.* **bains-ma·rie** (băn′mə-rē′). A large pan containing hot water in which smaller pans may be set to cook food slowly or to keep food warm. [French, from Medieval Latin *balneum Mariae,* bath of Maria, probably after *Maria,* an early alchemist.]

Baird (bârd), **John Logie.** 1888–1946. British electrical engineer and pioneer in the field of television, radar, and fiber optics.

Bai·ri·ki (bī-rē′kē). The administrative center of Kiribati, on Tarawa atoll in the northern Gilbert Islands of the west-central Pacific Ocean. Population, 1,956.

bairn (bârn) *n. Scots.* A child. [Middle English *barn,* from Old English *bearn.* See **bher-**[1] in Appendix.]

bait[1] (bāt) *n.* **1.a.** Food or other lure placed on a hook or in a trap and used in the taking of fish, birds, or other animals. **b.** Something, such as a worm, used for this purpose. **2.** An enticement; a temptation. **3.** *Archaic.* A stop for food or rest during a trip. —**bait** *v.* **bait·ed, bait·ing, baits.** —*tr.* **1.** To place a lure in (a trap) or on (a fishing hook). **2.** To entice, especially by trickery or strategy. **3.** To set dogs upon (a chained animal, for example) for sport. **4.** To attack or torment, especially with persistent insults, criticism, or ridicule. **5.** To tease. See Synonyms at **harass. 6.** To feed (an animal), especially on a journey. —*intr. Archaic.* To stop for food or rest during a trip. [Middle English, from Old Norse *beita,* food, fodder, fish bait. V., from Old Norse *beita,* to put animals to pasture, hunt with dogs. See **bheid-** in Appendix.] —**bait′er** *n.*

USAGE NOTE: The word *baited* is sometimes incorrectly substituted for the etymologically correct but unfamiliar word *bated* ("abated; suspended") in the expression *bated breath.*

bait[2] (bāt) *v.* Variant of **bate**[2]**.**

bait and switch *n.* A sales tactic in which a bargain-priced item is used to attract customers who are then encouraged to purchase a more expensive similar item.

♦ **bait·fish** (bāt′fĭsh′) *n. Chiefly Chesapeake Bay & North Atlantic Coast.* A small fish, such as a minnow, used for fishing bait.

bai·za (bī′zä) *n.* See table at **currency.** [Arabic, from Hindi *paisā.*]

baize (bāz) *n.* An often bright-green cotton or woolen material napped to imitate felt and used chiefly as a cover for gaming tables. [French *baies,* from pl. of *bai,* bay-colored, from Latin *badius.*]

Ba·ja Cal·i·for·nia (bä′hä kăl′ĭ-fôr′nyə, -fôr′nē-ə) also **Low·er California** (lō′ər). A mountainous peninsula of western Mexico extending south-southeast between the Pacific Ocean and the Gulf of California south of the U.S. border. It was first explored by the Spanish in the 1530's.

Ba·jer (bī′ər), **Fredrik.** 1837–1922. Danish pacifist who was a founder and president of the International Peace Bureau in Bern, Switzerland. He shared the 1908 Nobel Peace Prize.

bake (bāk) *v.* **baked, bak·ing, bakes.** —*tr.* **1.** To cook (food) with dry heat, especially in an oven. **2.** To harden or dry (something) by subjecting to heat in or as if in an oven: *bake bricks.* —*intr.* **1.** To cook food with dry heat. **2.** To become hardened or dry by or as if by having been subjected to the heat of an oven. —**bake** *n.* **1.a.** The act or process of baking. **b.** An amount baked. **2.** A social gathering at which food is cooked by baking and served. [Middle English *baken,* from Old English *bacan.*]

Ba·ke·lite (bā′kə-līt′, bāk′līt′). A trademark used for any of a group of synthetic resins and plastics found in a variety of manufactured articles.

bake-off (bāk′ôf′, -ŏf′) *adj.* Of, relating to, or being a bakery, as in a supermarket, that cooks preprepared pastry goods for public sale. —**bake′-off′** *n.*

Bake-Off (bāk′ôf′, -ŏf′). A service mark used for a contest in which cooks prepare their own recipes, usually of baked goods, and prizes are awarded for originality and taste. This service mark sometimes occurs in lowercase with the meaning "any contest among cooks": *"All the jockeying for support that has been going on recently has added a new dimension to the proceedings, as if there were a bake-off being held in the next room"* (New York Times).

bak·er (bā′kər) *n.* **1.** One that bakes bread, cakes, or pastries, especially commercially. **2.** One that bakes, especially a portable oven.

Ba·ker (bākər), **Ella.** 1903–1986. American social reformer whose organizational efforts were a major force behind the civil rights movement of the 1950's and 1960's.

Baker, George[1]. Known as "Father Divine." 1877–1965. American religious leader who founded (1919) a communal religious sect called the Peace Mission.

Baker, George[2]. 1915–1975. American cartoonist who created *Sad Sack* (1942), a comic strip about a hapless GI.

Baker, Josephine. 1906–1975. American-born French entertainer who became a popular jazz dancer and singer in Paris during the 1920's and 1930's. During World War II she worked for the French Resistance.

Baker, Mount. A peak, 3,287.3 m (10,778 ft) high, of northwest Washington in the Cascade Range east of Bellingham. It is in a popular resort area.

Baker, Newton Diehl. 1871–1937. American public official and lawyer who served as secretary of war under President Woodrow Wilson (1916–1921) and was appointed to the Permanent Court of Arbitration at The Hague (1928).

Baker, Russell Wayne. Born 1925. American writer. A longtime *New York Times* columnist, he won a Pulitzer Prize in 1979 for distinguished commentary and in 1983 for his autobiography *Growing Up*.

Baker, Sir **Samuel White.** 1821–1893. British explorer who founded a settlement at Ceylon (1848), explored the Blue Nile region (1861–1862), and discovered Lake Albert (1864).

Baker, Sara Josephine. 1873–1945. American pediatrician and public-health pioneer whose work helped reduce the infant mortality rate in New York City to the lowest level of any large American city.

Baker Lake. A lake of eastern Northwest Territories, Canada, near Chesterfield Inlet, an arm of Hudson Bay.

bak·er's dozen (bā′kərz) *n.* A group of 13. [From the former custom among bakers of adding an extra roll as a safeguard against the possibility of 12 weighing light.]

Ba·kers·field (bā′kərz-fēld′). A city of south-central California at the southern end of the fertile San Joaquin Valley north-northwest of Los Angeles. Gold was discovered in the region in 1855 and petroleum in 1899. Population, 105,735.

♦ **bak·er·sheet** (bā′kər-shēt′) *n. Maine.* See **drip pan.**

baker's yeast *n.* A commercial preparation consisting of dried cells of one or more strains of the fungus *Saccharomyces cerevisiae*, used as a leavening in baking.

bak·er·y (bā′kə-rē) *n., pl.* **-ies.** A place where products such as bread, cake, and pastries are baked or sold. Also called *bakeshop*.

bake·shop (bāk′shŏp′) *n.* See **bakery.**

Bakh·ta·ran (băk′tə-răn′, bäKH′tä-). Formerly **Ker·man·shah** (kĕr-män′shä′, -shô′). A city of western Iran west-southwest of Tehran. Founded in the fourth century A.D., it was later a frontier fortress against the Ottoman Turks. Population, 532,000.

bak·ing powder (bā′kĭng) *n.* A mixture of baking soda, starch, and at least one slightly acidic compound such as cream of tartar that works as a leavening agent in baking by releasing carbon dioxide when mixed with a liquid, such as milk or water.

baking soda *n.* A white crystalline compound, $NaHCO_3$, with a slightly alkaline taste, used in making effervescent salts and beverages, artificial mineral water, pharmaceuticals, and fire extinguishers. Also called *bicarbonate of soda, sodium bicarbonate.*

ba·kla·va (bä′klə-vä′, bä′klə-vä′) *n.* A dessert made of paper-thin layers of pastry, chopped nuts, and honey. [Turkish.]

bak·sheesh (băk′shēsh′, băk-shēsh′) *n., pl.* **baksheesh.** A gratuity or tip, paid to expedite service especially in some Near Eastern countries. [Persian *bakhshish*, present, from Middle Persian *bakhshishn*, from *bakhshīdan, bakhsh-*, to give presents, from Avestan *bakhsh-*. See **bhag-** in Appendix.]

Bakst (bäkst), **Léon Nikolaevich.** 1866–1924. Russian painter and scenic designer who modernized theater design. His best-known works were for ballets produced by Sergei Diaghilev in Paris.

Ba·ku (bä-ko͞o′). A city of eastern Azerbaijan on the western shore of the Caspian Sea. Frequently under Persian rule, the city was incorporated into Russia in 1806. It has been a center of oil production since the 1870's. Population, 1,104,000.

Ba·ku·nin (bə-ko͞o′nĭn, -nyĭn), **Mikhail Aleksandrovich.** 1814–1876. Russian anarchist and political theorist who was imprisoned and later exiled to Siberia for his revolutionary activities. He escaped to London (1861), where he opposed Karl Marx.

BAL *abbr.* British anti-lewisite.

bal·a·cla·va (băl′əklä′və) *n.* **1.** A woolen hood almost completely covering the head and neck, worn by mountain climbers and skiers in cold climates. **2.** A similar hood often covering the shoulders, worn by soldiers and sailors. [After BALAKLAVA.]

Bal·a·cla·va (băl′ə-klăv′ə, -klä′və). See **Balaklava.**

Ba·la·ki·rev (bə-lä′kĭ-rəf), **Mili Alekseevich.** 1837–1910. Russian composer whose works combine romanticism with folk music. The symphonic poems *Tamara* and *Russia* are among his best-known compositions.

Bal·a·kla·va also **Bal·a·cla·va** (băl′ə-klăv′ə, -klä′və). A section of Sevastopol in the Crimea of southern Ukraine. During the Crimean War Balaklava became famous for the doomed charge of the British Light Brigade against heavy Russian fire (October 25, 1854).

bal·a·lai·ka (băl′ə-lī′kə) *n. Music.* A Russian instrument with a triangular body and three strings that produces sounds like those of a mandolin. [Russian *balalaĭka*, of Turkic origin.]

bal·ance (băl′əns) *n.* **1.** A weighing device, especially one consisting of a rigid beam horizontally suspended by a low-friction support at its center, with identical weighing pans hung at either end, one of which holds an unknown weight while the effective weight in the other is increased by known amounts until the beam is level and motionless. **2.** A state of equilibrium or parity characterized by cancellation of all forces by equal opposing forces. **3.** The power or means to decide. **4.** A state of bodily equilibrium. **5.** A stable mental or psychological state; emotional stability. **6.** A harmonious or satisfying arrangement or proportion of parts or elements, as in a design. **7.** An influence or force tending to produce equilibrium; counterpoise. **8.** The difference in magnitude between opposing forces or influences. **9.** *Accounting.* **a.** Equality of totals in the debit and credit sides of an account. **b.** The difference between such totals, either on the credit or the debit side. **10.** Something that is left over; a remainder. **11.** *Chemistry.* Equality of mass and net electric charge of reacting species on each side of an equation. **12.** *Mathematics.* Equality with respect to the net number of reduced symbolic quantities on each side of an equation. **13.** A balance wheel. **—balance** *v.* **-anced, -anc·ing, -anc·es.** —*tr.* **1.** To determine the weight of (something) in or as if in a weighing device. **2.** To compare by or as if by turning over in the mind: *balanced the pros and cons before making a final decision.* **3.** To bring into or maintain in a state of equilibrium. **4.** To act as an equalizing weight or force to; counterbalance. **5.** *Accounting.* **a.** To compute the difference between the debits and credits of (an account). **b.** To reconcile or equalize the sums of the debits and credits of (an account). **c.** To settle (an account, for example) by paying what is owed. **6.** To bring into or keep in equal or satisfying proportion or harmony. **7.** *Mathematics.* To bring (an equation) into balance. **8.** *Chemistry.* To bring (an equation) into balance. **9.** To move toward and then away from (a dance partner). —*intr.* **1.** To be in or come into equilibrium. **2.** To be equal or equivalent. **3.** To sway or waver as if losing or regaining equilibrium. **4.** To move toward and then away from a dance partner. **—*idioms.* in the balance.** In an undetermined and often critical position: *Our plans were left hanging in the balance. Resolution of these matters is still in the balance.* **on balance.** Taking everything into consideration; all in all. [Middle English *balaunce*, from Old French, from Vulgar Latin **bilancia*, having two scale pans, from Latin *bilanx* : *bi-*, two; see **dwo-** in Appendix + *lanx*, scale.]

SYNONYMS: *balance, equilibrium, equipoise, poise.* The central meaning shared by these nouns is "a state of stability resulting from the cancellation of all forces by equal opposing forces": *upsetting the balance of nature through the use of insecticides; equilibrium of power between Western and Eastern countries; the weights of a scale in equipoise; a poise between disparate and contradictory emotions.* See also Synonyms at **proportion, remainder.**
ANTONYM: *imbalance.*

Bal·ance (băl′əns) *n.* See **Libra** (senses 1, 2a).

balance beam *n. Sports.* **1.** A horizontal, raised beam with a width of 10 centimeters (4 inches) and a length of 5 meters (16 feet) that is used in gymnastic competition for balancing exercises. **2.** A competitive gymnastics event in which various balancing feats are performed on this beam.

balance of payments *n.* A systematic record of a nation's total payments to foreign countries, including the price of imports, the outflow of capital and gold, and the total receipts from abroad, including the price of exports and the inflow of capital and gold.

balance of power *n.* Distribution of power in which no single nation is able to dominate or interfere with others.

balance of terror *n.* Evenly distributed military power between two or more potentially belligerent nations such that the equilibrium constitutes a deterrent to nuclear or limited war: *"Will the balance of terror ever end? Will it end in a balance free from terror, or a terror lacking all balance?"* (Edward Teller).

balance of trade *n.* The difference in value between the total exports and total imports of a nation during a specific period of time.

bal·anc·er (băl′ən-sər) *n.* See **halter[2].**

balance sheet *n. Abbr.* **B.S.** A statement of a business or an institution that lists the assets, debts, and owners' investment as of a specified date.

balance wheel *n.* **1.** A wheel that regulates rate of movement

balalaika
20th-century Russian

balance
16th-century
German or Flemish

balance beam

ă pat	oi boy
ā pay	ou out
âr care	o͝o took
ä father	o͞o boot
ĕ pet	ŭ cut
ē be	ûr urge
ĭ pit	th thin
ī pie	*th* this
îr pier	hw which
ŏ pot	zh vision
ō toe	ə about, item
ô paw	♦ regionalism

Stress marks: ′ (primary); ′ (secondary), as in **dictionary** (dĭk′shə-nĕr′ē)

in machine parts, as in a watch. **2.** A stabilizing influence.

Bal·an·chine (băl′ən-chēn′, băl′ən-chēn′), **George.** Originally Georgi Balanchivadze. 1904–1983. Russian-born American ballet director and choreographer who became artistic director of the New York City Ballet in 1948 and choreographed more than 100 ballets, including *Firebird* (1950) and *Don Quixote* (1965).

bal·as (băl′əs) *n.* A rose-red to orange spinel used as a semiprecious gem, once confused with the ruby. [Middle English, from Old French *balais* and from Old Spanish *balax;* both akin to Medieval Latin *balascus,* from Arabic *balakhš,* from Persian *Badakhshān,* a region of northeast Afghanistan.]

ba·la·ta (bə-lä′tə) *n.* The nonelastic rubber obtained from the latex of the South American tree *Manilkara bidentata.* It has been used in the manufacture of golf-ball covers and machine belts. [American Spanish, from Tupi and Galibi.]

Bal·a·ton (băl′ə-tŏn′, bŏl′ŏ-tôn′), **Lake.** A lake of west-central Hungary southwest of Budapest. It is the largest lake in central Europe, with many tourist and health resorts.

bal·bo·a (băl-bō′ə) *n.* See table at **currency.** [After Vasco Núñez de BALBOA.]

Bal·bo·a (băl-bō′ə), **Vasco Núñez de.** 1475–1517. Spanish explorer and colonial governor who discovered (1513) the Pacific Ocean and claimed it for Spain.

bal·brig·gan (băl-brĭg′ən) *n.* A knitted, unbleached cotton fabric for underwear. [After *Balbriggan,* a seaport of eastern Ireland.]

Balch (bôlch), **Emily Greene.** 1867–1961. American economist and sociologist. A founder of the Women's International League for Peace and Freedom (1919), she shared the 1946 Nobel Peace Prize.

balcony
Apartment complex

bal·co·ny (băl′kə-nē) *n., pl.* **-nies. 1.** A platform that projects from the wall of a building and is surrounded by a railing, balustrade, or parapet. **2.** A gallery that projects over the main floor in a theater or an auditorium. [Italian *balcone,* from Old Italian, scaffold, of Germanic origin.]

bald (bôld) *adj.* **bald·er, bald·est. 1.** Lacking hair on the head. **2.** Lacking a natural or usual covering: *a bald spot on the lawn.* **3.** *Zoology.* Having white feathers or markings on the head, as in some birds or mammals. **4.** Lacking ornamentation; unadorned. **5.** Undisguised; blunt: *a bald statement of policy.* [Middle English *balled,* probably from *bal,* ball. See BALL[1].] **—bald′ly** *adv.* **—bald′ness** *n.*

bal·da·chin (bôl′də-kĭn, băl′-) also **bal·da·chi·no** (băl′də-kē′nō) *n., pl.* **-chins** also **-chi·nos. 1.** A rich fabric of silk and gold brocade. **2.** A canopy of fabric carried in church processions or placed over an altar, a throne, or a dais. **3.** *Architecture.* A stone or marble structure built in the form of a canopy, especially over the altar of a church. [Italian *baldacchino,* from Old Italian, from *Baldacco,* Baghdad.]

bald eagle
Haliaeetus leucocephalus

bald cypress *n.* **1.** A deciduous, coniferous tree *(Taxodium distichum)* native to the swamps and streamsides of the southeast United States, having alternate, awl-shaped leaves, globose cones, and sometimes aerial root knees. **2.** The decay-resistant wood of this plant, used in construction and boat building.

bald eagle *n.* A North American eagle *(Haliaeetus leucocephalus)* characterized by a brownish-black body and a white head and tail in the adult. Also called *American eagle.*

bal·der·dash (bôl′dər-dăsh′) *n.* Nonsense. [Possibly alteration of Medieval Latin *balductum,* posset.]

bald-faced (bôld′fāst′) *adj.* **1.** Brash; undisguised: *a bald-faced lie.* **2.** *Zoology.* Having a white face or face markings.

bald·head (bôld′hĕd′) *n.* **1.** A person whose head is bald. Also called *baldpate.* **2.** Any of several birds having white markings on the head.

bald·ing (bôl′dĭng) *adj.* Becoming bald.

USAGE NOTE: The word *balding* was popularized by the newsmagazines of the 1930's and was for a long time associated with breezy, journalistic style. It has since passed into general usage, however, and has lost its earlier association with journalism.

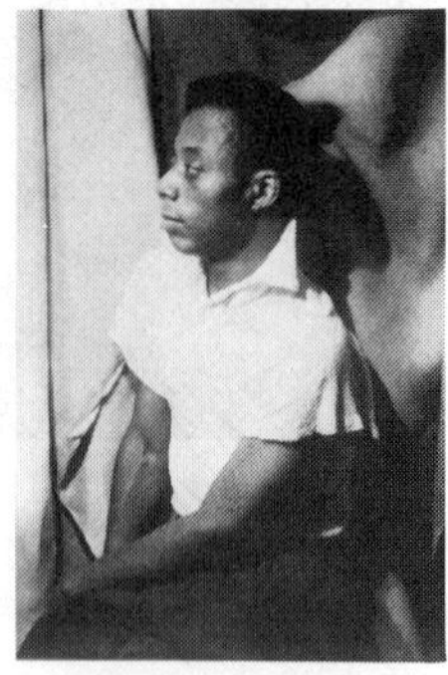

James Baldwin
1983 photogravure by Carl Van Vechten, from a 1955 negative

bald·pate (bôld′pāt′) *n.* **1.** See **baldhead** (sense 1). **2.** The widgeon of North America.

bal·dric (bôl′drĭk) *n.* A belt, usually of ornamented leather, worn across the chest to support a sword or bugle. [Middle English *baudrik,* from Old French *baudre* and from Middle High German *balderich.*]

ă pat	oi boy
ā pay	ou out
âr care	ŏŏ took
ä father	ōō boot
ĕ pet	ŭ cut
ē be	ûr urge
ĭ pit	th thin
ī pie	*th* this
îr pier	hw which
ŏ pot	zh vision
ō toe	ə about, item
ô paw	♦ regionalism

Stress marks: **′** (primary); ′ (secondary), as in **dictionary** (dĭk′shə-nĕr′ē)

Bald·win[1] (bôld′wĭn). A borough of southwest Pennsylvania, a suburb of Pittsburgh on the Monongahela River. Population, 24,712.

Bald·win[2] (bôld′wĭn) *n.* An American variety of apple with red or yellow and red skin. [After Loammi BALDWIN.]

Baldwin I. 1058–1118. King of Jerusalem (1100–1118) who was appointed to the throne after taking part in the First Crusade (1096–1099).

Baldwin, Henry. 1780–1844. American jurist who served as an associate justice of the U.S. Supreme Court (1830–1844).

Baldwin, James Arthur. 1924–1987. American writer and outspoken critic of racism whose works include *Go Tell It on the Mountain* (1953), a novel, and *Notes of a Native Son* (1955), a collection of essays.

Baldwin, James Mark. 1861–1934. American psychologist and editor who founded and edited (1894–1909) the *Psychological Review.*

Baldwin, Loammi. 1745–1807. American engineer who built (1794–1804) the Middlesex Canal in Massachusetts and developed the Baldwin apple.

Baldwin, Roger Nash. 1884–1981. American civil rights activist. In 1918 he helped found the American Civil Liberties Union, which he directed from 1920 to 1950.

Baldwin, Stanley. First Earl Baldwin of Bewdley. 1867–1947. British prime minister (1923–1929 and 1935–1937) who responded to the General Strike of 1926 with the Trade Disputes Act of 1927, an antiunion bill, and facilitated the abdication of Edward VIII (1936).

Baldwin Park. A city of southern California, a residential suburb of Los Angeles near the San Gabriel Mountains. Population, 50,554.

bale[1] (bāl) *n.* A large package of raw or finished material tightly bound with twine or wire and often wrapped. **—bale** *tr.v.* **baled, bal·ing, bales.** To wrap in a bale or in bales. [Middle English, from Old French. See **bhel-[2]** in Appendix.] **—bal′er** *n.*

bale[2] (bāl) *n.* **1.** Evil: *"Tidings of bale she brought"* (William Cullen Bryant). **2.** Mental suffering; anguish: *"Relieve my spirit from the bale that bows it down"* (Benjamin Disraeli). [Middle English, from Old English *bealu.*]

Bal·e·ar·ic Islands (băl′ē-ăr′ĭk). An archipelago in the western Mediterranean Sea off the eastern coast of Spain. Noted for their scenery and mild climate, the islands are a major tourist center.

ba·leen (bə-lēn′) *n.* See **whalebone** (sense 1). [Middle English *balene,* from Old French *baleine,* from Latin *balaena,* whale, from Greek *phalaina.* See **bhel-[2]** in Appendix.]

baleen whale *n.* Any of several usually large whales of the suborder Mysticeti, such as the right whale and rorquals, having a symmetrical skull, two blowholes, and whalebone plates instead of teeth. Also called *mysticete, whalebone whale.*

bale·ful (bāl′fəl) *adj.* **1.** Portending evil; ominous. See Synonyms at **sinister. 2.** Harmful or malignant in intent or effect. **—bale′ful·ly** *adv.* **—bale′ful·ness** *n.*

USAGE NOTE: *Baleful* and *baneful* overlap in meaning, but *baleful* usually applies to that which menaces or foreshadows evil: *a baleful look. Baneful* is said most often of that which is actually harmful or destructive: *baneful effects of their foreign policy.*

Bal·four (băl′fŏŏr′, -fôr′, -fōr′), **Arthur James.** First Earl of Balfour. 1848–1930. British prime minister (1902–1905) who later served as foreign secretary under David Lloyd George (1916–1919). In 1917 he promised British support for a national homeland for Jews in Palestine, provided that the rights of existing communities would be safeguarded.

Ba·li (bä′lē). An island of southern Indonesia in the Lesser Sundas just east of Java. Largely mountainous with a tropical climate and fertile soil, it is sometimes called the "the Jewel of the East."

Ba·lik·pa·pan (bä′lĭk-pä′pän). A city of Indonesia in southeast Borneo on an inlet of Makassar Strait. It is a major port and oil center. Population, 208,040.

Ba·li·nese (bä′lə-nēz′, -nēs′) *adj.* Of or relating to Bali or its people, language, or culture. **—Balinese** *n., pl.* **Balinese. 1.** A native or inhabitant of Bali. **2.** The Indonesian language of Bali.

Balinese cat *n.* A domestic cat that is a hybrid between the Persian and Siamese and that closely resembles the Siamese in appearance but has long, silky fur.

balk also **baulk** (bôk) *—v.* **balked, balk·ing, balks** also **baulked, baulk·ing, baulks.** *—intr.* **1.** To stop short and refuse to go on: *The horse balked at the jump.* **2.** To refuse obstinately or abruptly: *She balked at the very idea of compromise.* **3. a.** *Sports.* To make an incomplete or misleading motion. **b.** *Baseball.* To make an illegal motion before pitching, allowing one or more base runners to advance one base. *—tr.* **1.** To put obstacles in the way of; check or thwart. See Synonyms at **frustrate. 2.** *Archaic.* To let go by; miss. *—n.* **1.** A hindrance, check, or defeat. **2.** *Sports.* An incomplete or misleading motion, especially an illegal move made by a baseball pitcher. **3.** *Games.* One of the spaces between the cushion and the balk line on a billiard table. **4. a.** An unplowed strip of land. **b.** A ridge between furrows. **5.** A wooden beam or rafter. [Middle English *balken,* to plow up in ridges, from *balk,* ridge, from Old English *balca* and from Old Norse *balkr,* beam.] **—balk′er** *n.*

Bal·kan (bôl′kən) *adj.* **1.** Of or relating to the Balkan Peninsula or the Balkan Mountains. **2.** Of or relating to the Balkan States or their inhabitants.

Bal·kan·ize or **bal·kan·ize** (bôl′kə-nīz′) *tr.v.* **-ized, -iz·ing, -iz·es.** To divide (a region or territory) into small, often hostile units. [From the political division of the Balkans in the early 20th century.] **—Bal′kan·i·za′tion** *n.*

Balkan Mountains also **Bal·kans** (bôl′kənz). A major mountain system of southeast Europe extending about 563 km (350 mi) from eastern Yugoslavia through central Bulgaria to the Black Sea. The Balkans are a continuation of the Carpathian Mountains and rise to 2,377.2 m (7,794 ft).

Balkan Peninsula also **Balkans.** A peninsula of southeast Europe bounded by the Black Sea, the Sea of Marmara, and the Aegean, Mediterranean, Ionian, and Adriatic seas. The **Balkan**

States include Albania, Bulgaria, continental Greece, southeast Romania, European Turkey, and most of Yugoslavia. Formerly part of the Roman and Byzantine empires, the region fell to the Ottoman Turks by 1500. Nationalist movements, the Balkan Wars (1912–1913 and 1913), and treaties signed after World War I led to the present country boundaries.

Balkh (bälk). Formerly **Bac·tra** (băk′trə). An ancient city in present-day northern Afghanistan. One of the world's oldest settlements, it was the capital of Bactria and is the legendary birthplace of the prophet Zoroaster.

Bal·khash (băl-kăsh′, bäl-käsh′, -KHäsh′), **Lake.** A shallow lake of southeast Kazakhstan. It has saline water in the east and fresh water in the west.

balk line also **balk·line** (bôk′līn′) *n. Games.* A line parallel to one end of a billiard table, from behind which opening shots with the cue ball are made.

balk·y (bô′kē) *adj.* **-i·er, -i·est. 1.** Given to stopping and refusing to go on: *a balky horse; a balky client.* See Synonyms at **contrary. 2.** Difficult to operate or start: *a balky switch; a balky engine.* **—balk′i·ness** *n.*

ball[1] (bôl) *n.* **1.a.** A spherical or almost spherical body: *a ball of flame.* **b.** A spherical object or entity: *a steel ball.* **2.** *Sports & Games.* **a.** Any of various rounded, movable objects used in various athletic activities and games. **b.** Such an object moving, thrown, hit, or kicked in a particular manner: *a low ball; a fair ball.* **c.** A game, especially baseball, played with such an object. **d.** A pitched baseball that does not pass through the strike zone and is not swung at by the batter. **3.a.** A solid spherical or pointed projectile, such as one shot from a cannon. **b.** Projectiles of this kind considered as a group. **4.** A rounded part or protuberance, especially of the body: *the ball of the foot.* **5. balls.** *Vulgar Slang.* **a.** The testicles. **b.** Courage, especially when reckless. **c.** Great presumptuousness. **—ball** *v.* **balled, ball·ing, balls.** *—tr.* **1.** To form into a ball. **2.** *Vulgar Slang.* To have sexual intercourse with. *—intr.* **1.** To become formed into a ball. **2.** *Vulgar Slang.* To have sexual intercourse. ***—phrasal verb.*** **ball up.** To confuse; bungle. ***—idiom.*** **on the ball.** *Informal.* **1.** Alert, competent, or efficient: *a teacher who is really on the ball.* **2.** Relating to qualities, such as competence, skill, or knowledge, that are necessary for success: *a manager who has a lot on the ball; a student who has nothing on the ball.* [Middle English *bal,* probably from Old English **beall.* See **bhel-**[2] in Appendix.]

ball[2] (bôl) *n.* **1.** A formal gathering for social dancing. **2.** *Slang.* An extremely enjoyable time or experience: *We had a ball during our vacation.* [French *bal,* from Old French, from *baller,* to dance, from Late Latin *ballāre,* from Greek *ballizein.* See **gʷelə-** in Appendix.]

Ball (bôl), **John.** Called "the Mad Priest." Died 1381. English social agitator who was executed for his role in the Peasants' Revolt (1381).

Ball, Lucille. 1911–1989. American actress best known as the star of the popular situation comedy *I Love Lucy* (1951–1956).

bal·lad (băl′əd) *n.* **1.a.** A narrative poem, often of folk origin and intended to be sung, consisting of simple stanzas and usually having a recurrent refrain. **b.** The music for such a poem. **2.** *Music.* A popular song especially of a romantic or sentimental nature. *—attributive.* Often used to modify another noun: *a ballad singer; ballad compositions.* [Middle English *balade,* poem or song in stanza form, from Old French *ballade,* from Old Provençal *balada,* song sung while dancing, from *balar,* to dance, from Late Latin *ballāre,* to dance. See BALL[2].] **—bal·lad′ic** (bə-lăd′ĭk, bă-) *adj.*

bal·lade (bə-läd′, bă-) *n.* **1.** A verse form usually consisting of three stanzas of eight or ten lines each along with a brief envoy, with all three stanzas and the envoy ending in the same one-line refrain. **2.** *Music.* A composition, usually for the piano, having the romantic or dramatic quality of a ballad. [Middle English *balade.* See BALLAD.]

bal·lad·eer (băl′ə-dîr′) *n. Music.* A singer of ballads.

bal·lad·ist (băl′ə-dĭst′) *n.* A singer or composer of ballads.

bal·lad·ry (băl′ə-drē) *n.* Ballads considered as a group.

ballad stanza *n.* A four-line stanza often used in ballads, rhyming in the second and fourth lines and having four metrical feet in the first and third lines and three in the second and fourth.

ball-and-sock·et joint (bôl′ən-sŏk′ĭt) *n.* **1.** A synovial joint, such as the shoulder or hip joint, in which a spherical knob or knoblike part of one bone fits into a cavity or socket of another, so that some degree of rotary motion is possible in every direction. Also called *enarthrosis.* **2.** A joint, as in a mechanical device, that permits rotary movement in all directions through the movement of a ball in a socket.

bal·last (băl′əst) *n.* **1.** Heavy material that is placed in the hold of a ship or the gondola of a balloon to enhance stability. **2.a.** Coarse gravel or crushed rock laid to form a bed for roads or railroads. **b.** The gravel ingredient of concrete. **3.** Something that gives stability, especially in character. **—ballast** *tr.v.* **-last·ed, -last·ing, -lasts. 1.** To stabilize or provide with ballast. **2.** To fill (a railroad bed) with or as if with ballast. [Perhaps from Old Swedish or Old Danish *barlast* : *bar,* mere, bare; see **bhoso-** in Appendix + *last,* load.]

ball bearing *n. Abbr.* **bb, b.b. 1.** A friction-reducing bearing consisting essentially of a ring-shaped track containing freely revolving hard metal balls against which a rotating shaft or other part turns. **2.** A hard ball used in such a bearing.

ball boy *n. Sports.* **1.** A male attendant on a tennis court who collects the ball when it is out of play. **2.** A boy who is in charge of the extra balls used in practice or those that are out of play, especially in baseball.

ball carrier or **ball·car·ri·er** (bôl′kăr′ē-ər) *n. Football.* A player who carries the ball on an offensive play.

ball cock *n.* A self-regulating device controlling the supply of water in a tank, cistern, or toilet by means of a float connected to a valve that opens or closes with a change in water level.

bal·le·ri·na (băl′ə-rē′nə) *n.* **1.** A principal woman dancer in a ballet company. **2.** A woman ballet dancer. [Italian, from *ballare,* to dance, from Late Latin *ballāre,* from Greek *ballizein.* See BALL[2].]

bal·let (bă-lā′, băl′ā′) *n.* **1.** A classical dance form characterized by grace and precision of movement and elaborate formal technique, often but not always performed on point by the women dancers. **2.** A theatrical presentation of group or solo dancing to a musical accompaniment, usually with costume and scenic effects, conveying a story or theme. **3.** A musical composition written or used for this dance form. **4.** A company or group that performs ballet. [French, from Italian *balletto,* diminutive of *ballo,* dance, from *ballare,* to dance. See BALLERINA.] **—bal·let′ic** (bă-lĕt′ĭk) *adj.*

bal·let·o·mane (bă-lĕt′ə-mān′) *n.* An ardent admirer of the ballet. [French : *ballet,* ballet; see BALLET + *-mane,* ardent admirer (from Greek *-manēs;* see MANIA).] **—bal·let′o·ma′ni·a** (-mā′nē-ə, -mān′yə) *n.*

ball·flow·er (bôl′flou′ər) *n. Architecture.* An ornament in the form of a ball cupped in the petals of a circular flower.

ball game also **ball·game** (bô′gām′) *n.* **1.** *Sports.* A game, especially baseball, that is played with a ball. **2.** *Slang.* **a.** A competition: *"But in the winner-take-all world of politics, the contest for the undecided 2 or 3 percent can be the whole ballgame"* (Brad Edmondson). **b.** A particular condition, situation, or set of circumstances. **3.** *Anthropology.* A game with religious and political significance in Maya and other Mesoamerican societies before the Spanish conquest, played with a rubber ball on a walled court.

ball girl *n. Sports.* **1.** A woman attendant on a tennis court who collects the ball when it is out of play. **2.** A girl who is in charge of the extra balls used in practice or those that are out of play, especially in baseball.

bal·lis·ta (bə-lĭs′tə) *n., pl.* **-tae** (-tē′). An ancient and medieval engine of warfare used to hurl heavy projectiles at a target. [Latin, from Greek *ballistēs,* from *ballein,* to throw. See **gʷelə-** in Appendix.]

bal·lis·tic (bə-lĭs′tĭk) *adj.* **1.a.** Of or relating to the study of the dynamics of projectiles. **b.** Of or relating to the study of the internal action of firearms. **2.** Of or relating to projectiles, their motion, or their effects. [From BALLISTA.] **—bal·lis′ti·cal·ly** *adv.*

ballistic missile *n.* A projectile that assumes a free-falling trajectory after an internally guided, self-powered ascent.

bal·lis·tics (bə-lĭs′tĭks) *n. (used with a sing. verb).* **1.a.** The study of the dynamics of projectiles. **b.** The study of the flight characteristics of projectiles. **2.a.** The study of the functioning of firearms. **b.** The study of the firing, flight, and effects of ammunition. **—ballistics** *adj.* Of, relating to, or engaging in the study of ballistics: *a ballistics lab; ballistics experts.* **—bal′lis·ti′cian** (băl′ĭ-stĭsh′ən) *n.*

bal·lis·to·car·di·o·gram (bə-lĭs′tō-kär′dē-ə-grăm′) *n.* A recording made by a ballistocardiograph. [BALLIST(IC) + CARDIOGRAM.]

bal·lis·to·car·di·o·graph (bə-lĭs′tō-kär′dē-ə-grăf′) *n.* A device used to determine the volume of blood passing through the heart in a specific period of time and the force of cardiac contraction by measuring the body's recoil as blood is ejected from the ventricles with each heartbeat. [BALLIST(IC) + CARDIOGRAPH.] **—bal·lis′to·car′di·og′ra·phy** (-ŏg′rə-fē) *n.*

ball lightning *n.* A rare form of lightning in the shape of a glowing red ball, associated with thunderstorms and thought to consist of ionized gas.

ball of fire *n., pl.* **balls of fire.** A highly energetic or dynamic person. Also called *fireball.*

ball of wax *n. Slang.* An unspecified set of items or circumstances: *shopped, had dinner, saw a play—the whole ball of wax.*

bal·lo·net (băl′ə-nā′) *n.* One of several small, auxiliary gasbags placed inside a balloon or a nonrigid airship that can be inflated or deflated during flight to control and maintain shape and buoyancy. [French *ballonnet,* diminutive of *ballon,* balloon. See BALLOON.]

bal·loon (bə-lo͞on′) *n.* **1.a.** A flexible, nonporous bag inflated with a gas, such as helium, that is lighter than the surrounding air, that causes the bag to rise and float in the atmosphere. **b.** Such a bag with sufficient capacity to lift a suspended gondola or other payload. **2.** Any of variously shaped, brightly colored inflatable rubber bags used as toys. **3.** *Medicine.* A sac that is inserted into a body cavity or tube and distended with air or gas for therapeutic purposes, such as angioplasty. **4.** A rounded or irregularly shaped outline containing the words that a character in a cartoon is represented to be saying. **—balloon** *v.* **-looned, -loon·ing, -loons.** *—intr.* **1.** To ascend or ride in a balloon. **2.** To expand or swell out like a balloon. See Synonyms at **bulge. 3.** To in-

ballast
On the gondola of a hot-air balloon

ball cock

ballet

balloon
Hot-air balloons

crease or rise quickly. —*tr.* To cause to expand by or as if by inflating. —**balloon** *adj.* Suggestive of a balloon, as in shape: *balloon curtains.* [French *ballon,* from Italian dialectal *ballone,* augmentative of *balla,* ball, of Germanic origin. See **bhel-**[2] in Appendix.] —**bal·loon′ist** *n.*

balloon flower *n.* An east Asian perennial herb *(Platycodon grandiflorus),* having large, star-shaped, often violet-blue flowers and grown as an ornamental.

balloon mortgage *n.* A mortgage with periodic payments that are insufficient to pay back a note, thereby requiring a large final payment.

balloon sail *n. Nautical.* A comparatively large foresail used when going before the wind to supplement or replace a jib.

balloon tire *n.* A wide pneumatic tire, inflated to low pressure.

balloon vine *n.* A tendril-bearing vine *(Cardiospermum halicacabum)* widespread in warm regions and having small, whitish flowers and bladderlike fruits.

bal·lot (băl′ət) *n.* **1.** A sheet of paper or a card used to cast or register a vote, especially a secret one. **2.** The act, process, or method of voting, especially in secret. **3.** A list of candidates running for office; a ticket. **4.** The total of all votes cast in an election. **5.** The right to vote; franchise. **6.** A small ball once used to register a secret vote. —**ballot** *intr.v.* **-lot·ed, -lot·ing, -lots. 1.** To cast a ballot; vote. **2.** To draw lots. [Italian *ballotta,* a small ball used to register a vote, diminutive of dialectal *balla,* ball, of Germanic origin. See **bhel-**[2] in Appendix.] —**bal·lot·er** *n.*

bal·lotte·ment (bə-lŏt′mənt) *n. Medicine.* A palpatory technique for detecting or examining a floating object in the body, as: **a.** The use of a finger to push sharply against the uterus and detect the presence or position of a fetus by its return impact. **b.** Palpation of the abdominal wall while a kidney is being pushed sharply from the backside, used as a test for determining the presence of a floating kidney. [French, from *ballotter,* to toss, from Italian *ballotta,* diminutive of dialectal *balla,* ball. See BALLOON.]

balsam fir
Abies balsamea

ball·park (bôl′pärk′) *n.* **1.** *Sports.* A park or stadium in which ball games are played. **2.** *Slang.* The approximately proper range, as of possibilities or alternatives: *Your estimate is right in the ballpark.* —**ballpark** *adj.* **1.** *Sports.* Of, relating to, or used in a park or stadium: *ballpark lights; ballpark seating.* **2.** *Slang.* Being approximately proper in range: *gave a ballpark estimate of future unit sales.*

ball-peen hammer (bôl′pēn′) *n.* A hammer having one end of the head hemispherical and used in working metal.

ball·point pen (bôl′point′) *n.* A pen having as its writing point a small ball bearing that transfers ink stored in a cartridge onto a writing surface.

ball·room (bôl′ro͞om′, -ro͝om′) *n.* A large room for dancing.

ballroom dance *n.* Any of various social dances, such as the fox trot, tango, or waltz, in which couples follow a conventional pattern of steps. —**ballroom dancing** *n.*

baluchithere

balls·y (bôl′zē) *adj.* **-i·er, -i·est.** *Vulgar Slang.* Very tough and courageous, often recklessly or presumptuously so.

ball valve *n.* A valve regulated by the position of a free-floating ball that moves in response to fluid or mechanical pressure.

bal·ly·hoo (băl′ē-ho͞o′) *n., pl.* **-hoos. 1.** Sensational or clamorous advertising. **2.** Noisy shouting or uproar. —**ballyhoo** *tr.v.* **-hooed, -hoo·ing, -hoos.** To advertise by sensational methods. [Origin unknown.]

WORD HISTORY: The origin of *ballyhoo* has been the subject of much speculation. This spelling has actually graced four different words: *ballyhoo,* "sensational advertising"; *ballyhoo,* a spelling of *balao,* a kind of fish; *ballyhoo,* a part of the name *ballyhoo bird,* about which more later; and *ballyhoo,* a sailor's epithet for a disliked ship. This last *ballyhoo* (first recorded in 1836) was thought to be related to, or the same as, the word *ballahou,* from Spanish *balahú,* "a type of schooner common in the Antilles." First recorded in 1867, *ballahou,* besides being a term for a specific kind of ship, was also used contemptuously of inferior ships. But the connection between these sailing terms or the name of the fish and our word *ballyhoo,* first recorded in 1901, has not been established. There may, however, be a tie between *ballyhoo* and the creature called a *ballyhoo bird.* According to a July 1880 article in *Harper's,* the bird had four wings and two heads and could whistle through one bill while singing through the other. Anyone who has ever hunted a snipe will know what hunting ballyhoo birds was like.

balustrade

bal·ly·rag (băl′ē-răg′) *v.* Variant of **bullyrag.**

balm (bäm) *n.* **1.a.** A chiefly Mediterranean perennial herb *(Melissa officinalis)* in the mint family, grown for its lemon-scented foliage, which is used as a seasoning or for tea. Also called *lemon balm.* **b.** Any of several related plants in the mint family, such as the bee balm and the horse balm. **2.** Any of various aromatic resins exuded from several trees and shrubs, especially the balm of Gilead *(Commiphora)* and related plants. **3.** An aromatic salve or oil. **4.** A pleasing aromatic fragrance. **5.** A soothing, healing, or comforting agent or quality. [Middle English *baume, balsam,* from Old French *basme,* from Latin *balsamum.* See BALSAM.]

Honoré de Balzac
1845 drawing by Carl Christian Vogel von Vogelstein (1788–1868)

bal·ma·caan (băl′mə-kăn′, -kän′) *n.* A loose, full overcoat with raglan sleeves, originally made of rough woolen cloth. [After *Balmacaan,* an estate near Inverness, Scotland.]

balm of Gil·e·ad (gĭl′ē-əd, -ăd′) *n.* **1.a.** Any of several trees or shrubs of the genus *Commiphora,* especially *C. opobalsamum,* of Arabia and Somalia. **b.** See **myrrh** (sense 1). **2.** A poplar tree of hybrid origin, with sticky, aromatic, resinous buds and heart-shaped leaves, cultivated as a shade tree. **3.** A shrubby plant *(Cedronella canariensis)* in the mint family, native to Madeira and the Canary Islands, having a large, lilac-to-violet corolla with two lips. [After GILEAD, known for its balm.]

Bal·mor·al (băl-môr′əl, -mŏr′-) *n.* **1.** A brimless Scottish cap with a flat, round top. **2.** Often **balmoral.** A heavy, laced walking shoe. [After *Balmoral* Castle in northeast Scotland.]

bal mu·sette (bäl′ mo͞o-zĕt′) *n.* A dance hall in France, with the music provided by an accordion band. [French : *bal,* dance + *musette,* musette.]

balm·y[1] (bä′mē) *adj.* **-i·er, -i·est. 1.** Having the quality or fragrance of balm; soothing. **2.** Mild and pleasant: *a balmy breeze.* —**balm′i·ly** *adv.* —**balm′i·ness** *n.*

balm·y[2] (bä′mē) *adj.* **-i·er, -i·est.** *Slang.* Eccentric in behavior. [Alteration of BARMY.] —**balm′i·ly** *adv.* —**balm′i·ness** *n.*

bal·ne·al (băl′nē-əl) *adj.* Of or relating to baths or bathing. [From Latin *balneum,* bath. See BAGNIO.]

bal·ne·ol·o·gy (băl′nē-ŏl′ə-jē) *n.* The science of baths or bathing, especially the study of the therapeutic use of mineral baths. [Latin *balneum,* bath; see BAGNIO + –LOGY.]

ba·lo·ney[1] (bə-lō′nē) *n., pl.* **-neys.** Variant of **bologna.**

ba·lo·ney[2] (bə-lō′nē) *n., pl.* **-neys.** *Slang.* Nonsense. [Probably variant of BOLOGNA.]

bal·sa (bôl′sə) *n.* **1.a.** A tropical American tree *(Ochroma pyramidale)* having wood that is soft, very light in weight, and that is used as a substitute for cork in insulation, floats, and crafts such as model airplanes. **b.** The wood of this tree. Also called *corkwood.* **2.** A raft consisting of a frame fastened to buoyant cylinders of wood or metal. [Spanish.]

bal·sam (bôl′səm) *n.* **1.a.** Any of several aromatic resins, such as balsam of Peru and Tolu balsam, that contain considerable amounts of benzoic acid, cinnamic acid, or both, or their esters. **b.** Any of several other fragrant plant resins, such as Canada balsam. **c.** A similar substance, especially a fragrant ointment used as medication; a balm. **2.** Any of various trees, especially the balsam fir, yielding an aromatic resinous substance. **3.** See **jewelweed.** [Latin *balsamum,* from Greek *balsamon.*]

balsam apple *n.* A tendril-bearing annual Old World vine *(Momordica balsamina),* grown as an ornamental for its yellow flowers and ovoid, orange, warty fruits that open at maturity to expose red-coated seeds.

balsam fir *n.* A North American tree *(Abies balsamea)* having a pyramidal shape and flattened needles. It is widely used as a Christmas tree and yields Canada balsam and pulpwood.

bal·sam·ic (bôl-săm′ĭk) *adj.* **1.** Of, relating to, or resembling balsam. **2.** Containing or yielding balsam.

bal·sam·if·er·ous (bôl′sə-mĭf′ər-əs) *adj.* Yielding balsam.

balsam of Pe·ru (pə-ro͞o′) *n.* The thick, brown, aromatic resin of a tropical American tree *(Myroxylon balsamum)* used medically in skin lotions and cough preparations and in the manufacture of perfumes. Also called *balsam of Tolu.*

balsam of To·lu (tə-lo͞o′) *n.* See **balsam of Peru.** [After *Tolú,* a seaport of northwest Colombia.]

balsam pear *n.* **1.** A tropical, Old World, tendril-bearing, annual vine *(Momordica charantia),* having yellow flowers and orange, warty fruits that open at maturity to expose red-coated seeds. **2.** The immature fruit of this plant, used as a vegetable in Asian cuisine. The ripe fruit is not eaten. In this sense, also called *bitter gourd.*

balsam poplar *n.* A poplar tree of northern North America *(Populus balsamifera)* having ovate leaves and large buds coated with a sticky, fragrant resin. Also called *hackmatack, tacamahac.*

bal·sam·root (bôl′səm-ro͞ot′, -ro͝ot′) *n.* Any of several western North American perennial herbs of the genus *Balsamorhiza* in the composite family, having radiate heads of yellow flowers. The large roots of some species were used as food by certain Native American peoples.

Bal·sas (bôl′səs, bäl′-). A river flowing about 724 km (450 mi) from south-central Mexico to the Pacific Ocean.

Balt (bôlt) *n.* **1.** A speaker of a Baltic language. **2.** A native or inhabitant of Lithuania, Latvia, or Estonia.

Bal·tha·zar also **Bal·tha·sar** (băl-thā′zər, băl′thə-zär′). In the New Testament, one of the three wise men from the East who came bearing gifts for the infant Jesus, guided by the Star of Bethlehem.

Bal·tic (bôl′tĭk) *adj.* **1.** Of or relating to the Baltic Sea, the Baltic States, or a Baltic-speaking people. **2.** Of or relating to the branch of the Indo-European language family that contains Latvian, Lithuanian, and Old Prussian. —**Baltic** *n.* The Baltic language branch.

Baltic Sea. An arm of the Atlantic Ocean in northern Europe bounded by Denmark, Sweden, Finland, Russia, Estonia, Latvia, Lithuania, Poland, and Germany. It opens to the North Sea via channels and canals, is mostly shallow, with relatively low salinity, and often freezes for three to five months of the year.

Baltic States. Estonia, Latvia, and Lithuania, on the eastern coast of the Baltic Sea. Formerly Russian provinces, they became independent countries after World War I and were incorporated into the U.S.S.R. as constituent republics in 1940. They became independent again in 1991.

Bal·ti·more (bôl′tə-môr′, -mōr′). A city of northern Maryland on an arm of Chesapeake Bay northeast of Washington, D.C. It has been a busy port since the 18th century. Population, 786,775. **—Bal′ti·mor′e·an** *n.*

Baltimore, Lord. See **Calvert.**

Baltimore oriole *n.* A subspecies of the northern oriole in its eastern range, of which the male is bright orange and black and the female olive brown with white wing bars. [After Lord BALTIMORE.]

Bal·to-Sla·vic (bôl′tō-slä′vĭk, -slăv′ĭk) *n.* A subfamily of the Indo-European language family that consists of the Baltic and Slavic branches. **—Bal′to-Sla′vic** *adj.*

Ba·lu·chi (bə-lo͞o′chē) also **Ba·luch** (-lo͞och′) *n., pl.* **Baluchi** or **-chis** also **Baluch** or **-lu·ches** (-lo͞o′chəz). **1.** A member of a traditionally nomadic Moslem people of Baluchistan. **2.** The Iranian language of the Baluchi.

Ba·lu·chi·stan (bə-lo͞o′chĭ-stăn′). A desert region of western Pakistan bounded by Iran, Afghanistan, and the Arabian Sea.

ba·lu·chi·there (bə-lo͞o′chĭ-thîr′) *n.* A very large, extinct rhinoceroslike mammal of the genus *Baluchitherium,* of the Oligocene and Miocene epochs. [BALUCHI(STAN) + *-there,* an extinct mammal (from New Latin *-therium,* from Greek *thērion,* wild beast; see TREACLE).]

bal·us·ter (băl′ə-stər) *n.* **1.a.** One of the upright, usually rounded or vase-shaped supports of a balustrade. **b.** An upright support, such as a furniture leg, having a similar shape. **2.** One of the supporting posts of a handrail. [French *balustre,* from Italian *balaustro,* from *balaustra,* pomegranate flower (from a resemblance to the post), from Latin *balaustium,* from Greek *balaustion.*]

bal·us·trade (băl′ə-strād′) *n.* A rail and the row of balusters or posts that support it, as along the front of a gallery. [French, from Italian *balaustrata,* from *balaustro,* baluster. See BALUSTER.]

Bal·zac (bôl′zăk′, băl′-, băl-zăk′), **Honoré de.** 1799–1850. French writer who portrayed the panorama of French society in *La Comédie Humaine.* **—Bal·zac′i·an** *adj.*

B.A.M. *abbr.* **1.** Bachelor of Applied Mathematics. **2.** Bachelor of Arts in Music.

Ba·ma·ko (bä′mə-kō′). The capital and largest city of Mali, in the southwest on the Niger River. It was a leading center of Moslem learning under the Mali empire (c. 11th–15th century). Population, 502,000.

Bam·ba·ra (bäm-bä′rä) *n., pl.* **-ra** or **-ras. 1.** A member of a people of the upper Niger River valley. **2.** The Mandingo language of the Bambara, used as a lingua franca in Mali.

bam·bi·no (băm-bē′nō, bäm-) *n., pl.* **-nos** or **-ni** (-nē). **1.** A child; a baby. **2.** A representation of the infant Jesus. [Italian, diminutive of *bambo,* child.]

bam·boo (băm-bo͞o′) *n., pl.* **-boos. 1.** Any of various usually woody, temperate or tropical grasses of the genera *Arundinaria, Bambusa, Dendrocalamus, Phyllostachys,* or *Sasa.* **2.** The hard or woody stems of these plants, used in construction, crafts, and fishing poles. *—attributive.* Often used to modify another noun: *bamboo furniture; bamboo sticks.* [Malay *bambu,* of Indic origin.]

Bam·boo Curtain (băm-bo͞o′) *n.* A political and ideological barrier between the West and the Communist countries of Asia after the Chinese revolution of 1949.

bamboo shoot *n.* The young shoot of certain species of the bamboo genera *Dendrocalamus* and *Phyllostachys,* sliced, cooked, and eaten as a vegetable, especially in east Asian cuisine.

bam·boo·zle (băm-bo͞o′zəl) *tr.v.* **-zled, -zling, -zles.** *Informal.* To take in by elaborate methods of deceit; hoodwink. See Synonyms at **deceive.** [Origin unknown.] **—bam·boo′zle·ment** *n.*

ban¹ (băn) *tr.v.* **banned, ban·ning, bans. 1.** To prohibit, especially by official decree. See Synonyms at **forbid. 2.** *South African.* To deprive (a person suspected of illegal activity) of the right of free movement and association with others. **3.** *Archaic.* To curse. **—ban** *n.* **1.** An excommunication or condemnation by church officials. **2.** A prohibition imposed by law or official decree. **3.** Censure, condemnation, or disapproval expressed especially by public opinion. **4.** A curse; an imprecation. **5.** A summons to arms in feudal times. [Middle English *bannen,* to summon, banish, curse, from Old English *bannan,* to summon, and from Old Norse *banna,* to prohibit, curse; see **bhā-²** in Appendix.]

ban² (bän) *n., pl.* **ba·ni** (bä′nē). See table at **currency.** [Romanian, from Serbo-Croatian *bān,* lord, from Turkic *bayan,* very rich person : *bay,* rich; akin to Turkish *bay,* rich, gentleman + *-an,* intensive suff.]

ba·nal (bə-năl′, bā′nəl, bə-näl′) *adj.* Drearily commonplace and often predictable; trite. See Synonyms at **trite.** [French, from Old French, shared by tenants in a feudal jurisdiction, from *ban,* summons to military service, of Germanic origin. See **bhā-²** in Appendix.] **—ba·nal′ize′** *v.* **—ba·nal′ly** *adv.*

USAGE NOTE: The pronunciation of *banal* is not settled among educated speakers of American English. Sixty years ago, H.W. Fowler recommended the pronunciation BAN-al (rhyming with *panel*), but this pronunciation is now regarded as recondite by most Americans: it is preferred by only 2 percent of the Usage Panel. Other possibilities are BANE-al (rhyming with *anal*), preferred by 38 percent of the Panel; ba-NAL (rhyming with *canal*), preferred by 46 percent; and ba-NAHL (the last syllable rhyming with *doll*), preferred by 14 percent (this last pronunciation is more common in British English). Some panelists admit to being so vexed by the problem that they tend to avoid the word in conversation. Speakers can perhaps take comfort in knowing that any one of the last three pronunciations will have the support of a substantial minority, and that none of them is incorrect. When several pronunciations of a word are widely used, there is really no right or wrong one.

ba·nal·i·ty (bə-năl′ĭ-tē, bā-) *n.* **1.** The condition or quality of being banal; triviality. **2.** Something that is trite, obvious, or predictable; a commonplace.

ba·nan·a (bə-năn′ə) *n.* **1.** Any of several treelike Asian herbs of the genus *Musa,* especially *M. acuminata,* having a terminal crown of large, entire leaves and a hanging cluster of fruits. **2.** The elongated, edible fruit of these plants, having a thick yellowish to reddish skin and white, aromatic, seedless pulp. [Portuguese and Spanish, from Wolof, Mandingo, and Fulani.]

banana oil *n.* **1.** A liquid mixture of amyl acetate and usually nitrocellulose, having a bananalike odor and used as a solvent or flavoring agent. **2.** See **amyl acetate. 3.** *Slang.* Insincere flattery; nonsensical exaggeration.

banana republic *n.* A small country that is economically dependent on a single crop, such as bananas, or a single product, such as tin. It is often governed by a dictator or officers of the armed forces: *"America has begun to take on certain . . . characteristics of a banana republic. In those countries, savings are hoarded rather than invested in productive enterprises"* (Richard B. Hoey).

ba·nan·as (bə-năn′əz) *adj. & adv. Slang.* Crazy: *"That's the horrible thing when you're bananas—nobody can know the awful things that are going on in your head"* (Otto Friedrich). *"City dwellers . . . are subjected to so much noise it drives them bananas"* (New Yorker).

banana seat *n.* An elongated bicycle seat that usually curves upward in the back. [From its shape.]

♦ **banana split** *n.* Several scoops of ice cream and usually flavored syrups or sauces, nuts, fruit, and whipped cream served on a banana that has been split lengthwise. Also called ♦*houseboat.*

Ba·na·ras (bə-när′əs, -ēz). See **Varanasi.**

Ba·nat (bə-nät′, bä′nät′). A region of southeast-central Europe extending across western Romania, northeast Yugoslavia, and southern Hungary.

ba·nau·sic (bə-nô′sĭk, -zĭk) *adj.* **1.** Merely mechanical; routine: *"a sensitive, self-conscious creature . . . in sad revolt against uncongenially banausic employment"* (London Magazine). **2.** Of or relating to a mechanic. [Greek *banausikos,* from *banausos,* mechanic.]

ban·co (băng′kō, bäng′-) *n., pl.* **-cos.** *Games.* A bet in certain gambling games for the entire amount the banker offers to accept. **—banco** *interj.* Used to announce a bet in certain gambling games. [Italian, masculine of *banca,* bank. See BANK².]

Ban·croft (băn′krôft′, -krŏft′, băng′-), **George.** 1800–1891. American historian and diplomat whose published works include the ten-volume *History of the United States* (1834–1874). As secretary of the navy (1845–1846) he established the naval academy at Annapolis.

band¹ (bănd) *n.* **1.** A thin strip of flexible material used to encircle and bind one object or to hold a number of objects together: *a metal band around the bale of cotton.* **2.** A strip or stripe that contrasts with something else in color, texture, or material. **3.** A narrow strip of fabric used to trim, finish, or reinforce articles of clothing. **4.** Something that constrains or binds morally or legally: *the bands of marriage and family.* **5.** A simple ungrooved ring, especially a wedding ring. **6.a.** A neckband or collar. **b. bands.** The two strips hanging from the front of a collar as part of the dress of certain clerics, scholars, and lawyers. **c.** A high collar popular in the 16th and 17th centuries. **7.a.** *Biology.* A chromatically, structurally, or functionally differentiated strip or stripe in or on an organism. **b.** *Anatomy.* A cordlike tissue that connects or holds structures together. **8.** *Physics.* **a.** A specific range of wavelengths or frequencies of electromagnetic radiation. **b.** A range of very closely spaced electron energy levels in solids, the distribution and nature of which determine the electrical properties of a material. **9.** Any of the distinct grooves on a long-playing phonograph record that contains an individual selection or a separate section of a whole. **10.** *Computer Science.* Circular tracks on a storage device such as a disk. **11.** The cords across the back of a book to which the sheets or quires are attached. **—band** *tr.v.* **band·ed, band·ing, bands. 1.** To tie, bind, or encircle with or as if with a band. **2.** To mark or identify with or as if with a band: *a program to band migrating birds.* [Middle English, from Old Norse *band,* band, fetter, and from Old French *bande,* band, strip, of Germanic origin. See **bhendh-** in Appendix.]

band² (bănd) *n.* **1.a.** A group of people. **b.** A group of animals. **2.** *Music.* A group of players who perform as an ensemble. **—band** *v.* **band·ed, band·ing, bands.** *—tr.* To assemble or unite in a group. *—intr.* To form a group; unite: *banded together for protection.* [Old French, probably of Germanic origin.]

bamboo

banana

ă pat	oi boy
ā pay	ou out
âr care	o͝o took
ä father	o͞o boot
ĕ pet	ŭ cut
ē be	ûr urge
ĭ pit	th thin
ī pie	*th* this
îr pier	hw which
ŏ pot	zh vision
ō toe	ə about, item
ô paw	♦ regionalism

Stress marks: ′ (primary); ′ (secondary), as in **dictionary** (dĭk′shə-nĕr′ē)

bandoleer
Worn across the chest

band shell
Concert at the Hatch Shell, Boston

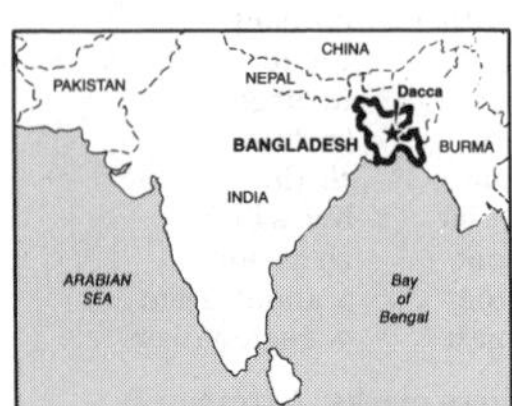

Bangladesh

SYNONYMS: *band, company, corps, party, troop, troupe.* The central meaning shared by these nouns is "a group of individuals acting together in a shared activity or enterprise": *a band of thieves; a company of scientists; a corps of drummers; a party of tourists; a troop of students on a field trip; a troupe of actors.*

band·age (băn′dĭj) *n.* A strip of material such as gauze used to protect, immobilize, compress, or support a wound or injured body part. **—bandage** *tr.v.* **-aged, -ag·ing, -ag·es.** To apply a bandage to. [French, from Old French *bande,* band, strip. See BAND[1].] **—band′ag·er** *n.*

Band-Aid (bănd′ād′). A trademark used for an adhesive bandage with a gauze pad in the center, employed to protect minor wounds. This trademark sometimes occurs in print in figurative uses: *"True welfare reform is being bypassed for Band-Aid solutions"* (Los Angeles Times). *"Many critics contend that these measures are mere Band-Aids"* (U.S. News & World Report).

ban·dan·na or **ban·dan·a** (băn-dăn′ə) *n.* A large handkerchief usually figured and brightly colored. [Probably Portuguese, from Hindi *bāndhnū,* tie-dyeing, from *bāndhnā,* to tie, from Sanskrit *bandhati,* he ties. See **bhendh-** in Appendix.]

Ban·dar Se·ri Be·ga·wan (bŭn′dər sĕr′ē bə-gä′wən). The capital of Brunei, on the northern coast of Borneo. Population, 63,868.

Ban·da Sea (băn′də, bän′-). An arm of the Pacific Ocean in eastern Indonesia southeast of Sulawesi and north of Timor. It includes the **Banda Islands,** a group of volcanic islands in the Moluccas south of Ceram.

B & B *abbr.* Bed-and-breakfast.

band·box (bănd′bŏks′) *n.* A lightweight cylindrical box used to hold small articles of apparel.

B and E *abbr. Law.* Breaking and entering.

ban·deau (băn-dō′) *n., pl.* **-deaux** (-dōz′) or **-deaus. 1.** A narrow band for the hair. **2.** A brassiere. [French, from Old French *bandel,* diminutive of *bande,* band, strip. See BAND[1].]

Ban·del·lo (băn-dĕl′ō, bän-), **Matteo.** 1485?–1561. Italian prelate and writer whose tales form the basis of many plays, including Shakespeare's *Much Ado about Nothing* and *Twelfth Night.*

ban·de·ri·lla (băn′də-rē′ə, -rēl′yə) *n.* A decorated barbed dart that is thrust into the bull's neck or shoulder muscles by a banderillero in a bullfight. [Spanish, diminutive of *bandera,* banner, from Vulgar Latin **bandāria.* See BANNER.]

ban·de·ri·lle·ro (băn′də-rē-âr′ō, -rēl-yâr′ō) *n., pl.* **-ros.** One who implants decorated barbed darts into the bull's neck or shoulder muscles during a bullfight. [Spanish, from *banderilla,* banderilla. See BANDERILLA.]

ban·de·role or **ban·de·rol** (băn′də-rōl′) also **ban·ne·rol** (băn′ə-rōl′) *n.* **1.** A narrow forked flag or streamer attached to a staff or lance or flown from a ship's masthead. **2.** A representation of a ribbon or scroll bearing an inscription. [French, from Italian *banderuola,* diminutive of *bandiera,* banner, from Vulgar Latin **bandāria.* See BANNER.]

ban·di·coot (băn′dĭ-ko͞ot′) *n.* **1.** Any of several large Indian rats of the genera *Bandicota* and *Nesokia,* of southeast Asia. **2.** Any of several ratlike marsupials of the family Peramelidae, of Australia and adjacent islands, that feed on insects and plants and have a long, tapering snout and elongated hind legs. [Telugu *bantikoku* : *banti,* ball + *kokku,* long beak.]

ban·dit (băn′dĭt) *n.* **1.** A robber, especially one who robs at gunpoint. **2.** An outlaw; a gangster. **3.** One who cheats or exploits others. **4.** *Slang.* A hostile aircraft, especially a fighter aircraft. ***—idiom.* make out like a bandit** (or **like bandits).** *Slang.* To be highly successful in a given enterprise. [Italian *bandito,* from *bandire,* to band together, probably of Germanic origin. See **bhā-**[2] in Appendix.] **—ban′dit·ry** *n.*

Ban·djar·ma·sin (bän′jər-mä′sĭn, bän′-). See **Banjarmasin.**

band·lead·er (bănd′lē′dər) *n. Music.* One who conducts a band, especially a dance band.

band·mas·ter (bănd′măs′tər) *n. Music.* One who conducts a band.

ban·dog (băn′dôg′, -dŏg′) *n.* A dog, such as a mastiff, kept chained as a watchdog or because of its ferocious aggressiveness. [Middle English *band-dogge* : *band,* leash, chain; see BAND[1] + *dogge,* dog; see DOG.]

ban·do·leer or **ban·do·lier** (băn′də-lîr′) *n.* A belt fitted with small pockets or loops for carrying cartridges and worn across the chest by soldiers. [French *bandoulière,* from Spanish *bandolera,* diminutive of *banda,* band, of Germanic origin. See **bhā-**[1] in Appendix.]

ban·do·ne·on (băn-dō′nē-ŏn′) *n. Music.* A small accordion especially popular in Latin America. [American Spanish *bandoneón,* from German *Bandonion, Bandoneon* : after H. Band (1821–1860), German inventor + *Akkordion,* accordion; see ACCORDION.] **—ban·do′ne·on·ist** (-ə-nĭst) *n.*

ban·dore (băn′dôr′, -dōr′) also **ban·do·ra** (băn-dôr′ə, -dōr′ə) *n. Music.* An ancient instrument resembling a guitar. Also called *pandore.* [Portuguese *bandurra,* from Late Latin *pandūra,* from Greek *pandoura.*]

band saw *n.* A power saw used in woodworking, consisting essentially of a toothed metal band coupled to and continuously driven around the circumferences of two wheels.

band shell also **band·shell** (bănd′shĕl′) *n. Music.* A bandstand with a concave, almost hemispheric wall at the rear that serves as a sounding board.

bands·man (băndz′mən) *n. Music.* A player in a band.

band·stand (bănd′stănd′) *n. Music.* **1.** A stand or platform, often roofed, for a band or orchestra. **2.** An indoor stand or platform for musicians and other performers.

Ban·dung (bän′do͝ong′). A city of Indonesia in western Java southeast of Jakarta. Founded by the Dutch in 1810, it is an industrial and cultural center and a resort known for its cool, healthful climate. Population, 1,462,637.

band·wag·on (bănd′wăg′ən) *n.* **1.** *Music.* An elaborately decorated wagon used to transport musicians in a parade. **2.** *Informal.* A cause or party that attracts increasing numbers of adherents: *young voters jumping onto the party's bandwagon.* **3.** *Informal.* A current trend: *tobacco companies that were hard hit by the nonsmoking bandwagon.* **—band′wag′on·ing** *n.*

band·width (bănd′wĭdth′, -wĭth′) *n.* The numerical difference between the upper and lower frequencies of a band of electromagnetic radiation, especially an assigned range of radio frequencies.

ban·dy (băn′dē) *tr.v.* **-died, -dy·ing, -dies. 1.a.** To toss or throw back and forth. **b.** To hit (a ball, for example) back and forth. **2.a.** To give and receive (words, for example); exchange: *The old friends bandied compliments when they met.* **b.** To discuss in a casual or frivolous manner: *bandy an idea about.* **—bandy** *adj.* Bowed or bent in an outward curve: *bandy legs.* **—bandy** *n., pl.* **-dies.** *Sports.* **1.** A game similar to modern field hockey. **2.** A stick, bent at one end, used in playing this game. [Origin unknown.]

ban·dy-leg·ged (băn′dē-lĕg′ĭd, - lĕgd′) *adj.* Bowlegged.

bane (bān) *n.* **1.** Fatal injury or ruin: *"Hath some fond lover tic'd thee to thy bane?"* (George Herbert). **2.** A cause of death, destruction, or ruin: *"Obedience,/Bane of all genius, virtue, freedom, truth,/Makes slaves of men"* (Percy Bysshe Shelley). **3.** A deadly poison. [Middle English, destroyer, from Old English *bana.* See **gʷhen-** in Appendix.]

bane·ber·ry (bān′bĕr′ē) *n.* **1.** Any of several perennial herbs of the genus *Actaea,* native to northern temperate regions, having terminal clusters of red, white, or blackish berries. **2.** The poisonous berry of a plant of this genus.

bane·ful (bān′fəl) *adj.* Causing death, destruction, or ruin; harmful. See Usage Note at **baleful. —bane′ful·ly** *adv.*

Banff (bămf). A town of southwest Alberta, Canada, in the Rocky Mountains near Lake Louise. It is a popular winter resort. Population, 4,208.

bang[1] (băng) *n.* **1.** A sudden loud noise, as of an explosion. **2.** A sudden loud blow or bump. **3.** *Informal.* A sudden burst of action: *The campaign started off with a bang.* **4.** *Slang.* A sense of excitement; a thrill: *We got a bang out of watching the old movies.* **—bang** *v.* **banged, bang·ing, bangs.** *—tr.* **1.** To strike heavily and often repeatedly; bump. **2.** To close suddenly and loudly; slam. **3.** To handle noisily or violently: *banged the pots in the kitchen.* **4.** *Vulgar Slang.* To have sexual intercourse with. *—intr.* **1.** To make a sudden loud, explosive noise. **2.** To crash noisily against or into something: *My elbow banged against the door.* **—bang** *adv.* Exactly; precisely: *The arrow hit bang on the target.* ***—phrasal verbs.* bang away. 1.** To assail insistently, especially with questions. **2.** To work diligently and often at length: *banged away at the project until it was finished.* **bang up.** To damage extensively: *banged up the car.* [Probably from Old Norse *bang,* a hammering.]

bang[2] (băng) *n.* A fringe of hair cut short and straight across the forehead. Often used in the plural. **—bang** *tr.v.* **banged, bang·ing, bangs.** To cut (hair) in bangs. [Perhaps short for BANGTAIL.]

bang[3] (băng) *n.* Variant of **bhang.**

♦**bang**[4] (bĕn-yā′) *n. Southern Louisiana.* Variant of **beignet.**

Ban·ga·lore (băng′gə-lôr′, -lōr′). A city of south-central India west of Madras. Founded in 1537, it is a major industrial center and transportation hub. Population, 2,476,355.

ban·ga·lore torpedo (băng′gə-lôr′, -lōr′) *n.* A piece of metal pipe filled with an explosive, used primarily to clear a path through barbed wire or to detonate land mines. [After BANGALORE.]

bang·er (băng′ər) *n. Chiefly British.* **1.** A sausage. **2.** A noisy old car. **3.** A firework that explodes with a sudden loud noise.

Bang·ka or **Ban·ka** (băng′kə). An island of western Indonesia in the Java Sea separated from Sumatra by the narrow **Strait of Bangka.** Tin was discovered here in the early 1700's.

bang·kok (băng′kŏk′, băng-kŏk′) *n.* A hat made of finely woven straw. [After BANGKOK.]

Bang·kok (băng′kŏk′, băng-kŏk′) also **Krung Thep** (gro͞ong tĕp′). The capital and largest city of Thailand, in the southwest on the Chao Phraya River near the Gulf of Siam. It is a leading port and industrial center with a major jewelry market. Population, 5,174,682.

Bang·la·desh (băng′glə-dĕsh′, bäng′-). A country of southern Asia on the Bay of Bengal. Formerly part of Bengal, it became East Pakistan when India achieved independence in 1947. After a savage civil war with West Pakistan (1971), Bangladesh formed a separate nation. Dacca is the capital and the largest city. Population, 87,052,000. **—Bang′la·desh′i** *adj. & n.*

ban·gle (băng′gəl) *n.* **1.** A rigid bracelet or anklet, especially one with no clasp. **2.** An ornament that hangs from a bracelet or necklace. [Hindi *baṅgrī,* glass bracelet.]

Ban·gor (băng′gôr, -gər). A city of south-central Maine on the Penobscot River. Settled in 1769, it was occupied by the British during the War of 1812. Population, 31,643.

Bang's disease (băngz) *n.* See **brucellosis** (sense 2). [After Bernhard L.F. *Bang* (1848–1932), Danish veterinarian.]

bang·tail (băng′tāl′) *n.* **1.** A racehorse. **2.** A detachable extension to the back of an envelope, having a perforated edge and special marketing information or an order form on it. [BANG[1] + TAIL[1].]

Ban·gui (bäng-gē′, bäN-). The capital and largest city of Central African Republic, in the southern part of the country on the Ubangi River. It is a major port and trade center. Population, 340,000.

bang-up (băng′ŭp′) *adj. Informal.* Very good; excellent. [From BANG[1].]

Bang·we·u·lu (băng′wē-o͞o′lo͞o), **Lake.** A shallow lake bordered by swamps on a plateau of northeast Zambia. It was discovered by David Livingstone in 1868.

ba·ni (bä′nē) *n.* Plural of **ban**[2].

ban·ian (băn′yən) *n.* Variant of **banyan.**

ban·ish (băn′ĭsh) *tr.v.* **-ished, -ish·ing, -ish·es. 1.** To force to leave a country or place by official decree; exile. **2.** To drive away; expel: *We banished all our doubts and fears.* [Middle English *banishen,* from Old French *banir, baniss-,* of Germanic origin. See **bhā-**[2] in Appendix.] **—ban′ish·er** *n.* **—ban′ish·ment** *n.*

SYNONYMS: *banish, exile, expatriate, deport, transport, extradite.* These verbs mean to send away from a country or state. *Banish* applies to forced departure from a country by official decree: *was convicted of heresy and banished from the kingdom. Exile* specifies departure from one's own country, either involuntarily because of legal expulsion or voluntarily because of adverse circumstances: *When the government was overthrown, the royal family was exiled. Expatriate* pertains to departure that is sometimes forced but often voluntary and may imply change of citizenship: *an immigrant whose citizenship was revoked and who was expatriated because he had concealed his criminal record. Deport* denotes the act of sending an alien abroad by governmental order: *was deported for entering the country illegally. Transport* pertains to the sending abroad, usually to a penal colony, of one convicted of a crime: *Offenders are no longer transported to Devil's Island. Extradite* applies to the delivery of an accused or convicted person to the state or country having jurisdiction over him or her: *The court refused to extradite political refugees.*

ban·is·ter also **ban·nis·ter** (băn′ĭ-stər) *n.* **1.** A handrail, along with all of its supporting structures. **2.** One of the vertical supports of a handrail on a staircase. [Variant of BALUSTER.]

Ban·ja Lu·ka (bän′yə lo͞o′kə). A city of northwest-central Yugoslavia northwest of Sarajevo. Ruled at various times by Turkey and Austria, Banja Luka became part of Yugoslavia after World War I. Population, 104,000.

Ban·jar·ma·sin also **Ban·djar·ma·sin** (băn′jər-mä′sĭn, bän′-). A city of Indonesia on a delta island of southern Borneo. An important deep-water port, Banjarmasin was part of a Hindu kingdom in the 14th century and passed to Moslem rulers in the 15th century. Population, 381,286.

ban·jo (băn′jō) *n., pl.* **-jos** or **-joes.** *Music.* A fretted stringed instrument having a narrow neck and a hollow circular body with a stretched diaphragm of vellum upon which the bridge rests. [Akin to Jamaican English *banja,* fiddle, probably akin to Kimbundu, Tshiluba *mbanza,* a plucked stringed instrument.] **—ban′jo·ist** *n.*

Ban·jul (bän′jo͞ol′). Formerly **Bath·urst** (băth′ərst). The capital and largest city of Gambia, on an island at the mouth of the Gambia River on the Atlantic Ocean. It was founded as a trading post by the British in 1816. Population, 44,536.

bank[1] (băngk) *n.* **1.** A piled-up mass, as of snow or clouds. See Synonyms at **heap. 2.** A steep natural incline. **3.** An artificial embankment. **4.** Often **banks.** The slope of land adjoining a body of water, especially adjoining a river, lake, or channel. **5.** Often **banks.** A large elevated area of a sea floor. **6.** *Games.* The cushion of a billiard or pool table. **7.** The lateral inward tilting, as of a motor vehicle or an aircraft, in turning or negotiating a curve. **—bank** *v.* **banked, bank·ing, banks.** —*tr.* **1.** To border or protect with a ridge or embankment. **2.** To pile up; amass: *banked earth along the wall.* **3.** To cover (a fire), as with ashes or fresh fuel, to ensure continued low burning. **4.** To construct with a slope rising to the outside edge: *The turns on the racetrack were steeply banked.* **5.a.** To tilt (an aircraft) laterally and inwardly in flight. **b.** To tilt (a motor vehicle) laterally and inwardly when negotiating a curve. **6.** *Games.* To strike (a billiard ball) so that it rebounds from the cushion of the table. **7.** *Sports.* To play (a ball) in such a way as to make it glance off a surface, such as a backboard or wall. —*intr.* **1.** To rise in or take the form of a bank. **2.** To tilt an aircraft or a motor vehicle laterally when turning. [Middle English, of Scandinavian origin.]

bank[2] (băngk) *n. Abbr.* **bk. 1.a.** A business establishment in which money is kept for saving or commercial purposes or is invested, supplied for loans, or exchanged. **b.** The offices or building in which such an establishment is located. **2.** *Games.* **a.** The funds of a gambling establishment. **b.** The funds held by a dealer or banker in some gambling games. **c.** The reserve pieces, cards, chips, or play money in some games, such as poker, from which the players may draw. **3.a.** A supply or stock for future or emergency use: *a grain bank.* **b.** *Medicine.* A supply of human tissues or other materials, such as blood, skin, or sperm, held in reserve for future use. **4.** A place of safekeeping or storage: *a computer's memory bank.* **5.** *Obsolete.* A moneychanger's table or place of business. **—bank** *v.* **banked, bank·ing, banks.** —*tr.* To deposit in or as if in a bank. —*intr.* **1.** To transact business with a bank or maintain a bank account. **2.** To operate a bank. ***—phrasal verb.*** **bank on.** To have confidence in; rely on. [French *banque,* from Old Italian *banca,* bench, moneychanger's table, from Old High German *banc.*]

bank[3] (băngk) *n.* **1.** A set of similar or matched things arranged in a row, especially: **a.** A set of elevators. **b.** A row of keys on a keyboard. **2.** *Nautical.* **a.** A bench for rowers in a galley. **b.** A row of oars in a galley. **3.** *Printing.* The lines of type under a headline. **—bank** *tr. v.* **banked, bank·ing, banks.** To arrange or set up in a row: *"Every street was banked with purple-blooming trees"* (Doris Lessing). [Middle English, bench, from Old French *banc,* from Late Latin *bancus,* of Germanic origin.]

Ban·ka (băng′kə). See **Bangka.**

bank·a·ble (băng′kə-bəl) *adj.* **1.** Acceptable to or at a bank: *bankable funds.* **2.** Guaranteed to bring profit: *a bankable movie star.* **—bank′a·bil′i·ty** *n.*

bank acceptance *n.* A draft or bill of exchange drawn upon and accepted by a bank. Also called *banker's acceptance.*

bank account *n.* Funds deposited in a bank that are credited to and subject to withdrawal by the depositor.

bank annuity *n. Chiefly British.* See **consol.**

bank barn *n.* A barn built into a hillside as protection against wind and cold, with a back entrance at the second-floor level.

bank bill *n.* See **bank note.**

bank·book (băngk′bo͝ok′) *n.* A book held by a depositor in which his or her deposits and withdrawals are recorded by the bank. Also called *passbook.*

bank·card (băngk′kärd′) *n.* A card issued by a bank especially to identify the holder, used for receiving credit or for operating an automated teller machine.

bank discount *n.* The interest on a loan computed in advance and deducted at the time the loan is made.

bank·er[1] (băng′kər) *n.* **1.** One serving as an officer or owner of a bank. **2.** *Games.* The player in charge of the bank in some gambling games. **—bank′er·ly** *adj.*

bank·er[2] (băng′kər) *n.* One engaged in cod fishing off Newfoundland.

bank·er[3] (băng′kər) *n.* A workbench used by a mason or sculptor. [From BANK[3], bench (obsolete).]

bank·er's acceptance (băng′kərz) *n.* See **bank acceptance.**

bank·ers' hours (băng′kərz) *pl.n.* A short working day.

Bank·head (băngk′hĕd′), **Tallulah Brockman.** 1903–1968. American actress noted for her wit, glamour, and performances in plays, such as *The Little Foxes* (1939), and motion pictures, including *Lifeboat* (1943).

bank holiday *n.* **1.** A day on which banks are legally closed. **2.** *Chiefly British.* A legal holiday when banks are ordered to remain closed.

bank·ing (băng′kĭng) *n. Abbr.* **bkg. 1.** The business of a bank. **2.** The occupation of a banker.

♦**ban·kit** (băng′kĭt) *n. Southern Louisiana & East Texas.* Variant of **banquette** (sense 2).

bank note *n.* A note issued by a bank representing its promise to pay a specific sum to the bearer on demand and acceptable as money. Also called *bank bill.*

bank paper *n.* **1.** Bank notes considered as a group. **2.** Securities, drafts, bills of exchange, and other commercial paper acceptable by a bank.

bank rate *n.* The rate of discount established by a country's central bank.

bank·roll (băngk′rōl′) *n.* **1.** A roll of paper money. **2.** *Informal.* One's ready cash. **—bankroll** *tr.v.* **-rolled, -roll·ing, -rolls.** *Informal.* To underwrite the expense of (a business venture, for example). **—bank′roll′er** *n.*

bank·rupt (băngk′rŭpt′, -rəpt) *n. Abbr.* **bkpt. 1.** *Law.* A debtor that, upon voluntary petition or one invoked by the debtor's creditors, is judged legally insolvent. The debtor's remaining property is then administered for the creditors or is distributed among them. **2.** A person who is totally lacking in a specified resource or quality: *an intellectual bankrupt.* **—bankrupt** *adj.* **1.a.** Having been legally declared financially insolvent. **b.** Financially ruined; impoverished. **2.a.** Depleted of valuable qualities or characteristics: *a morally and ethically bankrupt politician.* **b.** Totally depleted; destitute: *was bankrupt of new ideas.* **c.** Being in a ruined state: *a bankrupt foreign policy.* **—bankrupt** *tr.v.* **-rupt·ed, -rupt·ing, -rupts. 1.** To cause to become financially bankrupt. **2.** To ruin: *an administration that bankrupted its credibility by seeking to manipulate the news.* [French *banqueroute,* from Italian *bancarotta* : *banca,* moneychanger's table;

banjo

ă pat	oi boy
ā pay	ou out
âr care	o͝o took
ä father	o͞o boot
ĕ pet	ŭ cut
ē be	ûr urge
ĭ pit	th thin
ī pie	*th* this
îr pier	hw which
ŏ pot	zh vision
ō toe	ə about, item
ô paw	♦ regionalism

Stress marks: **′** (primary); ′ (secondary), as in **dictionary** (dĭk′shə-nĕr′ē)

see BANK[2] + *rotta,* past participle of *rompere,* to break (from Latin *rumpere;* see **reup-** in Appendix).] **—bank′rupt·cy** (-rəpt-sē, -rəp-sē) *n.* **—bank·rup′tive** *adj.*

Banks (băngks), Sir **Joseph.** 1743–1820. British botanist noted for his circumnavigation of the globe (1768–1771) with James Cook, during which he discovered and cataloged many species of plant and animal life.

bank·si·a (băngk′sē-ə) *n.* Any of various Australian evergreen shrubs or trees of the genus *Banksia,* having narrow, spiny or toothed leaves, showy, dense clusters of usually yellow flowers, and small fruits in conelike clusters. [After Sir Joseph BANKS.]

Banks Island. An island of northwest Northwest Territories, Canada, in the Arctic Ocean west of Victoria Island. It is the westernmost island of the Arctic Archipelago.

Ban-Lon (băn′lŏn′). A trademark used for knitted and woven fabrics made from artificially crimped yarns.

Ban·ne·ker (băn′ĭ-kər), **Benjamin.** 1731–1806. American mathematician and astronomer who published an almanac (1792–1802) containing ephemerides that he had calculated.

banquette
Louis XVI style banquette by Jean Baptiste Claude Sene (1748–1803)

ban·ner (băn′ər) *n.* **1.a.** A piece of cloth attached to a staff and used as a standard by a monarch, military commander, or knight. **b.** The flag of a nation, a state, or an army. **2.** A piece of cloth bearing a motto or legend, as of a club. **3.** A headline spanning the width of a newspaper page. **4.** *Botany.* See **standard** (sense 8). **—banner** *adj.* Unusually good; outstanding: *a banner year for the company.* **—banner** *tr.v.* **-nered, -ner·ing, -ners.** *Informal.* To give a banner headline to (a story or an item) in a newspaper. [Middle English *banere,* from Old French *baniere,* from Vulgar Latin **bandāria,* from Late Latin *bandum,* of Germanic origin. See **bhā-**[1] in Appendix.]

ban·ner·et[1] (băn′ər-ĭt, -ə-rĕt′) also **ban·ner·ette** (băn′ə-rĕt′) *n.* A small banner. [Middle English *baneret,* from Old French *banerete,* diminutive of *baniere,* banner. See BANNER.]

ban·ner·et[2] (băn′ər-ĭt, -ə-rĕt′) *n.* A feudal knight ranking between a knight bachelor and a baron, who was entitled to lead men into battle under his own standard. [Middle English *baneret,* from Old French, from *baniere,* banner. See BANNER.]

ban·ner·ette (băn′ə-rĕt′) *n.* Variant of **banneret**[1].

ban·ne·rol (băn′ə-rōl′) *n.* Variant of **banderole.**

ban·nis·ter (băn′ĭ-stər) *n.* Variant of **banister.**

Ban·nis·ter (băn′ĭ-stər), **Roger.** Born 1929. British runner who in 1954 became the first human being to run the mile in under four minutes.

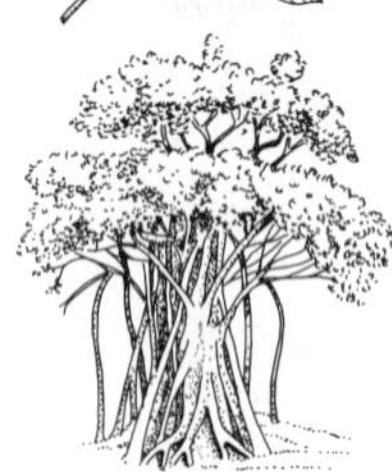

banyan
Ficus benghalensis

♦**ban·nock** (băn′ək) *n.* **1.** A flat, usually unleavened bread made of oatmeal or barley flour. **2.** *New England.* Thin cornbread baked on a griddle. [Middle English *bannok,* from Old English *bannuc,* of Celtic origin.]

Ban·nock (băn′ək) *n., pl.* **Bannock** or **-nocks. 1.a.** A Native American people inhabiting southeast Idaho and western Wyoming. **b.** A member of this people. **2.** The variety of Northern Paiute spoken by the Bannock.

Ban·nock·burn (băn′ək-bûrn′, băn′ək-bûrn′). A town of central Scotland north-northeast of Glasgow on the **Bannock River,** a tributary of the Forth. It was the site of Robert the Bruce's defeat of the English under Edward II on June 23, 1314.

banns also **bans** (bănz) *pl.n.* An announcement, especially in a church, of an intended marriage. [Middle English *banes,* pl. of *ban,* proclamation, from Old English *gebann* and from Old French *ban* (of Germanic origin; see **bhā-**[2] in Appendix).]

ban·quet (băng′kwĭt) *n.* **1.** An elaborate, sumptuous repast. **2.** A ceremonial dinner honoring a particular guest or occasion. **—banquet** *tr. & intr. v.* **-quet·ed, -quet·ing, -quets.** To honor at or partake of a banquet. [Old French, diminutive of *banc,* bench. See BANK[3].] **—ban′quet·er** *n.*

baobab
Adansonia digitata

WORD HISTORY: The linguistic stock of the word *banquet* has been fluctuating for a long time. The Old French word *banquet,* the likely source of our word, is derived from Old French *banc,* "bench," ultimately of Germanic origin. The sense development in Old French seems to have changed from "little bench" to "a meal taken on the family workbench" to "feast." The English word *banquet* is first recorded in a work possibly composed before 1475 with reference to a feast held by the god Apollo, and the word appears to have been used from the 15th to the 18th century to refer to the feasts of the powerful and the wealthy. Perhaps this association led a 19th-century newspaper editor to label the word "grandiloquent" because it was being appropriated by those lower down on the social scale.

ă pat	oi boy
ā pay	ou out
âr care	o͝o took
ä father	o͞o boot
ĕ pet	ŭ cut
ē be	ûr urge
ĭ pit	th thin
ī pie	*th* this
îr pier	hw which
ŏ pot	zh vision
ō toe	ə about, item
ô paw	♦ regionalism

Stress marks: **′** (primary); ′ (secondary), as in **dictionary** (dĭk′shə-nĕr′ē)

banquet room *n.* A large room, as in a restaurant, suitable for banquets.

♦**ban·quette** (băng-kĕt′) *n.* **1.** A platform lining a trench or parapet wall on which soldiers may stand when firing. **2.** Also **ban·kit** (băng′kĭt). *Southern Louisiana & East Texas.* A sidewalk: *"The flower of loafers . . . was found stretched on the banquette on Tuesday night"* (New Orleans Daily Picayune). See Regional Note at **beignet. 3.** A long upholstered bench placed against or built into a wall. **4.** A ledge or shelf, as on a buffet. [French, from Provençal *banqueta,* diminutive of *banca,* bench, of Germanic origin.]

bans (bănz) *pl.n.* Variant of **banns.**

ban·shee also **ban·shie** (băn′shē) *n.* A female spirit in Gaelic folklore believed to presage, by wailing, a death in a family. [Irish Gaelic *bean sídhe,* woman of the fairies, banshee : *bean,* woman (from Old Irish *ben;* see **gʷen-** in Appendix) + *sídhe,* fairy (from Old Irish *síde*).]

ban·tam (băn′təm) *n.* **1.** Any of various breeds of very small domestic fowl that are often miniatures of members of larger breeds. **2.** A small but aggressive and spirited person. **—bantam** *adj.* **1.** Diminutive; miniature. **2.** Aggressive and spirited. [After *Bantam,* Indonesia.]

ban·tam·weight (băn′təm-wāt′) *n. Sports.* **1.** A professional boxer weighing between 112 and 118 pounds (approximately 51–53.5 kilograms), heavier than a flyweight and lighter than a featherweight. **2.** A contestant in various other sports in a similar weight class.

ban·ter (băn′tər) *n.* Good-humored, playful conversation. **—banter** *v.* **-tered, -ter·ing, -ters.** —*tr.* To speak to in a playful or teasing way. —*intr.* To exchange mildly teasing remarks. [Origin unknown.] **—ban′ter·er** *n.* **—ban′ter·ing·ly** *adv.*

SYNONYMS: banter, chaff, josh, kid, rag, razz, rib. The central meaning shared by these verbs is "to poke fun at good-humoredly": *bantered with her colleagues about their long coffee breaks; chaffed her for forgetting the appointment; joshed his brother about his strange new haircut; thought you were kidding me; ragged her about being so stubborn; razzed the teammate who missed the shot; ribbing a friend for being helplessly in love.*

Ban·ting (băn′tĭng), Sir **Frederick Grant.** 1891–1941. Canadian physiologist. He shared a 1923 Nobel Prize for the discovery of insulin.

bant·ling (bănt′lĭng) *n.* A young child. [Origin unknown.]

Ban·tu (băn′to͞o) *n., pl.* **Bantu** or **-tus. 1.** A member of any of a large number of linguistically related peoples of central and southern Africa. **2.** A group of over 400 closely related languages spoken in central, east central, and southern Africa, belonging to the South Central subgroup of the Niger-Congo language family and including Swahili, Kinyarwanda, Kirundi, Zulu, and Xhosa. [From Proto-Bantu **bantu,* people : *ba-,* pl. human pref. + *ntu,* entity.] **—Ban′tu** *adj.*

ban·yan also **ban·ian** (băn′yən) *n.* A tropical Indian fig tree *(Ficus benghalensis),* often widely spreading because of the many aerial roots that descend from the branches and develop into additional trunks. It is planted for ornament and shade. [Short for *banyan tree,* merchants' tree, from Portuguese *banian,* Hindu merchant, from Gujarati *vāṇiyo,* from Sanskrit *vāṇijaḥ.* See **wen-**[1] in Appendix.]

ban·zai (bän-zī′) *n.* A Japanese battle cry or patriotic cheer. [Japanese, (may you live) ten thousand years, from Chinese (Mandarin) *wàn suì* : *wàn,* ten thousand + *suì,* years.]

banzai attack *n.* A desperate attack by Japanese troops in World War II. Also called *banzai charge.*

ba·o·bab (bā′ō-băb′, bä′-) *n.* A tropical African tree *(Adansonia digitata)* having a swollen trunk that stores water, palmately compound leaves, and long, hanging, hard-shelled fruits. [Possibly from North African Arabic *bū ḥibab,* fruit of many seeds.]

Bao·ding also **Pao·ting** (bou′dĭng′). A city of northeast China south-southwest of Beijing. The city wall was built during the Ming period. Population, 400,000.

Bao·tou also **Pao·tow** (bou′tō′). A city of northern China on the Huang He (Yellow River) west of Hohhot. It is a major manufacturing center. Population, 866,200.

Bap. *abbr.* Baptist.

Bapt. *abbr.* Baptist.

bap·tism (băp′tĭz′əm) *n.* **1.** A religious sacrament marked by the symbolic use of water and resulting in admission of the recipient into the community of Christians. **2.** A ceremony, a trial, or an experience by which one is initiated, purified, or given a name. **3.** *Christian Science.* A submergence in Spirit or purification by Spirit. [Middle English *baptisme,* from Old French, from Late Latin *baptismus,* from Greek *baptismos,* from *baptizein,* to baptize. See BAPTIZE.] **—bap·tis′mal** *adj.* **—bap·tis′mal·ly** *adv.*

baptism of fire *n.* **1.** A soldier's first experience of actual combat conditions. **2.** A severe ordeal experienced for the first time.

Bap·tist (băp′tĭst) *n.* **1.** *Abbr.* **Bap., Bapt.** A member of an evangelical Protestant church of congregational polity, following the reformed tradition in worship, and believing in individual freedom, in the separation of church and state, and in baptism of voluntary, conscious believers. **2. baptist.** One that baptizes. [Middle English, baptizer, from Old French *baptiste,* from Late Latin *baptista,* from Greek *baptistēs,* from *baptizein,* to baptize. See BAPTIZE.] **—Bap′tist** *adj.*

bap·tis·ter·y also **bap·tis·try** (băp′tĭ-strē) *n., pl.* **-ies** also **-tries. 1.** A part of a church or a separate building used for baptizing. **2.** A font used for baptism. [Middle English *baptisterie,* from Old French, from Late Latin *baptistērium,* from Greek *baptistērion,* from *baptizein,* to baptize. See BAPTIZE.]

bap·tize (băp-tīz′, băp′tīz′) *v.* **-tized, -tiz·ing, -tiz·es.** —*tr.* **1.** To admit into Christianity by means of baptism. **2.a.** To cleanse or purify. **b.** To initiate. **3.** To give a first or Christian name to; christen. —*intr.* To administer baptism. [Middle English *baptizen,* from Old French *baptiser,* from Late Latin *baptizāre,* from Greek *baptizein,* from *baptein,* to dip.] **—bap·tiz′er** *n.*

bar[1] (bär) *n.* **1.** A relatively long, straight, rigid piece of solid material used as a fastener, support, barrier, or structural or mechanical member. **2.a.** A solid oblong block of a substance, such as soap or candy. **b.** A rectangular block of a precious metal. **3.** Something that impedes or prevents action or progress. See Synonyms at **obstacle.** **4.** A ridge, as of sand or gravel, on a shore or streambed, that is formed by the action of tides or currents. **5.** A narrow marking, as a stripe or band. **6.** *Heraldry.* A pair of horizontal parallel lines drawn across a shield. **7.** *Law.* **a.** The nullification, defeat, or prevention of a claim or action. **b.** The process by which nullification, defeat, or prevention is achieved. **8.** The railing in a courtroom enclosing the part of the room where the judges and lawyers sit, witnesses are heard, and prisoners are tried. **9.** A place of judgment; a tribunal. **10.** *Law.* **a.** Attorneys considered as a group. **b.** The profession of law. **11.** *Music.* **a.** A vertical line dividing a staff into equal measures. **b.** A measure. **12.a.** A counter at which drinks, especially alcoholic drinks, and sometimes food, are served. **b.** An establishment or room having such a counter. **—bar** *tr.v.* **barred, bar•ring, bars. 1.** To fasten securely with a long, straight, rigid piece of material. **2.** To shut in or out with or as if with bars. **3.** To obstruct or impede; block. **4.** To keep out; exclude. See Synonyms at **hinder[1]. 5.** To rule out; except. **6.** To mark with stripes or bands. **7.** *Law.* To stop (a claim or action) by objection. **—bar** *prep.* Except for; excluding: *This was your best performance, bar none.* **—*idiom.* behind bars.** In prison. [Middle English *barre,* from Old French, from Vulgar Latin *barra.]

bar[2] (bär) *n.* A unit of pressure equal to one million (10^6) dynes per square centimeter. [Greek *baros,* weight. See **g^werə-[1]** in Appendix.]

BAR *abbr.* Browning automatic rifle.

bar. *abbr.* **1.a.** Barometer. **b.** Barometric. **2.** Barrel.

bar– *pref.* Variant of **baro–.**

Bar•a (băr′ə), **Theda.** 1890?–1955. American actress of the silent film era. She appeared in sensational, highly publicized films, including *Cleopatra* (1917) and *Salome* (1918).

Ba•rab•bas (bə-răb′əs). In the New Testament, the condemned thief whose release, instead of that of Jesus, was demanded of Pilate by the multitude.

Ba•ra•cal•do (băr′ə-käl′dō, bä′rä). A city of northern Spain, an industrial suburb of Bilbao. Population, 118,692.

Ba•ra•co•a (băr′ə-kō′ə, bä′rä-). A city of southeast Cuba on the coast near the eastern end of the island. It is the oldest settlement in Cuba. Population, 35,754.

Ba•ra•ka (bə-rä′kə), **Imamu Amiri.** Originally LeRoi Jones. Born 1934. American writer whose poems and plays, such as *Slave Ship* (1967), focus on racial conflict.

Ba•ra•nof Island (băr′ə-nôf′, -nŏf′, bə-rä′nəf). An island off southeast Alaska in the Alexander Archipelago. It was named after Aleksandr Baranov, who founded the town of Sitka on the island.

Ba•ra•nov (bə-rä′nəf), **Aleksandr Andreevich.** 1746–1819. Russian fur trader and first governor of the Russian colony of Alaska.

Ba•ra•no•vi•chi (bə-rä′nə-vĭch′ē). A city of southwest Belorussia west of Bobruisk. Founded in 1870, it passed to Poland in 1920 and was reincorporated into the U.S.S.R. in 1939. Population, 149,000.

bar•a•the•a (băr′ə-thē′ə) *n.* A soft fabric of silk and cotton, silk and wool, or all wool. [Origin unknown.]

barb[1] (bärb) *n.* **1.** A sharp point projecting in reverse direction to the main point of a weapon or tool, as on an arrow or fishhook. **2.** A cutting remark. **3.** *Zoology.* One of the parallel filaments projecting from the main shaft of a feather. **4.** *Botany.* A short, sharply hooked bristle or hairlike projection. **5.** See **barbel[1]. 6.** Any of various Old World freshwater fishes of the genus *Barbus* or *Puntius* and related genera. **7.** A linen covering for a woman's head, throat, and chin worn in medieval times. **—barb** *tr.v.* **barbed, barb•ing, barbs.** To provide or furnish with a barb. [Middle English *barbe,* from Old French, beard, from Latin *barba.* See **bhardh-ā-** in Appendix.]

barb[2] (bärb) *n.* **1.** A horse of a breed introduced by the Moors into Spain from northern Africa that resembles the Arabians and is known for its speed and endurance. **2.** One of a breed of domestic pigeons that is similar to the carrier and has dark plumage. [French *barbe,* from Italian *barbero,* Berber, from Vulgar Latin **Barbaria,* Barbary States. See BARBARIAN.]

Bar•ba•dos (bär-bā′dōs′, -dōz′, -dəs). *Abbr.* **Barb.** A country occupying the easternmost island of the West Indies. Probably first visited by the Portuguese, who named it Los Barbados ("the bearded") for its numerous bearded fig trees, the island gained its independence from Great Britain in 1966. Bridgetown is the capital and the largest city. Population, 248,983. **—Bar•ba′di•an** *adj. & n.*

Barbados cherry *n.* **1.** A tropical American evergreen shrub *(Malpighia glabra),* having red or rose flowers in umbels and red cherrylike edible fruits. **2.** The fruit of this plant, used to make desserts, preserves, and jellies.

Barbados gooseberry *n.* **1.** A tropical American cactus *(Pereskia aculeata)* with climbing or trailing spiny stems, broad leaves, and clusters of fragrant whitish, pale yellow, or pinkish flowers. **2.** The small, globular, yellow edible fruit of this plant, used to make jellies and preserves. Also called *blade apple.*

bar•bar•i•an (bär-bâr′ē-ən) *n.* **1.** A member of a people considered by those of another nation or group to have a primitive civilization. **2.** A fierce, brutal, or cruel person. **3.** An insensitive, uncultured person; a boor. See Synonyms at **boor.** [French *barbarien,* from *barbare,* from Latin *barbarus,* barbarous. See BARBAROUS.] **—bar•bar′i•an•ism** *n.*

bar•bar•ic (bär-băr′ĭk) *adj.* **1.** Of, relating to, or characteristic of barbarians. **2.** Marked by crudeness or lack of restraint in taste, style, or manner. [Latin *barbaricus,* from Greek *barbarikos,* from *barbaros,* foreign.] **—bar•bar′i•cal•ly** *adv.*

bar•ba•rism (bär′bə-rĭz′əm) *n.* **1.** An act, trait, or custom characterized by ignorance or crudity. **2.a.** The use of words, forms, or expressions considered incorrect or unacceptable. **b.** A specific word, form, or expression so used. [Latin *barbarismus,* use of a foreign tongue or of one's own tongue amiss, barbarism, from Greek *barbarismos,* from *barbarizein,* to behave or speak like a barbarian, from *barbaros,* non-Greek, foreign.]

USAGE NOTE: There is a significant difference in meaning between *barbarism* and *barbarity.* Both denote some absence of civilization, but the word *civilization* itself has several different senses, one the opposite of *barbarism,* the other the opposite of *barbarity.* On the one hand *civilization* may refer to the scientific, artistic, and cultural attainments of advanced societies; and it is this sense that figures in the meaning of *barbarism.* The English word *barbarism* originally referred to incorrect use of language, but it is now used more generally to refer to ignorance or crudity in matters of taste, including verbal expression: *The* New Yorker *would never tolerate such barbarisms.* On the other hand, *civilization* may refer to the basic social order that allows people to resolve their differences peaceably, and it is this sense—that is, civilization as opposed to savagery—that figures in the meaning of *barbarity,* which refers to savage brutality or cruelty in actions, as in *The accounts of the emperor's barbarity shocked the world.*

bar•bar•i•ty (bär-băr′ĭ-tē) *n., pl.* **-ties. 1.** Savage brutality or cruelty in actions or conduct. **2.** A cruel or savage act. **3.** *Usage Problem.* Crudity; coarseness. See Usage Note at **barbarism.**

bar•ba•rize (bär′bə-rīz′) *tr. & intr.v.* **-rized, -riz•ing, -riz•es.** To make or become crude, savage, or barbarous. **—bar′ba•ri•za′tion** (-rĭ-zā′shən) *n.*

Bar•ba•ros•sa[1] (bär′bə-rŏs′ə, -rôs′ə). European name for Khair ed-Din. Died 1546. Greek-born Turkish corsair who with his brother **Arouj** (died 1518) ravaged the coasts of Spain, Italy, and Greece.

Bar•ba•ros•sa[2] (bär′bə-rŏs′ə, -rôs′ə). See **Frederick I.**

bar•ba•rous (bär′bər-əs) *adj.* **1.** Primitive in culture and customs; uncivilized. **2.** Lacking refinement or culture; coarse. **3.** Characterized by savagery; very cruel. See Synonyms at **cruel. 4.** Marked by the use or occurrence of barbarisms in spoken or written language. [From Latin *barbarus,* from Greek *barbaros,* non-Greek, foreign.] **—bar′ba•rous•ly** *adv.* **—bar′ba•rous•ness** *n.*

Bar•ba•ry (bär′bə-rē, -brē). A region of northern Africa on the Mediterranean coast between Egypt and the Atlantic Ocean. Settled by Berbers in the 2nd millennium B.C., it fell to the Arabs in the 7th century A.D. From the 16th to the 19th century it was used as a base by pirates who raided ships in the Mediterranean Sea and extracted tribute from the European powers trading in the area.

Barbary ape *n.* A tailless monkey *(Macaca sylvana)* of Gibraltar and northern Africa. Also called *magot.*

Barbary Coast. 1. The Mediterranean coastal area of Barbary and the Barbary States. **2.** A waterfront area of San Francisco, California, in the years after the 1849 gold rush. It was notorious for its gambling dens, saloons, brothels, and disreputable boarding houses.

Barbary sheep *n.* See **aoudad.**

Barbary States. The North African states of Algeria, Tunisia, Tripoli, and Morocco, especially from the 16th to the 19th century.

bar•bas•co (bär-bäs′kō) *n., pl.* **-cos. 1.** Any of several tropical American plants, as in the genus *Lonchocarpus,* that contain a substance that can stun or paralyze fish. **2.** Any of several Mexican plants of the genus *Dioscorea* having a large, inedible root that yields an extract used as a raw material for synthetic steroid hormones. [American Spanish, from Spanish *barbasco,* mullein, alteration (possibly influenced by *barba,* beard) of *verbasco,* from Latin *verbascum.*]

bar•bate (bär′bāt′) *adj.* Having a beard; bearded. [Latin *barbātus,* from *barba,* beard. See BARB[1].]

bar•be•cue (bär′bĭ-kyo͞o′) *n.* **1.** A grill, pit, or outdoor fireplace for roasting meat. **2.a.** A whole animal carcass or section thereof roasted or broiled over an open fire or on a spit. **b.** A social gathering, usually held outdoors, at which food is cooked over an open flame. **—barbecue** *tr.v.* **-cued, -cu•ing, -cues.** To roast, broil, or grill (meat or seafood) over live coals or an open fire, often basting with a seasoned sauce. [American Spanish *barbacoa,* of Taino origin.]

barbed (bärbd) *adj.* **1.** Having barbs. **2.** Cutting; stinging: *barbed criticism; barbed statements.* **—barb′ed•ness** (bär′bĭd-nĭs) *n.*

barbed wire *n.* Twisted strands of fence wire with barbs at regular intervals.

baptistery
Top: The Baptistery, Pisa, Italy
Bottom: 15th-century German

barb[1]

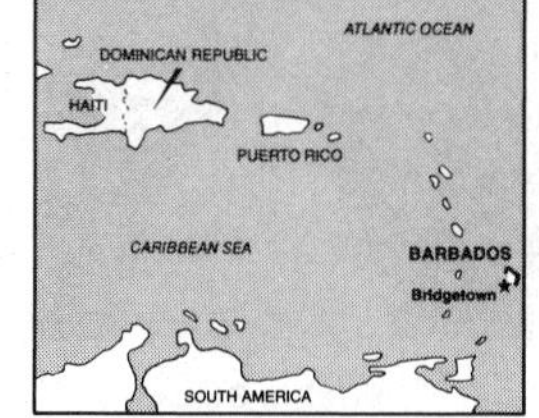

Barbados

bar·bel¹ (bär′bəl) *n.* One of the slender, whiskerlike tactile organs extending from the head of certain fishes, such as catfishes. Also called *barb.* [Obsolete French, from Old French, from Medieval Latin *barbula,* diminutive of Late Latin *barbus,* beard, from Latin *barba.* See **bhardh-ā-** in Appendix.]

bar·bel² (bär′bəl) *n.* Any of several Old World freshwater fish of the genus *Barbus,* especially *B. barbus,* having four barbels on its upper jaw. [Middle English, from Old French, from Medieval Latin **barbellus,* diminutive of *barbus,* from Latin *barba,* beard. See BARBEL¹.]

bar·bell (bär′bĕl′) *n.* A bar with adjustable weights at each end, lifted for sport or exercise. [BAR¹ + (DUMB)BELL.]

barbell
Kazushito Manabe of Japan at the 1984 Summer Olympics, Los Angeles

bar·bel·late (bär′bə-lāt′, bär-bĕl′ĭt, -āt′) *adj. Botany.* Finely or minutely barbed: *barbellate stems.* [From New Latin *barbella,* diminutive of Latin *barba,* beard. See **bhardh-ā-** in Appendix.]

bar·ber (bär′bər) *n.* One whose business is to cut hair and to shave or trim beards. **—barber** *v.* **-bered, -ber·ing, -bers.** *—tr.* **1.** To cut the hair of. **2.** To shave or trim the beard of. *—intr.* To work as a barber. [Middle English, from Old French *barbour,* from Medieval Latin *barbātor,* from Latin *barba,* beard. See **bhardh-ā-** in Appendix.]

Bar·ber (bär′bər), **Samuel.** 1910–1981. American composer whose works include *Adagio for Strings* (1936) and the opera *Vanessa* (1958), for which he won a Pulitzer Prize.

bar·ber·ry (bär′bĕr′ē) *n.* Any of various shrubs of the genus *Berberis* having leaves that are often clustered, small yellow flowers, and red, orange, or blackish berries. They are grown as specimen or hedge plants. [Middle English *berberie,* from Medieval Latin *berberis.*]

bar·ber·shop (bär′bər-shŏp′) *n.* The place of business of a barber. **—barbershop** *adj. Music.* Of, consisting of, or relating to the performance of sentimental songs in four-part harmony: *a barbershop quartet.*

bar·ber's itch (bär′bərz) *n.* Any of various skin eruptions on the face and neck, especially ringworm of the beard. Also called *tinea barbae.*

Bar·ber·ton (bär′bər-tən). A city of northeast Ohio, an industrial suburb of Akron. Population, 29,751.

bar·bet (bär′bĭt) *n.* Any of various brightly colored tropical birds of the family Capitonidae that have a broad bill with bristles at the base and are related to the toucans. [Probably from BARB¹.]

bar·bette (bär-bĕt′) *n.* **1.** A platform or mound of earth within a fort from which guns are fired over the parapet. **2.** An armored protective cylinder around a revolving gun turret on a warship. [French, diminutive of *barbe,* beard. See BARB¹.]

bar·bi·can (bär′bĭ-kən) *n.* A tower or other fortification on the approach to a castle or town, especially one at a gate or drawbridge. [Middle English, from Old French *barbacane,* from Medieval Latin *barbacana,* from Persian *barbārkhāna* : *barbār,* guard (from Old Iranian **parivāraka-,* protective; see **wer-⁴** in Appendix) + *khāna,* house (from Middle Persian *khānak*).]

bar·bi·cel (bär′bĭ-sĕl′) *n. Zoology.* One of the minute, hooked projections extending from and interlocking the barbules of a feather. [New Latin *barbicella,* diminutive of Latin *barba,* beard. See **bhardh-ā-** in Appendix.]

bar·bi·tal (bär′bĭ-tôl′, -tăl′) *n.* A barbiturate, $C_8H_{12}N_2O_3$, that is a white crystalline powder and is used as a sedative and hypnotic especially in the form of its soluble salt, sodium barbital. [From BARBITURIC ACID.]

bar·bi·tu·rate (bär-bĭch′ər-ĭt, -ə-rāt′, bär′bĭ-to͝or′ĭt, -āt′, -tyo͝or′-) *n.* **1.** A salt or ester of barbituric acid. **2.** Any of a group of barbituric acid derivatives that act as central nervous system depressants and are used as sedatives or hypnotics. [BARBITUR(IC ACID) + -ATE².]

bar·bi·tu·ric acid (bär′bĭ-to͝or′ĭk, -tyo͝or′-) *n.* An organic acid, $C_4H_4O_3N_2$, used in the manufacture of barbiturates and some plastics. [Partial translation of German *Barbitursäure.*]

Bar·bi·zon (bär′bĭ-zŏn′) *adj.* Of, relating to, or characteristic of a 19th-century group of landscape painters in France that included Corot, Daubigny, Millet, and Rousseau. [After *Barbizon,* a village of north-central France.]

bard²

Bar·bour (bär′bər), **Philip Pendleton.** 1783–1841. American jurist who served as an associate justice of the U.S. Supreme Court (1836–1841).

Bar·bu·da (bär-bo͞o′də). An island of Antigua and Barbuda in the West Indies north of Antigua. It was privately owned from 1691 to 1872. **—Bar·bu′dan** *adj. & n.*

bar·bule (bär′byo͞ol) *n. Zoology.* A small barb or pointed projection, especially one of the small projections fringing the edges of the barbs of feathers. [Latin *barbula,* diminutive of *barba,* beard. See **bhardh-ā-** in Appendix.]

barb·wire (bärb′wīr′) *n.* Barbed wire.

bar·ca (bär′kə) *n. Nautical.* A double-ended boat, skiff, or barge used in the Mediterranean. [Italian *barca.* See BARK³.]

bar·ca·role also **bar·ca·rolle** (bär′kə-rōl′) *n. Music.* **1.** A Venetian gondolier's song with a rhythm suggestive of rowing. **2.** A composition imitating a Venetian gondolier's song. [French, from Italian *barcaruola,* from *barcaruolo,* gondolier, from *barca,* boat, from Latin.]

Brigitte Bardot
Photographed in 1970

Bar·ce·lo·na (bär′sə-lō′nə). A city of northeast Spain on the Mediterranean Sea. Founded by the Carthaginians, it prospered under the Romans and Visigoths, fell to the Moors in 713, and was taken by Charlemagne's Frankish troops in 801. It has long been a center of Catalan separatism and of anarchic, socialist, and syndicalist movements. Population, 1,770,296.

Barcelona chair A trademark used for a wide armless chair with leather cushions on a double X-shaped frame formed of gently curving stainless steel bars.

B.Arch. *abbr.* Bachelor of Architecture.

bar chart *n.* See **bar graph.**

Bar·clay (bär′klē), **Robert.** 1648–1690. Scottish Quaker apologist whose *Truth Triumphant* (1692), a collection of his writings, describes and defends the tenets of Quakerism.

bar code *n.* See **Universal Product Code.**

bard¹ (bärd) *n.* **1.** One of an ancient Celtic order of minstrel poets who composed and recited verses celebrating the legendary exploits of chieftains and heroes. **2.** A poet, especially a lyric poet. See Synonyms at **poet.** [Middle English, from Irish and Scottish Gaelic *bard* and from Welsh *bardd;* see **gʷerə-²** in Appendix.] **—bard′ic** *adj.*

bard² also **barde** (bärd) *—n.* A piece of armor used to protect or ornament a horse. *—tr.v.* **bard·ed, bard·ing, bards.** To equip (a horse) with bards. [Middle English *barde,* from Old French, from Old Italian *barda,* from Arabic *barda'ah,* packsaddle, from Persian *pardah.* See PURDAH.]

♦**bar·da·cious** (bär′dā′shəs) *adj. & adv. Southern & South Midland U.S.* Variant of **bodacious.**

barde (bärd) *n. & tr.v.* Variant of **bard².**

Bar·deen (bär-dēn′), **John.** 1908–1991. American physicist. He shared a Nobel Prize in 1956 for the development of the electronic transistor and in 1972 for a theory of superconductivity.

Bar·do·li·no (bär′dl-ē′nō) *n., pl.* **-nos.** An Italian red wine with a dry, light taste. [After *Bardolino,* a village of northern Italy.]

Bar·dot (bär-dō′), **Brigitte.** Born 1935? French actress whose best-known films are *And God Created Woman* (1956) and *Shaloko* (1968).

bare¹ (bâr) *adj.* **bar·er, bar·est. 1.** Lacking the usual or appropriate covering or clothing; naked: *a bare arm.* **2.** Exposed to view; undisguised: *bare fangs.* **3.** Lacking the usual furnishings, equipment, or decoration: *bare walls.* **4.** Having no addition, adornment, or qualification: *the bare facts.* See Synonyms at **empty. 5.** Just sufficient; mere: *the bare necessities.* **6.** *Obsolete.* Bareheaded. **—bare** *tr.v.* **bared, bar·ing, bares. 1.** To make bare; uncover or reveal: *bared their heads; baring secrets.* See Synonyms at **strip¹. 2.** To expose: *The dog bared its teeth.* [Middle English *bar,* from Old English *bær.* See **bhoso-** in Appendix.] **—bare′ness** *n.*

bare² (bâr) *v. Archaic.* A past tense of **bear¹.**

bare·back (bâr′băk′) also **bare·backed** (-băkt′) *adv. & adj.* On a horse, pony, or other animal with no saddle: *rode bareback; a bareback rider.*

bare bones *pl.n. Informal.* The basic elements or essentials: *outlined the bare bones of the proposal.* **—bare′-bones′** (bâr′bōnz′) *adj.*

bare·faced (bâr′fāst′) *adj.* **1.a.** Having no covering over the face. **b.** Having no beard. **2.** Without disguise; unconcealed. **3.** Undisguisedly bold; brazen. See Synonyms at **shameless. —bare′fac′ed·ly** (-fā′sĭd-lē, -fāst′lē) *adv.* **—bare′fac′ed·ness** *n.*

bare·foot (bâr′fo͝ot′) also **bare·foot·ed** (-fo͝ot′ĭd) *adv. & adj.* With nothing on the feet: *walking barefoot in the grass; a barefoot boy.*

barefoot doctor *n.* A lay health care worker, especially in rural China, trained in such activities as first aid, childbirth assistance, the dispensing of drugs, and preventive medicine.

ba·rege also **ba·rège** (bə-rĕzh′) *n.* A sheer fabric woven of silk or cotton and wool, used for women's apparel. [French *barège,* after *Barèges,* a town in France.]

bare·hand·ed (bâr′hăn′dĭd) *adv. & adj.* With no covering on the hands: *fought barehanded; barehanded boxing.* **—bare′hand′ed·ness** *n.*

bare·head·ed (bâr′hĕd′ĭd) *adv. & adj.* With no covering on the head: *walking bareheaded in the rain; a bareheaded pedestrian.* **—bare′head′ed·ness** *n.*

Ba·reil·ly also **Ba·re·li** (bə-rā′lē). A city of northern India east-southeast of Delhi. It was founded in the 16th century. Population, 386,734.

bare-knuck·le (bâr′ nŭk′əl) *adv.* Without gloves: *boxers fighting bare-knuckle.* **—bare-knuckle** *adj.* **1.** Wearing no gloves: *an undefeated bare-knuckle champion.* **2.** *Slang.* Of a fiercely implacable character: *the bare-knuckle world of commercial real estate.*

bare-knuck·led (bâr′nŭk′əld) *adv. & adj.* Bare-knuckle.

bare·leg·ged (bâr′lĕg′ĭd, -lĕgd′) *adv. & adj.* With the legs uncovered: *ran barelegged through the surf; barelegged children on the beach.* **—bare′leg′ged·ness** *n.*

Ba·re·li (bə-rā′lē). See **Bareilly.**

bare·ly (bâr′lē) *adv.* **1.** By a very little; hardly: *could barely see the road in the fog.* **2.** In a scanty manner; sparsely: *a barely furnished room.*

♦**bare-na·ked** (bâr′nā′kĭd, -nĕk′ĭd) *adv. & adj. Chiefly Northern U.S.* With no clothes on.

♦ ***REGIONAL NOTE:*** Regional expressions abound for the meaning "entirely unclothed." The chiefly Northern U.S. expression *bare-naked* illustrates the linguistic process of redundancy, not normally acceptable in Standard English but productive in regional dialect speech. A redundant expression combines two words that mean the same thing, thereby intensifying the effect. The expression *buck-naked,* used chiefly in the South Atlantic and Gulf States, is not as clear as *bare-naked* with respect to its origin; *buck* is possibly an alteration of *butt,* "buttocks." If so, *bum-naked* and *bare-ass(ed),* attested in the Northeastern U.S., represent the same idea.

Bar·ents (băr′ənts, bär′-), **Willem.** 1550?–1597. Dutch Arctic explorer who led several expeditions (1594–1597) in search of the Northeast Passage.

Barents Sea. A shallow section of the Arctic Ocean north of Norway and northwest Russia. The North Atlantic Current keeps its southern ports ice-free all year.

barf (bärf) *tr. & intr.v.* **barfed, barf·ing, barfs.** *Slang.* To vomit. [Probably imitative.] **—barf** *n.*

barf bag *n. Slang.* A disposable plastic or paper bag provided to a passenger by an airline for use in case of airsickness.

bar·fly (bär′flī′) *n. Slang.* One who frequents drinking establishments.

bar·gain (bär′gĭn) *n.* **1.** An agreement between parties fixing obligations that each promises to carry out. **2.a.** An agreement establishing the terms of a sale or exchange of goods or services: *finally reached a bargain with the antique dealer over the lamp.* **b.** Property acquired or services rendered as a result of such an agreement. **3.** Something offered or acquired at a price advantageous to the buyer. **—bargain** *v.* **-gained, -gain·ing, -gains.** *—intr.* **1.** To negotiate the terms of an agreement, as to sell or exchange. **2.** To engage in collective bargaining. **3.** To arrive at an agreement. *—tr.* To exchange; trade: *bargained my watch for a meal.* ***—phrasal verb.*** **bargain for** (or **on**). To count on; expect: *"I never bargained for this tearing feeling inside me"* (Anne Tyler). ***—idiom.*** **into** (or **in**) **the bargain.** Over and above what is expected; in addition. [Middle English, from Old French *bargaigne,* haggling, from *bargaignier,* to haggle, of Germanic origin. See **bhergh-**[1] in Appendix.] **—bar′gain·er** *n.*

SYNONYMS: *bargain, compact, contract, covenant, deal.* The central meaning shared by these nouns is "an agreement arrived at after discussion in which the parties involved promise to honor their respective obligations": *kept his end of the bargain and mowed the lawn; made a compact to correspond regularly; a legally binding contract to install new windows in the house; a covenant for mutual defense; annoyance that wasn't part of the deal.*

bargain basement *n.* A basement floor or floors in a department store where goods and apparel are sold at reduced prices. **—bar′gain-base′ment** (bär′gĭn-bās′mənt) *adj.*

bar·gain·ing chip (bär′gə-nĭng) *n.* Leverage, typically in the form of an inducement or a concession, useful in successful negotiations: *"A bargaining chip is ultimately worthless if you're not willing to bargain it away"* (New Republic).

barge (bärj) *n. Nautical.* **1.a.** A long, large, usually flat-bottomed boat for transporting freight that is generally unpowered and towed or pushed by other craft. **b.** A large, open pleasure boat used for parties, pageants, or formal ceremonies. **2.** A powerboat reserved for the use of an admiral. **—barge** *v.* **barged, barg·ing, barg·es.** *—tr. Nautical.* To carry by barge. *—intr.* **1.** To move about clumsily. **2.** To enter rudely and abruptly; intrude: *barged into the meeting.* [Middle English, from Old French, from Latin *barca,* boat.]

barge·board (bärj′bôrd′, -bōrd′) *n. Architecture.* A board, often ornately carved, attached along the projecting edge of a gable roof. [Origin unknown.]

barg·ee (bär-jē′) *n. Chiefly British.* A bargeman. [BARGE + -EE[2].]

bar·gel·lo (bär-zhĕl′ō) *n., pl.* **-los.** A needlepoint stitch that produces zigzag lines. [After the *Bargello,* a museum in Florence, Italy, which contains chairs upholstered in fabric worked in this stitch.]

barge·man (bärj′mən) *n.* The master or a crew member of a barge.

bar·ghest also **bar·guest** (bär′gĕst) *n.* A goblin in English folklore, often appearing in the shape of a large dog and believed to portend imminent death or misfortune. [*bar* (perhaps from BARROW[2]) + *ghest,* ghost (dialectal variant of GHOST).]

bar·girl (bär′gûrl′) *n.* **1.** A B-girl. **2.** A barmaid.

bar graph *n.* A graph consisting of parallel, usually vertical bars or rectangles with lengths proportional to the frequency with which specified quantities occur in a set of data. Also called *bar chart.*

bar·guest (bär′gĕst) *n.* Variant of **barghest.**

Bar Harbor (bär). A town of southeast Maine on Mount Desert Island. It is a summer resort. Population, 2,685.

bar·hop (bär′hŏp′) *intr.v.* **-hopped, -hop·ing, -hops.** *Slang.* To patronize a series of bars during an evening.

Ba·ri (bä′rē). A city of southeast Italy on the Adriatic Sea. Controlled successively by the Greeks, Romans, Goths, Lombards, Byzantines, Normans, and Venetians, it became part of the kingdom of Naples in 1557. Population, 370,781.

bar·i·at·rics (băr′ē-ăt′rĭks) *n. (used with a sing. verb).* The branch of medicine that deals with the causes, prevention, and treatment of obesity. [BAR(O)- + -IATRICS.] **—bar′i·at′ric** *adj.* **—bar′i·a·tri′cian** (-ə-trĭsh′ən) *n.*

ba·ril·la (bə-rēl′yə, -rē′yə) *n.* **1.** Either of two Mediterranean saltworts *(Salsola kali* or *S. soda)* or a similar plant *(Halogeton sativus),* burned to obtain a crude soda ash. **2.** The crude sodium carbonate ash obtained from these plants. [Spanish *barrilla.*]

Bar·ing (bâr′ĭng), **Alexander.** First Baron Ashburton. 1774–1848. British financier and public official who concluded the treaty between Great Britain and the United States that defined the border between Canada and Maine (1842).

Ba·ri·sal (băr′ĭ-sôl′, bŭr′ĭ-säl′). A city of southern Bangladesh on the Ganges River delta. The phenomenon known as "the Barisal guns," unexplained sounds resembling distant thunder or cannon fire, may be seismic in origin. Population, 159,298.

bar·ite (bâr′īt, băr′-) also **ba·ry·tes** (bə-rī′tēz) *n.* A yellow, white, or colorless crystalline mineral of barium sulfate, $BaSO_4$, that is used in paint and as the chief source of barium chemicals. Also called *heavy spar.* [Greek *barus,* heavy see **gʷerə-**[1] in Appendix + -ITE[1].]

bar·i·tone also **bar·y·tone** (băr′ĭ-tōn′) *n. Music.* **1.a.** A male singer or voice with a range higher than a bass and lower than a tenor. **b.** A part written for a voice with such a range. **2.** A brass wind instrument with a range similar to that of a baritone voice. *—attributive.* Often used to modify another noun: *baritone voices; baritone parts.* [Italian *baritono,* from Greek *barutonos,* deep sounding : *barus,* heavy; see **gʷerə-**[1] in Appendix + *tonos,* tone; see TONE.]

bar·i·um (bâr′ē-əm, băr′-) *n. Symbol* **Ba** A soft, silvery-white alkaline-earth metal, used to deoxidize copper and in various alloys. Atomic number 56; atomic weight 137.34; melting point 725°C; boiling point 1,140°C; specific gravity 3.50; valence 2. See table at **element.** [BAR(YTA) + -IUM.] **—bar′ic** (-ĭk) *adj.*

barium sulfate *n.* A fine white powder, $BaSO_4$, used as a pigment, as a filler for textiles, rubbers, and plastics, and as a contrast medium in x-ray photography of the digestive tract.

bark[1] (bärk) *n.* **1.** The harsh, abrupt sound uttered by a dog. **2.** A sound, such as a cough, that is similar to a dog's bark. **—bark** *v.* **barked, bark·ing, barks.** *—intr.* **1.** To utter the harsh, abrupt sound of a dog. **2.** To make a sound similar to a bark: *"The birds bark softly, sounding almost like young pups"* (Charleston SC News and Courier). **3.** To speak sharply; snap: *"It is power that can often be misused—as when an obscure lieutenant colonel can bark at a Pentagon general, commanding him to do something questionable 'because the White House wants it done'"* (John Hughes). **4.** To work as a barker, as at a carnival. *—tr.* To utter in a loud, harsh voice: *The quarterback barked out the signals.* ***—idiom.*** **bark up the wrong tree.** To misdirect one's energies or attention. [From Middle English *berken,* to bark, from Old English *beorcan.*]

bark[2] (bärk) *n.* **1.** The tough outer covering of the woody stems and roots of trees, shrubs, and other woody plants. It includes all tissues outside the vascular cambium. **2.** A specific kind of bark used for a special purpose, as in tanning or medicine. **—bark** *tr.v.* **barked, bark·ing, barks.** **1.** To remove bark from (a tree or log). **2.** To rub off the skin of; abrade: *barked my shin on the car door.* **3.** To treat medically, tan, or dye using bark. [Middle English, from Old Norse *börkr.*]

bark[3] also **barque** (bärk) *n. Nautical.* **1.** A sailing ship with from three to five masts, all of them square-rigged except the after mast, which is fore-and-aft rigged. **2.** A small vessel that is propelled by oars or sails. [Middle English *barke,* boat, from Old French *barque,* from Old Italian *barca,* from Latin.]

bark beetle *n.* Any of various small, cylindrical beetles of the family Scolytidae that burrrow along the surface wood directly beneath the bark of trees, causing extensive damage.

bar·keep·er (bär′kē′pər) also **bar·keep** (-kēp′) *n.* **1.** A person who owns or operates a bar for the sale of alcoholic beverages. **2.** See **bartender.**

bar·ken·tine also **bar·quen·tine** (bär′kən-tēn′) *n. Nautical.* A sailing ship with from three to five masts of which only the foremast is square-rigged, the others being fore-and-aft rigged. [Probably BARK[3] + (BRIG)ANTINE.]

bark·er[1] (bär′kər) *n.* **1.** One, such as a dog, that makes a bark or a barking sound. **2.** An employee who stands before the entrance to a show, as at a carnival, and solicits customers with a loud, colorful sales spiel.

bark·er[2] (bär′kər) *n.* One that removes bark from trees or logs or prepares it for tanning.

Bar·kley (bär′klē), **Alben William.** 1877–1956. Vice President of the United States (1949–1953) under Harry S. Truman.

bar-le-duc also **Bar-le-Duc** (bär′lĭ-do͝ok′) *n.* A savory preserve made of white currants or gooseberries. [After *Bar-le-Duc,* a town of northeast France.]

Bar·let·ta (bär-lĕt′ə). A city of southern Italy on the Adriatic Sea west-northwest of Bari. It passed to the Goths after the fall of the Roman Empire. Population, 83,719.

bar·ley (bär′lē) *n.* **1.** A grass in the genus *Hordeum,* native to temperate regions, having flowers in terminal, often long-awned spikes. **2.** The grain of *H. vulgare* or its varieties, used for live-

barge
On the Mississippi River

bargeboard
Kingscote Mansion,
Newport, Rhode Island

ă pat	oi boy
ā pay	ou out
âr care	o͝o took
ä father	o͞o boot
ĕ pet	ŭ cut
ē be	ûr urge
ĭ pit	th thin
ī pie	*th* this
îr pier	hw which
ŏ pot	zh vision
ō toe	ə about, item
ô paw	♦ regionalism

Stress marks: ′ (primary); ′ (secondary), as in **dictionary** (dĭk′shə-nĕr′ē)

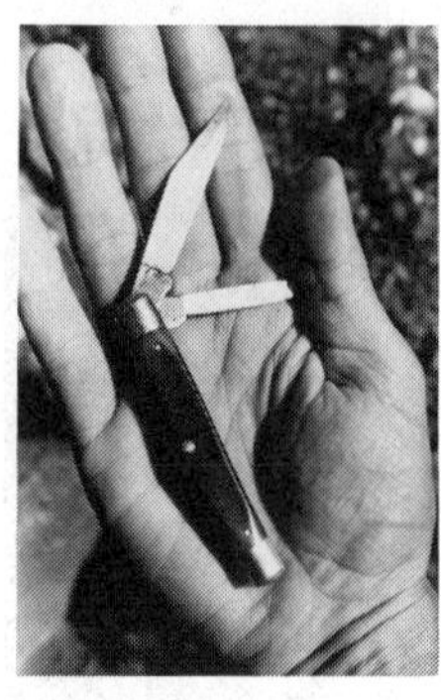
Barlow knife

Christiaan Barnard

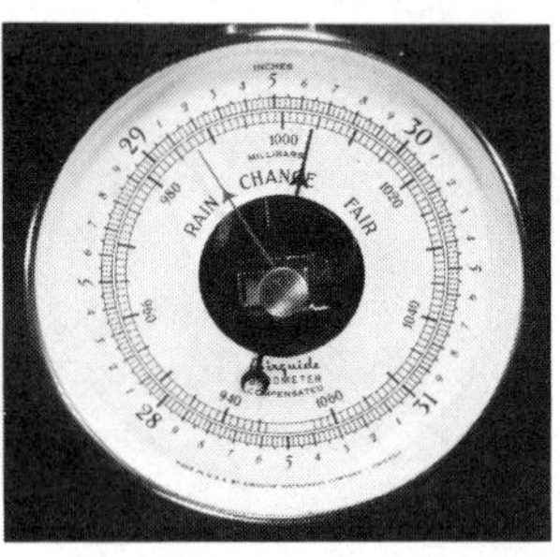

barometer

baroque

stock feed, malt production, and cereal. [Middle English *barli,* from Old English *bærlic.* See **bhares-** in Appendix.]

bar·ley·corn (bär′lē-kôrn′) *n.* **1.** The grain of barley. **2.** A unit of measure equal to the width of a grain of barley, or about ⅓ inch (0.85 centimeter).

barley sugar *n.* A clear, hard candy made by boiling down sugar, formerly with an extract of barley added.

Bar·low (bär′lō′), **Joel.** 1754–1812. American poet and diplomat in Algiers (1795–1797). Among his noted poetic works are "The Hasty Pudding" (1796) and the epic *Columbiad* (1807).

Barlow knife *n.* A two-bladed pocketknife with a short, spear-shaped blade for prying and gouging and a long, fine blade for carving and slicing. [After *Barlow,* the family name of its makers, two brothers in Sheffield, England.]

barm (bärm) *n.* The yeasty foam that rises to the surface of fermenting malt liquors. [Middle English *berme,* from Old English *beorma,* yeast. See **bhreu-** in Appendix.]

bar·maid (bär′mād′) *n.* A woman who serves drinks in a bar.

bar·man (bär′mən) *n.* A man who serves drinks in a bar.

Bar·me·cid·al (bär′mĭ-sīd′l) also **Bar·me·cide** (bär′mĭ-sīd′) *adj.* Plentiful or abundant in appearance only; illusory: *a Barmecidal feast.* [After *Barmecide,* a nobleman in *The Arabian Nights,* who served an imaginary feast to a beggar.]

bar mitz·vah or **bar miz·vah** (bär mĭts′və) —*n.* **1.** A 13-year-old Jewish boy, considered an adult and responsible for his moral and religious duties. **2.** The ceremony that initiates and recognizes a boy as a bar mitzvah. —*tr.v.* **-vahed, -vah·ing, -vahs.** To confirm in the ceremony of bar mitzvah. [Hebrew *bar miṣwâ : bar,* son + *miṣwâ,* command, commandment.]

barm·y (bär′mē) *adj.* **-i·er, -i·est. 1.** Full of barm; foamy. **2.** Eccentric; daft.

barn (bärn) *n.* **1.** A large farm building used for storing farm products and sheltering livestock. **2.** A large shed for the housing of vehicles, such as railroad cars. **3.** A particularly large, typically bare building: *lived in a barn of a country house.* **4.** *Abbr.* **b** *Physics.* A unit of area equal to 10^{-24} square centimeter, used to measure collision cross sections. [Middle English *bern,* from Old English *berærn : bere,* barley; see **bhares-** in Appendix + *ærn,* house.]

Bar·na·bas (bär′nə-bəs), Saint. Originally Joses or Joseph the Levite. fl. first century A.D. Christian convert and missionary with Saint Paul to Cyprus and Asia Minor.

bar·na·cle (bär′nə-kəl) *n.* **1.** Any of various marine crustaceans of the subclass Cirripedia that in the adult stage form a hard shell and remain attached to submerged surfaces, such as rocks and ships' bottoms. **2.** The barnacle goose. [Middle English, barnacle goose, from Old French *bernacle,* from Medieval Latin *bernacula,* diminutive of *bernaca,* perhaps from Old Irish *báirneach,* limpet.] —**bar′na·cled** *adj.*

barnacle goose *n.* A waterfowl *(Branta leucopsis)* of northern Europe and Greenland that breeds in the Arctic and has a white face with a black streak between the eyes and bill.

Bar·nard (bär′nərd, bär-närd′), **Christiaan Neethling.** Born 1923. South African surgeon who performed the first human heart transplant (1967).

Bar·nard (bär′nərd), **Edward Emerson.** 1857–1923. American astronomer and pioneer in photography noted for the discovery of Jupiter's fifth satellite (1892) and Barnard's star (1916), the second-nearest star system to the sun.

Barnard, Frederick Augustus Porter. 1809–1889. American educator and advocate of higher educational opportunities for women. He was the president of Columbia University from 1864 to 1889. Barnard College is named in his honor.

Barnard, George Grey. 1863–1938. American sculptor whose early works, such as *Struggle of Two Natures in Man* (1894), were influenced by Rodin. A colossal statue of Abraham Lincoln (1917) is perhaps his best-known work.

Bar·na·ul (bär′nə-o͞ol′). A city of south-central Russia on the Ob River south of Novosibirsk. It is an industrial center in a mining and agricultural region. Population, 578,000.

barn·burn·er (bärn′bûr′nər) *n. Informal.* An extremely impressive event or successful outcome: *"September will not be any barnburner* [for car sales]" (Lee Iacocca).

barn dance *n.* A social gathering, often held in a barn, with music and square dancing.

Barnes (bärnz), **Albert Coombs.** 1873–1951. American physician and art collector noted for his discovery of Argyrol and his collection of modern French paintings.

Bar·ne·veldt or **Bar·ne·veld** (bär′nə-vĕlt′), **Jan van Olden.** 1547–1619. Dutch public official who negotiated a treaty with Spain (1609) and opposed certain Calvinist doctrines, both of which actions led to his arrest and execution for treason.

barn owl *n.* A predatory nocturnal bird *(Tyto alba)* having a white, heart-shaped face, buff-brown upper plumage, and pale underparts, often nesting in barns and other buildings. Also called *monkey-faced owl.*

Barns·ley (bärnz′lē). A municipal borough of northern England north of Sheffield. It is a transportation and industrial center in a coal-mining area. Population, 225,800.

Barn·sta·ble (bärn′stə-bəl). A town of southeast Massachusetts on central Cape Cod. It is a resort community with many fine beaches. Population, 30,898.

barn·storm (bärn′stôrm′) *v.* **-stormed, -storm·ing, -storms.** —*intr.* **1.** To travel around the countryside making political speeches, giving lectures, or presenting plays. **2.** To appear at county fairs and carnivals in exhibitions of stunt flying and parachute jumping. —*tr.* To travel across while engaging in barnstorming. —**barn′storm′er** *n.*

barn swallow *n.* A widely distributed bird *(Hirundo rustica)* that nests in barns and caves and has a deeply forked tail, a dark-blue back, and tan underparts.

Bar·num (bär′nəm), **P(hineas) T(aylor).** 1810–1891. American showman who established The Greatest Show on Earth (1871), which was merged with its major competition (1881) to form the Barnum and Bailey Circus.

barn·yard (bärn′yärd′) *n.* The area surrounding a barn, often enclosed by a fence. —**barnyard** *adj.* Smutty; earthy: *barnyard humor.*

barnyard grass *n.* Any of certain grasses in the genus *Echinochloa,* especially the Old World annual species *E. crusgalli,* used sometimes for forage and widespread as a weed.

baro– or **bar–** *pref.* Weight; pressure: *barometer.* [From Greek *baros,* weight. See **gʷerə-¹** in Appendix.]

Ba·ro·da (bə-rō′də). A city of west-central India southeast of Ahmadabad. Once the capital of the princely state of **Baroda,** it is noted for its public buildings, palaces, and Hindu temples. Population, 734,473.

bar·o·gram (băr′ə-grăm′) *n.* A record produced by a barograph.

bar·o·graph (băr′ə-grăf′) *n.* A recording barometer. —**bar′o·graph′ic** *adj.*

Ba·ro·ja y Nes·si (bə-rō′hə ē nĕs′ē, bä-rô′hä), **Pío.** 1872–1956. Spanish writer whose novels largely concern the intellectual and political climate of his homeland.

Ba·ro·lo (bä-rō′lō′, bə-rō′-) *n.* A full-bodied red wine produced in Italy. [After *Barolo* in the Piedmont region of Italy.]

ba·rom·e·ter (bə-rŏm′ĭ-tər) *n.* **1.** *Abbr.* **bar.** An instrument for measuring atmospheric pressure, used especially in weather forecasting. **2.** Something that registers or responds to fluctuations; an indicator: *Opinion polls serve as a barometer of the public mood.* —**bar′o·met′ric** (băr′ə-mĕt′rĭk), **bar′o·met′ri·cal** *adj.* —**bar′o·met′ri·cal·ly** *adv.* —**ba·rom′e·try** *n.*

bar·on (băr′ən) *n.* **1.a.** A British nobleman of the lowest rank. **b.** A nobleman of continental Europe, ranked differently in various countries. **c.** A Japanese nobleman of the lowest rank. **d.** *Also* **Baron.** *Abbr.* **Bn., bn.** Used as the title for such a nobleman. **2.a.** A feudal tenant holding his rights and title directly from a king or another feudal superior. **b.** A lord or nobleman; a peer. **3.** One having great wealth, power, and influence in a specified sphere of activity: *an oil baron.* **4.** A cut of beef consisting of a double sirloin. [Middle English, from Old French, probably of Germanic origin.]

bar·on·age (băr′ə-nĭj) *n.* **1.** The peers of a kingdom considered as a group. **2.** Barons considered as a group. **3.** The rank or dignity of a baron. **4.** A list of barons.

bar·on·ess (băr′ə-nĭs) *n.* **1.a.** The wife or widow of a baron. **b.** A woman holding the title to a barony. **2.** Also **Baroness.** Used as the title for such a noblewoman.

bar·on·et (băr′ə-nĭt, băr′ə-nĕt′) *n.* **1.** A man holding a British hereditary title of honor reserved for commoners, ranking immediately below the barons and above all orders of knighthood except the Garter. **2.** Also **Baronet.** *Abbr.* **Bart., Bt.** Used as the title for such a man. [Middle English, diminutive of *baron,* baron. See BARON.]

bar·on·et·age (băr′ə-nĭ-tĭj, -nĕt′ĭj) *n.* **1.** Baronets considered as a group. **2.** The rank or dignity of a baronet. **3.** A list of baronets.

bar·on·et·cy (băr′ə-nĭt-sē, -nĕt′sē) *n., pl.* **-cies.** The rank or dignity of a baronet or a baronetess.

bar·on·et·ess (băr′ə-nĭ-tĭs, băr′ə-nĕt′ĭs) *n.* **1.** A woman holding a British hereditary title of honor reserved for commoners, ranking immediately below the barons and above all orders of knighthood except the Garter. **2. Baronetess.** *Abbr.* **Btss.** Used as the title for such a woman.

ba·rong (bə-rông′, -rŏng′) *n.* A large, broad-bladed knife used by the Moros of the Philippines. [Native word in the Philippines.]

ba·ro·ni·al (bə-rō′nē-əl) *adj.* **1.** Of or relating to a baron or barony. **2.** Suited for or befitting a baron; stately and grand: *a baronial mansion.*

bar·o·ny (băr′ə-nē) *n., pl.* **-nies. 1.** The domain of a baron. **2.** The rank or dignity of a baron.

ba·roque (bə-rōk′) *adj.* **1.** Also **Baroque.** Of, relating to, or characteristic of a style in art and architecture developed in Europe from about 1550 to 1700, emphasizing dramatic, often strained effect and typified by bold, curving forms, elaborate ornamentation, and overall balance of disparate parts. **2.** Also **Baroque.** *Music.* Of, relating to, or characteristic of a style of composition that flourished in Europe from about 1600 to 1750, marked by chromaticism, strict forms, and elaborate ornamentation. **3.** Marked by rich and sometimes bizarre or incongruous ornamentation. See Synonyms at **ornate. 4.** Irregular in shape: *baroque pearls.* —**baroque** also **Baroque** *n.* The baroque style or period in art, architecture, or music. [French, from Italian *barocco* and from Portuguese *barroco.*] —**ba·roque′ly** *adv.*

bar·o·re·cep·tor (băr′ə-rĭ-sĕp′tər) *n.* A sensory nerve ending that is stimulated by changes in pressure, especially one in the walls of blood vessels such as the carotid sinus.

Ba·rot·se·land (bə-rŏt′sē-lănd′). A former kindgom of central Africa, now the western part of Zambia.

ba·rouche (bə-ro͞osh′) *n.* A four-wheeled carriage with a collapsible top, two double seats inside opposite each other, and a box seat outside in front for the driver. [German *Barutsche,* from Italian *biroccio,* from Vulgar Latin **birotium,* from Late Latin *birotus,* two-wheeled : Latin *bi-,* bi-; see **dwo-** in Appendix + Latin *rota,* wheel; see **ret-** in Appendix.]

barque (bärk) *n. Nautical.* Variant of **bark**[3].

bar·quen·tine (bär′kən-tēn′) *n. Nautical.* Variant of **barkentine.**

Bar·qui·si·me·to (bär′kə-sə-mā′tō, -kē-sē-mĕ′tô). A city of northwest Venezuela west-southwest of Caracas. It was founded in 1552 and rebuilt after a major earthquake in 1812. Population, 504,000.

bar·rack[1] (băr′ək) *tr.v.* **-racked, -rack·ing, -racks.** To house (soldiers, for example) in quarters. **—barrack** *n. Abbr.* **bks. 1.** Often **bar·racks** (băr′əks). A building or group of buildings used to house military personnel. **2.** Often **barracks.** A large, unadorned building used for temporary occupancy. [From French *baraques,* barracks, from Spanish *barracas,* soldiers' tents or huts.]

bar·rack[2] (băr′ək) *v.* **-racked, -rack·ing, -racks.** —*intr.* **1.** *Chiefly British.* To jeer or shout at a player, speaker, or team. **2.** *Australian.* To shout support for a team. —*tr. Chiefly British.* To shout against; jeer at. [Perhaps from Irish dialectal *barrack,* to brag; akin to *brag.*] **—bar′rack·er** *n.*

barracks bag *n.* A cloth bag, usually with a drawstring, for the storage of clothing or laundry.

bar·ra·coon (băr′ə-ko͞on′) *n.* A barracks in which slaves or convicts were formerly held in temporary confinement. [Spanish *barracón,* augmentative of *barraca,* hut. See BARRACK[1].]

bar·ra·cu·da (băr′ə-ko͞o′də) *n., pl.* **barracuda** or **-das.** Any of various fierce, mostly tropical marine fishes of the genus *Sphyraena* that resemble pike, have a projecting lower jaw with fanglike teeth, and include some edible species. [American Spanish, from Spanish dialectal *barraco,* overlapping tooth.]

bar·rage[1] (bär′ĭj) *n.* An artificial obstruction, such as a dam or an irrigation channel, built in a watercourse to increase its depth or to divert its flow. [French, from *barrer,* to bar, from *barre,* bar, from Old French. See BAR[1].]

bar·rage[2] (bə-räzh′) *n.* **1.a.** A heavy curtain of artillery fire directed in front of friendly troops to screen and protect them. **b.** A rapid, concentrated discharge of missiles, as from small arms. **2.** An overwhelming, concentrated outpouring, as of words: *a barrage of criticism.* **—barrage** *tr.v.* **-raged, -rag·ing, -rag·es.** To direct a barrage at. [French *(tir de) barrage,* barrier (fire). See BARRAGE[1].]

SYNONYMS: *barrage, bombard, pepper, shower.* The central meaning shared by these verbs is "to direct a concentrated outpouring, as of missiles or words, at something or someone": *barraging the speaker with questions; bombarded the box office with ticket orders; peppered the senator with protests; showered the child with gifts.*

bar·rage balloon (bə-räzh′) *n.* A balloon anchored singly or in a series over a military objective to support nets that hinder the passage of enemy aircraft.

bar·ra·mun·da (băr′ə-mŭn′də) also **bar·ra·mun·di** (-dē) *n., pl.* **barramunda** or **-das** also **barramundi** or **-dis.** Any of several Australian food fishes, such as the lungfish. Also called *ceratodus.* [Probably of Aboriginal origin.]

♦ **bar·ran·ca** (bə-răng′kə) also **bar·ran·co** (-kō) *n. Southwestern U.S.* **1.** A deep ravine or gorge. **2.** A bluff. [Spanish, probably of Iberian origin.]

Bar·ran·quil·la (bär′ən-kē′ə, -yä, bä′rän-). A city of northern Colombia on the Magdalena River near the Caribbean Sea. Founded in 1629, it is Colombia's chief port. Population, 891,545.

bar·ra·tor also **bar·ra·ter** (băr′ə-tər) *n. Law.* One that persistently instigates lawsuits. [Middle English *baratour,* from Old French *barateour,* swindler, from *barater,* to cheat, perhaps from Vulgar Latin **prattāre,* from Greek *prattein,* to do.]

bar·ra·try (băr′ə-trē) *n., pl.* **-tries. 1.** *Law.* The offense of persistently instigating lawsuits, typically groundless ones. **2.** An unlawful breach of duty on the part of a ship's master or crew resulting in injury to the ship's owner: *"Gross misconduct of the officers is . . . barratry"* (Tom Clancy). **3.** Sale or purchase of positions in church or state. [Middle English *barratrie,* the sale of church offices, from Old French *baraterie,* deception, malversation, from *barater,* to cheat. See BARRATOR.] **—bar′ra·trous** (-trəs) *adj.* **—bar′ra·trous·ly** *adv.*

Barr body (bär) *n. Genetics.* The condensed, inactive, single X chromosome found in the nuclei of somatic cells of most female mammals. Its presence is the basis of sex determination tests that are performed, for example, on athletes. Also called *sex chromatin.* [After Murray L. *Barr* (born 1908), Canadian anatomist.]

barred (bärd) *adj.* Marked with bars or stripes: *barred prison cells; barred plumage on a bird.*

barred owl *n.* A large North American owl *(Strix varia)* having barred, brownish plumage across the breast, a streaked belly, and a strident, hooting cry.

bar·rel (băr′əl) *n.* **1.** A large, cylindrical container, usually made of staves bound together with hoops, with a flat top and bottom of equal diameter. **2.** The quantity that a barrel with a given or standard capacity will hold. **3.** *Abbr.* **bar., bbl, bbl., bl.** Any of various units of volume or capacity. In the U.S. Customary System it varies, as a liquid measure, from 31 to 42 gallons (120 to 159 liters) as established by law or usage. See table at **measurement. 4.** The cylindrical part or hollow shaft of any of various mechanisms, as: **a.** The metal, cylindrical part of a firearm through which the bullet travels. **b.** A cylinder that contains a movable piston. **c.** The drum of a capstan. **d.** The cylinder within the mechanism of a timepiece that contains the mainspring. **5.** *Informal.* A large quantity: *a barrel of fun.* **6.** *Slang.* An act or an instance of moving rapidly, often recklessly, in a motor vehicle. **—barrel** *adj.* Likened to a barrel, as in shape: *a barrel chest; barrel hips.* **—barrel** *v.* **-reled, -rel·ing, -rels** or **-relled, -rel·ling, -rels.** —*tr.* To put or pack in a barrel. —*intr. Slang.* To move at a high speed. **—*idioms.* on the barrel** (or **barrelhead).** Granting, giving, or requesting no credit: *paid cash on the barrel for the car.* **over a barrel.** In a very awkward position from which extrication is difficult: *During the negotiations the opposing faction had us over a barrel.* [Middle English *barel,* from Old French *baril.*]

barrel cactus *n.* Any of several cacti, especially in the genera *Ferocactus* and *Echinocactus,* having unbranched, globular to columnar, ribbed spiny stems.

barrel chair *n.* A large upholstered chair having a high, rounded back resembling a half barrel.

bar·rel·ful (băr′əl-fo͝ol′) *n., pl.* **-fuls.** The amount that a barrel can hold.

bar·rel·head (băr′əl-hĕd′) *n.* The flat top of a barrel.

bar·rel·house (băr′əl-hous′) *n.* **1.** A disreputable old-time saloon or bawdyhouse. **2.** *Music.* An early style of jazz characterized by free group improvisation and an accented two-beat rhythm.

barrel organ *n. Music.* A mechanical instrument on which a tune is played by the action of a revolving cylinder fitted with pegs or pins that open pipe valves supplied by a bellows.

barrel roll *n.* A flight maneuver in which an airplane makes a complete rotation on its longitudinal axis while approximately maintaining its original direction.

bar·ren (băr′ən) *adj.* **1.a.** Not producing offspring. **b.** Incapable of producing offspring. See Synonyms at **sterile. 2.** Lacking vegetation, especially useful vegetation. **3.** Unproductive of results or gains; unprofitable: *barren efforts.* See Synonyms at **futile. 4.** Devoid of something specified: *writing barren of insight.* See Synonyms at **empty. 5.** Lacking in liveliness or interest. **—barren** *n.* A tract of unproductive land, often with a scrubby growth of trees. Often used in the plural. [Middle English *barreine,* from Old French *brahaigne,* perhaps of Germanic origin.] **—bar′ren·ly** *adv.* **—bar′ren·ness** *n.*

Bar·ren Grounds (băr′ən). A treeless, sparsely inhabited region of northern Canada northwest of Hudson Bay and east of the Mackenzie River basin.

barren strawberry *n.* A low-growing, eastern North American perennial herb *(Waldsteinia fragarioides)* having strawberry-like leaves, yellow flowers, and small, dry, inedible fruit.

Bar·rès (bä-rĕs′), **Auguste Maurice.** 1862–1923. French writer and politician whose written works trace his metamorphosis from egocentric to nationalist.

bar·rette (bə-rĕt′) *n.* A small clasp used by women and girls for holding the hair in place. [French, diminutive of *barre,* bar, from Old French. See BAR[1].]

bar·ri·cade (băr′ĭ-kād′, băr′ĭ-kād′) *n.* **1.** A structure set up across a route of access to obstruct the passage of an enemy. **2.** Something that serves as an obstacle; a barrier. See Synonyms at **bulwark. —barricade** *tr.v.* **-cad·ed, -cad·ing, -cades. 1.** To close off or block with a barricade. **2.** To keep in or out by means of a barricade. [French, from *barrique,* barrel, from Old Provençal *barrica,* from Vulgar Latin **barrīca.* See EMBARGO.] **—bar′ri·cad′er** *n.*

Bar·rie (băr′ē). A city of southern Ontario, Canada, on Lake Simcoe north-northwest of Toronto. It is a manufacturing center and summer resort. Population, 38,423.

Barrie, Sir **J(ames) M(atthew).** 1860–1937. British writer whose whimsical and fantastic works include the play *Peter Pan* (1904).

bar·ri·er (băr′ē-ər) *n.* **1.** A structure, such as a fence, built to bar passage. **2.** Something immaterial that obstructs or impedes: *Intolerance is a barrier to understanding.* See Synonyms at **obstacle. 3.** *Ecology.* A physical or biological factor that limits the migration, interbreeding, or free movement of individuals or populations. **4.** A boundary or limit. **5.** Something that separates or holds apart. **6.** A movable gate that keeps racehorses in line before the start of a race. **7.** The palisades or fences enclosing the lists of a medieval tournament. Often used in the plural. **8.** *Geology.* An ice barrier. [Middle English *barrer,* from Old French *barriere,* from Vulgar Latin **barrāria,* from **barra,* bar.]

barrier reef *n.* A long, narrow ridge of coral or rock parallel to and relatively near a coastline, separated from the coastline by a lagoon too deep for coral growth.

barouche
c. 1870

barracuda
Great barracuda
Sphyraena barracuda

ă pat	oi boy
ā pay	ou out
âr care	o͝o took
ä father	o͞o boot
ĕ pet	ŭ cut
ē be	ûr urge
ĭ pit	th thin
ī pie	*th* this
îr pier	hw which
ŏ pot	zh vision
ō toe	ə about, item
ô paw	♦ regionalism

Stress marks: ′ (primary); ′ (secondary), as in **dictionary** (dĭk′shə-nĕr′ē)

bartizan
El Morro fortress,
San Juan, Puerto Rico

Clara Barton

Mikhail Baryshnikov

bar·ring (bär′ĭng) *prep.* Apart from the occurrence of; excepting: *Barring strong headwinds, the plane will arrive on schedule.*

Bar·ring·ton (băr′ĭng-tən). A town of eastern Rhode Island southeast of Providence. It was part of Massachusetts until 1746. Population, 16,174.

bar·ri·o (bä′rē-ō′, băr′-) *n., pl.* **-os. 1.** An urban district or quarter in a Spanish-speaking country. **2.** A chiefly Spanish-speaking community or neighborhood in a U.S. city. [Spanish, from Arabic *barrī,* of an open area, from *barr,* open area.]

bar·ris·ter (băr′ĭ-stər) *n. Chiefly British.* A lawyer admitted to plead at the bar in the superior courts. See Synonyms at **lawyer.** [Probably blend of BAR[1] and obsolete *legister,* legist; see LEGIST.]

bar·room (bär′ro͞om′, -ro͝om′) *n.* A room or building in which alcoholic beverages are sold at a bar.

bar·row[1] (băr′ō) *n.* **1.** A flat, rectangular tray or cart with handles at each end. **2.** A wheelbarrow. [Middle English *barowe,* from Old English *bearwe.* See **bher-**[1] in Appendix.]

bar·row[2] (băr′ō) *n.* A large mound of earth or stones placed over a burial site. [Middle English *bergh,* from Old English *beorg,* hill. See **bhergh-**[2] in Appendix.]

bar·row[3] (băr′ō) *n.* A pig that has been castrated before reaching sexual maturity. [Middle English *barow,* from Old English *bearg.*]

Bar·row (băr′ō), **Isaac.** 1630–1677. English theologian, scholar, and mathematician who wrote about trigonometry, optics, and papal supremacy.

Barrow, Point. The northernmost point of Alaska, in the northwest on the Arctic Ocean. The nearby city of **Barrow** has research and government facilities. Population, 2,207.

Bar·row-in-Fur·ness (băr′ō-ĭn-fûr′nĭs). A borough of northwest England on a peninsula in an inlet of the Irish Sea northwest of Manchester. It is a shipbuilding center. Population, 72,800.

Bar·ry (băr′ē), **John.** 1745–1803. Irish-born American Revolutionary naval officer who commanded the *Lexington* in the capture (1776) of the *Edward,* the first British ship taken during the war.

Barry, Leonora Marie Kearney. Known as "Mother Lake." 1849–1930. Irish-born American labor leader who campaigned for better factory wages and working conditions for women and children.

Barry, Philip. 1896–1949. American playwright whose works, mostly comedies about the wealthy, include *The Philadelphia Story* (1939).

Bar·ry·more (băr′ĭ-môr′, -mōr′). Family of American actors, including **Lionel** (1878–1954), who won an Oscar in 1931 for *Free Soul;* his sister **Ethel** (1879–1959), who appeared mainly on stage but also won an Academy Award in 1944 for *None but the Lonely Heart;* and their brother **John** (1882–1942), known as "the Great Profile," who appeared on stage as Hamlet and Richard III and in many motion pictures, including *Dinner at Eight* (1933).

bar sinister *n.* **1.** *Heraldry.* A bend or baton sinister held to signify bastardy. **2.** A hint or proof of illegitimate birth.

bar·stool (bär′sto͞ol′) *n.* A usually high stool with a cushioned seat, used chiefly as seating for patrons at a bar.

Bar·stow (bär′stō). A city of southeast California northeast of Los Angeles. It was founded in the 1880's as a silver-mining town. Population, 17,690.

Bart. *abbr.* Baronet.

bar·tend·er (bär′tĕn′dər) *n.* One who mixes and serves alcoholic drinks at a bar. Also called *barkeeper.*

bar·ter (bär′tər) *v.* **-tered, -ter·ing, -ters.** —*intr.* To trade goods or services without the exchange of money. —*tr.* To trade (goods or services) without the exchange of money. —**barter** *n.* **1.** The act or practice of bartering. **2.** Something bartered. —**barter** *adj.* Of, relating to, or being something based on bartering: *a barter economy.* [Middle English *barteren,* probably from Old French *barater.* See BARRATOR.] —**bar′ter·er** *n.*

Barth (bärth), **John Simmons.** Born 1930. American writer whose novels, including *The Sot-Weed Factor* (1960, revised 1967), often examine the relationship between language and reality.

Barth (bärt, bärth), **Karl.** 1886–1968. Swiss Protestant theologian who advocated a return to the principles of the Reformation and the teachings of the Bible. His published works include *Church Dogmatics* (1932). —**Barth′i·an** *adj.*

Bar·thel·me (bär′thəl-mē′), **Donald.** 1931–1989. American writer whose sometimes surrealistic stories of modern American life have been published in collections such as *Unspeakable Practices, Unnatural Acts* (1968).

Barthes (bärt), **Roland.** 1915–1980. French critic who applied semiology, the study of signs and symbols, to literary and social criticism.

Bar·thol·di (bär-thŏl′dē, -tôl-dē′), **Frédéric Auguste.** 1834–1904. French sculptor best known for his monumental figure of *Liberty Enlightening the World,* the Statue of Liberty in New York Harbor, presented to the United States by France and dedicated in 1886.

Bar·tho·lin's gland (bär′tl-ĭnz, -thə-lĭnz) *n. Anatomy.* Either of two small compound racemose glands located on either side of the vaginal orifice that secrete a lubricating mucus and are homologous to the bulbourethral glands in the male. [After Caspar *Bartholin* (1585–1629), Danish physician.]

Bar·thol·o·mew (bär-thŏl′ə-myo͞o′), Saint. Sometimes called **Na·than·ael** (nə-thăn′yəl). One of the 12 Apostles. According to tradition, he visited India and Ethiopia and was martyred in Armenia.

bar·ti·zan also **bar·ti·san** (bär′tĭ-zən, bär′tĭ-zăn′) *n.* A small, overhanging turret on a wall or tower. [Alteration of *bratticing,* timberwork, from BRATTICE.] —**bar′ti·zaned** *adj.*

Bar·tles·ville (bär′tlz-vĭl′). A city of northeast Oklahoma north of Tulsa. It is a trade center in a ranching and oil-producing region. Population, 34,568.

Bart·lett[1] (bärt′lĭt). A town of southwest Tennessee, a suburb of Memphis. Population, 17,170.

Bart·lett[2] (bärt′lĭt) *n.* A widely grown variety of pear with yellowish skin and soft, juicy white flesh, eaten fresh or often canned. [After Enoch *Bartlett* (1779–1860).]

Bartlett, John. 1820–1905. American publisher and editor who compiled *Familiar Quotations* (1855) and a Shakespearean concordance (1894).

Bartlett, Robert Abram. Known as "Captain Bob." 1875–1946. American explorer who accompanied Robert E. Peary's expedition to the North Pole (1909) and led numerous other Arctic voyages.

Bar·tók (bär′tŏk′, -tôk′), **Béla.** 1881–1945. Hungarian pianist and composer whose works, including the music for the opera *Duke Bluebeard's Castle* (1911) and *Concerto for Orchestra* (1943), combine Eastern European folk music with dissonant harmonies. —**Bar·tók′i·an** *adj.*

Bar·to·lom·me·o (bär-tōl′ə-mā′ō, -tô′lô-), **Fra.** Originally Bartolommeo di Pagolo del Fattorino. 1475?–1517. Italian painter of the Florentine school whose works include *The Vision of Saint Bernard* (1500–1507) and *Madonna della Misericordia* (1515).

Bar·ton (bär′tn), **Clara.** Full name Clarissa Harlowe Barton. 1821–1912. American administrator who did battlefield relief work during the Civil War and organized the American Red Cross (1881).

Barton, Sir **Derek Harold Richard.** Born 1918. British chemist. He shared a 1969 Nobel Prize for the study of organic molecules.

Bar·tram (bär′trəm), **John.** 1699–1777. American botanist who established the first botanical garden in the colonies (1728) and corresponded with European botanists, thus introducing many American species to Europe. His son **William Bartram** (1739–1823) was also a botanist.

Bar·uch (bâr′ək, bə-ro͞ok) *n. Bible.* See table at **Bible.**

Ba·ruch (bə-ro͞ok′), **Bernard Mannes.** 1870–1965. American stock broker, public official, and political adviser for every President from Woodrow Wilson to John F. Kennedy.

bar·ware (bär′wâr′) *n.* The glassware and other items used in preparing alcoholic drinks.

bar·y·cen·ter (băr′ĭ-sĕn′tər) *n.* See **center of mass.** [Greek *barus,* heavy; see **gʷerə-**[1] in Appendix + CENTER.]

bar·y·on (băr′ē-ŏn′) *n.* Any of a family of subatomic particles, including the nucleon and hyperon multiplets, that participate in strong interactions, are composed of three quarks, and are generally more massive than mesons. Also called *heavy particle.* See table at **subatomic particle.** [Greek *barus,* heavy; see **gʷerə-**[1] in Appendix + -ON[1].] —**bar′y·on′ic** *adj.*

baryon number *n.* A quantum number equal to the difference between the number of baryons and the number of antibaryons in a system of subatomic particles. It remains the same throughout any reaction.

Ba·rysh·ni·kov (bə-rĭsh′nĭ-kôf′), **Mikhail Nikolayavich.** Born 1948. Russian-born ballet dancer and choreographer who after performing with the Kirov Ballet in Leningrad defected to the United States (1974), where he has danced for the American Ballet Theater, appeared in independent productions, and choreographed many works.

bar·y·sphere (băr′ĭ-sfîr) *n.* See **centrosphere** (sense 2). [Greek *barus,* heavy; see **gʷerə-**[1] in Appendix + SPHERE.]

ba·ry·ta (bə-rī′tə) *n.* Any of several barium compounds, such as barium sulfate. [New Latin, from Greek *barutēs,* weight, from *barus,* heavy. See **gʷerə-**[1] in Appendix.]

ba·ry·tes (bə-rī′tēz) *n.* Variant of **barite.**

bar·y·tone (băr′ĭ-tōn′) *n. Music.* Variant of **baritone.**

Bar·zun (bär′zŭn), **Jacques Martin.** Born 1907. French-born American educator, author, and historian whose works include *Darwin, Marx, Wagner* (1941), *The American University* (1968), and *The Use and Abuse of Art* (1974).

B.A.S. *abbr.* **1.** Bachelor of Agricultural Science. **2.** Bachelor of Applied Science.

bas·al (bā′səl, -zəl) *adj.* **1. a.** Of, relating to, located at, or forming a base. **b.** *Botany.* Located at or near the base of a plant stem, or at the base of any other plant part: *basal placentation.* **2.** Of primary importance; basic. —**bas′al·ly** *adv.*

basal body *n.* A cellular organelle associated with the formation of cilia and flagella and similar to the centriole in structure. Also called *basal granule, kinetosome.*

basal cell *n. Biology.* A type of cell found in the deepest layer of the epithelium.

basal ganglion *n. Anatomy.* Any of several masses of gray matter embedded in the cerebral hemispheres that are involved in the regulation of voluntary movement.

basal granule *n.* See **basal body.**

basal metabolic rate *n. Abbr.* **BMR** *Physiology.* The rate at which energy is used by an organism at complete rest, measured in human beings by the heat given off per unit time, and expressed as the calories released per kilogram of body weight or per square meter of body surface per hour.

basal metabolism *n. Abbr.* **BM** *Physiology.* The minimum amount of energy required to maintain vital functions in an organism at complete rest, measured by the basal metabolic rate in a fasting individual who is awake and resting in a comfortably warm environment.

ba·salt (bə-sôlt′, bā′sôlt′) *n.* **1.** A hard, dense, dark volcanic rock composed chiefly of plagioclase, pyroxene, and olivine, and often having a glassy appearance. **2.** A kind of hard unglazed pottery. [Latin *basaltēs,* alteration of *basanītēs,* touchstone, from Greek *basanitēs (lithos),* from *basanos,* of Egyptian origin.] **—ba·sal′tic** (-sôl′tĭk) *adj.*

B.A.Sc. *abbr.* **1.** Bachelor of Agricultural Science. **2.** Bachelor of Applied Science.

bas·cule (băs′kyo͞ol) *n.* A device or structure, such as a drawbridge, counterbalanced so that when one end is lowered the other is raised. [French, seesaw : *bas,* low (from Medieval Latin *bassus*) + *cul,* bottom (from Latin *cūlus,* rump; see **(s)keu-** in Appendix).]

base¹ (bās) *n. Abbr.* **b., B. 1.a.** The lowest or bottom part: *the base of a cliff; the base of a lamp.* **b.** *Biology.* The part of an animal or plant organ nearest its point of attachment. **2.a.** A supporting part or layer; a foundation: *a skyscraper built on a base of solid rock.* **b.** A basic or underlying element; infrastructure: *the nation's industrial base.* **3.** The fundamental principle or underlying concept of a system or theory; a basis. **4.** A fundamental ingredient; a chief constituent: *a paint with an oil base.* **5.** The fact, observation, or premise from which a reasoning process is begun. **6.a.** *Games.* A starting point, safety area, or goal. **b.** *Baseball.* Any one of the four corners of an infield, marked by a bag or plate, that must be touched by a runner before a run can be scored. **7.** A center of organization, supply, or activity; a headquarters. **8.a.** A fortified center of operations. **b.** A supply center for a large force of military personnel. **9.** *Architecture.* The lowest part of a structure, such as a wall, considered as a separate unit: *the base of a column.* **10.** *Heraldry.* The lower part of a shield. **11.** *Linguistics.* A morpheme or morphemes regarded as a form to which affixes or other bases may be added. **12.** *Mathematics.* **a.** The side or face of a geometric figure to which an altitude is or is thought to be drawn. **b.** The number that is raised to various powers to generate the principal counting units of a number system. **c.** The number raised to the logarithm of a designated number in order to produce that designated number. **13.** A line used as a reference for measurement or computations. **14.** *Chemistry.* **a.** Any of a large class of compounds, including the hydroxides and oxides of metals, having a bitter taste, a slippery solution, the ability to turn litmus blue, and the ability to react with acids to form salts. **b.** A molecular or ionic substance capable of combining with a proton to form a new substance. **c.** A substance that provides a pair of electrons for a covalent bond with an acid. **15.** *Electronics.* **a.** The region in a transistor between the emitter and the collector. **b.** The electrode attached to this region. **16.** One of the purines (adenine and guanine) or pyrimidines (cystosine, thymine, and uracil) that occurs attached to the sugar component of DNA or RNA. **—base** *adj.* **1.** Forming or serving as a base: *a base layer of soil.* **2.** Situated at or near the base or bottom: *a base camp for the mountain climbers.* **—base** *tr.v.* **based, bas·ing, bas·es. 1.** To form or provide a base for: *based the new company in Portland.* **2.** To find a basis for; establish: *based her conclusions on the report; a film based on a best-selling novel.* **3.** To assign to a base; station: *troops based in the Middle East.* **—*idiom.* off base.** Badly mistaken. [Middle English, from Old French, from Latin *basis,* from Greek. See **gʷā-** in Appendix.]

SYNONYMS: *base, basis, foundation, ground, groundwork.* These nouns all pertain to what underlies and supports. *Base* is applied chiefly to material objects: *amazed by the size of the monument's base. Basis* is used in a nonphysical sense: *"The basis of a democratic state is liberty"* (Aristotle). *Foundation* applies physically *(the foundation of a house)* and figuratively *(a statement without foundation in fact).* It often stresses firmness of support for something of relative magnitude: *"Our flagrant disregard for the law attacks the foundation of this society"* (Peter D. Relic). *Ground* may denote an actual working surface, as in art *(a white design on a blue ground)*; more often it is used figuratively in the sense of a justifiable reason: *grounds for divorce. Groundwork* is most often applied figuratively, in the sense of a necessary preliminary: *laid the groundwork for future negotiations.*

base² (bās) *adj.* **bas·er, bas·est. 1.a.** Having or showing a contemptible, mean-spirited, or selfish lack of human decency. See Synonyms at **mean². b.** Devoid of high values or ethics: *a base, degrading way of life.* **c.** Inferior in value or quality. **2.** Containing inferior substances: *a base metal.* **3.** *Archaic.* Of low birth, rank, or position. **4.** *Obsolete.* Short in stature. **—base** *n. Obsolete.* A bass singer or voice. [Middle English *bas,* low, from Old French, from Medieval Latin *bassus.*] **—base′ly** *adv.*

base·ball (bās′bôl′) *n.* **1.** *Sports.* **a.** A game played with a bat and ball by two opposing teams of nine players, each team playing alternately in the field and at bat, the players at bat having to run a course of four bases laid out in a diamond pattern in order to score. **b.** The ball that is used in this game. **2.** *Games.* A game of darts in which the players attempt to score points by throwing the darts at a target laid out in the form of a baseball diamond. **—*attributive.*** Often used to modify another noun: *a baseball hat; baseball gloves.*

base·board (bās′bôrd′, -bōrd′) *n.* A molding that conceals the joint between an interior wall and a floor. Also called *mopboard.*

base·born (bās′bôrn′) *adj.* **1.** Ignoble; contemptible. **2.a.** Born of unwed parents; illegitimate. **b.** Of humble birth.

base·burn·er (bās′bûr′nər) *n.* A coal stove with a hopper that automatically replenishes itself from above as lower layers of fuel are consumed.

base community *n. Roman Catholic Church.* A lay group, especially in South America, practicing nonliturgical religious devotions and striving for socioeconomic improvement in the community.

Base Exchange (bās). *Abbr.* **BX** A service mark used for general merchandise store services for government employees on a naval or air force base. This service mark, often lowercased, sometimes occurs in print with the meaning "a general merchandise store on a military base": *"The products are distributed at Army and Air Force base exchanges"* (Washington Post).

base hit *n. Baseball.* A hit by which the batter reaches base safely without incurring an error, a fielder's choice, or a force play.

base house *n. Slang.* A crack house. [(FREE)BASE + HOUSE.]

BASE jump (bās) *n. Sports.* A parachute jump from extremely high structures and earth formations, typically involving heights under 305 meters (1,000 feet). [B(UILDING) + *a(ntenna tower)* + S(PAN)¹ + E(ARTH) + JUMP.]

BASE-jump (bās′jŭmp′) *intr.v.* **-jumped, -jump·ing, -jumps.** *Sports.* To engage in the sport of parachuting off extremely high structures and earth formations. **—BASE jumper** *n.*

Ba·sel (bä′zəl) also **Basle** (bäl). A city of northern Switzerland on the Rhine River. It is one of the oldest intellectual centers in Europe. Population, 176,200.

base·less (bās′lĭs) *adj.* Having no basis or foundation in fact; unfounded.

SYNONYMS: *baseless, groundless, idle, unfounded, unwarranted.* The central meaning shared by these adjectives is "being without a basis or foundation in fact": *a baseless accusation; groundless rumors; idle gossip; unfounded suspicions; unwarranted jealousy.*

base level *n.* The lowest level to which a land surface can be reduced by the action of running water.

base line *n.* **1.** A line serving as a basis, as for measurement, calculation, or location. **2.** *Baseball.* An area within which a base runner must stay when running between bases. **3.** *Sports.* The boundary line at either end of a court, as in badminton or tennis.

base·man (bās′mən) *n. Baseball.* A player assigned to first, second, or third base.

♦**base·ment** (bās′mənt) *n.* **1.** The substructure or foundation of a building. **2.** The lowest habitable story of a building, usually below ground level. **3.** *New England.* A public toilet, especially one in a school. [Perhaps obsolete Dutch, foundation, possibly from Italian *basamento,* base of a column, from *basare,* to found, from *base,* bottom, from Latin *basis.* See BASIS.]

basement membrane *n.* A thin, delicate layer of connective tissue underlying the epithelium of many organs. Also called *basement lamina.*

base·ness (bās′nĭs) *n.* The quality or state of being contemptible, mean-spirited, or selfish.

ba·sen·ji (bə-sĕn′jē) *n.* A dog of a breed originally from Africa, having a short, smooth, reddish-brown coat and characterized by the absence of a bark. [Of Bantu origin; akin to Tshiluba *basenji,* inhabitants of the hinterland : *ba-,* pl. pref + *-senji.*]

base on balls *n. Baseball.* An advance to first base that is awarded to a batter who takes four pitches that are balls.

base pair *n.* The pair of nitrogenous bases, consisting of a purine linked by hydrogen bonds to a pyrimidine, that connects the complementary strands of a DNA molecule or of a double-stranded RNA molecule. The base pairs are adenine-thymine and guanine-cytosine in DNA, and adenine-uracil and guanine-cytosine in RNA.

base pay *n.* An amount or a rate of compensation for a specified position of employment or activity excluding any other payments or allowances.

base runner *n. Baseball.* A member of the team at bat who has safely reached or is trying to reach a base.

ba·ses (bā′sēz′) *n.* Plural of **basis.**

bash (băsh) *v.* **bashed, bash·ing, bash·es.** **—*tr.* 1.** To strike with a heavy, crushing blow. **2.** *Informal.* To criticize (another) harshly, accusatorially, and threateningly: *"He bashed the . . . government unmercifully over the . . . spy affair"* (Lally Weymouth). **—*intr. Informal.*** To engage in harsh, accusatory, threatening criticism. **—bash** *n.* **1.** *Informal.* A heavy, crushing blow. **2.** *Slang.* A celebration; a party. [Origin unknown.] **—bash′er** *n.*

bascule
Tower Bridge, London

basenji

ă pat	oi boy
ā pay	ou out
âr care	o͝o took
ä father	o͞o boot
ĕ pet	ŭ cut
ē be	ûr urge
ĭ pit	th thin
ī pie	*th* this
îr pier	hw which
ŏ pot	zh vision
ō toe	ə about, item
ô paw	♦ regionalism

Stress marks: **′** (primary); ′ (secondary), as in **dictionary** (dĭk′shə-nĕr′ē)

Count Basie

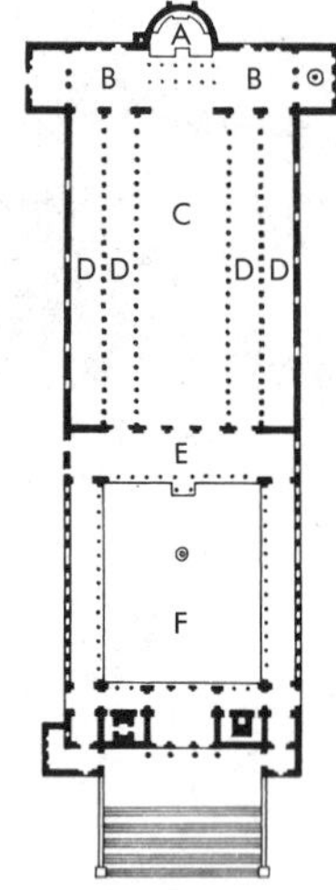

basilica
Plan of fourth-century A.D. Saint Peter's, Rome
A. Apse
B. Transept
C. Nave
D. Aisle
E. Narthex
F. Atrium

basketball
Boston Celtics and Philadelphia 76ers

Ba·shan (bā′shən). An ancient region of Palestine northeast of the Sea of Galilee.

ba·shaw (bə-shô′) *n.* A pasha. [Arabic *bāšā,* from Turkish *paşa,* from Persian *pādshāh.* See PADISHAH.]

bash·ful (băsh′fəl) *adj.* **1.** Shy, self-conscious, and awkward in the presence of others. See Synonyms at **shy**[1]. **2.** Characterized by, showing, or resulting from shyness, self-consciousness, or awkwardness. [From Middle English *basshe,* from *basshed,* past participle of *basshen,* to be discomfited, probably variant of *abaishen.* See ABASH.] **—bash′ful·ly** *adv.* **—bash′ful·ness** *n.*

Bash·kir·i·a (băsh-kîr′ē-ə). A region of southwest Russia in the southern Ural Mountains. It came under Russian control in the 16th century.

basi– or **baso–** *pref.* **1.** Base; lower part: *basipetal.* **2.** Chemical base; chemically basic: *basophil.* [From Latin *basis,* base. See BASIS.]

ba·sic (bā′sĭk) *adj.* **1.** Of, relating to, or forming a base; fundamental: *"Basic changes in public opinion often occur because of shifts in concerns and priorities"* (Atlantic). **2.** Of, being, or serving as a starting point or basis: *a basic course in Russian; a set of basic woodworking tools.* **3.** *Chemistry.* **a.** Producing, resulting from, or relating to a base. **b.** Containing a base, especially in excess of acid. **c.** Containing oxide or hydroxide anions. Used of a salt. **4.** *Geology.* Containing little silica, as igneous rocks. **—basic** *n.* **1.** An essential, fundamental element or entity: *the basics of math.* **2.** Basic training. **—ba′si·cal·ly** *adv.* **—ba·sic′i·ty** (-sĭs′ĭ-tē) *n.*

BA·SIC or **Ba·sic** (bā′sĭk) *n. Computer Science.* A simplified user-level programming language often employed with remote or time-sharing computer centers. [*b(eginner's) a(ll-purpose) s(ymbolic) i(nstruction) c(ode).*]

ba·si·chro·mat·ic (bā′sĭ-krō-măt′ĭk) *adj.* Easily stained with basic dye.

basic process *n.* A method of steel production that uses a furnace lined with a basic refractory material.

basic training *n.* The initial period of training of a recruit in the armed forces.

ba·sid·i·a (bə-sĭd′ē-ə) *n.* Plural of **basidium.**

ba·sid·i·o·carp (bə-sĭd′ē-ə-kärp′) *n.* A basidium-bearing structure found in such basidiomycetous fungi as mushrooms and puffballs. [BASIDI(UM) + –CARP.]

ba·sid·i·o·my·cete (bə-sĭd′ē-ō-mī′sēt′, -mī-sēt′) *n.* Any of various members of a large group of fungi bearing sexually produced spores on a basidium. The group includes puffballs, shelf fungi, rusts, smuts, and mushrooms. [BASIDI(UM) + –MYCETE.] **—ba·sid′i·o·my·ce′tous** (-mī-sē′təs) *adj.*

ba·sid·i·o·spore (bə-sĭd′ē-ə-spôr′, -spōr′) *n.* A sexually produced fungal spore borne on a basidium. **—ba·sid′i·o·spo′rous** *adj.*

ba·sid·i·um (bə-sĭd′ē-əm) *n., pl.* **-i·a** (-ē-ə). A small, specialized club-shaped structure typically bearing four basidiospores at the tips of minute projections. The basidium is unique to basidiomycetes and distinguishes them from other kinds of fungi. [BAS(I)– + *–idium,* diminutive suff. (from Greek *-idion*).] **—ba·sid′i·al** *adj.*

Ba·sie (bā′sē), **William.** Known as "Count Basie." 1904–1984. American musician. A pianist, band leader, and composer, he was a major force in jazz music and was especially famous for his Big Band sound.

ba·si·fixed (bā′sə-fĭkst′) *adj. Botany.* Attached by the base, as certain anthers are to their filaments.

ba·si·fy (bā′sə-fī′) *tr.v.* **-fied, -fy·ing, -fies.** *Chemistry.* **1.** To convert into a base. **2.** To make alkaline. **—ba′si·fi·ca′tion** (-fĭ-kā′shən) *n.* **—ba′si·fi′er** *n.*

bas·il (băz′əl, bā′zəl) *n.* **1.** An Old World aromatic annual herb *(Ocimum basilicum)* in the mint family, cultivated for its leaves, which are a popular seasoning. Also called *sweet basil.* **2.** Any of various plants in the genus *Ocimum,* native to warm regions, having aromatic foliage and terminal clusters of small, usually white flowers. [Middle English, from Old French *basile,* from Medieval Latin *basilicum,* from Greek *basilikon,* from neuter of *basilikos,* royal. See BASILICA.]

Bas·il (băz′əl, băs′-, bā′zəl, -səl), Saint. Known as "the Great." A.D. 330?–379? Greek Christian leader who was bishop of Caesarea in Cappadocia after A.D. 370 and a vigorous opponent of Arianism.

Ba·si·lan Islands (bä-sē′län′). A group of islands in the southern Philippines separated from southwest Mindanao by the narrow **Basilan Strait. Basilan Island** is the largest island in the group.

bas·i·lar (băs′ə-lər) also **bas·i·lar·y** (-lĕr′ē) *adj.* Of, relating to, or located at or near the base, especially the base of the skull: *the basilar artery.* [New Latin *basilāris,* from Latin *basis,* base. See BASIS.]

basilar membrane *n. Anatomy.* A membranous portion of the cochlea in the mammalian inner ear that supports the organ of Corti.

Bas·il·don (băz′əl-dən, bā′zəl-). An urban district of southeast England east-northeast of London. It has varied light industries. Population, 153,200.

ba·sil·i·ca (bə-sĭl′ĭ-kə) *n.* **1.a.** A public building of ancient Rome having a central nave with an apse at one or both ends and two side aisles formed by rows of columns, which was used as a courtroom or assembly hall. **b.** A Christian church building of a similar design, having a nave with a semicircular apse, two or four side aisles, a narthex, and a clerestory. **2.** *Roman Catholic Church.* A church that has been accorded certain privileges by the pope. [Latin, from Greek *basilikē,* from feminine of *basilikos,* royal, from *basileus,* king.] **—ba·sil′i·can** (-kən) *adj.*

Ba·si·li·ca·ta (bə-zĭl′ĭ-kä′tə, bä-zē′lē-kä′tä). A region of southern Italy bordering on the Tyrrhenian Sea and the Gulf of Taranta. It forms the instep of the Italian "boot."

bas·i·lisk (băs′ə-lĭsk′, băz′-) *n.* **1.** A legendary serpent or dragon with lethal breath and glance. **2.** Any of various tropical American lizards of the genus *Basiliscus,* characterized by a crest on the head, back, and tail and the ability to run on the hind legs. [Middle English, from Old French *basilisc,* from Latin *basiliscus,* from Greek *basiliskos,* diminutive of *basileus,* king.]

ba·sin (bā′sĭn) *n.* **1.a.** An open, shallow, usually round container used especially for holding liquids. **b.** The amount that such a vessel can hold. **2.** A washbowl; a sink. **3.a.** An artificially enclosed area of a river or harbor designed so that the water level remains unaffected by tidal changes. **b.** A small enclosed or partly enclosed body of water. **4.** A region drained by a single river system: *the Amazon basin.* **5.** *Geology.* **a.** A broad tract of land in which the rock strata are tilted toward a common center. **b.** A large, bowl-shaped depression in the surface of the land or ocean floor. [Middle English, from Old French *bacin,* from Vulgar Latin **baccīnum,* from **baccus,* container, of Celtic origin.] **—ba′sin·al** *adj.*

bas·i·net (băs′ə-nĕt′, băs′ə-nĭt) *n.* A small, light, rounded steel helmet, terminating in a point and often closed in front with a visor. [Middle English, from Old French *bacinet,* diminutive of *bacin,* basin. See BASIN.]

ba·sip·e·tal (bā-sĭp′ĭ-tl, -zĭp′-) *adj. Botany.* Of or relating to the development or maturation of tissues or organs or the movement of substances, such as hormones, from the apex downward toward the base. **—ba·sip′e·tal·ly** *adv.*

ba·sis (bā′sĭs) *n., pl.* **-ses** (-sēz′). **1.** A foundation upon which something rests. **2.** The chief constituent; the fundamental ingredient. **3.** The fundamental principle. See Synonyms at **base**[1]. [Middle English, from Latin, from Greek. See **g^{w}ā-** in Appendix.]

basis point *n.* One one-hundredth of a percent, used in measuring yield differences among bonds.

bask (băsk) *intr.v.* **basked, bask·ing, basks. 1.** To expose oneself to pleasant warmth. **2.** To take great pleasure or satisfaction: *She basked in her teacher's praise.* [Middle English *basken.*]

Bas·ker·ville (băs′kər-vĭl′), **John.** 1706–1775. British printer and typographer. He produced a notable edition of Virgil in 1757 and designed the typeface that bears his name.

bas·ket (băs′kĭt) *n.* **1.** *Abbr.* **bsk. a.** A container made of interwoven material, such as rushes or twigs. **b.** The amount that a basket can hold. **2.** An item resembling such a container in shape or function. **3.** A usually open gondola suspended from a hot-air balloon. **4.** *Basketball.* **a.** Either of the two elevated goals, each consisting of a metal hoop from which an open-bottomed circular net is suspended. **b.** The score, normally worth two points, made by throwing the ball through this goal. **5.** *Sports.* A circular structure at the base of a ski pole, used to prevent the pole from sinking too deeply into the snow. [Middle English, from Anglo-Norman, from Vulgar Latin **baskauta,* of Celtic origin.] **—bas′ket·ful′** *n.*

bas·ket·ball (băs′kĭt-bôl′) *n. Sports.* **1.** A game played between two teams of five players each, the object being to throw the ball through an elevated basket on the opponent's side of the rectangular court. **2.** The ball that is used in this game.

basket case *n. Informal.* **1.** One that is in a completely hopeless or useless condition: *"He immediately becomes a psychological basket case, embittered to the point of craziness"* (New York). *"After World War I, when the Hapsburg empire was split up, little Austria seemed a basket case"* (Paul A. Samuelson). **2.** A person, especially a soldier, who has had all four limbs amputated.

basket fish *n.* See **basket star.**

basket hilt *n.* A sword hilt with a basket-shaped guard serving to cover and protect the hand.

Bas·ket Maker (băs′kĭt) *n.* **1.** Any of several early periods of Anasazi culture preceding the Pueblo periods and characterized by the use of wicker basketry, dry farming, and coiled pottery. **2.** A member of the Anasazi people who produced this culture.

bas·ket-of-gold (băs′kĭt-əv-gōld′) *n.* A shrubby perennial European herb *(Aurinia saxatilis)* widely grown for its grayish foliage and profusion of small, golden-yellow flowers.

bas·ket·ry (băs′kĭ-trē) *n.* **1.** The craft or process of making baskets. **2.** Baskets considered as a group.

basket star *n.* Any of various marine organisms of the class Ophiuroidea, related to the starfishes and having slender, branching, interlaced arms. Also called *basket fish.*

basket weave *n.* A textile weave consisting of double threads interlaced to produce a checkered pattern similar to that of a woven basket.

bask·ing shark (băs′kĭng) *n.* A very large shark *(Cetorhinus maximus)* that measures up to about 12 meters (40 feet) in length, feeds on plankton, and often floats near the surface of water.

Basle (bäl). See **Basel.**

bas mitz·vah or **bas miz·vah** (bäs mĭts′və) —*n. & v.* Variants of **bat mitzvah.**

baso– *pref.* Variant of **basi–.**

ba·so·phil (bā′sə-fĭl, -zə-) *n.* A cell, especially a white blood cell, having granules that stain readily with basic dyes.

ba·so·phil·i·a (bā′sə-fĭl′ē-ə, -zə-) *n.* **1.** The affinity of cellular structures for basic dyes, such as methylene blue. **2.** An increase in the number of basophils in the circulating blood. **3.** An abnormal stippling of red blood cells with basic staining granules.

ba·so·phil·ic (bā′sə-fĭl′ĭk, -zə-) also **ba·soph·i·lous** (bə-sŏf′ə-ləs) *adj.* Relating to tissue components that stain readily with basic dyes.

Ba·sov (bä′sôf′, -səf), **Nikolai Gennadievich.** Born 1922. Russian physicist. He shared a 1964 Nobel Prize for developing the maser and laser principle of producing high-intensity radiation.

basque (băsk) *n.* A woman's close-fitting bodice. [French, skirt of a garment, alteration (perhaps influenced by *Basque,* Basque; see BASQUE) of Old French *baste,* from Italian *basta,* tuck, possibly of Germanic origin.]

Basque (băsk) *n.* **1.** A member of a people of unknown origin inhabiting the western Pyrenees and the Bay of Biscay in France and Spain. **2.** The language of the Basques, of no known linguistic affiliation. [French, probably from Latin *Vascō,* perhaps from Basque *Euskadi.*] **—Basque** *adj.*

Basque Provinces. A region comprising three provinces of northern Spain on the Bay of Biscay. It borders on France in the northeast along the western Pyrenees.

Bas·ra (bäs′rə, bŭs′-). A city of southeast Iraq on the Shatt al Arab near the Persian Gulf. It is the only port in the country. Population, 616,700.

bas-re·lief (bä′rĭ-lēf′) *n.* See **low relief.** [French, from Italian *bassorilievo* : *basso,* low (from Medieval Latin *bassus*) + *rilievo,* relief (from *rilevare,* to raise, from Latin *relevāre;* see RELIEVE).]

bass¹ (băs) *n., pl.* **bass** or **bass·es. 1.** Any of several North American freshwater fishes of the family Centrarchidae, related to but larger than the sunfishes. **2.** Any of various marine fishes of the family Serranidae, such as the sea bass and the striped bass. [Middle English **bars,* perch, from Old English *bærs.*]

bass² (bās) *n. Music.* **1.** A low-pitched sound or tone. **2.** The tones in the lowest register of an instrument. **3.** The lowest part in vocal or instrumental part music. **4. a.** A male singing voice of the lowest range. **b.** A singer who has such a voice. **5.** An instrument, especially a double bass, that produces tones in a low register. **—bass** *adj.* **1.** Having a deep tone. **2.** Low in pitch. [Middle English *bas,* lowest musical part, from *bas,* low. See BASE².]

bass clef (bās) *n. Music.* A symbol indicating that the fourth line from the bottom of a staff represents the pitch of F below middle C. Also called *F clef.*

bass drum (bās) *n. Music.* A large drum having a cylindrical body and two heads and producing a low, resonant sound.

Basse·terre (băs-târ′, bäs-). The capital of St. Christopher–Nevis, on St. Christopher Island in the Leeward Islands of the West Indies. Population, 14,725.

Basse-Terre (băs-târ′, bäs-). The capital of the French overseas department of Guadeloupe, on the southern end of **Basse-Terre Island** in the Leeward Islands of the West Indies. Population, 13,656.

basset hound (băs′ĭt) *n.* A short-haired hunting dog of a breed originating in France and having a long body, short legs, and long, drooping ears. [French, short, basset hound, diminutive of *basse,* feminine adjective of *bas,* low. See BASE².]

bass fiddle (bās) *n. Music.* See **double bass.**

bas·si (bä′sē) *n. Music.* A plural of **basso.**

bas·si·net (băs′ə-nĕt′, băs′ə-nĕt′) *n.* An oblong basketlike bed for an infant. [French, small basin, diminutive of *bassin,* basin, from Old French, bacin. See BASIN.]

bas·si pro·fun·di (bä′sē prə-fo͝on′dē) *n. Music.* A plural of **basso profundo.**

bass·ist (bā′sĭst) *n. Music.* One who plays a bass instrument, especially a double bass.

bas·so (băs′ō, bä′sō) *n., pl.* **bas·sos** or **bas·si** (bä′sē). *Abbr.* **b., B.** *Music.* A bass singer, especially an operatic bass. [Italian, from Medieval Latin *bassus,* low.]

bas·soon (bə-so͞on′, bă-) *n. Music.* A low-pitched woodwind instrument with a double reed, having a long wooden body attached to a U-shaped lateral tube that leads to the mouthpiece. The range of this instrument is typically two octaves lower than that of the oboe. [French *basson,* from Italian *bassone,* augmentative of *basso,* bass. See BASSO.] **—bas·soon′ist** *n.*

bas·so pro·fun·do (băs′ō prə-fŭn′dō, bä′sō prə-fo͞on′dō) *n., pl.* **basso pro·fun·dos** or **bas·si pro·fun·di** (bä′sē prə-fo͞on′dē). *Music.* **1.** A deep bass singing voice. **2.** A singer who has such a voice. [Italian : *basso,* bass + *profondo,* deep.]

bas·so-re·lie·vo (băs′ō-rĭ-lē′vō) *n., pl.* **-vos.** See **low relief.** [Italian *bassorilievo.* See BAS-RELIEF.]

Bass Strait (băs). A channel between Tasmania and southeast Australia connecting the Indian Ocean with the Tasman Sea. Its discovery in 1798 by the British explorer George Bass (died c. 1812) proved that Tasmania was not part of the Australian continent.

bass viol (bās) *n. Music.* **1.** See **double bass. 2.** See **viola da gamba.**

bass·wood (băs′wo͝od′) *n.* **1.** See **linden. 2.** The soft, light-colored wood of any species of linden. It is used in making crates and boxes, in carving, and in millwork. [*bass,* linden bark (alteration of BAST) + WOOD¹.]

bast (băst) *n. Botany.* Bast fiber. [Middle English, from Old English *bæst.*]

bas·tard (băs′tərd) *n.* **1.** An illegitimate child. **2.** Something that is of irregular, inferior, or dubious origin. **3.** *Vulgar Slang.* A person, especially one who is held to be mean or disagreeable. **—bastard** *adj.* **1.** Born of unwed parents; illegitimate. **2.** Not genuine; spurious: *a bastard style of architecture.* **3.** Resembling a known kind or species but not truly such. [Middle English, from Old French, probably of Germanic origin; akin to Old Frisian *bōst,* marriage.] **—bas′tard·ly** *adj.*

bas·tard·ize (băs′tər-dīz′) *tr.v.* **-ized, -iz·ing, -iz·es.** To lower in quality or character; debase. **—bas′tard·i·za′tion** (-tər-dĭ-zā′shən) *n.*

bastard toadflax *n.* Any of various hemiparasitic plants of the genus *Comandra,* having clusters of small, whitish or greenish flowers.

bastard wing *n.* See **alula.**

bas·tard·y (băs′tər-dē) *n.* **1.** The condition of being of illegitimate birth; illegitimacy. **2.** The begetting of a bastard.

baste¹ (bāst) *tr.v.* **bast·ed, bast·ing, bastes.** To sew loosely with large running stitches so as to hold together temporarily. [Middle English *basten,* from Old French *bastir,* of Germanic origin.] **—bast′er** *n.*

baste² (bāst) *tr.v.* **bast·ed, bast·ing, bastes.** To moisten (meat, for example) periodically with a liquid, such as melted butter or a sauce, especially while cooking. [Middle English *basten.*] **—bast′er** *n.*

baste³ (bāst) *tr.v.* **bast·ed, bast·ing, bastes. 1.** To beat vigorously; thrash. See Synonyms at **beat. 2.** To lambaste. [Probably of Scandinavian origin; akin to Old Norse *beysta.* See **bhau-** in Appendix.]

bast fiber *n. Botany.* Any of various durable fibers obtained from the phloem or from tissues outside the phloem. These fibers include flax, hemp, jute, and ramie and are used for textiles and cordage.

bas·tille (bă-stēl′) *n.* A prison; a jail. [French, from Old French, fortress, alteration of *bastide,* from Old Provençal *bastida,* from *bastir,* to build, of Germanic origin.]

Bas·tille Day (bă-stēl′) *n.* July 14, observed in France in commemoration of the storming of the Paris Bastille in 1789, a citizens' victory at the outset of the French Revolution.

bas·ti·na·do (băs′tə-nā′dō, -nä′-) also **bas·ti·nade** (-nād′, -näd′) *—n., pl.* **-does** also **-nades. 1.** A beating with a stick or cudgel, especially on the soles of the feet. **2.** A stick or cudgel. *—tr.v.* **-doed, -do·ing, -does** also **-nad·ed, -nad·ing, -nades.** To subject to a beating; thrash. [Alteration of Spanish *bastonada,* from *baston,* stick, from Vulgar Latin **bastō,* **bastōn-.*]

bas·tion (băs′chən, -tē-ən) *n.* **1.** A projecting part of a fortification. **2.** A well fortified position. **3.** One that is considered similar to a defensive stronghold: *You are a bastion of strength.* See Synonyms at **bulwark.** [French, from Old French *bastillon,* from *bastille,* fortress. See BASTILLE.] **—bas′tioned** *adj.*

bast·naes·ite (băst′nə-sīt′) *n.* A yellowish to reddish-brown mineral, $(Ce,La)CO_3(F,OH)$, that is a source of rare-earth elements, including gadoloinium, samarium, and neodymium. [After *Bastnäs,* a mine in south-central Sweden.]

Bas·togne (bă-stōn′, bă-stôn′yə). A town of southeast Belgium near the Luxembourg border. It was a crucial point in the U.S. defensive line during the World War II Battle of the Bulge (December 1944–January 1945). Population, 11,386.

Ba·su·to·land (bə-so͞o′tō-lănd′). See **Lesotho.**

bat¹ (băt) *n.* **1.** A stout wooden stick; a cudgel. **2.** A blow, such as one delivered with a stick. **3.** *Baseball.* A rounded, often wooden club, wider and heavier at the hitting end and tapering at the handle, used to strike the ball. **4.** *Sports.* **a.** A club used in cricket, having a broad, flat-surfaced hitting end and a distinct, narrow handle. **b.** The racket used in various games, such as table tennis or racquets. **—bat** *v.* **bat·ted, bat·ting, bats.** *—tr.* **1.** To hit with or as if with a bat. **2.** *Baseball.* **a.** To cause (a run) to be scored while at bat: *batted in the winning run with a double.* **b.** To have (a certain percentage) as a batting average. **3.** *Informal.* To produce in a hurried or an informal manner: *bat out a speech; bat out dance music.* **4.** *Informal.* To discuss or consider at length: *bat an idea around.* *—intr.* **1.** *Baseball.* **a.** To use a bat. **b.** To have a turn at bat. **2.** *Slang.* To wander about aimlessly. *—idioms.* **at bat.** *Sports.* Taking one's turn to bat, as in baseball or cricket. **go to bat for.** To give assistance to; defend. **off the bat.** Without hesitation; immediately: *They responded right off the bat.* [Middle English, perhaps partly of Celtic origin, and partly from Old French *batte,* pounding implement, flail (from *batre,* to beat; see BATTER¹).]

bat² (băt) *n.* Any of various nocturnal flying mammals of the order Chiroptera, having membranous wings that extend from the forelimbs to the hind limbs or tail and anatomical adaptations for

basket star
Astrophyton muricatum

bass clef

bat²
Mouse-eared bat

ă pat	oi boy
ā pay	ou out
âr care	o͝o took
ä father	o͞o boot
ĕ pet	ŭ cut
ē be	ûr urge
ĭ pit	th thin
ī pie	*th* this
îr pier	hw which
ŏ pot	zh vision
ō toe	ə about, item
ô paw	♦ regionalism

Stress marks: **′** (primary); ′ (secondary), as in **dictionary** (dĭk′shə-nĕr′ē)

echolocation, by which they navigate and hunt prey. ***—idiom.*** **have bats in (one's) belfry.** To behave in an eccentric, bizarre manner. [Alteration of Middle English *bakke,* of Scandinavian origin.]

bat³ (băt) *tr.v.* **bat·ted, bat·ting, bats.** To wink or flutter: *bat one's eyelashes.* [Probably a variant of BATE².]

bat⁴ (băt) *n. Slang.* A binge; a spree. [Probably from *batter,* spree.]

bat. *abbr.* Battalion.

B.A.T. *abbr.* Bachelor of Arts in Teaching.

Ba·taan (bə-tăn′, -tän′). A peninsula of western Luzon, Philippines, between Manila Bay and the South China Sea. After an extended siege U.S. and Philippine World War II troops surrendered to the Japanese in April 1942. U.S. forces recaptured the peninsula in February 1945.

Ba·ta·vi·a (bə-tā′vē-ə). **1.** A city of western New York west-southwest of Rochester. It is an industrial center in a farming region. Population, 16,703. **2.** See **Jakarta.**

bat·boy (băt′boi′) *n. Baseball.* A boy who is employed by a baseball team to look after its equipment, especially the bats.

batch¹ (băch) *n.* **1.** An amount produced at one baking: *a batch of cookies.* **2.** The quantity produced as the result of one operation: *mixed a batch of cement.* **3.** The quantity needed for one operation: *a batch of dough.* **4.** A group of persons or things: *a batch of tourists; a whole new batch of problems.* **5.** *Computer Science.* A set of data or jobs to be processed in a single program run. **—batch** *tr.v.* **batched, batch·ing, batch·es.** To assemble or process as a batch. [Middle English *bache,* probably from Old English **bæcce,* from *bacan,* to bake.]

batch² (băch) *v. Informal.* Variant of **bach.**

bate¹ (bāt) *tr.v.* **bat·ed, bat·ing, bates. 1.** To lessen the force or intensity of; moderate: *"To his dying day he bated his breath a little when he told the story"* (George Eliot). See Usage Note at **bait².** **2.** To take away; subtract. [Middle English *baten,* short for *abaten.* See ABATE.]

bate² also **bait** (bāt) *intr.v.* **bat·ed, bat·ing, bates** also **bait·ed, bait·ing, baits.** To flap the wings wildly or frantically. Used of a falcon. [Middle English *baten,* from Old French *batre,* to beat. See BATTER¹.]

ba·teau (bă-tō′) *n., pl.* **-teaux** (-tōz′). *Nautical.* **1.** A long, light, flat-bottomed boat with a sharply pointed bow and stern, used especially in Canada and the northeast United States. **2.** A small, light, flat-bottomed rowboat used chiefly in Louisiana. [Canadian and Louisiana French, from French, boat, from Old French *batel,* from Old English *bāt.* See **bheid-** in Appendix.]

bateau bridge *n.* See **pontoon bridge.**

Bates (bāts), **Herbert Ernest.** 1905–1974. British writer who served with the Royal Air Force during World War II and under the pen name Flying Officer X wrote many short stories based on his experiences.

Bates, Katherine Lee. 1859–1929. American educator and writer best known for her poem "America the Beautiful," written in 1893 and revised in 1904 and 1911.

Bates·i·an mimicry (bāt′sē-ən) *n.* A form of protective mimicry in which an unprotected species, especially of an insect, closely resembles an unpalatable or harmful species and therefore is similarly avoided by predators. [After Henry W. *Bates* (1825–1892), British naturalist.]

Bate·son (bāt′sən), **William.** 1861–1926. British biologist who was one of the founders of the science of genetics. He experimentally proved Gregor Mendel's theories on heredity and published the first English translation of Mendel's work in 1900.

bat·fish (băt′fĭsh′) *n., pl.* **batfish** or **-fish·es.** Any of various marine anglerfishes of the family Ogcocephalidae, having a retractable appendage above the mouth.

bat·fowl (băt′foul′) *intr.v.* **-fowled, -fowl·ing, -fowls.** To catch roosting birds at night by blinding them with a light and then hitting or netting them.

bat·girl (băt′gûrl′) *n. Baseball.* A girl who is employed by a baseball team to look after its equipment, especially the bats.

bath¹ (băth, bäth) *n., pl.* **baths** (băthz, bäthz, băths, bäths). **1.a.** The act of soaking or cleansing the body, as in water or steam. **b.** The water used for cleansing the body. **2.a.** A bathtub. **b.** A bathroom. **3.** A building equipped for bathing. **4.** Often **baths.** A resort providing therapeutic baths; a spa. **5.** A liquid or a liquid and its container in which something is dipped or soaked in order to process it: *an acid bath; a bath of dye.* [Middle English, from Old English *bæth.*]

bath² (băth) *n.* An ancient Hebrew unit of liquid measure, equal to about 38 liters (10 U.S. gallons). [Hebrew.]

Bath (băth, bäth). A city of southwest England southeast of Bristol. Famous for its Georgian architecture and its hot mineral springs, tapped by the Romans in the first century A.D., it is a popular resort. Population, 84,100.

Bath chair (băth, bäth) *n.* A hooded wheelchair used especially for invalids, typically at a spa. [After BATH.]

bathe (bāth) *v.* **bathed, bath·ing, bathes.** *—intr.* **1.** To take a bath. **2.** To go into the water for swimming or other recreation. **3.** To become immersed in or as if in liquid. *—tr.* **1.** To immerse in liquid; wet. **2.** To wash in a liquid. **3.** To apply a liquid to for healing or soothing purposes: *bathed the wound with iodine.* **4.** To seem to wash or pour over; suffuse: *a room that was bathed in sunlight.* [Middle English *bathen,* from Old English *bathian.*] **—bath′er** *n.*

ba·thet·ic (bə-thĕt′ĭk) *adj.* Marked by bathos. See Synonyms at **sentimental.** [Probably a blend of BATHOS and PATHETIC.]

bath·house (băth′hous′, bäth′-) *n.* **1.** A building with facilities for bathing. **2.** A building with dressing rooms for swimmers.

Bath·i·nette (băth′ə-nĕt′, bä′thə). A trademark used for portable bathing devices for infants.

bath·ing cap (bā′thĭng) *n.* A snug elastic cap worn in the water especially to keep the hair dry.

bathing suit *n.* See **swimsuit.**

bath·mat (băth′măt′, bäth′-) *n.* A mat used in front of a bathtub or shower, as to absorb water or prevent slipping.

batho– *pref.* Variant of **bathy–.**

bath·o·lith (băth′ə-lĭth′) *n.* A large mass of igneous rock that has melted and intruded surrounding strata at great depths. **—bath′o·lith′ic** *adj.*

ba·thom·e·ter (bə-thŏm′ĭ-tər) *n.* An instrument used to measure the depth of water.

bath·o·pho·bi·a (băth′ə-fō′bē-ə) *n.* An abnormal fear of depths.

ba·thos (bā′thŏs′, -thôs′) *n.* **1.a.** An abrupt, unintended transition in style from the exalted to the commonplace, producing a ludicrous effect. **b.** An anticlimax. **2.a.** Insincere or grossly sentimental pathos: *"a richly textured man who . . . can be . . . sentimental to the brink of bathos"* (Kenneth L. Woodward). **b.** Banality; triteness. [Greek, depth, from *bathus,* deep.]

bath·robe (băth′rōb′, bäth′-) *n.* A loose-fitting robe worn before and after bathing and for lounging.

bath·room (băth′ro͞om′, -ro͝om′, bäth′-) *n.* A room equipped with facilities for taking a bath or shower and usually also containing a sink and toilet.

bath salts (băth, bäth) *pl.n.* A perfumed crystalline substance for softening bathwater.

Bath·she·ba (băth-shē′bə, băth′shə-). In the Old Testament, the wife of Uriah and later of David. Her second son by David was Solomon.

bath·tub (băth′tŭb′, bäth′-) *n.* A tub for bathing, especially one installed in a bathroom.

Bath·urst (băth′ərst). See **Banjul.**

bath water (băth, bäth) *n.* The water used for a bath.

bathy– or **batho–** *pref.* **1.** Deep; depth: *batholith.* **2.** Deep-sea: *bathysphere.* [From Greek *bathus,* deep, and from Greek *bathos,* depth (from *bathus*).]

ba·thym·e·try (bə-thĭm′ĭ-trē) *n.* Measurement of the depth of large bodies of water. **—bath′y·met′ric** (băth′ə-mĕt′rĭk), **bath′y·met′ri·cal** *adj.* **—bath′y·met′ri·cal·ly** *adv.*

bath·y·pe·lag·ic (băth′ə-pə-lăj′ĭk) *adj.* Of, relating to, or living in the depths of the ocean, especially between about 600 and 3,000 meters (2,000 and 10,000 feet).

bath·y·scaph (băth′ĭ-skăf′) also **bath·y·scaphe** (-skăf′, -skāf′) *n.* A free-diving, self-contained deep-sea research vessel consisting essentially of a large flotation hull with a crewed observation capsule fixed to its underside, capable of reaching depths of 10 kilometers (6.2 miles) or more. [BATHY– + Greek *skaphos,* boat.]

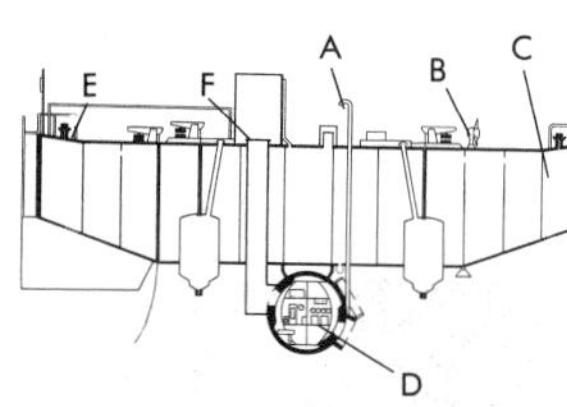

bathyscaph
Top: The *Trieste*
Bottom: Diagram of a bathyscaph vessel
A. Snorkel
B. Propellers
C. Water ballast tank
D. Observation gondola
E. Vents
F. Hatch

bath·y·sphere (băth′ĭ-sfîr′) *n.* A reinforced spherical deep-diving chamber in which persons are lowered by a cable to study the oceans. The bathysphere, limited to depths of about 900 meters (3,000 feet), has been supplanted by the safer and more navigable bathyscaph.

ba·tik (bə-tēk′, băt′ĭk) *n.* **1.a.** A method of dyeing a fabric by which the parts of the fabric not intended to be dyed are covered with removable wax. **b.** A design that is created by this method. **2.** Fabric dyed by this method. [Malay *batek,* of Javanese origin, from Proto-Austronesian **beCík,* tattoo (from the fact that the original process of piercing the waxed cloth prior to soaking was similar to tattooing).]

Ba·tis·ta y Zal·dí·var (bə-tēs′tə ē zäl-dē′vär′, bä-tē′stä), **Fulgencio.** 1901–1973. Cuban dictator (1933–1940) and president (1940–1944 and 1954–1958). His corrupt authoritarian regime was overthrown on New Year's Day, 1959, by a revolutionary movement led by Fidel Castro.

ba·tiste (bə-tēst′, bă-) *n.* A fine, plain-woven fabric made from various fibers and used especially for clothing. [French, from Old French, perhaps after *Baptiste* of Cambrai, 13th-century textile maker.]

bat·man (băt′mən) *n.* A British military officer's orderly. [Obsolete *bat* (from French *bât,* from Old French *bast,* from Late Latin *bastum*) + MAN.]

bat mitz·vah or **bat miz·vah** (bät mĭts′və) or **bas mitz·vah** or **bas miz·vah** (bäs) *—n.* **1.** In Conservative and Reform Judaism, a Jewish girl of 12 to 14 years of age, considered an adult and responsible for her moral and religious duties. **2.** The ceremony that initiates and recognizes a girl as having achieved this status. *—tr.v.* **-vahed, -vah·ing, -vahs.** To confirm in the ceremony of bat mitzvah. [Hebrew *bat miṣwâ* : *bat,* daughter + *miṣwâ,* commandment.]

ba·ton (bə-tŏn′, bă-, băt′n) *n.* **1.** *Music.* A slender wooden stick or rod used by a conductor to direct an orchestra or band. **2.** A hollow metal rod with a heavy rubber tip or tips that is wielded and twirled by a drum major or drum majorette. **3.** A short staff carried by certain public officials as a symbol of office. **4.** *Sports.* The hollow cylinder that is carried by each member of a relay team and passed to the next runner. **5.** A club or truncheon. **6.** *Heraldry.* A shortened narrow bend, often signifying bastardy. [French *bâton,* from Old French *baston,* stick, from Vulgar Latin **bastō,* **bastōn-*.]

Bat·on Rouge (băt′n ro͞ozh′). The capital of Louisiana, in the southeast-central part of the state on a bluff above the Mississippi River. It has notable antebellum houses. Population, 219,419.

bat·o·pho·bi·a (băt′ə-fō′bē-ə) *n.* An abnormal fear of being near an object of great height, such as a skyscraper or mountain. [Greek *batos,* passable (from *bainein,* to go; see **gʷā-** in Appendix) + -PHOBIA.]

ba·tra·chi·an (bə-trā′kē-ən) *adj.* Of or relating to vertebrate amphibians without tails, such as frogs and toads. **—batrachian** *n.* A vertebrate amphibian. [From Greek *batrakhos,* frog.]

ba·tra·cho·tox·in (bə-trăk′ə-tŏk′sĭn, băt′rə-kō-) *n.* A steroid alkaloid derived from skin secretions of the *Phyllobates* and *Dendrobates* genera of South American arrow-poison frogs. It is one of the most potent venoms known. [Greek *batrakhos,* frog + TOXIN.]

bats (băts) *adj. Slang.* Crazy; insane. [From *bats in the belfry.*]

bats·man (băts′mən) *n. Sports.* The player at bat in cricket and baseball.

Bat·swa·na (bŏt-swä′nə) *n., pl.* **Batswana** or **-nas.** See **Tswana** (sense 1).

batt (băt) *n.* Pieces of fabric used for stuffing; batting. [Variant of BAT[1], cotton or wool fiber wadded into rolls or sheets.]

bat·tal·ion (bə-tăl′yən) *n.* **1.** *Abbr.* **bat., batt., bn., Bn. a.** An army unit typically consisting of a headquarters and two or more companies, batteries, or similar subunits. **b.** A large body of organized troops. **2.** A great number: *battalions of ants.* [French *bataillon,* from Old French, from Italian *battaglione,* augmentative of *battaglia,* from Vulgar Latin **battalia.* See BATTLE.]

Bat·ta·ni (bə-tä′nē), **al-.** 858?–929. Arab astronomer and mathematician. Considered the greatest astronomer of his time, he proved the possibility of annular eclipses and introduced an organized table of sines.

bat·ten[1] (băt′n) *intr.v.* **-tened, -ten·ing, -tens. 1.** To become fat. **2.** To thrive and prosper, especially at another's expense: *slumlords who batten on the poor.* [Ultimately from Old Norse *batna,* to improve. See **bhad-** in Appendix.]

bat·ten[2] (băt′n) *n.* **1.** *Nautical.* **a.** One of several flexible strips of wood placed in pockets at the outer edge of a sail to keep it flat. **b.** A narrow strip of wood used to fasten down the edges of the material that covers hatches in foul weather. **2.** *Chiefly British.* A narrow strip of wood used especially for flooring. **—batten** *tr.v.* **-tened, -ten·ing, -tens.** *Nautical.* To furnish, fasten, or secure with battens: *batten down the hatches.* [Middle English *batent,* from Old French *bataunt,* wooden strip, clapper, from present participle of *batre,* to beat. See BATTER[1].]

Bat·ten (băt′n), **Jean.** 1909–1982. New Zealand aviator who was the first woman to fly a solo round trip between England and Australia (1935).

bat·ter[1] (băt′ər) *v.* **-tered, -ter·ing, -ters.** *—tr.* **1.** To hit heavily and repeatedly with violent blows. **2.** To damage, as by heavy wear. *—intr.* To pound repeatedly with heavy blows. **—batter** *n. Printing.* A damaged area on the face of type or on a plate. [Middle English *bateren,* from Old French *batre,* from Late Latin *battere,* from Latin *battuere.*]

SYNONYMS: *batter, maim, mangle, maul, mutilate.* The central meaning shared by these verbs is "to damage, injure, or disfigure by beating, abuse, or hard use": *a house battered by a hurricane; a wrist maimed in an accident; a mangled corpse; a tent mauled by a hungry bear; mutilated the painting with a razor blade.* See also Synonyms at **beat.**

bat·ter[2] (băt′ər) *n. Sports.* The player at bat in baseball and cricket.

bat·ter[3] (băt′ər) *n.* A liquid or semiliquid mixture, as of flour, milk, and eggs, used in cooking. [Middle English *bater,* probably from Old French *bateure,* a beating, from *batre,* to beat. See BATTER[1].]

bat·ter[4] (băt′ər) *n.* A slope, as of the outer face of a wall, that recedes from bottom to top. **—batter** *tr.v.* **-tered, -ter·ing, -ters.** To construct so as to create an upwardly receding slope. [Origin unknown.]

♦ **bat·ter·cake** (băt′ər-kāk′) *n. Chiefly Southern U.S.* **1.** See **pancake. 2.** See **johnnycake.** See Regional Note at **johnnycake.**

bat·tered child (băt′ərd) *n.* A child upon whom multiple, continuing, often serious nonaccidental injuries have been inflicted usually by parents, guardians, or other caregivers.

battered child syndrome *n.* A combination of continuing, often serious physical injuries, such as bruises, scratches, hematomas, burns, or malnutrition, inflicted on a child through gross abuse usually by parents, guardians, or other caregivers.

battered woman syndrome *n.* A pattern of signs and symptoms commonly appearing in women who are physically and mentally abused over an extended period by a husband or other dominant male figure. Characteristics of this syndrome are helplessness, constant fear, and a perceived inability to escape.

bat·ter·ing parent syndrome (băt′ər-ĭng) *n.* A group of signs and symptoms characterizing a psychological disorder in a child's parent or other caregiver, resulting in a tendency or disposition to abuse the child. Elements contributory to this syndrome include a history of abuse upon the parent or other caregiver during childhood, unreasonable behavioral expectations of young children, and stress.

battering ram *n.* **1.** A very heavy metal bar used by firefighters and law enforcement officers to break down walls and doors. **2.** A heavy beam used in ancient warfare to batter down the walls and gates of a place under siege.

battering ram

bat·ter·y (băt′ə-rē) *n., pl.* **-ies. 1. a.** The act of beating or pounding. **b.** *Law.* The unlawful and unwanted touching or striking of one person by another, with the intention of bringing about a harmful or offensive contact. **2. a.** An emplacement for one or more pieces of artillery. **b.** A set of guns or other heavy artillery, on a warship, for example. **c.** *Abbr.* **btry.** An army artillery unit, corresponding to a company in the infantry. **3. a.** An array of similar things intended for use together: *took a battery of achievement tests.* **b.** An impressive body or group: *a battery of political supporters.* **4.** *Baseball.* The pitcher and catcher. **5.** *Music.* The percussion section of an orchestra. **6.** *Electricity.* **a.** Two or more connected cells that produce a direct current by converting chemical energy to electrical energy. **b.** A single cell, such as a dry cell, that produces an electric current. [Middle English *batri,* forged metal ware, from Old French *baterie,* a beating, from *batre,* to batter. See BATTER[1].]

Bat·ter·y (băt′ə-rē) also **Battery Park.** A park at the southern tip of Manhattan Island at the upper end of New York Bay in southeast New York. It is the site of early Dutch and English fortifications and of Castle Clinton, built in 1808 for the defense of the harbor.

bat·ting (băt′ĭng) *n.* **1.** The act of one who bats. **2.** Cotton, wool, or synthetic fiber wadded into rolls or sheets, used for stuffing furniture and mattresses and for lining quilts. [Sense 2, from the beating of raw cotton to clean it.]

batting average *n. Baseball.* A measure of a batter's performance obtained by dividing the total of base hits by the number of times at bat.

bat·tle (băt′l) *n.* **1. a.** An encounter between opposing forces: *an important battle in the Pacific campaign.* **b.** Armed fighting; combat: *wounded in battle.* **2.** A match between two combatants: *trial by battle.* **3. a.** A protracted controversy or struggle: *won the battle of the budget.* **b.** An intense competition: *a battle of wits.* **—battle** *v.* **-tled, -tling, -tles.** *—intr.* To engage in or as if in battle. *—tr.* To fight against: *battled the enemy; battled cancer.* [Middle English *batel,* from Old French *bataille,* from Vulgar Latin **battālia,* from Late Latin *battuālia,* fighting and fencing exercises, from Latin *battuere,* to beat.] **—bat′tler** *n.*

Bat·tle (băt′l). A town of southeast England, site of the Battle of Hastings (1066). William the Conqueror built Battle Abbey to commemorate his victory here. Population, 4,987.

bat·tle-ax or **bat·tle-axe** (băt′l-ăks′) *n.* **1.** A heavy broadheaded ax formerly used as a weapon. **2.** *Informal.* A woman held to be antagonistic or overbearing.

Battle Creek. A city of southern Michigan east of Kalamazoo. Breakfast cereals and other food products are important to its economy. Population, 35,724.

battle cruiser *n.* A large warship with lighter armor but greater maneuverability than a battleship.

battle cry *n.* **1.** A rallying cry uttered in combat, especially while attacking. **2.** A slogan used by the proponents of a cause.

bat·tle·dore (băt′l-dôr′) *n. Sports.* **1. a.** An early form of badminton played with a flat wooden paddle and a shuttlecock. **b.** The paddle used in this game. **2.** A badminton racket. [Middle English *batildore,* perhaps blend of *betel,* bat; see BEETLE[3], and Old Provençal *batedor,* bat (from *battre,* to beat, from Late Latin *battere;* see BATTER[1]).]

battle fatigue *n.* The debilitating psychiatric breakdown caused by the stress of combat. Also called *combat fatigue.*

bat·tle·field (băt′l-fēld′) *n.* **1.** An area where a battle is fought. **2.** A sphere of contention. Also called *battleground.*

bat·tle·front (băt′l-frŭnt′) *n.* **1.** The line or sector in which armed forces engage in combat. **2.** The area where opponents meet or clash: *a struggle on the economic battlefront.*

bat·tle·ground (băt′l-ground′) *n.* See **battlefield.**

battle group *n.* **1.** A U.S. army unit usually composed of five companies. **2.** A naval force composed of a variable number of warships, escorts, and supply vessels, depending on the nature of the mission: *"A carrier battle group . . . consists of an aircraft carrier, 10 escort combatants, and four support ships"* (Defense & Foreign Affairs Daily).

bat·tle·ment (băt′l-mənt) *n.* A parapet built on top of a wall, with indentations for decoration or defense. Also called *embattlement.* [Middle English *batelment,* alteration (influenced by *batel,* battle; see BATTLE) of Old French *batillement,* tower, turret, from *bastille.* See BASTILLE.] **—bat′tle·ment′ed** (-mĕn′tĭd) *adj.*

battle royal *n., pl.* **battles royal. 1.** An intense altercation. **2.** A battle involving many combatants. **3.** A fight to the finish. [BATTLE + ROYAL, grand in scale.]

bat·tle·ship (băt′l-shĭp′) *n.* Any one of a class of warships of the largest size, carrying the greatest number of weapons and clad

ă pat	oi boy
ā pay	ou out
âr care	o͝o took
ä father	o͞o boot
ĕ pet	ŭ cut
ē be	ûr urge
ĭ pit	th thin
ī pie	*th* this
îr pier	hw which
ŏ pot	zh vision
ō toe	ə about, item
ô paw	♦ regionalism

Stress marks: ′ (primary); ′ (secondary), as in **dictionary** (dĭk′shə-nĕr′ē)

with the heaviest armor. Also called *battlewagon.* [Short for *line-of-battle ship.*]

battleship gray *n. Color.* A medium shade of gray. **—bat′tle·ship-gray′** *adj.*

bat·tle·wag·on (băt′l-wăg′ən) *n.* See **battleship.**

bat·ty (băt′ē) *adj.* **-ti·er, -ti·est.** *Slang.* Crazy; insane. [From *bats in the belfry.*] **—bat′ti·ness** *n.*

Ba·tu·mi (bə-to͞o′mē) also **Ba·tum** (-to͞om′). A city of southwest Georgia on the Black Sea near the Turkish border. On the site of an ancient Greek colony, it is an important petroleum refining and shipping center. Population, 132,000.

Bat Yam (bät′ yäm′). A city of west-central Israel on the Mediterranean Sea near Tel Aviv–Jaffa. It is a resort and an industrial center. Population, 131,200.

bau·ble (bô′bəl) *n.* **1.** A small, showy ornament of little value; a trinket. **2.** *Archaic.* A mock scepter carried by a court jester. [Middle English *babel,* from Old French, plaything.]

Bau·cis (bô′sĭs) *n. Greek Mythology.* A peasant woman of Phrygia who together with her husband Philemon received with great hospitality Zeus and Hermes disguised as men. The gods rewarded the couple by turning them in their old age into intertwining linden and oak trees.

baud (bôd) *n. Computer Science.* A unit of speed in data transmission usually equal to one bit per second. [After Jean Maurice Emile *Baudot* (1845–1903), French engineer.]

Baude·laire (bōd-lâr′), **Charles Pierre.** 1821–1867. French writer, translator, and critic. His only volume of poetry, *Les Fleurs du Mal* (1857, expanded 1861), was publicly condemned as obscene but exerted an enormous influence over later symbolist and modernist poets such as T.S. Eliot.

Bau·douin I (bō-dwăN′). Born 1930. King of Belgium. Although he exercised the prerogative of rule after August 11, 1950, when the Belgian parliament accepted Leopold III's offer to abdicate, he did not formally ascend the throne until July 17, 1951.

Bau·haus (bou′hous′) *adj.* Of, relating to, or characteristic of a 20th-century school of design, the aesthetic of which was influenced by and derived from techniques and materials employed especially in industrial fabrication and manufacture. [German, an architecture school founded by Walter Gropius (1883–1969) : *Bau,* construction, architecture (from Middle High German *bū,* building, from Old High German, from *būan,* to dwell, settle; see **bheuə-** in Appendix) + *Haus,* house (from Middle High German *hūs,* from Old High German).]

bau·hin·i·a (bô-hĭn′ē-ə, bō-ĭn′-) *n.* Any of various tropical or subtropical trees, shrubs, or woody vines of the genus *Bauhinia* in the pea family, having two-part or deeply cleft leaves and showy, variously colored flowers. [New Latin, after Jean *Bauhin* (1541–1612) and Gaspard *Bauhin* (1560–1624), Swiss botanists.]

baulk (bôk) *v. & n.* Variant of **balk.**

Baum (bôm, bäm), **Lyman Frank.** 1856–1919. American writer known especially for *The Wonderful Wizard of Oz* (1900) and 13 other Oz stories, including *Ozma of Oz* (1917).

Baum (boum), **Vicki.** 1896–1960. Austrian-born American writer whose best-known work is *Grand Hotel* (published in German in 1929 and in English in 1931), a tale of tangled relationships set in a luxurious European hotel.

Bau·mé (bō-mā′), **Antoine.** 1728–1804. French pharmacist who invented a process for making sal ammonia and in 1768 devised an improved hydrometer using the scale that now bears his name.

Baumé scale *n. Abbr.* **B., Bé** A hydrometer scale used to measure the specific gravity of liquids. [After Antoine BAUMÉ.]

Bau·ru (bou-ro͞o′). A city of southeast Brazil northwest of São Paulo. It is a railroad junction and commercial center. Population, 180,093.

baux·ite (bôk′sīt′) *n.* The principal ore of aluminum, composed mainly of hydrous aluminum oxides and aluminum hydroxides. [After Les *Baux,* a commune of southeast France.] **—baux·it′ic** (-sĭt′ĭk) *adj.*

Ba·var·i·a (bə-vâr′ē-ə). A region and former duchy of southern Germany. Conquered by the Romans in 15 B.C., the region became one of the five preeminent duchies of medieval Germany but was later overrun and ruled by numerous factions and powers.

Ba·var·i·an (bə-vâr′ē-ən) *n.* **1.** A native or inhabitant of Bavaria. **2.** The High German dialect of Bavaria and Austria. **—Ba·var′i·an** *adj.*

Bavarian Alps. A range of the Alps between southern Bavaria in Germany and the Tyrol in western Austria. It rises to 2,964.9 m (9,721 ft) at Zugspitze on the southern border of Germany.

bawd (bôd) *n.* **1.** A woman who keeps a brothel; a madam. **2.** A prostitute. [Middle English, probably from Old French *baud,* gay, licentious, from Old Low German *bald,* bold, merry. See **bhel-**[2] in Appendix.]

bawd·ry (bô′drē) *n.* Risqué, coarse, or obscene language. [Middle English *bawdery,* pandering, from *bawd,* bawd. See BAWD.]

bawd·y (bô′dē) *adj.* **-i·er, -i·est. 1.** Humorously coarse; risqué. **2.** Vulgar; lewd. **—bawd′i·ly** *adv.* **—bawd′i·ness** *n.*

bawd·y·house (bô′dē-hous′) *n.* A house of prostitution.

bawl (bôl) *v.* **bawled, bawl·ing, bawls.** *—intr.* **1.** To cry or sob loudly; wail. **2.** To cry out loudly and vehemently; shout. *—tr.* To utter in a loud, vehement voice. See Synonyms at **shout.** **—bawl** *n.* A loud, bellowing cry; a wail. ***—phrasal verb.* bawl out.** *Informal.* To reprimand loudly or harshly. [Middle English *bawlen,* to bark, from Medieval Latin *baulāre,* to bark (probably of Scandinavian origin) or from Old Norse *baula,* to low (of imitative origin).] **—bawl′er** *n.*

bay[1] (bā) *n. Abbr.* **b. 1.** A body of water partially enclosed by land but with a wide mouth, affording access to the sea: *the Bay of Biscay.* **2.** An area of land, such as an arm of prairie partially enclosed by woodland, that resembles in shape or formation a partially enclosed body of water. [Middle English, from Old French *baie,* perhaps from *baer,* to open out, gape. See BAY[2].]

bay[2] (bā) *n.* **1.** *Architecture.* A part of a building marked off by vertical elements, such as columns or pilasters: *an arcade divided into ten bays.* **2.** *Architecture.* **a.** A bay window. **b.** An opening or recess in a wall. **3.** A section or compartment, as in a service station, barn, or aircraft, that is set off for a specific purpose: *a cargo bay; an engine bay.* **4.** A sickbay. [Middle English, from Old French *baee,* an opening, from *baer,* to gape, from Vulgar Latin **badāre.*]

bay[3] (bā) *adj. Color.* Reddish-brown: *a bay colt.* **—bay** *n.* **1.** *Color.* A reddish brown. **2.** A reddish-brown animal, especially a horse having a black mane and tail. [Middle English, from Old French *bai,* from Latin *badius.*]

bay[4] (bā) *n.* **1.** A deep, prolonged bark, such as the sound made by hounds. **2.** The position of one cornered by pursuers and forced to turn and fight at close quarters: *The hunters brought their quarry to bay.* **3.** The position of having been checked or held at a distance: *"He has seen the nuclear threat held at bay for 40 years"* (Earl W. Foell). **—bay** *v.* **bayed, bay·ing, bays.** *—intr.* To utter a deep, prolonged bark. *—tr.* **1.** To pursue or challenge with barking: *"I had rather be a dog, and bay the moon"* (Shakespeare). **2.** To express by barking or howling: *a mob baying its fury.* **3.** To bring to bay: *"too big for the dogs which tried to bay it"* (William Faulkner). [Middle English, from *abai,* cornering a hunted animal, from Old French, from *abaiier,* to bark, perhaps from Vulgar Latin **abbaiāre* : Latin *ad-,* ad- + Vulgar Latin **badāre,* to gape, yawn. V., from Middle English *baien,* to bark, from *abaien,* from Old French *abaiier.*]

bay[5] (bā) *n.* **1.** See **laurel** (sense 1). **2.** Any of certain other trees or shrubs with aromatic foliage, such as the California laurel. **3.** A crown or wreath made especially of the leaves and branches of the laurel and given as a sign of honor or victory. **4.** Often **bays.** Honor; renown. [Middle English, from Old French *baie,* berry, from Latin *bāca.*]

ba·ya·dere (bī′ə-dîr′, -dâr′) *n.* A fabric with contrasting horizontal stripes. [French *bayadère,* from Portuguese *bailadeira,* dancer, from *bailar,* to dance, from Late Latin *ballāre,* from Greek *ballizein.* See **gʷelə-** in Appendix.]

Ba·ya·món (bä′yä-môn′). A town of northeast Puerto Rico, a residential and industrial suburb of San Juan. Founded in 1772, it is one of the oldest settlements on the island. Population, 185,087.

Bay·ard (bā′ərd, bī′-, bä-yär′), Seigneur de. Originally Pierre Terrail. 1473–1524. French military hero known for his fearlessness and chivalry in the Italian campaigns of Charles VII, Louis XII, and Francis I. He was called *"le chevalier sans peur et sans reproche."*

bay·ber·ry (bā′bĕr′ē) *n.* **1.** A deciduous, eastern North American shrub *(Myrica pensylvanica)* having aromatic foliage and small, globose fruits with a waxy covering used for making fragrant candles. **2.** The fruit of this tree.

Bay City (bā). **1.** A city of eastern Michigan on Saginaw Bay north-northwest of Detroit. It is a port of entry and industrial center. Population, 41,593. **2.** A city of southeast Texas near the Colorado River and the Gulf of Mexico southwest of Houston. There are oil wells and sulfur mines in the area. Population, 17,837.

Ba·yeux (bī-yo͞o′, bā-, bä-yœ′). A town of northwest France near the English Channel. The famed Bayeux tapestry, housed in a museum here, depicts incidents in the Norman Conquest (1066). Population, 14,721.

Bay·kal (bī-kôl′, -kŏl′), **Lake.** See Lake **Baikal.**

bay laurel *n.* See **laurel** (sense 1).

Bayle (bāl, bĕl), **Pierre.** 1647–1706. French philosopher and critic. Considered the progenitor of 18th-century rationalism, he compiled the famous *Dictionnaire Historique et Critique* (1697) and championed the cause of religious tolerance.

bay leaf *n.* The dried aromatic leaf of the laurel or bay *(Laurus nobilis)* used as a seasoning in cooking.

bay lynx *n.* See **bobcat.**

Bay of. For names of actual bays, see the specific element of the name; for example, **Biscay, Bay of; Pigs, Bay of.**

Bay of Pigs *n.* An invasion of another country that ends in failure and a rout: *"A President who finally is afraid to risk a Bay of Pigs . . . will be reluctant to . . . intercept . . . terrorists"* (Hugh Sidey).

bay·o·net (bā′ə-nĭt, -nĕt′, bā′ə-nĕt′) *n.* A blade adapted to fit the muzzle end of a rifle and used as a weapon in close combat. **—bayonet** *tr.v.* **-net·ed, -net·ing, -nets** or **-net·ted, -net·ting, -nets.** To prod, stab, or kill with this weapon. [French *baïonnette,* after BAYONNE[1].]

WORD HISTORY: It is not unusual for a word to come from a place name. *Cheddar,* from the name of a village in southwest England; *hamburger,* after Hamburg, Germany; and *mayonnaise,*

ă pat	oi boy
ā pay	ou out
âr care	o͝o took
ä father	o͞o boot
ĕ pet	ŭ cut
ē be	ûr urge
ĭ pit	th thin
ī pie	*th* this
îr pier	hw which
ŏ pot	zh vision
ō toe	ə about, item
ô paw	♦ regionalism

Stress marks: **′** (primary); ′ (secondary), as in **dictionary** (dĭk′shə-nĕr′ē)

possibly from Mahón, the capital of Minorca, are often found together on our tables. The word *bayonet*, a very undomestic sort of word, also derives from a place name, that of Bayonne, a town in southwest France where the weapon was first made. The French word *baïonnette* could mean "a dagger or a knife" as well, and the English word *bayonet* is first found in 1672 with this meaning. The word is first recorded in its present sense in 1704.

Ba·yonne¹ (bä-ōn′, bä-yôn′). A town of southwest France near the Bay of Biscay and the Spanish border. French, Spanish, and Basque are all spoken here. Population, 41,381.

Bay·onne² (bā-yōn′). A city of northeast New Jersey on a peninsula in Upper New York Bay across from Staten Island. First colonized by the Dutch, it passed to the English in 1664. Population, 65,047.

bay·ou (bī′o͞o, bī′ō) *n.* **1.** A body of water, such as a creek or small river, that is a tributary of a larger body of water. **2.** A sluggish stream that meanders through lowlands, marshes, or plantation grounds. [Louisiana French *bayouque, bayou,* possibly from Choctaw *bayuk*.]

Bay·reuth (bī-roit′, bī′roit). A city of east-central Germany northeast of Nuremberg. Richard Wagner lived here from 1872 to 1883 and designed the opera house used for the city's internationally famous music festivals. Population, 71,811.

bay rum *n.* An aromatic liquid originally prepared by distilling the leaves of the bay rum tree in rum and water but now usually made by mixing the oil from those leaves with other solvents.

bay rum tree *n.* A tropical American evergreen tree *(Pimenta racemosa)* having leathery leaves that yield a fragrant oil used in bay rum, perfumes, and soaps.

bay·side (bā′sīd′) *adj.* Situated very close to or on the shore of a bay: *bayside cottages.*

Bay·town (bā′toun′). A city of southeast Texas at the head of Galveston Bay on the Houston Ship Channel. It is an oil-refining and industrial center. Population, 56,923.

Bay Village. A city of northeast Ohio, a suburb of Cleveland on Lake Erie. Population, 17,846.

bay window *n.* **1.** *Architecture.* A large window or series of windows projecting from the outer wall of a building and forming a recess within. **2.** *Slang.* A protruding belly; a paunch.

ba·zaar also **ba·zar** (bə-zär′) *n.* **1.** A market consisting of a street lined with shops and stalls, especially one in the Middle East. **2.** A shop or a part of a store in which miscellaneous articles are sold. **3.** A fair or sale at which miscellaneous articles are sold, often for charitable purposes. [From Italian *bazarro* and from Urdu *bāzār,* both from Persian. See **wes-³** in Appendix.]

ba·zoo·ka (bə-zo͞o′kə) *n.* A shoulder-held weapon consisting of a long metal smoothbore tube for firing armor-piercing rockets at short range. [After the *bazooka,* a crude wind instrument made of pipes, invented and named by Bob Burns (1896–1956), American comedian, probably from *bazoo,* kazoo.]

bb also **b.b.** *abbr.* Ball bearing.

BB (bē′bē) *n.* A standard size of lead pellet that measures 7/40 of an inch (.44 centimeter) in diameter, and that is used in air rifles.

B.B.A. *abbr.* Bachelor of Business Administration.

BBC (bē′bē-sē′) *abbr.* British Broadcasting Corporation.

BBC English *n.* See **Received Pronunciation.**

BB gun *n.* A small air rifle that shoots BB's.

bbl or **bbl.** *abbr.* Barrel.

B.C. *abbr.* **1.** Bachelor of Chemistry. **2.** Also **B.C.** Before Christ. **3.** Or **BC** British Columbia.

B.C.B.G. *abbr. French.* Bon chic, bon genre (stylish and well-to-do).

BCD or **bcd** *abbr. Computer Science.* Binary coded decimal.

B.C.E. *abbr.* **1.** Bachelor of Chemical Engineering. **2.** Bachelor of Civil Engineering. **3.** Or **B.C.E.** Before the Common Era.

B cell *n.* A type of lymphocyte that plays a major role in the body's humoral immune response. When stimulated by a particular foreign antigen, these lymphocytes differentiate into plasma cells that synthesize the antibodies that circulate in the blood and react with the specific antigens. Also called *B lymphocyte.* [*b(ursa-dependent) cell.*]

BCG *abbr.* Bacillus Calmette-Guérin vaccine.

B.Ch.E. *abbr.* Bachelor of Chemical Engineering.

B.C.L. *abbr.* **1.** Bachelor of Canon Law. **2.** Bachelor of Civil Law.

B complex *n.* See **vitamin B complex.**

bd *abbr.* Bundle.

BD *abbr.* **1.** Bank draft. **2.** Bomb disposal.

bd. *abbr.* **1.** Board. **2.** Bond. **3.** Bound.

B.D. *abbr.* Bachelor of Divinity.

b/d *abbr.* Barrels per day.

bdel·li·um (dĕl′ē-əm) *n.* An aromatic gum resin similar to myrrh, produced by certain Asian and African shrubs or trees of the genus *Commiphora.* [Middle English, from Latin, from Greek *bdellion*; akin to Hebrew *bĕdōlaḥ*.]

bd. ft. *abbr.* Board foot.

bdl *abbr.* Bundle.

bdle. *abbr.* Bundle.

bdrm. *abbr.* Bedroom.

bds. *abbr.* Bound in boards.

B.D.S. *abbr.* Bachelor of Dental Surgery.

be (bē) *v.* First and third person singular past indicative **was** (wŭz, wŏz; wəz *when unstressed*), second person singular and plural and first and third person plural past indicative **were** (wûr), past subjunctive **were,** past participle **been** (bĭn), present participle **be·ing** (bē′ĭng), first person singular present indicative **am** (ăm), second person singular and plural and first and third person plural present indicative **are** (är), third person singular present indicative **is** (ĭz), present subjunctive **be.** —*intr.* **1.** To exist in actuality; have life or reality: *I think, therefore I am.* **2.a.** To occupy a specified position: *The food is on the table.* **b.** To remain in a certain state or situation undisturbed, untouched, or unmolested: *Let the children be.* **3.** To take place; occur: *The test was yesterday.* **4.** To go or come: *Have you ever been to Italy? Have you been home recently?* **5.** *Usage Problem.* Used as a copula in such senses as: **a.** To equal in identity: *"To be a Christian was to be a Roman"* (James Bryce). **b.** To have a specified significance: *A is excellent, C is passing. Let n be the unknown quantity.* **c.** To belong to a specified class or group: *The human being is a primate.* **d.** To have or show a specified quality or characteristic: *She is lovely. All men are mortal.* **e.** To seem to consist or be made of: *The yard is all snow. He is all bluff and no bite.* **6.** To belong; befall: *Peace be unto you. Woe is me.* —*aux.* **1.** Used with the past participle of a transitive verb to form the passive voice: *The mayoral election is held annually.* **2.** Used with the present participle of a verb to express a continuing action: *We are working to improve housing conditions.* **3.** Used with the infinitive of a verb to express intention, obligation, or future action: *She was to call before she left. You are to make the necessary changes.* **4.** *Archaic.* Used with the past participle of certain intransitive verbs to form the perfect tense: *"Where be those roses gone which sweetened so our eyes?"* (Philip Sidney). [Middle English *ben,* from Old English *bēon.* See **bheuə-** in Appendix. See *am¹, is,* etc. for links to other Indo-European roots.]

SYNONYMS: *be, breathe, exist, live, subsist.* The central meaning shared by these verbs is "to have life or reality": *Her parents are no more. A nicer person has never breathed. He is one of the worst actors who ever existed. Human beings cannot live without food and water. The benevolence subsisting in her character draws her friends closer to her.*

USAGE NOTE: Traditional grammar requires the nominative form of the pronoun in the predicate of the verb *be*: *It is I* (not *me*); *That must be they* (not *them*), and so forth. Even literate speakers of Modern English have found the rule difficult to conform to, but the stigmatization of *It is me* is by now so deeply lodged among the canons of correctness that there is little likelihood that the construction will ever be entirely acceptable in formal writing. Adherence to the traditional rule in informal speech, however, has come to sound increasingly pedantic, and begins to sound absurd when the verb is contracted, as in *It's we.* • The traditional rule creates particular problems when the pronoun following *be* also functions as the object of a verb or preposition in a relative clause, as in *It is not them/they that we have in mind when we talk about "crime in the streets" nowadays,* where the plural pronoun serves as both the predicate of *is* and the object of *have.* In this example, 57 percent of the Usage Panel preferred the nominative form *they,* 33 percent preferred the accusative *them,* and 10 percent accepted both versions. But H.W. Fowler, like other authorities, argued that the use of the nominative here is an error caused by "the temptation . . . to assume, perhaps from hearing *It is me* corrected to *It is I,* that a subjective [nominative] case cannot be wrong after the verb *to be.*" Writers can usually find a way to avoid this problem: *They are not the ones we have in mind, We have someone else in mind,* and so on. See Usage Notes at **I¹, we.**

bay window

Be The symbol for the element **beryllium.**

BE *abbr.* **1.** Also **B.E.** Bachelor of Education. **2.** Also **B.E.** Bachelor of Engineering. **3.** Board of Education.

B/E *abbr.* **1.** Bill of entry. **2.** Bill of exchange.

be– *pref.* **1.** Completely; thoroughly; excessively. Used as an intensive: *bemuse.* **2.** On; around; over: *besmear.* **3.** About; to: *bespeak.* **4.** Used to form transitive verbs from nouns, adjectives, and intransitive verbs, as: **a.** To make; cause to become: *bedim* **b.** To affect, cover, or provide: *bespectacled.* [Middle English *bi-, be-,* from Old English *be-, bi-.* See **ambhi** in Appendix.]

Bé *abbr.* Baumé scale.

beach (bēch) *n.* **1.** The shore of a body of water, especially when sandy or pebbly. **2.** The sand or pebbles on a shore. —**beach** *tr.v.* **beached, beach·ing, beach·es.** To haul or run ashore: *beached the rowboat in front of the cabin.* [Perhaps Middle English *beche,* stream, from Old English *bece.*]

Beach (bēch), **Alfred Ely.** 1826–1896. American editor and inventor who built a demonstration pneumatic subway under Broadway in New York City in 1870.

Beach, Moses Yale. 1800–1868. American publisher whose aggressive journalism established the *New York Sun* as a leading daily newspaper. He is also credited with publishing the first syndicated news story. His son **Moses Sperry Beach** (1822–1892) invented a cutting device that allowed printing on a continuous roll of paper and a process for printing both sides of a newspaper sheet at one time.

bazaar
Outdoor market in Jerusalem

Beach, Sylvia Woodbridge. 1887–1962. American bookseller. From 1919 to 1941 her shop in Paris, Shakespeare and Company, was a gathering place for authors such as Hemingway and Fitzgerald. She published the first edition of James Joyce's *Ulysses* in 1922.

beach ball *n.* A large inflatable ball used for games especially at a beach or swimming pool.

beach buggy *n.* See **dune buggy.**

beach bum *n. Informal.* A person who habitually loafs or idles on beaches.

beach-burn·er (bēch′ bûr′nər) *n. Informal.* A small, self-propelled watercraft for recreational use close to shore.

beach·comb·er (bēch′kō′mər) *n.* **1.** One who scavenges along beaches or in wharf areas. **2.** A seaside vacationer.

beach flea *n.* Any of various small, jumping crustaceans of the family Orchestiidae, living on sandy beaches at or near the tide line. Also called *sand hopper.*

beagle

beach·front (bēch′frŭnt′) *n.* A strip of land facing or running along a beach. **—beachfront** *adj.* Situated along or having direct access to a beach: *beachfront hotels; beachfront property.*

beach grass *n.* A perennial grass of the genus *Ammophila,* especially *A. breviligulata,* native to sandy shores along the Great Lakes and Atlantic coast of North America, and having spikelets in long, erect, crowded clusters. It is commonly planted as a sand-binder to stabilize dunes and combat beach erosion. Also called *marram.*

beach·head (bēch′hĕd′) *n.* **1.** A position on an enemy shoreline captured by troops in advance of an invading force. **2.** A first achievement that opens the way for further developments; a foothold.

Beach-la-Mar (bēch′lə-mär′) *n.* See **Bislama.**

beach·less (bēch′lĭs) *adj.* Having no beach, especially because of increased ocean level and wave action: *beachless seaside towns.*

beach pea or **beach-pea** (bēch′pē′) *n.* Any of certain perennial herbs of the genus *Lathyrus* in the pea family, especially *L. japonicus,* native to shores in the Northern Hemisphere, having pinnately compound leaves and purplish flowers.

beach plum *n.* A seacoast shrub *(Prunus maritima)* in the rose family, native to northeast North America and having white flowers and edible, plumlike fruits used in jams, jellies, and pies.

beach·scape (bēch′skā′) *n.* A view of shore scenery or an artistic representation of it.

beach·side (bēch′sīd′) *adj.* Situated on or along a beach.

beach·wear (bēch′wâr′) *n.* Clothing appropriate for swimming, boating, or sunning.

beach wormwood *n.* An Asian perennial seacoast plant *(Artemisia stelleriana)* in the composite family, densely covered with grayish-white felty hairs and having elongate clusters of heads with tiny yellow flowers.

Beach·y Head (bē′chē). Chalk cliffs, 175.4 m (575 ft) high, on the southeast coast of England. In 1690 Beachy Head was the scene of a French naval victory over Anglo-Dutch forces.

beak
Bald eagle
Haliaeetus leucocephalus (*top left*);
Evening grosbeak
Hesperiphona vespertina (*top right*); and
black skimmer
Rynchops niger (*bottom*)

bea·con (bē′kən) *n.* **1.** A signaling or guiding device, such as a lighthouse, located on a coast. **2.** A radio transmitter that emits a characteristic guidance signal for aircraft. **3.** A source of guidance or inspiration. **4.** A signal fire, especially one used to warn of an enemy's approach. **—beacon** *tr. & intr.v.* **-coned, -con·ing, -cons.** To provide with or shine as a beacon. [Middle English *beken,* from Old English *bēacen.* See **bhā-**[1] in Appendix.]

Bea·con Hill (bē′kən). An area of Boston, Massachusetts, noted for its historic residences, brick sidewalks, and picturesque mews.

Bea·cons·field (bē′kənz-fēld′). A town of southern Quebec, Canada, a residential suburb of Montreal on Montreal Island. Population, 19,613.

bead (bēd) *n.* **1.a.** A small, often round piece of material, such as glass, plastic, or wood, that is pierced for stringing or threading. **b. beads.** A necklace made of such pieces. **c. beads.** *Roman Catholic Church.* A rosary. **d.** *Obsolete.* A prayer. Often used in the plural. **2.** A small, round object, especially: **a.** A drop of moisture: *beads of sweat.* **b.** A bubble of gas in a liquid. **c.** A small metal knob on the muzzle of a firearm, such as a rifle, used for sighting. **3.** A strip of material, usually wood, with one molded edge placed flush against the inner part of a door or window frame. **4.** *Architecture.* **a.** A decoration consisting of a usually continuous series of small spherical shapes, as on a convex molding. **b.** Beading. **5.** A projecting rim or lip, as on a pneumatic tire. **6.** A line of continuously-applied ductile material, such as solder or caulking compound. **7.** *Chemistry.* A globule of fused borax or other flux used in a bead test. **—bead** *tr. & intr.v.* **bead·ed, bead·ing, beads.** To furnish with or collect into beads. **—*idiom.* draw** (or **get**) **a bead on.** To take careful aim at. [Middle English *bede,* rosary bead, prayer, from Old English *bed, bedu, gebed,* prayer. See **g**ʷ**hedh-** in Appendix.]

beaker
Filtering liquid into a beaker

bead·ing (bē′dĭng) *n.* **1.** Beads or the material used for making them. **2.** Ornamentation with beads. Also called *beadwork.* **3.** *Architecture.* A narrow, half-rounded molding; a bead. **4.** A narrow piece of openwork lace through which ribbon may be run. **5.** Tiny drops of condensation, as on the outside of a glass.

bea·dle (bēd′l) *n.* A minor parish official formerly employed in an English church to usher and keep order during services. [Middle English *bedel,* herald (from Old English *bydel*) and from Old French *bedel* (from Medieval Latin *bedellus,* from Old High German *butil;* see **bheudh-** in Appendix).]

Bea·dle (bēd′l), **Erastus Flavel.** 1821–1894. American publisher who in 1860 published the first dime novel, initiating a popular series of almost 3,000 books with virtually indistinguishable plots, implausible dialogue, and lashings of violence and suspense.

Beadle, George Wells. 1903–1989. American biologist. He shared a 1958 Nobel Prize for discovering how genes transmit hereditary characteristics.

bead plant *n.* An evergreen, mat-forming plant *(Nertera granadensis)* chiefly of the Southern Hemisphere, grown especially as a houseplant for its abundant, long-lasting, orange drupes.

bead test *n. Chemistry.* A test to identify the metal constituents of a mineral in which a bead covered with the mineral is heated in a flame and cooled to observe its characteristic color and other properties.

bead·work (bēd′wûrk′) *n.* **1.** See **beading** (sense 2). **2.** *Architecture.* Beaded molding.

bead·y (bē′dē) *adj.* **-i·er, -i·est. 1.** Small, round, and shiny: *beady eyes.* **2.** Decorated or covered with beads.

bea·gle (bē′gəl) *n.* One of a breed of small hounds having short legs, drooping ears, and a smooth coat with white, black, and tan markings. [Middle English *begle,* possibly from Old French *bee gueule,* loudmouth : *beer,* to gape (variant of *baer;* see BAY[2]) + *gueule,* gullet (from Latin *gula*).]

beak (bēk) *n.* **1.a.** The horny, projecting structure forming the mandibles of a bird, especially one that is strong, sharp, and useful in striking and tearing; a bill. **b.** A similar structure in other animals, such as turtles, insects, or fish. **2.** A usually firm, tapering tip on certain plant structures, such as some seeds and fruits. **3.** A beaklike structure or part, as: **a.** The spout of a pitcher. **b.** A metal or metal-clad ram projecting from the bow of an ancient warship. **4.** *Informal.* The human nose. **5.** *Chiefly British.* **a.** A schoolmaster. **b.** A judge. [Middle English *bek,* from Old French *bec,* from Latin *beccus,* of Celtic origin.] **—beaked** *adj.*

beaked salmon *n.* See **sandfish** (sense 2).

beak·er (bē′kər) *n.* **1.** A wide cylindrical glass vessel with a pouring lip, used as a laboratory container and mixing jar. **2.** A large drinking cup with a wide mouth. [Middle Dutch *bēker,* drinking vessel, and Middle English *bekir,* both from Medieval Latin *bicārius, bicārium,* probably from Greek *bikos,* jug, possibly of Egyptian origin.]

be all and end all or **be-all and end-all** (bē′ôl′ ənd ĕnd′-ôl′) *n.* The quintessential or all-important element: *"Not that the more spectacular athleticism is the be all and end all of free skating. Spins . . . and intricate step sequences are also important"* (Howard Bass).

beam (bēm) *n. Abbr.* **bm. 1.** A squared-off log or a large, oblong piece of timber, metal, or stone used especially as a horizontal support in construction. **2.** *Nautical.* **a.** A transverse structural member of a ship's frame, used to support a deck and to brace the sides against stress. **b.** The breadth of a ship at the widest point. **c.** The side of a ship: *sighted land off the starboard beam.* **3.** *Informal.* The widest part of a person's hips: *broad in the beam.* **4.** A steel tube or wooden roller on which the warp is wound in a loom. **5.** An oscillating lever connected to an engine piston rod and used to transmit power to the crankshaft. **6.a.** The bar of a balance from which weighing pans are suspended. **b.** *Sports.* A balance beam. **7.** The main horizontal bar on a plow to which the share, colter, and handles are attached. **8.** One of the main stems of a deer's antlers. **9.a.** A ray or shaft of light. **b.** A concentrated stream of particles or a similar propagation of waves: *a beam of protons; a beam of light.* **10.** A radio beam. **—beam** *v.* **beamed, beam·ing, beams.** —*intr.* **1.** To radiate light; shine. **2.** To smile expansively. —*tr.* **1.** To emit or transmit: *beam a message via satellite.* **2.** To express by means of a radiant smile: *He beamed his approval of the new idea.* **—*idiom.* on the beam. 1.** Following a radio beam. Used of aircraft. **2.** On the right track; operating correctly. [Middle English *bem,* from Old English *bēam.* See **bheuə-** in Appendix.]

beam-ends (bēm′ĕndz′) *pl.n. Nautical.* The ends of a ship's beams.

beam·ish (bē′mĭsh) *adj.* Smiling, as with happiness or optimism. **—beam′ish·ly** *adv.*

beam·y (bē′mē) *adj.* **-i·er, -i·est. 1.** Broad in the beam. **2.** Emitting beams, as of light; radiant.

bean (bēn) *n.* **1.a.** Any of various New World twining herbs of the genus *Phaseolus* in the pea family, having leaves with three leaflets, variously colored flowers, and edible pods and seeds. **b.** A seed or pod of any of these plants. **2.** Any of several related plants or their seeds or pods, such as the adzuki bean, broad bean, or soybean. **3.** Any of various other plants or their seeds or fruits, especially those suggestive of beans, such as the coffee bean or the vanilla bean. **4.** *Slang.* A person's head. **5. beans.** *Slang.* A small amount: *I don't know beans about the stock market.* **6.** *Chiefly British.* A fellow; a chap. **—bean** *tr.v.* **beaned, bean·ing, beans.** *Slang.* To hit (another) on the head with a thrown object, especially a pitched baseball. **—*idioms.* full of beans. 1.** Energetic; frisky: *The children were too full of beans to sit still.* **2.** Badly mistaken: *Don't believe him; he's full of beans.* **spill the beans.** To disclose a secret. [Middle English *ben,* broad bean, from Old English *bēan.* See **bha-bhā-** in Appendix.]

bean·bag (bēn′băg′) *n.* **1.** A small bag filled with dried beans and used for throwing in games. **2.** A small folded bag filled with lead pellets, used as ammunition in a stun gun. **3.** An article, such as a chair or the base of an ashtray, that is constructed as a bag filled with small pellets.

bean ball *n. Baseball.* A pitch aimed at the batter's head.

bean beetle *n.* The Mexican bean beetle.

bean counter *n. Slang.* A financial executive, especially an accountant: *"Companies tended to recognize two cultures—that of the technologist and that of the bean counter"* (Financial Times).

bean curd *n.* Tofu.

bean·er·y (bē′nə-rē) *n., pl.* **-ies.** *Informal.* An inexpensive restaurant or café.

bean family *n.* The pea family.

bean·ie (bē′nē) *n.* A small brimless cap. [Probably from BEAN, head.]

bean·o (bē′nō) *n., pl.* **-os.** *Games.* A form of bingo, especially one using beans as markers. [Blend of BEAN and (BING)O.]

bean·pole (bēn′pōl′) *n.* **1.** A thin pole used to support bean vines. **2.** *Informal.* A very tall, thin person.

bean sprouts *pl.n.* The tender, edible seedlings of certain bean plants, especially those of the mung bean.

bean·stalk (bēn′stôk′) *n.* The stem of a bean plant.

bear[1] (bâr) *v.* **bore** (bôr, bōr), **borne** (bôrn, bōrn) or **born** (bôrn), **bear·ing, bears.** —*tr.* **1.** To hold up; support. **2.** To carry on one's person; convey. **3.** To carry in the mind; harbor: *bear a grudge.* **4.** To transmit at large; relate: *bearing glad tidings.* **5.** To have as a visible characteristic: *bore a scar on the left arm.* **6.** To have as a quality; exhibit: *"A thousand different shapes it bears"* (Abraham Cowley). **7.** To carry (oneself) in a specified way; conduct: *She bore herself with dignity.* **8.** To be accountable for; assume: *bearing heavy responsibilities.* **9.** To have a tolerance for; endure: *couldn't bear his lying.* **10.** To call for; warrant: *This case bears investigation.* **11.** To give birth to. **12.** To produce; yield: *plants bearing flowers.* **13.** To offer; render: *I will bear witness to the deed.* **14.** To move by or as if by steady pressure; push: *"boats against the current, borne back ceaselessly into the past"* (F. Scott Fitzgerald). —*intr.* **1.** To yield fruit; produce: *peach trees that bear every summer.* **2.** To have relevance; apply: *They studied the ways in which the relativity theory bears on the history of science.* **3.** To exert pressure, force, or influence. **4.a.** To force oneself along; forge. **b.** To endure something with tolerance and patience: *Bear with me while I explain matters.* **5.** To extend or proceed in a specified direction: *The road bears to the right at the bottom of the hill.* —***phrasal verbs.*** **bear down. 1.** To overwhelm; vanquish. **2.** To apply maximum effort and concentration: *If you really bear down, you will finish the task.* **bear out.** To prove right or justified; confirm: *The test results bear out our claims.* **bear up.** To withstand stress, difficulty, or attrition: *The patient bore up well during the long illness.* —***idioms.*** **bear down on.** To effect in a harmful or adverse way: *Financial pressures are bearing down on them.* **bear fruit.** To come to a satisfactory conclusion or to fruition. **bear in mind.** To hold in one's mind; remember: *Bear in mind that bridges freeze before roads.* [Middle English *beren,* from Old English *beran.* See **bher-**[1] in Appendix.]

SYNONYMS: *bear, endure, stand, abide, suffer, tolerate.* These verbs are compared in the sense of withstanding or sustaining what is difficult or painful to undergo. *Bear* pertains broadly to capacity to withstand: *"Man performs, engenders, so much more than he can or should have to bear. That's how he finds that he can bear anything"* (William Faulkner). *Endure* specifies a continuing capacity to face pain or hardship: *"Human life is everywhere a state in which much is to be endured and little to be enjoyed"* (Samuel Johnson). *Stand* implies resoluteness of spirit: *The pain was too intense to stand. Actors who can't stand criticism shouldn't perform in public. Abide* and the more emphatic *suffer* suggest resignation and forbearance: *She couldn't abide fools. He suffered their insults in silence. Tolerate,* in its principal application to something other than pain, connotes reluctant acceptance despite reservations: *"A decent . . . examination of the acts of government should be not only tolerated, but encouraged"* (William Henry Harrison). See also Synonyms at **produce.**

bear[2] (bâr) *n.* **1.a.** Any of various usually omnivorous mammals of the family Ursidae that have a shaggy coat and a short tail and walk with the entire lower surface of the foot touching the ground. **b.** Any of various other animals, such as the koala, that resemble a true bear. **2.** A large, clumsy, or ill-mannered person. **3.a.** One, such as an investor, that sells securities or commodities in expectation of falling prices. **b.** A pessimist, especially regarding business conditions. **4.** *Slang.* Something that is difficult or unpleasant: *The final exam was a bear.* **5.** *Slang.* A police officer, especially one using radar to apprehend speeding motorists. [Middle English *bere,* from Old English *bera.* See **bher-**[2] in Appendix. Sense 3, probably from proverb *To sell the bear's skin before catching the bear.*]

Bear (bâr), **Mount.** A peak, 4,523.5 m (14,831 ft) high, in the Wrangell Mountains of southern Alaska near the British Columbia border.

bear·a·ble (bâr′ə-bəl) *adj.* That can be endured: *bearable pain.* —**bear′a·bil′i·ty** *n.* —**bear′a·bly** *adv.*

bear·bait·ing (bâr′bā′tĭng) *n.* The practice of setting dogs on a chained bear.

bear·ber·ry (bâr′bĕr′ē) *n.* Any of certain mat-forming shrubs of the genus *Arctostaphylos* especially *A. uva-ursi,* native to North America and Eurasia, having small leathery leaves, white or pinkish urn-shaped flowers, and red berrylike fruits. Also called *kinnikinnick.*

bear·cat (bâr′kăt′) *n.* See **binturong.**

beard (bîrd) *n.* **1.** The hair on a man's chin, cheeks, and throat. **2.** A hairy or hairlike growth such as that on or near the face of certain mammals. **3.** A tuft or group of hairs or bristles on certain plants, such as barley and wheat. **4.** One that serves to divert suspicion or attention from another. —**beard** *tr.v.* **beard·ed, beard·ing, beards. 1.** To furnish with a beard. **2.** To confront boldly. See Synonyms at **defy.** [Middle English *berd,* from Old English *beard.* See **bhardh-ā-** in Appendix.] —**beard′ed** *adj.* —**beard′ed·ness** *n.* —**beard′less** *adj.* —**beard′less·ness** *n.*

Beard (bîrd), **Charles Austin.** 1874–1948. American historian and educator who explored the economic aspects of history in works such as *An Economic Interpretation of the Constitution* (1913). His view that the document was based on its formulators' economic self-interests profoundly affected the study of American history.

Beard, Daniel Carter. Known as "Dan." 1850–1941. American writer and illustrator. In 1905 he founded the Sons of Daniel Boone, which in 1910 became the first Boy Scout organization in the United States.

Beard, James Andrew. 1903–1985. American cookery expert widely considered to be one of the foremost authorities on American cuisine.

Beard, Mary Ritter. 1876–1958. American historian and feminist. She shared her husband Charles's economic view of history and collaborated with him on *The Rise of American Civilization* (first volume 1927), in which they characterized the Civil War as the "second American Revolution," perpetrated by Northern capitalists over Southern plantation owners for economic gain.

beard·ed iris (bîr′dĭd) *n.* Any of various irises characterized by a conspicuous region of hairs or hairlike structures on the lower parts of the three outer drooping perianth segments.

bearded vulture *n.* See **lammergeier.**

Beards·ley (bîrdz′lē), **Aubrey Vincent.** 1872–1898. British illustrator whose black and white, often erotic drawings were both highly individual and typical of the art nouveau style.

beard·tongue or **beard-tongue** (bîrd′tŭng′) *n.* See **penstemon.** [After its bearded, tonguelike stamen.]

bear·er (bâr′ər) *n.* **1.** One that carries or supports, as: **a.** A porter. **b.** A pallbearer. **2.** One that holds a check or other redeemable note for payment. **3.** A fruit- or flower-bearing plant.

bearer bond *n.* A bond payable to the holder.

bear grass *n.* **1.** A western North American perennial herb *(Xerophyllum tenax)* in the lily family, having a dense clump of basal grasslike leaves and a tall stalk bearing a terminal raceme of small whitish flowers. **2.** Any of several similar North American plants, especially species of the genera *Nolina* and *Yucca.*

bear hug *n.* A rough, tight hug.

bear·ing (bâr′ĭng) *n.* **1.** The manner in which one carries or conducts oneself: *the poise and bearing of a champion.* **2.a.** A machine or structural part that supports another part. **b.** A device that supports, guides, and reduces the friction of motion between fixed and moving machine parts. **3.** Something that supports weight. **4.** The part of an arch or beam that rests on a support. **5.a.** The act, power, or period of producing fruit or offspring. **b.** The quantity produced; yield. **6.** Direction, especially angular direction measured from one position to another using geographical or celestial reference lines. **7.** Often **bearings.** Awareness of one's position or situation relative to one's surroundings: *lost my bearings after taking the wrong exit.* **8.** Relevant relationship or interconnection: *Those issues have no bearing on our situation.* **9.** *Heraldry.* A charge or device on a field.

SYNONYMS: *bearing, manner, demeanor, mien, presence.* These nouns pertain to a person's behavior as it reveals such distinctive personal qualities as his or her individuality or upbringing. *Bearing,* the most inclusive, applies to both physical posture and general conduct: *has the erect bearing of a soldier. "That is Claudio. I know him by his bearing"* (Shakespeare). *Manner* is a person's characteristic conduct or comportment: *her pleasant, shy manner; their arrogant, overbearing manner. Demeanor* is behavior that reveals to others one's personality or attitude: *"The President's outward demeanor was genial and relaxed"* (Edmund S. Muskie). *Mien* pertains to bearing especially as it reflects an inner state of mind: *She maintained her serious mien until the interview was over. Presence* denotes the quality of commanding respectful attention: "[Sir Thomas] *More was a man of stately and handsome presence"* (Horace Walpole).

bearing rein *n.* A rein for a horse; a checkrein.

bear·ish (bâr′ĭsh) *adj.* **1.** Clumsy, boorish, and surly. **2.a.** Causing, expecting, or characterized by falling stock-market prices. **b.** Pessimistic: *"Whether or not the* [Coast Guard] *cutter's presence made bearish the prospects of illicit trade in the outlying islands, there was a prompt mass migration of their inhabitants to the mainland"* (Springfield MA Sunday Republican). —**bear′ish·ly** *adv.* —**bear′ish·ness** *n.*

Bé·arn (bā-ärn′). A historical region and former province of

ă pat	oi boy
ā pay	ou out
âr care	o͝o took
ä father	o͞o boot
ĕ pet	ŭ cut
ē be	ûr urge
ĭ pit	th thin
ī pie	*th* this
îr pier	hw which
ŏ pot	zh vision
ō toe	ə about, item
ô paw	♦ regionalism

Stress marks: **′** (primary); **′** (secondary), as in **dictionary** (dĭk′shə-nĕr′ē)

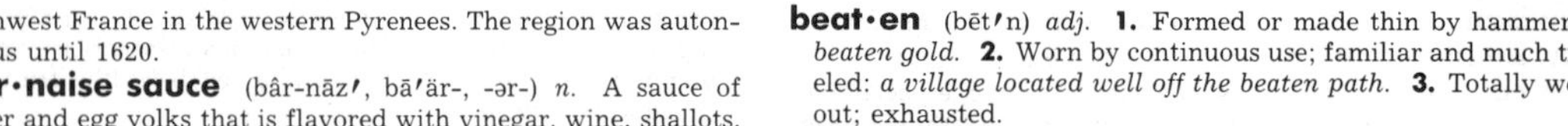

southwest France in the western Pyrenees. The region was autonomous until 1620.

bé·ar·naise sauce (bâr-nāz′, bā′är-, -ər-) *n.* A sauce of butter and egg yolks that is flavored with vinegar, wine, shallots, tarragon, and chervil. [From *béarnaise,* feminine of *béarnais,* of Béarn.]

Bear River. A river rising in northeast Utah and flowing about 563 km (350 mi) in a U-shaped course northwest through southwest Wyoming and southeast Idaho then south into Utah again. It empties into Great Salt Lake.

bear's breech (bârz) *n.* See **acanthus** (sense 1).

bear's ear *n.* See **auricula** (sense 1).

bear·skin (bâr′skĭn′) *n.* **1.** Something, such as a rug, made from the skin of a bear. **2.** A tall military hat made of black fur.

Be·as (bē′äs′). A river, about 402 km (250 mi) long, of northern India rising in the Himalaya Mountains. It is one of the five rivers of the Punjab that form a major tributary of the Indus River.

bearskin

♦**beast** (bēst) *n.* **1.a.** An animal other than a human being, especially a large four-footed mammal. **b.** *New England & Southern U.S.* A large domestic animal, especially a horse or bull. **2.** Animal nature as opposed to intellect or spirit: *"So far the beast in us has insisted upon having its full say"* (William Dean Howells). **3.** A brutal, contemptible person. [Middle English *beste,* from Old French, from Latin *bēstia.*]

beast epic *n.* A long, usually allegorical verse narrative in which the characters are animals with human feelings and motives.

beast·ings (bē′stĭngz) *pl.n. (used with a sing. or pl. verb).* Variant of **beestings.**

beast·ly (bēst′lē) *adj.* **-li·er, -li·est. 1.** Of or resembling a beast; bestial. See Synonyms at **brute. 2.** Very disagreeable; unpleasant. **—beastly** *adv. Chiefly British.* To an extreme degree; very. **—beast′li·ness** *n.*

beast of burden *n., pl.* **beasts of burden.** An animal, such as a donkey, an ox, or an elephant, used for transporting loads or doing other heavy work.

beat (bēt) *v.* **beat, beat·en** (bēt′n) or **beat, beat·ing, beats.** *—tr.* **1.a.** To strike repeatedly. **b.** To punish by hitting or whipping; flog. **2.a.** To strike against repeatedly and with force; pound: *waves beating the shore.* **b.** To flap, especially wings. **c.** To strike so as to produce music or a signal: *beat a drum.* **d.** *Music.* To mark or count (time or rhythm) with the hands or with a baton. **3.a.** To shape or break by repeated blows; forge: *beat the glowing metal into a dagger.* **b.** To make by pounding or trampling: *beat a path through the jungle.* **4.** To mix rapidly with a utensil: *beat two eggs in a bowl.* **5.a.** To defeat or subdue, as in a contest. **b.** To force to withdraw or retreat: *beat back the enemy.* **c.** To dislodge from a position: *I beat him down to a lower price.* **6.** *Informal.* To be superior to or better than: *Riding beats walking.* **7.** *Slang.* To perplex or baffle: *It beats me; I don't know the answer.* **8.** *Informal.* **a.** To avoid or counter the effects of, often by thinking ahead; circumvent: *beat the traffic.* **b.** To arrive or finish before (another): *We beat you home by five minutes.* **c.** To deprive, as by craft or ability: *He beat me out of 20 dollars with his latest scheme.* *—intr.* **1.** To inflict repeated blows. **2.** To pulsate; throb. **3.** *Physics.* To cause beating by superposing waves of different frequencies. **4.a.** To emit sound when struck: *The gong beat thunderously.* **b.** To strike a drum. **5.** To flap repeatedly. **6.** To be victorious or successful; win. **7.** To hunt through woods or underbrush in search of game. **8.** *Nautical.* To sail in the direction from which the wind blows. **—beat** *n.* **1.** A stroke or blow, especially one that produces a sound or serves as a signal. **2.** A pulsation or throb. **3.** *Physics.* A pulsation produced by beating. **4.** *Music.* **a.** A regular, rhythmical unit of time. **b.** The gesture used by a conductor to indicate this unit of time. **c.** The symbol representing this unit of time. **5.** The measured, rhythmical sound of verse; meter. **6.a.** The area regularly covered by a reporter, a police officer, or a sentry: *television's culture beat.* **b.** The reporting of a news item obtained ahead of one's competitors. **—beat** *adj.* **1.** *Informal.* Worn-out; fatigued. **2.** Of, relating to, or being a beatnik: *the beat generation.* ***—phrasal verbs.*** **beat off. 1.** To drive away. **2.** *Vulgar Slang.* To masturbate. **beat out.** *Baseball.* To reach base safely on (a bunt or ground ball). ***—idioms.*** **beat a retreat.** To make a hasty withdrawal. **beat around** (or **about**) **the bush.** To fail to confront a subject directly. **beat it.** *Slang.* To leave hurriedly. **beat the bushes.** To make an exhaustive search. **beat the drum** (or **drums**). To give enthusiastic public support or promotion: *a politician who beats the drum for liberalism.* **to beat the band.** With great vigor; in a fast and furious manner. [Middle English *beten,* from Old English *bēaten.* See **bhau-** in Appendix.]

Beatrix
Photographed in 1982

SYNONYMS: *beat, baste, batter, belabor, buffet, hammer, lambaste, pound, pummel, thrash.* The central meaning shared by these verbs is "to hit heavily and repeatedly with violent blows": *was mugged and beaten; basted him with a stick; was battered and bloodied in the prize ring; rioting students belabored by squads of police officers; buffeted him around the face with her open palm; hammered the opponent with his fists; lambasting a horse thief with a riding crop; troops being pounded with mortar fire; pummeled the bully soundly; an unruly child who was thrashed with a birch cane.* See also Synonyms at **defeat, pulsate.**

beat·en (bēt′n) *adj.* **1.** Formed or made thin by hammering: *beaten gold.* **2.** Worn by continuous use; familiar and much traveled: *a village located well off the beaten path.* **3.** Totally worn-out; exhausted.

beat·er (bē′tər) *n.* **1.** One that beats, especially a device for beating: *a carpet beater.* **2.** A person who drives wild game from under cover for a hunter.

be·a·tif·ic (bē′ə-tĭf′ĭk) *adj.* Showing or producing exalted joy or blessedness; angelic: *a beatific smile.* [Latin *beātificus* : *beātus,* happy, from past participle of *beāre,* to bless; see **deu-**[2] in Appendix + *-ficus,* -fic.] **—be′a·tif′i·cal·ly** *adv.*

be·at·i·fy (bē-ăt′ə-fī′) *tr.v.* **-fied, -fy·ing, -fies. 1.** To make blessedly happy. **2.** *Roman Catholic Church.* To proclaim (a deceased person) to be one of the blessed and thus worthy of public religious veneration in a particular region or religious congregation. **3.** To exalt above all others. [French *beatifier,* from Late Latin *beātificāre* : Latin *beātus,* happy; see BEATIFIC + Latin *-ficāre,* -fy.] **—be·at′i·fi·ca′tion** (-fĭ-kā′shən) *n.*

beat·ing (bē′tĭng) *n.* **1.** Punishment by whipping or flogging. **2.** A sound defeat. **3.** A throbbing or pulsation, as of the heart. **4.** *Physics.* The periodic variation in amplitude of a wave produced by the superposition of two waves of different frequencies.

be·at·i·tude (bē-ăt′ĭ-to͞od′, -tyo͞od′) *n.* **1.** Supreme blessedness or happiness. **2. Beatitude.** Any of the declarations of blessedness made by Jesus in the Sermon on the Mount. **3. Beatitude.** Used as a title and form of address for a patriarch in the Armenian Church or a metropolitan in the Russian Orthodox Church: *Your Beatitude.* [Middle English, from Old French, from Latin *beātitūdō,* from *beātus,* happy. See BEATIFIC.]

Beat·les (bēt′lz). A former British pop group comprising John Lennon, Ringo Starr, Paul McCartney, and George Harrison. The group first gained international fame in 1962 and disbanded in 1970.

beat·nik (bēt′nĭk) *n.* A person who acts and dresses with pointed, often exaggerated disregard for what is generally thought proper and who is given to radical and extravagant social criticism or self-expression. [From *beat generation,* a group of unconventional young people of the 1950's + –NIK.]

Bea·ton (bēt′n), **Cecil Walter Hardy.** 1904–1980. British photographer, diarist, and theatrical designer noted for his sets and costumes for *My Fair Lady* (stage, 1956; film, 1964).

Be·a·trix (bā′ə-trĭks′, bē′-). Born 1938. Queen of the Netherlands who ascended the throne in April 1980 after the abdication of her mother, Juliana.

Beat·tie (bā′tē, bē′-), **James.** 1735–1803. Scottish philosopher and poet best known as the author of *The Minstrel* (1771–1774), which detailed in Spenserian stanzas the evolution of poetic genius.

beat-up (bēt′ŭp′) *adj. Slang.* Damaged or worn because of neglect or heavy use.

beau (bō) *n., pl.* **beaus** or **beaux** (bōz). **1.** The boyfriend of a woman or girl. **2.** A dandy; a fop. [French, from *beau, bel,* handsome, from Latin *bellus.* See **deu-**[2] in Appendix.]

Beau Brum·mell (bō brŭm′əl) *n.* A dandy; a fop. [After George Bryan *("Beau")* BRUMMELL.]

♦**beau·coup** (bō′ko͞o′, bo͞o′-, bō-ko͞o′) also **boo·coo** or **boo·koo** (bo͞o′-) *Chiefly Southern U.S.* *—adj.* Many; much: *beaucoup money.* *—n., pl.* **-coups** also **-coos** or **-koos.** An abundance; a lot. *—adv.* In abundance; galore: *money beaucoup.* [French : *beau, bel,* fine, handsome; see BEAU + *coup,* stroke; see COUP.]

Beau·fort (bō′fərt), **Henry.** 1377?–1447. English prelate and diplomat who was papal legate to a crusade against the Hussites (1427–1431) and crowned Henry VI king of France and England (1431).

Beaufort scale *n.* A scale on which successive ranges of wind velocities are assigned code numbers from 0 (calm) to 12 (hurricane), corresponding to wind speeds of from less than 1 mile per hour (0–1 kilometer per hour) to over 74 miles per hour (over 117 kilometers per hour). [After Sir Francis *Beaufort* (1774–1857), British naval officer.]

Beaufort Sea. A part of the Arctic Ocean north of northeast Alaska and northwest Canada extending from Point Barrow, Alaska, to the Canadian Arctic Archipelago. Covered with pack ice year-round, it was first explored in 1914.

beau geste (bō zhĕst′) *n., pl.* **beaux gestes** or **beau gestes** (bō zhĕst′). **1.** A gracious gesture. **2.** A gesture noble in form but meaningless in substance. [French : *beau,* noble + *geste,* gesture.]

Beau·har·nais (bō-är-nā′), **Alexandre de.** 1760–1794. French soldier who fought with Rochambeau's troops in the American Revolution and later in France with the French Revolutionary army. He was guillotined during the Reign of Terror.

Beauharnais, Eugène de. 1781–1824. French soldier and statesman. Son of Alexandre and Josephine de Beauharnais, he was later adopted by Napoleon I and became viceroy and then heir apparent to the throne of Italy (1806).

Beauharnais, Josephine de. 1763–1814. Empress of the French (1804–1809) as the wife of Napoleon I. Married first to Alexandre de Beauharnais, she wed Napoleon Bonaparte in 1796.

beau i·de·al (bō′ ī-dē′əl) *n., pl.* **beau ideals. 1.** The concept of perfect beauty. **2.** An idealized type or model: *the beau ideal of an American army officer.* [French *beau idéal* : *beau,* perfect + *ideal,* ideal.]

Beau·jo·lais¹ (bō′zhə-lā′). A hilly region of east-central France west of the Saône River between Mâcon and Lyon. It is noted for its wine.

Beau·jo·lais² (bō′zhə-lā′) *n.* A light red table wine. [After BEAUJOLAIS¹.]

Beau·mar·chais (bō-mär-shā′), **Pierre Augustin Caron de.** 1732–1799. French writer whose best-known works are the comic plays *Le Barbier de Séville* (1775) and *Le Mariage de Figaro* (1784), which inspired operas by Rossini and Mozart.

beau monde (bō mŏnd′, môɴd′) *n., pl.* **beaux mondes** (bō môɴd′) or **beau mondes** (bō mŏndz′). The world of fashionable society. [French : *beau,* good + *monde,* world, society.]

Beau·mont (bō′mŏnt′). A city of southeast Texas north-northeast of Houston. A ship canal links the city with the Gulf of Mexico. Population, 118,102.

Beau·mont (bō′mŏnt′, -mənt), **Francis.** 1584–1616. English poet and playwright. He wrote his major works, including *The Maid's Tragedy* (1611), *The Coxcomb* (1612), and *The Knight of Malta* (1619), with John Fletcher.

Beau·mont (bō′mŏnt′), **William.** 1785–1853. American surgeon whose *Physiology of Digestion* (1833) revolutionized the study of gastric digestion.

Beau·port (bō-pôr′). A city of southern Quebec, Canada, a suburb of Quebec City on the St. Lawrence River. Settled in 1634, it is one of the oldest communities in Canada. Population, 60,447.

Beau·re·gard (bō′rĭ-gärd′, bō-rə-gär′), **Pierre Gustave Toutant.** 1818–1893. American Confederate general known for his flamboyant personal style and dashing but not always successful strategic campaigns. He ordered the bombardment of Fort Sumter in April 1861.

beaut (byo͞ot) *n. Slang.* Something outstanding of its kind: *"When I make a mistake, it's a beaut!"* (Fiorello H. La Guardia). [Short for BEAUTY.]

beau·te·ous (byo͞o′tē-əs) *adj.* Beautiful, especially to the sight. **—beau′te·ous·ly** *adv.* **—beau′te·ous·ness** *n.*

beau·ti·cian (byo͞o-tĭsh′ən) *n.* One skilled in giving cosmetic treatments.

beau·ti·ful (byo͞o′tə-fəl) *adj.* **1.** Having qualities that delight the senses, especially the sense of sight. **2.** Exciting intellectual or emotional admiration. **—beau′ti·ful·ly** *adv.* **—beau′ti·ful·ness** *n.*

SYNONYMS: *beautiful, lovely, pretty, handsome, comely, fair.* All these adjectives apply to what excites aesthetic admiration. *Beautiful,* the most comprehensive, applies to what stirs a heightened response both of the senses *(a beautiful child; beautiful country; a beautiful painting)* and of the mind on its highest level *(a persuasive and beautiful theory; a beautiful mathematical proof). Lovely* applies to what inspires emotion rather than intellectual appreciation: *"They were lovely, your eyes, but you didn't know where to look"* (George Seferis). *"Every man feels instinctively that all the beautiful sentiments in the world weigh less than a single lovely action"* (James Russell Lowell). What is *pretty* is beautiful but in a delicate or graceful way; the word rarely applies to what is imposing: *a pretty face; a pretty song; a pretty room. Handsome* stresses visual appeal by reason of conformity to ideals of form and proportion: *a very large, handsome paneled library. "She is very pretty, but not so* extraordinarily *handsome"* (Thackeray). *Comely* is usually restricted to wholesome physical attractiveness: *"Mrs. Hurd is a large woman with a big, comely, simple face"* (Ernest Hemingway). *Fair* in this context emphasizes visual appeal deriving from freshness or purity: *"In the highlands, in the country places,/Where the old plain men have rosy faces,/And the young fair maidens/Quiet eyes"* (Robert Louis Stevenson).

beautiful people also **Beautiful People** *pl.n. Abbr.* **bp, BP** Wealthy, prominent people, especially in international society.

beau·ti·fy (byo͞o′tə-fī′) *tr. & intr.v.* **-fied, -fy·ing, -fies.** To make or become beautiful. **—beau′ti·fi·ca′tion** (-fĭ-kā′shən) *n.* **—beau′ti·fi′er** *n.*

beau·ty (byo͞o′tē) *n., pl.* **-ties. 1.** A delightful quality associated with harmony of form or color, excellence of craftsmanship, truthfulness, originality, or another property. **2.** One that is beautiful, especially a beautiful woman. **3.** A quality or feature that is most effective, gratifying, or telling: *The beauty of the venture is that we stand to lose nothing.* **4.** An outstanding or conspicuous example: *"Hammett's gun went off. The shot was a beauty, just slightly behind the eyes"* (Lillian Hellman). [Middle English *beaute,* from Old French *biaute,* from Vulgar Latin **bellitās,* from Latin *bellus,* pretty. See **deu-²** in Appendix.]

beau·ty·ber·ry (byo͞o′tē-bĕr′ē) *n.* Any of various shrubs of the genus *Callicarpa* cultivated for their axillary clusters of showy, often lavender-pink to violet berrylike fruits.

beau·ty·bush (byo͞o′tē-bo͝osh′) *n.* A deciduous Chinese ornamental shrub (*Kolkwitzia amabilis*) cultivated for its profusion of showy pink flowers with yellow throats.

beauty mark *n.* See **beauty spot** (sense 1).

beauty parlor *n.* An establishment providing women with services that include hair treatment, manicures, and facials. Also called *beauty salon, beauty shop.*

beauty quark *n.* See **bottom quark.**

beauty salon *n.* See **beauty parlor.**

beauty shop *n.* See **beauty parlor.**

beauty spot *n.* **1.** A mole or birthmark. Also called *beauty mark.* **2.** A small black mark penciled or glued on a woman's face or shoulders to accentuate the fairness of her skin or to conceal a blemish.

Beau·vais (bō-vā′). A town of northern France north-northwest of Paris. Its tapestry works, established in the 17th century, were destroyed in June 1940 during World War II. Population, 52,365.

Beau·voir (bō-vwär′), **Simone de.** 1908–1986. French writer, existentialist, and feminist whose works include *The Second Sex* (1949) and *The Coming of Age* (1970), a study of how different cultures view old age.

beaux (bōz) *n.* A plural of **beau.**

Beaux (bō), **Cecilia.** 1863–1942. American artist who excelled in portraits, especially those of women and children.

beaux-arts (bō-zär′, -zärt′) *pl.n.* The fine arts. [French : *beau,* fine + *art,* art.]

beaux es·prits (bō′zĕ-sprē′) *n.* Plural of **bel esprit.**

beaux gestes (bō zhĕst′) *n.* A plural of **beau geste.**

beaux mondes (bō môɴd′) *n.* A plural of **beau monde.**

bea·ver¹ (bē′vər) *n.* **1.a.** A large aquatic rodent of the genus *Castor,* having thick brown fur, webbed hind feet, a broad flat tail, and sharp incisors adapted for gnawing bark, felling trees, and constructing dams and underwater lodges. **b.** The fur of this rodent. **c.** A top hat originally made of the underfur of this rodent. **2.** A napped wool fabric, similar to felt, used for outer garments. **3.a.** *Offensive & Vulgar Slang.* The female genitalia. **b.** *Offensive & Vulgar Slang.* A woman or girl. **—beaver** *adj.* **1.** Of or relating to a beaver or beavers: *beaver fur; a beaver hat.* **2.** Constructed by beavers: *beaver dams.* **—beaver** *intr.v.* **-vered, -ver·ing, -vers.** To work diligently and energetically. [Middle English *bever,* from Old English *beofor.* See **bher-²** in Appendix.]

bea·ver² (bē′vər) *n.* **1.** A piece of armor attached to a helmet or breastplate to protect the mouth and chin. **2.** The visor on a helmet. [Middle English *bavier,* from Old French *baviere,* child's bib, beaver, from *bave,* saliva.]

bea·ver·board (bē′vər-bôrd′, -bōrd′) *n.* A light, semirigid building material of compressed wood pulp, used for walls and partitions. [Originally a trademark.]

Bea·ver·brook (bē′vər-bro͝ok′), First Baron. Originally William Maxwell Aitken. 1879–1964. Canadian-born British publisher, financier, and politician. He founded his press empire on the *Daily Express* (1916) and the *Evening Standard* (1923), held many cabinet positions during the 1940's, and was a confidant of Winston Churchill.

Bea·ver·creek (bē′vər-krēk′). A village of southwest Ohio, a residential suburb of Dayton. Population, 31,589.

Bea·ver River (bē′vər). **1.** A river rising in central Alberta, Canada, and flowing about 491 km (305 mi) eastward into Saskatchewan then north to the headwaters of the Churchill River. **2.** A name for the North Canadian River as it flows about 450 km (280 mi) through northwest Oklahoma.

Bea·ver·ton (bē′vər-tən). A city of northwest Oregon west of Portland. It was founded in 1868. Population, 30,582.

Be·bel (bā′bəl), **(Ferdinand) August.** 1840–1913. German socialist leader who was a cofounder and leader of the Social Democratic Party, organized in 1869.

be·bop (bē′bŏp′) *n. Music.* Bop. [Imitation of a two-beat phrase in this music.] **—be′bop′per** *n.*

be·calm (bĭ-käm′) *tr.v.* **-calmed, -calm·ing, -calms. 1.** To render motionless for lack of wind. **2.** To make calm or still; soothe.

be·came (bĭ-kām′) *v.* Past tense of **become.**

be·cause (bĭ-kôz′, -kŭz′) *conj.* For the reason that; since. [Middle English. See BECAUSE OF.]

USAGE NOTE: A traditional rule holds that the construction *the reason is because* is redundant, and should be avoided in favor of *the reason is that.* The usage is well established, however, and can be justified by analogy to constructions such as *His* purpose *in calling her was* so that *she would be forewarned of the change in schedule* or *The last* time *I saw her was* when *she was leaving for college.* All three constructions are somewhat less than graceful, however. • When *because* follows a negated verb phrase, it should be preceded by a comma when the *because* clause explains why the event did *not* occur. *He didn't marry her, because she was frivolous* means roughly, "Her frivolity was his reason for not marrying her." When no comma is used, the *because* clause is understood as part of what is being negated. *He didn't marry her because she was frivolous* means roughly, "His reason for marrying her was independent of her frivolity." See Usage Note at **as¹.**

because of *prep.* On account of; by reason of. [Middle English *bi cause of,* by reason of : *bi,* by; see BY¹ + *cause,* reason; see CAUSE + *of,* of; see OF.]

bec·ca·fi·co (bĕk′ə-fē′kō) *n., pl.* **-cos.** A small songbird or warbler of various genera, especially the European garden warbler (*Sylvia hortensis*), that is eaten as a delicacy in Italy and France. [Italian : *beccare,* to peck (from *becco,* beak, from Latin *beccus;* see BEAK) + *fico,* fig (from Latin *fīcus*).]

bé·cha·mel sauce (bā′shə-mĕl′) *n.* A white sauce of butter, flour, and milk or cream. [French *sauce béchamel,* after Louis de *Béchamel* (1603–1703), chief steward of Louis XIV.]

Simone de Beauvoir

beaver¹
North American beaver
Castor canadensis

ă pat	oi boy
ā pay	ou out
âr care	o͝o took
ä father	o͞o boot
ĕ pet	ŭ cut
ē be	ûr urge
ĭ pit	th thin
ī pie	*th* this
îr pier	hw which
ŏ pot	zh vision
ō toe	ə about, item
ô paw	♦ regionalism

Stress marks: **′** (primary); ′ (secondary), as in **dictionary** (dĭk′shə-nĕr′ē)

be·chance (bĭ-chăns′) *intr. & tr.v.* **-chanced, -chanc·ing, -chanc·es.** *Archaic.* To happen or happen to.

bêche-de-mer (bĕsh′də-mâr′) *n., pl.* **bêches-de-mer** (bĕsh′də-mâr′). See **trepang.** [French, alteration (influenced by *bêche,* grub) of *biche-de-mer,* from Portuguese *bicho do mar* : *bicho,* worm (from Late Latin *bēstulus,* diminutive of Latin *bēstia,* beast) + *do,* of the + *mar,* sea (from Latin *mare;* see **mori-** in Appendix).]

Bêche-de-Mer (bĕsh′ də-mâr′) *n.* See **Bislama.** [From the commercial importance of *bêche-de-mer* where the language is spoken.]

Bech·u·a·na (bĕch′o͞o-ä′nə) *n., pl.* **Bechuana** or **-nas.** See **Tswana** (sense 1).

Bech·u·a·na·land (bĕch′wän′ə-lănd′, bĕch′o͞o-ä′nə-). See **Botswana.**

beck[1] (bĕk) *n.* A gesture of beckoning or summons. **—*idiom.* at (one's) beck and call.** Ready to comply with any wish or command. [Middle English *bek,* from *bekken,* to beckon, alteration of *bekenen.* See BECKON.]

beck[2] (bĕk) *n. Chiefly British.* A small brook; a creek. [Middle English, from Old Norse *bekkr.* See **bhegʷ-** in Appendix.]

beck·et (bĕk′ĭt) *n. Nautical.* A device, such as a looped rope, hook and eye, strap, or grommet, used to hold or fasten loose ropes, spars, or oars in position. [Origin unknown.]

Thomas à Becket
The Martyrdom of Thomas à Becket, mid 13th-century miniature from the Carrow Psalter

Beck·et (bĕk′ĭt), Saint **Thomas à.** 1118?–1170. English Roman Catholic martyr. Chancellor to Henry II after 1154, he was appointed archbishop of Canterbury (1162) and fell into disfavor with the king. Charged with misappropriating crown funds (1164), Becket fled the country. Upon his return (1170) he was embroiled in the controversy surrounding Henry's appointment of his son as archbishop of York and was murdered by four knights in Canterbury Cathedral. He was canonized in 1173.

Beck·ett (bĕk′ĭt), **Samuel.** 1906–1989. Irish-born writer whose novels include *Murphy* (1938) and *Malone Dies* (1951). Beckett is known to a wider audience for his absurdist plays, such as *Waiting for Godot* (1952) and *Krapp's Last Tape* (1959). He won the 1969 Nobel Prize for literature.

Beck·ford (bĕk′fərd), **William.** 1759?–1844. British writer and collector noted for his Arabian tale *Vathek* (1782), written in French, and for his magnificent residences.

Beck·ley (bĕk′lē). A city of southern West Virginia southeast of Charleston. It is a trade center in a coal-mining region. Population, 20,492.

Beck·mann (bĕk′män), **Max.** 1884–1950. German artist whose early expressionistic manner yielded to his lasting style, the painting of brutal, often grotesque figurative canvases, such as *Night* (1919).

beck·on (bĕk′ən) *v.* **-oned, -on·ing, -ons.** *—tr.* **1.** To signal or summon, as by nodding or waving. **2.** To attract because of an inviting or enticing appearance: *"a lovely, sunny country that seemed to beckon them on to the Emerald City"* (L. Frank Baum). *—intr.* **1.** To make a signaling or summoning gesture. **2.** To be inviting or enticing. **—beckon** *n.* A gesture of summons. [Middle English *bekenen,* from Old English *bēcnan.* See **bhā-**[1] in Appendix.] **—beck′on·er** *n.* **—beck′on·ing·ly** *adv.*

be·cloud (bĭ-kloud′) *tr.v.* **-cloud·ed, -cloud·ing, -clouds.** To darken with or as if with clouds; obscure: *a development that beclouds the real issues.*

be·come (bĭ-kŭm′) *v.* **-came** (-kām′), **-come, -com·ing, -comes.** *—intr.* To grow or come to be: *became more knowledgeable; will become clearer in the morning.* *—tr.* **1.** To be appropriate or suitable to: *"It would not become me . . . to interfere with parties"* (Jonathan Swift). **2.** To show to advantage; look good with: *The new suit becomes you.* **—*phrasal verb.* become of.** To be the fate of; happen to: *What has become of the old garden?* [Middle English *bicomen,* from Old English *becuman.* See **gʷā-** in Appendix.]

Bedlington terrier

be·com·ing (bĭ-kŭm′ĭng) *adj.* **1.** Appropriate, suitable, or proper. **2.** Pleasing or attractive to the eye. **—be·com′ing·ly** *adv.* **—be·com′ing·ness** *n.*

Bec·que·rel (bĕ-krĕl′, bĕk′ə-rĕl′). Family of French physicists, including **Antoine César** (1788–1878), one of the first investigators of electrochemistry; his son **Alexandre Edmond** (1820–1891), noted for his research on phosphorescence and spectroscopy; and his grandson **Antoine Henri** (1852–1908), who shared a 1903 Nobel Prize for basic work in nuclear physics.

bed (bĕd) *n.* **1.a.** A piece of furniture for reclining and sleeping, typically consisting of a flat, rectangular frame and a mattress resting on springs. **b.** A bedstead. **c.** A mattress. **2.a.** A place where one may sleep; lodging: *found bed and board at an inn.* **b.** Accommodations for a single person at a hospital or institution: *a maternity ward with 30 beds.* **3.** A time at which one goes to sleep: *drank milk before bed.* **4.** A place for lovemaking. **5.** A marital relationship with its rights and intimacies. **6.a.** A small plot of cultivated or planted land: *a flower bed.* **b.** An underwater or intertidal area in which a particular organism is established in large numbers: *a clam bed; an oyster bed.* **7.** The bottom of a body of water, such as a stream. **8.** A supporting, underlying, or securing part, especially: **a.** A layer of food surmounted by another kind of food: *tomatoes on a bed of lettuce.* **b.** A foundation of crushed rock or a similar substance for a road or railroad; a roadbed. **c.** A layer of mortar upon which stones or bricks are laid. **9.** *Printing.* The heavy table of a printing press in which the type form is placed. **10.** The part of a truck, trailer, or freight car designed to carry loads. **11.** *Geology.* **a.** A rock mass of large horizontal extent bounded, especially above, by physically different material. **b.** A deposit, as of ore, parallel to local stratification. **12.** A heap of material: *a bed of wood chips.* **—bed** *v.* **bed·ded, bed·ding, beds.** *—tr.* **1.** To furnish with a bed or sleeping quarters: *We bedded our guests down in the study.* **2.** To put or send to bed. **3.** To have sexual relations with. **4.** To plant in a prepared plot of soil. **5.** To lay flat or arrange in layers. **6.a.** To embed. **b.** To establish; base. *—intr.* **1.** To go to bed. **2.** *Geology.* To form layers or strata. **—*idioms.* get into bed with.** *Slang.* To become closely involved with another person or group, as in an intrigue: *"The Israelis were experienced at* [covert] *work, but it was essential that the administration not get into bed with them on this"* (Bob Woodward). **go to bed with.** To have sexual relations with. [Middle English, from Old English.]

B.Ed. *abbr.* Bachelor of Education.

Be·da (bē′də). See **Bede.**

bed-and-break·fast or **bed and breakfast** (bĕd′n-brĕk′fəst) *n. Abbr.* **B & B** A private residence, several rooms of which are set aside for overnight guests whose paid accommodations include breakfast. **—bed′-and-break′fast** *adj.*

be·daub (bĭ-dôb′) *tr.v.* **-daubed, -daub·ing, -daubs. 1.** To smear; soil. **2.** To ornament in a vulgar, showy fashion.

be·daz·zle (bĭ-dăz′əl) *tr.v.* **-zled, -zling, -zles. 1.** To dazzle so completely as to make blind. **2.** To please irresistibly; enchant. **—be·daz′zle·ment** *n.*

♦ **bed·bug** also **bed bug** (bĕd′bŭg′) *n.* A wingless, odorous insect *(Cimex lectularius)* with a flat, reddish body that infests dwellings and bedding and feeds on human blood. Also called ♦*chinch,* ♦*chinch bug.*

bed·cham·ber (bĕd′chām′bər) *n.* A bedroom.

bed check *n.* An inspection held at night in order to ensure that certain people, such as students or military personnel, are in bed as required by rules and regulations.

bed·clothes (bĕd′klōz′, -klōthz′) *pl.n.* Coverings, such as sheets and blankets, that are ordinarily used on a bed.

bed·ding (bĕd′ĭng) *n.* **1.** Bedclothes. **2.** Material, especially straw, on which animals sleep. **3.** A bottom layer; a foundation. **4.** *Geology.* Stratification of rocks into beds.

bedding plant *n.* A plant that has already been grown to blooming or near-blooming size before being planted out in a usually formal area for seasonal display of colorful flowers or foliage.

Bed·does (bĕd′ōz′), **Thomas Lovell.** 1803–1849. British poet whose often macabre works include *The Bride's Tragedy* (1822) and *Death's Jest-Book* (1850), published posthumously.

Bede (bēd) also **Bae·da** or **Be·da** (bē′də). Known as "the Venerable Bede." 673?–735. Anglo-Saxon theologian and historian whose major work, *Ecclesiastical History of the English Nation* (731), written in Latin, remains an important source of ancient English history. He introduced the method of dating events from the birth of Christ.

be·deck (bĭ-dĕk′) *tr.v.* **-decked, -deck·ing, -decks.** To adorn or ornament in a showy fashion.

be·dev·il (bĭ-dĕv′əl) *tr.v.* **-iled, -il·ing, -ils** or **-illed, -il·ling, -ils. 1.** To torment mercilessly; plague. **2.** To worry, annoy, or frustrate. **3.** To possess with or as if with a devil; bewitch. **4.** To spoil; ruin. **—be·dev′il·ment** *n.*

be·dew (bĭ-do͞o′, -dyo͞o′) *tr.v.* **-dewed, -dew·ing, -dews.** To wet with or as if with dew.

bed·fast (bĕd′făst′) *adj.* Confined to bed; bedridden.

bed·fel·low (bĕd′fĕl′ō) *n.* **1.** A bedmate. **2.** One closely associated or allied with another: *"Stupidity here makes an easy bedfellow, as always, with racialism"* (Christopher Hitchens).

Bed·ford (bĕd′fərd). **1.** A municipal borough of south-central England on the Ouse River west of Cambridge. It was the site of a British victory over the Saxons in 571. Population, 74,500. **2.** A city of northern Texas northeast of Fort Worth. It was settled c. 1843. Population, 20,821.

Bedford, Duke of. See **John of Lancaster.**

Bedford cord *n.* A heavy fabric with a lengthwise ribbed weave that resembles corduroy. [After BEDFORD, England.]

be·dight (bĭ-dīt′) *tr.v.* **-dight** or **-dight·ed, -dight·ing, -dights.** *Archaic.* To dress or array. [Middle English *bidighten* : *bi-,* be- + *dighten,* adorn; see DIGHT.]

be·dim (bĭ-dĭm′) *tr.v.* **-dimmed, -dim·ming, -dims.** To make dim.

be·di·zen (bĭ-dī′zən, -dĭz′ən) *tr.v.* **-zened, -zen·ing, -zens.** To ornament or dress in a showy or gaudy manner. [BE– + DIZEN.] **—be·di′zen·ment** *n.*

bed·lam (bĕd′ləm) *n.* **1.** A place or situation of noisy uproar and confusion. **2.** Often **Bedlam.** *Archaic.* An insane asylum. [Middle English *Bedlem,* Hospital of Saint Mary of *Bethlehem,* an institution in London for the mentally ill.]

bed·lam·ite (bĕd′lə-mīt′) *n.* A mentally ill person.

Bed·ling·ton terrier (bĕd′lĭng-tən) *n.* A dog of a breed developed in England, having a woolly grayish or brownish coat. [After *Bedlington,* a town of northeast England.]

Bed·loe's Island (bĕd′lōz). See **Liberty Island.**

bed·mate (bĕd′māt′) *n.* One with whom a bed is shared.

bed molding *n.* **1.** The molding between the corona and frieze of an entablature. **2.** A molding below a projecting part.

bed of roses *n.* A state of great comfort or luxury.

Bed·ou·in also **Bed·u·in** (bĕd′o͞o-ĭn, bĕd′wĭn) *n., pl.* **Bed·ouin** or **-ins** also **Beduin** or **-ins.** An Arab of any of the nomadic tribes of the Arabian, Syrian, Nubian, or Sahara deserts. [Middle English *Bedoin,* from Old French *beduin,* from Arabic *badāwīn,* pl. of *badāwī,* from *badw,* desert.]

bed·pan (bĕd′păn′) *n.* A metal, glass, or plastic receptacle for the urinary and fecal discharges of persons confined to bed.

bed·plate (bĕd′plāt′) *n.* A plate, frame, or platform serving as a base or support for a machine.

bed·post (bĕd′pōst′) *n.* A vertical post at the corner of a bed.

be·drag·gle (bĭ-drăg′əl) *tr.v.* **-gled, -gling, -gles.** To make wet and limp. [BE– + DRAGGLE.]

be·drag·gled (bĭ-drăg′əld) *adj.* **1.a.** Wet; limp. **b.** Soiled by or as if by having been dragged through mud. **2.** Being in a condition of deterioration; dilapidated: *a street of bedraggled tenements.*

bed·rid·den (bĕd′rĭd′n) also **bed·rid** (-rĭd′) *adj.* Confined to bed because of illness or infirmity. [Middle English *bedreden,* from Old English *bedrida* : *bed,* bed; see BED + *rida,* rider (from *rīdan,* to ride; see RIDE).]

bed·rock (bĕd′rŏk′) *n.* **1.** The solid rock that underlies loose material, such as soil, sand, clay, or gravel. **2.a.** The very basis; the foundation: *Ownership of land is the bedrock of democracy.* **b.** The lowest point: *personal finances that were at bedrock.*

bed·roll (bĕd′rōl′) *n.* A portable roll of bedding used especially by campers and others who sleep outdoors.

bed·room (bĕd′ro͞om′, -ro͝om′) *n. Abbr.* **bdrm., BR** A room in which to sleep. **—bedroom** *adj.* **1.** Sexually suggestive: *a bedroom comedy; bedroom eyes.* **2.** Relating to or inhabited by commuters: *bedroom suburbs.*

bed·side (bĕd′sīd′) *n.* The side of a bed or the space alongside it. **—bedside** *adj.* **1.** Near a bed: *a bedside table.* **2.** Of, relating to, or carried out near a bed: *a physician's bedside conversation with a patient.*

bedside manner *n.* The attitude and conduct of a physician in the presence of a patient.

bed-sit·ter (bĕd′sĭt′ər) *n. Chiefly British.* A one-room apartment that serves as a bedroom and a living room. [From BED + SITTING ROOM.]

bed·so·ni·a (bĕd-sō′nē-ə) *n., pl.* **-ni·ae** (-nē-ī′). Any of a group of microorganisms of the genus *Chlamydia* that are obligate intracellular parasites and include the causative agents of trachoma, psittacosis, and lymphogranuloma venereum. [New Latin, after Sir Samuel P. *Bedson* (died 1969), British bacteriologist.]

bed·sore (bĕd′sôr′, -sōr′) *n.* A pressure-induced ulceration of the skin occurring in persons confined to bed for long periods of time. Also called *decubitus ulcer.*

bed·spread (bĕd′sprĕd′) *n.* A usually decorative covering for a bed.

bed·spring (bĕd′sprĭng′) *n.* One of the springs supporting the mattress of a bed. Often used in the plural.

bed·stead (bĕd′stĕd′) *n.* The frame supporting a bed.

bed·straw (bĕd′strô′) *n.* Any of several weedy or ornamental plants of the genus *Galium,* having whorled leaves, clusters of small white or yellow flowers, and prickly stems. Also called *cleavers.* [Short for *Our Lady's Bedstraw,* name for a plant of the genus *Galium,* whose foliage was used to stuff mattresses in medieval times.]

bed·time (bĕd′tīm′) *n.* The time at which one goes to bed.

bedtime story *n.* A story that is read or told to a child just before bedtime.

Bed·u·in (bĕd′o͞o-ĭn, bĕd′wĭn) *n.* Variant of **Bedouin.**

bed-wet·ting (bĕd′wĕt′ĭng) *n.* Enuresis, especially when occurring nocturnally during sleep. **—bed wetter** *n.*

Bę·dzin (bĕn′jĕn′). A town of southern Poland northeast of Katowice. It was part of Russia from 1815 to 1919. Population, 77,100.

bee¹ (bē) *n.* **1.a.** Any of several winged, hairy-bodied, usually stinging insects of the superfamily Apoidea in the order Hymenoptera, including both solitary and social species and characterized by sucking and chewing mouthparts for gathering nectar and pollen. **b.** A bumblebee. **c.** A honeybee. **2.** A social gathering where people combine work, competition, and amusement: *a quilting bee.* ***—idiom.* a bee in (one's) bonnet.** An impulsive, often eccentric turn of mind; a notion. [Middle English, from Old English *bēo.* See **bhei-** in Appendix. Sense 2 perhaps also alteration of dialectal *bean,* voluntary help given to a farmer by his neighbors, from Middle English *bene,* extra service by a tenant to his lord, from Old English *bēn,* prayer. See **bhā-²** in Appendix.]

bee² (bē) *n. Nautical.* A bee block. [Middle English *be,* a ring, from Old English *bēag.* See **bheug-** in Appendix.]

bee³ (bē) *n.* The letter *b.*

bee balm *n.* An aromatic eastern North American herb *(Monarda didyma)* in the mint family, having variously colored, tubular bilabiate flowers grouped in dense, showy heads. Also called *bergamot.*

Bee·be (bē′bē), **(Charles) William.** 1877–1962. American naturalist, explorer, and author whose numerous expeditions include a record oceanic descent in a bathysphere he helped design (1934).

bee block *n. Nautical.* A piece of hardwood on either side of a bowsprit through which forestays are reeved.

bee·bread (bē′brĕd′) *n.* A brownish substance consisting of a mixture of pollen and honey and used by bees as food.

beech (bēch) *n.* **1.a.** A deciduous tree of the genus *Fagus* having smooth, gray bark, alternate, simple leaves, and three-angled nuts enclosed in prickly burs. The best-known species are *F. grandifolia* of eastern North America and the European species *F. sylvatica* and its numerous cultivated forms. **b.** The wood of any of these trees, used for flooring, containers, plywood, and tool handles. **2.** Any of several other woody plants, as in the genera *Carpinus* and *Nothofagus.* [Middle English *beche,* from Old English *bēce.* See **bhāgo-** in Appendix.]

Bee·cham (bē′chəm), Sir **Thomas.** 1879–1961. British conductor who founded the London Philharmonic (1932) and the Royal Philharmonic (1947) orchestras and helped popularize the works of Frederick Delius.

beech·drops or **beech-drops** (bēch′drŏps′) *pl.n. (used with a sing. or pl. verb).* A brownish eastern North American annual plant *(Epifagus virginiana)* having scalelike leaves and whitish tubular flowers with brown-purple stripes. It is parasitic on the roots of the beech tree.

Bee·cher (bē′chər). A city of east-central Michigan, a suburb of Flint. Population, 17,178.

Beecher, Lyman. 1775–1863. American cleric. A fiery preacher, moderate Calvinist theologian, and resolute abolitionist, he was the father of **Catharine Esther Beecher** (1800–1878), who promoted equal educational opportunities for women; **Edward Beecher** (1803–1895), a clergyman and educator noted for his abolitionist views and writings; and **Henry Ward Beecher** (1813–1887), a clergyman and newspaper editor famous for his abolitionist orations. Harriet Beecher Stowe was another of Lyman's children.

beech fern *n.* Either of two woodland ferns with deeply cut triangular blades, *Thelypteris hexagonoptera* of eastern North America and *T. phegopteris* of North America and Eurasia.

beech mast *n.* The nuts of the beech tree; beechnuts.

beech·nut (bēch′nŭt′) *n.* The small, three-angled nut of a beech tree.

bee-eat·er (bē′ē′tər) *n.* Any of various chiefly tropical Old World birds of the family Meropidae that have brightly colored plumage and feed on bees and wasps.

beef (bēf) *n., pl.* **beeves** (bēvz) or **beef. 1.a.** A full-grown steer, bull, ox, or cow, especially one intended for use as meat. **b.** The flesh of a slaughtered full-grown steer, bull, ox, or cow. **2.** *Informal.* Human muscle; brawn. **3.** *pl.* **beefs.** *Slang.* A complaint. **—beef** *intr.v.* **beefed, beef·ing, beefs.** *Slang.* To complain. ***—phrasal verb.* beef up.** *Informal.* To make or become greater or stronger: *beef up the budget.* [Middle English, from Old French *buef,* from Latin *bōs, bov-.* See **gʷou-** in Appendix.]

beef·a·lo (bē′fə-lō′) *n., pl.* **beefalo** or **-los** or **-loes.** A hybrid that results from a cross between the American buffalo, or bison, and beef cattle and is typically ⅜ buffalo and ⅝ bovine. Beefalo yields leaner beef than conventional breeds of cattle. Also called *cattalo.* [BEEF + (BUFF)ALO.]

beef bour·gui·gnon (bo͝or′gēn-yôn′, -yôɴ′) *n.* Braised beef cubes simmered in a seasoned red wine sauce with mushrooms, carrots, and onions. [French *boeuf bourguignon,* from *Bourgogne,* Burgundy, a region of eastern France.]

beef·cake (bēf′kāk′) *n. Informal.* Minimally attired men with muscular physiques, as in photographs or motion pictures. [BEEF + (CHEESE)CAKE.]

beef·eat·er (bēf′ē′tər) *n.* A yeoman of the British monarch's royal guard.

WORD HISTORY: Tourists in England who have seen the warders of the Tower of London and the Yeomen of the Guard know that these men dressed in 15th-century uniforms are called *beefeaters.* Not all tourists are aware, however, that the original use of the term (recorded in 1610) was pejorative, referring to a well-fed servant. In a work published before 1628 the word was also said to have been used contemptuously by the French for an Englishman or an English soldier. The word *beefeater* has thus risen in the world, for the well-fed, well-muscled beefeaters of today (this use was first recorded in 1671) are considered by many to be a national treasure.

beefed-up (bēft′ŭp′) *adj. Informal.* Having been made greater or stronger: *"Beefed-up sales efforts* [by competitors] *overwhelmed them"* (Wall Street Journal).

bee fly *n.* Any of various flies of the family Bombyliidae that resemble bees, feed on nectar and pollen, and have larvae that are parasitic on bees, wasps, and other insects.

beef·steak (bēf′stāk′) *n.* A slice of beef, such as one taken from the loin or the hindquarters, suitable for broiling or frying.

beefsteak fungus *n.* An edible fungus *(Fistulina hepatica),* growing on living tree trunks, such as oak and ash, and having a large, irregularly shaped reddish cap.

beef stro·ga·noff (strō′gə-nôf′, -nŏf′) *n.* Thinly sliced beef fillet sautéed and mixed with onions, mushrooms, sour cream, and herbs, often served on a bed of noodles or rice. [After Count Paul *Stroganoff,* 19th-century Russian diplomat.]

beef Well·ing·ton (wĕl′ĭng-tən) *n.* A fillet of beef covered

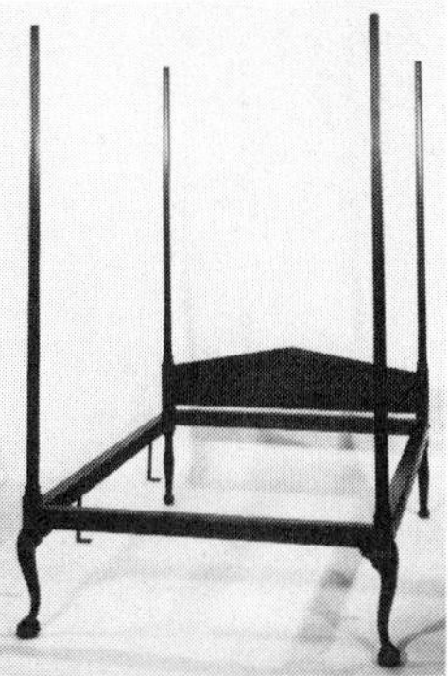

bedstead

beefeater
Yeoman Warder at the Tower of London

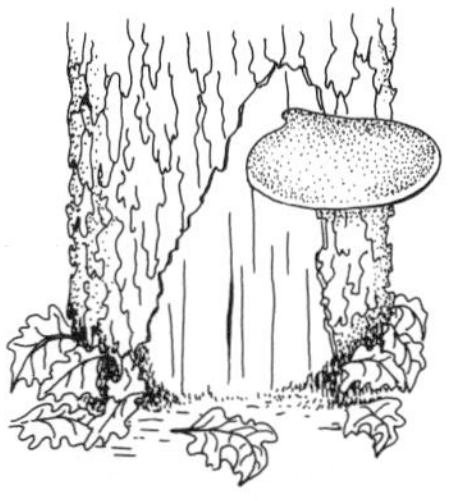

beefsteak fungus
Fistulina hepatica

ă pat	oi boy
ā pay	ou out
âr care	o͝o took
ä father	o͞o boot
ĕ pet	ŭ cut
ē be	ûr urge
ĭ pit	th thin
ī pie	*th* this
îr pier	hw which
ŏ pot	zh vision
ō toe	ə about, item
ô paw	♦ regionalism

Stress marks: **′** (primary); ′ (secondary), as in **dictionary** (dĭk′shə-nĕr′ē)

with pâté de foie gras, encased in pastry, and baked. [Probably from the name *Wellington.*]

beef·wood (bēf′wo͝od′) *n.* **1.** Any of various Australian evergreen trees or shrubs of the genus *Casuarina,* having jointed stems, scalelike whorled leaves, and small fruits grouped in woody, conelike structures. **2.** The wood of any of these plants, often used in construction. Also called *Australian pine, casuarina.*

beef·y (bē′fē) *adj.* **-i·er, -i·est. 1.a.** Muscular in build; brawny: *a beefy wrestler.* **b.** Substantial; filling: *"a rather . . . beefy, densely colored wine"* (Robert M. Parker, Jr.). **2.** Filled with beef. **—beef′i·ness** *n.*

♦ **bee gum** *n. Chiefly Southern U.S.* **1.** A beehive located in a hollow tree or log. **2.** Any beehive. [BEE[1] + *gum,* a hollowed-out log (from GUM[1]).]

bee·hive (bē′hīv′) *n.* A hive for bees.

beehive

bee·keep·er (bē′kē′pər) *n.* See **apiarist.**

bee·line (bē′līn′) *n.* A direct, straight course. [From the belief that a bee returns to its hive in a straight course.]

Be·el·ze·bub (bē-ĕl′zə-bŭb′) *n. Theology.* **1.** The Devil; Satan. **2.** One of the fallen angels in Milton's *Paradise Lost.* Beelzebub was next to Satan in power. **3.** An evil spirit; a demon. [Probably ultimately alteration of *ba'al zebûl,* exalted Baal : *ba'al,* Baal + *zebûl,* exalted.]

bee moth *n.* A moth *(Galleria mellonella)* that lays its eggs in beehives, where the larvae feed on the wax and debris of the honeycombs. Also called *wax moth.*

been (bĭn) *v.* Past participle of **be.**

beep (bēp) *n.* A sound or a signal, as from a horn or an electronic device. **—beep** *v.* **beeped, beep·ing, beeps.** *— intr.* To make a beep. *—tr.* **1.** To cause to make a beep. **2.** To call, summon, or warn by means of a beeper. [Imitative.]

beep·er (bē′pər) *n.* **1.** One that beeps. **2.** A small portable electronic device that emits a beeping signal when the person carrying it is being paged. In this sense, also called *pager.*

bee plant *n.* Any of numerous plants that attract bees for nectar or pollen.

beer (bîr) *n.* **1.a.** A fermented alcoholic beverage brewed from malt and flavored with hops. **b.** A fermented beverage brewed by traditional methods that is then dealcoholized so that the finished product contains no more than 0.5 percent alcohol. **c.** A carbonated beverage produced by a method in which the fermentation process is either circumvented or altered, resulting in a finished product having an alcohol content of no more than 0.01 percent. **2.** A beverage made from extracts of roots and plants: *birch beer.* [Middle English *ber,* from Old English *bēor,* from West Germanic, probably from Latin *bibere,* to drink. See **pō(i)-** in Appendix.]

Beer·bohm (bîr′bōm′), Sir **Henry Maximilian.** Known as "Max." 1872–1956. British caricaturist, writer, and wit whose *Caricatures of Twenty-five Gentlemen* appeared in 1896. He spent most of his later years in Italy.

Beer·naert (bâr′närt), **Auguste Marie François.** 1829–1912. Belgian diplomat active in the peace conferences at The Hague (1899 and 1907). He shared the 1909 Nobel Peace Prize.

Beer·she·ba (bîr-shē′bə, bĕr-shĕv′ə). A city of southern Israel southwest of Jerusalem. In biblical times it marked the southern boundary of Palestine. Population, 114,300.

beer·y (bîr′ē) *adj.* **-i·er, -i·est. 1.** Smelling or tasting of beer: *beery breath.* **2.** Affected or produced by beer: *beery humor.*

beest·ings also **beast·ings** (bē′stĭngz) *pl.n. (used with a sing. or pl. verb).* The first milk secreted by a mammal, especially a cow, after parturition; colostrum. [Middle English *bestinggis,* pl. of *besting,* from Old English *bӯsting,* from *bēost,* beestings.]

bees·wax (bēz′wăks′) *n.* **1.** The yellow to grayish-brown wax secreted by the honeybee for constructing honeycombs. **2.** Commercial wax obtained by processing and purifying the crude wax of the honeybee and used in making candles, crayons, and polishes.

beet (bēt) *n.* **1.** A biennial Eurasian plant *(Beta vulgaris)* grown as a crop plant for the edible roots and leaves. **2.** The swollen root of this plant eaten as a vegetable, typically having reddish flesh. **3.** The sugar beet. [Middle English *bete,* from Old English *bēte,* from Latin *bēta.*]

beet armyworm *n.* An armyworm *(Spodoptera exigua)* that feeds primarily on the foliage of alfalfa, beets, and other crops.

Ludwig van Beethoven

Bee·tho·ven (bā′tō′vən), **Ludwig van.** 1770–1827. German composer. The greatest composer of his day, he began to lose his hearing in 1801 and was deaf by 1819. His music, which formed a transition from classical to romantic composition, includes 9 symphonies, 5 piano concertos, a violin concerto, 32 piano sonatas, several other sonatas, 2 Masses, and an opera.

bee·tle[1] (bēt′l) *n.* **1.** Any of numerous insects of the order Coleoptera, having biting mouthparts and forewings modified to form horny coverings that protect the underlying pair of membranous hind wings when at rest. **2.** An insect resembling a member of the order Coleoptera. **—beetle** *intr.v.* **-tled, -tling, -tles.** To make one's way or move like a beetle: *"Chambermaids . . . beetled from bedroom to bedroom loaded with . . . champagne"* (Vanity Fair). [Middle English *betil,* from Old English *bitela,* from *bītan,* to bite. See **bheid-** in Appendix.]

bee·tle[2] (bēt′l) *adj.* Jutting; overhanging: *beetle brows.* **—beetle** *intr.v.* **-tled, -tling, -tles.** To jut; overhang: *"The rocks often beetled over the road"* (Washington Irving). [From Middle English *bitel-brouwed,* grim-browed : *bitel,* sharp (probably from Old English **bitol,* biting, from Old English *bite,* bite; see BIT[2]) + *brouwed* (from *brow,* brow; see BROW).]

bee·tle[3] (bēt′l) *n.* **1.** A heavy mallet with a large wooden head. **2.** A small wooden household mallet. **3.** A machine with revolving wooden hammers that gives fabrics a lustrous sheen. [Middle English *betel,* from Old English *bӯtl.* See **bhau-** in Appendix.]

beet leafhopper *n.* A small insect *(Eutettix tenellus)* that transmits a destructive viral disease to plants, especially sugar beets, in the United States.

bee·tle·weed (bēt′l-wēd′) *n.* See **galax.**

bee tree *n.* **1.** Any of various trees, such as the basswood, having nectar-rich flowers that are especially attractive to bees. **2.** A hollow tree in which bees form nests.

beet·root (bēt′ro͞ot′, -ro͝ot′) *n. Chiefly British.* The edible root of the beet.

beetroot purple *n. Color.* A deep to very deep purplish red.

beeves (bēvz) *n.* A plural of **beef.**

bef. *abbr.* Before.

be·fall (bĭ-fôl′) *v.* **-fell** (-fĕl′), **-fall·en** (-fô′lən), **-fall·ing, -falls.** *—intr.* To come to pass; happen. *—tr.* To happen to. See Synonyms at **happen.** [Middle English *bifallen,* from Old English *befeallan,* to fall.]

be·fit (bĭ-fĭt′) *tr.v.* **-fit·ted, -fit·ting, -fits.** To be suitable to or appropriate for: *formal attire that befits the occasion.*

be·fit·ting (bĭ-fĭt′ĭng) *adj.* Appropriate; suitable; proper. **—be·fit′ting·ly** *adv.*

be·fog (bĭ-fôg′, -fŏg′) *tr.v.* **-fogged, -fog·ging, -fogs. 1.** To cover or obscure with or as if with fog. **2.** To cause confusion in; muddle.

be·fool (bĭ-fo͞ol′) *tr.v.* **-fooled, -fool·ing, -fools. 1.** To make a fool of. **2.** To hoodwink; deceive.

be·fore (bĭ-fôr′, -fōr′) *adv.* **1.** Earlier in time: *They called me the day before.* **2.** In front; ahead. **—before** *prep. Abbr.* **bef. 1.** Previous to in time; earlier than. **2.** In front of. **3.** In store for; awaiting: *A young person's whole life lies before him.* **4.** Into or in the presence of: *She asked that the visitor be brought before her.* **5.** Under the consideration or jurisdiction of: *The case is now before the court.* **6.** In a position superior to: *The prince is before his brother in the line of succession.* **—before** *conj.* **1.** In advance of the time when: *See me before you leave.* **2.** Rather than; sooner than: *I will die before I will betray my country.* [Middle English *bifore,* from Old English *beforan.* See **per[1]** in Appendix.]

before Christ *adv. Abbr.* **B.C.** In a specified year of the pre-Christian era.

be·fore·hand (bĭ-fôr′hănd′, -fōr′-) *adv. & adj.* **1.** In anticipation. **2.** In advance; early.

be·fore·time (bĭ-fôr′tīm′, -fōr′-) *adv. Archaic.* Formerly.

be·foul (bĭ-foul′) *tr.v.* **-fouled, -foul·ing, -fouls. 1.** To make dirty; soil. See Synonyms at **contaminate. 2.** To cast aspersions upon; speak badly of.

be·friend (bĭ-frĕnd′) *tr.v.* **-friend·ed, -friend·ing, -friends.** To behave as a friend to.

be·fud·dle (bĭ-fŭd′l) *tr.v.* **-dled, -dling, -dles. 1.** To confuse; perplex. See Synonyms at **confuse. 2.** To stupefy with or as if with alcoholic drink.

beg (bĕg) *v.* **begged, beg·ging, begs.** *—tr.* **1.** To ask for as charity: *begged money while sitting in a doorway.* **2.** To ask earnestly for or of; entreat: *begged me for help.* **3.a.** To evade; dodge: *a speech that begged the real issues.* **b.** To take for granted without proof: *beg the point in a dispute.* *—intr.* **1.** To solicit alms. **2.** To make a humble or urgent plea. ***—phrasal verb.*** **beg off.** To ask to be released from something, such as an obligation: *We were invited to stay for dinner, but we had to beg off.* [Middle English *beggen,* possibly from Anglo-Norman *begger,* from Old French *begart,* lay brother, one who prays. See BEGGAR.]

SYNONYMS: *beg, crave, beseech, implore, entreat, importune.* These verbs mean to make an earnest request. *Beg* and *crave* apply to the act of asking in a serious and sometimes humble manner, especially for something one cannot claim as a right: *I begged her to forgive me. The attorney craved the court's indulgence. Beseech* emphasizes earnestness and often implies anxiety: *Be silent, we beseech you. Implore* intensifies the senses of urgent supplication and anxiety: *The child, with tears in his eyes, implored his father not to be angry. Entreat* pertains to persuasive pleading calculated to overcome opposition: *"Ask me no questions, I entreat you"* (Charles Dickens). *Importune* adds the sense of persistent and sometimes irksome pleading: *The foundation was being importuned by fundraisers to contribute to new charities.* See also Synonyms at **cadge.**

be·gan (bĭ-găn′) *v.* Past tense of **begin.**

be·get (bĭ-gĕt′) *tr.v.* **-got** (-gŏt′), **-got·ten** (-gŏt′n) or **-got, -get·ting, -gets. 1.** To father; sire. **2.** To cause to exist or occur; produce: *Violence begets more violence.* [Middle English *biyeten, bigeten,* from Old English *begetan.* See **ghend-** in Appendix.] **—be·get′ter** *n.*

beg·gar (bĕg′ər) *n.* **1.** One who solicits alms for a living. **2.** An impoverished person; a pauper. **3.** *Informal.* A man or a boy. **—beggar** *tr.v.* **-gared, -gar·ing, -gars. 1.** To make a beggar of; impoverish. **2.** To exceed the limits, resources, or capabilities of: *beauty that beggars description.* [Middle English, from Old

French *begart,* ultimately from Middle Dutch *beggaert,* one who rattles off prayers.]

beg·gar·ly (bĕg′ər-lē) *adj.* **1.** Of, relating to, or befitting a beggar; very poor: *a beggarly existence in the slums.* **2.** So mean, petty, or paltry as to deserve contempt. **—beg′gar·li·ness** *n.*

beg·gar's lice (bĕg′ərz) *n.* *(used with a sing. or pl. verb).* **1.** Any of several plants, such as the stickseed, having small, often prickly fruits that cling readily to clothing or animal fur. **2.** The fruit of any of these plants.

beggar's purse *n.* A buckwheat crepe filled with caviar and crème fraîche, tied with strips of chives into the shape of a purse, and served as an appetizer.

beggar ticks also **beggar's ticks** *pl.n.* *(used with a sing. or pl. verb).* **1.a.** Any of various weeds of the genus *Bidens* in the composite family, having heads of usually yellow flowers and small, dry fruits. Also called *bur marigold, Spanish needles, sticktight, tickseed.* **b.** The fruit of any of these plants, typically having barbed awns and clinging readily to clothing and animal fur. **2.** Any of certain other plants or their clinging fruits, especially species of the tick trefoil.

beg·gar·y (bĕg′ə-rē) *n.* **1.** Extreme poverty; penury. **2.** The state or condition of being a beggar. **3.** Beggars considered as a group.

be·gin (bĭ-gĭn′) *v.* **-gan** (-găn′), **-gun** (-gŭn′), **-gin·ning, -gins.** *—intr.* **1.** To take the first step in performing an action; start. **2.** To come into being: *when life began.* **3.** To do or accomplish in the least degree: *Those measures do not even begin to address the problem.* *—tr.* **1.** To take the first step in doing; start: *began work.* **2.** To cause to come into being; originate. **3.** To come first in: *The numeral 1 begins the sequence.* [Middle English *biginnen,* from Old English *beginnan.*]

SYNONYMS: *begin, commence, start, initiate, inaugurate.* These verbs are compared as they denote coming or putting into operation, being, or motion or setting about taking the first step, as in a procedure. *Begin* and *commence* are equivalent in meaning, though *commence* is more formal: *began the race; a play that begins at eight o'clock; commenced her career as a scientist; festivities that commenced with the national anthem. Start* is often interchangeable with *begin* and *commence* but can also imply setting out from a specific point, frequently following inaction: *Stand and visit with me for a few minutes until the train starts. The telephone started ringing. Initiate* applies to the act of taking the first steps in a process, without reference to what follows: *The public hoped the government would initiate restrictions on imported goods. Inaugurate* often connotes a formal beginning: *"The exhibition inaugurated a new era of cultural relations between the Soviet Union and United States"* (Serge Schmemann).

Be·gin (bā′gĭn), **Menachem.** 1913–1992. Russian-born Israeli politician. He led (1943–1948) Irgun, the Zionist underground movement in Palestine. After the establishment of Israel, Begin became a political leader known for his hard-line views on the Arabs, but as prime minister (1977–1983) he strove to resolve the Arab-Israel conflict. He shared the 1978 Nobel Peace Prize with Anwar el-Sadat of Egypt.

be·gin·ner (bĭ-gĭn′ər) *n.* One who is just starting to learn or do something; a novice.

be·gin·ning (bĭ-gĭn′ĭng) *n.* **1.** The act or process of bringing or being brought into being; a start. **2.** The time when something begins or is begun: *the beginning of the war.* **3.** The place where something begins or is begun: *at the beginning of the road.* **4.** A source; an origin: *What was the beginning of the dispute?* **5.** The first part: *The front matter is at the beginning of the book.* **6.** Often **beginnings.** An early or rudimentary phase: *the beginnings of human life on this planet.*

SYNONYMS: *beginning, birth, dawn, genesis, nascence, rise.* The central meaning shared by these nouns is "the initial stage of a developmental process": *the beginning of a new era in computer technology; the birth of generative grammar; the dawn of civilization; the genesis of quantum mechanics; the nascence of classical sculpture; the rise and decline of an ancient city-state.*
ANTONYM: *end.*

beginning rhyme *n.* **1.** Rhyme at the beginning of consecutive lines of verse. Also called *initial rhyme.* **2.** See **head rhyme.**

be·gird (bĭ-gûrd′) *tr.v.* **-girt** (-gûrt′) or **-gird·ed, -girt, -gird·ing, -girds.** To encircle with or as if with a band.

be·gone (bĭ-gôn′, -gŏn′) *v.* Used chiefly in the imperative to express an order of dismissal. [Middle English *begone* : *be,* imperative of *ben,* to be; see BE + *gone,* past participle of *gon,* to go; see GO[1].]

be·go·nia (bĭ-gōn′yə) *n.* Any of various tropical or subtropical plants of the genus *Begonia,* widely cultivated as ornamentals for their usually asymmetrical, brightly colored leaves. [New Latin *Begonia,* genus name, after Michel *Bégon* (1638–1710), French governor in the West Indies.]

be·gor·ra (bĭ-gôr′ə, -gŏr′ə) *interj.* *Irish.* Used as a mild oath. [Alteration of *by God.*]

be·got (bĭ-gŏt′) *v.* Past tense and a past participle of **beget.**

be·got·ten (bĭ-gŏt′n) *v.* A past participle of **beget.**

be·grime (bĭ-grīm′) *tr.v.* **-grimed, -grim·ing, -grimes.** To smear or soil with or as if with dirt.

be·grudge (bĭ-grŭj′) *tr.v.* **-grudged, -grudg·ing, -grudg·es.** **1.a.** To envy the possession or enjoyment of: *She begrudged his youth.* **b.** To envy for the possession of: *She begrudged him his youth.* See Synonyms at **envy.** **2.** To give or expend with reluctance: *begrudged every penny spent.* **—be·grudg′er** *n.* **—be·grudg′ing·ly** *adv.*

be·guile (bĭ-gīl′) *tr.v.* **-guiled, -guil·ing, -guiles.** **1.** To deceive by guile; delude. See Synonyms at **deceive.** **2.** To take away from by or as if by guile; cheat: *a disease that has beguiled me of strength.* **3.** To distract the attention of; divert: *"to beguile you from the grief of a loss so overwhelming"* (Abraham Lincoln). **4.** To pass (time) pleasantly. **5.** To amuse or charm; delight. See Synonyms at **charm.** [Middle English *bigilen* : *bi-,* be- + *gilen,* to deceive; see GUILE.] **—be·guile′ment** *n.* **—be·guil′er** *n.* **—be·guil′ing·ly** *adv.*

be·guine (bĭ-gēn′) *n.* **1.** A ballroom dance similar to the rumba, based on a dance of Martinique and St. Lucia. **2.** The music for this dance. [French (West Indies) *béguine,* from French *béguin,* hood, flirtation, from *beguine,* Beguine. See BEGUINE.]

Beg·uine (bā′gēn′, bā-gēn′) *n.* *Roman Catholic Church.* A member of any of several lay sisterhoods founded in the Netherlands in the 13th century. [Middle English *begine,* from Old French *beguine,* from Middle Dutch *beg-,* root of *beggaert,* one who rattles off prayers.]

be·gum (bā′gəm, bē′-) *n.* **1.** A Moslem woman of rank. **2.** Used as a form of address for such a woman. [Urdu *begam,* from East Turkic *begüm,* first person sing. possessive of *beg,* master, mistress, from Old Turkic.]

be·gun (bĭ-gŭn′) *v.* Past participle of **begin.**

be·half (bĭ-hăf′, -häf′) *n.* Interest, support, or benefit. ***—idioms.*** **in behalf of.** For the benefit of; in the interest of. **on behalf of.** As the agent of; on the part of. [Middle English, from Old English *be healfe,* by (his) side : *be,* by, at; see BY[1] + *healf,* side, half; see HALF.]

USAGE NOTE: Traditionally, *in behalf of* and *on behalf of* have distinct senses. *In behalf of* means "for the benefit of," as in *We raised money in behalf of the earthquake victims. On behalf of* means "as the agent of; on the part of," as in *The guardian signed the contract on behalf of the minor child.* The two senses are quite close, however, and are often confused, even by reputable writers.

Be·han (bē′ən), **Brendan Francis.** 1923–1964. Irish writer whose early association with the Irish Republican Army and experiences in prison influenced his works, including the play *The Quare Fellow* (1954) and the autobiographical *Borstal Boy* (1958).

be·have (bĭ-hāv′) *v.* **-haved, -hav·ing, -haves.** *—intr.* **1.a.** To conduct oneself in a specified way: *The child behaved badly at the party.* **b.** To conduct oneself in a proper way: *I told the child to behave.* **2.** To act, react, function, or perform in a particular way: *This fabric behaves well even in hot weather.* *—tr.* **1.** To conduct (oneself) properly: *Did you behave yourself at the party?* **2.** To conduct (oneself) in a specified way: *The witness behaved herself with great calmness.* [Middle English *behaven* : *be-,* be- + *have,* have; see HAVE.]

be·hav·ior (bĭ-hāv′yər) *n.* **1.** The manner in which one behaves. **2.** *Psychology.* The actions or reactions of persons or things in response to external or internal stimuli. [Middle English *behavour,* from *behaven,* to behave (on the model of *havour,* behavior, from Old French *avoir,* from *avoir,* to have). See BEHAVE.] **—be·hav′ior·al** *adj.* **—be·hav′ior·al·ly** *adv.*

SYNONYMS: *behavior, conduct, deportment.* These nouns all pertain to a person's actions as they constitute a means of evaluation by others. *Behavior* is the most general: *time off for good behavior; on their best behavior; guilty of contemptible behavior. Conduct* applies to actions considered from the standpoint of morality and ethics: *"The fate of unborn millions will now depend . . . on the courage and conduct of this army"* (George Washington). *"Life, not the parson, teaches conduct"* (Oliver Wendell Holmes, Jr.). *Deportment* more narrowly pertains to actions measured by a prevailing code of social behavior: "[Old Mr. Turveydrop] *was not like anything in the world but a model of Deportment"* (Charles Dickens).

behavioral medicine *n.* The application of behavior therapy techniques, such as biofeedback, relaxation training, and hypnosis, to the prevention and treatment of medical and psychosomatic disorders and to the treatment of undesirable behaviors, such as overeating and substance abuse. Also called *behavior medicine.*

behavioral psychophysics *n.* *Psychology.* A branch of psychology dealing primarily with the measurement of sensory capacities in nonaberrant animals.

behavioral science *n.* A scientific discipline, such as sociology, anthropology or psychology, in which the actions and reactions of human beings and animals are studied through observational and experimental methods. **—behavioral scientist** *n.*

behavioral therapy *n.* See **behavior therapy.**

be·hav·ior·ism (bĭ-hāv′yə-rĭz′əm) *n.* *Psychology.* A school of psychology that confines itself to the study of observable and quantifiable aspects of behavior and excludes subjective phenom-

ă pat	oi boy
ā pay	ou out
âr care	ŏŏ took
ä father	ōō boot
ĕ pet	ŭ cut
ē be	ûr urge
ĭ pit	th thin
ī pie	*th* this
îr pier	hw which
ŏ pot	zh vision
ō toe	ə about, item
ô paw	♦ regionalism

Stress marks: **′** (primary); ′ (secondary), as in **dictionary** (dĭk′shə-nĕr′ē)

ena, such as emotions or motives. **—be·hav′ior·ist** *n.* **—be·hav′ior·is′tic** *adj.*

behavior medicine *n.* See **behavioral medicine.**

behavior modification *n. Psychology.* **1.** The use of basic learning techniques, such as conditioning, biofeedback, reinforcement, or aversion therapy, to alter human behavior. **2.** See **behavior therapy. —behavior modifier** *n.*

behavior therapy *n. Psychology.* A form of psychotherapy that uses basic learning techniques to modify maladaptive behavior patterns by substituting new responses to given stimuli for undesirable ones. Also called *behavioral therapy, behavior modification.* **—behavior therapist** *n.*

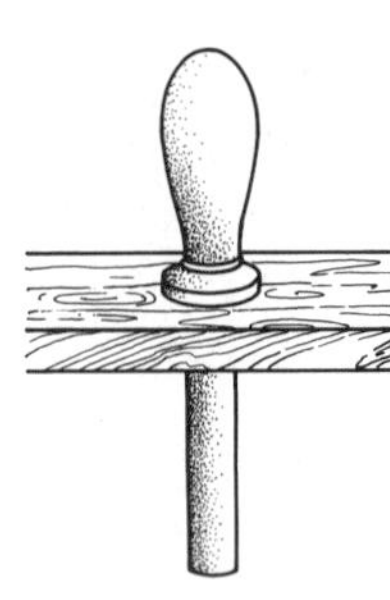
belaying pin

be·hav·iour (bĭ-hāv′yər) *n. Chiefly British.* Variant of **behavior.**

be·head (bĭ-hĕd′) *tr.v.* **-head·ed, -head·ing, -heads.** To separate the head from; decapitate. [Middle English *biheden,* from Old English *beheāfdian* : *be-,* away from; see BE– + *hēafod,* head; see HEAD.]

be·held (bĭ-hĕld′) *v.* Past tense and past participle of **behold.**

be·he·moth (bĭ-hē′məth, bē′ə-məth) *n.* **1.** Something enormous in size or power. **2.** Often **Behemoth.** *Bible.* A huge animal, possibly the hippopotamus, described in the Old Testament. [Hebrew *bĕhēmôt,* intensive pl. of *bĕhēmâ,* beast.]

be·hest (bĭ-hĕst′) *n.* **1.** An authoritative command. **2.** An urgent request: *I called the office at the behest of my secretary.* [Middle English *bihest,* vow, from Old English *behǣs.* See **kei-**[2] in Appendix.]

belemnite
Fossilized belemnites
Belemnitella americana

be·hind (bĭ-hīnd′) *adv.* **1.** In, to, or toward the rear: *We walked behind.* **2.** In a place or condition that has been passed or left: *I left my gloves behind.* **3.** In arrears; late: *I fell behind in my payments.* **4.** Below the standard level; in or into an inferior position: *Don't fall behind in class.* **5.** Slow: *My watch is running behind.* **6.** *Archaic.* Yet to come. **—behind** *prep.* **1.** At the back of or in the rear of: *He sat behind her.* **2.** On the farther side or other side of; beyond: *The broom is behind the door.* **3.** In a place or time that has been passed or left by: *Their worries are behind them.* **4. a.** Later than: *The plane was behind schedule.* **b.** Used to indicate deficiency in performance: *behind us in technological develpment.* **5. a.** Hidden or concealed by: *hatred hidden behind a bland smile.* **b.** In the background of; underlying: *Behind your every action is self-interest.* **6.** In a position of support; at the back of: *The leaders have the army behind them.* **7.** In pursuit of: *The police were hard behind the escapees.* **—behind** *n. Informal.* The buttocks. [Middle English *bihinde,* from Old English *behindan.* See **ko-** in Appendix.]

be·hind·hand (bĭ-hīnd′hănd′) *adj.* **1.** Being in arrears. **2.** Being behind time; slow. See Synonyms at **tardy. —be·hind′hand′** *adv.*

be·hind-the-scenes (bĭ-hīnd′thə-sēnz′) *adj.* Done, maintained, or held in secret.

be·hold (bĭ-hōld′) *v.* **-held** (-hĕld′), **-hold·ing, -holds.** *—tr.* **1. a.** To perceive by the visual faculty; see: *beheld a tiny figure in the distance.* **b.** To perceive through use of the mental faculty; comprehend: *"Behold the man of the future"* (Jerry Adler). **2.** To look upon; gaze at: *We beheld a beautiful vista before us.* See Synonyms at **see**[1]. *—intr.* Used in the imperative for the purpose of calling attention. [Middle English *biholden,* from Old English *behaldan* : *be-,* be- + *haldan,* to hold; see HOLD[1].] **—be·hold′er** *n.*

belfry

be·hold·en (bĭ-hōl′dən) *adj.* Owing something, such as gratitude, to another; indebted. [Middle English *biholden,* past participle of *biholden,* to observe. See BEHOLD.]

be·hoof (bĭ-ho͞of′) *n.* Benefit; advantage: *a sitting room that had been converted to a bedroom on my behoof.* [Middle English *bihove,* from Old English *behōf.* See **kap-** in Appendix.]

be·hoove (bĭ-ho͞ov′) *v.* **-hooved, -hoov·ing, -hooves.** *—tr.* To be necessary or proper for: *It behooves you at least to try.* *—intr.* To be necessary or proper. [Middle English *behōven,* from Old English *behōfian.* See **kap-** in Appendix.]

Beh·ring (bâr′ĭng, bĕr′-, bā′rĭng), **Emil Von.** 1854–1917. German physiologist. He won a 1901 Nobel Prize for work on serum immunization against diphtheria and tetanus.

Behr·man (bâr′mən), **S(amuel) N(athaniel).** 1893–1973. American playwright whose works include *The Second Man* (1927) and *No Time for Comedy* (1939).

Bei·der·becke (bī′dər-bĕk′), **Leon Bismark.** Known as "Bix." 1903–1931. American jazz composer and musician. A self-taught pianist and cornet player, he was the first white musician to be recognized by Black musicians as a luminary of the jazz world.

beige (bāzh) *n.* **1.** *Color.* A light grayish brown or yellowish brown to grayish yellow. **2.** A soft fabric of undyed, unbleached wool. **—beige** *adj. Color.* Light grayish-brown or yellowish-brown to grayish-yellow. [French, fine woolen fabric left in its natural color, from Old French *bege,* perhaps from Old Italian *bambagia,* cotton wool, from feminine of Late Latin *bombax.* See BOMBAST.]

♦**bei·gnet** also **bai·gnet** or **bei·gné** or **bang** (bĕn-yā′) *n. Southern Louisiana.* **1.** A square doughnut with no hole: *"a New Orleans coffeehouse selling beignets, an insidious Louisianian cousin of the doughnut that exists to get powdered sugar on your face"* (Los Angeles Times). **2.** A seafood fritter. [French, fritter, of Celtic origin.]

♦ ***REGIONAL NOTE:*** New Orleans, Louisiana, has been a rich contributor of French loan words and local expressions to American English. One variety of speech in this city is so distinctive that it has a name: *yat.* Many of the words, such as *beignet, café au lait, faubourg, lagniappe,* and *krewe,* reflect the New World French cuisine and culture characterizing this city and much of southern Louisiana. Other words reflect distinctive physical characteristics of the city: *banquette,* a raised sidewalk, and *camelback* and *shotgun,* distinctive architectural styles found among New Orleans houses.

Bei·jing (bā′jĭng′) also **Pe·king** (pē′kĭng′, pā′-). Formerly (1928–1949) **Pei·ping** (pā′pĭng′). The capital of China, in the northeast part of the country. Founded c. 700 B.C., it is a major commercial, industrial, and cultural center. The Inner City contains the Imperial, or Forbidden, City. Population, 5,860,000.

be·ing (bē′ĭng) *n.* **1.** The state or quality of having existence. See Synonyms at **existence. 2. a.** Something, such as an object, an idea, or a symbol, that exists, is thought to exist, or is represented as existing. **b.** The totality of all things that exist. **3. a.** A person: *"The artist after all is a solitary being"* (Virginia Woolf). **b.** All the qualities constituting one that exists; the essence. **c.** One's basic or essential nature; personality.

Bei·ra (bā′rə). A city of east-central Mozambique on the Mozambique Channel, an arm of the Indian Ocean. It is a commercial center and a popular resort. Population, 230,744.

Bei·rut[1] (bā-ro͞ot′). The capital and largest city of Lebanon, in the western part of the country on the Mediterranean Sea. Founded by the Phoenicians, it was an important Greek and Roman trade center. The city has long been the scene of bitter factional fighting. Population, 509,000.

Bei·rut[2] (bā-ro͞ot′, bā′ro͞ot′) *n.* A place or situation characterized by ongoing, widespread, highly destructive strife: *"Right now,* [this state] *is the Beirut of the medical malpractice system, with all the players in an angry state of turmoil and factionalism"* (Hatfield MA Valley Advocate).

Be·ja (bā′jə) *n., pl.* **Beja. 1.** A member of a people living primarily as pastoral nomads in the area between the Nile River and the Red Sea. **2.** The Cushitic language of the Beja.

be·je·sus (bĭ-jē′zəs, -jā′-) *n. Slang.* Used as an intensive: *The bear scared the bejesus out of us.* [Alteration of *by Jesus.*]

be·jew·eled (bĭ-jo͞o′əld) *adj.* Decorated with or as if with jewels.

bel (bĕl) *n. Abbr.* **b, B** Ten decibels. [After Alexander Graham BELL.]

be·la·bor (bĭ-lā′bər) *tr.v.* **-bored, -bor·ing, -bors. 1.** To attack with blows; hit, beat, or whip. See Synonyms at **beat. 2.** To assail verbally. **3.** To discuss repeatedly or at length; harp on: *Don't belabor the point.*

Be·las·co (bə-lăs′kō), **David.** 1853–1931. American playwright and theatrical producer known for his realistic stage settings and innovative lighting effects. Among his productions were *Madame Butterfly* (1900) and *Laugh, Clown, Laugh* (1923).

be·lat·ed (bĭ-lā′tĭd) *adj.* Having been delayed; done or sent too late: *a belated birthday card.* [BE– + LATED.] **—be·lat′ed·ly** *adv.* **—be·lat′ed·ness** *n.*

Be·lau (bə-lou′) also **Pa·lau** (pä-, pə-) or **Pe·lew** (pə-lo͞o′, pē-). A group of volcanic islands and islets in the Caroline Islands of the western Pacific Ocean. When the Carolines became part of the Federated States of Micronesia in 1978, Belau chose to form a republic in free association with the United States, which is responsible for its defense until 1996.

be·lay (bĭ-lā′) *v.* **-layed, -lay·ing, -lays.** *—tr.* **1.** *Nautical.* To secure or make fast (a rope, for example) by winding on a cleat or pin. **2.** To secure (a mountain climber, for example) at the end of a length of rope. **3.** To cause to stop. *—intr.* **1.** To be made secure. **2.** Used in the imperative as an order to stop: *Belay there!* **—belay** *n.* **1.** The securing of a rope on a rock or other projection during mountain climbing. **2.** An object, such as a rock, to which a mountain climber's rope can be secured. [Middle English *bileggen,* to surround, from Old English *belecgan.* See **legh-** in Appendix.]

Be·la·ya (bĕl′ə-yə). A river of southwest Russia rising in the Ural Mountains and flowing about 1,416 km (880 mi) generally northwest to the Kama River.

be·lay·ing pin (bĭ-lā′ĭng) *n. Nautical.* A short, removable wooden or metal pin fitted in a hole in the rail of a boat and used for securing running gear.

bel can·to (bĕl kän′tō) *n. Music.* A style of operatic singing characterized by rich tonal lyricism and brilliant display of vocal technique. [Italian : *bel, bello,* beautiful + *canto,* singing.]

belch (bĕlch) *v.* **belched, belch·ing, belch·es.** *—intr.* **1.** To expel gas noisily from the stomach through the mouth; burp. **2.** To erupt or explode. **3.** To gush forth. *—tr.* **1.** To expel (gas) noisily from the stomach through the mouth; burp. **2.** To eject violently. [Middle English *belchen,* from Old English *bealcettan* or from **bealcian;* akin to *bealcan.*] **—belch** *n.*

bel·dam or **bel·dame** (bĕl′dəm, -dăm) *n.* An old woman, especially one who is considered ugly. [Middle English, grandmother : *bel,* indicating respect (from Old French *bel,* fine, from Latin *bellus;* see **deu-**[2] in Appendix) + *dame,* lady; see DAME.]

be·lea·guer (bĭ-lē′gər) *tr.v.* **-guered, -guer·ing, -guers.**

ă pat	oi boy
ā pay	ou out
âr care	o͝o took
ä father	o͞o boot
ĕ pet	ŭ cut
ē be	ûr urge
ĭ pit	th thin
ī pie	*th* this
îr pier	hw which
ŏ pot	zh vision
ō toe	ə about, item
ô paw	♦ regionalism

Stress marks: ′ (primary); ′ (secondary), as in **dictionary** (dĭk′shə-nĕr′ē)

1. To harass; beset: *We are beleaguered by problems.* 2. To surround with troops; besiege. See Synonyms at **besiege.** [Probably Dutch *belegeren* : *be-*, around (from Middle Dutch *bie;* see **ambhi** in Appendix) + *leger,* camp; see **legh-** in Appendix.] —**be·lea′guer·ment** *n.*

Be·lém (bə-lĕm′, -lăN′). Formerly **Pa·rá** (pə-rä′). A city of northern Brazil on the Pará River. It is the chief port and commercial center of the vast Amazon River basin. Population, 933,287.

bel·em·nite (bĕl′əm-nīt′) *n.* A cone-shaped, fossilized internal shell of any of an extinct genus of cephalopods related to the cuttlefish. [New Latin *belemnītēs,* from Greek *belemnon,* dart. See **gʷele-** in Appendix.]

bel es·prit (bĕl′ ĕ-sprē′) *n., pl.* **beaux es·prits** (bō′zĕ-sprē′). A cultivated, highly intelligent person. [French : *bel,* fine + *esprit,* mind.]

Bel·fast (bĕl′făst′, bĕl-făst′). The capital and largest city of Northern Ireland, in the eastern part of the country on **Belfast Lough,** an inlet of the North Channel of the Irish Sea. Conflict between Protestants and Catholics has divided the city since the 19th century. Population, 318,600.

Bel·fort (bĕl-fôr′). A city of northeast France commanding the strategic **Belfort Gap** between the Vosges and the Jura Mountains, thus dominating the land approaches from France, Germany, and Switzerland. Population, 51,206.

bel·fry (bĕl′frē) *n., pl.* **-fries.** 1. A bell tower, especially one attached to a building. 2. The part of a tower or steeple in which bells are hung. [Middle English *belfrei,* from Old North French *belfroi,* alteration of Old French *berfrei, berfroi.* See **bhergh-**[2] in Appendix.] —**bel′fried** *adj.*

WORD HISTORY: The words *bell* and *belfry* seem obviously related, but in fact the *bel-* portion of *belfry* had nothing to do with bells until comparatively recently. *Belfry* goes back to a compound formed in prehistoric Common Germanic. It is generally agreed that the second part of this compound is the element **frij-*, meaning "peace, safety." The first element is either **bergan,* "to protect," which would yield a compound meaning "a defensive place of shelter," or **berg-*, "a high place," which would yield a compound meaning "a high place of safety, tower." Whatever the meaning of the original Germanic source, its Old French descendant *berfrei,* which first meant "siege tower," came to mean "watchtower." Presumably because bells were used in these towers, the word was applied to bell towers as well. The Old North French alteration *belfroi,* which reminded English speakers of their native word *belle* (our *bell*), entered Middle English with the sense "bell tower," first recorded in 1272.

Belg. *abbr.* Belgian; Belgium.

Bel·gae (bĕl′gī′, -jē′) *pl.n.* A people who formerly inhabited northeast Gaul and areas of southeast England. Belgium is named for them. [Latin.]

Bel·gian (bĕl′jən) *adj. Abbr.* **Belg.** Of or relating to Belgium or its people or culture. —**Belgian** *n.* 1. A native or inhabitant of Belgium. 2. Any of a breed of characteristically large, reddish-brown or chestnut-colored draft horses.

Belgian Con·go (kŏng′gō). See **Zaire.**

Belgian East Af·ri·ca (ăf′rĭ-kə). The former Belgian trust territory of Ruanda-Urundi, now divided into the independent countries of Rwanda and Burundi.

Belgian endive *n.* The endive.

Belgian hare *n.* A large reddish-brown rabbit of a domestic breed developed in England from Belgian stock.

Belgian Mal·in·ois (măl′ən-wä′) *n.* See **Belgian sheep dog** (sense 2).

Belgian sheep dog *n.* 1. Any of a breed of hardy black sheep dogs developed in Belgium. 2. Any of a breed of working dogs closely related to the Belgian sheep dog. In this sense, also called *Belgian Malinois, Belgian Tervuren.*

Belgian Ter·vu·ren (tĕr-vyo͝or′ən, tər-) *n.* See **Belgian sheep dog** (sense 2).

Bel·gic (bĕl′jĭk) *adj.* 1. Of or relating to Belgium or the Belgians. 2. Of or relating to the Belgae.

Bel·gium (bĕl′jəm). *Abbr.* **Belg.** A country of northwest Europe on the North Sea. It has long been a strategic crossroads of Europe and the scene of heavy fighting in numerous wars. The country is culturally divided into Dutch-speaking Flanders to the north of Brussels and French-speaking Wallonia to the south. Brussels is the capital and the largest city. Population, 9,858,017.

Bel·go·rod (bĕl′gə-rŏd′, byĕl′gə-rət). A city of southwest Russia on the Donets River. It is a transportation and industrial center. Population, 280,000.

Bel·grade (bĕl′grād′, -gräd′, bĕl-grād′) also **Be·o·grad** (bĕ′ô-gräd). The capital and largest city of Yugoslavia, in the eastern part of the country at the confluence of the Danube and Sava rivers. Founded in the 3rd century B.C., it was the primary city of Serbia from the 12th century until the formation of Yugoslavia in the 20th century. Population, 936,200.

Bel·gra·vi·a (bĕl-grā′vē-ə). A fashionable residential district of southwest London, England, centered on Belgrave Square. It was laid out in the 1820's.

Be·li·al (bē′lē-əl, bēl′yəl) *n.* 1. *Bible.* A personification of wickedness and ungodliness alluded to in the Old and New Testaments. 2. One of the fallen angels who rebelled against God in Milton's *Paradise Lost.*

be·lie (bĭ-lī′) *tr.v.* **-lied, -ly·ing, -lies.** 1. To picture falsely; misrepresent: *"He spoke roughly in order to belie his air of gentility"* (James Joyce). 2. To show to be false: *Their laughter belied their outward grief.* 3. To be counter to; contradict: *At first glance, life at the boarding school seemed to belie all the bad things I had heard about it.* [Middle English *bilien,* from Old English *belēogan,* to deceive with lies. See **leugh-** in Appendix.] —**be·li′er** *n.*

be·lief (bĭ-lēf′) *n.* 1. The mental act, condition, or habit of placing trust or confidence in another. 2. Mental acceptance of and conviction in the truth, actuality, or validity of something. 3. Something believed or accepted as true, especially a particular tenet or a body of tenets accepted by a group. [Middle English *bileve,* alteration (influenced by *belȳfan, belēfan,* to believe; see BELIEVE) of Old English *gelēafa.* See **leubh-** in Appendix.]

SYNONYMS: *belief, credence, credit, faith.* The central meaning shared by these nouns is "mental acceptance of the truth, actuality, or validity of something": *a statement unworthy of belief; an idea steadily gaining credence; testimony meriting credit; put no faith in a liar's assertions.* See also Synonyms at **opinion.**
ANTONYM: *disbelief.*

be·liev·a·ble (bĭ-lē′və-bəl) *adj.* Capable of eliciting belief or trust. See Synonyms at **plausible.** —**be·liev′a·bil′i·ty** *n.* —**be·liev′a·bly** *adv.*

be·lieve (bĭ-lēv′) *v.* **-lieved, -liev·ing, -lieves.** —*tr.* 1. To accept as true or real: *Do you believe the news stories?* 2. To credit with veracity: *I believe you.* 3. To expect or suppose; think: *I believe they will arrive shortly.* —*intr.* 1. To have firm faith, especially religious faith. 2. To have faith, confidence, or trust: *I believe in your ability to solve the problem.* 3. To have confidence in the truth or value of something: *We believe in free speech.* 4. To have an opinion; think: *They have already left, I believe.* [Middle English *bileven,* from Old English *belȳfan, belēfan, gelēfan.* See **leubh-** in Appendix.] —**be·liev′er** *n.*

be·like (bĭ-līk′) *adv. Archaic.* Probably; perhaps. [Probably *be-* (from BY[1]) + LIKE[2], what is likely; see LIKE.]

Bel·i·sar·i·us (bĕl′ĭ-sâr′ē-əs). 505?–565. Byzantine general under Emperor Justinian I who led campaigns against the barbarians in North Africa and Italy.

be·lit·tle (bĭ-lĭt′l) *tr.v.* **-tled, -tling, -tles.** 1. To represent or speak of as contemptibly small or unimportant; disparage: *a person who belittled our efforts to do the job right.* 2. To cause to seem less than another or little: *The size of the office tower belittles the surrounding buildings.* See Synonyms at **decry.** —**be·lit′tle·ment** *n.* —**be·lit′tler** *n.*

Be·li·tung (bə-lē′to͝ong) also **Bil·li·ton** (bə-lē′tŏn′). An island of western Indonesia in the Java Sea between Sumatra and Borneo. It has important tin mines.

Be·lize (bə-lēz′). 1. Formerly **Brit·ish Hon·du·ras** (brĭt′ĭsh hŏn-do͝or′əs, -dyo͝or′-). A country of Central America on the Caribbean Sea. A British colony in the late 19th century, it became self-governing in 1964 and independent in 1981. Belmopan is the capital. Population, 145,353. 2. Also **Belize City.** The largest city of Belize, in the eastern part of the country on the Caribbean Sea at the mouth of the **Belize River.** It was devastated by a hurricane in 1961. The capital was moved to Belmopan in 1970. Population, 39,771.

bell[1] (bĕl) *n.* 1. A hollow metal instrument, usually cup-shaped with a flared opening, that emits a metallic tone when struck. 2. Something resembling this hollow metal instrument in shape or sound, as: a. *Music.* The round, flared mouth of a wind instrument. b. **bells.** *Music.* A percussion instrument consisting of metal tubes or bars that emit tones when struck. c. A hollow, usually inverted vessel, such as one used for diving deep below the surface of a body of water. d. The corolla of a flower: *"In a cowslip's bell I lie"* (Shakespeare). 3. *Nautical.* a. A stroke on a hollow metal instrument to mark the hour. b. The time indicated by the striking of this instrument, divided into half hours. —**bell** *v.* **belled, bell·ing, bells.** —*tr.* 1. To put a bell on. 2. To cause to flare like a bell. —*intr.* To assume the form of a bell; flare. —***idiom.*** **bell the cat.** To perform a daring act. [Middle English *belle,* from Old English.]

bell[2] (bĕl) *n.* The bellowing or baying cry of certain animals, such as a deer in rut or a beagle on the hunt. —**bell** *intr.v.* **belled, bell·ing, bells.** To utter long, deep, resonant sounds; bellow. [From Middle English *bellen,* to bellow, from Old English *bellan.*]

Bell (bĕl). A city of southern California, a suburb of Los Angeles. Population, 25,450.

Bell, Alexander Graham. 1847–1922. Scottish-born American inventor of the telephone. The first demonstration of electrical transmission of speech by his apparatus took place in 1876. Bell also invented the audiometer, an early hearing aid, and improved the phonograph.

Bell, (Arthur) Clive (Howard). 1881–1964. British critic who proposed his aesthetic theory of significant form in *Art* (1914).

Bel·la Coo·la (bĕl′ə ko͞o′lə) *n., pl.* **Bella Coola** or **-las.** 1.a. A Native American people inhabiting the coast of British Columbia along the Bella Coola River, a short stream flowing westward into a channel of Queen Charlotte Sound. b. A member

Belgian sheep dog

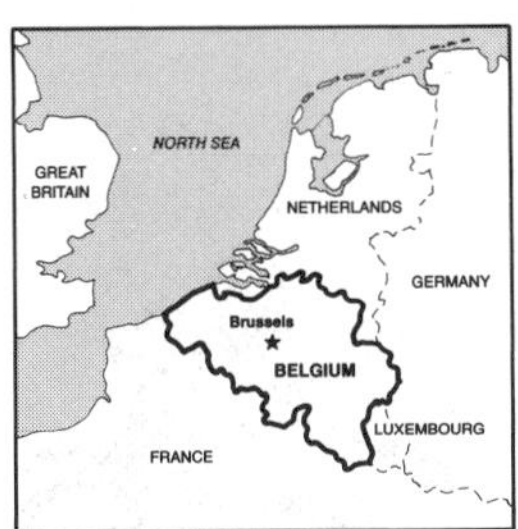

Belgium

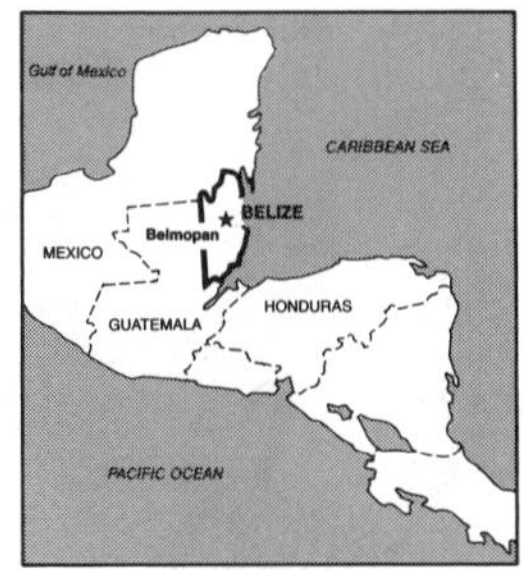

Belize

Alexander Graham Bell
Calling Chicago from New York City, 1892

of this people. **2.** The Salishan language of the Bella Coola.

bel·la·don·na (bĕl′ə-dŏn′ə) *n.* **1.** A poisonous Eurasian perennial herb *(Atropa belladonna)* having usually solitary, nodding, purplish-brown, bell-shaped flowers and glossy black berries. Also called *deadly nightshade.* **2.** An alkaloidal extract or tincture derived from this plant and used in medicine. [Italian : *bella,* feminine of *bello,* beautiful (from Latin *bellus;* see **deu-**[2] in Appendix) + *donna,* lady; see DONNA.]

belladonna alkaloids *pl.n.* A group of alkaloids, including atropine and scopolamine, found in plants such as belladonna and jimsonweed. They are used in medicine to dilate the pupils of the eyes, dry respiratory passages, prevent motion sickness, and relieve cramping of the intestines and bladder.

belladonna lily *n.* A bulbous, perennial southern African herb *(Amaryllis belladonna),* having showy umbels of large, trumpet-shaped flowers that appear in the fall after the spring leaves die back. Also called *amaryllis.*

Bel·la·my (bĕl′ə-mē), **Edward.** 1850–1898. American writer and utopian socialist who publicized his political views through his popular novel *Looking Backward* (1888).

Bel·lay (bə-lā′, bĕ-lā′), **Joachim du.** 1522?–1560. French poet. A founder of a group of poets known as the Pléiade, he wrote sonnets, satires on literary conventions, and a manifesto of the group's poetic principles.

bell·bird (bĕl′bûrd′) *n.* Any of various tropical American birds of the family Cotingidae, having a bell-like call.

bell-bot·tom (bĕl′bŏt′əm) *adj.* Having legs that flare out at the bottom: *bell-bottom trousers.*

bell-bot·toms (bĕl′bŏt′əmz) *pl.n.* Trousers with legs that flare at the bottom.

bell·boy (bĕl′boi′) *n.* A bellhop.

bell buoy *n. Nautical.* A buoy fitted with a warning bell that is activated by the movement of the waves.

bell captain *n.* The supervisor of a group of bellhops.

belle (bĕl) *n.* A popular, attractive girl or woman, especially the most attractive one of a group: *the belle of the ball.* [French, beautiful, belle, from Latin *bella,* feminine of *bellus.* See **deu-**[2] in Appendix.]

Bellerophon

Bel·leau Wood (bĕ-lō′, bĕl′ō). A forested area of northern France east of Château-Thierry. In World War I it was the site of a hard-fought victory over the Germans (June 1918).

belle é·poque (ā-pŭk′) *n.* An era of artistic and cultural refinement in a society, especially in France at the beginning of the 20th century. [French : *belle,* beautiful + *époque,* era.]

Belle Fourche (bĕl′ fo͞osh′). A river rising in northeast Wyoming and flowing about 467 km (290 mi) to the Cheyenne River in western South Dakota.

Belle Glade. A city of southeast Florida on Lake Okeechobee west of West Palm Beach. It was rebuilt after a hurricane in 1928. Population, 16,535.

Belle Isle, Strait of. A channel between southeast Labrador and northwest Newfoundland, Canada. It is the northern entrance to the Gulf of St. Lawrence.

Bel·ler·o·phon (bə-lĕr′ə-fən, -fŏn′) *n. Greek Mythology.* The Corinthian hero who, with the aid of the winged horse Pegasus, slew the Chimera.

belles-let·tres (bĕl-lĕt′rə) *pl.n. (used with a sing. verb).* **1.** Literature regarded for its aesthetic value rather than its didactic or informative content. **2.** Light, stylish writings, usually on literary or intellectual subjects. [French : *belles,* fine + *lettres,* letters, literature.]

bel·let·rist (bĕl-lĕt′rĭst) *n.* A writer of belles-lettres. —**bel·let′rism** *n.* —**bel′le·tris′tic** (bĕl′ĭ-trĭs′tĭk) *adj.*

Belle·ville (bĕl′vĭl′). **1.** A city of southeast Ontario, Canada, near Lake Ontario east-northeast of Toronto. Founded in 1790, it is a processing and manufacturing center. Population, 34,881. **2.** A city of southwest Illinois southeast of East St. Louis. It is in a coal-mining region and has diverse industries. Population, 41,580. **3.** A town of northeast New Jersey on the Passaic River near Newark. It was settled by the Dutch c. 1680. Population, 35,367.

Belle·vue (bĕl′vyo͞o′). **1.** A city of eastern Nebraska, a suburb of Omaha on the Missouri River. Population, 21,813. **2.** A city of west-central Washington on Lake Washington opposite Seattle. It is a manufacturing and residential community. Population, 73,903.

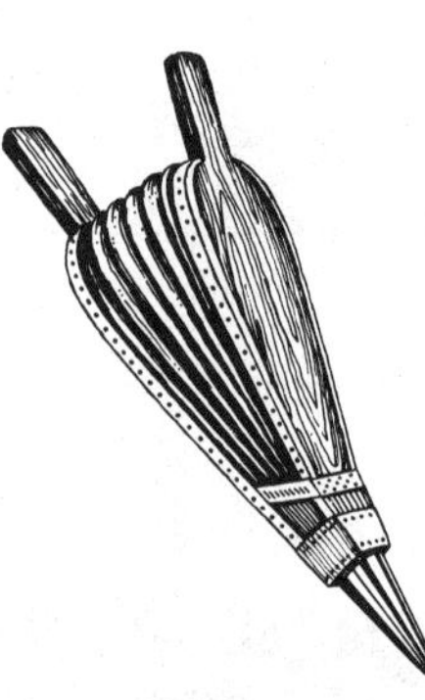
bellows

bell·flow·er (bĕl′flou′ər) *n.* **1.** Any of various herbs of the genus *Campanula,* native chiefly to the Northern Hemisphere and often having showy, bell-shaped, violet or blue flowers. **2.** Any of several other plants, especially one with bell-shaped flowers.

Bell·flow·er (bĕl′flou′ər). A city of southern California, a suburb in the Los Angeles–Long Beach metropolitan area. Population, 53,441.

Bell Gardens. A city of southern California, a suburb of Los Angeles. Population, 34,117.

bell·hop (bĕl′hŏp′) *n.* A person employed by a hotel to assist guests, as by carrying luggage and doing errands. [Probably short for *bell-hopper.*]

bel·li·cose (bĕl′ĭ-kōs′) *adj.* Warlike in manner or temperament; pugnacious. See Synonyms at **belligerent.** [Middle English, from Latin *bellicōsus,* from *bellicus,* of war, from *bellum,* war.] —**bel′li·cose′ly** *adv.* —**bel′li·cos′i·ty** (-kŏs′ĭ-tē), **bel′li·cose′ness** *n.*

bel·lig·er·ence (bə-lĭj′ər-əns) *n.* A hostile or warlike attitude, nature, or inclination; belligerency.

bel·lig·er·en·cy (bə-lĭj′ər-ən-sē) *n.* **1.** The state of being at war or being engaged in a warlike conflict. **2.** Belligerence.

bel·lig·er·ent (bə-lĭj′ər-ənt) *adj.* **1.** Inclined or eager to fight; hostile or aggressive. **2.** Of, pertaining to, or engaged in warfare. —**belligerent** *n.* One that is hostile or aggressive, especially one that is engaged in war. [Latin *belligerāns, belligerant-,* present participle of *belligerāre,* to wage war, from *belliger,* warlike : *bellum,* war + *gerere,* to make.] —**bel·lig′er·ent·ly** *adv.*

SYNONYMS: *belligerent, bellicose, pugnacious, contentious, quarrelsome.* These adjectives are compared as they mean having or showing an eagerness to fight. *Belligerent* may specify actual engagement in combat (*tried to arrange a truce between the belligerent nations*), or it may refer to a tendency to hostile behavior (*A belligerent reporter badgered the President for the facts*). *Bellicose* and *pugnacious* suggest a natural disposition to fight: *"All successful newspapers are ceaselessly querulous and bellicose."* (H.L. Mencken). *A retired litigator misses the challenge to her pugnacious intellect. Contentious* implies chronic argumentativeness: *"His style has been described variously as abrasive and contentious, overbearing and pompous"* (Victor Merina). *Quarrelsome* suggests bad temper and a perverse readiness to quarrel: *"On the days they worked they were good-natured and cheerful, and . . . they spent the evening jollily; but on our idle days they were mutinous and quarrelsome"* (Benjamin Franklin).

♦**bell·ing** (bĕl′ĭng) *n. Pennsylvania, West Virginia & Ohio.* See **shivaree.** See Regional Note at **shivaree.** [From BELL[1].]

Bel·ling·ham (bĕl′ĭng-hăm′). A city of northwest Washington on **Bellingham Bay** south of the British Columbia, Canada, border. It is a port of entry with shipbuilding and processing industries. Population, 45,794.

Bel·lings·hau·sen (bĕl′ĭngz-hou′zən), **Fabian Gottlieb von.** 1778–1852. Russian naval officer and explorer who led an expedition that circumnavigated Antarctica (1819–1821).

Bellingshausen Sea. An arm of the southern Pacific Ocean off the coast of Antarctica extending from Alexander I Island to Thurston Island.

Bel·li·ni (bə-lē′nē). Family of Venetian painters, including **Jacopo** (1400?–1470?), most of whose works have been lost, and his two sons, **Gentile** (1429?–1507) and **Giovanni** (1430?–1516). Giovanni, the most illustrious of the three, profoundly influenced the Venetian school of painting with his interest in light and color. His works include *Saint Francis in Ecstasy.*

Bellini, Vincenzo. 1801–1835. Italian composer whose operas include *La Sonnambula* and *Norma* (both 1831).

bell jar *n.* A cylindrical glass vessel with a rounded top and an open base, used to protect and display fragile objects or to establish a vacuum or a controlled atmosphere in experiments.

bell·man (bĕl′mən) *n.* **1.** A bellhop. **2.** A town crier.

bell metal *n.* An alloy of tin and copper used to make bells.

Bel·loc (bĕl′ŏk′, -ək), **Hilaire.** 1870–1953. French-born British writer. Considered a master of light English prose, he was also known widely for his droll verse, especially *The Bad Child's Book of Beasts* (1896).

Bel·lo·na (bə-lō′nə) *n. Roman Mythology.* The goddess of war.

bel·low (bĕl′ō) *v.* **-lowed, -low·ing, -lows.** —*intr.* **1.** To make the deep roaring sound characteristic of a bull. **2.** To shout in a deep voice. —*tr.* To utter in a loud, powerful voice. See Synonyms at **shout.** —**bellow** *n.* **1.** The roar of a large animal, such as a bull. **2.** A very loud utterance or other sound. [Middle English *belwen,* perhaps from Old English *belgan,* to be enraged, and *bylgan,* to bellow.] —**bel′low·er** *n.*

Bel·low (bĕl′ō), **Saul.** Born 1915. Canadian-born American writer whose novels, including *The Dangling Man* (1944) and *Humboldt's Gift* (1975), often concern an alienated individual within an indifferent society. He won the 1976 Nobel Prize for literature.

bel·lows (bĕl′ōz, -əz) *pl.n. (used with a sing. or pl. verb).* **1.a.** An apparatus for producing a strong current of air, as for sounding a pipe organ or increasing the draft to a fire, consisting of a flexible, valved air chamber that is contracted and expanded by pumping to force the air through a nozzle. **b.** Something, such as the pleated windbag of an accordion, that resembles this apparatus. **2.** The lungs. [Middle English *belowes,* from Old English *belgas,* pl. of *belg.* See **bhelgh-** in Appendix.]

Bel·lows (bĕl′ōz), **George Wesley.** 1882–1925. American artist noted for his energetic paintings of sporting scenes, such as *Stag at Sharkey's* (1907).

bell pepper *n.* **1.** An annual pepper *(Capsicum annuum)* widely cultivated for its edible fruit. **2.** The large, crisp, bell-shaped red, yellow, or green fruit of this plant.

Bell's Law (bĕlz) *n. Anatomy.* **1.** An axiom stating that the anterior or ventral roots of the spinal nerves are motor and the posterior or dorsal roots are sensory. **2.** The neurological law that, in any reflex arc, nerve impulses are conducted in only one direction. [After Sir Charles *Bell* (1774–1842), Scottish anatomist.]

bells of Ire·land (īr′lənd) *n.* An annual western Asian plant

(Moluccella laevis) in the mint family, grown for its long stems covered with persistent shell-shaped calyxes. It is especially popular in flower arrangements.

Bell's palsy *n.* A unilateral facial muscle paralysis of sudden onset, resulting from trauma, compression, or infection of the facial nerve and characterized by muscle weakness and a distorted facial expression. [After Sir Charles *Bell* (1774–1842), Scottish anatomist.]

bell·weth·er (bĕl′wĕth′ər) *n.* One that serves as a leader or as a leading indicator of future trends: *"The degree to which the paper is censored is a political bellwether"* (Justine De Lacy). [Middle English *bellewether,* wether with a bell hung from its neck, leader of the flock : *belle,* bell; see BELL[1] + *wether,* wether; see WETHER.]

Bell·wood (bĕl′wo͝od′). A village of northeast Illinois, a residential and manufacturing suburb of Chicago. Population, 19,811.

bell·wort (bĕl′wûrt′, -wôrt′) *n.* Any of various perennial plants of the genus *Uvularia* in the lily family, native to eastern North America and having solitary, nodding, yellow bell-shaped flowers. Also called *merry-bells.*

bel·ly (bĕl′ē) *n., pl.* **-lies. 1.** See **abdomen** (sense 1). **2.** The underside of the body of certain vertebrates, such as snakes and fish. **3.** *Informal.* **a.** The stomach. **b.** An appetite for food. **4.** The womb; the uterus. **5. a.** A part that bulges or protrudes: *the belly of a sail.* **b.** *Anatomy.* The bulging, central part of a muscle. **6.** A deep, hollow interior: *the belly of a ship.* **—belly** *intr. & tr.v.* **-lied, -ly·ing, -lies.** To bulge or cause to bulge. See Synonyms at **bulge.** [Middle English *beli,* from Old English *belg,* bag. See **bhelgh-** in Appendix.]

bel·ly·ache (bĕl′ē-āk′) *n.* **1.** Pain in the stomach or abdomen; colic. **2.** *Slang.* A whining complaint. **—bellyache** *intr.v.* **-ached, -ach·ing, -aches.** *Slang.* To complain, especially in a whining manner. **—bel′ly·ach′er** *n.*

bel·ly·band (bĕl′ē-bănd′) *n.* **1.** A band passed around the belly of an animal to secure something, such as a saddle. **2.** An encircling band for holding in a baby's protruding navel.

bel·ly·but·ton (bĕl′ē-bŭt′n) *n. Informal.* The navel; the umbilicus.

belly dance *n.* A dance in which the performer makes sinuous hip and abdominal movements. **—bel′ly-dance′** (bĕl′ē-dăns′) *v.* **—belly dancer** *n.*

belly flop *n. Informal.* A dive in which the front of the body hits flat against a surface, especially of water. **—bel′ly-flop′** (bĕl′ē-flŏp′) *v.*

bel·ly·ful (bĕl′ē-fo͝ol′) *n. Informal.* An undesirable or unendurable amount: *a bellyful of criticism.*

bel·ly-land (bĕl′ē-lănd′) *intr.v.* **-land·ed, -land·ing, -lands.** To land an aircraft on its underside without aid of landing gear. **—belly landing** *n.*

belly laugh *n.* A deep laugh.

bel·ly-up (bĕl′ē-ŭp′) *adj. Informal.* Bankrupt: *The company is belly-up.*

belly wash *n. Slang.* A soft drink, especially soda.

Bel·mont (bĕl′mŏnt′). **1.** A city of western California, a residential suburb midway between San Francisco and San Jose. Population, 24,505. **2.** A town of eastern Massachusetts, a residential suburb of Boston. Population, 26,100.

Belmont, Alva Ertskin Smith Vanderbilt. 1853–1933. American socialite and suffragist who won acceptance into New York's high society through extravagant spending and entertaining. She later promoted women's suffrage and was president of the National Women's Party (1921–1933).

Belmont, August. 1816–1890. German-born American banker, public official, and art collector who secured financial support for President Abraham Lincoln from European businessmen during the Civil War.

Bel·mon·te (bĕl-môn′tā), **Juan.** 1892–1962. Spanish matador who introduced modern bullfighting techniques and completed 109 corridas.

Bel·mo·pan (bĕl′mō-păn′). The capital of Belize, in the north-central part of the country. It became the capital in 1970 after a hurricane devastated Belize City (1961). Population, 2,935.

Bel·oeil (bə-lĭl′, bĕl-œy′). A town of southern Quebec, Canada, on the Richelieu River northeast of Montreal. It has varied light industries. Population, 17,540.

Be·lo Ho·ri·zon·te (bĕl′ō hôr′ĭ-zôn′tē, bĕ′lo͞o ô′rĭ-zôɴ′-thĭ). A city of eastern Brazil north of Rio de Janeiro. An important manufacturing and marketing center, it was built (1895–1897) as the first of Brazil's planned communities. Population, 1,780,855.

Be·loit (bə-loit′). A city of southern Wisconsin on the Illinois border south-southeast of Madison. Beloit College was founded in 1846. Population, 35,207.

bel·o·ne·pho·bi·a (bĕl′ə-nə-fō′bē-ə) *n.* An abnormal fear of sharply pointed objects, especially needles. [Greek *belonē,* needle; see **gʷelə-** in Appendix + –PHOBIA.]

be·long (bĭ-lông′, -lŏng′) *intr.v.* **-longed, -long·ing, -longs. 1. a.** To be proper, appropriate, or suitable: *A napkin belongs at every place setting.* **b.** To be in an appropriate situation or environment: *That plant belongs outdoors.* **2. a.** To be a member of a group, such as a club. **b.** To fit into a group naturally: *No matter what I did, I just didn't belong.* **3.** To be the property of: *"The earth belongs to the living"* (Thomas Jefferson). **4.** To be a part of something else: *These blades belong to the food processor.* [Middle English *bilongen* : probably *bi-,* be- + *longen,* to belong (probably from *long,* dependent, from Old English *gelang,* along, depending; see **del-**[1] in Appendix).]

♦ **Be·long·er** (bĭ-lông′ər, -lŏng′-) *n. Caribbean.* A Black native-born island resident: *"Resentment for what many Belongers consider Britain's parsimonious attitude has rekindled a 13-year-old debate in the islands"* (Maclean's).

be·long·ing (bĭ-lông′ĭng, -lŏng′-) *n.* **1.** Often **belongings.** Personal items that one owns; possessions. **2.** Close, secure relationship: *a sense of belonging.*

Be·lo·rus·sia (bĕl′ō-rŭsh′ə) also **Bye·lo·rus·sia** (byĕl′ō-). Popularly known as **White Rus·sia** (rŭsh′ə). A region of eastern Europe east of Poland, south of Lithuania and Latvia, and north of the Ukraine. Colonized originally by Slavs, it was controlled at various times by Lithuania and Poland and became part of the U.S.S.R. in 1922. Minsk is the capital. Population, 9,942,000.

Bel·o·rus·sian (bĕl′ō-rŭsh′ən, byĕl′-) *adj.* Of or relating to Belorussia or its people, language, or culture. **—Belorussian** *n.* **1.** A native or inhabitant of Belorussia. **2.** The Slavic language of the Belorussians.

be·lov·ed (bĭ-lŭv′ĭd, -lŭvd′) *adj.* Dearly loved. [Middle English *biloved,* past participle of *beloven,* to love : *bi-,* be- + *loven,* to love; see LOVE.] **—be·lov′ed** *n.*

be·low (bĭ-lō′) *adv.* **1.** In or to a lower place; beneath. **2. a.** On or to a lower floor; downstairs. **b.** *Nautical.* On or to a lower deck. **3.** In a later part of a given text: *figures quoted below.* **4.** Farther down, as along a slope or valley. **5.** In or to hell or Hades. **6.** On earth. **7. a.** In a lower rank or class. **b.** Below zero in temperature: *40° below.* **—below** *prep.* **1.** Underneath; beneath. **2.** Lower than, as on a graduated scale. **3.** Unsuitable to the rank or dignity of: *Such petty behavior is below me.* [Middle English *biloghe* : *bi,* by; see BY[1] + *loghe,* low; see LOW[1].]

be·low·ground (bĭ-lō′ground′) *adv. & adj.* Into or under the ground.

Bel·sen (bĕl′zən). In full **Ber·gen-Bel·sen** (bûr′gən-bĕl′sən, bĕr′gən-bĕl′zən). A village of northern Germany north of Hanover. It was the site of a Nazi concentration camp during World War II.

Bel·shaz·zar (bĕl-shăz′ər). Son of Nebuchadnezzar II and last king of Babylon, who in the Old Testament was warned of his doom by handwriting on the wall that was interpreted by Daniel.

belt (bĕlt) *n.* **1. a.** A flexible band, as of leather or cloth, worn around the waist to support clothing, secure tools or weapons, or serve as decoration. **b.** Something that resembles this type of band: *a belt of trees.* **2.** An encircling route. **3.** A seat belt. **4.** A continuous band or chain for transferring motion or power or conveying materials from one wheel or shaft to another. **5.** A band of tough reinforcing material beneath the tread of a tire. **6.** A geographic region that is distinctive in a specific respect: *"This is America's rural poverty belt"* (Charles Kuralt). See Synonyms at **area. 7.** *Slang.* A powerful blow; a wallop. **8.** *Slang.* A strong emotional reaction. **9.** *Slang.* A drink of hard liquor. **—belt** *tr.v.* **belt·ed, belt·ing, belts. 1.** To encircle; gird. **2.** To attach with or as if with an encircling band. **3.** To mark with or as if with an encircling band. **4.** *Slang.* To strike forcefully; punch. **5.** *Slang.* To sing in a loud and forceful manner: *belt out a song.* **6.** *Slang.* To swig (an alcoholic beverage). **—*idioms.* below the belt.** Not according to the rules; unfairly. **tighten (one's) belt.** To begin to exercise thrift and frugality. **under (one's) belt.** In one's possession or experience: *"By his mid-teens, Liszt had three years of intensive concertizing under his belt"* (Musical Heritage Review). [Middle English, from Old English, ultimately from Latin *balteus.*]

Bel·tane (bĕl′tān, -tən) *n.* **1.** An ancient Celtic feast marked by the lighting of bonfires and the performance of various rites of purification. **2.** May 1, the day on which this feast was held. [Middle English, from Scottish Gaelic *bealltainn.*]

belt highway *n.* See **beltway.**

belt·ing (bĕl′tĭng) *n.* **1.** Belts considered as a group. **2.** The material used to make belts.

belt-tight·en·ing (bĕlt′ tīt′n-ĭng) *n.* Increased thrift and frugality; a reduction in spending.

belt·way (bĕlt′wā′) *n.* A high-speed highway that encircles or skirts an urban area. Also called *belt highway.*

be·lu·ga (bə-lo͞o′gə) *n.* **1.** See **white whale. 2.** A large white sturgeon *(Huso huso)* of the Black and Caspian seas, whose roe is processed into caviar. In this sense, also called *beluga sturgeon, whitefish.* [Russian *byelukha,* white whale, and *byeluga,* sturgeon : *byeliĭ,* white; see **bhel-**[1] in Appendix + *-uga, -ukha,* augmentative suff.]

bel·ve·dere (bĕl′vĭ-dîr′) *n.* A structure, such as an open, roofed gallery or a summerhouse, situated so as to command a view. Also called *gazebo.* [Italian : *bel, bello,* beautiful (from Latin *bellus;* see **deu-**[2] in Appendix) + *vedere,* to see, view (from Latin *vidēre,* to see; see **weid-** in Appendix).]

Bel·ve·dere Park (bĕl′vĭ-dîr′). A city of northwest Georgia, a suburb of Atlanta. Population, 17,766.

be·ma (bē′mə) *n., pl.* **-ma·ta** (-mə-tə). **1.** *Judaism.* The platform from which services are conducted in a synagogue. Also called *almemar.* **2.** *Eastern Orthodox Church.* The area of a church in which the altar is located; the sanctuary. [Ultimately from Greek *bēma,* step, platform. See **gʷā-** in Appendix.]

ă pat	oi boy
ā pay	ou out
âr care	o͝o took
ä father	o͞o boot
ĕ pet	ŭ cut
ē be	ûr urge
ĭ pit	th thin
ī pie	*th* this
îr pier	hw which
ŏ pot	zh vision
ō toe	ə about, item
ô paw	♦ regionalism

Stress marks: ′ (primary); ′ (secondary), as in **dictionary** (dĭk′shə-nĕr′ē)

benchmark

bench press

bend²

bend sinister

Bem·ba (bĕm′bə) *n.* A Bantu language spoken in Zambia. Also called *Chibemba.*

be·med·aled or **be·med·alled** (bĭ-mĕd′ld) *adj.* Decorated with or wearing medals.

Be·mel·mans (bē′məl-mənz, bĕm′əl-), **Ludwig.** 1898–1962. Austrian-born American illustrator and writer of children's books, such as *Madeleine* (1939), and adult fiction, including *Hotel Splendide* (1940), which was based on his experiences in the hotel and restaurant business.

be·mire (bĭ-mīr′) *tr.v.* **-mired, -mir·ing, -mires. 1.** To soil with mud. **2.** To cause to sink into mud.

be·moan (bĭ-mōn′) *tr.v.* **-moaned, -moan·ing, -moans. 1.** To mourn over; lament. **2.** To express pity or grief for. [Middle English *bimonen,* alteration (influenced by *mone,* moan; see MOAN) of *bimenen,* from Old English *bemǣnan* : *be-,* be- + *mǣnan,* to complain of; see **mei-no-** in Appendix.]

be·muse (bĭ-myo͞oz′) *tr.v.* **-mused, -mus·ing, -mus·es. 1.** To cause to be bewildered; confuse. See Synonyms at **daze. 2.** To cause to be engrossed in thought. **—be·mus′ed·ly** (-myo͞o′zĭd-lē) *adv.* **—be·muse′ment** *n.*

ben (bĕn) *Scots. n.* The inner room or parlor of a house with two rooms. **—ben** *adv.* Inside; within. **—ben** *prep.* Within. [Middle English, variant of *binne,* within, from Old English *binnan.* See **en** in Appendix.]

Be·na·res (bə-när′əs, -ēz). See **Varanasi.**

Be·na·ven·te y Mar·tí·nez (bĕn′ə-vĕn′tē ē mär-tē′nəs, bĕ′nä-vĕn′tĕ ē mär-tē′nĕth), **Jacinto.** 1866–1954. Spanish playwright. He won the 1922 Nobel Prize for literature for his subtly satirical plays.

Ben Bel·la (bĕn bĕl′ə), **Ahmed.** Born 1919. Algerian revolutionary leader. Active in the Algerian nationalist movement after World War II, he became independent Algeria's first prime minister (1962) and its first elected president (1963) but was ousted in a coup (1965).

Bence-Jones protein (bĕns′jōnz′) *n.* A protein occurring in the serum and urine of patients with certain diseases, especially multiple myeloma. [After Henry *Bence-Jones* (1813–1873), British physician.]

bench (bĕnch) *n.* **1.** A long seat, often without a back, for two or more persons. **2.** *Nautical.* A thwart in a boat. **3.** *Law.* **a.** The seat for judges in a courtroom. **b.** The office or position of a judge. **c.** *Often* **Bench.** The judge or judges composing a court. **4.a.** A seat occupied by a person in an official capacity. **b.** The office of such a person. **5.** A strong worktable, such as one used in carpentry or in a laboratory. **6.** A platform on which animals, especially dogs, are exhibited. **7.** *Sports.* **a.** The place where the players on a team sit when not participating in a game. **b.** The reserve players on a team. **8.a.** A level, narrow stretch of land interrupting a declivity. **b.** A level elevation of land along a shore or coast, especially one marking a former shoreline. **—bench** *tr.v.* **benched, bench·ing, bench·es. 1.** To furnish with benches. **2.** To seat on a bench. **3.** To show (dogs) in a bench show. **4.** *Sports.* To keep out of or remove from a game: *benched the goalie for fighting.* [Middle English, from Old English *benc.*]

bench·er (bĕn′chər) *n.* **1.** One that sits on a bench. **2.** *Chiefly British.* A member of the inner or higher bar who acts as a governor of one of the Inns of Court. **3.** One, such as a magistrate, who occupies a bench.

Bench·ley (bĕnch′lē), **Robert Charles.** 1889–1945. American humorist, critic, and actor whose works, including the film *How to Sleep* (1935) and the book *My Ten Years in a Quandary* (1936), often pitted an average American against the complexities of modern life.

bench·mark (bĕnch′märk′) *n.* **1.** A standard by which something can be measured or judged: *"Inflation . . . is a great distorter of seemingly fixed economic ideas and benchmarks"* (Benjamin M. Friedman). See Synonyms at **standard. 2.** Often **bench mark.** A surveyor's mark made on a stationary object of previously determined position and elevation and used as a reference point in tidal observations and surveys. **—benchmark** *tr.v.* **-marked, -mark·ing, -marks.** To measure (a rival's product) according to specified standards in order to compare it with and improve one's own product. [From the use of the mark as a place to insert an angle iron that serves as a support for a leveling rod.]

bench press *n. Sports.* A lift that is executed from a horizontal position on a bench, in which the weight is lifted from the chest to arm's length and then lowered back to the chest.

bench-press (bĕnch′prĕs′) *tr.v.* **-pressed, -press·ing, -press·es.** *Sports.* To lift (barbells, for example) from a horizontal position on a bench.

bench show *n.* An indoor exhibition of small animals, especially a competitive dog show. [From the benches or platforms on which the dogs are displayed.]

bench·warm·er (bĕnch′wôr′mər) *n. Sports.* A substitute player.

bench warrant *n. Law.* A warrant issued by a judge or court ordering the apprehension of an offender.

bend¹ (bĕnd) *v.* **bent** (bĕnt), **bend·ing, bends.** *—tr.* **1.** To bring (something) into a state of tension: *bend a bow.* **2.a.** To cause to assume a curved or angular shape: *bend a piece of iron into a horseshoe.* **b.** To force to assume a different direction or shape, according to one's own purpose: *"Few will have the greatness to bend history itself, but each of us can work to change a small portion of events"* (Robert F. Kennedy). **3.** To cause to swerve from a straight line; deflect. **4.** To render submissive; subdue. **5.** To apply (the mind) closely: *"The weary naval officer goes to bed at night having bent his brain all day to a scheme of victory"* (Jack Beatty). **6.** *Nautical.* To fasten: *bend a mainsail onto the boom.* *—intr.* **1.a.** To deviate from a straight line or position: *The lane bends to the right at the bridge.* **b.** To assume a curved, crooked, or angular form or direction: *The saplings bent in the wind.* **2.** To incline the body; stoop. **3.** To make a concession; yield. **4.** To apply oneself closely; concentrate: *She bent to her task.* **—bend** *n.* **1.a.** The act or fact of bending. **b.** The state of being bent. **2.** Something bent: *a bend in the road.* **3. bends.** *Nautical.* The thick planks in a ship's side; wales. **4. bends.** *(used with a sing. or pl. verb).* A manifestation of decompression sickness that is caused by the formation of nitrogen bubbles in the blood and tissues after a rapid reduction in the surrounding pressure and is characterized by pain in the joints and abdomen. ***—idioms.*** **around the bend.** *Slang.* Insane; crazy. **bend (someone's) ear.** *Slang.* To talk to at length, usually excessively. [Middle English *benden,* from Old English *bendan.* See **bhendh-** in Appendix.]

SYNONYMS: *bend, crook, curve, round.* The central meaning shared by these verbs is "to swerve or cause to swerve from a straight line": *bent his knees and knelt; crooks her little finger when she holds a teacup; claws that curve under; rounding the lips to articulate an "o."*
ANTONYM: *straighten.*

bend² (bĕnd) *n.* **1.** *Heraldry.* A band passing from the upper dexter corner of an escutcheon to the lower sinister corner. **2.** *Nautical.* A knot that joins a rope to a rope or another object. [Middle English, from Old English *bend,* band, and from Old French *bende,* band (of Germanic origin; see **bhendh-** in Appendix).]

Bend (bĕnd). A city of central Oregon at the eastern foot of the Cascade Range east of Eugene. Lumbering and tourism are important to its economy. Population, 17,263.

Ben Day also **ben·day** or **Ben·day** (bĕn-dā′) *n.* A method of adding a tone to a printed image by imposing a transparent sheet of dots or other patterns on the image at some stage of a photographic reproduction process. [After Benjamin DAY.]

bend·er (bĕn′dər) *n.* **1.** One that bends: *a bender of iron bars; a bender of the truth.* **2.** *Slang.* A drinking spree.

Ben·de·ry (bĕn-dĕr′ē, bĭn-dyĕ′rē). A city of southern Moldavia on the Dniester River near Odessa. A historically strategic gateway to Bessarabia, the city has been controlled at various times by Turkey, Russia, Romania, and the Soviet Union. Population, 122,000.

Ben·di·go (bĕn′dĭ-gō′). A city of southeast Australia north-northwest of Melbourne. It was founded in 1851 during the Australian gold rush. Population, 31,841.

bend sinister *n. Heraldry.* A band passing from the upper sinister corner of an escutcheon to the lower dexter corner.

be·neath (bĭ-nēth′) *adv.* **1.** In a lower place; below. **2.** Underneath. **—beneath** *prep.* **1.** Lower than; below. **2.** Covered or concealed by: *The earth lay beneath a blanket of snow.* **3.** Under the force, control, or influence of. **4.a.** Lower than, as in rank or station. **b.** Unworthy of; unbefitting: *It was beneath me to beg.* [Middle English *binethe,* from Old English *beneothan* : *be,* by; see BY¹ + *neothan,* below.]

ben·e·dict (bĕn′ĭ-dĭkt′) *n.* A newly married man who was previously considered a confirmed bachelor. [After *Benedick,* a character in *Much Ado About Nothing* by Shakespeare.]

Ben·e·dict XIV (bĕn′ĭ-dĭkt′). Originally Prospero Lambertini. 1675–1758. Pope (1740–1758) who condemned the use of native rituals by Indian and Chinese converts to Catholicism.

Benedict XV. Originally Giacomo della Chiesa. 1854–1922. Pope (1914–1922) who sponsored World War I relief efforts and sought to mediate peace.

Benedict, Ruth Fulton. 1887–1948. American anthropologist noted for her study of Native American and Japanese cultures.

Ben·e·dic·tine (bĕn′ĭ-dĭk′tĭn, -tēn′) *n. Roman Catholic Church.* A monk or nun belonging to the order founded by Saint Benedict of Nursia. **—Ben′e·dic′tine** *adj.*

ben·e·dic·tion (bĕn′ĭ-dĭk′shən) *n.* **1.** A blessing. **2.** An invocation of divine blessing, usually at the end of a church service. **3.** Often **Benediction.** *Roman Catholic Church.* A short service consisting of prayers, the singing of a Eucharistic hymn, and the blessing of the congregation with the host. [Middle English *benediccioun,* from Old French *benedicion,* from Latin *benedictiō, benedictiōn-,* from *benedictus,* past participle of *benedicere,* to bless : *bene,* well; see **deu-²** in Appendix + *dīcere,* to speak; see **deik-** in Appendix.] **—ben′e·dic′tive, ben′e·dic′to·ry** (-dĭk′tə-rē) *adj.*

Benedict of Nur·si·a (nûr′shē-ə, -shə), Saint. A.D.480?–547? Italian monk who as founder of the Benedictine order (c. 529) is considered the patriarch of Western monasticism.

Ben·e·dict's solution (bĕn′ĭ-dĭkts) *n.* A solution of sodium citrate, sodium carbonate, and copper sulfate that changes from blue to yellow or red in the presence of reducing sugars, such as glucose. Also called *Benedict's reagent.* [After Stanley Rossiter *Benedict* (1884–1936), American chemist.]

Benedict's test *n.* A laboratory test using Benedict's solution to detect sugar in a sample.

Ben·e·dic·tus (bĕn′ĭ-dĭk′təs) *n.* **1.** A canticle that begins *Benedictus qui venit in nomine Domini* ("Blessed is he that cometh in the name of the Lord"). **2.** A canticle that begins *Benedictus Dominus Deus Israel* ("Blessed be the Lord God of Israel"). [Latin, past participle of *benedīcere,* to bless. See BENEDICTION.]

ben·e·fac·tion (bĕn′ə-făk′shən, bĕn′ə-făk′-) *n.* **1.** The act of conferring aid of some sort. **2.** A charitable gift or deed. [Late Latin *benefactiō, benefactiōn-,* from Latin *benefactus,* past participle of *benefacere,* to do a service : *bene,* well; see **deu-**[2] in Appendix + *facere,* to do; see **dhē-** in Appendix.]

ben·e·fac·tor (bĕn′ə-făk′tər) *n.* One that gives aid, especially financial aid. [Middle English, from Late Latin, from Latin *benefacere.* See BENEFACTION.]

ben·e·fac·tress (bĕn′ə-făk′trĭs) *n.* A woman who gives aid, especially financial aid.

be·nef·ic (bə-nĕf′ĭk) *adj.* Beneficent. [Latin *beneficus* : *bene,* well; see BENEFACTION + *-ficus,* -fic.]

ben·e·fice (bĕn′ə-fĭs) *n.* **1.** *Ecclesiastical.* **a.** A church office endowed with fixed capital assets that provide a living. **b.** The revenue from such assets. **2.** A landed estate granted in feudal tenure. [Middle English, from Old French, from Latin *beneficium,* benefit, from *beneficus,* benefic. See BENEFIC.] **—ben′e·fice** *v.*

be·nef·i·cence (bə-nĕf′ĭ-səns) *n.* **1.** The state or quality of being kind, charitable, or beneficial. **2.** A charitable act or gift. [Latin *beneficentia,* from *beneficus, beneficent-,* benefic. See BENEFIC.]

be·nef·i·cent (bə-nĕf′ĭ-sənt) *adj.* **1.** Characterized by or performing acts of kindness or charity. **2.** Producing benefit; beneficial. [Probably from BENEFICENCE, on the model of such pairs as *benevolent, benevolence.*] **—be·nef′i·cent·ly** *adv.*

ben·e·fi·cial (bĕn′ə-fĭsh′əl) *adj.* **1.** Producing or promoting a favorable result; advantageous. **2.** *Law.* Receiving or having the right to receive proceeds or other advantages. [Middle English, from Old French *beneficial,* from Late Latin *beneficiālis,* from Latin *beneficium,* benefit. See BENEFICE.] **—ben′e·fi′cial·ly** *adv.* **—ben′e·fi′cial·ness** *n.*

SYNONYMS: *beneficial, profitable, advantageous.* These adjectives apply to what promotes benefit or gain. *Beneficial* is said of what enhances well-being: *a temperate climate beneficial to the health; an arms limitation agreement beneficial to all countries. Profitable* refers to what yields material gain or useful compensation: *profitable speculation on the stock market; a profitable meeting to resolve difficulties.* Something *advantageous* affords improvement in relative position or in chances of success: *signed a contract that is advantageous to our company; found it socially advantageous to entertain often and well.*

ben·e·fi·ci·ar·y (bĕn′ə-fĭsh′ē-ĕr′ē, -fĭsh′ə-rē) *n., pl.* **-ies. 1.** One that receives a benefit: *I am the beneficiary of your generosity.* **2.** The recipient of funds, property, or other benefits, as from an insurance policy or will. **3.** *Ecclesiastical.* The holder of a benefice. [Medieval Latin *beneficiārius,* holder of a feudal benefice, from Latin, soldier granted privileges, from *beneficium,* benefit. See BENEFICE.] **—ben′e·fi′ci·ar′y** *adj.*

ben·e·fit (bĕn′ə-fĭt) *n.* **1.a.** Something that promotes or enhances well-being; an advantage. **b.** Help; aid. **2.** A payment made or an entitlement available in accordance with a wage agreement, an insurance policy, or a public assistance program. **3.** A public entertainment, performance, or social event held to raise funds for a person or cause. **4.** *Archaic.* A kindly deed. **—benefit** *v.* **-fit·ed, -fit·ing, -fits** also **-fit·ted, -fit·ting, -fits.** *—tr.* To be helpful or useful to. *—intr.* To derive benefit: *You will benefit from her good example.* [Middle English, from Old French *bienfait,* good deed, from Latin *benefactum,* from *benefacere,* to do a service. See BENEFACTION.]

SYNONYMS: *benefit, capitalize, profit.* The central meaning shared by these verbs is "to derive advantage from something": *benefited from the stock split; capitalized on her adversary's blunder; profiting from experience.*

benefit of clergy *n.* **1.** The authorized sanction of a religious rite: *cohabiting without benefit of clergy.* **2.** Exemption from trial or punishment in a civil court, given to the clergy in the Middle Ages.

benefit of the doubt *n.* A favorable judgment granted in the absence of full evidence.

Be·ne·lux (bĕn′ə-lŭks′). An economic union of Belgium, the Netherlands, and Luxembourg, originally established as a customs union in 1948.

Be·neš (bĕn′ĕsh′), **Eduard.** 1884–1948. Czechoslovakian politician who was foreign minister (1918–1935) and president (1935–1938) until the German occupation forced him to flee the country. On his return he was again elected president (1946) but resigned after refusing to sign a Communist constitution (1948).

Be·nét (bĭ-nā′), **William Rose.** 1886–1950. American writer and editor whose works include poetry, novels, and *The Reader's Encyclopedia* (1948). His brother **Stephen Vincent Benét** (1898–1943), also a writer, is best known for his Civil War narrative poem *John Brown's Body* (1928).

be·nev·o·lence (bə-nĕv′ə-ləns) *n.* **1.** An inclination to perform kind, charitable acts. **2.a.** A kindly act. **b.** A gift given out of generosity. **3.** A compulsory tax or payment exacted by some English sovereigns without the consent of Parliament.

be·nev·o·lent (bə-nĕv′ə-lənt) *adj.* **1.** Characterized by or suggestive of doing good. **2.** Of, concerned with, or organized for the benefit of charity. [Middle English, from Old French, from Latin *benevolēns, benevolent-* : *bene,* well; see **deu-**[2] in Appendix + *volēns,* present participle of *velle,* to wish; see **wel-**[1] in Appendix.] **—be·nev′o·lent·ly** *adv.*

SYNONYMS: *benevolent, charitable, eleemosynary, philanthropic.* The central meaning shared by these adjectives is "of, concerned with, providing, or provided by charity": *a benevolent fund; a charitable foundation; eleemosynary relief; philanthropic contributions.* See also Synonyms at **kind**[1].

Ben·fleet (bĕn′flēt′). An urban district of southeast England on an inlet of the Thames estuary east of London. Population, 86,000.

B.Eng. *abbr.* Bachelor of Engineering.

Ben·gal (bĕn-gôl′, bĕng-, bĕn′gəl, bĕng′-). A region of eastern India and Bangladesh. It was a province of India until 1947, when the eastern part became East Pakistan, and later (1971) Bangladesh, and the western section was included in independent India. **—Ben′ga·lese′** (bĕn′gə-lēz′, -lēs′, bĕng′-) *adj. & n.*

Bengal, Bay of. An arm of the Indian Ocean bordered by Sri Lanka and India on the west, Bangladesh on the north, and Burma and Thailand on the east.

Ben·ga·li (bĕn-gô′lē, bĕng-) *adj.* Of or relating to Bengal or its people, language, or culture. **—Bengali** *n.* **1.** A native or inhabitant of Bengal. **2.** The modern Indic language of West Bengal and Bangladesh.

ben·ga·line (bĕng′gə-lēn′) *n.* A fabric having a crosswise ribbed effect made of silk, wool, or synthetic fibers. [French, from *Bengale,* Bengal.]

Bengal light *n.* **1.** A colored flare or light. **2.** A blue light, formerly used for signaling.

Ben·ga·si (bĕn-gä′zē, bĕng-). See **Benghazi.**

Beng·bu (bŭng′bo͞o′) also **Peng·pu** (pŭng′po͞o′). A city of eastern China northwest of Nanjing. It was a government base during the civil war (1946–1949). Population, 425,000.

Ben·gha·zi also **Ben·ga·si** (bĕn-gä′zē, bĕng-). A city of northeast Libya on the Gulf of Sidra. Inhabited since Greek and Roman times, it is a major port and was a capital of Libya from 1951 to 1972. Population, 367,600.

B.Engr. *abbr.* Bachelor of Engineering.

B.Eng.Sci. *abbr.* Bachelor of Engineering Science.

Ben Gur·i·on (bĕn go͝or′ē-ən), **David.** Originally David Grün. 1886–1973. Polish-born Israeli political leader. Active in the Zionist movement, he founded the Mapai Party in 1930 and organized the resistance against the British after World War II. Upon Israel's independence, he became prime minister (1948–1953 and 1955–1963).

Be·ni (bĕ′nē). A river of central and northwest Bolivia rising in the Andes and flowing about 1,599 km (994 mi) to the Mamoré River.

be·night·ed (bĭ-nī′tĭd) *adj.* **1.** Overtaken by night or darkness. **2.** Being in a state of moral or intellectual darkness; unenlightened. **—be·night′ed·ly** *adv.* **—be·night′ed·ness** *n.*

be·nign (bĭ-nīn′) *adj.* **1.** Of a kind and gentle disposition. **2.** Showing gentleness and mildness. See Synonyms at **kind**[1]. **3.** Tending to exert a beneficial influence; favorable: *the benign influence of pure air.* See Synonyms at **favorable. 4.** *Medicine.* Of no danger to health; not recurrent or progressive; not malignant: *a benign tumor.* [Middle English *benigne,* from Old French, from Latin *benignus.* See **gene-** in Appendix.] **—be·nign′ly** *adv.*

be·nig·nan·cy (bĭ-nĭg′nən-sē) *n., pl.* **-cies.** Benignity.

be·nig·nant (bĭ-nĭg′nənt) *adj.* **1.** Favorable; beneficial. **2.** Kind and gracious. **—be·nig′nant·ly** *adv.*

be·nig·ni·ty (bĭ-nĭg′nĭ-tē) *n., pl.* **-ties. 1.** The quality or condition of being kind and gentle. **2.** A kindly or gracious act.

Be·nin (bə-nĭn′, bĕ-nēn′). **1.** A former kingdom of western Africa, now part of Nigeria. It flourished from the 14th to the 17th century. **2.** Formerly **Da·ho·mey** (də-hō′mē, dä-ō-mā′) A country of western Africa. Originally made up of several ancient kingdoms colonized by France, it became independent in 1960. Port-Novo is the capital and Cotonou the largest city. Population, 3,567,000. **3.** Also **Benin City.** A city of southern Nigeria on the **Benin River,** about 161 km (100 mi) long. The city is known for its bronze works of art. Population, 161,700.

Benin, Bight of. A wide indentation of the Gulf of Guinea in western Africa.

ben·i·son (bĕn′ĭ-zən, -sən) *n.* A blessing; a benediction. [Middle English, from Old French *beneison,* from Latin *benedictiō, benedictiōn-,* praising. See BENEDICTION.]

ben·ja·min (bĕn′jə-mən) *n.* See **benzoin** (sense 1). [Alteration of *benjoin, bengewyne,* early forms of BENZOIN.]

Ben·ja·min (bĕn′jə-mən). In the Old Testament, the younger son of Jacob and Rachel and the forebear of one of the tribes of Israel.

Benjamin, Judah Philip. 1811–1884. British-born American politician who served as Confederate secretary of war (1861–1862) and secretary of state (1862–1865).

David Ben Gurion

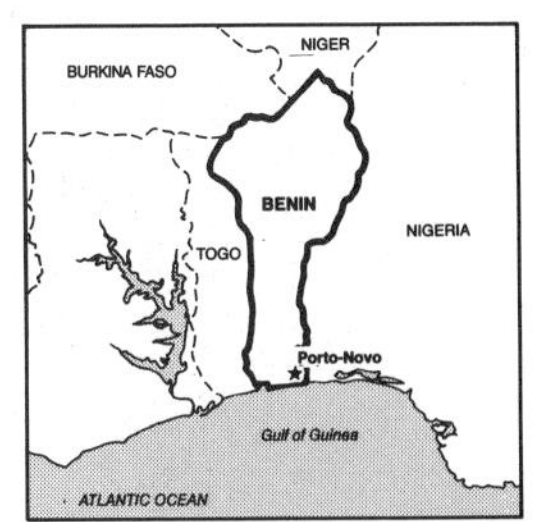

Benin

ă pat	oi boy
ā pay	ou out
âr care	o͝o took
ä father	o͞o boot
ĕ pet	ŭ cut
ē be	ûr urge
ĭ pit	th thin
ī pie	*th* this
îr pier	hw which
ŏ pot	zh vision
ō toe	ə about, item
ô paw	♦ regionalism

Stress marks: **′** (primary); ′ (secondary), as in **dictionary** (dĭk′shə-nĕr′ē)

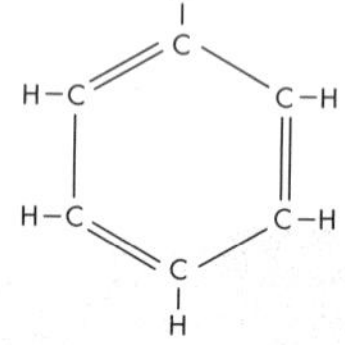

benzene ring

Ben Lo·mond (lō′mənd). A mountain, 973.6 m (3,192 ft) high, of south-central Scotland on the eastern shore of Loch Lomond.

ben·net (bĕn′ĭt) *n.* Herb bennet.

Ben·nett (bĕn′ĭt), **(Enoch) Arnold.** 1867–1931. British writer whose plays and novels, such as *The Old Wives' Tale* (1908), were influenced by the French realists and depict life among the lower middle classes.

Bennett, Floyd. 1890–1928. American aviator and Arctic explorer who piloted with Richard E. Byrd the first flight over the North Pole (1926).

Bennett, James Gordon. 1795–1872. American journalist and publisher who founded and edited (1835–1867) the *New York Herald.*

Bennett, Richard Bedford. Viscount Bennett. 1870–1947. Canadian prime minister (1930–1935) who convened the 1932 economic conference in Ottawa.

Ben Ne·vis (nē′vĭs, nĕv′ĭs). The highest mountain of Great Britain, rising to 1,343.8 m (4,406 ft) in the Grampian Mountains of western Scotland.

Ben·ning·ton (bĕn′ĭng-tən). A town of southwest Vermont east of Brattleboro. It is a tourist center and the seat of Bennington College (established 1925). Population, 9,349.

ben·ny (bĕn′ē) *n., pl.* **-nies.** *Slang.* An amphetamine tablet taken as a stimulant. [From BENZEDRINE.]

Ben·ny (bĕn′ē), **Jack.** 1894–1974. American comedian known for his delayed comic delivery and for his shows on radio (1932–1955) and television (1950–1965), which featured sketches based on his fictitious miserliness, constant age of 39, and inexpert violin playing.

Be·noît de Sainte-Maure (bən-wä′ də sănt-môr′). fl. 12th century. French trouvère whose *Roman de Troie* was a source for later works set during the Trojan War, such as Chaucer's *Troilus and Criseyde.*

Ben·sen·ville (bĕn′sən-vĭl′). A village of northeast Illinois, a suburb of Chicago. Population, 16,124.

bent[1] (bĕnt) *v.* Past tense and past participle of **bend**[1]. **—bent** *adj.* **1.** Altered from an originally straight or even condition: *pieces of bent wire.* **2.** Determined to take a course of action: *I was bent on going to the theater.* **3.** *Chiefly British.* Corrupt; venal. **—bent** *n.* **1.** A tendency, disposition, or inclination: *"The natural bent of my mind was to science"* (Thomas Paine). **2.** A transverse structural member or framework used for strengthening a bridge or trestle.

bent[2] (bĕnt) *n.* **1.** Bent grass. **2.** The stiff stalk of various grasses. **3.** An area of grassland unbounded by hedges or fences. [Middle English, from Old English *beonet* (attested only in place names).]

bent grass also **bent·grass** (bĕnt′grăs′) *n.* Any of various usually weedy grasses of the genus *Agrostis* native to chiefly temperate regions. Some are grown for pasture, turf, or putting greens on golf courses.

Ben·tham (bĕn′thəm), **Jeremy.** 1748–1832. British writer, reformer, and philosopher who systematically analyzed law and legislation, thereby laying the foundations of utilitarianism.

Ben·tham·ism (bĕn′thə-mĭz′əm) *n. Philosophy.* The utilitarian philosophy of Jeremy Bentham, holding that pleasure is the chief end of life and that the greatest happiness for the greatest number should be the ultimate goal of human beings. **—Ben′tham·ite′** (-mīt′) *n.*

ben·thos (bĕn′thŏs′) *n.* **1.** The collection of organisms living on or in sea or lake bottoms. **2.** The bottom of a sea or a lake. [Greek.] **—ben′thic** (-thĭk), **ben·thon′ic** (bĕn-thŏn′ĭk) *adj.*

Ben·tinck (bĕn′tĭngk), **William Henry Cavendish.** Third Duke of Portland. 1738–1809. British politician who served as prime minister (1783 and 1807–1809) and home secretary (1794–1801).

ben·to (bĕn′tō) *n.* Variant of **obento.**

Ben·ton (bĕn′tən). A city of central Arkansas southwest of Little Rock. There are bauxite deposits in the area. Population, 17,717.

Benton, Thomas Hart[1]. Called "Old Bullion." 1782–1858. American legislator. A U.S. senator (1821–1851) and representative (1853–1855) from Missouri, he staunchly opposed the use of paper currency.

Benton, Thomas Hart[2]. 1889–1975. American artist whose paintings and murals, such as *The History of Missouri,* were executed in a flat, realistic style known as regionalism and portrayed life in the Midwest and South.

ben·ton·ite (bĕn′tə-nīt′) *n.* An absorbent aluminum silicate clay formed from volcanic ash and used in various adhesives, cements, and ceramic fillers. [After *Benton* Formation (formerly Fort Benton Formation) of the Rock Creek district in eastern Wyoming.] **—ben′ton·it′ic** (-nĭt′ĭk) *adj.*

bent·wood (bĕnt′wo͝od′) *n.* Wood that has been steamed until pliable and then bent into shape. *—attributive.* Often used to modify another noun: *a bentwood rocker; bentwood chairs.*

Be·nue (bān′wā) also **Bin·ue** (bĭn′-). A river of western Africa rising in Cameroon and flowing about 1,078 km (670 mi) to the Niger River in central Nigeria.

be·numb (bĭ-nŭm′) *tr.v.* **-numbed, -numb·ing, -numbs. 1.** To make numb, especially by cold. **2.** To make inactive; dull: *"The anesthetic afternoon benumbs, sickens our senses"* (Karl Shapiro). See Synonyms at **daze.** [Middle English *binomen,* from past participle of *binimen,* to take away, from Old English *beniman* : *be-,* away; see BE– + *niman,* to take; see NUMB.] **—be·numb′ment** *n.*

Ben·xi (bŭn′shē′) also **Pen·ki** (-jē′). A city of northeast China south-southeast of Shenyang. It was founded as a metallurgical center in 1915. Population, 678,500.

Benz (bĕnts), **Karl Friedrich.** 1844–1929. German automobile pioneer credited with manufacturing the first vehicle powered with an internal-combustion engine, patented in 1886.

benz– *pref.* Variant of **benzo–.**

benz·al·de·hyde (bĕn-zăl′də-hīd′) *n.* A normally colorless aromatic oil, C_6H_5CHO, obtained naturally, as from the bitter almond, or made synthetically and used in perfumes and as a solvent and a flavoring.

ben·zal·ko·ni·um chloride (bĕn′zăl-kō′nē-əm) *n.* A yellow-white powder prepared in an aqueous solution and used as a detergent, fungicide, bactericide, and spermicide. [BENZ(O)– + ALK(YL) + (AMM)ONIUM.]

Ben·ze·drine (bĕn′zĭ-drēn′). A trademark used for a brand of amphetamine.

ben·zene (bĕn′zēn′, bĕn-zēn′) *n. Abbr.* **BHC** A clear, colorless, highly refractive flammable liquid, C_6H_6, derived from petroleum and used in or to manufacture a wide variety of chemical products, including DDT, detergents, insecticides, and motor fuels. Also called *benzine, benzol.*

benzene hexachloride *n. Abbr.* **BHC** A musty-smelling crystalline substance, $C_6H_6Cl_6$, prepared by the chlorination of benzene, occurring in several isomeric forms, and used as a powerful insecticide.

benzene ring *n.* The hexagonal ring structure in the benzene molecule, C_6H_6, and its substitutional derivatives, each vertex of which is occupied and distinguished by a carbon atom.

ben·zi·dine (bĕn′zĭ-dēn′) *n.* A yellowish, white, or reddish-gray crystalline powder, $NH_2C_6H_4C_6H_4NH_2$, used in dyes and to detect blood stains. [BENZ(ENE) + –ID(E) + –INE[2].]

ben·zim·id·az·ole (bĕn′zə-mĭ-dăz′ōl′, -mĭd′ə-zōl′) *n.* A crystalline compound, $C_7H_6N_2$, that is used in organic synthesis and inhibits the growth of certain microorganisms.

ben·zine (bĕn′zēn′, bĕn-zēn′) also **ben·zin** (bĕn′zĭn) *n.* **1.** A colorless, flammable, liquid mixture of hydrocarbons obtained in distilling petroleum, used in cleaning and dyeing and as a motor fuel. **2.** See **benzene.**

benzo– or **benz–** *pref.* Benzene; benzoic acid: *benzophenone.* [From BENZOIN.]

ben·zo·ate (bĕn′zō-āt′) *n.* A salt or ester of benzoic acid.

benzoate of soda *n.* See **sodium benzoate.**

ben·zo·caine (bĕn′zə-kān′) *n.* A white, odorless, tasteless crystalline ester, ethyl-para-aminobenzoate ($C_6H_4NH_2CO_2C_2H_5$), used as a local anesthetic.

ben·zo·di·az·e·pine (bĕn′zō-dī-ăz′ə-pēn′, -pĭn) *n.* Any of a group of chemical compounds with a common molecular structure and similar pharmacological effects, used as antianxiety agents, muscle relaxants, sedatives, and hypnotics. [BENZO– + DIAZEP(AM) + –INE[2].]

ben·zo·ic acid (bĕn-zō′ĭk) *n.* An aromatic white crystalline acid, C_6H_5COOH, used to season tobacco and in perfumes, dentifrices, and germicides. [From BENZOIN.]

ben·zo·in (bĕn′zō-ĭn, -zoin′) *n.* **1.** A balsamic resin obtained from certain tropical Asian trees of the genus *Styrax* and used in perfumery and medicine. Also called *benjamin, gum benjamin, gum benzoin.* **2.** A white or yellowish crystalline compound, $C_{14}H_{12}O_2$, derived from benzaldehyde. [French *benjoin* and Italian *benzoino,* both from Arabic *lubān jāwīy,* frankincense of Java.]

ben·zol (bĕn′zôl′, -zōl′, zŏl′) *n.* See **benzene.** [BENZ(O)– + –OL[1].]

ben·zo·phe·none (bĕn′zō-fĭ-nōn′, -fē′nōn) *n.* A white crystalline compound, $C_6H_5COC_6H_6$, used in perfumery and in medicine. Also called *diphenylketone.*

ben·zo·py·rene (bĕn′zō-pī′rēn′, -pī-rēn′) *n.* A yellow, crystalline, aromatic hydrocarbon, $C_{20}H_{12}$, that is a carcinogen found in coal tar and cigarette smoke.

ben·zo·yl (bĕn′zō-ĭl′) *n.* The univalent radical $C_6H_5ICO^-$, derived from benzoic acid.

benzoyl peroxide *n.* A flammable white granular solid, $(C_6H_5CO)_2O_2$, used as a bleaching agent for flour, fats, waxes, and oils, as a polymerization catalyst, and in pharmaceuticals.

ben·zyl (bĕn′zĭl, -zēl′) *n.* The univalent radical $C_6H_5CH_2^-$, derived from toluene.

Be·o·grad (bĕ′ô-gräd). See **Belgrade.**

Be·o·wulf (bā′ə-wo͝olf′) *n.* The legendary hero of an anonymous Old English epic poem believed to have been composed in the early eighth century. Beowulf slays the monster Grendel and its mother, becomes king of the Geats, and dies fighting a dragon.

be·queath (bĭ-kwēth′, -kwēth′) *tr.v.* **-queathed, -queath·ing, -queaths. 1.** *Law.* To leave or give (property) by will. **2.** To pass (something) on to another; hand down: *bequeathed to their children a respect for hard work.* [Middle English *biquethen,* from Old English *becwethan* : *be-,* be- + *cwethan,* to say; see **g**[w]**et-** in Appendix.] **—be·queath′al, be·queath′ment** *n.* **—be·queath′er** *n.*

be·quest (bĭ-kwĕst′) *n.* **1.** The act of giving, leaving by will, or passing on to another. **2.** Something that is bequeathed; a legacy.

[Middle English *biquest* (influenced by *biquethen,* to bequeath) : *bi-,* be- + *quist,* will (from Old English *-cwis,* as in *andcwis,* answer; see **gʷet-** in Appendix).]

Be·rar (bā-rär′, bə-). A region of west-central India. It was one of the early kingdoms of the Deccan.

be·rate (bĭ-rāt′) *tr.v.* **-rat·ed, -rat·ing, -rates.** To rebuke or scold angrily and at length. See Synonyms at **scold.**

Ber·ber (bûr′bər) *n.* **1.** A member of a North African, primarily Moslem people living in settled or nomadic tribes from Morocco to Egypt. **2.** Any of the Afro-Asiatic languages of the Berbers. [Arabic *Barbar.*] **—Ber′ber** *adj.*

ber·ber·ine (bûr′bə-rēn′) *n.* A bitter-tasting yellow alkaloid, $C_{20}H_{19}NO_5$, obtained from several plants such as goldenseal and having medical uses as an antipyretic and antibacterial agent. [New Latin *Berberis,* barberry genus (from Medieval Latin *berberis,* barberry, from Arabic *barbārīs*) + -INE[2].]

ber·ceuse (bĕr-sœz′) *n., pl.* **-ceuses** (-sœz′). *Music.* **1.** A lullaby. **2.** A soothing composition. [French, feminine of *berceur,* cradle rocker, from *bercer,* to rock, from Vulgar Latin **bertiāre.*]

Berch·tes·ga·den (bĕrk′təs-gäd′n, bĕrKH′-). A town of southeast Germany in the Bavarian Alps. It is a popular winter and summer resort. The site of Adolf Hitler's wartime villa is on a peak overlooking the town. Population, 8,126.

ber·dache (bər-dăsh′) *n.* Among certain Native American peoples, a person, usually a male, who assumes the sexual identity and is granted the social status of the opposite sex. [North American French, from French *bardache,* catamite, from Italian dialectal *bardascia,* from Arabic *bardaj,* slave, from Persian *bardah,* prisoner, from Middle Persian *vartak,* from Old Iranian **varta-.* See **wela-** in Appendix.] **—ber·dach′ism** *n.*

Ber·dya·ev (bər-dyä′yəf), **Nikolai Aleksandrovich.** 1874–1948. Russian philosopher whose spiritual ideals undercut his Marxist leanings and led to his expulsion from the Soviet Union (1922). His works include *The Spiritual Crisis of the Intelligentsia* (1910).

Be·re·a (bə-rē′ə). A city of northeast Ohio, a suburb of Cleveland. Population, 19,567.

be·reave (bĭ-rēv′) *tr.v.* **-reaved** or **-reft** (-rĕft′), **-reav·ing, -reaves. 1.** To leave desolate or alone, especially by death: *"Cry aloud for the man who is dead, for the woman and children bereaved"* (Alan Paton). **2.** *Archaic.* To take (something valuable or necessary), typically by force. [Middle English *bireven,* to deprive, from Old English *berēafian.* See **reup-** in Appendix.] **—be·reave′ment** *n.* **—be·reav′er** *n.*

be·reaved (bĭ-rēvd′) *adj.* Suffering the loss of a loved one: *the bereaved family.* **—bereaved** *n.* One or those bereaved: *The bereaved has entered the church. The bereaved were comforted by their friends.*

be·reft (bĭ-rĕft′) *v.* A past tense and a past participle of **bereave. —bereft** *adj.* **1.a.** Deprived of something: *They are bereft of their dignity.* **b.** Lacking something needed or expected: *"Today's graduates seem keenly aware that the future is bereft of conventional expectations"* (Bruce Weber). **2.** Suffering the death of a loved one; bereaved: *the bereft parents.*

Ber·en·gar·i·a (bĕr′ən-gâr′ē-ə). 1165–1230. Castilian-born queen of England as the wife of Richard I.

Ber·e·ni·ce's Hair (bĕr′ə-nī′sēz) *n.* See **Coma Berenices.**

Ber·en·son (bĕr′ĭn-sən), **Bernard** also **Bernhard.** 1865–1959. Lithuanian-born American art critic and historian particularly noted for his writings on the Italian Renaissance, including *Venetian Painters of the Renaissance* (1894).

be·ret (bə-rā, bĕr′ā′) *n.* **1.** A round, soft, brimless cap that fits snugly and is often worn angled to one side. **2. Beret.** A Green Beret. [French *béret,* from French dialectal *berret* and from Old Provençal *berret,* cap, both from Late Latin *birrus,* hooded cloak. See BIRETTA.]

be·ret·ta or **ber·ret·ta** (bə-rĕt′ə) *n.* Variants of **biretta.**

Be·re·zi·na (bə-rĕ′zĭ-nə, byə-ryĕ-zyĭ-nä′). A river of Belorussia rising in the northwest and flowing about 611 km (380 mi) generally southward to the Dnieper River.

Be·rez·ni·ki (bə-rĕz′nĭ-kē, byə-ryŏz′nyĭ-kē′). A city of western Russia on the Kama River. It is an important industrial center. Population, 195,000.

berg (bûrg) *n.* A mass of floating or stationary ice; an iceberg.

Berg (bĕrg, bĕrk), **Alban.** 1885–1935. Austrian composer. A pupil of Arnold Schönberg, he applied an atonal manner to classical forms in works such as the opera *Wozzeck* (1925) and *Violin Concerto* (1935).

Ber·ga·ma (bər-gä′mə, bûr′gə-). A town of western Turkey north of Izmir. It occupies the site of ancient Pergamum. Population, 34,716.

Ber·ga·mo (bĕr′gə-mō′). A city of northern Italy in the foothills of the Alps northeast of Milan. Originally a Gallic settlement, it later became a Lombard duchy and was ruled by Austria from 1814 to 1859. Population, 121,846.

ber·ga·mot (bûr′gə-mŏt′) *n.* **1.a.** A small tree *(Citrus aurantium* subsp. *bergamia)* commercially grown chiefly in southern Italy for its sour citrus fruits, the rinds of which yield an aromatic oil. Also called *bergamot orange.* **b.** The oil itself, used extensively in perfumery. Also called *bergamot oil.* **2.** See **bee balm.** [French *bergamote,* from Italian *bergamotta,* from Turkish dialectal *beg-armudu,* bey's pear : *beg,* bey; see BEY + *armud,* pear + *-u,* possessive suff.]

Ber·gen (bûr′gən, bĕr′-). A city of southwest Norway on inlets of the North Sea. Founded c. 1070, it was the largest and most important city of medieval Norway. Population, 207,232.

Ber·gen-Bel·sen (bûr′gən-bĕl′sən, bĕr′gən-bĕl′zən). See **Belsen.**

Ber·gen·field (bûr′gən-fēld′). A borough of northeast New Jersey east of Paterson. It has varied light industries. Population, 25,568.

Bergh (bûrg), **Henry.** 1811–1888. American reformer who founded the American Society for the Prevention of Cruelty to Animals (1866).

Ber·gisch-Glad·bach (bĕr′gĭsh-glät′bäk′, -bäKH′). A town of western Germany near Cologne. Chartered in 1856, it is an industrial center. Population, 100,749.

Berg·man (bûrg′mən), **Ingmar.** Born 1918. Swedish director whose critically acclaimed films, such as *The Silence* (1963) and *Fanny and Alexander* (1983), are characterized by slow pace, laconic dialogue, and heavy use of symbolism to explore the psychological states of the characters.

Bergman, Ingrid. 1915–1982. Swedish actress who won an Academy Award in 1944 for *Gaslight,* in 1956 for *Anastasia,* and in 1974 for *Murder on the Orient Express.*

Berg·mann's rule (bûrg′mənz) *n.* *Ecology.* The principle holding that in a warm-blooded, polytypic, wide-ranging animal species, the body size of the members of each geographic group varies with the average environmental temperature. According to this principle, warm-blooded animals living in cold climates tend to be larger than animals of the same species living in warm climates. [After Karl *Bergmann* (died 1865), German biologist.]

beret

Berg·son (bĕrg′sən, bĕrg-sôN′), **Henri Louis.** 1859–1941. French philosopher and writer whose widely influential works, including *Creative Evolution* (1907) and *The Creative Mind* (1934), largely concern the importance of intuition as a means of attaining knowledge and the élan vital present in all living things. He won the 1927 Nobel Prize for literature.

Berg·son·ism (bĕrg′sə-nĭz′əm) *n.* The philosophy of Henri Bergson, which asserts that the flow of time personally experienced is free and unrestricted rather than measured on a clock and contends that all living forms arise from a persisting natural force, the élan vital. **—Berg·so′ni·an** (-sō′nē-ən) *adj. & n.*

Ber·i·a (bĕr′ē-ə), **Lavrenti Pavlovich.** 1899–1953. Soviet secret police chief (1938–1953) during the brutal regime of Joseph Stalin. In the power struggle following Stalin's death, Beria was convicted of conspiracy and executed.

ber·i·ber·i (bĕr′ē-bĕr′ē) *n.* A disease caused by a deficiency of thiamine, endemic in eastern and southern Asia and characterized by neurological symptoms, cardiovascular abnormalities, and edema. [Singhalese, reduplication of *beri,* weakness.]

Ber·ing (bîr′ĭng, bâr′-, băr′- bā′rĭng), **Vitus.** 1681–1741. Danish navigator and explorer who in 1728 sailed through the Bering Strait, proving (though he did not realize it at the time) that Asia and North America are separate continents.

Bering Sea. A northward extension of the Pacific Ocean between Siberia and Alaska, lying north of the Aleutian Islands and connected with the Arctic Ocean by the Bering Strait. It was first explored in the 17th century.

Bering Standard Time *n.* Standard time in the 11th time zone west of Greenwich, England, reckoned at 165° west and used, for example, in the Midway Islands. Also called *Bering Time.* [After the BERING (SEA) or BERING (STRAIT).]

Bering Strait. A narrow stretch of water separating Alaska from Siberia and connecting the Arctic Ocean with the Bering Sea. It is believed that during prehistoric times the strait formed a land bridge by which the original inhabitants of North America arrived from Asia.

Bering Time *n.* See **Bering Standard Time.**

Berke·le·ian·ism (bärk′lē-ə-nĭz′əm, bûr′-) *n.* George Berkeley's philosophy of subjective idealism, which holds that material objects have no independent being but exist only as concepts in God's mind and as perceptions of those concepts in other minds. **—Berke′le·ian** *adj. & n.*

Berke·ley (bûrk′lē). A city of western California on San Francisco Bay north of Oakland. Founded as Oceanview on land purchased from a Spanish family in 1853, it was renamed Berkeley in 1866. A branch of the University of California is here (established 1872). Population, 103,328.

Berkeley, Busby. 1895–1976. American choreographer and film director noted for lavish, synchronized dance routines in films such as *42nd Street* (1933).

Berke·ley (bärk′lē, bûrk′-), **George.** 1685–1753. Irish prelate and philosopher whose basic theory, directed against the materialism of Thomas Hobbes, is that to be is to perceive or to be perceived. His works include *Treatise Concerning the Principles of Human Knowledge* (1710).

Berke·ley (bûrk′lē, bärk′-), Sir **William.** 1606–1677. English colonial governor of Virginia (1641–1649 and 1660–1677) whose policies led to Bacon's Rebellion (1676).

ber·ke·li·um (bər-kē′lē-əm, bûrk′lē-əm) *n.* *Symbol* **Bk** A synthetic transuranic radioactive element having 9 isotopes with mass numbers from 243 to 250 and half-lives from 3 hours to 1,380

ă pat	oi boy
ā pay	ou out
âr care	ŏŏ took
ä father	ōō boot
ĕ pet	ŭ cut
ē be	ûr urge
ĭ pit	th thin
ī pie	*th* this
îr pier	hw which
ŏ pot	zh vision
ō toe	ə about, item
ô paw	♦ regionalism

Stress marks: ′ (primary); ′ (secondary), as in **dictionary** (dĭk′shə-nĕr′ē)

years. Atomic number 97; melting point 986°C; valence 3, 4. See table at **element.** [After BERKELEY, California.]

Berk·ley (bûrk′lē). A city of southeast Michigan, a residential suburb of Detroit. Population, 18,637.

Berk·shire (bûrk′shîr′, -shər) *n.* One of a domestic breed of medium-sized black swine with white markings on the feet, legs, and face. [After *Berkshire,* a county of south-central England.]

Berkshire Hills also **Berk·shires** (bûrk′shîrz′, -shərz). A region of wooded hills in western Massachusetts rising to 1,064.8 m (3,491 ft).

ber·lin (bər-lĭn′) *n.* **1.** Berlin wool. **2.** Often **berline.** A four-wheeled closed carriage having an open, hooded seat behind. [After BERLIN, Germany.]

Ber·lin (bûr-lĭn′). The capital and largest city of Germany, in the northeast part of the country. Divided between 1945 and 1990 into **East Berlin** and **West Berlin,** it was the center of the Prussian state and after 1871 was the capital of the German Empire. The division of the city grew out of the zones of occupation established at the end of World War II. The **Berlin Wall,** a wire and concrete barrier, was erected by the East German government in August 1961 and dismantled in November 1989. Population, 3,034,118.

Berlin, Irving. Originally Israel Baline. 1888–1989. Russian-born American songwriter who wrote more than 1,500 songs, including "Alexander's Ragtime Band" (1911), and several musical comedies, such as *Annie Get Your Gun* (1946).

ber·line (bər-lĭn′) *n.* Variant of **berlin** (sense 2).

Ber·lin·er (bûr′lə-nər), **Emile.** 1851–1929. German-born American inventor who greatly improved the telephone and invented the gramophone (1887).

Berlin wool *n.* A light wool yarn used in making clothing, especially gloves.

Ber·li·oz (bĕr′lē-ōz′, -ōs′), **(Louis) Hector.** 1803–1869. French composer and leading representative of romanticism in French music. His works include *Symphonie Fantastique* (1830), *Romeo and Juliet* (1839), and the opera *The Trojans* (1855–1858).

Bernese mountain dog

berm also **berme** (bûrm) *n.* **1.a.** A narrow ledge or shelf, as along the top or bottom of a slope. **b.** The shoulder of a road. **c.** A raised bank or path, such as one along a canal. **2.** A terrace formed by wave action along the backshore of a beach. **3.** A mound or bank of earth placed against the wall of a building to provide protection or insulation. **4.** A ledge between the parapet and the moat in a fortification. [French *berme,* from Dutch *berm,* from Middle Dutch *bærm, berme.*]

Ber·me·jo (bər-mā′hō, bĕr-). A river of northern Argentina rising near the Bolivian border and flowing about 1,046 km (650 mi) generally southeast to the Paraguay River at the Paraguay border.

Sarah Bernhardt
Photographed by
Napoleon Sarony
(1821–1896)

Ber·mu·da (bər-myo͞o′də). A self-governing British colony comprising about 300 coral islands in the Atlantic Ocean southeast of Cape Hatteras. The first settlement was made in 1609 by British colonists shipwrecked on their way to Virginia. Tourism is crucial to its economy. Hamilton, on **Bermuda Island,** the largest in the archipelago, is the capital. Population, 56,000. —**Ber·mu′di·an, Ber·mu′dan** *adj. & n.*

Bermuda bag *n.* An oval handbag with wooden handles and decorative removable covers.

Bermuda buttercup *n.* A southern African herb *(Oxalis pes-caprae)* having umbels of bright yellow flowers and compound leaves with three leaflets.

Bermuda grass *n.* A mat-forming perennial grass *(Cynodon dactylon),* widespread in warm regions and important as a lawn and pasturage grass in the southern United States. It is also common as a weed. Also called *scutch grass.*

Bermuda lily *n.* See **Easter lily.**

Bermuda onion *n.* Any of several varieties of mild-flavored onions shaped like a flattened sphere.

Bermuda petrel *n.* See **cahow.**

Bermuda rig *n. Nautical.* A fore-and-aft rig distinguished by a tall triangular mainsail and a sharply raked mast, widely used on cruising and racing vessels. Also called *Marconi rig.*

Ber·mu·das (bər-myo͞o′dəz) *pl.n.* Bermuda shorts.

Bermuda shorts *pl.n.* Short pants that end slightly above the knee.

Leonard Bernstein

Bern or **Berne** (bûrn, bĕrn). The capital of Switzerland, in the west-central part of the country on the Aare River. Founded as a military post in 1191, it became part of the Swiss Confederation in 1353 and its capital in 1848. Population, 140,600.

Ber·na·dette of Lourdes (bûr′nə-dĕt′; lo͝ord, lo͝ordz), Saint. Originally Marie Bernarde Soubirous. 1844–1879. French peasant girl whose visions of the Virgin Mary led to the establishment of the shrine at Lourdes, France.

Bernadotte (bûr′nə-dŏt′), Count **Folke.** 1895–1948. Swedish diplomat who as a leader of the Swedish Red Cross (1943–1948) helped save thousands of people from Nazi concentration camps. As United Nations mediator in Palestine (1948) he attempted to end Israeli-Arab hostilities but was assassinated by terrorists.

Ber·nard (bĕr-när′), **Claude.** 1813–1878. French physiologist noted for his study of the digestive and nervous systems.

Ber·nar·din de Saint-Pierre (bĕr-när-dăN′ də săN-pyĕr′), **Jacques Henri.** 1737–1814. French writer whose works, including the novel *Paul et Virginie* (1787), praise nature and lament civilization.

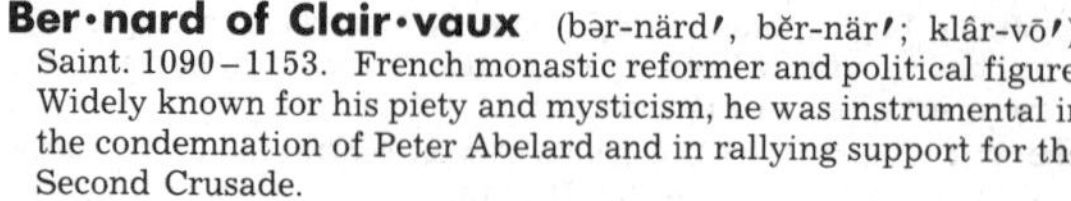

Ber·nard of Clair·vaux (bər-närd′, bĕr-när′; klâr-vō′), Saint. 1090–1153. French monastic reformer and political figure. Widely known for his piety and mysticism, he was instrumental in the condemnation of Peter Abelard and in rallying support for the Second Crusade.

Berne (bûrn, bĕrn). See **Bern.**

Ber·nese Alps (bûr′nēz, -nēs, bûr-nēz′, -nēs′). A range of the Alps in south-central Switzerland rising to 4,276.7 (14,022 ft).

Ber·nese mountain dog (bûr′nēz, -nēs, bûr-nēz′, -nēs′) *n.* Any of a Swiss breed of large, muscular dogs having a soft, silky black coat with russet or tan markings on the forelegs, over each eye, and on both sides of a white chest. The dogs were formerly used for draft.

Bern·hardt (bûrn′härt′, bĕr-när′), **Sarah.** Originally Henrietta Rosine Bernard. Known as "the Divine Sarah." 1844–1923. French actress. Considered the romantic and tragic actress of her day, she first achieved fame for her performance in *Phèdre* (1874).

Ber·ni·ci·a (bər-nĭsh′ē-ə, -nĭsh′ə, bĕr-). A sixth-century A.D. Anglian kingdom in present-day northeast England. It was later part of the kingdom of Northumbria.

Ber·ni·na Alps (bər-nē′nə, bĕr-). A mountain group of southeast Switzerland in the Rhaetian Alps on the Swiss-Italian border. The highest elevation is **Piz Bernina,** rising to 4,051.6 m (13,284 ft). **Bernina Pass** connects Switzerland and Italy by road and rail.

Ber·ni·ni (bər-nē′nē, bĕr-), **Giovanni Lorenzo** or **Gianlorenzo.** 1598–1680. Italian sculptor, painter, and architect. An outstanding exponent of the Italian baroque, he is noted for his flowing, dynamic sculpture, such as *Apollo and Daphne* (1622–1624), and his designs for many churches, including Saint Peter's Basilica.

Ber·noul·li (bər-no͞o′lē). Family of Swiss mathematicians and scientists, including **Jakob** or **Jacques** (1654–1705), an important theorist of ordinary calculus and the calculus of variations. His brother **Johann** or **Jean** (1667–1748) developed integral and exponential calculus. Johann's son **Daniel** (1700–1782) anticipated the law of conservation of energy, did pioneering work in the molecular theory of gases, and contributed to probability theory and the theory of differential equations.

Bernoulli distribution *n.* See **binomial distribution.** [After Jakob BERNOULLI.]

Bernoulli effect *n.* The phenomenon of internal pressure reduction with increased stream velocity in a fluid. [After Daniel BERNOULLI.]

Ber·noul·li's law (bər-no͞o′lēz) *n. Statistics.* See **law of large numbers.** [After Jakob BERNOULLI.]

Bernoulli trial *n. Statistics.* An experiment having only two possible outcomes, usually denoted *success* and *failure,* with the properties that the probability of occurrence of each outcome is the same in each trial and the occurrence of one excludes the occurrence of the other in any given trial. [After Jakob BERNOULLI.]

Bern·stein (bûrn′stīn′, -stēn′), **Leonard.** 1918–1990. American conductor and composer who has written numerous choral and symphonic works but is best known for his musical comedies, including *West Side Story* (1957).

Bern·storff (bĕrn′shtôrf), Count **Johann Heinrich von.** 1862–1939. German diplomat who as ambassador to the United States (1908–1917) warned his government against the use of unrestricted submarine warfare, a practice that precipitated American entry into World War I.

Ber·ra (bĕr′ə), **Lawrence Peter.** Known as "Yogi." Born 1925. American baseball player and manager. Considered among the best catchers in baseball history, he played for the New York Yankees from 1946 to 1963.

ber·ried (bĕr′ēd) *adj.* **1.** Having or bearing berries: *berried branches; a berried plant.* **2.** Resembling a berry or berries: *"an off-dry, berried flavor"* (New York Times). **3.** Bearing eggs. Used especially of egg-bearing crustaceans or fishes: *a berried lobster.*

ber·ry (bĕr′ē) *n., pl.* **-ries. 1.a.** *Botany.* An indehiscent fruit derived from a single ovary and having the whole wall fleshy, such as the grape or tomato. **b.** A small, juicy, fleshy fruit, such as a blackberry or raspberry, regardless of its botanical structure. **2.** The small, dark egg of certain crustaceans or fishes. —**berry** *intr.v.* **-ried, -ry·ing, -ries. 1.** To hunt for or gather berries: *went berrying in July.* **2.** To bear or produce berries. [Middle English *berye,* from Old English *berie.* See **bhā-**[1] in Appendix.]

Ber·ry (bĕ-rē′). A historical region and former province of central France. Purchased by the French crown in 1101, it became an independent duchy in 1360 and reverted to the crown in 1601.

Ber·ry (bĕr′ē), **Charles Edward Anderson.** Known as "Chuck." Born 1926. American musician and singer considered among the earliest and most influential **rock 'n' roll** performers.

Ber·ry·man (bĕr′ē-mən), **John.** 1914–1972. American poet whose dramatic, personal, and complex works include *Homage to Mistress Bradstreet* (1956) and the collection *77 Dream Songs* (1964).

ber·seem (bər-sēm′) *n.* A yellowish-flowered annual clover *(Trifolium alexandrinum),* native to the Mediterranean region and Asia and grown for forage in warm areas such as Florida. Also called *Egyptian clover.* [Arabic *birsīm,* from Coptic *bersīm.*]

ber·serk (bər-sûrk′, -zûrk′) *adj.* **1.** Destructively or frenetically violent: *a berserk worker who started smashing all the windows.* **2.** Mentally or emotionally upset; deranged: *berserk with* *grief.* **3.** *Informal.* Unrestrained, as with enthusiasm or appetite; wild: *berserk over chocolates.* **—berserk** *n.* **1.** One that is violent, upset, or unrestrained. **2.** A berserker. **—ber·serk′** *adv.* **—ber·serk′ly** *adv.*

WORD HISTORY: When we say that we are going berserk, we may not realize how extreme a state this might be. Our adjective comes from the noun *berserker,* or *berserk,* which is from the Old Norse word *berserkr,* "a wild warrior or champion." Such warriors wore hides of bears, which explains the probable origins of *berserkr* as a compound of **bera,* "bear," and *serkr,* "shirt, coat." These *berserkers* became frenzied in battle, howling like animals, foaming at the mouth, and biting the edges of their iron shields. *Berserker* is first recorded in English in the early 19th century, long after these wild warriors ceased to exist.

ber·serk·er (bər-sûr′kər, -zûr′-) *n.* One of a band of ancient Norse warriors legendary for their savagery and reckless frenzy in battle. [Old Norse *berserkr* : **bera,* feminine of *björn,* bear; see **bher-**[2] in Appendix + *serkr,* shirt.]

berth (bûrth) *n.* **1.** Sufficient space for a ship to maneuver; sea room: *kept a clear berth of the reefs.* **2.** A space for a ship to dock or anchor: *a steamship moored to its berth at the pier.* **3.a.** Employment on a ship: *sought an officer's berth in the merchant marine.* **b.** A job: *a comfortable berth as head of the department.* **4.a.** A built-in bed or bunk, as on a ship or a train. **b.** A place to sleep or stay; accommodations: *found a berth in a nearby hotel.* **5.** A space where a vehicle can be parked, as for loading. **—berth** *v.* **berthed, berth·ing, berths.** *—tr.* **1.** To bring (a ship) to a berth. **2.** To provide with a berth. *—intr.* To come to a berth; dock. **—*idiom.* a wide berth.** Ample space or distance to avoid an unwanted consequence: *gave their angry colleague a wide berth.* [Middle English *birth;* perhaps akin to *beren,* to bear. See BEAR[1].]

ber·tha (bûr′thə) *n.* A wide, deep collar, often of lace, that covers the shoulders of a dress. [French *berthe,* after *Bertha* (died 783), Carolingian queen as the wife of Pepin the Short.]

Ber·the·lot (bĕr-tə-lō′), **Pierre Eugène Marselin.** 1827–1907. French chemist and public official who was a founder of thermochemistry, studied explosives, and was the first to synthesize organic compounds.

Ber·til·lon (bûr′tl-ŏn′, bĕr-tē-yôɴ′), **Alphonse.** 1853–1914. French anthropologist and criminologist who devised the Bertillon system (1880).

Bertillon system *n.* A system formerly used for identifying persons by means of a detailed record of body measurements, physical description, and photographs. The Bertillon system was superseded by the more accurate procedure of fingerprinting. [After Alphonse BERTILLON.]

Ber·wyn (bûr′wĭn). A city of northeast Illinois, a residential suburb of Chicago. Population, 46,849.

ber·yl (bĕr′əl) *n.* A transparent to translucent glassy mineral, essentially aluminum beryllium silicate, $Be_3Al_2Si_6O_{18}$, occurring in hexagonal prisms and constituting the chief source of beryllium. Transparent varieties in white, green, blue, yellow, or pink are valued as gems. [Middle English, from Old French, from Latin *bēryllus,* from Greek *bērullos,* from *bērullion,* from Prakrit *veruliya,* from Pali *veḷuriya;* perhaps akin to Tamil *veḷiru* or *viḷar,* to whiten, become pale.] **—ber′yl·line** (-ə-lĭn, -līn′) *adj.*

be·ryl·li·um (bə-rĭl′ē-əm) *n. Symbol* **Be** A high-melting, lightweight, corrosion-resistant, rigid, steel-gray metallic element used as an aerospace structural material, as a moderator and reflector in nuclear reactors, and in a copper alloy used for springs, electrical contacts, and nonsparking tools. Atomic number 4; atomic weight 9.0122; melting point 1,278°C; boiling point 2,970°C; specific gravity 1.848; valence 2. See table at **element.** [From BERYL.]

Ber·ze·li·us (bər-zē′lē-əs, bĕr-sā′lē-ŏŏs′), Baron **Jöns Jakob.** 1779–1848. Swedish chemist who published a table of atomic weights (1828); discovered cerium (1803), zirconium (1824), and titanium (1825); and isolated silicon (1823).

Bes (bĕs) *n. Mythology.* The Egyptian god of music and revelry.

Be·san·çon (bĭ-zäɴ-sôɴ′). A city of eastern France east of Dijon. It is an industrial center noted for the manufacture of clocks and watches. Population, 113,283.

Bes·ant (bĕz′ənt), **Annie Wood.** 1847–1933. English theosophist, philosopher, and political figure who advocated home rule and educational reforms in India.

be·seech (bĭ-sēch′) *tr.v.* **-sought** (-sôt′) or **-seeched, -seech·ing, -seech·es. 1.** To address an earnest or urgent request to; implore: *beseech them for help.* **2.** To request earnestly; beg for: *beseech help.* See Synonyms at **beg.** [Middle English *bisechen,* from Old English *besēcan* : *be-,* be- + *sēcan,* to seek; see SEEK.] **—be·seech′er** *n.*

be·seem (bĭ-sēm′) *tr.v.* **-seemed, -seem·ing, -seems.** *Archaic.* To be appropriate for; befit. [Middle English *bisemen* : *bi-,* be- + *semen,* to seem; see SEEM.]

be·set (bĭ-sĕt′) *tr.v.* **-set, -set·ting, -sets. 1.** To attack from all sides. **2.** To trouble persistently; harass. See Synonyms at **attack. 3.** To hem in; surround: *"the mountains which beset it round"* (Nathaniel Hawthorne). **4.** To stud, as with jewels. [Middle English *bisetten,* from Old English *besettan.* See **sed-** in Appendix.] **—be·set′ment** *n.*

be·set·ting (bĭ-sĕt′ĭng) *adj.* Constantly troubling.

be·shrew (bĭ-shro͞o′) *tr.v.* **-shrewed, -shrew·ing, -shrews.** *Archaic.* To invoke evil upon; curse. [Middle English *bishrewen* : *bi-,* be- + *shrew,* wicked person; see SHREW.]

be·side (bĭ-sīd′) *prep.* **1.** At the side of; next to. **2.a.** In comparison with: *a proposal that seems quite reasonable beside the others.* **b.** On an equal footing with: *has earned a place beside the best performers in the business.* **3.** In addition to: *"Many creatures beside man live in communities"* (Stuart Chase). See Usage Note at **besides. 4.** Except for. See Usage Note at **besides. 5.** Not relevant to: *a remark that was beside the point.* **—beside** *adv. Archaic.* **1.** In addition. **2.** Nearby. **—*idiom.* beside (oneself).** In a state of extreme excitement or agitation: *They were beside themselves with glee.* [Middle English *biside,* from Old English *be sīdan* : *be,* by; see BY[1] + *sīde,* side.]

be·sides (bĭ-sīdz′) *adv.* **1.** In addition; also. **2.** Moreover; furthermore. See Synonyms at **also. 3.** Otherwise; else: *has been to Mexico but nowhere besides.* **—besides** *prep.* **1.** In addition to. **2.** Except for; other than. [Middle English : *biside,* at the side; see BESIDE + *-es,* adv. suff.; see –S[3].]

USAGE NOTE: In modern usage the senses "in addition to" and "except for" are conveyed more often by *besides* than *beside.* Thus: *He had few friends besides us.* See Usage Note at **together.**

be·siege (bĭ-sēj′) *tr.v.* **-sieged, -sieg·ing, -sieg·es. 1.** To surround with hostile forces. **2.** To crowd around; hem in. **3.** To harass or importune, as with requests: *Reporters besieged the winner for interviews.* **4.** To cause to feel distressed or worried: *She was besieged by problems.* [Middle English *besegen,* probably (with substitution of *bi-,* be-) from *assegen,* from Old French *assegier,* from Vulgar Latin **assedicāre* : Latin *ad-,* ad- + Vulgar Latin **sedicāre,* to sit (from Latin *sedēre;* see SIEGE).] **—be·siege′ment** *n.* **—be·sieg′er** *n.*

SYNONYMS: *besiege, beleaguer, blockade, invest, siege.* The central meaning shared by these verbs is "to surround with hostile forces": *besiege a walled city: a beleaguered settlement; blockaded the harbor; investing a fortress; a castle sieged by foot soldiers and cavalry.*

Bes·kids (bĕs′kĭdz′, bĕs-kēdz′). A mountain range of the western Carpathians extending about 322 km (200 mi) along the Polish-Czechoslovakian border and rising to 1,726 m (5,659 ft) at Babia Góra. The range is divided into the **East Beskids** and the **West Beskids.**

be·smear (bĭ-smîr′) *tr.v.* **-smeared, -smear·ing, -smears.** To smear. [Middle English *bismeorwen,* to make filthy, from Old English *besmirwan,* to besmear : *be-,* be- + *smierwan,* to smear.]

be·smirch (bĭ-smûrch′) *tr.v.* **-smirched, -smirch·ing, -smirch·es. 1.** To stain; sully: *a reputation that was besmirched by slander.* **2.** Make dirty; soil. **—be·smirch′er** *n.* **—be·smirch′ment** *n.*

be·som (bē′zəm) *n.* **1.** A bundle of twigs attached to a handle and used as a broom. **2.** *Sports.* The broom used to sweep the ice from the path of a curling stone. [Middle English, from Old English *besma.*]

besom pocket *n.* A flapless pocket trimmed with welting or stitching. [*besom,* reinforcement around pocket opening.]

be·sot (bĭ-sŏt′) *tr.v.* **-sot·ted, -sot·ting, -sots.** To muddle or stupefy, as with alcoholic liquor or infatuation. [BE– + *sot,* to stupefy (from *sot,* fool; see SOT) or from *assot,* to befool (from Old French *assoter,* from *sot,* foolish).]

be·sought (bĭ-sôt′) *v.* A past tense and a past participle of **beseech.**

be·spake (bĭ-spāk′) *v. Archaic.* A past tense of **bespeak.**

be·spat·ter (bĭ-spăt′ər) *tr.v.* **-tered, -ter·ing, -ters.** To spatter with or as if with mud: *"a thoughtful, anti-activist judge being bespattered with charges of racism, sexism, hypocrisy and dishonesty"* (William Safire).

be·speak (bĭ-spēk′) *tr.v.* **-spoke** (-spōk′), **-spo·ken** (-spō′kən) or **-spoke, -speak·ing, -speaks. 1.** To be or give a sign of; indicate. See Synonyms at **indicate. 2.** To engage, hire, or order in advance. See Synonyms at **book. 3.** To foretell; portend: *fearful weapons that bespeak great loss of life.* **4.** *Archaic.* To speak to; address. [Middle English *bispeken,* to speak out, from Old English *besprecan,* to speak about.]

be·spec·ta·cled (bĭ-spĕk′tə-kəld) *adj.* Wearing eyeglasses.

be·spoke (bĭ-spōk′) *v.* Past tense and a past participle of **bespeak.**

be·spo·ken (bĭ-spō′kən) *v.* A past participle of **bespeak.**

be·sprent (bĭ-sprĕnt′) *adj. Archaic.* Sprinkled over. [Middle English *bispreint,* past participle of *bisprenkle,* to besprinkle, from Old English *besprengan* : *be-,* be- + *sprengan,* to sprinkle.]

be·sprin·kle (bĭ-sprĭng′kəl) *tr.v.* **-kled, -kling, -kles.** To sprinkle. [Probably from Middle English *bisprenklen,* from *bisprengen.* See BESPRENT.]

Bes·sa·ra·bi·a (bĕs′ə-rā′bē-ə). A region of Moldavia and western Ukraine. As the gateway from Russia into the Danube River valley, it was for centuries an invasion route from Asia to Europe. The region became part of Russia in 1812 but declared itself independent in 1918 and later voted for union with Romania, which was forced to cede it to the U.S.S.R. in 1940. **—Bes′sa·ra′bi·an** *adj. & n.*

ă pat	oi boy
ā pay	ou out
âr care	o͝o took
ä father	o͞o boot
ĕ pet	ŭ cut
ē be	ûr urge
ĭ pit	th thin
ī pie	*th* this
îr pier	hw which
ŏ pot	zh vision
ō toe	ə about, item
ô paw	♦ regionalism

Stress marks: **′** (primary); ′ (secondary), as in **dictionary** (dĭk′shə-nĕr′ē)

Bes·sel (bĕs′əl), **Friedrich Wilhelm.** 1784–1846. Prussian astronomer who recalculated the orbit of Halley's comet (1804), verified by parallax the distance from the earth to the twin star 61 Cygni (1838), and developed a class of mathematical functions based on his study of planetary perturbation.

Bes·se·mer (bĕs′ə-mər). A city of north-central Alabama south-southwest of Birmingham. Founded as a mining town, it was named after Sir Henry Bessemer. Population, 31,729.

Bessemer, Sir **Henry.** 1813–1898. British inventor and metallurgist who received more than 100 patents, most notably for the Bessemer process.

Bessemer converter *n.* A large pear-shaped container in which molten iron is converted to steel by the Bessemer process.

Bessemer process *n.* A method for making steel by blasting compressed air through molten iron to burn out excess carbon and impurities. [After Sir Henry BESSEMER.]

Bes·sie (bĕs′ē) *n.* An award given annually since 1984 by the Dance Theater Workshop in New York City for achievement in dance and the performing arts. [After *Bessie* Schönberg (born 1906), German-born American dance teacher.]

best (bĕst) *adj.* Superlative of **good. 1.** Surpassing all others in excellence, achievement, or quality; most excellent: *the best performer; the best grade of ore.* **2.** Most satisfactory, suitable, or useful; most desirable: *the best solution; the best time for planting.* **3.** Greatest; most: *He spoke for the best part of an hour.* **—best** *adv.* Superlative of **well**[2]. **1.** In a most excellent way; most creditably or advantageously. **2.** To the greatest degree or extent; most: *"He was certainly the best hated man in the ship"* (W. Somerset Maugham). **—best** *n.* **1.** One that surpasses all others. **2.** The best part, moment, or value: *The best is still to come. Let's get the best out of life.* **3.** The optimum condition or quality: *look your best. She was at her best in the freestyle competition.* **4.** One's nicest or most formal clothing. **5.** The supreme effort one can make: *doing our best.* **6.** One's warmest wishes or regards: *Give them my best.* **—best** *tr.v.* **best·ed, best·ing, bests.** To get the better of; beat: *"I'm a rough customer, I expect, but I know when I'm bested"* (Nathanael West). ***—idioms.* at best. 1.** Interpreted most favorably; at the most: *no more than 40 people at best in attendance.* **2.** Under the most favorable conditions: *has a top speed of 20 miles per hour at best.* **for the best.** With an ultimately positive or preferable result. **get** (or **have) the best of.** To outdo or outwit; defeat: *My opponent got the best of me in the debate.* [Middle English, from Old English *betst.* See **bhad-** in Appendix.]

Bessemer converter
Pouring molten iron into Bessemer converter and liquid steel into molds

USAGE NOTE: According to rule, *better* should be used in comparisons between two things: *Which house of Congress has the better* (not *best*) *attendance record?* In certain fixed expressions, however, *best* is used idiomatically for comparisons between two: *Put your best foot forward. May the best man win!* See Usage Note at **better**[1], **rather.**

Best (bĕst), **Charles Herbert.** 1899–1978. American-born Canadian physiologist noted for his work on the discovery and application of insulin.

best boy *n.* The chief assistant to the gaffer on a movie or television set.

best-case (bĕst′kās′) *adj.* Most favorable; optimum: *"the best-case scenario of a mild recession"* (Business Week).

be·stead (bĭ-stĕd′) *Archaic. tr.v.* **-stead·ed** or **-stead, -stead·ing, -steads. 1.** To be of service to; aid. **2.** To be of use to; avail. **—bestead** *adj.* Having been placed; located. [Probably BE– + STEAD, to help. Adj., from Middle English *bistad,* placed : *bi-,* be- + *-stad* (ultimately from Old Norse *staddr,* placed, past participle of *stedhja,* to stop, from *stadhr,* place; see **stā-** in Appendix).]

bes·tial (bĕs′chəl, bēs′-) *adj.* **1.** Beastly. **2.** Marked by brutality or depravity. See Synonyms at **brute. 3.** Lacking in intelligence or reason; subhuman. [Middle English, from Old French, from Late Latin *bēstiālis,* from Latin *bēstia,* beast.] **—bes′tial·ly** *adv.*

bes·ti·al·i·ty (bĕs′chē-ăl′ĭ-tē, bēs′-) *n., pl.* **-ties. 1.** The quality or condition of being an animal or like an animal. **2.** Conduct or an action marked by depravity or brutality. **3.** Sexual relations between a human being and an animal.

bes·ti·ar·y (bĕs′chē-ĕr′ē, bēs′-) *n., pl.* **-ies. 1.** A medieval collection of stories providing physical and allegorical descriptions of real or imaginary animals along with an interpretation of the moral significance each animal was thought to embody. A number of common misconceptions relating to natural history were preserved in these popular accounts. **2.** A modern version of such a collection. [Medieval Latin *bēstiārium,* from Latin *bēstia,* beast.]

be·stir (bĭ-stûr′) *tr.v.* **-stirred, -stir·ring, -stirs.** To cause to become active; rouse: *finally bestirred himself to look for work.* [Middle English *bistiren* : probably *bi-,* be- + *stiren,* to rouse; see STIR[1].]

best man *n.* The bridegroom's chief attendant at a wedding.

be·stow (bĭ-stō′) *tr.v.* **-stowed, -stow·ing, -stows. 1.** To present as a gift or an honor; confer: *bestowed high praise on the winners.* **2.** To apply; use: *"On Hester Prynne's story . . . I bestowed much thought"* (Nathaniel Hawthorne). **3.** To store or house. [Middle English *bistowen* : *bi-,* be- + *stowen,* to place; see STOW.] **—be·stow′a·ble** *adj.* **—be·stow′al, be·stow′ment** *n.*

ă pat	oi boy
ā pay	ou out
âr care	o͝o took
ä father	o͞o boot
ĕ pet	ŭ cut
ē be	ûr urge
ĭ pit	th thin
ī pie	*th* this
îr pier	hw which
ŏ pot	zh vision
ō toe	ə about, item
ô paw	♦ regionalism

Stress marks: **′** (primary); ′ (secondary), as in **dictionary** (dĭk′shə-nĕr′ē)

be·strew (bĭ-stro͞o′) *tr.v.* **-strewed, -strewed** or **-strewn** (-stro͞on′), **-strew·ing, -strews. 1.** To strew (a surface) with things so as to cover it: *The crowd bestrewed the streets with confetti.* **2.** To lie scattered over or about: *Books and papers bestrewed the desk.* [Middle English *bistrewen,* from Old English *bestrēowian* : *be-,* be- + *strēowian,* to strew; see STREW.]

be·stride (bĭ-strīd′) *tr.v* **-strode** (-strōd′), **-strid·den** (-strĭd′n), **-strid·ing, -strides. 1.** To sit or stand on with the legs astride; straddle. **2.** To dominate by position; tower over: *"Hitler's ghost, the specter that . . . bestrides mid-twentieth-century history"* (Economist). **3.** *Archaic.* To step or stride across. [Middle English *bistriden,* from Old English *bestrīdan* : *be-,* be- + *strīdan,* to mount a horse; see STRIDE.]

best·sell·er (bĕst′sĕl′ər) *n.* A product, such as a book, that is among those sold in the largest numbers. *—attributive.* Often used to modify another noun: *bestseller lists; a bestseller candidate.* **—best′sell′er·dom** *n.* **—best′-sell′ing** *adj.*

bet (bĕt) *n.* **1.** An agreement usually between two parties that the one who has made an incorrect prediction about an uncertain outcome will forfeit something stipulated to the other; a wager. **2.** An amount or object risked in a wager; a stake. **3.** One on which a stake is or can be placed: *Our team is a sure bet to win.* **4. a.** A plan or an option considered with regard to its probable consequence: *Your best bet is to make reservations ahead of time.* **b.** *Informal.* A view; an opinion: *My bet is that the rain will hold off.* **—bet** *v.* **bet** or **bet·ted, bet·ting, bets.** *—tr.* **1.** To stake (an amount, for example) in a bet. **2.** To make a bet with: *I bet them that we would be first.* **3.** To make a bet on (a contestant or an outcome). **4.** To maintain confidently, as if making a bet: *I bet they were surprised by the news. —intr.* To make or place a bet. ***—idiom.* you bet.** *Informal.* Of course; surely. [Origin unknown.]

SYNONYMS: *bet, ante, pot, stake, wager.* The central meaning shared by these nouns is "something valuable risked on an uncertain outcome": *placed a 50-dollar bet on a horse in the first race; raising the ante in a poker game; won the whole pot in bridge; defeated her opponent and took the stakes; laid a wager on who would get the role.*

bet. *abbr.* Between.

be·ta (bā′tə, bē′-) *n.* **1.** The second letter of the Greek alphabet. See table at **alphabet. 2.** The second item in a series or system of classification. **3.** A mathematical measure of the sensitivity of rates of return on a portfolio or a given stock compared with rates of return on the market as a whole. A high degree of such sensitivity indicates moderate or high price volatility. **4.** *Physics.* **a.** A beta particle. **b.** A beta ray. **5.** *Chemistry.* **a.** The second position from a designated carbon atom in an organic molecule at which an atom or a radical may be substituted. **b.** An isomeric variation of a chemical compound. Used in combination: *beta-estradiol.* [Greek *bēta,* from Canaanite *bēt,* house. See BETH.]

be·ta-ad·re·ner·gic (bā′tə-ăd′rə-nûr′jĭk, bē′-) *adj.* Of, relating to, or being a beta-receptor.

beta-adrenergic block·ing agent (blŏk′ĭng) *n.* See **beta-blocker.**

beta-adrenergic receptor *n.* See **beta-receptor.**

be·ta-block·er (bā′tə-blŏk′ər, bē′-) *n. Physiology.* A drug, such as propanolol, that opposes the excitatory effects of norepinephrine released from sympathetic nerve endings at beta-receptors and is used for the treatment of angina, hypertension, arrhythmia, and migraine. Also called *beta-adrenergic blocking agent.*

be·ta-car·o·tene (bā′tə-kăr′ə-tēn′, bē′-) *n.* One of the isomeric forms of carotene that is widely distributed in nature.

beta cell *n. Physiology.* **1.** Any of the insulin-producing cells of the islets of Langerhans in the pancreas. **2.** Any of the basophilic chromophil cells located in the anterior lobe of the adenohypophysis.

be·ta-en·dor·phin (bā′tə-ĕn-dôr′fĭn, bē′-) *n.* An endorphin produced by the pituitary gland that is a potent pain suppressant.

beta globulin *n. Biochemistry.* A type of globulin in blood plasma that in electrically charged solutions exhibits colloidal mobility between that of the alpha and gamma globulins.

be·ta·ine (bē′tə-ēn′, -ĭn) *n.* **1.** A sweet crystalline alkaloid, $C_5H_{11}NO_2$, occurring in sugar beets and other plants and used in the treatment of muscular degeneration. **2.** Any of several alkaloids with similar structures. [Latin *bēta,* beet + –INE[2].]

be·take (bĭ-tāk′) *tr.v.* **-took** (-to͝ok′), **-tak·en** (-tā′kən), **-tak·ing, -takes. 1.** To cause (oneself) to go or move. **2.** *Archaic.* To commit. [Middle English *bitaken* : *bi-,* be- + *taken,* to take; see TAKE.]

be·ta·meth·a·sone (bā′tə-mĕth′ə-sōn′, bē′-) *n.* A synthetic glucocorticoid, $C_{22}H_{29}FO_5$, that occurs as a white crystalline powder and is used as a topical anti-inflammatory agent for the treatment of dermatological conditions. [BETA + METH(YL) + (PREDNI)S(OL)ONE.]

be·ta-naph·thol (bā′tə-năf′thôl′, -thōl′, -năp′-) *n.* An isomeric form of naphthol, $C_{10}H_7OH$, occurring as white crystals and used in making antioxidants, pigments, and dyes.

be·ta-ox·i·da·tion (bā′tə-ŏk′sĭ-dā′shən, bē′-) *n. Biochemistry.* The oxidative degradation of saturated fatty acids in which two-carbon units are sequentially removed from the molecule with each turn of the cycle.

beta particle *n.* A high-speed electron or positron, especially one emitted in radioactive decay.

beta ray *n.* A stream of beta particles, especially of electrons.

be·ta-re·cep·tor (bā′tə-rĭ-sĕp′tər, bē′-) *n.* A site in the autonomic nervous system in which inhibitory responses occur when adrenergic agents, such as norepinephrine and epinephrine, are released. Activation of beta-receptors causes various physiological reactions, such as relaxation of the bronchial muscles and an increase in the rate and force of cardiac contraction. Also called *beta-adrenergic receptor.*

beta rhythm *n.* See **beta wave.**

be·ta·tron (bā′tə-trŏn′, bē′-) *n.* A magnetic induction electron accelerator capable of accelerating electrons to energies of several hundred million electron volts.

beta wave *n.* The second most common waveform occurring in electroencephalograms of the adult brain, characteristically having a frequency from 13 to 30 cycles per second. It is associated with an alert waking state but can also occur as a sign of anxiety or apprehension. Also called *beta rhythm.*

be·tel (bēt′l) *n.* An evergreen Indo-Malayan climbing or trailing shrub *(Piper betle),* having usually ovate leaves used to wrap betel nuts. [Portuguese, from Malayalam *vettila, verrila,* from Tamil *verrilai.*]

Be·tel·geuse (bēt′l-jo͞oz′, bĕt′l-jœz′) *n.* A bright-red intrinsic variable star, 527 light-years from Earth, in the constellation Orion. [French *Bételgeuse,* probably from Arabic *bayt al-jauzā.*]

betel nut also **be·tel·nut** (bēt′l-nŭt′) *n.* The seed of the betel palm, chewed with betel leaves, lime, and flavorings as a mild stimulant. Also called *areca nut.*

betel palm *n.* A tropical Asian feather-leaved palm *(Areca catechu)* cultivated for its seeds. Also called *catechu.*

bête noire (bĕt nwär′) *n.* One that is particularly disliked or that is to be avoided: *"Tax shelters had long been the bête noire of reformers"* (Irwin Ross). [French : *bête,* beast + *noire,* black.]

beth (bĕt) *n.* The second letter of the Hebrew alphabet. See table at **alphabet.** [Hebrew *bêt,* from *bayit,* house.]

be·than·e·chol (bĕ-thăn′ĭ-kôl′, -kōl′) *n.* A cholinergic drug, $C_7H_{17}CLN_2O_2$, that acts principally by stimulating the parasympathetic nervous system and is used in the form of its chloride to treat abdominal distention and urinary retention. [Perhaps *beth* (blend of BETA and METHYL) + -ANE + CHOL(INE).]

Beth·a·ny (bĕth′ə-nē). **1.** A village of ancient Palestine at the foot of the Mount of Olives near Jerusalem. According to the New Testament, it was the site of the resurrection of Lazarus. **2.** A city of central Oklahoma west of Oklahoma City. It was settled in 1906. Population, 22,130.

Be·the (bā′tə), **Hans Albrecht.** Born 1906. German-born American physicist. He won a 1967 Nobel Prize for research on the energy production of stars.

beth·el (bĕth′əl) *n.* **1.** A hallowed or holy place. **2.a.** A chapel for seafarers. **b.** *Chiefly British.* A Nonconformist chapel, especially a Baptist or Methodist one. [Hebrew *bêt'el,* house of God : *bêt,* house + *'el,* God.]

Beth·el (bĕth′əl). **1.** (*also* bĕth′ĕl′). A town of ancient Palestine north of Jerusalem. It is now a major archaeological site. **2.** A town of southwest Connecticut southeast of Danbury. It has varied light industries. Population, 16,004.

Bethel Park. A borough of southwest Pennsylvania, an industrial suburb of Pittsburgh. Population, 34,755.

Be·thes·da (bə-thĕz′də). An unincorporated city of west-central Maryland, a residential suburb of Washington, D.C. The National Institutes of Health and Naval Medical Center are here. Population, 63,022.

be·think (bĭ-thĭngk′) *v.* **-thought** (-thôt′), **-think·ing, -thinks.** —*tr.* **1.** To cause (oneself) to reflect on or consider. **2.** To remind (oneself); remember. See Synonyms at **remember.** —*intr. Archaic.* To meditate; ponder. [Middle English *bithinken,* from Old English *bethencan.* See **tong-** in Appendix.]

Beth·le·hem (bĕth′lĭ-hĕm′, -lē-əm). **1.** A town in the West Bank south of Jerusalem. It is the traditional birthplace of Jesus. Population, 25,000. **2.** A city of eastern Pennsylvania on the Lehigh River north-northwest of Philadelphia. It is an important steel-producing center. Population, 70,419.

Beth·mann-Holl·weg (bĕt′mən-hôl′väg′, -män-), **Theobald von.** 1856–1921. German politician who as chancellor (1909–1917) was opposed to but unable to prevent unrestricted submarine warfare during World War I.

be·thought (bĭ-thôt′) *v.* Past tense and past participle of **bethink.**

Be·thune (bə-tho͞on′, -thyo͞on′), **Mary McLeod.** 1875–1955. American educator who sought improved racial relations and educational opportunities for Black Americans. She was part of the U.S. delegation to the first United Nations meeting (1945).

be·tide (bĭ-tīd′) *v.* **-tid·ed, -tid·ing, -tides.** —*tr.* To happen to. —*intr.* To take place; befall. See Synonyms at **happen.** [Middle English *bitiden* : *bi-,* be- + *tiden,* to happen (from Old English *tīdan;* see TIDE[2]).]

be·times (bĭ-tīmz′) *adv.* **1.** In good time; early: *"A beneficent microclimate brings out the camellias betimes"* (John Russell). **2.** Once in a while; on occasion. **3.** *Archaic.* Quickly; soon. [Middle English *bitimes* : *bi,* by; see BY[1] + *time,* time; see TIME + *-es,* adv. suff.; see -S[3].]

bê·tise (bā-tēz′) *n., pl.* **-tises** (-tēz′). **1.** Stupidity; folly: *"The bêtise of our human community is everywhere"* (Thornton Wilder). **2.** A stupid or foolish act or remark. [French, from *bête,* beast, fool, foolish, from Old French *beste,* beast. See BEAST.]

Bet·je·man (bĕch′ə-mən), Sir **John.** 1906–1984. British poet and poet laureate (1972–1984) whose often nostalgic works, in collections such as *A Few Late Chrysanthemums* (1955), praise the English countryside.

be·to·ken (bĭ-tō′kən) *tr.v.* **-kened, -ken·ing, -kens.** To be or give a sign or portent of. See Synonyms at **indicate.** [Middle English *bitokenen* : *bi-,* be- + *toknen,* to signify (from Old English *tācnian;* see **deik-** in Appendix).]

bet·o·ny (bĕt′n-ē) *n., pl.* **-nies. 1.** Any of several plants of the widespread genus *Stachys* in the mint family, especially *S. officinalis,* native chiefly to Europe and having spikes of usually reddish-purple flowers. It was once popular in herbal medicine. Also called *woundwort.* **2.** The lousewort. [Middle English, from Old French *betoine,* from Medieval Latin *betōnia,* both from Latin *vettōnica,* probably from *Vettōnēs,* an ancient Iberian tribe.]

be·took (bĭ-to͝ok′) *v.* Past tense of **betake.**

be·tray (bĭ-trā′) *tr.v.* **-trayed, -tray·ing, -trays. 1.a.** To give aid or information to an enemy of; commit treason against: *betray one's country.* **b.** To deliver into the hands of an enemy in violation of a trust or allegiance: *betrayed Christ to the Romans.* **2.** To be false or disloyal to: *betrayed their cause; betray one's better nature.* **3.** To divulge in a breach of confidence: *betray a secret.* **4.** To make known unintentionally: *Her hollow laugh betrayed her contempt for the idea.* **5.** To reveal against one's desire or will. See Synonyms at **reveal[1]. 6.** To lead astray; deceive. See Synonyms at **deceive.** [Middle English *bitrayen* : *bi-,* be- + *trayen,* to betray (from Old French *trair,* from Latin *trādere,* to hand over; see TRADITION).] —**be·tray′al** *n.* —**be·tray′er** *n.*

be·troth (bĭ-trōth′, -trôth′) *tr.v.* **-trothed, -troth·ing, -troths. 1.** To promise to give in marriage: *was betrothed to a member of the royal family.* **2.** To promise to marry. [Middle English *bitrouthen* : *bi-,* be- + *trouth,* troth (from Old English *trēowth;* see **deru-** in Appendix).]

be·troth·al (bĭ-trō′*th*əl, -trô′thəl) *n.* **1.** The act of betrothing or the fact of being betrothed. **2.** A mutual promise to marry; an engagement: *announced their betrothal the next day.*

be·trothed (bĭ-trō*th*d′, -trôtht′) *adj.* Engaged to be married. —**betrothed** *n.* A person to whom one is engaged to be married.

bet·ta (bĕt′ə) *n.* Any of various species of small, brightly colored, long-finned freshwater fishes of the genus *Betta,* found in southeast Asia. [New Latin *Betta,* genus name.]

Bet·ten·dorf (bĕt′n-dôrf′). A city of eastern Iowa, an industrial suburb of Davenport on the Mississippi River. Population, 27,381.

bet·ter[1] (bĕt′ər) *adj.* Comparative of **good. 1.** Greater in excellence or higher in quality than another of the same class, set, or kind. **2.** More useful, suitable, or desirable than another or others: *found a better way to go; a suit with a better fit than that one.* **3.** More highly skilled or adept than another or others: *I am better at math than English.* **4.** Greater or larger: *argued for the better part of an hour.* **5.** More advantageous or favorable than others; improved: *a better chance of success.* **6.** Healthier or more fit than before: *The patient is better today.* —**better** *adv.* Comparative of **well[2]. 1.** In a more excellent way. **2.a.** To a greater extent or degree: *better suited to the job; likes it better without sauce.* **b.** To greater advantage; preferably: *a deed better left undone.* **3.** More: *It took me better than a year to recover.* —**better** *n.* **1.** One that is greater in excellence or higher in quality than another or others. **2.** A superior, as in standing, competence, or intelligence. —**better** *v.* **-tered, -ter·ing, -ters.** —*tr.* **1.** To make better; improve: *trying to better conditions in the prison; bettered myself by changing jobs.* See Synonyms at **improve. 2.** To surpass or exceed. —*intr.* To become better. —***idioms.* for the better.** Resulting in or aiming at an improvement: *Her condition took a turn for the better.* **had better.** *Usage Problem.* Ought to; must: *We had better go before the storm becomes worse.* **think better of.** To change one's mind about (a course of action) after reconsideration. [Middle English, from Old English *betera.* See **bhad-** in Appendix.]

USAGE NOTE: The phrase *had better* is acceptable, as long as the *had* or its contraction is preserved: *You had better do it* or *You'd better do it,* but not *You better do it.* See Usage Notes at **best, rather.**

bet·ter[2] (bĕt′ər) *n.* Variant of **bettor.**

better half *n. Informal.* One's spouse. [From *my better half,* the larger part of me, that is, a close friend.]

bet·ter·ment (bĕt′ər-mənt) *n.* **1.** An improvement over what has been the case: *financial betterment.* **2.** *Law.* An improvement beyond normal upkeep and repair that adds to the value of real property.

bet·ter-off (bĕt′ər-ôf′, -ŏf′) *adj.* Being in a better or more prosperous condition.

bet·tor also **bet·ter** (bĕt′ər) *n.* One that bets or places a bet.

be·tween (bĭ-twēn′) *prep. Abbr.* **bet. 1.a.** In or through the position or interval separating: *between the trees; between 11 o'clock and 12 o'clock.* **b.** Intermediate to, as in quantity,

Mary McLeod Bethune

betony

amount, or degree: *It costs between 15 and 20 dollars.* **2.** *Usage Problem.* Connecting spatially: *a railroad between the two cities.* **3.** *Usage Problem.* Associating or uniting in a reciprocal action or relationship: *an agreement between workers and management; a certain resemblance between the two stories.* **4.a.** By the combined effort or effect of: *Between them they succeeded.* **b.** In the combined ownership of: *They had only a few dollars between them.* **5.** As measured against. Often used to express a reciprocal relationship: *choose between riding and walking.* **—between** *adv.* In an intermediate space, position, or time; in the interim. **—*idioms.* between you and me.** In the strictest confidence. **in between.** In an intermediate situation: *My roommates disagreed and I was caught in between.* **in between times.** During an intervening period: *has written several books and teaches in between times.* [Middle English *bitwene,* from Old English *betwēonum.* See **dwo-** in Appendix.] **—between′ness** *n.*

USAGE NOTE: According to a widely repeated but unjustified tradition, "*between* is used for two, and *among* for more than two." It is true that *between* is the only choice when exactly two entities are specified: *the choice between* (not *among*) *good and evil, the rivalry between* (not *among*) *Great Britain and France.* When more than two entities are involved, however, or when the number of entities is unspecified, the choice of one or the other word depends on the intended sense. *Between* is used when the entities are considered as distinct individuals; *among,* when they are considered as a mass or collectivity. Thus in the sentence *The bomb landed between the houses,* the houses are seen as points that define the boundaries of the area of impact (so that we presume that none of the individual houses was hit). In *The bomb landed among the houses,* the area of impact is considered to be the general location of the houses, taken together (in which case it is left open whether any houses were hit). By the same token, we may speak of *a series of wars between the Greek cities,* which suggests that each city was an independent belligerent, or of *a series of wars among the Greek cities,* which allows as well the possibility that the belligerents were shifting alliances of cities. For this reason, *among* is most appropriate to indicate inclusion in a group: *She is among the best of our young sculptors. There is a spy among you* (this last is arguably appropriate even when there are only two addressees; certainly *between* would be impossible). *Between* is the preferred choice when the entities are seen as determining the limits or endpoints of a range: *The plane went down somewhere between Quito, Lima, and La Paz. The truck driver had obviously been drinking between stops.*

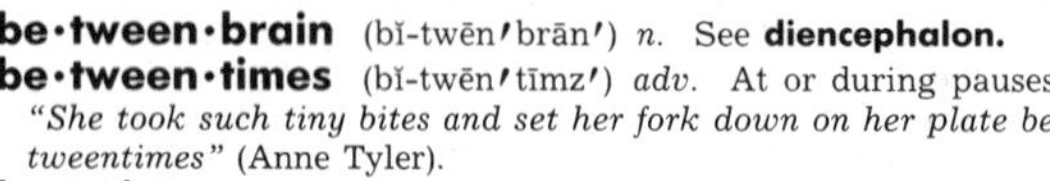

be·tween·brain (bĭ-twēn′brān′) *n.* See **diencephalon.**

be·tween·times (bĭ-twēn′tīmz′) *adv.* At or during pauses: *"She took such tiny bites and set her fork down on her plate betweentimes"* (Anne Tyler).

be·twixt (bĭ-twĭkst′) *adv. & prep.* Between. **—*idiom.* betwixt and between.** In an intermediate position; neither wholly one thing nor another. [Middle English *bitwixt,* from Old English *betwix.* See **dwo-** in Appendix.]

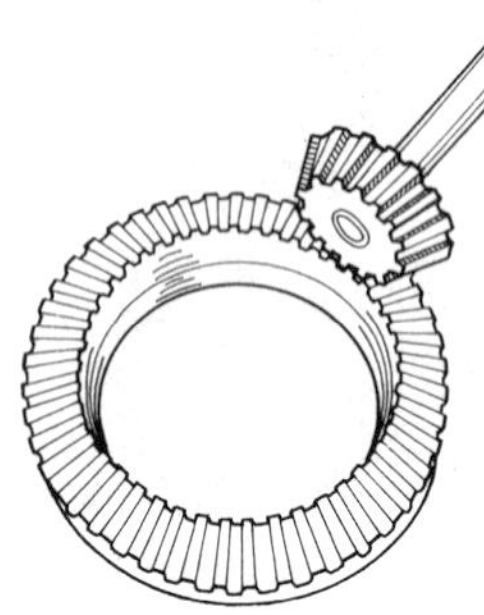
bevel gear

Beu·lah (byo͞o′lə) *n.* **1.** *Bible.* The land of Israel in the Old Testament. **2.** The land of peace described in John Bunyan's *Pilgrim's Progress.*

beurre blanc (bûr′ blängk′, bœr bläN′) *n.* A sauce made with butter, shallots, and vinegar or lemon juice, often served with seafood. [French : *beurre,* butter + *blanc,* white, not browned.]

Beuys (boiz, bois), **Joseph.** 1921–1986. German artist who attempted to convey his highly politicized views through sculpture, drawings, and performance art.

BeV *abbr.* Billion electron volts.

Bev·an (bĕv′ən), **Aneurin.** 1897–1960. Welsh-born British politician who as minister of health (1945–1951) was the chief architect of the National Health Service.

bev·el (bĕv′əl) *n.* **1.** The angle or inclination of a line or surface that meets another at any angle but 90°. **2.** Two rules joined together as adjustable arms used to measure or draw angles of any size or to fix a surface at an angle. In this sense, also called *bevel square.* **—bevel** *v.* **-eled, -el·ing, -els** or **-elled, -el·ling, -els.** *—tr.* To cut at an inclination that forms an angle other than a right angle: *beveled the edges of the table.* *—intr.* To be inclined; slant. [Possibly from Old French **bevel,* perhaps from *baif,* open-mouthed, from *baer,* to gape, from Vulgar Latin **badāre.*]

bevel gear *n.* Either of a pair of gears with teeth surfaces cut so that they can connect unparallel gear shafts.

bevel square *n.* See **bevel** (sense 2).

bev·er·age (bĕv′ər-ĭj, bĕv′rĭj) *n.* Any one of various liquids for drinking, usually excluding water. [Middle English, from Old French *bevrage,* from *beivre,* to drink, from Latin *bibere.* See **pō(i)-** in Appendix.]

Bev·er·idge (bĕv′ər-ĭj, bĕv′rĭj), **Albert Jeremiah.** 1862–1927. American politician and historian. A U.S. senator from Indiana (1899–1911), he is best known for his historical works, most notably *The Life of John Marshall* (1916–1919).

Bev·er·ly (bĕv′ər-lē). A city of northeast Massachusetts northeast of Boston. It was settled in 1626. The schooner *Hannah,* the first ship of the Continental Navy, was outfitted here (1775). Population, 37,655.

Beverly Hills. A city of southern California surrounded by Los Angeles. It adjoins Hollywood and is famous as a fashionable residential area for show business personalities. Population, 32,367.

Bev·in (bĕv′ĭn), **Ernest.** 1884–1951. British labor leader and politician who served as minister of labor (1940–1945) and foreign minister (1945–1951) and was instrumental in postwar diplomacy, notably the NATO treaty of 1949.

bev·y (bĕv′ē) *n., pl.* **-ies. 1.** A group of animals or birds, especially larks or quail. **2.** A group or an assemblage: *a bevy of beauties.* See Synonyms at **flock**[1]. [Middle English, from Anglo-Norman *bevee.*]

be·wail (bĭ-wāl′) *tr.v.* **-wailed, -wail·ing, -wails. 1.** To cry over; lament: *bewail the dead.* **2.** To express sorrow or unhappiness over: *"bewailing the possible effects of double-digit unemployment"* (Washington Post). [Middle English *biwailen* : *bi-,* be- + *wailen;* see WAIL.] **—be·wail′er** *n.* **—be·wail′ment** *n.*

be·ware (bĭ-wâr′) *v.* **-wared, -war·ing, -wares.** *—tr.* To be on guard against; be cautious of: *"Beware the ides of March"* (Shakespeare). *—intr.* To be cautious; exert caution: *We had to beware of the icy patches on the road. Beware of the dog.* [Middle English *ben war* : *ben,* to be; see BE + *war,* on one's guard; see WARE[2].]

be·whis·kered (bĭ-hwĭs′kərd, -wĭs′-) *adj.* Having whiskers.

be·wigged (bĭ-wĭgd′) *adj.* Wearing a wig.

be·wil·der (bĭ-wĭl′dər) *tr.v.* **-dered, -der·ing, -ders. 1.** To confuse or befuddle, especially with numerous conflicting situations, objects, or statements. See Synonyms at **puzzle. 2.** To cause to lose one's bearings; disorient: *The twists and turns in the cave soon bewildered us.* **—be·wil′dered·ly** *adv.* **—be·wil′dered·ness** *n.* **—be·wil′der·ing·ly** *adv.*

WORD HISTORY: The word *bewilder* is probably used much more commonly in its figurative sense "to confuse" than in its literal sense "to cause to lose one's bearings; disorient." Yet the latter sense is most likely the clue to the original source of this word. *Bewilder,* first recorded in 1684, is made up of the prefix *be-,* here meaning "completely," and the verb *wilder,* meaning "to cause to lose one's way," first found in 1613. *Wilder* may in turn be a back-formation from *wilderness,* a much older word than *wilder.* Users of English might have erroneously thought that *wilderness* was derived from an older verb *wilder,* which they then used with reference to the loss of one's way that can occur in a wilderness.

be·wil·der·ment (bĭ-wĭl′dər-mənt) *n.* **1.** The condition of being confused or disoriented. **2.** A situation of perplexity or confusion; a tangle: *a bewiderment of lies and half-truths.*

be·witch (bĭ-wĭch′) *tr.v.* **-witched, -witch·ing, -witch·es. 1.** To place under one's power by or as if by magic; cast a spell over. **2.** To captivate completely; entrance. See Synonyms at **charm.** [Middle English *biwicchen* : probably *bi-,* be- + *wicche,* witch; see WITCH.] **—be·witch′er** *n.* **—be·witch′er·y** *n.*

be·witch·ing (bĭ-wĭch′ĭng) *adj.* Enchanting as if with a magic spell; fascinating. **—be·witch′ing·ly** *adv.*

be·witch·ment (bĭ-wĭch′mənt) *n.* **1.a.** The act of bewitching. **b.** The power to bewitch. **c.** The state of being bewitched. **2.** A bewitching spell.

be·wray (bĭ-rā′) *tr.v.* **-wrayed, -wray·ing, -wrays.** *Archaic.* To disclose or betray. [Middle English *biwreien* : *bi-,* be- + *wreien,* to accuse (from Old English *wrēgan*).]

bey (bā) *n.* **1.** A provincial governor in the Ottoman Empire. **2.a.** A ruler of the former kingdom of Tunis. **b.** Used as the title for such a ruler. **3.** Used formerly as a title for various Turkish and Egyptian dignitaries. [Turkish, from Old Turkic *beg,* ruler, prince.]

be·yond (bē-ŏnd′, bĭ-yŏnd′) *prep.* **1.** On the far side of; past: *Just beyond the fence.* **2.** Later than; after: *beyond midnight.* **3.** To a degree that is past the understanding, reach, or scope of: *an evil beyond remedy.* **4.** To a degree or amount greater than: *rich beyond his wildest dreams.* **5.** In addition to: *asked for nothing beyond peace and quiet.* **—beyond** *adv.* **1.** Farther along or away. **2.** In addition; more: *wanted her share but nothing beyond.* **—beyond** *n.* **1.** That which is past or to a degree greater than knowledge or experience; the unknown: *"Sputnik, the first satellite to enter the great beyond of space"* (Dale Russakoff). **2.** The world beyond death; the hereafter. [Middle English *biyonde,* from Old English *begeondan* : *be,* by; see BY[1] + *geondan,* on the far side of; see **i-** in Appendix.]

bez·ant (bĕz′ənt, bə-zănt′) *n.* **1.** See **solidus** (sense 1). **2.** *Architecture.* A flat disk used as an ornament. [Middle English *besant,* from Old French, from Medieval Latin *Bȳzantius,* from Latin, of Byzantium.]

bez·el (bĕz′əl) *n.* **1.** A slanting surface or bevel on the edge of a cutting tool, such as a chisel. **2.** The upper, faceted portion of a cut gem, above the girdle and below the table. **3.** A groove or flange designed to hold a beveled edge, as of a watch crystal or a gem. [Probably French dialectal; akin to French *biseau,* from *bis,* two times, from Latin. See **dwo-** in Appendix.]

Bé·ziers (bāz-yā′). A city of southern France southwest of Montpellier. An ancient Gallic fortress, it is an industrial center with an important trade in wines. Population, 76,647.

be·zique (bə-zēk′) *n.* *Games.* A card game similar to pinochle that is played with a deck of 64 cards. [French *bésigue,* possibly from Italian *bazzica,* a kind of card game.]

be·zoar (bē′zôr′, -zōr′) *n.* A hard indigestible mass of material, such as hair, vegetable fibers, or fruits, found in the stomachs or intestines of animals, especially ruminants, and human beings.

It was formerly considered to be an antidote to poisons and to possess magic properties. [Middle English *bezear,* stone used as antidote to poison, probably from Old French *bezahar,* gastric or intestinal mass used as antidote to poison, from Arabic *bāzahr,* from Persian *pādzahr* : *pād-,* protector (from Avestan *pātar-;* see **pā-** in Appendix) + *zahr,* poison (from Middle Persian; see **g^when-** in Appendix).]

Bez·wa·da (bĕz-wä′də). See **Vijayawada.**

bf also **b.f.** or **bf** *abbr.* **1.** Board foot. **2.** Boldface.

b.f. or **B/F** *abbr. Accounting.* Brought forward.

B.F.A. *abbr.* Bachelor of Fine Arts.

BG or **B.G.** *abbr.* Brigadier general.

bg. *abbr.* **1.** Background. **2.** Bag.

BGH *abbr.* Bovine growth hormone.

B-girl (bē′gûrl′) *n.* A woman employed by a bar to encourage customers to spend money freely. [B(AR)[1] + GIRL.]

BH *abbr.* Bill of health.

BHA (bē′ăch-ā′) *n.* A white, waxy phenolic antioxidant, $C_{11}H_{16}O_2$, used to preserve fats and oils, especially in foods. [B(UTYLATED) H(YDROXY)A(NISOLE).]

Bha·ga·vad-Gi·ta (bä′gə-väd-gē′tə) *n. Hinduism.* A sacred Hindu text that is incorporated into the *Mahabharata,* an ancient Sanskrit epic. It takes the form of a philosophical dialogue in which Krishna instructs the prince Arjuna in ethical matters and the nature of God. [Sanskrit *bhagavad-gītā,* song of the Blessed One (Krishna) : *bhagavant-,* fortunate, blessed (from *bhagaḥ,* good fortune; see **bhag-** in Appendix) + *gītā,* song (from *gāyati,* he sings).]

bhak·ti (bŭk′tē) *n. Hinduism.* The devotional way of achieving salvation, emphasizing the loving faith of a devotee for a deity and open to all persons irrespective of sex or caste. [Sanskrit *bhaktiḥ,* devotion, from *bhajati,* to apportion. See BHAGAVAD-GITA.]

bhang also **bang** (băng) *n.* A preparation from the leaves and seed capsules of the cannabis plant, smoked, chewed, eaten, or infused and drunk to obtain mild euphoria. [Ultimately from Sanskrit *bhaṅgā.*]

Bhat·pa·ra (bät-pä′rə). A city of northeast India on the Hooghly River north of Calcutta. Once a center of Sanskrit learning, it is now part of a vast industrial complex. Population, 260,761.

Bhav·na·gar (bou-nŭg′ər, bäv-). A city of western India on the Gulf of Cambay south of Ahmadabad. It is a manufacturing center and major port. Population, 307,121.

BHC *abbr.* Benzene hexachloride.

bhd. *abbr.* Bulkhead.

Bhi·lai·na·gar (bĭ-lī′nə-gər) or **Bhi·lai** (bĭ-lī′). A city of east-central India east of Nagpur. It is the site of a large state-owned steel industry built with Soviet assistance. Population, 290,090.

Bhn. *abbr.* Brinell hardness number.

Bho·pal[1] (bō-päl′). A city of central India north-northwest of Nagpur. Founded in the early 18th century, it is an industrial and trade center. In 1984 a toxic gas leak at an insecticide plant killed more than 2,000 people. Population, 671,018.

Bho·pal[2] (bō-päl′). An industrial disaster, especially in a developing country, that causes significant damage to the surrounding population and environment: *"How inevitable . . . were future Bhopals?"* (Fergus M. Bordewich).

B-ho·ri·zon (bē′hə-rī′zən) *n.* In ABC soil, the second or subsurface zone of soil made of clay and oxidized materials and organic matter obtained from the A-horizon by leaching; subsoil. Also called *zone of accumulation, zone of illuviation.*

bhp or **b.hp.** *abbr.* Brake horsepower.

BHT (bē′ăch-tē′) *n.* A crystalline phenolic antioxidant, $C_{15}H_{24}O$, used to preserve fats and oils, especially in foods. [B(UTYLATED) H(YDROXY)T(OLUENE).]

Bhu. *abbr.* Bhutan.

Bhu·ba·nes·war (bo͞o′bə-nĕsh′wər). A city of east-central India southwest of Calcutta. It is known for its Hindu and Buddhist shrines. Population, 219,211.

Bhu·tan (bo͞o-tăn′, -tän′). *Abbr.* **Bhu.** An isolated country of central Asia in the eastern Himalaya Mountains. Great Britain and India have long exerted influence over the kingdom. Thimbu is the capital and the largest city. Population, 1,232,000.

Bhu·tan·ese (bo͞o′tə-nēz′, -nēs′) *adj.* Of or relating to Bhutan or its people, language, or culture. **—Bhutanese** *n., pl.* **Bhutanese. 1.** A native or inhabitant of Bhutan. **2.** The Sino-Tibetan language of Bhutan.

Bhut·to (bo͞o′tō), **Benazir.** Born 1953. Pakistani politician who served as prime minister (1988–1990).

Bhutto, Zulfikar Ali. 1928–1979. Pakistani politician who formed the Pakistan People's Party (1967) and became president (1971) and prime minister (1973). In 1977 he was deposed by a coup d'état and later executed.

bi (bī) *Slang. n., pl.* **bi's.** A bisexual person. **—bi** *adj.* Bisexual.

Bi The symbol for the element **bismuth.**

bi–[1] or **bin–** *pref.* **1.a.** Two: *biform.* **b.** Both: *binaural.* **c.** Both sides, parts, or directions: *biconcave.* **2.a.** Occurring at intervals of two: *bicentennial.* **b.** *Usage Problem.* Occurring twice during: *biweekly.* **3.a.** Containing twice the proportion of a specified chemical element or group necessary for stability: *bicarbonate.* **b.** Containing two chemical atoms, radicals, or groups: *biphenyl.* [Latin *bis, bi-,* twice, and *bīnī,* two by two; see **dwo-** in Appendix.]

USAGE NOTE: *Bimonthly* and *biweekly* mean "once every two months" and "once every two weeks." For "twice a month" and "twice a week," the words *semimonthly* and *semiweekly* should be used. Since there is a great deal of confusion over the distinction, a writer is well advised to substitute expressions like *every two months* or *twice a month* where possible. However, used as nouns to denote "a publication that appears every two months," the words with *bi–* are unavoidable.

bi–[2] *pref.* Variant of **bio–.**

BIA *abbr.* Bureau of Indian Affairs.

Bi·a·fra (bē-ăf′rə, -ä′frə). A region of eastern Nigeria on the **Bight of Biafra,** an arm of the Gulf of Guinea stretching from the Niger River delta to northern Gabon. It formed a secessionist state from May 1967 to January 1970. **—Bi·a′fran** *adj. & n.*

Bi·ak (bē-yäk′). The largest of the Schouten Islands of Indonesia, off the northwest coast of New Guinea. In World War II it was the scene of heavy fighting from May 27 to June 20, 1944.

bi·a·ly (bē-ä′lē) *n., pl.* **-lys.** A flat, round baked roll topped with onion flakes. [After BIALYSTOK.]

Bia·ly·stok (bē-ä′lĭ-stôk′, byä′wĭ-). A city of northeast Poland near the border of Belorussia. About half the city's population was killed by Nazi occupation forces (1941–1944). Today it is an industrial and transportation center. Population, 245,400.

bi·an·nu·al (bī-ăn′yo͞o-əl) *adj.* Happening twice each year; semiannual. **—bi·an′nu·al·ly** *adv.*

Biar·ritz (bē′ə-rĭts′, bē′ə-rĭts′). A city of southwest France on the Bay of Biscay near the Spanish border. It is a fashionable resort. Population, 26,598.

bi·as (bī′əs) *n.* **1.** A line going diagonally across the grain of fabric: *Cut the cloth on the bias.* **2.** *Usage Problem.* **a.** A preference or an inclination, especially one that inhibits impartial judgment. **b.** An unfair act or policy stemming from prejudice. **3.** A statistical sampling or testing error caused by systematically favoring some outcomes over others. **4.** *Sports.* **a.** A weight or irregularity in a ball that causes it to swerve, as in lawn bowling. **b.** The tendency of such a ball to swerve. **5.** The fixed voltage applied to an electrode. **—bias** *adj.* Slanting or diagonal; oblique: *a bias fold.* **—bias** *tr.v.* **-ased, -as·ing, -as·es** or **-assed, -as·sing, -as·ses. 1.** To influence in a particular, typically unfair direction; prejudice. **2.** To apply a small voltage to (a grid). [French *biais,* slant, from Provençal, perhaps ultimately from Greek *epikarsios,* slanted.]

Bhutan

SYNONYMS: *bias, color, jaundice, prejudice, warp.* The central meaning shared by these verbs is "to influence unfavorably or detrimentally": *past experiences that have biased his outlook; behavior that has colored my opinion of her; a view of campaign promises that have become jaundiced; lying that has prejudiced the public against the administration; bitterness that has warped your judgment.* See also Synonyms at **incline, predilection.**

USAGE NOTE: In its sense of "a preference or an inclination," *bias* can, in principle, be used with equal appropriateness for an inclination that is beneficial or for one that is adverse. But in a development similar to the one undergone by *discrimination, bias* has come to be used most commonly when it is believed that some injustice is involved. Thus, 90 percent of the Usage Panel accepts the sentence *The court's ruling provided a strong endorsement of affirmative action programs as a means to counter the effect of decades of racial bias in police hiring practices.* Moreover, it has become increasingly acceptable to use *bias* to refer not just to an unfair preference but to an unfair act or policy based on such a preference, as in *"The report also notes 'remarkably consistent' biases in administration R&D budget requests. These included emphasis on military R&D and civil basic research"* (Christian Science Monitor).

bias-ply tire

bi·ased also **bi·assed** (bī′əst) *adj. Usage Problem.* Marked by or exhibiting bias; prejudiced: *gave a biased account of the trial.* See Usage Note at **bias.**

bi·as-ply tire (bī′əs-plī′) *n.* A pneumatic tire having crossed layers of ply cord running diagonally to the tread.

bi·ath·lon (bī-ăth′lən, -lŏn′) *n. Sports.* A competition that combines events in cross-country skiing and rifle shooting. [BI–[1] + Greek *athlon,* prize of contest.] **—bi·ath′lete** (-lēt) *n.*

bi·ax·i·al (bī-ăk′sē-əl) *adj.* Having two axes. **—bi·ax′i·al′i·ty** (-ăl′ĭ-tē) *n.* **—bi·ax′i·al·ly** *adv.*

bib (bĭb) *n.* **1.** A piece of cloth or plastic secured under the chin and worn, especially by small children, to protect the clothing while eating. **2.a.** The part of an apron or pair of overalls worn over the chest. **b.** Bibbed overalls worn while skiing. **—bib** *tr. & intr.v.* **bibbed, bib·bing, bibs.** To drink or to indulge in drinking. [Probably from Middle English *bibben,* to drink heartily, from Latin *bibere.* See **pō(i)-** in Appendix.]

bib. or **Bib.** *abbr.* Biblical.

Bib. *abbr.* Bible.

bib and tucker *n. Informal.* Clothing: *put on my best bib and tucker for the reception.*

bibb (bĭb) *n.* **1.** *Nautical.* A bracket on the mast of a ship to support the trestletrees. **2.** A bibcock. [Alteration of BIB.]

ă pat	oi boy
ā pay	ou out
âr care	o͝o took
ä father	o͞o boot
ĕ pet	ŭ cut
ē be	ûr urge
ĭ pit	th thin
ī pie	*th* this
îr pier	hw which
ŏ pot	zh vision
ō toe	ə about, item
ô paw	♦ regionalism

Stress marks: **′** (primary); ′ (secondary), as in **dictionary** (dĭk′shə-nĕr′ē)

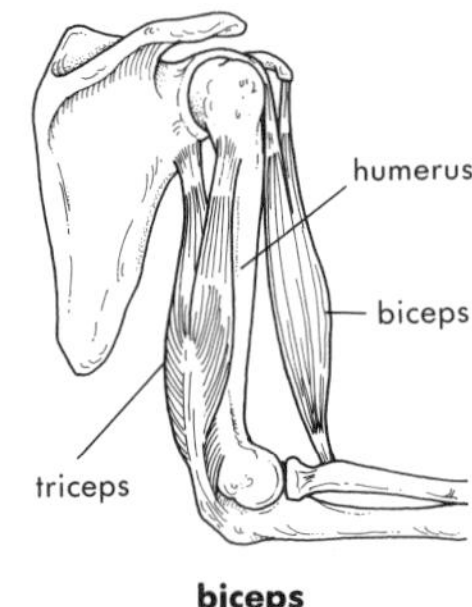

biceps

bibbed (bĭbd) *adj.* Having a bib: *bibbed overalls.*

bib·ber (bĭb′ər) *n.* A tippler; a drinker. [From BIB.]

Bibb lettuce (bĭb) *n.* A kind of lettuce forming a small, loose head and having tender, dark green leaves. [After Jack *Bibb,* 19th-century American vegetable grower.]

bib·cock (bĭb′kŏk′) *n.* A faucet with a nozzle that is bent downward; a bibb. [Probably BIB + COCK[1].]

bi·be·lot (bē′bə-lō′, bē-blō′) *n.* **1.** A small decorative object; a trinket. **2.** A miniature book, especially one that is finely crafted. [French, from Old French *beubelet,* from a reduplication of *bel,* beautiful, from Latin *bellus,* handsome. See BELLE.]

bibl. or **Bibl.** *abbr.* Biblical.

Bi·ble (bī′bəl) *n.* **1.a.** *Abbr.* **B., Bib.** The sacred book of Christianity, a collection of ancient writings including the books of both the Old Testament and the New Testament. **b.** *Abbr.* **B., Bib.** The Hebrew Scriptures, the sacred book of Judaism. **c.** A particular copy of a Bible: *the old family Bible.* **d.** A book or collection of writings constituting the sacred text of a religion. **2.** Often **bible.** A book considered authoritative in its field: *the bible of French cooking.* [Middle English, from Old French, from Late Latin *biblia,* from Greek, pl. of *biblion,* book, diminutive of *biblos,* papyrus, book, from *Bublos,* Byblos.]

Bible belt *n.* Those sections of the United States, especially in the South and Middle West, where Protestant fundamentalism is widely practiced. **—Bible belter** *n.*

Bible paper *n.* A thin, strong, opaque printing paper used for Bibles and reference books. Also called *India paper.*

bib·li·cal also **Bib·li·cal** (bĭb′lĭ-kəl) *adj.* **1.** *Abbr.* **bib., Bib., bibl., Bibl.** Of, relating to, or contained in the Bible. **2.** Being in keeping with the nature of the Bible, especially: **a.** Suggestive of the personages or times depicted in the Bible. **b.** Suggestive of the prose or narrative style of the King James Bible. [From Medieval Latin *biblicus,* from Late Latin *biblia,* Bible. See BIBLE.] **—Bib′li·cal·ly** *adv.*

Bib·li·cist (bĭb′lĭ-sĭst) *n.* **1.** An expert on the Bible. **2.** One who interprets the Bible literally. **—Bib′li·cism** *n.*

biblio– *pref.* Book: *bibliophile.* [From Greek *biblion,* book. See BIBLE.]

bib·li·o·film (bĭb′lē-ō-fĭlm′) *n.* A type of microfilm used especially to photograph the pages of books.

bibliog. *abbr.* Bibliographer; bibliography.

bib·li·og·ra·pher (bĭb′lē-ŏg′rə-fər) *n.* *Abbr.* **bibliog. 1.** One trained in the description and cataloging of printed matter. **2.** One who compiles a bibliography.

bib·li·og·ra·phy (bĭb′lē-ŏg′rə-fē) *n., pl.* **-phies.** *Abbr.* **bibliog. 1.** A list of the works of a specific author or publisher. **2.a.** A list of writings relating to a given subject: *a bibliography of Latin American history.* **b.** A list of writings used or considered by an author in preparing a particular work. **3.a.** The description and identification of the editions, dates of issue, authorship, and typography of books or other written material. **b.** A compilation of such information. **—bib′li·o·graph′i·cal** (-ə-grăf′ĭ-kəl), **bib′li·o·graph′ic** (-ĭk) *adj.* **—bib′li·o·graph′i·cal·ly** *adv.*

bib·li·ol·a·try (bĭb′lē-ŏl′ə-trē) *n.* **1.** Excessive adherence to a literal interpretation of the Bible. **2.** Extreme devotion to or concern with books. **—bib′li·ol′a·ter** *n.* **—bib′li·ol′a·trous** *adj.*

bib·li·o·man·cy (bĭb′lē-ə-măn′sē) *n., pl.* **-cies.** Divination by interpretation of a passage chosen at random from a book, especially the Bible.

bib·li·o·ma·ni·a (bĭb′lē-ə-mā′nē-ə, -mān′yə) *n.* An exaggerated liking for the acquisition and ownership of books. **—bib′li·o·ma′ni·ac′** (-ăk′) *n.* **—bib′li·o·ma·ni′a·cal** (-mə-nī′ə-kəl) *adj.*

bib·li·o·phile (bĭb′lē-ə-fīl′) also **bib·li·o·phil** (-fĭl′) or **bib·li·oph·i·list** (bĭb′lē-ŏf′ə-lĭst) *n.* **1.** A lover of books. **2.** A collector of books. **—bib′li·oph′i·lism** *n.* **—bib′li·oph′i·lis′tic** *adj.*

bib·li·o·pole (bĭb′lē-ə-pōl′) also **bib·li·op·o·list** (bĭb′lē-ŏp′ə-lĭst) *n.* A dealer in rare books. [Latin *bibliopōla,* bookseller, from Greek *bibliopōlēs* : *biblio-,* biblio- + *pōlein,* to sell; see **pel-**[4] in Appendix.] **—bib′li·o·pol′ic** (-pŏl′ĭk), **bib′li·o·pol′i·cal** *adj.*

bib·li·o·the·ca (bĭb′lē-ə-thē′kə) *n.* **1.** A collection of books; a library. **2.** A catalog of books. [Latin *bibliothēca,* from Greek *bibliothēkē* : *biblio-,* biblio- + *thēkē,* case; see **dhē-** in Appendix.] **—bib′li·o·the′cal** *adj.*

bib·li·o·ther·a·py (bĭb′lē-ō-thĕr′ə-pē) *n.* A form of supportive psychotherapy in which carefully selected reading materials are used to assist a subject in solving personal problems or for other therapeutic purposes.

bib·li·ot·ics (bĭb′lē-ŏt′ĭks) *n. (used with a sing. verb).* Examination of documents to determine authorship or authenticity.

bib·u·lous (bĭb′yə-ləs) *adj.* **1.** Given to or marked by the consumption of alcoholic drink: *a bibulous fellow; a bibulous evening.* **2.** Very absorbent, as paper or soil. [From Latin *bibulus,* from *bibere,* to drink. See **pō(i)-** in Appendix.] **—bib′u·lous·ly** *adv.* **—bib′u·lous·ness** *n.*

bi·cam·er·al (bī-kăm′ər-əl) *adj.* Composed of or based on two legislative chambers or branches: *a bicameral legislature.* [BI–[1] + Latin *camera,* chamber; see CAMERA + –AL[1].] **—bi·cam′er·al·ism** *n.*

bi·car·bon·ate (bī-kär′bə-nāt′, -nĭt) *n.* The radical group HCO_3^- or a compound, such as sodium bicarbonate, containing it.

bicarbonate of soda *n.* See **baking soda.**

bi·cau·dal (bī-kôd′l) *adj. Zoology.* Having two tails.

bice blue (bīs) *n. Color.* A moderate blue. [Middle English *bis,* blue-gray (sense uncertain), from Old French *bis,* dark (in *azur bis,* dark blue, and *vert bis,* dark green).]

bice green *n. Color.* A moderate yellow green. [See BICE BLUE.]

bi·cel·lu·lar (bī-sĕl′yə-lər) *adj.* Having two cells.

bi·cen·ten·a·ry (bī′sĕn-tĕn′ə-rē, bī-sĕn′tə-nĕr′ē) *n., pl.* **-ries.** See **bicentennial.** **—bi′cen·ten′a·ry** *adj.*

bi·cen·ten·ni·al (bī′sĕn-tĕn′ē-əl) *adj.* **1.** Happening once every 200 years. **2.** Lasting for 200 years. **3.** Relating to a 200th anniversary. **—bicentennial** *n.* A 200th anniversary or its celebration. Also called *bicentenary.*

bi·cen·tric (bī-sĕn′trĭk) *adj.* Having two centers. **—bi′cen·tric′i·ty** (-trĭs′ĭ-tē) *n.*

bi·ceph·a·lous (bī-sĕf′ə-ləs) *adj. Zoology.* Having two heads.

bi·ceps (bī′sĕps′) *n., pl.* **biceps** or **-ceps·es** (-sĕp′sĭz). **1.** A muscle with two heads or points of origin. **2.a.** The muscle at the front of the upper arm that flexes the forearm. Also called *biceps brachii.* **b.** The muscle at the back of the thigh that flexes the knee joint. Also called *biceps femoris.* [Latin, two-headed : *bi-,* two; see BI–[1] + *caput,* head; see **kaput-** in Appendix.]

BOOKS OF THE BIBLE

Books of the Hebrew Scriptures appear as listed in the translation by the Jewish Publication Society of America. Books of the Christian Bible appear as listed in the Jerusalem Bible, a 1966 translation of the 1956 French Roman Catholic version. The Old Testament books shown in italic are considered aprocryphal in most Christian churches, but they are accepted as canonical in the Roman Catholic Church, the Eastern Orthodox Churches, and the Armenian and the Ethiopian Oriental Orthodox Churches. The Christian Old Testament parallels the Hebrew Scriptures with the exception of these books.

HEBREW	CHRISTIAN	
THE TORAH	**OLD TESTAMENT**	**NEW TESTAMENT**
Genesis	Genesis	Matthew
Exodus	Exodus	Mark
Leviticus	Leviticus	Luke
Numbers	Numbers	John
Deuteronomy	Deuteronomy	Acts of the Apostles
	Joshua	Romans
THE PROPHETS	Judges	I Corinthians
	Ruth	II Corinthians
Joshua	I Samuel	Galatians
Judges	II Samuel	Ephesians
I Samuel	I Kings	Philippians
II Samuel	II Kings	Colossians
I Kings	I Chronicles	I Thessalonians
II Kings	II Chronicles	II Thessalonians
Isaiah	Ezra	I Timothy
Jeremiah	Nehemiah	II Timothy
Ezekiel	*Tobit*	Titus
Hosea	*Judith*	Philemon
Joel	Esther	Hebrews
Amos	*I Maccabees*	James
Obadiah	*II Maccabees*	I Peter
Jonah	Job	II Peter
Micah	Psalms	I John
Nahum	Proverbs	II John
Habakkuk	Ecclesiastes	III John
Zephaniah	Song of Songs	Jude
Haggai	(Song of Solomon)	Revelation
Zechariah	*Wisdom of Solomon*	
Malachi	*Ecclesiasticus*	
	Isaiah	
THE WRITINGS	Jeremiah	
Psalms	Lamentations	
Proverbs	*Baruch*	
Job	Ezekiel	
Song of Songs	Daniel	
Ruth	Hosea	
Lamentations	Joel	
Ecclesiastes	Amos	
Esther	Obadiah	
Daniel	Jonah	
Ezra	Micah	
Nehemiah	Nahum	
I Chronicles	Habakkuk	
II Chronicles	Zephaniah	
	Haggai	
	Zechariah	
	Malachi	

biceps bra·chi·i (brā′kē-ī′, -kē-ē′, brăk′-ē-ī′, -ē-ē′) *n.* See **biceps** (sense 2a). [New Latin *biceps brāchii* : *biceps,* biceps + Latin *brāchii,* genitive of *brāchium,* arm.]

biceps fem·o·ris (fĕm′ər-ĭs) *n.* See **biceps** (sense 2b). [New Latin : *biceps,* biceps + Latin *femoris,* genitive of *femur,* thigh.]

bi·chlo·ride (bī-klôr′īd, -klōr′-) *n.* See **dichloride.**

bichon frisé (bē-shŏn′ frē-zā′, frēz, bē′shŏn) *n., pl.* **bi·chons fri·sés** (bē-shŏn′ frē-zā′, frēz, bē′shŏn). Any of a European breed of small, sturdy dogs, originating in the Mediterranean area and having a thick, wavy white coat, drooping ears, and an upwardly curved tail. [French : *bichon,* lapdog + *frisé,* curly.]

bi·chro·mate (bī-krō′māt′, -mĭt) *n.* See **dichromate.**

bi·cip·i·tal (bī-sĭp′ĭ-tl) *adj.* **1.** Having two heads or points of origin, as a muscle. **2.** Of or relating to a biceps. [From New Latin *biceps, bicipit-,* biceps. See BICEPS.]

bick·er (bĭk′ər) *intr.v.* **-ered, -er·ing, -ers. 1.** To engage in a petty, bad-tempered quarrel; squabble. See Synonyms at **argue. 2.** To flicker; quiver: *"and bicker like a flame"* (Robert Browning). **—bicker** *n.* A petty quarrel; a squabble. [Middle English *bikeren,* to attack.] **—bick′er·er** *n.*

bi·coas·tal or **bi·coast·al** (bī-kō′stəl) *adj.* **1.** Relating to both the east and west coasts of the United States, as: **a.** Traveling frequently between coasts as part of a business or living arrangement: *"the early generation of bicoastal airline commuters"* (Elizabeth Mehren). **b.** Located or developed chiefly along the two coasts: *a bicoastal economy.* **2.** Coast-to-coast: *bicoastal telephone calls.*

bi·col·or (bī′kŭl′ər) or **bi·col·ored** (-ərd) *adj.* Having two colors, as an animal.

bi·con·cave (bī′kŏn-kāv′, bī-kŏn′kāv′) *adj.* Concave on both sides or surfaces: *a biconcave lens.* **—bi′con·cav′i·ty** (-kăv′ĭ-tē) *n.*

bi·con·vex (bī′kŏn-vĕks′, bī-kŏn′vĕks′) *adj.* Convex on both sides or surfaces: *a biconvex disk.* **—bi′con·vex′i·ty** (-vĕk′sĭ-tē) *n.*

bi·cor·nu·ate (bī-kôr′nyo͞o-ĭt, -āt′) also **bi·corn** (bī′kôrn′) *adj.* **1.** Having two horns or horn-shaped parts. **2.** Shaped like a crescent. [From BI–[1] + Latin *cornū,* horn; see **ker-**[1] in Appendix.]

bi·cul·tur·al (bī-kŭl′chər-əl) *adj.* Of or relating to two distinct cultures in one nation or geographic region: *bicultural education.* **—bi·cul′tur·al·ism** *n.*

bi·cus·pid (bī-kŭs′pĭd) *adj.* Having two points or cusps, as the crescent moon. **—bicuspid** *n.* A bicuspid tooth, especially a premolar. [New Latin *bicuspis, bicuspid-* : Latin *bi-,* two; see BI–[1] + Latin *cuspis,* sharp point.]

bicuspid valve *n.* See **mitral valve.**

bi·cy·cle (bī′sĭk′əl, -sĭ-kəl, -sī′kəl) *n.* **1.** A vehicle consisting of a light frame mounted on two wire-spoked wheels one behind the other and having a seat, handlebars for steering, brakes, and two pedals or a small motor by which it is driven. **2.** An exercise bicycle. *—attributive.* Often used to modify another noun: *a bicycle shop; bicycle paths.* **—bicycle** *intr.v.* **-cled, -cling, -cles.** To ride or travel on a bicycle. [Probably BI–[1] + *-cycle* (on the model of TRICYCLE, three-wheeled coach).] **—bi′cy·cler** (-klər), **bi′cy·clist** (-klĭst) *n.*

bicycle motocross *n. Abbr.* **BMX** *Sports.* A cross-country bicycle race, especially one involving young people riding bicycles designed for rough terrain.

bi·cy·clic (bī-sī′klĭk, -sĭk′lĭk) also **bi·cy·cli·cal** (-sī′klĭ-kəl, -sĭk′lĭ-) *adj.* **1.** Consisting of or having two cycles. **2.** *Botany.* Composed of or arranged in two distinct whorls, as the petals of a flower. **3.** *Chemistry.* Containing molecules consisting of two fused rings.

bid (bĭd) *v.* **bade** (băd, bād) or **bid, bid·den** (bĭd′n) or **bid, bid·ding, bids.** *—tr.* **1.** To issue a command to; direct. **2.** To utter (a greeting or salutation). **3.** To invite to attend; summon. **4.** *past tense and past participle* **bid.** *Games.* To state one's intention to take (tricks of a certain number or suit in cards): *bid four hearts.* **5.** *past tense and past participle* **bid.** To offer or propose (an amount) as a price. **6.** *past tense and past participle* **bid.** To offer (someone) membership, as in a group or club: *"glancing around to be sure that he had been bid by a society that he wanted"* (Louis Auchincloss). *—intr.* **1.** *past tense and past participle* **bid.** To make an offer to pay or accept a specified price: *decided not to bid on the roll-top desk.* **2.** *past tense and past participle* **bid.** To seek to win or attain something; strive. **—bid** *n.* **1. a.** An offer or proposal of a price. **b.** The amount offered or proposed: *They lost the contract because their bid was too high.* **2.** An invitation, especially one offering membership in a group or club. **3.** *Games.* **a.** The act of bidding in cards. **b.** The number of tricks or points declared. **c.** The trump or no-trump declared. **d.** The turn of a player to bid. **4.** An earnest effort to win or attain something: *made a bid for the presidency.* ***—phrasal verbs.*** **bid in.** To outbid on one's own property at an auction in order to raise the final selling price. **bid up.** To increase the amount bid: *bid up the price of wheat.* ***—idioms.*** **bid defiance.** To refuse to submit; offer resistance to. **bid fair.** To appear likely. [Middle English *bidden,* to ask, command (from Old English *biddan;* see **gʷhedh-** in Appendix) and Middle English *beden,* to offer, proclaim (from Old English *bēodan;* see **bheudh-** in Appendix).] **—bid′der** *n.*

b.i.d. *abbr. Latin.* Bis in die (twice a day).

bi·dar·ka (bī-där′kə) *n.* A one- or two-hole kayak used by the Aleut and various Alaskan Eskimo groups. [Russian *baidarka,* diminutive of *baidara.*]

bid·da·ble (bĭd′ə-bəl) *adj.* **1.** *Games.* Strong enough to be bid. Used of a hand of cards. **2.** Following directions or obeying commands; docile. See Synonyms at **obedient.**

Bid·de·ford (bĭd′ə-fərd). A city of southwest Maine on the Saco River southwest of Portland. The first permanent settlement was established in 1630. Population, 19,638.

bid·den (bĭd′n) *v.* A past participle of **bid.**

bid·ding (bĭd′ĭng) *n.* **1.** A demand that something be done; a command. **2.** A request to appear; a summons. **3.** Bids considered as a group, as at an auction or in card games: *The bidding was higher than expected.*

Bid·dle (bĭd′l), **Francis.** 1886–1968. French-born American jurist and public official who was U.S. attorney general (1941–1945) and a judge at the Nuremberg trials (1945–1946).

Biddle, John. 1615–1662. English theologian and founder of English Unitarianism who was several times imprisoned for his rejection of Trinitarian doctrine.

Biddle, Nicholas. 1786–1844. American financier and scholar who was president of the Bank of the United States (1822–1839).

bid·dy[1] (bĭd′ē) *n., pl.* **-dies.** A hen; a fowl. [Origin unknown.]

bid·dy[2] (bĭd′ē) *n., pl.* **-dies.** *Slang.* A woman, especially a garrulous old one. [Nickname for *Bridget.*]

Bid·dy Basketball (bĭd′ē). A service mark used for organized children's basketball games.

bide (bīd) *v.* **bid·ed** or **bode** (bōd), **bid·ed, bid·ing, bides.** *—intr.* **1.** To remain in a condition or state. **2. a.** To wait; tarry. **b.** To stay: *bide at home.* **c.** To be left; remain. *—tr. past tense* **bided.** To await; wait for. ***—idiom.*** **bide (one's) time.** To wait for further developments. [Middle English *biden,* from Old English *bīdan.* See **bheidh-** in Appendix.]

bi·den·tate (bī-dĕn′tāt′) *adj.* Having two teeth or toothlike parts.

bi·det (bē-dā′) *n.* A fixture similar in design to a toilet that is straddled for bathing the genitals and the posterior parts. [French, bidet, pony, probably from Old French *bider,* to trot.]

bi·di·a·lec·tal (bī′dī-ə-lĕk′təl) *adj.* Using two dialects of a language. **—bi′di·a·lec′tal·ism** *n.* **—bi′di·a·lec′tal·ist** *n.*

bi·don·ville (bē′dôɴ-vēl′) *n.* A shantytown on the outskirts of a city, especially in France or North Africa. [French : *bidon,* gas can, oildrum (from Old French, bottle, tankard, probably of Scandinavian origin) + *ville,* town; see VILLAGE.]

Bie·der·mei·er (bē′dər-mī′ər) *adj.* Of or relating to a type of furniture developed in Germany during the first half of the 19th century and modeled after French Empire styles. [After Gottlieb *Biedermeier,* the unsophisticated imaginary author of poems written by Ludwig Eichrodt (1827–1892) and others.]

Biel (bēl) also **Bi·enne** (bē-ĕn′). A city of northwest Switzerland at the northeast end of the **Lake of Biel** at the foot of the Jura Mountains. It is noted for its clocks. Population, 52,600.

Bie·le·feld (bē′lə-fĕlt′). A city of northwest Germany east of Münster. It is an industrial center long known for its fine linens. Population, 301,460.

Biel·sko-Bia·la (byĕl′skô-byä′lä, -byä′wä). A city of southern Poland south of Katowice. Founded in the 13th century, it passed to Austria in 1772 and was returned to Poland in 1919. Population, 174,100.

Bi·enne (bē-ĕn′). See **Biel.**

bi·en·ni·a (bī-ĕn′ē-ə) *n.* A plural of **biennium.**

bi·en·ni·al (bī-ĕn′ē-əl) *adj.* **1.** Lasting or living for two years. **2.** Happening every second year. **3.** *Botany.* Having a life cycle that normally takes two growing seasons to complete. **—biennial** *n.* **1.** An event that occurs every two years. **2.** *Botany.* **a.** A plant that normally requires two seasons to complete its life cycle, growing usually as a rosette in the first season and producing flowers and fruits and then dying in the second season. **b.** A perennial plant, such as the English daisy, cultivated as a biennial. **—bi·en′ni·al·ly** *adv.*

bi·en·ni·um (bī-ĕn′ē-əm) *n., pl.* **-en·ni·ums** or **-en·ni·a** (-ĕn′ē-ə). A two-year period. [Latin : *bi-,* two; see BI–[1] + *annus,* year; see **at-** in Appendix.]

Bien·ville (byĕn′vĭl′, byăɴ-vēl′), Sieur **Jean Baptiste Lemoyne de.** 1680–1768. French colonial administrator who as governor of Louisiana founded New Orleans (1718).

bier (bîr) *n.* **1.** A stand on which a corpse or a coffin containing a corpse is placed before burial. **2.** A coffin along with its stand: *followed the bier to the cemetery.* [Alteration (influenced by French *bière,* coffin, from Old French *biere,* bier, of Germanic origin) of Middle English *ber,* from Old English *bēr.* See **bher-**[1] in Appendix.]

Bierce (bîrs), **Ambrose Gwinett.** 1842–1914? American writer whose caustic wit and sense of realistic horror characterize his works, including *In the Midst of Life* (1891–1892) and *The Devil's Dictionary* (1906).

Bier·stadt (bîr′stăt′, -shtät′), **Albert.** 1830–1902. German-born American landscape painter whose romanticized works include *Domes of the Yosemite* (1864).

Bierstadt, Mount. A peak, 4,288.3 m (14,000 ft) high, of north-

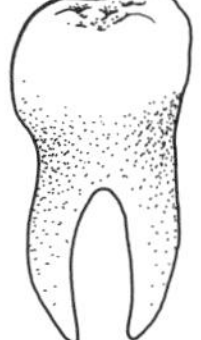

bicuspid

bicycle

ă pat	oi boy
ā pay	ou out
âr care	o͝o took
ä father	o͞o boot
ĕ pet	ŭ cut
ē be	ûr urge
ĭ pit	th thin
ī pie	*th* this
îr pier	hw which
ŏ pot	zh vision
ō toe	ə about, item
ô paw	♦ regionalism

Stress marks: ′ (primary); ′ (secondary), as in **dictionary** (dĭk′shə-nĕr′ē)

central Colorado in the Front Range of the Rocky Mountains.

bi·fa·cial (bī-fā′shəl) *adj.* **1.** Having two faces, fronts, or façades. **2.** Having two opposing surfaces that are alike.

biff¹ (bĭf) *Informal. tr.v.* **biffed, biff·ing, biffs.** To strike or punch. **—biff** *n.* A blow or punch. [From English *biff,* interjection, probably of imitative origin.]

♦**biff²** (bĭf) *n. Upper Midwest.* Variant of **biffy.**

♦**bif·fy** (bĭf′ē) also **biff** (bĭf) *n., pl.* **-fies** also **biffs.** *Upper Midwest.* **1.** An outdoor toilet; an outhouse. **2.** An indoor toilet. [Perhaps alteration of PRIVY.]

bi·fid (bī′fĭd) *adj.* Forked or cleft into two parts: *a bifid petal.* **—bi·fid′i·ty** (-fĭd′ĭ-tē) *n.* **—bi′fid·ly** *adv.*

bi·fi·lar (bī-fī′lər) *adj.* Fitted with or involving the use of two threads or wires. **—bi·fi′lar·ly** *adv.*

bi·flag·el·late (bī-flăj′ə-lĭt, -lāt′) *adj.* Having two flagella: *a biflagellate protozoan.*

bi·fo·cal (bī-fō′kəl, bī′fō′-) *adj.* **1.** Having two focal lengths. **2.** Having one section that corrects for distant vision and another that corrects for near vision, as an eyeglass lens. **3.** Embodying two distinct and often conflicting goals, interests, or courses of action: *"a smoothly functioning bifocal mind"* (John McPhee). *"A bifocal monetary policy . . . has kept one eye on the money supply and the other on interest rates"* (Edward Meadows). **—bi·fo·cals** (bī-fō′kəlz, bī′fō′-) *pl.n.* Eyeglasses with bifocal lenses. **—bi·fo′cal·ism** *n.*

bi·fo·caled (bī-fō′kəld) *adj.* Wearing bifocals: *"the thin, bifocaled woman"* (Los Angeles Times).

bi·fo·li·o·late (bī-fō′lē-ə-lāt′, -lĭt) *adj. Botany.* Having two leaflets.

bi·form (bī′fôrm′) *adj.* Having a combination of features or qualities of two distinct forms. [Latin *biformis* : *bi-,* two; see BI–¹ + *forma,* form; see FORM.]

bi·func·tion·al (bī-fŭngk′shə-nəl) *adj.* **1.** Having two functions: *bifunctional neurons.* **2.** *Chemistry.* Having or involving two functional groups or binding sites: *bifunctional reagents.*

bi·fur·cate (bī′fər-kāt′, bī-fûr′-) *v.* **-cat·ed, -cat·ing, -cates.** *—tr.* To divide into two parts or branches. *—intr.* To separate into two parts or branches; fork. **—bifurcate** (-kāt′, -kĭt) *adj.* Forked or divided into two parts or branches. [Medieval Latin *bifurcāre, bifurcāt-,* to divide, from Latin *bifurcus,* two-pronged : *bi-,* two; see BI–¹ + *furca,* fork.] **—bi′fur·cate′ly** *adv.* **—bi′fur·ca′tion** *n.*

big (bĭg) *adj.* **big·ger, big·gest. 1.** Of considerable size, number, quantity, magnitude, or extent; large. See Synonyms at **large. 2.a.** Of great force; strong: *a big wind; in a big rage.* **b.** *Obsolete.* Of great strength. **3.** Grown-up; adult. **4.** Pregnant: *big with child.* **5.** Filled up; brimming over: *felt big with love.* **6.** Having or exercising considerable authority, control, or influence: *a big official; a big chief.* **7.** Conspicuous in position, wealth, or importance; prominent: *a big figure in the peace movement.* **8.** Of great significance; momentous: *a big decision; a big victory.* **9.** *Informal.* Self-important; cocky: *You're too big for your own good.* **10.** Loud and firm; resounding: *a big voice.* **11.** Bountiful; generous: *had a big heart.* **—big** *adv.* **1.** In a pretentious or boastful way: *talked big about the new job.* **2.** *Informal.* **a.** With considerable success: *made it big with their recent best-selling album.* **b.** In a thorough or unmistakable way; emphatically: *failed big at the box office.* ***—idiom.*** **big on.** Enthusiastic about; partial to: *"The Japanese are big on ranking things and deciding which is Number One"* (James Fallows). [Middle English, perhaps of Scandinavian origin.] **—big′gish** *adj.* **—big′ly** *adv.* **—big′ness** *n.*

bighorn
American bighorn ram
Ovis canadensis

big·a·mous (bĭg′ə-məs) *adj.* **1.** Involving bigamy. **2.** Guilty of bigamy. **—big′a·mous·ly** *adv.*

big·a·my (bĭg′ə-mē) *n., pl.* **-mies.** *Law.* The criminal offense of marrying one person while still legally married to another. [Middle English *bigamie,* from Old French, from Medieval Latin *bigamia,* from Late Latin *bigamus,* twice married : Latin *bi-,* two; see BI–¹ + Greek *gamos,* marriage; see –GAMOUS.] **—big′a·mist** *n.*

bi·ga·rade (bē′gä-räd′) *n.* **1.** See **sour orange. 2.** A rich sauce served with duck, consisting of thickened duck stock flavored with the rind of bitter oranges, lemon juice, and sugar. [French, from Provençal *bigarrado,* from past participle of *bigarrar,* to variegate, from Old French *bigarrer* : *bi-,* two (from Latin *bi-;* see BI–¹) + *garrer,* to variegate (from *garre,* of two colors).]

big band (bĭg) or **Big Band** *n.* A large dance or jazz band usually featuring improvised solos by lead players.

big bang *n.* The cosmic explosion that marked the origin of the universe according to the big bang theory.

big bang theory *n.* A cosmological theory holding that the universe originated approximately 20 billion years ago from the violent explosion of a very small agglomeration of matter of extremely high density and temperature.

big beat *n. Music.* Popular music, especially rock 'n' roll, having a strong backbeat.

Big Bend (bĕnd). A region of southwest Texas on the Mexican border in a triangle formed by a bend in the Rio Grande. The area includes deep river canyons, desert wilderness, mountains rising to 2,386.6 m (7,825 ft), archaeological remains, and rare forms of plant and animal life.

Big Black River (blăk). A river rising in north-central Mississippi and flowing about 531 km (330 mi) generally southwest to the Mississippi River below Vicksburg.

Big Blue River (blo͞o). A river rising in southeast Nebraska and flowing about 483 km (300 mi) east and southeast to the Kansas River in northeast Kansas near Manhattan.

big brother *n.* **1.** An older brother. **2.** A man who assumes the role of an older brother, as by providing guidance or protection. **3.a.** Also **Big Brother.** An omnipresent, seemingly benevolent figure representing the oppressive control over individual lives exerted by an authoritarian government. **b.** A state, an organization, or a leader regarded in this manner. [Sense 3, after *Big Brother,* a character in the novel *Nineteen Eighty-Four* by George Orwell.] **—big′-broth′er·ly** (bĭg′brŭth′ər-lē) *adj. & adv.*

Big Broth·er·ism (brŭth′ə-rĭz′əm) *n.* Authoritarian efforts at total control, as of a person or nation: *"the frightening totalitarian Big Brotherism that launched the privacy scare"* (Newsweek).

big bucks *pl.n. Slang.* A large amount of money: *worked for big bucks in a large corporation.*

big business *n.* Commercial operations organized and financed on a large scale: *clashes between labor and big business.*

big daddy or **Big Daddy** *n. Slang.* **1.** One that is predominant, as in size, influence, or priority: *"The big daddy of them all has always been the Frankfurt Fair"* (Saturday Review). **2.** One that exercises a paternalistic authority or control.

big deal *n. Slang.* **1.** Something of great importance or consequence: *made a big deal out of getting there on time; losing one penny was no big deal.* **2.** An important person: *She was a big deal in local politics.* **—big′-deal′** (bĭg′dēl′) *adj.*

Big Di·o·mede Island (dī′ə-mēd′). See **Diomede Islands.**

Big Dipper *n.* A cluster of seven stars in the constellation Ursa Major, four forming the bowl and three the handle of a dipper-shaped configuration. Also called *Charles's Wain, Plow.*

bi·gem·i·nal (bī-jĕm′ə-nəl) *adj.* Occurring in pairs; doubled or twinned: *a bigeminal pulse.* [Possibly from Late Latin *bigeminus,* doubled : Latin *bi-,* two; see BI–¹ + Latin *geminus,* double.]

bi·gem·i·ny (bī-jĕm′ə-nē) *n. Medicine.* **1.** An association in pairs. **2.** An abnormal pulse characterized by two beats in rapid succession followed by a pause.

big enchilada or **Big Enchilada** *n. Slang.* **1.** One who is in charge: "[the President's] *big enchilada on both foreign and domestic policy"* (Mary McGrory). **2.** Something of the highest value or importance: "[The team] *won the big enchilada in 1980 and 1982"* (Scott Ostler). [On the model of such expressions as *big cheese.*]

bi·ge·ner·ic (bī′jə-nĕr′ĭk) *adj.* **1.** Relating to a hybrid that results from a cross between plants of different genera. **2.** Having the characteristics of two different genera.

big·eye (bĭg′ī′) *n.* Any of several small, tropical marine fishes of the family Priacanthidae, having large eyes and reddish scales.

Big·foot (bĭg′fo͝ot′) *n.* A very large, hairy, humanlike creature purported to inhabit the Pacific Northwest and Canada. Also called *Sasquatch.* [From the size of the footprints believed to belong to it.]

big game *n.* **1.** Large animals or fish hunted or caught for sport. **2.** *Informal.* An important objective. **—big′-game′** (bĭg′gām′) *adj.*

big·ge·ty (bĭg′ĭ-tē) *adj. Informal.* Variant of **biggity.**

big·gie (bĭg′ē) *n. Slang.* **1.** A very important person: *"hassles between executive biggies"* (New York). **2.** Something that is considered big or important: *Her new movie is expected to be a biggie.*

big·gi·ty also **big·ge·ty** (bĭg′ĭ-tē) *adj. Informal.* Self-important; conceited. [Probably alteration of BIG + –Y¹.]

big gun *n. Slang.* One that is powerful or influential: *The big guns for the prosecution were its expert witnesses.*

big·head (bĭg′hĕd′) *n.* **1.** *Informal.* Conceit; egotism. **2.** Also **big head.** Any of various diseases of animals, especially rams, characterized by swelling of the head, face, or neck. **—big′-head′ed** *adj.* **—big′head′ed·ness** *n.*

big-heart·ed (bĭg′här′tĭd) *adj.* Generous; kind. **—big′-heart′ed·ly** *adv.* **—big′-heart′ed·ness** *n.*

big·horn (bĭg′hôrn′) *n., pl.* **-horn** or **-horns.** A wild sheep *(Ovis canadensis)* of the mountains of western North America, the male of which has massive, curved horns. Also called *mountain sheep, Rocky Mountain sheep.*

Big·horn Mountains (bĭg′hôrn′). A section of the Rocky Mountains of northern Wyoming and southern Montana rising to 4,018.4 m (13,175 ft) at Cloud Peak in Wyoming.

Bighorn River. A river rising in west-central Wyoming and flowing about 742 km (461 mi) north to join the Yellowstone River in southern Montana northeast of Billings.

big house *n. Slang.* A penitentiary.

bight (bīt) *n.* **1.a.** A loop in a rope. **b.** The middle or slack part of an extended rope. **2.a.** A bend or curve, especially in a shoreline. **b.** A wide bay formed by such a bend or curve. [Middle English, bend, angle, from Old English *byht.* See **bheug-** in Appendix.]

big league *n.* **1.** *Sports.* A major league. **2.** *Informal.* The most prestigious level of accomplishment. **—big leaguer** *n.*

big-league (bĭg′lēg′) *adj.* **1.** *Sports.* Major-league. **2.** *Informal.* Outstanding or influential in one's field: *a big-league politician; one of the big-league banking institutions.*

big lie *n.* Intentional distortion of the truth, especially for political or official purposes: *released falsified documents to bolster the big lie that no government troops were involved in the other country's internal problems.*

big money *n. Slang.* **1.** A large amount of money, as in profits or salary: *made big money on the transaction.* **2.** A large-scale commercial enterprise. **—big′-mon′ey** (bĭg′mŭn′ē) *adj.*

big·mouth (bĭg′mouth′) *n.* **1.** *Slang.* A loud-mouthed or gossipy person. **2.** Any of various fishes having unusually large mouths.

big·mouthed (bĭg′mouthd′, -moutht′) *adj.* **1.** *Slang.* Speaking loudly or indiscreetly; loud-mouthed. **2.** Having a large mouth.

big-name (bĭg′nām′) *adj. Informal.* **1.** Widely recognized or acclaimed; famous: *a big-name performer; a big-name college.* **2.** Of or involving one that is widely recognized or acclaimed: *big-name politics.*

big·no·ni·a (bĭg-nō′nē-ə) *n.* An evergreen, tendril-bearing woody vine *(Bignonia capreolata),* native chiefly to the southeast United States and having showy red-orange, trumpet-shaped flowers. Also called *cross vine.* [New Latin *Bignonia,* genus name, after Jean Paul *Bignon* (died 1743), French royal librarian.]

bigos (bē′gōs) *n.* A Polish stew made with meat and cabbage, traditionally simmered for several days before serving. [Polish.]

big·ot (bĭg′ət) *n.* One who is strongly partial to one's own group, religion, race, or politics and is intolerant of those who differ. [French, from Old French.]

WORD HISTORY: A bigot may have more in common with God than one might think. Legend has it that Rollo, the first duke of Normandy, refused to kiss the foot of the French king Charles III, uttering the phrase *bi got,* his borrowing of the assumed Old English equivalent of our expression *by God.* Although this story is almost certainly apocryphal, it is true that *bigot* was used by the French as a term of abuse for the Normans, but not in a religious sense. Later, however, the word, or very possibly a homonym, was used abusively in French for the Beguines, members of a Roman Catholic lay sisterhood. From the 15th century on Old French *bigot* meant "an excessively devoted or hypocritical person." *Bigot* is first recorded in English in 1598 with the sense "a superstitious hypocrite."

big·ot·ed (bĭg′ə-tĭd) *adj.* Being or characteristic of a bigot: *a bigoted person; an outrageously bigoted viewpoint.* **—big′ot·ed·ly** *adv.* **—big′ot·ed·ness** *n.*

big·ot·ry (bĭg′ə-trē) *n.* The attitude, state of mind, or behavior characteristic of a bigot; intolerance.

Big San·dy Creek (săn′dē). A river rising in central Colorado and flowing about 322 km (200 mi) east-northeast and southeast to the Arkansas River.

big shot *n. Slang.* An important or influential person. **—big′shot′, big′-shot′** (bĭg′shŏt′) *adj.*

Big Sioux River (so͞o). A river rising in northeast South Dakota and flowing about 676 km (420 mi) southward, partly along the South Dakota–Iowa border, to the Missouri River at Sioux City, Iowa.

Big Spring. A city of west-central Texas west-southwest of Abilene. It is a trade center in an agricultural region. Population, 24,804.

big stick *n.* A display or threat, especially of military force: *a foreign policy that relied on the big stick.* **—big′stick′** (bĭg′stĭk′) *adj.*

Big Sur (sûr). A rugged, picturesque resort region along the Pacific coast of California south of Carmel and Monterey.

big-tick·et (bĭg′tĭk′ĭt) *adj. Informal.* Having a high price or cost: *big-ticket items such as cars and stereos; a big-ticket government program.*

big·time or **big-time** (bĭg′tīm′) *adj. Informal.* Significant or important; major: *a bigtime comedian.*

big time *n. Informal.* The most prestigious level of attainment in a competitive field: *made it to the big time with his latest film.* **—big′-time′** *adj.* **—big′-tim′er** *n.*

big toe *n.* The largest and innermost toe of the human foot.

big top *n.* **1.** The main tent of a circus. **2.** The circus.

big tree *n.* See **giant sequoia.**

big wheel *n. Slang.* A very important person.

big·wig (bĭg′wĭg′) *n. Slang.* A very important person.

Bi·har (bē-här′). A region of east-central India crossed by the Ganges River. Buddha spent his early days in the area.

Bi·ha·ri (bĭ-hä′rē) *n., pl.* **Bihari** or **-ris.** **1.** A native or inhabitant of Bihar. **2.** The Indic language of the Bihari.

bi·jou (bē′zho͞o′) *n., pl.* **-joux** (-zho͞o′, -zho͞oz′). A small, exquisitely wrought trinket. [French, from Breton *bizou,* jeweled ring, from *biz,* finger.]

bi·jou·te·rie (bē-zho͞o′tə-rē) *n.* **1.** A collection of trinkets or jewelry. **2.** Decoration. [French, from *bijou,* piece of jewelry. See BIJOU.]

bi·joux (bē′zho͞o′, -zho͞oz′) *n.* Plural of **bijou.**

bi·ju·gate (bī′jə-gāt′, -gĭt, -bī-jo͞o′-) also **bi·ju·gous** (bī′jə-gəs, bī-jo͞o′-) *adj. Botany.* Relating to a pinnate leaf with two pairs of leaflets.

Bi·ka·ner (bē′kə-nîr′, -nâr′). A city of northwest India in the Thar Desert near the Pakistan border west-southwest of Delhi. It has several 16th-century Rajput palaces built of red sandstone. Population 253,174.

bike (bīk) *n.* **1.** A bicycle. **2.** A motorcycle. **3.** A motorbike. **—bike** *intr.v.* **biked, bik·ing, bikes.** To ride a bike. [Shortening and alteration of BICYCLE.]

bik·er (bī′kər) *n.* **1.** One who rides a bicycle or a motorbike. **2.** A motorcyclist, especially a member of a motorcycle gang.

bike·way (bīk′wā′) *n.* A bicycle lane or path.

bi·ki·ni (bĭ-kē′nē) *n.* **1.a.** A very brief, close-fitting two-piece bathing suit worn by women. **b.** A very brief, close-fitting bathing suit worn by men. **2.** Often **bikinis.** Brief underpants that reach to the hips rather than to the waist. [French, after BIKINI.] **—bi·ki·′nied** (-nēd) *adj.*

Bi·ki·ni (bĭ-kē′nē). An atoll in the Ratak Chain of the Marshall Islands in the west-central Pacific Ocean. The area was the site of U.S. nuclear tests between 1946 and 1958, including the first aerial detonation of a hydrogen bomb (May 21, 1956).

bi·la·bi·al (bī-lā′bē-əl) *adj.* **1.** Pronounced or articulated with both lips, as the consonants *b, p, m,* and *w.* **2.** Relating to both lips. **—bilabial** *n.* A bilabial sound or consonant. **—bi·la′bi·al·ly** *adv.*

bi·la·bi·ate (bī-lā′bē-ĭt, -āt′) *adj. Botany.* Having two lips, as the corollas of the snapdragon.

bil·an·der (bĭl′ən-dər, bī′lən-) *n. Nautical.* A small two-masted sailing vessel, used especially on canals in the Low Countries. [Dutch *billander,* probably from *binlander,* inlander, from *binnenlander* : *binnen,* within (from Middle Dutch; see **en** in Appendix) + *land,* land; see **lendh-** in Appendix.]

bi·lat·er·al (bī-lăt′ər-əl) *adj.* **1.** Having or formed of two sides; two-sided. **2.** Affecting or undertaken by two sides equally; binding on both parties: *a bilateral agreement; bilateral negotiations.* **3.** Having or marked by bilateral symmetry. **—bi·lat′er·al·ism** *n.* **—bi·lat′er·al·ly** *adv.* **—bi·lat′er·al·ness** *n.*

bilateral symmetry *n.* Symmetrical arrangement, as of an organism or a body part, along a central axis, so that the body is divided into equivalent right and left halves by only one plane.

bi·lay·er (bī′lā′ər) *n.* A structure, such as a film or membrane, consisting of two molecular layers: *a phospholipid bilayer.*

Bil·ba·o (bĭl-bä′ō, -bou′). A city of northern Spain near the Bay of Biscay. Founded c. 1300, it is a major port and industrial center. Population, 397,541.

bil·ber·ry (bĭl′bĕr′ē) *n.* See **blueberry.** [*bil-,* probably of Scandinavian origin; see **bhel-**[2] in Appendix + BERRY.]

bil·bo[1] (bĭl′bō) *n., pl.* **-boes.** An iron bar to which sliding fetters are attached, formerly used to shackle the feet of prisoners. [Origin unknown.]

bil·bo[2] (bĭl′bō) *n., pl.* **-boes.** *Archaic.* A sword, especially one having a well-tempered blade. [After BILBAO.]

bil·dungs·ro·man (bĭl′do͝ongz-rō-män′, -do͝ongks-) or **Bil·dungs·ro·man** *n.* A novel whose principal subject is the moral, psychological, and intellectual development of a usually youthful main character. [German : *Bildung,* formation (from Middle High German *bildunge,* from Old High German *bildunga,* from *bilodi,* form, shape) + *Roman,* novel (from French, a story in the vernacular, novel; see ROMAN).]

bile (bīl) *n.* **1.** A bitter, alkaline, brownish-yellow or greenish-yellow fluid that is secreted by the liver, stored in the gallbladder, and discharged into the duodenum and aids in the emulsification, digestion, and absorption of fats. Also called *gall.* **2.** Bitterness of temper; ill humor; irascibility. **3.** Either of two bodily humors, black bile or yellow bile, in medieval physiology. [French, from Latin *bīlis.*]

bile acid *n.* Any of the liver-generated steroid acids, such as cholic acid, that commonly occur in the bile in combination with glycine and taurine as sodium salts.

bile duct *n.* Any of the excretory passages in the liver that carry bile to the hepatic duct, which joins with the cystic duct to form the common bile duct opening into the duodenum.

bile salt *n.* **1.** Any of the sodium salts of the bile acids occurring in bile. **2.** A mixture, such as a commercial preparation derived from the bile of the ox, that is used medicinally as a hepatic stimulant or laxative.

bi-lev·el or **bi·lev·el** (bī′lĕv′əl) —*adj.* **1.** Having or existing on two levels: *a bi-level passenger coach; a bi-level marketing campaign.* **2.** Divided vertically into two ground-floor levels: *a bi-level home.* —*n.* A dwelling that is divided vertically into two ground-floor levels.

bilge (bĭlj) *n.* **1.** *Nautical.* **a.** The rounded portion of a ship's hull, forming a transition between the bottom and the sides. **b.** The lowest inner part of a ship's hull. **2.** Bilgewater. **3.** *Slang.* Stupid talk or writing; nonsense. **4.** The bulging part of a barrel or cask. **—bilge** *v.* **bilged, bilg·ing, bilg·es.** —*intr.* **1.** *Nautical.* To spring a leak in the bilge. **2.** To bulge or swell. —*tr.* *Nautical.* To break open the bilge of. [Probably alteration of BULGE.] **—bilg′y** *adj.*

bilge keel *n. Nautical.* Either of two beams or fins fastened lengthwise along the outside of a ship's bilge to inhibit rolling.

bilge water *n.* **1.** Water that collects and stagnates in the bilge of a ship. **2.** *Slang.* Nonsense.

ă **pat**	oi **boy**
ā **pay**	ou **out**
âr **care**	o͝o **took**
ä **father**	o͞o **boot**
ĕ **pet**	ŭ **cut**
ē **be**	ûr **urge**
ĭ **pit**	th **thin**
ī **pie**	*th* **this**
îr **pier**	hw **which**
ŏ **pot**	zh **vision**
ō **toe**	ə **about, item**
ô **paw**	♦ **regionalism**

Stress marks: **′** (primary); ′ (secondary), as in **dictionary** (dĭk′shə-nĕr′ē)

bil·har·zi·a (bĭl-här′zē-ə) *n.* See **schistosome.** [New Latin *Bilharzia,* genus name, after Theodor *Bilharz* (1825–1862), German physician.]

bil·har·zi·a·sis (bĭl′här-zī′ə-sĭs) *n.* See **schistosomiasis.** [BILHARZ(IA) + –IASIS.]

bil·i·ar·y (bĭl′ē-ĕr′ē) *adj.* **1.** Of or relating to bile, the bile ducts, or the gallbladder. **2.** Transporting bile.

biliary cirrhosis *n.* A progressive inflammatory disease of the liver characterized by obstruction of the bile duct.

bi·lim·bi (bə-lĭm′bē) *n.* **1.** An evergreen tree *(Averrhoa bilimbi),* native to tropical Asia and grown for its edible fruits. **2.** The small, sour, greenish or yellowish cucumber-shaped fruit of this tree, eaten as a pickle or used in relishes and various dishes. [New Latin, species name, ultimately from Malay *bĕlimbing.*

bi·lin·e·ar (bī-lĭn′ē-ər) *adj. Mathematics.* Linear with respect to each of two variables or positions. Used of functions or equations.

bi·lin·gual (bī-lĭng′gwəl) *adj.* **1.a.** Using or able to use two languages, especially with equal or nearly equal fluency. **b.** Using two languages in some proportion in order to facilitate learning by students who have a native proficiency in one language and are acquiring proficiency in the other: *bilingual training; bilingual education.* **2.** Of, relating to, or expressed in two languages: *a bilingual dictionary.* —**bilingual** *n.* A person who uses or is able to use two languages, especially with equal fluency. —**bi·lin′gual·ism** *n.* —**bi·lin′gual·ly** *adv.*

bil·ious (bĭl′yəs) *adj.* **1.** Of, relating to, or containing bile; biliary. **2.a.** Characterized by an excess secretion of bile. **b.** Relating to, characterized by, or experiencing gastric distress caused by a disorder of the liver or gallbladder. **c.** Appearing as if affected by such a disorder; sickly. **3.** Resembling bile, especially in color: *a bilious green.* **4.** Having a peevish disposition; ill-humored. —**bil′ious·ly** *adv.* —**bil′ious·ness** *n.*

bil·i·ru·bin (bĭl′ĭ-ro͞o′bĭn, bĭl′ĭ-ro͞o′-) *n.* A reddish-yellow bile pigment, $C_{33}H_{36}N_4O_6$, derived from the degradation of heme. [Latin *bīlis,* bile + *ruber,* red; see **reudh-** in Appendix + –IN.]

bil·i·ver·din (bĭl′ĭ-vûr′dĭn, bĭl′ĭ-vûr′-) *n.* A green pigment, $C_{33}H_{34}N_4O_6$, occurring in bile and sometimes formed by oxidation of bilirubin. [German : Latin *bīlis,* bile + German *verd-* (from French *verdir,* to make green; see VERDANT).]

bilk (bĭlk) *tr.v.* **bilked, bilk·ing, bilks. 1.a.** To defraud, cheat, or swindle: *made millions bilking wealthy clients on art sales.* **b.** To evade payment of: *bilk one's debts.* **2.** To thwart or frustrate: *"Fate . . . may be to a certain extent bilked"* (Thomas Carlyle). **3.** To elude. —**bilk** *n.* **1.** One who cheats. **2.** *Obsolete.* A hoax or swindle. [Perhaps an alteration of BALK.] —**bilk′er** *n.*

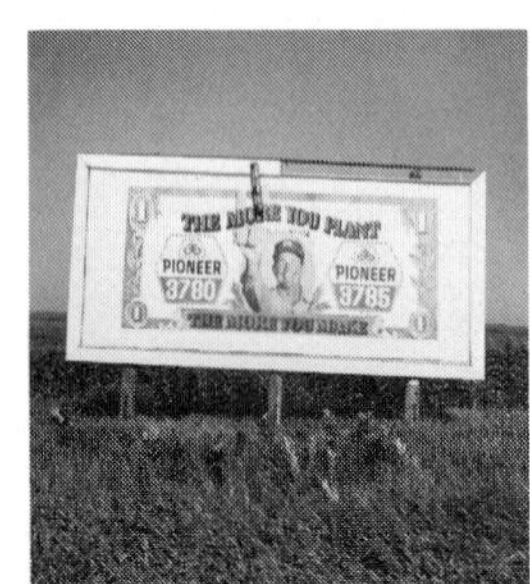

billboard[1]

bill[1] (bĭl) *n.* **1.** An itemized list or statement of fees or charges. **2.** A statement or list of particulars, such as a theater program or menu. **3.** The entertainment offered by a theater. **4.** A public notice, such as an advertising poster. **5.a.** A piece of legal paper money: *a ten-dollar bill.* **b.** *Slang.* One hundred dollars. **6.a.** A bill of exchange. **b.** *Obsolete.* A promissory note. **7.a.** A draft of a proposed law presented for approval to a legislative body. **b.** The law enacted from such a draft: *a bottle bill in effect in three states; the GI Bill.* **8.** *Law.* A document presented to a court and containing a formal statement of a case, complaint, or petition. —**bill** *tr.v.* **billed, bill·ing, bills. 1.** To present a statement of costs or charges to. **2.** To enter on a statement of costs or on a particularized list. **3.a.** To advertise or schedule by public notice or as part of a program. **b.** To declare or describe officially; proclaim: *a policy that was billed as an important departure for the administration.* [Middle English *bille,* from Norman French, from Medieval Latin *billa,* alteration of *bulla,* seal on a document, from Latin, bubble.] —**bill′a·ble** *adj.*

bill[2] (bĭl) *n.* **1.** The horny part of the jaws of a bird; a beak. **2.** A beaklike mouth part, such as that of a turtle. **3.** The visor of a cap. **4.** *Nautical.* The tip of the fluke of an anchor. —**bill** *intr.v.* **billed, bill·ing, bills.** To touch beaks together. [Middle English, from Old English *bile.*]

bill[3] (bĭl) *n.* **1.** A billhook. **2.** A halberd or similar weapon with a hooked blade and a long handle. [Middle English *bil,* from Old English *bill.*]

bil·la·bong (bĭl′ə-bông′, -bŏng′) *n. Australian.* **1.** A dead-end channel extending from the main stream of a river. **2.** A streambed filled with water only in the rainy season. **3.** A stagnant pool or backwater. [Wiradhuri (Aboriginal language of southeast Australia) *bila,* river + *-baŋ,* watercourse filled only after rain.]

bill·board[1] (bĭl′bôrd′, -bōrd′) *n.* **1.** A panel for the display of advertisements in public places, such as alongside highways or on the sides of buildings. **2.** The advertisement or message posted on such a panel. **3.** An introductory list of highlights from the program or text that follows, as in a broadcast or magazine. —**billboard** *tr.v.* **-board·ed, -board·ing, -boards.** To advertise or proclaim on or as if on a billboard: *was billboarded as the workers' candidate.* [BILL[1] + BOARD.]

bill·board[2] (bĭl′bôrd′, -bōrd′) *n. Nautical.* A ledge on the bow of a ship on which the bill of an anchor rests when the anchor is secured to the cathead. [BILL[2] + BOARD.]

bill·bug (bĭl′bŭg′) *n.* Any of several weevils, especially of the genera *Calendra* or *Sitophilus,* whose larvae feed on plants such as corn and other cereal grasses. [BILL[2] + BUG.]

bill·er (bĭl′ər) *n.* One that bills, as: **a.** A clerk who prepares bills. **b.** A machine used in preparing bills.

Bille·ric·a (bĭl-rĭk′ə, bĕl′ə-). A town of northeast Massachusetts south of Lowell. Settled in 1637, it is primarily residential. Population, 36,727.

bil·let[1] (bĭl′ĭt) *n.* **1.a.** Lodging for troops. **b.** A written order directing that such lodging be provided. **2.** A position of employment; a job. **3.** *Archaic.* A short letter; a note. —**billet** *v.* **-let·ed, -let·ing, -lets.** —*tr.* **1.a.** To lodge (soldiers). **b.** To serve (a person) with a written order to provide lodging for soldiers. **2.** To assign lodging to. —*intr.* To be quartered; lodge. [Middle English, official register, from Old French *billette,* from *bullette,* diminutive of *bulle,* document, from Medieval Latin *bulla,* document, seal. See BILL[1].]

bil·let[2] (bĭl′ĭt) *n.* **1.** A short, thick piece of wood, especially one used as firewood. **2.** One of a series of regularly spaced, log-shaped segments used horizontally as ornamentation in the moldings of Norman architecture. **3.a.** A small, usually rectangular bar of iron or steel in an intermediate stage of manufacture. **b.** A small ingot of nonferrous metal. **4.a.** The part of a harness strap that passes through a buckle. **b.** A loop or pocket for securing the end of a buckled harness strap. [Middle English, from Old French *billette,* diminutive of *bille,* log, from Vulgar Latin **bilia,* possibly of Celtic origin.]

bil·let-doux (bĭl′ā-do͞o′) *n., pl.* **bil·lets-doux** (bĭl′ā-do͞oz′). A love letter. [French : *billet,* short note; see BILLET[1] + *doux,* sweet (from Latin *dulcis*).]

bill·fish (bĭl′fĭsh′) *n., pl.* **billfish** or **-fish·es. 1.** Any of various fishes of the family Istiophoridae, such as a marlin or sailfish, having an elongated, swordlike or spearlike snout and upper jaw. **2.** Any of various other fishes having long, pointed jaws.

bill·fold (bĭl′fōld′) *n.* A folding pocket-sized case for carrying paper money, small personal documents, and sometimes change.

bill·head (bĭl′hĕd′) *n.* A sheet of paper with a business name and address printed at the top, used for billing costs or charges.

bill·hook (bĭl′ho͝ok′) *n.* An implement with a curved blade attached to a handle, used especially for clearing brush and for rough pruning.

bil·liard (bĭl′yərd) *Games. n.* See **carom** (sense 2a).

bil·liards (bĭl′yərdz) *pl.n.* *(used with a sing. verb). Games.* **1.** A game played on a rectangular cloth-covered table with raised cushioned edges, in which a cue is used to hit three small, hard balls against one another or the side cushions of the table. **2.** One of several similar games, sometimes using a table with pockets, as in pool. [French *billard,* from *bille,* log. See BILLET[2].]

bill·ing (bĭl′ĭng) *n.* **1.** The relative importance of performers as indicated by the position and type size in which their names are listed on programs, theater marquees, or advertisements: *top billing.* **2.** Advertising; promotion: *The product needed better billing to outsell its competition.* **3.** Often **billings.** The total amount of business done in a specific period, as by an advertising agency or a law firm.

Bil·lings (bĭl′ĭngz). A city of southern Montana on the Yellowstone River east-southeast of Helena. A trade and manufacturing center, it is the largest city in the state. Population, 66,842.

Billings, Josh. See Henry Wheeler **Shaw.**

bil·lings·gate (bĭl′ĭngz-gāt′, -gĭt) *n.* Foul, abusive language. [After *Billingsgate,* a former fish market in London, England.]

bil·lion (bĭl′yən) *n. Abbr.* **b. 1.** The cardinal number equal to 10^9. **2.** *Chiefly British.* The cardinal number equal to 10^{12}. **3.** An indefinitely large number. [French, a million million : blend of *bi-,* second power; see BI–[1], and MILLION.] —**bil′lion** *adj. & pron.*

bil·lion·aire (bĭl′yə-nâr′, bĭl′yə-nâr′) *n.* A person whose wealth amounts to at least a billion dollars, pounds, or the equivalent in other currency. [BILLION + (MILLION)AIRE.]

bil·lionth (bĭl′yənth) *n.* **1.** The ordinal number matching the number one billion in a series. **2.** One of a billion equal parts. —**bil′lionth** *adj. & adv.*

Bil·li·ton (bə-lē′tŏn′). See **Belitung.**

bill of attainder *n., pl.* **bills of attainder.** A legislative act pronouncing a person guilty of a crime, usually treason, without trial and subjecting that person to capital punishment and attainder. Such acts are prohibited by the U.S. Constitution.

bill of entry *n., pl.* **bills of entry.** *Abbr.* **B/E** A listing of goods received at a customhouse as imports or for export.

bill of exchange *n., pl.* **bills of exchange.** *Abbr.* **B/E** A written order directing that a specified sum of money be paid to a specified person.

bill of fare *n., pl.* **bills of fare. 1.** A list of dishes offered; a menu. **2.** A list of items or events in a presentation; a program.

bill of goods *n., pl.* **bills of goods. 1.** A consignment of items for sale. **2.** *Informal.* A plan, promise, or offer, especially one that is dishonest or misleading: *"The salesman himself . . . is often depicted as the ultimate sucker, who has fallen for his own cheesy bill of goods"* (Walter Goodman).

bill of health *n., pl.* **bills of health.** *Abbr.* **BH 1.** A certificate stating whether there is infectious disease aboard a ship or in a port of departure, given to the ship's master to present at the next port of arrival. **2.** *Informal.* An attestation as to condition, especially a favorable one: *gave the structure a clean bill of health in spite of its age.*

bill of lading *n., pl.* **bills of lading.** *Abbr.* **B/L** A document issued by a carrier to a shipper, listing and acknowledging receipt of goods for transport and specifying terms of delivery.

bill of particulars *n., pl.* **bills of particulars.** *Law.* An itemization of charges, claims, or counterclaims in an action.

bill of rights *n., pl.* **bills of rights. 1.** A formal summary of those rights and liberties considered essential to a people or group of people: *a consumer bill of rights.* **2.** Also **Bill of Rights.** The first ten amendments to the U.S. Constitution, added in 1791 to protect certain rights of citizens. **3.** Also **Bill of Rights.** A declaration of certain rights of subjects, enacted by the English Parliament in 1689.

bill of sale *n., pl.* **bills of sale.** *Abbr.* **B.S.** A document that attests a transfer of the ownership of personal property.

bil·lon (bĭl′ən) *n.* **1.** An alloy of gold or silver with a greater proportion of another metal, such as copper, used in making coins. **2.** An alloy of silver with a high percentage of copper, used in making medals and tokens. [French, from Old French, ingot, from *bille,* log. See BILLET[2].]

bil·low (bĭl′ō) *n.* **1.** A large wave or swell of water. **2.** A great swell, surge, or undulating mass, as of smoke or sound. **—billow** *v.* **-lowed, -low·ing, -lows.** *—intr.* **1.** To surge or roll in billows. **2.** To swell out or bulge: *sheets billowing in the breeze.* *—tr.* To cause to billow: *wind that billowed the sails.* [From Old Norse *bylgja,* a wave. See **bhelgh-** in Appendix.] **—bil′low·i·ness** *n.* **—bil′low·y** *adj.*

bill·post·er (bĭl′pō′stər) *n.* One that posts notices, posters, or advertisements. Also called *billsticker.* **—bill′post′ing** *n.*

bil·ly[1] (bĭl′ē) *n., pl.* **-lies.** A billy club. [Short for BILLY CLUB.]

bil·ly[2] (bĭl′ē) *n., pl.* **-lies.** *Australian.* A metal pot or kettle used in camp cooking. [Probably short for *billypot,* from *Billy,* nickname for *William.*]

billy club *n.* A short wooden club, especially a police officer's club. [Perhaps alteration of *bully club; see BULLY[1], or from BILLET[2].]

bil·ly·cock (bĭl′ē-kŏk′) *n. Chiefly British.* A felt hat with a low, rounded crown, similar to a derby. [Perhaps alteration of *bullycocked* : BULLY[1] + COCK[1].]

billy goat *n. Informal.* A male goat.

Bil·ly the Kid (bĭl′ē). See William H. **Bonney.**

bi·lo·bate (bī-lō′bāt′) also **bi·lo·bat·ed** (-bā′tĭd) or **bi·lobed** (bī′-lōbd′) *adj.* Divided into or having two lobes: *a bilobate leaf.*

bi·lob·u·lar (bī-lŏb′yə-lər, -lō′byə-) *adj.* Having two lobules.

bi·lo·ca·tion (bī′lō-kā′shən) *n.* Existence or the ability to exist simultaneously in two places.

bi·loc·u·lar (bī-lŏk′yə-lər) also **bi·loc·u·late** (-lĭt, -lāt′) *adj.* Divided into or containing two chambers.

Bi·lox·i[1] (bə-lŭk′sē, -lŏk′-) *n., pl.* **Biloxi** or **-is. 1.a.** A Native American people formerly inhabiting territory around Biloxi Bay in southeast Mississippi on the Gulf of Mexico. **b.** A member of this people. **2.** The extinct Siouan language of the Biloxi.

Bi·lox·i[2] (bə-lŭk′sē, -lŏk′-). A city of southeast Mississippi on a peninsula between **Biloxi Bay** and Mississippi Sound on the Gulf of Mexico. Old Biloxi was settled by the French in 1699. Population, 49,311.

bil·tong (bĭl′tŏng′, -tông′) *n. South African.* Narrow strips of meat dried in the sun. [Afrikaans : *bil,* buttock (from Middle Dutch *bille;* see **bhel-**[2] in Appendix) + *tong,* tongue (from Middle Dutch *tonghe;* see **dn̥ghū-** in Appendix).]

bi·man·u·al (bī-măn′yo͞o-əl) *adj.* Using or requiring the use of both hands. **—bi·man′u·al·ly** *adv.*

bi·max·il·lar·y (bī-măk′sə-lĕr′ē) *adj.* Relating to or affecting both jaws.

bim·bo (bĭm′bō) *n., pl.* **-bos. 1.** *Offensive Slang.* A woman, especially one who is perceived as vacuous or as having an exaggerated interest in sexuality: *"Bimbos had become major role models for young girls everywhere"* (Ellen Goodman). **2.** *Slang.* A vacuous person: *"a male bimbo . . . who even has to be tutored . . . in the clichés that comprise the basic interview"* (George F. Will). [Perhaps from Italian *bimbo,* baby.]

bi·mes·tri·al (bī-mĕs′trē-əl) *adj.* **1.** Occurring every two months; bimonthly. **2.** Lasting two months. [From Latin *bimēstris* : *bi-,* two; see BI–[1] + *mēnsis,* month; see **mē-**[2] in Appendix.]

bi·me·tal·lic (bī′mə-tăl′ĭk) *adj.* **1.** Consisting of two metals, often bonded together and having different rates of thermal expansion. **2.** Of, based on, or using the principles of bimetallism.

bi·met·al·lism (bī-mĕt′l-ĭz′əm) *n.* **1.** The use of a monetary standard consisting of two metals, especially gold and silver, in a fixed ratio of value. **2.** The doctrine advocating bimetallism. **—bi·met′al·list** *n.* **—bi·met′al·lis′tic** *adj.*

bi·mil·le·nar·y (bī-mĭl′ə-nĕr′ē, bī′mə-lĕn′ə-rē) *n., pl.* **-ies.** A bimillenium. **—bi·mil·len·a·ry** *adj.*

bi·mil·len·i·um (bī′mə-lĕn′ē-əm) *n., pl.* **-len·ni·ums** or **-len·ni·a** (-lĕn′ē-ə). **1.** A span of 2,000 years. **2.** A 2,000th anniversary. **—bi·mil·len·i·al** *adj.* **—bi·mil·len·i·al·ly** *adv.*

Bim·i·nis (bĭm′ə-nēz). A group of small islands of the western Bahamas in the Straits of Florida. According to legend, the islands are the site of the Fountain of Youth sought by Juan Ponce de León.

bi·mod·al (bī-mōd′l) *adj.* **1.** Having two distinct statistical modes. **2.** Designed for operation on either railroads or highways. Used of vehicles. **—bi′mo·dal′i·ty** (bī′mō-dăl′ĭ-tē) *n.*

bi·mo·lec·u·lar (bī′mə-lĕk′yə-lər) *adj.* Relating to, consisting of, or affecting two molecules. **—bi′mo·lec′u·lar·ly** *adv.*

bi·month·ly (bī-mŭnth′lē) *adj.* **1.** Happening every two months. **2.** Happening twice a month; semimonthly. **—bimonthly** *adv.* **1.** Once every two months. **2.** Twice a month; semimonthly. **—bimonthly** *n., pl.* **-lies.** A bimonthly publication. See Usage Note at **bi–[1].**

bi·mor·phe·mic (bī′môr-fē′mĭk) *adj.* Consisting of two morphemes.

bin (bĭn) *n.* A container or enclosed space for storage. **—bin** *tr.v.* **binned, bin·ning, bins.** To place or store in a bin. [Middle English *binne,* from Old English, probably of Celtic origin.]

bin– *pref.* Variant of **bi–[1].**

bi·nal (bī′nəl) *adj.* Twofold; double. [New Latin *bīnālis,* twin, from Latin *bīnī,* two by two. See **dwo-** in Appendix.]

bi·na·ry (bī′nə-rē) *adj.* **1.** Characterized by or consisting of two parts or components; twofold. **2.** Of or relating to a system of numeration having 2 as its base. **3.** *Chemistry.* Consisting of or containing only molecules consisting of two kinds of atoms. **4.** Of or employing two comparatively nontoxic chemicals that combine to produce a deadly poison: *binary weapons; a binary nerve gas.* **5.** *Music.* Having two sections or subjects. **—binary** *n., pl.* **-ries.** Something that is binary, especially a binary star. [Middle English *binarie,* from Late Latin *bīnārius,* from Latin *bīnī,* two by two. See **dwo-** in Appendix.]

binary cod·ed decimal (kō′dĭd) *n. Abbr.* **BCD, bcd** *Computer Science.* A code in which a string of four binary digits represents a decimal number.

binary digit *n.* Either of the digits 0 or 1, used in the binary number system.

binary fission *n.* A method of asexual reproduction that involves the splitting of a parent cell into two approximately equal parts.

binary number system *n.* A method of representing numbers in which only the digits 0 and 1 are used. Successive units are powers of 2. Also called *binary system.*

binary operation *n.* An operation, such as addition, that is applied to two elements of a set to produce a third element of the set.

binary star *n.* A stellar system consisting of two stars orbiting about a common center of mass and often appearing as a single visual or telescopic object. Also called *double star.*

binary system *n.* See **binary number system.**

bi·na·tion·al (bī-năsh′ə-nəl, -năsh′nəl) *adj.* Of, relating to, or involving two nations.

bin·au·ral (bī-nôr′əl, bĭn-ôr′-) *adj.* **1.a.** Having or relating to two ears. **b.** Having to do with the perception of sound with both ears: *binaural hearing.* **2.** Of or relating to sound transmission from two sources, which may vary acoustically, as in tone or pitch, to give a stereophonic effect. **—bin·au′ral·ly** *adv.*

bind (bīnd) *v.* **bound** (bound), **bind·ing, binds.** *—tr.* **1.** To tie or secure, as with a rope or cord. **2.** To fasten or wrap by encircling, as with a belt or ribbon. **3.** To bandage: *bound up their wounds.* **4.** To hold or restrain with or as if with bonds. **5.** To compel, obligate, or unite: *bound by a deep sense of duty; bound by a common interest in sports.* **6.** *Law.* To place under legal obligation by contract or oath. **7.** To make certain or irrevocable: *bind the deal with a down payment.* **8.** To apprentice or indenture: *was bound out as a servant.* **9.** To cause to cohere or stick together in a mass: *Bind the dry ingredients with milk and eggs.* **10.** To enclose and fasten (a book or other printed material) between covers. **11.** To furnish with an edge or border for protection, reinforcement, or ornamentation. **12.** To constipate. **13.** To form a chemical bond with. *—intr.* **1.** To tie up or fasten something. **2.** To stick or become stuck: *applied a lubricant to keep the moving parts from binding.* **3.** To be uncomfortably tight or restricting, as clothes. **4.** To become compact or solid; cohere. **5.** To be compelling or unifying: *the ties that bind.* **6.** To form a chemical bond. **—bind** *n.* **1.a.** The act of binding. **b.** The state of being bound. **c.** Something that binds. **d.** A place where something binds: *a bind halfway up the seam of the skirt.* **2.** *Informal.* A difficult, restrictive, or unresolvable situation: *found themselves in a bind when their car broke down.* **3.** *Music.* A tie, slur, or brace. ***—phrasal verbs.*** **bind off.** To cast off in knitting. **bind over.** *Law.* To hold on bail or place under bond. [Middle English *binden,* from Old English *bindan.* See **bhendh-** in Appendix.]

bind·er (bīn′dər) *n.* **1.** One that binds, especially a bookbinder. **2.** Something, such as a cord, used to bind. **3.** A notebook cover with rings or clamps for holding sheets of paper. **4.** Something, such as the latex in certain paints, that creates uniform consistency, solidification, or cohesion. **5.a.** A machine that reaps and ties grain. **b.** An attachment on a reaping machine that ties grain in bundles. **6.** *Law.* A payment or written statement making an agreement legally binding until the completion of a formal contract, especially an insurance contract.

bind·er·y (bīn′də-rē) *n., pl.* **-ies.** A place where books are bound.

bind·ing (bīn′dĭng) *n.* **1.** The action of one that binds. **2.** Something that binds or is used as a binder. **3.** The cover that holds together the pages of a book. **4.** A strip sewn or attached

billy club

ă pat	oi boy
ā pay	ou out
âr care	o͝o took
ä father	o͞o boot
ĕ pet	ŭ cut
ē be	ûr urge
ĭ pit	th thin
ī pie	*th* this
îr pier	hw which
ŏ pot	zh vision
ō toe	ə about, item
ô paw	♦ regionalism

Stress marks: **′** (primary); ′ (secondary), as in **dictionary** (dĭk′shə-nĕr′ē)

over or along an edge for protection, reinforcement, or ornamentation. **5.** *Sports.* Fastenings on a ski for securing the boot. **—binding** *adj.* **1.** Serving to bind. **2.** Uncomfortably tight and confining. **3.** Imposing or commanding adherence to a commitment, an obligation, or a duty: *binding arbitration; a binding agreement.* **—bind′ing·ly** *adv.* **—bind′ing·ness** *n.*

binding energy *n.* **1.** The net energy required to decompose a molecule, an atom, or a nucleus into its components. **2.** The net energy required to remove an atomic electron to an infinitely remote position from its orbit.

bin·dle·stiff (bĭn′dl-stĭf′) *n.* A hobo, especially one who carries a bedroll. [English *bindle,* bundle (probably from German dialectal *bindel,* from Middle High German *bündel,* from *binden,* to bind, from Old High German *binten;* see **bhendh-** in Appendix) + STIFF.]

bind·weed (bīnd′wēd′) *n.* **1.** Any of various trailing or twining, often weedy plants of the genera *Calystegia* and *Convolvulus,* having white, pink, or purple bell-shaped or funnel-shaped flowers. **2.** Any of various similar trailing or twining plants, such as the black bindweed.

bine (bīn) *n.* The flexible twining or climbing stem of certain plants, such as the hop, woodbine, or bindweed. [Alteration of BIND, vine.]

Bi·net-Si·mon scale (bĭ-nā′sē-mōN′, -sī′mən) *n.* An evaluation of the relative mental development of children by a series of psychological tests of intellectual ability. Also called *Binet scale, Binet-Simon test, Binet test.* [After Alfred *Binet* (1857–1911) and Théodore *Simon* (1873–1961), French psychologists.]

Bing (bĭng), Sir **Rudolf.** Born 1902. Austrian-born impresario who managed (1950–1972) the Metropolitan Opera in New York City.

Bing cherry *n.* A variety of cherry with juicy, sweet, deep red to nearly black fruit. [Perhaps after an employee of the cherry's originator.]

binge (bĭnj) *n.* **1.** A drunken spree or revel. **2. a.** A period of unrestrained, immoderate self-indulgence. **b.** A period of excessive or uncontrolled indulgence in food or drink: *an eating binge.* **—binge** *intr.v.* **binged, bing·ing** or **binge·ing, bing·es. 1.** To be immoderately self-indulgent and unrestrained: *"The story is like a fever dream that a disturbed and imaginative city-dweller might have after binging on comics"* (Lloyd Rose). **2.** To engage in excessive or uncontrolled indulgence in food or drink. [Dialectal *binge,* to soak.] **—bing′er** *n.*

SYNONYMS: *binge, fling, jag, orgy, spree.* The central meaning shared by these nouns is "a period of uncontrolled self-indulgence": *a gambling binge; had a fling between commencement and graduate school; a crying jag; an eating orgy; a shopping spree.*

binge-eat·ing syndrome (bĭnj′ē′tĭng) *n.* See **bulimia** (sense 2).

binge-purge syndrome (bĭnj′pûrj′) *n.* See **bulimarexia.**

binge-vom·it syndrome (bĭnj′vŏm′ĭt) *n.* See **bulimarexia.**

Bing·ham (bĭng′əm), **George Caleb.** 1811–1879. American painter noted for his portraits and genre paintings of the American frontier.

Bing·ham·ton (bĭng′əm-tən). A city of south-central New York near the Pennsylvania border south-southeast of Syracuse. It was settled in 1787. Population, 55,860.

bin·go (bĭng′gō) *n., pl.* **-goes.** *Games.* A game of chance in which each player has one or more cards printed with differently numbered squares on which to place markers when the respective numbers are drawn and announced by a caller. The first player to mark a complete row of numbers is the winner. **—bingo** *interj.* Used to express the sudden occurrence of an event or completion of an action. [Origin unknown.]

bin·na·cle (bĭn′ə-kəl) *n.* *Nautical.* A case that supports and protects a ship's compass, located near the helm. [Alteration of Middle English *bitakille,* from Old Spanish *bitácula* or from Old Portuguese *bitácola,* both from Latin *habitāculum,* habitation, from *habitāre,* to inhabit. See **ghabh-** in Appendix.]

binocular

bin·oc·u·lar (bə-nŏk′yə-lər, bī-) *adj.* **1.** Relating to, used by, or involving both eyes at the same time: *binocular vision.* **2.** Having two eyes arranged to produce stereoscopic vision. **—binocular** *n.* An optical device, such as a pair of field glasses or opera glasses, designed for simultaneous use by both eyes and consisting of two small telescopes joined with a single focusing device. Often used in the plural. **—bin·oc′u·lar′i·ty** (-lăr′ĭ-tē) *n.* **—bin·oc′u·lar·ly** *adv.*

bi·no·mi·al (bī-nō′mē-əl) *adj.* Consisting of or relating to two names or terms. **—binomial** *n.* **1.** *Mathematics.* A polynomial with two terms. **2.** *Biology.* A taxonomic name in binomial nomenclature. [From New Latin *binōmius,* having two names : BI–[1] + French *nom,* name (from Latin *nōmen;* see NOMINAL).] **—bi·no′mi·al·ly** *adv.*

binomial distribution *n.* The frequency distribution of the probability of a specified number of successes in an arbitrary number of repeated independent Bernoulli trials. Also called *Bernoulli distribution.*

binomial nomenclature *n.* The scientific naming of species whereby each species receives a Latin or Latinized name of two parts, the first indicating the genus and the second being the specific epithet. For example, *Juglans regia* is the English walnut; *Juglans nigra,* the black walnut.

binomial theorem *n.* *Mathematics.* A theorem that specifies the expansion of a binomial to any power without requiring the explicit multiplication of the binomial terms.

bint (bĭnt) *n.* *Chiefly British & Offensive.* A woman or girl: *"As the R.A.F. friend would have put it, you could never tell with these foreign bints"* (Kingsley Amis). [Arabic, daughter.]

bin·tu·rong (bĭn-to͝or′ông, -ŏng) *n.* A civet *(Arctictis binturong)* of southeast Asia with a long, prehensile tail. Also called *bearcat.* [Malay *bĕnturong, binturong.*]

bi·nu·cle·ar (bī-no͞o′klē-ər, -nyo͞o′-) *adj.* Variant of **binucleate.**

binuclear family *n.* The extended family, usually consisting of two separate households, formed by the children and subsequent spouses of the partners in a divorce.

bi·nu·cle·ate (bī-no͞o′klē-ĭt, -āt′, -nyo͞o′-) also **bi·nu·cle·at·ed** (-ā′tĭd) or **bi·nu·cle·ar** (-klē-ər, -nyo͞o′-) *adj.* Having two nuclei.

Bin·ue (bĭn′wā). See **Benue.**

bi·o (bī′ō) *n., pl.* **-os.** *Informal.* **1.** A biography. **2.** A biographical sketch or outline. *—attributive.* Often used to modify another noun: *bio cards; bio information.*

bio– or **bi–** *pref.* **1.** Life; living organism: *biome.* **2.** Biology; biological: *biophysics.* [Greek, from *bios,* life. See **gʷei-** in Appendix.]

bio·ac·cu·mu·la·tion (bī′ō-ə-kyo͞om′yə-lā′shən) *n.* The accumulation of a substance, such as a toxic chemical, in various tissues of a living organism: *the bioaccumulation of mercury in fish.* **—bi′o·ac·cu′mu·la′tive** *adj.*

bi·o·a·cous·tics (bī′ō-ə-ko͞o′stĭks) *n.* *(used with a sing. verb).* The study of sounds produced by or affecting living organisms, especially those sounds involved in communication.

bi·o·ac·tive (bī′ō-ăk′tĭv) *adj.* Of or relating to a substance that has an effect on living tissue: *bioactive compounds.*

bi·o·ac·tiv·i·ty (bī′ō-ăk-tĭv′ĭ-tē) *n.* The effect of a given agent, such as a vaccine, on a living organism or living tissue.

bi·o·as·say (bī′ō-ăs′ā′, -ă-sā′) *n.* Determination of the strength or biological activity of a substance, such as a drug or hormone, by comparing its effects with those of a standard preparation on a test organism.

bi·o·as·tro·nau·tics (bī′ō-ăs′trə-nô′tĭks) *n.* *(used with a sing. verb).* The study of the biological and medical effects of space flight on living organisms. **—bi′o·as′tro·nau′ti·cal** *adj.*

bi·o·a·vail·a·bil·i·ty (bī′ō-ə-vā′lə-bĭl′ĭ-tē) *n.* The degree to which a drug or other substance becomes available at the physiological site of activity after administration.

bi·o·bib·li·og·ra·phy or **bi·o·bib·li·og·ra·phy** (bī′ō-bĭb′lē-ŏg′rə-fē) *n., pl.* **-phies.** A book or article combining an account of a person's life with a discussion of works written by or about that person.

Bí·o-Bí·o (bē′ō-bē′ō). A river of central Chile flowing about 386 km (240 mi) generally northwest from the Andes to the Pacific Ocean near Concepción.

bi·o·cat·a·lyst (bī′ō-kăt′l-ĭst) *n.* A substance, especially an enzyme, that initiates or modifies the rate of a chemical reaction in a living body; a biochemical catalyst. **—bi′o·cat′a·lyt′ic** (-kăt′l-ĭt′ĭk) *adj.*

bi·o·ce·nol·o·gy (bī′ō-sə-nŏl′ə-jē) *n.* *Ecology.* The study of communities in nature and of interactions among their members.

bi·o·ce·no·sis also **bi·o·coe·no·sis** (bī′ō-sĭ-nō′sĭs) or **bi·o·ce·nose** (-sē′nōs) *n., pl.* **-ses** (-sēz). A group of interacting organisms that live in a particular habitat and form an ecological community.

biochemical oxygen demand *n.* *Abbr.* **B.O.D.** *Microbiology.* The amount of oxygen required by aerobic microorganisms to decompose the organic matter in a sample of water, such as that polluted by sewage. It is used as a measure of the degree of water pollution. Also called *biological oxygen demand.*

bi·o·chem·is·try (bī′ō-kĕm′ĭ-strē) *n.* **1.** The study of the chemical substances and vital processes occurring in living organisms; biological chemistry; physiological chemistry. **2.** The chemical composition of a particular living system or biological substance: *viral biochemistry.* **—bi′o·chem′i·cal** (-ĭ-kəl) *adj.* & *n.* **—bi′o·chem′i·cal·ly** *adv.* **—bi′o·chem′ist** *n.*

bi·o·chip (bī′ō-chĭp′) *n.* *Computer Science.* A computer chip made from organic molecules rather than silicon or germanium.

bi·o·cide (bī′ə-sīd′) *n.* A chemical agent, such as a pesticide, that is capable of destroying living organisms. **—bi′o·cid′al** (-sīd′l) *adj.*

bi·o·cli·ma·tol·o·gy (bī′ō-klī′mə-tŏl′ə-jē) *n.* The study of the effects of climatic conditions on living organisms. **—bi′o·cli·mat′ic** (-klī-măt′ĭk) *adj.*

bio·coe·no·sis (bī′ō-sĭ-nō′sĭs) *n.* Variant of **biocenosis.**

bi·o·com·pat·i·bil·i·ty (bī′ō-kəm-păt′ə-bĭl′ĭ-tē) *n.* The property of being biologically compatible by not producing a toxic, injurious, or immunological response in living tissue: *As a result of its strength and biocompatibility, the material is often used in medical devices.* **—bi′o·com·pat′i·ble** *adj.*

bi·o·con·ver·sion (bī′ō-kən-vûr′zhən, -shən) *n.* The conversion of organic materials, such as plant or animal waste, into usable products or energy sources by biological processes or agents, such as certain microorganisms.

bi·o·de·grad·a·ble (bī′ō-dĭ-grā′də-bəl) *adj.* Capable of being decomposed by biological agents, especially bacteria: *a biodegradable detergent.* **—bi′o·de·grad′a·bil′i·ty** *n.* **—bi′o·deg′ra·da′tion** (-dĕg′rə-dā′shən) *n.* **—bi′o·de·grade′** *v.*

bi·o·dy·nam·ic (bī′ō-dī-năm′ĭk, -dĭ-) *adj.* **1.** Of or relating to the study of the effects of dynamic processes, such as motion or acceleration, on living organisms. **2.** Of or relating to a system of organic crop cultivation: *biodynamic farming.*

bi·o·dy·nam·ics (bī′ō-dī-năm′ĭks, -dĭ-) *n.* *(used with a sing. verb).* **1.** The study of the effects of dynamic processes, such as motion or acceleration, on living organisms. **2.** The science of the force or energy of living matter and physiological processes. **3.** A method of organic gardening and crop cultivation in which certain factors, such as planetary and seasonal cycles, are considered.

bi·o·e·lec·tric (bī′ō-ĭ-lĕk′trĭk) also **bi·o·e·lec·tri·cal** (-trĭ-kəl) *adj.* **1.** Of or having to do with the electric current generated by living tissue. **2.** Of or relating to the effects of electricity on living tissue.

bi·o·e·lec·tric·i·ty (bī′ō-ĭ-lĕk-trĭs′ĭ-tē, -ē′lĕk-) *n.* An electric current that is generated by living tissue, such as nerve and muscle.

bi·o·e·lec·tron·ics (bī′ō-ĭ-lĕk-trŏn′ĭks, -ē-lĕk-) *n.* *(used with a sing. verb).* **1.** The application of the principles of electronics to biology and medicine. **2.** The study of the role of intermolecular electron transfer in physiological processes. **—bi′o·e·lec·tron′ic** *adj.*

bi·o·en·er·get·ics (bī′ō-ĕn′ər-jĕt′ĭks) *n.* *(used with a sing. verb).* **1.** *Biochemistry.* The study of the flow and transformation of energy in and between living organisms and between living organisms and their environment. **2.** *Psychology.* A therapeutic approach that incorporates breathing, movement, body exercises, psychotherapy, and free expression of feelings to enhance self-awareness and well-being and relieve physical and emotional tension. **—bi′o·en·er·get′ic** *adj.*

bi·o·en·gi·neer·ing (bī′ō-ĕn′jə-nîr′ĭng) *n.* **1.** The application of engineering principles to the fields of biology and medicine, as in the development of aids or replacements for defective or missing body organs. Also called *biomedical engineering.* **2.** Genetic engineering. **—bi′o·en′gi·neer′** *n.*

bi·o·en·vi·ron·men·tal (bī′ō-ĕn-vī′rən-mĕn′tl, -vī′ərn-) *adj.* Having to do with the relationship between the environment and living organisms: *Bioenvironmental engineers are studying the effects of toxic chemicals on life in the area.*

bi·o·eth·ics (bī′ō-ĕth′ĭks) *n.* *(used with a sing. verb).* The study of the ethical and moral implications of new biological discoveries and biomedical advances, as in the fields of genetic engineering and drug research. **—bi′o·eth′i·cal** *adj.* **—bi′o·eth′i·cist** (-ĭ-sĭst) *n.*

bi·o·feed·back (bī′ō-fēd′băk′) *n.* The technique of using monitoring devices to furnish information regarding an autonomic bodily function, such as heart rate or blood pressure, in an attempt to gain some voluntary control over that function. It may be used clinically to treat certain conditions, such as hypertension and migraine headache.

bi·o·fla·vo·noid (bī′ō-flā′və-noid′) *n.* Any of a group of biologically active substances found in plants and functioning in the maintenance of the walls of small blood vessels in mammals.

biog. *abbr.* Biographer; biographical; biography.

bi·o·gas (bī′ō-găs′) *n.* A mixture of methane and carbon dioxide produced by bacterial degradation of organic matter and used as a fuel.

bi·o·gen·e·sis (bī′ō-jĕn′ĭ-sĭs) also **bi·og·e·ny** (bī-ŏj′ə-nē) *n.* **1.** The principle that living organisms develop only from other living organisms and not from nonliving matter. **2.** Generation of living organisms from other living organisms. **3.** See **biosynthesis. 4.** The supposed recurrence of the evolutionary stages of a species during the embryonic development and differentiation of a member of that species. In this sense, also called *recapitulation.* **—bi′o·ge·net′ic** (-jə-nĕt′ĭk), **bi′o·ge·net′i·cal** (-ĭ-kəl) *adj.* **—bi′o·ge·net′i·cal·ly** *adv.*

biogenetic law *n.* The theory that the stages in an organism's embryonic development and differentiation correspond to the stages of evolutionary development characteristic of the species. Also called *Haeckel's law, recapitulation theory.*

bi·o·gen·ic (bī′ō-jĕn′ĭk) *adj.* **1.** Produced by living organisms or biological processes. **2.** Necessary for the maintenance of life processes.

biogenic amine *n.* Any of a group of naturally occurring, biologically active amines, such as norepinephrine, histamine, and serotonin, that act primarily as neurotransmitters and are capable of affecting mental functioning.

bi·og·e·nous (bī-ŏj′ə-nəs) *adj.* **1.** Originating from living things. **2.** Producing life.

bi·og·e·ny (bī-ŏj′ə-nē) *n.* Variant of **biogenesis.**

bi·o·ge·o·chem·is·try (bī′ō-jē′ō-kĕm′ĭ-strē) *n.* The study of the relationship between the geochemistry of a region and the animal and plant life in that region. **—bi′o·ge′o·chem′i·cal** (-ĭ-kəl) *adj.*

bi·o·ge·og·ra·phy (bī′ō-jē-ŏg′rə-fē) *n.* The study of the geographic distribution of organisms. **—bi′o·ge·og′ra·pher** *n.* **—bi′o·ge′o·graph′ic** (-jē′ə-grăf′ĭk), **bi′o·ge′o·graph′i·cal** (-ĭ-kəl) *adj.*

bi·og·ra·phee (bī-ŏg′rə-fē′, bē-) *n.* The subject of a biography.

bi·og·ra·pher (bī-ŏg′rə-fər, bē-) *n.* *Abbr.* **biog.** One who writes, composes, or produces biography.

bi·o·graph·i·cal (bī′ə-grăf′ĭ-kəl) also **bi·o·graph·ic** (-grăf′ĭk) *adj.* *Abbr.* **biog. 1.** Containing, consisting of, or relating to the facts or events in a person's life. **2.** Of or relating to biography as a literary form. **—bi′o·graph′i·cal·ly** *adv.*

bi·og·ra·phy (bī-ŏg′rə-fē, bē-) *n., pl.* **-phies.** *Abbr.* **biog. 1.** An account of a person's life written, composed, or produced by another: *a film biography of Adlai Stevenson; an oral biography.* **2.** Biographies considered as a group, especially when regarded as a genre. **3.** The writing, composition, or production of biographies: *a career entirely devoted to biography.* [Late Greek *biographia* : Greek *bio-*, bio- + Greek *-graphia*, -graphy.]

bi·o·haz·ard (bī′ō-hăz′ərd) *n.* **1.** A biological agent, such as an infectious microorganism, or a condition that constitutes a threat to human beings, especially in biological research or experimentation. **2.** The potential danger, risk, or harm from exposure to such an agent or condition.

bi·o·in·or·gan·ic (bī′ō-ĭn′ôr-găn′ĭk) *adj.* Of or having to do with inorganic compounds and their role in biochemical processes.

bi·o·in·stru·men·ta·tion (bī′ō-ĭn′strə-mĕn-tā′shən) *n.* **1.** Use of instruments for the recording or transmission of physiological information, such as breathing rate or heart rate. **2.** The instruments so used.

Bi·o·ko (bē-ō′kō). Formerly **Fer·nan·do Po** (fər-năn′dō pō′). An island of Equatorial Guinea in the Gulf of Guinea.

biol. *abbr.* **1.** Biological; biology. **2.** Biologist.

bi·o·log·i·cal (bī′ə-lŏj′ĭ-kəl) also **bi·o·log·ic** (-lŏj′ĭk) —*adj.* *Abbr.* **biol. 1.** Of, relating to, caused by, or affecting life or living organisms. **2.** Having to do with biology. **3.** Related by blood: *the child's biological parents; his biological sister.* —*n.* A preparation, such as a drug, a vaccine, or an antitoxin, that is synthesized from living organisms or their products and used medically as a diagnostic, preventive, or therapeutic agent. **—bi′o·log′i·cal·ly** *adv.*

biological clock *n.* An innate mechanism in living organisms that controls the periodicity or rhythm of various physiological functions or activities.

biological control *n.* Control of pests through the use of organisms that are natural predators, parasites, or pathogens.

biological half-life *n.* *Biology.* See **half-life** (sense 2a).

biological oxygen demand *n.* See **biochemical oxygen demand.**

biological warfare *n.* *Abbr.* **BW** The use of disease-producing microorganisms, toxic biological products, or organic biocides to cause death or injury to humans, animals, or plants.

bi·ol·o·gy (bī-ŏl′ə-jē) *n.* *Abbr.* **biol. 1.** The science of life and of living organisms, including their structure, function, growth, origin, evolution, and distribution. It includes botany and zoology and all their subdivisions. **2.** The life processes or characteristic phenomena of a group or category of living organisms: *the biology of viruses.* **3.** The plant and animal life of a specific area or region. [German *Biologie* : Greek *bio-*, bio- + Greek *-logia*, -logy.] **—bi·ol′o·gist** *n.*

bi·o·lu·mi·nes·cence (bī′ō-lo͞o′mə-nĕs′əns) *n.* Emission of visible light by living organisms such as the firefly and various fish, fungi, and bacteria. **—bi′o·lu′mi·nes′cent** *adj.*

bi·ol·y·sis (bī-ŏl′ĭ-sĭs) *n.* **1.** Death of a living organism or tissue caused or accompanied by lysis. **2.** The decomposition of organic material by living organisms, such as microorganisms. **—bi′o·lyt′ic** (bī′ə-lĭt′ĭk) *adj.*

bi·o·mark·er (bī′ō-mär′kər) *n.* *Medicine.* **a.** See **marker** (sense 9). **b.** A specific physical trait used to measure or indicate the effects or progress of a disease or condition: *Biomarkers of aging include thinning of the hair and diminished elasticity of the skin.*

bi·o·mass (bī′ō-măs′) *n.* **1.** The total mass of living matter within a given unit of environmental area. **2.** Plant material, vegetation, or agricultural waste used as a fuel or energy source.

bi·o·ma·ter·i·al (bī′ō-mə-tîr′ē-əl) *n.* A biocompatible material that is used to construct artificial organs, rehabilitation devices, or prostheses and replace natural body tissues. [BIO(COMPATIBLE) + MATERIAL.]

bi·o·math·e·mat·ics (bī′ō-măth′ə-măt′ĭks) *n.* *(used with a sing. verb).* The application of mathematical principles to biological processes. **—bi′o·math′e·mat′i·cal** *adj.* **—bi′o·math′e·ma·ti′cian** (-mə-tĭsh′ən) *n.*

bi·ome (bī′ōm′) *n.* A major regional or global biotic community, such as a grassland or desert, characterized chiefly by the dominant forms of plant life and the prevailing climate.

bi·o·me·chan·ics (bī′ō-mĭ-kăn′ĭks) *n.* **1.** *(used with a sing. verb).* The study of the mechanics of a living body, especially of the forces exerted by muscles and gravity on the skeletal structure. **2.** *(used with a pl. verb).* The mechanics of a part or function of a living body, such as of the heart or of locomotion. **—bi′o·me·chan′i·cal** *adj.* **—bi′o·me·chan′i·cal·ly** *adv.*

biomedical engineering *n.* See **bioengineering.**

bi·o·med·i·cine (bī′ō-mĕd′ĭ-sĭn) *n.* **1.** The branch of med-

ă pat	oi boy
ā pay	ou **out**
âr care	o͝o **took**
ä father	o͞o **boot**
ĕ pet	ŭ **cut**
ē be	ûr **urge**
ĭ pit	th **thin**
ī pie	*th* **this**
îr **pier**	hw **which**
ŏ pot	zh vision
ō toe	ə about, item
ô **paw**	♦ regionalism

Stress marks: ′ (primary); ′ (secondary), as in **dictionary** (dĭk′shə-nĕr′ē)

ical science that deals with the ability of human beings to tolerate environmental stresses and variations, as in space travel. **2.** The application of the principles of the natural sciences, especially biology and physiology, to clinical medicine. **—bi′o·med′i·cal** (-ĭ-kəl) *adj.*

bi·o·me·te·or·ol·o·gy (bī′ō-mē′tē-ə-rŏl′ə-jē) *n.* The study of the relationship between atmospheric conditions, such as temperature and humidity, and living organisms.

bi·o·met·rics (bī′ō-mĕt′rĭks) *n.* *(used with a sing. verb).* The statistical study of biological phenomena. **—bi′o·met′ric, bi′-o·met′ri·cal** *adj.* **—bi′o·met′ri·cal·ly** *adv.*

bi·om·e·try (bī-ŏm′ĭ-trē) *n.* Biometrics.

bi·on·ic (bī-ŏn′ĭk) *adj.* **1.** Of or relating to bionics. **2.** Having anatomical structures or physiological processes that are replaced or enhanced by electronic or mechanical components. **3.** Having extraordinary strength, powers, or capabilities; superhuman. [BI(O)– + (ELECTR)ONIC.]

bi·on·ics (bī-ŏn′ĭks) *n.* *(used with a sing. verb).* Application of biological principles to the study and design of engineering systems, especially electronic systems. [BI(O)– + (ELECTR)ONICS.]

bi·o·nom·ics (bī′ə-nŏm′ĭks) *n.* *(used with a sing. verb).* See **ecology** (sense 1a). [From French *bionomique,* pertaining to ecology, from *bionomie,* ecology : Greek *bio-,* bio- + Greek *-nomia,* -nomy.] **—bi′o·nom′ic, bi′o·nom′i·cal** *adj.* **—bi′o·nom′-i·cal·ly** *adv.*

–bi·ont (bī′ŏnt′) *suff.* Living organism; mode of living: *symbiont.* [BI(O)– + –ONT.]

bi·o·or·gan·ic (bī′ō-ôr-găn′ĭk) *adj.* Of or having to do with organic compounds and their role in biochemical processes.

bi·o·phys·ics (bī′ō-fĭz′ĭks) *n.* *(used with a sing. verb).* The science that deals with the application of physics to biological processes and phenomena. **—bi′o·phys′i·cal** *adj.* **—bi′o·phys′i·cal·ly** *adv.* **—bi′o·phys′i·cist** *n.*

bi·o·pic (bī′ō-pĭk′) *n.* A film or television biography, often with fictionalized episodes.

bi·o·pol·y·mer (bī′ō-pŏl′ə-mər) *n.* A macromolecule, such as a protein or nucleic acid, that is formed in a living organism.

bi·o·proc·ess (bī′ō-prŏs′ĕs, -prō′sĕs) *n.* **a.** A technique that produces a biological material, such as a genetically engineered microbial strain, for commercial use. **b.** Production of a commercially useful chemical or fuel by a biological process, such as microbial fermentation or degradation. *—attributive.* Often used to modify another noun: *bioprocess technology; the bioprocess market.* **—bioprocess** *tr.v.* **-essed, -ess·ing, -ess·es.** To prepare, produce, or treat (a substance) by means of a bioprocess.

bi·op·sy (bī′ŏp′sē) *n., pl.* **-sies.** The removal and examination of a sample of tissue from a living body for diagnostic purposes. **—bi·op′sic** (bī-ŏp′sĭk), **bi·op′tic** (-tĭk) *adj.*

bi·o·psy·chic (bī′ō-sī′kĭk) *adj.* **1.** Having to do with the relationship between psychological and biological phenomena. **2.** Involving both psychological and biological phenomena.

bi·o·psy·chol·o·gy (bī′ō-sī-kŏl′ə-jē) *n.* See **psychobiology** (sense 1).

bi·o·re·ac·tor (bī′ō-rē-ăk′tər) *n.* **1.** A container, such as a large fermentation chamber, for growing living organisms that are used in the industrial production of substances such as pharmaceuticals, antibodies, or vaccines. **2.** A living organism, such as a bacterium or yeast, that is used in the biotechnological production of substances such as pharmaceuticals, antibodies, or vaccines.

bi·o·re·gion (bī′ō-rē′jən) *n.* An area constituting a natural ecological community with characteristic flora, fauna, and environmental conditions and bounded by natural rather than artificial borders. **—bi′o·re′gion·al** *adj.*

bi·o·re·gion·al·ism (bī′ō-rē′jə-nə-lĭz′əm) *n.* The belief that social organization and environmental policies should be based on the bioregion rather than on a region determined by political or economic boundaries. **—bi′o·re′gion·al·ist** *n.*

bi·o·re·search (bī′ō-rĭ-sûrch′, -rē′sûrch) *n.* Research in the biological sciences.

bi·o·rhythm (bī′ō-rĭth′əm) *n.* An innate, cyclical biological process or function. **—bi′o·rhyth′mic** (-rĭth′mĭk) *adj.*

bi·o·sat·el·lite (bī′ō-săt′l-īt′) *n.* An artificial, recoverable satellite that is designed to carry and support humans, animals, or other living organisms.

bi·o·sci·ence (bī′ō-sī′əns) *n.* See **life science. —bi′o·sci′-en·tif′ic** (-sī′ən-tĭf′ĭk) *adj.* **—bi′o·sci′en·tist** *n.*

bi·o·scope (bī′ə-skōp′) *n.* An early movie projector.

bi·os·co·py (bī-ŏs′kə-pē) *n., pl.* **-pies.** Medical examination of a body to determine the presence or absence of life.

bi·o·sen·sor (bī′ō-sĕn′sər, -sôr) *n.* **1.** A device that detects, records, and transmits information regarding a physiological change or process. **2.** A device that uses biological materials to monitor the presence of various chemicals in a substance.

–biosis *suff.* A way of living: *parabiosis.* [From Greek *biōsis,* way of life, from *bioun,* to live, from *bios,* life. See BIO–.]

bi·o·so·cial (bī′ō-sō′shəl) *adj.* Of or having to do with the interaction of biological and social forces: *the biosocial aspects of disease.* **—bi′o·so′cial·ly** *adv.*

bi·o·sphere (bī′ə-sfîr′) *n.* **1.** The part of the earth and its atmosphere in which living organisms exist or that is capable of supporting life. **2.** The living organisms and their environment composing the biosphere. **—bi′o·spher′ic** (-sfîr′ĭk, -sfĕr′-) *adj.*

bi·o·sta·tis·tics (bī′ō-stə-tĭs′tĭks) *n.* *(used with a sing. verb).* Application of statistics to the analysis of biological and medical data.

bi·o·syn·the·sis (bī′ō-sĭn′thĭ-sĭs) *n.* Formation of a chemical compound by a living organism. Also called *biogenesis.* **—bi′o·syn·thet′ic** (-thĕt′ĭk) *adj.* **—bi′o·syn·thet′i·cal·ly** *adv.*

bi·o·sys·tem·at·ics (bī′ō-sĭs′tə-măt′ĭks) *n.* *(used with a sing. verb).* The use of data obtained from cytogenetic, biochemical, and other experimental studies to assess the taxonomic relationships of organisms or populations, especially within an evolutionary framework. **—bi′o·sys′tem·at′ic** *adj.*

bi·o·ta (bī-ō′tə) *n.* The combined flora and fauna of a region. [New Latin, from Greek *biotē,* way of life, from *bios,* life. See **gʷei-** in Appendix.]

bi·o·tech (bī′ō-tĕk′) *n.* *Informal.* Biotechnology.

bi·o·tech·nol·o·gy (bī′ō-tĕk-nŏl′ə-jē) *n.* **1.** The use of microorganisms, such as bacteria or yeasts, or biological substances, such as enzymes, to perform specific industrial or manufacturing processes. Applications include the production of certain drugs, synthetic hormones, and bulk foodstuffs as well as the bioconversion of organic waste and the use of genetically altered bacteria in the cleanup of oil spills. **2. a.** The application of the principles of engineering and technology to the life sciences; bioengineering. **b.** See **ergonomics** (sense 1). **—bi′o·tech′ni·cal** (-nĭ-kəl) *adj.* **—bi′o·tech′no·log′i·cal** (-nə-lŏj′ĭ-kəl) *adj.*

bi·o·te·lem·e·try (bī′ō-tə-lĕm′ĭ-trē) *n.* The monitoring, recording, and measuring of a living organism's basic physiological functions, such as heart rate, muscle activity, and body temperature, by the use of telemetry techniques.

bi·o·ther·a·py (bī′ō-thĕr′ə-pē) *n., pl.* **-pies.** Treatment of disease with biologicals, such as certain drugs, vaccines, or antitoxins.

bi·ot·ic (bī-ŏt′ĭk) *adj.* **1.** Of or having to do with life or living organisms. **2.** Produced or caused by living organisms. [Probably Greek *biōtikos,* from *biōtos,* life, from *bioun,* to live, from *bios,* life. See **gʷei-** in Appendix.]

–biotic *suff.* A mode of living: *endobiotic.* [Probably New Latin *-biōticus,* from Greek *biōtikos.* See BIOTIC.]

biotic potential *n.* An estimate of the maximum capacity of living things to survive and reproduce under optimal environmental conditions.

bi·o·tin (bī′ə-tĭn) *n.* A colorless crystalline vitamin, $C_{10}H_{16}N_2O_3S$, of the vitamin B complex, essential for the activity of many enzyme systems and found in large quantities in liver, egg yolk, milk, and yeast. [Greek *biotos,* life; see BIOTIC + –IN.]

bi·o·tite (bī′ə-tīt′) *n.* A dark-brown to black mica, $K_2(Mg,Fe,Al)_6(Si,Al)_8O_{20}(OH)_4$, found in igneous and metamorphic rocks. [After Jean Baptiste *Biot* (1774–1862), French physicist.] **—bi′o·tit′ic** (-tĭt′ĭk) *adj.*

bi·o·tope (bī′ə-tōp′) *n.* An area that is uniform in environmental conditions and in its distribution of animal and plant life. [BIO– + Greek *topos,* place.]

bi·o·trans·for·ma·tion (bī′ō-trăns′fər-mā′shən) *n.* Chemical alteration of a substance within the body, as by the action of enzymes.

bi·o·tron (bī′ə-trŏn′) *n.* A climate-control chamber used for studying a living organism's response to specific environmental conditions.

bi·o·type (bī′ə-tīp′) *n.* A group of organisms having the same genotype. **—bi′o·typ′ic** (-tĭp′ĭk) *adj.*

bi·pa·ren·tal (bī′-pə-rĕn′tl) *adj.* Of or derived from two parents: *biparental inheritance.*

bip·a·rous (bĭp′ər-əs) *adj.* *Zoology.* Producing two offspring in a single birth.

bi·par·ti·san (bī-pär′tĭ-zən, -sən) *adj.* Of, consisting of, or supported by members of two parties, especially two major political parties: *a bipartisan resolution.* **—bi·par′ti·san·ism** *n.* **—bi·par′ti·san·ship′** *n.*

bi·par·tite (bī-pär′tīt′) *adj.* **1.** Having or consisting of two parts. **2. a.** Having two corresponding parts, one for each party: *a bipartite contract.* **b.** Having two participants; joint: *a bipartite agreement.* **3.** *Botany.* Divided into two portions almost to the base, as certain leaves. [Latin *bipartītus,* past participle of *bipartīre,* to divide into two parts : *bi-,* two; see BI–¹ + *partīre,* to part (from *pars,* a share; see **perə-²** in Appendix).] **—bi·par′-tite′ly** *adv.* **—bi′par·ti′tion** (-tĭsh′ən) *n.*

bi·ped (bī′pĕd′) *n.* An animal with two feet. **—biped** also **bi·ped·al** (bī-pĕd′l) *adj.* Having two feet; two-footed. [Latin *bipēs, biped-,* two-footed : *bi-,* two; see BI–¹ + *pēs,* foot; see PEDESTRIAN.]

bi·phen·yl (bī-fĕn′əl, -fē′nəl) *n.* A colorless crystalline compound, $C_{12}H_{10}$, used as a heat-transfer agent, in fungicides, and in organic synthesis. Also called *diphenyl.*

bi·pin·nate (bī-pĭn′āt′) *adj.* *Botany.* Decompound. **—bi·pin′nate′ly** *adv.*

bi·plane (bī′plăn′) *n.* An airplane having two pairs of wings fixed at different levels, especially one above and one below the fuselage.

biplane

birch
Paper birch
Betula papyrifera

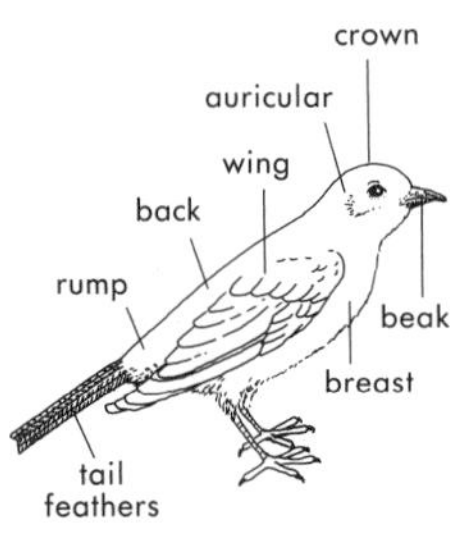

bird

ă pat	oi boy
ā pay	ou out
âr care	ŏŏ took
ä father	ōō boot
ĕ pet	ŭ cut
ē be	ûr urge
ĭ pit	th thin
ī pie	*th* this
îr pier	hw which
ŏ pot	zh vision
ō toe	ə about, item
ô paw	♦ regionalism

Stress marks: **′** (primary); ′ (secondary), as in **dictionary** (dĭk′shə-nĕr′ē)

bi·pod (bī′pŏd′) *n.* A stand having two legs, as for the support of an instrument or weapon.

bi·po·lar (bī-pō′lər) *adj.* **1.** Relating to or having two poles. **2.** Relating to or involving both of the earth's polar regions. **3.** Having two opposite or contradictory ideas or natures: *the bipolar world of the postwar period.* **4.** *Biology.* Having two poles or opposite extremities: *a bipolar neuron.* **5.** *Psychology.* Relating to a major affective disorder that is characterized by episodes of mania and depression. **—bi′po·lar′i·ty** (-lăr′ĭ-tē) *n.*

bipolar disorder *n. Psychiatry.* See **manic-depressive illness.**

bipolar illness *n. Psychiatry.* See **manic-depressive illness.**

bi·po·ten·ti·al·i·ty (bī′pə-tĕn′shē-ăl′ĭ-tē) *n.* **1.a.** The capacity to act, function, or develop in either of two possible ways. **b.** The capacity to function either as a male or a female. **2.** The condition of having both male and female reproductive organs; hermaphroditism.

bi·pro·pel·lant (bī′prə-pĕl′ənt) *n.* A two-component rocket propellant, such as liquid hydrogen and liquid oxygen, fed separately to the combustion chamber as fuel and oxidizer. Also called *dipropellant.*

bi·quad·rat·ic (bī′kwŏ-drăt′ĭk) *Mathematics. adj.* Of or relating to the fourth degree. **—biquadratic** *n.* An algebraic equation of the fourth degree.

bi·quar·ter·ly (bī-kwôr′tər-lē) *adj.* Happening or appearing two times during each three-month period of a year. **—bi·quar′ter·ly** *adv.*

bi·ra·cial (bī-rā′shəl) *adj.* Of, for, or consisting of members of two races. **—bi·ra′cial·ism** *n.*

bi·ra·mous (bī-rā′məs) *adj.* Consisting of or having two branches, as the appendages of an arthropod.

birch (bûrch) *n.* **1.a.** Any of various deciduous trees or shrubs of the genus *Betula,* native to the Northern Hemisphere and having unisexual flowers in catkins, alternate, simple, toothed leaves, and bark that often peels in thin papery layers. **b.** The hard, close-grained wood of any of these trees, used especially in furniture, interior finishes, and plywood. **2.** A rod from a birch, used to administer a whipping. **—birch** *tr.v.* **birched, birch·ing, birch·es.** To whip with or as if with a birch. [Middle English, from Old English *birce.* See **bherəg-** in Appendix.]

Birch·er (bûr′chər) also **Birch·ist** (-chĭst) or **Birch·ite** (-chīt′) *n.* A member or supporter of the John Birch Society, an anti-Communist organization founded in 1958. [After John *Birch* (died 1945), American missionary and intelligence officer.] **—Birch′ism** *n.* **—Birchist, Birchite** *adj.*

birch partridge *n.* See **ruffed grouse.**

bird (bûrd) *n.* **1.a.** Any of the class Aves of warm-blooded, egg-laying, feathered vertebrates with forelimbs modified to form wings. **b.** Such an animal hunted as game. **c.** Such an animal, especially a chicken or turkey, used as food: *put the bird in the oven.* **2.** See **clay pigeon. 3.** *Sports.* See **shuttlecock. 4.** *Slang.* A rocket, guided missile, satellite, or airplane. **5.** *Slang.* A person, especially one who is odd or remarkable: *a sly old bird.* **6.** *Chiefly British.* A young woman. **7.** *Slang.* **a.** A loud sound expressing disapproval; a raspberry. **b.** Discharge from employment: *lost a big sale and nearly got the bird.* **8.** An obscene gesture of anger, defiance, or derision made by pointing or jabbing the middle finger upward. **—bird** *intr.v.* **bird·ed, bird·ing, birds. 1.** To observe and identify birds in their natural surroundings. **2.** To trap, shoot, or catch birds. ***—idiom.* for the birds.** Objectionable or worthless. [Middle English, from Old English *brid,* young bird.] **—bird′ing** *n.*

bird·bath (bûrd′băth′, -bäth′) *n.* A basin filled with water for birds to drink and bathe in.

bird·brain (bûrd′brān′) *n. Slang.* A person regarded as silly or stupid. **—bird′brained′** *adj.*

bird·cage (bûrd′kāj′) *n.* **1.** A cage for birds. **2.** *Slang.* The controlled air traffic space near an airport.

bird·call (bûrd′kôl′) *n.* **1.** The song or cry of a bird. **2.a.** An imitation of the song or cry of a bird. **b.** A small device for producing this sound.

bird cherry *n.* Any of several cherry trees, especially the Eurasian *Prunus padus,* having clusters of white flowers and small black fruits.

bird colonel *n. Slang.* A full colonel. [From the eagle of the insignia.]

bird dog *n.* **1.** A dog used to hunt game birds; a gun dog. **2.** *Informal.* One that bird-dogs.

bird-dog also **bird·dog** (bûrd′dôg′, -dŏg′) *—v.* **-dogged, -dog·ging, -dogs.** *Informal. —intr.* To follow a subject of interest, such as a person or trend, with persistent attention. *—tr.* **1.** To observe or follow closely; monitor: *Police bird-dogged the suspect's movements.* **2.** To seek out (talent or clients, for example): *bird-dogs recruits for the team.*

bird·er (bûr′dər) *n.* **1.** A bird watcher. **2.a.** A breeder of birds. **b.** A hunter of birds.

bird feed or **bird·feed** (bûrd′fēd′) *n.* Food given to birds, especially dried food of mixed seeds.

bird feeder also **bird·feed·er** (bûrd′fē′dər) *n.* An outdoor container for bird feed, used to attract wild birds.

bird-foot violet (bûrd′fo͝ot′) *n.* Variant of **bird's-foot violet.**

bird·house (bûrd′hous′) *n.* **1.** A box with one or more small entry holes, made as a nesting place for birds. **2.** An aviary.

bird·ie (bûr′dē) *n.* **1.** *Informal.* A small bird. **2.** *Sports.* **a.** One stroke under par for a hole in golf. **b.** See **shuttlecock. —birdie** *tr.v.* **-ied, -ie·ing, -ies.** *Sports.* To shoot (a hole in golf) in one stroke under par.

bird·lime (bûrd′līm′) *n.* **1.** A sticky substance that is smeared on branches or twigs to capture small birds. **2.** Something that captures or ensnares. **—birdlime** *tr.v.* **-limed, -lim·ing, -limes. 1.** To smear with birdlime. **2.** To catch with or as if with birdlime.

bird louse *n.* See **biting louse.**

bird·man (bûrd′mən) *n.* **1.** (*also* -măn′). One, such as an ornithologist, who works with birds. **2.** *Slang.* An aviator.

bird of paradise *n., pl.* **birds of paradise. 1.** Any of various birds of the family Paradisaeidae, native to New Guinea and adjacent islands, usually having brilliant plumage and long tail feathers in the male. **2.** Any of several southern African herbs of the genus *Strelitzia,* especially *S. reginae,* having orange and blue flowers grouped above a boat-shaped bract.

bird of paradise
Strelitzia reginae

bird of passage *n., pl.* **birds of passage. 1.** A migratory bird. **2.** A person who moves from place to place frequently.

bird of prey *n., pl.* **birds of prey.** Any of various predatory carnivorous birds such as the eagle or hawk.

bird pepper *n.* **1.** A variety of pepper *(Capiscum annum* var. *glabriusculum)* that includes the wild forms native to the southern United States and Mexico south to Colombia. **2.** The small, pungent fruit of this plant.

bird·seed (bûrd′sēd′) *n.* A mixture of various kinds of seeds used for feeding birds, especially caged birds.

bird's-eye (bûrdz′ī′) *n.* **1.** A fabric woven with a pattern of small diamonds, each having a dot in the center. **2.** The pattern of such a fabric. **—bird's-eye** *adj.* **1.** Marked with a spot or spots resembling a bird's eye or eyes, as the bird's-eye maple or a blue flower having a small circular yellow center. **2.** Derived from or as if from an altitude or distance; comprehensive: *a bird's-eye survey; a bird's-eye view.*

bird's-eye maple *n.* A form of wood, chiefly of the sugar maple, that is patterned with small rounded figures and is especially popular for making musical instruments.

bird's-foot trefoil (bûrdz′fo͝ot′) *n.* A perennial Old World herb *(Lotus corniculata)* in the pea family, having golden-yellow flowers and clusters of pods arranged like the claws of a bird.

bird's-foot violet also **bird-foot violet** (bûrd′fo͝ot′) *n.* An eastern North American violet *(Viola pedata)* having large blue or purple flowers and palmately divided leaves that are shaped somewhat like a bird's foot.

bird·shot (bûrd′shŏt′) *n.* A small lead shot for shotgun shells.

bird's-nest fern (bûrdz′nĕst′) *n.* An Old World tropical fern *(Asplenium nidus),* having undivided leaves arranged in a clump resembling a bird's nest and popular as a houseplant.

bird's-nest fungus *n.* Any of various fungi having a cuplike body containing several round, egglike stuctures that enclose the spores.

bird watcher or **bird·watch·er** also **bird-watch·er** (bûrd′wŏch′ər) *n.* A person who observes and identifies birds in their natural surroundings. **—bird watching** *n.*

bi·re·frin·gence (bī′rĭ-frĭn′jəns) *n.* The resolution or splitting of a light wave into two unequally reflected waves by an optically anisotropic medium such as calcite or quartz. Also called *double refraction.* **—bi′re·frin′gent** *adj.*

bi·reme (bī′rēm′) *n.* An ancient galley equipped with two tiers of oars on each side. [Latin *birēmis* : *bi-,* two; see BI-[1] + *rēmus,* oar; see **erə-** in Appendix.]

bireme

bi·ret·ta also **be·ret·ta** or **ber·ret·ta** (bə-rĕt′ə) *n.* A stiff square cap with three or four ridges across the crown. Birettas are worn especially by Roman Catholic clergy and are black for priests, purple for bishops, and red for cardinals. [Italian *berretta,* from Old Provençal *berret,* cap, from Late Latin *birrus,* hooded cloak, probably of Celtic origin.]

bi·ri·a·ni (bĭ′rē-ä′nē) *n.* Variant of **biryani.**

birk (bûrk) *n. Scots.* Birch. [Middle English *birk,* from Old English *birce.* See BIRCH.]

Bir·ken·head (bûr′kən-hĕd′). A borough of northwest England at the mouth of the Mersey River near Liverpool. It has extensive docks and is a shipbuilding center. Population, 341,000.

birk·ie (bûr′kē) *Scots. n.* A man, especially one who is spirited and energetic. **—birkie** *adj.* Lively; spirited; cocky. [Possibly akin to Middle English *berken,* to bark, from Old English *beorcan.*]

birl (bûrl) *v.* **birled, birl·ing, birls.** *—tr.* To cause (a floating log) to spin rapidly by rotating with the feet. *—intr.* **1.** To participate in birling. **2.** To spin. **—birl** *n.* A whirring noise; a hum. [Blend of BIRR[1] and WHIRL.] **—birl′er** *n.*

birl·ing (bûr′lĭng) *n.* A game of skill, especially among lumberjacks, in which two competitors try to balance on a floating log while spinning it with their feet. Also called *logrolling.*

Bir·ming·ham (bûr′mĭng-hăm′). **1.** (*also* -əm). A city of central England northwest of London. It is a major industrial center and transportation hub. Population, 1,022,300. **2.** A city of north-central Alabama northeast of Tuscaloosa. The largest city in the state, it is in a mining and industrial region. Population,

biretta

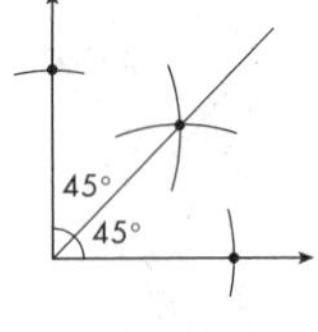

bisector

bishop
Chess piece

Otto von Bismarck

286,799. **3.** A city of southeast Michigan, a residential suburb of Detroit. Population, 21,689.

birr¹ (bûr) *n.* **1.** A whirring sound. **2.** Strong forward momentum; driving force. —**birr** *intr.v.* **birred, birr·ing, birrs.** To make a whirring sound. [Middle English *bir,* favorable wind, from Old Norse *byrr.* See **bher-¹** in Appendix.]

birr² (bîr) *n., pl.* **birr** or **birrs.** See table at **currency.** [Probably of Amharic origin.]

♦**birth** (bûrth) *n.* **1.a.** The emergence and separation of offspring from the body of the mother. **b.** The act or process of bearing young; parturition: *the mare's second birth.* **c.** The circumstances or conditions relating to this event, as its time or location: *an incident that took place before my birth; a Bostonian by birth.* **2.a.** The set of characteristics or circumstances received from one's ancestors; inheritance: *strong-willed by birth; acquired their wealth through birth.* **b.** Origin; extraction: *of Swedish birth; of humble birth.* **c.** Noble or high status: *persons of birth.* **3.** A beginning or commencement. See Synonyms at **beginning.** —**birth** *tr.v.* **birthed, birth·ing, births.** *Chiefly Southern U.S.* **1.** To deliver (a baby). **2.** To bear (a child). [Middle English, probably of Scandinavian origin. See **bher-¹** in Appendix.]

♦***REGIONAL NOTE:*** Until recently, the use of *birth* as a verb meaning "to bear (a child)" has been confined to Southern speech: *"Heap o' good it do a woman to birth a mess o' young uns and raise 'em and then have 'em all go off to oncet"* (Marjorie K. Rawlings). Recently, however, the nonstandard Southern usage has coincided with widespread usage of verbs derived from nouns, such as *parent, network,* and *microwave. Birth* in this new usage is most commonly found as a gerund, as in the compound *birthing room.*

birth canal *n.* The passageway through which the fetus is expelled during parturition, leading from the uterus through the cervix, vagina, and vulva.

birth certificate *n.* An official record of the date and place of a person's birth, usually including the names of the parents.

birth control *n.* Voluntary limitation or control of the number of children conceived, especially by planned use of contraceptive techniques.

birth control pill *n.* See **oral contraceptive.**

birth·day (bûrth′dā′) *n.* **1.** The day of one's birth. **2.** The anniversary of one's birth. —*attributive.* Often used to modify another noun: *a birthday cake; birthday parties.*

birthday suit *n.* The state of being nude; nakedness.

birth defect *n.* A physiological or structural abnormality that develops at or before birth and is present at the time of birth, especially as a result of faulty development, infection, heredity, or injury. Also called *congenital anomaly.*

birth family *n.* A family consisting of one's biological as opposed to adoptive parents and their offspring.

birth father also **birth·fa·ther** (bûrth′fä′*th*ər) *n.* A biological father.

birth·ing (bûr′thĭng) *adj.* Having to do with or used during birth: *a birthing counselor.* —**birthing** *n.* The act of giving birth.

birthing center *n.* A medical facility, often associated with a hospital, that is designed to provide a comfortable, homelike setting during childbirth and that is generally less restrictive than a hospital in its regulations, as in permitting midwifery or allowing family members or friends to attend the delivery.

♦**birthing room** *n.* An area of a hospital or outpatient medical facility equipped for labor, delivery, and recovery and designed as a natural, homelike environment. See Regional Note at **birth.**

birth·mark (bûrth′märk′) *n.* A mole or blemish present on the skin from birth; a nevus.

birth mother also **birth·moth·er** (bûrth′mŭ*th*′ər) *n.* A biological mother.

birth pang *n.* **1.** Often **birth pangs.** One of the repetitive pains occurring in childbirth. **2. birth pangs.** Difficulty or turmoil associated with a development or transition: *the birth pangs of an emergent democracy.*

birth parent also **birth·par·ent** (bûrth′pâr′ənt, -păr′-) *n.* A biological parent.

birth·place (bûrth′plās′) *n. Abbr.* **bp., bpl** The place where someone is born or where something originates.

birth·rate also **birth rate** (bûrth′rāt′) *n.* The ratio of total live births to total population in a specified community or area over a specified period of time. The birthrate is often expressed as the number of live births per 1,000 of the population per year. Also called *natality.*

birth·right (bûrth′rīt′) *n.* **1.** A right, possession, or privilege that is one's due by birth. See Synonyms at **right. 2.** A special privilege accorded a first-born.

birth·root (bûrth′ro͞ot′, -ro͝ot′) *n.* See **trillium.**

birth·stone (bûrth′stōn′) *n.* A gemstone associated with a particular month and customarily worn by persons born during that month.

birth trauma *n.* **1.** A physical injury sustained by an infant during birth. **2.** The psychological shock experienced by an infant during birth.

birth·wort (bûrth′wûrt′, -wôrt′) *n.* Any of several herbs or woody vines of the genus *Aristolochia* having showy, malodorous, purplish-brown to yellowish flowers with peculiar or unusual shapes. The European species *A. clematitis* was used as a folk medicine to aid childbirth.

bi·ry·a·ni also **bi·ri·a·ni** (bĭr′ē-ä′nē) *n.* An Indian dish containing meat, fish, or vegetables and rice flavored with saffron or turmeric. [Hindi or Urdu.]

bis (bĭs) *adv. Music.* Again; twice. Used as a direction to repeat a passage. —**bis** *interj.* Used to request an additional performance. [French or Italian, both from Latin, twice. See **dwo-** in Appendix.]

Bis·cay (bĭs′kā), **Bay of.** An arm of the Atlantic Ocean indenting the western coast of Europe from Brittany in northwest France southward to northwest Spain.

Bis·cayne Bay (bĭs-kān′, bĭs′kān′). A narrow inlet of the Atlantic Ocean in southwest Florida. Miami and Miami Beach are on the northern shore.

bis·cot·to (bĭ-skŏt′ō, bē-skôt′tô) *n., pl.* **bis·cot·ti** (bĭ-skŏt′ē, bē-skôt′tē). A crisp Italian cookie flavored with anise and often containing almonds or filberts. [Italian, from Medieval Latin *bis coctus,* twice cooked. See BISCUIT.]

bis·cuit (bĭs′kĭt) *n., pl.* **-cuits. 1.** A small cake of shortened bread leavened with baking powder or soda. **2.** *Chiefly British.* **a.** A thin, crisp cracker. **b.** A cookie. **3.** *Color.* A pale brown. **4.** *pl.* **biscuit.** Clay that has been fired once but not glazed. In this sense, also called *bisque.* [Middle English *bisquit,* from Old French *biscuit,* from Medieval Latin *bis coctus* : Latin *bis,* twice; see **dwo-** in Appendix + Latin *coctus,* past participle of *coquere,* to cook; see **pekʷ-** in Appendix.]

bise (bēz) *n.* A cold north wind of the Swiss Alps and nearby regions of France and Italy. [Middle English, from Old French, of Germanic origin.]

bi·sect (bī′sĕkt′, bī-sĕkt′) *v.* **-sect·ed, -sect·ing, -sects.** —*tr.* To cut or divide into two parts, especially two equal parts. —*intr.* To split; fork. —**bi·sec′tion** *n.* —**bi·sec′tion·al** *adj.* —**bi·sec′tion·al·ly** *adv.*

bi·sec·tor (bī′sĕk′tər, bī-sĕk′-) *n.* Something that bisects, especially a ray that bisects an angle.

bi·se·ri·ate (bī-sîr′ē-ĭt, -āt′) *adj.* Arranged in two rows or in two cycles: *a biseriate perianth composed of both a calyx and a corolla.*

bi·ser·rate (bī-sĕr′āt′) *adj.* **1.** *Botany.* Having serrations that are themselves serrated; doubly serrate: *a biserrate leaf margin.* **2.** *Zoology.* Serrated on both sides: *biserrate antennae.*

bi·sex·u·al (bī-sĕk′sho͞o-əl) *adj.* **1.** Of or relating to both sexes. **2.a.** Having both male and female reproductive organs; hermaphroditic. **b.** *Botany.* Denoting a single flower that contains functional staminate and pistillate structures; perfect. **3.** Of, relating to, or having a sexual orientation to persons of either sex. —**bisexual** *n.* **1.** A bisexual organism; a hermaphrodite. **2.** A bisexual person. —**bi′sex·u·al′i·ty** (-ăl′ĭ-tē) *n.* —**bi·sex′u·al·ly** *adv.*

bish·op (bĭsh′əp) *n.* **1.** A high-ranking Christian cleric, in modern churches usually in charge of a diocese and in some churches regarded as having received the highest ordination in unbroken succession from the apostles. **2.** *Abbr.* **B, bp.** *Games.* A usually miter-shaped chess piece that can move diagonally across any number of unoccupied spaces. **3.** Mulled port spiced with oranges, sugar, and cloves. [Middle English, from Old English *bisceope,* from Vulgar Latin **ebiscopus,* from Late Latin *episcopus,* from Late Greek *episkopos,* from Greek, overseer : *epi-,* epi- + *skopos,* watcher; see **spek-** in Appendix.]

Bish·op (bĭsh′əp), **Elizabeth.** 1911–1979. American poet noted for her spare, largely descriptive works, such as "Filling Station" (1965).

bish·op·ric (bĭsh′ə-prĭk) *n.* **1.** The office or rank of a bishop. **2.** The diocese of a bishop. [Middle English *bishoprik,* from Old English *bisceoprīce,* the diocese of a bishop : *bisceop,* bishop; see BISHOP + *rīce,* realm; see **reg-** in Appendix.]

bish·op's cap (bĭsh′əps) *n.* See **miterwort.**

bishop's weed *n.* **1.** See **goutweed. 2.** A chiefly Mediterranean annual plant *(Ammi magus)* in the parsley family, grown as a source of psoralens used in medicine and as an ornamental for its compound umbels of small white flowers.

Bisk (bĭsk, bēsk). See **Biysk.**

Bis·la·ma (bĭs-lä′mə) *n.* A lingua franca that combines Malay and English, spoken in the southwest Pacific, especially in the Papua New Guinea area. Also called *Beach-la-Mar, Bêche-de-Mer.* [Pidgin or native variant of BÊCHE-DE-MER.]

Bis·marck (bĭz′märk′). The capital of North Dakota, in the south-central part of the state on hills overlooking the Missouri River. It was originally a camp for laborers building the Northern Pacific Railroad. Population, 44,485.

Bismarck, Prince **Otto Eduard Leopold von.** Called "the Iron Chancellor." 1815–1898. Creator and first chancellor of the German Empire (1871–1890). —**Bis·marck′i·an** *adj.*

Bismarck Archipelago. A group of volcanic islands and islets of Papua New Guinea in the southwest Pacific Ocean. The islands were discovered by Dutch explorers in the early 1700's.

Bismarck Sea. A section of the southwest Pacific Ocean northeast of New Guinea and northwest of New Britain.

bis·muth (bĭz′məth) *n. Symbol* **Bi** A white, crystalline, brittle, highly diamagnetic metallic element used in alloys to form sharp castings for objects sensitive to high temperatures and in various low-melting alloys for fire-safety devices. Atomic number 83;

atomic weight 208.980; melting point 271.3°C; boiling point 1,560°C; specific gravity 9.747; valence 3, 5. See table at **element.** [Obsolete German *Bismut,* from New Latin *bisemūtum,* alteration of Medieval Latin *wismutum,* from obsolete German *Wismut* : Middle High German *wise,* meadow (from Old High German *wisa*) + *Mut, Muth,* claim to a mine (from *muten,* to stake a claim, demand, from Middle High German *muoten,* from Old High German, from *muot,* mind, spirit; see **mē-**[1] in Appendix).] **—bis′muth·al** *adj.*

bi·son (bī′sən, -zən) *n.* **1.** A bovine mammal *(Bison bison)* of western North America, having large forequarters, a shaggy mane, and a massive head with short, curved horns; a buffalo. **2.** An animal *(B. bonasus)* of Europe, similar to but somewhat smaller than the bison; a wisent. [Latin *bisōn,* of Germanic origin; akin to Old High German *wisunt.*]

bisque[1] (bĭsk) *n.* **1.a.** A rich, creamy soup made from meat, fish, or shellfish. **b.** A thick cream soup made of puréed vegetables. **2.** Ice cream mixed with crushed macaroons or nuts. [Perhaps from French dialectal, sour soup, from *Biscaye,* Bay of Biscay.]

bisque[2] (bĭsk) *n.* **1.** See **biscuit** (sense 4). **2.** *Color.* **a.** A pale orange-yellow to yellowish gray. **b.** A color ranging in various industries from moderate yellowish pink to grayish yellow. [From BISCUIT.]

bisque[3] (bĭsk) *n.* *Sports.* An advantage allowed an inferior player in certain games, such as a free point in tennis, an extra turn in croquet, or an additional stroke in golf. [French.]

Bis·sau (bĭ-sou′). The capital and largest city of Guinea-Bissau, on an estuary of the Atlantic Ocean. Founded by the Portuguese in 1687, the city has been a free port since 1869. Population, 109,486.

bis·sex·tile (bī-sĕk′stĭl, -stīl′, bĭ-) *adj.* **1.** Of or relating to a leap year. **2.** Of or relating to the extra day falling in a leap year. **—bissextile** *n.* A leap year. [Late Latin *bissextilis,* containing an intercalary day, from Latin *bissextus,* an intercalary day : *bi-,* twice; see BI–[1] + *sextus,* sixth, because the sixth day before the Calends of March (February 24) occurred twice every leap year; see SEXT.]

bi·state (bī′stāt′) *adj.* Of, relating to, or involving two states: *bistate cooperation in combating crime.*

bis·ter or **bis·tre** (bĭs′tər) *n.* **1.** A water-soluble, yellowish-brown pigment. **2.** *Color.* A grayish to yellowish brown. [French *bistre.*] **—bis′tered** *adj.*

bis·tort (bĭs′tôrt′) *n.* **1.** A Eurasian perennial herb *(Polygonum bistorta)* having cylindrical spikes of usually pink flowers and a rhizome used as an astringent in folk medicine. **2.** Any of certain related plants of the genus *Polygonum.* [French *bistorte,* from Old French, from Medieval Latin **bistorta* : Latin *bis,* twice; see BIS + *torta,* past participle of *torquēre,* to twist; see TORQUE[1].]

bis·tou·ry (bĭs′tə-rē) *n., pl.* **-ries.** A long, narrow surgical knife for minor incisions. [French *bistouri,* perhaps from Italian dialectal *bistori,* from *bistorino,* of Pistoia, from *Pistōrium,* Pistoia.]

bis·tre (bĭs′tər) *n.* Variant of **bister.**

bis·tro (bē′strō, bĭs′trō) *n., pl.* **-tros. 1.** A small bar, tavern, or nightclub. **2.** A small, informal restaurant serving wine. [French *bistro* or *bistrot,* tavern owner, tavern.]

WORD HISTORY: According to a popular story, *bistro* came into existence as a French word when Russian soldiers entered Parisian restaurants and cafés after the fall of Napoleon in 1815 shouting *"bystro, bystro,"* Russian for "quickly, quickly." Bistros seem to have been named not for this desire for quick service but possibly for a commodity to be found in at least some of them, since the French word *bistro* may be related to the word *bistouille,* "raw spirits, rotgut." Another possibility is that the word *bistro* comes from the dialectal word *bistraud,* "young cowherd." In Standard French the term may have come to mean "wine merchant's helper" and then "an establishment selling wine." Although the French word *bistro* is first recorded in 1884, evidence for the English word *bistro* is not found until the early 1920's.

bi·sul·cate (bī-sŭl′kāt′) *adj.* Cleft or cloven, as a hoof.

bi·sul·fate (bī-sŭl′fāt′) *n.* The univalent inorganic acid group HSO_4 or a salt of sulfuric acid containing it.

bi·sul·fide (bī-sŭl′fīd′) *n.* See **disulfide.**

bi·sul·fite (bī-sŭl′fīt′) *n.* The univalent inorganic acid group HSO_3 or a salt of sulfurous acid containing it.

bit[1] (bĭt) *n.* **1.** A small portion, degree, or amount: *a bit of lint; a bit of luck.* **2.** A brief amount of time; a moment: *Wait a bit.* **3.a.** A short scene or episode in a theatrical performance. **b.** A bit part. **4.** An entertainment routine given regularly by a performer; an act. **5.** *Informal.* **a.** A particular kind of action, situation, or behavior: *got tired of the macho bit.* **b.** A matter being considered: *What's this bit about inflation?* **6.** *Informal.* An amount equal to ⅛ of a dollar: *two bits.* **7.** *Chiefly British.* A small coin: *a threepenny bit.* **—*idioms.* a bit.** To a small degree; somewhat: *a bit warm.* **bit by bit.** Little by little; gradually. [Middle English *bite,* morsel, from Old English *bita.* See **bheid-** in Appendix.]

bit[2] (bĭt) *n.* **1.** The sharp part of a tool, such as the cutting edge of a knife or ax. **2.** A pointed and threaded tool for drilling and boring that is secured in a brace, bitstock, or drill press. **3.** The part of a key that enters the lock and engages the bolt and tumblers. **4.** The tip of the mouthpiece on a pipe or a cigarette or cigar holder. **5.** The metal mouthpiece of a bridle, serving to control, curb, and direct an animal. **6.** Something that controls, guides, or curbs. **—bit** *tr.v.* **bit·ted, bit·ting, bits. 1.** To place a bit in the mouth of (a horse, for example). **2.** To check or control with or as if with a bit. **3.** To make or grind a bit on (a key). **—*idiom.* have** (or **take) the bit in one's teeth.** To be uncontrollable, as a horse is when it clenches its teeth on the bit; to cast off or refuse restraint. [Middle English *bite,* from Old English, act of biting. See **bheid-** in Appendix.]

bit[3] (bĭt) *n.* *Computer Science.* **1.** A single character of a language having just two characters, as either of the binary digits 0 or 1. **2.** A unit of information equivalent to the choice of either of two equally likely alternatives. **3.** A unit of information storage capacity, as of memory. [Blend of B(INARY) and (DIG)IT.]

bit[4] (bĭt) *v.* Past tense and a past participle of **bite.**

bi·tar·trate (bī-tär′trāt′) *n.* The group $C_4H_5O_6^-$ or a salt of tartaric acid containing it.

bitch (bĭch) *n.* **1.** A female canine animal, especially a dog. **2.** *Offensive.* **a.** A woman considered to be spiteful or overbearing. **b.** A lewd woman. **3.** *Slang.* A complaint. **4.** *Slang.* Something very unpleasant or difficult. **—bitch** *v.* **bitched, bitch·ing, bitch·es.** *Slang.* —*intr.* To complain; grumble. —*tr.* To botch; bungle. [Middle English *bicche,* from Old English *bicce.*]

bitch·er·y (bĭch′ə-rē) *n.* Malicious remarks or spiteful behavior: *"the rapidly escalating and darkening volley of nasty political bitchery"* (Joe Brown).

bitch goddess *n.* Material success.

bitch·y (bĭch′ē) *adj.* **-i·er, -i·est.** *Slang.* Malicious, spiteful, or overbearing. **—bitch′i·ly** *adv.* **—bitch′i·ness** *n.*

bite (bīt) *v.* **bit** (bĭt), **bit·ten** (bĭt′n) or **bit, bit·ing, bites.** —*tr.* **1.** To cut, grip, or tear with or as if with the teeth. **2.a.** To pierce the skin of with the teeth, fangs, or mouthparts. **b.** To sting with a stinger. **3.** To cut into with or as if with a sharp instrument: *The sword bit straight through the wooden shield.* **4.** To grip, grab, or seize: *bald treads that couldn't bite the icy road; bitten by a sudden desire to travel.* **5.** To eat into; corrode. **6.** To cause to sting or be painful: *cold that bites the skin; a conscience bitten by remorse.* —*intr.* **1.** To grip, cut into, or injure something with or as if with the teeth. **2.** To have a stinging effect. **3.** To have a sharp taste. **4.** To take or swallow bait. **5.** To be taken in by a ploy or deception: *tried to sell the Brooklyn Bridge, but no one bit.* **—bite** *n.* **1.** The act of biting. **2.** A skin wound or puncture produced by an animal's teeth or mouthparts: *the bite of an insect.* **3.a.** A stinging or smarting sensation. **b.** An incisive, penetrating quality: *the bite of satire.* **4.** An amount removed by or as if by an act of biting: *Rezoning took a bite out of the town's residential area.* **5.a.** An amount of food taken into the mouth at one time; a mouthful. **b.** *Informal.* A light meal or snack. **6.** The act or an instance of taking bait: *fished all day without a bite; an ad that got a few bites but no final sales.* **7.a.** A secure grip or hold applied by a tool or machine upon a working surface. **b.** The part of a tool or machine that presses against and maintains a firm hold on a working surface. **8.** *Dentistry.* The angle at which the upper and lower teeth meet; occlusion. **9.** The corrosive action of acid upon an etcher's metal plate. **10.** *Slang.* An amount of money appropriated or withheld: *trying to avoid the tax bite.* **—*idioms.* bite off more than one can chew.** To decide or agree to do more than one can finally accomplish. **bite the bullet.** *Slang.* To face a painful situation bravely and stoically. **bite the dust.** *Slang.* **1.** To fall dead, especially in combat. **2.** To be defeated. **3.** To come to an end. **bite the hand that feeds (one).** To repay generosity or kindness with ingratitude and injury. [Middle English *biten,* from Old English *bītan.* See **bheid-** in Appendix.] **—bit′a·ble, bite′a·ble** *adj.* **—bit′er** *n.*

SYNONYMS: *bite, champ, gnaw.* The central meaning shared by these verbs is "to seize and tear or grind something with the teeth": *bite into a ripe tomato; horses champing grain; a dog gnawing a bone.*

bite·plate also **bite plate** (bīt′plāt′) *n.* A removable dental appliance, fabricated of wire and plastic, that is worn in the palate and used as a diagnostic or therapeutic aid in orthodontics or prosthodontics.

bite·wing (bīt′wĭng′) *n.* A dental x-ray film with a central projection on which the teeth can close, holding it in position for the radiographic examination of several upper and lower teeth simultaneously.

Bi·thyn·i·a (bĭ-thĭn′ē-ə). An ancient country of northwest Asia Minor in present-day Turkey. Originally inhabited by Thracians, it was absorbed into the Roman Empire by the end of the first century B.C. **—Bi·thyn′i·an** *adj. & n.*

bit·ing (bī′tĭng) *adj.* **1.** Causing a stinging sensation. **2.** Capable of gripping and affecting or wounding: *a biting aphorism.* See Synonyms at **incisive. —bit′ing·ly** *adv.*

biting louse *n.* Any of several small, wingless, biting insects of the order Mallophaga that are external parasites on birds. Also called *bird louse.*

biting midge *n.* See **punkie.**

bi·tok (bē′tŏk) *n.* A dish made from ground meat mixed with milk, bread, and onions to form patties that are fried and served with a sour-cream sauce. [Russian, from French *bifteck (haché),* (ground) beef, from BEEFSTEAK.]

bison
American Plains bison
Bison bison

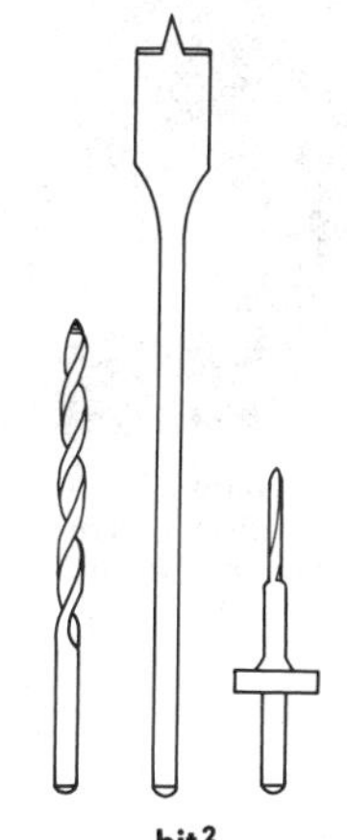

bit[2]
Left to right: Pilot, spade, and twist

ă pat	oi boy
ā pay	ou out
âr care	ŏŏ took
ä father	ōō boot
ĕ pet	ŭ cut
ē be	ûr urge
ĭ pit	th thin
ī pie	*th* this
îr pier	hw which
ŏ pot	zh vision
ō toe	ə about, item
ô paw	♦ regionalism

Stress marks: **′** (primary); ′ (secondary), as in **dictionary** (dĭk′shə-nĕr′ē)

bit part *n.* A small or insignificant role, as in a play or movie, usually having a few spoken lines.

bit·stock (bĭt′stŏk′) *n.* A handle used to secure and turn a drilling or boring bit; a brace.

bitt (bĭt) *Nautical. n.* A vertical post, usually one of a pair, set on the deck of a ship and used to secure ropes or cables. **—bitt** *tr.v.* **bitt·ed, bitt·ing, bitts.** To wind (a cable) around a bitt. [Perhaps of Dutch or Low German origin; akin to Old Norse *biti,* crossbeam.]

bit·ten (bĭt′n) *v.* A past participle of **bite.**

bit·ter (bĭt′ər) *adj.* **-er, -est. 1.** Having or being a taste that is sharp, acrid, and unpleasant. **2.** Causing a sharply unpleasant, painful, or stinging sensation; harsh: *enveloped in bitter cold; a bitter wind.* **3.** Difficult or distasteful to accept, admit, or bear: *the bitter truth; bitter sorrow.* **4.** Proceeding from or exhibiting strong animosity: *a bitter struggle; bitter foes.* **5.** Resulting from or expressive of severe grief, anguish, or disappointment: *cried bitter tears.* **6.** Marked by resentment or cynicism: *"He was already a bitter elderly man with a gray face"* (John Dos Passos). **—bitter** *adv.* In an intense or harsh way; bitterly: *a bitter cold night.* **—bitter** *tr.v.* **-tered, -ter·ing, -ters.** To make bitter. **—bitter** *n.* **1.** That which is bitter: *"all words . . . /Failing to give the bitter of the sweet"* (Tennyson). **2. bitters.** A bitter, usually alcoholic liquid made with herbs or roots and used in cocktails or as a tonic. **3.** *Chiefly British.* A sharp-tasting beer made with hops. [Middle English, from Old English. See **bheid-** in Appendix.] **—bit′ter·ly** *adv.* **—bit′ter·ness** *n.*

SYNONYMS: *bitter, acerbic, acrid.* The central meaning shared by these adjectives is "unpleasantly sharp or pungent in taste or smell": *a bitter cough syrup; acerbic barberries; acrid resin.*

bitter almond *n.* A variety of almond *(Prunus dulcis* var. *amara)* having kernels that yield an oil consisting mostly of benzaldehyde and some hydrocyanic acid. The detoxified oil can be used for flavoring.

bitter aloes *pl.n. (used with a sing. verb).* See **aloe** (sense 3).

bitter apple *n.* See **colocynth.**

bit·ter·brush (bĭt′ər-brŭsh′) *n.* A shrub of the genus *Purshia,* especially *P. tridentata* of western North America.

bitter cress *n.* Any of several herbs of the genus *Cardamine* in the mustard family, having racemes of white, pink, or purplish flowers, usually divided leaves, and pods that dehisce explosively.

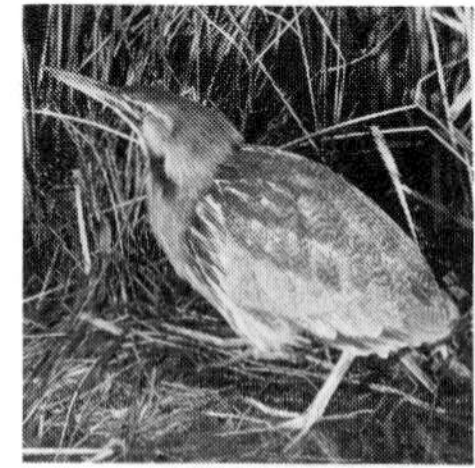

bittern[1]
American bittern
Botaurus lentiginosus

bitter end *n.* **1.** A final, painful, or disastrous extremity. **2.** *Nautical.* The inboard end of a chain, rope, or cable, especially the end of a rope or cable that is wound around a bitt. [English *bitter,* bitt (BITT + –ER[1]) + END. Sense 1, influenced by BITTER.]

bit·ter·end·er or **bit·ter-end·er** (bĭt′ər-ĕn′dər) *n.* One who persists in an action, attitude, or state despite difficult circumstances, until it becomes impossible to continue.

bitter gourd *n.* See **balsam pear** (sense 2).

bit·tern[1] (bĭt′ərn) *n.* Any of several wading birds of the genera *Botaurus* and *Ixobrychus,* having mottled, brownish plumage and a deep, booming cry in the male. [Middle English *bitour* (with *-n* perhaps from HERON), from Old French *butor,* possibly from Vulgar Latin **buti-taurus* : Latin *būtiō,* buzzard + Latin *taurus,* bull (after its cry); see **tauro-** in Appendix.]

bit·tern[2] (bĭt′ərn) *n.* The bitter water solution of bromides, magnesium, and calcium salts remaining after sodium chloride is crystallized out of seawater. [From BITTER.]

bit·ter·nut (bĭt′ər-nŭt′) *n.* A hickory tree *(Carya cordiformis)* of eastern North America, having thin-shelled nuts with bitter kernels.

bitter orange *n.* See **sour orange.**

bit·ter·root (bĭt′ər-ro͞ot′, -ro͝ot′) *n.* A perennial herb *(Lewisia rediviva),* native to western North America and having showy pink or whitish flowers and an edible, fleshy root.

Bit·ter·root Range (bĭt′ər-ro͞ot′, -ro͝ot′). A rugged chain of the Rocky Mountains along the Idaho-Montana border. It rises to 3,474.9 m (11,393 ft) at Scott Peak.

bit·ter·sweet (bĭt′ər-swēt′) *n.* **1.** A woody vine of the genus *Celastrus,* especially the North American species *C. scandens* and the eastern Asian species *C. orbiculata,* having small, round, yellow-orange fruits that open at maturity to expose red seeds. Also called *staff tree.* **2.** See **bittersweet nightshade. 3.** *Color.* A dark to deep reddish orange. **—bittersweet** *adj.* **1.** Bitter and sweet at the same time: *bittersweet chocolate.* **2.** Producing or expressing a mixture of pain and pleasure: *a movie with a bittersweet ending.* **3.** *Color.* Dark to deep reddish-orange. [After its roots, which are said to taste bitter, then sweet when chewed.]

bittersweet nightshade *n.* A poisonous climbing or trailing plant *(Solanum dulcamara)* native to Eurasia and a widespread weed in North America, having violet flowers with recurved corolla lobes and red berries. Also called *bittersweet, deadly nightshade.* [After its roots, which are said to taste bitter, then sweet when chewed.]

bit·ty (bĭt′ē) *adj.* **-ti·er, -ti·est. 1.** *Informal.* Tiny. **2.** *Chiefly British.* Composed of small segments lacking cohesion; fragmented: *"The play finally jerks its disjointed and bitty way to an arbitrary conclusion"* (Martin Hoyle). **—bit·ti·ness** *n.*

bi·tu·men (bĭ-to͞o′mən, -tyo͞o′-, bī-) *n.* Any of various flammable mixtures of hydrocarbons and other substances, occurring naturally or obtained by distillation from coal or petroleum, that are a component of asphalt and tar and are used for surfacing roads and for waterproofing. [Middle English *bithumen,* a mineral pitch from the Near East, from Latin *bitūmen,* perhaps of Celtic origin.] **—bi·tu′mi·noid′** (-mə-noid′) *adj.*

bi·tu·mi·nize (bĭ-to͞o′mə-nīz′, -tyo͞o′-, bī-) *tr.v.* **-nized, -niz·ing, -niz·es.** To treat with bitumen. **—bi·tu′mi·ni·za′·tion** (-nĭ-zā′shən) *n.*

bi·tu·mi·nous (bĭ-to͞o′mə-nəs, -tyo͞o′-, bī-) *adj.* **1.** Like or containing bitumen. **2.** Of or relating to bituminous coal.

bituminous coal *n.* A mineral coal with a high percentage of volatile matter that burns with a smoky yellow flame. Also called *soft coal.*

bi·va·lent (bī-vā′lənt) *adj.* **1.** *Chemistry.* Divalent. **2.** *Biology.* Consisting of a pair of homologous, synapsed chromosomes, as occurs during meiosis; double. **—bivalent** *n. Biology.* A pair of homologous, synapsed chromosomes associated together during meiosis. **—bi·va′lence, bi·va′len·cy** *n.*

bi·valve (bī′vălv′) *n.* A mollusk, such as an oyster or a clam, that has a shell consisting of two hinged valves. **—bivalve** *adj.* **1.** Having a shell consisting of two hinged valves. **2.** Consisting of two similar separable parts. **—bi′valved′** *adj.*

bi·var·i·ate (bī-vâr′ē-ĭt, -āt′) *adj. Mathematics.* Having two variables: *bivariate binomial distribution.*

biv·ou·ac (bĭv′o͞o-ăk′, bĭv′wăk′) *n.* A temporary encampment often in an unsheltered area. **—bivouac** *intr.v.* **-acked, -ack·ing, -acs** also **-acks.** To camp in a bivouac. [French, from German dialectal *beiwacht,* supplementary night watch : *bei-,* beside (from Middle High German *bi-,* from Old High German; see **ambhi** in Appendix) + *Wacht,* watch, vigil (from Middle High German *wahte,* from Old High German *wahta;* see **weg-** in Appendix).]

Bi·wa (bē′wä). A lake of southern Honshu, Japan, west of Nagoya. It is the largest lake in the country and a popular scenic resort area.

bi·week·ly (bī-wēk′lē) *adj.* **1.** Happening every two weeks. **2.** Happening twice a week; semiweekly. **—biweekly** *n., pl.* **-lies.** A publication issued every two weeks. **—biweekly** *adv.* **1.** Every two weeks. **2.** Twice a week; semiweekly. See Usage Note at **bi–[1].**

bi·year·ly (bī-yîr′lē) *adj.* **1.** Happening every two years. **2.** Happening twice a year; semiyearly. **—biyearly** *adv.* **1.** Every two years. **2.** Twice a year; semiyearly.

Bi·ysk (bē′ĭsk, bēsk) or **Bisk** (bĭsk, bēsk). A city of south-central Russia east-southeast of Barnaul. It was founded as a fortress in 1709. Population, 226,000.

biz (bĭz) *n. Slang.* Business.

bi·zarre (bĭ-zär′) *adj.* Strikingly unconventional and far-fetched in style or appearance; odd. See Synonyms at **fantastic.** [French, from Spanish *bizarro,* brave, probably from Basque *bizar,* beard.] **—bi·zarre′ly** *adv.* **—bi·zarre′ness** *n.*

Bi·zet (bē-zā′), **Alexandre César Léopold.** Known as "Georges Bizet." 1838–1875. French composer known especially for his opera *Carmen* (1875).

bi·zon·al (bī-zō′nəl) *adj.* Of or relating to the affairs of a zone under the joint administration of two powers.

B.J. *abbr.* Bachelor of Journalism.

Björn·son (byûrn′sən), **Björnstjerne.** 1832–1910. Norwegian writer who sought to revive the literary language and character of Norway. His works include the novel *The Fisher Girl* (1868) and the epic poem *Arnljot Gelline* (1870). He won the 1903 Nobel Prize for literature.

Bk The symbol for the element **berkelium.**

bk. *abbr.* **1.** Bank. **2.** Book.

bkg. *abbr.* Banking.

bkgd. *abbr.* Background.

bklr. *abbr. Printing.* Black letter.

bkpg. *abbr.* Bookkeeping.

bkpt. *abbr.* Bankrupt.

bks. *abbr.* **1.** Barracks. **2.** Books.

bl. *abbr.* **1.** Barrel. **2.** Black. **3.** Blue.

B.L. *abbr.* **1.** Bachelor of Laws. **2.** Bachelor of Letters. **3.** Bachelor of Literature.

B/L *abbr.* Bill of lading.

B.L.A. *abbr.* Bachelor of Liberal Arts.

blab (blăb) *v.* **blabbed, blab·bing, blabs.** *—tr.* To reveal (secret matters) especially through indiscreet or unreserved talk. *—intr.* **1.** To reveal secret matters. **2.** To chatter thoughtlessly or indiscreetly. See Synonyms at **gossip. —blab** *n.* **1.** An incessant or indiscreet talker. **2.** Lengthy chatter. [Middle English *blabben,* to talk foolishly, back-formation from *blaberen.*] **—blab′by** *adj.*

blab·ber (blăb′ər) *intr.v.* **-bered, -ber·ing, -bers.** To chatter; babble. **—blabber** *n.* **1.** Idle chatter. **2.** A blabbermouth. [Middle English *blaberen.*]

blab·ber·mouth (blăb′ər-mouth′) *n. Informal.* One who talks indiscreetly or incessantly.

black (blăk). *Abbr.* **bl., blk.** *adj.* **black·er, black·est. 1.** *Color.* Being of the color black, producing or reflecting comparatively little light and having no predominant hue. **2.** Having little or no light: *a black, moonless night.* **3.** Often **Black. a.** Of, relating to, or belonging to a racial group having brown to black skin, especially one of African origin: *the Black population of South Africa.*

b. Of, relating to, or belonging to an American ethnic group descended from African peoples having dark skin; African American; Afro-American: *"When the history books are written in future generations, the historians will . . . say, 'There lived a great people—a black people—who injected new meaning and dignity into the veins of civilization' "* (Martin Luther King, Jr.). *"Despite the exposure, being young, gifted and Black in the corridors of power has its trying moments"* (Ebony). **4.** Very dark in color: *rich black soil; black, wavy hair.* **5.** Soiled, as from soot; dirty: *feet black from playing outdoors.* **6.** Evil; wicked: *the pirates' black deeds.* **7.** Cheerless and depressing; gloomy: *black thoughts.* **8.** Marked by anger or sullenness: *gave me a black look.* **9.** Often **Black.** Attended with disaster; calamitous: *the stock market crash on Black Friday.* **10.** Deserving of, indicating, or incurring censure or dishonor: *"Man . . . has written one of his blackest records as a destroyer on the oceanic islands"* (Rachel Carson). **11.** Wearing clothing of the darkest visual hue: *the black knight.* **12.** Served without milk or cream: *black coffee.* **13.** Appearing to emanate from a source other than the actual point of origin. Used chiefly of intelligence operations: *black propaganda; black radio transmissions.* **14.** Disclosed, for reasons of security, only to an extremely limited number of authorized persons; very highly classified: *black programs in the Defense Department; the Pentagon's black budget.* **15.** *Chiefly British.* Boycotted as part of a labor union action. **—black** *n.* **1.** *Color.* **a.** The achromatic color value of minimum lightness or maximum darkness; the color of objects that absorb nearly all light of all visible wavelengths; one extreme of the neutral gray series, the opposite being white. Although strictly a response to zero stimulation of the retina, the perception of black appears to depend on contrast with surrounding color stimuli. **b.** A pigment or dye having this color value. **2.** Complete or almost complete absence of light; darkness. **3.** Clothing of the darkest hue, especially such clothing worn for mourning. **4.** Often **Black.** **a.** A member of a racial group having brown to black skin, especially one of African origin. **b.** An American descended from peoples of African origin having brown to black skin; an African American; an Afro-American: *"Many blacks and Hispanics cannot borrow money from banks on subjective grounds"* (Jesse Jackson). **5.** Something that is colored black. **6.** *Games.* **a.** The black-colored pieces, as in chess or checkers. **b.** The player using these pieces. *—tr.* **blacked, black·ing, blacks. 1.** To make black: *blacked their faces with charcoal.* **2.** To apply blacking to: *blacked the stove.* **3.** *Chiefly British.* To boycott as part of a labor union action. *—intr.* To become black. ***—phrasal verb.* black out. 1.a.** To lose consciousness or memory temporarily: *blacked out at the podium.* **b.** To suppress (a fact or memory, for example) from conscious recognition: *blacked out many of my wartime experiences.* **2.** To prohibit the dissemination of, especially by censorship: *blacked out the news issuing from the rebel provinces.* **3.** To extinguish or conceal all lights that might help enemy aircraft find a target during an air raid. **4.** To extinguish all the lights on (a stage). **5.** To cause a failure of electrical power in: *Storm damage blacked out much of the region.* **6.a.** To withhold (a televised event or program) from a broadcast area: *blacked out the football game on local stations.* **b.** To withhold a televised event or program from: *will black out the entire state to increase ticket sales for the game.* ***—idiom.* in the black.** On the credit side of a ledger; prosperous. [Middle English *blak,* from Old English *blæc.* See **bhel-**[1] in Appendix.] **—black′ish** *adj.* **—black′ly** *adv.* **—black′ness** *n.*

USAGE NOTE: *Black* is often capitalized in its use to denote persons, though the lowercased form *black* is still widely used by authors of all races: *"Together, blacks and whites can move our country beyond racism"* (Whitney Moore Young, Jr.). Use of the capitalized form has the advantage of acknowledging the parallel with other ethnic groups and nationalities, such as *Italian* and *Sioux.* It can be argued that *black* is different from these other terms because it was derived from an adjective rather than from a proper name. However, a precedent exists for the capitalization of adjectives used to denote specific groups, as in the *Reds* and the *Whites* (of the Russian Civil War) or the *Greens* (the European political party). The capitalization of *Black* does raise ancillary problems for the treatment of the term *white.* Orthographic evenhandedness would seem to require the use of the uppercase form *White,* but this form might be taken to imply that whites constitute a single ethnic group, an issue that is certainly debatable. On the other hand, the use of the lowercase form *white* in the same context as the uppercase form *Black* will obviously raise questions as to how and why the writer has distinguished between the two groups. There is no entirely happy solution to this problem. In all likelihood, uncertainty as to the mode of styling of *white* has dissuaded many publications from adopting the capitalized form *Black.* See Usage Note at **color.**

Black (blăk), **Hugo La Fayette.** 1886–1971. American jurist who served as an associate justice of the U.S. Supreme Court (1937–1971). He was noted for his ardent support of civil rights.

Black, Joseph. 1728–1799. British chemist who rediscovered carbon dioxide (1756) and formulated the concepts of latent heat and specific heat.

Black, Shirley Temple. Born 1927? American actress and public official. As Shirley Temple she was an immensely popular child actress of the 1930's, starring in films such as *Bright Eyes* (1934).

black alder *n.* **1.** A deciduous shrub or small tree *(Ilex verticillata),* the most widespread of North American hollies, growing in many variable forms from Minnesota to Texas and Georgia. Also called *winterberry.* **2.** A Eurasian alder tree *(Alnus glutinosa)* that is sometimes cultivated in North America, especially for its ability to grow in soils too wet for many other trees.

black·a·moor (blăk′ə-mo͝or′) *n. Offensive.* A dark-skinned person, especially a person from northern Africa. [BLACK + *-a-,* of unknown origin + MOOR.]

black-and-blue (blăk′ən-blo͞o′) *adj.* Discolored from coagulation of blood below the surface of the skin.

black-and-tan (blăk′ən-tăn′) *adj.* **1.** Having a black coat with tannish markings. Used of a dog. **2.** Involving, recognizing, or admitting Black and white people equally: *a black-and-tan organization.*

Black and Tan *n., pl.* **Black and Tans.** A member of the Royal Irish Constabulary, a force of British soldiers sent to Ireland to suppress the Sinn Fein rebellion of 1919 to 1921. [From the color of their uniform.]

black-and-tan coonhound *n.* Any of an American breed of large, strong coonhounds that have pendulous ears and a short black coat with tan markings above the eyes and on the chest, legs, and muzzle.

black-and-tan terrier *n.* See **Manchester terrier.**

black and white *n. Abbr.* **BW, b/w 1.** Writing or print: *saw their words in black and white.* **2.** A visual medium, as in photography or printmaking, employing only black and white or black, white, and values of gray: *a film shot in black and white; a painting reproduced in black and white.*

black-and-white (blăk′ən-hwīt′, -wīt′) *adj.* **1.** Partially black and partially white: *a black-and-white cow.* **2.** Being in writing or print: *black-and-white proof.* **3.a.** Rendered in black and white or in achromatic colors: *a black-and-white drawing.* **b.** Of or relating to the reproduction or presentation of visual images in black and white: *black-and-white television; black-and-white photography.* **4.** Expressing, recognizing, or based on two mutually exclusive sets of ideas or values: *black-and-white categories; a black-and-white point of view.*

Black Ang·us (ăng′gəs) *n.* See **Aberdeen Angus.**

black art *n.* Black magic; witchcraft.

black-a-vised (blăk′ə-vīst′, -vīzd′) *adj.* Having a dark complexion. [From dialectal *black a vice* : BLACK + dialectal *a,* of (from Middle English, unstressed variant of *of;* see OF) + *vice,* face (from Old French *vis,* face, from Latin *vīsus,* past participle of *vidēre,* to see; see **weid-** in Appendix).]

black bag job also **black-bag job** (blăk′băg′) *n. Slang.* An act of entry, search, and sometimes removal or photographing of property, conducted by federal investigators without a warrant.

black·ball (blăk′bôl′) *n.* **1.** A negative vote, especially one that blocks the admission of an applicant to an organization. **2.** A small black ball used as a negative ballot. **—blackball** *tr.v.* **-balled, -ball·ing, -balls. 1.** To vote against, especially to veto the admission of. **2.** To shut out from social or commercial participation; ostracize or boycott. **—black′ball′er** *n.*

SYNONYMS: *blackball, blacklist, boycott, ostracize.* The central meaning shared by these verbs is "to exclude from social, professional, or commercial activities": *blackballed from membership in the club; the movie industry blacklisting suspected Communists; winegrowers hiring union grape pickers for fear of being boycotted; ostracized by the community for immoral activities.*
ANTONYM: *admit.*

black bass (băs) *n.* Any of several North American freshwater game fishes of the genus *Micropterus.*

black bear *n.* **1.** The common North American bear *(Euarctos* or *Ursus americanus)* that lives in forests, is omnivorous, and has a glossy black or dark brown coat. **2.** Any of several black or dark brown Asiatic bears, especially *Selenarctos thibetanus,* with a pointed snout, a black coat, and a white, V-shaped mark on the chest.

Black·beard (blăk′bîrd′). See Edward **Teach.**

black belt *n.* **1.a.** The rank of expert in a martial art such as judo or karate. **b.** The black sash that symbolizes this rank of proficiency. **c.** A person who has attained this rank. **2.** A region of rich, black soil. **3.** Often **Black Belt.** An area having a predominantly Black population.

black·ber·ry (blăk′bĕr′ē) *n.* **1.** Any of various shrubs of the genus *Rubus,* having usually prickly stems, compound leaves, and an aggregate fruit of small drupelets. **2.** The fruit of these plants, usually black, purple, or deep red.

blackberry lily *n.* A medicinal Chinese perennial herb *(Belamcanda chinensis)* having sword-shaped leaves, usually orange showy flowers with red spots, and dehiscent fruits with shiny seeds in clusters resembling blackberries. Also called *leopard flower.*

black bile *n.* One of the four humors of medieval physiology, supposed to cause melancholy.

black bindweed or **black-bind·weed** (blăk′bīnd′wēd′) *n.* A twining annual vine *(Polygonum convolvulus),* native to Eurasia but widespread as a weed and having heart-shaped leaves and clusters of small, greenish-white flowers.

black birch *n.* **1.** See **sweet birch. 2.** See **river birch.**

black·bird (blăk′bûrd′) *n.* **1.** Any of various New World birds

black bear
American black bear
Ursus americanus

blackberry

ă pat	oi boy
ā pay	ou out
âr care	o͝o took
ä father	o͞o boot
ĕ pet	ŭ cut
ē be	ûr urge
ĭ pit	th thin
ī pie	*th* this
îr pier	hw which
ŏ pot	zh vision
ō toe	ə about, item
ô paw	♦ regionalism

Stress marks: **′** (primary); ′ (secondary), as in **dictionary** (dĭk′shə-nĕr′ē)

of the family Icteridae, such as the grackle or red-winged blackbird, the male of which has black or predominantly black plumage. **2.** An Old World songbird *(Turdus merula),* the male of which is black with a yellow bill. In this sense, also called *merle.*

black•board (blăk′bôrd′, -bōrd′) *n.* A smooth, hard, dark-colored panel for writing on with chalk.

blackboard

black•bod•y (blăk′bŏd′ē) *n.* A theoretically perfect absorber of all incident radiation.

black book *n.* A book containing names of people and organizations to blacklist.

black box *n.* **1. a.** A device or theoretical construct with known or specified performance characteristics but unknown or unspecified constituents and means of operation. **b.** Something that is mysterious, especially as to function. **2.** The flight recorder, as on a military or commercial aircraft, that documents preflight checks, in-flight procedures, and the landing.

black bryony *n.* A poisonous, perennial twining herb *(Tamus communis),* native to Eurasia and sometimes grown as an ornamental for its red berries.

black•buck (blăk′bŭk′) *n.* An antelope *(Antilope cervicapra)* of India that inhabits open grasslands and in the male has long, spiraled horns and a black coat with white underparts.

Black•burn (blăk′bûrn′). A borough of northwest England north-northwest of Manchester. The city's textile industry dates to the early 17th century. Population, 141,700.

Blackburn, Mount. A peak, 5,039.5 m (16,523 ft) high, of the Wrangell Mountains in southern Alaska.

black•cap (blăk′kăp′) *n.* **1.** See **black raspberry** (sense 1). **2. a.** A small European warbler *(Sylvia atricapilla),* the male of which is gray with a black crown. **b.** Any of various other black-crowned birds, such as the chickadee.

black cherry *n.* **1. a.** A deciduous North American tree *(Prunus serotina)* having drooping, elongate clusters of white flowers and blackish, somewhat poisonous fruits. **b.** The close-grained, reddish-brown wood of this tree, used especially for furniture, cabinets, and musical instruments. **2.** Any of various dark-fruited kinds of cherry.

black•cock (blăk′kŏk′) *n.* The male of the black grouse.

black cod *n.* See **sablefish.**

black cohosh *n.* An eastern North American perennial herb *(Cimicifuga racemosa)* having large, pinnately compound leaves and racemes of small white flowers. Also called *black snakeroot.*

black comedy *n.* Comedy that uses black humor.

♦ **black cow** *n. Chicago.* A float made with root beer and vanilla ice cream. See Regional Note at **milk shake.** [BLACK + COW[1] (from the ice cream used in making it).]

black crappie *n.* An edible North American sunfish *(Pomoxis nigromaculatus)* having dark mottled coloring. Also called *calico bass, strawberry bass.*

black cumin *n.* An annual Eurasian herb *(Nigella sativa)* having bluish-white flowers and pungent black seeds used as a seasoning in Asian cuisines.

black•damp (blăk′dămp′) *n.* A noncombustible gas that consists of a mixture of carbon dioxide and nitrogen, found in mines after fires or explosions and incapable of supporting life. Also called *chokedamp.* [BLACK + DAMP, gas.]

Black Death *n.* A form of bubonic plague, caused by the bacillus *Yersinia* (or *Pasturella*) *pestis,* that was pandemic throughout Europe and much of Asia in the 14th century. [From the dark splotches it causes on its victims.]

black diamond *n.* **1.** See **carbonado[2].** **2.** Also **black diamonds.** Coal.

black diet *n.* Deprivation of all food and water as a form of prison punishment and torture, usually resulting in death of the prisoners.

black-eyed Susan
Rudbeckia hirta

black duck *n.* A common duck *(Anas rubripes)* of the northeast United States and Canada, characterized by black or dusky brown plumage and often found in saltwater marshes.

black economy *n.* A sizable hidden segment of a country's economy that operates on numerous unreported private cash transactions.

black•en (blăk′ən) *v.* **-ened, -en•ing, -ens.** —*tr.* **1.** To make black. **2.** To sully or defame: *a scandal that blackened the mayor's name.* **3.** To coat (fish or meat, for example) with pepper and other spices and then sear in a hot skillet, thereby producing meat that is black on the outside but tender on the inside. —*intr.* To become dark or black: *The day blackened into night.* —**black′en•er** *n.*

Black English *n.* The range of varieties of English spoken by American Black people.

USAGE NOTE: In linguistic usage *Black English* refers to the entire range of varieties of English spoken by American Black people of any educational or social level. When reference is made to the nonstandard varieties of English used by certain Black speakers, the preferred terms are *Vernacular Black English* or *Black English Vernacular.*

Black•ett (blăk′ĭt), Baron **Patrick Maynard Stuart.** 1897–1974. British physicist. He won a 1948 Nobel Prize for contributions to the study of cosmic radiation.

black eye *n.* **1.** A bruised discoloration of the flesh surrounding the eye. **2.** A dishonored reputation; a bad name.

black-eyed pea (blăk′īd′) *n.* See **cowpea.**

black-eyed Su•san (so͞o′zən) *n.* **1.** Any of several North American herbs of the genus *Rudbeckia* in the composite family, especially *R. hirta,* having hairy stems and leaves and showy flower heads with orange-yellow rays and dark purple or brown centers. **2.** A tropical African twining herb *(Thunbergia alata)* cultivated for its showy, usually yellow to orange tubular flowers with dark purple centers.

black•face (blăk′fās′) *n.* **1.** Makeup for a conventionalized comic travesty of Black people, especially in a minstrel show. **2.** An actor wearing such makeup in a minstrel show.

black•fish (blăk′fĭsh′) *n., pl.* **blackfish** or **-fish•es. 1.** Any of various dark-colored fishes, such as: **a.** A small, edible, freshwater fish *(Dallia pectoralis)* that inhabits streams and ponds of Alaska and Siberia and is noted for its ability to withstand freezing. **b.** See **tautog. 2.** See **pilot whale.**

black flag *n.* A Jolly Roger.

black-flag (blăk′flăg′) *tr.v.* **-flagged, -flag•ging, -flags.** *Sports.* To signal (the driver of a racing car) to proceed immediately to the pits.

black fly *n.* Any of various small, dark-colored biting flies of the family Simuliidae, the larvae of which attach to rocks in running streams. Also called *buffalo gnat.*

Black•foot (blăk′fo͝ot′) *n., pl.* **Blackfoot** or **-feet** (-fēt′). **1. a.** A Native American confederacy located on the northern Great Plains, composed of the Blackfoot, Blood, and Piegan tribes. Traditional Blackfoot life was based on nomadic buffalo hunting. **b.** A member of this confederacy. **2. a.** The northernmost tribe of the Blackfoot confederacy, inhabiting central Alberta. **b.** A member of this tribe. **3.** The Algonquian language of the Blackfoot, Blood, and Piegan. **4.** See **Sihasapa.** —**Black′foot′** *adj.*

black-foot•ed albatross (blăk′fo͝ot′ĭd) *n.* An albatross *(Diomedea nigripes)* of the Pacific coastal islands that is blackish and dusky with black feet and legs and a whitish face.

black-footed ferret *n.* A North American weasel *(Mustela nigripes)* that is yellowish above, mixed with brown on the head and neck, and has a blackish mask and feet. It is related to the European polecat.

Blackfoot Sioux *n., pl.* **Blackfoot Sioux.** See **Sihasapa.**

Black Forest. A mountainous region of southwest Germany between the Rhine and Neckar rivers. It is a year-round resort area that is famous for its clock and toy industries.

black frost *n.* A dry freeze without the protective formation of hoarfrost that results in the internal freezing and death of vegetation.

black gold *n. Informal.* Petroleum.

black grouse *n.* A Eurasian game bird *(Lyrurus tetrix)* with black plumage and white wing markings in the male and brownish, barred plumage in the female.

black•guard (blăg′ərd, -ärd′) *n.* **1.** A thoroughly unprincipled person; a scoundrel. **2.** A foul-mouthed person. —**blackguard** *tr.v.* **-guard•ed, -guard•ing, -guards.** To abuse verbally; revile. —**black′guard•ism** *n.* —**black′guard•ly** *adj. & adv.*

black gum *n.* See **sour gum.**

Black Hand *n.* A secret society organized for acts of terrorism and blackmail that was active in the United States in the early 20th century.

black haw *n.* Either of two deciduous plants *(Viburnum lentago* or *V. prunifolium),* native to the eastern United States and having clusters of white flowers and blue-black berrylike fruits.

Black Hawk. Originally Makataimeshekiakiak. 1767–1838. Sauk leader. Resenting an 1804 treaty that ceded all Sauk and Fox lands east of the Mississippi River to the United States, he led 1,000 Fox and Sauk warriors in the Black Hawk War (1832).

black•head (blăk′hĕd′) *n.* **1.** *Medicine.* A plug of keratin and sebum within a hair follicle that is blackened at the surface. Also called *comedo.* **2.** An infectious disease of turkeys and some wildfowl that is caused by a protozoan *(Histomonas meleagridis)* and results in lesions of the intestine and liver. Also called *enterohepatitis, histomoniasis, infectious enterohepatitis.* **3.** Any of various birds, such as the scaup, with dark head markings.

black heroin *n.* A dark, sticky, extremely potent and highly addictive form of heroin, the purity of which is often as high as 60 to 70 percent.

Black Hills. A group of rugged mountains of southwest South Dakota and northeast Wyoming rising to 2,208.8 m (7,242 ft) at Harney Peak. The Black Hills are a major recreational area.

black hole *n.* **1.** An extremely small region of space-time with a gravitational field so intense that nothing can escape, not even light. **2.** A great void; an abyss: *The government created a bureaucratic black hole that swallows up individual initiative.*

black horehound *n.* A Eurasian perennial herb *(Ballota nigra)* in the mint family, having hairy, strong-smelling foliage and clusters of pinkish-purple flowers.

black humor *n.* **1.** The juxtaposition, as in writing or drama, of morbid or absurd elements with comical or farcical ones, especially so as to produce a shocking or disturbing effect. **2.** The literary genre employing this technique. —**black humorist** *n.*

black ice *n.* A thin, nearly invisible coating of ice, as on the surface of a road or a sidewalk, that is usually caused by freezing mist and is extremely hazardous.

black·ing (blăk′ĭng) *n.* **1.** See **lampblack. 2.** A preparation, such as a shoe or stove polish, that is used to impart a black color.

black·jack (blăk′jăk′) *n.* **1.** A leather-covered bludgeon with a short, flexible shaft or strap, used as a hand weapon. **2.** The blackjack oak. **3.** *Games.* A card game in which the object is to accumulate cards with a higher count than that of the dealer but not exceeding 21. In this sense, also called *twenty-one, vingt-et-un.* **4.** Sphalerite. **—blackjack** *tr.v.* **-jacked, -jack·ing, -jacks. 1.** To hit or beat with a leather-covered bludgeon. **2.** To coerce by threats. [BLACK + JACK.]

blackjack oak *n.* A deciduous oak tree *(Quercus marilandica),* native mostly to the southeastern United States and having blackish bark and leaves with three shallow lobes at the widened apex.

black knot *n.* A disease of the plum, the cherry, and related plants caused by the fungus *Apiosporina morbosa* and resulting in black, knotlike swellings on the branches.

black lead (lĕd) *n.* See **graphite.**

black·leg (blăk′lĕg′) *n.* **1.** An infectious, usually fatal bacterial disease of cattle and sometimes of sheep, goats, and swine, caused by *Clostridium chauvoe* and characterized by gas-containing swellings in the musculature. **2.** A bacterial or fungal disease of certain plants, such as the cabbage and potato, that causes the stems to turn black at the soil line. **3.** One who cheats at cards; a cardsharp. **4.** *Chiefly British.* A worker who is opposed to trade unions; a scab.

black letter *n. Abbr.* **bklr.** *Printing.* A heavy typeface with very broad counters and thick, ornamental serifs. Also called *gothic, Old English.*

black light *n.* Invisible ultraviolet or infrared radiation. Black light causes fluorescent materials to emit visible light and is used to take pictures in the dark.

black·light trap (blăk′līt′) *n.* An insect trap that attracts a wide variety of insects by the use of a form of black light.

black·list (blăk′lĭst′) *n.* A list of persons or organizations that have incurred disapproval or suspicion or are to be boycotted or otherwise penalized. **—blacklist** *tr.v.* **-list·ed, -list·ing, -lists.** To place on or as if on a blacklist. See Synonyms at **blackball. —black′list′er** *n.*

black locust *n.* A deciduous tree *(Robinia pseudoacacia)* in the pea family, native to the eastern and central United States and having alternate, pinnately compound leaves, spiny stipules, and hanging clusters of fragrant, creamy-white flowers.

black lung *n.* Pneumoconiosis caused by the long-term inhalation of coal dust. Also called *anthracosis.*

black magic *n.* Magic practiced for evil purposes or in league with supposed evil spirits; witchcraft.

black·mail (blăk′māl′) *n.* **1.a.** Extortion of money or something else of value from a person by the threat of exposing a criminal act or discreditable information. **b.** Something of value extorted in this manner. **2.** Tribute formerly paid to freebooters along the Scottish border for protection from pillage. [BLACK + MAIL[3].] **—black′mail′** *v.* **—black′mail′er** *n.*

Black Ma·ri·a (mə-rī′ə) *n.* A patrol wagon. [BLACK + the name *Maria.*]

black market *n.* **1.** The illegal business of buying or selling goods or currency in violation of restrictions such as price controls or rationing. **2.** A place where these illegal operations are carried on. **—black′-mar′ket** (blăk′mär′kĭt) *adj.* **—black′-mar′ket·er, black′-mar′ket·eer′** (-mär′kĭ-tîr′) *n.* **—black′-mar′ket·eer′ing** *n.*

black-mar·ket (blăk′mär′kĭt) *tr.v.* **-ket·ed, -ket·ing, -kets.** To trade (something) in the black market.

black mass *n.* **1.** A travesty of the Roman Catholic Mass, ascribed to reputed worshipers of Satanism. **2. Black Mass.** *Informal.* A Requiem Mass.

black measles *n. (used with a sing. or pl. verb).* A severe form of measles characterized by dark, hemorrhagic skin eruptions. Also called *hemorrhagic measles.*

black medic or **black medick** *n.* A cloverlike Eurasian plant *(Medicago lupulina)* in the pea family, having dense clusters of small yellow flowers and black pods. It is cultivated for forage. Also called *nonesuch.* [BLACK + MEDIC[1].]

black money *n.* Income, as from illegal activities, that is not reported to the government for tax purposes.

Black Mountains. A range of the Blue Ridge in western North Carolina rising to 2,038.6 km (6,684 ft) at Mount Mitchell.

Black·mun (blăk′mən), **Harry Andrew.** Born 1908. American jurist who was appointed an associate justice of the U.S. Supreme Court in 1970.

Black Muslim *n.* A member of a chiefly Black American group, the Nation of Islam, that professes Islamic religious beliefs.

black mustard *n.* A weedy, annual Eurasian plant *(Brassica nigra)* in the mustard family, having racemes of yellow flowers and pungent seeds formerly used to prepare the condiment mustard.

Black Nationalist *n.* A member of a group of militant Black people who urge separatism from white people and the establishment of self-governing Black communities. **—Black Nationalism** *n.*

black nightshade *n.* A poisonous, annual Eurasian plant *(Solanum nigrum),* widespread as a weed and having clusters of white, star-shaped flowers and usually blackish berries.

black oak *n.* A deciduous North American tree *(Quercus velutina)* having divided leaves with pointed lobes, a blackish outer bark, a yellowish inner bark, and durable wood.

black·out (blăk′out′) *n.* **1.** The concealment or extinguishment of lights that might be visible to enemy aircraft during an air raid. **2.** Lack of illumination caused by an electrical power failure. **3.a.** The sudden extinguishment of all stage lights in a theater to indicate the passage of time or to mark the end of an act or a scene. **b.** A short, comic vaudeville skit that ends with lights off. **4.** A temporary loss of memory or consciousness. **5.a.** A suppression, as of news, by censorship. **b.** Restriction or prohibition of telecasting a sports event in order to ensure ticket sales.

SYNONYMS: *blackout, faint, swoon, syncope.* The central meaning shared by these nouns is "a temporary loss of consciousness": *suffers blackouts at high altitudes; fell in a dead faint at the sight of the cadaver; sank to the ground in a swoon; was taken to the emergency room in a state of syncope.*

Black Panther *n.* A member of an organization of militant Black Americans.

black pepper *n.* The small, dark, unripe fruit of the pepper plant *(Piper nigrum),* used whole or ground as a pungent spice.

black·poll (blăk′pōl′) *n.* A North American warbler *(Dendroica striata),* the male of which has a black cap. [BLACK + POLL, head.]

Black·pool (blăk′po͞ol′). A borough of northwest England on the Irish Sea north of Liverpool. It is a popular seaside resort. Population, 148,700.

black poplar *n.* A Eurasian shade tree *(Populus nigra)* with spreading branches.

Black Power *n.* A movement among Black Americans emphasizing racial pride and social equality through the creation of Black political and cultural institutions: *"Black Power . . . calls for black people to consolidate behind their own, so that they can bargain from a position of strength"* (Stokely Carmichael and Charles Hamilton).

black pudding *n.* A French black sausage made of pork and seasoned pig's blood. Also called *boudin noir.*

black racer *n.* A North American blacksnake *(Coluber constrictor)* commonly found in the eastern United States.

black raspberry *n.* **1.** A prickly eastern North American shrub *(Rubus occidentalis)* having an aggregate, edible, juicy, purple-black fruit. Also called *blackcap.* **2.** The fruit of this plant.

black rat snake *n.* A North American blacksnake *(Elaphe obsoleta)* that resembles the black racer.

Black River. 1. Or in China **Ba·bian Jiang** (bä′byän′ jyäng′) and in Vietnam **Song Da** (sông′ dä′). A river of southeast Asia rising in southern China and flowing about 805 km (500 mi) generally southeast to the Red River in northern Vietnam. **2.** A river rising in southeast Missouri and flowing about 483 km (300 mi) to the White River in northeast Arkansas.

Black Rod *n.* The chief usher of the British House of Lords. [After the rod carried as symbol of the office.]

black rot *n.* Any of several fungal or bacterial plant diseases resulting in dark brown to black discoloration and decay of affected plant parts.

black salsify *n.* A European plant *(Scorzonera hispanica)* in the composite family, having heads of yellow ray flowers and a large, edible, fleshy root.

black sa·po·te (sə-pō′tē, -tā) *n.* **1.** A tropical American tree *(Diospyros digyna)* closely related to the persimmon, having edible, olive-green fruit that blackens when ripe and has a soft, chocolate-brown pulp. **2.** The fruit of this plant. [BLACK + American Spanish *zapote,* persimmonlike fruit (from Nahuatl *tzapotl*).]

Blacks·burg (blăks′bûrg′). A town of southwest Virginia in the Allegheny Mountains west of Roanoke. Virginia Polytechnic Institute and State University (established 1872) is located here. Population, 30,638.

Black Sea. An inland sea between Europe and Asia. It is connected with the Aegean Sea by the Bosporus, the Sea of Marmara, and the Dardanelles.

black sheep *n.* A member of a family or other group who is considered undesirable or disreputable.

Black Shirt *n.* A member of a fascist party organization having a black shirt as part of its uniform, especially an Italian fascist.

black skimmer *n.* A skimmer *(Rynchops niger)* of North and South America that is black above and white below and has a scissorlike bill, bright red legs and feet, and dark brown eyes with vertical pupils.

black·smith (blăk′smĭth′) *n.* **1.** One that forges and shapes iron with an anvil and hammer. **2.** One that makes, repairs, and fits horseshoes. [From the color of iron.] **—black′smith′ing** *n.*

black·snake (blăk′snāk′) *n.* **1.** Any of various dark-colored, chiefly nonvenomous snakes, such as the black racer or the black rat snake of North America. **2.** A long, tapering, braided rawhide or leather whip with a snapper on the end.

black snakeroot *n.* See **black cohosh.**

black spot *n.* Any of various fungal or bacterial diseases of plants, resulting in small black spots on the leaves or on other parts.

blackjack

black letter

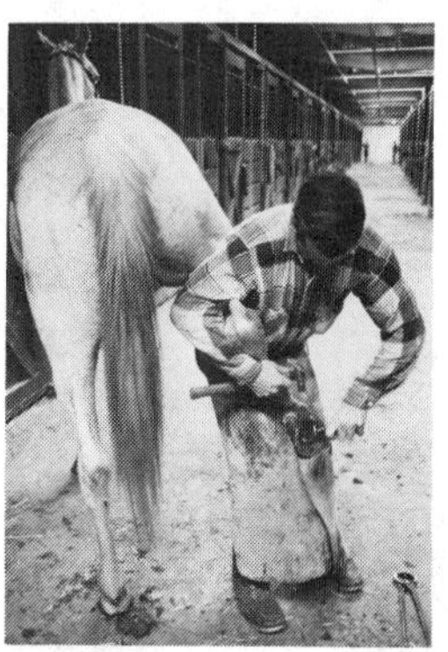

blacksmith

ă pat	oi boy
ā pay	ou out
âr care	o͝o took
ä father	o͞o boot
ĕ pet	ŭ cut
ē be	ûr urge
ĭ pit	th thin
ī pie	*th* this
îr pier	hw which
ŏ pot	zh vision
ō toe	ə about, item
ô paw	♦ regionalism

Stress marks: ′ (primary); ′ (secondary), as in **dictionary** (dĭk′shə-nĕr′ē)

black spruce *n.* A northern North American spruce *(Picea mariana)* having blue-green needles and small egg-shaped cones.

Black·stone (blăk′stōn′, -stən), Sir **William.** 1723–1780. British jurist and educator who wrote *Commentaries on the Laws of England* (1765–1769), the most comprehensive single treatment of the body of English law.

black·strap (blăk′străp′) *n.* A dark, very thick molasses, especially a residual product of sugar refining that is used in the manufacture of industrial alcohol and as an ingredient in cattle feed. [From its color and texture.]

black studies also **Black Studies** *pl.n.* Studies that deal with Afro-American culture.

black-tailed deer (blăk′tāld′) also **black·tail deer** (-tāl′) *n.* See **mule deer.**

black tar *n. Slang.* Black heroin.

black tea *n.* A dark tea prepared from fresh tea leaves that have been fully fermented before being dried.

black·thorn (blăk′thôrn′) *n.* A thorny, deciduous Eurasian shrub *(Prunus spinosa),* having white flowers and small, bluish-black, plumlike fruits used chiefly for flavoring alcoholic beverages such as sloe gin. Also called *sloe.*

black tie *n.* **1.** A black bow tie worn with a dinner jacket. **2.** Semiformal evening wear typically for men, usually requiring a dinner jacket. **—black′-tie′** (blăk′tī′) *adj.*

black·top (blăk′tŏp′) *n.* A bituminous material, such as asphalt, used to pave roads. *—tr.* **-topped, -top·ping, -tops.** To pave with a bituminous material.

Black Vol·ta (vŏl′tə, vōl′-, vôl′-). A river of western Africa rising in western Burkina Faso and flowing about 1,352 km (840 mi) to the White Volta in Ghana.

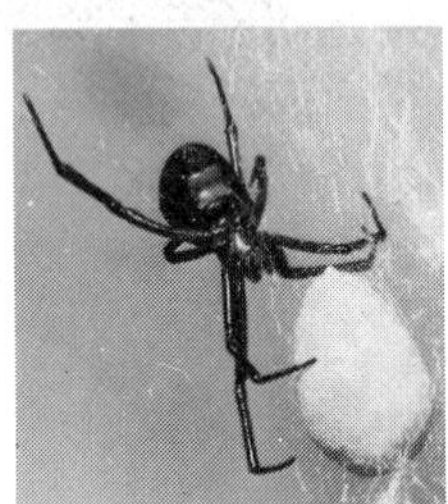
black widow
Latrodectus mactans

black vomit *n.* **1.** Dark vomit consisting of digested blood and gastric contents. **2.** Severe yellow fever with symptomatic regurgitation of dark vomited matter.

black vulture *n.* A carrion-eating bird *(Coragyps atratus)* of central North America and South America, having black plumage and a bald, black head.

black walnut *n.* **1.** An eastern North American tree *(Juglans nigra),* having dark brown wood and a deeply furrowed nut enclosed in a globose, aromatic husk. **2.** The wood of this tree, used especially for veneer, cabinets, furniture, and gunstocks. **3.** The nut of this tree, having an edible kernel used especially in confections.

black·wash (blăk′wŏsh′, -wôsh′) *tr.v.* **-washed, -wash·ing, -wash·es.** To bring from concealment; disclose. [BLACK + (WHITE)WASH.]

black·wa·ter fever (blăk′wô′tər, -wŏt′ər) *n.* A serious, often fatal complication of chronic malaria, characterized by the passage of bloody, dark red or black urine.

Black·well (blăck′wĕl′, -wəl), **Antoinette Louisa Brown.** 1825–1921. American social reformer. The first formally appointed (1852) woman pastor in America, she advocated abolition, temperance, and women's rights.

Blackwell, Elizabeth. 1821–1910. British-born American physician who was the first woman to be awarded a medical doctorate in modern times (1849).

black widow *n.* A poisonous New World spider *(Latrodectus mactans),* the female of which produces extremely toxic venom and has a black, shiny body with red markings. [From the fact that the female eats its mate.]

Black·wood (blăk′wo͝od′), **William.** 1776–1834. Scottish publisher and editor (1817–1834) of *Blackwood's Magazine,* a Tory literary review that published Wordsworth and Shelley among others.

blad·der (blăd′ər) *n.* **1.a.** *Anatomy.* Any of various distensible membranous sacs, such as the urinary bladder or the swim bladder, that serve as receptacles for fluid or gas. **b.** An item resembling one of the membranous sacs in animals: *the bladder of a football.* **2.** *Botany.* Any of various hollow or inflated saclike organs or structures, such as the floats of certain seaweeds or the specialized traps of bladderworts. **3.** *Pathology.* A blister, pustule, or cyst filled with fluid or air; a vesicle. [Middle English *bladdre,* from Old English *blǣdre.* See **bhlē-** in Appendix.]

William Blake

bladder campion *n.* A weedy Eurasian perennial herb *(Silene vulgaris)* having white flowers with deeply notched petals and a balloonlike, inflated calyx.

bladder fern *n.* Any of various ferns of the widespread genus *Cystopteris,* having pinnately compound fronds and often growing in rocky areas. [After its bladder-like indusium.]

blad·der·nose (blăd′ər-nōz′) *n.* See **hooded seal.**

blad·der·nut (blăd′ər-nŭt′) *n.* **1.** Any of various deciduous shrubs or small trees of the genus *Staphylea,* native to north temperate regions and having opposite compound leaves and terminal panicles of white flowers and bladderlike fruits. **2.** The fruit of such a plant.

bladder worm *n.* The bladderlike, encysted larva of the tapeworm that is characteristic of the cysticercus stage.

blad·der·wort (blăd′ər-wûrt′, -wôrt′) *n.* Any of various mostly aquatic carnivorous plants of the genus *Utricularia,* having small, specialized, urn-shaped bladders that trap minute insects and crustaceans.

bladder wrack *n.* Any of certain rockweeds, especially the widely distributed *Fucus vesiculosus,* having forked, brownish-green branches with gas-filled bladders.

blad·der·y (blăd′ə-rē) *adj.* **1.** Resembling or like a bladder. **2.** Possessing a bladder or bladders.

blade (blād) *n.* **1.** The flat-edged cutting part of a sharpened weapon or tool. **2.a.** A sword. **b.** A swordsman. **3.** A dashing youth. **4.** A flat, thin part or section: *the blade of an oar; the blade of a food processor.* **5.** The metal runner of an ice skate. **6.** A wide flat bone or bony part. **7.** The flat upper surface of the tongue just behind the tip. **8.** *Botany.* The expanded part of a leaf or petal. The term is often loosely used to include the entire leaf of grasses and similar plants. [Middle English, from Old English *blæd.* See **bhel-**[3] in Appendix.] **—blad′ed** *adj.*

blade apple *n.* See **Barbados gooseberry.** [From the shape of its leaves.]

♦ **blaff** (blăf) *n. Caribbean.* A West Indian stew consisting of fish or occasionally pork, seasonings such as lime and garlic, and often fruits and vegetables. [Probably from Dominican English *braff,* from BROTH.]

♦ **blag·ging** (blăg′ĭng) *n. Caribbean.* Informal talk, usually among men, occurring in a public place: *"the street corner, the rum shop, the crossroads, wherever hanging out, or . . . blagging, takes place"* (Roger D. Abrahams). [From French *blaguer,* to talk through one's hat, from *blague,* bladder, pouch, of Germanic origin, ultimately from Latin *bulga,* leather bag. See BULGE.]

Bla·go·vesh·chensk (blä′gə-vĕsh′chĕnsk, blə-gə-vyĕsh′-chĭsk). A city of eastern Russia at the confluence of the Amur and Zeya rivers. It is a port and railroad hub. Population, 195,000.

blah (blä) *Informal. n.* **1.** Worthless nonsense; drivel. **2. blahs.** A general feeling of discomfort, dissatisfaction, or depression: *"Monday morning Oscar woke up with the blahs"* (New Yorker). **—blah** *adj.* **1.** Dull and uninteresting. **2.** Low in spirit or health; down: *sat around all day feeling blah.* [Imitative of meaningless talk.] **—blah** *adv.*

blain (blān) *n.* A skin swelling or sore; a blister; a blotch. [Middle English, from Old English *blegen.*]

Blaine (blān). A city of eastern Minnesota, an industrial suburb of St. Paul. Population, 28,558.

Blaine, James Gillespie. Known as "the Plumed Knight." 1830–1893. American politician. A U.S. representative (1863–1876) and senator (1876–1881) from Maine, he was U.S. secretary of state (1881 and 1889–1892) and lost the 1884 presidential election to Grover Cleveland.

Blair (blâr), **John.** 1732–1800. American jurist who was a member of the Constitutional Convention (1787) and served as an associate justice of the U.S. Supreme Court (1789–1796).

Blake (blāk), **James Herbert.** Known as "Eubie." 1883–1983. American pianist and composer noted for his popular songs and Broadway productions, such as *Shuffle Along* (1921), which included "I'm Just Wild about Harry."

Blake, Robert. 1599–1657. English admiral who was a Parliamentarian during the English Civil War and pursued the Royalist fleet to the Mediterranean Sea, where he defeated it (1650).

Blake, William. 1757–1827. British poet and artist whose paintings and poetic works, such as *Songs of Innocence* (1789) and *The Marriage of Heaven and Hell* (c. 1790), have a mystical, visionary quality.

blam·a·ble also **blame·a·ble** (blā′mə-bəl) *adj.* Deserving blame; culpable. See Synonyms at **blameworthy. —blam′a·ble·ness** *n.* **—blam′a·bly** *adv.*

blame (blām) *tr.v.* **blamed, blam·ing, blames. 1.** To hold responsible. **2.** To find fault with; censure. **3.** To place responsibility for (something): *blamed the crisis on poor planning.* **—blame** *n.* **1.** The state of being responsible for a fault or an error; culpability. **2.** Censure; condemnation. ***—idiom.* to blame. 1.** Deserving censure; at fault. **2.** Being the cause or source of something: *A freak storm was to blame for the power outage.* [Middle English *blamen,* from Old French *blasmer, blamer,* from Vulgar Latin **blastēmāre,* alteration of Late Latin *blasphēmāre,* to reproach. See BLASPHEME.] **—blam′er** *n.*

SYNONYMS: *blame, fault, guilt.* These nouns are compared in the sense of responsibility for an offense. *Blame* stresses censure or punishment for a lapse or misdeed for which one is held accountable: *The police laid the blame for the accident squarely on the driver's shoulders. Fault* is culpability for causing or failing to prevent the occurrence of something detrimental: *The student failed the examination, but not through any fault of his teacher. Guilt* applies to serious, willful breaches of conduct and stresses moral culpability: *The case was dismissed because the prosecution did not have sufficient evidence of the defendant's guilt.* See also Synonyms at **criticize.**

blame·a·ble (blā′mə-bəl) *adj.* Variant of **blamable.**

blamed (blāmd) *adv.* & *adj. Informal.* Used as an intensive: *drove so blamed slow that we were late; called me a blamed fool.*

blame·ful (blām′fəl) *adj.* Deserving of blame; blameworthy. See Synonyms at **blameworthy. —blame′ful·ly** *adv.* **—blame′ful·ness** *n.*

blame·less (blām′lĭs) *adj.* Free of blame or guilt; innocent. **—blame′less·ly** *adv.* **—blame′less·ness** *n.*

blame·wor·thy (blām′wûr′thē) *adj.* **-thi·er, -thi·est.** Deserving blame; reprehensible. —**blame′wor′thi·ness** *n.*

SYNONYMS: *blameworthy, blamable, blameful, censurable, culpable, guilty, reprehensible.* The central meaning shared by these adjectives is "meriting reproof or punishment": *blameworthy if not criminal behavior; blamable but understandable resentment; blameful capriciousness; censurable misconduct; culpable negligence; secret guilty deeds; reprehensible arrogance.*
ANTONYM: *blameless.*

Blanc (blăngk, bläɴ), **Mont.** The highest peak of the Alps, rising to 4,810.2 m (15,771 ft) in the Savoy Alps of southeast France on the Italian border.

Blan·ca Peak (blăng′kə). A mountain, 4,375.2 m (14,345 ft) high, in the Sangre de Cristo Mountains of southern Colorado. It is the highest elevation in the range.

blanc fixe (blăngk′ fĭks′, bläɴ fēks′) *n.* Powdered barium sulfate used as a base for watercolor pigments and as a filler in paper. [French : *blanc,* white + *fixe,* fixed.]

blanch (blănch) also **blench** (blĕnch) *—v.* **blanched, blanch·ing, blanch·es** also **blenched, blench·ing, blench·es.** *—tr.* **1.** To take the color from; bleach. **2.** To whiten (a growing plant or plant part) by covering to cut off direct light. **3.** To whiten (a metal) by soaking in acid or by coating with tin. **4.a.** To scald (almonds, for example) in order to loosen the skin. **b.** To scald (food) briefly, as before freezing or as a preliminary stage in preparing a dish. **5.** To cause to turn white or become pale. *—intr.* To turn white or become pale: *Their faces blanched in terror.* [Middle English *blaunchen,* to make white, from Old French *blanchir,* from *blanche,* feminine of *blanc,* white, of Germanic origin. See **bhel-**[1] in Appendix.] —**blanch′er** *n.*

blanc·mange (blə-mänj′, -mäɴzh′) *n.* A flavored and sweetened milk pudding thickened with cornstarch. [Middle English *blankmanger,* a dish made with almond milk, from Old French *blanc mangier* : *blanc,* white (of Germanic origin; see **bhel-**[1] in Appendix) + *mangier,* to eat, food (from Latin *mandūcāre;* see MANGER).]

bland (blănd) *adj.* **bland·er, bland·est. 1.** Characterized by a moderate, unperturbed, or tranquil quality, especially: **a.** Pleasant in manner; smooth: *a bland smile.* **b.** Not irritating or stimulating; soothing: *a bland diet.* **c.** Exhibiting no personal worry, embarrassment, or concern: *told a series of bland lies.* **2.** Dull and insipid: *a bland little drama.* [Latin *blandus,* caressing, flattering. See **mel-**[1] in Appendix.] —**bland′ly** *adv.* —**bland′ness** *n.*

bland·i·fy (blăn′də-fī′) *tr.v.* **-fied, -fy·ing, -fies.** *Informal.* To make bland. —**blan′di·fi·ca′tion** (-fĭ-kā′shən) *n.*

blan·dish (blăn′dĭsh) *tr.v.* **-dished, -dish·ing, -dish·es.** To coax by flattery or wheedling; cajole. [Middle English *blandishen,* from Old French *blandir, blandiss-,* from Latin *blandīrī,* from *blandus,* flattering. See **mel-**[1] in Appendix.] —**blan′dish·er** *n.* —**blan′dish·ment** *n.*

blank (blăngk) *adj.* **blank·er, blank·est. 1.a.** Devoid of writing, images, or marks: *a blank page; a blank screen.* **b.** Containing no information; unrecorded or erased: *a blank tape; a blank diskette.* **2.** Not completed or filled in: *a blank questionnaire.* **3.** Not having received final processing; unfinished: *a blank key.* **4.a.** Lacking expression; expressionless: *"Although his gestures were elaborate, his face was blank"* (Nathanael West). See Synonyms at **empty. b.** Appearing or seeming to appear dazed or confused: *greeted me with a blank stare.* **5.** Devoid of thought or impression: *a blank mind.* **6.** Devoid of activity, interest, or distinctive character; empty: *tried to fill the blank hours of the day.* **7.** Absolute; complete: *a blank refusal.* —**blank** *n.* **1.** An empty space or place; a void: *During the exam my mind was a blank.* **2.a.** An empty space on a document to be filled in. **b.** A document with one or more such spaces. **3.** A manufactured article of a standard shape or form that is ready for final processing, as by stamping or cutting: *a key blank.* **4.** A blank cartridge. **5.** Something worthless, such as a losing lottery ticket. **6.** A mark, usually a dash (—), indicating the omission of a word or of a letter or letters. **7.** The white circle in the center of a target; a bull's eye. —**blank** *v.* **blanked, blank·ing, blanks.** *—tr.* **1.** To remove, as from view; obliterate: *"At times the strong glare of the sun blanked it from sight"* (Richard Wright). **2.** To block access to: *blank off a subway tunnel.* **3.** *Sports.* To prevent (an opponent) from scoring. **4.** To punch or stamp from flat stock, especially with a die. *—intr.* **1.** To become abstracted: *My mind blanked out for a few seconds.* **2.** To fade away: *The music gradually blanked out.* [Middle English, white, having spaces to be filled in, from Old French *blanc,* white, of Germanic origin. See **bhel-**[1] in Appendix.] —**blank′ly** *adv.* —**blank′ness** *n.*

blank cartridge *n.* A gun cartridge with a charge of powder but no bullet.

blank check *n.* **1.** A signed check with no amount to be paid filled in. **2.** Total freedom of action; carte blanche.

blank endorsement *n.* An endorsement on a check or negotiable note that names no payee, making it payable to the bearer. Also called *endorsement in blank.*

blan·ket (blăng′kĭt) *n.* **1.** A large piece of woven material used as a covering for warmth, especially on a bed. **2.** A layer that covers or encloses: *a thick blanket of snow.* —**blanket** *adj.* **1.** Applying to or covering all conditions or instances: *a blanket insurance policy.* **2.** Applying to or covering all members of a class: *blanket sanctions against human-rights violators.* —**blanket** *tr.v.* **-ket·ed, -ket·ing, -kets. 1.** To cover with or as if with a blanket: *leaves that blanket the ground.* **2.** To cover so as to inhibit, suppress, or extinguish: *blanketed the grease fire with sand.* **3.** To apply to generally and uniformly without exception: *high telephone service charges that blanketed our region.* [Middle English, from Old French, an unbleached soft cloth, from *blanc,* white, of Germanic origin. See **bhel-**[1] in Appendix.]

blanket flower *n.* See **gaillardia.**

blanket stitch *n.* A buttonhole stitch used for edging around heavy material.

blan·ket-stitch (blăng′kĭt-stĭch′) *tr.v.* **-stitched, -stitch·ing, -stitch·es.** To sew with a buttonhole stitch.

blank verse *n.* Verse consisting of unrhymed lines, usually of iambic pentameter.

Blan·tyre (blăn-tīr′). A city of southern Malawi. It is the largest city and chief commercial center of the country. Population, 229,000.

blare (blâr) *v.* **blared, blar·ing, blares.** *—intr.* To sound loudly and stridently: *a stereo blaring in the next apartment.* *—tr.* **1.** To cause to sound loudly and stridently: *Don't blare the stereo.* **2.** To proclaim loudly and flamboyantly: *headlines blaring the scandal.* —**blare** *n.* **1.** A loud, strident noise. **2.** Flamboyance. [Middle English *bleren.*]

blar·ney (blär′nē) *n.* **1.** Smooth, flattering talk. **2.** Deceptive nonsense. [After the BLARNEY Stone in Blarney Castle, Blarney, Ireland.] —**blar′ney** *v.*

Blar·ney (blär′nē). A village of southern Ireland near Cork. Blarney Castle (dating from the 15th century) is the site of the Blarney Stone, said to impart powers of eloquence and persuasion.

Blas·co I·bá·ñez (blä′skō ē-bän′yās, -ē-vän′yĕth), **Vicente.** 1867–1928. Spanish writer of naturalistic novels concerning his homeland, such as *The Cabin* (1898), and several highly popular but less literary novels, including *The Four Horsemen of the Apocalypse* (1916).

bla·sé (blä-zā′) *adj.* **1.** Uninterested because of frequent exposure or indulgence. **2.** Unconcerned; nonchalant: *had a blasé attitude about housecleaning.* **3.** Very sophisticated. [French, from past participle of *blaser,* to cloy, from French dialectal, to be chronically hung over, probably from Middle Dutch *blāsen,* to blow up, swell. See **bhlē-** in Appendix.]

blas·pheme (blăs-fēm′, blăs′fēm′) *v.* **-phemed, -phem·ing, -phemes.** *—tr.* **1.** To speak of (God or a sacred entity) in an irreverent, impious manner. **2.** To revile; execrate. *—intr.* To speak blasphemy. [Middle English *blasfemen,* from Old French *blasfemer,* from Late Latin *blasphēmāre,* from Greek *blasphēmein* : *blas-,* of unknown meaning + *phēmē,* speech; see **bhā-**[2] in Appendix.] —**blas·phem′er** (blăs-fē′mər, blăs′fə-) *n.*

blas·phe·mous (blăs′fə-məs) *adj.* Impiously irreverent. See Synonyms at **profane.** [Middle English *blasfemous,* from Late Latin *blasphēmus,* from Greek *blasphēmos,* from *blasphēmein,* to blaspheme. See BLASPHEME.] —**blas′phe·mous·ly** *adv.* —**blas′phe·mous·ness** *n.*

blas·phe·my (blăs′fə-mē) *n., pl.* **-mies. 1.a.** A contemptuous or profane act, utterance, or writing concerning God or a sacred entity. **b.** The act of claiming for oneself the attributes and rights of God. **2.** An irreverent or impious act, attitude, or utterance in regard to something considered inviolable or sacrosanct. [Middle English *blasfemie,* from Late Latin *blasphēmia,* from Greek, from *blasphēmein,* to blaspheme. See BLASPHEME.]

blast (blăst) *n.* **1.a.** A very strong gust of wind or air. **b.** The effect of such a gust. **2.** A forcible stream of air, gas, or steam from an opening, especially one in a blast furnace to aid combustion. **3.a.** A sudden loud sound, especially one produced by a stream of forced air: *a piercing blast from the steam whistle.* **b.** The act of producing such a sound: *gave a blast on his trumpet.* **4.a.** A violent explosion, as of dynamite or a bomb. **b.** The violent effect of such an explosion, consisting of a wave of increased atmospheric pressure followed immediately by a wave of decreased pressure. **c.** An explosive charge. **5.** *Botany.* Any of several plant diseases of diverse causes, resulting in sudden death of buds, flowers, foliage, or young fruits. **6.** A destructive or damaging influence. **7.** A powerful hit, blow, or shot. **8.** A violent verbal assault or outburst: *The candidate leveled a blast at her opponent.* **9.** *Slang.* A highly exciting or pleasurable experience or event, such as a big party. —**blast** *v.* **blast·ed, blast·ing, blasts.** *—tr.* **1.** To knock down or shatter by or as if by explosion; smash. **2.** To play or sound loudly: *The referees blasted their whistles.* **3.a.** To hit with great force: *The batter blasted the ball to right field.* **b.** To kill or destroy by hitting or shooting. **4.** To have a harmful or destructive effect on. **5.** To cause to shrivel, wither, or mature imperfectly by or as if by blast or blight: *crops that were blasted by frost.* **6.** To make or open by or as if by explosion: *blast a tunnel through the mountains.* **7.** To criticize or attack vigorously. *—intr.* **1.** To use or detonate explosives. **2.** To emit a loud, intense sound; blare: *speakers blasting at full volume.* **3.** To wither or shrivel or mature imperfectly. **4.** To criticize or attack with vigor. **5.** To shoot. **6.** *Electronics.* To distort sound recording or transmission by overloading a microphone or loudspeaker. —***phrasal verb.* blast off.** To take off, as a rocket. —***idiom.* full blast.** At full speed, volume, or capacity: *turned the radio up full blast; played the stereo at full blast.* [Middle English, from Old English *blǣst.* See **bhlē-** in Appendix.] —**blast′er** *n.*

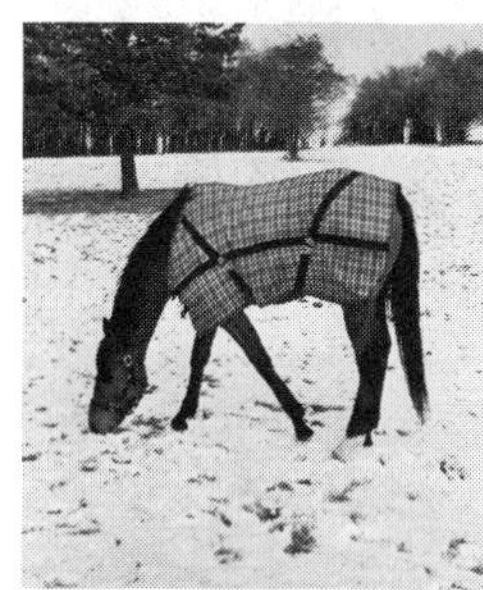

blanket
Horse blanket

ă **pat**	oi **boy**
ā **pay**	ou **out**
âr **care**	o͝o **took**
ä **father**	o͞o **boot**
ĕ **pet**	ŭ **cut**
ē **be**	ûr **urge**
ĭ **pit**	th **thin**
ī **pie**	*th* **this**
îr **pier**	hw **which**
ŏ **pot**	zh **vision**
ō **toe**	ə **about, item**
ô **paw**	♦ **regionalism**

Stress marks: ′ (primary); ′ (secondary), as in **dictionary** (dĭk′shə-nĕr′ē)

SYNONYMS: *blast, blight, dash, nip, wreck.* The central meaning shared by these verbs is "to have a pernicious, destructive, or ruinous effect on something": *prospects for peace blasted; blighted hopes; dashed ambitions; plans that were nipped in the bud; a wrecked life.*

blast– *pref.* Variant of **blasto–.**

–blast *suff.* An immature, embryonic stage in the development of cells or tissues: *erythroblast.* [From Greek *blastos,* bud.]

blast cell *n.* **1.** A precursor of a human blood cell. **2.** An immature, undifferentiated cell. [–BLAST + CELL.]

blast·ed (blăs′tĭd) *adj.* **1.** Used as an intensive: *I hate these blasted flies.* **2.** *Slang.* Intoxicated; drunk. **3.** Blighted, withered, or shriveled.

blas·te·ma (blă-stē′mə) *n., pl.* **-mas** or **-ma·ta** (-mə-tə). **1.** The formative, undifferentiated material from which cells are formed. **2.** A mass of embryonic cells from which an organ or a body part develops, either in normal development or in the regeneration of a lost body part. [Greek *blastēma,* offspring, sprout, from *blastos,* bud.] **—blas·te′mal, blas′te·mat′ic** (blăs′tə-măt′ĭk), **blas·te′mic** (blă-stē′mĭk) *adj.*

blast furnace *n.* A furnace in which combustion is intensified by a blast of air.

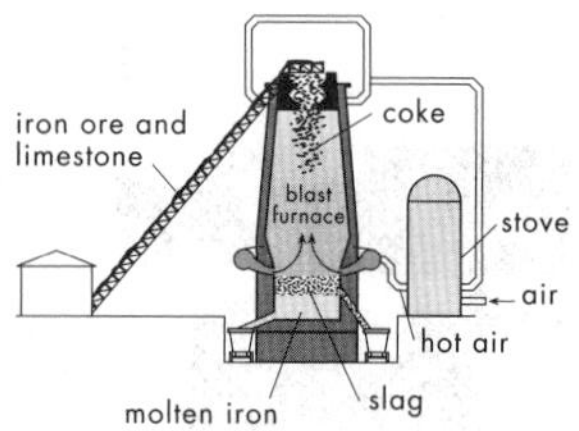

blast furnace

–blastic *suff.* Having a specified number or kind of formative elements such as buds, germs, cells, or cell layers: *meroblastic.* [From –BLAST.]

blasto– or **blast–** *pref.* Bud; germ; budding; germination: *blastocyst.* [From Greek *blastos,* bud.]

blas·to·coel or **blas·to·coele** (blăs′tə-sēl′) *n.* The fluid-filled, central cavity of a blastula. Also called *segmentation cavity.* **—blas′to·coe′lic** *adj.*

blas·to·cyst (blăs′tə-sĭst′) *n. Embryology.* The modified blastula that is characteristic of placental mammals. Also called *blastodermic vesicle.* **—blas′to·cys′tic** *adj.*

blas·to·derm (blăs′tə-dûrm′) *n. Embryology.* **1.** The layer of cells that develops on the surface of the yolk in an avian or reptilian egg and gives rise to the germinal disk from which the embryo develops. **2.** The layer of cells formed by the cleavage of a fertilized mammalian egg. It later divides into the three germ layers from which the embryo develops. **—blas′to·der′mic, blas′to·der·mat′ic** (-dər-măt′ĭk) *adj.*

blastodermic vesicle *n.* See **blastocyst.**

blas·to·disk or **blas·to·disc** (blăs′tə-dĭsk′) *n.* See **germinal disk.**

blast·off also **blast-off** (blăst′ôf′, -ŏf′) *n.* The launch, especially of a rocket.

blastoff
Apollo 16 voyage to the moon, April 16, 1972

blas·to·gen·e·sis (blăs′tə-jĕn′ĭ-sĭs) *n.* **1.** The theory that inherited characteristics are transmitted from parent to offspring by germ plasm. **2.** Reproduction of an organism by budding. **3.** The transformation of small lymphocytes into larger undifferentiated cells that are capable of undergoing mitosis. **—blas′to·ge·net′ic** (-jə-nĕt′ĭk), **blas′to·gen′ic** (-jĕn′ĭk) *adj.*

blas·to·ma (blă-stō′mə) *n., pl.* **-mas** or **-ma·ta** (-mə-tə). A neoplasm composed of immature and undifferentiated cells.

blas·to·mere (blăs′tə-mîr′) *n. Embryology.* Any of the cells resulting from the cleavage of a fertilized ovum during early embryonic development. **—blas′to·mer′ic** (-mîr′ĭk, -mĕr′-) *adj.*

blas·to·my·cete (blăs′tə-mī′sēt, -mī-sēt′) *n.* Any of various yeastlike, budding fungi of the genus *Blastomyces* that cause diseases in humans and animals.

blas·to·my·cin (blăs′tə-mī′sĭn) *n.* A preparation that is derived from a culture of the fungus *Blastomyces dermatitidis* and is injected intracutaneously as a diagnostic test for blastomycosis.

blas·to·my·co·sis (blăs′tō-mī-kō′sĭs) *n.* A fungal infection caused by a blastomycete and characterized by multiple inflammatory lesions of the skin, mucous membranes, or internal organs.

blas·to·pore (blăs′tə-pôr′, -pōr′) *n. Embryology.* The opening of the archenteron. [BLASTO– + PORE[2].] **—blas′to·por′ic, blas′to·por′al** (-pôr′əl, -pōr′-) *adj.*

blas·to·sphere (blăs′tə-sfîr′) *n.* See **blastula.**

blas·to·spore (blăs′tə-spôr′, -spōr′) *n.* A fungal spore produced by budding.

blas·tu·la (blăs′chə-lə) *n., pl.* **-las** or **-lae** (-lē′). *Embryology.* An early embryonic form produced by cleavage of a fertilized ovum and consisting of a spherical layer of cells surrounding a fluid-filled cavity. Also called *blastosphere.* [New Latin, from Greek *blastos,* bud.] **—blas′tu·lar** *adj.* **—blas′tu·la′tion** (-lā′shən) *n.*

blat (blăt) *v.* **blat·ted, blat·ting, blats.** *—tr.* To utter without thinking; blurt. *—intr.* **1.** To cry, especially like a sheep; bleat. **2.** To make a harsh or raucous noise. [Imitative.] **—blat** *n.*

bla·tant (blāt′nt) *adj.* **1.** Unpleasantly loud and noisy: *"There are those who find the trombones blatant and the triangle silly, but both add effective color"* (Musical Heritage Review). See Synonyms at **vociferous. 2.** *Usage Problem.* Totally or offensively conspicuous or obtrusive: *a blatant lie.* [From Latin *blatīre,* to blab (on the model of words such as RAMPANT).] **—bla′tan·cy** *n.* **—bla′tant·ly** *adv.*

USAGE NOTE: It is natural that *blatant* and *flagrant* are often confused, since the words overlap in meaning. Both attribute conspicuousness and offensiveness to certain acts. But *blatant* emphasizes the failure to conceal the act: *a blatant appeal to vanity; a blatant attempt to whitewash his country's misdeeds. Flagrant,* on the other hand, tends to emphasize a serious wrongdoing in the offense itself: *flagrant child abuse; a flagrant violation of human rights.* Certain contexts may admit either word depending on what is meant: a violation of international law might be either *blatant* or *flagrant.* But writers who refer to *the blatant torturing of animals* or *the flagrant liberal bias of the media* have implied something other than what they presumably intended. In the first case, the writer is probably more troubled by the enormity of the mistreatment of animals than by the failure to conceal it, so that *flagrant* would have been the better choice. In the second case, by contrast, the writer probably wants to draw attention to a moral failing in the media's unapologetic refusal to hide its bias, rather than to the iniquity of the bias itself, an implication that would have been conveyed more successfully by *blatant. Blatant* should not be used to mean simply "obvious," as in *the blatant danger of such an approach.*

Blatch·ford (blăch′fərd), **Samuel.** 1820–1893. American jurist who served as an associate justice of the U.S. Supreme Court (1882–1893).

blath·er (blăth′ər) also **bleth·er** (blĕth′-) *—intr.v.* **-ered, -er·ing, -ers.** To talk nonsensically. *—n.* Nonsensical talk. [Old Norse *bladhra.* See **bhlē-** in Appendix.] **—blath′er·er** *n.*

blath·er·skite (blăth′ər-skīt′) *n.* **1.** A babbling, foolish person. **2.** Blather. [BLATHER + dialectal *skite,* a contemptible person (from Middle English *shit,* from Old English; see SHIT).]

Bla·vat·sky (blə-văt′skē, -vät′-), **Helena Petrovna Hahn.** 1831–1891. Russian-born theosophist who founded (1875) the Theosophical Society in New York City and wrote books of occult lore, such as *Isis Unveiled* (1877).

blax·ploi·ta·tion (blăk′sploi-tā′shən) *n.* Exploitation of Black people, especially in the American film industry, by casting them in negative, stereotypical roles and by failing to depict in the films the realities of Black life. *—attributive.* Often used to modify another noun: *blaxploitation movies; the blaxploitation genre.* [Blend of BLACK and EXPLOITATION.]

blaze[1] (blāz) *n.* **1.a.** A brilliant burst of fire; a flame. **b.** A destructive fire. **2.** A bright or steady light or glare: *the blaze of the desert sun.* **3.** A brilliant, striking display: *flowers that were a blaze of color.* **4.** A sudden outburst, as of emotion: *a blaze of anger.* **5. blazes.** Used as an intensive: *Where in blazes are my keys?* **—blaze** *v.* **blazed, blaz·ing, blaz·es.** *—intr.* **1.** To burn with a bright flame. **2.** To shine brightly. **3.** To be resplendent: *a garden blazing with flowers.* **4.** To flare up suddenly: *My neighbor's temper blazed.* **5.** To shoot rapidly and continuously: *Machine guns blazed.* *—tr.* To shine or be resplendent with: *eyes that blazed hatred.* [Middle English *blase,* from Old English *blæse.* See **bhel-[1]** in Appendix.] **—blaz′ing·ly** *adv.*

SYNONYMS: *blaze, flame, flare, flash, glare, incandescence, glow.* These nouns denote bright light, especially when it is a visible sign of combustion. *Blaze* stresses intensity of burning and implies brilliance of illumination: *We warmed our hands near the blaze of the campfire. Flame* pertains to a jet or tongue of fire: *The paper burned with a yellow and blue flame and then disintegrated. Flare* applies to a dazzling but unsteady burst of light: *Flares of brilliant red shot up from the smokestack. Flash* denotes a sudden momentary burst: *The flash of strobe lights and the insistent beat of the music made the disco a favorite gathering place for young people. Glare* emphasizes intensely and often intolerably bright light: *The glare of the oncoming headlights temporarily blinded me. Incandescence* suggests the brilliance of something white-hot: *"When heated to incandescence in the furnace of stars, each element marks the spectrum of light it emits with a characteristic set of lines"* (Malcolm W. Browne). *Glow* stresses light in the absence of visible flame; it particularly suggests steadiness of radiation without intense brilliance: *When the electric stove is turned on, the burners give off a red glow.*

blaze[2] (blāz) *n.* **1.** A white or light-colored spot on the face of an animal, such as a horse. **2.** A mark cut or painted on a tree to indicate a trail. **—blaze** *tr.v.* **blazed, blaz·ing, blaz·es. 1.** To mark (a tree) with or as if with blazes. **2.** To indicate (a trail) by marking trees with blazes. [Of Germanic origin.]

blaze[3] (blāz) *tr.v.* **blazed, blaz·ing, blaz·es.** To make known publicly; proclaim: *Headlines blazed the news.* [Middle English *blasen,* from Middle Dutch *blāsen,* to blow up, swell. See **bhlē-** in Appendix.]

blaz·er (blā′zər) *n.* A lightweight, often striped or brightly colored sports jacket having pockets and notched lapels.

blaz·ing star (blā′zĭng) *n.* **1.** A rhizomatous dioecious herb *(Chamaelirium luteum)* in the lily family, having long racemes of small flowers. Also called *devil's bit.* **2.** Any of various North American plants of the genus *Liatris* in the composite family, having small, discoid flower heads grouped in a dense raceme or panicle. Also called *button snakeroot, gay feather.* **3.** A biennial plant *(Mentzelia laevicaulis)* of western North America, having large, star-shaped, pale-yellow flowers.

bla·zon (blā′zən) *tr.v.* **-zoned, -zon·ing, -zons. 1.** *Heraldry.* **a.** To describe (a coat of arms) in proper terms. **b.** To paint or depict (a coat of arms) with accurate detail. **2.** To adorn or embellish with or as if with a coat of arms: *"the stars and moons and suns blazoned on that sacred wall"* (G.K. Chesterton). **3.** To proclaim widely. **—blazon** *n.* **1.** *Heraldry.* **a.** A coat of arms. **b.** The description or representation of a coat of arms. **2.** An ostentatious display. [Probably from Middle English *blasoun,* shield, from Old French *blason.*] **—bla′zon·er** *n.* **—bla′zon·ment** *n.*

bla·zon·ry (blā′zən-rē) *n., pl.* **-ries. 1.** *Heraldry.* **a.** The art of properly and accurately describing or representing armorial bearings. **b.** A coat of arms. **2.** An ostentatious display.

bld. *abbr.* **1.** Blood. **2.** *Printing.* Boldface.

bldg. *abbr.* Building.

bldr. *abbr.* Builder.

bleach (blēch) *v.* **bleached, bleach·ing, bleach·es.** *—tr.* **1.** To remove the color from, as by means of chemical agents or sunlight. **2.** To make white or colorless. *—intr.* To become white or colorless. **—bleach** *n.* **1.** A chemical agent used for bleaching. **2.a.** The act of bleaching. **b.** The degree of bleaching obtained. [Middle English *blechen,* from Old English *blǣcan.* See **bhel-**[1] in Appendix.]

bleach·er (blē′chər) *n.* **1.** One that bleaches or is used in bleaching. **2.** Often **bleachers.** An often unroofed outdoor grandstand for seating spectators. [Sense 2, from comparing a person's exposure to the sun when sitting on them with the exposure of linens bleaching on a clothesline.]

bleach·ing powder (blē′chĭng) *n.* A powder containing calcium chloride and calcium hypochlorite, used in solution as a bleach. Also called *chloride of lime, chlorinated lime.*

bleak[1] (blēk) *adj.* **bleak·er, bleak·est. 1.a.** Gloomy and somber; dreary: *"Life in the Aran Islands has always been bleak and difficult"* (John Millington Synge). **b.** Providing no encouragement; depressing: *a bleak prospect.* **2.** Cold and cutting; raw: *bleak winds of the North Atlantic.* **3.** Exposed to the elements; unsheltered and barren: *the bleak, treeless regions of the high Andes.* [Middle English *bleik,* pale, from Old Norse *bleikr,* white. See **bhel-**[1] in Appendix.] **—bleak′ly** *adv.* **—bleak′ness** *n.*

bleak[2] (blēk) *n., pl.* **bleak** or **bleaks.** A small European freshwater fish of the genus *Alburnus* that is related to the carp and has silvery scales used in the manufacture of artificial pearls. [Middle English *bleke,* probably alteration (influenced by *bleke,* pale; see BLEAK[1]) of **blay,* from Old English *blǣge.*]

blear (blîr) *tr.v.* **bleared, blear·ing, blears. 1.** To blur or redden (the eyes). **2.** To blur; dim. **—blear** *adj.* Bleary. [Middle English *bleren.*]

blear-eyed (blîr′īd′) *adj.* Variant of **bleary-eyed.**

blear·y (blîr′ē) *adj.* **-i·er, -i·est. 1.** Blurred or dimmed by or as if by tears: *bleary eyes.* **2.** Vaguely outlined; indistinct. **3.** Exhausted; worn-out. **—blear′i·ly** *adv.* **—blear′i·ness** *n.*

blear·y-eyed (blîr′ē-īd′) also **blear-eyed** (blîr′īd′) *adj.* **1.** With eyes blurred or reddened, as from exhaustion or lack of sleep. **2.** Dull of mind or perception.

bleat (blēt) *n.* **1.a.** The characteristic cry of a goat or sheep. **b.** A sound similar to this cry. **2.** A whining, feeble complaint. **—bleat** *v.* **bleat·ed, bleat·ing, bleats.** *—intr.* **1.** To utter the characteristic cry of a goat or sheep. **2.** To utter a sound similar to this cry, especially a whine. *—tr.* To utter in a whining way. [Middle English *blet,* from *bleten,* to bleat, from Old English *blǣtan.*] **—bleat′er** *n.*

bleb (blĕb) *n.* **1.** A small blister or pustule. **2.** An air bubble. [Probably alteration of BLOB.] **—bleb′by** *adj.*

bleed (blēd) *v.* **bled** (blĕd), **bleed·ing, bleeds.** *—intr.* **1.** To emit or lose blood. **2.** To be wounded, especially in battle. **3.** To feel sympathetic grief or anguish: *My heart bleeds for the victims of the air crash.* **4.** To exude a fluid such as sap. **5.** To pay out money, especially an exorbitant amount. **6.a.** To run together or be diffused, as dyes in wet cloth. **b.** To undergo or be subject to such a diffusion of color: *The madras skirt bled when it was first washed.* **7.** To show through a layer of paint, as a stain or resin in wood. **8.** To be printed so as to go off the edge or edges of a page after trimming. *—tr.* **1.a.** To take or remove blood from. **b.** To extract sap or juice from. **2.a.** To draw liquid or gaseous contents from; drain. **b.** To draw off (liquid or gaseous matter) from a container. **3.a.** To obtain money from, especially by improper means. **b.** To drain of all valuable resources: *"Politicians . . . never stop inventing illicit enterprises of government that bleed the national economy"* (David A. Stockman). **4.a.** To cause (an illustration, for example) to bleed. **b.** To trim (a page, for example) so closely as to mutilate the printed or illustrative matter. **—bleed** *n.* **1.** Illustrative matter that bleeds. **2.a.** A page trimmed so as to bleed. **b.** The part of the page that is trimmed off. [Middle English *bleden,* from Old English *blēdan,* from *blōd,* blood. See **bhel-**[3] in Appendix.]

WORD HISTORY: It seems only common sense that *bleed* should be related to *blood,* but one needs some knowledge of historical linguistics to understand the relationship fully. In prehistoric Common Germanic, the hypothetical predecessor of Germanic languages such as English, German, and Swedish, the word **blōdha–,* "blood," the ancestor of our word *blood,* is assumed to have existed. From this noun was derived the verb **blōdhjan,* "to bleed." A change of sound then came into play in Old English, that is, the *j,* pronounced like the *y* in *your,* caused the vowel *ō,* pronounced as in *go,* to become pronounced like the *ö* in German *schön.* Later in Old English this *ō* changed to *ē,* pronounced like the *a* in *labor,* eventually becoming like the *e* in *bee* by 1500. By this change, as well as others, **blōdhjan* became Modern English *bleed.*

bleed·er (blē′dər) *n.* **1.** A person, such as a hemophiliac, who bleeds freely or is subject to frequent hemorrhages. **2.a.** *Slang.* A blood vessel from which there is uncontrolled bleeding. **b.** A blood vessel severed by trauma or surgery that requires cautery or ligature to arrest the flow of blood. **3.** A person who draws blood from another; a phlebotomist.

bleed·ing heart (blē′dĭng) *n.* **1.** Any of various perennial herbs of the genus *Dicentra,* especially the Old World *D. spectabilis,* having arching clusters of showy, pink to red or sometimes white, heart-shaped flowers. **2.** A person who is considered excessively sympathetic toward those who claim to be underprivileged or exploited. **—bleed′ing-heart′** (-härt′) *adj.*

bleep (blēp) *n.* A brief high-pitched sound, as from an electronic device. **—bleep** *v.* **bleeped, bleep·ing, bleeps.** *—intr.* To emit a bleep or bleeps. *—tr.* To edit out (spoken material) from a broadcast or recording, especially by replacing with an electronic sound: *The station bleeped out the expletives from the taped interview.* [Imitative.] **—bleep′er** *n.*

blem·ish (blĕm′ĭsh) *tr.v.* **-ished, -ish·ing, -ish·es.** To mar or impair by a flaw. **—blemish** *n.* An imperfection that mars or impairs; a flaw or defect. [Middle English *blemisshen,* from Old French *blesmir, blemir, blemiss-,* to make pale, of Germanic origin. See **bhel-**[1] in Appendix.] **—blem′ish·er** *n.*

SYNONYMS: *blemish, imperfection, fault, defect, flaw.* All of these nouns denote loss or absence of perfection. *Blemish* applies to something, such as a blotch, that is held to mar the appearance or impair the character of a thing: *Cosmetics are often used to conceal facial blemishes. "Industry in art is a necessity—not a virtue—and any evidence of the same, in the production, is a blemish"* (James McNeill Whistler). *Imperfection* and *fault* apply more comprehensively to any deficiency or shortcoming: *"A true critic ought to dwell rather upon excellencies than imperfections"* (Joseph Addison). *"His independence and love of the English were his only faults"* (David Livingstone). *Defect* denotes a serious functional or structural shortcoming: *"Ill breeding . . . is not a single defect, it is the result of many"* (Henry Fielding). *Flaw* refers to an often small but always fundamental weakness: *Flaws in emeralds greatly reduce their value. Experiments revealed a very basic flaw in the theory.*

blench[1] (blĕnch) *intr.v.* **blenched, blench·ing, blench·es.** To draw back or shy away, as from fear; flinch. See Synonyms at **recoil.** [Middle English *blenchen,* from Old English *blencan,* to deceive. See **bhel-**[1] in Appendix.] **—blench′er** *n.*

blench[2] (blĕnch) *v.* Variant of **blanch.**

blend (blĕnd) *v.* **blend·ed** or **blent** (blĕnt), **blend·ing, blends.** *—tr.* **1.** To combine or mix so that the constituent parts are indistinguishable from one another: *"He has no difficulty blending his two writing careers: novels and films"* (Charles E. Claffey). **2.** To combine (varieties or grades) to obtain a mixture of a particular character, quality, or consistency: *blend tobaccos.* *—intr.* **1.** To form a uniform mixture; intermingle: *"The smoke blended easily into the odor of the other fumes"* (Norman Mailer). **2.** To become merged into one; unite. **3.** To create a harmonious effect or result: *picked a tie that blended with the jacket.* See Synonyms at **mix. —blend** *n.* **1.a.** The act of blending. **b.** Something, such as an effect or a product, that is created by blending: *"His face shows, as he stares at the fire, a blend of fastidiousness and intransigence"* (John Fowles). See Synonyms at **mixture. 2.** *Linguistics.* A word produced by combining parts of other words, as *smog* from *smoke* and *fog.* [Middle English *blenden,* probably from Old Norse *blanda, blend-.* See **bhel-**[1] in Appendix.]

bleeding heart

blende (blĕnd) *n.* **1.** Any of various shiny minerals composed chiefly of metallic sulfides. **2.** See **sphalerite.** [German, from *blenden,* to deceive (because it resembles lead ore), from Middle High German *blenden,* from Old High German *blentan,* to blind, deceive. See **bhel-**[1] in Appendix.]

blend·ed whiskey (blĕn′dĭd) *n.* Whiskey that is either a blend of two or more straight whiskeys or a blend of whiskey and neutral spirits.

blend·er (blĕn′dər) *n.* One that blends, especially an electrical appliance with whirling blades for chopping, mixing, or liquefying foods.

blend·ing inheritance (blĕn′dĭng) *n.* *Genetics.* The inheritance pattern of a system involving incomplete dominance, whereby characters are inherited in heterozygous individuals that show the effects of both alleles. As a result the inherited characters in the offspring are intermediate between those of the parents.

blen·ny (blĕn′ē) *n., pl.* **-nies.** Any of several widely distributed, chiefly marine fishes that are primarily of the families Blenniidae and Clinidae and have small, elongated, often scaleless bodies. [Latin *blennius,* a kind of sea fish, from Greek *blennos,* slime, blenny. See **mel-**[1] in Appendix.]

blent (blĕnt) *v.* A past tense and a past participle of **blend.**

ble·o·my·cin (blē′ə-mī′sĭn) *n.* An antibiotic that is obtained from cultures of the bacterium *Streptomyces verticillus* and used in the form of its sulfate for the treatment of various neoplasms. [*bleo-,* of unknown meaning + –MYCIN.]

ă pat	oi boy
ā pay	ou out
âr care	o͝o took
ä father	o͞o boot
ĕ pet	ŭ cut
ē be	ûr urge
ĭ pit	th thin
ī pie	*th* this
îr pier	hw which
ŏ pot	zh vision
ō toe	ə about, item
ô paw	♦ regionalism

Stress marks: ′ (primary); ′ (secondary), as in **dictionary** (dĭk′shə-nĕr′ē)

bleph·ar– *pref.* Variant of **blepharo–**.

bleph·a·ri·tis (blĕf′ə-rī′tĭs) *n.* Inflammation of the eyelids.

blepharo– or **blephar–** *pref.* **1.** Eyelid; eyelids: *blepharospasm.* **2.** Cilium; flagellum: *blepharoplast.* [Greek, from Greek *blepharon,* eyelid.]

bleph·a·ro·plast (blĕf′ər-ə-plăst′) *n.* A basal body in certain flagellated protozoans that consists of a minute mass of chromatin embedded in the cytoplasm at the base of the flagellum.

bleph·a·ro·plas·ty (blĕf′ər-ə-plăs′tē) *n.* Plastic surgery of the eyelids.

bleph·a·ro·spasm (blĕf′ə-rō-spăz′əm) *n.* Spasmodic winking caused by the involuntary contraction of an eyelid muscle.

Blé·riot (blā′rē-ō, blā-ryō′), **Louis.** 1872–1936. French inventor and aviator who was the first to cross the English Channel by airplane (1909).

bles·bok (blĕs′bŏk′) *n., pl.* **blesbok** or **-boks.** A South African antelope *(Damaliscus albifrons)* having curved horns and a large white mark on its face. [Afrikaans : *bles,* white mark on an animal's face (from Middle Dutch; see **bhel-**[1] in Appendix) + *bok,* buck (from Middle Dutch *boc*).]

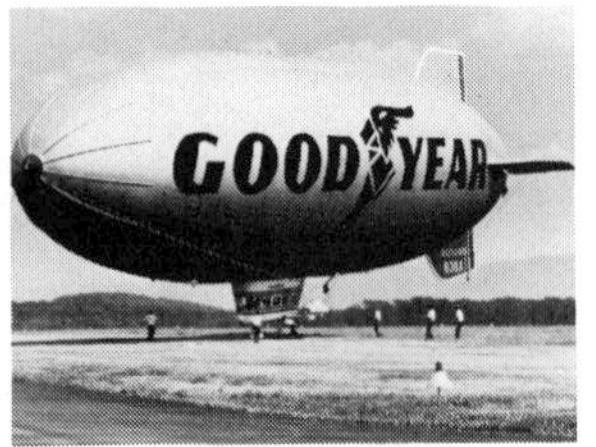

blimp
The Goodyear blimp
Mayflower

bless (blĕs) *tr.v.* **blessed** or **blest** (blĕst), **bless·ing, bless·es. 1.** To make holy by religious rite; sanctify. **2.** To make the sign of the cross over so as to sanctify. **3.** To invoke divine favor upon. **4.** To honor as holy; glorify: *Bless the Lord.* **5.** To confer well-being or prosperity on. **6.** To endow, as with talent. [Middle English *blessen,* from Old English *blētsian,* to consecrate. See **bhel-**[3] in Appendix.] **—bless′er** *n.*

bless·ed (blĕs′ĭd) also **blest** (blĕst) *adj.* **1.a.** Worthy of worship; holy. **b.** Held in veneration; revered. **2. Blessed.** *Roman Catholic Church.* Used as a title before the name of one who has been beatified. **3.** Bringing happiness, pleasure, or contentment. **4. blessed.** Used as an intensive: *I don't have a blessed dime.* **—bless′ed·ly** *adv.* **—bless′ed·ness** *n.*

Blessed Sacrament *n. Roman Catholic Church.* The consecrated host.

blessed thistle *n.* An annual, yellow-flowered, thistlelike Mediterranean herb *(Cnicus benedictus)* in the composite family, used in herbal medicine.

Blessed Virgin Mary *n. Abbr.* **B.V.M.** The Virgin Mary.

bless·ing (blĕs′ĭng) *n.* **1.** The act of one that blesses. **2.** A short prayer said before or after a meal. **3.** Something promoting or contributing to happiness, well-being, or prosperity; a boon. **4.** Approbation; approval: *This plan has my blessing.*

blest (blĕst) *v.* A past tense and a past participle of **bless.** **—blest** *adj.* Variant of **blessed.**

bleth·er (blĕth′ər) *v.* & *n.* Variant of **blather.**

bleu cheese (blo͞o) *n.* See **blue cheese.** [French, blue, from Old French. See BLUE.]

blew[1] (blo͞o) *v.* Past tense of **blow**[1].

blew[2] (blo͞o) *v.* Past tense of **blow**[3].

blinders

Bligh (blī), **William.** 1754–1817. British naval officer who as captain of the H.M.S. *Bounty* was set adrift by his mutinous crew during a voyage to Tahiti (1789).

blight (blīt) *n.* **1.a.** Any of numerous plant diseases resulting in sudden conspicuous wilting and dying of affected parts, especially young, growing tissues. **b.** The condition or causative agent, such as a bacterium, fungus, or virus, that results in blight. **2.** An extremely adverse environmental condition, such as air pollution. **3.** Something that impairs growth, withers hopes and ambitions, or impedes progress and prosperity. **—blight** *v.* **blight·ed, blight·ing, blights.** —*tr.* **1.** To cause (a plant, for example) to undergo blight. **2.** To have a deleterious effect on; ruin. See Synonyms at **blast.** —*intr.* To suffer blight. [Origin unknown.]

blight·er (blī′tər) *n. Chiefly British.* A fellow, especially one held in low esteem.

blimp (blĭmp) *n.* A nonrigid, buoyant airship. Modern blimps use helium instead of hydrogen to maintain buoyancy. [Perhaps from LIMP.]

blindfold

Blimp (blĭmp) *n. Chiefly British.* A pompous, reactionary, ultranationalistic person. [After Colonel *Blimp,* a cartoon character invented by David Low (1891–1963).] **—Blimp′ish** *adj.*

blin (blĭn) *n., pl.* **bli·ni** (blē′nē, blĭn′ē). A small, light pancake served with hot melted butter, sour cream, and various other garnishes such as caviar or lox. [Russian, from Old Russian *mlinŭ, blinŭ.* See **melə-** in Appendix.]

blind (blīnd) *adj.* **blind·er, blind·est. 1.a.** Sightless. **b.** Having a maximal visual acuity of the better eye, after correction by refractive lenses, of one-tenth normal vision or less (20/200 or less on the Snellen test). **c.** Of, relating to, or for sightless persons. **2.a.** Performed or made without the benefit of background information that might prejudice the outcome or result: *blind taste tests used in marketing studies.* **b.** Performed without preparation, experience, or knowledge: *made a blind stab at answering the question.* **c.** Performed by instruments and without the use of sight: *blind navigation.* **3.** Unable or unwilling to perceive or understand: *blind to a lover's faults.* **4.** Not based on reason or evidence; unquestioning: *put blind faith in their leaders.* **5.** *Slang.* Drunk. **6.** Independent of human control: *blind fate.* **7.a.** Difficult to comprehend or see; illegible. **b.** Incompletely or illegibly addressed: *blind mail.* **c.** Hidden from sight: *a blind seam.* **d.** Screened from the view of oncoming motorists: *a blind driveway.* **e.** Secret or otherwise undisclosed: *a blind item in a military budget.* **8.** Closed at one end: *a blind socket; a blind passage.* **9.** Having no opening: *a blind wall.* **10.** *Botany.* Failing to produce flowers or fruits: *a blind bud.* **—blind** *n.* **1.** Something, such as a window shade or a Venetian blind, that hinders vision or shuts out light. **2.** A shelter for concealing hunters, especially duck hunters. **3.** Something intended to conceal the true nature, especially of an activity; a subterfuge. **—blind** *adv.* **1.a.** Without seeing; blindly. **b.** Without the aid of visual reference: *flew blind through the fog.* **2.** Without forethought or provision; unawares: *entered into the scheme blind.* **3.** *Informal.* Into a stupor: *drank themselves blind.* **4.** Used as an intensive: *Thieves in the bazaar robbed us blind.* **—blind** *tr.v.* **blind·ed, blind·ing, blinds. 1.** To deprive of sight: *was blinded in an industrial accident.* **2.** To dazzle: *skiers temporarily blinded by sunlight on snow.* **3.** To deprive of perception or insight: *prejudice that blinded them to the merits of the proposal.* **4.** To withhold light from: *Thick shrubs blinded our downstairs windows.* [Middle English, from Old English. See **bhel-**[1] in Appendix.] **—blind′ing·ly** *adv.* **—blind′ly** *adv.* **—blind′ness** *n.*

blind alley *n.* **1.** An alley or passage that is closed at one end. **2.** A mistaken, unproductive undertaking.

blind date *n.* **1.** A social engagement between two persons who have not previously met, usually arranged by a mutual acquaintance. **2.** Either of the persons participating in such a social engagement.

blind·er (blīn′dər) *n.* **1. blinders.** A pair of leather flaps attached to a horse's bridle to curtail side vision. Also called *blinkers.* **2.** Something that serves to obscure clear perception and discernment.

blind·fish (blīnd′fĭsh′) *n., pl.* **blindfish** or **-fish·es.** Any of various small fishes, such as the cavefish, that have rudimentary, nonfunctioning eyes and inhabit the waters of caves and underground streams.

blind·fold (blīnd′fōld′) *tr.v.* **-fold·ed, -fold·ing, -folds. 1.** To cover the eyes of with or as if with a bandage. **2.** To prevent from seeing and especially from comprehending. **—blindfold** *n.* **1.** A bandage to cover the eyes. **2.** Something that serves to obscure clear perception. [From Middle English *blindfolde,* past participle of *blindfellen,* to strike blind, cover the eyes, from Old English *geblindfellian* : *blind,* blind; see BLIND + *fellian,* to strike down.] **—blind′fold′ed** *adj.*

blind gut *n.* **1.** A digestive cavity having only one opening. **2.** See **cecum** (sense 2).

blind·man's buff (blīnd′mănz′) *n. Games.* A game in which a blindfolded player tries to catch and identify one of the other players. Also called *blindman's bluff.* [*buff,* short for BUFFET[2].]

♦**blind pig** *n. Pacific Northwest.* See **blind tiger.**

blind pool *n.* A start-up company that sells stock in a public offering without specifying how the investors' money will be spent.

blind side *n.* **1.** The side on which one's vision, especially the peripheral vision, is limited or obstructed. **2.** The side away from which one is directing one's attention.

blind-side or **blind·side** (blīnd′sīd′) *tr.v.* **-sid·ed, -sid·ing, -sides. 1.** To hit or attack on or from the blind side. **2.** To catch or take unawares, especially with harmful or detrimental results: *"The recent recession, with its wave of corporate cost-cutting, blind-sided many lawyers"* (Aric Press).

blind spot *n.* **1.** *Anatomy.* The small, circular, optically insensitive region in the retina where fibers of the optic nerve emerge from the eyeball. It has no rods or cones. Also called *optic disk.* **2.** A part of an area that cannot be directly observed under existing circumstances. **3.** An area where radio reception is weak or nonexistent. **4.** A subject about which one is markedly ignorant or prejudiced: *"Of course, all of us . . . have our crotchets and our blind spots. I abhor novels written in the present tense"* (Mordecai Richler).

blind staggers *pl.n. (used with a sing. verb).* See **stagger** (sense 3).

♦**blind tiger** *n. Chiefly Southern & Midland U.S.* A place where alcoholic beverages are sold illegally; a speakeasy. Also called ♦*blind pig.* [After the early custom of exhibiting animal curiosities in speakeasies.]

blind trust *n.* A financial arrangement in which a person, such as a high-ranking elected official, avoids possible conflict of interest by relegating his or her financial affairs to a fiduciary who has sole discretion as to their management. The person choosing the trust also gives up the right to information regarding the status of the assets.

blind·worm (blīnd′wûrm′) *n.* See **slowworm.** [From its small eyes.]

bli·ni (blē′nē, blĭn′ē) *n.* Plural of **blin.**

blink (blĭngk) *v.* **blinked, blink·ing, blinks.** —*intr.* **1.** To close and open one or both of the eyes rapidly. **2.** To look through half-closed eyes, as in a bright glare; squint. **3.** To shine with intermittent gleams; flash on and off. **4.a.** To be startled or dismayed. **b.** To waver or back down, as in a contest of wills: *"This was the first genuine, direct confrontation between this administration and the Soviets. It was the U.S.A. that blinked"* (Zbigniew Brzezinski). **5.** To look with feigned ignorance: *a mayor who blinks at the corruption in city government.* —*tr.* **1.** To cause to blink. **2.** To hold back or remove from the eyes by blinking: *blinked back the tears.* **3.** To refuse to recognize or face: *blink ugly facts.* **4.** To transmit (a message) with a flashing light.

—**blink** *n.* **1.** The act or an instance of rapidly closing and opening the eyes or an eye. **2.** An instant: *I'll be back in a blink.* **3.** *Scots.* A quick look or glimpse; a glance. **4.** A flash of light; a twinkle. **5.** See **iceblink** (sense 1). —***idiom.*** **on the blink.** Out of working order. [Probably Middle English *blinken,* to move suddenly, variant of *blenchen.* See BLENCH[1].]

SYNONYMS: *blink, nictitate, twinkle, wink.* The central meaning shared by these verbs is "to open and close the eyelids or an eyelid rapidly": *a dog blinking lazily at the fire; reptiles nictitating; twinkled, then laughed and responded; winking conspiratorially at his chum.*

blink·er (blĭngʹkər) *n.* **1.** One that blinks, especially a light that blinks in order to convey a message or warning. **2. blinkers.** See **blinder** (sense 1). —**blinker** *tr.v.* **-ered, -er·ing, -ers.** To put blinders on.

blink·ered (blĭngʹkərd) *adj.* Subjective and limited, as in viewpoint or perception: *"He grasped the meaning of a blinkered youth"* (Benjamin DeMott). *"The characters have a blinkered view and, misinterpreting what they see, sometimes take totally inexpedient action"* (Pauline Kael).

blintz (blĭnts) also **blin·tze** (blĭnʹtsə) *n.* A thin, rolled blin, usually filled with cottage cheese, that is folded and then sautéed or baked and often served with sour cream. [Yiddish *blintse,* from Belorussian *blintsy,* pl. of *blinets,* diminutive of *blin,* pancake, from Old Russian *mlinŭ, blinŭ.* See **melə-** in Appendix.]

blip (blĭp) *n.* **1.** A spot of light on a radar or sonar screen indicating the position of a detected object, such as an aircraft or a submarine. Also called *pip.* **2.** A high-pitched electronic sound; a bleep. **3.** A temporary or insignificant phenomenon, especially a brief departure from the normal: *"The decline in the share of GNP going to health . . . appears to be a one-time blip in the historic trend rather than the start of a new trend"* (Atlantic). —**blip** *tr.v.* **blipped, blip·ping, blips.** To bleep. [Imitative.]

bliss (blĭs) *n.* **1.** Extreme happiness; ecstasy. **2.** The ecstasy of salvation; spiritual joy. —***phrasal verb.*** **bliss out.** *Slang.* To go into a state of ecstasy. [Middle English *blisse,* from Old English *bliss,* from *blīths,* from *blīthe,* joyful. See BLITHE.] —**blissʹful** *adj.* —**blissʹful·ly** *adv.* —**blissʹful·ness** *n.*

bliss-out or **bliss·out** (blĭsʹoutʹ) *n. Slang.* Ecstasy; bliss.

blis·ter (blĭsʹtər) *n.* **1. a.** A local swelling of the skin that contains watery fluid and is caused by burning or irritation. **b.** A similar swelling on a plant. **2. a.** A raised bubble, as on a painted or laminated surface. **b.** A rounded, bulging, usually transparent structure, such as one used for observation on certain aircraft or for display and protection of packaged products. —**blister** *v.* **-tered, -ter·ing, -ters.** —*tr.* **1.** To cause a blister to form on. **2.** To reprove harshly. —*intr.* To break out in or as if in blisters. [Middle English, probably from Old French *blestre,* of Germanic origin.] —**blisʹter·y** *adj.*

blister beetle *n.* Any of various soft-bodied beetles of the family Meloidae, such as the cantharis, that secrete a substance capable of blistering the skin. Also called *meloid.*

blister copper *n.* An almost pure copper produced in an intermediate stage of copper refining. [From its blistered appearance.]

blis·ter·ing (blĭsʹtər-ĭng) *adj.* **1.** Intensely hot: *a blistering sun.* **2.** Harsh; severe: *blistering criticism.* **3.** Very rapid: *a blistering pace.* **4.** Producing a blister or blisters: *a blistering agent.* —**blisʹter·ing·ly** *adv.*

blister pack *n.* A form of displaying and packaging an item of merchandise in which the merchandise is sealed into a transparent plastic blister backed by foil or cardboard. Also called *bubble pack.*

blister rust *n.* Any of several diseases of pine trees caused by certain fungi of the genus *Cronartium,* resulting in conspicuous blistering and often dieback of affected areas.

B.Lit. *abbr. Latin.* Baccalaureus Litterarum (Bachelor of Literature).

blithe (blīth, blīth) *adj.* **blith·er, blith·est.** **1.** Carefree and lighthearted. **2.** Lacking or showing a lack of due concern; casual: *spoke with blithe ignorance of the true situation.* See Synonyms at **jolly.** [Middle English, from Old English *blīthe.*] —**blitheʹly** *adv.* —**blitheʹness** *n.*

blith·er (blĭthʹər) *intr.v.* **-ered, -er·ing, -ers.** To blather. [Alteration of BLATHER.]

blithe·some (blīthʹsəm, blīthʹ-) *adj.* Cheerful; merry. —**blitheʹsome·ly** *adv.* —**blithʹsome·ness** *n.*

B.Litt. *abbr. Latin.* Baccalaureus Litterarum (Bachelor of Literature).

blitz (blĭts) *n.* **1. a.** A blitzkrieg. **b.** A heavy aerial bombardment. **2.** An intense campaign: *a media blitz focused on young voters.* **3.** *Football.* A defensive play in which one or more linebackers or defensive backs charge through the line of scrimmage at the snap in an attempt to overwhelm the quarterback, especially in a passing situation. In this sense, also called *red-dog.* —**blitz** *v.* **blitzed, blitz·ing, blitz·es.** —*tr.* **1.** To subject to a blitz. **2.** *Football.* To rush (the quarterback) in a blitz. —*intr. Football.* To carry out a blitz. [Short for BLITZKRIEG.]

blitz·krieg (blĭtsʹkrēgʹ) *n.* A swift, sudden military offensive, usually by combined air and mobile land forces. [German : *Blitz,* lightning (from Middle High German *blitze,* from *bliczen,* to flash, from Old High German *blëcchazzen;* see **bhel-**[1] in Appendix) + *Krieg,* war (from Middle High German *kriec,* from Old High German *chrēg,* stubbornness; see **gʷerə-**[1] in Appendix).]

Blitz·stein (blĭtsʹstīnʹ), **Marc.** 1905–1964. American composer whose works include operas, such as *Triple Sec* (1928), and musical plays, including *The Cradle Will Rock* (1937).

bliv·it (blĭvʹĭt) *n. Slang.* **1.** Something annoying, superfluous, or pointless. **2.** Something difficult or impossible to name. [Origin unknown.]

Blix·en (blĕkʹsən, blĭkʹ-), Baroness **Karen.** See Isak **Dinesen.**

bliz·zard (blĭzʹərd) *n.* **1. a.** *Meteorology.* A violent snowstorm with winds blowing at a minimum speed of 35 miles (56 kilometers) per hour and visibility of less than one-quarter mile (400 meters) for three hours. **b.** A very heavy snowstorm with high winds. **2.** A torrent; a superabundance: *The White House received a blizzard of phone calls.* [Origin unknown.]

blk. *abbr.* **1.** Black. **2.** Block. **3.** Bulk.

bloat (blōt) *v.* **bloat·ed, bloat·ing, bloats.** —*tr.* **1.** To cause to swell up or inflate, as with liquid or gas. **2.** To cure (fish) by soaking in brine and half-drying in smoke. —*intr.* To become swollen or inflated: *"Government had bloated out of control"* (Lance Morrow). —**bloat** *n.* **1.** A swelling of the rumen or intestinal tract of cattle and domestic animals that is caused by excessive gas formation following fermentation of ingested watery legumes or green forage. **2.** An excess or surfeit, as of employees, expenses, or procedures: *corporate bloat.* [From Middle English *blout,* soft, puffed, from Old Norse *blautr,* soft, soaked. See **bhleu-** in Appendix.]

bloat·ed (blōʹtĭd) *adj.* **1.** Being much bigger than desired: *a bloated bureaucracy; a bloated budget.* **2.** *Medicine.* Swollen or distended beyond normal size by fluid or gaseous material.

bloat·er[1] (blōʹtər) *n.* A large mackerel or herring, lightly smoked and salted. [From obsolete dialectal *bloat,* a soft, moist cured fish, probably from BLOAT.]

bloat·er[2] (blōʹtər) *n.* A small whitefish *(Coregonus hoyi)* of the Great Lakes and the lakes of eastern Canada.

blob (blŏb) *n.* **1.** A soft, amorphous mass. **2.** A daub, as of color. —*tr.v.* **blobbed, blob·bing, blobs.** To splash or daub with blobs; splotch. [From Middle English *blober,* bubble.]

bloc (blŏk) *n.* **1.** A group of nations, parties, or persons united for common action: *nations in the Communist bloc.* **2.** An often bipartisan coalition of legislators acting together for a common purpose or interest: *the farm bloc in the U.S. Senate.* [French, from Old French, block. See BLOCK.]

Bloch (blŏk, blôk, blôKH), **Ernest.** 1880–1959. Swiss-born American composer noted for his chamber music, such as *Quintet for Piano and Strings* (1923), and for works with Jewish themes, including *Israel Symphony* (1916).

Bloch, Felix. 1905–1983. Swiss-born American physicist. He shared a 1952 Nobel Prize for work concerning the measurement of magnetic fields in atomic nuclei.

Bloch, Konrad Emil. Born 1912. German-born American biochemist. He shared a 1964 Nobel Prize for research on cholesterol and fatty acid metabolism.

♦**block** (blŏk) *n. Abbr.* **blk.** **1. a.** A solid piece of a hard substance, such as wood, having one or more flat sides. **b.** Such a piece used as a construction member or as a support. **c.** Such a piece upon which chopping or cutting is done: *a butcher's block.* **d.** Such a piece upon which persons are beheaded. **e.** A small wooden or plastic cube used as a building toy: *a set of blocks.* **f.** *Printing.* A large amount of text. **g.** *Sports.* A starting block. **2.** A stand from which articles are displayed and sold at an auction: *Many priceless antiques went on the block.* **3.** A mold or form on which an item is shaped or displayed: *a hat block.* **4.** A substance, such as wood or stone, that has been prepared for engraving. **5. a.** A pulley or a system of pulleys set in a casing. **b.** An engine block. **6.** A bloc. **7.** A set of like items, such as shares of stock, sold or handled as a unit. **8.** A group of four or more unseparated postage stamps forming a rectangle. **9.** *Canadian.* A group of townships in an unsurveyed area. **10. a.** A usually rectangular section of a city or town bounded on each side by consecutive streets. **b.** A segment of a street bounded by consecutive cross streets and including its buildings and inhabitants. **11.** A large building divided into separate units, such as apartments. **12.** A length of railroad track controlled by signals. **13.** The act of obstructing. **14.** Something that obstructs; an obstacle. **15. a.** *Sports.* An act of bodily obstruction, as of a player or ball. **b.** *Football.* Legal interference with an opposing player to clear the path of the ball carrier. **16.** *Medicine.* Interruption, especially obstruction, of a normal physiological function: *nerve block.* **17.** *Psychology.* Sudden cessation of speech or a thought process without an immediate observable cause, sometimes considered a consequence of repression. **18.** *Slang.* The human head: *threatened to knock my block off.* **19.** A blockhead. —**block** *v.* **blocked, block·ing, blocks.** —*tr.* **1.** To shape into a block or blocks. **2.** To support, strengthen, or retain in place by means of a block. **3.** To shape, mold, or form with or on a block: *block a hat.* **4. a.** To stop or impede the passage of or movement through; obstruct: *block traffic.* **b.** To shut out from view: *a curtain blocking the stage.* **5.** To indicate broadly without great detail; sketch: *block out a plan of action.* **6.** *Sports.* To impede the movement of (an opponent or the ball) by physical interference. **7.** *Medicine.* To interrupt the proper functioning of (a nervous, muscular, or other physiological process), especially by the use of anesthesia. **8.** *Psychology.* To fail to remember. **9.** To run (trains) on a block

ă pat	oi boy
ā pay	ou out
âr care	ŏŏ took
ä father	ōō boot
ĕ pet	ŭ cut
ē be	ûr urge
ĭ pit	th thin
ī pie	*th* this
îr pier	hw which
ŏ pot	zh vision
ō toe	ə about, item
ô paw	♦ regionalism

Stress marks: **ʹ** (primary); ʹ (secondary), as in **dictionary** (dĭkʹshə-nĕrʹē)

system. —*intr.* *Sports.* To obstruct the movement of an opponent. —***idiom.*** **out of the blocks.** From a starting position, as in a race or contest: *The company has in the past been slow out of the blocks to adapt to consumer tastes.* [Middle English *blok,* from Old French, from Middle Dutch.] —**block′er** *n.*

SYNONYMS: *block, hide, obscure, obstruct, screen, shroud.* The central meaning shared by these verbs is "to cut off from sight": *trees that block the view; a road hidden by brush; mist that obscures the mountain peak; skyscrapers obstructing the sky; a fence that screens the alley; a face shrouded by a heavy veil.* See also Synonyms at **hinder¹, obstacle.**

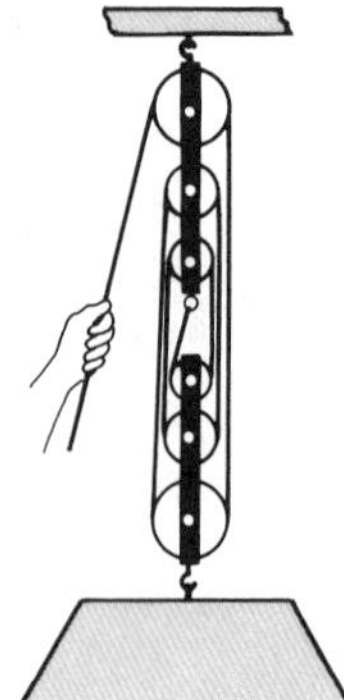

block and tackle
Multiple block and tackle

block•ade (blŏ-kād′) *n.* **1.** The isolation of a nation, an area, a city, or a harbor by hostile ships or forces in order to prevent the entrance and exit of traffic and commerce. **2.** The forces used to effect this isolation. —**blockade** *tr.v.* **-ad•ed, -ad•ing, -ades.** To set up a blockade against. See Synonyms at **besiege.** —**block•ad′er** *n.*

block•ade-run•ner (blŏ-kād′rŭn′ər) *n.* One that penetrates or evades a blockade. —**block•ade′-run′ning** *n.*

block•age (blŏk′ĭj) *n.* **1.** The act of obstructing. **2.** An obstruction.

block and tackle *n.* An apparatus of pulley blocks and ropes or cables used for hauling and hoisting heavy objects.

block•bust•er (blŏk′bŭs′tər) *n.* **1.** *Informal.* Something, such as a film or book, that sustains widespread popularity and achieves enormous sales. **2.** A high-explosive bomb used for demolition purposes. **3.** One that engages in the practice of blockbusting.

block•bust•ing (blŏk′bŭs′tĭng) *n.* *Informal.* The practice of persuading white homeowners to sell quickly and usually at a loss by appealing to the fear that minority groups and especially Black people will move into the neighborhood, causing property values to decline. The property is then resold at inflated prices.

block grant *n.* An unrestricted federal grant, as to a locality.

block•head (blŏk′hĕd′) *n.* A person regarded as very stupid; a dolt.

block•house (blŏk′hous′) *n.* **1.** A military fortification constructed of sturdy material, such as concrete, and designed with ports for defensive firing or observation. **2.** A heavily reinforced building used for launch operations of missiles and space launch vehicles. **3.** A fort made of squared timbers with a projecting upper story.

block•ish (blŏk′ĭsh) *adj.* Resembling a block, as in shape. —**block′ish•ly** *adv.* —**block′ish•ness** *n.*

Block Island. An island off southern Rhode Island at the eastern entrance to Long Island Sound. Visited by Dutch explorers in 1614, it was settled in 1661.

blockhouse
On the site of Fort Neilson, New York

block letter *n.* *Printing.* **1.** A letter printed or written sans serif. **2.** A sans-serif style of type.

block plane *n.* A small plane used by carpenters for cutting across the grain of wood.

block signal *n.* A fixed signal at the entrance to a railroad block, indicating whether or not trains may enter.

block system *n.* A system for controlling and safeguarding the flow of railway trains in which track is divided into blocks, each controlled by automatic signals.

block•y (blŏk′ē) *adj.* **-i•er, -i•est.** Blockish.

Bloem•fon•tein (blo͞om′fŏn-tān′). A city of central South Africa east-southeast of Kimberley. It is unofficially called the judicial capital of the country because the appellate division of the national supreme court sits here. Population, 102,600.

Blois (blwä). A town of central France on the Loire River northeast of Tours. It was the seat of the powerful counts of Blois and a favorite residence of French royalty. Population, 47,243.

bloke (blōk) *n.* *Chiefly British.* A fellow; a man. [Origin unknown.]

blond also **blonde** (blŏnd) —*adj.* **blond•er, blond•est. 1.** Having fair hair and skin and usually light eyes: *blond Scandinavians.* **2.** Of a flaxen or golden color or of any light shade of auburn or pale yellowish brown: *blond hair.* **3.** Light-colored through bleaching: *blond furniture.* —*n.* **1.** A person with fair hair and skin and usually light eyes. **2.** *Color.* A light yellowish brown to dark grayish yellow. [Middle English *blounde,* from Old French *blonde,* of Germanic origin. See **bhel-¹** in Appendix.] —**blond′ish** *adj.* —**blond′ness** *n.*

bloodhound

USAGE NOTE: It is usual in English to treat *blond* as if it required gender marking, as in French, spelling it *blonde* when referring to women and *blond* elsewhere. But this practice is in fact a relatively recent innovation, and some have suggested that it has sexist implications and that the form *blond* should be used for both sexes. There is certainly a measure of justice to the claim that the two forms are not used symmetrically. Since English does not normally mark adjectives according to the gender of the nouns they modify, it is natural to interpret the final *–e* as expressing some additional meaning, perhaps because it implies that hair color provides a primary category of classification for women but not men. This association of hair color and a particular perception of feminine identity is suggested in phrases such as *dumb blonde* and *Is it true blondes have more fun?* or in Susan Brownmiller's depiction of Hollywood's *"pantheon of celebrated blondes who have fed the fantasies of men and fueled the aspirations of women."* The corresponding masculine form *blond,* by contrast, is not ordinarily used to refer to men in contexts in which hair color is not specifically at issue; there is something arch in a reference to *Leslie Howard, Robert Redford, and other celebrated blonds.* See Usage Note at **brunette.**

blood (blŭd) *n.* *Abbr.* **bld. 1.a.** The fluid consisting of plasma, blood cells, and platelets that is circulated by the heart through the vertebrate vascular system, carrying oxygen and nutrients to and waste materials away from all body tissues. **b.** A functionally similar fluid in animals other than vertebrates. **c.** The juice or sap of certain plants. **2.** A vital or animating force; lifeblood. **3.** Bloodshed; murder. **4.** Temperament or disposition: *a person of hot blood and fiery temper.* **5.a.** Descent from a common ancestor; parental lineage. **b.** Family relationship; kinship. **c.** Descent from noble or royal lineage: *a princess of the blood.* **d.** Recorded descent from purebred stock. **e.** National or racial ancestry. **6.a.** A dandy. **b.** *Slang.* A youth who is a member of a city gang. —*attributive.* Often used to modify another noun: *a blood transfusion; a Red Cross blood drive.* —**blood** *tr.v.* **blood•ed, blood•ing, bloods. 1.** To give (a hunting dog) its first taste of blood. **2.** To subject (troops) to experience under fire: *"The measure of an army is not known until it has been blooded"* (Tom Clancy). —***idiom.*** **in cold blood.** Deliberately, coldly, and dispassionately. [Middle English *blod,* from Old English *blōd.* See **bhel-³** in Appendix.]

Blood (blŭd) *n., pl.* **Blood** or **Bloods. 1.** A tribe of the Blackfoot confederacy inhabiting southern Alberta. **2.** A member of this tribe.

blood agar *n.* *Microbiology.* A nutrient culture medium that is enriched with whole blood and used for the growth of certain strains of bacteria.

blood alcohol concentration *n.* *Abbr.* **BAC** The concentration of alcohol in the blood, expressed as the weight of alcohol in a fixed volume of blood and used as a measure of the degree of intoxication in an individual. The concentration depends on body weight, the quantity and rate of alcohol ingestion, and the rates of alcohol absorption and metabolism.

blood bank *n.* **1.** A place where whole blood or plasma is typed, processed, and stored for future use in transfusion. **2.** Blood or plasma stored in such a place.

blood•bath also **blood bath** (blŭd′băth′, -bäth′) *n.* Savage, indiscriminate killing; a massacre.

blood boost•ing or **blood-boost•ing** (blŭd′bo͞o′stĭng) *n.* See **blood doping.**

blood-brain barrier (blŭd′brān′) *n.* A physiological mechanism that alters the permeability of brain capillaries, so that some substances, such as certain drugs, are prevented from entering brain tissue, while other substances are allowed to enter freely.

blood brother *n.* **1.** A brother by birth. **2.** One of two individuals who vow mutual fidelity and trust by a ceremony involving the mingling of each other's blood. —**blood brotherhood** *n.*

blood cell *n.* Any of the cells contained in blood; an erythrocyte or leukocyte; a blood corpuscle.

blood clot *n.* *Physiology.* A semi-solid, gelatinous mass of coagulated blood that consists of red blood cells, white blood cells, and platelets entrapped in a fibrin network.

blood count *n.* **1.** The number of red blood cells, white blood cells, and platelets in a definite volume of blood. **2.** The determination of such a count. **3.** Complete blood count.

blood•cur•dling (blŭd′kûrd′lĭng) *adj.* Causing great horror; terrifying. —**blood′cur′dling•ly** *adv.*

blood dop•ing or **blood-dop•ing** (blŭd′dō′pĭng) *n.* The process of transfusing an athlete with a quantity of blood that has been previously removed from the same athlete, allowing the buildup of extra red blood cells by the body in the interim. The goal of this controversial technique is to increase the oxygen-carrying capacity of the blood and athletic endurance. Also called *blood boosting, blood packing.*

blood•ed (blŭd′ĭd) *adj.* **1.** Having blood or a temperament of a specified kind. Used only in combination: *a cold-blooded reptile; a hot-blooded person.* **2.** Thoroughbred: *blooded breeding stock.*

blood feud *n.* A feud involving the members of a family or clan.

blood fluke *n.* See **schistosome.**

blood group *n.* Any of several immunologically distinct, genetically determined classes of human blood that are based on the presence or absence of certain antigens and are clinically identified by characteristic agglutination reactions. Also called *blood type.*

blood•guilt (blŭd′gĭlt′) *n.* The fact or state of being guilty of murder or bloodshed.

blood heat *n.* The normal temperature (about 37.0°C or 98.6°F) of human blood.

blood•hound (blŭd′hound′) *n.* **1.** One of a breed of hounds with a smooth coat, drooping ears, sagging jowls, and a keen sense of smell. **2.** *Informal.* A relentless pursuer.

blood•less (blŭd′lĭs) *adj.* **1.** Deficient in or lacking blood. **2.** Pale and anemic in color: *smiled with bloodless lips.* **3.** Achieved without bloodshed: *a bloodless coup.* **4.** Lacking vivacity or spirit: *a long, bloodless speech.* **5.** Devoid of human emotion or feeling: *charts of bloodless economic indicators.* **—blood′less·ly** *adv.* **—blood′less·ness** *n.*

blood·let·ting (blŭd′lĕt′ĭng) *n.* **1.** Bloodshed. **2.** The removal of blood, usually from a vein, as a therapeutic measure. **3.** The laying off of personnel or the elimination of resources. **—blood′let′ter** *n.*

blood lily *n.* Any of several bulbous plants of the African genus *Haemanthus* grown for their dense clusters of red, white, or pink flowers with protruding stamens.

blood·line (blŭd′līn′) *n.* Direct line of descent; pedigree.

blood meal *n.* The dried and powdered blood of animals, used in animal feeds and as a nitrogen-rich fertilizer for plants.

blood·mo·bile (blŭd′mə-bēl′) *n.* A motor vehicle equipped for collecting blood from donors. [BLOOD + (AUTO)MOBILE.]

blood money *n.* **1.** Money paid by a killer as compensation to the next of kin of a murder victim. **2.** Money gained at the cost of another's life or livelihood.

blood pack·ing or **blood-pack·ing** (blŭd′ păk′ĭng) *n.* See **blood doping.**

blood plasma *n.* The pale yellow or gray-yellow, protein-containing fluid portion of the blood in which the blood cells and platelets are normally suspended.

blood platelet *n.* See **platelet.**

blood poi·son·ing (poi′zə-nĭng) *n.* **1.** See **septicemia. 2.** See **toxemia.**

blood pressure *n. Abbr.* **BP, B.P.** The pressure exerted by the blood against the walls of the blood vessels, especially the arteries. It varies with the strength of the heartbeat, the elasticity of the arterial walls, the volume and viscosity of the blood, and a person's health, age, and physical condition.

blood profile *n.* See **complete blood count.**

blood red *n. Color.* A moderate to vivid red. **—blood′-red′** (blŭd′rĕd′) *adj.*

blood relation *n.* A person who is related to another by birth rather than by marriage. **—blood relationship** *n.*

blood·root (blŭd′ro͞ot′, -ro͝ot′) *n.* A perennial wildflower *(Sanguinaria canadensis),* native to forests in eastern North America and having a fleshy rootstock exuding a poisonous red sap, a single lobed leaf, and a solitary white flower in early spring. Also called *red puccoon.*

blood serum *n.* See **serum** (sense 1).

blood·shed (blŭd′shĕd′) *n.* The shedding of blood, especially the injury or killing of human beings.

blood·shot (blŭd′shŏt′) *adj.* Red and inflamed as a result of locally congested blood vessels: *bloodshot eyes.* [From obsolete *bloodshotten* : BLOOD + *shotten,* suffused, past participle of SHOOT.]

blood·stain (blŭd′stān′) *n.* A stain caused by blood. **—bloodstain** *tr.v.* **-stained, -stain·ing, -stains.** To stain with blood.

blood·stone (blŭd′stōn′) *n.* A variety of deep-green chalcedony flecked with red jasper. Also called *heliotrope.*

blood·stream also **blood stream** (blŭd′strēm′) *n.* The flow of blood through the circulatory system of an organism.

blood·suck·er (blŭd′sŭk′ər) *n.* **1.** An animal, such as a leech, that sucks blood. **2.** An extortionist or a blackmailer. **3.** A person who is intrusively or overly dependent upon another; a parasite. **—blood′suck′ing** *adj.*

blood sugar *n.* **1.** Sugar in the form of glucose in the blood. **2.** The concentration of glucose in the blood, measured in milligrams of glucose per 100 milliliters of blood.

blood test *n.* **1.** An examination of a sample of blood to determine its chemical, physical, or serologic characteristics. **2.** A serologic test for certain diseases, such as syphilis or AIDS.

blood·thirst·y (blŭd′thûr′stē) *adj.* **1.** Eager to shed blood. **2.** Characterized by great carnage. **—blood′thirst′i·ly** *adv.* **—blood′thirst′i·ness** *n.*

blood type *n.* See **blood group.**

blood typ·ing or **blood-typ·ing** (blŭd′tī′pĭng) *n.* The process of identifying an individual's blood group by serologic testing of a sample of blood.

blood vessel *n.* An elastic tubular channel, such as an artery, a vein, or a capillary, through which the blood circulates.

blood·worm (blŭd′wûrm′) *n.* **1.** Any of various red, segmented marine worms of the genera *Polycirrus* and *Enoplobranchus* that have bright red bodies and are often used for bait. **2.** The freshwater larvae of certain midges that are red as a result of the high hemoglobin content of their blood.

blood·y (blŭd′ē) *adj.* **-i·er, -i·est. 1.** Stained with blood. **2.** Of, characteristic of, or containing blood. **3.** Accompanied by or giving rise to bloodshed: *a bloody fight.* **4.** Bloodthirsty. **5.** Suggesting the color of blood; blood-red. **6.** Used as an intensive: *"Everyone wants to have a convict in his bloody family tree"* (Robert Hughes). **—bloody** *adv.* Used as an intensive: *bloody well right.* **—bloody** *tr.v.* **-ied, -y·ing, -ies. 1.** To stain, spot, or color with or as if with blood. **2.** To make bleed, as by injuring or wounding: *The troops were bloodied in the skirmish.* **—blood′i·ly** *adv.* **—blood′i·ness** *n.*

SYNONYMS: *bloody, gory, sanguinary, sanguineous.* The central meaning shared by these adjectives is "attended by or causing bloodshed": *a bloody battle; a gory murder; a sanguinary struggle; a sanguineous victory.*

bloody mary also **Bloody Mary** *n., pl.* **bloody marys** or **bloody mary's.** A cocktail usually made of vodka, tomato juice, and seasonings. [After MARY I.]

blood·y-mind·ed (blŭd′ē-mīn′dĭd) *adj.* **1.** Ready and willing to accept bloodshed or to resort to violence: *"forging alliances with bloody-minded tyrants"* (Lewis H. Lapham). **2.** *Chiefly British.* Perversely cantankerous: *"The . . . unions . . . have never been as bloody-minded about demarcation as the shipbuilders"* (Spectator). **—blood′y-mind′ed·ness** *n.*

bloom[1] (blo͞om) *n.* **1.a.** The flower of a plant. **b.** Something resembling the flower of a plant: *"Her hair was caught all to one side in a great bloom of frizz"* (Anne Tyler). **2.a.** The condition of being in flower: *a rose in full bloom.* **b.** A condition or time of vigor, freshness, and beauty; prime: *"the radiant bloom of Greek genius"* (Edith Hamilton). **3.** A fresh, rosy complexion: *"She was short, plump, and fair, with a fine bloom"* (Jane Austen). **4.a.** A waxy or powdery whitish to bluish coating sometimes occurring on the surface of plant parts, such as on the fruits of certain plums. **b.** A similar coating, as on newly minted coins. **c.** *Chemistry.* See **efflorescence** (sense 3a). **5.** Glare that is caused by a shiny object reflecting too much light into a television camera. **6.** A visible, colored area on the surface of bodies of water caused by excessive planktonic growth. **—bloom** *v.* **bloomed, bloom·ing, blooms.** —*intr.* **1.a.** To bear a flower or flowers. **b.** To support plant life in abundance: *rains that made the yard bloom.* **2.** To shine; glow. **3.** To grow or flourish with youth and vigor. **4.** To appear or expand suddenly: *White vapor bloomed from the side of the rocket's fuel tank.* —*tr.* **1.** To cause to flourish. **2.** *Obsolete.* To cause to flower. [Middle English *blom,* from Old Norse *blōm.* See **bhel-[3]** in Appendix.] **—bloom′y** *adj.*

SYNONYMS: *bloom, blossom, efflorescence, florescence, flower, flush, prime.* The central meaning shared by these nouns is "a condition or time of greatest vigor and freshness": *beauty in its full bloom; classical sculpture in its blossom; the efflorescence of humanitarianism; the florescence of baroque music; in the flower of her womanhood; in the flush of his popularity; the prime of life.*

bloodroot
Sanguinaria canadensis

bloom[2] (blo͞om) *n.* **1.** A bar of steel prepared for rolling. **2.** A mass of wrought iron ready for further working. [Middle English *blome,* lump of metal, from Old English *blōma.* See **bhel-[3]** in Appendix.]

bloom·er[1] (blo͞o′mər) *n.* **1.a.** A plant that blooms. **b.** A person who attains full maturity and competence: *a late bloomer.* **2.** *Slang.* A blunder.

bloom·er[2] (blo͞o′mər) *n.* **1.** A costume formerly worn by women and girls that was composed of loose trousers gathered about the ankles and worn under a short skirt. **2. bloomers. a.** Wide, loose trousers gathered at the knee and formerly worn by women and girls as an athletic costume. **b.** Girls' underpants of similar design. [After Amelia Jenks BLOOMER.]

bloomer[2]

Bloom·er (blo͞o′mər), **Amelia Jenks.** 1818–1894. American social reformer who founded and edited the feminist newspaper *Lily* (1849–1855), wrote about unjust marriage laws and women's suffrage, and advocated a new style of dress for women.

Bloom·field (blo͞om′fēld′). **1.** A town of north-central Connecticut, a suburb of Hartford. Population, 18,608. **2.** A town of northeast New Jersey, an industrial and residential suburb of Newark. It was settled c. 1660. Population, 47,792.

Bloomfield, Leonard. 1887–1949. American linguist who introduced a behavioristic approach to linguistics in his text *Language* (1933).

bloom·ing (blo͞o′mĭng) *adv. & adj. Chiefly British.* Used as an intensive: *a blooming hot day; a blooming idiot.* [Probably a euphemism for BLOODY.]

Bloo·ming·ton (blo͞o′mĭng-tən). **1.** A city of central Illinois east-southeast of Peoria. It is a commercial and industrial center. Population, 44,189. **2.** A city of south-central Indiana south-southwest of Indianapolis. Indiana University (established 1820) is located here. Population, 52,044. **3.** A city of eastern Minnesota, a suburb of Minneapolis. Population, 81,831.

Blooms·bur·y (blo͞omz′bĕr′-ē, -bə-rē, -brē). A residential district of north-central London, England, famous for its associations with members of the intelligentsia, including Virginia Woolf, E.M. Forster, and John Maynard Keynes, in the early 20th century.

bloop (blo͞op) *Baseball. n.* A blooper. **—bloop** *tr.v.* **blooped, bloop·ing, bloops.** To hit (a ball) into the air just beyond the infield. **—bloop** *adj.* Hit just beyond the infield.

bloop·er (blo͞o′pər) *n.* **1.** *Informal.* A clumsy mistake, especially one made in public; a faux pas. **2.** *Baseball.* **a.** A weakly hit ball that carries just beyond the infield. **b.** A high pitch that is lobbed to the batter. [From BLOOP, to make the high-pitched sound of interference in a radio signal, and from the sound made by hitting a ball weakly.]

blos·som (blŏs′əm) *n.* **1.** A flower or cluster of flowers. **2.** The condition or time of flowering: *peach trees in blossom.* **3.** A period or condition of maximum development. See Synonyms at

ă **pat**	oi **boy**
ā **pay**	ou **out**
âr **care**	o͝o **took**
ä **father**	o͞o **boot**
ĕ **pet**	ŭ **cut**
ē **be**	ûr **urge**
ĭ **pit**	th **thin**
ī **pie**	*th* **this**
îr **pier**	hw **which**
ŏ **pot**	zh **vision**
ō **toe**	ə **about, item**
ô **paw**	♦ **regionalism**

Stress marks: ′ (primary); ′ (secondary), as in **dictionary** (dĭk′shə-nĕr′ē)

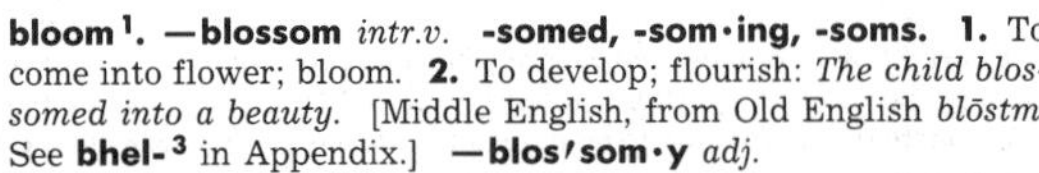
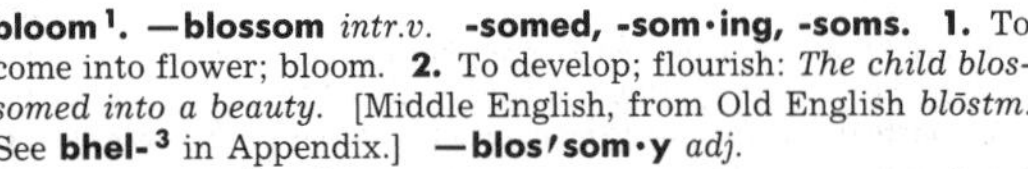

bloom[1]. **—blossom** *intr.v.* **-somed, -som·ing, -soms. 1.** To come into flower; bloom. **2.** To develop; flourish: *The child blossomed into a beauty.* [Middle English, from Old English *blōstm.* See **bhel-**[3] in Appendix.] **—blos′som·y** *adj.*

blos·som-end rot (blŏs′əm-ĕnd′) *n.* A disease, especially of tomato, pepper, squash, or melon, caused by a deficiency of calcium and characterized by brown or black decay at the distal part of the fruit.

blot[1] (blŏt) *n.* **1.** A spot or a stain caused by a discoloring substance: *a blot of paint.* **2.** A stain on one's character or reputation; a disgrace. See Synonyms at **stain. —blot** *v.* **blot·ted, blot·ting, blots.** —*tr.* **1.** To spot or stain, as with a discoloring substance. **2.** To bring moral disgrace to. **3.** To obliterate (writing, for example). **4.** To make obscure; hide: *clouds blotting out the moon.* **5.** To destroy utterly; annihilate: *War blotted out their traditional way of life.* **6.** To soak up or dry with absorbent material. —*intr.* **1.** To spill or spread in a spot or stain. **2.** To become blotted, soaked up, or absorbed. [Middle English.]

blowgun

blot[2] (blŏt) *n.* **1.** *Games.* An exposed piece in backgammon. **2.** *Archaic.* A weak point. [Possibly from Low German *blat,* naked, unprotected.]

blotch (blŏch) *n.* **1.** A spot or blot; a splotch. **2.** A discoloration on the skin; a blemish. **3.** Any of several plant diseases caused by fungi and resulting in brown or black dead areas on leaves or fruit. **—blotch** *tr. & intr.v.* **blotched, blotch·ing, blotch·es.** To mark or become marked with blotches. [Probably blend of BLOT[1] and BOTCH.] **—blotch′i·ly** *adv.* **—blotch′i·ness** *n.* **—blotch′y** *adj.*

blot·ter (blŏt′ər) *n.* **1.** A piece or pad of blotting paper. **2.** A book containing daily records of occurrences or transactions: *a police blotter.*

blot·ting paper (blŏt′ĭng) *n.* Absorbent paper used to blot a surface by soaking up excess ink.

blot·to (blŏt′ō) *adj. Slang.* Intoxicated; drunk.

blouse (blous, blouz) *n.* **1.** A woman's or child's loosely fitting shirt that extends to the waist or slightly below. **2.** A loosely fitting garment resembling a long shirt, worn especially by European workmen. **3.** The service coat or tunic worn by the members of some branches of the U.S. armed forces. **—blouse** *intr. & tr.v.* **bloused, blous·ing, blous·es.** To hang or cause to hang loosely and fully. [French, possibly alteration (influenced by *blousse,* wool scraps, of Germanic origin) of obsolete French *blaude,* from Old French *bliaut,* probably of Germanic origin.]

blou·son (blou′sŏn′, blōō′zŏn′) *n.* A woman's garment, such as a dress or blouse, with a fitted waistband over which material blouses. [French, diminutive of *blouse,* blouse. See BLOUSE.]

blowhole
Of a bottle-nosed dolphin
Tursiops truncatus

blow[1] (blō) *v.* **blew** (blōō), **blown** (blōn), **blow·ing, blows.** —*intr.* **1.** To be in a state of motion. Used of the air or of wind. **2.** To move along or be carried by or as if by the wind: *Her hat blew away.* **3.** To expel a current of air, as from the mouth or from a bellows. **4.** To produce a sound by expelling a current of air, as in sounding a wind instrument or a whistle. **5.** To breathe hard; pant. **6.** To storm: *It blew all night.* **7.** To melt or otherwise become disabled. Used of a fuse. **8.** To burst suddenly: *The tire blew.* **9.** To spout moist air from the blowhole. Used of a whale. **10.** *Informal.* To boast. **11.** *Slang.* To go away; depart. —*tr.* **1.** To cause to move by means of a current of air. **2.** To expel (air) from the mouth. **3.** To cause air to be expelled suddenly from: *blew a tire.* **4.** To drive a current of air on, in, or through: *blew my hair dry after I shampooed it.* **5.** To clear out or make free of obstruction by forcing air through: *constantly blowing his nose in allergy season.* **6.** To shape or form (glass, for example) by forcing air or gas through at the end of a pipe. **7.** *Music.* **a.** To cause (a wind instrument) to sound. **b.** To sound: *a bugle blowing taps.* **8. a.** To cause to be out of breath. **b.** To allow (a winded horse) to regain its breath. **9.** To demolish by the force of an explosion: *An artillery shell blew our headquarters apart.* **10.** To lay or deposit eggs in. Used of certain insects. **11.** To melt or otherwise disable (a fuse). **12.** *Slang.* **a.** To spend (money) freely and rashly. See Synonyms at **waste. b.** To spend money freely on; treat: *blew me to a sumptuous dinner.* **13.** *Vulgar Slang.* To perform fellatio on. **14. a.** *Slang.* To spoil or lose through ineptitude. See Synonyms at **botch. b.** To cause (a covert intelligence operation or operative) to be revealed and thereby jeopardized: *a story in the press that blew their cover; an agent who was blown by the opposition.* **15.** *Slang.* To depart (a place) in a great hurry: *Let's blow this city no later than noon.* **—blow** *n.* **1.** The act or an instance of blowing. **2. a.** A blast of air or wind. **b.** A storm. **3.** *Informal.* An act of bragging. **4.** *Slang.* Cocaine. ***—phrasal verbs.*** **blow away.** *Slang.* **1.** To kill by shooting, especially with a firearm. **2.** To affect intensely; overwhelm: *That concert blew me away.* **blow in.** *Slang.* To arrive, especially when unexpected. **blow off.** To relieve or release (pressure); let off. **blow out. 1.** To extinguish or be extinguished by a gust of air: *blow out a candle.* **2.** To fail, as an electrical apparatus. **3.** To erupt in an uncontrolled manner. Used of a gas or oil well. **blow over.** To subside, wane, or pass over with little lasting effect: *The storm blew over quickly. The scandal will soon blow over.* **blow up. 1.** To come into being: *A storm blew up.* **2.** To fill with air; inflate: *blow up a tire.* **3.** To enlarge (a photographic image or print). **4.** To explode: *bombs blowing up.* **5.** To lose one's temper. ***—idioms.*** **blow a gasket.** *Slang.* To explode with anger. **blow hot and cold.** To change one's opinion often on a matter; vacillate. **blow off steam.** To give vent to pent-up emotion. **blow (one's) cool.** *Slang.* To lose one's composure. **blow (one's) mind.** *Slang.* To affect with intense emotion, such as amazement, excitement, or shock. **blow (one's) top** (or **stack**). *Informal.* To lose one's temper. [Middle English *blowen,* from Old English *blāwan.* See **bhlē-** in Appendix.]

blow[2] (blō) *n.* **1.** A sudden hard stroke or hit, as with the fist or an object. **2.** An unexpected shock or calamity. **3.** An unexpected attack; an assault. [Middle English *blaw.*]

blow[3] (blō) *n.* **1.** A mass of blossoms: *peach blow.* **2.** The state of blossoming. **—blow** *intr. & tr.v.* **blew** (blōō), **blown** (blōn), **blow·ing, blows.** To bloom or cause to bloom. [From Middle English *blowen,* to bloom, from Old English *blōwan.* See **bhel-**[3] in Appendix.]

blow·back (blō′băk′) *n.* **1.** The backpressure in an internal-combustion engine or a boiler. **2.** Powder residue that is released upon automatic ejection of a spent cartridge or shell from a firearm. **3.** The effect caused by recirculation into the source country of disinformation previously planted abroad by that country's intelligence service in an effort to mislead the government of another country.

blow-by-blow (blō′-bī-blō′) *adj.* Exhibiting great detail: *a blow-by-blow description of the accident.*

blow-dry (blō′drī′) *tr.v.* **-dried, -dry·ing, -dries.** To dry and often style (hair) with a hand-held dryer. **—blow dryer** *n.*

blow·er (blō′ər) *n.* **1.** One that blows, especially a mechanical device, such as a fan, that produces a current of air. **2.** *Slang.* A braggart. **3.** *Chiefly British.* A telephone.

blow·fish (blō′fĭsh′) *n., pl.* **blowfish** or **-fish·es.** See **puffer.**

blow·fly (blō′flī′) *n.* Any of several flies of the family Calliphoridae that deposit their eggs in carcasses or carrion or in open sores and wounds.

blow·gun (blō′gŭn′) *n.* A long, narrow pipe through which darts or pellets may be blown. Also called *blowpipe.*

blow·hard (blō′härd′) *n. Informal.* A boaster or braggart.

blow·hole (blō′hōl′) *n.* **1.** An opening or one of a pair of openings for breathing, located on the top of the head of cetaceans, such as whales and dolphins. The blowhole is opened by muscles upon surfacing and closed by the pressure of water upon diving. **2.** A hole in ice to which aquatic mammals, such as dolphins, come to breathe. **3.** A vent to permit the escape of air or other gas.

blow·job (blō′jŏb′) *n. Vulgar Slang.* The act or an instance of fellatio.

blown[1] (blōn) *v.* Past participle of **blow**[1]. **—blown** *adj.* **1.** Swollen or inflated; distended. **2.** Out of breath; panting. **3.** Flyblown. **4.** Formed by blowing: *blown glass.*

blown[2] (blōn) *v.* Past participle of **blow**[3].

blow·off (blō′ôf′, -ŏf′) *n.* **1.** Something, such as a gas, that is blown off. **2.** A device or channel for blowing off something.

blow·out (blō′out′) *n.* **1. a.** A sudden rupture or bursting, as of an automobile tire. **b.** The hole made by such a rupture. **2.** A sudden escape of a confined gas or liquid, as from a well. **3.** *Slang.* A large party or other social affair: *"Lunch was a billion-calorie blowout beside the pool, accompanied by folkloric dancing"* (Vanity Fair).

blow·pipe (blō′pīp′) *n.* **1.** A metal tube in which a flow of gas is mixed with a controlled flow of air to concentrate the heat of a flame, used especially in the identification of minerals. **2.** See **blowgun. 3.** A long, narrow iron pipe used to gather, work, and blow molten glass.

blow·sy (blou′zē) *adj.* Variant of **blowzy.**

blow·torch (blō′tôrch′) *n.* A portable burner for mixing gas and oxygen to produce a very hot flame, used for soldering, welding, and glass blowing.

blow·up (blō′ŭp′) *n.* **1.** An explosion. **2.** An outburst of temper. **3.** A photographic enlargement.

blow·y (blō′ē) *adj.* **-i·er, -i·est.** Windy or breezy.

blow·zy also **blow·sy** (blou′zē) *adj.* **-zi·er, -zi·est** also **-si·er, -si·est. 1.** Having a coarsely ruddy and bloated appearance. **2.** Disheveled and frowzy; unkempt: *blowzy hair.* [From obsolete *blowze,* beggar wench.] **—blow′zi·ly** *adv.* **—blow′zi·ness** *n.*

BLS *abbr.* Bureau of Labor Statistics.

B.L.S. *abbr.* Bachelor of Library Science.

BLT (bē′ĕl-tē′) *n., pl.* **BLT's** or **BLTs.** A bacon, lettuce, and tomato sandwich.

blub·ber[1] (blŭb′ər) *v.* **-bered, -ber·ing, -bers.** —*intr.* To sob noisily. See Synonyms at **cry.** —*tr.* **1.** To utter while crying and sobbing. **2.** To make wet and swollen by weeping. **—blubber** *n.* A loud sobbing. [Middle English *bluberen,* to bubble, from *bluber,* foam.] **—blub′ber·er** *n.* **—blub′ber·ing·ly** *adv.*

blub·ber[2] (blŭb′ər) *n.* **1.** The thick layer of fat between the skin and the muscle layers of whales and other marine mammals, from which an oil is obtained. **2.** Excessive body fat. **3.** A large sea nettle or medusa. **—blubber** *adj.* Swollen and protruding: *blubber cheeks.* [Middle English *bluber,* foam.] **—blub′ber·y** *adj.*

blu·cher (blōō′chər, -kər) *n.* **1.** A high shoe or half boot. **2.** A shoe having the vamp and tongue made of one piece and the quarters lapping over the vamp. [After Gebhard Leberecht von BLÜCHER.]

Blü·cher (blōō′kər, -chər, -KHər), **Gebhard Leberecht von.**

Prince of Wahlstatt. 1742–1819. Prussian field marshal whose leadership of the Prussian army was crucial in the campaigns against Napoleon.

bludg·eon (blŭj′ən) *n.* A short, heavy club, usually of wood, that is thicker or loaded at one end. **—bludgeon** *tr.v.* **-eoned, -eon·ing, -eons. 1.** To hit with or as if with a heavy club. **2.** To overcome by or as if by using a heavy club. See Synonyms at **intimidate.** [Origin unknown.] **—bludg′eon·er, bludg′eon·eer′** (-ə-nîr′) *n.*

WORD HISTORY: The origin of some words is simply not known, and *bludgeon* is one such word. An interesting suggestion is that this word for a club used as a weapon comes from cant, the secret jargon of people such as thieves and beggars, and is related to the word *blood.* We do know that *bludgeon* is first recorded in a dictionary in 1730, while its first recorded use in running text (1755) is simple and to the point: "These villains . . . knocked him down with a bludgeon."

blue (blo͞o) *n.* **1.** *Abbr.* **bl.** *Color.* The hue of that portion of the visible spectrum lying between green and indigo, evoked in the human observer by radiant energy with wavelengths of approximately 450 to 490 nanometers; any of a group of colors that may vary in lightness and saturation, whose hue is that of a clear daytime sky; one of the additive or light primaries; one of the psychological primary hues. **2. a.** A pigment or dye imparting this hue. **b.** Bluing. **3. a.** An object having this hue. **b.** Dress or clothing of this hue: *The ushers wore blue.* **4. a.** A person who wears a blue uniform. **b. blues.** A dress blue uniform, especially that of the U.S. Army. **5.** Often **Blue. a.** A member of the Union Army in the Civil War. **b.** The Union Army. **6.** A bluefish. **7.** A small blue butterfly of the family Lycaenidae. **8. a.** The sky. **b.** The sea. **—blue** *adj.* **blu·er, blu·est. 1.** *Color.* Of the color blue. **2.** Bluish or having parts that are blue or bluish, as the blue spruce and the blue whale. **3.** Having a gray or purplish color, as from cold or contusion. **4.** Wearing blue. **5. a.** Gloomy; depressed. See Synonyms at **depressed. b.** Dismal; dreary: *a blue day.* **6.** Puritanical; strict. **7.** Aristocratic; patrician. **8.** Indecent; risqué: *a blue joke; a blue movie.* **—blue** *tr. & intr.v.* **blued, blu·ing, blues.** To make or become blue. **—*idioms.* blue in the face.** To the point or at the point of extreme exasperation: *I argued with them until I was blue in the face.* **into the blue.** At a far distance; into the unknown. **out of the blue. 1.** From an unexpected or unforeseen source: *criticism that came out of the blue.* **2.** At a completely unexpected time: *arrived out of the blue.* [Middle English *blue, bleu,* from Old French *bleu,* of Germanic origin. See **bhel-**[1] in Appendix.] **—blue′ly** *adv.* **—blue′ness** *n.*

blue angel *n. Slang.* A blue devil.

blue baby *n.* An infant born with cyanosis as a result of a congenital cardiac or pulmonary defect that causes inadequate oxygenation of the blood.

blue·back salmon (blo͞o′băk′) *n.* See **sockeye salmon.**

blue·beard (blo͞o′bîrd′) *n.* A man who first marries and then murders one wife after another. [After *Blue Beard,* translation of French *Barbe Bleue,* a character in a story by Charles Perrault (1628–1703).]

blue·bell (blo͞o′bĕl′) also **blue·bells** (-bĕlz′) *n.* **1.** Any of several bulbous plants of the genus *Endymion* in the lily family, native to western Europe and northwest Africa and having racemes of usually blue to pink bell-shaped flowers. Also called *wood hyacinth.* **2.** Any of numerous plants of the genus *Mertensia,* especially the Virginia bluebells. **3.** See **harebell. 4.** Any of several other plants having bluish, usually bell-shaped flowers.

blue·ber·ry (blo͞o′bĕr′ē) *n.* **1.** Any of numerous plants of the genus *Vaccinium,* having white to reddish, urn-shaped or tubular flowers and edible blue to blue-black berries. **2.** The fruit of any of these plants. Also called *bilberry.*

blue·bill (blo͞o′bĭl′) *n.* See **scaup.**

blue·bird (blo͞o′bûrd′) *n.* Any of several North American songbirds of the genus *Sialia,* having blue plumage and usually a rust-colored breast in the male.

blue-black (blo͞o′blăk′) *adj. Color.* Very dark blue.

blue blood also **blue·blood** (blo͞o′blŭd′) *n.* **1.** Noble or aristocratic descent. **2.** A member of the aristocracy. [Translation of Spanish *sangre azul* : *sangre,* blood + *azul,* blue (probably from the visible veins of fair-complexioned aristocrats).] **—blue′-blood′ed** *adj.*

blue·bon·net (blo͞o′bŏn′ĭt) *n.* **1.** Either of two annual lupines *(Lupinus texensis* and *L. subcarnosus),* native to Texas and having palmately compound leaves and light blue flowers. Also called *Texas bluebonnet.* **2. a.** A broad, blue woolen cap worn in Scotland. **b.** A person wearing such a cap.

blue book also **blue·book** (blo͞o′bo͝ok′) *n.* **1.** An official list of persons in the employ of the U.S. government. **2.** A book listing the names of socially prominent people. **3.** A blank notebook with blue covers in which to write the answers to examination questions.

blue·bot·tle (blo͞o′bŏt′l) *n.* Any of several flies of the genus *Calliphora* that have a bright metallic-blue body and breed in decaying organic matter.

blue box blue-box (blo͞o′bŏks′) *n. Slang.* An electronic device having a tone pulsator that prevents telephone equipment from registering long-distance charges.

blue catfish *n.* A large, bluish freshwater catfish *(Ictalurus furcatus)* of the Mississippi River valley, often weighing more than 45 kilograms (100 pounds). Also called *blue cat.*

blue cheese *n.* A semisoft cheese made of cow's milk and having a greenish-blue mold and flavor similar to Roquefort cheese. Also called *bleu cheese.*

blue chip also **blue-chip·per** (blo͞o′chĭp′ər) *n.* **1.** A stock that sells at a high price because of public confidence in its long record of steady earnings. **2.** An extremely valuable asset or property. **3.** *Games.* A blue poker chip of high value. **—blue′-chip′** *adj.*

blue·coat (blo͞o′kōt′) *n.* A person who wears a blue uniform, especially a police officer. **—blue′coat′ed** *adj.*

blue cohosh *n.* A perennial herb *(Caulophyllum thalictroides)* of eastern North America, having a ternately compound leaf, small yellow-green or purplish flowers, and blue berrylike seeds.

blue-col·lar (blo͞o′kŏl′ər) *adj.* Of or relating to wage earners, especially as a class, whose jobs are performed in work clothes and often involve manual labor. **—blue′-col′lar** *n.*

blue crab *n.* An edible, bluish swimming crab *(Callinectes sapidus)* that has a wide distribution along the Atlantic and Gulf coasts of North America.

blue·curls also **blue curls** (blo͞o′kûrlz′) *pl.n. (used with a sing. or pl. verb).* Any of several North American plants of the genus *Trichostema* in the mint family, having clusters of mostly bluish or purplish flowers with long, curved stamens.

blue devil *n.* **1.** *Slang.* A blue capsule or tablet containing barbiturate amobarbital or its sodium derivative. **2. blue devils.** *Informal.* A feeling of depression; despondency.

blue-eyed grass (blo͞o′īd′) *n.* Any of various New World perennial herbs of the genus *Sisyrinchium* having grasslike leaves and small blue, white, or yellow flowers.

blue-eyed Mary *n.* An annual North American herb *(Collinsia verna)* having bicolored flowers with two lips. Also called *innocence.*

Blue·field (blo͞o′fēld′). A city of southern West Virginia in the Allegheny Mountains south-southeast of Charleston. It is a trade and shipping center in a coal-mining region. Population, 16,060.

blue·fin tuna (blo͞o′fĭn′) *n.* A very large tuna *(Thunnus thynnus)* of temperate waters. It is an important commercial and eating variety.

blue·fish (blo͞o′fĭsh′) *n., pl.* **bluefish** or **-fish·es. 1.** A voracious food and game fish *(Pomatomus saltatrix)* of temperate and tropical waters of the Atlantic and Indian oceans. **2.** Any of various fishes that are predominantly blue, such as the pollack.

blue flag *n.* Any of several irises having blue or blue-violet flowers, especially *Iris versicolor* of eastern North America.

blue flu *n.* A sickout, especially by uniformed police officers. [From the blue color of most police officers' uniforms.]

blue fox *n.* **1.** An arctic fox whose fur is bluish gray during a color phase typically occurring in the summer or extending throughout the year. **2.** The fur of such a fox.

blue·gill (blo͞o′gĭl′) *n.* A common edible sunfish *(Lepomis macrochirus)* of North American lakes and streams.

blue·grass (blo͞o′grăs′) *n.* **1.** Also **blue grass.** Any of various grasses of the genus *Poa,* including many valuable lawn and pasture plants, such as Kentucky bluegrass, and also some weeds. **2.** *Music.* A type of folk music that originated in the southern United States, typically played on banjos and guitars and characterized by rapid tempos and jazzlike improvisation.

Blue·grass also **Blue·grass Country** or **Blue·grass Region** (blo͞o′grăs′). A region of central Kentucky noted for its lushly growing bluegrass and the breeding of thoroughbred horses.

blue-green alga (blo͞o′grēn′) *n.* See **cyanobacterium.**

blue grouse *n.* A wildfowl *(Dendragapus obscurus)* of western North America, having predominantly gray plumage. Also called *dusky grouse, sooty grouse.*

blue gum *n.* A tall timber tree *(Eucalyptus globulus)* of Australia, having smooth, bluish deciduous bark, and lance-shaped aromatic leaves.

blue heaven *n. Slang.* A blue devil.

blue heron *n.* Any of several varieties of heron with blue or blue-gray plumage.

blue·ing (blo͞o′ĭng) *n.* Variant of **bluing.**

blue·ish (blo͞o′ĭsh) *adj.* Variant of **bluish.**

Blue Island (blo͞o). A city of northeast Illinois, a residential and industrial suburb of Chicago. Population, 21,855.

blue·jack·et (blo͞o′jăk′ĭt) *n.* An enlisted person in the U.S. or British Navy; a sailor.

blue jay *n.* A North American bird *(Cyanocitta cristata)* having a crested head, predominantly blue plumage, and a harsh, noisy cry.

blue-jeaned (blo͞o′jēnd′) *adj.* **1.** Wearing blue jeans. **2.** Characteristic or suggestive of blue jeans: *a blue-jeaned look and a down-home attitude.*

blue jeans also **blue·jeans** (blo͞o′jēnz′) *pl.n.* Clothes, especially pants, made of blue denim.

blue law *n.* **1.** A law designed to regulate Sunday activities, such as shopping in retail stores. **2.** One of a body of laws in colonial New England designed to enforce certain moral standards and particularly to prohibit specified forms of entertainment or recreation on Sundays.

bluebell
Virginia cowslip
Mertensia virginica

blueberry
Highbush blueberry
Vaccinium corymbosum

blue grouse
Female blue grouse
Dendragapus obscurus

ă pat	oi boy
ā pay	ou out
âr care	o͝o took
ä father	o͞o boot
ĕ pet	ŭ cut
ē be	ûr urge
ĭ pit	th thin
ī pie	*th* this
îr pier	hw which
ŏ pot	zh vision
ō toe	ə about, item
ô paw	♦ regionalism

Stress marks: **′** (primary); ′ (secondary), as in **dictionary** (dĭk′shə-nĕr′ē)

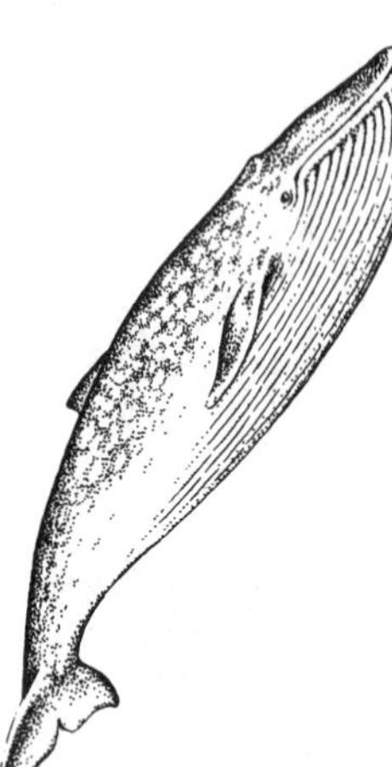
blue whale
Sibbaldus musculus

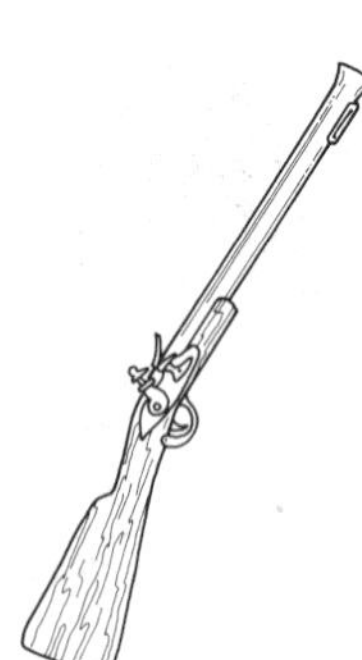
blunderbuss

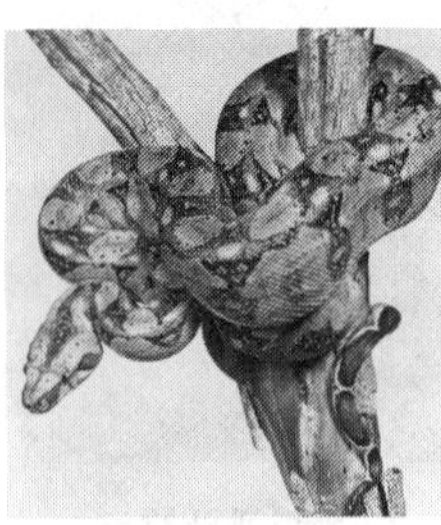
boa constrictor
Constrictor constrictor

ă pat oi boy
ā pay ou out
âr care o͝o took
ä father o͞o boot
ĕ pet ŭ cut
ē be ûr urge
ĭ pit th thin
ī pie *th* this
îr pier hw which
ŏ pot zh vision
ō toe ə about, item
ô paw ♦ regionalism

Stress marks: **ʹ** (primary); ʹ (secondary), as in **dictionary** (dĭkʹshə-nĕrʹē)

Blue Lodge *n.* A Freemasonry lodge in which the first three degrees, bearing blue decorations, are conferred.

blue moon *n. Informal.* A relatively long period of time: *I haven't seen you in a blue moon.*

Blue Mountains. A range of northeast Oregon and southeast Washington consisting of an uplifted, eroded part of the Columbia Plateau. It rises to 2,777.3 m (9,106 ft) at Rock Creek Butte in Oregon.

Blue Nile (nīl). A river of northeast Africa. It is the chief headstream of the Nile and flows about 1,609 km (1,000 mi) from northwest Ethiopia to Sudan. At Khartoum it merges with the White Nile to form the Nile River proper.

blue·nose (blo͞oʹnōzʹ) *n.* A puritanical person: *"Bluenoses demand restraint against the porn and violence that are the staple of popular culture"* (Charles Krauthammer). **—blueʹnosedʹ** *adj.*

blue note *n. Music.* A flatted note, especially the third or seventh note of a chord, in place of an expected major interval. [From its use in blues music.]

blue-pen·cil (blo͞oʹpĕnʹsəl) *tr.v.* **-ciled, -cil·ing, -cils** also **-cilled, -cil·ling, -cils.** To edit, revise, or correct with or as if with a blue pencil.

blue pe·ter (pēʹtər) *n. Nautical.* A blue flag with a white square in the center, flown to signal that a ship is ready to sail. [From the fact that it represents the letter P in the International Code of Symbols.]

blue pike *n.* A freshwater food and game fish *(Strizostedion vitreum glaucum)* found in the Great Lakes. It is a variety of the walleye. Also called *blue pikeperch, blue walleye.*

blue-plate (blo͞oʹplātʹ) *adj.* Being a main course of a restaurant meal usually offered at a special price: *a blue-plate lunch.* [Perhaps from the blue-patterned plate on which such meals were originally served.]

blue·point also **blue point** (blo͞oʹpointʹ) *n.* A type of small oyster found chiefly in eastern coastal waters and usually eaten raw. [After *Blue Point,* a locality on Great South Bay, Long Island, New York.]

blue point *n.* A variety of a domestic cat, especially the Siamese, with a bluish-white coat and darker bluish-gray points.

blue·print (blo͞oʹprĭntʹ) *n.* **1.** A photographic reproduction, as of architectural plans or technical drawings, rendered as white lines on a blue background. Also called *cyanotype.* **2.** A detailed plan of action. See Synonyms at **plan.** **—blueprint** *tr.v.* **-print·ed, -print·ing, -prints. 1.** To make a blueprint of. **2.** To lay a plan for.

blue racer *n.* A bluish-green, harmless variety *(Coluber constrictor flaviventris)* of the blacksnake, found in the central United States.

blue ribbon *n.* **1.** An emblem, badge, or rosette made of blue ribbon that is awarded as the first prize in a competition. **2.** An award or honor given for excellence. **—blueʹ-ribʹbon** (blo͞oʹrĭbʹən) *adj.*

blue-ribbon jury *n. Law.* A jury whose members have been selected for their special qualifications, such as higher education, that supposedly enable them to deal with complex legal issues. Also called *blue-ribbon panel, special jury.*

Blue Ridge also **Blue Ridge Mountains.** A range of the Appalachian Mountains extending from southern Pennsylvania to northern Georgia. It rises to 2,038.6 m (6,684 ft) at Mount Mitchell in the Black Mountains of western North Carolina.

blue runner *n.* See **runner** (sense 16).

blues (blo͞oz) *pl.n. (used with a sing. or pl. verb).* **1.** A state of depression or melancholy: *The blues has finally gotten me today. I really have the blues today.* **2.** *Music.* A style of music evolved from southern Black American secular songs and usually distinguished by slow tempo and flatted thirds and sevenths. [Short for BLUE DEVILS.] **—bluesʹman** *n.* **—bluesʹy** *adj.*

blue shark *n.* A pelagic shark *(Prionace glauca)* of tropical and temperate oceans that is a brilliant dark blue on top. It occasionally attacks people.

blue shift *n.* A decrease in the wavelength of radiation emitted by an approaching celestial body as a consequence of the Doppler effect. [From the fact that the shorter wavelengths of light are at the blue end of the visible spectrum.]

blue-sky (blo͞oʹskīʹ) *adj.* Unrealistic and impractical: *blue-sky marketing plans; blue-sky corporate planners.*

blue-sky law *n.* A law designed to protect the public from buying fraudulent securities.

Blue Springs. A city of western Missouri, a suburb of Kansas City. Population, 25,927.

blue spruce *n.* A Rocky Mountain tree *(Picea pungens)* having silvery-blue or blue-green, four-angled, needlelike leaves and cylindrical cones. It is extensively cultivated as an ornamental. Also called *Colorado blue spruce.*

blues-rock (blo͞ozʹrŏkʹ) *n. Music.* A style of music that combines blues and rock 'n' roll.

blue·stem (blo͞oʹstĕmʹ) *n.* Any of several chiefly North American grasses of the genera *Andropogon, Bothriochloa,* and *Schizachyrium,* some of which are important prairie grasses.

blue·stock·ing (blo͞oʹstŏkʹĭng) *n.* A woman with strong scholarly or literary interests. [After the *Blue Stocking* Society, a nickname for a predominantly female literary club of 18th-century London.] **—blueʹstockʹing** *adj.*

blue·stone (blo͞oʹstōnʹ) *n.* **1.** A bluish-gray sandstone used for paving and building. **2.** A stone similar to this kind of sandstone.

blue streak *n. Informal.* **1.** Something moving very fast. **2.** A rapid and seemingly interminable stream of words. [Probably in allusion to a bolt of lightning.]

blue·tongue (blo͞oʹtŭngʹ) *n.* A viral disease of sheep and cattle that is transmitted by biting insects and is characterized by fever, the formation of oral lesions, and swelling and cyanosis of the lips and tongue.

blu·ets (blo͞oʹĭts) *pl.n. (used with a sing. or pl. verb).* Any of several herbs of the genus *Hedyotis,* especially the low-growing *H. caerulea* of eastern North America, which has blue flowers with yellow centers. Also called *Quaker-ladies.* [Middle English, from *bleu,* blue. See BLUE.]

blue vitriol *n.* A blue, crystalline hydrous solution of copper sulfate, $CuSO_4{\cdot}5H_2O$, one of the most important industrial copper salts, used in insecticides, germicides, and hair dyes and in the processing of leather and textiles.

blue walleye *n.* See **blue pike.**

blue·weed (blo͞oʹwēdʹ) *n.* A biennial Eurasian plant *(Echium vulgare)* naturalized as a weed in eastern North America and having usually blue flowers.

blue whale *n.* A very large whalebone whale *(Sibbaldus musculus)* having a bluish-gray back, yellow underparts, and several ventral throat grooves. It is considered the largest living animal, sometimes reaching a length of 30.5 meters (100 feet). Also called *sulphur-bottom.*

bluff¹ (blŭf) *v.* **bluffed, bluff·ing, bluffs.** *—tr.* **1.** To mislead or deceive. **2.** To impress, deter, or intimidate by a false display of confidence. **3.** *Games.* To try to mislead (opponents) in a card game by heavy betting on a poor hand or by little or no betting on a good one. *—intr.* To engage in a false display of strength or confidence. **—bluff** *n.* **1.** The act or practice of bluffing. **2.** One that bluffs. [Probably from Dutch *bluffen,* from Low German.] **—bluffʹa·ble** *adj.* **—bluffʹer** *n.*

bluff² (blŭf) *n.* A steep headland, promontory, riverbank, or cliff. **—bluff** *adj.* **bluff·er, bluff·est. 1.** Rough and blunt but not unkind in manner. See Synonyms at **gruff. 2.** Having a broad, steep front. [Probably from obsolete Dutch *blaf* or Middle Low German *blaff,* broad.] **—bluffʹly** *adv.* **—bluffʹness** *n.*

blu·ing also **blue·ing** (blo͞oʹĭng) *n.* **1.** Any of various coloring agents used to counteract the yellowing of laundered fabrics. **2.** A rinsing agent used to give a silver tint to gray or graying hair.

blu·ish also **blue·ish** (blo͞oʹĭsh) *adj.* Somewhat blue. **—bluʹish·ness** *n.*

Blum (blo͞om), **Léon.** 1872–1950. French socialist politician who served as premier (1936–1937, 1938, and 1946–1947). He was imprisoned (1940–1945) by the Vichy government during World War II.

blun·der (blŭnʹdər) *n.* A usually serious mistake typically caused by ignorance or confusion. **—blunder** *v.* **-dered, -der·ing, -ders.** *—intr.* **1.** To move clumsily or blindly. **2.** To make a usually serious mistake. *—tr.* **1.** To make a stupid, usually serious error in; botch. **2.** To utter (something) stupidly or thoughtlessly. [From Middle English *blunderen,* to go blindly, perhaps from Old Swedish *blundra,* have one's eyes closed, from Old Norse *blunda.*] **—blunʹder·er** *n.* **—blunʹder·ing·ly** *adv.*

SYNONYMS: *blunder, bumble, flounder, lumber, lurch, stumble.* The central meaning shared by these verbs is "to move awkwardly or unsteadily": *blundered into the room and fell; flies bumbling against the open jam jar; floundered up the muddy mountain trail; a wagon lumbering along an unpaved road; twisted her ankle and lurched home; stumbled but regained his balance.*

blun·der·buss (blŭnʹdər-bŭsʹ) *n.* **1.** A short musket of wide bore and flaring muzzle, formerly used to scatter shot at close range. **2.** A person regarded as clumsy and stupid. [Alteration of Dutch *donderbus* : *donder,* thunder (from Middle Dutch *doner;* see **(s)tenə-** in Appendix) + *bus,* gun (from Middle Dutch *busse,* tube, from Latin *buxis,* box; see BOX¹).]

blunt (blŭnt) *adj.* **blunt·er, blunt·est. 1.** Having a dull edge or end; not sharp. **2.** Abrupt and often disconcertingly frank in speech: *"Onscreen, John Wayne was a blunt talker and straight shooter"* (Time). See Synonyms at **gruff. 3.** Slow to understand or perceive; dull. **4.** Lacking in feeling; insensitive. **—blunt** *v.* **blunt·ed, blunt·ing, blunts.** *—tr.* **1.** To dull the edge of. **2.** To make less effective; weaken: *blunting the criticism with a smile.* *—intr.* To become blunt. [Middle English.] **—bluntʹly** *adv.* **—bluntʹness** *n.*

blur (blûr) *v.* **blurred, blur·ring, blurs.** *—tr.* **1.** To make indistinct and hazy in outline or appearance; obscure. **2.** To smear or stain; smudge. **3.** To lessen the perception of; dim: *"For street children . . . drugs offer the chance to blur their hopeless poverty"* (Alma Guillermoprieto). *—intr.* **1.** To become indistinct. **2.** To make smudges or stains by smearing. **—blur** *n.* **1.** A smear or blot; a smudge. **2.** Something that is hazy and indistinct to the sight or mind. [Probably akin to Middle English *bleren,* to blear.] **—blurʹri·ness** *n.* **—blurʹry** *adj.*

blurb (blûrb) *n.* A brief publicity notice, as on a book jacket. [Coined by Gelett Burgess (1866–1951), American humorist.] **—blurb** *v.*

blurt (blûrt) *tr.v.* **blurt·ed, blurt·ing, blurts.** To utter suddenly and impulsively: *blurt a confession.* [Probably imitative.] **—blurt′er** *n.*

blush (blŭsh) *intr.v.* **blushed, blush·ing, blush·es. 1.** To become red in the face, especially from modesty, embarrassment, or shame; flush. **2.** To become red or rosy. **3.** To feel embarrassed or ashamed: *blushed at his own audacity.* **—blush** *n.* **1.** A reddening of the face, especially from modesty, embarrassment, or shame. **2.** A red or rosy color: *the blush of dawn.* **3.** A glance, look, or view: *thought the painting genuine at first blush.* **4.** Blusher. [Middle English *blushen,* from Old English *blyscan.* See **bhel-**[1] in Appendix.] **—blush′ful** *adj.* **—blush′ing·ly** *adv.*

blush·er (blŭsh′ər) *n.* Makeup used on the face and especially on the cheekbones to give a usually rosy tint.

blush wine *n.* Any of several wines having a slightly pink tinge, similar in style to a dry white wine and made from red-white grapes.

blus·ter (blŭs′tər) *v.* **-tered, -ter·ing, -ters.** *—intr.* **1.** To blow in loud, violent gusts, as the wind during a storm. **2. a.** To speak in a loudly arrogant or bullying manner. **b.** To brag or make loud, empty threats. *—tr.* To force or bully with swaggering threats. **—bluster** *n.* **1.** A violent, gusty wind. **2.** Turbulence or noisy confusion. **3.** Loud, arrogant speech, often full of empty threats. [Middle English *blusteren,* from Middle Low German *blüsteren.*] **—blus′ter·er** *n.* **—blus′ter·y, blus′ter·ous** *adj.*

blvd. or **Blvd.** *abbr.* Boulevard.

Bly (blī), **Nellie.** See Elizabeth Cochrane **Seaman.**

B lymphocyte also **B-lym·pho·cyte** (bē′lĭm′fə-sīt′) *n.* See **B cell.** [*b(ursa-dependent)* + LYMPHOCYTE.]

Blyth (blī, blīth). A municipal borough of northeast England on the North Sea at the mouth of the **Blyth River.** It is an industrial center and a seaport. Population, 78,200.

Blythe·ville (blī′vəl, blīth′vĭl′). A city of northeast Arkansas near the Mississippi River north of Memphis, Tennessee. It is a trade center in a cotton-growing area. Population, 23,844.

BM *abbr. Physiology.* Basal metabolism.

bm. *abbr.* Beam.

b.m. *abbr.* **1.** Board measure. **2.** Bowel movement.

B.M. *abbr.* **1.** Bachelor of Medicine. **2.** Bachelor of Music.

B.M.E. *abbr.* **1.** Bachelor of Mechanical Engineering. **2.** Bachelor of Mining Engineering. **3.** Bachelor of Music Education.

B movie *n.* See **B picture.**

BMR *abbr. Physiology.* Basal metabolic rate.

B.M.S. *abbr.* Bachelor of Marine Science.

B.Mus. *abbr.* Bachelor of Music.

BMX *abbr. Sports.* Bicycle motocross.

Bn. or **bn.** *abbr.* **1.** Baron. **2.** Battalion.

B'nai B'rith (bnā′ brĭth′) *n.* A Jewish international service organization. [Hebrew *bĕnê bĕrît,* sons of the covenant.]

bo·a (bō′ə) *n.* **1.** Any of various large, nonvenomous, chiefly tropical snakes of the family Boidae, which includes the python, anaconda, boa constrictor, and other snakes that coil around and suffocate their prey. **2.** A long fluffy scarf made of soft material, such as fur or feathers. [Middle English, from Latin *boa,* a large water snake.]

Bo·ab·dil (bō′əb-dēl′, bô′äb-*th*ēl′). Originally Abu Abdallah. Died c. 1527. Last Moorish king of Granada (1482–1483 and 1486–1492).

boa constrictor *n.* A large boa *(Constrictor constrictor)* of tropical America that has brown markings and kills its prey by constriction.

Bo·ad·i·ce·a (bō′ăd-ĭ-sē′ə). See **Boudicca.**

boar (bôr, bōr) *n.* **1. a.** An uncastrated male pig. **b.** The adult male of any of several mammals, such as the beaver, raccoon, or guinea pig. **2.** The wild boar. [Middle English *bor,* from Old English *bār.*]

board (bôrd, bōrd) *n. Abbr.* **bd. 1.** A long, flat slab of sawed lumber; a plank. **2.** A flat piece of wood or similarly rigid material adapted for a special use. **3.** *Games.* A flat surface on which a game is played. **4.** The hard cover of a book. **5. boards.** A theater stage. **6. a.** A table, especially one set for serving food. **b.** Food or meals considered as a whole: *board and lodging.* **7.** A table at which official meetings are held; a council table. **8.** An organized body of administrators or investigators: *a board of trustees; a board of directors.* **9.** An electrical-equipment panel. **10.** *Computer Science.* A circuit board. **11.** *Sports.* **a.** A scoreboard. **b.** *Basketball.* A backboard. **c. boards.** The wooden structure enclosing an ice hockey rink. **d.** A diving board. **e.** A surfboard. **12.** *Nautical.* **a.** The side of a ship. **b.** A leeboard. **c.** A centerboard. **13.** *Obsolete.* A border or an edge. **—board** *v.* **board·ed, board·ing, boards.** *—tr.* **1.** To cover or close with boards: *board up a broken window.* **2. a.** To furnish with meals in return for pay. **b.** To house where board is furnished: *board a horse at a stable.* **3. a.** To enter or go aboard (a vehicle or ship). **b.** *Nautical.* To come alongside (a ship). **4.** *Obsolete.* To approach. *—intr.* To receive meals in return for pay. ***—idiom.*** **on board. 1.** Aboard. **2.** On the job. [Middle English *bord,* from Old English.]

board certification *n.* The process by which a person is tested and approved to practice in a specialty field, especially medicine, after successfully completing the requirements of a board of specialists in that field. For a physician, board certification is required in order to have the privilege of practicing in a hospital.

board-cer·ti·fied (bôrd′sûr′tə-fīd′, bōrd′-) *adj.* Having completed the process of board certification in a specialty field. Used chiefly of physicians: *The hospital maintains a staff of board-certified surgeons and anesthesiologists.*

board·er[1] (bôr′dər, bōr′-) *n.* One who boards, especially one who pays a stipulated sum in return for regular meals or for meals and lodging.

board·er[2] (bôr′dər, bōr′-) *n. Sports.* **1.** A person who skies. **2.** One who rides a skateboard. **3.** One who uses a snowboard.

boarder baby *n.* An infant, often the offspring of drug addicts or AIDS victims, who remains for months, sometimes up to a year, at the hospital where he or she was born, waiting for placement in a home.

board foot *n., pl.* **board feet.** *Abbr.* **bd. ft., bf, b.f., bf.** A unit of cubic measure for lumber, equal to one foot square by one inch thick.

board game *n. Games.* A game of strategy, such as chess or backgammon, played by moving pieces on a board and sometimes involving dice.

board·ing house also **board·ing·house** (bôr′dĭng-hous′, bōr′-) *n.* A house where paying guests are provided with meals and lodging.

boarding school *n.* A school where pupils are provided with meals and lodging.

board measure *n. Abbr.* **b.m.** Measurement in board feet.

board of education *n., pl.* **boards of education.** A school board.

board of trade *n., pl.* **boards of trade.** An association of bankers and business people to promote common commercial interests.

board·room (bôrd′ro͞om′, -ro͝om′, bōrd′-) *n.* The room where the members of a board meet.

board rule *n.* A measuring stick for determining board feet.

board·sail·ing (bôrd′sā′lĭng, bōrd′-) *n. Sports.* See **windsurfing. —board sailor** *n.*

board·walk (bôrd′wôk′, bōrd′-) *n.* **1.** A walk made of wooden planks. **2.** A promenade, especially of planks, along a beach or waterfront.

boar·fish (bôr′fĭsh, bōr′-) *n., pl.* **boarfish** or **-fish·es.** Any of several marine fishes of the genus *Antigonia,* having a deep, flattened body, a projecting snout, and bright red coloring.

boar·hound (bôr′hound′, bōr′-) *n.* A large dog, such as the Great Dane, used originally for hunting wild boars.

Bo·as (bō′ăz), **Franz.** 1858–1942. German-born American anthropologist who emphasized the systematic analysis of culture and language structures.

boast[1] (bōst) *v.* **boast·ed, boast·ing, boasts.** *—intr.* To glorify oneself in speech; talk in a self-admiring way. *—tr.* **1.** To speak of with excessive pride. **2.** *Usage Problem.* To possess or own (a desirable feature): "[the] *capital of a region in the southeast that boasts bountiful coal fields"* (US Air). **3.** To contain; have. **—boast** *n.* **1.** The act or an instance of bragging. **2.** A source of pride. [Middle English *bosten,* from *bost,* a brag.] **—boast′er** *n.* **—boast′ful** *adj.* **—boast′ful·ly** *adv.* **—boast′ful·ness** *n.*

SYNONYMS: *boast, brag, crow, vaunt.* These verbs all mean to speak with pride, often excessive pride, about oneself or something, such as one's possessions, related to oneself. *Boast* is the most general: *"We confide* [i.e., have confidence] *in our strength, without boasting of it; we respect that of others, without fearing it"* (Thomas Jefferson). *Brag* implies exaggerated claims and often an air of insolent superiority: *He bragged that his father was the most successful stockbroker on Wall Street. Crow* stresses exultation and loud rejoicing, as over a victory: *No candidate should crow until the votes have been counted. Vaunt* suggests ostentatiousness and lofty extravagance of expression: *"an elite that . . . vaunts diplomacy over national security concerns"* (Jim Hoagland).

USAGE NOTE: Some have objected to the use of *boast* as a transitive verb meaning "to possess or own (a desirable feature)," as in *This network boasts an audience with a greater concentration of professionals and managers than any other broadcast vehicle.* This usage is by now well established, however, and is acceptable to 62 percent of the Usage Panel.

boast[2] (bōst) *tr.v.* **boast·ed, boast·ing, boasts.** To shape or form (stone) roughly with a broad chisel. [Origin unknown.]

boat (bōt) *n.* **1.** *Nautical.* **a.** A relatively small, usually open craft of a size that might be carried aboard a ship. **b.** An inland vessel of any size. **c.** A ship or submarine. **2.** A dish shaped like a boat: *a sauce boat.* **—boat** *v.* **boat·ed, boat·ing, boats.** *Nautical. —intr.* **1.** To travel by boat. **2.** To ride a boat for pleasure. *—tr.* **1.** To transport by boat. **2.** To place in a boat. ***—idiom.*** **in the same boat.** In the same situation as another or others. [Middle English *bot,* from Old English *bāt.* See **bheid-** in Appendix.]

boat·bill (bōt′bĭl′) *n.* A tropical American wading bird *(Cochlearius cochlearius)* having a large bill shaped like an inverted boat. Also called *boat-billed heron.*

boat-billed heron (bōt′bĭld′) *n.* See **boatbill.**

boat·er (bō′tər) *n.* **1.** *Nautical.* One that drives or rides in a

boar
European wild boar
Sus scrofa

boardwalk
Atlantic City, New Jersey

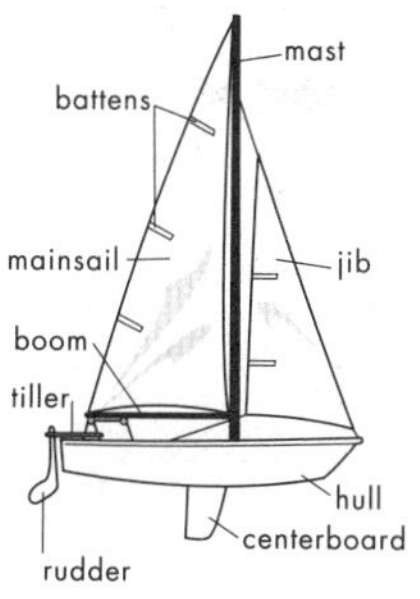

boat
Bermuda-rigged sloop

boatbill
Cochlearius cochlearius

boat, especially a pleasure craft. **2.** A stiff straw hat with a flat crown.

boat hook *n.* A pole with a metal point and hook at one end used especially to maneuver logs, rafts, and boats.

boat·house (bōt′hous′) *n.* A building at the water's edge in which boats are kept.

boat·lift (bōt′lĭft′) *n.* An unofficial system of transporting supplies and people, especially refugees, from one country to another by boats that are often dangerously overcrowded. [BOAT + (AIR)LIFT.] **—boat′lift′** *v.*

boat·load (bōt′lōd′) *n.* The number of passengers or the amount of cargo that a boat can hold.

boat·man (bōt′mən) *n.* One who works on, deals with, or operates boats. **—boat′man·ship′** *n.*

boat people *pl.n.* Refugees, usually political ones, who attempt to flee from their native country to other countries by boat: *"hundreds of thousands of boat people descending on the nation, arms outstretched in need"* (Jerry Adler).

boat·swain also **bo's'n** or **bos'n** or **bo·sun** (bō′sən) *n.* A warrant officer or petty officer in charge of a ship's rigging, anchors, cables, and deck crew. [Middle English *botswein* : *bot,* boat; see BOAT + *swein,* mate; see SWAIN.]

boat·swain's chair (bōsənz) *n. Nautical.* A short board secured by ropes and used as a seat by sailors when working aloft or over a ship's side.

boat train *n.* A train that regularly carries passengers between a city and a port.

Bo·az (bō′ăz). In the Old Testament, the husband of Ruth.

bob[1] (bŏb) *v.* **bobbed, bob·bing, bobs.** *—tr.* **1.** To hit lightly and quickly; tap. **2.** To cause to move up and down: *bobbed my head in response to the question.* *—intr.* **1.** To move up and down: *a cork bobbing on the water.* **2.** To grab at floating or hanging objects with the teeth: *bobbed for apples.* **3.** To curtsy or bow. **—bob** *n.* **1.** A tap or light blow. **2.** A quick, jerky movement of the head or body. ***—phrasal verb.*** **bob up.** To appear or arise unexpectedly or suddenly. [Middle English *bobben.*]

bobwhite
Male and female bobwhite quail
Colinus virginianus

bob[2] (bŏb) *n.* **1.** A small, knoblike pendent object, such as a plumb bob. **2.** A fishing float or cork. **3.** A small lock or curl of hair. **4.** A woman's or child's short haircut. **5.** *Informal.* Surgical shortening or reshaping of the nose. **6.** The docked tail of a horse. **7.a.** A bobsled. **b.** A bob skate. **—bob** *v.* **bobbed, bob·bing, bobs.** *—intr.* To fish with a bob. *—tr.* To cut short or reshape: *bobbed her hair; had his nose bobbed.* [Middle English *bobbe,* cluster of fruit.] **—bob′ber** *n.*

bob[3] (bŏb) *n., pl.* **bob.** *Chiefly British.* A shilling. [Origin unknown.]

bob·bin (bŏb′ĭn) *n.* **1.** A spool or reel that holds thread or yarn for spinning, weaving, knitting, sewing, or making lace. **2.** Narrow braid formerly used as trimming. [French *bobine.*]

bob·bi·net (bŏb′ə-nĕt′) *n.* A machine-woven net fabric with hexagonal meshes. [BOBBI(N) + NET[1].]

bobbin lace *n.* An intricate handmade lace made by interlacing thread around small notched pins or bobbins stuck into a pillow. Also called *pillow lace, point.*

bob·ble (bŏb′əl) *v.* **-bled, -bling, -bles.** *—intr.* To bob up and down. *—tr.* To lose one's grip on (a ball, for example) momentarily. **—bobble** *n.* A mistake or blunder. [From BOB[1].]

bob·by (bŏb′ē) *n., pl.* **-bies.** *Chiefly British.* A police officer. [After Sir Robert PEEL, home secretary of England when the Metropolitan Police Force was created in 1829.]

bobby pin *n.* A small metal hair clip with the ends pressed tightly together. [From BOB[2].]

bobby socks also **bobby sox** *pl.n. Informal.* Ankle socks worn by girls or women. [Possibly from BOB[2] (influenced by BOBBY PIN).]

bob·by·sox·er also **bobby sox·er** (bŏb′ē-sŏk′sər) *n. Informal.* A teenage girl.

bob·cat (bŏb′kăt′) *n.* A wild cat *(Lynx rufus)* of North America, having spotted reddish-brown fur, tufted ears, and a short tail. Also called *bay lynx.* [BOB(TAIL) + CAT.]

♦**bob·o·link** (bŏb′ə-lĭngk′) *n.* An American migratory songbird *(Dolichonyx oryzivorus),* the male of which has black, white, and yellowish plumage. Also called *reedbird,* ♦*ricebird.* [Imitative of its song.]

Bo·bruisk also **Bo·bruysk** (bə-bro͞o′ĭsk). A city of southern Belorussia southeast of Minsk. It was founded in the 16th century. Population, 223,000.

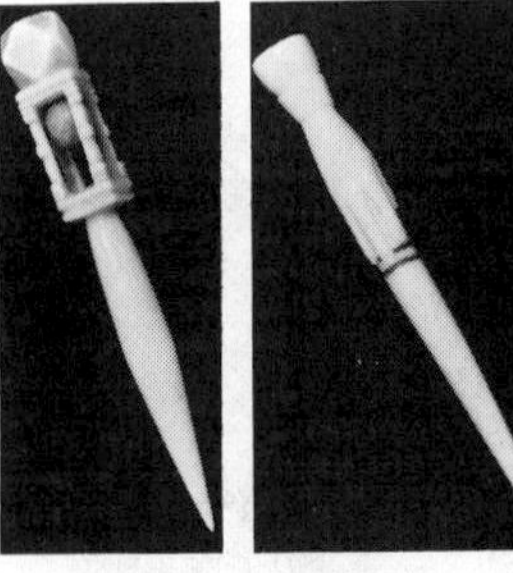
bodkin
Left: Ivory sewing implement with "ball in cage" design
Right: Ivory implement with red wax inlay

bob skate *n. Sports.* An ice skate with two parallel bearing edges. [Possibly BOB(SLED) + SKATE[1].]

bob·sled (bŏb′slĕd′) *Sports. n.* **1.** A long racing sled with a steering mechanism controlling the front runners. **2.a.** A long sled made of two shorter sleds joined in tandem. **b.** Either of these two smaller sleds. **—bobsled** *intr.v.* **-sled·ded, -sled·ding, -sleds.** To ride or race in or as if in a bobsled. [BOB[2] + SLED.]

bob·stay (bŏb′stā′) *n. Nautical.* A rope or chain used to steady the bowsprit of a ship.

bob·tail (bŏb′tāl′) *n.* **1.** A short or shortened tail. **2.** An animal, such as a horse, having a short or shortened tail. **3.** Something that has been cut short or abbreviated. **—bob′tailed′** *adj.*

bob·white (bŏb-hwīt′, -wīt′) *n.* A small North American quail *(Colinus virginianus)* having brown plumage with white markings. [Imitative of its call.]

bo·cac·cio (bə-kä′chō, -chē-ō′) *n., pl.* **-cios.** A large, edible rockfish *(Sebastes paucispinis)* of American Pacific waters. [Italian *bocaccio,* ugly mouth, diminutive of *bocca,* mouth, from Latin *bucca.*]

Bo·ca Ra·ton (bō′kə rə-tōn′). A city of southeast Florida on the Atlantic Ocean south of Palm Beach. It is a resort and industrial center. Population, 49,505.

Boc·cac·cio (bō-kä′chē-ō′, -chō′), **Giovanni.** 1313–1375. French-born Italian poet and writer whose classic work, the *Decameron* (1351–1353), is a collection of 100 tales set against the melancholic background of the Black Death.

boc·ce or **boc·ci** or **boc·cie** (bŏch′ē) *n. Sports.* A game of Italian origin similar to bowling that is played with wooden balls on a long, narrow court covered with fine gravel. [Italian *bocce,* bowls, pl. of *boccia,* ball.]

Boc·che·ri·ni (bō′kə-rē′nē, bŏk′ə-, bôk′kĕ-), **Luigi.** 1743–1805. Italian composer noted for his chamber music and cello concertos.

Boc·cio·ni (bŏ-chō′nē, bôt-chô′-), **Umberto.** 1882–1916. Italian artist whose works embodied futurism.

Boche also **boche** (bŏsh, bôsh) *n. Offensive Slang.* Used as a disparaging term for a German. [French, alteration of *Alboche,* blend of Allemand, German; see ALLEMANDE, and French dialectal *caboche,* cabbage, blockhead; see CABBAGE.]

Bo·chum (bō′kəm, -ᴋʜo͝om). A city of west-central Germany in the Ruhr Valley east of Essen. Chartered in 1321, it is an industrial and commercial center. Population, 384,774.

bock beer (bŏk) *n.* A strong dark beer, the first that is drawn from the vats in springtime. [German *Bockbier,* alteration of *Einbeckisch Bier,* after *Einbeck,* a town of north-central West Germany.]

bod (bŏd) *n. Slang.* **1.** The physical human body; build: *"likes brainy men who maintain a good bod"* (Catherine Breslin). **2.** A person: *"When his ancient tank had broken down . . . he had jumped on the back of mine with a few other bods"* (Robert Crisp).

B.O.D. *abbr.* Biochemical oxygen demand.

♦**bo·da·cious** also **bow·da·cious** (bō-dā′shəs) or **bar·da·cious** (bär-) *Southern & South Midland U.S.* *—adj.* **1.** Remarkable; prodigious. **2.** Audacious; gutsy. *—adv.* **1.** Completely; extremely. **2.** Audaciously; boldly. [Probably from dialectal *boldacious,* blend of BOLD and AUDACIOUS.]

♦***REGIONAL NOTE:*** Popularized in the comic strip *Snuffy Smith, bodacious* is probably a blend of the words *bold* and *audacious,* whose combined senses are evident in the following description of Sevier County, Tennessee, as *"the most bodacious display of tourisma this side of Anaheim"* (Los Angeles Times). A more traditional meaning is "remarkable, prodigious": *"a bodacious amount of smoke"* (Springfield MA Morning Union); *"the most bodacious tale of hidden treasure"* (Lawrence E. Will). *Bodacious* can also be an adverbial intensifier: *"She's so bowdacious unreasonable when she's raised* [irritated]*"* (William T. Thompson). Black speech in New York City retains this Southernism as *bardacious.* Joseph Wright's *English Dialect Dictionary* cites the form *boldacious,* which, as the likely source for *bodacious,* strengthens the theory that some archaic British expressions are preserved in the speech of the American South.

bode[1] (bōd) *tr.v.* **bod·ed, bod·ing, bodes.** **1.** To be an omen of: *heavy seas that boded trouble for small craft.* **2.** *Archaic.* To predict; foretell. [Middle English *boden,* from Old English *bodian,* to announce. See **bheudh-** in Appendix.]

bode[2] (bōd) *v.* A past tense of **bide.**

bo·de·ga (bō-dā′gə) *n.* **1.** A small Hispanic grocery store, sometimes combined with a wineshop. **2.** A warehouse for the storage of wine. [Spanish, from Latin *apothēca,* storehouse. See APOTHECARY.]

Bo·den·see (bōd′n-zā′). See Lake of **Constance.**

bo·dhi·satt·va (bō′dĭ-sŭt′və) *n. Buddhism.* An enlightened being who, out of compassion, forgoes nirvana in order to save others. [Sanskrit *bodhisattvaḥ,* one whose essence is enlightenment : *bodhiḥ,* perfect knowledge; see **bheudh-** in Appendix + *sattvam,* essence, being (from *sat-,* existing; see **es-** in Appendix).]

bod·ice (bŏd′ĭs) *n.* **1.** The fitted part of a dress that extends from the waist to the shoulder. **2.** A woman's laced outer garment, worn like a vest over a blouse. **3.** *Obsolete.* A corset. [Alteration of *bodies,* pl. of BODY.]

bod·ied (bŏd′ēd) *adj.* Having a body, especially of a specified kind. Often used in combination: *strong-bodied; weak-bodied.*

bod·i·less (bŏd′ē-lĭs) *adj.* Having no body, form, or substance; incorporeal.

bod·i·ly (bŏd′l-ē) *adj.* **1.** Of, relating to, or belonging to the body. **2.** Physical as opposed to mental or spiritual: *bodily welfare.* **—bodily** *adv.* **1.** In the flesh; in person: *bodily but not mentally present.* **2.** As a complete physical entity: *carried the child bodily from the room.*

SYNONYMS: *bodily, corporal, corporeal, fleshly, physical, somatic.* The central meaning shared by these adjectives is "of or relating to the human body": *a bodily organ; a corporal defect; cor-*

poreal suffering; fleshly frailty; physical robustness; a somatic symptom.

bod·ing (bō′dĭng) *n.* An omen or foreboding, especially of evil.

bod·kin (bŏd′kĭn) *n.* **1.** A small, sharply pointed instrument for making holes in fabric or leather. **2.** A blunt needle for pulling tape or ribbon through a series of loops or a hem. **3.** A long hairpin, usually with an ornamental head. **4.** *Printing.* An awl or pick for extracting letters from set type. **5.** A dagger or stiletto. [Middle English *boidekin.*]

Bo·do·ni (bō-dō′nē, bə-), **Gianbattista.** 1740–1813. Italian printer and designer of the Bodoni typeface.

bod·y (bŏd′ē) *n., pl.* **-ies. 1.a.** The entire material or physical structure of an organism, especially of a human being or an animal. **b.** The physical part of a person. **c.** A corpse or carcass. **2.a.** The trunk or torso of a human being or an animal. **b.** The part of a garment covering the torso. **3.a.** A human being; a person. **b.** A group of individuals regarded as an entity; a corporation. **4.** A number of persons, concepts, or things regarded as a group: *We walked out in a body.* **5.** The main or central part, as: **a.** *Anatomy.* The largest or principal part of an organ; corpus. **b.** The nave of a church. **c.** The content of a book or document exclusive of prefatory matter, codicils, indexes, or appendices. **d.** The passenger- and cargo-carrying part of an aircraft, ship, or other vehicle. **e.** *Music.* The sound box of an instrument. **6.** A mass or collection of material that is distinct from other masses: *a body of water.* **7.** Consistency of substance, as in paint, textiles, or wine: *a sauce with body.* **8.** *Printing.* The part of a block of type underlying the impression surface. **—body** *tr.v.* **-ied, -y·ing, -ies. 1.** To furnish with a body. **2.** To give shape to: *"Imagination bodies forth the forms of things unknown"* (Shakespeare). [Middle English *bodi,* from Old English *bodig.*]

SYNONYMS: *body, corpse, carcass, cadaver.* These nouns denote the physical organism of a person or an animal. *Body* refers to material substance, living or dead, especially of a person: *"my body to be buried obscurely"* (Francis Bacon). *Those who smoke abuse their bodies.* The word is often used to point up the distinction between material structure and spirit: *The battle to keep body and soul together was long and difficult. Corpse* refers to the physical remains of a dead person: *The corpse of the victim could be removed only after the police had finished photographing the scene of the crime. Carcass* primarily denotes the body of a dead animal: *"Close to the western summit there is the dried and frozen carcass of a leopard"* (Ernest Hemingway). The word is applied to a person, alive or dead, only derogatorily or humorously: *He exercised strenuously to keep his carcass in good condition. Cadaver* is a corpse used for dissection and study: *cadavers in the pathology department of the medical school.*

body bag *n.* A zippered bag, usually of rubber, for transporting a human corpse.

body blow *n.* **1.** *Sports.* A blow delivered to the front of the torso above the waist in boxing. **2.** A serious setback; a major disappointment.

bod·y·build·ing (bŏd′ē-bĭl′dĭng) *n.* *Sports.* The process of developing the musculature of the body through specific types of diet and physical exercise, such as weightlifting, especially for competitive exhibition. **—body′y·build′er** *n.*

body bunker *n.* A portable bulletproof shield used especially by riot police. Also called *body shield.*

body cavity *n.* See **coelom.**

body cell *n.* See **somatic cell.**

body clock *n.* An internal mechanism of the body that is thought to regulate physical and mental functions in rhythm with normal daily activities.

body corporate *n.* See **corporation** (sense 2).

body count *n.* A count of individual bodies, such as those of troops killed in combat operations.

body English *n.* **1.** The natural or instinctive tendency of a person to try to influence the movement of a propelled object, such as a ball, by twisting his or her body toward the desired goal. **2.** The usually irregular movement or spin of a propelled object as if it were influenced by this twisting.

body fluid *n.* **1.** A natural bodily fluid or secretion of fluid such as blood, semen, or saliva. **2.** Total body water, contained principally in blood plasma and in intracellular and interstitial fluids.

bod·y·guard (bŏd′ē-gärd′) *n.* A person or group of persons, usually armed, responsible for the physical safety of one or more other persons.

body image *n.* The subjective concept of one's physical appearance based on self-observation and the reactions of others.

body language *n.* The bodily gestures, postures, and facial expressions by which a person communicates nonverbally with others.

body louse *n.* A parasitic louse *(Pediculus humanus corporis)* that infests the body and clothes of human beings.

body mechanics *n. (used with a sing. or pl. verb).* The application of kinesiology to the use of proper body movement in daily activities, to the prevention and correction of problems associated with posture, and to the enhancement of coordination and endurance.

body packer *n.* A drug smuggler who swallows bags, usually filled with cocaine, to elude drug enforcement officers or customs officials. The bags may rupture and poison the carrier.

body politic *n.* The people of a politically organized nation or state considered as a group.

body pop·ping (pŏp′ĭng) *n.* *Slang.* A type of dancing characterized by convulsive body movements and mimed robotic gestures.

body search (bŏd′ē-sûrch′) *n.* A physical search of a person made usually by patting the body with the hands and often by exploring bodily orifices in an attempt to find concealed weapons, explosives, drugs, or other contraband. **—bod′y-search′** (bŏd′ē-sûrch′) *v.*

body shield *n.* **1.** Any of variously configured devices used to protect the body of a corrections or law enforcement officer, as in a riot. **2.** See **body bunker.**

body shirt *n.* **1.** A woman's garment for the torso that is made with a sewn-in or snapped crotch. **2.** A tight-fitting shirt or blouse.

body shop *n.* A shop or garage where the bodies of automotive vehicles are repaired.

body snatcher *n.* **1.** A person who steals corpses from graves and sells them, usually for purposes of dissection. **2.** *Slang.* A corporate recruiter. **—bod′y·snatch′ing** (bŏd′ē-snăch′ĭng) *n.*

body stocking *n.* A tight-fitting, usually one-piece garment that covers the torso and sometimes has sleeves and legs.

body suit *n.* A tight-fitting one-piece garment for the torso.

bod·y·surf (bŏd′ē-sûrf′) *intr.v.* **-surfed, -surf·ing, -surfs.** *Sports.* To ride the waves to shore without a surfboard. **—bod′y·surf′er** *n.*

body wall *n.* The portion of an animal body that consists of ectoderm and mesoderm, forms the external body surface, and encloses the body cavity.

bod·y·work (bŏd′ē-wûrk′) *n.* **1.** The metal or plastic external structure of a motor vehicle. **2.** The act or process of repairing the bodies of motor vehicles.

Boeh·me (bœ′mə) or **Boehm** (bœm), **Jakob.** See Jakob **Böhme.**

boehm·ite (bā′mīt′, bō′-) *n.* A white to dark reddish-brown orthorhombic mineral, AlO(OH), present in bauxite. [German *Böhmit,* after J. *Böhm* (1858–1930), German scientist.]

Boe·o·tia (bē-ō′shə, -shē-ə). An ancient region of Greece north of Attica and the Gulf of Corinth. The cities of the region formed the **Boeotian League** in the seventh century B.C. but were usually under the dominance of Thebes. **—Boe·o′tian** *adj. & n.*

Boer (bôr, bôr, bŏŏr) *n.* A Dutch colonist or descendant of a Dutch colonist in South Africa. [Afrikaans, from Dutch, farmer, from Middle Dutch *gheboer,* peasant. See **bheue-** in Appendix.]

Bo·e·thi·us (bō-ē′thē-əs), **Anicius Manlius Severinus.** A.D.480?–524? Roman philosopher. Falsely accused of treason, he wrote *The Consolation of Philosophy,* an account of classical thought, while awaiting his execution.

boff (bŏf) *n.* *Slang.* **1.** A line in a play or film, for example, that elicits a big laugh: *"He doesn't go for the big boffs, artificially inflated, but lets his comedy build through a leisurely accumulation of bizarre details"* (Vincent Canby). **2.** A big laugh. **3.** A conspicuous success. Also called *boffo, boffola.* [Probably from B(OX) OFF(ICE).]

bof·fin also **Bof·fin** (bŏf′ĭn) *n.* *Chiefly British.* A scientist, especially one engaged in research. [Origin unknown.]

bof·fo (bŏf′ō) *Slang. adj.* Extremely successful; great. **—boffo** *n.* See **boff.** [Alteration of BOFF.]

bof·fo·la (bŏf-ō′lə) *n.* *Slang.* See **boff.** [From BOFF.]

Bo·fors gun (bō′fôrz′, bōō′-) *n.* A double-barreled, automatic antiaircraft gun. [After *Bofors,* a city of south-central Sweden.]

bog (bôg, bŏg) *n.* **1.a.** An area having a wet, spongy, acidic substrate composed chiefly of sphagnum moss and peat in which characteristic shrubs and herbs and sometimes trees usually grow. **b.** Any of certain other wetland areas, such as a fen, having a peat substrate. Also called *peat bog.* **2.** An area of soft, naturally waterlogged ground. **—bog** *v.* **bogged, bog·ging, bogs.** *—tr.* To cause to sink in or as if in a bog: *We worried that the heavy rain across the prairie would soon bog our car. Don't bog me down in this mass of detail.* *—intr.* To be hindered and slowed. [Irish Gaelic *bogach,* from *bog,* soft. See **bheug-** in Appendix.] **—bog′gi·ness** *n.* **—bog′gy** *adj.*

Bo·ga·lu·sa (bō′gə-lōō′sə). A city of southeast Louisiana near the Mississippi border north-northeast of New Orleans. It was founded in 1906. Population, 16,976.

Bo·gart (bō′gärt), **Humphrey DeForest.** 1899–1957. American actor who played reticent, tough, but ultimately kind-hearted heroes in films such as *Casablanca* (1942) and *The African Queen* (1951), for which he won an Academy Award.

bog asphodel or **bog-as·pho·del** (bôg′ăs′fə-dĕl′, bŏg′-) *n.* Any of several perennial herbs of the genus *Narthecium* in the lily family, native to boggy areas in northern temperate regions and having grasslike leaves and clusters of yellow flowers.

bo·gey (bō′gē) also **bo·gy** or **bo·gie** *n., pl.* **-geys** also **-gies. 1.** *(also* bŏŏg′ē, bōō′gē). An evil or mischievous spirit; a hobgoblin. **2.** *(also* bŏŏg′ē, bōō′gē). A cause of annoyance or harassment. **3.** *Sports.* **a.** An estimated standard golf score. **b.** One

body bunker

body language

Humphrey Bogart

ă pat	oi boy
ā pay	ou out
âr care	ŏŏ took
ä father	ōō boot
ĕ pet	ŭ cut
ē be	ûr urge
ĭ pit	th thin
ī pie	*th* this
îr pier	hw which
ŏ pot	zh vision
ō toe	ə about, item
ô paw	♦ regionalism

Stress marks: ′ (primary); ′ (secondary), as in **dictionary** (dĭk′shə-nĕr′ē)

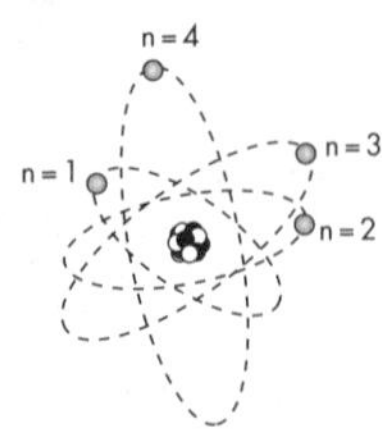

Bohr theory
n=1 through n=4 representing four orbits traveled by an electron around a nucleus

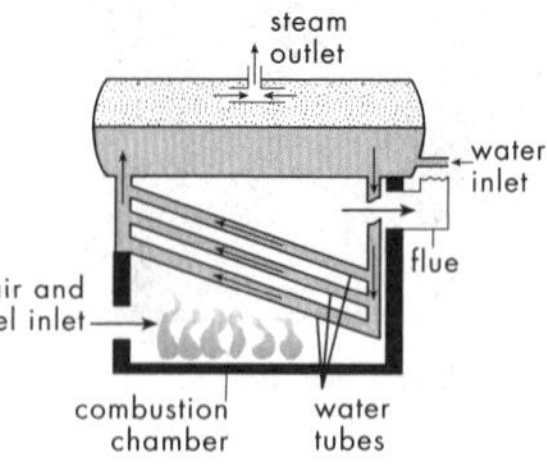

boiler
Water-tube boiler

bolero

Anne Boleyn
Detail of a portrait by an unknown artist

ă pat	oi boy
ā pay	ou out
âr care	o͝o took
ä father	o͞o boot
ĕ pet	ŭ cut
ē be	ûr urge
ĭ pit	th thin
ī pie	*th* this
îr pier	hw which
ŏ pot	zh vision
ō toe	ə about, item
ô paw	♦ regionalism

Stress marks: **ʹ** (primary); ʹ (secondary), as in **dictionary** (dĭkʹshə-nĕrʹē)

golf stroke over par on a hole. **4.** *Slang.* An unidentified flying aircraft. **5.** *Slang.* A detective or police officer. **—bogey** *tr.v.* **-geyed, -gey·ing, -geys.** *Sports.* To shoot (a hole in golf) in one stroke over par. [Possibly variant of BOGLE.]

bog·ey·man or **bo·gy·man** also **boog·ey·man** or **boog·y·man** or **boog·ie·man** (bo͝ogʹē-mănʹ, bōʹgē-, bo͞oʹ-gē-) *n.* A terrifying specter; a hobgoblin.

bog·gle (bŏgʹəl) *v.* **bog·gled, bog·gling, bog·gles.** *—intr.* **1.** To hesitate as if in fear or doubt. **2.** To shy away or be overcome with fright or astonishment: *"The mind now boggling at all the numbers on the table, both sides agreed to a recess of an hour"* (Henry A. Kissinger). **3.** To botch; bungle. *—tr.* To cause to be overcome, as with fright or astonishment. [Probably from *boggle,* dialectal variant of BOGLE.] **—bogʹgle** *n.* **—bogʹgler** *n.*

bog hole *n.* A hole containing soft mud or quicksand.

bo·gie[1] also **bo·gy** (bōʹgē) *n., pl.* **-gies. 1.** A railroad car or locomotive undercarriage with two, four, or six wheels that swivels so curves can be negotiated. **2.** One of several wheels or supporting and aligning rollers inside the tread of a tractor or tank. [Origin unknown.]

bo·gie[2] (bōʹgē, bo͝ogʹē, bo͞oʹgē) *n.* A variant of **bogey.**

bo·gle (bōʹgəl) *n.* A hobgoblin; a bogey. [Scots *bogill.*]

Bo·gor (bōʹgôrʹ). A city of western Java, Indonesia, south of Jakarta. It is a resort and agricultural research center with notable botanical gardens. Population, 247,409.

Bo·go·tá (bōʹgə-täʹ). The capital and largest city of Colombia, in the central part of the country on a high plain in the eastern Andes. It was a center of Chibcha culture before the Spanish established a settlement in 1538. Population, 3,967,988.

bog rosemary *n.* Any of several evergreen shrubs of the genus *Andromeda,* having pink or white urn-shaped flowers grouped in nodding umbels.

Bogsat (bôgʹsătʹ, bŏgʹ-) or **BOGSAT** *n. Slang.* A decision-making process that involves ad hoc judgments made by relatively inexperienced people, typically political or corporate staff members: *"Bogsat is, more often than not, an innocent form of cronyism"* (John W. Macy). *"Most important decisions are still made by BOGSAT"* (Dawn Marie Driscoll). [*B(unch) o(f) g(uys) s(itting) a(round a) t(able).*]

bog spavin *n.* A condition in horses in which lymph collects in the hock joint, causing a puffy swelling.

bog·trot·ter (bôgʹtrŏtʹər, bŏgʹ-) *n.* **1.** A person who lives in or frequents bogs. **2.** *Offensive Slang.* Used as a disparaging term for an Irishman.

bo·gus (bōʹgəs) *adj.* Counterfeit or fake. [From English *bogus,* a device for making counterfeit money.]

bog·wood (bôgʹwo͝odʹ, bŏgʹ-) *n.* Wood that has been preserved in a peat bog.

bo·gy[1] (bōʹgē, bo͝ogʹē, bo͞oʹgē) *n.* Variant of **bogey.**

bo·gy[2] (bōʹgē) *n.* Variant of **bogie**[1]**.**

bo·gy·man (bo͝ogʹē-mănʹ, bōʹgē-, bo͞oʹgē-) *n.* Variant of **bogeyman.**

Bo Hai also **Po Hai** (bōʹ hīʹ). An inlet of the Yellow Sea on the northeast coast of China west of the Shandong and Liaodong peninsulas.

bo·hea (bō-hēʹ) *n.* A black Chinese tea, originally the choicest grade but later an inferior variety. [After the Fujian pronunciation of Chinese (Mandarin) *wǔ yí (shān),* the Wuyi mountain range on the border of Jiangxi and Fujian provinces.]

bo·he·mi·a (bō-hēʹmē-ə) *n.* **1.** A community of persons with artistic or literary tastes who adopt manners and mores conspicuously different from those expected or approved of by the majority of society. **2.** The district in which bohemians live. [Back-formation from BOHEMIAN.]

Bo·he·mi·a (bō-hēʹmē-ə). A historical region and former kingdom of present-day western Czechoslovakia. The Czechs, a Slavic people, settled in the area between the 1st and 5th centuries A.D. A later principality was independent until the 15th century, when it passed to Hungary and then to the Hapsburgs. Bohemia became the core of the new state of Czechoslovakia in 1918.

bo·he·mi·an (bō-hēʹmē-ən) *n.* A person with artistic or literary interests who disregards conventional standards of behavior. [French *bohémien,* from *Bohême,* Bohemia (from the unconventional life style of its Gypsy inhabitants).] **—bo·heʹmi·an** *adj.* **—bo·heʹmi·an·ism** *n.*

Bo·he·mi·an (bō-hēʹmē-ən) *n.* **1.** A native or inhabitant of Bohemia. **2.** A Gypsy. **3.** The Czech dialects of Bohemia. **—Bo·heʹmi·an** *adj.*

Bohemian Brethren *n.* A religious society organized in the 15th century by the Hussites.

Böh·me also **Boeh·me** (bœʹmə) or **Boehm** (bœm), **Jakob.** 1575–1624. German theosophist and mystic whose works, including *Mysterium Magnum* (1623), describe evil as a necessary antithesis to good. He is considered the founder of modern theosophy.

Bo·hol (bō-hôlʹ). An island in the Visayan Islands of central Philippines north of Mindanao in the **Bohol Sea.**

Bohr (bôr, bōr), **Niels Henrik David.** 1885–1962. Danish physicist. He won a 1922 Nobel Prize for investigating atomic structure and radiations. His son **Aage Niels Bohr** (born 1922), also a physicist, shared a 1975 Nobel Prize for discovering the asymmetry of atomic nuclei.

Bohr effect *n. Biochemistry.* An effect by which an increase of carbon dioxide in the blood results in the dissociation of oxygen from hemoglobin and other respiratory compounds. [After Christian *Bohr* (1855–1911), Danish physiologist.]

Bohr theory *n.* An early model of atomic structure in which electrons travel around the nucleus in a number of discrete stable orbits determined by quantum conditions. [After Niels Henrik David BOHR.]

bo·hunk (bōʹhŭngk) *n. Offensive Slang.* Used as a disparaging term for a person from east-central Europe, especially a laborer. [Blend of BO(HEMIAN) and HUNG(ARIAN).]

Bo·iar·do (boi-ärʹdō, bō-yärʹ-), **Matteo Maria.** 1440?–1494. Italian lyric poet known for his unfinished romantic epic *Orlando Innamorato* (1487).

♦ **boil**[1] (boil) *v.* **boiled, boil·ing, boils.** *—intr.* **1. a.** To change from a liquid to a vapor by the application of heat: *All the water boiled away and left the kettle dry.* **b.** To reach the boiling point. **c.** To undergo the action of boiling, especially in being cooked. **2.** To be in a state of agitation; seethe: *a river boiling over the rocks.* **3.** To be stirred up or greatly excited: *The mere idea made me boil. —tr.* **1. a.** To vaporize (a liquid) by the application of heat. **b.** To heat to the boiling point. **2.** To cook or clean by boiling. **3.** To separate by evaporation in the process of boiling: *boil the maple sap.* **—boil** *n.* **1.** The condition or act of boiling. **2.** *Lower Southern U.S.* A picnic featuring shrimp, crab, or crayfish boiled in large pots with spices, and then shelled and eaten by hand. **3.** An agitated, swirling, roiling mass of liquid: *"Those tumbling boils show a dissolving bar and a changing channel there"* (Mark Twain). ***—phrasal verbs.*** **boil down. 1.** To reduce in bulk or size by boiling. **2.** To condense; summarize: *boiled down the complex document.* **3.** To constitute the equivalent of in summary: *The scathing editorial simply boils down to an exercise in partisan politics.* **boil over. 1.** To overflow while boiling. **2.** To lose one's temper. [Middle English *boillen,* from Old French *boillir,* from Latin *bullīre.*]

SYNONYMS: *boil, simmer, seethe, stew.* To *boil* is to cook in a liquid heated to a temperature at which it bubbles up and gives off vapor: *boil potatoes.* Figuratively *boil* pertains to intense agitation: *She boiled with resentment. Simmer* denotes gentle cooking just at or below the boiling point (*Let the stock simmer for several hours*); figuratively it refers to a state of gentle ferment (*Plans were simmering in his mind*). *Seethe* emphasizes in both senses the turbulence of steady boiling at high temperature: *Water seethed in the caldron. "The city had all through the interval been seething with discontent"* (John R. Green). *Stew* refers literally to slow boiling and figuratively to a persistent but not violent state of agitation: *I always add a little Madeira to the liquid when I stew prunes. "They don't want a man to fret and stew about his work"* (William H. Whyte, Jr.).

boil[2] (boil) *n.* A painful, circumscribed pus-filled inflammation of the skin and subcutaneous tissue usually caused by a local staphylococcal infection. Also called *furuncle.* [Middle English *bile,* from Old English *bȳle.*]

Boi·leau-Des·pré·aux (bwä-lōʹdĕ-prā-ōʹ), **Nicolas.** 1636–1711. French critic and poet whose *Art of Poetry* (1674), a treatise in verse, is a summation of the rules and conventions in French literature.

boil·er (boiʹlər) *n.* **1.** An enclosed vessel in which water is heated and circulated, either as hot water or as steam, for heating or power. **2.** A container, such as a kettle, for boiling liquids. **3.** A storage tank for hot water.

boil·er·mak·er (boiʹlər-māʹkər) *n.* **1.** One that makes or repairs boilers. **2.** *Slang.* A drink of whiskey with a beer chaser.

boil·er·plate (boiʹlər-plātʹ) *n.* **1.** A steel plate used in making the shells of steam boilers. **2.** Journalistic material, such as syndicated features, available in plate or mat form. **3.** Inconsequential, formulaic, or stereotypical language: *The provisions of the lease included no new elements and amounted to nothing more than boilerplate.*

boiler room *n.* An area, as in a building or on a ship, that houses one or more steam boilers or hot-water tanks.

boil·er-room (boiʹlər-ro͞omʹ, -ro͝omʹ) *adj. Informal.* Of, relating to, or involving often illegal, high-pressure telephone sales tactics, such as those used in selling stock, commodities, or land.

boil·ing point (boiʹlĭng) *n.* **1.** *Abbr.* **bp** The temperature at which a liquid boils at a fixed pressure, especially under standard atmospheric conditions. **2.** *Informal.* The point at which one loses one's temper.

boil·off (boilʹôfʹ, -ŏfʹ) *n.* The vaporization of liquid, such as rocket fuel.

Bois de Bou·logne (bwäʹ də bo͞o-lōnʹ, -lônʹyə). A park in Paris, France, bordering on the suburb of Neuilly-sur-Seine. A popular recreation area since the 17th century, it is the site of Auteuil and Longchamps racecourses.

bois de rose (bwäʹ də rōzʹ) *n. Color.* A grayish red. [French, rosewood : *bois,* wood + *de,* of + *rose,* rose.]

Boi·se (boiʹsē, -zē). The capital and largest city of Idaho, in the southwest part of the state on the **Boise River,** about 257 km (160 mi) long. The city was founded in 1863 after gold was discovered in the river valley. Population, 102,160.

bois·ter·ous (boiʹstər-əs, -strəs) *adj.* **1.** Rough and stormy; violent. **2.** Loud, noisy, and lacking in restraint or discipline. See

Synonyms at **vociferous.** [Middle English *boistres,* variant of *boistous,* rude, rough, perhaps from Old French *boisteus,* lame, limping, from *boiste,* knee joint.] **—bois′ter·ous·ly** *adv.* **—bois′ter·ous·ness** *n.*

boîte (bwät) *n.* A small restaurant or nightclub. [French, from Old French *boiste,* box, from Late Latin *buxida,* from *buxis.* See BOX[1].]

Bo·i·to (bō′ē-tō′), **Arrigo.** 1842–1918. Italian composer, librettist, and writer best known for his romantic opera *Mefistofele* (1868).

bok choy also **pak choi** (bŏk′ choi′) *n.* A Chinese vegetable *(Brassica rapa* var. *Chinensis)* in the mustard family, having a leafy head similar to that of the common cabbage. [Chinese (Mandarin) *bái cài* : *bái,* white + *cài,* vegetable.]

Bo·kha·ra (bō-kär′ə, -här′ə, -KHä′rə). See **Bukhara.**

Bok·mål (bo͝ok′môl′, bōk′-) *n.* See **Dano-Norwegian.** [Norwegian : *bok,* book; see **bhāgo-** in Appendix + *mål,* language.]

Bol. *abbr.* **1.** Bolivia. **2.** Bolivian.

bo·la (bō′lə) also **bo·las** (-ləs) *n.* A rope with weights attached, used especially in South America to catch cattle or game by entangling their legs. [From American Spanish *bolas,* pl. of Spanish *bola,* ball, probably from Latin *bulla.*]

bola tie *n.* Variant of **bolo tie.**

bold (bōld) *adj.* **bold·er, bold·est. 1.** Fearless and daring; courageous. **2.** Requiring or exhibiting courage and bravery. See Synonyms at **brave. 3.** Unduly forward and brazen in manner: *a bold, impudent child.* **4.** Clear and distinct to the eye; conspicuous: *a bold handwriting.* **5.** Steep or abrupt in grade or terrain: *bold cliffs.* **6.** *Printing.* Boldface. [Middle English, from Old English *bald.* See **bhel-[2]** in Appendix.] **—bold′ly** *adv.* **—bold′ness** *n.*

bold·face (bōld′fās′) *Printing. n. Abbr.* **bf, b.f., bf., bld.** Type with thick, heavy lines. **—boldface** *adj. Abbr.* **bf, b.f., bf., bld.** Printed in thick, heavy type. **—boldface** *tr.v.* **-faced, -fac·ing, -fac·es. 1.** To mark (copy) for printing in this type. **2.** To set or print in this type.

bold-faced (bōld′fāst′) *adj.* Impudent; brazen: *a bold-faced lie.*

bole[1] (bōl) *n.* The trunk of a tree. [Middle English, from Old Norse *bolr.* See **bhel-[2]** in Appendix.]

bole[2] (bōl) *n.* **1.** Any of various soft, fine clays, especially a reddish-brown variety used as a pigment. **2.** *Color.* A moderate reddish brown. [Middle English, from Medieval Latin *bōlus.* See BOLUS.] **—bole** *adj.*

bo·lec·tion (bō-lĕk′shən) *n. Architecture.* A molding that projects from the surface of a panel. [Origin unknown.]

bo·le·ro (bō-lâr′ō, bə-) *n., pl.* **-ros. 1.** A very short jacket worn open in the front. **2.a.** A Spanish dance in triple meter. **b.** The music for this dance. [Spanish, from *bola,* ball. See BOLA.]

bo·le·tus (bō-lē′təs) *n., pl.* **-tus·es** or **-ti** (-tī′). A fungus of the genus *Boletus,* having an umbrella-shaped cap with spore-bearing tubules on the underside and including both edible and poisonous species. [Latin *bōlētus,* mushroom.]

Bol·eyn (bo͝ol′ĭn, bo͝o-lĭn′), **Anne.** 1507–1536. Queen of England (1533–1536) as the second wife of Henry VIII. The mother of Elizabeth I, she produced no male heir and was subsequently tried for adultery and beheaded.

bo·lide (bō′līd, -lĭd) *n.* A meteoric fireball or something held to resemble it: *"a world-class sports car—quick, agile, lively—in short, everything car magazines . . . have ever wanted in a bolide of this type"* (Automobile). [French, from Latin *bolis, bolid-,* from Greek *bolis,* missile, javelin, from *ballein,* to throw. See **g**[w]**ele-** in Appendix.]

Bol·ing·broke (bŏl′ĭng-bro͝ok′, bo͝ol′-, bō′lĭng-), First Viscount. Originally Henry Saint John. 1678–1751. English statesman, orator, and writer. A Jacobite, he spent much of his life in exile and wrote influential political treatises, notably *The Idea of a Patriot King* (1749).

Bo·ling·brook (bō′lĭng-bro͝ok′). A village of northeast Illinois, a suburb of Chicago. Population, 37,261.

bo·li·var (bō-lē′vär, bŏl′ə-vər) *n., pl.* **bo·li·vars** or **bo·li·var·es** (bō′lē′vä-rĕs′). *Abbr.* **b.** See table at **currency.** [American Spanish *bolívar,* after Simón BOLÍVAR.]

Bo·lí·var (bō′lə-vär′, bŏl′ə-, bō-lē′vär), **Pico.** A mountain, 5,005.4 m (16,411 ft) high, of western Venezuela in the Cordillera Mérida south of Lake Maracaibo. It is the highest elevation in the range and in the country.

Bolívar, Simón. Known as "the Liberator." 1783–1830. South American revolutionary leader who defeated the Spanish in 1819, was made president of Greater Colombia (now Colombia, Venezuela, and Ecuador), and helped liberate (1823–1834) Peru and Bolivia.

Bo·liv·i·a (bə-lĭv′ē-ə, bō-). *Abbr.* **Bol.** A landlocked country of western South America. It was named after Simón Bolívar who helped win its independence from Spain in 1825. Sucre is the legal capital and the seat of the judiciary. La Paz is the administrative center and the largest city. Population, 6,429,226. **—Bo·liv′i·an** *adj. & n.*

bo·li·vi·a·no (bə-lĭv′ē-ä′nō, bō-) *n., pl.* **-nos.** See table at **currency.** [Spanish, Bolivian, boliviano, from BOLIVIA.]

boll (bōl) *n.* The seed-bearing capsule of certain plants, especially cotton and flax. [Middle English, from Middle Dutch *bolle,* round object. See **bhel-[2]** in Appendix.]

Böll (bœl), **Heinrich.** 1917–1985. German writer whose works, such as *The Clown* (1963), examine the psychological and societal effects of World War II on the German people. He won the 1972 Nobel Prize for literature.

bol·lard (bŏl′ərd) *n. Nautical.* A thick post on a ship or wharf, used for securing ropes and hawsers. [Middle English, probably from *bole,* tree trunk. See BOLE[1].]

bol·li·to mis·to (bō-lē′tō mĭs′tō) *n., pl.* **bol·li·ti mis·ti** (bō-lē′tē mĭs′tē). A mixture of vegetables and various meats, such as chicken, veal, beef, and sausage, cooked in a broth and usually served with a mustard-fruit sauce. [Italian, mixed stew : *bollito,* stew + *misto,* mixed.]

bol·lix also **bol·lox** (bŏl′ĭks) *tr.v.* **-lixed, -lix·ing, -lix·es** also **-loxed, -lox·ing, -lox·es.** *Informal.* To throw into confusion; botch or bungle: *managed to bollix up the whole project.* [Alteration of *ballocks,* testicles, from Middle English *balloks,* from Old English *beallucas.* See **bhel-[2]** in Appendix.]

boll weevil *n.* **1.** A small, grayish, long-snouted beetle *(Anthonomus grandis)* of Mexico and the southern United States, having adults that puncture cotton buds and larvae that hatch in and damage cotton bolls. **2.** *Informal.* A conservative Southern Democrat in the U.S. House of Representatives.

boll·worm (bōl′wûrm′) *n.* **1.** The pink bollworm. **2.** See **corn earworm.**

bo·lo (bō′lō) *n., pl.* **-los.** A long, heavy, single-edged machete originally used in the Philippines. [Spanish, of Philippine origin.]

bo·lo·gna (bə-lō′nē, -nə, -nyə) also **ba·lo·ney** or **bo·lo·ney** (-nē) *n.* A seasoned smoked sausage made of mixed meats, such as beef, pork, and veal. [After BOLOGNA.]

Bo·lo·gna (bə-lōn′yə). A city of north-central Italy at the foot of the Apennines north-northeast of Florence. It was originally an Etruscan town and became a Roman colony in the second century B.C. Its famed university was founded as a law school in A.D. 425. Population, 455,853. **—Bo·lo′gnan, Bo′lo·gnese′** (bō′lə-nēz′, -nēs′, -lən-yēz′, -yēs′) *adj. & n.*

bolo knife *n.* A bolo.

bo·lom·e·ter (bō-lŏm′ĭ-tər) *n.* An instrument that measures radiant heat by correlating the radiation-induced change in electrical resistance of a blackened metal foil with the amount of radiation absorbed. [Greek *bolē,* ray; see **g**[w]**ele-** in Appendix + -METER.] **—bo′lo·met′ric** (bō′lə-mĕt′rĭk) *adj.*

bo·lo·ney (bə-lō′nē) *n.* Variant of **bologna.**

bolo tie also **bola tie** *n.* A necktie consisting of a piece of cord fastened with an ornamental bar or clasp. [Alteration of BOLA + TIE.]

Bol·she·vik (bōl′shə-vĭk′, bŏl′-) *n., pl.* **-viks** or **-vi·ki** (-vē′kē). **1.a.** A member of the left-wing majority group of the Russian Social Democratic Workers' Party that adopted Lenin's theses on party organization in 1903. **b.** A member of the Russian Social Democratic Workers' Party that seized power in that country in November 1917. **c.** A member of a Marxist-Leninist party or a supporter of one; a Communist. Also called *Bolshevist.* **2.** Often **bolshevik.** An extreme radical: *a literary bolshevik.* [Russian *Bol'shevik,* from *bol'she,* comparative of *bol'shoĭ,* large. See **bel-** in Appendix.] **—Bol′she·vik′** *adj.*

WORD HISTORY: The word *Bolshevik,* an emotionally charged term in English, is derived from a very common word in Russian, *bol'she,* "bigger, more," the comparative form of *bol'shoĭ,* "big." The name *Bol'shevik* was given to the faction in the majority at the Second Congress of the Russian Social Democratic Workers' Party in 1903 (the term is first recorded in English in 1907). The smaller faction was known as *Men'sheviki,* from *men'she,* "less, smaller," the comparative of *malyĭ,* "little, few." The *Bol'sheviki,* who sided with Lenin in the split that followed the Congress, subsequently became the Russian Communist Party. In 1952 the word *Bol'shevik* was dropped as an official term in the Soviet Union, but it had long since passed into other languages, including English. It had even spawned the slang term *bolshie,* though there is no *menshie.*

Bol·she·vism also **bol·she·vism** (bōl′shə-vĭz′əm, bŏl′-) *n.* **1.** The strategy developed by the Bolsheviks between 1903 and 1917 with a view to seizing state power and establishing a dictatorship of the proletariat. **2.** Soviet Communism.

Bol·she·vist also **bol·she·vist** (bōl′shə-vĭst, bŏl′-) *n.* See **Bolshevik** (sense 1). **—Bol′she·vis′tic** *adj.*

♦**bol·son** (bōl-sōn′) *n. Chiefly Southwestern U.S.* A flat, arid valley surrounded by mountains and draining into a shallow central lake. [American Spanish *bolsón,* augmentative of Spanish *bolsa,* purse, pouch, from Late Latin *bursa.* See BURSA.]

bol·ster (bōl′stər) *n.* A long, narrow pillow or cushion. **—bolster** *tr.v.* **-stered, -ster·ing, -sters. 1.** To support or prop up with or as if with a long, narrow pillow or cushion. **2.** To buoy up: *Visitors bolstered the patient's morale.* [Middle English, from Old English. See **bhelgh-** in Appendix.] **—bol′ster·er** *n.*

bolt[1] (bōlt) *n.* **1.** A bar made of wood or metal that slides into a socket and is used to fasten doors and gates. **2.** A metal bar or rod in the mechanism of a lock that is thrown or withdrawn by turning the key. **3.** A fastener consisting of a threaded pin or rod with a head at one end, designed to be inserted through holes in assembled parts and secured by a mated nut that is tightened by applying torque. **4.a.** A sliding metal bar that positions the cartridge in breechloading rifles, closes the breech, and ejects the

Simón Bolívar

Bolivia

bollard

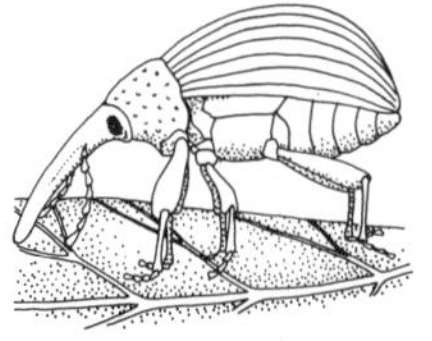

boll weevil
Anthonomus grandis

spent cartridge. **b.** A similar device in any breech mechanism. **5.** A short, heavy arrow with a thick head, used especially with a crossbow. **6.** A flash of lightning; a thunderbolt. **7.** A sudden or unexpected event: *The announcement was a veritable bolt.* **8.** A sudden movement toward or away. **9.** A large roll of cloth of a definite length, especially as it comes from the loom. **—bolt** *v.* **bolt·ed, bolt·ing, bolts.** *—tr.* **1.** To secure or lock with or as if with a bolt. **2.** To arrange or roll (lengths of cloth, for example) on or in a bolt. **3.** To eat (food) hurriedly and with little chewing; gulp. **4.** To desert or withdraw support from (a political party). **5.** To utter impulsively: blurt. **6.** *Archaic.* To shoot or discharge (a missile, such as an arrow). *—intr.* **1.** To move or spring suddenly. **2.** To start suddenly and run away: *The horse bolted at the sound of the shot. The frightened child bolted from the room.* **3.** To break away from a political party or its policies. **4.** *Botany.* To flower or produce seeds prematurely or develop a flowering stem from a rosette. ***—idiom.*** **bolt from the blue.** A sudden, shocking surprise or turn of events. [Middle English, from Old English, heavy arrow.]

bolt² (bōlt) *tr.v.* **bolt·ed, bolt·ing, bolts.** To pass (flour, for example) through a sieve. [Middle English *bulten,* from Old French *buleter,* from Middle High German *biuteln,* from *biutel,* bag, purse.]

bolt-action (bōlt′ăk′shən) *adj.* Loaded by a manually operated bolt. Used of a firearm.

bolt·er¹ (bōl′tər) *n.* **1.** A horse given to bolting. **2.** One who gives up membership in or withdraws support from a political party.

bolt·er² (bōl′tər) *n.* **1.** A machine used for sifting, especially for sifting flour. **2.** One who operates a sifting machine.

bolt·hole (bōlt′hōl′) *n.* **1.** A hole through which to bolt: *found a bolthole in the fencing.* **2.** A means of escape: *"The book offered exotic escape, but one could imagine more alluring boltholes than an ascetic all-male community"* (Anthony Burgess).

Bol·ton (bōl′tən). A borough of northwest England northwest of Manchester. It was a center of the woolen trade from the 14th to the 18th century. Population, 263,000.

bol·to·ni·a (bōl-tō′nē-ə) *n.* Any of several perennial herbs of the genus *Boltonia* in the composite family, having flower heads with white to purplish rays and yellow centers. [New Latin, genus name, after James *Bolton,* 18th-century British botanist.]

bolt·rope (bōlt′rōp′) *n. Nautical.* A rope sewn into the outer edge of a sail to prevent it from tearing.

bo·lus (bō′ləs) *n., pl.* **-lus·es.** **1.** A round mass: *"A dense bolus of trapped dolphins fills the frame"* (Kenneth Browser). **2.** *Pharmacology.* A round medicinal preparation, such as a large pill or tablet, that is usually of a soft consistency and not prepackaged. **3.** A soft mass of chewed food within the mouth or alimentary canal. [Medieval Latin *bōlus,* from Greek *bōlos,* lump of earth.]

Bol·za·no (bōl-zä′nō, bôl-tsä′nô). A city of northern Italy near the Austrian border north-northwest of Venice. It is a tourist center and health resort noted for its Alpine scenery. Population, 104,606.

bomb (bŏm) *n.* **1.a.** An explosive weapon detonated by impact, proximity to an object, a timing mechanism, or other means. **b.** An atomic or a nuclear bomb. Used with *the.* **2.** Any of various weapons detonated to release destructive material, such as smoke or gas. **3.** *Football.* A very long forward pass intended to gain great yardage in a single play. **4.a.** A container capable of withstanding high internal pressure. **b.** A vessel for storing compressed gas. **c.** A portable, manually operated container that ejects a spray, foam, or gas under pressure. **5.** *Slang.* A dismal failure; a fiasco. **6.** *Slang.* An old car. **7.** *Chiefly British.* A large amount of money. **—bomb** *v.* **bombed, bomb·ing, bombs.** *—tr.* To attack, damage, or destroy with or as if with bombs. *—intr.* **1.** To drop a bomb or bombs. **2.** *Slang.* To fail miserably: *The play bombed.* **3.** *Slang.* To paint a graffito. [French *bombe,* from Italian *bomba,* probably from Latin *bombus,* a booming sound, from Greek *bombos.*]

bom·bard (bŏm-bärd′, bŏm′bärd′) *tr.v.* **-bard·ed, -bard·ing, -bards.** **1.** To attack with bombs, shells, or missiles. **2.** To assail persistently, as with requests. See Synonyms at **attack, barrage².** **3.** To irradiate (an atom). **4.** To attack with a cannon firing stone balls. **—bombard** *n.* An early form of cannon that fired stone balls. [From Middle English, a bombard, from Old French *bombarde,* from Medieval Latin *bombarda,* probably from Latin *bombus,* a booming sound. See BOMB.] **—bom·bard′er** *n.* **—bom·bard′ment** *n.*

bom·bar·dier (bŏm′bər-dîr′) *n.* **1.** The member of a combat aircraft crew who operates the bombsight and drops the bombs. **2.** *Chiefly British.* A noncommissioned artillery officer. **3.** *Archaic.* A soldier in the artillery. [French, from Old French *bombarde,* bombard. See BOMBARD.]

bombardier beetle *n.* Any of various beetles of the genus *Brachinus* and related genera that expel an acrid, volatile secretion from the abdomen when disturbed, making an audible sound.

bom·bar·don (bŏm′bər-dŏn′, bŏm-bär′dn) *n. Music.* **1.** A brass instrument resembling a tuba but with a lower pitch; a bass or contrabass tuba. **2.** A 16-foot reed stop on an organ. [French, from Italian *bombardone,* augmentative of *bombardo,* alteration of *bombarda,* bombard, from Medieval Latin. See BOMBARD.]

bom·bast (bŏm′băst′) *n.* Grandiloquent, pompous speech or writing. [Alteration of obsolete *bombace,* cotton padding, from Old French, from Late Latin *bombax,* cotton. See BOMBAZINE.] **—bom′bast′er** *n.* **—bom·bas′tic** *adj.* **—bom·bas′ti·cal·ly** *adv.*

SYNONYMS: *bombast, rant, fustian, claptrap, rodomontade.* All these nouns designate speech or writing marked by an extravagance or affectation of style that the content does not warrant. *Bombast* stresses inflation of style but does not always imply insubstantiality of thought: *"Their eloquence is all bombast"* (Charles Kingsley). *Rant,* used chiefly of speech, emphasizes turgidity and violence of style: *"He sometimes . . . in his rants, talked with Norman haughtiness of the Celtic barbarians"* (Macaulay). *Fustian* stresses a contrast between pretentious style in writing or speech and absurd or commonplace content: *"They flounder about between fustian in expression, and bathos in sentiment"* (William Hazlitt). *Claptrap* is insincere, empty speech or writing: *"I hate . . . that air/Of claptrap, which your recent poets prize"* (Byron). *Rodomontade* is boastful speech and bluster: *"a detestable compound of vulgarity and rodomontade"* (John Morley).

Bom·bay (bŏm-bā′). A city of west-central India on coastal **Bombay Island** and adjacent Salsette Island. It is India's main port and commercial center. Population, 8,243,405.

Bombay duck *n.* **1.** A small, edible lizardfish *(Harpodon nehereus)* of Asia, having a thin, nearly transparent body. **2.** The dried, salted flesh of this fish that is used in India as a relish, usually with curry. In this sense, also called *bummalo.* [Alteration of Marathi *bombīla, bombil.*]

bom·ba·zine (bŏm′bə-zēn′) *n.* A fine twilled fabric of silk and worsted or cotton, often dyed black and used for mourning clothes. [French *bombasin,* from Late Latin *bambacīnum,* cotton fabric, from *bombax,* cotton, from Latin *bombȳx,* silk, silkworm, from Greek *bombux,* silkworm.]

bomb bay *n.* The compartment in the fuselage of a combat aircraft into which bombs are loaded and from which they are dropped.

bombe (bŏm, bôɴb) *n.* A dessert consisting of two or more layers of variously flavored ice cream frozen in a round or melon-shaped mold. [French (from its shape). See BOMB.]

bombed (bŏmd) *adj. Slang.* Intoxicated; drunk.

♦**bomb·er** (bŏm′ər) *n.* **1.** A combat aircraft designed to carry and drop bombs. **2.** One who makes and sets off bombs. **3.** *Upstate New York & Illinois.* See **submarine** (sense 2). See Regional Note at **submarine.**

bomb·let (bŏm′lĭt) *n.* One of a number of small bombs usually contained in a cluster bomb and released in midair.

bomb·proof (bŏm′pro͞of′) *adj.* Designed and constructed to resist destruction by a bomb.

bomb rack *n.* A framework or mechanical holder for bombs on a combat aircraft.

bomb·shell (bŏm′shĕl′) *n.* **1.** An explosive bomb. **2.** A shocking surprise.

bomb·sight (bŏm′sīt′) *n.* A device in a combat aircraft for determining the point at which to drop a bomb in order to strike a target.

bom·by·cid (bŏm′bĭ-sĭd) *n.* A moth of the family Bombycidae, which includes the silkworms. [From New Latin *Bombycidae,* family name, from Latin *bombȳx,* silkworm. See BOMBAZINE.]

Bo·mu (bō′mo͞o). A river of central Africa rising in southeast Central African Republic and flowing about 805 km (500 mi) generally west along the boundary with Zaire to merge with the Uele and form the Ubangi River.

Bo·na (bō′nə), **Mount.** A peak, 5,032.5 m (16,500 ft) high, of southern Alaska at the southern end of the Wrangell Mountains near the Canadian border. It is the highest elevation in the range.

bo·na fide (bō′nə fīd′, fī′dē, bŏn′ə) *adj.* **1.** Made or carried out in good faith; sincere: *a bona fide offer.* **2.** Authentic; genuine: *a bona fide Rembrandt.* See Synonyms at **authentic.** [Latin *bonā fidē* : *bonā,* feminine ablative of *bonus,* good + *fidē,* ablative of *fidēs,* faith.]

bona fi·des (fī′dēz, fīdz) *n. (used with a pl. verb).* Information that serves to guarantee a person's good faith, standing, and reputation; authentic credentials: *"Sakharov's bona fides within the Soviet system . . . have given added weight to his message"* (Christian Science Monitor). [Latin *bona fidēs,* good faith : *bona,* feminine of *bonus,* good + *fidēs,* faith.]

Bo·naire (bô-nâr′). An island of the Netherlands Antilles in the Caribbean Sea off the northern coast of Venezuela.

Bo·nam·pak (bō-näm′päk). A ruined Mayan city near present-day Tuxtla Gutiérrez in southern Mexico. The ruins, with temples and well-preserved frescoes, were discovered in 1946.

bo·nan·za (bə-năn′zə) *n.* **1.** A rich mine, vein, or pocket of ore. **2.** A source of great wealth or prosperity. [Spanish, from Medieval Latin *bonacia,* calm sea, blend of Latin *bonus,* good; see **deu-²** in Appendix, and Medieval Latin *malacia,* calm sea (from Greek *malakia,* from *malakos,* soft; see **mel-¹** in Appendix).]

Bo·na·parte (bō′nə-pärt′). Corsican family, all brothers of Napoleon I, including **Joseph** (1768–1844), king of Naples (1806–1808) and Spain (1808–1813); **Lucien** (1775–1840), who disapproved of Napoleon's policies; **Louis** (1778–1846), who was king of Holland (1806–1810) and fought with Napoleon in Italy (1796–1797) and Egypt (1798–1799); and **Jérôme** (1784–1860), who was king of Westphalia (1807–1813), fought at Waterloo (1815), became marshal of France (1850), and was president of the senate under Napoleon III.

Bo·na·part·ist (bō′nə-pär′tĭst) *n.* A follower or supporter of Napoleon I and his policies and dynastic claims or of the Bonaparte family. —**Bo′na·part′ism** *n.*

Bon·a·ven·ture (bŏn′ə-vĕn′chər) also **Bon·a·ven·tu·ra** (bŏn′ə-vĕn-cho͝or′ə, -to͝or′ə, -tyo͝or′ə), Saint. Originally Giovanni di Fidanza. Known as "the Seraphic Doctor." 1217?–1274. Italian theologian and philosopher who taught that the goal of all the arts and sciences is the direct contemplation of God.

bon·bon (bŏn′bŏn′) *n.* A candy that often has a center of fondant, fruit, or nuts and is coated with chocolate or fondant. [French, reduplication of *bon,* good, from Latin *bonus.* See **deu-**[2] in Appendix.]

bon·bon·nière (bŏn′bŏn-yâr′) *n.* **1.** A small, ornate box or dish for candy. **2.** A confectioner's store. [French, from *bonbon.* See BONBON.]

bond (bŏnd) *n. Abbr.* **bd. 1.** Something, such as a fetter, cord, or band, that binds, ties, or fastens things together. **2.** Often **bonds.** Confinement in prison; captivity. **3.** A uniting force or tie; a link: *the bonds of friendship, the familial bond.* **4.** A binding agreement; a covenant. **5.** A duty, a promise, or another obligation by which one is bound. **6. a.** A substance or an agent that causes two or more objects or parts to cohere. **b.** The union or cohesion brought about by such a substance or agent. **7.** A chemical bond. **8.** An overlapping arrangement of bricks or other masonry components in a wall. **9.** *Law.* **a.** A written and sealed obligation, especially one requiring payment of a stipulated amount of money on or before a given day. **b.** A sum of money paid as bail or surety. **c.** A bail bondsman. **10.** A certificate of debt issued by a government or corporation guaranteeing payment of the original investment plus interest by a specified future date. **11.** The condition of taxable goods being stored in a warehouse until the taxes or duties owed on them are paid. **12.** An insurance contract in which an agency guarantees payment to an employer in the event of unforeseen financial loss through the actions of an employee. **13.** Bond paper. —**bond** *v.* **bond·ed, bond·ing, bonds.** —*tr.* **1.** To mortgage or place a guaranteed bond on. **2.** To furnish bond or surety for. **3.** To place (an employee, for example) under bond or guarantee. **4.** To join securely, as with glue or cement. **5.** To join (two or more individuals) in or as if in a nurturing relationship: *"What bonded* [the two men]*—who spoke rarely and have little personal rapport—was patience and a conviction that uncontrolled inflation endangers . . . society"* (Robert J. Samuelson). **6.** To lay (bricks, for example) in an overlapping pattern for solidity. —*intr.* **1.** To cohere with or as if with a bond. **2.** To form a close personal relationship. [Middle English, variant of *band,* from Old Norse. See **bhendh-** in Appendix.] —**bond′a·ble** *adj.* —**bond′er** *n.*

Bond (bŏnd), **Julian.** Born 1940. American politician and civil rights leader who was elected to the Georgia legislature (1966) but temporarily barred from taking office because of his opposition to the Vietnam War.

bond·age (bŏn′dĭj) *n.* **1.** The state of one who is bound as a slave or serf. See Synonyms at **servitude. 2.** A state of subjection to a force, a power, or an influence. **3.** The practice of being physically restrained, as with cords or handcuffs, as a means of attaining sexual gratification. **4.** Villeinage. [Middle English, from Anglo-Norman, from Middle English *bonde,* serf, from Old English *bōnda,* husbandman, from Old Norse *bōndi,* present participle of *būa,* to live. See **bheuə-** in Appendix.]

bond·hold·er (bŏnd′hōl′dər) *n.* One that owns a bond certificate of a government or corporation.

bond·ing (bŏn′dĭng) *n.* **1. a.** The formation of close, specialized human relationships, such as those that link spouse with spouse or friend with friend: *"He says he has rediscovered the comforts of male bonding in a Washington men's group"* (Marilyn Chase). **b.** The attachment process occurring between a parent and offspring that usually begins at the time of birth, is the basis for further emotional affiliation, and influences the child's physical and psychological development. **2.** *Dentistry.* A technique for the restoration, repair, or cosmetic improvement of a tooth that involves the application of a high-impact resinous material to the tooth surface, where it adheres to the existing enamel.

bond·maid (bŏnd′mād′) *n.* A woman bondservant. [BOND(WOMAN) + MAID.]

bond·man (bŏnd′mən) *n.* A male bondservant. [Middle English, from *bonde,* serf. See BONDAGE.]

bond paper *n.* A superior grade of strong white paper made wholly or in part from rag pulp.

bond·ser·vant (bŏnd′sûr′vənt) *n.* **1.** A person obligated to service without wages. **2.** A slave or serf. [BOND(MAN) + SERVANT.]

bonds·man (bŏndz′mən) *n.* **1.** A person who provides bond or surety for another. **2.** A male bondservant.

bond·wom·an (bŏnd′wo͝om′ən) *n.* A woman bondservant. [Middle English *bondewomman,* from *bonde,* serf. See BONDAGE.]

bone (bōn) *n.* **1. a.** The dense, semirigid, porous, calcified connective tissue forming the major portion of the skeleton of most vertebrates. It consists of a dense organic matrix and an inorganic, mineral component. **b.** Any of numerous anatomically distinct structures making up the skeleton of a vertebrate animal. There are more than 200 different bones in the human body. **c.** A piece of bone. **2. bones. a.** The skeleton. **b.** The body. **c.** Mortal remains. **3.** An animal structure or material, such as ivory, resembling bone. **4.** Something made of bone or of material resembling bone, especially: **a.** A piece of whalebone or similar material used as a corset stay. **b. bones.** *Informal.* Dice. **5. bones.** The fundamental plan or design, as of the plot of a book. **6. a. bones.** Flat clappers made of bone or wood originally used by the end man in a minstrel show. **b. Bones.** *(used with a sing. verb).* The end man in a minstrel show. —**bone** *v.* **boned, bon·ing, bones.** —*tr.* **1.** To remove the bones from. **2.** To stiffen (a piece of clothing) with stays, as of whalebone. —*intr. Informal.* To study intensely, usually at the last minute: *"He's boning up on the role of Tevya"* (Douglas Watt). —***idioms.*** **bone of contention.** The subject of a dispute. **bone to pick.** Grounds for a complaint or dispute. [Middle English *bon,* from Old English *bān.*]

bone ash *n.* The white, powdery calcium phosphate ash of burned bones, used as a fertilizer, in making ceramics, and in cleaning and polishing compounds.

bone·black also **bone black** (bōn′blăk′) *n.* A black pigment containing about 10 percent charcoal, made by roasting bones in an airtight container and used in polishes, as a filtering medium, and in decolorizing sugar. Also called *bone charcoal.*

bone china *n.* Porcelain made of clay mixed with bone ash.

bone conduction *n.* The process by which sound waves are transmitted to the inner ear by the cranial bones without traveling through the air in the ear canal.

bone-dry (bōn′drī′) *adj.* Having no trace of moisture.

bone·fish (bōn′fĭsh′) *n., pl.* **bonefish** or **-fish·es.** A marine game fish *(Albula vulpes)* of warm, shallow waters, having silvery scales. [From its many small bones.]

bone·head (bōn′hĕd′) *n. Informal.* A stupid person; a dunce. —**bone′head′ed** *adj.* —**bone′head′ed·ness** *n.*

bone marrow *n.* The soft, fatty, vascular tissue that fills most bone cavities and is the source of red blood cells and many white blood cells.

bone marrow transplant *n.* A technique used to enhance or restore a person's immune response or supply of blood cells or to replace diseased or destroyed bone marrow, as by radiation, with normally functioning bone marrow. The technique involves the removal of bone marrow from a donor's pelvic bone and intravenous administration of it to a patient.

bone meal *n.* A substance made of crushed and coarsely ground bones that is used as a plant fertilizer and in animal feed.

bon·er (bō′nər) *n. Informal.* A blunder or an error. [BONE(HEAD) + –ER[1].]

bone·set (bōn′sĕt′) *n.* Any of several plants of the genus *Eupatorium* in the composite family, especially the eastern North American species *E. perfoliatum,* having opposite leaves united around the stem and clusters of small, white flower heads. Also called *thoroughwort.* [From its use as a folk medicine.]

bone spavin *n.* A condition in horses caused by the deposition of new bone in the hock joint and sometimes producing lameness.

bon·ey (bō′nē) *adj.* Variant of **bony.**

bon·fire (bŏn′fīr′) *n.* A large outdoor fire. [Middle English *bonnefire* : *bon,* bone; see BONE + *fir,* fire; see FIRE.]

bong[1] (bŏng, bông) *n.* A deep ringing sound, as of a bell. —**bong** *v.* **bonged, bong·ing, bongs.** —*tr.* To cause to sound with a deep ringing noise. —*intr.* To make a deep ringing noise. [Imitative.]

bong[2] (bŏng, bông) *n.* A water pipe that consists of a bottle or a vertical tube partially filled with liquid and a smaller tube ending in a bowl, used often in smoking narcotic substances. [Thai *baung.*]

bon·go[1] (bŏng′gō, bông′-) *n.* **-gos.** A large, forest-dwelling antelope *(Boocercus eurycerus)* of central Africa, having a reddish-brown coat with white stripes and spirally twisted horns. [Probably of Bantu origin; akin to Lingala *mongu,* antelope.]

bon·go[2] (bŏng′gō, bông′-) *n., pl.* **-gos** or **-goes.** *Music.* One of a pair of connected tuned drums that are played by beating with the hands. [American Spanish *bongó.*]

Bon·heur (bô-nûr′, -nœr′), **Rosa.** 1822–1899. French artist known for her animal paintings, such as *The Horse Fair.*

bon·ho·mie (bŏn′ə-mē′) *n.* A pleasant and affable disposition; geniality. [French, from *bonhomme,* good-natured man : *bon,* good (from Latin *bonus;* see **deu-**[2] in Appendix) + *homme,* man (from Latin *homō;* see **dhghem-** in Appendix).]

bon·i·face (bŏn′ə-fəs, -fās′) *n.* The keeper of an inn, a hotel, a nightclub, or an eating establishment. [After *Boniface,* an innkeeper in *The Beaux' Strategem* by George Farquhar (1678–1707).]

Bon·i·face (bŏn′ə-fās′), Saint. Originally Winfrid or **Wynfrith.** 675?–754. English Roman Catholic missionary active in Germany.

Boniface VIII. Originally Benedetto Caetani. 1235?–1303. Pope (1294–1303) who struggled to assert authority over England, France, and Sicily.

bon·ing knife (bō′nĭng) *n.* A knife with a narrow blade and a sharp point, used for removing the bones from poultry, meat, and fish.

Bo·nin Islands (bō′nĭn). An archipelago of volcanic islands in the western Pacific Ocean south of Japan. The islands formed a major Japanese military stronghold in World War II.

bongo[1]
Boocercus eurycerus

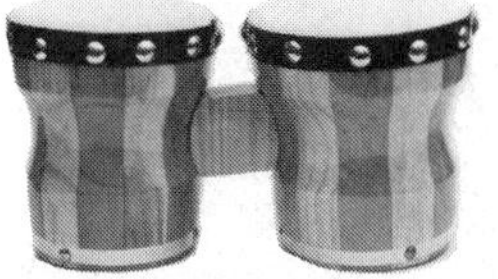

bongo[2]
Bongo drums

ă pat	oi boy
ā pay	ou out
âr care	o͝o took
ä father	o͞o boot
ĕ pet	ŭ cut
ē be	ûr urge
ĭ pit	th thin
ī pie	*th* this
îr pier	hw which
ŏ pot	zh vision
ō toe	ə about, item
ô paw	♦ regionalism

Stress marks: ′ (primary); ′ (secondary), as in **dictionary** (dĭk′shə-nĕr′ē)

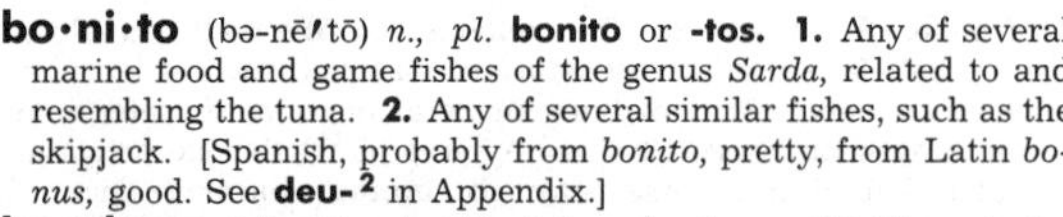

bo·ni·to (bə-nē′tō) *n., pl.* **bonito** or **-tos. 1.** Any of several marine food and game fishes of the genus *Sarda,* related to and resembling the tuna. **2.** Any of several similar fishes, such as the skipjack. [Spanish, probably from *bonito,* pretty, from Latin *bonus,* good. See **deu-**[2] in Appendix.]

bon·kers (bŏng′kərz) *adj. Informal.* Crazy: *"Yet here in the capital of the energy state, when word spread that free gas was to be found, the populace, as expected, went bonkers"* (Washington Post). [Origin unknown.]

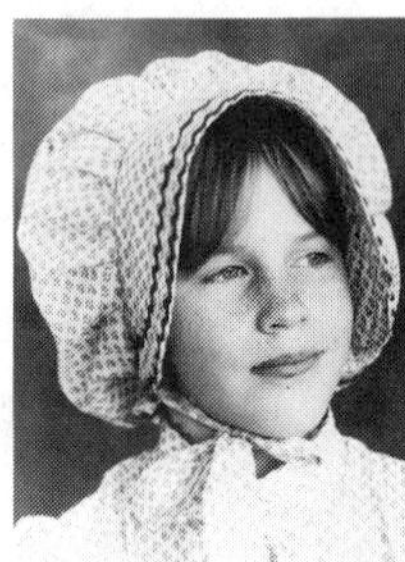

bonnet

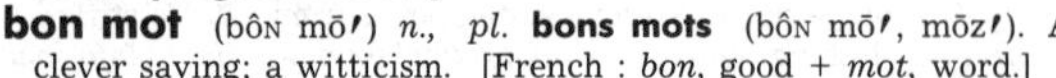

bon mot (bôɴ mō′) *n., pl.* **bons mots** (bôɴ mō′, mōz′). A clever saying; a witticism. [French : *bon,* good + *mot,* word.]

Bonn (bŏn, bôn). The former capital of West Germany, in the western part of the country on the Rhine River. It was founded as a Roman garrison in the first century A.D. and since 1990 has been the seat of the reunified German government. Population, 291,291.

Bon·nard (bô-när′), **Pierre.** 1867–1947. French painter who adhered to an impressionistic style in works such as *The Bath.*

bon·net (bŏn′ĭt) *n.* **1.a.** A hat of cloth or straw, held in place by ribbons tied under the chin, that is worn by women and children. **b.** *Scots.* A brimless cap worn by men. **2.** A removable metal plate over a machine part, such as a valve. **3.** *Chiefly British.* The hood of an automobile. **4.a.** A windscreen for a chimney. **b.** A cover for a fireplace. **5.** *Nautical.* A strip of canvas laced to a fore-and-aft sail to increase sail area. —**bonnet** *tr.v.* **-net·ed, -net·ing, -nets.** To put a bonnet on. [Middle English *bonet,* cap, from Old French, material for a headdress, perhaps from Medieval Latin *obbonis,* probably of Germanic origin.]

Bon·ne·ville Salt Flats (bŏn′ə-vĭl′). A plain of northwest Utah west of Great Salt Lake in the bed of prehistoric **Lake Bonneville.** The flats are often used for speed-test trials.

Bon·ney (bŏn′ē), **William H.** Known as "Billy the Kid." 1859–1881. American outlaw who murdered 21 men and was shot dead by Sheriff Pat Garrett (1850–1908).

bonsai

bon·ny also **bon·nie** (bŏn′ē) *adj.* **-ni·er, -ni·est.** *Scots.* **1.** Physically attractive or appealing; pretty. **2.** Excellent. [Origin unknown.] —**bon′ni·ly** *adv.* —**bon′ni·ness** *n.*

♦ **bon·ny·clab·ber** (bŏn′ē-klăb′ər) *n. New England & Central Atlantic U.S.* Thick, soured milk eaten with cream and sugar, honey, or molasses. [Irish Gaelic *bainne clabair* : *bainne,* milk (from Middle Irish, drop, milk, from Old Irish *bannae,* drop) + probably *clabair,* genitive of *clabar,* dasher of a churn.]

bon·sai (bŏn-sī′, bŏn′sī′, -zī′) *n., pl.* **bonsai. 1.** The art of growing dwarfed, ornamentally shaped trees or shrubs in small shallow pots or trays. **2.** A tree or shrub grown by this method. [Japanese, potted plant : *bon,* basin (from Chinese *pén*) + *sai,* to plant (from Chinese *zāi*).]

bons mots (bôɴ mō′, mōz′) *n.* Plural of **bon mot.**

bon·spiel (bŏn′spēl′) *n. Scots.* A curling tournament or match. [Probably Dutch *bonspel, league game : *bon,* league, perhaps from *bonne,* precinct of a city + *spel,* game, from Middle Dutch.]

bons vi·vants (bôɴ′ vē-väɴ′) *n.* Plural of **bon vivant.**

bon·te·bok (bŏn′tə-bŏk′) *n.* A rare South African antelope *(Damaliscus dorcas* or *D. pygargus)* having a dark reddish coat, a white rump, and a white mark on the face. [Afrikaans : *bont,* spotted (from Middle Dutch, probably from Latin *punctus;* see POINT) + *bok,* buck (from Middle Dutch *boc*).]

bontebok
Damaliscus dorcas

Bon·temps (bôɴ-täɴ′), **Arna Wendell.** 1902–1973. American writer whose works explore Black life and heritage.

bon ton (bŏn tŏn′) *n.* **1.a.** A sophisticated manner or style. **b.** The proper thing to do. **2.** High society. [French : *bon,* good + *ton,* tone.]

bo·nus (bō′nəs) *n., pl.* **-nus·es. 1.** Something given or paid in addition to what is usual or expected. **2.a.** A sum of money or the equivalent given to an employee in addition to the employee's usual compensation. **b.** A sum of money in addition to salary that is given to a professional athlete for signing up with a team. **3.** A subsidy from a government to an industry. **4.** A premium, as of stock, that is given by a corporation to another party, such as a purchaser of its securities. **5.** A sum of money that is paid by a corporation in excess of interest or royalties charged for the granting of a privilege or a loan to that corporation. [From Latin, good. See **deu-**[2] in Appendix.]

SYNONYMS: *bonus, bounty, subsidy, premium, prize, reward, gratuity.* Each of these nouns denotes a form of extra payment. *Bonus* usually applies to money in excess of what is normally received or strictly due, given especially in recognition of superior effort or achievement or as a share in profits: *Those who put in many hours of overtime will receive a percentage of their salary as a bonus.* A *bounty* is a sum of money offered by a government for the performance of a special service considered to be desirable: *The sheriff announced a bounty of 15 dollars for the pelt of every coyote killed. Subsidy* refers to a grant from a government in support of an enterprise regarded as being in the public interest: *The university will receive a subsidy for research in artificial intelligence.* A *premium* is generally something given as an incentive: *"Brown & Williamson . . . has been a pioneer in direct mail since it began offering premiums for coupons on its . . . packages"* (ADWEEK). A *prize* is awarded for superiority or victory, as in a contest or competition: *"Every compulsion is put upon writers to become safe, polite, obedient, and sterile. In protest . . . I must decline the Pulitzer Prize"* (Sinclair Lewis). *Reward* refers broadly to payment for a specific meritorious service: *A $10,000 reward*

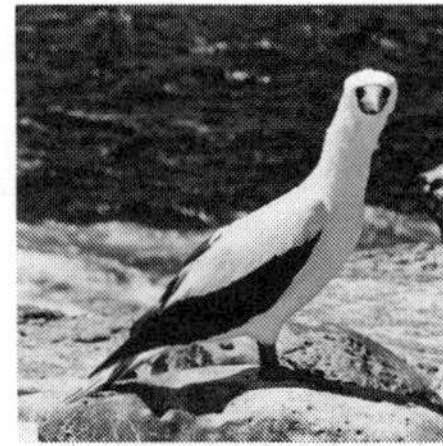

booby[1]

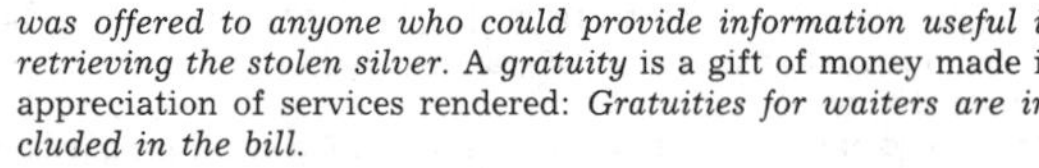

was offered to anyone who could provide information useful in retrieving the stolen silver. A *gratuity* is a gift of money made in appreciation of services rendered: *Gratuities for waiters are included in the bill.*

bonus issue *n.* See **scrip issue.**

bon vi·vant (bôɴ′ vē-väɴ′) *n., pl.* **bons vi·vants** (bôɴ′ vē-väɴ′). A person with refined taste, especially one who enjoys superb food and drink. [French : *bon,* good + *vivant,* present participle of *vivre,* to live.]

bon voy·age (bôɴ′ vwä-yäzh′) *interj.* Used to express farewell and good wishes to a departing traveler. [French : *bon,* good + *voyage,* journey.]

bon·y or **bon·ey** (bō′nē) *adj.* **-i·er, -i·est** or **-ey·er, -ey·est. 1.** Of, relating to, resembling, or consisting of bone. **2.** Having an internal skeleton of bones. **3.** Full of bones: *a bony fillet of fish.* **4.a.** Having prominent or protruding bones: *a bony wrist.* **b.** Lean; scrawny. —**bon′i·ness** *n.*

bony fish *n.* A fish having a bony rather than cartilaginous skeleton; a teleost.

bonze (bŏnz) *n.* A Buddhist monk, especially of China, Japan, or nearby countries. [French, from Portuguese *bonzo,* from Japanese *bonsō,* from Chinese *fán sēng* : *fán,* ordinary + *sēng,* monk.]

boo[1] (bo͞o) *n., pl.* **boos. 1.** A sound uttered to show contempt, scorn, or disapproval. **2.** *Informal.* Any sound or anything at all: *You never said boo to me about overtime.* —**boo** *interj.* Used to express contempt, scorn, or disapproval or to frighten or surprise another. —**boo** *v.* **booed, boo·ing, boos.** —*intr.* To utter a boo. —*tr.* To express contempt, scorn, or disapproval of by booing: *booed the singer off the stage.* [Imitative.]

boo[2] (bo͞o) *n. Slang.* Marijuana. [Origin unknown.]

boob[1] (bo͞ob) *n. Slang.* A stupid or foolish person; a dolt. [Short for BOOBY[1].]

boob[2] (bo͞ob) *n. Vulgar Slang.* A woman's breast. [Short for BOOBY[2].]

boob·oi·sie (bo͞ob′wä-zē′) *n.* A class of people regarded as stupid and gullible. [BOOB[1] + (BOURGE)OISIE.]

boo-boo also **boo·boo** (bo͞o′bo͞o) *n., pl.* **-boos.** *Informal.* **1.** A stupid mistake; a blunder: *"the petty talking points, peripheral issues, tactical boo-boos, and small-bore scandals that regularly intrude on campaigns"* (New Republic). **2.** A slight physical injury, such as a scratch. [Perhaps alteration of *boohoo,* to weep noisily.]

boob tube *n. Slang.* Television: *"Parents complain about the quality of the shows but don't prevent their children from gluing themselves to the boob tube"* (David Owen). [BOOB[1] + TUBE, television set.]

boo·by[1] (bo͞o′bē) *n., pl.* **-bies. 1.** A person regarded as stupid. **2.** Any of several tropical sea birds of the genus *Sula,* resembling and related to the gannets. [Probably Spanish *bobo,* from Latin *balbus,* stammering.]

boo·by[2] (bo͞o′bē) *n., pl.* **-bies.** *Vulgar Slang.* A woman's breast. [Perhaps alteration of obsolete English *bubby.*]

booby hatch *n.* **1.** *Nautical.* A raised covering over a small hatchway. **2.** *Slang.* A mental health facility.

booby prize *n.* **1.** *Sports & Games.* An award given to the one who scores lowest in a game or contest. **2.** *Informal.* Acknowledgment of great inferiority, as in ability.

booby trap *n.* **1.** A concealed, often explosive device that is triggered by an unsuspecting victim when a harmless-looking object is touched. **2.** A situation that catches one off guard; a pitfall. —**boo′by-trap′** (bo͞o′bē-trăp′) *v.*

♦ **boo·coo** (bo͞o′ko͞o′) *adj., n., & adv. Chiefly Southern U.S.* Variant of **beaucoup.**

boo·dle (bo͞od′l) *n. Slang.* **1.a.** Money, especially counterfeit money. **b.** Money accepted as a bribe. **2.** Stolen goods; swag. **3.** A crowd of people; caboodle. [Dutch *boedel,* estate, from Middle Dutch *bōdel.* See **bheuə-** in Appendix.]

boog·er (bo͝og′ər) *n.* **1.** A bogeyman. **2.** *Slang.* Dried nasal mucus. **3.** *Slang.* An item that is unnamed or unnameable: *"It's . . . like a pop-top . . . one of those sharp little boogers you pull off the beer cans"* (Hunter S. Thompson). **4.** *Slang.* **a.** A worthless, despicable person. **b.** A person; a fellow. [Origin unknown.]

boog·ey·man (bo͝og′ē-măn′, bō′gē-, bo͞o′gē-) *n.* Variant of **bogeyman.**

boog·ie (bo͝og′ē, bo͞o′gē) *Slang. intr.v.* **-ied, -y·ing, -ies.** To dance to the sound of rock music. —**boogie** *n.* **1.** Strongly rhythmic rock music. **2.** Boogie-woogie. [From BOOGIE-WOOGIE.]

boog·ie·man (bo͝og′ē-măn′, bō′gē-, bo͞o′gē-) *n.* Variant of **bogeyman.**

boog·ie-woog·ie (bo͝og′ē-wo͝og′ē, bo͞o′gē-wo͞o′gē) *n. Music.* A style of jazz piano characterized by a repeated rhythmic and melodic pattern in the bass and a series of improvised variations in the treble. [Possibly from Black West African English (Sierra Leone) *bogi(-bogi),* to dance; possibly akin to Hausa *buga,* to beat drums.]

boog·y·man (bo͝og′ē-măn′, bō′gē-, bo͞o′gē-) *n.* Variant of **bogeyman.**

boo·jum tree (bo͞o′jəm) *n.* A deciduous tree *(Idria columnaris),* native to Baja California and having a thick, tapering, columnar trunk, slender spiny branches, and yellow flowers. [After the *boojum,* an imaginary character in the poem *The Hunting of the Snark* by Lewis Carroll.]

book (bo͝ok) *n. Abbr.* **bk., b. 1.** A set of written, printed, or blank pages fastened along one side and encased between protective covers. **2.a.** A printed or written literary work. **b.** A main division of a larger printed or written work: *a book of the Old Testament.* **3.a.** A volume in which financial or business transactions are recorded. **b. books.** Financial or business records considered as a group: *checked the expenditures on the books.* **4.a.** A libretto. **b.** The script of a play. **5. Book.** The Bible. **6.a.** A set of prescribed standards or rules on which decisions are based: *runs the company by the book.* **b.** Something regarded as a source of knowledge or understanding. **c.** The total amount of experience, knowledge, understanding, and skill that can be used in solving a problem or performing a task: *We used every trick in the book to finish the project on schedule.* **7.** A packet of like or similar items bound together: *a book of matches.* **8.** A record of bets placed on a race. **9.** *Games.* The number of card tricks needed before any tricks can have scoring value, as the first six tricks taken by the declaring side in bridge. —*attributive.* Often used to modify another noun: *a book report; book learning.* **—book** *tr.v.* **booked, book·ing, books. 1.** To list or register in or as if in a book. **2.** To record charges against (a person) on a police blotter. **3.** To arrange for (tickets or lodgings, for example) in advance; reserve. **4.** To hire or engage: *The manager booked a magic show for Saturday night.* **5.** To allocate time for. ***—idioms.* bring to book.** To demand an explanation from; call to account. **in one's book.** In one's opinion: *In my book they both are wrong.* **like a book.** Thoroughly; completely: *I know my child like a book.* **one for the books.** A noteworthy act or occurrence. **throw the book at. 1.** To make all possible charges against (a lawbreaker, for example). **2.** To reprimand or punish severely. [Middle English *bok,* from Old English *bōc.* See **bhāgo-** in Appendix.] **—book′er** *n.*

SYNONYMS: *book, bespeak, engage, reserve.* The central meaning shared by these verbs is "to cause something to be set aside, as for one's use or possession, in advance": *will book a hotel room; bespoken merchandise; engaged a box for the opera season; reserving a table at a restaurant.*

book·bind·er·y (bo͝ok′bīn′də-rē) *n.* An establishment where books are bound.

book·bind·ing (bo͝ok′bīn′dĭng) *n.* The art, trade, or profession of binding books. **—book′bind′er** *n.*

book·case (bo͝ok′kās′) *n.* A piece of furniture with shelves for holding books.

book club *n.* A commercial organization that sells books to its members on a regular, usually monthly, basis and typically at a discount.

book·end (bo͝ok′ĕnd′) *n.* A prop placed at the end of a row of books to keep them upright.

book·ie (bo͝ok′ē) *n.* See **bookmaker** (sense 2).

book·ing (bo͝ok′ĭng) *n.* **1.** An engagement, as for a performance by an entertainer. **2.** A reservation, as for accommodations at a hotel.

book·ish (bo͝ok′ĭsh) *adj.* **1.** Of, relating to, or resembling a book. **2.** Fond of books; studious. **3.** Relying chiefly on book learning: *took a bookish rather than a pragmatic approach in solving the problem.* **4.** Pedantic; dull. See Synonyms at **pedantic. 5.** Literary and formal in tone. Used of words. **—book′ish·ly** *adv.* **—book′ish·ness** *n.*

book·keep·ing (bo͝ok′kē′pĭng) *n. Abbr.* **bkpg.** The practice or profession of recording the accounts and transactions of a business. **—book′keep′er** *n.*

book·let (bo͝ok′lĭt) *n.* A small bound book or pamphlet, usually having a paper cover.

book·lore (bo͝ok′lôr′, -lōr′) *n.* Knowledge gained from books.

book·louse or **book louse** (bo͝ok′lous′) *n.* Any of various small, often wingless insects of the order Psocoptera (or Corrodentia), some species of which feed on stored flour products, paper, or bookbindings.

book lung *n.* A sacculate respiratory organ found in some arachnids, such as scorpions and spiders, consisting of several parallel membranous folds arranged like the pages in a book.

book·mak·er (bo͝ok′mā′kər) *n.* **1.** One that edits, prints, publishes, or binds books. **2.** One who accepts and pays off bets, as on a horserace. In this sense, also called *bookie.* **—book′mak′ing** *n.*

book·mark (bo͝ok′märk′) *n.* A strip of material, as of ribbon or leather, or a metal clamp, that is placed between the pages of a book to mark the reader's place.

book·mo·bile (bo͝ok′mō-bēl′) *n.* A truck, trailer, or van equipped to serve as a mobile lending library. [BOOK + (AUTO)MOBILE.]

Book of Common Prayer *n.* The book of services and prayers used in the Anglican Church.

♦**boo·koo** (bo͞o′ko͞o′) *adj., n., & adv. Chiefly Southern U.S.* Variant of **beaucoup.**

book·plate (bo͝ok′plāt′) *n.* A label bearing the owner's name or other identification that is pasted usually on the inside cover of a book. Also called *ex libris.*

book·rack (bo͝ok′răk′) *n.* **1.** A small rack for books. **2.** A rack for supporting an open book.

book·sell·er (bo͝ok′sĕl′ər) *n.* One that sells books, especially the owner of a bookstore.

book·shelf (bo͝ok′shĕlf′) *n.* A shelf or set of shelves for holding books.

book·shop (bo͝ok′shŏp′) *n.* A bookstore.

book·stall (bo͝ok′stôl′) *n.* A stall where books are sold, as on a street.

book·stand (bo͝ok′stănd′) *n.* **1.** A small counter where books are sold. **2.** A bookrack.

book·store (bo͝ok′stôr′, -stōr′) *n.* A store where books are sold.

book value *n.* The monetary amount by which an asset is valued in business records, a figure not necessarily identical to the amount the asset could bring on the open market.

book·worm (bo͝ok′wûrm′) *n.* **1.** One who spends much time reading or studying. **2.** Any of various insects, especially booklice and silverfish, that infest books and feed on the paste in the bindings.

Boole (bo͞ol), **George.** 1815–1864. British mathematician and logician who developed a calculus of symbolic logic.

Bool·e·an (bo͞o′lē-ən) *adj.* Of or relating to a logical combinatorial system treating variables, such as propositions and computer logic elements, through the operators AND, OR, NOT, IF, THEN, and EXCEPT: *information retrieval involving Boolean searching.* [After George BOOLE.]

Boolean algebra *n.* An algebraic system with two binary operations and an identity element that is used in symbolic logic and in logic circuits in computer science.

boom¹ (bo͞om) *v.* **boomed, boom·ing, booms.** —*intr.* **1.** To make a deep, resonant sound. **2.** To grow or develop rapidly; flourish: *Business is booming.* —*tr.* **1.** To utter or give forth with a deep, resonant sound: *a field commander booming out orders.* **2.** To cause to grow or flourish; boost. **—boom** *n.* **1.** A deep resonant sound, as of an explosion. **2.** A time of economic prosperity. **3.** A sudden increase, as in popularity. [Middle English *bomben,* imitative of a loud noise.]

boom² (bo͞om) *n.* **1.** *Nautical.* A long spar extending from a mast to hold or extend the foot of a sail. **2.** A long pole extending upward at an angle from the mast of a derrick to support or guide objects lifted or suspended. **3.a.** A barrier composed of a chain of floating logs enclosing other free-floating logs, typically used to catch floating debris or to obstruct passage. **b.** A floating barrier serving to contain an oil spill. **4.** A long movable arm used to maneuver and support a microphone. **5.a.** A spar that connects the tail surfaces and the main structure of an airplane. **b.** A long hollow tube attached to a tanker aircraft, through which fuel flows to another aircraft being refueled in flight. [Dutch, tree, pole, from Middle Dutch. See **bheuə-** in Appendix.]

boom box *n. Slang.* A portable audio system, usually consisting of a cassette player and radio, with speakers capable of producing loud sound: *"The notorious boom box . . . is no longer just a street noisemaker: in its latest refinement it has built-in CD players and speakers able to handle digital sound"* (Hans Fantel).

boom·er (bo͞o′mər) *n.* **1.** *Informal.* A nuclear submarine armed with ballistic missiles. **2.** *Informal.* A baby boomer. **3.** A transient worker, especially in bridge construction. **4.** *Australian.* A large, fully grown male kangaroo.

boo·mer·ang (bo͞o′mə-răng′) *n.* **1.** A flat, curved, usually wooden missile configured so that when hurled it returns to the thrower. **2.** A statement or course of action that backfires. **—boomerang** *intr.v.* **-anged, -ang·ing, -angs.** To have the opposite effect from the one intended; backfire. [Dharuk (Aboriginal language of southeast Australia) *bumarin^y.*]

WORD HISTORY: The words we have borrowed from native languages of Australia, such as *billabong, budgerigar, dingo, kangaroo, koala, kookaburra, waddy,* and *wallaby,* generally have the exotic sound of down under, and *boomerang* is no exception. In a book about the languages of New South Wales published in 1790 is found the native term *boo-mer-rit,* glossed "the scimitar," because of the curved shape of the boomerang. In 1825 in a passage containing the first recorded instance of the English form *boomerang* we are told it is "a short crested weapon which the natives of Port Jackson [now part of Sydney] project with accurate aim into a rotary motion." In 1827 another commentator says that this term "may be retained for want of a more descriptive name."

boom·let (bo͞om′lĭt) *n.* A small boom, as in business, politics, or the birth rate.

boom·town (bo͞om′toun′) *n.* A town experiencing an economic or a population boom.

boom·y (bo͞o′mē) *adj.* **-i·er, -i·est. 1.** Of, relating to, characterized by, or resulting from a flourishing economy: *"Things aren't as boomy as forecasters thought they would be"* (U.S. News & World Report). **2.** *Acoustics.* Exhibiting excessive accentuation on lower-pitched tones in reproduced sound: *"This mode of bass reinforcement by resonance often causes boomy obfuscation of the true musical pitch—something akin to singing into a barrel"* (New York Times).

boon¹ (bo͞on) *n.* **1.** A benefit bestowed, especially one bestowed in response to a request. **2.** A timely blessing or benefit: *A spank-*

boojum tree
Idria columnaris

ă pat	oi boy
ā pay	ou out
âr care	o͝o took
ä father	o͞o boot
ĕ pet	ŭ cut
ē be	ûr urge
ĭ pit	th thin
ī pie	*th* this
îr pier	hw which
ŏ pot	zh vision
ō toe	ə about, item
ô paw	♦ regionalism

Stress marks: ′ (primary); ′ (secondary), as in **dictionary** (dĭk′shə-nĕr′ē)

ing breeze is a boon to sailors. [Middle English *bone,* from Old Norse *bōn,* prayer. See **bhā-[2]** in Appendix.]

boon[2] (bo͞on) *adj.* **1.** Convivial; jolly: *a boon companion to all.* **2.** *Archaic.* Favorable. [Middle English *bon,* good, from Old French, from Latin *bonus.* See **deu-[2]** in Appendix.]

boon·docks (bo͞on′dŏks′) *pl.n. Slang.* **1.** Wild and dense brush; jungle. **2.** Rural country; the backwoods. [From Tagalog *bundok,* mountain.]

boon·dog·gle (bo͞on′dô′gəl, -dŏg′əl) *Informal. n.* Unnecessary, wasteful, and often counterproductive work. **—boondoggle** *intr.v.* **-gled, -gling, -gles.** To waste time or money on unnecessary and often counterproductive work. [From *boondoggle,* a plaited leather cord worn by Boy Scouts (coined by R.H. Link, 20th-century American scoutmaster).] **—boon′dog′gler** *n.*

Boone (bo͞on), **Daniel.** 1734–1820. American frontiersman, folk hero, and central figure in the settlement of Kentucky.

boon·ies (bo͞o′nēz) *pl.n. Slang.* Rural country or a jungle. [Shortening and alteration of BOONDOCKS.]

boor (bo͝or) *n.* **1.** A person with rude, clumsy manners and little refinement. **2.** A peasant. [Dutch *boer,* from Middle Dutch *ghe-boer.* See **bheuə-** in Appendix.]

SYNONYMS: *boor, barbarian, churl, lout, vulgarian, yahoo.* The central meaning shared by these nouns is "an uncouth and uncultivated person": *tourists acting like boors; a barbarian on the loose in a museum; consideration wasted on a churl; is both a lout and a bully; married a parvenu vulgarian; a yahoo and a blowhard.*

Daniel Boone

boor·ish (bo͝or′ĭsh) *adj.* Resembling or characteristic of a boor; rude and clumsy in behavior. **—boor′ish·ly** *adv.* **—boor′ish·ness** *n.*

boost (bo͞ost) *v.* **boost·ed, boost·ing, boosts.** *—tr.* **1.** To raise or lift by pushing up from behind or below. See Synonyms at **lift. 2.a.** To increase; raise: *boost prices; efforts to boost participation in the program.* **b.** To assist in further development or progress: *a bill intended to boost local charities.* **3.** To stir up enthusiasm for; promote vigorously: *boosted their school with rallies and fund drives.* **4.** *Electricity.* To increase the voltage of (a circuit). **5.** *Slang.* To shoplift. *—intr. Slang.* To engage in shoplifting. **—boost** *n.* **1.** A push upward or ahead. **2.** An increase: *a big boost in salary.* [Perhaps from dialectal *boostering,* bustling, active.]

boost·er (bo͞o′stər) *n.* **1.** One that boosts, as: **a.** A device for increasing power or effectiveness. **b.** An enthusiastic promoter, as of a sports team or school. **c.** *Electronics.* A radio-frequency amplifier. **d.** The primary stage of a multistage rocket that provides the main thrust for launch, liftoff, and initial flight. **2.** A booster shot. **3.** *Slang.* One who steals goods on display in a store.

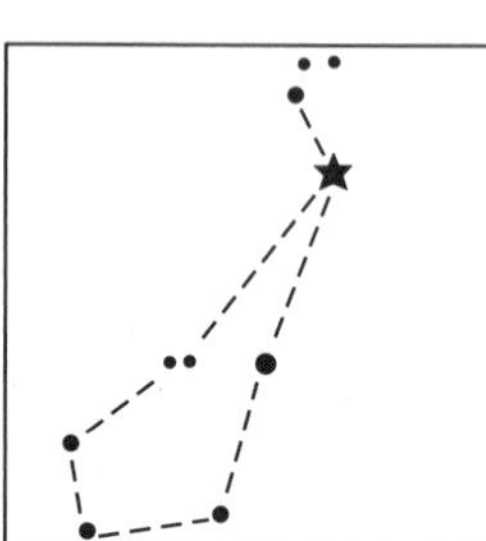
Boötes

booster cable *n.* An electric cable used to connect a discharged battery to a power source for charging. Also called *jumper cable.*

booster dose *n.* See **booster shot.**

boost·er·ish (bo͞o′stər-ĭsh) *adj.* Highly supportive, as of a product, project, or cause.

boost·er·ism (bo͞o′stə-rĭz′əm) *n.* The highly supportive attitudes and activities of boosters: *"the civic pride and heady boosterism that often accompany rising property values"* (New York).

booster seat *n.* **1.** A car seat for small children that lifts the child by several inches, designed for use with an adult seat belt. **2.** A seat placed on top of the seat of a chair, used to elevate a small child at a table.

booster shot *n.* An additional dose of an immunizing agent, such as a vaccine or toxoid, given at a time after the initial dose to sustain the immune response elicited by the previous dose of the same agent. Also called *booster dose.*

boost phase *n.* The period during which the rockets of a ballistic missile operate to bring it near or to peak velocity.

boot[1] (bo͞ot) *n.* **1.** Protective footgear, as of leather or rubber, covering the foot and part or all of the leg. **2.** A protective covering, especially a sheath to enclose the base of a floor-mounted gear shift lever in a car or truck. **3.** *Chiefly British.* An automobile trunk. **4.a.** A kick. **b.** *Slang.* An unceremonious dismissal, as from a job. **c.** *Slang.* A swift, pleasurable feeling; a thrill. **5.** A Denver boot. **6.** A marine or navy recruit in basic training. **7. boots.** An instrument of torture, used to crush the foot and leg. **—boot** *tr.v.* **boot·ed, boot·ing, boots. 1.** To put boots on. **2.** To kick. **3.** *Slang.* To discharge unceremoniously. See Synonyms at **dismiss. 4.** *Computer Science.* To enter (a program) into a computer using a few initial instructions. **5.** To disable (a vehicle) by attaching a Denver boot. [Middle English *bote,* from Old French.]

John Wilkes Booth
Photographed c. 1862

♦**boot[2]** (bo͞ot) *intr.v.* **boot·ed, boot·ing, boots.** To be of help or advantage; avail. **—boot** *n.* **1.** *Chiefly Southern U.S.* See **lagniappe. 2.** *Archaic.* Advantage; avail. ***—idiom.* to boot.** In addition; besides. [Middle English *boten,* to be of help, from Old English *bōtian,* from *bōt,* help. See **bhad-** in Appendix.]

boot·black (bo͞ot′blăk′) *n.* A person who cleans and polishes shoes for a living.

boot camp *n.* A training camp for military recruits.

boot·ed (bo͞o′tĭd) *adj.* Wearing boots.

boo·tee also **boo·tie** (bo͞o′tē) *n.* **1.** A soft, usually knitted shoe for a baby. **2.** An ankle-length disposable foot covering, used by medical personnel and others in sterile environments.

Bo·ö·tes (bō-ō′tēz) *n.* A constellation in the Northern Hemisphere near Virgo and Canes Venatici, containing the bright star Arcturus. Boötes is one of the earliest recorded constellations. [Latin *Boōtēs,* from Greek *boōtēs,* plowman, Boötes, from *boōtein,* to plow, from *bous,* ox. See **gʷou-** in Appendix.]

booth (bo͞oth) *n., pl.* **booths** (bo͞othz, bo͞oths). **1.a.** A small, often enclosed compartment, usually accommodating only one person: *a voting booth; a projection booth.* **b.** A small enclosed compartment with a window, used to separate the occupant from others: *a ticket booth.* **2.** A seating area in a restaurant that has a table and seats whose high backs serve as partitions. **3.** A small stall or stand for the display and sale of goods. [Middle English *bothe,* of Scandinavian origin. See **bheuə-** in Appendix.]

Booth[1] (bo͞oth). Family of actors, including **Junius Brutus** (1796–1852), a British-born Shakespearean actor who in 1821 immigrated to the United States, and his sons **Edwin Thomas** (1833–1893), noted for his portrayal of Hamlet, and **John Wilkes** (1838–1865), the assassin of President Abraham Lincoln.

Booth[2] (bo͞oth). Family of reformers, including **William** (1829–1912), a British religious leader who founded the Salvation Army (1878) with his wife, **Catherine Mumford Booth** (1829–1890), and served as its first general (1896–1912). His children **William Bramwell** (1856–1929); **Ballington** (1857–1940), who with his wife, **Maud Ballington Booth** (1865–1948), founded the Volunteers of America (1896); and **Evangeline Cory** (1865–1950) were active in the Salvation Army.

Boo·thi·a Peninsula (bo͞o′thē-ə). The northernmost tip of the North American mainland, in northeast Northwest Territories, Canada. It is connected with the Canadian mainland by the narrow **Isthmus of Boothia** and separated from Baffin Island to the east by the **Gulf of Boothia,** an arm of the Arctic Ocean.

boo·tie (bo͞o′tē) *n.* Variant of **bootee.**

boot·jack (bo͞ot′jăk′) *n.* A forked device for holding a boot secure while the foot is being withdrawn.

boot·leg (bo͞ot′lĕg′) *v.* **-legged, -leg·ging, -legs.** *—tr.* **1.** To make, sell, or transport (alcoholic liquor) for sale illegally. **2.** To produce, distribute, or sell without permission or illegally: *a clandestine outfit that bootlegs record albums and tapes.* *—intr.* **1.** To engage in the bootlegging of alcoholic liquor or another product. **2.** To attach a transmitter to a dish antenna, creating an uplink via which a signal is sent to a satellite without the knowledge of the satellite's owner. **3.** *Football.* To fake a hand-off, conceal the ball on the hip, and roll out in order to pass or especially to rush around the end. Used of a quarterback. **—bootleg** *n.* **1.** A product, especially alcoholic liquor, that is illicitly produced, distributed, or sold. **2.** The part of a boot above the instep. **3.** *Football.* A play in which the quarterback bootlegs. **—bootleg** *adj.* Produced, sold, or transported illegally: *bootleg gin; bootleg tapes.* [From a smuggler's practice of carrying liquor in the legs of boots.] **—boot′leg′ger** *n.*

boot·less (bo͞ot′lĭs) *adj.* Without advantage or benefit; useless. See Synonyms at **futile.** [BOOT[2] + -LESS.] **—boot′less·ly** *adv.* **—boot′less·ness** *n.*

boot·lick (bo͞ot′lĭk′) *v.* **-licked, -lick·ing, -licks.** *—tr.* To behave toward in a servile or obsequious manner. *—intr.* To behave in a servile or obsequious manner. See Synonyms at **fawn[1]. —boot′lick′er** *n.*

boot·strap (bo͞ot′străp′) *n.* **1.** A loop of leather, cloth, or synthetic material that is sewn at the side or the top rear of a boot to help in pulling the boot on. **2.** *Computer Science.* A subroutine used to establish the full routine or another routine. **—bootstrap** *tr.v.* **-strapped, -strap·ping, -straps. 1.** To promote and develop by use of one's own initiative and work without reliance on outside help: *"We've bootstrapped our way back with aggressive tourism and recruiting high tech industries"* (John Corrigan). **2.** *Computer Science.* To establish (a program) with a bootstrap. **—bootstrap** *adj.* **1.** Undertaken or accomplished with minimal outside resources or help. **2.** *Computer Science.* Being or relating to a process that is self-initiating or self-sustaining. ***—idiom.* by one's (own) bootstraps.** By one's own efforts.

bootstrap loader *n.* *Computer Science.* A short program that loads other loaders in a computer.

bootstrap memory *n.* *Computer Science.* A memory that allows new programs to be entered without erasing instructions already in the computer.

boo·ty (bo͞o′tē) *n., pl.* **-ties. 1.** Plunder taken from an enemy in time of war. **2.** Goods or property seized by force or piracy. **3.** A valuable prize, award, or gain. [Middle English *botye* (influenced by *bote,* advantage; see BOOT[2]), probably from Middle Low German *būte,* exchange.]

booze (bo͞oz) *Slang. n.* **1.a.** Hard liquor. **b.** An alcoholic beverage. **2.** A drinking spree. **—booze** *intr.v.* **boozed, booz·ing, booz·es.** To drink alcoholic beverages excessively or chronically. [Alteration of obsolete *bouse,* liquor, drinking bout, from Middle English *bousen,* to drink to excess, from Middle Dutch *būsen.*] **—booz′er** *n.* **—booz′y** *adj.*

booze·hound (bo͞oz′hound′) *n. Slang.* A very heavy drinker: *"All old . . . boozehounds are alike, aren't they?"* (Jimmy Breslin).

bop[1] (bŏp) *Informal. tr.v.* **bopped, bop·ping, bops.** To hit or strike. **—bop** *n.* A blow; a punch. [Imitative.]

bop[2] (bŏp) *n. Music.* A style of jazz characterized by rhythmic and harmonic complexity, improvised solos, and a brilliant style of execution. **—bop** *intr.v.* **bopped, bop·ping, bops. 1.** To dance or move to the beat of this music. **2.** *Slang.* To go: *bopped off to the movies.* [Short for BEBOP.] **—bop′per** *n.*

Bo·phu·tha·tswa·na (bō′po͞o-tät-swä′nə). An autonomous Black homeland within South Africa. It was granted nominal independence in December 1977. Mmabatho is the capital. Population, 1,347,000.

Bopp (bŏp), **Franz.** 1791–1867. German philologist whose *Comparative Grammar* (1833–1852) illustrated the similarities among Indo-European languages.

bop·pish (bŏp′ĭsh) *n. Music.* In the style of bop: *"a spirited boppish essay, full of harmonic twists and darting single-note runs"* (Washington Post).

BOQ *abbr.* Bachelor Officers' Quarters.

bor. *abbr.* Borough.

bor– *pref.* Variant of **boro–.**

bo·ra (bôr′ə, bōr′ə) *n.* A violent, cold, northeasterly winter wind on the Adriatic Sea. [Italian dialectal, from Latin *Boreās,* Boreas. See BOREAS.]

Bo·ra Bo·ra (bôr′ə bôr′ə, bōr′ə bōr′ə). A volcanic island of French Polynesia in the Leeward group of the Society Islands in the southern Pacific Ocean.

bo·rac·ic (bə-răs′ĭk) *adj.* Variant of **boric.** [From Medieval Latin *borāx, borāc-,* borax. See BORAX[1].]

bor·age (bôr′ĭj, bŏr′-) *n.* An annual, bristly European herb *(Borago officinalis)* having blue or puplish star-shaped flowers. [Middle English, from Old French *bourage,* from Medieval Latin *borāgō,* probably from Arabic *bū'araq,* from *abū'araq,* father of sweat (from its use as a sudorific).]

Bo·rah (bôr′ə, bōr′ə), **William Edgar.** 1865–1940. American politician. A Republican U.S. senator from Idaho (1907–1940), he was noted for his independent opinions.

bo·rane (bôr′ān′, bōr′-) *n.* Any of a series of boron-hydrogen compounds or a substance such as BCL that may be considered a derivative of such a compound.

Bo·rås (bo͞o-rôs′). A city of southwest Sweden east of Göteborg. It was founded in 1632. Population, 99,945.

bo·rate (bôr′āt′, bōr′-) *n.* A salt or an ester of boric acid.

bo·rax[1] (bôr′ăks′, -əks, bōr′-) *n.* **1.** A hydrated sodium borate, $Na_2B_4O_7 \cdot 10H_2O$, an ore of boron, that is used as a cleaning compound. **2.** An anhydrous sodium borate used in the manufacture of glass and various ceramics. [Middle English, from Medieval Latin, from Arabic *būraq,* from Middle Persian *būrak.*]

bo·rax[2] (bôr′ăks′, bōr′-) *n.* Cheap merchandise, especially tasteless furnishings: *"today's glinty borax"* (New Yorker). [Perhaps from the custom of giving away borax soap as a premium for the sale of cheap furniture.]

Bo·ra·zon (bôr′ə-zŏn′, bōr′-). A trademark used for an abrasive of boron nitride granules.

bor·bo·ryg·mus (bôr′bə-rĭg′məs) *n., pl.* **-mi** (-mī′). A rumbling noise produced by the movement of gas through the intestines. [New Latin, from Greek *borborugmos,* of imitative origin.]

Bor·deaux[1] (bôr-dō′). A city of southwest France on the Garonne River. It was under English rule from 1154 to 1453 and was the seat of the French government in 1914 and again in 1940. Bordeaux is the trading center of a notable wine-producing region. Population, 208,159.

Bor·deaux[2] (bôr-dō′) *n., pl.* **Bor·deaux** (bôr-dō′, -dōz′). A red or white wine originally produced in the region around Bordeaux, France.

Bordeaux mixture *n.* A mixture of copper sulfate, lime, and water that is sprayed as a fungicide on trees and plants. [Translation of French *bouillie bordelaise* : *bouillie,* gruel, mixture + *bordelaise,* of Bordeaux.]

bor·del·lo (bôr-dĕl′ō) *n., pl.* **-los.** A house of prostitution. [Italian, from Old French *bordel,* from *borde,* wooden hut, of Germanic origin.]

Bor·den (bôr′dn), **Gail.** 1801–1874. American surveyor and inventor who developed condensed milk (1853) and other food products.

Borden, Lizzie Andrew. 1860–1927. American woman accused and acquitted of the ax murder of her parents (1892).

Borden, Sir **Robert Laird.** 1854–1937. Canadian prime minister (1911–1920) during World War I.

bor·der (bôr′dər) *n.* **1.** A part that forms the outer edge of something. **2.** A decorative strip around the edge of something, such as fabric. **3.** A strip of ground, as at the edge of a garden or walk, in which ornamental plants or shrubs are planted. **4.** The line or frontier area separating political divisions or geographic regions; a boundary. **—border** *v.* **-dered, -der·ing, -ders.** *—tr.* **1.** To put a border on. **2.** To lie along or adjacent to the border of: *Canada borders the United States.* *—intr.* **1.** To lie adjacent to another: *The United States borders on Canada.* **2.** To be almost like another in character: *an act that borders on heroism.* [Middle English *bordure,* from Old French *bordeure,* from *border,* to border, from *bort,* border, of Germanic origin.] **—bor′der·er** *n.*

SYNONYMS: *border, margin, edge, verge, brink, rim, brim.* All these nouns refer to the line or narrow area that marks the outside limit of something such as a surface. *Border* refers either to the boundary line (*erected a fence along the border of the property*) or to the area that is immediately inside the boundary (*a picture frame with a wide border*). *Margin* is a border of more or less precisely definable width that is often distinguishable in other respects from the rest of the surface: *a boathouse near the margin of the pond; the margin of a little clearing in the forest. Edge* refers specifically to the precise bounding line formed by the continuous convergence of two surfaces: *sat on the edge of the chair. Verge* is an extreme terminating line or edge (*the sun's afterglow on the verge of the horizon*); figuratively it indicates a point at which something is likely to begin or to happen (*an explorer on the verge of a great discovery*). *Brink* denotes the edge of a steep place (*stood on the brink of the cliff*); in an extended sense it indicates the likelihood or imminence of a sudden change (*on the brink of falling in love*). *Rim* most often denotes the edge of something, such as a wheel, that is circular or curved: *a crack in the rim of the lens. Brim* applies to the upper edge or inner side of the rim of a container, such as a cup, or of something shaped like a basin: *lava issuing from the brim of the crater.* See also Synonyms at **boundary.**

Bor·der collie (bôr′dər) *n.* A British sheepdog that has a wavy, usually black coat with white markings and is used for herding. [From the border country of England and Scotland where it was first bred.]

bor·der·land (bôr′dər-lănd′) *n.* **1.a.** Land located on or near a frontier. **b.** The fringe: *a shadowy figure who lived on the borderland of the drug scene.* **2.** An indeterminate area, situation, or condition: *the borderland between sanity and insanity.*

bor·der·line (bôr′dər-līn′) *n.* **1.** A line that establishes or marks a border. **2.** An indefinite area intermediate between two qualities or conditions: *The borderline between love and hate is often thin.* **—borderline** *adj.* **1.a.** Verging on a given quality or condition: *borderline poverty.* **b.** Of a questionable nature or quality; dubious: *an applicant with borderline qualifications.* **2.a.** *Psychology.* Relating to any phenomenon that is intermediate between two groups and not clearly categorized in either group: *a borderline state showing the characteristics of both neurotic and psychotic reactions.* **b.** Relating to a condition characterized by a pattern of instability in mood, interpersonal relations, and self-image and manifested by self-destructive, manipulative, and inconsistent behavior: *the borderline personality disorder; the borderline syndrome.*

borage
Borago officinalis

Border States. The slave states of Delaware, Maryland, Virginia, Kentucky, and Missouri that were adjacent to the free states of the North during the Civil War.

Border terrier *n.* A small, hardy, rough-coated terrier bred to hunt foxes in the border country of England and Scotland.

bor·de·tel·la (bôr′də-tĕl′ə) *n. Microbiology.* Any of various small, gram-negative coccobacilli of the genus *Bordetella,* some of which are pathogenic in the human respiratory tract. It includes *B. partussis,* the causative agent of whooping cough. [New Latin *Bordetella,* genus name, after Jules Jean Baptiste Vincent BORDET.]

bor·dure (bôr′jər) *n. Heraldry.* A border around a shield. [Middle English. See BORDER.]

bore[1] (bôr, bōr) *v.* **bored, bor·ing, bores.** *—tr.* **1.** To make a hole in or through, with or as if with a drill. **2.** To form (a tunnel, for example) by drilling, digging, or burrowing. *—intr.* **1.** To make a hole in or through something with or as if with a drill. **2.** To proceed or advance steadily or laboriously: *a destroyer boring through heavy seas.* **—bore** *n.* **1.** A hole or passage made by or as if by use of a drill. **2.** A hollow, usually cylindrical chamber or barrel, as of a firearm. **3.** The interior diameter of a hole, tube, or cylinder. **4.** The caliber of a firearm. **5.** A drilling tool. [Middle English *boren,* from Old English *borian.*]

Lizzie Borden

bore[2] (bôr, bōr) *tr.v.* **bored, bor·ing, bores.** To make weary by being dull, repetitive, or tedious: *The play bored us.* **—bore** *n.* One that arouses boredom. [Origin unknown.]

bore[3] (bôr, bōr) *n.* A high, often dangerous wave caused by the surge of a flood tide upstream in a narrowing estuary or by colliding tidal currents. Also called *eagre.* [Middle English *bare,* wave, from Old Norse *bāra.* See **bher-[1]** in Appendix.]

bore[4] (bôr, bōr) *v.* Past tense of **bear[1].**

bo·re·al (bôr′ē-əl, bōr′-) *adj.* **1.** Of or relating to the north; northern. **2.** Of or concerning the north wind. **3. Boreal.** Of or relating to the forest areas of the northern North Temperate Zone, dominated by coniferous trees such as spruce, fir, and pine. [Middle English, from Late Latin *Boreālis,* from Latin *Boreās,* Boreas. See BOREAS.]

Bo·re·as (bôr′ē-əs, bōr′-) *n.* **1.** *Greek Mythology.* The god of the north wind. **2. boreas.** The north wind. [Middle English, from Latin *Boreās,* from Greek, from *boreios,* coming from the north.]

bore·cole (bôr′kōl′, bōr′-) *n.* See **kale** (sense 1). [Dutch *boerenkool* : *boren,* plural of *boer,* peasant; see BOOR + *kool,* cabbage, from Middle Dutch *cōle,* from Latin *caulis,* stalk. See KALE.]

bore·dom (bôr′dəm, bōr′-) *n.* The condition of being bored; ennui.

SYNONYMS: *boredom, ennui, tedium.* The central meaning shared by these nouns is "a condition of mental weariness, listlessness, and discontent": *a party so dull we thought we'd perish*

ă pat	oi boy
ā pay	ou out
âr care	o͝o took
ä father	o͞o boot
ĕ pet	ŭ cut
ē be	ûr urge
ĭ pit	th thin
ī pie	*th* this
îr pier	hw which
ŏ pot	zh vision
ō toe	ə about, item
ô paw	♦ regionalism

Stress marks: ′ (primary); ′ (secondary), as in **dictionary** (dĭk′shə-nĕr′ē)

of boredom; took up a hobby to relieve the ennui of retirement; the oppressive tedium of routine tasks.
ANTONYM: *amusement.*

bore·hole (bôr′hōl′, bōr′-) *n.* A hole that is drilled into the earth, as in exploratory well drilling or in building construction.

bor·er (bôr′ər, bōr′-) *n.* **1.** A tool used for drilling. **2.** An insect or insect larva, such as the corn borer, that bores into the woody parts of plants. **3.** Any of various mollusks that bore into soft rock or wood.

Bor·ges (bôr′hĕs), **Jorge Luis.** 1899–1986. Argentinian writer particularly known for his short stories, which have a metaphysical, fantastic quality.

Bor·gia (bôr′jə, -zhə). Italian family, influential from the 14th to the 16th century, that included the son and daughter of Pope Alexander VI. **Cesare** (1475?–1507), a religious, military, and political leader, was the model for Machiavelli's *The Prince.* **Lucrezia** (1489–1519), the Duchess of Ferrara, was a patron of learning and the arts.

Bor·glum (bôr′gləm), **Gutzon.** Originally John Gutzon de la Mothe Borglum. 1867–1941. American sculptor noted for his monumental works, particularly the busts of four U.S. Presidents on Mount Rushmore.

bo·ric (bôr′ĭk, bōr′-) also **bo·rac·ic** (bə-răs′ĭk) *adj.* Of, relating to, derived from, or containing boron.

boric acid *n.* A water-soluble white or colorless crystalline compound, H_3BO_3, used as an antiseptic and preservative and in fireproofing compounds, cosmetics, cements, and enamels.

bo·ride (bôr′īd′, bōr′-) *n.* A binary compound of boron with a more electropositive element or radical.

bor·ing (bôr′ĭng, bōr′-) *adj.* Uninteresting and tiresome; dull. **—bor′ing·ly** *adv.* **—bor′ing·ness** *n.*

SYNONYMS: *boring, monotonous, tedious, irksome, tiresome, humdrum.* These adjectives refer to what is so lacking in interest as to cause mental weariness. *Boring* implies feelings of listlessness and discontent: *I had expected the book to be boring, but on the contrary it was fascinating.* What is *monotonous* bores because of lack of variety: *"There is nothing so desperately monotonous as the sea"* (James Russell Lowell). *Tedious* suggests dull slowness or long-windedness: *When we travel from coast to coast, we take a plane to avoid spending tedious days on the train. Irksome* describes what is demanding of time and effort and yet is dull and often unrewarding: *"I know and feel what an irksome task the writing of long letters is"* (Edmund Burke). Something *tiresome* fatigues because it seems to be interminable or to be marked by unremitting sameness: *"What a tiresome being is a man who is fond of talking"* (Benjamin Jowett). *Humdrum* refers to what is commonplace, trivial, or unexcitingly routine: *She led a humdrum existence—all work and no play.*

Cesare Borgia
Portrait by Raphael

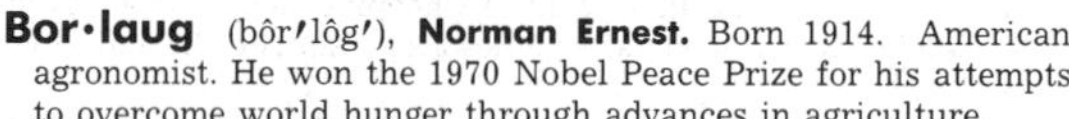

Bor·laug (bôr′lôg′), **Norman Ernest.** Born 1914. American agronomist. He won the 1970 Nobel Peace Prize for his attempts to overcome world hunger through advances in agriculture.

Bor·mann (bôr′män′), **Martin Ludwig.** 1900–1945? German Nazi official who served as Hitler's private secretary (1941–1945). He is believed to have died in May 1945.

born (bôrn) *v.* A past participle of **bear**[1]. **—born** *adj.* **1. a.** *Abbr.* **b.** Brought into life by birth. **b.** Brought into existence; created: *A new nation was born with the revolution.* **2. a.** Having from birth a particular quality or talent: *a born artist.* **b.** Destined, or seemingly destined, from birth: *a person born to lead.* **3.** Resulting or arising: *wisdom born of experience.* **4.** Native to a particular country, region, or place. Often used in combination: *Irish-born; Southern born and bred; Boston-born.*

Born (bôrn), **Max.** 1882–1970. German-born physicist. He shared a 1954 Nobel Prize for his pioneering work in quantum mechanics.

born-a·gain (bôrn′ə-gĕn′) *adj.* **1. a.** Of, relating to, or being a person who has made a conversion or has renewed a commitment to Jesus Christ as his or her personal savior: *a born-again Christian.* **b.** Of or relating to evangelical Christianity: *born-again evangelism.* **2.** Characterized by renewal, resurgence, or return: *born-again patriotism; a born-again fiscal conservative.* [From *born again* in John 3:3 and 3:7.] **—born′-a·gain′, born′-a·gain′er** *n.*

borne (bôrn, bōrn) *v.* A past participle of **bear**[1].

Bor·ne·o (bôr′nē-ō′). An island of the western Pacific Ocean in the Malay Archipelago between the Sulu and Java seas southwest of the Philippines. It is the third-largest island in the world. The sultanate of Brunei is on the northwest coast; the rest of the island is divided between Indonesia and Malaysia. **—Bor′ne·an** *adj. & n.*

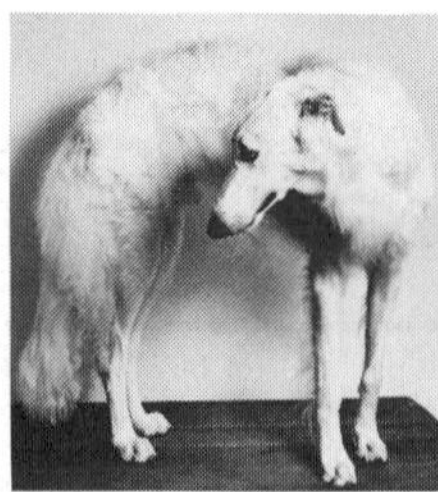

borzoi

Born·holm (bôrn′hōm′, -hōlm′, -hôlm′). An island of eastern Denmark in the Baltic Sea near Sweden. It was held for varying periods by Denmark, Sweden, and Lübeck merchants before becoming part of Denmark in the 1600's.

born·ite (bôr′nīt′) *n.* A brownish-bronze, lustrous copper ore with the composition Cu_5FeS_4 that tarnishes to purple when exposed to air. [After Ignaz von *Born* (1742–1791), Austrian mineralogist.]

Bor·nu (bôr′no͞o). A region and former Moslem kingdom of western Africa occupying a vast plain in present-day northeast Nigeria. Founded in the 11th century, the kingdom reached the height of its power in the late 16th century.

boro– or **bor–** *pref.* Boron: *borosilicate.* [From BORON.]

Bo·ro·bu·dur (bôr′ə-bə-do͝or′, bōr′-). A ruined Buddhist shrine in central Java, Indonesia. Dating probably from the ninth century, the ruins include intricately carved stone blocks illustrating episodes in the life of Buddha.

Bo·ro·din (bôr′ə-dēn′, bär′-, bə-rə-dēn′), **Aleksandr Porfirevich.** 1833–1887. Russian composer and chemist whose musical works were based on Russian folk themes and include the opera *Prince Igor,* unfinished at his death.

Bo·ro·di·no (bôr′ə-dē′nō, bŏr′-, bə-rə-dyĕ-nô′). A village of western Russia west of Moscow. Nearby, Napoleon defeated the Russian troops defending Moscow on September 7, 1812.

bo·ron (bôr′ŏn′, bōr′-) *n. Symbol* **B** A soft, brown, amorphous or crystalline nonmetallic element, extracted chiefly from kernite and borax and used in flares, propellant mixtures, nuclear reactor control elements, abrasives, and hard metallic alloys. Atomic number 5; atomic weight 10.811; melting point 2,300°C; sublimation point 2,550°C; specific gravity (crystal) 2.34; valence 3. See table at **element.** [BOR(AX)[1] + (CARB)ON.]

boron carbide *n.* A compound of boron and carbon, especially B_4C, an extremely hard, black crystalline compound or solid solution. It is used as an abrasive, in control rods for nuclear reactors, and as a reinforcing filament in composite structural materials.

bo·ro·sil·i·cate (bôr′ō-sĭl′ĭ-kĭt, -kāt′, bōr′) *n.* A salt that is derived from both boric acid and silicic acid and occurs naturally in dumortierite.

borosilicate glass *n.* A strong heat-resistant glass that contains a minimum of 5 percent boric oxide.

bor·ough (bûr′ō, bŭr′-ō) *n. Abbr.* **bor. 1.** A self-governing incorporated town in some U.S. states, such as New Jersey. **2.** One of the five administrative units of New York City. **3.** A civil division of the state of Alaska that is the equivalent of a county in most other U.S. states. **4.** *Chiefly British.* **a.** A town having a municipal corporation and certain rights, such as self-government. **b.** A town that sends a representative to Parliament. **5.** A medieval group of fortified houses that formed a town having special privileges and rights. [Middle English *burgh,* city, from Old English *burg,* fortified town. See **bhergh-**[2] in Appendix.]

bor·ough-Eng·lish (bûr′ō-ĭng′glĭsh, bŭr′-) *n.* An old custom in certain English boroughs whereby the right to inherit an estate intestate went to the youngest son or, in default of issue, to the youngest brother. [Partial translation of Anglo-Norman *tenure en burgh Engloys,* tenure in an English borough. See BOROUGH.]

bor·rel·i·a (bə-rĕl′ē-ə, -rē′lē-ə) *n. Microbiology.* Any of various irregularly coiled helical spirochetes of the genus *Borrelia,* some species of which cause relapsing fever in humans, other mammals, and birds. [New Latin, after Amédée *Borrel* (1867–1936), French bacteriologist.]

bor·row (bŏr′ō, bôr′ō) *v.* **-rowed, -row·ing, -rows.** *—tr.* **1.** To obtain or receive (something) on loan with the promise or understanding of returning it or its equivalent. **2.** To adopt or use as one's own: *I borrowed your good idea.* **3.** In subtraction, to take a unit from the next larger denomination in the minuend so as to make a number larger than the number to be subtracted. *—intr.* **1.** To obtain or receive something. **2.** *Linguistics.* To adopt words from one language for use in another. ***—idiom.*** **borrow trouble.** To take an unnecessary action that will probably engender adverse effects. [Middle English *borwen,* from Old English *borgian.* See **bhergh-**[1] in Appendix.] **—bor′row·er** *n.*

bor·rowed time (bŏr′ōd, bôr′-) *n.* An uncertain, typically uncontrolled extension of time that is the result of postponing or attempting to postpone the occurrence of something inevitable and often unpleasant. Often used with *on*: *cancer patients living on borrowed time; an unstable government that existed for months on borrowed time.*

bor·row·ing (bŏr′ō-ĭng, bôr′-) *n.* Something that is borrowed, especially a word borrowed from one language for use in another.

borscht also **borsht** (bôrsht) or **borsch** (bôrsh) *n.* A beet soup served hot or cold, usually with sour cream. [Yiddish *borsht,* from Russian *borshch,* cow parsnip (the original base of the soup), borscht.]

borscht belt *n. Informal.* The predominantly Jewish resort hotels of the Catskill Mountains. Also called *borscht circuit.* [From the popularity of BORSCHT in the cuisine of these hotels.]

borsht (bôrsht) *n.* Variant of **borscht.**

bort (bôrt) *n.* **1.** Poorly crystallized diamonds used for industrial cutting and abrasion. **2.** A carbonado. [Probably from Dutch *boort.*] **—bort′y** *adj.*

bor·zoi (bôr′zoi′) *n.* Any of a breed of tall, slender dogs having a narrow, pointed head and a silky, predominantly white coat, originally developed in Russia for hunting wolves. Also called *Russian wolfhound.* [Russian *borzoĭ,* swift.]

Bosc (bŏsk) *n.* A variety of pear having a long neck, greenish-yellow skin overlaid with reddish-brown color, and juicy sweet flesh. [After Louis Auguste Guillaume *Bosc,* 19th-century Belgian horticulturist.]

bos·cage also **bos·kage** (bŏs′kĭj) *n.* A mass of trees or shrubs; a thicket. [Middle English *boskage,* from Old French *boscage,* from *bosc,* forest, of Germanic origin.]

Bosch (bŏsh, bôsh, bŏs, bôs), **Hieronymus.** 1450?–1516. Dutch painter whose largely religious works are characterized by grotesque, fantastic creatures mingling with human figures.

bosh (bŏsh) *Informal. n.* Nonsense. **—bosh** *interj.* Used to express disbelief or annoyance. [Turkish *boş,* empty.]

bosk (bŏsk) *n.* A small wooded area. [Back-formation from BOSKY.]

bos·kage (bŏs′kĭj) *n.* Variant of **boscage.**

bosk·y (bŏs′kē) *adj.* **-i·er, -i·est. 1.** Having an abundance of bushes, shrubs, or trees: *"a bosky park leading to a modest yet majestic plaza"* (Jack Beatty). **2.** Of or relating to woods. [From Middle English *bosk,* bush, from Medieval Latin *bosca,* of Germanic origin.] **—bosk′i·ness** *n.*

bo's'n or **bos'n** (bō′sən) *n.* Variants of **boatswain.**

Bos·ni·a (bŏz′nē-ə). A region of west-central Yugoslavia. It was settled by Serbs in the 7th century and became an independent state in the 12th century. Bosnia was controlled by Turkey after 1483 and was later annexed by the Austro-Hungarian Empire. **—Bos′ni·an** *adj. & n.*

bos·om (bo͝oz′əm, bo͞o′zəm) *n.* **1.a.** The chest of a human being: *He held the sleepy child to his bosom.* **b.** A woman's breast or breasts. **2.** The part of a garment covering the chest or breasts. **3.** The security and closeness likened to being held in a warm familial embrace: *We welcomed the stranger into the bosom of our family.* **4.** The chest considered as the source of emotion. **—bosom** *adj.* Beloved; intimate: *a bosom friend.* [Middle English, from Old English *bōsm.*]

bo·son (bō′sŏn) *n.* Any of a class of particles, such as the photon, pion, or alpha particle, that have zero or integral spin and obey statistical rules permitting any number of identical particles to occupy the same quantum state. [After Satyendra Nath *Bose* (1894–1974), Indian physicist.]

Bos·po·rus (bŏs′pər-əs). A narrow strait separating European and Asian Turkey and joining the Black Sea with the Sea of Marmara. It has been an important trade route since ancient times.

bos·quet (bŏs′kĭt) *n.* A small grove; a thicket. [French, from Italian *boschetto,* diminutive of *bosco,* forest, of Germanic origin.]

boss[1] (bôs, bŏs) *n.* **1.a.** An employer or a supervisor. **b.** One who makes decisions or exercises authority. **2.** A professional politician who controls a party or a political machine. **—boss** *v.* **bossed, boss·ing, boss·es.** *—tr.* **1.** To supervise or control. See Synonyms at **supervise. 2.** To give orders to, especially in an arrogant or domineering manner: *bossing us around. —intr.* To be or act as a supervisor or controlling element. **—boss** *adj. Slang.* First-rate; topnotch. [Dutch *baas,* master.]

boss[2] (bôs, bŏs) *n.* **1.** A circular protuberance or knoblike swelling, as on the horns of certain animals. **2.** A raised area used as ornamentation. **3.** *Architecture.* A raised ornament, such as one at the intersection of the ribs in a vaulted roof. **4.a.** An enlarged part of a shaft to which another shaft is coupled or to which a wheel or gear is keyed. **b.** A hub, especially of a propeller. **—boss** *tr.v.* **bossed, boss·ing, boss·es.** To emboss. [Middle English *boce,* from Old French.]

boss[3] (bôs, bŏs) *n.* A cow or calf. [Perhaps ultimately from Latin *bōs.* See BOVINE.]

bos·sa no·va (bŏs′ə nō′və, bô′sə) *n.* **1.** A lively Brazilian dance similar to the samba. **2.** Music that is a blend of jazz and samba. [Portuguese : *bossa,* trend + *nova,* new.]

Bos·sier City (bō′zhər). A city of northwest Louisiana, an industrial suburb of Shreveport on the opposite bank of the Red River. Population, 50,817.

boss·ism (bô′sĭz′əm, bŏs′ĭz′-) *n.* The domination of a political organization by a boss.

Bos·suet (bôs-wā′), **Jacques Bénigne.** 1627–1704. French prelate and historian noted for his funereal orations and a philosophical treatise on history.

boss·y[1] (bô′sē, bŏs′ē) *adj.* **-i·er, -i·est.** Given to ordering others around; domineering. **—boss′i·ly** *adv.* **—boss′i·ness** *n.*

boss·y[2] (bô′sē, bŏs′ē) *adj.* Decorated with raised ornaments.

boss·y[3] (bô′sē, bŏs′ē) *n., pl.* **-ies.** *Informal.* A cow or calf. [From BOSS[3].]

Bos·ton (bô′stən, bŏs′tən). The capital and largest city of Massachusetts, in the eastern part of the state on **Boston Bay,** an arm of Massachusetts Bay. Founded in the 17th century, it was a leading center of agitation against England in the 18th century and a stronghold of abolitionist thought in the 19th century. Today it is a major commercial, financial, and educational hub. Population, 562,994. **—Bos·to′ni·an** (bô-stō′nē-ən, bŏs-) *adj. & n.*

Boston bull *n.* See **Boston terrier.**

Boston cream pie *n.* A round cake with a custard or cream filling.

Boston fern *n.* **1.** A cultivar of sword fern *(Nephrolepis exaltata* cv. *Bostoniensis)* having arching or drooping pinnate fronds. It is a popular houseplant. **2.** Any of numerous other forms derived from the sword fern.

Boston ivy *n.* A high-climbing woody vine *(Parthenocissus tricuspidata),* native to eastern Asia and having three-lobed deciduous leaves. It frequently covers the outer walls of buildings and has attractive fall coloration. Also called *Japanese ivy.*

Boston lettuce *n.* A type of cultivated lettuce forming a rounded head and having soft-textured, yellow-green inner leaves.

Boston rocker *n.* A rocking chair having a high back with spindles, a decorative panel at the top, and a seat and arms that curve downward in front.

Boston terrier *n.* Any of a breed of small dogs originating in New England as a cross between a bull terrier and a bulldog and having a smooth, brindled or black coat with white markings. Also called *Boston bull.*

bo·sun (bō′sən) *n.* Variant of **boatswain.**

Bos·well (bŏz′wĕl′, -wəl) *n.* An assiduous and devoted admirer, student, and recorder of another's words and deeds. [After James BOSWELL.] **—Bos′well·ize′** (-īz′) *v.*

Boswell, James. 1740–1795. Scottish lawyer, diarist, and writer renowned as the biographer of Samuel Johnson. **—Bos·well′i·an** *adj. & n.*

Bos·worth Field (bŏz′wərth). A locality in central England near Leicester. It was the site of the final battle (August 22, 1485) of the Wars of the Roses, in which Henry Tudor (afterward Henry VII) defeated Richard III, the last king of the Plantagenet line. Richard was killed in the battle.

bot also **bott** (bŏt) *n.* **1.** The parasitic larva of a botfly. **2. bots.** *(used with a sing. or pl. verb).* A disease of mammals, especially cattle and horses, caused by infestation of the stomach or intestines with botfly larvae. [Middle English, probably of Low German origin.]

bot. *abbr.* **1.** Botanical; botanist; botany. **2.** Bottle. **3.** Bottom.

bo·tan·i·cal (bə-tăn′ĭ-kəl) also **bo·tan·ic** (-tăn′ĭk) *—adj. Abbr.* **bot. 1.** Of or relating to plants or plant life. **2.** Of or relating to the science of botany. *—n.* A drug, medicinal preparation, or similar substance obtained from a plant or plants. [From Late Latin *botanicus,* from Greek *botanikos,* from *botanē,* fodder, plants.] **—bo·tan′i·cal·ly** *adv.*

botanical garden or **botanic garden** *n.* A place where a wide variety of plants are cultivated for scientific, educational, and ornamental purposes, often including a library, a herbarium, and greenhouses; an aboretum.

bot·a·nist (bŏt′n-ĭst) *n. Abbr.* **bot.** One who specializes in botany.

bot·a·nize (bŏt′n-īz′) *v.* **-nized, -niz·ing, -niz·es.** *—intr.* **1.** To collect plants for scientific study. **2.** To investigate or study plants scientifically. *—tr.* To investigate or explore the plant life of (a region). **—bot′a·niz′er** *n.*

bot·a·ny (bŏt′n-ē) *n., pl.* **-nies.** *Abbr.* **bot. 1.a.** The science or study of plants. **b.** A book or scholarly work on this subject. **2.** The plant life of a particular area: *the botany of the Ohio River valley.* **3.** The characteristic features and biology of a particular kind of plant or plant group. [From BOTANICAL.]

Bot·a·ny Bay (bŏt′n-ē). An inlet of the Tasman Sea in southeast Australia south of Sydney. It was visited by Capt. James Cook in 1770 and named by Sir Joseph Banks, the botanist in his crew, for the wide variety of exotic flora found on its shores.

botch (bŏch) *tr.v.* **botched, botch·ing, botch·es. 1.** To ruin through clumsiness. **2.** To make or perform clumsily; bungle. **3.** To repair or mend clumsily. **—botch** *n.* **1.** A ruined or defective piece of work: *"I have made a miserable botch of this description"* (Nathaniel Hawthorne). **2.** A hodgepodge. [Middle English *bocchen,* to mend.] **—botch′er** *n.* **—botch′y** *adj.*

SYNONYMS: *botch, blow, bungle, fumble, muff.* The central meaning shared by these verbs is "to harm or spoil through inept or clumsy handling": *botch a repair; blow an opportunity; a bungled performance; fumbled my chance for a promotion; an actor muffing his lines.*

bot·fly also **bot fly** (bŏt′flī′) *n.* Any of various stout, two-winged flies, chiefly of the genera *Gasterophilus* and *Oestrus,* having larvae that are parasitic on various animals, especially horses and sheep, and sometimes on humans.

both (bōth) *adj.* One and the other; relating to or being two in conjunction: *Both guests have arrived. Both the books are torn. Both her fingers are broken.* **—both** *pron.* The one and the other: *Both were candidates. We are both candidates. Both of us are candidates.* **—both** *conj.* Used with *and* to indicate that each of two things in a coordinated phrase or clause is included: *both men and women; an attorney well regarded for both intelligence and honesty.* [Middle English *bothe,* from Old English *bā thā,* both those : *bā,* neuter of *bēgen,* both + *thā,* plural of *thæt,* that; see THAT.]

USAGE NOTE: *Both* is used to indicate that the action or state denoted by the verb applies individually to each of two entities. *Both books weigh more than five pounds,* for example, means that each book weighs more than five pounds by itself, not that the two books weighed together come to more than five pounds. *Both* is inappropriate where the verb does not apply to each of the entities by itself. • In possessive constructions *of both* is usually preferred: *the mothers of both* (rather than *both their mothers*); *the fault of both* (rather than *both their fault* or *both's fault*). • When *both* is used with *and* to link parallel elements in a sentence, the words or phrases that follow them should correspond grammatically: *in*

boss[2]

Boston fern
Nephrolepis exaltata

Boston rocker

ă pat	oi boy
ā pay	ou out
âr care	o͝o took
ä father	o͞o boot
ĕ pet	ŭ cut
ē be	ûr urge
ĭ pit	th thin
ī pie	*th* this
îr pier	hw which
ŏ pot	zh vision
ō toe	ə about, item
ô paw	♦ regionalism

Stress marks: ′ (primary); ′ (secondary), as in **dictionary** (dĭk′shə-nĕr′ē)

both India and China or *both in India and in China* (not *both in India and China*). See Usage Note at **and.**

Bo·tha (bō′tə, -tä′), **Louis.** 1862–1919. South African general in the Boer War (1899–1902) and first prime minister of the Union of South Africa (1910–1919).

Botha, Pieter Willem. Born 1916. South African prime minister (1978–1989) who defended and upheld apartheid despite international protest.

both·er (bŏth′ər) *v.* **-ered, -er·ing, -ers.** —*tr.* **1.** To disturb or anger, especially by minor irritations; annoy. See Synonyms at **annoy. 2.a.** To make agitated or nervous; fluster. **b.** To make confused or perplexed; puzzle. **3.** To intrude on without invitation or warrant; disturb. **4.** To give trouble to: *a back condition that bothers her constantly.* —*intr.* **1.** To take the trouble; concern oneself. **2.** To cause trouble. —**bother** *n.* A cause or state of disturbance. —**bother** *interj.* Used to express annoyance or mild irritation. [Probably from dialectal *bodder,* possibly of Celtic origin.]

both·er·a·tion (bŏth′ə-rā′shən) *n.* The act of bothering or the state of being bothered. —**botheration** *interj.* Used to express annoyance or irritation.

both·er·some (bŏth′ər-səm) *adj.* Causing bother; troublesome.

Both·ni·a (bŏth′nē-ə), **Gulf of.** An arm of the Baltic Sea between Sweden and Finland. It is icebound for nearly half the year.

Both·well (bŏth′wĕl′, -wəl, bŏth′-), Fourth Earl of. Title of James Hepburn. 1536?–1578. Scottish Protestant nobleman and third husband of Mary Queen of Scots, whose second husband, Lord Darnley, he murdered (1567).

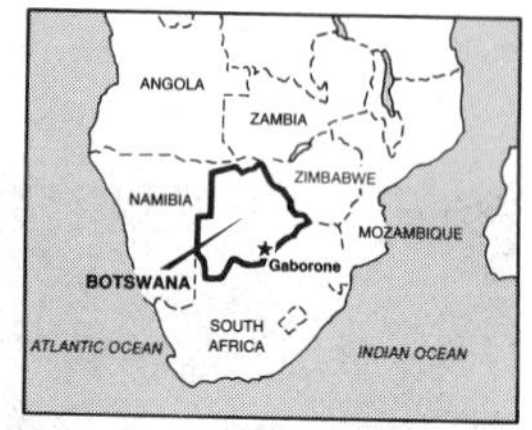

Botswana

bo tree (bō) *n.* See **peepul.** [Partial translation of Singhalese *bo-gaha,* tree of wisdom, from Pali *bodhi,* from Sanskrit *bodhiḥ,* enlightenment. See **bheudh-** in Appendix.]

bot·ry·oid·al (bŏt′rē-oid′l) also **bot·ry·oid** (bŏt′rē-oid′) *adj.* Shaped like a bunch of grapes. Used especially of mineral formations: *botryoidal hematite.* [From Greek *botruoeidēs* : *botrus,* bunch of grapes + *-oeidēs,* -oid.] —**bot′ry·oid′al·ly** *adv.*

bo·try·tis (bō-trī′tĭs) *n.* **1.** Any of various fungi of the genus *Botrytis* responsible for numerous diseases of fruits and vegetables. **2.** Noble rot. [New Latin, genus name, from Greek *botrus,* bunch of grapes.]

Bot·swa·na (bŏt-swä′nə). Formerly **Bech·u·a·na·land** (bĕch′wän′ə-lănd′, bĕch′ə-). A country of south-central Africa. A British protectorate after 1885, it gained full independence in 1966. Gaborone is the capital and Francistown the largest city. Population, 973,000.

bott (bŏt) *n.* Variant of **bot.**

Bot·ti·cel·li (bŏt′ĭ-chĕl′ē), **Sandro.** Originally Alessandro di Mariano dei Filipepi. 1444?–1510. Italian painter of the Florentine school whose flowing draftsmanship is evident in his masterpieces, *Primavera* (c. 1477) and *Birth of Venus* (c. 1485).

bot·tle (bŏt′l) *n. Abbr.* **bot. 1.** A receptacle having a narrow neck, usually no handles, and a mouth that can be plugged, corked, or capped. **2.** The quantity that a bottle holds. **3.** A receptacle filled with milk or formula that is fed, as to babies, in place of breast milk. **4.** *Informal.* **a.** Intoxicating liquor: *Don't take to the bottle.* **b.** The practice of drinking large quantities of intoxicating liquor: *Her problem is the bottle.* —*attributive.* Often used to modify another noun: *bottle soda; a bottle recycling program.* —**bottle** *tr.v.* **-tled, -tling, -tles. 1.** To place in a bottle. **2.** To hold in; restrain: *bottled up my emotions.* [Middle English *botel,* from Old French *botele,* from Medieval Latin *butticula,* diminutive of Late Latin *buttis,* cask.] —**bot′tler** *n.*

bot·tle·brush (bŏt′l-brŭsh′) *n.* Any of various Australian shrubs or trees of the genera *Callistemon* and *Melaleuca,* having densely flowered, cylindrical spikes with numerous, long, protruding stamens that suggest a brush used to clean bottles.

bot·tled gas (bŏt′ld) *n.* Gas, such as butane or propane, stored under pressure in portable tanks.

bot·tle-feed (bŏt′l-fēd′) *tr.v.* **-fed** (-fĕd′), **-feed·ing, -feeds.** To feed (a baby, for example) with a bottle.

bottle gourd *n.* See **calabash** (sense 1).

bottle green *n. Color.* A dark to moderate or grayish green. —**bot′tle-green′** (bŏt′l-grēn′) *adj.*

bot·tle·neck (bŏt′l-nĕk′) *n.* **1.a.** A narrow or obstructed section, as of a highway or a pipeline. **b.** A point or an area of traffic congestion. **2.** A hindrance to progress or production. **3.** The narrow part of a bottle near the top. **4.** *Music.* A style of guitar playing in which an object, such as a piece of glass or metal, is passed across the strings to achieve a gliding sound. —**bottleneck** *tr.v.* **-necked, -neck·ing, -necks.** To slow down or impede by creating an obstruction.

bot·tle-nosed dolphin (bŏt′l-nōzd′) *n.* Any of several marine mammals of the genus *Tursiops,* especially *T. truncatus,* widely distributed in temperate and tropical waters and characterized by a short, protruding beak, a large, stocky body, and a prominent falcate dorsal fin. Also called *bottlenose.*

bottle tree *n.* Any of certain Australian trees of the genus *Brachychiton,* having a swollen, sometimes bottle-shaped trunk and cultivated in warm regions as an ornamental.

bot·tom (bŏt′əm) *n. Abbr.* **bot. 1.** The deepest or lowest part: *the bottom of a well; the bottom of the page.* **2.** The underside: *scraped the bottom of the car on a rock.* **3.** The supporting part; the base. **4.** The far end or part: *at the bottom of the bed.* **5.a.** The last place, as on a list. **b.** The lowest or least favorable position: *started at the bottom of the corporate hierarchy.* **6.** The basic underlying quality; the source: *Let's get to the bottom of the problem.* **7.** The solid surface under a body of water. **8.** Often **bottoms.** Low-lying alluvial land adjacent to a river. Also called *bottomland.* **9.a.** *Nautical.* The part of a ship's hull below the water line. **b.** A ship; a boat: *"English merchants did much of their overseas trade in foreign bottoms"* (G.M. Trevelyan). **10.** Often **bottoms.** The trousers or short pants of pajamas. **11.** *Informal.* The buttocks. **12.** The seat of a chair. **13.** *Baseball.* The second or last half of an inning. **14.** Staying power; stamina. Used of a horse. —*attributive.* Often used to modify another noun: *a bottom drawer; the bottom stair.* —**bottom** *v.* **-tomed, -tom·ing, -toms.** —*tr.* **1.** To provide with an underside. **2.** To provide with a foundation. **3.** To get to the bottom of; fathom. —*intr.* **1.** To be or become based or grounded. **2.** To rest on or touch the bottom. —***phrasal verb.*** **bottom out.** To descend to the lowest point possible, after which only a rise may occur: *Sales of personal computers have bottomed out.* —***idiom.*** **at bottom.** Basically. [Middle English *botme,* from Old English *botm.*] —**bot′tom·er** *n.*

bottom break *n.* A branch arising from the stem base of a plant. [BOTTOM + BREAK, branch formed by pinching or disbudding.]

bot·tom·land (bŏt′əm-lănd′) *n.* See **bottom** (sense 8).

bot·tom·less (bŏt′əm-lĭs) *adj.* **1.** Having no bottom. **2.** Too deep to be measured: *a bottomless glacier lake.* **3.** Difficult or impossible to understand; unfathomable: *one of the bottomless mysteries of life.* **4.** Having no limitations or bounds; limitless: *a bottomless supply of money.* **5.a.** Nude, especially unclothed below the waist: *bottomless dancers.* **b.** Featuring such dancers as entertainment: *bottomless bars.* —**bot′tom·less·ly** *adv.*

bottom line *n.* **1.** The line in a financial statement that shows net income or loss. **2.** The final result or statement; upshot: *"The bottom line, however, is that he has escaped"* (David Wise). **3.** The main or essential point: *"A lot can happen between now and December, but the bottom line—for now—is that the city is still heading toward default"* (New York).

bot·tom-line (bŏt′əm-līn′) *adj.* **1.** Concerned exclusively with costs and profits: *bottom-line issues.* **2.** Ruthlessly realistic; pragmatic: *a bottom-line political strategy.* —**bot′tom-line′** *v.*

bot·tom·most (bŏt′əm-mōst′) *adj.* **1.** Sited at the very bottom: *the bottommost rung of a ladder.* **2.** Being or coming after all others; last: *Fleeing was the bottommost thought in my mind.* **3.** Forming the very basis: *Freedom of speech is one of the bottommost principles of democracy.*

bottom quark *n. Abbr.* **b** A quark with a charge of −⅓ and a mass about 10,000 times that of the electron. Also called *beauty quark.* See table at **subatomic particle.**

bottom round *n.* A cut of meat, such as steak, taken from the outer section of a round of beef.

Bot·trop (bŏt′rŏp′, bôt′rôp′). A city of northwest Germany in the Ruhr Valley northwest of Essen. It developed as a coal-mining center after the 1860's. Population, 112,353.

bot·u·lin (bŏch′ə-lĭn) *n.* Any of several potent neurotoxins produced by botulinum and resistant to proteolytic digestion. [Latin *botulus,* sausage + -IN.]

bot·u·li·num (bŏch′ə-lī′nəm) also **bot·u·li·nus** (-nəs) *n.* An anaerobic, rod-shaped bacterium *(Clostridium botulinum)* that secretes botulin and inhabits soils. [New Latin, from Latin *botulus,* sausage.] —**bot′u·li′nal** *adj.*

bot·u·lism (bŏch′ə-lĭz′əm) *n.* A severe, sometimes fatal food poisoning caused by ingestion of food containing botulin and characterized by nausea, vomiting, disturbed vision, muscular weakness, and fatigue. [German *Botulismus,* from Latin *botulus,* sausage.]

Bou·cher (bo͞o-shā′), **François.** 1703–1770. French artist whose paintings and tapestries are representative of the rococo style.

Bou·cher·ville (bo͞o′shər-vĭl′, bo͞o′shā-vēl′). A town of southern Quebec, Canada, an industrial suburb of Montreal on the St. Lawrence River. Population, 29,704.

Bou·ci·cault (bo͞o′sē-kō′), **Dion.** Originally Dionysius Lardner Boursiquot. 1820?–1890. Irish-born American actor and playwright whose original and adapted works include *The Octoroon* (1859) and *The Colleen Bawn* (1860).

bou·clé or **bou·cle** (bo͞o-klā′) *n.* **1.** A type of yarn, usually three-ply and having one thread looser than the others, that produces a rough-textured cloth. **2.** Fabric woven or knitted from this yarn. [French, from past participle of *boucler,* to curl, from Old French *boucler,* from *boucle,* buckle, curl of hair. See BUCKLE.]

Bou·dain (bo͞o-dăN′, -dăN′) *n.* Variant of **boudin.**

Bou·dic·ca (bo͞o-dĭk′ə) also **Bo·ad·i·ce·a** (bō′ăd-ĭ-sē′ə). First century A.D. Queen of ancient Britain who led a temporarily successful revolt against the Roman army that had claimed her deceased husband's kingdom.

bou·din also **Bou·dain** (bo͞o-dăN′, -dăN′) *n., pl.* **-dins -dains** (-dăN′, -dănz′). A highly seasoned link sausage of pork, pork liver, and rice that is a typical element of Louisiana Creole cuisine. [French, from Old French *bodine,* intestines.]

boudin blanc (bläN) *n., pl.* **boudins blancs** (bläN). A French white sausage made of pork, chicken, or veal. [French : *boudin,* boudin + *blanc,* white.]

boudin noir (nwär) *n., pl.* **boudins noirs** (nwär). See **black pudding.** [French : *boudin,* boudin + *noir,* black.]

bou·doir (bo͞o′dwär′, -dwôr′) *n.* A woman's private sitting room, dressing room, or bedroom. [French, from Old French *bouder,* to sulk.]

bouf·fant (bo͞o-fänt′) *adj.* Puffed-out; full: *a bouffant hair style.* [French, from present participle of *bouffer,* to puff up, from Old French.]

bouffe (bo͞of) *n.* See **comic opera.** [Short for OPÉRA BOUFFE.]

bou·gain·vil·lae·a (bo͞o′gən-vĭl′ē-ə, -vĭl′yə, -vē′ə, bō′-) *n.* Variant of **bougainvillea.**

Bou·gain·ville (bo͞o′gən-vĭl′, bo͞o-găn-vēl′). A volcanic island of Papua New Guinea in the Solomon Islands of the southwest Pacific Ocean.

Bougainville, Louis Antoine de. 1729–1811. French explorer who circumnavigated the globe (1766–1769) with a crew that included astronomers and naturalists.

bou·gain·vil·le·a also **bou·gain·vil·lae·a** (bo͞o′gən-vĭl′ē-ə, -vĭl′yə, -vē′ə, bō′-) *n.* Any of several South American woody shrubs or vines of the genus *Bougainvillea* having groups of three petallike, showy, variously colored bracts attached to the flowers. [New Latin *Bougainvillea,* genus name, after Louis Antoine de BOUGAINVILLE.]

bough (bou) *n.* A tree branch, especially a large or main branch. [Middle English, from Old English *bōh.* See **bhāghu-** in Appendix.]

♦**bought** (bôt) *v.* Past tense and past participle of **buy.** See Regional Note at **boughten.**

♦**bought·en** (bôt′n) *Chiefly Northern U.S. v.* A past participle of **buy.** —**boughten** *adj.* **1.** Commercially made; purchased, as opposed to homemade: *boughten bread.* **2.** Artificial; false. Used of teeth.

♦ ***REGIONAL NOTE:*** American regional dialects allow freer adjectival use of certain past participles of verbs than does Standard English. Time-honored examples are *boughten* (Chiefly Northern U.S.) and *bought* (Chiefly Southern U.S.) to mean "purchased rather than homemade": *boughten sugar, a boughten dress, bought bread.* The Northern form *boughten* (as in *store boughten*) features the participial ending *-en,* added to *bought,* the participial form, probably by analogy with more common participial adjectives such as *frozen.* Another development, analogous with *homemade,* is evident in *bought-made,* cited in *DARE* from a Texas informant.

bou·gie (bo͞o′zhē, -jē) *n.* **1.** *Medicine.* **a.** A slender, flexible, cylindrical instrument that is inserted into a bodily canal, such as the urethra, to dilate, examine, or medicate. **b.** See **suppository.** **2.** A wax candle. [French, from Old French, a fine wax, after *Bougie* (Bejaïa), a city of northern Algeria.]

bouil·la·baisse (bo͞o′yə-bās′, bo͞ol′yə-bās′) *n.* **1.** A highly seasoned fish stew made of several kinds of fish and shellfish. **2.** A combination of various different, often incongruous elements: *a bouillabaisse of special interests.* [French, from Provençal *bouiabaisso* : *boui,* imperative of *bouie,* to boil (from Latin *bullīre,* from *bulla,* bubble) + *abaisso,* imperative of *abeissa,* to lower (from Vulgar Latin *abbassiāre : Latin *ad-,* ad- + Medieval Latin *bassus,* low).]

bouil·lon (bo͞ol′yŏn′, -yən, bo͞o′yŏn′) *n.* A clear, thin broth made typically by simmering beef or chicken in water with seasonings. [French, from Old French, from *boulir,* to boil, from Latin *bullīre,* from *bulla,* bubble.]

bouillon cube *n.* A small cube of evaporated seasoned meat, poultry, or vegetable stock, used in making broth or to add flavor to soups or stews.

boul. *abbr.* Boulevard.

Bou·lan·ger (bo͞o-län-zhā′), **Georges Ernest Jean Marie.** 1837–1891. French military and political leader who after serving in the Franco-Prussian War (1870–1871) envisioned himself dictator and was accused of treason.

Boulanger, Nadia Juliette. 1887–1979. French music teacher of several modern American composers, including Virgil Thomson and Aaron Copland.

boul·der also **bowl·der** (bōl′dər) *n.* A large rounded mass of rock lying on the surface of the ground or embedded in the soil. [Middle English *bulder,* of Scandinavian origin. See **bhel-**[2] in Appendix.]

Boul·der (bōl′dər). A city of north-central Colorado northwest of Denver. It is a major Rocky Mountains resort and the seat of the University of Colorado (opened 1877). Population, 76,685.

bould·er·ing (bōl′dər-ĭng) *n. Sports.* Basic or intermediate climbing carried out on relatively small rocks that can be traversed without great risk of bodily harm in case of a fall. —**bould′er·er** *n.*

bou·le[1] (bo͞o′lē, bo͞o-lā′) *n.* **1.** The lower house of the modern Greek legislature. **2. a.** The senate of 400 founded by Solon in ancient Athens. **b.** A legislative assembly in any one of the ancient Greek states. [Greek *boulē.* See **gʷelə-** in Appendix.]

boule[2] (bo͞ol) *n.* A pear-shaped synthetic sapphire, ruby, or other alumina-based gem, produced by fusing and tinting alumina. [French, ball, from Old French, bubble, from Latin *bulla.*]

boule[3] (bo͞ol) *n.* Variant of **buhl.**

♦**boul·e·vard** (bo͝ol′ə-värd′, bo͞o′lə-) *n. Abbr.* **blvd., Blvd., boul. 1.** A broad city street, often tree-lined and landscaped. **2.** *Upper Midwest.* See **median strip.** See Regional Note at **neutral ground.** [French, from Old French *bollevart,* rampart converted to a promenade, from Middle Dutch *bolwerc,* bulwark. See BULWARK.]

bou·le·vard·ier (bo͞o′lə-vär-dyā′, -dîr′) *n.* A man about town. [Obsolete French, from *boulevard,* boulevard. See BOULEVARD.]

♦**boulevard strip** *n. Upper Midwest.* See **median strip.** See Regional Note at **neutral ground.**

bou·le·ver·se·ment (bo͞o′lə-vĕr′sə-mäN′) *n.* **1.** A violent uproar; a tumult. **2.** A reversal. [French, from Old French *bouleverser,* to overturn : *boule,* ball (from Latin *bulla*) + *verser,* to overturn (from Old French, from Latin *versāre,* frequentative of *vertere,* to turn; see **wer-**[2] in Appendix).]

Bou·lez (bo͞o-lĕz′), **Pierre.** Born 1925. French conductor and composer of atonal, avant-garde works, notably *Le Marteau sans Maître* (1955).

boulle (bo͞ol) *n.* Variant of **buhl.**

Bou·logne (bo͞o-lōn′, -lôn′yə) also **Bou·logne-sur-Mer** (-sûr-mĕr′). A city of northern France on the English Channel north-northwest of Amiens. Of Celtic origin, it is the leading fishing port of France. Population, 47,653.

Bou·logne-Bil·lan·court (bo͞o-lôn′yə-bē-yäN-ko͞or′). A city of north-central France, an industrial suburb of Paris. Population, 102,582.

Bou·logne-sur-Mer (bo͞o-lōn′sûr-mĕr′, -lôn′yə-). See **Boulogne.**

bounce (bouns) *v.* **bounced, bounc·ing, bounc·es.** —*intr.* **1.** To rebound after having struck an object or a surface. **2.** To move jerkily; bump: *The car bounced over the potholes.* **3.** To recover quickly, as from a setback: *The patient bounced back to good health.* **4.** To bound: *children bouncing into the room.* **5.** *Informal.* To be sent back by a bank as valueless: *a check that bounced.* **6.** *Baseball.* To hit a ground ball that rebounds before reaching an infielder: *The batter bounced out to the shortstop.* —*tr.* **1.** To cause to strike an object or a surface and rebound: *bounce a ball on the sidewalk.* **2.** *Slang.* **a.** To expel by force. **b.** To dismiss from employment. See Synonyms at **dismiss.** **3.** To write (a check) on an overdrawn bank account. —**bounce** *n.* **1.** A rebound. **2.** A sudden bound, spring, or leap. **3.** The capacity to rebound; spring: *a ball with bounce.* **4.** Spirit; liveliness. **5.** *Slang.* Expulsion; dismissal. **6.** *Chiefly British.* Loud, arrogant speech; bluster. [Probably from Middle English *bounsen,* to beat.]

bounc·er (boun′sər) *n.* **1.** *Slang.* A person employed to expel disorderly persons from a public place, especially a bar. **2.** *Baseball.* A ground ball hit in such a way that it bounces.

bounc·ing (boun′sĭng) *adj.* **1.** Vigorous; healthy: *a bouncing baby.* **2.** Spirited; lively: *a bouncing gait.* —**bounc′ing·ly** *adv.*

bouncing Bet (bĕt) *n.* A perennial Eurasian herb *(Saponaria officinalis)* having dense clusters of pink to whitish flowers. Also called *soapwort.* [From *Bet,* nickname for *Elizabeth.*]

bounc·y (boun′sē) *adj.* **-i·er, -i·est. 1.** Tending to bounce. **2.** Springy; elastic: *clean, bouncy hair.* **3.** Lively; energetic: *bouncy tunes.* —**bounc′i·ly** *adv.*

bound[1] (bound) *intr.v.* **bound·ed, bound·ing, bounds. 1.** To leap forward or upward; spring. **2.** To progress by forward leaps or springs. —**bound** *n.* **1.** A leap; a jump. **2.** A rebound; a bounce. [French *bondir,* to bounce, from Old French, to resound, perhaps from Vulgar Latin *bombitīre, from Latin *bombitāre,* to hum, from *bombus,* a humming sound, from Greek *bombos.*]

bound[2] (bound) *n.* **1.** Often **bounds.** A boundary; a limit: *Our joy knew no bounds. Your remarks exceed the bounds of reason.* **2. bounds.** The territory on, within, or near limiting lines: *the bounds of the kingdom.* —**bound** *v.* **bound·ed, bound·ing, bounds.** —*tr.* **1.** To set a limit to; confine: *a high wall that bounded the prison yard; lives that were bounded by poverty.* **2.** To constitute the boundary or limit of: *a city park that was bounded by busy streets.* **3.** To identify the boundaries of; demarcate. —*intr.* To border on another place, state, or country. [Middle English, from Old French *bodne, bonde* and Anglo-Norman *bunde,* both from Medieval Latin *bodina,* of Celtic origin.]

bound[3] (bound) *v.* Past tense and past participle of **bind.** —**bound** *adj.* **1.** Confined by bonds; tied: *bound and gagged hostages.* **2.** Being under legal or moral obligation: *bound by my promise.* **3.** *Abbr.* **bd.** Equipped with a cover or binding: *bound volumes.* **4.** Predetermined; certain: *We're bound to be late.* **5.** Determined; resolved: *She's bound to be mayor.* **6.** Constipated.

bound[4] (bound) *adj.* Headed or intending to head in a specified direction: *commuters bound for home; a south-bound train.* [Alteration of Middle English *boun,* ready, from Old Norse *būinn,* past participle of *būa,* to get ready. See **bheuə-** in Appendix.]

bound·a·ry (boun′də-rē, -drē) *n., pl.* **-ries. 1.** Something that indicates a border or limit. **2.** The border or limit so indicated.

SYNONYMS: *boundary, border, frontier, limit.* These nouns all denote a line or an area separating one piece of territory from another. A *boundary* is a limiting line: *A stone wall marked the boundary between the two farms.* A *border* is a line that separates

ă pat	oi boy
ā pay	ou out
âr care	o͝o took
ä father	o͞o boot
ĕ pet	ŭ cut
ē be	ûr urge
ĭ pit	th thin
ī pie	*th* this
îr pier	hw which
ŏ pot	zh vision
ō toe	ə about, item
ô paw	♦ regionalism

Stress marks: ′ (primary); ′ (secondary), as in **dictionary** (dĭk′shə-nĕr′ē)

political entities: *Customs officers inspected our luggage when we crossed the border.* *Frontier* denotes the part of a country that faces toward or fronts an adjoining country: *"that long* [Canadian] *frontier from the Atlantic to the Pacific Oceans, guarded only by neighborly respect and honorable obligations"* (Winston S. Churchill). *Limit* denotes a boundary that surrounds an area: *Cars cannot exceed 35 miles per hour within city limits.*

boundary condition *n. Mathematics.* The conditions specified for the solution to a set of differential equations.

boundary layer *n.* The layer of reduced velocity in fluids, such as air and water, that is immediately adjacent to the surface of a solid past which the fluid is flowing.

bound·en (boun′dən) *adj.* **1.** Obligatory: *their bounden duty.* **2.** *Archaic.* Being under obligation; obliged. [Middle English, past participle of *binden,* to bind, from Old English *bindan.* See BIND.]

bound·er (boun′dər) *n. Chiefly British.* An ill-bred, unscrupulous man; a cad.

bound form *n.* A linguistic element that always occurs as part of another word, such as *-ly* in *lovely.*

bound·less (bound′lĭs) *adj.* Being without boundaries or limits; infinite. See Synonyms at **infinite.** —**bound′less·ly** *adv.* —**bound′less·ness** *n.*

boun·te·ous (boun′tē-əs) *adj.* **1.** Giving or inclined to give generously. **2.** Generously and copiously given. See Synonyms at **liberal.** [Middle English *bountevous,* from Old French *bontive,* benevolent, from *bonte,* bounty. See BOUNTY.] —**boun′te·ous·ly** *adv.* —**boun′te·ous·ness** *n.*

boun·ti·ful (boun′tə-fəl) *adj.* **1.** Giving freely and generously; liberal. **2.** Marked by abundance; plentiful. See Synonyms at **liberal.** —**boun′ti·ful·ly** *adv.* —**boun′ti·ful·ness** *n.*

Boun·ti·ful (boun′tə-fəl). A city of north-central Utah, a residential suburb of Salt Lake City. Population, 32,877.

boun·ty (boun′tē) *n., pl.* **-ties. 1.** Liberality in giving. **2.** Something that is given liberally. **3.** A reward, inducement, or payment, especially one given by a government for acts deemed beneficial to the state, such as killing predatory animals, growing certain crops, starting certain industries, or enlisting for military service. See Synonyms at **bonus.** [Middle English *bounte,* from Old French *bonte,* from Latin *bonitās,* goodness, from *bonus,* good. See **deu-**[2] in Appendix.]

bounty hunter *n.* **1.** One who hunts predatory animals in order to collect a bounty. **2.** One who pursues a criminal or fugitive for whom a reward is offered.

bou·quet (bō-kā′, bo͞o-) *n.* **1.** A cluster of flowers; a nosegay. **2.** The fragrance typical of a wine or liqueur. [French, from Old French *bosquet,* thicket, diminutive of *bosc,* forest, of Germanic origin.]

SYNONYMS: *bouquet, nosegay, posy.* The central meaning shared by these nouns is "a bunch of cut flowers": *a bouquet of roses; a bride carrying a nosegay of lilies of the valley; gathered a posy of violets.* See also Synonyms at **fragrance.**

bouquet gar·ni (gär-nē′) *n., pl.* **bou·quets gar·nis** (bō-kāz′ gär-nē′, bo͞o-). A bunch of herbs tied together, wrapped in cheesecloth or enclosed in a small cloth sack, and immersed during cooking, as in a soup or stew. [French : *bouquet,* bunch + *garni,* past participle of *garnir,* to garnish.]

bou·quet·ier (bo͞o′kə-tyĕr′,-tîr′) *n.* A small container for holding flowers in a nosegay, shaped like a trumpet or a cup and having a deep handle to hold the stems of the flowers, the heads of which are kept in place by a strong pin inserted through holes in the side of the cup. Also called *porte bouquet.* [French, from *bouquet,* bouquet. See BOUQUET.]

bour·bon (bûr′bən) *n.* A whiskey distilled from a fermented mash containing not less than 51 percent corn in addition to malt and rye. [After *Bourbon* County in northeast Kentucky.]

Bour·bon[1] (bo͝or′bən, bo͝or-bôN′). French royal family descended from Louis I, Duke of Bourbon (1270?–1342), whose members have ruled in France (1589–1793 and 1814–1830), Spain (1700–1868, 1874–1931, and since 1975), and Naples and Sicily (1734–1860).

Bour·bon[2] (bûr′bən) *n.* A sociopolitical reactionary, especially a southern Democrat with highly conservative views. [After the Bourbon family.]

Bour·bon (bo͝or′bən, bo͝or-bôN′), Duc **Charles de.** 1490–1527. French general who served Holy Roman Emperor Charles V, led a failed invasion of France (1524), and was killed while leading a German-Spanish assault on Rome.

Bour·bon·nais (bo͝or-bôN-nā′). A historical region and former province of central France in the Massif Central. It was held by the counts (later dukes) of Bourbon until 1527, when Francis I added it to the French crown lands.

bour·don (bo͝or′dn) *n. Music.* **1.** The monotonic drone bass of a bagpipe. **2.** An organ stop, commonly of the 16-foot pipes. [Middle English *burdoun,* bass, from Old French *bourdon.*]

bourg (bo͝org) *n.* **1.** A market town. **2.** A medieval village, especially one situated near a castle. [French, from Old French, from Late Latin *burgus,* fortress, of Germanic origin. See **bhergh-**[2] in Appendix.]

bour·geois (bo͝or-zhwä′, bo͝or′zhwä′) *n., pl.* **bourgeois. 1.** A person belonging to the middle class. **2.** A person whose attitudes and behavior are marked by conformity to the standards and conventions of the middle class. **3.** In Marxist theory, a member of the property-owning class; a capitalist. —**bourgeois** *adj.* **1.** Of, relating to, or typical of the middle class. **2.** Held to be preoccupied with respectability and material values. [French, from Old French *burgeis,* citizen of a town, from *bourg,* bourg. See BOURG.]

Bour·geois (bo͝or-zhwä′), **Léon Victor Auguste.** 1851–1925. French statesman who was a member of the Permanent Court of Arbitration at The Hague (1903–1925) and helped draft the Covenant of the League of Nations (1919). He won the 1920 Nobel Peace Prize.

bour·geoise (bo͝or-zhwäz′, bo͝or′zhwäz′) *n., pl.* **-geois·es** (-zhwä′zĭz). A woman belonging to the middle class. [French, feminine of *bourgeois,* bourgeois. See BOURGEOIS.] —**bour·geoise′** *adj.*

bour·geoi·sie (bo͝or′zhwä-zē′) *n.* **1.** The middle class. **2.** In Marxist theory, the social group opposed to the proletariat in the class struggle. [French, from *bourgeois,* bourgeois. See BOURGEOIS.]

bourg·eoi·si·fi·ca·tion (bo͝or-zhwä′zə-fĭ-kā′shən) *n.* The act or process of adopting or the condition of having adopted the characteristics attributed to the bourgeoisie: *"Bourgeoisification, deplorable as it is, has good points too"* (Robert M. Adams).

bour·geoi·si·fy (bo͝or-zhwä′zə-fī′) *tr.v.* **-fied, -fy·ing, -fies.** To cause to adopt the characteristics attributed to the bourgeoisie: *"Rock 'n' roll . . . had become cozy and bourgeoisified"* (Stephen Schiff).

bour·geon (bûr′jən) *v.* Variant of **burgeon.**

Bourges (bo͝orzh). A city of central France south-southeast of Orléans. It was a Roman provincial capital under Augustus and the site of a notable university that was founded by Louis XI in 1463 but abolished during the French Revolution. Population, 76,432.

Bour·gogne (bo͝or-gôn′yə). See **Burgundy**[2]**.**

Bourke-White (bûrk′hwīt′, -wīt′), **Margaret.** 1906–1971. American photographer and writer. An editor of *Life* magazine (1936–1969), she photographed such diverse subjects as the rural South, Soviet life, and the release of concentration camp victims.

bourn[1] also **bourne** (bôrn, bōrn, bo͝orn) *n.* A small stream; a brook. [Middle English, from Old English *burna.* See **bhreu-** in Appendix.]

bourn[2] also **bourne** (bôrn, bōrn, bo͝orn) *n. Archaic.* **1.** A destination; a goal. **2.** A boundary; a limit. [French *bourne,* from French dialectal *bosne, borne,* from Old French *bodne,* limit, boundary marker, from Medieval Latin *bodina,* of Celtic origin.]

Bourne·mouth (bôrn′məth, bōrn′-, bo͝orn′-). A borough of southern England on an inlet of the English Channel southwest of Southampton. It is a popular resort and fine-arts center. Population, 143,000.

bour·rée (bo͞o-rā′, bo͞o-) *n.* **1.a.** An old French dance resembling the gavotte, usually in quick duple time beginning with an upbeat. **b.** The music for this dance. **2.** A pas de bourrée. [French, from *bourrer,* to stuff, from *bourre,* hair, fluff, from Late Latin *burra,* a shaggy garment.]

bourse (bo͝ors) *n.* A stock exchange, especially one in a continental European city. [French, purse, bourse, from Late Latin *bursa,* bag. See BURSA.]

bouse also **bowse** (bouz) *Nautical.*—*v.* **boused, bous·ing, bous·es** also **bowsed, bows·ing, bows·es.** —*tr.* To pull or hoist with a tackle. —*intr.* To hoist. [Origin unknown.]

bou·stro·phe·don (bo͞o′strə-fēd′n, -fē′dŏn′) *n.* An ancient method of writing in which the lines are inscribed alternately from right to left and from left to right. [From Greek *boustrophēdon,* turning like an ox while plowing : *bous,* ox; see **g**[w]**ou-** in Appendix + *strophē,* a turning, from *strephein,* to turn. See **streb(h)-** in Appendix.] —**bou·stroph′e·don′ic** (-strŏf′ĭ-dŏn′ĭk) *adj.*

bout (bout) *n.* **1.** A contest between antagonists; a match: *a wrestling bout.* **2.** A period of time spent in a particular way; a spell: *"His tremendous bouts of drinking had wrecked his health"* (Thomas Wolfe). [From obsolete English *bought,* a turning (influenced by ABOUT), from Middle English, from *bowen,* to bend, turn. See BOW[2].]

bou·tique (bo͞o-tēk′) *n.* **1.a.** A small retail shop that specializes in gifts, fashionable clothes, accessories, or food, for example. **b.** A small shop located within a large department store or supermarket. **2.** An investment boutique. —*attributive.* Often used to modify another noun: *boutique clothes; boutique food.* [French, from Old French *botique,* small shop, from Old Provençal *botica,* from Latin *apothēca,* storehouse. See APOTHECARY.]

boutique brewery *n.* See **microbrewery.**

bou·ton (bo͞o-tôn′) *n.* A knoblike enlargement at the end of an axon, where it synapses with other neurons. [French, button, from Old French. See BUTTON.]

bou·ton·niere also **bou·ton·nière** (bo͞o′tə-nîr′, -tən-yâr′) *n.* A flower or small bunch of flowers worn in a buttonhole. [French *boutonnière,* from Old French, buttonhole, from *bouton,* button. See BOUTON.]

bou·var·di·a (bo͞o-vär′dē-ə) *n.* Any of several Mexican and Central American shrubs or herbs of the genus *Bouvardia* cultivated for their showy, narrowly tubular, variously colored flowers

boutonniere

bouzouki

ă pat	oi boy
ā pay	ou out
âr care	o͝o took
ä father	o͞o boot
ĕ pet	ŭ cut
ē be	ûr urge
ĭ pit	th thin
ī pie	*th* this
îr pier	hw which
ŏ pot	zh vision
ō toe	ə about, item
ô paw	♦ regionalism

Stress marks: ′ (primary); ′ (secondary), as in **dictionary** (dĭk′shə-nĕr′ē)

grouped in terminal cymes. [New Latin *Bouvardia,* genus name, after Charles *Bouvard* (1572–1658), French physician.]

Bou·vier des Flan·dres (bo͞o-vyā′ də flăn′dərz, dā fläɴ′-drə) *n.* Any of a breed of large, strong dogs developed in Belgium, having a rough, fawn to black coat and originally used for herding and guarding cattle. [French : *bouvier,* cowherd + *des,* of + *Flandres,* Flanders.]

bou·zou·ki (bo͞o-zo͞o′kē, bə-) *n. Music.* A Greek stringed instrument resembling a mandolin. [Modern Greek *mpouzouki,* probably of Turkish origin.]

Bo·vet (bō-vā′, -vĕt′), **Daniel.** Born 1907. Swiss-born Italian physiologist. He won a 1957 Nobel Prize for the development of muscle relaxants and the first synthetic antihistamine.

bo·vid (bō′vĭd) *adj.* Of or belonging to the family Bovidae, which includes hoofed, hollow-horned ruminants such as cattle, sheep, goats, and buffaloes. **—bovid** *n.* A member of the family Bovidae. [From New Latin *Bovidae,* family name, from Latin *bōs,* cow. See BOVINE.]

bo·vine (bō′vīn′, -vēn′) *adj.* **1.** Of, relating to, or resembling a ruminant mammal of the genus *Bos,* such as an ox, cow, or buffalo. **2.** Sluggish, dull, and stolid. **—bovine** *n.* An animal of the genus *Bos.* [Late Latin *bovīnus,* from Latin *bōs,* cow. See **gʷou-** in Appendix.]

bovine growth hormone *n. Abbr.* **BGH** A naturally occurring hormone of cattle that regulates growth and milk production. It may also be produced artificially by genetic engineering techniques and administered to cows to increase milk production. Also called *bovine somatotropin.*

bow¹ (bou) *n. Nautical.* **1.** The front section of a ship or boat. **2.** The oar or the person wielding the oar closest to the bow. [Middle English *boue,* probably of Low German origin. See **bheug-** in Appendix.]

bow² (bou) *v.* **bowed, bow·ing, bows.** *—intr.* **1.** To bend or curve downward; stoop. **2.** To incline the body or head or bend the knee in greeting, consent, courtesy, acknowledgment, submission, or veneration. **3.** To yield in defeat or out of courtesy; submit. See Synonyms at **yield.** *—tr.* **1.** To bend (the head, knee, or body) to express greeting, consent, courtesy, acknowledgment, submission, or veneration. **2.** To convey (greeting, for example) by bending the body. **3.** To escort deferentially: *bowed us into the restaurant.* **4.** To cause to acquiesce; submit. **5.** To overburden: *Grief bowed them down.* **—bow** *n.* An inclination of the head or body, as in greeting, consent, courtesy, acknowledgment, submission, or veneration. ***—phrasal verb.* bow out.** To remove oneself; withdraw. ***—idiom.* bow and scrape.** To behave obsequiously. [Middle English *bowen,* from Old English *būgan.* See **bheug-** in Appendix.]

bow³ (bō) *n.* **1.** A bent, curved, or arched object. **2.** A weapon consisting of a curved, flexible strip of material, especially wood, strung taut from end to end and used to launch arrows. **3.a.** An archer. **b.** Archers considered as a group. **4.a.** *Music.* A rod having horsehair drawn tightly between its two raised ends, used in playing instruments of the violin and viol families. **b.** A stroke made by this rod. **5.** A knot usually having two loops and two ends; a bowknot. **6.a.** A frame for the lenses of a pair of eyeglasses. **b.** The part of such a frame passing over the ear. **7.** A rainbow. **8.** An oxbow. **—bow** *v.* **bowed, bow·ing, bows.** *—tr.* **1.** To bend (something) into the shape of a bow. **2.** *Music.* To play (a stringed instrument) with a bow. *—intr.* **1.** To bend into a curve or bow. **2.** *Music.* To play a stringed instrument with a bow. [Middle English *bowe,* from Old English *boga.* See **bheug-** in Appendix.]

Bow (bō), **Clara.** Known as "the It Girl." 1905–1965. American actress whose roles in silent films, such as *Mantrap* (1926) and *It* (1927), made her a symbol of the Roaring Twenties.

bow compass *n.* A drawing compass with legs that are connected by an adjustable metal spring band.

♦ **bow·da·cious** (bō′dā′shəs) *adj. & adv. Southern & South Midland U.S.* Variant of **bodacious.**

Bow·ditch (bou′dĭch), **Nathaniel.** 1773–1838. American mathematician and astronomer noted for his works concerning navigation.

bowd·ler·ize (bōd′lə-rīz′, boud′-) *tr.v.* **-ized, -iz·ing, -iz·es.** **1.** To expurgate (a book, for example) prudishly. **2.** To modify, as by shortening or simplifying or by skewing the content in a certain manner. [After Thomas *Bowdler* (1754–1825), who published an expurgated edition of Shakespeare in 1818.] **—bowd′ler·ism** *n.* **—bowd′ler·i·za′tion** (-lər-ĭ-zā′shən) *n.* **—bowd′ler·iz′er** *n.*

bow·el (bou′əl, boul) *n.* **1.a.** *Often* **bowels.** The intestine. **b.** A part or division of the intestine: *the large bowel.* **2. bowels.** The interior of something: *in the bowels of the ship.* **3. bowels.** *Archaic.* The seat of pity or the gentler emotions. [Middle English, from Old French *boel,* from Latin *botellus,* small intestine, diminutive of *botulus,* sausage.]

Bow·ell (bō′əl), Sir **Mackenzie.** 1823–1917. British-born Canadian prime minister (1894–1896) who later led the Conservative opposition (1896–1906).

bowel movement *n. Abbr.* **b.m.** **1.** The discharge of waste matter from the large intestine; defecation. **2.** The waste matter discharged from the large intestine; feces.

Bow·en (bō′ən), **Catherine Drinker.** 1897–1973. American writer of semifictional biographies, such as *The Lion and the Throne* (1957), a life of Sir Edward Coke.

bow·er¹ (bou′ər) *n.* **1.** A shaded, leafy recess; an arbor. **2.** A woman's private chamber in a medieval castle; a boudoir. **3.** A rustic cottage; a country retreat. **—bower** *tr.v.* **-ered, -er·ing, -ers.** To enclose in or as if in a bower; embower. [Middle English *bour,* a dwelling, from Old English *būr.* See **bheue-** in Appendix.] **—bow′er·y** *adj.*

bow·er² (bou′ər) *n. Nautical.* An anchor carried at the bow.

bow·er·bird (bou′ər-bûrd′) *n.* Any of various birds of the family Ptilonorhynchidae of Australia and New Guinea, the males of which build large, elaborate structures of grasses, twigs, and brightly colored materials to attract females.

Bow·er·y (bou′ə-rē, bou′rē). A section of lower Manhattan in New York City. The street that gives the area its name was once the road to Peter Stuyvesant's *bouwerij,* or farm.

bow·fin (bō′fĭn′) *n.* A primitive, bony freshwater fish *(Amia calva)* of central and eastern North America, with a long, spineless dorsal fin. Also called *dogfish, mudfish.*

bow·front (bō′frŭnt′) *adj.* **1.** Having an outward-curving front: *a bowfront bureau.* **2.** Designed or constructed with a bow window in front: *a bowfront house.*

bow·head (bō′hĕd′) *n.* A whalebone whale *(Balaena mysticetus)* of Arctic seas, having a very large head and an arched upper jaw.

Bow·ie (bo͞o′ē). A city of west-central Maryland northeast of Washington, D.C. It is primarily residential. Population, 33,695.

Bow·ie (bo͞o′ē, bō′ē), **James.** 1796–1836. American-born Mexican colonist who joined the Texan forces during the struggle for independence from Mexico. He died during the defense of the Alamo.

bow·ie knife (bō′ē, bo͞o′ē) *n.* A single-edged steel hunting knife, about 15 inches (38 centimeters) in length, having a hilt and a crosspiece. [After James BOWIE.]

bow·knot (bō′nŏt′) *n.* A knot with large, decorative loops.

bowl¹ (bōl) *n.* **1.a.** A hemispherical vessel, wider than it is deep, used for holding food or fluids. **b.** The contents of such a vessel. **2.** A drinking goblet. **3.** A bowl-shaped part, as of a spoon or pipe. **4.a.** A bowl-shaped topographic depression. **b.** A bowl-shaped stadium or outdoor theater. **5.** *Football.* Any of various postseason games played between specially selected teams. [Middle English *bowle,* from Old English *bolla.* See **bhel-²** in Appendix.]

bowie knife

bowl² (bōl) *n.* **1.** A large wooden ball weighted or slightly flattened so as to roll with a bias. **2.** *Sports.* A roll or throw of the ball, as in bowling. **3. bowls.** *(used with a sing. verb). Sports & Games.* See **lawn bowling.** **4.** A revolving cylinder or drum in a machine. **—bowl** *v.* **bowled, bowl·ing, bowls.** *—intr.* **1.** *Sports.* **a.** To participate in a game of bowling. **b.** To throw or roll a ball in bowling. **c.** To hurl a cricket ball from one end of the pitch toward the batsman at the other, keeping the arm straight throughout the delivery. **2.** To move quickly and smoothly, especially by rolling: *The children bowled along on their bicycles.* *—tr.* **1.** To throw or roll (a ball). **2.** *Sports.* **a.** To achieve (a specified score) by bowling. **b.** To perform (a specified amount, as a string or game) in bowling. **3.** To move quickly and smoothly by or as if by rolling: *bowled a tire from the garage.* **4.** To meet or strike with or as if with the force of a rapidly rolling object. ***—phrasal verbs.* bowl out.** *Sports.* To retire (a batsman in cricket) with a bowled ball that knocks the bails off the wicket. **bowl over.** **1.** To take by surprise. **2.** To make a powerful impression on; overwhelm. [Middle English *boule,* from Old French, from Latin *bulla,* round object.]

bowl·der (bōl′dər) *n.* Variant of **boulder.**

bow·leg (bō′lĕg′) *n.* **1.** A leg having an outward curvature in the region of the knee. **2.** The condition of such a curvature of the legs.

bow·leg·ged (bō′lĕg′ĭd, -lĕgd′) *adj.* Having bowlegs.

bowl·er¹ (bō′lər) *n. Sports.* One that bowls, as in cricket or bowling.

bowl·er² (bō′lər) *n.* A derby hat. [Probably from BOWL².]

bow·line (bō′lĭn, -līn′) *n.* **1.** *Nautical.* A rope attached to the weather leech of a square sail to hold the leech forward when sailing close-hauled. **2.** A knot forming a loop that does not slip. ***—idiom.* on a bowline.** *Nautical.* Close-hauled. [Middle English *bouline,* probably from Middle Danish *bovline* or Middle Low German *bōlīne,* both from *bōch līne* : *bōch,* bow + *līne,* line (from Latin *līnea*; see LINE¹).]

bowl·ing (bō′lĭng) *n. Sports & Games.* **1.a.** A game played by rolling a ball down a wooden alley in order to knock down a triangular group of ten pins. Also called *tenpins.* **b.** A similar game, such as duckpins or ninepins. **2.** Lawn bowling **3.** The playing of one of these games.

bowling alley

bowling alley *n. Sports.* **1.** A smooth, level wooden lane used in bowling. **2.** A building or room containing lanes for bowling.

bowling ball *n. Sports.* A large spherical ball, usually of rubber or plastic, having one or more indentations for the thumb and fingers.

bowling green *n. Sports & Games.* A level grassy area for lawn bowling.

Bowl·ing Green (bō′lĭng grēn′). **1.** A city of southern Kentucky southeast of Owensboro. It was occupied by the Confederates from the start of the Civil War until 1862. Population, 40,450. **2.** A city of northwest Ohio south-southwest of Toledo. Bowling

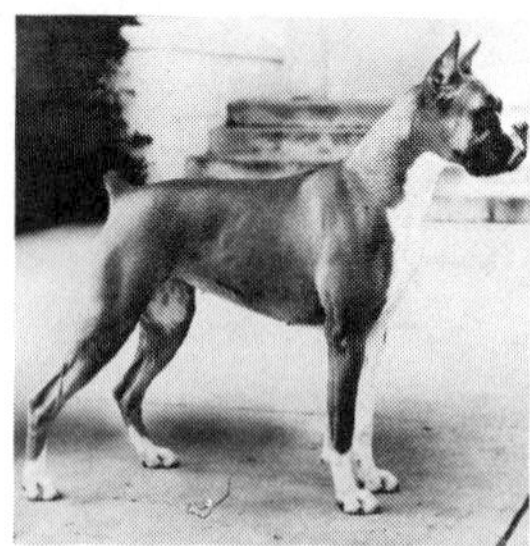
boxer³

boxing²
Muhammad Ali and Jimmy Young at the Capital Centre in Landover, Maryland, on April 30, 1976

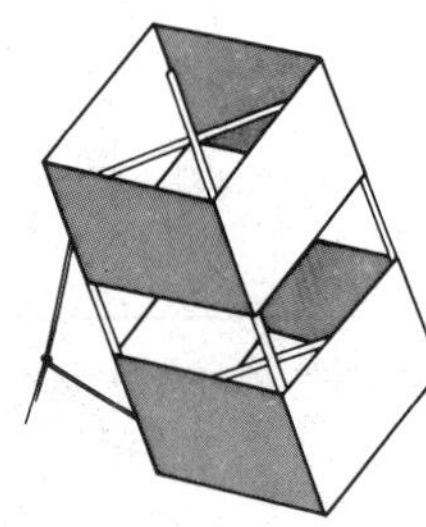
box kite

box turtle
Eastern box turtle
Terrapene carolina

Green State University (established 1910) is located here. Population, 25,728.

bow·man¹ (bō′mən) *n.* An archer.

bow·man² (bou′mən) *n. Nautical.* A person who oars, rows, or paddles at the bow of a boat.

Bow·man's capsule (bō′mənz) *n. Anatomy.* A double-walled, cup-shaped structure around the glomerulus of each nephron of the vertebrate kidney. It serves as a filter to remove organic wastes, excess inorganic salts, and water. [After Sir William *Bowman* (1816–1892), British surgeon.]

bow pen (bō) *n.* A bow compass with a pen at the end of one leg.

bow saw (bō) *n.* A saw with a slender blade connected at each end to a narrow handle that curves outward like an archer's bow.

bowse (bouz) *v.* Variant of **bouse.**

Bow·ser (bou′zər). A trademark used for a mobile fuel tank and pump employed in refueling aircraft and other vehicles.

bow·shot (bō′shŏt′) *n.* The distance that an arrow can be shot.

bow·sprit (bou′sprĭt′, bō′-) *n. Nautical.* A spar, extending forward from the stem of a ship, to which the stays of the foremast are fastened. [Middle English *bouspret,* possibly from Middle Low German *bōchsprēt* : *bōch,* bow + *sprēt,* sprit; see **sper-** in Appendix.]

bow·string (bō′strĭng′) *n.* The cord attached to both ends of an archer's bow.

bowstring hemp *n.* **1.** Any of several tropical African and Asian perennial plants of the genus *Sansevieria,* having thick, swordlike, spine-tipped leaves grouped in rosettes. **2.** The fibers of any of these plants, used for bowstrings, cordage, mats, and nets.

bow tie (bō) *n.* A short necktie fashioned into a bowknot close to the throat.

bow window (bō) *n.* A bay window built in a curve.

bow-wow or **bow·wow** (bou′wou′) —*n.* **1.a.** The bark of a dog. **b.** *Informal.* A dog. **2.** Outcry; clamor. **3.** An overbearing manner. —*adj.* Commanding, especially in an arrogant manner; overbearing. [Imitative.]

bow·yer (bō′yər) *n.* **1.** One who makes or sells bows for archery. **2.** *Archaic.* An archer.

box¹ (bŏks) *n.* **1.** *Abbr.* **bx., bx a.** A container typically constructed with four sides perpendicular to the base and often having a lid or cover. **b.** The amount or quantity that such a container can hold. **2.** A square or rectangle: *Draw a box around your answer.* **3.a.** A separated compartment in a public place of entertainment, such as a theater or stadium, for the accommodation of a small group. **b.** An area of a public place, such as a courtroom or stadium, marked off and restricted for use by persons performing a specific function: *a jury box.* **4.** A small structure serving as a shelter: *a sentry box.* **5.** *Chiefly British.* A small country house used as a sporting lodge: *a shooting box.* **6.** A box stall. **7.** The raised seat for the driver of a coach or carriage. **8.** *Baseball.* **a.** An area on a diamond marked by lines designating where the batter may stand. **b.** Any of various designated areas for other team members, such as the pitcher, catcher, and coaches. **9.** *Sports.* A penalty box. **10.** *Printing.* Featured printed matter enclosed by hairlines, a border, or white space and placed within or between text columns. **11.** A hollow made in the side of a tree for the collection of sap. **12.** A post office box. **13.a.** An insulating, enclosing, or protective casing or part in a machine. **b.** A signaling device enclosed in a casing: *an alarm box.* **14.a.** *Informal.* A television. **b.** A very large portable radio. **15.** *Chiefly British.* A gift or gratuity, especially one given at Christmas. **16.** An awkward or perplexing situation; a predicament. **17.** *Vulgar Slang.* The vulva and the vagina. —**box** *tr.v.* **boxed, box·ing, box·es. 1.** To pack in a box. **2.** To confine in or as if in a box. **3.** To border or enclose with or as if with a box: *Key sections of the report are boxed off.* **4.** To provide a housing or case for (a machine part, for example). **5.a.** To limit the activity or influence of by or as if by creating a restrictive structure or outlining a territory: *The legislature was boxed in by its earlier decisions.* **b.** *Sports.* To block (a competitor or opponent) from advancing, especially to hinder an opponent from getting a rebound in basketball by placing oneself between the opponent and the basket: *was boxed out by the tallest player on the team; was boxed in on the homestretch.* **6.** *Nautical.* To boxhaul. **7.** To cut a hole in (a tree) for the collection of sap. **8.** To blend (paint) by pouring alternately between two containers. **9.** To change the shape of (a structure, such as a wall) by applying lath and plaster or boarding. —***idioms.* box the compass. 1.** To name the 32 points of the compass in proper order. **2.** To make a complete revolution or reversal. **in a box.** *Informal.* In a very difficult or restrictive situation. [Middle English, from Old English, from Late Latin *buxis,* from Greek *puxis,* from *puxos,* box tree.]

box² (bŏks) *n.* A slap or blow with the hand or fist: *a box on the ear.* —**box** *v.* **boxed, box·ing, box·es.** —*tr.* **1.** To hit with the hand or fist. **2.** *Sports.* To take part in a boxing match with. —*intr.* To fight with the fists or in a boxing match. [Middle English.]

box³ (bŏks) *n., pl.* **box** or **box·es. 1.a.** Any of several evergreen shrubs or trees of the genus *Buxus,* especially the Eurasian species *B. sempervirens,* having opposite, leathery, simple leaves and clusters of unisexual flowers. It is widely grown as a hedge plant. **b.** The hard, light yellow wood of these plants, used to make musical instruments, rulers, inlays, and engraving blocks. **2.** Any of several other shrubs or trees with similar foliage or timber. [Middle English, from Old English, from Latin *buxus,* from Greek *puxos.*]

box·board (bŏks′bôrd′, -bōrd′) *n.* A firm cardboard used for making boxes.

box calf *n.* Calfskin treated with chromium salts and having square markings on the grain. [After Joseph *Box,* a 19th-century London bootmaker.]

box camera *n.* A simple camera shaped like a box and usually having a fixed focus and a single shutter speed.

box·car (bŏks′kär′) *n.* **1.** A fully enclosed railroad car, typically having sliding side doors, used to transport freight. **2. boxcars.** *Games.* A pair of sixes on the first throw in craps.

box coat *n.* **1.** A coat designed to hang loosely from the shoulders. **2.** A heavy overcoat formerly worn by coachmen. [BOX¹ + COAT.]

box elder *n.* A North American maple tree *(Acer negundo)* having pinnately compound leaves with coarsely toothed to lobed leaflets. Also called *ash-leaved maple.*

box·er¹ (bŏk′sər) *n. Sports.* One who fights with the fists as a sport.

box·er² (bŏk′sər) *n.* One that packs items in boxes.

box·er³ (bŏk′sər) *n.* A medium-sized, short-haired dog of a breed developed in Germany, having a brownish coat and a short, square-jawed muzzle. [German, from English BOXER¹ (from its pugnacious nature).]

Box·er (bŏk′sər) *n.* A member of a secret society in China that unsuccessfully attempted in 1900 to drive foreigners from the country by violence and force Chinese Christians to renounce their religion. [Approximate translation of Chinese (Mandarin) *yì hé quán,* righteous harmonious fists, alteration of *yì hé tuán,* righteous harmonious society : *yì,* righteous + *hé,* harmonious + *tuán,* society.]

boxer shorts *pl.n.* Men's full-cut undershorts.

box·fish (bŏks′fĭsh′) *n., pl.* **boxfish** or **-fish·es.** See **trunkfish.**

box·haul (bŏks′hôl′) *tr.v.* **-hauled, -haul·ing, -hauls.** *Nautical.* To turn (a square-rigged ship) about on the heel by bracing the sails aback. [BOX¹, to confine, reverse + HAUL.]

box·ing¹ (bŏk′sĭng) *n.* **1.** Material used for boxes. **2.** A boxlike covering or enclosure. **3.** The act of enclosing in a box.

box·ing² (bŏk′sĭng) *n. Sports.* The act, activity, or sport of fighting with the fists.

Box·ing Day (bŏk′sĭng) *n.* The first weekday after Christmas, celebrated as a holiday in parts of the British Commonwealth, when Christmas gifts are traditionally given to service workers.

boxing glove *n. Sports.* A heavily padded leather mitten worn for boxing.

box kite *n.* A tailless kite formed from or as if from two or more open-ended boxes connected at the corners by shafts spanning an interval of open space.

box lunch *n.* An individually portioned lunch packed in a small box.

box office *n.* **1.** A booth, as in a theater or stadium, where tickets are sold. **2.a.** The drawing power of a theatrical entertainment or of a performer; popular appeal. **b.** A factor influencing this power: *Notoriety is usually good box office.* **3.** Total attendance for an entertainment; turnout. **4.** The amount of money received from ticket sales for an entertainment. [So named because it was originally an office for the booking of boxes in a theater.] —**box′-of′fice** (bŏks′ô′fĭs, -ŏf′ĭs) *adj.*

box pleat *n.* A double pleat having two upper folds facing in opposite directions and two under folds facing each other.

box score *n. Sports.* A printed summary of a game, especially in baseball, in the form of a table listing the players and their positions and recording individual performance.

box seat *n.* **1.** A seat in a box at a public place of entertainment, such as a theater or stadium. **2.** A storage box on a coach, the lid of which serves as a seat for the driver.

box set *n.* A stage set with a ceiling and three walls.

box social *n.* A fund-raising event in which donated box lunches are auctioned off.

box spring *n.* A bedspring consisting of a cloth-covered frame containing rows of coil springs.

box stall *n.* A large enclosed stall for a single animal.

box step *n.* A dance step in which the feet are moved in a pattern approximating a square.

box·thorn (bŏks′thôrn′) *n.* See **matrimony vine.**

box top *n.* The top surface, as a flap or strip, of a box containing a commercial product, typically bearing identification and used to prove the date or fact of purchase.

box turtle *n.* Any of several North American land turtles of the genus *Terrapene* having a hinged plastron that pulls up against the carapace, allowing the animal to become completely encased within its shell. Also called *box tortoise.*

box·wood (bŏks′wŏŏd′) *n.* **1.** The box plant. **2.** The wood of the box plant.

box·y (bŏk′sē) *adj.* **-i·er, -i·est.** Resembling a box, especially in simplicity or rectangularity. —**box′i·ness** *n.*

boy (boi) *n.* **1.** A male child. **2.** An immature or inexperienced man, especially a young man. **3.** A son: *his youngest boy.* **4.** *Informal.* A grown man; a fellow: *a night out with the boys.* **5.** A male who comes from or belongs to a particular place: *a city boy.* **6.** *Offensive.* A male servant, such as a valet. **—boy** *interj.* Used to express mild astonishment, elation, or disgust: *Oh boy—what a surprise!* [Middle English *boi,* possibly from Old French *embuié,* servant, past participle of *embuier,* to fetter.] **—boy′hood′** *n.*

bo•yar (bō-yär′, boi′ər) *n.* A member of a class of higher Russian nobility that until the time of Peter I headed the civil and military administration of the country and participated in an early duma. [From *boiaren,* from Russian *boyarin,* from Old Russian *boljarin,* from Turkic *baylar,* pl. of *bay,* rich; akin to Turkish *bay,* rich, gentleman.]

boy•cott (boi′kŏt′) *tr.v.* **-cott•ed, -cott•ing, -cotts. 1.** To act together in abstaining from using, buying, or dealing with as an expression of protest or disfavor or as a means of coercion. See Synonyms at **blackball. 2.** To abstain from or unite with others in abstaining from using, buying, or dealing with. **—boycott** *n.* The act or an instance of boycotting. [After Charles C. *Boycott* (1832–1897), English land agent in Ireland.] **—boy′cott′er** *n.*

WORD HISTORY: Charles C. Boycott seems to have been forced by his strong sense of duty into becoming a household word. Boycott was the estate agent of the Earl of Erne in County Mayo, Ireland. The earl was one of the absentee landowners who as a group held most of the land in Ireland. Boycott was chosen in the fall of 1880 to be the test case for a new policy advocated by Charles Parnell, an Irish politician who wanted land reform. Any landlord who would not charge lower rents or any tenant who took over the farm of an evicted tenant would be given the complete cold shoulder by Parnell's supporters. Boycott, a former British soldier, refused to charge lower rents and ejected his tenants. At this point members of Parnell's Irish Land League stepped in, and Boycott and his family found themselves isolated—without servants, farmhands, service in stores, or mail delivery. Boycott's name was quickly adopted as the term for this treatment, not just in English but in other languages such as French, Dutch, German, and Russian.

Boyd Orr (boid′ ôr′, ōr′), Lord **John.** 1880–1971. British nutritionist. He won the 1949 Nobel Peace Prize for his efforts to alleviate world hunger.

boy•friend also **boy friend** (boi′frĕnd′) *n.* **1.** A favored male companion or sweetheart. **2.** A male friend.

boy•ish (boi′ĭsh) *adj.* Characteristic of or befitting a boy: *boyish charm.* **—boy′ish•ly** *adv.* **—boy′ish•ness** *n.*

Boyle (boil), **Kay.** Born 1903. American writer whose works examine the relationships between Europeans and Americans.

Boyle, Robert. 1627–1691. Irish-born British physicist and chemist whose precise definitions of chemical elements and reactions began the separation of chemistry from alchemy.

Boyle's law (boilz) *n.* The principle that at a constant temperature the volume of a confined ideal gas varies inversely with its pressure. [After Robert BOYLE.]

Boyne (boin). A river of eastern Ireland flowing about 113 km (70 mi) to the Irish Sea. In the Battle of the Boyne on July 1, 1690, the armies of King William III defeated the forces of James II, who fled to France.

Boyn•ton Beach (boin′tən). A city of southeast Florida on the Atlantic Ocean north of Boca Raton. It is a seaside resort. Population, 35,624.

Boy Scout (boi) *n.* **1.** A member of a worldwide organization of young men and boys, founded in England in 1908, for character development and citizenship training. **2.** Often **boy scout.** *Slang.* A man whose attitudes and behavior are felt to be naive.

boy•sen•ber•ry (boi′zən-bĕr′ē) *n.* **1.** A prickly bramble of uncertain origin but ultimately derived from a western North American blackberry *(Rubus ursinus).* **2.** The edible, dark wine-red to nearly black fruit of this plant, having a taste suggestive of raspberries. [After Rudolph *Boysen* (died 1950), American botanist.]

boy wonder *n.* An extremely talented and accomplished young man.

Boz•ca•a•da (bōz′jä-ä-dä′). An island of Turkey in the northeast Aegean Sea south of the Dardanelles. According to tradition, it was the site of a Greek naval station during the Trojan War.

Boze•man (bōz′mən). A city of southwest Montana east-southeast of Butte. Settled in the 1860's, it is a gateway to Yellowstone National Park. Population, 21,645.

bo•zo (bō′zō) *n., pl.* **-zos.** *Slang.* **1.** A fellow; a guy. **2.** A dunce; a fool. [Origin unknown.]

bp[1] *abbr.* Boiling point.

bp[2] also **BP** *abbr.* Beautiful people.

BP *abbr.* **1.** Or **B/P.** Bills payable. **2.** Or **B.P.** Blood pressure.

bp. *abbr.* **1.** Birthplace. **2.** *Games.* Bishop.

B.P. *abbr.* **1.** Bachelor of Pharmacy. **2.** Bachelor of Philosophy.

bpd *abbr.* Barrels per day.

B.Pd. *abbr.* Bachelor of Pedagogy.

B.P.E. *abbr.* Bachelor of Physical Education.

B.Ph. *abbr.* Bachelor of Philosophy.

B.Phil. *abbr.* Bachelor of Philosophy.

bpi *abbr. Computer Science.* **1.** Bits per inch. **2.** Bytes per inch.

B picture *n.* A movie produced on a low budget, originally made to accompany the main feature in a double billing. Also called *B movie.*

bpl *abbr.* Birthplace.

BPOE or **B.P.O.E.** *abbr.* Benevolent and Protective Order of Elks.

Br The symbol for the element **bromine.**

BR *abbr.* **1.** Bedroom. **2.** Or **B/R.** Bills receivable.

br. *abbr.* **1.** Branch. **2.** *Law.* Brief. **3.** Bronze. **4.** Or **Br.** Brother. **5.** Brown.

Br. *abbr.* **1.** Britain. **2.** British.

bra (brä) *n.* A brassiere.

Bra•bant (brə-bănt′, -bänt′, brä′bənt, -bänt′). A region and former duchy of the Netherlands. It became an independent duchy in 1190 and is now divided between the southern Netherlands and north-central Belgium.

brab•ble (brăb′əl) *intr.v.* **-bled, -bling, -bles.** To quarrel noisily, especially over a small matter; wrangle. **—brabble** *n.* A petty dispute; a squabble. [Probably from Middle Dutch *brabbelen,* to squabble.] **—brab′bler** *n.*

bra burner *n. Slang.* A woman perceived as having militant feminist views.

brace (brās) *n.* **1.** A device that holds or fastens two or more parts together or in place; a clamp. **2.** A device, such as a supporting beam in a building or a connecting wire or rope, that steadies or holds something else erect. **3. braces.** *Chiefly British.* Suspenders. **4.** An orthopedic appliance used to support, align, or hold a bodily part in the correct position. **5.** Often **braces.** A dental appliance, constructed of bands and wires that is fixed to the teeth to correct irregular alignment. **6.** An extremely stiff, erect posture. **7.** A cause or source of renewed physical or spiritual vigor. **8.** A protective pad strapped to the bow arm of an archer. **9.** *Nautical.* A rope by which a yard is swung and secured on a square-rigged ship. **10.** A cranklike handle with an adjustable aperture at one end for securing and turning a bit. **11.** *Music.* A leather loop that slides to change the tension on the cord of a drum. **12.** *Music.* **a.** A vertical line, usually accompanied by the symbol {, connecting two or more staffs. **b.** A set of staffs connected in this way. **13.** A symbol, { or }, enclosing two or more lines of text or listed items to show that they are considered as a unit. **14.** *Mathematics.* Either of a pair of symbols, { }, used to indicate aggregation or to clarify the grouping of quantities when parentheses and square brackets have already been used. Also called *bracket.* **15.** *pl.* **brace.** A pair of like things: *three brace of partridges.* See Synonyms at **couple. —brace** *v.* **braced, brac•ing, brac•es.** *—tr.* **1.** To furnish with a brace. **2.** To support or hold steady with or as if with a brace; reinforce. **3.** To prepare or position so as to be ready for impact or danger: *Union members braced themselves for a confrontation with management.* **4.** To confront with questions or requests. **5.** To increase the tension of. **6.** To invigorate; stimulate: *"The freshness of the September morning inspired and braced him"* (Thomas Hardy). **7.** *Nautical.* To turn (the yards of a ship) by the braces. *—intr.* To get ready; make preparations. ***—phrasal verb.* brace up.** To summon one's strength or endurance. [Middle English, from Old French, two arms, from Latin *brācchia,* pl. of *brācchium,* arm, from Greek *brakhīōn,* upper arm. See **mregh-u-** in Appendix. V., partly from Old French *bracier,* from Old French *brace.*]

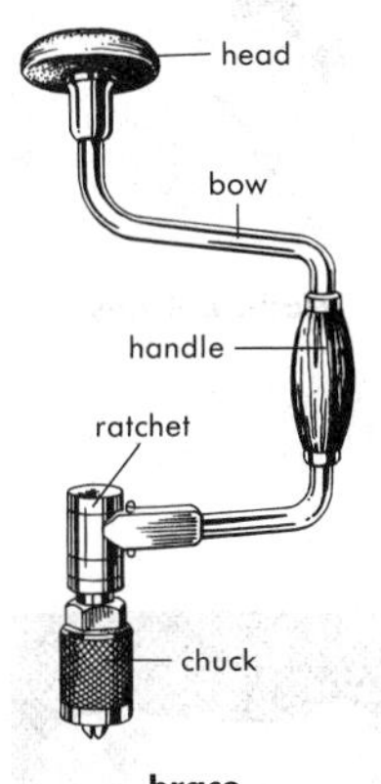

brace

brace•let (brās′lĭt) *n.* **1.** An ornamental band or chain encircling the wrist or arm. **2.** Something, such as a handcuff, that resembles a wrist ornament. [Middle English, from Old French, diminutive of *bracel,* armlet, from Latin *brācchiāle,* from *brācchium,* arm. See BRACE.]

brac•er[1] (brā′sər) *n.* **1.** One that braces, especially one that supports or holds something steady. **2.** *Informal.* A stimulating drink, especially of an alcoholic beverage.

bra•cer[2] (brā′sər) *n.* An arm or wrist guard worn by archers and fencers. [Middle English, probably from Anglo-Norman, from Old French *braceure,* from *bras,* arm, from Latin *brācchium.* See BRACE.]

bra•ce•ro (brə-sâr′ō) *n., pl.* **-ros.** A Mexican laborer permitted to enter the United States and work for a limited period of time, especially in agriculture. [Spanish, laborer, from *brazo,* arm, from Latin *brācchium,* from Greek *brakhīōn,* upper arm. See **mregh-u-** in Appendix.]

brace root *n.* See **prop root.**

bra•chi•a (brā′kē-ə, brăk′ē-ə) *n.* Plural of **brachium.**

bra•chi•al (brā′kē-əl, brăk′ē-) *adj.* Of, relating to, or resembling the arm or a similar or homologous part, such as the foreleg, wing, or other forelimb of a vertebrate: *the brachial artery.* [From Latin *brācchiālis,* from *brācchium,* arm. See BRACHIUM.]

brachial plexus *n. Anatomy.* A network of nerves located in the neck and axilla, composed of the anterior branches of the lower four cervical and first two thoracic spinal nerves and supplying the chest, shoulder, and arm.

bra•chi•ate (brā′kē-ĭt, -āt′, brăk′ē-) *adj. Zoology.* Having arms or armlike appendages. **—brachiate** (-āt′) *intr.v.* **-at•ed, -at•ing, -ates.** To move by swinging with the arms from one hold to another, as certain apes do. [Latin *brācchiātus,* from *brācchium,* arm. V., from New Latin *brāchiāre, brāchiāt-,* from *brācchium.* See BRACHIUM.] **—bra′chi•a′tion** *n.*

ă pat	oi boy
ā pay	ou out
âr care	o͝o took
ä father	o͞o boot
ĕ pet	ŭ cut
ē be	ûr urge
ĭ pit	th thin
ī pie	*th* this
îr pier	hw which
ŏ pot	zh vision
ō toe	ə about, item
ô paw	♦ regionalism

Stress marks: ′ (primary); ′ (secondary), as in **dictionary** (dĭk′shə-nĕr′ē)

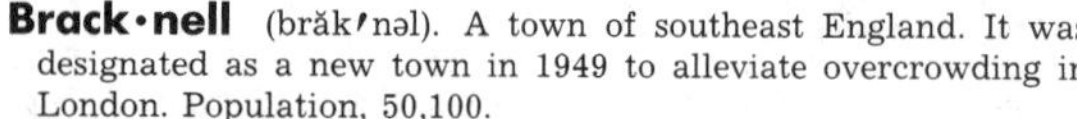

bracken
Pteridium aquilinum

Mathew Brady

Brahman
Brahman cow
Bos indicus

Johannes Brahms
Photographed c. 1880 by
Fritz Luckhardt

bra·chi·o·ce·phal·ic (brā′kē-ō-sə-făl′ĭk, brăk′ē-) *adj. Anatomy.* Of or involving the arm and the head. [BRACHI(UM) + CEPHALIC.]

brachiocephalic artery *n.* See **innominate artery.**

brachiocephalic trunk *n.* See **innominate artery.**

brachiocephalic vein *n.* See **innominate vein.**

bra·chi·o·pod (brā′kē-ə-pŏd′, brăk′ē) *n.* Any of various marine invertebrates of the phylum Brachiopoda, having bivalve dorsal and ventral shells enclosing a pair of tentacled, armlike structures that are used to sweep minute food particles into the mouth. Also called *lampshell.* [From New Latin *Brāchiopoda,* phylum name : Latin *brācchium,* arm; see BRACHIUM + New Latin *-poda,* -pod.] **—brach′i·o·pod′** *adj.*

bra·chi·um (brā′kē-əm, brăk′ē-) *n., pl.* **bra·chi·a** (brā′-kē-ə, brăk′ē-ə). **1.** The part of the upper arm or forelimb extending from the shoulder to the elbow. **2.** An arm or a homologous anatomical structure, such as a flipper or wing. **3.** The part of a limb or process corresponding to an arm. [Latin *brācchium,* arm, from Greek *brakhiōn,* upper arm. See **mregh-u-** in Appendix.]

brachy– *pref.* Short: *brachydactylic.* [Greek *brakhu-,* from *brakhus,* short. See **mregh-u-** in Appendix.]

brach·y·ce·phal·ic (brăk′ĭ-sə-făl′ĭk) also **brach·y·ceph·a·lous** (-sĕf′ə-ləs) *adj.* Having a short, broad head with a cephalic index over 80. **—brach′y·ceph′a·ly** (-sĕf′ə-lē), **brach′y·ceph′a·lism** *n.*

brach·y·dac·tyl·ic (brăk′ĭ-dăk-tĭl′ĭk) also **brach·y·dac·ty·lous** (-dăk′tə-ləs) *adj.* Having abnormally short fingers or toes. **—brach′y·dac·tyl′i·a** (-tĭl′ē-ə), **brach′y·dac′ty·ly** (-dăk′tə-lē) *n.*

bra·chyl·o·gy (brə-kĭl′ə-jē) *n., pl.* **-gies. 1.** Brevity of speech; conciseness. **2.** A shortened or condensed phrase or expression. [Medieval Latin *brachylogia,* from Greek *brakhulogia* : *brakhu-,* brachy- + *logos,* speech; see –LOGY.]

bra·chyp·ter·ous (brə-kĭp′tər-əs) *adj.* Having very short or rudimentary wings, as certain insects. [From Greek *brakhupteros* : *brakhu-,* brachy- + *pteron,* wing; see –PTER.] **—bra·chyp′ter·ism** (-tə-rĭz′əm) *n.*

brach·y·u·ran (brăk′ē-yo͝or′ən) also **brach·y·u·ral** (-yo͝or′əl) or **brach·y·u·rous** (-yo͝or′əs) *—adj.* Of or belonging to the Brachyura, a group of crustaceans including the true crabs, characterized by a short abdomen concealed under the cephalothorax. *—n.* A member of the Brachyura. [From New Latin *Brachyura,* suborder name : Greek *brakhu-,* brachy- + Greek *oura,* tail; see –UROUS.]

brac·ing (brā′sĭng) *adj.* Invigorating or refreshing; strengthening: *a bracing tonic.* **—bracing** *n.* **1.** A support; a brace. **2.** Braces considered as a group. **—brac′ing·ly** *adv.*

bra·ci·o·la (brä′chē-ō′lə, brä-chō′-) or **bra·ci·o·le** (-lā′, -lĕ′) *n.* A thin slice of meat, usually wrapped around a stuffing and cooked with wine. [Italian, probably from dialectal *bras'ola,* from *bras'a,* glowing ember, of Germanic origin. See **bhreu-** in Appendix.]

brack·en (brăk′ən) *n.* **1.** A widespread, often weedy fern *(Pteridium aquilinum)* having large, triangular, pinnately compound fronds and often forming dense thickets. **2.** An area overgrown with this fern. [Middle English *braken,* probably of Scandinavian origin. See **bhreg-** in Appendix.]

brack·et (brăk′ĭt) *n.* **1.a.** A simple rigid structure in the shape of an L, one arm of which is fixed to a vertical surface, the other projecting horizontally to support a shelf or other weight. **b.** A small shelf or shelves supported by such structures. **2.** *Architecture.* A decorative or weight-bearing structural unit, two sides of which form a right angle with one arm flush against a wall and the other flush beneath a projecting surface; a console or corbel. **3.** A wall-anchored fixture for gas or electricity. **4.a.** One of a pair of marks, [ ], used to enclose written or printed material or to indicate a mathematical expression considered in some sense a single quantity. Also called *square bracket.* **b.** See **angle bracket. c.** *Mathematics.* See **brace** (sense 14). **5.** *Chiefly British.* One of a pair of parentheses. **6.** A classification or grouping, especially within a sequence of numbers or grades, as a category of incomes sharing the same tax rate. **7.a.** The distance between two impacting shells, the first aimed beyond a target and the second aimed short of it, used to determine the range for artillery fire. **b.** The shells fired in such a manner. **—bracket** *tr.v.* **-et·ed, -et·ing, -ets. 1.** To furnish or support with a bracket or brackets. **2.** To place within or as if within brackets. **3.** To classify or group together. **4.** To include or exclude by establishing specific boundaries. **5.** To fire beyond and short of (a target) in order to determine artillery range. [Possibly French *braguette,* codpiece, diminutive of *brague,* breeches, from Old Provençal *braga,* from Latin *brācae,* of Celtic origin.]

bracket creep *n. Informal.* A shift of personal income into a higher tax bracket when the taxable income increases over time.

bracket fungus *n.* Any of various fungi that form shelflike growths on tree trunks and wood structures. Also called *shelf fungus.*

brack·ish (brăk′ĭsh) *adj.* **1.** Having a somewhat salty taste, especially from containing a mixture of seawater and fresh water: *"You could cut the brackish winds with a knife/Here in Nantucket"* (Robert Lowell). **2.** Distasteful; unpalatable: *a thin, brackish gruel.* [From Dutch *brak.*] **—brack′ish·ness** *n.*

Brack·nell (brăk′nəl). A town of southeast England. It was designated as a new town in 1949 to alleviate overcrowding in London. Population, 50,100.

brac·o·nid (brăk′ə-nĭd) *n.* Any of several ichneumon flies of the family Braconidae, the larvae of which are parasitic on other insects. [From New Latin *Braconidae,* family name, possibly from Greek *brakhus,* short. See BRACHY–.]

bract (brăkt) *n.* A leaflike or scalelike plant part, usually small, sometimes showy or brightly colored, and located just below a flower, a flower stalk, or an inflorescence. [From Latin *bractea,* gold leaf, perhaps from Greek *brakhein,* to rattle.] **—brac′te·al** (brăk′tē-əl) *adj.*

brac·te·ate (brăk′tē-ĭt, -āt′) *adj.* Bearing bracts. [New Latin *bracteātus,* from Latin *bractea,* gold leaf. See BRACT.]

brac·te·o·late (brăk′tē-ə-lĭt, -lāt′) *adj.* Bearing bracteoles.

brac·te·ole (brăk′tē-ōl′) *n.* A small bract. [Latin *bracteola,* gold leaf, diminutive of *bractea.* See BRACT.]

brad (brăd) *n.* A thin wire nail with a small head or a slight side projection instead of a head. [Middle English, from Old Norse *broddr,* spike.] **—brad** *v.*

brad·awl (brăd′ôl′) *n.* An awl with a beveled tip, used to make holes in wood for brads or screws.

Brad·bur·y (brăd′bĕr′ē, -bə-rē), **Ray Douglas.** Born 1920. American writer of science fiction mingled with social commentary. His works include *The Martian Chronicles* (1950) and *Fahrenheit 451* (1953).

Brad·dock (brăd′ək), **Edward.** 1695–1755. British general in America during the French and Indian War. He was mortally wounded during his unsuccessful expedition against Fort Duquesne (now Pittsburgh).

Bra·den·ton (brād′n-tən). A city of west-central Florida on an inlet of Tampa Bay south of Tampa. Hernando de Soto is believed to have landed near here in 1539. Population, 30,170.

Brad·ford (brăd′fərd). A borough of north-central England west of Leeds. Its worsted industry dates from the Middle Ages. Population, 464,100.

Bradford, Roark. 1896–1948. American writer whose works, such as *John Henry* (1931), reflect Black folklore.

Bradford, William[1]. 1590–1657. English Puritan colonist in America. A signer of the Mayflower Compact and a settler of Plymouth Plantation, he was elected governor for 30 one-year terms and led the colony through its difficult early years.

Bradford, William[2]. 1663–1752. English-born American colonial printer whose press produced the first American Book of Common Prayer (1710), New York City's first newspaper (1725), and numerous other items.

Brad·ley (brăd′lē), **Francis Herbert.** 1846–1924. British philosopher who, like Hegel, maintained that the mind is more fundamental than matter.

Bradley, Joseph P. 1813–1892. American jurist who served as an associate justice of the U.S. Supreme Court (1870–1892).

Bradley, Omar Nelson. 1893–1981. American general who played a major part in the Allied victory in World War II.

Bradley, Thomas. Born 1917. American policeman and politician who became the first Black mayor of Los Angeles in 1973.

Brad·street (brăd′strēt′), **Anne Dudley.** 1612–1672. English-born colonial poet who wrote several collections of verse, including *The Tenth Muse Lately Sprung Up in America* (1650).

Bra·dy (brā′dē), **James Buchanan.** Known as "Diamond Jim." 1856–1917. American financier and philanthropist who gained his nickname because of his attraction to diamonds and his extravagant lifestyle.

Brady, Mathew B. 1823–1896. American pioneer photographer who was famous for his portraits and was appointed official Union photographer of the Civil War in 1861.

brady– *pref.* Slow: *bradycardia.* [Greek *bradu-,* from *bradus,* slow.]

brad·y·car·di·a (brăd′ĭ-kär′dē-ə) *n.* Slowness of the heart rate, usually fewer than 60 beats per minute in an adult human being. [BRADY– + Greek *kardia,* heart; see CARDIA.] **—brad′y·car′dic** (-dĭk) *adj.*

brad·y·ki·nin (brăd′ĭ-kī′nĭn, -kĭn′ĭn) *n.* A biologically active polypeptide, consisting of nine amino acids, that forms from a blood plasma globulin and mediates the inflammatory response, increases vasodilation, and causes contraction of smooth muscle.

brad·y·lo·gia (brăd′ə-lō′jə, -jē-ə) *n.* Abnormally slow speech. [BRADY– + Greek *logos,* speech; see –LOGY + –IA[1].]

brae (brā) *n. Scots.* A hillside; a slope. [Middle English *bra,* from Old Norse *brā,* eyelash.]

brag (brăg) *v.* **bragged, brag·ging, brags.** *—intr.* To talk boastfully. See Synonyms at **boast**[1]. *—tr.* To assert boastfully. **—brag** *n.* **1.** A boast. **2.** Arrogant or boastful speech or manner. **3.** Something boasted of. **4.** A braggart; a boaster. **5.** *Games.* A card game similar to poker. **—brag** *adj.* **brag·ger, brag·gest.** Exceptionally fine. [Middle English *braggen,* from *brag,* ostentatious.] **—brag′ger** *n.*

Bra·ga (brä′gə). A city of northwest Portugal north-northeast of Oporto. Said to have been founded by the Carthaginians, it was an important settlement in Roman times. Population, 63,033.

Bra·gan·za (brə-găn′zə) also **Bra·gan·ça** (-gän′sä). A dynasty of Portuguese rulers (1640–1910) who also controlled Brazil from 1822 to 1889.

Bragg (brăg), **Braxton.** 1817–1876. American Confederate general in the Civil War who was defeated in the Chattanooga Campaign (1863).

Bragg, Sir **William Henry.** 1862–1942. British physicist. He shared a 1915 Nobel Prize with his son Sir **William Lawrence Bragg** (1890–1971) for an analysis of x-ray spectra and the structure of crystals.

brag·ga·do·ci·o (brăg′ə-dō′sē-ō′, -shē-ō′, -shō) *n., pl.* **-os. 1.** A braggart. **2. a.** Empty or pretentious bragging **b.** A swaggering, cocky manner. [Alteration of *Braggadocchio* (probably from BRAG), the personification of vainglory in *The Faerie Queene* by Edmund Spenser (1552?–1599).]

Bragg angle *n.* The angle between an incident x-ray beam and a set of crystal planes for which the secondary radiation displays maximum intensity as a result of constructive interference. [After Sir William Henry BRAGG and Sir William Lawrence BRAGG.]

brag·gart (brăg′ərt) *n.* One given to loud, empty boasting; a bragger. **—braggart** *adj.* Boastful. [French *bragard,* from *braguer,* to brag, perhaps from Middle English *braggen.* See BRAG.]

Bragg's law (brăgz) *n.* The fundamental law of x-ray crystallography, nl = 2dsinQ, where *n* is an integer, l is the wavelength of a beam of x-rays incident on a crystal with lattice planes separated by distance *d,* and Q is the Bragg angle. [After Sir William Henry BRAGG and Sir William Lawrence BRAGG.]

Brahe (brä, brä′hē, brä′ə), **Tycho.** 1546–1601. Danish astronomer whose accurate astronomical observations formed the basis for Johannes Kepler's laws of planetary motion.

Brah·ma[1] (brä′mə) *n.* **1.** *Hinduism.* **a.** The creator god, conceived chiefly as a member of the triad including also Vishnu and Shiva. **b.** Variant of **Brahman** (sense 1). **2.** Variant of **Brahman** (sense 3). [Sanskrit *brahmā.*]

Brah·ma[2] also **brah·ma** (brä′mə, brā′-) *n.* A large domestic fowl of a breed originating in Asia and having feathered legs and small wings and tail. [After BRAHMAPUTRA.]

Brah·man (brä′mən) *n.* **1.** Also **Brah·ma** (-mə). *Hinduism.* **a.** A religious formula or prayer and the holy or sacred power in it and in the officiating priest. **b.** The holy or sacred power that is the source and sustainer of the universe. **c.** The single absolute being pervading the universe and found within the individual; atman. **2.** *Hinduism.* Variant of **Brahmin** (sense 1). **3.** Also **Brah·ma** (-mə) or **Brah·min** (-mĭn). One of a breed of domestic cattle developed in the southern United States from stock originating in India and having a hump between the shoulders and a pendulous dewlap. Well adapted to hot climates, it is used chiefly for crossbreeding. [Sanskrit. Sense 2, from *brāhmaṇa-,* brahmanic, from *brahman.*] **—Brah·man′ic** (-măn′ĭk), **Brah·man′i·cal** *adj.*

Brah·man·ism (brä′mə-nĭz′əm) also **Brah·min·ism** (brä′-mĭ-) *n.* *Hinduism.* **1.** The religious practices and beliefs of ancient India as reflected in the Vedas. **2.** The social and religious system of orthodox Hindus, especially of the Brahmans, based on a caste structure and various forms of pantheism. **—Brah′man·ist** *n.*

Brah·ma·pu·tra (brä′mə-po͞o′trə). A river of southern Asia rising in the Himalaya Mountains of southwest Tibet and flowing about 2,896 km (1,800 mi) east then south and west through northeast India to join the Ganges River and form a vast delta in central Bangladesh.

Brah·min (brä′mĭn) *n.* **1.** Also **Brah·man** (-mən). *Hinduism.* **a.** The first of the four Hindu classes, responsible for officiating at religious rites and studying and teaching the Vedas. **b.** A member of this class. **2.** A member of a cultural and social elite, especially of that formed by descendants of old New England families: *a Boston Brahmin.* **3.** Variant of **Brahman** (sense 3). [Probably alteration of Sanskrit *brāhmaṇaḥ,* from *brāhmaṇa-,* brahminic. See BRAHMAN.] **—Brah·min′ic** (-mĭn′ĭk), **Brah·min′i·cal** *adj.*

Brah·min·ism (brä′mə-nĭz′əm) *n.* **1.** The attitude or conduct typical of a social or cultural elite. **2.** *Hinduism.* **Brahmanism.**

Brahms (brämz), **Johannes.** 1833–1897. German composer. His works, blending classical tradition with the new romantic impulse, include concertos, four symphonies, chamber music, and choral compositions. **—Brahms′i·an** *adj.*

braid (brād) *v.* **braid·ed, braid·ing, braids.** *—tr.* **1. a.** To interweave three or more strands, strips, or lengths of in a diagonally overlapping pattern: *braided the rags into a strong rope.* **b.** To create (something) by such interweaving: *braid a rug.* **c.** To style (the hair) by such interweaving. **d.** To mingle (discrete elements, for example) as if by such interweaving: *braided the ideas into a complex thesis.* **2.** To decorate or edge (something) with a trim of interwoven strands: *finished the jacket by braiding the collar and cuffs.* **3.** To fasten or decorate (hair) with a band or ribbon. *—intr.* To flow, twist, or wind as if interwoven: *a stream braiding through the woods.* **—braid** *n.* **1.** A braided segment or length, as of hair, fabric, or fiber. **2.** Ornamental cord or ribbon, used especially for decorating or edging fabrics. **3.** A ribbon or band used to fasten the hair. **4.** *Slang.* Naval officers of high rank. [Middle English *braiden,* from Old English *bregdan,* to weave.] **—braid′er** *n.*

braid·ed (brā′dĭd) *adj.* **1. a.** Produced by or as if by braiding. **b.** Having braids. **2.** Decorated with braid. **3.** Flowing in an interconnected network of channels that divide and reunite: *a braided stream.*

braid·ing (brā′dĭng) *n.* **1.** Braided embroidery or trim. **2.** Braids considered as a group.

brail (brāl) *Nautical. n.* **1.** One of several small ropes attached to the leech of a sail for drawing the sail in or up. **2.** A small net for drawing fish from a trap or a larger net into a boat. **—brail** *tr.v.* **brailed, brail·ing, brails. 1.** To gather in (a sail) with brails. **2.** To haul in (fish) with a brail. [Middle English *braile,* from Old French *brail,* belt, from Medieval Latin *brācale,* from Latin *brācae,* breeches, of Celtic origin.]

Bră·i·la (brə-ē′lə). A city of southeast Romania on the Danube River near the Ukrainian border. It was taken by the Turks c. 1550 and awarded to Romania in 1829. Population, 224,998.

Braille or **braille** (brāl) *—n.* A system of writing and printing for visually impaired or sightless people, in which varied arrangements of raised dots representing letters and numerals are identified by touch. *—tr.v.* **Brailled, Braill·ing, Brailles** or **brailled, braill·ing, brailles.** To print or transliterate using this system. [After Louis BRAILLE.]

Braille, Louis. 1809–1852. French musician, educator, and inventor of a writing and printing system for visually impaired or sightless people (1829). He lost his sight at the age of three.

Braill·er or **braill·er** (brā′lər) *n.* A machine analogous to a typewriter, used for printing in Braille. Also called *Braillewriter.*

Braille·writ·er or **braille·writ·er** (brāl′rī′tər) *n.* See **Brailler.**

brain (brān) *n.* **1. a.** The portion of the vertebrate central nervous system that is enclosed within the cranium, continuous with the spinal cord, and composed of gray matter and white matter. It is the primary center for the regulation and control of bodily activities, receiving and interpreting sensory impulses, and transmitting information to the muscles and body organs. It is also the seat of consciousness, thought, memory, and emotion. **b.** A functionally similar portion of the invertebrate nervous system. **2. a.** Intellectual ability; mind: *a dull brain; a quick brain.* **b.** Often **brains.** Intellectual power; intelligence: *brains and good looks.* See Synonyms at **mind. 3.** A highly intelligent person. **4.** Often **brains.** The primary director or planner, as of an organization or movement. **5.** The control center, as of a ship, aircraft, or spacecraft. **—brain** *tr.v.* **brained, brain·ing, brains.** *Slang.* **1.** To smash in the skull of. **2.** To hit on the head. ***—idioms.*** **beat (one's) brains (out).** *Informal.* To exert or expend great mental effort: *She beat her brains out during the examination.* **on the brain.** Obsessively in mind: *The coach has winning on the brain.* **pick (someone's) brain** (or **brains).** To explore another's ideas through questioning. **rack (one's) brain.** *Informal.* To think long and hard: *I racked my brain for hours trying to recall her name.* [Middle English, from Old English *brægen.*]

brain·case also **brain case** (brān′kās′) *n.* The part of the skull that encloses the brain; the cranium. Also called *brainpan.*

brain·child (brān′chīld′) *n.* An original idea or plan attributed to a person or group.

brain coral *n.* Any of several reef-building corals of the genus *Meandrina,* forming rounded colonies that resemble the convolutions of the human brain.

brain damage *n.* Injury to the brain that is caused by various conditions, such as head trauma, inadequate oxygen supply, infection, or intracranial hemorrhage, and that may be associated with a behavioral or functional abnormality. **—brain′-dam′-aged** (brān′dăm′ĭjd) *adj.*

brain death *n.* Irreversible brain damage and loss of brain function, as evidenced by cessation of breathing and other vital reflexes, unresponsiveness to stimuli, absence of muscle activity, and a flat electroencephalogram for a specific length of time. **—brain′-dead′** (brān′dĕd′) *adj.*

brain drain *n.* The loss of skilled intellectual and technical labor through the movement of such labor toward more favorable geographic, economic, or professional environments. **—brain-drain** (brān′drān′) *v.*

Braine (brān), **John.** 1922–1986. British writer whose best-selling novel *Room at the Top* (1957) established him as one of Britain's Angry Young Men.

brain fever *n.* Inflammation of the brain or meninges, as in encephalitis or meningitis.

brain hormone *n.* Any of various hormones produced in the hypothalamic region of the brain, especially those acting on the pituitary gland to release other hormones.

brain·ish (brā′nĭsh) *adj. Archaic.* Headstrong; impetuous.

brain·less (brān′lĭs) *adj.* Unintelligent; stupid. **—brain′less·ly** *adv.* **—brain′less·ness** *n.*

brain·pan (brān′păn′) *n.* See **braincase.**

brain-pick·ing (brān′pĭk′ing) *n.* The act of exploring another's ideas through questioning. **—brain′-pick′er** *n.*

brain·pow·er (brān′pou′ər) *n.* **1.** Intellectual capacity. **2.** People of well-developed mental abilities: *a country that doesn't value its brainpower.*

brain scan *n.* A scintigram of the brain, used to identify cerebral blood flow and to detect intracranial masses, lesions, tumors, or infarcts.

brain·sick (brān′sĭk′) *adj.* Of, relating to, or induced by a mental disorder; insane or mad. **—brain′sick′ly** *adv.* **—brain′sick′ness** *n.*

A B C D E
F G H I J
K L M N O
P Q R S T
U V W X Y
Z and for the with
numeral sign
1 2 3 4 5
6 7 8 9 0

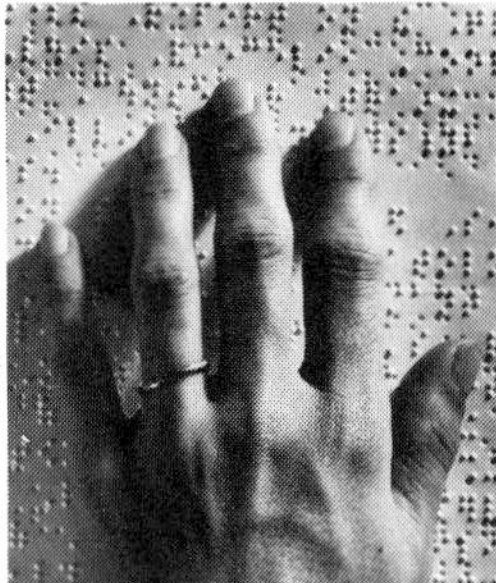

Braille
Top: Alphabet and numerals
Bottom: Printed material

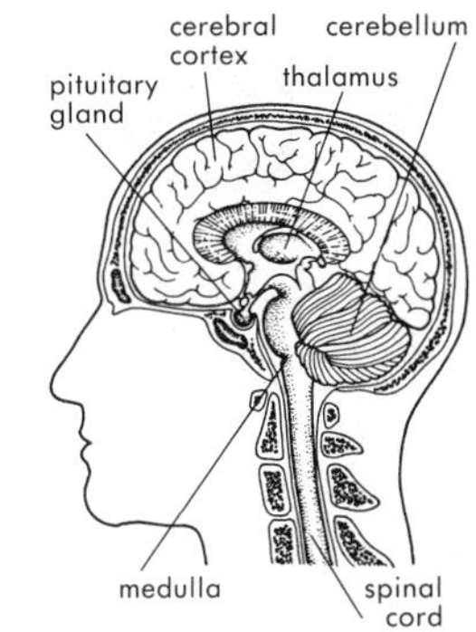

brain

ă pat	oi boy
ā pay	ou out
âr care	o͝o took
ä father	o͞o boot
ĕ pet	ŭ cut
ē be	ûr urge
ĭ pit	th thin
ī pie	*th* this
îr pier	hw which
ŏ pot	zh vision
ō toe	ə about, item
ô paw	♦ regionalism

Stress marks: ′ (primary); ′ (secondary), as in **dictionary** (dĭk′shə-nĕr′ē)

brain stem also **brain·stem** (brān′stĕm′) *n.* The portion of the brain, consisting of the medulla oblongata, pons Varolii, and mesencephalon, that connects the spinal cord to the forebrain and cerebrum.

brain·storm (brān′stôrm′) *n.* **1.** A sudden clever plan or idea. **2.** A sudden, violent disturbance of the mind. **—brainstorm** *v.* **-stormed, -storm·ing, -storms.** *—intr.* To engage in or organize shared problem solving. *—tr.* **1.** To consider or investigate (an issue, for example) by engaging in shared problem solving. **2.** To think of or produce (a solution to a problem, for example) by this method. **—brain′storm′er** *n.*

brain·storm·ing (brān′stôr′mĭng) *n.* **1.** A method of shared problem solving in which all members of a group spontaneously contribute ideas. **2.** A similar process undertaken by a person to solve a problem by rapidly generating a variety of possible solutions.

brain·teas·er (brān′tē′zər) *n.* A mentally challenging problem or puzzle.

Brain·tree (brān′trē′). A town of eastern Massachusetts, a residential and industrial suburb of Boston. Population, 36,337.

brain trust *n.* **1.** A group of experts who serve, usually unofficially, as advisers and policy planners, especially in a government. **2.** Often **Brain Trust.** Such a group associated with the administration of President Franklin D. Roosevelt and the development of the New Deal. **3. brains trust.** *Chiefly British.* A group of experts gathered to discuss issues informally in public, especially on radio or television. **—brain truster** *n.*

brain·wash (brān′wŏsh′, -wôsh′) *tr.v.* **-washed, -wash·ing, -wash·es.** To subject to brainwashing. **—brainwash** *n.* The process or an instance of brainwashing. [Back-formation from BRAINWASHING.]

brain·wash·ing (brān′wŏsh′ĭng, -wô′shĭng) *n.* **1.** Intensive, forcible indoctrination, usually political or religious, aimed at destroying a person's basic convictions and attitudes and replacing them with an alternative set of fixed beliefs. **2.** The application of a concentrated means of persuasion, such as an advertising campaign or repeated suggestion, in order to develop a specific belief or motivation. [Translation of Chinese (Mandarin) *xǐ naǒ* : *xǐ,* to wash + *naǒ,* brain.]

brain wave *n.* **1.** A rhythmic fluctuation of electric potential between parts of the brain, as seen on an electroencephalogram. **2.** *Informal.* A sudden inspiration.

brain·work (brān′wûrk′) *n.* Intellectual activity, especially as an aspect of a person's profession.

brain·work·er (brān′wûr′kər) *n.* One whose profession primarily involves intellectual activity.

brain·y (brā′nē) *adj.* **-i·er, -i·est.** *Informal.* Intelligent; smart. **—brain′i·ly** *adv.* **—brain′i·ness** *n.*

braise (brāz) *tr.v.* **braised, brais·ing, brais·es.** To cook (meat or vegetables) by browning in fat, then simmering in a small quantity of liquid in a covered container. [French *braiser,* from *braise,* hot charcoal, from Old French *brese,* of Germanic origin. See **bhreu-** in Appendix.]

brake¹ (brāk) *n.* **1.** A device for slowing or stopping motion, as of a vehicle, especially by contact friction. **2.** Something that slows or stops action. *—attributive.* Often used to modify another noun: *brake fluid; a brake job.* **—brake** *v.* **braked, brak·ing, brakes.** *—tr.* To reduce the speed of with or as if with a brake. *—intr.* **1.** To operate or apply a brake. **2.** To be slowed or stopped by or as if by the operation of a brake. [Probably *brake,* bridle, curb, from Middle Dutch or Middle Low German, nose ring, curb, flax brake; see BRAKE².]

ROTATING

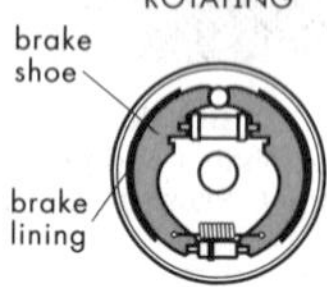

STOPPED

brake¹
Shoe brake

WORD HISTORY: Brakes, which are constantly becoming more technologically advanced, may take their name from a device associated with an earlier mode of transportation. It is thought that the term *brake* may come from an earlier English word *brake,* meaning "a bridle or curb," first recorded in the 16th century. In any case, the first recorded occurrence of our word *brake* is found in 1772, well before the advent of the automobile.

brake² (brāk) *n.* **1.** A toothed device for crushing and beating flax or hemp. **2.** A heavy harrow for breaking clods of earth. **3.** An apparatus for kneading large amounts of dough. **4.** A machine for bending and folding sheet metal. **—brake** *tr.v.* **braked, brak·ing, brakes. 1.** To crush (flax or hemp) in a toothed device. **2.** To break up (clods of earth) with a harrow. [Middle English, from Middle Dutch, from Middle Low German. See **bhreg-** in Appendix.]

brake³ (brāk) *n.* A lever or handle on a machine such as a pump. [Middle English, from Old French *brac,* from oblique form of *bras,* arm. See BRACER².]

brake⁴ (brāk) *n.* **1.** Any of various ferns of the genus *Pteris* having pinnately compound leaves and including several popular houseplants. **2.** Any of certain other ferns, such as the bracken or the cliff brake. [Middle English, probably back-formation from *braken.* See BRACKEN.]

brake⁵ (brāk) *n.* An area overgrown with dense brushwood, briers, and undergrowth; a thicket. [Middle English, from Middle Low German. See **bhreg-** in Appendix.]

brake⁶ (brāk) *n.* Variant of **break** (sense 28). **—brake** *v. Archaic.* A past tense of **break.**

brake drum *n.* A metal cylinder to which pressure is applied by a braking mechanism in order to arrest rotation of the wheel or shaft to which the cylinder is attached.

brake horsepower *n. Abbr.* **bhp, b.hp.** The actual or useful horsepower of an engine, usually determined from the force exerted on a friction brake or dynamometer connected to the drive shaft.

brake light *n.* See **stoplight** (sense 1).

brake lining *n.* The covering of a brake shoe.

brake·man (brāk′mən) *n.* One who operates, inspects, or repairs brakes, especially a railroad employee who assists the conductor and checks on the operation of a train's brakes.

brake pad *n.* A flat block that presses against the disk of a disc brake.

brake shoe *n.* A curved metal block that presses against and arrests the rotation of a wheel or brake drum.

brak·ing distance (brā′kĭng) *n.* The distance required for a vehicle moving at a specified velocity to come to a complete stop after its brakes have been activated.

braking time *n.* The time required for a vehicle moving at a specified velocity to come to a complete stop after its brakes have been activated.

bra·less (brä′lĭs) *adj. & adv.* Wearing no brassiere. **—bra′less·ness** *n.*

Bra·man·te (brə-män′tā, brä-män′tĕ), **Donato.** 1444–1514. Italian architect who evolved the style known as High Renaissance. He provided the original central plan for the new Saint Peter's Basilica (begun in 1506).

bram·ble (brăm′bəl) *n.* **1.** A prickly shrub of the genus *Rubus,* including the blackberry and the raspberry. **2.** A prickly shrub or bush. [Middle English *brembel,* from Old English *bræmbel.*] **—bram′bly** *adj.*

bram·ble·ber·ry (brăm′bəl-bĕr′ē) *n.* The fruit of a bramble *(Rubus).*

bram·bling (brăm′blĭng) *n.* A finch *(Fringilla montifringilla)* of northern Eurasia, having black, white, and rust-brown plumage. [Probably from Old English **bræmbling* : *bræmbel,* bramble + *-ling,* one connected with; see –LING¹.]

Bramp·ton (brămp′tən). A city of southern Ontario, Canada, an industrial suburb of Toronto. Population, 149,030.

bran (brăn) *n.* The outer layers of the grain of cereals such as wheat, removed during the process of milling and used as a source of dietary fiber. [Middle English, from Old French, of Celtic origin.] **—bran′ny** *adj.*

Bran (brăn) *n. Mythology.* A gigantic Celtic god and ruler of Britain.

◆**branch** (brănch) *n. Abbr.* **br. 1.a.** A secondary woody stem or limb growing from the trunk or main stem of a tree or shrub or from another secondary limb. **b.** A lateral division or subdivision of certain other plant parts, such as a root or flower cluster. **2.** Something that resembles a branch of a tree, as in form or function, as: **a.** A secondary outgrowth or subdivision of a main axis, such as the tine of a deer's antlers. **b.** *Anatomy.* An offshoot or a division of the main portion of a structure, especially that of a nerve, blood vessel, or lymphatic vessel; a ramus. **3.** A limited part of a larger or more complex unit or system, especially: **a.** An area of specialized skill or knowledge, especially academic or vocational, that is related to but separate from other areas: *the judicial branch of government; the branch of medicine called neurology.* **b.** A division of a business or other organization. **c.** A division of a family, categorized by descent from a particular ancestor. **d.** *Linguistics.* A subdivision of a family of languages, such as the Germanic branch of Indo-European. **4.a.** A tributary of a river. **b.** *Chiefly Southern U.S.* See **creek** (sense 1). See Regional Note at **run. c.** *Chiefly Southern U.S.* See **branch water** (sense 1). **d.** A divergent section of a river, especially near the mouth. **5.** *Mathematics.* A part of a curve that is separated, as by discontinuities or extreme points. **6.** *Computer Science.* **a.** A sequence of program instructions to which the normal sequence of instructions relinquishes control, depending on the value of certain variables. **b.** The instructions executed as the result of such a passing of control. **—branch** *v.* **branched, branch·ing, branch·es.** *—intr.* **1.** To put forth a branch or branches; spread by dividing. **2.a.** To come forth as a branch or subdivision; develop or diverge from: *an unpaved road that branches from the main road; a theory that branches from an older system of ideas.* **b.** To enlarge the scope of one's interests, business, or activities: *branch out from physics into related scientific fields.* **3.** *Computer Science.* To relinquish control to another set of instructions or another routine as a result of the presence of a branch. *—tr.* **1.** To separate (something) into or as if into branches. **2.** To embroider (something) with a design of foliage or flowers. [Middle English, from Old French *branche,* from Late Latin *branca,* paw, perhaps of Celtic origin.] **—branch′less** *adj.* **—branch′y** *adj.*

SYNONYMS: *branch, arm, fork, offshoot.* The central meaning shared by these nouns is "something resembling or structurally analogous to a limb of a tree": *a branch of a railroad; an arm of the sea; the western fork of the river; an offshoot of a mountain range.*

bran·chi·a (brăng′kē-ə) *n., pl.* **-chi·ae** (-kē-ē). A gill or similar organ of respiration. [Latin, from Greek *brankhia,* gills.]

bran·chi·al (brăng′kē-əl) *adj.* Of, relating to, or resembling the gills of a fish, their homologous embryonic structures, or the derivatives of their homologous parts in higher animals: *branchial muscles.*

branchial arch *n.* See **gill arch.**

branchial cleft *n.* See **gill slit** (sense 1).

branchial groove *n.* See **gill slit** (sense 2).

bran·chi·o·pod (brăng′kē-ə-pŏd′) *n.* Any of various aquatic crustaceans of the subclass Branchiopoda, such as the fairy shrimp and water flea, characterized by a segmented body and flattened, leaflike thoracic appendages. [From New Latin *Branchiopoda,* subclass name : Latin *branchia,* gills; see BRANCHIA + New Latin *poda,* -pod; see –POD.] **—bran′chi·o·pod′, bran′chi·op′o·dan** (-ŏp′ə-dən) , **bran′chi·op′a·dous** (-dəs) *adj.*

branch·let (brănch′lĭt) *n.* A small branch or the terminal or ultimate subdivision of a branch.

♦**branch water** *n.* **1.** Plain water, especially when mixed with a liquor such as whiskey. Also called ♦*branch.* **2.** *Chiefly Southern U.S.* Water from a stream. [BRANCH, stream + WATER.]

Bran·cu·si (brăn-ko͞o′zē, brăng-ko͞osh′), **Constantin.** 1876–1957. Romanian-born sculptor who settled in Paris in 1904. He broke sharply with the realist tradition, making abstract sculptures, chiefly in metal and stone, of great geometric simplicity.

brand (brănd) *n.* **1.a.** A trademark or distinctive name identifying a product or a manufacturer. **b.** A product line so identified: *a popular brand of soap.* **c.** A distinctive category; a particular kind: *a brand of comedy that I do not care for.* **2.** A mark indicating identity or ownership, burned on the hide of an animal with a hot iron. **3.** A mark burned into the flesh of criminals. **4.** A mark of disgrace or notoriety; a stigma. See Synonyms at **stain.** **5.** A branding iron. **6.** A piece of burning or charred wood. **7.** A sword: *"So flashed and fell the brand Excalibur"* (Tennyson). **—brand** *tr.v.* **brand·ed, brand·ing, brands. 1.** To mark with or as if with a hot iron. See Synonyms at **mark**[1]. **2.** To mark with disgrace or infamy; stigmatize. **3.** To impress firmly; fix ineradicably: *Imagery of the war has branded itself into the national consciousness.* [Middle English, torch, from Old English. See **gʷher-** in Appendix.] **—brand′er** *n.*

bran·dade (bräN-däd′) *n.* A dish of Provençal origin prepared from salted cod. [French, from Provençal *brandado,* from Old Provençal, past participle of *brandar,* to shake, from *brand,* sword, of Germanic origin. See **gʷher-** in Appendix.]

Bran·deis (brăn′dīs′, -dīz′), **Louis Dembitz.** 1856–1941. American jurist who served as an associate justice of the U.S. Supreme Court (1916–1939). His opposition to monopolies and defense of individual human rights formed the basis of many of his high court decisions.

Bran·den·burg (brăn′dən-bûrg′, brän′dən-bo͝ork′). **1.** A historical region and former duchy of north-central Germany around which the kingdom of Prussia developed. The region is now divided between Poland and Germany. **2.** A city of northeast Germany on the Havel River west-southwest of Berlin. It is an industrial center. Population, 95,133.

brand·ing iron (brăn′dĭng) *n.* An iron that is heated and used for indicating identity or ownership.

bran·dish (brăn′dĭsh) *tr.v.* **-dished, -dish·ing, -dish·es. 1.** To wave or flourish (a weapon, for example) menacingly. **2.** To display ostentatiously. See Synonyms at **flourish.** **—brandish** *n.* A menacing or defiant wave or flourish. [Middle English *brandissen,* from Old French *brandir, brandiss-,* from *brand,* sword, of Germanic origin. See **gʷher-** in Appendix.] **—bran′dish·er** *n.*

brand·ling (brănd′lĭng) *n.* A common reddish-brown earthworm *(Eisenia foetida)* often used as fish bait. [BRAND (from its markings) + –LING[1].]

brand name *n.* **1.** See **trade name** (sense 1). **2.** A commodity, service, or process having a trade name. **—brand-name** (brănd′nām′) *adj.*

brand-new (brănd′no͞o′, -nyo͞o′) *adj.* Being in a fresh and unused condition; completely new.

Bran·do (brăn′dō), **Marlon.** Born 1924. American actor widely known for his film appearances, most notably as Stanley Kowalski in *A Streetcar Named Desire* (1951).

Bran·don (brăn′dən). A city of southwest Manitoba, Canada, on the Assiniboine River west of Winnipeg. It is an industrial and transportation center. Population, 36,242.

Brandt (brănt, bränt), **Willy.** Born 1913. German political leader. He served as chancellor of West Germany (1969–1974) and won the 1971 Nobel Peace Prize for his efforts to reduce tension between the East and the West.

bran·dy (brăn′dē) *n., pl.* **-dies.** An alcoholic liquor distilled from wine or fermented fruit juice. **—brandy** *tr.v.* **-died, -dy·ing, -dies.** To preserve, flavor, or mix with brandy. [Short for *brandy-wine,* from Dutch *brandewijn* : *brandende,* present participle of *branden,* to burn; see **gʷher-** in Appendix + *wijn,* wine; see WINE.]

Bran·dy·wine (brăn′dē-wīn′). A creek of southeast Pennsylvania and northern Delaware. It was the site of a major defeat of the Continental Army on September 11, 1777, thus allowing British troops to enter Philadelphia on September 27.

Bran·gus (brăng′gəs). A trademark used for any of a breed of beef cattle developed from a cross between the Brahman and the Aberdeen Angus.

brank (brăngk) *n.* A device consisting of a metal frame for the head and a bit to restrain the tongue, formerly used to punish scolds. Usually used in the plural. [Possibly from Dutch *branken,* legs (of a compass, scissors, etc.), pl. of *branke,* branch, from Late Latin *branca,* paw. See BRANCH.]

bran·ni·gan (brăn′ĭ-gən) *n.* **1.** A noisy or confused quarrel. **2.** A drinking spree; a binge. [Probably from the name *Brannigan.*]

brant (brănt) *n., pl.* **brant** or **brants.** Any of several small, dark wild geese of the genus *Branta* that breed in arctic regions, especially *B. bernicla,* having a black neck and head. [Variant of *brent(-goose),* possibly from Middle English *brende,* brindled. See BRINDLED.]

Brant (brănt), **Joseph.** Originally Thayendanegea. 1742–1807. Mohawk leader who supported the British in the French and Indian War and the American Revolution.

Brant·ford (brănt′fərd). A city of southern Ontario, Canada, southwest of Toronto. It was named for the Mohawk leader Joseph Brant, who is buried nearby. Alexander Graham Bell performed some of his early experiments in sound transmission here in the 1870's. Population, 74,315.

Bran·ting (brăn′tĭng, brän′-), **Karl Hjalmar.** 1860–1925. Swedish political leader who served as premier (1920, 1921–1923, and 1924–1925). He shared the 1921 Nobel Peace Prize.

Braque (bräk, brăk), **Georges.** 1882–1963. French painter who was a leading exponent and theorist of the cubist movement.

brash[1] (brăsh) *adj.* **brash·er, brash·est. 1.a.** Hasty and unthinking; impetuous. **b.** Rash. **2.** Lacking in sensitivity or tact. **3.** Presumptuously forward; impudent. See Synonyms at **shameless.** **4.** Brittle: *brash timbers.* [Possibly imitative (influenced by RASH[1]) or from *brash,* attack.] **—brash′ly** *adv.* **—brash′ness** *n.*

brash[2] (brăsh) *n.* A mass or pile of rubble, refuse, or fragments, as of stone, brush, or ice. [Perhaps an alteration of French *brèche,* breach in a wall, from Italian *breccia.* See BRECCIA.]

bra·sier[1] (brā′zhər) *n.* Variant of **brazier**[1].

bra·sier[2] (brā′zhər) *n.* Variant of **brazier**[2].

Bra·sí·lia (brə-zĭl′yə). The capital of Brazil, in the central plateau northwest of Rio de Janeiro. The city, laid out in the shape of an airplane, was officially inaugurated in 1960. Population, 1,176,935.

Bra·şov (brä-shôv′). A city of central Romania in the foothills of the Transylvanian Alps north-northwest of Bucharest. It was founded in 1211 by the Teutonic Knights. Population, 331,240.

brass (brăs) *n.* **1.a.** A yellowish alloy of copper and zinc, sometimes including small amounts of other metals, but usually 67 percent copper and 33 percent zinc. **b.** Ornaments, objects, or utensils made of this alloy. **2.** Often **brasses.** *Music.* **a.** The section of a band or an orchestra composed of brass instruments. **b.** Brass instruments or their players considered as a group. **3.** A memorial plaque or tablet made of brass, especially one on which an effigy is incised. **4.** A bushing or similar lining for a bearing, made from a copper alloy. **5.** *Informal.* Bold self-assurance; effrontery. **6.** *Slang.* High-ranking military officers or other high officials. **7.** *Chiefly British.* Money. [Middle English *bras,* from Old English *bræs.*] **—brass** *adj.*

bras·sard (brə-särd′, brăs′ärd′) *n.* **1.** A band or badge worn around the upper arm. **2.** Also **bras·sart** (brə-särt′, brăs′ärt′). A piece of armor covering the arm, especially from elbow to shoulder. [French, from Old French *bras,* arm, from Latin *brācchium,* from Greek *brakhīōn,* upper arm. See **mregh-u-** in Appendix.]

brass band *n. Music.* A band composed of brass and sometimes percussion instruments.

brass·bound (brăs′bound′) *adj.* **1.** Banded or trimmed with brass or a similar metal, such as bronze. **2.** Inflexible; rigid: *brassbound party loyalists.* **3.** Bold and impudent; brazen.

brass-col·lar (brăs′kŏl′ər) *adj.* Unwavering in political allegiance; consistently voting a straight party ticket.

bras·se·rie (brăs′ə-rē′, brăs-rē′) *n.* A restaurant serving alcoholic beverages, especially beer, as well as food. [French, from *brasser,* to malt, brew, from Old French *bracier,* from Vulgar Latin **braciāre,* from Latin *brace,* malt, of Celtic origin.]

brass hat *n. Slang.* **1.** A high-ranking military officer. **2.** A high-ranking civilian official. [From the gold braid on the hat.]

brass·ie also **brass·y** (brăs′ē) *n., pl.* **-ies.** *Sports.* A golf club with a brass-plated sole and a wooden head, used for long low shots; a two wood.

bras·siere (brə-zîr′) *n.* A woman's undergarment worn to support and give contour to the breasts. [French, child's jacket with sleeves, brassiere : Old French *bras,* arm (from Latin *brācchium,* from Greek *brakhīōn,* upper arm; see **mregh-u-** in Appendix) + *-iere,* one associated with; see –ER[1].]

brass instrument *n. Music.* A wind instrument, such as the French horn or the trombone, made of brass or other metal. Sound is produced through vibration of the lips and adjustment of the length of the sound tube by means of valves or a slide.

brass knuckles *pl.n. (used with a sing. or pl. verb).* A metal chain or a set of rings attached to a bar that can be fitted over the fingers to increase the impact of a blow with the fist.

brass ring *n. Slang.* An opportunity to achieve wealth or success; a prize or reward.

brass tacks *pl.n. Informal.* Essential facts; basics: *getting down to brass tacks.*

brass-tacks (brăs′tăks′) *adj. Informal.* Concerned with essential matters; practical: *a brass-tacks leader.*

brass·ware (brăs′wâr′) *n.* Articles made from brass.

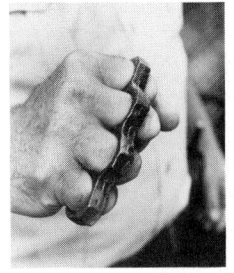

brass knuckles

ă pat	oi boy
ā pay	ou out
âr care	o͝o took
ä father	o͞o boot
ĕ pet	ŭ cut
ē be	ûr urge
ĭ pit	th thin
ī pie	*th* this
îr pier	hw which
ŏ pot	zh vision
ō toe	ə about, item
ô paw	♦ regionalism

Stress marks: ′ (primary); ′ (secondary), as in **dictionary** (dĭk′shə-nĕr′ē)

brass·y¹ (brăs′ē) *adj.* **-i·er, -i·est. 1.** Made of or decorated with brass. **2.** Resembling brass, as in color. **3.** *Music.* Resembling or characterized by the sound of brass instruments: *"The band was now playing some brassy march"* (Robert Penn Warren). **4.** Cheap and showy; flashy. **5.** *Informal.* Brazen; insolent. **—brass′i·ly** *adv.* **—brass′i·ness** *n.*

brass·y² (brăs′ē) *n. Sports.* Variant of **brassie.**

brat¹ (brăt) *n.* A child, especially a spoiled or ill-mannered one. [Possibly from *brat,* coarse garment, from Middle English, from Old English *bratt,* of Celtic origin.] **—brat′tish** *adj.* **—brat′tish·ness** *n.*

brat² (brăt) *n.* Bratwurst.

Bra·ti·sla·va (brăt′ĭ-slä′və, brä′tĭ-). A city of southern Czechoslovakia on the Danube River near the Austrian and Hungarian borders. It was the capital of Hungary from 1541 to 1784. Population, 409,100.

brat pack *n. Slang.* A group of highly successful young people engaged in the same profession: *"the kind of overnight fame that characterizes the literary brat pack—that covey of under-30 novelists"* (Christian Science Monitor). [On the model of *rat pack.*]

Bratsk (brätsk). A city of south-central Russia on the Angara River north-northwest of Irkutsk. It has hydroelectric power installations. Population, 240,000.

brat·tice (brăt′ĭs) *n.* **1.** A partition, typically of wood or cloth, erected in a mine for ventilation. **2.** A breastwork erected during a siege. [Middle English *bretice,* defensive structure, from Old French *bretesche,* from Medieval Latin *bretescha (turris),* British-style (tower), probably from Old English *bryttisc,* British.] **—brat′tice** *v.*

brat·tle (brăt′l) *Scots. n.* **1.** A rattling or clattering sound. **2.** A movement that produces such a sound. **—brattle** *intr.v.* **-tled, -tling, -tles.** To make a rattling or clattering sound, especially by rushing or scampering. [Imitative.]

brat·ty (brăt′ē) *adj.* **-ti·er, -ti·est.** Characteristic of or being a brat; ill-mannered. **—brat′ti·ness** *n.*

brat·wurst (brăt′wûrst′, -vo͝orst′) *n.* A small sausage of highly seasoned fresh pork, usually served fried. [German, from Middle High German *brātwurst,* from Old High German : *brāto,* meat; see **bhreu-** in Appendix + *wurst,* sausage; see WURST.]

Braun (broun), **Eva.** 1912–1945. German lover and later wife of Adolf Hitler. They began living together in 1936, but the liaison was kept secret, and she was never seen in public with him. They were married hours before their double suicide on April 30, 1945.

Braun (brôn, broun), **Wernher Magnus Maximilian von.** 1912–1977. German-born American rocket engineer, who was director of the U.S. Army team that put the first American satellite, Explorer I, into space (1958).

Braun·schwei·ger (broun′shwī′gər) *n.* A smoked liver sausage. [German, after *Braunschweig* (Brunswick), West Germany.]

bra·va (brä′vä, brä-vä′) *interj.* Used to express approval of a woman, especially for a performance. **—brava** *n.* A shout or cry of "brava." [Italian, feminine of *bravo,* bravo. See BRAVO¹.]

bra·va·do (brə-vä′dō) *n., pl.* **-dos** or **-does. 1.a.** Defiant or swaggering behavior: *strove to prevent our courage from turning into bravado.* **b.** A pretense of courage; a false show of bravery. **2.** A disposition toward showy defiance or false expressions of courage. [Spanish *bravada,* from *bravo,* brave. See BRAVE.]

brave (brāv) *adj.* **brav·er, brav·est. 1.** Possessing or displaying courage; valiant. **2.** Making a fine display; impressive or showy: *"a coat of brave red lipstick on a mouth so wrinkled that it didn't even have a clear outline"* (Anne Tyler). **3.** Excellent; great: *"The Romans were like brothers/In the brave days of old"* (Macaulay). **—brave** *n.* **1.** A Native American warrior. **2.** A courageous person. **3.** *Archaic.* A bully. **—brave** *v.* **braved, brav·ing, braves.** *—tr.* **1.** To undergo or face courageously. **2.** To challenge; dare: *"Together they would brave Satan and all his legions"* (Emily Brontë). **3.** *Obsolete.* To make showy or splendid. *—intr. Archaic.* To make a courageous show or to put up a stalwart front. [Middle English, from Old French, from Old Italian or Old Spanish *bravo,* wild, brave, excellent, probably from Vulgar Latin **brabus,* from Latin *barbarus.* See BARBAROUS.] **—brave′ly** *adv.* **—brave′ness** *n.*

SYNONYMS: *brave, courageous, fearless, intrepid, bold, audacious, valiant, valorous, doughty, mettlesome, plucky, dauntless, undaunted.* These adjectives all mean having or showing courage under difficult or dangerous conditions. *Brave,* the least specific, is frequently associated with an innate quality: *"Familiarity with danger makes a brave man braver, but less daring"* (Herman Melville). *Courageous* implies an act of consciously rising to a specific test by drawing on a reserve of inner strength: *The young platoon leader set a courageous example for his soldiers by leading them safely into and out of jungle territory held by the enemy. Fearless* emphasizes absence of fear and resolute self-possession: *"world-class* [boating] *races for fearless loners willing to face the distinct possibility of being run down, dismasted, capsized, attacked by whales"* (Jo Ann Morse Ridley). *Intrepid* sometimes suggests invulnerability to fear: *Intrepid pioneers settled the American West. Bold* stresses not only readiness to meet danger or difficulty but often also a tendency to seek it out: *"If we shrink from the hard contests where men must win at the hazard of their lives . . . then bolder and stronger peoples will pass us by"* (Theodore Roosevelt). *Audacious* implies extreme confidence and boldness: *"To demand these God-given rights is to seek black power—what I call audacious power"* (Adam Clayton Powell, Jr.). *Valiant,* said principally of persons, suggests the bravery of a hero or a heroine: *"a sympathetic and detailed biography that sees Hemingway as a valiant and moral man"* (New York Times). *Valorous* applies to the deeds of heros and heroines: *"Her passengers, the other hostages, will never forget her calm, confident, valorous work"* (William W. Bradley). *Doughty,* a bit old-fashioned in flavor and often used humorously, suggests stalwartness: *The doughty old man battled his illness with fierce determination. Mettlesome* stresses spirit and love of challenge: *The mettlesome actress resumed her career after recovering from a stroke. Plucky* emphasizes spirit and heart in the face of unfavorable odds: *"Everybody was . . . anxious to show these Belgians what England thought of their plucky little country"* (H.G. Wells). *Dauntless* refers to courage that resists subjection or intimidation: *"So faithful in love, and so dauntless in war,/There never was knight like the young Lochinvar"* (Sir Walter Scott). *Undaunted* suggests courage and resolve that persist after being put to the test: *"Death and sorrow will be the companions of our journey; hardship our garment; constancy and valor our only shield. We must be united, we must be undaunted, we must be inflexible"* (Winston S. Churchill). See also Synonyms at **defy.**

brave new world *n.* A vision or the realization of a radically transformed human existence, especially one in which scientific and technological change has a strong, adverse impact on social, political, and economic structures: *"This brave new world of science . . . offered broader opportunities for greater success to more people. At the same time, it scarred those who could not reap its benefits"* (W. Bruce Lincoln). [After *Brave New World,* title of a novel by Aldous Huxley (1894–1963).]

brav·er·y (brā′və-rē, brāv′rē) *n., pl.* **-ies. 1.** The condition or quality of being brave; courage. **2.** Splendor or magnificence; show.

bra·vis·si·mo (brä-vĭs′ə-mō′) *interj.* Used to express great approval, especially of a performance. [Italian, superlative of *bravo,* fine. See BRAVO¹.]

bra·vo¹ (brä′vō, brä-vō′) *interj.* Used to express approval, especially of a performance. **—bravo** *n., pl.* **-vos.** A shout or cry of "bravo." **—bravo** *v.* **-voed, -vo·ing, -voes.** *—tr.* To express approval of by shouting "bravo." *—intr.* To shout "bravo." [Italian. See BRAVE.]

bra·vo² (brä′vō) *n., pl.* **-voes** or **bra·vos.** A villain, especially a hired killer. [Italian, from *bravo,* wild, excellent. See BRAVE.]

bra·vu·ra (brə-vo͝or′ə, -vyo͝or′ə) *n.* **1.** *Music.* **a.** Brilliant technique or style in performance. **b.** A piece or passage that emphasizes a performer's virtuosity. **2.** A showy manner or display. [Italian, from *bravo,* excellent. See BRAVE.]

braw (brô) *adj.* **-er, -est.** *Scots.* **1.** Fine; splendid. **2.** Dressed in a fine or showy manner. [Scots, variant of BRAVE.]

brawl (brôl) *n.* **1.** A noisy quarrel or fight. **2.** A loud party. **3.** A loud, roaring noise. **—brawl** *intr.v.* **brawled, brawl·ing, brawls. 1.** To quarrel or fight noisily. **2.** To flow noisily, as water. [Middle English *braul,* from *braullen,* to quarrel.] **—brawl′er** *n.* **—brawl′ing·ly** *adv.*

SYNONYMS: *brawl, broil, donnybrook, fracas, fray, free-for-all, melee, row, ruction.* The central meaning shared by these nouns is "a very noisy, disorderly, and often violent quarrel or fight": *a barroom brawl; a protest march that degenerated into a general broil between the demonstrators and the police; an incident that turned into a vicious legal donnybrook; putting down a violent fracas among prison inmates; eager for the fray; a regular free-for-all in the schoolyard; police plunging into the melee; a terrific domestic row; a senseless ruction over trivia.*

brawl·y (brô′lē) *adj.* **-i·er, -i·est. 1.** Engaged in brawling. **2.** Tending to brawl.

brawn (brôn) *n.* **1.** Solid and well-developed muscles, especially of the arms and legs. **2.** Muscular strength and power. **3.** *Chiefly British.* The meat of a boar. **4.** Headcheese. [Middle English, muscle, from Old French *braon,* meat, of Germanic origin. See **bhreu-** in Appendix.]

brawn·y (brô′nē) *adj.* **-i·er, -i·est. 1.** Strong and muscular. See Synonyms at **muscular. 2.** Hardened; calloused. **—brawn′i·ly** *adv.* **—brawn′i·ness** *n.*

bray¹ (brā) *v.* **brayed, bray·ing, brays.** *—intr.* **1.** To utter the loud, harsh cry of a donkey. **2.** To sound loudly and harshly: *The foghorn brayed all night.* *—tr.* To emit (an utterance or a sound) loudly and harshly. **—bray** *n.* **1.** The loud, harsh cry of a donkey. **2.** A sound resembling that of a donkey: *"an endless bray of pointless jocosity"* (Louis Auchincloss). [Middle English *braien,* from Old French *braire,* of Celtic origin.]

bray² (brā) *tr.v.* **brayed, bray·ing, brays. 1.** To crush and pound to a fine consistency, as in a mortar. **2.** To spread (ink) thinly over a surface. [Middle English *braien,* from Old French *breier,* of Germanic origin. See **bhreg-** in Appendix.]

bray·er¹ (brā′ər) *n.* One that brays, especially a donkey.

bray·er² (brā′ər) *n. Printing.* A small hand roller used to spread ink thinly and evenly.

Braz. *abbr.* **1.** Brazil. **2.** Brazilian.

braze¹ (brāz) *tr.v.* **brazed, braz·ing, braz·es. 1.** To make of or decorate with brass. **2.** To make hard like brass. [Middle

English *brasen,* from Old English *brasian,* from *bræs,* brass.]

braze² (brāz) *tr.v.* **brazed, braz·ing, braz·es.** To solder (two pieces of metal) together using a hard solder with a high melting point. [Probably from French *braser,* from Old French, to burn, from *brese,* hot coal, of Germanic origin. See **bhreu-** in Appendix.] **—braz′er** *n.*

bra·zen (brā′zən) *adj.* **1.** Marked by flagrant and insolent audacity. See Synonyms at **shameless. 2.** Having a loud, usually harsh, resonant sound. **3.** Made of brass. **4.** Resembling brass, as in color or strength. **—brazen** *tr.v.* **-zened, -zen·ing, -zens.** To face with bold self-assurance: *brazened out the crisis.* [Middle English *brasen,* made of brass, from Old English *bræsen,* from *bræs,* brass.] **—bra′zen·ly** *adv.* **—bra′zen·ness** *n.*

bra·zen·faced (brā′zən-fāst′) *adj.* Flagrantly and insolently audacious.

bra·zier¹ also **bra·sier** (brā′zhər) *n.* One that works in brass. [Middle English *brasier,* from *bras,* brass. See BRASS.]

bra·zier² also **bra·sier** (brā′zhər) *n.* **1.** A metal pan for holding burning coals or charcoal. **2.** A cooking device consisting of a charcoal or electric heating source over which food is grilled. [French *brasier,* from *braise,* hot coals. See BRAISE.]

Bra·zil (brə-zĭl′). *Abbr.* **Braz.** A country of eastern South America. The largest country in the continent, it was ruled by Portugal from 1500 to 1822 and was an empire until 1889, when a republic was established. Brasília has been the capital since 1960; São Paulo is the largest city. Population, 119,002,706. **—Bra·zil′i·an** *adj. & n.*

Brazilian pepper tree *n.* An evergreen Brazilian tree *(Schinus terebinthifolius)* having aromatic foliage and clusters of red, berrylike fruits used for Christmas decorations. It is naturalized in warm regions and a serious pest in Hawaii and Florida. Also called *Christmas berry tree.*

Brazil nut *n.* **1.** A tropical South American evergreen tree *(Bertholletia excelsa)* having, globose, woody fruit and edible, dark brown, three-sided seeds. **2.** The seed of this tree. [After BRAZIL.]

bra·zil·wood (brə-zĭl′wo͝od′) *n.* The reddish wood of certain tropical trees or shrubs in the pea family, especially a Brazilian tree *Caesalpinia echinata,* whose wood is used for violin bows and as a source of a red or purplish dye. [Obsolete *brazil,* brazilwood (from Middle English *brasil,* from Old French *bresil,* perhaps from **bresiller,* to glow red, from *brese,* hot coal; see BRAISE) + WOOD¹.]

Braz·os (brăz′əs). A river rising as a tributary in eastern New Mexico and flowing about 1,400 km (870 mi) generally southeast across Texas to the Gulf of Mexico southwest of Galveston.

Braz·za·ville (brăz′ə-vĭl′, brä-zä-vēl′). The capital and largest city of Congo, in the southern part of the country on the Congo River across from Kinshasa, Zaire. Founded by the French in the 1880's, it is a trade center and major port. Population, 595,102.

B.R.E. *abbr.* Bachelor of Religious Education.

Bre·a (brā′ə). A city of southern California north of Anaheim. It is a residential community with varied light industries. Population, 27,913.

breach (brēch) *n.* **1.a.** An opening, a tear, or a rupture. **b.** A gap or rift, especially in or as if in a solid structure such as a dike or fortification. **2.** A violation or infraction, as of a law, a legal obligation, or a promise. **3.** A breaking up or disruption of friendly relations; an estrangement. **4.** A leap of a whale from the water. **5.** The breaking of waves or surf. **—breach** *v.* **breached, breach·ing, breach·es.** —*tr.* **1.** To make a hole or gap in; break through. **2.** To break or violate (an agreement, for example). —*intr.* To leap from the water: *waiting for the whale to breach.* [Middle English *breche,* from Old English *brēc.* See **bhreg-** in Appendix.]

SYNONYMS: *breach, infraction, violation, transgression, trespass, infringement.* These nouns denote an act or instance of breaking a law or regulation or failing to fulfill a duty, obligation, or promise. *Breach* and *infraction* are the least specific: *Revealing the secret would be a breach of trust. Infractions of the rules will not be tolerated.* A *violation* is an infraction committed willfully and with complete lack of regard for legal, moral, or ethical considerations: *She failed to appear for the rehearsal, in flagrant violation of her contract. Transgression* refers most often to a violation of divine or moral law: *"The children shall not be punished for the father's transgression"* (Daniel Defoe). As it refers to the breaking of a statute, *trespass* implies willful intrusion on another's rights, possessions, or person: *"In the limited and confined sense* [trespass] *signifies no more than an entry on another man's ground without a lawful authority"* (William Blackstone). *Infringement* is most frequently used specifically to denote encroachment on another's rights, such as those granted by a copyright: *"Necessity is the plea for every infringement of human freedom"* (William Pitt the Younger).

breach of promise *n.* Failure to fulfill a promise, especially a promise to marry.

bread (brĕd) *n.* **1.** A staple food made from flour or meal mixed with other dry and liquid ingredients, usually combined with a leavening agent, and kneaded, shaped into loaves, and baked. **2.a.** Food in general, regarded as necessary for sustaining life: *"If bread is the first necessity of life, recreation is a close second"* (Edward Bellamy). **b.** Something that nourishes; sustenance: *"My bread shall be the anguish of my mind"* (Edmund Spenser). **3.a.** Means of support; livelihood: *earn one's bread.* **b.** *Slang.* Money. **—bread** *tr.v.* **bread·ed, bread·ing, breads.** To coat with bread crumbs, as before cooking: *breaded the fish fillets.* [Middle English, from Old English *brēad.* See **bhreu-** in Appendix. N., sense 3b, possibly from Cockney rhyming slang *bread and honey.*]

bread and butter *n.* **1.** Means of support; livelihood. **2.** The essential sustaining element or elements; the mainstay: *"As ever, politics, vulgarity and sentimentality were the bread and butter of the Academy Awards"* (David Ansen).

bread-and-but·ter (brĕd′n-bŭt′ər) *adj.* **1.a.** Influenced by or undertaken out of necessity: *a bread-and-butter job.* **b.** Reliable, especially for producing income; basic: *Household appliances are the company's bread-and-butter goods.* **2.** Expressive of gratitude for hospitality: *a bread-and-butter note.*

bread·bas·ket (brĕd′băs′kĭt) *n.* **1.** A basket for serving bread. **2.** A geographic region serving as a principal source of grain supply. **3.** *Slang.* The stomach.

bread·board (brĕd′bôrd′, -bōrd′) *n.* **1.** A board on which bread is sliced or dough is kneaded. **2.** An experimental model, as of an electric circuit. **—breadboard** *tr.v.* **-board·ed, -board·ing, -boards.** To construct an experimental model of (an electric circuit, for example). **—bread′board′ing** *n.*

bread·box (brĕd′bŏks′) *n.* A container in which baked goods are stored to maintain their freshness.

bread·fruit (brĕd′fro͞ot′) *n.* **1.** A Malaysian evergreen timber tree *(Artocarpus altilis)* having large, round, yellowish, edible fruits. **2.** The fruit of this tree.

bread line *n.* A line of people waiting to receive food given by a charitable organization or public agency.

bread mold *n.* Any of various fungi of the genus *Rhizopus,* that form a dense, cottony growth on bread and other foods.

bread·nut (brĕd′nŭt′) *n.* **1.** A large tree *(Brosimum alicastrum)* native to Mexico, Central America, and the West Indies, having yellow fruits each with a large, edible seed. **2.** The seed of this tree.

bread·root (brĕd′ro͞ot′, -ro͝ot′) *n.* A perennial herb *(Psoralea esculenta)* in the pea family, native to prairies and plains in central North America, and having a tuberous, starchy root that was an important food for many Native Americans. Also called *prairie potato.*

bread·stuff (brĕd′stŭf′) *n.* **1.** Bread in any form or shape. **2.** Flour, meal, or grain used in the baking of bread.

breadth (brĕdth) *n.* **1.** *Abbr.* **b.** The measure or dimension from side to side; width. **2.** A piece usually produced in a standard width: *a breadth of canvas.* **3.a.** Wide range or scope: *breadth of knowledge.* **b.** Tolerance; broadmindedness: *a jurist of great breadth and wisdom.* **4.** An effect of unified, encompassing vision in an artistic composition. [Middle English *breth,* from *brede,* on the model of *length,* length.]

breadth·ways (brĕdth′wāz′) or **breadth·wise** (-wīz′) *adv. & adj.* In the direction of the breadth.

bread·win·ner (brĕd′wĭn′ər) *n.* One whose earnings are the primary source of support for one's dependents.

break (brāk) *v.* **broke** (brōk), **bro·ken** (brō′kən), **break·ing, breaks.** —*tr.* **1.** To cause to separate into pieces suddenly or violently; smash. **2.** To divide into pieces, as by bending or cutting: *break crackers for a baby.* **3.** To snap off or detach: *broke a twig from the tree.* **4.a.** To fracture a bone of: *I broke my leg.* **b.** To fracture (a bone): *I broke my femur.* **5.** To crack without separating into pieces. **6.a.** To destroy the completeness of (a group of related items): *broke the set of books by giving some away.* **b.** To exchange for smaller monetary units: *break a dollar.* **7.** To vary or disrupt the uniformity or continuity of: *a plain that was broken by low hills; caught the ball without breaking stride.* **8.** *Electricity.* To open: *break a circuit.* **9.a.** To force or make a way through; puncture or penetrate: *The blade barely broke the skin.* **b.** To part or pierce the surface of: *a dolphin breaking water.* **10.** To cause to burst. **11.** To force one's way out of; escape from: *break jail.* **12.a.** To find an opening or flaw in: *They couldn't break my alibi.* **b.** To find the solution or key to; uncover the basic elements and arrangement of: *break a code; break a spy ring.* **13.** To make known, as news: *break a story.* **14.** To surpass or outdo: *broke the league's home-run record.* **15.** To overcome (a force or resistance): *break the sound barrier.* **16.** To put an end to by force or strong opposition, especially to end (a strike) by means other than negotiation. **17.** To lessen in force or effect: *break a fall.* **18.** To render useless or inoperative: *We accidentally broke the radio.* **19.** To weaken or destroy, as in spirit or health; overwhelm with adversity: *"For a hero loves the world till it breaks him"* (William Butler Yeats). **20.** To cause the ruin or failure of (an enterprise, for example): *Indiscretion broke both marriage and career.* **21.** To reduce in rank; demote. **22.** To cause to be without money or go into bankruptcy. **23.** To fail to fulfill; cancel: *break an engagement; break one's vacation plans.* **24.** To fail to conform to; violate: *break the speed limit.* **25.** *Law.* To invalidate (a will) by judicial action. **26.a.** To give up (a habit). **b.** To cause to give up a habit: *They managed to break themselves of smoking.* **27.** To train to obey; tame: *The horse was difficult to break.* —*intr.* **1.** To become separated into pieces or fragments. **2.** To become cracked or split. **3.** To become unusable or inoperative: *The television broke.* **4.** To give way; collapse. **5.** To burst: *The blister has finally broken.* **6.a.** To become punctured or penetrated. **b.** To intrude on: *They broke in*

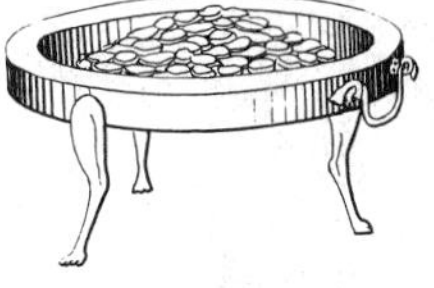
brazier²

Brazil

Brazil nut
Bertholletia excelsa

ă pat	oi boy
ā pay	ou out
âr care	o͝o took
ä father	o͞o boot
ĕ pet	ŭ cut
ē be	ûr urge
ĭ pit	th thin
ī pie	*th* this
îr pier	hw which
ŏ pot	zh vision
ō toe	ə about, item
ô paw	♦ regionalism

Stress marks: **′** (primary); ′ (secondary), as in **dictionary** (dĭk′shə-nĕr′ē)

break dancing

upon a heady conversation. **c.** To filter in or penetrate: *Sunlight broke into the room.* **7.** To become fractured. **8.** To scatter or disperse; part: *The clouds broke after the storm.* **9.** *Games.* To make the opening shot that scatters the grouped balls in billiards or pool. **10.** *Sports.* To separate from a clinch in boxing. **11.** To move away or escape suddenly. **12.** To come forth or begin from a state of latency; come into being or emerge: *A storm was breaking over Miami. Crocuses broke from the soil.* **13.** To emerge above the surface of water. **14.** To become known or noticed: *The big story broke on Friday.* **15.** To change direction suddenly. **16.** *Baseball.* To curve near or over the plate: *The pitch broke away from the batter.* **17.** To change suddenly from one tone quality or musical register to another: *My voice broke to a whisper.* **18.** *Linguistics.* To undergo breaking. **19.** To change to a gait different from the one set. Used of a horse. **20.** To interrupt or cease an activity: *We'll break for coffee at ten.* **21.** To discontinue an association, an agreement, or a relationship: *The partners broke over a financial matter. One hates to break with an old friend.* **22.** To diminish or discontinue abruptly: *The fever is breaking.* **23.** To diminish in or lose physical or spiritual strength; weaken or succumb: *Their good cheer broke after repeated setbacks.* **24.** To decrease sharply in value or quantity: *Stock prices broke when the firm suddenly announced layoffs.* **25.** To come to an end: *The cold spell broke yesterday.* **26.** To collapse or crash into surf or spray: *waves that were breaking along the shore.* **27.** *Informal.* To take place or happen; proceed: *Things have been breaking well for them.* **28.** To break dance. **—break** *n.* **1.** The act or an occurrence of breaking. **2.** The result of breaking, as a crack or separation. **3.** A beginning or an opening: *the break of day; a break in the clouds.* **4.** A sudden movement; a dash: *The dog made a break toward the open field.* **5.** An escape: *a prison break.* **6.** An interruption or a disruption in continuity or regularity: *television programming without commercial breaks.* **7.** A pause or an interval, as from work: *a coffee break.* **8.** A sudden or marked change. **9.** A violation: *a security break.* **10.** An often sudden piece of luck, especially good luck: *finally got the big break in life.* **11.** *Informal.* **a.** An allowance or indulgence; accommodating treatment: *The boss gave me a break because I'd been sick.* **b.** A favorable price or reduction: *a tax break for charitable contributions.* **12.** A severing of ties: *made a break with the past; a break between the two families.* **13.** *Informal.* A faux pas. **14.** A sudden decline in prices. **15.** A caesura. **16.** *Printing.* **a.** The space between two paragraphs. **b.** A series of three dots (. . .) used to indicate an omission in a text. **c.** The place where a word is or should be divided at the end of a line. **17.** *Electricity.* Interruption of a flow of current. **18.** *Geology.* A marked change in topography such as a fault or deep valley. **19.** *Nautical.* The point of discontinuity between two levels on the deck of a ship. **20.** *Music.* **a.** The point at which one register or a tonal quality changes to another. **b.** The change itself. **c.** A solo jazz cadenza played during the pause between the regular phrases or choruses of a melody. **21.** A change in a horse's gait to one different from that set by the rider. **22.** *Sports.* The swerving of a ball from a straight path of flight, as in baseball or cricket. **23.** *Sports.* The beginning of a race. **24.** *Sports.* The separation after a clinch in boxing. **25.** *Games.* The opening shot that scatters the grouped balls in billiards or pool. **26.** *Games.* A run or unbroken series of successful shots, as in billiards or croquet. **27.** *Sports & Games.* Failure to score a strike or a spare in a given bowling frame. **28.** Also **brake.** A high horse-drawn carriage with four wheels. **29.** Break dancing. ***—phrasal verbs.*** **break down. 1.** To cause to collapse; destroy: *break down a partition; broke down our resolve.* **2. a.** To become or cause to become distressed or upset. **b.** To have a physical or mental collapse. **3.** To give up resistance; give way: *broke down and bought a new car; prejudices that break down slowly.* **4.** To fail to function; cease to be useful, effective, or operable: *The elevator broke down.* **5.** To render or become weak or ineffective: *Opposition to the king's rule gradually broke down his authority.* **6. a.** To divide into or consider in parts; analyze. **b.** To be divisible; admit of analysis: *The population breaks down into three main groups.* **7.** To decompose or cause to decompose chemically. **8.** *Electricity.* To undergo a breakdown. **break in. 1.** To train or adapt for a purpose. **2.** To loosen or soften with use: *break in new shoes.* **3.** To enter premises forcibly or illegally: *a prowler who was trying to break in.* **4. a.** To interrupt a conversation or discussion. **b.** To intrude. **break into. 1.** To interrupt: *"No one would have dared to break into his abstraction"* (Alan Paton). **2.** To begin suddenly: *The horse broke into a wild gallop. The child broke into a flood of tears.* **3.** To enter (a field of activity): *broke into broadcast journalism at an early age.* **break off. 1.** To separate or become separated, as by twisting or tearing. **2.** To stop suddenly, as in speaking. **3. a.** To discontinue (a relationship). **b.** To cease to be friendly. **break out. 1.** To become affected with a skin eruption, such as pimples. **2.** To develop suddenly and forcefully: *Fighting broke out in the prison cells.* **3. a.** To ready for action or use: *Break out the rifles!* **b.** To bring forth for consumption: *Let's break out the champagne.* **4.** To emerge or escape. **5.** To be separable or classifiable into categories, as data. **6.** To isolate (information) from a large body of data. **break through.** To make a sudden, quick advance, as through obstruction or opposition. **break up. 1. a.** To separate into pieces; divide: *break up a chocolate bar.* **b.** To interrupt the uniformity or continuity of: *An impromptu visit broke up the long afternoon.* **2.** To scatter; disperse: *The crowd broke up after the game.* **3.** To bring or come to an end: *Guards broke up the fight. The marriage broke up.* **4.** *Informal.* To burst or cause to burst into laughter. ***—idioms.*** **break a leg.** Used to wish someone, such as an actor, success in a performance. **break bread.** To eat together. **break camp.** To pack up equipment and leave a campsite. **break cover.** To emerge from a protected location or hiding place: *The platoon broke cover and headed down the road.* **break even.** To gain an amount equal to that invested, as in a commercial venture. **break new ground.** To advance beyond previous achievements: *a company that broke new ground in the field of computers.* **break (one's) neck.** To make the utmost possible effort. **break rank** (or **ranks**). **1.** To fall into disorder, as a formation of soldiers. **2.** To fail to conform to a prevailing or expected pattern or order: *"Architectural experts have criticized the plaza in the past because it breaks rank with the distinctive façades of neighboring Fifth Avenue blocks, whose buildings are flush with the sidewalk"* (Sharon Churcher). **break (someone's) heart.** To disappoint or dispirit severely. **break (someone's) service.** *Sports.* To win a game, as in tennis, served by one's opponent. **break the ice. 1.** To make a start. **2.** To relax a tense or unduly formal atmosphere or social situation. **break wind.** To expel intestinal gas. [Middle English *breken,* from Old English *brecan.* See **bhreg-** in Appendix.]

breastplate

SYNONYMS: *break, crack, fracture, burst, split, splinter, shatter, shiver, smash.* These verbs are compared as they mean to separate or cause to separate into parts or pieces. *Break* is the most general and like the other members of the set implies either the sudden application of force or the build-up of internal stress: *a window broken by vandals; broke her leg; a delicate chair that will break under a great weight.* To *crack* is to break, often with a sharp snapping sound, without dividing into parts: *I cracked the platter when I knocked it against the table. The foundation of the house cracked during the earthquake. The soil cracked from the drought. Fracture* applies to a break or crack in a rigid body: *fractured her skull in the accident; a vertebra that fractured in the fall. Burst* implies a sudden coming apart, especially from internal pressure, and the dispersion of contents: *The child burst the balloon with a pin. Her appendix burst. Split* refers to a division into sections longitudinally or along the direction of the grain: *split the log with an ax; frost that caused the rock to split. Splinter* implies splitting into long, thin, sharp pieces: *The tree was struck by lightning and splintered. Repeated blows splintered the door.* To *shatter* is to break into many loose scattered pieces: *The bottle will shatter if you drop it. An exploding gas main shattered the tiles in the courtyard. Shiver* is a term rarely encountered outside literary contexts; like *shatter,* it indicates sudden force that causes fragmentation: *"Every statue was hurled from its niche . . . every painted window* [was] *shivered to atoms"* (John Lothrop Motley). *"The panels shivering in, like potsherds"* (Thomas Carlyle). *Smash* stresses force of blow or impact and suggests complete destruction: *My glasses slipped from my hand and smashed on the floor. The boat was smashed on the rocks.* See also Synonyms at **demote, opportunity.**

break·a·ble (brā′kə-bəl) *adj.* Liable to break or to be broken. See Synonyms at **fragile.** **—breakable** *n.* An article that can be broken easily: *We put the breakables away before the toddlers arrived.* **—break′a·ble·ness** *n.*

break·age (brā′kĭj) *n.* **1.** The act of breaking. **2.** A quantity broken. **3.** Loss or damage as a result of breaking. **4.** A commercial allowance for loss or damage.

break·a·way (brāk′ə-wā′) *adj.* **1.** Designed to break, bend, or fall apart easily upon impact, especially to create an illusion, as with a theater prop, or for safety, as with a highway sign or barrier. **2.** Severing or having severed alliance with another entity, policy, or attitude: *a group of breakaway political reformers.* **—breakaway** *n.* **1.** One that breaks away. **2.** The act of breaking away. **3.** An object designed to break away.

break·bone fever (brāk′bōn′) *n.* See **dengue.**

break-bulk (brāk′bŭlk′) *adj.* Having, being, or related to shipments of goods packed in small, separable units.

break dance *n.* A performance of break dancing.

break danc·ing also **break·danc·ing** (brāk′dăn′sĭng) *n.* A style of dancing in which agility, and often spectacular gymnastic skills, are combined with pantomime and performed especially to the rhythms of rap music. **—break′-dance′** *v.* **—break dancer, break′-danc′er** *n.*

break·down (brāk′doun′) *n.* **1. a.** The act or process of failing to function or continue. **b.** The condition resulting from this: *a breakdown in communication.* **2.** *Electricity.* The abrupt failure of an insulator or insulating medium to restrict the flow of current. **3.** A typically sudden collapse in physical or mental health. **4.** An analysis, an outline, or a summary consisting of itemized data or essentials. **5.** Disintegration or decomposition into parts or elements. **6.** A noisy, energetic American country dance.

break·er¹ (brā′kər) *n.* **1.** One that breaks, as a machine for breaking up or crushing a substance, such as rock, coal, or plant fibers. **2.** A circuit breaker. **3.** A wave that crests or breaks into foam, especially against a shoreline. **4.** One who break dances.

bre·ker² (brā′kər) *n.* *Nautical.* A small water cask, often used in lifeboats. [Alteration of Spanish *barrica.* See BARRICADE.]

break-e·ven (brāk′ē′vən) *adj.* Also **break·e·ven.** Marked by or indicating a balance of investment and return; having or showing neither profit nor loss. **—break-even** *n.* The point, especially the level of sales of a good or service, at which the return on investment is exactly equal to the amount invested. Also called *break-even point.*

break·fast (brĕk′fəst) *n.* The first meal of the day, usually eaten in the morning. —*attributive.* Often used to modify another noun: *a breakfast nook; the breakfast dishes.* —**breakfast** *v.* **-fast·ed, -fast·ing, -fasts.** —*intr.* To eat breakfast: *We breakfasted on the terrace.* —*tr.* To provide breakfast for. [Middle English *brekfast* : *breken,* to break; see BREAK + *faste,* a fast (from Old Norse *fasta,* to fast; see **past-** in Appendix).] —**break′fast·er** *n.*

break·front (brāk′frŭnt′) *n.* A piece of furniture, such as a cabinet or a bookcase, in which the frontal plane is interrupted horizontally by a projecting central section. —*attributive.* Often used to modify another noun: *a breakfront sideboard; a breakfront dresser.*

break-in (brāk′ĭn′) *n.* **1.** Forcible entry, as into a building or room, for an illegal purpose, especially theft. **2.** An initial period of employment or operation during which the performance of a person or thing may be evaluated and adjusted.

break·ing¹ (brā′kĭng) *n. Linguistics.* The change of a simple vowel to a diphthong, often caused by the influence of neighboring consonants. [Translation of German *Brechung.*]

break·ing² (brā′kĭng) *n.* Break dancing.

breaking and en·ter·ing (ĕn′tər-ĭng) *n. Abbr.* **B and E** *Law.* The gaining of unauthorized, illegal access to another's premises, as by forcing a lock.

breaking point *n.* **1.** The point at which physical, mental, or emotional strength gives way under stress. **2.** The point at which a condition or situation becomes critical.

break·neck (brāk′nĕk′) *adj.* **1.** Dangerously fast: *a breakneck pace.* **2.** Likely to cause an accident: *a breakneck curve.*

break·off (brāk′ôf′, -ŏf′) *n.* The act or an instance of breaking off; discontinuance.

break·out (brāk′out′) *n.* **1.** A forceful emergence from a restrictive condition or situation. **2.** A classified summary of statistical data.

break·point (brāk′point′) *n.* **1.** Or **break point.** A point of discontinuity, change, or cessation. **2.** *Computer Science.* A point in a program at which operation may be interrupted for manual intervention.

break·through (brāk′thro͞o′) *n.* **1.** An act of overcoming or penetrating an obstacle or restriction. **2.** A military offensive that penetrates an enemy's lines of defense. **3.** A major achievement or success that permits further progress, as in technology.

break·up (brāk′ŭp′) *n.* **1.** The act or an instance of breaking up, as a division, dispersal, or disintegration. **2.** The discontinuance of a relationship, as a marriage or a friendship. **3.** The cracking and shifting of ice in rivers or harbors during the spring. **4.** A loss of control or composure.

break·wa·ter (brāk′wô′tər, -wŏt′ər) *n.* A barrier that protects a harbor or shore from the full impact of waves.

bream¹ (brēm, brĭm) *n., pl.* **bream** or **breams.** **1.** Any of several European freshwater fishes of the genus *Abramis,* especially *A. brama,* having a flattened body and silvery scales. **2.** A similar fish, especially: **a.** Any one of various saltwater fishes in the family Sparidae, such as the porgy. **b.** Any one of various freshwater sunfishes of the genus *Lepomis* and related genera, such as the bluegill. [Middle English *breme,* from Old French, of Germanic origin.]

bream² (brēm) *tr.v.* **breamed, bream·ing, breams.** *Nautical.* To clean (a wooden ship's hull) by applying heat to soften the pitch and then scraping. [From Middle Dutch *brem(e),* furze, broom.]

breast (brĕst) *n.* **1.a.** Either of two milk-secreting, glandular organs on the chest of a woman; the human mammary gland. **b.** A corresponding organ in other mammals. **c.** A corresponding rudimentary gland in the male. **2.a.** The superior ventral surface of the human body, extending from the neck to the abdomen. **b.** A corresponding part in other animals. **3.** The part of a garment that covers the chest. **4.** The seat of affection and emotion: *"Griefs of mine own lie heavy in my breast"* (Shakespeare). **5.** A source of nourishment. **6.** Something likened to the human breast: *the breast of a hill.* **7.** The face of a mine or tunnel. —**breast** *tr.v.* **breast·ed, breast·ing, breasts.** **1.** To rise over; climb: *"He breasted a rise and looked down. He was at the head of a small valley"* (Ken Follett). **2.** To encounter or advance against resolutely; confront boldly. **3.** To push against with or as if with the breast. [Middle English *brest,* from Old English *brēost.*]

breast-beat·ing (brĕst′bē′tĭng) *n.* A loud, self-conscious demonstration of emotion, especially of remorse. —**breast′-beat′ing** *adj.*

breast·bone (brĕst′bōn′) *n.* See **sternum.**

breast-feed (brĕst′fēd′) *tr.v.* **-fed** (-fĕd′), **-feed·ing, -feeds.** To feed (a baby) mother's milk from the breast; suckle.

breast·plate (brĕst′plāt′) *n.* **1.** A piece of armor that covers the breast. **2.** *Judaism.* A square cloth set with 12 precious stones representing the 12 tribes of Israel, worn over the breast by ancient high priests.

breast·stroke (brĕst′strōk′) *n. Sports.* A swimming stroke in which a person lies face down in the water and extends the arms in front of the head, then sweeps them both back laterally under the surface of the water while performing a frog kick. —**breast′stroke′** *v.* —**breast′strok′er** *n.*

breast·work (brĕst′wûrk′) *n.* A temporary, quickly constructed fortification, usually breast-high. See Synonyms at **bulwark.**

breath (brĕth) *n.* **1.** The air inhaled and exhaled in respiration. **2.** The act or process of breathing; respiration. **3.** The capacity to breathe, especially in a natural and unlabored manner. **4.** Spirit or vitality; life. **5.** A single respiration: *a deep breath.* **6.** Exhaled air, as evidenced by vapor, odor, or heat. **7.** A momentary pause or rest. **8.a.** A momentary stirring of air. **b.** A slight gust of fragrant air. **9.** A trace or suggestion. **10.** A softly spoken sound; a whisper. **11.** *Linguistics.* Exhalation of air without vibration of the vocal cords, as in the articulation of *p* and *s.* —***idioms.*** **in one** (or **the same**) **breath.** At or almost at the same time. **out of breath.** Breathing with difficulty, as from exertion; gasping. **under (one's) breath.** In a muted voice or whisper. [Middle English *breth,* from Old English *brǣth.* See **gʷhrē-** in Appendix.]

breath·a·ble (brē′thə-bəl) *adj.* **1.** Suitable or pleasant for breathing: *breathable air.* **2.** Permitting air to pass through: *a breathable fabric.* —**breath′a·bil′i·ty** *n.*

Breath·a·lyz·er (brĕth′ə-lī′zər). A trademark used for a device that detects and measures alcohol in expired air so as to determine the concentration of alcohol in a person's blood. This trademark, often used attributively, sometimes occurs in print in lowercase: *"An arrestee requests to speak with or call an attorney, or anyone else, when requested to take a breathalyzer test"* (National Law Journal). *"The solution is the breathalyzer"* (Legal Times).

breathe (brēth) *v.* **breathed, breath·ing, breathes.** —*intr.* **1.** To inhale and exhale air, especially when naturally and freely. **2.** To be alive; live. See Synonyms at **be.** **3.** To pause to rest or regain breath: *Give me a moment to breathe.* **4.** To move or blow gently, as air. **5.** To allow air to pass through: *a natural fabric that breathes.* **6.** To be exhaled or emanated, as a fragrance. **7.** To be manifested or suggested, as an idea or feeling: *A sense of calm breathed from the landscape.* **8.** To reach fullness of flavor and aroma through exposure to air. Used chiefly of wine. **9.** To require air in the combustion process. Used of an internal-combustion engine. —*tr.* **1.** To inhale and exhale (air, for example) during respiration. **2.** To inhale (an aroma, for example): *breathe the lush scent of lilacs.* **3.** To impart as if by breathing; instill: *an artist who knows how to breathe life into a portrait.* **4.** To exhale (something); emit. **5.** To utter, especially quietly; whisper: *Don't breathe a word of this.* **6.** To make apparent or manifest; suggest: *Their manner breathed self-satisfaction.* **7.** To allow (a person or animal) to rest or regain breath. **8.** *Linguistics.* To utter with a voiceless exhalation of air. **9.** To draw in (air) for the combustion process. Used of an internal-combustion engine. —***idioms.*** **breathe down (someone's) neck.** **1.** To threaten by proximity, especially by pursuing closely. **2.** To watch or monitor closely, often annoyingly: *The boss was breathing down my neck all morning.* **breathe easily** (or **easy** or **freely**). To be relaxed or relieved, especially after a period of tension. **breathe (one's) last.** To die. [Middle English *brethen,* from *breth,* breath. See BREATH.] —**breath′a·ble** *adj.*

breathed (brĕtht) *adj.* **1.** (*also* brēthd). *Linguistics.* Voiceless. **2.** Having breath of a specified kind. Often used in combination: *sour-breathed.*

breath·er (brē′thər) *n.* **1.** One that breathes, especially in a specified manner: *a shallow breather.* **2.** *Informal.* A short rest period: *took a breather after skiing for two hours.* **3.** *Informal.* An activity, such as strenuous exercise, that causes difficult breathing. **4.** A small vent allowing the passage of gas or liquid to or from an enclosed area.

breath·ing (brē′thĭng) *n.* **1.a.** The act or process of respiration. **b.** A single breath. **2.** The time required to take one's breath. **3.a.** Either of two marks used in Greek to indicate aspiration of an initial vowel or diphthong (ʽ) or the absence of such aspiration (ʼ). **b.** The presence or absence of aspiration indicated by these marks.

breathing room *n.* Sufficient room to permit ease of breathing or movement: *no breathing room on the crowded airplane; bought property in the countryside to get a little breathing room.*

breathing space *n.* **1.** Breathing room. **2.** A breathing spell.

breathing spell *n.* An opportunity to rest or give thought to a situation.

breath·less (brĕth′lĭs) *adj.* **1.** Breathing with difficulty; gasping: *was breathless from running.* **2.** Marked by the suspension of regular breathing, as from tension or excitement: *a breathless audience.* **3.** Causing or capable of causing the suspension of regular breathing; tense or exciting: *a breathless flight.* **4.a.** Not breathing; without breath. **b.** Dead. **5.** Having no air or breeze; still: *a breathless summer day.* —**breath′less·ly** *adv.* —**breath′less·ness** *n.*

breath·tak·ing (brĕth′tā′kĭng) *adj.* Inspiring awe; exciting. —**breath′tak′ing·ly** *adv.*

breath·y (brĕth′ē) *adj.* **-i·er, -i·est.** Marked by or as if by audible or noisy breathing: *a breathy voice.* —**breath′i·ly** *adv.* —**breath′i·ness** *n.*

brec·ci·a (brĕch′ē-ə, brĕch′ə, brĕsh′-) *n.* Rock composed of sharp-angled fragments embedded in a fine-grained matrix. [Italian, of Germanic origin. See **bhreg-** in Appendix.]

ă pat	oi boy
ā pay	ou out
âr care	o͝o took
ä father	o͞o boot
ĕ pet	ŭ cut
ē be	ûr urge
ĭ pit	th thin
ī pie	*th* this
îr pier	hw which
ŏ pot	zh vision
ō toe	ə about, item
ô paw	♦ regionalism

Stress marks: **′** (primary); ′ (secondary), as in **dictionary** (dĭk′shə-nĕr′ē)

brec·ci·ate (brĕch′ē-āt′, brĕsh′-) *tr.v.* **-at·ed, -at·ing, -ates.** To form (rock) into breccia. **—brec′ci·a′tion** *n.*

Brecht (brĕkt, brĕKHt), **Bertolt.** 1898–1956. German poet and playwright who developed "epic drama," a style that relies on the audience's reflective detachment rather than the production's atmosphere and action. His works include *The Threepenny Opera* (1928) and *The Caucasian Chalk Circle* (1948). **—Brecht′i·an** *adj.*

Breck·in·ridge (brĕk′ĭn-rĭj′), **John Cabell.** 1821–1875. Vice President of the United States (1857–1861) under James Buchanan. In 1860 Breckinridge ran as the proslavery candidate for the presidency and was defeated by Abraham Lincoln.

bred (brĕd) *v.* Past tense and past participle of **breed.**

Bre·da (brā-dä′). A city of southern Netherlands south-southeast of Dordrecht. It was founded in the 11th century. Charles II of England lived here before the Restoration in 1660. Population, 118,662.

brede (brēd) *n. Archaic.* Ornamental embroidery or braiding. [Variant of BRAID.]

bred-in-the-bone (brĕd′n-*th*ə-bōn′) *adj.* **1.** Deeply instilled; firmly established: *bred-in-the-bone loyalty.* **2.** Persistent; habitual: *a bred-in-the-bone liberal.*

breech (brēch) *n.* **1.** The lower rear portion of the human trunk; the buttocks. **2. breeches. a.** Trousers extending to or just below the knee. **b.** *Informal.* Trousers. **3.** The part of a firearm behind the barrel. **4.** The lower part of a pulley block. [Middle English *brech,* from Old English *brēc,* pl. of *brōc,* leg covering; akin to Gaulish *brāca,* hose, trousers.]

breech birth *n.* See **breech delivery.**

breech·block (brēch′blŏk′) *n.* The metal part that closes the breech end of the barrel of a breechloading gun and that is removed to insert a cartridge and replaced before firing.

breech·cloth (brēch′klôth′, -klŏth′) also **breech·clout** (-klout′) *n.* A cloth worn to cover the loins; a loincloth.

breech delivery *n.* Delivery of a fetus with the buttocks or feet appearing first. Also called *breech birth.*

breeches buoy

breech·es buoy (brĭch′ĭz, brē′chĭz) *n. Nautical.* An apparatus used for rescues and transfers at sea, consisting of sturdy canvas breeches attached at the waist to a ring buoy that is suspended from a pulley running along a rope from ship to shore or from ship to ship.

breech·ing (brē′chĭng, brĭch′ĭng) *n.* **1.** The strap of a harness that passes behind a draft animal's haunches. **2.** The short wool or hair on the rump and hind legs of a sheep, goat, or dog. **3.** The parts of a gun that make up the breech. **4.** A rope formerly used to secure the breech of a cannon to the side of a ship to control the recoil.

breech·load·er (brēch′lō′dər) *n.* A gun or other firearm loaded at the breech.

breech·load·ing (brēch′lō′dĭng) *adj.* Designed to be loaded at the breech. Used of a gun or other firearm.

breech presentation *n.* The position of a fetus during labor in which the buttocks or feet appear first.

♦**breed** (brēd) *v.* **bred** (brĕd), **breed·ing, breeds.** *—tr.* **1.** To produce (offspring); give birth to or hatch. **2.** To bring about; engender. **3. a.** To cause to reproduce, especially by controlled mating and selection: *breed cattle.* **b.** To develop new or improved strains in (organisms), chiefly through controlled mating and selection of offspring for desirable traits. **c.** To mate with. **4.** To rear or train; bring up. **5.** To produce (fissionable material) in a breeder reactor. **6.** To be the place of origin of. *—intr.* **1.** To produce offspring. **2.** To originate and thrive: *Fads breed in empty heads and full purses.* **—breed** *n.* **1.** A group of organisms having common ancestors and certain distinguishable characteristics, especially a group within a species developed by artificial selection and maintained by controlled propagation. **2.** A kind; a sort: *a new breed of politician; a new breed of computer.* **—*idioms.* breed a scab** (or **scabs**) **on (one's) nose.** *Regional.* To stir up trouble for oneself. **breed up a storm.** *New England.* To become cloudy. See Regional Note at **fair[1].** [Middle English *breden,* from Old English *brēdan.* See **bhreu-** in Appendix.]

breed·er (brē′dər) *n.* **1.** A person who breeds animals or plants. **2.** An animal kept to produce offspring. **3.** *Offensive Slang.* Used as a disparaging term for a heterosexual person. **4.** A source or cause: *social injustice—a breeder of revolutions.* **5.** A breeder reactor.

breeder reactor *n.* A nuclear reactor that produces as well as consumes fissionable material, especially one that produces more fissionable material than it consumes.

breed·ing (brē′dĭng) *n.* **1.** One's line of descent; ancestry: *a person of noble breeding.* **2.** Training in the proper forms of social and personal conduct. **3.** Production of offspring or young. **4.** The propagation of animals or plants.

breeding ground *n.* **1.** A place where animals breed. **2.** A place or set of circumstances that encourages the development of certain ideas or conditions: *the university as a breeding ground for new scientific theories.*

Breed's Hill (brēdz). A hill in Charlestown, a section of Boston, Massachusetts. It was the site of the Battle of Bunker Hill on June 17, 1775.

breeks (brēks) *pl.n. Scots.* Breeches. [Middle English, pl. of *brek,* from Old English *brēc.* See BREECH.]

breeze[1] (brēz) *n.* **1.** A light current of air; a gentle wind. **2.** *Meteorology.* Any of five winds with speeds of from 4 to 31 miles (6 to 50 kilometers) per hour, according to the Beaufort scale. **3.** *Informal.* Something, such as a task, that is easy to do. **—breeze** *intr.v.* **breezed, breez·ing, breez·es. 1.** To blow lightly. **2.** *Informal.* To progress swiftly and effortlessly: *We breezed through the test.* **3.** To sprint around a racetrack as a means of exercise. Used of a racehorse. **—*idiom.* shoot the breeze.** *Slang.* To engage in idle conversation. [Perhaps from Old Spanish *briza,* northeast wind.]

SYNONYMS: *breeze, cinch, pushover, snap, walkaway, walkover.* The central meaning shared by these nouns is "something that is easily accomplished": *The exam was a breeze. Chopping onions is a cinch with a food processor. Winning the playoffs was no pushover. The new computer program was a snap to learn. Getting elected to the council was a walkaway. It wasn't any walkover to alphabetize all those names.*

breeze[2] (brēz) *n.* The refuse left when coke or charcoal is made. [Probably from French *braise,* hot coals, from Old French *brese,* of Germanic origin. See **bhreu-** in Appendix.]

breeze·way (brēz′wā′) *n.* A roofed, open-sided passageway connecting two structures, such as a house and a garage.

breez·y (brē′zē) *adj.* **-i·er, -i·est. 1.** Exposed to breezes; windy. **2.** Fresh and animated; lively: *a breezy prose style.* **—breez′i·ly** *adv.* **—breez′i·ness** *n.*

breg·ma (brĕg′mə) *n., pl.* **-ma·ta** (-mə-tə). The junction of the sagittal and coronal sutures at the top of the skull. [Latin, top of the head, from Greek.] **—breg·mat′ic** (-măt′ĭk) *adj.*

Bre·men (brĕm′ən, brā′mən). A city of northwest Germany on the Weser River southwest of Hamburg. It is a major port and was a leading member of the Hanseatic League in the Middle Ages. Population, 530,520.

Bre·mer·ha·ven (brĕm′ər-hä′vən, -hä′-, brā′mər-hä′fən). A city of northwest Germany at the mouth of the Weser River near the North Sea. It has a deep natural harbor and is an important shipping center. Transatlantic service to the United States was inaugurated here in 1847. Population, 135,095.

Brem·er·ton (brĕm′ər-tən). A city of west-central Washington on an arm of Puget Sound west of Seattle. It was laid out in 1891 after its selection as the site of a U.S. naval shipyard. Population, 36,208.

brems·strah·lung (brĕm′shträ′ləng) *n.* The electromagnetic radiation produced by an accelerated electrically charged subatomic particle, such as an electron, as when it is deflected by another charged particle. [German : *Bremse,* brake (from Middle Low German *premse,* from *pramen,* to press) + *Strahlung,* radiation (from *Strahl,* ray, from Middle High German *strāle,* from Old High German *strāla,* stripe, piece; see **ster-[2]** in Appendix).]

Bren·nan (brĕn′ən), **William Joseph, Jr.** Born 1906. American jurist who served as an associate justice of the U.S. Supreme Court (1956–1990).

Bren·ner Pass (brĕn′ər). An Alpine pass, 1,371 m (4,495 ft) high, connecting Innsbruck, Austria, with Bolzano, Italy. It has been a strategic trade and invasion route since Roman times.

brent (brĕnt) *n. Chiefly British.* Variant of **brant.**

Brent (brĕnt), **Margaret.** 1600–1671? English-born colonist and feminist. She immigrated to Maryland in 1638 and was the first woman to obtain a land grant there.

bre·sao·la (brĕ-sō′lə, brĭ-zō′-) *n.* Sliced salt-cured, air-dried beef that is dressed with olive oil, lemon juice, and black pepper before serving. [Italian, diminutive of Italian dialectal *bresada, past participle of *brasare,* to braise, from French *braiser.* See BRAISE.]

Bre·scia (brĕsh′ə). A city of northern Italy east of Milan. It was a Gallic town, a Roman stronghold, and a free city from 936 to 1426. Population, 206,460.

Bres·lau (brĕs′lou). See **Wroclaw.**

Brest (brĕst). **1.** A city of northwest France on an inlet of the Atlantic Ocean. Its large landlocked harbor was built in 1631 by Cardinal Richelieu as a military base and arsenal. Population, 156,060. **2.**. Formerly **Brest-Li·tovsk** (-lĭ-tôfsk′). A city of southwest Belorussia on the Bug River near the Polish border. The Treaty of Brest-Litovsk, ending World War I on the eastern front, was signed here by Russia and Germany on March 3, 1918. Population, 222,000.

Bret. *abbr.* Breton.

Bre·tagne (brə-tän′yə). See **Brittany.**

breth·ren (brĕ*th*′rən) *n.* A plural of **brother** (senses 2, 3, 4c).

Bret·on (brĕt′n) *adj. Abbr.* **Bret.** Of or relating to Brittany or its people, language, or culture. **—Breton** *n.* **1.** A native or inhabitant of Brittany. **2.** *Abbr.* **Bret.** The Celtic language of Brittany. In this sense, also called *Armoric.* [Middle English, from Old French. See BRITON.]

Bre·ton (brĭ-tôN′), **André.** 1896–1966. French poet and literary theorist. He began to write after World War I, at first linking himself with Dadaism but breaking with that movement to write the first manifesto of surrealism (1924).

Breu·er (broi′ər), **Marcel Lajos.** 1902–1981. Hungarian-born American architect and furniture designer who was associated with the Bauhaus in the 1920's. He is known for his chairs with tubular steel frames.

ă pat	oi boy
ā pay	ou out
âr care	ŏŏ took
ä father	ōō boot
ĕ pet	ŭ cut
ē be	ûr urge
ĭ pit	th thin
ī pie	*th* this
îr pier	hw which
ŏ pot	zh vision
ō toe	ə about, item
ô paw	♦ regionalism

Stress marks: ′ (primary); ′ (secondary), as in **dictionary** (dĭk′shə-nĕr′ē)

Breu·ghel (broiʹgəl, brōōʹ-, brœʹ-). See **Brueghel.**

brev. *abbr.* Brevet.

breve (brĕv, brēv) *n.* **1.** A symbol (˘) placed over a vowel to show that it has a short sound, as the *a* in *bat.* **2.** A curved mark used to indicate a short or unstressed syllable of verse. **3.** *Music.* A note equivalent to two whole notes. [Middle English, written communication, from Old French, from Medieval Latin, short syllable, from Latin, neuter of *brevis,* short. See BRIEF.]

bre·vet (brə-vĕtʹ, brĕvʹĭt) *n. Abbr.* **brev., bvt.** A commission promoting a military officer in rank without an increase in pay. **—brevet** *tr.v.* **-vet·ted, -vet·ting, -vets** or **-vet·ed, -vet·ing, -vets.** To promote by brevet. [Middle English, official letter, from Anglo-Norman, diminutive of *bref,* letter, from Latin *brevis,* short. See BRIEF.] **—bre·vetʹcy** (brə-vĕtʹsē) *n.*

bre·vi·ar·y (brēʹvē-ĕrʹē, brĕvʹē-) *n., pl.* **-ies.** *Ecclesiastical.* A book containing the hymns, offices, and prayers for the canonical hours. [Middle English *breviarie,* from Old French *breviaire,* from Medieval Latin *breviārium,* from Latin, summary, from *brevis,* short. See BRIEF.]

brev·i·ty (brĕvʹĭ-tē) *n.* **1.** The quality or state of being brief in duration. **2.** Concise expression; terseness. [Latin *brevitās,* from *brevis,* short. See BRIEF.]

brew (brōō) *v.* **brewed, brew·ing, brews.** *—tr.* **1.** To make (ale or beer) from malt and hops by infusion, boiling, and fermentation. **2.** To make (a beverage) by boiling, steeping, or mixing various ingredients: *brew tea.* **3.** To concoct; devise: *brew a plot to overthrow the government.* *—intr.* **1.** To make ale or beer as an occupation. **2.** To be imminent; impend: *"storms brewing on every frontier"* (John Dos Passos). **—brew** *n.* **1.a.** A beverage made by brewing. **b.** A serving of such a beverage. **2.** Something produced as if by brewing; a mix: *Their politics were a strange brew of idealism and self-interest.* [Middle English *brewen,* from Old English *brēowan.* See **bhreu-** in Appendix.] **—brewʹage** *n.* **—brewʹer** *n.*

Brew·er (brōōʹər), **David Josiah.** 1837–1910. American jurist who served as an associate justice of the U.S. Supreme Court (1889–1910).

brew·er's yeast (brōōʹərz) *n.* A yeast of the genus *Saccharomyces,* used as a ferment in brewing and also as a source of B-complex vitamins.

brew·er·y (brōōʹə-rē, brŏŏrʹē) *n., pl.* **-ies.** An establishment for the manufacture of malt liquors, such as beer and ale.

♦ **brew·is** (brōōʹĭs, brōōz) *n. New England.* Bread soaked in liquid, usually milk, and eaten as a pudding or as a side dish with meat. [Middle English *brewes,* from Old French *broez,* pl. of *broet,* diminutive of *breu,* broth, from Vulgar Latin **brodum,* of Germanic origin. See **bhreu-** in Appendix.]

brew·pub (brōōʹpŭbʹ) *n.* **1.** See **microbrewery. 2.** A saloon where the owners make their own beer and serve it on the premises.

Brew·ster (brōōʹstər), **William.** 1567–1644. English Pilgrim colonist who sailed to America on the *Mayflower* (1620) and was the religious leader of Plymouth Colony.

Brezh·nev (brĕzhʹnĕf, -nyĭf), **Leonid Ilyich.** 1906–1982. Soviet leader. He served as the chairman of the Presidium (now the Politburo) and secretary of the Communist Party before becoming president of the U.S.S.R. in 1977.

Bri·an Bo·ru (brīʹən bə-rōōʹ, bô-rōʹ, brĕn). 926–1014. Irish king (1002–1014) who spent most of his life fighting the Danes and the Norse. He was killed after the final defeat of a Danish coalition, which ended Norse power in Ireland.

Bri·and (brē-ändʹ, -äɴʹ), **Aristide.** 1862–1932. French politician who became prime minister for the first of 11 times in 1909. As foreign minister he was the chief architect of the Locarno Pact (1925), which guaranteed the borders of Belgium, France, and Germany. He also drew up the Kellogg-Briand Pact (1928) and shared the 1926 Nobel Peace Prize.

Bri·ansk (brē-änskʹ). See **Bryansk.**

bri·ar¹ also **bri·er** (brīʹər) *n.* **1.** A Mediterranean shrub or small tree *(Erica arborea)* whose hard, woody roots are used to make tobacco pipes. **2.** A pipe made from the root of this plant or from a similar wood. [French *bruyère,* heath, from Old French, from Vulgar Latin **brūcāria,* from Late Latin *brūcus,* heather, of Celtic origin. See **wer-²** in Appendix.]

bri·ar² (brīʹər) *n.* Variant of **brier¹.**

bri·ard (brē-ärʹ, -ärdʹ) *n.* Any of an ancient French breed of sturdily built, rough-coated dogs. [French, from *Brie,* a region of northern France.]

bri·ar·root (brīʹər-rōōtʹ, -rŏŏtʹ) *n.* The hard woody root of the briar.

bri·ar·wood (brīʹər-wŏŏdʹ) *n.* Wood from briarroot.

bribe (brīb) *n.* **1.** Something, such as money or a favor, offered or given to a person in a position of trust to influence that person's views or conduct. **2.** Something serving to influence or persuade. **—bribe** *v.* **bribed, brib·ing, bribes.** *—tr.* **1.** To give, offer, or promise a bribe to. **2.** To gain influence over or corrupt by bribery. *—intr.* To give, offer, or promise bribes. [Middle English, from Old French, piece of bread given as alms.] **—bribʹa·ble** *adj.* **—bribʹer** *n.*

brib·er·y (brīʹbə-rē) *n., pl.* **-ies.** The act or practice of offering, giving, or taking a bribe.

bric-a-brac (brĭkʹə-brăkʹ) *n.* Small, usually ornamental objects valued for their antiquity, rarity, originality, or sentimental associations. [French *bric-à-brac,* expressive of confusion.]

Brice (brīs), **Fannie.** 1891–1951. American entertainer who appeared in a number of films as well as the Ziegfield Follies.

brick (brĭk) *n., pl.* **bricks** or **brick. 1.** A molded rectangular block of clay baked by the sun or in a kiln until hard and used as a building and paving material. **2.** An object shaped like such a block: *a brick of cheese.* **3.** *Informal.* A helpful, reliable person. *—attributive.* Often used to modify another noun: *a brick wall; brick ice cream.* **—brick** *tr.v.* **bricked, brick·ing, bricks. 1.** To construct, line, or pave with bricks. **2.** To close or wall with brick: *bricked up the windows of the old house.* ***—idiom.* drop a brick.** *Informal.* To make a clumsy social error. [Middle English *brike,* from Middle Dutch *bricke.*] **—brickʹy** *adj.*

brick·bat (brĭkʹbătʹ) *n.* **1.** A piece, especially of brick, used as a weapon or missile. **2.** An unfavorable remark; criticism. [BRICK + BAT¹, piece of brick.]

WORD HISTORY: The earliest sense of *brickbat,* recorded in a work first published in 1563, was "a piece of brick." Such pieces of brick have not infrequently been thrown at others in the hope of injuring them; hence, the figuratively *brickbats* (first recorded in 1929) that critics hurl at performances they dislike. The appearance of *bat* as the second part of this compound is explained by the fact that the word *bat,* "war club, cudgel," developed in Middle English the sense "chunk, clod, wad," and in the 16th century came to be used specifically for a piece of brick that was unbroken on one end.

Leonid Brezhnev
Photographed in 1978

brick·lay·er (brĭkʹlāʹər) *n.* A person skilled in building with bricks. **—brickʹlayʹing** *n.*

brick red *n. Color.* A moderate to strong reddish brown. **—brickʹ-redʹ** (brĭkʹrĕdʹ) *adj.*

brick·work (brĭkʹwûrkʹ) *n.* **1.** The technique or work of constructing with bricks and mortar. **2.** A structure made of bricks.

brick·yard (brĭkʹyärdʹ) *n.* A place where bricks are made.

bri·co·lage (brēʹkō-läzhʹ, brĭkʹō-) *n.* Something made or put together using whatever materials happen to be available: *"Even the decor is a bricolage, a mix of this and that"* (Los Angeles Times). [French, from *bricole,* trifle, from Old French, catapult, from Italian *briccola,* of Germanic origin.]

bri·dal (brīdʹl) *n.* A marriage ceremony; a wedding. **—bridal** *adj.* **1.** Of or relating to a bride or a marriage ceremony; nuptial. **2.** Designed for a bride or a newly married couple: *a bridal shop; the hotel's bridal suite.* [Middle English *bridale,* wedding, wedding feast, from Old English *brȳdealo* : *brȳd,* bride; see BRIDE + *ealu,* ale; see ALE.]

bridal wreath or **bri·dal-wreath** (brīdʹl-rēth) *n.* Any of various shrubs of the genus *Spiraea,* such as *S. prunifolia,* having arching branches covered with white bloom. Bridal wreath is popular as an ornamental and in flower arrangements.

bride (brīd) *n.* A woman who is about to be married or has recently been married. [Middle English, from Old English *brȳd.*]

bride·groom (brīdʹgrōōmʹ, -grŏŏmʹ) *n.* A man who is about to be married or has recently been married. [Alteration of Middle English *bridegome,* from Old English *brȳdguma* : *brȳd,* bride; see BRIDE + *guma,* man; see **dhghem-** in Appendix.]

bride price *n.* A payment in the form of money, property, or other valuable asset that is made by or on behalf of a prospective husband to the bride's family in certain cultures or societies.

brides·maid (brīdzʹmādʹ) *n.* A woman who attends the bride at a wedding.

bridge¹ (brĭj) *n.* **1.** A structure spanning and providing passage over a gap or barrier, such as a river or roadway. **2.** Something resembling or analogous to this structure in form or function: *a land bridge between the continents; a bridge of understanding between two countries.* **3.a.** The upper bony ridge of the human nose. **b.** The part of a pair of eyeglasses that rests against this ridge. **4.** A fixed or removable replacement for one or several but not all of the natural teeth, usually anchored at each end to a natural tooth. **5.** *Music.* **a.** A thin, upright piece of wood in some stringed instruments that supports the strings above the soundboard. **b.** A transitional passage connecting two subjects or movements. **6.** *Nautical.* A crosswise platform or enclosed area above the main deck of a ship from which the ship is controlled. **7.** *Games.* **a.** A piece of wood used to steady the cue in billiards. Also called *rest.* **b.** The hand used as a support to steady the cue. **8.** *Electricity.* **a.** Any of various instruments for measuring or comparing the characteristics, such as impedance or inductance, of a conductor. **b.** An electrical shunt. **9.** *Chemistry.* An intramolecular connection that spans atoms or groups of atoms. **—bridge** *tr.v.* **bridged, bridg·ing, bridg·es. 1.** To build a bridge over. **2.** To cross by or as if by a bridge. [Middle English *brigge,* from Old English *brycg.* See **bhrū-** in Appendix.] **—bridgeʹa·ble** *adj.*

bridge¹
Top: San Francisco–Oakland Bay suspension bridge
Bottom: Bridge of the Cunard *Princess*

bridge² (brĭj) *n. Games.* Any of several card games derived from whist and played with one deck of cards divided equally among usually four people. [From earlier *biritch* (influenced by BRIDGE¹), from Russian *birich,* a call.]

bridge·board (brĭjʹbôrdʹ, -bōrdʹ) *n.* A notched board at either side of a staircase that supports the treads and risers.

bridge·head (brĭjʹhĕdʹ) *n.* **1.a.** A fortified position from which troops defend the end of a bridge nearest the enemy. **b.** A forward position seized by advancing troops in enemy territory as a foothold for further advance. **2.** The area immediately adjacent to the end of a bridge. [Translation of French *tête de pont* : *tête,* head + *de,* of + *pont,* bridge.]

bridge loan *n.* A short-term loan intended to provide or extend financing until a more permanent arrangement is made.

Bridge·port (brĭj′pôrt′, -pōrt′). A city of southwest Connecticut on Long Island Sound southwest of New Haven. Settled in 1639, it grew as a fishing community and is today the leading industrial center of the state. Population, 142,546.

Bridg·es (brĭj′ĭz), **Harry.** 1901–1990. American labor leader. He organized the International Longshoremen's and Warehousemen's Union (ILWU) and served as its president for 40 years.

Bridges, Robert Seymour. 1844–1930. British poet and essayist who was appointed poet laureate in 1913. He is best known for his philosophical poem *The Testament of Beauty* (1929).

Bridge·ton (brĭj′tən). **1.** A city of eastern Missouri on the Missouri River northwest of St. Louis. It is a manufacturing center. Population, 18,445. **2.** A city of southwest New Jersey near the mouth of the Delaware River south of Philadelphia. Settled by Quakers c. 1686, it is now highly industrialized. Population, 18,795.

Bridge·town (brĭj′toun′). The capital of Barbados, in the West Indies. It was founded by the British in 1628. Population, 7,466.

Bridge·wa·ter (brĭj′wô′tər, -wŏt′ər). A town of eastern Massachusetts south of Boston. It had an iron industry in colonial times. Population, 17,202.

bridge·work (brĭj′wûrk′) *n.* **1.** A dental bridge. **2.** Dental prosthetics involving a bridge or bridges.

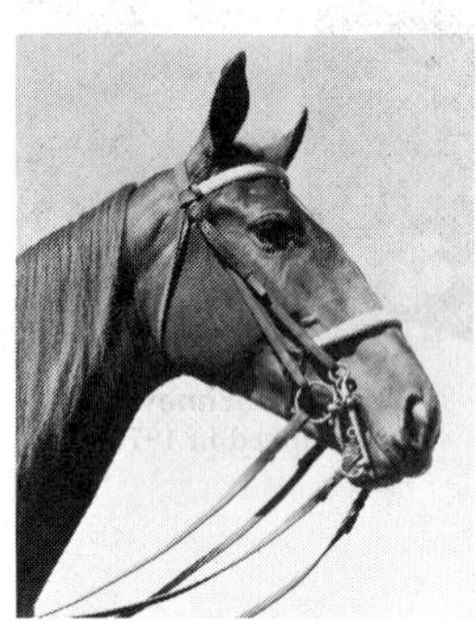

bridle

bri·dle (brīd′l) *n.* **1.** A harness, consisting of a headstall, bit, and reins, fitted about a horse's head and used to restrain or guide the animal. **2.** A curb or check: *put a bridle on spending.* **3.** *Nautical.* A span of chain, wire, or rope that can be secured at both ends to an object and slung from its center point. **—bridle** *v.* **-dled, -dling, -dles.** *—tr.* **1.** To put a bridle on. **2.** To control or restrain with or as if with a bridle. See Synonyms at **restrain.** *—intr.* **1.** To lift the head and draw in the chin as an expression of scorn or resentment. **2.** To show anger or resentment; take offense: *bridling at the criticism.* [Middle English *bridel,* from Old English *brīdel.*] **—bri′dler** *n.*

bridle path *n.* A trail for horseback riding.

Brie (brē) *n.* A mold-ripened, whole-milk cheese with a whitish rind and a soft, light yellow center. [After *Brie,* a region of northern France.]

brief (brēf) *adj.* **brief·er, brief·est. 1.** Short in time, duration, length, or extent. **2.** Succinct; concise: *a brief account of the incident.* **3.** Curt; abrupt. **—brief** *n.* **1.** A short, succinct statement. **2.** A condensation or an abstract of a larger document or series of documents. **3.** *Abbr.* **br.** *Law.* **a.** A formal outline listing main contentions along with supporting evidence and documentation. **b.** A document containing all the facts and points of law pertinent to a specific case, filed by an attorney before arguing the case in court. **4.** *Roman Catholic Church.* A papal letter that is not as formal as a bull. **5.** A briefing. **6. briefs.** Short, tight-fitting underpants. **—brief** *tr.v.* **briefed, brief·ing, briefs. 1.** To summarize. **2.** To give concise preparatory instructions, information, or advice to: *briefed the astronauts before the mission.* **—*idiom.* in brief.** In short. [Middle English *bref,* from Old French, from Latin *brevis.* N., Middle English *bref,* written communication, from Old French, from Medieval Latin *breve,* from Latin, neuter of *brevis,* short. See **mregh-u-** in Appendix.] **—brief′er** *n.* **—brief′ly** *adv.* **—brief′ness** *n.*

brief·case (brēf′kās′) *n.* A portable, often flat case with a handle, used for carrying papers or books. [*brief,* document + CASE[2].]

brief·ing (brē′fĭng) *n.* **1.** The act or procedure of giving or receiving concise preparatory instructions, information, or advice. **2.** The information conveyed in this manner.

Bri·enz (brē-ĕnts′), **Lake of.** A lake of central Switzerland near Interlaken. It is noted for its scenic beauty.

bri·er[1] also **bri·ar** (brī′ər) *n.* Any of several prickly plants, such as certain rosebushes or the greenbrier. [Middle English *brer,* from Old English *brēr.*] **—bri′er·y** *adj.*

bri·er[2] (brī′ər) *n.* Variant of **briar[1].**

brig (brĭg) *n.* **1.** *Nautical.* A two-masted sailing ship, square-rigged on both masts, carrying two or more headsails and a quadrilateral gaff sail or spanker aft of the mizzenmast. **2.** A jail or prison on board a U.S. Navy or Coast Guard vessel. **3.** A jail or guardhouse, especially on the premises of a U.S. military installation. [Short for BRIGANTINE. Senses 2 and 3, from the use of ships as prisons.]

brig. *abbr.* Brigade.

bri·gade (brĭ-gād′) *n.* **1.** *Abbr.* **brig. a.** A military unit consisting of a variable number of combat battalions. **b.** A U.S. Army administrative and tactical unit composed of a headquarters unit, at least one unit of infantry or armor or both, and designated support units. A brigade can be commanded by a brigadier general or by a colonel. **2.** A group of persons organized for a specific purpose: *formed a bucket brigade to carry water to the fire.* **—brigade** *tr.v.* **-gad·ed, -gad·ing, -gades.** To form into a brigade. [French, from Old French, company, from Old Italian *brigata,* from *brigare,* to fight, from *briga,* strife, of Celtic origin. See **g^were-[1]** in Appendix.]

brig·a·dier (brĭg′ə-dîr′) *n.* A brigadier general. [French, from *brigade,* brigade. See BRIGADE.]

brigadier general *n., pl.* **brigadier generals.** *Abbr.* **B.G., BG, Brig. Gen. 1.** A commissioned rank in the U.S. Army, Air Force, or Marine Corps that is above colonel and below major general. **2.** One who holds this rank.

brig·and (brĭg′ənd) *n.* A robber or bandit, especially one of an outlaw band. [Middle English *brigaunt,* from Old French, from Old Italian *brigante,* skirmisher, from present participle of *brigare,* to fight. See BRIGADE.] **—brig′and·age** (-ən-dĭj), **brig′and·ism** *n.*

brig·an·tine (brĭg′ən-tēn′) *n.* *Nautical.* A two-masted sailing ship, square-rigged on the foremast and having a fore-and-aft mainsail with square main topsails. [French *brigantin,* from Old French *brigandin,* from Old Italian *brigantino,* skirmishing ship, from *brigante,* skirmisher. See BRIGAND.]

Brig. Gen. *abbr.* Brigadier general.

Briggs (brĭgz), **Henry.** 1561–1630. English mathematician who devised the decimal-based system of logarithms and invented the modern method of long division.

bright (brīt) *adj.* **bright·er, bright·est. 1. a.** Emitting or reflecting light readily or in large amounts; shining. **b.** Comparatively high on the scale of brightness. **c.** Full of light or illumination: *a bright sunny day; a stage bright with spotlights.* **2.** Characterizing a dyestuff that produces a highly saturated color; brilliant. **3.** Glorious; splendid: *one of the bright stars of stage and screen; a bright moment in history.* **4.** Full of promise and hope; auspicious: *had a bright future in publishing.* **5.** Happy; cheerful: *bright faces.* **6.** Animatedly clever; intelligent. **7.** High and clear: *the bright sound of the trumpet section.* [Middle English, from Old English *beorht.* See **bhereg-** in Appendix.] **—bright, bright′ly** *adv.*

SYNONYMS: *bright, brilliant, radiant, lustrous, lambent, luminous, incandescent, effulgent.* These adjectives refer to what emits or reflects light. *Bright* is the most general: *bright sunshine; a bright blue; bright teeth. Brilliant* implies intense brightness and often suggests sparkling, glittering, or gleaming light: *a brilliant color; a brilliant gemstone.* Something that is *radiant* radiates or seems to radiate light: *a radiant sunrise; a radiant smile.* A *lustrous* object originates no light but reflects an agreeable sheen: *thick, lustrous auburn hair; a necklace of lustrous pearls. Lambent* applies to a soft, flickering light: *"its tranquil streets, bathed in the lambent green of budding trees"* (James C. McKinley). *Luminous* refers broadly to what shines with light but is said especially of something that glows in the dark: *The watch has a luminous dial. Incandescent* stresses burning brilliance, as of something white-hot: *Flames consist of incandescent gases. Effulgent* suggests splendid radiance: *"The crocus, the snowdrop, and the effulgent daffodil are considered bright harbingers of spring"* (John Gould). See also Synonyms at **intelligent.**

Bright (brīt), **John.** 1811–1889. British politician and noted orator who was a founder of the Anti-Corn Law League (1839).

bright·en (brīt′n) *tr. & intr.v.* **-ened, -en·ing, -ens.** To make or become bright or brighter. **—bright′en·er** *n.*

bright·ness (brīt′nĭs) *n.* **1.** The state or quality of being bright. **2.** The effect or sensation by means of which an observer is able to distinguish differences in luminance. **3.** *Color.* The dimension of a color that represents its similarity to one of a series of achromatic colors ranging from very dim (dark) to very bright (dazzling).

Brigh·ton (brīt′n). A borough of southeast England on the English Channel south of London. It became a fashionable resort after 1783 when the Prince of Wales (later George IV) began to patronize it. The Royal Pavilion, in a combination of Chinese and Mogul styles, was designed by the noted architect John Nash (1752–1835). Population, 150,200.

Bright's disease (brīts) *n.* Any of several diseases of the kidney marked by the presence of albumin in the urine. [After Richard *Bright* (1789–1858), British physician.]

bright·work (brīt′wûrk′) *n.* Metal parts or fixtures made bright by polishing.

brill (brĭl) *n., pl.* **brill** or **brills.** An edible flatfish *(Bothas rhombus)* of European waters. [Origin unknown.]

Bril·lat-Sa·va·rin (brē-yä′ sä-vä-răɴ′), **Anthelme.** 1755–1826. French politician and gourmet, who is noted for his *Physiologie de Goût* (1825), a witty dissertation on the art of dining.

bril·liance (brĭl′yəns) *n.* **1.** The state or quality of being brilliant, as: **a.** Extreme brightness. **b.** Exceptional clarity and agility of intellect or invention. **2.** Splendor; magnificence. **3.** *Music.* Sharpness and clarity of tone.

bril·lian·cy (brĭl′yən-sē) *n.* Brilliance, as of intellect or artistic performance.

bril·liant (brĭl′yənt) *adj.* **1.** Full of light; shining. See Synonyms at **bright. 2.** *Color.* Relating to or being a hue that has a combination of high lightness and strong saturation. **3.** Sharp and clear in tone. **4.** Glorious; magnificent: *the brilliant court life at Versailles.* **5.** Superb; wonderful: *The soloist gave a brilliant performance.* **6.** Marked by unusual and impressive intellectual acuteness: *a brilliant mind; a brilliant solution to the problem.* See Synonyms at **intelligent. —brilliant** *n.* A precious gem, especially a diamond, finely cut in any of various forms with numerous facets. [French *brillant,* present participle of *briller,* to shine, from Italian *brillare*, perhaps from *brillo*, beryl, from Latin *beryllus*. See BERYL.] —**bril′liant·ly** *adv.* —**bril′liant·ness** *n.*

bril·lian·tine (brĭl′yən-tēn′) *n.* **1.** An oily, perfumed hairdressing. **2.** A glossy fabric made from cotton and worsted or cotton and mohair. [French *brillantine,* from *brillant,* brilliant. See BRILLIANT.]

brim (brĭm) *n.* **1.** The rim or uppermost edge of a hollow container or natural basin. **2.** A projecting rim or edge: *the brim of a hat.* **3.** A border or an edge. See Synonyms at **border.** —**brim** *v.* **brimmed, brim·ming, brims.** —*intr.* **1.** To be full to the brim. **2.** To overflow: *The cup is brimming over with chowder.* —*tr.* To fill to the brim. [Middle English *brimme.*]

brim·ful (brĭm′fo͝ol′) *adj.* Full to overflowing.

brim·stone (brĭm′stōn′) *n.* **1.** Sulfur. **2.a.** Damnation to hell; hellfire. **b.** Fiery or passionate rhetoric: *"the great American evangelist of Yankee bargain-hunting, converting us . . . with the brimstone of his secular preaching"* (Rushworth M. Kidder). [Middle English *brimston,* from Old English *brynstān.* See **gʷher-** in Appendix.]

Brin·di·si (brĭn′dĭ-zē, brēn′-). A city of southern Italy on the Adriatic Sea southeast of Bari. It was an ancient center of trade with the eastern Mediterranean and an embarkation point for the Crusaders during the Middle Ages. Population, 88,947.

brin·dle (brĭn′dl) *n.* **1.** A brindled color. **2.** A brindled animal. [Back-formation from BRINDLED.]

brin·dled (brĭn′dld) *adj.* Tawny or grayish with streaks or spots of a darker color. [Alteration of Middle English *brended,* probably from *brende,* past participle of *brennen,* to burn, from Old Norse *brenna.* See **gʷher-** in Appendix.]

brine (brīn) *n.* **1.** Water saturated with or containing large amounts of a salt, especially of sodium chloride. **2.a.** The water of a sea or an ocean. **b.** A large body of salt water. **3.** Salt water used for preserving and pickling foods. —**brine** *tr.v.* **brined, brin·ing, brines.** To immerse, preserve, or pickle in salt water. [Middle English, from Old English *brīne.*] —**brin′er** *n.*

Bri·nell hardness (brĭ-nĕl′) *n.* The relative hardness of metals and alloys, determined by forcing a steel ball into a test piece under standard conditions and measuring the surface area of the resulting indentation. [After Johan August *Brinell* (1849–1925), Swedish engineer.]

Brinell hardness number *n. Abbr.* **Bhn.** The numerical value assigned to the Brinell hardness of metals and alloys. Also called *Brinell number.*

brine shrimp *n.* Any of various small crustaceans of the genus *Artemia.*

bring (brĭng) *tr.v.* **brought** (brôt), **bring·ing, brings. 1.** To take with oneself to a place: *brought enough money with me.* **2.** To carry as an attribute or contribution: *You bring many years of experience to your new post.* **3.** To lead or force into a specified state, situation, or location: *bring the water to a boil; brought the meeting to a close.* **4.a.** To persuade; induce: *The defendant's testimony brought others to confess.* **b.** To get the attention of; attract: *Smoke and flames brought the neighbors.* **5.** To cause to occur as a consequence or concomitant: *Floods brought destruction to the valley. A chill can bring on a cold.* **6.** To cause to become apparent to the mind; recall: *This music brings back memories.* **7.** *Law.* To advance or set forth (charges) in a court. **8.** To sell for: *a portrait that brought a million dollars.* —***phrasal verbs.*** **bring around** (or **round**). **1.** To cause to adopt an opinion or take a certain course of action. **2.** To cause to recover consciousness. **bring down. 1.** To cause to fall or collapse. **2.** To kill. **bring forth. 1.** To give rise to; produce: *plants bringing forth fruit.* **2.** To give birth to (young). **bring forward. 1.** To present; produce: *bring forward proof.* **2.** *Accounting.* To carry (a sum) from one page or column to another. **bring in. 1.** *Law.* To give or submit (a verdict) to a court. **2.** To produce, yield, or earn (profits or income). **bring off.** To accomplish: *bring off a successful advertising campaign.* **bring on.** To cause to appear: *brought on the dessert.* **bring out. 1.a.** To reveal or expose: *brought out the facts.* **b.** To introduce (a debutante) to society. **2.** To produce or publish: *bring out a new book.* **3.** To nurture and develop (a quality, for example) to best advantage: *You bring out the best in me.* **bring to. 1.** To cause to recover consciousness. **2.** *Nautical.* To cause (a ship) to turn into the wind or come to a stop. **bring up. 1.** To take care of and educate (a child); rear. **2.** To introduce into discussion; mention. **3.** To vomit. **4.** To cause to come to a sudden stop. —***idioms.*** **bring down the house.** To win overwhelming approval from an audience. **bring home.** To make perfectly clear: *a lecture that brought home several important points.* **bring to bear. 1.** To exert; apply: *bring pressure to bear on the student's parents.* **2.** To put (something) to good use: *"All of one's faculties are brought to bear in an effort to become fully incorporated into the landscape"* (Barry Lopez). **bring to light.** To reveal or disclose: *brought the real facts to light.* **bring to mind.** To cause to be remembered: *Thoughts of fishing brought to mind our youth.* **bring to (one's) knees.** To reduce to a position of subservience or submission. **bring to terms.** To force (another) to agree. **bring up the rear.** To be the last in a line or sequence. [Middle English *bringen,* from Old English *bringan.* See **bher-**[1] in Appendix.] —**bring′er** *n.*

USAGE NOTE: In most dialects of American English *bring* is used to denote motion toward the place of speaking or the place from which the action is regarded: *Bring it over here. The prime minister brought a large retinue to Washington with her. Take* is used to denote motion away from such a place: *Take it over there. The President will take several advisers with him when he goes to Moscow.* When the relevant point of focus is not the place of speaking itself, the difference obviously depends on the context. We can say either *The labor leaders brought* or *took their requests to the mayor's office,* depending on whether we want to describe things from the point of view of the labor leaders or the mayor. Perhaps for this reason, the distinction between *bring* and *take* has been blurred in some areas; a parent may say of a child, for example, *She always takes a pile of books home with her from school.* This usage may sound curious to those who are accustomed to observe the distinction more strictly, but it bears no particular stigma of incorrectness or illiteracy. • The form *brung* is common in colloquial use in many areas, even among educated speakers, but it is not acceptable for use in formal writing.

bring·down (brĭng′doun′) *n.* Something disappointing; a letdown.

brink (brĭngk) *n.* **1.a.** The upper edge of a steep or vertical slope: *the brink of a cliff.* **b.** The margin of land bordering a body of water. **2.** The point at which something is likely to begin; the verge: *"Time and again the monarchs and statesmen of Europe approached the brink of conflict"* (W. Bruce Lincoln). See Synonyms at **border.** [Middle English, probably of Scandinavian origin.]

brink·man·ship (brĭngk′mən-shĭp′) also **brinks·man·ship** (brĭngks′-) *n.* The practice, especially in international politics, of seeking advantage by creating the impression that one is willing and able to push a highly dangerous situation to the limit rather than concede.

Brin·ton (brĭn′tən), **Daniel Garrison.** 1837–1899. American anthropologist who was the first to attempt a systematic classification of Native American languages.

brin·y (brī′nē) *adj.* **-i·er, -i·est.** Of, relating to, or resembling brine; salty. —**brin′i·ness** *n.*

bri·o (brē′ō) *n.* Vigor; vivacity. [Italian, from Spanish *brio* or Provençal *briu,* both of Celtic origin. See **gʷerə-**[1] in Appendix.]

bri·oche (brē-ôsh′, -ōsh′) *n.* A soft, light-textured bread made from eggs, butter, flour, and yeast and formed into a roll or a bun. [French, from Old French, from *broyer, brier,* to knead, of Germanic origin. See **bhreg-** in Appendix.]

bri·o·lette (brē′ə-lĕt′) *n.* A pear-shaped or oval gem, especially a diamond, cut in long triangular facets. [French, perhaps alteration (influenced by *brillant,* brilliant) of *brignolette,* diminutive of *brignole,* dried plum, from *Brignoles,* a town of southeast France.]

bri·quette also **bri·quet** (brĭ-kĕt′) *n.* A block of compressed coal dust, charcoal, or sawdust and wood chips, used for fuel and kindling. [French, diminutive of *brique,* brick, from Middle Dutch *bricke.*]

bri·sance (brĭ-zäns′, -zäɴs′) *n.* The shattering effect of the sudden release of energy in an explosion. [French, from *brisant,* present participle of *briser,* to break, from Old French *brisier,* from Vulgar Latin **brisiāre,* perhaps of Celtic origin.] —**bri·sant′** (-zänt′, -zäɴt′) *adj.*

Bris·bane (brĭz′bən, -bān′). A city of eastern Australia on the **Brisbane River,** about 346 km (215 mi) long, near its mouth on Moreton Bay, an inlet of the Pacific Ocean. The area was settled in 1824 as a penal colony. Population, 734,750.

brisk (brĭsk) *adj.* **brisk·er, brisk·est. 1.** Marked by speed, liveliness, and vigor; energetic: *had a brisk walk in the park.* See Synonyms at **nimble. 2.** Keen or sharp in speech or manner: *a brisk greeting.* **3.** Stimulating and invigorating: *a brisk wind.* **4.** Pleasantly zestful: *a brisk tea.* [Probably of Scandinavian origin.] —**brisk′ly** *adv.* —**brisk′ness** *n.*

bris·ket (brĭs′kĭt) *n.* **1.** The chest of an animal. **2.** The ribs and meat taken from the chest of an animal. [Middle English *brusket,* perhaps of Scandinavian origin.]

bris·ling (brĭz′lĭng, brĭs′-) *n.* See **sprat** (sense 1). [Norwegian, alteration (influenced by Norwegian *brisa,* to flash) of Low German *bretling,* from *bret,* broad.]

bris·tle (brĭs′əl) *n.* A stiff hair. —**bristle** *v.* **-tled, -tling, -tles.** —*intr.* **1.** To stand stiffly on end like bristles: *The hair on the dog's neck bristled.* **2.** To raise the bristles: *The cat bristled at the sight of the large dog.* **3.** To react in an angry or offended manner: *The author bristled at the suggestion of plagiarism.* **4.** To be covered or thick with or as if with bristles: *The path bristled with thorns.* See Synonyms at **teem**[1]. —*tr.* **1.** To cause to stand erect like bristles; stiffen. **2.** To furnish or supply with bristles. **3.** To ruffle; disturb. [Middle English *bristel,* probably from Old English **byrstel,* from *byrst,* bristle.]

bris·tle·cone pine (brĭs′əl-kōn′) *n.* A small slow-growing pine *(Pinus aristata),* native to the western United States and having needles in fascicles of five. It is among the oldest living trees.

bris·tle·tail (brĭs′əl-tāl′) *n.* Any of various wingless insects of the order Thysanura, such as the silverfish, having bristlelike posterior appendages.

bris·tly (brĭs′lē) *adj.* **-tli·er, -tli·est. 1.a.** Consisting of or similar to bristles. **b.** Thick with bristles. **2.** Tending to react with agitation or anger; belligerent: *some bristly exchanges between the White House and the press.*

Bris·tol (brĭs′təl). **1.** A city of southwest England west of London. It has been an important trading center since the 12th cen-

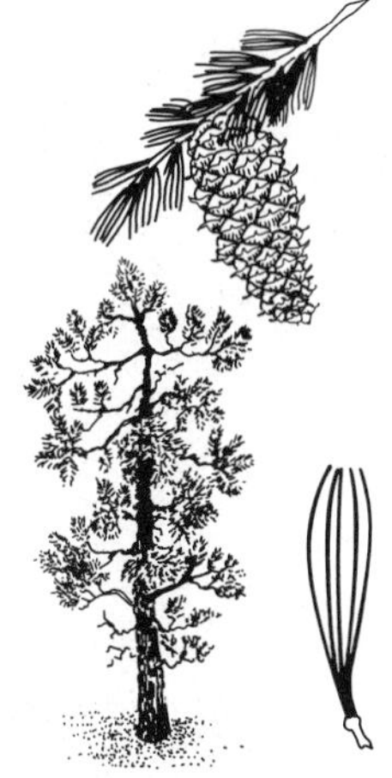

bristlecone pine
Pinus aristata

ă pat	oi boy
ā pay	ou out
âr care	o͝o took
ä father	o͞o boot
ĕ pet	ŭ cut
ē be	ûr urge
ĭ pit	th thin
ī pie	*th* this
îr pier	hw which
ŏ pot	zh vision
ō toe	ə about, item
ô paw	♦ regionalism

Stress marks: ′ (primary); ′ (secondary), as in **dictionary** (dĭk′shə-nĕr′ē)

tury. Population, 400,300. **2.** A city of central Connecticut north of Waterbury. Its clockmaking industry dates from 1790. Population, 57,370. **3.** A town of eastern Rhode Island on Narragansett Bay southeast of Providence. In the 18th and 19th centuries its port was a base for slave trading, privateering, whaling, and shipbuilding. Population, 20,128. **4.** Two cities on the Tennessee-Virginia line east-northeast of Kingsport, Tennessee. The communities, though politically independent, are an economic unit and share a main thoroughfare along the state boundary. Population, 23,986 (Tennessee) and 19,042 (Virginia).

Bristol Bay. An arm of the Bering Sea in southwest Alaska between the mainland and the Alaska Peninsula. It is a rich salmon-fishing area.

Bristol board *n.* A smooth, heavy pasteboard of fine quality. [After BRISTOL, England.]

Bristol Channel. An inlet of the Atlantic Ocean stretching west from the Severn River and separating Wales from southwest England. It is a major shipping route.

brit also **britt** (brĭt) *n.* **1.** The young of herring and similar fish. **2.** Minute marine organisms, such as crustaceans of the genus *Calanus,* that are a major source of food for right whales. [Perhaps from Cornish *brȳthel,* mackerel (from Old Cornish *breithil,* from **breith,* speckled) or from Welsh *brithyll,* trout, from *brith,* speckled).]

Brittany spaniel

Brit (brĭt) *n. Informal.* A British person: *"Americans approaching this new work of his are confronting not a hidebound Brit but a full-fledged citizen of Anglophonia"* (Anthony Burgess).

Brit. *abbr.* Britain; British.

Brit·ain¹ (brĭt′n). The island of Great Britain during pre-Roman, Roman, and early Anglo-Saxon times before the reign of Alfred the Great (871–899). The name is derived from *Brittania,* which the Romans used for the portion of the island that they occupied.

Brit·ain² (brĭt′n). *Abbr.* **Brit., Br.** See **United Kingdom.**

Bri·tan·nia (brĭ-tăn′yə, -tăn′ē-ə) *n.* **1.** A female personification of Great Britain or the British Empire. **2.** Also **britannia.** Britannia metal. [Latin, Britain, from *Brittannī,* the Britons. See BRITON.]

bri·tan·nia metal (brĭ-tăn′yə, -tăn′ē-ə) *n.* A white alloy of tin with copper, antimony, and sometimes bismuth and zinc that resembles pewter and is used in utensils and tableware.

Bri·tan·nic (brĭ-tăn′ĭk) *adj.* British.

britch·es (brĭch′ĭz) *pl.n.* Breeches. **—*idiom.* too big for (one's) britches.** Overconfident; cocky. [Alteration of *breeches,* pl. of BREECH.]

Brit·i·cism (brĭt′ĭ-sĭz′əm) also **Brit·ish·ism** (-shĭz′əm) *n.* A word, a phrase, or an idiom characteristic of or peculiar to English as it is spoken in Great Britain. [From BRITI(SH), on the model of words such as GALLICISM.]

Brit·ish (brĭt′ĭsh) *adj. Abbr.* **Brit., Br.** **1.a.** Of or relating to Great Britain or its people, language, or culture. **b.** Of or relating to the United Kingdom or the Commonwealth of Nations. **2.** Of or relating to the ancient Britons. **—British** *n.* **1.** The people of Great Britain. **2.** *Abbr.* **Brit., Br.** British English. **3.** The Celtic language of the ancient Britons. [Middle English *Brittish,* from Old English *Bryttisc,* relating to the ancient Britons, from *Bryttas,* Britons, of Celtic origin.]

British Ant·arc·tic Territory (ănt-ärk′tĭk, -är′tĭk). A British territory of the extreme Southern Hemisphere, including the South Orkney and South Shetland island groups in the southern Atlantic Ocean and Graham Land on the Antarctic Peninsula.

British an·ti-lew·is·ite (ăn′tē-lo͞o′ĭ-sīt′, ăn′tī-) *n. Abbr.* **BAL** See **dimercaprol.**

British Cam·e·roons (kăm′ə-ro͞onz′). A former British trust territory of western Africa, divided in 1961 between Nigeria and Cameroon.

British Co·lum·bi·a (kə-lŭm′bē-ə). *Abbr.* **BC, B.C.** A province of western Canada bordering on the Pacific Ocean. It joined the confederation in 1871. The coastal area was first explored by Capt. James Cook in 1778. Victoria Island was a separate colony from 1849 until 1866, when it was combined with the mainland territory. Victoria is the capital and Vancouver the largest city. Population, 2,744,467.

British Com·mon·wealth (kŏm′ən-wĕlth′). See **Commonwealth of Nations.**

British East Af·ri·ca (ăf′rĭ-kə). The former British territories of eastern Africa, including Kenya, Uganda, Tanganyika, and Zanzibar.

British Empire. The geographic and political units formerly under British control, including dominions, colonies, dependencies, trust territories, and protectorates. At the height of its power in the late 19th and early 20th centuries, it encompassed territories on all continents, comprising about one quarter of the world's land area and population.

British English *n.* The English language used in England as distinguished from that used elsewhere.

Brit·ish·er (brĭt′ĭ-shər) *n. Informal.* A native or inhabitant of Great Britain.

British Gui·a·na (gē-ăn′ə, -ä′nə). See **Guyana.**

British Hon·du·ras (hŏn-do͝or′əs, -dyo͝or′-). See **Belize** (sense 1).

British In·di·a (ĭn′dē-ə). The part of the Indian subcontinent under direct British administration until 1947.

British In·di·an Ocean Territory (ĭn′dē-ən). A British colony comprising small islands in the western Indian Ocean. It was formed in 1965 by agreement with Mauritius and Seychelles.

British Isles. A group of islands off the northwest coast of Europe comprising Great Britain, Ireland, and adjacent smaller islands.

Brit·ish·ism (brĭt′ĭ-shĭz′əm) *n.* Variant of **Briticism.**

British So·ma·li·land (sō-mä′lē-lănd′, sə-). A former British protectorate of eastern Africa on the Gulf of Aden. It has been part of Somaliland since 1960.

British thermal unit *n. Abbr.* **Btu** **1.** The quantity of heat required to raise the temperature of one pound of water from 60° to 61°F at a constant pressure of one atmosphere. **2.** The quantity of heat equal to 1/180 of the heat required to raise the temperature of one pound of water from 32° to 212°F at a constant pressure of one atmosphere.

British Vir·gin Islands (vûr′jĭn). A British colony in the eastern Caribbean east of Puerto Rico and the U.S. Virgin Islands. Road Town, on Tortola Island, is the capital. Population, 12,034.

British West In·dies (ĭn′dēz). *Abbr.* **B.W.I.** The islands of the West Indies that were formerly under British control, including Jamaica, Barbados, Trinidad and Tobago, and the Bahamas.

Brit·on (brĭt′n) *n.* **1.** A native or inhabitant of Great Britain. **2.** One of a Celtic people inhabiting ancient Britain at the time of the Roman invasion. [Middle English *Britoun,* Celt, Briton, from Anglo-Norman *Britun,* from Latin *Brittonēs,* Britons, of Celtic origin.]

britt (brĭt) *n.* Variant of **brit.**

Brit·ta·ny (brĭt′n-ē) also **Bre·tagne** (brə-tän′yə). A historical region and former province of northwest France on a peninsula between the English Channel and the Bay of Biscay. It was settled c. 500 by Britons driven out of their homeland by the Anglo-Saxons. The region was formally incorporated into France in 1532.

Brittany spaniel *n.* A large pointing spaniel of a breed originating in France.

Brit·ten (brĭt′n), **(Edward) Benjamin.** 1913–1976. British composer known for his song cycles, such as *Les Illuminations* (1939), and operas, including *Peter Grimes* (1945) and *Death in Venice* (1973).

brit·tle (brĭt′l) *adj.* **-tler, -tlest.** **1.a.** Likely to break, snap, or crack, as when subjected to pressure: *brittle bones.* **b.** Easily disrupted: *a brittle relationship between husband and wife.* See Synonyms at **fragile.** **2.a.** Difficult to deal with; snappish: *a brittle disposition.* **b.** Lacking warmth of feeling; cold: *The duchess, though well-known as a society hostess, conveyed an unmistakably brittle air.* **3.** Brilliantly sharp, as in percussive sound. **4.a.** Perishable. **b.** Fleeting; transitory. **—brittle** *n.* A confection of caramelized sugar to which nuts are added: *walnut brittle.* [Middle English *britel,* probably from Old English **brytel,* from *bryttian,* to shatter.] **—brit′tle·ly** (brĭt′l-ē) *adv.* **—brit′tle·ness** *n.*

brit·tle·bush (brĭt′l-bo͝osh′) *n.* A shrub *(Encelia farinosa)* in the composite family, native to Mexico and the southwest United States and having grayish foliage and showy flower heads with yellow rays.

brittle star *n.* Any of various marine organisms of the class Ophiuroidea, related to and resembling the starfish but having long, slender arms. Also called *ophiuroid.*

Brit·ton·ic (brĭ-tŏn′ĭk) also **Bry·thon·ic** (-thŏn′-) *n.* The branch of the Celtic languages that includes Welsh, Breton, and Cornish. [Ultimately from Latin *Brittonēs,* Britons. See BRITON.]

Brix scale (brĭks) *n.* A hydrometer scale for measuring the sugar content of a solution at a given temperature. [After Adolf F. *Brix* (1798–1870), German scientist.]

Br·no (bûr′nō). A city of central Czechoslovakia southeast of Prague. Founded in the tenth century, it became a free imperial city in 1243. Population, 383,443.

bro. *abbr.* Brother.

broach¹ (brōch) *tr.v.* **broached, broach·ing, broach·es.** **1.a.** To bring up (a subject) for discussion or debate. **b.** To announce: *We broached our plans for the new year.* **2.** To pierce in order to draw off liquid: *broach a keg of beer.* **3.** To draw off (a liquid) by piercing a hole in a cask or other container. **4.** To shape or enlarge (a hole) with a tapered, serrated tool. **—broach** *n.* **1.a.** A tapered, serrated tool used to shape or enlarge a hole. **b.** The hole made by such a tool. **2.** A spit for roasting meat. **3.** A mason's narrow chisel. **4.** A gimlet for tapping or broaching casks. **5.** Variant of **brooch.** [Middle English *brochen,* to pierce, probably from *broche,* pointed weapon or implement, from Old French, from Vulgar Latin **brocca,* from Latin *broccus,* projecting.] **—broach′er** *n.*

SYNONYMS: *broach, introduce, moot, raise.* The central meaning shared by these verbs is "to bring forward a point, topic, or question for consideration or discussion": *didn't know how to broach the subject tactfully; introduce a tax bill before the legislature; an idea that was approved when it was first mooted before the committee; raised the problem of dropouts with the faculty.*

broach² (brōch) *intr. & tr.v.* **broached, broach·ing, broach·es.** *Nautical.* To veer or cause to veer broadside to the wind and waves: *tried to keep the boat from broaching to.* [Probably from BROACH¹.]

broad (brôd) *adj.* **broad·er, broad·est. 1.** Wide in extent from side to side: *a broad river; broad shoulders.* **2.** Large in expanse; spacious: *a broad lawn.* **3.** Having a certain width from side to side: *A sidewalk three feet broad.* **4.** Full; open: *broad daylight.* **5.** Covering a wide scope; general: *a broad rule.* **6.** Liberal; tolerant: *had broad views regarding social services.* See Synonyms at **broad-minded. 7.** Relating to or covering the main facts or the essential points. **8.** Plain and clear; obvious: *gave us a broad hint to leave.* **9.** *Obsolete.* Outspoken. **10.** Vulgar; ribald: *a broad joke.* **11.** Heavily regional: *a broad Southern accent.* **12.** *Linguistics.* Pronounced with the tongue placed low and flat and with the oral cavity wide open, like the *a* in *bath* when pronounced like the *a* in *father.* Used of vowels. **—broad** *n.* **1.** A wide, flat part, as of one's hand. **2.** *Slang.* A woman or girl: *"I use 'broad' as a moniker of respect for a woman who* [knows] *how to throw a mean right"* (James Wolcott). **—broad** *adv.* Fully; completely. [Middle English *brod,* from Old English *brād.*] **—broad′ly** *adv.* **—broad′ness** *n.*

broad arrow *n.* **1.** An arrow with a wide barbed head. **2.** *Chiefly British.* A wide arrowhead mark identifying government property.

broad·ax broad·axe (brôd′ăks′) *n.* An ax with a wide, flat head and a short handle; a battle-ax.

broad·band (brôd′bănd′) *adj.* Of, relating to, or having a wide band of electromagnetic frequencies: *broadband communications.* **—broad′band′** *n.*

broad bean also **broad·bean** (brôd′bēn′) *n.* **1.** An annual Old World plant *(Vicia faba)* in the pea family, having pinnately compound leaves, white flowers with lateral purplish blotches, and long, thick pods. **2.** The edible seed or green pod of this plant. It is the bean of antiquity. Also called *fava bean, horse bean.*

broad-brush (brôd′brŭsh′) *adj.* Sweepingly general in scope or thrust: *an unfair, broad-brush indictment of all public officials.*

broad·cast (brôd′kăst′) *v.* **-cast** or **-cast·ed, -cast·ing, -casts.** *—tr.* **1.** To transmit (a radio or television program) for public or general use. **2.** To send out or communicate, especially by radio or television: *The agency broadcast an urgent appeal for medical supplies.* **3.** To make known over a wide area: *broadcast rumors.* See Synonyms at **announce. 4.** To sow (seed) over a wide area, especially by hand. *—intr.* **1. a.** To transmit a radio or television program for public or general use. **b.** To be on the air: *The station begins broadcasting at 6* A.M. **2.** To participate in a radio or television program. **3.** To send a transmission or signal; transmit. **—broadcast** *n.* **1.** Transmission of a radio or television program or signal for public use. **2. a.** A radio or television program: *watched the morning news broadcast.* **b.** The duration of such a program. **3.** The act of scattering seed. **—broadcast** *adj.* **1. a.** Communicated by means of television or radio. **b.** Of or relating to television or radio communications: *broadcast journalism; the print and broadcast media.* **2.** Widely known. **3.** Scattered over a wide area. **—broadcast** *adv.* In a scattered manner. **—broad′cast′er** *n.*

Broad-Church (brôd′chûrch′) *adj.* Of or relating to members of the Anglican Communion in the late 19th century who favored liberalization of ritual and doctrine.

broad·cloth (brôd′klôth′, -klŏth′) *n.* **1.** A densely textured woolen cloth with a plain or twill weave and a lustrous finish. **2.** A closely woven silk, cotton, or synthetic fabric with a narrow crosswise rib. [Middle English *brode clothe,* cloth woven in strips of double width : *brode,* broad; see BROAD + *clothe,* cloth; see CLOTH.]

broad·en (brôd′n) *tr. & intr.v.* **-ened, -en·ing, -ens.** To make or become broad or broader. **—broad′en·er** *n.*

broad gauge *n.* **1.** A distance between the rails of a railroad track that is greater than the standard width of 56½ inches (143.5 centimeters). **2.** A locomotive, car, or railway line of this gauge.

broad-gauge (brôd′gāj′) *adj.* **1.** Having a broad gauge. Used of a railroad track. **2.** *Informal.* Having a wide scope: *broad-gauge criticism.*

broad jump *n. Sports.* See **long jump.**

broad·leaf (brôd′lēf′) *adj.* Broad-leaved.

broad-leaved (brôd′lēvd′) also **broad-leafed** (-lēft′) *adj.* Having broad or relatively broad leaves rather than needlelike or scalelike leaves.

broad·loom (brôd′lo͞om′) *adj.* Woven on a wide loom: *a broadloom carpet.* **—broad′loom′** *n.*

broad-mind·ed (brôd′mīn′dĭd) *adj.* Having or characterized by tolerant or liberal views. **—broad′-mind′ed·ly** *adv.* **—broad′-mind′ed·ness** *n.*

SYNONYMS: *broad-minded, broad, liberal, open-minded, tolerant.* The central meaning shared by these adjectives is "having or showing an inclination to respect views and beliefs that differ from one's own": *a broad-minded but evenhanded judge; showed generous and broad sympathies; a liberal cleric; open-minded impartiality; a tolerant attitude.*
ANTONYM: *narrow-minded.*

Broads (brôdz). A low-lying region of eastern England with wide, shallow lakes interconnected by rivers and small streams. The Broads is a wildlife sanctuary and recreational center.

broad·sheet (brôd′shēt′) *n.* See **broadside** (sense 4).

broad·side (brôd′sīd′) *n.* **1.** The side of a ship above the water line. **2. a.** All the guns on one side of a warship. **b.** The simultaneous discharge of these guns. **3.** A forceful verbal attack, as in a speech or editorial. **4. a.** A large sheet of paper usually printed on one side. **b.** Something, such as an advertisement or public notice, that is printed on a broadside. Also called *broadsheet.* **5.** A broad, unbroken surface. **—broadside** *adv.* With the side turned to a given object: *The wave caught the canoe broadside and sank it.* **—broadside** *tr.v.* **-sid·ed, -sid·ing, -sides.** To strike or collide with full on the side: *were killed when an intoxicated driver broadsided their car.*

broad-spec·trum (brôd′spĕk′trəm) *adj.* Widely applicable or effective: *a broad-spectrum antibiotic.*

broad·sword (brôd′sôrd′, -sōrd′) *n.* A sword with a wide, usually two-edged blade that is designed for slashing rather than thrusting.

broad·tail (brôd′tāl′) *n.* **1.** See **karakul. 2.** The black pelt of a prematurely born karakul sheep, having a flat surface with wavy markings.

Broad·way (brôd′wā′). **1.** A thoroughfare of New York, the longest street in the world. It begins at the southern tip of Manhattan and extends about 241 km (150 mi) north to Albany. **2.** The principal theater and amusement district of New York City, on the West Side of midtown Manhattan centered on Broadway.

broad-winged hawk (brôd′wĭngd′) *n.* A crow-sized forest hawk *(Buteo platypterous)* of eastern North America.

Brob·ding·nag·i·an (brŏb′dĭng-năg′ē-ən) *adj.* Immense; enormous. [After *Brobdingnag,* a country in *Gulliver's Travels* by Jonathan Swift, where everything was enormous.]

bro·cade (brō-kād′) *n.* A heavy fabric interwoven with a rich, raised design. [Spanish or Portuguese *brocado,* from Italian *broccato,* from *brocco,* twisted thread, from Vulgar Latin **brocca,* spike, from Latin *brocchus,* projecting, of Celtic origin.] **—bro·cade′** *tr.v.*

broc·a·tel also **broc·a·telle** (brŏk′ə-tĕl′) *n.* A heavy fabric with highly raised designs. [French *brocatelle,* from Italian *broccatello,* diminutive of *broccato,* brocade. See BROCADE.]

broc·co·li (brŏk′ə-lē) *n.* **1.** A vegetable *(Brassica oleracea* var. *italica)* in the mustard family, closely related to the cauliflower and having dense clusters of numerous green flower buds. **2.** The flower clusters of this plant, eaten as a vegetable before the flower buds open. [Italian, pl. of *broccolo,* flowering sprout of a turnip, diminutive of *brocco,* shoot, sprout, from Vulgar Latin **brocca,* spike. See BROCADE.]

broccoli
Brassica oleracea

broccoli raab or **broccoli rabe** (räb) *n.* A vegetable plant *(Brassica rapa)* related to the turnip and grown for its pungent leafy shoots. [Italian *broccoli di rapa* : *broccoli,* pl. diminutive of *brocco,* sprout, shoot; see BROCCOLI + *di,* of (from Latin *dē;* see DE–) + *rapa,* turnip; see RAPE[2].]

bro·chette (brō-shĕt′) *n.* **1.** A small skewer or spit used to broil or roast meat, fish, or vegetables. **2.** Food broiled or roasted on a small skewer or spit. [French, from Old French, diminutive of *broche,* spit. See BROACH[1].]

bro·chure (brō-sho͝or′) *n.* A small booklet or pamphlet, often containing promotional material or product information. [French, from *brocher,* to stitch, from *broche,* knitting needle, from Old French, spit, needle. See BROACH[1].]

brock (brŏk) *n. Chiefly British.* A badger. [Middle English *brok,* from Old English *broc,* of Celtic origin.]

Brock·en (brŏk′ən). A granite peak, 1,142.8 m (3,747 ft) high, of the Harz Mountains in central Germany. It is the legendary site of the witches' Sabbath on Walpurgis Night.

brock·et (brŏk′ĭt) *n.* **1.** A two-year-old red deer with its first horns. **2.** Any of several small South American deer of the genus *Mazama,* having short, unbranched horns. [Middle English *broket,* from Old French *brocard,* from *broque,* animal's horn, dialectal variant of *broche,* spit. See BROACH[1].]

Brock·ton (brŏk′tən). A city of eastern Massachusetts south of Boston. It was settled in 1700. Population, 95,172.

Brock·ville (brŏk′vĭl′). A city of southeast Ontario, Canada, on the St. Lawrence River south of Ottawa. It is a summer resort. Population, 19,896.

Brod·sky, Joseph. Born 1940. Russian poet and essayist who was exiled from the Soviet Union in 1972. He won the 1987 Nobel Prize for literature.

bro·gan (brō′gən) *n.* A heavy, ankle-high work shoe. [Irish Gaelic *brōgan,* diminutive of *brōg,* brogue. See BROGUE[1].]

Bro·glie (brô-glē′), **Louis Victor de.** 1892–1987. French physicist who demonstrated (1927) that particles exhibit wavelike properties, thus establishing the field of wave mechanics. He won a 1929 Nobel Prize.

brogue[1] (brōg) *n.* **1.** A heavy shoe of untanned leather, formerly worn in Scotland and Ireland. **2.** A strong oxford shoe, usually with ornamental perforations and wing tips. [Irish and Scottish Gaelic *brōg,* from Old Irish *brōc,* shoe, possibly from Old Norse *brōk,* legging, or from Old English *brōc,* sing. of *brēc,* trousers; akin to Gaulish *brāca,* hose, trousers.]

brogue[2] (brōg) *n.* A strong dialectal accent, especially a strong Irish accent. [Probably from the brogues worn by peasants.]

broi·der (broi′dər) *tr.v.* **-dered, -der·ing, -ders.** To ornament with needlework; embroider. [Alteration (influenced by Middle English *broiden,* braided) of Middle English *brouderen,* from Old French *brosder, brouder.* See EMBROIDER.] **—broi′der·y** *n.*

ă pat	oi boy
ā pay	ou out
âr care	o͝o took
ä father	o͞o boot
ĕ pet	ŭ cut
ē be	ûr urge
ĭ pit	th thin
ī pie	*th* this
îr pier	hw which
ŏ pot	zh vision
ō toe	ə about, item
ô paw	♦ regionalism

Stress marks: **′** (primary); ′ (secondary), as in **dictionary** (dĭk′shə-nĕr′ē)

broil¹ (broil) *v.* **broiled, broil·ing, broils.** —*tr.* **1.** To cook by direct radiant heat, as over a grill or under an electric element. **2.** To expose to great heat. —*intr.* To be exposed to great heat. —**broil** *n.* **1.** The act of broiling or the condition of being broiled. **2.** Food, especially meat, that is broiled. [Middle English *broilen,* from Old French *brusler, bruler,* perhaps from *usler,* to burn (with *br-* from *bruir,* to burn), from Latin *ustulāre,* to scorch, from *ūrere,* to burn.]

broil² (broil) *n.* A rowdy argument; a brawl. See Synonyms at **brawl.** —**broil** *intr.v.* **broiled, broil·ing, broils.** To engage in a rowdy argument. [From obsolete *broil,* to brawl, from Middle English *broilen,* from Anglo-Norman *broiller,* mix up, confuse, from *breu,* broth, brew, from Vulgar Latin **brodum,* of Germanic origin. See **bhreu-** in Appendix.]

broil·er (broi′lər) *n.* **1.** One that broils, especially a small oven or the part of a stove used for broiling food. **2.** A tender young chicken suitable for broiling.

broke (brōk) *v.* **1.** Past tense of **break. 2.** *Non-Standard.* A past participle of **break.** —**broke** *adj. Informal.* **1.** Bankrupt. **2.** Lacking funds: *"Following the election, the Democrats were demoralized, discredited, and broke"* (Thomas P. O'Neill, Jr.).

Brontë
Detail of a portrait of Anne, Emily, and Charlotte, painted by Patrick Branwell Brontë (1817–1848), who obliterated his image between Emily and Charlotte

bro·ken (brō′kən) *v.* Past participle of **break.** —**broken** *adj.* **1. a.** Forcibly separated into two or more pieces; fractured: *a broken arm; broken glass.* **b.** Sundered by divorce, separation, or desertion of a parent or parents: *children from broken homes; a broken marriage.* **2.** Having been violated: *a broken promise.* **3. a.** Incomplete: *a broken set of books.* **b.** Being in a state of disarray; disordered: *troops fleeing in broken ranks.* **4. a.** Intermittently stopping and starting; discontinuous: *a broken cable transmission.* **b.** Varying abruptly, as in pitch: *broken sobs.* **c.** Spoken with gaps and errors: *broken English.* **5.** Topographically rough; uneven: *broken terrain.* **6. a.** Subdued totally; humbled: *a broken spirit.* **b.** Weakened and infirm: *broken health.* **7.** Crushed by grief: *died of a broken heart.* **8.** Financially ruined; bankrupt. **9.** Not functioning; out of order: *a broken washing machine.* —**bro′ken·ly** *adv.* —**bro′ken·ness** *n.*

Bro·ken Arrow (brō′kən). A city of northeast Oklahoma, a suburb of Tulsa. Population, 35,761.

bro·ken-down (brō′kən-doun′) *adj.* **1.** Out of working order. **2.** In poor condition, as from old age; infirm.

bro·ken-field (brō′kən-fēld′) *adj. Football.* Accomplished by a ball carrier against opposition that is widely scattered over the field: *broken-field running.*

bro·ken·heart·ed (brō′kən-här′tĭd) *adj.* Grievously sad.

bro·ker (brō′kər) *n.* **1.** One that acts as an agent for others, as in negotiating contracts, purchases, or sales in return for a fee or commission. **2.** A stockbroker. **3.** A power broker. —**broker** *tr.v.* **-kered, -ker·ing, -kers.** To arrange or manage as a broker: *broker an agreement among opposing factions.* [Middle English, from Anglo-Norman *brocour, abrocour*; possibly akin to Spanish *alboroque,* ceremonial gift at conclusion of business deal.]

WORD HISTORY: Giving gifts to one's broker might be justifiable from an etymological point of view because the word *broker* may be connected through its Anglo-Norman source *brocour, abrocour,* with Spanish *alboroque,* meaning "ceremony or ceremonial gift after the conclusion of a business deal." If this connection does exist, "business deal" is the notion shared by the Spanish and Anglo-Norman words because *brocour* referred to the middleman in transactions. The English word *broker* is first found in Middle English in 1355, several centuries before we find instances of its familiar compounds *pawnbroker,* first recorded in 1687, and *stockbroker,* first recorded in 1706.

brontosaur

bro·ker·age (brō′kər-ĭj) *n.* **1.** The business of a broker. **2.** A fee or commission paid to a broker. **3.** A firm engaged in buying and selling stocks and bonds for clients.

brol·ly (brŏl′ē) *n., pl.* **-lies.** *Chiefly British.* An umbrella. [Shortening and alteration of UMBRELLA.]

brom– *pref.* Variant of **bromo–.**

bro·mate (brō′māt′) *n.* **1.** A salt of bromic acid. **2.** An ion of bromic acid, BrO_3. —**bromate** *tr.v.* **-mat·ed, -mat·ing, -mates.** To treat (a substance) chemically with a bromate.

brome (brōm) *n.* Any of various grasses of the genus *Bromus,* native to temperate regions and including several weeds and ornamentals and some species important for forage. [New Latin *Bromus,* genus name, from Latin *bromos,* oats, from Greek.]

bro·me·li·ad (brō-mē′lē-ăd′) *n.* Any of various mostly epiphytic tropical American plants of the family Bromeliaceae, usually having long, stiff leaves, colorful flowers, and showy bracts. Bromeliads include the pineapple, the Spanish moss, and numerous ornamentals. [From New Latin *Bromelia,* type genus, after Olaf *Bromelius* (1639–1705), Swedish botanist.]

bro·mic acid (brō′mĭk) *n.* A corrosive, colorless liquid, $HBrO_3$, used in making dyes and pharmaceuticals.

bro·mide (brō′mīd′) *n.* **1. a.** A binary compound of bromine with another element, such as silver. **b.** Potassium bromide. **2. a.** A commonplace remark or notion; a platitude. See Synonyms at **cliché. b.** A tiresome person; a bore. —**bro·mid′ic** (-mĭd′ĭk) *adj.*

bro·mi·nate (brō′mə-nāt′) *tr.v.* **-nat·ed, -nat·ing, -nates.** To combine (a substance) with bromine or a bromine compound. —**bro′mi·na′tion** *n.*

bro·mine (brō′mēn) *n. Symbol* **Br** A heavy, volatile, corrosive, reddish-brown, nonmetallic liquid element, having a highly irritating vapor. It is used in producing gasoline antiknock mixtures, fumigants, dyes, and photographic chemicals. Atomic weight 79.904; atomic number 35; melting point 7.2°C; boiling point 58.78°C; valence 1, 3, 5, 7. See table at **element.** [French *brome* (from Greek *brōmos,* stench) + –INE².]

bro·mism (brō′mĭz′əm) also **bro·min·ism** (brō′mə-nĭz′əm) *n.* A toxic condition caused by the chronic overuse of bromides, characterized by mental dullness, loss of muscular coordination, and sometimes skin eruptions.

bromo– or **brom–** *pref.* Bromine: *bromide.* [From BROMINE and BROMIDE.]

bronch– *pref.* Variant of **broncho–.**

bron·chi (brŏng′kī′, -kē′) *n.* Plural of **bronchus.**

bron·chi·a (brŏng′kē-ə) *n.* Plural of **bronchium.**

bron·chi·al (brŏng′kē-əl) *adj.* Of or relating to the bronchi, the bronchia, or the bronchioles. —**bron′chi·al·ly** *adv.*

bronchial asthma *n.* Asthma that is caused by spasmodic contraction of the muscular walls of the bronchial tubes.

bronchial tube *n.* A bronchus or any of its branches.

bron·chi·ec·ta·sis (brŏng′kē-ĕk′tə-sĭs) *n.* Chronic dilatation of the bronchial tubes. [Greek *bronkhia,* bronchial tubes (from *bronkhos,* windpipe) + Greek *ektasis,* extension (*ek-,* out; see ECTO– + *tasis,* a stretching, from *teinein,* to stretch; see **ten-** in Appendix).]

bron·chi·ole (brŏng′kē-ōl′) *n.* Any of the fine, thin-walled, tubular extensions of a bronchus. [French : *bronchi* (from New Latin, pl. of *bronchus*; see BRONCHUS) + *-ole,* diminutive suff. (from Latin *-ola*).] —**bron′chi·o′lar** (-ō′lər) *adj.*

bron·chi·tis (brŏn-kī′tĭs, brŏng-) *n.* **1.** Chronic or acute inflammation of the mucous membrane of the bronchial tubes. **2.** A disease marked by this inflammation. —**bron·chit′ic** (-kĭt′ĭk) *adj.*

bron·chi·um (brŏng′kē-əm) *n., pl.* **-chi·a** (-kē-ə). A bronchial tube that is smaller than a bronchus and larger than a bronchiole. [New Latin, sing. of Late Latin *bronchia,* bronchial tubes, from Greek *bronkhia,* from *bronkhos,* windpipe.]

broncho– or **bronch–** *pref.* Bronchus; bronchial: *bronchoscope.* [Late Latin, from Greek *bronkho-,* from *bronkhos,* windpipe.]

bron·cho·di·la·tor (brŏng′kō-dī-lā′tər, -dĭ-, -dī′lā-) *n.* A drug that widens the air passages of the lungs and eases breathing by relaxing bronchial smooth muscle.

bron·cho·pneu·mon·ia (brŏng′kō-no͞o-mōn′yə, -nyo͞o-) *n.* A pneumonia involving inflammation of the lungs that spreads from and after infection of the bronchi.

bron·cho·scope (brŏng′kə-skōp′) *n.* A slender tubular instrument with a small light on the end for inspection of the interior of the bronchi. —**bron′cho·scop′ic** (-skŏp′ĭk) *adj.* —**bron′cho·scop′i·cal·ly** *adv.* —**bron·chos′co·pist** (brŏn-kŏs′kə-pĭst, brŏng-) *n.* —**bron·chos′co·py** (-kə-pē) *n.*

bron·chus (brŏng′kəs) *n., pl.* **-chi** (-kī′, -kē′). Either of two main branches of the trachea, leading directly to the lungs. [New Latin, from Greek *bronkhos,* windpipe.]

bron·co (brŏng′kō) *n., pl.* **-cos.** A wild or semiwild horse or pony of western North America. [American Spanish, from Spanish, wild, perhaps from Vulgar Latin **bruncus,* knot in a tree, perhaps from Latin *broccus,* projecting (influenced by *truncus,* stump).]

bron·co·bust·er (brŏng′kō-bŭs′tər) *n.* One who breaks wild horses to the saddle.

Bron·të (brŏn′tē). Family of British novelists and poets, including **Charlotte** (1816–1855), **Emily,** (1818–1848); and **Anne** (1820–1849). In 1846 their first publication was issued, a volume of poetry entitled *Poems by Currer, Ellis and Acton Bell.* In 1847 Charlotte published *Jane Eyre*; Emily, *Wuthering Heights*; and Anne, *Agnes Gray.*

bron·to·saur (brŏn′tə-sôr′) or **bron·to·sau·rus** (brŏn′tə-sôr′əs) *n.* A very large herbivorous dinosaur of the genus *Apatosaurus* (or *Brontosaurus*), of the Jurassic period. [New Latin *Brontosaurus,* genus name : Greek *brontē,* thunder + Greek *sauros,* lizard.]

Bronx (brŏngks). A borough of New York City in southeast New York on the mainland north of Manhattan. It was first settled by Jonas Bronck (died c. 1643), a Dane in the service of the Dutch West India Company, and became part of Greater New York in 1898. Population, 1,168,972.

Bronx cheer *n. Slang.* A loud sound expressing disapproval; a raspberry. [After the BRONX.]

bronze (brŏnz) *n.* **1.** *Abbr.* **br. a.** Any of various alloys of copper and tin in various proportions, sometimes with traces of other metals. **b.** Any of various alloys of copper, with or without tin, and antimony, phosphorus, or other components. **2.** A work of art made of one of these alloys. **3. a.** *Color.* A moderate yellowish to olive brown. **b.** A pigment of this color. —**bronze** *adj.* **1.** Made of or consisting of bronze. **2.** *Color.* Of a moderate yellowish to olive brown. —**bronze** *tr.v.* **bronzed, bronz·ing, bronz·es.** To give the color or appearance of bronze to. [French, from Italian *bronzo.*] —**bronz′er** *n.* —**bronz′y** *adj.*

Bronze Age (brŏnz) *n.* A period of human culture between the Stone Age and the Iron Age, characterized by weapons and implements made of bronze.

Bronze Star *n.* A U.S. military decoration awarded either for heroism or for meritorious achievement in ground combat. The Bronze Star awarded for heroism is distinguished by a metallic "V" device signifying valor.

brooch (brōch, bro͞och) also **broach** (brōch) *n.* A relatively large decorative pin or clasp. [Middle English *broche,* pointed tool, brooch, pin. See BROACH[1].]

brood (bro͞od) *n.* **1.** The young of certain animals, especially a group of young birds or fowl hatched at one time and cared for by the same mother. **2.** The children in one family. **—brood** *v.* **brood·ed, brood·ing, broods.** *—tr.* **1.** To sit on or hatch (eggs). **2.** To protect (young) by or as if by covering with the wings. *—intr.* **1.** To sit on or hatch eggs. **2.** To hover envelopingly; loom. **3.a.** To be deep in thought; meditate. **b.** To focus the attention on a subject persistently and moodily; worry: *brooded over the insult for several days.* **c.** To be depressed. **—brood** *adj.* Kept for breeding: *a brood hen; a brood mare.* [Middle English, from Old English *brōd.* See **bhreu-** in Appendix.] **—brood′ing·ly** *adv.*

SYNONYMS: *brood, dwell, fret, mope, stew, worry.* The central meaning shared by these verbs is "to turn over in the mind moodily and at length": *brooding about his decline in popularity; dwelled on her defeat; fretting over the loss of their jobs; moping about his illness; stewing over her upcoming trial; worrying about the unpaid bills.* See also Synonyms at **flock[1].**

brood·er (bro͞o′dər) *n.* **1.** One, such as an animal or a person, that broods: *a flock of brooders; a constant brooder over trifles.* **2.** A heated enclosure in which fowls are raised.

brood·y (bro͞o′dē) *adj.* **-i·er, -i·est. 1.a.** Meditative; contemplative. **b.** Oppressive: *"The room's air was broody and sullen, like the season's own, full of storm clouds"* (Nicholas Proffitt). **2.** Disposed to sit on eggs to hatch them: *a broody hen.* **—brood′i·ness** *n.*

♦ **brook[1]** (bro͝ok) *n.* See **creek** (sense 1). See Regional Note at **run.** [Middle English, from Old English *brōc.*]

brook[2] (bro͝ok) *tr.v.* **brooked, brook·ing, brooks.** To put up with; tolerate: *We will brook no further argument.* [Middle English *brouken,* from Old English *brūcan,* to use, enjoy.]

Brooke, Rupert. 1887–1915. British poet known for his war poetry suffused with a romantic patriotic quality.

Brook·field (bro͝ok′fēld′). **1.** A village of northeast Illinois, a residential suburb of Chicago. Population, 19,395. **2.** A city of southeast Wisconsin, a suburb of Milwaukee. Population, 34,035.

brook·ie (bro͝ok′ē) *n.* A brook trout.

brook·ite (bro͝ok′īt′) *n.* A mineral form of titanium dioxide, TiO_2, having characteristic orthorhombic crystals and a red-brown to black color. [After Henry James *Brooke* (1771–1857), British mineralogist.]

brook·let (bro͝ok′lĭt) *n.* A small brook.

brook·lime (bro͝ok′līm′) *n.* Either of two related trailing plants, *Veronica americana* of North America and *V. beccabunga* of Eurasia, growing in wet or moist places and having clusters of small blue or purplish flowers. [Alteration of Middle English *brokelemok* : *broke,* brook; see BROOK[1] + *lemok,* a kind of brooklime (from Old English *hleomoc*).]

Brook·line (bro͝ok′līn′). A town of eastern Massachusetts, a residential suburb of Boston. Population, 55,062.

Brook·lyn (bro͝ok′lĭn). A borough of New York City in southeast New York on western Long Island. Dutch colonists first settled the area in 1636 and 1637 and in 1645 established the hamlet of Breuckelen near the present-day site of borough hall. Renamed Brooklyn by the English, the expanded community became part of Greater New York City in 1898. Population, 2,230,936.

Brooklyn Center. A city of southeast Minnesota, a suburb of Minneapolis. Population, 31,230.

Brooklyn Park. A city of southeast Minnesota, a suburb of Minneapolis. Population, 43,332.

Brook Park (bro͝ok). A city of northeast Ohio, a suburb of Cleveland. Population, 26,195.

Brooks (bro͝oks), **Gwendolyn Elizabeth.** Born 1917. American poet known for her verses detailing the dreams and struggles of Black Americans.

Brooks, Phillips. 1835–1893. American Episcopal bishop noted for his intelligent and positive sermons. He wrote the Christmas hymn "O Little Town of Bethlehem" (1868).

Brooks, Van Wyck. 1886–1963. American literary historian, critic, and translator who wrote many books on the literary history of America, including *The Flowering of New England* (1936), for which he won a Pulitzer Prize.

Brooks Range. A mountain chain of northern Alaska within the Arctic Circle. The northernmost section of the Rocky Mountains, it rises to about 2,763 m (9,060 ft) in the eastern part of the range.

brook trout *n.* A freshwater game fish *(Salvelinus fontinalis)* of eastern North America. Also called *speckled trout, squaretail.*

broom (bro͞om, bro͝om) *n.* **1.** A bunch of twigs, straw, or bristles bound together, attached to a stick or handle, and used for sweeping. **2.a.** Any of various Mediterranean shrubs of the genus *Cytisus* in the pea family, especially *C. Scoparius,* having mostly compound leaves with three leaflets and showy, usually bright yellow flowers. **b.** Any of several similar or related shrubs, especially in the genera *Genista* and *Spartium.* **—broom** *tr.v.* **broomed, broom·ing, brooms.** To sweep with or as if with a broom. [Middle English, from Old English *brōm.*] **—broom′y** *adj.*

Broom·all (bro͞o′môl). A community of southeast Pennsylvania, a suburb of Philadelphia. Population, 23,642.

broom·ball (bro͞om′bôl′, bro͝om′-) *n. Sports.* A kind of ice hockey that is played on ice with the players using brooms and a soccer ball instead of hockey sticks and a puck and wearing shoes or boots instead of ice skates. **—broom′ball′er** *n.*

broom·corn (bro͞om′kôrn′, bro͝om′-) *n.* A variety of sorghum *(Sorghum bicolor)* having a stiff, erect, much-branched flower cluster, the stalks of which are used to make brooms.

Broom·field (bro͞om′fēld′). A city of north-central Colorado, a suburb of Denver. Population, 20,730.

broom·rape (bro͞om′rāp′, bro͝om′-) *n.* Any of various parasitic herbs of the genus *Orobanche,* having purplish or yellowish flowers and small scalelike leaves that lack chlorophyll. Broomrape grows on the roots of various plants. [Translation of Medieval Latin *rāpum genistae* : Latin *rāpum,* underground stock of a tree + Latin *genistae,* genitive of *genista,* broom (from the growth of these tubers on the roots of broom).]

broom·stick (bro͞om′stĭk′, bro͝om′-) *n.* The handle of a broom.

bros. *abbr.* Brothers.

Bros·sard (brô-sär′, -särd′). A town of southern Quebec, Canada, a residential suburb of Montreal on the St. Lawrence River. Population, 52,232.

broth (brôth, brŏth) *n., pl.* **broths** (brôths, brŏths, brô*th*z, brŏ*th*z). **1.** The water in which meat, fish, or vegetables have been boiled; stock. **2.** A thin, clear soup based on stock, to which rice, barley, meat, or vegetables may be added. [Middle English, from Old English. See **bhreu-** in Appendix.]

broth·el (brŏth′əl, brô′thəl) *n.* A house of prostitution. [Short for *brothel-house,* from Middle English *brothel,* prostitute, from *brothen,* past participle of *brethen,* to go to ruin, from Old English *brēothan,* to decay.]

broth·er (brŭ*th*′ər) *n., pl.* **-ers.** *Abbr.* **bro., br., b. 1.** A male having the same parents as another or one parent in common with another. **2.** *pl.* Often **breth·ren** (brĕ*th*′rən) One who shares a common ancestry, allegiance, character, or purpose with another or others, especially: **a.** A kinsman. **b.** A fellow man. **c.** A fellow member, as of a fraternity, trade union, or panel of judges on a court. **d.** A close male friend; a comrade. **e.** A soul brother. **3.** *pl.* Often **brethren.** Something, such as a corporation or an institution, that is regarded as a member of a class: *"A station that . . . relies on corporate contributions or advertising to survive runs the risk of becoming virtually indistinguishable from its commercial brethren"* (W. John Moore). **4.** *Abbr.* **Br.** *Ecclesiastical.* **a.** A member of a men's religious order who is not in holy orders but engages in the work of the order. **b.** A lay member of a religious order of men. **c.** *pl.* Often **brethren.** A fellow member of the Christian church. [Middle English, from Old English *brōthor.* See **bhrāter-** in Appendix.]

broth·er·hood (brŭ*th*′ər-ho͝od′) *n.* **1.** The state or relationship of being brothers. **2.** Fellowship. **3.** *Abbr.* **B.** An association of men, such as a fraternity or union, united for common purposes. **4.** All the members of a profession or trade.

broth·er-in-law (brŭ*th*′ər-ĭn-lô′) *n., pl.* **broth·ers-in-law** (brŭ*th*′ərz-). **1.** The brother of one's husband or wife. **2.** The husband of one's sister. **3.** The husband of the sister of one's husband or wife.

broth·er·ly (brŭ*th*′ər-lē) *adj.* Characteristic of or befitting brothers; fraternal. **—broth′er·li·ness** *n.* **—broth′er·ly** *adv.*

broth·ers-in-law (bru*th*′ərz-ĭn-lô′) *n.* Plural of **brother-in-law.**

brougham (bro͞om, bro͞o′əm, brōm, brō′əm) *n.* **1.** A closed four-wheeled carriage with an open driver's seat in front. **2.** An automobile with an open driver's seat. **3.** An electrically powered automobile resembling a coupé. [After Henry Peter *Brougham,* First Baron Brougham and Vaux (1778–1868), Scottish-born jurist.]

brought (brôt) *v.* Past tense and past participle of **bring.**

brou·ha·ha (bro͞o′hä-hä′) *n.* An uproar; a hubbub. [French, of imitative origin.]

brow (brou) *n.* **1.a.** The superciliary ridge over the eyes. **b.** The eyebrow. **c.** The forehead. **2.** A facial expression; countenance: *"Speak you this with a sad brow?"* (Shakespeare). **3.** The projecting upper edge of a steep place: *the brow of a hill.* [Middle English, from Old English *brū.* See **bhrū-** in Appendix.]

bro·wal·li·a (brə-wä′lē-ə) *n.* Any of various tropical American herbs of the genus *Browallia,* having blue, violet, or white flowers with united petals. [New Latin, after Bishop John *Browall* (1707–1755), Swedish botanist.]

brow·beat (brou′bēt′) *tr.v.* **-beat, -beat·en** (-bēt′n), **-beat·ing, -beats.** To intimidate or subjugate by an overbearing manner or domineering speech; bully. See Synonyms at **intimidate.** **—brow′beat′er** *n.*

brown (broun) *n. Abbr.* **br.** *Color.* Any of a group of colors between red and yellow in hue that are medium to low in lightness and low to moderate in saturation. **—brown** *adj.* **brown·er, brown·est. 1.** *Color.* Of the color brown. **2.** Deeply suntanned. **—brown** *tr. & intr.v.* **browned, brown·ing, browns. 1.** To

brooch

Gwendolyn Brooks

brougham
c. 1901–1909

ă pat	oi boy
ā pay	ou out
âr care	o͝o took
ä father	o͞o boot
ĕ pet	ŭ cut
ē be	ûr urge
ĭ pit	th thin
ī pie	*th* this
îr pier	hw which
ŏ pot	zh vision
ō toe	ə about, item
ô paw	♦ regionalism

Stress marks: **′** (primary); ′ (secondary), as in **dictionary** (dĭk′shə-nĕr′ē)

make or become brown. **2.** To cook until brown. ***—phrasal verb.*** **brown off.** *Chiefly British.* To make or become angry or irritated. [Middle English, from Old English *brūn.* See **bher-**[2] in Appendix.] **—brown′ish** *adj.* **—brown′ness** *n.*

Brown (broun), **Charles Brockden.** 1771–1810. American writer and editor who is considered America's first professional novelist. Brown is best known for his Gothic romances, such as *Wieland* (1798), *Ormund* (1799), and *Jane Talbot* (1801).

Brown, Henry Billings. 1836–1913. American jurist who served as an associate justice of the U.S. Supreme Court (1890–1906).

Brown, Herbert Charles. Born 1912. British-born American chemist. He shared a 1979 Nobel Prize for discoveries in the chemistry of boron and phosphorus.

Brown, James. Born 1933. American singer. First popular in the 1950's with hits like "Please, Please, Please," he is often called the "Godfather of Soul."

Brown, John. 1800–1859. American abolitionist. In 1859 Brown and 21 followers captured the U.S. arsenal at Harper's Ferry as part of an effort to liberate Southern slaves. His group was defeated, and Brown was hanged after a trial in which he won sympathy as an abolitionist martyr.

Brown, Olympia. 1835–1926. American minister and suffragist who was the first woman in the United States to be ordained in the ministry of an established denomination (1863).

Brown, Robert. 1773–1858. Scottish botanist known for his investigation of the sexual behavior of plants. His discovery of the irregular movement of pollen grains led to the concept known as Brownian movement.

brown alga *n.* Any of a large group of chiefly marine plants of the division Phaeophyta, including the rockweeds and the kelps, having brown and yellow pigments that mask the chlorophyll.

brown bagging *n.* **1.** The practice of taking one's lunch to work, typically in a brown paper bag. **2.** The practice of taking one's own liquor into a public establishment, such as a restaurant, where setups are available. **—brown bagger** *n.*

brown bear *n.* Any of several large bears of the genus *Ursus,* such as the grizzly and Kodiak bears, inhabiting western North America and northern Eurasia and having brown to yellowish fur. Brown bears are sometimes categorized as the single species *U. arctos.*

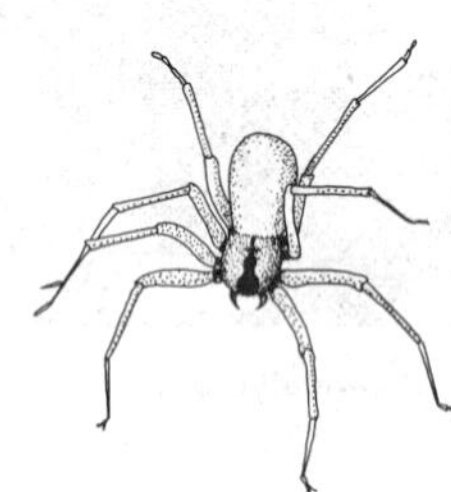

brown recluse spider
Loxosceles reclusa

brown Bet·ty (bĕt′ē) *n.* A baked pudding of chopped or sliced apples, bread crumbs, raisins, sugar, butter, and spices.

brown bread *n.* **1.** A bread made of a dark flour, such as graham or whole-wheat flour. **2.** A steamed bread usually made of cornmeal, flour, and molasses.

brown coal *n.* See lignite.

Browne (broun), **Charles Farrar.** Pen name Artemus Ward. 1834–1867. American humorist who used backwoods characters and local dialect to comment on current events in his fictional tales of an itinerant showman.

Browne, Sir **Thomas.** 1605–1682. English physician and writer known for the richness of his prose in works such as *Religio Medici* (1642), an attempt to reconcile Christian faith with scientific knowledge.

brown fat *n.* A dark-colored, mitochondrion-rich adipose tissue in many mammals that generates heat to regulate body temperature, especially in hibernating animals.

Brown·i·an movement (brou′nē-ən) *n.* The random movement of microscopic particles suspended in a liquid or gas, caused by collisions with molecules of the surrounding medium. Also called *Brownian motion.* [After Robert BROWN.]

brown thrasher
Toxostoma rufum

brown·ie (brou′nē) *n.* **1. Brownie.** A member of the Girl Scouts from six through eight years of age. **2.** A bar of moist, usually chocolate cake with nuts. **3.** A small sprite thought to do helpful work at night. **4.** A brown trout. [Sense 3, from the notion of the sprite as a tiny brown man.]

Brownie point also **brownie point** *n.* Credit considered as earned, especially by favorably impressing a superior. [From the practice of awarding points for achievement to Brownies in the Girl Scouts.]

Brown·ing (brou′nĭng), **Elizabeth Barrett.** 1806–1861. British poet. Overcoming ill health and the jealous objections of her tyrannical father, she eloped to Italy with Robert Browning and married him in 1846. Her greatest work, *Sonnets from the Portuguese* (1850), is a sequence of love poems written to her husband.

Browning, John Moses. 1855–1926. American firearms inventor whose designs include repeating rifles, automatic pistols, and a machine gun dubbed "the Peacemaker" that was used in the Spanish-American War and adapted for aerial warfare in World War I.

Browning, Robert. 1812–1889. British poet best known for dramatic monologues such as "My Last Duchess," "Fra Lippo Lippi," and "The Bishop Orders His Tomb." His work, including his masterpiece, *The Ring and the Book* (1868–1869), explored new ways of using diction and poetic rhythm.

Browning automatic rifle *n.* *Abbr.* **BAR** A .30 caliber air-cooled, automatic or semiautomatic, gas-operated, magazine-fed rifle used by U.S. troops in World Wars I and II and the Korean War. [After John Moses BROWNING.]

Browning machine gun *n.* A .30 or .50 caliber automatic belt-fed, air-cooled or water-cooled machine gun capable of firing ammunition at a rate of more than 500 rounds per minute, used by U.S. troops in World War II and the Korean War. [After John Moses BROWNING.]

brown lung disease *n.* See **byssinosis.**

brown mustard *n.* **1.** See **Indian mustard. 2.** The black mustard.

brown·nose or **brown-nose** (broun′nōz′) *tr.v.* **-nosed, -nos·ing, -nos·es.** *Informal.* To curry favor with in an obsequious manner. **—brown′nose′** *n.* **—brown′nos′er** *n.*

brown·out (broun′out′) *n.* A reduction or cutback in electric power, especially as a result of a shortage, a mechanical failure, or overuse by consumers. [BROWN + (BLACK)OUT.]

brown patch *n.* A disease of turf grasses caused by a fungus of the genus *Rhizoctonia* and resulting in circular patches of dead leaves.

brown rat *n.* See **Norway rat.**

brown recluse spider *n.* A venomous spider *(Loxosceles reclusa)* having a violin-shaped mark on the cephalothorax, introduced into the southern United States from South America.

brown rice *n.* The whole grain of rice, from which the germ and outer layers containing the bran have not been removed; unpolished rice.

brown rot *n.* Any of several plant diseases, especially a disease of peach, plum, apricot, cherry, and related plants, characterized by wilting and browning of the flowers and leaves and rotting of the fruits.

Brown Shirt or **brown·shirt** (broun′shûrt′) *n.* **1.** A Nazi, especially a storm trooper. **2.** A racist, especially a violent, right-wing one. [Translation of German *Braunhemd* : *braun,* brown + *Hemd,* shirt.]

brown·stone (broun′stōn′) *n.* **1.** A brownish-red sandstone used as a building material. **2.** A house built or faced with brownish-red sandstone.

brown study *n.* A state of deep thought. [BROWN, gloomy + STUDY, mental state.]

brown sugar *n.* **1.** Unrefined or incompletely refined sugar that still retains some molasses, which imparts a brownish color to it. **2.** A commercial product made by the addition of molasses to white sugar.

Browns·ville (brounz′vĭl′, -vəl). A city of southern Texas on the Rio Grande near its mouth on the Gulf of Mexico. It is a major port of entry served by a deepwater channel that accommodates oceangoing ships. Population, 84,997.

Brown Swiss *n.* One of a hardy breed of large brown dairy cattle that originated in Switzerland.

brown-tail moth (broun′tāl′) *n.* A small white and brown tussock moth *(Euproctis phaeorrhoea)* whose caterpillars defoliate shade trees and produce a poison capable of causing a skin rash on contact.

brown thrasher *n.* A North American bird *(Toxostoma rufum)* related to the mockingbird and having a reddish-brown back and a dark-streaked breast.

brown trout *n.* A European freshwater game fish *(Salmo trutta)* that is dark olive to purple-black above and yellow-brown with reddish spots on the sides. It is naturalized in North America.

Brown·wood (broun′wo͝od′). A city of central Texas west of Waco. It is an industrial center in an agricultural region. Population, 19,396.

browse (brouz) *v.* **browsed, brows·ing, brows·es.** *—intr.* **1.a.** To inspect something in a leisurely and casual way: *browsed through the record collection for items of interest.* **b.** To read something superficially by selecting passages at random: *browsed through the report during lunch.* **2.** To feed on leaves, young shoots, and other vegetation; graze. *—tr.* **1.** To look through or over (something) casually: *browsed the evening paper; browsing the gift shops for souvenirs.* **2.a.** To nibble; crop. **b.** To graze on. **—browse** *n.* **1.** Young twigs, leaves, and shoots that are fit for animals to eat. **2.** An act of browsing. [Probably from obsolete French *broust,* young shoot, from Old French *brost,* of Germanic origin.] **—brows′er** *n.*

Broz (brōz, brôz), **Josip.** See Marshal **Tito.**

Bru·beck (bro͞o′bĕk), **David Warren.** Known as "Dave." Born 1920. American jazz pianist and composer considered to be one of the foremost exponents of progressive jazz.

Bruce (bro͞os), **Blanche Kelso.** 1841–1898. American political leader who was the first Black politician to serve a full term in the U.S. Senate (1875–1881).

Bruce, Sir **David.** 1855–1931. Australian physician and bacteriologist known for his description (1887) of the bacterium that causes undulant fever, or brucellosis.

Bruce, Robert the. See **Robert I**[2].

Bruce, Stanley Melbourne. First Viscount Bruce of Melbourne. 1883–1967. Australian politician who was prime minister (1923–1929) and a delegate (1933–1936) to the League of Nations.

bru·cel·la (bro͞o-sĕl′ə) *n., pl.* **-cel·lae** (-sĕl′ē) or **-cel·las.** *Microbiology.* Any of various aerobic, short, rod-shaped bacteria of the genus *Brucella* that are pathogenic to human beings and domestic animals. [After Sir David BRUCE.]

bru·cel·lo·sis (bro͞o′sə-lō′sĭs) *n.* **1.** An infectious bacterial disease of human beings that is caused by brucellae, transmitted by contact with infected animals, and characterized by fever, malaise, and headache. Also called *Gibraltar fever, Malta fever, Med-*

iterranean fever, Rock fever, undulant fever. **2.** A disease of domestic animals, such as cattle, sheep, goats, and dogs, that is caused by brucellae and sometimes results in spontaneous abortions in newly infected animals. Also called *Bang's disease.* [BRUCELL(A) + –OSIS.]

bru·cine (bro͞o′sēn′, -sĭn) *n.* A poisonous white crystalline alkaloid, $C_{23}H_{26}N_2O_4$, derived from the seeds of nux vomica and closely related plants and used to denature alcohol. [After James *Bruce* (1730–1794), Scottish explorer.]

Bruck·ner (bro͝ok′nər), **Anton.** 1824–1896. Austrian organist and composer whose major works include nine symphonies, a Requiem (1848–1849), and a Te Deum (1881).

Brue·ghel or **Brue·gel** also **Breu·ghel** (broi′gəl, bro͞o′-, brœ′-), **Pieter.** Known as "the Elder." 1525?–1569. Flemish painter noted for his landscapes and his lively genre scenes, including *Peasant Wedding* (c. 1567). His son **Pieter** (1564–1638?), known as "the Younger," is primarily remembered for his copies of his father's works, while another son, **Jan** (1568–1625), is frequently called "the Flower Brueghel" or "the Velvet Brueghel" for the silky detail of his still-life paintings.

Bruges (bro͞ozh). A city of northwest Belgium connected by canal with the North Sea. It was founded in the 9th century and was a leading member of the Hanseatic League in the 13th century. Today the old city is a popular tourist center known as "the City of Bridges." Population, 118,218.

bru·in (bro͞o′ĭn) *n.* A bear. [Middle English *bruin,* name of the bear in *History of Reynard the Fox,* translated by William Caxton, from Middle Dutch *bruun, bruin,* brown, name of the bear in Middle Dutch version of the fable. See **bher-**[2] in Appendix.]

bruise (bro͞oz) *v.* **bruised, bruis·ing, bruis·es.** —*tr.* **1.a.** To injure the underlying soft tissue or bone of (part of the body) without breaking the skin, as by a blow. **b.** To damage (plant tissue), as by abrasion or pressure: *bruised the fruit by careless packing.* **2.** To dent or mar. **3.** To pound (berries, for example) into fragments; crush. **4.** To hurt, especially psychologically. —*intr.* To experience or undergo bruising: *Peaches bruise easily.* —**bruise** *n.* **1.** An injury to underlying tissues or bone in which the skin is not broken, often characterized by ruptured blood vessels and discolorations. **2.** A similar injury to plant tissue, often resulting in discoloration or spoilage. **3.** An injury, especially to one's feelings. [Middle English *bruisen,* from Old English *brȳsan,* to crush, and from Old North French *bruisier* (of Germanic origin).]

bruis·er (bro͞o′zər) *n. Informal.* A large, heavyset man.

bruit (bro͞ot) *tr.v.* **bruit·ed, bruit·ing, bruits.** To spread news of; repeat. —**bruit** *n.* **1.** (*also* bro͞o′ē). *Medicine.* An abnormal sound heard in auscultation. **2.** *Archaic.* **a.** A rumor. **b.** A din; a clamor. [From Middle English, noise, from Old French, past participle of *bruire,* to roar, from Vulgar Latin **brūgīre* (from Latin *rūgīre,* and from Vulgar Latin **bragere*).]

Bru·lé (bro͞o-lā′) *n., pl.* **Brulé** or **-lés.** **1.** A Native American people constituting a subdivision of the Teton Sioux, inhabiting northwest Nebraska and southwest South Dakota. **2.** A member of this people. [French *brûlé,* burnt (partial translation of their own name for themselves).]

bru·mal (bro͞o′məl) *adj.* Of, relating to, or occurring in winter. [Latin *brūmālis,* from *brūma,* winter, from **brevima (diēs),* the shortest (day) or winter solstice, archaic superlative of *brevis,* short. See **mregh-u-** in Appendix.]

brume (bro͞om) *n.* Fog or mist. [French, from Old French, perhaps from Provençal, from Latin *brūma,* winter. See BRUMAL.] —**bru′mous** (bro͞o′məs) *adj.*

brum·ma·gem (brŭm′ə-jəm) *adj.* Cheap and showy; meretricious. [Alteration of BIRMINGHAM, England (from the counterfeit coins made there in the 17th century).] —**brum′ma·gem** *n.*

Brum·mell (brŭm′əl), **George Bryan.** Known as "Beau Brummell." 1778–1840. British dandy who popularized new men's fashions, including simply cut clothing, trousers rather than breeches, and elaborate neckwear.

brunch (brŭnch) *n.* A meal typically eaten late in the morning as a combination of a late breakfast and an early lunch. [BR(EAKFAST) + (L)UNCH.]

Bru·nei (bro͞o-nī′). A sultanate of northwest Borneo on the South China Sea. Formerly a self-governing British protectorate, it became fully independent on January 1, 1984. Bandar Seri Begawan is the capital. Population, 191,765.

Bru·nel·le·schi (bro͞o′nə-lĕs′kē), **Filippo.** 1377–1446. Italian architect celebrated for his work during the Florentine Renaissance. His greatest achievement is the octagonal ribbed dome of the Florence cathedral.

bru·net (bro͞o-nĕt′) *adj.* **1.** Of a dark complexion or coloring. **2.** Having dark brown or black hair or eyes. —**brunet** *n.* A person with dark brown hair. See Usage Note at **brunette.** [French, from Old French, diminutive of *brun,* brown, of Germanic origin. See **bher-**[2] in Appendix.]

bru·nette (bro͞o-nĕt′) *adj.* Having dark or brown hair. —**brunette** *n.* A girl or woman with dark or brown hair. [French, feminine of *brunet.* See BRUNET.]

USAGE NOTE: *Brunette* was for a long time used to denote a woman having a dark complexion; now it is used chiefly in reference to hair color. The general practice is to use the form *brunette* to refer only to women, with *brunet* as a less frequently used variant that can be applied as well to men and mixed groups. The distinction, like the one between *blonde* and *blond,* has been regarded as carrying sexist implications. In this case, however, it is difficult to see how the problem can be easily resolved. It is unlikely that *brunette* could be pressed into service as a neutral term, since the suffix *–ette* is too closely associated with marked feminine gender. *Brunet* is theoretically available for both sexes but is rarely applied to men, whose corresponding coloration is typically described simply as "brown." It would, of course, be possible to use *brown* for the hair color of both sexes, if only that word could be redeemed from the associations of drabness that led to the adoption of the substitute *brunette* in the first place. See Usage Notes at **blond, -ette.**

brung (brŭng) *v. Usage Problem.* A past tense and a past participle of **bring.** See Usage Note at **bring.**

Brun·hild (bro͞on′hĭlt′) *n.* A queen in the *Nibelungenlied* who is won as a bride by Gunther.

Bru·no (bro͞o′nō), **Giordano.** 1548?–1600. Italian philosopher who used Copernican principles in formulating his cosmic theory of an infinite universe. Condemned by the Inquisition for heresy, immoral conduct, and blasphemy, he was burned at the stake.

Bruno of Co·logne (kə-lōn′), Saint. 1030?–1101. German monk who established a monastery at Chartreuse in southern France (1084) and founded the Carthusian order.

Bruns·wick (brŭnz′wĭk). **1.** A region and former duchy of north-central Germany. Established in the 13th century, the duchy became independent in 1918 before joining the Weimar Republic. **2.** A city of north-central Germany east-southeast of Hanover. Reputedly founded in 861, it is an industrial and commercial center. Population, 253,057. **3.** A city of southeast Georgia south-southwest of Savannah near the Atlantic coast. It is a port of entry. Population, 17,605. **4.** A town of southwest Maine on the Androscoggin River northeast of Portland. Bowdoin College (established 1794) is here. Population, 17,336. **5.** A city of northeast Ohio, a suburb of Cleveland and Akron. Population, 28,104.

Brunswick stew *n.* A stew that usually contains chicken and rabbit or squirrel meat cooked with vegetables. [After *Brunswick,* a county of southern Virginia.]

brunt (brŭnt) *n.* **1.** The main impact or force, as of an attack. **2.** The main burden: *bore the brunt of the household chores.* [Middle English, perhaps of Scandinavian origin.]

brush[1] (brŭsh) *n.* **1.a.** A device consisting of bristles fastened into a handle, used in scrubbing, polishing, or painting. **b.** The act of using this device. **2.** A light touch in passing; a graze. **3.** A bushy tail: *the brush of a fox.* **4.** A sliding connection completing a circuit between a fixed and a moving conductor. **5.** A snub; a brushoff. —**brush** *v.* **brushed, brush·ing, brush·es.** —*tr.* **1.a.** To clean, polish, or groom with a brush. **b.** To apply with or as if with motions of a brush. **c.** To remove with or as if with motions of a brush. **2.** To dismiss abruptly or curtly: *brushed the matter aside; brushed an old friend off.* **3.** To touch lightly in passing; graze against. —*intr.* **1.** To use or apply a brush. **2.** To move past something so as to touch it lightly. —***phrasal verb.* brush up.** **1.** To refresh one's memory. **2.** To renew a skill. [Middle English *brusshe,* from Old French *brosse,* brushwood, brush. See BRUSH[2].] —**brush′er** *n.* —**brush′y** *adj.*

SYNONYMS: *brush, flick, glance, graze, shave, skim.* The central meaning shared by these verbs is "to make light and momentary contact with something in passing": *her arm brushing mine; flicked the paper with his finger; an arrow that glanced off the tree; a knife blade grazing the countertop; a taxi that shaved the curb; an oar skimming the surface of the pond.*

brush[2] (brŭsh) *n.* **1.a.** A dense growth of bushes or shrubs. **b.** Land covered by such a growth. **2.** Cut or broken branches. [Middle English *brusshe,* from Old French *brosse,* brushwood, from Vulgar Latin **bruscia,* perhaps from Latin *bruscum,* knot on a maple.] —**brush′y** *adj.*

brush[3] (brŭsh) *n.* A brief, often hostile or alarming encounter: *a brush with the law; a brush with death.* [Middle English, from *brushen,* to hasten, rush, probably from *brusshe,* brush. See BRUSH[1].]

brush discharge *n.* A faintly visible, relatively slow crackling discharge of electricity without sparking.

brushed (brŭsht) *adj.* Having a nap produced by brushing: *a dress made of brushed cotton.*

brush·fire also **brush fire** (brŭsh′fīr′) —*n.* **1.** A fire in low-growing, scrubby trees and brush. **2.** A relatively minor crisis. —*adj.* Minor enough to involve only small-scale mobilization of counteracting resources: *brushfire wars.*

brush·off also **brush-off** (brŭsh′ôf′, -ŏf′) *n.* An abrupt dismissal or snub.

brush·wood (brŭsh′wo͝od′) *n.* **1.** Branches that have been cut or broken off. **2.a.** Dense undergrowth. **b.** An area covered by such growth.

brush·work (brŭsh′wûrk′) *n.* **1.** Work done with a brush. **2.** The manner in which a painter applies paint with a brush.

brusque also **brusk** (brŭsk) *adj.* Abrupt and curt in manner or speech; discourteously blunt. See Synonyms at **gruff.** [French, lively, fierce, from Italian *brusco,* coarse, rough, from Late Latin

Pieter Brueghel the Elder
Self-portrait

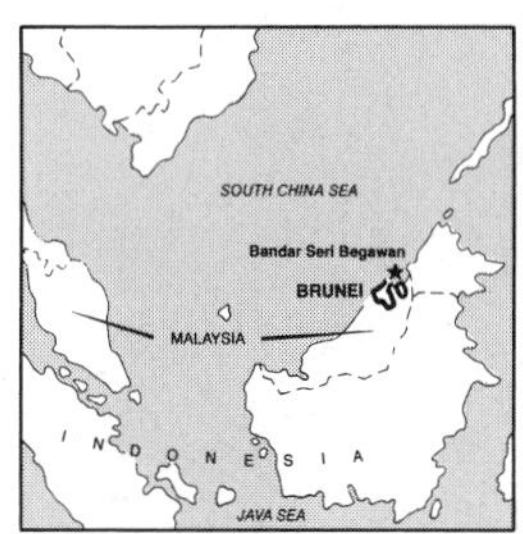

Brunei

ă pat	oi boy
ā pay	ou out
âr care	o͝o took
ä father	o͞o boot
ĕ pet	ŭ cut
ē be	ûr urge
ĭ pit	th thin
ī pie	*th* this
îr pier	hw which
ŏ pot	zh vision
ō toe	ə about, item
ô paw	♦ regionalism

Stress marks: **′** (primary); ′ (secondary), as in **dictionary** (dĭk′shə-nĕr′ē)

brūscum, perhaps blend of Latin *rūscus,* butcher's broom, and Late Latin *brūcus,* heather; see BRIAR[1].] **—brusque′ly** *adv.* **—brusque′ness** *n.*

brus·que·rie (brüs′kə-rē′) *n.* Curtness or bluntness of manner. [French, from *brusque,* brusque. See BRUSQUE.]

Brus·sels (brŭs′əlz). The capital and largest city of Belgium, in the central part of the country. Officially bilingual (Flemish and French), it became capital of Belgium in 1830. Metropolitan area population, 2,395,000.

Brussels carpet *n.* A machine-made carpet consisting of small, colored woolen loops that form a heavy, patterned pile.

Brussels griffon *n.* See **griffon** (sense 1).

Brussels lace *n.* Net lace with an appliqué design, formerly made by hand but now usually made by machine.

Brussels sprouts *pl.n. (used with a sing. or pl. verb).* **1.** A vegetable *(Brassica oleracea* var. *gemmifera)* in the mustard family, having long, stout cabbagelike buds. **2.** The edible buds of this plant.

Brussels sprouts
Brassica oleracea

brut (bro͞ot) *adj.* Very dry. Used of champagne. [French, from Old French, rough, from Latin *brūtus,* heavy. See **gʷerə-**[1] in Appendix.]

bru·tal (bro͞ot′l) *adj.* **1.** Extremely ruthless or cruel. See Synonyms at **brute. 2.** Crude or unfeeling in manner or speech. **3.** Harsh; unrelenting: *a brutal winter in the Arctic.* **4.** Disagreeably precise or penetrating: *spoke with brutal honesty.* **—bru′tal·ly** *adv.*

bru·tal·ism (bro͞ot′l-ĭz′əm) *n.* A style of architecture characterized by massive or monolithic forms typically unrelieved by exterior decoration. **—bru′tal·ist** *n.*

bru·tal·i·ty (bro͞o-tăl′ĭ-tē) *n., pl.* **-ties. 1.** The state or quality of being ruthless, cruel, harsh, or unrelenting. **2.** A ruthless, cruel, harsh, or unrelenting act.

bru·tal·ize (bro͞ot′l-īz′) *tr.v.* **-ized, -iz·ing, -iz·es. 1.** To make cruel, harsh, or unfeeling. **2.** To treat cruelly or harshly. **—bru′tal·i·za′tion** (-ĭ-zā′shən) *n.*

brute (bro͞ot) *n.* **1.** An animal; a beast. **2.** A brutal, crude, or insensitive person. **—brute** *adj.* **1.** Of or relating to beasts; animal: *"None of the brute creation requires more than food and shelter"* (Henry David Thoreau). **2.** Characteristic of a brute, especially: **a.** Entirely physical: *brute force.* **b.** Lacking or showing a lack of reason or intelligence: *a brute impulse.* **c.** Savage; cruel: *brute coercion.* **d.** Unremittingly severe: *was driven to steal food through brute necessity.* **3.** Coarse; brutish. [From Middle English, nonhuman, from Old French *brut,* from Latin *brūtus,* stupid. See **gʷerə-**[1] in Appendix.] **—brut′ism** *n.*

SYNONYMS: *brute, animal, brutish, brutal, beastly, bestial.* These adjectives apply to what is more characteristic of lower animals than of human beings. *Brute,* the least derogatory, stresses a lack of the understanding or sensibility regarded as distinguishing people from animals: *brute force. Animal* emphasizes physical nature as opposed to intellect or spirit: *animal vitality. Brutish* stresses marked lack of human refinement and sensitivity: *He had the look of a dull and brutish man. Brutal* emphasizes unfeeling cruelty: *"the brutal amusements of the bullbaiting or the cockpit"* (William Howitt). Both *beastly* and *bestial* imply degeneracy or moral degradation: *indulging beastly desires; bestial and sordid drunkenness. Beastly,* however, is often used to characterize what is merely very disagreeable: *What a beastly storm!*

brut·ish (bro͞o′tĭsh) *adj.* **1.** Of or characteristic of a brute. **2.** Crude in feeling or manner. **3.** Sensual; carnal. **4.** Rough; uncivilized: *"the Mesabi Iron Range, a brutish stretch of maroon hillocks"* (John McCormick). See Synonyms at **brute. —brut′ish·ly** *adv.* **—brut′ish·ness** *n.*

Brut·ti·um (bro͞ot′ē-əm, brŭt′-). An ancient region of southern Italy roughly occupying present-day Calabria in the toe of the Italian "boot."

Bru·tus (bro͞o′təs), **Marcus Junius.** 85?–42 B.C. Roman politician and general who conspired to assassinate Julius Caesar. In the subsequent power struggle with Mark Antony and Octavian, Brutus was defeated at the Battle of Philippi and committed suicide.

brux·ism (brŭk′sĭz′əm) *n.* The habitual, involuntary grinding or clenching of the teeth, usually during sleep, as from anger, tension, fear, or frustration. [From New Latin *brūxis,* a gnashing, from Greek *brūkein,* to gnash.]

Bry·an (brī′ən). A city of east-central Texas northwest of Houston. It is an industrial community and a research center. Population, 44,337.

Bryan, William Jennings. Called "the Great Commoner" or "the Boy Orator of the Platte." 1860–1925. American lawyer and politician who campaigned unsuccessfully for the presidency in 1896, 1900, and 1908. He is famous for his impassioned "Cross of Gold" speech advocating free silver (1896) and for his defense of fundamentalism in the Scopes trial (1925).

Bry·ansk also **Bri·ansk** (brē-änsk′). A city of western Russia southwest of Moscow. It was part of Lithuania until the 16th century. Population, 430,000.

Bry·ant (brī′ənt), **William Cullen.** 1794–1878. American poet, critic, and editor known especially for his early nature poems, such as "Thanatopsis" (1817) and "To a Waterfowl" (1821). As editor and part owner (1829–1878) of the *New York Evening Post* he advocated reforms ranging from abolitionism to free trade.

Bryce (brīs), **James.** First Viscount Bryce of Dechmont. 1838–1922. British diplomat and historian whose *American Commonwealth* (1888) is a classic study of government and politics.

Bryn·hild (brĭn′hĭld′) *n.* A Valkyrie who is revived from an enchanted sleep by Sigurd.

bryo– *pref.* Moss: *bryology.* [New Latin, from Greek *bruon,* moss, from *bruein,* to swell, teem.]

bry·ol·o·gy (brī-ŏl′ə-jē) *n.* The study of bryophytes. **—bry′o·log′i·cal** (-ə-lŏj′ĭ-kəl) *adj.*

bry·o·ny (brī′ə-nē) *n., pl.* **-nies. 1.** Any of various Eurasian tendril-bearing vines of the genus *Bryonia,* having red or black berries and tuberous roots formerly used as medicine. **2.** The black bryony. [Latin *bryōnia,* from Greek *bruōnia,* from *bruein,* to swell, teem.]

bry·o·phyte (brī′ə-fīt′) *n.* A plant of the Bryophyta, a division of photosynthetic, chiefly terrestrial, nonvascular plants, including the mosses, liverworts, and hornworts. **—bry′o·phyt′ic** (-fĭt′ĭk) *adj.*

bry·o·zo·an (brī′ə-zō′ən) *n.* Any of various small aquatic animals of the phylum Bryozoa that reproduce by budding and form mosslike or branching colonies permanently attached to stones or seaweed. Also called *moss animal, polyzoan.* **—bryozoan** *adj.* Of or belonging to the Bryozoa. [From New Latin *Bryozoa,* phylum name : BRYO– + Greek *zōia,* pl. of *zōion,* animal; see –ZOON.]

Bryth·on (brĭth′ən, -ŏn′) *n.* **1.** An ancient Celtic Briton of Cornwall, Wales, or Cumbria. **2.** One who speaks a Brittonic language. [Welsh, from Latin *Brittonēs,* Britons. See BRITON.]

Bry·thon·ic (brĭ-thŏn′ĭk) *adj.* Of or relating to the Brythons or their language or culture. **—Brythonic** *n.* Variant of **Brittonic.**

B.S. *abbr.* **1.** Bachelor of Science. **2.** Balance sheet. **3.** Bill of sale. **4.** *Obscene.* Bullshit.

BSA *abbr.* Boy Scouts of America.

B.S.A. *abbr.* Bachelor of Science in Agriculture.

B.S.A.A. *abbr.* Bachelor of Science in Applied Arts.

B.S.Arch. *abbr.* Bachelor of Science in Architecture.

B.Sc. *abbr.* Bachelor of Science.

B.S.Ch. *abbr.* Bachelor of Science in Chemistry.

B.S.Ec. *abbr.* Bachelor of Science in Economics.

B.S.Ed. *abbr.* Bachelor of Science in Education.

B.S.E.E. *abbr.* Bachelor of Science in Electrical Engineering.

B.S.For. *abbr.* Bachelor of Science in Forestry.

B.S.F.S. *abbr.* Bachelor of Science in Foreign Service.

bsh. *abbr.* Bushel.

BSI *abbr.* British Standards Institution.

B-side (bē′sīd′) *n.* The reverse side of a phonograph record, especially a single. [From the *B* on the record's label.]

bsk. *abbr.* Basket.

B.S.N. *abbr.* Bachelor of Science in Nursing.

BT (bē′tē′) *n.* A bacterium, lethal to and used to control many kinds of caterpillars that are pests of ornamental, crop, and other plants. [B(ACILLUS) T(HURINGIENSIS).]

Bt. *abbr.* Baronet.

B.T. *abbr.* Bachelor of Theology.

B.Th. *abbr.* Bachelor of Theology.

btry. *abbr.* Battery.

Btss. *abbr.* Baronetess.

Btu *abbr.* British thermal unit.

bu. *abbr.* **1.** Bureau. **2.** Or **bu.** Bushel.

bub (bŭb) *n. Slang.* Fellow. Used as a term of familiar address: *See you around, bub.* [Probably short for BROTHER.]

Bu·bas·tis (byo͞o-băs′tĭs). An ancient city of northeast Egypt in the Nile delta. It was a religious center for the worship of the cat-headed god Bast.

bub·ble (bŭb′əl) *n.* **1.** A thin, usually spherical or hemispherical film of liquid filled with air or gas: *a soap bubble.* **2.** A globular body of air or gas formed within a liquid: *air bubbles rising to the surface.* **3.** A pocket formed in a solid by air or gas that is trapped, as during cooling or hardening. **4. a.** The act or process of forming bubbles. **b.** A sound made by or as if by the forming and bursting of bubbles. **5.** Something insubstantial, groundless, or ephemeral, especially: **a.** A fantastic or impracticable idea or belief; an illusion: *didn't want to burst the new volunteers' bubble.* **b.** A speculative scheme that comes to nothing: *lost money in the real estate bubble.* **6.** Something light or effervescent: *"Macon—though terribly distressed—had to fight down a bubble of laughter"* (Anne Tyler). **7.** A usually transparent glass or plastic dome. **8.** A protective, often isolating envelope or cover: *"The Secret Service will talk of tightening protection, but no President wants to live in a bubble"* (Anthony Lewis). **—bubble** *v.* **-bled, -bling, -bles.** *—intr.* **1.** To form or give off bubbles. **2.** To move or flow with a gurgling sound: *a brook bubbling along its course.* **3.** To rise to or as if to the surface; emerge: *"Since then, the revolution has bubbled up again in many forms"* (Jonathan Schell). **4.** To display irrepressible activity or emotion: *bubbling over with excitement. —tr.* To cause to form bubbles. [From Middle English *bubelen,* to bubble.]

bubble and squeak *n. Chiefly British.* Cabbage and potatoes fried together. [Imitative of the sounds made as it cooks.]

bubble bath *n.* **1.** A perfumed preparation, such as powdered crystals or a liquid, added to bath water to make it foam. **2.** A bath to which such a preparation has been added.

bubble car *n.* A small, usually three-wheeled automobile with a transparent bubble top.

bubble chamber *n.* An apparatus in which the movement and collision of ionizing particles is determined by the examination of trails of gas bubbles that form in the paths of the particles as they move through a superheated liquid.

bubble gum *n.* Chewing gum that can be blown into bubbles.

bub·ble-gum also **bub·ble·gum** (bŭb′əl-gŭm′) *adj. Informal.* **1.** Marked by or displaying an adolescent immaturity, as in style or taste. **2.** Vapid; bland: *"Bubblegum news . . . is information packaged like a Krazy Kat cartoon"* (Tom Shales).

bub·ble·head (bŭb′əl-hĕd′) *n.* A foolish or empty-headed person: *"He presents antiwar protesters . . . as bubbleheads who didn't even know where Southeast Asia was"* (Frank Rich).

bubble memory *n. Computer Science.* A memory in which binary digits are represented by the presence or absence of magnetic bubbles.

bubble pack *n.* See **blister pack.**

♦**bub·bler** (bŭb′lər) *n. Northern U.S.* A drinking fountain. Used especially in Wisconsin.

bubble top *n.* **1.** A transparent glass or plastic dome, such as one constructed over a swimming pool or courtyard. **2.** A transparent, often bulletproof enclosure forming the top of an automobile. **—bub′ble·top′** (bŭb′əl-tŏp′) *adj.*

bub·bly (bŭb′lē) *adj.* **1.** Full of or producing bubbles: *a bubbly drink; a bubbly soap.* **2.** Resembling bubbles: *big, bubbly clouds.* **3.** Full of high spirits; effervescent: *bright, bubbly children.* **—bubbly** *n., pl.* **-blies.** *Informal.* Champagne.

bub·by (bo͝ob′ē, bo͝ob′ē) *n., pl.* **-bies.** *Slang.* A woman's breast. [Origin unknown.]

Bu·ber (bo͞o′bər), **Martin.** 1878–1965. Austrian-born Judaic scholar and philosopher whose influential *I and Thou* (1923) posits a direct personal dialogue between God and the individual.

bu·bo (bo͞o′bō, byo͞o′-) *n., pl.* **-boes.** An inflamed, tender swelling of a lymph node, especially in the area of the armpit or groin, that is characteristic of certain infections, such as plague and syphilis. [Middle English, from Late Latin *bubō, bubōn-*, from Greek *boubōn.*]

bu·bon·ic plague (bo͞o-bŏn′ĭk, byo͞o-) *n.* A contagious, often fatal epidemic disease caused by the bacterium *Yersinia pestis,* transmitted from person to person or by the bite of fleas from an infected host, especially a rat, and characterized by chills, fever, vomiting, diarrhea, and the formation of buboes.

bu·bon·o·cele (bo͞o-bŏn′ə-sēl′, byo͞o-) *n.* A partial hernia of the groin, characterized by swelling in the groin area. [Greek *boubōnokēlē* : *boubōn,* groin + *kēlē,* rupture.]

Bu·ca·ra·man·ga (bo͞o′kə-rə-măng′gə, -kä-rä-mäng′gä). A city of north-central Colombia in the Cordillera Oriental of the Andes. Founded in 1622, it is a leading commercial center. Population, 342,169.

buc·cal (bŭk′əl) *adj.* Of or relating to the cheeks or the mouth cavity. [From Latin *bucca,* cheek.]

buc·ca·neer (bŭk′ə-nîr′) *n.* **1.** A pirate, especially one of the freebooters who preyed on Spanish shipping in the West Indies during the 17th century. **2.** A ruthless speculator or adventurer. [French *boucanier,* from *boucaner,* to cure meat, from *boucan,* barbecue frame, possibly from Arawakan or Tupinamba (a Tupian language) *bocan,* rack.] **—buc′ca·neer′** *v.*

WORD HISTORY: The Errol Flynn–like figure of the buccaneer pillaging the Spanish Main may seem less dashing if we realize that the term *buccaneer* corresponds to the word *barbecuer.* The first recorded use of the French word *boucanier,* which was borrowed into English, referred to a person on the islands of Hispaniola and Tortuga who hunted wild oxen and boars and smoked the meat in a barbecue frame known in French as a *boucan.* This French word came from an Arawakan or Tupinamba word meaning "a rack, sometimes used for roasting or for storing things, or a racklike platform supporting an Indian house." The original barbecuers seem to have subsequently adapted a more remunerative way of life, piracy, which accounts for the new meaning given to the word. *Buccaneer* is recorded first in 1661 in its earlier sense in English; the sense we are familiar with is recorded in 1690.

buc·ca·neer·ing (bŭk′ə-nîr′ĭng) *adj.* Showing boldness and enterprise, as in business, often to the point of recklessness or unscrupulousness.

Bu·ceph·a·lus (byo͞o-sĕf′ə-ləs) *n.* Alexander the Great's war horse.

Buch·an (bŭk′ən, bŭKH′-), Sir **John.** First Baron Tweedsmuir. 1875–1940. Scottish writer and government official who was governor-general of Canada (1935–1940) but is best known for his adventure novels, such as *The Thirty-Nine Steps* (1915).

Bu·chan·an (byo͞o-kăn′ən, bə-), **James.** 1791–1868. The 15th President of the United States (1857–1861). He tried to maintain a balance between proslavery and antislavery factions, but his moderate views angered radicals in both North and South, and he was unable to forestall the secession of South Carolina on December 20, 1860.

Bu·cha·rest (bo͞o′kə-rĕst′, byo͞o′-). The capital and largest city of Romania, in the southeast part of the country on a tributary of the Danube River. Founded in the 14th century, it soon became a fortress and commercial center on the trade route to Constantinople. Population, 1,995,156.

Bu·chen·wald (bo͞o′kən-wôld′, -KHən-vält′). A village of central Germany near Weimar. It was the site of a Nazi concentration camp during World War II.

Buch·man (bo͝ok′mən, bŭk′-), **Frank Nathan Daniel.** 1878–1961. American evangelist who preached at Oxford University in the 1920's, where he founded the Oxford Group, or Buchmanism, which later became the nucleus of Moral Re-Armament.

bu·chu (bo͞o′ko͞o, byo͞o′kyo͞o) *n.* Any of various shrubs of the southern African genus *Agathosma,* especially *A. betulina* and *A. crenulata,* whose leaves are used as a mild diuretic and also yield an aromatic oil used for flavoring. [Afrikaans *boegoe,* probably from Zulu *bucu,* perhaps ultimately of Khoikhoin origin.]

buck¹ (bŭk) *n.* **1.a.** The adult male of some animals, such as the deer, antelope, or rabbit. **b.** Antelope considered as a group: *a herd of buck.* **2.a.** A robust or high-spirited young man. **b.** A fop. **3.** *Offensive.* Used as a disparaging term for a Native American or Black man. **4.** An act or instance of bucking: *a horse that unseated its rider on the first buck.* **5.a.** Buckskin. **b. bucks.** Buckskin breeches or shoes. **—buck** *v.* **bucked, buck·ing, bucks.** *—intr.* **1.** To leap upward arching the back: *The horse bucked in fright.* **2.** To charge with the head lowered; butt. **3.** To make sudden jerky movements; jolt: *The motor bucked and lurched before it finally ran smoothly.* **4.** To resist stubbornly and obstinately; balk. **5.** *Informal.* To strive with determination: *bucking for a promotion.* *—tr.* **1.** To throw or toss by bucking: *buck off a rider; bucked the packsaddle off its back.* **2.** To oppose directly and stubbornly; go against: *"Los Angeles County, the most populous county in the country, is bucking the trend"* (American Demographics). **3.** *Football.* To charge into (an opponent's line) carrying the ball. **4.** *Archaic.* To butt against with the head. **—buck** *adj.* Of the lowest rank in a specified military category: *a buck private; a buck sergeant.* ***—phrasal verb.*** **buck up.** To summon one's courage or spirits; hearten: *My friends tried to buck me up after I lost the contest.* [Middle English *bukke,* from Old English *buc,* male deer, and *bucca,* male goat.] **—buck′er** *n.*

buck² (bŭk) *n.* **1.** A sawhorse or sawbuck. **2.** A leather-covered frame used for gymnastic vaulting. [Alteration (influenced by BUCK¹) of Dutch *bok,* male goat, trestle, from Middle Dutch *boc.*]

buck³ (bŭk) *n. Informal.* **1.** A dollar. **2.** An amount of money: *working overtime to make an extra buck.* [Short for BUCKSKIN (from its use in trade).]

buck⁴ (bŭk) *n. Games.* A counter or marker formerly passed from one poker player to another to indicate an obligation, especially one's turn to deal. ***—idiom.*** **the buck stops here.** *Slang.* The ultimate responsibility rests here. [Short for *buckhorn knife* (from its use as a marker in poker).]

Buck (bŭk), **Pearl Sydenstricker.** 1892–1973. American writer whose life as a missionary in China lent a vivid immediacy to her novels, including *The Good Earth* (1931). She won the 1938 Nobel Prize for literature.

♦**buck·a·roo** also **buck·er·oo** (bŭk′ə-ro͞o′) *n., pl.* **-roos** or **-oos.** *Chiefly California.* See **cowboy** (sense 1). [Alteration (perhaps influenced by BUCK¹) of Spanish *vaquero,* from *vaca,* cow, from Latin *vacca.*]

buck·bean (bŭk′bēn′) *n.* A perennial herb *(Menyanthes trifoliata)* native to the Northern Hemisphere and having trifoliate leaves and clusters of white, pink, or purplish flowers. [Translation of Flemish *bocks boonen,* goat's beans : *bocks,* goat's + *boonen,* beans.]

buck·board (bŭk′bôrd′, -bōrd′) *n.* A four-wheeled open carriage with the seat or seats attached to a flexible board running between the front and rear axles. [Obsolete *buck,* body of a wagon (from Middle English *bouk,* belly, from Old English *būc*) + BOARD.]

♦**buck·er·oo** (bŭk′ə-ro͞o′) *n. Chiefly California.* Variant of **buckaroo.**

buck·et (bŭk′ĭt) *n.* **1.a.** A cylindrical vessel used for holding or carrying liquids or solids; a pail. **b.** The amount that a bucket can hold: *One bucket of paint will be enough for the ceiling.* **2.** A unit of dry measure in the U.S. Customary System equal to 2 pecks (17.6 liters). See table at **measurement. 3.** A receptacle on various machines, such as the scoop of a power shovel or the compartments on a water wheel, used to gather and convey material. **4.** *Basketball.* A basket. **—bucket** *v.* **-et·ed, -et·ing, -ets.** *—tr.* **1.** To hold, carry, or put in a bucket: *bucket up water from a well.* **2.** To ride (a horse) long and hard. *—intr.* **1.** To move or proceed rapidly and jerkily: *bucketing over the unpaved lane.* **2.** To make haste; hustle. ***—idiom.*** **a drop in the bucket.** An insufficient or inconsequential amount in comparison with what is required. [Middle English, from Old French *buket,* of Germanic origin.]

bucket brigade *n.* A line of people formed to fight a fire by passing buckets of water from a source to the fire.

bucket seat *n.* A single, usually low seat with a contoured back, typically used in some automobiles.

bucket shop *n.* A fraudulent brokerage operation in which orders to buy and sell are accepted but no executions take place. Instead, the operators expect to profit when customers close out their positions at a loss. [From *bucket shop,* a saloon selling small amounts of liquor in buckets, from its resemblance to the fore-

James Buchanan

buckboard
Adirondack buckboard

ă pat	oi boy
ā pay	ou out
âr care	o͝o took
ä father	o͞o boot
ĕ pet	ŭ cut
ē be	ûr urge
ĭ pit	th thin
ī pie	*th* this
îr pier	hw which
ŏ pot	zh vision
ō toe	ə about, item
ô paw	♦ regionalism

Stress marks: ′ (primary); ′ (secondary), as in **dictionary** (dĭk′shə-nĕr′ē)

runner of such brokerage operations, which dealt in small units of stocks and commodities.]

buck·eye (bŭk′ī′) *n.* **1.** Any of various North American trees or shrubs of the genus *Aesculus,* having palmately compound, opposite leaves, erect panicles of white to red or yellow flowers, and large, shiny seeds with a large attachment scar. All parts of the plant are poisonous. **2.** The spiny or smooth fruit of any of these plants. **3.** The large, shiny brown seed of such a fruit. [BUCK[1] + EYE.]

buck fever *n.* Nervous excitement felt by a novice hunter at the first sight of game.

buck·horn (bŭk′hôrn′) *n.* **1.** The horn of a buck. **2.** The material of such a horn, used especially to make handles for knives and tools.

buck·hound (bŭk′hound′) *n.* A hound used for coursing deer.

Buck·ing·ham (bŭk′ĭng-əm, -hăm′), First Duke of. Originally George Villiers. 1592–1628. English courtier and statesman whose military and political policies caused continual friction with Parliament. He was assassinated by a disgruntled naval officer.

Buckingham, Second Duke of. Originally George Villiers. 1628–1687. English courtier who was a prominent member of the influential group known as the Cabal that formed the ministry of Charles II after the Restoration. A vain and ambitious individual, Buckingham was dismissed for misconduct in 1674.

buck·jump (bŭk′jŭmp′) *intr.v.* **-jumped, -jump·ing, -jumps. 1.** To buck, as a horse or mule does. **2.** To move in sudden jerks; lurch. **—buck′jump·er** *n.*

buck·le (bŭk′əl) *n.* **1.** A clasp for fastening two ends, as of straps or a belt, in which a device attached to one of the ends is fitted or coupled to the other. **2.** An ornament that resembles this clasp, such as a metal square on a shoe or hat. **3.** An instance of bending, warping, or crumpling; a bend or bulge. **—buckle** *v.* **-led, -ling, -les.** —*tr.* **1.** To fasten with a buckle. **2.** To cause to bend, warp, or crumple. —*intr.* **1.** To become fastened with a buckle. **2.** To bend, warp, or crumple, as under pressure or heat. **3.** To give way; collapse: *My knees buckled with fear.* **4.** To succumb, as to exhaustion or authority; give in: *finally buckled under the excessive demands of the job.* **—*phrasal verbs.* buckle down.** To apply oneself with determination. **buckle up.** To use a safety belt, especially in an automobile. [Middle English *bokel,* from Old French *boucle,* from Latin *buccula,* cheek strap of a helmet, diminutive of *bucca,* cheek.]

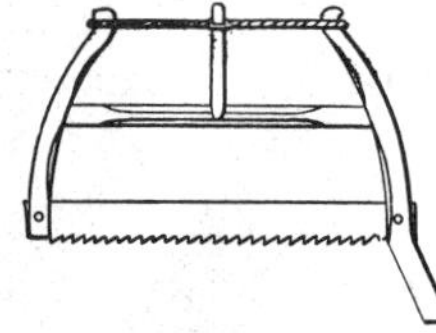

bucksaw

buck·ler (bŭk′lər) *n.* **1.** A small, round shield either carried or worn on the arm. **2.** A means of protection; a defense: *"has enjoyed a reputation as a shield and buckler for . . . the academic avant-garde"* (Donal Henahan). **—buckler** *tr.v.* **-lered, -ler·ing, -lers.** To shield; protect. [Middle English *bokeler,* from Old French *bouclier,* from *boucle,* boss on a shield, from Latin *buccula,* diminutive of *bucca,* cheek.]

♦**buck-na·ked** (bŭk′nĕk′ĭd) *adv. & adj. Chiefly Southern U.S.* Bare-naked. [Origin unknown.]

buck·o (bŭk′ō) *n., pl.* **-oes. 1.** A blustering or bossy person. **2.** *Irish.* A young man; a lad. [Alteration of BUCK[1].]

buck-pass·ing (bŭk′păs′ĭng) *n. Informal.* The shifting of responsibility or blame to another: *"smothered in avalanches of recriminations and orgies of buck-passing"* (Forbes). [BUCK[4] (from a poker player's passing the marker, or buck, to the next player when not wanting to deal).] **—buck′-pass′er** *n.*

buck·ram (bŭk′rəm) *n.* **1.** A coarse cotton fabric heavily sized with glue, used for stiffening garments and in bookbinding. **2.** *Archaic.* Rigid formality. **—buckram** *adj.* Resembling or suggesting buckram, as in stiffness or formality: *"a wondrous buckram style"* (Thomas Carlyle). **—buckram** *tr.v.* **-ramed, -ram·ing, -rams.** To stiffen with or as if with buckram. [Middle English *bukeram,* fine linen, from Old French *boquerant* and from Old Italian *bucherame,* both after BUKHARA, from which fine linen was once imported.]

Buddha[1]
Sandstone carved Buddha, Yungang, China

buck·saw (bŭk′sô′) *n.* A woodcutting saw, usually set in an H-shaped frame. [From BUCK[2].]

buck·shee (bŭk′shē) *Chiefly British. n.* **1.** Something extra or left over that is obtained free. **2.** An extra ration. **—buckshee** *adj.* **1.** Free of charge; gratis: *"If they deposit these shares, too, in the scheme, they will get further buckshee shares on a one-for-one basis"* (Economist). **2.** Unsolicited; gratuitous: *"The title was a bit of buckshee deceit, and had little to do with the plot"* (Financial Times). [Variant of BAKSHEESH.]

buck·shot (bŭk′shŏt′) *n.* A large lead shot for shotgun shells, used especially in hunting big game.

buck·skin (bŭk′skĭn′) *n.* **1.a.** The skin of a male deer. **b.** A soft, grayish-yellow leather usually having a suede finish, once made from deerskins but now generally made from sheepskins. **2. buckskins.** Clothing, especially breeches or shoes, made from buckskin. **3.** A person who wears buckskins, especially an American backwoodsman or soldier in the Revolutionary War. **4.** A horse of a grayish-yellow color. **—buck′skin′** *adj.*

buck·thorn (bŭk′thôrn′) *n.* Any of various shrubs or small trees of the genus *Rhamnus,* which includes several ornamentals and a few medicinal species such as the cascara buckthorn. [Translation of New Latin *cervī spīna* : *cervī,* genitive of *cervus,* buck + *spīna,* thorn.]

buck·tooth (bŭk′to͞oth′) *n.* A prominent, projecting upper front tooth. [BUCK[1] + TOOTH.] **—buck′toothed′** (-to͞otht′) *adj.*

buck·wheat (bŭk′hwēt′, -wēt′) *n.* **1.a.** An annual Asian plant *(Fagopyrum esculentum)* having clusters of small whitish or pinkish flowers and small, seedlike, triangular fruits. **b.** The edible fruits of this plant, used either whole or ground into flour. **2.** Any of several similar or related plants. [Probably partial translation of Middle Dutch *boecweite* : *boek,* beech; see **bhāgo-** in Appendix + *weite,* wheat.]

bu·col·ic (byo͞o-kŏl′ĭk) *adj.* **1.** Of or characteristic of the countryside or its people; rustic. See Synonyms at **rural. 2.** Of or characteristic of shepherds or flocks; pastoral. **—bucolic** *n.* **1.** A pastoral poem. **2.** A farmer or shepherd; a rustic. [Latin *būcolicus,* pastoral, from Greek *boukolikos,* from *boukolos,* cowherd : *bous,* cow; see **g[w]ou-** in Appendix + *-kolos,* herdsman; see **k[w]el-[1]** in Appendix.] **—bu·col′i·cal·ly** *adv.*

Bu·co·vi·na (bo͞o′kə-vē′nə). See **Bukovina.**

bud[1] (bŭd) *n.* **1.** *Botany.* **a.** A small protuberance on a stem or branch, sometimes enclosed in protective scales and containing an undeveloped shoot, leaf, or flower. **b.** The stage or condition of having buds: *branches in full bud.* **2.** *Biology.* **a.** An asexual reproductive structure, as in yeast or a hydra, that consists of an outgrowth capable of developing into a new individual. **b.** A small, rounded organic part, such as a taste bud, that resembles a plant bud. **3.** A person or thing that is not yet fully developed: *the bud of a new idea.* **—bud** *v.* **bud·ded, bud·ding, buds.** —*intr.* **1.** To put forth or produce buds: *a plant that buds in early spring.* **2.** To develop or grow from or as if from a bud: *"listened sympathetically for a moment, a bemused smile budding forth"* (Washington Post). **3.** To be in an undeveloped stage or condition. **4.** To reproduce asexually by forming a bud. —*tr.* **1.** To cause to put forth buds. **2.** To graft a bud onto (a plant). [Middle English *budde.*] **—bud′der** *n.*

bud[2] (bŭd) *n. Informal.* Friend; chum. Used as a form of familiar address for a man or boy: *Move along, bud.* [Short for BUDDY.]

Bu·da·pest (bo͞o′də-pĕst′, -pĕsht′). The capital and largest city of Hungary, in the north-central part of the country on the Danube River. It was formed in 1873 by the union of Buda on the right bank of the river with Pest on the left bank. The city was the center of the Hungarian uprising in 1956. Population, 2,071,484.

Bud·dha[1] (bo͞o′də, bo͝od′ə). Originally Siddhartha Gautama. 563?–483? B.C. Indian mystic and founder of Buddhism. He began preaching after achieving supreme enlightenment at the age of 35.

Bud·dha[2] (bo͞o′də, bo͝od′ə) *n.* **1.** One who has achieved a state of perfect spiritual enlightenment in accordance with the teachings of Buddha. **2.** A representation or likeness of Buddha. [Sanskrit *buddha-,* enlightened, past participle of *bodhati,* he awakes. See **bheudh-** in Appendix.]

Bud·dha·hood (bo͞o′də-ho͝od′, bo͝od′ə-) *n.* A state of spiritual enlightenment in accordance with Buddhist teachings.

Bud·dhism (bo͞o′dĭz′əm, bo͝od′ĭz′-) *n.* **1.** The doctrine, attributed to Buddha, that suffering is inseparable from existence but that inward extinction of the self and of worldly desire culminates in a state of spiritual enlightenment beyond both suffering and existence. **2.** The religion represented by the many groups, especially numerous in Asia, that profess varying forms of this doctrine and that venerate Buddha. **—Bud′dhist** *adj. & n.* **—Bud·dhis′tic** *adj.*

bud·ding (bŭd′ĭng) *n.* A form of asexual reproduction in which an outgrowth developing on a parent organism detaches to produce a new individual.

bud·dle (bŭd′l) *n.* An inclined trough in which crushed ore is washed with running water to flush away impurities. [Probably from Low German *buddeln,* to agitate.]

bud·dle·ia (bŭd′lē-ə, bŭd-lē′ə) *n.* See **butterfly bush.** [New Latin, after Adam *Buddle* (died 1715), British botanist.]

bud·dy (bŭd′ē) *Informal. n., pl.* **-dies. 1.** A good friend; a comrade. **2.** A partner, especially one of a pair or team associated under the buddy system. **3.** Friend or comrade; chum. Used as a form of familiar address, especially for a man or boy: *Watch it, buddy.* **—buddy** *intr.v.* **-died, -dy·ing, -dies.** To associate as a buddy or buddies: *buddied around with the older guys.* **—*phrasal verb.* buddy up.** To ingratiate oneself, as by presuming friendship: *buddied up to the coach in hopes of making the team.* [Probably alteration of BROTHER.]

bud·dy-bud·dy (bŭd′ē-bŭd′ē) *adj. Informal.* Showing or marked by great outward friendship.

buddy stores *pl.n.* Aircraft fuel tanks designed to transfer fuel from the host plane to another plane, such as a fighter, during flight.

buddy system *n.* An arrangement in which persons are paired, as for mutual safety or assistance.

budge[1] (bŭj) *v.* **budged, budg·ing, budg·es.** —*intr.* **1.** To move or stir slightly: *The child was stuck tight and couldn't budge.* **2.** To alter a position or attitude: *had made the decision and wouldn't budge.* —*tr.* **1.** To cause to move slightly. **2.** To cause to alter a position or attitude: *an adamant critic who couldn't be budged.* [Old French *bouger,* from Vulgar Latin **bullicāre,* to bubble, from Latin *bullīre,* to boil.]

budge[2] (bŭj) *n.* Fur made from lambskin dressed with the wool outside, formerly used to trim academic robes. **—budge** *adj. Ar-*

chaic. Overformal; pompous. [Middle English *bouge,* from Anglo-Norman, from Medieval Latin *bugia,* probably from Latin *bulga,* leather bag. See BUDGET.]

budg·er·i·gar (bŭj′ə-rē-gär′, bŭj′ə-rē′-) *n.* A parakeet *(Melopsittacus undulatus)* native to Australia and having green, yellow, or blue plumage. It is a popular cage bird bred in a variety of colors not found in wild populations. Also called *shell parakeet.* [Yuwaalaraay (Aboriginal language of southeast Australia) *gijirrigaa.*]

budg·et (bŭj′ĭt) *n.* **1.a.** An itemized summary of estimated or intended expenditures for a given period along with proposals for financing them: *submitted the annual budget to Congress.* **b.** A systematic plan for the expenditure of a usually fixed resource, such as money or time, during a given period: *A new car will not be part of our budget this year.* **c.** The total sum of money allocated for a particular purpose or period of time: *a project with an annual budget of five million dollars.* **2.** A stock or collection with definite limits: *"his budget of general knowledge"* (William Hazlitt). **—budget** *v.* **-et·ed, -et·ing, -ets.** *—tr.* **1.** To plan in advance the expenditure of: *needed help budgeting our income; budgeted my time wisely.* **2.** To enter or account for in a budget: *forgot to budget the car payments.* *—intr.* To make or use a budget. **—budget** *adj.* **1.** Of or relating to a budget: *budget items approved by Congress.* **2.** Appropriate to a budget; inexpensive: *a budget car; budget meals.* [Middle English *bouget,* wallet, from Old French *bougette,* diminutive of *bouge,* leather bag, from Latin *bulga,* of Celtic origin. See **bhelgh-** in Appendix.] **—budg′et·ar′y** (bŭj′ĭ-tĕr′ē) *adj.* **—budg′et·er, budg′et·eer′** (-ĭ-tîr′) *n.*

budg·ie (bŭj′ē) *n. Informal.* A budgerigar.

bud·worm (bŭd′wûrm′) *n.* A larva of several tortricid moths, especially the spruce budworm, that devours plant buds.

Bue·na Park (bwā′nə). A city of southern California west-northwest of Anaheim. Knott's Berry Farm, a re-created gold rush town, is here. Population, 64,165.

Bue·na·ven·tu·ra (bwā′nə-vĕn-to͝or′ə, -tyo͝or′ə, bwĕ′nä-vĕn-to͞o′rä). A city of western Colombia on **Buenaventura Bay,** an inlet of the Pacific Ocean. The city was originally settled in the 1540's. Population, 157,528.

Bue·na Vis·ta (bwā′nə vĭs′tə, bwĕ′nä vēs′tä). A locality in northern Mexico just south of Saltillo. In the Mexican War U.S. forces led by Zachary Taylor defeated a Mexican army commanded by Santa Anna on February 22–23, 1847.

Bue·nos Ai·res (bwā′nəs âr′ēz, ī′rĭz, bwĕ′nôs ī′rĕs). The capital and largest city of Argentina, in the eastern part of the country on the Río de la Plata. Founded by the Spanish in 1536, it became the national capital in 1862. The highly industrialized city is also a major port. Population, 2,922,829.

buff¹ (bŭf) *n.* **1.** A soft, thick, undyed leather made chiefly from the skins of buffalo, elk, or oxen. **2.** A military uniform coat made of such leather. **3.** *Color.* A pale, light, or moderate yellowish pink to yellow, including moderate orange yellow to light yellowish brown. **4.** *Informal.* Bare skin: *swimming in the buff.* **5.** A piece of soft material, such as velvet or leather, often mounted on a block and used for polishing. **—buff** *adj.* **1.** Made or formed of buff: *a buff jacket.* **2.** *Color.* Of the color buff. **—buff** *tr.v.* **buffed, buff·ing, buffs. 1.** To polish or shine with a piece of soft material. **2.** To soften the surface of (leather) by raising a nap. **3.** To make the color of buff. [From obsolete *buffle,* buffalo, from French *buffle,* from Late Latin *būfalus.* See BUFFALO.]

buff² (bŭf) *n. Informal.* One that is enthusiastic and knowledgeable about a subject: *a Civil War buff.* [From the buff-colored uniform worn by New York volunteer firemen around 1920, originally applied to an enthusiast of fires and fire fighting.]

buf·fa·lo (bŭf′ə-lō′) *n., pl.* **buffalo** or **-loes** or **-los. 1.a.** Any of several oxlike Old World mammals of the family Bovidae, such as the water buffalo and Cape buffalo. **b.** The North American bison, *Bison bison.* **2.** The buffalo fish. **—buffalo** *tr.v.* **-loed, -lo·ing, -loes. 1.** To intimidate, as by a display of confidence or authority: *"The board couldn't buffalo the federal courts as it had the Comptroller"* (American Banker). **2.** To deceive; hoodwink: *"Too often . . . job seekers have buffaloed lenders as to their competency and training"* (H. Jane Lehman). **3.** To confuse; bewilder. [Italian *bufalo* or Portuguese or Spanish *búfalo,* from Late Latin *būfalus,* from Latin *būbalus,* from Greek *boubalos.*]

WORD HISTORY: The buffalo is so closely associated with the Wild West that it would seem natural to assume that its name comes from a Native American word, as is the case with the words *moose* and *skunk.* In fact, however, *buffalo* can probably be traced back by way of one or more of the Romance languages, such as Portuguese, Spanish, or Italian, through Vulgar Latin and Latin and ultimately to the Greek word *boubalos,* meaning "an antelope or a buffalo." The buffalo referred to by the Greek and Latin words was, of course, not the American one but rather an Old World mammal, such as the water buffalo of southern Asia. Applied to the North American mammal, *buffalo* is in fact a misnomer, *bison* being the preferred term. As far as everyday usage is concerned, however, *buffalo,* first recorded for the American mammal in 1635, is older than *bison,* first recorded in 1774.

Buf·fa·lo (bŭf′ə-lō′). A city of western New York at the eastern end of Lake Erie on the Canadian border. It is a major Great Lakes port of entry and an important manufacturing and milling center. Population, 357,870.

buffalo berry *n.* **1.** Any of three North American shrubs or small trees of the genus *Shepherdia,* having small yellowish flowers, drupelike fruits, and foliage that is covered with silvery scales. **2.** The berry of any of these plants.

Buffalo Bill (bĭl). See William Frederick **Cody.**

buffalo bug *n.* See **carpet beetle.**

buffalo fish *n.* Any of several suckers of the genus *Ictiobus,* having a humped back and found mostly in the Mississippi Valley.

buffalo gnat *n.* See **black fly.**

buffalo grass *n.* A mat-forming perennial grass *(Buchloe dactyloides)* native to the plains of central North America, important as a forage grass and sometimes used for lawns.

Buffalo Grove. A village of northeast Illinois, a suburb of Chicago. Population, 22,230.

buffalo robe *n.* The dressed skin of the North American bison, used as a lap robe, cape, or blanket.

Buffalo wings *pl.n.* Fried chicken wings served with hot sauce and blue cheese dressing. [After BUFFALO, where they were first served.]

buff·er¹ (bŭf′ər) *n.* **1.** One that buffs, especially a piece of soft leather or cloth used to shine or polish. **2.** A buffing wheel.

buff·er² (bŭf′ər) *n.* **1.** Something that lessens or absorbs the shock of an impact. **2.** One that protects by intercepting or moderating adverse pressures or influences: *"A sense of humor . . . may have served as a buffer against the . . . shocks of disappointment"* (James Russell Lowell). **3.** Something that separates potentially antagonistic entities, as an area between two rival powers that serves to lessen the danger of conflict. **4.** *Chemistry.* A substance that minimizes change in the acidity of a solution when an acid or base is added to the solution. **5.** *Computer Science.* A device or area used to store data temporarily and deliver it at a rate different from that at which it was received. **—buffer** *tr.v.* **-ered, -er·ing, -ers. 1.** To act as a buffer for or between. **2.** *Chemistry.* To treat (a solution) with a buffer. [Perhaps from *buff,* blow, buffet, from Middle English *buffe,* short for *buffet,* from Old French. See BUFFET².]

buffer state *n.* A neutral state lying between two rival or potentially hostile states and serving to prevent conflict between them.

buffer zone *n.* A neutral area between hostile or belligerent forces that serves to prevent conflict.

buf·fet¹ (bə-fā′, bo͞o-) *n.* **1.** A large sideboard with drawers and cupboards. **2.a.** A counter or table from which meals or refreshments are served. **b.** A restaurant having such a counter. **3.** A meal at which guests serve themselves from various dishes displayed on a table or sideboard. **—buffet** *adj.* Informally served: *a buffet luncheon.* [French.]

buf·fet² (bŭf′ĭt) *n.* A blow or cuff with or as if with the hand. **—buffet** *v.* **-fet·ed, -fet·ing, -fets.** *—tr.* **1.** To hit or beat, especially repeatedly. **2.** To strike against forcefully; batter: *winds that buffeted the tent.* See Synonyms at **beat. 3.** To drive or force with or as if with repeated blows: *was buffeted about from job to job by the vagaries of the economy.* **4.** To force (one's way) with difficulty. *—intr.* To force one's way with difficulty: *a ship buffeting against the wind.* [Middle English, from Old French *buffet,* diminutive of *buffe,* blow.] **—buf′fet·er** *n.*

buf·fi (bo͞o′fē) *n.* A plural of **buffo.**

buff·ing wheel (bŭf′ĭng) *n.* A wheel covered with a soft material, such as velvet or leather, for shining and polishing metal.

buffing wheel

buf·fle·head (bŭf′əl-hĕd′) *n.* A small North American diving duck *(Bucephala albeola)* having black and white plumage and a densely feathered, rounded head. Also called *butterball.* [Obsolete *buffle,* buffalo (from French, from Late Latin *būfalus;* see BUFFALO) + HEAD.]

buf·fo (bo͞o′fō) *n., pl.* **-fi** (-fē) or **-fos.** *Music.* A man who sings comic opera roles. [Italian, from *buffare,* to puff, of imitative origin.]

Buf·fon (bo͞o-fôɴ′), Comte **Georges Louis Leclerc de.** 1707–1788. French naturalist whose monumental *Histoire Naturelle* (36 volumes, 1749–1788; 8 additional volumes completed by assistants and published in 1804) laid the foundation for later studies in biology, zoology, and comparative anatomy.

buf·foon (bə-fo͞on′) *n.* **1.** A clown; a jester: *a court buffoon.* **2.** A person given to clowning and joking. **3.** A ludicrous or bumbling person; a fool. [French *bouffon,* from Old Italian *buffone,* from *buffa,* jest, from *buffare,* to puff, of imitative origin.] **—buf·foon′er·y** (bə-fo͞o′nə-rē) *n.*

bug (bŭg) *n.* **1.** A true bug. **2.** An insect or similar organism, such as a centipede or an earwig. **3.a.** A disease-producing microorganism: *a flu bug.* **b.** The illness or disease so produced: *"stomach flu, a cold, or just some bug going around"* (David Smollar). **4.a.** A defect or difficulty, as in a system or design. **b.** *Computer Science.* A defect in the code or routine of a program. **5.** An enthusiasm or obsession: *got bitten by the writing bug.* **6.** An enthusiast or devotee; a buff: *a model train bug.* **7.** An electronic listening device, such as a hidden microphone or wiretap, used in surveillance: *planted a bug in the suspect's room.* **—bug** *v.* **bugged, bug·ging, bugs.** *—intr.* To grow large; bulge: *My eyes bugged when I saw the mess.* *—tr.* **1.a.** To annoy; pester. **b.**

ă pat	oi boy
ā pay	ou out
âr care	o͝o took
ä father	o͞o boot
ĕ pet	ŭ cut
ē be	ûr urge
ĭ pit	th thin
ī pie	*th* this
îr pier	hw which
ŏ pot	zh vision
ō toe	ə about, item
ô paw	♦ regionalism

Stress marks: **′** (primary); ′ (secondary), as in **dictionary** (dĭk′shə-nĕr′ē)

To prey on; worry: *a memory that bugged me for years.* **2.** To equip (a room or telephone circuit, for example) with a concealed electronic listening device. **3.** To make (the eyes) bulge or grow large. —***phrasal verbs.* bug off.** *Slang.* To leave someone alone; go away. **bug out.** *Slang.* **1.** To leave or quit, usually in a hurry. **2.** To avoid a responsibility or duty. Often used with *on* or *of: bugged out on his partners at the first sign of trouble.* —***idiom.* put a bug in (someone's) ear.** *Informal.* To impart useful information to (another) in a subtle, discreet way. [Origin unknown.] —**bug′ger** *n.*

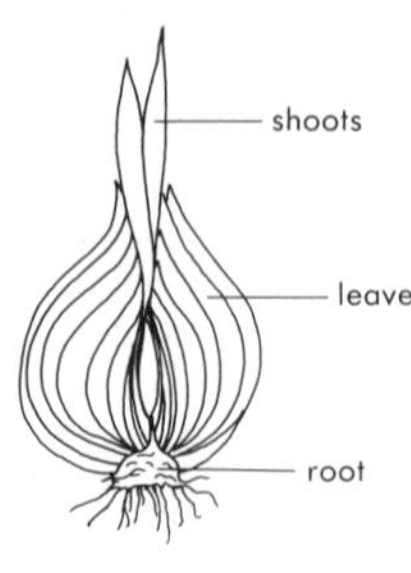

bulb

Bug (bo͝og, bo͝ok). **1.** Also **Western Bug.** A river of eastern Europe rising in the southwest Ukraine and flowing about 772 km (480 mi) through Poland to the Vistula River near Warsaw. **2.** Also **Southern Bug.** A river of southern Ukraine rising in the southwest part and flowing about 853 km (530 mi) generally southeast to the Black Sea.

bug·a·boo (bŭg′ə-bo͞o′) *n., pl.* **-boos. 1.** An object of obsessive, usually exaggerated fear or anxiety: *"Boredom, laziness and failure . . . These bugaboos, magnified by imagination, keep* [the workaholic] *running"* (Dun's Review). **2.** A recurring or persistent problem: *"the bugaboos that have plagued vision systems: high price and slow throughput"* (Lawrence A. Goshorn). [Perhaps of Celtic origin.]

Bu·gan·da (bo͞o-găn′də, byo͞o-). A region and former kingdom of eastern Africa on the northern shore of Lake Victoria in present-day Uganda. It was a British protectorate from 1900 until 1962, when it joined independent Uganda.

bug·bane (bŭg′bān′) *n.* Any of several plants of the genus *Cimicifuga,* native to northern temperate regions and including the black cohosh.

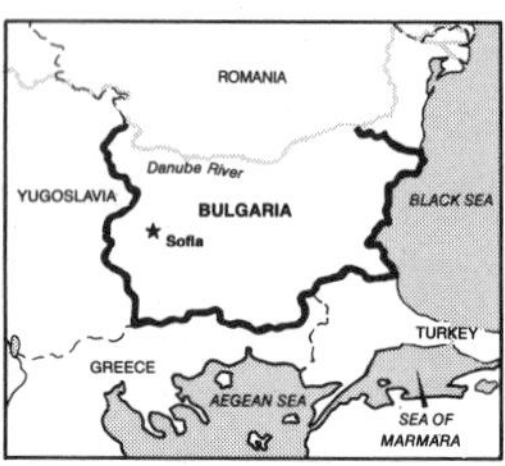

Bulgaria

bug·bear (bŭg′bâr′) *n.* **1.** A bugaboo. **2.** A fearsome imaginary creature, especially one evoked to frighten children. [Obsolete *bug,* hobgoblin (from Middle English *bugge*) + BEAR[2].]

bug-eyed (bŭg′īd′) *adj.* **1.** Having protruding eyes. **2.** Wide-eyed, as with astonishment or curiosity; agog.

bug·ger (bŭg′ər, bo͝og′-) *n.* **1.** *Vulgar.* A sodomite. **2.** A contemptible or disreputable person. **3.** A fellow; a chap: *"He's a silly little bugger, then"* (John le Carré). —**bugger** *v.* **-gered, -ger·ing, -gers.** *Vulgar.* —*intr.* To practice sodomy. —*tr.* To practice sodomy with. [Middle English *bougre,* heretic, from Old French *boulgre,* from Medieval Latin *Bulgarus.* See BULGAR.]

bug·ger·y (bŭg′ə-rē, bo͝og′-) *n. Vulgar.* Sodomy.

♦**bug·gy**[1] (bŭg′ē) *n., pl.* **-gies. 1.** A small, light, one-horse carriage usually having four wheels in the United States and two wheels in Great Britain. **2.** A baby carriage. **3.** *Informal.* An automobile. **4.** *Chiefly Southern U.S.* A shopping cart, especially for groceries. [Origin unknown.]

bug·gy[2] (bŭg′ē) *adj.* **-gi·er, -gi·est. 1.** Infested with bugs. **2.** *Slang.* Crazy. —**bug′gi·ness** *n.*

bug·house (bŭg′hous′) *n. Slang.* A mental health facility. [Probably from BUG, enthusiast.]

bug juice *n. Slang.* A sweet flavored drink, such as punch, that is usually not carbonated. [After its unattractive color and flavor.]

bu·gle[1] (byo͞o′gəl) *n. Music.* A brass wind instrument somewhat shorter than a trumpet and lacking keys or valves. —*intr.* **-gled, -gling, -gles. 1.** *Music.* To sound a bugle. **2.** To give forth a deep, prolonged sound similar to the bay of a hound. [Middle English, from Old French, from Latin *būculus,* steer, diminutive of *bōs,* ox. See **gʷou-** in Appendix.] —**bu′gler** *n.*

bu·gle[2] (byo͞o′gəl) *n.* A tubular glass or plastic bead used to trim clothing. [Origin unknown.]

bu·gle[3] (byo͞o′gəl) *n.* Bugleweed.

bu·gle·weed (byo͞o′gəl-wēd′) *n.* Any of several herbs of the genera *Ajuga* and *Lycopus* in the mint family, having opposite leaves, square stems, and axillary clusters of purplish to white flowers. [From Middle English *bugle,* from Old French, from Late Latin *būgula* (perhaps influenced by *būglōssa,* bugloss; see BUGLOSS), from Latin *būgillō.*]

bu·gloss (byo͞o′glôs′, -glŏs′) *n.* Any of several usually hairy Old World plants, especially in the genera *Anchusa, Brunnera,* and *Echium,* having blue or violet flowers. [Middle English *buglosse,* from Old French, from Late Latin *būglōssa,* from Latin *būglōssos,* from Greek *bouglōssos* : *bous,* ox; see **gʷou-** in Appendix + *glōssa,* tongue.]

buhl also **boule** or **boulle** (bo͞ol) *n.* An elaborate inlay of tortoiseshell, ivory, and metal, used especially in decorating furniture. [After André Charles *Boulle* or *Buhl* (1642–1732), French woodcarver.]

buhr·stone also **burr·stone** (bûr′stōn′) *n.* A tough, silicified limestone formerly used to make millstones. It is typified by the presence of multiple cavities that originally housed fossilized shells. [Variant of BURR[1] + STONE.]

bull[1]
Top: Hereford bull
Bottom: Longhorn bull

build (bĭld) *v.* **built** (bĭlt), **build·ing, builds.** —*tr.* **1.** To form by combining materials or parts; construct. **2.** To order, finance, or supervise the construction of: *The administration built several new housing projects.* **3.** To develop or give form to according to a plan or process; create: *build a nation; built a successful business out of their corner grocery store.* **4.** To increase or strengthen by adding gradually to: *money building interest in a savings account; build support for a political candidate.* **5.** To establish a basis for; found or ground: *build an argument on fact.* —*intr.* **1.** To make something by combining materials or parts. **2.** To engage in the construction or design of buildings: *"Each of the three architects built in a different style"* (Dwight Macdonald). **3.** To develop in magnitude or extent: *clouds building on the horizon.* **4.** To progress toward a maximum, as of intensity: *suspense building from the opening scene to the climax.* —**build** *n.* The physical makeup of a person or thing: *an athletic build.* See Synonyms at **physique.** —***phrasal verbs.* build in** (or **into**). To construct or include as an integral part of: *a wall with shelving that was built in; build stability into the economy.* **build on** (or **upon**). To use as a basis or foundation: *We must build on our recent success.* **build up. 1.** To develop or increase in stages or by degrees: *built up the business; building up my endurance for the marathon.* **2.** To accumulate or collect: *sediment building up on the ocean floor.* **3.** To bolster: *build up the product with a massive ad campaign; built up my hopes after the interview.* **4.** To fill up (an area) with buildings. [Middle English *bilden,* from Old English *byldan.* See **bheuə-** in Appendix.]

build·a·ble (bĭl′də-bəl) *adj.* Suitable or available for building: *"The problem was finding a site that was well located, appropriately zoned . . . and buildable"* (Sam Hall Kaplan).

build·down also **build-down** (bĭld′doun′) *n.* A systematic numerical reduction, especially of nuclear weapons, in which more than one weapon or warhead is destroyed for every new one that is built. [On the model of BUILDUP.] —**build′-down′** *adj.*

build·er (bĭl′dər) *n.* **1.** *Abbr.* **bldr.** One that builds, especially a person who contracts for and supervises the construction of a building. **2.** An abrasive or filler used in a soap or detergent.

build·er·ing (bĭl′dər-ĭng) *n. Sports.* The art or practice of climbing tall buildings, especially skyscrapers. [On the model of BOULDERING.] —**build′er·er** *n.*

build·ing (bĭl′dĭng) *n.* **1.** *Abbr.* **bldg.** Something that is built, as for human habitation; a structure. **2.** The act, process, art, or occupation of constructing.

SYNONYMS: *building, structure, edifice, pile.* All these nouns denote something, such as a house or school, constructed for human habitation or use. *Building* is the basic, broadly applicable term of the group: *an office building; condemned buildings being razed. "The essential thing in a building . . . is that it be strongly built, and fit for its uses"* (John Ruskin). *Structure* is sometimes interchangeable with *building* (*The ranch was a long, low wooden structure*); more often, though, the word implies considerable size: *In time their modest house was superseded by an elegant structure of glass and steel. Edifice* most frequently implies something large and imposing: *The legislature is housed in an impressive granite edifice. Pile* suggests the massiveness of stone and frequently denotes a cluster of buildings: *"Philip testified his joy . . . by raising the magnificent pile of the Escorial"* (William Hickling Prescott).

building society *n. Chiefly British.* A savings and loan association.

build·up also **build-up** (bĭld′ŭp′) *n.* **1.** The act or process of amassing or increasing: *a military buildup; a buildup of tension during the strike.* **2.** The result of building up: *a pipe clogged by rust buildup.* **3.a.** Widely favorable publicity, especially by a systematic campaign: *The new movie was given a tremendous buildup in the media.* **b.** Extravagant praise.

built (bĭlt) *v.* Past tense and past participle of **build.** —**built** *adj.* **1.** Having a specified physique: *a heavily built boxer.* **2.** *Informal.* Having a well-developed or attractive body: *a dancer who is really built.*

built-in (bĭlt′ĭn′) *adj.* **1.** Constructed as part of a larger unit; not detachable: *a built-in cabinet.* **2.** Forming a permanent or essential element or quality: *a built-in escape clause.* —**built′-in′** *n.*

built-up (bĭlt′ŭp′) *adj.* **1.** Made by fastening several layers or sections one on top of the other: *a built-up roof.* **2.** Filled with buildings; developed: *a built-up neighborhood.*

Buis·son (bwē-sôɴ′), **Ferdinand Édouard.** 1841–1932. French educator. An ardent pacifist, he shared the 1927 Nobel Peace Prize.

Bu·jum·bu·ra (bo͞o′jəm-bo͝or′ə). The capital and largest city of Burundi, in the western part of the country on Lake Tanganyika. Originally called Usumbura, it was renamed when Burundi became independent in 1962. Population, 229,980.

Bu·kha·ra (bo͞o-kär′ə, -här′ə, -ᴋʜä′rə) also **Bo·kha·ra** (bō-). A city of southern Uzbekistan west of Samarkand. It is one of the oldest cultural and trade centers of Asia and was capital of the former emirate of **Bukhara** from the 16th to the 19th century. Population, 209,000.

Bu·kha·rin (bo͞o-kär′ĭn, -ᴋʜär′-), **Nikolai Ivanovich.** 1888–1938. Bolshevik revolutionary and Soviet politician who advocated gradual agricultural collectivization. He was executed for treason after the last of the Moscow "show trials" of the 1930's.

Bu·ko·vi·na also **Bu·co·vi·na** (bo͞o′kə-vē′nə). A historical region of eastern Europe in western Ukraine and northeast Romania. A part of the Roman province of Dacia, it was overrun by barbarian hordes after the third century A.D.

bul. *abbr.* Bulletin.

Bu·la·wa·yo (bo͞o′lə-wā′yō, -wä′-). A city of southwest Zimbabwe near the Botswana border. It was founded by the British in 1893. Population, 413,814.

bulb (bŭlb) *n.* **1.** *Botany.* **a.** A short, modified, underground stem surrounded by usually fleshy modified leaves that contain stored food for the shoot within: *an onion bulb; a tulip bulb.* **b.** A similar underground stem or root, such as a corm, rhizome, or tuber. **c.** A plant that grows from a bulb. **2.** A rounded projection or part: *the bulb of a syringe.* **3.** An incandescent lamp or its glass housing. **4.** *Anatomy.* A rounded dilation or expansion of a canal, vessel, or organ. [Latin *bulbus,* from Greek *bolbos,* bulbous plant.]

bul·bar (bŭl′bər, -bär′) *adj.* Of, relating to, or characteristic of a bulb, especially of the medulla oblongata: *bulbar poliomyelitis.*

bul·bel (bŭl′bəl, -bĕl′) *n.* **1.** A smaller bulb produced from a larger bulb. **2.** A bulblet. [French *bulbille.* See BULBIL.]

bul·bif·er·ous (bŭl-bĭf′ər-əs) *adj.* Bearing or producing bulbs or bulbils.

bul·bil (bŭl′bəl, -bĭl′) *n.* **1.** A small bulb or bulblike structure in the place of a flower or in a leaf axil, as in a tiger lily. **2.** A bulblet. [French *bulbille,* diminutive of *bulbe,* bulb, from Latin *bulbus.* See BULB.]

bulb·let (bŭlb′lĭt) *n.* A small bulb.

bul·bo·u·re·thral gland (bŭl′bō-yo͝o-rē′thrəl) *n. Anatomy.* Either of two small racemose glands that are located below the prostate and discharge a component of the seminal fluid into the urethra. They are homologous to the Bartholin's glands in the female. Also called *Cowper's gland.* [BULBO(US) + URETHRAL + GLAND[1].]

bul·bous (bŭl′bəs) *adj.* **1.** Resembling a bulb in shape; rounded or swollen: *a bulbous nose; a bulbous stem base.* **2.** *Botany.* Bearing bulbs or growing from a bulb. **—bul′bous·ly** *adv.*

bul·bul (bo͝ol′bo͝ol′) *n.* **1.** Any of various passerine, chiefly tropical Old World songbirds of the family Pycnonotidae, having grayish or brownish plumage. **2.** A songbird often mentioned in Persian poetry and thought to be a nightingale. [Persian, from Arabic.]

Bul·finch (bo͝ol′fĭnch′), **Charles.** 1763–1844. American architect whose major works include the Massachusetts State House in Boston (1798) and the completion of the U.S. Capitol (1830).

Bulfinch, Thomas. 1796–1867. American writer best known for his books popularizing Greek, Roman, Scandinavian, and Celtic mythology.

Bulg. *abbr.* Bulgaria; Bulgarian.

Bul·ga·nin (bo͝ol-găn′ĭn, -gä′nyĭn), **Nikolai Aleksandrovich.** 1895–1975. Soviet military and political leader who was premier from 1955 to 1958, when he was ousted by Nikita Khrushchev for "anti-Party" activities.

Bul·gar (bŭl′gär′, bo͝ol′-) *n.* See **Bulgarian** (sense 1). [Medieval Latin *Bulgarus,* from Greek *Boulgaros,* from Turkic *bulghar,* of mixed origin, promiscuous, from *bulgamakq,* to mix.]

Bul·gar·i·a (bŭl-gâr′ē-ə, bo͝ol-). *Abbr.* **Bulg.** A country of southeast Europe on the Black Sea. Settled in the 6th century A.D. by Slavic tribes, it was ruled by Turkey from the late 14th to the early 20th century. Sofia is the capital and the largest city. Population, 8,960,679.

Bul·gar·i·an (bŭl-gâr′ē-ən, bo͝ol-). *Abbr.* **Bulg.** *adj.* Of or relating to Bulgaria or its people, language, or culture. **—Bulgarian** *n.* **1.** A native or inhabitant of Bulgaria. Also called *Bulgar.* **2.** The Slavic language of the Bulgarians.

bulge (bŭlj) *n.* **1.** A protruding part; an outward curve or swelling. **2.** *Nautical.* A bilge. **3.** A sudden, usually temporary increase in number or quantity: *The baby boom created a bulge in school enrollment.* **4.** An advantage. **—bulge** *v.* **bulged, bulg·ing, bulg·es.** *—tr.* To cause to curve outward. *—intr.* **1.** To curve outward. **2.** To swell up. **3.** To stick out; protrude. [Middle English, pouch, from Old French *bulge, bouge,* from Latin *bulga,* bag, of Celtic origin. See **bhelgh-** in Appendix.] **—bulg′i·ness** *n.* **—bulg′y** *adj.*

SYNONYMS: *bulge, balloon, belly, jut, overhang, project, protrude.* The central meaning shared by these verbs is "to curve, spread, or extend outward past the normal or usual limit": *a wallet bulging with money; expenses ballooning; a sail bellying in the wind; a pipe jutting from his mouth; overhanging eaves; projecting teeth; a head protruding from the window.*

bul·gur also **bul·ghur** (bo͝ol-go͝or′, bŭl′gər) *n.* Cracked wheat grains, often used in Middle Eastern dishes. Also called *bulgur wheat.* [Ottoman Turkish *bulghūr.*]

bu·lim·a·rex·i·a (byo͞o-lĭm′ə-rĕk′sē-ə, -lē′mə-, bo͞o-) *n.* An eating disorder in which one alternates between abnormal craving for and aversion to food. It is characterized by episodes of excessive food intake followed by periods of fasting and self-induced vomiting or diarrhea. Also called *binge-purge syndrome, binge-vomit syndrome, bulimia nervosa.* [BULIM(IA) + (AN)OREXIA.]

bu·lim·i·a (byo͞o-lĭm′ē-ə, -lē′mē-ə, bo͞o-) *n.* **1.** Insatiable appetite. **2.** An eating disorder common among young women of normal or nearly normal weight that is characterized by episodic, uncontrolled binge eating and followed by feelings of guilt, depression, and self-condemnation. It is often associated with measures taken to prevent weight gain, such as dieting or fasting. In this sense, also called *binge-eating syndrome.* [New Latin, from Greek *boulimia* : *bous,* ox; see **g**ʷ**ou-** in Appendix + *limos,* hunger.] **—bu·lim′ic** *adj. & n.*

bulimia ner·vo·sa (nûr-vō′sə) *n.* See **bulimarexia.** [New Latin : BULIMIA + *nervosa,* consisting of nerves.]

bulk (bŭlk) *n.* **1.** Size, mass, or volume, especially when very large. **2.a.** A distinct mass or portion of matter, especially a large one: *the dark bulk of buildings against the sky.* **b.** The body of a human being, especially when large. **3.** The major portion or greater part: *"The great bulk of necessary work can never be any-thing but painful"* (Bertrand Russell). **4.** See **fiber** (sense 6). **5.** Thickness of paper or cardboard in relation to weight. **6.** *Abbr.* **blk.** *Nautical.* A ship's cargo. **—bulk** *v.* **bulked, bulk·ing, bulks.** *—intr.* **1.** To be or appear to be massive in terms of size, volume, or importance; loom: *Safety considerations bulked large during development of the new spacecraft.* **2.** To grow or increase in size or importance. **3.** To cohere or form a mass: *Certain paper bulks well.* *—tr.* **1.** To cause to swell or expand. **2.** To cause to cohere or form a mass. **—bulk** *adj.* Being large in mass, quantity, or volume: *a bulk buy; a bulk mailing.* **—*idiom.* in bulk. 1.** Unpackaged; loose. **2.** In large numbers, amounts, or volume. [Middle English, perhaps partly alteration of *bouk,* belly, trunk of the body (from Old English *būc*) and partly from Old Norse *bulki,* cargo, heap; see **bhel-**[2] in Appendix.]

♦**bulk·head** (bŭlk′hĕd′) *n. Abbr.* **bhd. 1.a.** *Nautical.* One of the upright partitions dividing a ship into compartments and serving to add structural rigidity and to prevent the spread of leakage or fire. **b.** A partition or wall serving a similar purpose in a vehicle, such as an aircraft or spacecraft. **2.** A wall or embankment, as in a mine or along a waterfront, that acts as a protective barrier. **3.** *Chiefly New England.* A horizontal or sloping structure providing access to a cellar stairway. [*bulk,* stall, partition (perhaps of Scandinavian origin) + HEAD.]

bulk·y (bŭl′kē) *adj.* **-i·er, -i·est. 1.** Having considerable bulk. **2.** Of large size for its weight: *a bulky knit.* **3.** Clumsy to manage; unwieldy. **—bulk′i·ly** *adv.* **—bulk′i·ness** *n.*

bull[1] (bo͝ol) *n.* **1.a.** An adult male bovine mammal. **b.** The uncastrated adult male of domestic cattle. **c.** The male of certain other large animals, such as the alligator, elephant, or moose. **2.** An exceptionally large, strong, and aggressive person. **3.a.** An optimist, especially regarding business conditions. **b.** A person who buys commodities or securities in anticipation of a rise in prices or who tries by speculative purchases to effect such a rise. **4.** *Slang.* A police officer or detective. **5.** *Vulgar.* Empty, foolish, or pretentious talk. **—bull** *v.* **bulled, bull·ing, bulls.** *—tr.* To push; force. *—intr.* To push ahead or through forcefully: *"He bulls through the press horde that encircles the car"* (Scott Turow). **—bull** *adj.* **1.** Male. **2.** Large and strong like a bull. **3.** Characterized by rising prices: *a bull market.* **—*idiom.* grab** (or **take) the bull by the horns.** To deal with a problem directly and resolutely. [Middle English *bule,* from Old English *bula,* probably from Old Norse *boli.* See **bhel-**[2] in Appendix.]

bull[2] (bo͝ol) *n.* **1.** An official document issued by the pope and sealed with a bulla. **2.** The bulla with which such a document is sealed. [Middle English *bulle,* from Old French, from Medieval Latin *bulla.* See BULLA.]

bull[3] (bo͝ol) *n.* A gross blunder in logical speech or expression. [Origin unknown.]

Bull (bo͝ol) *n.* See **Taurus.**

bull. *abbr.* Bulletin.

bul·la (bo͝ol′ə) *n., pl.* **bul·lae** (bo͝ol′ē). **1.** A round seal affixed to a papal bull. **2.** *Pathology.* A large blister or vesicle. [Medieval Latin, from Latin, bubble, seal.]

bul·lace plum (bo͝ol′ĭs) *n.* See **damson** (sense 1). [Middle English *bolas,* from Anglo-Norman *bullace,* from Medieval Latin *bolluca.*]

bul·lae (bo͝ol′ē) *n.* Plural of **bulla.**

bul·late (bo͝ol′āt′, bŭl′-) *adj.* Having a puckered or blistered appearance: *bullate leaves.* [Latin *bullātus,* from *bulla,* bubble.]

bull·bait·ing (bo͝ol′bā′tĭng) *n.* The formerly popular sport of setting dogs to attack a chained bull and especially to seize it by the nose.

bull·bat (bo͝ol′băt′) *n.* See **nighthawk** (sense 1a). [From its roaring sound in flight.]

bull·boat (bo͝ol′bōt′) *n. Nautical.* A shallow, saucer-shaped skin boat used especially by Plains Indians for transporting possessions and sometimes persons across rivers or streams.

♦**bull·dog** (bo͝ol′dôg′, -dŏg′) *n.* **1.** Any of a breed of short-haired dog characterized by a large head, strong, square jaws with dewlaps, and a stocky body. It was originally bred for bullbaiting. **2.** A short-barreled, large-caliber revolver or pistol. **3.** A heat-resistant material used to line puddling furnaces. **4.** *Chiefly British.* A proctor's assistant at Oxford University or Cambridge University. **—bulldog** *adj.* Stubborn. **—bulldog** *tr.v.* **-dogged, -dog·ging, -dogs.** *Western U.S.* To throw (a calf or steer) by seizing its horns and twisting its neck until the animal falls. **—bull′dog′ger** *n.*

bull·doze (bo͝ol′dōz′) *v.* **-dozed, -doz·ing, -doz·es.** *—tr.* **1.** To clear, dig up, or move with a bulldozer. **2.** To treat in an abusive manner; bully. **3.** To coerce in an unsympathetic or cruel way. See Synonyms at **intimidate. 4.** To do away with; demolish: *"A massive bipartisan majority voted . . . to bulldoze the social programs of decades in the next 30 days"* (Peter Goldman). *—intr.* **1.** To operate a bulldozer. **2.** To proceed forcefully or insensitively: *"intends to bulldoze ahead with plans for extensive reconstruction"* (New York Times). [Perhaps alteration of obsolete *bulldose,* severe beating : BULL[1] + DOSE.]

bull·doz·er (bo͝ol′dō′zər) *n.* **1.** A heavy, driver-operated machine for clearing and grading land, usually having continuous

bullboat
On the Missouri River

bulldog

bulldozer

ă pat	oi boy
ā pay	ou out
âr care	o͝o took
ä father	o͞o boot
ĕ pet	ŭ cut
ē be	ûr urge
ĭ pit	th thin
ī pie	*th* this
îr pier	hw which
ŏ pot	zh vision
ō toe	ə about, item
ô paw	♦ regionalism

Stress marks: **′** (primary); ′ (secondary), as in **dictionary** (dĭk′shə-nĕr′ē)

treads and a broad hydraulic blade in front. **2.** An overbearing person; a bully.

bull dyke *n. Offensive.* Used as a disparaging term for a lesbian.

bul·let (bo͝ol′ĭt) *n.* **1.a.** A usually metal projectile in the shape of a pointed cylinder or a ball that is expelled from a firearm, especially a rifle or a handgun. **b.** Such a projectile in a metal casing; a cartridge. **2.** An object resembling a projectile in shape, action, or effect. **3.** *Printing.* A heavy dot (•) used to highlight a particular passage. [French *boulette,* diminutive of *boule,* ball, from Old French, from Latin *bulla.*]

bul·le·tin (bo͝ol′ĭ-tn, -tĭn) *n. Abbr.* **bul., bull. 1.** A brief report, especially an official statement on a matter of public interest issued for immediate publication or broadcast. **2.** A brief update or summary of current news, as on television or radio or in a newspaper. **3.** A periodical, especially one published by an organization or society. **4.** A printed program, especially one listing the order of worship for a religious service: *a church bulletin.* **—bulletin** *tr.v.* **-tined, -tin·ing, -tins.** To inform by bulletin. [French, probably from Italian *bullettino,* diminutive of *bolletta,* bill, diminutive of *bolla,* bubble, bull. See BULL[2].]

bulletin board *n.* **1.** A board on which notices are posted. **2.** *Computer Science.* A system that enables users to send or read messages that are of general interest and addressed to no particular person.

bul·let·proof (bo͝ol′ĭt-pro͞of′) *adj.* Impenetrable by bullets. **—bulletproof** *tr.v.* **-proofed, -proof·ing, -proofs.** To make impenetrable by bullets.

bullet train *n.* A high-speed passenger train.

bullet train

bull fiddle *n.* See **double bass.**

bull·fight (bo͝ol′fīt′) *n.* A public spectacle, performed especially in Spain, Portugal, and parts of Latin America, in which a fighting bull is engaged in a series of traditional maneuvers culminating usually with the ceremonial execution of the bull by sword. In Portugal the bull is often fought from horseback and is not killed. **—bull′fight′er** *n.* **—bull′fight′ing** *n.*

bull·finch (bo͝ol′fĭnch′) *n.* **1.** A European bird *(Pyrrhula pyrrhula)* having a short, thick bill and in the male a red breast, blue-gray back, and black head, wings, and tail. **2.** Any of several similar finches.

bull·frog (bo͝ol′frôg′, -frŏg′) *n.* Any of several large, heavy-bodied frogs, chiefly of the genus *Rana* and especially *R. catesbeiana,* native to North America and having a characteristic deep, resonant croak.

♦**bull·head** (bo͝ol′hĕd′) *n.* **1.** Any of several large-headed North American freshwater catfishes of the genus *Ictalurus.* **2.** Any of several fishes of the family Cottidae, such as the sculpin and the miller's thumb. **3.** *Upper Northern U.S.* See **catfish.**

bull·head·ed (bo͝ol′hĕd′ĭd) *adj.* Foolishly or irrationally stubborn; headstrong. See Synonyms at **obstinate. —bull′head′ed·ly** *adv.* **—bull′head′ed·ness** *n.*

bull·horn (bo͝ol′hôrn′) *n.* A portable device consisting of a microphone attached to a loudspeaker, used especially to amplify the voice.

Bul·lins (bo͝ol′ĭnz), **Ed.** Born 1935. American writer known primarily for his dramatic works that explore the Black experience, including *In the Wine Time* (1968).

bul·lion (bo͝ol′yən) *n.* **1.a.** Gold or silver considered with respect to quantity rather than value. **b.** Gold or silver in the form of bars, ingots, or plates. **2.** A heavy lace trimming made of twisted gold or silver threads. [Middle English, ingot of precious metal, from Anglo-Norman, from Old French *billon* (from *bille,* stick; see BILLON) and from Old French *bouillon,* bubble on the surface of boiling liquid (from *boilir,* to boil; see BOIL[1]).]

bull·ish (bo͝ol′ĭsh) *adj.* **1.a.** Having a heavy, muscular physique. **b.** Bullheaded. **2.a.** Causing, expecting, or characterized by rising stock market prices: *"Cheaper energy is bullish because it stimulates growth"* (Eric Gelman). **b.** Optimistic or confident: *bullish on the prospects of reaching a negotiated settlement.* **—bull′ish·ly** *adv.* **—bull′ish·ness** *n.*

bull terrier

bull·mas·tiff (bo͝ol′măs′tĭf) *n.* A large, heavy-set, powerful dog of a breed developed from the bulldog and the mastiff.

Bull Moose *n.* A member or supporter of the U.S. Progressive Party founded to support the presidential candidacy of Theodore Roosevelt in 1912. [From the party's emblem.]

Bull Moose Party *n.* See **Progressive Party** (sense 1).

bull·necked (bo͝ol′nĕkt′) *adj.* Having a short, thick neck.

bul·lock (bo͝ol′ək) *n.* **1.** A castrated bull; a steer. **2.** A young bull. [Middle English *bullok,* from Old English *bulluc.* See **bhel-[2]** in Appendix.]

bul·lock's heart (bo͝ol′əks) *n.* See **custard apple.**

Bul·lock's oriole (bo͝ol′əks) *n.* A subspecies of the northern oriole in its western range, distinguished from the Baltimore oriole in the male by its orange cheeks and large white wing patches and in the female by its whiter belly. [After William *Bullock,* 19th-century British naturalist.]

bull·pen (bo͝ol′pĕn′) *n.* **1.** A fenced enclosure for confining bulls. **2.** A place for the temporary detention of prisoners. **3.** *Baseball.* **a.** An area where relief pitchers warm up during a game. **b.** The relief pitchers of a team considered as a group.

bull·ring (bo͝ol′rĭng′) *n.* A circular arena for bullfights.

bull·roarer (bo͝ol′rôr′ər, -rōr′-) *n.* A small wooden slat attached to a string that makes a roaring noise when whirled.

Bull Run. A small stream of northeast Virginia southwest of Washington, D.C., near Manassas. It was the site of two important Civil War battles (July 21, 1861, and August 29–30, 1862), both Confederate victories. They are also known as the Battles of Manassas.

bull session *n. Informal.* An informal group discussion.

bull's-eye or **bull's eye** (bo͝olz′ī′) *n.* **1.a.** The small central circle on a target. **b.** A shot that hits this circle. **2.a.** A direct hit: *scored a bull's-eye on the window with a snowball.* **b.** The precise accomplishment of a goal or purpose: *"With his overflowing style,* [he] *almost always hits the bull's-eye of universality"* (William Zimmer). **3.** A thick, circular piece of glass set, as in a roof or ship's deck, to admit light. **4.** A circular opening or window. **5.a.** A planoconvex lens used to concentrate light. **b.** A lantern or lamp having such a lens. **6.** A piece of round, hard candy.

bull·shit (bo͝ol′shĭt′) *Obscene. n. Abbr.* **B.S.** Foolish, insolent talk; nonsense. **—bullshit** *v.* **-shit** also **-shat** (-shăt) or **-shit·ted** (-shĭt′ĭd), **-shit·ting, -shits.** *—intr.* **1.** To speak foolishly or insolently. **2.** To engage in idle conversation. *—tr.* To attempt to mislead or deceive by talking nonsense. **—bullshit** *interj.* Used to express displeasure or exasperation. **—bull′shit′ter** *n.*

bull snake *n.* Any of several large, nonvenomous North American snakes of the genus *Pituophis* that have yellow and brown or black markings and feed chiefly on rodents. Also called *gopher snake.*

bull terrier *n.* Any of a breed of dog having a short, usually white coat and a tapering muzzle, developed in England by crossing a bulldog with a now extinct breed of terrier.

bull thistle *n.* A biennial Eurasian thistle *(Cirsium vulgare)* in the composite family, naturalized in North America and having heads of purplish flowers and spiny stems and leaves. [From its large head.]

bull tongue *n.* A large, detachable plowshare with a single blade, used chiefly for breaking or clearing heavy soil. [From its resemblance to a bull's tongue.]

bull·whip (bo͝ol′hwĭp′, -wĭp′) *n.* A long, plaited rawhide whip with a knotted end. **—bullwhip** *tr.v.* **-whipped, -whip·ping, -whips.** To whip or heat with a bullwhip.

bul·ly[1] (bo͝ol′ē) *n., pl.* **-lies. 1.** A person who is habitually cruel or overbearing, especially to smaller or weaker people. **2.** A hired ruffian; a thug. **3.** A pimp. **4.** *Archaic.* A fine person. **5.** *Archaic.* A sweetheart. **—bully** *v.* **-lied, -ly·ing, -lies.** *—tr.* **1.** To treat in an overbearing or intimidating manner. See Synonyms at **intimidate. 2.** To make (one's way) aggressively. *—intr.* **1.** To behave like a bully. **2.** To force one's way aggressively or by intimidation: *"They bully into line at the gas pump"* (Martin Gottfried). **—bully** *adj.* Excellent; splendid: *did a bully job of persuading the members.* **—bully** *interj.* Used to express approval: *Bully for you!* [Possibly from Middle Dutch *boele,* sweetheart, probably alteration of *broeder,* brother. See **bhrāter-** in Appendix.]

bul·ly[2] (bo͝ol′ē) *n.* Canned or pickled beef. Also called *bully beef.* [Perhaps French *bouilli,* boiled meat, label on canned beef, from past participle of *bouillir,* to boil, from Old French *boilir.* See BOIL[1].]

bul·ly·boy (bo͝ol′ē-boi′) *n.* **1.** An aggressive or pugnacious fellow; a tough. **2.** A hired thug; a goon.

bully pulpit *n.* An advantageous position, as for making one's views known or rallying support: *"The presidency had been transformed from a bully pulpit on Pennsylvania Avenue to a stage the size of the world"* (Hugh Sidey).

bul·ly·rag (bo͝ol′ē-răg′) also **bal·ly·rag** (băl′ē-) *tr.v.* **-ragged, -rag·ging, -rags.** To mistreat or intimidate by bullying. [From dialectal *ballarag.*]

Bü·low (byo͞o′lō), Prince **Bernhard Heinrich Martin Karl von.** 1849–1929. German politician and diplomat who was chancellor from 1900 to 1909. As ambassador to Rome (1914) he tried unsuccessfully to keep Italy out of World War I.

Bülow, Hans Guido von. 1830–1894. German pianist and conductor considered to be the first modern virtuoso conductor.

bul·rush (bo͝ol′rŭsh′) *n.* **1.** Any of various aquatic or wetland herbs of the genus *Scirpus,* having grasslike leaves and usually clusters of small, often brown spikelets. **2.** Any of several wetland plants of similar aspect, such as the papyrus and the cattail. [Middle English *bulrish* : perhaps alteration (influenced by *bule,* bull; see BULL[1]) of *bole,* stem; see BOLE[1] + *rish,* rush; see RUSH[2].]

bul·wark (bo͝ol′wərk, -wôrk′, bŭl′-) *n.* **1.** A wall or embankment raised as a defensive fortification; a rampart. **2.** Something serving as a defense or safeguard: *"We have seen the necessity of the Union, as our bulwark against foreign danger"* (James Madison). **3.** A breakwater. **4.** Often **bulwarks.** *Nautical.* The part of a ship's side that is above the upper deck. **—bulwark** *tr.v.* **-warked, -wark·ing, -warks. 1.** To fortify with a wall, an embankment, or a rampart. **2.** To provide defense or protection for. [Middle English *bulwerk,* from Middle Dutch *bolwerk,* from Middle High German *bolwerc* : *bole,* plank; see **bhel-[2]** in Appendix + *werc,* work (from Old High German; see **werg-** in Appendix).]

SYNONYMS: *bulwark, barricade, breastwork, earthwork, rampart, bastion, parapet.* All of these nouns refer literally to structures used as a defense against attack. A *bulwark* can be a mound of earth, an embankment, or a wall-like fortification. *Barricade* pertains broadly to a barrier to passage but usually implies hasty construction to meet an imminent threat. *Breastwork* denotes a low defensive wall, especially a temporary one hurriedly built. *Earthwork* is a defensive construction of earth. A *rampart,* the main defensive structure around a guarded place, is permanent, high, and broad. A *bastion* is a projecting section of a fortification from which defenders have a wide range of view and fire. *Parapet* applies to any low fortification, typically a wall atop a rampart. Of these words *bulwark, barricade, rampart,* and *bastion* are the most frequently used to refer figuratively to something regarded as being a safeguard or a source of protection: *"The only sure bulwark of continuing liberty is a government strong enough to protect the interests of the people, and a people strong enough and well enough informed to maintain its sovereign control over its government"* (Franklin D. Roosevelt). *It was impossible to break through her barricade of reticence. "There is no rampart that will hold out against malice"* (Molière). *A free press is one of the bastions of a democracy.*

Bul·wer (bo͝ol′wər), **William Henry Lytton Earle.** Baron Dalling and Bulwer. 1801–1872. British politician and diplomat who negotiated the Clayton-Bulwer Treaty (1850) guaranteeing Anglo-American protection of a canal in Central America.

Bul·wer-Lyt·ton (bo͝ol′wər-lĭt′n), **Edward George Earle Lytton.** First Baron Lytton. 1803–1873. British writer best known for his popular historical novels, especially *The Last Days of Pompeii* (1834), and for his seemingly endless convoluted sentences.

bum[1] (bŭm) *n.* **1.** A tramp; a vagrant. **2.** A lazy or shiftless person, especially one who seeks to live solely by the support of others. **3.** An incompetent, insignificant, or obnoxious person: *The batter called the pitcher a bum.* **4.** One who is devoted to a particular activity or milieu: *a beach bum.* **—bum** *v.* **bummed, bum·ming, bums.** *—intr.* **1.** To live by begging and scavenging from place to place. Often used with *around.* **2.** To loaf. *—tr.* To acquire by begging; cadge. See Synonyms at **cadge. —bum** *adj.* **1.** Inferior; worthless: *gave me bum advice; did a bum job of fixing the car.* **2.** Disabled; malfunctioning: *a bum shoulder.* **3.** Unfavorable or unfair: *got a bum deal on my final grade for the course.* **4.** Unpleasant; lousy: *had a bum time at the party.* ***—idiom.*** **on the bum. 1.** Living as a vagrant or a tramp. **2.** Out of order; broken. [Back-formation from BUMMER.]

bum[2] (bŭm) *n. Chiefly British.* The buttocks. [Middle English *bom.*]

bum·ber·shoot (bŭm′bər-sho͞ot′) *n.* An umbrella. [Alteration of UMBRELLA + alteration of (PARA)CHUTE.]

bum·ble[1] (bŭm′bəl) *v.* **-bled, -bling, -bles.** *—intr.* **1.** To speak in a faltering manner. **2.** To move or proceed clumsily. See Synonyms at **blunder.** *—tr.* To bungle; botch. [Perhaps blend of BUNGLE and STUMBLE.]

bum·ble[2] (bŭm′bəl) *intr.v.* **-bled, -bling, -bles.** To make a humming or droning sound; buzz. **—bumble** *n.* A humming or droning sound; a buzz. [Middle English *bomblen,* of imitative origin.]

bum·ble·bee (bŭm′bəl-bē′) *n.* Any of various large, hairy, social bees of the genus *Bombus* that nest underground. Also called *humblebee.* [BUMBLE[2] + BEE[1].]

bum·boat (bŭm′bōt′) *n. Nautical.* A small boat used to peddle provisions to ships anchored offshore. [Probably partial translation of Low German *bumboot,* ship's boat, partial translation of Dutch dialectal *bomschuit,* small fishing boat : *bom,* ship's bottom (from Dutch *bodem,* from Middle Dutch) + *schuit,* ship.]

bumf or **bumph** (bŭmf) *n. Chiefly British.* **1.** Printed matter, such as pamphlets, forms, or memorandums, especially of an official nature and deemed of little interest or importance. **2.** Toilet paper. [Short for *bum fodder.*]

♦ **bum·fuz·zle** (bŭm′fŭz′əl) *tr.v.* **-zled, -zling, -zles.** *Chiefly Southern U.S.* To confuse. [Probably *bum-* (probably alteration of BAMBOOZLE) + *fuzzle* (perhaps blend of FUDDLE, and FUZZY).]

bum·ma·lo (bŭm′ə-lō) *n., pl.* **-los.** See **Bombay duck** (sense 2). [Marathi *bombīla.*]

bum·mer (bŭm′ər) *n. Slang.* **1.a.** An adverse reaction to a hallucinogenic drug. **b.** A disagreeable person, event, or situation. **2.** A failure: *"Now, the bad news: the book is a bummer"* (Newsweek). **3.** One who bums, especially for a living. [From BUM[1], adj. Senses 2 and 3, probably from German *Bummler,* loafer, from *bummeln,* to loaf.]

bump (bŭmp) *v.* **bumped, bump·ing, bumps.** *—tr.* **1.** To strike or collide with. **2.** To cause to knock against an obstacle. **3.a.** To knock to a new position; shift: *bumped the crate out of the way.* **b.** To shake up and down; jolt: *bumped the child on her knee; was bumped about on a rough flight.* **4.a.** To displace from a position within a group or organization. **b.** To deprive (a passenger) of a reserved seat because of overbooking. **5.** To raise; boost: *bump up the price of gasoline.* *—intr.* **1.** To hit or knock against something. **2.** To proceed with jerks and jolts: *bumped along slowly over the rocky terrain.* **—bump** *n.* **1.a.** A blow, collision, or jolt. **b.** The sound of something bumping: *heard a loud bump in the dark.* **2.a.** A raised or rounded spot; a bulge. **b.** A slight swelling or lump. **c.** Something, such as unevenness or a hole in a road, that causes a bump. **3.** A rise or increase, as in prices or enrollment. **4.** One of the natural protuberances on the human skull, considered to have significance in phrenology. **5.** A forward thrust of the pelvis, as in a burlesque striptease. **6.** *Slang.* A shot of hard liquor, sometimes accompanied by a beer chaser. ***—phrasal verbs.*** **bump into.** To meet by chance: *I often bump into him at the supermarket.* **bump off.** *Slang.* To murder. [Imitative.]

bump·er[1] (bŭm′pər) *n.* **1.** A usually metal or rubber bar attached to either end of a motor vehicle, such as a truck or car, to absorb impact in a collision. **2.** A protective device for absorbing shocks or impeding contact.

bump·er[2] (bŭm′pər) *n.* **1.** A drinking vessel filled to the brim. **2.** Something extraordinarily large. **—bumper** *adj.* Extraordinarily abundant or full: *a bumper crop of corn.* [Perhaps from BUMP.]

bumper sticker *n.* A sticker bearing a printed message for display on a vehicle's bumper.

bump·er-to-bump·er (bŭm′pər-tə-bŭm′pər) *adj.* **1.** Traveling close together with bumpers almost touching: *The cars were bumper-to-bumper in the tunnel.* **2.** Moving slowly or stalled as a result of tight spacing between vehicles: *bumper-to-bumper traffic.* **—bump′er-to-bump′er** *adv.*

bumph (bŭmf) *n.* Variant of **bumf.**

bump·kin[1] (bŭmp′kĭn, bŭm′-) *n.* An awkward, unsophisticated person; a yokel. [Perhaps from Flemish *boomken,* shrub, diminutive of *boom,* tree; see **bheuə-** in Appendix, or from Middle Dutch *bommekijn,* diminutive of *bomme,* barrel.]

WORD HISTORY: The term *bumpkin* may at one time have been directed at an entire people rather than that segment of the population living in a rural area. The first recorded appearance of the word in 1570 is glossed by the Latin word *Batavus,* "Dutchman," thus making plausible the suggestion that *bumpkin* may come from either the Middle Dutch word *bommekijn,* "little barrel," or the Flemish word *boomken,* "shrub." The connection would be between a squat object and the short, rotund figure of the Dutchman in the popular imagination. Any bumpkin would surely prefer this etymology to another suggestion that *bumpkin* is a derivative of *bum,* "the rear end."

---

bump·kin[2] (bŭmp′kĭn, bŭm′-) *n. Nautical.* A short spar projecting from the deck of a ship, used to extend a sail or secure a block or stay. [Probably from Dutch *boomken,* diminutive of *boom,* tree. See BOOM[2].]

bump·tious (bŭmp′shəs) *adj.* Crudely or loudly assertive; pushy. [Perhaps blend of BUMP and PRESUMPTUOUS.] **—bump′tious·ly** *adv.* **—bump′tious·ness** *n.*

bump·y (bŭm′pē) *adj.* **-i·er, -i·est. 1.** Covered with or full of bumps: *a bumpy country road.* **2.** Marked by bumps and jolts; rough: *a bumpy flight.* **—bump′i·ly** *adv.* **—bump′i·ness** *n.*

bum's rush (bŭmz) *n.* Forcible ejection from a place.

bun[1] (bŭn) *n.* **1.** A small bread roll, often sweetened or spiced and sometimes containing dried fruit. **2.** A tight roll of hair worn at the back of the head. [Middle English *bunne,* probably from Old French *bugne,* boil, of Celtic origin.]

bun[2] (bŭn) *n. Slang.* A drunken spree. [Origin unknown.]

bun[3] (bŭn) *n. Slang.* One of the buttocks. [Dialectal, hind part of a rabbit or squirrel, from Scottish Gaelic, stump, bottom, from Old Irish.]

bumblebee

bu·na (bo͞o′nə, byo͞o′-) *n.* A synthetic rubber made from the polymerization of butadiene and sodium. [Originally a trademark.]

bunch (bŭnch) *n.* **1.a.** A group of things growing close together; a cluster or clump: *a bunch of grapes; grass growing in bunches.* **b.** A group of like items or individuals gathered or placed together: *a bunch of keys on a ring; people standing around in bunches.* **2.** *Informal.* A group of people usually having a common interest or association: *My brother and his bunch are basketball fanatics.* **3.** *Informal.* A considerable number or amount; a lot: *a bunch of trouble; a whole bunch of food.* **4.** A small lump or swelling; a bump. **—bunch** *v.* **bunched, bunch·ing, bunch·es.** *—tr.* **1.** To gather or form into a cluster: *bunched my fingers into a fist.* **2.** To gather together into a group. **3.** To gather (fabric) into folds. *—intr.* **1.** To form a cluster or group: *runners bunching up at the starting line.* **2.** To be gathered together in folds, as fabric. **3.** To swell; protrude. [Middle English *bonche,* probably from Flemish *bondje,* diminutive of *bont,* bundle, from Middle Dutch. See BUNDLE.] **—bunch′i·ness** *n.* **—bunch′y** *adj.*

bunch·ber·ry (bŭnch′bĕr′ē) *n.* See **dwarf cornel.**

Bunche (bŭnch), **Ralph Johnson.** 1904–1971. American diplomat. He won the 1950 Nobel Peace Prize for his work on the United Nations Palestine Commission.

bunch·flow·er (bŭnch′flou′ər) *n.* A perennial herb *(Melanthium virginicum)* in the lily family, native to the eastern United States and having narrow leaves and a branched cluster of cream-colored or greenish flowers.

bunch grass or **bunch·grass** (bŭnch′grăs′) *n.* Any of various grasses in many different genera that grow in clumplike fashion rather than forming a sod or mat.

bunch·ing onion (bŭn′chĭng) *n.* Any of certain kinds of onion plants, such as the Welsh onion, that does not form a well-developed bulb and is grown for its multiple stems, which are used as scallions.

bun·co also **bun·ko** (bŭng′kō) *Informal.* *—n., pl.* **-cos** also **-kos.** A swindle in which an unsuspecting person is cheated; a confidence game. *—tr.v.* **-coed, -co·ing, -cos** also **-koed, -ko·ing, -kos.** To swindle. [Probably alteration of Spanish *banca,*

ă pat	oi boy
ā pay	ou out
âr care	o͝o took
ä father	o͞o boot
ĕ pet	ŭ cut
ē be	ûr urge
ĭ pit	th thin
ī pie	*th* this
îr pier	hw which
ŏ pot	zh vision
ō toe	ə about, item
ô paw	♦ regionalism

Stress marks: ′ (primary); ′ (secondary), as in **dictionary** (dĭk′shə-nĕr′ē)

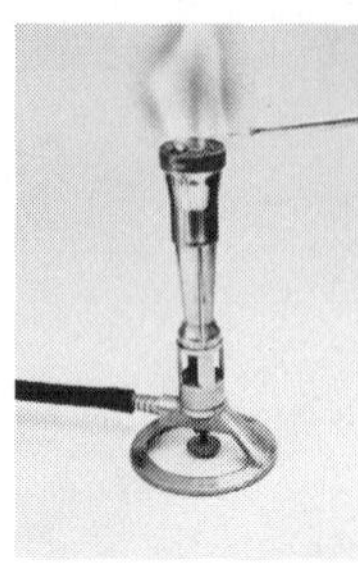
Bunsen burner

Luis Buñuel

buoy

card game, from Italian *banca,* bank, of Germanic origin. See BANK[2].]

bun·combe (bŭng′kəm) *n.* Variant of **bunkum.**

bund[1] (bŭnd) *n.* **1.** An embankment or dike, especially in India. **2.** A street running along a harbor or waterway, especially in the Far East. [Hindi *band,* from Persian, from Middle Persian, from Avestan *banda-,* from Old Iranian. See **bhendh-** in Appendix.]

bund[2] (bo͝ond, bŭnd) *n.* **1.** An association, especially a political association. **2.** Often **Bund.** A pro-Nazi German-American organization of the 1930's. **3.** Often **Bund.** A European Jewish socialist movement founded in Russia in 1897. [German, from Middle High German *bunt.* See **bhendh-** in Appendix.]

bun·dle (bŭn′dl) *n. Abbr.* **bd., bdl, bdle. 1.** A group of objects held together, as by tying or wrapping. **2.** Something wrapped or tied up for carrying; a package. **3.** *Biology.* A cluster or strand of closely bound muscle or nerve fibers. **4.** *Botany.* A vascular bundle. **5.** *Informal.* **a.** A large amount; a lot: *had a bundle of fun at the dance.* **b.** A large sum of money: *made a bundle selling real estate.* **—bundle** *v.* **-dled, -dling, -dles.** —*tr.* **1.** To tie, wrap, or gather together. **2.** To dispatch or dispense of quickly and with little fuss; hustle: *bundled the child off to school.* **3.** To dress (a person) warmly: *bundled them up in winter clothes.* —*intr.* **1.** To hurry; hasten: *The children came bundling in from outside.* **2.** To dress oneself warmly. **3.** To sleep in the same bed while fully clothed, a custom formerly practiced by engaged couples in New England and in Wales. [Middle English *bundel,* probably from Middle Dutch *bondel.* See **bhendh-** in Appendix.] **—bun′dler** *n.*

bundle of nerves *n. Informal.* An extremely nervous person.

bundle scar *n.* A small mark on a leaf scar indicating a point where a vein from the leaf was once connected with the stem.

bundle sheath *n.* A layer or region of cells surrounding a vascular bundle.

bundt cake (bŭnt, bo͝ont) *n.* A ring-shaped cake baked in a tube pan that has fluted sides. [Originally a trademark.]

bung (bŭng) *n.* **1.** A stopper especially for the hole through which a cask, keg, or barrel is filled or emptied. **2.** A bunghole. **—bung** *tr.v.* **bunged, bung·ing, bungs. 1.** To close with or as if with a cork or stopper. **2.** *Informal.* To injure or damage: *fell on skis and bunged up my leg.* **3.** *Chiefly British.* To fling; toss: *"The Hungarian director bungs star Klaus Maria Brandauer once more into the breaches of past Teuton history"* (Nigel Andrews). [Middle English *bunge,* from Middle Dutch *bonge,* from Late Latin *puncta,* hole, from Latin, feminine past participle of *pungere,* to prick. See **peuk-** in Appendix.]

bun·ga·low (bŭng′gə-lō′) *n.* **1.** A small house or cottage usually having a single story and sometimes an additional attic story. **2.** A thatched or tiled one-story house in India surrounded by a wide verandah. [Hindi *baṅglā,* Bengali (house), from *Bengali,* of Bengal.]

bun·gee (bŭn′jē) *n.* An elasticized rubber cord used to fasten, bear weight, or absorb shock.

bung·hole (bŭng′hōl′) *n.* The hole in a cask, keg, or barrel through which liquid is poured in or drained out.

bun·gle (bŭng′gəl) *v.* **-gled, -gling, -gles.** —*intr.* To work or act ineptly or inefficiently. —*tr.* To handle badly; botch. See Synonyms at **botch. —bungle** *n.* A clumsy or inept performance; a botch: *made a bungle of the case due to inexperience.* [Perhaps of Scandinavian origin.] **—bun′gler** *n.* **—bun′gling·ly** *adv.*

Bu·nin (bo͞o′nĭn, -nyĭn), **Ivan Alekseevich.** 1870–1953. Russian writer best known for his short stories. He won the 1933 Nobel Prize for literature.

bun·ion (bŭn′yən) *n.* A painful, inflamed swelling of the bursa at the first joint of the big toe, characterized by enlargement of the joint and lateral displacement of the toe. [Probably alteration of obsolete *bunny,* swelling, from Middle English *bony,* perhaps from Old French *bugne.* See BUN[1].]

bunk[1] (bŭngk) *n.* **1.** A narrow bed built like a shelf into or against a wall, as in a ship's cabin. **2.** A bunk bed. **3.** A place for sleeping. **—bunk** *v.* **bunked, bunk·ing, bunks.** —*intr.* **1. a.** To sleep in a bunk or bed. **b.** To stay the night; sleep: *bunk over at a friend's house.* **2.** To go to bed: *bunked down early.* —*tr.* To provide with sleeping quarters. [Perhaps short for BUNKER.]

bunk[2] (bŭngk) *n.* Empty talk; nonsense. [Short for BUNKUM.]

bunk bed *n.* Either of a pair of narrow beds stacked one on top of the other.

bun·ker (bŭng′kər) *n.* **1. a.** A bin or tank especially for fuel storage, as on a ship. **b.** *Often* **bunkers.** Fuel, such as coal or fuel oil, used especially in ships. **2. a.** An underground defensive position with a fortified projection above ground level for gun emplacements. **b.** A protective chamber: *watched the missile launch from a bunker.* **3.** *Sports.* A sand trap serving as an obstacle on a golf course. **—bunker** *tr.v.* **-kered, -ker·ing, -kers. 1.** To store or place (fuel) in a bunker. **2.** *Sports.* To hit (a golf ball) into a bunker. [Scots *bonker,* chest, perhaps of Scandinavian origin.] **—bun′ker** *adj.*

Bun·ker Hill (bŭng′kər). A low elevation, 32.6 m (107 ft) high, in Charlestown, a section of Boston, Massachusetts. The first major Revolutionary War battle took place on nearby Breed's Hill on June 17, 1775.

bun·ker·ing (bŭng′kər-ĭng) *n. Nautical.* The act or process of supplying a ship with fuel.

bunk·house (bŭngk′hous′) *n.* A building providing sleeping quarters on a ranch or in a camp.

bunk·mate (bŭngk′māt′) *n.* A person with whom one shares sleeping quarters.

bun·ko (bŭng′kō) *n. & v.* Variant of **bunco.**

bunk·room (bŭngk′ro͞om′, -ro͝om′) *n.* A room providing usually temporary sleeping quarters, as for workers or travelers.

bun·kum also **bun·combe** (bŭng′kəm) *n.* Empty or insincere talk; claptrap. [After *Buncombe,* a county of western North Carolina, from a remark made around 1820 by its congressman, who felt obligated to give a dull speech "for Buncombe."]

bun·ny (bŭn′ē) *n., pl.* **-nies.** A rabbit, especially a young one. [Dialectal *bun,* tail of a rabbit. See BUN[3].]

Bun·ra·ku (bo͞on-rä′ko͞o, bo͞on′rä′-) *n.* A traditional Japanese puppet theater featuring large puppets operated by on-stage puppeteers with a narrative recited from off-stage. The puppets have heads, hands, and feet of wood attached to a bodiless cloth costume. [Japanese : after the *Bunraku-za* theater built in the early 19th century by Bunraku-ken Oemurea (died 1810).]

Bun·sen (bŭn′sən), **Robert Wilhelm.** 1811–1899. German chemist who pioneered in spectrum analysis and codiscovered the elements casium and rubidium. He introduced the Bunsen burner in 1855.

Bunsen burner *n.* A small laboratory burner consisting of a vertical metal tube connected to a gas source and producing a very hot flame from a mixture of gas and air let in through adjustable holes at the base. [After Robert Wilhelm BUNSEN.]

bunt[1] (bŭnt) *v.* **bunt·ed, bunt·ing, bunts.** —*tr.* **1.** *Baseball.* To bat (a pitched ball) by tapping it lightly so that the ball rolls slowly in front of the infielders. **2.** To push or strike with or as if with the head; butt. —*intr.* **1.** *Baseball.* To bat a pitched ball by tapping it lightly, causing it to roll slowly in front of the infielders. **2.** To butt. **—bunt** *n.* **1.** *Baseball.* **a.** The act of bunting. **b.** A bunted ball. **2.** A butt with or as if with the head. [Dialectal, to push, strike.] **—bunt′er** *n.*

bunt[2] (bŭnt) *n.* **1.** *Nautical.* The middle portion of a sail, especially a square one, that is shaped like a pouch to increase the effect of the wind. **2.** The pouchlike midsection of a fishing net in which the catch is concentrated. [Perhaps from Swedish *bunt* or Danish *bundt,* both of Low German origin.]

bunt[3] (bŭnt) *n.* A smut disease of wheat and other cereal grasses, caused by fungi of the genus *Tilletia* and resulting in grains filled with foul-smelling, sooty black spores. [Origin unknown.]

bunt·ing[1] (bŭn′tĭng) *n.* **1.** A light cotton or woolen cloth used for making flags. **2.** Flags considered as a group. **3.** Strips of cloth or material usually in the colors of the national flag, used especially as drapery or streamers for festive decoration. [Perhaps from German *bunt,* colored.]

bunt·ing[2] (bŭn′tĭng) *n.* Any of various birds of the family Fringillidae, having short, cone-shaped bills and brownish or grayish plumage. [Middle English.]

bunt·ing[3] (bŭn′tĭng) *n.* A snug-fitting, hooded sleeping bag of heavy material for infants. [Perhaps from Scots *buntin,* plump, short.]

bunt·line (bŭnt′lĭn, -līn′) *n. Nautical.* A rope that keeps a square sail from bellying when it is being hauled up for furling. [BUNT[2] + LINE[1].]

Bunt·line (bŭnt′lĭn, -līn′), **Ned.** See Edward Zane Carroll **Judson.**

Bu·ñu·el (bo͞o-nyo͞o-ĕl′), **Luis.** 1900–1983. Spanish director known for his studies of modern social manners in films such as *Belle de Jour* (1966) and *The Discreet Charm of the Bourgeoisie* (1972).

bun·ya-bun·ya also **bun·ya·bun·ya** (bŭn′yə-bŭn′yə) *n.* An Australian evergreen coniferous tree *(Araucaria bidwilli)* having tiers of nearly whorled branches, sharp-pointed leaves, and large cones. Also called *bunya pine.* [From Wiradhuri (Aboriginal language of southeast Australia) *bunya.*]

Bun·yan (bŭn′yən), **John.** 1628–1688. English preacher and writer celebrated for his *Pilgrim's Progress* (two parts, 1678 and 1684), the allegorical tale of Christian's journey from the City of Destruction to the Celestial City.

Bun·yan·esque (bŭn′yə-nĕsk′) *adj.* **1.** Of, relating to, or suggestive of the allegorical writings of John Bunyan. **2. a.** Of, relating to, or suggestive of the legend of Paul Bunyan. **b.** Of astonishingly large size: *"Bunyanesque waves . . . crunched homes and municipal piers into little more than kindling wood"* (Time).

bun·ya pine (bŭn′yə) *n.* See **bunya-bunya.**

bun·yip (bŭn′yĭp) *n. Australian.* **1.** An imaginary monster inhabiting swamps and lagoons. **2.** An imposter; a fake. [Wemba (Aboriginal language of southwestern Australia) *banib.*]

buoy (bo͞o′ē, boi) *n.* **1.** *Nautical.* A float, often having a bell or light, moored in water as a warning of danger or as a marker for a channel. **2.** A life buoy. **—buoy** *tr.v.* **buoyed, buoy·ing, buoys. 1.** To keep afloat or aloft: *a glider buoyed by air currents.* **2. a.** To maintain at a high level; support: *"the persistent . . . takeover speculation, which has buoyed up the shares of banks"* (Financial Times). **b.** To hearten or inspire; uplift: *"buoyed up by the team spirit and the pride of the older generation back at home"* (Judith Martin). **3.** To mark with or as if with a buoy. [Middle English *boie,* from Old French *boue,* probably of Germanic origin. See **bhā-[1]** in Appendix.]

buoy·ance (boi′əns, bo͞o′yəns) *n.* Buoyancy.

buoy·an·cy (boi′ən-sē, bo͞o′yən-) *n.* **1.a.** The tendency or capacity to remain afloat in a liquid or rise in air or gas. **b.** The upward force that a fluid exerts on an object less dense than itself. **2.** Ability to recover quickly from setbacks; resilience. **3.** Lightness of spirit; cheerfulness.

buoy·ant (boi′ənt, bo͞o′yənt) *adj.* **1.** Having or marked by buoyancy: *a buoyant balloon; buoyant spirits.* **2.** Lighthearted; gay: *in a buoyant mood.* [Spanish *boyante,* present participle of *boyar,* to refloat a boat, from *boya,* buoy, from Old French *boue.* See BUOY.] **—buoy′ant·ly** *adv.*

bu·pres·tid (byo͞o-prĕs′tĭd) *n.* Any of various beetles of the family Buprestidae, which are destructive wood borers as larvae and often have a metallic red, green, or blue color. [From New Latin *Būprēstidae,* family name, from *Būprēstis,* type genus, from Latin *būprēstis,* beetle harmful to cattle, from Greek *bouprēstis* : *bous,* ox; see **g^wou-** in Appendix + *prēthein,* to swell up.]

bur[1] also **burr** (bûr) *n.* **1.a.** A rough, prickly husk or covering surrounding the seeds or fruits of plants such as the chestnut or the burdock. **b.** A plant producing such husks or coverings. **2.** A persistently clinging or nettlesome person or thing. **3.** A rough protuberance, especially a burl on a tree. **4.** Any of various rotary cutting tools designed to be attached to a drill. [Middle English *burre,* of Scandinavian origin.]

bur[2] (bûr) *n. & v.* Variant of **burr[2]**.

bur[3] (bûr) *n.* Variant of **burr[3]**.

bur. *abbr.* Bureau.

Bur. *abbr.* Burma; Burmese.

bu·ran (bo͞o-rän′) *n.* A violent windstorm of the Eurasian steppes, accompanied in summer by dust and in winter by snow. [Russian, probably from Tatar.]

′burb also **burb** (bûrb) *n. Informal.* A suburb: *"when the condos get so dense out in those 'burbs that the deer have to run right through hot tubs"* (Russell Baker). [Short for SUBURB.]

Bur·bage (bûr′bĭj), **Richard.** 1567?–1619. English actor and theater manager. The foremost tragedian of his day, he was the first to play the title roles in Shakespeare's *Hamlet, King Lear, Othello,* and *Richard III.*

Bur·bank (bûr′băngk′). **1.** A city of southern California near Los Angeles. There are several motion picture and television studios here. Population, 84,625. **2.** A city of northeast Illinois, a suburb of Chicago. Population, 28,462.

Burbank, Luther. 1849–1926. American horticulturist who developed countless new varieties of fruits, vegetables, and flowers, including the Burbank potato and the Shasta daisy.

Bur·bidge (bûr′bĭj), **(Eleanor) Margaret.** Born 1919. British-born American astronomer who worked on the composition of the interior of the stars. She was director of the Royal Greenwich Observatory (1972–1973).

bur·ble (bûr′bəl) *n.* **1.** A gurgling or bubbling sound, as of running water. **2.** A rapid, excited flow of speech. **3.** A separation in the boundary layer of fluid about a moving streamlined body, such as the wing of an airplane, causing a breakdown in the smooth flow of fluid and resulting in turbulence. **—burble** *intr.v.* **-bled, -bling, -bles. 1.** To bubble; gurgle. **2.** To speak quickly and excitedly; gush. [Middle English *burblen,* to bubble.] **—bur′bler** *n.* **—bur′bly** *adj.*

bur·bot (bûr′bət) *n., pl.* **burbot** or **-bots.** A freshwater fish *(Lota lota)* of the Northern Hemisphere, related to and resembling the cod and having barbels on the nose and chin. Also called *cusk, eelpout.* [Middle English, from Old French *borbote,* from *borbeter,* to move about in mud.]

Burch·field (bûrch′fēld′), **Charles Ephraim.** 1893–1967. American painter whose works, usually in watercolor, include landscapes and somber urban scenes.

bur cucumber *n.* **1.** A weedy, annual, tendril-bearing vine *(Sicyos angulatus)* native to North America and having small whitish flowers and clusters of small fruits covered with long, slender prickles. **2.** The fruit of this vine.

bur·den[1] (bûr′dn) *n.* **1.** Something that is carried. **2.a.** Something that is emotionally difficult to bear. **b.** A source of great worry or stress; weight: *The burden of economic sacrifice rests on the workers of the plant.* **3.** A responsibility or duty: *The burden of organizing the campaign fell to me.* **4.** *Nautical.* **a.** The amount of cargo that a vessel can carry. **b.** The weight of the cargo carried by a vessel at one time. **—burden** *tr.v.* **-dened, -den·ing, -dens. 1.** To weigh down; oppress. **2.** To load or overload. [Middle English, from Old English *byrthen.* See **bher-[1]** in Appendix.]

SYNONYMS: *burden, affliction, cross, trial, tribulation.* The central meaning shared by these nouns is "something that is onerous or troublesome": *the burden of a guilty conscience; indebtedness that is an affliction; illness that is her cross; sitting still, a trial to the very young; domestic tribulations.* See also Synonyms at **substance.**

bur·den[2] (bûr′dn) *n.* **1.** A principal or recurring idea; a theme: *"The burden of what he said was to defend enthusiastically the conservative aristocracy"* (J.A. Froude). **2.** *Music.* **a.** The chorus or refrain of a composition. **b.** The drone of a bagpipe. **c.** *Archaic.* The bass accompaniment to a song. [Variant of BOURDON.]

burden of proof *n. Law.* The responsibility of proving a disputed charge or allegation.

bur·den·some (bûr′dn-səm) *adj.* Of or like a burden; onerous. **—bur′den·some·ly** *adv.* **—bur′den·some·ness** *n.*

SYNONYMS: *burdensome, onerous, oppressive, arduous, demanding, rigorous, exacting.* These adjectives all apply to what imposes a severe test of bodily or spiritual strength. *Burdensome* is associated with both mental and physical hardship: *The burdensome task of preparing her income tax return awaited her. Onerous* adds to *burdensome* the connotation of the figuratively heavy load imposed by something irksome or annoying: *My duties weren't onerous; I only had to greet the guests.* Something *oppressive* weighs one down in body or spirit, as by subjection to an overpowering natural influence or to the harsh or unjust exercise of power: *oppressive humidity. "Old forms of government finally grow so oppressive that they must be thrown off"* (Herbert Spencer). *Arduous* emphasizes the expenditure of sustained and often exhausting labor: *Learning a new role is a long and arduous undertaking. Demanding, rigorous,* and *exacting* imply the imposition of severe and uncompromising demands: *Music is a demanding art. "Yet out of this unflattering, rigorous realism . . . Swift made great art"* (M.D. Aeschliman). *Making a petit point pillow is exacting work.*

bur·dock (bûr′dŏk′) *n.* Any of several weedy, chiefly biennial plants of the genus *Arctium* in the composite family, having pink or purplish flower heads surrounded by prickly bracts and forming a bur in fruit. [BUR[1] + DOCK[4].]

bu·reau (byo͝or′ō) *n., pl.* **-reaus** or **-reaux** (-ōz). **1.** A chest of drawers, especially a dresser for holding clothes. **2.** *Chiefly British.* A writing desk or writing table with drawers. **3.** *Abbr.* **bur., bu. a.** A government department or a subdivision of a department. **b.** An office, usually of a large organization, that is responsible for a specific duty: *a news bureau.* **c.** A business that offers information of a specified kind: *a travel bureau.* [French, cloth cover for desks, desk, office, from Old French *burel,* woolen cloth, probably from Vulgar Latin **būra,* from Late Latin *burra,* shaggy garment.]

bu·reauc·ra·cy (byo͝o-rŏk′rə-sē) *n., pl.* **-cies. 1.a.** Administration of a government chiefly through bureaus or departments staffed with nonelected officials. **b.** The departments and their officials as a group: *promised to reorganize the federal bureaucracy.* **2.** Management or administration marked by diffusion of authority among numerous offices and adherence to inflexible rules of operation: *"knew something about bureaucracy and those nameless, faceless forces that can crush the life's blood from the individual"* (Rollene W. Saal). **3.** An administrative system in which the need or inclination to follow complex procedures impedes effective action: *innovative ideas that get bogged down in red tape and bureaucracy.* [French *bureaucratie* : *bureau,* office; see BUREAU + *-cratie,* rule (from Old French; see –CRACY).]

bu·reau·crat (byo͝or′ə-krăt′) *n.* **1.** An official of a bureaucracy. **2.** An official who is rigidly devoted to the details of administrative procedure. **—bu′reau·crat′ic** *adj.* **—bu′reau·crat′i·cal·ly** *adv.*

bu·reau·crat·ese (byo͝or′ə-kră-tēz′, -tēs′) *n.* A style of language characterized by jargon and euphemism that is used especially by bureaucrats: *"Soviet bureaucratese, especially the tongue-twisting acronyms and alien-sounding portmanteau words of the state security apparatus"* (Strobe Talbott).

bu·reau·cra·tize (byo͝o-rŏk′rə-tīz′) *tr.v.* **-tized, -tiz·ing, -tiz·es.** To make into a bureaucracy or bring under bureaucratic control: *"The failure of communication is built—or . . . bureaucratized—into the legal system"* (Anatole Broyard). **—bu·reau′cra·ti·za′tion** (-tĭ-zā′shən) *n.*

bu·reaux (byo͝or′ōz) *n.* A plural of **bureau.**

bu·rette also **bu·ret** (byo͝o-rĕt′) *n.* A uniform-bore glass tube with fine gradations and a stopcock at the bottom, used especially in laboratory procedures for accurate fluid dispensing and measurement. [French, diminutive of *buire,* vase for liquors, from Old French, probably of Germanic origin.]

burg (bûrg) *n.* **1.** *Informal.* A city or town: *"There are no more opportunities for you in this burg"* (Damon Runyon). **2.** A fortified or walled town in early or medieval Europe. [Probably from *-burg* in place names, such as *Plattsburg, Harrisburg,* from Middle English *burgh,* town, from Old English *burg.* Sense 2, ultimately from Germanic **burgs,* hill fort. See **bhergh-[2]** in Appendix.]

bur·gage (bûr′gĭj) *n.* A tenure in England and Scotland under which property of the king or a lord in a town was held in return for a yearly rent or the rendering of a service. [Middle English, from Old French *bourgage,* from Medieval Latin *burgāgium,* from Late Latin *burgus,* fortified town, of Germanic origin. See BURGESS.]

bur·gee (bər-jē′, bûr′jē) *n. Nautical.* A small distinguishing flag displayed by a yacht. [Perhaps from French dialectal *bourgeais,* shipowner, from Old French *burgeis,* citizen, from *bourg,* bourg. See BOURG.]

bur·geon also **bour·geon** (bûr′jən) *intr.v.* **-geoned, -geon·ing, -geons. 1.a.** To put forth new buds, leaves, or greenery; sprout. **b.** To begin to grow or blossom. **2.** *Usage Problem.* To grow and flourish. [Middle English *burgeonen,* from Old French *borjoner,* from *burjon,* a bud, from Vulgar Latin **burriōnem,* from Late Latin *burra,* a shaggy garment.]

Luther Burbank

burdock
Smaller burdock
Arctium minus

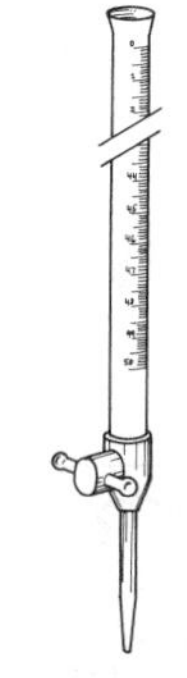

burette

ă pat	oi boy
ā pay	ou out
âr care	o͝o took
ä father	o͞o boot
ĕ pet	ŭ cut
ē be	ûr urge
ĭ pit	th thin
ī pie	*th* this
îr pier	hw which
ŏ pot	zh vision
ō toe	ə about, item
ô paw	♦ regionalism

Stress marks: **′** (primary); ′ (secondary), as in **dictionary** (dĭk′shə-nĕr′ē)

USAGE NOTE: *Burgeon* has gained greater acceptance in recent years in its use to mean not just "to put forth buds" but more generally "to grow and flourish." In 1969 only 49 percent of the Usage Panel accepted the phrase *the burgeoning population of Queens;* in our most recent survey 74 percent accepted the same phrase. However, it should be noted that in this use *burgeon* is more acceptable when it takes the form of the present participle. Only 29 percent of the current Panel accepts the sentence *News programs are less expensive to produce than entertainment series, and the public's appetite for them has burgeoned.*

burg•er (bûr′gər) *n.* **1.** A sandwich consisting of a bun, a cooked beef patty, and often other ingredients such as cheese, onion slices, lettuce, or condiments. Often used in combination: *a cheeseburger.* **2.** A sandwich with a nonbeef filling. Often used in combination: *a crab burger.* [Short for HAMBURGER.]

Bur•ger (bûr′gər), **Warren Earl.** Born 1907. American jurist who served as the chief justice of the U.S. Supreme Court (1969–1986).

bur•gess (bûr′jĭs) *n.* **1.** A freeman or citizen of an English borough. **2.** A member of the English Parliament who once represented a town, borough, or university. **3.** A member of the lower house of the legislature of colonial Virginia or Maryland. [Middle English *burgeis,* from Old French, from Late Latin *burgēnsis,* from *burgus,* fortified town. See **bhergh-**[2] in Appendix.]

Bur•gess (bûr′jĭs), **Anthony.** Born 1917. British writer and critic noted for his comic novels, including the futuristic classic *A Clockwork Orange* (1962).

Burgess, (Frank) Gelett. 1866–1951. American writer and illustrator whose works include *Are You a Bromide?* (1907) and *Look Eleven Years Younger* (1937). He also wrote the famous quatrain beginning "Have you ever seen a purple cow?"

burgh (bûrg) *n.* A chartered town or borough in Scotland. [Scots, variant of BOROUGH.]

burgh•er (bûr′gər) *n.* **1.** A citizen of a town or borough. **2.** A comfortable or complacent member of the middle class. **3.a.** A member of the mercantile class of a medieval European city. **b.** A citizen of a medieval European city. [German *Bürger* or Dutch *burger,* both from Middle High German *burgaere,* from Old High German *burgārī,* from *burg,* city. See **bhergh-**[2] in Appendix.]

Burgh•ley (bûr′lē), First Baron. See William **Cecil.**

Martha Jane Burk
"Calamity Jane"
Photographed in 1895

bur•glar (bûr′glər) *n.* One who commits burglary. [Anglo-Norman *burgler* (alteration of *burgesur,* probably from Old French *burg,* borough) and Medieval Latin *burgulātor* (alteration of *burgātor,* from Medieval Latin *burgāre,* to commit burglary in, from Late Latin *burgus,* fortified town), both of Germanic origin. See **bhergh-**[2] in Appendix.]

bur•glar•i•ous (bər-glâr′ē-əs) *adj.* Of or relating to burglary. **—bur•glar′i•ous•ly** *adv.*

bur•glar•ize (bûr′glə-rīz′) *v.* **-ized, -iz•ing, -iz•es.** *—tr.* **1.** To enter and steal from (a building or other premises). **2.** To commit burglary against: *The second-floor tenants have been burglarized twice.* *—intr.* To commit burglary.

bur•glar•proof (bûr′glər-pro͞of′) *adj.* Secure against burglars or burglary.

bur•gla•ry (bûr′glə-rē) *n., pl.* **-ries.** The act of entering a building or other premises with the intent to commit theft.

bur•gle (bûr′gəl) *tr.v. & intr.v.* **-gled, -gling, -gles.** To burglarize. [Back-formation from BURGLAR.]

bur•go•mas•ter (bûr′gə-măs′tər) *n.* The principal magistrate, comparable to a mayor, of a city or town in the Netherlands, Flanders, Austria, or Germany. [Partial translation of Dutch *burgemeester* : *burg,* town (from Middle Dutch *burch;* see **bhergh-**[2] in Appendix) + *meester,* master.]

bur•go•net (bûr′gə-nĭt, bûr′gə-nĕt′) *n.* A light steel helmet with a peak and hinged flaps covering the cheeks, worn in the 16th century. [Old French *bourguignotte,* probably from *Bourgogne,* Burgundy, a region of eastern France.]

Burkina Faso

♦ **bur•goo** (bûr′go͞o′, bər-go͞o′) *n., pl.* **-goos. 1.** *New England.* Any of several thick stews, originally an oatmeal porridge. **2.** *Kentucky.* **a.** A spicy stew made of poultry, game, other meats, and vegetables, usually cooked outdoors. **b.** A picnic featuring such a stew. [Perhaps alteration of RAGOUT.]

Bur•gos (bo͝or′gōs′). A city of northern Spain on a high plateau south-southwest of Bilbao. Founded c. 884, it was the capital of the kingdom of Castile in the 11th century. Population, 155,849.

Bur•goyne (bər-goin′, bûr′goin′), **John.** Known as "Gentleman Johnny." 1722–1792. British general and playwright. In the American Revolution he captured Fort Ticonderoga (July 6, 1777) but lost the Battle of Saratoga (October 17, 1777). *The Heiress* (1786) was his most popular play.

Bur•gun•dy[1] (bûr′gən-dē). **1.** A ducal house of Burgundy split into the Capetian line (1032–1361) and the Cadet, or Valois, line (1363–1477). **2.** A Portuguese dynasty (1139–1383) beginning with Alfonso I, who made Portugal an independent kingdom.

Bur•gun•dy[2] (bûr′gən-dē) also **Bour•gogne** (bo͞or-gôn′yə). A historical region and former province of eastern France. The area was first organized into a kingdom by the Burgundii in the 5th century A.D. At the height of its later power in the 14th and 15th centuries, Burgundy controlled vast territories in present-day Netherlands, Belgium, and northeast France. It was incorporated into the French crown lands by Louis XI in 1477. **—Bur•gun′di•an** (bər-gŭn′dē-ən) *adj. & n.*

Bur•gun•dy[3] (bûr′gən-dē) *n., pl.* **-dies. 1.a.** Any of various red or white wines produced in Burgundy, France. **b.** Any of various similar wines produced elsewhere. **2. burgundy.** *Color.* A dark grayish or blackish red to dark purplish red or reddish brown.

bur•i•al (bĕr′ē-əl) *n.* The act or process of burying. [Middle English *buriel,* back-formation from *buriels* (taken as pl.), from Old English *byrgels.* See **bhergh-**[1] in Appendix.] **—bur′i•al** *adj.*

bu•rin (byo͝or′ĭn, bûr′-) *n.* **1.** A steel cutting tool with a sharp beveled point, used in engraving or carving stone. **2.** The style or technique of an engraver's work. **3.** *Archaeology.* An early flint tool with a head like a chisel. [French, probably from obsolete Italian *burino,* of Germanic origin.]

Burk or **Burke** (bûrk), **Martha Jane.** Known as "Calamity Jane." 1852?–1903. American frontierswoman and legendary figure of the Wild West. Often dressed in men's clothing, she was reputed to be a crack shot and an expert rider.

burke (bûrk) *tr.v.* **burked, burk•ing, burkes. 1.** To suppress or extinguish quietly; stifle: *burked the investigation by failing to reappoint the commission.* **2.** To avoid; disregard: *"To make* The Tempest *a tragic and depressing play he was willing to burke all the elements that made it the exact opposite"* (Robert M. Adams). **3.** To execute (someone) by suffocation so as to leave the body intact and suitable for dissection. [After William *Burke* (1792–1829), Irish-born grave robber and murderer.]

Burke (bûrk), **Billie.** 1886–1970. American actress who appeared frequently with John Drew and made numerous motion pictues, including *The Wizard of Oz* (1939).

Burke, Edmund. 1729–1797. Irish-born British politician and writer. Famous for his oratory, he pleaded the cause of the American colonists in Parliament and was instrumental in developing the notions of party responsibility and a loyal opposition within the parliamentary system. His major work, *Reflections on the Revolution in France* (1790), voices his opposition to the excesses of the French experience.

Burke, Martha Jane. See Martha Jane **Burk.**

Bur•ki•na Fa•so (bər-kē′nə fä′sō). Formerly **Up•per Vol•ta** (ŭp′ər vŏl′tə, vōl′-, vôl′-). A landlocked country of western Africa. It was a French protectorate from 1896 until 1960, when it gained its independence. The name of the country was officially changed on August 4, 1984. Ouagadougou is the capital and the largest city. Population, 6,965,886.

Bur•kitt's lymphoma (bûr′kĭts) *n.* An undifferentiated malignant lymphoma usually occurring among children in central Africa, characterized by a large osteolytic lesion in the mandible or by a mass in the retroperitoneal area and associated with the Epstein-Barr virus. Also called *Burkitt's tumor.* [After Denis Parsons *Burkitt,* 20th-century Ugandan physician.]

burl (bûrl) *n.* **1.** A knot, lump, or slub in yarn or cloth. **2.a.** A large, rounded outgrowth on the trunk or branch of a tree. **b.** The wood cut from such an outgrowth, often used decoratively as a veneer. **—burl** *tr.v.* **burled, burl•ing, burls.** To dress or finish (cloth) by removing knots, lumps, slubs, or loose threads. [Middle English *burle,* from Old French *bourle,* tuft of wool, diminutive of *bourre,* coarse wool, from Late Latin *burra,* shaggy garment.] **—burl′er** *n.*

bur•lap (bûr′lăp′) *n.* A strong, coarsely woven cloth made of fibers of jute, flax, or hemp and used to make bags, to reinforce linoleum, and in interior decoration. [Origin unknown.]

Bur•leigh (bûr′lē), First Baron. See William **Cecil.**

Burleigh, Harry Thacker. 1866–1949. American singer, composer, and arranger who devoted much of his lifework to preserving the musical heritage of Black Americans.

bur•lesque (bər-lĕsk′) *n.* **1.** A literary or dramatic work that makes a subject appear ridiculous by treating it in an incongruous way, as by presenting a lofty subject with vulgarity or an inconsequential one with mock dignity. See Synonyms at **caricature. 2.** A ludicrous or mocking imitation; a travesty: *The antics of the defense attorneys turned the trial into a burlesque of justice.* **3.** A variety show characterized by broad ribald comedy, dancing, and striptease. **—burlesque** *v.* **-lesqued, -lesqu•ing, -lesques.** *—tr.* To imitate mockingly or humorously: *"always bringing junk . . . home, as if he were burlesquing his role as provider"* (John Updike). *—intr.* To use the methods or techniques of burlesque. [From French, comical, from Italian *burlesco,* from *burla,* joke, probably from Spanish, from Vulgar Latin **burrula,* diminutive of Late Latin *burrae,* nonsense, from *burra,* wool.] **—bur•lesque′** *adj.* **—bur•lesque′ly** *adv.* **—bur•lesqu′er** *n.*

bur•ley (bûr′lē) *n., pl.* **-leys.** A light-colored tobacco grown chiefly in Kentucky and used especially in making cigarettes. [Probably from the name *Burley.*]

Bur•lin•game (bûr′lĭn-găm′, -lĭng-). A city of western California on the western shore of San Francisco Bay. It is mainly residential. Population, 26,173.

Bur•ling•ton (bûr′lĭng-tən). **1.** A city of southern Ontario, Canada, a suburb of Hamilton on Lake Ontario. Population, 114,853. **2.** A city of southeast Iowa on hills overlooking the Mississippi River. Settled in the 1830's, it was the temporary capital of Iowa Territory (1838–1840). Population, 29,529. **3.** A town of northeast Massachusetts, a residential suburb of Boston. Population, 23,486. **4.** A city of north-central North Carolina east of

Greensboro. It is a textile center in an industrialized area. Population, 37,266. **5.** A city of northwest Vermont on Lake Champlain west-northwest of Montpelier. The largest city in the state, it was the site of a military and naval base during the War of 1812. Population, 37,712.

bur·ly (bûr′lē) *adj.* **-li·er, -li·est.** Heavy, strong, and muscular; husky. See Synonyms at **muscular.** [Middle English *burlich,* from Old English *borlic, excellent. See **bher-¹** in Appendix.] **—bur′li·ly** *adv.* **—bur′li·ness** *n.*

Bur·ma (bûr′mə). Officially (since 1989) **Myan·mar** (myän-mä′). *Abbr.* **Bur.** A country of southeast Asia on the Bay of Bengal and the Andaman Sea. Site of an ancient kingdom, Burma was a province of British India from 1886 until 1948, when it gained its independence. Rangoon is the capital and the largest city. Population, 35,313,905.

Bur·man (bûr′mən) *adj.* Variant of **Burmese. —Burman** *n.* Variant of **Burmese** (sense 1).

bur marigold *n.* See **beggar ticks** (sense 1a).

Burma Road. A highway extending about 1,126 km (700 mi) generally northeastward through mountainous country from northeast Burma to Kunming, China. It was a vital transportation route for wartime supplies to the Chinese government from 1938 to 1946.

Bur·mese (bər-mēz′, -mēs′) also **Bur·man** (bûr′mən) *adj.* *Abbr.* **Bur.** Of or relating to Burma or its people, language, or culture. **—Burmese** *n., pl.* **Burmese. 1.** Also **Burman.** A native or inhabitant of Burma. **2.** The Sino-Tibetan language of Burma.

burn¹ (bûrn) *v.* **burned** or **burnt** (bûrnt), **burn·ing, burns.** *—tr.* **1.a.** To cause to undergo combustion. **b.** To destroy with fire: *burned the trash; burn a house down.* **c.** To consume (fuel or energy, for example): *burned all the wood that winter.* **2.** *Physics.* To cause to undergo nuclear fission or fusion. **3.** To damage or injure by fire, heat, radiation, electricity, or a caustic agent: *burned the toast; burned my skin with the acid.* **4.a.** To execute or kill with fire: *burning heretics at the stake.* **b.** To execute by electrocution. **5.a.** To make or produce by fire or heat: *burn a hole in the rug.* **b.** To dispel; dissipate: *The sun burned off the fog.* **6.a.** To use as a fuel: *a furnace that burns coal.* **b.** To metabolize (glucose, for example) in the body. **7.** To impart a sensation of intense heat to: *The chili burned my mouth.* **8.a.** To irritate or inflame, as by chafing or sunburn. **b.** To let (oneself or a part of one's body) become sunburned. **9.** To brand (an animal). **10.** To harden or impart a finish to by subjecting to intense heat; fire: *burn clay pots in a kiln.* **11.** To make angry: *That remark really burns me.* **12.a.** To defeat in a contest, especially by a narrow margin. **b.** To inflict harm or hardship on; hurt: *"Huge loan losses have burned banks in recent years"* (Christian Science Monitor). **c.** To swindle or deceive; cheat: *We really got burned on the used car we bought.* *—intr.* **1.a.** To undergo combustion. **b.** To admit of burning: *Wood burns easily.* **2.** To consume fuel: *a rocket stage designed to burn for three minutes before being jettisoned.* **3.** *Physics.* To undergo nuclear fission or fusion. **4.a.** To emit heat or light by or as if by fire: *campfires burning in the dark; the sun burning brightly in the sky.* **b.** To become dissipated or to be dispelled by or as if by heat: *The fog burned off as the sun came up.* **5.** To give off light; shine: *a light burning over the door.* **6.** To be destroyed, injured, damaged, or changed by or as if by fire: *a house that burned to the ground; eggs that burned and stuck to the pan.* **7.a.** To be very hot; bake: *a desert burning under the midday sun.* **b.** To feel or look hot: *a child burning with fever.* **c.** To impart a sensation of heat: *a liniment that burns when first applied.* **8.a.** To become irritated or painful, as by chafing or inflammation: *eyes burning from the smoke.* **b.** To become sunburned or windburned. **9.** To be consumed with strong emotion, especially: **a.** To be or become angry: *an insult that really made me burn.* **b.** To be very eager: *was burning with ambition.* **10.** To penetrate by or as if by intense heat or flames: *enemy ground radar burning through the fighters' electronic jammers; a look that burned into them.* **11.** To be vividly or painfully present: *shame burning in my heart.* **12.a.** To suffer punishment or death by or as if by fire: *souls burning in hell.* **b.** To be electrocuted. **—burn** *n.* **1.** An injury produced by fire, heat, radiation, electricity, or a caustic agent. **2.** A burned place or area: *a cigarette burn in the tablecloth.* **3.** The process or result of burning: *The fire settled down to a steady burn.* **4.** A stinging sensation: *the burn of alcohol on an open wound.* **5.** A sunburn or windburn. **6.** *Aerospace.* A firing of a rocket. **7.** A swindle. ***—phrasal verbs.*** **burn out. 1.** To stop burning from lack of fuel. **2.** To wear out or make or become inoperative as a result of heat or friction: *The short circuit burned out the fuse.* **3.** To cause (a property owner or a resident) to have to evacuate the premises because of fire: *The shopkeeper was burned out by arsonists.* **4.** To make or become exhausted, especially as a result of long-term stress: *"Hours are long, stress is high, and many recruits drop out or burn out"* (Robert J. Samuelson). **burn up. 1.** To make angry: *Their rudeness really burns me up.* **2.** To travel over or through at high speed: *drag racers burning up the track.* ***—idioms.*** **burn (one's) bridges.** To eliminate the possibility of return or retreat. **burn the** (or **one's**) **candle at both ends.** To exhaust oneself or one's resources by leading a hectic or extravagant life. **burn the midnight oil.** To work or study very late at night. **to burn.** In great amounts: *They had money to burn.* [Middle English *burnen,* from Old English *beornan,* to be on fire, and from *bærnan,* to set on fire; see **gʷher-** in Appendix.]

SYNONYMS: *burn, scorch, singe, sear, char, parch.* These verbs mean to injure or alter by means of intense heat or flames. *Burn,* the most general, applies to the effects of exposure to a source of heat or to something that can produce a similar effect: *burned the rug with a cigarette; left the onions on the stove and burned them; burned my fingers by handling dry ice. Scorch* usually refers to contact with flame or heated metal and involves superficial burning that discolors or damages the texture of something: *afraid that the iron might scorch the sheet; trees that were scorched in a forest fire. Singe* specifies superficial burning by brief exposure to flame and especially the deliberate removal of projections such as bristles or feathers from a carcass, such as a plucked fowl, before cooking: *a grease fire that singed my eyelashes; singed the Thanksgiving turkey, then roasted it. Sear* applies to surface burning of organic tissue, as by branding or cauterizing: *Sear the lamb over high heat before lowering the flame and adding liquid.* To *char* is most often to reduce a substance to carbon or charcoal by means of fire: *The timbers of the house were charred by the raging fire. Parch* in this sense emphasizes the drying and often fissuring of a surface from exposure to flame, the sun, or hot wind: *The torrid rays of the sun parched the soil.*

burn² (bûrn) *n.* *Scots.* A small stream; a brook. [Middle English, from Old English *burna.* See **bhreu-** in Appendix.]

Bur·na·by (bûr′nə-bē). A city of southwest British Columbia, Canada, a suburb of Vancouver. Population, 136,494.

burn bag *n.* A bag into which secret or highly sensitive documents are placed before they are burned.

burn center *n.* A multidisciplinary health care facility in which victims of burns are treated.

burned-out (bûrnd′out′) or **burnt-out** (bûrnt′-) *adj.* Worn out or exhausted, especially as a result of long-term stress.

Burne-Jones (bûrn′jōnz′), Sir **Edward Coley.** 1833–1898. British painter and member of the Pre-Raphaelite Brotherhood who is known for the mystical, dreamlike settings of his paintings and stained-glass designs.

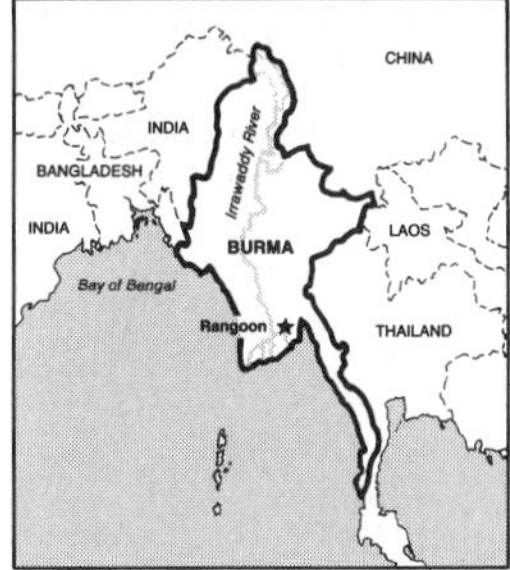

Burma

burn·er (bûr′nər) *n.* **1.** One that burns, especially: **a.** A device, as in a furnace, stove, or gas lamp, that is lighted to produce a flame. **b.** A device on a stovetop, such as a gas jet or electric element, that produces heat. **2.a.** A unit, such as a furnace, in which something is burned: *an oil burner.* **b.** An incinerator. **3.** *Slang.* **a.** An elaborate mural painted by a graffiti artist, usually on the wall of an abandoned building. **b.** A large, multicolored graffito.

bur·net (bər-nĕt′, bûr′nĭt) *n.* A perennial plant of the genus *Sanguisorba,* having pinnately compound leaves and apetalous flowers. The young leaves are sometimes added to salads as a garnish. [Middle English, from Medieval Latin *burneta,* from Old French *brunete,* dark brown, diminutive of *brun,* brown, of Germanic origin. See **bher-²** in Appendix.]

Bur·nett (bûr-nĕt′, bûr′nĭt), **Frances Eliza Hodgson.** 1849–1924. British-born American writer famous for her popular children's books, especially *Little Lord Fauntleroy* (1886), whose priggish title character dressed in black velvet with ruffled lace collars and sported long golden curls.

Bur·ney (bûr′nē), **Frances.** Known as "Fanny." 1752–1840. British writer best known for her witty and sophisticated letters and diaries covering the years from 1768 until her death.

Burn·ham (bûr′nəm), **Daniel Hudson.** 1846–1912. American architect and city planner. He did his major work in Chicago, including the general design for the Columbian Exposition (1893) and several early skyscrapers.

burnoose

burn·ing (bûr′nĭng) *adj.* **1.** Marked by flames or intense heat: *a burning sun.* **2.** Characterized by intense emotion; passionate: *a burning desire for justice.* **3.** Of immediate import; urgent: *"the issues that seem so burning in Washington"* (John F. Kennedy). **—burn′ing·ly** *adv.*

burning bush also **burn·ing-bush** (bûr′nĭng-bo͝osh′) *n.* **1.** Any of several shrubs or shrubby plants, such as the summer cypress and certain species of euonymous, having foliage that turns bright red in autumn. **2.** See **gas plant.**

bur·nish (bûr′nĭsh) *tr.v.* **-nished, -nish·ing, -nish·es. 1.** To make smooth or glossy by or as if by rubbing; polish. **2.** To rub with a tool that serves especially to smooth or polish. **—burnish** *n.* A smooth, glossy finish or appearance; luster. [Middle English *burnishen,* from Old French *burnir, burniss-,* variant of *brunir,* from *brun,* shining, of Germanic origin. See **bher-²** in Appendix.] **—bur′nish·er** *n.*

Burn·ley (bûrn′lē). A borough of northwest England north of Manchester. It grew as a coal-mining and textile center. Population, 93,700.

bur·noose also **bur·nous** (bər-no͞os′) *n.* A hooded cloak worn especially by Arabs. [French *burnous,* from Arabic *burnus,* from Greek *birros,* hooded cloak, from Late Latin *birrus.*]

burn·out (bûrn′out′) *n.* **1.** A failure in a device attributable to burning, excessive heat, or friction. **2.** *Aerospace.* **a.** The termination of rocket or jet-engine operation because of fuel exhaustion or shutoff. **b.** The point at which this termination occurs. **3.a.** Physical or emotional exhaustion, especially as a result of long-term stress or dissipation. **b.** One who is worn out physically or emotionally, as from long-term stress.

Burns (bûrnz), **Arthur Frank.** Born 1904. Austrian-born Amer-

ă pat	oi boy
ā pay	ou out
âr care	o͝o took
ä father	o͞o boot
ĕ pet	ŭ cut
ē be	ûr urge
ĭ pit	th thin
ī pie	*th* this
îr pier	hw which
ŏ pot	zh vision
ō toe	ə about, item
ô paw	♦ regionalism

Stress marks: ′ (primary); ′ (secondary), as in **dictionary** (dĭk′shə-nĕr′ē)

ican economist and influential adviser to several presidential administrations.

Burns, George. Born 1896. American comedian and actor. From 1922 to 1964 he and Gracie Allen were a popular husband-and-wife comedy team. Since her death in 1964 he has appeared in both comic and dramatic roles, winning an Academy Award in 1975 for *The Sunshine Boys.*

George Burns
Photographed in 1986

Burns, Robert. 1759–1796. Scottish poet considered the major poetic voice of his nation. His lyrics celebrate love, patriotism, and rustic life. **—Burns′i·an** *adj.*

Burn·side (bûrn′sīd′), **Ambrose Everett.** 1824–1881. American general and politician known more for his side-whiskers (or sideburns) than for his career in the Union Army, which included defeats at Fredericksburg (1862) and Petersburg (1864).

burn·sides (bûrn′sīdz′) *pl.n.* Heavy side-whiskers worn with the chin clean-shaven. [After Ambrose Everett BURNSIDE.]

Burns·ville (bûrnz′vĭl′). A city of southeastern Minnesota, a suburb of Minneapolis. Population, 35,674.

burnt (bûrnt) *v.* A past tense and a past participle of **burn[1].**

burnt offering *n.* A slaughtered animal or other offering burned on an altar as a religious sacrifice.

burnt-out (bûrnt′out′) *adj.* Variant of **burned-out.**

burnt sienna *n.* **1.** A reddish-brown pigment prepared by calcining raw sienna. **2.** *Color.* A dark reddish orange.

bur oak *n.* An oak tree *(Quercus macrocarpa)* of eastern North America, having pinnately lobed leaves, acorns enclosed within a deep fringed cup, and hard, durable wood.

burp (bûrp) *n.* A belch. **—burp** *v.* **burped, burp·ing, burps.** *—intr.* To belch. *—tr.* To cause (a baby) to expel gas from the stomach, as by patting the back after feeding. [Imitative.]

burp gun *n.* A lightweight portable submachine gun.

burr[1] (bûr) *n.* **1.** A rough edge or area remaining on material, such as metal, after it has been cast, cut, or drilled. **2.** Variant of **bur[1]. —burr** *tr.v.* **burred, burr·ing, burrs. 1.** To form a burr on. **2.** To remove burrs from. [Variant of BUR[1].]

burr[2] also **bur** (bûr) *—n.* **1.** A trilling of the letter *r,* usually made with the tip of the tongue and characteristic of Scottish speech. **2.** A buzzing or whirring sound. *—v.* **burred, burr·ing, burrs** also **burs.** *—tr.* To pronounce with a burr. *—intr.* **1.** To speak with a burr. **2.** To make a buzzing or whirring sound. [Imitative.]

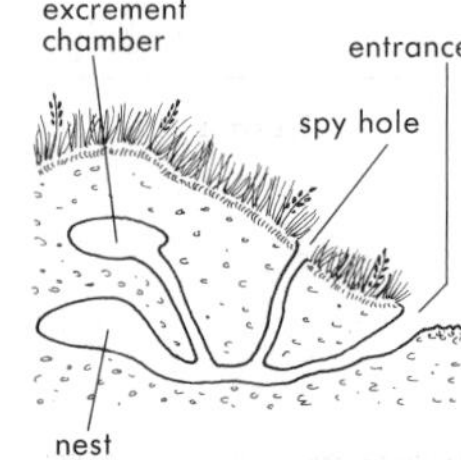

burrow
Of a woodchuck

burr[3] also **bur** (bûr) *n.* A washer that fits around the smaller end of a rivet. [Middle English *burre,* ring, disk, alteration of *burwhe,* circle, disk.]

Burr (bûr), **Aaron.** 1756–1836. American politician who became Vice President of the United States (1801–1805) under Thomas Jefferson after a deadlock in the electoral college was broken by the House of Representatives. On July 11, 1804, Burr mortally wounded his rival Alexander Hamilton in a duel and later fled south where he was involved in a mysterious conspiracy to establish an independent nation in Mexico and the Southwest. Tried for treason, he was acquitted for lack of evidence.

bur reed or **bur-reed** (bûr′rēd′) *n.* Any of various aquatic or wetland plants of the genus *Sparganium,* having elongated leaves and ball-like clusters of tiny, beaked fruits.

bur·ri·to (bo͞o-rē′tō, bə-) *n., pl.* **-tos.** A flour tortilla wrapped around a filling, as of beef, beans, or cheese. [American Spanish, from Spanish, diminutive of *burro,* burro. See BURRO.]

bur·ro (bûr′ō, bo͝or′ō, bŭr′ō) *n., pl.* **-ros.** A small donkey, especially one used as a pack animal. [Spanish, back-formation from *borrico,* donkey, from Late Latin *burrīcus,* small horse.]

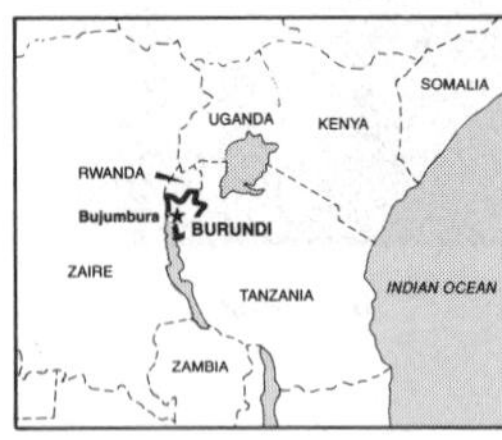

Burundi

bur·ro's tail (bûr′ōz, bo͝or′-, bŭr′-) *n.* A Mexican plant *(Sedum morganianum)* grown chiefly as a houseplant for its hanging, taillike stems covered with succulent, overlapping leaves. Also called *donkey's tail.*

Bur·roughs (bûr′ōz, bŭr′-), **Edgar Rice.** 1875–1950. American writer best known for creating the character Tarzan in his novel *Tarzan of the Apes* (1914).

Burroughs, John. 1837–1921. American naturalist and writer whose vivid essays gained him wide popularity as a benign sage of nature.

Burroughs, William Seward[1]. 1855–1898. American inventor who in the early 1890's designed and patented the first practical adding machine.

Burroughs, William Seward[2]. Born 1914. American writer noted especially for *Naked Lunch* (1959), a surrealist portrait of drug addiction.

bur·row (bûr′ō, bŭr′ō) *n.* **1.** A hole or tunnel dug in the ground by a small animal, such as a rabbit or a mole, for habitation or refuge. **2.** A narrow or snug place. **—burrow** *v.* **-rowed, -row·ing, -rows.** *—intr.* **1.a.** To dig a hole or tunnel for habitation or refuge. **b.** To live or hide in such a place. **2.** To move or progress by or as if by digging or tunneling: *"Suddenly the train is burrowing through the pinewoods"* (William Styron). *—tr.* **1.** To make by or as if by tunneling. **2.** To dig a hole or tunnel in or through. **3.** *Archaic.* To hide in or as in a burrow. [Middle English *borow.*] **—bur′row·er** *n.*

bur·row·ing owl (bûr′ō-ĭng, bŭr′-) *n.* A small, long-legged owl *(Speotyto cunicularia)* of American prairies that nests in burrows dug by animals such as prairie dogs or rabbits.

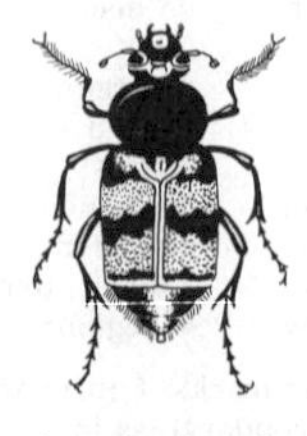
burying beetle

burr·stone (bûr′stōn′) *n.* Variant of **buhrstone.**

bur·ry (bûr′ē) *adj.* **-ri·er, -ri·est.** Having burs; prickly.

bur·sa (bûr′sə) *n., pl.* **-sae** (-sē) or **-sas.** *Anatomy.* A sac or saclike bodily cavity, especially one containing a viscous lubricating fluid and located between a tendon and a bone or at points of friction between moving structures. [Late Latin, purse, pouch, from Greek, skin, wineskin.] **—bur′sal** *adj.*

Bur·sa (bûr′sə, bo͝or-sä′). A city of northwest Turkey west of Ankara. It dates from the third century B.C. and was a capital of the Ottoman Turks in the 1300's. Population, 445,113.

bursa of Fa·bri·ci·us (fə-brĭsh′ē-əs, -brĭsh′əs) *n.* A thymuslike lymphoid gland in birds that is an outgrowth of the cloaca and the site of B cell maturation. [After Hieronymus *Fabricius* (1537–1619), Italian anatomist.]

bur·sar (bûr′sər, -sär′) *n.* An official in charge of funds, as at a college or university; a treasurer. [Middle English *burser,* from Medieval Latin *bursārius,* from Late Latin *bursa,* purse. See BURSA.]

bur·sa·ry (bûr′sə-rē) *n., pl.* **-ries. 1.** A treasury, especially of a public institution or religious order. **2.** *Chiefly British.* A scholarship granted to a university student in need. [Medieval Latin *bursāria,* from *bursa,* purse. See BURSA.] **—bur·sar′i·al** (bər-sâr′ē-əl) *adj.*

burse (bûrs) *n.* **1.** A purse. **2.** *Ecclesiastical.* A flat cloth case for carrying the corporal that is used in celebrating the Eucharist. [Late Latin *bursa.* See BURSA.]

bur·si·tis (bər-sī′tĭs) *n.* Inflammation of a bursa, especially in the shoulder, elbow, or knee joint.

burst (bûrst) *v.* **burst, burst·ing, bursts.** *—intr.* **1.a.** To come open or fly apart suddenly or violently, especially from internal pressure. **b.** To explode. **2.** To be or seem to be full to the point of breaking open: *The sacks were bursting with grain.* **3.** To emerge, come forth, or arrive suddenly: *burst out of the door.* **4.** To come apart or seem to come apart because of overwhelming emotion: *thought his heart would burst with happiness.* **5.** To give sudden utterance or expression: *burst out laughing; burst into tears.* *—tr.* **1.** To cause to burst: *burst the balloon.* See Synonyms at **break. 2.** To exert strong pressure in order to force (something) open. **3.** *Computer Science.* To separate (a continuous form or printout) into individual sheets. **—burst** *n.* **1.** A sudden outbreak or outburst; an explosion. **2.** The result of bursting, especially the explosion of a projectile or bomb on impact or in the air. **3.a.** The number of bullets fired from an automatic weapon by one pull of the trigger. **b.** A volley of bullets fired from an automatic weapon: *The machine gunner fired a quick burst.* **4.** An abrupt, intense increase; a rush: *a burst of speed; wind blowing in fitful bursts.* [Middle English *bursten,* from Old English *berstan.*]

burst·er (bûr′stər) *n.* *Computer Science.* An offline device used to burst computer printout.

bur·then (bûr′*th*ən) *n.* A burden.

bur·ton (bûr′tn) *n.* *Nautical.* A light tackle having double or single blocks, used to hoist or tighten rigging. [Origin unknown.]

Bur·ton (bûr′tn). A city of southeast-central Michigan, a suburb of Flint. Population, 29,976.

Burton, Harold Hitz. 1888–1964. American jurist who served as an associate justice of the U.S. Supreme Court (1945–1958).

Burton, Sir **Richard Francis.** 1821–1890. British explorer and Orientalist. Disguised as a Pathan, he journeyed (1853) to the forbidden cities of Mecca and Medina and in 1858 tried unsuccessfully to discover the source of the Nile River. His best-known work is a translation of *The Arabian Nights* (1885–1888), which was considered scandalous at the time.

Burton, Robert. 1577–1640. English cleric and writer known chiefly for his *Anatomy of Melancholy* (1621), a treatise on the causes, symptoms, and cure of melancholy that ranges far afield in its lively depiction of everyday life.

Burton upon Trent or **Burton on Trent** (trĕnt′). A borough of west-central England south-southwest of Derby. It is the center of a brewing industry begun by Benedictine monks who built an abbey on the site in 1002. Population, 48,500.

Bu·ru (bo͞or′o͞o). An island of eastern Indonesia in the Moluccas west of Ceram.

Bu·run·di (bo͞o-ro͞on′dē, -ro͞on′-). A country of east-central Africa with a coastline on Lake Tanganyika. It was part of German East Africa and later of Ruanda-Urundi before it gained its independence in 1962. Bujumbura is the capital and the largest city. Population, 4,523,513. **—Bu·run′di·an** *adj. & n.*

bur·y (bĕr′ē) *tr.v.* **-ied, -y·ing, -ies. 1.** To place in the ground: *bury a bone.* **2.** To place (a corpse) in a grave, a tomb, or the sea; inter. **3.** To conceal by or as if by covering over with earth; hide: *buried her face in the pillow; buried the secret deep within himself.* See Synonyms at **hide[1]. 4.** To occupy (oneself) with deep concentration; absorb: *buried myself in my studies.* **5.** To put an end to; abandon: *buried their quarrel and shook hands.* **—*idiom.* bury the hatchet.** To stop fighting; resolve a quarrel. [Middle English *burien,* from Old English *byrgan.* See **bhergh-[1]** in Appendix.] **—bur′i·er** *n.*

Bur·y (bĕr′ē). A borough of northwest England north-northwest of Manchester. It was founded on the site of a Saxon settlement and has been a textile center since the 14th century. Population, 177,600.

bur·y·ing beetle (bĕr′ē-ĭng) *n.* Any of various black or black and orange beetles of the genus *Necrophorus* that bury dead mice and other small animals on which they feed and lay their eggs. Also called *sexton beetle.*

Bury Saint Ed•munds (ĕd′məndz). A municipal borough of east-central England east of Cambridge. In 903 the remains of King Edmund were interred in the town's monastery (founded c. 630), which became a famous shrine and Benedictine abbey. Population, 28,914.

bus (bŭs) *n., pl.* **bus•es** or **bus•ses. 1.** A long motor vehicle for carrying passengers, usually along a fixed route. **2.** *Informal.* A large or ungainly automobile. **3.** A four-wheeled cart for carrying dishes in a restaurant. **4.** *Electricity.* A bus bar. **5.** *Computer Science.* A parallel circuit that connects the major components of a computer, allowing the transfer of electric impulses from one connected component to any other. —*attributive.* Often used to modify another noun: *a bus station; a bus tour.* **—bus** *v.* **bused, bus•ing, bus•es** or **bussed, bus•sing, bus•ses.** —*tr.* **1.** To transport in a bus. **2.** To transport (schoolchildren) by bus to schools outside their neighborhoods, especially as a means of achieving racial integration. **3.** To carry or clear (dishes) in a restaurant. —*intr.* **1.** To travel in a bus. **2.** To work as a busboy. [Short for OMNIBUS. V., intr., sense 2, back-formation from BUSBOY.]

bus. *abbr.* Business.

bus bar *n. Electricity.* A conducting bar that carries heavy currents to supply several electric circuits.

bus•boy also **bus boy** (bŭs′boi′) *n.* A restaurant employee who clears away dirty dishes, sets tables, and serves as an assistant to a waiter or waitress. [(OMNI)BUS + BOY.]

bus•by (bŭz′bē) *n., pl.* **-bies.** A tall, full-dress fur hat worn in certain guards regiments of the British army. [Possibly from the name *Busby.*]

bush¹ (bo͝osh) *n.* **1.** A low shrub with many branches. **2.** A thick growth of shrubs; a thicket. **3.a.** Land covered with dense vegetation or undergrowth. **b.** Land remote from settlement: *the Australian bush.* **4.** A shaggy mass, as of hair. **5.** A fox's tail. **6.a.** *Archaic.* A clump of ivy hung outside a tavern to indicate the availability of wine inside. **b.** *Obsolete.* A tavern. **—bush** *v.* **bushed, bush•ing, bushes.** —*intr.* **1.** To grow or branch out like a bush. **2.** To extend in a bushy growth. —*tr.* To decorate, protect, or support with bushes. **—bush** *adj. Slang.* Bush-league; second-rate: *"Reviewers here have tended to see in him a kind of bush D.H. Lawrence"* (Saturday Review). [Middle English, partly from Old English *busc,* partly from Old French *bois,* wood (of Germanic origin) and partly of Scandinavian origin (akin to Danish *busk*). N., sense 3, possibly from Dutch *bosch.*]

bush² (bo͝osh) *tr.v.* **bushed, bush•ing, bush•es.** To furnish or line with a bushing. [From *bush,* bushing, possibly alteration of Dutch *bus,* box.]

Bush (bo͝osh), **Barbara.** Born 1925. First Lady of the United States (since 1989) as the wife of President George Bush. She has been active in promoting literacy.

Bush, George Herbert Walker. Born 1924. The 41st President of the United States (since 1989). He was previously U.S. ambassador to the United Nations (1971–1972) and China (1974–1975), director of the Central Intelligence Agency (1976–1977), and Vice President (1981–1989) under Ronald Reagan.

Bush, Vannevar. 1890–1974. American electrical engineer and physicist who designed (1928) the differential analyzer, an early computer, and directed the World War II effort to develop the first atomic bomb.

bush baby *n.* Any of several small, nocturnal African primates of the genera *Galago* and *Euoticus,* having dense, woolly fur, large round eyes, prominent ears, and a long tail. Also called *galago.*

bush bean *n.* **1.** A shrubby variety of the snap bean. **2.** Any bean plant with an upright, bushy growth not requiring an artificial support.

bush•buck (bo͝osh′bŭk′) *n.* An African antelope *(Tragelaphus scriptus)* having a reddish-brown coat with white markings and twisted horns. Also called *harnessed antelope.* [Translation of Afrikaans *bosbok* : *bos,* bush + *bok,* buck.]

bush clover *n.* Any of various plants of the genus *Lespedeza* in the pea family, having compound leaves with three leaflets and various colored flowers and often grown for forage, soil improvement, erosion control, or ornament. Also called *lespedeza.*

bushed (bo͝osht) *adj. Informal.* Extremely tired; exhausted: *"I once stayed awake seven years on end. Not even a nap. Boy, was I bushed"* (Martin Amis). [Possibly from Australian slang, lost in the bush.]

bush•el¹ (bo͝osh′əl) *n. Abbr.* **bsh., bu., bu 1.a.** A unit of volume or capacity in the U.S. Customary System, used in dry measure and equal to 4 pecks, 2,150.42 cubic inches, or 35.24 liters. **b.** A unit of volume or capacity in the British Imperial System, used in dry and liquid measure and equal to 2,219.36 cubic inches or 36.37 liters. See table at **measurement. 2.** A container with the capacity of a bushel. **3.** *Informal.* A large amount; a great deal. [Middle English, from Anglo-Norman *bussel,* variant of Old French *boissiel,* from *boisse,* one sixth of a bushel, of Celtic origin.]

bush•el² (bo͝osh′əl) *tr.v.* **-eled, -el•ing, -els** or **-elled, -el•ling, -els.** To alter or mend (clothing). [Probably from German *bosseln,* to do odd jobs, alteration (perhaps influenced by *bosseln,* to emboss) of *basteln,* to putter.] **—bush′el•er, bush′el•ler** *n.* **—bush′el•man** (-mən) *n.*

bush honeysuckle *n.* **1.** Any of three eastern North American shrubs of the genus *Diervilla,* having opposite, deciduous leaves and clusters of yellow flowers. **2.** Any of several shrubby honeysuckle plants of the genus *Lonicera,* especially *L. tatarica* and *L. xylosteum.*

Bu•shi•do also **bu•shi•do** (bo͝osh′ĭ-dō′, bo͞o′shĭ-) *n.* The traditional code of the Japanese samurai, stressing honor, self-discipline, bravery, and simple living. [Japanese *bushidō* : *bushi,* warrior (from Chinese *wǔ shì,* knight, warrior : *wǔ,* military + *shì,* brave warrior) + *dō,* way (from Chinese *dào*).]

bush•ing (bo͝osh′ĭng) *n.* **1.** A fixed or removable cylindrical metal lining used to constrain, guide, or reduce friction. **2.** *Electricity.* An insulating lining for an aperture through which a conductor passes. **3.** An adapter threaded to permit joining of pipes with different diameters. [From BUSH².]

bush jacket *n.* A long, cotton shirtlike jacket usually with four flat pockets and a belt.

bush league *n. Baseball.* A minor league. **—bush leaguer** *n.*

bush-league (bo͝osh′lēg′) *adj.* **1.** *Baseball.* Of or belonging to a minor league. **2.** *Slang.* Of inferior or unprofessional quality; second-rate: *a bush-league advertising campaign.*

Bush•man (bo͝osh′mən) *n.* **1.** See **San. 2. bushman.** *Australian.* One who lives or travels in the wilderness, especially in the outback. [Translation of Afrikaans *boschjeman* : *boschje,* bush + *man,* man.]

Bushman, Francis Xavier. 1883–1966. American actor whose classic profile and impressive physique made him a matinee idol of the silent-film era.

bush•mas•ter (bo͝osh′măs′tər) *n.* A large venomous snake *(Lachesis mutus)* of tropical America, having brown and grayish markings.

Bush•nell (bo͝osh′nəl), **David.** 1742–1824. American inventor who designed (1775) a man-propelled submarine for use against British ships in the Revolution. The device proved ineffectual (it was ridiculed as "Bushnell's Turtle") but earned him later regard as "the Father of the Submarine."

bush pig *n.* A hog *(Potamochoerus porcus)* of southern Africa, having long tufts of hair on the face and ears. [Translation of Afrikaans *bosvark* : *bos,* bush + *vark,* pig.]

bush pilot *n.* A person who flies a small airplane to and from areas inaccessible to larger aircraft or other means of transportation.

bush•rang•er (bo͝osh′rān′jər) *n.* **1.** One who lives in the wilderness. **2.** *Australian.* An outlaw living in the bush.

bush•tit (bo͝osh′tĭt′) *n.* Either of two small, long-tailed birds *(Psaltriparus minimus* or *P. melanotis)* of western North America, having predominantly gray plumage.

bush•whack (bo͝osh′hwăk′, -wăk′) *v.* **-whacked, -whack•ing, -whacks.** —*intr.* **1.** To make one's way through thick woods by cutting away bushes and branches. **2.** To travel through or live in the woods. **3.** To fight as a guerrilla in the woods. —*tr.* To attack suddenly from a place of concealment; ambush. See Synonyms at **ambush. —bush′whack′er** *n.*

bush•y (bo͝osh′ē) *adj.* **-i•er, -i•est. 1.** Overgrown with bushes. **2.** Thick and shaggy: *a bushy head of hair.* **—bush′i•ly** *adv.* **—bush′i•ness** *n.*

busi•ness (bĭz′nĭs) *n. Abbr.* **bus. 1.a.** The occupation, work, or trade in which a person is engaged: *the wholesale food business.* **b.** A specific occupation or pursuit: *the best designer in the business.* **2.** Commercial, industrial, or professional dealings: *new systems now being used in business.* **3.** A commercial enterprise or establishment: *bought his uncle's business.* **4.** Volume or amount of commercial trade: *Business had fallen off.* **5.** Commercial dealings; patronage: *took her business to a trustworthy salesperson.* **6.a.** One's rightful or proper concern or interest: *"The business of America is business"* (Calvin Coolidge). **b.** Something involving one personally: *It's none of my business.* **7.** Serious work or endeavor: *got right down to business.* **8.** An affair or matter: *"We will proceed no further in this business"* (Shakespeare). **9.** An incidental action performed by an actor on the stage to fill a pause between lines or to provide interesting detail. **10.** *Informal.* Verbal abuse; scolding: *gave me the business for being late.* **11.** *Obsolete.* The condition of being busy. —*attributive.* Often used to modify another noun: *a business computer; a business suit.* [Middle English *businesse,* from *bisi,* busy. See BUSY.]

SYNONYMS: *business, industry, commerce, trade, traffic.* These nouns apply to forms of activity that have the objective of supplying commodities. *Business* pertains broadly to commercial, financial, and industrial activity: *decided to go into the oil business. Industry* is the production and manufacture of goods or commodities, especially on a large scale: *the computer industry; the arms industry. Commerce* and *trade* refer to the exchange and distribution of goods or commodities: *laws regulating interstate commerce; involved in the domestic fur trade; foreign commerce* (or *trade*). *Traffic* pertains broadly to commercial dealings but in particular to businesses engaged in the transportation of goods or passengers: *renovated the docks to attract shipping traffic.* The word may also suggest illegal trade, as in narcotics: *Traffic in stolen goods was brisk.* See also Synonyms at **affair.**

business administration *n.* A college or university course

Barbara Bush
Photographed in 1989

George Bush

ă pat	oi boy
ā pay	ou out
âr care	o͝o took
ä father	o͞o boot
ĕ pet	ŭ cut
ē be	ûr urge
ĭ pit	th thin
ī pie	*th* this
îr pier	hw which
ŏ pot	zh vision
ō toe	ə about, item
ô paw	♦ regionalism

Stress marks: **′** (primary); ′ (secondary), as in **dictionary** (dĭk′shə-nĕr′ē)

of studies that offers instruction in general business principles and practices.

business card *n.* A small card printed or engraved with a person's name and business affiliation, including such information as title, address, and telephone number.

business cycle *n.* A sequence of economic activity typically characterized by recession, fiscal recovery, growth, and fiscal decline.

busi·ness·like (bĭzʹnĭs-līkʹ) *adj.* **1.** Showing or having characteristics advantageous to or of use in business; methodical and systematic. **2.** Purposeful; earnest. **3.** Practical; unemotional: *The couple maintained a businesslike attitude toward their divorce.*

busi·ness·man (bĭzʹnĭs-mănʹ) *n.* A man engaged in business. See Usage Note at **man.**

busi·ness·per·son (bĭzʹnĭs-pûrʹsən) *n.* One engaged in business. See Usage Note at **man.**

busi·ness·wom·an (bĭzʹnĭs-wo͝omʹən) *n.* A woman engaged in business. See Usage Note at **man.**

bus·ing or **bus·sing** (bŭsʹĭng) *n.* The transportation of schoolchildren by bus to schools outside their neighborhoods, especially as a means of achieving racial integration.

busk·er (bŭsʹkər) *n.* A street musician or public entertainer, especially one who solicits money during a performance: *"A sun-warmed busker fiddles some Vivaldi near the subway exit north of the White House"* (New York Times). [From *busk,* to entertain by singing and dancing, of unknown origin.]

bus·kin (bŭsʹkĭn) *n.* **1.** A foot and leg covering reaching halfway to the knee, resembling a laced half boot. **2.a.** A thick-soled laced half boot worn by actors of Greek and Roman tragedies. **b.** Tragedy, especially that which resembles a Greek tragedy. [Perhaps alteration (influenced by BUCKSKIN) of obsolete French *broisequin,* small leather boot.]

bus·load (bŭsʹlōdʹ) *n.* The number of passengers or the quantity of cargo that a bus can carry.

bus·man (bŭsʹmən) *n.* One who drives a bus.

bus·man's holiday (bŭsʹmənz) *n. Informal.* A vacation during which one engages in activity that is similar to one's usual work.

bust[1]
Early 19th-century bust of Joachim Murat by Antonio Canova

Bu·so·ni (bo͞o-zōʹnē, byo͞o-), **Ferruccio Benvenuto.** 1866–1924. Italian pianist, conductor, and composer known for his flamboyant style.

buss (bŭs) *tr. & intr.v.* **bussed, buss·ing, buss·es.** To kiss. **—buss** *n.* A kiss. [Possibly blend of obsolete *bass* (akin to French *baiser*) and obsolete *cuss* (akin to Middle English *kissen,* to kiss; see KISS) or from Scottish Gaelic *bus,* lips, mouth; see PUSS[2].]

bus·ses (bŭsʹĭz) *n.* A plural of **bus.**

bus·sing (bŭsʹĭng) *n.* Variant of **busing.**

bust[1] (bŭst) *n.* **1.** A sculpture representing a person's head, shoulders, and upper chest. **2.a.** A woman's bosom. **b.** The human chest. [French *buste,* from Italian *busto,* possibly from Latin *bustum,* sepulchral monument.]

bust[2] (bŭst) *v.* **bust·ed, bust·ing, busts.** —*tr.* **1.** *Slang.* **a.** To smash or break, especially forcefully: *"Mr. Luger worked it with a rake, busting up the big clods, making a flat brown table"* (Garrison Keillor). **b.** To render inoperable or unusable: *busted the vending machine by putting in foreign coins.* **2.** To cause to come to an end; break up: *an attempt to bust the union.* **3.** To break or tame (a horse). **4.** To cause to become bankrupt or short of money: *"Too often, the promise of a high-tech design leads to a weapon that busts the budget"* (Business Week). **5.** *Slang.* To reduce in rank. See Synonyms at **demote. 6.** To hit; punch. **7.** *Slang.* **a.** To place under arrest. **b.** To make a raid on. —*intr.* **1.** *Slang.* **a.** To undergo breakage; become broken. **b.** To burst; break: *"Several companies have threatened to bust out of their high-wage contracts by the dubious technique of declaring bankruptcy"* (Washington Post). **2.** To become bankrupt or short of money. **3.** *Games.* To lose at blackjack by exceeding a score of 21. **—bust** *n.* **1.** A failure; a flop: *"The home-style bean curd is a bust, oily and rubbery"* (Mark and Gail Barnett). **2.** A state of bankruptcy. **3.** A time or period of widespread financial depression: *"Bankers consider the region's diversified economy to be good protection against a possible real estate bust"* (American Banker). **4.** A punch; a blow. **5.** A spree: *a fraternity beer bust.* **6.** *Slang.* **a.** An arrest. **b.** A raid. [Variant of BURST.]

Bus·ta·man·te (bo͞osʹtə-mänʹtā), Sir **(William) Alexander.** 1884–1977. Jamaican labor leader and politician who opposed federation with other West Indian states and was the first prime minister (1962–1967) of independent Jamaica.

bustard
Kori bustard
Ardeotis kori

bus·tard (bŭsʹtərd) *n.* Any of various large, long-legged Old World game birds of the family Otididae that frequent dry, open, grassy plains. [Middle English, from blend of Old French *bistarde* and Old French *oustarde,* both from Latin *avis tarda* : *avis,* bird; see **awi-** in Appendix + *tardus,* feminine of *tardus,* slow.]

bust·er (bŭsʹtər) *n.* **1.** One that breaks up something: *a crime buster.* **2.** A broncobuster. **3.** A particularly robust child. **4.** *Informal.* Fellow. Used as a form of familiar address: *Say, buster, where are you going?*

♦**bus·ti·cate** (bŭsʹtĭ-kātʹ) *tr.v.* **-cat·ed, -cat·ing, -cates.** *Northern U.S.* To break into pieces. See Regional Note at **absquatulate.** [BUST[2] + *-icate* (as in MEDICATE).]

bus·tier (bo͞os-tyāʹ, bŭs-) *n.* A formfitting sleeveless and usually strapless woman's top, worn as lingerie and often as evening attire. [French, from *buste,* bust. See BUST[1].]

bus·tle[1] (bŭsʹəl) *intr. & tr.v.* **-tled, -tling, -tles.** To move or cause to move energetically and busily. **—bustle** *n.* Excited and often noisy activity; a stir. [Possibly variant of obsolete *buskle,* frequentative of *busk,* to prepare oneself, from Old Norse *būask.* See **bheuə-** in Appendix.]

bus·tle[2] (bŭsʹəl) *n.* **1.** A frame or pad to support and expand the fullness of the back of a woman's skirt. **2.** A bow, peplum, or gathering of material at the back of a woman's skirt below the waist. [Origin unknown.]

Bu·sto Ar·si·zio (bo͞oʹstō är-sēʹtsyō). A city of northern Italy northwest of Milan. It is a center of Italy's cotton industry. Population, 76,769.

bust·y (bŭsʹtē) *adj.* **-i·er, -i·est.** Full-bosomed.

bu·sul·fan (byo͞o-sŭlʹfən) *n.* An alkylating agent, $C_6H_{14}O_6S_2$, that is used as an antineoplastic drug in the treatment of chronic myelocytic leukemia. [Blend of BUTANE and SULFONYL.]

bus·y (bĭzʹē) *adj.* **-i·er, -i·est. 1.** Engaged in activity, as work; occupied. **2.** Sustaining much activity: *a busy morning; a busy street.* **3.** Meddlesome; prying. **4.** Being in use, as a telephone line. **5.** Cluttered with detail to the point of being distracting: *a busy design.* **—busy** *tr.v.* **-ied, -y·ing, -ies.** To make busy; occupy: *busied myself preparing my tax return.* [Middle English *bisi, busi,* from Old English *bisig.*] **—busʹi·ly** *adv.* **—busʹy·ness** *n.*

SYNONYMS: *busy, industrious, diligent, assiduous, sedulous.* All these adjectives suggest active or sustained effort to accomplish something. *Busy,* the most general, often refers simply and nonspecifically to engagement in activity: *Don't bother me–I'm busy.* The word sometimes indicates constant and customary work or activity: *a busy lawyer; a busy day. Industrious* implies steady application that is often habitual or the result of a natural inclination: *The raspberries were harvested by industrious workers. Diligent* suggests constant painstaking effort, often toward the achievement of a specific goal: *A diligent detective investigates all clues. Assiduous* emphasizes sustained application: *She is assiduous in her efforts to learn French. Sedulous* adds to *assiduous* the sense of persistent, thoroughgoing endeavor: *"the sedulous pursuit of legal and moral principles"* (Ernest van den Haag); *"the innovative specialty store and oasis of elegant gadgets to the sedulous and casual collector alike"* (Time).

bus·y·bod·y (bĭzʹē-bŏdʹē) *n.* A person who meddles or pries into the affairs of others.

busy signal *n.* A series of sharp buzzing tones heard over a telephone when the line dialed is already in use.

bus·y·work (bĭzʹē-wûrkʹ) *n.* Activity, such as schoolwork or office work, meant to take up time but not necessarily yield productive results.

but (bŭt; bət *when unstressed*) *conj.* **1.** On the contrary: *the plan caused not prosperity but ruin.* **2.** Contrary to expectation; yet: *She organized her work but accomplished very little. He is tired but happy.* **3.** *Usage Problem.* Used to indicate an exception: *No one but she saw the prowler.* **4.** With the exception that; except that. Used to introduce a dependent clause: *would have resisted but that they lacked courage.* **5.** *Informal.* Without the result that: *It never rains but it pours.* **6.** *Informal.* That. Often used after a negative: *There is no doubt but right will prevail.* **7.** That . . . not. Used after a negative or question: *There never is a tax law presented but someone will oppose it.* **8.** If not; unless: *"Ten to one but the police have got them"* (Charlotte M. Yonge). **9.** *Informal.* Than: *They had no sooner arrived but they turned around and left.* **—but** *prep. Usage Problem.* Except. **—but** *adv.* **1.** Merely; just; only: *hopes that lasted but a moment.* **2.** Used as an intensive: *Get out of here but fast!* [Middle English, from Old English *būtan.* See **ud-** in Appendix.]

USAGE NOTE: Traditional grammarians have worried over what form the pronoun ought to take when *but* is used to indicate an exception in sentences such as *No one but I* (or *No one but me*) *has read it.* Some have argued that *but* is a conjunction in these sentences and therefore should be followed by the nominative form *I.* However, many of these grammarians have gone on to argue somewhat inconsistently that the accusative form *me* is appropriate when the *but* phrase occurs at the end of a sentence, as in *No one has read it but me.* While this treatment of the construction has a considerable weight of precedent on its side and cannot be regarded as incorrect, a strong case can be made on grammatical grounds for treating this use of *but* as a preposition. For one thing, if *but* were truly a conjunction here, we would expect the verb to agree in person and number with the noun or pronoun following *but;* we would then say *No one but the students have read it.* What is more, if *but* were a true conjunction here we would not expect that it could be moved to the end of a clause, as in *No one has read it but the students.* Note that we cannot use the conjunction *and* in a similar way, saying *John left and everyone else in the class* in place of *John and everyone else in the class left.* These observations suggest that *but* is best considered as a preposition here and followed by accusative forms such as *me* and *them* in all positions: *No one but me has read it. No one has read it but me.* These recommendations are supported by 73 percent of the Usage Panel when the *but* phrase precedes the verb and by 93 percent when the *but* phrase follows the verb. • *But* is redundant when used together with *however,* as in *But the army, however, went on with its plans;* one or the other word should be eliminated. • *But* is generally not followed by a comma. Correct written style requires *Kim wanted to go, but we stayed,* not *Kim wanted to go, but, we stayed.* • *But* may be used to begin a sentence at all levels of style. See Usage Notes at **and, cannot, doubt, however, I[1].**

but– *pref.* Containing a group of four carbon atoms: *butyl.* [From BUTYRIC.]

bu·ta·di·ene (byo͞o′tə-dī′ēn′, -dī-ēn′) *n.* A colorless, highly flammable hydrocarbon, C_4H_6, obtained from petroleum and used in the manufacture of synthetic rubber. [BUTA(NE) + DI–[1] + –ENE.]

bu·tane (byo͞o′tān′) *n.* Either of two isomers of a gaseous hydrocarbon, C_4H_{10}, produced synthetically from petroleum and used as a household fuel, refrigerant, and aerosol propellant and in the manufacture of synthetic rubber. [BUT(YL) + –ANE.]

bu·ta·no·ic acid (byo͞o′tə-nō′ĭk) *n.* See **butyric acid.** [BUTAN(E) + –OIC.]

bu·ta·nol (byo͞o′tə-nôl′, -nōl′, nŏl′) *n.* Either of two butyl alcohols derived from butane and used as solvents and in organic synthesis. [BUTAN(E) + –OL[1].]

bu·ta·none (byo͞o′tə-nōn′) *n.* A colorless, flammable ketone, $CH_3COCH_2CH_3$, used in lacquers, paint removers, cements and adhesives, cleaning fluids, and celluloid. Also called *methyl ethyl ketone.* [BUTAN(E) + –ONE.]

Bu·ta·zol·i·din (byo͞o′tə-zŏl′ĭ-dĭn). A trademark used for a preparation of phenylbutazone, an anti-inflammatory and analgesic drug.

butch (bo͝och) *n.* **1.** A butch haircut. **2.** *Offensive Slang.* Used as a disparaging term for a lesbian. **—butch** *adj.* Unusually or markedly masculine in appearance or manner. [Probably from the male nickname *Butch.*] **—butch** *adj.*

butch·er (bo͝och′ər) *n.* **1. a.** One that slaughters and dresses animals for food or market. **b.** One that sells meats. **2.** One who kills brutally or indiscriminately. **3.** A vender, especially one on a train or in a theater. **4.** One who bungles something. **—butcher** *tr.v.* **-ered, -er·ing, -ers. 1.** To slaughter or prepare (animals) for market. **2.** To kill brutally or indiscriminately. **3.** To botch; bungle: *butcher a project; butchered the language.* [Middle English *bucher,* from Old French *bouchier,* from *bouc, boc,* he-goat, probably of Celtic origin.] **—butch′er·er** *n.*

butch·er·bird (bo͝och′ər-bûrd′) *n.* Any of various birds, especially the shrike, that impale their prey on thorns.

butch·er-block (bo͝och′ər-blŏk′) *adj.* Made of or resembling a board of thick strips of hardwood like that on which butchers chop meat: *a butcher-block counter.*

butcher knife *n.* A heavy-duty knife with a broad, sharp blade used for cutting meat.

butch·er's broom (bo͝och′ərz) *n.* An evergreen shrub *(Ruscus aculeatus)* native to Europe and the Mediterranean region, having leaflike stems, greenish flowers, and usually red berries.

butch·er·y (bo͝och′ə-rē) *n., pl.* **-ies. 1.** Wanton or cruel killing; carnage. **2.** Something botched; a bungle. **3.** The trade of a butcher. **4.** *Chiefly British.* A slaughterhouse.

butch haircut *n.* A haircut in which the hair is cropped close to the head.

Bute (byo͞ot). An island of southwest Scotland in the Firth of Clyde.

Bu·te·nandt (bo͞ot′n-änt′), **Adolf Friedrich.** Born 1903. German chemist. He shared a 1939 Nobel Prize for his work on sexual hormones but declined the honor following a Nazi edict prohibiting acceptance.

bu·te·o (byo͞o′tē-ō′) *n., pl.* **-os.** Any of various broad-winged, soaring hawks of the genus *Buteo.* [Latin *būteō,* a kind of hawk or falcon.]

but·ler (bŭt′lər) *n.* The head servant in a household who is usually in charge of food service, the care of silverware, and the deportment of the other servants. [Middle English, from Old French *bouteillier,* bottle bearer, from *bouteille, botele,* bottle. See BOTTLE.]

But·ler (bŭt′lər). A city of western Pennsylvania north of Pittsburgh. It is a manufacturing center in a highly industrialized region. Population, 17,026.

Butler, Benjamin Franklin. 1818–1893. American army officer and politician. His harsh rule as military governor of New Orleans (May–December 1862) led to charges of corruption and Butler's removal.

Butler, Nicholas Murray. 1862–1947. American educator who advocated peace through education. He shared the 1931 Nobel Peace Prize.

Butler, Pierce. 1866–1939. American jurist who served as an associate justice of the U.S. Supreme Court (1923–1939).

Butler[1], Samuel. 1612–1680. English poet remembered primarily for his three-part work *Hudibras* (1663–1678), a venomous mock-heroic satire on the Puritans.

Butler[2], Samuel. 1835–1902. British writer best known for *The Way of All Flesh* (1903), a semiautobiographical novel satirizing family life in mid-Victorian England.

but·ler's pantry (bŭt′lərz) *n.* A serving and storage room between a kitchen and dining room.

butt[1] (bŭt) *v.* **butt·ed, butt·ing, butts.** *—tr.* To hit or push against with the head or horns; ram. *—intr.* **1.** To hit or push something with the head or horns. **2.** To project forward or out. **—butt** *n.* A push or blow with the head or horns. ***—phrasal verb.* butt in.** To interfere or meddle in other people's affairs. [Middle English *butten,* from Old French *bouter,* to strike, of Germanic origin. See **bhau-** in Appendix.] **—butt′er** *n.*

butt[2] (bŭt) *tr. & intr.v.* **butt·ed, butt·ing, butts.** To join or be joined end to end; abut. **—butt** *n.* **1.** A butt joint. **2.** A butt hinge. [Middle English *butten,* from Anglo-Norman *butter* (variant of Old French *bouter;* see BUTT[1]) and from *but,* end; see BUTT[4].]

butt[3] (bŭt) *n.* **1.** One that serves as an object of ridicule or contempt: *I was the butt of their jokes.* **2. a.** A target. **b. butts.** A target range. **c.** An obstacle behind a target for stopping the shot. **3.** An embankment or hollow used as a blind by hunters of wildfowl. **4. a.** *Archaic.* A goal. **b.** *Obsolete.* A bound; a limit. [Middle English *butte,* target, from Old French, from *but,* goal, end, target. See BUTT[4].]

butt[4] (bŭt) *n.* **1.** The larger or thicker end of an object: *the butt of a rifle.* **2. a.** An unburned end, as of a cigarette. **b.** *Informal.* A cigarette. **3.** A short or broken remnant; a stub. **4.** *Informal.* The buttocks; the rear end. [Middle English *butte,* from Old French *but,* end, of Germanic origin.]

butt[5] (bŭt) *n.* **1.** A large cask. **2.** A unit of volume equal to two hogsheads, usually the equivalent of 126 U.S. gallons (about 477 liters). [Middle English, from Old French *boute,* from Late Latin **buttia,* variant of *buttis.*]

♦ **butte** (byo͞ot) *n.* *Chiefly Western U.S.* A hill that rises abruptly from the surrounding area and has sloping sides and a flat top. [French, from Old French *butte,* mound behind targets. See BUTT[3].]

Butte (byo͞ot). A city of southwest Montana south-southwest of Helena. It has been a mining center since its settlement in the 1860's and enjoyed its greatest importance after the discovery of copper deposits in 1880. Population, 37,205.

but·ter (bŭt′ər) *n.* **1.** A soft yellowish or whitish emulsion of butterfat, water, air, and sometimes salt, churned from milk or cream and processed for use in cooking and as a food. **2.** Any of various substances similar to butter, especially: **a.** A spread made from fruit, nuts, or other foods: *apple butter.* **b.** A vegetable fat having a nearly solid consistency at ordinary temperatures. **3.** Flattery. **—butter** *tr.v.* **-tered, -ter·ing, -ters.** To put butter on or in. ***—phrasal verb.* butter up.** To praise or flatter excessively: *You're always buttering up the boss.* [Middle English *butere,* from Old English, from Latin *butyrum,* from Greek *bouturon* : *bous,* cow; see **gʷou-** in Appendix + *turos,* cheese; see **teuə-** in Appendix.]

but·ter-and-eggs (bŭt′ər-ən-ĕgz′) *pl.n. (used with a sing. or pl. verb).* A weedy, perennial herb *(Linaria vulgaris)* native to Eurasia, having narrow leaves and racemes of showy, long-spurred yellow and orange flowers. Also called *toadflax.*

but·ter·ball (bŭt′ər-bôl′) *n.* **1.** *Informal.* A chubby or fat person. **2.** See **bufflehead.**

♦ **butter bean** *n.* **1.** *Chiefly Southern & Midland U.S.* See **lima bean. 2.** *New England.* See **wax bean.**

but·ter·bur (bŭt′ər-bûr′) *n.* Any of several perennial herbs of the genus *Petasites* in the composite family, native to northern temperate regions and having large basal leaves and dense clusters of usually whitish or purplish flower heads.

butter clam *n.* A large, delicately flavored clam of the genus *Saxidomus,* found on the Pacific coast of North America and having a distinctive shell that was formerly used as money by Native Americans. Also called *money shell.*

but·ter·cup (bŭt′ər-kŭp′) *n.* Any of numerous herbs of the genus *Ranunculus,* native chiefly to temperate and cold regions and having acrid juice, often toothed or lobed leaves, and usually yellow or white flowers with numerous pistils.

buttercup squash *n.* A type of winter squash *(Cucurbita maxima)* shaped somewhat like a drum and having a dark green rind marked with silver or gray and yellowish to orange flesh.

but·ter·fat (bŭt′ər-făt′) *n.* The natural fat of milk from which butter is made, consisting largely of the glycerides of oleic, stearic, and palmitic acids.

but·ter·fin·gers (bŭt′ər-fĭng′gərz) *pl.n. (used with a sing. verb).* A person who tends to drop things. **—but′ter·fin′gered** *adj.*

but·ter·fish (bŭt′ər-fĭsh′) *n., pl.* **butterfish** or **-fish·es. 1.** A marine food fish *(Poronotus triacanthus)* of the North American Atlantic coast, having a flattened body. **2.** Any of various similar or related fishes, such as the moonfish and gunnel. [From its slippery mucous coating.]

but·ter·fly (bŭt′ər-flī′) *n.* **1.** Any of various insects of the order Lepidoptera, characteristically having slender bodies, knobbed antennae, and four broad, usually colorful wings. **2.** A person interested principally in frivolous pleasure: *a social butterfly.* **3.** *Sports.* The butterfly stroke. **4. butterflies.** A feeling of unease or mild nausea caused especially by fearful anticipation. *—attributive.* Often used to modify another noun: *a butterfly knife; a butterfly hinge.* **—butterfly** *tr.v.* **-flied, -fly·ing, -flies.** To cut and spread open and flat, as shrimp. [Middle English *butterflye,* from Old English *butorflēoge* : *butor, butere,* butter; see BUTTER + *flēoge,* fly; see FLY[2].]

butte

ă pat	oi boy
ā pay	ou out
âr care	o͝o took
ä father	o͞o boot
ĕ pet	ŭ cut
ē be	ûr urge
ĭ pit	th thin
ī pie	*th* this
îr pier	hw which
ŏ pot	zh vision
ō toe	ə about, item
ô paw	♦ regionalism

Stress marks: ′ (primary); ′ (secondary), as in **dictionary** (dĭk′shə-nĕr′ē)

WORD HISTORY: Is a butterfly named for the color of its excrement or because it was really a thieving witch? The first suggestion rests on the fact that an early Dutch name for the butterfly was *boterschijte.* This name is as astonishing a phenomenon as the fact that anyone ever noticed the color of butterfly excrement. Apparently, however, when the butterfly was not busy leaving colorful traces of itself, it was stealing milk and butter. This was not because of its thievish nature but because it was really a mischievous witch in the form of a winged insect. So the second suggestion is that this predilection for butter larceny gave rise to the colorful insect's name.

butterfly bush *n.* Any of various shrubs of the genus *Buddleja* native chiefly to warm regions and cultivated for their showy clusters of small, variously colored flowers. Also called *buddleia.*

butterfly fish *n.* **1.** Any of various small, brightly colored tropical marine fishes of the family Chaetodontidae, having deep, flattened bodies and a single dorsal fin. **2.** Any of various fishes with broad, winglike fins.

butterfly orchid *n.* Any of certain orchids, including *Epidendrum tampense* of Florida, *Habenaria psycodes* of eastern North America, and *Oncidium krameranum* and *O. pupilio* of tropical America, having showy, brightly colored flowers.

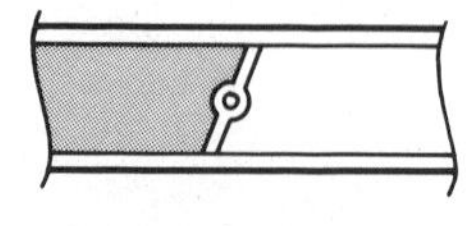

butterfly valve
Top: Closed
Bottom: Open

butterfly pea *n.* Any of several plants of the genera *Centrosema* and *Clitoria* in the pea family, having blue or lavender flowers and flat pods.

butterfly stroke *n. Sports.* A swimming stroke in which both arms are drawn upward out of the water and forward with a simultaneous up-and-down kick of the feet.

butterfly valve *n.* **1.** A disk turning on a diametrical axis inside a pipe, used as a throttle valve or damper. **2.** A valve composed of two semicircular plates hinged on a common spindle, used to permit flow in one direction only.

butterfly weed *n.* A North American milkweed *(Asclepias tuberosa)* having showy clusters of usually bright orange flowers and a root that was formerly used in medicine. Also called *orange milkweed, pleurisy root.*

but·ter·milk (bŭt′ər-mĭlk′) *n.* **1.** The sour liquid that remains after the butterfat has been removed from whole milk or cream by churning. **2.** A cultured sour milk made by adding certain microorganisms to sweet milk.

♦**buttermilk sky** *n. Chiefly Southern U.S.* See **mackerel sky.** [From the resemblance of the clouds to the texture of cultured milk.]

butternut
Juglans cinerea

but·ter·nut (bŭt′ər-nŭt′) *n.* **1.a.** An eastern North American walnut *(Juglans cinerea)* having light-brown wood, pinnately compound leaves, and a deeply furrowed nut enclosed in an egg-shaped, sticky, aromatic husk. Also called *white walnut.* **b.** The nut of this tree, having an edible sweet kernel. **c.** The wood of this tree, used for furniture, boxes, and interior finishes. **d.** The bark of this tree. **e.** A brownish dye obtained from the husks of the fruits of this tree. **2.a. butternuts.** Clothing dyed with butternut extract, especially the uniforms of Confederate soldiers in the Civil War. **b.** *Informal.* A Confederate soldier or partisan in the Civil War. **3.** See **souari nut.** [From the nut's oiliness.]

butternut squash *n.* A type of winter squash *(Cucurbita moschata)* shaped somewhat like a bell and having a smooth, tan rind and edible yellowish to orange flesh.

but·ter·scotch (bŭt′ər-skŏch′) *n.* A syrup, sauce, candy, or flavoring made by melting butter, brown sugar, and sometimes artificial flavorings. [Alteration of *butterscot* : BUTTER + *scot,* of unknown origin.]

but·ter·weed (bŭt′ər-wēd′) *n.* **1.** A succulent annual or biennial plant *(Senecio glabellus),* native to the eastern United States and having pinnately divided leaves and bright yellow, radiate flower heads. **2.** The horseweed.

but·ter·wort (bŭt′ər-wûrt′, -wôrt′) *n.* Any of numerous carnivorous plants of the genus *Pinguicula,* having a rosette of basal leaves that are coated with a sticky secretion that traps small insects for digestion.

but·ter·y¹ (bŭt′ə-rē) *adj.* **1.** Resembling, containing, or spread with butter. **2.** Marked by effusive and insincere flattery. **—but′ter·i·ness** *n.*

but·ter·y² (bŭt′ə-rē, bŭt′rē) *n., pl.* **-ies. 1.** A room in which liquors are stored. **2.** *Chiefly British.* A place in colleges and universities where students may buy provisions. [Middle English *buttrie,* from Anglo-Norman *buterie,* alteration of *botelerie,* from Old French *botele,* bottle. See BOTTLE.]

butt hinge *n.* A hinge composed of two plates attached to abutting surfaces of a door and door jamb and joined by a pin. [From BUTT².]

butt·in·sky (bŭt-ĭn′skē) *n., pl.* **-skies.** *Slang.* One who is prone to butting in; a meddler. [BUTT¹ + IN¹ + *-sky,* last syllable in many Slavic surnames.]

butt joint *n.* A joint formed by two abutting surfaces placed squarely together. [From BUTT².]

but·tock (bŭt′ək) *n.* **1.a.** Either of the two rounded prominences on the human torso that are posterior to the hips and formed by the gluteal muscles and underlying structures. **b.** The analogous part of the body on certain mammals. **2. buttocks.** The rear pelvic area of the human body. [Middle English, from Old English *buttuc,* strip of land, end. See **bhau-** in Appendix.]

but·ton (bŭt′n) *n.* **1.a.** A generally disk-shaped fastener used to join two parts of a garment by fitting through a buttonhole or loop. **b.** Such an object used for decoration. **2.** Any of various objects resembling a button, especially: **a.** A push-button switch. **b.** The blunt tip of a fencing foil. **c.** A fused metal or glass globule. **3.** Any of various knoblike structures of a plant or animal, especially: **a.** An immature, unexpanded mushroom. **b.** The tip of a rattlesnake's rattle. **4.** A usually round flat badge that bears a design or printed information and is typically pinned to a garment: *a campaign button.* **5.** *Informal.* The end of the chin, regarded as the point of impact for a punch. **—button** *v.* **-toned, -ton·ing, -tons.** *—tr.* **1.** To fasten with buttons: *buttoned his shirt; buttoned up her raincoat.* **2.** To decorate or furnish with buttons. **3.** *Informal.* To close (the lips or mouth): *Button your lip.* *—intr.* To be or be capable of being fastened with buttons: *The blouse buttons up the back.* **—*idiom.* on the button.** Exactly; precisely. [Middle English, from Old French *bouton,* from *bouter,* to thrust, of Germanic origin. See **bhau-** in Appendix.] **—but′ton·er** *n.* **—but′ton·y** *adj.*

but·ton·ball (bŭt′n-bôl′) *n.* See **sycamore** (sense 1). [From its button-shaped fruit.]

but·ton·bush (bŭt′n-bo͝osh′) *n.* A deciduous North American shrub *(Cephalanthus occidentalis)* having opposite leaves and spherical clusters of small white flowers.

but·ton-down (bŭt′n-doun′) *adj.* **1.** Having the ends of the collar fastened down by buttons: *a button-down shirt.* **2.** Also **but·toned-down** (bŭt′nd-). Conservative, conventional, or unimaginative: *"a colorful character in the buttoned-down, dull-gray world of business"* (Newsweek).

button fern *n.* A New Zealand fern *(Pellaea rotundifolia)* cultivated as a houseplant for its arching or trailing leaves with round, dark green, buttonlike leaflets.

but·ton·hole (bŭt′n-hōl′) *n.* **1.** A small slit in a garment or piece of fabric for fastening a button. **2.** *Chiefly British.* A boutonniere. *—tr.* **-holed, -hol·ing, -holes. 1.** To make a buttonhole in. **2.** To sew with a buttonhole stitch. **3.** To accost and detain (a person) in conversation by or as if by grasping the person's outer garments: *"He was also frequently buttonholed by White House lobbyists . . . who seemed to be permanently assigned to shadow the burly Democrat"* (Terence Moran). [Sense 3, probably alteration of *button-hold.*] **—but′ton·hol′er** *n.*

buttonhole stitch *n.* A loop stitch that forms a reinforced edge, as around a buttonhole.

but·ton·hook (bŭt′n-ho͝ok′) *n.* A small hook for fastening a button on shoes or gloves.

button mangrove *n.* See **buttonwood** (sense 2).

but·ton·mold (bŭt′n-mōld′) *n.* A piece of wood, plastic, or metal that is covered with fabric to form a button.

but·ton·quail (bŭt′n-kwāl′) *n.* Any of various small, quail-like Old World birds of the family Turnicidae that lack a hind toe and are related to the crane and the bustard.

button snakeroot *n.* **1.** See **rattlesnake master. 2.** See **blazing star** (sense 2).

but·ton·wood (bŭt′n-wo͝od′) *n.* **1.** See **sycamore** (sense 1). **2.** An evergreen shrub or tree *(Conocarpus erectus),* growing in mangrove forests of tropical America and western Africa and having alternate leathery leaves and small buttonlike heads of greenish flowers. Also called *button mangrove.*

but·tress (bŭt′rĭs) *n.* **1.** A structure, usually brick or stone, built against a wall for support or reinforcement. **2.** Something resembling a buttress, as: **a.** The flared base of certain tree trunks. **b.** A horny growth on the heel of a horse's hoof. **3.** Something that serves to support, prop, or reinforce: *"The law is by its very nature a buttress of the status quo"* (J. William Fulbright). **—buttress** *tr.v.* **-tressed, -tress·ing, -tress·es. 1.** To support or reinforce with a buttress. **2.** To sustain, prop, or bolster: *"The author buttresses her analysis with lengthy dissections of several of Moore's poems"* (Warren Woessner). [Middle English *buteras,* from Old French *bouterez,* from *bouter,* to strike against, of Germanic origin. See **bhau-** in Appendix.]

butt shaft *n.* A blunt arrow used for target practice. [Probably from BUTT⁴.]

butt weld *n.* A welded butt joint.

butt-weld (bŭt′wĕld′) *tr.v.* **-weld·ed, -weld·ing, -welds.** To join by a butt weld.

bu·tut (bo͞o′to͞ot′) *n., pl.* **butut** or **-tuts.** See table at **currency.** [Wolof.]

bu·tyl (byo͞ot′l) *n.* A hydrocarbon radical, C_4H_9, with the structure of butane and valence 1.

butyl alcohol *n.* Any of four isomeric alcohols, C_4H_9OH, widely used as solvents and in organic synthesis.

bu·tyl·ate (byo͞ot′l-āt′) *tr.v.* **-at·ed, -at·ing, -ates.** To bring a butyl group into (a compound). **—bu′tyl·a′tion** *n.*

bu·tyl·at·ed hy·drox·y·an·i·sole (byo͞ot′l-ā′tĭd hī-drŏk′sē-ăn′ĭ-sōl′) *n.* BHA.

butylated hy·drox·y·tol·u·ene (hī-drŏk′sē-tŏl′yo͞o-ēn′) *n.* BHT.

bu·tyl·ene (byo͞ot′l-ēn′) *n.* Any of three gaseous isomeric ethylene hydrocarbons, C_4H_8, used principally in making synthetic rubbers.

butyl rubber *n.* A synthetic rubber produced by copolymerization of a butylene with isoprene, nearly impermeable to air and used in tires, inner tubes, and insulation.

bu·ty·ra·ceous (byo͞o′tə-rā′shəs) *adj.* Resembling butter in appearance, consistency, or chemical properties. [Latin *butyrum,* butter; see BUTTER + –ACEOUS.]

bu·tyr·al·de·hyde (byo͞o′tə-răl′də-hīd′) *n.* A transparent, highly flammable liquid, C_4H_8O, used in synthesizing resins. [BUTYR(IC) + ALDEHYDE.]

bu·ty·rate (byo͞o′tə-rāt′) *n.* A salt or ester of butyric acid. [BUTYR(IC) + –ATE².]

bu·tyr·ic (byo͞o-tîr′ĭk) *adj.* **1.** Relating to, containing, or derived from butter. **2.** Relating to or derived from butyric acid. [From Latin *butyrum,* butter. See BUTTER.]

butyric acid *n.* Either of two colorless isomeric acids, C_3H_7COOH, occurring in animal milk fats and used in disinfectants, emulsifying agents, and pharmaceuticals. Also called *butanoic acid.*

bu·ty·rin (byo͞o′tər-ĭn) *n.* Any of three isomeric glyceryl esters of butyric acid, naturally present in butter. [French *butyrine,* from Latin *butyrum,* butter. See BUTTER.]

bu·ty·ro·phe·none (byo͞o-tîr′ō-fə-nōn′, byo͞o′tə-rō-) *n.* Any of a group of neuroleptic drugs, such as haloperidol, administered in the treatment of acute psychotic episodes, schizophrenia, and other psychiatric disorders. [BUTYR(IC) + PHEN– + –ONE.]

bux·om (bŭk′səm) *adj.* **1.a.** Healthily plump and ample of figure: *"A generation ago, fat babies were considered healthy and buxom actresses were popular, but society has since come to worship thinness"* (Robert A. Hamilton). **b.** Full-bosomed. **2.** *Archaic.* Lively, vivacious, and gay. **3.** *Obsolete.* Obedient; yielding; pliant. [Middle English, obedient, from Old English **būhsum,* from *būgan,* to bend, submit. See **bheug-** in Appendix.] **—bux′om·ly** *adv.* **—bux′om·ness** *n.*

Bux·te·hu·de (bo͝ok′stə-ho͞o′də), **Dietrich.** 1637–1707. Swedish-born organist and composer in Germany.

♦**buy** (bī) *v.* **bought** (bôt), **buy·ing, buys.** —*tr.* **1.** To acquire in exchange for money or its equivalent; purchase. See Regional Note at **boughten. 2.** To be capable of purchasing: *"Certainly there are lots of things in life that money won't buy"* (Ogden Nash). **3.** To acquire by sacrifice, exchange, or trade: *wanted to buy love with gifts.* **4.** To bribe: *tried to buy a judge.* **5.** *Slang.* To accept the truth or feasibility of: *The officer didn't buy my lame excuse for speeding.* —*intr.* **1.** To purchase goods; act as a purchaser. **2.** To believe in a person or movement or subscribe to an idea or theory: *couldn't buy into that brand of conservatism.* **—buy** *n.* **1.** Something bought or for sale; a purchase. **2.** *Informal.* Something that is underpriced; a bargain. ***—phrasal verbs.* buy off.** To bribe in order to proceed without interference or be exempted from an obligation or from prosecution. **buy out.** To purchase the entire stock, business rights, or interests of. **buy up.** To purchase all that is available of. ***—idioms.* buy time.** To increase the time available for a specific purpose: *"A moderate recovery thus buys time for Congress and the Administration to whittle the deficit"* (G. David Wallace). **buy the farm.** *Slang.* To die, especially suddenly or violently. [Middle English, from Old English *bycgan.*] **—buy′a·ble** *adj.*

buy·er (bī′ər) *n.* One that buys, especially a purchasing agent for a retail store.

buy·er's market also **buy·ers' market** (bī′ərz) *n.* A market condition characterized by low prices and a supply of commodities exceeding demand.

buy·out also **buy-out** (bī′out′) *n.* **1.** The purchase of the entire holdings or interests of an owner or investor. **2.** The purchase of a company or business: *"If the workers do approve the buyout, their company will become the nation's largest employee-owned enterprise"* (Harry Anderson).

Bu·zău (bə-zou′, bo͞o-zü′o͞o). A city of southeast Romania northeast of Bucharest. It is an important transportation hub. Population, 126,780.

buzz (bŭz) *v.* **buzzed, buzz·ing, buzz·es.** —*intr.* **1.** To make a low droning or vibrating sound like that of a bee. **2.a.** To talk, often excitedly, in low tones. **b.** To be abuzz; hum: *The department was buzzing with rumors.* **3.** To move quickly and busily; bustle. **4.** To make a signal with a buzzer. —*tr.* **1.** To cause to buzz. **2.** To utter in a rapid, low voice: *"What is he buzzing in my ears?"* (Robert Browning). **3.** *Informal.* To fly low over: *The plane buzzed the control tower.* **4.** To signal with a buzzer. **5.** To make a telephone call to. **—buzz** *n.* **1.** A vibrating, humming, or droning sound. **2.** A low murmur: *a buzz of talk.* **3.** A telephone call: *Give me a buzz at nine.* **4.** *Slang.* Pleasant intoxication, as from alcohol. ***—phrasal verb.* buzz off.** *Informal.* To leave quickly; go away: *I told them in no uncertain terms to buzz off.* [Middle English *bussen,* of imitative origin.]

buz·zard (bŭz′ərd) *n.* **1.** Any of various North American vultures, such as the turkey vulture. **2.** *Chiefly British.* A hawk of the genus *Buteo,* having broad wings and a broad tail. **3.** An avaricious or otherwise unpleasant person. [Middle English *busard,* hawk of the genus *Buteo,* from Old French, from Latin *būteō.*]

Buz·zards Bay (bŭz′ərdz). An inlet of the Atlantic Ocean in southeast Massachusetts connected with Cape Cod Bay by the Cape Cod Canal.

buzz bomb *n.* See **robot bomb.**

buzz·er (bŭz′ər) *n.* An electric signaling device, such as a doorbell, that makes a buzzing sound.

buzz saw *n.* See **circular saw.**

buzz·word (bŭz′wûrd′) *n.* A usually important-sounding word or phrase connected with a specialized field or group that is used primarily to impress laypersons: *"'Sensitivity' is the buzzword in the beauty industry this fall"* (ADWEEK).

B.V.D. also **BVD** (bē′vē′dē′). A trademark used for undershirts and underpants. This trademark sometimes occurs in print with a final *s*: *"He will be under constant scrutiny, right down to his BVD's"* (Los Angeles Times).

B vitamin *n.* A member of the vitamin B complex group of vitamins.

B.V.M. *abbr.* Blessed Virgin Mary.

bvt. *abbr.* **1.** Brevet. **2.** Brevetted.

BW *abbr.* **1.** Biological warfare. **2.** Also **b/w.** Black and white.

bwa·na (bwä′nə) *n.* Used as a form of respectful address in parts of Africa. [Swahili, from Arabic *'abūnā,* our father.]

B.W.I. *abbr.* British West Indies.

BX *abbr.* Base Exchange.

bx. also **bx** *abbr.* Box.

by¹ (bī) *prep.* **1.** Close to; next to: *the window by the door.* **2.** With the use or help of; through: *We came by the back road.* **3.** Up to and beyond; past: *We drove by the house.* **4.** In the period of; during: *sleeping by day.* **5.** Not later than: *by 5:30 P.M.* **6.a.** In the amount of: *letters by the thousands.* **b.** To the extent of: *shorter by two inches.* **7.a.** According to: *played by the rules.* **b.** With respect to: *siblings by blood.* **8.** In the name of: *swore by the Bible to tell the truth.* **9.** Through the agency or action of: *was killed by a bullet.* **10.** Used to indicate a succession of specified individuals, groups, or quantities: *One by one they left. They were persuaded little by little.* **11.a.** Used in multiplication and division: *Multiply 4 by 6 to get 24.* **b.** Used with measurements: *a room 12 by 18 feet.* **c.** Used to express direction with points of the compass: *south by southeast.* **—by** *adv.* **1.** On hand; nearby: *Stand by.* **2.** Aside; away: *We put it by for later.* **3.** Up to, alongside, and past: *The car raced by.* **4.** Into the past: *as years go by.* [Middle English, from Old English *bī, be.* See **ambhi** in Appendix.]

by² (bī) *n.* Variant of **bye.**

b.y. *abbr.* Billion years.

by– or **bye–** *pref.* **1.** By: *bygone.* **2.** Secondary, incidental: *byway.*

by and by *adv.* After a while; soon.

by-and-by (bī′ən-bī′) *n.* Some future time or occasion.

by and large *adv.* For the most part; generally: *By and large, the play was a success.*

by-bid·der (bī′bĭd′ər) *n.* A person who bids at an auction to raise prices for the owner. **—by′-bid′ding** *n.*

Byb·los (bĭb′ləs, -lŏs′). An ancient city of Phoenicia north-northeast of present-day Beirut, Lebanon. It was the chief city of Phoenicia in the second millennium B.C. and was noted for its papyruses.

by-blow (bī′blō′) *n.* **1.** An indirect or chance blow. **2.** An illegitimate child; a bastard.

Byd·goszcz (bĭd′gôsh, -gôshch). A city of north-central Poland northeast of Poznań. Chartered in 1346, it developed during the Middle Ages around the site of a prehistoric fort. Population, 361,400.

bye also **by** (bī) *n.* **1.** A secondary matter; a side issue. **2.** *Sports.* The position of one who draws no opponent for a round in a tournament and so advances to the next round. ***—idiom.* by the bye.** By the way; incidentally. [From BY¹.]

bye– *pref.* Variant of **by–.**

bye-bye (bī′bī′, bī-bī′) *interj.* Used to express farewell. **—bye-bye** *adv. Informal.* **1.** Away. **2.** To bed; to sleep: "[Live Senate television is] *a great way to go bye-bye. Pretty soon you're asleep"* (William Proxmire). [Reduplication of (GOOD-)BYE.]

by-e·lec·tion also **bye-e·lec·tion** (bī′ĭ-lĕk′shən) *n.* A special election held between general elections to fill a vacancy, as for a parliamentary seat.

Bye·lo·rus·sia (byĕl′ō-rŭsh′ə). See **Belorussia. —Bye′lo·rus′sian** *adj. & n.*

by·gone (bī′gôn′, -gŏn′) *adj.* Gone by; past: *bygone days.* **—bygone** *n.* One, especially a grievance, that is past: *Let bygones be bygones.*

by·law (bī′lô′) *n.* **1.** A law or rule governing the internal affairs of an organization. **2.** A secondary law. [Middle English *bilawe,* body of local regulations; akin to Danish *by-lag,* township ordinance : Old Norse *bȳr,* settlement; see **bheue-** in Appendix + Old Norse **lagu,* law; see **legh-** in Appendix.]

WORD HISTORY: A casual glance at the word *bylaw* might make one think that the element *by–* means "secondary, subsidiary," especially since *bylaw* can mean "a secondary law." It is possible that *by–,* as in *byway,* has influenced *bylaw* in the sense "secondary law"; however, *bylaw* existed long before the sense in question. The word is first recorded in 1283 with the meaning "a body of customs or regulations, as of a village, manor, religious organization, or sect." *By–* in this word comes from Old Norse, as may the word *bylaw,* and is related to if not identical with the element *–by* in the names of many places, such as Whitby, where Scandinavians settled when they invaded England during the early Middle Ages. We get the sense of this *–by* if we compare the related word entered as *bær, bœr, bȳr,* in the standard dictionary

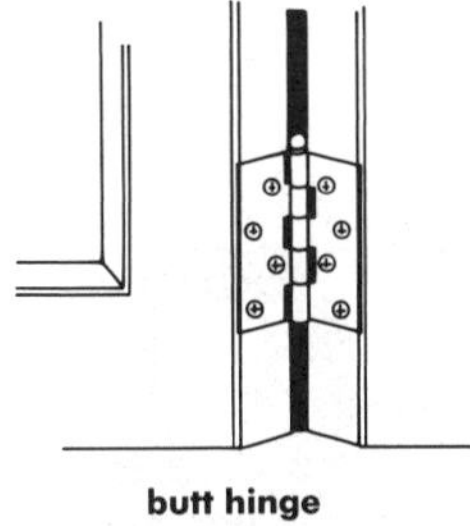
butt hinge

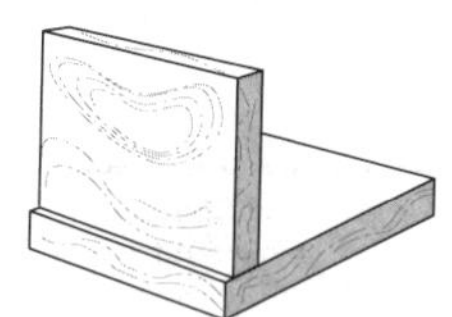
butt joint

buzzard
Turkey vulture
Cathartes aura

ă pat	oi boy
ā pay	ou out
âr care	o͝o took
ä father	o͞o boot
ĕ pet	ŭ cut
ē be	ûr urge
ĭ pit	th thin
ī pie	*th* this
îr pier	hw which
ŏ pot	zh vision
ō toe	ə about, item
ô paw	♦ regionalism

Stress marks: **′** (primary); ′ (secondary), as in **dictionary** (dĭk′shə-nĕr′ē)

of Old Icelandic, meaning "a town or village" in Norway, Sweden, and Denmark and "a farm or landed estate" in Iceland. We thus see why *bylaw* would mean "a body of customs of a village or manor" and why we use the word to mean "a law or rule governing the internal affairs of an organization."

by·line also **by-line** (bī′līn′) —*n.* A line at the head of a newspaper or magazine article carrying the writer's name. —*tr.v.* **-lined, -lin·ing, -lines.** To write (a newspaper or magazine article) under a byline. —**by′lin′er** *n.*

by-name (bī′nām′) *n.* **1.** A surname. **2.** A nickname.

BYOB or **B.Y.O.B** *abbr.* Bring your own booze; bring your own bottle.

by·pass also **by-pass** (bī′păs′) —*n.* **1.** A highway that passes around or to one side of an obstructed or congested area. **2.** A pipe or channel used to conduct gas or liquid around another pipe or a fixture. **3.** A means of circumvention. **4.** *Electricity.* See **shunt** (sense 3). **5.** *Medicine.* **a.** An alternative passage created surgically to divert the flow of blood or other bodily fluid or circumvent an obstructed or diseased organ. **b.** A surgical procedure to create such a channel: *a coronary artery bypass; a gastric bypass.* —*tr.v.* **-passed, -pass·ing, -pass·es. 1.** To avoid (an obstacle) by using an alternative channel, passage, or route. **2.** To be heedless of; ignore: *bypassed standard office procedures.* **3.** To channel (piped liquid, for example) through a bypass.

Richard E. Byrd
Photographed c. 1933

by·past (bī′păst′) *adj.* Past; bygone.

by-path (bī′păth′, -päth′) *n.* An indirect or rarely used path.

by-play (bī′plā′) *n.* Secondary action or speech taking place while the main action proceeds, as during a theatrical performance.

by·prod·uct or **by-prod·uct** (bī′prŏd′əkt) *n.* **1.** Something produced in the making of something else. **2.** A secondary result; a side effect.

Byrd (bûrd), **Richard Evelyn.** 1888–1957. American naval officer and explorer. After being the first to fly over the North Pole (with Floyd Bennett in 1926), he turned his attention to Antarctica, leading five expeditions between 1929 and 1956 and establishing a base for scientific discovery at Little America.

Byrd, William. 1674–1744. American planter and colonial official whose diaries (written in shorthand) provide a rare and humorous account of daily life in pre-Revolutionary Virginia.

byre (bīr) *n. Chiefly British.* A barn for cows. [Middle English, from Old English *bȳre.* See **bheue-** in Appendix.]

Byrnes (bûrnz), **James Francis.** 1879–1972. American politician who served as an associate justice of the U.S. Supreme Court (1941–1942).

by·road (bī′rōd′) *n.* See **byway** (sense 1).

By·ron (bī′rən), **George Gordon.** Sixth Baron Byron of Rochdale. 1788–1824. British poet acclaimed as one of the leading figures of the romantic movement. The "Byronic hero"—lonely, rebellious, and brooding—first appeared in *Manfred* (1817). Among his other works are *Childe Harold* (1812–1818), *The Prisoner of Chillon* (1816), and the epic satire *Don Juan* (1819–1824). Byron was notorious for his love affairs and unconventional lifestyle. He died while working to secure Greek independence from the Turks. —**By·ron′ic** (bī-rŏn′ĭk) *adj.*

ă pat	oi boy
ā pay	ou out
âr care	o͝o took
ä father	o͞o boot
ĕ pet	ŭ cut
ē be	ûr urge
ĭ pit	th thin
ī pie	*th* this
îr pier	hw which
ŏ pot	zh vision
ō toe	ə about, item
ô paw	♦ regionalism

Stress marks: **′** (primary); ′ (secondary), as in **dictionary** (dĭk′shə-nĕr′ē)

bys·si (bĭs′ī′) *n.* A plural of **byssus.**

bys·si·no·sis (bĭs′ĭ-nō′sĭs) *n.* An occupational respiratory disease caused by the long-term inhalation of cotton, flax, or hemp dust and characterized by shortness of breath, coughing, and wheezing. Also called *brown lung disease.* [Late Latin *byssinum,* linen garment (from Latin *byssus,* linen cloth) + -OSIS.]

bys·sus (bĭs′əs) *n., pl.* **bys·sus·es** or **bys·si** (bĭs′ī′). **1.** *Zoology.* A mass of strong, silky filaments by which certain bivalve mollusks, such as mussels, attach themselves to rocks and other fixed surfaces. **2.** A fine-textured linen of ancient times, used by the Egyptians for wrapping mummies. [Middle English *bissus,* linen cloth, from Latin, from Greek *bussos,* linen, ultimately from Egyptian *w'ḏ,* linen.]

by·stand·er (bī′stăn′dər) *n.* A person who is present at an event without participating in it.

by·street (bī′strēt′) *n.* A side street.

byte (bīt) *n.* **1.** A sequence of adjacent bits operated on as a unit by a computer. **2.** The amount of computer memory needed to store one character of a specified size, usually 8 bits for a microcomputer and 16 bits for a larger computer. [Alteration and blend of BIT[3] and BITE.]

by the way *adv.* Incidentally.

By·tom (bē′tôm′, bī′-). A city of southwest Poland northwest of Katowice. It became part of Prussia in 1742 and was incorporated into Poland in 1945. Population, 239,200.

by·way (bī′wā′) *n.* **1.** A side road. Also called *byroad.* **2.** A secondary or arcane field of study.

by·word also **by-word** (bī′wûrd′) *n.* **1.a.** A proverbial expression; a proverb. **b.** An often-used word or phrase. **2.** One that represents a type, class, or quality: *"Polyester got its déclassé reputation in the 1970s after cheap, poorly made double-knit leisure suits became a byword for bad taste"* (Fortune). **3.** An object of notoriety or interest: *The eccentric poet was a byword in literary circles.* **4.** An epithet. [Middle English *byworde,* from Old English *bīword,* translation of Latin *prōverbium.*]

Byz·an·tine (bĭz′ən-tēn′, -tīn′, bĭ-zăn′tĭn) *adj.* **1.a.** Of or relating to the ancient city of Byzantium. **b.** Of or relating to the Byzantine Empire. **2.** Of or belonging to the style of architecture developed from the fifth century A.D. in the Byzantine Empire, characterized by a central dome resting on a cube formed by four round arches and their pendentives and by the extensive use of surface decoration, especially veined marble panels, low relief carving, and colored glass mosaics. **3.** Of the painting and decorative style developed in the Byzantine Empire, characterized by formality of design, frontal stylized presentation of figures, rich use of color, especially gold, and generally religious subject matter. **4.a.** Of the Eastern Orthodox Church or the rites performed in it. **b.** Of a Uniat church that maintains the worship of the Eastern Orthodox Church or the rites performed in it. **5.** Often **byzantine. a.** Of, relating to, or characterized by intrigue; scheming or devious: *"a fine hand for Byzantine deals and cozy arrangements"* (New York). **b.** Highly complicated; intricate and involved: *a bill to simplify the Byzantine tax structure.* —**Byzantine** *n.* A native or inhabitant of Byzantium or the Byzantine Empire.

Byzantine Empire. The eastern part of the later Roman Empire, dating from A.D. 330 when Constantine I rebuilt Byzantium and made it his capital. Its extent varied greatly over the centuries, but its core remained the Balkan Peninsula and Asia Minor. The empire collapsed when Constantinople fell to the Ottoman Turks in 1453.

By·zan·ti·um (bĭ-zăn′shē-əm, -tē-əm). **1.** The Byzantine Empire. **2.** An ancient city of Thrace on the site of present-day Istanbul, Turkey. It was founded by the Greeks in the seventh century B.C. and taken by the Romans in A.D. 196. Constantine I ordered the rebuilding of the city in 330 and renamed it Constantinople.

BZ (bē′zē′) *n.* Used by the U.S. Army as a code word for a gas, $C_{21}H_{23}NO_3$, that produces incapacitating disorientation and hallucination when inhaled. [Possibly abbr. of *benzilic,* from BENZOIN.]

Cc

c[1] or **C** (sē) *n., pl.* **c's** or **C's.** **1.** The third letter of the modern English alphabet. **2.** Any of the speech sounds represented by the letter *c.* **3.** The third in a series. **4. C.** The third best or third highest in quality or rank: *a mark of C on a term paper.* **5.** *Music.* **a.** The first tone in the scale of C major or the third tone in the relative minor scale. **b.** A key or scale in which the tone of C is the tonic. **c.** A written or printed note representing this tone. **d.** A string, key, or pipe tuned to the pitch of this tone.

c[2] *abbr.* **1.** *Physics.* Candle. **2.** Carat. **3.** *Physics.* Charm quark. **4.** Also **C.** *Mathematics.* Constant. **5.** Cubic.

C[1] (sē) *n.* A computer programming language widely used on microcomputers.

C[2] **1.** The symbol for the element **carbon** (sense 1). **2.** Also **c.** The symbol for the Roman numeral one hundred. **3. c.** The symbol for the speed of light in a vacuum. **4.** *Electricity.* The symbol for **capacitance** (senses 1, 2). **5.** *Physics.* The symbol for **charge conjugation.**

C[3] *abbr.* **1.** Celsius. **2.** Centigrade. **3. C.** *Physics.* Charm. **4.** *Slang.* Cocaine. **5.** Coulomb.

c. or **C.** *abbr.* **1.** Capacity. **2.** Cape. **3.** Carton. **4.** Case. **5.** Catcher. **6.** Cent. **7.** Centavo. **8.** Centime. **9.** Century. **10.** Chapter. **11.** Church. **12.** Circa. **13.** *Latin.* Congius (gallon). **14.** Consul. **15.** Copy. **16.** Copyright. **17.** Corps. **18.** Cup.

C. *abbr.* **1.** Catholic. **2.** Celtic. **3.** Chancellor. **4.** Chief. **5.** City. **6.** Companion. **7.** Congress. **8.** Conservative. **9.** Court.

ca *abbr.* **1.** Centare. **2.** Circa.

Ca The symbol for the element **calcium.**

CA *abbr.* **1.** California. **2.** Also **C.A.** Chronological age.

C.A. *abbr.* **1.a.** Central America. **b.** Central American. **2.** Also **c.a.** Chartered accountant.

c/a *abbr.* Current account.

CAA or **C.A.A.** *abbr.* Civil Aeronautics Administration.

cab[1] (kăb) *n.* **1.** A taxicab. **2.** The covered compartment of a heavy vehicle or machine, such as a truck or locomotive, in which the operator or driver sits. **3.** A one-horse vehicle for public hire. **—cab** *v.* **cabbed, cab·bing, cabs.** *—intr.* **1.** To ride or travel in a taxicab: *We cabbed to the opera.* **2.** To drive a taxicab: *a student who cabbed for a living.* *—tr.* To transport or convey in a taxicab: *cabbed the package to the airport.* [Short for CABRIOLET.]

cab[2] also **kab** (kăb) *n.* An ancient Hebrew unit of measure equal to about 2 liters (2.1 quarts). [Hebrew *qab,* hollow vessel.]

CAB *abbr.* Civil Aeronautics Board.

ca·bal (kə-băl′) *n.* **1.** A conspiratorial group of plotters or intriguers: *"Espionage is quite precisely it—a cabal of powerful men, working secretly"* (Frank Conroy). **2.** A secret scheme or plot. See Synonyms at **conspiracy.** **—cabal** *intr.v.* **-balled, -bal·ling, -bals.** To form a cabal; conspire. [French *cabale,* from Medieval Latin *cabala.* See CABALA.]

WORD HISTORY: The history of *cabal* reveals how a word can be transferred from one sphere of activity to another while retaining only a tenuous connection with its past. Ultimately from Hebrew but transmitted to English probably by way of Medieval Latin and French, *cabal* is first recorded in English in 1616 in the sense "cabala." *Cabala* was the name for the Hebrew oral tradition transmitted by Moses and also the name for a Jewish religious philosophy based on an esoteric interpretation of the Hebrew Scriptures. The notion "esoteric" is central to the development of this word in English, for *cabal,* probably following the sense development in French, came to mean "a tradition, special interpretation, or secret," "a private intrigue" (first recorded in 1646–1647), and "a small body of intriguers" (first recorded in 1660). It is probably not coincidental that *cabal* is found with these latter meanings during the mid-17th century, that time of plots and counterplots by Royalists and Parliamentarians. The word gained a false etymology when it was noticed that the five most influential ministers of Charles II were named Clifford, Arlington, Buckingham, Ashley, and Lauderdale.

cab·a·la or **cab·ba·la** also **kab·a·la** or **kab·ba·la** (kăb′ə-lə, kə-bä′-) *n.* **1.** Often **Cabala.** A body of mystical teachings of rabbinical origin, often based on an esoteric interpretation of the Hebrew Scriptures. **2.** A secret doctrine resembling these teachings. [Medieval Latin, from Hebrew *qabbālâ,* received doctrine, tradition, from *qibbēl,* to receive.] **—cab′a·lism** *n.* **—cab′a·list** *n.*

ca·ba·let·ta (kăb′ə-lĕt′ə, kä′bə-) *n., pl.* **-let·tas** or **-let·te** (-lĕt′ē). **1.** *Music.* **a.** A short aria that has a repetitive rhythm and a simple style. **b.** The final section of an aria or duet marked by a quick uniform rhythm. **2.** Something likened to such a short aria or a final section of a piece: *"And a chronic chorus of cascades and birds/Cuts loose in a wild cabaletta"* (W.H. Auden). [Italian, alteration of *coboletta,* stanza, diminutive of *cobola, cobla,* from Old Provençal *cobla,* from Latin *cōpula,* link.]

cab·a·lis·tic (kăb′ə-lĭs′tĭk) *adj.* **1.** Having a secret or hidden meaning; occult: *cabalistic symbols engraved in stone.* **2.** Of or relating to the cabala. **—cab′a·lis′ti·cal·ly** *adv.*

cab·al·le·ro (kăb′ə-lâr′ō, -əl-yâr′ō, kä′bä-yĕ′rō) *n., pl.* **-ros.** **1.** A Spanish gentleman; a cavalier. **2.** One who is skilled in riding and managing horses; a horseman. [Spanish, from Late Latin *caballārius,* horse groom, from Latin *caballus,* horse.]

ca·ban·a also **ca·ba·ña** (kə-băn′ə, -băn′yə) *n.* A shelter on a beach or at a swimming pool used as a bathhouse. [Spanish *cabaña,* from Late Latin *capanna,* hut.]

Ca·ba·na·tuan (kä′bə-nə-twän′, -bä-nä-). A city of central Luzon, Philippines, north of Manila. It was the site of a World War II Japanese prison camp for American and Filipino soldiers captured at Bataan and Corregidor. Population, 38,400.

cab·a·ret (kăb′ə-rā′) *n.* **1.** A restaurant or nightclub providing short programs of live entertainment. **2.** The floor show presented by such a restaurant or nightclub. [French, tap-room, from Middle Dutch *cabret,* from Old North French *camberette,* from Late Latin *camera,* room. See CHAMBER.]

cab·bage (kăb′ĭj) *n.* **1.** Any of several forms of a European vegetable *(Brassica oleracea* var. *capitata)* of the mustard family, having a globose head consisting of a short stem and tightly overlapping green to purplish leaves. **2.** Any of several similar or related plants, such as Chinese cabbage. **3.** The terminal bud of several species of palm, eaten as a vegetable. **4.** *Slang.* Money, especially in the form of bills. **5.** *Informal.* Sweetheart; dear. Used as a term of endearment. [Middle English *caboche,* from Old North French, head, possibly from alteration of Latin *caput.* See CAPITAL[1].] **—cab′bag·y** *adj.*

cabbage butterfly *n.* Any of several white butterflies of the genus *Pieris,* having larvae that feed on cabbage.

cabbage palm *n.* **1.** Any of several palms, such as the assai, with edible terminal buds. **2.** See **cabbage palmetto.**

cabbage palmetto *n.* A species of palmetto *(Sabal palmetto)* native to the southeast United States and the Bahamas, having an edible terminal bud and leaves used in religious services on Palm Sunday. Also called *cabbage palm.*

cabbage rose *n.* A coarse, prickly shrub *(Rosa centifolia)* native to the Caucasus, having fragrant, pink, double-petaled flowers and widely cultivated as a source of attar of roses.

cab·bage·worm (kăb′ĭj-wûrm′) *n.* A larva that feeds on and is destructive to cabbage, especially the bright-green larva of the cabbage butterfly.

cab·ba·la (kăb′ə-lə, kə-bä′-) *n.* Variant of **cabala.**

cab·by or **cab·bie** (kăb′ē) *n., pl.* **-bies.** A cabdriver. [CAB[1] + -Y[3].]

cab·driv·er also **cab driver** (kăb′drī′vər) *n.* One who drives a taxicab for hire.

Cab·ell (kăb′əl), **James Branch.** 1879–1958. American writer best known for a series of satirical novels, including *Jurgen* (1919), set in a fictitious medieval French province called Poictesme.

ca·ber (kā′bər) *n.* *Sports.* A long, heavy wooden pole tossed end over end as a demonstration of strength in Scottish highland games. [Scottish Gaelic *cabar,* pole, beam, rafter, from Vulgar Latin **capriō,* from Latin *capra,* she-goat. See CHEVRON.]

cab·er·net (kăb′ər-nā′) *n.* A dry red wine made from the black grape variety *Cabernet sauvignon.* [French.]

Phoenician
The third letter of the Phoenician alphabet stood for the sound of *g* in *gīmel* or *gaml,* "camel."

Early Greek
Adopting the letter with little change, the Greeks called it *gamma.*

Roman
The Romans at first used their version of this sign for both *g* (writing *Caius* or *C.,* for the name *Gaius*) and *k* and only later developed the modified form G for the sound *g.* The modern "soft" value of C results from changes in the pronunciation of *k* before *e, i,* and *y* in Latin, the Romance languages, and Old English.

cab[1]

Ca·be·za de Va·ca (kə-bā′zə də vä′kə, kä-vĕ′thä *thĕ* vä′kä), **Álvar Núñez.** 1490?–1557? Spanish explorer and colonial administrator who explored parts of present-day Florida, Texas, and Mexico and aroused Spain's interest in the region with his vivid stories of riches and opportunities.

CABG *abbr.* Coronary artery bypass graft.

Ca·bi·mas (kə-bē′məs, kä-vē′mäs). A town of northwest Venezuela on the northeast shore of Lake Maracaibo. It is a center for oil producing and refining. Population, 183,000.

cab·in (kăb′ĭn) *n.* **1.** A small, roughly built house; a cottage. **2.** *Nautical.* **a.** A room in a ship used as living quarters by an officer or a passenger. **b.** An enclosed compartment in a boat that serves as a shelter or as living quarters. **3.** The enclosed space in an aircraft or spacecraft for the crew, passengers, or cargo. —**cabin** *tr. & intr.v.* **-ined, -in·ing, -ins.** To confine or live in or as if in a small space or area. [Middle English *caban,* from Old French *cabane,* from Old Provençal *cabana,* from Late Latin *capanna.*]

cabin

cabin boy *n.* A boy servant aboard a ship.

cabin class *n. Nautical.* A class of accommodations on some passenger ships, lower than first class and higher than tourist class.

cabin cruiser *n. Nautical.* A powerboat with a cabin that has living accommodations.

Ca·bin·da (kə-bĭn′də). A territory of Angola forming an exclave on the Atlantic Ocean between Congo and Zaire. It was separated from Angola proper when the Belgian Congo (now Zaire) acquired a corridor to the sea along the lower Congo River.

♦**cab·i·net** (kăb′ə-nĭt) *n.* **1.** An upright, cupboardlike repository with shelves, drawers, or compartments for the safekeeping or display of a collection of objects or materials. **2.** Often **Cabinet.** A body of persons appointed by a head of state or a prime minister to head the executive departments of the government and to act as official advisers. **3.** *Archaic.* A small or private room set aside for a specific activity. **4.** *Rhode Island & Southeastern Massachusetts.* See **milk shake** (sense 1). See Regional Note at **milk shake.** —**cabinet** *adj.* **1.** Suitable for storage or display in a cabinet, as because of size or decorative quality. **2.** Of, relating to, or being a member of a governmental cabinet: *cabinet matters; a cabinet minister.* **3.** Used in the making of cabinets: *teak and other heavy cabinet wood.* [French, partly from diminutive of Old North French *cabine,* gambling-room (perhaps alteration of Old French *cabane,* small house; see CABIN) and partly from Italian *gabinetto,* closet, chest of drawers; akin to Old North French *cabine.* N., sense 4, possibly from the square wooden container in which the mixer was encased.] —**cab′i·net·ful** *n.*

cable car

cab·i·net·mak·er (kăb′ə-nĭt-mā′kər) *n.* An artisan specializing in making fine articles of wooden furniture. —**cab′i·net·mak′ing** *n.*

cab·i·net·ry (kăb′ĭ-nĭ-trē) *n.* Cabinetwork: *finely detailed cabinetry.*

cab·i·net·work (kăb′ə-nĭt-wûrk′) *n.* Finished woodwork fashioned by a cabinetmaker.

cabin fever *n.* Uneasiness or distress that results from a lack of environmental stimulation, as when living in a remote, sparsely populated region or in a small, enclosed space.

ca·ble (kā′bəl) *n.* **1.a.** A strong, large-diameter, heavy steel or fiber rope. **b.** Something that resembles such steel or fiber rope. **2.** *Electricity.* A bound or sheathed group of mutually insulated conductors. **3.** *Nautical.* **a.** A heavy rope or chain for mooring or anchoring a ship. **b.** A cable length. **4.** A cablegram. **5.** Cable television. —**cable** *v.* **-bled, -bling, -bles.** —*tr.* **1.a.** To send a cablegram to. **b.** To transmit (a message) by telegraph. **2.** To supply or fasten with a cable or cables. —*intr.* To send a cablegram. [Middle English, from Old North French, from Late Latin *capulum,* lasso, from Latin *capere,* to seize. See **kap-** in Appendix.] —**ca′bler** *n.*

Ca·ble (kā′bəl), **George Washington.** 1844–1925. American writer whose works, including short stories and the novel *The Grandissimes* (1880), concern social order and racial discord in the South.

cable car *n.* A car designed to operate on a cableway or cable railway.

ca·ble·cast (kā′bəl-kăst′) *n.* A telecast by cable television. [CABLE + (BROAD)CAST.] —**ca′ble·cast′** *v.* —**ca′ble·cast′er** *n.*

ca·ble·gram (kā′bəl-grăm′) *n.* A telegram sent by submarine cable. [CABLE + (TELE)GRAM.]

ca·ble-laid (kā′bəl-lād′) *adj.* Made of three ropes of three strands each, twisted together counterclockwise.

cable length also **ca·ble's length** (kā′bəlz) *n. Nautical.* A unit of length equal to 720 feet (220 meters) in the United States and 608 feet (185 meters) in England.

cable railway *n.* A railroad on which the cars are moved by an endless cable driven by a stationary engine.

ca·ble's length (kā′bəlz) *n. Nautical.* Variant of **cable length.**

cable stitch *n.* A stitch in knitting that produces a twisted, ropelike design.

ca·blet (kā′blĭt) *n.* A cable-laid rope with a circumference of less than 10 inches (25 centimeters).

cable television *n.* A television distribution system in which station signals, picked up by elevated antennas, are delivered by cable to the receivers of subscribers. Also called *cable TV, cablevision, community antenna television.*

Mother Cabrini

ca·ble·vi·sion (kā′bəl-vĭzh′ən) *n.* See **cable television.**

ca·ble·way (kā′bəl-wā′) *n.* A suspended cable used as a track typically for a cable car.

cab·man (kăb′mən) *n.* A man who drives a taxicab.

cab·o·chon (kăb′ə-shŏn′) *n.* **1.** A highly polished, convex-cut, unfaceted gem. **2.** A convex style of cutting gems. —**cabochon** *adv.* In a highly polished, convex-cut, unfaceted style: *a sapphire that was cut cabochon.* [French, from Old North French, augmentative of *caboche,* head. See CABBAGE.]

Ca·bo·clo or **ca·bo·clo** (kə-bô′klo͞o, -klō) *n., pl.* **-clos.** A person, especially a Brazilian, whose descent is traced entirely or partially to the Indian peoples inhabiting Brazil: *"got to know some caboclos, the Amazonian backwoods people who are some of the warmest people on earth"* (Alex Shoumatoff). [Portuguese, of Tupian origin.]

ca·bom·ba (kə-bŏm′bə) *n.* See **fanwort.** [American Spanish.]

ca·boo·dle (kə-bo͞od′l) *n. Informal.* **1.** The lot, group, or bunch: *donated the whole caboodle.* **2.** A crowd or collection of people. [Alteration of BOODLE.]

ca·boose (kə-bo͞os′) *n.* **1.** The last car on a freight train, having kitchen and sleeping facilities for the train crew. **2.** *Obsolete.* **a.** A ship's galley. **b.** Any of various cast-iron cooking ranges used in such galleys during the early 19th century. **c.** An outdoor oven or fireplace. [Possibly from obsolete Dutch *cabūse,* ship's galley, from Middle Low German *kabūse* : perhaps **kab-,* cabin; akin to Old French *cabane;* see CABIN + Middle High German *hūs,* house.]

Cab·ot (kăb′ət), **John.** Originally Giovanni Caboto. 1450?–1498? Italian-born explorer who commanded the English expedition that discovered the North American mainland (1497).

Cabot, Sebastian. 1476?–1557. Italian-born explorer and cartographer who led an English expedition in search of the Northwest Passage (1509) and a Spanish expedition to South America (1525–1528). He published a map of the world in 1544.

cab·o·tage (kăb′ə-täzh′) *n.* **1.** Trade or navigation in coastal waters. **2.** The exclusive right of a country to operate the air traffic within its territory. [French, from *caboter,* to sail along a coast, perhaps from Spanish *cabo,* cape, from Latin *caput,* head. See CAPE[2].]

ca·bret·ta (kə-brĕt′ə) *n.* A soft, kidlike leather used for gloves and shoes and made from sheepskin having coarse, hairlike wool. [Spanish and Portuguese *cabra,* she-goat (both from Latin *capra,* feminine of *caper,* goat) + Italian *-etta,* diminutive suff.]

ca·bril·la (kə-brē′yə, -brĭl′ə) *n.* Any of various sea basses, especially *Epinephelus guttatus* of tropical waters, such as the Mediterranean. [Spanish, diminutive of *cabra,* she-goat. See CABRETTA.]

Ca·bri·ni (kə-brē′nē), Saint **Frances Xavier.** Known as "Mother Cabrini." 1850–1917. Italian-born American religious leader who founded the Missionary Sisters of the Sacred Heart (1880) and was the first American to be canonized (1946).

cab·ri·ole (kăb′rē-ōl′) *n.* A form of furniture leg that curves outward and then narrows downward into an ornamental foot, characteristic of Queen Anne and Chippendale furniture. [French, caper (from its resemblance to the foreleg of a capering animal). See CABRIOLET.]

cab·ri·o·let (kăb′rē-ə-lā′) *n.* **1.** A two-wheeled, one-horse carriage that has two seats and a folding top. **2.** An automobile with a folding top; a convertible coupe. [French, diminutive of *cabriole,* caper, from obsolete *capriole,* from Italian *capriola,* from *capriolo,* roebuck, from Latin *capreolus,* masculine diminutive of *caprea,* roe deer, from *caper,* he-goat.]

cab·stand (kăb′stănd′) *n.* A place designated for taxicabs waiting for hire.

cac– *pref.* Variant of **caco–.**

ca·ca·o (kə-kä′ō, -kā′ō) *n., pl.* **-os. 1.** An evergreen tropical American tree *(Theobroma cacao)* having leathery, ellipsoid, ten-ribbed fruits borne on the trunks and older branches. Also called *chocolate tree.* **2.** The seed of this plant, used in making chocolate, cocoa, and cocoa butter. In this sense, also called *cacao bean, cocoa bean.* [Spanish, from Nahuatl *cacahuatl.*]

cacao butter *n.* See **cocoa butter.**

ca·cha·ca also **ca·cha·ça** (kə-shä′sə) *n.* A light Brazilian rum made from sugar cane. [Portuguese *cachaça.*]

cach·a·lot (kăsh′ə-lŏt′, -lō′) *n.* See **sperm whale.** [French, from Spanish or Portuguese *cachalote,* augmentative of *cachola,* big head.]

cache (kăsh) *n.* **1.a.** A hiding place used especially for storing provisions. **b.** A place for concealment and safekeeping, as of valuables. **c.** The store of goods or valuables concealed in a hiding place. **2.** *Computer Science.* A fast storage buffer in the central processing unit of a computer. In this sense, also called *cache memory.* —**cache** *tr.v.* **cached, cach·ing, cach·es.** To hide or store in a cache. See Synonyms at **hide**[1]. [French, from *cacher,* to hide, from Old French, to press, hide, from Vulgar Latin **coācticāre,* to store, pack together, frequentative of Latin *coāctāre,* to constrain, from *coāctus,* past participle of *cōgere,* to force. See COGENT.]

ca·chec·tic (kə-kĕk′tĭk) *adj.* Affected by or relating to cachexia. [French *cachectique,* from Latin *cachecticus,* from Greek *kakhektikos,* from *kakhexia,* bad condition of the body. See CACHEXIA.]

cache memory *n. Computer Science.* See **cache** (sense 2).

cache•pot (kăsh′pŏt′, -pō′) *n.* An ornamental container for a flowerpot. [French : *cacher,* to hide; see CACHE + *pot,* pot (from Old French, from Vulgar Latin **pottus*).]

ca•chet (kă-shā′) *n.* **1.** A mark or a quality, as of distinction, individuality, or authenticity: *"Federal courts have a certain cachet which state courts lack"* (Christian Science Monitor). **2.** A seal on a document, such as a letter. **3.a.** A commemorative design stamped on an envelope to mark a postal or philatelic event. **b.** A motto forming part of a postal cancellation. **4.** A kind of wafer capsule formerly used by pharmacists for presenting an unpleasant-tasting drug. [French, from Old French, from *cacher,* to press. See CACHE.]

ca•chex•i•a (kə-kĕk′sē-ə) *n.* Weight loss, wasting of muscle, loss of appetite, and general debility that can occur during a chronic disease. [Late Latin, from Greek *kakhexia* : *kako-,* caco- + *hexis,* condition (from *ekhein,* to have; see **segh-** in Appendix).]

cach•in•nate (kăk′ə-nāt′) *intr.v.* **-nat•ed, -nat•ing, -nates.** To laugh hard, loudly, or convulsively; guffaw. [Latin *cachinnāre, cachinnāt-,* probably of imitative origin.] **—cach′in•na′tion** *n.* **—cach′in•na′tor** *n.*

ca•chou (kă-sho͞o′, kăsh′o͞o) *n.* A pastille used to sweeten the breath. [French, from Portuguese *cachu,* from Malayalam *kāccu,* from Tamil *kāyccu.*]

ca•chu•cha (kə-cho͞o′chə) *n.* An Andalusian solo dance in 3/4 time. [Spanish, small boat, cachucha, possibly from diminutive of *cacho,* shard, saucepan, probably from Vulgar Latin **cacculus,* alteration of Latin *caccabus,* pot, from Greek *kakkabos,* probably of Semitic origin; akin to Akkadian *kukubu,* vessel.]

ca•cique (kə-sēk′) *n.* **1.** An Indian chief, especially in the Spanish West Indies and other parts of Latin America during colonial and postcolonial times. **2.** A local political boss in Spain or Latin America. [American Spanish, from Arawak *kassequa,* chieftain.]

cack-hand•ed (kăk′hăn′dĭd) *adj. Chiefly British.* **1.** Left-handed. **2.** Awkward; clumsy. [Perhaps from Old Norse *keikr,* bent backwards; akin to Danish *keite,* left-handed.]

cack•le (kăk′əl) *v.* **-led, -ling, -les.** *—intr.* **1.** To make the shrill cry characteristic of a hen after laying an egg. **2.** To laugh or talk in a shrill manner. *—tr.* To utter in cackles. **—cackle** *n.* **1.** The act or sound of cackling. **2.** Shrill laughter. **3.** Foolish chatter. [Middle English *cakelen,* probably from Middle Low German *kākeln,* of imitative origin.] **—cack′ler** *n.*

caco– or **cac–** *pref.* Bad: *cacography.* [Greek *kako-,* from *kakos,* bad. See **kakka-** in Appendix.]

cac•o•dyl (kăk′ə-dĭl′) *n.* **1.** The arsenic group $(CH_3)_2As^-$. **2.** A poisonous oil, $As_2(CH_3)_4$, with an obnoxious garlicky odor. [Greek *kakōdēs,* bad-smelling (*kakos,* bad; see **kakka-** in Appendix + *-ōdēs,* -smelling, from *ozein, ōd-,* to smell) + –YL.] **—cac′o•dyl′ic** *adj.*

cac•o•ë•thes (kăk′ō-ē′thēz) *n.* An irresistible compulsion; a mania. [Latin *cacoēthes,* from neuter of Greek *kakoēthēs,* ill-disposed : *kakos,* bad; see **kakka-** in Appendix + *ēthos,* disposition; see **s(w)e-** in Appendix.]

ca•cog•ra•phy (kə-kŏg′rə-fē) *n.* **1.** Bad handwriting. **2.** Bad spelling.

cac•o•mis•tle (kăk′ə-mĭs′əl) *n.* A small, carnivorous mammal *(Bassariscus astutus)* of the southwest United States, having grayish or brownish fur and a black-banded tail and resembling the raccoon. [American Spanish *cacomiztle,* from Nahuatl *tlacomiztli* : *tlaco,* half, part + *miztli,* mountain lion.]

cac•o•nym (kăk′ə-nĭm) *n.* An erroneous name, especially in taxonomic classification; a misnomer. **—ca•con′y•my** (kə-kŏn′ə-mē) *n.*

ca•coph•o•nous (kə-kŏf′ə-nəs) *adj.* Having a harsh, unpleasant sound; discordant. [From Greek *kakophōnos* : *kakos,* bad; see **kakka-** in Appendix + *phōnē,* sound; see **bhā-**[2] in Appendix.] **—ca•coph′o•nous•ly** *adv.*

ca•coph•o•ny (kə-kŏf′ə-nē) *n., pl.* **-nies. 1.** Jarring, discordant sound; dissonance: *heard a cacophony of horns during the traffic jam.* **2.** The use of harsh or discordant sounds in literary composition, as for poetic effect. [French *cacophonie,* from Greek *kakophōnia,* from *kakophōnos,* cacophonous. See CACOPHONOUS.]

cac•tus (kăk′təs) *n., pl.* **-ti** (-tī′) or **-tus•es. 1.** Any of various succulent, spiny, usually leafless plants native mostly to arid regions of the New World, having variously colored, often showy flowers with numerous stamens and petals. **2.** Any of several similar plants. [Latin, cardoon, from Greek *kaktos.*]

cactus pear *n.* See **tuna**[2].

ca•cu•mi•nal (kə-kyo͞o′mə-nəl) *adj.* Articulated with the tip of the tongue turned back and up toward the roof of the mouth; retroflex. [From Latin *cacūmen, cacūmin-,* summit, point.]

cad (kăd) *n.* An unprincipled, ungentlemanly man. [Short for CADDIE.] **—cad′dish** *adj.* **—cad′dish•ly** *adv.*

CAD *abbr.* Computer-aided design.

ca•das•tre also **ca•das•ter** (kə-dăs′tər) *n.* A public record, survey, or map of the value, extent, and ownership of land as a basis of taxation. [French, from Provençal *cadastro,* from Italian *catastro,* alteration of Old Italian *catastico,* from Late Greek *katastikhon,* register : Greek *kata-,* by; see CATA– + Greek *stikhos,* line; see **steigh-** in Appendix.] **—ca•das′tral** *adj.*

ca•dav•er (kə-dăv′ər) *n.* A dead body, especially one intended for dissection. See Synonyms at **body.** [Middle English, from Latin *cadāver,* from *cadere,* to fall, die. See **kad-** in Appendix.] **—ca•dav′er•ic** (-ər-ĭk) *adj.*

ca•dav•er•ine (kə-dăv′ə-rēn′) *n.* A syrupy, colorless, fuming ptomaine, $C_5H_{14}N_2$, formed by the carboxylation of lysine by bacteria in decaying animal flesh.

ca•dav•er•ous (kə-dăv′ər-əs) *adj.* **1.** Suggestive of death; corpselike: *a cadaverous odor.* **2.a.** Of corpselike pallor; pallid: *"I saw a cadaverous face appear at a small window"* (Charles Dickens). **b.** Emaciated; gaunt: *a cadaverous mongrel picking through the garbage.* **—ca•dav′er•ous•ly** *adv.* **—ca•dav′er•ous•ness** *n.*

cad•dice (kăd′ĭs) *n.* Variant of **caddis.**

caddice fly *n.* Variant of **caddis fly.**

caddice worm *n.* Variant of **caddis worm.**

cad•die also **cad•dy** (kăd′ē) *—n., pl.* **-dies. 1.** *Sports.* One hired to serve as an attendant to a golfer, especially by carrying the golf clubs. **2.** *Scots.* A boy who does odd jobs. *—intr.v.* **-died, -dy•ing, -dies.** To serve as a caddie. [Scots, from French *cadet,* cadet, caddie. See CADET.]

cad•dis also **cad•dice** (kăd′ĭs) *n.* A coarse woolen fabric, yarn, or ribbon binding. [Probably from Middle English *cadace,* cotton wool (from Anglo-Norman, from Old Provençal *cadarz*) and from French *cadis,* woolen cloth (from Old Provençal).]

caddis fly also **caddice fly** *n.* Any of various four-winged insects of the order Trichoptera, found near lakes and streams. [Perhaps from obsolete *cad* (influenced by CADDIS), variant of COD[2] (from the tube in which the larva lives).]

caddis worm also **caddice worm** *n.* The aquatic, wormlike larva of the caddis fly, enclosed in a cylindrical case covered with grains of sand, fragments of shell, and other debris.

Cad•do (kăd′ō) *n., pl.* **Caddo** or **-dos. 1.a.** A Native American confederacy composed of numerous small tribes formerly inhabiting the Red River area of Louisiana, Arkansas, and eastern Texas and now located in central Oklahoma. **b.** A member of this confederacy. **2.** The Caddoan language of the Caddo. [French, from Caddo *kaduhdā·čuʔ,* a major tribe of the Caddo confederacy.]

Cad•do•an (kăd′ō-ən) *n.* A family of North American Indian languages formerly spoken in the Dakotas, Kansas, Nebraska, Texas, Oklahoma, Arkansas, and Louisiana, and presently in North Dakota and Oklahoma.

cad•dy[1] (kăd′ē) *n., pl.* **-dies.** A small container, such as a box, used especially for holding tea. [Alteration of CATTY[1].]

cad•dy[2] (kăd′ē) *n. & v.* Variant of **caddie.**

cade (kād) *adj.* Left by its mother and reared by hand: *a cade calf.* [Middle English, pet lamb.]

Cade (kād), **Jack.** Died 1450. English rebel who led an unsuccessful rebellion against Henry VI (1450).

–cade *suff.* Procession: *motorcade.* [From CAVALCADE.]

ca•delle (kə-dĕl′) *n.* A small blackish beetle *(Tenebroides mauritanicus),* both the larval and adult forms of which damage stored grain. [French, from Provençal *cadello,* from Latin *catella,* feminine of *catellus,* puppy, from *catulus,* the young of animals. See **kat-** in Appendix.]

ca•dence (kād′ns) *n., pl.* **-denc•es. 1.** Balanced, rhythmic flow, as of poetry or oratory. See Synonyms at **rhythm. 2.** The measure or beat of movement, as in dancing or marching. **3.a.** A falling inflection of the voice, as at the end of a sentence. **b.** General inflection or modulation of the voice. **4.** *Music.* A progression of chords moving to a harmonic close or point of rest. [Middle English, from Old French **cadence,* from Old Italian *cadenza,* from Vulgar Latin **cadentia,* a falling, from Latin *cadēns, cadent-,* present participle of *cadere,* to fall. See **kad-** in Appendix.] **—ca′denced** *adj.*

ca•den•cy (kād′n-sē) *n., pl.* **-cies.** Cadence.

ca•dent (kād′nt) *adj.* **1.** Having cadence or rhythm. **2.** *Archaic.* Falling, as water or tears. [Latin *cadēns, cadent-,* present participle of *cadere,* to fall. See **kad-** in Appendix.]

ca•den•tial (kə-dĕn′shəl) *adj.* **1.** Of or relating to a cadence. **2.** *Music.* Of or having to do with a cadenza: *"At certain cadential points,* [he] *inserts brief cadenzas that add an improvisational touch"* (Boris Schwarz).

ca•den•za (kə-dĕn′zə) *n. Music.* **1.** An elaborate, ornamental melodic flourish interpolated into an aria or other vocal piece. **2.** An extended virtuosic section for the soloist near the end of a movement of a concerto. [Italian, from Old Italian, cadence. See CADENCE.]

cade oil *n.* See **juniper tar.** [French *cade,* a species of juniper, from Provençal, from Old Provençal; akin to Late Latin *catanum,* possibly of Celtic origin.]

ca•det (kə-dĕt′) *n.* **1.** A student at a military school who is training to be an officer. **2.a.** A younger son or brother. **b.** A youngest son. **3.** *Slang.* A pimp. [French, from dialectal *capdet,* captain, from Late Latin *capitellum,* diminutive of Latin *caput, capit-,* head. See **kaput-** in Appendix.] **—ca•det′ship′** *n.*

cadge (kăj) *intr. & tr.v.* **cadged, cadg•ing, cadg•es.** To beg or get by begging. [Perhaps back-formation from obsolete *cadger,* peddler, from Middle English *cadgear.*] **—cadg′er** *n.*

SYNONYMS: *cadge, beg, bum, mooch, panhandle.* The central meaning shared by these verbs is "to ask, ask for, or get as charity": *cadged a cigarette; derelicts begging for change; bum a*

cabriole
Late 18th-century American side chair

cachepot
c. 1730 French

cacomistle
Bassariscus astutus

caddis fly

ă pat	oi boy
ā pay	ou out
âr care	o͝o took
ä father	o͞o boot
ĕ pet	ŭ cut
ē be	ûr urge
ĭ pit	th thin
ī pie	*th* this
îr pier	hw which
ŏ pot	zh vision
ō toe	ə about, item
ô paw	♦ regionalism

Stress marks: ′ (primary); ′ (secondary), as in **dictionary** (dĭk′shə-nĕr′ē)

drink; mooching food; homeless people forced to panhandle in subway stations.

Cad·il·lac (kăd′l-ăk′, kä-dē-yäk′), Sieur **Antoine de la Mothe.** 1658–1730. French explorer and colonial administrator who founded Detroit (1701).

Cá·diz (kə-dĭz′, kā′dĭz, kä′-, kä′thĕth, -thĕs). A city of southwest Spain northwest of Gibraltar on the **Gulf of Cádiz,** an inlet of the Atlantic Ocean. Cádiz was founded c. 1100 B.C. by Phoenicians and passed to the Carthaginians (c. 500 B.C.), Romans (third century A.D.), Moors (711), and the kingdom of Castile (1262). Population, 160,839.

cad·mi·um (kăd′mē-əm) *n. Symbol* **Cd** A soft, bluish-white metallic element occurring primarily in zinc, copper, and lead ores, that is easily cut with a knife and is used in low-friction, fatigue-resistant alloys, solders, dental amalgams, nickel-cadmium storage batteries, nuclear reactor shields, and in rust-proof electroplating. Atomic number 48; atomic weight 112.40; melting point 320.9°C; boiling point 765°C; specific gravity 8.65; valence 2. See table at **element.** [Latin *cadmīa,* calamine (from its being found with calamine in zinc ore) (from Greek *kadmeia (gē),* Theban (earth), from *Kadmos,* Cadmus) + -IUM.] **—cad′mic** (-mĭk) *adj.*

cadmium sulfate *n.* A compound, $CdSO_4$, that forms colorless crystals, is water soluble, and is used as an antiseptic.

Cad·mus (kăd′məs) *n. Greek Mythology.* A Phoenician prince who killed a dragon and sowed its teeth, from which sprang up an army of men who fought one another until only five survived. With these five men Cadmus founded the city of Thebes.

cad·re (kăd′rē, kä′drā) *n.* **1.** A nucleus of trained personnel around which a larger organization can be built and trained: *a cadre of sergeants and corporals who train recruits.* **2. a.** A tightly knit group of zealots who are active in advancing the interests of a revolutionary party. **b.** A member of such a group. **3.** A framework. [French, from Italian *quadro,* frame, from Latin *quadrum,* a square, from neuter of *quadrus,* square. See **kʷetwer-** in Appendix.]

caduceus

ca·du·ce·us (kə-do͞o′sē-əs, -shəs, -dyo͞o′-) *n., pl.* **-ce·i** (-sē-ī′). **1. a.** A herald's wand or staff, especially in ancient times. **b.** *Greek Mythology.* A winged staff with two serpents twined around it, carried by Hermes. **2.** An insignia modeled on Hermes' staff and used as the symbol of the medical profession. [Latin *cādūceus,* alteration of Greek *karukeion,* from *karux,* herald.] **—ca·du′ce·an** (-sē-ən, -shən) *adj.*

ca·du·ci·ty (kə-do͞o′sĭ-tē, -dyo͞o′-) *n.* **1.** The frailty of old age; senility. **2.** The quality or state of being perishable; impermanence. [French *caducité,* from *caduc,* frail, falling, from Latin *cadūcus.* See CADUCOUS.]

ca·du·cous (kə-do͞o′kəs, -dyo͞o′-) *adj.* Dropping off or shedding at an early stage of development, as the gills of most amphibians or the sepals or stipules of certain plants. [From Latin *cadūcus,* falling, from *cadere,* to fall. See **kad-** in Appendix.]

cae·cil·ian (sə-sĭl′yən, -sĭl′ē-ən, -sēl′-) *n.* Any of various legless, burrowing, wormlike amphibians of the order Gymnophiona, of tropical regions. [From Latin *caecilia,* a kind of lizard, from *caecus,* blind (from its small eyes).]

cae·cum (sē′kəm) *n.* Variant of **cecum.**

Caed·mon (kăd′mən). Died c. 680. The earliest English poet. According to Bede, he was an elderly herdsman who received the power of song in a vision.

Cae·li·an (sē′lē-ən). One of the seven hills of ancient Rome. The most southeasterly of the hills, it was densely populated until much of it was devastated by a fire in A.D. 27. **—Cae′li·an** *adj.*

Cae·lum (sē′ləm) *n.* A constellation in the Southern Hemisphere near Columba and Eridanus. [Latin *caelum,* sculptor's chisel. See **kae-id-** in Appendix.]

Caen (käN). A city of northern France southwest of Le Havre. A Huguenot stronghold in the 16th and 17th centuries, it is the burial place of William the Conqueror. Population, 114,068.

Caer·nar·von (kär-när′vən). A municipal borough of northwest Wales on a narrow strait of the Irish Sea opposite Anglesey Island. The investiture of Charles as Prince of Wales took place in the castle here in 1969. Population, 9,506.

caer·phil·ly (kär-fĭl′ē) *n.* A mild white Welsh cheese. [After *Caerphilly,* a district of southeast Wales.]

cae·sar also **Cae·sar** (sē′zər) *n.* **1.** Used as a title and form of address for Roman emperors. **2.** A dictator or an autocrat. [Middle English *cesar,* from Latin *Caesar,* after Julius CAESAR.]

Caesar, Julius. In full Gaius Julius Caesar. 100–44 B.C. Roman general, statesman, and historian who invaded Britain (55), crushed the army of his political enemy Pompey (48), pursued other enemies to Egypt, where he installed Cleopatra as queen (47), returned to Rome, and was given a mandate by the people to rule as dictator for life (45). On March 15 of the following year he was murdered by a group of republicans led by Cassius and Brutus, who feared he intended to establish a monarchy ruled by himself. **—Cae·sar′e·an, Cae·sar′i·an** (sĭ-zâr′ē-ən) *adj.*

Cae·sa·re·a (sē′zə-rē′ə, sĕs′ə-, sĕz′ə-). **1.** Also **Caesarea Pal·e·sti·nae** (păl′ĭ-stī′nē). An ancient seaport of Palestine south of present-day Haifa, Israel. It was founded (30 B.C.) by Herod the Great and later became the capital of Roman Judea. The city was destroyed by Moslems in 1265. **2.** Also **Caesarea Phil·ip·pi** (fĭl′ĭ-pī, fĭ-lĭp′ī). An ancient city of northern Palestine near Mount Hermon in present-day southwest Syria. It was built in the first century A.D. on the site of a center for the worship of Pan. **3.** Also **Caesarea Maz·a·ca** (măz′ə-kə). An ancient city of Cappadocia on the site of present-day Kayseri in central Turkey. It was destroyed by Persians in A.D. 260.

cae·sar·e·an (sĭ-zâr′ē-ən) *adj. & n.* Variant of **cesarean.**

caesarean section *n.* Variant of **cesarean section.**

cae·sar·i·an (sĭ-zâr′ē-ən) *adj. & n.* Variant of **cesarean.**

Cae·sar·ism (sē′zə-rĭz′əm) *n.* Military or imperial dictatorship; political authoritarianism. **—Cae′sar·ist** *n.* **—Cae′sar·is′tic** *adj.*

caesar salad *n.* A tossed salad of greens, anchovies, croutons, and grated cheese with a dressing of olive oil, lemon juice, and a raw or coddled egg. [Possibly after *Caesar's,* a restaurant in Tijuana, Mexico.]

cae·si·um (sē′zē-əm) *n.* Variant of **cesium.**

caes·tus (sĕs′təs) *n.* Variant of **cestus².**

cae·su·ra also **ce·su·ra** (sĭ-zho͝or′ə, -zo͝or′ə) *n., pl.* **-su·ras** or **-su·rae** (-zho͝or′ē, -zo͝or′ē). **1.** A pause in a line of verse dictated by sense or natural speech rhythm rather than by metrics. **2.** A pause or an interruption, as in conversation: *After another weighty caesura the senator resumed speaking.* **3.** In Latin and Greek prosody, a break in a line caused by the ending of a word within a foot, especially when this coincides with a sense division. **4.** *Music.* A pause or breathing at a point of rhythmic division in a melody. [Latin *caesūra,* a cutting, from *caesus,* past participle of *caedere,* to cut off. See **kae-id-** in Appendix.] **—cae·su′ral, cae·su′ric** *adj.*

C.A.F. *abbr.* Cost and freight.

ca·fé also **ca·fe** (kă-fā′, kə-) *n.* A coffee house, restaurant, or bar. [French, coffee, café, from Italian *caffè,* coffee, from Ottoman Turkish *qahveh.* See COFFEE.]

♦ **ca·fé au lait** (kă-fā′ ō lā′) *n.* **1.** Coffee served with hot milk. **2.** *Color.* A light coffee hue. See Regional Note at **beignet.** [French : *café,* coffee + *à,* with + *lait,* milk.]

café fil·tre (fĭl′trə) *n.* A beverage made by passing boiling water through ground coffee held in a filtering device that fits on top of a cup or pot. [French : *café,* coffee + *filtre,* filter.]

café noir (nwär′) *n.* Coffee served without cream or milk. [French : *café,* coffee + *noir,* black.]

café society *n.* The group of socialites and celebrities that frequents fashionable nightclubs and resorts and attends fashionable events: *"the glittering café society that revolves around the city's elite cultural institutions"* (Business Week).

caf·e·te·ri·a (kăf′ĭ-tîr′ē-ə) *n.* A restaurant in which the customers are served at a counter and carry their meals on trays to tables. [Spanish *cafetería,* coffee shop, cafeteria, from *café,* coffee, from Ottoman Turkish *qahveh.* See COFFEE.]

cafeteria benefit *n.* A particular employee benefit selected from a company plan offering a variety of choices that can be balanced to suit individual needs.

caf·e·te·ri·a-style (kăf′ĭ-tîr′ē-ə-stīl′) *adj.* **1.** Arranged in the manner of a cafeteria: *a cafeteria-style student dining hall.* **2.** Designed, established, or arranged in such a way that one may choose or select from a group, body, or collection only those things deemed desirable: *cafeteria-style medical benefits.*

caf·e·to·ri·um (kăf′ĭ-tôr′ē-əm, -tōr′-) *n., pl.* **-to·ri·ums** or **-to·ri·a** (-tôr′ē-ə, -tōr′-). A large room, usually in an educational institution, that serves both as a cafeteria and as an auditorium. [CAFE(TERIA) + (AUDI)TORIUM.]

caf·feine also **caf·fein** (kă-fēn′, kăf′ēn′, kăf′ē-ĭn) *n.* A bitter white alkaloid, $C_8H_{10}N_4O_2$, often derived from tea or coffee and used in medicine chiefly as a mild stimulant and to treat certain kinds of headache. [German *Kaffein* (from *Kaffee,* coffee) or French *caféine,* both from French *café,* coffee. See CAFÉ.] **—caf′fein·at′ed** (kăf′ə-nā′tĭd) *adj.*

caf·fein·ism (kă-fē′nĭz′əm, kăf′ē-, kăf′ē-ə-) *n.* A toxic condition marked by diarrhea, elevated blood pressure, rapid breathing, heart palpitations, and insomnia, caused by excessive ingestion of coffee and other caffeine-containing substances.

caf·tan or **kaf·tan** (kăf′tăn′, -tən, kăf-tăn′) *n.* **1.** A full-length garment with elbow-length or long sleeves, worn chiefly in eastern Mediterranean countries. **2.** A westernized version of this garment consisting of a loose, usually brightly colored waist-length or ankle-length tunic. [Russian *kaftan,* from Ottoman Turkish *qaftān.*]

cage (kāj) *n.* **1.** A structure for confining birds or animals, enclosed on at least one side by a grating of wires or bars that lets in air and light. **2.** A barred room or fenced enclosure for confining prisoners. **3.** An enclosing openwork structure: *placed a protective cage over the sapling; a bank teller's cage.* **4.** An elevator car. **5. a.** *Baseball.* A large wire screen placed behind home plate to stop balls in batting practice. **b.** *Sports.* A hockey or soccer goal made of a network frame. **c.** *Basketball.* The basket. **—cage** *tr.v.* **caged, cag·ing, cag·es.** To put or confine in or as if in a cage. See Synonyms at **enclose.** [Middle English, from Old French, from Latin *cavea.*]

Cage (kāj), **John Milton, Jr.** Born 1912. American composer of avant-garde works, such as *Sonatas and Interludes* for a piano with its strings damped by wood and metal (1946–1948).

cage·ling (kāj′lĭng) *n.* A bird kept as a pet in a cage.

ca·gey also **ca·gy** (kā′jē) *adj.* **-gi·er, -gi·est.** **1.** Wary; careful: *a cagey avoidance of a definite answer.* **2.** Crafty;

shrewd: *a cagey lawyer.* [Origin unknown.] **—ca′gi·ly** *adv.* **—ca′gi·ness** *n.*

Ca·glia·ri (käl′yə-rē′). A city of Sardinia, Italy, on the southern coast on the **Gulf of Cagliari,** an inlet of the Mediterranean Sea. The city was taken by the Romans in 238 B.C. Population, 232,785.

Ca·glio·stro (kăl-yō′strō, kä-lyô′strô), Count **Alessandro di.** Originally Giuseppe Balsamo. 1743–1795. Italian adventurer who was famous throughout Europe as a magician and alchemist.

Cag·ney (kăg′nē), **James.** Known as "Jimmy." 1899–1986. American actor noted for his portrayals of tough, often maleficent characters in films such as *Public Enemy* (1931).

C.A.G.S. *abbr.* Certificate of Advanced Graduate Studies.

Ca·guas (kä′gwäs′). A city of east-central Puerto Rico south-southeast of San Juan. It is an industrial center in an agricultural region. Population, 87,214.

ca·gy (kā′jē) *adj.* Variant of **cagey.**

ca·hier (kä-yā′) *n.* A report, especially one concerning the policy or proceedings of a parliamentary group. [French, notebook, from Old French *quaier,* from Vulgar Latin **quaternum,* from Latin *quaternī,* group of four, from *quater,* four times. See **k^{w}etwer-** in Appendix.]

Ca·ho·ki·a (kə-hō′kē-ə). A village of southwest Illinois, a residential suburb of East St. Louis. Nearby are the **Cahokia Mounds,** a group of approximately 85 prehistoric Native American earthworks. Population, 18,904.

ca·hoots (kə-ho͞ots′) *pl.n. Informal.* Questionable collaboration; secret partnership: *an accountant in cahoots with organized crime.* [Perhaps from French *cahute,* cabin, from Old French, possibly blend of *cabane;* see CABIN, and *hutte;* see HUT.]

ca·how (kə-hou′) *n.* An earth-burrowing, nocturnal bird *(Pterodroma cahow),* once abundant in Bermuda but now nearly extinct, with a hooked black beak, brown and white plumage, and a gray underside. Also called *Bermuda petrel.* [Imitative of its cry.]

Ca·huil·la (kə-wē′ə) *n., pl.* **Cahuilla** or **-las. 1.a.** A Native American people inhabiting parts of southeast California. **b.** A member of this people. **2.** The Uto-Aztecan language of the Cahuilla. [American Spanish.]

CAI *abbr.* Computer-aided instruction.

Cai·a·phas (kā′ə-fəs, kī′-), **Joseph.** fl. first century A.D. In the New Testament, the Jewish high priest who presided over the counsel that condemned Jesus.

Cai·cos Islands (kā′kəs, -kōs). One of the island groups constituting the Turks and Caicos Islands in the Atlantic Ocean southeast of the Bahamas.

cai·man also **cay·man** (kā′mən) *n., pl.* **-mans.** Any of various tropical American crocodilians of the genus *Caiman* and related genera, resembling and closely related to the alligators. [Spanish *caimán,* from Carib *acayuman.*]

Cain (kān). In the Old Testament, the eldest son of Adam and Eve, who murdered his brother Abel out of jealousy and was condemned to be a fugitive.

-caine *suff.* A synthetic alkaloid anesthetic: *eucaine.* [From COCAINE.]

cai·no·to·pho·bi·a (kā-nō′tə-fō′bē-ə) *n.* An abnormal fear of newness. [Greek *kainotēs,* newness (from *kainos,* new; see **ken-** in Appendix) + -PHOBIA.]

ca·ïque (kä-ēk′) *n. Nautical.* **1.** A long, narrow rowboat used in the Middle East. **2.** A small sailing vessel used in the eastern Mediterranean. [French, from Italian *caicco,* from Ottoman Turkish *qayïq,* from Old Turkic *qayghuq.*]

caird (kârd) *n. Scots.* An itinerant tinker. [Scottish Gaelic *ceard,* tinker, smith, from Old Irish *cerd,* artisan, skill.]

cairn (kârn) *n.* A mound of stones erected as a memorial or marker. [Middle English *carne,* from Scottish Gaelic *carn,* from Old Irish.] **—cairned** *adj.*

cairn·gorm (kârn′gôrm′) *n.* See **smoky quartz.** [After the CAIRNGORM (MOUNTAINS).]

Cairn·gorm Mountains (kârn′gôrm′). A range of the Grampian Mountains in central Scotland rising to 1,310.3 m (4,296 ft) at Ben Macdhui. It is a popular winter sports area.

Cairn terrier (kârn) *n.* A small dog of a breed developed in Scotland, having a broad head and a rough, shaggy coat. [So called because it hunts among cairns.]

Cai·ro (kī′rō). The capital and largest city of Egypt, in the northeastern part of the country on the Nile River. Old Cairo was built c. 642 as a military camp; the new city was founded c. 968 by the Fatimid dynasty and reached its greatest prosperity under the Mameluke sultans (13th–16th century). Population, 6,205,000.

cais·son (kā′sŏn′, -sən) *n.* **1.** A watertight structure within which construction work is carried on under water. **2.** See **camel** (sense 2). **3.** A large box open at the top and one side, designed to fit against the side of a ship and used to repair damaged hulls under water. **4.** A floating structure used to close off the entrance to a dock or canal lock. **5.a.** A horse-drawn vehicle, usually two-wheeled, used to carry artillery ammunition and coffins at military funerals. **b.** A large box used to hold ammunition. [French, from Old French, large box, alteration (influenced by *caisse,* chest, from Old Provençal *caissa,* from Vulgar Latin **capsea,* from Latin *capsa,* box) of *casson,* from Italian *cassone,* augmentative of *cassa,* box, from Latin *capsa.*]

caisson disease *n.* See **decompression sickness.**

Caith·ness (kāth′nĕs, kāth-nĕs′). A historical region and former county of northeast Scotland. Settled by the Picts, it was overrun by the Vikings in the ninth century and did not revert to Scottish rule until 1202.

cai·tiff (kā′tĭf) *n.* A despicable coward; a wretch. **—caitiff** *adj.* Despicable and cowardly. [Middle English *caitif,* from Norman French, from Latin *captīvus,* prisoner. See CAPTIVE.]

Ca·ius (kā′əs, kī′-). See **Gaius.**

Ca·jan (kā′jən) *n. & adj.* Variant of **Cajun.**

ca·jan pea (kā′jən) *n.* **1.** A tropical African shrub *(Cajanus cajan)* of the pea family, having trifoliolate leaves, yellow or orange flowers, hairy pods, and small edible seeds. **2.** A seed of this plant. Also called *catjang, dahl, pigeon pea.* [Malay *kachang,* bean, pea.]

ca·jole (kə-jōl′) *tr.v.* **-joled, -jol·ing, -joles.** To urge with gentle and repeated appeals, teasing, or flattery; wheedle. [French *cajoler,* possibly blend of Old French *cageoler,* to chatter like a jay (from *geai, jai,* jay; see JAY[2]) and Old French *gaioler,* to lure into a cage (from *gaiole, jaiole,* cage; see JAIL).] **—ca·jol′er** *n.* **—ca·jol′er·y** (-jō′lə-rē) *n.* **—ca·jol′ing·ly** *adv.*

Ca·jun also **Ca·jan** (kā′jən) *—n.* **1.** A member of a group of people in southern Louisiana descended from French colonists exiled from Acadia in the 18th century. **2.** Often **Cajan.** A member of a group living in southern Alabama and southeast Mississippi, of mixed white, Black, and Native American ancestry. *—adj.* Of or relating to the Cajuns. [Alteration of ACADIAN.]

cake (kāk) *n.* **1.** A sweet baked food made of flour, liquid, eggs, and other ingredients, and usually served in rectangular, square, or rounded layer form. **2.** A flat, rounded mass of dough or batter, such as a pancake that is baked or fried. **3.** A flat, rounded mass of hashed or chopped food that is baked or fried; a patty. **4.** A shaped or molded piece, as of soap or ice. **5.** A layer or deposit of compacted matter: *a cake of grime in the oven.* **—cake** *v.* **caked, cak·ing, cakes.** *—tr.* To cover or fill with a thick layer, as of compacted matter: *a miner whose face was caked with soot.* *—intr.* To become formed into a compact or crusty mass: *As temperatures dropped, the wet snow caked.* [Middle English, from Old Norse *kaka.*]

cake·walk (kāk′wôk′) *n.* **1.** Something easily accomplished: *The diving championship was a cakewalk for her.* **2.** A 19th-century public entertainment among American Black people in which walkers performing the most accomplished or amusing steps won cakes as prizes. **3.a.** A strutting dance, often performed in minstrel shows. **b.** The music for this dance. **—cakewalk** *intr.v.* **-walked, -walk·ing, -walks.** To perform a strutting dance. **—cake′walk′er** *n.*

cairn

cal or **Cal** *abbr.* **1. Cal.** Calorie (large calorie). **2.** Calorie (mean calorie). **3.** Calorie (small calorie).

cal. *abbr.* **1.** Calendar. **2.** Caliber.

Cal. *abbr.* California.

Cal·a·bar bean (kăl′ə-bär) *n.* The poisonous seed of a tropical western African woody vine *(Physostigma venenosum)* in the pea family, which has been used as an ordeal poison and is the source of the drug physostigmine. Also called *ordeal bean.* [After *Calabar,* a town of southeast Nigeria.]

cal·a·bash (kăl′ə-băsh′) *n.* **1.** An annual vine *(Lagenaria siceraria)* having white flowers and smooth, large, hard-shelled gourds. Also called *bottle gourd, white-flowered gourd.* **2.** A tropical American tree *(Crescentia cujete)* bearing hard-shelled, gourdlike fruits on the trunk and main branches. Also called *calabash tree.* **3.** Any of certain similar or related plants. **4.** The fruit of any of these plants. **5.** A utensil or container made from the dried, hollowed-out shell of any of these fruits. **6.** A smoking pipe with a curved stem and a large bowl made from the shell of a gourd. [French *calebasse,* gourd, from Spanish *calabaza,* from Catalan *carabaça,* perhaps from Arabic *qar'ah yābisah,* dry gourd : *qar'ah,* gourd + *yābisah,* dry.]

Cal·a·bash (kăl′ə-băsh′) *n.* A style of cooking in the southeast United States in which various seafoods, such as deviled crab, shrimp, oysters, and flounder, are deep-fried and then heaped onto dinner plates for serving. [Perhaps from *calabash,* a turtle cooked in its shell, from CALABASH.]

calabash tree *n.* See **calabash** (sense 2).

♦**cal·a·boose** (kăl′ə-bo͞os′) *n. Chiefly Southern & Western U.S.* A jail. [Louisiana French *calabouse,* from Spanish *calabozo,* dungeon.]

Cal·a·bre·se (kăl′ə-brā′zē) *n.* A type of broccoli, introduced from Italy and grown extensively in North America, bearing clusters of blue-green to dark green flower buds. [Italian, Calabrian, from *Calabria,* Calabria.]

Ca·la·bri·a (kə-lā′brē-ə, kä-lä′brē-ä). A region of southern Italy forming the toe of the Italian "boot." Founded as a Greek colony, it was taken by the Romans in 268 B.C. and by the Byzantine Empire in the ninth century A.D.

ca·la·di·um (kə-lā′dē-əm) *n.* Any of various tropical American plants of the genus *Caladium* widely cultivated for their ornamental foliage, variously patterned in white, green, pink, or red. [New Latin *Caladium,* genus name, from Malay *kĕladi,* an aroid.]

Ca·lah (kā′lə) also **Ka·lakh** (kä′läKH). An ancient city of Assyria on the Tigris River south of present-day Mosul, Iraq. It was probably built in the 13th century B.C.

Ca·lais (kă-lā′, kăl′ā). A city of northern France on the Strait

ă pat	oi boy
ā pay	ou out
âr care	o͝o took
ä father	o͞o boot
ĕ pet	ŭ cut
ē be	ûr urge
ĭ pit	th thin
ī pie	*th* this
îr pier	hw which
ŏ pot	zh vision
ō toe	ə about, item
ô paw	♦ regionalism

Stress marks: ′ (primary); ′ (secondary), as in **dictionary** (dĭk′shə-nĕr′ē)

of Dover opposite Dover, England. The city fell to the English in 1347 after a siege of 11 months and was retaken by the French in 1558. Population, 76,527.

cal·a·man·co (kăl′ə-măng′kō) *n., pl.* **-coes.** A glossy woolen fabric with a checked pattern on one side. [Perhaps from Spanish *calamaco,* from Late Latin *calamaucus,* felt cap.]

cal·a·man·der (kăl′ə-măn′dər) *n.* The hard, black-and-brown-striped wood of certain tropical Asian trees of the genus *Diospyros,* especially *D. quaesita* of Sri Lanka, used for making furniture. [Probably from Dutch *kalamanderhout,* calamander wood, perhaps from alteration of COROMANDEL COAST.]

cal·a·mar·i (kä′lə-mä′rē, kăl′ə-) *n.* Squid prepared as food. [Italian, pl. of *calamaro,* from Late Latin *calamārium,* pen-case, from Latin *calamārius,* relating to a reed pen, from *calamus,* reed pen (perhaps from the "ink" the squid secretes). See CALAMUS.]

cal·a·mi (kăl′ə-mī′) *n.* Plural of **calamus.**

cal·a·mine (kăl′ə-mīn′, -mĭn) *n.* **1.** See **hemimorphite. 2.** A pink, odorless, tasteless powder of zinc oxide with a small amount of ferric oxide, dissolved in mineral oils and used in skin lotions. **3.** An alloy composed of lead, tin, and zinc. [French, from Medieval Latin *calamīna,* alteration of Latin *cadmīa.* See CADMIUM.]

cal·a·mint (kăl′ə-mĭnt′) *n.* Any of several plants of the genera *Calamintha* or *Satureja* in the mint family, cultivated for their aromatic foliage and clusters of pink, lilac, or white flowers. [Middle English *calaminte,* from Old French *calamente,* from Medieval Latin *calamentum,* from Latin *calaminthē,* from Greek *kalaminthē.*]

calash

cal·a·mite (kăl′ə-mīt′) *n.* Any of various extinct, chiefly carboniferous trees of the genus *Calamites,* related to the modern-day herbaceous horsetails *(Equisetum).* [New Latin *Calamītēs,* genus name, from Late Greek *kalamitēs,* reedlike, from Greek *kalamos,* reed.]

ca·lam·i·tous (kə-lăm′ĭ-təs) *adj.* Causing or involving calamity; disastrous. **—ca·lam′i·tous·ly** *adv.* **—ca·lam′i·tous·ness** *n.*

ca·lam·i·ty (kə-lăm′ĭ-tē) *n., pl.* **-ties. 1.** An event that brings terrible loss, lasting distress, or severe affliction; a disaster: *A hurricane would be a calamity for this low-lying coastal region.* See Synonyms at **disaster. 2.** Dire distress resulting from loss or tragedy. [Middle English *calamite,* from Old French, from Latin *calamitās.*]

Ca·lam·i·ty Jane (kə-lăm′ĭ-tē jān′). See Martha Jane **Burk.**

cal·a·mon·din (kăl′ə-mŏn′dĭn) *n.* **1.** A small evergreen citrus tree (×*Citrofortunella mitis*), widely cultivated as a houseplant for its glossy foliage and ornamental fruits. **2.** The sour fruit of this plant, resembling a small tangerine and sometimes used as a flavoring or for beverages, sauces, or marmalades. [Tagalog *kalamunding.*]

cal·a·mus (kăl′ə-məs) *n., pl.* **-mi** (-mī′). **1.a.** See **sweet flag. b.** The aromatic, underground stem of the sweet flag, yielding an oil used in perfumery. **2.** Any of various chiefly tropical Asian climbing palms of the genus *Calamus,* having strong, flexible stems used as a source of rattan. **3.** See **quill** (sense 1). [Latin, reed, from Greek *kalamos.*]

ca·lan·do (kə-län′dō) *adv. & adj. Music.* With a gradual decrease in tempo and volume. Used chiefly as a direction. [Italian, present participle of *calare,* to slacken, from Latin *calāre,* from Greek *khalan.*]

ca·lash (kə-lăsh′) also **ca·lèche** (-lĕsh′) *n.* **1.a.** A light carriage with two or four low wheels and a collapsible top. **b.** A top for this or a similar carriage. **2.** A woman's folding bonnet of the late 18th century. [French *calèche,* from German *Kalesche,* from Czech *kolesa,* from pl. of *kolo, koles-,* wheel. See **kʷel-**[1] in Appendix.]

cal·a·the·a (kăl′ə-thē′ə) *n.* Any of various tropical American evergreen plants of the genus *Calathea* widely cultivated indoors for their attractively marked leaves. [New Latin *calathea,* genus name, from Latin *calathus,* basket. See CALATHUS.]

cal·a·thus (kăl′ə-thəs) *n., pl.* **-thi** (-thī′). A vase-shaped basket represented in Greek painting and sculpture. [Latin, from Greek *kalathos.*]

calc. *abbr.* **1.** Calculation. **2.** *Mathematics.* Calculus.

calc– *pref.* Variant of **calci–.**

cal·ca·ne·o·cu·boid ligament (kăl-kā′nē-ō-kyo͞o′boid′) *n.* The ligament that connects the calcaneus and the cuboid bones.

cal·ca·ne·us (kăl-kā′nē-əs) also **cal·ca·ne·um** (-nē-əm) *n., pl.* **-ne·i** (-nē-ī′) also **-ne·a** (-nē-ə). The quadrangular bone at the back of the tarsus. Also called *heel bone.* [Late Latin *calcāneus,* heel, from Latin *calcāneum,* from *calx, calc-.*] **—cal·ca′ne·al** *adj.*

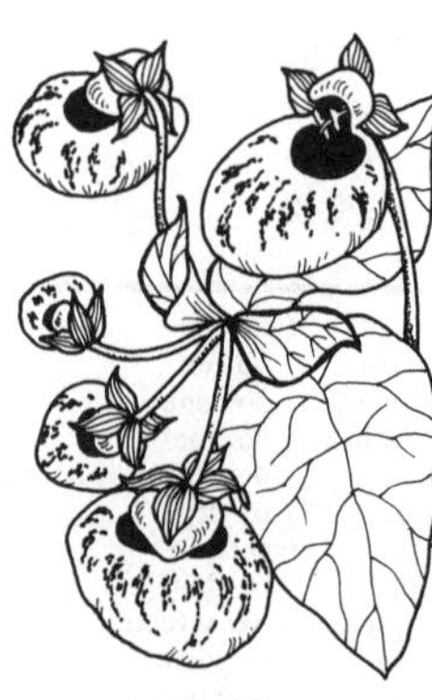
calceolaria

cal·car[1] (kăl′kär′) *n., pl.* **cal·car·i·a** (kăl-kâr′ē-ə). A spur or spurlike projection, such as one found on the base of a petal or on the wing or leg of a bird. [Latin, spur, from *calx, calc-,* heel.]

cal·car[2] (kăl′kär′) *n.* A furnace formerly used in glassmaking for calcination of materials into frit. [Italian *calcara,* from Late Latin *calcāria (fornāx),* lime(-kiln), from Latin, feminine of *calcārius,* of lime. See CALCAREOUS.]

cal·car·e·ous (kăl-kâr′ē-əs) *adj.* Composed of, containing, or characteristic of calcium carbonate, calcium, or limestone; chalky. [From Latin *calcārius,* from *calx, calc-,* lime. See CALX.] **—cal·car′e·ous·ly** *adv.*

cal·car·i·a (kăl-kâr′ē-ə) *n.* Plural of **calcar**[1].

cal·car·ine sulcus (kăl′kə-rīn′) *n.* A sulcus on the occipital lobe of the brain. Also called *calcarine fissure.* [CALCAR[1] + –INE[1].]

cal·ced·o·ny (kăl-sĕd′n-ē) *n.* Variant of **chalcedony.**

cal·ce·o·lar·i·a (kăl′sē-ə-lâr′ē-ə) *n.* Any of various plants of the genus *Calceolaria* native from Mexico to South America and widely cultivated for their showy, speckled, slipper-shaped flowers. Also called *slipper flower, slipperwort.* [New Latin *Calceolaria,* genus name, from Latin *calceolus,* small shoe. See CALCEOLATE.]

cal·ce·o·late (kăl′sē-ə-lāt′) *adj.* Shaped like a slipper, as the pouchlike petal of the flower of the lady's slipper. [From Latin *calceolus,* diminutive of *calceus,* shoe, from *calx, calc-,* heel.]

cal·ces (kăl′sēz′) *n.* A plural of **calx.**

calci– or **calc–** *pref.* Calcium; calcium salt; lime: *calciferous.* [From Latin *calx, calc-,* lime. See CALX.]

cal·cic (kăl′sĭk) *adj.* Composed of, containing, derived from, or relating to calcium or lime.

cal·ci·cole (kăl′sĭ-kōl′) *n.* A plant that thrives in soil rich in lime. [French : *calci-,* calcium (from Latin *calx, calc-,* lime; see CALX) + *-cole,* -dwelling (from Latin *-cola;* see –COLOUS).] **—cal·cic′o·lous** (-sĭk′ə-ləs) *adj.*

cal·cif·er·ol (kăl-sĭf′ə-rôl′, -rōl′, -rŏl′) *n.* See **vitamin D_2.** [CALCIFER(OUS) + –OL[1].]

cal·cif·er·ous (kăl-sĭf′ər-əs) *adj.* Of, forming, or containing calcium or calcium carbonate.

cal·cif·ic (kăl-sĭf′ĭk) *adj.* Producing salts of lime, as in the formation of eggshells in birds and reptiles.

cal·ci·fi·ca·tion (kăl′sə-fĭ-kā′shən) *n.* **1.a.** Impregnation with calcium or calcium salts, as with calcium carbonate. **b.** Hardening, as of tissue, by such impregnation. **2.** A calcified substance or part. **3.** An inflexible, unchanging state: *calcification of negotiations.*

cal·ci·fuge (kăl′sə-fyo͞oj′) *n.* A plant that does not grow well in lime-rich soil. **—cal·cif′u·gal** (-sĭf′yə-gəl), **cal·cif′u·gous** (-yə-gəs) *adj.*

cal·ci·fy (kăl′sə-fī′) *tr. & intr.v.* **-fied, -fy·ing, -fies. 1.** To make or become stony or chalky by deposition of calcium salts. **2.** To make or become inflexible and unchanging.

cal·ci·mine also **kal·so·mine** (kăl′sə-mīn′) —*n.* A white or tinted liquid containing zinc oxide, water, glue, and coloring matter, used as a wash for walls and ceilings. —*tr.v.* **-mined, -min·ing, -mines.** To cover or wash with calcimine. [Originally a trademark.]

cal·cine (kăl-sīn′, kăl′sīn′) *v.* **-cined, -cin·ing, -cines.** —*tr.* To heat (a substance) to a high temperature but below the melting or fusing point, causing loss of moisture, reduction, or oxidation and the decomposition of carbonates and other compounds. —*intr.* To undergo calcination. [Middle English *calcinen,* from Old French *calciner,* from Medieval Latin *calcīnāre,* from Late Latin *calcīna,* quicklime, from Latin *calx, calc-,* lime. See CALX.] **—cal′ci·na′tion** (-sə-nā′shən) *n.*

cal·ci·no·sis (kăl′sə-nō′sĭs) *n.* An abnormal condition in which calcium salts are deposited in a part or tissue of the body. [CALC(I)– (influenced by CALCINE) + –OSIS.]

cal·cite (kăl′sīt′) *n.* A common crystalline form of natural calcium carbonate, $CaCO_3$, that is the basic constituent of limestone, marble, and chalk. Also called *calcspar.* **—cal·cit′ic** (-sĭt′ĭk) *adj.*

cal·ci·to·nin (kăl′sĭ-tō′nĭn) *n.* A peptide hormone, produced by the thyroid gland in human beings, that lowers plasma calcium and phosphate levels without augmenting calcium accretion. Also called *thyrocalcitonin.* [CALCI– + TON(E) + –IN.]

cal·ci·um (kăl′sē-əm) *n. Symbol* **Ca** A silvery, moderately hard metallic element that constitutes approximately 3 percent of the earth's crust and is a basic component of most animals and plants. It occurs naturally in limestone, gypsum, and fluorite, and its compounds are used to make plaster, quicklime, Portland cement, and metallurgic and electronic materials. Atomic number 20; atomic weight 40.08; melting point 842 to 848°C; boiling point 1,487°C; specific gravity 1.55; valence 2. See table at **element.** [Latin *calx, calc-,* lime; see CALX + –IUM.]

calcium carbide *n.* A grayish-black crystalline compound, CaC_2, obtained by heating pulverized limestone or quicklime with carbon and used to generate acetylene gas, as a dehydrating agent, and in the manufacture of graphite and hydrogen.

calcium carbonate *n.* A colorless or white crystalline compound, $CaCO_3$, occurring naturally as chalk, limestone, marble, and other forms and used in a wide variety of manufactured products including commercial chalk, medicines, and dentifrices.

calcium chloride *n.* A white deliquescent compound, $CaCl_2$, used chiefly as a drying agent, refrigerant, and preservative and for controlling dust and ice on roads.

calcium cyanamide *n.* A gray-black compound, $CaCN_2$, used as a fertilizer and weed killer.

calcium cyanide *n.* A gray or black compound, $Ca(CN)_2$, used to kill insects and rodents.

calcium cyclamate *n.* An artificially prepared salt of cyclamic acid, $C_{12}H_{24}O_6N_2S_2Ca_2H_2O$, formerly used as a nonnutritive low-calorie sweetener but now banned because of possible carcinogenic effects of its metabolic products.

calcium fluoride *n.* A colorless powder, CaF_2, used in emery wheels, carbon electrodes, and cements.

calcium hydroxide *n.* A soft white powder, $Ca(OH)_2$, used in making mortar, cements, calcium salts, paints, hard rubber products, and petrochemicals. Also called *slaked lime.*

calcium hypochlorite *n.* A white crystalline solid, $Ca(OCl)_2 \cdot 4H_2O$, used as a bactericide, fungicide, and bleaching agent.

calcium light *n.* See **limelight** (sense 2).

calcium nitrate *n.* Colorless crystals, $Ca(NO_3)_2 \cdot 4H_2O$, used in explosives.

calcium oxide *n.* A white, caustic, lumpy powder, CaO, used as a refractory, as a flux, in manufacturing steel and paper, in glassmaking, in waste treatment, in insecticides, and as an industrial alkali. Also called *lime.*

calcium phosphate *n.* **1.** A colorless deliquescent powder, $Ca(H_2PO_4)_2$, used in baking powders, as a plant food and a plastic stabilizer, and in glass. **2.** A white crystalline powder, $CaHPO_4$, used as an animal food, as a plastic stabilizer, and in glass and toothpaste. **3.** A white amorphous powder, $Ca_3(PO_4)_2$, used in ceramics, rubber, fertilizers, and plastic stabilizers and as a food supplement.

calc·spar or **calc-spar** (kălk′spär′) *n.* See **calcite.** [Partial translation of Swedish *kalkspat* : *kalk,* lime (from Old Swedish *kalker,* from Middle Low German *kalk,* from Latin *calx, calc-,* lime; see CALX) + *spat,* spar (mineral).]

calc-tu·fa (kălk′to͞o′fə, -tyo͞o′-) also **calc-tuff** (-tŭf′) *n.* Calcareous tufa, a porous or spongy deposit of calcium carbonate found in calcareous mineral springs. [CALC(AREOUS) + TUFA.]

cal·cu·la·ble (kăl′kyə-lə-bəl) *adj.* **1.** That can be calculated or estimated: *calculable odds.* **2.** Readily relied on; dependable: *a calculable assistant.* **—cal′cu·la·bil′i·ty** *n.*

♦ **cal·cu·late** (kăl′kyə-lāt′) *v.* **-lat·ed, -lat·ing, -lates.** *—tr.* **1.** To ascertain by computation; reckon: *calculating the area of a circle; calculated their probable time of arrival.* **2.** To make an estimate of; evaluate: *calculating the team's chances of winning.* **3.** To make for a deliberate purpose; design: *a sturdy car that is calculated to last for years; a choice that was calculated to please.* **4.** Also **cal'late** (kăl′ăt′, -lăt′). *Chiefly New England & Upper Southern U.S.* **a.** To suppose: *"I cal'late she's a right smart cook"* (Dialect Notes). **b.** To plan, intend, or count on. *—intr.* **1.** To perform a mathematical process; figure: *We must measure and calculate to determine how much paint will be needed.* **2.** To predict consequences. **3.** *Regional.* **a.** To suppose; guess. **b.** To count, depend, or rely on someone or something: *We're calculating on your help.* [Late Latin *calculāre, calculāt-,* from Latin *calculus,* small stone used in reckoning, diminutive of *calx, calc-,* small stone for gaming. See CALX.]

SYNONYMS: *calculate, compute, reckon, cipher, figure.* These verbs refer to the determination of a result, such as expense, through the use of mathematical methods. *Calculate,* the most comprehensive, often implies a relatively high level of abstraction or procedural complexity: *astronomers calculating the positions of the planets. Compute* applies in general to essentially straightforward though possibly lengthy arithmetic operations: *computing fees according to time spent. Reckon, cipher,* and *figure* suggest the use of simple arithmetic: *reckoned the number of hours before her departure; had to be taught to read and to cipher; trying to figure my share of the bill.*

cal·cu·lat·ed (kăl′kyə-lā′tĭd) *adj.* **1.** Determined by mathematical calculation. **2.** Undertaken after careful estimation of the likely outcome: *took a calculated risk.* **3.** Made or planned to accomplish a certain purpose; deliberate: *insincere, calculated modesty.* **4.** Likely; apt. **—cal′cu·lat′ed·ly** *adv.*

cal·cu·lat·ing (kăl′kyə-lā′tĭng) *adj.* **1.** Capable of performing calculations: *a calculating machine.* **2. a.** Shrewd; crafty. **b.** Coldly scheming or conniving. **—cal′cu·lat′ing·ly** *adv.*

cal·cu·la·tion (kăl′kyə-lā′shən) *n.* **1.** *Abbr.* **calc. a.** The act, process, or result of calculating. **b.** An estimate based on probabilities. **2.** Careful, often cunning estimation and planning of likely outcomes, especially to advance one's own interests. **—cal′cu·la′tive** *adj.*

cal·cu·la·tor (kăl′kyə-lā′tər) *n.* **1.** One that calculates, as: **a.** An electronic or a mechanical device for the performance of mathematical computations. **b.** A person who operates such a machine or otherwise makes calculations. **2.** A set of mathematical tables used to aid in calculating.

cal·cu·li (kăl′kyə-lī′) *n.* A plural of **calculus.**

cal·cu·lous (kăl′kyə-ləs) *adj.* Relating to, caused by, or having a calculus or calculi.

cal·cu·lus (kăl′kyə-ləs) *n., pl.* **-li** (-lī′) or **-lus·es. 1.** *Pathology.* An abnormal concretion in the body, usually formed of mineral salts and found in the gallbladder, kidney, or urinary bladder, for example. **2.** *Dentistry.* Tartar. **3.** *Abbr.* **calc.** *Mathematics.* **a.** The branch of mathematics that deals with limits and the differentiation and integration of functions of one or more variables. **b.** A method of analysis or calculation using a special symbolic notation. **c.** The combined mathematics of differential calculus and integral calculus. **4.** A system or method of calculation: "[a] *dazzling grasp of the nation's byzantine budget calculus"* (David M. Alpern). [Latin, small stone used in reckoning. See CALCULATE.]

calculus of variations *n.* Mathematical analysis of the maxima and minima of definite integrals, the integrands of which are functions of independent variables, dependent variables, and the derivatives of one or more dependent variables.

Cal·cut·ta (kăl-kŭt′ə). A city of eastern India on the Hooghly River in the Ganges delta. Founded c. 1690 as a British East India Company trading post, it is India's largest city and a major port and industrial center. Population, 3,305,006.

Cal·der (kôl′dər, kŏl′-), **Alexander.** 1898–1976. American sculptor who created the mobile in Paris in the early 1930's and also produced immobile abstract sculptures known as stabiles.

cal·de·ra (kăl-dâr′ə, -dîr′ə, kôl-) *n.* A large crater formed by volcanic explosion or by collapse of a volcanic cone. [Spanish, caldron, caldera, from Late Latin *caldāria.* See CALDRON.]

Cal·de·rón de la Bar·ca (käl′də-rôn′ dā lə bär′kə, käl′-*th*ĕ-rôn′ *th*ĕ lä bär′kä), **Pedro.** 1600–1681. Spanish playwright. One of the greatest dramatists of Spain's Golden Age, he wrote more than 120 plays, including *Life is a Dream* (1635).

cal·dron also **caul·dron** (kôl′drən) *n.* **1.** A large vessel, such as a kettle or vat, used for boiling. **2.** A state or situation of great distress or unrest felt to resemble a boiling kettle or vat: *a caldron of conflicting corporate politics.* [Middle English, alteration of *cauderon,* from Norman French, diminutive of *caudiere,* cooking pot, from Late Latin *caldāria,* from feminine of Latin *caldārius,* suitable for warming, from *calidus,* warm. See **kelə-¹** in Appendix.]

Cald·well (kôld′wĕl′, -wəl, kŏld′-). A city of southwest Idaho on the Boise River west of Boise. It was built on the site of an Oregon Trail camping ground. Population, 17,699.

Caldwell, Erskine Preston. 1903–1987. American writer best known for his graphic novels about poverty and degeneration, such as *Tobacco Road* (1932).

Caldwell, Sarah. Born 1928. American conductor and opera producer noted for her ingenious stagings of classical and modern works.

ca·lèche (kə-lĕsh′) *n.* Variant of **calash.**

Cal·e·don (kăl′ĭ-dən). A town of southeast Ontario, Canada, northwest of Toronto. Pop. 26,645.

Cal·e·do·ni·a (kăl′ĭ-dō′nē-ə, -dōn′yə). Roman Britain north of the Antonine Wall, which stretched from the Firth of Forth to the Firth of Clyde. Today the term is used as a poetic appellation for all of Scotland. **—Cal′e·do′ni·an** *adj. & n.*

Caledonian Canal. A waterway, about 97 km (60 mi) long, cutting diagonally across northern Scotland from Loch Linnhe on the southwest to Moray Firth on the northeast. Opened in 1822, it is used today mainly by pleasure craft.

cal·en·dar (kăl′ən-dər) *n. Abbr.* **cal. 1.** Any of various systems of reckoning time in which the beginning, length, and divisions of a year are defined. **2.** A table showing the months, weeks, and days in at least one specific year. **3.** A schedule of events. **4.** An ordered list of matters to be considered: *a calendar of court cases; the bills on a legislative calendar.* **5.** *Chiefly British.* A catalogue of a university. **—calendar** *tr.v.* **-dared, -dar·ing, -dars.** To enter in a calendar; schedule. [Middle English *calender,* from Old French *calendier,* from Late Latin *kalendārium,* from Latin, account book, from *kalendae,* calends (from the fact that monthly interest was due on the calends). See **kelə-²** in Appendix.]

calendar month *n.* See **month** (sense 2).

calendar year *n. Abbr.* **CY** See **year** (sense 1a).

cal·en·der (kăl′ən-dər) *n.* A machine in which paper or cloth is made smooth and glossy by being pressed through rollers. **—calender** *tr.v.* **-dered, -der·ing, -ders.** To press (paper or cloth) in the rollers of such a machine. [French *calandre,* from Vulgar Latin **colendra,* alteration (possibly influenced by Latin *columna,* column) of Latin *cylindrus,* roller. See CYLINDER.] **—cal′en·der·er** *n.*

ca·len·dri·cal (kə-lĕn′drĭ-kəl) also **ca·len·dric** (-drĭk) *adj.* Of, relating to, or used in a calendar.

cal·ends also **kal·ends** (kăl′əndz, kā′ləndz) *n., pl.* **calends** also **kalends.** The day of the new moon and the first day of the month in the ancient Roman calendar. [Middle English *kalendes,* from Latin *kalendae.* See **kelə-²** in Appendix.] **—ca·len′dal** (kə-lĕn′dəl) *adj.*

ca·len·du·la (kə-lĕn′jə-lə) *n.* A Mediterranean annual plant *(Calendula officinalis)* in the composite family, widely cultivated for its showy, yellow or orange, rayed flower heads that were formerly used in medicine, coloring, and flavoring of food. Also called *pot marigold.* [Medieval Latin, marigold, from Latin *kalendae,* calends. See CALENDS.]

cal·en·ture (kăl′ən-cho͝or′) *n.* A tropical fever once believed to be caused by the heat. [Spanish *calentura,* from *calentar,* to heat, from Latin *calēns, calent-,* present participle of *calēre,* to be warm. See **kelə-¹** in Appendix.]

calf¹ (kăf, käf) *n., pl.* **calves** (kăvz, kävz). **1. a.** A young cow or bull. **b.** The young of certain other mammals, such as the elephant or whale. **2.** Calfskin leather. **3.** A large floating chunk of ice split off from a glacier, an iceberg, or a floe. **4.** An awkward, callow youth. [Middle English, from Old English *cealf.*]

calf² (kăf, käf) *n., pl.* **calves** (kăvz, kävz). The fleshy, muscular back part of the human leg between the knee and ankle. [Middle English, from Old Norse *kālfi.*]

caldron
Late 12th-century Persian

ă pat	oi boy
ā pay	ou out
âr care	o͝o took
ä father	o͞o boot
ĕ pet	ŭ cut
ē be	ûr urge
ĭ pit	th thin
ī pie	*th* this
îr pier	hw which
ŏ pot	zh vision
ō toe	ə about, item
ô paw	♦ regionalism

Stress marks: ′ (primary); ′ (secondary), as in **dictionary** (dĭk′shə-nĕr′ē)

THREE PRINCIPAL CALENDARS

In use throughout most of the modern world, the **Gregorian calendar** was first introduced in 1582 by Pope Gregory XIII as a corrected form of the **Julian calendar** of the first century B.C. The **Jewish calendar** is used to mark the dates of annual religious events and is the official calendar of the Jewish religious community. The **Moslem calendar** is used throughout the Islamic world to mark the religious festivals and is the official calendar in many Moslem countries. The following lists begin with the first month of the year.

GREGORIAN

The solar year of the **Gregorian calendar** consists of 365 days, except in a leap year, which has 366 days and occurs every fourth, even-numbered year. Centenary years are leap years only if they are evenly divisible by 400.

MONTHS	NUMBER OF DAYS
January	31
February	28
in leap year	29
March	31
April	30
May	31
June	30
July	31
August	31
September	30
October	31
November	30
December	31

JEWISH

The **Jewish calendar** is based on both the solar and lunar cycles. The average lunar year of 354 days is adjusted to the solar year by the periodic introduction of leap years, which contain an intercalary month and ensure that the major religious festivals fall in their proper season.

MONTHS	NUMBER OF DAYS
Tishri (September-October)*	30
Heshvan (October-November)	29
in some years	30
Kislev (November-December)	29
in some years	30
Tevet (December-January)	29
Shevat (January-February)	30
Adar (February-March)	29
in some years	30
Adar Sheni intercalary month in leap year only	29
Nisan (March-April)	30
Iyar (April-May)	29
Sivan (May-June)	30
Tammuz (June-July)	29
Av (July-August)	30
Elul (August-September)	29

*The months correspond approximately to those of the Gregorian calendar shown in parentheses.

MOSLEM

The **Moslem calendar** is based on the lunar year and consists of 354 or 355 days. The number of days in each month is adjusted throughout the year in accordance with each lunar cycle. The beginning of the Moslem year retrogresses through the solar year, completing a full cycle every 32½ years.

MONTHS	NUMBER OF DAYS
Muharram	29 or 30
Safar	29 or 30
Rabi I	29 or 30
Rabi II	29 or 30
Jumada I	29 or 30
Jumada II	29 or 30
Rajab	29 or 30
Sha'ban	29 or 30
Ramadan	29 or 30
Shawwal	29 or 30
Dhu'l-Qa'dah	29 or 30
Dhu'l-Hijjah	29 or 30

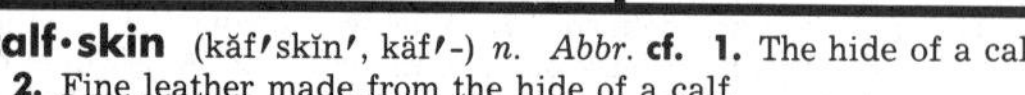

calf•skin (kăf′skĭn′, käf′-) *n.* *Abbr.* **cf. 1.** The hide of a calf. **2.** Fine leather made from the hide of a calf.

Cal•ga•ry (kăl′gə-rē). A city of southern Alberta, Canada, south of Edmonton. Site of the annual Calgary Stampede, a famous rodeo dating from 1912, the city is the center of Canada's petroleum industry. The 1988 Winter Olympics were held here. Population, 592,743. **—Cal•gar′i•an** (-gâr′ē-ən, -găr′-) *n.*

Cal•houn (kăl-ho͞on′), **John Caldwell.** 1782–1850. Vice President of the United States (1825–1832) under John Quincy Adams and Andrew Jackson. In his political philosophy he maintained that the states had the right to nullify federal legislation that they deemed unconstitutional.

Ca•li (kä′lē). A city of western Colombia on the **Cali River** southwest of Bogotá. It was founded in 1536. Population, 1,347,810.

Cal•i•ban (kăl′ə-băn′) *n.* The grotesque, deformed slave in Shakespeare's *The Tempest.*

calico
Calico cat

cal•i•ber (kăl′ə-bər) *n.* **1.** *Abbr.* **cal. a.** The diameter of the inside of a round cylinder, such as a tube. **b.** The diameter of the bore of a firearm, usually shown in hundredths or thousandths of an inch and expressed in writing or print in terms of a decimal fraction: *.45 caliber.* **c.** The diameter of a large projectile, such as an artillery shell, measured in millimeters or in inches. **2.** Degree of worth; quality: *a school of high caliber; an executive of low caliber.* [French *calibre.*]

cal•i•brate (kăl′ə-brāt′) *tr.v.* **-brat•ed, -brat•ing, -brates. 1.** To check, adjust, or determine by comparison with a standard (the graduations of a quantitative measuring instrument): *calibrate a thermometer.* **2.** To determine the caliber of (a tube). **3.** To make corrections in; adjust: *calibrated the polling procedures to ensure objectivity.* **—cal′i•bra′tor** *n.*

cal•i•bra•tion (kăl′ə-brā′shən) *n.* **1.** The act or process of calibrating or the state of being calibrated. **2.** Often **calibrations.** A set of gradations that show positions or values: *the calibrations on a pressure gauge.*

cal•i•bre (kăl′ə-bər) *n.* *Chiefly British.* Variant of **caliber.**

ca•li•ces (kā′lĭ-sēz′, kăl′ĭ-) *n.* Plural of **calix.**

ca•li•che (kə-lē′chē) *n.* **1.a.** A crude sodium nitrate occurring naturally in Chile, Peru, and the southwest United States, used as fertilizer. **b.** See **sodium nitrate. 2.** See **hardpan** (sense 1). [American Spanish, from Spanish, pebble in a brick, flake of lime, from *cal,* lime, from Latin *calx, calc-,* lime. See CALX.]

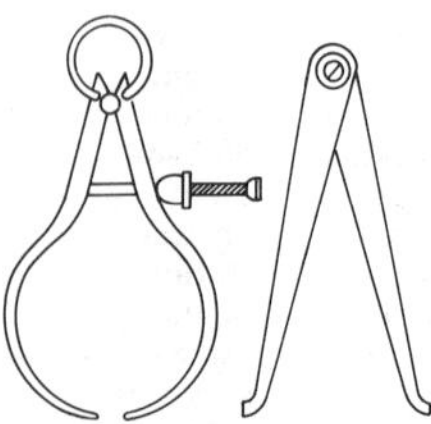

caliper
Left: Outside spring calipers
Right: Inside firm-joint calipers

cal•i•co (kăl′ĭ-kō′) *n., pl.* **-coes** or **-cos. 1.a.** A coarse, brightly printed cloth. **b.** *Chiefly British.* A plain white cotton cloth, heavier than muslin. **2.** An animal, such as a cat, having a coat that is mottled in tones of white with red and black. [After CALICUT.] **—cal′i•co** *adj.*

cal•i•co•back (kăl′ĭ-kō-băk′) *n.* See **harlequin bug.**

calico bass *n.* See **black crappie.** [From the colored spots on its body.]

calico bush *n.* See **mountain laurel.**

Cal•i•cut (kăl′ĭ-kŭt′) also **Ko•zhi•kode** (kō′zhĭ-kōd′). A city of southwest India on the Malabar Coast southwest of Bangalore. It was the site of Vasco da Gama's first landfall in India (1498) and was later occupied by Portuguese, British, French, and Danish trading colonies. Population, 394,447.

ca•lif (kā′lĭf, kăl′ĭf) *n.* Variant of **caliph.**

Cal•i•for•nia (kăl′ĭ-fôr′nyə, -fôr′nē-ə). *Abbr.* **CA, Cal., Calif.** A state of the western United States on the Pacific Ocean. It was admitted as the 31st state in 1850. The area was colonized by the Spanish and formally ceded to the United States by the Treaty of Guadalupe Hidalgo (1848). Sacramento is the capital and Los Angeles the largest city. Population, 23,667,837. **—Cal′i•for′nian** *adj. & n.*

California, Gulf of. An arm of the Pacific Ocean in northwest Mexico separating Baja California from the mainland.

California bay *n.* See **California laurel.**

California condor *n.* A very large vulture *(Gymnogyps californianus),* related to the condor of South America, found in the southern California mountains and nearly extinct.

California laurel *n.* An aromatic evergreen tree *(Umbellularia californica)* native to California and southern Oregon and having clusters of small yellowish-green flowers, olivelike yellowish-green to purple fruits, and light brown wood valued for use in fine woodwork. Also called *California bay, Oregon myrtle.*

California nutmeg *n.* An evergreen tree *(Torreya californica)* native to California, having yewlike linear leaves and solitary drupelike seeds surrounded by a green, purple-streaked, fleshy aril.

California pepper tree *n.* See **pepper tree.**

California poppy *n.* An herb *(Eschscholzia californica)* native to western North America and having finely divided leaves and showy, often orange or yellow flowers.

California quail *n.* A plump, chunky bird *(Lophortyx californicus)* of western North America, having gray and brown plumage and a curving black plume on the crown of the head.

cal•i•for•nite (kăl′ə-fôr′nīt) *n.* A massive green vesuvianite. [After CALIFORNIA (where it is found).]

cal•i•for•ni•um (kăl′ə-fôr′nē-əm) *n.* *Symbol* **Cf** A synthetic element produced in trace quantities by helium isotope bombardment of curium. All isotopes are radioactive, chiefly by emission of alpha particles. Atomic number 98; mass numbers 244 to 254; half-lives varying from 25 minutes to 800 years. See table at **element.** [After CALIFORNIA.]

ca•lig•i•nous (kə-lĭj′ə-nəs) *adj.* Dark, misty, and gloomy. [From Latin *cālīginōsus,* from *cālīgō, cālīgin-,* darkness.]

Ca•lig•u•la (kə-lĭg′yə-lə). Originally Gaius Caesar. A.D. 12–41. Emperor of Rome (37–41) who succeeded his adoptive father, Tiberius. After a severe illness, he displayed the ruthlessness, extravagance, and megalomania that led to his assassination.

Ca•li•na•go (kăl′ĭ-nä′gō, kä′lĭ-) *n., pl.* **Calinago** or **-gos. 1.** A member of a Caribbean Indian people inhabiting the Lesser Antilles. **2.** The language of the Calinago. [Spanish *calinago, calino, caribal,* alterations of *karinako,* from Carib, brave men : *ka,* sky, spirit + *na,* group + *-ko,* group place.]

cal•i•pash (kăl′ə-păsh′, kăl′ə-păsh′) *n.* An edible, gelatinous, greenish substance lying beneath the upper shell of a turtle. [Possibly alteration of Spanish *carapacho,* carapace.]

cal•i•pee (kăl′ə-pē′, kăl′ə-pē′) *n.* An edible, gelatinous, yellowish substance lying beneath the lower shell of a turtle. [Possibly alteration of CALIPASH.]

cal•i•per also **cal•li•per** (kăl′ə-pər) *n.* **1.** Often **calipers.** An instrument consisting essentially of two curved hinged legs, used to measure thickness and distances. **2.** A large instrument having a fixed and a movable arm on a graduated stock, used for measuring the diameters of logs and similar objects. **3.** A vernier caliper. [Alteration of CALIBER.] **—cal′i•per** *v.*

ca•liph also **ca•lif** or **kha•lif** (kā′lĭf, kăl′ĭf) *n.* A male leader of an Islamic polity. [Middle English *calife,* from Old French, from Arabic *ḫalīfah,* successor (to Mohammed), caliph, from *ḫalafa,* to succeed.]

ca•liph•ate (kā′lĭ-fāt′, -fĭt, kăl′ĭ-) *n.* The office or jurisdiction of a caliph.

cal•is•then•ics (kăl′ĭs-thĕn′ĭks) *n.* *Sports.* **1.** *(used with a pl. verb).* Gymnastic exercises designed to develop muscular tone and promote physical well-being: *Sit-ups, trunk twists, and other calisthenics are demonstrated on the videotape.* **2.** *(used with a sing. verb).* The practice or art of such exercises: *Calisthenics is recommended to relax the muscles before a run.* [From Greek *kalli-,* beautiful (from *kallos,* beauty) + *sthenos,* strength.] **—cal′is•then′ic** *adj.*

ca•lix (kā′lĭks, kăl′ĭks) *n., pl.* **ca•li•ces** (kā′lĭ-sēz′, kăl′ĭ-). *Ecclesiastical.* A chalice. [Latin *calix, calic-,* cup.]

Ca•lix•tus III (kə-lĭk′stəs). Originally Alfonso Borgia. 1378–

1458. Pope (1455–1458) whose nepotism empowered the Borgia family in Italy.

calk¹ (kôk) *n.* **1.** A pointed extension on the toe or heels of a horseshoe, designed to prevent slipping. **2.** A spiked plate fixed on the bottom of a shoe to prevent slipping and preserve the sole. [Probably back-formation from obsolete *calkin,* from Middle English *kakun,* possibly from Middle Dutch *kalkoen,* hoof, or from Old French *calcain,* heel (Middle Dutch, from Old French), from Latin *calcāneum,* heel-bone. See CALCANEUS.] **—calk** *v.*

calk² (kôk) *v.* Variant of **caulk.**

call (kôl) *v.* **called, call·ing, calls.** *—tr.* **1.** To say in a loud voice; announce: *called my name from across the street; calling out numbers.* **2.** To demand or ask for the presence of: *called the children to dinner; call the police.* **3.** To demand or ask for a meeting of; convene or convoke: *call the legislature into session.* **4.** To order or request to undertake a particular activity or work; summon: *She was called for jury duty. He was called to the priesthood.* **5.** To give the command for; order: *call a work stoppage.* **6.** To communicate or try to communicate with by telephone: *called me at nine.* **7.** To lure (prey) by imitating the characteristic cry of an animal: *call ducks.* **8.** To cause to come to the mind or to attention: *a story that calls to mind an incident in my youth.* **9.** To name: *What will you call the baby?* **10.** To consider or regard as being of a particular type or kind; characterize: *Let's call the game a draw. I'd hardly call him a good manager.* **11.** To designate; label: *Nobody calls me a liar.* **12.a.** To demand payment of: *call a loan.* **b.** To require the presentation of (a bond) for redemption before maturity. **13.** *Sports.* **a.** To stop or postpone (a game) because of bad weather, darkness, or other adverse conditions. **b.** To declare in the capacity of an umpire or referee: *call a runner out; call a foul on a boxer; call a penalty for holding.* **c.** To indicate a decision in regard to: *calling balls and strikes behind the plate; called a close play.* **d.** To give the orders or signals for: *a quarterback who called a poor play.* **14.** *Games.* **a.** To describe the intended outcome of (one's billiard shot) before playing. **b.** To equal the bet of (the preceding bet or bettor) in a poker game. **15.** To indicate or characterize accurately in advance; predict: *It is often difficult to call the outcome of an election.* See Synonyms at **predict. 16.** To challenge the truthfulness or genuineness of: *called the debater on a question of fact.* **17.** To shout directions in rhythm for (a square dance). *—intr.* **1.a.** To speak loudly; shout: *a swimmer who was calling for help.* **b.** To utter a characteristic cry. Used of an animal: *geese calling in early morning.* **2.** To communicate or try to communicate with someone by telephone: *I called twice, but no one answered.* **3.** To pay a short visit: *We called to pay our respects.* **—call** *n.* **1.** A loud cry; a shout. **2.a.** The characteristic cry of an animal. **b.** A sound or an instrument made to imitate such a cry, used as a lure: *a moose call.* **3.** A telephone communication or connection. **4.** Need or occasion: *There was no call for an apology.* **5.** Demand: *There isn't much call for buggy whips today.* **6.** A claim on a person's time or life: *the call of duty.* **7.** A short visit, especially one made as a formality or for business or professional purposes. **8.** A summons or an invitation. **9.a.** A signal, such as that made by a horn or bell. **b.** The sounding of a horn to encourage hounds during a hunt. **10.a.** A strong inner urge or prompting; a vocation: *a call to the priesthood.* **b.** The strong attraction or appeal of a given activity or environment: *the call of the wild; answered the call of the desert.* **11.** A roll call. **12.** A notice of rehearsal times posted in a theater. **13.** *Sports.* A decision made by an umpire or a referee. **14.** A direction or series of directions rhythmically called out to square dancers. **15.a.** A demand for payment of a debt. **b.** A demand to submit bonds to the issuer for redemption before the maturity date. **c.** An option to buy a certain quantity of a stock or commodity for a specified price within a specified time. **d.** A demand for payment due on stock bought on margin when the value has shrunk. ***—phrasal verbs.*** **call back. 1.** To communicate the need for (someone) to return from one situation or location to a previous one: *Management called the laid-off workers back.* **2.** To telephone or radio (a person) who has called previously: *I called her back at noon.* **3.** To recall (a defective product) for repair: *The company has called back all such models built in 1990.* **call down. 1.** To find fault with; reprimand: *The teacher called me down for disobedience.* **2.** To invoke, as from heaven. **call for. 1.** To appear, as on someone else's premises, in order to get: *My chauffeur will call for you at seven.* **2.** To be an appropriate occasion for: *This news calls for champagne.* **3.** To require; demand: *work that calls for patience.* **call forth.** To evoke; elicit: *a love song that calls forth sad memories.* **call in. 1.** To take out of circulation: *calling in silver dollars.* **2.** To summon for assistance or consultation: *call in a specialist.* **3.** To communicate with another by telephone: *Has the boss called in today?* **call off. 1.** To cancel or postpone: *call off a trip; called the trip off.* **2.** To restrain or recall: *Call off your dogs.* **call out. 1.** To cause to assemble; summon: *call out the guard.* **2.** To challenge to a duel. **call up. 1.** To summon to active military service: *called up reserve troops for active duty.* **2.** To cause one to remember; bring to mind: *stories that call up old times.* **3.** To bring forth for action or discussion; raise. **call upon. 1.** To order; require: *I call upon you to tell the truth.* **2.** To make a demand or a series of demands on: *Social institutions are now being called upon to provide assistance to the homeless.* ***—idioms.*** **call a spade a spade.** To speak directly, precisely, and forthrightly. **call in** (or **into) question.** To raise doubts about. **call it a day.** *Informal.* To stop whatever one has been doing, for the remainder of the day or at least for the present. **call it quits.** *Informal.* To stop working or trying; quit. **call names.** To speak to or about another in offensive terms. **call (someone's) bluff.** To challenge another with a display of strength or confidence. **call the shots** (or **tune).** *Informal.* To exercise authority; be in charge. **on call. 1.** Available when summoned for service or use: *physicians who were on call for 48 hours.* **2.** Subject to payment on demand. **within call.** Close enough to come if summoned: *The nurse is within call if you need him.* [Middle English *callen,* probably from Old Norse *kalla.* See **gal-** in Appendix.]

SYNONYMS: *call, convene, convoke, muster, summon.* The central meaning shared by these verbs is "to demand or request to appear, come, or assemble": *called the doctor; convene a meeting; convoke the legislature; mustering the militia; summon a witness.*

cal·la (kăl′ə) *n.* **1.** A calla lily. **2.** A marsh plant *(Calla palustris)* of the North Temperate zone, having small, densely clustered, greenish flowers partly enclosed in a spreading white spathe. In this sense, also called *water arum.* [New Latin *Calla,* genus name, from Greek *kallaia,* wattle of a cock, perhaps from *kallos,* beauty.]

Cal·la·ghan (kăl′ə-hən, -hăn′), **(Leonard) James.** Born 1912. British prime minister (1976–1979) who as Chancellor of the Exchequer (1964–1967) introduced controversial tax measures

calla lily *n.* Any of several chiefly southern African plants of the genus *Zantedeschia,* widely cultivated as ornamentals and cut flowers for their showy white, yellow, pink, or purple spathes.

Cal·la·o (kə-yä′ō, käyou′). A city of west-central Peru on the Pacific Ocean near Lima. Founded in 1537, it is Peru's largest port. Population, 264,133.

Maria Callas

Cal·las (kăl′əs, kä′ləs), **Maria Meneghini.** 1923–1977. American coloratura soprano known for her dramatic intensity. Among her notable operatic roles was Bellini's *Norma.*

♦**cal'late** (kăl′āt′, -lāt′) *v. Chiefly New England & Upper Southern U.S.* Variant of **calculate** (sense 4).

call·back (kôl′băk′) *n.* **1.** The act or an instance of calling back from one location or situation to the previous one: *a callback of laid-off auto workers.* **2.** A return telephone or radio call. **3.** A recall of a recently sold product by the manufacturer to correct a defect.

call·board (kôl′bôrd′, -bōrd′) *n.* A bulletin board backstage in a theater for posting instructions and notices.

call box *n.* **1.** A roadside telephone used for reporting motorists' emergencies, such as collisions and automotive breakdowns. **2.** *Chiefly British.* A public telephone booth.

call·boy (kôl′boi′) *n.* **1.** One who tells performers when it is time for them to go on stage. **2.** A bellhop. **3.** A male prostitute hired by telephone.

call·er¹ (kô′lər) *n.* **1.** One that calls, especially a party placing a telephone call. **2.** A person paying a short social visit. **3.** A person who calls out numbers or directions, as at a bingo game or a square dance.

calligraphy

cal·ler² (kăl′ər) *adj. Scots.* **1.** Fresh. **2.** Cool and refreshing. [Middle English *calour,* alteration of *calver.*]

call girl *n.* A woman prostitute hired by telephone.

call house *n.* A house of prostitution.

cal·lig·ra·phy (kə-lĭg′rə-fē) *n.* **1.a.** The art of fine handwriting. **b.** Works in fine handwriting considered as a group. **2.** Handwriting. [French *calligraphie,* from Greek *kalligraphia,* beautiful writing : *kalli-,* beautiful (from *kallos,* beauty) + *-graphia,* -graphy.] **—cal·lig′ra·pher, cal·lig′ra·phist** *n.* **—cal′li·graph′ic** (kăl′ĭ-grăf′ĭk) *adj.*

Cal·lim·a·chus¹ (kə-lĭm′ə-kəs). Fifth century B.C. Greek sculptor who reputedly designed the Corinthian column.

Cal·lim·a·chus² (kə-lĭm′ə-kəs). Third century B.C. Greek poet and scholar whose extant works include 64 epigrams and a catalog of the library at Alexandria.

call-in (kôl′ĭn′) *adj.* Being in a format such that listeners or viewers are invited to have their telephone conversations with the host or guests on a show broadcast to other listeners: *a call-in radio show.* **—call-in** *n.* **1.** A viewer or listener's telephone conversation with or telephone call to the host of such a show. **2.** A viewer or listener making such a call.

calliope

call·ing (kô′lĭng) *n.* **1.** An inner urge; a strong impulse. **2.** An occupation, a profession, or a career.

calling card *n.* An engraved card bearing one's full name. Also called *visiting card.*

cal·li·o·pe (kə-lī′ə-pē′, kăl′ē-ōp′) *n. Music.* An instrument fitted with steam whistles, played from a keyboard. [From CALLIOPE.]

Cal·li·o·pe (kə-lī′ə-pē′) *n. Greek Mythology.* The Muse of epic poetry. [Latin, from Greek *Kalliopē* : *kalli-,* beautiful (from *kallos,* beauty) + *ops, op-,* voice; see **wekʷ-** in Appendix.]

cal·li·op·sis (kăl′ē-ŏp′sĭs) *n.* A North American annual plant *(Coreopsis tinctoria)* widely cultivated for its showy flower heads with yellow rays and purple-red to brownish centers. [New Latin : Greek *kalli-,* beautiful (from *kallos,* beauty) + Greek *opsis,* appearance; see -OPSIS.]

cal·li·per (kăl′ə-pər) *n.* Variant of **caliper.**

cal·li·pyg·i·an (kăl′ə-pĭj′ē-ən) also **cal·li·py·gous** (-pī′gəs) *adj.* Having beautifully proportioned buttocks. [From Greek *kallipugos* : *kalli-,* beautiful (from *kallos,* beauty) + *pugē,* buttocks.]

ă pat	oi boy
ā pay	ou out
âr care	ŏŏ took
ä father	ōō boot
ĕ pet	ŭ cut
ē be	ûr urge
ĭ pit	th thin
ī pie	*th* this
îr pier	hw which
ŏ pot	zh vision
ō toe	ə about, item
ô paw	♦ regionalism

Stress marks: ′ (primary); ′ (secondary), as in **dictionary** (dĭk′shə-nĕr′ē)

Cal·lis·to (kə-lĭs′tō) *n.* **1.** *Greek Mythology.* A nymph, beloved of Zeus and hated by Hera. Hera changed her into a bear, and Zeus then placed her in the sky as the constellation Ursa Major. **2.** One of the four brightest satellites of Jupiter and the sixth in distance from the planet. Originally sighted by Galileo, it is the largest planetary satellite. [Latin, from Greek *Kallistō,* perhaps from *kallistos,* superlative of *kalos,* beautiful.]

call letters *pl.n.* The identifying code letters or numbers of a radio or television transmitting station, assigned by a regulatory body. Also called *call sign.*

call loan *n.* A loan repayable on demand at any time. Also called *demand loan.*

call number *n.* A number used in libraries to classify a book and indicate its location on the shelves.

cal·lose (kăl′ōs′) *n. Botany.* A complex branched carbohydrate commonly associated with sieve areas of sieve elements. [From Latin *callōsus,* callous. See CALLOUS.]

cal·los·i·ty (kə-lŏs′ĭ-tē) *n., pl.* **-ties. 1.** The condition of being calloused. **2.** Hardheartedness; insensitivity. **3.** See **callus** (sense 1a). [Middle English *callosite,* from Old French, from Late Latin *callōsitās,* from Latin *callōsus,* callous. See CALLOUS.]

cal·lous (kăl′əs) *adj.* **1.** Having calluses; toughened: *callous skin on the elbow.* **2.** Emotionally hardened; unfeeling: *a callous indifference to the suffering of others.* **—callous** *tr. & intr.v.* **-loused, -lous·ing, -lous·es.** To make or become callous. [Middle English, from Old French *cailleux,* from Latin *callōsus,* from *callum,* hard skin.] **—cal′lous·ly** *adv.* **—cal′lous·ness** *n.*

USAGE NOTE: Do not confuse the adjective *callous,* as in *Years of dealing with criminals had left her callous,* with the noun *callus,* as in *I have a callus on my thumb.* The verbs *callous* and *callus* mean respectively "to make or become callous" and "to form or develop hardened tissue."

cal·low (kăl′ō) *adj.* Lacking adult maturity or experience; immature: *a callow youth.* [Middle English *calwe,* bald, from Old English *calu.*] **—cal′low·ness** *n.*

Cal·lo·way (kăl′ə-wā′), **Cabell.** Known as "Cab." Born 1907. American jazz musician and bandleader noted for his scat singing.

call sign *n.* See **call letters.**

call to quarters *n.* A signal by a bugle that calls troops to their barracks just before taps.

call-up (kôl′ŭp′) *n.* The act or an instance of summoning reserve military personnel to active service.

cal·lus (kăl′əs) *n., pl.* **-lus·es. 1.a.** A localized thickening and enlargement of the horny layer of the skin. Also called *callosity.* **b.** The hard bony tissue that develops around the ends of a fractured bone during healing. **2.** *Botany.* **a.** Undifferentiated tissue that develops on or around an injured or cut plant surface or in tissue culture. **b.** The hardened, sometimes sharp base of the floret of certain grasses. **—callus** *intr.v.* **-lused, -lus·ing, -lus·es.** To form or develop such hardened tissue. See Usage Note at **callous.** [Latin, masculine of *callum.*]

calm (käm) *adj.* **calm·er, calm·est. 1.** Nearly or completely motionless; undisturbed: *the calm surface of the lake.* **2.** Not excited or agitated; composed: *The President was calm throughout the global crisis.* **—calm** *n.* **1.** An absence or cessation of motion; stillness. **2.** Serenity; tranquillity; peace. **3.** A condition of no wind or a wind with a speed of less than 1 mile (2 kilometers) per hour, according to the Beaufort scale. **—calm** *tr. & intr.v.* **calmed, calm·ing, calms.** To make or become calm or quiet: *A warm bath will calm you. After the storm, the air calmed.* [Middle English *calme,* from Old French, from Old Italian *calmo,* from Late Latin *cauma,* heat of the day, resting place in the heat of the day, from Greek *kauma,* burning heat, from *kaiein,* to burn. N., from Middle English *calme,* from Italian *calma,* from Vulgar Latin **calma,* from Late Latin.] **—calm′ly** *adv.* **—calm′ness** *n.*

SYNONYMS: *calm, tranquil, placid, serene, halcyon, peaceful.* These adjectives denote absence of excitement or disturbance. *Calm* implies freedom from emotional agitation: *calm acceptance of the inevitable. Tranquil* suggests a more enduring calm: *hoped for a more tranquil life in the country. Placid* suggests a pleasant, often phlegmatic calm: *"Not everyone shared his placid temperament. Several cursed the delays"* (Samuel G. Freedman). *Serene* denotes a lofty, even spiritual repose: *remained serene in the midst of turbulence. Halcyon* suggests happy tranquillity: *halcyon days of youth. Peaceful* implies undisturbed serenity: *"I am . . . peaceful as old age tonight"* (Robert Browning).

calm·a·tive (kä′mə-tĭv, kăl′mə-) *adj.* Having relaxing or pacifying properties; sedative. **—calmative** *n.* A sedative.

cal·o·mel (kăl′ə-mĕl′, -məl) *n.* A colorless, white or brown tasteless compound, Hg_2Cl_2, used as a purgative and an insecticide. Also called *mercurous chloride.* [Probably from New Latin *kalomelas* : Greek *kalos,* beautiful + *melas,* black.]

Ca·lo·o·can (kăl′ə-ō′kän, kä′lä-). A city of southwest Luzon, Philippines, a suburb of Manila. Population, 467,816.

cal·o·re·cep·tor (kăl′ə-rĭ-sĕp′tər) *n.* A sensory receptor that detects warmth. [Latin *calor,* heat; see **kelə-¹** in Appendix + RECEPTOR.]

ca·lor·ic (kə-lôr′ĭk, -lŏr′-) *adj.* **1.** Of or relating to heat: *the caloric effect of sunlight.* **2.** Of or relating to calories: *the caloric content of foods.* **—caloric** *n.* A hypothetically indestructible, uncreatable, highly elastic, self-repellent, all-pervading fluid formerly thought responsible for the production, possession, and transfer of heat. [French *calorique,* from Latin *calor,* heat. See **kelə-¹** in Appendix.] **—ca·lor′i·cal·ly** *adv.*

cal·o·rie (kăl′ə-rē) *n.* **1.** *Abbr.* **cal** Any of several approximately equal units of heat, each measured as the quantity of heat required to raise the temperature of 1 gram of water by 1°C from a standard initial temperature, especially from 3.98°C, 14.5°C, or 19.5°C, at 1 atmosphere pressure. Also called *gram calorie, small calorie.* **2.** *Abbr.* **cal** The unit of heat equal to 1/100 the quantity of heat required to raise the temperature of 1 gram of water from 0 to 100°C at 1 atmosphere pressure. Also called *mean calorie.* **3.a.** *Abbr.* **Cal** The unit of heat equal to the amount of heat required to raise the temperature of 1 kilogram of water by 1°C at 1 atmosphere pressure. Also called *kilocalorie, kilogram calorie, large calorie.* **b.** A unit of energy-producing potential equal to this amount of heat that is contained in food and released upon oxidation by the body. Also called *nutritionist's calorie.* [French, from Latin *calor,* heat. See **kelə-¹** in Appendix.]

cal·o·rif·ic (kăl′ə-rĭf′ĭk) *adj.* Relating to or generating heat or calories. [French *calorifique,* from Latin *calōrificus* : *calor,* heat; see **kelə-¹** in Appendix + *-ficus,* -fic.]

calorific value *n.* The calories or thermal units contained in one unit of a substance and released when the substance is burned.

cal·o·rim·e·ter (kăl′ə-rĭm′ĭ-tər) *n.* **1.** An apparatus for measuring the heat generated by a chemical reaction, change of state, or formation of a solution. **2.** The part of this apparatus, usually a container for holding a sample, in which the heat measured causes a change of state. [Latin *calor,* heat; see **kelə-¹** in Appendix + -METER.] **—ca·lor′i·met′ric** (kə-lôr′ə-mĕt′rĭk, -lŏr′-) *adj.* **—ca·lor′i·met′ri·cal·ly** *adv.*

cal·o·rim·e·try (kăl′ə-rĭm′ĭ-trē) *n.* Measurement of the amount of heat evolved or absorbed in a chemical reaction, change of state, or formation of a solution. [Latin *calor,* heat; see **kelə-¹** in Appendix + -METRY.]

ca·lotte (kə-lŏt′) *n.* A skullcap, especially one worn by Roman Catholic priests. [French, from Provençal *calota* or Italian *callotta.*]

cal·pac or **cal·pack** also **kal·pac** (kăl′păk′, kăl-păk′) *n.* A large black cap, usually of sheepskin or felt, worn in Turkey, the Caucasus, Iran, and neighboring regions. [Ottoman Turkish *qalpāq,* from Old Turkic, probably ultimately from Middle Persian *kulāfak,* cap, diminutive of *kulāf,* hat.]

calpac

Cal·pe (kăl′pē). Ancient Gibraltar. Calpe was one of the Pillars of Hercules at the entrance to the Mediterranean Sea.

calque (kălk) *n.* See **loan translation.** [French, from *calquer,* to trace, copy, from Italian *calcare,* to press, from Latin *calcāre,* to tread on, from *calx,* heel.]

cal·trop (kăl′trəp, kôl′-) *n.* **1.** Any of various plants of the genera *Tribulus* and *Kallstroemia,* having spiny or tuberculate fruits. **2.** A Mediterranean species of star thistle *(Centaurea calcitrapa)* naturalized in North America. **3.** See **water chestnut** (sense 1). **4.** A metal device with four projecting spikes so arranged that when three of the spikes are on the ground, the fourth points upward, used as a hazard to pneumatic tires or to the hooves of horses. [Middle English *calketrappe,* from Norman French and from Old English *calcatrippe,* thistle, both from Medieval Latin *calcatrippa,* thistle : possibly from Latin *calcāre,* to tread on; see CALQUE + *trappa,* trap (of Germanic origin).]

cal·u·met (kăl′yə-mĕt′, -mĭt, kăl′yə-mĕt′) *n.* A long-stemmed sacred or ceremonial tobacco pipe used by certain Native Americans. [Canadian French, from French dialectal, straw, from Late Latin *calamellus,* diminutive of Latin *calamus,* reed, from Greek *kalamos.*]

calumet
Mandan

Cal·u·met (kăl′yə-mĕt′, -mĭt). A major industrial region of northeast Illinois and northwest Indiana on Lake Michigan adjacent to Chicago.

Calumet City. A city of northeast Illinois, an industrial suburb of Chicago. Population, 39,697.

ca·lum·ni·ate (kə-lŭm′nē-āt′) *tr.v.* **-at·ed, -at·ing, -ates.** To make maliciously or knowingly false statements about. See Synonyms at **malign.** [Latin *calumniārī, calumniāt-,* from *calumnia,* calumny. See CALUMNY.] **—ca·lum′ni·a′tion** *n.* **—ca·lum′ni·a′tor** *n.*

ca·lum·ni·ous (kə-lŭm′nē-əs) *adj.* Containing or implying calumny; slanderous or defamatory. **—ca·lum′ni·ous·ly** *adv.*

cal·um·ny (kăl′əm-nē) *n., pl.* **-nies. 1.** A false statement maliciously made to injure another's reputation. **2.** The utterance of maliciously false statements; slander. [Middle English *calumnie,* from Old French *calomnie,* from Latin *calumnia,* from *calvī,* to deceive.]

cal·va·dos (kăl′və-dōs′, kăl′və-dōs′) *n.* A French brandy made from apples. [French, after *Calvados,* a department of northwest France.]

cal·var·i·um (kăl-vâr′ē-əm) *n., pl.* **-i·ums** or **-i·a** (-ē-ə). A skull that lacks the lower jaw or the lower jaw and the facial parts. [Latin *calvāria,* skull, from *calva,* scalp, from *calvus,* bald.]

Cal·va·ry¹ (kăl′və-rē, kăl′vrē) also **Gol·go·tha** (gŏl′gə-thə, gŏl-gŏth′ə). A hill outside ancient Jerusalem where Jesus was crucified.

Calvary cross

Cal·va·ry² also **cal·va·ry** (kăl′və-rē) *n., pl.* **-ries. 1.** A sculptured depiction of the Crucifixion. **2. calvary.** A great or-

ă pat	oi boy
ā pay	ou out
âr care	ŏŏ took
ä father	ōō boot
ĕ pet	ŭ cut
ē be	ûr urge
ĭ pit	th thin
ī pie	*th* this
îr pier	hw which
ŏ pot	zh vision
ō toe	ə about, item
ô paw	♦ regionalism

Stress marks: ′ (primary); ′ (secondary), as in **dictionary** (dĭk′shə-nĕr′ē)

deal. [French *calvaire,* from *Calvaire,* Calvary. Sense 2, from CALVARY[1].]

Calvary cross *n. Heraldry.* A Latin cross set on three steps.

calve (kăv, käv) *v.* **calved, calv·ing, calves.** —*intr.* **1.** To give birth to a calf. **2.** To break at an edge, so that a portion separates. Used of a glacier or an iceberg. —*tr.* **1.** To give birth to (a calf). **2.** To set loose (a mass of ice). Used of a glacier or an iceberg. [Middle English *calven,* from Old English **calfian,* from *calf,* calf.]

Cal·vert (kăl′vərt). Family of English colonists in America, including **George** (1580?–1632), First Baron Baltimore; his son **Cecilius** (1605–1675), Second Baron and recipient of the Maryland charter; another son, **Leonard** (1606–1647), first governor of Maryland (1634–1647); and Cecilius's son **Charles** (1637–1715), Third Baron and governor (1661–1675) and proprietor (1675–1689) of Maryland.

calves[1] (kăvz, kävz) *n.* Plural of **calf[1].**

calves[2] (kăvz, kävz) *n.* Plural of **calf[2].**

Cal·vin (kăl′vĭn), **John.** 1509–1564. French-born Swiss Protestant theologian who broke with the Roman Catholic Church (1533) and set forth the tenets of his theology, known today as Presbyterianism, in *Institutes of the Christian Religion* (1536).

John Calvin

Calvin, Melvin. Born 1911. American chemist. He won a 1961 Nobel Prize for discovering the series of chemical reactions in photosynthesis.

Cal·vin·ism (kăl′vĭ-nĭz′əm) *n.* The religious doctrines of John Calvin, emphasizing the omnipotence of God and the salvation of the elect by God's grace alone. **—Cal′vin·ist** *adj. & n.* **—Cal′vin·is′tic** *adj.* **—Cal′vin·is′ti·cal·ly** *adv.*

calx (kălks) *n., pl.* **calx·es** or **cal·ces** (kăl′sēz′). The crumbly residue left after a mineral or metal has been calcined or roasted. [Middle English, from Latin, lime, limestone, pebble, from Greek *khalix,* pebble.]

ca·ly·ces (kā′lĭ-sēz′, kăl′ĭ-) *n.* A plural of **calyx.**

ca·ly·cine (kā′lĭ-sīn′, -sĭn, kăl′ĭ-) *adj.* Of, relating to, or resembling a calyx.

ca·lyc·u·lus (kə-lĭk′yə-ləs) *n., pl.* **-li** (-lī′). **1.** *Biology.* A small cup-shaped structure. **2.** *Botany.* A group of small bracts that resembles a calyx. [Latin, diminutive of *calyx, calyc-,* calyx. See CALYX.] **—ca·lyc′u·lar** *adj.* **—ca·lyc′u·late** (-lĭt, lāt′) *adj.*

Cal·y·don (kăl′ĭ-dŏn′, -dən). An ancient city of west-central Greece near the Gulf of Patras. According to legend, the Calydonian boar, a gigantic beast sent by Artemis to devastate the city, was slain by Meleager, the son of the king of Calydon. **—Cal′y·do′ni·an** (-dō′nē-ən, -dōn′yən) *adj. & n.*

ca·lyp·so (kə-lĭp′sō) *n., pl.* **-sos.** A terrestrial orchid *(Calypso bulbosa)* native to north temperate regions, having a rose-pink flower with an inflated pouchlike lip usually marked with white, purple, and yellow. [Probably Latin *Calypsō,* Calypso. See CALYPSO[1].]

Ca·lyp·so[1] (kə-lĭp′sō) *n.* **1.** *Greek Mythology.* A sea nymph who delayed Odysseus on her island, Ogygia, for seven years. **2.** The satellite of Saturn that is tenth in distance from the planet. [Latin, from Greek *Kalupsō,* from *kaluptein,* to conceal. See **kel-[1]** in Appendix.]

Ca·lyp·so[2] or **ca·lyp·so** (kə-lĭp′sō) *n., pl.* **-sos** also **-soes.** *Music.* A type of music that originated in the West Indies, notably in Trinidad, and is characterized by improvised lyrics on topical or broadly humorous subjects. [Origin unknown.] **—Ca·lyp·so′ni·an** (kə-lĭp-sō′nē-ən, kăl′ĭp-) *n.*

ca·lyp·tra (kə-lĭp′trə) *n.* **1.** The protective cap or hood covering the spore case of a moss or related plant. **2.** A similar hoodlike, lidlike, or caplike structure, such as a root cap. [Medieval Latin, from Greek *kaluptra,* veil, from *kaluptein,* to cover. See **kel-[1]** in Appendix.] **—ca·lyp′trate′** (-trāt′) *adj.*

ca·lyx (kā′lĭks, kăl′ĭks) *n., pl.* **ca·lyx·es** or **ca·ly·ces** (kā′lĭ-sēz′, kăl′ĭ-). **1.** The sepals of a flower considered as a group. **2.** A cuplike structure or organ, such as one of the cuplike divisions of the pelvis or of the kidney. **3.** A collecting structure in the kidney. [Latin *calyx, calyc-,* from Greek *kalux.*]

cam (kăm) *n.* An eccentric or multiply curved wheel mounted on a rotating shaft, used to produce variable or reciprocating motion in another engaged or contacted part. [Dutch *kam,* cog, comb. See **gembh-** in Appendix.]

Cam (kăm). A river, about 64 km (40 mi) long, of east-central England. It flows past Cambridge to join the Ouse River south of Ely.

CAM *abbr. Computer Science.* Computer-aided manufacturing.

Ca·ma·güey (kăm′ə-gwā′, kä′mä-). A city of east-central Cuba. Founded in 1514, it was moved to its present site in 1528. Population, 244,091.

ca·ma·ra·der·ie (kä′mə-rä′də-rē, kăm′ə-răd′ə-) *n.* Good will and lighthearted rapport between or among friends; comradeship. [French, from *camarade,* comrade, from Old French, roommate. See COMRADE.]

cam·a·ril·la (kăm′ə-rĭl′ə, -rē′yə) *n.* A group of confidential, often scheming advisers; a cabal. [Spanish, diminutive of *cámara,* room, from Late Latin *camera.* See CHAMBER.]

Cam·a·ril·lo (kăm′ə-rē′ō). A city of southern California west of Los Angeles. It is a manufacturing center in a fertile farming area. Population, 37,797.

cam·as or **cam·ass** (kăm′əs) *n.* **1.** Any of several plants of the genus *Camassia* in the lily family, especially *C. quamash* of western North America, having grasslike leaves, a raceme of blue flowers, and a bulb that was an important food for various Native American peoples. Also called *quamash.* **2.** Death camas. [Chinook Jargon, perhaps of Nootka origin.]

Cam·bay (kăm-bā′), **Gulf of.** An inlet of the Arabian Sea on the northwest coast of India.

cam·ber (kăm′bər) *n.* **1.a.** A slightly arched surface, as of a road, a ship's deck, an airfoil, or a snow ski. **b.** The condition of having an arched surface. **2.** A setting of automobile wheels in which they are closer together at the bottom than at the top. **—camber** *intr. & tr.v.* **-bered, -ber·ing, -bers.** To arch or cause to arch slightly. [From Middle English *caumber,* curved, from Old North French dialectal *caumbre,* from Latin *camur,* perhaps from Greek *kamara,* vault.]

Cam·ber·well beauty (kăm′bər-wĕl′, -wəl) *n. Chiefly British.* The mourning cloak. [After *Camberwell,* a former borough of London, England.]

cam·bi·um (kăm′bē-əm) *n.* A lateral meristem in most vascular plants that forms parallel rows of cells resulting in secondary tissues either as secondary growth or as cork. [Medieval Latin, exchange, from Late Latin *cambīre, cambiāre,* to exchange, of Celtic origin.] **—cam′bi·al** *adj.*

Cam·bo·di·a (kăm-bō′dē-ə) or **Kam·pu·che·a** (kăm′po͞o-chē′ə). Formerly (1970–1975) **Khmer Republic** (kmâr). A country of southeast Asia on the Gulf of Siam. During the time of the Khmer emperors, it ruled the entire Mekong River valley but fell under the sway of its stronger neighbors after the 15th century. Cambodia became part of French Indochina in the 19th century and proclaimed its independence in 1953. Phnom Penh is the capital and the largest city. Population, 5,756,141. **—Cam·bo′di·an** *adj. & n.*

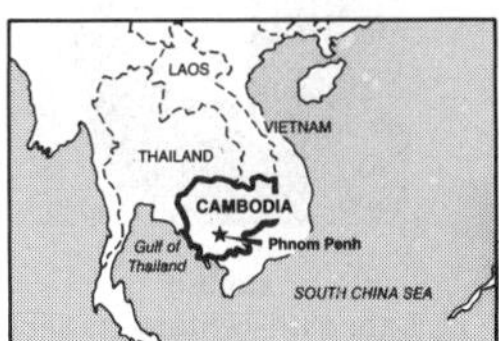

Cambodia

Cam·bri·a (kăm′brē-ə). Wales during Roman times. The term is now used as a poetic appellation.

Cam·bri·an (kăm′brē-ən) *adj.* **1.** Of or relating to Wales; Welsh. **2.** Of, relating to, or belonging to the geologic time, system of rocks, and sedimentary deposits of the first period of the Paleozoic Era, characterized by warm seas and desert land areas. See table at **geologic time.** **—Cambrian** *n.* **1.** A native of Wales; a Welshman. **2.** The Cambrian Period. [From Medieval Latin *Cambria,* Wales, alteration of *Cumbria,* from Welsh *Cymry.* Adj., sense 2, and n., sense 2, after CAMBRIA.]

cam·bric (kăm′brĭk) *n.* A finely woven white linen or cotton fabric. [Obsolete Flemish *kameryk,* from *Kameryk,* Cambrai, a city of northern France.]

cambric tea *n.* A drink for children, made of hot water, milk, sugar, and usually a small amount of tea. [So called because it is thin and white like cambric.]

Cam·bridge (kām′brĭj). **1.** A city of southeast Ontario, Canada, west-northwest of Hamilton. Population 77,183. **2.** A municipal borough of east-central England on the Cam River north-northeast of London. It is an ancient market town and the site of Cambridge University, established in the 12th to 13th century. Population, 100,200. **3.** A city of eastern Massachusetts on the Charles River opposite Boston. Settled in 1630 as New Towne, it is known for its research and educational facilities, including Harvard University (founded in 1636), Radcliffe College (1879), and Massachusetts Institute of Technology (1861). Population, 95,322.

Cam·by·ses (kăm-bī′sēz). Died 522 B.C. King of Persia (529–522) who extended Persian rule throughout the Nile Valley.

cam·cord·er (kăm′kôr′dər) *n.* A self-contained unit of communications equipment made up of a lightweight, hand-held television camera and a videocassette recorder. [CAM(ERA) + (RE)CORDER.]

Cam·den (kăm′dən). A city of western New Jersey on the Delaware River opposite Philadelphia. Walt Whitman lived here from 1873 to 1892. Population, 84,910.

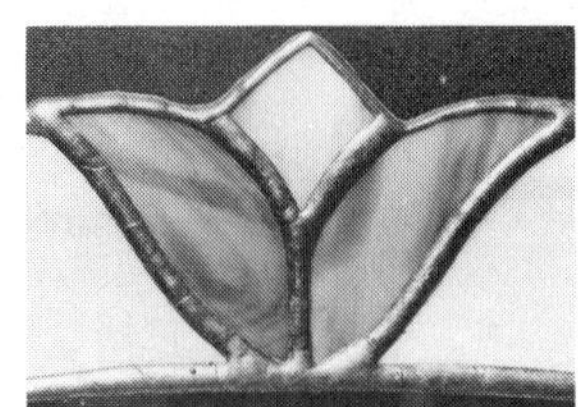
came[1]
In stained glass

came[1] (kăm) *n.* A slender, grooved lead bar used to hold together the panes in stained glass or latticework windows. [Possibly dialectal *kame,* ridge. See KAME.]

came[2] (kām) *v.* Past tense of **come.**

cam·el (kăm′əl) *n.* **1.** A humped, long-necked ruminant mammal of the genus *Camelus,* domesticated in Old World desert regions as a beast of burden and as a source of wool, milk, and meat. **2.** A device used to raise sunken objects, consisting of a hollow structure that is submerged, attached tightly to the object, and pumped free of water. Also called *caisson.* **3.** *Sports.* A spin in figure skating that is performed in an arabesque or modified arabesque position. [Middle English, from Old English and from Anglo-Norman *cameil,* both from Latin *camēlus,* from Greek *kamēlos,* of Semitic origin.]

♦**cam·el·back** (kăm′əl-băk′) *adj.* Shaped like a hump or an arching curve. **—camelback** *n. New Orleans.* A narrow house with one story in front and two in the rear. See Regional Note at **beignet.**

cam·el·eer (kăm′ə-lîr′) *n.* A person who drives or rides a camel.

camel
Bactrian camel
Camelus bactrianus

ca·mel·lia (kə-mēl′yə) *n.* Any of several evergreen shrubs or small trees of the genus *Camellia* native to eastern Asia, especially *C. japonica,* having shiny leaves and showy roselike flowers that are usually red, white, or pink. [New Latin *Camellia,* genus name, after Georg Josef *Kamel* (1661–1706), Moravian Jesuit missionary.]

ca·mel·o·pard (kə-mĕl′ə-pärd′) *n.* **1.** A giraffe. **2.** *Herald-*

ry. A bearing resembling a giraffe but represented with long, curved horns. [Middle English, from Medieval Latin *camēlopardus,* from Latin *camēlopardalis,* from Greek *kamēlopardalis : kamēlos,* camel; see CAMEL + *pardalis,* pard (so called because the giraffe has a head like a camel's and the spots of a leopard).]

Ca·mel·o·par·da·lis (kə-mĕl′ō-pär′dl-ĭs) *n.* A constellation in the Northern Hemisphere in the large space between Ursa Major, Ursa Minor, and Perseus. [Latin *camēlopardalis,* camelopard. See CAMELOPARD.]

Cam·e·lot (kăm′ə-lŏt′) *n.* **1.** In Arthurian legend, the site of King Arthur's court. **2.** A place or time of idealized beauty, peacefulness, and enlightenment.

cam·el's hair (kăm′əlz) *n.* **1.** The soft, fine hair of the camel or a substitute for it. **2.** A soft, heavy, usually light tan cloth, made chiefly of the hair of camel.

Cam·em·bert (kăm′əm-bâr′) *n.* A creamy, mold-ripened cheese that softens on the inside as it matures. [French, after *Camembert,* a village of northwest France.]

cam·e·o (kăm′ē-ō′) *n., pl.* **-os. 1.a.** A gem or shell carved in relief, especially one in which the raised design and the background consist of layers of contrasting colors. **b.** The technique of carving in this way. **c.** A medallion with a profile cut in raised relief. **2.** A brief, vivid portrayal or depiction: *a literary cameo.* **3.** A brief but dramatic appearance of a prominent actor, as in a single scene of a motion picture. In this sense, also called *cameo role.* **—cameo** *v.* **-oed, -o·ing, -os.** *—tr.* **1.** To make into or like a gem or shell carved in relief. **2.** To portray in sharp, delicate relief, as in a literary composition. *—intr.* To make a brief but dramatic appearance, as in a film: *She cameoed as Anne Boleyn in* A Man for All Seasons. [Italian and Middle English *cameu* (from Old French *camaieu,* and from Medieval Latin *camahūtus*).]

cameo
Late 19th-century Italian

cam·er·a (kăm′ər-ə, kăm′rə) *n.* **1.** An apparatus for taking photographs, generally consisting of a lightproof enclosure having an aperture with a shuttered lens through which the image of an object is focused and recorded on a photosensitive film or plate. **2.** The part of a television transmitting apparatus that receives the primary image on a light-sensitive cathode tube and transforms it into electrical impulses. **3.** Camera obscura. **4.** *pl.* **-er·ae** (-ə-rē) A judge's private chamber. ***—idioms.* in camera.** In private. **off camera.** Outside the field of view of a television or movie camera. **on camera.** Within the field of view of a television or movie camera. [Late Latin, room. See CHAMBER.]

camera lu·ci·da (lo͞o′sĭ-də) *n., pl.* **camera lu·ci·das.** An optical device that projects a virtual image of an object onto a plane surface, especially for tracing. [New Latin : Latin *camera,* chamber + Latin *lucida,* light.]

cam·er·a·man (kăm′ər-ə-măn′, kăm′rə-) *n.* A man who operates a movie or television camera.

camera ob·scu·ra (əb-skyo͝or′ə) *n., pl.* **camera ob·scu·ras.** A darkened chamber in which the real image of an object is received through a small opening or lens and focused in natural color onto a facing surface rather than recorded on a film or plate. [New Latin : Latin *camera,* chamber + Latin *obscura,* dark.]

cam·er·a·per·son (kăm′ər-ə-pûr′sən, kăm′rə-) *n.* One who operates a movie or television camera.

cam·er·a-read·y (kăm′ər-ə-rĕd′ē, kăm′rə-) *adj.* Prepared in such a way as to be appropriate for photographing prior to being made into a printing plate: *camera-ready art; camera-ready text copy.*

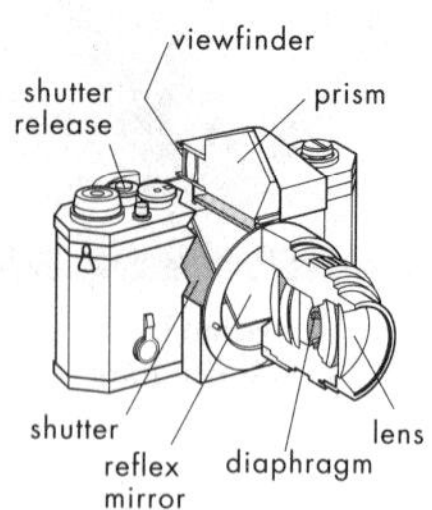

camera

cam·er·a·wo·man (kăm′ər-ə-wo͝om′ən, kăm′rə-) *n.* A woman who operates a movie or television camera.

cam·er·lin·go (kăm′ər-lĭng′gō) also **cam·er·len·go** (-lĕng′gō) *n., pl.* **-gos.** The cardinal who manages the pope's secular affairs. [Italian *camarlingo,* of Germanic origin.]

Cam·er·on (kăm′ər-ən), **Mount.** A peak, 4,342.6 m (14,238 ft) high, in the Rocky Mountains of central Colorado.

Cam·e·roon (kăm′ə-ro͞on′) also **Came·roun** (kăm-ro͞on′). A country of west-central Africa on the Bight of Biafra. Comprising the former French Cameroons and the southern part of British Cameroons, it became independent in 1960. Yaoundé is the capital and Douala the largest city. Population, 9,542,400.

Cam·e·roons (kăm′ə-ro͞onz′). A region and former German protectorate of west-central Africa. After World War I the territory was divided into British Cameroons and French Cameroons.

Came·roun (kăm-ro͞on′). See **Cameroon.**

cam·i (kăm′ē) *n., pl.* **-is.** A camisole worn as an undergarment.

cam·i·on (kăm′ē-ən, kăm-yôN′) *n.* **1.** A truck. **2.** A bus. [French, from Old French *chamion,* three-wheeled cart.]

cam·i·sa·do (kăm′ĭ-sä′dō, -sā′-) *n., pl.* **-does.** *Archaic.* A surprise attack by night. [Probably from obsolete Spanish *encamisado,* shirted, surprise attack, from *camisa,* shirt (so called because the attackers wore white shirts over their armor for identification), from Late Latin *camisia, camīsa.*]

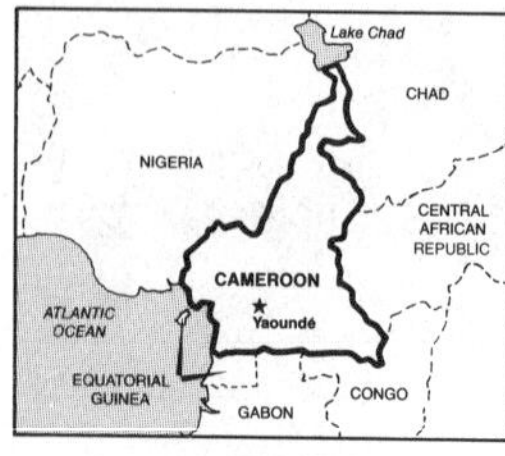

Cameroon

ca·mise (kə-mēz′, -mēs′) *n.* A loose shirt, shift, or tunic. [Arabic *qamīṣ,* from Late Latin *camisia, camīsa,* shirt.]

cam·i·sole (kăm′ĭ-sōl′) *n.* **1.** A woman's sleeveless undergarment, now usually worn under a sheer blouse. **2.** A short negligee. [French (from Italian *camiciola,* diminutive of *camicia,* shirt) or from Old Provençal *camisolla,* diminutive of *camisa,* shirt, both from Late Latin *camisia, camīsa.*]

Cam·lan (kăm′lən) *n.* In Arthurian legend, the battlefield where King Arthur was mortally wounded.

cam·let (kăm′lĭt) *n.* **1.** A rich cloth of Asian origin, supposed originally to have been made of camel's hair and silk and later made of goat's hair and silk or other combinations. **2.** A garment made from this cloth. [Middle English *chamelet,* from Old French *chamelot,* perhaps from Arabic *ḥamlah,* nap, fibers.]

cam·o (kăm′ō) *n., pl.* **-os.** *Informal.* Camouflage fabric or a garment made of it. [Short for CAMOUFLAGE.]

Ca·mões (kə-moiNsh) also **Ca·mo·ëns** (kăm′ō-ənz, kə-mō′-), **Luiz Vaz de.** 1524?–1580. Portuguese writer whose epic poem *Os Lusíadas* (1572) is among Portugal's greatest literary works.

cam·o·mile (kăm′ə-mīl′, -mēl′) *n.* Variant of **chamomile.**

Ca·mor·ra (kə-môr′ə, -mŏr′ə) *n.* **1.** A Neapolitan secret society organized about 1820, notorious for practicing violence and blackmail. **2. camorra.** An unscrupulous, clandestine group. [Italian, perhaps from *camorra,* a kind of smock, said to have been worn by members of the society.]

cam·ou·flage (kăm′ə-fläzh′, -fläj′) *n.* **1.** The method or result of concealing personnel or equipment from an enemy by making them appear to be part of the natural surroundings. **2.** Concealment by disguise or protective coloring. **3.** Fabric or a garment dyed in splotches of green, brown, tan, and black so as to make the wearer indistinguishable from the surrounding environment. **—camouflage** *v.* **-flaged, -flag·ing, -flag·es.** *—tr.* **1.** To conceal by the use of disguise or by protective coloring or garments that blend in with the surrounding environment. **2.** To conceal, usually through misrepresentation or other artifice: *camouflaged their hatred with professions of friendship.* See Synonyms at **disguise.** *—intr.* To use protective coloring or garments for concealment. [French, from *camoufler,* to disguise, alteration (influenced by *camouflet,* snub, smoke blown in one's face) of Italian *camuffare.*] **—cam′ou·flag′er** *n.*

camp¹ (kămp) *n.* **1.a.** A place where tents, huts, or other temporary shelters are set up, as by soldiers, nomads, or travelers. **b.** A cabin or shelter or group of such buildings: *gathered branches and grasses for a makeshift camp; had a fishing camp in Vermont.* **c.** The people using such shelters: *a howl that awakened the whole camp.* **2.a.** A place in the country that offers simple group accommodations and organized recreation or instruction, as for vacationing children: *a girls' summer camp; a tennis camp.* **b.** *Sports.* A place where athletes engage in intensive training, especially preseason training. **c.** The people attending the programs at such a place. **3.** Military service; army life. **4.** A group of people who think alike or share a cause; side: *The council members disagreed, falling into liberal and conservative camps.* **—camp** *v.* **camped, camp·ing, camps.** *—intr.* **1.** To make or set up a camp. **2.** To live in or as if in a camp; settle: *We camped in the apartment until the furniture arrived.* *—tr.* To shelter or lodge in a camp; encamp: *They camped themselves by a river.* [Obsolete French, perhaps from Italian or Spanish *campo,* all from Latin *campus,* field.]

camp² (kămp) *n.* **1.** An affectation or appreciation of manners and tastes commonly thought to be artificial, vulgar, or banal. **2.** Banality, vulgarity, or artificiality when deliberately affected or when appreciated for its humor: *"Camp is popularity plus vulgarity plus innocence"* (Indra Jahalani). **—camp** *adj.* Having deliberately artificial, vulgar, banal, or affectedly humorous qualities or style: *played up the silliness of their roles for camp effect.* **—camp** *v.* **camped, camp·ing, camps.** *—intr.* To act in a deliberately artificial, vulgar, or banal way. *—tr.* To give a deliberately artificial, vulgar, or banal quality to: *camped up their cowboy costumes with chaps, tin stars, and ten-gallon hats.* [Origin unknown.] **—camp′y** *adj.*

Camp (kămp), **Walter Chauncey.** 1859–1925. American football coach and promoter who developed many of the sport's basic rules.

Cam·pa·gna di Ro·ma (kăm-pän′yə dē rō′mə, -mä, kăm-). A low-lying region surrounding Rome, Italy. It was a favorite residential area during ancient times but was largely abandoned for centuries because of the prevalence of malaria.

cam·paign (kăm-pān′) *n.* **1.** A series of military operations undertaken to achieve a large-scale objective during a war: *Grant's Vicksburg campaign secured the entire Mississippi for the Union.* **2.** An operation or series of operations energetically pursued to accomplish a purpose: *an advertising campaign for a new product; a candidate's political campaign.* **—campaign** *intr.v.* **-paigned, -paign·ing, -paigns.** To engage in an operation planned to achieve a certain goal: *campaigned through the jungles of Vietnam; campaigned for human rights.* [French *campagne,* from Italian *campagna,* military operation, from Late Latin *campānia,* open country, battlefield, from *campus,* field.] **—cam·paign′er** *n.*

SYNONYMS: *campaign, crusade, drive, push.* The central meaning shared by these nouns is "a vigorous concerted effort to accomplish a purpose": *a fund-raising campaign; a crusade for improved social services; a drive to sell bonds; a push to get the bill through Congress.*

Cam·pa·ni·a (kăm-pā′nē-ə, -pān′yə, käm-pä′nyä). A region of southern Italy on the Tyrrhenian Sea. Inhabited in ancient times by Italic tribes, Greek colonists, Etruscans, and Samnites, it was conquered by Rome in the fourth century B.C.

cam·pa·ni·le (kăm′pə-nē′lē) *n., pl.* **-les** (-lēz) or **-li** (-lē). A bell tower, especially one near but not attached to a church or other public building. [French, from Italian, from *campana,* bell, from Late Latin *campāna,* bell (made of metal produced in Campania), from Latin *campānus,* of Campania, from CAMPANIA.]

cam·pa·nol·o·gy (kăm′pə-nŏl′ə-jē) *n.* The art or study of bell casting and ringing. [Late Latin *campāna,* bell; see CAMPANILE + –LOGY.] —**cam′pa·nol′o·gist** *n.*

cam·pan·u·la (kăm-păn′yə-lə) *n.* Any of various plants of the genus *Campanula,* which includes the harebell, bellflower, and Canterbury bells. [New Latin *Campanula,* genus name, diminutive of Late Latin *campāna,* bell. See CAMPANILE.]

cam·pan·u·late (kăm-păn′yə-lĭt, -lāt′) *adj. Botany.* Shaped like a bell, as certain flowers are.

Camp·bell (kăm′bəl). A city of west-central California southwest of San Jose. It has an electronics industry. Population, 26,910.

Campbell, John Archibald. 1811–1889. American jurist and public official who served as an associate justice of the U.S. Supreme Court (1853–1861) and as assistant secretary of war (1862–1865) in the Confederate cabinet.

Campbell, Joseph. 1904–1987. American mythologist who wrote numerous works, including *The Hero with a Thousand Faces* (1949) and the four-volume *Masks of God* (1959–1967).

Campbell, Mrs. **Patrick.** Originally Beatrice Stella Tanner. 1865–1940. British actress who was the first to portray Eliza in *Pygmalion* (1913), a part written for her by George Bernard Shaw.

Campbell, Thomas¹. 1763–1854. Irish-born American religious leader who with his son **Alexander** (1788–1866) founded the Disciples of Christ (1809).

Campbell, Thomas². 1777–1844. British poet and editor best known for his ballad "Lord Ullin's Daughter" (1809).

Camp·bell-Ban·ner·man (kăm′bəl-băn′ər-mən, kăm′əl-), Sir **Henry.** 1836–1908. British politician who was the Liberal Party leader during the Boer War (1899–1902) and later served as prime minister (1905–1908).

Camp Da·vid (dā′vĭd). A presidential retreat in the Catoctin Mountains of northern Maryland north-northwest of Washington, D.C. It was established by Franklin D. Roosevelt in 1942 as Shangri-La. Dwight D. Eisenhower renamed it Camp David in honor of his grandson.

Cam·pe·che (kăm-pē′chē, käm-pĕ′-). A city of southeast Mexico on the **Bay of Campeche,** a section of the Gulf of Mexico west of Yucatán. Founded in 1540, Campeche was frequently sacked by buccaneers in the 17th century. Population, 128,434.

camp·er (kăm′pər) *n.* **1.** One that camps, such as a person lodging temporarily in a tent or cabin. **2.a.** A motor vehicle with space and equipment, either in a rear compartment or in an attached trailer, for sleeping and simple housekeeping, used for camping and recreational travel. **b.** The rear compartment or attached trailer of such a vehicle.

cam·pe·si·no (käm′pĭ-sē′nō, kăm′-) *n., pl.* **-nos.** A farmer or farm worker in a Latin American country. [Spanish, from *campo,* field, from Latin *campus.*]

cam·pes·tral (kăm-pĕs′trəl) *adj.* Of, relating to, or growing in uncultivated land or open fields. [From Latin *campester,* of a field, from *campus,* field.]

camp·fire (kămp′fīr′) *n.* **1.** An outdoor fire in a camp, used for cooking or warmth. **2.** A meeting held around such a fire.

Camp Fire Girl *n.* A member of an organization for girls aged 7 through 18 that strives to instill good values and character and teach practical skills. [From *Camp Fire Girls,* Inc.]

camp follower *n.* **1.** A civilian who follows a military unit from place to place, especially as a vendor of supplies or as a prostitute. **2.** One who follows but does not belong to a main body or group.

camp·ground (kămp′ground′) *n.* An area used for setting up a camp or holding a camp meeting.

cam·phene (kăm′fēn′) *n.* A colorless crystalline terpene, $C_{10}H_{16}$, used in the manufacture of synthetic camphor and insecticides. [CAMPH(OR) + –ENE.]

cam·phor (kăm′fər) *n.* An aromatic crystalline compound, $C_{10}H_{16}O$, obtained naturally from the wood or leaves of the camphor tree or synthesized and used as an insect repellent, in the manufacture of film, plastics, lacquers, and explosives, and in medicine chiefly in external preparations to relieve mild pain and itching. [Middle English *caumfre,* from Anglo-Norman, from Medieval Latin *camphora,* from Arabic *kāfūr,* possibly from Malay *kapur;* akin to Sanskrit *karpūraḥ.*] —**cam′phor·a′ceous** (kăm′fə-rā′shəs) *adj.* —**cam·phor′ic** (-fôr′ĭk, -fŏr′-) *adj.*

cam·phor·ate (kăm′fə-rāt′) *tr.v.* **-at·ed, -at·ing, -ates.** To treat or impregnate with camphor.

camphor oil *n.* The oil obtained by steam distillation from the wood of the camphor tree and used to produce natural camphor.

camphor tree *n.* An east Asian evergreen tree *(Cinnamomum camphora)* naturalized and cultivated as an ornamental in the southern United States, having aromatic wood and leathery leaves that are a source of camphor.

cam·phor·weed (kăm′fər-wēd′) *n.* Either of two eastern North American herbs *Heterotheca subaxillaris* or *Pluchea camphorata,* of the composite family, having numerous small flower heads.

Cam·pi·na Gran·de (kăm′pē-nə grăn′də, -dē, kän-pē′nə grän′də). A city of extreme eastern Brazil northwest of Recife. It is a commercial and financial center. Population, 222,102.

Cam·pi·nas (kăm-pē′nəs, kän-). A city of southeast Brazil north-northwest of São Paulo. It grew as the center of a coffee-producing region in the 19th century. Population, 566,627.

cam·pi·on (kăm′pē-ən) *n.* Any of several plants of the genera *Lychnis* and *Silene* native chiefly to the Northern Hemisphere and having variously colored flowers with notched or fringed petals. [Origin unknown.]

Cam·pi·on (kăm′pē-ən), **Thomas.** 1567–1620. English poet and composer of songs for voice and lute.

camp meeting *n.* An evangelistic gathering held in a tent or outdoors and often lasting several days.

cam·po (kăm′pō, käm′-) *n., pl.* **-pos.** A large grassy plain in South America, with scattered bushes and small trees. [Spanish, field, from Latin *campus.*]

Cam·po·bel·lo Island (kăm′pə-bĕl′ō). An island of southwest New Brunswick, Canada, off the coast of Maine. A popular resort area, the island became part of Canada in 1817.

Cam·po Gran·de (kăm′pō grăn′də, -dē, käɴ′pŏŏ gräɴ′də). A city of southwest Brazil west-northwest of São Paulo. It is a major processing and shipping center. Population, 282,857.

camp·o·ree (kăm′pə-rē′) *n.* An assembly or gathering of Boy Scouts or Girl Scouts on a local or district level. [Probably CAMP¹ + (JAMB)OREE.]

Cam·pos (kăm′pəs, käɴ′pŏŏs). A city of southeast Brazil on the Paraíba River northeast of Rio de Janeiro. It was founded in the 17th century. Population, 178,457.

camp robber *n.* See **gray jay.**

camp·site (kămp′sīt′) *n.* An area suitable or used for camping.

Camp Springs. A city of west-central Maryland, a suburb of Washington, D.C. Population, 16,118.

camp·stool (kămp′stōōl′) *n.* A light folding stool.

cam·pus (kăm′pəs) *n., pl.* **-pus·es.** The grounds of a school, college, university, or hospital. [Latin, field.]

cam·py·lo·bac·ter·o·sis (kăm′pə-lō-băk′tə-rō′sĭs) *n.* A gastrointestinal condition characterized by diarrhea, abdominal cramps, and fever, caused by eating raw meat or unpasteurized milk contaminated with *Campylobacter jejuni,* a bacterium that infects poultry, cattle, and sheep. [New Latin *Campylobacter,* genus name (Greek *kampulos,* curved + BACTER(IUM)) + –OSIS.]

cam·py·lot·ro·pous (kăm′pə-lŏt′rə-pəs) *adj. Botany.* Having an ovule partially inverted and curved such that the micropyle nearly meets the funiculus. [Greek *kampulos,* curved + –TROPOUS.]

Cam·ranh Bay or **Cam Ranh Bay** (kăm′răn′, käm′rän′). An inlet of the South China Sea in southeast Vietnam. Formerly a French naval base, it was the site of a large U.S. military installation during the Vietnam War.

cam·shaft (kăm′shăft′) *n.* An engine shaft fitted with a cam or cams.

Ca·mus (kä-mōō′, -mü′), **Albert.** 1913–1960. French writer and philosopher whose works, such as *The Stranger* (1942) and *The Plague* (1947), concern the absurdity of the human condition. He won the 1957 Nobel Prize for literature.

can¹ (kăn; kən *when unstressed*) Past tense *aux.v.* **could** (kŏŏd). **1.a.** Used to indicate physical or mental ability: *I can carry both suitcases. Can you remember the war?* **b.** Used to indicate possession of a specified power, right, or privilege: *The President can veto congressional bills.* **c.** Used to indicate possession of a specified capability or skill: *I can tune the harpsichord as well as play it.* **2.a.** Used to indicate possibility or probability: *I wonder if my long lost neighbor can still be alive. Such things can and do happen.* **b.** Used to indicate that which is permitted, as by conscience or feelings: *One can hardly blame you for being upset.* **c.** Used to indicate probability or possibility under the specified circumstances: *They can hardly have intended to do that.* **3.** *Usage Problem.* Used to request or grant permission: *Can I be excused?* [Middle English, first and third person singular present tense of *connen,* to know how, from Old English *cunnan.* See **gnō-** in Appendix.]

USAGE NOTE: Generations of grammarians and schoolteachers have insisted that *can* should be used only to express the capacity to do something, and that *may* must be used to express permission. Technically, correct usage therefore requires *The supervisor said that anyone who wants an extra day off may* (not *can*) *have one,* or *May* (not *can*) *I take another week to submit the application?* Only 21 percent of the Usage Panel accepts *can* in the latter sentence. But *can* has a long history of use by educated speakers to express permission, particularly in British English. What is more, the blurring of the line between *can* and *may* is socially and historically inevitable, since politeness often makes the use of *can* preferable in the "permission" sense. For example, the sentence *You can borrow my car if you like* is a more gracious offer than *You may borrow my car;* the first presumes the granting of permission, while the second makes a point of it. Still, it is understandable that insistence on the use of *may* should become a traditional schoolroom ritual, particularly in first-person requests such as *May I leave the room?* since it requires the pupil to distinguish explicitly between what is possible and what is allowed, a difference not always apparent to younger children. And even in later life, observance of the distinction is often advisable in the interests of clarity. Thus, the sentence *Students can take no more than three courses* allows the possibility that a student who is unusually capable may take more, whereas *Students may take no more than three courses* does not. • The use of *can* to express

camouflage
United States Army camouflage

campanile
Saint Mark's Square, Venice, Italy

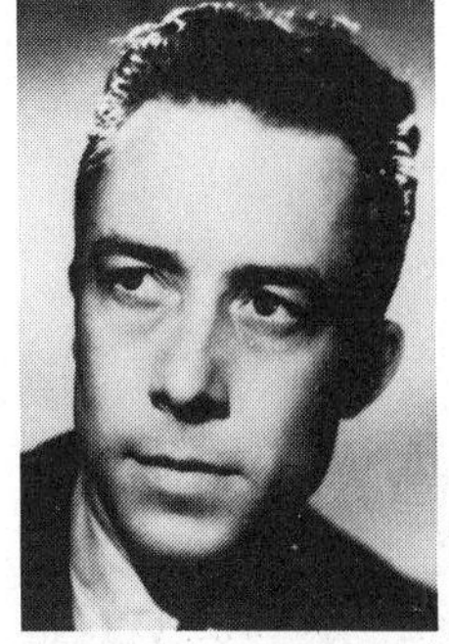

Albert Camus
Photographed in 1956

ă pat	oi boy
ā pay	ou out
âr care	ŏŏ took
ä father	ōō boot
ĕ pet	ŭ cut
ē be	ûr urge
ĭ pit	th thin
ī pie	*th* this
îr pier	hw which
ŏ pot	zh vision
ō toe	ə about, item
ô paw	♦ regionalism

Stress marks: ′ (primary); ′ (secondary), as in **dictionary** (dĭk′shə-nĕr′ē)

permission is better tolerated in negative questions, as in *Can't I have the car tonight?*, probably because the alternative contraction *mayn't* is felt to be awkward.

can² (kăn) *n.* **1.** A usually cylindrical metal container. **2.a.** An airtight container, usually made of tin-coated iron, in which foods or beverages are preserved. **b.** The contents of such a container. **3.** *Slang.* A jail or prison. **4.** *Slang.* A toilet or restroom. **5.** *Slang.* The buttocks. **—can** *tr.v.* **canned, can·ning, cans. 1.** To seal in an airtight container for future use; preserve: *canning peaches.* **2.** *Slang.* To make a recording of: *can the audience's applause for a TV comedy show.* **3.** *Slang.* To dismiss from employment or school. See Synonyms at **dismiss. 4.** *Slang.* To put a stop to; quit: *Let's can the chatter.* [Middle English *canne,* a water container, from Old English.] **—can′ner** *n.*

can. *abbr.* **1.a.** Canceled. **b.** Cancellation. **2.** Cannon. **3.** Canon. **4.** Canto.

Can. *abbr.* **1.** Canada. **2.** Canadian.

Ca·na (kā′nə). A village of northern Palestine near Nazareth. In the New Testament, Jesus performed his first miracle here, changing water into wine.

Ca·naan (kā′nən). An ancient region made up of Palestine or the part of it between the Jordan River and the Mediterranean Sea. In the Old Testament, it was referred to as the Promised Land.

Ca·naan·ite (kā′nə-nīt′) *n.* **1.** A member of a Semitic people inhabiting Canaan from late prehistoric times and who were conquered by the Israelites around 1,000 B.C. **2.** The Semitic language of the Canaanites. **—Canaanite** *adj.* Of or relating to ancient Canaan or its people, language, or culture.

Canada

Can·a·da (kăn′ə-də). *Abbr.* **Can.** A country of northern North America. Eastern Canada was settled by both English and French colonists and was ceded to England in 1763 after the Seven Years' War. The Dominion of Canada was formed in 1867 and extended to the western provinces in 1905; Newfoundland formally joined the federation in 1949. Ottawa is the capital and Montreal the largest city. Population, 23,343,181. **—Ca·na′di·an** (kə-nā′dē-ən) *adj. & n.*

Canada balsam *n.* A viscous, yellowish, transparent resin obtained from the balsam fir and used as a cement for glass lenses and for mounting specimens on microscopic slides.

Canada goose or **Canadian goose** *n.* A common wild goose *(Branta canadensis)* of North America, having grayish plumage, a black neck and head, and a white throat patch.

Canada goose
Branta canadensis

Canada jay *n.* See **gray jay.**

Canada thistle *n.* A perennial herb *(Cirsium arvense)* in the composite family, native to Europe and naturalized as a noxious weed in North America, having spiny-margined leaves and rose-purple or sometimes white flower heads.

Canadian bacon *n.* Cured rolled bacon from the loin of a pig.

Canadian Falls also **Horse·shoe Falls** (hôrs′sho͞o′, hôrsh′-). A section, about 48 m (158 ft) high, of Niagara Falls within Ontario, Canada.

Canadian French *n.* The French language as used in Canada.

Canadian goose *n.* Variant of **Canada goose.**

Canadian hemlock *n.* A coniferous evergreen monoecious tree *(Tsuga canadensis)* native from Nova Scotia to Alaska and valuable for its timber, as a pulpwood, for tanning, and as an ornamental.

Canadian River. A river rising in northeast New Mexico and flowing about 1,458 km (906 mi) eastward across the Texas Panhandle to the Arkansas River in eastern Oklahoma.

Canadian Shield. See **Laurentian Plateau.**

ca·nai·gre (kə-nī′grē) *n.* A perennial herb *(Rumex hymenosepalus)* native chiefly to southwest North America, having tannin-rich, tuberous roots formerly used for tanning and in herbal medicine. [Spanish.]

ca·naille (kə-nī′, -nāl′) *n.* **1.** The masses of the people; the proletariat. **2.** Rabble; riffraff. [French, from Italian *canaglia,* pack of dogs, rabble, from *cane,* dog, from Latin *canis.* See **kwon-** in Appendix.]

canal
Miraflores Locks on the Panama Canal, 1923

ca·nal (kə-năl′) *n.* **1.** An artificial waterway or artificially improved river used for travel, shipping, or irrigation. **2.** *Anatomy.* A tube, duct, or passageway. **3.** *Astronomy.* One of the faint, hazy markings resembling straight lines on early telescopic images of the surface of Mars. **—canal** *tr.v.* **-nalled, -nal·ling, -nals** or **-naled, -nal·ing, -nals. 1.** To dig an artificial waterway through: *canal an isthmus.* **2.** To provide with an artificial waterway or waterways. [Partly French, channel, and partly Middle English, tube (from Medieval Latin *canāle*), both from Latin *canālis,* tube, channel, probably from *canna,* small reed. See CANE.]

Ca·na·let·to (kăn′ə-lĕt′ō). Originally Giovanni Antonio Canal. 1697–1768. Italian painter noted for his detailed and precisely proportioned views of Venice.

can·a·lic·u·late (kăn′ə-lĭk′yə-lĭt, -lāt′) *adj.* Having one or more longitudinal grooves or channels. [Latin *canāliculātus,* from *canāliculus,* diminutive of *canālis,* channel. See CANAL.]

can·a·lic·u·lus (kăn′ə-lĭk′yə-ləs) *n., pl.* **-li** (-lī′). A small canal or duct in the body, such as the minute channels in compact bone. [Latin, diminutive of *canālis,* conduit. See CANAL.] **—can′a·lic′u·lar** (-lər) *adj.*

can·a·li·za·tion (kăn′ə-lĭ-zā′shən) *n.* **1.** The act or an instance of canalizing. **2.** A system of canals.

can·a·lize (kăn′ə-līz′) *tr.v.* **-lized, -liz·ing, -liz·es. 1.** To furnish with or convert into a canal or canals. **2.** To provide an outlet for; channel.

Ca·nal Zone (kə-năl′) also **Pan·a·ma Canal Zone** (păn′ə-mä′, -mô′). *Abbr.* **CZ, C.Z.** A strip of land, about 16 km (10 mi) wide, across the Isthmus of Panama. Formerly administered by the United States for the operation of the Panama Canal, it was turned over to Panama in 1979.

Can·an·dai·gua Lake (kăn′ən-dā′gwə). A glacial lake of west-central New York. One of the Finger Lakes, it is in a popular resort area.

can·a·pé (kăn′ə-pā′, -pē) *n.* A cracker or a small, thin piece of bread or toast spread with cheese, meat, or relish and served as an appetizer. [French, from *canapé,* couch, from Medieval Latin *canāpēum,* mosquito net. See CANOPY.]

ca·nard (kə-närd′) *n.* **1.** An unfounded or false, deliberately misleading story. **2.a.** A short, winglike control surface projecting from the fuselage of an aircraft, such as a space shuttle, mounted forward of the main wing and serving as a horizontal stabilizer. **b.** An aircraft whose horizontal stabilizing surfaces are forward of the main wing. [French, duck, canard, probably from the phrase *vendre un canard à moitié,* to half-sell a duck, to swindle, from Old French *quanart,* duck, from *caner,* to cackle, of imitative origin.]

ca·nar·y (kə-nâr′ē) *n., pl.* **-ies. 1.** A small finch *(Serinus canaria)* native to the Canary Islands that is greenish to yellow and has long been bred as a cage bird. **2.** *Slang.* **a.** A woman singer. **b.** An informer; a stool pigeon. **3.** A sweet white wine from the Canary Islands, similar to Madeira. **4.** A lively 16th-century court dance. **5.** *Color.* A light to moderate or vivid yellow. [French *canari,* from Spanish *canario,* of the Canary Islands, from *(Islas) Canarias,* Canary (Islands), from Late Latin *Canāriae (Īnsulae),* (islands) of dogs, from Latin *canārius,* pertaining to dogs, canine, from *canis,* dog. See **kwon-** in Appendix.]

ca·nar·y-bird flower (kə-nâr′ē-bûrd′) *n.* A Peruvian climbing plant *(Tropaeolum peregrinum)* cultivated for its showy, spurred yellow flowers. Also called *canary-bird vine.*

canary grass *n.* **1.** An annual Mediterranean grass *(Phalaris canariensis)* having grains used as food for caged birds, such as canaries. **2.** Any of several related grasses, such as reed canary grass.

Ca·nar·y Islands (kə-nâr′ē). A group of Spanish islands in the Atlantic Ocean off the northwest coast of Africa. The Canaries have been part of Spain since 1479 and are a major tourist center.

ca·nas·ta (kə-năs′tə) *n.* *Games.* A card game for two to six players, related to rummy and requiring two decks of cards. [Spanish, from *canasto,* basket, from Latin *canistrum.* See CANISTER.]

Ca·nav·er·al (kə-năv′ər-əl, -năv′rəl), **Cape.** Formerly (1963–1973) **Cape Ken·ne·dy** (kĕn′ĭ-dē). A sandy promontory extending into the Atlantic Ocean from a barrier island on the east-central coast of Florida. It is the site of NASA's Kennedy Manned Space Flight Center.

Can·ber·ra (kăn′bər-ə, -bĕr′ə). The capital of Australia, in the southeast part of the country. Settled in 1824, it replaced Melbourne as the capital in 1908. Population, 243,450.

canc. *abbr.* **1.** Canceled. **2.** Cancellation.

can·can (kăn′kăn′) *n.* An exuberant dance that originated in France, performed by women and marked by high kicking. [French.]

can·cel (kăn′səl) *v.* **-celed, -cel·ing, -cels** also **-celled, -cel·ling, -cels.** —*tr.* **1.** To cross out with lines or other markings. See Synonyms at **erase. 2.** To annul or invalidate. **3.** To mark or perforate (a postage stamp or check, for example) to indicate that it may not be used again. **4.** To equalize or make up for; offset: *Today's decline in stock price canceled out yesterday's gain.* **5.** *Mathematics.* **a.** To remove (a common factor) from the numerator and denominator of a fractional expression. **b.** To remove (a common factor or term) from both sides of an equation or inequality. **6.** *Printing.* To omit or delete. —*intr.* To neutralize one another; counterbalance: *two opposing forces that canceled out.* **—cancel** *n.* **1.** The act or an instance of canceling; a cancellation. **2.** *Printing.* **a.** Deletion of typed or printed matter. **b.** The matter deleted. **c.** A replacement for deleted matter. [Middle English *cancellen,* from Old French *canceller,* from Latin *cancellāre,* to cross out, from *cancellus,* lattice, diminutive of *cancer,* lattice.] **—can′cel·a·ble** *adj.* **—can′cel·er** *n.*

can·ce·la·tion (kăn′sə-lā′shən) *n.* Variant of **cancellation.**

can·cel·late (kăn-sĕl′ĭt, kăn′sə-lāt′) also **can·cel·lat·ed** (-lā′tĭd) *adj.* *Anatomy.* Cancellous. [Latin *cancellātus,* past participle of *cancellāre,* to make in a crisscross pattern. See CANCEL.]

can·cel·la·tion also **can·ce·la·tion** (kăn′sə-lā′shən) *n.* *Abbr.* **can., canc. 1.** The act or an instance of canceling. **2.** A mark or a perforation indicating canceling. **3.** Something canceled, especially a released accommodation or an unfilled appointment.

can·cel·lous (kăn-sĕl′əs, kăn′sə-ləs) *adj.* *Anatomy.* Having an open, latticed, or porous structure. Used especially of bone. [From Latin *cancellus,* lattice. See CANCEL.]

can·cer (kăn′sər) *n.* **1.a.** Any of various malignant neoplasms characterized by the proliferation of anaplastic cells that tend to invade surrounding tissue and metastasize to new body sites. **b.** The pathological condition characterized by such growths. **2.** A pernicious, spreading evil: *A cancer of bigotry spread through the community.* [Middle English. See CANKER.] **—can′cer·ous** (kăn′sər-əs) *adj.*

Can·cer (kăn′sər) *n.* **1.** A constellation in the Northern Hemisphere near Leo and Gemini. **2. a.** The fourth sign of the zodiac in astrology. **b.** One who is born under this sign. Also called *Crab.* [Middle English, from Latin. See CANKER.]

Can·cer·i·an (kăn-sĕr′ē-ən) *n.* One who is born under the sign of Cancer. **—Cancerian** *adj.*

can·croid (kăng′kroid′) *n.* See **squamous cell carcinoma.** **—cancroid** *adj.* **1.** Of or relating to squamous cell carcinoma. **2.** Resembling a crab. [Latin *cancer, cancr-;* see CANCER + –OID.]

Can·cún (kăn-ko͞on′, käng-). An island community of southeast Mexico off the northeast tip of the Yucatán Peninsula. It is a popular Caribbean resort. Population, 33,273.

can·del·a (kăn-dĕl′ə) *n. Abbr.* **cd** A unit of luminous intensity equal to 1/60 of the luminous intensity per square centimeter of a blackbody radiating at the temperature of solidification of platinum (2,046°K). Also called *candle.* See table at **measurement.** [Latin *candēla,* candle. See CANDLE.]

can·de·la·bra (kăn′dl-ä′brə, -ăb′rə, -ā′brə) *n.* A candelabrum. [From Latin *candēlābra,* pl. of *candēlābrum.* See CANDELABRUM.]

can·de·la·brum (kăn′dl-ä′brəm, -ăb′rəm, -ā′brəm) *n., pl.* **-bra** (-brə) or **-brums.** A large decorative candlestick having several arms or branches. [Latin *candēlābrum,* candlestick, from *candēla,* candle. See CANDLE.]

can·de·lil·la (kăn′dl-ē′ə) *n.* A shrubby spurge *(Euphorbia antisyphilitica)* native to southwest Texas and Mexico, having densely clustered, erect, essentially leafless stems that yield a multipurpose wax. [American Spanish, diminutive of Spanish *candela,* from Latin *candēla.* See CANDLE.]

can·dent (kăn′dənt) *adj.* Having a white-hot glow; incandescent. [Latin *candēns, candent-,* present participle of *candēre,* to shine. See **kand-** in Appendix.]

can·des·cence (kăn-dĕs′əns) *n.* The state of being white hot; incandescence. [From Latin *candēscēns, candēscent-,* present participle of *candēscere,* inchoative of *candēre,* to shine. See CANDID.] **—can·des′cent** *adj.* **—can·des′cent·ly** *adv.*

Can·di·a[1] (kăn′dē-ə). A name used by Italian colonizers (13th–17th century) for the island of Crete.

Can·di·a[2] (kăn′dē-ə). See **Iráklion.**

can·did (kăn′dĭd) *adj.* **1.** Free from prejudice; impartial. **2.** Characterized by openness and sincerity of expression; unreservedly straightforward: *In private, I gave them my candid opinion.* See Synonyms at **frank**[1]. **3.** Not posed or rehearsed: *a candid snapshot.* **—candid** *n.* An unposed informal photograph. [Latin *candidus,* glowing, white, pure, guileless, from *candēre,* to shine. See **kand-** in Appendix.] **—can′did·ly** *adv.* **—can′did·ness** *n.*

can·di·da (kăn′dĭ-də) *n.* Any of the pathogenic yeastlike imperfect fungi of the genus *Candida.* [Latin, feminine of *candidus,* white. See CANDID.]

can·di·date (kăn′dĭ-dāt′, -dĭt) *n.* **1.** A person who seeks or is nominated for an office, prize, or honor. **2.** One that seems likely to gain a certain position or come to a certain fate: *young actors who are candidates for stardom; a memorandum that is a good candidate for the trash can.* [Latin *candidātus,* clothed in white (from the white togas worn by Romans seeking office), candidate, from *candidus,* white. See CANDID.] **—can′di·da·cy** (-də-sē), **can′di·da·ture′** (-də-cho͝or′, -chər) *n.*

candid camera *n.* A small, easily operated camera with a fast lens for taking unposed or informal photographs.

can·di·di·a·sis (kăn′dĭ-dī′ə-sĭs) *n.* A fungous infection caused by a member of the genus *Candida,* especially *Candida albicans,* that can involve various parts of the body, such as the skin and mucous membranes. Also called *moniliasis.*

can·died (kăn′dēd) *adj.* Permeated, covered, encrusted, or cooked with sugar: *candied sweet potatoes.*

can·dle (kăn′dl) *n.* **1. a.** A solid, usually cylindrical mass of tallow, wax, or other fatty substance with an axially embedded wick that is burned to provide light. **b.** Something resembling this object in shape or use. **2.** *Abbr.* **c** *Physics.* **a.** An obsolete unit of luminous intensity, originally defined in terms of a wax candle with standard composition and equal to 1.02 candelas. Also called *international candle.* **b.** See **candela.** **—candle** *tr.v.* **-dled, -dling, -dles.** To examine (an egg) for freshness or fertility by holding it before a bright light. [Middle English *candel,* from Old English and from Anglo-Norman *candele,* both from Latin *candēla,* from *candēre,* to shine. See **kand-** in Appendix.] **—can′dler** *n.*

can·dle·ber·ry (kăn′dl-bĕr′ē) *n.* **1.** Any of certain bayberries, the wax myrtle, or the fruit of these plants. **2.** See **candlenut.**

can·dle·fish (kăn′dl-fĭsh′) *n., pl.* **candlefish** or **-fish·es.** An oily, edible fish *(Thaleichthys pacificus)* of northern Pacific waters, formerly dried and used as a torch by Native Americans. Also called *eulachon.*

can·dle·hold·er (kăn′dl-hōl′dər) *n.* A candlestick.

can·dle·light (kăn′dl-līt′) *n.* **1.** Illumination from a candle or candles. **2.** Dusk; twilight.

Can·dle·mas (kăn′dl-məs) *n.* **1.** A Christian feast commemorating the purification of the Virgin Mary and the presentation of the infant Jesus in the temple. **2.** February 2, the day on which this feast is observed. [Middle English *candelmasse,* from Old English *candelmæsse : candel,* candle; see CANDLE + *mæsse,* mass (from the blessing of candles at the feast); see MASS.]

can·dle·nut (kăn′dl-nŭt′) *n.* **1.** A tropical southeast Asian tree *(Aleurites moluccana)* bearing nutlike seeds that are used to make candles and yield a drying oil used in paints, varnishes, lacquer, and soft soap. **2.** The seed of this tree. Also called *candleberry.*

can·dle·pin (kăn′dl-pĭn′) *n. Sports.* **1.** A slender bowling pin used in a variation of the game of tenpins. **2.** Also **candlepins.** *(used with a sing. verb).* A bowling game using slender pins and a ball smaller than that used in tenpins.

can·dle·pow·er (kăn′dl-pou′ər) *n. Abbr.* **cp** Luminous intensity expressed in standard candles.

can·dle·snuff·er (kăn′dl-snŭf′ər) *n.* An implement with a bell-shaped cup and often a long, slender handle, used to extinguish the flame of a candle.

can·dle·stick (kăn′dl-stĭk′) *n.* A holder with a cup or spike for a candle.

can·dle·wick (kăn′dl-wĭk′) *n.* **1.** The wick of a candle. **2. a.** A soft, heavy cotton thread similar to that used to make wicks for candles. **b.** Embroidery made of tufts of this thread.

can·dle·wood (kăn′dl-wo͝od′) *n.* **1.** Any of several trees or shrubs yielding a usually resinous wood. **2.** The wood of such a plant, burned for light or fuel. **3.** The ocotillo.

can-do (kăn′do͞o′) *adj. Informal.* Marked by a willingness to tackle a job and get it done: *"the city's indomitable optimism and can-do spirit"* (Christian Science Monitor).

can·dor (kăn′dər) *n.* **1.** Frankness or sincerity of expression; openness. **2.** Freedom from prejudice; impartiality. [Middle English, from Old French, from Latin, from *candēre,* to shine. See **kand-** in Appendix.]

C & W or **C and W** *abbr.* Country and western.

can·dy (kăn′dē) *n., pl.* **-dies.** **1.** A rich, sweet confection made with sugar and often flavored or combined with fruits or nuts. **2.** A piece of such a confection. **—candy** *v.* **-died, -dy·ing, -dies.** *—tr.* **1.** To reduce to sugar crystals. **2.** To cook, preserve, saturate, or coat with sugar or syrup. **3.** To make pleasant or agreeable; sweeten. *—intr.* **1.** To become crystallized into sugar. **2.** To become coated with sugar or syrup. [Middle English *candi,* crystallized cane sugar, short for *sugre-candi,* translation of Old French *sucre candi* and Old Italian *zucchero candi,* both from Arabic *sukkar qandīy : sukkar,* sugar; see SUGAR + *qandīy,* candied (from *qand,* cane sugar, probably from Dravidian *kaṇṭu,* lump).]

can·dy-ass or **candy ass** (kăn′dē-ăs′) *n. Vulgar Slang.* A sissy; a wimp. **—can′dy-ass′** *adj.*

candy striper *n.* A volunteer worker in a hospital. [From the resemblance of the volunteer's red and white striped uniform to a candy cane.]

can·dy·tuft (kăn′dē-tŭft′) *n.* Any of several plants of the genus *Iberis* in the mustard family, native to Europe and the Mediterranean region and widely cultivated for their showy clusters of white, pink, crimson, or purple flowers. [Obsolete *Candy* (variant of CANDIA[1]) + TUFT.]

cane (kān) *n.* **1. a.** A slender, strong but often flexible stem, as of certain bamboos, reeds, or rattans. **b.** A plant having such a stem. **c.** Such stems or strips of such stems used for wickerwork or baskets. **2.** A bamboo *(Arundinaria gigantea)* native to the southeast United States, having long stiff stems and often forming canebrakes. **3.** The stem of a raspberry, blackberry, certain roses, or similar plants. **4.** Sugar cane. **5.** A stick used as an aid in walking or carried as an accessory. **6.** A rod used for flogging. **—cane** *tr.v.* **caned, can·ing, canes.** **1.** To make, supply, or repair with flexible woody material. **2.** To hit or beat with a rod. [Middle English, from Old French, from Latin *canna,* small reed, from Greek *kanna,* of Semitic origin.] **—can′er** *n.*

cane·brake (kān′brāk′) *n.* A dense thicket of cane.

ca·nes·cent (kə-nĕs′ənt) *adj.* **1.** *Biology.* Covered with short, fine whitish or grayish hairs or down; hoary. **2.** Turning white or grayish. [Latin *cānēscēns, cānēscent-,* present participle of *cānēscere,* inchoative of *cānēre,* to be white, from *cānus,* white. See **kas-** in Appendix.] **—ca·nes′cence** *n.*

cane sugar *n.* Sucrose obtained from sugar cane.

Ca·nes Ve·nat·i·ci (kā′nēz vĭ-năt′ĭ-sī′) *n.* A constellation in the Northern Hemisphere near Ursa Major and Boötes, under the handle of the Big Dipper. [Latin *canēs,* pl. of *canis* + *vēnāticī,* pl. of *vēnāticus,* hunting.]

Ca·net·ti (kä-nĕt′ē), **Elias.** Born 1905. Bulgarian-born writer whose works, all written in German, include a novel, *The Tower of Babel* (1935), and *Crowds and Power* (1960), a study of mass psychology. He won the 1981 Nobel Prize for literature.

can·field (kăn′fēld′) *n. Games.* A form of solitaire. [After Richard Albert Canfield (1855–1914), American gambler.]

cangue (kăng) *n.* A heavy wooden yoke borne on the shoulders and enclosing the neck and arms, formerly used in China for punishing petty criminals. [French, from Portuguese *canga.*]

Can·i·a·pis·cau also **Kan·i·a·pis·kau** (kăn′ē-ə-pĭs′kō, -kou). A river of northern Quebec, Canada, rising in **Lake Can-**

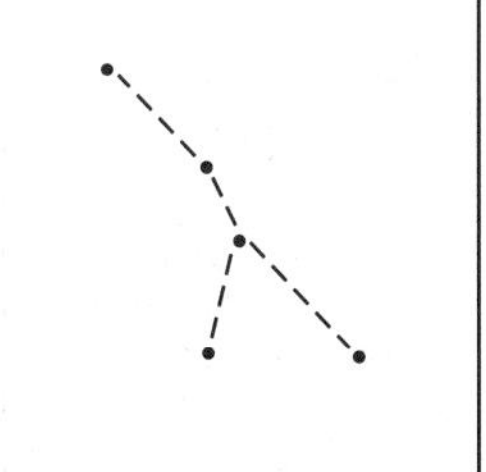
Cancer

candelabrum
Early 19th-century French candelabra

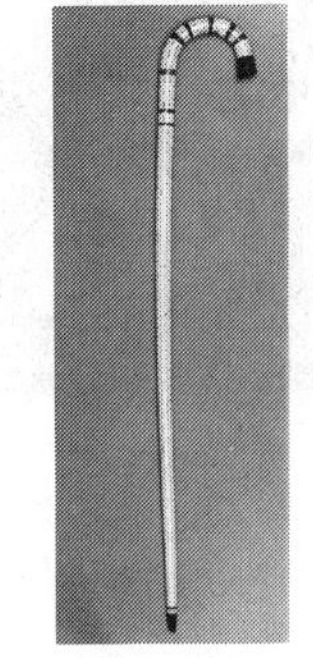
cane
Made of shark vertebrae

ă pat	oi boy
ā pay	ou out
âr care	o͝o took
ä father	o͞o boot
ĕ pet	ŭ cut
ē be	ûr urge
ĭ pit	th thin
ī pie	*th* this
îr pier	hw which
ŏ pot	zh vision
ō toe	ə about, item
ô paw	♦ regionalism

Stress marks: **′** (primary); ′ (secondary), as in **dictionary** (dĭk′shə-nĕr′ē)

iapiscau (or **Lake Kaniapiskau**) and flowing about 925 km (575 mi) generally northward to the Larch River.

ca·nic·u·lar (kə-nĭk′yə-lər) *adj.* **1.** Of or relating to Sirius or Procyon. **2.** Of or relating to the dog days. [Late Latin *canīculāris,* of Sirius, from Latin *Canīcula,* Sirius, diminutive of *canis,* dog. See **kwon-** in Appendix.]

ca·nid (kăn′ĭd, kā′nĭd) *n.* Any of various widely distributed carnivorous mammals of the family Canidae, which includes the foxes, wolves, dogs, jackals, and coyotes. [From New Latin *Canidae,* from *Canis,* type genus (from Latin. See CANINE).]

ca·nine (kā′nīn) *adj.* **1.** Of, relating to, or characteristic of the canids. **2.** Of, relating to, or being one of the pointed conical teeth located between the incisors and the first bicuspids. **—canine** *n.* **1.** An animal of the family Canidae, especially a dog. **2.** One of the pointed, conical teeth located between the incisors and the first bicuspids. In this sense, also called *cuspid.* [Latin *canīnus,* from *canis,* dog. See **kwon-** in Appendix.]

canine distemper *n.* See **distemper**[1] (sense 1a).

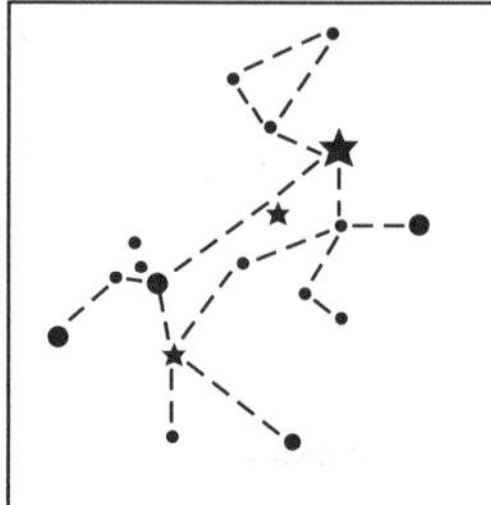

Canis Major

Ca·nis Ma·jor (kā′nĭs mā′jər, kăn′ĭs) *n.* A constellation in the Southern Hemisphere near Puppis and Lepus, containing the star Sirius. [Latin *canis,* dog + *maior,* larger.]

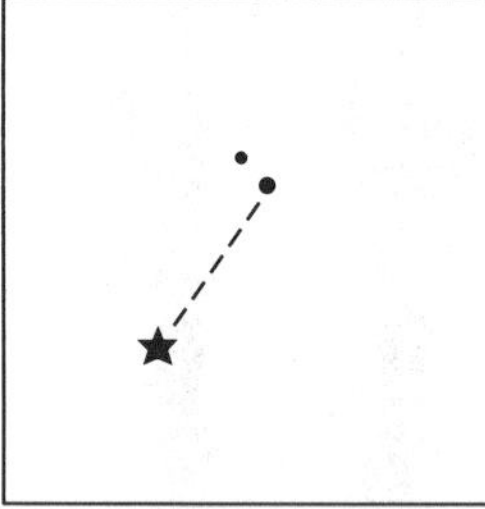

Canis Minor

Canis Mi·nor (mī′nər) *n.* A constellation in the equatorial region of the Southern Hemisphere near Hydra and Monoceros, containing the star Procyon. [Latin *canis,* dog + *minor,* smaller.]

can·is·tel (kăn′ĭ-stĕl′) *n.* **1.** A tree *(Pouteria campechiana),* native to Mexico, Central America, and the Caribbean and having very sweet oval fruit with a musky odor. **2.** The fruit of this tree. Also called *eggfruit.* [American Spanish.]

can·is·ter (kăn′ĭ-stər) *n.* **1.** A box or can of thin metal or plastic used for holding dry cooking ingredients, such as flour, sugar, or tea. **2.** A metallic cylinder packed with shot that are scattered when the cylinder is fired; case shot. **3.** The part of a gas mask that contains the filter for removing toxic agents from the air. [Latin *canistrum,* basket, from Greek *kanastron,* from *kanna,* reed. See CANE.]

can·ker (kăng′kər) *n.* **1.** Ulceration of the mouth and lips. **2.** An inflammation or infection of the ear and auditory canal, especially in dogs and cats. **3.** A condition in horses similar to but more advanced than thrush. **4. a.** A localized diseased or necrotic area on a plant part, especially on a trunk, branch, or twig of a woody plant, usually caused by fungi or bacteria. **b.** Any of several diseases of plants characterized by the presence of such lesions. **5.** A source of spreading corruption or decay. **—canker** *v.* **-kered, -ker·ing, -kers.** *—tr.* **1.** To attack or infect with canker. **2.** To infect with corruption or decay. *—intr.* To become infected with or as if with canker. [Middle English, from Old English *cancer* and from Old French *cancre,* both from Latin *cancer.* See **kar-** in Appendix.]

canker brake *n.* See **Christmas fern.**

canoe

can·ker·ous (kăng′kər-əs) *adj.* **1.** Marked by or infected with canker; ulcerous. **2.** Causing canker; ulcerating.

can·ker·root (kăng′kər-ro͞ot′, -ro͝ot′) *n.* The goldthread.

canker sore *n.* A small, painful ulcer or sore, usually of the mouth.

can·ker·worm (kăng′kər-wûrm′) *n.* The larva of either of two moths *(Paleacrita vernata* or *Alsophila pometaria),* destructive to fruit and shade trees.

can·na (kăn′ə) *n.* Any of various perennial tropical herbs of the genus *Canna,* having clusters of large, showy flowers and including an edible variety. [Latin *canna,* cane. See CANE.]

can·na·bi·di·ol (kăn′ə-bĭ-dī′ôl′, -ōl′, -ŏl′) *n.* A chemical constituent of cannabis, $C_{21}H_{28}(OH)_2$. [CANNABI(S) + DI-[1] + -OL[1].]

can·na·bin (kăn′ə-bĭn) *n.* A resinous material extracted from cannabis. [CANNAB(IS) + -IN.]

can·na·bis (kăn′ə-bĭs) *n.* **1.** A tall, annual dioecious plant *(Cannabis sativa),* native to central Asia and having alternate, palmately divided leaves and tough bast fibers. **2.** Any of several mildly euphoriant, intoxicating hallucinogenic drugs, such as ganja, hashish, or marijuana, prepared from various parts of this plant. [Latin, from Greek *kannabis.*] **—can′na·bic** (-bĭk) *adj.*

Can·nae (kăn′ē). An ancient town of southeast Italy where Carthaginians under Hannibal defeated the Romans in 216 B.C.

canned (kănd) *adj.* **1.** Preserved and sealed in a can or jar. **2.** *Informal.* Recorded or taped for repeated use on television or radio: *canned laughter.* **3.** *Informal.* **a.** Used repeatedly with little or no change: *a canned speech.* **b.** Totally unoriginal; devoid of individuality: *"Most* [soundtrack albums] *contain homogenized dance tracks that provide little more than canned excitement"* (Boston Globe).

Canned Heat (kănd). A trademark used for solid alcohol or paraffin fuel that is packed in small cans and used to heat food.

can·nel (kăn′əl) *n.* A bituminous coal that burns brightly with much smoke. [Perhaps short for *cannel coal,* dialectal variant of *candle coal* (from its bright flame).]

can·nel·lo·ni (kăn′ə-lō′nē) *n.* Large-sized tubes of pasta stuffed with meat or cheese and baked in a tomato or cream sauce. [Italian, plural of *cannellone,* tubular soup noodle, from *cannello,* small tube, diminutive of *canna,* reed, from Latin. See CANE.]

can·ne·lure (kăn′ə-lo͝or′) *n.* A groove around the cylinder of a bullet. [French, alteration of *cannelature,* from Old Italian *cannellatura,* from *cannello,* small tube. See CANNELLONI.]

can·ner·y (kăn′ə-rē) *n., pl.* **-ies.** A factory where fish, vegetables, or other foods are canned.

Cannes (kăn, kănz, kän). A city of southeast France on the Mediterranean Sea near Nice. It is a fashionable resort and the site of an annual international film festival. Population, 72,259.

can·ni·bal (kăn′ə-bəl) *n.* **1.** A person who eats the flesh of other human beings. **2.** An animal that feeds on others of its own kind. [From Spanish *Caníbalis,* name (as recorded by Christopher Columbus) of the man-eating Caribs of Cuba and Haiti, variant of *caríbalis,* from Arawak *caniba, carib,* an ethnic name.] **—can′ni·bal·ism** *n.* **—can′ni·bal·is′tic** *adj.*

can·ni·bal·ize (kăn′ə-bə-līz′) *tr.v.* **-ized, -iz·ing, -iz·es. 1.** To remove serviceable parts from (damaged airplanes, for example) for use in the repair of other equipment of the same kind. **2.** To deprive of vital elements or resources, such as personnel, equipment, or funding, for use elsewhere: *"It becomes necessary to cannibalize unsuccessful projects to fund those which can proceed"* (Daily Report for Executives). **3.** To draw on as a major source: *"cannibalizes the lives of his wife and friends for his second-rate novels"* (Washington Post). **—can′ni·bal·i·za′tion** (-bə-lĭ-zā′shən) *n.*

can·ni·kin (kăn′ĭ-kĭn) *n.* **1.** A small can or cup. **2.** A small wooden bucket. [Dutch *kanneken* (from Middle Dutch *cannekijn,* diminutive of *canne,* can) and Flemish *cannikin,* diminutive of *cann,* can.]

Can·ning (kăn′ĭng), Earl **Charles John.** 1812–1862. British colonial administrator who was governor-general (1856–1858) and first viceroy (1858–1862) of India.

Canning, George. 1770–1827. British politician who served as foreign secretary (1807–1809 and 1822–1827) and prime minister (1827).

Can·nock (kăn′ək). An urban district of west-central England north-northwest of Birmingham. It is the center of a mining area based at **Cannock Chase,** a nearby moorland. Population, 84,900.

can·no·li (kə-nō′lē, kă-) *n.* A fried pastry roll with a sweet, creamy filling. [Italian, pl. of *cannolo,* tube, diminutive of *canna,* reed. See CANNELLONI.]

can·non (kăn′ən) *n., pl.* **cannon** or **-nons.** *Abbr.* **can. 1.** A large, mounted weapon that fires heavy projectiles. Cannon include guns, howitzers, and mortars. **2.** The loop at the top of a bell by which it is hung. **3.** A round bit for a horse. **4.** *Zoology.* The section of the lower leg in some hoofed mammals between the hock or knee and the fetlock, containing the cannon bone. **5.** *Chiefly British.* A carom made in billiards. **—cannon** *v.* **-noned, -non·ing, -nons.** *—tr.* **1.** To bombard with cannon. **2.** *Chiefly British.* To cause to carom in billiards. *—intr.* **1.** To fire cannon. **2.** *Chiefly British.* To make a carom in billiards. [Middle English *canon,* from Old French, from Old Italian *cannone,* augmentative of *canna,* tube, from Latin, reed. See CANE.]

Can·non (kăn′ən), **Annie Jump.** 1863–1941. American astronomer noted for her work on classifying stellar spectra.

Cannon, Joseph Gurney. Known as "Uncle Joe." 1836–1926. American politician who as Republican speaker of the U.S. House of Representatives (1903–1911) was known for his strongly partisan and autocratic use of authority.

can·non·ade (kăn′ə-nād′) *v.* **-ad·ed, -ad·ing, -ades.** *—tr.* To assault with heavy artillery fire. *—intr.* To deliver heavy artillery fire. **—cannonade** *n.* **1.** An extended, usually heavy discharge of artillery. **2.** A harsh verbal or physical attack. [From French *canonade,* discharge of artillery, from Italian *cannonata,* from *cannone,* cannon, from Old Italian. See CANNON.]

can·non·ball also **cannon ball** (kăn′ən-bôl′) *—n.* **1.** A round projectile fired from a cannon. **2.** A jump into water made with the arms grasping the upraised knees. **3.** Something, such as a fast train, moving with great speed. **4.** *Sports.* A fast low serve in tennis. *—intr.v.* **-balled, -ball·ing, -balls. 1.** To travel with great speed. **2.** To jump into water while grasping one's upraised knees with one's arms.

cannonball tree *n.* A South American tree *(Couroupita guianensis)* bearing globose, woody fruits on its trunk and main branches. The hard shells of the fruits are used to make containers and utensils.

cannon bone *n.* A supporting bone of the leg in some hoofed mammals, analogous to the metacarpus of the hand or the metatarsus of the foot in human beings.

can·non·eer (kăn′ə-nîr′) *n.* A soldier in the artillery; a gunner.

cannon fodder *n.* Soldiers, sailors, or other military personnel regarded as likely to be killed or wounded in combat.

can·non·ry (kăn′ən-rē) *n., pl.* **-ries. 1.** A battery of cannons; artillery. **2.** Artillery fire.

can·not (kăn′ŏt, kə-nŏt′, kă-) *aux.v.* The negative form of **can**[1].

USAGE NOTE: The idiomatic phrase *cannot but* has sometimes been criticized as a double negative, perhaps because it has been confused with *can but.* The *but* of *cannot but,* however, means "except," as it does in phrases such as *no one but,* while the *but* of *can but* has the sense *only,* as it does in the sentence *We had but a single bullet left.* Both *cannot but* and *can but* are established as standard expressions. • The construction *cannot help* is used with a present participle to roughly the same effect as *cannot but* in a sentence such as *We cannot help admiring his courage.* But this

ă pat	oi boy
ā pay	ou out
âr care	o͝o took
ä father	o͞o boot
ĕ pet	ŭ cut
ē be	ûr urge
ĭ pit	th thin
ī pie	*th* this
îr pier	hw which
ŏ pot	zh vision
ō toe	ə about, item
ô paw	♦ regionalism

Stress marks: **′** (primary); ′ (secondary), as in **dictionary** (dĭk′shə-nĕr′ē)

construction is generally restricted to contexts in which a person is unable to affect an outcome that would normally be under his or her control. It would be more precise to say *With all the public interest in the affair, the book cannot but attract the attention of reviewers* (or . . . *can but gain* . . .) than to say *the book cannot help attracting the attention of reviewers,* which suggests that the book might have had a say in the matter. • The construction *cannot help but* probably arose as a blend of *cannot help* and *cannot but;* it has the meaning of the first and the syntax of the second: *We cannot help but admire his courage.* The construction has sometimes been criticized as a redundancy, but it is by now an established idiom with reputable precedent on its side. • The expression *cannot* (or *can't*) *seem to* has occasionally been criticized as illogical, and so it is. *Brian can't seem to get angry* does not mean "Brian is incapable of appearing to get angry," as its syntax would seem to dictate; rather, it means "Brian appears to be unable to get angry." But the idiom serves a useful purpose, since the syntax of English does not allow a logical equivalent like *Brian seems to cannot* . . . , and the *cannot seem to* construction is so widely used that it would be pedantic to object to it. See Usage Notes at **but, care, help.**

---

can·nu·la also **can·u·la** (kăn′yə-lə) *n., pl.* **-las** or **-lae** (-lē′). A flexible tube, usually containing a trocar at one end, that is inserted into a bodily cavity, duct, or vessel to drain fluid or administer a substance such as a medication. [Latin, diminutive of *canna,* reed. See CANE.]

can·nu·lar also **can·u·lar** (kăn′yə-lər) *adj.* Of, relating to, or resembling a tube; tubular.

can·nu·late also **can·u·late** (kăn′yə-lāt′) *—tr.v.* **-lat·ed, -lat·ing, -lates.** To insert a cannula into (a bodily cavity, duct, or vessel), as for the drainage of fluid or the administration of medication. *—adj.* Tubular; hollow. **—can′nu·la′tion** *n.*

can·ny (kăn′ē) *adj.* **-ni·er, -ni·est. 1.** Careful and shrewd, especially where one's own interests are concerned. **2.** Cautious in spending money; frugal. **3.** *Scots.* **a.** Steady, restrained, and gentle. **b.** Snug and quiet. [From CAN[1].] **—can′ni·ly** *adv.* **—can′ni·ness** *n.*

Ca·no·as (kə-nō′əs, kä-nô′äs). A city of southern Brazil, a suburb of Pôrto Alegre. Population, 213,999.

ca·noe (kə-no͞o′) *Nautical. n.* A light, slender boat that has pointed ends and is propelled by paddles. **—canoe** *v.* **-noed, -noe·ing, -noes.** *—tr.* To carry or send by canoe. *—intr.* To travel in or propel a canoe. [French *canoe* and Spanish *canoa* (French, from Spanish), of Cariban origin.] **—ca·noe′ist** *n.*

canoe birch *n.* See **paper birch.**

can of worms *n., pl.* **cans of worms.** *Informal.* A source of unforeseen and troublesome complexity.

ca·no·la (kə-nō′lə) *n.* A rapeseed oil that is very low in erucic acid content. [Origin unknown.]

can·on[1] (kăn′ən) *n. Abbr.* **can. 1.** An ecclesiastical law or code of laws established by a church council. **2.** A secular law, rule, or code of law. **3. a.** An established principle: *the canons of polite society.* **b.** A basis for judgment; a standard or criterion. **4.** The books of the Bible officially accepted as Holy Scripture. **5.** The works of a writer that have been accepted as authentic: *the entire Sherlock Holmes canon.* **6. Canon.** The part of the Mass beginning after the Preface and Sanctus and ending just before the Lord's Prayer. **7.** The calendar of saints accepted by the Roman Catholic Church. **8.** *Music.* A composition or passage in which the same melody is repeated by one or more voices, overlapping in time in the same or a related key. [Middle English *canoun,* from Old English *canon* and from Old French, both from Latin *canōn,* rule, from Greek *kanōn,* measuring rod, rule.]

can·on[2] (kăn′ən) *n.* **1.** A member of a chapter of priests serving in a cathedral or collegiate church. **2.** A member of certain religious communities living under a common rule and bound by vows. [Middle English *canoun,* from Norman French *canun,* from Late Latin *canōnicus,* one living under a rule, from *canōn,* rule. See CANON[1].]

ca·ñon (kăn′yən) *n.* Variant of **canyon.**

can·on·ess (kăn′ə-nĭs) *n.* A member of a religious community of women living under a common rule but not bound by vows.

ca·non·i·cal (kə-nŏn′ĭ-kəl) also **ca·non·ic** (-ĭk) *adj.* **1.** Of, relating to, or required by canon law. **2.** Of or appearing in the biblical canon. **3.** Conforming to orthodox rules, as of procedure. **4.** Of or belonging to a cathedral chapter. **5.** *Music.* Having the form of a canon. **—ca·non′i·cal·ly** *adv.* **—can′on·ic′i·ty** (kăn′ə-nĭs′ĭ-tē) *n.*

canonical hours *pl.n. Ecclesiastical.* **a.** The times of day at which canon law prescribes certain prayers to be said. These times are matins with lauds, prime, tierce, sext, nones, vespers, and complin. **b.** The prayers said at these times.

ca·non·i·cals (kə-nŏn′ĭ-kəlz) *pl.n.* The dress prescribed by canon for officiating clergy.

can·on·ist (kăn′ə-nĭst) *n.* A person specializing in canon law. **—can′on·is′tic, can′on·is′ti·cal** *adj.*

can·on·ize (kăn′ə-nīz′) *tr.v.* **-ized, -iz·ing, -iz·es. 1.** To declare (a deceased person) to be a saint and entitled to be fully honored as such. **2.** To include in the biblical canon. **3.** To approve as being within canon law. **4.** To treat as sacred; glorify. **—can′on·i·za′tion** (-ĭ-zā′shən) *n.* **—can′on·iz′er** *n.*

canon law *n.* The body of officially established rules governing the faith and practice of the members of a Christian church.

can·on·ry (kăn′ən-rē) *n., pl.* **-ries. 1.** The office or dignity of a canon. **2.** Canons considered as a group.

ca·noo·dle (kə-no͞od′l) *v.* **-dled, -dling, -dles.** *Informal. —intr.* To engage in caressing, petting, or lovemaking. *—tr.* To win over or convince by cajoling or flattering; wheedle: *"his matchless ability to charm, bamboozle, or canoodle most of his political associates"* (Timothy Garton Ash). [Of unknown origin; akin to English dialectal *canoodle,* donkey, fool, one who is foolish in love.]

Ca·no·pic or **ca·no·pic** (kə-nō′pĭk, -nŏp′ĭk) *adj.* Relating to or being an ancient Egyptian vase, urn, or jar used to hold the viscera of an embalmed body. [After CANOPUS[1].]

Ca·no·pus[1] (kə-nō′pəs). An ancient city of northern Egypt east of Alexandria. It was the site of a great temple honoring Serapis.

Ca·no·pus[2] (kə-nō′pəs) *n.* A star, 650 light-years from Earth, in the constellation Carina. It is the second-brightest star in the sky. [Latin, from Greek *kanōpos,* perhaps of Egyptian origin.]

can·o·py (kăn′ə-pē) *n., pl.* **-pies. 1.** A covering, usually of cloth, suspended over a throne or bed or held aloft on poles above an eminent person or a sacred object. **2.** *Architecture.* An ornamental, rooflike projection over a niche, an altar, or a tomb. **3.** A protective rooflike covering, often of canvas, mounted on a frame over a walkway or door. **4.** A high, overarching covering, such as the sky: *"I just look up at the stars and let the vastness of that black and twinkling canopy fill my soul"* (Margaret Mason). **5.** The uppermost layer in a forest, formed by the crowns of the trees. Also called *crown canopy.* **6.** The transparent enclosure over the cockpit of an aircraft. **7.** The part of a parachute that opens up to catch the air. **—canopy** *tr.v.* **-pied, -py·ing, -pies.** To cover with or as if with a canopy. [Middle English *canape,* from Medieval Latin *canapēum,* mosquito net, from Latin *cōnōpēum,* from Greek *kōnōpeion,* bed with mosquito netting, from *kōnōps,* mosquito.]

ca·no·rous (kə-nôr′əs, -nōr′-, kăn′ər-əs) *adj.* Richly melodious; tuneful: *"Edward R. Murrow's canorous broadcasts of the blitz of London"* (Newsweek). [From Latin *canōrus,* from *canor,* tune, from *canere,* to sing. See **kan-** in Appendix.] **—ca·no′rous·ly** *adv.* **—ca·no′rous·ness** *n.*

Ca·no·va (kə-nō′və), **Antonio.** 1757–1822. Italian sculptor who was an important figure in the development of neoclassicism.

Can·so (kăn′sō), **Strait of** or **Gut of.** A narrow channel between Cape Breton Island and the northeast mainland of Nova Scotia, Canada.

canst (kănst) *aux.v. Archaic.* A second person singular present tense of **can**[1].

cant[1] (kănt) *n.* **1.** Angular deviation from a vertical or horizontal plane or surface; an inclination or a slope. **2.** A slanted or oblique surface. **3. a.** A thrust or motion that tilts something. **b.** The tilt caused by such a thrust or motion. **4.** An outer corner, as of a building. **—cant** *v.* **cant·ed, cant·ing, cants.** *—tr.* **1.** To set at an oblique angle; tilt. **2.** To give a slanting edge to; bevel. **3.** To change the direction of suddenly. *—intr.* **1.** To lean to one side; slant. **2.** To take an oblique direction or course; swing around, as a ship. [Middle English, side, from Old North French, from Vulgar Latin **cantus,* corner, from Latin *canthus,* rim of wheel, tire, of Celtic origin.]

cant[2] (kănt) *n.* **1.** Monotonous talk filled with platitudes. **2.** Hypocritically pious language. **3.** The special vocabulary peculiar to the members of an underworld group; argot. **4.** Whining speech, such as that used by beggars. **5.** The special terminology understood among the members of a profession, discipline, or class but obscure to the general population; jargon. See Synonyms at **dialect. —cant** *intr.v.* **cant·ed, cant·ing, cants. 1.** To speak tediously or sententiously; moralize. **2.** To speak in argot or jargon. **3.** To speak in a whining, pleading tone. [Anglo-Norman *cant,* song, singing, from *canter,* to sing, from Latin *cantāre.* See **kan-** in Appendix.] **—cant′ing·ly** *adv.* **—cant′ing·ness** *n.*

Cant. *abbr. Bible.* Canticle of Canticles.

can't (kănt). Cannot.

can·ta·bi·le (kän-tä′bĭ-lā′) *Music. adv. & adj.* In a smooth, lyrical, flowing style. Used chiefly as a direction. **—cantabile** *n.* A cantabile passage or movement. [Italian, from Late Latin *cantābilis,* worthy to be sung, from Latin *cantāre,* to sing. See **kan-** in Appendix.]

Can·ta·bri·an Mountains (kăn-tā′brē-ən). A range of northern Spain extending about 483 km (300 mi) along the coast of the Bay of Biscay from the Pyrenees to Cape Finisterre. It rises to 2,649.8 m (8,688 ft) at Torre de Cerredo.

Can·ta·brig·i·an (kăn′tə-brĭj′ē-ən) *adj.* **1.** Of or relating to Cambridge, England, or Cambridge, Massachusetts. **2.** Of or relating to Cambridge University. **—Cantabrigian** *n.* **1.** A native or resident of Cambridge, England, or Cambridge, Massachusetts. **2.** A student or graduate of Cambridge University. [From Medieval Latin *Cantabrigia,* Cambridge, England.]

can·ta·la (kăn-tä′lə) *n.* **1.** A species of agave *(Agave cantula)* cultivated chiefly in warm regions of the Old World for its leaf fibers. **2.** The fiber of this plant, used for twine, rope, and nets. [Origin unknown.]

can·ta·loupe also **can·ta·loup** (kăn′tl-ōp′) *n.* **1.** A variety of melon *(Cucumis melo* var. *reticulatus)* having a tan rind with netlike ridges and a sweet, fragrant orange flesh. **2.** Any of several other related or similar melons. [French *cantaloup,* perhaps

canopy
Top: Early 19th-century four-poster bed
Bottom: At an Israeli wedding

cantaloupe
Cucumis melo

from Italian *cantalupo* (from *Cantalupo,* a former papal villa near Rome) or from *Cantaloup,* a village of southern France.]

can·tan·ker·ous (kăn-tăng′kər-əs) *adj.* **1.** Ill-tempered and quarrelsome; disagreeable. **2.** Difficult to handle: *"had to use liquid helium, which is supercold, costly and cantankerous"* (Boston Globe). [Perhaps from Middle English *contek,* dissension (influenced by words such as *rancorous, cankerous*), from Anglo-Norman *contec,* possibly from Latin *contāctus,* past participle of *contingere,* to touch. See CONTACT.] **—can·tan′ker·ous·ly** *adv.* **—can·tan′ker·ous·ness** *n.*

can·ta·ta (kən-tä′tə) *n. Music.* A vocal and instrumental piece composed of choruses, solos, and recitatives. [Italian *(aria) cantata,* sung (aria), feminine past participle of *cantare,* to sing, from Latin *cantāre.* See **kan-** in Appendix.]

can·teen (kăn-tēn′) *n.* **1.a.** A snack bar or small cafeteria, as on a military installation. **b.** A bar or small general store formerly established for the patronage of soldiers. **2.** A recreation hall or social club where refreshments are available. **3.** A temporary or mobile eating place, especially one set up in an emergency. **4.** A flask for carrying drinking water, as on a hike. **5.a.** A box with compartments for carrying cooking gear and eating utensils. **b.** A soldier's mess kit. **6.** *Chiefly British.* A box used to store silverware. [French *cantine,* from Italian *cantina,* wine cellar.]

can·ter (kăn′tər) *n.* A smooth gait, especially of a horse, that is slower than a gallop but faster than a trot. **—canter** *v.* **-tered, -ter·ing, -ters.** *—intr.* **1.** To ride a horse at a canter. **2.** To go or move at a canter. *—tr.* To cause (a horse) to go at a canter. [Ultimately from phrases such as *Canterbury gallop,* after CANTERBURY, England, toward which pilgrims rode at an easy pace.]

WORD HISTORY: Most of those who have majored in English literature, and many more besides, know that Chaucer's *Canterbury Tales* were told by a group of pilgrims on their way to Canterbury to visit the shrine of England's famous martyr Thomas à Becket. Many pilgrims other than Chaucer's visited Canterbury on horse, and phrases such as *Canterbury gallop, Canterbury pace,* and *Canterbury trot* described the easy gait at which they rode to their destination. The first recorded instance of one of these phrases, *Canterbury pace,* is found in a work published before 1636. However, in a work written in 1631 we find a shortened form, the noun *Canterbury,* meaning "a canter," and later, in 1673, the verb *Canterbury,* meaning "to canter." This verb, or perhaps the noun, was further shortened, giving us the verb *canter,* first recorded in 1706, and the noun *canter,* first recorded in 1755.

Can·ter·bur·y (kăn′tər-bĕr′ē, -brē, -tə-). **1.** A city of southeast Australia, a suburb of Sydney. Population, 128,000. **2.** A borough of southeast England on the Stour River east-southeast of London. Canterbury Cathedral (11th–16th century) is the seat of the archbishop and primate of the Anglican Communion. Population, 36,000.

Canterbury bells *pl.n. (used with a sing. or pl. verb).* A European biennial herb *(Campanula medium)* widely cultivated for its showy, bell-shaped, blue, pink, or white flowers. [From the association of the flowers with the bells on the horses of Canterbury pilgrims.]

cantilever
Cantilevered bridge

can·tha·ris (kăn′thər-ĭs) *n., pl.* **can·thar·i·des** (kăn-thăr′ĭ-dēz′). **1.** A brilliant green blister beetle *(Lytta vesicatoria* or *Cantharis vesicatoria)* of central and southern Europe. **2. cantharides.** *(used with a sing. or pl. verb).* A toxic preparation of the crushed, dried bodies of this beetle, formerly used as a counterirritant for skin blisters and as an aphrodisiac. Also called *Spanish fly.* [Latin *cantharis, cantharid-,* from Greek *kantharis,* from *kantharos.*]

can·thi (kăn′thī′) *n.* Plural of **canthus.**

can·thi·tis (kăn-thī′tĭs) *n.* Inflammation of the canthus.

cant hook *n.* A wooden lever with a movable metal hook near one end, used for handling logs. It is similar to a peavey but has a blunt tip, often with teeth. [From CANT[1].]

can·thus (kăn′thəs) *n., pl.* **-thi** (-thī′). The angle formed by the meeting of the upper and lower eyelids at either side of the eye. [Late Latin, from Greek *kanthos.*]

can·ti·cle (kăn′tĭ-kəl) *n.* **1.** *Music.* A song or chant, especially a nonmetrical hymn with words taken from a biblical text. **2. Canticles.** *Bible.* The Song of Songs. [Middle English, from Latin *canticulum,* diminutive of *cantus,* song, from past participle of *canere,* to sing. See **kan-** in Appendix.]

Canticle of Can·ti·cles (kăn′tĭ-kəlz) *n. Abbr.* **Cant.** *Bible.* The Song of Songs.

Can·ti·gny (käɴ-tē-nyē′). A village of northern France south of Amiens. It was the site of the first U.S. offensive (May 1918) in World War I.

can·ti·le·na (kăn′tl-ē′nə) *n. Music.* A sustained, smooth-flowing melodic line. [Italian, from Latin *cantilēna,* song, from *cantus.* See CANTICLE.]

canvasback
Male canvasback
Aythya valisineria

can·ti·le·ver (kăn′tl-ē′vər, -ĕv′ər) *n.* **1.** A projecting structure, such as a beam, that is supported at only one end. **2.** A member, such as a beam, that projects beyond a fulcrum and is supported by a balancing member or a downward force behind the fulcrum. **3.** A bracket or block supporting a balcony or cornice. **—cantilever** *v.* **-vered, -ver·ing, -vers.** *—tr.* To construct as or in the manner of a cantilever. *—intr.* To extend outward as or in the manner of a cantilever. [Perhaps CANT[1] + LEVER.]

cantilever bridge *n.* A bridge formed by two projecting beams or trusses that are joined in the center by a connecting member and are supported on piers and anchored by counterbalancing members.

can·til·late (kăn′tl-āt′) *tr. & intr.v.* **-lat·ed, -lat·ing, -lates.** To chant or recite in a musical monotone. [Latin *cantilāre, cantilāt-,* to sing, from *cantāre,* to sing. See **kan-** in Appendix.] **—can′til·la′tion** *n.*

♦ **can·ti·na** (kăn-tē′nə) *n. Southwestern U.S.* A bar that serves liquor. [Spanish, canteen, from Italian, wine cellar.]

can·tle (kăn′tl) *n.* **1.** The raised rear part of a saddle. **2.** A corner, segment, or portion; a piece: *a cantle of land.* [Middle English *cantel,* corner, from Old French, from Medieval Latin *cantellus,* from Vulgar Latin **cantus.* See CANT[1].]

can·to (kăn′tō) *n., pl.* **-tos.** *Abbr.* **can.** One of the principal divisions of a long poem. [Italian, from Latin *cantus,* song. See CANTICLE.]

can·ton (kăn′tən, -tŏn′) *n.* **1.a.** A small territorial division of a country, especially one of the states of Switzerland. **b.** A subdivision of an arrondissement in France. **2.** *Heraldry.* A small, square division of a shield, usually in the upper right corner. **3.** A usually rectangular division of a flag, occupying the upper corner next to the staff. [French, from Old French, from Old Italian *cantone,* augmentative of *canto,* corner, from Vulgar Latin **cantus.* See CANT[1].] **—can′ton·al** (kăn′tə-nəl, kăn-tŏn′əl) *adj.*

Can·ton (kăn′tən). **1.** A town of eastern Massachusetts, a residential and industrial suburb of Boston. Population, 18,182. **2.** A city of northeast Ohio south-southeast of Akron. It was the home of President William McKinley. Population, 93,077. **3.** (kăn′tŏn′, kăn′tŏn′). See **Guangzhou.**

Can·ton crepe (kăn′tŏn′) *n.* A soft, silk or rayon fabric with a finely crinkled texture, similar to but heavier than crêpe de Chine. [After *Canton* (Guangzhou), China.]

Can·ton·ese (kăn′tə-nēz′, -nēs′) *n.* The dialect of Chinese spoken in and around Guangzhou (formerly Canton), China. **—Can′ton·ese′** *adj.*

Can·ton flannel (kăn′tŏn′) *n.* Flannelette. [After *Canton* (Guangzhou), China.]

can·ton·ment (kăn-tōn′mənt, -tŏn′-) *n.* **1.a.** A group of temporary billets for troops. **b.** Assignment of troops to temporary quarters. **2.** A permanent military installation in India. [From CANTON, to quarter soldiers.]

Can·ton porcelain (kăn′tŏn′) *n.* Porcelain having a blue or white underglaze, decorated in the enameling workshops of Canton (now Guangzhou) and exported from China during the 18th and early 19th centuries. Also called *Chinese export porcelain.* [After *Canton* (Guangzhou), China.]

Can·ton River (kăn′tŏn′, kăn′tŏn′). See **Zhu Jiang.**

can·tor (kăn′tər) *n.* **1.** The Jewish religious official who leads the musical part of a service. **2.** The person who leads a church choir or congregation in singing; a precentor. [Latin, singer, from *canere,* to sing. See **kan-** in Appendix.] **—can·to′ri·al** (kăn-tôr′ē-əl, -tōr′-) *adj.*

Can·tor (kăn′tər), **Eddie.** 1892–1964. American entertainer known especially for his energetic, goggle-eyed performances in vaudeville and Broadway reviews.

can·trip (kăn′trĭp) *n.* **1.** *Scots.* A magic spell; a witch's trick. **2.** *Chiefly British.* A deceptive move; a sham. [Origin unknown.]

can·tus fir·mus (kăn′təs fîr′məs, fûr′-) *n. Music.* A plainsong melody serving as the basis of a polyphonic composition by the addition of contrapuntal voices, as in 15th-century polyphony. [Medieval Latin : Latin *cantus,* song + Latin *firmus,* fixed.]

Ca·nuck (kə-nŭk′) *n. Offensive Slang.* Used as a disparaging term for a Canadian, especially a French Canadian. [Probably alteration of CANADIAN.]

can·u·la (kăn′yə-lə) *n.* Variant of **cannula.**

can·u·lar (kăn′yə-lər) *adj.* Variant of **cannular.**

can·u·late (kăn′yə-lāt′) *v. & adj.* Variant of **cannulate.**

Ca·nute also **Cnut** or **Knut** (kə-no͞ot′, -nyo͞ot′). Known as "the Great." 994?–1035. King of England (1016–1035), Denmark (1018–1035), and Norway (1028–1035) whose reign, at first brutal, was later marked by wisdom and temperance.

can·vas (kăn′vəs) *n.* **1.** A heavy, coarse, closely woven fabric of cotton, hemp, or flax, used for tents and sails. **2.a.** A piece of such fabric on which a painting, especially an oil painting, is executed. **b.** A painting executed on such fabric. **3.** A fabric of coarse open weave, used as a foundation for needlework. **4.** The background against which events unfold, as in a historical narrative: *a grim portrait of despair against the bright canvas of the postwar economy.* **5.** *Nautical.* A sail or set of sails. **6.a.** A tent or group of tents. **b.** A circus tent. **7.** *Sports.* The floor of a ring in which boxing or wrestling takes place. ***—idiom.* under canvas. 1.** *Nautical.* With sails spread. **2.** In a tent or tents. [Middle English *canevas,* from Old French and from Medieval Latin *canavāsium,* both ultimately from Latin *cannabis,* hemp. See CANNABIS.]

can·vas·back (kăn′vəs-băk′) *n.* A North American wild duck *(Aythya valisineria)* having a reddish-brown head and neck and a whitish back.

canvas duck *n.* A fabric made of lightweight cotton or linen.

can·vass (kăn′vəs) *v.* **-vassed, -vass·ing, -vass·es.** *—tr.* **1.** To examine carefully or discuss thoroughly; scrutinize: *"The evidence had been repeatedly canvassed in American courts"* (Anthony Lewis). **2. a.** To go through (a region) or go to (persons) to solicit votes or orders. **b.** To conduct a survey of (public opinion); poll. —*intr.* **1.** To make a thorough examination or conduct a detailed discussion. **2.** To solicit voters, orders, or opinions. **—canvass** *n.* **1.** An examination or discussion. **2.** A solicitation of votes or orders. **3.** A survey of public opinion. [From obsolete *canvass,* to toss in a canvas sheet as punishment, from CANVAS.] **—can′vass·er** *n.*

can·yon also **ca·ñon** (kăn′yən) *n.* A narrow chasm with steep cliff walls, cut into the earth by running water; a gorge. [Spanish *cañon,* augmentative of *caña,* tube, cane, from Latin *canna,* reed, from Greek *kanna.* See CANE.]

can·zo·ne (kăn-zō′nē, känt-sô′nĕ) *n., pl.* **-nes** (-nēz, -nāz) or **-ni** (-nē). **1.** A medieval Italian or Provençal lyric of varying stanzaic form, usually with a concluding envoy. **2.** *Music.* A polyphonic song evolving from this form of poetry and resembling the madrigal in style. [Italian, from Latin *cantiō, cantiōn-,* song, from *cantus,* past particple of *canere,* to sing. See **kan-** in Appendix.]

can·zo·net (kăn′zə-nĕt′) *n. Music.* A short, lighthearted air or song. [From Italian *canzonetta,* diminutive of *canzone.* See CANZONE.]

caou·tchouc (kou′cho͝ok′, -cho͞ok′) *n.* See **rubber**[1] (sense 1). [French, probably from Spanish *caucho,* from Tupi *cau-ucha.*]

cap[1] (kăp) *n.* **1.** A usually soft and close-fitting head covering, either having no brim or with a visor. **2. a.** A special head covering worn to indicate rank, occupation, or membership in a particular group: *a cardinal's cap; a sailor's cap.* **b.** An academic mortarboard. Used especially in the phrase *cap and gown.* **3. a.** A protective cover or seal, especially one that closes off an end or a tip: *a bottle cap; a 35-millimeter lens cap.* **b.** A crown for covering or sealing a tooth. **c.** A tread for a worn pneumatic tire. **d.** A fitted covering used to seal a well or large pipe. **4.** A summit or top, as of a mountain. **5.** An upper limit; a ceiling: *placed a cap on mortgage rates.* **6.** *Architecture.* The capital of a column. **7.** *Botany.* **a.** The top part, or pileus, of a mushroom. **b.** A calyptra. **8. a.** A percussion cap. **b.** A small explosive charge enclosed in paper for use in a toy gun. **9.** Any of several sizes of writing paper, such as foolscap. **—cap** *tr.v.* **capped, cap·ping, caps. 1.** To cover, protect, or seal with a cap. **2.** To award a special cap to as a sign of rank or achievement: *capped the new women nurses at graduation.* **3.** To lie over or on top of; cover: *hills capped with snow.* **4.** To apply the finishing touch to; complete: *cap a meal with dessert.* **5.** To follow with something better; surpass or outdo: *capped his last trick with a disappearing act that brought the audience to its feet.* **6.** To set an upper limit on: *decided to cap cost-of-living increases.* **—*idioms.* cap in hand.** Respectfully or humbly; unpretentiously. **set (one's) cap for.** To attempt to attract and win as a mate. [Middle English *cappe,* from Old English *cæppe,* from Late Latin *cappa.*]

cap[2] (kăp) *Informal. n.* A capital letter. **—cap** *tr.v.* **capped, cap·ping, caps.** To capitalize. [Shortened form of CAPITAL[1].]

CAP *abbr.* Civil Air Patrol.

cap. *abbr.* **1.** Capacity. **2.** Capital.

ca·pa·bil·i·ty (kā′pə-bĭl′ĭ-tē) *n., pl.* **-ties. 1.** The quality of being capable; ability. **2.** Often **capabilities.** A talent or ability that has potential for development or use: *a student of great capabilities.* **3.** The capacity to be used, treated, or developed for a specific purpose: *nuclear capability.*

ca·pa·ble (kā′pə-bəl) *adj.* **1.** Having capacity or ability; efficient and able: *a capable administrator.* **2.** Having the ability required for a specific task or accomplishment; qualified: *capable of winning.* **3.** Having the inclination or disposition: *capable of violence.* **4.** Susceptible; permitting: *an error capable of remedy.* [Late Latin *capābilis,* from *capere,* to take. See **kap-** in Appendix.] **—ca′pa·ble·ness** *n.* **—ca′pa·bly** *adv.*

ca·pa·cious (kə-pā′shəs) *adj.* Capable of containing a large quantity; spacious or roomy. See Synonyms at **spacious.** [From Latin *capāx, capāc-,* from *capere,* to take. See **kap-** in Appendix.] **—ca·pa′cious·ly** *adv.* **—ca·pa′cious·ness** *n.*

ca·pac·i·tance (kə-păs′ĭ-təns) *n.* **1.** *Symbol* **C** The ratio of charge to potential on an electrically charged, isolated conductor. **2.** *Symbol* **C** The ratio of the electric charge transferred from one to the other of a pair of conductors to the resulting potential difference between them. **3. a.** The property of a circuit element that permits it to store charge. **b.** The part of the circuit exhibiting capacitance. [CAPACIT(Y) + -ANCE.] **—ca·pac′i·tive** (-tĭv) *adj.* **—ca·pac′i·tive·ly** *adv.*

ca·pac·i·tate (kə-păs′ĭ-tāt′) *tr.v.* **-tat·ed, -tat·ing, -tates. 1.** To render fit or make qualified; enable. **2.** *Biology.* To cause (spermatozoa) to undergo the physical changes needed to penetrate and fertilize an egg. [CAPACIT(Y) + -ATE[1].] **—ca·pac′i·ta′tion** *n.*

ca·pac·i·tor (kə-păs′ĭ-tər) *n.* An electric circuit element used to store charge temporarily, consisting in general of two metallic plates separated and insulated from each other by a dielectric. Also called *condenser.*

ca·pac·i·ty (kə-păs′ĭ-tē) *n., pl.* **-ties.** *Abbr.* **c., C., cap. 1. a.** The ability to receive, hold, or absorb. **b.** A measure of this ability; volume. **2.** The maximum amount that can be contained: *a trunk filled to capacity.* **3. a.** Ability to perform or produce; capability. **b.** The maximum or optimum amount that can be produced: *factories operating below capacity.* **4.** The power to learn or retain knowledge; mental ability. **5.** Innate potential for growth, development, or accomplishment; faculty. See Synonyms at **ability. 6.** The quality of being suitable for or receptive to specified treatment: *the capacity of elastic to be stretched.* **7.** The position in which one functions; role: *in your capacity as sales manager.* **8.** Legal qualification or authority: *the capacity to make an arrest.* **9.** *Electricity.* Capacitance. **—capacity** *adj.* Filling a space with the most it can hold: *a capacity crowd at the concert.* [Middle English *capacite,* from Old French, from Latin *capācitās,* from *capāx, capāc-,* spacious. See CAPACIOUS.]

ca·par·i·son (kə-păr′ĭ-sən) *n.* **1.** An ornamental covering for a horse or for its saddle or harness; trappings. **2.** Richly ornamented clothing; finery. **—caparison** *tr.v.* **-soned, -son·ing, -sons. 1.** To outfit (a horse) with an ornamental covering. **2.** To dress (another) in rich clothing. [Obsolete French *caparasson,* from Old Spanish *caparazón,* from Medieval Latin *cappa,* cloak. See CAPE[1].]

Cap de la Ma·de·leine or **Cap-de-la-Ma·de·leine** (kăp′də lä măd-lān′, -lĕn′). A city of southern Quebec, Canada, on the St. Lawrence River northeast of Montreal. It is a manufacturing center with a shrine that is an important pilgrimage site. Population, 32,626.

cape[1] (kāp) *n.* A sleeveless outer garment fastened at the throat and worn hanging over the shoulders. [Middle English *cape,* partly variant of *cope,* cope; see COPE[2], and partly from Anglo-Norman *cape* (from Medieval Latin *cāpa,* variant of Late Latin *cappa*).]

cape[2] (kāp) *n. Abbr.* **c., C.** A point or head of land projecting into a body of water. [Middle English *cap,* from Old French, from Old Provençal, from Latin *caput,* head. See **kaput-** in Appendix.]

Cape (kāp) or **Cape of.** For names of actual capes, see the specific element of the names, for example, **Hatteras, Cape; Good Hope, Cape of.**

Cape Bret·on Island (brĕt′n, brĭt′n). An island forming the northeast part of Nova Scotia, Canada. It was under French sovereignty from 1632 to 1763.

Cape buffalo *n.* A large, often fierce buffalo *(Syncerus caffer)* of Africa, having massive downward-curving horns.

Cape Cod Canal (kŏd). A waterway, about 28 km (17.5 mi) long, of southeast Massachusetts connecting Buzzards Bay with **Cape Cod Bay,** the southern part of Massachusetts Bay.

Cape Cod cottage *n.* A compact house of one or one-and-a-half stories with a gabled roof and a central chimney.

Cape Coral. A city of southwest Florida on the estuary of the Caloosahatchee River southwest of Fort Myers. It grew rapidly during the 1970's. Population, 32,103.

Cape Fear River. A river rising in central North Carolina and flowing about 325 km (202 mi) southeast to the Atlantic Ocean north of Cape Fear.

Cape Gi·rar·deau (jə-rär′dō, -rä′-). A city of southeast Missouri on the Mississippi River south-southeast of St. Louis. It was founded in 1793. Population, 34,361.

Cape gooseberry *n.* A tropical South American plant *(Physalis peruviana)* having yellow flowers with purple centers and an inflated calyx enclosing an edible yellow berry used to make jam, sauces, and desserts.

Cape jasmine *n.* See **gardenia.**

Ča·pek (chä′pĕk′), **Karel.** 1890–1938. Czechoslovakian writer noted for his science fiction, such as the play *R.U.R.* (1921).

cap·e·lin (kăp′ə-lĭn, kăp′lĭn) also **cap·lin** (kăp′lĭn) *n.* A small, edible marine fish *(Mallotus villosus)* of northern Atlantic and Pacific waters, related to and resembling the smelt. [Canadian French *capelan,* from French, codfish, from Old Provençal, from Medieval Latin *cappelānus.* See CHAPLAIN.]

Ca·pel·la (kə-pĕl′ə) *n.* A double star in Auriga, the brightest star in the constellation, approximately 46 light-years from Earth. [Latin, diminutive of *caper,* goat.]

Cape primrose *n.* Any of various chiefly African plants of the genus *Streptocarpus,* widely cultivated as houseplants for their attractive foliage and clusters of showy, colorful flowers. Also called *streptocarpus.*

Cape Province. Officially Cape of Good Hope Province; formerly (before 1910) Cape Colony. *Abbr.* **C.P.** A province and historical region of southern South Africa on the Atlantic and Indian oceans. Settled by the Dutch in 1652, it was ceded to Great Britain in 1814 and became part of the newly formed Union of South Africa in 1910.

ca·per[1] (kā′pər) *n.* **1.** A playful leap or hop. **2.** A frivolous escapade or prank. **3.** *Slang.* An illegal plot or enterprise, especially one involving theft. **—caper** *intr.v.* **-pered, -per·ing, -pers.** To leap or frisk about; frolic. [Alteration of CAPRIOLE.]

ca·per[2] (kā′pər) *n.* **1.** A usually spiny Mediterranean shrub *(Capparis spinosa)* having white to pale lilac flowers and dehiscent fruits with reddish pulp. **2.** A pickled flower bud of this plant, used as a pungent condiment in sauces, relishes, and various other dishes. [Middle English *caperis, capar,* from Latin *capparis,* from Greek *kapparis.*]

cap·er·cail·lie (kăp′ər-kāl′yē, -kā′lē) also **cap·er·cail·zie** (-kāl′zē) *n.* A large grouse *(Tetrao urogallus),* native to northern Europe and having dark plumage and a fanlike tail. Also called *wood grouse.* [Scottish Gaelic *capull coille* : *capull,* horse (from Middle Irish *capall,* from Old Irish, ultimately from Latin *caballus,* of Celtic origin) + *coille,* genitive of *coille,* forest (from Old Irish *caill*).]

Ca·per·na·um (kə-pûr′nē-əm). A city of ancient Palestine on

ă pat	oi boy
ā pay	ou out
âr care	o͝o took
ä father	o͞o boot
ĕ pet	ŭ cut
ē be	ûr urge
ĭ pit	th thin
ī pie	*th* this
îr pier	hw which
ŏ pot	zh vision
ō toe	ə about, item
ô paw	♦ regionalism

Stress marks: **′** (primary); ′ (secondary), as in **dictionary** (dĭk′shə-nĕr′ē)

the northwest shore of the Sea of Galilee. It was Jesus's home for much of his ministry and the site of many events in the New Testament. A nearby elevation is said to have been the setting for the Sermon on the Mount.

caper spurge *n.* An ornamental European spurge *(Euphorbia lathyris)* having a latex considered to be a potential source of hydrocarbons that can be converted into fuel.

cape·skin (kăp′skĭn′) *n.* Soft leather made from sheepskin, used especially for gloves. [After Cape of GOOD HOPE.]

Ca·pet (kā′pĭt, kăp′ĭt, kä-pā′). A dynasty of French kings (987–1328), including **Hugh Capet** (940?–996), who was elected king in 987, thereby permanently removing the Carolingians from power, and ruled until his death.

Ca·pe·tian (kə-pē′shən) *adj.* Of or relating to the French dynasty founded by Hugh Capet. —**Capetian** *n.* A member of this dynasty.

Cape Town or **Cape·town** (kāp′toun′). The legislative capital of South Africa, in the extreme southwest part of the country on the Atlantic Ocean. It was founded in 1652 as a supply station for the Dutch East Indies Company. Population, 859,940.

Cape Verde (vûrd). *Abbr.* **C.V.** An island country of the Atlantic Ocean west of Senegal. The islands were settled by the Portuguese in the mid-15th century, became a colony in 1495 and an overseas province in 1951, and gained independence in 1975. Praia, on São Tiago Island, is the capital. Population, 296,093.

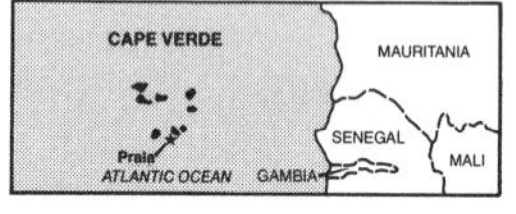

Cape Verde

Cape York Peninsula (yôrk). A peninsula of northeast Australia between the Gulf of Carpentaria and the Coral Sea.

cap·ful (kăp′fo͝ol′) *n., pl.* **-fuls.** The amount that a cap can hold.

cap gun *n.* A toy pistol with a hammer action that detonates a mildly explosive cap.

Cap Hai·tien (kăp′ hā′shən) or **Cap-Ha·ï·tien** (kä-pä-ē-syăN′). A city of northern Haiti on the Atlantic Ocean. Founded c. 1670, it is a tourist center. Population, 64,406.

ca·pi·as (kā′pē-əs) *n. Law.* A warrant for arrest. [Middle English, from Medieval Latin, from Latin, second person sing. present subjunctive of *capere,* to seize (from the first word of the writ). See **kap-** in Appendix.]

cap·il·lar·i·ty (kăp′ə-lăr′ĭ-tē) *n., pl.* **-ties.** The interaction between contacting surfaces of a liquid and a solid that distorts the liquid surface from a planar shape. Also called *capillary action.*

cap·il·lar·y (kăp′ə-lĕr′ē) *adj.* **1.** Relating to or resembling a hair; fine and slender. **2.** Having a very small internal diameter: *a capillary tube.* **3.** *Anatomy.* Of or relating to the capillaries. **4.** *Physics.* Of or relating to capillarity. —**capillary** *n., pl.* **-ies. 1.** *Anatomy.* One of the minute blood vessels that connect arterioles and venules. These blood vessels form an intricate network throughout the body for the interchange of various substances, such as oxygen and carbon dioxide, between blood and tissue cells. **2.** A tube with a very small internal diameter. [From Latin *capillāris,* from *capillus,* hair.]

capillary action *n.* See **capillarity.**

capillary attraction *n.* The force that results from greater adhesion of a liquid to a solid surface than internal cohesion of the liquid itself and that causes the liquid to be raised against a vertical surface, as water is in a clean glass tube. It is the force that allows a porous material to soak up a liquid.

capillary bed *n. Anatomy.* The network of capillaries in a particular area or organ of the body.

cap·i·tal¹ (kăp′ĭ-tl) *n.* **1. a.** *Abbr.* **cap.** A town or city that is the official seat of government in a political entity, such as a state or nation. **b.** A city that is the center of a specific activity or industry: *the financial capital of the world.* **2. a.** Wealth in the form of money or property, used or accumulated in a business by a person, partnership, or corporation. **b.** Material wealth used or available for use in the production of more wealth. **c.** Human resources considered in terms of their contributions to an economy: "[The] *swift unveiling of his . . . plans provoked a flight of human capital*" (George F. Will). **3.** *Accounting.* The remaining assets of a business after all liabilities have been deducted; net worth. **4.** Capital stock. **5.** Capitalists considered as a group or class. **6.** An asset or advantage: *"profited from political capital accumulated by others"* (Michael Mandelbaum). **7.** *Abbr.* **cap.** A capital letter. —**capital** *adj.* **1.** First and foremost; principal: *a decision of capital importance.* **2.** First-rate; excellent: *a capital idea.* **3.** Relating to or being a seat of government. **4.** Extremely serious: *a capital blunder.* **5.** Involving death or calling for the death penalty: *a capital offense.* **6.** Of or relating to financial assets, especially being or related to those financial assets that add to the net worth of a business: *made capital improvements at the plant site.* **7.** *Abbr.* **cap.** Relating to or being a capital letter. [From Middle English, principal, from Old French, from Latin *capitālis,* from *caput,* head, money laid out. See **kaput-** in Appendix.]

USAGE NOTE: The term for a town or city that serves as a seat of government is spelled *capital.* The term for the building in which a legislative assembly meets is spelled *capitol.*

cap·i·tal² (kăp′ĭ-tl) *n. Architecture.* The top part of a pillar or column. [Middle English, from Anglo-Norman, from Late Latin *capitellum,* diminutive of Latin *caput,* head. See **kaput-** in Appendix.]

capital account *n.* **1.** An account stating the amount of funds and assets invested in a business by the owners or stockholders, including retained earnings. **2.** A statement of the net worth of a business at a given time.

capital asset *n.* A long-term asset, such as land or a building.

capital expenditure *n.* Funds spent for the acquisition of a long-term asset.

capital flight *n.* Large-scale removal of individual and corporate investment capital and income from a country.

capital gain *n.* The amount by which proceeds from the sale of a capital asset exceed the original cost.

capital goods *pl.n.* Goods, such as machinery, used in the production of commodities; producer goods.

cap·i·tal-in·ten·sive (kăp′ĭ-tl-ĭn-tĕn′sĭv) *adj.* Requiring a large expenditure of capital in comparison to labor: *a capital-intensive industry.*

cap·i·tal·ism (kăp′ĭ-tl-ĭz′əm) *n.* An economic system in which the means of production and distribution are privately or corporately owned and development is proportionate to the accumulation and reinvestment of profits gained in a free market.

cap·i·tal·ist (kăp′ĭ-tl-ĭst) *n.* **1.** A supporter of capitalism. **2.** An investor of capital in business, especially one having a major financial interest in an important enterprise. **3.** A person of great wealth. —**capitalist** *adj.* Capitalistic.

cap·i·tal·is·tic (kăp′ĭ-tl-ĭs′tĭk) *adj.* **1.** Of or relating to capitalism or capitalists. **2.** Favoring or practicing capitalism: *a capitalistic country.* —**cap′i·tal·is′ti·cal·ly** *adv.*

cap·i·tal·i·za·tion (kăp′ĭ-tl-ĭ-zā′shən) *n.* **1. a.** The practice or act of capitalizing. **b.** The sum that results from capitalizing. **2. a.** The amounts and types of long-term financing used by a firm, including common stock, preferred stock, retained earnings, and long-term debt. **b.** The total par value or stated value of no-par capital stock issues. **3.** The use of capital letters in writing or printing.

cap·i·tal·ize (kăp′ĭ-tl-īz′) *v.* **-ized, -iz·ing, -iz·es.** —*tr.* **1.** To use as or convert into capital. **2.** To supply with capital or investment funds: *capitalize a new business.* **3.** To authorize the issue of a certain amount of capital stock of: *capitalize a corporation.* **4.** To convert (debt) into capital stock or shares. **5.** To calculate the current value of (a future stream of earnings or cash flows). **6.** To include (expenditures) in business accounts as assets instead of expenses. **7. a.** To write or print in capital letters. **b.** To begin a word with a capital letter. —*intr.* To turn something to one's advantage; benefit: *capitalize on an opponent's error.* See Synonyms at **benefit.** —**cap′i·tal·iz′a·ble** *adj.*

capital letter *n.* A letter written or printed in a size larger than and often in a form differing from its corresponding lowercase letter; an uppercase letter.

cap·i·tal·ly (kăp′ĭ-tl-ē) *adv.* In an excellent manner; admirably.

capital punishment *n.* The penalty of death for the commission of a crime.

capital ship *n.* A warship of the largest class, such as a battleship or an aircraft carrier.

capital stock *n. Abbr.* **CS 1.** The total amount of stock authorized for issue by a corporation, including common and preferred stock. **2.** The total stated or par value of the permanently invested capital of a corporation.

cap·i·tate (kăp′ĭ-tāt′) *adj.* **1.** *Anatomy.* Enlarged and globular at the tip, as a bone of the wrist having a rounded, knoblike end. **2.** *Botany.* Forming a headlike mass or dense cluster, as the flowers of plants in the composite family. [Latin *capitātus,* having a head, from *caput, capit-,* head. See **kaput-** in Appendix.]

cap·i·ta·tion (kăp′ĭ-tā′shən) *n.* **1.** A poll tax. **2.** A payment or fee of a fixed amount per person. [Late Latin *capitātiō, capitātiōn-,* from Latin *caput, capit-,* head. See **kaput-** in Appendix.] —**cap′i·ta′tive** *adj.*

cap·i·tel·lum (kăp′ĭ-tĕl′əm) *n., pl.* **-tel·la** (-tĕl′ə). *Anatomy.* The rounded protuberance at the lower end of the humerus that articulates with the radius. [Late Latin, diminutive of Latin *caput, capit-,* head. See **kaput-** in Appendix.]

cap·i·tol (kăp′ĭ-tl) *n.* **1.** A building or complex of buildings in which a state legislature meets. **2. Capitol.** The building in Washington, D.C., where the Congress of the United States meets. See Usage Note at **capital¹.** [Middle English *Capitol,* Jupiter's temple in Rome, from Old French *capitole,* from Latin *Capitōlium,* after *Capitōlīnus,* Capitoline, the hill on which Jupiter's temple stood, perhaps akin to *caput,* head. See CAPITAL¹.]

Capitol Hill *n. Informal.* The U.S. Congress.

Cap·i·to·line (kăp′ĭ-tə-līn′). The highest of the seven hills of ancient Rome. It was the historic and religious center of the city. —**Cap′i·to·line′** *adj.*

Capitol Peak. A mountain, 4,309.7 m (14,130 ft) high, in the Rocky Mountains of west-central Colorado.

ca·pit·u·la (kə-pĭch′ə-lə) *n.* Plural of **capitulum.**

ca·pit·u·lar (kə-pĭch′ə-lər) *adj.* Of or relating to a chapter, especially an ecclesiastical chapter. [Medieval Latin *capitulāris,* from *capitulum,* chapter. See CHAPTER.] —**ca·pit′u·lar·ly** *adv.*

ca·pit·u·lar·y (kə-pĭch′ə-lĕr′ē) *n., pl.* **-ies. 1.** A member of an ecclesiastical or similar chapter. **2. a.** An ecclesiastical or civil ordinance. **b.** A set of such ordinances, especially those promulgated by Charlemagne and his successors. [Medieval Latin *capitulārius,* from *capitulum,* chapter. See CHAPTER.]

ca·pit·u·late (kə-pĭch′ə-lāt′) *intr.v.* **-lat·ed, -lat·ing, -lates. 1.** To surrender under specified conditions; come to terms. **2.** To give up all resistance; acquiesce. See Synonyms at **yield.** [Medieval Latin *capitulāre, capitulāt-,* to draw up in chapters, from *capitulum,* chapter. See CHAPTER.] **—ca·pit′u·lant** *n.* **—ca·pit′u·la′tor** *n.*

ca·pit·u·la·tion (kə-pĭch′ə-lā′shən) *n.* **1.** The act of surrendering or giving up. See Synonyms at **surrender. 2.** A document containing the terms of surrender. **3.** An enumeration of the main parts of a subject; a summary. **—ca·pit′u·la·to′ry** (-lə-tôr′ē, -tōr′ē) *adj.*

ca·pit·u·lum (kə-pĭch′ə-ləm) *n., pl.* **-la** (-lə). **1.** *Botany.* See **flower head** (sense 1). **2.** *Biology.* A small knob or head-shaped part, such as a protuberance of a bone or the tip of an insect's antenna. [Latin, diminutive of *caput, capit-,* head. See **kaput-** in Appendix.]

cap·let (kăp′lĭt) *n.* A smooth, coated, oval-shaped medicine tablet intended to be tamper-resistant. [CAP(SULE) + (TAB)LET.]

cap·lin (kăp′lĭn) *n.* Variant of **capelin.**

ca·po[1] (kā′pō) *n., pl.* **-pos.** *Music.* A small movable bar placed across the fingerboard of a guitar or similar instrument so as to raise the pitch of all the strings uniformly. [Italian *capo (di tastiera),* head (of the fingerboard), from Latin *caput.* See **kaput-** in Appendix.]

ca·po[2] (kä′pō, kăp′ō) *n., pl.* **-pos.** The head of a branch of an organized crime syndicate. [Italian, from Latin *caput,* head. See CAPO[1].]

ca·pon (kā′pŏn′, -pən) *n.* A male chicken castrated when young to improve the quality of its flesh for food. [Middle English *capoun,* from Old English *capūn* and from Old French *capon,* both from Latin *cāpō, cāpōn-.*]

ca·po·na·ta (kä′pə-nä′tə) *n.* A seasoned mixture of eggplant and other vegetables served as an appetizer. [Italian, of Sicilian dialectal origin.]

Ca·pone (kə-pōn′), **Alphonse.** Known as "Al." Also called "Scarface." 1899–1947. Italian-born American gangster who ruthlessly ruled the Chicago underworld and was imprisoned (1931–1939) for tax evasion.

cap·o·ral (kăp′ər-əl, kăp′ə-răl′) *n.* A strong dark tobacco. [French, short for *(tabac de) caporal,* corporal('s tobacco), from Italian *caporale,* from *capo,* head. See CAPO[1].]

ca·pote (kə-pōt′) *n.* A long, usually hooded cloak or coat. [French, from Old French *capote, capette,* diminutive of *cape,* cloak, from Medieval Latin *cāpa.* See CAPE[1].]

Ca·po·te (kə-pō′tē), **Truman.** 1924–1984. American writer whose works, such as *In Cold Blood* (1966), concern alienated, sometimes psychopathic characters. He also wrote the novella *Breakfast at Tiffany's* (1958), detailing the New York life of an uninhibited playgirl, Holly Golightly.

Capp (kăp), **Al.** 1909–1979. American cartoonist noted for his comic strip *L'il Abner* (1934–1977).

Cap·pa·do·cia (kăp′ə-dō′shə, -shē-ə). An ancient region of Asia Minor in present-day east-central Turkey. Heart of a Hittite state and later a Persian satrapy, it was annexed by the Romans in A.D. 17. **—Cap′pa·do′cian** *adj. & n.*

cap·per (kăp′ər) *n.* **1.** One that caps or makes caps. **2.** *Informal.* Something that surpasses or completes what has gone before; a finishing touch or finale. **3.** *Slang.* One who acts as a decoy, as in a confidence game.

cap pistol *n.* A cap gun.

cap·puc·ci·no (kăp′ə-chē′nō, kä′pə-) *n., pl.* **-nos.** Espresso coffee mixed or topped with steamed milk or cream. [Italian, Capuchin, cappuccino (from the resemblance of its color to the color of the monk's habit). See CAPUCHIN.]

WORD HISTORY: The history of the word *cappuccino* exemplifies how words can develop new senses because of resemblances that the original coiners of the terms might not have dreamed possible. The Capuchin order of friars, established after 1525, played an important role in bringing Catholicism back to Reformation Europe. Its Italian name came from the long, pointed cowl, or *cappuccino,* derived from *cappuccio,* "hood," that was worn as part of the order's habit. The French version of *cappuccino* was *capuchin* (now *capucin*), from which came English *Capuchin.* The name of this pious order was later used as the name (first recorded in English in 1785) for a type of monkey with a tuft of black, cowllike hair. In Italian *cappuccino* went on to develop another sense, "espresso coffee mixed or topped with steamed milk or cream," so called because the color of the coffee resembled the color of the habit of a Capuchin friar. The first use of *cappuccino* in English is recorded in 1948 in a work about San Francisco.

Cap·ra (kăp′rə), **Frank.** 1897–1991. American filmmaker who won an Academy Award for his direction of *It Happened One Night* (1934), *Mr. Deeds Goes to Town* (1936), and *You Can't Take It with You* (1938).

cap·re·o·my·cin (kăp′rē-ō-mī′sĭn) *n.* An antibiotic derived from a bacterium *(Streptomyces capreolus)* that is effective against the microorganism responsible for tuberculosis in human beings. [Latin *capreolus,* diminutive of *caper, capr-,* goat + -MYCIN.]

Ca·pri (kə-prē′, kăp′rē, kä′prē). An island of southern Italy on the southern edge of the Bay of Naples. A popular resort since Roman times, it is famous for its Blue Grotto, a picturesque cave indenting the island's high, precipitous coast.

cap·ric acid (kăp′rĭk) *n.* A fatty acid, $CH_3(CH_2)_8COOH$, obtained from animal fats and oils and used in the manufacture of perfumes and fruit flavors. Also called *decanoic acid.* [From Latin *caper, capr-,* goat (from the acid's nasty smell).]

ca·pric·cio (kə-prē′chō, -chē-ō′) *n., pl.* **-cios. 1.** *Music.* An instrumental work with an improvisatory style and a free form. **2.** A prank; a caper. **3.** A whim. [Italian. See CAPRICE.]

ca·pric·cio·so (kə-prē′chē-ō′sō, kä′prē-chō′sō) *adj. Music.* Lively and free. Used chiefly as a direction. [Italian, from *capriccio,* caprice. See CAPRICE.]

ca·price (kə-prēs′) *n.* **1.a.** An impulsive change of mind. **b.** An inclination to change one's mind impulsively. **c.** A sudden, unpredictable action, change, or series of actions or changes: *A hailstorm in July is a caprice of nature.* **2.** *Music.* A capriccio. [French, from Italian *capriccio,* from *caporiccio,* fright, sudden start : *capo,* head (from Latin *caput;* see **kaput-** in Appendix) + *riccio,* curly (from Latin *ēricius,* hedgehog, from *ēr*).]

SYNONYMS: *caprice, whim, whimsy, vagary, freak.* These nouns are compared as they denote an impulsive or unexpected notion. *Caprice* strongly suggests lack of apparent motivation and can imply wanton and willful behavior: *Before the establishment of labor unions, a worker could be discharged at the caprice of any manager. Whim* and *whimsy* can both mean a quaint or fantastic idea, but *whim* more strongly suggests sudden inspiration, *whimsy* a playful or fanciful quality: *That suggestion was no whim of the moment. "Talk of space stations, space manufacturing or space defense will be whimsy until the cost of reaching orbit comes down"* (Gregg Easterbrook). *Vagary* emphasizes the erratic and unpredictable, even irresponsible nature of a notion or an act: *"This is a time of life when a solicitous family does well to watch affectionately over the vagaries of its unattached relatives, particularly of those who are comfortably off"* (J.P. Marquand). *Freak* is a sudden and seemingly motiveless turn of mind: *"Sometimes goldfinches one by one will drop/From low-hung branches . . . /Then off at once, as in a wanton freak"* (John Keats).

ca·pri·cious (kə-prĭsh′əs, -prē′shəs) *adj.* Characterized by or subject to whim; impulsive and unpredictable. See Synonyms at **arbitrary. —ca·pri′cious·ly** *adv.* **—ca·pri′cious·ness** *n.*

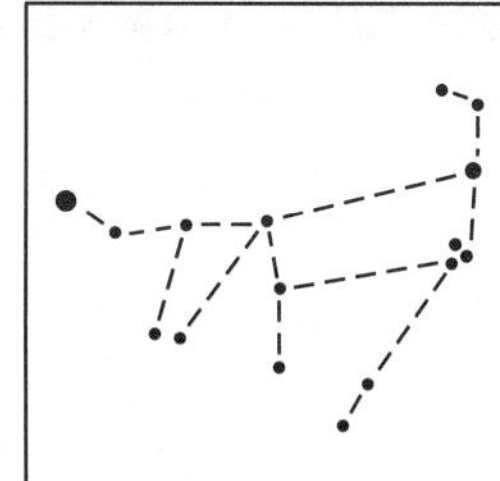

Capricorn

Cap·ri·corn (kăp′rĭ-kôrn′) also **Cap·ri·cor·nus** (kăp′rĭ-kôr′nəs) *n.* **1.** A constellation in the equatorial region of the Southern Hemisphere, near Aquarius and Sagittarius. **2.a.** The tenth sign of the zodiac in astrology. **b.** One who is born under this sign. Also called *Goat.* [Middle English *Capricorne,* from Latin *Capricornus* : *caper, capr-,* goat + *cornū,* horn; see **ker-[1]** in Appendix.]

Cap·ri·corn·i·an (kăp′rĭ-kôr′nē-ən) *n.* One who is born under the sign of Capricorn.

Cap·ri·cor·nus (kăp′rĭ-kôr′nəs) *n.* Variant of **Capricorn.**

cap·ri·fi·ca·tion (kăp′rə-fĭ-kā′shən) *n.* A method of assuring pollination of the Smyrna and other edible figs in which flower clusters of the caprifig are hung from trees of the edible fig, allowing wasps to carry pollen from the flowers of the caprifig to those of the edible varieties. [Latin *caprificātio, caprificātiōn-,* from *caprificātus,* past participle of *caprificāre,* to ripen figs by caprification, from *caprificus,* caprifig. See CAPRIFIG.]

cap·ri·fig (kăp′rə-fĭg′) *n.* A wild variety of Mediterranean fig *(Ficus carica* var. *sylvestris)* used in the caprification of certain edible figs. [Middle English, from Latin *caprificus* (influenced by Middle English *fig,* fig) : *caper, capr-,* goat + *fīcus,* fig; see FIG[1].]

cap·ri·ole (kăp′rē-ōl′) *n.* **1.** An upward leap made by a trained horse without going forward and with the hind legs kicked out. **2.** A playful leap or jump; a caper. **—capriole** *intr.v.* **-oled, -ol·ing, -oles.** To perform a capriole. [French, from Italian *capriola,* somersault, from *capriolo,* roebuck, wild goat, from Latin *capreolus,* diminutive of *caper, capr-,* goat.]

ca·pri pants (kä′prē, kə-prē′) *pl.n.* Tight-fitting, calf-length women's pants, often having a slit on the outside of the leg bottoms. [After CAPRI.]

ca·pris (kä′prēz, kə-prēz′) *pl.n.* Capri pants.

ca·pro·ic acid (kə-prō′ĭk, kă-) *n.* A liquid fatty acid, $CH_3(CH_2)_4COOH$, found in animal fats and oils or synthesized and used in the manufacture of pharmaceuticals and flavorings. [From Latin *caper, capr-,* goat (from the acid's goatlike smell).]

ca·pryl·ic acid (kə-prĭl′ĭk, kă-) *n.* A liquid fatty acid, $C_8H_{16}O_2$, found in butter and other fats and oils and having a rancid taste. It is used in the manufacture of dyes and perfumes. [CAPR(IC ACID) + -YL + -IC.]

caps. *abbr.* Capsule.

cap·sa·i·cin (kăp-sā′ĭ-sĭn) *n.* A colorless, pungent, crystalline compound, $C_{18}H_{27}NO_3$, that is derived from capsicum and is a strong irritant to skin and mucous membranes. [CAPSIC(UM) (perhaps influenced by Latin *capsa,* box; see CAPSICUM) + -IN.]

cap screw *n.* A long-threaded bolt, usually with a square head, used in fastening machine parts.

Cap·si·an (kăp′sē-ən) *adj.* Of, relating to, or being a Paleolithic culture of northern Africa and southern Europe. [French *capsien,* from Latin *Capsa,* Gafsa, a town of west-central Tunisia.]

ă pat	oi boy
ā pay	ou out
âr care	ŏŏ took
ä father	ōō boot
ĕ pet	ŭ cut
ē be	ûr urge
ĭ pit	th thin
ī pie	*th* this
îr pier	hw which
ŏ pot	zh vision
ō toe	ə about, item
ô paw	♦ regionalism

Stress marks: **′** (primary); ′ (secondary), as in **dictionary** (dĭk′shə-nĕr′ē)

cap·si·cum (kăp′sĭ-kəm) *n.* **1.** Any of various tropical American pepper plants of the genus *Capsicum,* especially any of the numerous cultivated forms of the species *C. annuum* and *C. frutescens.* **2.** The fruit of any of these plants, especially the dried pungent types used as a condiment and in medicine. [New Latin *Capsicum,* genus name, perhaps from Latin *capsa,* box (from its podlike fruit).]

cap·sid (kăp′sĭd) *n.* The protein shell that surrounds a virus particle. [From Latin *capsa,* box.]

cap·size (kăp′sīz′, kăp-sīz′) *intr. & tr.v.* **-sized, -siz·ing, -siz·es.** To overturn or cause to overturn: *The boat capsized. I capsized the canoe.* [Origin unknown.]

cap·so·mere (kăp′sə-mîr′) *n.* One of the individual subunits that makes up a capsid. [CAPS(ID) + -MERE.]

cap·stan (kăp′stən, -stăn′) *n.* **1.** *Nautical.* An apparatus used for hoisting weights, consisting of a vertical spool-shaped cylinder that is rotated manually or by machine and around which a cable is wound. **2.** A small cylindrical shaft used to drive magnetic tape at a constant speed in a tape recorder. [Middle English, from Norman French, from Old Provençal *cabestan,* from *cabestre,* noose, from Latin *capistrum,* halter, probably from *capere,* to seize. See **kap-** in Appendix.]

cap·stone (kăp′stōn′) *n.* **1.** The top stone of a structure or wall. **2.** The crowning achievement or final stroke; the culmination or acme.

capstone

cap·su·lar (kăp′sə-lər, -syo͞o-) *adj.* Of, relating to, or resembling a capsule.

cap·su·late (kăp′sə-lāt′, -lĭt, -syo͞o-) also **cap·su·lat·ed** (-lā′tĭd) *adj.* Enclosed in or formed into a capsule. **—cap′su·la′tion** *n.*

cap·sule (kăp′səl, -so͞ol) *n. Abbr.* **caps. 1.** A small soluble container, usually made of gelatin, that encloses a dose of an oral medicine or a vitamin. **2.** *Anatomy.* A fibrous, membranous, or fatty sheath that encloses an organ or part, such as the sac surrounding the kidney or the fibrous tissues that surround a joint. **3.** *Microbiology.* A mucopolysaccharide outer shell enveloping certain bacteria. **4.** *Botany.* **a.** A dry, dehiscent fruit that develops from two or more united carpels. **b.** The thin-walled, spore-containing structure of mosses and related plants. **5.** A space capsule. **6.** A brief summary; a condensation. **—capsule** *adj.* **1.** Highly condensed; very brief: *a capsule description.* **2.** Very small; compact. **—capsule** *tr.v.* **-suled, -sul·ing, -sules. 1.** To enclose in or furnish with a capsule. **2.** To condense or summarize: *capsuled the news.* [French, from Latin *capsula,* diminutive of *capsa,* box.]

cap·sul·ize (kăp′sə-līz′, -syo͞o-) *tr.v.* **-ized, -iz·ing, -iz·es.** To capsule: *capsulized the news every 30 minutes.*

cap·su·lot·o·my (kăp′sə-lŏt′ə-mē) *n.* Incision into a capsule, especially that of the crystalline lens of the eye, as to remove cataracts by surgery.

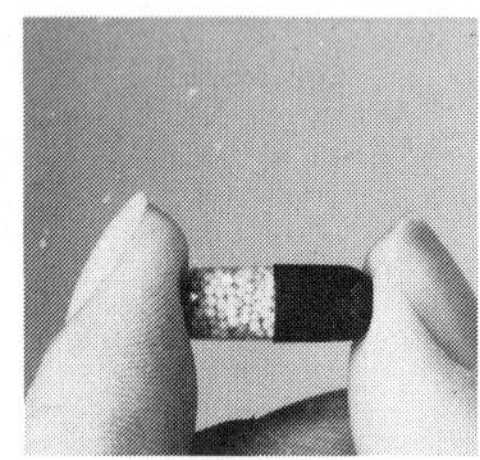
capsule
Medicinal

Capt. *abbr.* Captain.

cap·tain (kăp′tən) *n.* **1.** *Abbr.* **Capt.** One who commands, leads, or guides others, especially: **a.** The officer in command of a ship, aircraft, or spacecraft. **b.** A precinct commander in a police or fire department, usually ranking above a lieutenant and below a chief. **c.** The designated leader of a team or crew in sports. **2.** *Abbr.* **Capt., Cpt., CPT a.** A commissioned rank in the U.S. Army, Air Force, or Marine Corps that is above first lieutenant and below major. **b.** A commissioned rank in the U.S. Navy or Coast Guard that is above commander and below rear admiral. **c.** One who holds the rank of captain. **3.** A figure in the forefront; a leader: *a captain of industry.* **4.** One who supervises or directs the work of others, especially: **a.** A district official for a political party. **b.** A restaurant employee who is in charge of the waiters and usually attends to table seating. **c.** A bell captain. **—captain** *tr.v.* **-tained, -tain·ing, -tains.** To act as captain of; command or direct: *captained the football team.* [Middle English *capitain,* from Old French, from Late Latin *capitāneus,* chief, from Latin *caput, capit-,* head. See **kaput-** in Appendix.] **—cap′tain·cy** *n.* **—cap′tain·ship′** *n.*

cap·tain's chair (kăp′tənz) *n.* A wooden chair having a low back with spindles that curve forward to provide armrests.

captain's mast *n.* A disciplinary hearing during which the commanding officer of a naval unit studies and disposes of cases against the enlisted personnel in the unit.

cap·tan (kăp′tən, -tăn′) *n.* A white solid agricultural fungicide, $C_9H_8O_2NSCl_3$. [Short for MERCAPTAN.]

cap·tion (kăp′shən) *n.* **1.** A title, short explanation, or description accompanying an illustration or a photograph. **2.** A subtitle in a motion picture. **3.** A title or heading, as of a document or article. **4.** *Law.* The heading of a pleading or other document that identifies the parties, court, term, and number of the action. **—caption** *tr.v.* **-tioned, -tion·ing, -tions.** To furnish a caption for. [Middle English *capcioun,* arrest, from Old French *capcion,* from Latin *captiō, captiōn-,* from *captus,* past participle of *capere,* to seize. See **kap-** in Appendix.]

cap·tious (kăp′shəs) *adj.* **1.** Marked by a disposition to find and point out trivial faults. See Synonyms at **critical. 2.** Intended to entrap or confuse, as in an argument: *a captious question.* [Middle English *capcious,* from Old French *captieux,* from Latin *captiōsus,* from *captiō,* seizure, sophism, from *captus,* past participle of *capere,* to seize. See **kap-** in Appendix.] **—cap′tious·ly** *adv.* **—cap′tious·ness** *n.*

capuchin
White-throated capuchin
Cebus capucinus

cap·ti·vate (kăp′tə-vāt′) *tr.v.* **-vat·ed, -vat·ing, -vates. 1.** To attract and hold by charm, beauty, or excellence. See Synonyms at **charm. 2.** *Archaic.* To capture. [Late Latin *captivāre, captivāt-,* to capture, from Latin *captīvus,* prisoner. See CAPTIVE.] **—cap′ti·va′tion** *n.* **—cap′ti·va′tor** *n.*

cap·tive (kăp′tĭv) *n.* **1.** One, such as a prisoner of war, that is forcibly confined, subjugated, or enslaved. **2.** One held in the grip of a strong emotion or passion. **—captive** *adj.* **1.** Taken and held prisoner, as in war. **2.** Held in bondage; enslaved. **3.** Kept under restraint or control; confined: *captive birds.* **4.** Restrained by circumstances that prevent free choice: *a captive audience; a captive market.* **5.** Enraptured, as by beauty; captivated. [Middle English *captif,* from Old French, from Latin *captīvus,* from *captus,* past participle of *capere,* to seize. See **kap-** in Appendix.]

cap·tiv·i·ty (kăp-tĭv′ĭ-tē) *n., pl.* **-ties.** The state or period of being imprisoned, confined, or enslaved.

cap·to·pril (kăp′tə-prĭl′) *n.* A drug used in the treatment of hypertension that functions by inhibiting the enzymes that activate angiotensin. [(MER)CAPT(AN) + *pr(opano)-,* propane (from PROPANE) + -YL.]

cap·tor (kăp′tər, -tôr′) *n.* One that takes another as a captive. [Late Latin *captor,* hunter, from Latin *capere,* to seize. See **kap-** in Appendix.]

cap·ture (kăp′chər) *tr.v.* **-tured, -tur·ing, -tures. 1.** To take captive, as by force or craft; seize. **2.** To gain possession or control of, as in a game or contest: *capture the queen in chess; captured the liberal vote.* **3.** To attract and hold: *tales of adventure that capture the imagination.* **4.** To succeed in preserving in lasting form: *capture a likeness in a painting.* **—capture** *n.* **1.** The act of catching, taking, or winning, as by force or skill. **2.** One that has been seized, caught, or won; a catch or prize. **3.** *Physics.* The phenomenon in which an atom or a nucleus absorbs a subatomic particle, often with the subsequent emission of radiation. [From French, capture, from Old French, from Latin *captūra,* a catching of animals, from *captus,* past participle of *capere,* to seize. See **kap-** in Appendix.]

Cap·u·a (kăp′yo͞o-ə, kä′pwä). A town of southern Italy north of Naples. The strategically important ancient Roman city of **Capua** was located nearby on the Appian Way. Population, 18,053.

ca·puche (kə-po͞och′, -po͞osh′) *n.* A hood on a cloak, especially the long, pointed cowl worn by a Capuchin monk. [Italian *cappuccio,* from *cappa,* hood, from Late Latin, cloak.]

cap·u·chin (kăp′yə-chĭn, -shĭn, kə-pyo͞o′-) *n.* **1. Capuchin.** A monk belonging to the Order of Friars Minor Capuchin, an independent order of Franciscans founded in Italy in 1525–1528 and dedicated to preaching and missionary work. **2.** A hooded cloak worn by women. **3.** Any of several long-tailed monkeys of the genus *Cebus,* native to Central and South America and often having a hoodlike tuft of hair on the head. In this sense, also called *sapajou.* [Obsolete French, from Italian *cappuccino,* pointed cowl, Capuchin, from *cappuccio,* hood. See CAPUCHE.]

cap·y·ba·ra (kăp′ə-bär′ə, -băr′ə) *n.* A large semiaquatic rodent *(Hydrochoerus hydrochaeris)* of tropical South America, having short limbs and a vestigial tail and often attaining lengths of more than 1.2 meters (4 feet). [Portuguese *capybara,* from Tupi *capivara, capibara* : *capii,* grass + *urara,* eater.]

car (kär) *n.* **1.** An automobile. **2.** A vehicle, such as a streetcar, that runs on rails: *a railroad car.* **3.** A boxlike enclosure for passengers and freight on a conveyance: *an elevator car.* **4.** The part of a balloon or airship that carries people and cargo. **5.** *Archaic.* A chariot, carriage, or cart. [Middle English *carre,* cart, from Old North French, from Latin *carra,* pl. of *carrus, carrum,* a Gallic type of wagon. See **kers-** in Appendix.]

car. *abbr.* Carat.

car·a·bao (kăr′ə-bou′, kä′rə-) *n., pl.* **-baos.** See **water buffalo.** [Spanish, from Visayan *karabáw,* from Malay *kĕrbau.*]

car·a·bid (kăr′ə-bĭd, kə-răb′ĭd) *n.* Any of a large family (Carabidae) of chiefly black beetles that often inhabit the spaces under stones, logs, or piles of debris and feed on other insects. Also called *ground beetle.* [From New Latin *Cārabidae,* family name, from Latin *cārabus,* crustacean, from Greek *karabos,* horned beetle.] **—car′a·bid** *adj.*

car·a·bi·neer also **car·a·bi·nier** (kăr′ə-bə-nîr′) or **car·bi·neer** (kär′bə-) *n.* A soldier armed with a carbine. [French *carabinier,* from *carabine,* carbine. See CARBINE.]

car·a·bi·ner also **kar·a·bi·ner** (kăr′ə-bē′nər) *n.* An oblong metal ring with a spring clip, used in mountaineering to attach a running rope to a piton or similar device. [German *Karabiner,* short for *Karabinerhaken,* hook for a carbine, from *Karabiner,* carbine, from French *carabine.* See CARBINE.]

car·a·bi·nier (kăr′ə-bə-nîr′) *n.* Variant of **carabineer.**

ca·ra·bi·nie·re (kăr′ə-bĭn-yâr′ē, kä′rä-bē-nyĕ′rĕ) *n., pl.* **-bi·nie·ri** (-bĭn-yâr′ē, -bē-nyĕ′rē). A member of the Italian police force. [Italian, from French *carabinier.* See CARABINEER.]

car·a·cal (kăr′ə-kăl′) *n.* A wildcat *(Lynx caracal)* of Africa and southern Asia having short, fawn-colored fur and long, tufted ears. [French, from Ottoman Turkish *qaraqūlāq* : *qara,* black + *qūlāq,* ear.]

Car·a·cal·la (kăr′ə-kăl′ə). Real name Marcus Aurelius Antonius. A.D. 188–217. Emperor of Rome (211–217) who was obsessed with and sought to imitate Alexander the Great.

car·a·car·a (kăr′ə-kăr′ə, -kə-rä′) *n.* Any of several large, carrion-eating or predatory hawks of the subfamily Caracarinae, native to South and Central America and the southern United States. [Spanish and Portuguese *caracará,* both from Tupi *caracara.*]

Ca·ra·cas (kə-rä′kəs). The capital and largest city of Venezuela, in the northern part of the country near the Caribbean coast. It was founded by the Spanish in 1567 and grew rapidly during the oil boom of the 1950's. Population, 3,041,000.

car·ack (kăr′ək) *n. Nautical.* Variant of **carrack.**

car·a·cole (kăr′ə-kōl′) also **car·a·col** (-kŏl′) —*n.* A half turn to right or left performed by a horse and rider. —*intr.v.* **-coled, -col·ing, -coles.** To perform a caracole. [French, from Spanish *caracol,* snail.]

car·a·cul (kăr′ə-kəl) *n.* Variant of **karakul.**

ca·rafe (kə-răf′) *n.* **1.** A glass or metal bottle, often with a flared lip, used for serving water or wine. **2.** A glass pot with a pouring spout, used in making coffee. [French, from Italian *caraffa,* from Spanish *garrafa,* probably from Arabic *ġarafa,* to ladle, scoop.]

car·am·bo·la (kăr′əm-bō′lə) *n.* **1.** An ornamental evergreen tree *(Averrhoa carambola),* native to southeast Asia and having crisp, edible, yellow to orange, longitudinally ridged fruits that are star-shaped in cross section. **2.** The fruit of this plant, eaten fresh or used to make jams and juices. In this sense, also called *star fruit.* [Portuguese, perhaps from Marathi *karambal.*]

car·a·mel (kăr′ə-məl, -mĕl′, kär′məl) *n.* **1.** A smooth, chewy candy made with sugar, butter, cream or milk, and flavoring. **2.** Burnt sugar, used for coloring and sweetening foods. **3.** *Color.* A moderate yellow brown. [French, from Old French, from Old Spanish *caramel, caramelo,* from Portuguese *caramel,* from Late Latin *calamellus,* diminutive of Latin *calamus,* reed, cane, from Greek *kalamos.*]

car·a·mel·ize (kăr′ə-mə-līz′, kär′mə-) *tr. & intr.v.* **-ized, -iz·ing, -iz·es.** To convert or be converted into caramel. —**car′a·mel·i·za′tion** (-mə-lĭ-zā′shən) *n.*

ca·ran·gid (kə-răn′jĭd, -răng′gĭd) *n.* Any of a large family (Carangidae) of marine food and game fishes, such as the jacks and pompanos. [From New Latin *Carangidae,* family name, from French *carangue,* mackerel, from Spanish *caranga.*] —**ca·ran′gid** *adj.*

car·a·pace (kăr′ə-pās′) *n.* **1.** *Zoology.* A hard bony or chitinous outer covering, such as the fused dorsal plates of a turtle or the portion of the exoskeleton covering the head and thorax of a crustacean. **2.** A protective, shell-like covering likened to that of a turtle or crustacean: *"He used to worry that Sarah would age the same way, develop the same brittle carapace"* (Anne Tyler). [French, from Spanish *carapacho.*]

car·at (kăr′ət) *n.* **1.** *Abbr.* **c, car.** A unit of weight for precious stones, equal to 200 milligrams. **2.** Variant of **karat.** [Middle English, from Old French, from Medieval Latin *quarātus,* from Arabic *qīrāṭ,* weight of four grains, from Greek *keration,* a weight, diminutive of *keras,* horn. See **ker-**[1] in Appendix.]

Ca·ra·vag·gio (kăr′ə-vä′jō, kä′rä-väd′jô), **Michelangelo Merisi da.** 1573–1610. Italian painter of the baroque whose influential works, such as *Deposition of Christ* (1604), are marked by intense realism and revolutionary use of light.

car·a·van (kăr′ə-văn′) *n.* **1.** A company of travelers journeying together, as across a desert or through hostile territory. **2.** A single file of vehicles or pack animals. **3.** A large covered vehicle; a van. **4.** *Chiefly British.* A trailer or dwelling place on wheels. [French *caravane* or Italian *carovana,* both from Persian *kārvān.*]

car·a·van·sa·ry (kăr′ə-văn′sə-rē) also **car·a·van·se·rai** (-rī′) *n., pl.* **-ries** also **-rais. 1.** An inn built around a large court for accommodating caravans at night in the Near or Far East. **2.** A large inn or hostelry. [French *caravanserai,* from Persian *kārvānsarāy* : *kārvān,* caravan + *sarāy,* camp, palace; see **terə-**[2] in Appendix.]

car·a·vel or **car·a·velle** (kăr′ə-vĕl′) also **car·vel** (kär′vəl, -vĕl′) *n. Nautical.* Any of several types of small, light sailing ships, especially one with two or three masts and lateen sails used by the Spanish and Portuguese in the 15th and 16th centuries. [French *caravelle,* from Old French, from Old Portuguese *caravela,* diminutive of *cávaro,* ship, from Late Latin *cārabus,* a small wicker boat, from Late Greek *karabos,* light ship, from Greek, horned beetle.]

car·a·way (kăr′ə-wā′) *n.* **1.** A biennial Eurasian herb *(Carum carvi)* in the parsley family, having finely divided leaves and clusters of small, white or pinkish flowers. **2.** The seedlike fruit of this plant, widely used as a flavoring and seasoning in various foods. In this sense, also called *caraway seed.* [Middle English *carewei,* from Old French *carvi, caroi,* probably from Medieval Latin *carvi, carwi,* ultimately from Arabic *karāwiyā,* from Greek *karon.*]

Car·a·way (kăr′ə-wā′), **Hattie Ophelia Wyatt.** 1878–1950. American legislator. Appointed to fill out her husband's term in the U.S. Senate in 1931, she became in 1932 the first elected woman senator and served until 1945.

caraway seed *n.* See **caraway** (sense 2).

carb– *pref.* Variant of **carbo–.**

car·ba·mate (kär′bə-māt′, kär-băm′āt′) *n.* A salt or ester of carbamic acid, especially one used as an insecticide. [CARBAM(IC ACID) + –ATE[2].]

car·ba·maz·e·pine (kär′bə-măz′ə-pēn′) *n.* An anticonvulsant and analgesic drug, $C_{15}H_{12}N_2O$, used in the treatment of certain forms of epilepsy and to relieve pain associated with trigeminal neuralgia. [Rearrangement of chemical name *dibenzazepinecarboxamide.*]

car·bam·ic acid (kär-băm′ĭk) *n.* A hypothetical acid, NH_2COOH, that exists only in the form of its esters and salts. [CARBAM(IDE) + –IC.]

car·ba·mide (kär′bə-mīd′, kär-băm′ĭd) *n.* See **urea.** [CARB(O)– + AMIDE.]

car·bam·o·yl (kär-băm′ō-ĭl′) *n.* The radical NH_2CO. [CARBAM(IC ACID) + –YL.]

car·ban·i·on (kär-băn′ī′ən, -ī′ŏn′) *n.* An anion in which carbon carries a negative charge and an unshared pair of electrons.

car·ba·ryl (kär′bə-rĭl′) *n.* A carbamate, $C_{12}H_{11}NO_2$, used as a general-purpose insecticide. [CARB(AMATE) + AR(OMATIC) + –YL.]

car·ben·i·cil·lin (kär-bĕn′ĭ-sĭl′ĭn) *n.* A semisynthetic derivative of penicillin that is effective in the treatment of infections caused by certain susceptible strains of Gram-negative bacteria, such as *Pseudomonas* and *Proteus.* [*car(boxy)ben(zylpen)icillin,* semisynthetic penicillin.]

car·bide (kär′bīd′) *n.* **1.** A binary compound consisting of carbon and a more electropositive element, especially calcium. **2.** A hard material made of compacted binary compounds of carbon and heavy metals, used to make tools that cut metal.

car·bine (kär′bēn′, -bīn′) *n.* A lightweight rifle with a short barrel. [French *carabine,* from Old French *carabin,* soldier armed with a musket, perhaps from *escarrabin,* gravedigger, from *scarabee,* dung beetle. See SCARAB.]

car·bi·neer (kär′bə-nîr′) *n.* Variant of **carabineer.**

car·bi·nol (kär′bə-nôl′, -nōl′, -nŏl′) *n.* **1.** See **methanol. 2.** An alcohol derived from methanol.

carbo– or **carb–** *pref.* Carbon: *carbohydrate.* [French, from *carbone,* carbon. See CARBON.]

car·bo·cy·clic (kär′bō-sī′klĭk, -sĭk′lĭk) *adj. Chemistry.* Having a ring composed exclusively of carbon atoms, as benzene.

car·bo·hy·drase (kär′bō-hī′drās′, -drāz′) *n.* Any of various enzymes, such as amylase, that catalyze the hydrolysis of a carbohydrate.

car·bo·hy·drate (kär′bō-hī′drāt′) *n.* Any of a group of organic compounds that includes sugars, starches, celluloses, and gums and serves as a major energy source in the diet of animals. These compounds are produced by photosynthetic plants and contain only carbon, hydrogen, and oxygen, usually in the ratio 1:2:1.

carbohydrate loading *n.* A dietary practice that increases carbohydrate reserves in muscle tissue through the consumption of extra quantities of high-starch foods. Some marathoners and other endurance athletes follow this practice prior to competition.

car·bo·lat·ed (kär′bə-lā′tĭd) *adj.* Containing or treated with carbolic acid.

car·bol·ic acid (kär-bŏl′ĭk) *n.* See **phenol** (sense 1). [CARB(O)– + –OL[1] + –IC.]

car·bo-load·ing (kär′bō-lō′dĭng) *n. Informal.* Carbohydrate loading. —**car′bo-load′** *v.*

car bomb *n.* A car wired with explosives that are then detonated, as by remote control, so as to kill persons or destroy property nearby.

car·bon (kär′bən) *n.* **1.** *Symbol* **C** A naturally abundant nonmetallic element that occurs in many inorganic and in all organic compounds, exists freely as graphite and diamond and as a constituent of coal, limestone, and petroleum, and is capable of chemical self-bonding to form an enormous number of chemically, biologically, and commercially important molecules. Atomic number 6; atomic weight 12.01115; sublimation point above 3,500°C; boiling point 4,827°C; specific gravity of amorphous carbon 1.8 to 2.1, of diamond 3.15 to 3.53, of graphite 1.9 to 2.3; valence 2, 3, 4. See table at **element. 2.a.** A sheet of carbon paper. **b.** A copy made by using carbon paper. **3.** *Electricity.* **a.** Either of two rods through which current flows to form an arc, as in lighting or welding. **b.** A carbonaceous electrode in an electric cell. [French *carbone,* from Latin *carbō, carbōn-,* a coal, charcoal. See **ker-**[3] in Appendix.] —**car′bon·ous** (-bə-nəs) *adj.*

carbon 14 *n.* A naturally radioactive carbon isotope with atomic mass 14 and half-life 5,780 years, used in determining the age of ancient organic, geologic, or archaeological specimens.

car·bon-14 dating (kär′bən-fôr-tēn′, -fōr-) *n.* Carbon dating.

car·bo·na·ceous (kär′bə-nā′shəs) *adj.* Consisting of, containing, relating to, or yielding carbon.

car·bo·na·do[1] (kär′bə-nā′dō, -nä′-) *Archaic. n., pl.* **-does** or **-dos.** A piece of scored and broiled fish, fowl, or meat. —**carbonado** *tr.v.* **-doed, -do·ing, -dos. 1.** To score and broil (fish, fowl, or meat). **2.** To slice or cut. [From Spanish *carbonada,* from *carbón,* charcoal, from Latin *carbō, carbōn-.* See CARBON.]

car·bo·na·do[2] (kär′bə-nā′dō, -nä′-) *n., pl.* **-does.** A form of opaque or dark-colored diamond used for drills. Also called *black diamond.* [Portuguese, from *carbone,* carbon, from French. See CARBON.]

car·bo·na·ra (kär′bə-när′ə) *n.* A sauce for pasta containing eggs, minced bacon or ham, grated cheese, and seasonings. [Italian *(alla) carbonara,* (from) a charcoal grill, from *carbone,* charcoal, from Latin *carbō, carbōn-.* See CARBON.]

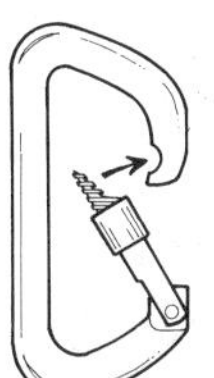

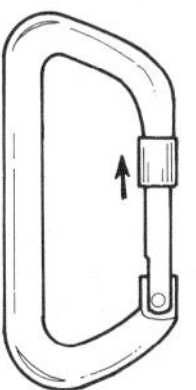

carabiner
Top: Open
Bottom: Closed

caravan

caravel

ă pat	oi boy
ā pay	ou out
âr care	o͝o took
ä father	o͞o boot
ĕ pet	ŭ cut
ē be	ûr urge
ĭ pit	th thin
ī pie	*th* this
îr pier	hw which
ŏ pot	zh vision
ō toe	ə about, item
ô paw	♦ regionalism

Stress marks: **′** (primary); ′ (secondary), as in **dictionary** (dĭk′shə-nĕr′ē)

car•bon•ate (kär′bə-nāt′) *tr.v.* **-at•ed, -at•ing, -ates. 1.** To charge (a beverage, for example) with carbon dioxide gas. **2.** To burn to carbon; carbonize. **3.** To change into a carbonate. **—carbonate** (-nāt′, -nĭt) *n.* A salt or ester of carbonic acid. **—car′bon•a′tion** *n.* **—car′bon•a′tor** *n.*

car•bon•at•ed water (kär′bə-nā′tĭd) *n.* See **soda water** (sense 1a).

carbon bisulfide *n.* Carbon disulfide.

carbon black *n.* Any of various finely divided forms of carbon derived from the incomplete combustion of natural gas or petroleum oil and used to reinforce rubber and as an ingredient in inks, paints, crayons, and polishes.

carbon copy *n.* **1.** *Abbr.* **cc** A duplicate, as of a letter, made by using carbon paper. **2.** A person or thing that closely resembles another.

carbon cycle *n.* **1.** *Physics.* See **carbon-nitrogen cycle. 2.** *Ecology.* The combined processes, including photosynthesis, decomposition, and respiration, by which carbon as a component of various compounds cycles between its major reservoirs—the atmosphere, oceans, and living organisms.

Car•bon•dale (kär′bən-dāl′). A city of southern Illinois southeast of East St. Louis. It is the seat of a branch of Southern Illinois University (established 1869). Population, 26,414.

carbon dating *n.* The determination of the approximate age of an ancient object, such as an archaeological specimen, by measuring the amount of carbon 14 it contains. **—car′bon-date′-** (kär′bən-dāt′) *v.*

carboy

carbon dioxide *n.* A colorless, odorless, incombustible gas, CO_2, formed during respiration, combustion, and organic decomposition and used in food refrigeration, carbonated beverages, inert atmospheres, fire extinguishers, and aerosols. Also called *carbonic acid gas.*

carbon disulfide *n.* A clear, flammable liquid, CS_2, used to manufacture viscose rayon and cellophane, as a solvent for fats, rubber, resins, waxes, and sulfur, and in matches, fumigants, and pesticides.

carbon fiber *n.* An extremely strong thin fiber made by pyrolyzing synthetic fibers, such as rayon, until charred. It is used to make high-strength composites.

car•bon•ic acid (kär-bŏn′ĭk) *n.* A weak, unstable acid, H_2CO_3, present in solutions of carbon dioxide in water.

carbonic acid gas *n.* See **carbon dioxide.**

Car•bon•if•er•ous (kär′bə-nĭf′ər-əs) *adj.* **1.** Of, belonging to, or denoting a geologic division of the Paleozoic Era following the Devonian and preceding the Permian, including the Mississippian Period and the Pennsylvanian Period and characterized, especially in the Pennsylvanian, by swamp formation and deposition of plant remains later hardened into coal. **2. carboniferous.** Producing or containing carbon or coal. **—Carboniferous** *n.* The Carboniferous Period. See table at **geologic time.**

car•bo•ni•um (kär-bō′nē-əm) *n.* An organic cation, such as H_3C, having one less electron than a corresponding free radical and with positive charge localized on the carbon atom.

car•bon•i•za•tion (kär′bə-nĭ-zā′shən) *n.* **1.** The process of carbonizing. **2.** The destructive distillation of bituminous coal, done in the absence of air in order to obtain coke and other fractions having a greater percentage of carbon than the original material.

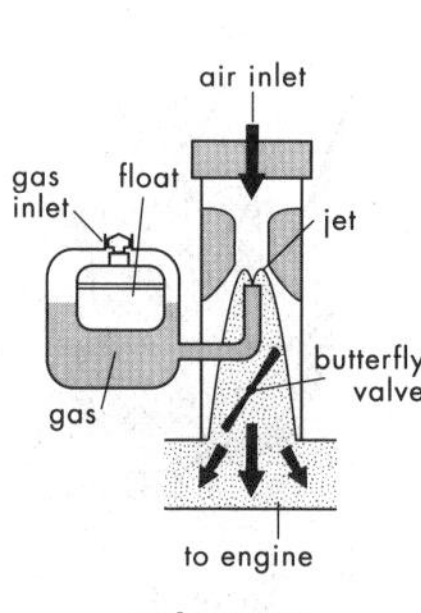

carburetor

car•bon•ize (kär′bə-nīz′) *tr.v.* **-ized, -iz•ing, -iz•es. 1.** To reduce or convert a carbon-containing substance to carbon, as by partial burning. **2.** To coat or combine with carbon. **—car′-bon•iz′er** *n.*

carbon monoxide *n.* A colorless, odorless, highly poisonous gas, CO, formed by the incomplete combustion of carbon or a carbonaceous material, such as gasoline.

car•bon-ni•tro•gen cycle (kär′bən-nī′trə-jən) *n. Physics.* A chain of thermonuclear reactions in which nitrogen isotopes are formed in intermediate stages and carbon acts essentially as a catalyst to convert four hydrogen atoms into one helium atom with the emission of two positrons. The entire sequence is thought to generate significant amounts of energy in the sun and certain other stars. Also called *carbon cycle, nitrogen cycle.*

carbon paper *n.* A lightweight paper coated on one side with a dark waxy pigment, placed between two sheets of blank paper so that the bottom sheet will receive a copy of what is typed or written on the top sheet.

carbon process *n.* A photographic printing process using permanent pigments, such as carbon, contained in a sensitized tissue or film of gelatin.

carbon star *n.* Any of a class of stars with high carbon-to-hydrogen ratios and primarily low temperatures.

carbon tetrachloride *n.* A poisonous, nonflammable, colorless liquid, CCl_4, used in fire extinguishers and as a dry-cleaning fluid.

car•bon•yl (kär′bə-nĭl′) *n.* **1.** The bivalent radical CO. Also called *carbonyl group.* **2.** A metal compound, such as $Ni(CO)_4$, containing the CO group. **—car′bon•yl′ic** *adj.*

car•bo•rane (kär′bə-rān′) *n.* Any of a class of stable compounds containing carbon, hydrogen, and boron. [Blend of CARBON and BORANE.]

Car•bo•run•dum (kär′bə-rŭn′dəm). A trademark used for an abrasive of silicon carbide crystals.

carboxy– *pref.* Carboxyl: *carboxyhemoglobin.* [From CARBOXYL.]

car•box•y•he•mo•glo•bin (kär-bŏk′sē-hē′mə-glō′bĭn) *n.* The compound that is formed when inhaled carbon monoxide combines with hemoglobin in the blood.

car•box•yl (kär-bŏk′səl) *n.* The univalent radical, COOH, the functional group characteristic of all organic acids. [CARB(O)– + OX(Y)– + –YL.] **—car′box•yl′ic** (-sĭl′ĭk) *adj.*

car•box•yl•ase (kär-bŏk′sə-lās′, -lāz′) *n.* An enzyme that catalyzes a carboxylation or decarboxylation reaction.

car•box•yl•a•tion (kär-bŏk′sə-lā′shən) *n.* The introduction of a carboxyl group into a compound or molecule.

car•box•yl•ic acid (kär′bŏk-sĭl′ĭk) *n.* An organic acid that contains one or more carboxyl groups.

car•box•y•meth•yl•cel•lu•lose (kär-bŏk′sē-mĕth′əl-sĕl′yə-lōs′) *n.* A derivative of cellulose whose sodium salt is used in the manufacture of processed foods as a stabilizing and emulsifying agent and in medicine as a laxative.

car•box•y•pep•ti•dase (kär-bŏk′sē-pĕp′tĭ-dās′, -dāz′) *n.* An enzyme that catalyzes the hydrolysis of a terminal amino acid from the end of a peptide or polypeptide that contains a free carboxyl group.

car•boy (kär′boi′) *n.* A large glass or plastic bottle, usually encased in a protective basket or crate and often used to hold corrosive liquids. [Persian *qarābah,* from Arabic *qarrābah,* big jug.]

car•bun•cle (kär′bŭng′kəl) *n.* **1.** A painful localized bacterial infection of the skin and subcutaneous tissue that usually has several openings through which pus is discharged. **2.a.** A deep-red garnet, unfaceted and convex. **b.** *Obsolete.* A red precious stone. [Middle English, from Old French, from Latin *carbunculus,* small glowing ember, carbuncle, diminutive of *carbō, carbōn-,* coal. See **ker-³** in Appendix.] **—car′bun′cled** *adj.* **—car•bun′cu•lar** (-kyə-lər) *adj.*

car•bu•ret (kär′bə-rāt′, -rĕt′, -byə-) *tr.v.* **-ret•ed, -ret•ing, -rets** or **-ret•ted, -ret•ting, -rets.** To combine or mix (a gas, for example) with volatile hydrocarbons, so as to increase available fuel energy. [From *carburet,* carbide, from French *carbure,* from Latin *carbō,* carbon. See CARBON.] **—car•bu•re′tion** *n.*

car•bu•re•tor (kär′bə-rā′tər, -byə-) *n.* A device used in internal-combustion engines to produce an explosive mixture of vaporized fuel and air. [From CARBURET.]

car•bu•rize (kär′bə-rīz′, -byə-) *tr.v.* **-rized, -riz•ing, -riz•es. 1.** To treat, combine, or impregnate with carbon, as when casehardening steel. **2.** To carburet. [CARBUR(ET) + –IZE.] **—car′bu•ri•za′tion** (-bər-ĭ-zā′shən, -byər-) *n.*

car•ca•jou (kär′kə-jo͞o′, -zho͞o′) *n.* See **wolverine** (sense 1). [Canadian French, from Montagnais *kuàkuàtsheu.*]

car•ca•net (kär′kə-nĕt′, -nĭt) *n. Archaic.* A jeweled necklace, collar, or headband. [From Old French *carcan,* collar, perhaps from Medieval Latin *carcannum,* perhaps of Germanic origin.]

car•cass (kär′kəs) *n.* **1.** The dead body of an animal, especially one slaughtered for food. **2.** The body of a human being. See Synonyms at **body. 3.** Remains from which the substance or character is gone: *the carcass of a once glorious empire.* **4.** A framework or basic structure: *the carcass of a burned-out building.* [Middle English *carcas,* from Anglo-Norman *carcais* and Medieval Latin *carcasium.*]

Car•cas•sonne (kär′-kə-sôn′, -sŏn′, -kä-). A city of southern France southeast of Toulouse. Its medieval stronghold is a major tourist attraction. Population, 41,153.

Car•che•mish (kär′kə-mĭsh′, kär-kē′mĭsh). An ancient Hittite and Assyrian city on the Euphrates River in present-day southern Turkey. Nebuchadnezzar II defeated the Egyptians here in 605 B.C.

carcino– *pref.* Cancer; cancerous: *carcinogen.* [Greek *karkino-,* from *karkinos,* crab, cancer. See **kar-** in Appendix.]

car•cin•o•gen (kär-sĭn′ə-jən, kär′sə-nə-jĕn′) *n.* A cancer-causing substance or agent. **—car′ci•no•gen′e•sis** (kär′sə-nə-jĕn′ĭ-sĭs) *n.* **—car′cin•o•gen′ic** (-jĕn′ĭk) *adj.* **—car′ci•no•ge•nic′i•ty** (-jə-nĭs′ĭ-tē) *n.*

car•ci•noid (kär′sə-noid′) *n.* A small tumor, usually found in the gastrointestinal tract, that secretes serotonin.

car•ci•no•ma (kär′sə-nō′mə) *n., pl.* **-mas** or **-ma•ta** (-mə-tə). An invasive malignant tumor derived from epithelial tissue that tends to metastasize to other areas of the body. [Latin, cancerous ulcer, from Greek *karkinōma,* from *karkinos,* cancer. See **kar-** in Appendix.] **—car′ci•no′ma•toid** (-nō′mə-toid′) *adj.* **—car′ci•nom′a•tous** (-nŏm′ə-təs, -nō′mə-) *adj.*

car•ci•no•ma•to•sis (kär′sə-nō′mə-tō′sĭs) *n.* A pathological condition characterized by the presence of carcinomas that have metastasized to many parts of the body. [Greek *karkinōma, karkinōmat-,* cancerous ulcer; see CARCINOMA + –OSIS.]

car coat *n.* An overcoat with a length extending to about the middle of the thighs.

card¹ (kärd) *n.* **1.** A flat, usually rectangular piece of stiff paper, cardboard, or plastic, especially: **a.** One of a set or pack bearing significant numbers, symbols, or figures, used in games and in divination. **b.** A greeting card. **c.** A post card. **d.** One bearing a person's name and other information, used for purposes of identification or classification. **e.** A business card. **f.** A credit card. **g.** A magnetic card. **h.** One used for recording information in a file: *an index card; a recipe card.* **2. cards.** *(used with a sing.*

or pl. verb). Games. **a.** A game played with cards. **b.** The playing of games with cards. **3.** A program, especially for a sports event. **4.a.** A menu, as in a restaurant. **b.** A wine list. **5.** *Computer Science.* **a.** A circuit board, especially for use in a microcomputer. **b.** A punch card. **6.** A compass card. **7.** *Informal.* An eccentrically amusing person. **8.** Something, such as an advantageous circumstance or tactical maneuver, that can be used to help gain an objective: "[He believed that] *Soviet Russia . . . had far more Iranian cards to play than had the United States*" (Theodore Draper). **—card** *tr.v.* **card·ed, card·ing, cards. 1.** To furnish with or attach to a card. **2.** To list (something) on a card; catalogue. **3.** To check the identification of, especially in order to verify legal age. ***—phrasal verbs.*** **card in.** To sign in, as at a place of business, by use of a magnetic card. **card out.** To sign out, as from a place of business, by use of a magnetic card. ***—idioms.*** **card up (one's) sleeve.** A secret resource or plan held in reserve: *a tough negotiator who had a number of cards up his sleeve.* **in the cards.** Likely or certain to happen: *My promotion to a higher position just isn't in the cards.* **put** (or **lay**) **(one's) cards on the table.** To make frank and clear revelation, as of one's motives or intentions. [Middle English *carde,* from Old French *carte,* from Latin *charta,* paper made from papyrus, from Greek *khartēs.*]

card² (kärd) *n.* **1.** A wire-toothed brush or a machine fitted with rows of wire teeth, used to disentangle fibers, as of wool, prior to spinning. **2.** A device used to raise the nap on a fabric. **—card** *tr.v.* **card·ed, card·ing, cards.** To comb out or brush with a card. [Middle English *carde,* from Medieval Latin *cardus,* from Latin *carduus,* thistle.] **—card′er** *n.*

Card. *abbr. Roman Catholic Church.* Cardinal.

car·da·mom (kär′də-məm) or **car·da·mon** (-mən) *n.* **1.a.** A rhizomatous Indian herb *(Elettaria cardamomum)* having capsular fruits with aromatic seeds used as a spice or condiment. **b.** The seed of this plant. **2.** Any of several plants of the related genus *Amomum,* used as a substitute for cardamom. [Middle English *cardamome,* from Old French *cardemome,* from Latin *cardamōmum,* from Greek *kardamōmon* : *kardamon,* cress + *amōmon,* an Indian spice.]

card·board (kärd′bôrd′, -bōrd′) *n.* A material similar to thick, stiff paper, that is made of pressed paper pulp or pasted sheets of paper. It is used for making cartons and signs, for example. **—cardboard** *adj.* **1.** Made of or consisting of cardboard. **2.a.** Flimsy; insubstantial. **b.** Lacking depth; superficial: *a movie with only cardboard caricatures of its historical subjects.*

card-car·ry·ing (kärd′kăr′ē-ĭng) *adj.* **1.** Being an enrolled member of a particular organization: *a card-carrying Communist.* **2.** Avidly devoted to a group or cause: *card-carrying fitness enthusiasts.* [From the assumption that such a person carries a membership card.]

card catalog *n.* An alphabetical listing, especially of books in a library, made with a separate card for each item.

Cár·de·nas (kär′dn-äs′, -thĕ-näs′). A city of northern Cuba on the **Bay of Cárdenas,** an inlet of the Straits of Florida. Cárdenas is a processing and shipping center. Population, 59,532.

Cárdenas, Lázaro. 1895–1970. Mexican soldier and politician who as president (1934–1940) distributed land to peasants, instituted social reforms, and expropriated foreign-held properties.

card·hold·er (kärd′hōl′dər) *n.* One that holds a card, especially a credit card. **—card′hold′ing** *adj.*

cardi– *pref.* Variant of **cardio–.**

car·di·a (kär′dē-ə) *n., pl.* **-di·ae** (-dē-ē′) or **-di·as. 1.** The opening of the esophagus into the stomach. **2.** The upper portion of the stomach that adjoins this opening. [Greek *kardia,* heart, cardiac orifice of the stomach. See **kerd-** in Appendix.]

car·di·ac (kär′dē-ăk′) *adj.* **1.** Of, near, or relating to the heart: *cardiac arteries.* **2.** Of or relating to the cardia. **—cardiac** *n.* A person with a heart disorder. [Middle English, from Latin *cardiacus,* from Greek *kardiakos,* from *kardia,* heart. See **kerd-** in Appendix.]

cardiac arrest *n.* Sudden cessation of heartbeat and cardiac function, resulting in the loss of effective circulation.

cardiac glycoside *n.* Any of several glycosides obtained chiefly from plant sources such as the foxglove, used medicinally to increase the force of contraction of heart muscle and to regulate heartbeats.

cardiac massage *n.* A resuscitative procedure that employs the rhythmic compression of the chest and heart in an effort to restore and maintain the circulation after cardiac arrest or ventricular fibrillation. Also called *heart massage.*

cardiac muscle *n.* The specialized striated muscle tissue of the heart; the myocardium.

car·di·ae (kär′dē-ē′) *n.* A plural of **cardia.**

car·di·al·gia (kär′dē-ăl′jə, -jē-ə) *n.* **1.** See **heartburn. 2.** Localized pain in the region of the heart. [Greek *kardialgia* : *kardia,* heart; see CARDIA + *-algia,* -algia.]

Car·diff (kär′dĭf). The capital and largest city of Wales, in the southeast part of the country on Bristol Channel. It was a prosperous coal-shipping port in the 19th and early 20th centuries. Population, 281,300.

car·di·gan (kär′dĭ-gən) *n.* A knitted upper garment, such as a sweater or a jacket, that opens down the front. [After the Seventh Earl of *Cardigan,* James Thomas Brudenell (1797–1868), British army officer.]

car·di·nal (kär′dn-əl, kärd′nəl) *adj.* **1.** Of foremost importance; paramount: *a cardinal rule; cardinal sins.* **2.** *Color.* Dark to deep or vivid red. **—cardinal** *n.* **1.** *Abbr.* **Card.** *Roman Catholic Church.* A high church official, ranking just below the pope, who has been appointed by a pope to membership in the College of Cardinals. **2.** *Color.* A dark to deep or vivid red. **3.** A North American finch *(Cardinalis cardinalis)* having a crested head, a short, thick bill, and bright red plumage in the male. **4.** A short, hooded cloak, originally of scarlet cloth, worn by women in the 18th century. **5.** A cardinal number. [Middle English, from Late Latin *cardinālis,* principal, pivotal, from Latin, serving as a hinge, from *cardō, cardin-,* hinge.] **—car′di·nal·ship′** *n.*

car·di·nal·ate (kär′dn-ə-lĭt, -lāt′, kärd′nə-) *n. Roman Catholic Church.* **1.** The position, rank, dignity, or term of a cardinal. **2.** The College of Cardinals.

cardinal flower *n.* A perennial lobelia *(Lobelia cardinalis)* native to central and eastern North America, having an elongate cluster of showy, brilliant red flowers.

cardinal number *n.* A number, such as 3 or 11 or 412, used in counting to indicate quantity but not order.

cardinal point *n.* One of the four principal directions on a compass: north, south, east, or west.

cardinal virtue *n.* One of the four paramount virtues in classical philosophy: justice, prudence, fortitude, or temperance.

cardio– or **cardi–** *pref.* Heart: *cardiovascular.* [Greek *kardio-,* from *kardia,* heart. See **kerd-** in Appendix.]

car·di·o·ac·cel·er·a·tor (kär′dē-ō′ăk-sĕl′ə-rā′tər) *n.* An agent, such as a drug, that increases the heart rate. **—car′di·o′ac·cel′er·a′tion** *n.*

car·di·o·gen·ic (kär′dē-ō-jĕn′ĭk, -jē′nĭk) *adj.* **1.** Having origin in the heart. **2.** Resulting from a disease or disorder of the heart.

car·di·o·gram (kär′dē-ə-grăm′) *n.* **1.** The curve traced by a cardiograph, used in the diagnosis of heart disorders. **2.** See **electrocardiogram.**

car·di·o·graph (kär′dē-ə-grăf′) *n.* **1.** An instrument used to record the mechanical movements of the heart. **2.** See **electrocardiograph. —car′di·og′ra·phy** (-ŏg′rə-fē) *n.*

car·di·oid (kär′dē-oid′) *n.* A heart-shaped plane curve, the locus of a fixed point on a circle that rolls on the circumference of another circle with the same radius.

car·di·ol·o·gy (kär′dē-ŏl′ə-jē) *n.* The medical study of the structure, function, and disorders of the heart. **—car′di·o·log′i·cal** (-ə-lŏj′ĭ-kəl) *adj.* **—car′di·ol′o·gist** *n.*

car·di·o·meg·a·ly (kär′dē-ō-mĕg′ə-lē) *n.* Enlargement of the heart. Also called *megalocardia.*

car·di·o·my·op·a·thy (kär′dē-ō-mī-ŏp′ə-thē) *n., pl.* **-thies.** A disease or disorder of the heart muscle, especially of unknown or obscure cause.

car·di·op·a·thy (kär′dē-ŏp′ə-thē) *n., pl.* **-thies.** A disease or disorder of the heart.

car·di·o·pul·mo·nar·y (kär′dē-ō-po͝ol′mə-nĕr′ē, -pŭl′-) *adj.* Of, relating to, or involving both the heart and the lungs.

cardiopulmonary bypass *n.* A procedure to circulate and oxygenate the blood while surgery is performed on the heart. It involves the diversion of blood from the heart and lungs through a heart-lung machine and the return of oxygenated blood to the aorta.

cardiopulmonary resuscitation *n. Abbr.* **CPR** An emergency procedure, often employed after cardiac arrest, in which cardiac massage, artificial respiration, and drugs are used to maintain the circulation of oxygenated blood to the brain.

car·di·o·res·pi·ra·to·ry (kär′dē-ō-rĕs′pər-ə-tôr′ē, -tōr′ē, -rĭ-spīr′ə-) *adj.* Of or relating to the heart and the respiratory system.

car·di·o·tho·rac·ic (kär′dē-ō-thə-răs′ĭk) *adj.* Of or relating to the heart and the chest.

car·di·o·vas·cu·lar (kär′dē-ō-văs′kyə-lər) *adj. Abbr.* **CV** Of, relating to, or involving the heart and the blood vessels: *cardiovascular disease.*

car·di·tis (kär-dī′tĭs) *n.* Inflammation of the muscle tissue of the heart.

car·doon (kär-do͞on′) *n.* A Mediterranean plant *(Cynara cardunculus)* closely related to the artichoke, cultivated for its edible leafstalks and roots. [Middle English *cardoun,* from Old French *cardon,* from Old Provençal, from Late Latin *cardō, cardōn-,* from Latin *carduus,* wild thistle.]

Car·do·zo (kär-dō′zō), **Benjamin Nathan.** 1870–1938. American jurist and writer who served as an associate justice of the U.S. Supreme Court (1932–1938).

card·sharp (kärd′shärp′) also **card·sharp·er** (-shär′pər) *n.* An expert in cheating at cards. **—card′sharp′ing** *n.*

Car·duc·ci (kär-do͞o′chē), **Giosuè.** 1835–1907. Italian poet considered the national poet of modern Italy. He won the 1906 Nobel Prize for literature.

care (kâr) *n.* **1.** A burdened state of mind, as that arising from heavy responsibilities; worry. **2.** Mental suffering; grief. **3.** An object or source of worry, attention, or solicitude: *the many cares of a working parent.* **4.** Caution in avoiding harm or danger: *handled the crystal bowl with care.* **5.a.** Close attention; painstaking application: *painting the window frames and sashes with care.* **b.** Upkeep; maintenance: *a product for the care of fine floors; hair care products.* **6.** Watchful oversight; charge or su-

cardinal
Cardinalis cardinalis

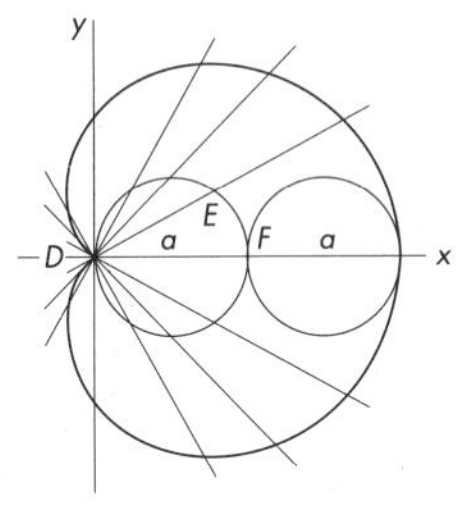

cardioid
Constructed from circle DEF and its secants through fixed point D

ă pat	oi boy
ā pay	ou out
âr care	o͝o took
ä father	o͞o boot
ĕ pet	ŭ cut
ē be	ûr urge
ĭ pit	th thin
ī pie	*th* this
îr pier	hw which
ŏ pot	zh vision
ō toe	ə about, item
ô paw	♦ regionalism

Stress marks: ′ (primary); ′ (secondary), as in **dictionary** (dĭk′shə-nĕr′ē)

pervision: *left the child in the care of a neighbor.* **7.** Attentive assistance or treatment to those in need: *a hospital that provides emergency care.* **—care** *v.* **cared, car•ing, cares.** *—intr.* **1.** To be concerned or interested: *Once inside, we didn't care whether it rained or not.* **2.** To provide needed assistance or watchful supervision: *cared for the wounded; caring for an aged relative at home.* **3.** To object or mind: *If no one cares, I'll smoke.* **4.a.** To have a liking or attachment: *didn't care for the movie.* **b.** To have a wish; be inclined: *Would you care for another helping?* *—tr.* **1.** To wish; desire: *Would you care to dance?* **2.** To be concerned to the degree of: *I don't care a bit what critics think.* [Middle English, from Old English *cearu.*]

SYNONYMS: *care, charge, custody, keeping, supervision, trust.* The central meaning shared by these nouns is "the function of watching, guarding, or overseeing": *left the house keys in my care; has charge of all rare books in the library; had custody of his friend's car during her absence; left the canary in the neighbors' keeping; assuming supervision of the first-grade pupils; documents that were committed to the bank's trust.* See also Synonyms at **anxiety.**
USAGE NOTE: It is true that a close examination of the syntax of the phrase *I could care less* reveals that it ought by rights to mean something like "I care more than I might," rather than "I don't care at all." But while the illogicality of a phrase may be reason enough for excluding it from formal writing, this illogicality cannot be invoked as grounds for keeping it out of the colloquial language, particularly when the phrase is itself an expression of casual indifference. See Usage Note at **cannot.**

CARE *abbr.* Cooperative for American Relief Everywhere.

ca•reen (kə-rēn′) *v.* **-reened, -reen•ing, -reens.** *—intr.* **1.** To lurch or swerve while in motion. **2.** To rush headlong or carelessly; career: *"He careened through foreign territories on a desperate kind of blitz"* (Anne Tyler). **3.** *Nautical.* **a.** To lean to one side, as a ship sailing in the wind. **b.** To turn a ship on its side for cleaning, caulking, or repairing. *—tr. Nautical.* **1.** To cause (a ship) to lean to one side; tilt. **2.a.** To lean (a ship) on one side for cleaning, caulking, or repairing. **b.** To clean, caulk, or repair (a ship in this position). **—careen** *n. Nautical.* **1.** The act or process of careening a ship. **2.** The position of a careened ship. [From French *(en) carène,* (on) the keel, from Old French *carene,* from Old Italian *carena,* from Latin *carīna.* See **kar-** in Appendix.] **—ca•reen′er** *n.*

USAGE NOTE: The implication of rapidity that most often accompanies the use of *careen* as a verb of motion may have arisen naturally through the extension of the nautical sense of the verb to apply to the motion of automobiles, which generally *careen,* that is, lurch or tip over, only when driven at high speed. There is thus no reason to conclude that this use of the verb is the result of a confusion of *careen* with *career,* "to rush." Whatever the origin of this use, however, it is by now so well established that it would be pedantic to object to it.

ca•reer (kə-rîr′) *n.* **1.a.** A chosen pursuit; a profession or occupation. **b.** The general course or progression of one's working life or one's professional achievements: *an officer with a distinguished career; a teacher in the midst of a long career.* **2.** A path or course, as of the sun through the heavens. **3.** Speed: *"My hasting days fly on with full career"* (John Milton). **—career** *adj.* Doing what one does as a permanent occupation or lifework: *career diplomats; a career criminal.* **—career** *intr.v.* **-reered, -reer•ing, -reers.** To move or run at full speed; rush. See Usage Note at **careen.** [French *carrière,* from Old French, racecourse, from Old Provençal *carriera,* street, from Medieval Latin *(via) carrāria,* (road) for carts, from Latin *carrus,* a Gallic type of wagon. See **kers-** in Appendix.]

ca•reer•ism (kə-rîr′ĭz′əm) *n.* Pursuit of professional advancement as one's chief or sole aim: *"Rampant careerism, which makes many a work place a joyless site, was in check"* (Mary McGrory). **—ca•reer′ist** *n.*

care•free (kâr′frē′) *adj.* Free of worries and responsibilities.

care•ful (kâr′fəl) *adj.* **1.** Attentive to potential danger, error, or harm; cautious: *was careful when crossing the busy street; gave a careful answer.* **2.** Thorough and painstaking in action or execution; conscientious: *a careful search; careful art restorers.* **3.** Protective; solicitous: *Be careful of his feelings.* **4.** Full of cares or anxiety: *"Thou art careful and troubled about many things"* (Luke 10:41). **—care′ful•ly** *adv.* **—care′ful•ness** *n.*

SYNONYMS: *careful, heedful, mindful, observant, watchful.* The central meaning shared by these adjectives is "cautiously attentive": *was careful not to get her shoes muddy; heedful of the danger; mindful of his health; observant to avoid giving offense; a watchful nurse tending a critically ill patient.* See also Synonyms at **meticulous.**
ANTONYM: *careless.*

care•giv•er (kâr′gĭv′ər) *n.* **1.** An individual, such as a physician, nurse, or social worker, who assists in the identification, prevention, or treatment of an illness or disability. **2.** An individual, such as a parent, foster parent, or head of a household, who attends to the needs of a child or dependent adult. **—care′giv′ing** *adj. & n.*

care•less (kâr′lĭs) *adj.* **1.** Taking insufficient care; negligent: *a careless housekeeper; careless proofreading.* **2.** Marked by or resulting from lack of forethought or thoroughness: *a careless mistake.* **3.** Showing a lack of consideration: *a careless remark.* **4.** Unconcerned or indifferent; heedless: *careless of the consequences.* **5.** Unstudied or effortless: *danced with careless grace.* **6.** Exhibiting a disposition that is free from cares; cheerful: *a careless grin; a careless wave of the hand.* **—care′less•ly** *adv.* **—care′less•ness** *n.*

SYNONYMS: *careless, heedless, thoughtless, inadvertent.* These adjectives apply to what is marked by insufficient care or attention. *Careless* often implies negligence: *"It is natural for careless writers to run into faults they never think of"* (George Berkeley). *Heedless* suggests often reckless inattentiveness: *"We have always known that heedless self-interest was bad morals; we know now that it is bad economics"* (Franklin D. Roosevelt). *Thoughtless* applies to actions taken without due thought or consideration: *"At length I recollected the thoughtless saying of a great princess, who, on being informed that the country people had no bread, replied, 'Let them eat cake'"* (Jean Jacques Rousseau). *Inadvertent* is used of actions marked by unintentional lack of care: *With an inadvertent gesture she swept the vase off the table onto the floor.*

ca•ress (kə-rĕs′) *n.* A gentle touch or gesture of fondness, tenderness, or love. **—caress** *tr.v.* **-ressed, -ress•ing, -ress•es. 1.** To touch or stroke in an affectionate or loving manner. **2.** To touch or move as if with a caress: *soft music that caressed the ears.* **3.** To treat fondly, kindly, or favorably; cherish. [French *caresse,* from Italian *carezza,* from *caro,* dear, from Latin *cārus.* See **kā-** in Appendix.] **—ca•ress′er** *n.* **—ca•ress′ing•ly** *adv.* **—ca•res′sive** *adj.*

SYNONYMS: *caress, cuddle, fondle, pet.* The central meaning shared by these verbs is "to touch or handle affectionately": *caressed the little boy's forehead; cuddled the kitten in her arms; fondling my hand; petting his pony.*

car•et (kăr′ĭt) *n.* A proofreading symbol (^) used to indicate where something is to be inserted in a line of printed or written matter. [Latin, there is lacking, third person sing. present tense of *carēre,* to lack. See **kes-** in Appendix.]

care•tak•er (kâr′tā′kər) *n.* **1.** One that is employed to look after or take charge of goods, property, or a person; a custodian. **2.** One that temporarily performs the duties of an office: *The government resigned, but the premier served as caretaker until new leaders could be elected.* *—attributive.* Often used to modify another noun: *a caretaker government; a caretaker administration.*

Ca•rew (kə-ro͞o′), **Thomas.** 1595?–1639? English poet whose amorous, light lyrics were favored by Charles I.

care•worn (kâr′wôrn′, -wōrn′) *adj.* Showing the effects of worry, anxiety, or burdensome responsibility: *the parent's careworn face.* See Synonyms at **haggard.**

car•fare (kär′fâr′) *n.* The fare charged a passenger, as on a streetcar or bus.

car•go (kär′gō) *n., pl.* **-goes** or **-gos.** The freight carried by a ship, an aircraft, or another vehicle. [Spanish, from *cargar,* to load, from Late Latin *carricāre,* from Latin *carrus,* a Gallic type of wagon. See **kers-** in Appendix.]

car•hop (kär′hŏp′) *n.* One who waits on customers at a drive-in restaurant.

Car•i•a (kâr′ē-ə). An ancient region of southwest Asia Minor with a coastline on the Aegean Sea. It was settled by Dorian and Ionian colonists and conquered by Alexander the Great in 334 B.C. **—Car′i•an** *adj. & n.*

Car•ib (kăr′ĭb) *n., pl.* **Carib** or **-ibs. 1.** Also **Car•i•ban** (kăr′ə-bən, kə-rē′bən′). A member of a group of American Indian peoples of northern South America, the Lesser Antilles, and the eastern coast of Central America. **2.** Any of the languages of the Carib. [Spanish *Caribe,* of Cariban origin.]

Car•i•ban (kăr′ə-bən, kə-rē′bən) *n., pl.* **Cariban** or **-bans. 1.** Variant of **Carib** (sense 1). **2.** A language family comprising the Carib languages. **—Car′i•ban** *adj.*

Car•ib•be•an (kăr′ə-bē′ən, kə-rĭb′ē-ən) *adj.* **1.** Of or relating to the Caribbean Sea, its islands, or its Central or South American coasts or to the peoples or cultures of this region. **2.** Of or relating to the Carib or their language or culture. **—Caribbean** *n.* A Carib.

Caribbean Sea. An arm of the western Atlantic Ocean bounded by the coasts of Central and South America and the West Indies. It has been an important shipping route since the opening of the Panama Canal in 1914. Its many islands and tropical climate make the Caribbean a major tourist area.

ca•ri•be (kə-rē′bē) *n.* See **piranha.** [American Spanish, from Spanish *Caribe,* Carib. See CARIB.]

Car•i•boo Mountains (kăr′ə-bo͞o′). A range of eastern British Columbia, Canada, parallel to and west of the Rocky Mountains. It rises to 3,583.8 m (11,750 ft) at Mount Sir Wilfred Laurier.

car•i•bou (kăr′ə-bo͞o′) *n., pl.* **caribou** or **-bous.** Any of several large reindeer native to northern North America. [Micmac *ĝalipu* (influenced by Canadian French *caribou,* also from Micmac), from Proto-Algonquin **mekālixpowa* : **mekāl-,* to scrape + *-*ixpo-,* snow.]

car•i•ca•ture (kăr′ĭ-kə-cho͝or′, -chər) *n.* **1.a.** A representation, especially pictorial or literary, in which the subject's distinctive features or peculiarities are deliberately exaggerated to produce a comic or grotesque effect. **b.** The art of creating such representations. **2.** A grotesque imitation or misrepresentation: *The trial was a caricature of justice.* **—caricature** *tr.v.* **-tured, -tur·ing, -tures.** To represent or imitate in an exaggerated, distorted manner. [French, from Italian *caricatura,* from *caricare,* to load, to exaggerate, from Late Latin *carricāre,* from Latin *carrus,* a Gallic type of wagon. See **kers-** in Appendix.] **—car′i·ca·tur′ist** *n.*

SYNONYMS: *caricature, burlesque, parody, travesty, satire, lampoon.* These nouns denote artistic forms in which someone or something is imitated in an amusing and generally critical manner. A *caricature* grossly exaggerates a distinctive or striking feature, as of a person or group, with intent to ridicule. *Burlesque,* which usually denotes a stage work, suggests outlandish mimicry and broad comedy to provoke laughter. *Parody, travesty,* and *satire* generally apply to written works. *Parody* is writing that employs the manner and style of a well-known work or writer for a ludicrous effect. A *travesty* is a harshly distorted imitation. *Satire* usually involves holding up to ridicule the follies and vices of a people or time. A *lampoon* is a malicious but broadly humorous satire.

WORD HISTORY: The history of the word *caricature* takes us back through the centuries to a time when the Romans occupied Gaul, offering the blessings of civilization to the Gauls but also borrowing from them as well. One such borrowing, the Gaulish word **karros,* meaning "a wagon or cart," became Latin *carrus,* "a Gallic type of wagon." This Latin word has continued to roll through the English language, giving us *car, career, cargo, carry,* and *charge,* among others. *Caricature,* another offspring of *carrus,* came to us via French from Italian, in which *caricatura,* the source of the French word, was derived from Italian *caricare,* "to load, burden, or exaggerate." *Caricare* in turn came from Late Latin *carricāre,* "to load," derived from the Romans' Gaulish borrowing *carrus.*

car·ies (kâr′ēz) *n., pl.* **caries.** Decay of a bone or tooth, especially dental caries. [Latin *cariēs.*]

car·il·lon (kăr′ə-lŏn′, -lən) *n. Music.* **1.** A stationary set of chromatically tuned bells in a tower, usually played from a keyboard. **2.** A composition written or arranged for these bells. **—carillon** *intr.v.* **-lonned, -lon·ning, -lons.** To play a carillon. [French, alteration of Old French *quarregnon,* from Late Latin *quaterniō, quaterniōn-,* set of four. See QUATERNION.]

car·il·lon·neur (kăr′ə-lə-nûr′) *n. Music.* A person who plays a carillon. [French, from *carillon,* carillon. See CARILLON.]

ca·ri·na (kə-rī′nə, -rē′-) *n., pl.* **-nae** (-nē). A keel-shaped ridge or structure, such as that on the breastbone of a bird or of the fused lower two petals of flowers of many members of the pea family. [Latin *carīna,* keel. See **kar-** in Appendix.]

Ca·ri·na (kə-rī′nə) *n.* A constellation in the Southern Hemisphere near Volans and Vela that contains the star Canopus. [Latin *carīna,* keel. See CARINA.]

ca·ri·nae (kə-rī′nē, -rē′-) *n.* Plural of **carina.**

car·i·nate (kăr′ə-nāt′, -nĭt) also **car·i·nat·ed** (-nā′tĭd) *adj.* Shaped like or having a carina or keel; ridged.

car·ing (kâr′ĭng) *adj. Usage Problem.* Feeling and exhibiting concern and empathy for others: *"We formed Generations United to argue for a caring society"* (Jack Ossofsky).

USAGE NOTE: Some critics have objected to the use of *caring* as an adjective, perhaps because it appears to treat compassion as a chronic condition. The acceptability of the usage may therefore vary according to the relation between the source and object of the caring. Thus 74 percent of the Usage Panel accepts the sentence *A child has a right to certain things: a secure home, a healthful environment, and caring parents.* A smaller majority, 58 percent, accepts *We are looking for a few caring people to help with this program,* where the adjective appears to ascribe an undiscriminating disposition to care about whatever object of concern may present itself. Finally, only 29 percent of the Panel accepts *A child has the right to grow up in a healthful, caring environment,* where *caring* is applied to circumstances rather than to persons.

Ca·rin·thi·a (kə-rĭn′thē-ə). A region and former duchy of central Europe in southern Austria. It was part of the Hapsburg domains after 1335. **—Ca·rin′thi·an** *adj.*

Car·i·o·ca (kăr′ē-ō′kə) *n.* **1.** A native or inhabitant of Rio de Janeiro, Brazil. **2. carioca. a.** A dance similar to the samba. **b.** The music for this dance. [Portuguese, of Tupian origin.] **—Car′i·o′can** *adj.*

car·i·ole also **car·ri·ole** (kăr′ē-ōl′) *n.* **1.** A small, open, two- or four-wheeled carriage drawn by one horse. **2.** A light covered cart. [French *carriole,* from Old Provençal *carriola,* diminutive of *carri,* chariot, from Latin *carrus,* a Gallic type of wagon. See **kers-** in Appendix.]

car·i·ous (kâr′ē-əs) *adj.* Having caries, especially of the teeth; decayed. **—car′i·os′i·ty** (-ŏs′ĭ-tē), **car′i·ous·ness** *n.*

cark (kärk) *tr. & intr.v.* **carked, cark·ing, carks.** To burden or be burdened with trouble; worry. **—cark** *n.* A worry; a trouble: *carks and cares.* [Middle English *carken,* from Norman French *carquier,* to burden, load, from Late Latin *carricāre.* See CARGO.]

Carl XVI Gus·tav (kärl gŭs′täv, -täf, go͝os′-). Born 1946. King of Sweden (since 1973).

Carle·ton (kärl′tən), Sir **Guy.** First Baron Dorchester. 1724–1808. British general and colonial administrator who repelled an American attack on Quebec (1775–1776) and captured the fort at Crown Point, New York (1776).

car·line or **car·lin** (kär′lĭn) *n. Scots.* A woman, especially an old one. [Middle English *kerling,* from Old Norse, from *karl,* man.]

car·ling (kär′lĭng, -lĭn) *n. Nautical.* One of the short timbers running fore and aft that connect the transverse beams supporting the deck of a ship. [Middle English, from Old French *calingue* and from Old Norse *kerling,* old woman (Old French, from Old Norse).]

Car·lisle (kär-līl′, kär′līl′). **1.** A borough of northwest England near the Scottish border. Mary Queen of Scots was imprisoned in Carlisle's 11th-century castle from May to July 1568. Population, 71,200. **2.** A borough of southern Pennsylvania west-southwest of Harrisburg. It was a headquarters for George Washington during the Whiskey Rebellion of 1794. Population, 18,314.

Car·list (kär′lĭst) *n.* A supporter of Don Carlos, the pretender to the Spanish throne, or his heirs. **—Car′list** *adj.*

car·load (kär′lōd′) *n. Abbr.* **c.l. 1.** The quantity that a car can hold. **2.** The official minimum weight necessary to ship freight at a reduced rate.

Car·los (kär′ləs, -lôs), Don Count of Molina. 1788–1855. Spanish pretender to the throne who claimed the title (1833) when his brother Ferdinand VII's daughter Isabella II inherited the crown because of Ferdinand's abrogation (1830) of the ancient Salic law prohibiting women from succeeding to the throne. Don Carlos waged an unsuccessful civil war until 1840. His claim was later revived by his heirs in 1860, 1869, and 1872.

Car·lo·ta (kär-lô′tə). 1840–1927. Belgian-born empress of Mexico (1864–1867) as the wife of Archduke Maximilian of Austria.

Car·lo·vin·gian (kär′lə-vĭn′jən, -jē-ən) *adj. & n.* Variant of **Carolingian.**

Carls·bad (kärlz′băd′). **1.** A city of southern California on the Pacific Ocean north-northwest of San Diego. It is a health resort and manufacturing center. Population, 35,490. **2.** A city of southeast New Mexico on the Pecos River near the Texas border. Large deposits of potash were discovered in the vicinity in 1931. Population, 25,496. **3.** (*also* kärls′bät′). See **Karlovy Vary.**

Carlsbad Caverns. A group of limestone caverns in the Guadalupe Mountains of southeast New Mexico including spectacular stalactite and stalagmite formations.

Carls·ru·he (kärlz′ro͞o′ə, kärls′-). See **Karlsruhe.**

Car·lyle (kär-līl′, kär′līl), **Thomas.** 1795–1881. British historian and essayist whose works, such as *The French Revolution* (1837), are characterized by his trenchant social and political criticism and his complex literary style.

car·mak·er (kär′mā′kər) *n.* A manufacturer of automotive vehicles, such as cars, trucks, and vans.

Car·mar·then (kär-mär′*th*ən). A municipal borough of southern Wales. One of the oldest towns in Wales, it was built on the site of a Roman fort. Population, 12,302.

Car·me (kär′mē) *n.* The satellite of Jupiter that is 15th in distance from the planet. [Greek *Karmē,* mother by Zeus of Britomartis, a Cretan goddess.]

Car·mel. 1. (kär-mĕl′). Also **Car·mel-by-the-Sea** (-bī-*th*ə-sē′) A city of western California on **Carmel Bay** at the southern end of the Monterey Peninsula. It is an artists' and writers' colony and a popular tourist spot. Population, 4,707. **2.** (kär′məl). A city of central Indiana, a suburb of Indianapolis. Population, 18,272.

Car·mel (kär′məl), **Mount.** A limestone ridge of northwest Israel extending about 24 km (15 mi) from the Plain of Esdraelon northwest to the Mediterranean Sea. It rises to approximately 546 m (1,790 ft).

Car·mel·ite (kär′mə-līt′) *n.* **1.** A monk or mendicant friar belonging to the order of Our Lady of Mount Carmel, founded in 1155. Also called *White Friar.* **2.** A member of a community of nuns of this order, founded in 1452. **—Car′mel·ite′** *adj.*

Car·mi·chael (kär′mī-kəl), **Hoagland Howard.** Known as "Hoagy." 1899–1981. American songwriter whose many popular works include "Stardust" (1929).

car·min·a·tive (kär-mĭn′ə-tĭv, kär′mə-nā′-) *adj.* Inducing the expulsion of gas from the stomach and intestines. **—carminative** *n.* A drug or agent that induces the expulsion of gas from the stomach or intestines. [Middle English *carminatif,* from Old French, from Latin *carminātus,* past participle of *carmināre,* to card wool, from **carmen,* card for wool, from *cārere,* to card.]

car·mine (kär′mĭn, -mīn′) *n.* **1.** *Color.* A strong to vivid red. **2.** A crimson pigment derived from cochineal. **—carmine** *adj. Color.* Strong to vivid red. [French *carmin,* from Medieval Latin *carminium,* probably blend of Arabic *qirmiz,* kermes; see KERMES, and Latin *minium,* cinnabar; see MINIUM.]

car·nage (kär′nĭj) *n.* **1.** Massive slaughter, as in war; a massacre. **2.** Corpses, especially of those killed in battle. [French, from Old French, from Old Italian *carnaggio,* from Medieval Latin *carnāticum,* meat, from Latin *carō, carn-,* flesh. See **sker-**[1] in Appendix.]

car·nal (kär′nəl) *adj.* **1.** Relating to the physical and especially

ă pat	oi boy
ā pay	ou out
âr care	o͝o took
ä father	o͞o boot
ĕ pet	ŭ cut
ē be	ûr urge
ĭ pit	th thin
ī pie	*th* this
îr pier	hw which
ŏ pot	zh vision
ō toe	ə about, item
ô paw	♦ regionalism

Stress marks: **′** (primary); ′ (secondary), as in **dictionary** (dĭk′shə-nĕr′ē)

sexual appetites: *carnal desire.* **2.** Worldly or earthly; temporal: *the carnal world.* **3.** Of or relating to the body or flesh; bodily: *carnal remains.* [Middle English, from Old North French *carnel,* from Latin *carnālis,* from Latin *carō, carn-,* flesh. See **sker-** [1] in Appendix.] **—car•nal′i•ty** (kär-năl′ĭ-tē) *n.* **—car′nal•ly** *adv.*

carnal knowledge *n.* Sexual intercourse.

car•nall•ite (kär′nə-līt′) *n.* A white, brownish, or reddish mineral, $KClMgCl_2 \cdot 6H_2O$, an ore of potassium, used to manufacture potash salts. [After Rudolf von *Carnall* (1804–1874), German mining engineer.]

car•nas•si•al (kär-năs′ē-əl) *adj.* Adapted for tearing apart flesh: *carnassial teeth.* **—carnassial** *n.* A tooth adapted for tearing apart flesh, especially one of the last upper premolar or first lower molar teeth in carnivorous mammals. [From French *carnassier,* carnivorous, from Provençal, from *carnasso,* meat in abundance, from *carn,* flesh, from Latin *carō, carn-.* See **sker-** [1] in Appendix.]

car•na•tion (kär-nā′shən) *n.* **1.a.** Any of numerous cultivated forms of a perennial plant *(Dianthus caryophyllus)* having showy, variously colored, usually double, often fragrant flowers with fringed petals. **b.** A flower of this plant. Also called *clove pink.* **2.** A pinkish tint once used in painting. [From obsolete French, flesh-colored, from Old French (from Old Italian *carnagione,* skin, complexion, from *carne,* flesh) or from Late Latin *carnātiō, carnātiōn-,* flesh, both from Latin *carō, carn-.* See **sker-** [1] in Appendix.]

car•nau•ba (kär-nô′bə, -nou′-, -no͞o′-) *n.* **1.** A Brazilian palm tree *(Copernicia prunifera)* having densely waxy, fan-shaped leaves and toothed leafstalks. **2.** A hard wax obtained from the leaves of this plant and used especially in polishes and floor waxes. In this sense, also called *carnauba wax.* [Portuguese, from Tupi *carnaúba.*]

Car•ne•gie (kär′nə-gē, kär-nā′gē, -nĕg′ē), **Andrew.** 1835–1919. Scottish-born American industrialist and philanthropist who amassed a fortune in the steel industry and donated millions of dollars for the benefit of the public.

Car•ne•gie (kär′nə-gē), **Dale.** 1888–1955. American educator known for his self-improvement book *How to Win Friends and Influence People* (1936).

car•nel•ian (kär-nēl′yən) also **cor•nel•ian** (kôr-) *n.* A pale to deep red or reddish-brown variety of clear chalcedony, used in jewelry. [Middle English *corneline,* from Old French, from *cornel,* cornel, from Latin *cornus.*]

car•net (kär-nā′) *n.* **1.** An official pass or permit, especially one for crossing national boundaries. **2.** A book of postage stamps. [French, notebook, carnet, from Old French *quernet,* pocket notebook, from *quaer,* quire. See QUIRE [1].]

car•ney (kär′nē) *n. Informal.* Variant of **carny.**

Car•nic Alps (kär′nĭk). A range of the eastern Alps in southern Austria and northeast Italy rising to about 2,782 m (9,121 ft).

Car•ni•o•la (kär′nē-ō′lə, kärn-yō′-). A mountainous region of northwest Yugoslavia. The earliest inhabitants, a Celtic people, were displaced by the Romans, who in turn were overrun by Slovenes in the sixth century A.D. **—Car′ni•o′lan** *adj. & n.*

car•ni•tine (kär′nĭ-tēn′) *n.* A betaine commonly occurring in the liver and in skeletal muscle that functions in fatty acid transport across mitochondrial membranes. [German *Karnitin,* from *Karnin,* a basic substance derived from meat, from Latin *carō, carn-,* flesh. See CARNAL.]

car•ni•val (kär′nə-vəl) *n.* **1.a.** A festival marked by merrymaking and feasting during the season just before Lent. **b.** Merrymaking and feasting just before Lent. **2.** A traveling amusement show usually including rides, games, and sideshows. **3.** A festival or revel: *winter carnival.* [Italian *carnevale,* from Old Italian *carnelevare,* Shrovetide : *carne,* meat (from Latin *carō, carn-;* see **sker-** [1] in Appendix) + *levare,* to remove (from Latin *levāre,* to raise; see **legʷh-** in Appendix).]

car•ni•vore (kär′nə-vôr′, -vōr′) *n.* **1.** A flesh-eating animal. **2.** Any of various predatory, flesh-eating mammals of the order Carnivora, including the dogs, cats, bears, weasels, hyenas, and raccoons. **3.** An insectivorous plant. [From French, meat-eating, from Latin *carnivorus.* See CARNIVOROUS.]

car•niv•o•rous (kär-nĭv′ər-əs) *adj.* **1.** Of or relating to carnivores. **2.** Flesh-eating or predatory: *a carnivorous bird.* **3.** *Botany.* Capable of trapping insects or other small organisms and absorbing nutrients from them; insectivorous. [From Latin *carnivorus* : *carō, carn-,* flesh; see **sker-** [1] in Appendix + *-vorus,* -vorous.] **—car•niv′o•rous•ly** *adv.* **—car•niv′o•rous•ness** *n.*

Car•not (kär-nō′), **Lazare Nicolas Marguerite.** 1753–1823. French military strategist for the Republican armies during the French Revolution. He later held high positions under Napoleon I.

Carnot, Nicolas Léonard Sadi. 1796–1832. French physicist and engineer who founded the science of thermodynamics.

car•no•tite (kär′nə-tīt′) *n.* A yellow ore of uranium and radium with composition $K(UO_2)_2(VO_4)_2 \cdot 3H_2O$. [French, after Marie Adolphe *Carnot* (died 1920), French mining engineer.]

car•ny also **car•ney** (kär′nē) *n., pl.* **-nies** also **-neys.** *Informal.* **1.** A carnival. **2.** A person who works with a carnival.

car•ob (kăr′əb) *n.* **1.** An eastern Mediterranean evergreen tree *(Ceratonia siliqua)* in the pea family, having pinnately compound leaves and large, dark, leathery pods. **2.** The pod of this plant, containing a sweet edible pulp and seeds that yield a gum used as a stabilizer in food products. Also called *algarroba.* **3.** An edible powder or flour made from the ground seeds and pods of this plant, often used as a substitute for chocolate. [Middle English *carabe,* from Old French *carobe,* from Medieval Latin *carrūbium,* from Arabic *ḫarrūbah.*]

ca•roche (kə-rōch′, -rōsh′) *n.* A stately carriage of the late 16th and 17th centuries. [Obsolete French *carroche,* from Old Italian *carrozza,* ultimately from *carro,* cart, from Latin *carrus,* a Gallic type of wagon. See **kers-** in Appendix.]

car•ol (kăr′əl) *n.* **1.** *Music.* A song of praise or joy, especially for Christmas. **2.** An old round dance often accompanied by singing. **—carol** *v.* **-oled, -ol•ing, -ols** also **-olled, -ol•ling, -ols.** *—intr.* **1.** To sing in a loud, joyous manner. **2.** To go from house to house singing Christmas songs. *—tr.* **1.** To celebrate in or as if in song: *caroling the victory.* **2.** To sing loudly and joyously. [Middle English *carole,* a kind of round dance with singing, from Old French *carole,* probably from Late Latin *choraula,* choral song, from Latin *choraulēs,* accompanist, from Greek *khoraulēs* : *khoros,* choral dance; see CHORUS + *aulos,* flute.] **—car′ol•er** *n.*

Car•ol II (kăr′əl). 1893–1953. King of Romania (1930–1940) who renounced his right of succession (1925) because of his love for a commoner, Magda Lupescu (1896?–1977), but reclaimed the throne in 1930. In 1940 he was ousted by a Nazi-influenced revolt.

Car•o•le•an (kăr′ə-lē′ən) *adj.* Of or relating to Charles I or Charles II of England. [From Medieval Latin *Carolus,* Charles.]

Ca•ro•li•na. **1.** (kăr′ə-lī′nə). An English colony of southeastern North America, first settled in 1653 and divided into North Carolina and South Carolina in 1729. **2.** (kä′rô-lē′nä). A city of northeast Puerto Rico east-southeast of San Juan. It is a processing center with a textile industry. Population, 147,835.

Carolina allspice *n.* A species of sweet shrub *(Calycanthus floridus)* native chiefly to the southeast United States. Also called *strawberry shrub.*

Carolina jasmine also **Carolina jessamine** *n.* Any of several poisonous, woody, evergreen vines of the genus *Gelsemium,* especially *G. sempervirens,* of the southeast United States, having fragrant, yellow, funnel-shaped flowers. Also called *Carolina yellow jasmine, evening trumpet flower, jasmine, yellow jessamine.*

Ca•ro•li•nas (kăr′ə-lī′nəz). The colonies (after 1729) or present-day states of North Carolina and South Carolina.

Carolina yellow jasmine *n.* See **Carolina jasmine.**

Car•o•line (kăr′ə-līn′, -lĭn) *adj.* Relating to the life and times of Charles I or Charles II of England. [Medieval Latin *Carolīnus,* from *Carolus,* Charles.]

Caroline Islands. An archipelago of the western Pacific Ocean east of the Philippines. The islands were controlled successively by Spain, Germany, and Japan before being included in the U.S. Trust Territory of the Pacific Islands in 1947.

Car•o•lin•gian (kăr′ə-lĭn′-jən, -jē-ən) also **Car•lo•vin•gian** (kär′lə-vĭn′jən, -jē-ən) *—adj.* Of or relating to the Frankish dynasty that was founded by Pepin the Short in 751 and that lasted until 987 in France and 911 in Germany. *—n.* A member of the Carolingian dynasty. [French *Carolingien,* alteration of *Carlovingien,* blend of Medieval Latin *Carolus,* Charles, and French *Mérovingien,* Merovingian.]

Car•o•lin•i•an (kăr′ə-lĭn′ē-ən) *adj.* **1.** Caroline. **2.** Of or relating to Charlemagne and his times. **3.** Of or relating to Carolina or the Carolinas. **—Carolinian** *n.* A native or inhabitant of Carolina or the Carolinas.

car•om (kăr′əm) *n.* **1.** A collision followed by a rebound. **2.** *Games.* **a.** A shot in billiards in which the cue ball successively strikes two other balls. Also called *billiard.* **b.** A similar shot in a related game, such as pool. **—carom** *v.* **-omed, -om•ing, -oms.** *—intr.* **1.** To collide and rebound; glance: *The car caromed off the guard rail into the ditch.* **2.** *Games.* To make a carom, as in billiards. *—tr.* To cause to carom. [Short for *carambole,* a stroke at billiards, from French, a billiard ball, from Spanish *carambola,* a stroke at billiards, perhaps from Portuguese, carambola. See CARAMBOLA.]

Ca•ro•ní (kär′ə-nē′). A river rising in southeast Venezuela near the Guyana border and flowing 885 km (550 mi) northward to join the Orinoco River.

car•o•tene (kăr′ə-tēn′) also **car•o•tin** (-tĭn) *n.* An orange-yellow to red crystalline pigment, $C_{40}H_{56}$, found in animal tissue and certain plants, such as carrots and squash. It exists in three isomeric forms and is converted to vitamin A in the liver. [German *Karotin,* from Latin *carōta,* carrot. See CARROT.]

car•o•te•ne•mi•a (kăr′ə-tə-nē′mē-ə) *n.* The presence of excess carotene in the blood, often resulting in yellowing of the skin.

ca•rot•e•noid (kə-rŏt′n-oid′) *n.* Any of a class of yellow to red pigments, including the carotenes and the xanthophylls. **—carotenoid** *adj.* Of or relating to such a pigment.

Ca•roth•ers (kə-rŭth′ərz), **Wallace Hume.** 1896–1937. American chemist who developed the synthetic material nylon, which was patented in 1937.

ca•rot•id (kə-rŏt′ĭd) *n.* Either of the two major arteries, one on each side of the neck, that carry blood to the head. **—carotid** *adj.* Of or relating to either of these arteries. [French *carotide,* from Greek *karōtides,* carotid arteries, from *karoun,* to stupefy. See **ker-** [1] in Appendix.]

carotid body *n.* A chemoreceptor located near the bifurcations of the carotid arteries that monitors changes in the oxygen content of the blood and helps control respiratory activity.

carotid sinus *n.* A dilated area located at the bifurcations of

ă pat	oi boy
ā pay	ou out
âr care	o͝o took
ä father	o͞o boot
ĕ pet	ŭ cut
ē be	ûr urge
ĭ pit	th thin
ī pie	*th* this
îr pier	hw which
ŏ pot	zh vision
ō toe	ə about, item
ô paw	♦ regionalism

Stress marks: ′ (primary); ′ (secondary), as in **dictionary** (dĭk′shə-nĕr′ē)

the carotid arteries and containing numerous baroreceptors that function in the control of blood pressure by mediating changes in the heart rate.

car·o·tin (kăr′ə-tĭn) *n.* Variant of **carotene.**

ca·rous·al (kə-rou′zəl) *n.* A riotous drinking party; boisterous merrymaking; revelry.

ca·rouse (kə-rouz′) *n.* Boisterous, drunken merrymaking; a carousal. **—carouse** *intr.v.* **-roused, -rous·ing, -rous·es. 1.** To engage in boisterous, drunken merrymaking. **2.** To drink excessively. [German *garaus,* all out, drink up : *gar,* completely (from Middle High German, from Old High German *garo*) + *aus,* out, up (from Middle High German *ūz,* from Old High German *ūz;* see **ud-** in Appendix).] **—ca·rous′er** *n.*

WORD HISTORY: The origin of the word *carouse* can be found in a German interjection that meant "time to leave the bar." German *garaus,* which is derived from the phrase *gar* ("all") *aus* ("out"), meaning "all out," then came to mean "drink up, bottoms up," and "a last drink before closing time." The English borrowed this noun, with the meaning "the practice of sitting around drinking until closing time," sometimes spelling the word *garaus* but usually spelling it closer to the way it is spelled today. Soon after the word is first recorded as a noun in 1559, we find the verb *carouse,* in 1567.

car·ou·sel or **car·rou·sel** (kăr′ə-sĕl′, -zĕl′) *n.* **1.** A merry-go-round, as one at an amusement park. **2.** A circular conveyor on which objects are displayed or rotated: *a baggage carousel in an airport.* **3.** A tournament in which knights or horsemen engaged in various exercises and races. [French *carrousel,* tilting match, carousel, from Italian *carosello,* tilting match.]

carp¹ (kärp) *intr.v.* **carped, carp·ing, carps.** To find fault in a disagreeable way; complain fretfully. See Synonyms at **quibble.** [Middle English *carpen,* from Old Norse *karpa,* to boast.] **—carp′er** *n.*

carp² (kärp) *n., pl.* **carp** or **carps. 1.** An edible freshwater fish *(Cyprinus carpio)* of Europe and Asia that is frequently bred in ponds and lakes. **2.** Any of various fishes of the family Cyprinidae. [Middle English *carpe,* from Old French *carpe,* from Medieval Latin *carpa,* of Germanic origin.]

-carp *suff.* Fruit; part of a fruit; fruitlike structure: *mesocarp.* [New Latin *-carpium,* from Greek *-karpion,* from *karpos,* fruit. See **kerp-** in Appendix.]

car·pac·cio (kär-pä′chō) *n.* Very thinly sliced raw beef or tuna garnished with a sauce. [Italian, after Vittore CARPACCIO, who favored red pigments.]

Car·pac·cio (kär-pä′chē-ō, -chô), **Vittore.** 1460?–1525? Italian painter noted for his vivid narrative series on religious subjects.

car·pal (kär′pəl) *adj.* Of, relating to, or near the carpus. **—carpal** *n.* A bone of the carpus. [New Latin *carpālis,* from Greek *karpos,* wrist.]

Car·pa·thi·an Mountains (kär-pā′thē-ən). A major mountain system of central Europe in eastern Czechoslovakia, southern Poland, western Ukraine, and northeast Romania. Extending in an arc about 2,253 km (1,400 mi) long, the range links the Alps with the Balkan Mountains.

car·pe di·em (kär′pĕ dē′ĕm′, -əm, dī′-) *n.* The admonition to seize the pleasures of the moment without thought for the future. [Latin : *carpe,* seize + *diem,* day.]

car·pel (kär′pəl) *n.* One of the structural units of a pistil, representing a modified, ovule-bearing leaf. [New Latin *carpellum,* from Greek *karpos,* fruit. See **kerp-** in Appendix.] **—car′pel·lar′y** (-pə-lĕr′ē) *adj.*

car·pel·late (kär′pə-lāt′, -lĭt) *adj. Botany.* Having carpels; pistillate.

Car·pen·tar·i·a (kär′pən-târ′ē-ə), **Gulf of.** A wide inlet of the Arafura Sea indenting the northern coast of Australia.

car·pen·ter (kär′pən-tər) *n.* A skilled worker who makes, finishes, and repairs wooden objects and structures. **—carpenter** *v.* **-tered, -ter·ing, -ters.** *—tr.* To make, finish, or repair (wooden structures). *—intr.* To work as a carpenter. [Middle English, from Anglo-Norman, from Latin *carpentārius (artifex),* (maker) of a carriage, from *carpentum,* a two-wheeled carriage. See **kers-** in Appendix.] **—car′pen·try** (-trē) *n.*

carpenter ant *n.* Any of various large ants of the genus *Camponotus* that nest in and are destructive to wood.

carpenter bee *n.* Any of various solitary bees of the family Apidae that bore tunnels into wood to lay their eggs.

Car·pen·ters·ville (kär′pən-tərz-vĭl′). A village of northeast Illinois west-northwest of Chicago. It was settled in 1834. Population, 23,272.

car·pet (kär′pĭt) *n.* **1.a.** A thick, heavy covering for a floor, usually made of woven wool or synthetic fibers; a rug. **b.** The fabric used for this floor covering. **2.** A surface or surface covering that is similar to a rug: *a carpet of leaves and pine needles on the forest floor.* **—carpet** *tr.v.* **-pet·ed, -pet·ing, -pets.** To cover with or as if with a carpet: *carpet the stairs; snow that carpeted the sidewalks.* **—*idiom.* on the carpet. 1.** In a position of being reprimanded by one in authority: *was called on the carpet for cheating.* **2.** Under discussion or consideration: *Several important matters will be on the carpet at today's meeting.* [Middle English, from Old French *carpite,* from Medieval Latin *carpīta,* from Old Italian *carpita,* from *carpire,* to pluck, from Latin *carpere.* See **kerp-** in Appendix.]

car·pet·bag (kär′pĭt-băg′) *n.* A traveling bag made of carpet fabric that was used chiefly in the United States during the 19th century. **—carpetbag** *adj.* Of or relating to carpetbaggers.

car·pet·bag·ger (kär′pĭt-băg′ər) *n.* **1.** A Northerner who went to the South after the Civil War for political or financial advantage. **2.** An outsider, especially a politician, who presumptuously seeks a position or success in a new locality. [So called because they carried their belongings in a carpetbag.] **—car′pet·bag′ger·y** *n.*

carpet beetle *n.* Any of various small beetles of the genera *Anthrenus* and *Attagenus* having larvae that are injurious to fabrics and furs. Also called *buffalo bug.*

car·pet-bomb (kär′pĭt-bŏm′) *tr. & intr.v.* **-bombed, -bomb·ing, -bombs.** To bomb in a systematic and extensive pattern, so as to devastate a large target area uniformly. **—car′pet-bomb′ing** *n.*

carpet grass or **car·pet·grass** (kär′pĭt-grăs′) *n.* Any of several coarse, sod-forming grasses of the chiefly New World genus *Axonopus,* especially *A. affinis,* cultivated for turf and pasture in warm, humid regions.

car·pet·ing (kär′pĭ-tĭng) *n.* **1.** Material used for carpets. **2.** A carpet or carpets.

car·pet·weed (kär′pĭt-wēd′) *n.* A prostrate, mat-forming annual plant *(Mollugo verticillata)* widespread as a weed throughout North America and having whorled leaves and small, greenish-white flowers.

car·pi (kär′pī′) *n.* Plural of **carpus.**

-carpic *suff.* Variant of **-carpous.**

carp·ing (kär′pĭng) *adj.* Naggingly critical or complaining. **—carp′ing·ly** *adv.*

carpo- *pref.* Fruit: *carpophore.* [Greek *karpo-,* from *karpos,* fruit. See **kerp-** in Appendix.]

car pool *n.* **1.** An arrangement whereby several participants or their children travel together in one vehicle, the participants sharing the costs and often taking turns providing the vehicle and driver. **2.** A group, as of commuters or parents, participating in a car pool.

car-pool (kär′po͞ol′) *v.* **-pooled, -pool·ing, -pools.** *—intr.* To travel in a car pool. *—tr.* To transport by means of a car pool: *car-pool the children to school.* **—car′-pool′er** *n.*

car·poph·a·gous (kär-pŏf′ə-gəs) *adj.* Feeding on fruit; fruit-eating.

car·po·phore (kär′pə-fôr′, -fōr′) *n.* A slender stalk that supports each half of a dehisced fruit in many members of the parsley family.

car·port (kär′pôrt′, -pōrt′) *n.* An open-sided shelter for an automotive vehicle, formed by a roof projecting from the side of a building.

-carpous or **-carpic** *suff.* A specified number or kind of carpel or fruit: *apocarpous.* [From New Latin *-carpus,* from Greek *karpos,* fruit. See **kerp-** in Appendix.]

car·pus (kär′pəs) *n., pl.* **-pi** (-pī′). **1.** The group of eight bones forming the joint between the forearm and the hand. Also called *wrist.* **2.** A joint in quadrupeds corresponding to the wrist. [New Latin, from Greek *karpos,* wrist.]

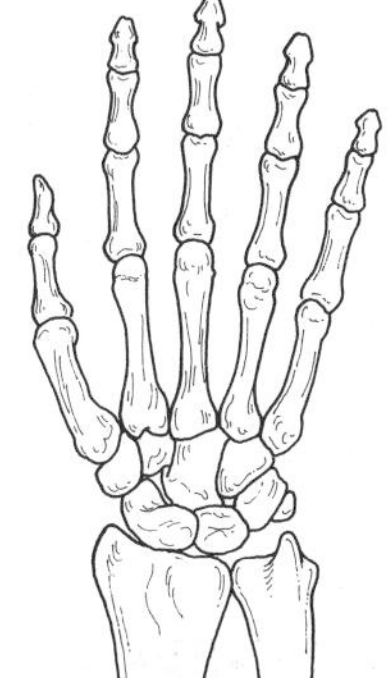

carpus

Car·rac·ci (kə-rä′chē, kä-rät′-). Family of Bolognese painters, including **Agostino** (1557–1602), his brother **Annibale** (1560–1609), and their cousin **Lodovico** (1555–1619). Their works and influence led a reform of Mannerism that provided a transition to the baroque style.

car·rack also **car·ack** (kăr′ək) *n. Nautical.* A large galleon used in the 14th, 15th, and 16th centuries. [Middle English *carike,* from Medieval Latin *carrica* and from Old French *caraque* (from Old Spanish *carraca*), both from Arabic *qarāqir,* pl. of *qurqūr.*]

carrack
Model of the late 16th-century Spanish carrack *Madre de Dios*

car·ra·geen also **car·ra·gheen** (kăr′ə-gēn′) *n.* See **Irish moss.** [After *Carragheen,* a village of southeast Ireland.]

car·ra·geen·an also **car·ra·geen·in** (kăr′ə-gē′nən) *n.* Any of a group of closely related colloids derived from Irish moss and several other red algae, widely used as a thickening, stabilizing, emulsifying, or suspending agent in industrial, pharmaceutical, and food products.

car·ra·gheen (kăr′ə-gēn′) *n.* Variant of **carrageen.**

Car·ran·za (kə-răn′zə, kä-rän′sä), **Venustiano.** 1859–1920. Mexican revolutionary politician who was the first president (1915–1920) of the new Mexican Republic after the overthrow of dictator Porfirio Díaz (1911).

Car·ra·ra (kə-rär′ə, kär-rä′rä). A city of northern Italy near the Ligurian Sea east of Genoa. It is famous for the white marble quarried nearby that was favored by Michelangelo. Population, 68,460.

car·re·four (kăr′ə-fo͝or′) *n.* **1.** A crossroads. **2.** A public square; a plaza. [French, from Old French *carrefor,* from Latin *quadrifurcus,* four-forked : *quadri-,* quadri- + *furca,* fork.]

car·rel also **car·rell** (kăr′əl) *n.* A partially partitioned nook in or near the stacks in a library, used for private study. [Middle English *carole,* round dance ring, circle, stall for study. See CAROL.]

carrel

Car·rel (kə-rĕl′, kăr′əl), **Alexis.** 1873–1944. French-born American surgeon and biologist. He won a 1912 Nobel Prize for

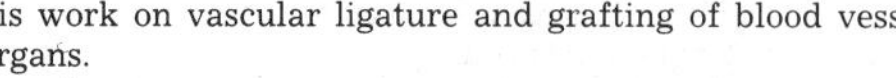

his work on vascular ligature and grafting of blood vessels and organs.

Car·rère (kə-râr′), **John Merven.** 1858–1911. American architect who with his partner Thomas Hastings designed the office buildings of the U.S. Senate (1905) and House of Representatives (1906) and the New York Public Library (1897–1911).

car·riage (kăr′ĭj) *n.* **1.** A wheeled vehicle, especially a four-wheeled horse-drawn passenger vehicle, often of an elegant design. **2.** *Chiefly British.* A railroad passenger car. **3.** A baby carriage. **4.** A wheeled support or frame for carrying a heavy object, such as a cannon. **5.** A moving part of a machine for holding or shifting another part: *the carriage of a typewriter.* **6.a.** The act or process of transporting or carrying. **b.** (kăr′ē-ĭj). The cost of or the charge for transporting. **7.** The manner of holding and moving one's head and body; bearing. See Synonyms at **posture. 8.** *Archaic.* Management; administration. [Middle English *cariage,* from Norman French, from *carier,* to carry. See CARRY.]

carriage

carriage dog *n.* See **Dalmatian** (sense 2).

carriage trade *n.* Wealthy patrons or customers, as of a store.

car·rick bend (kăr′ĭk) *n. Nautical.* A type of knot used to fasten two cables or hawsers together. [From obsolete *carrick,* variant of CARRACK.]

carrick bitt *n. Nautical.* Either of the two posts that support the windlass on a ship's deck. [Probably from obsolete *carrick,* variant of CARRACK.]

car·ri·er (kăr′ē-ər) *n.* **1.** One that transports or conveys: *baggage carriers; a message carrier.* **2.** One, such as a person, a business, or an organization, that deals in the transport of passengers or goods. **3.** A mechanism or device by which something is conveyed or conducted. **4.** *Medicine.* A person or an animal that shows no symptoms of a disease but harbors the infectious agent of that disease and is capable of transmitting it to others. **5.** *Genetics.* An individual that carries one gene for a particular recessive trait. A carrier does not express the trait but, when mated with another carrier, can produce offspring that do. **6.** *Electronics.* **a.** A carrier wave. **b.** A charge-carrying entity, especially an electron or a hole in a semiconductor. **7.** An aircraft carrier. **8.** A telecommunications company.

carrier pigeon *n.* **1.** A homing pigeon, especially one trained to carry messages. **2.** Any of various large domestic pigeons having a prominent wattle.

carrick bend

carrier wave *n.* An electromagnetic wave that can be modulated, as in frequency, amplitude, or phase, to transmit speech, music, images, or other signals.

car·ri·ole (kăr′ē-ōl′) *n.* Variant of **cariole.**

car·ri·on (kăr′ē-ən) *n.* Dead and decaying flesh. —**carrion** *adj.* **1.** Of or similar to dead and decaying flesh. **2.** Feeding on such flesh. [Middle English *careine,* from Anglo-Norman, from Vulgar Latin **carōnia,* from Latin *carō,* flesh. See **sker-**[1] in Appendix.]

carrion crow *n.* A common European crow *(Corvus corone)* having glossy black plumage.

carrion flower *n.* **1.** Any of several North American plants of the genus *Smilax,* especially *S. herbacea,* an herbaceous tendril-bearing vine having clusters of small greenish flowers with the odor of decaying flesh. **2.** See **starfish flower.**

Johnny Carson
Photographed in 1979

Car·roll (kăr′əl), **Charles.** Known as "Carroll of Carrollton." 1737–1832. American Revolutionary leader and legislator who was a member of the Continental Congress (1776–1778) and served as a U.S. senator (1789–1792).

Carroll, Lewis. See Charles Lutwidge **Dodgson.**

Car·roll·ton (kăr′əl-tən). A city of northern Texas, a residential and industrial suburb of Dallas. Population, 40,595.

car·rot (kăr′ət) *n.* **1.** A biennial Eurasian plant *(Daucus carota* subsp. *sativus)* in the parsley family, widely cultivated as an annual for its edible taproot. **2.** The usually tapering, elongate, fleshy orange root of this plant, eaten as a vegetable. **3.** Queen Anne's lace. **4.** A reward offered for desired behavior; an inducement: *"The U.S. should use a moratorium on* [strategic defense initiative] *development as a carrot to bring an acceptable offensive arms limitation"* (C. Peter Gall). [French *carotte,* from Old French *garroite,* from Latin *carōta,* from Greek *karōton.* See **ker-**[1] in Appendix.]

car·rot-and-stick (kăr′ət-ən-stĭk′) *adj.* Combining a promised reward with a threatened penalty: *took a carrot-and-stick approach to the rehabilitation of juvenile offenders.*

car·rot·y (kăr′ə-tē) *adj.* **1.** Bright orange in color. **2.** Having carrot-colored hair.

car·rou·sel (kăr′ə-sĕl′, -zĕl′) *n.* Variant of **carousel.**

♦**car·ry** (kăr′ē) *v.* **-ried, -ry·ing, -ries.** —*tr.* **1.** To hold or support while moving; bear: *carried the baby in my arms; carrying a heavy backpack.* See Synonyms at **convey. 2.a.** To take from one place to another; transport: *a train carrying freight; a courier carrying messages.* **b.** *Chiefly Southern U.S.* To transport (someone) in a motor vehicle, such as an automobile. **3.** To serve as a means for the conveyance of; transmit: *pipes that carry waste water; a bridge that carries traffic between the two cities.* **4.a.** To communicate; pass on: *The news was carried by word of mouth to every settlement.* **b.** To express or contain: *harsh words that carried a threat of violence.* **5.** To have (something) on the surface or skin; bear: *carries scars from acne.* **6.** To hold or be capable of holding: *The tank carries 16 gallons when full.* **7.** To support the weight or responsibility of: *carried a heavy academic load last semester.* **8.** To keep or have on one's person: *stopped carrying credit cards.* **9.** To be pregnant with. **10.a.** To hold and move (the body or a part of it) in a particular way: *carried her head proudly.* **b.** To behave or conduct (oneself) in a specified manner. **11.** To extend or continue in space, time, or degree: *carried the line to the edge of the page; carry a joke too far.* **12.a.** To give impetus to; propel: *The wind carried the ball over the fence.* **b.** To take further; advance: *carry a cause.* **13.** To take or seize, especially by force; capture. **14.a.** To be successful in; win: *lost the game but carried the match.* **b.** To gain victory, support, or acceptance for: *The motion was carried in a close vote.* **c.** To win a majority of the votes in: *Roosevelt carried all but two states in the 1936 presidential election.* **d.** To gain the sympathy of; win over: *The amateurs' enthusiasm carried the audience.* **15.** To include or keep on a list: *carried a dozen workers on the payroll.* **16.a.** To have as an attribute or accompaniment: *an appliance carrying a full-year guarantee.* **b.** To involve as a condition, consequence, or effect: *The crime carried a five-year sentence.* **17.** To transfer from one place, as a column, page, or book, to another: *carry a number in addition.* **18.** To keep in stock; offer for sale: *a store that carries a full line of electronic equipment.* **19.** To keep in one's accounts as a debtor: *carried the unemployed customer for 90 days.* **20.a.** To maintain or support (one that is weaker or less competent, for example). **b.** To compensate for (a weaker member or partner) by one's performance. **21.** To place before the public; print or broadcast: *The morning papers carried the story. The press conference was carried by all networks.* **22.** To produce as a crop. **23.** To provide forage for (livestock): *land that carries sheep.* **24.** To sing (a melody, for example) on key: *carry a tune.* **25.** *Sports.* **a.** To cover (a distance) or advance beyond (a point or object) in one golf stroke. **b.** *Football.* To hold and rush with (the ball). **c.** *Basketball.* To palm (the ball) in violation of the rules. —*intr.* **1.** To act as a bearer: *teach a dog to fetch and carry.* **2.** To be transmitted or conveyed; cover a range: *a voice that carries well.* **3.** To admit of being transported: *Unbalanced loads do not carry easily.* **4.** To hold the neck and head in a certain way. Used of a horse. **5.** To be accepted or approved: *The proposal carried by a wide margin.* —**carry** *n., pl.* **-ries. 1.** The act or process of carrying. **2.** A portage, as between two navigable bodies of water. **3.a.** The range of a gun or projectile. **b.** The distance traveled by a hurled or struck ball. **c.** Reach; projection: *"a voice that had far more carry to it than at any time in the term thus far"* (Jimmy Breslin). **4.** *Football.* An act of rushing with the ball: *a carry of two yards.* —***phrasal verbs.* carry away.** To move or excite greatly: *was carried away by desire.* **carry forward.** *Accounting.* To transfer (an entry) to the next column, page, or book, or to another account. **carry off. 1.** To cause the death of: *was carried off by a fever.* **2.** To handle successfully: *carried off the difficult situation with aplomb.* **carry on. 1.** To conduct; maintain: *carry on a thriving business.* **2.** To engage in: *carry on a love affair.* **3.** To continue without halting; persevere: *carry on in the face of disaster.* **4.** To behave in an excited, improper, or silly manner. **carry out. 1.** To put into practice or effect: *carry out a new policy.* **2.** To follow or obey: *carry out instructions.* **3.** To bring to a conclusion; accomplish: *carried out the mission successfully.* **carry over. 1.** *Accounting.* **a.** To transfer (an account) to the next column, page, or book relating to the same account. **b.** To retain (merchandise or other goods) for a subsequent, usually the next, season. **2.** To deduct (an unused tax credit or a loss, for example) for taxable income of a subsequent period. **3.** To persist to another time or situation: *The confidence gained in remedial classes carried over into the children's regular school work.* **carry through. 1.** To accomplish; complete: *carry a project through despite difficulties.* **2.** To survive; persist: *prejudices that have carried through over the centuries.* **3.** To enable to endure; sustain: *a faith that carried them through the ordeal.* —***idioms.* carry a** (or **the) torch.** To feel a painful, unreciprocated love: *still carrying a torch for an old sweetheart.* **carry the ball.** *Informal.* To assume the leading role; do most of the work. **carry the day.** To be victorious; win. [Middle English *carien,* from Old North French *carier,* from *carre,* cart. See CAR.]

♦ ***REGIONAL NOTE:*** A non-Southerner is always amused when a Southerner offers to "carry" rather than to drive him or her somewhere, imagining it to be an invitation to be picked up and bodily lugged to the destination. However, the verb *carry,* which to Southerners means "to transport (someone) in a motor vehicle, such as an automobile," is etymologically more precise in the Southern usage than anywhere else. *Carry* derives from the Latin noun *carrus,* "cart," from which we get the nouns *carriage* and our modern *car.* Therefore, *carry* is more closely related to *car* than is *drive,* which only makes literal sense if the vehicle is drawn by a team of animals.

car·ry·all (kăr′ē-ôl′) *n.* **1.** A large receptacle, such as a bag, basket, or pocketbook, used to carry things from one place to another. **2.** A closed automobile with two lengthwise seats facing each other. **3.** A covered one-horse carriage with two seats. [Alteration of CARIOLE.]

car·ry·ing capacity (kăr′ē-ĭng) *n.* **1.** The maximum number of persons or things that a vehicle or a receptacle can carry: *a van with a carrying capacity of 12.* **2.** *Ecology.* The maximum

ă pat	oi boy
ā pay	ou out
âr care	ŏŏ took
ä father	ōō boot
ĕ pet	ŭ cut
ē be	ûr urge
ĭ pit	th thin
ī pie	*th* this
îr pier	hw which
ŏ pot	zh vision
ō toe	ə about, item
ô paw	♦ regionalism

Stress marks: ′ (primary); ′ (secondary), as in **dictionary** (dĭk′shə-nĕr′ē)

number of individuals or inhabitants that a given environment can support without detrimental effects.

carrying charge *n.* The interest charged on the balance owed when paying in installments.

car·ry·on (kăr′ē-ŏn′) *adj.* Small or compact enough to be carried aboard an airplane, a train, or a bus by a passenger: *carryon luggage.* **—carryon** *n.* A bag, suitcase, or other item that can be carried aboard a commercial transport vehicle.

car·ry·out (kăr′ē-out′) *adj.* Intended to be consumed away from the place of sale; takeout: *a shop offering carryout sandwiches.* **—carryout** *n.* An item of food or a meal that is to be consumed away from the place of sale.

car·ry·o·ver (kăr′ē-ō′vər) *n.* **1.** Something that is transferred or extended from an earlier time or another place: *a showing of new fashions as well as carryovers from last spring; a carryover of good will from the previous meeting.* **2.** *Accounting.* A sum transferred to a new column, page, or book relating to the same account.

car seat *n.* A small removable seat, usually equipped with safety straps, that fastens to the seat of a vehicle and is used for securing young children.

car·sick (kär′sĭk′) *adj.* Suffering from motion sickness caused by travel in a motor vehicle. **—car′sick′ness** *n.*

Car·son (kär′sən). A city of southern California, a residential and industrial suburb of Los Angeles. Population, 81,221.

Carson, Christopher. Known as "Kit." 1809–1868. American frontiersman who was the renowned guide of John C. Frémont's western expeditions in the 1840's, an agent for the Ute (1853–1861), and a Union general in the Civil War.

Carson, Johnny. Born 1925. American comedian and host of *The Tonight Show* (1962–1992).

Carson, Rachel Louise. 1907–1964. American environmentalist and writer whose best-known work, *Silent Spring* (1962), condemns the use of pesticides hazardous to wildlife.

Carson City. The capital of Nevada, in the western part of the state near the California border. It was laid out in 1858 on the site of an earlier trading post and named in honor of Kit Carson. Population, 32,022.

cart (kärt) *n.* **1.** A small wheeled vehicle typically pushed by hand: *a shopping cart; a pastry cart.* **2.** A two-wheeled vehicle drawn by an animal and used in farm work and for transporting goods. **3. a.** An open two-wheeled carriage. **b.** A light motorized vehicle: *a golf cart.* **—cart** *tr.v.* **cart·ed, cart·ing, carts. 1.** To convey in a cart or truck: *cart away garbage.* **2.** To convey laboriously or unceremoniously; lug: *carted the whole gang off to jail.* [Middle English, wagon, from Old English *cræt* and from Old Norse *kartr.*] **—cart′a·ble** *adj.* **—cart′er** *n.*

cart·age (kär′tĭj) *n. Abbr.* **ctg., ctge. 1.** The act or process of carting. **2.** The cost of carting.

Car·ta·ge·na (kär′tə-gā′nə, -jē′-, -hĕ′nä). **1.** A city of northwest Colombia on the **Bay of Cartagena,** an inlet of the Caribbean Sea. Founded in 1533, Cartagena was once the richest port on the Spanish Main. Population, 495,028. **2.** A city of southeast Spain on the Mediterranean Sea south-southeast of Murcia. It was settled c. 225 B.C. and soon became the chief Carthaginian sea base in Spain. Population, 142,300.

Carte (kärt), **Richard D'Oyly.** 1844–1901. British theatrical producer associated with the works of W.S. Gilbert and Arthur Sullivan.

carte blanche (kärt bläNsh′, kärts blänch′, blănch) *n., pl.* **cartes blanches** (kärt bläNsh′, kärts blänch′, blănch′). Unrestricted power to act at one's own discretion; unconditional authority: *had given the interior decorator carte blanche and then detested the results.* [French : *carte,* ticket + *blanche,* blank.]

car·tel (kär-tĕl′) *n.* **1.** A combination of independent business organizations formed to regulate production, pricing, and marketing of goods by the members. **2.** An official agreement between governments at war, especially one concerning the exchange of prisoners. **3.** A group of parties, factions, or nations united in a common cause; a bloc. [German *Kartell,* from French *cartel,* from Italian *cartello,* placard, from Medieval Latin *cartellus,* charter, diminutive of Latin *charta, carta,* paper made from papyrus. See CARD[1].]

Car·ter (kär′tər), **Howard.** 1873–1939. British archaeologist who worked in Egypt after 1890 and discovered (1922) the tomb of Tutankhamen.

Carter, James Earl, Jr. Known as "Jimmy." Born 1924. The 39th President of the United States (1977–1981), who is credited with establishing energy-conservation measures, concluding the Panama Canal treaties (1978), and negotiating the Camp David accords between Egypt and Israel (1979).

Carter, Rosalynn Smith. Born 1928. First Lady of the United States (1977–1981) as the wife of President Jimmy Carter. She worked on better care for the elderly and for the mentally and emotionally disadvantaged.

Car·ter·et (kär′tə-rĕt′). A borough of northeast New Jersey south of Elizabeth opposite Staten Island. It is an industrial center. Population, 20,598.

Car·ter·et (kär′tər-ĭt), **John.** Earl Granville. 1690–1763. British statesman and diplomat who twice served as secretary of state (1721–1724 and 1742–1744).

Car·te·sian (kär-tē′zhən) *adj.* Of or relating to the philosophy or methods of Descartes. [French *cartésien* (from René DESCARTES) and New Latin *Cartesiānus* (from *Cartesius,* Latin form of Descartes).] **—Car·te′sian·ism** *n.*

Cartesian coordinate *n.* A member of the set of numbers that locates a point in a Cartesian coordinate system.

Cartesian coordinate system *n.* **1.** A two-dimensional coordinate system in which the coordinates of a point in a plane are its distances from two perpendicular lines that intersect at an origin, the distance from each line being measured along a straight line parallel to the other. **2.** A three-dimensional coordinate system in which the coordinates of a point in space are its distances from each of three perpendicular lines that intersect at an origin.

Cartesian plane *n.* A plane having all points described by Cartesian coordinates.

Cartesian product *n.* A set of all pairs of elements (x, y) that can be constructed from given sets, X and Y, such that x belongs to X and y to Y.

Car·thage (kär′thĭj). An ancient city and state of northern Africa on the Bay of Tunis northeast of modern Tunis. It was founded by the Phoenicians in the ninth century B.C. and became the center of Carthaginian power in the Mediterranean after the sixth century B.C. The city was destroyed by the Romans at the end of the Third Punic War (146 B.C.) but was rebuilt by Julius Caesar and later (A.D. 439–533) served as capital of the Vandals before its virtual annihilation by the Arabs (698). **—Car′tha·gin′i·an** (kär′thə-jĭn′ē-ən) *adj. & n.*

Kit Carson
Photographed in 1864

Car·thu·sian (kär-thōō′zhən) *Roman Catholic Church. n.* A member of a contemplative order founded during the 11th century by Saint Bruno. **—Carthusian** *adj.* Of or relating to the Carthusian order. [Medieval Latin *Carthusiānus,* from *Cartusia,* Chartreuse, France, where the order's first monastery was built.]

Car·tier (kär-tyā′, kär′tē-ā′), Sir **George Étienne.** 1814–1873. Prime minister of Canada (1858–1862) who served jointly with Sir John Macdonald. He persuaded French Canadians to accept Canada's confederation (1867).

Cartier, Jacques. 1491–1557. French explorer who navigated the St. Lawrence River (1535) and laid claim to the region for France.

Car·tier-Bres·son (kär-tyā′brĕ-sôN′), **Henri.** Born 1908. French photographer noted for his black-and-white documentary photographs of daily life.

Jimmy Carter

car·ti·lage (kär′tl-ĭj) *n.* A tough, elastic, fibrous connective tissue found in various parts of the body, such as the joints, outer ear, and larynx. A major constituent of the embryonic and young vertebrate skeleton, it is converted largely to bone with maturation. [Middle English, from Old French, from Latin *cartilāgō, cartilāgin-.*]

cartilage bone *n.* A bone developed from cartilage.

car·ti·lag·i·nous (kär′tl-ăj′ə-nəs) *adj.* **1.** Of, relating to, or consisting of cartilage. **2.** Having a skeleton consisting mainly of cartilage. **3.** Having the texture of cartilage; firm and tough, yet flexible.

cartilaginous fish *n.* A fish whose skeleton consists mainly of cartilage, especially a member of the class Chondrichthyes, such as a shark, skate, or ray.

cart·load (kärt′lōd′) *n.* The amount of something, such as dirt, that a cart can carry.

car·to·gram (kär′tə-grăm′) *n.* A presentation of statistical data in geographical distribution on a map. [French *cartogramme* : *carte,* map (from Old French, card, from Latin *charta, carta,* paper made from papyrus; see CARD[1]) + *-gramme,* a record (from Late Latin *gramma,* something written; see –GRAM).]

Rosalynn Carter

car·tog·ra·phy (kär-tŏg′rə-fē) *n.* The art or technique of making maps or charts. [French *cartographie* : *carte,* map (from Old French, from Latin *charta, carta,* paper made from papyrus; see CARD[1]) + *-graphie,* writing (from Greek *graphia;* see –GRAPHY).] **—car·tog′ra·pher** *n.* **—car′to·graph′ic** (kär′tə-grăf′ĭk), **car′to·graph′i·cal** *adj.*

car·ton (kär′tn) *n. Abbr.* **c., C., ctn. 1.** Any of various containers made from cardboard or coated paper: *cans packed in cartons; a milk carton.* **2.** The contents of a carton: *dyed the whole carton of eggs.* **—carton** *tr.v.* **-toned, -ton·ing, -tons.** To place (something) in a carton. [French, from Italian *cartone,* pasteboard, augmentative of *carta,* card, paper, from Latin *charta, carta,* paper made from papyrus. See CARD[1].]

car·toon (kär-tōōn′) *n.* **1.** A drawing depicting a humorous situation, often accompanied by a caption. **2.** A drawing representing current public figures or issues symbolically and often satirically: *a political cartoon.* **3.** A preliminary sketch similar in size to the work, such as a fresco, that is to be copied from it. **4.** An animated cartoon. **5.** A comic strip. **—cartoon** *v.* **-tooned, -toon·ing, -toons.** —*tr.* To draw a humorous or satirical representation of; caricature. —*intr.* To make humorous or satirical drawings. [French *carton,* drawing, from Italian *cartone,* pasteboard. See CARTON.] **—car·toon′ish** *adj.* **—car·toon′ist** *n.*

car·top (kär′tŏp′) *adj.* Designed for use or suitable for carrying on top of a vehicle: *a cartop luggage rack; a cartop boat.*

car·touche or **car·touch** (kär-tōōsh′) *n.* **1.** A structure or figure, often in the shape of an oval shield or oblong scroll, used as an architectural or graphic ornament or to bear a design or inscription. **2.** An oval or oblong figure in ancient Egyptian hieroglyphics that encloses characters expressing the names or epithets of royal or divine personages. **3.** A heavy paper cartridge

cartouche
Egyptian hieroglyphics

case. [French, from Italian *cartoccio,* paper cornet, from *carta,* card, paper. See CARTON.]

car·tridge (kär′trĭj) *n.* **1.a.** A cylindrical, usually metal casing containing the primer and charge of ammunition for firearms. **b.** Such a casing fitted with a bullet. **c.** A similar piece of ammunition, such as a shotgun shell. **2.** A case filled with high explosives, used in blasting. **3.** A small modular unit designed to be inserted into a larger piece of equipment: *an ink cartridge; a disposable cartridge of caulking compound.* **4.** A removable case containing the stylus and electric conversion circuitry in a phonograph pickup. **5.a.** A case containing magnetic tape in a reel; a cassette. **b.** A case containing a ribbon in a spool, for use in printers and electric typewriters. **6.** A lightproof case with photographic film that can be loaded directly into a camera. [Alteration of earlier *cartage,* alteration of French *cartouche,* from Italian *cartuccio,* variant of *cartoccio,* roll of paper. See CARTOUCHE.]

cartridge belt *n.* A belt with loops or pockets for carrying ammunition or other kinds of equipment.

cartridge clip *n.* A metal container or frame for holding cartridges to be loaded into an automatic rifle or pistol.

car·tu·lar·y also **char·tu·lar·y** (kär′chə-lĕr′ē) *n., pl.* **-ies.** A collection of deeds or charters, especially a register of titles to all the property of an estate or a monastery. [Middle English *cartularie,* collection of documents, from Medieval Latin *cartulārium,* from Latin *cartula, chartula,* document. See CHARTER.]

Enrico Caruso

cart·wheel (kärt′hwēl′, -wēl′) *n.* **1.** A handspring in which the body turns over sideways with the arms and legs spread like the spokes of a wheel. **2.** *Slang.* A large coin, such as a silver dollar.

Cart·wright (kärt′rīt′), **Edmund.** 1743–1823. British cleric and inventor of the power loom (1785–1790).

ca·run·cle (kə-rŭng′kəl, kăr′ŭng′-) *n.* **1.** *Biology.* A fleshy, naked outgrowth, such as a fowl's wattles. **2.** *Botany.* An outgrowth or appendage at or near the hilum of certain seeds, as of the castor-oil plant. [Obsolete French *caruncule,* from Latin *caruncula,* diminutive of *carō,* flesh. See **sker-**[1] in Appendix.] **—ca·run′cu·lar** (-kyə-lər) *adj.* **—ca·run′cu·late** (-lĭt, -lāt′), **ca·run′cu·lat′ed** (-lā′tĭd) *adj.*

George Washington Carver

Ca·ru·so (kə-ro͞o′sō, -zō), **Enrico.** 1873–1921. Italian operatic tenor who with his powerful, pure, emotive voice is considered one of the greatest singers ever.

car·va·crol (kär′və-krôl′, -krōl′) *n.* An aromatic phenolic compound, $C_{10}H_{14}O$, found in plants such as oregano and savory and used in flavorings and fungicides. [New Latin *carvi* (specific epithet of *(Carum) carvi,* caraway, from Medieval Latin; see CARAWAY) + Latin *ācer, acr-,* sharp; see **ak-** in Appendix + –OL[1].]

carve (kärv) *v.* **carved, carv·ing, carves.** —*tr.* **1.a.** To divide into pieces by cutting; slice: *carve a roast turkey.* **b.** To divide by parceling out: *carve up an estate.* **2.** To cut into a desired shape; fashion by cutting: *carve the wood into a figure.* **3.** To make or form by or as if by cutting: *carve initials in the bark; carved out an empire.* **4.** To decorate by cutting and shaping carefully. —*intr.* **1.** To engrave or cut figures as an art, a hobby, or a trade. **2.** To disjoint, slice, and serve meat or poultry. [Middle English *kerven,* from Old English *ceorfan.* See **gerbh-** in Appendix.] **—carv′er** *n.*

car·vel (kär′vəl, -vĕl′) *n.* Variant of **caravel.**

car·vel-built (kär′vəl-bĭlt′, -vĕl′-) *adj.* *Nautical.* Built with the hull planks lying flush or edge to edge rather than overlapping: *a carvel-built ship.*

carv·en (kär′vən) *v.* *Archaic.* A past tense and a past participle of **carve. —carven** *adj.* That has been wrought or decorated by carving.

caryatid
Detail of
Porch of the Maidens
at the Erechtheum,
Athens, Greece

Car·ver (kär′vər), **George Washington.** 1864?–1943. American botanist, agricultural chemist, and educator who developed hundreds of uses for the peanut, soybean, and sweet potato.

Carver, John. 1576?–1621. English-born Pilgrim colonist who was the first governor of Plymouth Colony (1620–1621).

carv·ing (kär′vĭng) *n.* **1.** The cutting of material such as stone or wood in order to form a figure or design. **2.** A figure or design formed by this kind of cutting.

car wash *n.* An area, place, or business equipped for cleaning and washing motor vehicles such as cars, vans, and small trucks.

Car·y (kăr′ē). A town of east-central North Carolina, an industrial suburb of Raleigh. Population, 21,763.

Cary, (Arthur) Joyce (Lunel). 1888–1957. British writer whose novels, including *The Horse's Mouth* (1944), concern the necessity of personal freedom.

Cary, Henry Francis. 1772–1844. British poet and translator (1805–1814) of Dante's *Divine Comedy.*

car·y·at·id (kăr′ē-ăt′ĭd) *n., pl.* **-ids** or **-i·des** (-ĭ-dēz′). *Architecture.* A supporting column sculptured in the form of a draped female figure. [From Latin *Caryātides,* maidens of Caryae, caryatids, from Greek *Karuatides,* from *Karuai,* Caryae, a village of Laconia in southern Greece.] **—car′y·at′i·dal** (-ĭ-dəl), **car′y·at′i·de′an** (-ĭ-dē′ən), **car′y·a·tid′ic** (-ə-tĭd′ĭk) *adj.*

cascade

caryo– *pref.* Variant of **karyo–.**

car·y·op·sis (kăr′ē-ŏp′sĭs) *n., pl.* **-op·ses** (-ŏp′sēz′) or **-op·si·des** (-ŏp′sĭ-dēz′). See **grain** (sense 1a). [*cary(o)-,* variant of KARYO– + –OPSIS.]

CAS *abbr.* Certificate of Advanced Study.

ca·sa·ba also **cas·sa·ba** (kə-sä′bə) *n.* A variety of winter melon *(Cucumis melo* var. *Inodorus)* having a yellow rind and sweet, whitish flesh. [After *Kasaba* (Turgutlu), a city of western Turkey.]

Cas·a·blan·ca (kăs′ə-blăng′kə, kä′sə-blăng′kə). A city of northwest Morocco on the Atlantic Ocean south-southwest of Tangier. Founded by the Portuguese in the 16th century, it became a center of French influence in Africa after 1907. It is now Morocco's largest city. Population, 2,139,204.

Ca·sals (kə-sälz′, -sälz′), **Pablo.** 1876–1973. Spanish cellist considered the greatest of his time.

Cas·a·no·va (kăs′ə-nō′və, kăz′-) *n.* **1.** A man who is amorously and gallantly attentive to women. **2.** A promiscuous man; a philanderer. [After Giovanni Jacopo CASANOVA DE SEINGALT.]

Cas·a·no·va de Sein·galt (kăs′ə-nō′və də săN-gält′, kăz′-, kä′sä-nô′vä), **Giovanni Jacopo.** 1725–1798. Italian adventurer who after his expulsion from a seminary wandered Europe, meeting luminaries, working in a variety of occupations, and establishing a legendary reputation as a lover.

Cas·bah also **Kas·bah** (kăz′bä′, käz′-) *n.* **1.** A castle or palace in northern Africa. **2.** Often **casbah.** The older section of a city in northern Africa or the Middle East. [French, from Arabic dialectal *qaṣbah,* from Arabic *qaṣabah,* fortress.]

cas·cade (kă-skād′) *n.* **1.** A waterfall or a series of small waterfalls over steep rocks. **2.** Something, such as lace, thought to resemble a waterfall or series of small waterfalls, especially an arrangement or fall of material. **3.** A succession of stages, processes, operations, or units. **4.** *Electronics.* A series of components or networks, the output of each of which serves as the input for the next. **—cascade** *intr. & tr.v.* **-cad·ed, -cad·ing, -cades.** To fall or cause to fall in or as if in a cascade. [French, from Italian *cascata,* from *cascare,* to fall, from Vulgar Latin **casicāre,* from Latin *cadere.* See **kad-** in Appendix.]

Cas·cade Range (kăs-kād′). A mountain chain of western Canada and the United States extending about 1,126 km (700 mi) south from British Columbia through western Washington and Oregon to northern California, where it joins the Sierra Nevada. Mount Rainier, 4,395.1 m (14,410 ft), is the highest peak.

cas·car·a (kă-skăr′ə) *n.* A buckthorn *(Rhamnus purshiana)* native to northwest North America, the bark of which is the source of cascara sagrada. [Spanish *cáscara,* bark, from *cascar,* to break off, from Vulgar Latin **quassicāre,* from Latin *quassāre,* frequentative of *quatere,* to shake. See **kwēt-** in Appendix.]

cascara sa·gra·da (sə-grä′də) *n.* The dried bark of the cascara buckthorn, used as a laxative. [American Spanish *cáscara sagrada* : Spanish *cáscara,* bark + Spanish *sagrada,* sacred.]

cas·ca·ril·la (kăs′kə-rĭl′ə) *n.* **1.** A tropical shrub or tree *(Croton eluteria)* native to the West Indies and northern South America, having a bark that yields an aromatic, spicy oil used as a flavoring and fragrance. **2.** The bark of this plant. [Spanish, diminutive of *cáscara,* bark. See CASCARA.]

Cas·co Bay (kăs′kō). A deep inlet of the Atlantic Ocean in southwest Maine. The bay, with its wooded, hilly islands, is a popular vacation area.

case[1] (kās) *n.* **1.** An instance of something; an occurrence; an example: *a case of mistaken identity.* See Synonyms at **example. 2.** An occurrence of a disease or disorder: *a mild case of flu.* **3.** A set of circumstances or a state of affairs; a situation: *It may rain, in which case the hike will be canceled.* **4.** Actual fact; reality: *We suspected the walls were hollow, and this proved to be the case.* **5.** A question or problem; a matter: *It is simply a case of honor.* **6.** A situation that requires investigation, especially by a formal or official body. **7.** *Law.* **a.** An action or a suit or just grounds for an action. **b.** The facts or evidence offered in support of a claim. **8.** A set of reasons or supporting facts; an argument: *presented a good case for changing the law.* **9.** A person or group of persons being assisted, treated, or studied, as by a physician, lawyer, or social worker. **10.** *Informal.* A peculiar or eccentric person; a character. **11.** *Linguistics.* **a.** The syntactic relationship of a noun, a pronoun or a determiner to the other words of a sentence, indicated by declensional endings, by the position of the words within the sentence, by prepositions, or by postpositions. **b.** The form or position of a word that indicates this relationship. **c.** Such forms, positions, and relationships considered as a group. **d.** A pattern of inflection of nouns, pronouns, and adjectives to express different syntactic functions in a sentence. **e.** The form of such an inflected word. **—case** *tr.v.* **cased, cas·ing, cas·es.** *Informal.* To examine carefully, as in planning a crime: *cased the bank before robbing it.* **—*idioms.* in any case.** Regardless of what has occurred or will occur. **in case. 1.** If it happens that; if. **2.** As a precaution: *took along an umbrella, just in case.* **in case of.** If there should happen to be: *a number to call in case of emergency.* [Middle English *cas,* from Old French, from Latin *cāsus,* from past participle of *cadere,* to fall. See **kad-** in Appendix.]

case[2] (kās) *n.* **1.** A container; a receptacle: *a jewelry case; meat-filled cases of dough.* **2.** *Abbr.* **c., C., cs.** A container with its contents. **3.** A decorative or protective covering or cover. **4.** A set or pair: *a case of pistols.* **5.** The frame or framework of a window, door, or stairway. **6.** The surface or outer layer of a metal alloy. **—case** *tr.v.* **cased, cas·ing, cas·es.** To put into or cover with a case; encase. [Middle English, from Norman French *casse,* from Latin *capsa.*]

ca·se·ate (kā′sē-āt′) *intr.v.* **-at·ed, -at·ing, -ates.** To undergo caseation. [Back-formation from CASEATION.]

ca·se·a·tion (kā′sē-ā′shən) *n.* Necrotic degeneration of bodily tissue into a soft, cheeselike substance. [From Latin *cāseus,* cheese.]

case·book (kās′bo͝ok′) *n.* A book containing source materials in a specific area, used as a reference and in teaching.

case goods *pl.n.* **1.a.** Furniture, such as bookcases or chests of drawers, that provide the user with interior storage space. **b.** Dining and bedroom furniture sold as sets. **2.** Food and beverage products sold by the case.

case·hard·en (kās′här′dn) *tr.v.* **-ened, -en·ing, -ens. 1.** To harden the surface or case of (iron or steel) by high-temperature shallow infusion of carbon followed by quenching. **2.** To make callous or insensitive.

case history *n.* A detailed account of the facts affecting the development or condition of a person or group under treatment or study, especially in medicine, psychiatry, or psychology.

ca·sein (kā′sēn′, -sē-ĭn) *n.* A white, tasteless, odorless protein precipitated from milk by rennin. It is the basis of cheese and is used to make plastics, adhesives, paints, and foods. [Ultimately from Latin *cāseus,* cheese.]

case in point *n., pl.* **cases in point.** A relevant illustrative example.

case knife *n.* **1.** A knife kept in a sheath or case. **2.** A table knife.

case law *n.* Law based on judicial decision and precedent rather than on statutes.

case·load (kās′lōd′) *n.* The number of cases handled in a given period, as by an attorney or a social services agency.

case·mate (kās′māt′) *n.* **1.** A fortified enclosure for artillery on a warship. **2.** An armored compartment for artillery on a rampart. [French, from Italian *casamatta* : perhaps *casa,* house (from Latin *cāsa*) + *matto,* mad, crazy (from Latin *mattus,* drunk, past participle of *madēre,* to be drunk).] **—case′mat′ed** *adj.*

case·ment (kās′mənt) *n.* **1.a.** A window sash that opens outward by means of hinges. **b.** A window with such sashes. **2.** A case or covering. [Middle English, a hollow molding, possibly from Middle English *case,* chest, frame. See CASE[2].] **—case′ment·ed** *adj.*

Case·ment (kās′mənt), Sir **Roger David.** 1864–1916. British diplomat who sought German assistance in the Irish nationalist cause during World War I and was executed for treason.

ca·se·ous (kā′sē-əs) *adj.* Resembling cheese. [From Latin *cāseus,* cheese.]

ca·sern also **ca·serne** (kə-zûrn′) *n.* A military barracks or garrison. [French *caserne,* from Old French, small room for the night watch, from Old Provençal *cazerna,* group of four men, from Latin *quaterna,* four together, from Latin *quaternī,* by four. See QUATERNION.]

case shot *n.* **1.a.** A shot-packed metallic cylinder used as ammunition in a firearm; a canister. **b.** The shot in such a cylinder. **2.** A shrapnel shell.

case study *n.* **1.** A detailed analysis of a person or group, especially as a model of medical, psychiatric, psychological, or social phenomena. **2.a.** A detailed, intensive study of a unit, such as a corporation or a division within a corporation, that stresses factors contributing to its success or failure. **b.** An exemplary or cautionary model; an instructive example: *"Before they lost their independence,* [the two companies] *were case studies in unsuccessful long-term planning"* (T. Boone Pickens, Jr.).

case system *n.* A method of teaching law that emphasizes the study of selected cases rather than textbooks.

case·work (kās′wûrk′) *n.* Social work devoted to the needs of individual clients or cases. **—case′work′er** *n.*

cash[1] (kăsh) *n.* **1.** Money in the form of bills or coins; currency. **2.** Payment for goods or services in currency or by check. **—cash** *tr.v.* **cashed, cash·ing, cash·es.** To exchange for or convert into ready money: *cash a check; cash in one's gambling chips.* ***—phrasal verbs.* cash in. 1.** To withdraw from a venture by or as if by settling one's account. **2.** *Informal.* To obtain a profit or other advantage by timely exploitation: *Profiteers cashed in during the gasoline shortage.* **3.** *Slang.* To die. **cash out.** To dispose of a long-held asset for profit: *Hard-pressed farmers are tempted to cash out by selling their valuable land.* [Obsolete French *casse,* money box (from Norman French; see CASE[2]) or from Italian *cassa* (from Latin *capsa,* case).] **—cash′less** *adj.*

cash[2] (kăsh) *n., pl.* **cash.** Any of various Asian coins of small denomination, especially a copper and lead coin with a square hole in its center. [Portuguese *caixa,* from Tamil *kācu,* a small coin.]

cash-and-car·ry (kăsh′ən-kăr′ē) *adj.* Sold for cash, usually without delivery service. **—cash-and-carry** *n.* The policy of selling goods for cash, usually without delivery service.

cash bar *n.* A bar, such as one at a large party, where drinks are sold by the glass.

cash·book (kăsh′bo͝ok′) *n.* A book in which a record of cash receipts and expenditures is kept.

cash cow *n. Slang.* A steady, dependable source of funds or income: *"a collapse of its profitable cash cow, the clusters of word-processing machines"* (Christian Science Monitor).

cash crop *n.* A crop, such as tobacco, grown for direct sale rather than for livestock feed.

cash discount *n. Abbr.* **c.d.** A reduction in the price of an item allowed if payment is made within a stipulated period.

cash·ew (kăsh′o͞o, kə-sho͞o′) *n.* **1.** A tropical American evergreen tree *(Anacardium occidentale)* widely cultivated for its edible nutlike kernels. **2.** The kidney-shaped seed of this tree, eaten after roasting. [Probably Portuguese *acajú,* from Tupi *acajú,* from *cajú,* yellow fruit, acidic.]

cashew apple *n.* The soft, swollen, pear-shaped edible stalk of the fruit of the cashew, used for beverages, preserves, or jams.

cashew nut *n.* The edible seed of the cashew tree.

cash flow *n.* **1.** The pattern of income and expenditures, as of a company or person, and the resulting availability of cash: *The city improved its cash flow by borrowing against future revenues.* **2.** The cash receipts or net income from one or more assets for a given period, reckoned after taxes and other disbursements, and often used as a measure of corporate worth. **—cash′-flow′** (kăsh′flō′) *adj.*

cash·ier[1] (kă-shîr′) *n.* **1.** The officer of a bank or business concern in charge of paying and receiving money. **2.** A store employee who handles cash transactions with customers. [Dutch *cassier* or French *caissier,* both from *caisse,* money box, from Old Provençal *caisa,* from Vulgar Latin **capsea,* from Latin *capsa,* case.]

ca·shier[2] (kă-shîr′) *tr.v.* **-shiered, -shier·ing, -shiers.** To dismiss from a position of command or responsibility, especially for disciplinary reasons. See Synonyms at **dismiss.** [Dutch *casseren,* from Old French *casser,* to dismiss, annul. See QUASH[1].]

ca·shier's check (kă-shîrz′) *n.* A check drawn by a bank on its own funds and signed by the bank's cashier.

cash machine *n.* See **automated teller machine.**

cash·mere (kăzh′mîr′, kăsh′-) *n.* **1.** Fine, downy wool growing beneath the outer hair of the Cashmere goat. **2.** A soft fabric made of this wool or of similar fibers. [After KASHMIR.]

Cash·mere (kăsh′mîr′, kăsh-mîr′). See **Kashmir.**

Cashmere goat also **Kashmir goat** *n.* A goat native to the Himalayan regions of India and Tibet and prized for its wool.

cash register *n.* A machine that tabulates the amount of sales transactions, makes a permanent and cumulative record of them, and has a drawer in which cash can be kept.

cas·i·mere (kăz′ə-mîr′, kăs′-) *n.* Variant of **cassimere.**

cas·ing (kā′sĭng) *n.* **1.** An outer cover: *a shell casing.* **2.** The frame or framework for a window or door. **3.** A metal pipe or tube used as a lining for a water, oil, or gas well. **4.** A membranous case, often made of animal intestine, used to contain sausage or other processed meat.

ca·si·no (kə-sē′nō) *n., pl.* **-nos. 1.** A public room or building for gambling and other entertainment. **2.** Also **cas·si·no.** *Games.* A card game for two to four players in which cards on the table are matched by cards in the hand. **3.** A summer or country house in Italy. [Italian, diminutive of *casa,* house, from Latin *casa.*]

WORD HISTORY: The history of the word *casino* reveals a transformation from a cottage to a gambling palace. The source of our word, Italian *casino,* is a diminutive of *casa,* "house," itself from Latin *cāsa,* "cottage, hut, hovel." Central to the transformation is the development of the senses of *casino* in Italian. The word was first applied to a country house and then came to be used for a social gathering place, a room or building where one could dance, listen to music, and gamble. This last pastime seems to have gained precedence over the others, at least as far as the development of the word is concerned, and *casino* took on the meaning "gambling establishment." These senses of the Italian word have all been borrowed into English, the sense "social gathering place" being recorded first in the 18th century, the sense "gambling establishment" first in 1851.

cask (kăsk) *n. Abbr.* **ck., csk. 1.** A sturdy cylindrical container for storing liquids; a barrel. **2.** The quantity that such a container can hold. [Middle English *caske,* possibly from Old Spanish *casco,* potsherd, helmet, from *cascar,* to break. See CASCARA.]

cas·ket (kăs′kĭt) *n.* **1.** A small case or chest, as for jewels and other valuables. **2.** A coffin. **—casket** *tr.v.* **-ket·ed, -ket·ing, -kets.** To enclose in a case, chest, or coffin. [Middle English, possibly alteration of Old French *cassette.* See CASSETTE.]

Cas·lon (kăz′lən), **William.** 1692–1766. English type designer whose typefaces, such as Caslon, were widely used in the 18th century.

Cas·par (kăs′pär′, -pər) also **Gas·par** (găs′-). In the New Testament, one of the three wise men from the East who came bearing gifts for the infant Jesus, guided by the Star of Bethlehem.

Cas·per (kăs′pər). A city of east-central Wyoming on the North Platte River northwest of Cheyenne. It was founded in 1888 with the coming of the railroad and grew rapidly after the discovery of oil nearby. Population, 51,016.

Cas·pi·an Sea (kăs′pē-ən). A saline lake between southeast Europe and western Asia. Its water level is decreasing because of dam construction on the Volga River, which feeds the lake.

casque (kăsk) *n.* **1.** A helmet, especially an ornate, visorless headpiece of the 16th century. **2.** *Zoology.* A helmetlike structure or protuberance. [French, from Spanish *casco.* See CASK.] **—casqued** (kăskt) *adj.*

Cass (kăs), **Lewis.** 1782–1866. American soldier, politician, and diplomat who held several governmental positions, including U.S.

case[2]
Type case

cashew
Anacardium occidentale

ă pat	oi boy
ā pay	ou out
âr care	o͝o took
ä father	o͞o boot
ĕ pet	ŭ cut
ē be	ûr urge
ĭ pit	th thin
ī pie	*th* this
îr pier	hw which
ŏ pot	zh vision
ō toe	ə about, item
ô paw	♦ regionalism

Stress marks: ′ (primary); ′ (secondary), as in **dictionary** (dĭk′shə-nĕr′ē)

secretary of war (1831–1836) during the Black Hawk and Seminole wars.

cas·sa·ba (kə-sä′bə) *n.* Variant of **casaba.**

Cas·san·dra (kə-săn′drə) *n.* **1.** *Greek Mythology.* A daughter of Priam, the king of Troy, endowed with the gift of prophecy but fated by Apollo never to be believed. **2.** One that utters unheeded prophecies. [Latin, from Greek *Kassandra.*]

cas·sa·tion (kă-sā′shən) *n.* Abrogation or annulment by a higher authority. [Middle English *cassatioun,* from Old French *cassation,* from Late Latin *cassātiō, cassātiōn-,* from *cassātus,* past participle of *cassāre,* to annul. See QUASH[1].]

Cas·satt (kə-săt′), **Mary Stevenson.** 1844?–1926. American painter noted for her studies of mothers and their children, such as *The Bath* (1891–1892).

Mary Cassatt
Self-portrait, 1880

cas·sa·va (kə-sä′və) *n.* **1.** A shrubby tropical American plant *(Manihot esculenta)* widely grown for its large, tuberous, starchy roots. **2.** The root of this plant, eaten as a staple food in the tropics only after leaching and drying to remove cyanide. Cassava starch is also the source of tapioca. Also called *manioc.* [Ultimately from Taino *casavi,* flour from manioc.]

Cas·sel (kăs′əl, kä′səl). See **Kassel.**

cas·se·na (kə-sē′nə) *n. Botany.* Variant of **cassina.**

cas·se·ne (kə-sē′nə) *n. Botany.* Variant of **cassina.**

cas·se·role (kăs′ə-rōl′) *n.* **1.a.** A dish, usually of earthenware, glass, or cast iron, in which food is both baked and served. **b.** Food prepared and served in such a dish. **2.** *Chemistry.* A small-handled, deep porcelain crucible used for heating and evaporating. [French, saucepan, diminutive of Old French *casse,* ladle, pan, from Old Provençal *cassa,* from Medieval Latin *cattia,* dipper, from Greek *kuathion,* diminutive of *kuathos,* ladle.]

cas·sette (kə-sĕt′, kă-) *n.* **1.** A small, flat case containing two reels and a length of magnetic tape that winds between them, used in audio or video tape recorders or players. **2.** A lightproof cartridge containing photographic film or plates, used in specially designed cameras. **3.** A cartridge for holding and winding typewriter or printer ribbon while in the machine. [French, small box, from Old French, diminutive of Norman French *casse,* case. See CASE[2].]

cassette deck *n.* A tape deck designed for recording or playing audiocassettes.

cassette memory *n. Computer Science.* A removable cartridge containing magnetic tape that stores programs.

cassette player *n.* A tape player designed to play recorded cassettes.

casserole
Pouring liquid sulfur from a porcelain casserole

cas·sia (kăsh′ə) *n.* **1.** Any of various chiefly tropical or subtropical trees, shrubs, or herbs of the genus *Cassia* in the pea family, having pinnately compound leaves, usually yellow flowers, and long, flat or cylindrical pods. **2.a.** A tropical Asian evergreen tree *(Cinnamomum cassia)* having aromatic bark used as a substitute for cinnamon. **b.** The bark of this tree. [Middle English, from Latin, a kind of plant, from Greek *kassia,* of Semitic origin.]

cas·si·mere also **cas·i·mere** (kăz′ə-mîr′, kăs′-) *n.* A plain or twilled woolen cloth used for suits. [Variant of CASHMERE.]

Cas·sin (kä-săN′), **René.** 1887–1976. French jurist and public official. He won the 1968 Nobel Peace Prize for his efforts to safeguard human rights.

cas·si·na also **cas·se·na** or **cas·se·ne** or **cas·si·ne** (kə-sē′nə) *n. Botany.* **1.** See **dahoon.** **2.** See **yaupon.** [American Spanish, yaupon, from Timucua *kasine.*]

Cas·sin·gle (kə-sĭng′gəl, kă-). A trademark used for a prerecorded magnetic tape cassette typically containing one song.

cas·si·no (kə-sē′nō) *n. Games.* Variant of **casino** (sense 2).

Cas·si·no (kə-sē′nō, käs-). A town of central Italy in the Apennines northwest of Naples. In World War II the town and nearby Benedictine monastery of Monte Cassino were reduced to rubble during fierce German-Allied fighting (February–May 1944). Population, 26,300.

cassowary
Southern cassowary
Casuarius casuarius

Cas·si·o·dor·us (kăs′ē-ə-dôr′əs, -dōr′-), **Flavius Magnus Aurelius.** Sixth century A.D. Roman statesman and historian who wrote *Chronicon,* a universal history to A.D. 519, and *Institutiones,* a broad course of study for a monastery.

Cas·si·o·pe·ia (kăs′ē-ə-pē′ə) *n.* A W-shaped constellation in the Northern Hemisphere between Andromeda and Cepheus. [Latin *Cassiopēa,* from Greek *Kassiepeia.*]

Cas·sir·er (kə-sîr′ər, kä-), **Ernst.** 1874–1945. German philosopher who was concerned with the formation of concepts in the mind and the theory of scientific knowledge.

cas·sis (kə-sēs′) *n.* **1.** A Eurasian currant *(Ribes nigrum)* bearing black berries. **2.** A cordial made from the berries of this plant. [French, from Latin *cassia,* a kind of plant. See CASSIA.]

cas·sit·er·ite (kə-sĭt′ə-rīt′) *n.* A light yellow, red-brown, or black mineral, SnO_2, that is an important tin ore. Also called *tinstone.* [French *cassitérite,* from Greek *kassiteros,* tin.]

Cas·sius Lon·gi·nus (kăsh′əs lŏn-jī′nəs), **Gaius.** Died 42 B.C. Roman general and politician who was a leading member of the conspiracy to assassinate Julius Caesar.

cas·sock (kăs′ək) *n.* An ankle-length garment with a close-fitting waist and sleeves, worn by the clergy and others assisting in church services. [French *casaque,* long coat, from Old French, perhaps from Italian *casacca,* from Persian *kazhāgand,* padded garment : *kazh,* raw silk + *āgand,* stuffed.]

castanet
A pair of castanets

cas·sou·let (kăs′o͞o-lā′) *n.* A casserole of white beans, various meats, vegetables, and herbs, slowly simmered or baked in a slow oven. [French, stove dish, diminutive of *cassolo,* earthenware vessel, from *casso,* from Old Provençal *cassa.* See CASSEROLE.]

cas·so·war·y (kăs′ə-wĕr′ē) *n., pl.* **-ies.** Any of several large flightless birds of the genus *Casuarius* of Australia, New Guinea, and adjacent areas, having a large, bony projection on the top of the head and brightly colored wattles. [Malay *kĕsuari.*]

cast (kăst) *v.* **cast, cast·ing, casts.** —*tr.* **1.a.** To throw (something, especially something light): *The angler cast the line.* **b.** To throw with force; hurl: *waves that cast driftwood far up on the shore.* See Synonyms at **throw. 2.** To shed; molt. **3.** To throw forth; drop: *cast anchor.* **4.** To throw on the ground, as in wrestling. **5.** To deposit or indicate (a ballot or vote). **6.** To turn or direct: *All eyes were cast upon the speaker.* **7.** To cause to fall onto or over something or in a certain direction, as if by throwing: *candles casting light; cast aspersions on my character; findings that cast doubt on our hypothesis.* **8.** To bestow; confer: *"The government I cast upon my brother"* (Shakespeare). **9.a.** To roll or throw (dice, for example). **b.** To draw (lots). **10.** To give birth to prematurely: *The cow cast a calf.* **11.** To cause (hunting hounds) to scatter and circle in search of a lost scent. **12.a.** To choose actors for (a play, for example). **b.** To assign a certain role to (an actor): *cast her as the lead.* **c.** To assign an actor to (a part): *cast each role carefully.* **13.** To form (liquid metal, for example) into a particular shape by pouring into a mold. **14.** To give a form to; arrange: *decided to cast the book in three parts.* **15.** To contrive; devise: *cast a plan.* **16.** To calculate or compute; add up (a column of figures). **17.** To calculate astrologically: *cast my horoscope.* **18.** To warp; twist: *floorboards cast by age.* **19.** *Nautical.* To turn (a ship); change to the opposite tack. —*intr.* **1.** To throw something, especially to throw out a lure or bait at the end of a fishing line. **2.** To add a column of figures; make calculations. **3.** To make a conjecture or a forecast. **4.** To receive form or shape in a mold. **5.** To search for a lost scent in hunting with hounds. **6.** *Nautical.* **a.** To veer to leeward from a former course; fall off. **b.** To put about; tack. **7.** To choose actors for the parts in a play, movie, or other theatrical presentation. **8.** *Obsolete.* To estimate; conjecture. —**cast** *n.* **1.a.** The act or an instance of casting or throwing. **b.** The distance thrown. **2.a.** A throwing of a fishing line or net into the water. **b.** The line or net thrown. **3.a.** A throw of dice. **b.** The number thrown. **4.** A stroke of fortune or fate; lot. **5.a.** A direction or expression of the eyes. **b.** A slight squint. **6.** Something, such as molted skin, that is thrown off, out, or away. **7.** The addition of a column of figures; calculation. **8.** A conjecture; a forecast. **9.a.** The act of pouring molten material into a mold. **b.** The amount of molten material poured into a mold at a single operation. **c.** Something formed by this means: *The sculpture was a bronze cast.* **10.** An impression formed in a mold or matrix; a mold: *a cast of her face made in plaster.* **11.** A rigid dressing, usually made of gauze and plaster of Paris, used to immobilize an injured body part, as in a fracture or dislocation. Also called *plaster cast.* **12.** The form in which something is made or constructed; arrangement: *the close-set cast of her features.* **13.** Outward form or look; appearance: *a suit of stylish cast.* **14.** Sort; type: *fancied himself to be of a macho cast.* **15.** An inclination; tendency: *her thoughtful cast of mind.* **16.** The actors in a theatrical presentation. **17.** A slight trace of color; a tinge. **18.** A distortion of shape. **19.** The circling of hounds to pick up a scent in hunting. **20.** A pair of hawks released by a falconer at one time. See Synonyms at **flock[1]**. —***phrasal verbs.* cast about. 1.** To make a search; look: *had to cast about for an hour, looking for a good campsite.* **2.** To devise means; contrive: *cast about for new ways to proceed.* **cast around.** To search about: *cast around for solutions to the problem.* **cast off. 1.** To discard; reject: *cast off old clothing.* **2.** To let go; set loose: *cast off a boat; cast off a line.* **3.** To make the last row of stitches in knitting. **4.** *Printing.* To estimate the space a manuscript will occupy when set into type. **cast on.** To make the first row of stitches in knitting. **cast out.** To drive out by force; expel. —***idiom.* cast (one's) lot with.** To join or side with for better or worse. [Middle English *casten,* from Old Norse *kasta.*]

cas·ta·net (kăs′tə-nĕt′) *n. Music.* A rhythm instrument consisting of a pair of slightly concave shells of ivory or hardwood, held in the palm of the hand by a connecting cord over the thumb and clapped together with the fingers. Often used in the plural. [Spanish *castañeta,* from *castaña,* chestnut, from Latin *castanea.* See CHESTNUT.]

cast·a·way (kăst′ə-wā′) *adj.* **1.** Cast adrift or ashore; shipwrecked. **2.** Discarded; thrown away. —**castaway** *n.* **1.** A shipwrecked person. **2.** A rejected or discarded person or thing.

caste (kăst) *n.* **1.a.** Any of four classes, comprising numerous subclasses, constituting Hindu society. **b.** Any of numerous hereditary, endogamous social subclasses stratified according to Hindu ritual purity. **2.** A social class separated from others by distinctions of hereditary rank, profession, or wealth. **3.a.** A social system or the principle of grading society based on castes. **b.** The social position or status conferred by a system based on castes: *lose caste by doing work beneath one's station.* **4.** A specialized level in a colony of social insects, such as ants, in which the members, such as workers or soldiers, carry out a specific function. [Spanish *casta,* race, and Portuguese *casta,* race, caste, both from feminine of *casto,* pure, from Latin *castus.* See **kes-** in Appendix.]

Cas·tel Gan·dol·fo (kä-stĕl′ gän-dôl′fō). A town of central

Italy on Lake Albano southeast of Rome. It is the site of the papal summer residence. Population, 3,600.

cas·tel·lan (kăs′tə-lən) *n.* The keeper or governor of a castle. [Middle English *castelain,* from Norman French, from Medieval Latin *castellānus,* from Latin, of a fortress, from *castellum,* stronghold. See CASTLE.]

cas·tel·lat·ed (kăs′tə-lā′tĭd) *adj.* **1.** Furnished with turrets and battlements in the style of a castle. **2.** Having a castle. [Medieval Latin *castellātus,* past participle of *castellāre,* to fortify as a castle, from Latin *castellum,* fort. See CASTLE.] **—cas′tel·la′tion** *n.*

Cas·tel·lón de la Pla·na (kăs′təl-yōn′ də lä plä′nə, kä′-stĕlyôn′ dĕ lä plä′nä). A city of eastern Spain on the Mediterranean Sea north-northeast of Valencia. A port and manufacturing center, it was captured from the Moors in 1233. Population, 129,518.

cast·er (kăs′tər) *n.* **1.** One that casts: *a caster of nets.* **2.** Also **cas·tor.** A small wheel on a swivel, attached under a piece of furniture or other heavy object to make it easier to move. **3.** Also **castor. a.** A small bottle, pot, or shaker for holding a condiment. **b.** A stand for a set of condiment containers.

cas·ti·gate (kăs′tĭ-gāt′) *tr.v.* **-gat·ed, -gat·ing, -gates. 1.** To inflict severe punishment on. See Synonyms at **punish. 2.** To criticize severely. [Latin *castīgāre, castīgāt-,* from *castus,* pure. See **kes-** in Appendix.] **—cas′ti·ga′tion** *n.* **—cas′ti·ga′tor** *n.*

Cas·ti·glio·ne (kä′stĭl-yō′nā, kä′stē-lyô′nĕ), Count **Baldassare.** 1478–1529. Italian diplomat and writer best known for *Il Cortegiano* (1528), which describes the perfect courtier.

Cas·tile (kăs-tēl′). A region and former kingdom of central and northern Spain. Autonomous from the tenth century, it joined with Aragon after the marriage of Isabella and Ferdinand in 1479, thus forming the nucleus of modern Spain.

Castile soap also **cas·tile soap** (kăs-tēl′) *n.* A fine, hard, white, odorless soap made with olive oil and sodium hydroxide. [After CASTILE.]

Cas·til·ian (kă-stĭl′yən) *n.* **1.** A native or inhabitant of Castile. **2. a.** The Spanish dialect of Castile. **b.** The standard literary and official form of Spanish, which is based on this dialect. **—Castilian** *adj.* Of or relating to Castile or its people, language, or culture.

cast·ing (kăs′tĭng) *n.* **1. a.** The act or process of making casts or molds. **b.** Something cast in a mold. **2.** The act of throwing a fishing line. **3.** Something cast off or out. **4.** Selection of actors or performers for the parts of a presentation.

casting vote *n.* The vote of a presiding officer in an assembly or council, given to break a tie.

cast iron *n.* A hard, brittle, nonmalleable iron-carbon alloy, cast into shape, containing 2 to 4.5 percent carbon, 0.5 to 3 percent silicon, and lesser amounts of sulfur, manganese, and phosphorus.

cast-i·ron (kăst′ī′ərn) *adj.* **1.** Made of cast iron. **2.** Rigid; inflexible: *a cast-iron rule.* **3.** Exceptionally strong or resistant: *a cast-iron stomach.*

cast-iron plant *n.* See **aspidistra.**

cas·tle (kăs′əl) *n.* **1. a.** A large fortified building or group of buildings with thick walls, usually dominating the surrounding country. **b.** A fortified stronghold converted to residential use. **c.** A large, ornate building similar to or resembling a fortified stronghold. **2.** A place of privacy, security, or refuge. **3.** *Games.* See **rook**[2]. **—castle** *v.* **-tled, -tling, -tles.** *—intr. Games.* To move the king in chess from its own square two empty squares to one side and then, in the same move, bring the rook from that side to the square immediately past the new position of the king. *—tr.* **1.** To place in or as if in a castle. **2.** *Games.* To move (the king in chess) by castling. [Middle English *castel,* from Old English and from Norman French, both from Latin *castellum,* diminutive of *castrum.* See **kes-** in Appendix.]

Cas·tle (kăs′əl), **Vernon Blythe.** 1887–1918. British-born dancer who together with his wife, **Irene Foote Castle** (1893–1969), gained recognition for innovative dancing.

cas·tled (kăs′əld) *adj.* Castellated.

Castle Peak. A mountain, 4,350.8 m (14,265 ft) high, in the Elk Mountains of west-central Colorado. It is the highest elevation in the range.

Cas·tle·reagh (kăs′əl-rā′), Viscount. Title of Robert Stewart, Second Marquis of Londonderry. 1769–1822. British politician who as chief secretary for Ireland (1798–1801) was able to quell the 1798 rebellion and form a political union between Ireland and Great Britain (1800).

cast·off (kăst′ôf′, -ŏf′) *n.* **1.** One that has been discarded. **2.** *Printing.* A calculation of the amount of space a manuscript will occupy when set into type.

cast-off (kăst′ôf′, -ŏf′) *adj.* Discarded; rejected.

cas·tor[1] (kăs′tər) *n.* **1.** An oily, brown, odorous substance obtained from glands in the groin of the beaver and used as a perfume fixative. **2.** A hat made of beaver fur or an imitation. **3.** A heavy wool fabric used especially for overcoats. [Middle English, from Latin, beaver, from Greek *kastōr.*]

cas·tor[2] (kăs′tər) *n.* Variant of **caster** (senses 2, 3).

Cas·tor (kăs′tər) *n.* **1.** *Greek Mythology.* One of the Dioscuri. **2.** A double star in the constellation Gemini, the brightest star in the group, approximately 46 light-years from Earth. [Latin, from Greek *Kastōr,* twin of Pollux.]

castor bean *n.* **1.** The castor-oil plant. **2.** The poisonous seed of the castor-oil plant, from which castor oil is obtained. [CASTOR (OIL) + BEAN.]

castor oil *n.* A colorless or pale yellowish oil extracted from the seeds of the castor-oil plant, used pharmaceutically as a laxative and skin softener and industrially as a lubricant. [Possibly from a former use as a substitute for castor in medicine.]

cas·tor-oil plant (kăs′tər-oil′) *n.* A poisonous, ornamental, tropical African herb or tree *(Ricinus communis)* having palmately lobed leaves and unisexual flowers and yielding a seed oil of commercial and medicinal value.

cas·trate (kăs′trāt′) *tr.v.* **-trat·ed, -trat·ing, -trates. 1.** To remove the testicles of (a male); geld or emasculate. **2.** To remove the ovaries of (a female); spay. **3.** To deprive of virility or spirit; emasculate. **—castrate** *n.* An individual who is incapable of reproduction as a result of removal, destruction, or inactivation of the gonads. [Latin *castrāre, castrāt-.* See **kes-** in Appendix.] **—cas′trat·er, cas′tra·tor** *n.* **—cas·tra′tion** *n.*

ca·stra·to (kă-strä′tō, kə-) *n., pl.* **-ti** (-tē) or **-tos.** *Music.* A male singer castrated before puberty so as to retain a soprano or alto voice. [Italian, from Latin *castrātus,* past participle of *castrāre,* to castrate. See CASTRATE.]

Cas·tries (kăs′trēz′, -trēs′). The capital of St. Lucia, in the Windward Islands of the British West Indies. It was founded by the French in 1650. Population, 50,798.

Cas·tro (kăs′trō, kä′strō), **Cipriano.** 1858?–1924. Venezuelan soldier and politician who was president from 1902 to 1908, when he was suspended by the congress for his dictatorial policies.

Castro, Fidel. Born 1927. Cuban revolutionary leader who overthrew the corrupt regime of the dictator Fulgencio Batista in 1959 and established a socialist state.

Cas·tro·ism (kăs′trō-ĭz′əm) *n.* The political and socioeconomic principles and policies of Fidel Castro. **—Cas′tro·ist, Cas′tro·ite′** (-īt′) *adj. & n.*

Cas·trop-Rau·xel (käs′trôp-rouk′səl). A city of western Germany in the Ruhr Valley south-southwest of Münster. It is a commercial and industrial center. Population, 76,428.

ca·su·al (kăzh′o͞o-əl) *adj.* **1.** Occurring by chance. See Synonyms at **chance. 2. a.** Occurring at irregular or infrequent intervals; occasional: *casual employment at a factory; a casual correspondence with a former teacher.* **b.** Unpremeditated; offhand: *a casual remark.* **3. a.** Being without ceremony or formality; relaxed: *a casual evening with friends.* **b.** Suited for everyday wear or use; informal. **4.** Not serious or thorough; superficial: *a casual inspection.* **5. a.** Showing little interest or concern; nonchalant: *a casual disregard for cold weather.* **b.** Lenient; permissive: *a casual attitude toward drugs.* **6.** Not close or intimate; passing: *a casual acquaintance with avant-garde music.* **—casual** *n.* **1.** One that serves or appears at irregular intervals, especially a temporary worker. **2.** Often **casuals.** Casual clothing. **3.** A soldier temporarily attached to a unit while awaiting permanent assignment. [Middle English *casuel,* from Old French, from Latin *cāsuālis,* from *cāsus,* event. See CASE[1].] **—ca′su·al·ly** *adv.* **—ca′su·al·ness** *n.*

ca·su·al·ty (kăzh′o͞o-əl-tē) *n., pl.* **-ties. 1.** An accident, especially one involving serious injury or loss of life. **2.** One injured or killed in an accident: *a train wreck with an unknown number of casualties.* **3. a.** One injured, killed, captured, or missing in action through engagement with an enemy. **b.** *Often* **casualties.** Loss in numbers especially through engagement with an enemy: *Battlefield casualties were high.* **4.** One that is harmed or eliminated as a result of an action or circumstance: *The corner grocery was a casualty of the expanding supermarkets.* [Middle English *casuelte,* from Old French, from Medieval Latin *cāsuālitās,* chance, accident, from Latin *cāsuālis,* fortuitous. See CASUAL.]

ca·su·a·ri·na (kăzh′o͞o-ə-rī′nə) *n.* See **beefwood.** [New Latin *Casuarina,* genus name, from Malay *kĕsuari,* cassowary (from the resemblance of its twigs to the drooping feathers of the cassowary).]

ca·su·ist (kăzh′o͞o-ĭst) *n.* A person who is expert in or given to casuistry. [French *casuiste,* from Spanish *casuista,* from Latin *cāsus,* case. See CASE[1].]

ca·su·is·tic (kăzh′o͞o-ĭs′tĭk) also **ca·su·is·ti·cal** (-tĭ-kəl) *adj.* Of or relating to casuists or casuistry. **—ca′su·is′ti·cal·ly** *adv.*

ca·su·ist·ry (kăzh′o͞o-ĭ-strē) *n., pl.* **-ries. 1.** Specious or excessively subtle reasoning intended to rationalize or mislead. **2.** The determination of right and wrong in questions of conduct or conscience by the application of general principles of ethics. [From CASUIST.]

ca·sus bel·li (kā′səs bĕl′ī, kä′səs bĕl′ē) *n., pl.* **casus belli.** An act or event that provokes or is used to justify war. [New Latin *cāsus bellī* : Latin *cāsus,* occasion + Latin *bellī,* genitive of *bellum,* war.]

cat (kăt) *n.* **1. a.** A small carnivorous mammal *(Felis catus* or *F. domesticus)* domesticated since early times as a catcher of rats and mice and as a pet and existing in several distinctive breeds and varieties. **b.** Any of various other carnivorous mammals of the family Felidae, which includes the lion, tiger, leopard, and lynx. **c.** The fur of a domestic cat. **2.** A woman who is regarded as spiteful. **3.** A cat-o'-nine-tails. **4.** A catfish. **5.** *Nautical.* **a.** A cathead. **b.** A device for raising an anchor to the cathead. **c.** A catboat. **d.** A catamaran. **6.** *Slang.* **a.** A person, especially a man. **b.** A player or devotee of jazz music. **—cat** *v.* **cat·ted,**

caster
c. 1778 American
by Jonathan Otis
(1723–1791)

castle
Neuschwanstein Castle,
Germany

Fidel Castro
Photographed in 1978

ă pat	oi boy
ā pay	ou out
âr care	o͝o took
ä father	o͞o boot
ĕ pet	ŭ cut
ē be	ûr urge
ĭ pit	th thin
ī pie	*th* this
îr pier	hw which
ŏ pot	zh vision
ō toe	ə about, item
ô paw	♦ regionalism

Stress marks: ′ (primary); ′ (secondary), as in **dictionary** (dĭk′shə-nĕr′ē)

cat·ting, cats. —*tr. Nautical.* To hoist an anchor to (the cathead). —*intr. Slang.* To look for sexual partners; have an affair or affairs: *"catting around with every lady in sight"* (Gore Vidal). —***idiom.*** **let the cat out of the bag.** To let a secret be known. [Middle English, from Old English *catt,* from Germanic **kattuz.*]

CAT (kăt) *abbr.* **1.** Clear-air turbulence. **2.** Computerized axial tomography.

cat. *abbr.* Catalog.

cata– *pref.* **1.** Down: *catadromous.* **2.** Reverse; backward; degenerative: *cataplasia.* [Greek *kata-,* from *kata,* down, downwards, thoroughly. See **kat-** in Appendix.]

ca·tab·o·lism (kə-tăb′ə-lĭz′əm) *n.* The metabolic breakdown of complex molecules into simpler ones, often resulting in a release of energy. [CATA– + (META)BOLISM.] —**cat′a·bol′ic** (kăt′ə-bŏl′ĭk) *adj.* —**cat′a·bol′i·cal·ly** *adv.*

ca·tab·o·lite (kə-tăb′ə-līt′) *n.* A substance produced by the process of catabolism. [CATABOL(ISM) + –ITE[2].]

ca·tab·o·lize (kə-tăb′ə-līz′) *intr. & tr.v.* **-lized, -liz·ing, -liz·es.** To undergo or cause to undergo catabolism.

cat·a·chre·sis (kăt′ə-krē′sĭs) *n., pl.* **-ses** (-sēz). **1.a.** Strained use of a word or phrase, as for rhetorical effect. **b.** A deliberately paradoxical figure of speech. **2.** The improper use of a word or phrase, especially in application to something it does not denote, as the use of *blatant* to mean "flagrant." [Latin *catachrēsis,* improper use of a word, from Greek *katakhrēsis,* excessive use, from *katakhrēsthai,* to misuse : *kata-,* completely; see CATA– + *khrēsthai,* to use; see **gher-[2]** in Appendix.] —**cat′a·chres′tic** (-krĕs′tĭk), **cat′a·chres′ti·cal** (-tĭ-kəl) *adj.* —**cat′a·chres′ti·cal·ly** *adv.*

cat·a·clysm (kăt′ə-klĭz′əm) *n.* **1.** A violent upheaval that causes great destruction or brings about a fundamental change. See Synonyms at **disaster. 2.** A violent and sudden change in the earth's crust. **3.** A devastating flood. [French *cataclysme,* from Latin *cataclysmos,* deluge, from Greek *kataklusmos,* from *katakluzein,* to inundate : *kata-,* intensive pref.; see CATA– + *kluzein,* to wash away.] —**cat′a·clys′mic** (-klĭz′mĭk), **cat′a·clys′mal** (-klĭz′məl) *adj.*

cat·a·comb (kăt′ə-kōm′) *n.* **1.** Often **catacombs.** An underground cemetery consisting of chambers or tunnels with recesses for graves. **2.** An underground burial place. [Probably French *catacombe,* from Old French, from Late Latin *catacumba.*]

ca·tad·ro·mous (kə-tăd′rə-məs) *adj.* Living in fresh water but migrating to marine waters to breed. Used of fish.

catafalque
Supporting a coffin

cat·a·falque (kăt′ə-fălk′, -fôlk′) *n.* **1.** A decorated platform or framework on which a coffin rests in state during a funeral. **2.** *Roman Catholic Church.* A coffin-shaped structure draped with a pall, used to represent the corpse at a requiem Mass celebrated after the burial. [French, from Italian *catafalco.*]

Cat·a·lan (kăt′l-ăn′, -ən, kăt′l-ăn′) *adj.* Of or relating to Catalonia or its people, language, or culture. —**Catalan** *n.* **1.** A native or inhabitant of Catalonia. **2.** The Romance language spoken especially in Catalonia, the Balearic Islands, Andorra, and the Roussillon region of France. [Middle English *Catalane,* possibly from Catalan *catalana,* from *Catalunya,* Catalonia.]

cat·a·lase (kăt′l-ās′, -āz′) *n.* An enzyme found in the blood and in most living cells that catalyzes the decomposition of hydrogen peroxide into water and oxygen. [CATAL(YSIS) + –ASE.] —**cat′a·lat′ic** (kăt′l-ăt′ĭk) *adj.*

cat·a·lec·tic (kăt′l-ĕk′tĭk) *adj.* Lacking one or more syllables, especially in the final foot. Used of verse. [Late Latin *catalēcticus,* from Greek *katalēktikos,* from *katalēgein,* to leave off : *kata-,* intensive pref.; see CATA– + *lēgein,* to cease, terminate; see **slēg-** in Appendix.]

catamaran
Engine-powered catamaran

cat·a·lep·sy (kăt′l-ĕp′sē) *n., pl.* **-sies.** A condition characterized by lack of response to external stimuli and by muscular rigidity, so that the limbs remain in whatever position they are placed. It is known to occur in a variety of physical and psychological disorders, such as epilepsy and schizophrenia, and can be induced by hypnosis. [Middle English *catalempsi,* from Late Latin *catalēmpsia,* from Greek *katalēpsis,* from *katalambanein,* to seize upon : *kata-,* intensive pref.; see CATA– + *lambanein, lēp-,* to seize.] —**cat′a·lep′tic** (kăt′l-ĕp′tĭk) *adj.*

cat·a·lex·is (kăt′l-ĕk′sĭs) *n.* The absence of one or more syllables in a line of verse, especially in the last foot. [Greek *katalēxis,* from *katalēgein,* to leave off. See CATALECTIC.]

Cat·a·li·na Island (kăt′l-ē′nə). See **Santa Catalina Island.**

cat·a·lo (kăt′l-ō′) *n.* Variant of **cattalo.**

cat·a·log or **cat·a·logue** (kăt′l-ôg′, -ŏg′) —*n. Abbr.* **cat. 1.a.** A list or itemized display, as of titles, course offerings, or articles for exhibition or sale, usually including descriptive information or illustrations. **b.** A publication, such as a book or pamphlet, containing such a list or display: *a catalog of fall fashions; a seed catalog.* **2.** A list or enumeration: *"the long catalogue of his concerns: unemployment, housing, race, drugs, the decay of the inner city, the environment and family life"* (Anthony Holden). **3.** A card catalog. —*v.* **-loged, -log·ing, -logs** or **-logued, -logu·ing, -logues.** —*tr.* **1.** To make an itemized list of: *catalog a record collection.* **2.a.** To list or include in a catalog. **b.** To classify (a book or publication, for example) according to a categorical system. —*intr.* **1.** To make a catalog. **2.** To be listed in a catalog: *an item that catalogs for 200 dollars.* [Middle English *cathaloge,* list, register, from Old French *catalogue,* from Late Latin *catalogus,* from Greek *katalogos,* from *katalegein,* to list : *kata-,* down, off; see CATA– + *legein,* to count; see **leg-** in Appendix.] —**cat′a·log′er, cat′a·logu′er** *n.*

ca·ta·logue rai·son·né (kăt′l-ôg′ rā′zə-nā′, -ŏg′, kä-tä-lôg′ rĕ-zô-nā′) *n., pl.* **ca·ta·logues rai·son·nés** (kăt′l-ôgz′ rā′zə-nā′, -ŏgz′, kä-tä-lôg′ rĕ-zô-nā′). A publication listing titles of articles or literary works, especially the contents of an exhibition, along with related descriptive or critical material. [French : *catalogue,* catalog + *raisonné,* methodical, descriptive, from past participle of *raisonner,* to reason, analyze.]

Cat·a·lo·nia (kăt′l-ōn′yə, -ō′nē-ə). A region of northeast Spain bordering on France and the Mediterranean Sea. In the late 19th and early 20th centuries it was a center of socialist and anarchist activity. The Catalans established a separate state in the 1930's. —**Cat′a·lo′nian** *adj. & n.*

ca·tal·pa (kə-tăl′pə, -tôl′-) *n.* Any of various, usually deciduous trees of the genus *Catalpa,* especially *C. bignonioides* or *C. speciosa,* native to the United States and having whorled, heart-shaped leaves, showy clusters of white flowers, and long, slender, cylindrical pods. Also called *Indian bean.* [Creek *katałpa* : *ka-,* head + *tałpa,* wing (from the shape of its flowers).]

ca·tal·y·sis (kə-tăl′ĭ-sĭs) *n., pl.* **-ses** (-sēz′). The action of a catalyst, especially an increase in the rate of a chemical reaction. [Greek *katalusis,* dissolution, from *kataluein,* to dissolve : *kata-,* intensive pref.; see CATA– + *luein,* to loosen; see **leu-** in Appendix.]

cat·a·lyst (kăt′l-ĭst) *n.* **1.** *Chemistry.* A substance, usually used in small amounts relative to the reactants, that modifies and increases the rate of a reaction without being consumed in the process. **2.** One that precipitates a process or event, especially without being involved in or changed by the consequences. [From CATALYSIS.]

SYNONYMS: *catalyst, ferment, leaven, leavening, yeast.* The central meaning shared by these nouns is "an agent that stimulates or precipitates a reaction, development, or change": *a serious breach of trust that was the catalyst for the divorce; love, the most powerful ferment; the leaven of reform working in their minds; a leavening of humor; the yeast of revolution.*

cat·a·lyt·ic (kăt′l-ĭt′ĭk) *adj.* Of, involving, or acting as a catalyst: *"Deregulation's catalytic power . . . is still reshaping the banking, communications, and transportation industries"* (Ellyn E. Spragins). [Greek *katalutikos,* able to dissolve, from *katalusis,* dissolution. See CATALYSIS.] —**cat′a·lyt′i·cal·ly** *adv.*

catalytic converter *n.* A reaction chamber typically containing a finely divided platinum-iridium catalyst into which exhaust gases from an automotive engine are passed together with excess air so that carbon monoxide and hydrocarbon pollutants are oxidized to carbon dioxide and water.

catalytic cracker *n.* An oil refinery unit in which the cracking of petroleum takes place in the presence of a catalyst.

cat·a·lyze (kăt′l-īz′) *tr.v.* **-lyzed, -lyz·ing, -lyz·es. 1.** To modify, especially to increase, the rate of (a chemical reaction) by catalysis. **2.** To bring about; initiate: *"The technology bred of science has catalyzed stupendous economic growth"* (Nature). **3.** To produce fundamental change in; transform: *changes in student enrollment that have catalyzed the educational system.* [From CATALYSIS.] —**cat′a·lyz′er** *n.*

cat·a·ma·ran (kăt′ə-mə-răn′) *n. Nautical.* **1.** A boat with two parallel hulls or floats, especially a light sailboat with a mast mounted on a transverse frame joining the hulls. **2.** A raft of logs or floats lashed together and propelled by paddles or sails. [Tamil *kaṭṭumaram* : *kaṭṭu,* to tie + *maram,* tree, log.]

cat·a·me·ni·a (kăt′ə-mē′nē-ə) *n.* See **menses.** [Greek *katamēnia,* from neuter pl. of *katamēnios,* monthly : *kata-,* according to, per; see CATA– + *mēn,* month; see **mē-[2]** in Appendix.] —**cat′a·me′ni·al** *adj.*

cat·a·mite (kăt′ə-mīt′) *n.* A boy who has a sexual relationship with a man. [Latin *catamītus,* from *Catamītus,* Ganymede, from Etruscan *Catmite,* from Greek *Ganumēdēs.*]

cat·a·mount (kăt′ə-mount′) *n.* See **mountain lion.** [Short for CATAMOUNTAIN.]

cat·a·moun·tain (kăt′ə-moun′tən) *n.* Any of various wild felines, such as the leopard or a wildcat. [Alteration of *cat of the mountain.*]

cat-and-mouse (kăt′n-mous′) *adj.* **1.** Playfully or teasingly cruel, as in prolonging the pain or torment of another: *the cat-and-mouse tactics of the interrogators.* **2.** Of or involving a suspenseful and sometimes alternating relation beween hunter and hunted: *"another cat-and-mouse thriller"* (New York Times).

Ca·ta·nia (kə-tān′yə, -tā′nē-ə, kä-tä′nyä). A city of eastern Sicily, Italy on the **Gulf of Catania,** an inlet of the Ionian Sea. Founded in the eighth century B.C., Catania was a flourishing Greek community and later a Roman colony. Population, 378,521.

Ca·tan·za·ro (kä′tän-zär′ō, -dzär′ō). A city of southern Italy near the Ionian Sea. It was founded in the tenth century. Population, 100,637.

cat·a·pho·re·sis (kăt′ə-fə-rē′sĭs) *n.* See **electrophoresis** (sense 1). —**cat′a·pho·ret′ic** (-rĕt′ĭk) *adj.* —**cat′a·pho·ret′i·cal·ly** *adv.*

cat·a·pla·sia (kăt′ə-plā′zhə, -zhē-ə) *n. Pathology.* Degenerative reversion of cells or tissue to a less differentiated form. —**cat′a·plas′tic** (-plăs′tĭk) *adj.*

ă pat	oi boy
ā pay	ou out
âr care	ŏŏ took
ä father	ōō boot
ĕ pet	ŭ cut
ē be	ûr urge
ĭ pit	th thin
ī pie	*th* this
îr pier	hw which
ŏ pot	zh vision
ō toe	ə about, item
ô paw	♦ regionalism

Stress marks: ′ (primary); ′ (secondary), as in **dictionary** (dĭk′shə-nĕr′ē)

cat·a·plasm (kăt′ə-plăz′əm) *n.* See **poultice.** [Middle English *cathaplasma* and French *cataplasme,* both from Latin *cataplasma,* from Greek *kataplasma,* from *kataplassein,* to plaster over : *kata-,* down, onto, over; see CATA– + *plassein,* to mold, form; see PLASMA.]

cat·a·plex·y (kăt′ə-plĕk′sē) *n.* A sudden loss of muscle tone and strength, usually caused by an extreme emotional stimulus. [From Greek *kataplēxis,* fixation (of the eyes), from *kataplēssein,* to astound, terrify : *kata-,* intensive pref.; see CATA– + *plēssein, plēk-,* to strike; see **plāk-²** in Appendix.] **—cat′a·plec′tic** (-plĕk′tĭk) *adj.*

cat·a·pult (kăt′ə-pŭlt′, -po͝olt′) *n.* **1.** A military machine for hurling missiles, such as large stones or spears, used in ancient and medieval times. **2.** A mechanism for launching aircraft at a speed sufficient for flight, as from the deck of a carrier. **3.** A slingshot. **—catapult** *v.* **-pult·ed, -pult·ing, -pults.** *—tr.* To hurl or launch from or as if from a catapult. *—intr.* To become catapulted; spring or bolt. [French *catapulte,* from Old French, from Latin *catapulta,* from Greek *katapaltēs* : *kata-,* cata- + *pallein,* to brandish, poise a weapon before hurling; see **pōl-** in Appendix.]

cat·a·ract (kăt′ə-răkt′) *n.* **1.** A large or high waterfall. **2.** A great downpour; a deluge. **3.** *Pathology.* Opacity of the lens or capsule of the eye, causing impairment of vision or blindness. [Middle English *cataracte,* from Old French, from Latin *cataracta,* from Greek *katarraktēs, kataraktēs,* probably from *katarassein,* to dash down (*kat-, kata-,* cata- + *arassein,* to strike).]

ca·tarrh (kə-tär′) *n.* Inflammation of mucous membranes, especially of the nose and throat. [Middle English *catarre,* from Old French *catarrhe,* from Late Latin *catarrhus,* from Greek *katarrous,* from *katarrein,* to flow down : *kata-,* cata- + *rhein,* to flow; see **sreu-** in Appendix.] **—ca·tarrh′al, ca·tarrh′ous** *adj.* **—ca·tarrh′al·ly** *adv.*

ca·tas·ta·sis (kə-tăs′tə-sĭs) *n., pl.* **-ses** (-sēz′). **1.** The intensified part of the action directly preceding the catastrophe in classical tragedy. **2.** The climax of a drama. [Greek *katastasis,* settled state, from *kathistanai,* to come into a certain state : *kat-, kata-,* cata- + *histanai,* to set; see **stā-** in Appendix.]

ca·tas·tro·phe (kə-tăs′trə-fē) *n.* **1.** A great, often sudden calamity. See Synonyms at **disaster. 2.** A complete failure; a fiasco: *The food was cold, the guests quarreled—the whole dinner was a catastrophe.* **3.** The concluding action of a drama, especially a classical tragedy, following the climax and containing a resolution of the plot. **4.** A sudden violent change in the earth's surface; a cataclysm. [Greek *katastrophē,* an overturning, ruin, conclusion, from *katastrephein,* to ruin, undo : *kata-,* cata- + *strephein,* to turn; see **streb(h)-** in Appendix.]

cat·a·stroph·ic (kăt′ə-strŏf′ĭk) *adj.* **1.** Of, relating to, or involving a catastrophe. **2.** Involving or resulting in substantial, often ruinous medical expense: *a catastrophic illness.* **—cat′a·stroph′i·cal·ly** *adv.*

ca·tas·tro·phism (kə-tăs′trə-fĭz′əm) *n.* **1.** *Geology.* The doctrine that major changes in the earth's crust result from catastrophes rather than evolutionary processes. **2.** The prediction or expectation of cataclysmic upheaval, as in political or social developments. **—ca·tas′tro·phist** *n.*

cat·a·to·ni·a (kăt′ə-tō′nē-ə) *n.* An abnormal condition variously characterized by stupor, stereotypy, mania, and either rigidity or extreme flexibility of the limbs. It is most often associated with schizophrenia. [New Latin, from German *Katatonie,* from Greek *katatonos,* stretching tight, from *katateinein,* to stretch tight : *kata-,* intensive pref.; see CATA– + *teinein,* to stretch; see **ten-** in Appendix.] **—cat′a·ton′ic** (-tŏn′ĭk) *adj. & n.* **—cat′a·ton′i·cal·ly** *adv.*

Ca·taw·ba¹ (kə-tô′bə) *n., pl.* **Catawba** or **-bas. a.** A Native American people formerly inhabiting territory along the Catawba River in North and South Carolina and now located in western South Carolina. **b.** A member of this people. **c.** The Siouan language of the Catawba.

Ca·taw·ba² (kə-tô′bə) *n., pl.* **-bas. 1.** A reddish North American grape developed from the fox grape. **2.** Wine made from such grapes. [After CATAWBA (RIVER).]

Catawba River. A river rising in the Blue Ridge of western North Carolina and flowing about 402 km (250 mi) generally southward into South Carolina, where it is called the Wateree River.

cat·bird (kăt′bûrd′) *n.* A North American songbird *(Dumetella carolinensis)* having predominantly slate plumage. [From the resemblance of one of its calls to the mewing of a cat.]

catbird seat *n.* A position of power or prominence.

cat·boat (kăt′bōt′) *n.* *Nautical.* A broad-beamed sailboat carrying a single sail on a mast stepped well forward and often fitted with a centerboard.

cat·bri·er (kăt′brī′ər) *n.* Any of several woody, usually prickly dioecious vines of the genus *Smilax,* having greenish, unisexual flowers, heart-shaped leaves, and usually bluish to black berries. Also called *greenbrier, smilax.*

cat burglar *n.* A burglar who is especially skilled at stealthy or undetected entry of a premises.

cat·call (kăt′kôl′) *n.* A harsh or shrill call or whistle expressing derision or disapproval. **—catcall** *v.* **-called, -call·ing, -calls.** *—tr.* To express derision or disapproval of with catcalls. *—intr.* To make catcalls.

catch (kăch, kĕch) *v.* **caught** (kôt), **catch·ing, catch·es.** *—tr.* **1.** To capture or seize, especially after a chase. **2.** To take by or as if by trapping or snaring. **3.a.** To discover or come upon suddenly, unexpectedly, or accidentally: *He was caught in the act of stealing.* **b.** To become cognizant or aware of suddenly: *caught her gazing out the window.* **4.a.** To take hold of, especially forcibly or suddenly; grasp: *caught me by the arm; caught the reins.* **b.** To grab so as to stop the motion of: *catch a ball.* **5.a.** To overtake: *The green car caught me on the straightaway.* **b.** To reach just in time; take: *caught the bus to town; catch a wave.* **6.a.** To hold, as by snagging or entangling. **b.** To cause to become suddenly or accidentally hooked, entangled, or fastened: *caught my hem on the stair.* **c.** To hold up; delay: *was caught in traffic for an hour.* **7.** To hit; strike: *a punch that caught me in the stomach.* **8.** To check (oneself) during an action: *I caught myself before replying.* **9.** To become subject to or to contract, as by exposure to a pathogen: *catch a cold.* **10.a.** To become affected by or infused with: *caught the joyous mood of the festival.* **b.** To suffer from the receipt of (criticism, for example): *caught hell for being late.* **11.** To take or get suddenly, momentarily, or quickly: *We caught a glimpse of the monarch. I caught a hint of sarcasm in your response.* **12.a.** To grasp mentally; apprehend: *I don't catch your meaning.* **b.** To apprehend and reproduce accurately by or as if by artistic means: *an impressionist who caught the effects of wind and water in his paintings.* **13.** To attract and fix; arrest: *couldn't catch their attention; caught the teacher's eye.* **14.** To charm; captivate. **15.a.** *Informal.* To go to see (a performance, for example): *caught the midnight show.* **b.** To get (something required), usually quickly or for a brief period: *catch some sleep.* *—intr.* **1.** To become held, entangled, or fastened: *My coat caught in the car door.* **2.** To act or move so as to hold or grab someone or something: *tried to catch at the life preserver.* **3.** To be communicable or infectious; spread. **4.** To ignite: *The fire caught.* **5.** *Baseball.* To act as catcher. **—catch** *n.* **1.** The act of catching; a taking and holding. **2.** Something that catches, especially a device for fastening or for checking motion. **3.a.** Something caught: *The mistake you found was a good catch.* **b.** *Informal.* One, such as a person or thing, that is worth catching. **4.** *Sports.* **a.** The grabbing and holding of a thrown, kicked, or batted ball before it hits the ground. **b.** A game of throwing and catching a ball. **5.** A quantity that is caught: *The catch amounted to 50 fish.* **6.** A choking or stoppage of the breath or voice. **7.** A stop or break in the operation of a mechanism. **8.** *Informal.* A tricky or previously unsuspected condition or drawback: *It sounds like a good offer, but there may be a catch.* **9.** A snatch; a fragment. **10.** *Music.* A canonical, often rhythmically intricate composition for three or more voices, popular especially in the 17th and 18th centuries. **—*phrasal verbs.* catch on. 1.** To understand; perceive. **2.** To become popular: *Skateboarding caught on quickly.* **catch out.** To detect (another) in the act or process of wrongdoing. **catch up. 1.** To snatch: *The mugger caught the wallet up and fled.* **2.** To detect (another) in a mistake or wrongdoing: *Auditors caught up with the embezzler.* **3.** To come up from behind; overtake. **4.a.** To become involved with, often unwillingly: *was caught up in the scandal.* **b.** To captivate; enthrall: *I was caught up in the mood of the evening.* **5.a.** To bring up to date; brief: *Let me catch you up on all the gossip.* **b.** To bring an activity nearer to completion: *I must catch up on my correspondence.* **—*idioms.* catch fire. 1.** To ignite. **2.** To become very enthusiastic. **3.** To become the subject of great interest and widespread enthusiasm: *an idea that caught fire all over the country.* **catch it.** *Informal.* To receive a punishment or scolding. **catch (one's) breath.** To rest so as to be able to continue an activity. [Middle English *cacchen,* from Old North French *cachier,* to chase, from Latin *captāre,* frequentative of *capere,* to seize. See **kap-** in Appendix.] **—catch′a·ble** *adj.*

SYNONYMS: *catch, enmesh, ensnare, entangle, entrap, snare, tangle, trap.* The central meaning shared by these verbs is "to take in and hold as if by using bait or a lure": *caught in her own lies; enmeshed in the neighbors' dispute; ensnaring an unsuspecting dupe with fast talk; became entangled in his own contradictions; entrapped by a skillful interviewer into making a damaging statement; snared by false hopes; tangled by his own duplicity; trapped into making an incriminating admission.*

Catch-22 also **catch-22** (kăch′twĕn-tē-to͞o′, kĕch′-) *n., pl.* **Catch-22's** or **Catch-22s** also **catch-22's** or **catch-22s. 1.a.** A situation in which a desired outcome or solution is impossible to attain because of a set of inherently illogical rules or conditions: *"In the Catch-22 of a closed repertoire, only music that is already familiar is thought to deserve familiarity"* (Joseph McLennan). **b.** The rules or conditions that create such a situation. **2.** A situation or predicament characterized by absurdity or senselessness. **3.** A contradictory or self-defeating course of action: *"The Catch-22 of his administration was that every grandiose improvement scheme began with community dismemberment"* (Village Voice). **4.** A tricky or disadvantageous condition; a catch: *"Of course, there is a Catch-22 with Form 4868—you are supposed to include a check if you owe any additional tax, otherwise you face some penalties"* (New York). [After *Catch-22,* a novel by Joseph Heller (born 1923), American writer.] **—Catch′-22′** *adj.*

catch·all (kăch′ôl′, kĕch′-) *n.* **1.** A receptacle or storage area for odds and ends. **2.** Something that encompasses a wide variety of items or situations: *a word that serves as a catchall for a bewildering array of computer accessories.* **—catch′all′** *adj.*

catapult

cataract

catboat
Oil painting
by Albert S. Bigelow

catcher
Left to right: Umpire, catcher, and batter

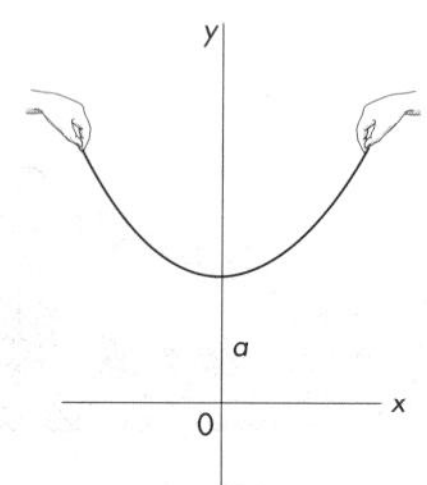

catenary
$y = \frac{a}{2}(e^{x/a} + e^{-x/a})$

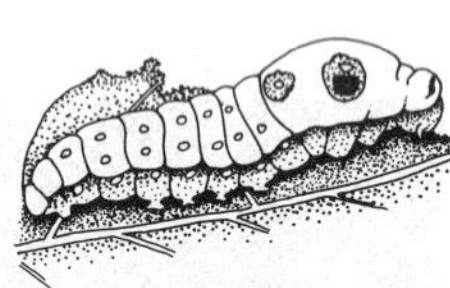
caterpillar
Of a spicebush swallowtail butterfly
Papilio troilus

catfish

catch-as-catch-can (kăch′əz-kăch-kăn′, kĕch′əz-kĕch-) *adj.* Using or making do with whatever means are available; irregular: *made a catch-as-catch-can living doing odd jobs.* **—catch-as-catch-can** *adv.* However or by whatever means possible: *"Reading was learned catch-as-catch-can, while reindeer farming was learned deeply and thoroughly through the daily rigors of survival"* (Bunny McBride).

catch basin *n.* **1.** A receptacle at the entrance to a sewer designed to keep out large or obstructive matter. **2.** A reservoir for collecting surface drainage or run-off.

♦ **catch colt** *n. Western U.S.* See **old-field colt.** See Regional Note at **old-field colt.**

catch·er (kăch′ər, kĕch′-) *n. Abbr.* **c., C.** One that catches, especially the baseball player positioned behind home plate who signals for and receives pitches.

catch·fly (kăch′flī′, kĕch′-) *n.* Any of several plants of the genera *Silene* and *Lychnis,* native chiefly to the Northern Hemisphere and having white, pink, red, or purplish flowers and sticky stems and calyxes on which small insects may become stuck.

catch·ing (kăch′ĭng, kĕch′-) *adj.* **1.** Infectious. **2.** Attractive; catchy.

catch·ment (kăch′mənt, kĕch′-) *n.* **1.** A catching or collecting of water, especially rainwater. **2.a.** A structure, such as a basin or reservoir, used for collecting or draining water. **b.** The amount of water collected in such structure. **3.** A catchment area.

catchment area *n.* **1.** The area drained by a river or body of water. Also called *catchment basin.* **2.** The surrounding area served by an institution, such as a hospital or school.

catch·pen·ny (kăch′pĕn′ē, kĕch′-) *adj.* Designed and made to sell without concern for quality; cheap. **—catchpenny** *n.* A cheap item.

catch phrase *n.* A phrase in wide or popular use, especially one serving as a slogan for a group or movement.

catch·pole also **catch·poll** (kăch′pōl′, kĕch′-) *n.* A sheriff's officer, especially one who arrests debtors. [Middle English *cacchepol,* from Norman French *cachepol,* probably from Old French *chacepol* : *chacier,* to chase; see CHASE[1] + *poul,* rooster (from Latin *pullus,* chicken; see **pau-** in Appendix).]

catch·up (kăch′əp, kĕch′-) *n.* Variant of **ketchup.**

catch-up (kăch′ŭp′, kĕch′-) *n.* **1.** An approach or strategy intended to overcome a disadvantage or lead: *The competition will be playing catch-up for the rest of the season.* **2.** An increase intended to bring an amount or rate up to a standard: *"the statutory catch-up of Social Security benefits with the cost of living"* (Nation). **—catch′-up′** *adj.*

catch·word (kăch′wûrd′, kĕch′-) *n.* **1.a.** A well-known word or phrase, especially one that exemplifies a notion, class, or quality: *"Glasnost has entered the international vocabulary as a catchword for a general liberalization of Soviet society"* (Bill Keller). **b.** A catchy name or slogan: *"the top management of major corporations . . . busy coining catchwords for their new management concepts"* (Japan Economic Journal). **2.** *Printing.* **a.** A guideword. **b.** The first word of a page printed in the bottom right-hand corner of the preceding page.

catch·y (kăch′ē, kĕch′ē) *adj.* **-i·er, -i·est. 1.** Attractive or appealing: *a catchy idea for a new television series.* **2.** Easily remembered: *a song with a catchy tune.* **3.** Tricky; deceptive: *a catchy question on an exam.* **4.** Fitful or spasmodic: *catchy breathing.* **—catch′i·ness** *n.*

cate (kāt) *n. Archaic.* A choice or dainty food; a delicacy. [Short for *acate,* from Middle English *acat,* a purchase, from Norman French, from *acater,* to buy. See CATER.]

cat·e·che·sis (kăt′ĭ-kē′sĭs) *n., pl.* **-ses** (-sēz). Oral instruction given to catechumens. [Late Latin *catēchēsis,* from Greek *katēkhēsis,* oral instruction, from *katēkhein,* to teach by word of mouth. See CATECHIZE.] **—cat′e·chet′i·cal** (-kĕt′ĭ-kəl) *adj.*

cat·e·chin (kăt′ĭ-kĭn′) *n.* A crystalline substance, $C_{15}H_{14}O_6$, derived from catechu and used in tanning and dyeing. Also called *catechol.* [CATECH(U) + -IN.]

cat·e·chism (kăt′ĭ-kĭz′əm) *n.* **1.** A book giving a brief summary of the basic principles of Christianity in question-and-answer form. **2.** A manual giving basic instruction in a subject, usually by rote or repetition. **3.** A body of fundamental principles or beliefs, especially when accepted uncritically: *"the core of the catechism of the antinuclear left, the notion that the threat to peace is technological, not political"* (George F. Will). **4.** A close questioning or examination, as of a political figure. [French *catechisme,* from Old French, from Late Latin *catēchismus,* from Late Greek *katēkhismos,* from *katēkhizein,* to teach by word of mouth. See CATECHIZE.]

cat·e·chist (kăt′ĭ-kĭst) *n.* A person who catechizes, especially one who instructs catechumens in preparation for admission into a Christian church. [French *catechiste,* from Old French, from Late Latin *catēchista,* from Late Greek *katēkhistēs,* from *katēkhizein,* to teach by word of mouth. See CATECHIZE.] **—cat′e·chis′tic, cat′e·chis′ti·cal** *adj.*

cat·e·chize (kăt′ĭ-kīz′) *tr.v.* **-chized, -chiz·ing, -chiz·es. 1.** To teach the principles of Christian dogma, discipline, and ethics by means of questions and answers. **2.** To question or examine closely or methodically: *"Boswell was eternally catechizing him on all kinds of subjects"* (Macaulay). [Middle English *catecizen,* from Old French *catechiser,* from Medieval Latin *catēchizāre,* from Late Greek *katēkhizein,* from Greek *katēkhein* : *kata-,* down, off, out; see CATA– + *ēkhein,* to sound (from *ēkhē,* sound).] **—cat′e·chi·za′tion** (-kĭ-zā′shən) *n.* **—cat′e·chiz′er** *n.*

cat·e·chol (kăt′ĭ-kôl′, -kōl′, -kŏl′) *n.* **1.** See **catechin. 2.** A biologically important organic phenol, having two hydroxyl groups attached to the benzene ring. [CATECH(U) + -OL[1].]

cat·e·cho·la·mine (kăt′ĭ-kō′lə-mēn′, -kô′-) *n.* Any of a group of amines derived from catechol that have important physiological effects as neurotransmitters and hormones and include epinephrine, norepinephrine, and dopamine.

cat·e·chu (kăt′ə-chōō′) *n.* **1.a.** A spiny Asian tree *(Acacia catechu)* having bipinnately compound leaves, spikes of yellow flowers, and dark heartwood. **b.** A raw material obtained from the heartwood of this plant, used in the preparation of tannins and brown dyes. Also called *cutch.* **2.** See **betel palm.** [Probably from Malay *kachu,* probably from Dravidian *karaiyal, karaiccal,* that which is dissolved, from *karai,* to melt.]

cat·e·chu·men (kăt′ĭ-kyōō′mən) *n.* **1.** One who is being taught the principles of Christianity. **2.** One who is being instructed in a subject at an elementary level. [Middle English *cathecumine,* from Old French *catechumene,* from Latin *catēchūmenus,* from Greek *katēkhoumenos,* present passive participle of *katēkhein,* to instruct. See CATECHIZE.]

cat·e·gor·i·cal (kăt′ĭ-gôr′ĭ-kəl, -gŏr′-) also **cat·e·gor·ic** (-ĭk) *adj.* **1.** Being without exception or qualification; absolute. See Synonyms at **explicit. 2.a.** Of or relating to a category or categories. **b.** According to or using categories: *a categorical arrangement of specimens.* **—cat′e·gor′i·cal·ly** *adv.* **—cat′e·gor′i·cal·ness** *n.*

categorical imperative *n.* In the ethical system of Immanuel Kant, an unconditional moral law that applies to all rational beings and is independent of any personal motive or desire.

cat·e·go·rize (kăt′ĭ-gə-rīz′) *tr.v.* **-rized, -riz·ing, -riz·es.** To put into a category or categories; classify. **—cat′e·go·riz′a·ble** *adj.* **—cat′e·go·ri·za′tion** (-gər-ĭ-zā′shən) *n.*

cat·e·go·ry (kăt′ĭ-gôr′ē, -gōr′ē) *n., pl.* **-ries. 1.** A specifically defined division in a system of classification; a class. **2.** A general class of ideas, terms, or things that mark divisions or coordinations within a conceptual scheme, especially: **a.** Aristotle's modes of objective being, such as quality, quantity, or relation, that are inherent in everything. **b.** Kant's modes of subjective understanding, such as singularity, universality, or particularity, that organize perceptions into knowledge. **c.** A basic logical type of philosophical conception in post-Kantian philosophy. [French *catégorie,* from Old French, from Late Latin *catēgoria,* class of predicables, from Greek *katēgoria,* accusation, charge, from *katēgorein,* to accuse, predicate : *kata-,* down, against; see CATA– + *agoreuein, ēgor-,* to speak in public (from *agora,* marketplace, assembly; see **ger-** in Appendix).]

category killer *n. Slang.* A large retail store or chain of stores specializing in a single kind of merchandise that is stocked in great quantity and variety and sold at discount prices.

ca·te·na (kə-tē′nə) *n., pl.* **-nae** (-nē) or **-nas.** A closely linked series, especially of excerpted writings or commentaries. [Latin *catēna,* chain.]

cat·e·nar·y (kăt′n-ĕr′ē, kə-tē′nə-rē) *n., pl.* **-ies. 1.** The curve theoretically formed by a perfectly flexible, uniformly dense, and inextensible cable suspended from its endpoints. **2.** Something having the general shape of this curve. [New Latin *catēnāria,* from Latin, feminine of *catēnārius,* relating to a chain, from *catēna,* chain.] **—cat′e·nar′y** *adj.*

cat·e·nate (kăt′n-āt′) *tr.v.* **-nat·ed, -nat·ing, -nates.** To connect in a series of ties or links; form into a chain. [Latin *catēnāre, catēnāt-,* from *catēna,* chain.]

ca·ter (kā′tər) *v.* **-tered, -ter·ing, -ters.** *—intr.* **1.** To provide food or entertainment. **2.** To be particularly attentive or solicitous; minister: *The nurses catered to my every need. The legislation catered to various special interest groups.* *—tr.* **1.** To provide food service for: *a business that caters banquets and weddings.* **2.** To attend to the wants or needs of. [From obsolete *cater,* a buyer of provisions, from Middle English *catour,* short for *acatour,* from Norman French, from *acater,* to buy, from Vulgar Latin **accaptāre* : Latin *ad-,* ad- + Latin *captāre,* to chase; see CATCH.] **—ca′ter·er** *n.*

cat·er-cor·nered (kăt′ər-kôr′nərd, kăt′ē-) also **cat·er-cor·ner** (-nər) or **cat·ty-cor·nered** (kăt′ē-kôr′nərd) or **cat·ty-cor·ner** (-nər) or **kit·ty-cor·nered** (kĭt′ē-kôr′nərd) or **kit·ty-cor·ner** (-kôr′nər) *—adj.* Diagonal. *—adv.* In a diagonal position. [From obsolete *cater,* four at dice, from Middle English, from Old French *catre,* four, from Latin *quattuor.* See **k^wetwer-** in Appendix.]

cat·er·pil·lar (kăt′ər-pĭl′ər, kăt′ə-) *n.* **1.** The wormlike, often brightly colored, hairy or spiny larva of a butterfly or moth. **2.** Any of various insect larvae similar to those of the butterfly or moth. [Middle English *catirpel, catirpeller,* probably alteration of Old North French **catepelose* : *cate,* cat (from Latin *cattus*) + *pelose,* hairy (from Latin *pilōsus;* see PILOSE).]

WORD HISTORY: It seems that the larvae of moths and butterflies are popularly seen as resembling other, larger animals. Consider the Italian dialect word *gatta,* "cat, caterpillar"; the German dialect term *tüfelskatz,* "caterpillar" (literally "devil's cat"); the French word *chenille,* "caterpillar" (from a Vulgar Latin diminutive, **canīcula,* of *canis,* "dog"); and last but not least, our own word *caterpillar,* which appears probably to have come through

ă pat	oi boy
ā pay	ou out
âr care	ŏŏ took
ä father	ōō boot
ĕ pet	ŭ cut
ē be	ûr urge
ĭ pit	th thin
ī pie	*th* this
îr pier	hw which
ŏ pot	zh vision
ō toe	ə about, item
ô paw	♦ regionalism

Stress marks: ′ (primary); ′ (secondary), as in **dictionary** (dĭk′shə-nĕr′ē)

Northern French from the Old French term *chatepelose,* meaning literally "hairy cat." Our word *caterpillar* is first recorded in English in 1440 in the form *catyrpel. Catyr,* the first part of *catyrpel,* may indicate the existence of an English word **cater,* meaning "tomcat," otherwise attested only in *caterwaul. Cater* would be cognate with Middle High German *kater* and Dutch *kater.* The latter part of *catyrpel* seems to have become associated with the word *piller,* "plunderer." By giving the variant spelling *–ar,* Johnson's *Dictionary* set the spelling *caterpillar* with which we are familiar today.

Cat•er•pil•lar (kăt′ər-pĭl′ər, kăt′ə-). A trademark used for a tractor equipped with continuous chain treads.

cat•er•waul (kăt′ər-wôl′) *intr.v.* **-wauled, -waul•ing, -wauls. 1.** To cry or screech like a cat in heat. **2.** To make a shrill, discordant sound. **3.** To have a noisy argument. **—caterwaul** *n.* A shrill, discordant sound. [Middle English **caterwawlen* : **cater,* tomcat; akin to Low German *kater* + *wawlen, wrawlen,* to yowl (ultimately of imitative origin).]

cat•fight (kăt′fīt′) *n.* **1.** A fight between or among cats. **2.** *Informal.* A vociferous dispute: *a catfight between farmers and the government over subsidies.*

♦**cat•fish** (kăt′fĭsh′) *n., pl.* **catfish** or **-fish•es.** Any of numerous scaleless, chiefly freshwater fishes of the suborder Siluroidei, characteristically having whiskerlike barbels extending from the upper jaw. Also called ♦*bullhead,* ♦*mud cat,* ♦*mud puppy.*

cat•gut (kăt′gŭt′) *n.* A tough, thin cord made from the treated and stretched intestines of certain animals, especially sheep, and used for stringing musical instruments and tennis rackets and for surgical ligatures.

cath. *abbr.* **1.** Cathedral. **2.** Cathode.

Cath•ar (kăth′är) *n., pl.* **-a•ri** (-ə-rī′) or **-ars.** A member of a heretical Christian sect that flourished in western Europe in the 12th and 13th centuries and professed a dualistic belief emphasizing ascetic renunciation of the world. [French *Cathare,* from sing. of Medieval Latin *Catharī,* from Late Greek *Katharoi,* from pl. of Greek *katharos,* pure.] **—Cath′ar** *adj.* **—Cath′a•rism** *n.* **—Cath′a•rist** *adj. & n.*

ca•thar•sis (kə-thär′sĭs) *n., pl.* **-ses** (-sēz). **1.** *Medicine.* Purgation, especially for the digestive system. **2.** A purifying or figurative cleansing of the emotions, especially pity and fear, described by Aristotle as an effect of tragic drama on its audience. **3.** A release of emotional tension, as after an overwhelming experience, that restores or refreshes the spirit. **4.** *Psychology.* **a.** A technique used to relieve tension and anxiety by bringing repressed feelings and fears to consciousness. **b.** The therapeutic result of this process; abreaction. [New Latin, from Greek *katharsis,* from *kathairein,* to purge, from *katharos,* pure.]

ca•thar•tic (kə-thär′tĭk) *adj.* Inducing catharsis; purgative. **—cathartic** *n.* An agent for purging the bowels, especially a laxative. [Late Latin *catharticus,* from Greek *kathartikos,* from *kathairein,* to purge. See CATHARSIS.]

Ca•thay (kă-thā′). A medieval name for China popularized by Marco Polo in accounts of his travels. It usually applied only to the area north of the Yangtze River (Chang Jiang).

cat•head (kăt′hĕd′) *n. Nautical.* A beam projecting outward from the bow of a ship and used as a support to lift the anchor.

ca•thect (kə-thĕkt′, kă-) *tr.v.* **-thect•ed, -thect•ing, -thects.** To concentrate emotional energy on (an object or idea). [Back-formation from CATHEXIS.] **—ca•thec′tic** *adj.*

ca•the•dra (kə-thē′drə) *n., pl.* **-drae** (-drē). **1.** A bishop's official chair or throne. **2.** The office or see of a bishop. **3.** The official chair of an office or position, as of a professor. [Middle English, from Latin, chair, from Greek *kathedra* : *kat-, kata-,* cata- + *hedra,* seat; see **sed-** in Appendix.]

ca•the•dral (kə-thē′drəl) *n. Abbr.* **cath. 1.** The principal church of a bishop's diocese, containing the episcopal throne. **2.** A large, important church. **3.** Something that resembles a cathedral, as in grandeur or authority. **—cathedral** *adj.* **1.** Of, relating to, or containing a bishop's throne: *a cathedral church.* **2.** Relating to or issuing from a chair of office or authority; authoritative. **3.** Of, relating to, or resembling a cathedral: *tall trees whose branches met to form cathedral arches over the path.* [Short for *cathedral church,* from Middle English *cathedral,* of a diocese, from Old French, from Medieval Latin *cathedrālis,* of a bishop's see, from Latin *cathedra,* chair. See CATHEDRA.]

cathedral ceiling *n.* A high, open, usually slanting or pointed ceiling.

ca•thep•sin (kə-thĕp′sĭn) *n.* Any of various proteolytic enzymes found in animal tissue that catalyze the hydrolysis of proteins into polypeptides. [German *Kathepsin,* from Greek *kathepsein,* to digest : *kat-, kata-,* cata- + *hepsein,* to boil.]

Cath•er (kăth′ər), **Willa Sibert.** 1873–1947 American author who wrote about frontier life. Her novel *One of Ours* (1922) won a Pulitzer Prize.

Cath•e•rine I (kăth′ər-ĭn, kăth′rĭn). 1684?–1727. Empress of Russia (1725–1727) as successor to her husband, Peter the Great. She founded the Russian Academy of Sciences (1725).

Catherine II. Known as "Catherine the Great." 1729–1796. Empress of Russia (1762–1796) after her husband, Peter III (1728–1762), was deposed by a group led by her lover. She vastly increased the territory of the empire through conquest and three partitions of Poland.

Cath•e•rine de Mé•di•cis (kăth′ər-ĭn də mĕd′ĭ-chē′, kăth′rĭn, kăt-rēn′ də mā-dē-sēs′). 1519–1589. Queen of France as the wife of Henry II and regent during the minority (1560–1563) of her son Charles IX. She continued to wield power until the end of Charles's reign (1574).

Cath•e•rine of Ar•a•gon (kăth′ər-ĭn, kăth′rĭn; ăr′ə-gŏn′). 1485–1536. The first wife of Henry VIII of England. Henry's insistence on a divorce from her (1533) caused his break with Roman Catholicism and the beginning of the English Reformation.

Catherine of Bra•gan•za (brə-găn′zə). 1638–1705. Portuguese princess and queen of England as the wife of Charles II.

cath•er•ine wheel (kăth′ər-ĭn, kăth′rĭn) *n.* See **pinwheel** (sense 2). [After Saint *Catherine* of Alexandria (died A.D. 307), who was condemned to be tortured on a wheel.]

cath•e•ter (kăth′ĭ-tər) *n.* A hollow, flexible tube for insertion into a body cavity, duct, or vessel to allow the passage of fluids or distend a passageway. Its uses include the drainage of urine from the bladder through the urethra or insertion through a blood vessel into the heart for diagnostic purposes. [Late Latin, from Greek *kathetēr,* from *kathienai,* to send down : *kat-, kata-,* cata- + *hienai, hē-,* to send; see **yē-** in Appendix.]

cath•e•ter•ize (kăth′ĭ-tə-rīz′) *tr.v.* **-ized, -iz•ing, -iz•es.** To introduce a catheter into. **—cath′e•ter•i•za′tion** (-rĭ-zā′shən) *n.*

ca•thex•is (kə-thĕk′sĭs) *n., pl.* **-thex•es** (-thĕk′sēz). Concentration of emotional energy on an object or idea. [Greek *kathexis,* holding, retention, from *katekhein,* to hold fast : *kat-, kata-,* intensive pref.; see CATA– + *ekhein,* to hold; see **segh-** in Appendix.]

cath•ode (kăth′ōd′) *n. Abbr.* **cath., ka 1.** A negatively charged electrode, as of an electrolytic cell, a storage battery, or an electron tube. **2.** The positively charged terminal of a primary cell or a storage battery that is supplying current. [Greek *kathodos,* descent : *kat-, kata-,* cata- + *hodos,* way, path.] **—ca•thod′ic** (kă-thŏd′ĭk) *adj.* **—ca•thod′i•cal•ly** *adv.*

cathode ray *n.* **1.** A stream of electrons emitted by the cathode in electrical discharge tubes. **2.** One of the electrons that is emitted in a stream from a cathode-ray tube.

cath•ode-ray tube (kăth′ōd-rā′) *n. Abbr.* **CRT** A vacuum tube in which a hot cathode emits electrons that are accelerated as a beam through a relatively high voltage anode, further focused or deflected electrostatically or electromagnetically, and allowed to fall on a phosphorescent screen.

cath•o•lic (kăth′ə-lĭk, kăth′lĭk) *adj.* **1.** Of broad or liberal scope; comprehensive: *"The 100-odd pages of formulas and constants are surely the most catholic to be found"* (Scientific American). **2.** Including or concerning all humankind; universal: *"what was of catholic rather than national interest"* (J.A. Froude). **3. Catholic.** *Abbr.* **C. a.** Of or involving the Roman Catholic Church. **b.** Of or relating to the universal Christian church. **c.** Of or relating to the ancient undivided Christian church. **d.** Of or relating to those churches that have claimed to be representatives of the ancient undivided church. **—Catholic** *n. Abbr.* **C.** A member of a Catholic church, especially a Roman Catholic. [Middle English *catholik,* universally accepted, from Old French *catholique,* from Latin *catholicus,* universal, from Greek *katholikos,* from *katholou,* in general : *kat-, kata-,* down, along, according to; see CATA– + *holou,* from neuter genitive of *holos,* whole; see **sol-** in Appendix.] **—ca•thol′i•cal•ly** (kə-thŏl′ĭk-lē) *adv.*

Catholic Church *n.* The Roman Catholic Church.

Catholic Epistles *pl.n. Bible.* The five New Testament epistles (James, I and II Peter, I John, and Jude) that were addressed to the universal church rather than to particular Christian communities.

Ca•thol•i•cism (kə-thŏl′ĭ-sĭz′əm) *n.* The faith, doctrine, system, and practice of a Catholic church, especially the Roman Catholic Church.

cath•o•lic•i•ty (kăth′ə-lĭs′ĭ-tē) *n.* **1.** The condition or quality of being catholic; breadth or inclusiveness. **2.** General application or acceptance; universality. **3. Catholicity.** Roman Catholicism.

ca•thol•i•cize (kə-thŏl′ĭ-sīz′) *tr. & intr.v.* **-cized, -ciz•ing, -ciz•es. 1.** To make or become catholic. **2.** To convert or be converted to Catholicism.

ca•thol•i•con (kə-thŏl′ĭ-kŏn′) *n.* A universal remedy; a panacea. [Middle English, from Old French, from Medieval Latin, from Greek *katholikon,* generic description, from neuter of *katholikos,* universal. See CATHOLIC.]

cat•house (kăt′hous′) *n. Slang.* A house of prostitution.

Cat•i•line (kăt′l-īn′). 108?–62 B.C. Roman politician and conspirator who led an unsuccessful revolt against the Roman Republic while Cicero was a consul.

cat•i•on (kăt′ī′ən) *n.* An ion or group of ions having a positive charge and characteristically moving toward the negative electrode in electrolysis. [Greek *kation,* something going down, from neuter of *katiōn,* present participle of *katienai* : *kat-, kata-,* cata- + *ienai,* to go; see **ei-** in Appendix.] **—cat′i•on′ic** (kăt′ī-ŏn′ĭk) *adj.*

cation exchange *n.* A chemical process in which cations of like charge are exchanged equally between a solid, such as zeolite, and a solution, such as water. The process is often used to soften water.

cathedral

Catherine de Médicis
Detail of a portrait by François Clouet (1505?–1572)

Catherine of Aragon
c. 1530 portrait by an unknown artist

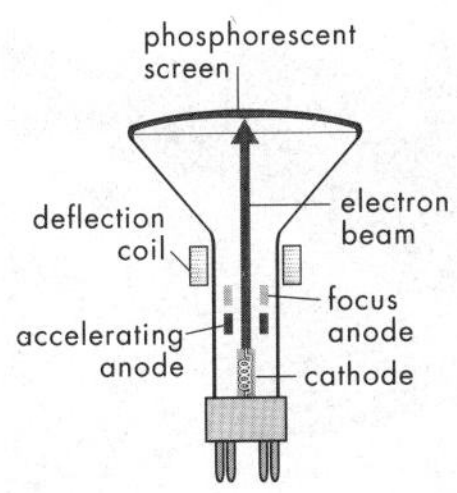

cathode-ray tube

cat·jang (kä-chăng′) *n.* **1.** See **cajan pea. 2.** See **cowpea.** [Dutch *katjang,* from Malay *kachang,* pea, bean.]

cat·kin (kăt′kĭn) *n.* A usually dense, cylindrical, often drooping cluster of unisexual, apetalous flowers found in willows, birches, and oaks. Also called *ament.* [From obsolete Dutch *katteken,* kitten, diminutive of *katte,* cat (from its resemblance to a kitten's tail), from Germanic **kattuz.*]

cat·like (kăt′līk′) *adj.* Resembling a cat, especially in being quiet or stealthy.

Cat·lin (kăt′lĭn), **George.** 1796–1872. American artist who painted portraits and tribal scenes in the American West and in South and Central America.

cat·mint (kăt′mĭnt′) *n.* **1.** Any of various aromatic, ornamental, annual or perennial plants of the genus *Nepeta,* having opposite leaves and variously colored flowers with two-lipped corollas. **2.** *Chiefly British.* Catnip.

cat·nap (kăt′năp′) *n.* A short nap; a light sleep. **—catnap** *intr.v.* **-napped, -nap·ping, -naps.** To take a short nap; doze lightly.

cat·nip (kăt′nĭp′) *n.* **1.** A hairy, aromatic perennial herb *(Nepeta cataria)* in the mint family, native to Eurasia and containing an aromatic oil to which cats are strongly attracted. **2.** Any of various other mostly aromatic plants in the genus *Nepeta,* cultivated for their ornamental foliage and clusters of blue, lavender, or white flowers. [CAT + *nip,* catnip (variant of *nep,* from Middle English *nept, nep,* from Old English *nepte,* from Latin *nepeta,* aromatic herb, perhaps of Etruscan origin).]

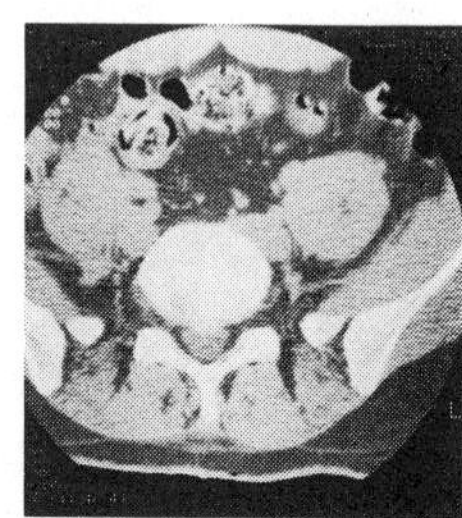

CAT scan
Cross section of the spine

Ca·to[1] (kā′tō), **Marcus Porcius.** Known as "the Elder" or "the Censor." 234–149 B.C. Roman politician and general who wrote the first history of Rome. As censor he attempted to restore simplicity to Roman life.

Ca·to[2] (kā′tō), **Marcus Porcius.** Known as "the Younger." 95–46 B.C. Roman politician and great-grandson of Cato the Elder. A conservative opponent of Julius Caesar's political ambitions, he supported Pompey against Caesar in the civil war and committed suicide after Caesar's decisive victory at Thapsus.

Ca·toc·tin Mountains (kə-tŏk′tĭn). A section of the Blue Ridge in northern Maryland extending from the Pennsylvania border south to Virginia.

cat-o'-nine-tails (kăt′ə-nīn′tālz′) *n., pl.* **cat-o'-nine-tails.** A whip consisting of nine knotted cords fastened to a handle, used in flogging. [So called because it leaves marks like the scratches of a cat.]

ca·top·tric (kə-tŏp′trĭk) also **ca·top·tri·cal** (-trĭ-kəl) *adj.* Of or relating to mirrors and reflected images. [Greek *katoptrikos,* from *katoptron,* mirror. See **ok**ʷ**-** in Appendix.] **—ca·top′trics** *n.*

cat rig *n. Nautical.* The rig of a catboat.

Cat·ron (kăt′rən), **John.** 1786?–1865. American jurist who served as an associate justice of the U.S. Supreme Court (1837–1865).

CAT scan (kăt) *n.* An image produced by a CAT scanner. Also called *CT scan.*

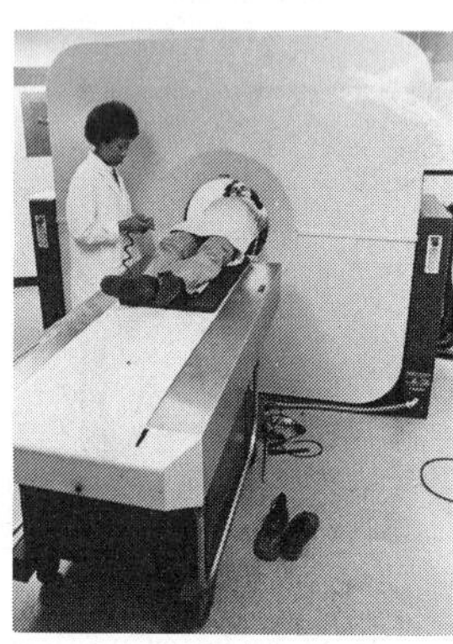

CAT scanner

CAT scanner *n.* A device that produces cross-sectional views of an internal body structure using computerized axial tomography. Also called *CT scanner.*

cat's cradle (kăts) *n.* **1.** A game in which a string is looped on the fingers to form an intricate pattern between a player's hands that can be successively varied or transferred to another player's hands. **2.** An intricate pattern: *"Their computers devised a cat's cradle of infinite complexity for the flight tracks of half a dozen space cameras around the globe's surface"* (Frederick Forsyth).

cat scratch disease *n.* A disease thought to be transmitted to humans by the scratch or bite of a cat and characterized by fever and swollen lymph nodes. Also called *cat scratch fever.*

cat's-eye (kăts′ī′) *n., pl.* **cat's-eyes. 1.** Any of various semiprecious gems such as chrysoberyl, $BeAl_2O_4$, reflecting a band of light that shifts position as the gem is turned. **2.** A glass or plastic reflector designed to glow in the beam of a headlight, used on a vehicle as a safety device or set in rows along a highway as lane markers. **3.** A marble having an eyelike design, such as concentric circles or a colored center set in clear glass.

Cats·kill Mountains (kăt′skĭl′). A range of the Appalachian Mountains in southeast New York just west of the Hudson River. The mountains, rising to 1,282.2 m (4,204 ft), include many popular resort areas.

cat's-paw also **cats·paw** (kăts′pô′) *n., pl.* **cat's-paws** also **cats·paws. 1.** A person used by another as a dupe or tool. **2.** A light breeze that ruffles small areas of a water surface. **3.** *Nautical.* A knot made by twisting a section of rope to form two adjacent eyes through which a hook is passed, used in hoisting. [From a fable about a monkey that used a cat's paw to pull chestnuts out of a fire.]

cat·sup (kăt′səp, kăch′əp, kĕch′-) *n.* Variant of **ketchup.**

cattle guard

Catt (kăt), **Carrie (Lane) Chapman.** 1859–1947. American suffragist who was an organizer and president (1900–1904 and 1915–1947) of the National American Woman Suffrage Association. She organized the League of Women Voters in 1919, the year before the 19th Amendment to the U.S. Constitution was ratified.

cat·tail (kăt′tāl′) *n.* Any of various perennial herbs of the genus *Typha,* widespread in marshy places and having long, straplike leaves and a dense, cylindrical cluster of minute flowers and fruits. Also called *reed mace.*

cat·ta·lo also **cat·a·lo** (kăt′l-ō′) *n., pl.* **-loes** or **-los.** See **beefalo.** [CATT(LE) + (BUFF)ALO.]

cat·tie (kăt′ē) *n.* Variant of **catty**[2].

cat·tle (kăt′l) *pl.n.* **1.** Any of various mammals of the genus *Bos,* including cows, steers, bulls, and oxen, often raised for meat and dairy products. **2.** Human beings, especially when viewed contemptuously or as a mob. [Middle English *catel,* property, livestock, from Old North French, from Old Provençal *capdal,* from Medieval Latin *capitāle,* holdings, funds, from neuter of Latin *capitālis,* principal, original, from *caput,* head. See **kaput-** in Appendix.]

cattle call *n. Informal.* An audition in which a large number of often inexperienced actors or performers try out.

cattle egret *n.* A small egret *(Bubulus ibis)* native to Africa and southern Eurasia that feeds among grazing cattle.

cattle grub *n.* The larva of a warble fly, especially of the genus *Hypoderma,* that parasitizes cattle and causes a boillike swelling under the hide.

cattle guard *n.* A grid, usually of parallel metal bars, set at ground level in a road or gateway as a barrier to cattle while allowing the passage of vehicles and pedestrians.

cat·tle·man (kăt′l-mən, -măn′) *n.* A man who raises or tends cattle.

cattle prod *n.* A usually electrified prod designed for driving cattle.

cattle tick *n.* A brown tick *(Boophilus annulatus)* whose bite transmits the causative agent of Texas fever in cattle.

cat·tle·ya (kăt′lē-ə) *n.* Any of various tropical American, mostly epiphytic orchids of the genus *Cattleya,* much hybridized and extensively cultivated for their showy, variously colored flowers. [New Latin *Cattleya,* genus name, after William *Cattley* (died 1832), British patron of botany.]

Cat·ton (kăt′n), **(Charles) Bruce.** 1899–1978. American historian and editor who wrote extensively on the Civil War and edited (1954–1959) *American Heritage* magazine.

cat·ty[1] (kăt′ē) *adj.* **-ti·er, -ti·est. 1.** Subtly cruel or malicious; spiteful: *a catty remark.* **2.** Catlike; stealthy. **—cat′ti·ly** *adv.* **—cat′ti·ness** *n.*

cat·ty[2] also **cat·tie** (kăt′ē) *n., pl.* **-ties.** Any of various units of weight used in Southeast Asia, especially a Chinese measure equal to 500 grams (approximately 1.1 pounds). [Malay *kati.*]

cat·ty-cor·nered (kăt′ē-kôr′nərd) or **cat·ty-cor·ner** (-nər) *adj. & adv.* Variants of **cater-cornered.**

Ca·tul·lus (kə-tŭl′əs), **Gaius Valerius.** 84?–54? B.C. Roman lyric poet known for his love poems to "Lesbia," an aristocratic Roman woman whose real name was Clodia.

CATV *abbr.* Community antenna television.

cat·walk (kăt′wôk′) *n.* A narrow, often elevated walkway, as on the sides of a bridge or in the flies above a theater stage.

Cau·ca (kou′kə). A river rising in the Cordillera Central of western Colombia and flowing about 965 km (600 mi) northward to the Magdalena River.

Cau·ca·sia (kô-kā′zhə, -shə). See **Caucasus.**

Cau·ca·sian (kô-kā′zhən, -kăzh′ən) *adj.* **1.** *Anthropology.* Of, relating to, or being a major human racial division traditionally distinguished by physical characteristics such as very light to brown skin pigmentation and straight to wavy or curly hair, and including peoples indigenous to Europe, northern Africa, western Asia, and India. No longer in scientific use. **2.** Of or relating to the Caucasus region or its peoples, languages, or cultures. **—Caucasian** *n.* **1.** *Anthropology.* A member of the Caucasian racial division. No longer in scientific use. **2.** A native or inhabitant of the Caucasus.

Cau·ca·soid (kô′kə-soid′) *Anthropology. adj.* Of or relating to the Caucasian racial division. No longer in scientific use. **—Caucasoid** *n.* A member of the Caucasian racial division. No longer in scientific use.

Cau·ca·sus (kô′kə-səs) also **Cau·ca·sia** (kô-kā′zhə, -shə). A region between the Black and Caspian seas that includes Russia, Georgia, Azerbaijan, and Armenia. The area has vast oil reserves.

Caucasus Mountains. A range extending from the north to the southeast in the Caucasus. Mount Elbrus, 5,645.6 m (18,510 ft), is the highest elevation.

cau·cus (kô′kəs) *n., pl.* **-cus·es** or **-cus·ses. 1.a.** A meeting of the local members of a political party especially to select delegates to a convention or register preferences for candidates running for office. **b.** A closed meeting of party members within a legislative body to decide on questions of policy or leadership. **c.** A group within a legislative or decision-making body seeking to represent a specific interest or influence a particular area of policy: *a minority caucus.* **2.** *Chiefly British.* A committee within a political party charged with determining policy. **—caucus** *v.* **-cused, -cus·ing, -cus·es** or **-cussed, -cus·sing, -cus·ses.** —*intr.* To assemble in or hold a caucus. —*tr.* To assemble or canvass (members of a caucus). [After the *Caucus* Club of Boston (in the 1760's), possibly from Medieval Latin *caucus,* drinking vessel.]

cau·dad (kô′dăd′) *adv. Anatomy.* Toward the tail or posterior end of the body; caudally. [Latin *cauda,* tail + -AD.]

cau·dal (kôd′l) *adj. Anatomy.* **1.a.** Of, at, or near the tail or hind parts; posterior: *the caudal fin of a fish.* **b.** Situated beneath or on the underside; inferior. **2.** *Zoology.* Taillike. [New Latin *caudālis,* from Latin *cauda,* tail.] **—cau′dal·ly** *adv.*

cau·date (kô′dāt′) also **cau·dat·ed** (-dā′tĭd) *adj.* Having a tail or taillike appendage. [Medieval Latin *caudātus,* from Latin *cauda,* tail.] **—cau·da′tion** *n.*

caudate nucleus *n.* A basal ganglion located in the lateral ventricle of the brain that has a curved, taillike extension and functions in motor control.

cau·dex (kô′dĕks′) *n., pl.* **-di·ces** (-dĭ-sēz′) or **-dex·es. 1.** The thickened, usually underground base of the stem of many perennial herbaceous plants, from which new leaves and flowering stems arise. **2.** The trunk of a palm or tree fern. [Latin *caudex,* tree trunk.]

cau·dil·lis·mo (kô′dēl-yēz′mō, -dē-yēz′-, kou′*th*ēl-, -*th*ē-) *n.* The practice or system of rule by a caudillo. [Spanish, from *caudillo,* leader. See CAUDILLO.]

cau·dil·lo (kô-dēl′yō, -dē′yō, kou-*th*ēl′-, -*th*ē′-) *n., pl.* **-los. 1.** A leader or chief, especially a military dictator. **2.** A political boss; an overlord. [Spanish, leader, from Late Latin *capitellum,* diminutive of Latin *caput,* head. See **kaput-** in Appendix.]

cau·dle (kôd′l) *n.* A warm drink consisting of wine or ale mixed with sugar, eggs, bread, and various spices, sometimes given to ill persons. [Middle English *caudel,* from Old North French, from Medieval Latin *caldellus,* from Latin *caldum,* hot drink, from *caldus, calidus,* warm, hot. See **kelə-[1]** in Appendix.]

caught (kôt) *v.* Past tense and past participle of **catch.**

caul (kôl) *n.* **1.** A portion of the amnion, especially when it covers the head of a fetus at birth. Also called *pileus.* **2.** See **greater omentum.** [Middle English *calle,* from Old English *cawl,* basket.]

caul·dron (kôl′drən) *n.* Variant of **caldron.**

cau·les·cent (kô-lĕs′ənt) *adj. Botany.* Having a well-developed aboveground stem. [Latin *caulis,* stem + –ESCENT.]

cau·li·flor·y (kô′lə-flôr′ē, -flōr′ē) *n.* The production of flowers and fruits on the older branches or trunks of woody plants, such as the redbud, and many mostly tropical plants, including cacao. [From Latin *caulis,* stem + *flōs, flōr-,* flower; see FLOWER.] **—cau′li·flor′ous** *adj.*

cau·li·flow·er (kô′lĭ-flou′ər, kŏl′ĭ-) *n.* An herb *(Brassica oleracea* var. *botrytis)* in the mustard family, related to the cabbage and broccoli and having a whitish undeveloped flower with a large, edible head. [Probably alteration (influenced by FLOWER) of New Latin *cauliflora* : Latin *caulis,* stem + Latin *flōs, flōr-,* flower; see FLOWER.]

cauliflower ear *n.* An ear swollen and deformed by repeated blows.

cau·line (kô′līn′) *adj. Botany.* Of, having, or growing on a stem. Used especially of leaves arising from the upper part of a stem. [Latin *caulis,* stem + –INE[1].]

caulk also **calk** (kôk) *—v.* **caulked, caulk·ing, caulks** also **calked, calk·ing, calks.** *—tr.* **1.** To make watertight or airtight by filling or sealing: *caulk a pipe joint; caulked the cracks between the boards with mud.* **2.** *Nautical.* To make (a boat) watertight by packing seams with a waterproof material, such as oakum or pitch. *—intr.* To apply caulking: *caulked all around the window frame.* *—n.* Caulking. [Middle English *cauken,* to press, from Old North French *cauquer,* from Latin *calcāre,* to tread, from *calx,* heel.] **—caulk′er** *n.*

caulk·ing (kô′kĭng) *n.* A usually impermeable substance used for caulking. Also called *caulking compound.*

caus. *abbr.* Causative.

caus·al (kô′zəl) *adj.* **1.** Of, involving, or constituting a cause: *a causal relationship between scarcity of goods and higher prices.* **2.** Indicative of or expressing a cause. **—causal** *n.* A word or grammatical element, such as *since* or *because,* expressing a cause or reason. **—caus′al·ly** *adv.*

cau·sal·i·ty (kô-zăl′ĭ-tē) *n., pl.* **-ties. 1.** The principle of or relationship between cause and effect. **2.** A causal agency, force, or quality.

cau·sa·tion (kô-zā′shən) *n.* **1.** The act or process of causing. **2.** A cause. **3.** Causality.

caus·a·tive (kô′zə-tĭv) *adj.* **1.** Functioning as an agent or cause. **2.** *Abbr.* **caus.** Expressing causation. Used of a verb or verbal affix. **—caus′a·tive** *n.* **—caus′a·tive·ly** *adv.*

cause (kôz) *n.* **1.a.** The producer of an effect, result, or consequence. **b.** The one, such as a person, an event, or a condition, that is responsible for an action or a result. **2.** A basis for an action or a response; a reason: *The doctor's report gave no cause for alarm.* **3.** A goal or principle served with dedication and zeal: *"the cause of freedom versus tyranny"* (Hannah Arendt). **4.** The interests of a person or group engaged in a struggle: *"The cause of America is in great measure the cause of all mankind"* (Thomas Paine). **5.** *Law.* **a.** A ground for legal action. **b.** A lawsuit. **6.** A subject under debate or discussion. **—cause** *tr.v.* **caused, caus·ing, caus·es. 1.** To be the cause of or reason for; result in. **2.** To bring about or compel by authority or force: *The moderator invoked a rule causing the debate to be ended.* [Middle English, from Old French, from Latin *causa,* reason, purpose.] **—caus′a·ble** *adj.* **—cause′less** *adj.* **—caus′er** *n.*

SYNONYMS: *cause, reason, occasion, antecedent.* These nouns denote what brings about or is associated with an effect or result. A *cause* is an agent or condition that permits the occurrence of an effect or necessarily or ineluctably leads to a result: *"He is not only dull in himself, but the cause of dullness in others"* (Samuel Foote). *Reason* refers to what explains the occurrence or nature of an effect: *There was no obvious reason for the accident. Occasion* is a situation that permits or stimulates existing causes to come into play: *"Such were the causes; but the immediate occasion of his departure . . . was the favorable opportunity . . . of migrating in a pleasant way"* (Thomas De Quincey). *Antecedent* refers to what has gone before and implies a relationship—but not necessarily a causal one—with what ensues: *Some of the antecedents of World War II lie in economic conditions in Europe following World War I.*

′cause (kôz, kŭz) *conj. Informal.* Because.

cause cé·lè·bre (kōz′ sā-lĕb′rə) *n., pl.* **causes cé·lè·bres** (kōz′ sā-lĕb′rə). **1.** An issue arousing widespread controversy or heated public debate. **2.** A celebrated legal case. [French : *cause,* case + *célèbre,* celebrated.]

cau·se·rie (kōz-rē′) *n.* **1.** An informal discussion or chat, especially of an intellectual nature. **2.** A short, conversational piece of writing or criticism. [French, from *causer,* to talk, from Latin *causārī,* to plead, discuss, from *causa,* case, cause.]

cause·way (kôz′wā′) *n.* **1.** A raised roadway, as across water or marshland. **2.** A paved highway. [Middle English *caucewei* : *cauce,* raised road (from Norman French *caucie,* from Medieval Latin *calciāta (via),* paved (road), from Latin *calx, calc-,* limestone; see CALX) + *wei,* road (variant of *way;* see WAY).]

causeway
Seven Mile Bridge crossing Pigeon Key in the Florida Keys

caus·tic (kô′stĭk) *adj.* **1.** Capable of burning, corroding, dissolving, or eating away by chemical action. **2.** Corrosive and bitingly trenchant; cutting. See Synonyms at **sarcastic. 3.** Causing a burning or stinging sensation, as from intense emotion: *"Most of all, there is caustic shame for my own stupidity"* (Scott Turow). **4.** Of or relating to light emitted from a point source and reflected or refracted from a curved surface. **—caustic** *n.* **1.** A caustic substance. **2.** A hydroxide of a light metal. **3.** A caustic curve or surface. [Middle English *caustik,* from Latin *causticus,* from Greek *kaustikos,* from *kaustos,* from *kaiein, kau-,* to burn.] **—caus′ti·cal·ly** *adv.* **—caus·tic′i·ty** (kô-stĭs′ĭ-tē) *n.*

caustic potash *n.* See **potassium hydroxide.**

caustic soda *n.* See **sodium hydroxide.**

cau·ter·ize (kô′tə-rīz′) *tr.v.* **-ized, -iz·ing, -iz·es. 1.** To burn or sear with a cautery. **2.** To deaden, as to feelings or moral scruples; callous. [Middle English *cauterizen,* from Late Latin *cautērizāre,* to cauterize, brand, from Latin *cautērium,* cautery. See CAUTERY.] **—cau′ter·i·za′tion** (-tər-ĭ-zā′shən) *n.*

cau·ter·y (kô′tə-rē) *n., pl.* **-ies. 1.** An agent or instrument used to destroy abnormal tissue by burning, searing, or scarring, including caustic substances, electric currents, lasers, and very hot or very cold instruments. **2.** The act or process of cauterizing. [Middle English *cauterie,* from Latin *cautērium,* branding iron, cautery, from Greek *kautērion,* from *kaiein, kau-,* to burn.]

cau·tion (kô′shən) *n.* **1.a.** Careful forethought to avoid danger or harm. **b.** Close attention or vigilance to minimize risk: *The car proceeded over the rickety bridge with caution.* **2.** Prudence or restraint in action or decision: *advised caution in choosing a school.* **3.** A warning or admonishment, especially to take heed: *I received a caution from the doctor about fat in my diet.* **4.** A cautious action; a precaution: *The climbers took the necessary cautions in preparing for the ascent.* **5.** *Informal.* One that is striking or alarming. **—caution** *tr.v.* **-tioned, -tion·ing, -tions.** To advise to take heed; warn or admonish. See Synonyms at **warn.** [Middle English *caucioun,* from Old French *caution,* from Latin *cautiō, cautiōn-,* from *cautus,* past participle of *cavēre,* to take care.]

cau·tion·ar·y (kô′shə-nĕr′ē) *adj.* Giving or serving as a warning; admonitory: *a cautionary tale; cautionary advice.*

cau·tious (kô′shəs) *adj.* **1.** Showing or practicing caution; careful. **2.** Tentative or restrained; guarded: *felt a cautious optimism that the offer would be accepted.* **—cau′tious·ly** *adv.* **—cau′tious·ness** *n.*

cav. *abbr.* **1.** Cavalier. **2.** Cavalry. **3.** Cavity.

cav·al·cade (kăv′əl-kād′, kăv′əl-kād′) *n.* **1.** A procession of riders or horse-drawn carriages. **2.** A ceremonial procession or display. **3.** A succession or series: *starred in a cavalcade of Broadway hits.* [French, from Old French, from Old Italian *cavalcata,* from *cavalcare,* to ride on horseback, from Medieval Latin *caballicāre,* from Latin *caballus,* horse.]

cav·a·lier (kăv′ə-lîr′) *n.* **1.** *Abbr.* **cav.** A gallant or chivalrous man, especially one serving as escort to a woman of high social position; a gentleman. **2.** *Abbr.* **cav.** A mounted soldier; a knight. **3. Cavalier.** A supporter of Charles I of England in his struggles against Parliament. Also called *Royalist.* **—cavalier** *adj.* **1.** Showing arrogant or offhand disregard; dismissive: *a cavalier attitude toward the suffering of others.* **2.** Carefree and nonchalant; jaunty. **3. Cavalier.** Of or relating to a group of 17th-century English poets associated with the court of Charles I. [French, horseman, from Old Italian *cavaliere,* from Medieval Latin *caballārius,* from Latin *caballus,* horse.] **—cav′a·lier′ly** *adv.*

ca·val·la (kə-văl′ə) *n., pl.* **-las** or **cavalla. 1.** Any of various tropical marine food fishes of the family Carangidae, which includes the jacks and pompanos. **2.** See **king mackerel.** [Spanish *caballa,* horse mackerel, from Late Latin, from Latin *caballus,* horse.]

cav·al·ry (kăv′əl-rē) *n., pl.* **-ries.** *Abbr.* **cav. 1.** A highly mobile army unit using vehicular transport, such as light armor

ă **pat**	oi **boy**
ā **pay**	ou **out**
âr **care**	o͝o **took**
ä **father**	o͞o **boot**
ĕ **pet**	ŭ **cut**
ē **be**	ûr **urge**
ĭ **pit**	th **thin**
ī **pie**	*th* **this**
îr **pier**	hw **which**
ŏ **pot**	zh **vision**
ō **toe**	ə **a**bout, **i**tem
ô **paw**	♦ regionalism

Stress marks: ′ (primary); ′ (secondary), as in **dictionary** (dĭk′shə-nĕr′ē)

and helicopters. **2.** Troops trained to fight on horseback. [French *cavalerie,* from Italian *cavalleria,* from *cavaliere,* cavalier. See CAVALIER.] **—cav′al·ry·man** *n.*

cav·a·tel·li (kăv′ə-tĕl′ē) *n.* Small shell-shaped or bullet-shaped pasta. [Italian, from pl. diminutive of *cavato,* past participle of *cavare,* to hollow out, from Latin *cavāre.* See EXCAVATE.]

cave (kāv) *n.* A hollow or natural passage under or into the earth with an opening to the surface. **—cave** *v.* **caved, cav·ing, caves.** *—tr.* **1.** To dig or hollow out. **2.** To cause to collapse or yield. **3.** To crumple or smash: *The top of the car was caved in by the impact.* *—intr.* **1.** To fall in; collapse: *The walls caved in during the earthquake.* **2.** To give up all opposition; yield: *The school committee finally caved in to the demands of parents and teachers.* **3.** To explore caves. [Middle English, from Old French, from Latin *cava,* from neuter pl. of *cavus,* hollow. See **keuə-** in Appendix.] **—cav′er** *n.*

ca·ve·at (kā′vē-ăt′, kăv′ē-, kä′vē-ät′) *n.* **1.a.** A warning or caution: *"A final caveat: Most experts feel that clients get unsatisfactory results when they don't specify clearly what they want"* (Savvy). **b.** A qualification or explanation. **2.** *Law.* A formal notice filed by an interested party with a court or officer, requesting the postponement of a proceeding until the filer is heard. **—caveat** *v.* **-at·ed, -at·ing, -ats** or **-at·ted, -at·ting, -ats.** *—intr. Law.* To enter a caveat. *—tr. Informal.* To qualify with a warning or clarification: *The spokesperson caveated the statement with a reminder that certain facts were still unknown.* [From Latin, let him beware, imperative of *cavēre,* to beware.]

caveat emp·tor (ĕmp′tôr′) *n.* The axiom or principle in commerce that the buyer alone is responsible for assessing the quality of a purchase before buying. [From Latin, let the buyer beware : *caveat,* imperative of *cavēre,* to beware + *emptor,* buyer.]

cave dweller *n.* One that dwells in a cave, especially a prehistoric human. **—cave′-dwell′ing** (kāv′dwĕl′ĭng) *adj.*

cave·fish (kāv′fĭsh′) *n., pl.* **cavefish** or **-fish·es.** Any of various freshwater fishes of the family Amblyopsidae, found in subterranean waters and having rudimentary, nonfunctioning eyes.

cave-in (kāv′ĭn′) *n.* **1.a.** A collapse, as of a tunnel or structure. **b.** A place where a cave-in has occurred. **2.** An act or instance of ceasing opposition or resistance: *The vote was seen as a cave-in to the demands of the administration.*

Cav·ell (kăv′əl, kə-vĕl′), **Edith Louisa.** 1865–1915. British nurse who remained in Brussels after the German occupation (1915) to help smuggle Allied troops to the Dutch border. She was caught by the Germans and executed.

cave·man also **cave man** (kāv′măn′) *n.* **1.** A prehistoric or primitive human living in caves. **2.** *Informal.* A man who is crude or brutal, especially toward women. **—cave′man′, cave′-man′** *adj.*

Cav·en·dish (kăv′ən-dĭsh), **Henry.** 1731–1810. British chemist and physicist who established that water is a compound of hydrogen and oxygen.

cav·ern (kăv′ərn) *n.* **1.** A large cave. **2.** A large underground chamber, as in a cave. **—cavern** *tr.v.* **-erned, -ern·ing, -erns. 1.** To enclose in or as if in a cavern. **2.** To hollow out. [Middle English *caverne,* from Old French, from Latin *caverna,* from *cavus,* hollow. See **keuə-** in Appendix.]

cav·er·nic·o·lous (kăv′ər-nĭk′ə-ləs) *adj.* Inhabiting caverns or caves: *cavernicolous animals.*

cav·ern·ous (kăv′ər-nəs) *adj.* **1.** Filled with caverns. **2.** Resembling a cavern, as in depth, vastness, or effect: *a cavernous yawn; cavernous echoes.* **3.** *Anatomy.* Filled with cavities or hollow areas; porous. **—cav′ern·ous·ly** *adv.*

ca·vet·to (kə-vĕt′ō) *n., pl.* **-vet·ti** (-vĕt′ē) or **-vet·tos.** A concave molding with a cross section that approximates a quarter circle. [Italian, diminutive of *cavo,* hollow, from Latin *cavus.* See **keuə-** in Appendix.]

cav·i·ar also **cav·i·are** (kăv′ē-är′, kä′vē-) *n.* The roe of a large fish, especially sturgeon, that is salted, seasoned, and eaten as a delicacy or relish. [Alteration of *caviarie* (probably from obsolete Italian *caviari,* pl. of *caviaro*) or from French *caviare,* both from Turkish *havyar,* from Persian *khāvyār*; akin to *khāyah,* egg, from Middle Persian *khāyak.* See **awi-** in Appendix.]

WORD HISTORY: Although caviar might seem to be something quintessentially Russian, the word *caviar* is not a native one, the Russian term being *ikra. Caviar* first came into English in the 16th century, probably by way of French and Italian, which, along with other European languages, borrowed it from Turkish *havyar.* The source of the Turkish word is apparently an Iranian dialectal form related to the Persian word for "egg," *khāyah,* and this in turn goes back to the same Indo-European root that gives us the English words *egg* and *oval.* This rather exotic etymology is appropriate to a substance that is not to everyone's taste, giving rise to Shakespeare's famous phrase, "'twas caviary to the general," the general public, that is.

cav·il (kăv′əl) *v.* **-iled, -il·ing, -ils** also **-illed, -il·ling, -ils.** *—intr.* To find fault unnecessarily; raise trivial objections. See Synonyms at **quibble.** *—tr.* To quibble about; detect petty flaws in. **—cavil** *n.* A carping or trivial objection. [French *caviller,* from Old French, from Latin *cavillārī,* to jeer, from *cavilla,* a jeering.] **—cav′il·er** *n.*

cav·i·ta·tion (kăv′ĭ-tā′shən) *n.* **1.** The sudden formation and collapse of low-pressure bubbles in liquids by means of mechanical forces, such as those resulting from rotation of a marine propeller. **2.** The pitting of a solid surface. **3.** *Medicine.* The formation of cavities in a body tissue or an organ, especially those formed in the lung as a result of tuberculosis. [From CAVITY.] **—cav′i·tate′** *v.*

Ca·vi·te (kə-vē′tē, kä-vē′tĕ). A city of southwest Luzon, Philippines, on Manila Bay southwest of Manila. It has been an important naval base since Spanish times. Population, 87,666.

cav·i·ty (kăv′ĭ-tē) *n., pl.* **-ties.** *Abbr.* **cav. 1.** A hollow; a hole. **2.** A hollow area within the body: *a sinus cavity.* **3.** A pitted area in a tooth caused by caries. See Synonyms at **hole.** [French *cavité,* from Late Latin *cavitās,* from Latin *cavus,* hollow. See **keuə-** in Appendix.]

ca·vort (kə-vôrt′) *intr.v.* **-vort·ed, -vort·ing, -vorts. 1.** To bound or prance about in a sprightly manner; caper. **2.** To have lively or boisterous fun; romp: *The children cavorted in the water, splashing and ducking each other.* [Possibly alteration of CURVET.]

Ca·vour (kə-vo͝or′, kä-vo͝or′), Conte **Camillo Benso di.** 1810–1861. Italian political leader who was premier of Sardinia (1852–1859 and 1860–1861) and assisted in the unification of Italy under Victor Emmanuel II, the king of Sardinia.

ca·vy (kā′vē) *n., pl.* **-vies. 1.** Any of various tailless South American rodents of the family Caviidae, which includes the guinea pig. **2.** Any of various similar or related rodents, such as the capybara, coypu, and agouti. [From New Latin *Cavia,* genus name, perhaps from Galibi *cabiai.*]

caw (kô) *n.* The hoarse, raucous sound characteristic of a crow or similar bird. **—caw** *intr.v.* **cawed, caw·ing, caws.** To utter such a hoarse, raucous sound. [Imitative.]

Cawn·pore (kôn′pôr′, -pōr′). See **Kanpur.**

Ca·xi·as (kə-shē′əs), Duke of. Title of Luiz Alves de Lima y Silva. 1803–1880. Brazilian general and statesman who commanded the Brazilian army that drove the Argentine dictator Juan Manuel de Rosas from Buenos Aires (1851).

Caxias do Sul (də so͞ol′). A city of southern Brazil north of Pôrto Alegre. It is an industrial center in a wine-producing region. Population, 198,683.

Cax·ton (kăk′stən), **William.** 1422?–1491. English printer who published the first book in English, *Recuyell of the Historyes of Troye* (c. 1475).

cay (kē, kā) *n.* A small, low island composed largely of coral or sand. [Alteration (influenced by QUAY) of Spanish *cayo,* probably from Taino.]

Cay·enne (kī-ĕn′, kā-). The capital of French Guiana, on **Cayenne Island** at the mouth of the **Cayenne River.** Founded by the French in 1643, it was the center of a penal colony from the 1850's until the 1940's. Population, 38,093.

cay·enne pepper (kī-ĕn′, kā-) *n.* An orange-red to dark red condiment consisting of the ground ripe fruits of any of several pungent varieties of capsicum. Also called *red pepper.* [Alteration (by folk etymology from CAYENNE) of *kian, chian,* from Tupi *quiinia,* hot pepper.]

cay·man (kā′mən) *n.* Variant of **caiman.**

Cay·man Islands (kā-măn′, kā′mən). A British-administered island group in the Caribbean Sea northwest of Jamaica, including **Grand Cayman, Little Cayman,** and **Cayman Brac.** The islands were discovered by Columbus in 1503. Georgetown, on Grand Cayman, is the capital. Population, 16,677.

Ca·yu·ga (kā-yo͞o′gə, kī-) *n., pl.* **Cayuga** or **-gas. 1.a.** A Native American people formerly inhabiting the shores of Cayuga Lake in west-central New York, with present-day populations in Ontario, western New York, Wisconsin, and Oklahoma. The Cayuga are one of the five original tribes of the Iroquois confederacy. **b.** A member of this people. **2.** The Iroquoian language spoken by the Cayuga.

Cayuga Lake. A lake of west-central New York. The longest of the Finger Lakes, it is a popular resort area.

♦ **cay·use** (kī-yo͞os′, kī′yo͞os′) *n. Pacific Northwest.* A horse, especially an Indian pony. [Short for *cayuse pony,* from CAYUSE.]

♦ ***REGIONAL NOTE:*** The noun *cayuse* comes from the name of the Cayuse people in the Pacific Northwest. *Cayuse* is used chiefly in the territory of the word's origin—the states of Washington, Oregon, and Idaho—although its use has also spread into other Western states. A verb meaning "to buck," derived from the noun, is cited by Ramon F. Adams in *Old-Time Cowhand* (1961): "What cowboys in other sections called *buckin',* the Texan called *pitchin',* and a term used in South Texas, though seldom heard in other sections, was *cayusein'* ".

Cay·use (kī-yo͞os′, kī′yo͞os′) *n., pl.* **Cayuse** or **-us·es. 1.a.** A Native American people inhabiting northeast Oregon and southeast Washington. **b.** A member of this people. **2.a.** The extinct traditional language of the Cayuse, not closely related to any other. **b.** The dialect of Nez Perce spoken by the Cayuse in the 19th and 20th centuries.

Cb The symbol for the element **columbium.**

CB (sē-bē′) *abbr.* Citizens band.

CBC *abbr.* **1.** Canadian Broadcasting Corporation. **2.** Complete blood count.

C.B.D. *abbr.* Cash before delivery.

ă pat	oi boy
ā pay	ou out
âr care	o͝o took
ä father	o͞o boot
ĕ pet	ŭ cut
ē be	ûr urge
ĭ pit	th thin
ī pie	*th* this
îr pier	hw which
ŏ pot	zh vision
ō toe	ə about, item
ô paw	♦ regionalism

Stress marks: ′ (primary); ′ (secondary), as in **dictionary** (dĭk′shə-nĕr′ē)

CB·er (sē-bē′ər) *n.* One that uses a CB radio.
CBI *abbr.* Cumulative book index.
CBW *abbr.* Chemical and biological warfare.
cc *abbr.* **1.** Carbon copy. **2.** Cubic centimeter.
cc. *abbr.* Chapters.
C.C.A. *abbr.* *Law.* Circuit Court of Appeals.
CCC *abbr.* **1.** Civilian Conservation Corps. **2.** Commodity Credit Corporation.
CCD *abbr.* Confraternity of Christian Doctrine.
CCF or **C.C.F.** *abbr.* Cooperative Commonwealth Federation of Canada.
CCK *abbr.* Cholecystokinin.
cckw. *abbr.* Counterclockwise.
C clef *n.* *Music.* A symbol indicating which line of a staff represents the pitch of middle C. On the bottom line it becomes the soprano clef, on the middle line the alto clef, and on the third line above the bottom the tenor clef.
CCS *abbr.* Combined chiefs of staff.
CCTV *abbr.* Closed-circuit television.
CCU *abbr.* Coronary care unit.
ccw. *abbr.* Counterclockwise.
cd *abbr.* Candela.
Cd The symbol for the element **cadmium.**
CD *abbr.* **1.** Also **C/D.** Certificate of deposit. **2.** Also **C.D.** Civil defense. **3.** Compact disk. **4.** *French.* Corps diplomatique (diplomatic corps).
cd. *abbr.* Cord.
c.d. *abbr.* Cash discount.
CDC *abbr.* Centers for Disease Control.
Cdr. or **CDR** *abbr.* Commander.
CD/ROM (sē′dē′rŏm′) *n.* *Computer Science.* A compact disk that functions as a read-only memory.
CDT or **C.D.T.** *abbr.* Central Daylight Time.
Ce The symbol for the element **cerium.**
C.E. *abbr.* **1.** Chemical engineer. **2.** Civil engineer. **3.** Common Era.
ce·a·no·thus (sē′ə-nō′thəs) *n.* Any of various shrubs or small trees of the genus *Ceanothus,* native mostly to western North America and often cultivated for their ornamental foliage and showy clusters of usually blue or whitish flowers. Also called *redroot.* [New Latin, genus name, from Greek *keanōthos,* cornthistle.]
cease (sēs) *v.* **ceased, ceas·ing, ceas·es.** —*tr.* To put an end to; discontinue: *The factory ceased production.* See Synonyms at **stop.** —*intr.* **1.** To come to an end; stop: *a process that never ceases.* **2.** To stop performing an activity or action; desist: *"fold our wings,/And cease from wanderings"* (Tennyson). —**cease** *n.* Cessation; pause: *We worked without cease to get the project finished on time.* [Middle English *cesen,* from Old French *cesser,* from Latin *cessāre,* to stop, frequentative of *cēdere,* to yield. See **ked-** in Appendix.]
cease-fire or **cease·fire** (sēs′fīr′) *n.* **1.** An order to stop firing. **2.** Suspension of active hostilities; a truce.
cease·less (sēs′lĭs) *adj.* Without stop or pause; constant. See Synonyms at **continual.** —**cease′less·ly** *adv.* —**cease′less·ness** *n.*
Ceau·ses·cu (chou-shĕs′ko͞o), **Nicolae.** 1918–1989. Romanian politician who was the absolute ruler after 1965. His regime was overthrown in December 1989, and Ceausescu was executed for crimes against the state.
Ce·bu (sĕ-bo͞o′). An island of the central Philippines in the Visayan Islands between Leyte and Negros. Magellan landed on the island in 1521. The city of **Cebu** is an important harbor on the eastern coast. Its population is 490,281.
ce·ca (sē′kə) *n.* Plural of **cecum.**
Cec·il (sĕs′əl), **(Edgar Algernon) Robert.** First Viscount Cecil of Chelwood. 1864–1958. British public official who helped draft the League of Nations Covenant and was president of the League of Nations Union (1923–1945). He won the 1937 Nobel Peace Prize.
Cecil, Robert. First Viscount Cranborne and First Earl of Salisbury. 1563?–1612. English statesman who helped secure the throne for James I after the death of Elizabeth I (1603).
Cecil, Robert Arthur Talbot Gascoyne. Third Marquis of Salisbury. 1830–1903. British politician who was foreign minister under Disraeli and prime minister (1885–1892 and 1895–1902).
Cecil, William. First Baron Burghley *or* Burleigh. 1520–1598. English statesman and chief adviser to Elizabeth I. He persuaded the queen to execute Mary Queen of Scots.
Ce·cil·ia (sĭ-sēl′yə), Saint. Third century A.D. Christian martyr traditionally regarded as the patron saint of music.
ce·cro·pi·a moth (sĭ-krō′pē-ə) *n.* A large North American silkworm moth *(Hyalophora cecropia)* having wings with red, white, and black markings. [New Latin *cecropia,* species name, from Latin, feminine of *Cecropius,* Athenian, from Greek *Kekropios,* from *Kekrops,* Cecrops, a legendary Athenian knight.]
ce·cum also **cae·cum** (sē′kəm) *n.* **-ca** (-kə). **1.** A saclike cavity with only one opening. **2.** *Anatomy.* The large blind pouch forming the beginning of the large intestine. In this sense, also called *blind gut.* [Middle English, from Latin *(intestīnum) caecum,* blind (intestine), from *caecus,* blind.] —**ce′cal** *adj.* —**ce′cal·ly** *adv.*
CED *abbr.* Committee for Economic Development.
ce·dar (sē′dər) *n.* **a.** Any of several Old World evergreen coniferous trees of the genus *Cedrus,* having stiff needles on short shoots and large, erect seed cones with broad deciduous scales. **b.** Any of several other evergreen coniferous trees or shrubs, such as the Alaska cedar, incense cedar, or red cedar. **c.** The durable, aromatic wood of any of these plants, especially that of the red cedar, often used to make chests. [Middle English *cedre,* from Old French, from Latin *cedrus,* from Greek *kedros.*]
ce·dar-ap·ple rust (sē′dər-ăp′əl) *n.* A disease caused by a rust fungus *(Gymnosporangium juniperi-virginianae)* that spends part of its life cycle on certain junipers, causing galls and twig dieback, and the remainder of its life cycle on susceptible apples or crab apples, causing lesions and early shedding of leaves or fruit.

C clef

ce·dar·bird (sē′dər-bûrd′) *n.* See **cedar waxwing.**
Ce·dar Falls (sē′dər). A city of northeast Iowa, a manufacturing suburb of Waterloo on the Cedar River. Population, 36,322.
cedar of Lebanon *n., pl.* **cedars of Lebanon.** A large, long-lived cedar *(Cedrus libani),* native to Lebanon and Turkey and having spreading horizontal branches at maturity.
Cedar Rapids. A city of east-central Iowa on the Cedar River west-northwest of Davenport. It is a major commercial, industrial, and transportation center. Population, 110,243.
Cedar River. A river rising in southeast Minnesota and flowing about 531 km (330 mi) southeastward to the Iowa River in southeast Iowa.
cedar waxwing *n.* A North American bird *(Bombycilla cedrorum)* having a crested head, a yellow-tipped tail, and predominantly brown plumage. Also called *cedarbird.* [Probably so called because it eats the berries of the red cedar.]
cede (sēd) *tr.v.* **ced·ed, ced·ing, cedes. 1.** To surrender possession of, especially by treaty. See Synonyms at **relinquish. 2.** To yield; grant: *The debater refused to cede the point to her opponent.* [French *céder,* from Old French, from Latin *cēdere.* See **ked-** in Appendix.]

cecropia moth
Hyalophora cecropia

ce·di (sā′dē) *n., pl.* **cedi** or **-dis.** See table at **currency.** [Possibly from Akan (Fante) *sedị,* small shell, cowry.]
ce·dil·la (sĭ-dĭl′ə) *n.* A mark (̧) placed beneath the letter *c,* as in the spelling of the French word *garçon,* to indicate that the letter is to be pronounced (s). [Obsolete Spanish, diminutive of *ceda,* the letter *z* (so called because a small *z* was formerly written after a *c,* and later below it, to indicate that the normal hard *c* was to be pronounced as a sibilant, like *s* or *z*), from Late Latin *zeta,* zeta. See ZETA.]
cee (sē) *n.* The letter *c.*
CEEB *abbr.* College Entry Examination Board.
cei·ba (sā′bə) *n.* The silk-cotton tree. [Spanish, probably from Arawakan.]
ceil (sēl) *tr.v.* **ceiled, ceil·ing, ceils. 1.** To provide or cover with a ceiling. **2.** *Nautical.* To provide (a ship) with interior planking or lining. [Middle English *celen,* probably from Old French **cęler,* from Latin *caelāre,* to carve, from *caelum,* chisel. See CAELUM.]
cei·lidh (kā′lē) *n.* An Irish or Scottish social gathering with traditional music, dancing, and storytelling. [Irish Gaelic *céilidhe,* from Old Irish *célide,* visit, from *céle,* companion. See **kei-**[1] in Appendix.]

ceil·ing (sē′lĭng) *n.* **1. a.** The upper interior surface of a room. **b.** Material used to cover this surface. **2.** Something resembling a ceiling: *a ceiling of leaves over the arbor.* **3.** An upper limit, especially as set by regulation: *wage and price ceilings.* **4. a.** The highest altitude under particular weather conditions from which the ground is still visible. **b.** The altitude of the lowest layer of clouds. **c.** Absolute ceiling. **5.** *Nautical.* The planking applied to the interior framework of a ship. [Middle English *celing,* from *celen,* to ceil. See CEIL.] —**ceil′inged** *adj.*

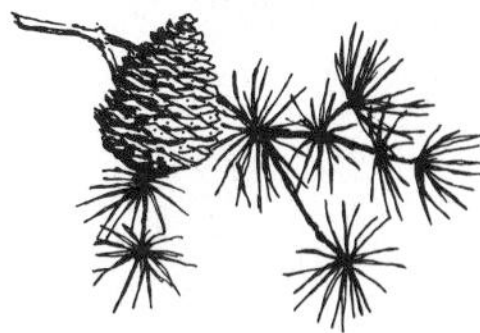
cedar of Lebanon
Cedrus libani

ceil·om·e·ter (sē-lŏm′ĭ-tər) *n.* A photoelectric instrument for ascertaining cloud heights. [CEIL(ING) + -METER.]
cel·a·don (sĕl′ə-dŏn′) *n.* **1.** *Color.* A pale to very pale green. **2.** A type of pottery having a pale green glaze, originally produced in China. [French, after *Céladon,* a character in *L'Astrée,* a romance by Honoré d'Urfé (1568–1625), French writer (after *Celadōn,* a character in Ovid's *Metamorphoses*).] —**cel′a·don′** *adj.*
cel·a·don·ite (sĕl′ə-dn-īt′) *n.* A soft mica having a green hue and a high iron content.
Ce·lae·no (sĭ-lē′nō) *n.* **1.** *Greek Mythology.* One of the Pleiades. **2.** One of the six stars in the Pleiades cluster visible to the naked eye. [Latin *Celaenō,* from Greek *Kelainō.*]
cel·an·dine (sĕl′ən-dīn′, -dēn′) *n.* **1.** A perennial Eurasian herb *(Chelidonium majus)* having deeply divided leaves, showy yellow flowers, and yellow-orange latex. Also called *swallowwort.* **2.** The lesser celandine. [Middle English *celidoine,* from Old French, from Medieval Latin *celidōnia,* from Latin *chelīdonia,* feminine of *chelīdonium,* from Greek *khelidonion,* from *khelidōn,* swallow (from the association by ancient writers of the blossoming of the plant with the return of the swallows in spring). See **ghel-**[1] in Appendix.]
celandine poppy *n.* A perennial herb *(Stylophorum diphyllum)* native to midwest North America and somewhat similar in appearance to the celandine.

cedar waxwing
Bombycilla cedrorum

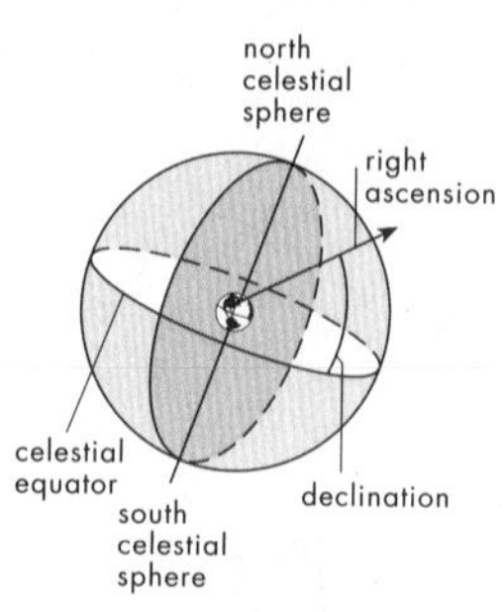

celestial sphere

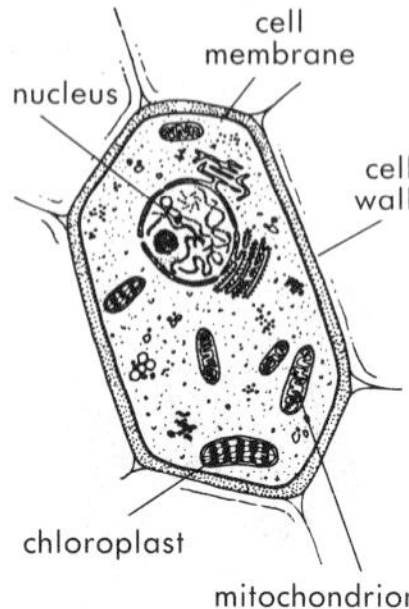

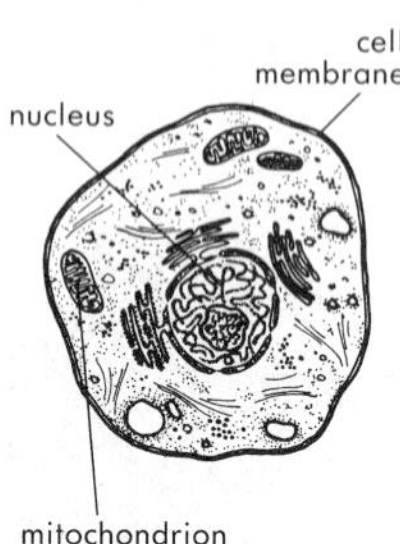

cell

cellarette
c. 1792–1796 American

–cele¹ *suff.* Tumor; hernia: *cystocele.* [From Greek *kēlē,* tumor.]

–cele² *suff.* See **–coel.**

ce·leb (sə-lĕb′) *n. Informal.* A celebrity.

Cel·e·bes (sĕl′ə-bēz′, sə-lē′bēz′, sĕ-lā′bĕs) also **Su·la·we·si** (so͞o′lä-wā′sē). An irregularly shaped island of central Indonesia on the equator east of Borneo. The Portuguese first visited Celebes in 1512 but were ousted by the Dutch in the 1600's.

Celebes Sea. A section of the western Pacific Ocean between Celebes and the southern Philippines. It is connected with the Java Sea by Makassar Strait.

cel·e·brant (sĕl′ə-brənt) *n.* **1.a.** A person who participates in a religious ceremony or rite. **b.** The priest officiating at the celebration of the Eucharist. **2.** A participant in a celebration.

USAGE NOTE: Strictly speaking, *celebrant* should be reserved for an official participant in a religious ceremony or rite. In an earlier survey, however, a majority of the Usage Panel accepted the use of *celebrant* to mean "a participant in a celebration" (as in *New Year's Eve celebrants*). In this more general sense, *celebrator* is an undisputed alternative.

cel·e·brate (sĕl′ə-brāt′) *v.* **-brat·ed, -brat·ing, -brates.** —*tr.* **1.** To observe (a day or event) with ceremonies of respect, festivity, or rejoicing. See Synonyms at **observe. 2.** To pĕrform (a religious ceremony): *celebrate Mass.* **3.** To extol or praise: *a sonnet that celebrates love.* **4.** To make widely known; display: *"a determination on the author's part to celebrate . . . the offenses of another"* (William H. Pritchard). —*intr.* **1.** To observe an occasion with appropriate ceremony or festivity. **2.** To perform a religious ceremony. **3.** To engage in festivities: *went out and celebrated after the victory.* [Middle English *celebraten,* from Latin *celebrāre, celebrāt-,* to frequent, celebrate, from *celeber, celebr-,* frequented, famous.] **—cel′e·bra′tion** *n.* **—cel′e·bra′tor** *n.* **—cel′e·bra·to′ry** (sĕl′ə-brə-tôr′ē, -tōr′ē, sə-lĕb′rə-) *adj.*

cel·e·brat·ed (sĕl′ə-brā′tĭd) *adj.* Known and praised widely; noted. See Synonyms at **noted.**

ce·leb·ri·ty (sə-lĕb′rĭ-tē) *n., pl.* **-ties. 1.** A famous person. **2.** Renown; fame. —*attributive.* Often used to modify another noun: *a celebrity fundraising dinner; celebrity exercise books.* [Middle English *celebrite,* fame, from Old French, from Latin *celebritās,* from *celeber, celebr-,* famous.] **—ce·leb′ri·ty·hood′** *n.*

SYNONYMS: *celebrity, hero, luminary, name, notable, personage.* The central meaning shared by these nouns is "a widely known person": *social celebrities; the heroes of science; a theatrical luminary; a big name in sports; a notable of the concert stage; a personage in the field of philosophy.*

ce·le·ri·ac (sə-lîr′ē-ăk′, -lĕr′-) *n.* An edible variety of celery *(Apium graveolens* var. *rapaceum)* cultivated for its swollen, knobby root. Also called *celery root, turnip-rooted celery.* [Alteration of CELERY.]

ce·ler·i·ty (sə-lĕr′ĭ-tē) *n.* Swiftness of action or motion; speed. See Synonyms at **haste.** [French *célérité,* from Old French, from Latin *celeritās,* from *celer,* swift.]

cel·er·y (sĕl′ə-rē) *n., pl.* **-ies. 1.** A biennial European plant *(Apium graveolens* var. *dulce)* in the parsley family, having edible roots, leafstalks, leaves, and fruits. **2.** The crisp, thick leafstalks of this plant. **3.** The seedlike fruits of this plant used as a flavoring. [French *céleri,* from Italian dialectal *seleri,* pl. of *selero,* alteration of Late Latin *selīnon,* parsley, from Greek *selinon.*]

celery cabbage *n.* See **Chinese cabbage.**

celery root *n.* See **celeriac.**

ce·les·ta (sə-lĕs′tə) also **ce·leste** (-lĕst′) *n. Music.* An instrument with a keyboard and metal plates struck by hammers that produce bell-like tones. [French *célesta,* from *céleste,* celestial, from Latin *caelestis.* See CELESTIAL.]

ce·les·tial (sə-lĕs′chəl) *adj.* **1.** Of or relating to the sky or the heavens: *Planets are celestial bodies.* **2.** Of or relating to heaven; divine: *celestial beings.* **3.** Supremely good; sublime: *celestial happiness.* **4. Celestial.** Of or relating to the Chinese people or to the former Chinese Empire. **—celestial** *n.* A heavenly being; a god or angel. [Middle English, from Old French, from Medieval Latin *celestiālis,* from Latin *caelestis,* from *caelum,* sky.] **—ce·les′tial·ly** *adv.*

Celestial Empire. An old name for China or the Chinese Empire.

celestial equator *n.* A great circle on the celestial sphere in the same plane as the earth's equator. Also called *equinoctial, equinoctial circle.*

celestial globe *n.* A model of the celestial sphere showing the positions of the stars and other celestial bodies.

celestial horizon *n.* A great circle on the celestial sphere having a plane that passes through the center of the earth and is parallel to an observer's horizon. Also called *rational horizon.*

celestial longitude *n.* The angular distance eastward from the vernal equinox to the great circle drawn through the pole of the ecliptic and a celestial body.

celestial mechanics *n. (used with a sing. verb).* The science of the motion of celestial bodies under the influence of gravitational forces.

celestial navigation *n.* Navigation of a ship or an aircraft based on the positions of celestial bodies. Also called *astronavigation.*

celestial pole *n.* Either of two diametrically opposite points at which the extensions of the earth's axis intersect the celestial sphere.

celestial sphere *n.* An imaginary sphere of infinite extent with the earth at its center on which the stars, planets, and other heavenly bodies appear to be located.

cel·es·tine (sĕl′ĭ-stīn′, -stīn′, sə-lĕs′tĭn, -tīn) *n.* See **celestite.** [German *Zölestin,* from Latin *caelestis,* celestial. See CELESTIAL.]

cel·es·tite (sĕl′ĭ-stīt′, sə-lĕs′tīt′) *n.* A white, red-brown, orange, or light blue principal strontium ore, essentially strontium sulfate, $SrSO_4$, found in sedimentary rock. Also called *celestine.* [CELESTINE + –ITE¹.]

ce·li·ac also **coe·li·ac** (sē′lē-ăk′) *adj.* Of or relating to the abdomen or abdominal cavity. [Latin *coeliacus,* from Greek *koiliakos,* from *koilia,* abdomen, from *koilos,* hollow. See **keuə-** in Appendix.]

celiac disease *n.* A chronic nutritional disturbance, usually of young children, caused by the inability to metabolize gluten, which results in malnutrition, a distended abdomen, muscle wasting, and the passage of stools having a high fat content. The disorder can be controlled by a special diet that emphasizes the elimination of all foods containing gluten.

cel·i·ba·cy (sĕl′ə-bə-sē) *n.* **1.** Abstinence from sexual intercourse, especially by reason of religious vows. **2.** The condition of being unmarried.

cel·i·bate (sĕl′ə-bĭt) *n.* **1.** One who abstains from sexual intercourse, especially by reason of religious vows. **2.** One who is unmarried. **—celibate** *adj.* **1.** Abstaining from sexual intercourse, especially by reason of religious vows. **2.** Unmarried; unwed. [Latin *caelibātus,* From *caelebs, caelib-,* unmarried.]

USAGE NOTE: Historically, *celibate* means only "unmarried"; its use to mean "abstaining from sexual intercourse" is a 20th-century development. But the new sense of the word appears more or less to have displaced the old, and the use of *celibate* to mean "unmarried" is now almost sure to invite misinterpretation in other than narrowly ecclesiastical contexts. Sixty-eight percent of the Usage Panel rejected the older use in the sentence *He remained celibate* [unmarried], *although he engaged in sexual intercourse.*

cell (sĕl) *n.* **1.** A narrow, confining room, as in a prison or convent. **2.** A small enclosed cavity or space, such as a compartment in a honeycomb or within a plant ovary or an area bordered by veins in an insect's wing. **3.** *Biology.* The smallest structural unit of an organism that is capable of independent functioning, consisting of one or more nuclei, cytoplasm, and various organelles, all surrounded by a semipermeable cell membrane. **4.** The smallest organizational unit of a centralized group or movement, especially of a political party of Leninist structure. **5.** *Electricity.* **a.** A single unit for electrolysis or conversion of chemical into electric energy, usually consisting of a container with electrodes and an electrolyte. Also called *electrochemical cell.* **b.** A single unit that converts radiant energy into electric energy: *a solar cell.* **6.** *Computer Science.* A basic unit of storage in a computer memory that can hold one unit of information, such as a character or word. **7.** A geographic area or zone surrounding a transmitter in a cellular telephone system. **8.** A small, humble abode, such as a hermit's cave or hut. **9.** A small religious house dependent on a larger one, such as a priory within an abbey. **—cell** *v.* **celled, cell·ing, cells.** —*tr.* **1.** To put or confine in a cell. **2.** To store in a honeycomb. —*intr.* To live in or share a cell. [Middle English *celle,* from Old English *cell* and from Old French, both from Latin *cella,* chamber. See **kel-¹** in Appendix.]

cel·la (sĕl′ə) *n., pl.* **cel·lae** (sĕl′ē). The inner room or sanctuary of an ancient Greek or Roman temple. [Latin. See **kel-¹** in Appendix.]

cel·lar (sĕl′ər) *n.* **1.** A room or enclosed space used for storage, usually beneath the ground or under a building. **2.** A basement. **3.** An underground shelter, as from storms. **4.** A wine cellar. **5.** *Slang.* The lowest level, especially in the standing of an athletic team: *The revitalized team came from the cellar to win the pennant.* **—cellar** *tr.v.* **-lared, -lar·ing, -lars.** To store in a cellar. [Middle English *celer,* from Old French, from Late Latin *cellārium,* pantry, from Latin *cella,* storeroom. See **kel-¹** in Appendix.]

cel·lar·age (sĕl′ər-ĭj) *n.* **1.** A fee charged for storage in a cellar. **2.** A cellar or several cellars.

cel·lar·er (sĕl′ər-ər) *n.* A person, as in a monastic community, who is responsible for maintaining the supply of food and drink. [Middle English *celerer,* from Old French, from Latin *cellārius,* steward, from *cella,* storeroom. See **kel-¹** in Appendix.]

cel·lar·ette also **cel·lar·et** (sĕl′ə-rĕt′) *n.* A cabinet for storing bottles of wine or liquor.

cell·block (sĕl′blŏk′) *n.* A group of cells that make up a section or unit of a prison.

cell body *n.* The portion of a nerve cell that contains the nucleus but does not incorporate the dendrites or axon. Also called *soma.*

cell cycle *n.* The series of events involving the growth, replication, and division of a eukaryotic cell.

cell division *n.* The process by which a cell divides to form two daughter cells. Upon completion of the process, each daughter cell contains the same genetic material as the original cell and roughly half of its cytoplasm.

Cel·li·ni (chə-lē′nē, chĕ-), **Benvenuto.** 1500–1571. Italian writer and sculptor who is known for his *Autobiography* and his sculpture of Perseus.

cell·mate (sĕl′māt′) *n.* A person with whom one shares a cell, especially in a prison.

cell-med·i·at·ed immune response (sĕl′mē′dē-ā′tĭd) *n.* The immune response produced when sensitized T cells directly attack foreign antigens and secrete lymphokines that initiate the body's humoral immune response. Also called *cellular immune response.*

cell membrane *n.* The semipermeable membrane that encloses the cytoplasm of a cell. Also called *cytomembrane, plasmalemma, plasma membrane.*

cel·lo[1] (chĕl′ō) *n., pl.* **-los.** *Music.* A four-stringed instrument of the violin family, pitched lower than the viola but higher than the double bass. [Short for VIOLONCELLO.] **—cel′list** (chĕl′ĭst) *n.*

cel·lo[2] (sĕl′ō) *n.* Cellophane. **—cel·lo** *adj.*

cel·lo·bi·ose (sĕl′ə-bī′ōs′, -ōz′) *n.* A disaccharide that is produced from the partial hydrolysis of cellulose. [CELL(ULOSE) + BI–[1] + –OSE[2].]

cel·loi·din (sə-loid′n) *n.* A pure form of pyroxylin in which specimens for microscopic examination are embedded. [CELL(ULOSE) + –OID + –IN.]

cel·lo·phane (sĕl′ə-fān′) *n.* A thin, flexible, transparent cellulose material made from wood pulp and used as a moistureproof wrapping. [Originally a trademark.] **—cel′lo·phane′** *adj.*

cellophane noodle *n.* A thin, transparent noodle.

cell plate *n.* A partition formed during cell division in plants and some algae that separates the two newly formed daughter cells.

cell sap *n.* The liquid contained within a vacuole of a plant cell.

cel·lu·lar (sĕl′yə-lər) *adj.* **1.** Of, relating to, or resembling a cell. **2.** Consisting of or containing a cell or cells: *the cellular construction of a beehive; the cellular nature of plant and animal tissue.* **3.** Of or involving the cells of an organization or movement: *"The assessment of opposition to any totalitarian regime . . . is notoriously difficult, for any effective movement must be secretive and cellular"* (Anthony Sampson). [From Latin *cellula.* See CELLULE.] **—cel′lu·lar′i·ty** (-lăr′ĭ-tē) *n.* **—cel′lu·lar·ly** *adv.*

cellular immune response *n.* See **cell-mediated immune response.**

cellular respiration *n.* The series of metabolic processes by which living cells produce energy through the oxidation of organic substances.

cellular slime mold *n.* See **slime mold** (sense 1).

cellular telephone *n.* A mobile radiotelephone, often in an automobile, that uses a network of short-range transmitters located in overlapping cells throughout a region, with calls automatically switched from one transmitter to the next as the caller enters an adjoining cell. A central station switches the calls and makes connections to regular telephone lines.

cel·lu·lase (sĕl′yə-lās′, -lāz′) *n.* Any of several enzymes produced chiefly by fungi, bacteria, and protozoans that catalyze the hydrolysis of cellulose. [CELLUL(OSE) + –ASE.]

cel·lule (sĕl′yo͞ol) *n.* A small cell. [French, from Latin *cellula,* diminutive of *cella,* chamber. See CELLA.]

cel·lu·lite (sĕl′yə-līt′) *n.* A fatty deposit causing a dimpled or uneven appearance, as around the thighs and buttocks. [French : *cellule,* cellule; see CELLULE + *-ite,* disease (from New Latin *-itis,* -itis).]

cel·lu·li·tis (sĕl′yə-lī′tĭs) *n.* A spreading inflammation of subcutaneous or connective tissue. [CELLUL(E) + –ITIS.]

cel·lu·loid (sĕl′yə-loid′) *n.* **1.** A colorless, flammable material made from nitrocellulose and camphor and used to make photographic film. **2. a.** Motion-picture film: *"a strange, anachronistic sight: theater pieces transferred to celluloid"* (David Ansen). **b.** The cinema; motion pictures: *"There are no heroes but in celluloid"* (Charles Langbridge Morgan). **—celluloid** *adj.* **1.** Made of or using a material made from nitrocellulose and camphor. **2.** Of or portrayed on film or in motion pictures. **3.** Artificial; synthetic: *a novel with flat, celluloid characters.* [Originally a trademark.]

cel·lu·lo·lyt·ic (sĕl′yə-lō-lĭt′ĭk) *adj.* Of, relating to, or causing the hydrolysis of cellulose: *cellulolytic organisms.* [CELLULO(SE) + –LYTIC.]

cel·lu·lose (sĕl′yə-lōs′, -lōz′) *n.* A complex carbohydrate, $(C_6H_{10}O_5)_n$, that is composed of glucose units, forms the main constituent of the cell wall in most plants, and is important in the manufacture of numerous products, such as paper, textiles, pharmaceuticals, and explosives. [French, from *cellule,* biological cell. See CELLULE.] **—cel′lu·lo′sic** (-lō′sĭk, -zĭk) *adj.*

cellulose acetate *n.* A cellulose resin used in lacquers, photographic film, transparent sheeting, and cigarette filters.

cellulose nitrate *n.* See **nitrocellulose.**

cell wall *n.* The rigid outermost cell layer found in plants and certain algae, bacteria, and fungi but characteristically absent from animal cells.

ce·lom (sē′ləm) *n.* Variant of **coelom.**

ce·lo·sia (sə-lō′zhə, -zhē-ə) *n.* See **cockscomb** (sense 3). [New Latin *Cēlosia,* genus name, from Greek *kēlos,* dry, burnt (from its color), from *kaiein,* to burn.]

Cel·o·tex (sĕl′ə-tĕks′). A trademark used for a building board that is employed as insulation or paneling.

Cel·si·us (sĕl′sē-əs, -shəs) *adj. Abbr.* **C** Of or relating to a temperature scale that registers the freezing point of water as 0° and the boiling point as 100° under normal atmospheric pressure. See table at **measurement.** [After Anders CELSIUS.]

Celsius, Anders. 1701–1744. Swedish astronomer who devised (1742) the centigrade thermometer.

celt (sĕlt) *n.* A common prehistoric tool of stone or metal, shaped like a chisel or ax head. [Late Latin **celtis,* chisel.]

Celt (kĕlt, sĕlt) also **Kelt** (kĕlt) *n.* **1.** One of an Indo-European people originally of central Europe and spreading to western Europe, the British Isles, and southeast to Galatia during pre-Roman times, especially a Briton or Gaul. **2.** A speaker of a modern Celtic language or a descendant of such a speaker, especially a modern Gael, Welshman, Cornishman, or Breton. [French *Celte,* sing. of *Celtes,* from Latin *Celtae,* from Greek *Keltoi.*]

Celt·i·ber·i·an (kĕl′tĭ-bîr′ē-ən, sĕl′-) *n.* **1.** One of an ancient Celtic people of northern Spain. **2.** The language of this people, known from place and personal names and from inscriptions. **—Celtiberian** *adj.* Of or relating to the Celtiberians or to their language or culture.

Celt·ic (kĕl′tĭk, sĕl′-) also **Kelt·ic** (kĕl′-) *—n. Abbr.* **C.** A subfamily of the Indo-European language family comprising the Brittonic and the Goidelic branches. *—adj.* Of or relating to the Celtic people and languages.

Celtic cross *n.* A Latin cross with a circle superimposed on its center.

Celt·i·cism (kĕl′tĭ-sĭz′əm, sĕl′-) *n.* **1.** A Celtic custom. **2.** A Celtic idiom. **3.** A fondness for Celtic culture.

Celt·i·cist (kĕl′tĭ-sĭst, sĕl′-) *n.* A specialist in Celtic culture or Celtic languages.

cem·ba·lo (chĕm′bə-lō′) *n., pl.* **-los.** *Music.* A harpsichord. [Italian, short for *clavicembalo,* from Medieval Latin *clāvicymbalum* : Latin *clāvis,* key + Latin *cymbalum,* cymbal; see CYMBAL.] **—cem′ba·list** (-bə-lĭst) *n.*

ce·ment (sĭ-mĕnt′) *n.* **1. a.** A building material made by grinding calcined limestone and clay to a fine powder, which can be mixed with water and poured to set as a solid mass or used as an ingredient in making mortar or concrete. **b.** Portland cement. **c.** Concrete. **2.** A substance that hardens to act as an adhesive; glue. **3.** Something that serves to bind or unite: *"Custom was in early days the cement of society"* (Walter Bagehot). **4.** *Geology.* A chemically precipitated substance that binds particles of clastic rocks. **5.** *Dentistry.* A substance used for filling cavities or anchoring crowns, inlays, or other restorations. **6.** Variant of **cementum.** **—cement** *v.* **-ment·ed, -ment·ing, -ments.** *—tr.* **1.** To bind with or as if with cement. **2.** To cover or coat with cement. *—intr.* To become cemented. ***—idiom.* in cement.** Firmly settled or determined; unalterable: *The administration's position on taxes was set in cement despite the unfavorable public response.* [Middle English, from Old French *ciment,* from Latin *caementum,* rough-cut stone, from *caedere,* to cut. See **kae-id-** in Appendix.] **—ce·ment′er** *n.*

ce·men·ta·tion (sē′mĕn-tā′shən) *n.* **1.** The act, process, or result of cementing. **2.** A metallurgical coating process in which iron or steel is immersed in a powder of another metal, such as zinc, chromium, or aluminum, and heated to a temperature below the melting point of either.

ce·ment·ite (sĭ-mĕn′tīt′) *n.* A hard, brittle iron carbide, Fe_3C, found in steel with more than 0.85 percent carbon. [From CEMENT.]

ce·men·ti·tious (sē′mĕn-tĭsh′əs) *adj.* Of or relating to a chemical precipitate, especially of carbonates, having the characteristics of cement.

cement mixer *n.* A machine, often mounted on a truck, having a revolving drum in which cement, sand, gravel, and water are combined into concrete.

ce·men·tum (sĭ-mĕn′təm) also **ce·ment** (-mĕnt′) *n.* A bonelike substance covering the root of a tooth. [New Latin, from Latin *caementum,* rough stone. See CEMENT.]

cem·e·ter·y (sĕm′ĭ-tĕr′ē) *n., pl.* **-ies.** A place for burying the dead; a graveyard. [Middle English *cimiterie,* from Old French *cimitiere,* from Medieval Latin *cimitērium,* from Late Latin *coemētērium,* from Greek *koimētērion,* from *koiman,* to put to sleep. See **kei-**[1] in Appendix.]

CEMF *abbr.* Counter-electromotive force.

cen. *abbr.* **1.** Central. **2.** Century.

cen·a·cle (sĕn′ə-kəl) *n.* **1.** A clique or circle, especially of writers. **2.** A small dining room, usually on an upper floor. [French *cénacle,* from Old French, the room where the Last Supper took place, from Latin *cēnāculum,* dining room, garret, from *cēna,* meal; see **sker-**[1] in Appendix. Sense 2, Middle English, from Old French, from Latin *cēnāculum.*]

Cen·ci (chĕn′chē), **Beatrice.** 1577–1599. Italian noblewoman who was hanged for patricide. She was the subject of a number of poems, including Shelley's *The Cenci* (1819).

–cene *suff.* Recent. Used in names of geological periods: *Oligocene.* [From Greek *kainos,* new. See **ken-** in Appendix.]

Ce·nis (sə-nē′), **Mont.** A mountain pass, 2,083.5 m (6,831 ft)

cello[1]

Celtic cross

cement mixer
Discharging cement

ă pat	oi boy
ā pay	ou out
âr care	o͝o took
ä father	o͞o boot
ĕ pet	ŭ cut
ē be	ûr urge
ĭ pit	th thin
ī pie	*th* this
îr pier	hw which
ŏ pot	zh vision
ō toe	ə about, item
ô paw	♦ regionalism

Stress marks: **′** (primary); ′ (secondary), as in **dictionary** (dĭk′shə-nĕr′ē)

high, in the Alps on the French-Italian border. It was long important as an invasion route.

ceno– *pref.* Variant of **coeno–.**

cen·o·bite also **coen·o·bite** (sĕn′ə-bīt′, sē′nə-) *n.* A member of a convent or other religious community. [Middle English, from Late Latin *coenobīta,* from *coenobium,* convent, from Greek *koinobion,* from *koinobios,* living in community : *koinos,* common; see **kom** in Appendix + *bios,* life; see **gʷei-** in Appendix.] **—cen′o·bit′ic** (-bĭt′ĭk), **cen′o·bit′i·cal** *adj.*

cenotaph
Honoring Leonardo da Vinci, Milan, Italy

ce·no·spe·cies (sē′nə-spē′shēz, -sēz, sĕn′ə-) *n.* A group of related ecospecies capable of interbreeding so as to produce at least partially fertile hybrids.

cen·o·taph (sĕn′ə-tăf′) *n.* A monument erected in honor of a dead person whose remains lie elsewhere. [French *cénotaphe,* from Old French, from Latin *cenotaphium,* from Greek *kenotaphion* : *kenos,* empty + *taphos,* tomb.] **—cen′o·taph′ic** *adj.*

Ce·no·zo·ic (sē′nə-zō′ĭk, sĕn′ə-) *adj.* Of, belonging to, or designating the latest era of geologic time, which includes the Tertiary Period and the Quaternary Period and is characterized by the formation of modern continents, glaciation, and the diversification of mammals, birds, and plants. See table at **geologic time.** **—Cenozoic** *n.* The Cenozoic Era. [Greek *kainos,* new; see **ken-** in Appendix + -ZOIC.]

cense (sĕns) *tr.v.* **censed, cens·ing, cens·es. 1.** To perfume with incense. **2.** To burn incense to. [Middle English *censen,* short for *encensen,* from *encens,* incense. See INCENSE[2].]

cen·ser (sĕn′sər) *n.* A vessel in which incense is burned, especially during religious services. [Middle English, short for *encenser,* from Anglo-Norman *encensier,* from *encens,* incense, from Old French. See INCENSE[2].]

censer

cen·sor (sĕn′sər) *n.* **1.** A person authorized to examine books, films, or other material and to remove or suppress what is considered morally, politically, or otherwise objectionable. **2.** An official, as in the armed forces, who examines personal mail and official dispatches to remove information considered secret or a risk to security. **3.** One that condemns or censures. **4.** One of two officials in ancient Rome responsible for taking the public census and supervising public behavior and morals. **5.** *Psychology.* The agent in the unconscious that is responsible for censorship. **—censor** *tr.v.* **-sored, -sor·ing, -sors.** To examine and expurgate. [Latin *cēnsor,* Roman censor, from *cēnsēre,* to assess. See **kens-** in Appendix.] **—cen′sor·a·ble** *adj.* **—cen·so′ri·al** (sĕn-sôr′ē-əl, -sōr′-) *adj.*

cen·so·ri·ous (sĕn-sôr′ē-əs, -sōr′-) *adj.* **1.** Tending to censure; highly critical. **2.** Expressing censure. See Synonyms at **critical.** [Latin *cēnsōrius,* of a censor, from *cēnsor,* Roman censor. See CENSOR.] **—cen·so′ri·ous·ly** *adv.* **—cen·so′ri·ous·ness** *n.*

cen·sor·ship (sĕn′sər-shĭp′) *n.* **1.** The act, process, or practice of censoring. **2.** The office or authority of a Roman censor. **3.** *Psychology.* Prevention of disturbing or painful thoughts or feelings from reaching consciousness except in a disguised form.

cen·sur·a·ble (sĕn′shər-ə-bəl) *adj.* Deserving of or open to censure. See Synonyms at **blameworthy.** **—cen′sur·a·ble·ness, cen′sur·a·bil′i·ty** *n.* **—cen′sur·a·bly** *adv.*

cen·sure (sĕn′shər) *n.* **1.** An expression of strong disapproval or harsh criticism. **2.** An official rebuke, as by a legislature of one of its members. **—censure** *tr.v.* **-sured, -sur·ing, -sures. 1.** To criticize severely; blame. See Synonyms at **criticize. 2.** To express official disapproval of: *"whether the Senate will censure one of its members for conflict of interest"* (Washington Post). [Middle English, from Latin *cēnsūra,* censorship, from *cēnsor,* Roman censor. See CENSOR.] **—cen′sur·er** *n.*

centaur
Black marble statue by Aristeas and Papias of Aphrodisias (first half of second century A.D.)

cen·sus (sĕn′səs) *n.* **1.** An official, usually periodic enumeration of a population, often including the collection of related demographic information. **2.** In ancient Rome, a count of the citizens and an evaluation of their property for taxation purposes. [Latin *cēnsus,* registration of citizens, from *cēnsēre,* to assess. See **kens-** in Appendix.]

cent (sĕnt) *n. Abbr.* **c., ct., C.** See table at **currency.** [Middle English, from Old French, hundred, from Latin *centum.* See **dekm̥** in Appendix.]

cent. *abbr.* **1.** Centigrade. **2.** Central. **3.** *Latin.* Centum (hundred). **4.** Century.

cen·tal (sĕn′tl) *n.* See **hundredweight** (sense 1). [From Latin *centum,* hundred. See **dekm̥** in Appendix.]

cen·taur (sĕn′tôr′) *n. Greek Mythology.* One of a race of monsters having the head, arms, and trunk of a man and the body and legs of a horse. [Middle English, from Latin *Centaurus,* from Greek *Kentauros.*]

Cen·tau·rus (sĕn-tôr′əs) *n.* A constellation in the Southern Hemisphere near Vela and Lupus. [Latin *Centaurus,* centaur. See CENTAUR.]

cen·tau·ry (sĕn′tôr′ē) *n., pl.* **-ries.** Any of several herbs of the genus *Centaurium,* especially a Eurasian species *(C. erythraea)* that has clusters of pink flowers and has long been used in herbal medicine. [Middle English, from Old English *centaurie,* from Latin *centaurēum,* from Greek *kentaureion,* from *Kentauros,* centaur (from the legend that the plant's medicinal properties were discovered by the centaur Chiron).]

cen·ta·vo (sĕn-tä′vō) *n., pl.* **-vos.** *Abbr.* **c., C.** See table at **currency.** [Spanish, hundredth, from Latin *centum,* hundred. See **dekm̥** in Appendix.]

cen·te·nar·i·an (sĕn′tə-nâr′ē-ən) *n.* One that is 100 years old or older. [From Latin *centēnārius,* of a hundred. See CENTENARY.] **—cen′te·nar′i·an** *adj.*

cen·ten·a·ry (sĕn-tĕn′ə-rē, sĕn′tə-nĕr′ē) *adj.* **1.** Of or relating to a 100-year period. **2.** Occurring once every 100 years. **—centenary** *n., pl.* **-ries. 1.** A 100-year period. **2.** A centennial. [Latin *centēnārius,* of a hundred, from *centum,* hundred. See **dekm̥** in Appendix.]

cen·ten·ni·al (sĕn-tĕn′ē-əl) *adj.* **1.** Of or relating to an age or period of 100 years. **2.** Occurring once every 100 years: *a centennial commemoration.* **3.** Of or relating to a 100th anniversary. **—centennial** *n.* A 100th anniversary or a celebration of it. [Latin *centum,* hundred; see **dekm̥** in Appendix + (BI)ENNIAL.] **—cen·ten′ni·al·ly** *adv.*

cen·ter (sĕn′tər) *n. Abbr.* **ctr. 1.** A point or place that is equally distant from the sides or outer boundaries of something; the middle: *the center of town; the center of a stage.* **2. a.** A point equidistant from the vertexes of a regular polygon. **b.** A point equidistant from all points on the circumference of a circle or on the surface of a sphere. **3.** A point around which something rotates or revolves: *The sun is the center of our solar system.* **4.** A part of an object that is surrounded by the rest; a core: *chocolates with soft centers.* **5. a.** A place where a particular activity or service is concentrated: *a medical center.* **b.** A point of origin, as of influence, ideas, or actions: *a center of power; a center of unrest.* **c.** An area of dense population: *a metropolitan center.* **6.** A person or thing that is the chief object of attention, interest, activity, or emotion. **7.** A person, object, or group occupying a middle position. **8.** Often **Center.** A political group or a set of policies representing a moderate view between those of the right and the left. **9.** *Physiology.* A group of neurons in the central nervous system that control a particular function: *the vasomotor center.* **10.** *Sports.* A player who holds a middle position on the field, court, or forward line in some team sports, such as football and basketball. **11.** *Baseball.* Center field. **12. a.** A small conical hole made in a piece of work with a center punch so that a drill can be accurately positioned within it. **b.** A bar with a conical point used to support work, as during turning on a lathe. **—center** *v.* **-tered, -ter·ing, -ters.** *—tr.* **1.** To place in or at the center: *centered the vase on the table.* **2.** To direct toward a center or central point; concentrate or focus: *tried to center the discussion on the main issues.* **3.** *Football.* To pass (the ball) back between the legs to begin a down. *—intr.* **1.** To be concentrated; cluster: *The epidemic centered in the urban areas.* **2.** To have a central theme or concern; be focused: *Her novels center on the problems of adolescence.* [Middle English *centre,* from Old French, from Latin *centrum,* from Greek *kentron,* center of a circle, from *kentein,* to prick. See **kent-** in Appendix.]

SYNONYMS: *center, focus, headquarters, heart, hub, seat.* The central meaning shared by these nouns is "a region, person, or thing around which something, such as an activity, is concentrated": *a great cultural center; the focus of research efforts; the headquarters of a multinational corporation; a town that is the heart of the colony; the hub of a steel empire; the seat of government.*

USAGE NOTE: According to traditional canons of usage, the verb *center* may be freely used with the prepositions *on, upon, in,* or *at;* but its use with *around* is excoriated as "ungrammatical," "illogical," "geometrically senseless," and "physically impossible." But the fact that writers persist in using this phrase in sentences such as *The discussion centered around the need for curriculum revision* (where traditionalists would require *revolved around*) suggests a widespread perception that *center around,* for all its apparent illogicality, may sometimes represent the true nature of experience. *Center* may denote a variety of relations involving having, finding, or turning about a center, and the choice of a preposition depends on what is intended. There is reputable precedent for usages such as *Our hope centered in the young sovereign; His thoughts centered on the long journey before him;* and *The trade is centered at Amsterdam;* as well as for usages such as *A storm of battle centered around the king,* in which example *around* seems to be the only appropriate choice. See Usage Note at **equal.**

center back *n. Sports.* The player in the back line during a volleyball or water polo game.

center bit *n.* A drill bit having a sharp center point, used in carpentry for boring holes.

cen·ter·board (sĕn′tər-bôrd′, -bōrd′) *n. Nautical.* A movable keel in a sailboat that can be pivoted upward to reduce the boat's draft in shallow water.

Cen·ter·each (sĕn′tə-rēch′). A community of southeast New York on central Long Island. It is mainly residential. Population, 34,600.

cen·tered (sĕn′tərd) *adj.* **1.** Being at or placed in the center. **2.** Having a specified center. Often used in combination: *a soft-centered candy; a yellow-centered daisy.* **3.** Self-confident and well-balanced: *"He's a centered guy. He's always seemed to know what he wanted, and gone after it in a concrete way"* (Vanity Fair).

center field *n. Abbr.* **CF** *Baseball.* **1.** The middle third of the outfield, behind second base. **2.** The position played by the center fielder.

center fielder *n. Abbr.* **CF** *Baseball.* The player who defends center field.

cen·ter·fold (sĕn′tər-fōld′) *n.* **1.** A magazine center spread, especially a foldout of an oversize photograph or feature. **2.a.** The subject of a photograph used as a centerfold, often a nude model. **b.** A feature, such as an advertisement or calender, inserted as a centerfold.

cen·ter·line (sĕn′tər-līn′) *n.* A painted line running along the center of a road or highway that divides it into two sections for traffic moving in opposite directions, or, in the case of a divided highway, for lines of traffic moving in the same direction at different speeds.

center of gravity *n., pl.* **centers of gravity.** **1.** *Abbr.* **c.g.** The point in or near a body at which the gravitational potential energy of the body is equal to that of a single particle of the same mass located at that point and through which the resultant of the gravitational forces on the component particles of the body acts. **2.** The point of greatest importance, interest, or activity: *"The center of gravity for the English language is no longer Britain. American English is the greatest influence on English everywhere"* (Robert W. Burchfield).

center of mass *n., pl.* **centers of mass.** *Abbr.* **c.m.** The point in a system of bodies at which the mass of the system may be considered to be concentrated and at which external forces may be considered to be applied. Also called *barycenter, centroid.*

cen·ter·piece (sĕn′tər-pēs′) *n.* **1.** Something in a central position, especially a decorative object or arrangement placed at the center of a table. **2.** The central or most important feature: *"Now comes decontrol, the centerpiece of* [the President's] *energy program"* (Tom Alexander).

center punch *n.* A tool with a sharp point used in metalworking to mark centers or center lines on pieces to be drilled.

center spread *n.* **1.** The two facing pages in the center of a magazine or newspaper. **2.** A feature that occupies the center of a magazine or newspaper: *a four-page center spread devoted to the championship playoffs.*

Cen·ter·ville (sĕn′tər-vĭl′). A city of southwest Ohio, a suburb of Dayton. Population, 18,886.

cen·tes·i·mal (sĕn-tĕs′ə-məl) *adj.* Relating to or divided into hundredths. [From Latin *centēsimus,* from *centum,* hundred. See **dekm̥** in Appendix.] **—cen·tes′i·mal·ly** *adv.*

cen·tes·i·mo[1] (sĕn-tĕs′ə-mō′) *n., pl.* **-mos** or **-mi** (-mē). See table at **currency.** [Italian, hundredth, from Latin *centēsimus.* See CENTESIMAL.]

cen·tes·i·mo[2] (sĕn-tĕs′ə-mō′) *n., pl.* **-mos.** See table at **currency.** [Spanish *centésimo,* hundredth, from Latin *centēsimus.* See CENTESIMAL.]

centi– *pref.* **1.** One hundredth part (10^{-2}): *centiliter.* **2.** One hundred: *centipede.* [French, from Latin *centi-,* hundred, from *centum.* See **dekm̥** in Appendix.]

cen·ti·grade (sĕn′tĭ-grād′) *adj. Abbr.* **C, cent.** Celsius. See table at **Measurement.** [French : *centi-,* centi- + *grade,* degree (from Italian *grado,* rank, degree, from Latin *gradus,* step; see **ghredh-** in Appendix).]

cen·ti·gram (sĕn′tĭ-grăm′) *n. Abbr.* **cg, cgm** A metric unit of mass equal to one hundredth (10^{-2}) of a gram.

cen·ti·li·ter (sĕn′tə-lē′tər) *n. Abbr.* **cl** A metric unit of volume equal to one hundredth (10^{-2}) of a liter.

cen·time (sän′tēm′, säɴ-tēm′) *n. Abbr.* **c., C.** See table at **currency.** [French, from Old French *centisme,* from Latin *centēsimus,* hundredth, from *centum,* hundred. See **dekm̥** in Appendix.]

cen·ti·me·ter (sĕn′tə-mē′tər) *n. Abbr.* **cm** A unit of length equal to one hundredth (10^{-2}) of a meter. See table at **measurement.**

cen·ti·me·ter-gram-sec·ond system (sĕn′tə-mē′tər-grăm′sĕk′ənd) *n. Abbr.* **cgs, CGS** An absolute metric system in which the basic units of length, mass, and time are the centimeter, gram, and second, in the United States used chiefly in science, medicine, and engineering.

cen·ti·mo (sĕn′tə-mō′) *n., pl.* **-mos.** See table at **currency.** [Spanish *céntimo,* from French *centime.* See CENTIME.]

cen·ti·pede (sĕn′tə-pēd′) *n.* Any of various wormlike arthropods of the class Chilopoda, having a flattened body composed of segments, each bearing a pair of jointed appendages. The appendages of the foremost body segment are modified into venomous biting organs with which it preys on insects, such as cockroaches. [Latin *centipeda* : *centi-,* centi- + *pēs, ped-,* foot; see –PED.]

centipede grass *n.* A low, mat-forming perennial grass *(Eremochloa ophiuroides)* native to southeast Asia and cultivated for lawns in warm regions such as the southeast United States.

cen·ti·poise (sĕn′tə-poiz′) *n. Abbr.* **cP** A centimeter-gram-second unit of dynamic viscosity equal to one hundredth (10^{-2}) of a poise.

cent·ner (sĕnt′nər) *n.* **1.a.** A unit of weight in Germany and Scandinavia corresponding to the hundredweight and equal to 50 kilograms (110.23 pounds). **b.** A unit of weight in the Soviet Union equal to 100 kilograms (220.46 pounds). **2.** An assaying unit equal to one dram. [German *Zentner,* from Old High German *cëntenāri,* from Latin *centēnārius,* of a hundred. See CENTENARY.]

cen·to (sĕn′tō) *n., pl.* **-tos.** A literary work pieced together from the works of several authors. [Latin *centō,* patchwork.]

centr– *pref.* Variant of **centro–.**

cen·tra (sĕn′trə) *n.* A plural of **centrum.**

cen·tral (sĕn′trəl) *adj. Abbr.* **cent., cen.** **1.** Situated at, in, or near the center: *the central states.* **2.** Forming the center. **3.** Having dominant or controlling power or influence: *the central office of the corporation.* **4.** Of basic importance; essential or principal: *"Performance, including technological invention and artistic creation, will become central to education at all levels"* (Frederick Turner). **5.** Easily reached from various points: *a central location for the new store.* **6.** Of or constituting a single source controlling all components of a system: *central air conditioning.* **7.** *Anatomy.* **a.** Of, relating to, or originating from the nervous system. **b.** Relating to a centrum. **8.** *Linguistics.* Neither front nor back. Used of vowels, as the *u* in *cut.* **—central** *n.* **1.a.** A telephone exchange. **b.** An operator at a telephone exchange. **2.** An office or agency that is at the center of a group of related activities and serves to control and coordinate them: *traffic central.* [Latin *centrālis,* from *centrum,* center. See CENTER.] **—cen′tral·ly** *adv.*

Cen·tral Af·ri·can Republic (sĕn′trəl ăf′rĭ-kən). Formerly (1976–1979) **Central African Empire.** A country of central Africa. Part of French Equatorial Africa after the 1890's, it became independent in 1960. Bangui is the capital and the largest city. Population, 2,395,000.

Central A·mer·i·ca (ə-mĕr′ĭ-kə). *Abbr.* **C.A.** A region of southern North America extending from the southern border of Mexico to the northern border of Colombia. It separates the Caribbean Sea from the Pacific Ocean and is linked to South America by the Isthmus of Panama. **—Central A·mer′i·can** *adj. & n.*

central angle *n. Mathematics.* An angle having its vertex at the center of a circle.

Central A·sian U.S.S.R. (ā′zhən, ā′shən). A historical region of the southern U.S.S.R. stretching from the Caspian Sea to just beyond the Irtysh River.

central bank *n.* A nation's principal monetary authority, such as the Federal Reserve Bank, which regulates the money supply and credit, issues currency, and manages the rate of exchange.

central city *n.* A heavily populated city at the core of a large metropolitan area.

Central Falls. A city of northeast Rhode Island, an industrial suburb of Providence. Population, 16,995.

Central I·slip (ī′slĭp). A community of southeast New York on central Long Island. It is mainly residential. Population, 26,000.

cen·tral·ism (sĕn′trə-lĭz′əm) *n.* Concentration of power and authority in a central organization, as in a political system. **—cen′tral·ist** *n.* **—cen′tral·is′tic** *adj.*

cen·tral·i·ty (sĕn-trăl′ĭ-tē) *n.* **1.** The state or quality of being central. **2.** A tendency to be or remain at the center.

cen·tral·ize (sĕn′trə-līz′) *v.* **-ized, -iz·ing, -iz·es.** *—tr.* **1.** To draw into or toward a center; consolidate. **2.** To bring under a single, central authority. *—intr.* To come together at a center; concentrate. **—cen′tral·i·za′tion** (-trə-lĭ-zā′shən) *n.* **—cen′tral·iz′er** *n.*

Central Kar·roo (kə-ro͞o′). See **Karroo.**

central nervous system *n. Abbr.* **CNS** The portion of the vertebrate nervous system consisting of the brain and spinal cord.

Central Park. An extensive recreational area of New York City extending north to south in central Manhattan. The land, acquired in 1856, was developed according to plans drawn up by the landscape artists Frederick Law Olmsted and Calvert Vaux.

central processing unit *n. Abbr.* **CPU** *Computer Science.* The part of a computer that interprets and executes instructions.

Central Provinces. The Canadian provinces of Ontario and Quebec.

Central Standard Time *n. Abbr.* **CST, C.S.T.** Standard time in the sixth time zone west of Greenwich, England, reckoned at 90° W and used in the central United States. Also called *Central Time.*

Central Valley. A rich agricultural valley of central California between the Sierra Nevada and the Coast Ranges.

cen·tre (sĕn′tər) *n. & v. Chiefly British.* Variant of **center.**

centri– *pref.* Variant of **centro–.**

cen·tric (sĕn′trĭk) also **cen·tri·cal** (-trĭ-kəl) *adj.* **1.** Situated at or near the center; central. **2.** Having a center. **3.** Of or relating to diatoms of the class Centrales, distinguished by their radially symmetrical form. **—cen′tri·cal·ly** *adv.* **—cen·tric′i·ty** (sĕn-trĭs′ĭ-tē) *n.*

–centric *suff.* **1.** Having a specified kind or number of centers: *polycentric.* **2.** Having a specified object as the center: *geocentric.*

cen·tri·cal (sĕn′trĭ-kəl) *adj.* Variant of **centric.**

cen·trif·u·gal (sĕn-trĭf′yə-gəl, -trĭf′ə-) *adj.* **1.** Moving or directed away from a center or axis. **2.** Operated by means of centrifugal force. **3.** *Physiology.* Transmitting nerve impulses away from the central nervous system; efferent. **4.** *Botany.* Developing or progressing outward from a center or axis, as in a flower cluster in which the oldest flowers are in the center and the youngest flowers are near the edge. **5.** Tending or directed away from centralization, as of authority: *"The division of Europe into two warring blocs, each ultimately dependent on a superpower patron, is subject to ever-increasing centrifugal stress"* (Scott Sullivan). [From New Latin *centrifugus* : Latin *centrum,* center; see CENTER + Latin *fugere,* to flee.] **—cen·trif′u·gal·ism** *n.* **—cen·trif′u·gal·ly** *adv.*

centrifugal force *n.* The component of apparent force on a body in curvilinear motion, as observed from that body, that is

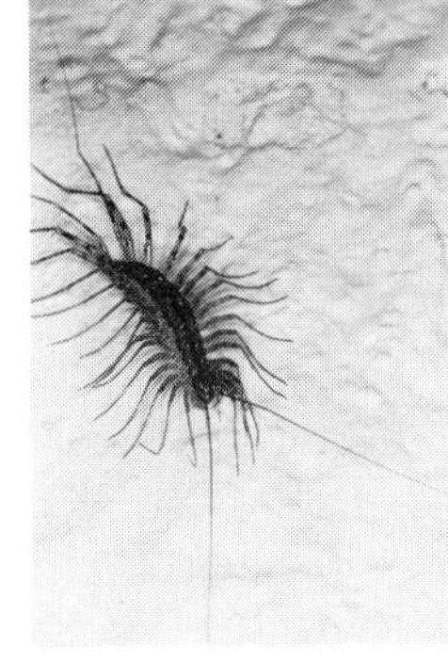

centipede

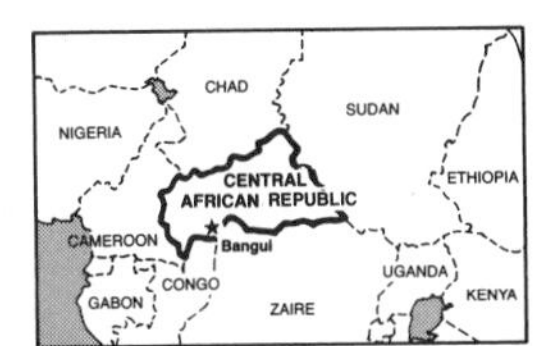

Central African Republic

ă pat	oi boy
ā pay	ou out
âr care	o͝o took
ä father	o͞o boot
ĕ pet	ŭ cut
ē be	ûr urge
ĭ pit	th thin
ī pie	*th* this
îr pier	hw which
ŏ pot	zh vision
ō toe	ə about, item
ô paw	♦ regionalism

Stress marks: ′ (primary); ′ (secondary), as in **dictionary** (dĭk′shə-nĕr′ē)

directed away from the center of curvature or axis of rotation.

cen·tri·fuge (sĕn′trə-fyo͞oj′) *n.* **a.** An apparatus consisting essentially of a compartment spun about a central axis to separate contained materials of different specific gravities, or to separate colloidal particles suspended in a liquid. **b.** An apparatus in which human beings or animals are enclosed and which is revolved to simulate the effects of acceleration in a spacecraft. **—centrifuge** *tr.v.* **-fuged, -fug·ing, -fug·es.** To rotate (something) in a centrifuge or to separate, dehydrate, or test by means of this apparatus. [French, centrifugal, from New Latin *centrifugus.* See CENTRIFUGAL.] **—cen·trif′u·ga′tion** (sĕn-trĭf′yə-gā′shən, -trĭf′ə-) *n.*

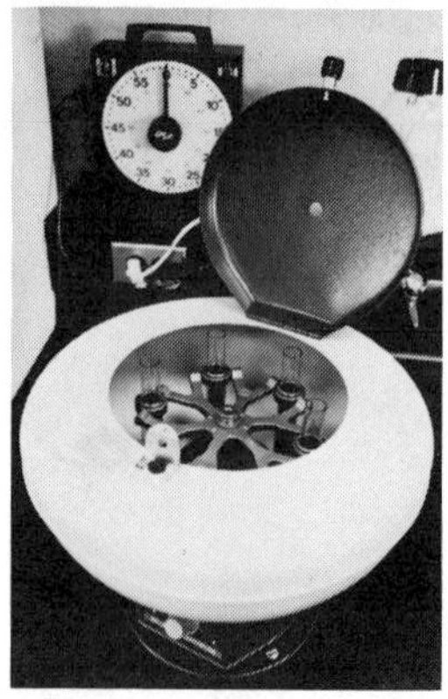

centrifuge

cen·tri·ole (sĕn′trē-ōl′) *n.* One of two cylindrical cellular structures that are composed of nine triplet microtubules and form the asters during mitosis. [New Latin *centriolum,* diminutive of Latin *centrum,* center. See CENTER.]

cen·trip·e·tal (sĕn-trĭp′ĭ-tl) *adj.* **1.** Moving or directed toward a center or axis. **2.** Operated by means of centripetal force. **3.** *Physiology.* Transmitting nerve impulses toward the central nervous system; afferent. **4.** *Botany.* Developing or progressing inward toward the center or axis, as in the head of a sunflower, in which the oldest flowers are near the edge and the youngest flowers are in the center. **5.** Tending or directed toward centralization: *the centripetal effects of a homogeneous population.* **—cen·trip′e·tal·ly** *adv.*

centripetal force *n.* The component of force acting on a body in curvilinear motion that is directed toward the center of curvature or axis of rotation.

cen·trism (sĕn′trĭz′əm) *n.* The political philosophy of avoiding the extremes of right and left by taking a moderate position.

cen·trist (sĕn′trĭst) *n.* One who takes a position in the political center; a moderate. **—centrist** *adj.* Marked by or adhering to a moderate political view: *"The deep pool of centrist opinion in the country, that essential guarantee against violent political upheavals, is being dangerously shaken"* (New York Times).

centro– or **centr–** or **centri–** *pref.* Center: *centroid.* [From Latin *centrum* and Greek *kentron;* see CENTER.]

cen·tro·bar·ic (sĕn′trə-băr′ĭk) *adj.* Of or relating to the center of gravity. [From Greek *kentrobarikē,* theory of the center of gravity : *kentron,* center; see CENTER + *baros,* weight; see **g^wera-** [1] in Appendix.]

cen·troid (sĕn′troid′) *n.* **1.** See **center of mass. 2.** The point in a system of masses each of whose coordinates is a weighted mean of coordinates of the same dimension of points within the system, the weights being determined by the density function of the system.

cen·tro·lec·i·thal (sĕn′trə-lĕs′ə-thəl) *adj. Biology.* Having the yolk located in the center: *a centrolecithal egg.* [CENTRO– + LECITH(IN) + –AL [1].]

cen·tro·mere (sĕn′trə-mîr′) *n.* The most condensed and constricted region of a chromosome to which the spindle fiber is attached during mitosis. **—cen′tro·mer′ic** (-mĕr′ĭk, -mîr′-) *adj.*

cen·tro·some (sĕn′trə-sōm′) *n.* A small region of cytoplasm adjacent to the nucleus that contains the centrioles and serves to organize microtubules. **—cen′tro·so′mic** (-sō′mĭk) *adj.*

cen·tro·sphere (sĕn′trə-sfîr′) *n.* **1.** The mass of cytoplasm surrounding the centriole in a centrosome. **2.** The central core of the earth. In this sense, also called *barysphere.*

cen·trum (sĕn′trəm) *n., pl.* **-trums** or **-tra** (-trə). The major part of a vertebra, exclusive of the bases of the neural arch. [Latin, center. See CENTER.]

cen·tum (kĕn′təm) *adj.* Of, relating to, or comprising the Indo-European languages that maintained a distinction between the reflexes of Indo-European velar *k, g, gh* and labiovelar k^w, g^w, g^wh. [Latin, hundred (a word whose initial sound in classical Latin illustrates the preservation of the Indo-European velar *k*). See **dekm̥** in Appendix.]

cen·tu·ri·on (sĕn-to͝or′ē-ən, -tyo͝or′-) *n.* The commander of a century in the Roman army. [Middle English, from Old French, from Latin *centuriō, centuriōn-,* from *centuria,* group of a hundred. See CENTURY.] **—cen·tu′ri·al** *adj.*

cen·tu·ry (sĕn′chə-rē) *n., pl.* **-ries. 1.** *Abbr.* **C., c., cen., cent. a.** A period of 100 years. **b.** Each of the successive periods of 100 years before or since the advent of the Christian era. **2. a.** A unit of the Roman army originally consisting of 100 men. **b.** One of the 193 electoral divisions of the Roman people. **3.** A group of 100 things. [Latin *centuria,* a group of a hundred, from *centum,* hundred. See **dekm̥** in Appendix.] **—cen′tu·ry·long′** *adj.*

century plant *n.* See **agave.**

CEO or **C.E.O.** *abbr.* Chief executive officer.

ce·orl (chā′ôrl) *n.* A freeman of the lowest class in Anglo-Saxon England. [Old English.]

cep or **cèpe** (sĕp) *n.* A species of edible mushroom *(Boleteus edulis)* widely distributed in woodlands. [French *cèpe,* from Gascon *cep,* tree trunk, cep, from Latin *cipus, cippus,* post, boundary marker.]

cephal– *pref.* Variant of **cephalo–.**

ceph·a·lad (sĕf′ə-lăd′) *adv. Biology.* Toward the head or anterior section.

ceph·al·al·gia (sĕf′ə-lăl′jə, -jē-ə) *n.* Pain in the head; a headache.

ceph·a·lex·in (sĕf′ə-lĕk′sĭn) *n.* A semisynthetic analogue of cephalosporin used especially in the treatment of respiratory and urinary tract infections. [CEPHAL(OSPORIN) + *-ex-,* of unknown origin + –IN.]

ce·phal·ic (sə-făl′ĭk) *adj.* **1.** Of or relating to the head. **2.** Located on, in, or near the head. [French *céphalique,* from Latin *cephalicus,* from Greek *kephalikos,* from *kephalē,* head. See **ghebh-el-** in Appendix.] **—ce·phal′i·cal·ly** *adv.*

–cephalic *suff.* Having a specified kind or number of heads: *dolichocephalic.*

cephalic index *n.* The ratio of the maximum width of the head to its maximum length, multiplied by 100.

ceph·a·lin (sĕf′ə-lĭn) also **keph·a·lin** (kĕf′-) *n.* Any of a group of phospholipids having hemostatic properties and found especially in the nervous tissue of the brain and spinal cord.

ceph·a·li·za·tion (sĕf′ə-lĭ-zā′shən) *n.* An evolutionary trend in the animal kingdom toward centralization of neural and sensory organs in the head or anterior region of the body.

cephalo– or **cephal–** *pref.* Head: *cephalothorax.* [New Latin, from Greek *kephalo-,* from *kephalē,* head. See **ghebh-el-** in Appendix.]

ceph·a·lo·chor·date (sĕf′ə-lə-kôr′dāt′) *n.* Any of various primitive chordate animals of the subphylum Cephalochordata, such as the lancet, that lack a true vertebral column. **—cephalochordate** *adj.* Of, relating to, or belonging to the subphylum Cephalochordata. [From New Latin *Cephalochordata,* subphylum name : CEPHALO– + *Chordata,* chordate phylum; see CHORDATE.]

ceph·a·lo·me·ter (sĕf′ə-lŏm′ĭ-tər) *n.* A device for measuring the head.

ceph·a·lom·e·try (sĕf′ə-lŏm′ĭ-trē) *n.* Scientific measurement of the head. **—ceph′a·lo·met′ric** (-lō-mĕt′rĭk) *adj.*

Ceph·a·lo·ni·a (sĕf′ə-lō′nē-ə, -lōn′yə) also **Ke·fal·li·ní·a** (kĕ′fä-lē-nē′ä). The largest of the Ionian Islands off the western coast of Greece. It was held by the British from 1809 to 1864.

ceph·a·lo·pod (sĕf′ə-lə-pŏd′) *n.* Any of various marine mollusks of the class Cephalopoda, such as the octopus, squid, cuttlefish, or nautilus, having a large head, large eyes, prehensile tentacles, and, in most species, an ink sac containing a dark fluid used for protection or defense. **—cephalopod** *adj.* Of, relating to, or belonging to the class Cephalopoda. [From New Latin *Cephalopoda,* class name : CEPHALO– + *-poda,* -pod.] **—ceph′a·lop′o·dan** (sĕf′ə-lŏp′ə-dən) *n. & adj.*

ceph·a·lo·spo·rin (sĕf-ə-lə-spôr′ĭn, -spōr′-) *n.* Any of various broad-spectrum antibiotics, closely related to the penicillins, that were originally derived from the fungus *Cephalosporium acremonium.* [New Latin *Cephalosporium,* genus name (CEPHALO– + *spora,* spore; see SPORE) + –IN.]

ceph·a·lo·thin (sĕf′ə-lə-thĭn) *n.* A semisynthetic analogue of cephalosporin having a broad spectrum of antibiotic activity that is administered parenterally and used especially to treat systemic infections caused by susceptible microorganisms. [CEPHALO(SPORIN) + THI(O)– + –(I)N.]

ceph·a·lo·tho·rax (sĕf′ə-lə-thôr′ăks′, -thōr′-) *n.* The anterior section of arachnids and many crustaceans, consisting of the fused head and thorax.

–cephalous *suff.* Having a specified kind of head or number of heads: *dicephalous.* [From Greek *-kephalos,* from *kephalē,* head. See **ghebh-el-** in Appendix.]

–cephaly *suff.* A specified condition of the head: *microcephaly.*

Ce·phe·id (sē′fē-ĭd, sĕf′ē-) *n.* Any of a class of intrinsically variable stars with exceptionally regular periods of light pulsation. [From CEPHEUS.]

Ce·pheus (sē′fyo͞os′, -fē-əs, sĕf′ē-) *n.* A constellation in the Northern Hemisphere near Cassiopeia and Draco. [Latin *Cēpheus,* from Greek *Kēpheus.*]

ce·ra·ceous (sə-rā′shəs) *adj.* Waxy or waxlike. [Latin *cēra,* wax; see CERATE + –ACEOUS.]

Ce·ram (sā′räm′, sĕ-rän′). An island of eastern Indonesia in the Moluccas west of New Guinea. It borders on the **Ceram Sea,** a section of the western Pacific Ocean.

ce·ram·al (sə-răm′əl) *n.* See **cermet.** [CERAM(IC) + AL(LOY).]

ce·ram·ic (sə-răm′ĭk) *n.* **1.** Any of various hard, brittle, heat-resistant and corrosion-resistant materials made by shaping and then firing a nonmetallic mineral, such as clay, at a high temperature. **2. a.** An object, such as earthenware, porcelain, or tile, made of ceramic. **b. ceramics.** *(used with a sing. verb).* The art or technique of making objects of ceramic, especially from fired clay. [From Greek *keramikos,* of pottery, from *keramos,* potter's clay. See **ker-** [3] in Appendix.] **—ce·ram′ic** *adj.*

ce·ram·ist (sə-răm′ĭst, sĕr′ə-mĭst) *n.* One who makes objects of ceramic.

ce·ras·tes (sə-răs′tēz) *n., pl.* **cerastes.** Any of several venomous snakes of the genus *Cerastes,* such as the horned viper, having hornlike projections over each eye. [Middle English, from Latin *cerastēs,* from Greek *kerastēs,* horned serpent, from *keras,* horn. See **ker-** [1] in Appendix.]

cerat– *pref.* Variant of **kerato–.**

ce·rate (sîr′āt′) *n.* A hard, unctuous, fat- or wax-based solid, sometimes medicated, formerly applied to the skin directly or on dressings. [Latin *cērātum,* from *cērātus,* past participle of *cērāre,* to cover with wax, from *cēra,* wax; akin to Greek *kēros.*]

ce·rat·ed (sîr′ā′tĭd) *adj.* **1.** Coated with wax or resin. **2.** Having a cere: *a cerated beak.* [From Latin *cērātus.* See CERATE.]

ă pat	oi boy
ā pay	ou out
âr care	o͝o took
ä father	o͞o boot
ĕ pet	ŭ cut
ē be	ûr urge
ĭ pit	th thin
ī pie	*th* this
îr pier	hw which
ŏ pot	zh vision
ō toe	ə about, item
ô paw	♦ regionalism

Stress marks: ′ (primary); ′ (secondary), as in **dictionary** (dĭk′shə-nĕr′ē)

cerato– *pref.* Variant of **kerato–.**

ce·rat·o·dus (sə-răt′ə-dəs) *n., pl.* **-dus·es. 1.** Any of various extinct lungfishes of the genus *Ceratodus,* of the Triassic and Cretaceous periods. **2.** See **barramunda.** [New Latin *Ceratodus,* genus name : Greek *keras, kerat-,* horn; see **ker-**[1] in Appendix + Greek *odous,* tooth; see **dent-** in Appendix.]

cer·a·toid (sĕr′ə-toid′) *adj.* Similar to a horn; hornlike.

Cer·ber·us (sûr′bər-əs) *n. Greek & Roman Mythology.* A three-headed dog guarding the entrance to Hades. **—Cer′ber·e′an** (sûr′bə-rē′ən) *adj.*

cer·car·i·a (sər-kâr′ē-ə) *n., pl.* **-i·ae** (-ē-ē′) or **-i·as.** The parasitic larva of a trematode worm, having a tail that disappears in the adult stage. [New Latin : Greek *kerkos,* tail + *-aria,* feminine of Latin *-arius,* -ary.] **—cer·car′i·al** *adj.*

cer·cus (sûr′kəs, kĕr′-) *n., pl.* **cer·ci** (sûr′sī, -kī, kĕr′kē). Either of a pair of terminal, dorsolateral sensory appendages of certain insects, such as the female mosquito. [New Latin, from Greek *kerkos,* tail.]

cere[1] (sîr) *tr.v.* **cered, cer·ing, ceres.** To wrap in or as if in cerecloth. [Middle English *ceren, ciren,* from Old French *cirer,* to cover with wax, from Latin *cērāre.* See CERATE.]

cere[2] (sîr) *n.* A fleshy or waxlike swelling at the base of the upper part of the beak in certain birds, such as parrots. [Middle English *sere,* from Old French *cire,* from Medieval Latin *cēra,* from Latin, wax. See CERATE.] **—cered** *adj.*

ce·re·al (sîr′ē-əl) *n.* **1. a.** A grass such as wheat, oats, or corn, the starchy grains of which are used as food. **b.** The grain of such a grass. **2.** Any of several other plants or their edible seed or fruit, such as buckwheat or grain amaranth. **3.** A food prepared from any of these plants, especially a breakfast food made from commercially processed grain. **—cereal** *adj.* Consisting of or relating to grain or to a plant producing grain. [From Latin *cereālis,* of grain, from *Cerēs,* Ceres. See **ker-**[2] in Appendix.]

cereal leaf beetle *n.* An Old World beetle *(Oulema melanopus)* now found in the United States, where it is a serious pest of grain crops as a result of its consumption of cereal grasses.

cer·e·bel·lum (sĕr′ə-bĕl′əm) *n., pl.* **-bel·lums** or **-bel·la** (-bĕl′ə). The trilobed structure of the brain, lying posterior to the pons and medulla oblongata and inferior to the occipital lobes of the cerebral hemispheres, that is responsible for the regulation and coordination of complex voluntary muscular movement as well as the maintenance of posture and balance. [Medieval Latin, from Latin, diminutive of *cerebrum,* brain. See **ker-**[1] in Appendix.] **—cer′e·bel′lar** (-bĕl′ər) *adj.*

cerebr– *pref.* Variant of **cerebro–.**

cer·e·bra (sĕr′ə-brə, sə-rē′brə) *n.* A plural of **cerebrum.**

cer·e·bral (sĕr′ə-brəl, sə-rē′-) *adj.* **1.** Of or relating to the brain or cerebrum. **2.** Appealing to or requiring the use of the intellect; intellectual rather than emotional: *"His approach is cerebral, analytical, cautious"* (Helen Dewar). **—cer·e′bral·ly** *adv.*

cerebral accident *n.* See **stroke**[1] (sense 6).

cerebral cortex *n.* The extensive outer layer of gray matter of the cerebral hemispheres, largely responsible for higher brain functions, including sensation, voluntary muscle movement, thought, reasoning, and memory.

cerebral hemisphere *n.* Either of the two symmetrical halves of the cerebrum, as divided by the longitudinal cerebral fissure.

cerebral palsy *n.* A disorder usually caused by brain damage occurring at or before birth and marked by muscular impairment. Often accompanied by poor coordination, it sometimes involves speech and learning difficulties. **—cer′e·bral-pal′sied** (sĕr′ə-brəl-pôl′zēd, sə-rē′-) *adj.*

cer·e·brate (sĕr′ə-brāt′) *intr.v.* **-brat·ed, -brat·ing, -brates.** To use the power of reason; think. See Synonyms at **think.** [Back-formation from *cerebration,* from Latin *cerebrum,* brain. See CEREBRUM.] **—cer′e·bra′tion** *n.*

cerebro– or **cerebr–** *pref.* Brain; cerebrum: *cerebroside.* [From CEREBRUM.]

cer·e·bro·side (sĕr′ə-brə-sīd′, sə-rē′-) *n.* Any of various lipid compounds containing glucose or galactose and glucose, and found in the brain and other nerve tissue. [CEREBR(O)– + –OS(E)[2] + –IDE.]

cer·e·bro·spi·nal (sĕr′ə-brō-spī′nəl, sə-rē′brō-) *adj.* Of or relating to the brain and spinal cord.

cerebrospinal fluid *n. Abbr.* **CSF** The serumlike fluid that circulates through the ventricles of the brain, the cavity of the spinal cord, and the subarachnoid space, functioning in shock absorption.

cerebrospinal meningitis *n.* Inflammation of the meninges of both the brain and the spinal cord.

cer·e·bro·vas·cu·lar (sĕr′ə-brō-văs′kyə-lər, sə-rē′brō-) *adj.* Of or relating to the blood vessels that supply the brain.

cerebrovascular accident *n. Abbr.* **CVA** See **stroke**[1] (sense 6).

cer·e·brum (sĕr′ə-brəm, sə-rē′-) *n., pl.* **-brums** or **-bra** (-brə). The large, rounded structure of the brain occupying most of the cranial cavity, divided into two cerebral hemispheres that are joined at the bottom by the corpus callosum. It controls and integrates motor, sensory, and higher mental functions, such as thought, reason, emotion, and memory. [Latin, brain. See **ker-**[1] in Appendix.]

cere·cloth (sîr′klôth′, -klŏth′) *n.* Cloth coated with wax, formerly used for wrapping the dead.

cer·e·ment (sĕr′ə-mənt, sîr′mənt) *n.* **1.** Cerecloth. **2.** Often **cerements.** A burial garment.

cer·e·mo·ni·al (sĕr′ə-mō′nē-əl) *adj.* **1.** Of, appropriate to, or characterized by ceremony; formal or ritual. **2.** Involved or used in ceremonies: *ceremonial garb.* **—ceremonial** *n.* **1.** A set of ceremonies prescribed for an occasion; a ritual. **2.** A ceremony or rite. **—cer′e·mo′ni·al·ism** *n.* **—cer′e·mo′ni·al·ist** *n.* **—cer′e·mo′ni·al·ly** *adv.*

cer·e·mo·ni·ous (sĕr′ə-mō′nē-əs) *adj.* **1.** Strictly observant of or devoted to ceremony, ritual, or etiquette; punctilious: *"borne on silvery trays by ceremonious world-weary waiters"* (Financial Times). **2. a.** Characterized by ceremony: *"Putting on a hat can be a ceremonious act, an elegant gesture in the ritual of dressing"* (Ruth La Ferla). **b.** In accord with prescribed or customary usage; rigidly formal: *Their ceremonious greetings did not seem heartfelt.* **—cer′e·mo′ni·ous·ly** *adv.* **—cer′e·mo′ni·ous·ness** *n.*

cer·e·mo·ny (sĕr′ə-mō′nē) *n., pl.* **-nies. 1.** A formal act or set of acts performed as prescribed by ritual or custom: *a wedding ceremony; the Japanese tea ceremony.* **2.** A conventional social gesture or act of courtesy: *the ceremony of shaking hands when introduced.* **3.** A formal act without intrinsic purpose; an empty form: *ignored the ceremony of asking for comments and suggestions from other committee members.* **4.** Strict observance of formalities or etiquette: *The head of state was welcomed with full ceremony.* [Middle English *ceremonie,* from Latin *caerimōnia,* religious rite.]

Ce·ren·kov (chə-rĕng′kôf, -kəf, chĭ-ryĭn-kôf′), **Pavel Alekseevich.** See Pavel Alekseevich **Cherenkov.**

Ce·ren·kov effect also **Che·ren·kov effect** (chə-rĕng′kôf, -kəf) *n.* The emission of light by a charged particle passing through a transparent nonconducting liquid or solid material at a speed greater than the speed of light in that material. [After Pavel Alekseevich CHERENKOV.]

Cerenkov radiation also **Cherenkov radiation** *n.* Light emitted in the Cerenkov effect.

Ce·res (sîr′ēz) *n.* **1.** *Roman Mythology.* The goddess of agriculture. **2.** The largest asteroid and the first to be discovered, having an orbit between Mars and Saturn. [Latin *Cerēs.* See **ker-**[2] in Appendix.]

ce·re·us (sîr′ē-əs) *n.* Any of several cacti of the genus *Cereus* or closely related genera, such as a night-blooming cereus. [New Latin *Cēreus,* genus name, from Latin *cēreus,* candle (from its shape), from *cēra,* wax. See CERATE.]

ce·ric (sîr′ĭk, sĕr′-) *adj.* Of, relating to, or containing cerium, especially with valence 4. [CER(IUM) + –IC.]

ceric oxide *n.* A pale yellow-white powder, CeO_2, used in ceramics, to polish glass, and to sensitize photosensitive glass.

cer·iph (sĕr′ĭf) *n. Chiefly British.* Variant of **serif.**

ce·rise (sə-rēs′, -rēz′) *n. Color.* A deep to vivid purplish red. [French, from Old French, cherry. See CHERRY.] **—ce·rise′** *adj.*

ce·ri·um (sîr′ē-əm) *n. Symbol* **Ce** A lustrous, iron-gray, malleable metallic rare-earth element that occurs chiefly in the minerals monazite and bastnaesite, exists in four allotropic states, is a constituent of lighter flint alloys, and is used in various metallurgical and nuclear applications. Atomic number 58; atomic weight 140.12; melting point 795°C; boiling point 3,468°C; specific gravity 6.67 to 8.23; valence 3, 4. See table at **element.** [CER(ES) + –IUM.]

cer·met (sûr′mĕt′) *n.* A material consisting of processed ceramic particles bonded with metal and used in high-strength and high-temperature applications. Also called *ceramal.* [CER(AMIC) + MET(AL).]

cer·nu·ous (sûr′nyo͞o-əs) *adj. Botany.* Nodding; drooping. [From Latin *cernuus,* bowing forward.]

ce·ro (sîr′ō, sĕr′ō) *n., pl.* **ce·ros** or **cero.** An edible fish *(Scomberomorus regalis)* of western Atlantic waters, having silvery sides and a dark-blue back. Also called *sierra.* [Alteration of Spanish *sierra,* saw, sawfish. See SIERRA.]

ce·ro·tic acid (sə-rō′tĭk, -rŏt′ĭk) *n.* A fatty acid, $CH_3(CH_2)_{24}COOH$, occurring in waxes, such as beeswax or carnauba wax. [From Latin *cērōtum,* wax plaster, from Greek *kērōton,* from neuter of *kēroun,* to wax, from *kēros,* wax.]

ce·ro·type (sîr′ə-tīp′, sĕr′ə-) *n.* The process of preparing a printing surface for electrotyping by first engraving on a wax-coated metal plate. [Greek *kēros,* wax + TYPE.]

ce·rous (sîr′əs) *adj.* Of, relating to, or containing cerium, especially with valence 3. [CER(IUM) + –OUS.]

Cer·ri·tos (sə-rē′təs). A city of southern California, a suburb of Los Angeles. Population, 53,020.

Cer·ro de Pun·ta (sĕr′ō də po͞on′tə, -tä). A peak, 1,338.6 m (4,389 ft) high, of central Puerto Rico in the Cordillera Central.

Cerro Gor·do (gôr′dō). A mountain pass of southeast Mexico between Veracruz and Mexico City. It was the site of a U.S. victory (April 18, 1847) in the Mexican War.

cert. *abbr.* **1.** Certificate; certification. **2.** Certified.

cer·tain (sûr′tn) *adj.* **1.** Definite; fixed: *set aside a certain sum each week.* **2.** Sure to come or happen; inevitable: *certain success.* **3.** Established beyond doubt or question; indisputable: *What is certain is that every effect must have a cause.* **4.** Capable of being relied on; dependable: *a quick and certain remedy.* **5.**

Cerberus
Orpheus and Cerberus
by Thomas Crawford

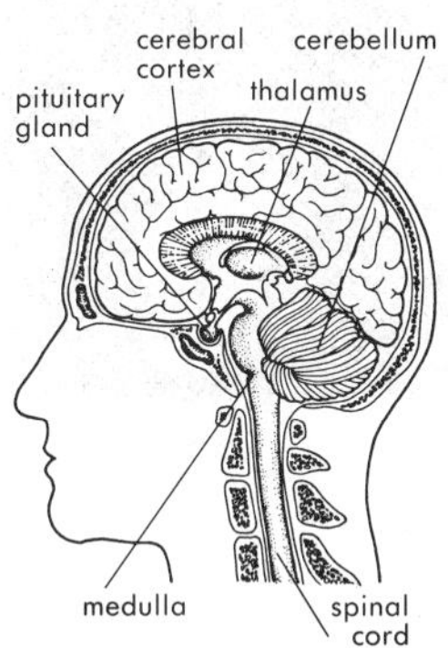

cerebellum

Ceres

Having or showing confidence; assured. **6.a.** Not specified or identified but assumed to be known: *a certain popular teacher; felt that certain breeds did not make good pets.* **b.** Named but not known or previously mentioned: *a certain Ms. Johnson.* **7.** Perceptible; noticeable: *a certain cozy charm; kept a certain air of mystery about him.* **8.** Not great; calculable: *to a certain degree; a certain delay in the schedule.* **—certain** *pron.* An indefinite but limited number; some: *Certain of the products are faulty.* **—*idiom.* for certain.** Without doubt; definitely. [Middle English, from Old French, from Vulgar Latin *certānus, from Latin *certus,* past participle of *cernere,* to determine. See **krei-** in Appendix.]

SYNONYMS: *certain, inescapable, inevitable, sure, unavoidable.* The central meaning shared by these adjectives is "impossible to avoid or evade": *certain death; an inescapable conclusion; an inevitable result; sudden but sure regret; an unavoidable accident.* See also Synonyms at **sure.**

USAGE NOTE: Although *certain* appears to be an absolute term, it is frequently qualified by adverbs, as in *fairly certain* or *quite certain.* In an earlier survey, a majority of the Usage Panel accepted the construction *Nothing could be more certain.*

cesta

cer·tain·ly (sûr′tn-lē) *adv.* **1.** Undoubtedly; definitely: *This is certainly not my writing.* **2.** By all means; of course: *You may certainly join us.* **3.** Surely: *They certainly are hard workers.*

cer·tain·ty (sûr′tn-tē) *n., pl.* **-ties. 1.** The fact, quality, or state of being certain: *the certainty of death.* **2.** Something that is clearly established or assured: *"On the field of battle there are no certainties"* (Tom Clancy).

SYNONYMS: *certainty, certitude, assurance, conviction.* These nouns mean freedom from doubt. *Certainty* implies an absence of doubt that is based on a thorough consideration of evidence: *"Jealousy feeds upon suspicion, and it turns into fury or it ends as soon as we pass from suspicion to certainty"* (La Rochefoucauld). *Certitude* is certainty that is based more on personal belief than on objective facts: *"Certitude is not the test of certainty"* (Oliver Wendell Holmes, Jr.). *Assurance* is a feeling of confidence resulting from subjective experience: *"There is no such thing as absolute certainty, but there is assurance sufficient for the purposes of human life"* (John Stuart Mill). *Conviction* is certainty arising from the vanquishment of doubt: *"The supreme happiness of life is the conviction that we are loved"* (Victor Hugo).

cer·tes (sûr′tēz, sûrts) *adv. Archaic.* Certainly; truly. [Middle English, from Old French *(a) certes,* perhaps from Latin *ad certās* or from Vulgar Latin **certānus,* both from Latin *certus,* certain. See CERTAIN.]

certif. *abbr.* Certificate.

cer·ti·fi·a·ble (sûr′tə-fī′ə-bəl) *adj.* **1.** That can be certified: *a certifiable fact; certifiable data.* **2.** Fit to be declared insane. **—cer′ti·fi′a·bly** *adv.*

cer·tif·i·cate (sər-tĭf′ĭ-kĭt) *n. Abbr.* **cert., certif., ctf., ct. 1.** A document testifying to the truth of something: *a certificate of birth.* **2.** A document issued to a person completing a course of study not leading to a diploma. **3.** A document certifying that a person may officially practice in certain professions. **4.** A document certifying ownership. **—certificate** (-kāt′) *tr.v.* **-cat·ed, -cat·ing, -cates.** To furnish with, testify to, or authorize by a certificate. [Middle English *certificat,* from Old French, from Medieval Latin *certificātum,* something certified, from neuter of Late Latin *certificātus,* past participle of *certificāre,* to certify. See CERTIFY.] **—cer·tif′i·ca·to′ry** (-kə-tôr′ē, -tōr′ē) *adj.*

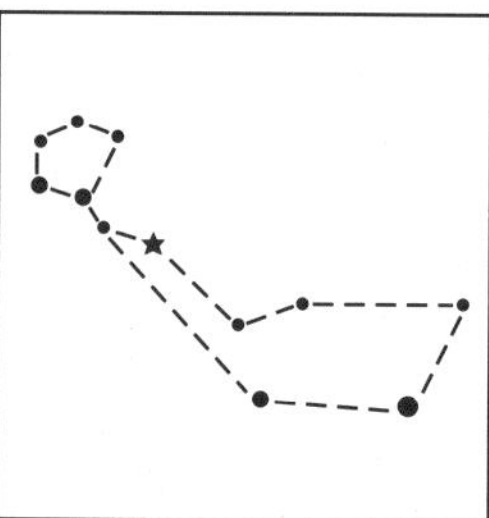
Cetus

certificate of deposit *n., pl.* **certificates of deposit.** *Abbr.* **CD, C/D** A certificate from a bank stating that the named party has a specified sum on deposit, usually for a given period of time at a fixed rate of interest.

cer·ti·fi·ca·tion (sûr′tə-fĭ-kā′shən) *n. Abbr.* **cert. 1.a.** The act of certifying. **b.** The state of being certified. **2.** A certified statement.

cer·ti·fied check (sûr′tə-fīd′) *n.* A check guaranteed by a bank to be covered by sufficient funds on deposit.

certified mail *n.* Uninsured first-class mail for which proof of delivery is obtained.

certified public accountant *n. Abbr.* **CPA, C.P.A.** A public accountant who has been certified by a state examining board as having met the state's legal requirements.

cer·ti·fy (sûr′tə-fī′) *v.* **-fied, -fy·ing, -fies.** *—tr.* **1.a.** To confirm formally as true, accurate, or genuine. **b.** To guarantee as meeting a standard: *butter that was certified Grade A.* See Synonyms at **approve. 2.** To acknowledge in writing on the face of (a check) that the signature of the maker is genuine and that there are sufficient funds on deposit for its payment. **3.** To issue a license or certificate to. **4.** To declare legally insane. **5.** *Archaic.* To inform positively; assure. *—intr.* To testify: *certify to the facts.* [Middle English *certifien,* from Old French *certifier,* from Late Latin *certificāre* : Latin *certus,* certain; see CERTAIN + Latin *-ficāre,* -fy.] **—cer′ti·fi′er** *n.*

cer·ti·o·rar·i (sûr′shē-ə-râr′ē, -rä′rē) *n. Law.* A writ from a higher court to a lower one requesting a transcript of the proceedings of a case for review. [Middle English, from Latin *certiorārī (volumus),* (we wish) to be informed (from the word's occurrence in the writ), passive of *certiōrāre,* to inform, apprise, from *certior,* comparative of *certus,* certain. See CERTAIN.]

ă pat	oi boy
ā pay	ou out
âr care	ŏŏ took
ä father	ōō boot
ĕ pet	ŭ cut
ē be	ûr urge
ĭ pit	th thin
ī pie	*th* this
îr pier	hw which
ŏ pot	zh vision
ō toe	ə about, item
ô paw	♦ regionalism

Stress marks: **′** (primary); ′ (secondary), as in **dictionary** (dĭk′shə-nĕr′ē)

cer·ti·tude (sûr′tĭ-to͞od′, -tyo͞od′) *n.* **1.** The state of being certain; complete assurance; confidence. **2.** Sureness of occurrence or result; inevitability. **3.** Something that is assured or unfailing: *"eager to swap the hazards of American freedom for the gray certitudes of Soviet life"* (Time). See Synonyms at **certainty.** [Middle English, from Late Latin *certitūdō,* from Latin *certus,* certain. See CERTAIN.]

ce·ru·le·an (sə-ro͞o′lē-ən) *adj. Color.* Azure; sky-blue. [From Latin *caeruleus,* dark blue; akin to *caelum,* sky.]

ce·ru·lo·plas·min (sə-ro͞o′lō-plăz′mĭn) *n.* A blood glycoprotein to which copper is bound during transport and storage. [CERUL(EAN) + PLASM(A) + -IN.]

ce·ru·men (sə-ro͞o′mən) *n.* See **earwax.** [New Latin, from Latin *cēra,* wax. See CERATE.] **—ce·ru′mi·nous** (-mə-nəs) *adj.*

ce·ruse (sə-ro͞os′, sîr′o͞os′) *n.* A white lead pigment, sometimes used in cosmetics. [Middle English, from Old French, from Latin *cērussa.*]

ce·rus·site (sə-rŭs′īt′) *n.* A colorless or white mineral, $PbCO_3$, that is an ore of lead; lead carbonate. [German *Zerussit,* from Latin *cērussa,* ceruse.]

Cer·van·tes Sa·a·ve·dra (sər-văn′tēz sä′ə-vā′drə, thĕr-bän′tĕs sä′ä-bĕ*th*′rä), **Miguel de.** 1547–1616. Spanish writer who is best known for his classic satirical novel *Don Quixote* (1605–1615).

cer·vi·cal (sûr′vĭ-kəl) *adj.* Of or relating to a neck or a cervix. [From Latin *cervīx, cervīc-,* neck. See CERVIX.]

cervical cap *n.* A small, rubber, cup-shaped contraceptive device that fits over the uterine cervix to prevent the entry of sperm.

cer·vi·ces (sûr′vĭ-sēz′, sər-vī′sēz) *n.* A plural of **cervix.**

cer·vi·ci·tis (sûr′vĭ-sī′tĭs) *n.* Inflammation of the cervix of the uterus.

cer·vine (sûr′vīn′) *adj.* Relating to, resembling, or characteristic of deer. [Latin *cervīnus,* from *cervus,* deer. See **ker-**[1] in Appendix.]

cer·vix (sûr′vĭks) *n., pl.* **cer·vix·es** or **cer·vi·ces** (sûr′vĭ-sēz′, sər-vī′sēz). **1.** The neck. **2.** A neck-shaped anatomical structure, such as the narrow outer end of the uterus. [Latin *cervīx,* neck. See **ker-**[1] in Appendix.]

ce·sar·e·an also **cae·sar·e·an** or **cae·sar·i·an** or **ce·sar·i·an** (sĭ-zâr′ē-ən) *—adj.* Of or relating to a cesarean section. *—n.* A cesarean section.

cesarean section also **caesarean section** *n.* A surgical incision through the abdominal wall and uterus, performed to deliver a fetus. [From the traditional belief that Julius Caesar (or his eponymous ancestor) was born by this operation.]

ce·sar·i·an (sĭ-zâr′ē-ən) *adj. & n.* Variant of **cesarean.**

Ce·se·na (chə-zā′nə, chĕ-zĕ′nä). A city of north-central Italy east-northeast of Florence. It flourished under the Malatesta family (1379–1465), who founded its Renaissance-style library. Population, 67,600.

ce·si·um also **cae·si·um** (sē′zē-əm) *n. Symbol* **Cs** A soft, silvery-white ductile metal, liquid at room temperature, the most electropositive and alkaline of the elements, used in photoelectric cells and to catalyze hydrogenation of some organic compounds. Atomic number 55; atomic weight 132.905; melting point 28.5°C; boiling point 690°C; specific gravity 1.87; valence 1. See table at **element.** [From Latin *caesius,* bluish gray (from its blue spectral lines).]

Čes·ké Bu·dě·jo·vi·ce (chĕs′kĕ bo͝od′yə-yô-vĭ-tsĕ). A city of southwest Czechoslovakia on the Vltava River south of Prague. It was founded in the 13th century. Population, 93,520.

ces·pi·tose (sĕs′pĭ-tōs′) *adj. Botany.* Growing in tufts or clumps. [New Latin *caespitōsus,* from Latin *caespes, caespit-,* turf.] **—ces′pi·tose′ly** *adv.*

cess (sĕs) *n. Irish.* Luck. [Possibly short for SUCCESS.]

ces·sa·tion (sĕ-sā′shən) *n.* A bringing or coming to an end; a ceasing: *a cessation of hostilities.* [Middle English *cessacioun,* from Old French *cessation,* from Latin *cessātiō, cessātiōn-,* from *cessātus,* past participle of *cessāre,* to stop. See CEASE.]

ces·sion (sĕsh′ən) *n.* **1.** A ceding or surrendering, as of territory to another country by treaty. **2.** Something, such as territory, that is ceded. [Middle English, from Old French, from Latin *cessiō, cessiōn-,* from *cessus,* past participle of *cēdere,* to yield. See **ked-** in Appendix.]

cess·pit (sĕs′pĭt′) *n.* A pit for refuse or sewage. [CESS(POOL) + PIT[1].]

cess·pool (sĕs′po͞ol′) *n.* **1.** A covered hole or pit for receiving drainage or sewage, as from a house. **2.** A filthy, disgusting, or morally corrupt place. [Perhaps alteration (influenced by POOL[1]) of obsolete *cesperalle,* drainpipe, from Middle English *suspiral,* vent, from Old French *sospirail,* breathing hole, from *souspirer,* to breathe, from Latin *suspīrāre,* to sigh. See SUSPIRE.]

ces·ta (sĕs′tə) *n. Sports.* A scoop-shaped wicker basket that is worn over the hand and used to catch and throw the ball in jai alai. [Spanish, basket, from Latin *cista,* chest. See CHEST.]

ces·ti (sĕs′tī) *n.* Plural of **cestus**[1].

ces·tode (sĕs′tōd′) *n.* Any of various parasitic flatworms of the class Cestoda, including the tapeworms, having a long, flat body equipped with a specialized organ of attachment at one end. **—cestode** *adj.* Of, relating to, or belonging to the class Cestoda. [From New Latin *Cestoda,* class name, from Latin *cestus,* belt, from Greek *kestos.* See CESTUS[1].]

ces·tus[1] (sĕs′təs) *n., pl.* **-ti** (-tī). A woman's belt or girdle, especially as worn in ancient Greece. [Latin, belt, from Greek *kestos.* See **kent-** in Appendix.]

ces·tus[2] also **caes·tus** (sĕs′təs) *n., pl.* **-tus·es.** A covering for the hand made of leather straps weighted with iron or lead and worn by boxers in ancient Rome. [Latin *caestus,* from *caedere,* to strike. See **kaə-id-** in Appendix.]

ce·su·ra (sĭ-zho͝or′ə, -zo͝or′ə) *n.* Variant of **caesura.**

CET or **C.E.T.** *abbr.* Central European Time.

CETA *abbr.* Comprehensive Employment and Training Act.

ce·ta·cean (sĭ-tā′shən) *n.* Any of various aquatic, chiefly marine mammals of the order Cetacea, including the whales, dolphins, and porpoises, characterized by a nearly hairless body, anterior limbs modified into broad flippers, vestigial posterior limbs, and a flat, notched tail. **—cetacean** also **ce·ta·ceous** (sĭ-tā′shəs) *adj.* Of or belonging to the order Cetacea. [From New Latin *Cētācea,* order name, from Latin *cētus,* whale. See CETUS.]

ce·tane (sē′tān′) *n.* A colorless liquid, $C_{16}H_{34}$, used as a solvent and in standardized hydrocarbons. [Latin *cētus,* whale (so called because it is found in sperm whale oil); see CETUS + -ANE.]

cetane number *n.* The performance rating of a diesel fuel, corresponding to the percentage of cetane in a cetane-methylnaphthalene mixture with the same ignition performance. A higher cetane number indicates greater fuel efficiency. Also called *cetane rating.*

cete (sēt) *n.* A company of badgers. See Synonyms at **flock[1].** [Middle English, possibly from Medieval Latin *cetus,* assembly, from Latin *coetus,* a coming together, variant of *coitus.* See COITUS.]

ce·ter·is par·i·bus (kā′tər-ĭs păr′ə-bəs) *adv. Abbr.* **cet. par.** With all other factors or things remaining the same. [New Latin *cēterīs pāribus,* with other things equal : Latin *cēterīs,* ablative pl. of *cēterus,* the other + Latin *pāribus,* ablative pl. of *pārs,* equal.]

ce·tol·o·gy (sĭ-tŏl′ə-jē) *n.* The zoology of whales and related aquatic mammals. [Latin *cētus,* whale; see CETUS + -LOGY.] **—ce′to·log′i·cal** (sēt′l-ŏj′ĭ-kəl) *adj.* **—ce·tol′o·gist** *n.*

cet. par. *abbr.* Ceteris paribus.

Ce·tus (sē′təs) *n.* A constellation in the equatorial region of the Southern Hemisphere near Aquarius and Eridanus. [Latin *cētus,* whale, from Greek *kētos.*]

ce·tyl alcohol (sēt′l) *n.* A waxy alcohol, $C_{15}H_{33}OH$, used in cosmetics and pharmaceuticals. [Latin *cētus,* whale; see CETUS + -YL.]

Ceu·ta (syo͞o′tə, thĕ′o͞o-tä, sĕ′-). A Spanish city of northwest Africa, an enclave in Morocco on the Strait of Gibraltar. A flourishing trade city under the Arabs, it was taken by the Portuguese in 1415 and passed to Spain in 1580. Population, 68,882.

Cé·vennes (sā-vĕn′). A mountain range of southern France west of the Rhone River, rising to 1,754.7 m (5,753 ft).

ce·vi·che or **se·vi·che** (sə-vē′chā, sĕ-) *n.* Raw fish marinated in lime or lemon juice with olive oil and spices and served as an appetizer. [American Spanish, from Spanish *cebiche,* fish stew, from *cebo,* fodder, bait, from Latin *cibus,* food.]

Cey·lon (sĭ-lŏn′, sā-). See **Sri Lanka.** **—Cey′lo·nese′** (-nēz′, -nēs′) *adj. & n.*

Ce·yx (sē′ĭks) *n. Greek Mythology.* The husband of Alcyone.

Cé·zanne (sā-zăn′, -zän′), **Paul.** 1839–1906. French artist and leading postimpressionist figure. His most famous paintings include *Mont Sainte-Victoire* (1885–1887) and *The Card Players* (1890–1892). **—Cé·zan′nesque′** (-zăn′ĕsk′) *adj.*

Cf The symbol for the element **californium.**

CF *abbr.* **1.** *Baseball.* Center field; center fielder. **2.** Cystic fibrosis.

cf. *abbr.* **1.** Calfskin. **2.** *Latin.* Confer (compare).

c.f. or **C.F.** *abbr.* Cost and freight.

C/F *abbr. Accounting.* Carried forward.

CFC *abbr.* Chlorofluorocarbon.

c.f.i. or **C.F.I.** *abbr.* Cost, freight, and insurance.

cfm or **c.f.m.** *abbr.* Cubic feet per minute.

cfs or **c.f.s.** *abbr.* Cubic feet per second.

cg *abbr.* Centigram.

c.g. *abbr.* **1.** Center of gravity. **2.** Or **C.G.** Consul general.

C.G. *abbr.* **1.** Coast guard. **2.** Commanding general.

cgm *abbr.* Centigram.

cgs or **CGS** *abbr.* Centimeter-gram-second system.

ch *abbr.* **1.** Chain (measurement). **2.** *Games.* Check (chess).

ch. *abbr.* **1.** Or **Ch.** Chaplain. **2.** Chapter. **3.** Check (bank order). **4.** Or **Ch.** Chief. **5.** Child; children. **6.** Or **Ch.** Church.

Ch. *abbr.* China.

c.h. or **C.H.** *abbr.* **1.** Clearing-house. **2.** Courthouse. **3.** Customhouse.

Cha·blis (shă-blē′, shä-, shăb′lē) *n.* **1.** A very dry white Burgundy wine originally from east-central France. **2.** A blended white table wine of California. [After *Chablis,* a village of north-central France.]

cha-cha (chä′chä) *n.* A rhythmic ballroom dance that originated in Latin America. **—cha-cha** *intr.v.* **-chaed, -cha·ing, -chas.** To perform this rhythmic ballroom dance. [American Spanish *chachachá.*]

chach·ka or **tchotch·ke** (chŏch′kə) also **tsats·ke** (tsäts′kə) *n. Slang.* A cheap, showy trinket. [Yiddish *tshatshke,* from Polish dialectal *czaczka.*]

chac·ma (chăk′mə) *n.* A grayish-black baboon *(Papio ursinus)* of southern and eastern Africa. [Possibly of Khokhoin origin.]

Cha·co (chä′kō). See **Gran Chaco.**

cha·conne (shă-kôn′, -kŏn′) *n.* **1.** A slow, stately dance of the 18th century or the music for it. **2.** *Music.* A form consisting of variations based on a reiterated harmonic pattern. [French, from Spanish *chacona,* a kind of dance.]

chad (chăd) *n.* Small pieces of paper or cardboard generated by punching holes in paper tape or data cards. [Origin unknown.] **—chad′less** *adj.*

Chad (chăd). A country of north-central Africa. Formerly part of French Equatorial Africa, it became independent in 1960. Ndjamena is the capital and the largest city. Population, 4,405,000. **—Chad′i·an** *adj. & n.*

Chad, Lake. A shallow lake of north-central Africa in Chad, Cameroon, Niger, and Nigeria. It was first explored by Europeans in 1823.

Chad·ic (chăd′ĭk) *n.* A branch of the Afro-Asiatic language family, spoken in west-central Africa and including Hausa as its best-known member.

cha·dor (chä-dôr′) *n.* A loose, usually black robe worn by Moslem women that covers the body from head to toe and most of the face. [Urdu *chādar,* cover, cloth, from Persian screen, tent, from Sanskrit *chattram,* screen, parasol. See CHUDDAR.]

Chad·wick (chăd′wĭk), **Henry.** 1824–1908. British-born American sportswriter who helped organize professional baseball. In 1869 he began an annual baseball handbook, which later became *Spalding's Official Baseball Guide.*

Chadwick, Sir **James.** 1891–1974. British physicist. He won a 1935 Nobel Prize for his discovery of the neutron.

Chaer·o·ne·a (kĕr′ə-nē′ə, kîr′-). An ancient city of eastern Greece. Philip of Macedon defeated a confederation of Greek states here in 338 B.C.

chae·ta (kē′tə) *n., pl.* **-tae** (-tē′). A bristle or seta, especially of an annelid worm. [New Latin, from Greek *khaitē,* long hair.]

chae·tog·nath (kē′tŏg-năth′) *n.* Any of various marine worms of the phylum Chaetognatha, which includes the arrow worms. **—chaetognath** *adj.* Of, relating to, or belonging to the phylum Chaetognatha. [From New Latin *Chaetognatha,* phylum name : *chaeta,* chaeta; see CHAETA + Greek *gnathos,* jaw; see **genu-[2]** in Appendix.] **—chae·tog′na·thous** (-nə-thəs) *adj.*

chafe (chāf) *v.* **chafed, chaf·ing, chafes.** *—tr.* **1.** To wear away or irritate by rubbing. **2.** To annoy; vex. **3.** To warm by rubbing, as with the hands. *—intr.* **1.** To rub and cause irritation or friction: *The high collar chafed against my neck.* **2.** To become worn or sore from rubbing. **3.** To feel irritated or impatient: *chafed at the delay.* **—chafe** *n.* **1.** Warmth, wear, or soreness produced by friction. **2.** Annoyance; vexation. [Middle English *chafen,* from Old French *chaufer,* to warm, from Vulgar Latin **calefāre,* alteration of Latin *calefacere* : *calēre,* to be warm; see **kelə-[1]** in Appendix + *facere,* to make; see **dhē-** in Appendix.]

SYNONYMS: *chafe, abrade, excoriate, fret, gall.* The central meaning shared by these verbs is "to wear down or rub away a surface by or as if by scraping": *chafed my skin; a swift stream abrading boulders; an excoriated elbow; rope that fretted a groove in the post; his heel galled by an ill-fitting shoe.*

cha·fer (chā′fər) *n.* Any of various beetles of the family Scarabaeidae, such as the cockchafer. [Middle English, a kind of beetle, from Old English *ceafor.*]

chaff[1] (chăf) *n.* **1.** *Botany.* Thin, dry bracts or scales, especially: **a.** The dry bracts enclosing mature grains of wheat and some other cereal grasses, removed during threshing. **b.** The scales or bracts borne on the receptacle among the small, individual flowers of many plants in the composite family. **2.** Finely cut straw or hay used as fodder. **3.** Trivial or worthless matter. **4.** Strips of metal, foil, or glass fiber with a metal content, cut into various lengths and having varying frequency responses, that are used to reflect electromagnetic energy as a radar countermeasure. These materials, usually dropped from aircraft, also can be deployed from shells or rockets. [Middle English *chaf,* from Old English *ceaf.*] **—chaff′y** *adj.*

chaff[2] (chăf) *v.* **chaffed, chaff·ing, chaffs.** *—tr.* To make fun of in a good-natured way; tease. *—intr.* To engage in playful teasing. See Synonyms at **banter.** **—chaff** *n.* Good-natured teasing; banter. [Possibly alteration of CHAFE or CHAFF[1].]

chaff·er[1] (chăf′ər) *n.* One who engages in banter or good-natured teasing.

chaf·fer[2] (chăf′ər) *v.* **-fered, -fer·ing, -fers.** *—intr.* **1.** To bargain or haggle. **2.** *Chiefly British.* To bandy words; engage in small talk. *—tr.* To bargain or haggle for. **—chaffer** *n. Archaic.* A bargaining or haggling. [Middle English *chaffaren,* to haggle, from *chaffare, cheapfare,* bargaining : *chep,* purchase; see CHEAP + *fare,* journey, business (from Old English *faru,* from *faran,* to travel; see FARE).] **—chaf′fer·er** *n.*

chaf·finch (chăf′ĭnch) *n.* A small European songbird *(Fringilla coelebs),* the male of which has predominantly reddish-brown plumage. [Middle English *chaffinche,* from Old English *ceaffinc* : *ceaf,* chaff, husk + *finch,* finch.]

chaf·ing dish (chā′fĭng) *n.* A metal dish or pan mounted

Paul Cézanne
Self-portrait

Chad

chafing dish
Mid 18th-century silver chafing dish

Marc Chagall
Photographed in the late 1970's

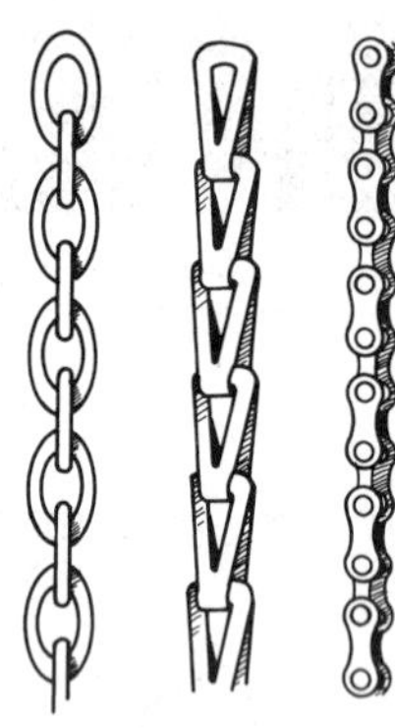

chain
Left to right: Straight, sash, and roller chains

chainlink fence

chain mail
16th-century chain mail maker

above a heating device and used to cook food or keep it warm at the table.

Cha·gall (shə-gäl′, -găl′, shä-), **Marc.** 1887–1985. Russian-born artist noted for his dreamlike, fanciful imagery and brilliantly colored canvases. Among his works are two huge murals designed for the New York City Metropolitan Opera House (1966).

Cha·gas' disease (shä′gəs) *n.* A South American form of trypanosomiasis caused by the protozoan *Trypanosoma cruzi* that is characterized by fever and enlargement of the spleen and lymph nodes. [After Carlos *Chagas* (1879–1934), Brazilian physician.]

Chag·a·tai (chăg′ə-tī′). See **Jagatai.**

Cha·gres (chä′grĕs). A river rising in central Panama, flowing southwest to Gatún Lake (formed by a dam on the river), then draining northwest to the Caribbean Sea.

cha·grin (shə-grĭn′) *n.* A keen feeling of mental unease, as of annoyance or embarrassment, caused by failure, disappointment, or a disconcerting event: *To her chagrin, the party ended just as she arrived.* **—chagrin** *tr.v.* **-grined, -grin·ing, -grins.** To cause to feel chagrin; mortify or discomfit: *He was chagrined at the poor sales of his book.* See Synonyms at **embarrass.** [French, possibly from dialectal French *chagraigner,* to distress, become gloomy, from Old French *graim,* sorrowful, gloomy, of Germanic origin.]

WORD HISTORY: The ultimate etymology of the word *chagrin,* which comes directly to us from French, is considered uncertain by many etymologists. At one time *chagrin* was thought to be the same word as *shagreen,* "a leather or skin with a rough surface," derived from French *chagrin.* The reasoning was that in French the word for this rough material, which was used to smooth and polish things, was extended to the notion of troubles that fret and annoy a person. It was later decided, however, that the sense "rough leather" and the sense "sorrow" each belonged to a different French word *chagrin.* Other etymologists have offered an alternative explanation, suggesting that the French word *chagrin,* "sorrow," is a loan translation of the German word *Katzenjammer,* "a morning-after-the-night-before feeling." A loan translation is a type of borrowing from another language in which the elements of a foreign word, as in *Katzen,* "cats," and *Jammer,* "distress, seediness," are assumed to be translated literally by corresponding elements in another language, in this case, *chat,* "cat," and *grigner,* "to grimace." The actual etymology is less colorful, with the word probably going back to a Germanic word, **gramī,* meaning "sorrow, trouble." *Chagrin* is first recorded in English in 1656 in the now obsolete sense "anxiety, melancholy."

chain (chān) *n.* **1.a.** A connected, flexible series of links, typically of metal, used especially for holding objects together or restraining or for transmitting mechanical power. **b.** Such a set of links, often of precious metal and with pendants attached, worn as an ornament or symbol of office. **2.** A restraining or confining agent or force. **3. chains. a.** Bonds, fetters, or shackles. **b.** Captivity or oppression; bondage: *threw off the chains of slavery.* **4.** A series of closely linked or connected things: *a chain of coincidences.* See Synonyms at **series. 5.** A number of establishments, such as stores, theaters, or hotels, under common ownership or management. **6.** A range of mountains. **7.** *Chemistry.* A group of atoms bonded in a spatial configuration like links in a chain. **8.a.** An instrument used in surveying, consisting of 100 linked pieces of iron or steel and measuring 66 feet (20.1 meters). Also called *Gunter's chain.* **b.** A similar instrument used in engineering, measuring 100 feet (30.5 meters). **c.** *Abbr.* **ch** A unit of measurement equal to the length of either of these instruments. **—chain** *tr.v.* **chained, chain·ing, chains. 1.** To bind or make fast with a chain or chains: *chained the dog to a tree.* **2.** To restrain or confine as if with chains: *workers who were chained to a life of dull routine.* [Middle English *chaine,* from Old French, from Latin *catēna.*]

Chain (chān), Sir **Ernst Boris.** 1906–1979. German-born British biochemist. He shared a 1945 Nobel Prize for isolating and purifying penicillin, discovered in 1928 by Sir Alexander Fleming.

chain fern *n.* Any of various terrestrial ferns of the genus *Woodwardia,* native chiefly to the Northern Hemisphere, having pinnately compound or divided leaves that when fertile bear chainlike rows of spore cases.

chain gang *n.* A group of convicts chained together, especially for outdoor labor.

chain letter *n.* A letter sent to a number of people asking each recipient to send copies with the same request to a specified number of others. The circulation of a chain letter increases in geometrical progression as long as the instructions are followed by all recipients.

chain·link fence (chān′lĭngk′) *n.* A fence made of thick steel wire interwoven in a diamond pattern.

chain mail *n.* Flexible armor made of joined metal links or scales.

chain·man (chān′mən) *n.* Either of the two persons who hold a surveyor's measuring chain.

chain of command *n., pl.* **chains of command.** A system whereby authority passes down from the top through a series of executive positions or military ranks in which each is accountable to the one directly superior.

chain pickerel *n.* A freshwater game and food fish *(Esox niger)* of eastern North America.

chain-re·act (chān′rē-ăkt′) *intr.v.* **-act·ed, -act·ing, -acts.** To undergo a chain reaction.

chain reaction *n.* **1.** A series of events in which each induces or influences the next. **2.** *Physics.* A multistage nuclear reaction, especially a self-sustaining series of fissions in which the release of neutrons from the splitting of one atom leads to the splitting of others. **3.** *Chemistry.* A series of reactions in which one product of a reacting set is a reactant in the following set.

chain saw *n.* A portable power saw with teeth linked in an endless chain. **—chain′-saw′** (chān′sô′) *v.*

chain-smoke (chān′smōk′) *v.* **-smoked, -smok·ing, -smokes.** —*intr.* To smoke continually, as by lighting the next cigarette from the previous one. —*tr.* To smoke (cigarettes, for example) in continuing succession. **—chain smoker** *n.*

chain stitch *n.* A decorative sewing stitch in which loops are connected like the links of a chain.

chain store *n.* One of a number of retail stores under the same ownership and dealing in the same merchandise.

chair (châr) *n.* **1.** A piece of furniture consisting of a seat, legs, back, and often arms, designed to accommodate one person. **2.** A seat of office, authority, or dignity, such as that of a bishop. **3.a.** An office or position of authority, such as a professorship. **b.** A person who holds an office or a position of authority, such as one who presides over a meeting or administers a department of instruction at a college; a chairperson. **4.** The position of a player in an orchestra. **5.** *Slang.* The electric chair. **6.** A seat carried about on poles; a sedan chair. **7.** Any of several devices that serve to support or secure, such as a metal block that supports and holds railroad track in position. **—chair** *tr.v.* **chaired, chair·ing, chairs. 1.** To install in a position of authority, especially as a presiding officer. **2.** To preside over as chairperson: *chair a meeting.* [Middle English *chaiere,* from Old French, from Latin *cathedra.* See CATHEDRA.]

chair car *n.* See **parlor car.**

chair lift *n.* A mechanized, cable-suspended, aerial chair assembly used to transport skiers and others up or down a mountain slope.

chair·man (châr′mən) *n. Abbr.* **chm., Chmn 1.** The presiding officer of an assembly, a meeting, a committee, or a board. **2.** The administrative head of a department of instruction, as at a college. See Usage Note at **man. —chairman** *tr.v.* **-manned, -man·ning, -mans.** To act as chairman of.

chair·man·ship (châr′mən-shĭp′) *n.* The office or term of a chairman.

chair·per·son (châr′pûr′sən) *n.* A chairman or chairwoman. See Usage Note at **man.**

chair·wom·an (châr′wo͝om′ən) *n.* **1.** A woman presiding officer of an assembly, meeting, committee, or board. **2.** A woman administrative head of a department of instruction, as at a college. See Usage Note at **man.**

chaise (shāz) *n.* **1.** Any of various light, open carriages, often with a collapsible hood, especially a two-wheeled carriage drawn by one horse. **2.** A post chaise. **3.** A chaise longue. [French, chair, variant of Old French *chaiere.* See CHAIR.]

chaise longue (shāz lông′) *n., pl.* **chaise longues** or **chaises longues** (shāz lông′). A reclining chair with a lengthened seat that supports the outstretched legs. [French : *chaise,* chair + *longue,* long.]

chak·ra (chŭk′rə) *n.* One of the seven centers of spiritual energy in the human body according to yoga philosophy. [Sanskrit *cakram,* wheel, circle. See **kʷel-¹** in Appendix.]

cha·lah (KHä′lə) *n.* Variant of **challah.**

cha·la·za (kə-lā′zə, -lăz′ə) *n., pl.* **-zae** (-zē) or **-zas. 1.** *Biology.* One of two spiral bands of tissue in an egg that connect the yolk to the lining membrane at either end of the shell. **2.** *Botany.* The region of an ovule that is opposite the micropyle, where the integuments and nucellus are joined. [Greek *khalaza,* hard lump, hailstone.] **—cha·la′zal** *adj.*

cha·la·zi·on (kə-lā′zē-ən, -ŏn′) *n., pl.* **-zi·a** (-zē-ə). A cyst of a tarsal gland. [Greek *khalazion,* diminutive of *khalaza,* hard lump, hailstone.]

Chal·ce·don (kăl′sĭ-dŏn′, kăl-sēd′n). An ancient Greek city of northwest Asia Minor on the Bosporus near present-day Istanbul. It was founded in 685 B.C. and passed to Rome in A.D. 74.

chal·ced·o·ny also **cal·ced·o·ny** (kăl-sĕd′n-ē) *n., pl.* **-nies.** A translucent to transparent milky or grayish quartz with distinctive microscopic crystals arranged in slender fibers in parallel bands. [Late Latin *chalcēdonius,* from Greek *khalkēdōn,* a mystical stone (Rev. 21:19), perhaps from *Khalkēdōn,* Chalcedon.] **—chal′ce·don′ic** (kăl′sĭ-dŏn′ĭk) *adj.*

chal·cid (kăl′sĭd) *n.* Any of various minute wasps of the superfamily Chalcidoidea, many of whose larvae parasitize the larvae of other insects. [From New Latin *Chalcis,* type genus, from Greek *khalkos,* copper (from the wasp's metallic color).]

Chal·cid·i·ce (kăl-sĭd′ĭ-sē) also **Khal·ki·dhi·kí** (käl-kē′-thē-kē′, KHäl-). A mountainous peninsula of northeast Greece projecting into the northern Aegean Sea with three fingerlike extensions. **—Chal·cid′i·an** *adj. & n.*

Chal·cis (kăl′sĭs) also **Khal·kís** (käl-kēs′, KHäl-). An ancient city of southeast Greece on the western coast of Euboea. It was a prosperous trading center after the eighth century B.C., establishing outposts in Italy, Syria, Sicily, and mainland Greece.

chal·co·cite (kăl′kə-sīt′) *n.* A dark gray mineral, essentially

Cu_2S, that is an important ore of copper. [Alteration of obsolete *chalcosine*, from Greek *khalkos*, copper.]

chal·co·py·rite (kăl′kə-pī′rīt′) *n.* A yellow mineral, essentially $CuFeS_2$, that is an important ore of copper. Also called *copper pyrites*. [New Latin *chalcopyrites* : Greek *khalkos*, copper + PYRITES.]

Chal·de·a or **Chal·dae·a** (kăl-dē′ə). An ancient region of southern Mesopotamia. Settled c. 1000 B.C., it reached the height of its power under Nebuchadnezzar II. The Chaldean empire was destroyed by Persians in 539 B.C.

Chal·de·an also **Chal·dae·an** (kăl-dē′ən) or **Chal·dee** (kăl′dē′) —*adj.* Of or relating to Chaldea or its people, language, or culture. —*n.* **1.** A member of an ancient Semitic people who ruled in Babylonia. **2.** See **Aramaic. 3.** A person versed in occult learning. —**Chal·da′ic** (-dā′ĭk) *adj. & n.*

chal·dron (chôl′drən) *n.* A unit of dry measure formerly used in England, equal to 4 quarters or about 32 bushels for grain and 36 bushels for coal. [Middle English, from Old French *chauderon*, augmentative of *chaudiere*, kettle, from Late Latin *caldāria*. See CALDRON.]

cha·let (shă-lā′, shăl′ā) *n.* **1.a.** A wooden dwelling with a sloping roof and widely overhanging eaves, common in Switzerland and other Alpine regions. **b.** A cottage or lodge built in this style. **2.** The hut of a herder in the Swiss Alps. [French, from Swiss French, possibly diminutive of *cala, shelter.]

Cha·leur Bay (shə-lo͝or′, -lûr′). An inlet of the Gulf of St. Lawrence between eastern Quebec and northern New Brunswick, Canada. It is an important fishing ground.

Cha·lia·pin (shä-lyä′pĭn), **Feodor Ivanovich.** 1873–1938. Russian-born French operatic basso who gained fame for his performance in Arrigo Boito's *Mefistofele*.

chal·ice (chăl′ĭs) *n.* **1.** A cup or goblet. **2.** A cup for the consecrated wine of the Eucharist. [Middle English, from Old French, from Latin *calix, calic-*.]

chal·i·co·there (kăl′ĭ-kə-thîr′) *n.* Any of various extinct ungulate mammals of the Eocene to Pleistocene epochs, having distinctive three-clawed, three-toed feet. [New Latin *Chalicotherium*, genus name : Greek *khalix, khalik-*, pebble + Greek *thērion*, diminutive of *thēr*, beast; see **ghwer-** in Appendix.]

chalk (chôk) *n.* **1.** A soft, compact calcite, $CaCO_3$, with varying amounts of silica, quartz, feldspar, or other mineral impurities, generally gray-white or yellow-white and derived chiefly from fossil seashells. **2.a.** A piece of chalk or chalklike substance in crayon form, used for marking on a blackboard or other surface. **b.** *Games.* A small cube of chalk used in rubbing the tip of a billiard or pool cue to increase its friction with the cue ball. **3.** A mark made with chalk. **4.** *Chiefly British.* A score or tally. —**chalk** *tr.v.* **chalked, chalk·ing, chalks. 1.** To mark, draw, or write with chalk: *chalked my name on the blackboard.* **2.** To rub or cover with chalk, as the tip of a billiard cue. **3.** To make pale; whiten. **4.** To treat (soil, for example) with chalk. —***phrasal verb.*** **chalk up. 1.** To earn or score: *chalk up points.* **2.** To credit or ascribe: *Chalk that up to experience.* [Middle English, from Old English *cealk*, from Latin *calx, calc-*, lime. See CALX.] —**chalk′i·ness** *n.* —**chalk′y** *adj.*

chalk·board (chôk′bôrd′, -bōrd′) *n.* A smooth, hard panel, usually green or black, for writing on with chalk; a blackboard.

chalk·stone (chôk′stōn′) *n. Pathology.* See **tophus** (sense 1).

chalk talk *n.* A lecture, often informal, illustrated with diagrams chalked on a blackboard.

chal·lah also **cha·lah** or **hal·lah** (KHä′lə, hä′-) *n.* A loaf of yeast-leavened, white egg bread, usually braided, traditionally eaten by Jews on the Sabbath, holidays, and other ceremonial occasions. [Hebrew *ḥallā*.]

chal·lenge (chăl′ənj) *n.* **1.a.** A call to engage in a contest, fight, or competition: *a challenge to a duel.* **b.** An act or statement of defiance; a call to confrontation: *a challenge to the government's authority.* **2.** A demand for explanation or justification; a calling into question: *a challenge to a theory.* **3.** A sentry's call to an unknown party for proper identification. **4.** A test of one's abilities or resources in a demanding but stimulating undertaking: *a career that offers a challenge.* **5.** A claim that a vote is invalid or that a voter is unqualified. **6.** *Law.* A formal objection to the inclusion of a prospective juror in a jury. **7.** *Immunology.* The induction or evaluation of an immune response in an organism by administration of a specific antigen to which it has been sensitized. —**challenge** *v.* **-lenged, -leng·ing, -leng·es.** —*tr.* **1.a.** To call to engage in a contest, fight, or competition: *challenged me to a game of chess.* **b.** To invite with defiance; dare: *challenged him to contradict her.* See Synonyms at **defy. 2.** To take exception to; call into question; dispute: *a book that challenges established beliefs.* **3.** To order to halt and be identified, as by a sentry. **4.** *Law.* To take formal objection to (a prospective juror). **5.** To question the qualifications of (a voter) or validity of (a vote). **6.** To have due claim to; call for: *events that challenge our attention.* **7.** To summon to action, effort, or use; stimulate: *a problem that challenges the imagination.* **8.** *Immunology.* To induce or evaluate an immune response in (an organism) by administering a specific antigen to which it has been sensitized. —*intr.* **1.** To make or give voice to a challenge. **2.** To begin barking upon picking up the scent. Used of hunting dogs. [Middle English *chalenge*, from Old French, from Latin *calumnia*, trickery, false accusation; see CALUMNY. V., from Middle English *chalengen*, from Old French *chalangier*, from Latin *calumniārī*, from *calumnia*, calumny.] —**chal′lenge·a·ble** *adj.*

chal·leng·er (chăl′ən-jər) *n.* **1.** One that challenges: *a challenger of established authority.* **2.** *Sports.* One who competes against the holder of a title or championship, as in boxing.

chal·leng·ing (chăl′ən-jĭng) *adj.* **1.** Calling for full use of one's abilities or resources in a difficult but stimulating effort: *a challenging course of study; a challenging role for an inexperienced performer.* **2.** Absorbing; intriguing: *a challenging idea.*

chal·lis (shăl′ē) *n.* A soft, lightweight, usually printed fabric of wool, cotton, or rayon. [Possibly from the surname *Challis*.]

Chal·mette (shăl-mĕt′). A village of extreme southeast Louisiana on the east bank of the Mississippi River just below New Orleans. It is a processing center. Population, 33,847.

cha·lone (kā′lōn′, kăl′ōn′) *n.* Any of several polypeptides that are produced by a body tissue and that cause the reversible inhibition of mitosis in the cells of that tissue. [From Greek *khalōn*, present participle of *khalan*, to slacken.]

Châ·lons-sur-Marne (shä-lôN′sûr′märn′, -sür-). A city of northeast France east of Paris. The Huns under Attila were defeated here in A.D. 451. Population, 51,137.

cha·lyb·e·ate (kə-lĭb′ē-ĭt, -lē′bē-) *adj.* **1.** Impregnated with or containing salts of iron. **2.** Tasting like iron, as water from a mineral spring. —**chalybeate** *n.* Water or medicine containing iron in solution. [New Latin *chalybeātus*, from Latin *chalybs*, steel, from Greek *khalups, khalub-*, possibly from *Khalups*, sing. of *Khalubes*, Chalybes, people of Asia Minor famous for their steel.]

cham (kăm) *n. Archaic.* A Tartar or Mogul khan. [French, from Turkish *khān*, lord, prince. See KHAN[1].]

Cha·mae·leon also **Cha·me·leon** (kə-mēl′yən, -mē′lē-ən) *n.* A constellation in the southern polar region near Apus and Mensa. [Latin *chamaeleōn*, chameleon. See CHAMELEON.]

cham·ae·phyte (kăm′ə-fīt′) *n.* A low-growing perennial plant whose dormant overwintering buds are borne at or just above the surface of the ground. [Greek *khamai*, on the ground; see **dhghem-** in Appendix + -PHYTE.]

cham·ber (chām′bər) *n.* **1.** A room in a house, especially a bedroom. **2.** A room where a person of authority, rank, or importance receives visitors. **3. chambers.** A room in which a judge may consult privately with attorneys or hear cases not taken into court. **4. chambers.** *Chiefly British.* A suite of rooms, especially one used by lawyers. **5.** A hall for the meetings of a legislative or other assembly. **6.** A legislative or judicial body. **7.** A board or council. **8.** A place where municipal or state funds are received and held; a treasury. **9.a.** An enclosed space or compartment: *the chamber of a pump; a compression chamber.* **b.** An enclosed space in the body of an organism; a cavity: *the four chambers of the heart.* **10.a.** A compartment in a firearm, as in the breech of a rifle or the cylinder of a revolver, that holds the cartridge in readiness for firing. **b.** An enclosed space in the bore of a gun that holds the charge. —**chamber** *tr.v.* **-bered, -ber·ing, -bers. 1.** To put in or as if in a chamber; enclose or confine. **2.** To furnish with a chamber. [Middle English *chaumbre*, from Old French *chambre*, from Late Latin *camera*, chamber, from Latin, vault, from Greek *kamara*.]

cham·bered nautilus (chām′bərd) *n.* See **nautilus** (sense 1).

cham·ber·lain (chām′bər-lən) *n.* **1.a.** An officer who manages the household of a sovereign or a noble; a chief steward. **b.** A high-ranking official in various royal courts. **2.** An official who receives the rents and fees of a municipality; a treasurer. **3.** *Roman Catholic Church.* An often honorary papal attendant. [Middle English *chaumberlein*, from Old French *chamberlenc*, from Frankish **kamerling* : Late Latin *camera*, chamber; see CHAMBER + Germanic *-*linga-*, one connected with; see -LING[1].]

Cham·ber·lain (chām′bər-lĭn), **(Arthur) Neville.** 1869–1940. British politician and prime minister (1937–1940) who advocated a policy of appeasement toward the fascist regimes of Europe.

Chamberlain, Joseph. 1836–1914. British politician who served as the mayor of Birmingham (1873–1876), president of the Board of Trade (1880–1885), and colonial secretary (1895–1903).

Chamberlain, Sir **(Joseph) Austen.** 1863–1937. British politician who helped establish the Locarno Pact. He won the 1925 Nobel Peace Prize.

Cham·ber·lin (chām′bər-lĭn), **Thomas Chrowder.** 1843–1928. American geologist who with the astronomer Forest Ray Moulton (1872–1952) proposed (1906) the planetismal hypothesis for the formation of the planets in the solar system.

cham·ber·maid (chām′bər-mād′) *n.* A maid who cleans and cares for bedrooms, as in a hotel.

chamber music *n. Music.* Compositions traditionally intended for performance in a private room or small concert hall and written for an instrumental ensemble, such as a trio or quartet, with one player for each part.

chamber of commerce *n., pl.* **chambers of commerce.** *Abbr.* **C. of C.** An association of businesspersons and merchants for the promotion of commercial interests in the community.

chamber pot *n.* A portable vessel used especially in a bedroom as a toilet.

Cham·bers (chām′bərz), **(Jay David) Whittaker.** 1901–1961. American journalist and onetime member of the Communist Party

chain saw

chair lift
Mount Sunapee, New Hampshire

chalice
Chalice of Tassilo, Merovingian, c. 780

ă pat	oi boy
ā pay	ou out
âr care	o͝o took
ä father	o͞o boot
ĕ pet	ŭ cut
ē be	ûr urge
ĭ pit	th thin
ī pie	*th* this
îr pier	hw which
ŏ pot	zh vision
ō toe	ə about, item
ô paw	♦ regionalism

Stress marks: ′ (primary); ′ (secondary), as in **dictionary** (dĭk′shə-nĕr′ē)

who testified before the House Un-American Activities Committee (1948), where he implicated Alger Hiss.

Cham•bers•burg (chăm′bərz-bûrg′). A borough of southern Pennsylvania southwest of Harrisburg. It was burned by the Confederate cavalry in July 1864 after the townspeople refused to pay an indemnity of $100,000 in gold. Population, 16,174.

Cham•bé•ry (shäN-bā-rē′). A city of eastern France east-southeast of Lyons. It is a manufacturing center in a popular tourist area. Population, 53,427.

Cham•bord (shäN-bôr′). A village of north-central France northeast of Tours. It is noted for its magnificent Renaissance château built by Francis I.

cham•bray (shăm′brā′) *n.* A fine, lightweight fabric woven with white threads across a colored warp. [Alteration of French *cambrai,* cambric, after *Cambrai,* a city of northern France.]

cha•me•leon (kə-mēl′yən, -mē′lē-ən) *n.* **1.** Any of various tropical Old World lizards of the family Chamaeleonidae, characterized by their ability to change color. **2.** See **anole. 3.** A changeable or inconstant person: *"In his testimony, the nominee came off as . . . a chameleon of legal philosophy"* (Joseph A. Califano, Jr.). [Middle English *camelioun,* from Latin *chamaeleōn,* from Greek *khamaileōn* : *khamai,* on the ground; see **dhghem-** in Appendix + *leōn,* lion (loan translation of Akkadian *nēš qaqqari,* ground lion, lizard); see LION.] **—cha•me′le•on′ic** (-lē-ŏn′ĭk) *adj.*

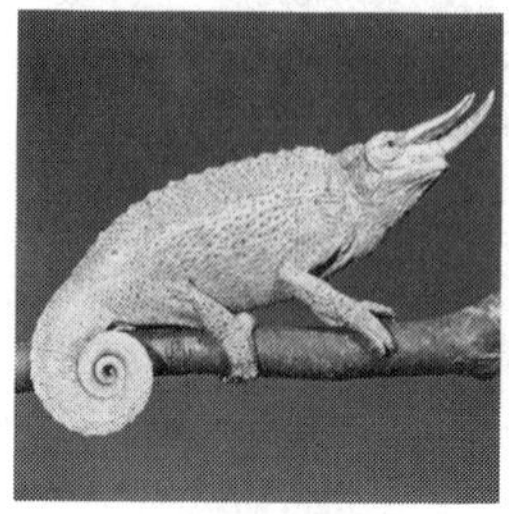

chameleon
Horned chameleon
Chamaeleo oweni

WORD HISTORY: The words referring to the animal chameleon and the plant chamomile are related etymologically by a reference to the place one would expect to find them, that is, on the ground. The first part of both words goes back to the Greek form *khamai,* meaning "on the ground." What is found on the ground in each case is quite different, of course. The *khamaileōn* is a "lion [*leōn*] on the ground," a term translating the Akkadian phrase *nēš qaqqari.* The *khamaimēlon* is "an apple [*mēlon*] on the ground," so named because the blossoms of at least one variety of this creeping herb have an applelike scent. Both words are first found in Middle English, *chameleon* in a work composed before 1382 and *chamomile* in a work written in 1373.

Cha•me•leon (kə-mēl′yən, -mē′lē-ən) *n.* Variant of **Chamaeleon.**

cham•fer (chăm′fər) *tr.v.* **-fered, -fer•ing, -fers. 1.** To cut off the edge or corner of; bevel. **2.** To cut a groove in; flute. **—chamfer** *n.* **1.** A flat surface made by cutting off the edge or corner of a block of wood or other material. **2.** A furrow or groove, as in a column. [Probably back-formation from *chamfering,* from French *chanfrein,* bevelled edge, from past participle of Old French *chanfreindre,* to bevel : *chant,* edge (from Latin *canthus,* iron tire; see CANT[1]) + *fraindre,* to break (from Latin *frangere;* see **bhreg-** in Appendix).]

cham•fron (chăm′frən) *n.* Armor used to protect the front of a war horse's head in medieval times. [Middle English *shamfron,* from Old French *chanfrein* : Latin *cāmus,* horse-muzzle, heavy necklace (from Greek *kēmos*) + Latin *frēnum,* bridle, bit; see FRENUM.]

cha•mi•se (chə-mēz′) also **cha•mi•so** (-mē′sō) *n., pl.* **-ses** also **-sos.** An evergreen shrub, *(Adenostoma fasciculatum)* in the rose family, native to California, having small needlelike leaves in fascicles and clusters of small white flowers. [Spanish *chamisa,* from Galician *chamiça,* dry brush, firewood, from *chama,* flame, from Latin *flamma.* See FLAME.]

cham•ois (shăm′ē) *n., pl.* **cham•ois** (shăm′ēz). **1.** An extremely agile goat antelope *(Rupicapra rupicapra)* of mountainous regions of Europe, having upright horns with backward-hooked tips. **2.** Also **cham•my** or **sham•my** (shăm′ē), *pl.* **-mies. a.** A soft leather made from the hide of this animal or other animals such as deer or sheep. **b.** A piece of such leather, or a cotton fabric made to resemble it, used as a polishing cloth or in shirts. **3.** *Color.* A moderate to grayish yellow. [French, from Old French, from Late Latin *camōx.*]

chamois
Rupicapra rupicapra

cham•o•mile or **cam•o•mile** (kăm′ə-mīl′, -mēl′) *n.* **a.** An aromatic perennial herb *(Chamaemelum nobile)* in the composite family, native to Europe and the Mediterranean region, having feathery foliage and flower heads with white rays and yellow centers. **b.** A similar, related Eurasian annual plant *(Matricaria recutita).* **c.** The dried flower heads of either one of these plants, used to make an herbal tea and yielding an oil used in commercial flavorings and perfumery. [Middle English *camomille,* from Old French, from Late Latin *chamomilla,* alteration of Latin *chamaemēlon,* from Greek *khamaimēlon* : *khamai,* on the ground; see **dhghem-** in Appendix + *mēlon,* apple.]

Cha•mo•nix (shăm′ə-nē′, shä-mô-). A valley of eastern France at the foot of Mont Blanc. It is a major winter sports resort and was the site of the 1924 Winter Olympics.

champ[1] (chămp) *v.* **champed, champ•ing, champs.** *—tr.* To bite or chew upon noisily. See Synonyms at **bite.** *—intr.* To work the jaws and teeth vigorously. ***—idiom.*** **champ at the bit.** To show impatience at being held back or delayed. [Probably imitative.]

champ[2] (chămp) *n. Informal.* A champion.

cham•pagne (shăm-pān′) *n.* **1.a.** A sparkling white wine produced in Champagne. **b.** A similar sparkling wine made elsewhere. **2.** *Color.* A pale orange yellow to grayish yellow or yellowish gray. [French, short for *(vin de) Champagne,* (wine from) Champagne, from Late Latin *campānia,* flat open country. See CAMPAIGN.]

Cham•pagne (shăm-pān′, shäN-pän′yə). A historical region and former province of northeast France. It was incorporated into the French royal domain in 1314. The sparkling wine champagne was first produced here c. 1700.

cham•paign (shăm-pān′) *n.* A stretch of level and open country; a plain. [Middle English *champain,* from Old French *champainge,* from Late Latin *campānia.* See CAMPAIGN.] **—cham•paign′** *adj.*

Cham•paign (shăm-pān′). A city of east-central Illinois adjoining Urbana. It was founded in 1855 with the coming of the railroad. Population, 58,133.

cham•pak also **cham•pac** (chăm′păk, chŭm′pŭk) or **cham•pa•ca** (chăm′pə-kə, chŭm′-) *n.* An evergreen timber tree *(Michelia champaca)* native to India and having fragrant orange-yellow flowers that yield an oil used in perfumery. [Hindi *campak,* from Sanskrit *campakaḥ.*]

cham•per•ty (chăm′pər-tē) *n., pl.* **-ties.** *Law.* A sharing in the proceeds of a lawsuit by an outside party who has promoted the litigation. [Middle English *champartie,* from Old French *champart,* the lord's share of the tenant's crop, from Medieval Latin *campars, campīpars* : Latin *campī,* genitive of *campus,* field + Latin *pars,* part; see PART.] **—cham′per•tous** (-təs) *adj.*

cham•pi•gnon (shăm-pĭn′yən) *n.* An edible mushroom, especially the much cultivated species *Agaricus bisporus.* [French, alteration of Old French *champigneul,* probably from Vulgar Latin **(fungus) campiniolus,* (fungus) growing in the fields, from Late Latin *campānia,* countryside. See CAMPAIGN.]

Cham•pi•gny-sur-Marne (shäN-pē-nyē′sûr-märn′, -sür-). A city of northern France, a suburb of Paris. Population, 76,176.

cham•pi•on (chăm′pē-ən) *n.* **1.** One that wins first place or first prize in a competition. **2.** One that is clearly superior or has the attributes of a winner: *a champion at teaching.* **3.** An ardent defender or supporter of a cause or another person: *a champion of the homeless.* **4.** One who fights; a warrior. **—champion** *tr.v.* **-oned, -on•ing, -ons. 1.** To fight for, defend, or support as a champion: *championed the cause of civil rights.* See Synonyms at **support. 2.** *Obsolete.* To defy or challenge. **—champion** *adj.* **1.** Holding first place or prize: *a champion show dog.* **2.** Superior to all others: *"the champion playboy of the Western World"* (John Millington Synge). [Middle English *champioun,* combatant, athlete, from Old French *champion,* from Medieval Latin *campiō, campiōn-,* from Latin *campus,* field.]

cham•pi•on•ship (chăm′pē-ən-shĭp′) *n.* **1.** The position or title of a winner. **2.** Defense or support; advocacy: *her championship of the elderly and their rights.* **3.** A competition or series of competitions held to determine a winner.

Cham•plain (shăm-plān′), **Lake.** A lake of northeast New York, northwest Vermont, and southern Quebec, Canada. It was the site of important battles in the French and Indian War, the American Revolution, and the War of 1812.

Cham•plain (shăm-plān′, shäN-plăN′), **Samuel de.** 1567?–1635. French explorer who founded Port Royal, now Annapolis Royal, in Nova Scotia (1605) and established a settlement (1608) on the site of present-day Quebec.

champ•le•vé (shäN-lə-vā′) *n.* A technique of decorating metal in which areas that have been hollowed out, as by incising, are filled with colored enamel and fired. [French : *champ,* field (from Old French, from Latin *campus*) + *levé,* raised; see LEVEE[2].] **—champ′le•vé′** *adj.*

Cham•pol•lion (shäN-pô-lyôN′), **Jean François.** 1790–1832. French Egyptologist. Working from the Rosetta stone, he became the first person to decipher Egyptian hieroglyphics (1821).

Champs É•ly•sées (shäN zā-lē-zā′). A tree-lined thoroughfare of Paris, France, leading from the Place de la Concorde to the Arc de Triomphe.

chan. *abbr.* Channel.

chance (chăns) *n.* **1.a.** The unknown and unpredictable element in happenings that seems to have no assignable cause. **b.** A force assumed to cause events that cannot be foreseen or controlled; luck: *Chance will determine the outcome.* **2.** Often **chances.** The likelihood of something happening; possibility or probability: *Chances are good that you will win. Is there any chance of rain?* **3.** An accidental or unpredictable event. **4.** A favorable set of circumstances; an opportunity: *a chance to escape.* **5.** A risk or hazard; a gamble: *took a chance that the ice would hold me.* **6.** *Games.* A raffle or lottery ticket. **7.** *Baseball.* An opportunity to make a putout or an assist that counts as an error if unsuccessful. **—chance** *adj.* Caused by or ascribable to chance; unexpected, random, or casual: *a chance encounter; a chance result.* **—chance** *v.* **chanced, chanc•ing, chanc•es.** *—intr.* To come about by chance; occur: *It chanced that the train was late that day.* *—tr.* To take the risk or hazard of: *not willing to chance it.* ***—phrasal verb.*** **chance on** (or **upon**). To find or meet accidentally; happen upon: *While in Paris we chanced on two old friends.* ***—idioms.*** **by chance. 1.** Without plan; accidentally: *They met by chance on a plane.* **2.** Possibly; perchance: *Is he, by chance, her brother?* **on the off chance.** In the slight hope or possibility. [Middle English, unexpected event, from Old French, from Vulgar Latin **cadentia,* from Latin *cadēns, cadent-,* present participle of *cadere,* to fall, befall. See **kad-** in Appendix.]

SYNONYMS: *chance, random, casual, haphazard, desultory.* These adjectives apply to what is determined not by deliberation or method but by accident. *Chance* stresses lack of premeditation: *a chance meeting with a friend. Random* implies the absence of a specific pattern or objective and suggests a lack of direction that might or could profitably be imposed: *struck by a random shot; took a random guess. Casual* stresses lack of deliberation and often suggests an absence of due concern: *made a casual observation. Haphazard* implies a carelessness or a willful leaving to chance: *offered a haphazard plan of action. Desultory* suggests a shifting about from one thing to another that reflects a lack of method: *engaged in a desultory conversation.* See also Synonyms at **happen, opportunity.**

chance·ful (chăns′fəl) *adj.* **1.** Eventful: *spent two chanceful months in England during the war.* **2.** *Archaic.* Casual.

chan·cel (chăn′səl) *n.* The space around the altar of a church for the clergy and sometimes the choir, often enclosed by a lattice or railing. [Middle English *chauncel,* from Old French *chancel,* from Late Latin *cancellus,* latticework, sing. of Latin *cancellī.* See CANCEL.]

chan·cel·ler·y or **chan·cel·lor·y** (chăn′sə-lə-rē, -slə-rē) *n., pl.* **-ies. 1.** The rank or position of a chancellor. **2. a.** The office or department of a chancellor. **b.** The building in which such an office or department is located. **3.** The official place of business of an embassy or consulate. [Middle English *chancelrie,* from Old French *chancelerie,* from *chancelier,* chancellor. See CHANCELLOR.]

chan·cel·lor (chăn′sə-lər, -slər) *n. Abbr.* **C. 1.** Any of various officials of high rank, especially: **a.** A secretary to a monarch or noble. **b.** *Chiefly British.* The chief secretary of an embassy. **c.** The chief minister of state in some European countries. **2. a.** The president of certain American universities. **b.** *Chiefly British.* The honorary or titular head of a university. **3.** *Law.* The presiding judge of a court of chancery or equity in some U.S. states. [Middle English *chaunceler,* from Old French *chancelier,* from Late Latin *cancellārius,* doorkeeper, from Latin *cancellī,* bars, latticework. See CANCEL.] **—chan′cel·lor·ship′** *n.*

Chan·cel·lor of the Exchequer (chăn′sə-lər, -slər) *n.* The senior finance minister in the British government and a member of the prime minister's cabinet.

Chan·cel·lors·ville (chăn′sə-lərz-vĭl′, -slərz-). A former town of northeast Virginia west of Fredericksburg. It was the site of a major Civil War battle (May 2–4, 1863) in which the Confederates under Robert E. Lee defeated the Union forces commanded by Joseph Hooker.

chan·cel·lor·y (chăn′sə-lə-rē, -slə-rē) *n.* Variant of **chancellery.**

chance-med·ley (chăns′mĕd′lē) *n.* A random, haphazard action or occurrence. [Middle English *chaunce medley,* manslaughter, from Norman French *chance medlee,* mixed accident : Old French *chance,* accident; see CHANCE + Old French *medlee,* mixed; see MEDLEY.]

chan·cer·y (chăn′sə-rē) *n., pl.* **-ies. 1.** *Law.* **a.** A court of chancery. **b.** The proceedings and practice of a court of chancery; equity. **c.** A court of public record; an office of archives. **d.** One of the five divisions of the High Court of Justice of Great Britain, presided over by the Lord High Chancellor. **2.** The office or department of a chancellor; a chancellery. [Middle English *chancerie,* alteration of *chancelrie.* See CHANCELLERY.]

Chan Chan (chän′ chän′). A ruined pre-Incan city of northern Peru, probably built after A.D. 800. It may once have had a population of 200,000.

Chan·chiang (jän′jyäng′). See **Zhanjiang.**

chan·cre (shăng′kər) *n.* **1.** A dull red, hard, insensitive lesion that is the first manifestation of syphilis. **2.** An ulcer located at the initial point of entry of a pathogen. [French, from Old French, from Latin *cancer,* tumor, crab. See **kar-** in Appendix.] **—chan′crous** (-krəs) *adj.*

chan·croid (shăng′kroid′) *n.* A soft, highly infectious, nonsyphilitic venereal ulcer of the genital region, caused by the bacillus *Hemophilus ducreyi.* Also called *soft chancre.* [French *chancroïde,* from *chancre,* chancre. See CHANCRE.] **—chan′-croid′al** (-kroid′l) *adj.*

chanc·y (chăn′sē) *adj.* **-i·er, -i·est. 1.** Uncertain as to outcome; risky; hazardous. **2.** Random; haphazard. **3.** *Scots.* Lucky; propitious. **—chanc′i·ness** *n.*

chan·de·lier (shăn′də-lîr′) *n.* A branched, decorative lighting fixture that holds a number of bulbs or candles and is suspended from a ceiling. [Middle English *chandeler,* from Old French *chandelier,* from Vulgar Latin **candēlārium,* alteration of Latin *candēlābrum,* candelabrum. See CANDELABRUM.]

chan·delle (shăn-dĕl′) *n.* A sudden, steep climbing turn of an aircraft, executed to alter flight direction and gain altitude simultaneously. [French, from *chandelle,* candle, from Old French, from Latin *candēla.* See CANDLE.]

Chan·di·garh (chŭn′dē-gər, chŭn′dĭ-gŭr′). A city of northern India north of Delhi. It was laid out by a European team of architects led by Le Corbusier. Population, 373,789.

chan·dler (chănd′lər) *n.* **1.** One that makes or sells candles. **2.** A retail dealer in specified goods or equipment: *a ship chandler.* [Middle English *chaundeler,* from Old French *chandelier,* from Vulgar Latin **candēlārius,* from Latin *candēla.* See CANDLE.] **—chan′dler·y** (chănd′lə-rē) *n.*

Chan·dler (chănd′lər). A city of south-central Arizona southeast of Phoenix. It is a residential community and winter resort. Population, 29,673.

Chandler, Raymond Thornton. 1888–1959. American novelist noted for creating the character Philip Marlowe, a tough and cynical detective. His works include *The Big Sleep* (1939) and *Farewell, My Lovely* (1940).

Chan·dra·gup·ta (chŭn′drə-go͝op′tə). Died c. 297 B.C. King of northern India (322?–298) and founder of a dynasty of Hindu kings of India that ruled until c. 185 B.C.

Cha·nel (shə-nĕl′), **Gabrielle Bonheur.** Known as "Coco." 1883–1971. French fashion designer famous for her tailored suits and dresses and her line of perfumes, particularly Chanel No. 5.

Cha·ney (chā′nē), **Lon.** 1883–1930. American actor known for his performances as monsters in horror movies, particularly *The Hunchback of Notre Dame* (1923).

Chang·chow (chäng′jō′). See **Changzhou.**

Chang·chun (chäng′cho͞on′). Formerly **Hsin·king** (shĭn′-kĭng′, -gĭng′). A city of northeast China south-southwest of Harbin. It was the capital of the Japanese puppet state of Manchukuo from 1932 until 1945. Changchun is the capital of Jilin province. Population, 1,480,000.

Chan Chan

change (chānj) *v.* **changed, chang·ing, chang·es.** *—tr.* **1. a.** To cause to be different: *change the spelling of a word.* **b.** To give a completely different form or appearance to; transform: *changed the yard into a garden.* **2.** To give and receive reciprocally; interchange: *change places.* **3.** To exchange for or replace with another, usually of the same kind or category: *change one's name; a light that changes colors.* **4. a.** To lay aside, abandon, or leave for another; switch: *change methods; change sides.* **b.** To transfer from (one conveyance) to another: *change planes.* **5.** To give or receive the equivalent of (money) in lower denominations or in foreign currency. **6.** To put a fresh covering on: *change a bed; change the baby.* *—intr.* **1.** To become different or undergo alteration: *He changed as he matured.* **2.** To undergo transformation or transition: *The music changed to a slow waltz.* **3.** To go from one phase to another, as the moon or the seasons. **4.** To make an exchange: *If you prefer this seat, I'll change with you.* **5.** To transfer from one conveyance to another: *She changed in Chicago on her way to the coast.* **6.** To put on other clothing: *We changed for dinner.* **7.** To become deeper in tone: *His voice began to change at age 13.* **—change** *n.* **1.** The act, process, or result of altering or modifying: *a change in facial expression.* **2.** The replacing of one thing for another; substitution: *a change of atmosphere; a change of ownership.* **3.** A transformation or transition from one state, condition, or phase to another: *the change of seasons.* **4.** Something different; variety: *ate early for a change.* **5.** A different or fresh set of clothing. **6.** *Abbr.* **chg. a.** Money of smaller denomination given or received in exchange for money of higher denomination. **b.** The balance of money returned when an amount given is more than what is due. **c.** Coins: *had change jingling in his pocket.* **7.** *Music.* A pattern or order in which bells are rung. **8.** A market or exchange where business is transacted. ***—phrasal verb.* change off. 1.** To alternate with another person in performing a task. **2.** To perform two tasks at once by alternating or a single task by alternate means. ***—idioms.* change hands.** To pass from one owner to another. **change (one's) mind.** To reverse a previously held opinion or an earlier decision. **change (one's) tune.** To alter one's attitude. [Middle English *changen,* from Norman French *chaunger,* from Latin *cambiāre, cambīre,* to exchange, probably of Celtic origin.]

chandelier
c. 1870 American gas-burning chandelier

change·a·ble (chān′jə-bəl) *adj.* **1.** Liable to change; capricious: *changeable weather.* **2.** Being such that alteration is possible: *changeable behavior.* **3.** Varying in color or appearance when seen from different angles: *changeable silk.* **—change′a·bil′i·ty, change′a·ble·ness** *n.* **—change′a·bly** *adv.*

change·ful (chānj′fəl) *adj.* Having the tendency or ability to change; variable. **—change′ful·ly** *adv.* **—change′ful·ness** *n.*

change·less (chānj′lĭs) *adj.* Unchanging; constant.

change·ling (chānj′lĭng) *n.* **1.** A child secretly exchanged for another. **2.** *Archaic.* A changeable, fickle person. **3.** *Archaic.* A person of deficient intelligence.

change of heart *n., pl.* **changes of heart.** A reversal of one's opinion, attitude, or feelings.

change of life *n.* Menopause.

change·o·ver (chānj′ō′vər) *n.* A conversion to a different purpose or from one system to another, as in equipment or production techniques.

chang·er (chānj′ər) *n.* **1.** One that changes something: *an inveterate changer of decor.* **2.** A record changer.

change ring·ing (rĭng′ĭng) *n. Music.* The ringing of a set of chimes or bells with every possible unrepeated variation.

change·up (chānj′ŭp′) *n. Baseball.* A pitch intended to look like a fastball, which actually approaches the plate at a slow speed, thereby causing the batter to swing prematurely. [Alteration of *change-of-pace.*]

Chang Jiang (chäng′ jyäng′). See **Yangtze River.**

Chang·sha (chäng′shä′). A city of southern China on the Xiang Jiang west-southwest of Shanghai. It was founded in the early third century B.C. and was long noted as a literary center. Changsha is the capital of Hunan province. Population, 1,123,900.

ă pat	oi boy
ā pay	ou out
âr care	o͝o took
ä father	o͞o boot
ĕ pet	ŭ cut
ē be	ûr urge
ĭ pit	th thin
ī pie	*th* this
îr pier	hw which
ŏ pot	zh vision
ō toe	ə about, item
ô paw	♦ regionalism

Stress marks: ′ (primary); ′ (secondary), as in **dictionary** (dĭk′shə-nĕr′ē)

Chang·zhou also **Chang·chow** (chäng′jō′). A city of eastern China on the Grand Canal west-northwest of Shanghai. It is an industrial center in an agricultural region. Population, 425,000.

Chan·kiang (chän′kyäng′, jän′jyäng′). See **Zhanjiang.**

chan·nel[1] (chăn′əl) *n. Abbr.* **chan. 1.** The bed of a stream or river. **2.** The deeper part of a river or harbor, especially a deep navigable passage. **3.** A broad strait, especially one that connects two seas. **4.** A trench, furrow, or groove. **5.** A tubular passage for liquids; a conduit. **6.** A course or passage through which something may move or be directed: *new channels of thought; a reliable channel of information.* **7.** Often **channels.** A route of communication or access: *took her request through official channels.* **8.** *Electronics.* A specified frequency band for the transmission and reception of electromagnetic signals, as for television signals. **9.** The medium through which a spirit guide purportedly communicates with the physical world. **10.** A rolled metal bar with a bracket-shaped section. **—channel** *tr.v.* **-neled, -nel·ing, -nels** also **-nelled, -nel·ling, -nels. 1.** To make or cut channels in. **2.** To form a groove or flute in. **3.** To direct or guide along some desired course: *channels her curiosity into research.* **4.** To serve as a medium for (a spirit guide). [Middle English *chanel,* from Old French, from Latin *canālis.* See CANAL.] **—chan′nel·er** *n.*

chan·nel[2] (chăn′əl) *n. Nautical.* A wood or steel ledge projecting from a sailing ship's sides to spread the shrouds and keep them clear of the gunwales. [Alteration of obsolete *chainwale* : CHAIN + WALE.]

channel bass *n.* See **red drum.**

channel black *n.* A type of carbon black formed by exposing an iron plate to a natural gas flame and collecting the deposited soot. [From CHANNEL[1].]

channel catfish *n.* A freshwater food fish *(Ictalurus punctatus)* common to the central United States. Also called *channel cat.*

chan·nel·ing (chăn′ə-lĭng) *n.* Purported communication by a disembodied entity through a living person, as by voice during a trance.

Chan·nel Islands (chăn′əl). A group of British islands in the English Channel off the coast of Normandy, France. Settled by Norse mariners, the islands became part of the duchy of Normandy in the tenth century and passed to England with the Norman Conquest of 1066.

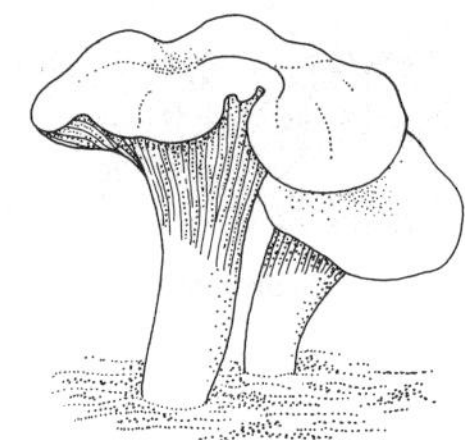
chanterelle
Cantharellus cibarius

chan·nel·ize (chăn′ə-līz′) *tr.v.* **-ized, -iz·ing, -iz·es. 1.** To make, form, or cut channels in. **2.** To direct through a channel. **—chan′nel·i·za′tion** (chăn′ə-lĭ-zā′shən) *n.*

Chan·nel·view (chăn′əl-vyo͞o′). A community of southeast Texas, a suburb of Houston. Population, 16,000.

Chan·ning (chăn′ĭng), **Edward.** 1856–1931. American historian whose major work was *A History of the United States* (six volumes, 1905–1925).

Channing, William Ellery. 1780–1842. American religious leader whose writings and sermons led to the emergence of Unitarianism.

cha·no·yu (chä′nô-yo͞o′) *n.* The Japanese tea ceremony, an ancient ritual for the preparation, serving, and drinking of tea. [Japanese : *cha,* tea + *no,* possessive particle + *yu,* hot water.]

chan·son (shäN-sôN′) *n., pl.* **-sons** (-sôN′, -sônz′). *Music.* A song, especially a French cabaret song. [French, from Old French, from Latin *cantiō, cantiōn-,* from *cantus,* past participle of *canāre,* to sing. See CHANT.]

chanson de geste (də zhĕst′) *n., pl.* **chansons de geste.** Any of more than 80 Old French epic poems of the 11th to the 14th centuries celebrating the deeds of historical or legendary figures, especially the exploits of Charlemagne and his successors. [French : *chanson,* song + *de,* of + *geste,* heroic exploit.]

chapel
Restored chapel,
Fort Ross, California

chant (chănt) *n.* **1.** *Music.* **a.** A short, simple melody in which a number of syllables or words are sung on or intoned to the same note. **b.** A canticle or prayer sung or intoned in this manner. **c.** A song or melody. **2.** A monotonous rhythmic call or shout, as of a slogan: *the chant of the crowd at the rally.* **—chant** *v.* **chant·ed, chant·ing, chants.** —*tr.* **1.** *Music.* To sing or intone to a chant: *chant a prayer.* **2.** *Music.* To celebrate in song: *chanting a hero's deeds.* **3.** To say in the manner of a chant: *chanted defiant slogans.* —*intr.* **1.** *Music.* To sing, especially in the manner of a chant: *chanted while a friend jumped rope.* **2.** To speak monotonously. [Probably from French, song, from Old French, from Latin *cantus,* from past participle of *canere,* to sing. V., from Middle English *chaunten,* to sing, from Old French *chanter,* from Latin *cantāre,* frequentative of *canere.* See **kan-** in Appendix.] **—chant′ing·ly** *adv.*

chant·er (chăn′tər) *n.* **1.** *Music.* A person, such as a chorister, who chants. **2.** *Music.* The pipe of a bagpipe on which the melody is played. **3.** A priest who sings in a chantry.

chan·te·relle (shăn′tə-rĕl′, shän′-) *n.* An edible mushroom *(Cantharellus cibarius)* that is yellow to orange in color, trumpet-shaped, and sometimes fragrant. [French, from New Latin *cantharella,* feminine diminutive of Latin *cantharus,* cup (from its shape), from Greek *kantharos.*]

chan·teuse (shäN-tœz′) *n. Music.* A woman singer, especially a nightclub singer. [French, feminine of *chanteur,* singer, from *chanter,* to sing. See CHANT.]

chan·tey also **chan·ty** (shăn′tē, chăn′-) or **shan·tey** or **shan·ty** (shăn′tē) *n., pl.* **-teys** also **-ties.** *Music.* A song sung by sailors to the rhythm of their movements while working. [Probably from French *chantez,* imperative pl. of *chanter,* to sing, from Old French. See CHANT.]

chan·ti·cleer (chăn′tĭ-klîr′, shăn′-) *n.* A rooster. [Middle English *chauntecler,* from Old French *chantecler,* the name of the rooster in the tale of Reynard the Fox : *chanter,* to sing; see CHANT + *cler,* clear; see CLEAR.]

Chan·til·ly (shăn-tĭl′ē, shäN-tē-yē′). A village of northern France north of Paris. It was long noted for its fine porcelain and delicate lace. Population, 10,065.

chan·try (chăn′trē) *n., pl.* **-tries.** *Ecclesiastical.* **1.** An endowment to cover expenses for the saying of masses and prayers, usually for the soul of the founder of the endowment. **2.** An altar or chapel endowed for the saying of such masses and prayers. [Middle English *chanterie,* from Old French, from *chanter,* to sing. See CHANT.]

chan·ty (shăn′tē, chăn′-) *n. Music.* Variant of **chantey.**

Cha·nu·kah (KHä′nə-kə, hä′-) *n.* Variant of **Hanukkah.**

Chao K'uang-yin (jou′ kwäng′yĭn′). See **Zhao Kuangyin.**

Chao Phra·ya (chou prä-yä′). A river of Thailand formed by the Nan and Ping rivers and flowing about 225 km (140 mi) southward past Bangkok to the Gulf of Thailand.

cha·os (kā′ŏs′) *n.* **1.** A condition or place of great disorder or confusion. **2.** A disorderly mass; a jumble: *The desk was a chaos of papers and unopened letters.* **3.** Often **Chaos.** The disordered state of unformed matter and infinite space supposed in some cosmogonic views to have existed before the ordered universe. **4.** *Obsolete.* An abyss; a chasm. [Middle English, formless primordial space, from Latin, from Greek *khaos.*] **—cha·ot′ic** (-ŏt′ĭk) *adj.* **—cha·ot′i·cal·ly** *adv.*

Chao Tzu-yang (jou′ dzo͞o-yäng′). See **Zhao Ziyang.**

chap[1] (chăp) *v.* **chapped, chap·ping, chaps.** —*tr.* To cause (the skin) to roughen, redden, or crack, especially as a result of cold or exposure: *The headwind chapped the cyclist's lips.* —*intr.* To split or become rough and sore: *skin that chaps easily in winter.* **—chap** *n.* A sore roughening or splitting of the skin, caused especially by cold or exposure. [Middle English *chappen.*]

chap[2] (chăp) *n. Informal.* A man or boy; a fellow. [Short for CHAPMAN.]

chap. *abbr.* Chapter.

Cha·pa·la (chə-pä′lə). A lake of west-central Mexico southeast of Guadalajara. It is the largest lake in the country and a popular resort area.

chap·ar·ral (shăp′ə-răl′) *n.* **1.** *Ecology.* A biome characterized by hot, dry summers and cool, moist winters and dominated by a dense growth of mostly small-leaved evergreen shrubs, as that found in the foothills of California. **2.** A dense thicket of shrubs and small trees. [Spanish, from *chaparro,* evergreen oak, from Basque *txapar,* diminutive of *saphar,* thicket.]

chaparral bird *n.* See **roadrunner.**

chaparral cock *n.* See **roadrunner.**

cha·pa·ti also **cha·pat·ti** (chə-pä′tē) *n.* A traditional flat, disk-shaped bread of northern India, made of wheat flour, water, and salt. [Hindi *capātī.*]

chap·book (chăp′bo͝ok′) *n.* A small book or pamphlet containing poems, ballads, stories, or religious tracts. [CHAP(MAN) + BOOK (so called because it was originally sold by chapmen).]

chape (chāp, chăp) *n.* A metal tip or mounting on a scabbard or sheath. [Middle English, from Old French, hood, head covering, from Late Latin *cappa,* hooded cloak.]

cha·peau (shă-pō′) *n., pl.* **-peaus** or **-peaux** (-pōz′). A hat. [French, from Old French *chapel,* from Vulgar Latin *cappellus,* diminutive of Late Latin *cappa,* hooded cloak.]

chap·el (chăp′əl) *n.* **1.a.** A place of worship that is smaller than and subordinate to a church. **b.** A place of worship in an institution, such as a prison, college, or hospital. **c.** A recess or room in a church set apart for special or small services. **d.** A place of worship for those not belonging to an established church. **e.** The services held at a chapel: *Students attend chapel each morning.* **2.** *Music.* A choir or orchestra connected with a place of worship at a royal court. **3.a.** A funeral home. **b.** A room in a funeral home used for conducting funeral services. [Middle English *chapele,* from Old French, from Medieval Latin *capella,* chapel, canopy, cape (perhaps from a shrine containing the cape of St. Martin of Tours), diminutive of *capa,* from Late Latin *cappa,* hooded cloak.]

Chap·el Hill (chăp′əl). A town of north-central North Carolina at the edge of the Piedmont west-northwest of Raleigh. It is the seat of the University of North Carolina (chartered 1789). Population, 32,421.

chap·er·on or **chap·er·one** (shăp′ə-rōn′) —*n.* **1.** A person, especially an older or married woman, who accompanies a young unmarried woman in public. **2.** An older person who attends and supervises a social gathering for young people. **3.** A guide or companion whose purpose is to ensure propriety or restrict activity: *"to see and feel the rough edges of the society . . . without the filter of official chaperones"* (Philip Taubman). —*tr.v.* **-oned, -on·ing, -ones.** To act as chaperon to or for. See Synonyms at **accompany.** [French, from *chaperon,* hood, from Old French, diminutive of *chape,* cape, head covering. See CHAPE.] **—chap′er·on′age** (-rō′nĭj) *n.*

WORD HISTORY: The chaperon at a high-school dance seems to have little relationship to what was first signified by the English word *chaperon,* "a hood for a hawk," and not even that much to what the word later meant, "a protectress of a young single woman." The sense "hood for a hawk," recorded in a Middle English text composed before 1400, reflects the original meaning of the Old French word *chaperon,* "hood, headgear." In order to understand why our *chaperon* came to have the sense "protectress," we need to know that in French the verb *chaperonner,* meaning "to cover with a hood," was derived from *chaperon* and that this verb subsequently developed the figurative sense "to protect." Under the influence of the verb sense the French noun *chaperon* came to mean "escort," a meaning that was borrowed into English, being found first in a work published in 1720. In its earlier use English *chaperon* referred to a person, commonly an older woman, who accompanied a young unmarried woman in public to protect her. The English verb *chaperon,* "to be a chaperon," is first recorded in Jane Austen's *Sense and Sensibility,* begun in 1796 as a sketch called "Elinor and Marianne" and published as a novel in 1811.

---

chap·fall·en (chăp′fô′lən) also **chop·fall·en** (chŏp′-) *adj.* Being in low spirits; dejected and disheartened. [From obsolete *chaps,* alteration of CHOPS.]

chap·i·ter (chăp′ĭ-tər) *n. Architecture.* The capital of a column. [Middle English *chapitre,* chapter, chapiter. See CHAPTER.]

chap·lain (chăp′lĭn) *n. Abbr.* **Ch., ch. 1.** A member of the clergy attached to a chapel. **2.a.** A member of the clergy who conducts religious services for an institution, such as a prison or hospital. **b.** A member of the clergy who is connected with a royal court or an aristocratic household. **3.** A member of the clergy attached to a branch of the armed forces. [Middle English *chapelein,* from Old French *chapelain,* from Medieval Latin *capellānus,* from *capella,* chapel. See CHAPEL.] **—chap′lain·cy, chap′lain·ship′** *n.*

chap·let (chăp′lĭt) *n.* **1.** A wreath or garland for the head. **2.** *Roman Catholic Church.* **a.** A rosary having beads for five decades of Hail Marys. **b.** The prayers counted on such a rosary. **3.** A string of beads. **4.** *Architecture.* A small molding carved to resemble a string of beads. [Middle English *chapelet,* from Old French, diminutive of *chapel,* hat, wreath. See CHAPEAU.] **—chap′let·ed** *adj.*

Chap·lin (chăp′lĭn), Sir **Charles Spencer.** Known as "Charlie." 1889–1977. British-born actor, director, and producer who gained fame for his role as a tramp in baggy trousers and a bowler hat. His productions include *The Kid* (1921), *The Gold Rush* (1925), and *City Lights* (1931).

chap·man (chăp′mən) *n.* **1.** *Chiefly British.* A peddler. **2.** *Archaic.* A dealer or merchant. [Middle English, from Old English *cēapman* : *cēap,* trade; see CHEAP + *man, mann,* man; see MAN.]

Chap·man (chăp′mən), **Frank Michler.** 1864–1945. American ornithologist who was curator of ornithology (1908–1942) at the American Museum of Natural History in New York City and compiled a number of bird studies, including *A Color Key to North American Birds* (1903).

Chapman, George. 1559?–1634. English writer, dramatist, and translator noted for his translations of Homer's *Iliad* (1598–1611) and *Odyssey* (1616).

Chapman, John. Known as "Johnny Appleseed." 1775?–1845. American pioneer and subject of many legends. He traveled widely in the Ohio River valley, planting apple seeds and pruning apple trees.

chaps (chăps, shăps) *pl.n.* Heavy leather trousers without a seat, worn over ordinary trousers by ranch hands to protect their legs. [Short for American Spanish *chaparreras,* from Spanish *chaparro,* chaparral. See CHAPARRAL.]

Chap Stick (chăp). A trademark used for a medicinal preparation for the prevention or treatment of chapped lips.

chap·ter (chăp′tər) *n. Abbr.* **chap., ch., c., C. 1.** One of the main divisions of a relatively lengthy piece of writing, such as a book, that is usually numbered or titled. **2.** A distinct period or sequence of events, as in history or a person's life: *Steamboat travel opened a new chapter in America's exploration of the West.* **3.** A local branch of an organization, such as a club or fraternity: *The Chicago chapter is admitting new members this year.* **4.** *Ecclesiastical.* **a.** An assembly of the canons of a church or of the members of a religious residence. **b.** The canons of a church or the members of a religious residence considered as a group. **5.** A short Scriptural passage read after the psalms in certain church services. [Middle English *chaptre,* variant of *chapitre,* chapter, chapiter, from Old French, alteration of *chapitle,* from Latin *capitulum,* diminutive of *caput,* head. See **kaput-** in Appendix.]

chapter and verse *n.* **1.** Full, detailed information on a subject or an issue: *recited the client's complaints by chapter and verse.* **2.** *Bible.* A specific passage.

chapter house *n.* **1.** A building in which the chapter of a church or religious residence assembles. **2.** A house in which a chapter of a fraternity or sorority lives and holds its meetings.

Cha·pul·te·pec (chə-po͝ol′tə-pĕk′). A rocky hill south of Mexico City, Mexico. It was the site of a major American victory (September 12–13, 1847) during the Mexican War.

char¹ (chär) *v.* **charred, char·ring, chars.** *—tr.* **1.** To burn the surface of; scorch. **2.** To reduce to carbon or charcoal by incomplete combustion. *—intr.* **1.** To become scorched. **2.** To become reduced to carbon or charcoal. See Synonyms at **burn¹**. **—char** *n.* A substance that has been scorched, burned, or reduced to charcoal. [Back-formation from CHARCOAL.]

char² also **charr** (chär) *n., pl.* **char** or **chars** also **charr** or **charrs.** Any of several fishes of the genus *Salvelinus,* especially the arctic char, related to the trout and salmon. [Origin unknown.]

char³ (chär) *Chiefly British. n.* A charwoman. **—char** *intr.v.* **charred, char·ring, chars.** To work as a charwoman. [Middle English, a piece of work, from Old English *cierr,* a turning.]

char. *abbr.* Charter.

char·a·banc (shăr′ə-băng′) *n. Chiefly British.* A large bus, typically used for sightseeing. [From French *char à bancs* : *char,* coach, carriage (from Old French, cart; see CHARIOT) + *à,* with (from Latin *ad,* toward; see AD–) + *bancs,* benches, pl. of *banc* (from Old French; see BANK³).]

char·a·cin (kăr′ə-sĭn) also **char·a·cid** (-sĭd) *n.* See **tetra.** [From New Latin *Characinidae,* former family name, from Greek *kharax, kharak-,* a kind of fish.]

char·ac·ter (kăr′ək-tər) *n.* **1.** The combination of qualities or features that distinguishes one person, group, or thing from another. See Synonyms at **disposition. 2.** A distinguishing feature or attribute, as of an individual, a group, or a category. See Synonyms at **quality, type. 3.** *Genetics.* A structure, function, or attribute determined by a gene or group of genes. **4.** Moral or ethical strength. **5.** A description of a person's attributes, traits, or abilities. **6.** A formal written statement as to competency and dependability, given by an employer to a former employee; a recommendation. **7.** Public estimation of someone; reputation: *personal attacks that damaged her character.* **8.** Status or role; capacity: *in his character as the father.* **9.a.** A notable or well-known person; a personage. **b.** A person, especially one who is peculiar or eccentric: *a shady character; catcalls from some character in the back row.* **10.a.** A person portrayed in an artistic piece, such as a drama or novel. **b.** Characterization in fiction or drama: *a script that is weak in plot but strong in character.* **11.** A mark or symbol used in a writing system. **12.** *Computer Science.* **a.** One of a set of symbols, such as letters or numbers, that are arranged to express information. **b.** The multi-bit code representing such a character. **13.** A style of printing or writing. **14.** A symbol used in secret writing; a cipher or code. **—character** *adj.* **1.** Of or relating to one's character. **2.a.** Specializing in the interpretation of often minor roles that emphasize fixed personality traits or specific physical characteristics: *a character actor.* **b.** Of or relating to the interpretation of such roles by an actor: *the character part of the hero's devoted mother.* **3.** Dedicated to the portrayal of a person with regard to distinguishing psychological or physical features: *a character sketch.* **4.** *Law.* Of or relating to a person who gives testimony as to the moral and ethical reputation or behavior of one engaged in a lawsuit: *a character witness.* **—character** *tr.v.* **-tered, -ter·ing, -ters.** *Archaic.* **1.** To write, print, engrave, or inscribe. **2.** To portray or describe. ***—idioms.*** **in character.** Consistent with someone's general character or behavior: *behavior that was totally in character.* **out of character.** Inconsistent with someone's general character or behavior: *a response so much out of character that it amazed me.* [Middle English *carecter,* distinctive mark, imprint on the soul, from Old French *caractere,* from Latin *charactēr,* from Greek *kharaktēr,* from *kharassein,* to inscribe, from *kharax,* pointed stick.] **—char′ac·ter·less** *adj.*

character assassination *n.* A vicious personal verbal attack, especially one intended to destroy or damage a public figure's reputation. **—character assassin** *n.*

char·ac·ter·ful (kăr′ək-tər-fəl) *adj.* Having or displaying remarkable, memorable character: *"It was easy to forget what a sensitive and characterful performance he could deliver"* (Charles Champlin).

char·ac·ter·is·tic (kăr′ək-tə-rĭs′tĭk) *adj.* Being a feature that helps to distinguish a person or thing; distinctive: *heard my friend's characteristic laugh; the stripes that are characteristic of the zebra.* **—characteristic** *n.* **1.** A feature that helps to identify, tell apart, or describe recognizably; a distinguishing mark or trait. **2.** *Mathematics.* The integral part of a logarithm as distinguished from the mantissa: *The characteristic of the logarithm 6.3214 is 6.* **—char′ac·ter·is′ti·cal·ly** *adv.*

char·ac·ter·i·za·tion (kăr′ək-tər-ĭ-zā′shən) *n.* **1.** The act or an instance of characterizing. **2.** A description of qualities or peculiarities: *a list of places of interest, with brief characterizations of each.* **3.** Representation of a character or characters on the stage or in writing, especially by imitating or describing actions, gestures, or speeches.

char·ac·ter·ize (kăr′ək-tə-rīz′) *tr.v.* **-ized, -iz·ing, -iz·es. 1.** To describe the qualities or peculiarities of: *characterized the warden as ruthless.* **2.** To be a distinctive trait or mark of; distinguish: *the rash and high fever that characterize this disease; a region that is characterized by its dikes and canals.* **—char′ac·ter·iz′er** *n.*

char·ac·ter·y (kăr′ək-tə-rē, kə-răk′-) *n., pl.* **-ies.** A system of characters or symbols used to express or convey thought and meaning.

cha·rade (shə-rād′) *n.* **1.** *Games.* **a. charades** *(used with a sing. or pl. verb).* A game in which words or phrases are represented in pantomime, sometimes syllable by syllable, until they are guessed by the other players. **b.** An episode in this game or a word or phrase so represented. **2.** A readily perceived pretense;

Charlie Chaplin
In character as *The Tramp*

ă pat	oi boy
ā pay	ou out
âr care	o͝o took
ä father	o͞o boot
ĕ pet	ŭ cut
ē be	ûr urge
ĭ pit	th thin
ī pie	*th* this
îr pier	hw which
ŏ pot	zh vision
ō toe	ə about, item
ô paw	♦ regionalism

Stress marks: ′ (primary); ′ (secondary), as in **dictionary** (dĭk′shə-nĕr′ē)

a travesty: *went through the charade of a public apology.* [French, probably from Provençal *charrado,* chat, from *charra,* to chat, chatter, perhaps from Italian *ciarlare.*]

char•broil (chär′broil′) *tr.v.* **-broiled, -broil•ing, -broils.** To broil over charcoal: *charbroil a steak.* [CHAR[1] + BROIL[1].]

char•coal (chär′kōl′) *n.* **1.** A black, porous, carbonaceous material, 85 to 98 percent carbon, produced by the destructive distillation of wood and used as a fuel, filter, and absorbent. **2. a.** A drawing pencil or crayon made from this material. **b.** A drawing executed with such a pencil or crayon. **3.** *Color.* A dark grayish brown to black or dark purplish gray. **—charcoal** *tr.v.* **-coaled, -coal•ing, -coals. 1.** To draw, write, or blacken with a black, carbonaceous material. **2.** To charbroil. [Middle English *charcol* : *char* (perhaps from Old French *charbon,* from Latin *carbō;* see CARBON) + *col,* charcoal, coal; see COAL.]

Char•cot (shär-kō′), **Jean Baptiste Étienne Auguste.** 1867–1936. French explorer who led two missions to the Antarctic (1903–1905 and 1908–1910).

Charcot, Jean Martin. 1825–1893. French neurologist known for his research into diseases of the nervous system.

char•cu•ter•ie (shär-ko͞o′tə-rē′, -ko͞o′tə-rē) *n.* **1.** Sausages, ham, pâtés, and other cooked or processed meat foods. **2.** A delicatessen specializing in such foods. [French, from *chaircuicterie* : *chair,* meat (from Latin *carō,* flesh; see CARNAGE) + *cuict, cuit,* cooked (from Latin *coctus,* past participle of *coquere;* see COOK).]

chard (chärd) *n.* Swiss chard. [Alteration (possibly influenced by French *chardon,* thistle) of French *carde,* from Provençal *cardon,* cardoon. See CARDOON.]

char•don•nay also **Char•don•nay** (shär′dn-ā′, shär′dn-ā′) *n.* A dry white table wine, originally from Burgundy, France.

Cha•rente (shə-ränt′, shä-räɴt′). A river of France rising in the foothills of the Massif Central and flowing about 354 km (220 mi) westward to the Bay of Biscay.

charge (chärj) *v.* **charged, charg•ing, charg•es.** *—tr.* **1.** To impose a duty, responsibility, or obligation on: *charged him with the task of watching the young swimmers.* **2.** To set or ask (a given amount) as a price: *charges ten dollars for a haircut.* **3.** To hold financially liable; demand payment from: *charged her for the balance due.* **4.** To postpone payment on (a purchase) by recording as a debt: *paid cash for the stockings but charged the new coat.* **5. a.** To load to capacity; fill: *charge a furnace with coal.* **b.** To saturate; impregnate: *The atmosphere was charged with tension.* **6.** To load (a gun or other firearm) with a quantity of explosive: *charged the musket with powder.* **7.** To instruct or urge authoritatively; command: *charged her not to reveal the source of information.* **8.** *Law.* To instruct (a jury) about the law, its application, and the weighing of evidence. **9.** To make a claim of wrongdoing against; accuse or blame: *The police charged him with car theft. Critics charged the writer with a lack of originality.* **10.** To put the blame for; attribute or impute: *charged the accident to the driver's inexperience.* **11.** To attack violently: *The troops charged the enemy line.* **12.** *Electricity.* **a.** To cause formation of a net electric charge on or in (a conductor, for example). **b.** To energize (a storage battery) by passing current through it in the direction opposite to discharge. **13.** To excite; rouse: *a speaker who knows how to charge up a crowd.* **14.** To direct or put (a weapon) into position for use; level. **15.** *Heraldry.* To place a bearing on. *—intr.* **1.** To rush forward in or as if in a violent attack: *dogs trained to charge at intruders; children charging through the house.* **2.** To demand or ask payment: *did not charge for the second cup of coffee.* **3.** To postpone payment for a purchase. **4.** *Accounting.* To consider or record as a loss. Often used with *off.* **—charge** *n.* **1.** *Abbr.* **chg. a.** Expense; cost. **b.** The price asked for something: *no charge for window-shopping.* **2. a.** A weight or burden; a load: *a freighter relieved of its charge of cargo.* **b.** The quantity that a container or apparatus can hold. **3.** A quantity of explosive to be set off at one time. **4.** An assigned duty or task; a responsibility: *The commission's charge was to determine the facts.* **5.** One that is entrusted to another's care or management: *the baby sitter's three young charges.* **6. a.** Supervision; management: *the scientist who had overall charge of the research project.* **b.** Care; custody: *a child put in my charge.* **7.** An order, a command, or an injunction. **8.** *Law.* Instruction given by a judge to a jury about the law, its application, and the weighing of evidence. **9.** A claim of wrongdoing; an accusation: *a charge of murder; pleaded not guilty to the charges.* **10. a.** A rushing, forceful attack: *repelled the charge of enemy troops; the charge of a herd of elephants.* **b.** The command to attack: *The bugler sounded the charge.* **11.** *Abbr.* **chg.** A debt or an entry in an account recording a debt: *Are you paying cash or is this a charge?* **12.** *Abbr.* **chg.** A financial burden, such as a tax or lien. **13.** *Symbol* **q** *Physics.* **a.** The intrinsic property of matter responsible for all electric phenomena, in particular for the force of the electromagnetic interaction, occurring in two forms arbitrarily designated *negative* and *positive.* **b.** A measure of this property. **c.** The net measure of this property possessed by a body or contained in a bounded region of space. **14.** *Informal.* A feeling of pleasant excitement; a thrill: *got a real charge out of the movie.* **15.** *Heraldry.* A bearing or figure. **—*idioms.* in charge. 1.** In a position of leadership or supervision: *the security agent in charge at the airport.* **2.** *Chiefly British.* Under arrest. **in charge of.** Having control over or responsibility for: *You're in charge of making the salad.* [Middle English *chargen,* to load, from Old French *chargier,* from Late Latin *carricāre,* from Latin *carrus,* cart, of Celtic origin. See **kers-** in Appendix.]

chariot
Late sixth-century B.C. bronze Etruscan ceremonial chariot

SYNONYMS: *charge, freight, imbue, impregnate, permeate, pervade, saturate, suffuse.* The central meaning shared by these verbs is "to cause to be filled with a particular mood or tone": *an atmosphere charged with excitement; a pause freighted with meaning; poetry imbued with grace; a spirit impregnated with lofty ideals; optimism that permeates a group; letters pervaded with gloom; a novel saturated with imagination; a heart suffused with love.* See also Synonyms at **care, price.**

charge•a•ble (chär′jə-bəl) *adj.* **1.** Suitable to be charged, as to an account: *chargeable expenses.* **2.** Liable to be accused or indicted. **—charge′a•ble•ness** *n.*

charge account *n.* A credit arrangement in which a customer receives purchased goods or services before paying for them.

charge card *n.* See **credit card.**

charge conjugation *n.* *Symbol* **C** *Physics.* **1.** A mathematical operator that changes the sign of the charge and of the magnetic moment of every particle in the system to which it is applied. **2.** The theoretical conversion of matter to antimatter or of antimatter to matter.

charge-coup•led device (chärj′kŭp′əld) *n.* A device made up of semiconductors arranged in such a way that the electric charge output of one semiconductor charges an adjacent one.

char•gé d'af•faires (shär-zhā′ də-fâr′, dä-) *n., pl.* **char•gés d'affaires** (-zhā′, -zhāz′). **1.** A diplomat who temporarily substitutes for an absent ambassador or minister. **2.** A diplomat of the lowest rank, accredited by one government to the minister of foreign affairs of another. [French : *chargé,* charged, in charge + *de,* with, of + *affaires,* affairs.]

charge density *n.* The electric charge per unit area or per unit volume of a body or of a region of space.

charged particle (chärjd) *n.* An elementary particle, such as a proton or an electron, with a positive or negative electric charge.

charg•er[1] (chär′jər) *n.* **1.** One that charges, such as an instrument that charges or replenishes storage batteries. **2.** A horse trained for battle; a cavalry horse.

charg•er[2] (chär′jər) *n.* A large shallow dish; a platter. [Middle English *chargeour,* from Old French *chargeor,* from *chargier,* to load. See CHARGE.]

Cha•ri (shä′rē, shä-rē′). See **Shari.**

Char•ing Cross (chăr′ĭng). A district of London, England, where Edward I erected (c. 1290) the last of a series of crosses in memory of his wife, Eleanor of Castile.

char•i•ot (chăr′ē-ət) *n.* **1.** An ancient horse-drawn two-wheeled vehicle used in war, races, and processions. **2.** A light four-wheeled carriage used for occasions of ceremony or for pleasure. **—chariot** *tr. & intr.v.* **-ot•ed, -ot•ing, -ots.** To convey or ride in a chariot. [Middle English, vehicle, from Old French, from *char,* cart, from Latin *carrus,* of Celtic origin. See **kers-** in Appendix.]

char•i•o•teer (chăr′ē-ə-tîr′) *n.* The driver of a chariot.

Char•i•o•teer (chăr′ē-ə-tîr) *n.* See **Auriga.**

char•ism (kăr′ĭz′əm) *n.* *Theology.* Charisma.

cha•ris•ma (kə-rĭz′mə) *n., pl.* **-ma•ta** (-mə-tə). **1. a.** A rare personal quality attributed to leaders who arouse fervent popular devotion and enthusiasm. **b.** Personal magnetism or charm: *a television news program famed for the charisma of its anchors.* **2.** *Theology.* An extraordinary power, such as the ability to perform miracles, granted to a Christian by the Holy Spirit. [Greek *kharisma,* divine favor, from *kharizesthai,* to favor, from *kharis,* favor. See **gher-[2]** in Appendix.]

char•is•mat•ic (kăr′ĭz-măt′ĭk) *adj.* **1.** Of, relating to, or characterized by charisma: *"the warmth of a naturally charismatic leader"* (Joyce Carol Oates). **2.** *Theology.* Of, relating to, or being a type of Christianity that emphasizes personal religious experience and divinely inspired powers, as of healing, prophecy, and the gift of tongues. **—charismatic** *n.* *Theology.* A member of a Christian charismatic group or movement.

char•i•ta•ble (chăr′ĭ-tə-bəl) *adj.* **1.** Generous in giving money or other help to the needy. **2.** Mild or tolerant in judging others; lenient. **3.** Of, for, or concerned with charity: *a charitable organization.* See Synonyms at **benevolent. —char′i•ta•ble•ness** *n.* **—char′i•ta•bly** *adv.*

Char•i•ton (shăr′ĭ-tn). A river rising in southern Iowa and flowing about 451 km (280 mi) east then south to the Missouri River in northern Missouri.

char•i•ty (chăr′ĭ-tē) *n., pl.* **-ties. 1.** Provision of help or relief to the poor; almsgiving. **2.** Something given to help the needy; alms. **3.** An institution, an organization, or a fund established to help the needy. **4.** Benevolence or generosity toward others or toward humanity. **5.** Indulgence or forbearance in judging others. See Synonyms at **mercy. 6.** Often **Charity.** *Theology.* The virtue defined as love directed first toward God but also toward oneself and one's neighbors as objects of God's love. [Middle English *charite,* from Old French, Christian love, from Latin *cāritās,* affection, from *cārus,* dear. See **kā-** in Appendix.]

♦ **cha•ri•va•ri** (shĭv′ə-rē′, shĭv′ə-rē′) *n., pl.* **-ris.** See **shivaree.** See Regional Note at **shivaree.** [French, from Old French, perhaps from Late Latin *carībaria,* headache, from Greek *karēbaria* : *karē,* head; see **ker-[1]** in Appendix + *barus,* heavy; see **g^werə-[1]** in Appendix.]

char•kha also **char•ka** (chûr′kə, chär′-) *n.* A spinning wheel used in India for spinning cotton. [Hindustani *carkhā,* from Persian *charkha,* diminutive of *charkh,* wheel, from Old Persian **carka-.* See **kʷel-¹** in Appendix.]

char·la·tan (shär′lə-tən) *n.* A person who makes elaborate, fraudulent, and often voluble claims to skill or knowledge; a quack or fraud. See Synonyms at **impostor.** [French, from Italian *ciarlatano,* probably alteration (influenced by *ciarlare,* to prattle) of *cerretano,* inhabitant of *Cerreto,* a city of Italy once famous for its quacks.] **—char′la·tan′ic** (-tăn′ĭk), **char′la·tan′i·cal** *adj.* **—char′la·tan·ism, char′la·tan·ry** *n.*

WORD HISTORY: A charlatan and chatter are inseparable, even perhaps in the etymology of *charlatan.* According to one explanation, *charlatan* goes back through French to Italian *ciarlatano,* "mountebank, fraud," from the word *ciarlare,* "to chatter." Another explanation would derive *charlatan* from the Italian word *cerretano,* "an inhabitant of Cerreto, a quack," the village of Cerreto being noted for its charlatans. It seems, however, that both *ciarlare* and *cerretano* have been involved in the formation of the Italian word. The first example of the English word and of its earliest recorded sense, "huckster, especially of medicines, who gives his pitch to a crowd; mountebank," is found in 1618. The sense familiar to us, "a person pretending to skill or knowledge," is first recorded in 1809.

Char·le·magne (shär′lə-măn′). 742?–814. King of the Franks (768–814) and founder of the first empire in western Europe after the fall of Rome. His court at Aix-la-Chapelle became the center of the Carolingian Renaissance.

Char·le·roi (shär′lə-roi′, shär-lə-rwä′). A city of southern Belgium south of Brussels. It was founded in 1666 and is now a commercial center and rail junction. Population, 216,144.

Charles (chärlz) Prince of Wales. Born 1948. The eldest son of Elizabeth II and heir to the British throne. He was invested as Prince of Wales in 1969.

Charles I¹. 1600–1649. King of England, Scotland, and Ireland (1625–1649). His power struggles with Parliament resulted in the English Civil War (1642–1648) in which Charles was defeated. He was tried for treason and beheaded in 1649.

Charles I². 1887–1922. Emperor of Austria (1916–1918) and king of Hungary as Charles IV (1916–1918). Deposed after World War I, he twice failed to regain the Hungarian throne (1921).

Charles I³. See **Charlemagne.**

Charles II. 1630–1685. King of England, Scotland, and Ireland (1660–1685) who reigned during the Restoration.

Charles V. 1500–1558. Holy Roman emperor (1519–1558) and king of Spain as Charles I (1516–1556). He summoned the Diet of Worms (1521) and the Council of Trent (1545–1563).

Charles VII. 1403–1461. King of France (1422–1461). He ended the Hundred Years' War (1453) by driving the English from most of France.

Charles IX. 1550–1574. King of France (1560–1574). His mother, Catherine de Médicis, controlled most of his decisions and persuaded him to order the massacre of French Protestants on Saint Bartholomew's Day in 1752.

Charles X. 1757–1836. King of France (1824–1830) who attempted to restore absolutism by dissolving the Chamber of Deputies and terminating freedom of the press. He abdicated as a result of the July Revolution of 1830 and later fled to England.

Charles XIV. Originally Jean Baptiste Jules Bernadotte. 1763–1844. King of Sweden and Norway (1818–1844). He served under Napoleon Bonaparte in the Italian campaign (1796–1797) and was elected crown prince in 1810, founding the present Swedish royal dynasty.

Charles, Jacques Alexandre César. 1746–1823. French physicist and inventor who formulated Charles's law (1787) and was the first to use hydrogen in balloons (1783).

Charles, Ray. Born 1930. American musician and composer whose songs, such as "I Can't Stop Loving You," are rooted in gospel music, blues, and jazz.

Charles·bourg (chärlz′bûrg′, shärl-bo͝or′). A city of southern Quebec, Canada, near Quebec City. It was settled in 1659. Population, 68,326.

Charles Ed·ward Stu·art (ĕd′wərd sto͞o′ərt, styo͞o′-). See Charles Edward **Stuart.**

Charles Mar·tel (mär-tĕl′). Known as "the Hammer." 688?–741. Frankish ruler of Austrasia (715–741) who in 732 halted the European invasion of the Moors. His grandson was Charlemagne.

Charles River. A river, about 97 km (60 mi) long, of eastern Massachusetts flowing into Boston harbor and separating Boston from Cambridge.

Charles's law (chärl′zĭz) *n.* The physical law that the volume of a fixed mass of gas held at a constant pressure varies directly with the absolute temperature. [After Jacques Alexandre César CHARLES.]

Charles's Wain *n.* See **Big Dipper.** [Middle English *charleswen,* Charles' (Charlemagne's) wain, probably reinterpreted from Old English *carles wægn,* churl's wain : *carl,* churl (from Old Norse *karl*) + *wægn,* wain; see WAIN.]

Charles·ton¹ (chärl′stən). **1.** A city of eastern Illinois east-southeast of Decatur. It is a trade and processing center. Population, 19,355. **2.** A city of southeast South Carolina northeast of Savannah. Charleston has been a major commercial and cultural center since colonial times. Population, 69,510. **3.** The capital and largest city of West Virginia, in the west-central part of the state. The city grew around the site of Fort Lee in the late 1780's. Population, 63,968.

Charles·ton² (chärl′stən) *n.* A fast ballroom dance in 4/4 time, popular during the 1920's. [After CHARLESTON¹, South Carolina.]

Charles·town (chärlz′toun′). A former city of eastern Massachusetts, the oldest part of present-day Boston. It was settled c. 1629. The Battle of Bunker Hill was fought here at Breed's Hill on June 17, 1775.

char·ley horse (chär′lē) *n. Informal.* A cramp or stiffness in a muscle, especially of the upper leg, caused by injury or excessive exertion. [Originally baseball slang, of unknown origin.]

char·lock (chär′lək, -lŏk′) *n.* An annual weed *(Sinapis arvensis)* in the mustard family, native to Eurasia and naturalized in North America, having racemes of yellow flowers and hairy stems and foliage. [Middle English *cherlok,* from Old English *cerlic.*]

char·lotte (shär′lət) *n.* A dessert consisting of a mold of sponge cake or bread with a filling, as of fruits, whipped cream, or custard. [French, from the personal name *Charlotte.*]

Char·lotte¹ (shär′lət). 1896–1985. Grand duchess of Luxembourg. Ascending to the throne in 1919, she took her government into exile during the Nazi occupation of Luxembourg and supported her people through regular radio broadcasts. She returned triumphantly in 1945 and ruled until 1984.

Char·lotte² (shär′lət). A city of southern North Carolina near the South Carolina border south-southwest of Winston-Salem. Settled c. 1750 and named for the wife of King George III of England, it is the largest city in the state. Population, 314,447.

Charlotte A·ma·lie (ə-mäl′yə). The capital of the U.S. Virgin Islands, on St. Thomas Island in the West Indies east of Puerto Rico. Population, 11,842.

charlotte russe (ro͞os′) *n.* A cold dessert of Bavarian cream set in a mold lined with ladyfingers. [French : *charlotte,* charlotte + *russe,* Russian.]

Char·lottes·ville (shär′ləts-vĭl′). An independent city of central Virginia northwest of Richmond. It is the seat of the University of Virginia (founded 1819). Thomas Jefferson's estate, Monticello, is nearby. Population, 39,916.

Char·lotte·town (shär′lət-toun′). The capital and largest city of Prince Edward Island, Canada, on the southern coast of the island. It was founded by the French c. 1720. Population, 15,282.

charm (chärm) *n.* **1.** The power or quality of pleasing or delighting; attractiveness: *a breezy tropical setting of great charm.* **2.** A particular quality that attracts; a delightful characteristic: *A mischievous grin was among the child's many charms.* **3.** A small ornament, such as one worn on a bracelet. **4.** An item worn for its supposed magical benefit, as in warding off evil; an amulet. **5.** An action or formula thought to have magical power. **6.** The chanting of a magic word or verse; incantation. **7.** *Abbr.* **C** *Physics.* A quantum property of the charm quark whose conservation explains the absence of certain strange-particle decay modes and that accounts for the longevity of the J particle. **—charm** *v.* **charmed, charm·ing, charms.** *—tr.* **1.** To attract or delight greatly: *the simple elegance of the meal charmed the guests.* **2.** To induce by using strong personal attractiveness: *charmed the guard into admitting them without invitations.* **3.** To cast or seem to cast a spell on; bewitch. *—intr.* **1.** To be alluring or pleasing. **2.** To function as an amulet or charm. **3.** To use magic spells. [Middle English *charme,* magic spell, from Old French, from Latin *carmen,* incantation. See **kan-** in Appendix.] **—charm′ing·ly** *adv.* **—charm′less** *adj.*

SYNONYMS: *charm, beguile, bewitch, captivate, enchant, entrance, fascinate.* The central meaning shared by these verbs is "to attract strongly or irresistibly": *grace and manners that charmed the old curmudgeon; delicacies that beguile even the most discerning gourmet; a performance that bewitched the audience; a novel that captivates its readers; an evening that enchanted all the guests; music that entrances its listeners; a celebrity who fascinated his fellow guests.*
ANTONYM: *repel.*

charmed life (chärmd) *n.* A life that seems to have been protected by a charm or spell.

charmed particle *n. Physics.* A particle with nonzero total charm.

charm·er (chär′mər) *n.* **1.** One that charms, especially a disarmingly attractive person. **2.** One who casts spells; an enchanter or a magician.

char·meuse (shär-mo͞oz′, -mo͞os′, -mœz′) *n.* A satin-finished silk fabric. [French, trade name, from *charmeuse,* charmer, seductress, from *charmer,* to charm, from *charme,* charm. See CHARM.]

char·mo·ni·um (chär-mō′nē-əm) *n.* Any of various elementary particles consisting of a charm quark and an antiquark. [From CHARM.]

charm quark *n. Abbr.* **c** A quark with a charge of +⅔, a mass about 2900 times that of the electron, and a charm of +1. See table at **subatomic particle.**

char·nel (chär′nəl) *n.* A repository for the bones or bodies of the dead; a charnel house. **—charnel** *adj.* Resembling, suggest-

Charles
Photographed in 1981 by Lord Snowdon to commemorate Charles's engagement to Lady Diana Spencer

ă pat	oi boy
ā pay	ou out
âr care	o͝o took
ä father	o͞o boot
ĕ pet	ŭ cut
ē be	ûr urge
ĭ pit	th thin
ī pie	*th* this
îr pier	hw which
ŏ pot	zh vision
ō toe	ə about, item
ô paw	♦ regionalism

Stress marks: **′** (primary); ′ (secondary), as in **dictionary** (dĭk′shə-nĕr′ē)

ing, or suitable for receiving the dead. [Middle English, from Old French, from Late Latin *carnāle,* from neuter of Latin *carnālis,* of the flesh, from *carō, carn-,* flesh. See **sker-**[1] in Appendix.]

charnel house *n.* **1.** A building, room, or vault in which the bones or bodies of the dead are placed; a charnel. **2.** A scene or place of great physical suffering and loss of life: *The bombing turned the barracks into a charnel house.*

Char·on (kâr′ən) *n. Greek Mythology.* **1.** The ferryman who conveyed the dead to Hades over the river Styx. **2.** The only satellite of Pluto.

char·qui (chär′kē) *n.* See **jerky**[2]. [American Spanish, from Quechua *ch'arki.*]

charr (chär) *n.* Variant of **char**[2].

chart (chärt) *n.* **1.** A map showing coastlines, water depths, or other information of use to navigators. **2.** An outline map on which specific information, such as scientific data, can be plotted. **3.** A sheet presenting information in the form of graphs or tables. **4.** See **graph**[1] (sense 2). **5.** Often **charts.** A listing of best-selling recorded music or other items. Often used with *the.* **—chart** *tr.v.* **chart·ed, chart·ing, charts. 1.** To make a chart of. **2.** To plan (something) in detail: *is charting a course to destruction.* [Obsolete French *charte,* from Latin *charta,* sheet of paper made from papyrus. See CARD[1].]

chase[1]
Fox hunters and hounds

char·ter (chär′tər) *n. Abbr.* **char. 1.** A document issued by a sovereign, legislature, or other authority, creating a public or private corporation, such as a city, college, or bank, and defining its privileges and purposes. **2.** A written grant from the sovereign power of a country conferring certain rights and privileges on a person, a corporation, or the people: *A royal charter exempted the Massachusetts colony from direct interference by the Crown.* **3.** A document outlining the principles, functions, and organization of a corporate body; a constitution. *the city charter.* **4.** An authorization from a central organization to establish a local branch or chapter. **5.** Special privilege or immunity. **6. a.** A contract for the commercial leasing of a vessel or space on a vessel. **b.** The hiring or leasing of an aircraft, a vessel, or other vehicle, especially for the exclusive, temporary use of a group of travelers. **7.** A written instrument given as evidence of agreement, transfer, or contract; a deed. **—charter** *tr.v.* **-tered, -ter·ing, -ters. 1.** To grant a charter to; establish by charter. **2.** To hire or lease by charter: *charter an oil tanker.* **3.** To hire (a bus or an airplane, for example) for the exclusive, temporary use of a group of travelers. [Middle English *chartre,* from Old French, from Latin *chartula,* diminutive of *charta,* paper made from papyrus. See CARD[1].] **—char′ter·er** *n.*

char·tered accountant (chär′tərd) *n. Abbr.* **C.A., c.a.** *Chiefly British.* A member of one of the institutes of accountants granted a royal charter.

char·ter·house (chär′tər-hous′) *n.* A Carthusian monastery. [By folk etymology from Anglo-Norman *chartrouse,* from Old French *chartreus.* See CHARTREUSE.]

charter member *n.* An original member or a founder of an organization.

Chart·ism (chär′tĭz′əm) *n.* The principles and practices of a party of political reformers, chiefly workingmen, active in England from 1838 to 1848. [From Medieval Latin *charta,* charter (referring to the "People's Charter" of 1837), from Latin, paper, document. See CARD[1].] **—Char′tist** *adj. & n.*

chart·ist (chär′tĭst) *n.* A stock-market specialist who uses charts and graphs to interpret market action, predict trends, or forecast price movements of individual stocks.

Char·tres (shärt, shär′trə). A city of northern France southwest of Paris. Its 13th-century cathedral is a masterpiece of Gothic architecture noted for its stained glass and asymmetrical spires. Population, 37,119.

char·treuse (shär-tro͞oz′, -tro͞os′, -trœz′) *n. Color.* A strong to brilliant greenish yellow to moderate or strong yellow green. [From CHARTREUSE.] **—char·treuse′** *adj.*

Char·treuse (shär-tro͞oz′, -tro͞os′, -trœz′). A trademark used for a usually yellow or green liqueur.

char·tu·lar·y (kär′chə-lĕr′ē) *n.* Variant of **cartulary.**

char·wom·an (chär′wo͝om′ən) *n.* A woman hired to do cleaning or similar work, usually in a large building.

char·y (châr′ē) *adj.* **-i·er, -i·est. 1.** Very cautious; wary: *was chary of the risks involved.* **2.** Not giving or expending freely; sparing: *was chary of compliments.* [Middle English *chari,* careful, sorrowful, from Old English *cearig,* sorrowful, from *cearu,* sorrow. See CARE.] **—char′i·ly** *adv.* **—char′i·ness** *n.*

Cha·ryb·dis (kə-rĭb′dĭs) *n. Greek Mythology.* A whirlpool off the Sicilian coast, personified as a ship-devouring sea monster and located opposite the cave of Scylla.

chasuble
Roman Catholic bishops

chase[1] (chās) *v.* **chased, chas·ing, chas·es.** *—tr.* **1.** To follow rapidly in order to catch or overtake; pursue: *chased the thief.* **2.** To follow (game) in order to capture or kill; hunt: *chase foxes.* **3.** *Informal.* To seek the favor or company of persistently: *still chasing members of the opposite sex.* **4.** To put to flight; drive: *chased the dog away.* *—intr.* **1.** To go or follow in pursuit. **2.** *Informal.* To go hurriedly; rush: *chased all over looking for us.* **—chase** *n.* **1.** The act of chasing; pursuit. **2. a.** The hunting of game: *the thrill of the chase.* **b.** Something that is hunted or pursued; quarry. **3.** *Chiefly British.* **a.** A privately owned, unenclosed game preserve. **b.** The right to hunt or keep game on the land of others. **—*idiom.* give chase.** To engage in pursuit of quarry: *Police gave chase to the speeding car.* [Middle English *chasen,* to hunt, from Old French *chacier,* from Vulgar Latin **captiāre,* from Latin *captāre,* to catch. See CATCH.]

chase[2] (chās) *n. Printing.* A rectangular steel or iron frame into which pages or columns of type are locked for printing or plate making. [Perhaps from French *châsse,* case, reliquary, from Old French *chasse,* from Latin *capsa.*]

chase[3] (chās) *n.* **1. a.** A groove cut in an object; a slot: *the chase for the quarrel on a crossbow.* **b.** A trench or channel for drainpipes or wiring. **2.** The part of a gun in front of the trunnions. **3.** The cavity of a mold. **—chase** *tr.v.* **chased, chas·ing, chas·es. 1.** To groove; indent. **2.** To cut (the thread of a screw). **3.** To decorate (metal) by engraving or embossing. [Possibly from obsolete French *chas,* groove, enclosure, from Old French, from Latin *capsa,* box. V., variant of ENCHASE.]

Chase (chās), **Mary Ellen.** 1887–1973. American writer and educator known for her novels about the seacoast of Maine, including *Silas Crockett* (1935).

Chase, Salmon Portland. 1808–1873. American jurist who served as the chief justice of the U.S. Supreme Court (1864–1873). He presided over the trial of President Andrew Johnson (1868).

Chase, Samuel. 1741–1811. American jurist and Revolutionary War leader who was a delegate to the Continental Congresses, signed the Declaration of Independence, and served as an associate justice of the U.S. Supreme Court (1796–1811).

chas·er[1] (chā′sər) *n.* **1.** One that chases or pursues another: *a chaser of criminals.* **2.** *Informal.* A drink, as of beer or water, taken after hard liquor.

chas·er[2] (chā′sər) *n.* **1.** One who decorates metal by engraving or embossing. **2.** A steel tool for cutting or finishing screw threads.

chasm (kăz′əm) *n.* **1.** A deep, steep-sided opening in the earth's surface; an abyss or a gorge. **2.** A sudden interruption of continuity; a gap. **3.** A pronounced difference of opinion, interests, or loyalty. [Latin *chasma,* from Greek *khasma.*] **—chas′mal** (kăz′məl) *adj.*

chas·mog·a·mous (kăz-mŏg′ə-məs) *adj.* Of or relating to a flower that opens to allow for pollination. [Greek *khasma,* an opening + -GAMOUS.]

chas·sé (shă-sā′) *n.* A ballet movement consisting of one or more quick, gliding steps with the same foot always leading. **—chassé** *intr.v.* **-séd, -sé·ing, -sés.** To perform this movement. [French, from past participle of *chasser,* to chase, from Old French *chacier.* See CHASE[1].]

chasse·pot (shăs′pō′) *n.* A breechloading rifle introduced into the French army in 1866. [French, after Antoine Alphonse *Chassepot* (1833–1905), French gunsmith.]

chas·seur (shă-sûr′) *n.* **1.** Any of certain light cavalry or infantry troops trained for rapid maneuvers. **2.** A hunter. **3.** A uniformed footman. [French, from Old French *chaceor,* from *chacier,* to pursue. See CHASE[1].]

Chas·sid (KHä′sĭd, KHô′-, hä′-) *n.* Variant of **Hasid. —Chas·si′dic** *adj.* **—Chas·si′dism** *n.*

chas·sis (shăs′ē, chăs′ē) *n., pl.* **chas·sis** (-ēz). **1.** The rectangular steel frame, supported on springs and attached to the axles, that holds the body and motor of an automotive vehicle. **2.** The landing gear of an aircraft, including the wheels, skids, floats, and other structures that support the aircraft on land or water. **3.** The frame on which a gun carriage moves forward and backward. **4.** The framework to which the components of a radio, television, or other electronic equipment are attached. [French *châssis,* frame, from Old French, from Vulgar Latin **capsīcium,* from Latin *capsa,* box.]

chaste (chāst) *adj.* **chast·er, chast·est. 1.** Morally pure in thought or conduct; decent and modest. **2. a.** Not having experienced sexual intercourse; virginal. **b.** Abstaining from unlawful sexual intercourse. **c.** Abstaining from sexual intercourse; celibate. **3.** Pure or simple design or style; austere. [Middle English, from Old French, from Latin *castus.* See **kes-** in Appendix.] **—chaste′ly** *adv.* **—chaste′ness** *n.*

chas·ten (chā′sən) *tr.v.* **-tened, -ten·ing, -tens. 1.** To correct by punishment or reproof; take to task. **2.** To restrain; subdue: *chasten a proud spirit.* **3.** To rid of excess; refine or purify: *chasten a careless writing style.* [Alteration of obsolete *chaste,* from Middle English *chasten, chastien,* from Old French *chastiier,* from Latin *castigāre.* See CASTIGATE.] **—chas′ten·er** *n.*

chaste tree *n.* Any of several shrubs or trees of the genus *Vitex,* especially two cultivated Old World species *(V. agnus-castus* and *V. negundo),* having aromatic, palmately compound leaves and clusters of usually lilac flowers.

chas·tise (chăs-tīz′, chăs′tīz′) *tr.v.* **-tised, -tis·ing, -tis·es. 1.** To punish, as by beating. See Synonyms at **punish. 2.** To criticize severely; rebuke. **3.** *Archaic.* To purify. [Middle English *chastisen,* alteration of *chasten, chastien.* See CHASTEN.] **—chas·tis′a·ble** *adj.* **—chas·tise′ment** (chăs-tīz′mənt, chăs′tĭz-mənt) *n.* **—chas·tis′er** *n.*

chas·ti·ty (chăs′tĭ-tē) *n.* **1.** The condition or quality of being pure or chaste. **2. a.** Virginity. **b.** Virtuous character. **c.** Celibacy. [Middle English *chastite,* from Old French *chastete,* from Latin *castitās,* from *castus,* pure. See CHASTE.]

chastity belt *n.* A beltlike device of medieval times designed to prevent the woman wearing it from having sexual intercourse.

chas·u·ble (chăz′ə-bəl, chăzh′ə-, chăs′ə-) *n.* A long, sleeveless vestment worn over the alb by a priest during services. [French, from Old French, from Late Latin *casubla,* hooded garment, from **casupula,* diminutive of *casa,* house.]

chat (chăt) *intr.v.* **chat·ted, chat·ting, chats.** To converse in an easy, familiar manner; talk lightly and casually. **—chat** *n.* **1.** An informal, light conversation. **2.** Any of several birds known for their chattering call, as of the genera *Saxicola* or *Icteria.* ***—phrasal verb.*** **chat up.** To engage (someone) in light, casual talk: *"He would be . . . chatting up folks from Kansas"* (Vanity Fair). [Middle English *chatten,* to jabber, alteration of *chateren.* See CHATTER.]

cha·teau also **châ·teau** (shă-tō′) *n., pl.* **-teaus** or **-teaux** (-tōz′). **1.a.** A French castle. **b.** A French manor house. **2.** A large country house. [French *château,* from Old French *chastel,* from Latin *castellum,* castle. See CASTLE.]

Cha·teau·bri·and also **cha·teau·bri·and** (shă-tō′-brē-äɴ′) *n.* A double-thick, tender center cut of beef tenderloin, sometimes stuffed with seasonings before grilling. [After Vicomte François René de CHÂTEAUBRIAND.]

Châ·teau·bri·and (shä-tō′brē-äɴ′, shă-), Vicomte **François René de.** 1768–1848. French political leader, diplomat, and writer considered a forerunner of romanticism. His works include *Atala* (1801), *The Genius of Christianity* (1802), and *Memoirs from beyond the Tomb,* published posthumously.

Châ·teau·guay (shăt′ə-gā′, shä-tō-gā′). A town of southern Quebec, Canada, southwest of Montreal. It is a port of entry and manufacturing center. Population, 36,928.

Châ·teau-Thier·ry (shă-tō-tyĕ-rē′). A town of northern France on the Marne River east-northeast of Paris. It was the site of the second Battle of the Marne (June 3–4, 1918), which ended the last major German offensive in World War I. Population, 14,557.

chat·e·lain (shăt′l-ān′) *n.* The master of a castle; a castellan. [Middle English *chatelein,* from Old French *chastelain,* from Latin *castellānus,* from *castellum,* castle. See CASTLE.]

chat·e·laine (shăt′l-ān′) *n.* **1.a.** The mistress of a castle. **b.** The mistress of a large, fashionable household. **2.** A clasp or chain worn at the waist for holding keys, a purse, or a watch. [French *châtelaine,* feminine of *châtelain,* chatelain, from Old French *chastelain.* See CHATELAIN.]

Chat·ham (chăt′əm). **1.** A city of southeast Ontario, Canada, on the Thames River east-northeast of Windsor. It is an industrial center in an agricultural region. Population, 40,952. **2.** A municipal borough of southeast England east of London. Elizabeth I established the first dockyard here in 1588. Population, 142,800.

Chatham, First Earl of. See William **Pitt**[1].

Chatham Islands. An island group of New Zealand in the southwest Pacific Ocean east of South Island. The islands were discovered in 1791.

cha·toy·ant (shə-toi′ənt) *adj.* Having a changeable luster. **—chatoyant** *n.* A chatoyant stone or gemstone, such as the cat's-eye. [French, present participle of *chatoyer,* to shimmer like cats' eyes, from *chat,* cat. See CAT.] **—cha·toy′an·cy** *n.*

chat show *n. Chiefly British.* A talk show.

Chat·ta·hoo·chee (chăt′ə-ho͞o′chē). A river rising in northern Georgia and flowing about 702 km (436 mi) generally southwest then south to the Flint River on the Georgia-Florida border.

Chat·ta·noo·ga (chăt′ə-no͞o′gə). A city of southeast Tennessee on the Georgia border southeast of Nashville. A port of entry on the Tennessee River, it was strategically important during the Civil War and was finally taken by Union forces in November 1863. Population, 169,558.

chat·tel (chăt′l) *n.* **1.** *Law.* An article of personal, movable property. **2.** A slave. [Middle English *chatel,* movable property, from Old French, from Medieval Latin *capitāle.* See CATTLE.]

chattel mortgage *n.* A mortgage using movable personal property rather than real estate as security.

chat·ter (chăt′ər) *v.* **-tered, -ter·ing, -ters.** *—intr.* **1.** To talk rapidly, incessantly, and on trivial subjects; jabber. **2.** To utter a rapid series of short, inarticulate, speechlike sounds: *birds chattering in the trees.* **3.** To click quickly and repeatedly: *Our teeth chattered from the cold.* **4.** To vibrate or rattle while in operation: *A power drill will chatter if the bit is loose.* *—tr.* To utter in a rapid, usually thoughtless way: *chattered a long reply.* **—chatter** *n.* **1.** Idle, trivial talk. **2.** The sharp, rapid sounds made by some birds and animals. **3.** A series of quick rattling or clicking sounds. [Middle English *chateren,* of imitative origin.] **—chat′ter·er** *n.*

chat·ter·box (chăt′ər-bŏks′) *n.* A very talkative person.

chatter mark also **chat·ter·mark** (chăt′ər-märk′) *n.* **1.** A riblike marking on wood or metal, caused by vibration of a cutting tool. **2.** *Geology.* One of a series of short scars made by glacial drift on a surface of bedrock.

Chat·ter·ton (chăt′ər-tən), **Thomas.** 1752–1770. British poet who fooled scholars by ascribing his poetry to a 15th-century monk, Thomas Rowley. Unable to support himself by writing, Chatterton became dejected and took his own life at age 18.

chat·ty (chăt′ē) *adj.* **-ti·er, -ti·est.** **1.** Inclined to chat; friendly and talkative. **2.** Full of or in the style of light informal talk: *a chatty letter.* **—chat′ti·ly** *adv.* **—chat′ti·ness** *n.*

Chau·cer (chô′sər), **Geoffrey.** 1340?–1400. English poet regarded as the greatest literary figure of medieval England. His works include *The Book of the Duchess* (1369), *Troilus and Criseyde* (c. 1385), and his masterwork, *The Canterbury Tales* (1387–1400). **—Chau·cer′i·an** (chô-sîr′ē-ən) *adj. & n.*

chauf·feur (shō′fər, shō-fûr′) *n.* One employed to drive a private automobile. **—chauffeur** *v.* **-feured, -feur·ing, -feurs.** *—tr.* **1.** To serve as a driver for (another). **2.** To transport in (a motor vehicle); drive: *chauffeured the guests around town.* *—intr.* To serve as a driver for another. [French, stoker, from *chauffer,* to heat, stoke, from Old French *chaufer.* See CHAFE.]

chaul·moo·gra (chôl-mo͞o′grə) *n.* Any of several tropical Asian trees of the genus *Hydnocarpus,* whose seeds contain an oil formerly used to treat skin lesions caused by leprosy and other diseases. [Bengali *cāulmugrā.*]

chaunt (chônt, chänt) *n. & v. Archaic.* Variant of **chant.**

Chau·tau·qua Lake (shə-tô′kwə, chə-). A lake of extreme southwest New York. The Chautauqua movement of adult education, offering a range of cultural, religious, and recreational activities, was founded in 1874 at the resort village of **Chautauqua** on the northwest shore of the lake.

chau·vin·ism (shō′və-nĭz′əm) *n.* **1.** Militant devotion to and glorification of one's country; fanatical patriotism. **2.** Prejudiced belief in the superiority of one's own gender, group, or kind: *"the chauvinism . . . of making extraterrestrial life in our own image"* (Henry S.F. Cooper, Jr.). [French *chauvinisme,* after Nicolas *Chauvin,* a legendary French soldier famous for his devotion to Napoleon.] **—chau′vin·ist** *n.* **—chau′vin·is′tic** *adj.* **—chau′vin·is′ti·cal·ly** *adv.*

Cha·vannes (shä-văn′), **Pierre Puvis de.** See Pierre **Puvis de Chavannes.**

Cha·vez (chä′vĕz′, shä′-), **Cesar Estrada.** Born 1927. American labor organizer who founded the National Farm Workers Association (1962).

♦**chaw** (chô) *Regional. intr. & tr.v.* **chawed, chaw·ing, chaws.** To chew. **—chaw** *n.* A chew, especially of tobacco. [Variant of CHEW.]

♦ ***REGIONAL NOTE:*** The use of *chaw* for *chew,* in both the verb and the noun, is remarkably wide in its U.S. distribution, occurring in pronunciations from New England south to the Gulf States, throughout the Midwest, and westward to Colorado and California. *Chaw* has a wide range of senses in regional expressions. One meaning of the verb is "to bawl someone out": *He chawed her good.* A Southern sense is "to get the best of someone in a bantering contest" or simply "to embarrass": *"That compliment sort of chawed me"* (Publication of the American Dialect Society). The noun *chaw* can mean "a twist of chewing tobacco" or "an attachment or hold (on someone)"; for example, a flirtatious girl in South Midland states is *"tryin' to git a chaw on a feller"* (Dialect Notes). In areas where Irish immigrants were seeking work at the turn of the century, *chaw* was a derogatory term for an Irishman.

Cha·yef·sky (chī-ĕf′skē, chä-), **Paddy.** 1923–1981. American playwright and screenwriter who adapted several of his acclaimed television dramas into movies. He won an Academy Award for *Marty* (1955) and *Hospital* (1971).

♦**cha·yo·te** (chä-yō′tā) *n.* **1.** A tropical American perennial herbaceous vine *(Sechium edule)* having tendrils, tuberous roots, and an edible, pear-shaped fruit cooked as a vegetable. **2.** The fruit of this plant. Also called ♦*mirliton.* [Spanish, from Nahuatl *chayotli.*]

cha·zan or **haz·zan** also **chaz·zen** (ᴋʜä′zən) *n.* A cantor in a synagogue. [Late Hebrew *ḥazzān.*]

Ch.E. *abbr.* Chemical engineer.

cheap (chēp) *adj.* **cheap·er, cheap·est.** **1.a.** Relatively low in cost; inexpensive or comparatively inexpensive. **b.** Charging low prices: *a cheap restaurant.* **2.a.** Obtainable at a low rate of interest. Used especially of money. **b.** Devalued, as in buying power: *cheap dollars.* **3.** Achieved with little effort: *a cheap victory; cheap laughs.* **4.** Of or considered of small value: *in wartime, when life was cheap.* **5.** Of poor quality; inferior: *a cheap toy.* **6.** Worthy of no respect; vulgar or contemptible: *a cheap gangster.* **7.** Stingy; miserly. **—cheap** *adv.* **cheaper, cheapest.** Inexpensively: *got the new car cheap.* ***—idioms.*** **cheap at twice the price.** Extremely inexpensive. **on the cheap.** By inexpensive means; cheaply: *traveled to Europe on the cheap.* [From Middle English *(god) chep,* (good) price, purchase, bargain, from Old English *cēap,* trade, from Latin *caupō,* shopkeeper.] **—cheap′ly** *adv.* **—cheap′ness** *n.*

cheap·en (chē′pən) *v.* **-ened, -en·ing, -ens.** *—tr.* **1.** To make cheap or cheaper. **2.** To lower in public estimation; debase or degrade: *misconduct that cheapened a high office.* *—intr.* To become cheap or cheaper. **—cheap′en·er** *n.*

cheap·ie (chē′pē) *n. Slang.* **1.** A cheap item. **2.** A stingy person.

cheap·jack (chēp′jăk′) *n.* A peddler or dealer of cheap goods. **—cheapjack** *adj.* Inferior in quality or value; tawdry: *"the cheapjack moviemaking . . . that feeds on the low taste of the mob"* (Judith Crist).

cheap shot *n.* An unfair or unsporting verbal attack on a vulnerable target.

Cheap·side (chēp′sīd′). A street and district in the City of London, England. It was the market center of medieval London and the site of the Mermaid Tavern, a gathering place for Elizabethan poets and playwrights.

chateau
Château de Chillon, Montreux, Switzerland

chatelaine
18th-century German

Cesar Chavez

ă pat	oi boy
ā pay	ou out
âr care	o͝o took
ä father	o͞o boot
ĕ pet	ŭ cut
ē be	ûr urge
ĭ pit	th thin
ī pie	*th* this
îr pier	hw which
ŏ pot	zh vision
ō toe	ə about, item
ô paw	♦ regionalism

Stress marks: ′ (primary); ′ (secondary), as in **dictionary** (dĭk′shə-nĕr′ē)

cheap·skate (chēp′skāt′) *n.* *Slang.* A stingy person; a miser.

cheat (chēt) *v.* **cheat·ed, cheat·ing, cheats.** —*tr.* **1.** To deceive by trickery; swindle: *cheated customers by overcharging them for purchases.* **2.** To deprive by trickery; defraud: *cheated them of their land.* **3.** To mislead; fool: *illusions that cheat the eye.* **4.** To elude; escape: *cheat death.* —*intr.* **1.** To act dishonestly; practice fraud. **2.** To violate rules deliberately, as in a game: *accused of cheating at cards.* **3.** *Informal.* To be sexually unfaithful: *young marrieds who cheat on their spouses.* —**cheat** *n.* **1.** An act of cheating; a fraud or swindle. **2.** One that cheats; a swindler. **3.** *Law.* Fraudulent acquisition of another's property. **4.** *Botany.* An annual European species of brome grass *(Bromus secalinus)* widely naturalized in temperate regions. [Middle English *cheten,* to confiscate, short for *acheten,* variant of *escheten,* from *eschete,* escheat. See ESCHEAT.] —**cheat′er** *n.* —**cheat′ing·ly** *adv.*

che·bec (chĭ-bĕk′) *n.* See **least flycatcher.** [Imitative of its call.]

Che·bok·sa·ry (chĭ-bŏk-sär′ē). A city of west-central Russia on the Volga River west of Kazan. It is a commercial and cultural center. Population, 389,000.

check (chĕk) *n.* **1.** An action or influence that stops motion or expression; a restraint: *Heavy rains were a check on the army's advance.* **2.** The condition of being stopped or held back; restraint: *kept my temper in check; holding agricultural pests in check with sprays.* **3.** An abrupt stop in forward movement or progress; a halt. **4.** The act or an instance of inspecting or testing, as for accuracy or quality; examination: *the careful check of each unit before sale; gave the car an oil check.* **5.** A standard for inspecting or evaluating; a test. **6.** A check mark. **7.** A ticket or slip of identification: *a baggage check.* **8.** A bill at a restaurant or bar. **9.** *Games.* A chip or counter used in gambling. **10.** *Abbr.* **ch., ck.** A written order to a bank to pay the amount specified from funds on deposit; a draft. **11.** A small crack; a chink. **12.a.** A pattern of small squares, as on a chessboard. **b.** One of the squares of such a pattern. **c.** A fabric patterned with squares: *a dress of pale green check.* **13.** *Abbr.* **ch** *Games.* **a.** A move in chess that directly attacks an opponent's king but does not constitute a checkmate. **b.** The position or condition of a king so attacked. **14.** *Sports.* The act of blocking or impeding an opponent in control of the puck in ice hockey, either with one's body or one's stick. —**check** *interj.* **1.** *Games.* Used to declare that a chess opponent's king is in check. **2.** *Informal.* Used to express agreement or understanding. —**check** *v.* **checked, check·ing, checks.** —*tr.* **1.** To arrest the motion of abruptly; halt: *checked the flow by shutting a valve.* **2.** To hold in restraint; curb: *check an impulse to laugh.* See Synonyms at **restrain. 3.** To slow the growth of; retard. **4.** To rebuke; rebuff. **5.** To inspect so as to determine accuracy, quality, or other condition; test: *checked the brakes and lights for defects; checked out the system to make sure there were no errors in the software.* **6.** To verify by consulting a source or authority: *checked her facts before speaking; check a spelling in the dictionary.* **7.** To put a check mark on or next to: *checked off each item on the shopping list.* **8.** To deposit for temporary safekeeping: *checked his coat at the door.* **9.** To consign (luggage, for example) for shipment on a transportation vehicle: *checked her bags and boarded the plane.* **10.** To make cracks or chinks in: *Sunlight dried and checked the paint.* **11.** *Games.* To move in chess so as to put (an opponent's king) under direct attack. **12.** *Sports.* To block or impede (an opposing player with the puck) in ice hockey by using one's body or one's stick. —*intr.* **1.** To come to an abrupt halt; stop. **2.** To agree point for point; correspond: *The fingerprints checked with the ones on file.* **3.** To be verified or confirmed; pass inspection: *The suspect's story checked out.* **4.** To make an examination or investigation; inquire: *phoned to check on the departure time; checked into the rumor.* **5.** To write a check on a bank account. **6.** To undergo cracking in a pattern of checks, as paint does. **7.** *Games.* To place a chess opponent's king in check. **8.a.** To pause to relocate a scent. Used of hunting dogs. **b.** To abandon the proper game and follow baser prey. Used of trained falcons. **9.** *Sports.* To block or impede an opposing player carrying the puck in ice hockey. —***phrasal verbs.*** **check in.** To register, as at a hotel. **check out. 1.** To settle one's bill and leave a hotel or other place of lodging. **2.** To withdraw (an item) after recording the withdrawal: *check out books.* **3.** To record and total up the prices of and receive payment for (items being purchased) at a retail store: *The cashier checked out and bagged my order.* **check over.** To look over; examine: *The teacher checked the students' papers over.* [Middle English *chek,* check in chess, from Old French *eschec,* from Arabic *shāh,* from Persian, king, king in chess. See SHAH.] —**check′a·ble** *adj.*

WORD HISTORY: The words *check, chess,* and *shah* are all related. *Shah,* as one might think, is a borrowing into English of the Persian title for the monarch of that country. The Persian word *shāh* was also a term used in chess, a game played in Persia long before it was introduced to Europe. One said *shāh* as a warning when the opponent's king was under attack. The Persian word in this sense, after passing through Arabic, probably Old Spanish, and then Old French, came into Middle English as *chek* about seven hundred years ago. *Chess* itself comes from a plural form of the Old French word that gave us the word *check. Checkmate,* the next stage after *check,* goes back to the Arabic phrase *shāh māt,* meaning "the king is stymied." Through a complex development having to do with senses that evolved from the notion of checking the king, *check* came to mean something used to ensure accuracy or authenticity. One such means was a counterfoil, a part of a check, for example, retained by the issuer as documentation of a transaction. *Check* first meant "counterfoil" and then came to mean anything, such as a bill or bank draft, with a counterfoil—or eventually even without one.

check·book (chĕk′bo͝ok′) *n.* A book containing blank checks issued by a bank.

checked (chĕkt) *adj.* **1.** Having a pattern of checks or squares: *checked cloth.* **2.** Held in check; restrained. **3.** *Linguistics.* Situated in a stopped or closed syllable: *a checked vowel.*

check·er (chĕk′ər) *n.* **1.a.** One, such as an inspector or examiner, that checks. **b.** One that receives items for temporary safekeeping or for shipment: *a baggage checker.* **2.** *Games.* **a. checkers** *(used with a sing. verb).* A game played on a checkerboard by two players, each using 12 pieces. **b.** One of the round, flat pieces used in this game. **3.a.** A pattern of checks or squares. **b.** One of the squares in such a pattern. **4.** A cashier. —**checker** *tr.v.* **-ered, -er·ing, -ers. 1.** To mark with a checked or squared pattern. **2.** To diversify (something) in color, shading, or character; variegate. [Middle English *cheker,* chessboard, alteration of *escheker,* from Old French *eschequier,* from *eschec,* check in chess. See CHECK.]

check·er·ber·ry (chĕk′ər-bĕr′ē) *n.* See **wintergreen** (sense 1a). [CHECKER(BOARD) + BERRY.]

check·er·bloom (chĕk′ər-blo͞om′) *n.* An ornamental herb *(Sidalcea malviflora)* native to the western coast of North America and cultivated for its showy clusters of pink to purple flowers. [CHECKER(BOARD) + BLOOM[1].]

check·er·board (chĕk′ər-bôrd′, -bōrd′) *n.* *Games.* A board on which chess and checkers are played, divided into 64 squares of two alternating colors.

check·ered (chĕk′ərd) *adj.* **1.** Divided into squares. **2.** Marked by light and dark patches; diversified in color. **3.** Marked by great changes or shifts in fortune: *a checkered career.*

check·ing account (chĕk′ĭng) *n.* A bank account in which checks may be written against amounts on deposit.

check·list (chĕk′lĭst′) *n.* A list of items to be noted, checked, or remembered.

check mark *n.* A mark placed next to an item to show that it has been noted, verified, or approved.

check·mate (chĕk′māt′) *tr.v.* **-mat·ed, -mat·ing, -mates. 1.** *Games.* To attack (a chess opponent's king) in such a manner that no escape or defense is possible, thus ending the game. **2.** To defeat completely. —**checkmate** *n.* **1.** *Abbr.* **chm.** *Games.* **a.** A move that constitutes an inescapable and indefensible attack on a chess opponent's king. **b.** The position or condition of a king so attacked. **2.** Utter defeat. —**checkmate** *interj.* *Games.* Used to declare the checkmate of an opponent's king in chess. [Middle English *chekmat,* from Old French *eschec mat,* from Arabic *shāh māt,* the king is dead : *shāh,* king (from Persian; see SHAH) + *māt,* dead.]

check·off (chĕk′ôf′, -ŏf′) *n.* Collection of dues from members of a union by authorized deduction from their wages.

check·out (chĕk′out′) *n.* **1.** The act, time, or place of checking out, as at a hotel, library, or supermarket. **2.** A test, as of a machine, for proper functioning. **3.** An investigation; an inspection.

check·point (chĕk′point′) *n.* A point where a check is performed: *Vehicles are stopped at checkpoints along the border.*

check·rein (chĕk′rān′) *n.* **1.** A short rein that extends from a horse's bit to the saddle to keep the horse from lowering its head. **2.** A rein joining the bit of one of a span of horses to the driving rein of the other horse.

check·room (chĕk′ro͞om′, -ro͝om′) *n.* A place where hats, coats, packages, or other items can be stored temporarily.

check·up (chĕk′ŭp′) *n.* **1.** An examination or inspection. **2.** A general physical examination.

Ched·dar also **ched·dar** (chĕd′ər) *n.* Any of several types of smooth, hard cheese varying in flavor from mild to extra sharp. [After *Cheddar,* a village of southwest England.]

cheek (chēk) *n.* **1.** The fleshy part of either side of the face below the eye and between the nose and ear. **2.** Something resembling the cheek in shape or position. **3.** Either of the buttocks. **4.** Cool impertinence. See Synonyms at **temerity.** —**cheek** *tr.v.* **cheeked, cheek·ing, cheeks.** *Informal.* To speak impudently to. —***idiom.*** **cheek by jowl.** Side by side; close together. [Middle English *cheke,* from Old English *cēace.*]

cheek·bone (chēk′bōn′) *n.* See **zygomatic bone.**

cheek pouch *n.* A pocketlike fold of skin in the cheeks of various animals, such as squirrels, gophers, and monkeys, that functions as a means of carrying food.

cheek·y (chē′kē) *adj.* **-i·er, -i·est.** Impertinently bold; impudent and saucy. —**cheek′i·ly** *adv.* —**cheek′i·ness** *n.*

cheep (chēp) *n.* A faint, shrill sound like that of a young bird; a chirp. —**cheep** *intr.v.* **cheeped, cheep·ing, cheeps.** To make a faint, shrill sound or sounds; chirp. [Imitative.] —**cheep′er** *n.*

cheer (chîr) *n.* **1.** Lightness of spirits or mood; gaiety or joy: *a happy tune, full of cheer.* **2.** A source of joy or happiness; comfort. **3.a.** A shout of approval, encouragement, or congratulation. **b.** A short, rehearsed jingle or phrase, shouted in unison by a squad of cheerleaders. **4.** Festive food and drink; refreshment. **—cheer** *v.* **cheered, cheer·ing, cheers.** *—tr.* **1.** To make happier or more cheerful: *a warm fire that cheered us.* **2.** To encourage with or as if with cheers; urge: *The fans cheered the runners on.* See Synonyms at **encourage. 3.** To salute or acclaim with cheers; applaud. See Synonyms at **applaud.** *—intr.* **1.** To shout cheers. **2.** To become cheerful: *had lunch and soon cheered up.* [Middle English *chere,* expression, mood, from Old French *chiere,* face, from Late Latin *cara,* from Greek *kara,* head. See **ker-**[1] in Appendix.] **—cheer′er** *n.* **—cheer′ing·ly** *adv.*

cheer·ful (chîr′fəl) *adj.* **1.** Being in good spirits; merry. See Synonyms at **glad**[1]. **2.** Promoting a feeling of cheer; pleasant: *a cozy, cheerful room.* **3.** Reflecting willingness or good humor: *cheerful labor.* **—cheer′ful·ly** *adv.* **—cheer′ful·ness** *n.*

cheer·i·o (chîr′ē-ō′) *interj. Chiefly British.* Used in greeting or parting. [Alteration of CHEER.]

cheer·lead (chîr′lēd′) *intr.v.* **-led** (-lĕd′), **-lead·ing, -leads. 1.** To lead organized cheering, as at sports events. **2.** To express or promote automatic or servile praise: *We want someone not just to cheerlead but to help us revamp our organization.* [Back-formation from CHEERLEADER.]

cheer·lead·er (chîr′lē′dər) *n.* **1.** One who leads the cheering of spectators, as at a sports contest. **2.** One who expresses or promotes thoughtless praise; an adulator.

cheer·led (chîr′lĕd′) *v.* Past tense and past participle of **cheerlead.**

cheer·less (chîr′lĭs) *adj.* Lacking cheer; depressing. **—cheer′less·ly** *adv.* **—cheer′less·ness** *n.*

cheers (chîz) *interj.* Used as a toast.

cheer·y (chîr′ē) *adj.* **-i·er, -i·est.** Showing or suggesting good spirits; cheerful: *a cheery hello.* **—cheer′i·ly** *adv.* **—cheer′i·ness** *n.*

cheese[1] (chēz) *n.* **1.a.** A solid food prepared from the pressed curd of milk, often seasoned and aged. **b.** A molded mass of this substance. **2.** Something resembling this substance in shape or consistency. [Middle English *chese,* from Old English *cȳse,* from Germanic **kasjus,* from Latin *cāseus.*]

cheese[2] (chēz) *tr.v.* **cheesed, chees·ing, chees·es.** *Slang.* To stop. ***—idiom.* cheese it.** *Slang.* **1.** To look out. Often used in the imperative. **2.** To get away fast; get going. Often used in the imperative. [Origin unknown.]

cheese[3] (chēz) *n. Slang.* An important person. [Perhaps from Urdu *chīz,* thing, from Persian, from Old Persian **ciš-ciy,* something. See **kʷo-** in Appendix.]

cheese·burg·er (chēz′bûr′gər) *n.* A hamburger topped with melted cheese.

cheese·cake (chēz′kāk′) *n.* **1.** A cake made of sweetened cottage cheese or cream cheese, eggs, milk, sugar, and flavorings. **2.** *Informal.* Photographs of minimally attired women.

cheese·cloth (chēz′klôth′, -klŏth′) *n.* A coarse, loosely woven cotton gauze, originally used for wrapping cheese.

cheese-par·ing (chēz′pâr′ĭng) *adj.* Miserly; stingy. **—cheese-paring** *n.* **1.** Something of little or no value. **2.** Stinginess; parsimony.

chees·y (chē′zē) *adj.* **-i·er, -i·est. 1.** Containing or resembling cheese. **2.** *Informal.* Of poor quality; shoddy. [Sense 2, possibly from *cheesy,* showy, from CHEESE[3].] **—chees′i·ness** *n.*

chee·tah also **che·tah** (chē′tə) *n.* A long-legged, swift-running wild cat *(Acinonyx jubatus)* of Africa and southwest Asia, having black-spotted, tawny fur and nonretractile claws. The cheetah, the fastest animal on land, can run for short distances at about 96 kilometers (60 miles) per hour. [Hindustani *cītā,* from Sanskrit *citrakāyaḥ,* tiger, leopard : *citra-,* variegated + *kāyaḥ,* body; see **kʷei-**[2] in Appendix.]

Chee·ver (chē′vər), **John.** 1912–1982. American writer who depicted life in American suburbs with humor and compassion in his short stories and novels.

chef (shĕf) *n.* A cook, especially the chief cook of a large kitchen staff. [French, short for *chef (de cuisine),* head (of the kitchen). See CHIEF.]

chef-d'oeu·vre (shā-dœ′vrə, -dûrv′) *n., pl.* **chefs-d'oeuvre** (-dœ′vrə, -dûrv′). A masterpiece, especially in literature or art. [French : *chef,* head, beginning + *de,* of + *oeuvre,* work.]

chef's salad (shĕfs) *n.* A tossed green salad that usually includes raw vegetables, hard-boiled eggs, and julienne strips of cheese and meat.

cheiro– *pref.* Variant of **chiro–.**

Che·ju (chĕ′jo͞o′). An island of South Korea separated from the southwest coast of the mainland by **Cheju Strait,** a channel linking the Yellow Sea and Korea Strait.

Che·khov also **Che·kov** (chĕk′ôf, -ŏf, -ŏv, chyĕ′KHəf), **Anton Pavlovich.** 1860–1904. Russian writer whose dramas, such as *The Seagull* (1896, revised 1898), and stories, including "A Dreary Story" (1889), concern the inability of human beings to communicate with one another. **—Che·kho′vi·an** (chĕ-kō′vē-ən) *adj.*

Che·kiang (chŭ′kyäng′, jə′gyäng′). See **Zhejiang.**

Che·kov (chĕk′ôf, -ŏf, -ŏv, chyĕ′KHəf), **Anton Pavlovich.** See Anton Pavlovich **Chekhov.**

che·la (kē′lə) *n., pl.* **-lae** (-lē). A pincerlike claw of a crustacean or an arachnid, such as a lobster, crab, or scorpion. [New Latin, from Greek *khēlē,* claw.]

Che·lan (shə-lăn′), **Lake.** A narrow lake of north-central Washington in the Cascade Range. It is the third-deepest freshwater lake in the United States.

che·late (kē′lāt′) *adj. Zoology.* Having chelae or resembling a chela. **—chelate** *n. Chemistry.* A chemical compound in the form of a heterocyclic ring, containing a metal ion attached by coordinate bonds to at least two nonmetal ions. **—chelate** *tr.v.* **-lat·ed, -lat·ing, -lates. 1.** *Chemistry.* To combine (a metal ion) with a chemical compound to form a ring. **2.** *Medicine.* To remove (a heavy metal, such as lead or mercury) from the bloodstream by means of a chelate, such as EDTA. **—che′lat·a·ble** *adj.* **—che′late′** *n.* **—che·la′tion** *n.* **—che′la′tor** *n.*

che·lic·er·a (kĭ-lĭs′ər-ə) *n., pl.* **-er·ae** (-ə-rē′). Either of the first pair of fanglike appendages near the mouth of an arachnid, such as a spider, often modified for grasping and piercing. [New Latin : CHELA + Greek *keras,* horn; see **ker-**[1] in Appendix.]

che·li·form (kē′lə-fôrm′) *adj.* Having the shape of a chela; pincerlike.

Chel·li·an or **Chel·le·an** (shĕl′ē-ən) *adj.* Abbevillian. [After *Chelles,* a city of north-central France.]

Chelms·ford (chĕmz′fərd). A town of northeast Massachusetts near Lowell. It is chiefly residential. Population, 31,174.

che·loid (kē′loid′) *n.* Variant of **keloid.**

che·lo·ni·an (kĭ-lō′nē-ən) *adj.* Of, relating to, or belonging to the order Chelonia, which includes the turtles and tortoises. **—chelonian** *n.* A reptile of the order Chelonia. [From New Latin *Chelonia,* order name, from Greek *khelōnē,* tortoise.]

Chel·sea (chĕl′sē). **1.** A district of western London, England, on the north bank of the Thames River, popular since the 18th century with writers and artists. **2.** A city of eastern Massachusetts, a suburb of Boston. It was settled in 1624 and set off from Boston in 1739. Population, 25,431.

Chel·ten·ham (chĕlt′nəm, chĕl′tən-əm). A municipal borough of west-central England south of Birmingham. It has been a popular resort since the discovery of mineral springs in 1716. Population, 86,100.

Che·lya·binsk (chĕl-yä′bĭnsk, chĭ-lyä′-). A city of southwest Russia south of Sverdlovsk. Founded in 1736 as a frontier outpost, it is a major metallurgical and industrial center. Population, 1,096,000.

Che·lyus·kin (chĕl-yo͞o′skĭn, chĭ-lyo͞o′-), **Cape.** A cape of north-central Russia on the Taimyr Peninsula. It is the northernmost point of Asia.

chem. *abbr.* Chemical; chemist; chemistry.

chem– or **chemi–** *pref.* Variant of **chemo–.**

chem·ic (kĕm′ĭk) *adj.* **1.** Chemical. **2.** *Archaic.* Alchemic. **—chemic** *n. Obsolete.* An alchemist.

chem·i·cal (kĕm′ĭ-kəl) *adj. Abbr.* **chem. 1.** Of or relating to chemistry. **2.** Of or relating to the properties or actions of chemicals. **—chemical** *n.* **1.** A substance with a distinct molecular composition that is produced by or used in a chemical process. **2.** A drug, especially an illicit or addictive one. [Obsolete *chimical,* from *chimic,* alchemist, from New Latin *chimicus,* from Medieval Latin *alchimicus,* from *alchymia,* alchemy. See ALCHEMY.] **—chem′i·cal·ly** *adv.*

chemical abuse *n.* See **substance abuse.**

chemical bond *n.* Any of several forces or mechanisms, especially the ionic bond, covalent bond, and metallic bond, by which atoms or ions are bound in a molecule or crystal.

chemical dependency *n.* A physical and psychological habituation to a mood- or mind-altering drug, such as alcohol or cocaine.

chemical engineering *n.* The branch of engineering that deals with the technology of large-scale chemical production and the manufacture of products through chemical processes. **—chemical engineer** *n.*

Chem·i·cal Mace (kĕm′ĭ-kəl). A trademark used for a temporarily disabling liquid packed in aerosol form and sprayed in self-defense into the face of an attacker, thereby causing dizziness, irritation of the eyes, and immobilization.

chemical warfare *n.* Warfare and associated military operations involving the employment of lethal and incapacitating munitions and agents, typically poisons, contaminants, and irritants.

chem·i·lu·mi·nes·cence (kĕm′ə-lo͞o′mə-nĕs′əns) *n.* Emission of light as a result of a chemical reaction at environmental temperatures. **—chem′i·lu′mi·nes′cent** *adj.*

che·min de fer (shə-măɴ′ də fâr′) *n. Games.* A variation of baccarat. [French *chemin de fer,* railroad : *chemin,* way + *de,* of + *fer,* iron.]

che·mise (shə-mēz′) *n.* **1.** A woman's loose, shirtlike undergarment. **2.** A loosely fitting dress that hangs straight, sometimes worn with a belt; a shift. [Middle English, from Old French, shirt, from Late Latin *camisia.*]

chem·i·sette (shĕm′ĭ-zĕt′) *n.* **1.** A short, sleeveless bodice, formerly worn by women. **2.** A blouse front formerly worn by women; a dickey. [French, diminutive of *chemise,* shirt, from Old French. See CHEMISE.]

chem·i·sorb (kĕm′ĭ-sôrb′) also **chem·o·sorb** (-ə-sôrb′) *tr.v.* **-sorbed, -sorb·ing, -sorbs.** To take up and chemically bind (a substance) onto the surface of another substance. [CHEMI– + (AB)SORB.] **—chem′i·sorp′tion** (-sôrp′shən) *n.*

chem·ist (kĕm′ĭst) *n. Abbr.* **chem. 1.** A scientist specializing in chemistry. **2.** *Chiefly British.* A pharmacist. **3.** *Obsolete.* An

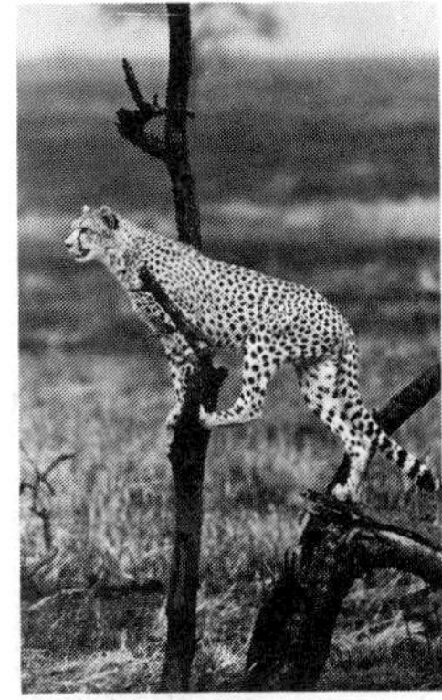

cheetah
Acinonyx jubatus

ă pat	oi boy
ā pay	ou out
âr care	o͝o took
ä father	o͞o boot
ĕ pet	ŭ cut
ē be	ûr urge
ĭ pit	th thin
ī pie	*th* this
îr pier	hw which
ŏ pot	zh vision
ō toe	ə about, item
ô paw	♦ regionalism

Stress marks: ′ (primary); ′ (secondary), as in **dictionary** (dĭk′shə-nĕr′ē)

alchemist. [Obsolete *chimist,* from New Latin *chimista,* from Medieval Latin *alchymista,* alchemist, from *alchymia,* alchemy. See ALCHEMY.]

chem·is·try (kĕm′ĭ-strē) *n., pl.* **-tries.** *Abbr.* **chem.** **1.** The science of the composition, structure, properties, and reactions of matter, especially of atomic and molecular systems. **2.** The composition, structure, properties, and reactions of a substance. **3.** The elements of a complex entity and their dynamic interrelation: *"Now that they had a leader, a restless chemistry possessed the group"* (John Updike). **4.** Mutual attraction or sympathy; rapport: *The chemistry was good between the partners.*

Chem·nitz (kĕm′nĭts). See **Karl-Marx-Stadt.**

che·mo (kē′mō, kĕm′ō) *n. Informal.* Chemotherapy or a chemotherapeutic treatment.

chemo– or **chemi–** or **chem–** *pref.* Chemicals; chemical: *chemotherapy.* [From CHEMICAL.]

che·mo·au·to·troph (kē′mō-ô′tə-trŏf′, -trōf′, kĕm′ō-) *n.* An organism, such as a bacterium or a protozoan, that obtains its nourishment through the oxidation of inorganic chemical compounds as opposed to photosynthesis. **—che′mo·au′to·tro′phic** (-trō′fĭk, -trŏf′ĭk) *adj.* **—che′mo·au′to·tro′phi·cal·ly** *adv.* **—che′mo·au·tot′ro·phy** (-ô-tŏt′rə-fē) *n.*

che·mo·pre·ven·tion (kē′mō-prĭ-vĕn′shən, kĕm′ō-) *n.* The use of chemical agents, drugs, or food supplements to prevent disease. Also called *chemoprophylaxis.* **—che′mo·pre·ven′tive** *adj. & n.*

che·mo·pro·phy·lax·is (kē′mō-prō′fə-lăk′sĭs, kĕm′ō-) *n.* See **chemoprevention. —che′mo·pro′phy·lac′tic** (-lăk′tĭk) *n. & adj.*

che·mo·re·cep·tion (kē′mō-rĭ-sĕp′shən, kĕm′ō-) *n.* The physiological response of a sense organ to a chemical stimulus. **—che′mo·re·cep′tive** *adj.* **—che′mo·re′cep·tiv′i·ty** (-rē′sĕp-tĭv′ĭ-tē) *n.*

che·mo·re·cep·tor (kē′mō-rĭ-sĕp′tər, kĕm′ō-) *n.* A sensory nerve cell or sense organ, as of smell or taste, that responds to chemical stimuli.

che·mo·sen·so·ry (kē′mō-sĕn′sə-rē, kĕm′ō-) *adj.* Relating to the perception of a chemical stimulus by sensory means. Used especially of olfactory reception.

chem·o·sorb (kĕm′ə-sôrb′) *v.* Variant of **chemisorb.**

che·mo·sphere (kē′mə-sfîr′, kĕm′ə-) *n.* The region of the atmosphere from 30 to 190 kilometers (20 to 120 miles) above Earth's surface, in which photochemical reactions initiated by solar radiation occur.

che·mo·sur·ger·y (kē′mō-sûr′jə-rē, kĕm′ō-) *n.* Selective destruction of tissue by use of chemicals, as for removing malignant skin lesions. **—che′mo·sur′gi·cal** (-jĭ-kəl) *adj.*

che·mo·syn·the·sis (kē′mō-sĭn′thĭ-sĭs, kĕm′ō-) *n.* Synthesis of carbohydrate from carbon dioxide and water using energy obtained from the chemical oxidation of simple inorganic compounds. This form of synthesis is limited to certain bacteria and fungi. **—che′mo·syn·thet′ic** (-sĭn-thĕt′ĭk) *adj.* **—che′mo·syn·thet′i·cal·ly** *adv.*

che·mo·sys·tem·at·ics (kē′mō-sĭs′tə-măt′ĭks, kĕm′ō-) *n.* *(used with a sing. or pl. verb).* See **chemotaxonomy.**

che·mo·tax·is (kē′mō-tăk′sĭs, kĕm′ō-) *n.* The characteristic movement or orientation of an organism or cell along a chemical concentration gradient either toward or away from the chemical stimulus. **—che′mo·tac′tic** (-tăk′tĭk) *adj.* **—che′mo·tac′ti·cal·ly** *adv.*

che·mo·tax·on·o·my (kē′mō-tăk-sŏn′ə-mē, kĕm′ō-) *n.* Classification of organisms based on differences at the biochemical level, especially in the amino acid sequences of common proteins. Also called *chemosystematics.* **—che′mo·tax′o·nom′ic** (-tăk′sə-nŏm′ĭk) *adj.* **—che′mo·tax′o·nom′i·cal·ly** *adv.* **—che′mo·tax·on′o·mist** *n.*

che·mo·ther·a·py (kē′mō-thĕr′ə-pē, kĕm′ō-) *n.* **1.** The treatment of cancer using specific chemical agents or drugs that are selectively destructive to malignant cells and tissues. **2.** The treatment of disease using chemical agents or drugs that are selectively toxic to the causative agent of the disease, such as a virus, bacterium, or other microorganism. **—che′mo·ther′a·peu′tic** (-pyo͞o′tĭk) *adj.* **—che′mo·ther′a·peu′ti·cal·ly** *adv.* **—che′mo·ther′a·pist** *n.*

che·mot·ro·pism (kĭ-mŏt′rə-pĭz′əm) *n.* Movement or growth of an organism or part of an organism in response to a chemical stimulus. **—che′mo·trop′ic** (kē′mō-trŏp′ĭk, kĕm′ō-) *adj.*

chem·ur·gy (kĕm′ər-jē, kĭ-mûr′-) *n.* The development of new industrial chemical products from organic raw materials, especially from those of agricultural origin. **—che·mur′gic** (kĭ-mûr′jĭk), **che·mur′gi·cal** *adj.*

Chen also **Ch'ên** (chŭn). A Chinese dynasty that ruled from 557 to 589.

Che·nab (chə-näb′). A river, about 1,086 km (675 mi) long, of northern India and eastern Pakistan. It is one of the five rivers of the Punjab.

Cheng·chow (jŭng′jō′, jœng′-). See **Zhengzhou.**

Cheng·du also **Cheng·tu** (chŭng′do͞o′). A city of south-central China west-northwest of Chongqing. Founded before 770 B.C., it is one of China's oldest cities. Population, 1,590,000.

che·nille (shə-nēl′) *n.* **1.** A soft, tufted cord of silk, cotton, or worsted used in embroidery or for fringing. **2.** Fabric made of this cord, commonly used for bedspreads or rugs. [French *chenille,* caterpillar, chenille, from Latin *canīcula,* diminutive of *canis,* dog. See **kwon-** in Appendix.]

Che·nin Blanc (shĕn′ĭn blängk′) *n.* **1.** A grape used in making white wine. **2.** The white wine so made.

che·no·pod (kē′nə-pŏd′, kĕn′ə-) *n.* Any plant of the goosefoot family, which includes spinach, beets, and pigweed. [From New Latin *Chenopodiaceae,* family name, from *Chenopodium,* type genus : Greek *khēn,* goose; see **ghans-** in Appendix + *-podium,* neuter of *-podius,* -pod.]

Che·ops (kē′ŏps). Originally **Khu·fu** (ko͞o′fo͞o′). 2590–2567 B.C. Second king of the IV Dynasty of Egypt, renowned as the builder of the Great Pyramid at Giza.

cheque (chĕk) *n. Chiefly British.* Variant of **check.**

cheq·uer (chĕk′ər) *n. Chiefly British.* Variant of **checker.**

Cher (shĕr). A river of central France flowing about 354 km (220 mi) to the Loire River near Tours.

Cher·bourg (shâr′bo͝org′, shĕr-bo͞or′). A city of northwest France on the English Channel. The site has been occupied since ancient times and was frequently contested by the French and English because of its strategic location. Population, 28,442.

Che·ren·kov also **Ce·ren·kov** (chə-rĕng′kôf, -kəf, chĭ-ryĭn-kôf′), **Pavel Alekseevich.** Born 1904. Russian physicist. He shared a 1958 Nobel Prize for work leading to the development of a cosmic-ray counter.

Che·ren·kov effect (chə-rĕng′kôf, -kəf) *n.* Variant of **Cerenkov effect.**

Cherenkov radiation *n.* Variant of **Cerenkov radiation.**

Che·re·po·vets (chĕr′ə-pə-vĕts′, chĭ-rĭ-pŭ-vyĕts′). A city of east-central Russia north of Moscow. It grew around a monastery established in the 14th century. Population, 299,000.

cher·i·moy·a (chĕr′ə-moi′ə) *n.* **1.** A tropical American tree *(Annona cherimola)* having heart-shaped, edible fruits with green skin and white, aromatic flesh. **2.** The fruit of this plant. [American Spanish *chirimoya,* from Quechua *chirimuya.*]

cher·ish (chĕr′ĭsh) *tr.v.* **-ished, -ish·ing, -ish·es. 1.** To treat with affection and tenderness; hold dear: *cherish one's family; fine rugs that are cherished by their owners.* **2.** To keep fondly in mind; entertain: *cherish a memory.* See Synonyms at **appreciate.** [Middle English *cherishen,* from Old French *cherir, cheriss-,* from *cher,* dear, from Latin *cārus.* See **kā-** in Appendix.] **—cher′ish·a·ble** *n.* **—cher′ish·er** *n.* **—cher′ish·ing·ly** *adv.*

Cher·kas·sy (chər-kä′sē). A city of central Ukraine on the Dnieper River south-southeast of Kiev. It was an important Cossack outpost before passing to Russia in the 1790's. Population, 273,000.

Cher·ni·gov (chər-nē′gəf, -nyĕ′-). A city of north-central Ukraine north-northeast of Kiev. First mentioned in 907, it was the capital of the Chernigov principality in the 11th century and later passed to Lithuania, Poland, and Russia (1868). Population, 278,000.

Cher·no·byl (chər-nō′bəl, chyĭr-nô′bĭl). A city of north-central Ukraine north-northwest of Kiev. It was the site of a major nuclear power plant accident on April 16, 1986.

Cher·nov·tsy (chər-nôft′sē, chyĭr-nŭf-tsĭ′). A city of southwest Ukraine in the foothills of the Carpathian Mountains near the Romanian border. It was a center of the Ukrainian nationalist movement in the 19th and early 20th centuries. Population, 244,000.

cher·no·zem (chĕr′nə-zĕm′, chîr′nə-zyôm′) *n.* A very black topsoil, rich in humus, typical of cool to temperate semiarid regions, such as the grasslands of European Russia. [Russian *chernozëm* : *chërnyĭ,* black + Old Russian *zemĭ,* earth; see **dhghem-** in Appendix.] **—cher′no·zem′ic** *adj.*

Cher·o·kee (chĕr′ə-kē′, chĕr′ə-kē′) *n., pl.* **Cherokee** or **-kees. 1.a.** A Native American people formerly inhabiting the southern Appalachian Mountains from the western Carolinas and eastern Tennessee to northern Georgia, with present-day populations in northeast Oklahoma and western North Carolina. The Cherokee were removed to Indian Territory in the 1830's after conflict with American settlers over rights to traditional lands. **b.** A member of this people. **2.** The Iroquoian language of the Cherokee. [From Cherokee *tsalaki.*] **—Cher′o·kee′** *adj.*

Cherokee rose *n.* A prickly, climbing, evergreen rose *(Rosa laevigata)* native to China and naturalized in the southeast United States, having showy, white, fragrant flowers.

Cherokee Strip or **Cherokee Outlet.** A plot of land in present-day northern Oklahoma. Purchased from the Cherokee Nation by the United States in 1891, it was opened to settlement in 1893.

che·root also **she·root** (shə-ro͞ot′) *n.* A cigar with square-cut ends. [French *cheroute,* ultimately from Tamil *curuṭṭu,* from *curi,* to be spiral.]

cher·ry (chĕr′ē) *n., pl.* **-ries. 1.a.** Any of several trees or shrubs of the genus *Prunus,* especially *P. avium* or *P. cerasus,* native chiefly to northern temperate regions and having pink or white flowers and small, juicy drupes. **b.** The yellow, red, or blackish fruit of any of these plants. **c.** The wood of any of these plants, especially black cherry. **d.** Any of various plants, such as the Barbados cherry or the cornelian cherry, having fruits resembling a cherry. **2.** *Color.* A moderate or strong red to purplish red. **3.** *Vulgar Slang.* The hymen considered as a symbol of virginity. **—cherry** *adj.* **1.** Containing or having the flavor of cher-

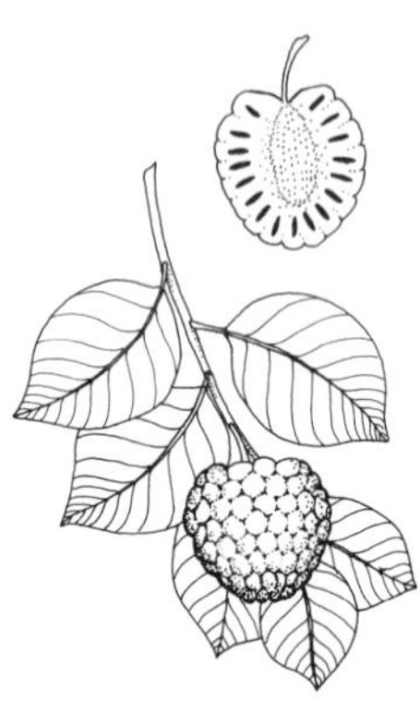
cherimoya
Annona cherimola

cherry

cherry picker

ă pat	oi boy
ā pay	ou **out**
âr care	o͝o took
ä father	o͞o boot
ĕ pet	ŭ cut
ē be	ûr **urge**
ĭ pit	th **thin**
ī pie	*th* this
îr pier	hw **which**
ŏ pot	zh vision
ō toe	ə about, item
ô paw	♦ regionalism

Stress marks: ′ (primary); ′ (secondary), as in **dictionary** (dĭk′shə-nĕr′ē)

ries. **2.** Made of the wood of a cherry tree: *a cherry cabinet.* **3.** *Color.* Of a moderate or strong red to purplish red. [Middle English *cheri,* from Anglo-Norman *cherise,* variant of Old French *cerise,* from Vulgar Latin **ceresia,* from **cerasia,* from Greek *kerasia,* cherry tree, from *kerasos,* of Semitic origin; akin to Assyrian *karšu.*]

cherry birch *n.* See **sweet birch.**

cherry bomb *n.* A red, ball-shaped firecracker that explodes with a loud bang.

Cher·ry Hill (chĕr′ē). An urban township of west-central New Jersey east-southeast of Camden. It is mainly residential. Population, 68,785.

cherry laurel *n.* A frequently cultivated Eurasian evergreen shrub or small tree *(Prunus laurocerasus)* in the rose family, having showy clusters of white flowers and glossy foliage that yields an oil similar to bitter almond oil.

cherry picker *n.* A mobile crane having a maneuverable vertical boom, at the top of which a passenger can do such work as tree pruning and street-light maintenance.

cherry plum *n.* A deciduous ornamental Eurasian shrub or small tree *(Prunus cerasifera)* in the rose family, having white flowers and small red to yellow edible fruits. Also called *myrobalan, myrobalan plum.*

cher·ry·stone (chĕr′ē-stōn′) *n.* The quahog clam when half-grown and of comparatively small size.

cherry tomato *n.* A variety of tomato *(Lycopersicon esculentum* var. *cerasiforme)* having small red to yellow fruits.

cher·so·nese (kûr′sə-nēz′, -nēs′) *n.* A peninsula. [Latin *chersonēsus,* from Greek *khersonēsos* : *khersos,* dry land + *nēsos,* island; see **snā-** in Appendix.]

chert (chûrt) *n.* **1.** A variety of silica that contains microcrystalline quartz. **2.** A siliceous rock of chalcedonic or opaline silica occurring in limestone. [Origin unknown.] **—chert′y** *adj.*

cher·ub (chĕr′əb) *n.* **1.** *pl.* **cher·u·bim** (chĕr′ə-bĭm′, -yə-bĭm′). **a.** A winged celestial being. **b.** One of the second order of angels. **2.** *pl.* **cher·ubs. a.** A representation of a small angel, portrayed as a child with a chubby, rosy face. **b.** A person, especially a child, with an innocent or chubby face. [Middle English, from Late Latin, from Hebrew *kĕrūb.*] **—che·ru′bic** (chə-ro͞o′bĭk) *adj.* **—che·ru′bi·cal·ly** *adv.*

Che·ru·bi·ni (kĕr′ə-bē′nē, kĕ′ro͞o-), **(Maria) Luigi Carlo Zenobio Salvatore.** 1760–1842. Italian composer whose 29 operas, including *Les Deux Journées* (1800), helped form the transition in music from classicism to romanticism.

cher·vil (chûr′vəl) *n.* **1.** An annual Eurasian herb *(Anthriscus cerefolium)* in the parsley family, having aromatic parsleylike leaves that are used as a seasoning or garnish. **2.** Any of several related plants, such as those of the genus *Chaerophyllum.* [Middle English, from Old English *cerfille,* from Latin *chaerephyllum,* from Greek *khairephullon* : *khairein,* to greet, delight in; see **gher-**[2] in Appendix + *phullon,* leaf; see **bhel-**[3] in Appendix.]

Ches·a·peake (chĕs′ə-pēk′). An independent city of southeast Virginia south of Norfolk. Its vast area includes residential communities, farmland, and a section of the Great Dismal Swamp. Population, 114,486.

Chesapeake Bay. An inlet of the Atlantic Ocean separating the Delmarva Peninsula from mainland Maryland and Virginia. Explored and charted by John Smith in 1608, it is an important link in the Intracoastal Waterway.

Chesapeake Bay retriever *n.* A hunting dog of a breed developed in the United States, and having a thick, short, wavy coat ranging from dark brown to tan in color and known for its skill in retrieving game from water.

Chesh·ire[1] (chĕsh′ər, -îr′). A town of south-central Connecticut north of New Haven. It is mainly residential. Population, 21,788.

Chesh·ire[2] also **chesh·ire** (chĕsh′ər) *n.* A hard, yellow English cheese made from cow's milk. [After *Cheshire,* a county of west-central England.]

Ches·hunt (chĕs′ənt). An urban district of southeast England, a residential suburb of London. Population, 79,700.

Ches·nutt (chĕs′nŭt′), **Charles Waddell.** 1858–1932. American writer whose works, such as *The Wife of His Youth* (1899), concern racial prejudice and life among Black Americans.

chess[1] (chĕs) *n. Games.* A board game for two players, each beginning with 16 pieces of six kinds that are moved according to individual rules, with the objective of checkmating the opposing king. [Middle English *ches,* short for Old French *esches,* pl. of *eschec,* check in chess. See CHECK.]

chess[2] (chĕs) *n.* Any of several species of brome grass, especially the cheat. [Origin unknown.]

chess[3] (chĕs) *n., pl.* **chess** or **chess·es.** One of the floorboards of a pontoon bridge. [Middle English *ches,* tier, perhaps from Old French *chasse,* frame, from Latin *capsa,* box.]

chess·board (chĕs′bôrd′, -bōrd′) *n. Games.* A board marked with 64 squares, used in playing chess.

chess·man (chĕs′măn′, -mən) *n. Games.* One of the pieces used in playing chess.

ches·sy·lite (shĕs′ə-līt′, chĕs′-) *n.* See **azurite.** [After *Chessy,* a town of east-central France.]

chest (chĕst) *n.* **1.** The part of the body between the neck and the abdomen, enclosed by the ribs and the breastbone; the thorax. **2.a.** A sturdy box with a lid and often a lock, used especially for storage. **b.** A small closet or cabinet with shelves for storing supplies: *a medicine chest above the bathroom sink.* **3.a.** The treasury of a public institution. **b.** The funds kept there. **4.a.** A box for the shipping of certain goods, such as tea. **b.** The quantity packed in such a box. **5.** A sealed receptacle for liquid, gas, or steam. **6.** A bureau; a dresser. ***—idiom.*** **get (something) off (one's) chest.** To vent one's pent-up feelings. [Middle English, from Old English *cest,* box, from West Germanic **kistā,* from Latin *cista,* from Greek *kistē.*] **—chest′ed** (chĕs′tĭd) *adj.*

Ches·ter (chĕs′tər). **1.** A borough of west-central England on the Dee River south-southeast of Liverpool. The Romans built a fort here to defend the river crossing into Wales and named the settlement Deva. Chester is known for its Rows, a double tier of shops and houses along its main streets. Population, 58,100. **2.** A city of southeast Pennsylvania on the Delaware River, an industrial suburb of Philadelphia. Established as Upland, it was the site of William Penn's first landing in America (1682) and is the oldest city in the state. Population, 45,794.

♦**ches·ter·field** (chĕs′tər-fēld′) *n.* **1.** A single- or double-breasted overcoat, usually with concealed buttons and a velvet collar. **2.** *Chiefly Northern California & Canada.* A large, overstuffed sofa with upright armrests. [After a 19th-century earl of *Chesterfield.*]

♦ ***REGIONAL NOTE:*** *Chesterfield,* a term for any type of sofa, was probably brought down from Canada, where it is common. According to Craig M. Carver in *American Regional Dialects,* this regionalism is "unique to northern California." The word probably comes from the name of a 19th-century earl of Chesterfield and originally referred "specifically to a couch with upright armrests at either end." It appears to have come into use in Canada around 1903 and in Northern California at about the same time.

Ches·ter·field (chĕs′tər-fēld′). A city of north-central England south of Sheffield. It is an important industrial center. Population, 96,300.

Chesterfield, Fourth Earl of. Title of Philip Dormer Stanhope. 1694–1773. English politician and writer best known for *Letters to His Son* (1774).

Ches·ter·ton (chĕs′tər-tən), **Gilbert Keith.** 1874–1936. British writer and critic known for his Roman Catholicism and his conservative political views. His works include essays, a series of detective novels featuring Father Brown, and volumes of criticism and polemics.

Chester White *n.* Any of a breed of large white hogs with drooping ears that were originally bred in Chester County in southeast Pennsylvania.

chest·nut (chĕs′nŭt′, -nət) *n.* **1.a.** Any of several deciduous trees of the genus *Castanea* native to northern temperate regions, having alternate, simple, toothed leaves, and nuts enclosed in a prickly husk. **b.** The often edible nut of any of these trees. **c.** The wood of any of these trees. **2.** Any of several other plants, such as the horse chestnut. **3.** *Color.* A moderate to deep reddish brown. **4.** A reddish-brown horse. **5.** A small, hard callus on the inner surface of a horse's foreleg. **6.** An old, frequently repeated joke, story, or song. **—chestnut** *adj. Color.* Of a moderate to deep reddish brown. [Earlier *chesten* (from Middle English *chesteine,* from Old French *chastaigne,* from Latin *castanea,* from Greek *kastanea,* chestnut tree) + NUT.]

chestnut blight *n.* A disease of chestnut trees caused by a fungus *(Cryphonectria parasitica)* that is especially destructive to the American chestnut, characterized by cankers that eventually kill the branches and trunk.

chestnut oak *n.* Either of two eastern North American deciduous oak trees *(Quercus prinus* and *Q. muehlenbergii)* having leaves that resemble those of the American chestnut.

chest of drawers *n., pl.* **chests of drawers.** A piece of furniture consisting of a set of drawers that fit within a frame.

chest·y (chĕs′tē) *adj.* **-i·er, -i·est.** *Informal.* **1.** Having a large or well-developed chest or bust. **2.** Arrogant or proud; conceited. **—chest′i·ness** *n.*

che·tah (chē′tə) *n.* Variant of **cheetah.**

chet·rum (chē′trəm, chĕt′rəm) *n.* See table at **currency.** [Native word in Bhutan.]

che·val-de-frise (shə-văl′də-frēz′) *n., pl.* **che·vaux-de-frise** (shə-vō′-). **1.** An obstacle composed of barbed wire or spikes attached to a wooden frame, used to block enemy advancement. **2.** An obstacle made of jagged glass or spikes set into masonry on top of a wall. [French, Frisian horse (from its use in Friesland to compensate for a lack of cavalry) : *cheval,* horse + *de,* of + *Frise,* Friesland.]

che·val·et (shə-văl′ā, shĕv′ə-lā′) *n. Music.* The bridge of a stringed instrument. [French, from diminutive of *cheval,* horse, from Latin *caballus.*]

che·val glass (shə-văl′) *n.* A long mirror mounted on swivels in a frame. [From French *cheval,* support, horse. See CHEVALET.]

chev·a·lier (shĕv′ə-lîr′) *n.* **1.** A member of certain male orders of knighthood or merit, such as the Legion of Honor in France. **2.a.** A French nobleman of the lowest rank. **b.** Used as a title for such a nobleman. **3.** A knight. **4.** A chivalrous man. [Middle English *chevaler,* from Old French *chevalier,* from Late Latin *caballārius,* horseman, from *caballus,* horse.]

Che·va·lier (shə-văl′yā, shə-vä-lyā′), **Maurice.** 1888–1972.

cherub

chess[1]

chestnut

cheval glass
c. 1815 American, attributed to the workshop of Duncan Phyfe or to Charles Honoré Lannuier (fl. 1803–1819)

French actor and singer best known for his cabaret appearances and his role in the musical film *Gigi* (1958).

che·vaux-de-frise (shə-vō′də-frēz′) *n.* Plural of **cheval-de-frise.**

che·ve·lure (shəv-lür′) *n.* A head of hair. [Middle English *cheveler,* from Old French *cheveleure,* from Latin *capillātūra,* from *capillus,* hair.]

Chev·i·ot (shĕv′ē-ət, chĕv′-) *n.* **1.** Any of a breed of hornless sheep with short, thick wool, originally raised in the Cheviot Hills. **2.** Also **cheviot.** A woolen fabric with a coarse twill weave, used chiefly for suits and overcoats and originally made from the wool of this breed of sheep. [After the CHEVIOT (HILLS).]

Cheviot Hills (chĕv′ē-ət, shĭv′-, chē′vē-). A range of hills extending about 56 km (35 mi) along the border between England and Scotland. **The Cheviot,** 816.2 m (2,676 ft), is the highest elevation.

chè·vre (shĕv′rə) *n.* Cheese made from goat's milk. [French, from Old French, from Latin *capra,* she-goat, feminine of *caper,* goat.]

chevron
On uniform of a 1980 West Point graduate

chev·ron (shĕv′rən) *n.* **1.** A badge or insignia consisting of stripes meeting at an angle, worn on the sleeve of a military or police uniform to indicate rank, merit, or length of service. **2.** *Heraldry.* A device shaped like an inverted V. **3.** A V-shaped pattern, especially a kind of fret used in architecture. [Middle English *cheveron,* from Old French *chevron,* rafter (from the meeting of rafters at an angle), probably from Vulgar Latin **capriō, capriōn-,* from Latin *caper, capr-,* goat.]

chev·ro·tain (shĕv′rə-tān′) *n.* Any of several small, deerlike, hornless ruminants of the genera *Hyemoschus* and *Tragulus* native to the tropical rain forests of central Africa, India, and southeast Asia. Also called *mouse deer.* [French *chevrotin,* from Old French, diminutive of *chevrot,* kid, diminutive of *chevre,* goat, from Latin *capra,* she-goat, feminine of *caper,* goat.]

chew (cho͞o) *v.* **chewed, chew·ing, chews.** —*tr.* **1.** To bite and grind with the teeth; masticate. **2.** To meditate on; ponder: *chew a problem over.* —*intr.* **1.** To make a crushing and grinding motion with the teeth. See Regional Note at **chaw. 2.** To cogitate; meditate: *chewed on the difficulties ahead.* **3.** *Informal.* To use chewing tobacco. —**chew** *n.* **1.** The act of chewing. **2.** Something held in the mouth and chewed, especially a plug of tobacco. —***phrasal verb.* chew out.** *Slang.* To reprimand; scold. —***idioms.* chew the cud.** *Slang.* To ponder over; meditate. **chew the fat** (or **rag**). *Slang.* To talk together in a friendly, leisurely way; chat at length. [Middle English *cheuen,* from Old English *cēowan.*] —**chew′a·ble** *adj.* —**chew′er** *n.*

Che·wa (chā′wä) *n.* A Bantu language spoken in Malawi, closely related to Nyanja.

chew·ing gum (cho͞o′ĭng) *n.* A sweetened, flavored preparation for chewing, usually made of chicle.

che·wink (chĭ-wĭngk′) *n.* See **towhee** (sense 1). [Imitative of its call.]

chew·y (cho͞o′ē) *adj.* **-i·er, -i·est.** Needing much chewing: *chewy candy.* —**chew′i·ness** *n.*

Chey·enne[1] (shī-ĕn′, -ăn′) *n., pl.* **Cheyenne** or **-ennes. 1.a.** A Native American people, divided after 1832 into the Northern and Southern Cheyenne, inhabiting respectively southeast Montana and southern Colorado, with present-day populations in Montana and Oklahoma. The Cheyenne became nomadic buffalo hunters after migrating to the Great Plains in the 18th century and figured prominently in the resistance by Plains Indians to white encroachment. **b.** A member of this people. **2.** The Algonquian language of the Cheyenne. [Canadian French, from Dakota *šahíyela.*] —**Chey·enne′** *adj.*

Chey·enne[2] (shī-ăn′, -ĕn′). The capital of Wyoming, in the southeast part of the state near the Nebraska and Colorado borders. It was founded in 1867 as a division point for the Union Pacific Railroad. Population, 47,283.

Cheyenne River. A river rising in eastern Wyoming and flowing about 848 km (527 mi) east then northeast to the Missouri River in central South Dakota.

Cheyne-Stokes respiration (chān′stōks′, chā′nē-stōks′) *n.* An abnormal type of breathing seen especially in comatose patients, characterized by alternating periods of shallow and deep breathing. [After John *Cheyne* (1777–1836), Scottish physician, and William *Stokes* (1804–1878), Irish physician.]

chez (shā) *prep.* At the home of; at or by. [French, from Old French, from Latin *casa,* cottage, hut.]

chg. *abbr.* **1.** Change. **2.** Charge.

chi also **khi** (kī) *n.* The 22nd letter of the Greek alphabet. See table at **alphabet.** [Greek *khi.*]

chi·a (chē′ə) *n.* An aromatic annual plant *(Salvia columbariae)* in the mint family, native to Mexico and the southwest United States and having clusters of blue or violet flowers and edible seedlike fruits. [American Spanish *chía,* from Nahuatl *chiah.*]

Chiang Kai-shek

Chi·ai or **Chia-i** (jē-ī′, jyä′ē′). A city of southwest Taiwan north of Kaohsiung. It is an agricultural market center. Population, 252,376.

Chia-ling (jyä′lĭng′). See **Jialing.**

Chia·mus·su (jyä′mo͞o′so͞o′). See **Jiamusi.**

Chiang Kai-shek (chăng′ kī′shĕk′, jyäng′). 1887–1975. Chinese military and political figure who led the Nationalists against the rising Communist forces and was driven from the mainland to Taiwan (1949), where he served as president of Nationalist China until his death.

Chi·an·ti (kē-än′tē, -ăn′-) *n.* A dry table wine, usually red, originally produced in northwest Italy. [After the *Chianti* Mountains, a range of the Apennines in central Italy.]

chiao (chyou) *n., pl.* **chiao.** Variant of **jiao.**

chi·a·ro·scu·ro (kē-är′ə-sko͝or′ō, -skyo͝or′ō) *n., pl.* **-ros. 1.** The technique of using light and shade in pictorial representation. **2.** The arrangement of light and dark elements in a pictorial work of art. Also called *claire-obscure.* [Italian : *chiaro,* bright, light (from Latin *clārus,* clear; see **kelə-[2]** in Appendix) + *oscuro,* dark (from Latin *obscūrus;* see **(s)keu-** in Appendix).] —**chi·a′ro·scu′rist** *n.*

chi·as·ma (kī-ăz′mə) also **chi·asm** (kī′ăz′əm) *n., pl.* **-ma·ta** (-mə-tə) or **-mas** also **-asms. 1.** *Anatomy.* A crossing or intersection of two tracts, as of nerves or ligaments. **2.** *Genetics.* The point of contact between paired chromatids during meiosis, resulting in a cross-shaped configuration and representing the cytological manifestation of crossing over. [Greek *khiasma,* crosspiece, from *khiazein,* to mark with an X, from *khi,* chi (from the letter's shape).] —**chi·as′mal, chi·as′mic, chi′as·mat′ic** (-măt′ĭk) *adj.*

chi·as·ma·ty·py (kī-ăz′mə-tī′pē) *n.* The meiotic twisting between paired chromatids that produces chiasmata. [CHIASMA + TYP(E) + -Y[2].]

chi·as·mus (kī-ăz′məs) *n., pl.* **-mi** (-mī′). A rhetorical inversion of the second of two parallel structures, as in *"Each throat/Was parched, and glazed each eye"* (Samuel Taylor Coleridge). [New Latin, from Greek *khiasmos,* syntactic inversion, from *khiazein,* to invert or mark with an X. See CHIASMA.]

chi·as·to·lite (kī-ăs′tə-līt′) *n.* A mineral variety of andalusite with carbonaceous impurities regularly arranged along the longer axis of the crystal. [From Greek *khiastos,* crossed, past participle of *khiazein,* to mark with an X. See CHIASMA.]

chiaus (chous, choush) *n.* An official Turkish messenger, emissary, or sergeant. [Turkish *çavuş,* from Old Turkic *chāv,* announcement.]

Chi·ba (chē′bä′). A city of east central Honshu, Japan, on the northeast shore of Tokyo Bay. It is a manufacturing center. Population, 788,920.

Chib·cha (chĭb′chə) *n., pl.* **Chibcha** or **-chas. 1.** A member of an extinct Indian people once inhabiting central Colombia. **2.** The extinct language of the Chibcha.

Chib·chan (chĭb′chən) *n.* **1.** A member of a widely scattered Indian people of Colombia and Central America. **2.** A language family comprising the Chibchan languages.

Chi·bem·ba (chĭ-bĕm′bə) *n.* See **Bemba.**

chi·bouk also **chi·bouque** (chĭ-bo͝ok′, shĭ-) *n.* A Turkish tobacco pipe with a long stem and a red clay bowl. [Turkish dialectal *çibuk,* from *çubuk,* shoot, twig, staff, from Old Turkic *chubuq, chībīq,* diminutive of *chīp, chīb-,* branch.]

chic (shēk) *adj.* **chic·er, chic·est. 1.** Conforming to the current fashion; stylish: *chic clothes; a chic boutique.* **2.** Adopting or setting current fashions and styles; sophisticated: *chic, well-dressed young executives.* See Synonyms at **fashionable.** —**chic** *n.* **1.** The quality or state of being stylish; fashionableness. **2.** Sophistication in dress and manner; elegance. [French, probably from German *Schick,* skill, fitness, elegance, from Middle High German *(sich) schicken,* to outfit (oneself); fit in.] —**chic′ly** *adv.* —**chic′ness** *n.*

Chi·ca·go (shĭ-kä′gō, -kô′-). The largest city of Illinois, in the northeast part of the state on Lake Michigan. It is a major port and the commercial, financial, industrial, and cultural center of the Middle West. The city was nearly destroyed by a disastrous fire in 1871. Population, 3,005,072. —**Chi·ca′go·an** *n.*

Chicago, Judy. Born 1939. American artist best known for *The Dinner Party* (1979), a ceramic and needlepoint project depicting the social history of women in the Western world.

Chicago Heights. A city of northeast Illinois south of Chicago. It is an industrial center. Population, 37,026.

Chicago River. A river formed at Chicago by the junction of northern and southern branches that total about 55 km (34 mi) in length. It is an important link in the Illinois Waterway.

Chi·ca·na (chĭ-kä′nə, shĭ-) *n.* *Usage Problem.* A Mexican-American woman or girl. See Usage Note at **Chicano.** [American Spanish, feminine of *chicano,* chicano. See CHICANO.] —**Chi·ca′na** *adj.*

chi·cane (shĭ-kān′, chĭ-) *v.* **-caned, -can·ing, -canes.** —*intr.* To resort to tricks or subterfuges; use chicanery. —*tr.* To trick; deceive. —**chicane** *n.* **1.** Chicanery. **2.** *Games.* A bridge or whist hand without trumps. [French *chicaner,* from Old French, to quibble.] —**chi·can′er** *n.*

chi·can·er·y (shĭ-kā′nə-rē, chĭ-) *n., pl.* **-ies. 1.** Deception by trickery or sophistry. **2.** A trick; a subterfuge.

Chi·ca·no (chĭ-kä′nō, shĭ-) *n., pl.* **-nos.** *Usage Problem.* A Mexican-American. —**Chicano** *adj.* Of or relating to Mexican-Americans or their culture. [American Spanish, dialectal variant of *Mexicano,* Mexican, from *México,* Mexico.]

USAGE NOTE: Care should be taken in using the term *Chicano* when referring to Mexican-Americans. In some regions of the

Southwest the term suggests ethnic pride; in others it may be felt to be derogatory. See Usage Note at **Hispanic.**

Chi·chén It·zá (chē-chĕn′ ē-tsä′, ēt′sə). An ancient Mayan city of central Yucatán in Mexico. It was founded c. A.D. 514 and abandoned in 1194.

chi·chi (shē′shē) *adj.* **-chi·er, -chi·est.** Ostentatiously stylish; deliberately chic. **—chichi** *n.* Ostentatious stylishness. [French.]

chick (chĭk) *n.* **1.a.** A young chicken. **b.** The young of any bird. **2.** A child. **3.** *Slang.* A girl or young woman. [Middle English *chike,* variant of *chiken,* chicken. See CHICKEN.]

chick·a·dee (chĭk′ə-dē′) *n.* Any of several small, plump North American birds of the genus *Parus,* having predominantly gray plumage and a dark-crowned head. [Imitative of its call.]

Chick·a·mau·ga (chĭk′ə-mô′gə). A city of extreme northwest Georgia south of Chattanooga, Tennessee. Confederate troops led by Braxton Bragg defeated Union forces here on September 19–20, 1863. Population, 2,232.

chick·a·ree (chĭk′ə-rē′) *n.* A small squirrel *(Tamiasciurus douglasi)* of the evergreen forests of northwest North America, resembling and closely related to the red squirrel. [Imitative.]

Chick·a·saw (chĭk′ə-sô′) *n., pl.* **Chick·a·saw** or **-saws. 1.a.** A Native American people formerly inhabiting northeast Mississippi and northwest Alabama, now located in south-central Oklahoma. The Chickasaw were removed to Indian Territory in the 1830's. **b.** A member of this people. **2.** The Muskogean language of the Chickasaw. **—Chick′a·saw′** *adj.*

Chick·a·sa·whay (chĭk′ə-sô′wā). A river, about 338 km (210 mi) long, of southeast Mississippi.

chick·en (chĭk′ən) *n.* **1.a.** The common domestic fowl *(Gallus domesticus)* or its young. **b.** Any of various similar or related birds. **c.** The flesh of the common domestic fowl. **2.** *Slang.* A coward. **3.** Any of various foolhardy competitions in which the participants persist in a dangerous course of action until one loses nerve and stops. **—chicken** *adj. Slang.* Afraid; cowardly. **—chicken** *intr.v.* **-ened, -en·ing, -ens.** *Slang.* To act in a cowardly manner; lose one's nerve: *chickened out at the last moment.* [Middle English *chiken,* from Old English *cīcen.*]

chicken breast *n. Pathology.* See **pigeon breast. —chick′en-breast′ed** (chĭk′ən-brĕs′tĭd) *adj.*

chicken feed *n. Slang.* A trifling amount of money.

chicken hawk *n.* **1.** Any of various hawks that prey on or have the reputation of preying on chickens. **2.** *Vulgar Slang.* A man who seeks out young boys as his sexual partners.

chick·en-heart·ed (chĭk′ən-här′tĭd) *adj.* Lacking courage; cowardly. **—chick′en·heart′ed·ness** *n.*

Chick·en Little (chĭk′ən) *n.* A confirmed pessimist, particularly one who warns of impending disaster. [After a character in a story who is hit on the head by an acorn and believes the sky is falling.]

chick·en-liv·ered (chĭk′ən-lĭv′ərd) *adj.* Cowardly.

chick·en·pox or **chicken pox** (chĭk′ən-pŏks′) *n.* An acute contagious disease, primarily of children, that is caused by the varicella-zoster virus and characterized by skin eruptions, slight fever, and malaise. Also called *varicella.*

chicken run *n.* An enclosed area in which chickens are allowed to walk and run about.

chicken shit *Obscene. n.* Contemptibly petty, insignificant nonsense. **—chicken shit** *adj.* **1.** Contemptibly unimportant; petty. **2.** Cowardly; afraid.

chicken snake *n.* See **rat snake.**

chicken wire *n.* A light-gauge galvanized wire fencing usually made with hexagonal mesh.

chick·pea (chĭk′pē′) *n.* **1.** An annual Asian plant *(Cicer arietinum)* in the pea family, widely cultivated for the edible seeds in its short, inflated pods. **2.** A seed of this plant. Also called *garbanzo.* [Obsolete *chichpease* : Middle English *chiche,* chickpea (from Old French, from Latin *cicer*) + *pease,* pea; see PEA.]

chick·weed (chĭk′wēd′) *n.* Any of various herbs of the genera *Cerastium* and *Stellaria,* especially *S. media,* a European weed naturalized worldwide. The herb has small white flowers, petals with two deep lobes, and opposite leaves. [So called because it is eaten by chickens.]

Chi·cla·yo (chĭ-klä′yō, chē-). A city of northwest Peru north-northwest of Lima. Situated on the coastal desert between the Andes and the Pacific Ocean, the city may go years at a time without rainfall. Population, 213,095.

chic·le (chĭk′əl) *n.* The coagulated milky juice of the sapodilla, used as the principal ingredient of chewing gum. [Spanish, from Nahuatl *chictli.*]

Chic·lets (chĭk′lĭts). A trademark used for chewing gum in the form of small, square, candy-coated pieces.

Chi·co (chē′kō). A city of northern California northwest of Oroville. It is a processing and packing center in an almond-growing region. Population, 26,603.

Chic·o·pee (chĭk′ə-pē). A city of southwest Massachusetts on the Connecticut River near Springfield. It was founded c. 1641 and set off from Springfield in 1848. Population, 55,112.

chic·o·ry (chĭk′ə-rē) *n., pl.* **-ries. 1.** A perennial herb *(Cichorium intybus)* of the composite family, native to the Old World, widely naturalized in North America, and having rayed flower heads with blue florets. Also called *succory.* **2.** Any of various forms of this plant having edible leaves, such as radicchio. **3.** The dried, roasted, ground roots of this plant, used as an adulterant of or substitute for coffee. [Middle English *cicoree* (from Old French *cichoree*) and French *chicorée,* both from Latin *cichorium, cichorēum,* from Greek *kikhoreia,* pl. diminutive of *kikhora, kikhorē.*]

Chi·cou·ti·mi (shĭ-ko͞o′tə-mē). A city of south-central Quebec, Canada, on the Saguenay River north of Quebec City. A Jesuit mission was established here in 1676. Population, 60,064.

chide (chīd) *v.* **chid·ed** or **chid** (chĭd), **chid·ed** or **chid** or **chid·den** (chĭd′n), **chid·ing, chid·es.** *—tr.* To scold mildly so as to correct or improve; reprimand: *chided the boy for his sloppiness. —intr.* To express disapproval. [Middle English *chiden,* from Old English *cīdan,* from *cīd,* strife, contention.] **—chid′er** *n.* **—chid′ing·ly** *adv.*

chief (chēf) *n. Abbr.* **ch., Ch., C. 1.** One who is highest in rank or authority; a leader. **2.** Often **Chief. a.** A chief petty officer. **b.** *Nautical.* The chief engineer of a ship. **3.** *Slang.* A boss. **4.** *Heraldry.* The upper section of a shield. **5.** The most important or valuable part. **—chief** *adj.* **1.** Highest in rank, authority, or office. **2.** Most important or influential. See Usage Note at **perfect. —chief** *adv. Archaic.* Chiefly. [Middle English *chef,* from Old French, from Latin *caput,* head. See **kaput-** in Appendix.] **—chief′dom** *n.* **—chief′ship′** *n.*

chief executive *n.* **1. Chief Executive.** The President of the United States. **2.** A principal executive official, such as the leader of a nation's government or the governor of a state.

chief executive officer *n. Abbr.* **CEO, C.E.O.** The highest-ranking executive in a company or organization, responsible for carrying out the policies of the board of directors on a day-to-day basis.

chief justice also **Chief Justice** *n. Abbr.* **C.J.** The presiding judge of a high court having several judges, especially the U.S. Supreme Court.

chief·ly (chēf′lē) *adv.* **1.** Above all; especially. **2.** Almost entirely; mainly. **—chiefly** *adj.* Of or relating to a chief: *chiefly responsibilities.*

chief master sergeant *n. Abbr.* **CMSGT 1.** A noncommissioned rank in the U.S. Air Force that is above senior master sergeant. **2.** One who holds this rank.

chief of staff *n., pl.* **chiefs of staff.** *Abbr.* **CS, C. of S. 1.** Often **Chief of Staff.** The ranking officer of the U.S. Army or Air Force, responsible to the secretary of his or her branch and to the President. **2.** The senior military staff officer at the division level or higher.

chief of state *n., pl.* **chiefs of state.** The formal head of a nation, distinct from the head of the government.

chief petty officer *n. Abbr.* **CPO 1.** An enlisted rank in the U.S. Navy that is above petty officer first class and below senior chief petty officer. **2.** One who holds this rank.

chief·tain (chēf′tən) *n.* The leader or head of a group, especially a clan or tribe. [Middle English *cheftain,* from Old French *chevetain,* from Late Latin *capitāneus,* from Latin *caput,* head. See **kaput-** in Appendix.] **—chief′tain·cy** *n.* **—chief′tain·ship′** *n.*

Ch'ien-lung (chyĕn′lo͝ong′). See **Qianlong.**

chiff·chaff (chĭf′chăf′) *n.* A small European warbler *(Phylloscopus collybita)* with yellowish-green plumage. [Imitative of its song.]

chif·fon (shĭ-fŏn′, shĭf′ŏn′) *n.* **1.** A fabric of sheer silk or rayon. **2.** Ornamental accessories, such as ribbons or laces, for women's clothing. **—chiffon** *adj.* **1.** Of, relating to, or resembling the fabric chiffon. **2.** Made light and fluffy by the addition of beaten egg whites or gelatin: *a lemon chiffon pie.* [French, rag, chiffon, from *chiffe,* old rag, perhaps variant of Old French *chipe,* of Germanic origin.]

chif·fo·nier (shĭf′ə-nîr′) *n.* A narrow, high chest of drawers or bureau, often with a mirror attached. [French, from *chiffon,* rag. See CHIFFON.]

♦ **chif·fo·robe** (shĭf′ə-rōb′, shĭf′rōb′) *n. Regional.* A tall piece of furniture typically having drawers on one side and space for hanging clothes on the other. [CHIFFO(NIER) + (WARD)ROBE.]

chig·ger (chĭg′ər) *n.* **1.** Any of various small, six-legged larvae of mites of the family Trombiculidae, parasitic on insects, humans, and other vertebrates. The chigger's bite produces a wheal that is usually accompanied by severe itching. Also called *chigoe, harvest bug, harvest mite, jigger, red bug.* **2.** See **chigoe** (sense 1). [Alteration of CHIGOE.]

chi·gnon (shēn-yŏn′, shēn′yŏn′) *n.* A roll or knot of hair worn at the back of the head or especially at the nape of the neck. [French, from Old French *chaignon,* chain, collar, nape, from Vulgar Latin **catēniō,* from Latin *catēna,* chain.]

chig·oe (chĭg′ō, chē′gō) *n.* **1.** A small tropical flea *(Tunga penetrans),* the fertilized female of which burrows under the skin of animals and humans, causing intense irritation and sores that may become severely infected. Also called *chigger, jigger, sand flea.* **2.** See **chigger** (sense 1). [Possibly from Galibi *chico,* or of African origin. See JIGGER².]

Chi·hua·hua¹ (chə-wä′wä, chē-). A city of northern Mexico south of Ciudad Juárez. It is the rail and commercial center for the vast northern section of the country. Population, 385,603.

Chi·hua·hua² (chĭ-wä′wä, -wə) *n.* A very small dog of a breed originating in Mexico, having pointed ears and a smooth

Chichén Itzá

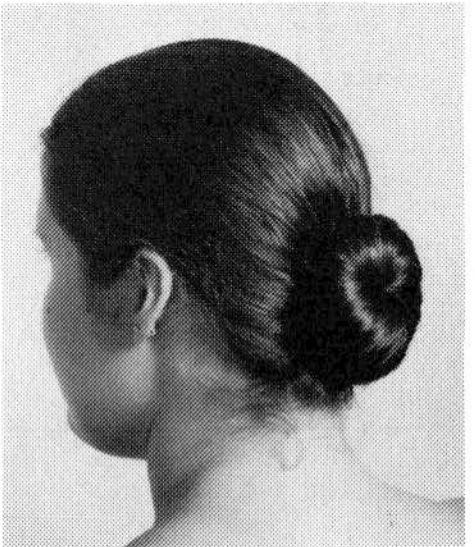

chignon

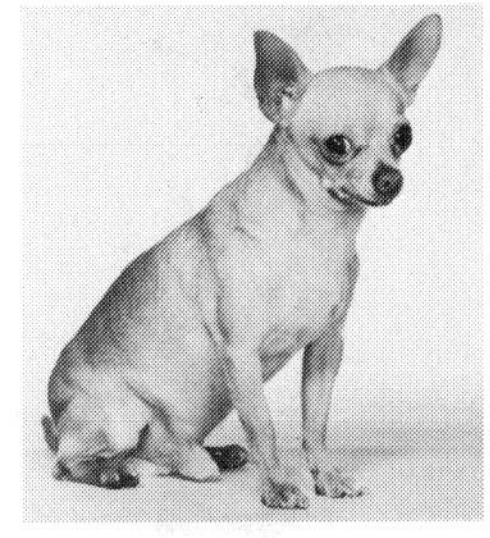

Chihuahua²

ă pat	oi boy
ā pay	ou out
âr care	o͝o took
ä father	o͞o boot
ĕ pet	ŭ cut
ē be	ûr urge
ĭ pit	th thin
ī pie	*th* this
îr pier	hw which
ŏ pot	zh vision
ō toe	ə about, item
ô paw	♦ regionalism

Stress marks: ′ (primary); ′ (secondary), as in **dictionary** (dĭk′shə-nĕr′ē)

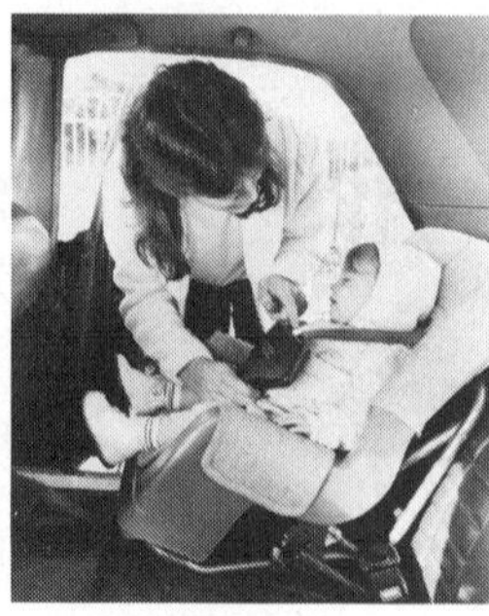

child restraint

Chile

chimney sweep

ă pat	oi boy
ā pay	ou out
âr care	o͝o took
ä father	o͞o boot
ĕ pet	ŭ cut
ē be	ûr urge
ĭ pit	th thin
ī pie	*th* this
îr pier	hw which
ŏ pot	zh vision
ō toe	ə about, item
ô paw	♦ regionalism

Stress marks: **′** (primary); ′ (secondary), as in **dictionary** (dĭk′shə-nĕr′ē)

coat. [After *Chihuahua,* a city and state of northern Mexico.]

Chi·ka·ma·tsu Mon·za·e·mon (chē′kä-mät′so͞o môn′-zä-ĕ-môn′). 1653–1724. Japanese playwright whose numerous plays, mostly written for the puppet theater, deeply influenced Japanese drama.

chil·blain (chĭl′blān′) *n.* An inflammation followed by itchy irritation on the hands, feet, or ears, resulting from exposure to moist cold. [CHIL(L) + BLAIN.] **—chil′blained′** *adj.*

child (chīld) *n., pl.* **chil·dren** (chĭl′drən). *Abbr.* **ch. 1.** A person between birth and puberty. **2. a.** An unborn infant; a fetus. **b.** An infant; a baby. **3.** One who is childish or immature. **4.** A son or daughter; an offspring. **5.** Often **children.** Members of a tribe; descendants: *children of Abraham.* **6. a.** An individual regarded as strongly affected by another or by a specified time, place, or circumstance: *a child of nature; a child of the Sixties.* **b.** A product or result of something specified: *"Times Square is a child of the 20th century"* (Richard F. Shepard). **—*idiom.* with child.** Pregnant. [Middle English, from Old English *cild.*] **—child′less** *adj.* **—child′less·ness** *n.*

Child (chīld), **Julia.** Born 1912. American cookery expert known for her books and her instructional television and video series.

Child, Lydia Maria Francis. 1802–1880. American abolitionist and writer of novels, children's books, and reform works.

child·bear·ing (chīld′bâr′ĭng) *n.* The human act or process of giving birth; parturition. **—child′bear′ing** *adj.*

child·bed (chīld′bĕd′) *n.* The condition of a woman in the process of giving birth.

childbed fever *n.* See **puerperal fever.**

child·birth (chīld′bûrth′) *n.* Parturition.

child-care or **child·care** (chīld′kâr′) *adj.* Of, relating to, or providing care for children, especially preschoolers: *a child-care center; child-care professionals.* **—child′care′** *n.*

childe (chīld) *n. Archaic.* A child of noble birth. [Middle English *childe, child,* child. See CHILD.]

child·free (chīld′frē′) *adj.* Without children, especially by choice: *childfree couples.*

child·hood (chīld′ho͝od′) *n.* **1.** The time or state of being a child. **2.** The early stage in the existence or development of something: *the childhood of Western civilization.*

child·ish (chīl′dĭsh) *adj.* **1.** Of, relating to, or suitable for a child or childhood: *a high, childish voice; childish nightmares.* **2. a.** Marked by or indicating a lack of maturity; puerile: *tired of your childish pranks.* **b.** Not complicated; simple. **c.** Affected mentally by old age; senile. **—child′ish·ly** *adv.* **—child′ish·ness** *n.*

child labor *n.* The full-time employment of children who are under a minimum legal age.

child·like (chīld′līk′) *adj.* Like or befitting a child, as in innocence, trustfulness, or candor.

child·proof (chīld′pro͞of′) *adj.* **1.** Designed to resist tampering by young children: *a childproof aspirin bottle.* **2.** Made safe for young children, as by the removal or alteration of potential hazards: *a childproof kitchen.* **—childproof** *tr.v.* **-proofed, -proof·ing, -proofs.** To make childproof: *childproof a house.*

chil·dren (chĭl′drən) *n. Abbr.* **ch.** Plural of **child.**

child restraint *n.* A device, such as a seat belt or small car seat with a seat belt, used to control and protect a child in a motor vehicle.

child's play (chīldz) *n.* **1.** Something very easy to do. **2.** A trivial matter.

Chil·e (chĭl′ē, chĕ′lĕ). A country of southwest South America with a long Pacific coastline. Colonized by Spain in 1541, it declared its independence in 1818. Santiago is the capital and the largest city. Population, 11,329,736. **—Chil′e·an** *adj. & n.*

Chil·e saltpeter (chĭl′ē) *n.* See **sodium nitrate.**

chil·i (chĭl′ē) *n., pl.* **-ies. 1.** The pungent fresh or dried fruit of any of several cultivated varieties of capsicum, used especially as a flavoring in cooking. Also called *chili pepper.* **2.** Chili con carne. [Spanish *chile, chili,* from Nahuatl *chilli.*]

chil·i·ad (kĭl′ē-ăd′, -əd) *n.* **1.** A group that contains 1,000 elements. **2.** One thousand years; a millennium. [Late Latin *chilias, chiliad-,* from Greek *khilias,* from *khilioi,* thousand. See **gheslo-** in Appendix.]

chil·i·asm (kĭl′ē-ăz′əm) *n. Theology.* The doctrine stating that Jesus will reign on earth for 1,000 years. [New Latin *chiliasmus,* from Late Latin *chilias,* chiliad. See CHILIAD.] **—chil′i·ast′** (-ăst′, -əst) *n.* **—chil′i·as′tic** *adj.*

chil·i·bur·ger (chĭl′ē-bûr′gər) *n.* A hamburger covered with chili con carne.

chili con car·ne (kŏn kär′nē) *n.* A highly spiced dish made of red peppers, meat, and often beans. [Spanish : *chili, chile,* chili + *con,* with + *carne,* meat.]

chil·i·dog (chĭl′ē-dôg′, -dŏg′) *n.* A hot dog covered with chili con carne, served in a long roll.

Chi·lin (jē′lĭn′). See **Jilin.**

chili pepper *n.* See **chili** (sense 1).

chili powder *n.* A condiment consisting of ground chilies mixed with several seasonings, such as cumin, oregano, and garlic.

chili sauce *n.* A spiced sauce made with chilies and tomatoes.

chill (chĭl) *n.* **1.** A moderate but penetrating coldness. **2.** A sensation of coldness, often accompanied by shivering and pallor of the skin. **3.** A checking or dampening of enthusiasm, spirit, or joy: *bad news that put a chill on the celebration.* **4.** A sudden numbing fear or dread. **—chill** *adj.* **1.** Moderately cold; chilly: *a chill wind.* **2.** Not warm and friendly; distant: *a chill greeting.* **3.** Discouraging; dispiriting: *"Chill penury repressed their noble rage"* (Thomas Gray). **—chill** *v.* **chilled, chill·ing, chills.** *—tr.* **1.** To affect with or as if with cold. **2.** To lower in temperature; cool. **3.** To make discouraged; dispirit. **4.** *Metallurgy.* To harden (a metallic surface) by rapid cooling. *—intr.* **1.** To be seized with cold. **2.** To become cold or set: *jelly that chills quickly.* **3.** *Metallurgy.* To become hard by rapid cooling. [Middle English *chile,* from Old English *cele.* See **gel-** in Appendix.] **—chill′ing·ly** *adv.* **—chill′ness** *n.*

Chil·lán (chē-yän′). A city of central Chile east-northeast of Concepción. Founded in the 16th century, it was twice destroyed by earthquakes (1835 and 1939). Population, 118,163.

chill·er (chĭl′ər) *n.* **1.** One that chills. **2.** A frightening story, especially one involving violence, evil, or the supernatural; a thriller.

chill factor *n.* Wind-chill factor.

Chil·li·coth·e (chĭl′ĭ-kŏth′ē, -kô′thē). A city of south-central Ohio south of Columbus. It became capital of the Northwest Territory in 1800 and served as Ohio's capital from 1803 to 1810 and from 1812 to 1816. Population, 23,420.

Chil·li·wack (chĭl′ə-wăk′). A city of southwest British Columbia, Canada, on the Fraser River east of Vancouver. It is a processing center. Population, 40,642.

chill·y (chĭl′ē) *adj.* **-i·er, -i·est. 1.** Cool or cold enough to cause shivering. See Synonyms at **cold. 2.** Seized with or feeling cold; shivering. **3.** Distant and cool; unfriendly: *a chilly look.* **—chill′i·ly** *adv.* **—chill′i·ness** *n.*

Chi·lo·é (chĭl′ō-ā′, chē′lô-ĕ′). An island off south-central Chile. It is the largest of the Chilean islands and the only one to be successfully settled.

chi·lo·pod (kī′lə-pŏd′) *n.* Any of various arthropods of the class Chilopoda, which includes the centipedes. [From New Latin *Chīlopoda,* class name : Greek *kheilos,* lip + *-poda,* -pod (so called because the foremost pair of legs are jawlike appendages).]

Chil·tern Hills (chĭl′tərn). A range of chalk hills in south-central England northeast of the upper Thames River.

Chiltern Hundreds *n. (used with a sing. verb). Chiefly British.* A merely formal office applied for by members of Parliament when they wish to resign from the House of Commons. [Short for *Stewardship of the Chiltern Hundreds,* tracts of crown lands in south-central England including the Chiltern Hills.]

Chi·lung (jē′lo͝ong′, chē′-). See **Keelung.**

chi·mae·ra (kī-mîr′ə, kĭ-) *n.* **1.** A deep-sea cartilaginous fish of the family Chimaeridae, having a smooth-skinned tapering body and a whiplike tail. **2.** *Genetics.* Variant of **chimera.** [New Latin *Chimaera,* type genus, from Latin *chimaera,* chimera. See CHIMERA.]

Chi·mae·ra (kī-mîr′ə, kĭ-) *n. Greek Mythology.* Variant of **Chimera.**

Chim·bo·ra·zo (chĭm′bə-rä′zō, -rā′-, chēm′bô-rä′sô). An inactive volcano, 6,271.1 m (20,561 ft) high, in central Ecuador. The highest elevation of the Cordillera Real, it was first scaled in 1880.

Chim·bo·te (chĭm-bō′tē, chēm-bô′tĕ). A city of western Peru on the Pacific Ocean north-northwest of Callao. It suffered severe earthquake damage in 1970. Population, 223,341.

chime¹ (chīm) *n.* **1.** An apparatus for striking a bell or set of bells to produce a musical sound. **2.** Often **chimes.** *Music.* A set of bells tuned to scale and used as an orchestral instrument. **3.** A single bell, as in the mechanism of a clock. **4.** The sound produced by or as if by a bell or bells. **5.** Agreement; accord: *a flawless chime of romance and reality.* **—chime** *v.* **chimed, chim·ing, chimes.** *—intr.* **1. a.** To sound with a harmonious ring when struck. **b.** To make a musical sound by striking a bell or set of bells. **2.** To be in agreement or accord: harmonize: *Their views chimed with ours. The seafood and wine chimed perfectly.* *—tr.* **1.** To produce (music) by striking bells. **2.** To strike (a bell) to produce music. **3. a.** To signal or make known by chiming: *The clock chimed noon.* **b.** To call, send, or welcome by chiming. **4.** To repeat insistently. **—*phrasal verb.* chime in. 1.** To interrupt the speech of others, especially with an unwanted opinion. **2.** To join in harmoniously. **3.** To go together harmoniously; agree. [From Middle English *chimbe (belle),* from Old French, variant of *cimble,* cymbal, from Latin *cymbalum.* See CYMBAL.] **—chim′er** *n.*

chime² (chīm) *n.* The rim of a cask. [Middle English *chimb,* from Old English *cim-, cimb-.* See **gembh-** in Appendix.]

chi·me·ra also **chi·mae·ra** (kī-mîr′ə, kĭ-) *n. Genetics.* **1.** An organism consisting of two or more tissues of different genetic composition, produced as a result of mutation, grafting, or the mixture of cell populations from different zygotes. **2.** An organism produced by genetic engineering, in which DNA from distinct parent species is combined to produce an individual with a double chromosome complement. [Middle English *chimere,* Chimera, from Old French, from Latin *chimaera,* from Greek *khimaira,* chimera, she-goat. See **ghei-** in Appendix.]

Chi·me·ra also **Chi·mae·ra** (kī-mîr′ə, kĭ-) *n.* **1.** *Greek Mythology.* A fire-breathing she-monster usually represented as a composite of a lion, goat, and serpent. **2.** An imaginary monster made up of grotesquely disparate parts.

chi·mer·i·cal (kī-mĕr′ĭ-kəl, -mîr′-, kĭ-) also **chi·mer·ic** (-mĕr′ĭk, -mîr′-) *adj.* **1.** Created by or as if by a wildly fanciful imagination; highly improbable. **2.** Given to unrealistic fantasies; fanciful. —**chi·mer′i·cal·ly** *adv.*

chi·mer·ism (kī-mîr′ĭz′əm, kī′mə-rĭz′-) *n.* The condition of being a genetic chimera.

chim·i·chan·ga (chĭm′ē-chăng′gə) *n.* A deep-fried burrito. [American Spanish.]

Chim·kent (chĭm-kĕnt′). A city of south-central Kazakhstan north of Tashkent. Founded in the 12th century, it was taken by Russia in 1864. Population, 369,000.

chim·ney (chĭm′nē) *n., pl.* **-neys. 1.a.** A passage through which smoke and gases escape from a fire or furnace; a flue. **b.** The usually vertical structure containing a chimney. **c.** The part of such a structure that rises above a roof. **2.** *Chiefly British.* A smokestack, as of a ship or locomotive. **3.** A glass tube for enclosing the flame of a lamp. **4.** Something, such as a narrow cleft in a cliff, resembling a chimney. [Middle English *chimenei,* from Old French *cheminee,* from Late Latin *camīnāta,* fireplace, from Latin *camīnus,* furnace, from Greek *kaminos.*]

chim·ney·piece (chĭm′nē-pēs′) *n.* **1.** The mantel of a fireplace. **2.** A decoration over a fireplace.

chimney pot *n.* A short, usually earthenware pipe placed on the top of a chimney to improve the draft.

chimney sweep *n.* A worker employed to clean soot from chimneys.

chimney swift *n.* A small, dark, swallowlike New World bird *(Chaetura pelagica)* that frequently nests in chimneys.

chimp (chĭmp) *n. Informal.* A chimpanzee.

chim·pan·zee (chĭm′păn-zē′, -pən-, chĭm-păn′zē) *n.* A gregarious anthropoid ape *(Pan troglodytes)* of tropical Africa, having long dark hair and somewhat arboreal habits and exhibiting humanlike behavior and a high degree of intelligence. It is now considered vulnerable to extinction in the wild. [Portuguese, from Kongo (Vili) *ci-mpenzi.*]

chin (chĭn) *n.* The central forward portion of the lower jaw. —**chin** *v.* **chinned, chin·ning, chins.** —*tr.* **1.** To pull (oneself) up with the arms while grasping an overhead horizontal bar until the chin is level with the bar. **2.** *Music.* To place (a violin) under the chin in preparation to play it. —*intr.* **1.** To chin oneself. **2.** *Informal.* To make idle conversation; chatter. [Middle English, from Old English *cin.* See **genu-**[2] in Appendix.] —**chin′less** *adj.*

Chin (jĭn). See **Jin.**

Chin. *abbr.* China; Chinese.

Ch'in (chĭn). See **Qin.**

chi·na (chī′nə) *n.* **1.** High-quality porcelain or ceramic ware, originally made in China. **2.** Porcelain or earthenware used for the table. [Short for *chinaware.*]

WORD HISTORY: Our term *china* for porcelain or ceramic ware is a shortening of *chinaware* and probably *china dishes.* Although the word *china* is identical in spelling to the name of the country, there are 16th- and 17th-century spellings like *chiney, cheny,* and *cheney* that reflect the borrowing into English of the Persian term for this porcelain, *chīnī.* The Persian word and the Sanskrit word *cīnāḥ,* "Chinese people," which gave us the English name for the country, go back to the Chinese word *Qin,* the name of the dynasty that ruled China from 221 to 206 B.C.

Chi·na (chī′nə). *Abbr.* **Ch., Chin.** A country of eastern Asia. Its ancient civilization traditionally dates to c. 2700 B.C.. After a bitter civil war (1946–1949) a people's republic led by Mao Zedong was established on the mainland, and the Nationalists fled to Taiwan. Beijing is the capital and Shanghai the largest city. Population, 1,008,175,288.

China, Republic of. See **Taiwan.**

China aster *n.* An annual Chinese plant *(Callistephus chinensis)* in the composite family, widely grown in several forms for its showy, variously colored flower heads.

chi·na·ber·ry (chī′nə-bĕr′ē) *n.* A deciduous Asian tree *(Melia azedarach),* widely cultivated and naturalized in the southern United States and having bipinnately compound leaves, clusters of purplish flowers, and yellow, globose, poisonous fruits. Also called *China tree.*

China jute *n.* See **velvetleaf.**

Chi·na·man (chī′nə-mən) *n. Offensive.* Used as a disparaging term for a Chinese man.

China rose *n.* A Chinese rose *(Rosa chinensis)* having mostly red, pink, or white flowers. It is an ancestor of many cultivated hybrid roses.

China Sea. The western part of the Pacific Ocean extending along the eastern coast of Asia from southern Japan to the Malay Peninsula. It is divided by Taiwan into the **East China Sea** and the **South China Sea.**

China syndrome *n.* The accidental melting of a nuclear reactor core so that its contents sink through the bottom of its container and into the earth.

Chi·na·town (chī′nə-toun′) *n.* A neighborhood or section of a city that is inhabited chiefly by Chinese people.

China tree *n.* See **chinaberry.**

chi·na·ware (chī′nə-wâr′) *n.* Tableware made of china.

Chi·na·wood oil (chī′nə-wŏŏd′) *n.* See **tung oil.**

♦**chinch** (chĭnch) *n. Chiefly Southern & Midland U.S.* See **bedbug.** [Spanish *chinche,* from Latin *cīmex, cīmic-,* bug.]

♦**chinch bug** also **cinch bug** *n.* **1.** A small black and white insect *(Blissus leucopterus)* that is very destructive to grains and grasses. **2.** *Chiefly Southern & Midland U.S.* See **bedbug.**

chin·che·rin·chee (chĭn′chə-rĭn-chē′, chĭng′kə-) *n.* A southern African bulbous plant *(Ornithogalum thyrsoides)* in the lily family, whose fragrant cluster of showy white blossoms is popular as a cut flower. [Probably Afrikaans *tjienkerientjee.*]

chin·chil·la (chĭn-chĭl′ə) *n.* **1.a.** A squirrellike rodent *(Chinchilla laniger)* native to the mountains of South America and widely raised in captivity for its soft, pale-gray fur. **b.** The fur of this animal. **2.** A thick, twilled cloth of wool and cotton used for overcoats. [Spanish, probably alteration of a native word in Aymara.]

Chin·chow (jĭn′jō′). See **Jinzhou.**

♦**chinch·y** (chĭn′chē) *adj.* **-i·er, -i·est.** *Chiefly Southern U.S.* Stingy; tightfisted; cheap. [Alteration of CHINTZY.]

Chin·co·teague Bay (shĭng′kə-tēg′, chĭng′-). A long, narrow bay off northeast Virginia and southeast Maryland. **Chincoteague Island** is at the southern end of the bay.

Chincoteague pony *n.* A type of small, inbred North American horse that runs wild on certain islands off the Virginia coast. [After CHINCOTEAGUE ISLAND.]

Chin·dwin (chĭn′dwĭn′). A river rising in the hills of northern Burma and flowing about 1,158 km (720 mi) generally south to the Irrawaddy River.

China

chine (chīn) *n.* **1.a.** The backbone or spine, especially of an animal. **b.** A cut of meat containing part of the backbone. **2.** A ridge or crest. **3.** *Nautical.* The line of intersection between the side and bottom of a flatbottom or V-bottom boat. [Middle English, from Old French *eschine,* of Germanic origin. See **skei-** in Appendix.]

Chi·nese (chī-nēz′, -nēs′) *adj. Abbr.* **Chin.** Of or relating to China or its peoples, languages, or cultures. —**Chinese** *n., pl.* **Chinese.** *Abbr.* **Chin. 1.a.** A native or inhabitant of China. **b.** A person of Chinese ancestry. **c.** See **Han**[1]. **2.a.** A branch of the Sino-Tibetan language family that consists of the various dialects spoken by the Chinese people. **b.** Any of the dialects spoken by the Chinese people. **3.** *Informal.* Chinese food.

Chinese anise *n.* An evergreen tree *(Illicium anisatum),* native to Japan and Korea and having aromatic leaves and fragrant white or yellow flowers.

Chinese artichoke *n.* A perennial Chinese herb *(Stachys affinis)* in the mint family, cultivated for its edible, tuberous underground stems that somewhat resemble a string of large, whitish beads.

Chinese black mushroom *n.* See **shiitake.**

Chinese cabbage *n.* Any of several forms of a plant *(Brassica rapa* var. *pekinensis)* of the mustard family, having an elongated head of overlapping, crinkled, broad-stalked leaves and eaten as a vegetable in eastern Asian cuisine. Also called *celery cabbage, napa, pe-tsai.*

chinchilla
Chinchilla laniger

Chinese calendar *n.* The traditional lunisolar calendar of the Chinese people, based on 24 seasonal segments each about 15 days long. An intercalary month is occasionally necessary to reconcile the lunar year with the solar year.

Chinese checkers *pl.n. (used with a sing. or pl. verb). Games.* A board game in which each player tries to move a set of marbles arranged in holes from one point of a six-pointed star to the opposite point by means of single moves or jumps.

Chinese chestnut *n.* A chestnut *(Castanea mollissima)* native to China and Korea, resistant to chestnut blight and cultivated as an ornamental and for its edible nuts.

Chinese chive *n.* An eastern Asian herb *(Allium tuberosum)* having flat leaves, small white flowers, and elongated bulbs covered with a fibrous coat. Often used in the plural. Also called *garlic chive, Oriental garlic.*

Chinese date *n.* See **jujube** (sense 1).

Chinese evergreen *n.* A Chinese evergreen plant *(Aglaonema modestum)* cultivated as a houseplant for its dark green or occasionally variegated foliage.

Chinese export porcelain *n.* See **Canton porcelain.**

Chinese gooseberry *n.* See **kiwi** (sense 2).

Chinese houses *pl.n. (used with a sing. or pl. verb).* Any of several chiefly Californian plants of the genus *Collinsia,* especially *C. heterophylla,* which has several widely spaced whorls of purple and white flowers suggestive of a pagoda.

Chinese ink *n.* See **India ink** (sense 2).

Chinese kale *n.* A Chinese vegetable *(Brassica oleracea* var. *alboglabra)* of the mustard family, related to the cabbage and grown for its leafy shoots used in eastern Asian cuisine.

Chinese lantern *n.* A decorative collapsible lantern of thin, brightly colored paper.

Chinese lantern plant *n.* See **winter cherry.**

Chinese mustard *n.* Any of several cultivated varieties of the Indian mustard, grown for their leafy shoots and eaten as a vegetable especially in eastern Asian cuisine.

Chinese parsley *n.* See **coriander** (sense 2).

Chinese pear *n.* See **sand pear.**

Chinese puzzle *n.* **1.** A very intricate puzzle. **2.** Something very difficult or complex.

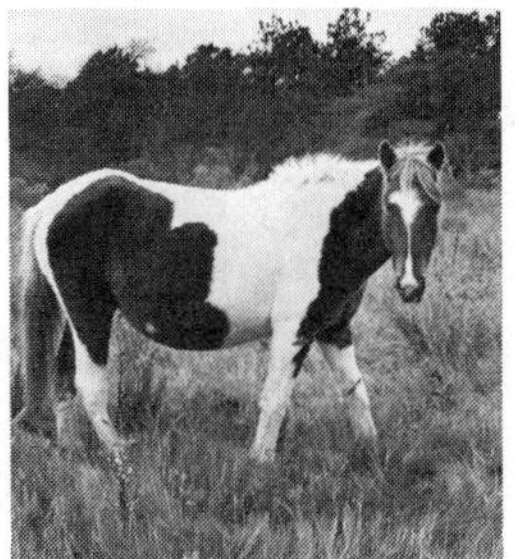
Chincoteague pony

chin-up

chipmunk
Eastern chipmunk
Tamias striatus

Chippendale
Bonnet-top mahogany highboy

Chi-Rho

Chinese radish *n.* See **daikon.**

Chinese red *n. Color.* See **vermilion** (sense 2).

Chinese restaurant syndrome *n.* A group of symptoms, including dizziness, facial pressure, sweating, and headache, that may occur after the ingestion of food containing large amounts of monosodium glutamate.

Chinese tallow tree *n.* An ornamental tree *(Sapium sebiferum),* native to China and Japan and naturalized in the southern United States and having a thick, waxy seed coat that is used in making candles and soap. Also called *vegetable tallow.*

Chinese wall *n.* A barrier, especially one that seriously hinders communication or understanding: *"still believe a Chinese wall can exist between public and private selves"* (Gail Sheehy). [After the GREAT WALL OF CHINA.]

Chinese water chestnut *n.* See **water chestnut** (sense 2).

Chinese white *n.* See **zinc oxide.**

Chinese windlass *n.* See **differential windlass.**

Ch'ing (chĭng). See **Qing.**

Ching·hai (chĭng′hī′). See **Qinghai.**

Chin Hills (chĭn). A range of hills in western Burma rising to 3,055.5 m (10,018 ft).

chink¹ (chĭngk) *n.* A narrow opening, such as a crack or fissure. **—chink** *tr.v.* **chinked, chink·ing, chinks. 1.** To make narrow openings in. **2.** To fill narrow openings in. [Probably alteration of obsolete *chine,* from Middle English, crack, from Old English *cine.*] **—chink′y** *adj.*

chink² (chĭngk) *n.* A slight, metallic sound, as of coins rattling in a pocket. **—chink** *intr. & tr.v.* **chinked, chink·ing, chinks.** To make or cause to make a slight, metallic sound. [Imitative.]

Chink (chĭngk) *n. Offensive Slang.* Used as a disparaging term for a Chinese person. [Probably alteration of CHINESE.]

Chin·kiang (chĭn′kyăng′, jĭn′gyăng′). See **Zhenjiang.**

chi·no (chē′nō, shē′-) *n., pl.* **-nos. 1.** A coarse, twilled cotton fabric used for uniforms and sometimes work or sports clothes. **2.** Trousers made of a coarse, twilled cotton. Often used in the plural. [American Spanish, mestizo, yellowish (from its original tan color), probably from Spanish *chino,* Chinese, from *China,* China.]

Chi·no (chē′nō). A city of southern California east of Los Angeles. It was founded in 1887. Population, 40,165.

chi·noi·se·rie (shēn′wäz-rē′) *n.* **1.** A style in art reflecting Chinese influence through use of elaborate decoration and intricate patterns. **2.** An object reflecting Chinese artistic influence. [French, from *chinois,* Chinese, from *Chine,* China.]

Chi·nook (shĭ-no͝ok′, chĭ-) *n., pl.* **Chinook** or **-nooks. 1.a.** A Native American people formerly inhabiting the lower Columbia River valley and adjoining coastal regions of Washington and Oregon, now located in western Washington. The Chinook traded widely throughout the Pacific Northwest. **b.** A member of this people. **c.** The Chinookan language of the Chinook. **2.a.** Any of various Chinookan-speaking peoples formerly inhabiting the Columbia River valley eastward to The Dalles and now located in southern Washington and northern Oregon. **b.** A member of any of these peoples. **3. chinook. a.** A moist, warm wind blowing from the sea on the northwest U.S. coast. **b.** A warm, dry wind that descends from the eastern slopes of the Rocky Mountains, causing a rapid rise in temperature. [Chehalis (Salishan) *c'inuk.*]

Chi·nook·an (shĭ-no͝ok′ən, chĭ-) *n.* A North American Indian language family of Washington and Oregon. **—Chi·nook′an** *adj.*

Chinook Jargon *n.* A pidgin language combining words from Nootka, Chinook, Salishan languages, French, and English, formerly used as a lingua franca in the Pacific Northwest.

Chinook salmon *n.* A very large, commercially valuable salmon *(Oncorhynchus tshawytscha)* of northern Pacific waters, characterized by irregular black spots on its back. Also called *king salmon, quinnat salmon.*

chin·qua·pin (chĭng′kə-pĭn′) *n.* **1.** Any of several deciduous shrubs or small trees related and similar to the chestnut, especially *Castanea pumila,* native to the eastern United States. **2.** A large evergreen tree *(Castanopsis chrysophylla)* of the Pacific Coast of North America. Also called *giant chinquapin, golden chinquapin.* **3.** The nut of any of these plants. [Of Algonquian origin; akin to Virginia Algonquin *chechinkamin,* chestnut.]

chinquapin oak *n.* A deciduous oak shrub *(Quercus prinoides)* of the eastern and central United States, having toothed leaves that resemble those of the chinquapin.

chintz (chĭnts) *n.* A printed and glazed cotton fabric, usually of bright colors. [Obsolete *chints,* pl. of *chint,* calico cloth, from Hindi *cīṇt,* from Sanskrit *citra-,* shiny, variegated.]

chintz·y (chĭnt′sē) *adj.* **-i·er, -i·est. 1.** Of, relating to, or decorated with chintz. **2.a.** Gaudy; trashy: *chintzy merchandise.* **b.** Stingy; miserly.

chin-up (chĭn′ŭp′) *n.* The act or an instance of chinning oneself, practiced especially as a fitness exercise. Also called *pull-up.*

Chin·wang·tao (chĭn′wäng′tou′). See **Qinhuangdao.**

Chi·os (kī′ŏs′, -ôs′, kē′-, KHē′ôs) also **Khí·os** (kē′ôs, KHē′-). An island of eastern Greece in the Aegean Sea off the western coast of Turkey.

chip¹ (chĭp) *n.* **1.** A small piece, as of wood, stone, or glass, broken or cut off. **2.** A crack or flaw caused by the removal of a small piece. **3.a.** *Games.* A small disk or counter used in poker and other games to represent money. **b. chips.** *Slang.* Money. **4.a.** *Electronics.* A minute slice of a semiconducting material, such as silicon or germanium, doped and otherwise processed to have specified electrical characteristics, especially before it is developed into an electronic component or integrated circuit. Also called *microchip.* **b.** An integrated circuit. **5.a. chips.** A thin, usually fried slice of food, especially a potato chip. **b.** Often **chips.** A very small piece of food or candy: *chocolate chips.* **c. chips.** *Chiefly British.* French fries. **6.** Wood, palm leaves, straw, or similar material cut and dried for weaving. **7.** A fragment of dried animal dung used as fuel. **8.** Something worthless. **9.** *Sports.* A chip shot. **—chip** *v.* **chipped, chip·ping, chips.** *—tr.* **1.** To chop or cut with an ax or other implement. **2.a.** To break a small piece from: *chip a tooth.* **b.** To break or cut off (a small piece): *chip ice from the car window.* **3.** To shape or carve by cutting or chopping: *chipped her name in the stone.* *—intr.* **1.** To become broken off into small pieces. **2.** *Sports.* To make a chip shot in golf. ***—phrasal verb.*** **chip in. 1.** To contribute money or labor: *We all chipped in for champagne.* **2.** To interrupt with comments; interject. **3.** *Games.* To put up chips or money as one's bet in poker and other games. ***—idioms.*** **chip off the old block.** A child whose appearance or character closely resembles that of one or the other parent. **chip on (one's) shoulder.** A habitually hostile or combative attitude. [Middle English, from Old English *cyp,* beam, from Latin *cippus.*]

chip² (chĭp) *intr.v.* **chipped, chip·ping, chips.** To cheep, as a bird. [Imitative.] **—chip** *n.*

chip³ (chĭp) *n. Sports.* A trick method of throwing one's opponent in wrestling. [Origin unknown.]

Chip·e·wy·an (chĭp′ə-wī′ən) *n., pl.* **Chipewyan** or **-ans. 1.a.** A Native American people made up of numerous autonomous bands inhabiting a large area of northern Canada north of the Churchill River. Formerly nomadic caribou hunters, the Chipewyan became settled fur traders during the 18th century. **b.** A member of this people. **2.** The Athabaskan language of the Chipewyan. [Cree *čīpwayān,* parka wearer : *cīpw-,* pointed + *ayān,* skin.]

chip·mak·er (chĭp′mā′kər) *n.* A manufacturer of electronic and integrated circuit chips.

chip·munk (chĭp′mŭngk′) *n.* Any of several small, striped, terrestrial squirrels of the genera *Tamias* and *Eutamias,* especially *T. striatus* of eastern North America. [Alteration of obsolete *chitmunk,* perhaps from Ojibwa *ajidamoonʔ,* red squirrel.]

chipped beef (chĭpt) *n.* Dried beef smoked and sliced very thin.

Chip·pen·dale (chĭp′ən-dāl′) *adj.* Of or relating to an 18th-century English style of furniture characterized by flowing lines and often rococo ornamentation. [After Thomas CHIPPENDALE.]

Chippendale, Thomas. 1718–1779. British cabinetmaker noted for his graceful neoclassical furniture, particularly chairs, which had wide influence on his contemporary artisans.

chip·per¹ (chĭp′ər) *n.* One that chips or cuts: *a wood chipper.*

chip·per² (chĭp′ər) *intr.v.* **-pered, -per·ing, -pers. 1.** To chirp or twitter, as a bird. **2.** To babble. [Frequentative of CHIP².]

chip·per³ (chĭp′ər) *adj.* In lively spirits; cheerful. [Possibly alteration of British dialectal *kipper,* lively.]

Chip·pe·wa (chĭp′ə-wô′, -wä′, -wā′, -wə) *n., pl.* **Chippewa** or **-was.** See **Ojibwa.**

chip·ping sparrow (chĭp′ĭng) *n.* A small North American sparrow *(Spizella passerina)* having a reddish-brown crown.

chip·py (chĭp′ē) *n., pl.* **-pies. 1.** A chipping sparrow. **2.** *Slang.* A woman prostitute. [From CHIP².]

chip shot *n. Sports.* A short, lofted golf stroke, used in approaching the green.

chi·ral (kī′rəl) *adj.* Of or relating to the structural characteristic of a molecule that makes it impossible to superimpose it on its mirror image. [CHIR(O)– + –AL¹.] **—chi·ral′i·ty** (kī-răl′ĭ-tē) *n.*

Chi-Rho (kī′rō′, kē′-) *n.* A monogram and symbol for Christ, consisting of the superimposed Greek letters *chi* (X) and *rho* (R), often embroidered on altar cloths and clerical vestments. Also called *Christogram.* [CHI + RHO, first two letters of Greek *Khristos,* Christ.]

Chir·i·ca·hua (chĭr′ĭ-kä′wə) *n., pl.* **Chiricahua** or **-huas. 1.** A formerly nomadic Apache tribe inhabiting southern New Mexico, southeast Arizona, and northern Mexico, with present-day populations in Oklahoma and New Mexico. **2.** A member of this tribe.

Chi·ri·co (kîr′ĭ-kō′, kē′rē-kô′), **Giorgio de.** 1888–1978. Italian painter whose works are characterized by deep shadow and perspective, barren landscapes, and elements of classical architecture and sculpture.

chirk (chûrk) *tr. & intr.v.* **chirked, chirk·ing, chirks.** To make or become cheerful. [Middle English *chirken,* to chirp, chirrup, from Old English *cearcian,* to chatter, alteration of *cracian,* to resound. See CRACK.]

chiro– or **cheiro–** *pref.* Hand: *chiropractic.* [Latin, from Greek *kheir,* hand. See **ghesor-** in Appendix.]

chi·rog·ra·phy (kī-rŏg′rə-fē) *n.* Penmanship. **—chi·rog′ra·pher** *n.* **—chi′ro·graph′ic** (kī′rə-grăf′ĭk), **chi′ro·graph′i·cal** *adj.*

chi·ro·man·cy (kī′rə-măn′sē) *n.* Palmistry. **—chi′ro·man′cer** *n.*

Chi·ron (kī′rŏn′) *n. Greek Mythology.* The wise centaur who tutored Achilles, Hercules, and Asclepius.

chi·rop·o·dy (kĭ-rŏp′ə-dē, shĭ-) *n.* See **podiatry.** [CHIRO– + –POD + –Y².] **—chi·rop′o·dist** *n.*

chi·ro·prac·tic (kī′rə-prăk′tĭk) *n.* A system of therapy in which disease is considered the result of abnormal function of the nervous system. Treatment usually involves manipulation of the spinal column and other body structures. [CHIRO– + Greek *praktikos,* practical; see PRACTICAL.] **—chi′ro·prac′tor** *n.*

chi·rop·ter·an (kī-rŏp′tər-ən) also **chi·rop·ter** (-rŏp′tər) *n.* A mammal, such as the bat, that is a member of the order Chiroptera and has forelimbs modified as wings. [From New Latin *Chiroptera,* order name : CHIRO– + –PTER.] **—chi·rop′ter·an** *adj.*

chirp (chûrp) *n.* A short, high-pitched sound, such as that made by a small bird or an insect. **—chirp** *intr.v.* **chirped, chirp·ing, chirps.** To make a short, high-pitched sound. [Middle English *chirpen, of imitative origin.]

chirr (chûr) *n.* A harsh, trilling sound, such as that made by crickets. **—chirr** *intr.v.* **chirred, chirr·ing, chirrs.** To make a harsh, trilling sound. [Imitative.]

♦ **chir·ren** (chĭr′ən) *n. Chiefly Southern U.S.* Children.

♦ ***REGIONAL NOTE:*** The linguistic process of ellipsis allows for the deletion within words of some internal sounds, such as weakly stressed syllables and less prominent consonants. This process caused Old English *heafod* ultimately to become Modern English *head,* losing its internal *v* sound (spelled *f* in Old English). Ellipsis is still an active process in American regional dialects. For example, in *chirren* both the *l* and the *d* of *children* are omitted in favor of the more conspicuous *r.*

chir·rup (chûr′əp, chĭr′-) *v.* **-ruped, -rup·ing, -rups.** *—intr.* **1.** To utter a series of chirps. **2.** To make clucking or clicking sounds with the lips, as in urging on a horse. *—tr.* **1.** To sound with chirps. **2.** To make clucking sounds to. **—chirrup** *n.* **1.** A series of chirps. **2.** A series of clucks or clicking sounds, such as those made to urge on a horse. [Variant of CHIRP.]

chi·rur·geon (kī-rûr′jən) *n. Archaic.* A surgeon. [Middle English *cirurgien,* from Old French, from Latin *chīrurgia,* surgery. See SURGERY.]

chis·el (chĭz′əl) *n.* A metal tool with a sharp beveled edge, used to cut and shape stone, wood, or metal. **—chisel** *v.* **-eled, -el·ing, -els** or **-elled, -el·ling, -els.** *—tr.* **1.** To shape or cut with a chisel. **2.** *Informal.* **a.** To cheat or swindle. **b.** To obtain by deception. *—intr.* **1.** To use a chisel. **2.** *Informal.* **a.** To use unethical methods; cheat: *"who's up, who's down and who's chiseling on the side"* (James Reston). **b.** To intrude oneself without welcome: *always tries to chisel in on our conversations.* [Middle English, from Old French *cisiel,* from Vulgar Latin *cīsellus, cutting tool, from diminutive of Latin *caesus,* past participle of *caedere,* to cut. See **kae-id-** in Appendix.] **—chis′el·er** *n.*

chis·eled or **chis·elled** (chĭz′əld) *adj.* Made or shaped with or as if with a chisel: *a finely chiseled nose.*

Chis·holm (chĭz′əm), **Shirley Anita Saint Hill.** Born 1924. American politician who as a U.S. representative from New York State (1969–1983) sought an end to the Vietnam War and advocated educational and social reforms.

Chisholm Trail. A former cattle trail from San Antonio, Texas, north to Abilene, Kansas. It was important after the Civil War until the expansion of the railroads and the introduction of barbed-wire fencing all but closed the trail.

chi-square (kī′skwâr′) *n.* A test statistic that is calculated as the sum of the squares of observed values minus expected values divided by the expected values.

chi-square test *n.* A test that uses the chi-square statistic to test the fit between a theoretical frequency distribution and a frequency distribution of observed data for which each observation may fall into one of several classes.

chit¹ (chĭt) *n.* **1.** A statement of an amount owed for food and drink; a check. **2.** A short letter; a note. **3.** A Brownie point: *earned vital chits with his party by making fundraising speeches.* [Obsolete *chitty,* from Hindi *ciṭṭhī,* note, letter, from Sanskrit *citrikā, *citritā, note.]

chit² (chĭt) *n.* **1.** A child. **2.** A saucy girl or young woman. [Middle English, young animal.]

Chi·ta (chĭ-tä′). A city of southeast Russia east of Irkutsk. It was founded in 1653. Population, 336,000.

chit·chat (chĭt′chăt′) *n.* **1.** Casual conversation; small talk. **2.** Gossip. **—chitchat** *intr.v.* **-chat·ted, -chat·ting, -chats.** To engage in small talk or gossip. [Reduplication of CHAT.]

chi·tin (kīt′n) *n.* A tough, protective, semitransparent substance, primarily a nitrogen-containing polysaccharide, forming the principal component of arthropod exoskeletons and the cell walls of certain fungi. [French *chitine,* from New Latin *chitōn,* mollusk, from Greek *khitōn,* chiton. See CHITON.] **—chi′tin·ous** *adj.*

chit·lin circuit or **chit·lin′ circuit** (chĭt′lĭn) *n. Informal.* A circuit of nightclubs and theaters that feature Black performers and cater especially to Black audiences: *"I was traveling up and down . . . with these little groups on what they call the chitlin' circuit"* (Carter Jefferson).

chit·lins or **chit·lings** (chĭt′lĭnz) *pl.n.* Variants of **chitterlings.**

chi·ton (kīt′n, kī′tŏn′) *n.* **1.** Any of various marine mollusks of the class Polyplacophora that live on rocks and have shells consisting of eight overlapping calcareous plates. Also called *sea cradle.* **2.** A tunic worn by men and women in ancient Greece. [Greek *khitōn,* tunic, of Semitic origin; akin to Hebrew *kuttōnet,* garment.]

Chit·ta·gong (chĭt′ə-gông′, -gŏng′). A city of southeast Bangladesh near the Bay of Bengal. It is a major port and industrial center. Population, 980,000.

chit·ter (chĭt′ər) *intr.v.* **-tered, -ter·ing, -ters.** To twitter or chatter, as a bird. [Middle English *chiteren,* of imitative origin.]

chit·ter·lings also **chit·lins** or **chit·lings** (chĭt′lĭnz) *pl.n.* The small intestines of pigs, especially when cooked and eaten as food. [From Middle English *chiterling,* probably diminutive of Old English *cieter, intestines.]

chi·val·ric (shĭ-văl′rĭk, shĭv′əl-) *adj.* Relating to chivalry.

chiv·al·rous (shĭv′əl-rəs) *adj.* **1.** Having the qualities of gallantry and honor attributed to an ideal knight. **2.** Of or relating to chivalry. **3.** Characterized by consideration and courtesy, especially toward women. **—chiv′al·rous·ly** *adv.* **—chiv′al·rous·ness** *n.*

chiv·al·ry (shĭv′əl-rē) *n., pl.* **-ries. 1.** The medieval system, principles, and customs of knighthood. **2. a.** The qualities idealized by knighthood, such as bravery, courtesy, honor, and gallantry toward women. **b.** A manifestation of any of these qualities. **3.** A group of knights or gallant gentlemen. [Middle English *chivalrie,* from Old French *chevalerie,* from *chevalier,* knight. See CHEVALIER.]

WORD HISTORY: The Age of Chivalry was also the age of the horse. Bedecked in elaborate armor and other trappings, horses were certainly well dressed although they might have wished for lighter loads. That the horse should be featured so prominently during the Age of Chivalry is etymologically appropriate, because *chivalry* goes back to the Latin word *caballus,* "horse, especially a riding horse or packhorse." Borrowed from French, as were so many other important words having to do with medieval English culture, the English word *chivalry* is first recorded in works composed around the beginning of the 14th century and is found in several senses, including "a body of armored mounted warriors serving a lord" and "knighthood as a ceremonially conferred rank in the social system." Our modern sense, "the medieval system of knighthood," could not exist until the passage of several centuries had allowed the perspective for such a conceptualization, with this sense being recorded first in 1765.

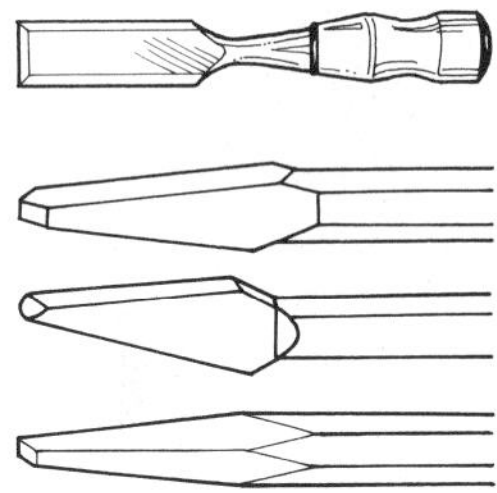

chisel
Top to bottom: Wood, cape, round-nose, and diamond-point chisels

chive (chīv) *n.* A Eurasian bulbous herb *(Allium schoenoprasum)* in the lily family, having pink to rose-violet flowers and cultivated for its long, slender, hollow leaves used as a mild onion-flavored seasoning. Often used in the plural. [Middle English *chive,* from Anglo-Norman, from Latin *cēpa,* onion.]

chiv·vy or **chiv·y** (chĭv′ē) *—v.* **-vied, -vy·ing, -vies** or **-ied, -y·ing, -ies.** *—tr.* **1.** To vex or harass with petty attacks: *political opponents who chivvied the senator.* **2.** To maneuver or secure gradually: *"had spent two weeks chivvying this division toward combat readiness"* (Tom Clancy). *—intr.* To scurry. *—n., pl.* **-vies** or **-ies. 1.** A hunt or chase. **2.** A hunting cry. [Variant of *chevy,* a hunt, hunting cry, from *Chevy Chase,* title of a ballad about a border skirmish, from *Cheviot Chase,* a large unenclosed hunting tract in the Cheviot Hills.]

Chka·lov (chə-kä′ləf, chkä′-). See **Orenburg.**

chl. *abbr.* Chloroform.

chlam·y·date (klăm′ĭ-dāt′) *adj.* Having a mantle. Used of mollusks. [Latin *chlamydātus,* cloaked, from *chlamys, chlamyd-,* mantle. See CHLAMYS.]

chla·myd·e·ous (klə-mĭd′ē-əs) *adj. Botany.* Having a perianth. [Latin *chlamys, chlamyd-,* mantle; see CHLAMYS + –EOUS.]

chlam·y·des (klăm′ĭ-dēz′) *n.* A plural of **chlamys.**

chla·myd·i·a (klə-mĭd′ē-ə) *n., pl.* **-i·ae** (-ē-ē′). *Microbiology.* **1.** Any of various gram-negative, coccoid microorganisms of the genus *Chlamydia,* especially *C. psittaci* and *C. trachomatis,* that are pathogenic to human beings and animals, causing diseases such as conjunctivitis in cattle and sheep and trachoma, nonspecific urethritis, and proctitis in human beings. **2.** Any of several common, often asymptomatic, sexually transmitted diseases caused by the microorganism *Chlamydia trachomatis,* including nonspecific urethritis in men. [New Latin, genus name, from Latin *chlamys, chlamyd-,* mantle. See CHLAMYS.] **—chla·myd′i·al** *adj.*

chla·myd·o·spore (klə-mĭd′ə-spôr′, -spōr′) *n.* A thick-walled, asexual fungal spore that is derived from a hyphal cell and can function as a resting spore. [Latin *chlamys, chlamyd-,* mantle; see CHLAMYS + SPORE.]

chlam·ys (klăm′ĭs, klā′mĭs) *n., pl.* **chlam·ys·es** or **chlam·y·des** (klăm′ĭ-dēz′). A short mantle fastened at the shoulder, worn by men in ancient Greece. [Latin, from Greek *khlamus.*]

chlo·as·ma (klō-ăz′mə) *n., pl.* **-ma·ta** (-mə-tə). A patchy brown or dark brown skin discoloration that usually occurs on a woman's face and may result from hormonal changes, as in pregnancy. [New Latin, from Greek *khloasma,* greenness, from *khloazein,* to be green, from *khloos,* greenish color. See **ghel-²** in Appendix.]

chiton
Ceres wearing a chiton

ă pat	oi boy
ā pay	ou out
âr care	o͝o took
ä father	o͞o boot
ĕ pet	ŭ cut
ē be	ûr urge
ĭ pit	th thin
ī pie	*th* this
îr pier	hw which
ŏ pot	zh vision
ō toe	ə about, item
ô paw	♦ regionalism

Stress marks: ′ (primary); ′ (secondary), as in **dictionary** (dĭk′shə-nĕr′ē)

chlor– *pref.* Variant of **chloro–.**

chlor·ac·ne (klôr-ăk′nē, klōr-) *n.* An acnelike skin disorder caused by prolonged exposure to chlorinated hydrocarbons.

chlo·ral (klôr′əl, klōr′-) *n.* A colorless, mobile, oily aldehyde, CCl_3CHO, a penetrating lung irritant, used to manufacture DDT and chloral hydrate. [CHLOR(INE) + AL(COHOL).]

chloral hydrate *n.* A colorless crystalline compound, $CCl_3CH(OH)_2$, used medicinally as a sedative and hypnotic.

chlo·ra·mine (klôr′ə-mēn′, klōr′-) *n.* Any of several compounds containing nitrogen and chlorine, especially an unstable colorless liquid, NH_2Cl, used to make hydrazine.

chlo·ram·phen·i·col (klôr′ăm-fĕn′ĭ-kôl′, -kŏl′, -kōl′, klōr′-) *n.* An antibiotic, $C_{11}H_{12}Cl_2N_2O_5$, derived from the soil bacterium *Streptomyces venezuelae* or produced synthetically and effective against a broad spectrum of microorganisms. [CHLOR(O)– + AM(IDE) + PHE(NO)– + NI(TRO)– + (GLY)COL.]

chlo·rate (klôr′āt′, klōr′-) *n.* The inorganic group ClO_3 or a compound containing it.

chlor·dane (klôr′dān′, klōr′-) also **chlor·dan** (-dăn′) *n.* A colorless, odorless, viscous liquid, $C_{10}H_6Cl_8$, used as an insecticide. It may be toxic to human beings and wildlife as a result of its effect on the nervous system. [CHLOR(O)– + (IN)D(ENE) + –ANE.]

chlor·di·az·e·pox·ide (klôr′dī-ăz′ə-pŏk′sīd′, klōr′-) *n.* A benzodiazepine drug, $C_{16}H_{14}ClN_3O$, whose hydrochloride is used as an antianxiety drug and in the treatment of chronic alcoholism and alcohol withdrawal. [CHLOR(O)– + DI–[1] + AZ(O) + EP(I)– + OXIDE.]

chlo·rel·la (klə-rĕl′ə) *n.* Any of various unicellular green algae of the genus *Chlorella,* easily cultured and often used in studies of photosynthesis and other experiments. [New Latin *Chlorella,* genus name, from Greek *khlōros,* green. See CHLORO–.]

chlo·ren·chy·ma (klə-rĕng′kə-mə) *n.* Plant tissue consisting of parenchyma cells that contain chloroplasts. [CHLOR(OPHYLL) + –ENCHYMA.]

chlo·ric (klôr′ĭk, klōr′-) *adj.* Of, relating to, or containing chlorine.

chloric acid *n.* A strongly oxidizing unstable acid, $HClO_3{\cdot}7H_2O$.

chlo·ride (klôr′īd′, klōr′-) *n.* A binary compound of chlorine. **—chlo·rid′ic** (klə-rĭd′ĭk) *adj.*

chloride of lime *n.* See **bleaching powder.**

chlo·ri·nate (klôr′ə-nāt′, klōr′-) *tr.v.* **-nat·ed, -nat·ing, -nates.** To treat or combine with chlorine or a chlorine compound. **—chlo′ri·na′tion** *n.* **—chlo′ri·na′tor** *n.*

chlo·ri·nat·ed lime (klôr′ə-nā′tĭd, klōr′-) *n.* See **bleaching powder.**

chlo·rine (klôr′ēn′, -ĭn, klōr′-) *n. Symbol* **Cl** A highly irritating, greenish-yellow gaseous halogen, capable of combining with nearly all other elements, produced principally by electrolysis of sodium chloride and used widely to purify water, as a disinfectant and bleaching agent, and in the manufacture of many important compounds including chloroform and carbon tetrachloride. Atomic number 17; atomic weight 35.45; freezing point −100.98°C; boiling point −34.6°C; specific gravity 1.56 (−33.6°C); valence 1, 3, 5, 7. See table at **element.**

chock

chlo·rite[1] (klôr′īt′, klōr′-) *n.* A generally green or black secondary mineral, $(Mg,Fe,Al)_6(Si,Al)_4O_{10}(OH)_8$, often formed by metamorphic alteration of primary dark rock minerals, that appears as a spot of green and resembles mica. [Latin *chlōrītis,* a green precious stone, from Greek *khlōritis,* from *khlōros,* green. See **ghel-**[2] in Appendix.]

chlo·rite[2] (klôr′īt′, klōr′-) *n.* The inorganic group ClO_2 or a salt containing it.

chloro– or **chlor–** *pref.* **1.** Green: *chlorosis.* **2.** Chlorine: *chloroform.* [From Greek *khlōros,* green. See **ghel-**[2] in Appendix.]

chlo·ro·ben·zene (klôr′ō-bĕn′zēn′, -bĕn-zēn′, klōr′-) *n.* A colorless, volatile flammable liquid, C_6H_5Cl, used to prepare phenol, DDT, and aniline and as a general solvent.

chlo·ro·car·bon (klôr′ō-kär′bən, klōr′-) *n.* A compound that consists of chlorine and halocarbon.

chlo·ro·fluor·o·car·bon (klôr′ō-flo͝or′ō-kär′bən, -flôr′-, -flōr′-, klōr′-) *n. Abbr.* **CFC** Any of various halocarbon compounds consisting of carbon, hydrogen, chlorine, and fluorine, once used widely as aerosol propellants and refrigerants. Chlorofluorocarbons are believed to cause depletion of the atmospheric ozone layer.

chlo·ro·form (klôr′ə-fôrm′, klōr′-) *n. Abbr.* **chl.** A clear, colorless, heavy, sweet-smelling liquid, $CHCl_3$, used in refrigerants, propellants, and resins, as a solvent, and sometimes as an anesthetic. Chloroform, once widely used in human and veterinary surgery, has generally been replaced by less toxic, more easily controlled agents. *—tr.* **-formed, -form·ing, -forms. 1.** To treat with chloroform to anesthetize, render unconscious, or kill. **2.** To apply chloroform to. [CHLORO– + FORM(YL).]

chlo·ro·hy·drin (klôr′ō-hī′drĭn, klōr′-) *n.* An aliphatic organic chemical compound that is both an alkyl chloride and an alcohol, frequently containing a single chlorine atom and a single hydroxyl group on adjacent carbon atoms.

Chlo·ro·my·ce·tin (klôr′ō-mī-sēt′n, klōr′-). A trademark used for an antibiotic preparation of chloramphenicol.

chlo·ro·phyll also **chlo·ro·phyl** (klôr′ə-fĭl, klōr′-) *n.* Any of a group of related green pigments found in photosynthetic organisms, especially: **a.** A waxy blue-black microcrystalline green-plant pigment, $C_{55}H_{72}MgN_4O_5$, with a characteristic blue-green alcohol solution. Also called *chlorophyll a.* **b.** A similar green-plant pigment, $C_{55}H_{70}MgN_4O_6$, having a brilliant green alcohol solution. Also called *chlorophyll b.*

chlo·ro·pic·rin (klôr′ə-pĭk′rĭn, klōr′-) *n.* An oily, colorless liquid, CCl_3NO_2, used as a lung irritant in poison gas and in dyestuffs, disinfectants, insecticides, and soil fumigants. Also called *nitrochloroform.* [CHLORO– + PICR(O)– + –IN.]

chlo·ro·plast (klôr′ə-plăst′, klōr′-) also **chlo·ro·plas·tid** (klôr′ə-plăs′tĭd, klōr′-) *n.* A chlorophyll-containing plastid found in algal and green plant cells. [CHLORO– + PLAST(ID).]

chlo·ro·prene (klôr′ə-prēn′, klōr′-) *n.* A colorless liquid, C_4H_5Cl, that polymerizes to neoprene. [CHLORO– + (ISO)PRENE.]

chlo·ro·quine (klôr′ə-kwīn′, -kwēn′, klōr′-) *n.* A drug, $C_{18}H_{26}ClN_3$, used mainly in the treatment and prevention of malaria. [CHLORO– + QUIN(OLIN)E.]

chlo·ro·sis (klə-rō′sĭs) *n.* **1.** *Botany.* The yellowing or whitening of normally green plant tissue because of a decreased amount of chlorophyll, often as a result of disease or nutrient deficiency. **2.** *Pathology.* An iron-deficiency anemia, primarily of young women, characterized by a greenish-yellow discoloration of the skin. In this sense, also called *greensickness.* **—chlo·rot′ic** (-rŏt′ĭk) *adj.* **—chlo·rot′i·cal·ly** *adv.*

chlo·ro·thi·a·zide (klôr′ə-thī′ə-zīd′, klōr′-) *n.* A thiazide diuretic used in the treatment of hypertension, heart failure, and edema to promote the excretion of excess salt and water from the body.

chlor·prom·a·zine (klôr-prŏm′ə-zēn′, -prō′mə-, klōr-) *n.* A drug, $C_{17}H_{19}ClN_2S$, derived from phenothiazine and used to suppress vomiting and as a sedative and a tranquilizer, especially in the treatment of schizophrenia and other psychotic states. [CHLOR(O)– + PRO(PYL) + M(ETHYL) + AZINE.]

chlor·tet·ra·cy·cline (klôr′tĕt-rə-sī′klēn′, -klĭn, klōr′-) *n.* A broad-spectrum antibiotic, $C_{22}H_{23}ClN_2O_8$, obtained from the soil bacterium *Streptomyces aureofaciens* and used in the treatment of a variety of infections.

chm. *abbr.* **1.** Chairman. **2.** Checkmate.

Chmn *abbr.* Chairman.

cho·an·o·cyte (kō-ăn′ə-sīt′) *n.* One of a layer of flagellated cells lining the body cavity of a sponge and characterized by a collar of cytoplasm surrounding the flagellum. Also called *collar cell.* [Greek *khoanē,* funnel (from *khein,* to pour; see **gheu-** in Appendix) + –CYTE.]

Choate (chōt), **Rufus.** 1799–1859. American politician who served as a U.S. representative (1831–1834) and senator (1841–1845) from Massachusetts.

chock (chŏk) *n.* **1.** A block or wedge placed under something else, such as a wheel, to keep it from moving. **2.** *Nautical.* A heavy fitting of metal or wood with two jaws curving inward, through which a rope or cable may be run. **—chock** *tr.v.* **chocked, chock·ing, chocks. 1.** To fit with or secure by a chock: *The plane's wheels were chocked and chained down.* **2.** *Nautical.* To place (a boat) on chocks. **—chock** *adv.* **1.** As completely as possible: *a report chock full of errors.* **2.** As close as possible: *had to stand chock up against the railing.* [Possibly from Old North French *choque,* log, from Gaulish **tsukka,* stump, of Germanic origin.]

chock-a-block or **chock·a·block** (chŏk′ə-blŏk′) *—adj.* **1.** Squeezed together; jammed: *The cheering fans were chock-a-block in the stands.* **2.** Completely filled; stuffed: *"I recommend the north shore chowder, chockablock with pieces of seasonal fish"* (Charles Monaghan). **3.** *Nautical.* Drawn so close as to have the blocks touching. Used of a ship's hoisting tackle. *—adv.* Chock: *a hall that was chock-a-block full.* [Alteration (influenced by CHOCK) of *block-a-block* : BLOCK + A–[2] + BLOCK.]

choc·o·hol·ic (chôk′ə-hô′lĭk, -hŏl′ĭk, chŏk′-) *n.* A person who craves chocolate. [CHOC(OLATE) + (ALC)OHOLIC.]

choc·o·late (chô′kə-lĭt, chôk′lĭt, chŏk′-) *n.* **1.** Fermented, roasted, shelled, and ground cacao seeds, often combined with a sweetener or flavoring agent. **2.** A beverage made by mixing water or milk with chocolate. **3.** A small, chocolate-covered candy with a hard or soft center. **4.** *Color.* A grayish to deep reddish brown to deep grayish brown. **—chocolate** *adj.* **1.** Made or flavored with chocolate: *chocolate pudding.* **2.** *Color.* Of a grayish to deep reddish brown to deep grayish brown. [Spanish, from Nahuatl *xocolatl* : *xococ,* bitter + *atl,* water.]

chocolate tree *n.* See **cacao** (sense 1).

Choc·taw (chŏk′tô) *n., pl.* **Choctaw** or **-taws. 1.a.** A Native American people inhabiting central and southern Mississippi and southwest Alabama, with present-day populations in Mississippi and southeast Oklahoma. The Choctaw were removed to Indian Territory in the 1830's. **b.** A member of this people. **2.** The Muskogean language of the Choctaw. [Choctaw *Chahta.*]

choice (chois) *n.* **1.** The act of choosing; selection. **2.** The power, right, or liberty to choose; option. **3.** One that is chosen. **4.** A number or variety from which to choose: *a wide choice of styles and colors.* **5.** The best or most preferable part. **6.** Care in choosing. **7.** An alternative. **—choice** *adj.* **choic·er, choic·est. 1.a.** Of very fine quality. **b.** Appealing to refined taste. **2.** Selected with care. **3.** Of the U.S. Government grade of meat higher than good and lower than prime. —***idiom.* of choice.** Preferred above others of the same kind or set: *"the much used leveraged buyout as the weapon of choice"* (Alison Leigh Cowan). [Middle English *chois,* from Old French, from *choisir,* to choose, from Vulgar Latin *causīre, of Germanic origin. See **geus-** in Appendix.] —**choice′ly** *adv.* —**choice′ness** *n.*

SYNONYMS: *choice, alternative, option, preference, selection, election.* Each of these nouns denotes the act, power, or right of choosing. *Choice* implies broadly the freedom to choose from a set, as of persons or things: *The store offers a wide choice of fruits and vegetables. I had no choice—their decision was final. Alternative* emphasizes a choosing between only two possibilities or courses of action: *"An unhappy alternative is before you, Elizabeth. . . . Your mother will never see you again if you do* not *marry Mr. Collins, and I will never see you again if you* do*"* (Jane Austen). *Option* often stresses a power or liberty to choose that has been granted, as by an authority: *The option lies between accepting the candidate the administration proposes and reconstituting the search committee. Preference* indicates choice based on one's values, bias, or predilections: *We were offered our preference of wines. Selection* suggests a variety of things or persons to choose from: *Parents should exercise care in their selection of the movies their young children see. Election* especially emphasizes the use of judgment in choosing: *The university recommends the election of courses in composition and literature.* See also Synonyms at **delicate.**

choir (kwīr) *n.* **1.** An organized company of singers, especially one performing church music or singing in a church. **2.a.** The part of a church used by such a company of singers. **b.** The part of the chancel in a cruciform church that is occupied by this company of singers. **3.** *Music.* **a.** A group of instruments of the same kind: *a string choir.* **b.** A division of some pipe organs, containing pipes suitable for accompanying a choir. **4.** An organized group: *a choir of dancers.* **5.** One of the orders of angels. —**choir** *intr.v.* **choired, choir·ing, choirs.** *Music.* To sing in chorus. [Middle English *quer, quire,* from Old French *cuer,* from Medieval Latin *chorus,* from Latin, choral dance. See CHORUS.]

choir·boy (kwīr′boi′) *n.* **1.** *Music.* A boy member of a choir. **2.** *Informal.* A young man who is considered to be of the highest character: *"They're . . . choirboys—clean, scrubbed nothings—so there's no dramatic or psychological preparation for the explosion of killing"* (Pauline Kael).

choir·girl (kwīr′gûrl′) *n.* *Music.* A girl member of a choir.

choir loft *n.* A gallery for a group of church singers.

choir·mas·ter (kwīr′măs′tər) *n.* The director of a group of church singers.

Choi·seul (shwä-zœl′). One of the Solomon Islands in the southwest Pacific Ocean southeast of Bougainville Island. It was under German control from 1886 to 1899.

choke (chōk) *v.* **choked, chok·ing, chokes.** —*tr.* **1.** To interfere with the respiration of by compression or obstruction of the larynx or trachea. **2.a.** To check or slow down the movement, growth, or action of: *a garden that was choked by weeds.* **b.** To block up or obstruct by filling or clogging: *Mud choked the drainpipe.* **c.** To fill up completely; jam: *Major commuter arteries were choked with stalled traffic.* **3.** To reduce the air intake of (a carburetor), thereby enriching the fuel mixture. **4.** *Sports.* To grip (a bat or racket, for example) at a point nearer the hitting surface. —*intr.* **1.** To have difficulty in breathing, swallowing, or speaking. **2.** To become blocked up or obstructed. **3.** *Sports.* To shorten one's grip on the handle of a bat or racket. **4.** To fail to perform effectively because of nervous agitation or tension: *"The only top official to choke up was the Secretary of State. . . . he created a problem by insisting on solving a problem that was not acute"* (William Safire). —**choke** *n.* **1.** The act or sound of choking. **2.a.** Something that constricts or chokes. **b.** A narrow part, such as the chokebore of a firearm. **3.** A device used in an internal-combustion engine to enrich the fuel mixture by reducing the flow of air to the carburetor. —***phrasal verbs.* choke back.** To hold back; suppress: *choked back his tears.* **choke off.** To bring to an end as if by choking: *"Treasury borrowing of existing savings would drive up the interest rate and choke off economic activity"* (Paul Craig Roberts). **choke up.** To be unable to speak because of strong emotion. [Middle English *choken,* short for *achoken,* from Old English *āceōcian* : *ā-,* intensive pref. + *cēoce, cēace,* jaw, cheek.]

choke·ber·ry (chōk′bĕr′ē) *n.* **1.** Any of various deciduous shrubs of the genus *Aronia* in the rose family, native to eastern North America and having clusters of small white or pinkish flowers and tiny red to black applelike fruit. **2.** The fruit of any of these plants. [From its bitter fruit.]

choke·bore (chōk′bôr′, -bōr′) *n.* **1.** A shotgun bore that narrows toward the muzzle to prevent wide scattering of the shot. **2.** A gun with a narrowed bore near the muzzle.

choke chain *n.* See **choke collar.**

choke·cher·ry (chōk′chĕr′ē) *n.* **1.** A deciduous North American shrub or small tree *(Prunus virginiana)* in the rose family, having elongate clusters of small white flowers and astringent, dark red to nearly black fruit. **2.** The fruit of this plant. [From its bitter fruit.]

choke coil *n.* *Electronics.* A circuit element used to suppress or limit the flow of alternating current without affecting the flow of direct current.

choke collar *n.* A chain collar that tightens like a noose when the leash is pulled, used in canine obedience training or to control untrained animals. Also called *choke chain.*

choke·damp (chōk′dămp′) *n.* See **blackdamp.** [So called because it causes suffocation in mines.]

choke·hold (chōk′hōld′) *n.* A restraining move in which one person seizes another around the neck in a tight grip, typically from behind.

choke·point or **choke point** (chōk′point′) *n.* **1.** A narrow passage, such as a strait, through which shipping must pass. **2.** A point of congestion or obstruction.

chok·er (chō′kər) *n.* **1.** One that chokes or suffocates another. **2.** Something that fits closely around the neck or throat, as: **a.** A tight-fitting necklace. **b.** A high, tight collar. **c.** A narrow neckpiece of fur.

chok·ing (chō′kĭng) *adj.* **1.** Causing a feeling of being choked or suffocated: *The hall was filled with choking clouds of smoke.* **2.** Having a strained or husky sound: *spoke in a choking voice.* —**chok′ing·ly** *adv.*

chok·y (chō′kē) *adj.* **-i·er, -i·est.** **1.** Likely to cause choking. **2.** Tending to become choked.

chol– *pref.* Variant of **chole–.**

cho·lan·gi·og·ra·phy (kō-lăn′jē-ŏg′rə-fē) *n.* X-ray examination of the bile ducts following administration of a radiopaque contrast medium. [CHOL(E)– + ANGIOGRAPHY.] —**cho·lan′gi·o·graph′ic** (-ə-grăf′ĭk) *adj.*

chole– or **chol–** *pref.* Bile: *cholesterol.* [From Greek *kholē,* bile. See **ghel-**[2] in Appendix.]

cho·le·cal·cif·er·ol (kō′lĭ-kăl-sĭf′ə-rôl′, -rōl′, -rŏl′) *n.* See **vitamin D_3.**

cho·le·cyst (kō′lĭ-sĭst′) *n.* The gallbladder.

cho·le·cys·tec·to·my (kō′lĭ-sĭ-stĕk′tə-mē) *n., pl.* **-mies.** Surgical removal of the gallbladder.

cho·le·cys·ti·tis (kō′lĭ-sĭ-stī′tĭs) *n.* Inflammation of the gallbladder.

cho·le·cys·to·ki·nin (kō′lĭ-sĭs′tə-kī′nĭn) *n.* *Abbr.* **CCK** A hormone produced principally by the small intestine in response to the presence of fats, causing contraction of the gallbladder, release of bile, and secretion of pancreatic digestive enzymes. Also called *pancreozymin.*

cho·le·li·thi·a·sis (kō′lə-lĭ-thī′ə-sĭs) *n.* The presence or formation of gallstones in the gallbladder or bile ducts.

chol·er (kŏl′ər, kō′lər) *n.* **1.** Anger; irritability. **2. a.** Archaic. One of the four humors of the body thought in the Middle Ages to cause anger and bad temper when present in excess; yellow bile. **b.** *Obsolete.* The quality or condition of being bilious. [Middle English *colre,* from Old French, from Latin *cholera,* cholera, jaundice, from Greek *kholera,* from *kholē,* bile. See **ghel-**[2] in Appendix.]

chol·er·a (kŏl′ər-ə) *n.* **1.** An acute infectious disease of the small intestine, caused by the bacterium *Vibrio cholerae* and characterized by profuse watery diarrhea, vomiting, muscle cramps, severe dehydration, and depletion of electrolytes. Also called *Asiatic cholera.* **2.** Any of various diseases of domesticated animals, such as chickens, turkeys, or hogs, marked by severe gastroenteritis. [Latin, cholera, jaundice. See CHOLER.] —**chol′e·ra′ic** (-ə-rā′ĭk) *adj.* —**chol′e·roid′** (-ə-roid′) *adj.*

cholera mor·bus (môr′bəs) *n.* Acute gastroenteritis occurring in summer and autumn and marked by severe cramps, diarrhea, and vomiting. No longer in scientific use. [New Latin : Latin *cholera,* jaundice + Latin *morbus,* disease.]

chol·er·ic (kŏl′ə-rĭk, kə-lĕr′ĭk) *adj.* **1.** Easily angered; bad-tempered. **2.** Showing or expressing anger. —**chol′er·i·cal·ly, chol′er·ic·ly** *adv.*

cho·le·sta·sis (kō′lĭ-stā′sĭs) *n.* Suppression of biliary flow.

cho·les·ter·in (kə-lĕs′tər-ĭn) *n.* Cholesterol.

cho·les·ter·ol (kə-lĕs′tə-rôl′, -rōl′) *n.* A white, crystalline substance, $C_{27}H_{45}OH$, found in animal tissues and various foods, that is normally synthesized by the liver and is important as a constituent of cell membranes and a precursor to steroid hormones. Its level in the bloodstream can influence the pathogenesis of certain conditions, such as the development of atherosclerotic plaque and coronary artery disease. [CHOLE– + Greek *stereos,* solid; see **ster-**[1] in Appendix + –OL[1] (so called because it was first found in gallstones).]

cho·le·styr·a·mine (kō′lĭ-stîr′ə-mēn′, kō-lĕs′tə-răm′ēn) *n.* A drug used to lower serum cholesterol levels and treat itching associated with jaundice through its ability to bind intestinal bile acids and promote their excretion. [CHOLE– + *styr-,* possibly alteration of STER(OL) + AMINE.]

cho·lic acid (kō′lĭk) *n.* An abundant crystalline bile acid, $C_{24}H_{40}O_5$ derived from cholesterol. [Greek *kholikos,* bilious, from *kholē,* bile. See CHOLE–.]

cho·line (kō′lēn′) *n.* A natural amine, $C_5H_{15}NO_2$, often classed in the vitamin B complex and a constituent of many other biologically important molecules, such as acetylcholine and lecithin.

cho·lin·er·gic (kō′lə-nûr′jĭk) *adj.* **1.** Activated by or capable of liberating acetylcholine, especially as related to nerve fibers of the parasympathetic nervous system. **2.** Having physiological effects similar to acetylcholine: *a cholinergic agent or drug.* [(ACETYL)CHOLIN(E) + Greek *ergon,* work; see **werg-** in Appendix.]

cho·lin·es·ter·ase (kō′lə-nĕs′tə-rās′, -rāz′) *n.* An enzyme

choir
High-school choir rehearsing

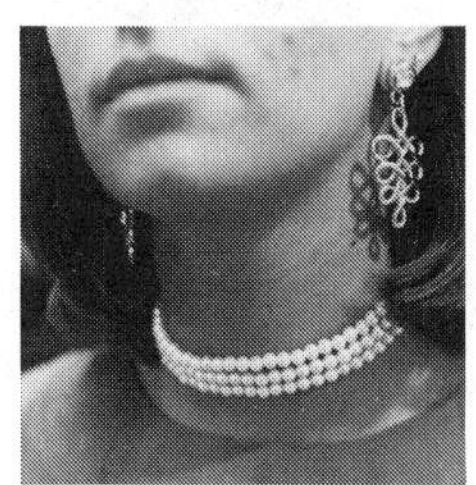

choker
Pearl necklace

ă pat	oi boy
ā pay	ou out
âr care	ŏŏ took
ä father	ōō boot
ĕ pet	ŭ cut
ē be	ûr urge
ĭ pit	th thin
ī pie	*th* this
îr pier	hw which
ŏ pot	zh vision
ō toe	ə about, item
ô paw	♦ regionalism

Stress marks: **′** (primary); ′ (secondary), as in **dictionary** (dĭk′shə-nĕr′ē)

found chiefly at nerve terminals that inactivates acetylcholine by hydrolyzing it to form acetic acid and choline. [CHOLIN(E) + ESTERASE.]

chol·la (choi′ə) *n.* Any of several spiny, shrubby, or treelike cacti of the genus *Opuntia* having cylindrical stem segments. [American Spanish, from obsolete Spanish, upper part of the head, possibly from Old French *cholle,* round lump, head, of Germanic origin.]

Cho·lu·la (chə-lo͞o′lə, chô-lo͞o′lä). A town of east-central Mexico west of Puebla. Site of an ancient Toltec center and a city sacred to the Aztecs, it was destroyed by Hernando Cortés in 1519. Population, 26,748.

Cho·mo Lha·ri (chō′mō lär′ē). A peak, 7,318.8 m (23,996 ft) high, of the southeast Himalaya Mountains on the Bhutan-China border.

Frédéric Chopin

chomp (chŏmp) *v.* **chomped, chomp·ing, chomps.** —*tr.* To chew or bite on noisily: *a horse chomping oats.* —*intr.* To chew or bite on something repeatedly: *chomping on a cigar.* **—chomp** *n.* The act or an instance of vigorous biting: *"He finished the last of his sandwich with a single chomp"* (Anne Tyler). [Variant of CHAMP¹.]

Chom·sky (chŏm′skē), **Noam.** Born 1928. American linguist who revolutionized the study of language with his theory of generative grammar, set forth in *Syntactic Structures* (1957).

chon (chŏn) *n., pl.* **chon.** See table at **currency.** [Korean.]

chondr– or **chondri–** *pref.* Variants of **chondro–.**

chon·dri·fy (kŏn′drə-fī′) *v.* **-fied, -fy·ing, -fies.** —*tr.* To change (a tissue) into cartilage. —*intr.* To develop into cartilage. **—chon′dri·fi·ca′tion** (-fĭ-kā′shən) *n.*

chon·dri·o·some (kŏn′drē-ə-sōm′) *n.* See **mitochondrion.**

chon·drite (kŏn′drīt′) *n.* A stone of meteoric origin characterized by chondrules. **—chon·drit′ic** (-drĭt′ĭk) *adj.*

chondro– or **chrondri–** or **chrondr–** *pref.* **1.** Cartilage: *chondrocranium.* **2.** Granule: *chondrite.* [From Greek *khondros,* granule, cartilage. See **ghrendh-** in Appendix.]

chon·dro·cra·ni·um (kŏn′drō-krā′nē-əm) *n., pl.* **-ni·ums** or **-ni·a** (-nē-ə). **1.** The cartilaginous cranium of an embryo before ossification. **2.** A portion of the embryonic cranium forming the bones of the base of the skull and eventually undergoing ossification.

chon·dro·i·tin sulfate (kŏn-drō′ĭ-tĭn) *n.* One of several classes of sulfated glycosaminoglycans that is a major constituent in various connective tissues, especially in the ground substance of blood vessels, bone, and cartilage. [From *chondroitic acid,* an acid occurring in cartilage.]

chon·dro·ma (kŏn-drō′mə) *n., pl.* **-mas** or **-ma·ta** (-mə-tə). A cartilaginous growth or tumor.

chon·dro·ma·la·cia (kŏn′drō-mə-lā′shə) *n.* Abnormal softening or degeneration of cartilage of the joints, especially of the knee. [CHONDRO– + Greek *malakia,* softness (from *malakos,* soft; see **mel-¹** in Appendix).]

chopine
Venetian, c. 1600

chon·dro·ma·ta (kŏn-drō′mə-tə) *n.* A plural of **chondroma.**

chon·drule (kŏn′dro͞ol) *n.* A small round granule of extraterrestrial origin found embedded in some meteorites.

Chong·jin (chông′jĭn′, chœng′-). A city of northeast North Korea on the Sea of Japan. It is a port and an industrial center. Population, 490,000.

Chong·qing (chông′chĭng′, cho͞ong′-) also **Chung·king** (cho͞ong′kĭng′, jo͞ong′gĭng′). A city of south-central China on the Yangtze River (Chang Jiang). It was the capital of China from 1937 to 1946. Population 2,080,000.

Chon·ju (chôn′jo͞o′, chœn′-). A city of southwest South Korea south of Seoul. It is a marketing center in a rice-growing region. Population, 305,000.

choose (cho͞oz) *v.* **chose** (chōz), **cho·sen** (chō′zən), **choos·ing, choos·es.** —*tr.* **1.** To select from a number of possible alternatives; decide on and pick out. **2.a.** To prefer above others: *chooses the supermarket over the neighborhood grocery store.* **b.** To determine or decide: *chose to fly rather than drive.* —*intr.* To make a choice; make a selection: *was used to doing as she chose.* **—*phrasal verb.* choose up.** To choose players and form sides or teams for a game, such as baseball or softball. [Middle English *chesen,* from Old English *cēosan.* See **geus-** in Appendix.] **—choos′er** *n.*

chopstick
Serving sushi with a pair of chopsticks

SYNONYMS: *choose, select, elect, pick.* These verbs mean to make a choice from a number of possibilities. *Choose* implies the use of judgment in taking one of several persons, things, or courses of action: *"We do not choose survival as a value; it chooses us"* (B.F. Skinner). *Select* stresses fastidiousness in choosing from a wide variety: *Four skiers will be selected to represent each country.* *Elect* strongly suggests deliberation in making a selection, usually between alternatives: *I elected not to go.* *Pick,* like *select,* indicates care in choosing: *"Not only do I knock 'em out, I pick the round"* (Muhammad Ali).

choos·y also **choos·ey** (cho͞o′zē) *adj.* **-i·er, -i·est.** Very careful in choosing; highly selective. **—choos′i·ness** *n.*

Cho O·yu (chō′ ō-yo͞o′). A peak, 8,158.8 m (26,750 ft) high, of the central Himalaya Mountains on the Nepal-China border.

chop¹ (chŏp) *v.* **chopped, chop·ping, chops.** —*tr.* **1.a.** To cut by striking with a heavy, sharp tool, such as an ax: *chop wood.* **b.** To shape or form by chopping: *chop a hole in the ice.* **c.** To cut into small pieces: *chop onions; chop up meat.* **d.** To curtail as if by chopping: *chopped off his sentence midway; are going to chop expenses.* **2.** *Sports.* To hit or hit at with a short, swift downward stroke. —*intr.* **1.** To make heavy, cutting strokes. **2.** *Archaic.* To move roughly or suddenly. **—chop** *n.* **1.** The act of chopping. **2.a.** A swift, short, cutting blow or stroke. **b.** *Sports.* A short, downward stroke. **3.** A piece that has been chopped off, especially a cut of meat, usually taken from the rib, shoulder, or loin and containing a bone. **4.a.** A short, irregular motion of waves. **b.** An area of choppy water, as on an ocean. [Middle English *choppen,* probably variant of *chappen,* to split. See CHAP¹.]

chop² (chŏp) *intr.v.* **chopped, chop·ping, chops.** To change direction suddenly, as a ship in the wind. [Obsolete, to exchange, from Middle English *choppen,* to barter, bargain, variant of *chapen,* from Old English *cēapian,* from *cēap,* bargain, trade. See CHEAP.]

chop³ (chŏp) *n.* **1.** An official stamp or permit in the Far East. **2.a.** A mark stamped on goods or coins to indicate their identity or quality. **b.** Quality; class: *first chop.* [Hindi *chāp,* seal.]

chop-chop (chŏp′chŏp′) *adv. Informal.* Right away; quickly. [Pidgin English, reduplication of *chop,* quick. See CHOPSTICK.]

chop·fall·en (chŏp′fô′lən) *adj.* Variant of **chapfallen.**

chop·house (chŏp′hous′) *n.* A restaurant that specializes in serving steaks and chops.

Cho·pin (shō-păn′, -pǎN′), **Frédéric François.** 1810–1849. Polish-born French composer and pianist of the romantic era. His music, written chiefly for the piano, was based on traditional Polish dance themes.

Cho·pin (shō′păn′), **Kate O'Flaherty.** 1851–1904. American writer whose works, such as *The Awakening* (1899), portray Creole life in Louisiana.

cho·pine (chō-pēn′, chŏ-, chŏp′ĭn) *n.* A woman's shoe worn in the 16th and 17th centuries that featured a very high, thick sole. [Obsolete French *chapin,* from Old Spanish, from *chapa,* plate, covering, from Old French. See CHAPE.]

chop·log·ic (chŏp′lŏj′ĭk) *n.* Complicated, often illogical or spurious argumentation. [From *to chop logic,* to bandy logic, from *chop,* to bandy, exchange. See CHOP².] **—chop′log′ic** *adj.*

chop·per (chŏp′ər) *n.* **1.** One that chops: *a vegetable chopper.* **2.** A device that interrupts an electric current or a beam of radiation. **3.** *Informal.* A helicopter. **4. choppers.** *Slang.* Teeth, especially a set of false teeth. **5.** *Informal.* A motorcycle, especially one that is customized. **—chopper** *intr. & tr.v.* **-pered, -per·ing, -pers.** *Informal.* To travel by helicopter or transport (someone or something) by helicopter.

chop·ping block (chŏp′ĭng) *n.* A wooden block on which food or wood is chopped.

chop·py¹ (chŏp′ē) *adj.* **-pi·er, -pi·est. 1.** Having many small waves: *choppy seas.* **2.** Marked by abrupt transitions; jerky: *choppy prose.* **—chop′pi·ly** *adv.* **—chop′pi·ness** *n.*

chop·py² (chŏp′ē) *adj.* **-pi·er, -pi·est.** Abruptly shifting; variable. Used of the wind.

♦**chops** (chŏps) *pl.n.* **1.** The jaws. **2.a.** The mouth. **b.** The lower cheeks or jowls. **3.** *Slang.* The technical skill with which a jazz or rock musician performs. **—*idiom.* slap** (or **bust**) **(someone's) chops.** *New England.* **1.a.** To scold or insult. **b.** To disappoint or defeat. **2.** To hold (a building contractor) to the letter of an agreement. [Possibly akin to CHOP¹.]

chop shop *n. Slang.* A place where stolen cars are disassembled for parts that are then sold.

chop·stick (chŏp′stĭk′) *n.* One of a pair of slender sticks made especially of wood or ivory, held between the thumb and fingers and used as an eating utensil in Asian countries and in restaurants serving Asian food. Often used in the plural. [Pidgin English *chop,* quick (probably from Chinese (Cantonese) *kuai*) + STICK.]

chop su·ey (so͞o′ē) *n.* **1.** A Chinese-American dish consisting of small pieces of meat or chicken cooked with bean sprouts and other vegetables and served with rice. **2.** *Informal.* A miscellany: *"His coterie of execs were up to their pin stripes in a chop suey of deals"* (TV Guide). [Chinese (Cantonese) *tsapsui,* mixed pieces : Chinese (Mandarin) *zá,* mixed + Chinese (Mandarin) *suì,* to break up, pieces.]

cho·ra·gus (kə-rā′gəs) *n., pl.* **-gi** (-jī′). **1.** One who undertook the expense of providing the chorus in ancient Greek drama. **2.** The leader of a group or movement. [Latin, from Greek *khoragos* : *khoros,* chorus; see **gher-¹** in Appendix + *agein,* to lead; see **ag-** in Appendix.] **—cho·rag′ic** (-răj′ĭk) *adj.*

cho·ral (kôr′əl, kōr′-) *adj. Music.* **1.** Of or relating to a chorus or choir. **2.** Performed or written for performance by a chorus. [Medieval Latin *chorālis,* from *chorus,* choral dance, from Latin. See CHORUS.] **—cho′ral·ly** *adv.*

cho·rale also **cho·ral** (kə-răl′, -räl′) *n. Music.* **1.** A Protestant hymn melody. **2.** A harmonized hymn, especially one for organ. **3.** A chorus or choir. [German, short for *Choralgesang,* choral song, translation of Medieval Latin *cantus chorālis.* See CHORAL.]

chorale prelude *n. Music.* A composition usually for organ, chiefly in baroque style and characterized by an elaborate contrapuntal structure based on the melody of a hymn or chorale.

choral speaking *n.* Recitation of poetry or prose by a chorus.

chord¹ (kôrd, kōrd) *n.* **1.** *Music.* A combination of three or more usually concordant tones sounded simultaneously. **2.** Harmony, as of color. **—chord** *v.* **chord·ed, chord·ing, chords.** *—intr.* **1.** To be in accord; agree. **2.** *Music.* To play chords on an instrument. *—tr.* **1.** *Music.* To play chords on. **2.** To harmonize. [Alteration (influenced by *chord,* musical instrument string; see CHORD[2]) of Middle English *cord,* from *accord,* agreement, from Old French *acorde,* from *acorder,* to agree. See ACCORD.]

chord² (kôrd, kōrd) *n.* **1.** A line segment that joins two points on a curve. **2.** A straight line connecting the leading and trailing edges of an airfoil. **3.** *Anatomy.* Variant of **cord** (sense 5). **4.** An emotional feeling or response: *Her words struck a sympathetic chord in her audience.* **5.** *Archaic.* The string of a musical instrument. [Alteration of CORD.]

chord·al (kôr′dl) *adj. Music.* **1.** Of or relating to the strings of an instrument. **2.** Relating to or consisting of a harmonic chord. **3.** Giving prominence to harmonic rather than contrapuntal structure: *chordal music.*

chor·date (kôr′dāt′, -dĭt) *n.* Any of numerous animals belonging to the phylum Chordata, having at some stage of development a dorsal nerve cord, a notochord, and gill slits and including all vertebrates and certain marine animals, such as the lancelets. [From New Latin *Chordāta,* phylum name, from Latin *chorda,* cord. See CORD.]

chord organ *n. Music.* An electronic or reed organ equipped with buttons for producing chords.

chore (chôr, chōr) *n.* **1.** A routine or minor duty. See Synonyms at **task. 2. chores. a.** Daily or routine domestic tasks. **b.** The routine morning and evening tasks of a farmer, such as the feeding of livestock. **3.** An unpleasant or burdensome task. [Variant of CHAR[3].]

–chore *suff.* A plant distributed by a specified agency: *zoochore.* [From Greek *khōrein,* to spread about. See **ghē-** in Appendix.]

cho·re·a (kô-rē′ə, kō-) *n.* Any of various disorders of the nervous system marked by uncontrollable and irregular muscle movements, especially of the arms, legs, and face. [New Latin *chorea (Sancti Viti),* (St. Vitus') dance, from Latin *chorēa,* from Greek *khoreia,* choral dance, from *khoros.* See CHORUS.]

cho·re·o·graph (kôr′ē-ə-grăf′, kōr′-) *v.* **-graphed, -graph·ing, -graphs.** *—tr.* **1.** To create the choreography of: *choreograph a ballet.* **2.** To plan out or oversee the movement, development, or details of; orchestrate: *advance people who choreographed the candidate's whistle-stop tour.* *—intr.* To specialize in choreography. **—cho′re·og′ra·pher** (-ŏg′rə-fər) *n.*

cho·re·og·ra·phy (kôr′ē-ŏg′rə-fē, kōr′-) *n., pl.* **-phies. 1.a.** The art of creating and arranging dances or ballets. **b.** A work created by this art. **2.** Something, such as a situation or series of situations or a plan or series of plans, likened to dance arrangements: *"There are times when the choreography of frustration and violence seems rather too rich"* (John Simon). [French *chorégraphie* : Greek *khoreia,* choral dance; see CHOREA + *-graphie,* writing (from Latin *-graphia,* -graphy).] **—cho′re·o·graph′ic** (-ə-grăf′ĭk) *adj.* **—cho′re·o·graph′i·cal·ly** *adv.*

cho·ri·amb (kôr′ē-ămb′, -ăm′, kōr′-) *n.* **1.** A metrical foot consisting of a trochee followed by an iamb, much used in Greek and Latin poetry. **2.** A foot of verse used in lyric poetry having two unstressed syllables flanked by the two rhythmic stresses marking the first and last syllables of the foot. [Late Latin *choriambus,* from Greek *khoriambos* : *khoreios,* of a chorus (from *khoros,* chorus; see CHORUS) + *iambos,* iamb.] **—cho′ri·am′bic** (-ăm′bĭk) *adj.*

cho·ric (kôr′ĭk, kōr′-, kŏr′-) *adj.* Of or relating to a chorus. [Late Latin *choricus,* from Greek *khorikos,* from *khoros,* choral dance. See **gher-¹** in Appendix.]

cho·rine (kôr′ēn′, kōr′-) *n.* A chorus girl. [CHOR(US) + -INE[1].]

cho·ri·o·al·lan·to·is (kôr′ē-ō′ə-lăn′tō-ĭs, kōr′-) *n. Embryology.* The highly vascular fetal membrane that consists of the fused chorion and allantois, found adjacent to the eggshell in reptiles and birds and constituting the placenta in most mammals. **—cho′ri·o·al′lan·to′ic** (-ō-ăl′ən-tō′ĭk) *adj.*

cho·ri·oid (kôr′ē-oid′, kōr′-) *n. & adj.* Variant of **choroid.** [Greek *khorioeidēs,* like an afterbirth : *khorion,* afterbirth + *-oeidēs,* -oid.]

cho·ri·on (kôr′ē-ŏn′, kōr′-) *n. Embryology.* The outer membrane enclosing the embryo in reptiles, birds, and mammals. In placental mammals it contributes to the development of the placenta. [Greek *khorion.* See **gherə-** in Appendix.] **—cho′ri·on′ic** (-ŏn′ĭk) *adj.*

chorionic villus *n.* One of the minute vascular projections of the fetal chorion that combines with maternal uterine tissue to form the placenta.

chorionic villus sampling *n.* A prenatal test to detect birth defects that is performed at an early stage of pregnancy and involves retrieval and examination of tissue from the chorionic villi. Also called *chorionic villus biopsy.*

cho·ri·pet·al·ous (kôr′ə-pĕt′l-əs, kōr′-) *adj.* Having separate petals; polypetalous. [Greek *khōri, khōris,* apart; see **ghē-** in Appendix + PETALOUS.]

cho·ris·ter (kôr′ĭ-stər, kōr′-, kŏr′-) *n. Music.* **1.** A singer in a choir, especially a choirboy or choirgirl. **2.** A leader of a choir. [Middle English *queristre,* from Anglo-Norman **cueristre,* from Medieval Latin *chorista,* from *chorus,* chorus, from Latin, choral dance. See CHORUS.]

cho·ri·zo (chə-rē′zō, -sō) *n., pl.* **-zos.** A very spicy pork sausage seasoned especially with garlic. [Spanish.]

C-ho·ri·zon (sē′hə-rī′zən) *n.* The third-deepest soil zone in ABC soil, unaltered by weathering and made up of the parent rock from which the two uppermost layers derive as well as other mineral materials.

cho·rog·ra·phy (kə-rŏg′rə-fē) *n.* **1.** The technique of mapping a region or district. **2.** A description or map of a region. [Latin *chōrographia,* from Greek *khōrographia* : *khōros,* place; see **ghē-** in Appendix + *-graphia,* -graphy.] **—cho·rog′ra·pher** *n.* **—cho′ro·graph′ic** (kôr′ə-grăf′ĭk, kōr′-), **cho′ro·graph′i·cal** *adj.* **—cho′ro·graph′i·cal·ly** *adv.*

cho·roid (kôr′oid′, kōr′-) or **cho·ri·oid** (kôr′ē-oid′, kōr′-) *—n.* The dark-brown vascular coat of the eye between the sclera and the retina. Also called *choroid coat, choroid membrane.* *—adj.* **1.** Resembling the chorion; membranous. **2.** Of or relating to the choroid. [From Greek *khoroeidēs,* like an afterbirth, alteration of *khorioeidēs* : *khorion,* afterbirth; see CHORION + *-oeidēs,* -oid.]

chor·tle (chôr′tl) *n.* A snorting, joyful laugh or chuckle. **—chortle** *intr. & tr.v.* **-tled, -tling, -tles.** To utter a chortle or express with a chortle. [Blend of CHUCKLE and SNORT.] **—chor′tler** *n.*

WORD HISTORY: "'O frabjous day! Callooh! Callay!' He chortled in his joy." Perhaps Lewis Carroll would chortle a bit himself to find that people are still using the word *chortle,* which he coined in *Through the Looking-Glass,* published in 1872. In any case, Carroll had constructed his word well, combining the words *chuckle* and *snort* to create it. This type of word is called a blend or a portmanteau word. In *Through the Looking-Glass* Humpty Dumpty uses *portmanteau* to describe the word *slithy,* saying, "It's like a portmanteau—there are two meanings packed up into one word" (the meanings being "lithe" and "slimy").

cho·rus (kôr′əs, kōr′-) *n., pl.* **-rus·es. 1.** *Music.* **a.** A composition in four or more parts written for a large number of singers. **b.** A refrain in which an audience joins a soloist in a song. **c.** A repeat of the opening statement of a popular song played by the whole group. **d.** A solo section based on the main melody of a popular song and played by a member of the group. **e.** A body of singers who perform choral compositions. **f.** A body of vocalists and dancers who support the soloists and leading performers in operas, musical comedies, and revues. **2.a.** A group of persons who speak or sing in unison a given part or composition in drama or poetry recitation. **b.** An actor in Elizabethan drama who recites the prologue and epilogue to a play and sometimes comments on the action. **3.a.** A group of masked dancers who performed ceremonial songs at religious festivals in early Greek times. **b.** The group in a classical Greek drama whose songs and dances present an exposition of or, in later tradition, a disengaged commentary on the action. **c.** The portion of a classical Greek drama consisting of choric dance and song. **4.** A group or performer in a modern drama serving a purpose similar to the Greek chorus. **5.** The performers of a choral ode, especially a Pindaric ode. **6.a.** A speech, song, or other utterance made in concert by many people. **b.** A simultaneous utterance by a number of people: *a chorus of jeers from the bystanders.* **c.** The sounds so made. **—chorus** *tr. & intr.v.* **-rused, -rus·ing, -rus·es** or **-russed, -rus·sing, -rus·ses.** To sing or utter in or as if in chorus. **—*idiom.* in chorus.** All together; in unison. [Latin, choral dance, from Greek *khoros.* See **gher-¹** in Appendix.]

chorus girl *n.* A young woman who dances in a chorus.

–chory *suff.* Plant dispersal by a specified agency: *zoochory.*

Cho·rzów (hô′zho͞of). A city of southern Poland northwest of Katowice. It is a mining center. Population, 144,200.

chose¹ (chōz) *v.* Past tense of **choose.**

chose² (shōz) *n. Law.* An item of personal property; a chattel. [French, from Latin *causa,* thing, case, reason.]

cho·sen (chō′zən) *v.* Past participle of **choose. —chosen** *adj.* **1.** Selected from or preferred above others: *the chosen few.* **2.** Having been selected by God; elect. **—chosen** *n., pl.* **chosen. 1.** One of the elect. **2.** The elect considered as a group.

Cho·sen (chō′sĕn′). A name used for Korea since the second millennium B.C.

chott also **shott** (shŏt) *n.* **1.** The depression surrounding a salt marsh or lake, especially in North Africa. **2.** The bed of a dried salt marsh. [French, from Arabic *šaṭṭ.*]

Chou (jō). See **Zhou.**

chou·croute (sho͞o-kro͞ot′) *n.* An Alsatian dish of sauerkraut with wine, sausages, pork, and juniper berries. [French *choucroute (garnie),* (garnished) sauerkraut, alteration (influenced by *chou,* cabbage, from Latin *caulis*) of German dialectal *sûrkrūt* : Old High German *sūr,* sour + Old High German *krūt,* cabbage, kraut.]

Chou En-lai (jō′ ĕn-lī′). See **Zhou Enlai.**

chough (chŭf) *n.* A crowlike Old World bird of the genus *Pyrrhocorax,* especially *P. pyrrhocorax,* having black plumage and red legs. [Middle English.]

chow¹ (chou) *n.* Any of a breed of heavy-set dog originating in China, having a long, dense, reddish-brown or black coat and a blue-black tongue. Also called *chow chow.* [Possibly from Chinese (Cantonese) *gǒu,* dog.]

chow¹

ă pat	oi boy
ā pay	ou out
âr care	o͝o took
ä father	o͞o boot
ĕ pet	ŭ cut
ē be	ûr urge
ĭ pit	th thin
ī pie	*th* this
îr pier	hw which
ŏ pot	zh vision
ō toe	ə about, item
ô paw	♦ regionalism

Stress marks: ′ (primary); ′ (secondary), as in **dictionary** (dĭk′shə-nĕr′ē)

chow² (chou) *Slang. n.* Food; victuals. **—chow** *intr.v.* **chowed, chow·ing, chows.** To eat: *chowed down on the meat and potatoes.* [Possibly from Chinese (Cantonese) *zab,* food, miscellany, from Chinese (Mandarin) *zá,* mixed.]

Chow (jō). See **Zhou.**

chow chow *n.* See **chow¹.**

chow-chow (chou′chou′) *n.* **1.** A Chinese preserve of fruits, peels, and ginger. **2.** A relish consisting of chopped vegetables pickled in mustard. [Pidgin English, possibly reduplication of Chinese (Cantonese) *zab,* food, mixture. See CHOW².]

chow·der (chou′dər) *n.* **1.** A thick soup containing fish or shellfish, especially clams, and vegetables, such as potatoes and onions, in a milk or tomato base. **2.** A soup similar to this seafood dish: *corn chowder.* [French *chaudière,* stew pot, from Old French, from Late Latin *caldāria.* See CALDRON.]

chow·hound (chou′hound′) *n. Slang.* A person who enjoys eating.

chow line *n. Slang.* A line of people waiting for food, as in a cafeteria.

chow mein (chou′ mān′) *n.* A Chinese-American dish consisting of a combination of stewed vegetables and meat served over fried noodles. [Chinese (Mandarin) *chǎo miàn* : *chǎo,* to stir-fry + *miàn,* noodles.]

Agatha Christie

Chr *abbr. Bible.* Chronicles.

Chr. *abbr.* Christ; Christian.

chres·ard (krĕs′ərd) *n.* Water present in the soil and available for plant absorption. [Greek *khrēsis,* use (from *khrēsthai,* to use; see **gher-²** in Appendix) + Greek *ardein,* to water.]

Chrés·tien de Troyes also **Chré·tien de Troyes** (krā-tyăN′də trwä′). fl. 1170. French trouvère who wrote the earliest surviving Arthurian romances, including *Perseval,* the first work to incorporate the quest for the Holy Grail into an Arthurian tale.

chres·tom·a·thy (krĕ-stŏm′ə-thē) *n., pl.* **-thies. 1.** A selection of literary passages, usually by one author. **2.** An anthology used in studying a language. [Greek *khrēstomatheia* : *khrēstos,* useful (from *khrēsthai,* to use; see **gher-²** in Appendix) + *-matheia,* body of learning (from *manthanein, math-,* to learn; see **mendh-** in Appendix).] **—chres′to·math′ic** (krĕs′tə-măth′ĭk) *adj.*

Chré·tien de Troyes (krā-tyăN′ də trwä′). See **Chréstien de Troyes.**

chrism (krĭz′əm) *n. Ecclesiastical.* **1.** A consecrated mixture of oil and balsam, used for anointing in church sacraments such as baptism and confirmation. Also called *holy oil.* **2.** A sacramental anointing, especially upon confirmation into the Eastern Orthodox Church. [Middle English *crisme,* chrism, chrisom, from Old English *crisma,* from Latin *chrīsma,* from Greek *khrisma,* an anointing, from *khriein,* to anoint. See **ghrēi-** in Appendix.] **—chris′mal** (krĭz′məl) *adj.*

chris·om (krĭz′əm) *n.* **1.** A white cloth or robe worn by an infant at baptism. **2.** *Archaic.* An infant wearing a baptismal robe; a baby. [Middle English *crisom,* variant of *crisme,* chrisom, chrism. See CHRISM.]

chrisom child *n. Archaic.* An infant that dies before one month of age.

Christ (krīst) *n. Abbr.* **Chr. 1.** The Messiah, as foretold by the prophets of the Old Testament. **2.** Jesus. **3.** *Christian Science.* "The divine manifestation of God, which comes to the flesh to destroy incarnate error" (Mary Baker Eddy). [Middle English *Crist,* from Old English *Crīst,* from Latin *Chrīstus,* from Greek *Khristos,* from *khristos,* anointed, past participle of *khriein,* to anoint. See **ghrēi-** in Appendix.] **—Christ′like′** *adj.* **—Christ′like′ness** *n.* **—Christ′li·ness** *n.* **—Christ′ly** *adj.*

Christ·church (krīst′chûrch′). A city of eastern South Island, New Zealand, near the Pacific coast. It is an important manufacturing center. Population, 161,700.

chris·ten (krĭs′ən) *tr.v.* **-tened, -ten·ing, -tens. 1.a.** To baptize into a Christian church. **b.** To give a name to at baptism. **2.a.** To name: *christened the kitten "Snowball."* **b.** To name and dedicate ceremonially: *christen a ship.* **3.** To use for the first time: *christened the new car by going for a drive.* [Middle English *cristnen,* from Old English *cristnian,* from *cristen,* Christian. See CHRISTIAN.]

Chris·ten·dom (krĭs′ən-dəm) *n.* **1.** Christians considered as a group. **2.** The Christian world. [Middle English *Cristendom,* from Old English *cristendōm* : *cristen,* Christian; see CHRISTIAN + *-dom,* -dom.]

chris·ten·ing (krĭs′ə-nĭng) *n.* The Christian sacrament of baptizing and naming an infant.

Chris·tian (krĭs′chən) *adj.* **1.** Professing belief in Jesus as Christ or following the religion based on the life and teachings of Jesus. **2.** Relating to or derived from Jesus or Jesus's teachings. **3.** Manifesting the qualities or spirit of Jesus; Christlike. **4.** Relating to or characteristic of Christianity or its adherents. **5.** Showing a loving concern for others; humane. **—Christian** *n. Abbr.* **Chr. 1.** One who professes belief in Jesus as Christ or follows the religion based on the life and teachings of Jesus. **2.** One who lives according to the teachings of Jesus. [Middle English *Cristen,* from Old English *cristen,* from Latin *Christiānus,* from Greek *Khristianos,* from *Khristos,* Christ. See CHRIST.] **—Chris′tian·ly** *adj. & adv.*

Christian X. 1870–1947. King of Denmark (1912–1947) noted for his passive resistance to the Nazi occupation of Denmark in World War II.

Christian Brother *n. Roman Catholic Church.* A member of the order of Brothers of the Christian Schools that was founded in France in 1684 by Saint Jean Baptiste de la Salle (1651–1719) and is dedicated primarily to education.

Christian era *n.* The period beginning with the birth of Jesus.

chris·ti·an·i·a (krĭs′tē-ăn′ē-ə, -ä′nē-ə, krĭs′chē-) *n. Sports.* A christie. [Norwegian, after *Christiania* (Oslo), Norway.]

Chris·ti·a·ni·a (krĭs′tē-ăn′ē-ə, -ä′nē-ə, krĭs′chē-). See **Oslo.**

Chris·ti·an·i·ty (krĭs′chē-ăn′ĭ-tē, krĭs′tē-) *n., pl.* **-ties. 1.** The Christian religion, founded on the life and teachings of Jesus. **2.** Christians as a group; Christendom. **3.** The state or fact of being a Christian.

Chris·tian·ize (krĭs′chə-nīz′) *tr.v.* **-ized, -iz·ing, -iz·es.** To convert (another) to Christianity; make Christian. **—Chris′tian·i·za′tion** (-chə-nĭ-zā′shən) *n.* **—Chris′tian·iz′er** *n.*

Christian name *n.* **1.** A name given at baptism or confirmation. **2.** A name that precedes a person's family name, especially the first name.

Christian Science *n. Abbr.* **CS** The church and the religious system founded by Mary Baker Eddy, emphasizing healing through spiritual means as an important element of Christianity and teaching pure divine goodness as underlying the scientific reality of existence. Also called *Church of Christ, Scientist.* **—Christian Scientist** *n.*

chris·tie or **chris·ty** (krĭs′tē) *n., pl.* **-ties.** *Sports.* A usually high-speed ski turn used for changing the direction of descent or stopping, performed by shifting the weight forward and turning with the skis kept parallel. [Short for CHRISTIANIA.]

Chris·tie (krĭs′tē), Dame **Agatha Mary Clarissa.** 1890–1976. British writer of more than 70 detective novels, including *The Murder of Roger Ackroyd* (1926), *And Then There Were None* (1940), and *The Pale Horse* (1961).

Chris·ti·na (krĭ-stē′nə). 1626–1689. Queen of Sweden (1632–1654). A patron of learning and the arts, she unexpectedly abdicated her throne, embraced Roman Catholicism, and spent much of the rest of her life in Rome.

Christ·mas (krĭs′məs) *n.* **1.** A Christian feast commemorating the birth of Jesus. **2.** December 25, the day on which this feast is celebrated. **3.** Christmastide. [Middle English *Cristemas,* from Old English *Crīstes mæsse,* Christ's festival : *Crīst,* Christ; see CHRIST + *mæsse,* festival; see MASS.] **—Christ′mas·sy, Christ′mas·y** *adj.*

Christmas berry *n.* See **toyon.**

Christmas berry tree *n.* See **Brazilian pepper tree.**

Christmas cactus *n.* An epiphytic cactus *(Schlumbergera ×bridgesii)* of Brazilian ancestry, widely cultivated as a houseplant and having jointed flat segments with crenate margins and showy, often magenta or rose-purple flowers that bloom in winter.

Christmas card *n.* A greeting card sent at Christmas to express good will.

Christmas club *n.* A savings account, as in a bank, requiring periodic deposits to ensure money for shopping at Christmas.

Christmas disease *n.* A type of hemophilia that is caused by a deficiency of factor IX. [After Stephen *Christmas,* a 20th-century British boy who was first diagnosed with it.]

Christmas Eve *n.* **1.** The evening before Christmas. **2.** The day before Christmas.

Christmas fern *n.* A North American evergreen fern *(Polystichum acrostichoides)* having pinnate leaves and dense clusters of lance-shaped fronds. Also called *canker brake, dagger fern.*

Christmas Island. 1. An Australian-administered island in the eastern Indian Ocean south of Java. It was annexed by Great Britain in 1888 and came under Australian sovereignty in 1958. **2.** The largest of the Line Islands in the central Pacific Ocean near the equator. Discovered by James Cook in 1777, the island is now part of Kiribati.

Christmas rose *n.* A European perennial evergreen herb *(Helleborus niger)* cultivated for its white or pinkish flowers that bloom in winter.

Christ·mas·tide (krĭs′məs-tīd′) *n.* A Christian festival observed from December 24, Christmas Eve, to January 5, the eve of Epiphany.

Christ·mas·time (krĭs′məs-tīm′) *n.* The season of Christmas.

Christmas tree *n.* An evergreen or artificial tree decorated, as with lights and ornaments, during the Christmas season.

Chris·to·gram (krĭs′tə-grăm′) *n.* See **Chi-Rho.**

Chris·tol·o·gy (krĭ-stŏl′ə-jē) *n., pl.* **-gies. 1.** The theological study of the person and deeds of Jesus. **2.** A doctrine or theory based on Jesus or Jesus's teachings. **—Chris′to·log′i·cal** (krĭs′tə-lŏj′ĭ-kəl) *adj.*

Chris·tophe (krē-stôf′), **Henri.** 1767–1820. King of Haiti (1811–1820) who before proclaiming himself monarch had been instrumental in the liberation of Haiti from France (1804).

Chris·to·pher (krĭs′tə-fər), Saint. fl. third century A.D. Christian martyr often depicted as a giant who converted to Christianity and thereafter devoted himself to carrying travelers across a river. His feast, July 25, was dropped from the Catholic liturgical calendar in 1969.

Christ's thorn (krīsts) also **Christ-thorn** (krīst′thôrn′) *n.* **1.**

Either of two similar and related Old World spiny shrubs *(Ziziphus spina-christi* or *Paliurus spina-christi)* popularly believed to have been used for Jesus's crown of thorns. **2.** Any of several other plants, such as the crown-of-thorns.

chris·ty (krĭs′tē) *n. Sports.* Variant of **christie.**

Chris·ty (krĭs′tē), **Edwin Pearce.** 1815–1862. American showman whose troupe, Christy's Minstrels, developed the standard minstrel show format.

Christy, Howard Chandler. 1873–1952. American artist noted for his portraits of political figures, including Calvin Coolidge and Benito Mussolini.

chrom– *pref.* Variant of **chromo–.**

chro·ma (krō′mə) *n.* The aspect of color in the Munsell color system by which a sample appears to differ from a gray of the same lightness or brightness and that corresponds to saturation of the perceived color. [Greek *khrōma,* color.]

chro·maf·fin (krō′mə-fĭn) *adj.* Readily stained with chromium salts: *chromaffin cells of the adrenal medulla.* [German : *Chrom,* chromium (from French *chrome;* see CHROME) + Latin *affīnis,* related; see AFFINED.]

chromat– *pref.* Variant of **chromato–.**

chro·mate (krō′māt′) *n.* A salt or ester of chromic acid.

chro·mat·ic (krō-măt′ĭk) *adj.* **1.a.** Relating to colors or color. **b.** Relating to color perceived to have a saturation greater than zero. **2.** *Music.* **a.** Of, relating to, or based on the chromatic scale. **b.** Relating to chords or harmonies based on nonharmonic tones. [Greek *khrōmatikos,* from *khrōma, khrōmat-,* color.] **—chro·mat′i·cal·ly** *adv.* **—chro·mat′i·cism** (-sĭz′əm) *n.*

chromatic aberration *n.* Color distortion in an image produced by a lens, caused by the inability of the lens to bring the various colors of light to focus at a single point.

chro·ma·tic·i·ty (krō′mə-tĭs′ĭ-tē) *n.* The aspect of color that includes consideration of its dominant wavelength and purity.

chro·mat·ics (krō-măt′ĭks) *n. (used with a sing. verb).* The scientific study of color. **—chro′ma·tist** (-mə-tĭst) *n.*

chromatic scale *n. Music.* A scale consisting of 12 semitones.

chro·ma·tid (krō′mə-tĭd) *n.* Either of the two daughter strands of a duplicated chromosome that are joined by a single centromere and separate during cell division to become individual chromosomes.

chro·ma·tin (krō′mə-tĭn) *n.* A complex of nucleic acids and proteins in the cell nucleus that stains readily with basic dyes and condenses to form chromosomes during cell division. **—chro′ma·tin′ic** *adj.*

chromato– or **chromat–** *pref.* **1.** Color: *chromatophore.* **2.** Chromatin: *chromatolysis.* [Greek *khrōma, khrōmat-,* color.]

chro·mat·o·gram (krō-măt′ə-grăm′) *n.* The pattern of separated substances obtained by chromatography.

chro·mat·o·graph (krō-măt′ə-grăf′) *n.* An instrument that produces a chromatogram. **—chromatograph** *tr.v.* **-graphed, -graph·ing, -graphs.** To separate and analyze by chromatography. **—chro·mat′o·graph′ic** *adj.* **—chro·mat′o·graph′i·cal·ly** *adv.*

chro·ma·tog·ra·phy (krō′mə-tŏg′rə-fē) *n.* Any of various techniques for the separation of complex mixtures that rely on the differential affinities of substances for a gas or liquid mobile medium and for a stationary adsorbing medium through which they pass, such as paper, gelatin, or magnesia. **—chro′ma·tog′ra·pher** *n.*

chro·ma·tol·y·sis (krō′mə-tŏl′ĭ-sĭs) *n. Biology.* The dissolution or disintegration of chromophil material, such as chromatin, within a cell. **—chro·mat′o·lyt′ic** (-măt′l-ĭt′ĭk) *adj.*

chro·mat·o·phil·ic (krō-măt′ə-fĭl′ĭk) *adj.* Staining readily. Used of a cell or cell structure.

chro·mat·o·phore (krō-măt′ə-fôr′, -fōr′) *n. Biology.* **1.** A pigment-containing or pigment-producing cell, especially in certain lizards, that by expansion or contraction can change the color of the skin. Also called *pigment cell.* **2.** A specialized pigment-bearing organelle in certain photosynthetic bacteria and cyanobacteria. **—chro·mat′o·phor′ic** (-fôr′ĭk, -fōr′-) *adj.*

chrome (krōm) *n.* **1.a.** Chromium or a chromium alloy. **b.** Something plated with a chromium alloy. **2.** A pigment containing chromium. **—chrome** *tr.v.* **chromed, chrom·ing, chromes. 1.** To plate with chromium. **2.** To tan or dye with a chromium compound. [French, from Greek *khrōma,* color (from the brilliant colors of chromium compounds).]

–chrome *suff.* **1.** Colored: *polychrome.* **2.** Color; pigment: *urochrome.* [From Greek *khrōma,* color.]

chrome alum *n.* A violet-red crystalline compound, $CrK(SO_4)_2 \cdot 12H_2O$, used in tanning, as a mordant, and in photography.

chrome green *n.* **1.** Any of a class of green pigments consisting of chrome yellow and iron blue in various proportions. **2.** *Color.* A very dark yellowish green to moderate or strong green.

chrome red *n.* A light orange to red pigment consisting of basic lead chromate, $PbCrO_4$, with varying amounts of lead oxide, PbO.

chrome yellow *n.* Lead chromate, $PbCrO_4$, a yellow pigment often combined with lead sulfate, $PbSO_4$, for lighter hues.

chro·mic (krō′mĭk) *adj.* Of, relating to, or containing chromium, especially with valence 3.

chromic acid *n.* **1.** A corrosive, oxidizing acid, H_2CrO_4, occurring only as salts or in solution. **2.** The anhydride of chromic acid, CrO_3, a purplish crystalline material that reacts explosively with reducing agents and is used in chromium plating, as an oxidizing agent, and to color glass and rubber.

chromic oxide *n.* A bright-green crystalline powder, Cr_2O_3, used in metallurgy and as a paint pigment.

chro·mite (krō′mīt′) *n.* A widely distributed black to brownish-black chromium ore, $FeCr_2O_4$.

chro·mi·um (krō′mē-əm) *n. Symbol* **Cr** A lustrous, hard, steel-gray metallic element, resistant to tarnish and corrosion and found primarily in chromite. It is used as a catalyst, to harden steel alloys and produce stainless steels, in corrosion-resistant decorative platings, and as a pigment in glass. Atomic number 24; atomic weight 51.996; melting point 1,890°C; boiling point 2,482°C; specific gravity 7.18; valence 2, 3, 6. See table at **element.** [From French *chrome.* See CHROME.]

chromo– or **chrom–** *pref.* **1.** Color: *chromoplast.* **2.** Chromium: *chromous.* [From Greek *khrōma,* color.]

chro·mo·dy·nam·ics (krō′mō-dī-năm′ĭks) *n. (used with a sing. verb).* The physics of the relationship between color-carrying quarks, especially the nature of their strong interaction, which is characterized by the exchange of gluons.

chro·mo·gen (krō′mə-jən) *n.* **1.** *Chemistry.* A substance capable of conversion into a pigment or dye. **2.** *Biology.* A strongly pigmented or pigment-generating organelle, organ, or microorganism. **—chro′mo·gen′ic** (-jĕn′ĭk) *adj.*

chro·mo·lith·o·graph (krō′mə-lĭth′ə-grăf′) *n.* A colored print produced by chromolithography.

chro·mo·li·thog·ra·phy (krō′mə-lĭ-thŏg′rə-fē) *n.* The art or process of printing color pictures from a series of stone or zinc plates by lithography. **—chro′mo·li·thog′ra·pher** *n.* **—chro′mo·lith′o·graph′ic** (-lĭth′ə-grăf′ĭk) *adj.*

chro·mo·mere (krō′mə-mîr′) *n.* One of the serially aligned beadlike granules of concentrated chromatin that constitutes a chromosome during the early phases of cell division. **—chro′mo·mer′ic** (-mĕr′ĭk, -mîr′-) *adj.*

chro·mo·ne·ma (krō′mə-nē′mə) *n., pl.* **-ma·ta** (-mə-tə). The spirally coiled central filament of a chromatid along which the chromomeres are aligned. [CHROMO(SOME) + Greek *nēma,* thread; see **(s)nē-** in Appendix.] **—chro′mo·ne′mal** (-nē′məl), **chro·mo′ne·mat′al** (-nē-măt′l), **chro′mo·ne·mat′ic** (-nə-măt′ĭk), **chro′mo·ne′mic** (-nē′mĭk) *adj.*

chro·mo·phil (krō′mə-fĭl′) *adj.* Readily stained with dyes: *chromophil cells.*

chro·mo·phore (krō′mə-fôr′, -fōr′) *n.* A chemical group capable of selective light absorption resulting in the coloration of certain organic compounds. **—chro′mo·phor′ic** (-fôr′ĭk, -fōr′-) *adj.*

chro·mo·plast (krō′mə-plăst′) *n. Botany.* A plastid that contains pigments other than chlorophyll, usually yellow or orange carotenoids.

chro·mo·pro·tein (krō′mə-prō′tēn, -tē-ĭn) *n.* A conjugated protein, such as hemoglobin, that contains a colored, metal-containing prosthetic group, such as heme.

chro·mo·some (krō′mə-sōm′) *n.* **1.** A threadlike linear strand of DNA and associated proteins in the nucleus of animal and plant cells that carries the genes and functions in the transmission of hereditary information. **2.** A circular strand of DNA in bacteria and cyanobacteria that contains the hereditary information necessary for cell life. **—chro′mo·so′mal** (-sō′məl), **chro′mo·so′mic** (-sō′mĭk) *adj.* **—chro′mo·so′mal·ly** *adv.*

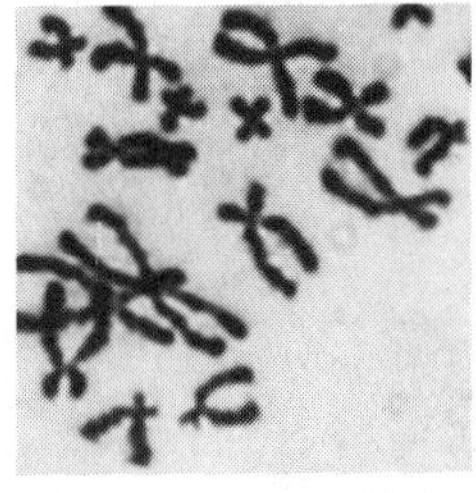

chromosome
Human chromosomes

chro·mo·sphere (krō′mə-sfîr′) *n.* **1.** An incandescent, transparent layer of gas, primarily hydrogen, several thousand miles in depth, lying above and surrounding the photosphere of a star, such as the sun, but distinctly separate from the corona. **2.** A gaseous layer similar to a chromosphere around a star. **—chro′mo·spher′ic** (-sfîr′ĭk, -sfĕr′-) *adj.*

chro·mous (krō′məs) *adj.* Of, relating to, or containing chromium, especially with valence 2.

chron. *abbr.* **1.** Chronicle. **2.** Chronological. **3.** Chronology.

Chron. *abbr. Bible.* Chronicles.

chron– *pref.* Variant of **chrono–.**

chro·nax·ie also **chro·nax·y** (krō′năk′sē, krŏn′ăk′-) *n., pl.* **-ies.** The minimum interval of time necessary to electrically stimulate a muscle or nerve fiber, using twice the minimum current needed to elicit a threshold response. [French : Greek *khronos,* time + Greek *axia,* value (from *axios,* worthy; see **ag-** in Appendix).]

chron·ic (krŏn′ĭk) *adj.* **1.** Of long duration; continuing: *chronic money problems.* **2.** Lasting for a long period of time or marked by frequent recurrence, as certain diseases: *chronic colitis.* **3.** Subject to a habit or pattern of behavior for a long time: *a chronic liar.* [French *chronique,* from Latin *chronicus,* from Greek *khronikos,* of time, from *khronos,* time.] **—chron′i·cal·ly** *adv.* **—chro·nic′i·ty** (krŏ-nĭs′ĭ-tē) *n.*

SYNONYMS: *chronic, confirmed, habitual, inveterate.* The central meaning shared by these adjectives is "having long had a habit or a disease": *a chronic complainer; a confirmed bachelor; a habitual cheat; an inveterate smoker.*

chron·i·cle (krŏn′ĭ-kəl) *n.* **1.** *Abbr.* **chron.** An extended account in prose or verse of historical events, sometimes including

ă pat	oi boy
ā pay	ou out
âr care	ŏŏ took
ä father	ōō boot
ĕ pet	ŭ cut
ē be	ûr urge
ĭ pit	th thin
ī pie	*th* this
îr pier	hw which
ŏ pot	zh vision
ō toe	ə about, item
ô paw	♦ regionalism

Stress marks: ′ (primary); ′ (secondary), as in **dictionary** (dĭk′shə-nĕr′ē)

legendary material, presented in chronological order and without authorial interpretation or comment. **2.** A detailed narrative record or report. **3. Chronicles** *(used with a sing. verb). Abbr.* **Chron., Chr** *Bible.* See table at **Bible.** **—chronicle** *tr.v.* **-cled, -cling, -cles.** To record in or in the form of a historical record. [Middle English *cronicle,* from Anglo-Norman, alteration of Old French *cronique,* from Latin *chronica,* from Greek *khronika (biblia),* chronological (books), annals, from *khronikos,* of time. See CHRONIC.] **—chron′i·cler** (-klər) *n.*

chronicle play *n.* A dramatization of historical material, especially any of the Elizabethan dramas based on the chronicle histories of England.

chrono– or **chron–** *pref.* Time: *chronometer.* [From Greek *khronos,* time.]

chron·o·bi·ol·o·gy (krŏn′ō-bī-ŏl′ə-jē) *n.* The study of the effects of time and rhythmical phenomena on life processes.

chron·o·gram (krŏn′ə-grăm′, krō′nə-) *n.* **1.** The record produced by a chronograph. **2.** An inscribed phrase in which certain letters can be read as Roman numerals indicating a specific date. **—chron′o·gram·mat′ic** (-grə-măt′ĭk) *adj.* **—chron′o·gram·mat′i·cal·ly** *adv.*

chron·o·graph (krŏn′ə-grăf′, krō′nə-) *n.* An instrument that registers or graphically records time intervals such as the duration of an event. **—chron′o·graph′ic** *adj.* **—chron′o·graph′i·cal·ly** *adv.*

chronol. *abbr.* **1.** Chronological. **2.** Chronology.

chron·o·log·i·cal (krŏn′ə-lŏj′ĭ-kəl, krō′nə-) also **chron·o·log·ic** (-lŏj′ĭk) *adj. Abbr.* **chron., chronol. 1.** Arranged in order of time of occurrence. **2.** Relating to or in accordance with chronology. **—chron′o·log′i·cal·ly** *adv.*

chronological age *n. Abbr.* **CA, C.A.** The number of years a person has lived, used especially in psychometrics as a standard against which certain variables, such as behavior and intelligence, are measured.

chro·nol·o·gy (krə-nŏl′ə-jē) *n., pl.* **-gies.** *Abbr.* **chron., chronol. 1.** The science that deals with the determination of dates and the sequence of events. **2.** The arrangement of events in time. **3.** A chronological list or table. **—chro·nol′o·gist** *n.*

chro·nom·e·ter (krə-nŏm′ĭ-tər) *n.* An exceptionally precise timepiece. **—chron′o·met′ric** (krŏn′ə-mĕt′rĭk, krō′nə-), **chron′o·met′ri·cal** *adj.* **—chron′o·met′ri·cal·ly** *adv.*

chro·nom·e·try (krə-nŏm′ĭ-trē) *n.* The scientific measurement of time.

chron·o·scope (krŏn′ə-skōp′, krō′nə-) *n.* An optical instrument for the precise measurement of very small time intervals. **—chron′o·scop′ic** (-skŏp′ĭk) *adj.*

chrys– *pref.* Variant of **chryso–.**

chrys·a·lid (krĭs′ə-lĭd) *n.* A chrysalis. **—chrysalid** *adj.* Relating to or resembling a chrysalis.

chrys·a·lis (krĭs′ə-lĭs) *n., pl.* **chrys·a·lis·es** or **chry·sal·i·des** (krĭ-săl′ĭ-dēz′). A pupa, especially of a moth or butterfly, enclosed in a firm case or cocoon. [Latin *chrȳsallis,* from Greek *khrusallis, khrusallid-,* gold-colored pupa of a butterfly, from *khrus-,* chryso-.]

WORD HISTORY: "All that is gold does not glitter" we may say when confronted with *khrus–* or *khruso–,* the combining form of the Greek word *khrusos,* "gold." We find this form, for example, in the Greek word *khrusallis,* "chrysalis," which refers specifically to a gold-colored pupa. This Greek word gave us our *chrysalis,* first recorded in English in the 17th century. As Modern English *chrys–* or *chryso–* the Greek form *khrus–* or *khruso–* has also been used to make words that did not exist in Greek. Among the more interesting of these are *chrysocracy,* "rule of the wealthy," and *chrysotherapy,* "the treatment of disease with gold compounds."

chrysanthemum
Top: Anemone-centered
Center: Incurved
Bottom: Reflexed

chry·san·the·mum (krĭ-săn′thə-məm, -zăn′-) *n.* **1.** Any of numerous, mostly Eurasian plants of the genus *Chrysanthemum* in the composite family, many of which are cultivated as ornamentals for their showy, radiate flower heads. **2.** A flower head of one of these plants. [Latin *chrȳsanthemum,* from Greek *khrusanthemon,* gold flower : *khrus-,* chryso- + *anthemon,* flower (from *anthos*).]

chrys·el·e·phan·tine (krĭ-sĕl′ə-făn′tēn′, -tīn′) *adj.* Made of gold and ivory, as certain pieces of sculpture or artwork in ancient Greece. [Greek *khruselephantinos* : *khrus-,* chryso- + *elephas, elephant-,* ivory; see ELEPHANT.]

chryso– or **chrys–** *pref.* Gold; golden: *chrysotherapy.* [Greek *khrus-, khruso-,* from *khrusos,* gold, of Semitic origin; akin to Hebrew *ḥārūṣ.*]

chrys·o·ber·yl (krĭs′ə-bĕr′əl) *n.* A gray, green to yellow, or brown vitreous mineral, $BeAl_2O_4$, relatively rare and used as a gemstone. [Latin *chrȳsobēryllus,* from Greek *khrusobērullos* : *khruso-,* chryso- + *bērullos,* beryl; see BERYL.]

chrys·o·lite (krĭs′ə-līt′) *n.* See **olivine.** [Middle English *crisolite,* from Old French, from Medieval Latin *crīsolitus,* from Latin *chrȳsolithus,* from Greek *khrusolithos,* topaz : *khruso-,* chryso- + *lithos,* stone.]

chrys·o·mel·id (krĭs′ə-mĕl′ĭd, -mē′lĭd) *n.* Any of various beetles of the family Chrysomelidae, which includes the Colorado potato beetle. **—chrysomelid** *adj.* Of or belonging to the family Chrysomelidae. [From New Latin *Chrysomela,* type genus, from Greek *khrusomēlon,* quince : *khruso-,* chryso- + *mēlon,* apple.]

chrys·o·prase (krĭs′ə-prāz′) *n.* An apple-green chalcedony used as a gemstone. [Middle English *crisopase,* from Old French *crisopras,* from Latin *chrȳsoprasus,* from Greek *khrusoprasos* : *khruso-,* chryso- + *prason,* leek; see PRASEODYMIUM.]

Chry·sos·tom (krĭs′əs-təm, krĭ-sŏs′-), Saint **John.** A.D. 347?–407. Antioch-born Greek prelate. Made patriarch of Constantinople (398), he elegantly criticized the wealthy and powerful, earning himself the name *Chrysostom,* "golden-mouthed."

chrys·o·ther·a·py (krĭs′ō-thĕr′ə-pē) *n.* The treatment of certain diseases, especially rheumatoid arthritis, with gold compounds.

chrys·o·tile (krĭs′ə-tĭl′) *n.* A fibrous mineral variety of serpentine forming part of commercial asbestos. [German *Chrysotil* : Greek *khruso-,* chryso- + Greek *tilos,* something plucked (from *tillein,* to pluck).]

chthon·ic (thŏn′ĭk) also **chtho·ni·an** (thō′nē-ən) *adj. Greek Mythology.* Of or relating to the gods and spirits of the underworld. [From Greek *khthonios,* of the earth, from *khthōn,* earth. See **dhghem-** in Appendix.]

Chu (cho͞o). A river of southern Kazakhstan flowing about 1,126 km (700 mi) eastward into Issyk-Kul.

chub (chŭb) *n., pl.* **chub** or **chubs. 1.** Any of various freshwater fishes of the family Cyprinidae related to the carps and minnows, especially a Eurasian species, *Leuciscus cephalus.* **2.** Any of various North American fishes, such as a freshwater whitefish of the genus *Coregonus* or a marine fish of the genus *Kyphosus.* [Middle English *chubbe.*]

chub·by (chŭb′ē) *adj.* **-bi·er, -bi·est.** Rounded and plump. See Synonyms at **fat.** [Probably from CHUB (from the plumpness of the fish).] **—chub′bi·ly** *adv.* **—chub′bi·ness** *n.*

Chu·but (chə-bo͝ot′, cho͞o-). A river rising in the Andes of southwest Argentina and flowing about 805 km (500 mi) eastward to the Atlantic Ocean.

chuck¹ (chŭk) *tr.v.* **chucked, chuck·ing, chucks. 1.** To pat or squeeze fondly or playfully, especially under the chin. **2.a.** To throw or toss: *chucked stones into the water.* **b.** *Informal.* To throw out; discard: *chucked my old sweater.* **c.** *Informal.* To force out; eject: *chucking out the troublemakers.* **3.** *Informal.* To give up; quit: *chucked her job.* **—chuck** *n.* **1.** An affectionate pat or squeeze under the chin. **2.** A throw, toss, or pitch. [Variant of *chock,* possibly from French *choc,* knock, blow. See SHOCK¹.]

chuck² (chŭk) *n.* **1.** A cut of beef extending from the neck to the ribs and including the shoulder blade. **2.a.** A clamp that holds a tool or the material being worked in a machine such as a lathe. **b.** A clamping device for holding a drill bit. [Dialectal *chuck,* lump, perhaps variant of CHOCK.]

chuck³ (chŭk) *intr.v.* **chucked, chuck·ing, chucks.** To make a clucking sound. **—chuck** *n.* A clucking sound. [Middle English *chukken,* of imitative origin.]

chuck-a-luck (chŭk′ə-lŭk′) *n. Games.* A gambling game in which players bet on the possible combinations of three thrown dice. [Probably CHUCK¹ + LUCK.]

chuck·hole (chŭk′hōl′) *n.* See **pothole** (sense 1). [Probably from CHUCK¹.]

chuck·le (chŭk′əl) *intr.v.* **-led, -ling, -les. 1.** To laugh quietly or to oneself. **2.** To cluck or chuck, as a hen. **—chuckle** *n.* A quiet laugh of mild amusement or satisfaction. [Probably frequentative of CHUCK³.] **—chuck′ler** *n.* **—chuck′le·some** *adj.* **—chuck′ling·ly** (-lĭng-lē) *adv.*

chuck·le·head (chŭk′əl-hĕd′) *n. Informal.* A stupid, gauche person; a blockhead. [Possibly from CHUCK².] **—chuck′le·head′ed** *adj.*

chuck wagon *n.* A wagon equipped with food and cooking utensils, as on a ranch or in a lumber camp.

chuck·wal·la (chŭk′wŏl′ə) *n.* A large herbaceous lizard *(Sauromalus obesus)* of the southwest United States and Mexico, related to the iguana. [American Spanish *chacahuala,* from Cahuilla *tcáxxwal.*]

chuck-will's-wid·ow (chŭk′wĭlz-wĭd′ō) *n.* A bird *(Caprimulgus carolinensis)* of the southern and central United States, resembling but larger than the whippoorwill. [Imitative of its call.]

chud·dar (chŭd′ər) *n.* **1.** A chador. **2.** A cotton shawl traditionally worn in India by men and women. [Urdu *chaddar,* cloth, from Sanskrit *chattram,* screen, parasol, from *chadati,* he covers, protects.]

chu·fa (cho͞o′fə) *n.* An Old World sedge *(Cyperus esculentus* var. *sativus)* having edible, nutlike tubers. [From Spanish *chufar,* to make fun of, alteration of *chuflar,* to whistle, ridicule, from Vulgar Latin **sufilāre,* alteration of Latin *sībilāre, sīfilāre,* to hiss, whistle at. See SIBILANT.]

chuff¹ (chŭf) *n.* A rude, insensitive person; a boor. [Middle English *chuffe.*]

chuff² (chŭf) *intr.v.* **chuffed, chuf·fing, chuffs.** To produce or move with noisy puffing or explosive sounds: *"Switch engines chuffed impatiently in busy rail yards"* (Robert Paul Jordan). **—chuff** *n.* A noisy puffing or explosive sound, such as one made by a locomotive. [Imitative.]

chug (chŭg) *n.* A dull explosive sound, usually short and repeated, made by or as if by a laboring engine. **—chug** *intr.v.* **chugged, chug·ging, chugs. 1.** To make dull, explosive sounds.

ă pat	oi boy
ā pay	ou out
âr care	o͝o took
ä father	o͞o boot
ĕ pet	ŭ cut
ē be	ûr urge
ĭ pit	th thin
ī pie	*th* this
îr pier	hw which
ŏ pot	zh vision
ō toe	ə about, item
ô paw	♦ regionalism

Stress marks: ′ (primary); ′ (secondary), as in **dictionary** (dĭk′shə-nĕr′ē)

2. To move or travel while making dull, explosive sounds. [Imitative.] **—chug′ger** *n.*

chug·a·lug (chŭg′ə-lŭg′) *Slang. v.* **-lugged, -lug·ging, -lugs.** *—tr.* To swallow the contents of (a container of beer, for example) without pausing. *—intr.* To swallow liquid, such as beer, without pausing. **—chugalug** *adv.* In continuous gulps: *drank the beer chugalug.* [Imitative.]

chu·kar (chə-kär′) *n.* A Eurasian partridge *(Alectoris graeca)* with grayish-brown plumage and red legs and bill, introduced into western North America as a game bird. [Hindi *cakor,* from Sanskrit *cakoraḥ.*]

Chuk·chi also **Chuk·chee** (cho͝ok′chē) *n., pl.* **Chukchi** or **-chis** also **Chukchee** or **-chees. 1.** A member of a people of northeast Siberia. **2.** The language of the Chukchi, noted for being pronounced differently by men and women. [Russian, pl. of *chukcha,* from Chukchi *chawchəw.*]

Chukchi Peninsula. A peninsula of extreme northeast Russia across the Bering Strait from northwest Alaska. It borders on the **Chukchi Sea,** a section of the Arctic Ocean.

Chu Kiang (cho͞o′ kyäng′, jo͞o′ gyäng′). See **Zhu Jiang.**

chuk·ka (chŭk′ə) *n.* A short, ankle-length boot, usually made of suede, having two or three pairs of eyelets. [Alteration of CHUKKER (so called because polo players wear a similar boot).]

chuk·ker also **chuk·kar** (chŭk′ər) *n. Sports.* One of the periods of play, lasting 7½ minutes, in a polo match. [Hindi *cakkar,* circle, turn, from Sanskrit *cakram.* See **kʷel-¹** in Appendix.]

Chu·la Vis·ta (cho͞o′lə vĭs′tə). A city of southern California south of San Diego. It is an industrial center. Population, 83,927.

Chu·lym also **Chu·lim** (chə-lĭm′, cho͞o-). A river of south-central Russia flowing about 1,730 km (1,075 mi) north and west to the Ob River.

chum¹ (chŭm) *n.* An intimate friend or companion. **—chum** *intr.v.* **chummed, chum·ming, chums. 1.a.** To be an intimate friend. **b.** To display good-natured friendliness: *chummed around with the other teammates.* **2.** To share the same room, as in a dormitory. [Perhaps short for *chamber fellow,* roommate.]

chum² (chŭm) *n.* Bait usually consisting of oily fish ground up and scattered on the water. **—chum** *v.* **chummed, chum·ming, chums.** *—intr.* To fish with such bait. *—tr.* To lure (fish) with such bait. [Origin unknown.]

chum³ (chŭm) *n.* A chum salmon.

Chu·mash (cho͞o′măsh) *n., pl.* **Chumash** or **-mash·es. 1.** A group of Hokan-speaking Native American peoples formerly inhabiting the southern California coastal region around and the channel islands off Santa Barbara, with a small present-day population near Santa Barbara. **2.** A member of any of these peoples.

chum·my (chŭm′ē) *adj.* **-mi·er, -mi·est.** Intimate; friendly. See Synonyms at **familiar. —chum′mi·ly** *adv.* **—chum′mi·ness** *n.*

chump¹ (chŭmp) *n.* A stupid or foolish person; a dolt. [Perhaps blend of CHUNK and LUMP¹ or STUMP.]

chump² (chŭmp) *tr. & intr.v.* **chumped, chump·ing, chumps.** To chew or make a chewing movement. [Variant of CHAMP¹.]

chum salmon *n.* A Pacific salmon *(Oncorhynchus keta)* with minute specks on its back that is fished for food and sport. [Chinook Jargon *cam,* spotted, striped, from Lower Chinook *c'ə́ám(·),* variegated.]

Chung·king (cho͝ong′kĭng′, jo͝ong′gĭng′). See **Chongqing.**

chunk (chŭngk) *n.* **1.** A thick mass or piece: *a chunk of ice.* **2.** *Informal.* A substantial amount: *won quite a chunk of money.* **3.** A strong, stocky horse. **—chunk** *v.* **chunked, chunk·ing, chunks.** *—tr.* To form into chunks. *—intr.* To make a dull clacking sound: *listened to the electronic printer chunk along.* [Perhaps variant of CHUCK².]

chunk·y (chŭng′kē) *adj.* **-i·er, -i·est. 1.** Short and thick; stocky. **2.** Containing small, thick pieces: *chunky peanut butter; chunky soup.* **—chunk′i·ly** *adv.* **—chunk′i·ness** *n.*

chun·nel (chŭn′əl) *n.* An underwater tunnel for the passage of motor vehicles, especially one under the English Channel. [CH(ANNEL)¹ + (T)UNNEL.]

church (chûrch) *n. Abbr.* **c., C., ch., Ch. 1.** A building for public, especially Christian worship. **2.** Often **Church. a.** The company of all Christians regarded as a mystic spiritual body. **b.** A specified Christian denomination: *the Presbyterian Church.* **c.** A congregation. **3.** Public divine worship in a church; a religious service: *goes to church at Christmas and Easter.* **4.** The clerical profession; clergy. **5.** Ecclesiastical power as distinguished from the secular: *the separation of church and state.* **6.** *Christian Science.* "The structure of Truth and Love" (Mary Baker Eddy). **—church** *tr.v.* **churched, church·ing, church·es.** To conduct a church service for, especially to perform a religious service for (a woman after childbirth). **—church** *adj.* Of or relating to the church; ecclesiastical. [Middle English *chirche,* from Old English *cirice,* ultimately from Medieval Greek *kurikon,* from Late Greek *kuriakon (dōma),* the Lord's (house), from Greek *kuriakos,* of the lord, from *kurios,* lord. See **keuə-** in Appendix.]

Church (chûrch), **Frederick Edwin.** 1826–1900. American painter and leader of the Hudson River School. His works include *Heart of the Andes* (1859).

church father or **Church Father** *n.* Any of the early writers in the Christian church who formulated doctrines and codified religious observances.

church·go·er (chûrch′gō′ər) *n.* One who attends church. **—church′go′ing** *adj. & n.*

Chur·chill (chûr′chĭl′, chûrch′hĭl′), **John.** First Duke of Marlborough. 1650–1722. English general and statesman during the reigns of James II, Anne, and George I. He is considered among history's greatest military commanders.

Churchill, Mount. A peak, 4,769.6 m (15,638 ft) high, in the Wrangell Mountains of southern Alaska.

Churchill, Randolph Henry Spencer. 1849–1895. British politician who led the so-called Fourth Party, a group of Conservative members of Parliament who advocated social and constitutional reform.

Churchill, Winston. 1871–1947. American writer known for his historical romance novels, such as *Richard Carvel* (1899).

Churchill, Sir **Winston Leonard Spenser.** 1874–1965. British politician and writer. As prime minister (1940–1945 and 1951–1955) he led Great Britain through World War II. Churchill published several works, including *The Second World War* (1948–1953), and won the 1953 Nobel Prize for literature. **—Chur·chill′i·an** (chûr-chĭl′ē-ən) *adj.*

Churchill Falls. Formerly **Grand Falls** (grănd). A waterfall, 74.7 m (245 ft) high, of the upper Churchill River in southwest Labrador, Canada.

Churchill River. 1. A river of eastern Canada flowing about 965 km (600 mi) across Labrador to the Atlantic Ocean. **2.** A river rising in northwest Saskatchewan, Canada, and flowing about 1,609 km (1,000 mi) eastward across Saskatchewan and northern Manitoba then northeast to Hudson Bay.

church key *n.* A can or bottle opener having a usually triangular head.

church·ly (chûrch′lē) *adj.* **1.** Of or relating to a church. **2.** Appropriate for or suggestive of a church: *"aspires to the pure fragrance of churchly incense"* (Martin Bernheimer). **—church′li·ness** *n.*

church·man (chûrch′mən) *n.* **1.** A man who is a cleric. **2.** A man who is a member of a church. **—church′man·ly** *adj.* **—church′man·ship′** *n.*

Church of Christ, Scientist *n.* See **Christian Science.**

Church of England *n. Abbr.* **C. of E.** The episcopal and liturgical national church of England, which has its see in Canterbury.

Church of Jesus Christ of Lat·ter-day Saints (lat′ər-dā′) *n.* See **Mormon Church.**

Church of Rome *n.* The Roman Catholic Church.

Church Slavonic *n.* See **Old Church Slavonic.**

church·war·den (chûrch′wôr′dn) *n.* **1.** A lay officer in the Anglican Church chosen annually by the vicar or the congregation to handle the secular and legal affairs of the parish. **2.** One of two elected chief lay officers of the vestry in the Episcopal Church.

church·wom·an (chûrch′wo͝om′ən) *n.* **1.** A woman who is a cleric. **2.** A woman who is a member of a church.

church·y (chûr′chē) *adj.* **-i·er, -i·est. 1.** Conforming or adhering rigorously to the practices or creeds of a church. **2.** Of, suitable for, or suggesting a church: *"two . . . ladies in churchy hats sipping pale pink drinks"* (Anne Tyler).

church·yard (chûrch′yärd′) *n.* **1.** A yard adjacent to a church, especially a cemetery. **2.** The ground on which a church stands.

churl (chûrl) *n.* **1.** A rude, boorish person. See Synonyms at **boor. 2.** A miserly person. **3.a.** A ceorl. **b.** A medieval English peasant. [Middle English, from Old English *ceorl,* peasant.]

churl·ish (chûr′lĭsh) *adj.* **1.** Of, like, or befitting a churl; boorish or vulgar. **2.** Having a bad disposition; surly: *"as valiant as the lion, churlish as the bear"* (Shakespeare). **3.** Difficult to work with, such as soil; intractable. **—churl′ish·ly** *adv.* **—churl′ish·ness** *n.*

churn (chûrn) *n.* A vessel or device in which cream or milk is agitated to separate the oily globules from the caseous and serous parts, used to make butter. **—churn** *v.* **churned, churn·ing, churns.** *—tr.* **1.a.** To agitate or stir (milk or cream) in order to make butter. **b.** To make by the agitation of milk or cream: *churn butter.* **2.** To shake or agitate vigorously: *wind churning up the piles of leaves.* See Synonyms at **agitate. 3.** To buy and sell (a client's securities) frequently, especially in order to generate commissions. *—intr.* **1.** To make butter by operating a device that agitates cream or milk. **2.** To move with or produce great agitation: *waves churning in the storm; so angry it made my stomach churn.* ***—phrasal verb.*** **churn out.** To produce in an abundant and automatic manner: *churns out four novels a year.* [Middle English *chirne,* from Old English *cyrn, cyrin.*] **—churn′er** *n.*

churr (chûr) *n.* The sharp whirring or trilling sound made by some insects and birds, such as the grasshopper and partridge. **—churr** *intr.v.* **churred, churr·ing, churrs.** To make a sharp whirring sound. [Imitative.]

Chur·ri·gue·resque (cho͝or′ĭ-gə-rĕsk′) *adj.* Of or relating to a style of baroque architecture of Spain and its Latin-American colonies, characterized by elaborate and extravagant decoration. [Spanish *churrigueresco,* after José Benito *Churriguera* (1665–1725), Spanish architect.]

chur·ro (cho͝or′ō) *n., pl.* **-ros.** A thick, coiled fritter of fried dough. [Spanish, perhaps from dialectal *xurro,* dirty, Valencian.]

church

Winston S. Churchill

churn
Detail of a wood engraving by Alexander Anderson (1775–1870)

Churrigueresque

chute

ciborium
c. 1670 English silver-gilt traveling ciborium

chute (sho͞ot) *n.* **1.** An inclined trough, passage, or channel through or down which things may pass. **2.** A waterfall or rapid. **3.** A parachute, such as one for pilots or skydivers. —**chute** *v.* **chut•ed, chut•ing, chutes.** —*tr.* To convey or deposit by a chute. —*intr.* To go or descend by a chute. [French, a fall, alteration (influenced by *chu*, from Vulgar Latin **cadūtum,* from **cadēre,* to fall) of Old French *cheoite,* feminine past participle of *cheoir,* to fall, from Vulgar Latin **cadēre,* from Latin *cadere;* see **kad-** in Appendix. Sense 3, short for PARACHUTE.]

Chu Teh (jo͞o′ də′). See **Zhu De.**

chute-the-chute (sho͞ot′*th*ə-sho͞ot′) *n.* Variant of **shoot-the-chute.**

chutist (sho͞o′tĭst) *n.* One who parachutes from an aircraft; a parachutist. [Short for PARACHUTIST.]

chut•ney (chŭt′nē) *n.* A pungent relish made of fruits, spices, and herbs. [Hindi *caṭnī.*]

chutz•pah also **hutz•pah** (KHo͞ot′spə, ho͞ot′-) *n.* Utter nerve; effrontery: *"has the chutzpah to claim a lock on God and morality"* (New York Times). [Yiddish *khutspe,* from Late Hebrew *ḥuṣpâ.*]

Chu•vash[1] (cho͞o-väsh′) *n., pl.* **Chuvash** or **-vash•es. 1.** A member of a people located in the middle Volga River valley, chiefly in the Chuvash region. **2.** The Turkic language spoken by the Chuvash. [Russian, from Chuvash *čăvaš.*]

Chu•vash[2] (cho͞o′väsh′, chyo͞o-väsh′). A region of western Russia in the Volga River valley. Conquered by the Mongols in the 13th and 14th centuries, it came under Russian rule in 1552.

chyle (kīl) *n.* A milky fluid consisting of lymph and emulsified fat extracted from chyme by the lacteals during digestion and passed to the bloodstream through the thoracic duct. [French, from Late Latin *chȳlus,* from Greek *khulos,* juice. See **gheu-** in Appendix.] —**chy•la′ceous** (kī-lā′shəs), **chy′lous** (kī′ləs) *adj.*

chy•lo•mi•cron (kī′lō-mī′krŏn′) *n.* One of the microscopic particles of emulsified fat found in the blood and lymph and formed during the digestion of fats. [CHYL(E) + Greek *mikron,* small thing, from neuter of *mikros,* small.]

chyme (kīm) *n.* The thick semifluid mass of partly digested food that is passed from the stomach to the duodenum. [Middle English *chime,* humors, body fluids, from Old French, from Late Latin *chȳmus,* from Greek *khumos,* juice. See **gheu-** in Appendix.] —**chy′mous** (kī′məs) *adj.*

chy•mo•pa•pa•in (kī′mō-pə-pā′ĭn, -pī′ĭn) *n.* A proteolytic enzyme obtained from the fruit of the tropical tree *Carica papaya* that resembles papain and is used in the treatment of herniated intervertebral disks. [CHYM(E) + PAPAIN.]

chy•mo•sin (kī′mə-sĭn) *n.* See **rennin.** [CHYM(E) + -OS(E)[2] + -IN.]

chy•mo•tryp•sin (kī′mə-trĭp′sĭn) *n.* A pancreatic digestive enzyme that catalyzes the hydrolysis of certain proteins in the small intestine into polypeptides and amino acids. [CHYM(E) + TRYPSIN.] —**chy′mo•tryp′tic** (-tĭk) *adj.*

Ci *abbr.* **1.** Cirrus. **2.** Curie.

CI *abbr.* **1.** Certificate of insurance. **2.** Cost and insurance.

CIA *abbr.* Central Intelligence Agency.

CIAA *abbr.* Central Intercollegiate Athletic Association.

Cia•no (chä′nō), Conte **Galeazzo.** 1903–1944. Italian fascist politician. Married (1930) to the daughter of Benito Mussolini, he urged Italy to join the Axis powers in World War II but later favored a separate peace with the Allies. He was tried for treason and executed on Mussolini's orders.

ciao (chou) *interj.* Used to express greeting or farewell. [Italian, from dialectal *ciau,* alteration of Italian *(sono vostro) schiavo,* (I am your) slave, from Medieval Latin *sclavus.* See SLAVE.]

Ciar•di (chär′dē), **John Anthony.** 1916–1986. American poet and critic noted for his clear, ironic poetry, works of literary criticism, such as *How Does a Poem Mean?* (1960), and a translation of Dante's *Divine Comedy* (1954–1970).

Cí•bo•la (sē′bə-lə). A vaguely defined historical region generally thought to be in present-day northern New Mexico. It included seven pueblos, the fabled Seven Cities of Cibola, which were sought by the earliest Spanish explorers for their supposed riches.

ci•bo•ri•um (sĭ-bôr′ē-əm, -bōr′-) *n., pl.* **-bo•ri•a** (-bôr′ē-ə, -bōr′-). **1.** A vaulted canopy permanently placed over an altar. **2.** A covered receptacle for holding the consecrated wafers of the Eucharist. [Medieval Latin *cibōrium,* from Latin, a drinking cup, from Greek *kibōrion,* probably of Egyptian origin.]

ci•ca•da (sĭ-kā′də, -kä′-) *n., pl.* **-das** or **-dae** (-dē′). Any of various insects of the family Cicadidae, having a broad head, membranous wings, and in the male a pair of resonating organs that produce a characteristic high-pitched, droning sound. Also called *cicala.* [Middle English, from Latin *cicāda.*]

cicada killer *n.* A large wasp *(Sphecius speciosus)* that preys on cicadas.

ci•ca•la (sĭ-kä′lə) *n.* See **cicada.** [Italian, from Latin *cicāda.* See CICADA.]

cic•a•trix (sĭk′ə-trĭks′, sĭ-kā′trĭks) *n., pl.* **cic•a•tri•ces** (sĭk′ə-trī′sēz, sĭ-kā′trĭ-sēz′). A scar left by the formation of new connective tissue over a healing sore or wound. [Middle English *cicatrice,* from Latin *cicātrīx, cicātrīc-.*] —**cic′a•tri′cial** (sĭk′ə-trĭsh′əl), **ci•cat′ri•cose′** (sĭ-kăt′rĭ-kōs′) *adj.*

cic•a•trize (sĭk′ə-trīz′) *tr. & intr.v.* **-trized, -triz•ing, -triz•es.** To heal or become healed by the formation of scar tissue. [Middle English *cicatrizen,* from Old French *cicatriser,* from Medieval Latin *cicātrīzāre,* from Late Latin *cicātrīcārī,* to scar over, from Latin *cicātrīx, cicātrīc-,* cicatrix.] —**cic′a•tri•za′tion** (-trĭ-zā′shən) *n.*

Cic•e•ro (sĭs′ə-rō′). A town of northeast Illinois, an industrial and residential suburb of Chicago. Population, 61,232.

Cicero, Marcus Tullius. 106–43 B.C. Roman statesman, orator, and philosopher. A major figure in the last years of the Republic, he is best known for his orations against Catiline and for his mastery of Latin prose. —**Cic′e•ro′ni•an** *adj.*

cic•e•ro•ne (sĭs′ə-rō′nē, chĭch′ə-, chē′chĕ-rô′nĕ) *n., pl.* **-nes** or **-ni** (nē). A guide for sightseers. [Italian, from Latin *Cicerō, Cicerōn-,* Marcus Tullius Cicero.]

cich•lid (sĭk′lĭd) *n.* Any of various tropical and subtropical freshwater fishes of the family Cichlidae, many of which are popular as aquarium fish. [From New Latin *Cichla,* type genus, from Greek *kikhlē,* a kind of fish. See **ghel-**[1] in Appendix.] —**cich′lid** *adj.*

Cid (sĭd), **the.** Originally Rodrigo Díaz de Vivar. 1043?–1099. Spanish soldier and national hero whose military exploits, including the capture of Valencia (1094), are recounted in several literary works.

CID also **C.I.D.** *abbr.* Criminal Investigation Department.

-cide *suff.* **1.** Killer: *bactericide.* **2.** Act of killing: *ecocide.* [Middle English, from Old French (from Latin *-cīda,* killer) and from Latin *-cīdium,* killing, both from *caedere,* to strike; kill. See **kaə-id-** in Appendix.]

ci•der (sī′dər) *n.* The juice pressed from fruits, especially apples, used as a beverage or to make other products, such as vinegar. [Middle English *sidre,* from Old French, from Late Latin *sīcera,* intoxicating drink, from Greek *sikera,* from Hebrew *šēkār.*]

cider vinegar *n.* Vinegar made from fermented cider.

ci-de•vant (sē′də-väN′) *adj.* Heretofore; former. [French : *ci,* here + *devant,* before.]

Cien•fue•gos (syĕn-fwā′gōs). A city of south-central Cuba on **Cienfuegos Bay,** a narrow-necked inlet of the Caribbean Sea. The city is a port and a trade and processing center. Population, 102,297.

c.i.f. or **C.I.F.** *abbr.* Cost, insurance, and freight.

ci•gar (sĭ-gär′) *n.* A compact roll of tobacco leaves prepared for smoking. [Spanish *cigarro,* possibly from Maya *sik'ar,* from *sik,* tobacco.]

ci•gar-box cedar (sĭ-gär′bŏks) *n.* See **Spanish cedar.**

cig•a•rette also **cig•a•ret** (sĭg′ə-rĕt′, sĭg′ə-rĕt′) *n.* **1.** A small roll of finely cut tobacco for smoking, enclosed in a wrapper of thin paper. **2.** A similar roll of another substance, such as a tobacco substitute or marijuana. [French, diminutive of *cigare,* cigar, from Spanish *cigarro.* See CIGAR.]

Cig•a•rette (sĭg′ə-rĕt′, sĭg′ə-rĕt′). A trademark used for a long, slender, high-powered offshore racing boat. This trademark often occurs in print as *cigarette boat*: *"The chipper hoisted a sailfish pennant and we steamed triumphantly back into the harbor past cigarette boats"* (Advertising Age). *"The Coast Guard . . . has let him pilot government cigarette boats off the Florida coast"* (U.S. News & World Report).

cigar flower *n.* A small bushy plant *(Cuphea ignea),* native to Mexico and Jamaica and widely cultivated as an ornamental and a houseplant for its red, tubular flowers that have white and dark tips that resemble lit cigars.

cig•a•ril•lo (sĭg′ə-rĭl′ō) *n., pl.* **-los.** A small, narrow cigar. [Spanish *cigarrillo,* diminutive of *cigarro,* cigar. See CIGAR.]

ci•gar-store Indian (sĭ-gär′stôr′, -stōr′) *n.* A wooden effigy of a Native American holding a cluster of cigars, formerly used as the emblem of a tobacconist.

ci•lan•tro (sĭ-lăn′trō) *n.* See **coriander** (sense 2). [Spanish, alteration of Late Latin *coliandrum,* from Latin *coriandrum.* See CORIANDER.]

cil•i•a (sĭl′ē-ə) *n.* Plural of **cilium.**

cil•i•ar•y (sĭl′ē-ĕr′ē) *adj.* **1.** Of, relating to, or resembling cilia. **2.** Of or relating to the ciliary body and associated structures of the eye.

ciliary body *n.* A thickened portion of the vascular tunic of the eye located between the choroid and the iris.

cil•i•ate (sĭl′ē-ĭt, -āt′) *adj.* Ciliated. —**ciliate** *n.* Any of various protozoans of the class Ciliata, characterized by numerous cilia. —**cil′i•ate•ly** *adv.* —**cil′i•a′tion** *n.*

cil•i•a•ted (sĭl′ē-ā′tĭd) *adj.* Having cilia.

cil•ice (sĭl′ĭs) *n.* A coarse cloth; haircloth. [French, from Latin *cilicium,* a covering made of Cilician goat's hair, from CILICIA.]

Ci•li•cia (sĭ-lĭsh′ə). An ancient region of southeast Asia Minor along the Mediterranean Sea south of the Taurus Mountains. The area was conquered by Alexander the Great and later became part of the Roman Empire. It was the site of an independent Armenian state from 1080 to 1375. —**Ci•li′cian** *adj. & n.*

Cilician Gates. A mountain pass in the Taurus Mountains of southern Turkey. The pass has served for centuries as a natural highway linking Anatolia with the Mediterranean coast.

cil•i•o•late (sĭl′ē-ə-lāt′) *adj.* Having minute cilia. [From New Latin *ciliolum,* diminutive of *cilium,* cilium, from Latin, eyelid. See CILIUM.]

cil•i•um (sĭl′ē-əm) *n., pl.* **-i•a** (-ē-ə). **1.** A microscopic hairlike process extending from the surface of a cell or unicellular organism. Capable of rhythmical motion, it acts in unison with other such structures to bring about the movement of the cell or of the surrounding medium. **2.** An eyelash. **3.** *Botany.* One of the hairs along the margin or edge of a structure, such as a leaf, usually forming a fringe. [Latin, eyelid. See **kel-**[1] in Appendix.]

Ci·ma·bu·e (chē′mä-bo͞o′ē), **Giovanni.** Originally Cenni di Pepo. 1240?–1302? Italian painter trained in the Byzantine style and considered the first master of the Florentine school.

Cim·ar·ron (sĭm′ə-rŏn′, -rōn′). A river rising in northeast New Mexico and flowing about 1,123 km (698 mi) eastward across southwest Kansas to the Arkansas River in northern Oklahoma.

ci·met·i·dine (sĭ-mĕt′ĭ-dēn′, -dīn′) *n.* A drug, $C_{10}H_{16}N_6S$, that inhibits acid secretion in the stomach and is used to treat gastrointestinal disorders, such as peptic ulcers. [*ci-* (alteration of CYANO–) + MET(HYL) + (GUAN)IDINE.]

ci·mex (sī′mĕks′) *n., pl.* **cim·i·ces** (sĭm′ĭ-sēz′). An insect of the genus *Cimex,* which includes the bedbugs. [Latin *cīmex,* bedbug.]

Cim·me·ri·an (sĭ-mîr′ē-ən) *adj.* Very dark or gloomy. —**Cimmerian** *n. Greek Mythology.* One of a mythical people described by Homer as inhabiting a land of perpetual darkness. [From Latin *Cimmerii,* the Cimmerians, from Greek *Kimmerioi.*]

CINC or **C in C** *abbr.* Commander in chief.

cinch (sĭnch) *n.* **1.** A girth for a pack or saddle. **2.** A firm grip. **3.** Something easy to accomplish. See Synonyms at **breeze**[1]. **4.** A sure thing; a certainty. —**cinch** *v.* **cinched, cinch·ing, cinch·es.** —*tr.* **1.** To put a saddle girth on. **2.** To get a tight grip on. **3.** *Informal.* To make certain of: *cinch a victory.* —*intr.* To tighten a saddle girth. Often used with *up.* [Spanish *cincha,* feminine of *cincho,* belt, from Latin *cīnctus,* from past participle of *cingere,* to gird. See **kenk-** in Appendix.]

♦**cinch bug** *n. Chiefly Southern & Midland U.S.* Variant of **chinch bug.**

cin·cho·na (sĭng-kō′nə, sĭn-chō′-) *n.* **1.** Any of several trees and shrubs of the genus *Cinchona,* native chiefly to the Andes and cultivated for bark that yields the medicinal alkaloids quinine and quinidine, which are used to treat malaria. **2.** The dried bark of any of these plants. In this sense, also called *Jesuit's bark, Peruvian bark.* [New Latin *Cinchona,* genus name, reputedly after Francisca Henríquez de Ribera (1576–1639), Countess of *Chinchón.*] —**cin·chon′ic** (sĭng-kŏn′ĭk, sĭn-chŏn′-) *adj.*

cin·cho·nine (sĭng′kə-nēn′, sĭn′chə-) *n.* An alkaloid, $C_{19}H_{22}N_2O$, derived from the bark of various cinchona trees and used as an antimalarial agent. [CINCHON(A) + –INE[2].]

cin·cho·nism (sĭng′kə-nĭz′əm, sĭn′chə-) *n.* A pathological condition resulting from an overdose of cinchona bark or its alkaloid derivatives and marked by headache, dizziness, hearing loss, and ringing in the ears.

Cin·cin·na·ti (sĭn′sə-năt′ē, -năt′ə). A city of extreme southwest Ohio on the Ohio River. Founded in 1788, it is a port of entry and an industrial, commercial, and cultural center for an extensive area in Ohio and Kentucky. Population, 385,457.

Cin·cin·na·tus (sĭn′sə-năt′əs, -nā′təs), **Lucius Quinctius.** 519?–438 B.C. Roman statesman who according to tradition was twice called away from his farm to assume the dictatorship of Rome (458 and 439).

Cin·co de Ma·yo (sēng′kō də mä′yō, thĕ) *n.* May 5, observed by Mexican communities in Latin America and Mexican-American communities in the United States in commemoration of the 1862 defeat of French troops at the Battle of Puebla. [Spanish : *cinco,* five + *de,* of + *Mayo,* May.]

cinc·ture (sĭngk′chər) *n.* **1.** The act of encircling or encompassing. **2. a.** Something that encircles or surrounds. **b.** A belt or sash, especially one worn with an ecclesiastical vestment or the habit of a monk or nun. —**cincture** *tr.v.* **-tured, -tur·ing, -tures.** To gird; encompass. [Latin *cīnctūra,* from *cīnctus,* past participle of *cingere,* to gird. See **kenk-** in Appendix.]

cin·der (sĭn′dər) *n.* **1. a.** A burned or partly burned substance, such as coal, that is not reduced to ashes but is incapable of further combustion. **b.** A partly charred substance that can burn further but without flame. **2. cinders.** Ashes. **3. cinders.** *Geology.* See **scoria** (sense 1). **4.** *Metallurgy.* See **scoria** (sense 2). **5.** Slag from a metal furnace. —**cinder** *tr.v.* **-dered, -der·ing, -ders.** To burn or reduce to cinders. [Alteration (influenced by Old French *cendre,* ashes, from Latin *cinis*) of Middle English *sinder,* from Old English, slag, dross.] —**cin′der·y** *adj.*

cinder block or **cin·der·block** (sĭn′dər-blŏk′) *n.* A usually hollow building block made with concrete and coal cinders.

Cin·der·el·la (sĭn′də-rĕl′ə) *n.* One that unexpectedly achieves recognition or success after a period of obscurity and neglect. [After *Cinderella,* the fairy-tale character who escapes from a life of drudgery and marries a prince, translation of French *Cendrillon.*]

cin·e·aste also **cin·e·ast** (sĭn′ē-ăst′) or **cin·é·aste** (sĭn′ā-ăst′) *n.* **1.** A film or movie enthusiast. **2.** A person involved in filmmaking. [French *cinéaste,* from *ciné,* cinema, short for *cinéma.* See CINEMA.]

cin·e·ma (sĭn′ə-mə) *n.* **1. a.** A film or movie. **b.** A movie theater. **2. a.** Films or movies considered as a group. **b.** The film or movie industry. **3.** The art or technique of making films or movies; filmmaking. [French *cinéma,* short for *cinématograph.* See CINEMATOGRAPH.] —**cin′e·mat′ic** (sĭn′ə-măt′ĭk) *adj.* —**cin′e·mat′i·cal·ly** *adv.*

cin·e·ma·go·er (sĭn′ə-mə-gō′ər) *n.* A filmgoer.

cin·e·ma·theque (sĭn′ə-mə-tĕk′) *n.* A small movie theater showing classic or avant-garde films. [French *cinémathèque,* blend of *cinéma,* cinema; see CINEMA, and *bibliothèque,* library (from Latin *bibliotheca;* see BIBLIOTHECA).]

cin·e·ma·tize (sĭn′ə-mə-tīz′) *tr.v.* **-tized, -tiz·ing, -tiz·es.** To adapt (a novel or a play, for example) for film or movies. —**cin′e·mat′i·za′tion** (-măt′ĭ-zā′shən) *n.*

cin·e·mat·o·graph (sĭn′ə-măt′ə-grăf′) *n. Chiefly British.* **1.** A movie camera or projector. **2.** The art or technique of making films or movies. [French *cinématographe* : Greek *kinēma, kinēmat-,* motion (from *kinein,* to move; see **kei-**[2] in Appendix) + *-graphe,* -graph.]

cin·e·ma·tog·ra·pher (sĭn′ə-mə-tŏg′rə-fər) *n.* **1.** A movie photographer, especially one who is in charge of shooting a movie. **2.** *Chiefly British.* A movie projectionist.

cin·e·ma·tog·ra·phy (sĭn′ə-mə-tŏg′rə-fē) *n.* The art or technique of movie photography. —**cin′e·mat′o·graph′ic** (-măt′ə-grăf′ĭk) *adj.* —**cin′e·mat′o·graph′i·cal·ly** *adv.*

ci·né·ma vé·ri·té (sē′nā-mä′ vā′rē-tā′) *n.* A style of filmmaking that stresses unbiased realism. [French *cinéma-vérité* : *cinéma,* cinema + *vérité,* truth.]

cin·e·ole also **cin·e·ol** (sĭn′ē-ōl′) *n.* See **eucalyptol.** [Alteration of New Latin *cinae oleum* : *cinae,* genitive of *cina,* wormseed + Latin *oleum,* oil; see OLEO–.]

cin·e·phile (sĭn′ə-fīl′) *n.* A film or movie enthusiast. [French *cinéphile* : *ciné,* cinema; see CINEASTE + *-phile,* -phile.]

cin·e·ra·di·og·ra·phy (sĭn′ō-rā′dē-ŏg′rə-fē) *n.* A diagnostic technique in which a movie camera is used to film the images, as of internal body structures, produced through radiography or fluoroscopy. [CINE(MA) + RADIOGRAPHY.]

Cin·er·am·a (sĭn′ə-răm′ə, -rä′mə). A trademark used for a motion-picture process designed to produce wide-screen, realistic images.

cin·e·rar·i·a[1] (sĭn′ə-râr′ē-ə) *n.* Plural of **cinerarium.**

cin·e·rar·i·a[2] (sĭn′ə-râr′ē-ə) *n.* Any of several hybrid ornamental plants *(Senecio ×hybridus)* in the composite family, derived from species native to the Canary Islands and widely grown as indoor or bedding plants for their showy, variously colored radiate flower heads and attractive silvery foliage. [New Latin *Cineraria,* genus name, from Latin *cinerārius,* of ashes (from the ash-colored down on its leaves). See CINERARIUM.]

cin·e·rar·i·um (sĭn′ə-râr′ē-əm) *n., pl.* **-i·a** (-ē-ə). A place for keeping the ashes of a cremated body. [Latin *cinerārium,* from neuter of *cinerārius,* of ashes, from *cinis, ciner-,* ashes.] —**cin′er·ar′y** (sĭn′ə-rĕr′ē) *adj.*

ci·ne·re·ous (sĭ-nîr′ē-əs) *adj.* **1.** Consisting of or resembling ashes. **2.** Of a gray color tinged with black. [From Latin *cinereus,* from *cinis, ciner-,* ashes.]

cin·er·in (sĭn′ər-ĭn) *n.* Either of two compounds, $C_{20}H_{28}O_3$ or $C_{21}H_{28}O_5$, used in insecticides. [Latin *cinis, ciner-,* ashes + –IN.]

cin·gu·lum (sĭng′gyə-ləm) *n., pl.* **-la** (-lə). *Biology.* A girdlelike marking or structure, such as a band or ridge, on an animal. [Latin, girdle, from *cingere,* to gird. See **kenk-** in Appendix.] —**cin′gu·late** (-lĭt), **cin′gu·la′ted** (-lā′tĭd) *adj.*

cin·na·bar (sĭn′ə-bär′) *n.* **1.** A heavy reddish mercuric sulfide, HgS, that is the principal ore of mercury. **2.** Red mercuric sulfide used as a pigment. **3.** *Color.* See **vermilion** (sense 2). [Middle English *cinabare,* from Latin *cinnabaris,* from Greek *kinnabari.*]

cinnamic acid *n.* A white crystalline acid, $C_6H_5CH_2COOH$, obtained from cinnamon or from balsams such as storax or made synthetically and used chiefly to manufacture perfumery compounds. [CINNAM(ON) + –IC.]

Cin·na·min·son (sĭn′ə-mĭn′sən). A community of southwest New Jersey near the Delaware River northeast of Camden. The destructive Japanese beetle was first discovered here in 1916. Population, 16,072.

cin·na·mon (sĭn′ə-mən) *n.* **1. a.** The dried aromatic inner bark of certain tropical Asian trees in the genus *Cinnamomum,* especially *C. verum* and *C. loureirii,* often ground and used as a spice. **b.** A plant yielding this bark. **2.** *Color.* A light reddish brown. —**cinnamon** *adj. Color.* Of a light reddish brown. [Middle English *cinamome,* from Old French, from Latin *cinnamōmum,* from Greek *kinnamōmon,* of Semitic origin; akin to Hebrew *qinnāmôn.*] —**cin·nam′ic** (sə-năm′ĭk) *adj.*

cinnamon bear *n.* A variety of the North American black bear *(Ursus americanus)* that has a reddish-brown coat.

cinnamon fern *n.* A New World fern *(Osmunda cinnamomea)* having narrow, spore-bearing, cinnamon-colored leaves in early spring, which are later encircled by wider, sterile green leaves.

cinnamon stone *n.* See **essonite.**

cin·quain (sĭng′kān′, săng′-) *n.* A five-line stanza. [French *cinq,* five (from Latin *quīnque;* see **penkʷe** in Appendix) + (QUATR)AIN.]

cinque (sĭngk, săngk) *n. Games.* The number five in cards or dice. [Middle English *cink,* from Old French, from Latin *quīnque,* five. See **penkʷe** in Appendix.]

cin·que·cen·tist (chĭng′kwĭ-chĕn′tĭst) *n.* An Italian, especially a poet or an artist, of the 16th century.

cin·que·cen·to (chĭng′kwĭ-chĕn′tō) *n.* The 16th century, especially in Italian art and literature. [Italian, from *(mil) cinquecento,* (one thousand) five hundred : *cinque,* five (from Latin *quīnque;* see **penkʷe** in Appendix) + *cento,* hundred (from Latin *centum;* see **dekm** in Appendix).]

cinque·foil (sĭngk′foil′, săngk′-) *n.* **1.** Any of several plants of the genus *Potentilla* in the rose family, native chiefly to temperate and cold regions and having yellow or sometimes white or red flowers and compound leaves that in some species bear five leaflets. **2.** *Architecture.* A design having five sides composed of converging arcs, usually used as a frame for glass or a panel. [Middle English *cinkfoil* : *cink,* five; see CINQUE + *foil,* leaf (translation of Old French *quintefeuille,* from Latin *quīnquefolium,* translation of Greek *pentaphullon*); see FOIL[2].]

cinquefoil

Cinque Ports (sĭngk′). A group of seaports of southeast England (originally Hastings, Romney, Hythe, Dover, and Sandwich) that formed a maritime and defensive association in the 11th century. They reached the height of their significance in the Anglo-French conflicts of the 14th century.

CIO also **C.I.O.** *abbr.* Congress of Industrial Organizations.

ci·on (sī′ən) *n.* Variant of **scion** (sense 2).

Ci·pan·go (sĭ-păng′gō). A poetic name for Japan, used by Marco Polo.

ci·pher also **cy·pher** (sī′fər) —*n.* **1.** The mathematical symbol (0) denoting absence of quantity; zero. **2.** An Arabic numeral or figure; a number. **3.** The Arabic system of numerical notation. **4.** One having no influence or value; a nonentity. **5. a.** A cryptographic system in which units of plain text of regular length, usually letters, are arbitrarily transposed or substituted according to a predetermined code. **b.** The key to such a system. **c.** A message written or transmitted in such a system. **6.** A design combining or interweaving letters or initials; a monogram. —*v.* **-phered, -pher·ing, -phers.** —*intr.* To solve problems in arithmetic; calculate. See Synonyms at **calculate.** —*tr.* **1.** To put in secret writing; encode. **2.** To solve by means of arithmetic. [Middle English *cifre,* from Old French, from Medieval Latin *cifra,* from Arabic *ṣifr,* from *ṣafira,* to be empty (translation of Sanskrit *śūnyam,* cipher, dot).]

cir *abbr.* **1.** Circle. **2.** Circuit. **3.** Circular **4.** Circumference.

circ. *abbr.* **1.** Circle. **2.** Circuit. **3.** Circular. **4.** Circulation. **5.** Circumference.

cir·ca (sûr′kə) *prep. Abbr.* **ca, c., C.** In approximately; about: *born circa 1900.* [Latin *circā,* from *circum,* around, from *circus,* circle. See CIRCLE.]

cir·ca·di·an (sər-kā′dē-ən, -kăd′ē-, sûr′kə-dī′ən, -dē′-) *adj. Biology.* Relating to or exhibiting approximately 24-hour periodicity. [Latin *circā,* around; see CIRCA + Latin *diēs,* day; see **deiw-** in Appendix.] —**cir·ca′di·an·ly** *adv.*

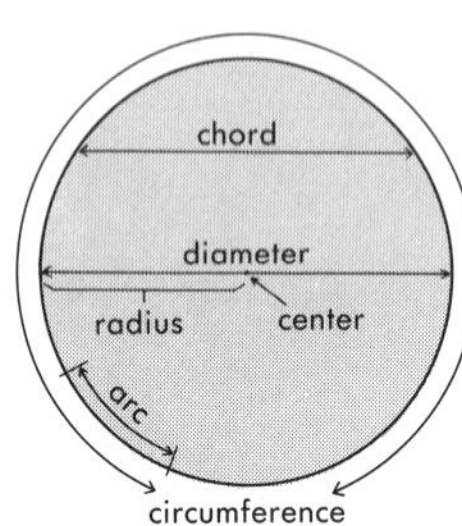

circle

circadian rhythm *n.* A daily rhythmic activity cycle, based on 24-hour intervals, that is exhibited by many organisms.

Cir·cas·sia (sər-kăsh′ə, -ē-ə). A historical region of southwest Russia on the northeast coast of the Black Sea north of the Caucasus Mountains. It was ceded to Russia by the Ottoman Turks in 1829.

Cir·cas·sian (sər-kăsh′ən, -kăsh′ē-ən) *n.* **1.** A native or inhabitant of Circassia. **2.** The non-Indo-European language of the Circassians. —**Circassian** *adj.* Of or relating to Circassia or its people, language, or culture.

Circassian walnut *n.* A type of English walnut, patterned with swirls and curves in shades of brown or with occasional black streaks, used for veneer and cabinetwork.

Cir·ce (sûr′sē) *n. Greek Mythology.* A goddess who turned Odysseus's men temporarily into swine but later gave him directions for their journey home. —**Cir′ce·an** (sûr′sē-ən, sər-sē′ən) *adj.*

cir·ci·nate (sûr′sə-nāt′) *adj.* **1.** Ring-shaped. **2.** *Botany.* Rolled up in the form of a coil with the tip in the center, as an unexpanded fern frond. [Latin *circinātus,* past participle of *circināre,* to make circular, from *circinus,* pair of compasses. See CIRCINUS.] —**cir′ci·nate′ly** *adv.*

Cir·ci·nus (sûr′sə-nəs) *n.* A constellation in the Southern Hemisphere near Musca and Triangulum Australe. [Latin *circinus,* pair of compasses, from *circus,* circle. See CIRCLE.]

cir·cle (sûr′kəl) *n. Abbr.* **cir, circ. 1.** A plane curve everywhere equidistant from a given fixed point, the center. **2.** A planar region bounded by a circle. **3.** Something, such as a ring, shaped like such a plane curve. **4.** A circular course, circuit, or orbit: *a satellite's circle around the earth.* **5.** A curved section or tier of seats in a theater. **6.** A series or process that finishes at its starting point or continuously repeats itself; a cycle. **7.** A group of people sharing an interest, activity, or achievement. **8.** A territorial or administrative division, especially of a province, in some European countries. **9.** A sphere of influence or interest; domain: *well-known in artistic circles.* **10.** *Logic.* A vicious circle. —**circle** *v.* **-cled, -cling, -cles.** —*tr.* **1.** To make or form a circle around; enclose. **2.** To move in a circle around. —*intr.* To move in a circle. [Middle English *cercle,* from Old French, from Latin *circulus,* diminutive of *circus,* circle, from Greek *kirkos, krikos.* See **sker-**[2] in Appendix.] —**cir′cler** (-klər) *n.*

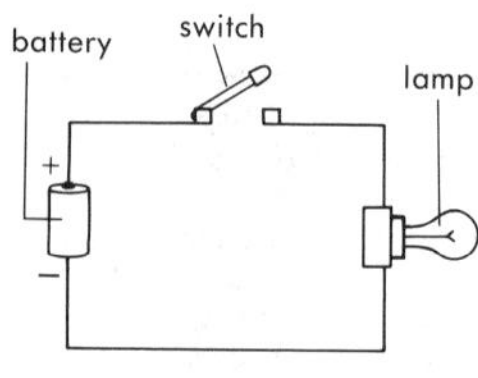

circuit
Electrical circuit

SYNONYMS: *circle, coterie, set, clique.* These nouns denote a group of people sharing an interest or activity. *Circle* connotes gravitation around a central point or element: *my circle of friends; prominent in financial circles. "For the most of us, if we do not talk of ourselves, or at any rate of the individual circles of which we are the centers, we can talk of nothing"* (Anthony Trollope). *Coterie* applies to a small, select group of congenial persons: *"a coterie of Wall Street bankers and their friends"* (Robert B. Reich). *Set* suggests a large, loosely bound group, especially of persons of the same social status who have similar interests and tastes: *"These men constituted the best set in the College. . . . All were reading men, and all good men"* (Walter Besant). A *clique* is an exclusive group, usually social and often participating in activities from which outsiders are barred: *"the narrow, often self-perpetuating cliques which control our lives, living standards and leisure"* (John Lloyd). See also Synonyms at **surround, turn.**

circle graph *n.* See **pie chart.**

cir·clet (sûr′klĭt) *n.* A small circle, especially a circular ornament. [Middle English *cerclet,* from Old French, diminutive of *cercle,* circle. See CIRCLE.]

cir·cuit (sûr′kĭt) *n. Abbr.* **cir, circ. 1. a.** A closed, usually circular line that goes around an object or area. **b.** The region enclosed by such a line. See Synonyms at **circumference. 2. a.** A path or route the complete traversal of which without local change of direction requires returning to the starting point. **b.** The act of following such a path or route. **c.** A journey made on such a path or route. **3.** *Electronics.* **a.** A closed path followed or capable of being followed by an electric current. **b.** A configuration of electrically or electromagnetically connected components or devices. **4. a.** A regular or accustomed course from place to place; a round: *a salesperson on the Detroit–Minneapolis–Chicago circuit; a popular speaker on the lecture circuit.* **b.** The area or district thus covered, especially a territory under the jurisdiction of a judge in which periodic court sessions are held. **5. a.** An association of theaters in which plays, acts, or films move from theater to theater for presentation. **b.** A group of nightclubs, show halls, or resorts at which entertainers appear in turn. **c.** An association of teams, clubs, or arenas of competition: *the downhill ski circuit.* —**circuit** *intr. & tr.v.* **-cuit·ed, -cuit·ing, -cuits.** To make a circuit or circuit of. [Middle English, circumference, from Old French, from Latin *circuitus,* a going around, from past participle of *circumīre,* to go around : *circum-,* circum- + *īre,* to go; see **ei-** in Appendix.]

circuit board *n. Computer Science.* An insulated board on which interconnected circuits and components such as microchips are mounted or etched.

circuit breaker *n.* An automatic switch that stops the flow of electric current in a suddenly overloaded or otherwise abnormally stressed electric circuit.

circuit court *n. Law.* A state court that holds sessions at several different places within a judicial district.

cir·cu·i·tous (sər-kyo͞o′ĭ-təs) *adj.* Being or taking a roundabout, lengthy course. See Synonyms at **indirect.** [From Medieval Latin *circuitōsus,* from Latin *circuitus,* a going around. See CIRCUIT.] —**cir·cu′i·tous·ly** *adv.* —**cir·cu′i·ty, cir·cu′i·tous·ness** *n.*

circuit rider *n.* A cleric who travels from church to church, especially in a rural district.

cir·cuit·ry (sûr′kĭ-trē) *n., pl.* **-ries. 1.** The design of or a detailed plan for an electric circuit. **2.** Electric circuits considered as a group.

cir·cu·lar (sûr′kyə-lər) *adj. Abbr.* **cir, circ. 1.** Of or relating to a circle. **2. a.** Shaped like or nearly like a circle; round. **b.** Moving in or forming a circle. **3.** Circuitous; roundabout: *took a circular route to the office.* **4.** Marked by reasoning in a circle: *a circular theory.* **5.** Addressed or distributed to a large number of persons. —**circular** *n.* A printed advertisement, directive, or notice intended for mass distribution. [Middle English *circuler,* from Anglo-Norman, from Latin *circulāris,* from *circulus,* circle. See CIRCLE.] —**cir′cu·lar′i·ty** (-lăr′ĭ-tē) *n.* —**cir′cu·lar·ly** *adv.*

circular file *n. Slang.* A wastebasket.

circular function *n.* See **trigonometric function.**

cir·cu·lar·ize (sûr′kyə-lə-rīz′) *tr.v.* **-ized, -iz·ing, -iz·es. 1.** To publicize with circulars. **2.** To canvass or poll using a questionnaire. —**cir′cu·lar·i·za′tion** (-lə-rĭ-zā′shən) *n.* —**cir′cu·lar·iz′er** *n.*

circular measure *n.* The measure of an angle in radians.

circular saw *n.* A power saw for cutting wood or metal consisting of a toothed disk rotated at high speed. Also called *buzz saw.*

cir·cu·late (sûr′kyə-lāt′) *v.* **-lat·ed, -lat·ing, -lates.** —*intr.* **1.** To move in or flow through a circle or circuit: *blood circulating through the body.* **2.** To move around, as from person to person or place to place: *a guest circulating at a party.* **3.** To move about or flow freely, as air. **4.** To spread widely among persons or places; disseminate: *Gossip tends to circulate quickly.* —*tr.* To cause to move about or be distributed: *Please circulate these fliers.* [From Middle English *circulat,* continuously distilled, from *circulātus,* past participle of *circulāre,* to make circular, from *circulus.* See CIRCLE.] —**cir′cu·la′tive** (-lā′tĭv) *adj.* —**cir′cu·la′tor** *n.*

cir·cu·lat·ing decimal (sûr′kyə-lā′tĭng) *n.* See **repeating decimal.**

circulating library *n.* See **lending library.**

cir·cu·la·tion (sûr′kyə-lā′shən) *n. Abbr.* **circ. 1.** Movement in a circle or circuit, especially the movement of blood through bodily vessels as a result of the heart's pumping action. **2. a.** Movement or passage through a system of vessels, as of water through pipes; flow. **b.** Free movement or passage. **3.** The passing of something, such as money or news, from place to place or person to person. **4. a.** The condition of being passed about and widely known; distribution. **b.** Dissemination of printed material, especially copies of newspapers or magazines, among readers. **c.** The number of copies of a publication sold or distributed.

cir·cu·la·tor·y (sûr′kyə-lə-tôr′ē, -tōr′ē) *adj.* **1.** Of or relating to circulation. **2.** Of or relating to the circulatory system.

circulatory system *n.* The system of structures, consisting of the heart, blood vessels, and lymphatics, by which blood and lymph are circulated throughout the body.

circum. *abbr.* Circumference.

circum– *pref.* Around; about: *circumlunar.* [Latin, from *circum,* around, accusative of *circus,* circle. See CIRCLE.]

cir·cum·am·bi·ent (sûr′kəm-ăm′bē-ənt) *adj.* Encompassing on all sides; surrounding. **—cir′cum·am′bi·ence, cir′cum·am′bi·en·cy** *n.* **—cir′cum·am′bi·ent·ly** *adv.*

cir·cum·am·bu·late (sûr′kəm-ăm′byə-lāt′) *tr.v.* **-lat·ed, -lat·ing, -lates.** To walk around (something), especially as part of a ritual: *"Circumambulate the city of a dreamy Sabbath afternoon"* (Herman Melville). **—cir′cum·am′bu·la′tion** *n.*

cir·cum·bo·re·al (sûr′kəm-bôr′ē-əl, -bōr′-) *adj.* Distributed or occurring chiefly throughout the boreal regions of North America and Eurasia. Used especially of plants.

cir·cum·cise (sûr′kəm-sīz′) *tr.v.* **-cised, -cis·ing, -cis·es. 1.** To remove the prepuce of (a male). **2.** To remove the prepuce or a part of the clitoris of (a female). [Middle English *circumcisen,* from Latin *circumcīdere, circumcīs-,* to cut around (translation of Greek *peritemnein*) : *circum-,* circum- + *caedere,* to cut; see **kaə-id-** in Appendix.] **—cir′cum·cis′er** *n.*

cir·cum·ci·sion (sûr′kəm-sĭzh′ən) *n.* **1.** The act of circumcising. **2.** A religious ceremony, as in the Jewish or Moslem faith, in which someone is circumcised. **3. Circumcision. a.** A Christian feast celebrating the circumcision of Jesus. **b.** January 1, the day on which this feast is celebrated. Used with *the.*

cir·cum·duc·tion (sûr′kəm-dŭk′shən) *n.* The circular movement of a limb such that the distal end of the limb delineates an arc. [Latin *circumductiō, circumductiōn-,* act of leading around, from *circumductus,* past participle of *circumdūcere,* to lead around : *circum-,* circum- + *dūcere,* to lead; see **deuk-** in Appendix.]

cir·cum·fer·ence (sər-kŭm′fər-əns) *n. Abbr.* **cir, circ., circum. 1.** The boundary line of a circle. **2. a.** The boundary line of a figure, area, or object. **b.** The length of such a boundary. [Middle English, from Old French *circonference,* from Latin *circumferentia,* from *circumferēns, circumferent-,* present participle of *circumferre,* to carry around : *circum-,* circum- + *ferre,* to carry; see **bher-**[1] in Appendix.] **—cir·cum′fer·en′tial** (-fə-rĕn′-shəl) *adj.*

SYNONYMS: *circumference, circuit, compass, perimeter, periphery.* The central meaning shared by these nouns is "a line around a closed figure or area": *the circumference of the earth; a park five acres in circuit; stayed within the compass of the schoolyard; the perimeter of a rectangle; erected a fence around the periphery of the property.*

cir·cum·flex (sûr′kəm-flĕks′) *n.* A mark (ˆ) used over a vowel in certain languages or in phonetic keys to indicate quality of pronunciation. **—circumflex** *adj.* **1.** Having this mark. **2.** Curving around: *a circumflex blood vessel.* [From Latin *circumflexus,* bent around, circumflex, past participle of *circumflectere,* to bend around : *circum-,* circum- + *flectere,* to bend.]

cir·cum·flu·ent (sər-kŭm′flo͞o-ənt) also **cir·cum·flu·ous** (-əs) *adj.* Flowing around or surrounding.

cir·cum·fuse (sûr′kəm-fyo͞oz′) *tr.v.* **-fused, -fus·ing, -fus·es. 1.** To pour or diffuse around; spread. **2.** To surround, as with liquid; suffuse. [Latin *circumfundere, circumfūs-* : *circum-,* circum- + *fundere,* to pour; see **gheu-** in Appendix.] **—cir′cum·fu′sion** *n.*

cir·cum·lo·cu·tion (sûr′kəm-lō-kyo͞o′shən) *n.* **1.** The use of unnecessarily wordy and indirect language. **2.** Evasion in speech or writing. **3.** A roundabout expression. [Middle English *circumlocucioun,* from Latin *circumlocūtiō, circumlocūtiōn-,* from *circumlocūtus,* past participle of *circumloquī* : *circum-,* circum- + *loquī,* to speak; see **tolkʷ-** in Appendix.] **—cir′cum·loc′u·to′ri·ly** (-lŏk′yə-tôr′ə-lē, -tōr′-) *adv.* **—cir′cum·loc′u·to′ry** (-tôr′ē, -tōr′ē) *adj.*

cir·cum·lu·nar (sûr′kəm-lo͞o′nər) *adj.* Revolving about or surrounding the moon.

cir·cum·nav·i·gate (sûr′kəm-năv′ĭ-gāt′) *tr.v.* **-gat·ed, -gat·ing, -gates. 1.** To proceed completely around: *circumnavigating the earth.* **2.** To go around; circumvent: *circumnavigate the downtown traffic.* **—cir′cum·nav′i·ga′tion** *n.* **—cir′cum·nav′i·ga′tor** *n.*

cir·cum·po·lar (sûr′kəm-pō′lər) *adj.* **1.** Located or found in one of the Polar Regions. **2.** *Astronomy.* Denoting a star that from a given observer's latitude does not go below the horizon.

cir·cum·ro·tate (sûr′kəm-rō′tāt′) *intr.v.* **-tat·ed, -tat·ing, -tat·es.** To turn like a wheel; revolve. **—cir′cum·ro·ta′tion** *n.* **—cir′cum·ro′ta·to′ry** (-tə-tôr′ē, -tōr′ē) *adj.*

cir·cum·scis·sile (sûr′kəm-sĭs′ĭl, -īl′) *adj. Botany.* Splitting or opening along a circumference, with the top coming off as a lid: *a circumscissile seed capsule.* [CIRCUM– + Latin *scissilis,* easily split, splitting; see SCISSILE.]

cir·cum·scribe (sûr′kəm-skrīb′) *tr.v.* **-scribed, -scrib·ing, -scribes. 1.** To draw a line around; encircle. **2.** To limit narrowly; restrict. **3.** To determine the limits of; define. See Synonyms at **limit. 4. a.** To enclose (a polygon or polyhedron) within a configuration of lines, curves, or surfaces so that every vertex of the enclosed object is incident on the enclosing configuration. **b.** To erect (such a configuration) around a polygon or polyhedron: *circumscribe a circle around a square.* [Middle English *circumscriben,* from Latin *circumscrībere* : *circum-,* circum- + *scrībere,* to write; see **skrībh-** in Appendix.] **—cir′cum·scrib′a·ble** *adj.* **—cir′cum·scrib′er** *n.*

cir·cum·scrip·tion (sûr′kəm-skrĭp′shən) *n.* **1.** The act of circumscribing or the state of being circumscribed. **2.** Something, such as a limit or restriction, that circumscribes. **3.** A circumscribed space or area. **4.** A circular inscription, as on a medallion. [Latin *circumscrīptiō, circumscrīptiōn-,* from *circumscrīptus,* past participle of *circumscrībere,* to circumscribe. See CIRCUMSCRIBE.] **—cir′cum·scrip′tive** *adj.* **—cir′cum·scrip′tive·ly** *adv.*

cir·cum·so·lar (sûr′kəm-sō′lər) *adj.* Revolving around or surrounding the sun.

cir·cum·spect (sûr′kəm-spĕkt′) *adj.* Heedful of circumstances and potential consequences; prudent. [Middle English, from Latin *circumspectus,* past participle of *circumspicere,* to take heed : *circum-,* circum- + *specere,* to look; see **spek-** in Appendix.] **—cir′cum·spect′ly** *adv.*

cir·cum·spec·tion (sûr′kəm-spĕk′shən) *n.* The state or quality of being circumspect. See Synonyms at **prudence.**

cir·cum·stance (sûr′kəm-stăns′) *n.* **1.** A condition or fact attending an event and having some bearing on it; a determining or modifying factor. **2.** A condition or fact that determines or must be considered in the determining of a course of action. **3.** Often **circumstances.** The sum of determining factors beyond willful control: *a victim of circumstance; work that will begin on Monday if circumstances permit.* **4. circumstances.** Financial status or means: *"Prior came of a good family, much reduced in circumstances"* (George Sherburn). **5.** Detail accompanying or surrounding an event, as in a narrative or series of events. **6.** Formal display; ceremony: *the pomp and circumstance of a coronation.* **7.** A particular incident or occurrence: *Your arrival was a fortunate circumstance.* See Synonyms at **occurrence. —circumstance** *tr.v.* **-stanced, -stanc·ing, -stanc·es.** To place in particular circumstances or conditions; situate. ***—idioms.* under no circumstances.** In no case; never. **under** (or **in**) **the circumstances.** Given these conditions; such being the case. [Middle English, from Old French *circonstance,* from Latin *circumstantia,* from *circumstāns, circumstant-,* present participle of *circumstāre,* to stand around : *circum-,* circum- + *stāre,* to stand; see **stā-** in Appendix.]

USAGE NOTE: Use of the idiom *under the circumstances* is justified by both logic and reputable precedent, and objections to it must be accounted at best overfussy if not also, as H.W. Fowler put it, "puerile."

cir·cum·stan·tial (sûr′kəm-stăn′shəl) *adj.* **1.** Of, relating to, or dependent on circumstances. **2.** Of no primary significance; incidental. **3.** Complete and particular; full of detail: *a circumstantial report about the debate.* See Synonyms at **detailed. 4.** Full of ceremonial display. **—cir′cum·stan′tial·ly** *adv.*

circumstantial evidence *n. Law.* Evidence not bearing directly on the fact in dispute but on various attendant circumstances from which the judge or jury might infer the occurrence of the fact in dispute.

cir·cum·stan·ti·al·i·ty (sûr′kəm-stăn′shē-ăl′ĭ-tē) *n., pl.* **-ties. 1.** The quality of being fully or minutely detailed. **2.** A particular detail or circumstance.

cir·cum·stan·ti·ate (sûr′kəm-stăn′shē-āt′) *tr.v.* **-at·ed, -at·ing, -ates.** To set forth or verify with circumstances; give detailed proof or description of. **—cir′cum·stan′ti·a′tion** *n.*

cir·cum·ter·res·tri·al (sûr′kəm-tə-rĕs′trē-əl) *adj.* Revolving around or surrounding the earth.

cir·cum·val·late (sûr′kəm-văl′āt′) *tr.v.* **-lat·ed, -lat·ing, -lates.** To surround with or as if with a rampart. **—circumvallate** *adj.* **1.** (*also* -ĭt). Surrounded with or as if with a rampart. **2.** *Anatomy.* Surrounded by a ridge or raised, wall-like structure. [Latin *circumvallāre, circumvallāt-* : *circum-,* circum- + *vallum,* rampart with palisades, from *vallus,* post, stake.] **—cir′cum·val·la′tion** *n.*

cir·cum·vent (sûr′kəm-vĕnt′) *tr.v.* **-vent·ed, -vent·ing, -vents. 1.** To surround (an enemy, for example); enclose or entrap. **2.** To go around; bypass: *circumvented the city.* **3.** To avoid or get around by artful maneuvering: *She planned a way to circumvent all the bureaucratic red tape.* [Middle English *circumventen,* from Latin *circumvenīre, circumvent-* : *circum-,* circum- + *venīre,* to go, come; see **gʷā-** in Appendix.] **—cir′cum·vent′er, cir′cum·ven′tor** *n.* **—cir′cum·ven′tion** *n.* **—cir′cum·ven′tive** *adj.*

cir·cum·vo·lu·tion (sər-kŭm′və-lo͞o′shən, sûr′kəm-vō-) *n.* **1.** An act of turning, coiling, or folding about a center, a core, or an axis. **2.** A single turn, coil, or fold; a convolution. [Middle English *circumvolucioun,* from Medieval Latin *circumvolūtiō,*

circular saw

ă pat	oi boy
ā pay	ou out
âr care	o͝o took
ä father	o͞o boot
ĕ pet	ŭ cut
ē be	ûr urge
ĭ pit	th thin
ī pie	*th* this
îr pier	hw which
ŏ pot	zh vision
ō toe	ə about, item
ô paw	♦ regionalism

Stress marks: ′ (primary); ′ (secondary), as in **dictionary** (dĭk′shə-nĕr′ē)

circumvolūtiōn-, from Latin *circumvolūtus,* past participle of *circumvolvere,* to roll around. See CIRCUMVOLVE.]

cir·cum·volve (sûr′kəm-vŏlv′) *intr. & tr.v.* **-volved, -volv·ing, -volves.** To revolve or cause to revolve. [Latin *circumvolvere : circum-,* circum- + *volvere,* to roll; see **wel-**[2] in Appendix.]

cir·cus (sûr′kəs) *n.* **1.a.** A public entertainment consisting typically of a variety of performances by acrobats, clowns, and trained animals. **b.** A traveling company that performs such entertainments. **c.** A circular arena, surrounded by tiers of seats and often covered by a tent, in which such shows are performed. **2.** A roofless, oval enclosure surrounded by tiers of seats that was used in antiquity for public spectacles. **3.** *Chiefly British.* An open circular place where several streets intersect. **4.** *Informal.* Something suggestive of a circus, as in frenetic activity or noisy disorder: *"The city is a circus of the senses"* (William H. Gass). [Middle English, round arena, from Latin, circus, circle. See CIRCLE.] **—cir′cus·y** *adj.*

cirrocumulus

WORD HISTORY: The modern circus owes its name but fortunately not its regular program of events to the amusement of ancient times. The Latin word *circus,* which comes from the Greek word *kirkos,* "circle, ring," referred to a circular or oval area enclosed by rows of seats for spectators. In the center ring, so to speak, was held a variety of events, including chariot races and gladiatorial combats, spectacles in which bloodshed and brutality were not uncommon. The first use of *circus* recorded in English, in a work by Chaucer written around 1380, probably refers to the Circus Maximus in Rome. Our modern circus, which dates to the end of the 18th century, was originally an equestrian spectacle as well, but the trick riders were soon joined in the ring by such performers as ropedancers, acrobats, and jugglers. Even though the circular shape of the arena and the equestrian nature of some of the performances are carried over from its Roman namesake, the modern circus, despite occasional accidental violence, has little connection with its brutal namesake of long ago.

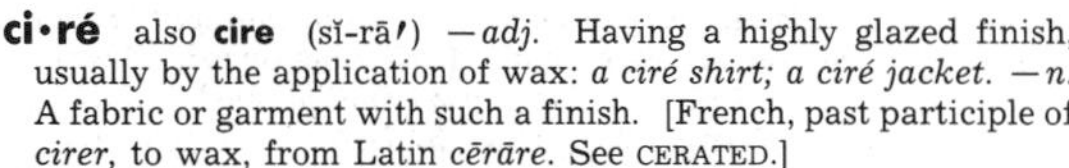

ci·ré also **cire** (sĭ-rā′) *—adj.* Having a highly glazed finish, usually by the application of wax: *a ciré shirt; a ciré jacket.* —*n.* A fabric or garment with such a finish. [French, past participle of *cirer,* to wax, from Latin *cērāre.* See CERATED.]

Ci·re·bon (chĭr′ə-bôn′). A city of south-central Indonesia on the northern coast of Java east-northeast of Bandung. It is a port on the Java Sea. Population, 223,776.

cirque (sûrk) *n.* A steep hollow, often containing a small lake, occurring at the upper end of a mountain valley. Also called *cwm.* [French, from Latin *circus,* circle. See CIRCLE.]

cir·rate (sĭr′āt′) *adj. Biology.* Having or resembling a cirrus or cirri. [Latin *cirrātus,* curled, from *cirrus,* curl of hair.]

cirrus

cir·rho·sis (sĭ-rō′sĭs) *n.* **1.** A chronic disease of the liver characterized by the replacement of normal tissue with fibrous tissue and the loss of functional liver cells. It can result from alcohol abuse, nutritional deprivation, or infection especially by the hepatitis virus. **2.** Chronic interstitial inflammation of any tissue or organ. [New Latin : Greek *kirros,* tawny (from the color of the diseased liver) + -OSIS.] **—cir·rhot′ic** (-rŏt′ĭk) *adj.*

cir·ri (sĭr′ī′) *n.* Plural of **cirrus.**

cirri– *pref.* Variant of **cirro–.**

cir·ri·ped (sĭr′ə-pĕd′) also **cir·ri·pede** (-pēd′) *n.* Any of various crustaceans of the subclass Cirripedia, which includes the barnacles and related organisms that attach themselves to objects or become parasitic in the adult stage. [From New Latin *Cirripedia,* order name : CIRR(US) + -PED.] **—cir′ri·ped′** *adj.*

cirro– or **cirri–** *pref.* Cirrus cloud: *cirrostratus.* [From CIRRUS.]

cir·ro·cu·mu·lus (sĭr′ō-kyo͞om′yə-ləs) *n.* A high-altitude cloud composed of a series of small, regularly arranged cloudlets in the form of ripples or grains.

cir·ro·stra·tus (sĭr′ō-strā′təs, -străt′əs) *n.* A high-altitude, thin hazy cloud, usually covering the sky and often producing a halo effect.

cir·rus (sĭr′əs) *n., pl.* **cir·ri** (sĭr′ī′). **1.** A high-altitude cloud composed of narrow bands or patches of thin, generally white, fleecy parts. **2.** *Botany.* A tendril or similar part. **3.** *Zoology.* A slender, flexible appendage, such as the fused cilia of certain protozoans. [Latin, curl of hair.]

cithara
Detail from mid fifth-century B.C. Greek vase showing Apollo holding a cithara

cis– *pref.* **1.** On this side: *cisatlantic.* **2.** Having a pair of identical atoms or groups on the same side of a plane that passes through two carbon atoms linked by a double bond. Used of a geometric isomer: cis-*butene.* [Latin, from *cis,* on this side of. See **ko-** in Appendix.]

cis·al·pine (sĭs-ăl′pīn′) *adj.* Relating to, living on, or coming from the southern side of the Alps. [Latin *Cisalpīnus : cis-,* cis- + *alpīnus,* alpine; see ALPINE.]

Cis·al·pine Gaul (sĭs-ăl′pīn′ gôl′). A section of ancient Gaul south and east of the Alps in present-day Italy.

cis·at·lan·tic (sĭs′ət-lăn′tĭk) *adj.* Situated on this side of the Atlantic Ocean.

Cis·cau·ca·sia (sĭs′kô-kā′zhə, -shə). A steppeland of southwest Russia in the Caucasus north of the main range of the Caucasus Mountains.

cis·co (sĭs′kō) *n., pl.* **-coes** or **-cos.** Any of several North American freshwater fishes of the genus *Coregonus* or *Leucichthys,* related to and resembling the whitefish. [From Canadian French *ciscoette,* from Ojibwa *bemidewiskawed,* the (fish) with oily skin.]

Cis·kei (sĭs′kī). A Black homeland of southeast South Africa. It was granted nominal independence in 1980. Zwelitsha is the capital. Population, 645,000.

cis·lu·nar (sĭs-lo͞o′nər) *adj.* Situated between the earth and the moon.

cis·mon·tane (sĭs-mŏn′tān′) *adj.* Situated on this side of the mountains, especially the Alps.

cist[1] (sĭst) *n.* A wicker receptacle used in ancient Rome for carrying sacred utensils in procession. [Latin *cista,* from Greek *kistē.*]

cist[2] (sĭst, kĭst) also **kist** (kĭst) *n.* A Neolithic stone coffin. [Welsh, chest, from Latin *cista,* basket. See CIST[1].]

Cis·ter·cian (sĭ-stûr′shən) *n.* A member of a contemplative monastic order founded by reformist Benedictines in France in 1098. [French *Cistertien,* from Medieval Latin *Cistercium,* Cîteaux, a village of eastern France, site of an abbey.] **—Cis·ter′cian** *adj.*

cis·tern (sĭs′tərn) *n.* **1.** A receptacle for holding water or other liquid, especially a tank for catching and storing rainwater. **2.** *Anatomy.* A cisterna. [Middle English *cisterne,* from Latin *cisterna,* from *cista,* box, from Greek *kistē,* basket.] **—cis·tern′al** (sĭ-stûr′nəl) *adj.*

cis·ter·na (sĭ-stûr′nə) *n., pl.* **-nae** (-nē). **1.** *Anatomy.* A fluid-containing sac or cavity in the body of an organism. Also called *reservoir.* **2.** *Cytology.* One of the saclike vesicles that comprise the endoplasmic reticulum. [Latin, cistern. See CISTERN.] **—cis·ter′nal** *adj.*

cis·tron (sĭs′trŏn′) *n.* A section of DNA that contains the genetic code for a single polypeptide and functions as a hereditary unit. [From *cis-trans test,* a genetic test (CIS– + TRANS–) + –ON[1].] **—cis·tron′ic** *adj.*

cit. *abbr.* **1.** Citation. **2.** Cited. **3.** Citizen.

cit·a·del (sĭt′ə-dəl, -dĕl′) *n.* **1.** A fortress in a commanding position in or near a city. **2.** A stronghold or fortified place; a bulwark. [French *citadelle,* from Italian *cittadella,* diminutive of *città,* city, from Latin *cīvitās.* See CITY.]

ci·ta·tion (sī-tā′shən) *n. Abbr.* **cit. 1.** The act of citing. **2.a.** A quoting of an authoritative source for substantiation. **b.** A source so cited; a quotation. **3.** *Law.* A reference to previous court decisions or authoritative writings. **4.** Enumeration or mention, as of facts, especially: **a.** An official commendation for meritorious action, especially in military service: *a citation for bravery.* **b.** A formal statement of the accomplishments of one being honored with an academic degree. **5.** An official summons, especially one calling for appearance in court. **—ci·ta′tion·al** *adj.* **—ci′ta·to′ry** (sī′tə-tôr′ē, -tōr′ē) *adj.*

cite (sīt) *tr.v.* **cit·ed, cit·ing, cites. 1.** To quote as an authority or example. **2.** To mention or bring forward as support, illustration, or proof: *cited several instances of insubordinate behavior.* **3.a.** To commend officially for meritorious action in military service. **b.** To honor formally. **4.** To summon before a court of law. [Middle English *citen,* to summon, from Old French *citer,* from Latin *citāre.* See **kei-**[2] in Appendix.] **—cit′a·ble** *adj.*

Ci·thae·ron (sĭ-thîr′ən). A mountain, 1,410 m (4,623 ft) high, of southeast Greece. It was considered sacred to Dionysus and the Muses.

cith·a·ra (sĭth′ər-ə, kĭth′-) *n. Music.* An ancient instrument resembling the lyre. [Latin, from Greek *kithara.*]

cith·er (sĭth′ər, sĭth′-) *n.* A cittern. [French *cithare, kitaire,* from Latin *cithara,* cithara. See CITHARA.]

cith·ern (sĭth′ərn, sĭth′-) *n.* Variant of **cittern.**

cit·ied (sĭt′ēd) *adj.* Having a city or cities.

cit·i·fied (sĭt′ĭ-fīd′) *adj.* Having or pretending to have the sophisticated style or manner associated with an urban way of life.

cit·i·fy (sĭt′ĭ-fī′) *tr.v.* **-fied, -fy·ing, -fies. 1.** To cause to become urban. **2.** To impart the styles and manners of a city to: *"Will the immigration of high-powered executives somehow citify the country?"* (Wharton Magazine). **—cit′i·fi·ca′tion** (-fĭ-kā′shən) *n.*

cit·i·zen (sĭt′ĭ-zən) *n. Abbr.* **cit. 1.** A person owing loyalty to and entitled by birth or naturalization to the protection of a state or nation. **2.** A resident of a city or town, especially one entitled to vote and enjoy other privileges there. **3.** A civilian. **4.** A native, inhabitant, or denizen of a particular place: *"We have learned to be citizens of the world, members of the human community"* (Franklin D. Roosevelt). [Middle English *citisein,* from Anglo-Norman *citesein,* probably alteration of Old French *citeain,* from *cite,* city. See CITY.] **—cit′i·zen·ly** *adj.*

SYNONYMS: *citizen, national, subject.* The central meaning shared by these nouns is "a person owing allegiance to a nation or state and entitled to its protection": *an American citizen; a British national; a French subject.*

cit·i·zen·ry (sĭt′ĭ-zən-rē) *n., pl.* **-ries.** Citizens considered as a group.

cit·i·zen's arrest (sĭt′ĭ-zənz) *n.* An arrest made by a citizen, for whom legal authority arises from the fact of citizenship, rather than by an officer of the law.

cit·i·zens band (sĭt′ĭ-zənz) *n. Abbr.* **CB** A radio-frequency band officially allocated for private radio communications.

cit·i·zen·ship (sĭt′ĭ-zən-shĭp′) *n.* The status of a citizen with its attendant duties, rights, and privileges.

Ci·tlal·té·petl (sē′tläl-tā′pĕt-l). Also **Mount O·ri·za·ba** (ôr′ĭ-zä′bə, ōr′-, ô′rē-sä′vä). An extinct volcanic peak, 5,702.6 m (18,697 ft) high, of southern Mexico between Mexico City and Veracruz. It is the highest elevation in the country.

cit·ral (sĭt′răl) *n.* A mobile pale-yellow liquid, $C_9H_{15}COH$, derived from lemon-grass oil and used in perfume and as a flavoring. [CITR(US) + –AL[3].]

cit·rate (sĭt′rāt′) *n.* A salt or ester of citric acid.

cit·ric (sĭt′rĭk) *adj.* Of or relating to citric acid.

citric acid *n.* A colorless translucent crystalline acid, $C_6H_8O_7{\cdot}H_2O$, principally derived by fermentation of carbohydrates or from lemon, lime, and pineapple juices and used in preparing citrates and in flavorings and metal polishes.

citric acid cycle *n.* See **Krebs cycle.**

cit·ri·cul·ture (sĭt′rĭ-kŭl′chər) *n.* The cultivation of citrus fruits. [CITR(US) + CULTURE.] **—cit′ri·cul′tur·ist** *n.*

ci·trine (sĭ-trēn′, sĭt′rēn′) *n.* **1.** A pale yellow variety of crystalline quartz resembling topaz. **2.** *Color.* A light to moderate olive. [Middle English, reddish yellow, from Old French *citrin,* from Medieval Latin *citrīnus,* from Latin *citrus,* citron tree.] **—ci·trine′** *adj.*

cit·ron (sĭt′rən) *n.* **1.a.** A thorny evergreen shrub or small tree *(Citrus medica)* native to India and widely cultivated for its large, lemonlike fruits that have a thick, warty rind. **b.** The fruit of this plant, whose rind is often candied and used in confections and fruitcakes. **2.** A globose watermelon *(Citrullus lanatus* var. *citroides)* having white flesh that is candied or pickled. **3.** *Color.* A grayish green yellow. [Middle English, from Old French, alteration (influenced by *limon,* lemon; see LEMON) of Latin *(mālum) citreum,* citron (fruit), from *citrus,* citron tree.] **—cit′ron** *adj.*

cit·ro·nel·la (sĭt′rə-nĕl′ə) *n.* **1.** A tropical Asian grass *(Cymbopogon nardus)* having bluish-green, lemon-scented leaves and an essential oil. **2.** A pale yellow to brownish aromatic oil obtained from this plant, used in perfumery and also in insect repellents and commercial flavorings. [New Latin, from French *citronnelle,* lemon oil, diminutive of *citron,* citron. See CITRON.]

cit·ro·nel·lal (sĭt′rə-nĕl′ăl′) *n.* A colorless aromatic liquid, $C_{10}H_{18}O$, obtained from citronella and certain other essential oils or produced synthetically and used in making perfumes and as a commercial flavoring. [CITRONELL(A) + –AL[3].]

cit·ro·nel·lol (sĭt′rə-nĕl′ôl, -ōl, -ŏl) *n.* A colorless liquid, $C_{10}H_{20}O$, with a roselike odor, derived from any of several essential oils or made synthetically and used extensively in perfumery. [CITRONELL(A) + –OL[1].]

cit·rul·line (sĭt′rə-lēn′) *n.* An amino acid, $C_6H_{13}N_3O_3$, originally isolated from watermelon, that is produced as an intermediate in the conversion of ornithine to arginine during urea formation in the liver. [New Latin *Citrullus,* watermelon genus (from Medieval Latin *citrullus,* watermelon, from Italian dialectal *citrulo,* from Late Latin *citrium,* from Latin *citrus,* citron) + –INE[2].]

cit·rus (sĭt′rəs) *n., pl.* **citrus** or **-rus·es. 1.** Any of various evergreen, usually spiny shrubs or trees of the genus *Citrus,* such as the grapefruit, lemon, or orange, native to southern and southeast Asia, having leathery, aromatic, unifoliolate compound leaves and widely cultivated for their juicy, edible fruits that have a leathery, aromatic rind. **2.** The fruit of any of these plants. **—citrus** *adj.* Of or relating to any of the citrus plants or their fruits. [Latin, citron tree.]

citrus canker *n.* A destructive bacterial disease of citrus plants that attacks seedlings and mature plants and causes defoliation and death.

Cit·rus Heights (sĭt′rəs). A community of north-central California, a suburb of Sacramento. Population, 85,911.

citrus red mite *n.* A large mite *(Panonychus citri)* that infests citrus plants and shrubs. Also called *citrus red spider.*

cit·tern (sĭt′ərn) also **cith·ern** (sĭth′ərn, sĭth′-) *n. Music.* A 16th-century guitar with a flat, pear-shaped body. [Perhaps blend of Latin *cithara,* cithara; see CITHARA, and obsolete English *gittern* (from Middle English, from Old French *guiterne,* from Latin *cithara*).]

cit·y (sĭt′ē) *n., pl.* **-ies.** *Abbr.* **C. 1.** A center of population, commerce, and culture; a town of significant size and importance. **2.a.** An incorporated municipality in the United States with definite boundaries and legal powers set forth in a charter granted by the state. **b.** A Canadian municipality of high rank, usually determined by population but varying by province. **c.** A large incorporated town in Great Britain, usually the seat of a bishop, with its title conferred by the Crown. **3.** The inhabitants of a city considered as a group. **4.** An ancient Greek city-state. **5. City.** An area or complex specializing in a particular type of merchandise. Often used in combination: *Car City on Route 1A; Bargain City.* **6.** *Slang.* Used in combination as an intensive: *The playing field was mud city after the big rain.* [Middle English *cite,* from Old French, from Latin *cīvitās,* from *cīvis,* citizen. See **kei-**[1] in Appendix.]

city council *n.* The governing body of a city.

city desk *n.* The newspaper department that handles local news.

city editor *n.* **1.** A newspaper editor responsible for handling local news and reporters' assignments. **2.** *Chiefly British.* A newspaper editor who handles commercial and financial news.

city father *n.* A municipal official, such as a council member.

city hall *n.* **1.** The building housing the administrative offices of a municipal government. **2.** The municipal government, especially its officials considered as a group. **3.** *Slang.* An entrenched and insensitive bureaucracy: *still trying to fight city hall.*

city manager *n.* An administrator appointed by a city council to manage the affairs of the municipality.

cit·y·scape (sĭt′ē-skāp′) *n.* **1.** An artistic representation, such as a painting or photograph, of a city. **2.** A city or section of a city regarded as a scene: *"the vast cityscape of lower Manhattan"* (New Yorker).

city slicker *n. Informal.* A person with the sophisticated manner and dress traditionally associated by rural people with city dwellers.

cit·y-state (sĭt′ē-stāt′) *n.* A sovereign state consisting of an independent city and its surrounding territory.

cit·y·wide (sĭt′ē-wīd′) *adj.* Including or occurring in all parts of a city: *citywide busing; a citywide strike.*

Ci·u·dad Bo·lí·var (sē′o͞o-däd′ bə-lē′vär, syo͞o-*thäth′* bô-lē′vär). A city of east-central Venezuela on the Orinoco River southeast of Caracas. It was founded in 1764 on the narrows (or *angosturas*) of the river and was popularly known as Angostura. Population, 151,000.

Ciudad Gua·ya·na (gwə-yä′nə, gwä-yä′nä). A city of eastern Venezuela on the Orinoco River. It was founded in 1961 as a planned community. Population, 212,000.

Ciudad Juá·rez (wär′ĕz, hwä′rĕs) also **Juárez.** A city of northern Mexico on the Rio Grande opposite El Paso, Texas. The two cities are connected by bridge. Population, 544,496.

Ciudad Tru·jil·lo (tro͞o-hē′yō). See **Santo Domingo.**

Ciudad Vic·to·ri·a (vĭk-tôr′ē-ə, -tōr′-, vĕk-tô′ryä). A city of east-central Mexico south-southeast of Monterrey. It was founded in 1750. Population, 140,161.

civ. *abbr.* Civil; civilian.

civ·et (sĭv′ĭt) *n.* **1.** Any of various carnivorous catlike mammals of the family Viverridae of Africa and Asia, having anal scent glands that secrete a fluid with a musky odor. Also called *civet cat.* **2.** The thick, yellowish, musky fluid secreted by one of these mammals, used in the manufacture of perfumes. **3.** The fur of one of these mammals. [French *civette,* from Old French, from Catalan *civetta,* from Medieval Latin *zibethus,* from Arabic *zabād,* civet perfume.]

civ·ic (sĭv′ĭk) *adj.* Of, relating to, or belonging to a city, a citizen, or citizenship; municipal or civil. [Latin *cīvicus,* from *cīvis,* citizen. See **kei-**[1] in Appendix.]

civ·ics (sĭv′ĭks) *n. (used with a sing. verb).* The branch of political science that deals with civic affairs and the rights and duties of citizens.

civ·ies (sĭv′ēz) *pl.n. Slang.* Variant of **civvies.**

civ·il (sĭv′əl) *adj. Abbr.* **civ. 1.** Of, relating to, or befitting a citizen or citizens: *civil duties.* **2.** Of or relating to citizens and their interrelations with one another or with the state: *civil society; the civil branches of government.* **3.** Of ordinary citizens or ordinary community life as distinguished from the military or the ecclesiastical: *civil authorities.* **4.** Of or in accordance with organized society; civilized. **5.** Sufficiently observing or befitting accepted social usages; not rude: *a civil reply.* See Synonyms at **polite. 6.** Being in accordance with or denoting legally recognized divisions of time: *a civil year.* **7.** *Law.* Relating to the rights of private individuals and legal proceedings concerning these rights as distinguished from criminal, military, or international regulations or proceedings. [Middle English, from Latin *cīvīlis,* from *cīvis,* citizen. See **kei-**[1] in Appendix.] **—civ′il·ly** *adv.*

civil death *n. Law.* Total deprivation of civil rights resulting from conviction for treason or other serious offense.

civil defense *n. Abbr.* **CD, C.D.** A range of emergency measures to be taken by an organized body of civilian volunteers for the protection of life and property in the event of natural disaster or enemy attack.

civil disobedience *n.* Refusal to obey civil laws in an effort to induce change in governmental policy or legislation, characterized by the use of passive resistance or other nonviolent means.

civil engineer *n. Abbr.* **C.E.** An engineer trained in the design and construction of public works, such as bridges or dams, and other large facilities. **—civil engineering** *n.*

ci·vil·ian (sĭ-vĭl′yən) *n. Abbr.* **civ. 1.** A person following the pursuits of civil life. **2.** A specialist in Roman or civil law. **—civilian** *adj.* Of or relating to civilians or civil life; nonmilitary: *civilian clothes; a civilian career.* [Middle English, civil law judge, from Old French *civilien,* from *civil,* civil, from Latin *cīvīlis.* See CIVIL.]

ci·vil·ian·ize (sĭ-vĭl′yə-nīz′) *tr.v.* **-ized, -iz·ing, -iz·es.** To convert to civilian operation or control. **—ci·vil′ian·i·za′tion** (-ĭ-zā′shən) *n.*

ci·vil·i·ty (sĭ-vĭl′ĭ-tē) *n., pl.* **-ties. 1.** Courteous behavior; politeness. **2.** A courteous act or utterance.

civ·i·li·za·tion (sĭv′ə-lĭ-zā′shən) *n.* **1.** An advanced state of intellectual, cultural, and material development in human society, marked by progress in the arts and sciences, the extensive use of writing, and the appearance of complex political and social institutions. **2.** The type of culture and society developed by a particular nation or region or in a particular epoch: *Mayan civiliza-*

cittern
Mid 18th-century German

civet
Otter civet
Cynogale bennettii

ă pat	oi boy
ā pay	ou out
âr care	o͝o took
ä father	o͞o boot
ĕ pet	ŭ cut
ē be	ûr urge
ĭ pit	th thin
ī pie	*th* this
îr pier	hw which
ŏ pot	zh vision
ō toe	ə about, item
ô paw	♦ regionalism

Stress marks: ′ (primary); ′ (secondary), as in **dictionary** (dĭk′shə-nĕr′ē)

tion; the civilization of ancient Rome. **3.** The act or process of civilizing or reaching a civilized state. **4.** Cultural or intellectual refinement; good taste. **5.** Modern society with its conveniences: *returned to civilization after camping in the mountains.*

civ·i·lize (sĭv′ə-līz′) *tr.v.* **-lized, -liz·ing, -liz·es. 1.** To raise from barbarism to an enlightened stage of development; bring out of a primitive or savage state. **2.** To educate in matters of culture and refinement; make more polished or sophisticated. **—civ′i·liz′a·ble** *adj.* **—civ′i·liz′er** *n.*

civ·i·lized (sĭv′ə-līzd′) *adj.* **1.** Having a highly developed society and culture. **2.** Showing evidence of moral and intellectual advancement; humane, ethical, and reasonable: *terrorist acts that shocked the civilized world.* **3.** Marked by refinement in taste and manners; cultured; polished.

civil law *n. Abbr.* **c.l., C.L.** *Law.* **1.** The body of laws of a state or nation dealing with the rights of private citizens. **2.** The law of ancient Rome as embodied in the Justinian code, especially that which applied to private citizens. **3.** A system of law having its origin in Roman law, as opposed to common law or canon law.

civil libertarian *n.* One who is actively concerned with the protection of those rights guaranteed to the individual by law: *"Civil libertarians tend to assume such tests must be an illegal invasion of privacy"* (Larry Martz).

civil lib·er·ties (lĭb′ər-tēz) *pl.n.* Fundamental individual rights, such as freedom of speech and religion, protected by law against unwarranted governmental or other interference.

civil marriage *n.* A marriage ceremony performed by a civil official.

civil rights *pl.n.* The rights belonging to an individual by virtue of citizenship, especially the fundamental freedoms and privileges guaranteed by the 13th and 14th Amendments to the U.S. Constitution and by subsequent acts of Congress, including civil liberties, due process, equal protection of the laws, and freedom from discrimination. **—civil rights** or **civ·il-rights** (sĭv′əl-rīts′) *adj.* **1.** Of or relating to such rights or privileges: *civil rights legislation.* **2.** Of or relating to a political movement, especially during the 1950's and 1960's, devoted to securing equal opportunity and treatment for members of minority groups. **—civil righter** *n.*

civil servant *n.* A person employed in the civil service.

civil service *n. Abbr.* **CS 1.** Those branches of public service that are not legislative, judicial, or military and in which employment is usually based on competitive examination. **2.** The entire body of persons employed by the civil branches of a government.

civil war *n.* **1.** A war between factions or regions of the same country. **2.** A state of hostility or conflict between elements within an organization: *"The broadcaster is in the midst of a civil war that has brought it to the brink of a complete management overhaul"* (Bill Powell). **3. Civil War.** The war in the United States between the Union and the Confederacy from 1861 to 1865. Also called *War Between the States.* **4. Civil War.** The war in England between the Parliamentarians and the Royalists from 1642 to 1648.

civ·vies also **civ·ies** (sĭv′ēz) *pl.n. Slang.* Civilian clothes. [Shortening and alteration of CIVILIAN.]

C.J. *abbr. Law.* Chief Justice.

ck. *abbr.* **1.** Cask. **2.** Check.

cl *abbr.* Centiliter.

Cl The symbol for the element **chlorine.**

cl. *abbr.* **1.** Class; classification. **2.** Clause. **3.** Clearance. **4.** Closet. **5.** Cloth.

c.l. *abbr.* **1.** Carload. **2.** Or **C.L.** Civil law. **3.** Common law.

♦ **clab·ber** (klăb′ər) *n.* Sour, curdled milk. Also called ♦ *thick milk.* **—clabber** *tr. & intr.v.* **-bered, -ber·ing, -bers.** To curdle. [Short for BONNYCLABBER.]

clack (klăk) *v.* **clacked, clack·ing, clacks.** *—intr.* **1.** To make an abrupt, sharp sound, as in the collision of two hard surfaces. **2.** To chatter thoughtlessly or at length. **3.** To cackle or cluck, as a hen. *—tr.* To cause to make an abrupt, sharp sound. **—clack** *n.* **1.** A clacking sound: *the clack of an old-fashioned typewriter.* **2.** Something that makes a clacking sound. **3.** Thoughtless, prolonged talk; chatter. [Middle English *clakken,* from Old Norse *klaka,* of imitative origin.] **—clack′er** *n.*

clack valve *n.* A hinged valve that permits fluids to flow in only one direction and clacks when the valve closes.

Clac·ton (klăk′tən) also **Clac·ton-on-Sea** (-ŏn-sē′, -ôn-). An urban district of southeast England on the North Sea. It is a resort situated on high cliffs overlooking the sea. Population, 44,000.

Clac·to·ni·an (klăk-tō′nē-ən) *adj. Archaeology.* Of or relating to a lower Paleolithic culture of northwest Europe. [After CLACTON.]

Clac·ton-on-Sea (klăk′tən-ŏn-sē′, -ôn-). See **Clacton.**

clad[1] (klăd) *tr.v.* **clad, clad·ding, clads. 1.** To sheathe or cover (a metal) with a metal. **2.** To cover with a protective or insulating layer of other material. [Back-formation from CLADDING.]

clad[2] (klăd) *v.* A past tense and a past participle of **clothe.**

clad·ding (klăd′ĭng) *n.* **1.** A metal coating bonded onto another metal under high pressure and temperature. **2.** A protective or insulating layer fixed to the outside of a building or another structure. [Earlier, clothing, possibly from CLAD[2].]

clade (klād) *n.* A group of organisms, such as a species, whose members share homologous features derived from a common ancestor. [From Greek *klados,* branch.]

cla·dist (klăd′ĭst, klā′dist) *n.* One who classifies organisms according to the principles of cladistics.

cla·dis·tics (klə-dĭs′tĭks) *n. (used with a sing. verb).* A system of classification based on the phylogenetic relationships and evolutionary history of groups of organisms. **—cla·dis′tic** *adj.* **—cla·dis′ti·cal·ly** *adv.*

cla·doc·er·an (klə-dŏs′ər-ən) *n.* Any of various small, mostly freshwater crustaceans of the order Cladocera, which includes the water fleas. **—cladoceran** *adj.* Of or belonging to the order Cladocera. [From New Latin *Cladocera,* order name : Greek *klados,* branch + Greek *keras,* horn; see **ker-**[1] in Appendix.]

clad·ode (klăd′ōd′) *n.* See **cladophyll.** [New Latin *cladōdium,* from Late Greek *kladōdēs,* many-branched, from Greek *klados,* branch.] **—cla·do′di·al** (klə-dō′dē-əl) *adj.*

clad·o·gen·e·sis (klăd′ə-jĕn′ĭ-sĭs) *n.* The evolutionary change and diversification resulting from the branching off of new taxa from common ancestral lineages. [Greek *klados,* branch + -GENESIS.] **—clad′o·ge·net′ic** (-jə-nĕt′ĭk) *adj.* **—clad′o·ge·net′i·cal·ly** *adv.*

clad·o·gram (klăd′ə-grăm′, klā′də-) *n.* A branching, treelike diagram in which the endpoints of the branches represent specific species of organisms. It is used to illustrate phylogenetic relationships and show points at which various species have diverged from common ancestral forms. [Greek *klados,* branch + -GRAM.]

clad·o·phyll (klăd′ə-fĭl′) *n.* A branch or portion of a stem that resembles and functions as a leaf. Also called *cladode.* [Greek *klados,* twig + -PHYLL.]

cla·fou·ti (klä-fo͞o-tē′) *n.* A fruit and custard pastry made with a thick batter. [French *clafoutis,* from Old French : *claufir,* to attach with nails (from Latin *clavō figere* : *clavō,* ablative sing. of *clavis,* nail + *figere,* to fix) + *foutis,* nominalized form of *foutre,* to stuff. See FOOTLE.]

claim (klām) *tr.v.* **claimed, claim·ing, claims. 1.** To demand or ask for as one's own or one's due; assert one's right to: *claim a reward.* **2.** To take in a violent manner as if by right: *a hurricane that claimed two lives.* **3.** To state to be true, especially when open to question; assert or maintain: *claimed he had won the race; a candidate claiming many supporters.* **4.** To deserve or call for; require: *problems that claim her attention.* **—claim** *n.* **1.** A demand for something as rightful or due. **2.** A basis for demanding something; a title or right. **3.** Something claimed in a formal or legal manner, especially a tract of public land staked out by a miner or homesteader. **4. a.** A demand for payment in accordance with an insurance policy or other formal arrangement. **b.** The sum of money demanded. **5.** A statement of something as a fact; an assertion of truth: *makes no claim to be a cure.* ***—idiom.*** **lay claim to.** To assert one's right to or ownership of. [Middle English *claimen,* from Old French *clamer, claim-,* from Latin *clāmāre,* to call. See **kelə-**[2] in Appendix.] **—claim′a·ble** *adj.* **—claim′er** *n.*

SYNONYMS: *claim, pretense, pretension, title.* The central meaning shared by these nouns is "a legitimate or asserted right to demand something as one's rightful due": *had a strong legal claim to the property; makes no pretense to scholarliness; pretensions to the chairmanship unjustified in every particular; has no title to our thanks.* See also Synonyms at **demand.**

claim·ant (klā′mənt) *n.* A party that makes a claim.

Clair (klâr), **René.** Originally René Chomette. 1898–1981. French filmmaker. An early exponent of productions with sound, he directed the classics *Sous les Toits de Paris* (1929) and *Le Million* (1931).

clair·au·di·ence (klâr-ô′dē-əns) *n.* The supposed power to hear things outside the range of normal perception. [CLAIR(VOYANCE) + AUDIENCE.] **—clair·au′di·ent** *adj. & n.*

clair de lune (klâr′ də lo͞on′) *n.* **1.** A pale, grayish-blue glaze applied to various kinds of Chinese porcelain. **2.** The color of such a glaze. [French : *clair,* light + *de,* of + *lune,* moon.]

claire-ob·scure (klâr′əb-skyo͝or′) *n.* See **chiaroscuro.** [French *clair-obscur,* translation of Italian *chiaroscuro.*]

clair·voy·ance (klâr-voi′əns) *n.* **1.** The supposed power to see objects or events that cannot be perceived by the senses. **2.** Acute intuitive insight or perceptiveness.

clair·voy·ant (klâr-voi′ənt) *adj.* **1.** Of or relating to clairvoyance. **2.** Having the supposed power to see objects or events that cannot be perceived by the senses. **—clairvoyant** *n.* A person, such as a medium, possessing the supposed power of clairvoyance. [French : *clair,* clear (from Latin *clārus;* see **kelə-**[2] in Appendix) + *voyant,* present participle of *voir,* to see (from Latin *vidēre;* see **weid-** in Appendix).]

clam[1] (klăm) *n.* **1. a.** Any of various usually burrowing marine and freshwater bivalve mollusks of the class Pelecypoda, including members of the genera *Venus* and *Mya,* many of which are edible. **b.** The soft, edible body of such a mollusk. **2.** *Informal.* A close-mouthed person, especially one who can keep a secret. **3.** *Slang.* A dollar: *set me back 75 clams.* **—clam** *intr.v.* **clammed, clam·ming, clams.** To hunt for clams. ***—phrasal verb.*** **clam up.** *Informal.* To refuse to talk. [From obsolete *clam-shell,* shell that clamps, clam, from CLAM[2].] **—clam′mer** *n.*

clam[2] (klăm) *n.* A clamp or vise. [Middle English, from Old English *clam, clamm,* bond, fetter.]

cla·mant (klā′mənt, klăm′ənt) *adj.* **1.** Clamorous; loud. **2.**

Demanding attention; pressing: *clamant needs.* [Latin *clāmāns, clāmant-,* present participle of *clāmāre,* to cry out. See **kelə-²** in Appendix.] **—cla′mant·ly** *adv.*

clam·bake (klăm′bāk′) *n.* **1.** A seashore picnic where clams, fish, corn, and other foods are traditionally baked on heated stones covered with seaweed. **2.** *Informal.* A party or gathering, especially a noisy and lively one.

clam·ber (klăm′bər, klăm′ər) *intr.v.* **-bered, -ber·ing, -bers.** To climb with difficulty, especially on all fours; scramble. **—clamber** *n.* A difficult, awkward climb. [Middle English *clambren,* probably frequentative of *climben,* to climb. See CLIMB.] **—clam′ber·er** *n.*

clam·ber·ing (klăm′bər-ĭng, klăm′ər-) *adj.* Of or relating to a plant, often one without tendrils, that sprawls or climbs.

clam chowder *n.* Any of various soups made with clams, salt pork, potatoes, onions, and milk or tomatoes.

clam dig·gers or **clam·dig·gers** (klăm′dĭg′ərz) *pl.n.* Casual pants in a mid-calf length.

♦**clam-flat** (klăm′flat′) *n. New England.* A level stretch of soft tidal mud where clams burrow.

clam·my (klăm′ē) *adj.* **-mi·er, -mi·est. 1.** Disagreeably moist, sticky, and cold to the touch: *a clammy handshake.* **2.** Damp and unpleasant: *clammy weather.* **3.** Uneasy; apprehensive: *The ghost town gave us a clammy feeling.* [Middle English, sticky, probably from *clam* (from Old English mud, clay) or from Middle Low German *klam,* stickiness.] **—clam′mi·ly** *adv.* **—clam′mi·ness** *n.*

clam·or (klăm′ər) *n.* **1.** A loud outcry; a hubbub. **2.** A vehement expression of discontent or protest: *a clamor in the press for pollution control.* **3.** A loud, sustained noise. See Synonyms at **noise. —clamor** *v.* **-ored, -or·ing, -ors.** *—intr.* **1.** To make a loud, sustained noise or outcry. **2.** To make insistent demands or complaints: *clamored for tax reforms.* *—tr.* **1.** To exclaim insistently and noisily: *The representatives clamored their disapproval.* **2.** To influence or force by clamoring: *clamored the mayor into resigning.* [Middle English *clamour,* from Old French, from Latin *clāmor,* shout, from *clāmāre,* to cry out. See **kelə-²** in Appendix.] **—clam′or·er** *n.*

clam·or·ous (klăm′ər-əs) *adj.* **1.** Making or marked by loud outcry or sustained din. **2.** Insistently demanding attention; importunate. See Synonyms at **vociferous. —clam′or·ous·ly** *adv.* **—clam′or·ous·ness** *n.*

clam·our (klăm′ər) *n. & v. Chiefly British.* Variant of **clamor.**

clamp (klămp) *n.* **1.** Any of various devices used to join, grip, support, or compress mechanical or structural parts. **2.** Any of various tools with opposing, often adjustable sides or parts for bracing objects or holding them together. **—clamp** *tr.v.* **clamped, clamp·ing, clamps. 1.** To fasten, grip, or support with or as if with a clamp. **2.** To establish by authority; impose: *clamped a tax on imports.* ***—phrasal verb.*** **clamp down.** To become more strict or repressive; impose controls: *clamping down on polluters.* [Middle English, from Middle Dutch *klampe.*]

clamp·down (klămp′doun′) *n.* An imposing of restrictions or controls: *"Advertisers and broadcasters would raise howls of protest against any strong clampdown"* (Wall Street Journal).

clamp·er (klăm′pər) *n.* One that clamps, especially a spiked plate attached to the sole of a shoe to prevent slipping on ice.

clam·shell (klăm′shĕl′) *n.* **1.** The shell of a clam. **2.** Any of various devices with two hinged jaws, used for dredging or digging.

clam·worm (klăm′wûrm′) *n.* Any of various segmented burrowing marine worms of the genus *Nereis,* commonly used as bait for fishing. Also called *nereis.*

clan (klăn) *n.* **1.** A traditional social unit in the Scottish Highlands, consisting of a number of families claiming a common ancestor and following the same hereditary chieftain. **2.** A division of a tribe tracing descent from a common ancestor. **3.** A large group of relatives, friends, or associates. [Middle English, from Scottish Gaelic *clann,* family, from Old Irish *cland,* offspring, from Latin *planta,* plant, sprout. See **plat-** in Appendix.]

clan·des·tine (klăn-dĕs′tĭn) *adj.* Kept or done in secret, often in order to conceal an illicit or improper purpose. See Synonyms at **secret.** [Latin *clandestīnus,* probably blend of **clam-de,* secretly (from *clam;* see **kel-¹** in Appendix) and *intestīnus,* internal; see INTESTINE.] **—clan·des′tine·ly** *adv.* **—clan·des′tine·ness, clan′des·tin′i·ty** *n.*

clang (klăng) *n.* **1.** A loud, resonant, metallic sound. **2.** The strident call of a crane or goose. **—clang** *intr. & tr.v.* **clanged, clang·ing, clangs.** To make or cause to make a clang. [Probably from Latin *clangere,* to ring, clang.]

clang·er (klăng′ər) *n. Chiefly British.* A blunder; a faux pas.

clan·gor (klăng′ər, klăng′gər) *n.* **1.** A clang or repeated clanging. **2.** A loud racket; a din. **—clangor** *intr.v.* **-gored, -gor·ing, -gors.** To make a clangor. [Latin, from *clangere,* to clang.] **—clan′gor·ous** *adj.* **—clan′gor·ous·ly** *adv.*

clan·gour (klăng′ər, klăng′gər) *n. & v. Chiefly British.* Variant of **clangor.**

clank (klăngk) *n.* A metallic sound, sharp and hard but not resonant: *the clank of chains.* **—clank** *intr.v.* **clanked, clank·ing, clanks.** To make a sharp, hard, metallic sound. [Probably imitative.] **—clank′y** *adj.*

clan·nish (klăn′ĭsh) *adj.* **1.** Of, relating to, or characteristic of a clan. **2.** Inclined to cling together as a group and exclude outsiders. **—clan′nish·ly** *adv.* **—clan′nish·ness** *n.*

clans·man (klănz′mən) *n.* A man belonging to a clan.

clans·wom·an (klănz′wo͝om′ən) *n.* A woman belonging to a clan.

clap¹ (klăp) *v.* **clapped, clap·ping, claps.** *—intr.* **1.** To strike the palms of the hands together with a sudden explosive sound, as in applauding. **2.** To come together suddenly with a sharp sound. *—tr.* **1.** To strike together with a sharp sound, as one hard surface on another: *clapped a book on the desk.* **2.** To strike (the hands) together with an abrupt, loud sound, usually repeatedly: *clapped hands in time to the music.* **3.** To strike lightly but firmly with the open hand, as in greeting: *clapped me on the shoulder.* **4.** To put or place quickly and firmly: *clapped the purse snatcher in jail; clapped a lid on the box.* **5.** To arrange hastily: *clapped together a plan.* **—clap** *n.* **1.** The act or sound of clapping the hands. **2.** A sudden, loud, explosive sound: *a clap of thunder.* **3.** A sharp blow with the open hand; a slap. **4.** *Obsolete.* A sudden stroke of fortune, especially of bad luck. [Middle English *clappen,* from Old English *clæppan, clappian,* to throb, and from Old Norse *klappa,* to clap, pat.]

clap² (klăp) *n. Vulgar Slang.* Gonorrhea. Often used with *the.* [Probably from obsolete French *clapoir,* bubo, from Old French *clapier,* brothel, from Old Provençal, rabbit warren, from *clap,* heap of stones, perhaps of Celtic origin.]

clap·board (klăb′ərd, klăp′bôrd′, -bōrd′) *n.* A long, narrow board with one edge thicker than the other, overlapped horizontally to cover the outer walls of frame structures. Also called *weatherboard.* *—attributive.* Often used to modify another noun: *a clapboard house; a clapboard roof.* **—clapboard** *tr.v.* **-board·ed, -board·ing, -boards.** To cover with clapboards. [Partial translation of Dutch *klaphout* : *klappen,* to split, crack + Middle Dutch *holt,* board.]

clap·per (klăp′ər) *n.* **1.** One who applauds. **2.** The tongue of a bell. **3.** *Slang.* The tongue of a garrulous person. **4. clappers.** Two flat pieces of wood held between the fingers and struck together rhythmically.

clapper rail *n.* A North American bird *(Rallus longirostris)* of coastal marshes, characterized by a henlike appearance, brownish plumage, long bill, and clattering cry.

clap·trap (klăp′trăp′) *n.* Pretentious, insincere, or empty language. See Synonyms at **bombast.** [Obsolete *claptrap,* a theatrical trick to win applause : CLAP¹ + TRAP¹.]

claque (klăk) *n.* **1.** A group of persons hired to applaud at a performance. **2.** A group of fawning admirers. [French, from *claquer,* to clap, of imitative origin.]

Clare·mont (klâr′mŏnt′). A city of southern California northeast of Pomona. It is mainly residential and the site of the associated Claremont Colleges. Population, 30,950.

clar·ence (klăr′əns) *n.* A four-wheeled closed carriage with seats for four passengers. [After the Duke of *Clarence* (1765–1837), later William IV of England.]

Clar·en·don (klăr′ən-dən), First Earl of. Title of Edward Hyde. 1609–1674. English politician and historian who was falsely accused of treason and banished (1667). While in France he wrote his major work, *The History of the Rebellion and Civil Wars in England* (1702–1704).

Clare of As·si·si (klâr; ə-sē′zē, -sē, ə-sĭs′ē), Saint. 1194–1253. Italian nun and religious leader who founded with Saint Francis of Assisi the first Franciscan order of nuns, the Poor Clares. She was canonized in 1255.

clar·et (klăr′ĭt) *n.* **1.a.** A dry red wine produced in the Bordeaux region of France. **b.** A similar wine made elsewhere. **2.** *Color.* A dark or grayish purplish red to dark purplish pink. [Middle English, light-colored wine, from Old French *(vin) claret,* diminutive of *clair,* clear, from Latin *clārus.* See CLEAR.]

claret cup *n.* A chilled drink made of claret mixed with soda, fruit juices, brandy, and sugar.

clar·i·fy (klăr′ə-fī′) *v.* **-fied, -fy·ing, -fies.** *—tr.* **1.** To make clear or easier to understand; elucidate: *clarified her intentions.* **2.** To clear of confusion or uncertainty: *clarify the mind.* **3.** To make clear by removing impurities or solid matter, as by heating gently: *clarify butter.* *—intr.* To become clear. [Middle English *clarifien,* from Old French *clarifier,* from Late Latin *clārificāre* : Latin *clārus,* clear; see CLEAR + Latin *-ficāre,* -fy.] **—clar′i·fi·ca′tion** (-fĭ-kā′shən) *n.* **—clar′i·fi′er** *n.*

clar·i·net (klăr′ə-nĕt′) *n. Music.* A woodwind instrument having a straight, cylindrical tube with a flaring bell and a single-reed mouthpiece, played by means of finger holes and keys. [French *clarinette,* feminine diminutive of Old French *clarin, clarion,* clarion; see CLARION, or of Provençal *clarin,* oboe (from Old Provençal *clar,* clear, from Latin *clārus;* see CLEAR).] **—clar′i·net′ist, clar′i·net′tist** *n.*

clar·i·on (klăr′ē-ən) *adj.* Loud and clear: *a clarion call to resistance.* **—clarion** *n. Music.* **1.** A medieval trumpet with a shrill, clear tone. **2.** The sound of this instrument or a sound resembling it. [Middle English *clarioun,* a clarion, from Old French *clarion,* from Medieval Latin *clāriō, clāriōn-,* from Latin *clārus,* clear. See CLEAR.]

clar·i·ty (klăr′ĭ-tē) *n.* **1.** Clearness of appearance: *the clarity of the mountain air.* **2.** Clearness of thought or style; lucidity: *writes with clarity and perception.* [Middle English *clarite,*

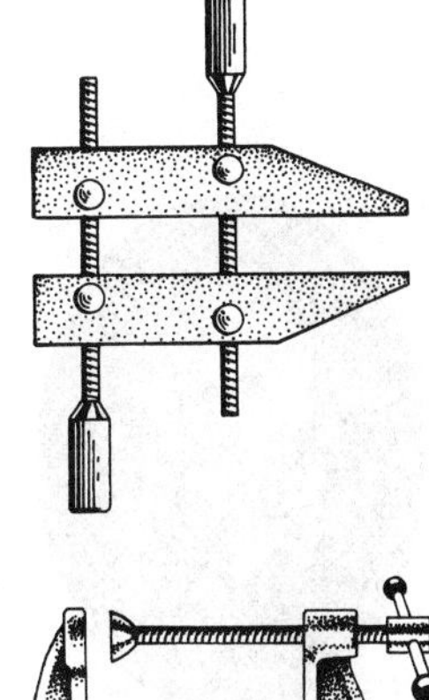

clamp

clarinet

ă pat	oi boy
ā pay	ou out
âr care	o͝o took
ä father	o͞o boot
ĕ pet	ŭ cut
ē be	ûr urge
ĭ pit	th thin
ī pie	*th* this
îr pier	hw which
ŏ pot	zh vision
ō toe	ə about, item
ô paw	♦ regionalism

Stress marks: **′** (primary); ′ (secondary), as in **dictionary** (dĭk′shə-nĕr′ē)

brightness, from Latin *clāritās,* clearness, from *clārus,* clear. See CLEAR.]

Clark, (klärk), **Charles Joseph.** Known as "Joe." Born 1939. Canadian politician who served as prime minister (1979–1980).

Clark, George Rogers. 1752–1818. American military leader and frontiersman who led numerous raids on British troops and Native Americans in the Northwest Territory during the Revolutionary War.

Clark, John Bates. 1847–1938. American economist known for his theory of marginal productivity. He wrote *The Philosophy of Wealth* (1885) and *The Distribution of Wealth* (1899).

Clark, Kenneth Bancroft. Born 1914. Panamanian-born American psychologist and author who demonstrated the psychological effects of racial segregation and ghetto life, influencing the Supreme Court ruling in *Brown* v. *Board of Education* (1954).

Clark, Mark Wayne. 1896–1984. American general who was Allied commander in North Africa and Italy in World War II and commander of United Nations forces in Korea (1952–1953).

Clark, Tom Campbell. 1899–1977. American jurist who served as an associate justice of the U.S. Supreme Court (1949–1967).

Clark, William. 1770–1838. American explorer who joined Meriwether Lewis in an expedition to the Pacific Ocean (1804–1806). Clark was responsible for the careful mapmaking en route.

William Clark

Clarke (klärk), **Charles Cowden.** 1787–1877. British Shakespearean scholar who collaborated with his wife **Mary Victoria Clarke** (1809–1898) on *Recollections of Writers* (1878) and *The Shakespeare Key* (1879).

Clarke, John Hessin. 1857–1945. American jurist who served as an associate justice of the U.S. Supreme Court (1916–1922).

Clark Fork. A river rising in southwest Montana near Butte and flowing about 579 km (360 mi) generally north then northwest to Pend Oreille Lake in the Idaho Panhandle.

clark·i·a (klär′kē-ə) *n.* Any of various annual, chiefly western North American plants of the genus *Clarkia,* several of which are cultivated for their showy red, purple, pink, or white flowers. [New Latin *Clarkia,* genus name, after William CLARK.]

Clarks·burg (klärks′bûrg′). A city of northern West Virginia south-southeast of Wheeling. It was an important Union supply base during the Civil War. Population, 22,371.

Clarks·dale (klärks′dāl′). A city of northwest Mississippi near the Arkansas border. It is a manufacturing center. Population, 21,137.

Clarks·ville (klärks′vĭl′). A city of northwest Tennessee on the Cumberland and Red rivers northwest of Nashville. An important tobacco market, it is also a manufacturing center. Population, 54,777.

clar·y (klâr′ē) *n., pl.* **-ies.** A stout aromatic Mediterranean herb *(Salvia sclarea)* in the mint family, having showy violet, pink, or white flower clusters and yielding an essential oil used as a flavoring and in perfumery. Also called *clary sage.* [Middle English *clare,* from Medieval Latin *sclarea* and from Old English *slaria.*]

clash (klăsh) *v.* **clashed, clash·ing, clash·es.** —*intr.* **1.** To collide with a loud, harsh, usually metallic noise: *cymbals clashing.* **2.** To come into conflict; be in opposition: *factions that clashed on a tax increase; an eyewitness account that clashed with published reports.* **3.** To create an unpleasant visual impression when placed together: *colors that clash.* —*tr.* To strike together with a loud, harsh, metallic noise. —**clash** *n.* **1.** A loud, harsh noise, such as that made by two metal objects in collision. **2.** A conflict, as between opposing or irreconcilable ideas. See Synonyms at **discord. 3.** An encounter between hostile forces; a battle or skirmish. [Imitative.]

clasp (klăsp) *n.* **1.** A fastening, such as a hook or buckle, used to hold two or more objects or parts together. **2. a.** An embrace or hug. **b.** A grip or grasp of the hand. **3.** A small metal bar or other device attached to the ribbon of a military decoration to indicate the action or service for which it was awarded or an additional award of the same medal. —**clasp** *tr.v.* **clasped, clasp·ing, clasps. 1.** To fasten with or as if with a clasp. **2.** To hold in a tight embrace. **3.** To grip firmly in or with the hand; grasp. [Middle English *claspe,* probably ultimately from Old English *clyppan,* to grasp, hold.]

clasp·er (klăs′pər) *n.* **1.** One that clasps. **2.** Any of the appendages of the male of certain insects and crustaceans that are used during copulation to hold the female. **3.** A posterior extension on each of the pelvic fins of male elasmobranch fishes that aids in the transmission of sperm during copulation.

clasp·ing (klăs′pĭng) *adj. Botany.* Denoting a leaf whose base partially or completely surrounds a stem.

clasp knife *n.* A pocketknife with a folding blade.

class (klăs) *n. Abbr.* **cl. 1.** A set, collection, group, or configuration containing members regarded as having certain attributes or traits in common; a kind or category. **2.** A division based on quality, rank, or grade, as: **a.** A grade of mail: *a package sent third class.* **b.** A quality of accommodation on public transport: *tourist class.* **3. a.** A social stratum whose members share certain economic, social, or cultural characteristics: *the lower-income classes.* **b.** Social rank or caste, especially high rank. **c.** *Informal.* Elegance of style, taste, and manner: *an actor with class.* **4. a.** A group of students or alumni who have the same year of graduation. **b.** A group of students who meet at a regularly scheduled time to study the same subject. **c.** The period during which such a group meets: *had to stay after class.* **5.** *Biology.* A taxonomic category ranking below a phylum or division and above an order. See table at **taxonomy. 6.** *Statistics.* An interval in a frequency distribution. —*attributive.* Often used to modify another noun: *class warfare; a class picnic.* —**class** *tr.v.* **classed, class·ing, class·es.** To arrange, group, or rate according to qualities or characteristics; assign to a class. [French *classe,* from Latin *classis,* class of citizens. See **kelə-**[2] in Appendix.]

class. *abbr.* **1.** Classic; classical. **2.** Classification; classified.

class act *n. Informal.* One of distinctive and superior quality: *"In this world of often tacky entertainment they have just witnessed the definition of a 'class act'"* (Linda Bird Francke).

class action *n. Law.* A lawsuit brought by one or more plaintiffs on behalf of a large group of others who have a common interest. —**class′-ac′tion** (klăs′ăk′shən) *adj.*

class-con·scious (klăs′kŏn′shəs) *adj.* **1.** Aware of belonging to a particular socioeconomic class. **2.** Supportive of class solidarity. —**class′-con′scious·ness** *n.*

clas·ses (klăs′ēz) *n.* Plural of **classis.**

clas·sic (klăs′ĭk) *adj.* **1. a.** Belonging to the highest rank or class. **b.** Serving as the established model or standard: *a classic example of colonial architecture.* **c.** Having lasting significance or worth; enduring. **2. a.** Adhering or conforming to established standards and principles: *a classic piece of research.* **b.** Of a well-known type; typical: *a classic mistake.* **3.** *Abbr.* **class.** Of or characteristic of the literature, art, and culture of ancient Greece and Rome; classical. **4. a.** Formal, refined, and restrained in style. **b.** Simple and harmonious; elegant: *the classic cut of a suit; the classic lines of a clipper ship.* **5.** Having historical or literary associations: *classic battlefields of the Civil War.* —**classic** *n.* **1.** An artist, author, or work generally considered to be of the highest rank or excellence, especially one of enduring significance. **2.** A work recognized as definitive in its field. **3. a.** A literary work of ancient Greece or Rome. **b. classics.** The languages and literature of ancient Greece and Rome. Used with *the.* **c.** One that is of the highest rank or class: *The car was a classic of automotive design.* **4.** A typical or traditional example. **5.** *Informal.* A superior or unusual example of its kind: *The reason he gave for being late was a classic.* **6.** A traditional event, especially a major sporting event that is held annually: *a golf classic.*

clas·si·cal (klăs′ĭ-kəl) *adj.* **1.** *Abbr.* **class. a.** Of or relating to the ancient Greeks and Romans, especially their art, architecture, and literature. **b.** Conforming to the artistic and literary models of ancient Greece and Rome. **c.** Versed in the classics: *a classical scholar.* **2.** Of or relating to the most artistically developed stage of a civilization: *Chinese classical poetry.* **3.** *Abbr.* **class.** *Music.* **a.** Of or relating to European music during the latter half of the 18th and the early 19th centuries: *a classical work by Mozart.* **b.** Of or relating to music in the educated European tradition, such as symphony and opera, as opposed to popular or folk music. **4.** Of, relating to, or being a variety of a language that is epitomized by a prestigious body of literature. **5. a.** Standard and authoritative rather than new or experimental: *classical methods of navigation.* **b.** Well-known; classic: *the classical argument between free trade and protectionism.* **6.** Of or relating to nonrelativistic or nonquantum physics: *classical mechanics.* **7.** Relating to or consisting of studies in the humanities and general sciences: *a classical curriculum.* —**clas′si·cal′i·ty** (-kăl′ĭ-tē), **clas′si·cal·ness** *n.* —**clas′si·cal·ly** *adv.*

classical conditioning *n. Psychology.* A process of behavior modification by which a subject comes to respond in a desired manner to a previously neutral stimulus that has been repeatedly presented along with an unconditioned stimulus that elicits the desired response.

clas·si·cism (klăs′ĭ-sĭz′əm) also **clas·si·cal·ism** (-kə-lĭz′əm) *n.* **1.** Aesthetic attitudes and principles manifested in the art, architecture, and literature of ancient Greece and Rome and characterized by emphasis on form, simplicity, proportion, and restraint. **2.** Adherence to the aesthetic values embodied in ancient Greek and Roman art and literature. **3.** Classical scholarship. **4.** A Greek or Latin expression or idiom.

clas·si·cist (klăs′ĭ-sĭst) *n.* **1.** One versed in the classics; a classical scholar. **2.** An adherent of classicism. **3.** An advocate of the study of ancient Greek and Latin.

clas·si·cize (klăs′ĭ-sīz′) *v.* **-cized, -ciz·ing, -ciz·es.** —*tr.* To make classic or classical. —*intr.* To conform to classic style.

clas·si·fi·ca·tion (klăs′ə-fĭ-kā′shən) *n. Abbr.* **cl., class. 1.** The act or result of classifying. **2.** A category or class. **3.** *Biology.* The systematic grouping of organisms into categories on the basis of evolutionary or structural relationships between them; taxonomy. —**clas′si·fi·ca·to′ri·ly** (klăs′ə-fĭ-kə-tôr′ə-lē, -tōr′-, klə-sĭf′ĭ-) *adv.* —**clas′si·fi·ca·to′ry** (klăs′ə-fĭ-kə-tôr′ē, -tōr′ē, klə-sĭf′ĭ-, klăs′ə-fĭ-kā′tə-rē) *adj.*

clas·si·fied (klăs′ə-fīd′) *adj. Abbr.* **class. 1.** Arranged in classes or categories. **2.** Available to authorized persons only, as for reasons of national security: *a classified document.*

classified advertisement *n.* An advertisement, usually brief and in small type, printed in a newspaper or magazine under headings with others of the same category.

clas·si·fi·er (klăs′ə-fī′ər) *n. Linguistics.* A word or morpheme used in some languages in certain contexts, such as counting, that indicates the semantic class to which an item belongs. For example, *hon* is used in Japanese in counting long, slender objects such as sticks or pencils.

ă pat	oi boy
ā pay	ou out
âr care	ŏŏ took
ä father	ōō boot
ĕ pet	ŭ cut
ē be	ûr urge
ĭ pit	th thin
ī pie	*th* this
îr pier	hw which
ŏ pot	zh vision
ō toe	ə about, item
ô paw	♦ regionalism

Stress marks: **′** (primary); ′ (secondary), as in **dictionary** (dĭk′shə-nĕr′ē)

clas·si·fy (klăs′ə-fī′) *tr.v.* **-fied, -fy·ing, -fies.** **1.** To arrange or organize according to class or category. **2.** To designate (a document, for example) as confidential, secret, or top secret. **—clas′si·fi′a·ble** *adj.*

clas·sis (klăs′ĭs) *n., pl.* **-ses** (-ēz). *Ecclesiastical.* **1.** A governing body of pastors and elders in certain Reformed churches, having jurisdiction over local churches. **2.** The district or churches governed by such a body. [Latin, class of citizens. See CLASS.]

class·ism (klăs′ĭz′əm) *n.* Bias based on social or economic class. **—class′ist** *adj. & n.*

class·less (klăs′lĭs) *adj.* **1.** Lacking social or economic distinctions of class: *a classless society.* **2.** Belonging to no particular social or economic class.

class·mate (klăs′māt′) *n.* A member of the same class at school.

clas·son (klăs′ŏn) *n.* Either of two massless bosons, the photon and the graviton, that are quanta of the two classical fields, electromagnetic and gravitational. See table at **subatomic particle.** [CLASS(ICAL) + (BOS)ON.]

class·room (klăs′ro͞om′, -ro͝om′) *n.* A room or place especially in a school in which classes are conducted: *a second-floor classroom; an outdoor classroom.* —*attributive.* Often used to modify another noun: *classroom teachers; classroom instruction.*

class·y (klăs′ē) *adj.* **-i·er, -i·est.** *Informal.* Highly stylish; elegant. **—class′i·ness** *n.*

clast (klăst) *n.* A rock fragment or grain resulting from the breakdown of larger rocks. [From Greek *klastos,* broken, from *klan,* to break.]

clas·tic (klăs′tĭk) *adj.* **1.** Separable into parts or having removable sections: *a clastic anatomical model.* **2.** *Geology.* Made up of fragments of preexisting rock; fragmental. [From Greek *klastos,* broken. See CLAST.] **—clas′tic** *n.*

clath·rate (klăth′rāt′) *adj.* **1.** *Biology.* Having a latticelike structure or appearance: *clathrate foliage.* **2.** *Chemistry.* Of or relating to inclusion complexes in which molecules of one substance are completely enclosed within the crystal structure of another. **—clathrate** *n. Chemistry.* A clathrate compound, such as urea. [Latin *clāthrātus,* past participle of *clāthrāre,* to furnish with a lattice, from *clāthrī, clātra,* lattice, from Greek *klēithra,* pl. of *klēithron,* door bar, from *kleiein,* to close.]

clat·ter (klăt′ər) *v.* **-tered, -ter·ing, -ters.** —*intr.* **1.** To make a rattling sound. **2.** To move with a rattling sound: *clattering along on roller skates.* **3.** To talk rapidly and noisily; chatter. —*tr.* To cause to make a rattling sound. **—clatter** *n.* **1.** A rattling sound: *the clatter of dishes in the kitchen.* **2.** A loud disturbance; a racket: *the clatter of the subway train.* **3.** Noisy talk; chatter. [Middle English *clateren,* from Old English **clatrian.* See **gal-** in Appendix.] **—clat′ter·er** *n.*

Clau·del (klō-dĕl′), **Paul Louis Charles.** 1868–1955. French diplomat and writer whose works include poetry and a number of plays, such as *Tidings Brought to Mary* (1912).

clau·di·ca·tion (klô′dĭ-kā′shən) *n.* A halt or lameness in a person's walk; a limp. [Middle English *claudicacioun,* from Latin *claudicātiō, claudicātiōn-,* from *claudicātus,* past participle of *claudicāre,* to limp, from *claudus,* lame.]

Clau·di·us I (klô′dē-əs). In full Tiberius Claudius Drusus Nero Germanicus. 10 B.C.–A.D. 54. Emperor of Rome (A.D. 41–54) who became ruler after Caligula was murdered. He was poisoned by his wife, Agrippina, after her son Nero was named as heir.

Claudius II. In full Marcus Aurelius Claudius Gothicus. A.D. 214–270. Emperor of Rome (268–270) who defeated the Goths in 269.

Claudius, Appius[1]. In full Appius Claudius Crassus. fl. fifth century B.C. Roman decemvir (451–449) whose actions provoked a plebian revolt and the overthrow of the decemvirs.

Claudius, Appius[2]. In full Appius Claudius Caecus. fl. fourth–third century B.C. Roman censor and consul who built the first Roman aqueduct and began construction of the Appian Way.

clause (klôz) *n. Abbr.* **cl.** **1.** *Grammar.* A group of words containing a subject and a predicate and forming part of a compound or complex sentence. **2.** A distinct article, stipulation, or provision in a document. [Middle English, from Old French, from Medieval Latin *clausa,* close of a rhetorical period, from feminine of Latin *clausus,* past participle of *claudere,* to close.] **—claus′al** (klô′zəl) *adj.*

Clau·se·witz (klou′zə-vĭts), **Karl von.** 1780–1831. Prussian army officer and military theorist who proposed the doctrines of total war and war as an instrument of policy. His treatise *On War* was published posthumously (1833).

claus·tral (klô′strəl) *adj.* Variant of **cloistral.**

claus·tro·pho·bi·a (klô′strə-fō′bē-ə) *n.* An abnormal fear of being in narrow or enclosed spaces. [Latin *claustrum,* enclosed place; see CLOISTER + –PHOBIA.] **—claus′tro·phobe′** *n.*

claus·tro·pho·bic (klô′strə-fō′bĭk) *adj.* **1.a.** Relating to or suffering from claustrophobia. **b.** Uncomfortably closed or hemmed in. **2.** *Usage Problem.* Tending to induce claustrophobia; uncomfortably confined or crowded: *a claustrophobic little room.* **—claus′tro·pho′bi·cal·ly** *adv.*

USAGE NOTE: Clinically speaking, *claustrophobic* denotes a pathological disposition to feel terror in closed spaces. But like other terms from clinical psychology (*narcissism* and *schizophrenic,* for example), the word has been applied more loosely in general usage: at first to refer to a temporary feeling of being closed in (as in *I felt claustrophobic in that tiny room*) and then to refer to a space that induces such sensations (as in *The staff members are jammed into a nest of claustrophobic offices*). This latter usage was unacceptable to 74 percent of the members of the Usage Panel, many of whom said that *claustrophobic* should be used only to describe a psychological state. In defense of this usage, however, it can be pointed out that it is well established and that it follows a general tendency to combine adjectives with nouns according to a progressively looser construal of the semantic connection between the two. Thus the phrase *topless swimsuit* came to be followed by *topless dancers,* which led in turn to *topless bars, topless districts,* and *topless ordinances.* By the same token, a room that induces a particular emotion may be described as *sad* or *cheerful* without objection, and there seems to be no principled basis for drawing the line at calling it *claustrophobic.*

cla·vate (klā′vāt′) *adj. Biology.* Having one end thickened; club-shaped: *clavate antennae.* [From Latin *clāva,* club.] **—cla′vate′ly** *adv.*

clave[1] (klāv) *v. Archaic.* A past tense of **cleave[1].**

clave[2] (klāv) *v. Archaic.* A past tense of **cleave[2].**

cla·ver (klā′vər) *Scots. intr.v.* **-vered, -ver·ing, -vers.** To gossip or talk idly. **—claver** *n.* Gossip; idle talk. [Perhaps of Celtic origin.]

clav·i·chord (klăv′ĭ-kôrd′) *n. Music.* An early keyboard instrument with a soft sound produced by small brass wedges striking horizontal strings. [Middle English *clavicord,* from Medieval Latin *clāvichordium* : Latin *clāvis,* key + Latin *chorda,* string; see CORD.] **—clav′i·chord′ist** *n.*

clavichord
Mid 16th-century Italian

clav·i·cle (klăv′ĭ-kəl) *n.* **1.** Either of two slender bones in human beings that extend from the manubrium of the sternum to the acromion of the scapula. Also called *collarbone.* **2.** One of the bones of the pectoral girdle in many vertebrates. [New Latin *clāvīcula,* from Latin, diminutive of *clāvis,* key (from its shape).] **—cla·vic′u·lar** (klə-vĭk′yə-lər) *adj.* **—cla·vic′u·late′** (-lāt′) *adj.*

cla·vier (klə-vîr′, klā′vē-ər, klăv′ē-) *n. Music.* **1.** A keyboard. **2.** A stringed keyboard instrument, such as a harpsichord. [German *Klavier,* from French *clavier,* from Old French, key-bearer, from Latin *clāvis,* key.]

cla·vus (klā′vəs, klä′-) *n.* See **corn[2].** [Latin, nail, callus.]

claw (klô) *n.* **1.** A sharp, curved nail on the toe of a mammal, reptile, or bird. **2.a.** A chela or similar pincerlike structure on the end of a limb of a crustacean or other arthropod. **b.** A limb terminating in such a structure. **3.** Something, such as the cleft end of a hammerhead, that resembles a claw. **4.** *Botany.* The narrowed, stalklike basal part of certain petals or sepals. **—claw** *tr. & intr.v.* **clawed, claw·ing, claws.** To scratch, dig, tear, or pull with or as if with claws. [Middle English *clawe,* from Old English *clawu.*] **—clawed** *adj.*

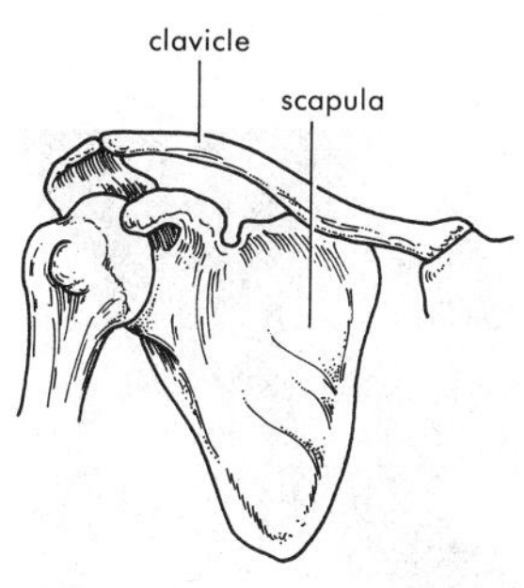

clavicle

claw hammer *n.* **1.** A hammer having a head with one end forked for removing nails. **2.** *Informal.* A swallow-tailed coat.

claw hatchet *n.* A hatchet having one end of the head forked.

clay (klā) *n.* **1.a.** A fine-grained, firm earthy material that is plastic when wet and hardens when heated, consisting primarily of hydrated silicates of aluminum and widely used in making bricks, tiles, and pottery. **b.** A hardening or nonhardening material having a consistency similar to clay and used for modeling. **2.** *Geology.* A sedimentary material with grains smaller than 0.002 millimeters in diameter. **3.** Moist, sticky earth; mud. **4.** The human body as opposed to the spirit. [Middle English *clei,* from Old English *clæg.*] **—clay′ey** (klā′ē), **clay′ish** *adj.*

Clay (klā), **Cassius Marcellus[1].** 1810–1903. American abolitionist and public official who was minister to Russia (1861–1862 and 1863–1869).

Clay (klā), **Cassius Marcellus[2].** See Muhammad **Ali.**

Clay, Henry. Known as "the Great Compromiser." 1777–1852. American politician who pushed the Missouri Compromise through the U.S. House of Representatives (1820–1821) in an effort to reconcile free and slave states.

Clay, Lucius DuBignon. 1897–1978. American army officer who commanded U.S. forces in Germany (1945–1949) and oversaw the Berlin airlift (1948).

Clay·ma·tion (klā-mā′shən). A service mark used for an animation process in which clay figurines are manipulated and filmed to produce an image of lifelike movement.

clay mineral *n.* Any of various hydrous silicates that have a fine crystalline structure and are components of clay.

clay·more (klā′môr′, -mōr′) *n.* **1.** A claymore mine. **2.** A large, double-edged broadsword formerly used by Scottish Highlanders. [Scottish Gaelic *claidheamh mōr,* Celtic sword : Old Irish *claideb,* sword + *mōr,* great; see **mē-[3]** in Appendix.]

claymore mine *n.* A lens-shaped, ground-emplaced antipersonnel mine whose blast is focused in the direction of the oncoming enemy.

clay pigeon *n.* A clay disk thrown as a flying target for skeet and trapshooting. Also called *bird.*

Clay·ton (klāt′n), **John Middleton.** 1796–1856. American public official who as secretary of state (1849–1850) negotiated the Clayton-Bulwer Treaty with Great Britain (1850), establishing the neutrality of a proposed canal across Central America.

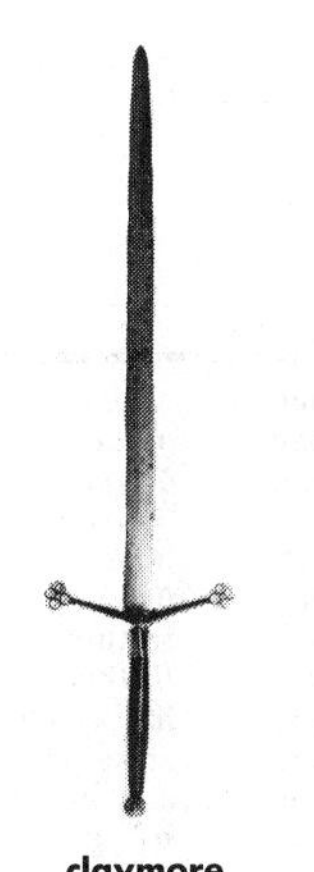

claymore

cld. *abbr.* **1.** Called. **2.** Cleared.

clean (klēn) *adj.* **clean·er, clean·est. 1.** Free from dirt, stain, or impurities; unsoiled. **2.a.** Free from foreign matter or pollution; unadulterated: *clean air; clean drinking water.* **b.** Not infected: *a clean wound.* **3.a.** Producing relatively little pollution: *a clean fuel; a cleaner, more efficient engine.* **b.** Producing relatively little radioactive fallout or contamination: *a clean nuclear bomb.* **4.** Having no imperfections or blemishes; regular: *a clean, straight line.* **5.** Free from clumsiness; deft; adroit: *a clean throw.* **6.** Devoid of restrictions or encumbrances: *a clean bill of health.* **7.** Thorough; complete: *a clean getaway.* **8.** Having few alterations or corrections; legible: *clean manuscript.* **9.** Blank: *a clean page.* **10.a.** Morally pure; virtuous: *led a clean life.* **b.** Having no marks of discredit or offense: *a clean voting record.* **11.** Fit for all readers, listeners, or audiences; not ribald or obscene: *a clean joke.* **12.** Honest or fair: *a clean fighter; a clean competition.* **13.** *Slang.* **a.** Not carrying concealed weapons or drugs. **b.** Free from narcotics addiction. **c.** Innocent of a suspected crime. **—clean** *adv.* **cleaner, cleanest. 1.** So as to be unsoiled: *wash the dishes clean.* **2.** In a fair manner: *played the game clean.* **3.** In a clean or nonpolluting manner: *a fuel that burns clean.* **4.** *Informal.* Entirely; wholly: *clean forgot the appointment.* **—clean** *v.* **cleaned, clean·ing, cleans.** *—tr.* **1.** To rid of dirt, rubbish, or impurities: *clean a room; clean a suit.* **2.** To get rid of (impurities or dirt, for example); remove: *cleaned up the trash; cleaned off the stains.* **3.** To prepare (fowl or other food) for cooking, as by removing the entrails or fat. **4.** To remove the contents from; empty: *cleaned my plate.* *—intr.* To undergo or perform an act of cleaning. ***—phrasal verbs.*** **clean out. 1.** To rid of dirt, rubbish, or impurities. **2.** To empty of contents or occupants. **3.** *Informal.* To drive or force out: *cleaned out the incompetent workers.* **4.** *Slang.* To deprive completely of money or material wealth: *The robbery cleaned us out.* **clean up. 1.** To make clean or orderly. **2.** To make oneself clean, neat, or presentable. **3.** To dispose of; settle: *cleaned up the unpaid bills.* **4.** *Slang.* To make a large profit, often in a short period of time: *cleaned up during the bull market.* ***—idiom.*** **clean house.** *Slang.* To eliminate or discard what is undesirable: *The scandal forced the company to clean house.* [Middle English *clene,* from Old English *clǣne.*] **—clean′a·ble** *adj.* **—clean′ness** *n.*

SYNONYMS: *clean, antiseptic, cleanly, immaculate, spotless.* The central meaning shared by these adjectives is "free from dirt": *clean clothing; antiseptic surgical instruments; cats, cleanly animals; an immaculate tablecloth; spotless gloves.*
ANTONYM: *dirty.*

clean and jerk *n. Sports.* A lift in weightlifting in which a weight is raised to shoulder height, held there briefly, and then pushed overhead in a rapid motion of the arms, typically accompanied by a spring or lunge from the legs.

clean-cut (klēn′kŭt′) *adj.* **1.** Clearly and sharply defined or outlined. **2.** Neat and trim in appearance.

clean·er (klē′nər) *n.* **1.** One whose work or business is cleaning. **2.** A machine or substance used in cleaning. **3.** Often **cleaners.** A dry-cleaning establishment.

clean-hand·ed (klēn′hăn′dĭd) *adj.* Innocent; guiltless.

clean-limbed (klēn′lĭmd′) *adj.* Having well-formed limbs; well-proportioned.

clean·ly (klĕn′lē) *adj.* **-li·er, -li·est.** Habitually and carefully neat and clean. See Synonyms at **clean. —cleanly** (klēn′lē) *adv.* In a clean manner. **—clean′li·ness** (klĕn′lē-nĭs) *n.*

clean room

clean room *n.* A room that is maintained virtually free of contaminants, such as dust or bacteria, used in laboratory work and in the production of precision parts for electronic or aerospace equipment. Also called *white room.*

cleanse (klĕnz) *tr.v.* **cleansed, cleans·ing, cleans·es.** To free from dirt, defilement, or guilt; purge or clean. [Middle English *clensen,* from Old English *clǣnsian,* from *clǣne,* pure, clean.]

cleans·er (klĕn′zər) *n.* **1.** A detergent, powder, or other chemical agent that removes dirt, grease, or stains. **2.** A skin lotion or cream that is used to clean the face.

clean-shav·en (klēn′shā′vən) *adj.* **1.** Having the beard or hair shaved off. **2.** Having recently shaved.

Cle·an·thes (klē-ăn′thēz). 331?–232? B.C. Greek philosopher who succeeded Zeno as head of the Stoic school.

clean·up (klēn′ŭp′) *n.* **1.** A thorough cleaning or ordering. **2.** *Informal.* The final, often routine tasks that complete a project. **3.** *Slang.* A very large profit; a killing. **4.** *Baseball.* The fourth position on a team's batting order, usually reserved for a strong hitter who can drive in extra runs. **—clean′up′** *adj.*

clear (klîr) *adj.* **clear·er, clear·est. 1.** Free from clouds, mist, or haze: *a clear day.* **2.** Free from what dims, obscures, or darkens; unclouded: *clear water; bright, clear colors.* **3.** Free from flaw, blemish, or impurity: *a clear, perfect diamond; a clear record with the police.* **4.** Free from impediment, obstruction, or hindrance; open: *a clear view; a clear path to victory.* **5.** Plain or evident to the mind; unmistakable: *a clear case of cheating.* **6.** Easily perceptible to the eye or ear; distinct. **7.** Discerning or perceiving easily; keen: *a clear mind.* **8.** Free from doubt or confusion; certain. **9.** Free from qualification or limitation; absolute: *a clear winner.* **10.** Free from guilt; untroubled: *a clear conscience.* **11.** Having been freed from contact, proximity, or connection: *At last we were clear of the danger. The ship was clear of the reef.* **12.** Free from charges or deductions; net: *a clear profit.* **13.** Containing nothing. **—clear** *adv.* **1.** Distinctly; clearly: *spoke loud and clear.* **2.** Out of the way; completely away: *stood clear of the doors.* **3.** *Informal.* All the way; completely: *slept clear through the night; read the book clear to the end.* **—clear** *v.* **cleared, clear·ing, clears.** *—tr.* **1.** To make light, clear, or bright. **2.** To rid of impurities, blemishes, muddiness, or foreign matter. **3.** To free from confusion, doubt, or ambiguity; make plain or intelligible: *cleared up the question of responsibility.* **4.a.** To rid of objects or obstructions: *clear the table; clear the road of debris.* **b.** To make (a way or clearing) by removing obstructions: *clear a path through the jungle.* **c.** To remove (objects or obstructions): *clear the dishes; clear snow from the road.* **5.a.** To remove the occupants of: *clear the theater.* **b.** To remove (people): *clear the children from the room.* **6.** *Computer Science.* **a.** To rid (a memory or buffer, for example) of instructions or data. **b.** To remove (instructions or data) from a memory. **7.** To free from a legal charge or imputation of guilt; acquit: *cleared the suspect of the murder charge.* **8.** To pass by, under, or over without contact: *The boat cleared the dock.* **9.** To settle (a debt). **10.** To gain (a given amount) as net profit or earnings. **11.** To pass (a bill of exchange, such as a check) through a clearing-house. **12.a.** To secure the approval of: *The bill cleared the Senate.* **b.** To authorize or approve: *cleared the material for publication.* **13.** To free (a ship or cargo) from legal detention at a harbor by fulfilling customs and harbor requirements. **14.** To give clearance or authorization to: *cleared the plane to land.* **15.** To free (the throat) of phlegm by making a rasping sound. *—intr.* **1.** To become clear: *The sky cleared.* **2.** To go away; disappear: *The fog cleared.* **3.a.** To exchange checks and bills or settle accounts through a clearing-house. **b.** To pass through the banking system and be debited and credited to the relevant accounts: *The check cleared.* **4.** To comply with customs and harbor requirements in discharging a cargo or in leaving or entering a port. **—clear** *n.* A clear or open space. ***—phrasal verb.*** **clear out.** *Informal.* To leave a place, usually quickly. ***—idioms.*** **clear the air.** To dispel differences or emotional tensions. **in the clear. 1.** Free from burdens or dangers. **2.** Not subject to suspicion or accusations of guilt: *The evidence showed that the suspect was in the clear.* [Middle English *cler,* from Old French, from Latin *clārus,* clear, bright. See **kelə-²** in Appendix.] **—clear′a·ble** *adj.* **—clear′er** *n.* **—clear′ly** *adv.* **—clear′ness** *n.*

SYNONYMS: *clear, limpid, lucid, pellucid, transparent.* The central meaning shared by these adjectives is "not opaque or clouded": *clear, sediment-free claret; limpid blue eyes; lucid air; a pellucid brook; transparent crystal.* See also Synonyms at **apparent.**
ANTONYM: *opaque.*

clear-air turbulence (klîr′âr′) *n. Abbr.* **CAT** A severe atmospheric turbulence that occurs under otherwise tranquil conditions and subjects aircraft to strong updrafts and downdrafts.

clear·ance (klîr′əns) *n.* **1.** The act or process of clearing. **2.** A space cleared; a clearing. **3.** *Abbr.* **cl. a.** The amount of space or distance by which a moving object clears something. **b.** The height or width of a passage: *an underpass with a 13-foot clearance.* **4.** An intervening space or distance allowing free play, as between machine parts. **5.** Permission for an aircraft, ship, or other vehicle to proceed, as after an inspection of equipment or cargo or during certain traffic conditions. **6.** Official certification of blamelessness, trustworthiness, or suitability. **7.** A sale, generally at reduced prices, to dispose of old merchandise. **8.** *Abbr.* **cl.** The passage of checks and other bills of exchange through a clearing-house. **9.** *Physiology.* **a.** The removal by the kidneys of a substance from blood plasma. **b.** Renal clearance.

Cle·ar·chus (klē-är′kəs). fl. fifth century B.C. Spartan military leader and governor of Byzantium (408). His rule was so severe that the people surrendered the city to the Athenians in his absence.

clear-cut (klîr′kŭt′) *adj.* **1.** Distinctly and sharply defined or outlined. **2.** Not ambiguous; clear and obvious. See Synonyms at **apparent, incisive. —clear-cut** *v.* **-cut, -cut·ting, -cuts.** *—tr.* To remove all of the trees in (a tract of timber) at one time. *—intr.* To log an area by removing all of the trees at one time. **—clear-cut** *n.* A tract of timberland that has been clear-cut.

clear-eyed (klîr′īd′) *adj.* **1.** Having sharp, bright eyes; keen-sighted. **2.** Mentally acute or perceptive.

Clear·field (klîr′fēld′). A city of northern Utah south of Ogden. It is a trade center in an irrigated agricultural area. Population, 17,982.

clear-head·ed (klîr′hĕd′ĭd) *adj.* Having a clear, orderly mind; sensible. **—clear′-head′ed·ly** *adv.* **—clear′-head′ed·ness** *n.*

clear·ing (klîr′ĭng) *n.* **1.** The act or process of making or becoming clear. **2.** A tract of land within a wood or other overgrown area from which trees and other obstructions have been removed. **3.** An open space: *a clearing in the fog.* **4.a.** The exchange among banks of checks, drafts, and notes and the settlement of consequent differences. **b. clearings.** The total of claims presented daily at a clearing-house.

clear·ing-house or **clear·ing·house** (klîr′ĭng-hous′) *n. Abbr.* **c.h., C.H.** An office where banks exchange checks and drafts and settle accounts.

clear-sight·ed (klîr′sī′tĭd) *adj.* **1.** Having sharp, clear vision. **2.** Perceptive; discerning. **—clear′-sight′ed·ly** *adv.* **—clear′-sight′ed·ness** *n.*

ă pat	oi boy
ā pay	ou out
âr care	o͝o took
ä father	o͞o boot
ĕ pet	ŭ cut
ē be	ûr urge
ĭ pit	th thin
ī pie	*th* this
îr pier	hw which
ŏ pot	zh vision
ō toe	ə about, item
ô paw	♦ regionalism

Stress marks: ′ (primary); ′ (secondary), as in **dictionary** (dĭk′shə-nĕr′ē)

clear·sto·ry (klîr′stôr′ē, -stōr′ē) *n.* Variant of **clerestory.**

Clear·wa·ter (klîr′wô′tər, -wŏt′ər). A city of west-central Florida west of Tampa. It is a residential and resort community. Population, 85,528.

Clearwater Mountains. A range of north-central Idaho between the Salmon River and the Bitterroot Range. The highest point is about 2,745 m (9,000 ft).

clear·weed (klîr′wēd′) *n.* Either of two eastern North American annual plants *(Pilea pumila* or *P. fontana)* having short, drooping clusters of tiny greenish-white flowers and translucent stems and leaves. Also called *richweed.*

clear·wing (klîr′wĭng′) *n.* Any of various diurnal moths of the family Sesiidae, having scaleless, transparent wings and a wasplike appearance.

cleat (klēt) *n.* **1.** A strip of wood or iron used to strengthen or support the surface to which it is attached. **2.a.** A projecting piece of metal or hard rubber attached to the underside of a shoe to provide traction. **b. cleats.** A pair of shoes with such projections on the soles. **3.** A piece of metal or wood having projecting arms or ends on which a rope can be wound or secured. **4.** A wedge-shaped piece of material, such as wood, that is fastened onto something, such as a spar, to act as a support or prevent slippage. **5.** A spurlike device used in gripping a tree or pole in climbing. **—cleat** *tr.v.* **cleat·ed, cleat·ing, cleats.** To supply, support, secure, or strengthen with a cleat. [Middle English *clete,* from Old English **clēat,* lump, wedge.]

cleav·age (klē′vĭj) *n.* **1.** The act of splitting or cleaving. **2.** The state of being split or cleft; a fissure or division. **3.** *Mineralogy.* The splitting or tendency to split of a crystallized substance along definite crystalline planes, yielding smooth surfaces. **4.** *Embryology.* **a.** The series of mitotic cell divisions that produces a blastula from a fertilized ovum. It is the basis of the multicellularity of complex organisms. Also called *segmentation.* **b.** Any single cell division in such a series. **5.** *Informal.* The hollow between a woman's breasts, especially as revealed by a low neckline.

cleave[1] (klēv) *v.* **cleft** (klĕft) or **cleaved** or **clove** (klōv), **cleft** or **cleaved** or **clo·ven** (klō′vən), **cleav·ing, cleaves.** —*tr.* **1.** To split with or as if with a sharp instrument. See Synonyms at **tear[1].** **2.** To make or accomplish by or as if by cutting: *cleave a path through the ice.* **3.** To pierce or penetrate. —*intr.* **1.** *Mineralogy.* To split or separate, especially along a natural line of division. **2.** To make one's way; penetrate. [Middle English *cleven,* from Old English *clēofan.* See **gleubh-** in Appendix.] **—cleav′a·ble** *adj.*

cleave[2] (klēv) *intr.v.* **cleaved, cleav·ing, cleaves. 1.** To adhere, cling, or stick fast. **2.** To be faithful: *cleave to one's principles.* [Middle English *cleven,* from Old English *cleofian.*]

cleav·er (klē′vər) *n.* A heavy, broad-bladed knife or hatchet used especially by butchers.

cleav·ers (klē′vərz) *pl.n. (used with a sing. or pl. verb).* See **bedstraw.** [Middle English *clivers,* probably blend of *clife,* burdock (from Old English *clīfe)* and *clivres,* claws (from Old English *clifras,* pl. of *clifer).*]

Cle·burne (klē′bərn). A city of northeast Texas south of Fort Worth. It is a market center in an agricultural region. Population, 19,218.

cleek (klēk) *n.* **1.** *Sports.* A number one golf iron, having very little loft to the club face. **2.** *Scots.* A large hook, such as one used to hang a pot over a fire. [Middle English *cleike,* large hook, from *cleken,* to grasp, variant of *clechen,* from Old English **clǣcan;* probably akin to *clyccan,* to clutch.]

clef (klĕf) *n. Music.* A symbol indicating the pitch represented by one line of a staff, in relation to which the other pitches of the staff can be determined. [French, key, from Old French, from Latin *clāvis.*]

cleft (klĕft) *v.* A past tense and a past participle of **cleave[1].** **—cleft** *adj.* **1.** Divided; split. **2.** *Botany.* Having indentations that extend about halfway to the center, as in certain leaves. **—cleft** *n.* **1.** A crack, crevice, or split. **2.** A split or indentation between two parts, as of the chin. [Middle English, past participle of *cleven,* to split. See CLEAVE[1]. N., from Middle English, alteration (influenced by *cleft)* of *clift,* from Old English *geclyft.* See **gleubh-** in Appendix.]

cleft palate *n.* A congenital fissure in the roof of the mouth, resulting from incomplete fusion of the palate during embryonic development. It may involve only the uvula or extend through the entire palate.

Cleis·the·nes (klīs′thə-nēz′) or **Clis·the·nes** (klĭs′-). fl. sixth century B.C. Greek tyrant of Sicyon who led the Ionian population of the region in a revolt against the Dorians.

cleis·tog·a·mous (klī-stŏg′ə-məs) also **cleis·to·gam·ic** (klī′stə-găm′ĭk) *adj. Botany.* Of or relating to a flower that does not open and is self-pollinated in the bud. [Greek *kleistos,* closed (from *kleiein,* to close) + -GAMOUS.] **—cleis·tog′a·mous·ly** *adv.* **—cleis·tog′a·my** (-mē) *n.*

cleis·to·the·ci·um (klī′stə-thē′sē-əm) *n., pl.* **-ci·a** (-sē-ə). *Botany.* A closed, spherical ascocarp. [New Latin : Greek *kleistos,* closed (from *kleiein,* to close) + Greek *thēkion,* small case, diminutive of *thēkē,* receptacle; see **dhē-** in Appendix.]

clem·a·tis (klĕm′ə-tĭs, klĭ-măt′ĭs) *n.* Any of various ornamental, mostly climbing plants of the genus *Clematis,* native chiefly to northern temperate regions and having showy, variously colored flowers or decorative fruit clusters. [Latin *clēmatis,* a creeping plant, from Greek *klēmatis,* from *klēma, klēmat-,* twig.]

Cle·men·ceau (klĕm′ən-sō′, klĕ-mäɴ-), **Georges.** 1841–1929. French politician who served as premier (1906–1909 and 1917–1920) and played a key role in negotiating the Treaty of Versailles (1919).

clem·en·cy (klĕm′ən-sē) *n., pl.* **-cies. 1.** A disposition to show mercy, especially toward an offender or enemy. See Synonyms at **mercy. 2.** A merciful, kind, or lenient act. **3.** Mildness, especially of weather.

Clem·ens (klĕm′ənz), **Samuel Langhorne.** Pen name Mark Twain. 1835–1910. American author and humorist who drew on his childhood along the Mississippi River to create masterpieces of humor and sarcasm, including *Tom Sawyer* (1876) and *The Adventures of Huckleberry Finn* (1884).

clem·ent (klĕm′ənt) *adj.* **1.** Inclined to be lenient or merciful. **2.** Mild: *clement weather.* [Middle English, from Latin *clēmēns, clēment-.*] **—clem′ent·ly** *adv.*

Clem·ent I (klĕm′ənt), Saint. Known as "Clement of Rome." Died c. A.D. 97. Pope (88–97) who was one of the Apostolic Fathers and the author of the First Epistle to the Corinthians (c. 96).

Clement V. Originally Bertrand de Got. 1264–1314. Pope (1305–1314) befriended by Philip IV of France, who arranged his election as pope and at whose request the papal residence was moved from Rome to Avignon (1309).

cleats

Clement VII. Originally Giulio de' Medici. 1475?–1534. Pope (1523–1534) who refused to grant the divorce of Henry VIII from Catherine of Aragon and was unable to stop Henry's break with the Roman Catholic Church.

clem·en·tine (klĕm′ən-tīn′, -tēn′) *n.* A deep red-orange, often seedless tangerinelike fruit. [French *clémentine,* perhaps after Père *Clément* (fl. 1902), French missionary in Africa.]

Clement of Al·ex·an·dri·a (ăl′ĭg-zăn′drē-ə), Saint. A.D. 150?–220? Greek Christian theologian who is considered the founder of the Alexandrian school of theology.

clench (klĕnch) *tr.v.* **clenched, clench·ing, clench·es. 1.** To close tightly: *clench one's teeth; clenched my fists in anger.* **2.** To grasp or grip tightly: *clenched the steering wheel.* **3.** To clinch (a bolt, for example). **4.** *Nautical.* To fasten with a clinch. **—clench** *n.* **1.** A tight grip or grasp. **2.** Something, such as a mechanical device, that clenches or holds fast. **3.** *Nautical.* See **clinch** (sense 4). [Middle English *clenchen,* from Old English *beclencan.*]

cle·o·me (klē-ō′mē) *n.* Any of various often strong-smelling plants of the genus *Cleome,* native chiefly to warm regions and including several ornamentals. Also called *spider flower.* [New Latin *Cleome,* genus name.]

Cleopatra
Roman sculpture

Cle·on (klē′ŏn). Died 422 B.C. Athenian political and military leader who led the democratic faction after the death of Pericles (429 B.C.).

Cle·o·pat·ra (klē′ə-păt′rə, -pä′trə, -pā′-). 69–30 B.C. Egyptian queen (51–49 and 48–30) noted for her beauty and charisma. Octavian defeated the forces led by Cleopatra and Mark Antony at Actium (31).

CLEP *abbr.* College Level Examination Program.

clepe (klēp) *tr.v.* **cleped** (klēpt, klĕpt), **cleped** or **clept** (klĕpt) or **y·clept** (ĭ-klĕpt′) or **y·cleped** (ĭ-klēpt′, ĭ-klĕpt′), **clep·ing, clepes.** *Archaic.* To call; name. [Middle English *clepen,* from Old English *cleopian,* to cry out.]

clep·sy·dra (klĕp′sĭ-drə) *n., pl.* **-dras** or **-drae** (-drē′). An ancient device that measured time by marking the regulated flow of water through a small opening. Also called *water glass.* [Latin, from Greek *klepsudra* : *kleptein, kleps-,* to steal + *hudōr,* water; see **wed-[1]** in Appendix.]

clept (klĕpt) *v.* A past participle of **clepe.**

clere·sto·ry also **clear·sto·ry** (klîr′stôr′ē, -stōr′ē) *n., pl.* **-ries. 1.** The upper part of the nave, transepts, and choir of a church, containing windows. **2.** An upper portion of a wall containing windows for supplying natural light to a building. [Middle English *clerestorie* : perhaps *cler,* giving light, clear; see CLEAR + *storie,* tier; see STORY[2].]

clerestory

cler·gy (klûr′jē) *n., pl.* **-gies.** The body of people ordained for religious service. See Usage Note at **collective noun.** [Middle English *clergie,* from Old French (from *clerc,* cleric, from Late Latin *clēricus;* see CLERK) and from Old French *clergé,* body of clerks (from Late Latin *clēricātus,* from *clēricus,* clerk, cleric).]

cler·gy·man (klûr′jē-mən) *n.* A man who is a member of the clergy.

cler·gy·wom·an (klûr′jē-wo͝om′ən) *n.* A woman who is a member of the clergy.

cler·ic (klĕr′ĭk) *n.* A member of the clergy. [Late Latin *clēricus.* See CLERK.]

cler·i·cal (klĕr′ĭ-kəl) *adj.* **1.** Of or relating to clerks or office workers or their work. **2.** Of, relating to, or characteristic of the clergy. **3.** Advocating clericalism. **—clerical** *n.* **1.** A member of the clergy. **2. clericals.** Garments worn by the clergy. **3.** An advocate of clericalism. **—cler′i·cal·ly** *adv.*

clerical collar

clerical collar *n.* A stiff white collar in the shape of a band fastened at the back of the neck, worn by certain members of the Christian clergy.

cler·i·cal·ism (klĕr′ĭ-kə-lĭz′əm) *n.* A policy of supporting the power and influence of the clergy in political or secular matters. **—cler′i·cal·ist** *n.*

cler·i·hew (klĕr′ə-hyo͞o′) *n.* A humorous verse, usually consisting of two unmatched rhyming couplets, about a person whose name generally serves as one of the rhymes. [After Edmund *Clerihew* Bentley (1875–1956), British writer.]

cler·i·sy (klĕr′ĭ-sē) *n.* Educated people considered as a group; the literati. [German *Klerisei,* clergy, from Medieval Latin *clēricia,* from Late Latin *clēricus,* priest. See CLERK.]

clerk (klûrk; *British* klärk) *n. Abbr.* **clk. 1.** A person who works in an office performing such tasks as keeping records, attending to correspondence, or filing. **2.a.** A person who keeps the records and performs the regular business of a court or legislative body. **b.** *Law.* A law clerk, as for a judge. **3.** A person who works at a sales counter or service desk, as at a store or hotel. **4.** A cleric. **5.** *Archaic.* A scholar. **—clerk** *intr.v.* **clerked, clerk·ing, clerks.** To work or serve as a clerk: *clerked in a store; clerks for a judge.* [Middle English, clergyman, secretary, from Old English *clerc* and Old French *clerc,* clergyman, both from Late Latin *clēricus,* from Greek *klērikos,* belonging to the clergy, from *klēros,* inheritance, lot.] **—clerk′dom** *n.* **—clerk′ship′** *n.*

Grover Cleveland

clerk·ly (klûrk′lē) *adj.* **-li·er, -li·est. 1.** Of or characteristic of a clerk. **2.** *Archaic.* Scholarly. **—clerk′li·ness** *n.*

Cler·mont-Fer·rand (klĕr-mōN′fə-räN′, -fĕ-). A city of central France west of Lyons. Clermont was founded in Roman times and merged with Montferrand, an 11th-century town, in 1731. Population, 147,361.

Cleve·land (klēv′lənd). **1.** A city of northeast Ohio on Lake Erie. A port of entry and industrial center, the city was laid out in 1796 by Moses Cleveland (1754–1806). Population, 573,822. **2.** A city of southeast Tennessee east-northeast of Chattanooga. It is a trade center with varied industries. Population, 26,415.

Cleveland, (Stephen) Grover. 1837–1908. The 22nd and 24th President of the United States (1885–1889 and 1893–1897). He was known as an honest, independent President opposed to corruption and the spoils system.

Cleveland Heights. A city of northeast Ohio, a residential suburb of Cleveland. Population, 56,438.

♦**clev·er** (klĕv′ər) *adj.* **-er·er, -er·est. 1.** Mentally quick and original; bright. **2.** Nimble with the hands or body; dexterous. **3.** Exhibiting quick-wittedness: *a clever story.* **4.** *New England.* Easily managed; docile: *"Oxen must be pretty clever to be bossed around the way they are"* (Dialect Notes). **5.** *New England.* Affable but not especially smart. **6.** *Chiefly Southern U.S.* Good-natured; amiable. See Regional Note at **ugly.** [Middle English *cliver;* akin to East Frisian *klifer, klüfer,* perhaps from *klüfen,* to gnaw apart, work assiduously, of Low German origin; akin to Old Saxon *klioban,* to split, cleave. See **gleubh-** in Appendix.] **—clev′er·ly** *adv.* **—clev′er·ness** *n.*

SYNONYMS: *clever, ingenious, shrewd.* These adjectives are compared as they refer to mental adroitness or to practical ingenuity and skill. *Clever,* the most comprehensive, stresses mental quickness or adeptness: *"If I ever felt inclined to be timid as I was going into a room full of people, I would say to myself, 'You're the cleverest member of one of the cleverest families in the cleverest class of the cleverest nation in the world, why should you be frightened?'"* (Beatrice Webb). *Ingenious* implies originality and inventiveness: *"an ingenious solution to the storage problem"* (Linda Greider). *Shrewd* emphasizes mental astuteness and practical understanding: *"a woman of shrewd intellect and masculine character"* (Leslie Stephen).

clevis

♦***REGIONAL NOTE:*** In the 17th and 18th centuries, in addition to its basic sense of "able to use the brain readily and effectively," the word *clever* acquired a constellation of imprecise but generally positive senses in regional British speech: "clean-limbed and handsome," "neat and convenient to use," and "of an agreeable disposition." Some of these British regional senses, brought over when America was colonized, are still found in American regional speech, as in the South, where *clever* can mean "good-natured, amiable," in old-fashioned speech. The speech of New England extends the meaning "good-natured" to animals in the specific sense of "easily managed, docile." Perhaps it was the association with animals that gave rise to another meaning, "affable but not especially smart," applicable to people when used in old-fashioned New England dialects.

WORD HISTORY: Being too clever is thought to be unwise, and support for this popular notion may be afforded by the fact that the devil seems to have been the first "clever" one in English. The source of our word *clever* is probably the Middle English word *cliver,* recorded only once in a work written before 1250, in which it is said that the devil is "cliver on sinnes." This means something like "skillful in respect to sins." *Cliver* probably goes back to the Indo-European root *gleubh–,* "to cut, cleave." Although the intermediate ancestry of *cliver* is unclear, the semantic connection has to do with penetration or incisiveness—that is, cutting through to the heart of the matter, just as a woodcarver cuts through material in order to realize a certain vision.

cliff dweller
Cliff Palace, the largest cliff dwelling in Mesa Verde National Park, Colorado

Cleves (klēvz). See **Kleve.**

clev·is (klĕv′ĭs) *n.* A U-shaped metal piece with holes in each end through which a pin or bolt is run, used as a fastening device. [From *clevi,* possibly of Scandinavian origin; akin to Old Norse *klofi,* cleft. See **gleubh-** in Appendix.]

clew¹ (klo͞o) *n.* **1.** A ball of yarn or thread. **2.** *Greek Mythology.* The ball of thread used by Theseus to find his way out of the labyrinth. **3. clews.** The cords by which a hammock is suspended. **4.** Also **clue.** *Nautical.* **a.** One of the two lower corners of a square sail. **b.** The lower aft corner of a fore-and-aft sail. **c.** A metal loop attached to the lower corner of a sail. **—clew** *tr.v.* **clewed, clew·ing, clews. 1.** To roll or coil into a ball. **2.** Also **clue.** *Nautical.* To raise the lower corners of (a square sail) by means of clew lines. Used with *up.* [Middle English *clewe,* from Old English *cliwen.*]

clew² (klo͞o) *n.* & *v. Chiefly British.* Variant of **clue¹.**

clew line *n. Nautical.* A rope used to raise the clew of a sail up to the yard or mast.

Cli·burn (klī′bərn), **Van.** Born 1934. American pianist who was the first American to win the Tchaikovsky Prize (1958).

cli·ché (klē-shā′) *n.* A trite or overused expression or idea: *"Even while the phrase was degenerating to cliché in ordinary public use . . . scholars were giving it increasing attention"* (Anthony Brandt). [French, past participle of *clicher,* to stereotype (imitative of the sound made when the matrix is dropped into molten metal to make a stereotype plate).]

SYNONYMS: *cliché, bromide, commonplace, platitude, truism.* The central meaning shared by these nouns is "an expression or idea that has lost its originality or force through overuse": *a short story weakened by clichés; the old bromide that we are what we eat; uttered the commonplace "welcome aboard"; taking comfort in the platitude that all will end well; a once-original thought that has become a truism.*

cli·chéd (klē-shād′) *adj.* Having become stale or commonplace through overuse; hackneyed: *"In the States, it might seem a little clichéd; in Paris, it seems fresh and original"* (Nina Martin).

Cli·chy (klē-shē′). A city of north-central France, a suburb of Paris. It was a residence of Merovingian royalty in the seventh century. Population, 46,895.

click (klĭk) *n.* **1.** A brief, sharp, nonresonant sound: *the click of a door latch.* **2.** A mechanical device, such as a pawl, that snaps into position. **3.** *Linguistics.* An implosive stop found in some African languages and produced by raising the back of the tongue to make contact with the soft palate and simultaneously closing the lips or touching the teeth or alveolar ridge with the tip and sides of the tongue. In this sense, also called *suction stop.* **—click** *v.* **clicked, click·ing, clicks.** —*intr.* **1.** To produce a click or series of clicks. **2.** *Slang.* **a.** To be a great success: *The play clicked on Broadway.* **b.** To function well together; hit it off. **c.** To become clear; fall into place. —*tr.* To cause to click, as by striking together: *clicked his heels.* [Imitative.] **—click′er** *n.*

click beetle *n.* Any of various beetles of the family Elateridae, characterized by the ability to right themselves from an overturned position by flipping into the air with a clicking sound. Also called *snapping beetle.*

cli·ent (klī′ənt) *n.* **1.** The party for which professional services are rendered, as by an attorney. **2.** A customer or patron: *clients of the hotel.* **3.** A person using the services of a social services agency. **4.** One that depends on the protection of another. **5.** A client state. [Middle English, from Old French, from Latin *cliēns, client-,* dependent, follower. See **klei-** in Appendix.] **—cli′ent·age** (-ən-tĭj) *n.* **—cli·en′tal** (klī-ĕn′tl, klī′ən-) *adj.*

cli·en·tele (klī′ən-tĕl′, klē′än-) *n.* **1.** The clients of a professional person or practice considered as a group. **2.** A body of customers or patrons: *a restaurant's clientele.* [French *clientèle,* from Latin *clientēla,* clientship, from *cliēns,* client. See CLIENT.]

client state *n.* A country that is dependent on the economic or military support of a larger, more powerful country: *"Each superpower continues to arm its client states"* (C.L. Sulzberger).

cliff (klĭf) *n.* A high, steep, or overhanging face of rock. [Middle English *clif,* from Old English.] **—cliff′y** *adj.*

cliff brake *n.* Any of several ferns in the widely distributed genus *Pellaea,* typically growing in relatively dry, rocky areas or on cliffs and having pinnately compound, often leathery leaves.

cliff dweller *n.* **1.** A member of certain Anasazi groups of the southwest United States who built rock or adobe dwellings on sheltered ledges in the sides of cliffs. **2.** *Informal.* A person who lives in a large apartment house, especially in a city. **—cliff dwelling** *n.*

cliff·hang·er (klĭf′hăng′ər) *n.* **1.** A melodramatic serial in which each episode ends in suspense. **2.** A suspenseful situation occurring at the end of a chapter, a scene, or an episode. **3.** A contest so closely matched that the outcome is uncertain until the end. **—cliff′hang′ing** *adj.*

Clif·ford (klĭf′ərd), **Nathan.** 1803–1881. American jurist who served as an associate justice of the U.S. Supreme Court (1858–1881).

Cliff·side Park (klĭf′sīd′). A borough of northeast New Jersey on the Palisades overlooking the Hudson River opposite New York City. It is mainly residential and has varied light industries. Population, 21,464.

cliff swallow *n.* A North American swallow *(Petrochelidon pyrrhonota)* that builds a bottle-shaped nest of mud, grass, and twigs on the face of a cliff or bluff or under the eaves of a roof.

Clift (klĭft), **Montgomery.** 1920–1966. American actor known for his performances in *Red River* (1948), *From Here to Eternity* (1953), and *Judgment at Nuremberg* (1961).

Clif·ton (klĭf′tən). A city of northeast New Jersey near Paterson. It was formerly part of Passaic. Population, 74,388.

cli·mac·ter·ic (klī-măk′tər-ĭk, klī′măk-tĕr′ĭk) *n.* **1.a.** A period of life characterized by physiological and psychic change that marks the end of the reproductive capacity of women and terminates with the completion of menopause. **b.** A corresponding period sometimes occurring in men that may be marked by a reduction in sexual activity, although fertility is retained. **2.** A critical period or year in a person's life when major changes in health or fortune are thought to take place. **3.** A critical stage, period, or year: *"before the end of the millennium, whether* [he] *lives to see that ecclesiastical climacteric or not"* (Conor Cruise O'Brien). **—climacteric** *adj.* **1.** Of or relating to a climacteric. **2.** Critical; crucial. [From Latin *clīmactēricus,* of a dangerous period in life, from Greek *klimaktērikos,* from *klimaktēr,* dangerous point, rung of a ladder, from *klimax,* ladder. See CLIMAX.]

cli·mac·tic (klī-măk′tĭk) also **cli·mac·ti·cal** (-tĭ-kəl) *adj.* Relating to or constituting a climax. **—cli·mac′ti·cal·ly** *adv.*

cli·mate (klī′mĭt) *n.* **1.** The meteorological conditions, including temperature, precipitation, and wind, that characteristically prevail in a particular region. **2.** A region of the earth having particular meteorological conditions: *lives in a cold climate.* **3.** A prevailing condition or set of attitudes in human affairs: *a climate of unrest.* [Middle English *climat,* from Old French, from Late Latin *clīma, clīmat-,* from Greek *klima,* surface of the earth, region. See **klei-** in Appendix.]

cli·mat·ic (klī-măt′ĭk) *adj.* **1.** Of or relating to climate. **2.** *Ecology.* Influenced by or resulting from the prevailing climate. **—cli·mat′i·cal·ly** *adv.*

cli·ma·tol·o·gy (klī′mə-tŏl′ə-jē) *n.* The meteorological study of climates and their phenomena. **—cli′ma·to·log′ic** (-mə-tl-ŏj′ĭk), **cli′ma·to·log′i·cal** (-ĭ-kəl) *adj.* **—cli′ma·to·log′i·cal·ly** *adv.* **—cli′ma·tol′o·gist** *n.*

cli·max (klī′măks′) *n.* **1.** The point of greatest intensity or force in an ascending series or progression; a culmination. See Synonyms at **summit. 2. a.** A series of statements or ideas in an ascending order of rhetorical force or intensity. **b.** The final statement in such a series. **3. a.** A moment of great or culminating intensity in a narrative or drama, especially the conclusion of a crisis. **b.** The turning point in a plot or dramatic action. **4.** See **orgasm** (sense 1). **5.** A stage in ecological development in which a community of organisms, especially plants, is stable and capable of perpetuating itself. Also called *climax community.* **—climax** *tr. & intr.v.* **-maxed, -max·ing, -max·es.** To bring to or reach a climax. [Latin *clīmax,* rhetorical climax, from Greek *klimax,* ladder. See **klei-** in Appendix.]

climb (klīm) *v.* **climbed, climb·ing, climbs.** *—tr.* **1.** To move upward on or mount, especially by using the hands and feet or the feet alone; ascend: *climb a mountain; climbed the stairs.* **2.** To grow in an upward direction on or over: *ivy climbing the walls.* *—intr.* **1.** To move oneself upward, especially by using the hands and feet. **2.** To rise slowly, steadily, or effortfully; ascend. See Synonyms at **rise. 3.** To move in a specified direction by using the hands and feet: *climbed down the ladder; climbed out the window.* **4.** To slant or slope upward: *The road climbs steeply to the top.* **5.** To engage in the activity or sport of mountain climbing. **6.** To grow in an upward direction, as some plants do, often by means of twining stems or tendrils. **—climb** *n.* **1.** An act of climbing; an ascent: *a long, exhausting climb to the top.* **2.** A place to be climbed: *The face of the cliff was a steep climb.* [Middle English *climben,* from Old English *climban.*] **—climb′a·ble** (klī′mə-bəl) *adj.*

climb-down or **climb·down** (klīm′doun′) *n.* A retreat from an earlier position or opinion; a backing down: *"Agreeing to give up their arms and to yield control of Tripoli represented a major climb-down"* (Jim Muir).

climb·er (clī′mər) *n.* **1.** One that climbs, especially a person who climbs mountains. **2.** *Sports.* A device, such as a crampon, used in mountain climbing. **3.** A plant that climbs. **4.** A person who avidly seeks a higher social or professional position.

climb·ing fern (klī′mĭng) *n.* Any of various terrestrial ferns of the genus *Lygodium,* having a single pinnately compound leaf that climbs by twining, including *L. palmatum* of the eastern United States.

climbing iron *n. Sports.* See **crampon** (sense 2).

climbing perch *n.* A freshwater fish *(Anabas testudineus)* of tropical Asia, having modified gills allowing it to breathe air and pectoral fins adapted for traveling on land.

clime (klīm) *n.* Climate: *in search of warmer climes.* [Middle English, region of the earth, from Late Latin *clīma,* from Greek *klima.* See CLIMATE.]

clin– *pref.* Variant of **clino–.**

–clinal *suff.* Sloping: *synclinal.* [From Greek *klinein,* to lean. See **klei-** in Appendix.]

cli·nan·dri·um (klĭ-năn′drē-əm) *n., pl.* **-dri·a** (-drē-ə). *Botany.* A hollow containing the anther in the upper part of the column of an orchid flower. [New Latin : Greek *klinē,* couch (from *klinein,* to recline; see **klei-** in Appendix) + New Latin *-andrium,* stamen (from Greek *anēr, andr-,* man; see –ANDRY).]

clinch (klĭnch) *v.* **clinched, clinch·ing, clinch·es.** *—tr.* **1. a.** To fix or secure (a nail or bolt, for example) by bending down or flattening the pointed end that protrudes. **b.** To fasten together in this way. **2.** To settle definitely and conclusively; make final: *"The cocktail circuit is a constant and more contracts are clinched over pâté than over paper"* (Ann L. Trebbe). **3.** *Nautical.* To fasten with a clinch. *—intr.* **1.** To be held together securely. **2.** *Sports.* To hold a boxing opponent's body with one or both arms to prevent or hinder his punches. **3.** *Slang.* To embrace amorously. **—clinch** *n.* **1.** Something, such as a clamp, that clinches. **2.** The clinched part of a nail, bolt, or rivet. **3.** *Sports.* An act or instance of clinching in boxing. **4.** *Nautical.* A knot in a rope made by a half hitch with the end of the rope fastened back by seizing. Also called *clench.* **5.** *Slang.* An amorous embrace. [Variant of CLENCH.]

clinch·er (klĭn′chər) *n.* **1.** One that clinches, as: **a.** A nail, screw, or bolt for clinching. **b.** A tool for clinching nails, screws, or bolts. **2.** *Informal.* A point, fact, or remark that settles something conclusively; a decisive factor.

Clinch River (klĭnch). A river rising in southwest Virginia and flowing about 483 km (300 mi) generally southwest across eastern Tennessee to the Tennessee River.

cline (klīn) *n. Ecology.* A gradual change in a character or feature across the distributional range of a species or population, usually correlated with an environmental or a geographic transition. [From Greek *klinein,* to lean. See **klei-** in Appendix.] **—clin′al** (klī′nəl) *adj.*

–cline *suff.* Slope: *anticline.* [Back-formation from –CLINAL.]

cling (klĭng) *intr.v.* **clung** (klŭng), **cling·ing, clings. 1.** To hold fast or adhere to something, as by grasping, sticking, embracing, or entwining: *clung to the rope to keep from falling; fabrics that cling to the body.* **2.** To remain close; resist separation: *We clung together in the storm.* **3.** To remain emotionally attached; hold on: *clinging to outdated customs.* **—cling** *n. Botany.* A clingstone. [Middle English *clingen,* from Old English *clingan.*] **—cling′er** *n.* **—cling′y** *adj.*

cling·fish (klĭng′fĭsh′) *n., pl.* **clingfish** or **-fish·es.** Any of various small marine fishes of the family Gobiesocidae, having a large sucking disk under the front part of the body by which they fasten themselves to rocks and seaweed.

cling·stone (klĭng′stōn′) *adj.* Of or relating to a fruit, especially a peach, having flesh that adheres closely to the stone. **—clingstone** *n.* A clingstone fruit, especially a peach.

clin·ic (klĭn′ĭk) *n.* **1.** A facility, often associated with a hospital or medical school, that is devoted to the diagnosis and care of outpatients. **2.** A medical establishment run by several specialists working in cooperation and sharing the same facilities. **3.** A group session offering counsel or instruction in a particular field or activity: *a vocational clinic; a tennis clinic.* **4. a.** A seminar or meeting of physicians and medical students in which medical instruction is conducted in the presence of the patient, as at the bedside. **b.** A place where such instruction occurs. **c.** A class or lecture of medical instruction conducted in this manner. [French *clinique,* from Greek *klinikē (tekhnē),* clinical (method), feminine of *klinikos,* from *klinē,* couch, bed. See **klei-** in Appendix.]

–clinic *suff.* **1.** Sloping: *isoclinic.* **2.** Having a specified number of oblique axial intersections: *triclinic.*

clin·i·cal (klĭn′ĭ-kəl) *adj.* **1.** Of, relating to, or connected with a clinic. **2.** Involving or based on direct observation of the patient: *a clinical diagnosis.* **3.** Very objective and devoid of emotion; analytical: *"He spoke in the clipped, clinical monotones typical of police testimony in court"* (Connie Paige). **4.** Suggestive of a medical clinic; austere and antiseptic: *a clinical style of decor.* **—clin′i·cal·ly** *adv.*

clinical thermometer *n.* A thermometer used to measure body temperature, especially a small glass thermometer designed with a narrowing above the bulb so that the mercury column stays in position when the instrument is removed from the body.

cli·ni·cian (klĭ-nĭsh′ən) *n.* **1.** A physician, psychologist, or psychiatrist specializing in clinical studies or practice. **2.** One who conducts sessions or teaches at a clinic. [French *clinicien,* from *clinique,* clinic. See CLINIC.]

clink[1] (klĭngk) *intr. & tr.v.* **clinked, clink·ing, clinks.** To make or cause to make a light, sharp ringing sound. **—clink** *n.* A light, sharp ringing sound, as of glass or metal. [Middle English *clinken,* probably from Middle Dutch *klinken,* of imitative origin.]

clink[2] (klĭngk) *n. Slang.* A prison or a prison cell; a jail: *spent the night in the clink.* [After *Clink,* a district of London famous for its prison.]

clink·er (klĭng′kər) *n.* **1.** The incombustible residue, fused into an irregular lump, that remains after the combustion of coal. **2.** A partially vitrified brick or a mass of bricks fused together. **3.** An extremely hard burned brick. **4.** Vitrified matter expelled by a volcano. **5.** *Slang.* **a.** A sour note in a musical performance: *hit a clinker.* **b.** A mistake; a blunder. **c.** Something of inferior quality; a conspicuous failure: *a clinker of a show.* **6.** *Chiefly British.* Something admirable or first-rate. **—clinker** *intr.v.* **-ered, -er·ing, -ers.** To form clinkers in burning. [Obsolete Dutch *klinckaerd,* from Middle Dutch *klinken,* to clink. See CLINK[1].]

clink·er-built (klĭng′kər-bĭlt′) *adj.* Built with overlapping planks or boards, as a ship. [From obsolete *clinker,* clinch-nail, from Middle English *clinken,* probably variant of *clenchen,* to clench, from Old English *beclencan.*]

clino– or **clin–** *pref.* Slope; slant: *clinometer.* [New Latin, from Greek *klinein,* to slope. See **klei-** in Appendix.]

cli·nom·e·ter (klī-nŏm′ĭ-tər) *n.* Any of various surveying instruments for measuring angles of elevation, slope, or incline, as of an embankment. Also called *inclinometer.* **—cli′no·met′ric** (-nə-mĕt′rĭk), **cli′no·met′ri·cal** *adj.* **—cli·nom′e·try** *n.*

clin·quant (klĭng′kənt, klăN-käN′) *adj.* Glittering with gold or

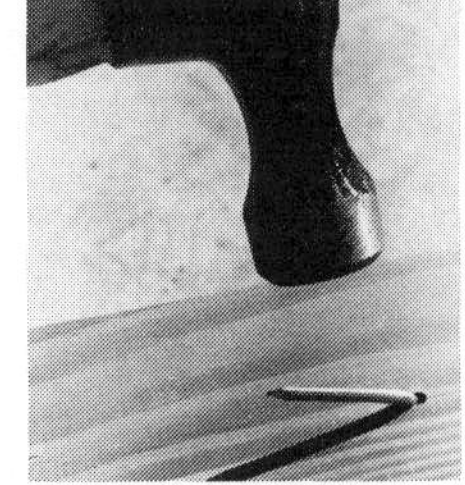
clinch

ă pat	oi boy
ā pay	ou out
âr care	ŏŏ took
ä father	ōō boot
ĕ pet	ŭ cut
ē be	ûr urge
ĭ pit	th thin
ī pie	*th* this
îr pier	hw which
ŏ pot	zh vision
ō toe	ə about, item
ô paw	♦ regionalism

Stress marks: **′** (primary); ′ (secondary), as in **dictionary** (dĭk′shə-nĕr′ē)

tinsel. **—clinquant** *n.* Imitation gold leaf; tinsel; glitter. [French, glistening, tinkling, present participle of obsolete *clinquer,* to clink, perhaps from Middle Dutch *klinken.* See CLINK[1].]

Clin·ton (klĭn′tən). A city of east-central Iowa on the Mississippi River northeast of Davenport. It is a manufacturing and trade center in an agricultural region. Population, 32,828.

Clinton, DeWitt. 1769–1828. American politician who as governor of New York (1817–1823 and 1825–1828) was a principal supporter of the Erie Canal (completed 1825).

Clinton, George[1]. 1686?–1761. British naval officer and colonial administrator who served as governor of Newfoundland (1732–1741) and New York (1741–1753).

Clinton, George[2]. 1739–1812. Vice President of the United States (1805–1812) under Thomas Jefferson and James Madison. As governor of New York (1777–1795) he was suspicious of centralized government and opposed New York's ratification of the U.S. Constitution.

Clinton, Sir **Henry.** 1738–1795. British general in the American Revolution who was commander in chief of British forces in North America (1778–1781).

clin·to·ni·a (klĭn-tō′nē-ə) *n.* Any of various perennial herbs of the genus *Clintonia* in the lily family, native to North America and eastern Asia and having broad basal leaves, white, greenish-yellow, or purplish flowers, and blue or black berries. [New Latin *Clintonia,* genus name, after DeWitt CLINTON.]

clipper
The *Agenor*

Cli·o (klī′ō) *n.* **1.** *Greek Mythology.* The Muse of history. **2.** (klē′ō), *pl.* **Cli·os.** A statuette awarded annually for outstanding achievement in radio and television advertising. [Latin, from Greek *Kleiō,* from *kleiein,* to tell. See **kleu-** in Appendix.]

cli·o·met·rics (klī′ə-mĕt′rĭks) *n. (used with a sing. verb).* The study of history using economic models and advanced mathematical methods of data processing and analysis. [CLIO + –METRICS.] **—cli′o·met′ric** *adj.* **—cli′o·me·tri′cian** (-mĭ-trĭsh′ən) *n.*

clip[1] (klĭp) *v.* **clipped, clip·ping, clips.** *—tr.* **1.** To cut, cut off, or cut out with or as if with shears: *clip coupons; clipped three seconds off the record.* **2.** To make shorter by cutting; trim: *clip a hedge.* **3.** To cut off the edge of: *clip a coin.* **4.** To cut short; curtail. **5. a.** To shorten (a word or words) by leaving out letters or syllables. **b.** To enunciate with clarity and precision: *clip one's words.* **6.** *Informal.* To hit with a sharp blow: *clipped me under the eye.* **7.** *Slang.* To cheat, swindle, or rob. *—intr.* **1.** To cut something. **2.** *Informal.* To move rapidly. **—clip** *n.* **1.** The act of clipping. **2.** Something clipped off, especially: **a.** The wool shorn at one shearing, as of sheep. **b.** A season's shearing. **3.** A short extract from a film or videotape. **4.** *Informal.* A quick, sharp blow: *a clip on the ear.* **5.** *Informal.* A pace or rate: *go at a fast clip.* **6.** A single occasion; a time: *could write nine pages at a clip.* **7. clips.** A pair of shears or clippers. [Middle English *clippen,* from Old Norse *klippa.*]

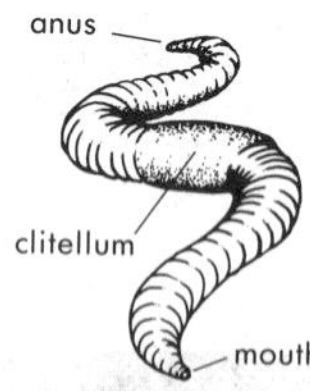

clitellum
Of an earthworm

clip[2] (klĭp) *n.* **1.** Any of various devices for gripping or holding things together; a clasp or fastener. **2.** A piece of jewelry that fastens with a clasp or clip; a brooch. **3.** A cartridge clip. **4.** *Football.* An act of clipping. **—clip** *tr.v.* **clipped, clip·ping, clips.** **1.** To fasten with or as if with a clip; hold tightly. **2.** *Football.* To block (an opponent who is not carrying the ball) illegally from the rear. **3.** *Archaic.* To embrace or encompass. [Middle English, hook, from *clippen,* to clasp, embrace, from Old English *clyppan.*]

clip·board (klĭp′bôrd′, -bōrd′) *n.* A small writing board with a spring clip at the top for holding papers or a writing pad.

clip joint *n.* *Slang.* A restaurant, nightclub, or other business where customers are regularly overcharged.

clip-on (klĭp′ŏn′, -ôn′) *adj.* Designed to attach by means of a clip: *clip-on earrings.* **—clip′-on′** *n.*

cloche

clipped form (klĭpt) *n.* A word formed by dropping one or more syllables from a polysyllabic word, such as *gas* from *gasoline* or *phone* from *telephone.*

clip·per (klĭp′ər) *n.* **1.** One that cuts, shears, or clips. **2.** An instrument or tool for cutting, clipping, or shearing. Often used in the plural: *nail clippers.* **3.** *Nautical.* A sharp-bowed sailing vessel of the mid-19th century, having tall masts and sharp lines and built for great speed. **4.** One that moves very fast. **5.** *Electronics.* See **limiter** (sense 2).

clip·ping (klĭp′ĭng) *n.* Something cut off or out, especially an item clipped from a newspaper or magazine.

clip·sheet (klĭp′shēt′) *n.* A sheet of paper containing news items and other newspaper material, usually printed on only one side for convenience in clipping and reprinting.

clique (klēk, klĭk) *n.* A small, exclusive group of friends or associates. See Synonyms at **circle.** **—clique** *intr.v.* **cliqued, cliqu·ing, cliques.** *Informal.* To form, associate in, or act as a clique. [French, from Old French, latch, or from obsolete French *cliquer,* to click, clink, of imitative origin.] **—cliqu′ey, cliqu′y, cliqu′ish** *adj.* **—cliqu′ish·ly** *adv.* **—cliqu′ish·ness** *n.*

Clis·the·nes (klĭs′thə-nēz′). See **Cleisthenes.**

cli·tel·lum (klī-tĕl′əm) *n., pl.* **-tel·la** (-tĕl′ə). A swollen, glandular, saddlelike region in the epidermis of certain annelid worms, such as the earthworm, that secretes a viscous fluid to form a cocoon for their eggs. [New Latin *clītellum,* sing. of Latin *clītellae,* packsaddle. See **klei-** in Appendix.]

clock[1]
Mid 18th-century French by Julien Le Roy

clit·o·ris (klĭt′ər-ĭs, klī′tər-) *n.* A small, elongated erectile organ at the anterior part of the vulva, homologous with the penis. [New Latin, from Greek *kleitoris.* See **klei-** in Appendix.] **—clit′o·ral** (-ər-əl) *adj.*

Clive (klīv), **Robert.** Baron Clive of Plassey. 1725–1774. British soldier and statesman who was instrumental in securing Great Britain's interests in India.

clk. *abbr.* Clerk.

clm. *abbr.* Column.

clo·a·ca (klō-ā′kə) *n., pl.* **-cae** (-sē′). **1.** A sewer or latrine. **2.** *Zoology.* **a.** The common cavity into which the intestinal, genital, and urinary tracts open in vertebrates such as fish, reptiles, birds, and some primitive mammals. **b.** The posterior part of the intestinal tract in various invertebrates. [Latin *cloāca,* sewer, canal.] **—clo·a′cal** (-kəl) *adj.*

cloak (klōk) *n.* **1.** A loose outer garment, such as a cape. **2.** Something that covers or conceals: *a cloak of secrecy.* **—cloak** *tr.v.* **cloaked, cloak·ing, cloaks.** To cover or conceal with or as if with a cloak. See Synonyms at **clothe, disguise, hide[1].** [Middle English *cloke,* from Old North French *cloque,* cloak, bell (from its shape), from Medieval Latin *clocca.* See CLOCK[1].]

cloak-and-dag·ger (klōk′ən-dăg′ər) *adj.* Marked by melodramatic intrigue and often espionage.

cloak fern *n.* Any of various ferns in the genus *Notholaena,* native chiefly to the temperate and tropical Americas, having pinnately compound leaves, and often found in dry, rocky areas.

cloak·room (klōk′ro͝om′, -ro͞om′) *n.* **1.** A room where coats and other articles may be left temporarily, as in a theater or school. Also called *coatroom.* **2.** A private lounge adjacent to a legislative chamber.

clob·ber (klŏb′ər) *tr.v.* **-bered, -ber·ing, -bers.** *Slang.* **1.** To strike violently and repeatedly; batter or maul. **2.** To defeat decisively. **3.** To criticize harshly. [Origin unknown.]

clo·chard (klō-shär′) *n., pl.* **-chards** (-shär′). A tramp; a vagrant. [French, from *clocher,* to limp, from Old French, from Vulgar Latin **cloppicāre,* from *cloppus,* lame person, alteration of Latin *claudus.*]

cloche (klōsh) *n.* **1.** A close-fitting woman's hat with a bell-like shape. **2.** A usually bell-shaped cover, used chiefly to protect plants from frost. [French, from Old French, bell, from Medieval Latin *clocca.* See CLOCK[1].]

clock[1] (klŏk) *n.* **1.** An instrument other than a watch for measuring or indicating time, especially a mechanical or electronic device having a numbered dial and moving hands or a digital display. **2.** A time clock. **3.** A source of regularly occurring pulses used to measure the passage of time, as in a computer. **4.** Any of various devices that indicate measurement, such as a speedometer or a taximeter. **5.** *Botany.* The downy flower head of a dandelion that has gone to seed. **—clock** *v.* **clocked, clock·ing, clocks.** *—tr.* **1.** To time, as with a stopwatch: *clock a runner.* **2.** To register or record with a mechanical device: *clocked the winds at 60 miles per hour.* *—intr.* To record working hours with a time clock: *clocks in at 8 A.M. and out at 4 P.M.* ***—idiom.*** **clean (someone's) clock.** *Slang.* To beat or defeat decisively: *"Immense linemen declared their intentions to clean the clocks of opposing players"* (Russell Baker). [Middle English *clokke,* from Old North French *cloque,* bell, or from Middle Dutch *clocke,* bell, clock, both from Medieval Latin *clocca,* of imitative origin.] **—clock′er** *n.*

clock[2] (klŏk) *n.* An embroidered or woven decoration on the side of a stocking or sock. [Perhaps from CLOCK[1], bell (obsolete), from its original bell-shaped appearance.]

clock radio *n.* A radio having a built-in alarm clock that can be set to turn the radio on automatically.

clock-watch·er (klŏk′wôch′ər) *n.* A person who is eager for the time to pass, as at work or school. **—clock′-watch′ing** *n.*

clock·wise (klŏk′wīz′) *adv. & adj.* *Abbr.* **cw.** In the same direction as the rotating hands of a clock.

clock·work (klŏk′wûrk′) *n.* A mechanism of geared wheels driven by a wound spring, as in a mechanical clock. ***—idiom.*** **like clockwork.** With machinelike regularity and precision; perfectly: *The project proceeded like clockwork.*

clod (klŏd) *n.* **1.** A lump or chunk, especially of earth or clay. **2.** Earth or soil. **3.** A dull, stupid person; a dolt. [Middle English, variant of *clot,* lump. See CLOT.] **—clod′dish** *adj.* **—clod′dish·ly** *adv.* **—clod′dish·ness** *n.*

clod·hop·per (klŏd′hŏp′ər) *n.* **1.** A clumsy, coarse person; a bumpkin. **2.** A big, heavy shoe.

clo·fi·brate (klō-fī′brāt, -fĭb′rāt) *n.* A synthetic drug, $C_{12}H_{15}ClO_3$, used primarily to reduce abnormally elevated levels of plasma cholesterol and triglyceride. [*clofibric acid* (perhaps C(H)LO(RO)– + FIBR(O)– + –IC) + –ATE[2].]

clog (klôg, klŏg) *n.* **1.** An obstruction or hindrance. **2.** A weight, such as a block, attached to the leg of an animal to hinder movement. **3.** A heavy, usually wooden-soled shoe. **—clog** *v.* **clogged, clog·ging, clogs.** *—tr.* **1.** To obstruct movement on or in; block up: *Heavy traffic clogged the freeways.* **2.** To hamper the function or activity of; impede: *"attorneys clogging our courts with actions designed to harass state and local governments"* (Roslyn L. Anderson and Patricia L. Irvin). *—intr.* **1.** To become obstructed or choked up: *The pipes had clogged with rust.* **2.** To thicken or stick together; clot. **3.** To do a clog dance. [Middle English, block attached to an animal's leg.]

clog dance *n.* A dance performed while wearing clogs and characterized by heavy, stamping steps. **—clog dancer** *n.*

cloi·son·né (kloi′zə-nā′, klə-wä′zə-) *n.* **1.** Enamelware in which the surface decoration is formed by different colors of enamel separated by thin strips of metal. **2.** The process or method of producing such enamelware. [French, past participle of *cloisonner,* to partition, from Old French *cloison,* partition, from Vulgar Latin **clausiō, clausiōn-,* from Latin *clausus,* past participle of *claudere,* to close, lock.] **—cloi·son·né′** *adj.*

clois·ter (kloi′stər) *n.* **1.** A covered walk with an open colonnade on one side, running along the walls of buildings that face a quadrangle. **2.a.** A place, especially a monastery or convent, devoted to religious seclusion. **b.** Life in a monastery or convent. **3.** A secluded, quiet place. **—cloister** *tr.v.* **-tered, -ter·ing, -ters. 1.** To shut away from the world in or as if in a cloister; seclude. **2.** To furnish (a building) with a cloister. [Middle English *cloistre,* from Old French, alteration (influenced by *cloison,* partition; see CLOISONNÉ) of *clostre,* from Latin *claustrum,* enclosed place, from *claudere,* to close.]

clois·tral (kloi′strəl) also **claus·tral** (klô′strəl) *adj.* **1.** Of or suggesting a cloister; secluded. **2.** Living in a cloister.

clomb (klōm) *v. Archaic.* A past tense and a past participle of **climb.**

clom·i·phene (klŏm′ə-fēn, klō′mə-) *n.* A synthetic drug, $C_{26}H_{28}ClNO$, that is used in its citrate form to stimulate ovulation. [C(H)LO(RO)– + (A)MI(NE) + PHEN(YL).]

clomp (klŏmp) *intr.v.* **clomped, clomp·ing, clomps.** To walk heavily and noisily. [Imitative.]

clone (klōn) *n.* **1.** A group of genetically identical cells descended from a single common ancestor, such as a bacterial colony whose members arose from a single original cell as a result of binary fission. **2.** An organism descended asexually from a single ancestor, such as a plant produced by layering or a polyp produced by budding. **3.** A replica of a DNA sequence, such as a gene, produced by genetic engineering. **4.** One that copies or closely resembles another, as in appearance or function: *"filled with business-school clones in gray and blue suits"* (Michael M. Thomas). **—clone** *v.* **cloned, clon·ing, clones.** *—tr.* **1.** To make multiple identical copies of (a DNA sequence). **2.a.** To establish and maintain pure lineages of (a cell) under laboratory conditions. **b.** To reproduce or propagate asexually: *clone a frog; clone a plant variety.* **3.** To produce a copy of; imitate: *"The look has been cloned into cliché"* (Cathleen McGuigan). *—intr.* To grow as a clone. [Greek *klōn,* twig.] **—clon′al** (klō′nəl) *adj.* **—clon′al·ly** *adv.* **—clon′er** *n.*

clon·i·dine (klŏn′ĭ-dēn′, klō′nĭ-) *n.* A synthetic drug, $C_9H_9Cl_2N_3$, used in the treatment of hypertension and for the prevention of migraine headaches. [C(H)LO(RO)– + (A)NI(LINE) + (IMI)D(E) + –INE[2].]

clo·nus (klō′nəs) *n., pl.* **-nus·es.** An abnormality in neuromuscular activity characterized by rapidly alternating muscular contraction and relaxation. [New Latin, from Greek *klonos,* turmoil.] **—clo′nic** (klō′nĭk, klŏn′ĭk) *adj.* **—clo·nic′i·ty** (klō-nĭs′ĭ-tē, klŏ-), **clo′nism** (klō′nĭz′əm, klŏn′ĭz′əm) *n.*

clop (klŏp) *n.* A sharp, hollow sound, as of a horse's hoof striking pavement. **—clop** *intr.v.* **clopped, clop·ping, clops.** To make or move with this sound. [Imitative.]

clo·que also **clo·qué** (klō-kā′) *n.* A cotton, silk, or rayon fabric with a raised woven pattern and a puckered or quilted look. [French *cloqué,* past participle of *cloquer,* to become blistered, from dialectal *cloque,* blister, from Medieval Latin *clocca,* bell. See CLOCK[1].]

close (klōs) *adj.* **clos·er, clos·est. 1.** Being near in space or time. **2.** Being near in relationship: *close relatives.* **3.** Bound by mutual interests, loyalties, or affections; intimate: *close friends.* **4.** Having little or no space between elements or parts; tight and compact: *a close weave.* **5.** Being near the surface; short: *a close haircut.* **6.** Being on the brink of: *close to tears.* **7.** Decided by a narrow margin; almost even: *a close election.* **8.** Faithful to the original: *a close copy.* **9.** Rigorous; thorough: *close attention; close supervision.* **10.** Shut; closed. **11.** Shut in; enclosed. **12.** Confining or narrow; crowded: *close quarters.* **13.** Fitting tightly: *close garments.* **14.** Lacking fresh air; stuffy: *a close room.* **15.** Confined to specific persons or groups: *a close secret.* **16.** Strictly confined or guarded: *kept under close custody.* **17.** Hidden from view; secluded. **18.** Secretive; reticent: *was close about her personal life.* **19.** Giving or spending with reluctance; stingy. **20.** Not easily acquired; scarce: *Money was close.* **21.** *Linguistics.* Pronounced with the tongue near the palate, as the *ee* in *meet.* Used of vowels. **22.** Marked by more rather than less punctuation, especially commas. **—close** (klōz) *v.* **closed, clos·ing, clos·es.** *—tr.* **1.** To move (a door, for example) so that an opening or passage is covered or obstructed; shut. **2.** To bar access to: *closed the road for repairs.* **3.** To fill or stop up: *closed the cracks with plaster.* **4.** To stop the operations of permanently or temporarily: *closed down the factory.* **5.** To bring to an end; terminate: *close a letter; close a bank account.* **6.** To bring together all the elements or parts of: *Management closed ranks and ostracized the troublemaker.* **7.** To join or unite; bring into contact: *close a circuit.* **8.** To draw or bind together the edges of: *close a wound.* **9.** To complete the final details or negotiations on: *close a deal.* **10.** *Archaic.* To enclose on all sides. *—intr.* **1.** To become shut: *The door closed quietly.* **2.** To come to an end; finish: *The book closes on a hopeful note.* **3.** To reach an agreement; come to terms. **4.** To cease operation: *The shop closes at six.* **5.a.** To engage at close quarters: *closed with the enemy.* **b.** To draw near: *The orbiter closed with the space station in preparation for docking.* **6.** To come together: *My arms closed around the little child.* **—close** (klōz) *n.* **1.** The act of closing. **2.** A conclusion; a finish: *The meeting came to a close.* **3.** *Music.* The concluding part of a phrase or theme; a cadence. **4.** (klōs). An enclosed place, especially land surrounding or beside a cathedral or other building. **5.** (klōs). *Chiefly British.* A narrow way or alley. **6.** *Archaic.* A fight at close quarters. **—close** (klōs) *adv.* **closer, closest.** In a close position or manner; closely: *stayed close together.* ***—phrasal verbs.*** **close in. 1.** To seem to be gathering in on all sides: *The problems closed in.* **2.** To advance on a target so as to block escape: *The police closed in on the sniper.* **3.** To surround so as to make unusable: *The airport was closed in by fog.* **close out. 1.** To dispose of (a line of merchandise) at reduced prices. **2.** To terminate, as by selling: *close out a business.* ***—idioms.*** **close to home.** So as to affect one's feelings or interests: *Her comment hit close to home.* **close to the wind.** *Nautical.* At a close angle into the direction from which the wind is blowing: *sailing close to the wind.* [Middle English *clos,* closed, from Old French, from Latin *clausus,* past participle of *claudere,* to close. V., from Middle English *closen,* from Old French *clore, clos-,* from Latin *claudere.*] **—close′ly** *adv.* **—close′ness** *n.* **—clos′er** (klō′zər) *n.* **—clos′ing** (klō′zĭng) *n.*

SYNONYMS: *close, immediate, near, nearby, nigh, proximate.* The central meaning shared by these adjectives is "not far from another in space, time, or relationship": *an airport close to town; her immediate family; his nearest relative; a nearby library; our nighest neighbor; a proximate neighborhood.* See also Synonyms at **familiar, stingy.**
ANTONYM: *far.*
USAGE NOTE: Strictly speaking, the phrase *close proximity* says nothing that is not said by *proximity* itself. Like other common redundancies, however (*old adage, mental telepathy*), this usage is too widespread and too innocuous to be worth objecting to. See Usage Note at **redundancy.**

close call (klōs) *n. Informal.* A narrow escape.

close corporation (klōs) *n.* See **closed corporation.**

closed (klōzd) *adj.* **1.** Having boundaries; enclosed: *a closed corridor between the two buildings.* **2.** Blocked or barred to passage or entry: *a closed port.* **3.** Explicitly limited; restricted: *closed membership.* **4.** Self-contained or self-sufficient: *a closed relationship.* **5.** Barred to the public; conducted in secrecy: *a closed session of the judiciary committee.* **6.** *Mathematics.* **a.** Of or relating to a curve, such as a circle, having no endpoints. **b.** Of or relating to a surface having no boundary curves. **c.** Of or relating to an interval containing both its endpoints. **d.** Characterized by or possessing the property by which an operation acting on an element in a set produces an element within the set. **7.** *Computer Science.* **a.** Of or relating to a file that cannot be accessed. **b.** Of or relating to a switch that is on. **8.** *Linguistics.* Ending in a consonant: *a closed syllable.*

closed book *n.* A person or thing that cannot be known or understood; something unfathomable or puzzling.

closed-cap·tioned (klōzd′kăp′shənd) *adj.* Broadcast with captions that can be seen only on a specially equipped receiver: *closed-captioned television for the hearing-impaired.*

closed chain *n. Chemistry.* See **ring**[1] (sense 14).

closed circuit *n.* **1.** An electric circuit providing an uninterrupted, endless path for the flow of current. **2.** A television transmission circuit with a limited number of reception stations and no broadcast facilities. **—closed′-cir′cuit** (klōzd′sûr′kĭt) *adj.*

closed corporation *n.* A corporation in which the shares of stock are held by relatively few persons and are not publicly traded. Also called *close corporation.*

closed couplet *n.* A rhymed couplet forming a complete thought or syntactic unit, for example, *"True wit is nature to advantage dressed,/What oft was thought, but ne'er so well expressed"* (Alexander Pope).

closed-door (klōzd′dôr′, -dōr′) *adj.* Not open to the public; held in privacy: *a series of closed-door meetings.*

closed-end investment company (klōzd′ĕnd′) *n.* A company with fixed capitalization whose shares are traded by investors and whose capital is invested in other companies.

closed interval *n. Mathematics.* See **interval** (sense 4).

closed-mind·ed (klōzd′mīn′dĭd) *adj.* Variant of **close-minded.**

close·down (klōz′doun′) *n.* A suspension or termination of operations: *a plant closedown.*

closed shop *n.* See **union shop.**

close-fist·ed (klōs′fĭs′tĭd) *adj.* Tightfisted; stingy. See Synonyms at **stingy.**

close-grained (klōs′grānd′) *adj.* Dense or compact in structure or texture, as a wood composed of small-diameter cells.

close-hauled (klōs′hôld′) *adv. & adj. Nautical.* With sails trimmed flat for sailing as close to the wind as possible.

close-knit (klōs′nĭt′) *adj.* Held tightly together, as by social or cultural ties: *a close-knit family.*

close-mind·ed (klōs′mīn′dĭd, klōz′-) or **closed-mind·ed** (klōzd′-) *adj.* Intolerant of the beliefs and opinions of others; unreceptive to new ideas. **—close′-mind′ed·ness** *n.*

close-mouthed (klōs′mouthd′, -moutht′) *adj.* Disposed not to talk; tightlipped.

close-or·der drill (klōs′ôr′dər) *n.* A military drill in marching, maneuvering, and formal handling of arms in which the participants perform at close intervals.

cloisonné
16th-century
Ming dynasty
incense burner

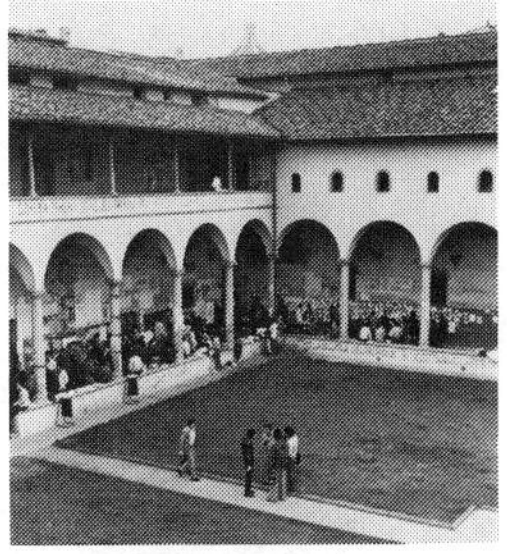

cloister
Palermo University

ă pat	oi boy
ā pay	ou out
âr care	ŏŏ took
ä father	ōō boot
ĕ pet	ŭ cut
ē be	ûr urge
ĭ pit	th thin
ī pie	*th* this
îr pier	hw which
ŏ pot	zh vision
ō toe	ə about, item
ô paw	♦ regionalism

Stress marks: **′** (primary); ′ (secondary), as in **dictionary** (dĭk′shə-nĕr′ē)

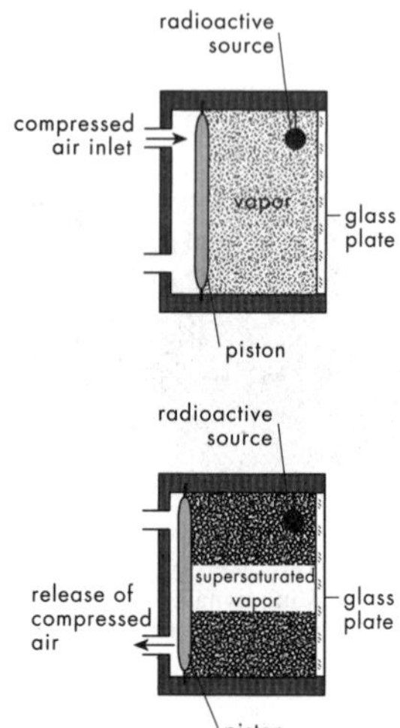

cloud chamber

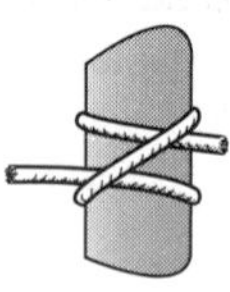
clove hitch

ă **pat**	oi **boy**
ā **pay**	ou **out**
âr **care**	o͝o **took**
ä **father**	o͞o **boot**
ĕ **pet**	ŭ **cut**
ē **be**	ûr **urge**
ĭ **pit**	th **thin**
ī **pie**	*th* **this**
îr **pier**	hw **which**
ŏ **pot**	zh **vision**
ō **toe**	ə **about, item**
ô **paw**	♦ regionalism

Stress marks: **′** (primary); ′ (secondary), as in **dictionary** (dĭk′shə-nĕr′ē)

close•out (klōz′out′) *n.* A sale in which all remaining stock is disposed of, usually at greatly reduced prices.

close shave (klōs) *n. Informal.* A narrow escape; a close call.

clos•et (klŏz′ĭt, klô′zĭt) *n.* **1.** *Abbr.* **cl.** A cabinet or enclosed recess for linens, household supplies, or clothing. **2.** A small private chamber, as for study or prayer. **3.** A water closet; a toilet. **4.** A state of secrecy or cautious privacy: *Two days before the election, the candidate suddenly came out of the closet and denounced the proposed law.* **—closet** *tr.v.* **-et•ed, -et•ing, -ets.** To enclose or shut up in a private room, as for discussion: *closeted themselves with their attorneys.* **—closet** *adj.* **1.** Private; confidential: *closet information.* **2.** Being so or engaging only in private; secret: *a closet proponent of a tax increase; a closet alcoholic.* **3.** Based on theory and speculation rather than practice. [Middle English, private room, from Old French, diminutive of *clos,* enclosure, from Latin *clausum,* from neuter of *clausus,* enclosed. See CLOSE.] **—clos′et•ful′** *n.*

closet drama *n.* A play to be read rather than performed.

closet queen *n. Offensive.* Used as a disparaging term for a gay or homosexual man who chooses not to reveal his sexual orientation.

close-up (klōs′ŭp′) *n.* **1.** A photograph or a film or television shot taken at close range. **2.** An intimate view or description. **—close′-up′** *adj.*

clos•ing transaction (klō′zĭng) *n.* **1.** The last transaction for a security during a trading day. **2.** An option order that will eliminate or decrease the size of an existing option position.

clos•trid•i•um (klŏ-strĭd′ē-əm) *n., pl.* **-i•a** (-ē-ə). Any of various rod-shaped, spore-forming, chiefly anaerobic bacteria of the genus *Clostridium,* such as the nitrogen-fixing bacteria found in soil and those causing botulism and tetanus. [New Latin *Clōstridium,* genus name, from Greek *klōstēr,* spindle, from *klōthein,* to spin.] **—clos•trid′i•al** (-əl) *adj.*

clo•sure (klō′zhər) *n.* **1.** The act of closing or the state of being closed: *closure of an incision.* **2.** Something that closes or shuts. **3.** A bringing to an end; a conclusion: *finally brought the project to closure.* **4.** See **cloture. 5.** The property of being mathematically closed. **—closure** *tr.v.* **-sured, -sur•ing, -sures.** To cloture (a debate). [Middle English, from Old French, from Late Latin *clausūra,* fortress, lock, from *clausus,* enclosed; see CLOSE. Sense 4, translation of French *clôture.* See CLOTURE.]

clot (klŏt) *n.* **1.** A thick, viscous, or coagulated mass or lump, as of blood. **2.** A clump, mass, or lump, as of clay. **3.** A compact group: *a clot of automobiles blocking the tunnel's entrance.* **—clot** *v.* **clot•ted, clot•ting, clots.** *—intr.* To form into a clot or clots; coagulate. *—tr.* **1.** To cause to form into a clot or clots. See Synonyms at **coagulate. 2.** To fill or cover with or as if with clots. [Middle English, from Old English *clott,* lump.]

cloth (klôth, klŏth) *n., pl.* **cloths** (klôths, klô*th*z, klŏths, klŏ*th*z). *Abbr.* **cl. 1.** Fabric or material formed by weaving, knitting, pressing, or felting natural or synthetic fibers. **2.** A piece of fabric or material used for a specific purpose, as a tablecloth. **3.** *Nautical.* **a.** Canvas. **b.** A sail. **4.** The characteristic attire of a profession, especially that of the clergy. **5.** The clergy: *a man of the cloth.* [Middle English, from Old English *clāth.*]

cloth•bound (klôth′bound′, klŏth′-) *adj.* Having a cover of thick paper boards covered with cloth. Used of a book.

clothe (klō*th*) *tr.v.* **clothed** or **clad** (klăd), **cloth•ing, clothes. 1.** To put clothes on; dress. **2.** To provide clothes for. **3.** To cover as if with clothing. [Middle English *clothen,* from Old English *clāthian,* from *clāth,* cloth.]

SYNONYMS: *clothe, cloak, drape, mantle, robe.* The central meaning shared by these verbs is "to cover as if with clothes": *trees clothed in leafy splendor; mist that cloaks the mountains; a beam draped with cobwebs; a boulder mantled with moss; snow robing fields and gardens.*
ANTONYM: *unclothe.*

clothes (klōz, klō*th*z) *pl.n.* **1.** Articles of dress; wearing apparel; garments. **2.** Bedclothes. [Middle English, from Old English *clāthas,* pl. of *clāth,* cloth.]

clothes•horse (klōz′hôrs′, klō*th*z′-) *n.* **1.** A frame on which clothes are hung to dry or air. **2.** A person excessively concerned with dress.

clothes•line (klōz′līn′, klō*th*z′-) *n.* A cord, rope, or wire on which clothes may be hung to dry or air. **—clothesline** *tr.v.* **-lined, -lin•ing, -lines.** *Sports.* To knock down (an opponent in an athletic contest) by hooking the neck with an outstretched arm.

clothes moth *n.* Any of various moths of the family Tineidae, whose larvae feed on wool, hair, fur, and feathers.

clothes•pin (klōz′pĭn′, klō*th*z′-) *n.* A clip of wood or plastic for fastening clothes to a clothesline.

clothes•press also **clothes press** (klōz′prĕs′, klō*th*z′-) *n.* A chest, closet, or wardrobe in which clothes are kept.

clothes tree *n.* An upright pole or stand with hooks or pegs on which to hang clothing. Also called *coat tree.*

cloth•ier (klō*th*′yər, klō′*th*ē-ər) *n.* One that makes or sells clothing or cloth.

cloth•ing (klō′*th*ĭng) *n.* **1.** Clothes considered as a group; wearing apparel. **2.** A covering.

Clo•tho (klō′thō) *n. Greek Mythology.* One of the three Fates, the spinner of the thread of destiny.

cloth yard *n.* The standard unit of cloth measurement, equal to 36 inches (0.914 meter).

clot•ted cream (klŏt′ĭd) *n.* A thick cream made primarily in England by heating and cooling milk on which cream has already been allowed to rise, and then by skimming the cream from the top. Also called *Devonshire cream.*

clo•ture (klō′chər) *n.* A parliamentary procedure by which debate is ended and an immediate vote is taken on the matter under discussion. Also called *closure.* **—cloture** *tr.v.* **-tured, -tur•ing, -tures.** To apply cloture to (a parliamentary debate). [French *clôture,* from Old French *closture,* probably alteration of *closure,* closure. See CLOSURE.]

cloud (kloud) *n.* **1. a.** A visible body of very fine water droplets or ice particles suspended in the atmosphere at altitudes ranging up to several miles above sea level. **b.** A mass, as of dust, smoke, or steam, suspended in the air or in outer space. **2.** A large moving body of things in the air or on the ground; a swarm: *a cloud of locusts.* **3.** Something that darkens or fills with gloom. **4.** A dark region or blemish, as on a polished stone. **5.** Something that obscures. **6.** Suspicion or a charge affecting a reputation. **7.** A collection of charged particles: *an electron cloud.* **—cloud** *v.* **cloud•ed, cloud•ing, clouds.** *—tr.* **1.** To cover with or as if with clouds: *Mist clouded the hills.* **2.** To make gloomy or troubled. **3.** To obscure: *cloud the issues.* **4.** To cast aspersions on; sully: *Scandal clouded the officer's reputation.* *—intr.* To become cloudy or overcast: *The sky clouded over.* **—*idiom.* in the clouds. 1.** Imaginary; unreal; fanciful. **2.** Impractical. [Middle English, hill, cloud, from Old English *clūd,* rock, hill.] **—cloud′less** *adj.*

cloud•ber•ry (kloud′bĕr′ē) *n.* A creeping perennial herb *(Rubus chamaemorus)* in the rose family, native to northern regions of North America and Eurasia and having white flowers and edible, yellowish fruit.

cloud•burst (kloud′bûrst′) *n.* A sudden, heavy rainstorm; a downpour.

cloud chamber *n.* A gas-filled device in which the path of charged subatomic particles can be detected by the formation of chains of droplets on ions generated by their passage. It is also used to infer the presence of neutral particles and to study certain nuclear reactions.

cloud forest *n.* A tropical forest, often near peaks of coastal mountains, that usually has constant cloud cover throughout the year.

cloud grass *n.* An annual grass *(Agrostis nebulosa)* native to Spain and Portugal, cultivated for its delicate, finely branched cluster of tiny spikelets and used in dried arrangements.

cloud•land (kloud′lănd′) *n.* A realm of imagination or fantasy.

cloud•let (kloud′lĭt) *n.* A small cloud or something resembling one.

cloud nine *n. Informal.* A state of elation or great happiness: *was on cloud nine after winning the marathon.*

cloud•scape (kloud′skāp′) *n.* **1.** A work of art representing a view of clouds: *an Impressionist painting that is a vast cloudscape of buoyant, floating forms.* **2.** A photograph showing a view of clouds, such as those surrounding a planet.

cloud seed•ing (sē′dĭng) *n.* The technique of stimulating rainfall, especially by distributing dry ice crystals or silver iodide smoke through clouds.

cloud•y (klou′dē) *adj.* **-i•er, -i•est. 1.** Full of or covered with clouds; overcast. **2.** Of or like a cloud or clouds. **3.** Marked with indistinct masses or streaks: *cloudy marble.* **4.** Not transparent, as certain liquids. **5. a.** Open to more than one interpretation. **b.** Not clearly perceived or perceptible. **6.** Troubled; gloomy. **—cloud′i•ly** *adv.* **—cloud′i•ness** *n.*

♦**clout** (klout) *n.* **1.** A blow, especially with the fist. **2. a.** *Baseball.* A long, powerful hit. **b.** *Sports.* An archery target. **3.** *Informal.* **a.** Influence; pull: *"All the evidence showed that Russia does not have that kind of clout in the Far East any more"* (Joseph Kraft). **b.** Power; muscle. **4.** *Regional.* A piece of cloth, especially a baby's diaper. **—clout** *tr.v.* **clout•ed, clout•ing, clouts.** To hit, especially with the fist. [Middle English, probably from Old English *clūt,* cloth patch.]

clove¹ (klōv) *n.* **1.** An evergreen tree *(Syzygium aromaticum)* native to the Moluccas and widely cultivated in warm regions for its aromatic dried flower buds. **2.** A flower bud of this plant, used whole or ground as a spice. Often used in the plural. [Middle English, from Old French *clou (de girofle),* nail (of the clove tree), from Latin *clāvus,* nail.]

clove² (klōv) *n.* One of the small sections of a separable bulb, as that of garlic. [Middle English, from Old English *clufu.* See **gleubh-** in Appendix.]

clove³ (klōv) *v.* **1.** A past tense of **cleave¹. 2.** *Archaic.* A past participle of **cleave¹.**

clove⁴ (klōv) *v. Archaic.* A past tense of **cleave².**

clove hitch *n.* A knot used to secure a line to a spar, post, or other object, consisting of two half hitches made in opposite directions. [Middle English *clove,* split, past participle of *cleven,* to split. See CLEAVE¹.]

clo•ven (klō′vən) *v.* A past participle of **cleave¹. —cloven** *adj.* Split; divided.

cloven foot *n.* See **cloven hoof** (sense 1).

clo•ven-footed (klō′vən-fo͝ot′ĭd) *adj.* Cloven-hoofed.

cloven hoof *n.* **1.** A divided or cleft hoof, as in deer or cattle. Also called *cloven foot.* **2.** Evil or Satan, often depicted as a figure with cleft hoofs.

clo·ven-hoofed (klō′vən-ho͝oft′, -ho͞oft′, -ho͝ovd′, -ho͞ovd′) *adj.* **1.** Having cloven hoofs, as deer or cattle do. **2.** Satanic; devilish.

clove oil *n.* An aromatic oil obtained from the buds, stems, or leaves of the clove tree, used in flavoring and perfumery, and as a temporary anesthetic for toothaches.

clove pink *n.* See **carnation** (sense 1).

clo·ver (klō′vər) *n.* **1.** Any of various herbs of the genus *Trifolium* in the pea family, having trifoliolate leaves and dense heads of small flowers and including species grown for forage, for erosion control, and as a source of nectar for honeybees. **2.** Any of several other plants in the pea family, such as bush clover and sweet clover. **3.** Any of several nonleguminous plants, such as owl's clover and water clover. **—*idiom.* in clover.** Living a carefree life of ease, comfort, or prosperity. [Middle English, from Old English *clāfre.*]

clo·ver·leaf (klō′vər-lēf′) *n.* A highway interchange at which two highways, one crossing over the other, have a series of entrance and exit ramps resembling the outline of a four-leaf clover and enabling vehicles to proceed in either direction on either highway. **—cloverleaf** *adj.* Resembling or shaped like a leaf of the clover plant.

Clo·vis[1] (klō′vĭs). **1.** A city of central California in the foothills of the Sierra Nevada near Fresno. It is a processing center. Population, 33,021. **2.** A city of eastern New Mexico near the Texas border. It is a trade center in a wheat and cattle area. Population, 31,194.

Clo·vis[2] (klō′vĭs) *adj.* Of or relating to a prehistoric human culture widespread throughout North America from about 12,000 to 9,000 B.C., distinguished by sharp, fluted projectile points made of chalcedony or obsidian. [After CLOVIS[1], New Mexico.]

Clovis I. A.D. 466?–511. King of the Franks (481–511) who unified Gaul as a single kingdom and established his capital at Paris. His name, Gallicized as "Louis," was given to 18 later French monarchs.

clown (kloun) *n.* **1.a.** A buffoon or jester who entertains by jokes, antics, and tricks in a circus, play, or other presentation. **b.** One who jokes and plays tricks. **2.** A coarse, rude, vulgar person; a boor. **3.** A peasant; a rustic. **—clown** *intr.v.* **clowned, clown·ing, clowns. 1.** To behave like a buffoon or jester. **2.** To perform as a buffoon or jester. [Of Scandinavian origin (akin to Icelandic *klunni,* clumsy person) or of Low German origin.] **—clown′ish** *adj.* **—clown′ish·ly** *adv.* **—clown′ish·ness** *n.*

clown anemone *n.* See **anemone fish.**

clown fish *n.* See **anemone fish.**

clox·a·cil·lin (klŏk′sə-sĭl′ĭn) *n.* A semisynthetic antibiotic of the penicillin group that is used primarily to treat infections caused by staphylococci, streptococci, or pneumococci. [C(H)L(ORO)– + OX(O)– + A(ZO)– + (PENI)CILLIN.]

cloy (kloi) *v.* **cloyed, cloy·ing, cloys.** *—tr.* To cause distaste or disgust by supplying with too much of something originally pleasant, especially something rich or sweet; surfeit. *—intr.* To cause to feel surfeited. See Synonyms at **satiate.** [Short for obsolete *accloy,* to clog, from Middle English *acloien,* from Old French *encloer,* to drive a nail into, from Medieval Latin *inclāvāre* : Latin *in-,* in; see IN–[2] + Latin *clāvāre,* to nail (from *clāvus,* nail).] **—cloy′ing·ly** *adv.* **—cloy′ing·ness** *n.*

cloze (klōz) *adj.* Based on or being a test of reading comprehension in which the test taker is asked to supply words that have been systematically deleted from a text. [Alteration of CLOSURE.]

CLU *abbr.* Chartered life underwriter.

club (klŭb) *n.* **1.** A stout, heavy stick, usually thicker at one end, suitable for use as a weapon; a cudgel. **2.** *Sports.* An implement used in some games to drive a ball, especially a stick with a protruding head used in golf. **3.** *Games.* **a.** A black figure shaped like a trefoil or clover leaf on certain playing cards. **b.** A playing card with this figure. **c. clubs** *(used with a sing. or pl. verb).* The suit of cards represented by this figure. **4.** A group of people organized for a common purpose, especially a group that meets regularly: *a garden club.* **5.** The building, room, or other facility used for the meetings of an organized group. **6.** *Sports.* An athletic team or organization. **7.** A nightclub. *—attributive.* Often used to modify another noun: *a club meeting; club regulations.* **—club** *v.* **clubbed, club·bing, clubs.** *—tr.* **1.** To strike or beat with or as if with a club. **2.** To use (a firearm) as a club by holding the barrel and hitting with the butt end. **3.** To gather or combine (hair, for example) into a clublike mass. **4.** To contribute to a joint or common purpose. *—intr.* To join or combine for a common purpose; form a club. [Middle English, from Old Norse *klubba.*]

club·ba·ble also **club·a·ble** (klŭb′ə-bəl) *adj. Informal.* Suited to membership in a social club; sociable.

clubbed (klŭbd) *adj.* Shaped like a club.

club·ber (klŭb′ər) *n.* **1.** One that wields a club. **2.** One who is active in a club.

club·by (klŭb′ē) *adj.* **-bi·er, -bi·est. 1.** Typical of a club or club members. **2.** Friendly; sociable. **3.** Clannish; exclusive. **—club′bi·ness** *n.*

club car *n.* A railroad passenger car equipped with lounge chairs, tables, a buffet or bar, and other comforts. Also called *lounge car.*

club chair *n.* A heavily upholstered easy chair with arms and a low back.

club·face (klŭb′fās′) *n. Sports.* The surface on the head of a golf club used to strike the ball directly.

club·foot (klŭb′fo͝ot′) *n.* **1.** A congenital deformity of the foot, usually marked by a curled shape or twisted position of the ankle, heel, and toes. Also called *talipes.* **2.** A foot so deformed. **—club′foot′ed** *adj.*

club·house (klŭb′hous′) *n.* **1.** A building occupied by a club. **2.** *Sports.* The locker room of an athletic team.

club·man (klŭb′mən, -măn′) *n.* A man who is a member of a club or clubs, especially one who is active in club life.

club moss or **club-moss** (klŭb′môs′, -mŏs′) *n.* Any of various mostly small vascular plants of the genus *Lycopodium,* often resembling mosses and reproducing by spores. [From the club-shaped strobiles on some species of this plant.]

club·room (klŭb′ro͞om′, ro͝om′) *n.* A room used for meetings or activities of a club.

club root *n.* A disease of cabbage and related plants, caused by a fungus *(Plasmodiophora brassicae)* and characterized by knobby or club-shaped swellings on the roots and wilting, yellowing, and stunted growth of aboveground parts.

cloverleaf

club sandwich *n.* A sandwich composed of two or three slices of bread with a filling of various meats, tomato, lettuce, and dressing.

club soda *n.* See **soda water** (sense 1a).

club steak *n.* See **Delmonico steak.**

club·wom·an (klŭb′wo͝om′ən) *n.* A woman who is a member of a club or clubs, especially one who is active in club life.

cluck (klŭk) *n.* **1.a.** The characteristic sound made by a hen when brooding or calling its chicks. **b.** A sound similar to this. **2.** *Informal.* A stupid or foolish person. **—cluck** *v.* **clucked, cluck·ing, clucks.** *—intr.* **1.** To utter the characteristic sound of a hen. **2.** To make a sound similar to that of a hen, as in coaxing a horse. *—tr.* **1.** To call by making the characteristic sound of a hen. **2.** To express by clucking: *He clucked disapproval.* [Middle English *clokken,* from Old English *cloccian.*]

clue[1] (klo͞o) *n.* Something that serves to guide or direct in the solution of a problem or mystery. **—clue** *tr.v.* **clued, clue·ing** or **clu·ing, clues.** To give (someone) guiding information: *Clue me in on what's happening.* [Variant of CLEW[1] (from Theseus's use of a ball of thread as a guide through the Cretan labyrinth).]

clue[2] (klo͞o) *Nautical. n.* Variant of **clew[1]** (sense 4). **—clue** *v.* Variant of **clew[1]** (sense 2).

Cluj-Na·po·ca (klo͞ozh′nä-pô′kä). A city of west-central Romania northwest of Bucharest. It was founded by German colonists in the 12th century and became part of Romania in 1920. Population, 301,244.

Clum·ber spaniel also **clum·ber spaniel** (klŭm′bər) *n.* A dog of a breed developed in England, having short legs, a stocky body, and a silky, predominantly white coat. [After *Clumber Park,* an estate in Nottinghamshire, a county of central England.]

clown

clump (klŭmp) *n.* **1.** A clustered mass; a lump: *clumps of soil.* **2.** A thick grouping, as of trees or bushes. **3.** A heavy, dull sound; a thud. **—clump** *v.* **clumped, clump·ing, clumps.** *—intr.* **1.** To form lumps or thick groupings. **2.** To walk or move so as to make a heavy, dull sound. *—tr.* To gather into or form lumps or thick groupings of. [Probably Low German *klump,* from Middle Low German *klumpe,* cluster of trees.] **—clump′y** *adj.*

clum·sy (klŭm′zē) *adj.* **-si·er, -si·est. 1.** Lacking physical coordination, skill, or grace; awkward. **2.** Awkwardly constructed; unwieldy: *clumsy wooden shoes; a clumsy sentence.* **3.** Gauche; inept: *a clumsy excuse.* See Synonyms at **awkward.** [From obsolete *clumse,* to be numb with cold, from Middle English *clomsen,* of Scandinavian origin.] **—clum′si·ly** *adv.* **—clum′si·ness** *n.*

clung (klŭng) *v.* Past tense and past participle of **cling.**

clunk (klŭngk) *n.* **1.** A dull sound; a thump. **2.** A blow that produces a dull sound. **3.** *Informal.* A stupid, dull person. **—clunk** *v.* **clunked, clunk·ing, clunks.** *—intr.* **1.** To make or move with a clunk. **2.** To strike something so as to make a dull sound. *—tr.* To strike so as to make a dull sound: *"Icy weather affected the clock's mechanism and for several hours Big Ben clunked instead of bonged the time changes"* (Christian Science Monitor). [Imitative.]

clunk·er (clŭng′kər) *n. Informal.* **1.** A decrepit machine, especially an old car; a rattletrap. **2.** A failure; a flop.

clunk·y (klŭng′kē) *adj.* **-i·er, -i·est.** Clumsy in form or manner; awkward: *clunky high-heel shoes.*

Clu·ny (klo͞o′nē, klo͞o-nē′, klü-). A town of east-central France north-northwest of Lyons. Its abbey, the center of an influential religious order, was founded in 910. Population, 4,335.

Clumber spaniel

clu·pe·id (klo͞o′pē-ĭd) *n.* Any of various widely distributed soft-finned fishes of the family Clupeidae, which includes the herrings, menhadens, and sardines. **—clupeid** *adj.* Of, relating to, or belonging to the family Clupeidae. [From New Latin *Clupeidae,* family name, from Latin *clupea,* a kind of small fish.]

clus·ter (klŭs′tər) *n.* **1.** A group of the same or similar elements gathered or occurring closely together; a bunch: *"She held out her hand, a small tight cluster of fingers"* (Anne Tyler). **2.** *Linguistics.* Two or more successive consonants in a word, as *cl* and *st* in the word *cluster.* —**cluster** *v.* **-tered, -ter·ing, -ters.** —*intr.* To gather or grow into bunches. —*tr.* To cause to grow or form into bunches. [Middle English, from Old English *clyster.*]

cluster bean *n.* See **guar.**

cluster bomb *n.* A projectile that, when dropped from an aircraft or fired through the air, releases explosive fragments over a wide area.

cluster headache *n.* A severe recurring headache that is associated with the release of histamine and is characterized by sudden sharp pain, watering of the eye, and runny nose on one side of the head.

cluster pine *n.* A Mediterranean pine tree *(Pinus pinaster)* having long needles in clusters of two, and large ovoid seed-bearing cones.

clutch[1] (klŭch) *v.* **clutched, clutch·ing, clutch·es.** —*tr.* **1.** To grasp and hold tightly. **2.** To seize; snatch. —*intr.* **1.** To attempt to grasp or seize: *clutch at a life raft.* **2.** To engage or disengage a motor vehicle's clutch. —**clutch** *n.* **1.** A hand, claw, talon, or paw in the act of grasping. **2.** A tight grasp. **3.** Often **clutches.** Control or power: *caught in the clutches of sin.* **4.** A device for gripping and holding. **5.a.** Any of various devices for engaging and disengaging two working parts of a shaft or of a shaft and a driving mechanism. **b.** The apparatus, such as a lever or pedal, that activates one of these devices. **6.** A tense, critical situation: *came through in the clutch.* **7.** A clutch bag. —**clutch** *adj. Informal.* **1.** Being or occurring in a tense or critical situation: *sank a clutch putt.* **2.** Tending to be successful in tense or critical situations: *The coach relied on her clutch pitcher.* [Middle English *clucchen,* from Old English *clyccan.*]

clutch bag

clutch[2] (klŭch) *n.* **1.** The complete set of eggs produced or incubated at one time. **2.** A brood of chickens. **3.** A group; a bunch. —**clutch** *tr.v.* **clutched, clutch·ing, clutch·es.** To hatch (chicks). [Variant of dialectal *cletch,* to hatch, from Middle English *clekken,* from Old Norse *klekja.*]

clutch bag *n.* A woman's purse that is usually strapless.

clut·ter (klŭt′ər) *n.* **1.** A confused or disordered state or collection; a jumble: *clutter in the attic.* **2.** A confused noise; a clatter. —**clutter** *v.* **-tered, -ter·ing, -ters.** —*tr.* To litter or pile in a disordered manner: *Tools and boxes cluttered the garage. I cluttered up my files with clippings.* —*intr.* **1.** To run or move with bustle and confusion. **2.** To make a clatter. [Probably from Middle English *cloteren,* to clot, from *clot,* lump, from Old English *clott.*]

Clyde (klīd). A river of southwest Scotland flowing about 171 km (106 mi) northwest to the **Firth of Clyde,** an estuary of the North Channel. The river is navigable to Glasgow for oceangoing vessels.

Clyde·bank (klīd′băngk′). A burgh of west-central Scotland on the north bank of the Clyde River. Many large ocean liners, including the *Queen Mary,* were built in its shipyards. Population, 52,385.

Clydesdale

Clydes·dale (klīdz′dāl′) *n.* A large, powerful draft horse of a breed developed in the Clyde valley of Scotland, having white, feathered hair on its fetlocks.

clyp·e·ate (klĭp′ē-ĭt) also **clyp·e·at·ed** (-ā′tĭd) *adj.* **1.** Shaped like a round shield. **2.** *Zoology.* Having a clypeus: *clypeate insects.*

clyp·e·us (klĭp′ē-əs) *n., pl.* **-e·i** (-ē-ī′). *Zoology.* A shieldlike plate on the front of the head of an insect. [New Latin, from Latin *clipeus,* round shield.] —**clyp′e·al** (-ē-əl) *adj.*

clys·ter (klĭs′tər) *n.* An enema. [Middle English *clister,* from Old French *clistere,* from Latin *clyster,* from Greek *klustēr,* clyster pipe, from *kluzein,* to wash out.]

Cly·tem·nes·tra also **Cly·taem·nes·tra** (klī′təm-nĕs′trə) *n. Greek Mythology.* The wife of Agamemnon who, with the assistance of her lover Aegisthus, murdered him on his return from the Trojan War and was later murdered by her son Orestes.

cm *abbr.* Centimeter.

Cm The symbol for the element **curium.**

CM *abbr.* Common market.

c.m. *abbr.* **1.** Center of mass. **2.** Circular mil. **3.** Court-martial.

CMA also **C.M.A.** *abbr.* Certified medical assistant.

cmd. *abbr.* **1.** Command. **2. Cmd.** Commander.

cmdg. *abbr.* Commanding.

Cmdr *abbr.* Commander.

cml. *abbr.* Commercial.

CMSGT *abbr.* Chief master sergeant.

CMV *abbr.* Cytomegalovirus.

C/N *abbr.* Credit note.

cni·do·blast (nī′də-blăst′) *n.* A cell in the epidermis of coelenterates in which a nematocyst is developed. [New Latin *cnīdă,* nematocyst (from Latin *cnīdē,* nettle, from Greek *knidē*) + -BLAST.]

Cni·dus also **Cni·dos** (nī′dəs). An ancient Greek city of Asia Minor in present-day southwest Asiatic Turkey. It was noted for its wealth and its magnificent buildings and statuary.

Cnos·sos or **Cnos·sus** (nŏs′əs). See **Knossos.**

CNS *abbr.* Central nervous system.

Cnut (kə-no͞ot′, -nyo͞ot′). See **Canute.**

Co[1] The symbol for the element **cobalt.**

Co[2] *abbr. Bible.* Corinthians.

CO *abbr.* **1.** Colorado. **2.** Or **C.O.** Commanding officer. **3.** Also **C.O.** Conscientious objector.

co. *abbr.* **1.** Or **co, Co.** Company. **2.** County.

c.o. *abbr.* **1.** *Accounting.* Carried over. **2.** Cash order.

c/o also **c.o.** *abbr.* Care of.

co– *pref.* **1.** Together; joint; jointly; mutually: *coeducation.* **2.a.** Partner or associate in an activity: *coauthor; cofounder.* **b.** Subordinate or assistant: *copilot.* **3.** To the same extent or degree: *coextensive.* **4.** Complement of an angle: *cotangent.* [Middle English, from Latin, variant of *com-,* com-.]

CoA *abbr.* Coenzyme A.

co·ac·er·vate (kō-ăs′ər-vāt′) *n.* A cluster of droplets separated out of a lyophilic colloid. —**coacervate** *adj.* **1.** Of or relating to a cluster of droplets. **2.** *Biology.* Growing in clusters. —**coacervate** *tr.v.* **-vated, -vat·ing, -vates.** To cause to form a coacervate. [From Latin *coacervātus,* past participle of *coacervāre,* to heap together : *co-,* co- + *acervāre,* to heap (from *acervus,* a heap).] —**co·ac′er·vate** *adj.* —**co·ac′er·va′tion** *n.*

coach (kōch) *n.* **1.a.** A motorbus. **b.** A railroad passenger car. **c.** A closed automobile, usually with two doors. **d.** A large, closed, four-wheeled carriage with an elevated exterior seat for the driver; a stagecoach. **2.** An economical class of passenger accommodations on a commercial airplane or a train. **3.** *Sports.* A person who trains or directs athletes or athletic teams. **4.a.** A person who gives instruction, as in singing or acting. **b.** A private tutor employed to prepare a student for an examination. —**coach** *tr. & intr.v.* **coached, coach·ing, coach·es. 1.** To train or tutor or to act as a trainer or tutor. **2.** To transport by or ride in a coach. [French *coche,* from obsolete German *Kotsche,* from Hungarian *kocsi,* after *Kocs,* a town of northwest Hungary (where such carriages were first made).] —**coach′a·ble** *adj.* —**coach′er** *n.*

coach dog *n.* See **Dalmatian** (sense 2). [So called because it was trained to run behind a coach.]

coach·man (kōch′mən) *n.* **1.** A man who drives a coach or carriage. **2.** An artificial fly used in angling.

co·ac·tion (kō-ăk′shən) *n.* **1.** An impelling or restraining force; a compulsion. **2.** Joint action. **3.** *Ecology.* Any of the reciprocal actions or effects, such as symbiosis, that can occur in a community. [Middle English *coaccioun,* from Latin *coāctiō, coāctiōn-,* a collecting, from *coāctus,* past participle of *cōgere,* to collect, condense; see COAGULUM. Senses 2 and 3 : CO– + ACTION.] —**co·ac′tive** *adj.* —**co·ac′tive·ly** *adv.*

co·a·dapt·ed (kō′ə-dăp′tĭd) *adj. Ecology.* Of or relating to characteristics that have become established through mutually beneficial interaction between organisms in a community. —**co′ad·ap·ta′tion** (-ăd-ăp-tā′shən) *n.*

co·ad·ju·tant (kō-ăj′ə-tənt) *n.* A helper; an assistant. See Synonyms at **assistant.**

co·ad·ju·tor (kō′ə-jo͞o′tər, kō-ăj′ə-tər) *n.* **1.** A coworker; an assistant. See Synonyms at **assistant. 2.** An assistant to a bishop, especially one designated to succeed the bishop. [Middle English *coadjutour,* assistant, from Latin *coadiūtor* : *co-,* co- + *adiūtor,* assistant (from *adiūtāre,* to aid; see ADJUTANT).]

co·ad·u·nate (kō-ăj′ə-nĭt, -nāt′) *adj.* Closely joined; grown together; united. [Late Latin *coadūnātus,* past participle of *coadūnāre,* to combine : Latin *co-,* co- + Latin *adūnāre,* to unite (*ad-,* ad- + *ūnus,* one; see **oi-no-** in Appendix).] —**co·ad′u·na′tion** (-nā′shən) *n.* —**co·ad′u·na′tive** *adj.*

co·ag·u·lant (kō-ăg′yə-lənt) *n.* An agent that causes a liquid or sol to coagulate. —**co·ag′u·lant** *adj.*

co·ag·u·lase (kō-ăg′yə-lās′, -lāz′) *n.* An enzyme, such as rennin or thrombin, that induces coagulation. [COAGUL(ATE) + -ASE.]

co·ag·u·late (kō-ăg′yə-lāt′) *v.* **-lat·ed, -lat·ing, -lates.** —*tr.* To cause transformation of (a liquid or sol, for example) into or as if into a soft, semisolid, or solid mass. —*intr.* To become coagulated. [Middle English *coagulaten,* from Latin *coāgulāre, coāgulāt-,* from *coāgulum,* coagulator. See COAGULUM.] —**co·ag′u·la·bil′i·ty** *n.* —**co·ag′u·la·ble** *adj.* —**co·ag′u·la′tion** *n.* —**co·ag′u·la′tor** *n.*

SYNONYMS: *coagulate, clot, congeal, curdle, jell, jelly, set.* The central meaning shared by these verbs is "to change or be changed from a liquid into a thickened mass": *egg white coagulating when heated; gravy clotting as it cools; water congealing into ice; milk that had curdled; used pectin to jell the jam; jellied consommé; allowed the aspic to set.*

co·ag·u·lum (kō-ăg′yə-ləm) *n., pl.* **-la** (-lə). A coagulated mass, as of blood; a clot. [Latin, coagulator, rennet, from *cōgere,* to condense : *co-,* co- + *agere,* to drive; see **ag-** in Appendix.]

coal (kōl) *n.* **1.a.** A natural dark brown to black graphitelike material used as a fuel, formed from fossilized plants and consisting of amorphous carbon with various organic and some inorganic compounds. **b.** A piece of this substance. **2.** A glowing or charred piece of solid fuel. **3.** Charcoal. —*attributive.* Often used to modify another noun: *coal miners; coal seams; coal haulers.* —**coal** *v.* **coaled, coal·ing, coals.** —*tr.* **1.** To burn (a combustible solid) to a charcoal residue. **2.** To provide with coal. —*intr.* To take on coal. [Middle English *col,* from Old English.]

coal·er (kō′lər) *n.* Something, such as a ship or train, used for carrying or supplying coal.

co·a·lesce (kō′ə-lĕs′) *intr.v.* **-lesced, -lesc·ing, -lesc·es. 1.** To grow together; fuse. **2.** To come together so as to form one whole; unite: *The rebel units coalesced into one army to fight the invaders.* See Synonyms at **mix.** [Latin *coalēscere* : *co-*, co- + *alēscere,* to grow, inchoative of *alere,* to nourish; see **al-**[2] in Appendix.] **—co′a·les′cence** *n.* **—co′a·les′cent** *adj.*

coal·field (kōl′fēld′) *n.* An area in which deposits of coal are found.

coal·fish (kōl′fĭsh′) *n.* Any of several black or dark-colored fishes, especially the pollock or sablefish.

coal gas *n.* **1.** A gaseous mixture produced by the destructive distillation of bituminous coal and used as a commercial fuel. **2.** The gaseous mixture released by burning coal.

coal·i·fi·ca·tion (kō′lə-fĭ-kā′shən) *n.* Compression and hardening over long periods of time, the processes by which coal is formed from plant materials.

co·a·li·tion (kō′ə-lĭsh′ən) *n.* **1.** An alliance, especially a temporary one, of people, factions, parties, or nations. **2.** A combination into one body; a union. [French, from Medieval Latin *coalitiō, coalitiōn-,* from Latin *coalitus,* past participle of *coalēscere,* to grow together. See COALESCE.] **—co′a·li′tion·ist** *n.*

coal measures *pl.n. Geology.* **1. Coal Measures.** A stratigraphic unit equivalent to the Pennsylvanian or Upper Carboniferous periods. **2.** Strata of the Carboniferous period containing coal deposits.

coal oil *n.* See **kerosene.**

Coal·sack (kōl′săk′) *n.* **1.** A dark nebula, one of the nearest to Earth, that appears in the southern Milky Way. **2.** A similar dark nebula in the Northern Hemisphere near the constellation Cygnus.

coal tar *n.* A viscous black liquid containing numerous organic compounds that is obtained by the destructive distillation of coal and used as a roofing, waterproofing, and insulating compound and as a raw material for many dyes, drugs, and paints.

coam·ing (kō′mĭng) *n. Nautical.* A raised rim or border around an opening, as in a ship's deck, designed to keep out water. [Origin unknown.]

co-an·chor or **co·an·chor** (kō-ăng′kər) —*n.* Either of two news commentators jointly narrating or coordinating a newscast. —*v.* **-chored, -chor·ing, -chors.** —*intr.* To narrate or coordinate a newscast with another person. —*tr.* To narrate or coordinate (a newscast) with another person.

co·arc·tate (kō-ärk′tāt′) *adj. Zoology.* **1.** Enclosed in an oval, horny case. Used of an insect pupa. **2.** Constricted, narrowed, or compressed, as a segment of a blood vessel. [Latin *coarctātus,* past participle of *coarctāre,* to compress, alteration of *coartāre* : *co-*, co- + *artāre,* to compress (from *artus,* tight, confined; see **ar-** in Appendix).]

co·arc·ta·tion (kō′ärk-tā′shən) *n.* **1.** A narrowing or constricting, especially of the aorta or of a blood vessel. **2.** The state of being enclosed in an oval, horny case. Used of an insect pupa.

coarse (kôrs, kōrs) *adj.* **coars·er, coars·est. 1.** Of low, common, or inferior quality. **2.a.** Lacking in delicacy or refinement: *coarse manners.* **b.** Vulgar or indecent: *coarse language.* **3.** Consisting of large particles; not fine in texture: *coarse sand.* **4.** Rough, especially to the touch: *a coarse tweed.* [Middle English *cors,* probably from *course,* custom. See COURSE.] **—coarse′ly** *adv.* **—coarse′ness** *n.*

SYNONYMS: *coarse, gross, indelicate, vulgar, obscene, ribald.* These adjectives apply to what is offensive to accepted standards of decency, propriety, morality, or good taste. *Coarse* implies roughness and crudeness: *A stand-up comedian performed a coarse imitation of the President. Gross* suggests a lack of refinement verging on brutishness: *"It is futile to expect a hungry and squalid population to be anything but violent and gross"* (Thomas H. Huxley). *Indelicate* implies a lack of delicacy, tact, or taste: *She bridled at the indelicate suggestion. Vulgar* emphasizes impropriety and suggests boorishness and poor breeding: *The movie is full of language so vulgar it should have been edited. Obscene* strongly stresses loathsome lewdness and indecency: *The book is racy rather than obscene. Ribald* implies vulgar, coarse, off-color language or behavior that provokes mirth: *"Peals of laughter were mingled with loud ribald jokes"* (Washington Irving).

coarse-grained (kôrs′grānd′, kōrs′-) *adj.* **1.** Having a rough, coarse texture. **2.** Not refined; indelicate and crude.

coars·en (kôr′sən, kōr′-) *tr. & intr.v.* **-ened, -en·ing, -ens.** To make or become coarse.

coast (kōst) *n.* **1.a.** Land next to the sea; the seashore. **b. Coast.** The Pacific Coast of the United States. **2.** A hill or other slope down which one may coast, as on a sled. **3.** The act of sliding or coasting; slide. **4.** *Obsolete.* The frontier or border of a country. —**coast** *v.* **coast·ed, coast·ing, coasts.** —*intr.* **1.a.** To slide down an incline through the effect of gravity. **b.** To move effortlessly and smoothly. See Synonyms at **slide. 2.** To move without further use of propelling power. **3.** To act or move aimlessly or with little effort: *coasted for a few weeks before applying for a job.* **4.** *Nautical.* To sail near or along a coast. —*tr. Nautical.* To sail or move along the coast or border of. [Middle English *coste,* from Old French, from Latin *costa,* side. See **kost-** in Appendix.] **—coast′al** (kō′stəl) *adj.*

coast·er (kō′stər) *n.* **1.** One that coasts, as: **a.** One who acts in an aimless manner. **b.** A sled or toboggan. **c.** One who rides a sled or toboggan. **2.** *Nautical.* A vessel engaged in coastal trade: *"dirty British coaster with a salt-caked smokestack"* (John Masefield). **3.** A roller coaster. **4.a.** A disk, plate, or small mat placed under a bottle, pitcher, or drinking glass to protect a table top or other surface beneath. **b.** A small tray, often on wheels, for passing something, such as a wine decanter, around a table. **5.** A resident of a coastal region.

coaster brake *n.* A brake and clutch on the rear wheel and drive mechanism of a bicycle operated through reverse pressure on the pedals.

coast guard also **Coast Guard** *n. Abbr.* **C.G. 1.** The branch of a nation's armed forces that is responsible for coastal defense, protection of life and property at sea, and enforcement of customs, immigration, and navigation laws. **2.** A member of a coast guard.

coast·guards·man (kōst′gärdz′mən) *n.* A member of a coast guard.

coast·land (kōst′lănd′) *n.* The land along a coast.

coast·line (kōst′līn′) *n.* The shape, outline, or boundary of a coast.

Coast Mountains. A range of western British Columbia, Canada, and southeast Alaska extending about 1,609 km (1,000 mi) parallel to the Pacific coast.

Coast Ranges. A series of mountain ranges of extreme western North America extending from southeast Alaska to Baja California along the coastline of the Pacific Ocean.

Coast Salish *n.* The Salish-speaking Native American peoples inhabiting the northwest Pacific coast from the Strait of Georgia to southwest Washington.

coast-to-coast (kōst′tə-kōst′) *adj.* Reaching, airing, or traveling from one coast to another, especially across a nation or continent: *a coast-to-coast flight; coast-to-coast coverage on TV.*

coast·ward (kōst′wərd) *adv. & adj.* Toward or directed toward a coast: *The schooner sailed coastward. We followed a coastward route.* **—coast′wards** (-wərdz) *adv.*

coast·wise (kōst′wīz′) *adv. & adj.* Along, by way of, or following a coast: *The winds blew coastwise. Coastwise winds contributed to the storm.*

coat (kōt) *n.* **1.a.** A sleeved outer garment extending from the shoulders to the waist or below. **b.** A garment extending to just below the waist and usually forming the top part of a suit. **2.** A natural outer covering, such as the fur of an animal; an integument. **3.** A layer of material covering something else; a coating: *a second coat of paint.* —**coat** *tr.v.* **coat·ed, coat·ing, coats. 1.** To provide or cover with a coat. **2.** To cover with a layer, as of paint. [Middle English *cote,* from Old French, of Germanic origin.] **—coat′ed** *adj.*

coat·dress (kōt′drĕs′) *n.* A dress that buttons up the front and is tailored somewhat like a coat.

coati
Nasua nasua

co·a·ti (kō-ä′tē) *n.* Any of four species of omnivorous mammals of the genera *Nasua* or *Nasuella* of South and Central America and the southwest United States, related to and resembling the raccoon but having a longer snout and tail. [Spanish and Portuguese *coatí,* from Tupi : *cua,* belt + *tim,* nose.]

co·a·ti·mun·di also **co·a·ti·mon·di** (kō-ä′tē-mŭn′dē) *n.* A coati. [Possibly Tupi *coati* + Tupi *mundé,* animal trap.]

coat·ing (kō′tĭng) *n.* **1.** A layer of a substance spread over a surface for protection or decoration; a covering layer. **2.** Cloth for making coats.

coat of arms *n., pl.* **coats of arms.** *Heraldry.* **1.** A tabard or surcoat blazoned with bearings. **2.a.** An arrangement of bearings, usually depicted on and around a shield, that indicates ancestry and distinctions. **b.** A representation of bearings.

coat of arms
MacGregor family

coat of mail *n., pl.* **coats of mail.** An armored coat made of chain mail, interlinked rings, or overlapping metal plates; a hauberk.

coat·room (kōt′ro͞om′, -ro͝om′) *n.* See **cloakroom** (sense 1).

coat·tail (kōt′tāl′) *n.* **1.** The loose back part of a coat that hangs below the waist. **2. coattails.** The skirts of a formal or dress coat. **—*idioms.* on (someone's) coattails.** With the assistance of another: *won the mayor's post on the senator's coattails.* **on the coattails of. 1.** As a result of the success of another: *elected to office on the coattails of a popular governor.* **2.** Immediately following or as a direct result of: *resigned on the coattails of the scandal.*

coat tree *n.* See **clothes tree.**

co·au·thor or **co-au·thor** (kō-ô′thər) —*n.* A collaborating or joint author. —*tr.v.* **-thored, -thor·ing, -thors.** To be a collaborating or joint author of: *"He and a colleague . . . co-authored a genetics text"* (Roger W. Pease, Jr.). See Usage Note at **author.**

coax[1] (kōks) *v.* **coaxed, coax·ing, coax·es.** —*tr.* **1.** To persuade or try to persuade by pleading or flattery; cajole. **2.** To obtain by persistent persuasion: *coaxed the secret out of the child.* **3.** *Obsolete.* To caress; fondle. —*intr.* To use persuasion or inducement. [Obsolete *cokes,* to fool, from *cokes,* fool.] **—coax′er** *n.* **—coax′ing·ly** *adv.*

co·ax[2] (kō′ăks, kō-ăks′) *n. Informal.* A coaxial cable.

co·ax·i·al (kō-ăk′sē-əl) *adj.* Having or mounted on a common axis.

coaxial cable *n.* A cable consisting of a conducting outer metal tube enclosing and insulated from a central conducting core, used for high-frequency transmission of telephone, telegraph, and television signals. Also called *coaxial line.*

cob (kŏb) *n.* **1.** A corncob: *corn on the cob.* **2.** A male swan. **3.**

ă pat	oi boy
ā pay	ou out
âr care	o͝o took
ä father	o͞o boot
ĕ pet	ŭ cut
ē be	ûr urge
ĭ pit	th thin
ī pie	*th* this
îr pier	hw which
ŏ pot	zh vision
ō toe	ə about, item
ô paw	♦ regionalism

Stress marks: ′ (primary); ′ (secondary), as in **dictionary** (dĭk′shə-nĕr′ē)

A thickset, stocky, short-legged horse. **4.** A small lump or mass, as of coal. **5.** A mixture of clay and straw used as a building material. [Probably from obsolete *cob,* round object, head, testicle.]

co·bal·a·min (kō-băl′ə-mĭn) also **co·bal·a·mine** (-mēn′) *n.* See **vitamin B_{12}.** [COBAL(T) + (VIT)AMIN.]

co·balt (kō′bôlt′) *n. Symbol* **Co** A hard, brittle metallic element, found associated with nickel, silver, lead, copper, and iron ores and resembling nickel and iron in appearance. It is used chiefly for magnetic alloys, high-temperature alloys, and in the form of its salts for blue glass and ceramic pigments. Atomic number 27; atomic weight 58.9332; melting point 1,495°C; boiling point 2,900°C; specific gravity 8.9; valence 2, 3. See table at **element.** [German *Kobalt,* from Middle High German *kobolt,* goblin (from the trouble it gave silver miners).]

cobalt 60 *n.* A radioactive isotope of cobalt with mass number 60 and exceptionally intense gamma-ray activity, used in radiotherapy, metallurgy, and materials testing.

cobalt blue *n.* **1.** A blue to green pigment consisting of a variable mixture of cobalt oxide and alumina. **2.** *Color.* A moderate to deep vivid blue or strong greenish blue.

co·balt·ic (kō-bôl′tĭk) *adj.* Of or containing cobalt, especially with a valence of 3.

co·balt·ite (kō′bôl-tīt′) also **co·balt·ine** (-tēn′) *n.* A rare silver-white to gray mineral, cobalt sulfarsenide, CoAsS, that is a cobalt ore and is used in ceramics.

co·balt·ous (kō-bôl′təs) *adj.* Of or containing cobalt, especially with a valence of 2.

Cobb (kŏb), **Irwin Shrewsbury.** 1876–1944. American humorist known for his books and short-story collections, especially *Old Judge Priest* (1915).

Cobb, Tyrus Raymond. Known as "Ty." 1886–1961. American baseball player and manager who was the first player elected to the National Baseball Hall of Fame (1936). He set a number of major league records, including a lifetime batting average of .367.

cob·ber (kŏb′ər) *n. Australian.* A pal; a buddy. [Possibly from dialectal *cob,* to take a liking to.]

Cob·bett (kŏb′ĭt), **William.** 1763?–1835. British journalist and social reformer noted for his *Rural Rides* (1830), a collection of essays showing the deterioration of rural life brought about by the Industrial Revolution.

cob·ble¹ (kŏb′əl) *n.* **1.** A cobblestone. **2.** *Geology.* A rock fragment between 64 and 256 millimeters in diameter, especially one that has been naturally rounded. **3. cobbles.** See **cob coal.** —**cobble** *tr.v.* **-bled, -bling, -bles.** To pave with cobblestones. [Short for COBBLESTONE.]

cob·ble² (kŏb′əl) *tr.v.* **-bled, -bling, -bles. 1.** To make or mend (boots or shoes). **2.** To put together clumsily; bungle: *cobbled a plan together at the last minute.* [Probably back-formation from COBBLER¹.]

cob·bler¹ (kŏb′lər) *n.* **1.** One that mends or makes boots and shoes. **2.** *Archaic.* One who is clumsy at work; a bungler. [Middle English *cobeler.*]

cob·bler² *n.* **1.** A deep-dish fruit pie with a thick top crust. **2.** An iced drink made of wine or liqueur, sugar, and citrus fruit. [Origin unknown.]

cob·ble·stone (kŏb′əl-stōn′) *n.* A naturally rounded paving stone. [Middle English *cobelston* : obsolete *cobel,* probably diminutive of *cob,* round object; see COB + Middle English *ston, stone,* stone; see STONE.]

cob coal *n.* Coal in rounded lumps of various sizes. Also called *cobbles.*

Cob·den (kŏb′dən), **Richard.** 1804–1865. British politician who was a leading supporter of free trade and an opponent of protectionism.

co·bel·lig·er·ent (kō′bə-lĭj′ər-ənt) *n.* One, such as a nation, that assists another or others in waging war, usually without entering a formal alliance.

Cobh (kōv). An urban district of southern Ireland on Cork Harbor. It is a popular seaside resort. Population, 6,587.

co·bi·a (kō′bē-ə) *n.* A large food and game fish *(Rachycentron canadum)* of tropical and subtropical seas. Also called *sergeant fish.* [Origin unknown.]

co·ble (kō′bəl) *n.* **1.** *Nautical.* A small, flat-bottomed fishing boat with a lugsail on a raking mast. **2.** *Scots.* A kind of flat-bottomed rowboat. [Middle English *cobel,* perhaps ultimately from Latin *caupulus,* a kind of small ship.]

Co·blenz (kō′blĕnts′). See **Koblenz.**

cob·nut (kŏb′nŭt′) *n.* **1.** The large edible nut of a cultivated variety of hazel. **2.** The plant bearing this fruit.

CO·BOL or **Co·bol** (kō′bôl′) *n. Computer Science.* A language based on English words and phrases, used in programming digital computers for various business applications. [*Co(mmon) B(usiness-)O(riented) L(anguage).*]

co·bra (kō′brə) *n.* **1.** Any of several venomous snakes, especially of the genus *Naja,* that are native to Asia and Africa and are capable of expanding the skin of the neck to form a flattened hood. **2.** Leather made from the skin of one of these snakes. [Short for Portuguese *cobra (de capello),* snake (with a hood), from Latin *colubra,* feminine of *coluber.*]

Co·burg (kō′bûrg′). A city of central Germany north of Nuremberg. It was first mentioned in the 11th century. Population, 44,239.

cob·web (kŏb′wĕb′) *n.* **1.a.** The web spun by a spider to catch its prey. **b.** A single thread spun by a spider. **2.** Something resembling the web of a spider in gauziness or flimsiness. **3.** An intricate plot; a snare: *caught in a cobweb of espionage and intrigue.* **4. cobwebs.** Confusion; disorder: *cobwebs on the brain.* —**cobweb** *tr.v.* **-webbed, -web·bing, -webs.** To cover with or as if with cobwebs. [Middle English *coppeweb* : *coppe,* spider (short for *attercoppe,* from Old English *āttercoppe* : *ātor,* poison + *copp,* head) + *web,* web (from Old English; see WEB).] —**cob′web′by** *adj.*

co·ca (kō′kə) *n.* **1.** Any of certain Andean evergreen shrubs or small trees of the genus *Erythroxylum,* especially *E. coca,* whose leaves contain cocaine and other alkaloids. **2.** The dried leaves of such a plant, chewed by people of the Andes for a stimulating effect and also used for extraction of cocaine and other alkaloids. [Spanish, from Quechua *kúka.*]

co·caine (kō-kān′, kō′kān′) *n. Abbr.* **C** A colorless or white crystalline alkaloid, $C_{17}H_{21}NO_4$, extracted from coca leaves, sometimes used in medicine as a local anesthetic especially for the eyes, nose, or throat and widely used as an illicit drug for its euphoric and stimulating effects. [French *cocaïne,* from *coca,* coca, from Spanish. See COCA.]

co·cain·ism (kō-kā′nĭz′əm) *n.* The habitual or excessive use of cocaine.

co·cain·ize (kō-kā′nīz′) *tr.v.* **-ized, -iz·ing, -iz·es.** To anesthetize (a body part) with cocaine. —**co·cain′i·za′tion** (-kā′nĭ-zā′shən) *n.*

co·car·cin·o·gen (kō′kär-sĭn′ə-jən, kō-kär′sĭn-ə-jĕn′) *n.* A substance or factor that will not promote cancer by itself but can potentiate cancer when acting with carcinogenic agents. —**co·car′cin·o·gen′ic** (-sə-nə-jĕn′ĭk) *adj.*

coc·ci (kŏk′sī, kŏk′ī) *n.* Plural of **coccus.**

coc·cid (kŏk′sĭd) *n.* Any of various insects of the superfamily Coccoidea, including the scale insects and mealybugs. [From New Latin *Coccidae,* family name, from *Coccus,* type genus, from Greek *kokkos,* grain.]

coc·cid·i·oi·do·my·co·sis (kŏk-sĭd′ē-oi′dō-mī-kō′sĭs) *n.* An infectious respiratory disease of human beings and other animals caused by inhaling the fungus *Coccidioides immitis.* It is characterized by fever and various respiratory symptoms. Also called *valley fever.* [New Latin *Coccidioides,* genus name (from *Coccidium,* coccidium; see COCCIDIUM + *-oides,* from Greek *-oeidēs,* -oid) + MYCOSIS.]

coc·cid·i·o·sis (kŏk-sĭd′ē-ō′sĭs) *n.* A parasitic disease of many animals, including cattle, swine, sheep, dogs, cats, and poultry, but rarely of human beings, resulting from infestation of the alimentary canal by protozoans of the order Coccidia. [New Latin *Coccidia,* order name, pl. of *coccidium,* coccidium; see COCCIDIUM + –OSIS.]

coc·cid·i·um (kŏk-sĭd′ē-əm) *n., pl.* **-i·a** (-ē-ə). Any of various parasitic protozoans belonging to the order Coccidia and responsible for a disease of the alimentary canal in livestock, fowl, and human beings. [New Latin *Coccidium,* originally a genus name : COCCUS + *-idium,* n. suff. (from Greek *-idion,* diminutive suff.).]

coc·co·ba·cil·lus (kŏk′ō-bə-sĭl′əs) *n., pl.* **-cil·li** (-sĭl′ī). A bacillus that is short and oval in shape. [COCC(US) + BACILLUS.]

coc·coid (kŏk′oid) *adj.* Shaped like or resembling a coccus; spherical. —**coccoid** *n.* A coccoid microorganism.

coc·co·lith (kŏk′ə-lĭth′) *n.* A microscopic skeletal plate made of calcite that protects certain marine phytoplankton and which, in a fossilized state, forms chalk and limestone deposits. [COCC(US) (from its shape) + –LITH.]

coc·cus (kŏk′əs) *n., pl.* **coc·ci** (kŏk′sī, kŏk′ī). **1.** A bacterium having a spherical or spheroidal shape. **2.** *Botany.* A division containing a single seed that splits apart from a many-lobed fruit. [New Latin, from Greek *kokkos,* grain, seed.] —**coc′coid′** (kŏk′oid′), **coc′cal** (kŏk′əl) *adj.*

–coccus *suff.* A microorganism of spherical or spheroidal shape: *streptococcus.* [From COCCUS.]

coc·cyg·e·al (kŏk-sĭj′ē-əl) *adj.* Of or relating to the coccyx: *coccygeal vertebra.* [From New Latin *coccyx, coccȳg-,* coccyx. See COCCYX.]

coc·cyx (kŏk′sĭks) *n., pl.* **coc·cy·ges** (kŏk-sī′jēz, kŏk′sĭ-jēz′). A small triangular bone at the base of the spinal column in human beings and tailless apes, consisting of several fused rudimentary vertebrae. Also called *tailbone.* [New Latin, from Greek *kokkux,* cuckoo, coccyx (from its resemblance to a cuckoo's beak).]

Co·cha·bam·ba (kō′chə-bäm′bə, kô′chä-bäm′bä). A city of west-central Bolivia north-northwest of Sucre. Founded in 1574 as Orpeza, it was renamed in 1786. Population, 317,251.

Co·chin¹ (kō′chĭn). A region and former princely state of southwest India on the Malabar Coast of the Arabian Sea. The city of **Cochin** was visited by Vasco da Gama in 1502 and colonized by the Portuguese in the following year. It was taken by the Dutch in 1663 and occupied by the British in 1795. Population, 513,249.

Co·chin² (kō′chĭn, kŏch′ĭn) *n.* See **Cochin China².**

Cochin Chi·na¹ (chī′nə). A region of southern Indochina including the rich delta area of the Mekong River. Originally a part

cobblestone
Acorn Street on
Beacon Hill, Boston

cobra
Indian cobra
Naja naja

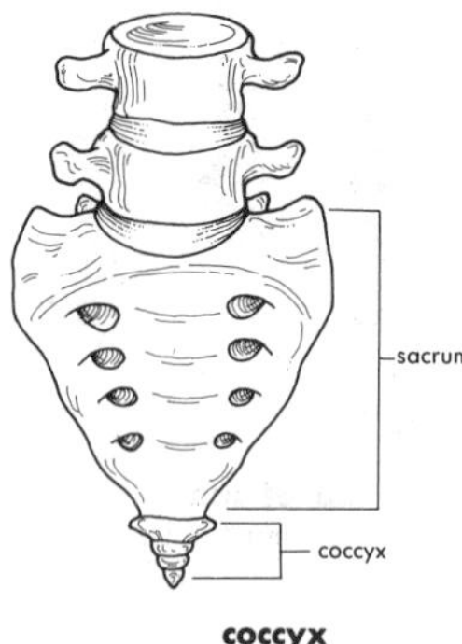

coccyx

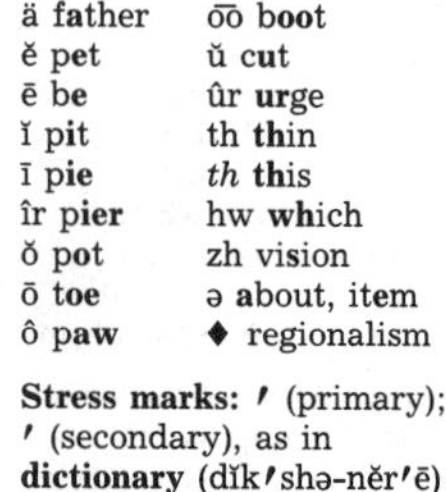

ă pat	oi boy
ā pay	ou out
âr care	ŏŏ took
ä father	ōō boot
ĕ pet	ŭ cut
ē be	ûr urge
ĭ pit	th thin
ī pie	*th* this
îr pier	hw which
ŏ pot	zh vision
ō toe	ə about, item
ô paw	♦ regionalism

Stress marks: **′** (primary); ′ (secondary), as in **dictionary** (dĭk′shə-nĕr′ē)

of the Khmer Empire, it fell to the Annamese in the 18th century and to the French in the 19th century.

Cochin Chi·na² (chī′nə) *n.* A large domestic fowl of a breed developed in Asia, having thickly feathered legs. Also called *Cochin, Shanghai.* [After COCHIN CHINA¹.]

coch·i·neal (kŏch′ə-nēl′, kŏch′ə-nēl′, kō′chə-, kō′chə-) *n.* **1.** A red dye made of the dried and pulverized bodies of female cochineal insects. It is used as a biological stain and as an indicator in acid-base titrations. **2.** *Color.* A vivid red. [French *cochenille,* from Spanish *cochinilla,* cochineal insect, probably from Vulgar Latin **coccinella,* from feminine diminutive of Latin *coccinus,* scarlet, from Greek *kokkinos,* from *kokkos,* kermes berry (from its use in making scarlet dye).] **—coch′i·neal′** *adj.*

cochineal insect *n.* Any of several red scale insects of the family Dactylopiidae that feed on cacti, especially the prickly pear, and range from the southwest United States to Central America.

Co·chise (kō-chēs′, -chēz′). 1812?–1874. Chiricahua Apache leader who directed Apache resistance to U.S. troops in Arizona (1861–1872).

coch·le·a (kŏk′lē-ə, kō′klē-ə) *n., pl.* **-le·ae** (-lē-ē′, -lē-ī′) also **-le·as.** A spiral-shaped cavity of the inner ear that resembles a snail shell and contains nerve endings essential for hearing. [Latin, snail shell, from Greek *kokhlias,* snail, from *kokhlos,* land snail.] **—coch′le·ar** *adj.*

cochlear nerve *n.* A division of the acoustic nerve that conducts auditory stimuli to the brain.

coch·le·ate (kŏk′lē-ĭt, -āt′, kō′klē-) also **coch·le·at·ed** (-ā′tĭd) *adj.* Shaped like a snail shell; spirally twisted. [Latin *cochleātus,* from *cochlea,* snail shell. See COCHLEA.]

Coch·ran (kŏk′rən), **Jacqueline.** 1910–1980. American aviator who held numerous national and international speed records and headed the Women's Air Force Service Pilots during World War II.

cock¹ (kŏk) *n.* **1.a.** An adult male chicken; a rooster. **b.** An adult male of various other birds. **2.** A weathervane shaped like a rooster; a weathercock. **3.** A leader or chief. **4.** A faucet or valve by which the flow of a liquid or gas can be regulated. **5.a.** The hammer of a firearm. **b.** The position of the hammer of a firearm when ready for firing. **6.** A tilting or jaunty turn upward: *the cock of a hat.* **7.** *Vulgar Slang.* The penis. **8.** *Archaic.* The characteristic cry of a rooster early in the morning. **—cock** *v.* **cocked, cock·ing, cocks.** *—tr.* **1.** To set the hammer of (a firearm) in a position ready for firing. **2.** To set (a device, such as a camera shutter) in a position ready for use. **3.** To tilt or turn up or to one side, usually in a jaunty or alert manner: *cocked an eyebrow in response to a silly question.* **4.** To raise in preparation to throw or hit: *cocked the bat before swinging at the pitch.* *—intr.* **1.** To set the hammer of a firearm in a position ready for firing. **2.** To turn or stick up. **3.** To strut; swagger. ***—idioms.*** **cock a snoot** (or **snook**). *Slang.* To express scorn or derision by or as if by placing the thumb on the nose and wiggling the fingers; thumb one's nose: "[He] *could cock a snoot at the rest of the . . . world and blithely go his own way*" (Elie Kedourie). **cock of the walk.** An overbearing or domineering person. [Middle English *cok,* from Old English *cocc,* probably from Late Latin *coccus,* from *coco,* a cackling, of imitative origin.]

cock² (kŏk) *n.* A cone-shaped pile of straw or hay. **—cock** *tr.v.* **cocked, cock·ing, cocks.** To arrange (straw or hay) into piles shaped like cones. [Middle English *cok.*]

cock·ade (kŏ-kād′) *n.* An ornament, such as a rosette or knot of ribbon, usually worn on the hat as a badge. [Alteration of obsolete *cockard,* from French *cocarde,* from Old French *coquarde,* feminine of *coquard,* vain, cocky, from *coq,* cock. See COCK¹.] **—cock·ad′ed** *adj.*

cock-a-hoop (kŏk′ə-hōōp′, -hŏŏp′) *adj.* **1.** Being in a state of boastful elation or exultation. **2.** Being askew. [From the phrase *to set cock on hoop,* to drink festively.] **—cock′-a-hoop′** *adv.*

Cock·aigne (kŏ-kān′) *n.* An imaginary land of easy and luxurious living. [Middle English *cokaigne,* from Old French, from *(pais de) cokaigne,* (land of) plenty, from Middle Low German *kōkenje,* diminutive of *kōke,* cake.]

cock-a-leek·ie also **cock·a·leek·ie** (kŏk′ə-lē′kē) *n.* A soup made with chicken broth and leeks. [Alteration of *cockie,* diminutive of COCK¹ + *leekie,* diminutive of LEEK.]

cock·a·lo·rum (kŏk′ə-lôr′əm, -lōr′-) *n.* **1.** A little man with an unduly high opinion of himself. **2.** Boastful talk; braggadocio. [Perhaps alteration (influenced by Latin *-ōrum,* nominal ending) of obsolete Flemish *kockeloeren,* to crow, of imitative origin.]

cock·a·ma·mie also **cock·a·ma·my** (kŏk′ə-mā′mē) *adj.* *Slang.* **1.** Trifling; nearly valueless. **2.** Ludicrous; nonsensical: *gave me a cockamamie reason for not going.* [Probably alteration of DECALCOMANIA.]

cock-and-bull story (kŏk′ən-bŏŏl′) *n.* An absurd or highly improbable tale passed off as being true.

cock·a·tiel also **cock·a·teel** (kŏk′ə-tēl′) *n.* A small crested Australian parrot *(Nymphicus hollandicus)* having gray and yellow plumage. [Dutch *kaketielje,* ultimately from Malay *kakatua,* cockatoo. See COCKATOO.]

cock·a·too (kŏk′ə-tōō′) *n., pl.* **-toos.** Any of various large parrots, especially of the genus *Kakatoe* of Australia and adjacent areas, characterized by a long, erectile crest. [Dutch *kaketoe,* from Malay *kakatua.*]

cock·a·trice (kŏk′ə-trĭs, -trīs′) *n.* *Mythology.* A serpent hatched from a cock's egg and having the power to kill by its glance. [Middle English *cocatrice,* basilisk, from Old French *cocatris,* from Medieval Latin *cocātrix, cocātric-,* possibly alteration of *calcātrix,* from Latin *calcāre,* to track, from *calx, calc-,* heel (translation of Greek *ikhneumōn,* tracker. See ICHNEUMON).]

cock·boat (kŏk′bōt′) *n.* *Nautical.* A small rowboat, especially one used to ferry supplies from ship to shore. Also called *cockleboat.* [Middle English *cokboot* : *cok,* cockboat (from Anglo-Norman *coque,* probably ultimately from Latin *caudica,* from *caudex, caudic-,* tree trunk) + *boot,* boat; see BOAT.]

cock·chaf·er (kŏk′chā′fər) *n.* Any of various European beetles of the family Scarabaeidae, especially *Melolontha melolontha,* which is destructive to plants. [Possibly COCK¹ + CHAFER.]

Cock·croft (kŏk′krôft′, -krŏft′), Sir **John Douglas.** 1897–1967. British physicist who with Ernest Walton succeeded in splitting the atom (1931). They shared a 1951 Nobel Prize for their contributions to nuclear physics.

cock·crow (kŏk′krō′) *n.* The very beginning of the day; dawn.

cocked hat (kŏkt) *n.* A hat with the brim turned up in two or three places, especially a three-cornered hat; a tricorn.

cock·er¹ (kŏk′ər) *n.* **1.** A cocker spaniel. **2.a.** A person who keeps or trains gamecocks. **b.** A person who promotes or attends cockfights.

cock·er² (kŏk′ər) *tr.v.* **-ered, -er·ing, -ers.** To pamper, spoil, or coddle. [Middle English *cokeren.*]

cock·er·el (kŏk′ər-əl) *n.* A young rooster. [Middle English *cokerel,* diminutive of *cok,* cock. See COCK¹.]

cocker spaniel *n.* A dog of a breed originally developed in England, having long, drooping ears and a variously colored silky coat. [From its original use in hunting woodcocks.]

cock·eye (kŏk′ī′) *n.* A squinting eye. [Possibly alteration (influenced by COCK¹) of Irish Gaelic *caoch,* one-eyed, squinting (from Old Irish *cáech*) + EYE.]

cock·eyed (kŏk′īd′) *adj.* *Informal.* **1.** Foolish; ridiculous; absurd: *a cockeyed idea.* **2.** Askew; crooked. **3.** Intoxicated; drunk.

Cock·eys·ville (kŏk′ēz-vĭl′). A community of northern Maryland, a manufacturing suburb of Baltimore. Population, 17,013.

cock·fight (kŏk′fīt′) *n.* A fight between gamecocks, often having their legs fitted with metal spurs, that is arranged as a spectacle. **—cock′fight′ing** *adj. & n.*

cock·horse (kŏk′hôrs′) *n.* **1.** Something used as a toy horse, such as the knee of an adult or a rocking horse. **2.** A horse added to a team of horses to assist a wagon through high water or over difficult terrain. [Origin unknown.]

cock·le¹ (kŏk′əl) *n.* **1.** Any of various bivalve mollusks of the family Cardiidae, having rounded or heart-shaped shells with radiating ribs. **2.** The shell of a cockle. **3.** A wrinkle; a pucker. **4.** *Nautical.* A cockleshell. **—cockle** *intr. & tr.v.* **-led, -ling, -les.** To become or cause to become wrinkled or puckered. ***—idiom.*** **cockles of (one's) heart.** One's innermost feelings: *The valentine warmed the cockles of my heart.* [Middle English *cokel,* from Old French *coquille,* shell, from Vulgar Latin **cochillia,* from Latin *conchylium,* from Greek *konkhulion,* diminutive of *konkhē,* mussel.]

cock·le² (kŏk′əl) *n.* Any of several weedy plants, especially the corn cockle. [Middle English *cokkel,* from Old English *coccel,* from Medieval Latin **cocculus,* diminutive of Latin *coccus,* kermes berry, from Greek *kokkos.*]

cock·le·boat (kŏk′əl-bōt′) *n.* *Nautical.* See **cockboat.**

cock·le·bur (kŏk′əl-bûr′) *n.* **1.** Any of several annual weeds of the genus *Xanthium* in the composite family, having small seedlike fruits enclosed within a prickly bur that clings readily to clothing or animal fur. **2.** A bur of this plant.

cock·le·shell (kŏk′əl-shĕl′) *n.* **1.a.** The shell of a cockle. **b.** A shell similar to that of a cockle. **2.** *Nautical.* A small, light boat.

cock·loft (kŏk′lôft′, -lŏft′) *n.* A small loft, garret, or attic. [Probably from its use as a roosting place.]

cock·ney (kŏk′nē) *n., pl.* **-neys.** **1.** Often **Cockney.** A native of the East End of London. **2.** The dialect or accent of the natives of the East End of London. **—cockney** *adj.* Of or relating to cockneys or their dialect. [Middle English *cokenei,* city dweller, pampered child, cock's egg : *coken,* cock (possibly blend of *cok;* see COCK¹, and *chiken,* chicken; see CHICKEN) + *ei,* egg (from Old English *ǣg;* see **awi-** in Appendix).]

cock-of-the-rock (kŏk′əv-thə-rŏk′) *n., pl.* **cocks-of-the-rock.** Either of two South American birds *(Rupicola rupicola* or *R. peruviana)* having a distinctive crest and bright-orange or reddish plumage in the male. [From its habit of nesting on rocks.]

cock·pit (kŏk′pĭt′) *n.* **1.a.** The space in the fuselage of a small airplane containing seats for the pilot, copilot, and sometimes passengers. **b.** The space set apart for the pilot and crew, as in a helicopter, large airliner, or transport aircraft. **2.** The driver's compartment in a racing car. **3.** A pit or enclosed area for cockfights. **4.** A place where many battles have been fought. **5.** *Nautical.* **a.** A compartment in an old warship below the water line, used as quarters for junior officers and as a station for the wounded during a battle. **b.** An area in a small decked vessel toward the

Jacqueline Cochran

cockatoo
Sulfur-crested cockatoo
Cacatua galerita

cock-of-the-rock

cockpit
Airplane

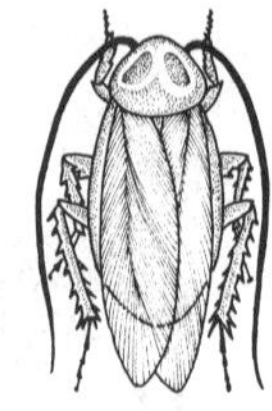

cockroach
American cockroach
Periplaneta americana

codpiece

stern, lower than the rest of the deck, from which the vessel is steered.

cock•roach (kŏk′rōch′) *n.* Any of numerous oval, flat-bodied insects of the family Blattidae, including several species that are common household pests. [By folk etymology from obsolete *cacarootch,* from Spanish *cucaracha,* from *cuca,* caterpillar.]

WORD HISTORY: The word for *cockroach* in Spanish is *cucaracha,* which should certainly set anyone with an eye for etymology to thinking. Users of English did not simply borrow the Spanish word, however. Instead, they made it conform in appearance to other English words: *cock,* the word for rooster, and *roach,* the name of a fish. We do not know exactly why these words were chosen other than their resemblance to the two parts of the original Spanish word. We do know that the first recorded use of the word comes from a 1624 work by the colonist John Smith. The form Smith used, *cacarootch,* is closer to the Spanish. A form more like our own, *cockroche,* is first recorded in 1657.

cocks•comb (kŏks′kōm′) *n.* **1.** The comb of a rooster. **2.** The cap of a jester, decorated to resemble the comb of a rooster. **3.** An annual plant *(Celosia cristata)* widely cultivated for its showy, fan-shaped or plumelike clusters of red or yellow flowers. Also called *celosia.* **4.** *Obsolete.* Variant of **coxcomb** (sense 1).

cocks•foot *n. Chiefly British.* Orchard grass.

cock•shy (kŏk′shī′) *n., pl.* **-shies.** *Chiefly British.* **1.** A mark aimed at in throwing contests. **2.** The throw in a throwing contest. [From an old game in which sticks were shied at a cock.]

cock•spur hawthorn (kŏk′spûr′) *n.* A small, thorny North American tree *(Crataegus crus-galli)* having white flowers and small red fruit. [From the resemblance of its thorn to a cock's spur.]

cock•suck•er (kŏk′sŭk′ər) *n. Obscene.* **1.** One who performs an act of fellatio. **2.** A mean or despicable person.

cock•sure (kŏk′sho͝or′) *adj.* **1.** Completely sure; certain. **2.** Too sure; overconfident. **—cock′sure′ly** *adv.* **—cock′sure′ness** *n.*

cock•tail (kŏk′tāl′) *n.* **1.** Any of various mixed alcoholic drinks consisting usually of brandy, whiskey, vodka, or gin combined with fruit juices or other liquors and often served chilled. **2.** An appetizer, such as mixed fruit served with some juice or seafood served with a sharp sauce: *fruit cocktail; shrimp cocktail.* **—cocktail** *adj.* **1.** Of or relating to cocktails: *a cocktail glass; a cocktail party.* **2.** Suitable for wear on semiformal occasions: *a cocktail dress.* [Origin unknown.]

cocktail table *n.* See **coffee table.**

cock-up (kŏk′ŭp′) *n. Chiefly British.* A blunder; a mess.

cock•y (kŏk′ē) *adj.* **-i•er, -i•est.** Overly self-assertive or self-confident. **—cock′i•ly** *adv.* **—cock′i•ness** *n.*

Co•co (kō′kō). A river rising in northern Nicaragua and flowing about 483 km (300 mi) northeast along the Nicaragua-Honduras border to the Caribbean Sea.

co•coa (kō′kō) *n.* **1.a.** A powder made from cacao seeds after they have been fermented, roasted, shelled, ground, and freed of most of their fat. **b.** A beverage made by mixing this powder with sugar in hot water or milk. **2.** *Color.* A moderate brown to reddish brown. [Alteration (influenced by *coco,* coconut palm; see COCONUT) of CACAO.] **—co′coa** *adj.*

Co•coa (kō′kō). A city of east-central Florida east-southeast of Orlando. It is a tourist center in a citrus-growing region. Population, 16,096.

cocoa bean *n.* See **cacao** (sense 2).

cocoa butter *n.* A yellowish-white fatty solid obtained from cacao seeds and used as an ingredient in cosmetics, tanning oils, chocolate, and soap. Also called *cacao butter.*

co•coa•nut (kō′kə-nŭt′, -nət) *n.* Variant of **coconut.**

co•co•bo•lo (kō′kə-bō′lō) *n., pl.* **-los. 1.** Any of certain trees of the genus *Dahlbergia* in the pea family, especially *D. retusa* of Central America and Mexico. **2.** The hard, durable wood of such a tree, deep orange-red with black streaking or mottling, used for small specialty items such as knife handles. [Spanish, from Arawak *kakabali.*]

co•co-de-mer (kō′kō-də-mâr′) *n.* **1.** A fan-leaved palm *(Lodoicea maldivica)* native to the Seychelles, bearing the largest seed of all plants, which is enclosed in a hard shell resembling a pair of coconuts joined in the middle. **2.** The hard-shelled seed of this plant. Also called *double coconut.* [French : *coco,* coconut + *de,* of + *mer,* sea.]

co•con•spir•a•tor (kō′kən-spîr′ə-tər) *n.* A joint conspirator.

co•co•nut also **co•coa•nut** (kō′kə-nŭt′, -nət) *n.* **1.** The fruit of the coconut palm, consisting of a fibrous husk surrounding a large seed. **2.** The large, brown, hard-shelled seed of the coconut, containing white flesh surrounding a partially fluid-filled central cavity. **3.** The edible white flesh of the coconut, often shredded and used in food and confections or for the extraction of coconut oil. **4.** A coconut palm. [*coco* (from Portuguese *côco,* grinning skull, goblin, coconut, probably from Late Latin *coccum,* shell; see COCOON) + NUT.]

coconut crab *n.* A large terrestrial hermit crab *(Birgus latro)* that can climb trees and that feeds on carrion and vegetation.

coconut milk *n.* **1.** A milky fluid extracted from the flesh of the coconut, used in foods or as a beverage. **2.** The watery fluid in the central cavity of the coconut, used chiefly as a beverage.

coconut oil *n.* A pale yellow to colorless oil or a white semisolid fat obtained from the flesh of the coconut, widely used in food products and in the production of cosmetics and soaps.

coconut palm *n.* A feather-leaved palm *(Cocos nucifera)* extensively cultivated in tropical regions for food, beverages, oil, thatching, fiber, utensils, or ornament.

co•coon (kə-ko͞on′) *n.* **1.a.** A protective case of silk or similar fibrous material spun by the larvae of moths and other insects that serves as a covering for their pupal stage. **b.** A similar natural protective covering or structure, such as the egg case of a spider. **2.** A protective plastic coating that is placed over stored military or naval equipment. **3.** Something suggestive of a cocoon in appearance or purpose: *"a congressionally mandated process that will gradually strip these institutions of a cocoon of regulations"* (Edward Meadows). **—cocoon** *v.* **-cooned, -coon•ing, -coons.** *—tr.* To envelop in or as if in a cocoon, as for protection from a harsh or unfriendly environment. *—intr.* To retreat as if into a cocoon, as for security from a harsh or unfriendly environment. [French *cocon,* from Provençal *coucoun,* diminutive of *coco,* shell, from Late Latin *coccum,* from Latin, berry, oak gall, from Greek *kokkos,* seed, berry.]

co•coon•ing (kə-ko͞o′nĭng) *n.* Retreat into the privacy of one's own home during leisure time as a means of insulating oneself from what is perceived to be a harsh, unpredictable world: *"The harassments of daily life—looming nuclear incineration, rude waiters—have driven people to cocooning. They have gone to ground in their dens . . . to keep at bay the modern world"* (George F. Will).

coco plum or **co•co•plum** (kō′kō-plŭm′) *n.* An evergreen shrub or small tree *(Chrysobalanus icaco)* native to the American and African tropics, having plumlike fruit used to make jellies and preserves. [Alteration of Spanish *icaco,* from Arawak *ikaku.*]

Co•cos Islands (kō′kōs) also **Kee•ling Islands** (kē′lĭng). An island group in the eastern Indian Ocean southwest of Sumatra. Discovered in 1609, the islands were settled by the British in 1826 and are today administered by Australia.

co•cotte (kô-kôt′) *n.* A woman prostitute. [French, chicken, prostitute, feminine diminutive of *coq,* cock, from Old French. See COCK[1].]

co•co•yam (kō′kō-yăm′) *n.* See **taro.** [COCO(A) + YAM (from its being planted in coconut groves).]

Coc•teau (kŏk-tō′, kôk-), **Jean.** 1889–1963. French author and filmmaker who worked in nearly every artistic medium but is best known for the novel *Les Enfants Terrible* (1929), the play *The Infernal Machine* (1934), and the film *Beauty and the Beast* (1945).

co•cur•ric•u•lar (kō′kə-rĭk′yə-lər) *adj.* Complementing but not part of the regular curriculum: *The civics class sponsored a voter registration drive as a cocurricular activity.*

Co•cy•tus (kō-kī′təs, -sī′-) *n. Greek Mythology.* One of the five rivers of Hades.

cod[1] (kŏd) *n., pl.* **cod** or **cods.** Any of various marine fishes of the family Gadidae, especially *Gadus morhua,* an important food fish of northern Atlantic waters. Also called *codfish.* [Middle English.]

cod[2] (kŏd) *n.* **1.** A husk or pod. **2.** *Archaic.* The scrotum. **3.** *Obsolete.* A bag. [Middle English, from Old English *codd.*]

Cod (kŏd), **Cape.** A hook-shaped peninsula of southeast Massachusetts extending east and north into the Atlantic Ocean.

COD or **C.O.D.** *abbr.* **1.** Cash on delivery. **2.** Collect on delivery.

co•da (kō′də) *n. Music.* A passage at the end of a movement or composition that brings it to a formal close. [Italian, from Latin *cauda,* tail.]

cod•dle (kŏd′l) *tr.v.* **-dled, -dling, -dles. 1.** To cook in water just below the boiling point: *coddle eggs.* **2.** To treat indulgently; baby. See Synonyms at **pamper.** [Possibly alteration of CAUDLE.] **—cod′dler** *n.*

code (kōd) *n.* **1.** A systematically arranged and comprehensive collection of laws. **2.** A systematic collection of regulations and rules of procedure or conduct: *a traffic code.* **3.a.** A system of signals used to represent letters or numbers in transmitting messages. **b.** A system of symbols, letters, or words given certain arbitrary meanings, used for transmitting messages requiring secrecy or brevity. **4.** A system of symbols and rules used to represent instructions to a computer. **5.** *Genetics.* The genetic code. **6.** *Slang.* A patient whose heart has stopped beating, as in cardiac arrest. **—code** *v.* **cod•ed, cod•ing, codes.** *—tr.* **1.** To systematize and arrange (laws and regulations) into a code. **2.** To convert (a message, for example) into code. *—intr.* **1.** *Genetics.* To specify the genetic code for an amino acid or a polypeptide. **2.** *Slang.* To go into cardiac arrest. [Middle English, from Old French, from Latin *cōdex,* book. See CODEX.]

code•book (kōd′bo͝ok′) *n.* A book that lists the symbols of a code and their meanings.

co•dec•li•na•tion (kō′dĕk-lə-nā′shən) *n. Astronomy.* The complement of the declination.

co•de•fen•dant (kō′dĭ-fĕn′dənt) *n. Law.* A joint defendant.

co•deine (kō′dēn′, -dē-ĭn) *n.* An alkaloid narcotic, $C_{18}H_{21}NO_3$, derived from opium or morphine and used as a cough suppressant, analgesic, and hypnotic. [French *codéine* : Greek *kōdeia,* poppy head (from *kōos,* cavity; see **keuə-** in Appendix) + *-ine,* alkaloid; see -INE[2].]

code name *n.* A name assigned to conceal the identity or existence of something or someone.

code-name (kōd′nām′) *tr.v.* **-named, -nam·ing, -names.** To assign a code name to.

co·de·ter·mi·na·tion (kō′dĭ-tûr′mə-nā′shən) *n.* Cooperation, especially between labor and management, in policymaking: *"The codetermination of labor with management, compulsory in large firms here, was applied to universities as well, with governing committees forced to share representation more evenly between professors, junior staff, and students"* (Elizabeth Pond).

code word *n.* **1.** A secret word or phrase used as a code name or password. **2.** A euphemism: *"The Democrats' 'populism' is a code word for bigger farm subsidies and protectionism"* (New Republic).

co·dex (kō′dĕks′) *n., pl.* **co·di·ces** (kō′dĭ-sēz′, kŏd′ĭ-). A manuscript volume, especially of a classic work or of the Scriptures. [Latin *cōdex, cōdic-,* tree trunk, wooden tablet, book, variant of *caudex,* stem, trunk.]

cod·fish (kŏd′fĭsh′) *n., pl.* **codfish** or **-fish·es.** See **cod**[1].

codg·er (kŏj′ər) *n. Informal.* A somewhat eccentric man, especially an old one. [Perhaps alteration of obsolete *cadger,* peddler. See CADGE.]

co·di·ces (kō′dĭ-sēz′, kŏd′ĭ-) *n.* Plural of **codex.**

cod·i·cil (kŏd′ə-sĭl) *n.* **1.** *Law.* A supplement or appendix to a will. **2.** A supplement or appendix. [Middle English, from Old French *codicille,* from Latin *cōdicillus,* diminutive of *cōdex, cōdic-,* codex. See CODEX.] **—cod′i·cil′la·ry** (kŏd′ə-sĭl′ə-rē) *adj.*

cod·i·fy (kŏd′ĭ-fī′, kō′də-) *tr.v.* **-fied, -fy·ing, -fies. 1.** To reduce to a code: *codify laws.* **2.** To arrange or systematize. **—cod′i·fi·ca′tion** (-fĭ-kā′shən) *n.* **—cod′i·fi′er** *n.*

co·di·rect (kō′dĭ-rĕkt′) *tr.v.* **-rected, -rect·ing, -rects.** To direct (a play, film, or other form of public entertainment) jointly with another or others. **—co·di·rect′or** *n.*

cod·ling[1] (kŏd′lĭng) also **cod·lin** (-lĭn) *n.* **1.** A greenish, elongated English apple used for cooking. **2.** A small, unripe apple. [Alteration of Middle English *querdlyng,* possibly from Anglo-Norman **querdelion,* lionheart : Old French *cuer,* heart; see COURAGE + *de,* of (from Latin *dē;* see DE–) + Old French *lion,* lion; see LION.]

cod·ling[2] (kŏd′lĭng) *n., pl.* **-lings** or **codling.** A young cod.

codling moth also **codlin moth** *n.* A small, grayish moth *(Carpocapsa pomonella)* whose larvae are destructive to various fruits, especially apples.

cod-liv·er oil (kŏd′lĭv′ər) *n.* An oil obtained from the liver of cod and related fishes and used as a dietary source of vitamins A and D.

co·dom·i·nance (kō-dŏm′ə-nəns) *n. Genetics.* A condition in which both alleles of a gene pair in a heterozygote are fully expressed, with neither one being dominant or recessive to the other.

co·dom·i·nant (kō-dŏm′ə-nənt) *adj.* **1.** *Genetics.* Of or relating to two alleles of a gene pair in a heterozygote that are both fully expressed. **2.a.** *Ecology.* Being one of two or more of the most characteristic species in a biotic community. **b.** Influencing the presence and type of other species in the community. **—codominant** *n. Ecology.* One of the most characteristic species in a biotic community.

co·don (kō′dŏn′) *n.* A sequence of three adjacent nucleotides constituting the genetic code that specifies the insertion of an amino acid in a specific structural position in a polypeptide chain during protein synthesis. [COD(E) + –ON[1].]

cod·piece (kŏd′pēs′) *n.* A pouch at the crotch of the tight-fitting breeches worn by men in the 15th and 16th centuries. [Middle English *codpece* : *cod,* bag, scrotum (from Old English *codd,* bag) + *pece,* piece; see PIECE.]

cods·wal·lop (kŏdz′wŏl′əp) *n. Chiefly British.* Nonsense; rubbish. [Origin unknown.]

Co·dy (kō′dē), **William Frederick.** Known as "Buffalo Bill." 1846–1917. American frontier scout and showman who after 1883 toured the United States and Europe with his Wild West Show.

co·ed or **co-ed** (kō′ĕd′) *Informal.* —*n.* A woman who attends a coeducational college or university. —*adj.* **1.** Of or relating to an education system in which both men and women attend the same institution or classes; coeducational: *a coed university.* **2.** Open to both sexes: *a coed dorm.* [Short for *coeducational.*]

co·ed·it (kō-ĕd′ĭt) *tr.v.* **-ed·it·ed, -ed·it·ing, -ed·its.** To edit (a print publication or a film) jointly with another or others. **—co·ed′i·tor** *n.*

co·ed·u·ca·tion (kō-ĕj′ə-kā′shən) *n.* The system of education in which both men and women attend the same institution or classes. **—co·ed′u·ca′tion·al** *adj.* **—co·ed′u·ca′tion·al·ly** *adv.*

co·ef·fi·cient (kō′ə-fĭsh′ənt) *n. Abbr.* **coef. 1.** *Mathematics.* A number or symbol multiplying a variable or an unknown quantity in an algebraic term, as 4 in the term $4x$, or x in the term $x(a+b)$. **2.** A numerical measure of a physical or chemical property that is constant for a system under specified conditions such as the coefficient of friction.

coefficient of correlation *n., pl.* **coefficients of correlation.** See **correlation coefficient.**

coefficient of friction *n., pl.* **coefficients of friction.** The ratio of the weight of an object being moved along a surface and the force that maintains contact between the object and the surface.

coefficient of self-induction *n., pl.* **coefficients of self-induction.** *Electricity.* See **self-inductance.**

coefficient of viscosity *n., pl.* **coefficients of viscosity.** The degree to which a fluid resists flow under an applied force, measured by the tangential friction force per unit area divided by the velocity gradient under conditions of streamline flow.

–coel or **–coele** or **–cele** *suff.* Chamber; cavity: *blastocoel.* [New Latin *-coela,* from Greek *koilos,* hollow. See **keuə-** in Appendix.]

coe·la·canth (sē′lə-kănth′) *n.* Any of various mostly extinct fishes of the order Coelacanthiformes, known only in fossil form until a single living species, *Latimeria chalumnae* of African marine waters, was identified in 1938. [New Latin *Coelacanthus,* former genus name : *coel-,* hollow (from Greek *koilos;* see –COEL) + *acanthus,* -spined (from Greek *akantha,* spine).] **—coe′la·can′thine′** (-kăn′thīn′, -thĭn) *adj.* **—coe′la·can′thous** (-thəs) *adj.*

–coele *suff.* Variant of **–coel.**

coe·len·te·ra (sĭ-lĕn′tər-ə) *n.* Plural of **coelenteron.**

coe·len·ter·ate (sĭ-lĕn′tə-rāt′, -tər-ĭt) *n.* Any of various invertebrate animals of the phylum Coelenterata, characterized by a radially symmetrical body with a saclike internal cavity, and including the jellyfishes, hydras, sea anemones, and corals. **—coelenterate** *adj.* Of, relating to, or belonging to the phylum Coelenterata. [From New Latin *Coelenterata,* phylum name : *coel-,* hollow; see COELACANTH + ENTER(ON) + –ATE[1].] **—coe·len·ter′ic** (-tĕr′ĭk) *adj.*

coe·len·ter·on (sĭ-lĕn′tə-rŏn′, -tər-ən) *n., pl.* **-te·ra** (-tər-ə). The saclike cavity within the body of a coelenterate. [New Latin : *coel-,* hollow; see COELACANTH + ENTERON.]

coe·li·ac (sē′lē-ăk′) *adj.* Variant of **celiac.**

coe·lom also **ce·lom** or **coe·lome** (sē′ləm) *n.* The cavity within the body of all animals higher than the coelenterates and certain primitive worms, formed by the splitting of the embryonic mesoderm into two layers. In mammals it forms the peritoneal, pleural, and pericardial cavities. Also called *body cavity.* [German *Koelom,* from Greek *koilōma,* cavity, from *koilos,* hollow. See **keuə-** in Appendix.] **—coe·lom′ic** (sĭ-lŏm′ĭk, -lō′mĭk) *adj.*

coe·lo·mate (sē′lə-māt′) *adj.* Possessing a coelom: *a coelomate animal.* **—coe′lo·mate** *n.*

coeno– or **ceno–** *pref.* Common: *coenocyte.* [New Latin, from Greek *koino-,* from *koinos.* See **kom** in Appendix.]

coen·o·bite (sĕn′ə-bīt′, sē′nə-) *n.* Variant of **cenobite.**

coe·no·cyte (sē′nə-sīt′) *n.* A multinucleate cytoplasmic mass enclosed by a single cell wall, as in slime molds and certain fungi and algae. **—coe′no·cyt′ic** (-sĭt′ĭk) *adj.*

coe·nu·rus (sĭ-no͝or′əs, -nyo͝or′-) *n., pl.* **-nu·ri** (-no͝or′ī′, -nyo͝or′ī′). The parasitic larval stage of the tapeworm *Taenia multiceps* that consists of a cyst in which the scolex develops and that infects the central nervous system of ruminants, especially sheep. [COEN(O)– + –UR(O)US.]

co·en·zyme (kō-ĕn′zīm′) *n.* A nonproteinaceous organic substance that usually contains a vitamin or mineral and combines with a specific protein, the apoenzyme, to form an active enzyme system. **—co′en·zy·mat′ic** (-zə-măt′ĭk) *adj.* **—co·en′zy·mat′i·cal·ly** *adv.*

coenzyme A *n. Abbr.* **CoA** A coenzyme present in all living cells that functions as an acyl group carrier and is necessary for fatty acid synthesis and oxidation, pyruvate oxidation, and other acetylation reactions.

coenzyme Q *n.* Ubiquinone.

co·e·qual (kō-ē′kwəl) *adj.* Equal with one another, as in rank or size. **—coequal** *n.* An equal. **—co′e·qual′i·ty** (-kwŏl′ĭ-tē) *n.* **—co·e′qual·ly** *adv.*

co·erce (kō-ûrs′) *tr.v.* **-erced, -erc·ing, -erc·es. 1.** To force to act or think in a certain way by use of pressure, threats, or intimidation; compel. **2.** To dominate, restrain, or control forcibly: *coerced the strikers into compliance.* See Synonyms at **force. 3.** To bring about by force or threat: *efforts to coerce agreement.* [Latin *coercēre,* to control, restrain : *co-,* co- + *arcēre,* to enclose, confine.] **—co·erc′er** *n.* **—co·erc′i·ble** *adj.*

co·er·cion (kō-ûr′zhən, -shən) *n.* **1.** The act or practice of coercing. **2.** Power or ability to coerce. **—co·er′cion·ar′y** (-zhə-nĕr′ē, -shə-) *adj.*

co·er·cive (kō-ûr′sĭv) *adj.* Characterized by or inclined to coercion. **—co·er′cive·ly** *adv.* **—co·er′cive·ness** *n.*

co·es·sen·tial (kō′ĭ-sĕn′shəl) *adj.* Having the same essence or nature. **—co′es·sen′ti·al′i·ty** (-shē-ăl′ĭ-tē), **co′es·sen′tial·ness** *n.* **—co′es·sen′tial·ly** *adv.*

co·e·ta·ne·ous (kō′ĭ-tā′nē-əs) *adj.* Of equal age, duration, or period; coeval. [From Late Latin *coaetāneus,* a contemporary : Latin *co-,* co- + Latin *aetās,* age; see **aiw-** in Appendix.] **—co′e·ta′ne·ous·ly** *adv.* **—co′e·ta′ne·ous·ness** *n.*

co·e·ter·nal (kō′ĭ-tûr′nəl) *adj.* Equally or jointly eternal. **—co′e·ter′nal·ly** *adv.*

co·e·ter·ni·ty (kō′ĭ-tûr′nĭ-tē) *n.* Existence for eternity with another or others.

Coeur d'A·lene (kôr′ də-lān′, kôrd′l-ān′, kûrd′-). A city of

William F. Cody
"Buffalo Bill"

coelacanth

ă pat	oi boy
ā pay	ou out
âr care	o͝o took
ä father	o͞o boot
ĕ pet	ŭ cut
ē be	ûr urge
ĭ pit	th thin
ī pie	*th* this
îr pier	hw which
ŏ pot	zh vision
ō toe	ə about, item
ô paw	♦ regionalism

Stress marks: ′ (primary); ′ (secondary), as in **dictionary** (dĭk′shə-nĕr′ē)

northern Idaho on **Coeur D'Alene Lake** in the Panhandle east of Spokane, Washington. The city is the gateway to a popular resort area. Population, 20,054.

Coeur de Li·on (kûr′ də lē′ən, kœr də lyôN′). See **Richard I.**

co·e·val (kō-ē′vəl) *adj.* Originating or existing during the same period; lasting through the same era. **—coeval** *n.* One of the same era or period; a contemporary. [From Late Latin *coaevus* : co-, co- + *aevum,* age; see **aiw-** in Appendix.] **—co·e′val·ly** *adv.*

co·ev·o·lu·tion (kō′ĕv-ə-lo͞o′shən, -ē-və-) *n.* The evolution of two or more interdependent species, each adapting to changes in the other. It occurs, for example, between predators and prey and between insects and the flowers that they pollinate. **—co′ev·o·lu′tion·ar·y** *adj.* **—co′e·volve′** (-ĭ-vŏlv′) *v.*

co·ex·ist (kō′ĭg-zĭst′) *intr.v.* **-ist·ed, -ist·ing, -ists. 1.** To exist together, at the same time, or in the same place. **2.** To live in peace with another or others despite differences, especially as a matter of policy: *"recognize and accept, as every President in the nuclear age has, that this means coexisting with the Soviet Union"* (McGeorge Bundy). **—co′ex·is′tence** *n.* **—co′ex·is′tent** *adj.*

co·ex·tend (kō′ĭk-stĕnd′) *intr. & tr.v.* **-tend·ed, -tend·ing, -tends.** To extend or cause to extend through the same space or duration. **—co′ex·ten′sion** *n.*

co·ex·ten·sive (kō′ĭk-stĕn′sĭv) *adj.* Having the same limits, boundaries, or scope. **—co′ex·ten′sive·ly** *adv.*

co·fac·tor (kō′făk′tər) *n.* A substance, such as a metallic iron or coenzyme, that must be associated with an enzyme for the enzyme to function.

C. of C. *abbr.* Chamber of commerce.

C. of E. *abbr.* Church of England.

cof·fee (kô′fē, kŏf′ē) *n.* **1.a.** Any of various tropical African shrubs or trees of the genus *Coffea,* especially *C. arabica,* widely cultivated in the tropics for their seeds that are dried, roasted, and ground to prepare a stimulating, aromatic drink. **b.** The beanlike seeds of this plant, enclosed within a pulpy fruit. **c.** The beverage prepared from the seeds of this plant. **2.** *Color.* A moderate brown to dark brown or dark grayish brown. **3.** An informal social gathering at which coffee and other refreshments are served. *—attributive.* Often used to modify another noun: *a coffee cup; a coffee grinder.* [Alteration (influenced by Italian *caffè,* from Turkish) of Ottoman Turkish *qahveh,* from Arabic *qahwah.*]

WORD HISTORY: Would one be as ready to drink *chaoua, kauhi,* or *coffa* as *coffee*? Most of these exotic early forms of our word reflect the fact that coffee, though a normal accompaniment to the life of many English speakers, was originally an exotic substance. Coffee came to Europe from the Middle East, where its name was *qahveh,* an Ottoman Turkish pronunciation of Arabic *qahwah,* the Turks having borrowed the word and the drink from the Arabs. The first three forms cited above show the influence of the Middle Eastern words for coffee. Our form *coffee* results from combining *caffè,* the Italian version of the Middle Eastern word, and the vowel of the Middle Eastern word, represented by *o. Coffee* is first recorded in English in 1601 with the spelling *coffe.*

coffee

coffee break *n.* A short break from work during which coffee or other refreshments may be consumed.

cof·fee·cake (kô′fē-kāk′, kŏf′ē-) *n.* A cake or sweetened bread, often containing nuts or raisins.

cof·fee·house also **coffee house** (kô′fē-hous′, kŏf′ē-) *n.* A restaurant where coffee and other refreshments are served, especially one where people gather for conversation, games, or musical entertainment.

coffee klatch or **coffee klatsch** (klăch, kläch) also **kaf·fee·klatsch** (kŏf′ē-klăch′, -kläch′, kô′fē-) *n.* A casual social gathering for coffee and conversation. [Partial translation of German *Kaffeeklatsch* : *Kaffee,* coffee + *Klatsch,* gossip.]

cof·fee·mak·er also **coffee maker** (kô′fē-mā′kər, kŏf′ē-) *n.* An apparatus used to brew coffee.

coffee mill *n.* A device for grinding roasted coffee beans.

cof·fee·pot (kô′fē-pŏt′, kŏf′ē-) *n.* A pot for brewing or serving coffee.

coffee shop *n.* A small restaurant in which coffee and light meals are served.

coffee table *n.* A long, low table, often placed before a sofa. Also called *cocktail table.*

cof·fee-ta·ble book (kô′fē-tā′bəl, kŏf′ē-) *n.* An oversize book of elaborate design that may be used for display, as on a coffee table.

cof·fer (kô′fər, kŏf′ər) *n.* **1.** A strongbox. **2.** Often **coffers. a.** Financial resources; funds. **b.** A treasury: *stole money from the union coffers.* **3.** *Architecture.* A decorative sunken panel in a ceiling, dome, soffit, or vault. **4.** The chamber formed by a canal lock. **5.** A cofferdam. **6.** A floating dock. **—coffer** *tr.v.* **-fered, -fer·ing, -fers. 1.** To put in a coffer. **2.** *Architecture.* To supply (a ceiling, for example) with decorative sunken panels. [Middle English *cofre,* from Old French, alteration of **cofne,* from Latin *cophinus,* basket. See COFFIN.]

cof·fer·dam (kô′fər-dăm′, kŏf′ər-) *n.* **1.** A temporary watertight enclosure that is pumped dry to expose the bottom of a body of water so that construction, as of piers, may be undertaken. **2.** A watertight chamber attached to the side of a ship to facilitate repairs below the water line.

cof·fin (kô′fĭn, kŏf′ĭn) *n.* **1.** An oblong box in which a corpse is buried. **2.** The horny part of a horse's hoof. **—coffin** *tr.v.* **-fined, -fin·ing, -fins.** To place in or as if in a coffin. [Middle English *cofin,* basket, from Old French, from Latin *cophinus,* from Greek *kophinos.*]

coffin bone *n.* The bone enclosed inside a horse's hoof.

coffin corner *n. Football.* Either corner of the field formed by the sideline and the defending team's goal line. The ball may be deliberately punted out of bounds in this area, thus forcing the receiving team to play very close to its goal line.

coffin nail *n. Slang.* A cigarette.

cof·fle (kô′fəl, kŏf′əl) *n.* A group of animals, prisoners, or slaves chained together in a line. **—coffle** *tr.v.* **-fled, -fling, -fles.** To fasten together in a coffle. [Arabic *qāfilah,* caravan.]

co·found (kō-found′) *tr.v.* **-found·ed, -found·ing, -founds.** To establish or found in concert with another or others. **—co·found′er** *n.*

C. of S. *abbr.* Chief of staff.

co·func·tion (kō′fungk′shən) *n.* The trigonometric function of the complement of an angle: *Cotan* ϕ *is cofunction of tan* ϕ.

cog[1] (kŏg, kôg) *n.* **1.** One of a series of teeth, as on the rim of a wheel or gear, whose engagement transmits successive motive force to a corresponding wheel or gear. **2.** A cogwheel. **3.** A subordinate member of an organization who performs necessary but usually minor or routine functions. [Middle English *cogge,* probably of Scandinavian origin; akin to Swedish *kugg, kugge.*] **—cogged** *adj.*

cog[2] (kŏg, kôg) *v.* **cogged, cog·ging, cogs.** *—tr.* To load or manipulate (dice) fraudulently. *—intr.* To cheat, especially at dice. **—cog** *n.* An instance of cheating; a swindle. [Origin unknown.]

cog[3] (kŏg, kôg) *n.* A tenon projecting from a wooden beam designed to fit into an opening in another beam to form a joint. **—cog** *tr.v.* **cogged, cog·ging, cogs.** To join with tenons. [Alteration (influenced by COG[1]) of *cock,* to join with tenons.]

cog. *abbr.* Cognate.

co·gen·er·a·tion (kō-jĕn′ə-rā′shən) *n.* A process in which an industrial facility uses its waste energy to produce heat or electricity.

co·gent (kō′jənt) *adj.* Appealing to the intellect or powers of reasoning; convincing: *a cogent argument.* See Synonyms at **valid.** [Latin *cōgēns, cōgent-,* present participle of *cōgere,* to force : *co-,* co- + *agere,* to drive; see **ag-** in Appendix.] **—co′gen·cy** (-jən-sē) *n.* **—co′gent·ly** *adv.*

cog·i·ta·ble (kŏj′ĭ-tə-bəl) *adj.* Thinkable; conceivable: *Since the discovery of the vaccine, annihilation of the disease is at last cogitable.*

cog·i·tate (kŏj′ĭ-tāt′) *intr. & tr.v.* **-tat·ed, -tat·ing, -tates.** To take careful thought or think carefully about; ponder. See Synonyms at **think.** [Latin *cōgitāre, cōgitāt-* : *co-,* intensive pref.; see CO– + *agitāre,* to consider; see AGITATE.] **—cog′i·ta′tor** *n.*

cog·i·ta·tion (kŏj′ĭ-tā′shən) *n.* **1.** Thoughtful consideration; meditation. **2.** A serious thought.

cog·i·ta·tive (kŏj′ĭ-tā′tĭv) *adj.* **1.** Of or relating to cogitation. **2.** Inclined to or capable of cogitation. **—cog′i·ta′tive·ly** *adv.* **—cog′i·ta′tive·ness** *n.*

co·gnac (kōn′yăk′, kŏn′-, kôn′-) *n.* A brandy distilled from white wine and produced in the vicinity of Cognac.

Co·gnac (kôn′yăk′, kŏn-, kô-nyăk′). A city of western France on the Charente River north-northeast of Bordeaux. It is famous for its distilleries, which have manufactured and exported cognac since the 18th century. Population, 20,660.

cog·nate (kŏg′nāt′) *adj. Abbr.* **cog. 1.** Related by blood; having a common ancestor. **2.** Related in origin, as certain words in genetically related languages descended from the same ancestral root; for example, English *name* and Latin *nōmen* from Indo-European **nŏ-men-*. **3.** Related or analogous in nature, character, or function. **—cognate** *n.* **1.** One related by blood or origin with another, especially a person sharing an ancestor with another. **2.** A word related to one in another language. [Latin *cognātus* : *co-,* co- + *gnātus,* born, past participle of *nāscī,* to be born; see **gene-** in Appendix.] **—cog·na′tion** *n.*

cog·ni·tion (kŏg-nĭsh′ən) *n.* **1.** The mental process or faculty of knowing, including aspects such as awareness, perception, reasoning, and judgment. **2.** That which comes to be known, as through perception, reasoning, or intuition; knowledge. [Middle English *cognicioun,* from Latin *cognitiō, cognitiōn-,* from *cognitus,* past participle of *cognōscere,* to learn : *co-,* intensive pref.; see CO– + *gnōscere,* to know; see **gnō-** in Appendix.] **—cog·ni′tion·al** *adj.*

cog·ni·tive (kŏg′nĭ-tĭv) *adj.* **1.** Of, characterized by, involving, or relating to cognition: *"Thinking in terms of dualisms is common in our cognitive culture"* (Key Reporter). **2.** Having a basis in or reducible to empirical factual knowledge. **—cog′ni·tive·ly** *adv.*

cognitive dissonance *n. Psychology.* A condition of conflict or anxiety resulting from inconsistency between one's beliefs and one's actions, such as opposing the slaughter of animals and eating meat.

cognitive science *n.* The study of the nature of various mental tasks and the processes that enable them to be performed.

cog·ni·za·ble (kŏg′nĭ-zə-bəl, kŏg-nī′-) *adj.* **1.** Knowable or perceivable. **2.** *Law.* That can be tried before a particular court. **—cog′ni·za·bly** *adv.*

cog·ni·zance (kŏg′nĭ-zəns) *n.* **1.** Conscious knowledge or recognition; awareness. **2.** The range of what one can know or understand. **3.** Observance; notice: *We will take cognizance of your objections at the proper time.* **4.** *Law.* Acknowledgment, recognition, or jurisdiction; the assumption of jurisdiction in a case. **5.** *Heraldry.* A crest or badge worn to distinguish the bearer. [Middle English *conissaunce,* from Old French *conoissance,* from *connoistre,* to know, from Latin *cognōscere,* to learn. See COGNITION.]

cog·ni·zant (kŏg′nĭ-zənt) *adj.* Fully informed; conscious. See Synonyms at **aware.** [From COGNIZANCE.]

cog·no·men (kŏg-nō′mən) *n., pl.* **-no·mens** or **-nom·i·na** (-nŏm′ə-nə). **1.a.** A family name; a surname. **b.** The third and usually last name of a citizen of ancient Rome, as *Caesar* in *Gaius Julius Caesar.* **2.** A name, especially a descriptive nickname or epithet acquired through usage over a period of time. See Synonyms at **name.** [Latin : *co-,* co- + *nōmen,* name; see **nō-men-** in Appendix.] **—cog·nom′i·nal** (-nŏm′ə-nəl) *adj.*

co·gno·scen·te (kŏn′yə-shĕn′tē, kŏg′nə-) *n., pl.* **-ti** (-tē). A person with superior, usually specialized knowledge or highly refined taste; a connoisseur. [Obsolete Italian, from Latin *cognōscēns, cognōscent-,* present participle of *cognōscere,* to know. See COGNITION.]

co·gon (kō-gōn′) *n.* An Old World perennial grass *(Imperata cylindrica),* widespread as a weed in warm regions and used for thatching. [Spanish *cogón,* from Tagalog *kúgon.*]

cog railway *n.* A railway designed to operate on steep slopes and having a locomotive with a center cogwheel that engages with a cogged center rail to provide traction. Also called *rack railway.*

Cogs·well chair (kŏgz′wĕl′, -wəl) *n.* An upholstered easy chair, open under the armrests, with a sloping back and cabriole front legs. [Probably from the name *Cogswell.*]

cog·wheel (kŏg′hwēl′, -wēl′, kôg′-) *n.* **1.** A toothed wheel. **2.** One of a set of cogged wheels within a mechanism.

co·hab·it (kō-hăb′ĭt) *intr.v.* **-it·ed, -it·ing, -its. 1.** To live together as spouses. **2.** To live together in a sexual relationship when not legally married. [Late Latin *cohabitāre* : Latin *co-,* co- + Latin *habitāre,* to dwell; see INHABIT.] **—co·hab′i·tant, co·hab′it·er** *n.* **—co·hab′i·ta′tion** *n.* **—co·hab′i·ta′tion·al** *adj.*

Co·han (kō′hăn′), **George Michael.** 1878–1942. American singer, songwriter, and playwright known for his flashy, patriotic Broadway productions. He wrote "Over There" and "I'm a Yankee Doodle Dandy."

co·heir (kō-âr′) *n.* A joint heir, as to an estate.

co·heir·ess (kō-âr′ĭs) *n.* A joint woman heir, as to an estate.

co·here (kō-hîr′) *v.* **-hered, -her·ing, -heres.** *—intr.* **1.** To stick or hold together in a mass that resists separation. **2.** To have internal elements or parts logically connected so that aesthetic consistency results: *"The movie as a whole failed to cohere"* (Robert Brustein). *—tr.* To cause to form a united, orderly, and aesthetically consistent whole. [Latin *cohaerēre* : *co-,* co- + *haerēre,* to cling.]

co·her·ence (kō-hîr′əns, -hĕr′-) *n.* **1.** The quality or state of cohering, especially a logical, orderly, and aesthetically consistent relationship of parts. **2.** *Physics.* The property of being coherent, as of waves.

co·her·en·cy (kō-hîr′ən-sē) *n., pl.* **-cies.** Coherence.

co·her·ent (kō-hîr′ənt, -hĕr′-) *adj.* **1.** Sticking together; cohering. **2.** Marked by an orderly, logical, and aesthetically consistent relation of parts: *a coherent essay.* **3.** *Physics.* Of, relating to, or having waves with a constant or nearly constant phase relationship that are capable of exhibiting interference. **4.** Of or relating to a system of units of measurement in which a small number of basic units are defined from which all others in the system are derived by multiplication or division only. **5.** *Botany.* Sticking to but not fused with a part or an organ of the same kind. **—co·her′ent·ly** *adv.*

co·he·sion (kō-hē′zhən) *n.* **1.** The act, process, or condition of cohering: *exhibited strong cohesion in the family unit.* **2.** *Physics.* The intermolecular attraction by which the elements of a body are held together. **3.** *Botany.* The congenital union of parts of the same kind, such as a calyx of five united sepals. [From Latin *cohaesus,* past participle of *cohaerēre,* to cling together. See COHERE.] **—co·he′sive** (-sĭv, -zĭv) *adj.* **—co·he′sive·ly** *adv.* **—co·he′sive·ness** *n.*

co·he·sion·less (kō-hē′zhən-lĭs) *adj.* Composed of particles that do not cohere. Used of soil.

Cohn (kōn), **Ferdinand Julius.** 1828–1898. German botanist who is considered the founder of bacteriology. He was the first to recognize bacteria as plants.

co·ho (kō′hō) *n., pl.* **co·hos** or **coho.** The coho salmon.

Co·hoes (kə-hōz′). A city of east-central New York on the Hudson River north of Albany. It was settled by the Dutch in 1665. Population, 18,144.

co·hort (kō′hôrt′) *n.* **1.** A group or band of people. **2.** A companion or an associate. **3.** A generational group as defined in demographics, statistics, or market research: *"The cohort of people aged 30 to 39 . . . were more conservative"* (American Demographics). **4.a.** One of the 10 divisions of a Roman legion, consisting of 300 to 600 men. **b.** A group of soldiers. [Middle English, from Old French *cohorte,* from Latin *cohors, cohort-.* See **gher-**[1] in Appendix.]

USAGE NOTE: The use of *cohort* to refer to an individual rather than a group has gained considerable currency in recent years, and seems now to be the predominant usage. Seventy-one percent of the Usage Panel accepts the sentence *The cashiered dictator and his cohorts have all written their memoirs,* while only 43 percent accepts *The gangster walked into the room surrounded by his cohort.* • Perhaps because of its original military meaning, *cohort* usually implies a somewhat negative judgment. A phrase such as *the President and his cohorts* might therefore be better used by critics of the President than by defenders.

coho salmon *n.* A small silver food and game fish *(Oncorhynchus kisutch)* native to North Pacific waters and introduced in the Great Lakes. Also called *silver salmon.* [Alteration of *cohose,* from Salish (Halkomelem) $k^{w}əx^{w}əθ$.]

co·hosh (kō′hŏsh′) *n.* Any of several North American plants, especially blue cohosh, black cohosh, and baneberry. [From Eastern Abenaki $kk^{w}\grave{a}has$.]

co·host or **co-host** (kō′hōst′) *—n.* A joint host, as of a social event. *—tr.v.* **-host·ed, -host·ing, -hosts.** To serve as a joint host of: *"In 1980,* [he] *co-hosted another event for large contributors"* (New Yorker). See Usage Note at **host**[1].

co·hune (kō-ho͞on′) *n.* A feather-leaved Central American palm *(Orbignya cohune)* having hard-shelled fruits that yield a useful oil. [New Latin, perhaps from American Spanish, from Mosquito *ókhún.*]

coif (koif) *n.* **1.** *(also* kwäf). A coiffure. **2.** A tight-fitting cap worn under a veil, as by nuns. **3.** A white skullcap formerly worn by English lawyers. **4.** A heavy skullcap of steel or leather, formerly worn under a helmet or mail hood. **—coif** *tr.v.* **coifed, coif·ing, coifs. 1.** *(also* kwäf). To arrange or dress (the hair). **2.** To cover with or as if with a coif. [Middle English, from Old French *coife,* from Late Latin *cofea,* helmet, of Germanic origin.]

coif·feur (kwä-fûr′) *n.* A male hairdresser. [French, from *coiffer,* to coif, from Old French *coife,* coif. See COIF.]

coif·feuse (kwä-fyo͞oz′, -fœz′) *n.* A woman hairdresser. [French, feminine of *coiffeur,* coiffeur. See COIFFEUR.]

coif·fure (kwä-fyo͝or′) *n.* A hairstyle. **—coiffure** *tr.v.* **-fured, -fur·ing, -fures.** To arrange or dress (hair). [French, from *coiffer,* to coif. See COIFFEUR.]

coign (koin, kwoin) *n. & v.* Variant of **quoin.**

coil[1] (koil) *n.* **1.a.** A series of connected spirals or concentric rings formed by gathering or winding: *a coil of rope; long coils of hair.* **b.** An individual spiral or ring within such a series. **2.** A spiral pipe or series of spiral pipes, as in a radiator. **3.** *Electricity.* **a.** A wound spiral of two or more turns of insulated wire, used to introduce inductance into a circuit. **b.** Any of various devices of which such a spiral is the major component. **4.** A roll of postage stamps prepared for use in a vending machine. **—coil** *v.* **coiled, coil·ing, coils.** *—tr.* **1.** To wind in concentric rings or spirals. **2.** To wind into a shape resembling a coil. *—intr.* **1.** To form concentric rings or spirals. **2.** To move in a spiral course: *black smoke coiling up into the sky.* [Probably from obsolete French *coillir,* to gather up, from Latin *colligere.* See COLLECT[1].] **—coil′er** *n.*

coil[2] (koil) *n.* A disturbance; a fuss. [Origin unknown.]

Coim·ba·tore (koim′bə-tōr′, -tôr′). A city of southern India south-southwest of Bangalore. It is a manufacturing center and an agricultural market. Population, 704,514.

coin (koin) *n.* **1.** A small piece of metal, usually flat and circular, authorized by a government for use as money. **2.** Metal money considered as a whole. **3.** A flat, circular piece or object felt to resemble metal money: *a pizza topped with coins of pepperoni.* **4.** *Architecture.* A corner or cornerstone. **5.** A mode of expression considered standard: *Two-word verbs are valid linguistic coin in the 20th century.* **—coin** *tr.v.* **coined, coin·ing, coins. 1.** To make (pieces of money) from metal; mint or strike: *coined silver dollars.* **2.** To make pieces of money from (metal): *coin gold.* **3.** To devise (a new word or phrase). **—coin** *adj.* Requiring one or more pieces of metal money for operation: *a coin washing machine.* **—*idiom.* the other side of the coin.** One of two differing or opposing views or sides. [Middle English, from Old French, die for stamping coins, wedge, from Latin *cuneus,* wedge.] **—coin′a·ble** *adj.* **—coin′er** *n.*

coin·age (koi′nĭj) *n.* **1.** The right or process of making coins. **2.a.** Metal currency. **b.** A system of metal currency. **3.a.** A new word or phrase. **b.** The invention of new words. **4.** Ancestry or social background: *"Count Gengler was of common coinage, but in coming to America he took on a royal name"* (Jimmy Breslin).

co·in·cide (kō′ĭn-sīd′) *intr.v.* **-cid·ed, -cid·ing, -cides. 1.** To occupy the same relative position or the same area in space. **2.** To happen at the same time or during the same period. **3.** To correspond exactly; be identical. **4.** To agree exactly, as in opinion; concur. See Synonyms at **agree.** [Medieval Latin *coincidere* : Latin *co-,* co- + Latin *incidere,* to occur; see INCIDENT.]

co·in·ci·dence (kō-ĭn′sĭ-dəns, -dĕns′) *n.* **1.** The state or fact of occupying the same relative position or area in space. **2.** A sequence of events that although accidental seems to have been planned or arranged.

co·in·ci·dent (kō-ĭn′sĭ-dənt) *adj.* **1.** Occupying the same area in space or happening at the same time: *a series of coincident*

cog railway

ă pat	oi boy
ā pay	ou out
âr care	o͝o took
ä father	o͞o boot
ĕ pet	ŭ cut
ē be	ûr urge
ĭ pit	th thin
ī pie	*th* this
îr pier	hw which
ŏ pot	zh vision
ō toe	ə about, item
ô paw	♦ regionalism

Stress marks: ′ (primary); ′ (secondary), as in **dictionary** (dĭk′shə-nĕr′ē)

events. See Synonyms at **contemporary.** **2.** Being very similar to another, as in nature: *testimony that was coincident with the actual facts.* **3.** Matching point for point; coinciding: *coincident circles.*

co·in·ci·den·tal (kō-ĭn′sĭ-dĕn′tl) *adj.* **1.** Occurring as or resulting from coincidence. **2.** Happening or existing at the same time. **—co·in′ci·den′tal·ly** *adv.*

co·in·sur·ance (kō′ĭn-shŏŏr′əns) *n.* **1.** Insurance held jointly by two or more insurers. **2.** A form of insurance in which a person insures property for less than its full value and agrees to be responsible for the difference.

co·in·sure (kō′ĭn-shŏŏr′) *tr.v.* **-sured, -sur·ing, -sures.** **1.** To insure jointly. **2.** To insure with coinsurance.

coir (koir) *n.* The fiber obtained from the husk of a coconut, used chiefly in making rope and matting. [Malayalam *kayar,* cord, from *kayaru,* to be twisted.]

co·i·tus (kō′ĭ-təs, kō-ē′-) *n.* Sexual union between a male and a female involving insertion of the penis into the vagina. [Latin, from past participle of *coīre,* to copulate : *co-,* co- + *īre,* to go, come; see **ei-** in Appendix.] **—co′i·tal** *adj.* **—co′i·tal·ly** *adv.*

coitus in·ter·rup·tus (ĭn′tə-rŭp′təs) *n.* Sexual intercourse deliberately interrupted by withdrawal of the penis from the vagina prior to ejaculation. [New Latin : Latin *coitus,* coitus + Latin *interruptus,* interrupted.]

coke[1] (kōk) *n.* The solid residue of impure carbon obtained from bituminous coal and other carbonaceous materials after removal of volatile material by destructive distillation. It is used as a fuel and in making steel. **—coke** *tr. & intr.v.* **coked, cok·ing, cokes.** To convert or be converted into coke. [Perhaps from Middle English *colk,* core.]

coke[2] (kōk) *n. Slang.* Cocaine.

♦ **Coke** (kōk). A trademark used for a soft drink. See Regional Note at **tonic.**

Coke (kŏŏk, kōk), Sir **Edward.** 1552–1634. English jurist who as chief justice of the Court of Common Pleas (1606–1616) ruled that the common law is supreme law, even when the Crown disagrees.

coke·head (kōk′hĕd′) *n. Slang.* A heavy user of cocaine: *"his fictional characters—the cokehead, wild-man producer, the celebrity exercise man"* (Wall Street Journal).

col (kŏl) *n.* A pass between two mountain peaks or a gap in a ridge. [French, from Old French, neck, from Latin *collum.* See **k^wel-[1]** in Appendix.]

Col or **Col.** *abbr. Bible.* Colossians.

col. *abbr.* **1.** Collect; collected; collector. **2.** College; collegiate. **3.** Colonial; colony. **4.** Color. **5.** Column.

Col. *abbr.* **1.** Colombia. **2.** Colonel. **3.** Colorado.

col–[1] *pref.* Variant of **com–.**

col–[2] *pref.* Variant of **colo–.**

♦ **co·la[1]** (kō′lə) *n.* A carbonated soft drink containing an extract of the cola nut and other flavorings. Also called ♦*dope.*

co·la[2] (kō′lə) *n.* Plural of **colon[1]** (sense 2).

co·la[3] (kō′lə) *n.* A plural of **colon[2].**

co·la[4] also **ko·la** (kō′lə) *n.* Either of two tropical African evergreen plants *(Cola acuminata* or *C. nitida)* having reddish, fragrant, nutlike seeds yielding an extract that contains caffeine and theobromine and is used in carbonated beverages and pharmaceuticals. [Of West African origin; akin to Temne *kōla,* kola nut.]

COLA *abbr.* Cost-of-living adjustment.

col·an·der (kŭl′ən-dər, kŏl′-) *n.* A bowl-shaped kitchen utensil with perforations for draining off liquids and rinsing food. [Middle English *colyndore,* probably alteration of Old Provençal *colador,* strainer, from Vulgar Latin *cōlātōrium,* from Latin *cōlātus,* past participle of *cōlāre,* to strain, from *cōlum,* sieve.]

Col·bert (kôl-bĕr′, kôl-), **Jean Baptiste.** 1619–1683. French politician who served as an adviser to Louis XIV. Colbert reformed taxes, centralized the administration, and improved roads and canals in an effort to encourage trade.

col·can·non (kŏl-kăn′ən) *n.* An Irish dish of mashed potatoes and cabbage, seasoned with butter. [Irish Gaelic *cāl ceannan* : *cál,* cabbage (from Old Irish *cāl,* from Latin *caulis*) + *ceannan,* white-headed (*ceann,* head, from Old Irish *cenn* + *fionn,* white, from Old Irish *find;* see **weid-** in Appendix).]

Col·ches·ter (kōl′chĕs′tər, -chĭ-stər). A municipal borough of southeast England near the North Sea. It was an important pre-Roman city and the site of the first Roman colony in Britain. Population, 83,900.

col·chi·cine (kŏl′chĭ-sēn′, kŏl′kĭ-) *n.* A poisonous, pale-yellow alkaloid, $C_{22}H_{25}NO_6$, obtained from the autumn crocus and used in plant breeding to induce chromosome doubling and in medicine to treat gout. [COLCHIC(UM) + –INE[2].]

col·chi·cum (kŏl′chĭ-kəm, kŏl′kĭ-) *n.* **1.** Any of various bulbous plants of the genus *Colchicum,* such as the autumn crocus. **2.** The dried ripe seeds or corms of the autumn crocus, both of which yield colchicine. [Latin, a plant with a poisonous root, from Greek *kolkhikon,* meadow saffron, after *Kolkhos,* Colchis.]

Col·chis (kŏl′kĭs). An ancient region on the Black Sea south of the Caucasus Mountains. It was the site of Jason's legendary quest for the Golden Fleece.

col·co·thar (kŏl′kə-thər, -thär′) *n.* A brownish-red ferric oxide obtained as a residue after heating ferrous sulfate, used in glass polishing and as a pigment. [Medieval Latin, from Spanish *colcótar,* from Arabic *qulquṭār,* possibly from Greek *khalkanthos,* copper sulfate : *khalkos,* copper + *anthos,* flower.]

cold (kōld) *adj.* **cold·er, cold·est.** **1.a.** Having a low temperature. **b.** Having a temperature lower than normal body temperature. **c.** Feeling no warmth; uncomfortably chilled. **2.a.** Marked by deficient heat: *a cold room.* **b.** Being at a temperature that is less than what is required: *cold oatmeal.* **c.** Chilled by refrigeration or ice: *cold beer.* **3.** Lacking emotion; objective: *cold logic.* **4.** Having no appeal to the senses or feelings: *a cold decor.* **5.a.** Not affectionate or friendly; aloof: *a cold person; a cold nod.* **b.** Exhibiting or feeling no enthusiasm: *a cold audience; a cold response to the new play; a concert that left me cold.* **c.** Devoid of sexual desire; frigid. **6.** *Color.* Designating a tone or color, such as pale gray, that suggests little warmth. **7.** Having lost all freshness or vividness through passage of time: *dogs attempting to catch a cold scent.* **8.a.** Marked by or sustaining a loss of body heat: *cold hands and feet.* **b.** Appearing to be dead; unconscious. **c.** Dead: *was cold in his grave.* **9.** Marked by unqualified certainty or sure familiarity. **10.** So intense as to be almost uncontrollable: *cold fury.* **—cold** *adv.* **1.** To an unqualified degree; totally: *was cold sober.* **2.** With complete finality: *We turned him down cold.* **3.** Without advance preparation or introduction: *took the exam cold and passed; walked in cold and got the new job.* **—cold** *n.* **1.a.** Relative lack of warmth. **b.** The sensation resulting from lack of warmth; chill. **2.** A condition of low air temperature; cold weather: *went out into the cold and got a chill.* **3.** A viral infection characterized by inflammation of the mucous membranes lining the upper respiratory passages and usually accompanied by malaise, fever, chills, coughing, and sneezing. In this sense, also called *common cold, coryza.* **—*idiom.* out in the cold.** Lacking benefits given to others; neglected. [Middle English, from Old English *ceald.* See **gel-** in Appendix.] **—cold′ly** *adv.* **—cold′ness** *n.*

SYNONYMS: *cold, arctic, chilly, cool, frigid, frosty, gelid, glacial, icy.* The central meaning shared by these adjectives is "marked by a low or an extremely low temperature": *cold air; an arctic climate; a chilly day; cool water; a frigid room; a frosty morning; gelid seas; glacial winds; icy hands.*
ANTONYM: *hot.*

cold bath *n. Informal.* A chilly reaction or response.

cold-blood·ed (kōld′blŭd′ĭd) *adj.* **1.a.** Lacking feeling or emotion: *a cold-blooded killer.* **b.** Executed without feeling or emotion: *a cold-blooded crime; a cold-blooded performance of the concerto.* **2.** Ectothermic. **—cold′-blood′ed·ly** *adv.* **—cold′-blood′ed·ness** *n.*

cold cash *n. Informal.* Money readily at hand.

cold chisel *n.* A chisel made of hardened, tempered steel and used for cutting cold metal.

cold·cock (kōld′kŏk′) *tr.v.* **-cocked, -cock·ing, -cocks.** *Slang.* To knock (another) unconscious.

cold comfort *n.* Extremely limited empathy, sympathy, or encouragement: *"I told him that the years would pass with remarkable celerity, but that appeared to be cold comfort"* (Nelson Bryant).

cold cream *n.* An emulsion for softening and cleansing the skin.

cold cut *n.* A slice of cold, cooked meat. Often used in the plural.

♦ **cold drink** *n.* **1.** A drink, as of water, served or taken cold. **2.** *Chiefly Southern U.S.* See **soft drink.** See Regional Note at **tonic.**

cold duck *n.* A beverage made of sparkling burgundy and champagne. [Translation of German *Kalte Ente,* a drink made from a mixture of wines.]

cold-eyed (kōld′īd′) *adj.* Cold-bloodedly dispassionate: *a cold-eyed appraisal of the situation.*

cold feet *pl.n. Slang.* Fearfulness or timidity preventing the completion of a course of action.

cold fish *n. Informal.* An aloof person.

cold frame *n.* An unheated outdoor structure consisting of a wooden or concrete frame and a top of glass or clear plastic, used for protecting and acclimatizing seedlings and plants.

cold front *n.* The leading portion of a cold atmospheric air mass moving against and eventually replacing a warm air mass.

Cold Harbor (kōld). A locality in eastern Virginia east-northeast of Richmond. Confederate forces defeated Union troops here in two Civil War battles (1862 and 1864).

cold-heart·ed (kōld′här′tĭd) *adj.* Devoid of sympathy or feeling. **—cold′-heart′ed·ly** *adv.* **—cold′-heart′ed·ness** *n.*

cold light *n.* **1.** Light producing little or no heat. **2.** Light emitted by a process other than incandescence.

cold pack *n.* **1.** A compress of gauze, cloth, or plastic filled or moistened with a cold fluid and applied externally to swollen or injured body parts to relieve pain and swelling. **2.** A canning process in which uncooked food is packed in jars or cans, then sterilized by heat.

cold rolling *n.* The rolling of steel or other metal at room temperature to preserve its original crystal structure.

cold rubber *n.* A durable, strong synthetic rubber polymerized at low temperatures.

cold·shoul·der (kōld′shōl′dər) *tr.v.* **-dered, -der·ing, -ders.** *Informal.* To slight or snub (someone).

cold shoulder *n. Informal.* Deliberate coldness or disregard;

ă pat	oi boy
ā pay	ou out
âr care	ŏŏ took
ä father	ōō boot
ĕ pet	ŭ cut
ē be	ûr urge
ĭ pit	th thin
ī pie	*th* this
îr pier	hw which
ŏ pot	zh vision
ō toe	ə about, item
ô paw	♦ regionalism

Stress marks: ′ (primary); ′ (secondary), as in **dictionary** (dĭk′shə-nĕr′ē)

a slight or a snub: *received the cold shoulder from several members of the club.*

cold shower *n. Informal.* A startlingly chilly, unenthusiastic reaction, response, or reception: *"The elections, however, amounted to a cold shower for the . . . authorities"* (Los Angeles Times).

cold sore *n.* A small blister occurring on the lips and face and caused by herpes simplex. Also called *fever blister, herpes labialis.*

cold storage *n.* **1.** Protective storage, as of foods or furs, in a refrigerated place. **2.** *Informal.* A state of being held in abeyance.

cold sweat *n.* A reaction to nervousness, fear, pain, or shock, characterized by simultaneous perspiration and chill and cold moist skin.

cold turkey *n. Slang.* **1.** Immediate, complete withdrawal from something on which one has become dependent, such as an addictive drug. **2.** Blunt language or procedural method. **3.** A cold fish.

cold type *n.* Typesetting, such as photocomposition, done without the casting of metal.

cold wall effect *n.* The chilly discomfort experienced by a person in a building as his or her body radiates heat to the cold surface of an uninsulated wall.

cold war or **Cold War** *n.* **1.** A state of political tension and military rivalry between nations that stops short of full-scale war. **2.** A state of rivalry and tension between two factions, groups, or individuals that stops short of open, violent confrontation. **—cold warrior** *n.*

cold water *n. Informal.* Deprecation, as of a proposal or an idea deemed silly or ill-advised: *"The President was careful not to throw cold water on the latest Soviet arms proposal"* (Christian Science Monitor).

cold-wa·ter (kōld′wô′tər, -wŏt′ər) *adj.* Lacking modern plumbing or heating facilities: *a cold-water flat.*

cold wave *n.* **1.** An onset of unusually cold weather within a 24-hour period. **2.** A form of permanent wave in which the hair is set by chemicals rather than by heat.

cold-weld (kōld′wĕld′) *tr.v.* **-weld·ed, -weld·ing, -welds.** To weld under high pressure or vacuum without heat.

cold weld·ing (wĕl′dĭng) *n.* The welding of two materials under high pressure or vacuum without the use of heat.

cole (kōl) *n.* See **kale** (sense 1). [Middle English *col,* from Old English *cāl,* from Latin *caulis,* cabbage.]

Cole (kōl), **Nat "King."** 1919–1965. American singer and pianist who recorded such popular ballads as "Unforgettable" and "Mona Lisa."

Cole, Thomas. 1801–1848. American painter acknowledged as the leader of the Hudson River School, America's first painting movement.

co·lec·to·my (kə-lĕk′tə-mē) *n., pl.* **-mies.** Surgical removal of part or all of the colon.

cole·man·ite (kōl′mə-nīt′) *n.* A natural white or colorless hydrated calcium borate, $Ca_2B_6O_{11}{\cdot}5H_2O$, a principal source of borax. [After William Tell *Coleman* (1824–1893), American merchant in California.]

co·le·op·ter·an (kō′lē-ŏp′tər-ən, kŏl′ē-) also **co·le·op·ter·on** (-tə-rŏn′) *—n.* Any of numerous insects of the order Coleoptera, characterized by forewings modified to form tough, protective covers for the membranous hind wings and including the beetles, weevils, and fireflies. *—adj.* Of, relating to, or belonging to the order Coleoptera. [From New Latin *Coleoptera,* order name, from Greek *koleopteros,* sheath-winged : *koleon,* sheath; see **kel-**[1] in Appendix + *pteron,* wing; see **pet-** in Appendix.] **—co′le·op′ter·ous** (-tər-əs) *adj.*

co·le·op·tile (kō′lē-ŏp′tĭl, kŏl′ē-) *n.* A protective sheath enclosing the shoot tip and embryonic leaves of grasses. [From New Latin *coleoptilum* : Greek *koleon,* sheath; see **kel-**[1] in Appendix + Greek *ptilon,* plume; see **pet-** in Appendix.]

co·le·o·rhi·za (kō′lē-ə-rī′zə, kŏl′ē-) *n., pl.* **-zae** (-zē). A protective sheath enclosing the embryonic root of grasses. [New Latin : Greek *koleon,* sheath; see **kel-**[1] in Appendix + Greek *rhiza,* root; see **wrād-** in Appendix.]

Cole·ridge (kōl′rĭj, kō′lə-rĭj), **Samuel Taylor.** 1772–1834. British poet and critic who was a leader of the romantic movement. With William Wordsworth he published *Lyrical Ballads* (1798), which contains "The Rime of the Ancient Mariner," his best-known poem.

cole·slaw also **cole slaw** (kōl′slô′) *n.* A salad of finely shredded raw cabbage and sometimes shredded carrots, dressed with mayonnaise. [Dutch *koolsla* : *kool,* cabbage (from Middle Dutch *cōle,* from Latin *caulis*) + *sla,* salad (short for *salade,* from French, from Old French; see SALAD).]

Col·et (kŏl′ət), **John.** 1467?–1519. English scholar and theologian who founded Saint Paul's School in London (1509) to promote classical as well as scriptural learning.

Co·lette (kŏ-lĕt′, kô-), **(Sidonie Gabrielle Claudine).** 1873–1954. French novelist known for her observations of women and nature. She wrote the *Claudine* series, as well as *Chéri* (1920) and *Gigi* (1945).

co·le·us (kō′lē-əs) *n.* Any of various Old World herbs of the genus *Coleus* in the mint family, widely cultivated for their multicolored decorative leaves. Also called *flame nettle.* [New Latin *Coleus,* genus name, from Greek *koleos,* sheath (from the way its filaments are joined). See **kel-**[1] in Appendix.]

cole·wort (kōl′wûrt′, -wôrt′) *n.* See **kale** (sense 1).

Col·fax (kōl′făks), **Schuyler.** 1823–1885. Vice President of the United States (1869–1873) under Ulysses S. Grant.

coli– *pref.* Variant of **colo–.**

col·ic (kŏl′ĭk) *n.* Severe abdominal pain caused by spasm, obstruction, or distention of any of the hollow viscera, such as the intestines. Often a condition of early infancy, colic is marked by chronic irritability and crying. **—colic** (kō′lĭk) *adj.* Of, relating to, or affecting the colon. [Middle English *colik,* affecting the colon, colic, from Old French *colique,* from Latin *cōlica (passiō),* (suffering) of the colon, feminine of *cōlicus,* from Greek *kōlikos,* from *kolon,* colon.] **—col′ick·y** (kŏl′ĭ-kē) *adj.*

col·i·cin (kŏl′ĭ-sĭn, kō′lĭ-) *n.* Any of various antibacterial proteins produced by certain strains of the colon bacillus that are lethal to other closely related strains of bacteria. [COL(ON)[2] + –IC + –IN.]

col·ic·root (kŏl′ĭk-ro͞ot′, -ro͝ot′) *n.* **1.** Any of certain perennial herbs of the genus *Aletris* in the lily family, especially *A. farinosa* of eastern North America, having racemes of small white flowers and rootstocks formerly used in medicine to treat colic. Also called *star grass.* **2.** Any of various other plants thought to relieve colic.

co·li·form (kō′lə-fôrm′, kŏl′ə-) *adj. Microbiology.* Of or relating to the bacilli that commonly inhabit the intestines of human beings and other vertebrates, especially the colon bacillus. **—co′li·form′** *n.*

Co·li·gny or **Co·li·gni** (kô-lē-nyē′), **Gaspard de.** 1519–1572. French general and Huguenot leader who was one of the first victims in the massacre of Protestants that took place on Saint Bartholomew's Day, 1572.

co·lin·e·ar (kō-lĭn′ē-ər) *adj.* **1.** Containing elements that correspond to one another and that are arranged in the same linear sequence. **2.** Collinear. **—co·lin′e·ar′i·ty** (-ăr′ĭ-tē) *n.*

col·i·se·um also **col·os·se·um** (kŏl′ĭ-sē′əm) *n.* A large amphitheater for public sports events, entertainment, or assemblies. [Medieval Latin *Colisēum,* an amphitheater in Rome, Italy, variant of Latin *Colossēum,* from neuter of *colossēus,* gigantic, from *colossus,* huge statue. See COLOSSUS.]

co·lis·tin (kə-lĭs′tĭn, kō-) *n. Microbiology.* An antibiotic produced by the bacterium *Bacillus polymyxa* or *B. colistinus* that is effective against a wide range of Gram-negative bacteria and is used especially in the treatment of infections of the gastrointestinal tract. [From New Latin *Colistīnus,* species name, from COLI–.]

co·li·tis (kə-lī′tĭs) *n.* Inflammation of the colon. Also called *colonitis.*

coll. *abbr.* **1.** Collateral. **2.** Collect; collection; collector. **3.** College; collegiate. **4.** Colloquial; colloquialism.

coll– *pref.* Variant of **collo–.**

col·lab·o·rate (kə-lăb′ə-rāt′) *intr.v.* **-rat·ed, -rat·ing, -rates. 1.** To work together, especially in a joint intellectual effort. **2.** To cooperate treasonably, as with an enemy occupation force. [Late Latin *collabōrāre, collabōrāt-* : Latin *com-,* com- + Latin *labōrāre,* to work (from *labor,* toil).] **—col·lab′o·ra′tion** *n.* **—col·lab′o·ra′tive** *adj.* **—col·lab′o·ra′tor** *n.*

coliseum
Partial view of the Colosseum, Rome, Italy

col·lab·o·ra·tion·ist (kə-lăb′ə-rā′shə-nĭst) *n.* One that collaborates with an enemy occupation force. **—col·lab′o·ra′tion·ism** *n.*

col·lage (kō-läzh′, kə-) *n.* **1.a.** An artistic composition of materials and objects pasted over a surface, often with unifying lines and color. **b.** The art of creating such compositions. **2.** An assemblage of diverse elements: *a collage of conflicting memories.* **—collage** *v.* **-laged, -lag·ing, -lages.** *—tr.* To paste (diverse materials) over a surface, thereby creating an artistic product. *—intr.* To create such an artistic product. [French, from *coller,* to glue, from *colle,* glue, from Vulgar Latin **colla,* from Greek *kolla.*] **—col·lag′ist** *n.*

collage film *n.* A film that has disparate scenes linked in series without transition.

col·la·gen (kŏl′ə-jən) *n.* The fibrous protein constituent of bone, cartilage, tendon, and other connective tissue. It is converted into gelatin by boiling. [Greek *kolla,* glue + –GEN.] **—col′la·gen′ic** (-jĕn′ĭk), **col·lag′e·nous** (kə-lăj′ə-nəs) *adj.*

col·lag·e·nase (kə-lăj′ə-nās′, -nāz′, kŏl′ə-jə-) *n.* Any of various enzymes that catalyze the hydrolysis of collagen and gelatin.

col·lapse (kə-lăps′) *v.* **-lapsed, -laps·ing, -laps·es.** *—intr.* **1.** To fall down or inward suddenly; cave in. **2.** To break down suddenly in strength or health and thereby cease to function: *a monarchy that collapsed.* **3.** To fold compactly: *chairs that collapse for storage.* *—tr.* To cause to fold, break down, or fall down or inward. **—collapse** *n.* **1.** The act of falling down or inward, as from loss of supports. **2.** An abrupt failure of function, strength, or health; a breakdown. **3.** An abrupt loss of perceived value or of effect: *the collapse of popular respect for the integrity of world leaders.* [Latin *collābī, collāps-,* to fall together : *com-,* com- + *lābī,* to fall.] **—col·laps′i·bil′i·ty** *n.* **—col·laps′i·ble, col·laps′a·ble** *adj.*

collage
Merz 163, with Woman Spraying,
$6\frac{1}{16}$″ x $4\frac{7}{8}$″, 1920
paper and cloth collage
by Kurt Schwitters
(1887–1948)

col·lar (kŏl′ər) *n.* **1.** The part of a garment that encircles the neck. **2.** A necklace. **3.a.** A restraining or identifying band of leather, metal, or plastic put around the neck of an animal. **b.** The cushioned part of a harness that presses against the shoulders of a draft animal. **4.** *Biology.* An encircling structure or bandlike marking, as around the neck of an animal, suggestive of a collar. **5.** Any of various ringlike devices used to limit, guide, or secure a machine part. **6.** *Slang.* An arrest, as of a criminal. **—collar** *tr.v.* **-lared, -lar·ing, -lars. 1.** To furnish with a collar. **2.** *Slang.* **a.** To seize or detain. **b.** To arrest (a criminal, for example). [Middle English *coler,* from Old French *colier,* from Latin *collāre,* from *collum,* neck. See **kʷel-¹** in Appendix.] **—col′lared** *adj.*

col·lar·bone (kŏl′ər-bōn′) *n.* See **clavicle** (sense 1).

collar cell *n.* See **choanocyte.**

col·lard (kŏl′ərd) *n.* **1.** See **kale** (sense 1). **2. collards.** The leaves of kale, used as a vegetable. [Variant of COLEWORT.]

collared peccary *n.* A small wild hog *(Tayassu tajacu)* with a range from the southwest United States to northern Argentina, having a gray and black coat with a white band from the back to the chest. Also called *javelina.*

collat. *abbr.* Collateral.

col·late (kə-lāt′, kŏl′āt′, kō′lāt′) *tr.v.* **-lat·ed, -lat·ing, -lates. 1.** To examine and compare carefully in order to note points of disagreement. **2.** To assemble in proper numerical or logical sequence. **3.** *Printing.* **a.** To examine (gathered sheets) in order to arrange them in proper sequence before binding. **b.** To verify the order and completeness of (the pages of a volume). **4.** *Ecclesiastical.* To admit (a cleric) to a benefice. [From Latin *collātus,* past participle of *cōnferre,* to bring together : *com-,* com- + *lātus,* brought; see **tele-** in Appendix.] **—col·la′tor** *n.*

col·lat·er·al (kə-lăt′ər-əl) *adj. Abbr.* **collat., coll. 1.** Situated or running side by side; parallel. **2.** Coinciding in tendency or effect; concomitant or accompanying. **3.** Serving to support or corroborate: *collateral evidence.* **4.** Of a secondary nature; subordinate: *collateral target damage from a bombing run.* **5.** Of, relating to, or guaranteed by a security pledged against the performance of an obligation: *a collateral loan.* **6.** Having an ancestor in common but descended from a different line. **—collateral** *n.* **1.** Property acceptable as security for a loan or other obligation. **2.** A collateral relative. [Middle English, from Medieval Latin *collāterālis* : Latin *com-,* com- + Latin *lātus, later-,* side.] **—col·lat′er·al·ly** *adv.*

col·lat·er·al·ize (kə-lăt′ər-ə-līz′) *tr.v.* **-ized, -iz·ing, -izes. 1.** To secure (a loan) through use of collateral. **2.** To pledge (property, for example) as collateral.

col·la·tion (kə-lā′shən, kŏ-, kō-) *n.* **1.** The act or process of collating. **2. a.** A light meal permitted on fast days. **b.** A light meal.

col·league (kŏl′ēg′) *n.* A fellow member of a profession, a staff, or an academic faculty; an associate. See Synonyms at **partner.** [French *collègue,* from Latin *collēga* : *com-,* com- + *lēgāre,* to depute; see **leg-** in Appendix.] **—col′league·ship′** *n.*

col·lect¹ (kə-lĕkt′) *v.* **-lect·ed, -lect·ing, -lects.** *—tr.* **1.** To bring together in a group or mass; gather. **2.** To accumulate as a hobby or for study. **3.** To call for and obtain payment of: *collect taxes.* **4.** To recover control of: *collect one's emotions.* **5.** To call for (someone); pick up: *collected the children and drove home.* *—intr.* **1.** To come together in a group or mass; gather. See Synonyms at **gather. 2.** To take in payments or donations: *collecting for charity.* **—collect** *adv. & adj. Abbr.* **col., coll.** With payment to be made by the receiver: *called collect; a collect phone call.* [Middle English *collecten,* from Latin *colligere, collēct-* : *com-,* com- + *legere,* to gather; see **leg-** in Appendix.]

col·lect² (kŏl′ĭkt, -ĕkt′) *n. Ecclesiastical.* A brief formal prayer that is used in various Western liturgies before the epistle and that varies with the day. [Middle English *collecte,* from Old French, from Medieval Latin *collēcta,* short for *(ōrātiō ad) collēctam,* (prayer at the) gathering, from Latin *collēctus,* gathered, past participle of *colligere,* to gather. See COLLECT¹.]

col·lect·a·ble (kə-lĕk′tə-bəl) *n.* Variant of **collectible.**

col·lec·ta·ne·a (kŏl′ĕk-tā′nē-ə) *pl.n.* A selection of passages from one or more authors; an anthology. [Latin, from neuter pl. of *collēctāneus,* collected, from *collēctus.* See COLLECT².]

col·lect·ed (kə-lĕk′tĭd) *adj.* **1.** Self-possessed; composed. See Synonyms at **cool. 2.** *Abbr.* **col.** Brought or placed together from various sources: *the collected poems of W.H. Auden.* **—col·lect′ed·ly** *adv.* **—col·lect′ed·ness** *n.*

col·lect·i·ble also **col·lect·a·ble** (kə-lĕk′tə-bəl) *n.* One of a group or class of objects, such as period glass or domestic utensils, prized by fanciers. **—col·lect′i·ble, col·lect′a·ble** *adj.*

col·lec·tion (kə-lĕk′shən) *n. Abbr.* **col., coll. 1.** The act or process of collecting. **2.** A group of objects or works to be seen, studied, or kept together. **3.** An accumulation; a deposit: *a collection of dust on the piano.* **4. a.** A collecting of money, as in church. **b.** The sum so collected.

col·lec·tive (kə-lĕk′tĭv) *adj.* **1.** Assembled or accumulated into a whole. **2.** Of, relating to, characteristic of, or made by a number of people acting as a group: *a collective decision.* **—collective** *n.* **1.** An undertaking, such as a business operation, set up on the principle of ownership and control of the means of production and distribution by the workers involved, usually under the supervision of a government. **2.** *Grammar.* A collective noun. **—col·lec′tive·ly** *adv.* **—col·lec′tive·ness** *n.*

collective bar·gain·ing (bär′gə-nĭng) *n.* Negotiation between the representatives of organized workers and their employer or employers to determine wages, hours, rules, and working conditions.

collective farm *n.* A farm or a group of farms organized as a unit and managed and worked cooperatively by a group of laborers under state supervision.

collective mark *n.* A trademark or service mark used by members of a cooperative, an association, or other collective group or organization, including marks used to indicate membership in a union, an association, or other organization.

collective noun *n. Grammar.* A noun that denotes a collection of persons or things regarded as a unit.

USAGE NOTE: In American usage, a collective noun takes a singular verb when it refers to the collection considered as a whole, as in *The family was united on this question. The enemy is suing for peace.* It takes a plural verb when it refers to the members of the group considered as individuals, as in *My family are always fighting among themselves. The enemy were showing up in groups of three or four to turn in their weapons.* (In British usage, however, collective nouns are more often treated as plurals: *The government have not announced a new policy. The team are playing in the test matches next week.*) A collective noun should not be treated as both singular and plural in the same construction; thus *The family is determined to press its* (not *their*) *claim.* Among the common collective nouns are *committee, clergy, company, enemy, group, family, flock, public,* and *team.* See Usage Note at **government, group.**

collective unconscious *n.* In Jungian psychology, a part of the unconscious mind, shared by a society, a people, or all humankind. The product of ancestral experience, it contains concepts of science, religion, and morality, for example.

col·lec·tiv·ism (kə-lĕk′tə-vĭz′əm) *n.* The principles or system of ownership and control of the means of production and distribution by the people collectively. **—col·lec′tiv·ist** *n.* **—col·lec′tiv·is′tic** *adj.* **—col·lec′tiv·is′ti·cal·ly** *adv.*

col·lec·tiv·i·ty (kŏl′ĕk-tĭv′ĭ-tē, kə-lĕk′-) *n.* **1.** The quality or condition of being collective. **2.** The people as a whole.

col·lec·tiv·ize (kə-lĕk′tə-vīz′) *tr.v.* **-ized, -iz·ing, -iz·es.** To organize (an economy, industry, or enterprise) on the basis of collectivism. **—col·lec′tiv·i·za′tion** (-tə-vĭ-zā′shən) *n.*

col·lec·tor (kə-lĕk′tər) *n.* **1.** One that collects: *a solar energy collector; a dust collector.* **2.** *Abbr.* **col., coll.** A person employed to collect taxes, duties, or other payments. **3.** A person who makes a collection, as of stamps. **4.** *Electronics.* An electrode in an electron tube that collects electrons which have finished carrying current. **—col·lec′tor·ship′** *n.*

col·leen (kŏ-lēn′, kŏl′ēn′) *n.* An Irish girl. [Irish Gaelic *cailín,* diminutive of *caile,* girl, from Old Irish.]

col·lege (kŏl′ĭj) *n. Abbr.* **col., coll. 1. a.** An institution of higher learning that grants the bachelor's degree in liberal arts or science or both. **b.** An undergraduate division or school of a university offering courses and granting degrees in a particular field. **c.** A school, sometimes but not always a university, offering special instruction in professional or technical subjects. **d.** The students, faculty, and administration of such a school or institution. **e.** The building or buildings occupied by such a school or institution. **f.** *Chiefly British.* A self-governing society of scholars for study or instruction, incorporated within a university. **g.** An institution in France for secondary education that is not supported by the state. **2. a.** A body of persons having a common purpose or shared duties: *a college of surgeons.* **b.** An electoral college. **3.** A body of clerics living together on an endowment. *—attributive.* Often used to modify another noun: *college courses; college faculty.* [Middle English, from Old French, from Latin *collēgium,* association. See COLLEGIUM.]

Col·lege Board (kŏl′ĭj). A service mark used for the administration of aptitude and achievement tests, used by some colleges and universities in admitting and placing students.

College of Cardinals *n. Roman Catholic Church.* The body of all the cardinals that elect the pope, assist him in governing the church, and administer the Holy See when the papacy is vacant.

College Park. 1. A city of northwest Georgia, a residential suburb of Atlanta. Population, 24,632. **2.** A city of west-central Maryland north-northeast of Washington, D.C. It is the seat of the University of Maryland (established 1807). Population, 23,614.

College Station. A city of east-central Texas northwest of Houston. Texas Agricultural and Mechanical University (opened 1876) is here. Population, 37,272.

college try *n. Informal.* A serious effort to do or achieve.

col·le·gi·a (kə-lē′jē-ə, -lĕg′ē-ə) *n.* A plural of **collegium.**

col·le·gi·al (kə-lē′jē-əl, -jəl) *adj.* **1. a.** Characterized by or having power and authority vested equally among colleagues: *"He . . . prefers a collegial harmony that will present him with a consensus on the issues"* (Time). **b.** *Roman Catholic Church.* Characterized by the equal sharing of power among the bishops. **2.** Of, relating to, characterized by, or likened to college life; collegiate: *"Law-school faculties have traditionally been thought of as collegial—academic extensions of the courtroom civility that calls for the enemy to be spoken of as 'my learned opponent'"* (Calvin Trillin). [Middle English, from Latin *collēgiālis,* of colleagues, from *collēgium,* association. See COLLEGIUM.] **—col·le′gi·al·ly** *adv.*

col·le·gi·al·i·ty (kə-lē′jē-ăl′ĭ-tē) *n.* **1.** Shared power and authority vested among colleagues. **2.** *Roman Catholic Church.* The doctrine that bishops collectively share collegiate power.

col·le·gian (kə-lē′jən, -jē-ən) *n.* A college student or recent college graduate. [Middle English, member of an endowed religious or scholarly body, from Medieval Latin *collēgiānus,* from Latin *collēgium,* association. See COLLEGIUM.]

col·le·giate (kə-lē′jĭt, -jē-ĭt) *adj. Abbr.* **col., coll. 1.** Of, relating to, or held to resemble a college. **2.** Of, for, or typical of college students. **3.** Of or relating to a collegiate church. [Middle English *collegiat,* from Late Latin *collēgiātus,* from Latin *collēgium,* association. See COLLEGIUM.]

collegiate church *n.* **1.** A Roman Catholic or Anglican church other than a cathedral, having a chapter of canons and presided over by a dean or provost. **2.a.** A church in the United States associated with others under a common body of pastors. **b.** An association of such churches. **3.** A church in Scotland served by two or more ministers at the same time.

col·le·gi·um (kə-lē′jē-əm, -lĕg′ē-) *n., pl.* **-le·gi·a** (-lē′jē-ə, -lĕg′ē-ə) or **-le·gi·ums. 1.** An executive council or committee of equally empowered members, especially one supervising an industry, a commissariat, or another organization in the Soviet Union. **2.** A group, the members of which pursue shared goals while working within a framework of mutual trust and respect: *"This standing firm . . . enables the college to be a community, a collegium of students and faculty working at common problems and possibilities from the shared perspective of the liberal arts"* (Robert A. Spivey). [Russian *kollegiya,* from Latin *collēgium,* association, from *collēga,* colleague. See COLLEAGUE.]

col·lem·bo·lan (kə-lĕm′bə-lən) *n.* See **springtail.** [COLL(O)– + Greek *embolos,* peg, stopper; see EMBOLUS.]

col·len·chy·ma (kə-lĕng′kə-mə) *n.* A supportive tissue of plants, consisting of elongated, living cells with unevenly thickened walls. [COLL(O)– + –ENCHYMA.] **—col′len·chym′a·tous** (kŏl′ən-kĭm′ə-təs) *adj.*

col·len·chyme (kŏl′ən-kīm′) *n.* A gelatinous mesenchyme that constitutes a layer in the body wall of many coelenterates and ctenophores. [From COLLENCHYMA.]

col·let (kŏl′ĭt) *n.* **1.** A cone-shaped sleeve used for holding circular or rodlike pieces in a lathe or other machine. **2.** A metal collar used in watchmaking to join one end of a balance spring to the balance staff. **3.** A circular flange or rim, as in a ring, into which a gem is set. [French, diminutive of *col,* collar, from Latin *collum,* neck. See **kʷel-** [1] in Appendix.]

col·lide (kə-līd′) *intr.v.* **-lid·ed, -lid·ing, -lides. 1.** To come together with violent, direct impact. **2.** To meet in opposition; conflict: *"When truths collide, compromise becomes the first casualty"* (Henry A. Kissinger). [Latin *collīdere : com-,* com- + *laedere,* to strike.]

col·lie (kŏl′ē) *n.* A large dog of a breed originating in Scotland as a sheepdog, having long hair and a long, narrow muzzle. [Scots, perhaps variant of *colly,* like coal, from Middle English *col,* coal. See COAL.]

col·lier (kŏl′yər) *n.* **1.** A coal miner. **2.** *Nautical.* A coal ship. [Middle English *colier,* from *col,* coal, from Old English.]

col·lier·y (kŏl′yə-rē) *n., pl.* **-ies.** A coal mine together with its physical plant and outbuildings.

col·li·gate (kŏl′ĭ-gāt′) *tr.v.* **-gat·ed, -gat·ing, -gates. 1.** To tie or group together. **2.** *Logic.* To bring (isolated facts) together by an explanation or hypothesis that applies to them all. [Latin *colligāre, colligāt- : com-,* com- + *ligāre,* to tie, bind; see **leig-** in Appendix.] **—col′li·ga′tion** *n.*

col·li·ga·tive (kŏl′ĭ-gā′tĭv) *adj. Chemistry.* Depending on the quantity of molecules but not on their chemical nature: *colligative properties.*

col·li·mate (kŏl′ə-māt′) *tr.v.* **-mat·ed, -mat·ing, -mates. 1.** To make parallel. **2.** To adjust the line of sight of (an optical device). [New Latin *collīmāre, collīmāt-,* alteration of Latin *collīneāre,* to aim : *com-,* intensive pref.; see COM– + *līneāre,* to make straight (from *līnea,* line; see LINE [1]).] **—col′li·ma′tion** *n.*

col·li·ma·tor (kŏl′ə-mā′tər) *n.* A device capable of collimating radiation, as a long narrow tube in which strongly absorbing or reflecting walls permit only radiation traveling parallel to the tube axis to traverse the entire length.

col·lin·e·ar (kə-lĭn′ē-ər, kō-) *adj.* **1.** Passing through or lying on the same straight line. **2.** Containing a common line; coaxial. **—col·lin′e·ar′i·ty** (-ăr′ĭ-tē) *n.*

col·lins (kŏl′ənz) *n.* A tall iced drink made with liquor, such as gin, and lemon or lime juice. [Probably from the name *Collins.*]

Col·lins (kŏl′ĭnz), **Michael** [1]**.** 1890–1922. Irish nationalist and Sinn Fein leader who helped negotiate the establishment of the Irish Free State (1921).

Col·lins (kŏl′ĭnz), **Michael** [2]**.** Born 1930. Italian-born American astronaut who as a crew member of Apollo 11 piloted the spacecraft during its historic mission to the moon (1969). He orbited the moon alone while Neil Armstrong and Buzz Aldrin made the first manned lunar landing.

Collins, William. 1721–1759. British poet best known for his melancholy *Odes* (1747).

Collins, (William) Wilkie. 1824–1889. British writer noted for his pioneering detective novels, including *The Woman in White* (1860) and *Moonstone* (1868).

col·lin·si·a (kə-lĭn′zē-ə) *n.* Any of various North American plants of the genus *Collinsia,* which includes blue-eyed Mary and Chinese houses. [New Latin *Collinsia,* genus name, after Zaccheus *Collins* (1764–1831), American botanist.]

Col·lins·ville (kŏl′ĭnz-vĭl′). A city of southwest Illinois east-northeast of East St. Louis. It was formerly a coal-mining center. Population, 19,613.

col·li·sion (kə-lĭzh′ən) *n.* **1.** The act or process of colliding; a crash or conflict. **2.** *Physics.* A brief dynamic event consisting of the close approach of two or more particles, such as atoms, resulting in an abrupt change of momentum or exchange of energy. [Middle English, from Late Latin *collīsiō, collīsiōn-,* from Latin *collīsus,* past participle of *collīdere,* to collide. See COLLIDE.] **— col·li′sion·al** *adj.*

SYNONYMS: *collision, concussion, crash, impact, jar, jolt, shock.* The central meaning shared by these nouns is "violent forcible contact between two or more things": *the midair collision of two light planes; the concussion caused by an explosion; the crash of a car into a tree; the impact of a sledgehammer on pilings; felt repeated jars as the train ground to a halt; a series of jolts as the baby carriage rolled down the steps; experienced the physical shock of a sudden fall to hard pavement.*

collision course *n.* A course, such as that of moving objects or opposing philosophies, that will end in impact or conflict if permitted to continue unchanged or unabated: *two planes on a collision course; dissidents on a collision course with the dictatorial regime.*

collision cross section *n.* See **cross section** (sense 2).

collo– or **coll–** *pref.* **1.** Glue: *collenchyma.* **2.** Colloid: *collotype.* [New Latin, from Greek *kolla,* glue.]

col·lo·cate (kŏl′ə-kāt′) *tr.v.* **-cat·ed, -cat·ing, -cates.** To place together or in proper order; arrange side by side. [Latin *collocāre, collocāt- : com-,* com- + *locāre,* to place; see LOCATE.]

col·lo·ca·tion (kŏl′ō-kā′shən) *n.* **1.** The act of collocating or the state of being collocated. **2.** An arrangement or juxtaposition, especially of linguistic elements, such as words. **—col′lo·ca′tion·al** *adj.*

collie
Tricolor collie

col·lo·di·on (kə-lō′dē-ən) *n.* A highly flammable, colorless or yellowish syrupy solution of pyroxylin, ether, and alcohol, used as an adhesive to close small wounds and hold surgical dressings, in topical medications, and for making photographic plates. [From New Latin *collodium,* from Greek *kollōdēs,* glutinous, gluelike : *kolla,* glue + *-oeidēs,* -oid.]

♦ **col·logue** (kə-lōg′) *intr.v.* **-logued, -logu·ing, -logues. 1.** To be on friendly or intimate terms with someone. **2.a.** To consult or confer with someone. **b.** To chat. **3.** *Chiefly Upper Southern U.S.* To conspire; intrigue: *"I'm satisfied they're colloguing to beat me out of my place"* (Dialect Notes). [Perhaps alteration (influenced by Latin *colloquī,* to converse; see COLLOQUIUM) of *colleague,* to enter into an alliance, from Old French *colleguer,* from Latin *colligāre,* to collect (influenced by Old French *collegue,* colleague. See COLLEAGUE). See COLLIGATE.]

col·loid (kŏl′oid′) *n.* **1.** *Chemistry.* **a.** A suspension of finely divided particles in a continuous medium in which the particles are approximately 5 to 5,000 angstroms in size, do not settle out of the substance rapidly, and are not readily filtered. **b.** The particulate matter so suspended. **2.** *Physiology.* The gelatinous product of the thyroid gland, consisting mainly of thyroglobulin, which serves as the precursor and storage form of thyroid hormone. **3.** *Pathology.* Gelatinous material resulting from colloid degeneration in diseased tissue. **—colloid** *adj.* Of, relating to, containing, or having the nature of a colloid. **—col·loid′al** (kə-loid′l, kō-) *adj.* **—col·loid′al·ly** *adv.*

col·lop (kŏl′əp) *n.* **1.** A small portion of food or a slice, especially of meat. **2.** A roll of fat flesh. [Middle English.]

colloq. *abbr.* Colloquial; colloquialism.

col·lo·qui·a (kə-lō′kwē-ə) *n.* A plural of **colloquium.**

col·lo·qui·al (kə-lō′kwē-əl) *adj. Abbr.* **coll., colloq. 1.** Characteristic of or appropriate to the spoken language or to writing that seeks the effect of speech; informal. **2.** Relating to conversation; conversational. [From COLLOQUY.] **—col·lo′qui·al** *n.* **—col·lo′qui·al·ly** *adv.* **—col·lo′qui·al·ness** *n.*

col·lo·qui·al·ism (kə-lō′kwē-ə-lĭz′əm) *n. Abbr.* **coll., colloq. 1.** Colloquial style or quality. **2.** A colloquial expression.

col·lo·qui·um (kə-lō′kwē-əm) *n., pl.* **-qui·ums** or **-qui·a** (-kwē-ə). **1.** An informal meeting for the exchange of views. **2.** An academic seminar on a broad field of study, usually led by a different lecturer at each meeting. [Latin, conversation, from *colloquī,* to talk together : *com-,* com- + *loquī,* to speak; see **tolkʷ-** in Appendix.]

col·lo·quy (kŏl′ə-kwē) *n., pl.* **-quies. 1.** A conversation, especially a formal one. **2.** A written dialogue. [From Latin *colloquium,* conversation. See COLLOQUIUM.]

col·lo·type (kŏl′ə-tīp′) *n.* **1.** A printing process employing a glass plate with a gelatin surface that carries the image to be reproduced. Also called *photogelatin process.* **2.** A print made by this process.

col·lude (kə-lo͞od′) *intr.v.* **-lud·ed, -lud·ing, -ludes.** To act together secretly to achieve a fraudulent, illegal, or deceitful purpose; conspire. [Latin *collūdere : com-,* com- + *lūdere,* to play; see **leid-** in Appendix.] **—col·lud′er** *n.*

col·lu·sion (kə-lo͞o′zhən) *n.* A secret agreement between two or more parties for a fraudulent, illegal, or deceitful purpose. See Synonyms at **conspiracy.** [Middle English, from Latin *collūsiō,*

ă pat	oi boy
ā pay	ou out
âr care	o͝o took
ä father	o͞o boot
ĕ pet	ŭ cut
ē be	ûr urge
ĭ pit	th thin
ī pie	*th* this
îr pier	hw which
ŏ pot	zh vision
ō toe	ə about, item
ô paw	♦ regionalism

Stress marks: ′ (primary); ′ (secondary), as in **dictionary** (dĭk′shə-nĕr′ē)

collūsiōn-, from *collūsus*, past participle of *collūdere*, to collude. See COLLUDE.]

col·lu·sive (kə-lo͞o′sĭv, -zĭv) *adj.* Acting in secret to achieve a fraudulent, illegal, or deceitful goal. —**col·lu′sive·ly** *adv.* —**col·lu′sive·ness** *n.*

col·lu·vi·um (kə-lo͞o′vē-əm) *n., pl.* **-vi·ums** or **-vi·a** (-vē-ə). A loose deposit of rock debris accumulated through the action of gravity at the base of a cliff or slope. [Latin, a collection of washings, dregs, from *colluere*, to wash thoroughly : *com-*, intensive pref.; see COM– + *-luere*, to wash; see **leu(ə)-** in Appendix.] —**col·lu′vi·al** *adj.*

col·lyr·i·um (kə-lîr′ē-əm) *n., pl.* **-i·ums** or **-i·a** (-ē-ə). A medicinal lotion applied to the eye; eyewash. [Latin, from Greek *kollurion*, eye salve, poultice, diminutive of *kollura*, roll of bread.]

col·ly·wob·bles (kŏl′ē-wŏb′əlz) *pl.n. (used with a sing. or pl. verb). Informal.* Pain in the stomach or bowels. [Probably alteration (influenced by COLIC and WOBBLE) of CHOLERA MORBUS.]

Col·mar also **Kol·mar** (kŏl′mär, kôl-mär′). A city of eastern France between the Vosges Mountains and the Rhine River. It became a free imperial city in 1226. Population, 62,483.

Colo. *abbr.* Colorado.

colo– or **coli–** or **col–** *pref.* Colon: *colostomy.* [From COLON[2].]

col·o·bo·ma (kŏl′ə-bō′mə) *n., pl.* **-ma·ta** (-mə-tə). An anomaly of the eye, usually a developmental defect, that often results in some loss of vision. [New Latin *colobōma*, from Greek *kolobōma*, part removed in mutilation, from *koloboun*, to mutilate, from *kolobos*, maimed.] —**col′o·bo′ma·tous** *adj.*

Colombia

col·o·bus monkey (kŏl′ə-bəs, kə-lō′-) *n.* Any of various large African monkeys of the genus *Colobus* having a long tail and vestigial thumbs. [New Latin *Colobus*, genus name, from Greek *kolobos*, maimed (from the appearance of its hands).]

col·o·cynth (kŏl′ə-sĭnth′) *n.* **1.** A tendril-bearing Old World vine *(Citrullus colocynthis)* bearing yellowish, green-mottled fruits the size of small lemons. **2.** The fruit of this plant, whose dried, bitter, spongy pulp is a very strong laxative. Also called *bitter apple.* [Latin *colocynthis*, from Greek *kolokunthis*, from *kolokunthē*, round gourd.]

co·logne (kə-lōn′) *n.* A scented liquid made of alcohol and various fragrant oils. Also called *eau de cologne.* [Short for *cologne (water)*, translation of French *(eau de) Cologne*, after COLOGNE.]

WORD HISTORY: The word *cologne*, denoting toilet water, is from *Cologne*, the French name of the city in Germany that in German is called *Köln*, where cologne has been made since the beginning of the 18th century. The first use of *cologne* for toilet water is recorded in English in 1814, with the word being used in the compound *cologne water*, a translation of *eau de cologne*, the French name for this liquid. With a history dating to the Roman Empire, a history reflected in its name, which comes from the Latin word *Colōnia*, meaning "colony," Cologne is memorialized in English, though in a hidden way, as the name of a minor luxury.

Co·logne (kə-lōn′) also **Köln** (kœln). A city of western Germany on the Rhine River north of Bonn. It was a Roman settlement called Colonia Agrippina after A.D. 50 and passed under Frankish control in the 5th century. During the 15th century it flourished as a member of the Hanseatic League. Population, 922,286.

Co·lombes (kə-lōm′, kô-lôɴb′). A city of north-central France, an industrial suburb of Paris on the Seine River. Population, 78,777.

colonnade
Colonnade of Amenhotep III at the Temple of Ammon, Luxor, Egypt

Co·lom·bi·a (kə-lŭm′bē-ə). *Abbr.* **Col.** A country of northwest South America with coastlines on the Pacific Ocean and the Caribbean Sea. It was settled by the Spanish in 1510 and formed the nucleus of the viceroyalty of New Granada after 1740. Colombia gained its independence from Spain in 1819 under the leadership of Simón Bolívar. Bogotá is the capital and the largest city. Population, 26,525,670. —**Co·lom′bi·an** *adj. & n.*

Co·lom·bo (kə-lŭm′bō). The capital and largest city of Sri Lanka, on the western coast of the island on the Indian Ocean. The city was probably known to Greco-Roman, Arab, and Chinese traders more than 2,000 years ago. It became capital of the crown colony of Ceylon in 1802 and of independent Ceylon in 1948. Population, 587,647.

co·lon[1] (kō′lən) *n., pl.* **-lons. 1.a.** A punctuation mark (:) used after a word introducing a quotation, an explanation, an example, or a series and often after the salutation of a business letter. **b.** The sign (:) used between numbers or groups of numbers in expressions of time (2:30 A.M.) and ratios (1:2). **2.** *pl.* **co·la** (-lə). A section of a metrical period in quantitative verse, consisting of two to six feet and in Latin verse having one principal accent. [Latin *cōlon*, part of a verse, from Greek *kōlon*, limb, member, metrical unit.]

co·lon[2] (kō′lən) *n., pl.* **-lons** or **-la** (-lə). The section of the large intestine extending from the cecum to the rectum. [Middle English, from Latin, from Greek *kolon*, large intestine.] —**co·lon′ic** (kə-lŏn′ĭk) *adj.*

co·lon[3] (kō-lōn′) *n., pl.* **-lons** or **-lo·nes** (-lō′nās′). See table at **currency.** [Spanish *colón*, after Cristóbal *Colón*, Christopher Columbus.]

Co·lón (kə-lō′, kô-lôn′). A city of northern Panama at the Caribbean entrance to the Panama Canal. The city was founded as Aspinwall in 1850 by Americans working on the Panama Railroad and was renamed in 1890. Population, 59,840.

co·lon bacillus (kō′lən) *n. Microbiology.* A rod-shaped bacterium, especially *Escherichia coli*, a normal, generally nonpathogenic commensal found in all vertebrate intestinal tracts, but which can be virulent, causing diarrhea and other dysenteric symptoms. Its presence in water is an indicator of fecal contamination.

colo·nel (kûr′nəl) *n. Abbr.* **Col. 1.a.** A commissioned rank in the U.S. Army, Air Force, or Marine Corps that is above lieutenant colonel and below brigadier general. **b.** One who holds this rank or a similar rank in another military organization. **2.** An honorary nonmilitary title awarded by some states of the United States. [Alteration of obsolete *coronel*, from French, from Old Italian *colonello*, from diminutive of *colonna*, column of soldiers, from Latin *columna*, column. See **kel-**[2] in Appendix.] —**colo′nel·cy, colo′nel·ship′** *n.*

Colonel Blimp *n. Chiefly British.* A pompous, reactionary, ultranationalistic person. [After *Colonel Blimp*, a cartoon character created by Sir David Low.]

co·lo·nes (kō-lō′nās′) *n.* A plural of **colon**[3].

co·lo·ni·al (kə-lō′nē-əl) *adj. Abbr.* **col. 1.** Of, relating to, possessing, or inhabiting a colony or colonies. **2.** Often **Colonial. a.** Of or relating to the 13 British colonies that became the original United States of America. **b.** Of or relating to the colonial period in the United States. **3.** Often **Colonial.** Of, relating to, or being a style of architecture and furniture prevalent in the American colonies just before and during the Revolution. **4.** Living in, consisting of, or forming a colony: *colonial organisms.* —**colonial** *n.* **1.** An inhabitant of a colony. **2.** A house designed in an architectural style reminiscent of the one prevalent in the American colonies just before and during the Revolution. —**co·lo′ni·al·ly** *adv.*

Colonial Heights. A city of southeast Virginia south of Richmond. It was Robert E. Lee's headquarters during the Battle of Petersburg (1864). Population, 16,509.

co·lo·ni·al·ism (kə-lō′nē-ə-lĭz′əm) *n.* A policy by which a nation maintains or extends its control over foreign dependencies. —**co·lo′ni·al·ist** *n.*

col·o·nist (kŏl′ə-nĭst) *n.* **1.** An original settler or founder of a colony. **2.** An inhabitant of a colony.

co·lon·i·tis (kō′lə-nī′tĭs) *n.* See **colitis.**

col·o·ni·za·tion (kŏl′ə-nĭ-zā′shən) *n.* The act or process of establishing a colony or colonies.

col·o·nize (kŏl′ə-nīz′) *v.* **-nized, -niz·ing, -niz·es.** —*tr.* **1.** To form or establish a colony or colonies in. **2.** To migrate to and settle in; occupy as a colony. **3.** To establish in a new settlement; form a colony of. —*intr.* **1.** To form or establish a colony. **2.** To settle in a colony or colonies. —**col′o·niz′er** *n.*

col·on·nade (kŏl′ə-nād′) *n. Architecture.* **1.** A series of columns placed at regular intervals. **2.** A structure composed of columns placed at regular intervals. [French, alteration of *colonnate*, from Italian *colonnato*, from *colonna*, column, from Latin *columna*. See **kel-**[2] in Appendix.] —**col′on·nad′ed** *adj.*

co·lon·o·scope (kō-lŏn′ə-skōp′, kə-) *n.* A long, flexible endoscope, often equipped with a device for obtaining tissue samples, that is used for visual examination of the colon. Also called *coloscope.*

co·lon·os·co·py (kō′lə-nŏs′kə-pē) *n.* Examination of the colon by means of a colonoscope. Also called *coloscopy.*

col·o·ny (kŏl′ə-nē) *n., pl.* **-nies. 1.a.** A group of emigrants or their descendants who settle in a distant territory but remain subject to or closely associated with the parent country. **b.** A territory thus settled. **2.** *Abbr.* **col.** A region politically controlled by a distant country; a dependency. **3.a.** A group of people with the same interests or ethnic origin concentrated in a particular area: *the American colony in Paris.* **b.** The area occupied by such a group. **4.** A group of people who have been institutionalized in a relatively remote area: *an island penal colony.* **5.** *Ecology.* A group of the same kind of animals, plants, or one-celled organisms living or growing together. **6.** *Microbiology.* A visible growth of microorganisms, usually in a solid or semisolid nutrient medium. [Middle English *colonie*, from Latin *colōnia*, from *colōnus*, settler, from *colere*, to cultivate. See **kʷel-**[1] in Appendix.]

col·o·phon (kŏl′ə-fŏn′, -fən) *n.* **1.** An inscription placed usually at the end of a book, giving facts about its publication. **2.** A publisher's emblem or trademark placed usually on the title page of a book. [Late Latin *colophōn*, from Greek *kolophōn*, summit, finishing touch. See **kel-**[2] in Appendix.]

Col·o·phon (kŏl′ə-fŏn′). An ancient Greek city of Asia Minor northwest of Ephesus. It was famous for its cavalry.

col·or (kŭl′ər) *n. Abbr.* **col. 1.** That aspect of things that is caused by differing qualities of the light reflected or emitted by them, definable in terms of the observer or of the light, as: **a.** The appearance of objects or light sources described in terms of the individual's perception of them, involving hue, lightness, and saturation for objects and hue, brightness, and saturation for light sources. **b.** The characteristics of light by which the individual is made aware of objects or light sources through the receptors of the eye, described in terms of dominant wavelength, luminance, and purity. **2.** A substance, such as a dye, pigment, or paint, that imparts a hue. **3.a.** The general appearance of the skin; complexion. **b.** A ruddy complexion. **c.** A reddening of the face; a blush. **4.** The skin pigmentation of a person not classed as white.

5. colors. A flag or banner, as of a country or military unit. **6. colors.** The salute made during the ceremony of raising or lowering a flag. **7. colors.** A distinguishing symbol, badge, ribbon, or mark: *the colors of a college.* **8. colors.** One's opinion or position: *Stick to your colors.* **9.** Often **colors.** Character or nature: *revealed their true colors.* **10.a.** Outward appearance, often deceptive: *a tale with only the slightest color of truth.* **b.** Appearance of authenticity: *testimony that lends color to an otherwise absurd notion.* **11.a.** Variety of expression. **b.** Vivid, picturesque detail: *a story with a great deal of color in it.* **12.** Traits of personality or behavior that attract interest. **13.** The use or effect of pigment in painting, as distinct from form. **14.** *Music.* Tonal quality. **15.** *Law.* A mere semblance of legal right. **16.** A particle or bit of gold found in auriferous gravel or sand. **17.** *Physics.* A quantum characteristic of quarks that determines their role in the strong interaction. —*attributive.* Often used to modify another noun: *color photography; color television.* **—color** *v.* **-ored, -or·ing, -ors.** —*tr.* **1.** To impart color to or change the color of. **2.a.** To give a distinctive character or quality to; modify. See Synonyms at **bias. b.** To exert an influence on; affect: *The war colored the lives of all of us.* **3.a.** To misrepresent, especially by distortion or exaggeration: *color the facts.* **b.** To gloss over; excuse: *a parent who colored the children's lies.* —*intr.* **1.a.** To take on color. **b.** To change color. **2.** To become red in the face; blush. [Middle English *colour,* from Old French, from Latin *color.* See **kel-**[1] in Appendix.] **—col′or·er** *n.*

USAGE NOTE: The terms *person of color* and *people of color* have been revived for use in formal contexts to refer to members or groups of non-European origin (e.g., Black people, Asians, Pacific Islanders, and Native Americans): *"These are profound tendencies which strike at the middle class as well as the poor, at whites as well as people of color"* (Jesse Jackson). Many people prefer *people of color* as a rough substitute for *minorities* because these groups are not in fact in the minority in many parts of America. See Usage Note at **black.**

col·or·a·ble (kŭl′ər-ə-bəl) *adj.* **1.** Meant to deceive; not genuine. **2.** Seemingly true or genuine; plausible. See Synonyms at **plausible. —col′or·a·bil′i·ty, col′or·a·ble·ness** *n.* **—col′or·a·bly** *adv.*

Col·o·ra·do (kŏl′ə-răd′ō, -rä′dō). *Abbr.* **CO, Col., Colo.** A state of the west-central United States. It was admitted as the 38th state in 1876. First explored by the Spanish in the 16th and 17th centuries, the region was added to the United States through the Louisiana Purchase (1803) and a cession by Mexico (1848). Denver is the capital and the largest city. Population, 2,889,735. **—Col′o·ra′dan** *adj. & n.*

Colorado blue spruce *n.* See **blue spruce.**

Colorado Desert. An arid region of southeast California west of the Colorado River.

Colorado potato beetle *n.* A small yellow-and-black striped beetle *(Leptinotarsa decemlineata)* that is a major agricultural pest.

Colorado River. 1. A river of central Argentina rising in the Andes and flowing about 853 km (530 mi) southeast to the Atlantic Ocean. **2.** A river of the southwest United States rising in the Rocky Mountains and flowing about 2,333 km (1,450 mi) southwest through the **Colorado Plateau** of western Colorado, southeast Utah, and western Arizona to the Gulf of California in northwest Mexico. In Arizona it flows along the borders of Nevada and California. The most spectacular of its many gorges is the Grand Canyon. **3.** A river rising in northwest Texas and flowing about 1,438 km (894 mi) southeast to an inlet of the Gulf of Mexico.

Colorado Springs. A city of central Colorado at the foot of Pikes Peak south of Denver. It is a popular tourist center near the site of the U.S. Air Force Academy (established here in 1958). Population, 214,821.

col·or·ant (kŭl′ər-ənt) *n.* Something, especially a dye, a pigment, an ink, or a paint, that colors or modifies the hue of something else. **—colorant** *adj. Color.* Of or being a subtractive primary color.

col·or·a·tion (kŭl′ə-rā′shən) *n.* **1.** Arrangement of colors. **2.** The sum of the beliefs or principles of a person, a group, or an institution.

col·or·a·tu·ra (kŭl′ər-ə-to͝or′ə, -tyo͝or′ə) *n. Music.* **1.** Florid, ornamental vocal trills and runs. **2.** Music characterized by florid, ornamental trills and runs. **3.** A singer, especially a soprano, specializing in such trills and runs. —*attributive.* Often used to modify another noun: *coloratura compositions; a coloratura performer.* [Obsolete Italian, from Late Latin *colōrātūra,* coloring, from Latin *colōrātus,* past participle of *colōrāre,* to color, from *color,* color. See COLOR.]

color bar *n.* See **color line.**

col·or·blind or **col·or-blind** (kŭl′ər-blīnd′) *adj.* **1.** Partially or totally unable to distinguish certain colors. **2.a.** Not subject to racial prejudices. **b.** Not recognizing racial or class distinctions: *"Our Constitution is color-blind, and neither knows nor tolerates classes among citizens"* (John M. Harlan). **—col′or·blind′ness** *n.*

col·or·breed (kŭl′ər-brēd′) *tr.v.* **-bred** (-brĕd′), **-breed·ing, -breeds.** To breed (plants or animals) selectively to produce new or desired colors.

col·or·cast (kŭl′ər-kăst′) *v.* **-cast** or **-cast·ed, -cast·ing, -casts.** —*tr.* To broadcast (a television program) in color. —*intr.* To televise a program in color. **—colorcast** *n.* A television program broadcast in color. [COLOR + (BROAD)CAST.]

col·or-code (kŭl′ər-kōd′) *tr.v.* **-cod·ed, -cod·ing, -codes.** To color, as wires or papers, according to a code for easy identification.

co·lo·rec·tal (kō′lə-rĕk′təl) *adj.* Associated with or involving both the colon and the rectum: *colorectal cancer.*

col·ored (kŭl′ərd) *adj.* **1.** Having color: *colored tissue paper.* **2.** Often **Colored.** *Offensive.* **a.** Of or belonging to a racial group not regarded as white: *"the huge shift that occurred when we stopped thinking of ourselves as colored people"* (Courtland Milloy). **b.** Of mixed racial strains. **3.** Distorted or biased, as by irrelevant or incorrect information. **—colored** also **Colored** *n., pl.* **colored** or **coloreds** also **Colored** or **Coloreds.** *Offensive.* **1.** A person of a racial group not regarded as white. **2.** A person of mixed racial strains. See Usage Note at **black.**

col·or·fast (kŭl′ər-făst′) *adj.* Having color that will not run or fade with washing or wear: *a colorfast fabric.* **—col′or·fast′ness** *n.*

color filter *n.* A photographic filter made of colored glass that modifies the light incident on a film by selectively absorbing colors. It is used when taking photographs through haze.

col·or·ful (kŭl′ər-fəl) *adj.* **1.** Full of color; abounding in colors: *colorful leaves in the fall.* **2.** Characterized by rich variety; vividly distinctive: *colorful language.* **—col′or·ful·ly** *adv.* **—col′or·ful·ness** *n.*

color guard *n.* The ceremonial escort for the flag, as of a country or an organization.

col·or·if·ic (kŭl′ə-rĭf′ĭk) *adj.* Producing or imparting color.

col·or·im·e·ter (kŭl′ə-rĭm′ĭ-tər) *n.* **1.** Any of various instruments used to determine or specify colors, as by comparison with spectroscopic or visual standards. **2.** An instrument that measures the concentration of a known constituent of a solution by comparison with colors of standard solutions of that constituent. **—col′or·i·met′ric** (-ər-ə-mĕt′rĭk) *adj.* **—col′or·i·met′ri·cal·ly** *adv.* **—col′or·im′e·try** *n.*

col·or·ing (kŭl′ər-ĭng) *n.* **1.** The art, manner, or process of applying color. **2.** A substance used to color something. **3.** Appearance with regard to color. **4.** Characteristic aspect, tone, or style. **5.** False or misleading appearance.

col·or·ist (kŭl′ər-ĭst) *n.* **1.** A painter skilled in achieving special effects with color: *a forceful colorist whose idiom was reminiscent of Cézanne.* **2.** A hairdresser who specializes in dyeing hair. **—col′or·is′tic** *adj.*

col·or·i·za·tion (kŭl′ər-ĭ-zā′shən) *n.* A computer-assisted process by which color is imparted to previously black-and-white film. The original film is first transferred to videotape, to which numerically coded colors are assigned, frame by frame, area by area. A graphics computer then applies the assigned colors to the appropriate areas of the images on each frame within a scene. The process continues until the entire film has been tinted.

col·or·ize (kŭl′ə-rīz′) *tr.v.* **-ized, -iz·ing, -iz·es.** To impart color to (black-and-white film) by means of a computer-assisted process: *"Be prepared . . . for the . . . colorized version of* Topper*"* (Vincent Canby). **—col′or·iz·er** *n.*

col·or·less (kŭl′ər-lĭs) *adj.* **1.** Lacking color. **2.** Weak in color; pallid. **3.** Lacking animation, variety, or distinction; dull. See Synonyms at **dull. —col′or·less·ly** *adv.* **—col′or·less·ness** *n.*

color line *n.* A barrier, created by custom, law, or economic differences, separating nonwhite persons from whites. Also called *color bar.*

co·lo·scope (kō′lə-skōp′) *n.* See **colonoscope.**

co·los·co·py (kə-lŏs′kə-pē) *n.* See **colonoscopy.**

Co·los·sae (kə-lŏs′ē). An ancient city of central Asia Minor. It was the site of an early Christian church to which Saint Paul addressed his Epistle to the Colossians. **—Co·los′sian** (-lŏsh′ən) *adj. & n.*

co·los·sal (kə-lŏs′əl) *adj.* Of a size, extent, or degree that elicits awe or taxes belief; immense. See Synonyms at **enormous.** [French, from Latin *colossus,* colossus. See COLOSSUS.] **—co·los′sal·ly** *adv.*

col·os·se·um (kŏl′ĭ-sē′əm) *n.* Variant of **coliseum.**

co·los·si (kə-lŏs′ī′) *n.* A plural of **colossus.**

Co·los·sians (kə-lŏsh′ənz) *pl.n.* *(used with a sing. verb). Abbr.* **Col, Col.** *Bible.* See table at **Bible.** [Latin *Colossēnses,* inhabitants of Colossae, from *Colossae,* Colossae, from Greek *Kolossai.*]

co·los·sus (kə-lŏs′əs) *n., pl.* **-los·si** (-lŏs′ī′) or **-los·sus·es. 1.** A huge statue. **2.** Something likened to a huge statue, as in size or importance: *a colossus of bureaucracy.* [Latin, from Greek *kolossos.*]

Co·los·sus of Rhodes (kə-lŏs′əs; rōdz). A huge statue of Apollo located at the entrance to the harbor of Rhodes. Built c. 280 B.C. and later destroyed by an earthquake, it was about 37 m (120 ft) high and was one of the Seven Wonders of the World.

co·los·to·my (kə-lŏs′tə-mē) *n., pl.* **-mies. 1.** Surgical construction of an artificial excretory opening from the colon. **2.** The opening created by such a surgical procedure.

co·los·trum (kə-lŏs′trəm) *n.* The thin, yellowish fluid secreted by the mammary glands at the time of parturition that is rich in antibodies and minerals, and precedes the production of true milk. Also called *foremilk.* [Latin.] **—co·los′tral** (-trəl) *adj.*

Colorado potato beetle
Leptinotarsa decemlineata

color guard

colossus

ă pat	oi boy
ā pay	ou out
âr care	o͝o took
ä father	o͞o boot
ĕ pet	ŭ cut
ē be	ûr urge
ĭ pit	th thin
ī pie	*th* this
îr pier	hw which
ŏ pot	zh vision
ō toe	ə about, item
ô paw	♦ regionalism

Stress marks: ′ (primary); ′ (secondary), as in **dictionary** (dĭk′shə-nĕr′ē)

col·our (kŭl′ər) *n. & v. Chiefly British.* Variant of **color.**

–colous *suff.* Having a specified kind of habitat: *arenicolous.* [From Latin *-cola,* tiller, inhabitant. See **kʷel-¹** in Appendix.]

col·pi·tis (kŏl-pī′tĭs) *n.* See **vaginitis.** [Greek *kolpos,* vagina + –ITIS.]

col·por·tage (kŏl′pôr′tĭj, -pōr′-) *n.* The work of a colporteur.

col·por·teur (kŏl′pôr′tər, -pōr′-) *n.* A peddler of devotional literature. [French, alteration (influenced by *col,* neck, from the idea that peddlers carry their wares on trays suspended from straps around their necks) of Old French *comporteur,* from *comporter,* to conduct, peddle. See COMPORT.]

col·po·scope (kŏl′pə-skōp′) *n.* A magnifying and photographic device used as an aid in the diagnostic examination of the vaginal and cervical epithelia. [Greek *kolpos,* vagina, womb + –SCOPE.] **—col′po·scop′ic** (-skŏp′ĭk) *adj.*

col·pos·co·py (kŏl-pŏs′kə-pē) *n., pl.* **-pies.** Examination of the vaginal and cervical epithelia by means of a colposcope. [Greek *kolpos,* vagina, womb + –SCOPY.]

colt (kōlt) *n.* **1.** A young male horse. **2.** A youthful or inexperienced person; a novice. [Middle English, from Old English.]

columbarium

Colt (kōlt), **Samuel.** 1814–1862. American firearms inventor and manufacturer who developed the first revolver.

colt·ish (kōl′tĭsh) *adj.* **1.** Relating to or suggestive of a colt. **2.** Lively and playful; frisky. **—colt′ish·ly** *adv.* **—colt′ish·ness** *n.*

Col·trane (kōl′trān), **John William.** 1926–1967. American jazz saxophonist and composer whose musical innovations broke through formal thematic and harmonic restrictions in jazz improvisation.

colts·foot (kōlts′fo͝ot′) *n., pl.* **-foots. 1.** A low perennial Eurasian herb *(Tussilago farfara)* in the composite family, naturalized in parts of North America and having dandelionlike flower heads and large, hoof-shaped basal leaves. **2.** The dried leaves or flower heads of this plant, long used in herbal medicine to treat coughs. **3.** See **galax.** [From the shape of its leaves.]

col·u·brid (kŏl′ə-brĭd, kŏl′yə-) *n.* Any of numerous, widely distributed, chiefly nonvenomous snakes of the family Colubridae, which includes the king snakes, garter snakes, and water snakes. **—colubrid** *adj.* Of, relating to, or belonging to the Colubridae. [From New Latin *Colubridae,* family name, from Latin *coluber, colubr-,* snake.]

col·u·brine (kŏl′ə-brīn′, kŏl′yə-) *adj.* **1.** Of, relating to, or resembling a snake. **2.** Colubrid.

co·lu·go (kə-lo͞o′gō) *n., pl.* **-gos.** See **flying lemur.** [Of Malayan origin.]

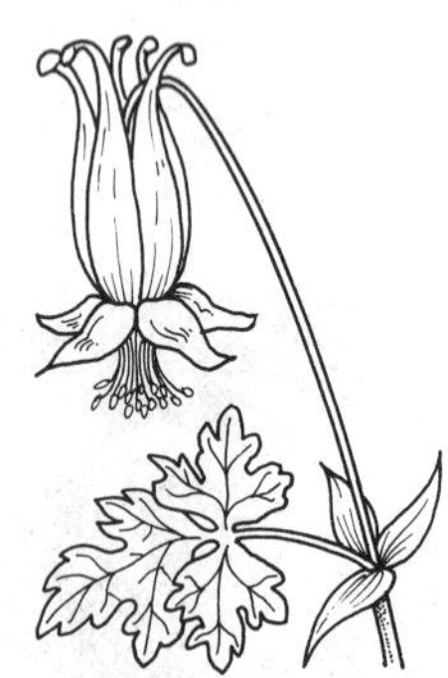
columbine

Col·um (kŭl′əm), Saint. See Saint **Columba.**

Col·um (kŏl′əm), **Padraic.** 1881–1972. Irish-American writer who was associated with the Irish Renaissance. His volumes of poetry include *Wild Earth* (1907) and *Images of Departure* (1968).

Co·lum·ba (kə-lŭm′bə) *n.* A constellation in the Southern Hemisphere near Caelum and Puppis. Also called *Dove.* [Latin *columba,* dove.]

Columba also **Col·um** (kŭl′əm), Saint. 521–597. Irish missionary who established a monastery on the island of Iona and subsequently Christianized northern Scotland.

col·um·bar·i·um (kŏl′əm-bâr′ē-əm) also **col·um·bar·y** (kŏl′əm-bĕr′ē) *n., pl.* **-i·a** (-ē-ə) also **-ies. 1.a.** A vault with niches for urns containing ashes of the dead. **b.** One of the niches in such a vault. **2.a.** A dovecote. **b.** A pigeonhole in a dovecote. [Latin *columbārium,* sepulchre for urns, dovecote, from *columba,* dove.]

Co·lum·bi·a¹ (kə-lŭm′bē-ə). **1.** A community of north-central Maryland west-southwest of Baltimore. It is mainly residential. Population, 52,518. **2.** A city of central Missouri north-northwest of Jefferson City. The main campus of the University of Missouri (established 1839) is here. Population, 62,061. **3.** The capital and largest city of South Carolina, in the central part of the state. It was chosen as the site of the new state's capital in 1786. Population, 100,385. **4.** A city of west-central Tennessee south-southwest of Nashville. It was first settled in 1807. Population, 26,571.

Christopher Columbus

Co·lum·bi·a² (kə-lŭm′bē-ə) *n.* The United States. [After Christopher COLUMBUS.]

Columbia, District of. See **District of Columbia.**

Columbia Heights. A city of eastern Minnesota, a residential suburb of Minneapolis. Population, 20,029.

Co·lum·bi·an (kə-lŭm′bē-ən) *adj.* **1.** Of or relating to the United States. **2.** Of or relating to Christopher Columbus.

Columbia River. A river rising in southeast British Columbia, Canada, and flowing about 1,947 km (1,210 mi) south then west through the **Columbia Plateau** and along the Washington-Oregon border to its outlet on the Pacific Ocean. It was discovered and named by the American explorer Robert Gray in 1792.

col·um·bine (kŏl′əm-bīn′) *n.* Any of various perennial herbs of the genus *Aquilegia* native to north temperate regions, cultivated for their showy, variously colored flowers that have petals with long, hollow spurs. Also called *aquilegia.* [Middle English, from Medieval Latin *columbīna,* from feminine of Latin *columbīnus,* dovelike (from the resemblance of the inverted flower to a cluster of doves), from *columba,* dove.]

co·lum·bite (kə-lŭm′bīt′) *n.* A black, red-brown, or colorless mineral, essentially (Fe, Mn)(Nb, Ta)$_2$O$_6$, the principal ore of niobium. [COLUMB(IUM) + –ITE¹.]

co·lum·bi·um (kə-lŭm′bē-əm) *n. Symbol* **Cb** Niobium. No longer in scientific use. [After COLUMBIA².]

Co·lum·bus (kə-lŭm′bəs). **1.** A city of western Georgia on the Chattahoochee River south-southwest of Atlanta. Settled in 1828 on the site of a Creek village, it is a port of entry and major industrial center. Population, 169,441. **2.** A city of south-central Indiana south-southeast of Indianapolis. It was a supply depot for Union troops during the Civil War. Population, 30,614. **3.** A city of northeast Mississippi near the Alabama border. There are many antebellum houses in the area. Population, 27,383. **4.** A city of east-central Nebraska at the confluence of the Loup and Platte rivers west of Omaha. It is a trade, processing, and manufacturing center. Population, 17,328. **5.** The capital of Ohio, in the central part of the state. Laid out in 1812, it is a major industrial, commercial, and cultural center. Population, 565,032.

Columbus, Christopher. 1451–1506. Italian explorer in the service of Spain who determined that the earth was round and attempted to reach Asia by sailing west from Europe, thereby discovering America (1492). He made three subsequent voyages to the Caribbean in his quest for a sea route to China.

Columbus Day *n.* October 12, observed in the United States in commemoration of the discovery in 1492 of the New World by Christopher Columbus. Columbus Day is now officially observed on the second Monday in October.

col·u·mel·la (kŏl′yə-mĕl′ə, kŏl′ə-) *n., pl.* **-mel·lae** (-mĕl′ē). Any small columnlike structure in various plants and animals, often forming the central axis of development for the organism or an anatomical structure. [Latin, diminutive of *columna,* column. See COLUMN.] **—col′u·mel′lar** (-mĕl′ər) *adj.* **—col′u·mel′late′** (-mĕl′āt′) *adj.*

col·umn (kŏl′əm) *n. Abbr.* **col., clm. 1.** *Architecture.* A supporting pillar consisting of a base, a cylindrical shaft, and a capital. **2.** Something resembling an architectural pillar in form or function: *a column of mercury in a thermometer.* **3.a.** *Printing.* One of two or more vertical sections of typed lines lying side by side on a page and separated by a rule or a blank space. **b.** A feature article that appears regularly in a publication, such as a newspaper. **4.** A formation, as of troops or vehicles, in which all elements follow one behind the other. **5.** *Botany.* A columnlike structure, especially one formed by the union of a stamen and the style in an orchid flower, or one formed by the united staminal filaments in flowers such as those of the hibiscus or mallow. **6.** *Anatomy.* Any of various tubular or pillarlike supporting structures in the body, each generally having a single tissue origin and function: *the vertebral column.* [Middle English *columne,* from Latin *columna.* See **kel-²** in Appendix.] **—col′umned** (kŏl′əmd) *adj.*

co·lum·nar (kə-lŭm′nər) *adj.* **1.** Having the shape of a column. **2.** Constructed with or having columns.

columnar epithelium *n.* Epithelium consisting of one or more cell layers, the most superficial of which is composed of elongated and somewhat cylindrical cells projecting toward the surface.

co·lum·ne·a (kə-lŭm′nē-ə) *n.* Any of various bushy or trailing tropical American plants of the genus *Columnea,* grown indoors for their showy, colorful, tubular flowers. [New Latin *Columnea,* genus name, after Fabius *Columna,* Latin name of Fabio Colonna (1567–1650?), Italian botanist.]

co·lum·ni·a·tion (kə-lŭm′nē-ā′shən) *n. Architecture.* The use or arrangement of columns in a building.

col·um·nist (kŏl′əm-nĭst, -ə-mĭst) *n.* A writer of a column in a publication, such as a newspaper.

Col·ville (kōl′vĭl′, kŏl′-). A river rising in the Brooks Range of northwest Alaska and flowing about 603 km (375 mi) east and north across the tundra to the Arctic Ocean.

col·za (kŏl′zə, kōl′-) *n.* See **rape².** [French, from Dutch *koolzaad* : *kool,* cabbage (from Middle Dutch *cōle,* from Latin *caulis*) + *zaad,* seed (from Middle Dutch *saet;* see **sē-** in Appendix).]

COM *abbr.* Computer-output microfilm; computer-output microfilmer.

com. *abbr.* **1.** Combining. **2.** Combustion. **3.** Comedy; comic. **4.** Comma. **5.** Commentary. **6.** Commerce; commercial. **7.** Or **Com.** Commission; commissioner. **8.** Or **Com.** Committee. **9.** Common. **10.** Commune. **11.** Communication. **12.** Community.

Com. *abbr.* **1.** Also **com.** Commander. **2.** Commodore. **3.** Communist.

com– or **col–** or **con–** *pref.* Together; with; joint; jointly: *commingle.* [Middle English, from Latin, from Old Latin *com.* See **kom** in Appendix.]

co·ma¹ (kō′mə) *n., pl.* **-mas.** A state of deep, often prolonged unconsciousness, usually the result of injury, disease, or poison, in which an individual is incapable of sensing or responding to external stimuli and internal needs. [Greek *kōma,* deep sleep.]

co·ma² (kō′mə) *n., pl.* **-mae** (-mē). **1.** *Astronomy.* The nebulous, luminescent cloud containing the nucleus and constituting the major portion of the head of a comet. **2.** *Botany.* A usually terminal tuft or cluster, especially a tuft of hairs on a seed, as on a willow or milkseed. **3.** *Physics.* A diffuse, pear-shaped image of a point source. [Latin, hair, from Greek *komē.*] **—co′mal** *adj.*

Co·ma Ber·e·ni·ces (kō′mə bĕr′ə-nī′sēz′) *n.* A constellation in the northern sky near Boötes and Leo that contains the north pole of the Milky Way. Also called *Berenice's Hair.* [New Latin *Coma Berenicēs,* Berenice's hair : Latin *coma,* hair + Latin *Berenicēs,* genitive of *Berenicē,* Berenice (a queen of Egypt who promised her hair to Venus).]

co·mae (kō′mē) *n.* Plural of **coma**[2].

Co·man·che (kə-măn′chē) *n., pl.* **Comanche** or **-ches. 1.a.** A Native American people formerly ranging over the southern Great Plains from western Kansas to northern Texas and now located in Oklahoma. The Comanche became nomadic buffalo hunters after migrating south from Wyoming in the 18th century. **b.** A member of this people. **2.** The Uto-Aztecan language of the Comanche. [Spanish, from Ute *kɨmmanči.*] **—Co·man′che** *adj.*

co·mate[1] (kō′māt′) *adj.* Comose. [Latin *comātus,* having long hair, from *coma,* hair. See COMA[2].]

co·mate[2] (kō-māt′, kō′māt′) *n.* A mate; a companion.

co·ma·tose (kō′mə-tōs′, kŏm′ə-) *adj.* **1.** Of, relating to, or affected with coma; unconscious. **2.** Marked by lethargy; torpid. **—co′ma·tose′ly** *adv.*

co·mat·u·lid (kə-măch′ə-lĭd) also **co·mat·u·la** (-lə) *n., pl.* **-lids** also **-lae** (-lē). Any of various marine invertebrates of the class Crinoidea, such as the sea lilies and feather stars, that are attached to a surface by a stalk when young but may be free-swimming as adults. [From New Latin *Comātulidae,* former family name, from Late Latin *comātulus,* having neatly curled hair, from Latin *comātus,* having long hair. See COMATE[1].]

comb (kōm) *n.* **1.a.** A thin toothed strip, as of plastic, used to smooth, arrange, or fasten the hair. **b.** An implement, such as a card for dressing and cleansing wool or other fiber, that resembles a hair comb in shape or use. **c.** A currycomb. **2.a.** The fleshy crest or ridge that grows on the crown of the head of domestic fowl and other birds and is most prominent in the male. **b.** Something suggesting a fowl's comb in appearance or position. **3.** A honeycomb. **—comb** *v.* **combed, comb·ing, combs.** *—tr.* **1.** To dress or arrange with or as if with a comb. **2.** To card (wool or other fiber). **3.** To search thoroughly; look through: *combed the dresser drawers for a lost bracelet.* *—intr.* To roll and break. Used of waves. [Middle English, from Old English. See **gembh-** in Appendix.]

comb. *abbr.* **1.** Combination. **2.** Combining. **3.** Combustion.

com·bat (kəm-băt′, kŏm′băt′) *v.* **-bat·ed, -bat·ing, -bats** or **-bat·ted, -bat·ting, -bats.** *—tr.* **1.** To oppose in battle; fight against. **2.** To oppose vigorously; struggle against. See Synonyms at **oppose.** *—intr.* To engage in fighting; contend or struggle. **—combat** (kŏm′băt′) *n.* Fighting, especially armed battle; strife. See Synonyms at **conflict. —combat** *adj.* **1.** Of or relating to combat: *flew 50 combat missions.* **2.** Intended for use or deployment in combat: *combat boots; combat troops.* [French *combattre,* from Old French, from Late Latin *combattere* : Latin *com-,* com- + Latin *battere,* to beat (alteration of *battuere*).]

com·bat·ant (kəm-băt′nt, kŏm′bə-tnt) *n.* One, such as a person or a combat vehicle, that takes part in armed strife. **—combatant** *adj.* Engaging in armed strife.

combat fatigue *n.* A nervous disorder, usually temporary but sometimes leading to a permanent neurosis, brought on by the exhaustion and stress of combat or similar situations and characterized by deep anxiety, depression, irritability, and other related symptoms. Also called *battle fatigue.*

com·bat·ive (kəm-băt′ĭv) *adj.* Eager or disposed to fight; belligerent. See Synonyms at **argumentative. —com·bat′ive·ly** *adv.* **—com·bat′ive·ness** *n.*

comb·er (kō′mər) *n.* **1.** One, such as a machine or a worker, that combs wool, for example. **2.** A long wave that has reached its peak or broken into foam; a breaker.

com·bi·na·tion (kŏm′bə-nā′shən) *n. Abbr.* **comb. 1.** The act of combining or the state of being combined. **2.** The result of combining. **3.** An alliance of persons or parties for a common purpose; an association. **4.** A sequence of numbers or letters used to open a combination lock. **5.** *Mathematics.* One or more elements selected from a set without regard to the order of selection. **—com′bi·na′tion·al** *adj.*

combination lock *n.* A lock that will open only when its dial is turned through a predetermined sequence of positions identified on the dial face by numbers or letters.

com·bi·na·tive (kŏm′bə-nā′tĭv, kəm-bī′nə-tĭv) *adj.* **1.** Of, relating to, or resulting from combination. **2.** Tending, serving, or able to combine.

com·bi·na·to·ri·al (kŏm′bə-nə-tôr′ē-əl, -tōr′-, kəm-bī′nə-) *adj.* **1.** Relating to or involving combinations. **2.** Relating to the arrangement and manipulation of mathematical elements in sets.

com·bi·na·tor·ics (kŏm′bə-nə-tôr′ĭks, -tōr′-, kəm-bī′nə-) *n. (used with a sing. verb).* Combinatorial mathematics.

com·bine (kəm-bīn′) *v.* **-bined, -bin·ing, -bines.** *—tr.* **1.** To bring into a state of unity; merge. **2.** To join (two or more substances) to make a single substance, such as a chemical compound; mix. **3.** To possess or exhibit in combination: *The choreography, which combines artistry and athletics, is extremely innovative.* **4.** (kŏm′bīn′). To harvest (a grain crop) using a cutting, threshing, and cleaning machine. *—intr.* **1.** To become united; coalesce. **2.** To join forces for a common purpose. See Synonyms at **join. 3.** *Chemistry.* To form a compound. **4.** (kŏm′bīn′). To harvest a grain crop using a cutting, threshing, and cleaning machine: *"Norwegian bachelor farmers combining in their antique McCormacks"* (Garrison Keillor). **—combine** (kŏm′bīn′) *n.* **1.** A power-operated harvesting machine that cuts, threshes, and cleans grain. **2.** An association of people or groups united for the furtherance of political or commercial interests. **3.** A combination. [Middle English *combinen,* from Old French *combiner,* from Late Latin *combīnāre* : Latin *com-,* com- + *bīnī,* two by two; see **dwo-** in Appendix.] **—com·bin′er** *n.*

comb·ings (kō′mĭngz) *pl.n.* Small loose pieces of material, such as hairs or wool, removed with a comb.

com·bin·ing (kəm-bī′nĭng) *n. Abbr.* **com., comb. 1.** The act or process of joining, merging, or mixing two or more things. **2.** (kŏm′bī-nĭng). The act or process of operating a combine.

combining form *n. Grammar.* A modified form of an independent word in English or in a language such as Greek or Latin from which English has borrowed that occurs only in combination with other forms. It combines with words, affixes, or other combining forms to form compounds or derivatives, as *electro-* (from *electric*) in *electromagnet* or *geo-* (from Greek *gēo-,* from *gē-,* "earth") in *geochemistry.*

comb jelly *n.* See **ctenophore.**

com·bo (kŏm′bō) *n., pl.* **-bos. 1.** *Music.* A small jazz band. **2.** *Informal.* The product or result of combining; a combination. [Short for COMBINATION.]

com·bus·ti·ble (kəm-bŭs′tə-bəl) *adj.* **1.** Capable of igniting and burning. **2.** Easily aroused or excited. **—combustible** *n.* A substance that ignites and burns readily. **—com·bus′ti·bil′i·ty** *n.* **—com·bus′ti·bly** *adv.*

com·bus·tion (kəm-bŭs′chən) *n. Abbr.* **com., comb. 1.** The process of burning. **2.** A chemical change, especially oxidation, accompanied by the production of heat and light. **3.** Violent anger or agitation: *Combustion within the populace slowly built up to the point of revolution.* [Middle English, from Late Latin *combustiō, combustiōn-,* from Latin *combustus,* past participle of *combūrere,* to burn up, blend of *com-,* intensive pref.; see COM–, and *ambūrere,* to burn around (*ambi-,* ambi- + *ūrere,* to burn).] **—com·bus′tive** (-tĭv) *adj.*

combustion chamber *n.* An enclosure in which combustion, especially of a fuel or propellant, is initiated and controlled.

com·bus·tor (kəm-bŭs′tər) *n.* A combustion chamber and its igniters, injectors, and other related apparatus in a jet engine or gas turbine.

comd. *abbr.* Command.

comdg. *abbr.* Commanding.

Comdr. *abbr.* Commander.

Comdt. *abbr.* Commandant.

come (kŭm) *intr.v.* **came** (kām), **come, com·ing, comes. 1.a.** To advance toward the speaker or toward a specified place; approach: *Come to me.* **b.** To advance in a specified manner: *The children came reluctantly when I insisted.* **2.a.** To make progress; advance: *a former drug addict who has come a long way.* **b.** To fare: *How are things coming today? They're coming fine.* **3.a.** To reach a particular point in a series or as a result of orderly progression: *At last we came to the chapter on ergonomics.* **b.** To arrive, as in due course: *Dawn comes at 5 A.M. in June.* **4.** To move into view; appear: *The moon came over the horizon.* **5.** To occur in time; take place: *"In the . . . saloon . . . the sawdust on the floor gets changed biweekly come fog, downpour or the occasional shard of sunlight"* (Paul A. Witteman). **6.a.** To arrive at a particular result or end: *come to an understanding.* **b.** To arrive at or reach a particular state or condition: *Come to your senses!* **c.** To move or be brought to a particular position: *The convoy came to an abrupt halt.* **7.** To extend; reach: *water that came to my waist.* **8.** To have priority; rank: *My work comes first.* **9.a.** To reach a particular condition or to arrive at a specified viewpoint: *I have come to view the issue in a different light. How did you come to know that?* **b.** To happen as a result: *This comes of your carelessness.* **10.** To fall to one: *No good can come of this.* **11.** To occur in the mind: *A good idea just came to me.* **12.a.** To issue forth: *A cry came from the frightened child.* **b.** To be derived; originate: *Oaks come from acorns.* **c.** To be descended: *They come from a good family.* **d.** To be within a given range or spectrum of reference or application: *This stipulation comes within the terms of your contract.* **13.** To be a native or resident of: *My friend comes from Chicago.* **14.** To add up to a certain amount: *Expenses came to more than income.* **15.a.** To become: *The knot came loose. This is a dream that has come true.* **b.** To turn out to be: *A good education doesn't come cheap.* **16.** To be available or obtainable: *shoes that come in all sizes.* **17.** *Vulgar Slang.* To experience orgasm. **—come** *n. Vulgar Slang.* Semen. ***—phrasal verbs.* come about. 1.** To take place; happen. **2.** To turn around. **3.** *Nautical.* To change tack. **come across. 1.** To meet or find by chance: *came across my old college roommate in town today.* **2.** *Slang.* **a.** To do what is wanted. **b.** To pay over money that is demanded: *came across with the check.* **3.** To give an impression: *"He comes across as a very sincere, religious individual"* (William L. Clay). **come along. 1.** To make advances to a goal; progress: *Things are coming along fine.* **2.** To go with someone else who takes the lead: *I'll come along on the hike.* **3.** To show up; appear: *Don't take the first offer that comes along.* **come around** (or **round**). **1.** To recover; revive: *fainted but soon came around.* **2.** To change one's opinion or position: *You'll come around after you hear the whole story.* **come at. 1.** To obtain; get: *come at an education through study.* **2.** To rush at; attack. **come back. 1.** To return to or regain past success after a period

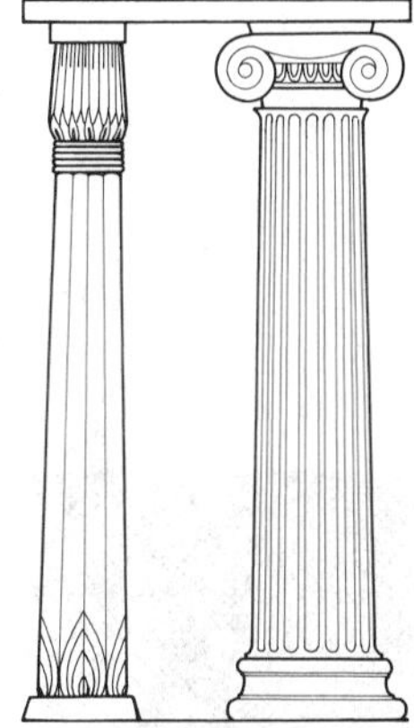

column
Left: Egyptian bundle/bud
Right: Greek Ionic

combine
Harvesting wheat

ă pat	oi boy
ā pay	ou out
âr care	ŏŏ took
ä father	ōō boot
ĕ pet	ŭ cut
ē be	ûr urge
ĭ pit	th thin
ī pie	*th* this
îr pier	hw which
ŏ pot	zh vision
ō toe	ə about, item
ô paw	♦ regionalism

Stress marks: ′ (primary); ′ (secondary), as in **dictionary** (dĭk′shə-nĕr′ē)

of misfortune. **2.** To retort; reply: *came back with a sharp riposte.* **3.** To recur to the memory: *When I saw the picture, happy memories came back.* **come by. 1.** To gain possession of; acquire: *Mortgages are hard to come by.* **2.** To pay a visit. **come down. 1.** To lose wealth or position: *He has really come down in the world.* **2.a.** To pass or be handed down by tradition: *customs that come down from colonial times.* **b.** To be handed down from a higher authority: *An indictment finally came down.* **3.** *Slang.* To happen; occur: *What's coming down tonight?* **come in. 1.a.** To arrive: *Fall clothes will be coming in soon.* **b.** To become available for use: *New weather information just came in.* **c.** To start producing. Used of an oil well. **2.** To arrive among those who finish a contest or race: *came in fifth.* **3.** To perform or function in a particular way: *A food processor comes in handy.* **4.** To reply in a specified manner to a call or signal: *The pilot's voice came in loud and clear.* **5.** To take on a specified role: *When editorial review commences, that's where you come in.* **come into.** To acquire, especially as an inheritance: *She came into a fortune on her 21st birthday.* **come off. 1.** To happen; occur: *The trip came off on schedule.* **2.** To acquit oneself: *She is sure to come off badly if challenged to explain.* **3.** To turn out to be successful: *a party that came off.* **come on. 1.** To convey a particular personal image: *comes on as an old-fashioned reactionary.* **2.** *Slang.* To show sexual interest in someone: *trying to come on to me during the party.* **3.a.** To progress or advance in increments: *Darkness came on after seven.* **b.** To begin in small increments or by degrees: *Sleet came on after one o'clock.* **4.** To hurry up; move rapidly. Often used in the imperative: *Would you please come on! We'll be late!* **5.** To stop an inappropriate behavior; abandon a position or an attitude; be obliging. Used chiefly in the imperative: *You've used the same feeble excuse for weeks. Come on!* **come out. 1.** To become known: *The whole story came out at the trial.* **2.** To be issued or brought out: *The author's new book just came out.* **3.** To make a formal social debut: *She came out at age 18 in New York City.* **4.** To end up; result: *Everything came out wrong.* **5.** To declare oneself publicly: *The governor came out in favor of tax breaks.* **6.** To reveal that one is gay or homosexual. **come over. 1.** To change sides, as in a controversy. **2.** To pay a casual visit. **come through. 1.** To do what is required or anticipated: *I asked for their help, and they came through.* **2.a.** To become manifest: *The parents' tenderness comes through in their facial expressions.* **b.** To be communicated in a specified manner: *The pilot's voice came through loud and clear.* **come to. 1.** To recover consciousness: *The fainting victim came to.* **2.** *Nautical.* **a.** To bring the bow into the wind. **b.** To anchor. **come up. 1.** To manifest itself; arise: *The question never came up.* **2.** To rise above the horizon: *The sun came up.* **3.** To rise, as in status or rank: *a general who came up from the ranks.* **4.** To draw near; approach: *came up and said hello.* **come upon.** To discover or meet by accident. —***idioms.*** **come a cropper.** To fail utterly. **come clean.** To confess all. **come down on.** To punish, oppose, or reprimand severely and often with force: *a district attorney who came down hard on drug dealers.* **come down to. 1.** To confront or deal with forthrightly: *When you come right down to it, you have to admit I'm correct.* **2.** To amount to in essence: *It comes down to this: the man is a cheat.* **come down with.** To become sick with (an illness): *came down with the flu.* **come in for.** To receive; be subjected to: *came in for harsh criticism.* **come into (one's) own. 1.** To get possession of what belongs to one. **2.** To obtain rightful recognition or prosperity: *a concert pianist who has at last come into his own.* **come off it.** *Slang.* To stop acting or speaking foolishly or pretentiously. Often used in the imperative. **come out with. 1.** To put into words; say: *always comes out with the truth.* **2.** To reveal publicly: *came out with a new tax package.* **come to blows.** To begin a physical fight. **come to grief.** To meet with disaster; fail. **come to grips with.** To confront squarely and attempt to deal decisively with: *"He had to come to grips with the proposition"* (Louis Auchincloss). **come to light** (or **hand).** To be clearly revealed or disclosed: *"A further problem . . . came to light last summer as a result of post-flight inspections"* (John Noble Wilford). **come to terms. 1.** To confront squarely and come to understand fully and objectively: *"He attempts to come to terms with his own early experiences . . . and with his father, a con man of extravagant dimensions"* (Peter S. Prescott). **2.** To reach mutual agreement: *The warring factions have at last come to terms.* **come true.** To happen as predicted: *My fondest dreams have at last come true.* **come up against.** To encounter, especially a difficulty or major problem. **come up with.** To bring forth or discover: *came up with a cure for the disease.* [Middle English *comen,* from Old English *cuman.* See **g**ʷ**ā-** in Appendix.]

come·back (kŭm′băk′) *n.* **1.a.** A return to formerly enjoyed status or prosperity: *The film star made an unexpected comeback.* **b.** A return to popularity: *Wide ties are making a comeback this year.* **2.** The act of making up a deficit, as in a contest or game. **3.** A reply, especially a quick, witty one; a retort.

co·me·di·an (kə-mē′dē-ən) *n.* **1.** A professional entertainer who tells jokes or performs various other comic acts. **2.** An actor in comedy. **3.** A writer of comedy. **4.** A person who amuses or tries to be amusing; a clown. [French *comédien,* player, comedian, from *comédie,* comedy, from Medieval Latin *cōmēdia.* See COMEDY.]

co·me·dic (kə-mē′dĭk) *adj.* Of or relating to comedy. —**co·me′di·cal·ly** *adv.*

co·me·di·enne (kə-mē′dē-ĕn′) *n.* A woman professional entertainer who tells jokes or performs various other comic acts. [French *comédienne,* feminine of *comédien,* comedian. See COMEDIAN.]

com·e·do (kŏm′ĭ-dō′) *n., pl.* **-dos** or **-do·nes** (-dō′nēz). See **blackhead** (sense 1). [Latin *comedō,* glutton, from *comedere,* to eat up : *com-,* intensive pref.; see COM– + *edere,* to eat; see **ed-** in Appendix.]

com·e·do·gen·ic (kŏm′ĭ-dō-jĕn′ĭk) *adj.* Tending to produce or aggravate acne. [COMEDO + –GENIC.]

come·down (kŭm′doun′) *n.* **1.** A decline to a lower status or level. **2.a.** A feeling of disappointment or depression. **b.** A cause of disappointment or depression.

com·e·dy (kŏm′ĭ-dē) *n., pl.* **-dies.** *Abbr.* **com. 1.a.** A dramatic work that is light and often humorous or satirical in tone and that usually contains a happy resolution of the thematic conflict. **b.** The genre made up of such works. **2.** A literary or cinematic work of a comic nature or that uses the themes or methods of comedy. **3.** Popular entertainment composed of jokes, satire, or humorous performance. **4.** The art of composing or performing comedy. **5.** A humorous element of life or literature: *the human comedy of political campaigns.* **6.** A humorous occurrence. —*attributive.* Often used to modify another noun: *a comedy writer; a comedy show.* —***idiom.*** **comedy of errors.** A ludicrous event or sequence of events: *The candidate's campaign turned out to be a political comedy of errors.* [Middle English *comedie,* from Medieval Latin *cōmēdia,* from Latin *cōmoedia,* from Greek *kōmōidia,* from *kōmōidos,* comic actor : *kōmos,* revel + *aoidos,* singer (from *aeidein,* to sing; see **wed-²** in Appendix).]

comedy of manners *n., pl.* **comedies of manners.** A comedy satirizing the attitudes and behavior of a particular social group, often of fashionable society.

come-hith·er (kŭm-hĭ*th*′ər) *adj.* Seductive; alluring: *a come-hither look.*

come·ly (kŭm′lē) *adj.* **-li·er, -li·est. 1.** Pleasing and wholesome in appearance; attractive. See Synonyms at **beautiful. 2.** Suitable; seemly: *comely behavior.* [Middle English *comli,* alteration (probably influenced by *bicomli,* seemly, from *bicomen,* to be suitable; see BECOME) of *cumli,* from Old English *cȳmlic,* lovely, delicate, from *cȳme,* beautiful.] —**come′li·ness** *n.*

Co·me·ni·us (kə-mē′nē-əs), **John Amos.** 1592–1670. Czechoslovakian theologian and educational reformer who held that science exalted divine majesty rather than threatened it.

come-on (kŭm′ŏn′, -ôn′) *n.* **1.** Something offered to allure or attract; an inducement, especially to buy. **2.** *Slang.* A sexual or romantic approach or proposal.

com·er (kŭm′ər) *n.* **1.** One that arrives or comes: *free food for all comers.* **2.** One showing promise of attaining success: *a political comer.*

co·mes·ti·ble (kə-mĕs′tə-bəl) *adj.* Fit to be eaten; edible. —**comestible** *n.* Something that can be eaten as food: *meat, cheese, and other comestibles.* [French, from Old French, from Late Latin *comēstibilis,* from Latin *comēstus,* alteration (influenced by *pōtus,* drunk; see POTION) of *comēsus,* past participle of *comedere,* to eat up : *com-,* intensive pref.; see COM– + *edere,* to eat; see **ed-** in Appendix.]

com·et (kŏm′ĭt) *n.* A celestial body, observed only in that part of its orbit that is relatively close to the sun, having a head consisting of a solid nucleus surrounded by a nebulous coma up to 2.4 million kilometers (1.5 million miles) in diameter and an elongated, curved vapor tail arising from the coma when sufficiently close to the sun. Comets are thought to consist chiefly of ammonia, methane, carbon dioxide, and water. [Middle English *comete,* from Old English *comēta,* from Latin, from Greek *(astēr) komētēs,* long-haired (star), from *komē,* hair.] —**com′et·ar′y** (-ĭ-tĕr′ē), **co·met′ic** (kə-mĕt′ĭk) *adj.*

comet

WORD HISTORY: Comets have been feared throughout much of human history, and even in our own time their goings and comings receive great attention. Perhaps a comet might seem less awesome if we realized that our name for it is based on a figurative resemblance between it and human beings. This figurative name is recorded first in the works of Aristotle, in which he uses *komē,* the Greek word for "hair of the head," to mean "luminous tail of a comet." Aristotle then uses the derived word *komētēs,* "wearing long hair," as a noun meaning "comet." The Greek word was adopted into Latin as *comētēs,* which was refashioned in Late Latin and given the form *comēta,* furnishing Old English with *comēta,* the earliest English ancestor of our word *comet.*

come·up·pance (kŭm′ŭp′əns) *n.* A punishment or retribution that one deserves; one's just deserts: *"It's a chance to strike back at the critical brotherhood and give each his comeuppance for evaluative sins of the past"* (Judith Crist).

com·fit (kŭm′fĭt, kŏm′-) *n.* A confection that consists of a piece of fruit, a seed, or a nut coated with sugar. [Middle English *confit,* from Old French, from Latin *cōnfectum,* thing prepared, neuter past participle of *cōnficere,* to prepare : *com-,* com- + *facere,* to make; see **dhē-** in Appendix.]

com·fort (kŭm′fərt) *tr.v.* **-fort·ed, -fort·ing, -forts. 1.** To soothe in time of affliction or distress. **2.** To ease physically; relieve. —**comfort** *n.* **1.** A condition or feeling of pleasurable ease, well-being, and contentment. **2.** Solace in time of grief or fear. **3.** Help; assistance: *gave comfort to the enemy.* **4.** One that brings or provides comfort. **5.** The capacity to give physical ease and well-being: *enjoying the comfort of my favorite chair.* [Middle English *comforten,* from Old French *conforter,* to strengthen, from Late Latin *cōnfortāre* : Latin *com-,* intensive pref.; see COM– + Latin *fortis,* strong; see **bhergh-**[2] in Appendix.] **—com′fort·ing·ly** *adv.*

SYNONYMS: *comfort, console, solace.* The central meaning shared by these verbs is "to give hope or help to in time of grief or pain": *comforted the distressed child; consoling a woman on the death of her husband; solaced myself with a hot cup of coffee.* See also Synonyms at **amenity, rest**[1].

com·fort·a·ble (kŭm′fər-tə-bəl, kŭmf′tə-bəl) *adj.* **1.** Providing physical comfort: *a comfortable chair.* **2.** Free from stress or anxiety; at ease: *not comfortable about the interview.* **3.** Sufficient to provide financial security: *comfortable earnings.* **—com′fort·a·ble·ness** *n.* **—com′fort·a·bly** *adv.*

SYNONYMS: *comfortable, cozy, snug, restful.* These words mean affording ease of mind or body. *Comfortable* implies the absence of sources of pain or distress: *sleeps in a comfortable bed; wears comfortable clothes.* The word may also suggest peace of mind: *felt comfortable with the decision; has a comfortable income. Cozy* evokes the image of a warm room in winter and suggests homey and reassuring ease: *sat in a cozy nook near the fire; had a cozy little chat. Snug* brings to mind the image of a warm, secure, compact shelter: *children snug in their beds. Restful* suggests a quiet conducive to tranquillity: *spent a restful hour reading; a room painted in restful colors.*

com·fort·er (kŭm′fər-tər) *n.* **1.** One that comforts: *the nurse as comforter of the sick.* **2. Comforter.** The Holy Spirit. **3.** A quilted bedcover. **4.** A narrow, long, typically woolen neck scarf.

comfort food *n.* Easily prepared plain food, such as macaroni and cheese, meat loaf, or puddings, sometimes prepackaged.

comfort station *n.* A public restroom or toilet.

com·frey (kŭm′frē) *n., pl.* **-freys.** Any of various hairy perennial Eurasian herbs of the genus *Symphytum,* especially *S. officinale,* having variously colored flowers in coiled cymes and long used in herbal medicine. Also called *healing herb.* [Middle English *comferi,* from Old French *cumfirie,* from Vulgar Latin **cōnfervia,* from Latin *cōnferva,* from *cōnfervēre,* to boil together : *com-,* com- + *fervēre,* to boil; see FERVENT.]

com·fy (kŭm′fē) *adj.* **-fi·er, -fi·est.** *Informal.* Comfortable.

com·ic (kŏm′ĭk) *adj. Abbr.* **com. 1.** Characteristic of or having to do with comedy. **2.** Of or relating to comic strips. **3.** Amusing; humorous: *a comic situation involving the family's pets.* **—comic** *n.* **1.a.** A comedian. **b.** A person whose behavior elicits laughter. **2.a. comics.** Comic strips. **b.** A comic book. **3.** A source of humor in art or life. [Latin *cōmicus,* from Greek *kōmikos,* from *kōmos,* revel.]

com·i·cal (kŏm′ĭ-kəl) *adj.* **1.** Provoking mirth or amusement; funny. **2.** Of or relating to comedy. **—com′i·cal′i·ty** (-kăl′ĭ-tē), **com′i·cal·ness** *n.* **—com′i·cal·ly** *adv.*

comic book *n.* A book of comic strips. Also called *funny book.*

Co·mice (kō-mēs′, kə-) *n.* A cultivated variety of pear having greenish-yellow skin blushed with russet-red and yellowish, juicy, fine-textured flesh. [From French *(Doyenne du) Comice,* (Dean of the) Show, from *comice (agricole),* (agricultural) show, from Old French, convention, from Latin *comitia.* See COMITIA.]

comic opera *n. Music.* An opera or operetta with a humorous plot, spoken dialogue, and usually a happy ending. Also called *bouffe, opéra comique.*

com·ic-op·er·a (kŏm′ĭk-ŏp′ər-ə, -ŏp′rə) *adj.* Not to be taken seriously: *comic-opera politics; a comic-opera style of uniform.*

comic relief *n.* A humorous or farcical interlude in a serious literary work, especially a tragedy, intended to relieve the dramatic tension or heighten the emotional impact by means of contrast.

comic strip *n.* A narrative series of cartoons.

Co·mines also **Com·mines** (kô-mēn′), **Philippe de.** 1447?–1511. French diplomat, political adviser, and historian whose *Mémoires* (1524) are among the most perceptive historical documents of the Middle Ages.

com·ing (kŭm′ĭng) *adj.* **1.** Approaching; forthcoming; next: *the coming season; a coming report on arms limitation.* **2.** Showing promise of fame or success. **—coming** *n.* Arrival; advent: *the coming of spring.*

com·ing-out (kŭm′ĭng-out′) *n.* A social debut.

Com·in·tern (kŏm′ĭn-tûrn′) *n.* An association of Communist parties of the world, established in 1919 by Lenin and dissolved in 1943. [Russian *komintern,* abbreviation of *Kommunisticheskiĭ Internatsional,* Communist International.]

co·mi·ti·a (kə-mĭsh′ē-ə, -mĭsh′ə) *n., pl.* **comitia.** A popular assembly in ancient Rome having legislative or electoral duties. [Latin, from pl. of *comitium,* assembly place : *com-,* com- + *itus,* past participle of *īre,* to go; see **ei-** in Appendix.] **—co·mi′tial** (-mĭsh′əl) *adj.*

com·i·ty (kŏm′ĭ-tē) *n., pl.* **-ties. 1.** An atmosphere of social harmony. **2.** See **comity of nations** (sense 2). **3.** The principle by which the courts of one jurisdiction may accede or give effect to the laws or decisions of another. [Latin *cōmitās,* from *cōmis,* friendly. See **smei-** in Appendix.]

comity of nations *n.* **1.** Courteous recognition accorded by one nation to the laws and institutions of another. **2.** The nations observing international comity. In this sense, also called *comity.*

com·ix (kŏm′ĭks) *pl.n.* Comic books and comic strips, especially of the underground press: *"the countercultural . . . comix of the sixties and early seventies, with their explicit criticism of American society"* (Lloyd Rose). [Alteration of *comics,* pl. of COMIC.]

coml. *abbr.* Commercial.

comm. *abbr.* **1.** Commerce. **2.** Commission; commissioner. **3.** Also **Comm.** Committee. **4.** Commonwealth. **5.** Communication.

com·ma (kŏm′ə) *n.* **1.** *Abbr.* **com.** *Grammar.* A punctuation mark (,) used to indicate a separation of ideas or of elements within the structure of a sentence. **2.** A pause or separation; a caesura. **3.** Any of several butterflies of the genus *Polygonia,* having wings with brownish coloring and irregularly notched edges. [Latin, from Greek *komma,* piece cut off, short clause, from *koptein,* to cut.]

comma
Hop merchant
comma butterfly
Polygonia comma

comma fault *n.* Improper use of a comma to join two independent clauses. Also called *comma splice.*

com·mand (kə-mănd′) *v.* **-mand·ed, -mand·ing, -mands.** —*tr.* **1.** To direct with authority; give orders to. **2.** To have control or authority over; rule: *a general who commands an army.* **3.** To have at one's disposal: *a person who commands seven languages.* **4.** To deserve and receive as due; exact: *The troops' bravery commanded respect.* **5.a.** To exercise dominating, authoritative influence over: *"He commands any room he enters"* (Stephen Schiff). **b.** To dominate by physical position; overlook: *a mountain commanding the valley below.* —*intr.* **1.** To give orders. **2.** To exercise authority or control as or as if one is a commander. **—command** *n.* **1.** The act of commanding. **2.** An order given with authority. **3.** *Computer Science.* A signal that initiates an operation defined by an instruction. **4.a.** The authority to command: *an admiral in command.* **b.** Possession and exercise of the authority to command: *command of the seas.* **5.** Ability to control or use; mastery: *command of four languages.* **6.** Dominance by location; extent of view. **7.** *Abbr.* **cmd. a.** The jurisdiction of a commander. **b.** A military unit, post, district, or region under the control of one officer. **c.** A unit of the U.S. Air Force that is larger than an air force. **—command** *adj.* **1.** Of, relating to, or constituting a command: *command headquarters; a command decision.* **2.** Done or performed in response to a command: *a command performance.* [Middle English *commaunden,* from Old French *comander,* from Late Latin *commandāre* : *com-,* intensive pref.; see COM– + *mandāre,* to entrust; see **man-**[2] in Appendix.]

com·man·dant (kŏm′ən-dănt′, -dänt′) *n. Abbr.* **Comdt.** The commanding officer of a military organization. [French, from present participle of *commander,* to command, from Old French *comander.* See COMMAND.]

com·man·deer (kŏm′ən-dîr′) *tr.v.* **-deered, -deer·ing, -deers. 1.** To force into military service. **2.** To seize for military use; confiscate. **3.** To take arbitrarily or by force. See Synonyms at **appropriate.** [Afrikaans *kommandeer,* from French *commander,* to command, from Old French *comander.* See COMMAND.]

com·mand·er (kə-măn′dər) *n.* **1.** A person who commands, especially a commanding officer. **2.** *Abbr.* **CDR, Cdr., Cmd., Cmdr, com., Com., Comdr. a.** A commissioned rank in the U.S. Navy or Coast Guard that is above lieutenant commander and below captain. **b.** One who holds this rank. **c.** The chief commissioned officer of a military unit regardless of his or her rank. **3.** An officer in some knightly or fraternal orders.

commander in chief *n., pl.* **commanders in chief.** *Abbr.* **CINC, C in C 1.** Often **Commander in Chief.** The supreme commander of all the armed forces of a nation. **2.** The officer commanding a major armed force.

com·mand·ing (kə-măn′dĭng) *adj.* **1.** *Abbr.* **cmdg., comdg.** Having command; controlling. **2.** Dominating, as by magnitude or position: *took a commanding lead at the polls; a commanding view of the ocean.* **—com·mand′ing·ly** *adv.* **—com·mand′ing·ness** *n.*

commanding officer *n. Abbr.* **CO, C.O.** A military officer in charge of a unit, post, camp, base, or station.

com·mand·ment (kə-mănd′mənt) *n.* **1.** A command; an edict. **2.** One of the Ten Commandments.

command module
Apollo 15

command module *n.* The portion of a spacecraft in which the astronauts live, communicate with a ground station, and operate controls during a flight.

com·man·do (kə-măn′dō) *n., pl.* **-dos** or **-does. 1.a.** A small fighting force specially trained for making quick, destructive raids against enemy-held areas. **b.** A member of such a force. **2.a.** An organized force of Boer troops in South Africa. **b.** A raid made by such a force. [Afrikaans *kommando,* from Dutch *commando,* unit of troops, from Spanish *comando,* from *comandar,* to command, from Late Latin *commandāre.* See COMMAND.]

command post *n. Abbr.* **CP, C.P. 1.** The field headquarters used by the commander of a military unit. **2.** A headquarters, as for communications, used by a team or an organization: *a mobile news command post for election night coverage.*

comma splice *n.* See **comma fault.**

com·me·dia dell'ar·te (kə-mā′dē-ə dĕl-är′tē, -tĕ, -mĕd′ē-ə) *n.* A type of comedy developed in Italy in the 16th and 17th centuries and characterized by improvisation from a standard plot outline and the use of stock characters, often in traditional masks and costumes. [Italian : *commedia,* comedy + *dell'arte,* of the guild, professional (from *arte,* art, craft, guild).]

ă pat	oi boy
ā pay	ou out
âr care	o͝o took
ä father	o͞o boot
ĕ pet	ŭ cut
ē be	ûr urge
ĭ pit	th thin
ī pie	*th* this
îr pier	hw which
ŏ pot	zh vision
ō toe	ə about, item
ô paw	♦ regionalism

Stress marks: ′ (primary); **′** (secondary), as in **dictionary** (dĭk′shə-nĕr′ē)

comme il faut (kŭm′ ēl fō′) *adj.* Being in accord with conventions or accepted standards; proper. [French : *comme,* as + *il faut,* it is necessary, proper.]

com·mem·o·rate (kə-mĕm′ə-rāt′) *tr.v.* **-rat·ed, -rat·ing, -rates. 1.** To honor the memory of with a ceremony. See Synonyms at **observe. 2.** To serve as a memorial to. [Latin *commemorāre, commemorāt-,* to remind : *com-,* intensive pref.; see COM– + *memorāre,* to remind (from *memor,* mindful; see **(s)mer-**[1] in Appendix).] **—com·mem′o·ra′tor** *n.*

com·mem·o·ra·tion (kə-mĕm′ə-rā′shən) *n.* **1.** The act of honoring the memory of or serving as a memorial to someone or something. **2.** Something that honors or preserves the memory of another.

com·mem·o·ra·tive (kə-mĕm′ər-ə-tĭv, -ə-rā′-) *adj.* Honoring or preserving the memory of another. **—commemorative** *n.* Something that honors or preserves the memory of another.

com·mem·o·ra·to·ry (kə-mĕm′ər-ə-tôr′ē, -tōr′ē) *adj.* Commemorative.

com·mence (kə-mĕns′) *v.* **-menced, -menc·ing, -menc·es.** *—tr.* To begin; start. *—intr.* To enter upon or have a beginning; start. See Synonyms at **begin.** [Middle English *commencen,* from Old French *comencier,* from Vulgar Latin **cominitiāre* : Latin *com-,* intensive pref.; see COM– + Late Latin *initiāre,* to begin (from Latin *initium,* beginning; see **ei-** in Appendix).] **—com·menc′er** *n.*

com·mence·ment (kə-mĕns′mənt) *n.* **1.** A beginning; a start. **2.a.** A ceremony at which academic degrees or diplomas are conferred. **b.** The day on which such a ceremony occurs.

com·mend (kə-mĕnd′) *tr.v.* **-mend·ed, -mend·ing, -mends. 1.** To represent as worthy, qualified, or desirable; recommend. **2.** To express approval of; praise. See Synonyms at **praise. 3.** To commit to the care of another; entrust. [Middle English *commenden,* from Latin *commendāre* : *com-,* intensive pref.; see COM– + *mandāre,* to entrust; see **man-**[2] in Appendix.] **—com·mend′a·ble** *adj.* **—com·mend′a·ble·ness** *n.* **—com·mend′a·bly** *adv.*

com·men·da·tion (kŏm′ən-dā′shən) *n.* **1.** The act of commending. **2.** Something, especially an official award or citation, that commends.

com·men·da·to·ry (kə-mĕn′də-tôr′ē, -tōr′ē) *adj.* Serving to commend.

com·men·sal (kə-mĕn′səl) *Biology. adj.* Of, relating to, or characterized by a symbiotic relationship in which one species is benefited while the other is unaffected. **—commensal** *n.* An organism participating in a symbiotic relationship in which one species derives some benefit while the other is unaffected. [Middle English, sharing a meal, from Medieval Latin *commēnsālis* : Latin *com-,* com- + Latin *mēnsa,* table.] **—com·men′sal·ly** *adv.*

com·men·sal·ism (kə-mĕn′sə-lĭz′əm) *n. Biology.* A symbiotic relationship between two organisms of different species in which one derives some benefit while the other is unaffected.

com·men·su·ra·ble (kə-mĕn′sər-ə-bəl, -shər-) *adj.* **1.** Measurable by a common standard. **2.** Commensurate; proportionate. **3.** *Mathematics.* Exactly divisible by the same unit an integral number of times. Used of two quantities. [Late Latin *commēnsūrābilis* : Latin *com-,* com- + *mēnsūrābilis,* measurable (from *mēsūrāre,* to measure; see COMMENSURATE).] **—com·men′su·ra·bil′i·ty** *n.* **—com·men′su·ra·bly** *adv.*

com·men·su·rate (kə-mĕn′sər-ĭt, -shər-) *adj.* **1.** Of the same size, extent, or duration as another. **2.** Corresponding in size or degree; proportionate: *a salary commensurate with my performance.* **3.** Measurable by a common standard; commensurable. [Late Latin *commēnsūrātus* : Latin *com-,* com- + *mēnsūrātus,* from past participle of *mēnsūrāre,* to measure (from Latin *mēnsūra,* measure; see MEASURE).] **—com·men′su·rate·ly** *adv.* **—com·men′su·ra′tion** *n.*

com·ment (kŏm′ĕnt) *n.* **1.a.** A written note intended as an explanation, an illustration, or a criticism of a passage in a book or other writing; an annotation. **b.** A series of annotations or explanations. **2.a.** A statement of fact or opinion, especially a remark that expresses a personal reaction or attitude. **b.** An implied conclusion or judgment: *a novel that is a comment on contemporary lawlessness.* **3.** Talk; gossip: *a divorce that caused much comment.* **4.** *Computer Science.* Text in a program that does not function in the program itself but is used by the programmer to explain instructions. **—comment** *v.* **-ment·ed, -ment·ing, -ments.** *—intr.* **1.** To make a comment; remark. **2.** To serve as a judgmental commentary: *"Her demise comments on* [the Upper East Side's] *entire way of life"* (Mark Muro). *—tr.* To make comments on; annotate. [Middle English, from Late Latin *commentum,* interpretation, from Latin, contrivance, from neuter past participle of *comminīscī,* to devise. See **men-**[1] in Appendix.]

SYNONYMS: *comment, observation, remark.* The central meaning shared by these nouns is "an expression of fact, opinion, or explanation": *made an unpleasant comment about my friend; a casual observation about the movie; an offensive personal remark.*

com·men·tar·y (kŏm′ən-tĕr′ē) *n., pl.* **-ies.** *Abbr.* **com. 1.** A series of explanations or interpretations. **2.** Often **commentaries.** An expository treatise or series of annotations; an exegesis. **3.** An apt explanation or illustration: *a scandal that is a sad commentary on national politics.* **4.** Often **commentaries.** A personal narrative; a memoir. **—com′men·tar′i·al** (-târ′ē-əl) *adj.*

com·men·tate (kŏm′ən-tāt′) *v.* **-tat·ed, -tat·ing, -tates.** *—intr.* To serve as commentator. *—tr. Usage Problem.* To make a running commentary on. [Back-formation from COMMENTATOR.]

USAGE NOTE: *Commentate,* in the sense "to make a running commentary on," as in *she commentated the fashion show,* was unacceptable to a majority of the Usage Panel in an earlier survey.

com·men·ta·tor (kŏm′ən-tā′tər) *n.* **1.** A broadcaster or writer who reports and analyzes events in the news. **2.** One who writes or delivers a commentary or commentaries.

com·merce (kŏm′ərs) *n.* **1.** *Abbr.* **com., comm.** The buying and selling of goods, especially on a large scale, as between cities or nations. See Synonyms at **business. 2.** Intellectual exchange or social interaction. **3.** Sexual intercourse. [French, from Old French, from Latin *commercium* : *com-,* com- + *merx, merc-,* merchandise.]

Com·merce City (kŏm′ərs). A city of north-central Colorado, an industrial suburb of Denver. Population, 16,234.

com·mer·cial (kə-mûr′shəl) *adj. Abbr.* **com., coml., cml. 1.a.** Of or relating to commerce: *a commercial loan; a commercial attaché.* **b.** Engaged in commerce: *a commercial trucker.* **c.** Involved in work that is intended for the mass market: *a commercial artist.* **2.** Of, relating to, or being goods, often unrefined, produced and distributed in large quantities for use by industry. **3.** Having profit as a chief aim: *a commercial book, not a scholarly tome.* **4.** Sponsored by an advertiser or supported by advertising: *commercial television.* **—commercial** *n.* An advertisement on television or radio. **—com·mer′cial·ly** *adv.*

commercial bank *n.* A bank whose principal functions are to receive demand deposits and to make short-term loans.

com·mer·cial·ism (kə-mûr′shə-lĭz′əm) *n.* **1.** The practices, methods, aims, and spirit of commerce or business. **2.** An attitude that emphasizes tangible profit or success. **—com·mer′cial·ist** *n.* **—com·mer′cial·is′tic** *adj.*

com·mer·cial·ize (kə-mûr′shə-līz′) *tr.v.* **-ized, -iz·ing, -iz·es. 1.** To apply methods of business to for profit. **2.a.** To do, exploit, or make chiefly for financial gain. **b.** To sacrifice the quality of for profit. **—com·mer′cial·i·za′tion** (-shə-lĭ-zā′shən) *n.*

commercial paper *n.* Short-term, unsecured, discounted, and negotiable notes sold by one company to another in order to satisfy immediate cash needs.

commercial traveler *n.* A traveling sales representative.

com·mie also **Com·mie** (kŏm′ē) *n. Informal.* A Communist. [Short for COMMUNIST.]

com·mi·na·tion (kŏm′ə-nā′shən) *n.* A formal denunciation. [Middle English *comminacioun,* from Latin *comminātiō, comminātiōn-,* from *comminātus,* past participle of *comminārī,* to threaten : *com-,* intensive pref.; see COM– + *minārī,* to threaten; see MENACE.] **—com·min′a·to′ry** (kə-mĭn′ə-tôr′ē, -tōr′ē, kŏm′ĭ-nə-) *adj.*

Com·mines (kô-mēn′), **Philippe de.** See Philippe de **Comines.**

com·min·gle (kə-mĭng′gəl) *v.* **-gled, -gling, -gles.** *—intr.* To become blended. *—tr.* To cause to blend together; mix.

com·mi·nute (kŏm′ə-no͞ot′, -nyo͞ot′) *tr.v.* **-nut·ed, -nut·ing, -nutes.** To reduce to powder; pulverize. [Latin *comminuere, comminūt-* : *com-,* intensive pref.; see COM– + *minuere,* to lessen; see **mei-**[2] in Appendix.] **—com′mi·nu′tion** *n.*

com·mis·er·ate (kə-mĭz′ə-rāt′) *v.* **-at·ed, -at·ing, -ates.** *—tr.* To feel or express sorrow or pity for; sympathize with. *—intr.* To feel or express sympathy: *commiserated over their failure.* [Latin *commiserārī, commiserāt-* : *com-,* com- + *miserārī,* to pity (from *miser,* wretched).] **—com·mis′er·a′tive** *adj.* **—com·mis′er·a′tive·ly** *adv.* **—com·mis′er·a′tor** *n.*

com·mis·er·a·tion (kə-mĭz′ə-rā′shən) *n.* The feeling or expression of pity or sorrow. See Synonyms at **pity.**

com·mis·sar (kŏm′ĭ-sär′) *n.* **1.a.** An official of the Communist Party in charge of political indoctrination and the enforcement of party loyalty. **b.** The head of a commissariat in the Soviet Union until 1946. **2.** A person who tries to control public opinion. [Russian *komissar,* from German *Kommissar,* deputy, from Medieval Latin *commissārius,* agent. See COMMISSARY.]

com·mis·sar·i·at (kŏm′ĭ-sâr′ē-ĭt) *n.* **1.** A department of an army in charge of providing food and other supplies for the troops. **2.** A food supply. **3.** A major government department in the Soviet Union until 1946. [French, from Medieval Latin *commissārius,* agent, see COMMISSARY. Sense 3, Russian *komissariat,* from French *commissariat.*]

com·mis·sar·y (kŏm′ĭ-sĕr′ē) *n., pl.* **-ies. 1.a.** A supermarket for military personnel and their dependents, usually located on a military installation. **b.** A store where food and equipment are sold, as in a mining camp. **2.** A lunchroom or cafeteria, especially one in a film or television studio. **3.** A person to whom a special duty is given by a higher authority; a deputy. [Middle English *commissarie,* agent, from Medieval Latin *commissārius,* from Latin *commissus,* entrusted. See COMMISSION.]

com·mis·sion (kə-mĭsh′ən) *n.* **1.a.** The act of granting certain powers or the authority to carry out a particular task or duty.

b. The authority so granted. **c.** The matter or task so authorized: *Investigation of fraud was their commission.* **d.** A document conferring such authorization. **2.a.** *Abbr.* **Com., com., comm.** A group of people officially authorized to perform certain duties or functions: *The Federal Trade Commission investigates false advertising.* **b.** Often **Commission.** A ruling council within the Mafia that adjudicates family disputes and regulates family activities. **3.** The act of committing or perpetrating: *the commission of a crime.* **4.** A fee or percentage allowed to a sales representative or an agent for services rendered. **5.a.** *Abbr.* **Com., com., comm.** An official document issued by a government, conferring on the recipient the rank of a commissioned officer in the armed forces. **b.** The rank and powers so conferred. **—commission** *tr.v.* **-sioned, -sion·ing, -sions. 1.** To grant a commission to. See Synonyms at **authorize. 2.** To place an order for: *commissioned a new symphony for the festival.* **3.** To put (a ship) into active service. **—*idioms.* in commission. 1.** In active service. Used of a ship. **2.** In use or in usable condition. **on commission.** With a sales commission serving as full or partial recompense for the work done: *sells boats on commission.* **out of commission. 1.** Not in active service. Used of a ship. **2.** Not in use or in working condition. [Middle English *commissioun,* from Latin *commissiō, commissiōn-,* from *commissus,* past participle of *committere,* to entrust. See COMMIT.] **—com·mis′sion·al** *adj.*

com·mis·sion·aire (kə-mĭsh′ə-nâr′) *n. Chiefly British.* A uniformed attendant, such as a doorman. [French, from Medieval Latin *commissiōnārius,* from Latin *commissiō, commissiōn-,* commission. See COMMISSION.]

com·mis·sioned officer (kə-mĭsh′ənd) *n.* An officer who holds a commission and ranks as a second lieutenant or above in the U.S. Army, Air Force, or Marine Corps, or as an ensign or above in the U.S. Navy or Coast Guard.

com·mis·sion·er (kə-mĭsh′ə-nər) *n. Abbr.* **Com., com., Comr., comm. 1.** A member of a commission. **2.** A person authorized by a commission to perform certain duties. **3.** A governmental official in charge of a department: *a police commissioner.* **4.** *Sports.* An official selected by an athletic association or league to exercise administrative or regulatory powers over it: *a baseball commissioner.* **—com·mis′sion·er·ship′** *n.*

commission merchant *n.* One that buys and sells goods for others on a commission basis.

commission plan *n.* Municipal government in which legislative and administrative functions and powers are vested in an elected commission rather than in a mayor and city council.

com·mis·sure (kŏm′ə-shŏŏr′) *n.* **1.** A line or place at which two things are joined. **2.** *Anatomy.* **a.** A tract of nerve fibers passing from one side to the other of the spinal cord or brain. **b.** The point or surface where two parts, such as the eyelids, lips, or cardiac valves, join or form a connection. **3.** *Botany.* The surface or place along which two structures, such as carpels, are joined. [Middle English, from Latin *commissūra,* from *commissus,* past participle of *committere,* to join. See COMMIT.] **—com′mis·su′ral** *adj.*

com·mis·sur·ot·o·my (kŏm′ə-shŏŏ-rŏt′ə-mē) *n., pl.* **-mies.** Surgical incision of a commissure in the body, as one made in the heart to relieve constriction of the mitral valve or one made in the brain to treat certain psychiatric disorders. [COMMISSUR(E) + -TOMY.]

com·mit (kə-mĭt′) *v.* **-mit·ted, -mit·ting, -mits.** *—tr.* **1.** To do, perform, or perpetrate: *commit a murder.* **2.** To put in trust or charge; entrust. **3.** To place officially in confinement or custody, as in a mental health facility. **4.** To consign for future use or reference or for preservation: *commit the verse to memory.* **5.** To put into a place to be kept safe or to be disposed of. **6.a.** To make known the views of (oneself) on an issue: *I never commit myself on such issues.* **b.** To bind or obligate, as by a pledge: *They were committed to follow orders.* **7.** To refer (a legislative bill, for example) to a committee. *—intr.* To pledge or obligate one's own self: *felt that he was too young to commit fully to marriage.* [Middle English *committen,* from Latin *committere* : *com-,* com- + *mittere,* to send.] **—com·mit′ta·ble** *adj.*

SYNONYMS: *commit, consign, entrust, confide, relegate.* These verbs mean to give over to another for a purpose such as care or safekeeping. *Commit* has the widest application and means to deliver to another to deal with: *The general sent the troops committed to his charge into battle.* The word can also refer to giving over for preservation or confinement: *I committed the sonata to memory. The patient was committed to the hospital.* To *consign* is to transfer to another's custody or charge: *The owner consigned the paintings to a dealer for sale. Entrust* and *confide* stress trust and confidence in another: *The task was too important to be entrusted to a child. She confided her plans to her family.* To *relegate* is to assign to a specific and especially an inferior category or position: *Some scientists relegate parapsychology to the sphere of quackery.*

com·mit·ment (kə-mĭt′mənt) *n.* **1.** The act or an instance of committing, especially: **a.** The act of referring a legislative bill to committee. **b.** Official consignment, as to a prison or mental health facility. **c.** A court order authorizing consignment to a prison. **2.a.** A pledge to do. **b.** Something pledged, especially an engagement by contract involving financial obligation. **3.** The state of being bound emotionally or intellectually to a course of action or to another person or persons: *a deep commitment to liberal policies; a profound commitment to the family.*

com·mit·tal (kə-mĭt′l) *n.* **1.** The act of entrusting: *committal of the property to an attorney.* **2.** The act or an instance of committing to confinement. **3.** The act of pledging oneself to a particular view or position: *articulated her strong committal to world peace.*

com·mit·tee (kə-mĭt′ē) *n. Abbr.* **com., Com., comm., Comm. 1.** A group of people officially delegated to perform a function, such as investigating, considering, reporting, or acting on a matter. See Usage Note at **collective noun. 2.** *Archaic.* A person to whom a trust or charge is committed. [From Middle English *committe,* trustee, from Anglo-Norman *comité,* past participle of *cometre,* to commit, from Latin *committere.* See COMMIT.]

com·mit·tee·man (kə-mĭt′ē-mən, -măn′) *n.* **1.** A man who is a member of a committee. **2.** A man who is a party leader of a ward or precinct.

committee of the whole *n.* The whole membership of a legislative body sitting as a committee to consider the details of a proposal.

com·mit·tee·wo·man (kə-mĭt′ē-wŏŏm′ən) *n.* **1.** A woman who is a member of a committee. **2.** A woman who is a party leader of a ward or precinct.

com·mix (kə-mĭks′, kŏ-) *v.* **-mixed, -mix·ing, -mix·es.** *—intr.* To be or become mixed. *—tr.* To cause to mix. [From Middle English *commixt,* mixed together, from Latin *commixtus,* past participle of *commiscēre,* to mix together : *com-,* com- + *miscēre,* to mix; see **meik-** in Appendix.]

com·mix·ture (kə-mĭks′chər, kŏ-) *n.* **1.** The act or process of mixing. **2.** The result of mixing; a mixture.

com·mode (kə-mōd′) *n.* **1.** A low cabinet or chest of drawers, often elaborately decorated and usually standing on legs or short feet. **2.a.** A movable stand or cupboard containing a washbowl. **b.** A chair enclosing a chamber pot. **c.** A toilet. **3.** A woman's ornate headdress, fashionable around 1700. [French, from *commode,* convenient, from Latin *commodus.* See COMMODIOUS.]

commode
18th-century German

com·mo·di·ous (kə-mō′dē-əs) *adj.* **1.** Spacious; roomy. See Synonyms at **spacious. 2.** *Archaic.* Suitable; handy. [Middle English, convenient, from Medieval Latin *commodiōsus,* from Latin *commodus* : *com-,* com- + *modus,* measure; see **med-** in Appendix.] **—com·mo′di·ous·ly** *adv.* **—com·mo′di·ous·ness** *n.*

com·mod·i·ty (kə-mŏd′ĭ-tē) *n., pl.* **-ties. 1.** Something useful that can be turned to commercial or other advantage. **2.** An article of trade or commerce, especially an agricultural or mining product, that can be transported. **3.** Advantage; benefit. **4.** *Obsolete.* A quantity; lot. [Middle English *commodite,* from Old French, convenience, from Latin *commoditās,* from *commodus,* convenient. See COMMODIOUS.]

com·mo·dore (kŏm′ə-dôr′, -dōr′) *n. Abbr.* **Com. 1.a.** A commissioned rank in the U.S. Navy that is above captain and below rear admiral. This rank, abolished in 1899, was restored temporarily during World War II and is currently in use as the lowest grade of admiral. **b.** One who holds this rank. **2.** Used as an unofficial designation for a captain in the British Navy temporarily in command of a fleet division or squadron. **3.a.** The senior captain of a naval squadron or merchant fleet. **b.** The presiding officer of a yacht club. [Obsolete *commandore,* probably from Dutch *komandeur,* commander, from French *commandeur,* from Old French, from *comander,* to command. See COMMAND.]

Com·mo·dus (kŏm′ə-dəs), **Lucius Aelius Aurelius.** A.D. 161–192. Emperor of Rome (180–192) who ruled in a cruel and violent manner. He was murdered in a conspiracy led by his mistress.

com·mon (kŏm′ən) *adj.* **-er, -est.** *Abbr.* **com. 1.a.** Belonging equally to or shared equally by two or more; joint: *common interests.* **b.** Of or relating to the community as a whole; public: *for the common good.* See Usage Note at **mutual. 2.** Widespread; prevalent. **3.a.** Occurring frequently or habitually; usual. **b.** Most widely known; ordinary: *the common housefly.* **4.** Having no special designation, status, or rank: *a common sailor.* **5.a.** Not distinguished by superior or noteworthy characteristics; average: *the common spectator.* **b.** Of no special quality; standard: *common procedure.* **c.** Of mediocre or inferior quality; second-rate: *common cloth.* **6.** Unrefined or coarse in manner; vulgar: *behavior that branded him as common.* **7.** *Grammar.* **a.** Either masculine or feminine in gender. **b.** Representing one or all of the members of a class; not designating a unique entity. **—common** *n. Abbr.* **com. 1. commons.** The common people; commonalty. **2. commons** *(used with a sing. or pl. verb).* **a.** The political class composed of commoners. **b.** The parliamentary representatives of this class. **3.** Often **Commons.** See **House of Commons. 4.** A tract of land, usually in a centrally located spot, belonging to or used by a community as a whole: *a band concert on the village common.* **5.** The legal right of a person to use the lands or waters of another, as for fishing. **6. commons** *(used with a sing. verb).* A building or hall for dining, typically at a university or college. **7.** Common stock. **8.** *Ecclesiastical.* A service used for a particular class of festivals. **—*idiom.* in common.** Equally with or by all. [Middle English *commune,* from Old French, from Latin *commūnis.* See **mei-**[1] in Appendix.] **—com′mon·ly** *adv.* **—com′mon·ness** *n.*

com·mon·age (kŏm′ə-nĭj) *n.* **1.** The right to pasture animals on common land. **2.** The state of being held in common.

com·mon·al·i·ty (kŏm′ə-năl′ĭ-tē) *n., pl.* **-ties. 1.** The possession, along with another or others, of a certain attribute or set

ă pat	oi boy
ā pay	ou out
âr care	ŏŏ took
ä father	ōō boot
ĕ pet	ŭ cut
ē be	ûr urge
ĭ pit	th thin
ī pie	*th* this
îr pier	hw which
ŏ pot	zh vision
ō toe	ə about, item
ô paw	♦ regionalism

Stress marks: **′** (primary); ′ (secondary), as in **dictionary** (dĭk′shə-nĕr′ē)

of attributes: *"First there needs to be an acknowledgment of some degree of commonality, mutuality, responsibility and opportunity with respect to fellow blacks"* (H. Naylor Fitzhugh). **2.** See **commonalty** (sense 1).

com·mon·al·ty (kŏm′ə-nəl-tē) *n., pl.* **-ties. 1.** The common people as opposed to the upper classes. Also called *commonality.* **2.** A body corporate; a corporation. **3.** An entire group: *the commonalty of laypeople.* [Middle English *communalte,* from Old French *comunalte,* from Medieval Latin *commūnālitās,* from Late Latin *commūnālis,* of the community. See COMMUNAL.]

common bile duct *n.* The duct formed by the union of the cystic duct and the hepatic duct that carries bile from the liver and the gallbladder to the duodenum.

common carrier *n.* **1.** One that is in the business of transporting the public, goods, or messages for a fee. **2.** A company that provides telecommunications services, as by telephone or satellite, to the public.

common cold *n.* See **cold** (sense 3).

common denominator *n.* **1.** *Mathematics.* A quantity into which all the denominators of a set of fractions may be divided without a remainder. **2.** A commonly shared theme or trait.

common divisor *n. Mathematics.* A quantity that is a factor of two or more quantities. Also called *common measure.*

com·mon·er (kŏm′ə-nər) *n.* **1.** One of the common people. **2.** A person without noble rank or title.

Com·mon Era (kŏm′ən) *n. Abbr.* **C.E.** The period coinciding with the Christian era.

common fraction *n. Mathematics.* A fraction having an integer as a numerator and an integer as a denominator.

common gender *n.* **1.** *Grammar.* In modern English, the gender of those nouns that apply to either sex, as *spouse, parent,* or *mouse.* **2.** *Linguistics.* In some languages, the gender of those nouns that may be either masculine or feminine but not neuter, as Latin *parēns,* "parent," or *bōs,* "ox, cow." **3.** *Linguistics.* In some languages, the gender of those nouns belonging to the single gender derived from the earlier masculine and feminine genders and separate from the neuter gender, as in Hittite or modern Danish.

common ground *n.* A foundation for mutual understanding: *"The leaders failed to find common ground on the defensive side of this possible bargain"* (McGeorge Bundy).

common law *n. Abbr.* **c.l.** *Law.* The system of laws originated and developed in England and based on court decisions, on the doctrines implicit in those decisions, and on customs and usages rather than on codified written laws.

com·mon-law marriage (kŏm′ən-lô′) *n.* A marriage existing by agreement between a man and a woman or the fact of their cohabitation, without a civil or religious ceremony.

common logarithm *n. Mathematics.* A logarithm to the base 10, especially as distinguished from a natural logarithm.

common market or **Common Market** *n. Abbr.* **CM** An economic unit, typically formed of nations, intended to eliminate or markedly reduce trade barriers among its members.

Common Market. Officially **Eu·ro·pe·an Economic Community** (yo͝or′ə-pē′ən). An economic union established in 1958 to reduce tariff barriers and promote trade and cooperation among the countries of western Europe.

common measure *n.* **1.** *Music.* See **common time. 2.** *Mathematics.* See **common divisor. 3.** A ballad stanza form in iambic meter, often rhyming in alternating pairs, that is typical of many church hymns. In this sense, also called *hymnal stanza.*

common multiple *n. Mathematics.* A quantity into which each of two or more other quantities may be divided with zero remainder: *The quantities 6, 12, and 24 are common multiples of 2 and 3.*

common noun *n. Grammar.* A noun, such as *book* or *dog,* that can be preceded by the definite article and that represents one or all of the members of a class.

com·mon·place (kŏm′ən-plās′) *adj.* Having no remarkable features, characteristics, or traits; ordinary. —**commonplace** *n.* **1.a.** A trite or obvious remark; a platitude: *"the solidified commonplaces of established wisdom"* (John Simon). See Synonyms at **cliché. b.** Something that is ordinary or common. **2.** *Archaic.* A passage marked for reference or entered in a commonplace book. [Translation of Latin *locus commūnis,* generally applicable literary passage, translation of Greek *koinos topos.*]

commonplace book *n.* A personal journal in which quotable passages, literary excerpts, and comments are written.

common pleas (plēz) *pl.n.* *(used with a sing. verb). Law.* In some states of the United States, a court of common pleas.

common room *n.* **1.** A faculty lounge in a college or university. **2.** A lounge for use by all members of a residential institution or community.

common salt *n.* **1.** See **salt** (sense 1). **2.** Sodium chloride.

common school *n.* A public elementary school.

com·mon·sense (kŏm′ən-sĕns′) *adj.* Having or exhibiting native good judgment: *"commonsense scholarship on the foibles and oversights of a genius"* (Times Literary Supplement). —**com′mon·sen′si·ble** *adj.* —**com′mon·sen′si·bly** *adv.*

common sense *n.* Native good judgment. [Translation of Latin *sēnsus commūnis,* common feelings of humanity.]

com·mon-si·tus pick·et·ing (kŏm′ən-sī′təs pĭk′ĭ-tĭng) also **com·mon-site picketing** (kŏm′ən-sīt′) *n.* Picketing by a labor union of an entire construction project as a result of a grievance held against a single subcontractor on the project, a tactic that can result in a shutdown of the project. [Latin *situs,* site. See SITE.]

common stock *n.* Ordinary capital shares of a corporation that have exclusive residual claim on the net assets and net income of the corporation after all prior claims have been paid.

common time *n. Music.* A meter with four quarter notes to the measure. Also called *common measure.*

common touch *n.* The ability to appeal to the interests and sensibilities of the ordinary person: *"an effective administrator and also an effective leader, with a common touch"* (Christian Science Monitor).

com·mon·weal (kŏm′ən-wēl′) *n.* **1.** The public good or welfare. **2.** *Archaic.* A commonwealth or republic.

com·mon·wealth (kŏm′ən-wĕlth′) *n.* **1.** The people of a nation or state; the body politic. **2.** *Abbr.* **comm.** A nation or state governed by the people; a republic. **3. Commonwealth. a.** Used to refer to some U.S. states, namely, Kentucky, Maryland, Massachusetts, Pennsylvania, and Virginia. **b.** Used to refer to a self-governing, autonomous political unit voluntarily associated with the United States, namely, Puerto Rico and the Northern Mariana Islands. **4.** Often **Commonwealth.** The Commonwealth of Nations. **5.** The English state and government from the death of Charles I in 1649 to the restoration of the monarchy in 1660, including the Protectorate of 1653 to 1659. **6.** *Archaic.* The public good; commonweal.

Commonwealth of Na·tions (nā′shənz) also **Brit·ish Commonwealth** (brĭt′ĭsh). An association comprising the United Kingdom, its dependencies, and many former British colonies that are now sovereign states with a common allegiance to the British Crown. It was formally established by the Statute of Westminster in 1931.

common wormwood *n.* See **absinthe** (sense 1).

com·mo·tion (kə-mō′shən) *n.* **1.** A condition of turbulent motion. **2.a.** An agitated disturbance; a hubbub: *heard a commotion in the hall.* **b.** Civil disturbance or insurrection; disorder. [Middle English *commocioun,* from Old French *commotion,* from Latin *commōtiō, commōtiōn-,* from *commōtus,* past participle of *commovēre,* to disturb : *com-,* intensive pref.; see COM– + *movēre,* to move; see **meuə-** in Appendix.]

com·move (kə-mo͞ov′) *tr.v.* **-moved, -mov·ing, -moves.** To agitate; disturb. [Middle English *commeven,* from Old French *commovoir, commeuv-,* from Latin *commovēre.* See COMMOTION.]

com·mu·nal (kə-myo͞o′nəl, kŏm′yə-) *adj.* **1.** Of or relating to a commune. **2.** Of or relating to a community. **3.a.** Of, belonging to, or shared by the people of a community; public. **b.** Marked by collective ownership and control of goods and property. [French, from Late Latin *commūnālis,* from Latin *commūnis,* common. See COMMON.] —**com′mu·nal′i·ty** (kŏm′yə-năl′ĭ-tē) *n.* —**com·mu′nal·ly** *adv.*

com·mu·nal·ism (kə-myo͞o′nə-lĭz′əm, kŏm′yə-nə-) *n.* **1.** Belief in or practice of communal ownership, as of goods and property. **2.** Strong devotion to the interests of one's own minority or ethnic group rather than those of society as a whole.

com·mu·nal·ist (kə-myo͞o′nə-lĭst) *n.* **1.** An advocate of communal living. **2.** One who is more interested in one's own minority or ethnic group than in society as a whole. **3.** One who is deeply concerned about the quality of community life. —**com·mu′nal·is′tic** *adj.*

com·mu·nal·ize (kə-myo͞o′nə-līz′, kŏm′yə-nə-) *tr.v.* **-ized, -iz·ing, -iz·es.** To convert into communal property.

Com·mu·nard (kŏm′yə-närd′) *n.* **1.** A member or advocate of the Commune of Paris of 1871. **2. communard.** One who lives in a commune. [French, from *commune,* commune. See COMMUNE[2].]

com·mune[1] (kə-myo͞on′) *intr.v.* **-muned, -mun·ing, -munes. 1.** To be in a state of intimate, heightened sensitivity and receptivity, as with one's surroundings: *hikers communing with nature.* **2.** To receive the Eucharist. [Middle English *communen,* from Old French *communier* (from Latin *commūnicāre;* see COMMUNICATE) and from Old French *communer,* to share (from *commun,* common; see COMMON).]

com·mune[2] (kŏm′yo͞on′, kə-myo͞on′) *n. Abbr.* **com. 1.a.** A relatively small, often rural community whose members share common interests, work, and income and often own property collectively. **b.** The people in such a community. **2.** The smallest local political division of various European countries, governed by a mayor and municipal council. **3.a.** A local community organized with a government for promoting local interests. **b.** A municipal corporation in the Middle Ages. [French, independent municipality, from Old French *comugne,* from Medieval Latin *commūnia,* community, from neuter of Latin *commūnis,* common. See **mei-[1]** in Appendix.]

com·mu·ni·ca·ble (kə-myo͞o′nĭ-kə-bəl) *adj.* **1.** Transmittable between persons or species; contagious: *communicable diseases.* **2.** Readily communicated: *communicable ideas.* **3.** Talkative. —**com·mu′ni·ca·bil′i·ty, com·mu′ni·ca·ble·ness** *n.* —**com·mu′ni·ca·bly** *adv.*

com·mu·ni·cant (kə-myo͞o′nĭ-kənt) *n.* **1.** A person who receives or is entitled to receive Communion. **2.** A person, especially an informant, who communicates something. —**com·mu′ni·cant** *adj.*

com·mu·ni·cate (kə-myo͞o′nĭ-kāt′) *v.* **-cat·ed, -cat·ing, -cates.** —*tr.* **1.a.** To convey information about; make known; impart: *communicated the new data to our office.* **b.** To reveal clearly; manifest: *"Music . . . can name the unnamable and communicate the unknowable"* (Leonard Bernstein). **2.** To spread (a disease, for example) to others; transmit: *a carrier who communicated typhus.* —*intr.* **1.** To have an interchange, as of ideas. **2.** To express oneself in such a way that one is readily and clearly understood: *"That ability to communicate was strange in a man given to long, awkward silences"* (Anthony Lewis). **3.** To receive Communion. **4.** To be connected: *apartments that communicate.* [Latin *commūnicāre, commūnicāt-,* from *commūnis,* common. See **mei-¹** in Appendix.] —**com·mu′ni·ca′tor** *n.*

com·mu·ni·ca·tion (kə-myo͞o′nĭ-kā′shən) *n. Abbr.* **com., comm. 1.** The act of communicating; transmission. **2.a.** The exchange of thoughts, messages, or information, as by speech, signals, writing, or behavior. **b.** Interpersonal rapport. **c. communications** *(used with a sing. or pl. verb).* The art and technique of using words effectively and with grace in imparting one's ideas. **3.** Something communicated; a message. **4. communications.** A means of communicating, especially: **a.** A system, such as mail, telephone, or television, for sending and receiving messages. **b.** A network of routes for sending messages and transporting troops and supplies. **5. communications.** The technology employed in transmitting messages. —*attributive.* Often used to modify another noun: *communication systems; communication technology; communications equipment; communications interface.* —**com·mu′ni·ca′tion·al** *adj.*

com·mu·ni·ca·tions satellite (kə-myo͞o′nĭ-kā′shənz) *n.* An artificial satellite used to aid telecommunications, as by reflecting or relaying a radio signal.

com·mu·ni·ca·tive (kə-myo͞o′nĭ-kā′tĭv, -kə-tĭv) *adj.* **1.** Inclined to communicate readily; talkative. **2.** Of or relating to communication. —**com·mu′ni·ca′tive·ly** *adv.* —**com·mu′ni·ca′tive·ness** *n.*

com·mun·ion (kə-myo͞on′yən) *n.* **1.** The act or an instance of sharing, as of thoughts or feelings. **2.** Religious or spiritual fellowship. **3.** A body of Christians with a common religious faith who practice the same rites; a denomination. **4. Communion. a.** The sacrament of the Eucharist received by a congregation. **b.** The consecrated elements of the Eucharist. **c.** The part of the Mass or a liturgy in which the Eucharist is received. [Middle English *communioun,* Christian fellowship, Eucharist, from Old French *communion,* from Late Latin *commūnio, commūniōn-,* from Latin, mutual participation, from *commūnis,* common. See COMMON.]

com·mu·ni·qué (kə-myo͞o′nĭ-kā′, -myo͞o′nĭ-kā′) *n.* An official announcement. [French, past participle of *communiquer,* to announce, from Latin *commūnicāre,* to communicate. See COMMUNICATE.]

com·mu·nism (kŏm′yə-nĭz′əm) *n.* **1.** A theoretical economic system characterized by the collective ownership of property and by the organization of labor for the common advantage of all members. **2. Communism. a.** A system of government in which the state plans and controls the economy and a single, often authoritarian party holds power, claiming to make progress toward a higher social order in which all goods are equally shared by the people. **b.** The Marxist-Leninist version of Communist doctrine that advocates the overthrow of capitalism by the revolution of the proletariat. [French *communisme,* from *commun,* common, from Old French, from Latin *commūnis.* See COMMUNE².]

Communism Peak. also **Mount** Communism. A mountain, 7,500 m (24,590 ft) high, of northeast Tadzhikistan in the Pamirs near the Chinese border.

Com·mu·nist (kŏm′yə-nĭst) *n. Abbr.* **Com. 1.a.** A member of a Marxist-Leninist party. **b.** A supporter of such a party or movement. **2.** A Communard. **3.** Often **communist.** A radical viewed as a subversive or revolutionary. —**Communist** *adj. Abbr.* **Com. 1.** Often **communist.** Relating to, characteristic of, or held to resemble communism or Communists. **2. communist.** Supporting, advocating, or serving to further communism: *communist propaganda.*

com·mu·nis·tic (kŏm′yə-nĭs′tĭk) *adj.* Of, characteristic of, or inclined to communism. —**com′mu·nis′ti·cal·ly** *adv.*

com·mu·ni·tar·i·an (kə-myo͞o′nĭ-târ′ē-ən) *n.* A member or supporter of a small cooperative or a collectivist community.

com·mu·ni·ty (kə-myo͞o′nĭ-tē) *n., pl.* **-ties.** *Abbr.* **com. 1.a.** A group of people living in the same locality and under the same government. **b.** The district or locality in which such a group lives. **2.** A group of people having common interests: *the scientific community; the international business community.* **3.a.** Similarity or identity: *a community of interests.* **b.** Sharing, participation, and fellowship. **4.** Society as a whole; the public. **5.** *Ecology.* **a.** A group of plants and animals living and interacting with one another in a specific region under relatively similar environmental conditions. **b.** The region occupied by a group of interacting organisms. —*attributive.* Often used to modify another noun: *community problems; community facilities.* [Middle English *communite,* citizenry, from Old French, from Latin *commūnitās,* fellowship, from *commūnis,* common. See COMMON.]

community antenna television *n. Abbr.* **CATV** See **cable television.**

community center *n.* A meeting place used by members of a community for social, cultural, or recreational purposes.

community chest *n.* A fund financed by private contributions for charitable organizations and welfare agencies.

community college *n.* A junior college without residential facilities that is often funded by the government.

community medicine *n.* Public health services emphasizing preventive medicine and epidemiology for members of a given community or region.

community property *n.* Property owned jointly by spouses.

com·mu·nize (kŏm′yə-nīz′) *tr.v.* **-nized, -niz·ing, -niz·es. 1.** To subject to public ownership or control. **2.** To convert to Communist principles or control. —**com′mu·ni·za′tion** (-nĭ-zā′shən) *n.*

com·mut·a·ble (kə-myo͞o′tə-bəl) *adj.* **1.** That can be substituted, interchanged, or revoked: *a commutable prison sentence.* **2.** Accessible to commuters: *"Seattle's next most commutable island is Vashon"* (Islands). —**com·mut′a·bil′i·ty** *n.*

com·mu·tate (kŏm′yə-tāt′) *tr.v.* **-tat·ed, -tat·ing, -tates.** To reverse the direction of (an alternating electric current) each half-cycle to produce a unidirectional current. [Back-formation from COMMUTATOR.]

com·mu·ta·tion (kŏm′yə-tā′shən) *n.* **1.** A substitution, an exchange, or an interchange. **2.a.** The substitution of one kind of payment for another. **b.** The payment substituted. **3.** The travel of a commuter. **4.** *Electricity.* **a.** Conversion of alternating to unidirectional current. **b.** Reversal of current direction. **5.** *Law.* Reduction of a penalty to a less severe one. [Middle English *commutacioun,* from Latin *commūtātiō, commūtātiōn-,* from *commūtātus,* past participle of *commūtāre,* to alter, exchange. See COMMUTE.]

commutation ticket *n.* A ticket issued at a reduced rate by a railroad or other transportation company for passage over a given route for a specified number of trips.

com·mu·ta·tive (kŏm′yə-tā′tĭv, kə-myo͞o′tə-tĭv) *adj.* **1.** Relating to, involving, or characterized by substitution, interchange, or exchange. **2.** Independent of order. Used of a logical or mathematical operation that combines objects or sets of objects two at a time. If $a \times b = b \times a$, the operation indicated by $\times$ is commutative. —**com·mu′ta·tiv′i·ty** (kə-myo͞o′tə-tĭv′ĭ-tē) *n.*

commutative group *n.* A mathematical group in which the result of multiplying one member by another is independent of the order of multiplication. Also called *Abelian group.*

com·mu·ta·tor (kŏm′yə-tā′tər) *n.* A cylindrical arrangement of insulated metal bars connected to the coils of a direct-current electric motor or generator, providing a unidirectional current from the generator or a reversal of current into the coils of the motor.

com·mute (kə-myo͞ot′) *v.* **-mut·ed, -mut·ing, -mutes.** —*intr.* **1.** To travel as a commuter. **2.a.** To make substitution or exchange. **b.** To serve as a substitute. **3.** To pay in gross, usually at a reduced rate, rather than in individual payments. **4.** *Mathematics & Logic.* To satisfy or engage in a commutative operation. —*tr.* **1.** To substitute (one thing for another); exchange. **2.** To change (a penalty, debt, or payment) to a less severe one. —**commute** *n.* An act or instance of commuting, especially the trip made by a commuter: *a 22-mile commute; an easy commute.* [Middle English *commuten,* to transform, from Latin *commūtāre* : *com-,* com- + *mūtāre,* to change; see **mei-¹** in Appendix.]

com·mut·er (kə-myo͞o′tər) *n.* One that travels regularly from one place to another, as from suburb to city and back.

Co·mo (kō′mō). A resort city of northern Italy near the Swiss border at the southwest end of **Lake Como.** The city was a Roman colony and became an independent commune in the 11th century. Population, 95,183.

co·mon·o·mer (kō-mŏn′ə-mər) *n. Chemistry.* One of the compounds that constitute a copolymer.

Com·o·rin (kŏm′ər-ĭn), **Cape.** A cape at the southernmost point of India projecting into the Indian Ocean.

Com·o·ros (kŏm′ə-rōz′). A country comprising the three main islands and numerous islets of the **Comoro Islands** in the Indian Ocean off southeast Africa between Mozambique and Madagascar. The islands declared their independence from France in 1975, although Mayotte, the largest of the group, voted to retain its status as a French territory. Moroni, on Grande Comoro Island, is the capital of the country. Population, 346,992.

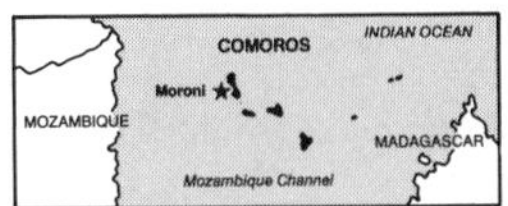

Comoros

co·mose (kō′mōs′) *adj. Botany.* Having a coma; comate.

comp¹ (kŏmp) *intr.v.* **comped, comp·ing, comps.** *Music.* To play a jazz accompaniment, as on a piano or guitar. [Short for ACCOMPANY.]

comp² (kŏmp) *n. Informal.* Something, such as a theater ticket or a book, given free of charge. [Short for COMPLIMENTARY.]

comp. *abbr.* **1.** Companion. **2.** Comparative. **3.** Compensation. **4.a.** Compilation; compiler. **b.** Compiled. **5.** Complete. **6.** Compose; composer. **7.** Composite; composition. compositor. **8.** Compound. **9.** Comprehensive. **10.** Comprising.

com·pact¹ (kəm-păkt′, kŏm-, kŏm′păkt′) *adj.* **1.** Closely and firmly united or packed together; dense: *compact clusters of flowers.* **2.** Occupying little space compared with others of its type: *a compact camera; a compact car.* **3.** Brief and to the point; concise: *a compact narration.* **4.** Marked by or having a short, solid physique: *a wrestler of compact build.* —**compact** (kəm-păkt′) *v.* **-pact·ed, -pact·ing, -pacts.** —*tr.* **1.** To press or join firmly together: *a kitchen device that compacted the trash.* **2.a.** To make by pressing or joining together; compose. **b.** To consoli-

ă pat	oi boy
ā pay	ou out
âr care	o͝o took
ä father	o͞o boot
ĕ pet	ŭ cut
ē be	ûr urge
ĭ pit	th thin
ī pie	*th* this
îr pier	hw which
ŏ pot	zh vision
ō toe	ə about, item
ô paw	♦ regionalism

Stress marks: **′** (primary); ′ (secondary), as in **dictionary** (dĭk′shə-nĕr′ē)

date; combine. —*intr.* To be capable of being pressed tightly together or to become so pressed: *garbage that compacts easily.* —**compact** (kŏm′păkt′) *n.* **1.** A small case containing a mirror, pressed powder, and a powder puff. **2.** An automobile that is bigger in size than a subcompact but smaller than an intermediate. [Middle English, from Latin *compāctus,* past participle of *compingere,* to put together : *com-,* com- + *pangere,* to fasten; see **pag-** in Appendix.] —**com·pact′ly** *adv.* —**com·pact′ness** *n.*

com·pact² (kŏm′păkt′) *n.* An agreement or a covenant. See Synonyms at **bargain.** [Latin *compactum,* neuter past participle of *compacīscī,* to make an agreement : *com-,* com- + *pacīscī,* to agree; see PACT.]

com·pact disk (kŏm′păkt′) or **compact disc** *n. Abbr.* **CD** A small optical disk on which matter such as data or music is encoded.

compact disk

com·pact·er (kəm-păk′tər, kŏm′păk′-) *n.* Variant of **compactor.**

com·pac·tion (kəm-păk′shən) *n.* The process of compacting or the state of being compacted.

com·pac·tor or **com·pact·er** (kəm-păk′tər, kŏm′păk′-) *n.* An apparatus that compresses refuse into relatively small packs for handy disposal.

com·pan·ion¹ (kəm-păn′yən) *n.* **1.** A person who accompanies or associates with another; a comrade. **2.** *Abbr.* **C., comp.** A person employed to assist, live with, or travel with another. **3.** One of a pair or set of things; a mate. —**companion** *tr.v.* **-ioned, -ion·ing, -ions.** To be a companion to; accompany. [Middle English *compaignyon,* from Old French *compaignon,* from Vulgar Latin *compāniō, compāniōn- : Latin *com-,* com- + Latin *pānis,* bread; see **pā-** in Appendix.]

com·pan·ion² (kəm-păn′yən) *n. Nautical.* A companionway.

com·pan·ion·a·ble (kəm-păn′yə-nə-bəl) *adj.* **1.** Having the qualities of a good companion; friendly. See Synonyms at **social. 2.** Suggestive of companionship: *reading together in companionable silence.* —**com·pan′ion·a·ble·ness** *n.* —**com·pan′ion·a·bly** *adv.*

com·pan·ion·ate (kəm-păn′yə-nĭt) *adj.* **1.** Having the qualities of a companion. **2.** Harmonious; suitable.

companionate marriage *n.* A marriage in which the partners agree not to have children and may divorce by mutual consent, with neither partner responsible for the financial welfare of the other.

companion cell *n.* A specialized parenchyma cell, located in the phloem of flowering plants and closely associated in development and function with a sieve-tube element.

companion plant·ing (plăn′tĭng) *n.* The cultivation of certain kinds of plants together in the same area, especially if one species will benefit from another, as planting an insect-repellent plant in a vegetable garden.

com·pan·ion·ship (kəm-păn′yən-shĭp′) *n.* The relationship of companions; fellowship.

com·pan·ion·way (kəm-păn′yən-wā′) *n. Nautical.* A staircase leading from a deck to the cabins or area below. [From *companion,* framed windows above a hatchway, companionway, probably alteration of obsolete Dutch *kompanje,* from Old French *compagne,* steward's cabin, storeroom, from Old Italian *(camera della) compagna,* (cabin for) provisions, pantry, from Vulgar Latin **compānia,* things eaten with bread : Latin *com-,* com- + Latin *pānis,* bread; see COMPANION¹.]

com·pa·ny (kŭm′pə-nē) *n., pl.* **-nies. 1.** A group of persons. See Synonyms at **band². 2.a.** One's companions or associates: *moved in fast company; is known by the company she keeps.* **b.** A guest or guests: *had company for the weekend.* **c.** The state of friendly companionship; fellowship: *was grateful for her company; friends who finally parted company.* **3.a.** A business enterprise; a firm. **b.** *Abbr.* **co., co, Co.** A partner or partners not specifically named in a firm's title: *Lee Rogers and Company.* **4.** A troupe of dramatic or musical performers: *a repertory company.* **5.a.** A subdivision of a military regiment or battalion that constitutes the lowest administrative unit. It is usually under the command of a captain and is made up of at least two platoons. **b.** A unit of firefighters. **6.** A ship's crew and officers. See Usage Note at **collective noun.** —*attributive.* Often used to modify another noun: *company policy; a company newsletter.* —**company** *tr.v.* **-nied, -ny·ing, -nies.** To accompany or associate with. [Middle English *compainie,* from Old French *compaignie,* from Vulgar Latin **compānia,* from **compāniō,* companion. See COMPANION¹.]

compass
Directional compass

com·pa·ny-grade officer (kŭm′pə-nē-grād′) *n.* A commissioned officer having the rank of second lieutenant, first lieutenant, or captain in the U.S. Army, Air Force, or Marine Corps. Also called *company officer.*

company town *n.* A town whose residents are dependent on the economic support of a single firm for maintenance of retail stores, schools, hospitals, and housing.

compar. *abbr.* Comparative.

com·pa·ra·ble (kŏm′pər-ə-bəl) *adj.* **1.** Admitting of comparison with another or others: *"The satellite revolution is comparable to Gutenberg's invention of movable type"* (Irvin Molotsky). **2.** Similar or equivalent: *pianists of comparable ability.* —**com′pa·ra·bil′i·ty, com′pa·ra·ble·ness** *n.* —**com′pa·ra·bly** *adv.*

comparable worth *n.* A theory holding that compensation for job classifications filled chiefly by women should be the same as for those classifications filled chiefly by men if the jobs, albeit dissimilar, are regarded as having equal value. According to this theory, workers' salaries should be calculated on a scale of socioeconomic value that transcends traditional supply and demand.

com·par·a·tist (kəm-păr′ə-tĭst) *n.* A person who employs the comparative method, as in studying literature. [French *comparatiste,* from *comparative,* comparative, from *comparer,* to compare. See COMPARE.]

com·par·a·tive (kəm-păr′ə-tĭv) *adj. Abbr.* **comp., compar. 1.** Relating to, based on, or involving comparison. **2.** Estimated by comparison; relative: *a comparative newcomer.* **3.** *Grammar.* Of, relating to, or being the intermediate degree of comparison of adjectives, as *better, sweeter,* or *more wonderful,* or adverbs, as *more softly.* **4.** *Linguistics.* **a.** Of or relating to the synchronic typological comparison of languages. **b.** Of or relating to the comparison of languages descended from a common ancestor: *comparative historical linguistics.* —**comparative** *n. Grammar.* **1.** The comparative degree. **2.** An adjective or adverb expressing the comparative degree. —**com·par′a·tive·ly** *adv.*

comparative method *n. Linguistics.* **1.** Comparison of languages with the goal of establishing their descent from a common ancestor. **2.** Comparison of phonemes, morphemes, words, or syntactic constructions in genetically related languages with the goal of reconstructing the sound system, grammar, or lexicon of the protolanguage.

com·pa·ra·tor (kŏm′pə-rā′tər, kəm-păr′ə-) *n.* Any of various instruments for comparing a measured property of an object, such as its shape, color, or brightness, with a standard.

com·pare (kəm-pâr′) *v.* **-pared, -par·ing, -pares.** —*tr.* **1.** To consider or describe as similar, equal, or analogous; liken. **2.** *Abbr.* **cp.** To examine in order to note the similarities or differences of. **3.** *Grammar.* To form the positive, comparative, or superlative degree of (an adjective or adverb). —*intr.* **1.** To be worthy of comparison; bear comparison: *two concert halls that just do not compare.* **2.** To draw comparisons. —**compare** *n.* Comparison: *a musician beyond compare.* —***idiom.* compare notes.** To exchange ideas, views, or opinions. [Middle English *comparen,* from Old French *comparer,* from Latin *comparāre,* from *compār,* equal : *com-,* com- + *pār,* equal; see **pere-²** in Appendix.] —**com·par′er** *n.*

USAGE NOTE: *Compare* usually takes the preposition *to* when it refers to the activity of describing the resemblances between unlike things: *He compared her to a summer day. Scientists sometimes compare the human brain to a computer.* It takes *with* when it refers to the act of examining two like things in order to discern their similarities or differences: *The police compared the forged signature with the original. The committee will have to compare the Senate's version of the bill with the version that was passed by the House.* When *compare* is used to mean "to liken (one) with another," *with* is traditionally held to be the correct form: *That little bauble is not to be compared with* (not *to*) *this enormous jewel.* But *to* is frequently used in this context and is not incorrect.

com·par·i·son (kəm-păr′ĭ-sən) *n.* **1.a.** The act of comparing or the process of being compared. **b.** A statement or estimate of similarities and differences. **2.** The quality of being similar or equivalent; likeness: *no comparison between the two books.* **3.** *Grammar.* The modification or inflection of an adjective or adverb to denote the positive, comparative, and superlative degrees. [Middle English *comparisoun,* from Old French *comparaison,* from Latin *comparātiō, comparātiōn-,* from *comparātus,* past participle of *comparāre,* to compare. See COMPARE.]

com·par·i·son-shop (kəm-păr′ĭ-sən-shŏp′) *intr.v.* **-shopped, -shop·ping, -shops.** To shop for bargains by comparing the prices of competing brands or stores.

com·part (kəm-pärt′) *tr.v.* **-part·ed, -part·ing, -parts.** To divide into parts. [Obsolete French *compartir,* from Italian *compartire,* from Late Latin *compartīrī,* to share : Latin *com-,* com- + Latin *partīrī,* to divide (from *pars, part-,* a part; see **pere-²** in Appendix).]

com·part·ment (kəm-pärt′mənt) *n. Abbr.* **compt. 1.** One of the parts or spaces into which an area is subdivided. **2.** A separate room, section, or chamber: *a storage compartment.* —**compartment** *tr.v.* **-ment·ed, -ment·ing, -ments.** To compartmentalize: *"The information has not been compartmented"* (John H. Cushman, Jr.). —**com′part·ment′al** (kŏm′pärt-mĕn′tl) *adj.*

com·part·men·tal·ize (kŏm′pärt-mĕn′tl-īz′, kəm-pärt′-) *tr.v.* **-ized, -iz·ing, -iz·es.** To separate into distinct parts, categories, or compartments: *"You learn . . . even the ability to compartmentalize ethics"* (Ellen Goodman). —**com′part·men′tal·i·za′tion** (-ĭ-zā′shən) *n.*

com·pass (kŭm′pəs, kŏm′-) *n.* **1.a.** A device used to determine geographic direction, usually consisting of a magnetic needle or needles horizontally mounted or suspended and free to pivot until aligned with the magnetic field of Earth. **b.** Another device, such as a radio compass or a gyrocompass, used for determining geographic direction. **2.** A V-shaped device for describing circles or circular arcs and for taking measurements, consisting of a pair of rigid, end-hinged legs, one of which is equipped with a pen, pencil, or other marker and the other with a sharp point providing a pivot about which the drawing leg is turned. Also called *pair of* *compasses.* **3.a.** An enclosing line or boundary; a circumference: *outside the compass of the fence.* See Synonyms at **circumference.** **b.** A restricted space or area: *four huge crates within the compass of the elevator.* **c.** Range or scope, as of understanding, perception, or authority: *"Lacking a coherent intellectual and moral commitment,* [he] *was forced to find his compass in personal experience"* (Doris Kearns Goodwin). See Synonyms at **range.** **—compass** *tr.v.* **-passed, -pass·ing, -pass·es. 1.** To make a circuit of; circle: *The sailboat compassed the island.* **2.** To surround; encircle. See Synonyms at **surround. 3.** To understand; comprehend. **4.** To succeed in carrying out; accomplish. See Synonyms at **reach. 5.** To scheme; plot. **—compass** *adj.* **1.** Forming a curved configuration. **2.** Semicircular. Used of bow windows. [Middle English *compas,* circle, compass, from Old French, from *compasser,* to measure, from Vulgar Latin **compassāre,* to pace off : Latin *com-,* com- + Latin *passus,* step; see PACE[1].] **—com′pass·a·ble** *adj.*

compass card *n.* A freely pivoting circular disk carrying the magnetic needles of a compass and marked with the 32 points of the compass and the 360 degrees of the circle.

com·pas·sion (kəm-păsh′ən) *n.* Deep awareness of the suffering of another coupled with the wish to relieve it. See Synonyms at **pity.** [Middle English *compassioun,* from Late Latin *compassiō, compassiōn-,* from *compassus,* past participle of *compatī,* to sympathize : Latin *com-,* com- + Latin *patī,* to suffer; see **pē(i)-** in Appendix.] **—com·pas′sion·less** *adj.*

com·pas·sion·ate (kəm-păsh′ə-nĭt) *adj.* Feeling or showing compassion; sympathetic. See Synonyms at **humane. —compassionate** (-nāt′) *tr.v.* **-at·ed, -at·ing, -ates.** To pity. **—com·pas′sion·ate·ly** *adv.* **—com·pas′sion·ate·ness** *n.*

compass plant *n.* A perennial herb *(Silphium laciniatum)* in the composite family, native to prairie regions of the Midwest United States and having radiate yellow flower heads and erect, basal, pinnately divided leaves.

com·pat·i·ble (kəm-păt′ə-bəl) *adj.* **1.** Capable of existing or performing in harmonious, agreeable, or congenial combination with another or others: *compatible family relationships.* **2.** Capable of orderly, efficient integration and operation with other elements in a system with no modification or conversion required. **3.** Capable of forming a chemically or biochemically stable system. **4.** Of or relating to a television system in which color broadcasts can be received in black and white by sets incapable of color reception. **5.** *Medicine.* Capable of being grafted, transfused, or transplanted from one individual to another without rejection: *compatible blood.* **—compatible** *n.* A device, such as a computer or computer software, that can be integrated into or used with another device or system of its type. [Middle English, from Medieval Latin *compatībilis,* from Late Latin *compatī,* to sympathize. See COMPASSION.] **—com·pat′i·bil′i·ty, com·pat′i·ble·ness** *n.* **—com·pat′i·bly** *adv.*

com·pa·tri·ot (kəm-pā′trē-ət, -ŏt′) *n.* **1.** A person from one's own country. **2.** A colleague. [French *compatriote,* from Late Latin *compatriōta* : Latin *com-,* com- + Late Latin *patriōta,* countryman; see PATRIOT.] **—com·pa′tri·ot′ic** (-ŏt′ĭk) *adj.*

compd. *abbr.* Compound.

com·peer (kŏm′pîr′, kəm-pîr′) *n.* **1.** A person of equal status or rank; a peer. **2.** A comrade, companion, or associate. [Middle English *comper,* from Old French, from Latin *compār,* equal. See COMPARE.]

com·pel (kəm-pĕl′) *tr.v.* **-pelled, -pel·ling, -pels. 1.** To force, drive, or constrain: *Duty compelled the soldiers to volunteer for the mission.* **2.** To necessitate or pressure by force; exact: *An energy crisis compels fuel conservation.* See Synonyms at **force. 3.** To exert a strong, irresistible force on; sway: *"The land, in a certain, very real way, compels the minds of the people"* (Barry Lopez). [Middle English *compellen,* from Latin *compellere* : *com-,* com- + *pellere,* to drive; see **pel-**[5] in Appendix.] **—com·pel′la·ble** *adj.* **—com·pel′la·bly** *adv.* **—com·pel′ler** *n.*

com·pel·la·tion (kŏm′pə-lā′shən) *n.* **1.** The act of addressing or designating someone by name. **2.** A name; an appellation. [Latin *compellātiō, compellātiōn-,* from *compellātus,* past participle of *compellāre,* to address. See **pel-**[5] in Appendix.]

com·pel·ling (kəm-pĕl′ĭng) *adj.* **1.** Urgently requiring attention: *a host of compelling socioeconomic problems.* **2.** Drivingly forceful: *compelling ambition and egotism.*

com·pend (kŏm′pĕnd′) *n.* A compendium.

com·pen·di·a (kəm-pĕn′dē-ə) *n.* A plural of **compendium.**

com·pen·di·ous (kəm-pĕn′dē-əs) *adj.* Containing or stating briefly and concisely all the essentials; succinct. [Middle English, from Late Latin *compendiōsus,* from Latin *compendium,* a shortening. See COMPENDIUM.] **—com·pen′di·ous·ly** *adv.* **—com·pen′di·ous·ness** *n.*

com·pen·di·um (kəm-pĕn′dē-əm) (-dē-ə)*n., pl.* **-di·ums** or **-di·a. 1.** A short, complete summary; an abstract. **2.** A list or collection of various items. [Latin, a shortening, from *compendere,* to weigh together : *com-,* com- + *pendere,* to weigh; see **(s)pen-** in Appendix.]

com·pen·sa·ble (kəm-pĕn′sə-bəl) *adj.* Being such as to entitle or warrant compensation: *compensable injuries.*

com·pen·sate (kŏm′pən-sāt′) *v.* **-sat·ed, -sat·ing, -sates.** *—tr.* **1.** To offset; counterbalance. **2.** To make satisfactory payment or reparation to; recompense or reimburse: *Management compensated us for the time we worked.* **3.** To stabilize the purchasing power of (a monetary unit) by changing the gold content in order to counterbalance price variations. *—intr.* To serve as or provide a substitute or counterbalance. [Latin *compēnsāre, compēnsāt-* : *com-,* com- + *pēnsāre,* to weigh; see **(s)pen-** in Appendix.] **—com′pen·sa′tive** (kŏm′pən-sā′tĭv, kəm-pĕn′sə-tĭv) *adj.* **—com′pen·sa′tor** *n.* **—com·pen′sa·to′ry** (kəm-pĕn′sə-tôr′ē, -tōr′ē) *adj.*

com·pen·sa·tion (kŏm′pən-sā′shən) *n. Abbr.* **comp. 1.** The act of compensating or the state of being compensated. **2.** Something, such as money, given or received as payment or reparation, as for a service or loss. **3.** *Biology.* The increase in size or activity of one part of an organism or organ that makes up for the loss or dysfunction of another. **4.** *Psychology.* Behavior that develops either consciously or unconsciously to offset a real or imagined deficiency, as in personality or physical ability. **—com′pen·sa′tion·al** *adj.*

com·pere (kŏm′pâr′) *Chiefly British. n.* The master of ceremonies, as of a television entertainment program or a variety show. **—compere** *v.* **-pered, -per·ing, -peres.** *—tr.* To serve as master of ceremonies for. *—intr.* To serve as the master of ceremonies. [French *compère,* godfather, companion, from Medieval Latin *compater* : Latin *com-,* com- + Latin *pater,* father; see PATER.]

com·pete (kəm-pēt′) *intr.v.* **-pet·ed, -pet·ing, -petes.** To strive with another or others to attain a goal, such as gaining an advantage or winning a victory. See Synonyms at **rival.** [Late Latin *competere,* to strive together, from Latin, to coincide, be suitable : *com-,* com- + Latin *petere,* to seek; see **pet-** in Appendix.]

com·pe·tence (kŏm′pĭ-təns) *n.* **1.a.** The state or quality of being adequately or well qualified; ability. See Synonyms at **ability. b.** A specific range of skill, knowledge, or ability. **2.** *Law.* The quality or condition of being legally qualified to perform an act. **3.** Sufficient means for a comfortable existence. **4.** *Microbiology.* The ability of bacteria to be genetically transformable. **5.** *Medicine.* The ability to respond immunologically to bacteria, viruses, or other antigenic agents.

com·pe·ten·cy (kŏm′pĭ-tən-se) *n., pl.* **-cies.** Competence.

com·pe·tent (kŏm′pĭ-tənt) *adj.* **1.** Properly or sufficiently qualified; capable: *a competent typist.* **2.** Adequate for the purpose: *a competent performance.* **3.** *Law.* Legally qualified or fit to perform an act. [Middle English, adequate, from Old French, from Latin *competēns, competent-,* present participle of *competere,* to be suitable. See COMPETE.] **—com′pe·tent·ly** *adv.*

com·pe·ti·tion (kŏm′pĭ-tĭsh′ən) *n.* **1.** The act of competing, as for profit or a prize; rivalry. **2.** A test of skill or ability; a contest: *a skating competition.* **3.** Rivalry between two or more businesses striving for the same customer or market. **4.** A competitor: *The competition has cornered the market.* **5.** *Ecology.* The simultaneous demand by two or more organisms for limited environmental resources, such as nutrients, living space, or light.

com·pet·i·tive (kəm-pĕt′ĭ-tĭv) *adj.* **1.** Of, involving, or determined by competition: *competitive games.* **2.** Liking competition or inclined to compete: *a highly competitive sales representative.* **3.** *Biochemistry.* Relating to the inhibition of enzyme activity that results from the reversible combination of an enzyme with an alternate compound and prevents normal substrate binding. **—com·pet′i·tive·ly** *adv.* **—com·pet′i·tive·ness** *n.*

com·pet·i·tor (kəm-pĕt′ĭ-tər) *n.* One that competes with another, as in sports or business; a rival.

Com·piégne (kōmp-yān′, kôN-pyĕn′yə). A city of northern France on the Oise River northeast of Paris. The armistice ending World War I was signed in a railroad car in a nearby forest on November 11, 1918. Adolf Hitler demanded that the same car be used for the formal surrender of France in World War II on June 22, 1940. Population, 40,384.

com·pi·la·tion (kŏm′pə-lā′shən) *n. Abbr.* **comp. 1.** The act of compiling. **2.** Something, such as a set of data, a report, or an anthology, that is compiled.

com·pile (kəm-pīl′) *tr.v.* **-piled, -pil·ing, -piles. 1.** To gather into a single book. **2.** To put together or compose from materials gathered from several sources: *compile an encyclopedia.* **3.** *Computer Science.* To translate (a program) into machine language. [Middle English *compilen,* from Old French *compiler,* probably from Latin *compīlāre,* to plunder : *com-,* com- + *pīla,* heap (of stones), pillar.]

com·pil·er (kəm-pī′lər) *n. Abbr.* **comp. 1.** One that compiles: *a compiler of anthologies.* **2.** *Computer Science.* A program that translates another program written in a high-level language into machine language so that it can be executed.

com·pla·cence (kəm-plā′səns) *n.* **1.** Contented self-satisfaction. **2.** Total lack of concern.

com·pla·cen·cy (kəm-plā′sən-sē) *n.* **1.** A feeling of contentment or self-satisfaction, especially when coupled with an unawareness of danger or trouble. **2.** An instance of contented self-satisfaction.

com·pla·cent (kəm-plā′sənt) *adj.* **1.** Contented to a fault; self-satisfied and unconcerned: *He had become complacent after years of success.* **2.** Eager to please; complaisant. [Latin *complacēns, complacent-,* present participle of *complacēre,* to please : *com-,* intensive pref.; see COM– + *placēre,* to please; see **plāk-**[1] in Appendix.] **—com·pla′cent·ly** *adv.*

com·plain (kəm-plān′) *intr.v.* **-plained, -plain·ing, -plains. 1.** To express feelings of pain, dissatisfaction, or resentment. **2.** To make a formal accusation or bring a formal charge. [Middle

compass plant
Silphium laciniatum

ă pat	oi boy
ā pay	ou out
âr care	o͝o took
ä father	o͞o boot
ĕ pet	ŭ cut
ē be	ûr urge
ĭ pit	th thin
ī pie	*th* this
îr pier	hw which
ŏ pot	zh vision
ō toe	ə about, item
ô paw	♦ regionalism

Stress marks: ′ (primary); ′ (secondary), as in **dictionary** (dĭk′shə-nĕr′ē)

English *compleinen,* from Old French *complaindre, complaign-,* from Vulgar Latin **complangere* : Latin *com-,* intensive pref.; see COM– + Latin *plangere,* to lament; see **plāk-²** in Appendix.] **—com·plain′er** *n.*

com·plain·ant (kəm-plā′nənt) *n. Law.* A party that makes a complaint or files a formal charge, as in court; a plaintiff.

com·plaint (kəm-plānt′) *n.* **1.** An expression of pain, dissatisfaction, or resentment. **2.** A cause or reason for complaining; a grievance. **3.a.** A bodily disorder or disease; a malady or an ailment. **b.** The symptom or distress about which a patient seeks medical assistance. **4.** *Law.* **a.** The presentation by the plaintiff in a civil action, setting forth the claim on which relief is sought. **b.** A formal charge, made under oath, of the commission of a crime or other such offense. [Middle English *compleinte,* from Old French *complainte,* from feminine past participle of *complaindre,* to complain. See COMPLAIN.]

com·plai·sance (kəm-plā′səns, -zəns) *n.* The inclination to comply willingly with the wishes of others; amiability.

com·plai·sant (kəm-plā′sənt, -zənt) *adj.* Exhibiting a desire or willingness to please; cheerfully obliging. [French, from Old French, present participle of *complaire,* to please, from Latin *complacēre.* See COMPLACENT.] **—com·plai′sant·ly** *adv.*

com·pleat (kəm-plēt′) *adj.* **1.** Of or characterized by a highly developed or wide-ranging skill or proficiency: *"The compleat speechwriter . . . comes to anonymity from Harvard Law"* (Israel Shenker). **2.** Being an outstanding example of a kind; quintessential: *"Here was the compleat modern misfit: the very air appeared to poison him; his every step looked treacherous and hard won"* (Stephen Schiff). [Variant of COMPLETE.]

com·plect (kəm-plĕkt′) *tr.v.* **-plect·ed, -plect·ing, -plects.** To join by weaving or twining together; interweave. [Latin *complectī,* to entwine : *com-,* com- + *plectere,* to plait; see **plek-** in Appendix.]

♦ **com·plect·ed** (kəm-plĕk′tĭd) *adj. Informal.* Marked by or having a particular facial complexion. Often used in combination: *"A white-haired and ruddy-complected priest stood on the deck of one of the trawlers"* (New York Times). *"Fewer still could fit the original job description of a raven-haired, smooth-complected, red-lipped innocent"* (Los Angeles Times). [Back-formation from *complection,* variant of COMPLEXION.]

♦ ***REGIONAL NOTE:*** *Complected* has a long history in American folk speech, showing up, for example, in 1806 in the journals of the Lewis and Clark Expedition: "[The Indians] *are . . . reather lighter complected . . . than the Indians of the Missouri"* (Meriwether Lewis). *Complected* has long been treated as a dialectal term in dictionaries, but it actually should be regarded as informal Standard English, since its wide distribution (including New England, the Midwest, the South, and elsewhere) disqualifies it as a true regionalism. Its use by one western Texas informant quoted in *DARE* extends its semantic domain beyond skin color to general appearance: *"a fat-complected man."*

com·ple·ment (kŏm′plə-mənt) *n.* **1.a.** Something that completes, makes up a whole, or brings to perfection. **b.** The quantity or number needed to make up a whole: *shelves with a full complement of books.* **c.** Either of two parts that complete the whole or mutually complete each other. **2.** An angle related to another so that the sum of their measures is 90°. **3.** *Grammar.* A word or words used after a verb to complete a predicate construction; for example, the phrase *to eat ice cream* in *We like to eat ice cream.* **4.** *Music.* An interval that completes an octave when added to a given interval. **5.** The full crew of officers and enlisted personnel required to run a ship. **6.** *Biochemistry.* A complex system of proteins found in normal blood serum that combines with antibodies to destroy pathogenic bacteria and other foreign cells. Also called *alexin.* **7.** *Mathematics & Logic.* For a universal set, the set of all elements in the set that are not in a specified subset. **—complement** (-mĕnt′) *tr.v.* **-ment·ed, -ment·ing, -ments.** To serve as a complement to: *Roses in a silver bowl complement the handsome cherry table.* [Middle English, from Old French, from Latin *complēmentum,* from *complēre,* to fill out. See COMPLETE.]

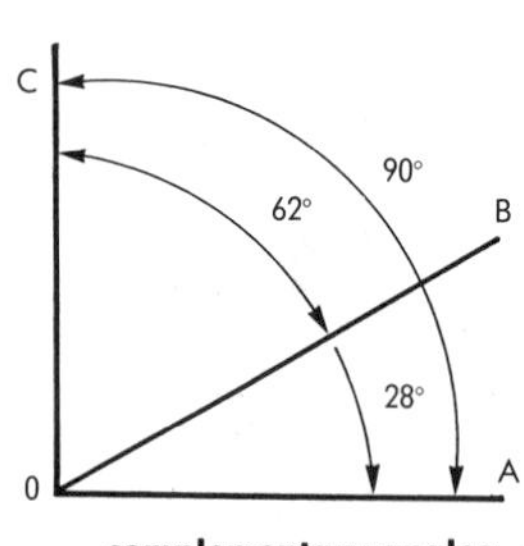

complementary angles

USAGE NOTE: *Complement* and *compliment,* though quite distinct in meaning, are sometimes confused because they are pronounced the same. *Complement* means "something that completes or brings to perfection": *The antique silver was a complement to the beautifully set table. Compliment* means "an expression or act of courtesy or praise": *They gave us a compliment on our beautifully set table.*

com·ple·men·tal (kŏm′plə-mĕn′tl) *adj.* Having to do with or being a complement. **—com′ple·men′tal·ly** *adv.*

com·ple·men·tar·i·ty (kŏm′plə-mĕn-tăr′ĭ-tē) *n.* The state or quality of being complementary: *"This is where the complementarity of the masculine and the feminine so acutely emerges. They are the necessary poles of a dialectic process"* (Therese Namenek).

com·ple·men·ta·ry (kŏm′plə-mĕn′tə-rē, -trē) *adj.* **1.** Forming or serving as a complement; completing. **2.** Supplying mutual needs or offsetting mutual lacks. **3.** *Genetics.* Of or relating to a group of genes that act in concert to produce a specific phenotype. **4.** *Biochemistry.* Of or relating to the specific pairing of the purines and pyrimidines between strands of a DNA or an RNA molecule. **—com′ple·men′ta·ri·ly** (-tə-rə-lē, -trə-lē, -mĕn-târ′ə-lē) *adv.* **—com′ple·men′ta·ri·ness** *n.*

complementary angles *pl.n. Mathematics.* Two angles whose sum is 90°.

complementary color *n.* Either one of two colors whose mixture in the right proportions produces white (in the case of light) or gray (in the case of pigment): *Red and green are complementary colors.*

complement fixation *n.* The binding of active serum complement to a specific antigen-antibody pair. It is used in various diagnostic tests, such as the Wasserman test, to detect the presence of a specific antigen or antibody.

com·plete (kəm-plēt′) *adj.* **-plet·er, -plet·est.** *Abbr.* **comp., cpl 1.** Having all necessary or normal parts, components, or steps; entire: *a complete meal.* **2.** *Botany.* Having all principal parts, namely, the sepals, petals, stamens, and pistil or pistils. Used of a flower. **3.** Having come to an end; concluded. **4.** Absolute; total: *"In Cairo I have seen buildings which were falling down as they were being put up, buildings whose incompletion was complete"* (William H. Gass). **5.a.** Skilled; accomplished: *a complete musician.* **b.** Thorough; consummate: *a complete coward.* **—complete** *tr.v.* **-plet·ed, -plet·ing, -pletes. 1.** To bring to a finish or an end: *She has completed her studies.* **2.** To make whole, with all necessary elements or parts: *A second child would complete their family.* [Middle English *complet,* from Latin *complētus,* past participle of *complēre,* to fill out : *com-,* intensive pref.; see COM– + *plēre,* to fill; see **pelə-¹** in Appendix.] **—com·plete′ly** *adv.* **—com·plete′ness** *n.* **—com·ple′tive** *adj.*

USAGE NOTE: *Complete* is sometimes held to be an absolute term like *perfect* or *chief,* which is not subject to comparison. Nonetheless, it can be qualified as *more* or *less,* for example. A majority of the Usage Panel accepts *His book is the most complete treatment of the subject.* See Usage Note at **perfect.**

complete blood count *n. Abbr.* **CBC** The determination of the quantity of each type of blood cell in a given sample of blood, often including the amount of hemoglobin, the hematocrit, and the proportions of various white cells. Also called *blood profile.*

complete metamorphosis *n. Zoology.* The complete form of metamorphosis in which an insect passes through for separate stages of growth, as embryo, larva, pupa, and imago. Also called *holometabolism.*

com·ple·tion (kəm-plē′shən) *n.* The act of completing or the state of being completed.

com·plex (kəm-plĕks′, kŏm′plĕks′) *adj.* **1.a.** Consisting of interconnected or interwoven parts; composite. **b.** Composed of two or more units: *a complex carbohydrate.* **2.** Involved or intricate, as in structure; complicated. **3.** *Grammar.* **a.** Consisting of at least one bound form. Used of a word. **b.** Consisting of an independent clause and at least one other independent or dependent clause. Used of a sentence. **—complex** (kŏm′plĕks′) *n.* **1.** A whole composed of interconnected or interwoven parts: *a complex of cities and suburbs; the military-industrial complex.* **2.** *Psychiatry.* A group of related, often repressed ideas and impulses that compel characteristic or habitual patterns of thought, feelings, and behavior. **3.** An exaggerated or obsessive concern or fear. **4.** *Medicine.* The combination of factors, symptoms, or signs of a disease or disorder that forms a syndrome. [Latin *complexus,* past participle of *complectī,* to entwine. See COMPLECT.] **—com·plex′ly** *adv.* **—com·plex′ness** *n.*

SYNONYMS: *complex, complicated, intricate, involved, tangled, knotty.* These adjectives mean having parts so interconnected as to make the whole perplexing. *Complex* implies a combination of many associated parts: *The composer transformed a simple folk tune into a complex set of variations. Complicated* stresses elaborate relationship of parts: *Middle Eastern politics is so complicated that even experts cannot agree on a cohesive policy. Intricate* refers to a pattern of intertwining parts that is difficult to follow or analyze: *"No one could soar into a more intricate labyrinth of refined phraseology"* (Anthony Trollope). *Involved* stresses confusion arising from the commingling of parts and the consequent difficulty of separating them: *The plot of the play has been criticized as being too involved. Tangled* strongly suggests the random twisting of many parts: *"Oh, what a tangled web we weave,/When first we practice to deceive!"* (Sir Walter Scott). *Knotty* stresses intellectual complexity leading to difficulty of solution or comprehension: *Even the professor couldn't clarify the knotty point.*

complex conjugate *n. Mathematics.* Either one of a pair of imaginary numbers whose real parts are identical, whose imaginary parts differ only in sign, and whose product is a real number; for example, $6 + 4i$ and $6 - 4i$ are complex conjugates whose product is 52.

complex fraction *n. Mathematics.* A fraction in which the numerator or the denominator or both contain fractions. Also called *compound fraction.*

com·plex·ion (kəm-plĕk′shən) *n.* **1.** The natural color, texture, and appearance of the skin, especially of the face. **2.** General character, aspect, or appearance: *findings that will alter the complexion of the problem.* **3.** The combination of the four humors of cold, heat, moistness, and dryness in specific proportions, thought in ancient and medieval physiology to control the temperament and the constitution of the body. [Middle English *complexioun,* physical constitution, from Old French *complexion,* from Late Latin *complexiō, complexiōn-,* balance of the humors, from Latin, combination, from *complexus,* past participle of *complectī,* to entwine. See COMPLECT.] **—com·plex′ion·al** *adj.*

com·plex·ioned (kəm-plĕk′shənd) *adj.* Of or having a specified complexion. Often used in combination: *fair-complexioned.*

com·plex·i·ty (kəm-plĕk′sĭ-tē) *n., pl.* **-ties. 1.** The quality or condition of being complex. **2.** Something complex: *a maze of bureaucratic and legalistic complexities.*

complex number *n. Mathematics.* Any number of the form $a + bi$, where a and b are real numbers and i is an imaginary number whose square equals -1.

complex plane *n. Mathematics.* A plane whose points have complex numbers as their coordinates.

complex variable *n. Mathematics.* An expression of the form $x + iy$, where x and y are real variables and $i^2 = -1$.

com·pli·ance (kəm-plī′əns) *n.* **1.a.** The act of complying with a wish, request, or demand. **b.** *Medicine.* Willingness to follow a prescribed course of treatment. **2.** A disposition or tendency to yield to the will of others. **3.a.** Extension or displacement of a loaded structure per unit load. **b.** Flexibility.

com·pli·an·cy (kəm-plī′ən-sē) *n.* Compliance.

com·pli·ant (kəm-plī′ənt) *adj.* Disposed or willing to comply; submissive. See Synonyms at **obedient. —com·pli′ant·ly** *adv.*

com·pli·ca·cy (kəm-plĭk′ə-sē) *n., pl.* **-cies. 1.** The state of being complicated. **2.** A complication.

com·pli·cate (kŏm′plĭ-kāt′) *tr. & intr.v.* **-cat·ed, -cat·ing, -cates. 1.** To make or become complex or perplexing. **2.** To twist or become twisted together. **—complicate** (-kĭt) *adj.* **1.** Complex, intricate, and involved. **2.** *Biology.* Folded longitudinally one or several times, as certain leaves or the wings of some insects. [Latin *complicāre, complicāt-,* to fold together : *com-,* com- + *plicāre,* to fold; see **plek-** in Appendix.]

com·pli·cat·ed (kŏm′plĭ-kā′tĭd) *adj.* **1.** Containing intricately combined or involved parts. **2.** Not easy to understand or analyze. See Synonyms at **complex, elaborate. —com′pli·cat′ed·ly** *adv.* **—com′pli·cat′ed·ness** *n.*

com·pli·ca·tion (kŏm′plĭ-kā′shən) *n.* **1.** The act of complicating. **2.** A confused or intricate relationship of parts. **3.** A factor, a condition, or an element that complicates. **4.** *Medicine.* A secondary disease, an accident, or a negative reaction occurring during the course of an illness and usually aggravating the illness.

com·plice (kŏm′plĭs) *n. Archaic.* An associate; an accomplice. [Middle English, from Old French, from Late Latin *complex, complic-,* one closely connected with : Latin *com-,* com- + Latin *plicāre,* to fold; see **plek-** in Appendix.]

com·plic·it (kəm-plĭs′ĭt) *adj.* Associated with or participating in a questionable act or a crime; having complicity: *newspapers complicit with the propaganda arm of a dictatorship.* [Back-formation from COMPLICITY.]

com·plic·i·ty (kəm-plĭs′ĭ-tē) *n., pl.* **-ties.** Involvement as an accomplice in a questionable act or a crime.

com·pli·er (kəm-plī′ər) *n.* One that complies: *a ready complier with all rules and regulations.*

com·pli·ment (kŏm′plə-mənt) *n.* **1.** An expression of praise, admiration, or congratulation. **2.** A formal act of civility, courtesy, or respect. **3. compliments.** Good wishes; regards: *Extend my compliments to your parents.* See Usage Note at **complement. —compliment** *tr.v.* **-ment·ed, -ment·ing, -ments. 1.** To pay a compliment to. **2.** To show fondness, regard, or respect for by giving a gift or performing a favor. [French, from Italian *complimento,* from Spanish *cumplimiento,* from *cumplir,* to complete, from Latin *complēre,* to fill up : *com-,* intensive pref.; see COM– + *plēre,* to fill; see **pele-**[1] in Appendix.]

com·pli·men·ta·ry (kŏm′plə-mĕn′tə-rē, -trē) *adj.* **1.** Expressing, using, or resembling a compliment: *a concert that received complimentary reviews.* **2.** Given free to repay a favor or as an act of courtesy: *complimentary copies of the new book.* **—com′pli·men′ta·ri·ly** *adv.*

complimentary close (klōz) *n.* Words, such as *Yours truly,* that appear at the end of a letter and just before the writer's signature, used as a polite termination of the letter.

com·plin (kŏm′plĭn) or **com·pline** (-plĭn, -plīn′) *n. Abbr.* **cpl** *Ecclesiastical.* **1.** The last of the seven canonical hours recited or sung just before retiring. **2.** The time of day appointed for this service. [Middle English, alteration (probably influenced by *matines,* matins; see MATINS) of *compli,* from Old French *complie,* from Medieval Latin *(hōra) complēta,* final (hour), from Latin *complētus,* past participle of *complēre,* to complete. See COMPLETE.]

com·ply (kəm-plī′) *intr.v.* **-plied, -ply·ing, -plies. 1.** To act in accordance with another's command, request, rule, or wish: *The patient complied with the physician's orders.* **2.** *Obsolete.* To be courteous or obedient. [Middle English *complien,* to carry out, fulfill, from Old French *complir,* from Latin *complēre.* See COMPLETE.]

com·po (kŏm′pō) *n., pl.* **-pos.** Any of various combined substances, such as mortar or plaster, formed by mixing ingredients. [Short for COMPOSITION.]

com·po·nent (kəm-pō′nənt) *n.* **1.** A constituent element, as of a system. See Synonyms at **element. 2.** A part of a mechanical or electrical complex. **3.** *Mathematics.* One of a set of two or more vectors having a sum equal to a given vector. **4.** Any of the minimum number of substances required to specify completely the composition of all phases of a chemical system. **—component** *adj.* Being or functioning as a constituent or an ingredient. [From Latin *compōnēns, compōnent-,* present participle of *compōnere,* to put together : *com-,* com- + *pōnere,* to put; see **apo-** in Appendix.] **—com′po·nen′tial** (kŏm′pə-nĕn′shəl) *adj.*

com·port (kəm-pôrt′, -pōrt′) *v.* **-port·ed, -port·ing, -ports.** *—tr.* To conduct or behave (oneself) in a particular manner: *Comport yourself with dignity.* *—intr.* To agree, correspond, or harmonize: *a foreign policy that comports with the principles of democracy.* [Middle English *comporten,* from Old French *comporter,* to conduct, from Latin *comportāre,* to bring together : *com-,* com- + *portāre,* to carry; see **per-**[2] in Appendix.]

com·port·ment (kəm-pôrt′mənt, -pōrt′-) *n.* Bearing; deportment.

com·pos (kŏm′pəs) *adj.* Compos mentis; sane: *"The well-being of the country, even the survival of the world, depends on the president's being compos"* (Morton Kondracke). [Short for COMPOS MENTIS.]

com·pose (kəm-pōz′) *v.* **-posed, -pos·ing, -pos·es.** *Abbr.* **comp.** *—tr.* **1.** To make up the constituent parts of; constitute or form: *an exhibit composed of French paintings; the many ethnic groups that compose our nation.* See Usage Note at **comprise. 2.** To make or create by putting together parts or elements. **3.** To create or produce (a literary or musical piece). **4.** To make (oneself) calm or tranquil: *Compose yourself and deal with the problems logically.* **5.** To settle or adjust; reconcile: *They managed to compose their differences.* **6.** To arrange aesthetically or artistically. **7.** *Printing.* To arrange or set (type or matter to be printed). *—intr.* **1.** To create a literary or a musical piece. **2.** *Printing.* To set type. [Middle English *composen,* from Old French *composer,* alteration (influenced by *poser,* to put, place; see POSE[1]) of Latin *compōnere.* See COMPONENT.]

com·posed (kəm-pōzd′) *adj.* Serenely self-possessed; calm. See Synonyms at **cool. —com·pos′ed·ly** (-pō′zĭd-lē) *adv.* **—com·pos′ed·ness** *n.*

com·pos·er (kəm-pō′zər) *n. Abbr.* **comp.** One that composes, especially a person who composes music.

com·pos·ing room (kəm-pō′zĭng) *n. Printing.* A room where typesetting is done.

composing stick *n. Printing.* A small, shallow tray, usually metal and with an adjustable end, in which type is set by hand. Also called *job stick.*

com·pos·ite (kəm-pŏz′ĭt) *adj. Abbr.* **comp. 1.** Made up of distinct components; compound. **2.** *Mathematics.* Having factors; factorable. **3.** *Botany.* Of, belonging to, or characteristic of the composite family. **4. Composite.** *Architecture.* Of, relating to, or being in the Composite order. **—composite** *n. Abbr.* **comp. 1.** A structure or an entity made up of distinct components. See Synonyms at **mixture. 2.** A complex material, such as wood or fiberglass, in which two or more distinct, structurally complementary substances, especially metals, ceramics, glasses, and polymers, combine to produce structural or functional properties not present in any individual component. **3.** *Botany.* A composite plant. [French, from Old French, from Latin *compositus,* past participle of *compōnere,* to put together. See COMPONENT.] **—com·pos′ite·ly** *adv.* **—com·pos′ite·ness** *n.*

composite family *n.* The largest family of flowering plants, the Compositae (Asteraceae), comprising about 1,100 genera and more than 20,000 species and characterized by many small flowers arranged in a head looking like a single flower and subtended by an involucre of bracts. A head may consist of both ray flowers and disk flowers, as in the sunflower, of disk flowers only, as in the burdock, or of ray flowers only, as in the dandelion.

composite number *n. Mathematics.* An integer exactly divisible by at least one number other than itself or 1.

Composite order *n. Architecture.* A Roman capital formed by superimposing Ionic volutes on a Corinthian capital.

composite photograph *n.* A photograph made by combining two or more separate photographs.

com·po·si·tion (kŏm′pə-zĭsh′ən) *n. Abbr.* **comp. 1.a.** The combining of distinct parts or elements to form a whole. **b.** The manner in which such parts are combined or related. **c.** General makeup: *the changing composition of the electorate.* **d.** The result or product of composing; a mixture or compound. **2.** Arrangement of artistic parts so as to form a unified whole. **3.a.** The art or act of composing a musical or literary work. **b.** A work of music, literature, or art, or its structure or organization. **4.** A short essay, especially one written as an academic exercise. **5.** *Law.* A settlement whereby the creditors of a debtor about to enter bankruptcy agree, in return for some financial consideration, usually proffered immediately, to the discharge of their respective claims on receipt of payment which is in a lesser amount than that actually owed on the claim. **6.** *Linguistics.* The formation of compounds from separate words. **7.** *Printing.* Typesetting. [Middle English *composicioun,* from Old French *composition,* from Latin *compositiō, compositiōn-,* from *compositus,* past participle of *compōnere,* to put together. See COMPONENT.] **—com′po·si′tion·al** *adj.* **—com′po·si′tion·al·ly** *adv.*

com·pos·i·tive (kəm-pŏz′ĭ-tĭv) *adj.* Synthetic; compounded.

com·pos·i·tor (kəm-pŏz′ĭ-tər) *n. Abbr.* **comp.** *Printing.* One that sets written material into type; a typesetter. [Middle English *compositur,* one who composes, settler of disputes, from

ă pat	oi boy
ā pay	ou out
âr care	ŏŏ took
ä father	ōō boot
ĕ pet	ŭ cut
ē be	ûr urge
ĭ pit	th thin
ī pie	*th* this
îr pier	hw which
ŏ pot	zh vision
ō toe	ə about, item
ô paw	♦ regionalism

Stress marks: **′** (primary); ′ (secondary), as in **dictionary** (dĭk′shə-nĕr′ē)

Anglo-Norman *compositour,* from Latin, writer, compiler, from *compōnere, composit-,* to put together. See COMPONENT.] **—com·pos′i·to′ri·al** (-tôr′ē-əl, -tōr′-) *adj.*

compos men·tis (mĕn′tĭs) *adj.* Of sound mind; sane. [Latin : *compos,* having mastery of + *mentis,* genitive of *mēns,* mind.]

com·post (kŏm′pōst′) *n.* **1.** A mixture of decaying organic matter, as from leaves and manure, used to improve soil structure and provide nutrients. **2.** A composition; a mixture. **—compost** *tr.v.* **-post·ed, -post·ing, -posts. 1.** To fertilize with a mixture of decaying organic matter. **2.** To convert (vegetable matter) to compost. [Middle English *compote,* from Old French, mixture, compost, from Latin *compositum,* mixture, from neuter past participle of *compōnere,* to put together. See COMPONENT.]

com·po·sure (kəm-pō′zhər) *n.* A calm or tranquil state of mind. See Synonyms at **equanimity.** [From COMPOSE.]

com·pote (kŏm′pōt) *n.* **1.** Fruit stewed or cooked in syrup. **2.** A long-stemmed dish used for holding fruit, nuts, or candy. [French, from Old French *composte,* mixture, from Latin *composita,* feminine past participle of *compōnere,* to put together. See COMPONENT.]

compote
Mid 19th-century American pressed glass compote made by the Boston and Sandwich Glass Company

com·pound¹ (kŏm-pound′, kəm-, kŏm′pound′) *v.* **-pound·ed, -pound·ing, -pounds.** *—tr.* **1.** To combine so as to form a whole; mix. **2.** To produce or create by combining two or more ingredients or parts: *pharmacists compounding prescriptions.* **3.** To settle (a debt, for example) by agreeing on an amount less than the claim; adjust. **4.** To compute (interest) on the principal and accrued interest. **5.** To add to; increase: *High winds compounded the difficulties of the firefighters.* *—intr.* **1.** To combine in or form a compound. **2.** To come to terms; agree. **—compound** (kŏm′pound′, kŏm-pound′, kəm-) *adj.* **1.** Consisting of two or more substances, ingredients, elements, or parts. **2.** *Botany.* Composed of more than one part. **—compound** (kŏm′pound′) *n.* *Abbr.* **comp., cpd. 1.** A combination of two or more elements or parts. See Synonyms at **mixture. 2.** *Linguistics.* A word that consists either of two or more elements that are independent words, such as *loudspeaker, baby-sit,* or *high school,* or of specially modified combining forms of words, such as Greek *philosophia,* from *philos,* "loving," and *sophia,* "wisdom." **3.** *Chemistry.* A pure, macroscopically homogeneous substance consisting of atoms or ions of two or more different elements in definite proportions that cannot be separated by physical means. A compound usually has properties unlike those of its constituent elements. **4.** *Botany.* **a.** A leaf whose blade is divided into two or more distinct leaflets. **b.** A pistil composed of two or more united carpels. [Alteration of Middle English *compounen,* from Old French *componre, compondre,* to put together, from Latin *compōnere.* See COMPONENT.] **—com·pound′a·ble** *adj.* **—com·pound′er** *n.*

com·pound² (kŏm′pound′) *n.* **1.** A building or buildings, especially a residence or group of residences, set off and enclosed by a barrier. **2.** An enclosed area used for confining prisoners of war. [Alteration of Malay *kampong,* village.]

com·pound-com·plex sentence (kŏm′pound-kŏm′plĕks) *n.* A sentence consisting of at least two coordinate independent clauses and one or more dependent clauses.

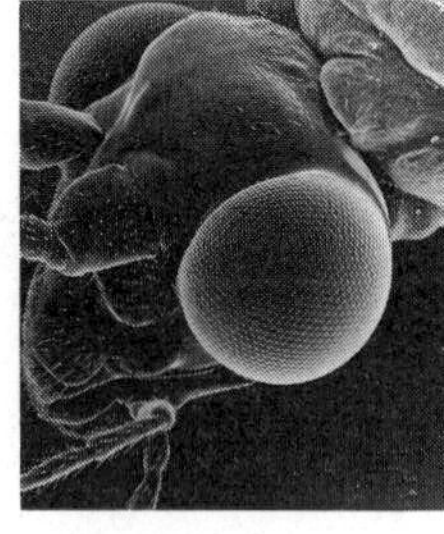

compound eye
Magnified compound eye of a green lacewing

compound eye *n.* The eye of most insects and some crustaceans, which is composed of many light-sensitive elements, each having its own refractive system and each forming a portion of an image.

compound fraction *n. Mathematics.* See **complex fraction.**

compound fracture *n.* A fracture in which broken bone fragments lacerate soft tissue and protrude through an open wound in the skin.

compound gland *n. Anatomy.* A gland composed of branching duct systems that combine, eventually to open into a secretory duct.

compound interest *n.* Interest computed on the accumulated unpaid interest as well as on the original principal.

compound lens *n.* See **lens** (sense 2).

compound microscope *n.* A microscope consisting of an objective and an eyepiece at opposite ends of an adjustable tube.

compound number *n. Mathematics.* A quantity that is expressed in terms of two or more different units, such as 10 pounds 5 ounces or 3 feet 4 inches.

compound sentence *n.* A sentence of two or more coordinate independent clauses, often joined by a conjunction or conjunctions, as *The problem was difficult, but I finally found the answer.*

compound sugar *n.* A sugar that yields two or more monosaccharides on hydrolysis.

com·pra·dor also **com·pra·dore** (kŏm′prə-dôr′) *n.* **1.** A go-between; an intermediary. **2.** A native-born agent in China and certain other Asian countries formerly employed by a foreign business to serve as a collaborator or an intermediary in commercial transactions. [Portuguese, from Late Latin *comparātor,* buyer, from Latin *comparāre,* to buy : *com-,* com- + *parāre,* to get; see **pere-¹** in Appendix.]

com·pre·hend (kŏm′prĭ-hĕnd′) *tr.v.* **-hend·ed, -hend·ing, -hends. 1.** To take in the meaning, nature, or importance of; grasp. See Synonyms at **apprehend. 2.** To take in as a part; include. See Synonyms at **include.** [Middle English *comprehenden,* from Latin *comprehendere* : *com-,* com- + *prehendere,* to grasp; see **ghend-** in Appendix.] **—com′pre·hend′i·ble** *adj.* **—com′pre·hend′ing·ly** *adv.*

com·pre·hen·si·ble (kŏm′prĭ-hĕn′sə-bəl) *adj.* Readily comprehended or understood; intelligible. [Latin *comprehēnsibilis,* from *comprehēnsus,* past participle of *comprehendere,* to comprehend. See COMPREHEND.] **—com′pre·hen′si·bil′i·ty, com′pre·hen′si·ble·ness** *n.* **—com′pre·hen′si·bly** *adv.*

com·pre·hen·sion (kŏm′prĭ-hĕn′shən) *n.* **1.a.** The act or fact of grasping the meaning, nature, or importance of; understanding. **b.** The knowledge that is acquired in this way. **2.** Capacity to include. **3.** *Logic.* The sum of meanings and corresponding implications inherent in a term. [Middle English *comprehensioun,* from Latin *comprehēnsiō, comprehēnsiōn-,* from *comprehēnsus,* past participle of *comprehendere,* to comprehend. See COMPREHEND.]

com·pre·hen·sive (kŏm′prĭ-hĕn′sĭv) *adj.* **1.** So large in scope or content as to include much: *a comprehensive history of the revolution.* **2.** Marked by or showing extensive understanding: *comprehensive knowledge.* **—comprehensive** *n.* **1.** Often **comprehensives.** Examinations covering the entire field of major study, given in the final undergraduate or graduate year of college. **2.** *Abbr.* **comp.** A preliminary layout showing all the elements planned for an advertisement. [Late Latin *comprehēnsīvus,* conceivable, from *comprehēnsus,* past participle of *comprehendere,* to comprehend. See COMPREHEND.] **—com′pre·hen′sive·ly** *adv.* **—com′pre·hen′sive·ness** *n.*

com·press (kəm-prĕs′) *tr.v.* **-pressed, -press·ing, -press·es. 1.** To press together: *compressed her lips.* **2.** To make more compact by or as if by pressing. See Synonyms at **contract. —compress** (kŏm′prĕs′) *n.* **1.** *Medicine.* A soft pad of gauze or other material applied with pressure to a part of the body to control hemorrhage or to supply heat, cold, moisture, or medication to alleviate pain or reduce infection. **2.** A machine for compressing material. [Middle English *compressen,* from Old French *compresser,* from Late Latin *compressāre,* frequentative of Latin *comprimere* : *com-,* com- + *premere,* to press; see **per-⁴** in Appendix.]

com·pressed (kəm-prĕst′) *adj.* **1.** Pressed together or into less volume or space. **2.** *Biology.* Flattened, especially laterally or lengthwise, as certain leafstalks or the bodies of many fishes.

compressed air *n.* Air under greater than atmospheric pressure, especially when used to power a mechanical device or to provide a portable supply of oxygen.

com·press·i·ble (kəm-prĕs′ə-bəl) *adj.* That can be compressed: *compressible packing materials; a compressible box.* **—com·press′i·bil′i·ty, com·press′i·ble·ness** *n.*

com·pres·sion (kəm-prĕsh′ən) *n.* **1.a.** The act or process of compressing. **b.** The state of being compressed. **2.a.** The process by which the working substance in a heat engine, such as the vapor mixture in the cylinder of an internal-combustion engine, is compressed. **b.** The engine cycle during which this process occurs. **—com·pres′sion·al** *adj.*

compression wave *n.* A wave propagated by means of the compression of a fluid, as a sound wave in air is.

com·pres·sive (kəm-prĕs′ĭv) *adj.* Serving to or able to compress. **—com·pres′sive·ly** *adv.*

com·pres·sor (kəm-prĕs′ər) *n.* One that compresses, especially a machine used to compress gases.

com·prise (kəm-prīz′) *tr.v.* **-prised, -pris·ing, -pris·es. 1.** To consist of; be composed of: *"The French got . . . French Equatorial Africa, comprising several territories"* (Alex Shoumatoff). **2.** To include; contain: *"The word 'politics' . . . comprises, in itself, a difficult study of no inconsiderable magnitude"* (Charles Dickens). See Synonyms at **include. 3.** *Usage Problem.* To compose; constitute: *"Put together the slaughterhouses, the steel mills, the freight yards . . . that comprised the city"* (Saul Bellow). [Middle English *comprisen,* from Old French *compris,* past participle of *comprendre,* to include, from Latin *comprehendere.* See COMPREHEND.] **—com·pris′a·ble** *adj.*

USAGE NOTE: The traditional rule states that the whole *comprises* the parts; the parts *compose* the whole. In strict usage: *The Union comprises 50 states. Fifty states compose* (or *constitute* or *make up*) *the Union.* While this distinction is still maintained by many writers, *comprise* is increasingly used, especially in the passive, in place of *compose: The Union is comprised of 50 states.* In an earlier survey, a majority of the Usage Panel found this use of *comprise* unacceptable. See Usage Note at **include.**

com·pro·mise (kŏm′prə-mīz′) *n.* **1.a.** A settlement of differences in which each side makes concessions. **b.** The result of such a settlement. **2.** Something that combines qualities or elements of different things: *The incongruous design is a compromise between high tech and early American.* **3.** A concession to something detrimental or pejorative: *a compromise of morality.* **—compromise** *v.* **-mised, -mis·ing, -mis·es.** *—tr.* **1.** To settle by concessions. **2.** To expose or make liable to danger, suspicion, or disrepute: *an embassy that was compromised by hidden listening devices.* **3.** *Obsolete.* To pledge mutually. *—intr.* To make a compromise. [Middle English *compromis,* from Old French, from Latin *comprōmissum,* mutual promise, from neuter past participle of *comprōmittere,* to promise mutually : *com-,* com- + *prōmittere,* to promise; see PROMISE.] **—com′pro·mis′er** *n.*

compt. *abbr.* Compartment.

Comp·ton (kŏmp′tən). A city of southern California, a residential and industrial suburb between Los Angeles and Long Beach. Population, 81,286.

Compton, **Arthur Holly.** 1892–1962. American physicist. He shared a 1927 Nobel Prize for his discovery of the Compton effect.

Compton effect *n.* The increase in wavelength of electromagnetic radiation, especially of an x-ray or a gamma-ray photon, scattered by an electron. [After Arthur Holly COMPTON.]

comp·trol·ler (kən-trō′lər) *n.* Variant of **controller** (sense 2).

com·pul·sion (kəm-pŭl′shən) *n.* **1.a.** The act of compelling. **b.** The state of being compelled. **2.a.** An irresistible impulse to act, regardless of the rationality of the motivation: *"The compulsion to protect the powerful from the discomfort of public disclosure feeds further abuse and neglect"* (Boston Globe). **b.** An act or acts performed in response to such an impulse. [Middle English, from Old French, from Late Latin *compulsiō, compulsiōn-,* from Latin *compulsus,* past participle of *compellere,* to compel. See COMPEL.]

com·pul·sive (kəm-pŭl′sĭv) *adj.* **1.** Having the capacity to compel: *a frightening, compulsive novel.* **2.** *Psychology.* Caused or conditioned by compulsion or obsession. **—compulsive** *n.* A person with behavior patterns governed by a compulsion. **—com·pul′sive·ly** *adv.* **—com·pul′sive·ness** *n.* **—com′pul·siv′i·ty** (kŏm′pŭl-sĭv′ĭ-tē, kəm-) *n.*

com·pul·so·ry (kəm-pŭl′sə-rē) *adj.* **1.** Obligatory; required: *a compulsory examination.* **2.** Employing or exerting compulsion; coercive. **—compulsory** *n., pl.* **-ries.** *Sports.* A school figure. Often used in the plural. **—com·pul′so·ri·ly** *adv.* **—com·pul′so·ri·ness** *n.*

com·punc·tion (kəm-pŭngk′shən) *n.* **1.** A strong uneasiness caused by a sense of guilt. See Synonyms at **penitence. 2.** A sting of conscience or a pang of doubt aroused by wrongdoing or the prospect of wrongdoing. See Synonyms at **qualm.** [Middle English *compunccioun,* from Old French *componction,* from Late Latin *compunctiō, compunctiōn-,* sting of conscience, puncture, from *compunctus,* past participle of *compungere,* to sting : *com-,* intensive pref.; see COM– + *pungere,* to prick; see **peuk-** in Appendix.] **—com·punc′tious** (-shəs) *adj.* **—com·punc′tious·ly** *adv.*

com·pur·ga·tion (kŏm′pər-gā′shən) *n. Law.* An ancient form of trial in which an accused person could call 11 people to swear to their belief in his innocence. [Late Latin *compūrgātiō, compūrgātiōn-,* complete purification, from Latin *compūrgātus,* past participle of *compūrgāre,* to purify completely : *com-,* intensive pref.; see COM– + *pūrgāre,* to purify; see **peuə-** in Appendix.]

com·pu·ta·tion (kŏm′pyo͞o-tā′shən) *n.* **1.a.** The act or process of computing. **b.** A method of computing. **2.** The result of computing. **3.** The act of operating a computer. **—com′pu·ta′tion·al** *adj.* **—com′pu·ta′tion·al·ly** *adv.*

com·pute (kəm-pyo͞ot′) *v.* **-put·ed, -put·ing, -putes.** *—tr.* **1.** To determine by mathematics, especially by numerical methods: *computed the tax due.* See Synonyms at **calculate. 2.** To determine by the use of a computer. *—intr.* **1.** To determine an amount or number. **2.** To use a computer. **—compute** *n.* Computation: *amounts beyond compute.* [Latin *computāre* : *com-,* com- + *putāre,* to reckon; see **peu-** in Appendix. N., from Late Latin *computus,* from Latin *computāre,* to compute.] **—com·put′a·bil′i·ty** *n.* **—com·put′a·ble** *adj.*

com·put·er (kəm-pyo͞o′tər) *n.* **1.** A device that computes, especially a programmable electronic machine that performs high-speed mathematical or logical operations or that assembles, stores, correlates, or otherwise processes information. **2.** One who computes. *—attributive.* Often used to modify another noun: *computer programming; computer software.*

computer crime *n.* Criminal activity directly related to the use of computers, specifically illegal trespass into the computer system or database of another, manipulation or theft of stored or on-line data, or sabotage of equipment and data. **—computer criminal** *n.*

com·put·er·dom (kəm-pyo͞o′tər-dəm) *n.* The world of computers and those who use them.

com·put·er·ese (kəm-pyo͞o′tə-rēz′, -rēs′) *n.* The technical language of those involved in computer technology.

com·put·er·ist (kəm-pyo͞o′tər-ĭst) *n.* One who uses or operates a computer.

com·put·er·ize (kəm-pyo͞o′tə-rīz′) *tr.v.* **-ized, -iz·ing, -iz·es.** *Usage Problem.* **1.** To furnish with a computer or computer system. **2.** To enter, process, or store (information) in a computer or system of computers. See Usage Note at **–ize. —com·put′er·iz′a·ble** *adj.* **—com·put′er·i·za′tion** (-pyo͞o′tər-ĭ-zā′shən) *n.*

com·put·er·ized (kəm-pyo͞o′tə-rīzd′) *adj.* Of or relating to a computer or the use of a computer.

computerized axial tomography *n. Abbr.* **CAT** Tomography in which computer analysis of a series of cross-sectional scans made along a single axis of a bodily structure or tissue is used to construct a three-dimensional image of that structure. The technique is used in diagnostic studies of internal bodily structures, as in the detection of tumors or brain aneurysms.

computerized tomography *n. Abbr.* **CT** Computerized axial tomography.

computer literacy *n.* The ability to operate a computer and to understand the language used in working with a specific system or systems. **—computer literate** *adj.*

computer virus *n.* A computer program that is designed to replicate itself by copying itself into the other programs stored in a computer. It may be benign or have a negative effect, such as causing a program to operate incorrectly or filling a computer's memory with unwanted codes.

Comr. *abbr.* Commissioner.

com·rade (kŏm′răd′, -rəd) *n.* **1.** A person who shares one's interests or activities; a friend or companion. **2.** Often **Comrade.** A fellow member of a group, especially a fellow member of the Communist Party. [French *camarade,* from Old French, roommate, from Old Spanish *camarada,* barracks company, roommate, from *camara,* room, from Late Latin *camera.* See CHAMBER.] **—com′rade·ship′** *n.*

WORD HISTORY: A comrade can be socially or politically close, a closeness that is found at the etymological heart of the word *comrade.* In Spanish the Latin word *camara,* with its Late Latin meaning "chamber, room," was retained, and the derivative *camarada,* with the sense "roommates, especially barrack mates," was formed. *Camarada* then came to have the general sense "companion." English borrowed the word from Spanish and French, English *comrade* being first recorded in the 16th century. The political sense of *comrade,* now associated with Communism, had its origin in the late-19th-century use of the word as a title by socialists and communists in order to avoid such forms of address as *mister.* This usage, which originated during the French Revolution, is first recorded in English in 1884.

Com·sat (kŏm′săt′). A trademark used for a communications satellite.

Com·stock (kŏm′stŏk′, kŭm′-), **Anthony.** 1844–1915. American reformer. As organizer and secretary of the New York Society for the Suppression of Vice, he became notorious for his moral crusades against literature and artwork that he considered obscene.

Com·stock·er·y (kŏm′stŏk′ə-rē, kŭm′-) *n.* Censorship of literature and other forms of expression because of perceived immorality or obscenity. [After Anthony COMSTOCK.]

WORD HISTORY: Bowdlerism, named after Dr. Thomas Bowdler (1754–1825), has been around longer than Comstockery, named for Anthony Comstock (1844–1915). All Bowdler did to enter the world of common nouns was to expurgate Shakespeare, the Bible, and Gibbon's *History of the Decline and Fall of the Roman Empire.* On the other hand, Comstock, the organizer and secretary of the New York Society for the Suppression of Vice, helped destroy 160 tons of literature and pictures that he deemed immoral. *Comstockery,* the word honoring his achievements, is first recorded in 1905 in a letter by George Bernard Shaw to the *New York Times:* "*Comstockery* is the world's standing Joke at the expense of the United States. . . . It confirms the deep-seated conviction of the Old World that America is a provincial place, a second rate country-town civilization after all."

Comstock Lode. A rich vein of gold and silver discovered in 1859 at Virginia City in western Nevada. Because of wasteful mining techniques, it was largely abandoned by 1898.

com·symp (kŏm′sĭmp′) *n. Slang.* A Communist Party sympathizer. [COM(MUNIST) + SYMP(ATHIZER).]

Comte (kôNt), **(Isidore) Auguste (Marie François).** 1798–1857. French philosopher known as the founder of positivism. He also established sociology as a systematic study.

Com·tism (kŏm′tĭz′əm) *n.* The philosophy of Auguste Comte; positivism. **—Com′tist** (kŏm′tĭst) *n.*

con¹ (kŏn) *adv.* In opposition or disagreement; against: *debated the issue pro and con.* **—con** *n.* **1.** An argument or opinion against something. **2.** One that holds an opposing opinion or view. [Middle English, short for *contra,* from Latin *contrā,* against. See CONTRA–.]

con² (kŏn) *tr.v.* **conned, con·ning, cons. 1.** To study, peruse, or examine carefully. **2.** To learn or commit to memory. [Middle English *connen,* to know, from Old English *cunnan.* See **gnō-** in Appendix.] **—con′ner** *n.*

con³ or **conn** (kŏn) *Nautical.—tr.v.* **conned, con·ning, cons** or **conns.** To direct the steering or course of (a vessel). *—n.* **1.** The station or post of the person who steers a vessel. **2.** The act or process of steering a vessel. [From *cond,* from Middle English *conduen,* from Old French *conduire,* from Latin *condūcere,* to lead together. See CONDUCE.]

con⁴ (kŏn) *Slang. tr.v.* **conned, con·ning, cons.** To swindle (a victim) by first winning his or her confidence; dupe. **—con** *n.* A swindle. **—con** *adj.* Of, relating to, or involving a swindle or a fraud: *a con artist; a con job.* [Short for CONFIDENCE.]

con⁵ (kŏn) *n. Slang.* A convict.

con. *abbr.* **1.** *Music.* Concerto. **2.** *Law.* Conclusion. **3.** *Latin.* Conjunx (wife). **4.** Connection. **5.** Consolidate; consolidated. **6.** Or **Con.** Consul. **7.** Continued.

con– *pref.* Variant of **com–.**

Con·a·kry (kŏn′ə-krē). The capital and largest city of Guinea, in the southwest part of the country on the Atlantic Ocean. It is on an island connected with the mainland by causeway. Population, 600,000.

con a·mo·re (kŏn′ ə-môr′ē, -mōr′ē, kôn′ ä-mô′rā) *adv.* **1.** *Music.* Lovingly; tenderly. Used chiefly as a direction. **2.** With devotion or zeal. [Italian : *con,* with + *amore,* love.]

computer
Personal computer with monitor, disk drive, and keyboard

ă pat	oi boy
ā pay	ou out
âr care	o͝o took
ä father	o͞o boot
ĕ pet	ŭ cut
ē be	ûr urge
ĭ pit	th thin
ī pie	*th* this
îr pier	hw which
ŏ pot	zh vision
ō toe	ə about, item
ô paw	♦ regionalism

Stress marks: ′ (primary); ′ (secondary), as in **dictionary** (dĭk′shə-nĕr′ē)

Co•nant (kō′nənt), **James Bryant.** 1893–1978. American educator who was president of Harvard University (1933–1953) and served as ambassador to West Germany (1955–1957).

co•na•tion (kō-nā′shən) *n. Psychology.* The aspect of mental processes or behavior directed toward action or change and including impulse, desire, volition, and striving. [Latin *cōnātiō, cōnātiōn-,* effort, from *cōnātus,* past participle of *cōnārī,* to try.] **—co•na′tion•al** *adj.* **—co′na•tive** (kō′nə-tĭv, kŏn′ə-) *adj.*

con bri•o (kŏn brē′ō, kôn) *adv. Music.* With great energy; vigorously. Used chiefly as a direction. [Italian : *con,* with + *brio,* vigor.]

conc. *abbr.* **1.** Concentrate. **2.** Concrete.

con•cat•e•nate (kŏn-kăt′n-āt′, kən-) *tr.v.* **-nat•ed, -nat•ing, -nates. 1.** To connect or link in a series or chain. **2.** *Computer Science.* To arrange (strings of characters) into a chained list. **—concatenate** (-nĭt, -nāt′) *adj.* Connected in a series. [Late Latin *concatēnāre, concatēnāt-* : *com-,* com- + *catēnāre,* to bind (from Latin *catēna,* chain).] **—con•cat′e•na′tion** *n.*

con•cave (kŏn-kāv′, kŏn′kāv′) *adj.* Curved like the inner surface of a sphere. **—concave** *n.* A concave surface, structure, or line. **—concave** *tr.v.* **-caved, -cav•ing, -caves.** To make concave. [Middle English, from Latin *concavus* : *com-,* intensive pref.; see COM– + *cavus,* hollow; see **keuə-** in Appendix.] **—con•cave′ly** *adv.* **—con•cave′ness** *n.*

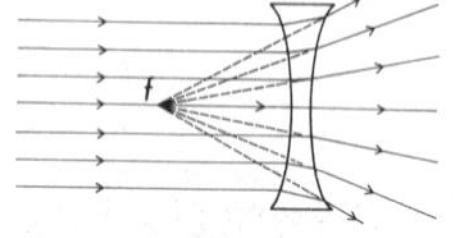

concave
Light passing through a double-concave lens, with f indicating the focus

con•cav•i•ty (kŏn-kăv′ĭ-tē) *n., pl.* **-ties. 1.** The state of being curved like the inner surface of a sphere. **2.** A surface or structure configured in such a curve: *"a perfect concavity of white sand lined with palm . . . trees"* (Islands).

con•ca•vo-con•cave (kŏn-kā′vō-kŏn-kāv′) *adj.* Concave on both surfaces; biconcave. Used of a lens.

con•ca•vo-con•vex (kŏn-kā′vō-kŏn-vĕks′) *adj.* **1.** Concave on one side and convex on the other. **2.** Having greater curvature on the concave side than on the convex side. Used of a lens.

con•ceal (kən-sēl′) *tr.v.* **-cealed, -ceal•ing, -ceals.** To keep from being seen, found, observed, or discovered; hide. See Synonyms at **hide**[1]. [Middle English *concelen,* from Old French *conceler,* from Latin *concēlāre* : *com-,* intensive pref.; see COM– + *cēlāre,* to hide; see **kel-**[1] in Appendix.] **—con•ceal′a•ble** *adj.* **—con•ceal′er** *n.* **—con•ceal′ment** *n.*

con•cede (kən-sēd′) *v.* **-ced•ed, -ced•ing, -cedes.** *—tr.* **1.** To acknowledge, often reluctantly, as being true, just, or proper; admit. See Synonyms at **acknowledge. 2.** To yield or grant (a privilege or right, for example). See Synonyms at **grant.** *—intr.* To make a concession: yield: *The losing candidate conceded at midnight after the polls had closed.* [French *concéder,* from Latin *concēdere* : *com-,* intensive pref.; see COM– + *cēdere,* to yield; see **ked-** in Appendix.] **—con•ced′ed•ly** (-sē′dĭd-lē) *adv.* **—con•ced′er** *n.*

con•ceit (kən-sēt′) *n.* **1.** A favorable and especially unduly high opinion of one's own abilities or worth. **2.** An ingenious or witty turn of phrase or thought. **3.a.** A fanciful poetic image, especially an elaborate or exaggerated comparison. **b.** A poem or passage consisting of such an image. **4.a.** The result of intellectual activity; a thought or an opinion. **b.** A fanciful thought or idea. **5.a.** A fancy article; a knickknack. **b.** An extravagant, fanciful, and elaborate construction or structure: *"An eccentric addition to the lobby is a life-size wooden horse, a 19th century conceit"* (Mimi Sheraton). **—conceit** *tr.v.* **-ceit•ed, -ceit•ing, -ceits. 1.** *Chiefly British.* To take a fancy to. **2.** *Obsolete.* To understand; conceive. [Middle English, mind, conception, from Anglo-Norman *conceite,* from Late Latin *conceptus.* See CONCEPT.]

SYNONYMS: *conceit, amour-propre, egoism, egotism, narcissism, vanity.* The central meaning shared by these nouns is "a regarding of oneself with often excessive favor": *constant boasting that reveals conceit; insulted her amour-propre; imperturbable egoism; arrogance and egotism betrayed by a glance; lack of consideration arising from narcissism; immoderate and incurable vanity.* ***ANTONYM:*** *humility.*

con•ceit•ed (kən-sē′tĭd) *adj.* Holding or characterized by an unduly high opinion of oneself; vain. **—con•ceit′ed•ly** *adv.* **—con•ceit′ed•ness** *n.*

con•ceive (kən-sēv′) *v.* **-ceived, -ceiv•ing, -ceives.** *—tr.* **1.** To become pregnant with (offspring). **2.** To form or develop in the mind; devise: *conceive a plan to increase profits.* **3.** To apprehend mentally; understand: *couldn't conceive the meaning of that sentence.* **4.** To be of the opinion that; think: *didn't conceive such a tragedy could occur.* *—intr.* **1.** To form or hold an idea: *Ancient peoples conceived of the earth as flat.* **2.** To become pregnant. [Middle English *conceiven,* from Old French *concevoir, conceiv-,* from Latin *concipere* : *com-,* intensive pref.; see COM– + *capere,* to take; see **kap-** in Appendix.] **—con•ceiv′a•bil′i•ty, con•ceiv′a•ble•ness** *n.* **—con•ceiv′a•ble** *adj.* **—con•ceiv′a•bly** *adv.* **—con•ceiv′er** *n.*

con•cel•e•brate (kən-sĕl′ə-brāt′) *v.* **-brat•ed, -brat•ing, -brates.** *—intr.* To take part in a concelebration of the Eucharist. *—tr.* To take part in (a Eucharist) as a joint celebrant. [Latin *concelebrāre, concelebrāt-* : *com-,* com- + *celebrāre,* to celebrate; see CELEBRATE.] **—con•cel′e•brant** (-brənt) *n.*

con•cel•e•bra•tion (kən-sĕl′ə-brā′shən) *n.* Celebration of the Eucharist by two or more officiants.

con•cen•ter (kən-sĕn′tər, kŏn-) *tr. & intr.v.* **-tered, -ter•ing, -ters.** To direct toward or come together at a common center. [Probably Italian *concentrare* or French *concentrer* : both from Latin *com-,* com- + Latin *centrum,* center; see CENTER.]

con•cen•trate (kŏn′sən-trāt′) *v.* **-trat•ed, -trat•ing, -trates.** *—tr.* **1.a.** To direct or draw toward a common center; focus. **b.** To bring into one main body: *Authority was concentrated in the president.* **2.** To make (a solution or mixture) less dilute. *—intr.* **1.a.** To converge toward or meet in a common center. **b.** To increase by degree; gather: *"Dusk began to concentrate into full night"* (Anthony Hyde). **2.** To direct one's thoughts or attention: *We concentrated on the task before us.* **—concentrate** *n. Abbr.* **conc.** A product that has been concentrated, especially a food that has been reduced in volume or bulk by the removal of liquid: *pineapple juice concentrate.* [From CONCENTER.] **—con′cen•tra′tive** *adj.* **—con′cen•tra′tive•ly** *adv.* **—con′cen•tra′tor** *n.*

con•cen•tra•tion (kŏn′sən-trā′shən) *n.* **1.a.** The act or process of concentrating, especially the fixing of close, undivided attention. **b.** The condition of being concentrated. **2.** Something that has been concentrated. **3.** *Chemistry.* The amount of a specified substance in a unit amount of another substance.

concentration camp *n.* **1.** A camp where prisoners of war, enemy aliens, and political prisoners are detained and confined, typically under harsh conditions. **2.** A place or situation characterized by extremely harsh conditions.

concentration gradient *n.* The graduated difference in concentration of a solute per unit distance through a solution.

con•cen•tric (kən-sĕn′trĭk) also **con•cen•tri•cal** (-trĭ-kəl) *adj.* Having a common center. [Middle English *concentrik,* from Medieval Latin *concentricus* : Latin *com-,* com- + Latin *centrum,* center; see CENTER.] **—con•cen′tri•cal•ly** *adv.* **—con′cen•tric′i•ty** (kŏn′sĕn-trĭs′ĭ-tē) *n.*

Con•cep•ción (kən-sĕp′sē-ōn′, -sĕp′shən, kôn′sĕp-syôn′). A city of west-central Chile near the Pacific coast south-southwest of Santiago. Founded in 1550, it has frequently suffered severe earthquake damage. Population, 267,891.

con•cept (kŏn′sĕpt′) *n.* **1.** A general idea derived or inferred from specific instances or occurrences. **2.** Something formed in the mind; a thought or notion. See Synonyms at **idea. 3.** *Usage Problem.* A scheme; a plan: *"began searching for an agency to handle a new restaurant concept"* (ADWEEK). [Late Latin *conceptus,* from Latin, past participle of *concipere,* to conceive. See CONCEIVE.]

USAGE NOTE: In fields such as entertainment and advertising, *concept* is often used loosely to mean "a scheme, plan," as in *The studio liked the concept for the new game show and decided to put it into development.* Perhaps this usage sounds most at home in these industries.

con•cep•ta•cle (kən-sĕp′tə-kəl) *n.* One of many specialized hollow chambers containing reproductive structures that appear as dark, dotlike bodies on the surface of receptacles in certain algae and fungi. [Latin *conceptāculum,* receptacle, from *conceptus,* past participle of *concipere,* to conceive. See CONCEIVE.]

concept art *n.* Conceptual art.

con•cep•tion (kən-sĕp′shən) *n.* **1.a.** Formation of a viable zygote by the union of the male sperm and the female ovum; fertilization. **b.** The entity formed by the union of the male sperm and the female ovum; an embryo or a zygote. **2.a.** The ability to form or understand mental concepts and abstractions. **b.** Something conceived in the mind; a concept, plan, design, idea, or thought. See Synonyms at **idea. 3.** *Archaic.* A beginning; a start. [Middle English *concepcioun,* from Old French *conception,* from Latin *conceptiō, conceptiōn-,* from *conceptus.* See CONCEPT.] **—con•cep′tion•al** *adj.* **—con•cep′tive** *adj.* **—con•cep′tive•ly** *adv.*

con•cep•tu•al (kən-sĕp′cho͞o-əl) *adj.* Of, consisting of, or relating to concepts or conception: *conceptual discussions that antedated development of the new product.* [Medieval Latin *conceptuālis,* from Late Latin *conceptus,* a thought. See CONCEPT.] **—con•cep′tu•al•ly** *adv.*

conceptual art *n.* Art that is intended to convey an idea or a concept to the perceiver and need not involve the creation or appreciation of a traditional art object such as a painting or a sculpture. **—conceptual artist** *n.*

con•cep•tu•al•ism (kən-sĕp′cho͞o-ə-lĭz′əm) *n.* **1.** *Philosophy.* The doctrine, intermediate between nominalism and realism, that universals exist only within the mind and have no external or substantial reality. **2.** A school of abstract art or an artistic doctrine that is concerned with the intellectual engagement of the viewer through conveyance of an idea and negation of the importance of the art object itself. **—con•cep′tu•al•ist** *n.* **—con•cep′tu•al•is′tic** *adj.* **—con•cep′tu•al•is′ti•cal•ly** *adv.*

con•cep•tu•al•ize (kən-sĕp′cho͞o-ə-līz′) *v.* **-ized, -iz•ing, -iz•es.** *—tr.* To form a concept or concepts of, and especially to interpret in a conceptual way: *"Efforts to conceptualize the history and structure of the universe were already running into trouble because . . . the universe was not as uniform as had been assumed"* (John Noble Wilford). *—intr.* To form concepts. **—con•cep′tu•al•i•za′tion** (-sĕp′cho͞o-ə-lĭ-zā′shən) *n.* **—con•cep′tu•al•iz′er** *n.*

ă pat	oi boy
ā pay	ou out
âr care	o͝o took
ä father	o͞o boot
ĕ pet	ŭ cut
ē be	ûr urge
ĭ pit	th thin
ī pie	*th* this
îr pier	hw which
ŏ pot	zh vision
ō toe	ə about, item
ô paw	♦ regionalism

Stress marks: ′ (primary); ′ (secondary), as in **dictionary** (dĭk′shə-nĕr′ē)

con·cep·tus (kən-sĕp′təs) *n.* The product of conception at any point between fertilization and birth. It includes the embryo or the fetus as well as the extraembryonic membranes. [Latin, something conceived. See CONCEPT.]

con·cern (kən-sûrn′) *v.* **-cerned, -cern·ing, -cerns.** —*tr.* **1.** To have to do with or relate to: *an article that concerns the plight of homeless people.* **2.** To be of interest or importance to: *This problem concerns all of us.* **3.** To engage the attention of; involve: *We concerned ourselves with accomplishing the task at hand.* **4.** To cause anxiety or uneasiness in: *The firm's weak financial posture is starting to concern its stockholders.* —*intr. Obsolete.* To be of importance. —**concern** *n.* **1.** A matter that relates to or affects one. See Synonyms at **affair. 2.** Regard for or interest in someone or something. **3.** A troubled or anxious state of mind arising from solicitude or interest. See Synonyms at **anxiety. 4.** A business establishment or enterprise; a firm. **5.** A contrivance; a gadget. [Middle English *concernen,* from Old French *concerner,* from Medieval Latin *concernere,* from Late Latin, to mingle together : *com-,* com- + *cernere,* to sift; see **krei-** in Appendix.]

con·cerned (kən-sûrnd′) *adj.* **1.** Interested and involved: *sent a memorandum to those concerned.* **2.** Anxious; troubled: *the concerned parents of youthful offenders.*

con·cern·ing (kən-sûr′nĭng) *prep.* In reference to. See Usage Note at **participle.**

con·cern·ment (kən-sûrn′mənt) *n.* **1.** A matter of concern. **2.** Reference, relation, or importance. **3.** Anxiety; worry.

con·cert (kŏn′sûrt′, -sərt) *n.* **1.** *Music.* A performance given by one or more singers or instrumentalists or both. **2. a.** Agreement in purpose, feeling, or action. **b.** Unity achieved by mutual communication of views, ideas, and opinions: *acted in concert on the issue.* **c.** Concerted action: *"One feels between them an accumulation of gentleness and strength, a concert of energies"* (Vanity Fair). —**concert** (kən-sûrt′) *v.* **-cert·ed, -cert·ing, -certs.** —*tr.* **1.** To plan or arrange by mutual agreement. **2.** To adjust; settle. —*intr.* To act together in harmony. [French, from Italian *concerto,* from Old Italian, agreement, harmony, possibly from Late Latin *concertus,* past participle of *concernere,* to mingle together. See CONCERN.]

con·cert·ed (kən-sûr′tĭd) *adj.* **1.** Planned or accomplished together; combined: *We made a concerted effort to solve the problem.* **2.** *Music.* Arranged in parts for voices or instruments. —**con·cert′ed·ly** *adv.*

con·cert·go·er (kŏn′sərt-gō′ər) *n.* One who attends a concert. —**con′cert·go′ing** *adj.* & *n.*

concert grand *n. Music.* The largest grand piano, being roughly 2.7 meters (9 feet) in length, and having the volume, tone, and timbre appropriate for use in concerts.

con·cer·ti·na (kŏn′sər-tē′nə) *n. Music.* A small, hexagonal accordion with bellows and with buttons for keys. [CONCERT + Italian *-ina,* feminine diminutive suff.]

con·cer·ti·no (kŏn′chĕr-tē′nō) *n., pl.* **-nos.** *Music.* **1.** A short concerto. **2.** The solo instrument group in a concerto grosso. [Italian, diminutive of *concerto,* concert. See CONCERT.]

con·cer·tize (kŏn′sər-tīz′) *intr.v.* **-tized, -tiz·ing, -tiz·es.** *Music.* To give concerts or perform in concerts: *"has worked extensively on Broadway, has also made several movies, starred in a television series and concertized regularly throughout the country"* (Jeremy Gerard).

con·cert·mas·ter (kŏn′sərt-măs′tər) *n. Music.* The first violinist and assistant conductor in a symphony orchestra.

con·cert·mis·tress (kŏn′sərt-mĭs′trĭs) *n. Music.* A woman who is the first violinist and assistant conductor in a symphony orchestra.

con·cer·to (kən-chĕr′tō) *n., pl.* **-tos** or **-ti** (-tē). *Abbr.* **con.** *Music.* A composition for an orchestra and one or more solo instruments, typically in three movements. [Italian, concert. See CONCERT.]

concerto gros·so (grō′sō) *n., pl.* **concerti grossi** (grō′sē). *Music.* A composition for a small group of solo instruments and a full orchestra. [Italian : *concerto,* concerto + *grosso,* large.]

concert pitch *n.* **1.** *Music.* See **international pitch. 2.** The state of being ready and tensely alert: *a diver whose mental and physical states were at concert pitch before executing the dive.*

con·ces·sion (kən-sĕsh′ən) *n.* **1.** The act of conceding. **2. a.** Something, such as a point previously claimed in argument, that is later conceded. **b.** An acknowledgment or admission. **3.** A grant of a tract of land made by a government or other controlling authority in return for stipulated services or a promise that the land will be used for a specific purpose. **4. a.** The privilege of maintaining a subsidiary business within certain premises. **b.** The space allotted for such a business. **c.** The business itself: *had an ice-cream concession in the subway station.* [Middle English, from Latin *concessiō, concessiōn-,* from *concessus,* past participle of *concēdere,* to concede. See CONCEDE.] —**con·ces′sion·al** *adj.* —**con·ces′sion·ar′y** (-sĕsh′ə-nĕr′ē) *adj.*

con·ces·sion·aire (kən-sĕsh′ə-nâr′) *n.* The holder or operator of a concession. [French, from *concession,* concession, from Latin *concessiō.* See CONCESSION.]

con·ces·sion·er (kən-sĕsh′ə-nər) *n.* A concessionaire.

con·ces·sive (kən-sĕs′ĭv) *adj.* **1.** Of the nature of or containing a concession. **2.** *Grammar.* Expressing concession, as the conjunction *though.* [Late Latin *concessīvus,* from Latin *concessus,* past participle of *concēdere,* to concede. See CONCEDE.] —**con·ces′sive·ly** *adv.*

conch (kŏngk, kŏnch) *n., pl.* **conchs** (kŏngks) or **conch·es** (kŏn′chĭz). **1.** Any of various tropical marine gastropod mollusks, especially of the genera *Strombus* and *Cassis,* having large, often brightly colored spiral shells and edible flesh. **2.** The shell of one of these gastropod mollusks, used as an ornament, in making cameos, or as a horn. **3.** *Anatomy.* See **concha** (sense 1). [Middle English *conche,* from Old French, from Latin *concha,* mussel, from Greek *konkhē.*]

conch– *pref.* Variant of **concho–.**

con·cha (kŏng′kə) *n., pl.* **-chae** (-kē′). **1.** *Anatomy.* Any of various structures, such as the external ear, that resemble a shell in shape. Also called *conch.* **2.** *Architecture.* The half dome over an apse. [Late Latin, semidome, from Latin, mussel shell. See CONCH.] —**con′chal** (-kəl) *adj.*

conchi– *pref.* Variant of **concho–.**

con·chif·er·ous (kŏng-kĭf′ər-əs) *adj.* Having or forming a shell.

con·chi·o·lin (kŏng-kī′ə-lĭn, kŏn-) *n.* A protein substance that is the organic basis of mollusk shells. [CONCH + –OL[1] + –IN.]

concho– or **conchi–** or **conch–** *pref.* Shell: *conchology.* [Greek *konkho-,* from *konkhos,* shell.]

Con·cho·bar (kŏn-kŭv′ər, -ko͝o′ho͝or, kŏn′ər) *n. Mythology.* The king of Ulster.

con·choi·dal (kŏng-koid′l) *adj.* Of, relating to, or being a surface characterized by smooth, shell-like convexities and concavities, as on fractured obsidian. [From Greek *konkhoeidēs,* mussellike : *konkho-,* concho- + *-eidēs, -oeidēs,* -oid.] —**con·choi′dal·ly** *adv.*

con·chol·o·gy (kŏng-kŏl′ə-jē) *n.* The branch of zoology that deals with the study of mollusks and shells. —**con′cho·log′i·cal** (-kə-lŏj′ĭ-kəl) *adj.* —**con·chol′o·gist** *n.*

con·cierge (kôN-syârzh′) *n.* **1.** A staff member of a hotel or apartment complex who assists guests or residents, as by handling the storage of luggage, taking and delivering messages, and making reservations for tours. **2.** A person, especially in France, who lives in an apartment house, attends the entrance, and serves as a janitor. [French, from Old French *cumcerges,* from Vulgar Latin **cōnservius,* alteration of Latin *cōnservus,* fellow slave : *com-,* com- + *servus,* slave.]

con·cil·i·ar (kən-sĭl′ē-ər) *adj.* Of, relating to, or generated by a council: *a conciliar appointment made by the governor; conciliar edicts.* [From Latin *concilium,* council. See COUNCIL.]

con·cil·i·ate (kən-sĭl′ē-āt′) *v.* **-at·ed, -at·ing, -ates.** —*tr.* **1.** To overcome the distrust or animosity of; appease. **2.** To regain or try to regain (friendship or goodwill) by pleasant behavior. **3.** To make or attempt to make compatible; reconcile. —*intr.* To gain or try to gain someone's friendship or goodwill. See Synonyms at **pacify.** [Latin *conciliāre, conciliāt-,* from *concilium,* meeting. See **kelə-[2]** in Appendix.] —**con·cil′i·a·ble** (-ə-bəl) *adj.* —**con·cil′i·a′tion** *n.* —**con·cil′i·a′tor** *n.* —**con·cil′i·a·to′ry** (-ə-tôr′ē, -tōr′ē) *adj.*

con·cin·ni·ty (kən-sĭn′ĭ-tē) *n., pl.* **-ties. 1.** Harmony in the arrangement or interarrangement of parts with respect to a whole. **2.** Studied elegance and facility in style of expression: *"He has what one character calls 'the gifts of concinnity and concision,' that deft swipe with a phrase that can be so devastating in children"* (Elizabeth Ward). **3.** An instance of harmonious arrangement or studied elegance and facility. [From Latin *concinnitās,* from *concinnāre,* to put in order, from *concinnus,* deftly joined.]

con·cise (kən-sīs′) *adj.* Expressing much in few words; clear and succinct. [Latin *concīsus,* past participle of *concīdere,* to cut up : *com-,* intensive pref.; see COM– + *caedere,* to cut; see **kaə-id-** in Appendix.] —**con·cise′ly** *adv.* —**con·cise′ness** *n.*

con·ci·sion (kən-sĭzh′ən) *n.* **1.** The state or quality of being concise: *"a role made . . . dramatically accessible by the concision of the form"* (George Steiner). **2.** *Archaic.* A cutting apart or off.

con·clave (kŏn′klāv′, kŏng′-) *n.* **1.** A secret or confidential meeting. **2.** *Roman Catholic Church.* **a.** The private rooms in which the cardinals meet to elect a new pope. **b.** The meeting held to elect a new pope. **3.** A meeting of family members or associates. [Middle English, private chamber, conclave of cardinals, from Latin *conclāve,* lockable room : *com-,* com- + *clāvis,* key.]

con·clude (kən-klo͞od′) *v.* **-clud·ed, -clud·ing, -cludes.** —*tr.* **1.** To bring to an end; close: *concluded the rally with the national anthem.* **2.** To bring about (a final agreement or settlement, for example): *conclude a peace treaty.* **3.** To reach a decision or form an opinion about. See Synonyms at **decide. 4.** To arrive at (a logical conclusion or end) by the process of reasoning; infer on the basis of convincing evidence: *The jury concluded that the defendant was innocent.* **5.** *Obsolete.* To confine; enclose. —*intr.* **1.** To come to an end; close. **2.** To come to a decision or an agreement. [Middle English *concluden,* from Latin *conclūdere* : *com-,* intensive pref.; see COM– + *claudere,* to close.] —**con·clud′er** *n.*

con·clu·sion (kən-klo͞o′zhən) *n.* **1.** The close or last part; the end or finish. **2.** The result or outcome of an act or process. **3.** A judgment or decision reached after deliberation. See Synonyms at **decision. 4.** A final arrangement or settlement, as of a treaty. **5.** *Abbr.* **con.** *Law.* The close of a plea or deed. **6.** *Logic.* **a.** The

concession

conch

proposition that must follow from the major and minor premises in a syllogism. **b.** The proposition concluded from one or more premises; a deduction. [Middle English *conclusioun,* from Old French *conclusion,* from Latin *conclūsiō, conclūsiōn-,* from *conclūsus,* past participle of *conclūdere,* to end. See CONCLUDE.]

con·clu·sive (kən-klo͞o′sĭv) *adj.* Serving to put an end to doubt, question, or uncertainty; decisive. See Synonyms at **decisive.** —**con·clu′sive·ly** *adv.* —**con·clu′sive·ness** *n.*

con·clu·so·ry (kən-klo͞o′sə-rē) *adj.* **1.** Conclusive. **2.** *Law.* Convincing, but not so much so that contradiction is impossible; not justified or supported by all the facts: *"Perfunctory and conclusory findings of the magistrate . . . did not comport with requirements of Federal Rules of Civil Procedure"* (National Law Journal).

con·coct (kən-kŏkt′) *tr.v.* **-coct·ed, -coct·ing, -cocts. 1.** To prepare by mixing ingredients, as in cooking. **2.** To devise, using skill and intelligence; contrive: *concoct a mystery story.* [Latin *concoquere, concoct-,* to boil together : *com-,* com- + *coquere,* to cook; see **pekʷ-** in Appendix.] —**con·coct′er, con·coc′tor** *n.* —**con·coc′tion** *n.*

con·com·i·tance (kən-kŏm′ĭ-təns) *n.* **1.** Occurrence or existence together or in connection with one another. **2.** A concomitant.

con·com·i·tant (kən-kŏm′ĭ-tənt) *adj.* Occurring or existing concurrently; attendant. See Synonyms at **contemporary.** —**concomitant** *n.* One that occurs or exists concurrently with another. [Late Latin *concomitāns, concomitant-,* present participle of *concomitārī,* to accompany : Latin *com-,* com- + Latin *comitārī,* to accompany (from *comes, comit-,* companion; see **ei-** in Appendix).] —**con·com′i·tant·ly** *adv.*

con·cord (kŏn′kôrd′, kŏng′-) *n.* **1.** Harmony or agreement of interests or feelings; accord. **2.** A treaty establishing peaceful relations. **3.** *Grammar.* Agreement between words in person, number, gender, and case. [Middle English *concorde,* from Old French, from Latin *concordia,* from *concors, concord-,* agreeing : *com-,* com- + *cor,* heart; see **kerd-** in Appendix.]

Con·cord (kŏng′kərd). **1.** A city of west-central California northeast of Oakland. It is a residential and manufacturing community. Population, 103,255. **2.** A town of eastern Massachusetts on the **Concord River** west-northwest of Boston. An early battle of the Revolutionary War was fought here on April 19, 1775. In the 19th century the town was noted as an intellectual and literary center. Population, 16,293. **3.** A community of east-central Missouri, a suburb of St. Louis. Population, 20,896. **4.** The capital of New Hampshire, in the south-central part of the state on the Merrimack River. It became the capital in 1808. Population, 30,400. **5.** (kŏn′kôrd′). A city of south-central North Carolina northeast of Charlotte. Population, 16,942.

con·cor·dance (kən-kôr′dns) *n.* **1.** Agreement; concord. **2.** An alphabetical index of all the words in a text or corpus of texts, showing every contextual occurrence of a word: *a concordance of Shakespeare's works.* **3.** *Genetics.* The presence of a given trait in both members of a pair of twins.

concordance rate *n.* A quantitative statistical expression for the concordance of a given genetic trait.

con·cor·dant (kən-kôr′dnt) *adj.* Harmonious; agreeing. [Middle English *concordaunt,* from Old French *concordant,* from Latin *concordāns, concordant-,* present participle of *concordāre,* to agree, from *concors, concord-,* agreeing. See CONCORD.] —**con·cor′dant·ly** *adv.*

con·cor·dat (kən-kôr′dăt′) *n.* **1.** A formal agreement; a compact. **2.** *Roman Catholic Church.* An agreement between the pope and a government for the regulation of church affairs. [French, from Medieval Latin *concordātum,* from neuter past participle of Latin *concordāre,* to agree. See CONCORDANT.]

Con·cord grape (kŏng′kərd) *n.* A cultivated variety of the fox grape having dark blue to purple-black skin, used for making jelly, juice, and wine. [After CONCORD, Massachusetts.]

con·course (kŏn′kôrs′, -kōrs′, kŏng′-) *n.* **1.** A large open space for the gathering or passage of crowds, as in an airport. **2.** A broad thoroughfare. **3.** A great crowd; a throng. **4.** The act of coming, moving, or flowing together. [Middle English *concours,* assembly, throng, from Old French, from Latin *concursus,* from past participle of *concurrere,* to assemble : *com-,* com- + *currere,* to run; see **kers-** in Appendix.]

concourse
Grand Central Station, New York City

con·cres·cence (kən-krĕs′əns) *n.* **1.** *Biology.* The growing together of related parts, tissues, or cells. **2.** The amassing of physical particles. [Latin *concrēscentia,* from *concrēscēns, concrēscent-,* present participle of *concrēscere,* to grow together. See CONCRETE.] —**con·cres′cent** *adj.*

con·crete (kŏn-krēt′, kŏng-, kŏn′krēt′, kŏng′-) *adj.* **1.** Of or relating to an actual, specific thing or instance; particular: *had the concrete evidence needed to convict.* **2.** Existing in reality or in real experience; perceptible by the senses; real: *concrete objects such as trees.* **3.** Of or relating to a material thing or group of things as opposed to an abstraction. **4.** Formed by the coalescence of separate particles or parts into one mass; solid. **5.** Made of hard, strong, conglomerate construction material. —**concrete** (kŏn′krēt′, kŏng′-, kŏn-krēt′, kŏng-) *n.* **1.** *Abbr.* **conc.** A hard, strong construction material consisting of sand, conglomerate gravel, pebbles, broken stone, or slag in a mortar or cement matrix. **2.** A mass formed by the coalescence of particles. —**concrete** (kŏn′krēt′, kŏng′-, kŏn-krēt′, kŏng-) *v.* **-cret·ed, -cret·ing, -cretes.** —*tr.* **1.** To build, treat, or cover with hard, strong conglomerate construction material. **2.** To form into a mass by coalescence or cohesion of particles or parts. —*intr.* To harden; solidify. [Middle English *concret,* from Latin *concrētus,* past participle of *concrēscere,* to grow together, harden : *com-,* com- + *crēscere,* to grow; see **ker-²** in Appendix.] —**con·crete′ly** *adv.* —**con·crete′ness** *n.*

concrete music *n.* Musique concrète.

concrete poetry *n.* Poetry that visually conveys the poet's meaning through the graphic arrangement of letters, words, or symbols on the page.

con·cre·tion (kən-krē′shən) *n.* **1.a.** The act or process of concreting into a mass; coalescence. **b.** The state of having been concreted: *a concretion of seminal ideas in her treatise.* **2.** A solid, hard mass. **3.** *Geology.* A rounded mass of mineral matter found in sedimentary rock. **4.** *Pathology.* A solid mass, usually composed of inorganic material, formed in a cavity or tissue of the body; a calculus. —**con·cre′tion·ar′y** (-shə-nĕr′ē) *adj.*

con·cret·ism (kŏn-krē′tĭz′əm, kŏng-) *n.* The practice of representing abstract concepts or qualities in concrete form, as in concrete poetry. —**con·cret′ist** *n.*

con·cre·tize (kŏn′krĭ-tīz′, kŏng′-) *tr.v.* **-tized, -tiz·ing, -tiz·es.** To make real or specific: *"The need to simplify and concretize . . . was hardly acceptable to a mind fascinated by the . . . suggestiveness of ideas"* (Arthur A. Cohen). —**con′cre·ti·za′tion** (-tĭ-zā′shən) *n.*

con·cu·bi·nage (kŏn-kyo͞o′bə-nĭj, kən-) *n.* **1.** *Law.* Cohabitation without legal marriage. **2.** The state of being a concubine.

con·cu·bine (kŏng′kyə-bīn′, kŏn′-) *n.* **1.** *Law.* A woman who cohabits with a man. **2.** In certain societies, such as imperial China, a woman contracted to a man as a secondary wife, often having few legal rights and low social status. [Middle English, from Old French, from Latin *concubīna* : *com-,* com- + *cubāre,* to lie down.]

con·cu·pis·cence (kŏn-kyo͞o′pĭ-səns) *n.* A strong desire, especially sexual desire; lust. [Middle English, from Old French, from Late Latin *concupīscentia,* from Latin *concupīscēns, concupīscent-,* present participle of *concupīscere,* inchoative of *concupere,* to desire strongly : *com-,* intensive pref.; see COM– + *cupere,* to desire.] —**con·cu′pis·cent** *adj.*

con·cur (kən-kûr′) *intr.v.* **-curred, -cur·ring, -curs. 1.** To be of the same opinion; agree. See Synonyms at **assent. 2.** To act together; cooperate. **3.** To occur at the same time; coincide. **4.** *Obsolete.* To converge; meet. [Middle English *concurren,* from Latin *concurrere,* to meet, coincide : *com-,* com- + *currere,* to run; see **kers-** in Appendix.]

con·cur·rence (kən-kûr′əns, -kŭr′-) *n.* **1.** Agreement in opinion. **2.** Cooperation, as of agents, circumstances, or events. **3.** Simultaneous occurrence; coincidence.

con·cur·ren·cy (kən-kûr′ən-sē, -kŭr′-) *n., pl.* **-cies.** Concurrence: *"Concurrency of development with deployment . . . has almost always proven counterproductive"* (Harold Brown).

con·cur·rent (kən-kûr′ənt, -kŭr′-) *adj.* **1.** Happening at the same time as something else. See Synonyms at **contemporary. 2.** Operating or acting in conjunction with another. **3.** Meeting or tending to meet at the same point; convergent. **4.** Being in accordance; harmonious. [Middle English, from Latin *concurrēns, concurrent-,* present participle of *concurrere,* to coincide. See CONCUR.] —**con·cur′rent** *n.* —**con·cur′rent·ly** *adv.*

concurrent resolution *n.* A resolution adopted by both houses of a bicameral legislature that does not have the force of law and does not require the signature of the chief executive.

con·cuss (kən-kŭs′) *tr.v.* **-cussed, -cuss·ing, -cuss·es.** To injure by concussion: *"a middle-aged woman concussed by a blow on the head"* (Manchester Guardian Weekly). [Latin *concutere, concuss-,* to strike together : *com-,* com- + *quatere,* to strike; see **kwēt-** in Appendix.]

con·cus·sion (kən-kŭsh′ən) *n.* **1.** A violent jarring; a shock. See Synonyms at **collision. 2.** An injury to an organ, especially the brain, produced by a violent blow and followed by a temporary or prolonged loss of function. [Middle English *concussioun,* bruise, contusion, from Latin *concussiō, concussiōn-,* concussion, from *concussus,* past participle of *concutere,* to strike together. See CONCUSS.] —**con·cus′sive** (-kŭs′ĭv) *adj.* —**con·cus′sive·ly** *adv.*

cond. *abbr.* **1.** Condition. **2.** Conductivity. **3.** Conductor.

Con·dé (kôɴ-dā′), Prince de. Title of Louis II de Bourbon. Known as "the Great Condé." 1621–1686. French general who won major victories in the Thirty Years' War.

con·demn (kən-dĕm′) *tr.v.* **-demned, -demn·ing, -demns. 1.** To express strong disapproval of: *condemned the needless waste of food.* **2.** To pronounce judgment against; sentence. **3.** To judge or declare to be unfit for use or consumption, usually by official order: *condemn an old building.* **4.** *Law.* To appropriate (property) for public use. [Middle English *condemnen,* from Old French *condemner,* from Latin *condemnāre* : *com-,* intensive pref.; see COM– + *damnāre,* to sentence (from *damnum,* penalty).] —**con·dem′na·ble** (-dĕm′nə-bəl) *adj.* —**con·dem′na·to′ry** (-nə-tôr′ē, -tōr′ē) *adj.* —**con·demn′er** *n.*

SYNONYMS: *condemn, damn, doom, sentence.* The central meaning shared by these verbs is "to fix the punishment or destiny of one found to be guilty or undeserving": *condemned the dissident to hard labor; damned to everlasting uncertainty; an attempt that* *was doomed to failure; sentenced the murderer to life in prison.* See also Synonyms at **criticize.**

con·dem·na·tion (kŏn′dĕm-nā′shən) *n.* **1.a.** The act of condemning. **b.** The state of being condemned. **2.** Severe reproof; strong censure. **3.** A reason or occasion for condemning.

con·den·sate (kŏn′dən-sāt′, -dĕn-, kən-dĕn′sāt′) *n.* A product of condensation. [From *condensate,* condensed, from Latin *condēnsātus,* past participle of *condēnsāre,* to condense. See CONDENSE.]

con·den·sa·tion (kŏn′dĕn-sā′shən, -dən-) *n.* **1.** The act of condensing. **2.** The state of being condensed. **3.** A condensate. **4.** *Physics.* **a.** The process by which a gas or vapor changes to a liquid. **b.** The liquid so formed. **5.** *Chemistry.* A chemical reaction in which water or another simple substance is released by the combination of two or more molecules. **6.** *Psychology.* The process by which a single symbol or word is associated with the emotional content of a group of ideas, feelings, memories, or impulses, especially as expressed in dreams. **—con′den·sa′tion·al** *adj.*

con·dense (kən-dĕns′) *v.* **-densed, -dens·ing, -dens·es.** *—tr.* **1.** To reduce the volume or compass of. See Synonyms at **contract. 2.** To make more concise; abridge or shorten. **3.** *Physics.* **a.** To cause (a gas or vapor) to change to a liquid. **b.** To remove water from (milk, for example). *—intr.* **1.** To become more compact. **2.** To undergo condensation. [Middle English *condensen,* from Old French *condenser,* from Latin *condēnsāre* : *com-,* intensive pref.; see COM– + *dēnsāre,* to thicken (from *dēnsus,* thick).] **—con·dens′a·bil′i·ty** *n.* **—con·dens′a·ble, con·dens′i·ble** *adj.*

con·densed milk (kən-dĕnst′) *n.* Cow's milk with sugar added, reduced by evaporation to a thick consistency.

con·dens·er (kən-dĕn′sər) *n.* **1.** One that condenses, especially an apparatus used to condense vapor. **2.** See **capacitor. 3.** A mirror, lens, or combination of lenses used to gather light and direct it upon an object or through a projection lens.

con·de·scend (kŏn′dĭ-sĕnd′) *intr.v.* **-scend·ed, -scend·ing, -scends. 1.** To descend to the level of one considered inferior; lower oneself. See Synonyms at **stoop[1]. 2.** To deal with people in a patronizingly superior manner. [Middle English *condescenden,* from Old French *condescendre,* from Late Latin *condēscendere* : Latin *com-,* intensive pref.; see COM– + *dēscendere,* to descend; see DESCEND.] **—con′de·scend′er** *n.*

con·de·scen·dence (kŏn′dĭ-sĕn′dəns) *n.* Condescension.

con·de·scend·ing (kŏn′dĭ-sĕn′dĭng) *adj.* Displaying a patronizingly superior attitude. **—con′de·scend′ing·ly** *adv.*

con·de·scen·sion (kŏn′dĭ-sĕn′shən) *n.* **1.** The act of condescending or an instance of it. **2.** Patronizingly superior behavior or attitude. [Late Latin *condēscēnsiō, condēscēnsiōn-,* from *condēscēnsus,* past participle of *condēscendere,* to condescend. See CONDESCEND.]

con·dign (kən-dīn′) *adj.* Deserved; adequate: *condign censure.* [Middle English *condigne,* from Old French, from Latin *condignus* : *com-,* intensive pref.; see COM– + *dignus,* worthy; see **dek-** in Appendix.] **—con·dign′ly** *adv.*

con·di·ment (kŏn′də-mənt) *n.* A sauce, relish, or spice used to season food. [Middle English, from Old French, from Latin *condīmentum,* from *condīre,* to season. See **dhē-** in Appendix.] **—con′di·men′tal** (-mĕn′tl) *adj.*

con·di·tion (kən-dĭsh′ən) *n.* *Abbr.* **cond. 1.** A mode or state of being: "The Organization Man *survives as a modern classic because it captures a permanent part of our social condition"* (Robert J. Samuelson). **2.a.** A state of health. **b.** A state of readiness or physical fitness. See Synonyms at **state. 3.** A disease or physical ailment: *a heart condition.* **4.** Social position; rank. **5.** One that is indispensable to the appearance or occurrence of another; prerequisite: *Compatibility is a condition of a successful marriage.* **6.** One that restricts or modifies another; a qualification. **7. conditions.** Existing circumstances: *Conditions in the office made concentration impossible.* **8.** *Grammar.* The dependent clause of a conditional sentence. **9.** *Logic.* A proposition on which another proposition depends; the antecedent of a conditional proposition. **10.** *Law.* **a.** A provision making the effect of a legal instrument contingent on the occurrence of an uncertain future event. **b.** The event itself. **11.** An unsatisfactory grade given to a student, serving notice that deficiencies can be made up by the completion of additional work. **12.** *Obsolete.* Disposition; temperament. **—condition** *tr.v.* **-tioned, -tion·ing, -tions. 1.** To make dependent on a condition or conditions. **2.** To stipulate as a condition. **3.** To render fit for work or use. **4.** To accustom (oneself or another) to; adapt: *had to condition herself to long hours of hard work; conditioned the troops to marches at high altitudes.* **5.** To air-condition. **6.** To give the unsatisfactory grade of condition to. **7.** *Psychology.* To cause an organism to respond in a specific manner to a conditioned stimulus in the absence of an unconditioned stimulus. **8.** To replace moisture or oils in (hair, for example) by use of a therapeutic product. [Middle English *condicioun,* from Old French *condicion,* from Latin *conditiō, conditiōn-,* from *condīcere,* to agree : *com-,* com- + *dīcere,* to talk; see **deik-** in Appendix.]

con·di·tion·al (kən-dĭsh′ə-nəl) *adj.* **1.** Imposing, depending on, or containing a condition. See Synonyms at **dependent. 2.** *Grammar.* Stating, containing, or implying a condition. **3.** *Psychology.* Brought about by conditioning. **—conditional** *n.* *Grammar.* A mood, tense, clause, or word expressing a condition. **—con·di′tion·al′i·ty** (-dĭsh′ə-năl′ĭ-tē) *n.* **—con·di′tion·al·ly** *adv.*

conditional probability *n.* The probability that an event will occur, given that one or more other events have occurred.

con·di·tioned (kən-dĭsh′ənd) *adj.* **1.** Subject to or dependent on a condition or conditions. **2.** Physically fit. **3.** Prepared for a specific action or process. **4.** *Psychology.* Exhibiting or trained to exhibit a conditioned response.

conditioned response *n.* *Abbr.* **CR** *Psychology.* A new or modified response elicited by a stimulus after conditioning. Also called *conditioned reflex.*

conditioned stimulus *n.* *Abbr.* **CS** *Psychology.* A previously neutral stimulus that, after repeated association with an unconditioned stimulus, elicits the response effected by the unconditioned stimulus itself.

con·di·tion·er (kən-dĭsh′ə-nər) *n.* One that conditions, especially an additive or application that improves the quality or usability of a substance: *a soil conditioner; a hair conditioner.*

con·di·tion·ing (kən-dĭsh′ə-nĭng) *n.* *Psychology.* A process of behavior modification by which a subject comes to associate a desired behavior with a previously unrelated stimulus.

con·do (kŏn′dō′) *n., pl.* **-dos.** *Informal.* A condominium. *—attributive.* Often used to modify another noun: *condo sales; condo advertisements.*

con·dole (kən-dōl′) *intr.v.* **-doled, -dol·ing, -doles.** To express sympathy or sorrow: *I condoled with him in his loss.* [Late Latin *condolēre,* to feel another's pain : Latin *com-,* com- + Latin *dolēre,* to grieve.] **—con·do′la·to′ry** (-dō′lə-tôr′ē, -tōr′ē) *adj.* **—con·dol′er** *n.*

con·do·lence (kən-dō′ləns) *n.* **1.** Sympathy with a person who has experienced pain, grief, or misfortune. See Synonyms at **pity. 2.** A formal declaration of condolence. **—con·do′lent** *adj.*

con·dom (kŏn′dəm, kŭn′-) *n.* A flexible sheath, usually made of thin rubber or latex, designed to cover the penis during sexual intercourse for contraceptive purposes or as a means of preventing sexually transmitted diseases. [Origin unknown.]

con·do·min·i·um (kŏn′də-mĭn′ē-əm) *n., pl.* **-min·i·ums** also **-min·i·a** (-mĭn′ē-ə). **1.a.** Real estate, such as a unit in an apartment complex or a parking space in a garage, that combines fee simple title to the unit and joint ownership in the common elements shared with other unit owners. **b.** A unit in such a complex. **2.a.** Joint sovereignty, especially joint rule of territory by two or more nations, or a plan to achieve it: *"The allies would fear that they were pawns in a superpower condominium"* (New Republic). **b.** A politically dependent territory. **—con′do·min′i·al** (-ē-əl) *adj.*

con·do·na·tion (kŏn′də-nā′shən, -dō-) *n.* The act of condoning, especially the implied forgiveness of an offense by ignoring it.

con·done (kən-dōn′) *tr.v.* **-doned, -don·ing, -dones.** To overlook, forgive, or disregard (an offense) without protest or censure. See Synonyms at **forgive.** [Latin *condōnāre* : *com-,* intensive pref.; see COM– + *dōnāre,* to give (from *dōnum,* gift; see **dō-** in Appendix).] **—con·don′er** *n.*

con·dor (kŏn′dôr′, -dər) *n.* **1.** Either of two New World vultures, *Vultur gryphus* of the Andes or *Gymnogyps californianus,* a nearly extinct vulture of the mountains of California, having a bare head and neck and dull black plumage containing variable amounts of white. With a wingspan of about three meters (ten feet), they are the largest birds in the Western Hemisphere. **2.** A gold coin of some South American countries bearing the figure of one of these vultures. [Spanish *cóndor,* from Quechua *cuntur.*]

condor
California condor
Gymnogyps californianus

Con·dor·cet (kôn-dôr-sĕ′), Marquis de. Title of Marie Jean Antoine Nicolas Caritat. 1743–1794. French mathematician and philosopher known for his work on the mathematical theory of probability and for his philosophical study *Sketch for a Historical Picture of the Progress of the Human Mind* (1795).

con·dot·tie·re (kŏn′də-tyâr′ē, -tyâr′ā) *n., pl.* **-tie·ri** (-tyâr′ē). A leader of mercenary soldiers between the 14th and 16th centuries. [Italian, from *condotta,* troop of mercenaries, from feminine past participle of *condurre,* to conduct, from Latin *condūcere,* to lead together. See CONDUCE.]

con·duce (kən-do͞os′, -dyo͞os′) *intr.v.* **-duced, -duc·ing, -duc·es.** To contribute or lead to a specific result: *"The quiet conduces to thinking about the darkening future"* (George F. Will). [Latin *condūcere* : *com-,* com- + *dūcere,* to lead; see **deuk-** in Appendix.] **—con·duc′er** *n.* **—con·duc′ing·ly** *adv.*

con·du·cive (kən-do͞o′sĭv, -dyo͞o′-) *adj.* Tending to bring about; contributive: *working conditions not conducive to productivity.* See Synonyms at **favorable. —con·du′cive·ness** *n.*

con·duct (kən-dŭkt′) *v.* **-duct·ed, -duct·ing, -ducts.** *—tr.* **1.** To direct the course of; manage or control. **2.** To lead or guide. See Synonyms at **conduct. 3.** *Music.* To lead (an orchestra, for example). **4.** To serve as a medium for conveying; transmit: *Some metals conduct heat.* **5.** To comport (oneself) in a specified way: *She conducted herself stoically in her time of grief.* *—intr.* **1.** To act as a conductor. **2.** To lead. **—conduct** (kŏn′dŭkt′) *n.* **1.** The way a person acts, especially from the standpoint of morality and ethics. See Synonyms at **behavior. 2.** The act of directing or controlling; management. **3.** *Obsolete.* A guide; an escort. [Middle English *conducten,* from Latin *condūcere, conduct-,* to lead

ă pat	oi boy
ā pay	ou out
âr care	o͝o took
ä father	o͞o boot
ĕ pet	ŭ cut
ē be	ûr urge
ĭ pit	th thin
ī pie	*th* this
îr pier	hw which
ŏ pot	zh vision
ō toe	ə about, item
ô paw	♦ regionalism

Stress marks: ′ (primary); ′ (secondary), as in **dictionary** (dĭk′shə-nĕr′ē)

together. See CONDUCE.] **—con·duct′i·bil′i·ty** *n.* **—con·duct′i·ble** *adj.*

con·duc·tance (kən-dŭk′təns) *n.* *Symbol* **G** A measure of a material's ability to conduct electric charge; the reciprocal of the resistance.

con·duc·tim·e·try (kŏn′dŭk-tĭm′ĭ-trē) *n.* The scientific measurement of solution conductance.

con·duc·tion (kən-dŭk′shən) *n.* The transmission or conveying of something through a medium or passage, especially the transmission of electric charge or heat through a conducting medium without perceptible motion of the medium itself.

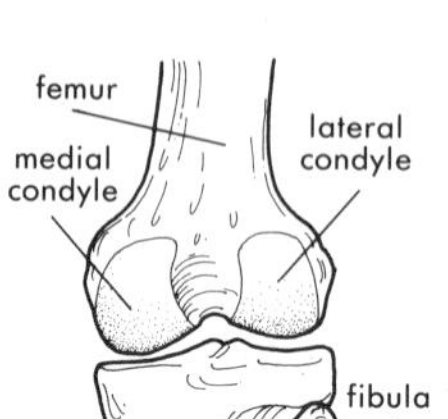
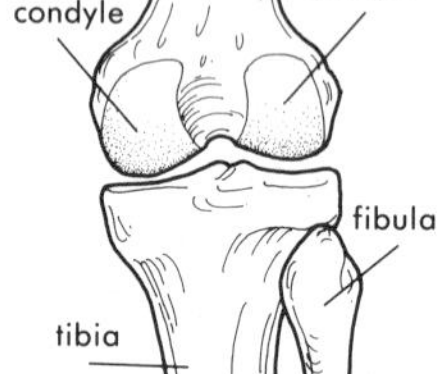

condyle
Posterior view of a right knee joint

con·duc·tive (kən-dŭk′tĭv) *adj.* Exhibiting conductivity.

con·duc·tiv·i·ty (kŏn′dŭk-tĭv′ĭ-tē) *n., pl.* **-ties.** *Abbr.* **cond. 1.** The ability or power to conduct or transmit heat, electricity, or sound. **2.** The conductance of a material. **3.** *Physiology.* The conductibility of a structure, especially the ability of a nerve to transmit a wave of excitation.

con·duc·to·met·ric titration (kən-dŭk′tə-mĕt′rĭk) *n.* Titration based on changes in the electrical conductance of a solution.

con·duc·tor (kən-dŭk′tər) *n.* *Abbr.* **cond. 1.** One who conducts, especially: **a.** One who is in charge of a railroad train, bus, or streetcar. **b.** *Music.* One who directs an orchestra or other such group. **2.** *Physics.* A substance or medium that conducts heat, light, sound, or especially an electric charge. **3.** A lightning rod, as on a house or barn. **—con′duc·to′ri·al** (kŏn′dŭk-tôr′ē-əl, -tōr′-) *adj.* **—con·duc′tor·ship′** *n.*

con·duit (kŏn′do͞o-ĭt, -dĭt) *n.* **1.** A pipe or channel for conveying fluids, such as water. **2.** A tube or duct for enclosing electric wires or cable. **3.** A means by which something is transmitted: *an arms dealer who served as a conduit for intelligence data.* **4.** *Archaic.* A fountain. [Middle English, from Old French, from Medieval Latin *conductus,* from Latin, past participle of *condūcere,* to lead together. See CONDUCE.]

con·du·pli·cate (kŏn-do͞o′plĭ-kĭt, -dyo͞o′-) *adj.* Folded together lengthwise, as certain leaves or certain petals in a bud. [Latin *conduplicātus,* past participle of *conduplicāre,* to double : *com-,* com- + *duplicāre,* to double (from *duplex, duplic-,* double; see **dwo-** in Appendix).] **—con′du·pli·ca′tion** (-kā′shən) *n.*

con·dyle (kŏn′dīl′, -dl) *n.* A rounded prominence at the end of a bone, most often for articulation with another bone. [Latin *condylus,* knuckle, from Greek *kondulos.*] **—con′dy·lar** (-də-lər) *adj.* **—con′dy·loid′** (-dl-oid′) *adj.*

con·dy·lo·ma (kŏn′dl-ō′mə) *n., pl.* **-mas** or **-ma·ta** (-mə-tə). A wartlike growth on the skin or mucous membrane, usually in the area of the anus or external genitalia. [Greek *kondulōma,* from *kondulos,* knuckle.] **—con′dy·lo′ma·tous** (-mə-təs) *adj.*

condyloma a·cu·mi·na·tum (ə-kyo͞o′mə-nā′təm) *n., pl.* **condylomata a·cu·mi·na·ta** (-nā′tə). See **genital wart.** [Latin *acūminātum,* pointed, neuter of *acūminātus.* See ACUMINATE.]

con·dy·lo·ma·ta (kŏn′dl-ō′mə-tə) *n.* A plural of **condyloma.**

cone (kōn) *n.* **1.** *Mathematics.* **a.** The surface generated by a straight line, the generator, passing through a fixed point, the vertex, and moving along a fixed curve, the directrix. **b.** A right circular cone. **2.a.** The figure formed by a cone, bound or regarded as bound by its vertex and a plane section taken anywhere above or below the vertex. **b.** Something having the shape of this figure: *"the cone of illuminated drops spilling beneath a street lamp"* (Anne Tyler). **3.** *Botany.* **a.** A unisexual reproductive structure of gymnospermous plants such as conifers and cycads, typically consisting of a central axis around which there are scaly, overlapping, spirally arranged sporophylls that develop pollen-bearing sacs or naked ovules or seeds. **b.** A similar structure that produces spores on club mosses, horsetails, and spike mosses. **c.** Any reproductive structure resembling a cone, such as a cluster of hop or alder fruits. **4.** *Physiology.* One of the photoreceptors in the retina of the eye that is responsible for daylight and color vision. These photoreceptors are most densely concentrated in the fovea centralis, creating the area of greatest visual acuity. **5.** Any of various gastropod mollusks of the family Conidae of tropical and subtropical seas, having a conical, often vividly marked shell and the ability to inflict a poisonous, sometimes fatal sting. **—cone** *tr.v.* **coned, con·ing, cones.** To shape (something) like a cone or a segment of one. [French *cône* and Middle English, angle of a quadrant, both from Latin *cōnus,* from Greek *kōnos.* See **kō-** in Appendix.]

vertex vertex element axis base directrix

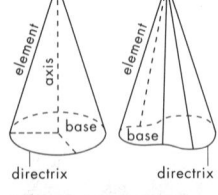

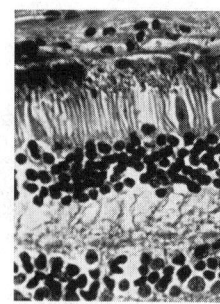

cone
Top: Right circular cone (*left*) and general cone (*right*)
Bottom: Cones and rods in a retina

cone·flow·er (kōn′flou′ər) *n.* Any of various North American plants of the genera *Rudbeckia, Ratibida,* and *Echinacea* in the composite family, having disk flowers on a cone-shaped central receptacle surrounded by colorful ray flowers.

cone·nose (kōn′nōz′) *n.* Any of various bloodsucking hemipterous insects of the family Reduviidae, especially *Triatoma sanguisuga* of Mexico and the southern and western United States, having sucking mouthparts and capable of inflicting a painful, toxic bite. Although they usually prey on insects, some suck the blood of mammals. Also called *cone-nosed bug, kissing bug.*

cone-nosed bug (kōn′nōzd′) *n.* See **conenose.**

Con·es·to·ga (kŏn′ĭ-stō′gə) *n., pl.* **Conestoga** or **-gas.** See **Susquehannock** (sense 1).

Conestoga wagon *n.* A heavy covered wagon with broad wheels, used by American pioneers for westward travel. [After *Conestoga,* a village of southeast Pennsylvania.]

Conestoga wagon

♦ **co·ney**[1] also **co·ny** (kō′nē, kŭn′ē) *n., pl.* **-neys** also **-nies. 1.** A rabbit, especially the European rabbit *(Oryctolagus cuniculus).* **2.** The fur of a rabbit. **3.** See **pika. 4.** See **hyrax. 5.a.** A grouper *(Epinephelus fulvus)* of the tropical Atlantic, having dark brown or sharply bicolored skin and a few blue and black spots. **b.** *Chiefly Florida Keys & West Indies.* Either of two related fish, the red hind or the graysby. **6.** *Archaic.* A dupe; a simpleton. [Middle English *coni,* from Old French *conis,* pl. of *conil,* from Latin *cunīculus,* possibly from *cunnus, cunus,* female pudenda.]

co·ney[2] (kō′nē) *n.* *Informal.* A Coney Island.

Co·ney Island[1] (kō′nē). A resort district of Brooklyn, New York, on the Atlantic Ocean, famous for its boardwalk and amusement park.

Co·ney Island[2] (kō′nē) *n.* *Informal.* A frankfurter served in a bun with condiments; a hot dog.

conf. *abbr.* **1.** Conference. **2.** Confidential.

con·fab (kŏn′făb′) *Informal. n.* A casual talk; confabulation. **—confab** (kən-făb′, kŏn′făb′) *intr.v.* **-fabbed, -fab·bing, -fabs.** To engage in casual talk.

con·fab·u·late (kən-făb′yə-lāt′) *intr.v.* **-lat·ed, -lat·ing, -lates. 1.** To talk casually; chat. **2.** *Psychology.* To replace fact with fantasy unconsciously in memory. [Latin *cōnfābulārī, cōnfābulāt-* : *com-,* com- + *fābulārī,* to talk (from *fābula,* conversation; see FABLE).] **—con·fab′u·la′tion** *n.* **—con·fab′u·la′tor** *n.* **—con·fab′u·la·to′ry** (-lə-tôr′ē, -tōr′ē) *adj.*

con·fect (kən-fĕkt′) *tr.v.* **-fect·ed, -fect·ing, -fects. 1.** To make into a confection or preserve. **2.** To put together by combining materials: *a group of writers who confected a television series.* **—confect** (kŏn′fĕkt′) *n.* A sweet confection, such as candy. [Middle English *confecten,* to prepare, from Latin *cōnficere, cōnfect-* : *com-,* intensive pref.; see COM– + *facere,* to make; see **dhē-** in Appendix.]

con·fec·tion (kən-fĕk′shən) *n.* **1.** The act or process of confecting or the result of it: *"These sentiments are not the confection of a consummate courtroom actor"* (Ron Rosenbaum). **2.** A sweet preparation, such as candy. **3.** A sweetened medicinal compound; an electuary. **4.** A piece displaying splendid craft, skill, and work: *The gown was a confection of satin and appliqué.* **—confection** *tr.v.* **-tioned, -tion·ing, -tions.** To make into a confection.

con·fec·tion·ar·y (kən-fĕk′shə-nĕr′ē) *n., pl.* **-ies. 1.** A confectioner's shop; a confectionery. **2.** Sweet preparations; confections. **3.** *Obsolete.* A confectioner. **—con·fec′tion·ar′y** *adj.*

con·fec·tion·er (kən-fĕk′shə-nər) *n.* One that makes or sells confections.

con·fec·tion·ers' sugar (kən-fĕk′shə-nərz) *n.* Finely pulverized sugar with cornstarch added.

con·fec·tion·er·y (kən-fĕk′shə-nĕr′ē) *n., pl.* **-ies. 1.** Candies and other confections considered as a group. **2.** The skill or occupation of a confectioner. **3.** A confectioner's shop.

confed. *abbr.* Confederation.

con·fed·er·a·cy (kən-fĕd′ər-ə-sē) *n., pl.* **-cies. 1.a.** A union of persons, parties, or states; a league. **b.** The persons, parties, or states joined in such a union. **c. Confederacy.** The 11 Southern states that seceded from the United States in 1860 and 1861. **2.** A group of people who have united for unlawful practices; a conspiracy. [Middle English *confederacie,* from Anglo-Norman, from Late Latin *cōnfoederātiō, cōnfoederātiōn-,* agreement, from *cōnfoederātus,* past participle of *cōnfoederāre,* to unite. See CONFEDERATE.]

con·fed·er·al (kən-fĕd′ər-əl, -fĕd′rəl) *adj.* **1.** Of or relating to confederation or a specific confederation. **2.** Of, relating to, or involving the activities of two or more nations: *"Can federal or confederal solutions be negotiated to limit ethnic strife?"* (Lincoln P. Bloomfield). **—con·fed′er·al·ist** *n.*

con·fed·er·ate (kən-fĕd′ər-ĭt) *n.* **1.** A member of a confederacy; an ally. **2.** One who assists in a plot; an accomplice. See Synonyms at **partner. 3. Confederate.** A supporter of the American Confederacy. **—confederate** *adj.* **1.** United in a confederacy; allied. **2. Confederate.** Of or having to do with the American Confederacy. **—confederate** (-ə-rāt′) *tr. & intr.v.* **-at·ed, -at·ing, -ates.** To form into or become part of a confederacy. [From Middle English *confederat,* allied, from Late Latin *cōnfoederātus,* past participle of *cōnfoederāre,* to unite : Latin *com-,* com- + Latin *foederāre,* to unite (from *foedus, foeder-,* league; see **bheidh-** in Appendix).] **—con·fed′er·a′tive** *adj.*

con·fed·er·a·tion (kən-fĕd′ə-rā′shən) *n.* *Abbr.* **confed. 1.a.** The act of forming into or becoming part of a confederacy. **b.** The state of being confederated. **2.** A group of confederates, especially of states or nations, united for a common purpose. **—con·fed′er·a′tion·ism** *n.* **—con·fed′er·a′tion·ist** *n.*

con·fer (kən-fûr′) *v.* **-ferred, -fer·ring, -fers.** —*tr.* **1.** To bestow (an honor, for example): *conferred a medal on the hero; conferred an honorary degree on her.* **2.** To invest with (a characteristic, for example): *a carefully worded statement that conferred an aura of credibility onto the administration's actions.* —*intr.* To meet in order to deliberate together or compare views. [Latin *cōnferre* : *com-,* com- + *ferre,* to bring; see **bher-**[1] in Appendix.] **—con·fer′ment** *n.* **—con·fer′ra·ble** *adj.* **—con·fer′ral** *n.* **—con·fer′rer** *n.*

SYNONYMS: *confer, advise, consult, parley, treat.* The central meaning shared by these verbs is "to exchange views in order to reach a decision or resolve differences": *a doctor conferring with a patient; a board chairperson advising with the members; has to consult with an attorney; parleyed with enemy representatives during the cease-fire; delegates treating for the recognition of their union.*

con·fer·ee also **con·fer·ree** (kŏn′fə-rē′) *n.* **1.** A participant in a conference. **2.** One upon whom something, such as an honor, is conferred.

con·fer·ence (kŏn′fər-əns, -frəns) *n. Abbr.* **conf.** **1.a.** A meeting for consultation or discussion. **b.** An exchange of views. **c.** A meeting of committees to settle differences between two legislative bodies. **2.** An assembly of clerical or of clerical and lay members from a particular district in various Protestant churches. **3.** *Sports.* An association of teams. **4.** The act of conferring, as of an academic degree. [Medieval Latin *cōnferentia,* from Latin *cōnferēns, cōnferent-,* present participle of *cōnferre,* to bring together. See CONFER.] **—con′fer·en′tial** (-fə-rĕn′shəl) *adj.*

conference call *n.* A conference by telephone in which three or more persons in different locations participate by means of a central switching unit.

con·fer·ree (kŏn′fə-rē′) *n.* Variant of **conferee.**

con·fess (kən-fĕs′) *v.* **-fessed, -fess·ing, -fess·es.** *—tr.* **1.** To disclose (something damaging or inconvenient to oneself); admit. See Synonyms at **acknowledge.** **2.** To acknowledge belief or faith in; profess. **3.a.** To make known (one's sins) to God or to a priest. **b.** To hear the confession of (a penitent). *—intr.* **1.** To admit or acknowledge something damaging or inconvenient to oneself: *The suspect confessed to the crime.* **2.a.** To disclose one's sins to a priest. **b.** To listen to a confession. [Middle English *confessen,* from Old French *confesser,* from Vulgar Latin **cōnfessāre,* from Latin *cōnfitērī, cōnfess-* : *com-,* intensive pref.; see COM– + *fatērī,* to admit; see **bhā-**[2] in Appendix.] **—con·fess′a·ble** *adj.* **—con·fess′ed·ly** (-ĭd-lē) *adv.*

con·fes·sion (kən-fĕsh′ən) *n.* **1.** The act or process of confessing. **2.** Something confessed, especially disclosure of one's sins to a priest for absolution. **3.** A written or an oral statement acknowledging guilt, made by one who has been accused or charged with an offense. **4.** An avowal of belief in the doctrines of a particular faith; a creed. **5.** A church or group of worshipers adhering to a specific creed.

con·fes·sion·al (kən-fĕsh′ə-nəl) *adj.* Of, relating to, or resembling confession. **—confessional** *n.* A small enclosed stall in which a priest hears confessions.

con·fes·sor (kən-fĕs′ər) *n.* **1.** One who confesses. **2.** One who confesses faith in Christianity in the face of persecution but does not suffer martyrdom. **3.a.** A priest who hears confession and gives absolution. **b.** A priest who is one's spiritual mentor.

con·fet·ti (kən-fĕt′ē) *pl.n. (used with a sing. verb).* Small pieces or streamers of colored paper that are scattered around during the course of festive occasions: *Confetti covers the floor every year on January 1.* [Italian, pl. of *confetto,* candy, from Medieval Latin *cōnfectum,* neuter of Latin *cōnfectus,* past participle of *cōnficere,* to prepare. See CONFECT.]

con·fi·dant (kŏn′fĭ-dănt′, -dänt′, kŏn′fĭ-dănt′, -dänt′) *n.* **1.** One to whom secrets or private matters are disclosed. **2.** A character in a drama or fiction, such as a trusted friend or servant, who serves as a device for revealing the inner thoughts or intentions of a main character. [French *confident,* from Italian *confidente,* from Latin *cōnfīdēns, cōnfīdent-,* present participle of *cōnfīdere,* to rely on. See CONFIDE.]

con·fi·dante (kŏn′fĭ-dănt′, -dänt′, kŏn′fĭ-dănt′, -dänt′) *n.* **1.** A woman to whom secrets or private matters are disclosed. **2.** A woman character in a drama or fiction, such as a trusted friend or servant, who serves as a device for revealing the inner thoughts or intentions of a main character. [French *confidente,* feminine of *confident,* confidant. See CONFIDANT.]

con·fide (kən-fīd′) *v.* **-fid·ed, -fid·ing, -fides.** *—tr.* **1.** To tell (something) in confidence. **2.** To put into another's keeping. *—intr.* To disclose private matters in confidence. See Synonyms at **commit.** [Middle English *confide,* to rely on, from Old French *confider,* from Latin *cōnfīdere* : *com-,* intensive pref.; see COM– + *fīdere,* to trust; see **bheidh-** in Appendix.] **—con·fid′er** *n.*

con·fi·dence (kŏn′fĭ-dəns) *n.* **1.** Trust or faith in a person or thing. **2.** A trusting relationship: *I took them into my confidence.* **3.a.** That which is confided; a secret: *A friend does not betray confidences.* **b.** A feeling of assurance that a confidant will keep a secret: *I am telling you this in strict confidence.* **4.** A feeling of assurance, especially of self-assurance. **5.** The state or quality of being certain: *I have every confidence in your ability to succeed.* **—confidence** *adj.* Of, relating to, or involving a swindle or fraud: *a confidence scheme; a confidence trickster.*

SYNONYMS: *confidence, assurance, aplomb, self-confidence, self-possession.* These nouns denote a feeling of emotional security resulting from faith in oneself. *Confidence* is a firm belief in one's powers, abilities, or capacities: *"You gain strength, courage and confidence by every experience in which you really stop to look fear in the face"* (Eleanor Roosevelt). *Assurance* even more strongly stresses certainty and can suggest arrogance: *How can a nonscientist explain an abstruse theory with such assurance? Aplomb* implies calm poise: *"It is native personality, and that alone, that endows a man to stand before presidents or generals, or in any distinguished collection, with* aplomb*"* (Walt Whitman). *Self-confidence* stresses trust in one's own self-sufficiency: *"The most vital quality a soldier can possess is self-confidence, utter, complete and bumptious"* (George S. Patton). *Self-possession* implies composure arising from control over one's own reactions: *"In life courtesy and self-possession . . . are the sensible impressions of the free mind, for both arise . . . from never being swept away, whatever the emotion, into confusion or dullness"* (William Butler Yeats). See also Synonyms at **trust.**

confidence game *n.* A swindle in which the victim is defrauded after his or her confidence has been won.

confidence interval *n.* A statistical range with a specified probability that a given parameter lies within the range.

confidence limit *n.* Either of the two numbers that specify the endpoints of a confidence interval.

confidence man *n.* A man who swindles his victims by using a confidence game.

con·fi·dent (kŏn′fĭ-dənt) *adj.* **1.** Marked by assurance, as of success. **2.** Marked by confidence in oneself; self-assured. See Synonyms at **sure.** **3.** Very bold; presumptuous. **4.** *Obsolete.* Confiding; trustful. [Latin *cōnfīdēns, cōnfīdent-,* present participle of *cōnfīdere,* to rely on. See CONFIDE.] **—con′fi·dent·ly** *adv.*

con·fi·den·tial (kŏn′fĭ-dĕn′shəl) *adj. Abbr.* **conf.** **1.** Done or communicated in confidence; secret. **2.** Entrusted with the confidence of another: *a confidential secretary.* **3.** Denoting confidence or intimacy: *a confidential tone of voice.* See Synonyms at **familiar.** **4.** Containing secret information, the unauthorized disclosure of which poses a threat to national security. **—con′fi·den′ti·al′i·ty** (-shē-ăl′ĭ-tē), **con′fi·den′tial·ness** *n.* **—con′fi·den′tial·ly** *adv.*

confidential communication *n. Law.* A statement made to someone, such as one's physician, attorney, priest, or spouse, who cannot be compelled to divulge the information.

con·fid·ing (kən-fī′dĭng) *adj.* Having a tendency to confide; trusting. **—con·fid′ing·ly** *adv.* **—con·fid′ing·ness** *n.*

con·fig·u·ra·tion (kən-fĭg′yə-rā′shən) *n.* **1.a.** Arrangement of parts or elements. **b.** The form, as of a figure, determined by the arrangement of its parts or elements. See Synonyms at **form.** **2.** *Psychology.* Gestalt. **3.** *Chemistry.* The structural arrangement of atoms in a compound or molecule. **—con·fig′u·ra′tion·al·ly** *adv.* **—con·fig′u·ra′tive, con·fig′u·ra′tion·al** *adj.*

con·fig·u·ra·tion·ism (kən-fĭg′yə-rā′shə-nĭz′əm) *n.* Gestalt psychology.

con·fig·ure (kən-fĭg′yər) *tr.v.* **-ured, -ur·ing, -ures.** To design, arrange, set up, or shape with a view to specific applications or uses: *an internal security vehicle that was configured for rough terrain.* [Middle English *configuren,* from Old French *configurer,* from Latin *cōnfigūrāre* : *com-,* com- + *figūrāre,* to form (from *figūra,* shape; see **dheigh-** in Appendix).]

con·fine (kən-fīn′) *v.* **-fined, -fin·ing, -fines.** *—tr.* **1.** To keep within bounds; restrict: *Please confine your remarks to the issues at hand.* See Synonyms at **limit.** **2.** To shut or keep in, especially to imprison. **3.** To restrict in movement: *The sick child was confined to bed.* *—intr. Archaic.* To border. **—confine** (kŏn′fīn′) *n.* **1. confines. a.** The limits of a space or an area; the borders: *within the confines of one county.* **b.** Restraining elements: *wanted to escape the confines of corporate politics and bureaucracy.* **c.** Purview; scope: *children who learned to work within the confines of the curriculum; a theory that has transcended the confines of science.* **2.a.** *Archaic.* A restriction. **b.** *Obsolete.* A prison. [French *confiner,* from Old French, from *confins,* boundaries, ultimately from Latin *cōnfīne,* from neuter of *cōnfīnis,* adjoining : *com-,* com- + *fīnis,* border.] **—con·fin′a·ble, con·fine′a·ble** *adj.* **—con·fin′er** *n.*

con·fine·ment (kən-fīn′mənt) *n.* **1.** The act of confining or the state of being confined. **2.** Lying-in.

con·firm (kən-fûrm′) *tr.v.* **-firmed, -firm·ing, -firms.** **1.** To support or establish the certainty or validity of; verify. **2.** To make firmer; strengthen: *The recent airplane crash confirms my belief that stronger safety regulations are needed.* **3.** To make valid or binding by a formal or legal act; ratify. **4.** To administer the religious rite of confirmation to. [Middle English *confirmen,* from Old French *confermer,* from Latin *cōnfirmāre* : *com-,* intensive pref.; see COM– + *firmāre,* to strengthen (from *firmus,* strong; see **dher-** in Appendix).] **—con·firm′a·bil′i·ty** *n.* **—con·firm′a·ble** *adj.* **—con·firm′a·to′ry** (-fûr′mə-tôr′ē, -tōr′ē) *adj.* **—con·firm′er** *n.*

SYNONYMS: *confirm, corroborate, substantiate, authenticate, validate, verify.* These verbs all mean to affirm the truth, accuracy, or genuineness of something. *Confirm* generally implies removal of all doubt about something considered uncertain or tentative: *"We must never make experiments to confirm our ideas, but simply to control them"* (Claude Bernard). *Corroborate* refers to strengthening or supporting something, such as a statement, by means of the evidence of another: *The witness is expected to corroborate the plaintiff's testimony.* To *substantiate* is to establish something by presenting substantial or tangible evidence: *"one of the most fully substantiated of historical facts"* (James Harvey Robinson). *Authenticate* implies the removal of doubt about the genuineness of something by the act of an authority or the testimony of an expert: *The museum made the mistake of accepting the painting before it had been authenticated. Validate* usually

confessional

confetti

ă **pat**	oi **boy**
ā **pay**	ou **out**
âr **care**	ŏŏ **took**
ä **father**	ōō **boot**
ĕ **pet**	ŭ **cut**
ē **be**	ûr **urge**
ĭ **pit**	th **thin**
ī **pie**	*th* **this**
îr **pier**	hw **which**
ŏ **pot**	zh **vision**
ō **toe**	ə **about, item**
ô **paw**	♦ **regionalism**

Stress marks: **′** (primary); ′ (secondary), as in **dictionary** (dĭk′shə-nĕr′ē)

implies formal action taken to give legal force to something (*validate a deed of sale*) but can also refer to establishing the validity of something, such as a theory, claim, or judgment (*The divorce validated my parents' original objection to the marriage*). *Verify* implies proving by comparison with an original or with established fact: *The bank refused to cash the check until the signature was verified.*

con·fir·ma·tion (kŏn′fər-mā′shən) *n.* **1.a.** The act of confirming. **b.** Something that confirms; verification. **2.a.** A Christian rite admitting a baptized person to full membership in a church. **b.** A ceremony in Judaism that marks the completion of a young person's religious training.

con·firmed (kən-fûrmd′) *adj.* **1.** Being firmly settled in habit; inveterate. See Synonyms at **chronic. 2.** Having been ratified; verified. **3.** Having received the rite of confirmation. **—con·firm′ed·ly** (-fûr′mĭd-lē) *adv.*

con·fis·ca·ble (kən-fĭs′kə-bəl) *adj.* Subject to confiscation: *confiscable goods.*

con·fis·cate (kŏn′fĭ-skāt′) *tr.v.* **-cat·ed, -cat·ing, -cates. 1.** To seize (private property) for the public treasury. **2.** To seize by or as if by authority. See Synonyms at **appropriate. —confiscate** (kŏn′fĭ-skāt′, kən-fĭs′kət) *adj.* **1.** Seized by a government; appropriated. **2.** Having lost property through confiscation. [Latin *cōnfiscāre, cōnfiscāt-* : *com-*, com- + *fiscus*, treasury.] **—con′fis·ca′tion** *n.* **—con′fis·ca′tor** *n.* **—con·fis′ca·to′ry** (kən-fĭs′kə-tôr′ē, -tōr′ē) *adj.*

Con·fi·te·or (kən-fē′tē-ər, -ôr′) *n.* A prayer in which confession of sins is made. [Latin *Cōnfiteor*, I confess, the first word of the prayer, first person sing. present tense of *cōnfitērī*, to acknowledge. See CONFESS.]

con·fi·ture (kŏn′fĭ-cho͝or′) *n.* A confection, preserve, or other sweetmeat. [French, from Old French, from *confit*, confection. See COMFIT.]

con·fla·grant (kən-flā′grənt) *adj.* Burning intensely; blazing. [Latin *cōnflagrāns, cōnflagrant-*, present participle of *cōnflagrāre*, to burn up : *com-*, intensive pref.; see COM– + *flagrāre*, to burn; see **bhel-**[1] in Appendix.]

con·fla·gra·tion (kŏn′flə-grā′shən) *n.* A large, destructive fire. [Latin *cōnflagrātiō, cōnflagrātiōn-*, from *cōnflagrātus*, past participle of *cōnflagrāre*, to burn up. See CONFLAGRANT.]

con·flate (kən-flāt′) *tr.v.* **-flat·ed, -flat·ing, -flates. 1.** To bring together; meld or fuse: *"They ingeniously conflated other characters and incidents to provide an opéra-comique setting"* (Andrew Porter). **2.** To combine (two variant texts, for example) into one whole. [Latin *cōnflāre, cōnflāt-* : *com-*, com- + *flāre*, to blow; see **bhlē-** in Appendix.] **—con·fla′tion** *n.*

con·flict (kŏn′flĭkt′) *n.* **1.** A state of open, often prolonged fighting; a battle or war. **2.** A state of disharmony between incompatible or antithetical persons, ideas, or interests; a clash. **3.** *Psychology.* A psychic struggle, often unconscious, resulting from the opposition or simultaneous functioning of mutually exclusive impulses, desires, or tendencies. **4.** Opposition between characters or forces in a work of drama or fiction, especially opposition that motivates or shapes the action of the plot. **—conflict** (kən-flĭkt′) *intr.v.* **-flict·ed, -flict·ing, -flicts. 1.** To be in or come into opposition; differ. **2.** *Archaic.* To engage in warfare. [Middle English, from Latin *cōnflīctus*, collision, from past participle of *cōnflīgere*, to strike together : *com-*, com- + *flīgere*, to strike.] **—con·flic′tion** *n.* **—con·flic′tive** *adj.* **—con·flic′tu·al** (kən-flĭk′cho͞o-əl) *adj.*

SYNONYMS: *conflict, contest, combat, fight, affray.* These nouns denote struggle between opposing forces for victory or supremacy. *Conflict* applies both to open fighting between hostile groups and to a struggle, often an inner struggle, between antithetical forces: *"The kind of victory MacArthur had in mind—victory by the bombing of Chinese cities, victory by expanding the conflict to all of China—would have been the wrong kind of victory"* (Harry S. Truman). *"Fortunately analysis is not the only way to resolve inner conflicts. Life itself still remains a very effective therapist"* (Karen Horney). *Contest* can refer either to friendly competition or to a hostile struggle to achieve an objective: *an archery contest; a spelling contest; the gubernatorial contest. Combat* most commonly implies an encounter between two armed persons or groups: *"Alexander had appeared to him, armed for combat"* (Connop Thirlwall). *Fight* usually refers to a clash, physical or figurative, involving individual adversaries: *A fight was scheduled between the world boxing champion and the challenger. "There is nothing I love as much as a good fight"* (Franklin D. Roosevelt). *Affray* suggests a public fight or brawl: *"Yet still the poachers came . . . for affrays in woods and on moors with liveried armies of keepers"* (Patricia Morison). See also Synonyms at **discord.**

con·flict·ed (kən-flĭk′tĭd) *adj. Usage Problem.* Made uneasy by conflicting impulses.

USAGE NOTE: The adjective *conflicted* is associated with the jargon of New Age psychology: 92 percent of the Usage Panel rejected its use in the sentence *Caught between loyalty to old employees and a recognition of the need to cut costs, many managers are conflicted about the reorganization plan.*

conflict of interest *n., pl.* **conflicts of interest.** A conflict between the private interests and the public obligations of a person in an official position.

con·flu·ence (kŏn′flo͞o-əns) *n.* **1.a.** A flowing together of two or more streams. **b.** The point of juncture of such streams. **c.** The combined stream formed by this juncture. **2.** A gathering, flowing, or meeting together at one juncture or point: *a confluence of artistry, superb choreography, and stage design.*

con·flu·ent (kŏn′flo͞o-ənt) *adj.* **1.** Flowing together; blended into one. **2.** *Pathology.* Merging or running together so as to form a mass, as sores in a rash. **—confluent** *n.* **1.** One of two or more confluent streams. **2.** A tributary. [Middle English, from Latin *cōnfluēns, cōnfluent-*, present participle of *cōnfluere*, to flow together : *com-*, com- + *fluere*, to flow; see **bhleu-** in Appendix.]

con·flux (kŏn′flŭks′) *n.* A confluence. [From Latin *cōnfluxus*, past participle of *cōnfluere*, to flow together. See CONFLUENT.]

con·fo·cal (kŏn-fō′kəl) *adj.* Having the same focus or foci. Used of a lens. **—con·fo′cal·ly** *adv.*

con·form (kən-fôrm′) *v.* **-formed, -form·ing, -forms.** —*intr.* **1.** To correspond in form or character; be similar. **2.** To act or be in accord or agreement; comply. See Synonyms at **agree. 3.** To act in accordance with current customs or modes. See Synonyms at **adapt.** —*tr.* To bring into agreement or correspondence; make similar. [Middle English *conformen*, from Old French *conformer*, from Latin *cōnformāre*, to shape after : *com-*, com- + *formāre*, to shape (from *forma*, shape).] **—con·form′er** *n.*

con·form·a·ble (kən-fôr′mə-bəl) *adj.* **1.** Corresponding; similar: *plans that are conformable to your wishes.* **2.** Quick to comply; submissive. **3.** *Geology.* Of, relating to, or being strata that are parallel to each other without interruption. **—con·form′a·bil′i·ty, con·form′a·ble·ness** *n.* **—con·form′a·bly** *adv.*

con·for·mal (kən-fôr′məl) *adj.* **1.** *Mathematics.* Designating or specifying a mapping of a surface or region upon another surface so that all angles between intersecting curves remain unchanged. **2.** Of or relating to a map projection in which small areas are rendered with true shape. [Late Latin *cōnformālis*, similar : Latin *com-*, com- + Latin *forma*, shape.]

con·for·mance (kən-fôr′məns) *n.* Conformity.

con·for·ma·tion (kŏn′fər-mā′shən) *n.* **1.** The act of conforming or the state of being conformed. **2.** The structure or outline of an item or entity, determined by the arrangement of its parts. **3.** A symmetrical arrangement of the parts of a thing. **4.** One of the spatial arrangements of atoms in a molecule that can come about through free rotation of the atoms about a single chemical bond. **—con′for·ma′tion·al** *adj.* **—con′for·ma′tion·al·ly** *adv.*

con·form·ist (kən-fôr′mĭst) *n.* A person who uncritically or habitually conforms to the customs, rules, or styles of a group. **—conformist** *adj.* Marked by conformity or convention: *"Underneath the image, teenagers today are surprisingly conformist"* (Selina S. Guber).

con·form·i·ty (kən-fôr′mĭ-tē) *n., pl.* **-ties. 1.** Similarity in form or character; agreement: *I acted in conformity with my principles.* **2.** Action or behavior in correspondence with current customs, rules, or styles: *conformity to university regulations.*

con·found (kən-found′, kŏn-) *tr.v.* **-found·ed, -found·ing, -founds. 1.** To cause to become confused or perplexed. See Synonyms at **puzzle. 2.** To fail to distinguish; mix up: *confound fiction and fact.* **3.** To make (something bad) worse: *Do not confound the problem by losing your temper.* **4.** To cause to be ashamed; abash: *an invention that confounded the skeptics.* **5.** To damn. **6.a.** To frustrate: *picayune demands that all but confounded the peace talks.* **b.** *Archaic.* To bring to ruination. [Middle English *confounden*, from Anglo-Norman *confundre*, from Latin *cōnfundere*, to mix together, confuse : *com-*, com- + *fundere*, to pour; see **gheu-** in Appendix.] **—con·found′er** *n.*

con·found·ed (kən-foun′dĭd, kŏn-) *adj.* **1.** Confused; befuddled: *A crowd of confounded bystanders stared at the appalling wreckage.* **2.** Used as an intensive: *a confounded fool.* **—con·found′ed·ly** *adv.* **—con·found′ed·ness** *n.*

con·fra·ter·ni·ty (kŏn′frə-tûr′nĭ-tē) *n., pl.* **-ties.** An association of persons united in a common purpose or profession. [Middle English *confraternite*, from Old French, from Medieval Latin *cōnfrāternitās*, from *cōnfrāter*, colleague. See CONFRERE.]

con·frere (kŏn′frâr′) *n.* A fellow member of a fraternity or profession; a colleague. [Middle English, from Old French, from Medieval Latin *cōnfrāter* : Latin *com-*, com- + Latin *frāter*, brother; see **bhrāter-** in Appendix.]

con·front (kən-frŭnt′) *v.* **-front·ed, -front·ing, -fronts.** —*tr.* **1.** To come face to face with, especially with defiance or hostility: *I wish to confront my accuser in a court of law.* **2.** To bring face to face with: *The defendant was confronted with incontrovertible evidence of guilt.* **3.** To come up against; encounter: *confronted danger at every turn.* —*intr.* To engage in confrontation: *"She got no child support. [She] didn't argue or confront"* (Gail Sheehy). [French *confronter*, from Old French, to adjoin, from Medieval Latin *cōnfrontāre* : Latin *com-*, com- + Latin *frōns, front-*, front.] **—con·front′er** *n.* **—con·front′ment** *n.*

con·fron·ta·tion (kŏn′frŭn-tā′shən) *n.* **1.** The act of confronting or the state of being confronted, especially a meeting face to face. **2.a.** A conflict involving armed forces: *a nuclear confrontation.* **b.** Discord or a clash of opinions and ideas: *an age of ideological confrontation.* **3.** A focused comparison: *an essay that brought elements of biography, autobiography, and general Euro-*

ă pat	oi boy
ā pay	ou out
âr care	o͝o took
ä father	o͞o boot
ĕ pet	ŭ cut
ē be	ûr urge
ĭ pit	th thin
ī pie	*th* this
îr pier	hw which
ŏ pot	zh vision
ō toe	ə about, item
ô paw	♦ regionalism

Stress marks: **′** (primary); ′ (secondary), as in **dictionary** (dĭk′shə-nĕr′ē)

pean history into powerful, meaningful confrontation. **—con′fron·ta′tion·al** *adj.* **—con′fron·ta′tion·ist** *n.* **—con′fron·ta′tive** *adj.*

Con·fu·cian (kən-fyo͞o′shən) *adj.* Of, relating to, or characteristic of Confucius, his teachings, or his followers. **—Confucian** *n.* An adherent of the teachings of Confucius. **—Con·fu′cian·ism** *n.* **—Con·fu′cian·ist** *n.*

Con·fu·cius (kən-fyo͞o′shəs). c. 551–479 B.C. Chinese philosopher whose *Analects* contain a collection of his sayings and dialogues compiled by disciples after his death.

Confucius

con·fuse (kən-fyo͞oz′) *v.* **-fused, -fus·ing, -fus·es.** *—tr.* **1.a.** To cause to be unable to think with clarity or act with intelligence or understanding; throw off. **b.** To cause to feel embarrassment. **2.a.** To mistake (one thing for another): *confused effusiveness with affection.* **b.** To make opaque; blur: *"The old labels . . . confuse debate instead of clarifying it"* (Christopher Lasch). **c.** To assemble without order or sense; jumble. **3.** *Archaic.* To bring to ruination. *—intr.* To make something unclear or incomprehensible: *a new tax code that only further confuses.* [Middle English *confusen,* from Old French *confus,* perplexed, from Latin *cōnfūsus,* past participle of *cōnfundere,* to mix together. See CONFOUND.] **—con·fus′ing·ly** *adv.*

SYNONYMS: *confuse, addle, befuddle, discombobulate, fuddle, muddle, throw.* The central meaning shared by these verbs is "to cause to be unclear in mind or intent": *heavy traffic that confused the novice driver; problems that addle my brain; a question that befuddled even the professor; was discombobulated by the staggering number of possibilities; a plot so complex that it fuddles one's comprehension; a head that was muddled by endless facts and figures; behavior that really threw me.*

con·fused (kən-fyo͞ozd′) *adj.* **1.** Being unable to think with clarity or act with understanding and intelligence. **2.a.** Lacking logical order or sense: *a confused set of instructions.* **b.** Chaotic; jumbled: *a confused mass of papers on the floor.* **—con·fus′ed·ly** (-fyo͞o′zĭd-lē) *adv.* **—con·fus′ed·ness** *n.*

con·fu·sion (kən-fyo͞o′zhən) *n.* **1.a.** The act of confusing or the state of being confused: *"To insist . . . that the plight of two, or six, or 52 individuals outweighs policies in which the credibility of the United States and the security of the Middle East are deeply involved, represents the worst kind of moral confusion"* (Moorhead Kennedy). **b.** An instance of being confused: *"Both John Cheever and James Michener . . . clarify some of the confusions of our times"* (Clifton Fadiman). **2.** *Psychology.* Impaired orientation with respect to time, place, or person; a disturbed mental state. **—con·fu′sion·al** *adj.*

con·fu·ta·tion (kŏn′fyo͞o-tā′shən) *n.* **1.** The act of confuting. **2.** Something that confutes. **—con·fu′ta·tive** (kən-fyo͞o′tə-tĭv) *adj.*

con·fute (kən-fyo͞ot′) *tr.v.* **-fut·ed, -fut·ing, -futes.** **1.** To prove to be wrong or in error; refute decisively. **2.** *Obsolete.* To confound. [Latin *cōnfūtāre.* See **bhau-** in Appendix.] **—con·fut′a·ble** *adj.* **—con·fut′er** *n.*

cong. *abbr. Pharmacology.* Congius (gallon).

Cong. *abbr.* **1.** Congregational. **2.** Congress. **3.** Congressional.

con·ga (kŏng′gə) *n.* **1.** A dance of Latin-American origin in which the dancers form a long, winding line. **2.** Music for this dance. **3.** A conga drum. **—conga** *intr.v.* **-gaed, -ga·ing, -gas.** To perform this dance. [American Spanish *(danza) Conga,* Congo (dance), from Spanish *Congo,* of the Congo, from Kongo *-kongo,* Kongo language and people.]

conga drum *n.* A tall, usually tapering single-headed drum typically played by beating with the hands.

conga drum
A pair of conga drums

con game *n. Slang.* A confidence game.

con·gé (kŏn′zhā′, -jā′, kôɴ-zhā′) also **con·gee** (kŏn′jē) *n.* **1.** Formal or authoritative permission to depart. **2.** An abrupt dismissal. **3.** A leave-taking. **4.** A formal bow. **5.** *Architecture.* A concave molding. [Middle English *conge* and French *congé,* both from Old French *congie,* from Latin *commeātus,* from past participle of *commeāre,* to come and go : *com-,* com- + *meāre,* to go; see **mei-**[1] in Appendix.]

con·geal (kən-jēl′) *v.* **-gealed, -geal·ing, -geals.** *—intr.* **1.** To solidify by or as if by freezing: *"My aim . . . was to take the Hill by storm before . . . opposition to spending cuts congealed"* (David A. Stockman). **2.** To coagulate; jell. *—tr.* To cause to solidify or coagulate or to undergo a process likened to solidification or coagulation. See Synonyms at **coagulate.** [Middle English *congelen,* from Old French *congeler,* from Latin *congelāre* : *com-,* com- + *gelāre,* to freeze; see **gel-** in Appendix.] **—con·geal′a·ble** *adj.* **—con·geal′er** *n.* **—con·geal′ment** *n.*

♦**con·gealed salad** (kən-jēld′) *n. Chiefly Southern U.S.* A molded salad made of flavored gelatin, chopped fruits or vegetables, and sometimes cottage cheese, sour cream, shredded coconut, marshmallows, or chopped nuts.

con·gee (kŏn′jē) *n.* Variant of **congé.**

con·ge·la·tion (kŏn′jə-lā′shən) *n.* The process of congealing or the state of being congealed.

con·ge·ner (kŏn′jə-nər) *n.* **1.** A member of the same kind, class, or group. **2.** An organism belonging to the same taxonomic genus as another organism. [From Latin, of the same race : *com-,* com- + *genus, gener-,* race; see **gene-** in Appendix.] **—con′ge·ner′ic** (-nĕr′ĭk), **con·gen′er·ous** (kən-jĕn′ər-əs, kŏn-) *adj.*

con·gen·ial (kən-jēn′yəl) *adj.* **1.** Having the same tastes, habits, or temperament; sympathetic. **2.** Of a pleasant disposition; friendly and sociable: *a congenial host and hostess.* **3.** Suited to one's needs or nature; agreeable: *congenial surroundings.* [Probably from CON– + Latin *genius,* the personification of one's natural inclinations; see GENIUS.] **—con·ge′ni·al′i·ty** (-jē′nē-ăl′ĭ-tē), **con·gen′ial·ness** *n.* **—con·gen′ial·ly** *adv.*

con·gen·i·tal (kən-jĕn′ĭ-tl) *adj.* **1.a.** Existing at or before birth. **b.** Acquired at birth or during uterine development, as a result of either hereditary or environmental influences. See Synonyms at **innate.** **2.** Being an essential characteristic as if by nature; inherent: *"the congenital American optimism that denies conflicts and imagines all stories having happy endings"* (Robert J. Samuelson). [From Latin *congenitus* : *com-,* com- + *genitus,* born, past participle of *gignere,* to bear; see **gene-** in Appendix.] **—con·gen′i·tal·ly** *adv.*

congenital anomaly *n.* See **birth defect.**

congenital myxedema *n.* See **cretinism.**

con·ger (kŏng′gər) *n.* Any of various large, scaleless marine eels of the family Congridae, especially *Conger oceanicus,* native to Atlantic waters. [Middle English *congre,* from Old French, probably from Late Latin *congrus,* from Latin *conger,* from Greek *gongros.*]

con·ge·ries (kən-jîr′ēz′, kŏn′jə-rēz′) *n. (used with a sing. verb).* A collection; an aggregation: *"Our city, it should be explained, is two cities, or more—an urban mass or congeries divided by the river"* (John Updike). [Latin *congeriēs,* from *congerere,* to heap up. See CONGEST.]

con·gest (kən-jĕst′) *v.* **-gest·ed, -gest·ing, -gests.** *—tr.* **1.** To overfill or overcrowd: *Trucks congested the tunnel.* **2.** *Pathology.* To cause the accumulation of excessive blood or tissue fluid in (a vessel or an organ). *—intr.* To become congested. [Latin *congerere, congest-,* to heap up, crowd together : *com-,* com- + *gerere,* to carry.] **—con·ges′tion** *n.* **—con·ges′tive** *adj.*

congestive heart failure *n.* A condition marked by weakness, edema, and shortness of breath that is caused by the inability of the heart to maintain adequate blood circulation in the peripheral tissues and the lungs.

con·gi·us (kŏn′jē-əs) *n., pl.* **-gi·i** (-jē-ī′). **1.** *Abbr.* **cong.** *Pharmacology.* A gallon. **2.** An ancient Roman measure for liquids, equal to about seven eighths of a U.S. gallon (3.3 liters). [Middle English, a liquid measure, from Latin, from Greek *konkhion,* diminutive of *konkhē, konkhos,* shellful.]

con·glo·bate (kŏn-glō′bāt′, kŏng′glō-) *tr.v.* **-bat·ed, -bat·ing, -bates.** To form into a globe or ball. [Latin *conglobāre, conglobāt-* : *com-,* com- + *globus,* ball.] **—con·glo′bate** *adj.* **—con′glo·ba′tion** *n.*

con·globe (kən-glōb′) *tr.v.* **-globed, -glob·ing, -globes.** To conglobate.

con·glom·er·ate (kən-glŏm′ə-rāt′) *intr. & tr.v.* **-at·ed, -at·ing, -ates.** To form or cause to form into an adhering or rounded mass. **—conglomerate** (-ər-ĭt) *n.* **1.** A corporation made up of a number of different companies that operate in diversified fields. **2.** A collected heterogeneous mass; a cluster: *a city-suburban conglomerate; a conglomerate of color, passion, and artistry.* **3.** *Geology.* A rock consisting of pebbles and gravel embedded in cement. **—conglomerate** (-ər-ĭt) *adj.* **1.** Gathered into a mass; clustered. **2.** *Geology.* Made up of loosely cemented heterogeneous material. [Latin *conglomerāre, conglomerāt-* : *com-,* com- + *glomerāre,* to wind into a ball (from *glomus,* ball).] **—con·glom′er·at′ic** (-ə-răt′ĭk), **con·glom′er·it′ic** (-ə-rĭt′ĭk) *adj.* **—con·glom′er·a′tor** *n.*

con·glom·er·a·tion (kən-glŏm′ə-rā′shən) *n.* **1.a.** The act or process of conglomerating. **b.** The state of being conglomerated. **2.** An accumulation of miscellaneous things.

con·glu·ti·nate (kən-glo͞ot′n-āt′, kŏn-) *intr. & tr.v.* **-nat·ed, -nat·ing, -nates.** **1.** To become or cause to become stuck or glued together. **2.** *Medicine.* To become or cause to become reunited, as bones or tissues. **—conglutinate** *adj.* Relating to the abnormal adhering of tissues to one another. [Middle English *conglutinaten,* from Latin *conglūtināre, conglūtināt-* : *com-,* com- + *glūtināre,* to glue (from *glūten,* glue).]

Con·go (kŏng′gō). **1.** A country of west-central Africa with a short coastline on the Pacific Ocean. It was part of French Equatorial Africa before becoming independent in 1960. Brazzaville is the capital and the largest city. Population, 1,912,429. **2.** See **Zaire.** **—Con′go·lese′** (-lēz′, -lēs′) *adj. & n.*

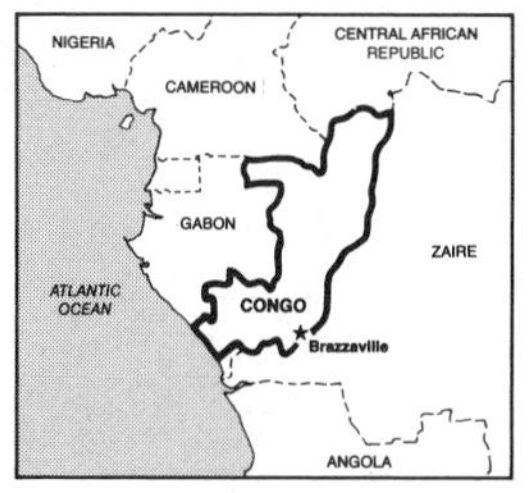

Congo

con·go dye (kŏng′gō) *n.* A nitrogen-containing dye that is usually derived from benzidine.

Congo eel *n.* An eellike amphibian *(Amphiuma means)* of the southeast United States, having two pairs of tiny, nonfunctioning legs. Although it is almost completely aquatic, it can move overland. Also called *Congo snake.*

Congo Free State. See **Zaire.**

Congo red *n.* A brownish-red powder, $C_{32}H_{22}N_6Na_2O_6S_2$, used in medicine and as a dye, an indicator, and a biological stain.

Congo River also **Zaire River** (zī′îr, zä-îr′). A river of central Africa flowing about 4,666 km (2,900 mi) north, west, and southwest through Zaire to the Atlantic Ocean.

Congo snake *n.* See **Congo eel.**

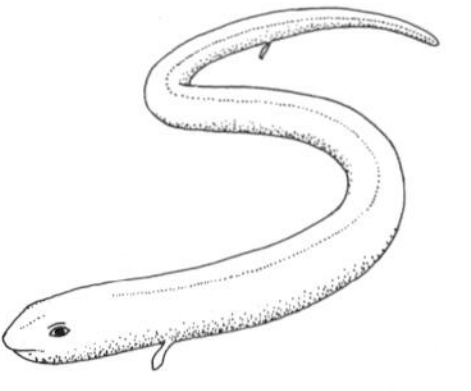

Congo eel
Amphiuma means

con·gou (kŏng′gō, -go͞o) *n.* A grade of Chinese black tea, obtained from the fifth and largest leaf gathered from a shoot tip of a tea plant. [Chinese (Amoy) *kong hu (te),* elaborately prepared (tea).]

con·grat·u·late (kən-grăch′ə-lāt′, -grăj′-, kəng-) *tr.v.* **-lat·ed, -lat·ing, -lates.** To express joy or acknowledgment, as for the achievement or good fortune of (another). [Latin *congrātulārī, congrātulāt-* : *com-,* com- + *grātulārī,* to rejoice (from *grātus,* pleasing; see **gʷerə-²** in Appendix).] **—con·grat′u·la′tor** *n.* **—con·grat′u·la·to′ry** (-lə-tôr′ē, -tōr′ē) *adj.*

con·grat·u·la·tion (kən-grăch′ə-lā′shən, -grăj′-, kəng-) *n.* **1.** The act of expressing joy or acknowledgment, as for the achievement or good fortune of another. **2.** Often **congratulations.** An expression of such joy or acknowledgment.

con·gre·gant (kŏng′grĭ-gənt) *n.* One who congregates, especially a member of a group of people gathered for religious worship.

con·gre·gate (kŏng′grĭ-gāt′) *tr. & intr.v.* **-gat·ed, -gat·ing, -gates.** To bring or come together in a group, crowd, or assembly. See Synonyms at **gather.** **—congregate** (-gĭt) *adj.* **1.** Gathered; assembled. **2.** Involving a group: *congregate living facilities for senior citizens.* [Middle English *congregaten,* from Latin *congregāre, congregāt-* : *com-,* com- + *gregāre,* to assemble (from *grex, greg-,* herd; see **ger-** in Appendix).] **—con′gre·ga′tive** *adj.* **—con′gre·ga′tive·ness** *n.* **—con′gre·ga′tor** *n.*

con·gre·ga·tion (kŏng′grĭ-gā′shən) *n.* **1.** The act of assembling. **2.** A body of assembled people or things; a gathering. **3. a.** A group of people gathered for religious worship. **b.** The members of a specific religious group who regularly worship at a church or synagogue. **4.** *Roman Catholic Church.* **a.** A religious institute in which only simple vows, not solemn vows, are taken. **b.** A division of the Curia.

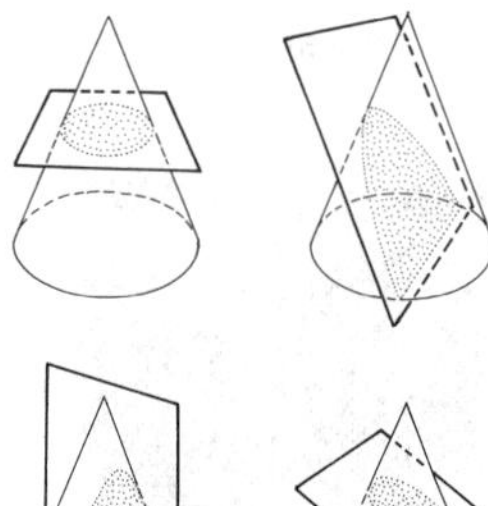
conic section

con·gre·ga·tion·al (kŏng′grĭ-gā′shə-nəl) *adj.* **1.** Of or relating to a congregation. **2. Congregational.** *Abbr.* **Cong.** Of or relating to Congregationalism or Congregationalists.

con·gre·ga·tion·al·ism (kŏng′grĭ-gā′shə-nə-lĭz′əm) *n.* **1.** A type of church government in which each local congregation is self-governing. **2. Congregationalism.** The system of government and religious beliefs of a Protestant denomination in which each member church is self-governing. **—con′gre·ga′tion·al·ist** *n.*

con·gress (kŏng′grĭs) *n.* **1.** A formal assembly of representatives, as of various nations, to discuss problems. **2.** The national legislative body of a nation, especially a republic. **3. Congress.** *Abbr.* **Cong., C. a.** The national legislative body of the United States, consisting of the Senate and the House of Representatives. **b.** The two-year session of this legislature between elections of the House of Representatives. **4. a.** The act of coming together or meeting. **b.** A single meeting, as of a political party or other group. **5.** Sexual intercourse. [Middle English *congresse,* body of attendants, from Latin *congressus,* meeting, from past participle of *congredī,* to meet : *com-,* com- + *gradī,* to go; see **ghredh-** in Appendix.] **—con·gres′sion·al** (kən-grĕsh′ə-nəl, kəng-) *adj.* **—con·gres′sion·al·ly** *adv.*

Congress boot *n.* An ankle-high shoe with elastic material in the sides. Also called *Congress gaiter.* [From its former popularity among members of the U.S. Congress.]

Congressional Medal of Honor *n.* The highest U.S. military decoration, awarded in the name of Congress to members of the armed forces for gallantry and bravery beyond the call of duty in action against an enemy.

con·gress·man (kŏng′grĭs-mən) *n.* A man who is a member of the U.S. Congress, especially of the House of Representatives.

con·gress·peo·ple (kŏng′grĭs-pē′pəl) *pl.n.* The members of the U.S. Congress considered as a group.

con·gress·per·son (kŏng′grĭs-pûr′sən) *n.* A congressman or congresswoman.

con·gress·wom·an (kŏng′grĭs-wo͝om′ən) *n.* A woman member of the U.S. Congress, especially of the House of Representatives.

Con·greve (kŏn′grēv′, kŏng′-), **William.** 1670–1729. English playwright known for his comedies, including *Love for Love* (1695) and *The Way of the World* (1700).

con·gru·ence (kŏng′gro͞o-əns, kən-gro͞o′-) *n., pl.* **-enc·es.** **1.** Agreement, harmony, conformity, or correspondence: *"What an extraordinary congruence of genius and era"* (Rita Rack). **2.** *Mathematics.* **a.** The state of being congruent. **b.** A statement that two quantities are congruent.

con·gru·en·cy (kŏng′gro͞o-ən-sē, kən-gro͞o′-) *n., pl.* **-cies.** Congruence.

con·gru·ent (kŏng′gro͞o-ənt, kən-gro͞o′-) *adj.* **1.** Corresponding; congruous. **2.** *Mathematics.* **a.** Coinciding exactly when superimposed: *congruent triangles.* **b.** Having a difference divisible by a modulus: *congruent numbers.* [Middle English, from Latin *congruēns, congruent-,* present participle of *congruere,* to agree.] **—con′gru·ent·ly** *adv.*

con·gru·i·ty (kən-gro͞o′ĭ-tē, kŏn-) *n., pl.* **-ties.** **1.** The quality or fact of being congruous. **2.** The quality or fact of being congruent. **3.** A point of agreement.

con·gru·ous (kŏng′gro͞o-əs) *adj.* **1.** Corresponding in character or kind; appropriate or harmonious. **2.** *Mathematics.* Congruent. [From Latin *congruus,* from *congruere,* to agree.] **—con′gru·ous·ly** *adv.* **—con′gru·ous·ness** *n.*

co·ni ar·te·ri·o·si (kō′nī är-tîr′ē-ō′sī, kō′nē är-tîr′ē-ō′sē) *n.* Plural of **conus arteriosus.**

con·ic (kŏn′ĭk) *adj.* Conical. **—conic** *n.* A conic section. [New Latin *cōnicus,* from Greek *kōnikos,* from *kōnos,* cone. See **kō-** in Appendix.]

con·i·cal (kŏn′ĭ-kəl) *adj.* Of, relating to, or shaped like a cone.

conic projection or **conical projection** *n.* A method of projecting maps of parts of the earth's spherical surface on a surrounding cone, which is then flattened to a plane surface having concentric circles as parallels of latitude and radiating lines from the apex as meridians.

conic section *n.* **a.** The intersection of a right circular cone and a plane, which generates one of a group of plane curves, including the circle, ellipse, hyperbola, and parabola. **b.** A graph of the general quadratic equation in two variables.

co·nid·i·a (kə-nĭd′ē-ə) *n.* Plural of **conidium.**

co·nid·i·o·phore (kə-nĭd′ē-ə-fôr′, -fōr′) *n.* A specialized fungal hypha that produces conidia. [CONIDI(UM) + –PHORE.] **—co·nid′i·oph′or·ous** (kə-nĭd′ē-ŏf′ər-əs) *adj.*

co·nid·i·um (kə-nĭd′ē-əm) *n., pl.* **-i·a** (-ē-ə). An asexually produced fungal spore, formed on a conidiophore. [New Latin, from Greek *konis,* dust.] **—co·nid′i·al** (-əl) *adj.*

con·i·fer (kŏn′ə-fər, kō′nə-) *n.* Any of various mostly needle-leaved or scale-leaved, chiefly evergreen, cone-bearing gymnospermous trees or shrubs such as pines, spruces, and firs. [From New Latin *Cōniferae,* family name, from Latin, feminine pl. of *cōnifer,* cone-bearing : *cōnus,* cone (from Greek *kōnos;* see **kō-** in Appendix) + *-fer,* -fer.] **—co·nif′er·ous** (kō-nĭf′ər-əs, kə-) *adj.*

co·ni·ine (kō′nē-ēn′) also **co·nin** (kō′nĭn) or **co·nine** (-nēn′) *n.* A poisonous, colorless liquid alkaloid, $C_5H_{10}NC_3H_7$, found in the poison hemlock. [Late Latin *cōnium,* conium; see CONIUM + –INE².]

co·ni·um (kō′nē-əm) *n.* The poison hemlock. [Late Latin *cōnium,* from Greek *kōneion,* probably from *kōna,* liquid pitch.]

conj. *abbr.* **1.** Conjugation. **2.** Conjunction. **3.** Conjunctive.

con·jec·tur·al (kən-jĕk′chər-əl) *adj.* **1.** Based on or involving conjecture. See Synonyms at **supposed.** **2.** Tending to conjecture. **—con·jec′tur·al·ly** *adv.*

con·jec·ture (kən-jĕk′chər) *n.* **1.** Inference or judgment based on inconclusive or incomplete evidence; guesswork. **2.** A statement, an opinion, or a conclusion based on guesswork: *The commentators made various conjectures about the outcome of the next election.* **—conjecture** *v.* **-tured, -tur·ing, -tures.** *—tr.* To infer from inconclusive evidence; guess. *—intr.* To make a conjecture. [Middle English, from Old French, from Latin *coniectūra,* from *coniectus,* past participle of *conicere,* to infer : *com-,* com- + *iacere,* to throw; see **yē-** in Appendix.] **—con·jec′tur·a·ble** *adj.* **—con·jec′tur·a·bly** *adv.* **—con·jec′tur·er** *n.*

SYNONYMS: *conjecture, surmise, guess, speculate, infer.* These verbs mean to reach a conclusion or judgment on the basis of uncertain evidence. *Conjecture* implies the formation of a conclusion without sufficient evidence: *It was impossible to conjecture from the expression on his face what his reaction was. Surmise* suggests a conclusion reached by intuition or by interpretation of slender evidence: *He was afraid she might surmise the truth. Guess* implies an inference drawn in a haphazard manner and suggests substantial grounds for doubt: *We can only guess what will happen next. Speculate* stresses a process of reasoning based on inconclusive evidence: *Scientists speculate on the origin of the universe. Infer* involves reasoning from evidence about which some doubt may be but is not necessarily suggested: *She quickly inferred from what I said that I had not heard the news.*

con·join (kən-join′) *tr. & intr.v.* **-joined, -join·ing, -joins.** To join or become joined together; unite. [Middle English *conjoinen,* from Old French *conjoindre, conjoign-,* from Latin *coniungere* : *com-,* com- + *iungere,* to join; see **yeug-** in Appendix.] **—con·join′er** *n.*

con·joint (kən-joint′) *adj.* **1.** Joined together; combined: *"social order and prosperity, the conjoint aims of government"* (John K. Fairbank). **2.** Of, consisting of, or involving two or more combined or associated entities; joint. [Middle English, from Old French, past participle of *conjoindre,* to conjoin. See CONJOIN.] **—con·joint′ly** *adv.*

con·ju·gal (kŏn′jə-gəl, kən-jo͞o′-) *adj.* Of or relating to marriage or the relationship of spouses. [Latin *coniugālis,* from *coniunx, coniug-,* spouse, from *coniungere,* to join in marriage. See CONJOIN.] **—con′ju·gal′i·ty** (-găl′ĭ-tē) *n.* **—con′ju·gal·ly** *adv.*

conjugal rights *pl.n.* The rights and privileges arising from the marriage relationship, especially the mutual rights of companionship, aid, and sexual relations.

con·ju·gant (kŏn′jə-gənt) *n.* Either of a pair of organisms, cells, or gametes undergoing conjugation. [From Latin *coniugāns, coniugant-,* present participle of *coniugāre,* to unite. See CONJUGATE.]

con·ju·gate (kŏn′jə-gāt′) *v.* **-gat·ed, -gat·ing, -gates.** *—tr.* **1.** *Grammar.* To inflect (a verb) in its forms for distinctions such as number, person, voice, mood, and tense. **2.** To join together. *—intr.* **1.** *Biology.* To undergo conjugation. **2.** *Grammar.* To be inflected. **—conjugate** (-gĭt, -gāt′) *adj.* **1.** Joined together, especially in a pair or pairs; coupled. **2.** *Mathematics & Physics.* Inversely or oppositely related with respect to one of a group of otherwise identical properties, especially designating either or both of a pair of complex numbers differing only in the sign of the imaginary term. **3.** *Chemistry.* Pertaining to an acid and a base that are related by the difference of a proton. **—conjugate** (-gĭt, -gāt′) *n. Mathematics & Physics.* Either of a pair of conjugate quantities. [Latin *coniugāre, coniugāt-,* to join together : *com-,* com- + *iugāre,* to join (from *iugum,* yoke; see **yeug-** in Appendix).] **—con′ju·gate′ly** *adv.* **—con′ju·ga′tive** *adj.* **—con′ju·ga′tor** *n.*

con·ju·gat·ed protein (kŏn′jə-gā′tĭd) *n.* A compound, such as hemoglobin, made up of a protein molecule and a nonprotein prosthetic group.

con·ju·ga·tion (kŏn′jə-gā′shən) *n. Abbr.* **conj. 1.a.** The act of conjugating. **b.** The state of being conjugated. **2.** *Grammar.* **a.** The inflection of a particular verb. **b.** A presentation of the complete set of inflected forms of a verb. **c.** A class of verbs having similar inflected forms. **3.** *Biology.* **a.** The temporary union of two bacterial cells during which one cell transfers part or all of its genome to the other. **b.** A process of sexual reproduction in which ciliate protozoans of the same species temporarily couple and exchange genetic material. **c.** A process of sexual reproduction in certain algae and fungi in which temporary or permanent fusion occurs, resulting in the union of the male and female gametes. **—con′ju·ga′tion·al** *adj.* **—con′ju·ga′tion·al·ly** *adv.*

conjugation tube *n.* A slender tube in certain bacteria and algae that connects two individuals during conjugation and through which the transfer of genetic material occurs.

con·junct (kən-jŭngkt′, kŏn′jŭngkt′) *adj.* **1.** Joined together; united. **2.** Acting in association; combined: *"the conjunct . . . influences of fire and strong drink"* (Thomas Love Peacock). **3.** *Music.* Of or relating to successive tones of the scale. **—conjunct** (kŏn′jŭngkt′) *n.* **1.** One that is in conjunction or association with another. **2.** *Logic.* One of the components of a conjunction. [Middle English, from Latin *coniūnctus,* past participle of *coniungere,* to join together. See CONJOIN.] **—con·junct′ly** *adv.*

con·junc·tion (kən-jŭngk′shən) *n.* **1.a.** The act of joining. **b.** The state of being joined. **2.** A joint or simultaneous occurrence; concurrence: *the conjunction of historical and economic forces that created a depression.* **3.** One resulting from or embodying a union; a combination: *"He is, in fact, a remarkable conjunction of talents"* (Jerry Adler). **4.** *Abbr.* **conj.** *Grammar.* A part of speech such as *and, but, as,* and *because* that serves to connect words, phrases, clauses, or sentences. **5.** *Abbr.* **conj.** *Astronomy.* The position of two celestial bodies on the celestial sphere when they have the same celestial longitude. **6.** *Logic.* **a.** *Abbr.* **conj.** A compound proposition that has components joined by the word *and* or its symbol and is true only if both or all the components are true. **b.** The relationship between the components of a conjunction. **—con·junc′tion·al** *adj.* **—con·junc′tion·al·ly** *adv.*

con·junc·ti·va (kŏn′jŭngk-tī′və) *n., pl.* **-vas** or **-vae** (-vē). The mucous membrane that lines the inner surface of the eyelid and the exposed surface of the eyeball. [Middle English, from Medieval Latin *(membrāna) coniūnctīva,* connective (membrane), feminine of Late Latin *coniūnctīvus,* connective, from Latin *coniūnctus,* past participle of *coniungere,* to join together. See CONJOIN.] **—con′junc·ti′val** (-vəl) *adj.*

con·junc·tive (kən-jŭngk′tĭv) *adj.* **1.** Joining; connective. **2.** Joined together; combined: *the conjunctive focus of political opposition.* **3.** *Grammar.* **a.** Of, relating to, or being a conjunction. **b.** Serving to connect elements of meaning and construction within sentences, as *and* and *since,* or between sentences, as *therefore.* **—conjunctive** *n. Abbr.* **conj.** *Grammar.* A connective word, especially a conjunction or conjunctive adverb. **—con·junc′tive·ly** *adv.*

conjunctive adverb *n. Grammar.* A function word that connects two sentences and provides adverbial emphasis, as *therefore* in *This intersection is dangerous; therefore motorists should approach it slowly.*

con·junc·ti·vi·tis (kən-jŭngk′tə-vī′tĭs) *n. Pathology.* Inflammation of the conjunctiva, characterized by redness and often accompanied by a discharge.

con·junc·ture (kən-jŭngk′chər) *n.* **1.** A combination, as of events or circumstances: *"the power that lies in the conjuncture of faith and fatherland"* (Conor Cruise O'Brien). **2.** A critical set of circumstances; a crisis: *"reports on the deteriorating world conjuncture and the disappointment of earlier hopes"* (Financial Times).

con·jun·to (kŏn-ho͞on′tō) *n., pl.* **-tos.** *Music.* A dance band, especially in Latin America, featuring brass, percussion, and rhythm instruments. [Spanish, from Latin *coniūnctus,* past participle of *coniungere,* to join together. See CONJOIN.]

con·ju·ra·tion (kŏn′jə-rā′shən) *n.* **1.** The act or art of conjuring. **2.** A magic spell or incantation. **3.** A magic trick or magical effect: *"a theatrical magician who knows how to make a dance program an evening of fantastic conjurations"* (New York Times). **4.** *Archaic.* A solemn appeal; an entreaty.

con·jure (kŏn′jər, kən-jo͝or′) *v.* **-jured, -jur·ing, -jures.** *—tr.* **1.a.** To summon (a devil or spirit) by magical or supernatural power. **b.** To influence or effect by or as if by magic: *tried to conjure away the doubts that beset her.* **2.a.** To call or bring to mind; evoke: *"Arizona conjures up an image of stark deserts for most Americans"* (American Demographics). **b.** To imagine; picture: *"a sight to store away, then conjure up someday when they were no longer together"* (Nelson DeMille). **3.** *Obsolete.* To call on or entreat solemnly, especially by an oath. *—intr.* **1.** To perform magic tricks, especially by sleight of hand. **2.a.** To summon a devil by magic or supernatural power. **b.** To practice black magic. **3.** *Obsolete.* To conspire. [Middle English *conjuren,* from Old French *conjurer,* to use a spell, from Late Latin *coniūrāre,* to pray by something holy, from Latin, to swear together : *com-,* com- + *iūrāre,* to swear; see **yewes-** in Appendix.]

con·jur·er also **con·jur·or** (kŏn′jər-ər, kŭn′-) *n.* **1.** One that performs magic tricks; a magician. **2.** A sorcerer or sorceress.

♦ **conjure woman** *n. Lower Southern U.S.* A Black woman who practices voodoo.

con·jur·or (kŏn′jər-ər, kŭn′-) *n.* Variant of **conjurer.**

conk¹ (kŏngk) *n.* **1.** *Slang.* **a.** The head. **b.** A blow, especially on the head. **2.** *Chiefly British.* The human nose. **—conk** *v.* **conked, conk·ing, conks.** *Slang. —tr.* To hit, especially on the head. *—intr.* **1.** To stop functioning; fail: *The engine conked out on the final lap.* **2.** To fall asleep, especially suddenly or heavily: *conked out on the couch watching television.* **3.** To pass out; faint. **4.** To die. [Origin unknown.]

conk² (kŏngk) *n.* A hard, shelflike, spore-bearing structure of certain wood-decaying fungi, found on stumps, logs, or trees. [Perhaps alteration of CONCH.]

conk³ (kŏngk) *n.* A hair style in which the hair is straightened, usually by chemical means. Also called *process.* **—conk** *tr.v.* **conked, conk·ing, conks.** To straighten (tightly curled hair) usually by chemical means. [Perhaps alteration of *congolene,* substance for straightening hair.]

Conk·ling (kŏngk′lĭng), **Roscoe.** 1829–1888. American politician who resigned from the U.S. Senate (1881) as a protest against President James A. Garfield's interference in New York patronage politics.

con man *n. Slang.* A confidence man.

conn (kŏn) *v. & n. Nautical.* Variant of **con³.**

Conn. *abbr.* Connecticut.

Con·nacht (kŏn′ət, -əKHt) also **Con·naught** (-ôt′). A historical region of west-central Ireland.

con·nate (kŏn′āt′, kŏ-nāt′) *adj.* **1.** Existing at birth or from the beginning; inborn or inherent. **2.** Originating at the same time; related. **3.** Being in close accord or sympathy; congenial: *"In the wilderness, I find something more dear and connate than in streets and villages"* (Ralph Waldo Emerson). **4.** *Biology.* United to a structure of the same kind, as one petal to another: *a connate tomato flower.* [Late Latin *connātus,* past participle of *connāscī,* to be born with : Latin *com-,* com- + Latin *nāscī,* to be born; see **genə-** in Appendix.] **—con′nate′ly** *adv.* **—con′nate′ness** *n.*

con·nat·u·ral (kə-năch′ər-əl, kŏ-) *adj.* **1.** Innate; inborn. **2.** Related or similar in nature; cognate. [Medieval Latin *connātūrālis* : Latin *com-,* com- + Latin *nātūrālis,* by birth; see NATURAL.] **—con·nat′u·ral′i·ty** (-ə-răl′ĭ-tē) *n.* **—con·nat′u·ral·ly** *adv.* **—con·nat′u·ral·ness** *n.*

Con·naught (kŏn′ôt′). See **Connacht.**

con·nect (kə-nĕkt′) *v.* **-nect·ed, -nect·ing, -nects.** *—tr.* **1.** To join or fasten together. **2.** To associate or consider as related: *no reason to connect the two events.* See Synonyms at **join. 3.** To join to or by means of a communications circuit: *Please connect me to the number in San Diego.* **4.** To plug in (an electrical cord or device) to an outlet. *—intr.* **1.** To become joined or united: *two streams connecting to form a river.* **2.** To be scheduled so as to provide continuing service, as between airplanes or buses. **3.** To establish a rapport or relationship; relate: *The candidate failed to connect with the voters.* **4.** *Sports.* To hit or play a ball successfully: *The batter connected for a home run.* [Middle English *connecten,* from Latin *cōnectere* : *cō-,* co- + *nectere,* to bind; see **ned-** in Appendix.] **—con·nect′i·ble, con·nect′a·ble** *adj.* **—con·nec′tor, con·nect′er** *n.*

con·nect·ed (kə-nĕk′tĭd) *adj.* **1.** Joined or fastened together. **2.** *Mathematics.* Having a continuous path between any two points. Used of a curve, set, or surface. **3.** Related; associated. **4.** Logically or intelligibly ordered or presented; coherent: *a stroke that left him incapable of connected speech.* **5.** Associated with or related to persons of influence or position: *a young photographer who was well connected in the fashion world.* **—con·nect′ed·ly** *adv.* **—con·nect′ed·ness** *n.*

Con·nect·i·cut (kə-nĕt′ĭ-kət). *Abbr.* **CT, Conn., Ct.** A state of the northeast United States. It was admitted as one of the original Thirteen Colonies in 1788. Connecticut's coastline was first explored by Dutch navigators after 1614, and in 1635 colonists from Massachusetts Bay began to settle in the Connecticut River valley. The Fundamental Orders, a constitution based on the consent of the governed, was adopted by the colony in 1639. Hartford is the capital and Bridgeport the largest city. Population, 3,107,576.

Connecticut River. A river of the northeast United States flowing about 655 km (407 mi) from northern New Hampshire southward along the Vermont–New Hampshire border and through central Massachusetts and Connecticut to its outlet on Long Island Sound.

con·nect·ing rod (kə-nĕk′tĭng) *n.* A rod that transmits motion or power from one moving part to another, especially the rod connecting the crankshaft of an automobile to a piston. Also called *pitman.*

con·nec·tion (kə-nĕk′shən) *n. Abbr.* **con. 1.a.** The act of connecting. **b.** The state of being connected. **2.** One that con-

ă **pat**	oi **boy**
ā **pay**	ou **out**
âr **care**	o͝o **took**
ä **father**	o͞o **boot**
ĕ **pet**	ŭ **cut**
ē **be**	ûr **urge**
ĭ **pit**	th **thin**
ī **pie**	*th* **this**
îr **pier**	hw **which**
ŏ **pot**	zh **vision**
ō **toe**	ə **about, item**
ô **paw**	♦ **regionalism**

Stress marks: ′ (primary); ′ (secondary), as in **dictionary** (dĭk′shə-nĕr′ē)

nects; a link: *a faulty connection in the circuit.* **3.** An association or a relationship: *There appeared to be no connection between the two crimes.* **4.** The logical or intelligible ordering of words or ideas; coherence. **5.** Reference or relation to something else; context: *In this connection, the agreement can be seen as a step toward peace.* **6.** A person, especially one of influence or position, with whom one is associated, as by kinship, interests in common, or marriage: *used her connections to land a job.* **7.** A conveyance or scheduled run providing continuing service between means of transportation: *missed my connection in Atlanta.* **8.** A line of communication between two points in a telephone or similar wired system. **9.** *Slang.* **a.** A drug dealer. **b.** A purchase of illegal drugs. **—con·nec′tion·al** *adj.*

con·nec·tive (kə-nĕk′tĭv) *adj.* Serving or tending to connect. **—connective** *n.* **1.** One that connects. **2.** *Grammar.* A word, such as a conjunction, that connects words, phrases, clauses, and sentences. **3.** *Botany.* The portion of a stamen that connects the halves of an anther. **—con·nec′tive·ly** *adv.* **—con′nec·tiv′i·ty** (kŏn′ĕk-tĭv′ĭ-tē) *n.*

connective tissue *n.* Tissue arising chiefly from the embryonic mesoderm that is characterized by a highly vascular matrix and includes collagenous, elastic, and reticular fibers, adipose tissue, cartilage, and bone. It forms the supporting and connecting structures of the body.

connect time *n. Computer Science.* The elapsed time during which a user of a remote terminal is connected with a time-sharing system.

Con·nel·ly (kŏn′ə-lē), **Marcus Cook.** Known as "Marc." 1890–1980. American playwright, producer, and director who won a Pulitzer Prize for *The Green Pastures* (1930), a play based on Southern Black interpretations of biblical stories.

Con·ne·ma·ra (kŏn′ə-mär′ə). A region of western Ireland on the coast of the Atlantic Ocean. The area is noted for its peat bogs and mountainous terrain.

Con·ners·ville (kŏn′ərz-vĭl′). A city of east-central Indiana east of Indianapolis. It was founded in 1813. Population, 17,023.

con·nex·ion (kə-nĕk′shən) *n. Chiefly British.* Variant of **connection.**

con·ning tower (kŏn′ĭng) *n.* **1.** A raised, enclosed observation post in a submarine, often used as a means of entrance and exit. **2.** The armored pilothouse of a warship. [From CON³.]

con·nip·tion (kə-nĭp′shən) *n. Informal.* A fit of violent emotion, such as anger or panic. Also called *conniption fit.* [Origin unknown.]

con·niv·ance also **con·niv·ence** (kə-nī′vəns) *n.* **1.** The act of conniving. **2.** *Law.* Knowledge of and tacit consent to the commission of an illegal act by another.

con·nive (kə-nīv′) *intr.v.* **-nived, -niv·ing, -nives. 1.** To cooperate secretly in an illegal or wrongful action; collude: *The dealers connived with customs officials to bring in narcotics.* **2.** To scheme; plot. **3.** To feign ignorance of or fail to take measures against a wrong, thus implying tacit encouragement or consent: *The guards were suspected of conniving at the prisoner's escape.* [Latin *cōnīvēre, connīvēre,* to close the eyes.] **—con·niv′er** *n.* **—con·niv′er·y** *n.*

con·niv·ence (kə-nī′vəns) *n.* Variant of **connivance.**

con·ni·vent (kə-nī′vənt) *adj. Biology.* Converging and touching but not fused, as stamens or an insect's wings. [Latin *connīvēns, connīvent-,* present participle of *connīvēre,* to be tightly closed.]

con·nois·seur (kŏn′ə-sûr′, -so͝or′) *n.* **1.** A person with expert knowledge or training, especially in the fine arts. **2.** A person of informed and discriminating taste: *a connoisseur of fine wines.* [Obsolete French, from Old French *connoisseor,* from *connoistre,* to know, from Latin *cognōscere,* to learn, know. See COGNITION.] **—con′nois·seur′ship′** *n.*

Con·nol·ly (kŏn′ə-lē), **Maureen Catherine.** Known as "Little Mo." 1934–1969. American tennis player who was the first to win the grand slam of U.S., British, French, and Australian women's championships (1953).

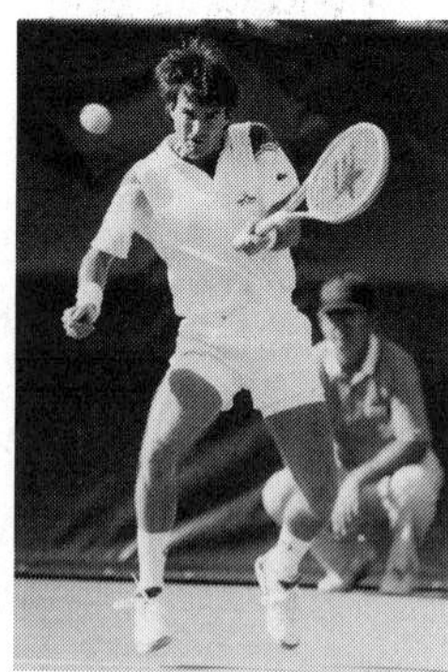

Jimmy Connors
At the U.S. Open semifinals in 1991

Con·nors (kŏn′ərz), **James Scott.** Known as "Jimmy." Born 1952. American tennis player who twice won both the U.S. and Wimbledon men's singles titles (1974 and 1982) and also won the U.S. title in 1976, 1978, and 1983.

con·no·ta·tion (kŏn′ə-tā′shən) *n.* **1.** The act or process of connoting. **2.a.** An idea or meaning suggested by or associated with a word or thing: *Hollywood holds connotations of romance and glittering success.* **b.** The set of associative implications constituting the general sense of a word in addition to its literal sense. **3.** *Logic.* The set of attributes constituting the meaning of a term; intension. **—con′no·ta′tive** *adj.* **—con′no·ta′tive·ly** *adv.*

con·note (kə-nōt′) *tr.v.* **-not·ed, -not·ing, -notes. 1.** To suggest or imply in addition to literal meaning: *"The term 'liberal arts' connotes a certain elevation above utilitarian concerns"* (George F. Will). See Usage Note at **denote. 2.** To have as a related or attendant condition: *For a political leader, hesitation is apt to connote weakness.* [Medieval Latin *connotāre,* to mark along with : Latin *com-,* com- + Latin *notāre,* to mark (from *nota,* mark; see **gnō-** in Appendix).]

con·nu·bi·al (kə-no͞o′bē-əl, -nyo͞o′-) *adj.* Relating to marriage or the married state; conjugal. [Latin *cōnūbiālis,* from *cōnūbium,* marriage : *com-,* com- + *nūbere,* to marry.] **—con·nu′bi·al·ism** *n.* **—con·nu′bi·al′i·ty** (-ăl′ĭ-tē) *n.* **—con·nu′bi·al·ly** *adv.*

co·no·dont (kō′nə-dŏnt′, kŏn′ə-) *n. Paleontology.* A Paleozoic microfossil usually having a toothlike shape and considered to be the remains of an extinct marine organism. [Greek *kōnos,* cone; see **kō-** in Appendix + -ODONT.]

co·noid (kō′noid′) also **co·noi·dal** (kō-noid′l) *adj.* Shaped like a cone. **—co′noid** *n.*

con·quer (kŏng′kər) *v.* **-quered, -quer·ing, -quers.** —*tr.* **1.** To defeat or subdue by force, especially by force of arms. **2.** To gain or secure control of by or as if by force of arms: *scientists battling to conquer disease; a singer who conquered the operatic world.* **3.** To overcome or surmount by physical, mental, or moral force: *I finally conquered my fear of heights.* See Synonyms at **defeat.** —*intr.* To be victorious; win. [Middle English *conqueren,* from Old French *conquerre,* from Vulgar Latin **conquaerere,* from Latin *conquīrere,* to procure : *com-,* intensive pref.; see COM- + *quaerere,* to seek.] **—con′quer·a·ble** *adj.* **—con′quer·or, con′quer·er** *n.*

con·quest (kŏn′kwĕst′, kŏng′-) *n.* **1.** The act or process of conquering. See Synonyms at **victory. 2.** Something, such as territory, acquired by conquering. **3.** One that has been captivated or overcome: *The pianist made a conquest of every audience for which she played.* [Middle English, from Old French, from Vulgar Latin **conquaesīta,* feminine past participle of **conquaerere.* See CONQUER.]

con·qui·an (kŏng′kē-ən) *n. Games.* Variant of **cooncan.**

con·quis·ta·dor (kŏn-kwĭs′tə-dôr′, kŏng-kē′stə-) *n., pl.* **-dors** or **-dor·es** (-dôr′ās, -ēz). A conqueror, especially one of the 16th-century Spanish soldiers who defeated the Indian civilizations of Mexico, Central America, or Peru. [Spanish, from *conquistar,* to conquer, from Vulgar Latin **conquīsītāre,* frequentative of Latin *conquīrere.* See CONQUER.]

Con·rad (kŏn′răd′), **Joseph.** 1857–1924. Polish-born British novelist noted as a master of atmosphere and narrative technique. His works include *Lord Jim* (1900), *Heart of Darkness* (1902), and *Nostromo* (1904).

Con·roe (kŏn′rō). A city of southeast Texas north of Houston. Oil was discovered in the area in 1932. Population, 18,034.

cons. *abbr.* **1.a.** Consigned. **b.** Consignment. **2.** Consonant. **3.** Also **Cons.** Constable. **4.** Constitution; constitutional. **5.** Construction. **6.** Also **Cons.** Consul.

con·san·guin·e·ous (kŏn′săn-gwĭn′ē-əs, -săng-) also **con·san·guine** (kŏn-săng′gwĭn, kən-) *adj.* Of the same lineage or origin; having a common ancestor. [From Latin *cōnsanguineus* : *com-,* com- + *sanguineus,* of blood; see SANGUINE.] **—con′san·guin′e·ous·ly** *adv.*

con·san·guin·i·ty (kŏn′săn-gwĭn′ĭ-tē, -săng-) *n., pl.* **-ties. 1.** Relationship by blood or by a common ancestor. **2.** A close affinity or connection.

con·science (kŏn′shəns) *n.* **1.a.** The awareness of a moral or ethical aspect to one's conduct together with the urge to prefer right over wrong: *Let your conscience be your guide.* **b.** A source of moral or ethical judgment or pronouncement: *a document that serves as the nation's conscience.* **c.** Conformity to one's own sense of right conduct: *a person of unflagging conscience.* **2.** The part of the superego in psychoanalysis that judges the ethical nature of one's actions and thoughts and then transmits such determinations to the ego for consideration. **3.** *Obsolete.* Consciousness. **—*idiom.* in (all good) conscience.** In all truth or fairness. [Middle English, from Old French, from Latin *cōnscientia,* from *cōnsciēns, cōnscient-,* present participle of *cōnscīre,* to be conscious of : *com-,* intensive pref.; see COM- + *scīre,* to know; see **skei-** in Appendix.] **—con′science·less** *adj.*

conscience clause *n.* A clause in a law that relieves persons whose conscientious or religious scruples forbid compliance.

conscience money *n.* Money paid in compensation or atonement, as for a dishonest or morally objectionable act.

con·sci·en·tious (kŏn′shē-ĕn′shəs) *adj.* **1.** Guided by or in accordance with the dictates of conscience; principled: *a conscientious decision to speak out about injustice.* **2.** Thorough and assiduous: *a conscientious worker; a conscientious effort to comply with the regulations.* [Obsolete French *conscientieux,* from Medieval Latin *cōnscientiōsus,* from Latin *cōnscientia,* conscience. See CONSCIENCE.] **—con′sci·en′tious·ly** *adv.* **—con′sci·en′tious·ness** *n.*

conscientious objector *n. Abbr.* **CO, C.O.** One who on the basis of religious or moral principles refuses to bear arms or participate in military service.

con·scio·na·ble (kŏn′shə-nə-bəl) *adj.* **1.** Acceptable or permissible according to conscience: *"Ignoring* [disadvantaged minorities] *is no more conscionable today than it was in the riot-scorched America of 20 years ago"* (Christian Science Monitor). **2.** Conscientious; principled. [Obsolete *conscions* (variant of CONSCIENCE) + -ABLE.]

con·scious (kŏn′shəs) *adj.* **1.a.** Having an awareness of one's environment and one's own existence, sensations, and thoughts. See Synonyms at **aware. b.** Mentally perceptive or alert; awake: *The patient remained fully conscious after the local anesthetic was administered.* **2.** Capable of thought, will, or perception: *The development of conscious life on the planet.* **3.** Subjectively known or felt: *conscious remorse.* **4.** Intentionally conceived or done; deliberate: *a conscious insult; made a conscious effort to speak more clearly.* **5.** Inwardly attentive or sensible; mindful: *was in-*

creasingly conscious of being stared at on the street. **6.** Especially aware of or preoccupied with. Often used in combination: *a cost-conscious approach to further development; a health-conscious diet.* **—conscious** *n.* In psychoanalysis, the component of waking awareness perceptible by a person at any given instant; consciousness. [From Latin *cōnscius* : *com-*, com- + *scīre,* to know; see **skei-** in Appendix.] **—con′scious·ly** *adv.*

con·scious·ness (kŏn′shəs-nĭs) *n.* **1.** The state or condition of being conscious. **2.** A sense of one's personal or collective identity, especially the complex of attitudes, beliefs, and sensitivities held by or considered characteristic of an individual or a group: *Love of freedom runs deep in the national consciousness.* **3.a.** Special awareness or sensitivity: *class consciousness; race consciousness.* **b.** Alertness to or concern for a particular issue or situation: *a movement aimed at raising the general public's consciousness of social injustice.* **4.** In psychoanalysis, the conscious.

con·scious·ness-rais·ing (kŏn′shəs-nĭs-rā′zĭng) *n.* **1.** A process, as by group therapy, of achieving greater awareness of one's needs in order to fulfill one's potential as a person. **2.** A method for making people aware of a political or social issue, especially discrimination or injustice. **—con′scious·ness-rais′er** *n.* **—con′scious·ness-rais′ing** *adj.*

con·script (kŏn′skrĭpt′) *n.* One compulsorily enrolled for service, especially in the armed forces; a draftee. **—conscript** *adj.* Enrolled compulsorily; drafted. **—conscript** (kən-skrĭpt′) *tr.v.* **-script·ed, -script·ing, -scripts.** To enroll compulsorily into service; draft. [Latin *cōnscrīptus,* past participle of *cōnscrībere,* to enroll : *com-*, com- + *scrībere,* to write; see **skribh-** in Appendix.]

con·scrip·tion (kən-skrĭp′shən) *n.* **1.** Compulsory enrollment, especially for the armed forces; draft. **2.** A monetary payment exacted by a government in wartime.

con·se·crate (kŏn′sĭ-krāt′) *tr.v.* **-crat·ed, -crat·ing, -crates. 1.** To declare or set apart as sacred: *consecrate a church.* **2.a.** To produce the ritual transformation of (the elements of the Eucharist) into the body and blood of Jesus. **b.** To sanctify (bread and wine) for use in Communion. **c.** To initiate (a priest) into the order of bishops. **3.** To dedicate solemnly to a service or goal. See Synonyms at **devote. 4.** To make venerable; hallow: *a tradition consecrated by time.* **—consecrate** *adj.* Dedicated to a sacred purpose; sanctified. [Middle English *consecraten,* from Latin *cōnsecrāre, cōnsecrāt-* : *com-*, intensive pref.; see COM– + *sacrāre,* to make sacred (from *sacer, sacr-*, sacred; see **sak-** in Appendix).] **—con′se·cra′tive** *adj.* **—con′se·cra′tor** *n.* **—con′se·cra·to′ry** (-krə-tôr′ē, -tōr′ē) *adj.*

con·se·cra·tion (kŏn′sĭ-krā′shən) *n.* **1.** The act, process, or ceremony of consecrating. **2.** The state of being consecrated.

con·se·cu·tion (kŏn′sĭ-kyo͞o′shən) *n.* **1.** A sequence or succession. **2.** *Logic.* The relation of consequent to antecedent; deduction. [Middle English *consecucioun,* attainment, from Latin *cōnsecūtiō, cōnsecūtiōn-*, orderly sequence, from *cōnsecūtus,* past participle of *cōnsequī,* to follow closely. See CONSEQUENT.]

con·sec·u·tive (kən-sĕk′yə-tĭv) *adj.* **1.** Following one after another without interruption; successive: *was absent on three consecutive days; won five consecutive games on the road.* **2.** Marked by logical sequence. **3.** *Grammar.* Expressing consequence or result: *a consecutive clause.* [French *consécutif,* from Old French, from Medieval Latin *cōnsecūtīvus,* from *cōnsecūtus,* past participle of Latin *cōnsequī,* to follow closely. See CONSEQUENT.] **—con·sec′u·tive·ly** *adv.* **—con·sec′u·tive·ness** *n.*

con·sen·su·al (kən-sĕn′sho͞o-əl) *adj.* **1.** Of or expressing a consensus: *a consensual decision.* **2.a.** *Law.* Existing or entered into by mutual consent without formalization by document or ceremony: *a consensual marriage; a consensual contract.* **b.** Involving the willing participation of both or all parties, especially in an illegal transaction or practice: *the consensual crimes of prostitution, drug abuse, and illegal gambling.* **3.** *Physiology.* **a.** Of or relating to a reflexive response of one body structure following stimulation of another, such as the concurrent constriction of one pupil in response to light shined in the other. **b.** Of or relating to involuntary movement of a body part accompanying voluntary movement of another. **—con·sen′su·al·ly** *adv.*

con·sen·sus (kən-sĕn′səs) *n.* **1.** An opinion or position reached by a group as a whole or by majority will: *The voters' consensus was that the measure should be adopted.* **2.** General agreement or accord: *government by consensus.* —*attributive.* Often used to modify another noun: *consensus politics; consensus management.* [Latin, from past participle of *cōnsentīre,* to agree. See CONSENT.]

USAGE NOTE: Many grammarians have maintained that the expression *consensus of opinion* is redundant, inasmuch as *consensus* itself denotes a judgment about which there is general agreement. *Consensus of opinion* has often been used by reputable writers, however, and has sometimes been defended on the grounds that a consensus may involve attitudes other than opinions; thus, one may speak of a *consensus of beliefs,* or a *consensus of usage.* Nonetheless, the qualifying phrase can usually be omitted with no loss of clarity. The sentence *It was the consensus of opinion among the sportswriters that the game should not have been played* says nothing that is not said by *It was the consensus of the sportswriters that the game should not have been played.* • Expressions such as *overall consensus* and *general consensus* are harder to defend against the charge of redundancy. In the most recent survey, *overall consensus* was judged redundant by 95 percent of the members of the Usage Panel. See Usage Note at **redundancy.**

con·sent (kən-sĕnt′) *intr.v.* **-sent·ed, -sent·ing, -sents. 1.** To give assent, as to the proposal of another; agree. See Synonyms at **assent. 2.** *Archaic.* To be of the same mind or opinion. **—consent** *n.* **1.** Acceptance or approval of what is planned or done by another; acquiescence. See Synonyms at **permission. 2.** Agreement as to opinion or a course of action: *She was chosen by common consent to speak for the group.* [Middle English *consenten,* from Old French *consentir,* from Latin *cōnsentīre* : *com-*, com- + *sentīre,* to feel; see **sent-** in Appendix.] **—con·sent′er** *n.*

con·sen·ta·ne·ous (kŏn′sĕn-tā′nē-əs) *adj.* **1.** Manifesting agreement; accordant. **2.** Unanimous. [From Latin *cōnsentāneus,* from *cōnsentīre,* to agree. See CONSENT.] **—con·sen′ta·ne′i·ty** (kən-sĕn′tə-nē′ĭ-tē), **con′sen·ta′ne·ous·ness** *n.* **—con′sen·ta′ne·ous·ly** *adv.*

consent decree *n. Law.* A judicial decree expressing a voluntary agreement between parties to a suit, especially an agreement by a defendant to cease activities alleged by the government to be illegal in return for an end to the charges.

con·se·quence (kŏn′sĭ-kwĕns′, -kwəns) *n.* **1.** Something that logically or naturally follows from an action or condition. See Synonyms at **effect. 2.** The relation of a result to its cause. **3.** A logical conclusion or inference. **4.** Importance in rank or position: *scientists of consequence.* **5.** Significance; importance: *an issue of consequence.* See Synonyms at **importance.** *—idiom.* **in consequence.** As a result; consequently.

con·se·quent (kŏn′sĭ-kwĕnt′, -kwənt) *adj.* **1.a.** Following as a natural effect, result, or conclusion: *tried to prevent an oil spill and the consequent damage to wildlife.* **b.** Following as a logical conclusion. **2.** Logically correct or consistent. **3.** *Geology.* Having a position or direction determined by the original form or slope of the earth's surface: *a consequent river; a consequent valley.* **—consequent** *n.* **1.** *Logic.* The conclusion, as of a syllogism or a conditional sentence. **2.** The second term of a ratio. [Middle English, from Old French, from Latin *cōnsequēns, cōnsequent-*, present participle of *cōnsequī,* to follow closely : *com-*, intensive pref.; see COM– + *sequī,* to follow; see **sek^w-[1]** in Appendix.]

con·se·quen·tial (kŏn′sĭ-kwĕn′shəl) *adj.* **1.** Following as an effect, result, or conclusion; consequent. **2.** Having important consequences; significant: *"The year's only really consequential legislation was the reform of Social Security"* (New York Times). **3.a.** Important; influential: *a consequential figure in the academic community.* **b.** Pompous; self-important. **—con′se·quen′ti·al′i·ty** (-shē-ăl′ĭ-tē), **con′se·quen′tial·ness** *n.* **—con′se·quen′tial·ly** *adv.*

con·se·quent·ly (kŏn′sĭ-kwĕnt′lē, -kwənt-lē) *adv.* As a result; therefore.

con·ser·van·cy (kən-sûr′vən-sē) *n., pl.* **-cies. 1.** Conservation, especially of natural resources. **2.a.** An organization dedicated to the conservation of wildlife and wildlife habitats in the United States. **b.** *Chiefly British.* A commission supervising fisheries and navigation.

con·ser·va·tion (kŏn′sûr-vā′shən) *n.* **1.** The act or process of conserving. **2.a.** Preservation from loss, damage, or neglect: *Valuable manuscripts were saved from deterioration under the program of library conservation.* **b.** The controlled use and systematic protection of natural resources, such as forests, soil, and water systems. **3.** The maintenance of a physical quantity, such as energy or mass, during a physical or chemical change. **—con′ser·va′tion·al** *adj.*

con·ser·va·tion·ist (kŏn′sûr-vā′shə-nĭst) *n.* One that practices or advocates conservation, especially of natural resources.

conservation of charge *n.* A principle stating that the total electric charge of an isolated system remains constant regardless of changes within the system.

conservation of energy *n.* A principle stating that the total energy of an isolated system remains constant regardless of changes within the system.

conservation of mass *n.* A principle in classical physics stating that the total mass of an isolated system is unchanged by interaction of its parts.

conservation of momentum *n.* A principle stating that the total linear momentum of an isolated system remains constant regardless of changes within the system.

con·ser·va·tism (kən-sûr′və-tĭz′əm) *n.* **1.** The inclination, especially in politics, to maintain the existing or traditional order. **2.** A political philosophy or attitude emphasizing respect for traditional institutions, distrust of government activism, and opposition to sudden change in the established order. **3. Conservatism.** The principles and policies of the Conservative Party in the United Kingdom or of the Progressive Conservative Party in Canada. **4.** Caution or moderation, as in behavior or outlook.

con·ser·va·tive (kən-sûr′və-tĭv) *adj.* **1.** Favoring traditional views and values; tending to oppose change. **2.** Traditional or restrained in style: *a conservative dark suit.* **3.** Moderate; cautious: *a conservative estimate.* **4.a.** Of or relating to the political philosophy of conservatism. **b.** Belonging to a conservative party, group, or movement. **5. Conservative.** Of or belonging to the Conservative Party in the United Kingdom or the Progressive Conservative Party in Canada. **6. Conservative.** Of or adhering

ă pat	oi boy
ā pay	ou out
âr care	o͝o took
ä father	o͞o boot
ĕ pet	ŭ cut
ē be	ûr urge
ĭ pit	th thin
ī pie	*th* this
îr pier	hw which
ŏ pot	zh vision
ō toe	ə about, item
ô paw	♦ regionalism

Stress marks: ′ (primary); ′ (secondary), as in **dictionary** (dĭk′shə-nĕr′ē)

to Conservative Judaism. **7.** Tending to conserve; preservative: *the conservative use of natural resources.* **—conservative** *n.* **1.** One favoring traditional views and values. **2.** A supporter of political conservatism. **3. Conservative.** *Abbr.* **C.** A member or supporter of the Conservative Party in the United Kingdom or the Progressive Conservative Party in Canada. **4.** *Archaic.* A preservative agent or principle. **—con·ser′va·tive·ly** *adv.* **—con·ser′va·tive·ness** *n.*

Conservative Judaism *n.* The branch of Judaism that allows for modifications in Jewish law when authorized by the Conservative rabbinate.

Conservative Party *n.* A major political party of the United Kingdom, characterized by moderate progressivism.

con·ser·va·tize (kən-sûr′və-tīz′) *tr.v.* **-tized, -tiz·ing, -tizes.** To make conservative or more conservative: *"He has prepared himself by . . . conservatizing his politics"* (Peter Goldman). [CONSERVATIVE + -IZE.]

con·ser·va·tor (kən-sûr′və-tər, kŏn′sər-vā′tər) *n.* **1.** A person in charge of maintaining or restoring valuable items, as in a museum or library. **2.** One that conserves or preserves from injury, violation, or infraction; a protector. **3.** *Law.* One that is responsible for the person and property of an incompetent. **—con·ser′va·to′ri·al** (-tôr′ē-əl, -tōr′-) *adj.* **—con·ser′va·tor·ship′** *n.*

con·ser·va·to·ry (kən-sûr′və-tôr′ē, -tōr′ē) *n.*, *pl.* **-ries.** **1.** A greenhouse, especially one in which plants are arranged aesthetically for display, as at a botanical garden. **2.** A school of music or dramatic art.

con·serve (kən-sûrv′) *v.* **-served, -serv·ing, -serves.** *—tr.* **1.a.** To protect from loss or harm; preserve: *calls to conserve our national heritage in the face of bewildering change.* **b.** To use carefully or sparingly, avoiding waste: *kept the thermostat lower to conserve energy.* **2.** To keep (a quantity) constant through physical or chemical reactions or evolutionary changes. **3.** To preserve (fruits) with sugar. *—intr.* To economize: *tried to conserve on fuel during the long winter.* **—conserve** (kŏn′sûrv′) *n.* A jam made of fruits stewed in sugar. [Middle English *conserven,* from Old French *conserver,* from Latin *cōnservāre* : *com-,* intensive pref.; see COM- + *servāre,* to preserve; see **ser-¹** in Appendix.] **—con·serv′a·ble** *adj.* **—con·serv′er** *n.*

con·sid·er (kən-sĭd′ər) *v.* **-ered, -er·ing, -ers.** *—tr.* **1.** To think carefully about. **2.** To think or deem to be; regard as. See Usage Note at **as¹**. **3.** To form an opinion about; judge: *considers waste to be criminal.* **4.** To take into account; bear in mind: *Her success is not surprising if you consider her excellent training.* **5.** To show consideration for: *failed to consider the feelings of others.* **6.** To esteem; regard. **7.** To look at thoughtfully. *—intr.* To think carefully; reflect. [Middle English *consideren,* from Old French, from Latin *cōnsīderāre* : *com-,* intensive pref.; see COM- + *sīdus, sīder-,* star.] **—con·sid′er·er** *n.*

SYNONYMS: *consider, deem, regard, account, reckon.* These verbs refer to holding opinions or views that are based on evaluation. *Consider* suggests objective reflection and reasoning: *She is considered an intelligent woman. He considers success of little importance. Deem* is more subjective through its emphasis on judgment as distinguished from contemplation: *The faculty deems the essay to be by far the best one submitted. Regard* often implies a personal attitude: *I regard your apology as the end of the matter. Account* and *reckon* in this sense are rather literary in flavor and imply calculated judgment: *"I account no man to be a philosopher who attempts to do more"* (John Henry Newman). *"I cannot reckon you as an admirer"* (Nathaniel Hawthorne).

con·sid·er·a·ble (kən-sĭd′ər-ə-bəl) *adj.* **1.** Large in amount, extent, or degree: *a writer of considerable influence.* **2.** Worthy of consideration; significant: *The economy was a considerable issue in the campaign.* **—considerable** *n.* *Informal.* A considerable amount, extent, or degree. **—con·sid′er·a·bly** *adv.*

con·sid·er·ate (kən-sĭd′ər-ĭt) *adj.* **1.** Having or marked by regard for the needs or feelings of others. See Synonyms at **thoughtful.** **2.** Characterized by careful thought; deliberate. [Middle English, observed, from Latin *cōnsīderātus,* past participle of *cōnsīderāre,* to consider. See CONSIDER.] **—con·sid′er·ate·ly** *adv.* **—con·sid′er·ate·ness** *n.*

con·sid·er·a·tion (kən-sĭd′ə-rā′shən) *n.* **1.a.** Careful thought; deliberation: *We will give your proposal consideration.* **b.** A result of considering; an opinion or a judgment: *Is it your consideration that I should apply?* **2.** A factor to be considered in forming a judgment or decision: *Safety is the most important consideration in choosing a car.* **3.** A treatment or account: *The essay begins with a brief consideration of the history of the problem.* **4.** Thoughtful concern for others; solicitude. **5.** High regard; esteem. **6.** Payment given in exchange for a service rendered; recompense: *agreed to do it for a small consideration.* **7.** *Law.* Something promised, given, or done that has the effect of making an agreement a legally enforceable contract. **—*idiom.* in consideration of.** **1.** In view of; on account of: *turned back in consideration of the worsening weather.* **2.** In return for: *an honorarium given in consideration of her contributions to the project.*

con·sid·ered (kən-sĭd′ərd) *adj.* **1.** Reached after or carried out with careful thought; deliberate: *my considered opinion; a considered policy involving a measured response to provocations.* **2.** Highly regarded; esteemed.

con·sid·er·ing (kən-sĭd′ər-ĭng) *prep.* In view of; taking into consideration: *You managed the project well, considering your inexperience.* See Usage Note at **participle.** **—considering** *adv.* *Informal.* All things considered: *We had a good trip, considering.*

con·si·glie·re (kŏn′sē-lyĕ′rĕ) *n.*, *pl.* **-ri** (-rē). An adviser, especially to a capo or leader of an organized crime syndicate. [Italian, from Latin *cōnsiliārius,* from *cōnsilium,* advice.]

con·sign (kən-sīn′) *v.* **-signed, -sign·ing, -signs.** *—tr.* **1.** To give over to the care of another; entrust. **2.** To turn over permanently to another's charge or to a lasting condition; commit irrevocably: *"Their desponding imaginations had already consigned him to a watery grave"* (William Hickling Prescott). **3.** To deliver (merchandise, for example) for custody or sale. **4.** To set apart, as for a special use or purpose; assign. See Synonyms at **commit.** *—intr. Obsolete.* To submit; consent. [Middle English *consignen,* to certify by seal, from Old French *consigner,* from Latin *cōnsignāre* : *com-,* intensive pref.; see COM- + *signāre,* to mark (from *signum,* mark; see **sekʷ-¹** in Appendix).] **—con·sign′a·ble** *adj.* **—con′sig·na′tion** (kŏn′sĭ-nā′shən, -sĭg-) *n.* **—con·sig′nor, con·sign′er** *n.*

con·sign·ee (kŏn′sī-nē′, kən-sī′nē′) *n.* The one to whom something, such as goods or merchandise, is consigned.

con·sign·ment (kən-sīn′mənt) *n.* *Abbr.* **cons.** **1.** The act of consigning. **2.** Something consigned. **—*idiom.* on consignment.** With the provision that payment is expected only on completed sales and that unsold items may be returned to the one consigning: *The retailer accepted the shipment on consignment.*

consignment store *n.* A retail store that stocks and sells merchandise on consignment.

con·sist (kən-sĭst′) *intr.v.* **-sist·ed, -sist·ing, -sists.** **1.** To be made up or composed: *New York City consists of five boroughs.* See Usage Note at **include.** **2.** To have a basis; reside or lie: *The beauty of the artist's style consists in its simplicity.* **3.** To be compatible; accord: *The information consists with her account.* [Latin *cōnsistere,* to stand still, to be composed of : *com-,* intensive pref.; see COM- + *sistere,* to cause to stand; see **stā-** in Appendix.]

con·sis·tence (kən-sĭs′təns) *n.* Consistency.

con·sis·ten·cy (kən-sĭs′tən-sē) *n.*, *pl.* **-cies.** **1.a.** Agreement or logical coherence among things or parts: *a rambling argument that lacked any consistency.* **b.** Correspondence among related aspects; compatibility: *questioned the consistency of the administration's actions with its stated policy.* **2.** Reliability or uniformity of successive results or events: *pitched with remarkable consistency throughout the season.* **3.** Degree or texture of density, firmness, or viscosity: *beat the mixture to the consistency of soft butter.*

con·sis·tent (kən-sĭs′tənt) *adj.* **1.** In agreement; compatible: *The testimony was consistent with the known facts.* **2.** Being in agreement with itself; coherent and uniform: *a consistent pattern of behavior.* **3.** Reliable; steady: *demonstrated a consistent ability to impress the critics.* **4.** *Mathematics.* Having at least one common solution, as of two or more equations or inequalities. [Latin *cōnsistēns, cōnsistent-,* present participle of *cōnsistere,* to stand still. See CONSIST.] **—con·sis′tent·ly** *adv.*

con·sis·to·ry (kən-sĭs′tə-rē) *n.*, *pl.* **-ries.** **1.a.** *Roman Catholic Church.* An assembly of cardinals presided over by the pope for the solemn promulgation of papal acts, such as the canonization of a saint. **b.** A governing body of a local congregation in certain Reformed churches. **c.** A court appointed to regulate ecclesiastical affairs in Lutheran state churches. **d.** An Anglican diocesan court presided over by a bishop's chancellor or commissary. **2.** The meeting of a consistory. **3.** A council; a tribunal. [Middle English *consistorie,* from Old French, from Latin *cōnsistōrium,* place of assembly, from *cōnsistere,* to stand together. See CONSIST.] **—con′sis·to′ri·al** (kŏn′sĭ-stôr′ē-əl, -stōr′-) *adj.*

con·so·ci·ate (kən-sō′shē-āt′) *tr. & intr.v.* **-at·ed, -at·ing, -ates.** To bring or come into friendly or cooperative association. **—consociate** (-ĭt) *adj.* Associated; united. **—consociate** (-ĭt) *n.* An associate or partner. [Latin *cōnsociāre, cōnsociāt-,* to associate : *com-,* com- + *sociāre,* to associate (from *socius,* companion; see **sekʷ-¹** in Appendix).]

con·so·ci·a·tion (kən-sō′shē-ā′shən) *n.* **1.** Friendly or cooperative association, as between groups or organizations. **2.** *Ecology.* A subdivision of an association having one dominant species of plant. **3.** A political arrangement in which various groups, such as ethnic or racial populations within a country or region, share power according to an agreed formula or mechanism. **—con·so′ci·a′tion·al** *adj.*

con·sol (kŏn′sŏl, kən-sŏl′) *n.* *Chiefly British.* A government bond in Great Britain that pays perpetual interest and has no date of maturity. Often used in the plural. Also called *bank annuity.* [Short for *Consolidated Annuity.*]

consol. *abbr.* Consolidated.

con·so·la·tion (kŏn′sə-lā′shən) *n.* **1.a.** The act or an instance of consoling. **b.** The state of being consoled. **2.** One that consoles; a comfort: *Your kindness was a consolation to me in my grief.*

consolation prize *n.* A prize given to a competitor who loses or does not win the first prize.

con·sole¹ (kən-sōl′) *tr.v.* **-soled, -sol·ing, -soles.** To allay the sorrow or grief of. See Synonyms at **comfort.** [French *consoler,* from Old French, from Latin *cōnsōlārī* : *com-,* intensive pref.; see COM- + *sōlārī,* to comfort.] **—con·sol′a·ble** *adj.*

ă pat	oi boy
ā pay	ou out
âr care	o͝o took
ä father	o͞o boot
ĕ pet	ŭ cut
ē be	ûr urge
ĭ pit	th thin
ī pie	*th* this
îr pier	hw which
ŏ pot	zh vision
ō toe	ə about, item
ô paw	♦ regionalism

Stress marks: **′** (primary); ′ (secondary), as in **dictionary** (dĭk′shə-nĕr′ē)

—**con·so′la·to′ry** (-sō′lə-tôr′ē, -tōr′ē, -sŏl′ə-) *adj.* —**con·sol′er** *n.* —**con·sol′ing·ly** *adv.*

con·sole² (kŏn′sōl′) *n.* **1.a.** A cabinet for a radio, television set, or phonograph, designed to stand on the floor. **b.** A small, freestanding storage cabinet. **2.** *Music.* The desklike part of an organ that contains the keyboard, stops, and pedals. **3.a.** A central control panel for a mechanical, electrical, or electronic system. **b.** An instrument panel. **4.** The portion of a computer or peripheral that houses the apparatus used to operate the machine manually and provides a means of communication between the computer operator and the central processing unit, often in the form of a keyboard. **5.** A small storage compartment mounted between bucket seats in an automobile. **6.** An often scroll-shaped bracket used for decoration or for supporting a projecting member, such as a cornice or shelf. **7.** A console table. [French, perhaps short for *consolider,* to strengthen, from Latin *cōnsolidāre.* See CONSOLIDATE.]

con·sole table (kŏn′sōl′) *n.* **1.** A table supported by decorative consoles fixed to a wall. **2.** A small table, often with curved legs resembling consoles, designed to be set against a wall.

con·sol·i·date (kən-sŏl′ĭ-dāt′) *v.* **-dat·ed, -dat·ing, -dates.** —*tr.* **1.** To unite into one system or whole; combine: *consolidated five separate agencies into a single department.* **2.** To make strong or secure; strengthen: *She consolidated her power during her first year in office.* **3.** To make firm or coherent; form into a compact mass. —*intr.* **1.** To become solidified or united. **2.** To join in a merger or union: *The two firms consolidated under a new name.* [Latin *cōnsolidāre, cōnsolidāt-* : *com-,* intensive pref.; see COM– + *solidāre,* to make firm (from *solidus,* firm; see **sol-** in Appendix).] —**con·sol′i·da′tor** *n.*

con·sol·i·dat·ed school (kən-sŏl′ĭ-dā′tĭd) *n.* A public school serving pupils from several adjacent, often rural districts.

con·sol·i·da·tion (kən-sŏl′ĭ-dā′shən) *n.* **1.a.** The act or process of consolidating. **b.** The state of being consolidated. **2.** The merger of two or more commercial interests or corporations.

con·so·lute (kŏn′sə-lo͞ot′) *adj.* Of or relating to liquid substances that are capable of being mixed in all proportions. [Late Latin *cōnsolūtus,* dissolved together : Latin *com-,* com- + Latin *solūtus,* past participle of *solvere,* to loosen, dissolve; see **leu-** in Appendix.]

con·som·mé (kŏn′sə-mā′, kŏn′sə-mā′) *n.* A clear soup made of strained meat or vegetable stock, served hot or as a cold jelly. [French, from past participle of *consommer,* to use up, from Latin *cōnsummāre,* to finish. See CONSUMMATE.]

con·so·nance (kŏn′sə-nəns) *n.* **1.** Agreement; harmony; accord. **2.a.** Close correspondence of sounds. **b.** The repetition of consonants or of a consonant pattern, especially at the ends of words, as in *blank* and *think* or *strong* and *string.* **3.** *Music.* A simultaneous combination of sounds conventionally regarded as pleasing and final in effect.

con·so·nant (kŏn′sə-nənt) *adj.* **1.** Being in agreement or accord: *remarks consonant with our own beliefs.* **2.** Corresponding or alike in sound, as words or syllables. **3.** Harmonious in sound or tone. **4.** Consonantal. —**consonant** *n.* *Abbr.* **cons. 1.** A speech sound produced by a partial or complete obstruction of the air stream by any of various constrictions of the speech organs. **2.** A letter or character representing such a speech sound. [Middle English, from Old French, from Latin *cōnsonāns, cōnsonant-,* present participle of *cōnsonāre,* to agree : *com-,* com- + *sonāre,* to sound; see **swen-** in Appendix.] —**con′so·nant·ly** *adv.*

con·so·nan·tal (kŏn′sə-năn′tl) *adj.* **1.** Of, relating to, or having the nature of a consonant. **2.** Containing a consonant or consonants. —**con′so·nan′tal·ly** *adv.*

con·sort (kŏn′sôrt′) *n.* **1.** A husband or wife, especially the spouse of a monarch. **2.** A companion or partner. **3.** A ship accompanying another in travel. **4.** Partnership; association: *governed in consort with her advisers.* **5.** A group; a company: *a consort of fellow diplomats.* **6.** *Music.* **a.** An ensemble of players. **b.** A group of instruments of the same family. —**consort** (kən-sôrt′) *v.* **-sort·ed, -sort·ing, -sorts.** —*intr.* **1.** To keep company; associate: *a politician known to consort with gangsters.* **2.** To be in accord or agreement. —*tr.* **1.** To unite in company; associate. **2.** *Obsolete.* **a.** To escort; accompany. **b.** To espouse. [Middle English, colleague, from Old French, from Latin *cōnsors, cōnsort-* : *com-,* com- + *sors,* fate; see **ser-²** in Appendix.]

con·sor·ti·um (kən-sôr′tē-əm, -shē-əm) *n., pl.* **-ti·a** (-tē-ə, -shē-ə). **1.a.** An association or a combination, as of businesses, financial institutions, or investors, for the purpose of engaging in a joint venture. **b.** A cooperative arrangement among groups or institutions: *a library consortium.* **2.** An association or a society. **3.** *Law.* The right of a spouse to the company of, help of, affection of, and sexual relations with his or her mate. [Latin, fellowship, from *cōnsors, cōnsort-,* partner. See CONSORT.] —**con·sor′ti·al** *adj.*

con·spe·cif·ic (kŏn′spĭ-sĭf′ĭk) *adj.* Of or belonging to the same species. —**conspecific** *n.* An organism belonging to the same species as another.

con·spec·tus (kən-spĕk′təs) *n., pl.* **-tus·es. 1.** A general survey of a subject. **2.** A synopsis. [Latin, from past participle of *cōnspicere,* to observe. See CONSPICUOUS.]

con·spic·u·ous (kən-spĭk′yo͞o-əs) *adj.* **1.** Easy to notice; obvious. **2.** Attracting attention, as by being unusual or remarkable; noticeable. See Synonyms at **noticeable.** [From Latin *cōnspicuus,* from *cōnspicere,* to observe : *com-,* intensive pref.; see COM– + *specere,* to look; see **spek-** in Appendix.] —**con·spic′u·ous·ly** *adv.* —**con·spic′u·ous·ness** *n.*

con·spir·a·cist (kən-spîr′ə-sĭst) *n.* One holding a conspiracy theory.

con·spir·a·cy (kən-spîr′ə-sē) *n., pl.* **-cies. 1.** An agreement to perform together an illegal, wrongful, or subversive act. **2.** A group of conspirators. **3.** *Law.* An agreement between two or more persons to commit a crime or accomplish a legal purpose through illegal action. **4.** A joining or acting together, as if by sinister design: *a conspiracy of wind and tide that devastated coastal areas.* [Middle English *conspiracie,* from Anglo-Norman *conspiracie,* probably alteration of Old French *conspiration,* from Latin *cōnspīrātiō, cōnspīrātiōn-,* from *cōnspīrātus,* past participle of *cōnspīrāre,* to conspire. See CONSPIRE.]

SYNONYMS: *conspiracy, plot, machination, collusion, intrigue, cabal.* Each of these nouns denotes a secret plan to achieve an evil or illegal end. *Conspiracy* refers to such a plan by a group intent usually on a treacherous purpose: *Several generals formed a conspiracy to overthrow the government. Plot* stresses sinister means and motives but may be small or large in number of participants and scope: *Several financiers joined the plot to take over the profitable company. Machination,* usually in the plural, strongly implies crafty, underhand dealing: *"the devious machinations of CIA operatives"* (Christian Science Monitor). *Collusion* is secret agreement for a fraudulent purpose: *If it had not been for collusion between criminals and a few corrupt police officers, the drug ring would have been exposed long ago. Intrigue* denotes a complex clandestine scheme; usually it implies selfish, petty actions rather than criminal ends: *Political intrigue prevented her from becoming her party's candidate. Cabal* refers to a conspiratorial group whose actions usually are directed against a government or political leader: *"The cabal against Washington found supporters exclusively in the north"* (George Bancroft).

conspiracy theory *n.* A theory seeking to explain a disputed case or matter as a plot by a secret group or alliance rather than an individual or isolated act. —**conspiracy theorist** *n.*

con·spir·a·tor (kən-spîr′ə-tər) *n.* One that engages in a conspiracy.

con·spir·a·to·ri·al (kən-spîr′ə-tôr′ē-əl, -tōr′-) *adj.* Of, relating to, or characteristic of conspirators or a conspiracy: *a conspiratorial act; a conspiratorial smile.* —**con·spir′a·to′ri·al·ly** *adv.*

con·spir·a·to·ri·al·ist (kən-spîr′ə-tôr′ē-ə-lĭst, -tōr′-) *n.* A conspiracist.

con·spire (kən-spīr′) *v.* **-spired, -spir·ing, -spires.** —*intr.* **1.** To plan together secretly to commit an illegal or wrongful act or accomplish a legal purpose through illegal action. **2.** To join or act together; combine: *factors that conspired to delay the project.* —*tr.* To plan or plot secretly. [Middle English *conspiren,* from Old French, from Latin *cōnspīrāre* : *com-,* com- + *spīrāre,* to breathe.] —**con·spir′er** *n.* —**con·spir′ing·ly** *adv.*

con spi·ri·to (kŏn spîr′ĭ-tō′, kôn) *adv. Music.* With spirit and vigor. Used chiefly as a direction. [Italian : *con,* with + *spirito,* spirit, soul.]

const. *abbr.* **1.** Also **Const.** Constable. **2.** Constant. **3.** Also **Const.** Constitution. **4.** Construction.

con·sta·ble (kŏn′stə-bəl, kŭn′-) *n.* *Abbr.* **cons., Cons., const., Const. 1.** A peace officer with less authority and smaller jurisdiction than a sheriff, empowered to serve writs and warrants and make arrests. **2.** A medieval officer of high rank, usually serving as military commander in the absence of a monarch. **3.** The governor of a royal castle. **4.** *Chiefly British.* A police officer. [Middle English, from Old French *conestable,* from Late Latin *comes stabulī,* officer of the stable : Latin *comes,* officer, companion; see **ei-** in Appendix + Latin *stabulī,* genitive of *stabulum,* stable; see **stā-** in Appendix.] —**con′sta·ble·ship′** *n.*

Con·sta·ble (kŭn′stə-bəl, kŏn′-), **John.** 1776–1837. British landscape painter whose use of broken color influenced later French painters. *The Hay Wain* (1821) is his best-known work.

con·stab·u·lar (kən-stăb′yə-lər) *adj.* Constabulary.

con·stab·u·lar·y (kən-stăb′yə-lĕr′ē) *n., pl.* **-ies. 1.** The body of constables of a district or city. **2.** The district under the jurisdiction of a constable. **3.** An armed police force organized like a military unit. —**constabulary** *adj.* Of or relating to constables, constabularies, or their jurisdictions.

Con·stance (kŏn′stəns). See **Konstanz.**

Constance, Lake of. Also **Bo·den·see** (bōd′n-zā′). An Alpine lake bordering on southern Germany, northern Switzerland, and western Austria.

con·stan·cy (kŏn′stən-sē) *n.* **1.** Steadfastness, as in purpose or affection; faithfulness. **2.** The condition or quality of being constant; changelessness.

con·stant (kŏn′stənt) *adj.* **1.** Continually occurring; persistent. **2.** Unchanging in nature, value, or extent; invariable. See Synonyms at **continual. 3.** Steadfast in purpose, loyalty, or affection; faithful. See Synonyms at **faithful, steady.** —**constant** *n.* **1.** Something that is unchanging or invariable. **2.** *Abbr.* **c, C, const. a.** A quantity assumed to have a fixed value in a specified mathematical context. **b.** An experimental or theoretical condition, factor, or quantity that does not vary or that is regarded as invariant in specified circumstances. [Middle English, from Old French, from Latin *cōnstāns, cōnstant-,* present participle of *cōn-*

console²

console table
Mid 18th-century French

stāre, to stand firm : *com-,* intensive pref.; see COM– + *stāre,* to stand; see **stā-** in Appendix.] **—con′stant·ly** *adv.*

Con·stan·ța (kən-stän′sə, kôn-stän′tsä). A city of southeast Romania on the Black Sea east of Bucharest. Founded in the seventh century B.C. as a Greek colony, it is the country's main seaport. Population, 315,662.

con·stan·tan (kŏn′stən-tăn′) *n.* An alloy of 45 percent nickel and 55 percent copper, used chiefly in electrical instruments because of its constant resistance. [From CONSTANT.]

Con·stant de Re·becque (kôN-stäN′ də rə-bĕk′), **Benjamin.** 1767–1830. French writer and politician who was exiled in 1802 for denouncing Napoleon's machinations. He is best known for the novel *Adolphe* (1816), inspired by his affair with Madame de Staël.

constant dollars *pl.n.* Dollars reported in terms of the value they had on a previous date: *The dividend of $5 per share that was paid in 1986 was worth only $2.50 in constant dollars of 1976, when the stock was purchased.*

Con·stan·tine (kŏn′stən-tēn′, kôN-stăN-tēn′). A city of northeast Algeria east of Algiers. It was founded by Carthaginians and was the capital and commercial center of Numidia. Destroyed in warfare in A.D. 311, it was rebuilt by Constantine I and named in his honor. Population, 344,454.

Con·stan·tine I[1] (kŏn′stən-tēn′, -tīn′). Known as "Constantine the Great." A.D. 285?–337. Emperor of Rome (306–337) who adopted the Christian faith and suspended the persecution of Christians. He rebuilt Constantinople (now Istanbul) as the new Rome (330).

Con·stan·tine I[2]**.** 1868–1923. King of Greece (1913–1917) who opposed the Allies in World War I and was forced to abdicate. He also ruled from 1920 to 1922.

Constantine II. Born 1940. King of Greece (1964–1967) who went into exile after a coup d'état by army officers. The Greek monarchy was officially abolished in 1974.

Con·stan·ti·no·ple (kŏn′stăn-tə-nō′pəl). See **Istanbul.**

con·stel·late (kŏn′stə-lāt′) *intr. & tr.v.* **-lat·ed, -lat·ing, -lates.** To form or cause to form a group or cluster. [Back-formation from CONSTELLATION.]

con·stel·la·tion (kŏn′stə-lā′shən) *n.* **1.** *Astronomy.* **a.** An arbitrary formation of stars perceived as a figure or design, especially one of 88 recognized groups named after characters from classical mythology and various common animals and objects. **b.** An area of the celestial sphere occupied by one of the 88 recognized constellations. **2.** The configuration of planets at the time of one's birth, regarded by astrologers as determining one's character or fate. **3.** A gathering or an assemblage, especially of prominent persons or things: *The symposium was attended by a constellation of artists and writers.* **4.** A set or configuration, as of related items, properties, ideas, or individuals: *a constellation of demands ranging from better food to improved health care; a constellation of feelings about the divorce.* [Middle English *constellacioun,* from Old French *constellation,* from Late Latin *cōnstellātiō, cōnstellātiōn-* : *com-,* com- + *stēlla,* star; see **ster-**[3] in Appendix.] **—con′stel·la′tion·al** *adj.* **—con·stel′la·to′ry** (-stĕl′ə-tôr′ē, -tōr′ē) *adj.*

con·ster·nate (kŏn′stər-nāt′) *tr.v.* **-nat·ed, -nat·ing, -nates.** To cause consternation in. [Latin *cōnsternāre, cōnsternāt-* : *com-,* intensive pref.; see COM– + *sternere,* to throw down; see **ster-**[2] in Appendix.]

con·ster·na·tion (kŏn′stər-nā′shən) *n.* A state of paralyzing dismay. See Synonyms at **fear.**

con·sti·pate (kŏn′stə-pāt′) *tr.v.* **-pat·ed, -pat·ing, -pates.** **1.** To cause constipation in. **2.** To clog or make sluggish; obstruct. [Latin *cōnstīpāre, cōnstīpāt-,* to crowd together : *com-,* com- + *stīpāre,* to cram.]

con·sti·pa·tion (kŏn′stə-pā′shən) *n.* **1.** Difficult, incomplete, or infrequent evacuation of dry, hardened feces from the bowels. **2.** Obstruction; stultification.

con·stit·u·en·cy (kən-stĭch′o͞o-ən-sē) *n., pl.* **-cies.** **1. a.** The body of voters represented by an elected legislator or official. **b.** The district so represented. **c.** The residents of an electoral district. **2. a.** A group of supporters or patrons. **b.** A group served by an organization or institution; a clientele: *The magazine changed its format to appeal to a broader constituency.*

con·stit·u·ent (kən-stĭch′o͞o-ənt) *adj.* **1.** Serving as part of a whole; component: *a constituent element.* **2.** Empowered to elect or designate. **3.** Authorized to make or amend a constitution: *a constituent assembly.* **—constituent** *n.* **1.** A constituent part; a component. See Synonyms at **element.** **2.** A resident of a district or member of a group represented by an elected official. **3.** One that authorizes another to act as a representative; a client. **4.** *Grammar.* One of two or more elements into which a construction or compound may be divided by analysis, being either immediate, as *He/ works on the railroad,* or ultimate, as *He/ work/s/ on/ the/ rail/road.* [Latin *cōnstituēns, cōnstituent-,* present participle of *cōnstituere,* to set up. See CONSTITUTE. N., from French, from Latin *cōnstituēns.*] **—con·stit′u·ent·ly** *adv.*

constituent structure *n. Grammar.* An analysis, often in the form of a schematic representation, of the constituents of a construction, such as a sentence.

con·sti·tute (kŏn′stĭ-to͞ot′, -tyo͞ot′) *tr.v.* **-tut·ed, -tut·ing, -tutes.** **1. a.** To be the elements or parts of; compose: *Correct grammar and sentence structure do not in themselves constitute good writing.* **b.** To amount to; equal: *an infraction that constitutes a punishable offense.* **2. a.** To set up or establish according to law or provision: *a body that is duly constituted under the charter.* **b.** To found (an institution, for example). **c.** To enact (a law or regulation). **3.** To appoint to an office, dignity, function, or task; designate. [Latin *cōnstituere, cōnstitūt-,* to set up : *com-,* com- + *statuere,* to set up; see **stā-** in Appendix.] **—con′sti·tut′er, con′sti·tu′tor** *n.*

con·sti·tu·tion (kŏn′stĭ-to͞o′shən, -tyo͞o′-) *n.* **1.** The act or process of composing, setting up, or establishing. **2. a.** The composition or structure of something; makeup. **b.** The physical makeup of a person: *She was born with a strong constitution.* See Synonyms at **physique.** **3.** *Abbr.* **cons., const., Const.** **a.** The system of fundamental laws and principles that prescribes the nature, functions, and limits of a government or another institution. **b.** The document on which such a system is recorded.

con·sti·tu·tion·al (kŏn′stĭ-to͞o′shə-nəl, -tyo͞o′-) *adj. Abbr.* **cons.** **1.** Of or relating to a constitution: *a constitutional amendment.* **2.** Consistent with, sanctioned by, or permissible according to a constitution: *a law that was declared constitutional by the court; the constitutional right of free speech.* **3.** Established by or operating under a constitution: *a constitutional government.* **4.** Of or proceeding from the basic structure or nature of a person or thing; inherent: *a constitutional inability to tell the truth.* **5.** Of or relating to one's physical makeup. **—constitutional** *n.* A walk taken regularly for one's health. **—con′sti·tu′tion·al·ly** *adv.*

con·sti·tu·tion·al·ism (kŏn′stĭ-to͞o′shə-nə-lĭz′əm, -tyo͞o′-) *n.* **1.** Government in which power is distributed and limited by a system of laws that must be obeyed by the rulers. **2. a.** A constitutional system of government. **b.** Advocacy of such a system. **—con′sti·tu′tion·al·ist** *n.*

con·sti·tu·tion·al·i·ty (kŏn′stĭ-to͞o′shə-năl′ĭ-tē, -tyo͞o′-) *n.* Accordance with the provisions or principles of a constitution: *The high court will rule on the constitutionality of the new law.*

con·sti·tu·tion·al·ize (kŏn′stĭ-to͞o′shə-nə-līz′, -tyo͞o′-) *tr.v.* **-ized, -iz·ing, -iz·es.** **1.** To provide with or make subject to a constitution. **2.** To incorporate into or sanction under a constitution: *"Today a like kind of wisdom might caution against constitutionalizing every grievance that might (or might not) appear tomorrow"* (Potter Stewart). **—con′sti·tu′tion·al·i·za′tion** (-shə-nə-lĭ-zā′shən) *n.*

constitutional monarchy *n.* A monarchy in which the powers of the ruler are restricted to those granted under the constitution and laws of the nation.

con·sti·tu·tive (kŏn′stĭ-to͞o′tĭv, -tyo͞o′-) *adj.* **1.** Making a thing what it is; essential. **2.** Having power to institute, establish, or enact. **3.** Of or relating to the synthesis of a protein or an enzyme at a constant rate regardless of physiological demand or the concentration of a substrate. **—con′sti·tu′tive·ly** *adv.*

con·strain (kən-strān′) *tr.v.* **-strained, -strain·ing, -strains.** **1.** To compel by physical, moral, or circumstantial force; oblige: *felt constrained to object.* See Synonyms at **force.** **2.** To keep within close bounds; confine: *a life that had been constrained by habit to the same few activities and friends.* **3.** To inhibit or restrain; hold back: *"Failing to control the growth of international debt will also constrain living standards"* (Ronald Brownstein). **4.** To produce in a forced or inhibited manner. [Middle English *constreinen,* from Old French *constraindre, constraign-,* from Latin *cōnstringere,* to restrain, compress : *com-,* com- + *stringere,* to bind, press together; see **streig-** in Appendix.] **—con·strain′a·ble** *adj.* **—con·strain′ed·ly** (-strā′nĭd-lē) *adv.* **—con·strain′er** *n.*

con·straint (kən-strānt′) *n.* **1.** The threat or use of force to prevent, restrict, or dictate the action or thought of others. **2.** The state of being restricted or confined within prescribed bounds: *soon tired of the constraint of military life.* **3.** One that restricts, limits, or regulates; a check: *ignored all moral constraints in his pursuit of success.* **4.** Embarrassed reserve or reticence; awkwardness: *"All constraint had vanished between the two, and they began to talk"* (Edith Wharton). [Middle English *constreinte,* from Old French, from feminine past participle of *constraindre.* See CONSTRAIN.]

con·strict (kən-strĭkt′) *v.* **-strict·ed, -strict·ing, -stricts.** *—tr.* **1.** To make smaller or narrower by binding or squeezing. **2.** To squeeze or compress. See Synonyms at **contract.** **3.** To restrict the scope or freedom of; cramp: *lives constricted by poverty.* *—intr.* To become constricted. [Latin *cōnstringere, cōnstrict-,* to compress. See CONSTRAIN.] **—con·stric′tive** *adj.* **—con·stric′tive·ly** *adv.*

con·stric·tion (kən-strĭk′shən) *n.* **1. a.** The act or process of constricting. **b.** The condition or result of being constricted. **c.** Something that constricts. **2.** A feeling of tightness or pressure: *Fear caused a sudden constriction in my chest.* **3.** A constricted or narrow part.

con·stric·tor (kən-strĭk′tər) *n.* **1.** One that constricts, as a muscle that contracts or compresses a part or organ of the body. **2.** Any of various snakes, such as the python or boa, that tightly coil around and asphyxiate their prey.

con·stringe (kən-strĭnj′) *tr.v.* **-stringed, -string·ing, -string·es.** To cause to contract; constrict. [Latin *cōnstringere,* to compress. See CONSTRAIN.] **—con·strin′gen·cy** *n.* **—con·strin′gent** *adj.*

con·struct (kən-strŭkt′) *tr.v.* **-struct·ed, -struct·ing, -structs.** **1.** To form by assembling or combining parts; build. **2.**

To create (an argument or a sentence, for example) by systematically arranging ideas or terms. **3.** *Mathematics.* To draw (a geometric figure) that meets specific requirements, usually with instruments limited to a straightedge and compass. **—construct** (kŏn′strŭkt′) *n.* **1.** Something formed or constructed from parts. **2.a.** A concept, model, or schematic idea: *a theoretical construct of the atom.* **b.** A concrete image or idea: "[He] *began to shift focus from the haunted constructs of terror in his early work*" (Stephen Koch). [Latin *cōnstruere, cōnstrūct-* : *com-*, com- + *struere*, to pile up; see **ster-**[2] in Appendix.] **—con·struct′i·ble** *adj.* **—con·struc′tor, con·struct′er** *n.*

con·struc·tion (kən-strŭk′shən) *n. Abbr.* **cons., const. 1.a.** The act or process of constructing. **b.** The art, trade, or work of building: *an engineer trained in highway construction; worked in construction for seven years.* **2.a.** A structure, such as a building, framework, or model. **b.** Something fashioned or devised systematically: *a nation that was glorious in its historical construction.* **c.** An artistic composition using various materials; an assemblage or a collage. **3.** The way in which something is built or put together: *a shelter of simple construction.* **4.** The interpretation or explanation given to an expression or a statement: *I was inclined to put a favorable construction on his reply.* **5.** *Grammar.* **a.** The arrangement of words to form a meaningful phrase, clause, or sentence. **b.** A group of words so arranged. **—con·struc′tion·al** *adj.* **—con·struc′tion·al·ly** *adv.*

con·struc·tion·ist (kən-strŭk′shə-nĭst) *n.* A person who construes a legal text or document in a specified way: *a strict constructionist.*

construction paper *n.* A heavy paper produced in a variety of colors and used in artwork especially for making folded or cut-out designs.

con·struc·tive (kən-strŭk′tĭv) *adj.* **1.** Serving to improve or advance; helpful: *constructive criticism.* **2.** Of or relating to construction; structural. **3.** *Law.* Based on an interpretation; not directly expressed. **—con·struc′tive·ly** *adv.* **—con·struc′tive·ness** *n.*

con·struc·tiv·ism (kən-strŭk′tə-vĭz′əm) *n.* A movement in modern art originating in Moscow in 1920 and characterized by the use of industrial materials such as glass, sheet metal, and plastic to create nonrepresentational, often geometric objects. **—con·struc′tiv·ist** *n.*

con·strue (kən-stro͞o′) *v.* **-strued, -stru·ing, -strues.** *—tr.* **1.** To adduce or explain the meaning of; interpret: *construed my smile as assent.* See Synonyms at **explain. 2.** *Grammar.* **a.** To analyze the structure of (a clause or sentence). **b.** To use syntactically: *The noun* fish *can be construed as singular or plural.* **3.** To translate, especially aloud. *—intr. Grammar.* **1.** To analyze grammatical structure. **2.** To be subject to grammatical analysis. **—construe** (kŏn′stro͞o′) *n.* An interpretation or translation. [Middle English *construen*, from Late Latin *cōnstruere*, from Latin, to build. See CONSTRUCT.]

con·sub·stan·tial (kŏn′səb-stăn′shəl) *adj.* Of the same substance, nature, or essence. [Middle English *consubstancial*, from Late Latin *cōnsubstantiālis* : Latin *com-*, com- + Late Latin *substantiālis*, substantial; see SUBSTANTIAL.]

con·sub·stan·ti·ate (kŏn′səb-stăn′shē-āt′) *tr. & intr.v.* **-at·ed, -at·ing, -ates.** To unite or become united in one common substance, nature, or essence.

con·sub·stan·ti·a·tion (kŏn′səb-stăn′shē-ā′shən) *n. Theology.* The doctrine that the substance of the body and blood of Jesus coexists with the substance of the bread and wine in the Eucharist.

con·sue·tude (kŏn′swĭ-to͞od′, -tyo͞od′) *n.* Custom; usage. [Middle English, from Latin *cōnsuētūdō*. See CUSTOM.] **—con′sue·tu′di·nar′y** (-to͞od′n-ĕr′ē, -tyo͞od′-) *adj.*

con·sul (kŏn′səl) *n. Abbr.* **c., C., cons., Cons. 1.** An official appointed by a government to reside in a foreign country and represent his or her government's commercial interests and assist its citizens there. See Usage Note at **council. 2.** Either of the two chief magistrates of the Roman Republic, elected for a term of one year. **3.** Any of the three chief magistrates of the French Republic from 1799 to 1804. [Middle English, Roman consul, from Latin *cōnsul*; possibly akin to *cōnsulere*, to take counsel.] **—con′su·lar** (-sə-lər) *adj.* **—con′sul·ship′** *n.*

con·su·late (kŏn′sə-lĭt) *n.* **1.** The residence or official premises of a consul. **2.** The office, term of office, or jurisdiction of a consul. **3.** Government by consuls. [Middle English *consulat*, consulship, from Latin *cōnsulātus*, from *cōnsul*, consul. See CONSUL.]

consulate general *n., pl.* **consulates general.** The consulate occupied by a consul general.

consul general *n., pl.* **consuls general.** *Abbr.* **c.g., C.G.** A consul of the highest rank serving at a principal location and usually responsible for other consular offices within a country.

con·sult (kən-sŭlt′) *v.* **-sult·ed, -sult·ing, -sults.** *—tr.* **1.a.** To seek advice or information of: *consult an attorney.* **b.** To refer to: *consulted a telephone directory for the number.* **2.** To take into account; consider: *consult one's checkbook before making a major purchase.* *—intr.* **1.** To exchange views; confer. See Synonyms at **confer. 2.** To work or serve as a consultant: *a retired executive who consults for several large companies.* **—consult** (kən-sŭlt′, kŏn′sŭlt′) *n.* A consultation, especially one involving physicians. [French *consulter*, from Latin *cōnsultāre*, frequentative of *cōnsulere*, to take counsel.] **—con·sult′er** *n.*

con·sul·tan·cy (kən-sŭl′tn-sē) *n., pl.* **-cies. 1.** The act or an instance of consulting. **2.** A business or agency offering expert or professional advice in a field: *opened a financial consultancy.* **3.** A position as a consultant: *accepted a three-year consultancy abroad.*

con·sult·ant (kən-sŭl′tənt) *n.* **1.** One that gives expert or professional advice. **2.** One that consults another. **—con·sult′ant·ship′** *n.*

con·sul·ta·tion (kŏn′səl-tā′shən) *n.* **1.** The act or process of consulting. **2.a.** A conference at which advice is given or views are exchanged. **b.** A meeting between physicians to discuss the diagnosis or treatment of a case.

con·sul·ta·tive (kən-sŭl′tə-tĭv) also **con·sul·tive** (-sŭl′-tĭv) or **con·sul·ta·to·ry** (-tôr′ē, -tōr′ē) *adj.* Of or relating to consultation; advisory.

con·sul·tor (kən-sŭl′tər) *n. Roman Catholic Church.* **1.** A priest or religious appointed to assist and advise a bishop. **2.** An adviser to a congregation of the Curia.

con·sum·a·ble (kən-so͞o′mə-bəl) *adj.* **1.** That can be consumed: *consumable energy.* **2.** That may be depleted or worn out by use: *consumable paper products.* **—consumable** *n.* A consumable good or service: *supplies of food, fuel, spare parts, and other consumables.*

con·sume (kən-so͞om′) *v.* **-sumed, -sum·ing, -sumes.** *—tr.* **1.** To eat or drink up; ingest. See Synonyms at **eat. 2.a.** To expend; use up: *engines that consume less fuel; a project that consumed most of my time and energy.* **b.** To purchase (goods or services) for direct use or ownership. **3.** To waste; squander. See Synonyms at **waste. 4.** To destroy totally; ravage: *flames that consumed the house; a body consumed by cancer.* **5.** To absorb; engross: *consumed with jealousy.* See Synonyms at **monopolize.** *—intr.* **1.** To be destroyed, expended, or wasted. **2.** To purchase economic goods and services: *a society that consumes as fast as it produces.* [Middle English *consumen*, from Latin *cōnsūmere* : *com-*, intensive pref.; see COM– + *sūmere*, to take; see **em-** in Appendix.]

con·sum·ed·ly (kən-so͞o′mĭd-lē) *adv.* To an excessive degree.

con·sum·er (kən-so͞o′mər) *n.* **1.** One that consumes, especially one that acquires goods or services for direct use or ownership rather than for resale or use in production and manufacturing. **2.** A heterotrophic organism that ingests other organisms or organic matter in a food chain. *—attributive.* Often used to modify another noun: *consumer questionnaires; consumer products.* **—con·sum′er·ship′** *n.*

consumer credit *n.* Credit granted to a consumer permitting the use or ownership of goods or services during a term of payment.

consumer goods *pl.n.* Goods, such as food and clothing, that satisfy human wants through their direct consumption or use.

con·sum·er·ism (kən-so͞o′mə-rĭz′əm) *n.* **1.** The movement seeking to protect and inform consumers by requiring such practices as honest packaging and advertising, product guarantees, and improved safety standards. **2.** The theory that a progressively greater consumption of goods is economically beneficial. **3.** Attachment to materialistic values or possessions: *deplored the rampant consumerism of contemporary society.* **—con·sum′er·ist** *n.* **—con·sum′er·is′tic** *adj.*

consumer price index *n. Abbr.* **CPI** An index of prices used to measure the change in the cost of basic goods and services in comparison with a fixed base period. Also called *cost-of-living index.*

con·sum·mate (kŏn′sə-māt′) *tr.v.* **-mat·ed, -mat·ing, -mates. 1.a.** To bring to completion or fruition; conclude: *consummate a business transaction.* **b.** To realize or achieve; fulfill: *a dream that was finally consummated with the publication of her first book.* **2.a.** To complete (a marriage) with the first act of sexual intercourse after the ceremony. **b.** To fulfill (a sexual desire or attraction) especially by intercourse. **—consummate** (kən-sŭm′ĭt, kŏn′sə-mət) *adj.* **1.** Complete or perfect in every respect: *consummate happiness.* See Synonyms at **perfect. 2.** Supremely accomplished or skilled: *"Sargent was now a consummate master of brushwork"* (Roberta Smith). **3.** Complete; utter: *a consummate bore.* [Middle English *consummaten*, from Latin *cōnsummāre, cōnsummāt-* : *com-*, com- + *summa*, sum; see SUM.] **—con·sum′mate·ly** (kən-sŭm′ĭt-lē) *adv.* **—con′sum·ma′tive, con·sum′ma·to′ry** (-sŭm′ə-tôr′ē, -tōr′ē) *adj.* **—con′sum·ma′tor** *n.*

con·sum·ma·tion (kŏn′sə-mā′shən) *n.* **1.** The act of consummating; a fulfillment. **2.** An ultimate goal or end.

con·sump·tion (kən-sŭmp′shən) *n.* **1.a.** The act or process of consuming. **b.** The state of being consumed. **c.** An amount consumed. **2.** *Economics.* The using up of goods and services by consumer purchasing or in the production of other goods. **3.** *Pathology.* **a.** A progressive wasting of body tissue. **b.** Pulmonary tuberculosis. No longer in scientific use. [Middle English *consumpcioun*, from Latin *cōnsūmptiō, cōnsūmptiōn-*, a consuming, from *cōnsūmptus*, past participle of *cōnsūmere*, to consume. See CONSUME.]

con·sump·tive (kən-sŭmp′tĭv) *adj.* **1.** Consuming or tending to consume. **2.** Of, relating to, or afflicted with consumption. **—consumptive** *n.* A person afflicted with consumption. **—con·sump′tive·ly** *adv.*

cont. *abbr.* **1.** Containing. **2.** Contents. **3.** Continent. **4.a.**

Continue. **b.** Continued. **5.** Contract. **6.** Contraction. **7.** Control.

con·tact (kŏn′tăkt′) *n.* **1.a.** A coming together or touching, as of objects or surfaces. **b.** The state or condition of touching or of immediate proximity: *Litmus paper turns red on contact with an acid.* **2.a.** Connection or interaction; communication: *in contact with the right people.* **b.** Visual observation: *The pilot made contact with the ship.* **c.** Association; relationship: *came into contact with new ideas at college.* **3.** A person who might be of use; a connection. **4.** *Electricity.* **a.** A connection between two conductors that permits a flow of current. **b.** A part or device that makes or breaks such a connection. **5.** *Medicine.* A person recently exposed to a contagious disease, usually through close association with an infected individual. **6.** A contact lens. **—contact** (kŏn′tăkt′, kən-tăkt′) *v.* **-tact·ed, -tact·ing, -tacts.** *—tr.* **1.** To bring or put in contact. **2.** To get in touch with; communicate with: *"This past January I was contacted by a lawyer who said he needed my help"* (Elizabeth Loftus). *—intr.* To be in or come into contact. **—contact** *adj.* **1.** Of, sustaining, or making contact. **2.** Caused or transmitted by touching: *a contact skin rash.* [Latin *contāctus,* from past participle of *contingere,* to touch : *com-,* com- + *tangere,* to touch; see **tag-** in Appendix.] **—con·tac′tu·al** (kən-tăk′cho͞o-əl) *adj.* **—con·tac′tu·al·ly** *adv.*

USAGE NOTE: In 1966 Wilson Follett wrote that "Persons old enough to have been repelled by the verb *contact* . . . may as well make up their minds that there is no way to arrest or reverse the tide of its popularity." His prophecy is proving correct: In 1969 only 34 percent of the Usage Panel accepted the use of *contact* as a verb, but in our most recent survey 65 percent of the Panel accepted the sentence *She immediately called an officer at the Naval Intelligence Service, who in turn contacted the FBI.* See Usage Note at **impact.**

contact dermatitis *n.* An acute or chronic skin inflammation resulting from contact with an irritating substance or allergen.

contact flight *n.* Aircraft navigation by visual observation of the horizon or of landmarks. Also called *contact flying.*

contact inhibition *n.* The cessation of cellular growth and division due to physical contact with other cells.

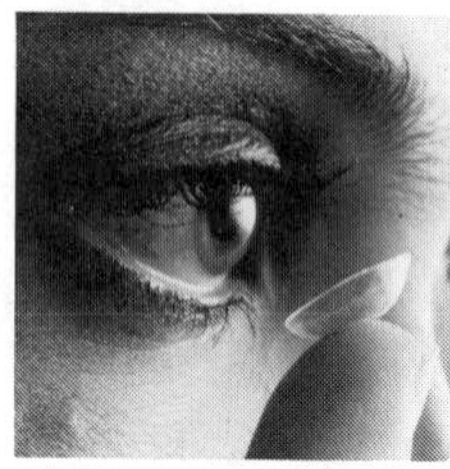

contact lens

contact lens *n.* A thin plastic or glass lens that is fitted over the cornea of the eye to correct various vision defects.

con·tac·tor (kŏn′tăk′tər, kən-tăk′-) *n.* An electrical relay used to control the flow of power in a circuit.

contact print *n.* A print made by exposing a photosensitive surface in direct contact with a photographic negative.

contact sport *n. Sports.* A sport, such as football, hockey, or boxing, that involves physical contact between players as part of normal play.

con·ta·gia (kən-tā′jə) *n.* Plural of **contagium.**

con·ta·gion (kən-tā′jən) *n.* **1.a.** Disease transmission by direct or indirect contact. **b.** A disease that is or may be transmitted by direct or indirect contact; a contagious disease. **c.** See **contagium. 2.** A harmful, corrupting influence: *feared that violence on television was a contagion affecting young viewers.* **3.** The tendency to spread, as of a doctrine, influence, or emotional state. [Middle English *contagioun,* from Latin *contāgiō, contāgiōn-,* from *contingere, contāct-,* to touch. See CONTACT.]

con·ta·gious (kən-tā′jəs) *adj.* **1.** Of or relating to contagion. **2.** Transmissible by direct or indirect contact; communicable: *a contagious disease.* **3.** Capable of transmitting disease; carrying a disease: *stayed at home until he was no longer contagious.* **4.** Spreading or tending to spread from one to another; infectious: *a contagious smile.* **—con·ta′gious·ly** *adv.* **—con·ta′gious·ness** *n.*

contagious abortion *n. Veterinary Medicine.* Brucellosis, especially in cattle.

con·ta·gium (kən-tā′jəm) *n., pl.* **-gia** (-jə). The direct cause, such as a bacterium or virus, of a communicable disease. Also called *contagion.* [Latin *contāgium,* contagion, contamination, from *contāgiō.* See CONTAGION.]

con·tain (kən-tān′) *tr.v.* **-tained, -tain·ing, -tains. 1.a.** To have within; hold. **b.** To be capable of holding. **2.** To have as component parts; include or comprise: *The album contains many memorable songs.* **3.a.** To hold or keep within limits; restrain: *I could hardly contain my curiosity.* **b.** To halt the spread or development of; check: *Science sought an effective method of containing the disease.* **4.** To check the expansion or influence of (a hostile power or ideology) by containment. **5.** *Mathematics.* To be exactly divisible by. [Middle English *conteinen,* from Old French *contenir,* from Latin *continēre* : *com-,* com- + *tenēre,* to hold; see **ten-** in Appendix.] **—con·tain′a·ble** *adj.*

SYNONYMS: *contain, hold, accommodate.* These verbs mean to have within or have the capacity for having within. *Contain* means to have within or have as a part or constituent: *This drawer contains all the cutlery we own. The book contains some amusing passages. Polluted water contains contaminants. Hold* can be used in that sense but primarily stresses capacity for containing: *The pitcher holds two pints but contains only one. Accommodate* refers to capacity for holding comfortably: *The restaurant accommodates 50 customers. Four hundred inmates were crowded into a prison intended to accommodate 200.*

con·tain·er (kən-tā′nər) *n.* **1.** A receptacle, such as a carton, can, or jar, in which material is held or carried. **2.** A large reusable receptacle that can accommodate smaller cartons or cases in a single shipment, designed for efficient handling of cargo.

con·tain·er·board (kən-tā′nər-bôrd′, -bōrd′) *n.* A corrugated or solid cardboard used to make containers.

con·tain·er·ize (kən-tā′nə-rīz′) *v.* *—tr.* **-ized, -iz·ing, -iz·es. 1.** To package (cargo) in large standardized containers for efficient shipping and handling. **2.** To adapt (an industry or shipping operation) to the use of such containers. *—intr.* To convert to the use of containerized cargo. **—con·tain′er·i·za′tion** (-tā′nər-ĭ-zā′shən) *n.*

con·tain·er·port (kən-tā′nər-pôrt′, -pōrt′) *n.* A port equipped to handle containerized cargo.

container ship *n. Nautical.* A ship fitted for transporting containerized cargo.

con·tain·ment (kən-tān′mənt) *n.* **1.** The act or condition of containing. **2.** A policy of checking the expansion or influence of a hostile power or ideology, as by the creation of strategic alliances or support of client states in areas of conflict or unrest. **3.** A structure or system designed to prevent the accidental release of radioactive materials from a reactor.

con·tam·i·nant (kən-tăm′ə-nənt) *n.* One that contaminates.

con·tam·i·nate (kən-tăm′ə-nāt′) *tr.v.* **-nated, -nat·ing, -nates. 1.** To make impure or unclean by contact or mixture. **2.** To expose to or permeate with radioactivity. **—contaminate** (-nĭt) *adj. Archaic.* Contaminated. [Middle English *contaminaten,* from Latin *contāmināre, contāmināt-.* See **tag-** in Appendix.] **—con·tam′i·na′tive** *adj.* **—con·tam′i·na′tor** *n.*

SYNONYMS: *contaminate, befoul, foul, poison, pollute, taint.* The central meaning shared by these verbs is "to make dirty or impure": *a contaminated reservoir; shoes that were befouled with mud; noxious fumes that foul the air; chemicals poisoning the lake; polluted streams; food that had been tainted through improper storage.*

con·tam·i·na·tion (kən-tăm′ə-nā′shən) *n.* **1.a.** The act or process of contaminating. **b.** The state of being contaminated. **2.** One that contaminates.

contd. *abbr.* Continued.

conte (kôɴt) *n., pl.* **contes** (kôɴt). **1.** A short story or novella. **2.** A medieval narrative tale. [French, from Old French *conter,* to relate, recount. See COUNT[1].]

con·temn (kən-tĕm′) *tr.v.* **-temned, -temn·ing, -temns.** To view with contempt; despise. See Synonyms at **despise.** [Middle English *contempnen,* to slight, from Latin *contemnere* : *com-,* intensive pref.; see COM– + *temnere,* to despise.] **—con·temn′er** (-tĕm′ər, -tĕm′nər) *n.*

contemp. *abbr.* Contemporary.

con·tem·plate (kŏn′təm-plāt′) *v.* **-plat·ed, -plat·ing, -plates.** *—tr.* **1.** To look at attentively and thoughtfully. See Synonyms at **see**[1]. **2.** To consider carefully and at length; meditate on or ponder: *contemplated the problem from all sides; contemplated the mystery of God.* **3.** To have in mind as an intention or possibility: *contemplate marriage; forced by the accident to contemplate retirement.* *—intr.* To ponder; meditate. [Latin *contemplārī, contemplāt-* : *com-,* intensive pref.; see COM– + *templum,* space for observing auguries; see **tem-** in Appendix.] **—con′tem·pla′tor** *n.*

con·tem·pla·tion (kŏn′təm-plā′shən) *n.* **1.** The act or state of contemplating. **2.** Thoughtful observation or study. **3.** Meditation on spiritual matters, especially as a form of devotion. **4.** Intention or expectation: *sought further information in contemplation of a career change.*

con·tem·pla·tive (kən-tĕm′plə-tĭv, kŏn′təm-plā′-) *adj.* Disposed to or characterized by contemplation. See Synonyms at **pensive. —contemplative** *n.* **1.** A person given to contemplation. **2.** A member of a religious order that emphasizes meditation. **—con·tem′pla·tive·ly** *adv.* **—con·tem′pla·tive·ness** *n.*

con·tem·po·ra·ne·ous (kən-tĕm′pə-rā′nē-əs) *adj.* Originating, existing, or happening during the same period of time: *the contemporaneous reigns of two monarchs.* See Synonyms at **contemporary.** [Latin *contemporāneus* : *com-,* com- + *tempus, tempor-,* time + *-āneus,* adj. suff.] **—con·tem′po·ra·ne′i·ty** (-pər-ə-nē′ĭ-tē, -nā′-), **con·tem′po·ra′ne·ous·ness** *n.* **—con·tem′po·ra′ne·ous·ly** *adv.*

con·tem·po·rar·y (kən-tĕm′pə-rĕr′ē) *adj. Abbr.* **contemp. 1.** Belonging to the same period of time: *a fact documented by two contemporary sources.* **2.** Of about the same age. **3.** Current; modern: *contemporary trends in design.* **—contemporary** *n., pl.* **-ies.** *Abbr.* **contemp. 1.** One of the same time or age: *Shelley and Keats were contemporaries.* **2.** A person of the present age. [Medieval Latin *contemporārius* : Latin *com-,* com- + Latin *tempus, tempor-,* time + Latin *-ārius,* -ary.] **—con·tem′po·rar′i·ly** (-tĕm′pə-râr′ə-lē) *adv.*

SYNONYMS: *contemporary, contemporaneous, simultaneous, synchronous, concurrent, coincident, concomitant.* These adjectives mean existing or occurring at the same time. *Contemporary* is used more often of persons, *contemporaneous* of events and

ă pat	oi boy
ā pay	ou out
âr care	o͝o took
ä father	o͞o boot
ĕ pet	ŭ cut
ē be	ûr urge
ĭ pit	th thin
ī pie	*th* this
îr pier	hw which
ŏ pot	zh vision
ō toe	ə about, item
ô paw	♦ regionalism

Stress marks: ′ (primary); ′ (secondary), as in **dictionary** (dĭk′shə-nĕr′ē)

facts: *The composer Salieri had the misfortune of being contemporary with Mozart. A rise in interest rates is often contemporaneous with an increase in inflation.* Only *contemporary* has the sense "modern" or "present-day": *I heard a concert of contemporary music. Simultaneous* more narrowly specifies occurrence of events at the same time: *Opponents of nuclear power tried to organize simultaneous demonstrations in all the major cities. Synchronous* refers to correspondence of events in time over a generally short period: *The animal uttered a series of low cries that seemed synchronous with its heartbeat. Concurrent* implies parallelism in character or length of time: *The mass murderer was given three concurrent life sentences. Coincident* applies to events occurring at the same time without implying a relationship between them: *"The resistance to the Pope's authority . . . is pretty nearly coincident with the rise of the Ottomans"* (John Henry Newman). *Concomitant* refers to coincidence in time of events so clearly related that one seems attendant on the other: *He is an adherent of the theories of Sigmund Freud and has a concomitant belief in the efficacy of psychoanalysis.*

USAGE NOTE: When *contemporary* is used in reference to something in the past, its meaning is not always clear. *Contemporary critics of Shakespeare* may mean critics in his time or critics in our time. When the context does not make the meaning clear, misunderstanding can be avoided by using phrases such as *critics in Shakespeare's time* or *modern critics.*

con·tem·po·rize (kən-tĕm′pə-rīz′) *v.* **-rized, -riz·ing, -riz·es.** *—tr.* **1.** To regard or place in the same time period; synchronize. **2.** To make modern or contemporary, as in style or décor. *—intr.* To be contemporary. [From CONTEMPORARY.] **—con·tem′po·ri·za′tion** (-tĕm′pər-ĭ-zā′shən) *n.*

con·tempt (kən-tĕmpt′) *n.* **1.** Disparaging or haughty disdain, as for something base or unworthy; scorn. **2.** The state of being despised or dishonored; disgrace. **3.** Open disrespect or willful disobedience of the authority of a court of law or legislative body. [Middle English, from Latin *contemptus,* past participle of *contemnere,* to despise. See CONTEMN.]

con·tempt·i·ble (kən-tĕmp′tə-bəl) *adj.* **1.** Deserving of contempt; despicable. **2.** *Obsolete.* Contemptuous. **—con·tempt′i·bil′i·ty, con·tempt′i·ble·ness** *n.* **—con·tempt′i·bly** *adv.*

con·temp·tu·ous (kən-tĕmp′cho͞o-əs) *adj.* Manifesting or feeling contempt; scornful. **—con·temp′tu·ous·ly** *adv.* **—con·temp′tu·ous·ness** *n.*

con·tend (kən-tĕnd′) *v.* **-tend·ed, -tend·ing, contends.** *—intr.* **1.** To strive in opposition or against difficulties; struggle: *armies contending for control of strategic territory; had to contend with long lines at the airport.* **2.** To compete, as in a race; vie. **3.** To strive in controversy or debate; dispute. See Synonyms at **discuss.** *—tr.* To maintain or assert: *The defense contended that the evidence was inadmissible.* [Middle English *contenden,* from Latin *contendere* : *com-,* com- + *tendere,* to stretch, strive; see **ten-** in Appendix.] **—con·tend′er** *n.*

con·tent¹ (kŏn′tĕnt′) *n.* **1.** Often **contents.** Something contained, as in a receptacle: *the contents of my desk drawer; the contents of an aerosol can.* **2.** Often **contents.** The subject matter of a written work, such as a book or magazine. **3.a.** The substantive or meaningful part: *"The brain is hungry not for method but for content, especially content which contains generalizations that are powerful, precise, and explicit"* (Frederick Turner). **b.** The meaning or significance of a literary or artistic work. **4.** The proportion of a specified substance: *Eggs have a high protein content.* [Middle English, from Medieval Latin *contentum,* neuter past participle of Latin *continēre,* to contain. See CONTAIN.]

con·tent² (kən-tĕnt′) *adj.* **1.** Desiring no more than what one has; satisfied. **2.** Ready to accept or acquiesce; willing: *She was content to step down after four years as chief executive.* **—content** *tr.v.* **-tent·ed, -tent·ing, -tents.** To make content or satisfied: *contented himself with one piece of cake.* **—content** *n.* Contentment; satisfaction. [Middle English, from Old French, from Latin *contentus,* past participle of *continēre,* to restrain. See CONTAIN.]

con·tent analysis (kŏn′tĕnt′) *n.* A systematic analysis of the content rather than the structure of a communication, such as a written work, speech, or film, including the study of thematic and symbolic elements to determine the objective or meaning of the communication.

con·tent·ed (kən-tĕn′tĭd) *adj.* Satisfied with things as they are; content: *a contented expression on the child's face.* **—con·tent′ed·ly** *adv.* **—con·tent′ed·ness** *n.*

con·ten·tion (kən-tĕn′shən) *n.* **1.** The act or an instance of striving in controversy or debate. See Synonyms at **discord. 2.** A striving to win in competition; rivalry: *The teams met in fierce contention for first place.* **3.** An assertion put forward in argument. [Middle English *contencioun,* from Old French *contention,* from Latin *contentiō, contentiōn-,* from *contentus,* past participle of *contendere,* to contend. See CONTEND.]

con·ten·tious (kən-tĕn′shəs) *adj.* **1.** Given to contention; quarrelsome. See Synonyms at **argumentative, belligerent. 2.** Involving or likely to cause contention; controversial: *"a central and contentious element of the book"* (Tim W. Ferguson). **—con·ten′tious·ly** *adv.* **—con·ten′tious·ness** *n.*

con·tent·ment (kən-tĕnt′mənt) *n.* **1.** The state of being contented; satisfaction. **2.** A source of satisfaction: *the contentments of a comfortable retirement.*

con·ter·mi·nous (kən-tûr′mə-nəs) also **co·ter·mi·nous** (kō-) *adj.* **1.** Having a boundary in common; contiguous. **2.** Contained in the same boundaries; coextensive. **3.** Having the same scope, range of meaning, or extent in time. [From Latin *conterminus* : *com-,* com- + *terminus,* boundary.] **—con·ter′mi·nous·ly** *adv.* **—con·ter′mi·nous·ness** *n.*

contes (kôNt) *n.* Plural of **conte.**

con·tes·sa (kən-tĕs′ə, kŏn-tĕs′sä) *n.* An Italian countess. [Italian, feminine of *conte,* count, from Late Latin *comes, comit-.* See COUNT².]

con·test (kŏn′tĕst′) *n.* **1.** A struggle for superiority or victory between rivals. **2.** A competition, especially one in which entrants perform separately and are rated by judges. See Synonyms at **conflict. —contest** (kən-tĕst′, kŏn′tĕst′) *v.* **-test·ed, -test·ing, -tests.** *—tr.* **1.** To compete or strive for. **2.** To call into question and take an active stand against; dispute or challenge: *contest a will.* See Synonyms at **oppose.** *—intr.* To struggle or compete; contend: *contested with other bidders for the antique.* [Probably from French *conteste,* from *contester,* to dispute, from Old French, to call to witness, from Latin *contestārī* : *com-,* com- + *testis,* witness; see **trei-** in Appendix.] **—con·test′a·ble** *adj.* **—con′tes·ta′tion** (kŏn′tĕ-stā′shən) *n.* **—con·test′er** *n.*

con·tes·tant (kən-tĕs′tənt, kŏn′tĕs′tənt) *n.* **1.** One taking part in a contest; a competitor. **2.** One that contests or disputes something, such as an election or a will.

con·text (kŏn′tĕkst′) *n.* **1.** The part of a text or statement that surrounds a particular word or passage and determines its meaning. **2.** The circumstances in which an event occurs; a setting. [Middle English, composition, from Latin *contextus,* from past participle of *contexere,* to join together : *com-,* com- + *texere,* to weave; see **teks-** in Appendix.]

con·tex·tu·al (kən-tĕks′cho͞o-əl, kŏn-) *adj.* Of, involving, or depending on a context. **—con·tex′tu·al·ly** *adv.*

con·tex·tu·al·ize (kən-tĕks′cho͞o-ə-līz′) *tr.v.* **-ized, -iz·ing, -iz·es.** To place (a word or idea, for example) in an appropriate context. **—con·tex′tu·al·i·za′tion** (-ə-lĭ-zā′shən) *n.*

con·tex·ture (kən-tĕks′chər, kŏn′tĕks′-) *n.* **1.** The act of weaving or assembling parts into a whole. **2.** An arrangement of interconnected parts; a structure. **—con·tex′tur·al** *adj.*

con·ti·gu·i·ty (kŏn′tĭ-gyo͞o′ĭ-tē) *n., pl.* **-ties. 1.** The state of being contiguous. **2.** A continuous mass or series.

con·tig·u·ous (kən-tĭg′yo͞o-əs) *adj.* **1.** Sharing an edge or boundary; touching. **2.** Neighboring; adjacent. **3.a.** Connecting without a break: *the 48 contiguous states.* **b.** Connected in time; uninterrupted: *served two contiguous terms in office.* [From Latin *contiguus,* from *contingere, contig-,* to touch. See CONTACT.] **—con·tig′u·ous·ly** *adv.* **—con·tig′u·ous·ness** *n.*

con·ti·nence (kŏn′tə-nəns) *n.* **1.** Self-restraint; moderation. **2.** Voluntary control over urinary and fecal discharge. **3.** Partial or complete abstention from sexual activity. See Synonyms at **abstinence.**

con·ti·nent¹ (kŏn′tə-nənt) *n.* **1.** *Abbr.* **cont.** One of the principal land masses of the earth, usually regarded as including Africa, Antarctica, Asia, Australia, Europe, North America, and South America. **2. Continent.** The mainland of Europe. Used with *the.* [Latin *(terra) continēns, continent-,* continuous (land), present participle of *continēre,* to hold together. See CONTAIN.]

con·ti·nent² (kŏn′tə-nənt) *adj.* Exercising continence. [Middle English, from Latin *continēns,* present participle of *continēre,* to restrain. See CONTAIN.] **—con′ti·nent·ly** *adv.*

con·ti·nen·tal (kŏn′tə-nĕn′tl) *adj.* **1.** Of, relating to, or characteristic of a continent. **2.** Often **Continental.** Of or relating to the mainland of Europe; European. **3. Continental.** Of or relating to the American colonies during and immediately after the Revolutionary War. **—continental** *n.* **1.** Often **Continental. a.** An inhabitant of a continent. **b.** An inhabitant of the mainland of Europe; a European. **2.** A native of the continental United States living or working in Puerto Rico or the U.S. Virgin Islands. **3. Continental.** A soldier in the American army during the Revolutionary War. **4.** A piece of paper money issued by the Continental Congress during the Revolutionary War. **—con′ti·nen′tal·ism** *n.* **—con′ti·nen′tal·ist** *n.* **—con′ti·nen·tal′i·ty** (-nĕn-tăl′ĭ-tē) *n.* **—con′ti·nen′tal·ly** *adv.*

continental breakfast *n.* Breakfast consisting usually of coffee or tea and a roll.

continental code *n.* A form of Morse code having no spaces between the dot and dash elements, commonly used for telegraphic communication outside the United States and Canada. Also called *international Morse code.*

A	B	C	D
•—	—•••	—•—•	—••
E	F	G	H
•	••—•	——•	••••
I	J	K	L
••	•———	—•—	•—••
M	N	O	P
——	—•	———	•——•
Q	R	S	T
——•—	•—•	•••	—
U	V	W	X
••—	•••—	•——	—••—
	Y	Z	
	—•——	——••	

continental code

continental divide *n.* An extensive stretch of high ground from each side of which the river systems of a continent flow in opposite directions.

Con·ti·nen·tal Di·vide (kŏn′tə-nĕn′tl dĭ-vīd′). A series of mountain ridges extending from Alaska to Mexico that forms the watershed of North America. Most of it runs along peaks of the Rocky Mountains and is often called the **Great Divide** in the United States.

continental drift *n.* The movement, formation, or reformation of continents described by the theory of plate tectonics.

continental shelf *n.* A submerged border of a continent that slopes gradually and extends to a point of steeper descent to the ocean bottom.

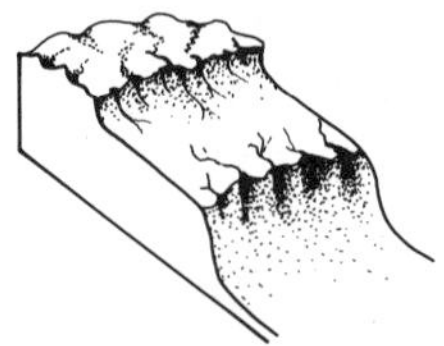

continental shelf

continental slope *n.* The descent from the continental shelf to the ocean bottom.

con·tin·gence (kən-tĭn′jəns) *n.* **1.** A joining or touching. **2.** Contingency.

con·tin·gen·cy (kən-tĭn′jən-sē) *n., pl.* **-cies. 1.a.** An event that may occur but that is not likely or intended; a possibility. **b.** A possibility that must be prepared for; a future emergency. **2.** The condition of being dependent on chance; uncertainty. **3.** Something incidental to something else. **—con·tin′gen·cy** *adj.*

contingency fee *n.* A fee, as for an attorney's services, that is payable only in the event of a successful or satisfactory outcome.

contingency table *n.* A statistical table that shows the observed frequencies of data elements classified according to two variables, with the rows indicating one variable and the columns indicating the other variable.

con·tin·gent (kən-tĭn′jənt) *adj.* **1.** Liable to occur but not with certainty; possible. **2.** Dependent on conditions or occurrences not yet established; conditional: *arms sales contingent on the approval of Congress.* See Synonyms at **dependent. 3.** Happening by chance or accident; fortuitous. See Synonyms at **accidental. 4.** *Logic.* True only under certain conditions; not necessarily or universally true: *a contingent proposition.* **—contingent** *n.* **1.** An event or condition that is likely but not inevitable. **2.** A share or quota, as of troops, contributed to a general effort. **3.** A representative group forming part of an assemblage. [Middle English, from Latin *contingēns, contingent-,* present participle of *contingere,* to touch. See CONTACT.] **—con·tin′gent·ly** *adv.*

con·tin·u·a (kən-tĭn′yo͞o-ə) *n.* A plural of **continuum.**

con·tin·u·al (kən-tĭn′yo͞o-əl) *adj.* **1.** Recurring regularly or frequently: *the continual need to pay the mortgage.* **2.** Not interrupted; steady: *continual noise; a continual diet of vegetables.* **—con·tin′u·al·ly** *adv.*

SYNONYMS: *continual, continuous, constant, ceaseless, incessant, perpetual, eternal, perennial, interminable.* These adjectives are compared as they mean occurring over and over during a long period of time. *Continual* can connote absence of interruption (*lived in continual fear*) but is chiefly restricted to what is intermittent or repeated at intervals (*the continual banging of the shutter in the wind*). *Continuous* implies lack of interruption in time, substance, or extent: *She suffered a continuous bout of illness lasting six months. The horizon is a continuous line. Constant* stresses steadiness or persistence of occurrence and unvarying nature: *the constant chatter of the monkeys in the zoo; constant repetition of the exercise. Ceaseless* and *incessant* pertain to uninterrupted activity: *the ceaseless thunder of the surf against the rocks; incessant questions. Perpetual* emphasizes both steadiness and duration: *a perpetual struggle; a perpetual stream of visitors. Eternal* refers to what is everlasting, especially to what is seemingly without temporal beginning or end: *"That freedom can be retained only by the eternal vigilance which has always been its price"* (Elmer Davis). *Perennial* describes existence that goes on year after year, often with the suggestion of self-renewal: *wished for perennial youth; the perennial problem of urban poverty. Interminable* refers to what is or seems to be endless and is often applied to something prolonged and wearisome: *interminable talk; an interminable argument.*

contortionist

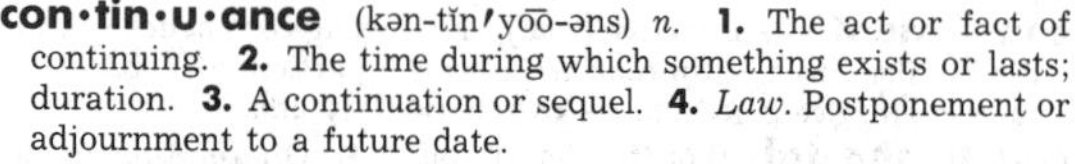

con·tin·u·ance (kən-tĭn′yo͞o-əns) *n.* **1.** The act or fact of continuing. **2.** The time during which something exists or lasts; duration. **3.** A continuation or sequel. **4.** *Law.* Postponement or adjournment to a future date.

USAGE NOTE: *Continuance* is interchangeable with *continuation* in some of its senses. However, only *continuance* is used to refer to the duration of a state or condition, as in *his continuance in office. Continuation* applies especially to prolongation or resumption of action (*a continuation of the meeting*) or to physical extension (*the continuation of the street*). The *continuation* of a story is that part of the story following a break in its narration.

con·tin·u·ant (kən-tĭn′yo͞o-ənt) *n. Linguistics.* A consonant, such as *s, z, m,* or *l,* that can be prolonged as long as the breath lasts without a change in quality.

con·tin·u·a·tion (kən-tĭn′yo͞o-ā′shən) *n.* **1.a.** The act or fact of continuing. **b.** The state of being continued. **2.** An extension by which something is carried to a further point. **3.** A resumption after an interruption. See Usage Note at **continuance.**

con·tin·u·a·tive (kən-tĭn′yo͞o-ā′tĭv, -ə-tĭv) *adj.* Of, relating to, or serving to cause continuation. **—continuative** *n.* Something that expresses or causes continuation. **—con·tin′u·a′tive·ly** *adv.*

con·tin·u·a·tor (kən-tĭn′yo͞o-ā′tər) *n.* One that continues, especially a person who carries on the work of another.

con·tin·ue (kən-tĭn′yo͞o) *v.* **-ued, -u·ing, -ues.** *Abbr.* **cont.** —*intr.* **1.** To go on with a particular action or in a particular condition; persist. **2.** To exist over a prolonged period; last. **3.** To remain in the same state, capacity, or place: *She continued as mayor for a second term.* **4.** To go on after an interruption; resume: *The negotiations continued after a break for lunch.* —*tr.* **1.** To carry forward; persist in: *The police will continue their investigation.* **2.** To carry further in time, space, or development; extend. **3.** To cause to remain or last. **4.** To carry on after an interruption. **5.** *Law.* To postpone or adjourn. [Middle English *continuen,* from Old French *continuer,* from Latin *continuāre,* from *continuus,* continuous, from *continēre,* to hold together. See CONTAIN.] **—con·tin′u·a·ble** *adj.* **—con·tin′u·er** *n.*

con·tin·ued fraction (kən-tĭn′yo͞od) *n.* A fraction whose numerator is a whole number and whose denominator is a whole number plus a fraction that has a denominator consisting of a whole number plus a fraction.

con·tin·u·ing education (kən-tĭn′yo͞o-ĭng) *n.* **1.** An instructional program that brings participants up to date in a particular area of knowledge or skills. **2.** Instructional courses designed especially for part-time, adult students.

con·ti·nu·i·ty (kŏn′tə-no͞o′ĭ-tē, -nyo͞o′-) *n., pl.* **-ties. 1.** The state or quality of being continuous. **2.** An uninterrupted succession or flow; a coherent whole. **3.a.** A detailed script or scenario consulted to avoid discrepancies from shot to shot in a film. **b.** Spoken matter serving to link parts of a radio or television program so that no break occurs.

con·tin·u·o (kən-tĭn′yo͞o-ō′) *n., pl.* **-os.** *Music.* A bass accompaniment, usually played on a keyboard instrument, in which numerals written underneath the notes indicate the kinds of harmony to be played. Also called *figured bass, thoroughbass.* [Italian, from Latin *continuus,* continuous. See CONTINUE.]

con·tin·u·ous (kən-tĭn′yo͞o-əs) *adj.* **1.** Uninterrupted in time, sequence, substance, or extent. See Synonyms at **continual. 2.** Attached together in repeated units: *a continuous form fed into a printer.* **3.** *Mathematics.* Of or relating to a line or curve that extends without a break or irregularity. [From Latin *continuus.* See CONTINUE.] **—con·tin′u·ous·ly** *adv.* **—con·tin′u·ous·ness** *n.*

continuous creation theory *n.* See **steady-state theory.**

continuous spectrum *n.* A spectrum having no lines or bands, especially a spectrum of radiation distributed over an uninterrupted range of wavelengths.

continuous variation *n. Genetics.* Variation within a population in which a graded series of intermediate phenotypes falls between the extremes.

continuous wave also **con·tin·u·ous-wave** (kən-tĭn′yo͞o-əs-wāv′) *adj. Abbr.* **cw, CW** Emitting or capable of emitting continuously; not pulsed: *a continuous wave laser; continuous wave radar.*

con·tin·u·um (kən-tĭn′yo͞o-əm) *n., pl.* **-tin·u·a** (-tĭn′yo͞o-ə) or **-tin·u·ums. 1.** A continuous extent, succession, or whole, no part of which can be distinguished from neighboring parts except by arbitrary division. **2.** *Mathematics.* A set having the same number of points as all the real numbers in an interval. [Latin, neuter of *continuus,* continuous. See CONTINUE.]

con·tort (kən-tôrt′) *v.* **-tort·ed, -tort·ing, -torts.** —*tr.* To twist, wrench, or bend severely out of shape: *pain that contorted their faces.* —*intr.* To become twisted into a strained shape or expression. See Synonyms at **distort.** [Latin *contorquēre, contort-,* to twist : *com-,* intensive pref.; see COM– + *torquēre,* to twist; see **terkʷ-** in Appendix.] **—con·tor′tion** *n.* **—con·tor′tive** *adj.*

con·tort·ed (kən-tôr′tĭd) *adj.* **1.** Twisted or strained out of shape. **2.** *Botany.* Twisted, bent, or partially rolled upon itself; convolute. **—con·tort′ed·ly** *adv.* **—con·tort′ed·ness** *n.*

con·tor·tion·ist (kən-tôr′shə-nĭst) *n.* One who contorts, especially an acrobat capable of twisting into extraordinary positions. **—con·tor′tion·is′tic** *adj.*

con·tour (kŏn′to͝or′) *n.* **1.a.** The outline of a figure, body, or mass. **b.** A line that represents such an outline. See Synonyms at **form, outline. 2.** Often **contours.** A surface, especially of a curving form. **3.** A contour line. **—contour** *tr.v.* **-toured, -tour·ing, -tours. 1.** To make or shape the outline of; represent in contour. **2.** To build (a road, for example) to follow the contour of the land. **—contour** *adj.* **1.** Following the contour lines of uneven terrain to limit erosion of topsoil: *contour plowing.* **2.** Shaped to fit the outline or form of something: *a contour sheet.* [French, alteration (influenced by *tour,* turn; see TOUR) of Italian *contorno,* from *contornare,* to draw in outline : Latin *com-,* intensive pref.; see COM– + Latin *tornāre,* to round off (from *tornus,* lathe, from Greek *tornos;* see **tere-**[1] in Appendix).]

contour feather *n.* Any of the outermost feathers of a bird, forming the visible body contour and plumage.

contour line *n.* A line on a map that joins points of equal elevation.

contour map *n.* A map showing elevations and surface configuration by means of contour lines.

contr. *abbr.* **1.** Contract. **2.** Contraction. **3.** *Music.* Contralto. **4.** Control.

contra– *pref.* **1.** Against; opposite; contrasting: *contraposition.* **2.** Lower in pitch: *contrabassoon.* [Middle English, from Latin *contrā-,* from *contrā,* against. See **kom** in Appendix.]

con·tra·band (kŏn′trə-bănd′) *n.* **1.** Goods prohibited by law or treaty from being imported or exported. **2.a.** Illegal traffic in contraband; smuggling. **b.** Smuggled goods. **3.** Goods that may be seized and confiscated by a belligerent if shipped to another belligerent by a neutral. **4.** An escaped slave during the Civil War who fled to or was taken behind Union lines. **—contraband** *adj.* Prohibited from being imported or exported. [Italian *contrabbando* : *contra-,* against (from Latin *contrā-;* see CONTRA–) + *bando,* legal proclamation (from Late Latin *bannus,* of Germanic origin; see **bhā-**[2] in Appendix).] **—con′tra·band′age** *n.* **—con′tra·band′ist** *n.*

con·tra·bass (kŏn′trə-bās′) *Music. n.* See **double bass.** **—contrabass** *adj.* Pitched an octave below the normal bass range. [Obsolete Italian *contrabasso* : *contra-*, against (from Latin *contrā-*; see CONTRA–) + *basso*, bass (from Late Latin *bassus*, low).] **—con′tra·bass′ist** *n.*

con·tra·bas·soon (kŏn′trə-bə-so͞on′, -bă-) *n. Music.* The largest and lowest pitched of the double-reed wind instruments, sounding an octave below the bassoon. Also called *double bassoon.*

con·tra·cep·tion (kŏn′trə-sĕp′shən) *n.* Intentional prevention of conception or impregnation through the use of various devices, agents, drugs, sexual practices, or surgical procedures. [CONTRA– + (CON)CEPTION.]

con·tra·cep·tive (kŏn′trə-sĕp′tĭv) *adj.* Capable of preventing conception. **—contraceptive** *n.* A device, drug, or chemical agent that prevents conception.

con·tract (kŏn′trăkt′) *n. Abbr.* **contr., cont. 1. a.** An agreement between two or more parties, especially one that is written and enforceable by law. **b.** The writing or document containing such an agreement. **2.** The branch of law dealing with formal agreements between parties. **3.** Marriage as a formal agreement; betrothal. **4.** *Games.* **a.** The last and highest bid of one hand in bridge. **b.** The number of tricks thus bid. **c.** Contract bridge. **5.** A paid assignment to murder someone: *put out a contract on the mobster's life.* **—contract** (kən-trăkt′, kŏn′trăkt′) *v.* **-tract·ed, -tract·ing, -tracts.** *—tr.* **1.** To enter into by contract; establish or settle by formal agreement: *contract a marriage.* **2.** To acquire or incur: *contract obligations; contract a serious illness.* **3. a.** To reduce in size by drawing together; shrink. **b.** To pull together; wrinkle. **4.** *Grammar.* To shorten (a word or words) by omitting or combining some of the letters or sounds. *—intr.* **1.** To enter into or make an agreement: *contract for garbage collection.* **2.** To become reduced in size by or as if by being drawn together: *The pupils of the patient's eyes contracted.* [Middle English, from Latin *contractus*, past participle of *contrahere*, to draw together, make a contract : *com-*, com- + *trahere*, to draw.] **—con·tract′i·bil′i·ty, con·tract′i·ble·ness** *n.* **—con·tract′i·ble** *adj.*

SYNONYMS: *contract, condense, compress, constrict, shrink.* These verbs mean to decrease in size or content. To *contract* is to draw together, especially by an internal force, with a resultant reduction in size, extent, or volume: *The bodybuilders contracted their biceps in unison. The pupil of the eye dilates and contracts in response to light. Condense* refers to a reduction in volume and an increase in compactness: *"To produce snow requires both heat and cold; the first to evaporate, the second to condense"* (John Lubbock). *The chairman condensed all the suggestions put forward into a single plan of action. Compress* applies to increased compactness brought about by pressing or squeezing; the term implies reduction in volume and change of form or shape: *compress dough into a circle with a rolling pin; sat on the lid of the suitcase to compress the clothes; trying to compress my thoughts into a few words.* To *constrict* is to make smaller or narrower, usually by binding or compression: *An accumulation of silt constricted the entrance to the harbor. Tight shoes constrict the feet. Shrink* refers to contraction that produces reduction in length, size, volume, or extent: *Wool jersey should be shrunk before being cut and stitched. Many once prosperous northern mill towns have shrunk as industry has moved to the South. His capital shrank as his business foundered.* See also Synonyms at **bargain.**

contract bridge *n. Games.* Auction bridge in which tricks in excess of the contract may not count toward game bonuses.

con·trac·tile (kən-trăk′təl, -tīl′) *adj.* Capable of contracting or causing contraction: *Muscle is a contractile tissue.* **—con′·trac·til′i·ty** (kŏn′trăk-tĭl′ĭ-tē) *n.*

contractile vacuole *n.* A membrane-bound organelle found in certain protists that pumps fluid in a cyclical manner from within the cell to the outside by alternately filling and then contracting to release its contents at various points on the surface of the cell. It functions in maintaining osmotic equilibrium.

con·trac·tion (kən-trăk′shən) *n.* **1.** The act of contracting or the state of being contracted. **2.** *Abbr.* **cont., contr. a.** A word, as *won't* from *will not*, or phrase, as *o'clock* from *of the clock*, formed by omitting or combining some of the sounds of a longer phrase. **b.** The formation of such a word. **3.** *Physiology.* The shortening and thickening of functioning muscle or muscle fiber. **4.** A period of decreased business activity.

con·trac·tor (kŏn′trăk′tər, kən-trăk′-) *n.* **1.** One that agrees to furnish materials or perform services at a specified price, especially for construction work. **2.** Something, especially a muscle, that contracts.

con·trac·tu·al (kən-trăk′cho͞o-əl) *adj.* Of, relating to, or having the nature of a contract. **—con·trac′tu·al·ly** *adv.*

con·trac·ture (kən-trăk′chər) *n.* **1.** An abnormal, often permanent shortening, as of muscle or scar tissue, that results in distortion or deformity, especially of a joint of the body. **2.** A deformity resulting from a contracture.

con·tra·cy·cli·cal (kŏn′trə-sī′klĭ-kəl, -sĭk′lĭ-) *adj.* Acting counter to an economic cycle.

con·tra·dance or **con·tra·danse** (kŏn′trə-dăns′) *n.* Variants of **contredanse.**

con·tra·dict (kŏn′trə-dĭkt′) *v.* **-dict·ed, -dict·ing, -dicts.** *—tr.* **1.** To assert or express the opposite of (a statement). **2.** To deny the statement of. See Synonyms at **deny. 3.** To be contrary to; be inconsistent with. *—intr.* To utter a contradictory statement. [Latin *contrādīcere, contrādict-*, to speak against : *contrā-*, contra- + *dīcere*, to speak; see **deik-** in Appendix.] **—con′tra·dict′a·ble** *adj.* **—con′tra·dict′er, con′tra·dic′tor** *n.*

con·tra·dic·tion (kŏn′trə-dĭk′shən) *n.* **1. a.** The act of contradicting. **b.** The state of being contradicted. **2.** A denial. **3.** Inconsistency; discrepancy. **4.** Something that contains contradictory elements.

con·tra·dic·to·ry (kŏn′trə-dĭk′tə-rē) *adj.* **1.** Involving, of the nature of, or being a contradiction. See Synonyms at **opposite. 2.** Given to contradicting. **—contradictory** *n., pl.* **-ries.** *Logic.* Either of two propositions related in such a way that it is impossible for both to be true or both to be false. **—con′tra·dic′to·ri·ly** *adv.* **—con′tra·dic′to·ri·ness** *n.*

con·tra·dis·tinc·tion (kŏn′trə-dĭ-stĭngk′shən) *n.* Distinction by contrasting or opposing qualities. **—con′tra·dis·tinc′tive** *adj.* **—con′tra·dis·tinc′tive·ly** *adv.*

con·tra·dis·tin·guish (kŏn′trə-dĭ-stĭng′gwĭsh) *tr.v.* **-guished, -guish·ing, -guish·es.** To distinguish by contrasting qualities.

con·tra·ges·tive (kŏn′trə-jĕs′tĭv) *adj.* Capable of preventing gestation, either by preventing implantation or by causing the uterine lining to shed after implantation. **—contragestive** *n.* A contragestive drug or agent. **—con′tra·ges·ta′tion** (-jĕ-stā′shən).

con·trail (kŏn′trāl′) *n.* A visible trail of streaks of condensed water vapor or ice crystals sometimes forming in the wake of an aircraft. Also called *vapor trail.* [CON(DENSATION) + TRAIL.]

con·tra·in·di·cate (kŏn′trə-ĭn′dĭ-kāt′) *tr.v.* **-cat·ed, -cat·ing, -cates.** To indicate the inadvisability of (a medical treatment, for example). **—con′tra·in·dic′a·tive** (-ĭn-dĭk′ə-tĭv) *adj.*

con·tra·in·di·ca·tion (kŏn′trə-ĭn′dĭ-kā′shən) *n.* A factor that renders the administration of a drug or the carrying out of a medical procedure inadvisable: *A previous allergic reaction to penicillin is a contraindication to the future use of that drug.*

con·tra·lat·er·al (kŏn′trə-lăt′ər-əl) *adj.* Taking place or originating in a corresponding part on an opposite side.

con·tral·to (kən-trăl′tō) *n., pl.* **-tos.** *Abbr.* **contr.** *Music.* **1.** The lowest female voice or voice part, intermediate in range between soprano and tenor. **2.** A woman having a contralto voice. *—attributive.* Often used to modify another noun: *a contralto part; contralto tones.* [Italian : *contra-*, below (from Latin *contrā*, contra-) + *alto*, alto; see ALTO.]

con·tra·po·si·tion (kŏn′trə-pə-zĭsh′ən) *n.* An opposite position; antithesis.

con·tra·pos·i·tive (kŏn′trə-pŏz′ĭ-tĭv) *n. Logic.* A proposition derived by negating and permuting the terms of another, equivalent proposition; for example, *All not-Y is not-X* is the contrapositive of *All X is Y.*

con·trap·pos·to (kōn′trə-pōs′tō) *n.* The position of a figure in painting or sculpture in which the hips and legs are turned in a different direction from that of the shoulders and head; the twisting of a figure on its own vertical axis. [Italian, past participle of *contrapporre*, to set opposite, contrast, from Latin *contrāpōnere* : *contrā-*, contra- + *pōnere*, to place; see **apo-** in Appendix.]

con·trap·tion (kən-trăp′shən) *n.* A mechanical device; a gadget. [Perhaps blend of CONTRIVE and TRAP[2].]

con·tra·pun·tal (kŏn′trə-pŭn′tl) *adj. Music.* Of, relating to, or incorporating counterpoint. [From obsolete Italian *contrapunto*, counterpoint : *contra-*, against (from Latin *contrā-*; see CONTRA–) + *punto*, point, note (from Latin *punctum*; see PUNCTUAL).] **—con′tra·pun′tal·ly** *adv.*

con·tra·pun·tist (kŏn′trə-pŭn′tĭst) *n. Music.* A specialist in counterpoint.

con·trar·i·an (kən-trâr′ē-ən) *n.* An investor who makes decisions that contradict prevailing wisdom, as in buying securities that are unpopular at the time.

con·tra·ri·e·ty (kŏn′trə-rī′ĭ-tē) *n., pl.* **-ties. 1.** The quality or condition of being contrary. **2.** Something that is contrary.

con·trar·i·ous (kən-trâr′ē-əs) *adj.* Perverse; inimical. **—con·trar′i·ous·ly** *adv.*

con·trar·i·wise (kŏn′trĕr′ē-wīz′, kən-trâr′-) *adv.* **1.** From a contrasting point of view. **2.** In the opposite way or reverse order. **3.** In a perverse manner.

con·trar·y (kŏn′trĕr′ē) *adj.* **1.** Opposed, as in character or purpose: *contrary opinions; acts that are contrary to our code of ethics.* **2.** Opposite in direction or position: *playing scales in contrary motion.* **3.** Adverse; unfavorable: *a contrary wind.* **4.** (*also* kən-trâr′ē). Given to recalcitrant behavior; willful or perverse. **—contrary** *n., pl.* **-ies. 1.** Something that is opposite or contrary. **2.** Either of two opposing or contrary things: *"Truth is perhaps . . . a dynamic compound of opposites, savage contraries for a moment conjoined"* (A. Bartlett Giamatti). **3.** *Logic.* A proposition related to another in such a way that if the latter is true, the former must be false, but if the latter is false, the former is not necessarily true. **—contrary** *adv.* In an opposite direction or manner; counter: *The judge ruled contrary to all precedent in the case. —idioms.* **by contraries.** *Obsolete.* In opposition to what is expected. **on the contrary.** In opposition to what has been

ă pat	oi boy
ā pay	ou out
âr care	o͝o took
ä father	o͞o boot
ĕ pet	ŭ cut
ē be	ûr urge
ĭ pit	th thin
ī pie	*th* this
îr pier	hw which
ŏ pot	zh vision
ō toe	ə about, item
ô paw	♦ regionalism

Stress marks: ′ (primary); ′ (secondary), as in **dictionary** (dĭk′shə-nĕr′ē)

stated or what is expected: *I'm not sick; on the contrary, I'm in the peak of health.* [Middle English *contrarie,* from Anglo-Norman, from Latin *contrārius* : *contrā,* against; see **kom** in Appendix + *-ārius,* -ary.] **—con′trar·i·ly** *adv.* **—con′trar·i·ness** *n.*

SYNONYMS: *contrary, balky, perverse, wayward, ornery.* These adjectives mean given to acting in opposition to others. *Contrary* applies especially to a person who is inherently self-willed and resistant to direction or counsel: *Who can reason with you when you're being contrary? Balky* describes an animal or a mechanical device that stops short and does not proceed or continue in operation; the word is also applicable to analogous human behavior: *The balky horse refused the jump. The balky engine sputtered and stopped. Even threats of indictment didn't loosen the tongue of the balky witness. Perverse* implies disposition or determination to contravene what is expected or desired: *He said no just to be perverse. Wayward* stresses a flouting of authority that leads to erratic, capricious, or reprehensible behavior: *"a lively child, who had been spoilt and indulged, and therefore was sometimes wayward"* (Charlotte Brontë). One who is *ornery* is marked by a mean-spirited, often defiant contrariety: *When I tried to get the car salesman to lower his prices, he became ornery and dug in his heels.* See also Synonyms at **opposite.**

con·trast (kən-trăst′, kŏn′trăst′) *v.* **-trast·ed, -trast·ing, -trasts.** *—tr.* To set in opposition in order to show or emphasize differences: *an essay that contrasts city and country life; contrasted this computer with inferior models.* *—intr.* To show differences when compared: *siblings who contrast sharply in interests and abilities; a color that contrasted clearly with the dark background.* **—contrast** (kŏn′trăst′) *n.* **1.a.** The act of contrasting; a setting off of dissimilar entities or objects. **b.** The state of being contrasted: *red berries standing in vivid contrast against the snow.* **2.** A difference, especially a strong dissimilarity, between entities or objects compared: *the contrast between Northern and Southern speech patterns.* **3.** One thing that is strikingly dissimilar to another: *My new school was a welcome contrast to the one before.* **4.** The use of opposing elements, such as colors, forms, or lines, in proximity to produce an intensified effect in a work of art. **5.** The difference in brightness between the light and dark areas of a picture, such as a photograph or video image. [French *contraster,* from Italian *contrastare,* from Medieval Latin *contrāstāre* : Latin *contrā-,* contra- + Latin *stāre,* to stand; see **stā-** in Appendix.] **—con·trast′a·ble** *adj.* **—con·trast′ing·ly** *adv.*

USAGE NOTE: The noun *contrast* may be followed by *between, with,* or *to*: *There is a sharp contrast between his earlier and later works. In contrast with* (or less frequently, *to*) *his early works, the later plays are brittle and highly theatrical.* When *contrast* is used as a transitive verb, both *with* and *to* may follow, though *with* is more common: *He contrasts the naturalistic early plays with* (or *to*) *the brittle later comedies.*

contrast medium *n.* A substance, such as barium or air, used in radiography to increase the contrast of an image. A positive contrast medium absorbs x-rays more strongly than the tissue or structure being examined; a negative contrast medium, less strongly.

con·trast·y (kŏn′trăs′tē) *adj.* Having or producing sharp contrasts between light and dark areas in photography.

con·tra·vene (kŏn′trə-vēn′) *tr.v.* **-vened, -ven·ing, -venes. 1.** To act or be counter to; violate: *contravene a direct order.* **2.** To oppose in argument; gainsay: *contravened the proposal.* See Synonyms at **deny.** [French *contrevenir,* from Medieval Latin *contrāvenīre,* to transgress, from Late Latin, to oppose : Latin *contrā-,* contra- + Latin *venīre,* to come; see **gʷā-** in Appendix.] **—con′tra·ven′er** *n.*

con·tra·ven·tion (kŏn′trə-vĕn′shən) *n.* The act of contravening; a violation.

con·tre·danse also **con·tre·dance** or **con·tra·dance** or **con·tra·danse** (kŏn′trə-dăns′) *n.* **1.** A folk dance performed in two lines with the partners facing each other. **2.** The music for a contredanse. [French, alteration (influenced by French *contre-,* opposite, from Latin *contrā-,* contra-) of COUNTRY-DANCE.]

con·tre·temps (kŏn′trə-täɴ′, kôɴ′trə-täɴ′) *n., pl.* **contretemps** (-täɴz′, -täɴz′). An unforeseen event that disrupts the normal course of things; an inopportune occurrence. [French : *contre-,* against (from Latin *contrā-;* see CONTRA–) + *temps,* time (from Latin *tempus*).]

contrib. *abbr.* **1.** Contribution. **2.** Contributor.

con·trib·ute (kən-trĭb′yo͞ot) *v.* **-ut·ed, -ut·ing, -utes.** *—tr.* **1.** To give or supply in common with others; give to a common fund or for a common purpose. **2.** To submit for publication: *contributed two stories to the summer issue.* *—intr.* **1.** To make a contribution: *contributes to several charities.* **2.** To help bring about a result; act as a factor: *Exercise contributes to better health.* **3.** To submit material for publication. [Latin *contribuere, contribūt-,* to bring together : *com-,* com- + *tribuere,* to grant; see TRIBUTE.] **—con·trib′u·tive** *adj.* **—con·trib′u·tive·ly** *adv.* **—con·trib′u·tive·ness** *n.* **—con·trib′u·tor** *n.*

con·tri·bu·tion (kŏn′trĭ-byo͞o′shən) *n.* **1.** The act of contributing. **2.** *Abbr.* **contrib.** Something contributed. **3.** A payment exacted for a special purpose; an impost or a levy.

con·trib·u·to·ry (kən-trĭb′yə-tôr′ē, -tōr′ē) *adj.* **1.** Of, relating to, or involving contribution. **2.** Helping to bring about a result. **3.** Subject to an impost or levy. **—contributory** *n., pl.* **-ries.** One that contributes.

con·trite (kən-trīt′, kŏn′trīt′) *adj.* **1.** Feeling regret and sorrow for one's sins or offenses; penitent. **2.** Arising from or expressing contrition: *contrite words.* [Middle English *contrit,* from Latin *contrītus,* past participle of *conterere,* to crush : *com-,* com- + *terere,* to grind; see **terə-¹** in Appendix.] **—con·trite′ly** *adv.* **—con·trite′ness** *n.*

con·tri·tion (kən-trĭsh′ən) *n.* Sincere remorse for wrongdoing; repentance. See Synonyms at **penitence.**

con·tri·vance (kən-trī′vəns) *n.* **1.a.** The act of contriving. **b.** The state of being contrived. **2.** Something contrived, as a mechanical device or a clever plan.

con·trive (kən-trīv′) *v.* **-trived, -triv·ing, -trives.** *—tr.* **1.** To plan with cleverness or ingenuity; devise: *contrive ways to amuse the children.* **2.** To invent or fabricate, especially by improvisation: *contrived a swing from hanging vines.* **3.** To plan with evil intent; scheme: *contrived a plot to seize power.* **4.** To bring about, as by scheming; manage: *somehow contrived to get past the guards unnoticed.* *—intr.* To form plans or schemes. [Middle English *contreven,* from Old French *controver, contreuv-,* from Medieval Latin *contropāre,* to compare : Latin *com-,* com- + Latin *tropus,* turn, manner, style (from Greek *tropos;* see **trep-** in Appendix).] **—con·triv′er** *n.*

con·trived (kən-trīvd′) *adj.* Obviously planned or calculated; not spontaneous; labored: *a novel with a contrived ending.* **—con·triv′ed·ly** (-trī′vĭd-lē, -trīvd′lē) *adv.*

con·trol (kən-trōl′) *tr.v.* **-trolled, -trol·ling, -trols. 1.** To exercise authoritative or dominating influence over; direct. See Synonyms at **conduct. 2.** To hold in restraint; check: *struggled to control my temper; regulations intended to control prices.* **3.a.** To verify or regulate (a scientific experiment) by conducting a parallel experiment or by comparing with another standard. **b.** To verify (an account, for example) by using a duplicate register for comparison. **—control** *n.* **1.** Authority or ability to manage or direct: *lost control of the skidding car; the leaders in control of the country.* **2.** *Abbr.* **cont., contr. a.** One that controls; a controlling agent, device, or organization. **b.** Often **controls.** An instrument or set of instruments used to operate, regulate, or guide a machine or vehicle. **3.** A restraining device, measure, or limit; a curb: *a control on prices; price controls.* **4.a.** A standard of comparison for checking or verifying the results of an experiment. **b.** An individual or group used as a standard of comparison in a control experiment. **5.** An intelligence agent who supervises or instructs another agent. **6.** A spirit presumed to speak or act through a medium. [Middle English *controllen,* from Anglo-Norman *contreroller,* from Medieval Latin *contrārotulāre,* to check by duplicate register, from *contrārotulus,* duplicate register : Latin *contrā-,* contra- + Latin *rotulus,* roll, diminutive of *rota,* wheel; see **ret-** in Appendix.] **—con·trol′la·bil′i·ty** *n.* **—con·trol′la·ble** *adj.*

control experiment *n.* An experiment that isolates the effect of one variable on a system by holding constant all variables but the one under observation.

con·trolled substance (kən-trōld′) *n.* A drug or chemical substance whose possession and use are regulated under the Controlled Substances Act.

con·trol·ler (kən-trō′lər) *n.* **1.** One that controls: *a controller, not an observer of events.* **2.** Also **comp·trol·ler** (kən-trō′lər). An officer who audits accounts and supervises the financial affairs of a corporation or of a governmental body. **3.** A regulating mechanism, as in a vehicle or electric device. **—con·trol′ler·ship′** *n.*

con·trol·ling interest (kən-trō′lĭng) *n.* Ownership of a sufficient number of shares of stock in a company to control company policy.

control rocket *n.* A vernier rocket or similar missile used to change the attitude or trajectory of a rocket or spacecraft.

control stick *n.* A lever used to control the motion of an aircraft by changing the angle of the elevators and ailerons.

control surface *n.* A movable airfoil, especially a rudder, an aileron, or an elevator, used to control or guide an aircraft, a guided missile, or a rocket.

control tower *n.* A tower at an airfield from which air traffic is controlled by radio and observed physically and by radar.

con·tro·ver·sial (kŏn′trə-vûr′shəl, -sē-əl) *adj.* **1.** Of, producing, or marked by controversy: *a controversial movie; a controversial stand on human rights.* **2.** Fond of controversy; disputatious. **—con′tro·ver′sial·ist** *n.* **—con′tro·ver′si·al′i·ty** (-shē-ăl′ĭ-tē, -sē-) *n.* **—con′tro·ver′sial·ly** *adv.*

con·tro·ver·sy (kŏn′trə-vûr′sē) *n., pl.* **-sies. 1.** A dispute, especially a public one, between sides holding opposing views. See Synonyms at **argument. 2.** The act or practice of engaging in such disputes: *writers skilled at controversy.* [Middle English *controversie,* from Latin *contrōversia,* from *contrōversus,* disputed : *contrā-,* contra- + *versus,* past participle of *vertere,* to turn; see **wer-²** in Appendix.]

con·tro·vert (kŏn′trə-vûrt′, kŏn′trə-vûrt′) *tr.v.* **-vert·ed, -vert·ing, -verts.** To raise arguments against; voice opposition to. [From CONTROVERSY.] **—con′tro·vert′i·ble** *adj.*

con·tu·ma·cious (kŏn′tə-mā′shəs, -tyə-) *adj.* Obstinately disobedient or rebellious; insubordinate. **—con′tu·ma′cious·ly** *adv.* **—con′tu·ma′cious·ness** *n.*

con·tu·ma·cy (kŏn′to͞o-mə-sē, -tyo͞o-) *n., pl.* **-cies.** Obstinate or contemptuous resistance to authority; stubborn rebelliousness. [Middle English *contumacie,* from Latin *contumācia,* from *contumāx,* insolent.]

con·tu·me·ly (kŏn′to͞o-mə-lē, -tyo͞o-, -təm-lē) *n., pl.* **-lies.** **1.** Rudeness or contempt arising from arrogance; insolence. **2.** An insolent or arrogant remark or act. [Middle English *contumelie,* from Old French, from Latin *contumēlia;* akin to *contumāx,* insolent.] **—con′tu·me′li·ous** (kŏn′tə-mē′lē-əs) *adj.* **—con′tu·me′li·ous·ly** *adv.*

con·tuse (kən-to͞oz′, -tyo͞oz′) *tr.v.* **-tused, -tus·ing, -tus·es.** To injure without breaking the skin; bruise. [Middle English *contusen,* from Latin *contundere, contūs-,* to beat : *com-,* intensive pref.; see COM– + *tundere,* to beat.]

con·tu·sion (kən-to͞o′zhən, -tyo͞o′-) *n.* An injury in which the skin is not broken; a bruise.

co·nun·drum (kə-nŭn′drəm) *n.* **1.** A riddle in which a fanciful question is answered by a pun. **2.** A paradoxical, insoluble, or difficult problem; a dilemma: *"the conundrum, thus far unanswered, of achieving full employment without inflation"* (Arthur M. Schlesinger, Jr.). [Origin unknown.]

con·ur·ba·tion (kŏn′ər-bā′shən) *n.* A predominantly urban region including adjacent towns and suburbs; a metropolitan area. [CON– + Latin *urbs,* city + –ATION.]

co·nus ar·te·ri·o·sus (kō′nəs är-tîr′ē-ō′səs) *n., pl.* **co·ni ar·te·ri·o·si** (kō′nī är-tîr′ē-ō′sī, kō′nē är-tîr′ē-ō′sē). **1.** A conical extension of the right ventricle in the heart of mammals, from which the pulmonary artery originates. **2.** An extension of the ventricle in the heart of amphibians and certain fish. [New Latin : Latin *conus,* cone + Latin *arteriōsus,* arterial.]

conv. *abbr.* **1.** Convention. **2.** Convertible. **3.** Convocation.

Conv. *abbr.* Conventual.

con·va·lesce (kŏn′və-lĕs′) *intr.v.* **-lesced, -lesc·ing, -lesc·es.** To return to health and strength after illness; recuperate. [Latin *convalēscere* : *com-,* intensive pref.; see COM– + *valēscere,* to grow strong, inchoative of *valēre,* to be strong; see **wal-** in Appendix.]

con·va·les·cence (kŏn′və-lĕs′əns) *n.* **1.** Gradual return to health and strength after illness. **2.** The period needed for returning to health after illness. **—con′va·les′cent** *adj. & n.*

con·vect (kən-vĕkt′) *v.* **-vect·ed, -vect·ing, -vects.** —*tr.* To transfer (heat) by convection. —*intr.* To undergo convection: *warm air convecting upward.* [Back-formation from CONVECTION.]

con·vec·tion (kən-vĕk′shən) *n.* **1.** The act or process of conveying; transmission. **2.** *Physics.* **a.** Heat transfer in a gas or liquid by the circulation of currents from one region to another. **b.** Fluid motion caused by an external force such as gravity. **3.** *Meteorology.* The transfer of heat or other atmospheric properties by massive motion within the atmosphere, especially by such motion directed upward. [Late Latin *convectiō, convectiōn-,* from *convectus,* past participle of *convehere,* to carry together : Latin *com-,* com- + Latin *vehere,* to carry; see **wegh-** in Appendix.] **—con·vec′tion·al** *adj.* **—con·vec′tive** *adj.* **—con·vec′tive·ly** *adv.*

con·vec·tor (kən-vĕk′tər) *n.* A partly enclosed, directly heated surface from which warm air circulates by convection.

con·vene (kən-vēn′) *v.* **-vened, -ven·ing, -venes.** —*intr.* To come together usually for an official or public purpose; assemble formally. —*tr.* **1.** To cause to come together formally; convoke: *convene a special session of Congress.* See Synonyms at **call.** **2.** To summon to appear, as before a tribunal. [Middle English *convenen,* from Old French *convenir,* from Latin *convenīre* : *com-,* com- + *venīre,* to come; see **gʷā-** in Appendix.] **—con·ven′a·ble** *adj.* **—con·ven′er, con·ven′or** *n.*

con·ven·ience (kən-vēn′yəns) *n.* **1.** The quality of being suitable to one's comfort, purposes, or needs: *the convenience of living near shops, schools, and libraries.* **2.** Personal comfort or advantage: *services that promote the customer's convenience.* **3.** Something that increases comfort or saves work: *household conveniences such as a washing machine, an electric can opener, and disposable diapers.* See Synonyms at **amenity.** **4.** *Chiefly British.* A lavatory.

convenience food *n.* A prepackaged food that can be prepared quickly and easily.

convenience store *n.* A small retail store that is open long hours and that typically sells staple groceries, snacks, and sometimes gasoline.

con·ven·ien·cy (kən-vēn′yən-sē) *n., pl.* **-cies.** *Archaic.* Convenience.

con·ven·ient (kən-vēn′yənt) *adj.* **1.** Suited or favorable to one's comfort, purpose, or needs: *a convenient time to receive guests; a convenient excuse for not going.* **2.a.** Easy to reach; accessible: *a bank with branches at six convenient locations.* **b.** Close at hand; near: *an apartment that is convenient to shopping and transportation.* **3.** *Obsolete.* Fitting and proper; suitable. [Middle English, from Latin *conveniēns, convenient-,* present participle of *convenīre,* to be suitable, fit. See CONVENE.] **—con·ven′ient·ly** *adv.*

con·vent (kŏn′vənt, -vĕnt′) *n.* **1.** A community, especially of nuns, bound by vows to a religious life under a superior. **2.** The building or buildings occupied by such a community. [Middle English *covent,* from Old French, from Medieval Latin *conventus,* from Latin, assembly, from past participle of *convenīre,* to assemble. See CONVENE.]

con·ven·ti·cle (kən-vĕn′tĭ-kəl) *n.* A religious meeting, especially a secret or illegal one, such as those held by Dissenters in England and Scotland in the 16th and 17th centuries. [Middle English, from Latin *conventiculum,* meeting, diminutive of *conventus,* assembly. See CONVENT.] **—con·ven′ti·cler** *n.*

con·ven·tion (kən-vĕn′shən) *n. Abbr.* **conv. 1.a.** A formal meeting of members, representatives, or delegates, as of a political party, fraternal society, profession, or industry. **b.** The body of persons attending such an assembly: *called the convention to order.* **2.** An agreement between states, sides, or military forces, especially an international agreement dealing with a specific subject, such as the treatment of prisoners of war. **3.** General agreement on or acceptance of certain practices or attitudes: *By convention, north is at the top of most maps.* **4.** A practice or procedure widely observed in a group, especially to facilitate social interaction; a custom: *the convention of shaking hands.* **5.** A widely used and accepted device or technique, as in drama, literature, or painting: *the theatrical convention of the aside.* [Middle English *convencioun,* from Latin *conventiō, conventiōn-,* meeting, from *conventus,* past participle of *convenīre,* to assemble. See CONVENE.]

con·ven·tion·al (kən-vĕn′shə-nəl) *adj.* **1.** Based on or in accordance with general agreement, use, or practice; customary: *conventional symbols; a conventional form of address.* **2.** Conforming to established practice or accepted standards; traditional: *a conventional church wedding.* **3.a.** Devoted to or bound by conventions to the point of artificiality; ceremonious. **b.** Unimaginative; conformist: *longed to escape from their conventional, bourgeois lives.* **4.** Represented, as in a work of art, in simplified or abstract form. **5.** *Law.* Based on consent or agreement; contractual. **6.** Of, relating to, or resembling an assembly. **7.** Using means other than nuclear weapons or energy: *conventional warfare; conventional power plants.* **—con·ven′tion·al·ism** *n.* **—con·ven′tion·al·ist** *n.* **—con·ven′tion·al·ly** *adv.*

con·ven·tion·al·i·ty (kən-vĕn′shə-năl′ĭ-tē) *n., pl.* **-ties.** **1.** The state, quality, or character of being conventional. **2.** A conventional act, idea, or practice. **3. conventionalities.** The rules of conventional social behavior.

con·ven·tion·al·ize (kən-vĕn′shə-nə-līz′) *tr.v.* **-ized, -iz·ing, -iz·es.** To make conventional. **—con·ven′tion·al·i·za′tion** (-vĕn′shə-nə-lĭ-zā′shən) *n.*

con·ven·tion·eer (kən-vĕn′shə-nîr′) *n.* One who attends a convention.

con·ven·tu·al (kən-vĕn′cho͞o-əl) *adj.* Of or relating to a convent. **—conventual** *n.* **1.** A member of a convent. **2. Conventual.** *Abbr.* **Conv.** A member of a branch of the Franciscan order that permits the accumulation and possession of common property. [Middle English, from Medieval Latin *conventuālis,* from *conventus,* convent. See CONVENT.]

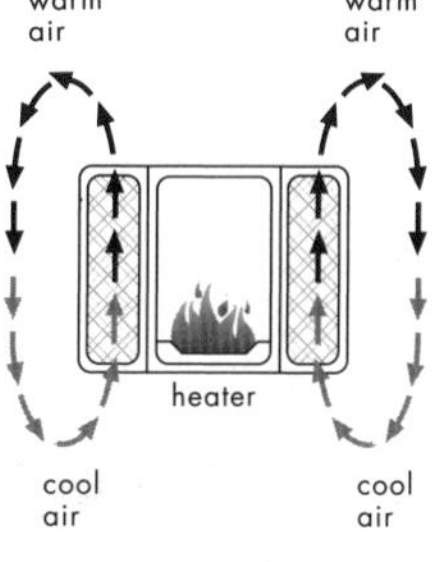

convection

con·verge (kən-vûrj′) *v.* **-verged, -verg·ing, -verg·es.** —*intr.* **1.a.** To tend toward or approach an intersecting point: *lines that converge.* **b.** To come together from different directions; meet: *The avenues converge at a central square.* **2.** To tend toward or achieve union or a common conclusion or result: *In time, our views and our efforts converged.* **3.** *Mathematics.* To approach a limit. —*tr.* To cause to converge. [Late Latin *convergere,* to incline together : Latin *com-,* com- + Latin *vergere,* to incline; see **wer-**[2] in Appendix.]

con·ver·gence (kən-vûr′jəns) *n.* **1.** The act, condition, quality, or fact of converging. **2.** *Mathematics.* The property or manner of approaching a limit, such as a point, line, surface, or value. **3.** The point of converging; a meeting place: *a town at the convergence of two rivers.* **4.** *Physiology.* The coordinated turning of the eyes inward to focus on an object at close range. **5.** *Biology.* The adaptive evolution of superficially similar structures, such as the wings of birds and insects, in unrelated species subjected to similar environments. In this sense, also called *convergent evolution.* **—con·ver′gent** *adj.*

con·ver·gen·cy (kən-vûr′jən-sē) *n., pl.* **-cies.** Convergence.

convergent evolution *n.* See **convergence** (sense 5).

con·ver·sance (kən-vûr′səns, kŏn′vər-) *n.* The state of being conversant; familiarity.

con·ver·san·cy (kən-vûr′sən-sē) *n., pl.* **-cies.** Conversance.

con·ver·sant (kən-vûr′sənt, kŏn′vər-) *adj.* Familiar, as by study or experience: *conversant with medieval history.* [Middle English *conversaunt,* associated with, from Old French *conversant,* present participle of *converser,* to associate with, from Latin *conversārī.* See CONVERSE[1].] **—con·ver′sant·ly** *adv.*

con·ver·sa·tion (kŏn′vər-sā′shən) *n.* **1.** A spoken exchange of thoughts, opinions, and feelings; a talk. **2.** An informal discussion of a matter by representatives of governments, institutions, or organizations. **3.** *Computer Science.* A real-time interaction with a computer. **—con′ver·sa′tion·al** *adj.* **—con′ver·sa′tion·al·ly** *adv.*

con·ver·sa·tion·al·ist (kŏn′vər-sā′shə-nə-lĭst) also **con·ver·sa·tion·ist** (-shə-nĭst) *n.* One given to or skilled at conversation.

conversation piece *n.* **1.** An unusual object that arouses comment or interest. **2.** A genre painting, popular especially in the 18th century, depicting a group of fashionable people.

con·ver·sa·zi·o·ne (kŏn′vər-sät′sē-ō′nē, kôn′vĕr-sä-

ă pat	oi boy
ā pay	ou out
âr care	o͝o took
ä father	o͞o boot
ĕ pet	ŭ cut
ē be	ûr urge
ĭ pit	th thin
ī pie	*th* this
îr pier	hw which
ŏ pot	zh vision
ō toe	ə about, item
ô paw	♦ regionalism

Stress marks: ′ (primary); ′ (secondary), as in **dictionary** (dĭk′shə-nĕr′ē)

tsyô′nĕ) *n.*, *pl.* **-nes** or **-ni** (-nē). A meeting for conversation or discussion, especially about art. [Italian, from Latin *conversātiō, conversātiōn-*, dealings with persons, from *conversātus*, past participle of *conversārī*, to associate with. See CONVERSE ¹.]

con·verse¹ (kən-vûrs′) *intr.v.* **-versed, -vers·ing, -vers·es. 1.** To engage in a spoken exchange of thoughts, ideas, or feelings; talk. See Synonyms at **speak. 2.** *Computer Science.* To interact with a computer on-line. **3.** *Archaic.* To be familiar; associate. **—converse** (kŏn′vûrs′) *n.* **1.** Spoken interchange of thoughts and feelings; conversation. **2.** *Obsolete.* Social interaction. [Middle English *conversen*, to associate with, from Old French *converser*, from Latin *conversārī* : *com-*, com- + *versārī*, to occupy oneself; see **wer-²** in Appendix.]

con·verse² (kən-vûrs′, kŏn′vûrs′) *adj.* Reversed, as in position, order, or action; contrary. **—converse** (kŏn′vûrs′) *n.* **1.** Something that has been reversed; an opposite. **2.** *Logic.* A proposition obtained by conversion. [Latin *conversus*, past participle of *convertere*, to turn around. See CONVERT.] **—con·verse′ly** *adv.*

con·ver·sion (kən-vûr′zhən, -shən) *n.* **1.a.** The act of converting. **b.** The state of being converted. **2.** A change in which one adopts a new religion, faith, or belief. **3.** Something that is changed from one use, function, or purpose to another. **4.** *Law.* **a.** The unlawful appropriation of another's property. **b.** The changing of real property to personal property or vice versa. **5.** The exchange of one type of security or currency for another. **6.** *Logic.* The interchange of the subject and predicate of a proposition. **7.** *Football.* A score made on a try for a point or points after a touchdown. **8.** *Psychiatry.* A defense mechanism in which repressed ideas, conflicts, or impulses are manifested by various bodily symptoms, such as paralysis or breathing difficulties, that have no physical cause. [Middle English *conversioun*, religious conversion, from Old French *conversion*, from Latin *conversiō, conversiōn-*, a turning around, from *conversus*, past participle of *convertere*, to turn around. See CONVERT.] **—con·ver′sion·al, con·ver′sion·ar′y** (-zhə-nĕr′ē, -shə-) *adj.*

convertible
1989 Cadillac Allanté

conversion disorder *n.* See **conversion reaction.**

conversion factor *n.* A numerical factor used to multiply or divide a quantity expressed in one system of units in a conversion to another system.

conversion reaction *n.* A neurosis characterized by the presence of bodily symptoms having no discernible physical cause but for which there is evidence of a psychological conflict or need. Also called *conversion disorder.*

con·vert (kən-vûrt′) *v.* **-vert·ed, -vert·ing, -verts.** *—tr.* **1.** To change (something) into another form, substance, state, or product; transform: *convert water into ice.* **2.** To change (something) from one use, function, or purpose to another; adapt to a new or different purpose: *convert a forest into farmland.* **3.** To persuade or induce to adopt a particular religion, faith, or belief: *convert pagans to Christianity; was converted to pacifism by the war.* **4.** To exchange for something of equal value: *convert assets into cash.* **5.** To exchange (a security, for example) by substituting an equivalent of another form. **6.** To express (a quantity) in alternative units: *converting feet into meters.* **7.** *Logic.* To transform (a proposition) by conversion. **8.** *Law.* **a.** To appropriate (another's property) without right to one's own use. **b.** To change (property) from real to personal or from joint to separate or vice versa. *—intr.* **1.** To undergo a conversion: *We converted to Islam several years ago.* **2.** To be converted: *a sofa that converts into a bed; arms factories converting to peacetime production.* **3.** *Football.* To make a conversion. **—convert** (kŏn′vûrt′) *n.* One who has been converted, especially from one religion or belief to another. [Middle English *converten*, from Old French *convertir*, from Latin *convertere*, to turn around : *com-*, intensive pref.; see COM– + *vertere*, to turn; see **wer-²** in Appendix.]

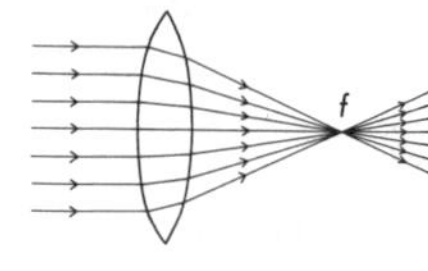

convex

SYNONYMS: *convert, metamorphose, transfigure, transform, transmogrify, transmute.* The central meaning shared by these verbs is "to change into a different form, substance, or state": *convert stocks into cash; misery metamorphosing into happiness; a bare stage that was transfigured into an enchanted forest; a gangling adolescent transformed into a handsome adult; a sleepy town transmogrified by the boom into a bustling city; impossible to transmute lead into gold.*

con·vert·a·plane (kən-vûr′tə-plăn′) *n.* Variant of **convertiplane.**

con·vert·ed rice (kən-vûr′tĭd) *n.* A white rice prepared from brown rice that has been soaked, steamed under pressure to force water-soluble nutrients into the starchy endosperm, and then dried and milled.

conveyer

con·vert·er also **con·ver·tor** (kən-vûr′tər) *n.* **1.** One that converts, especially: **a.** A furnace in which pig iron is converted into steel by the Bessemer process. **b.** A machine that converts electric current from one kind to another. **c.** An electronic device that converts one frequency of a radio signal to another. **d.** A device that converts data from one code to another. **2.** One that is employed in converting raw products into finished products.

con·vert·i·ble (kən-vûr′tə-bəl) *adj.* **1.** That can be converted: *a convertible sofa bed.* **2.** Having a top that can be folded back or removed: *a convertible automobile.* **3.** *Abbr.* **conv., cvt.** Lawfully exchangeable for gold or another currency: *dollars convertible into yen.* **—convertible** *n.* **1.** Something that can be converted. **2.** A convertible automobile. **3.** A convertible security. **—con·vert′i·bil′i·ty, con·vert′i·ble·ness** *n.* **—con·vert′i·bly** *adv.*

convertible security *n.* A security that, at the holder's option, may be exchanged for another asset, typically a fixed number of shares of common stock.

con·vert·i·plane also **con·vert·a·plane** (kən-vûr′tə-plăn′) *n.* An airplane built to fly vertically as well as forward.

con·ver·tor (kən-vûr′tər) *n.* Variant of **converter.**

con·vex (kŏn′vĕks′, kən-vĕks′) *adj.* Having a surface or boundary that curves or bulges outward, as the exterior of a sphere. [Latin *convexus.* See **wegh-** in Appendix.] **—con′vex′ly** *adv.*

con·vex·i·ty (kən-vĕk′sĭ-tē) *n.*, *pl.* **-ties. 1.** The state of being convex. **2.** A convex surface, body, part, or line.

con·vex·o-con·cave (kən-vĕk′sō-kən-kāv′) *adj.* **1.** Convex on one side and concave on the other. **2.** Having greater curvature on the convex side than on the concave side. Used of a lens.

con·vex·o-con·vex (kən-vĕk′sō-kən-vĕks′) *adj.* Convex on both sides; biconvex. Used of a lens.

con·vey (kən-vā′) *tr.v.* **-veyed, -vey·ing, -veys. 1.** To take or carry from one place to another; transport. **2.** To serve as a medium of transmission for; transmit: *wires that convey electricity.* **3.** To communicate or make known; impart: *"a look intended to convey sympathetic comprehension"* (Saki). **4.** *Law.* To transfer ownership of or title to. **5.** *Archaic.* To steal. [Middle English *conveien*, from Old French *conveier*, from Medieval Latin *conviāre*, to escort : Latin *com-*, com- + *via*, way; see **wegh-** in Appendix.] **—con·vey′a·ble** *adj.*

con·vey·ance (kən-vā′əns) *n.* **1.** The act of conveying. **2.** A means of conveying, especially a vehicle for transportation. **3.** *Law.* **a.** Transfer of title to property from one person to another. **b.** The document by which a property transfer is effected.

con·vey·anc·ing (kən-vā′ən-sĭng) *n.* *Law.* The branch of legal practice dealing with the conveyance of property or real estate. **—con·vey′anc·er** *n.*

con·vey·er also **con·vey·or** (kən-vā′ər) *n.* One that conveys, especially a mechanical apparatus, such as a continuous moving belt, that transports materials, packages, or items being assembled from one place to another.

con·vict (kən-vĭkt′) *v.* **-vict·ed, -vict·ing, -victs.** *—tr.* **1.** *Law.* To find or prove (someone) guilty of an offense or crime, especially by the verdict of a court: *The jury convicted the defendant of manslaughter.* **2.** To show or delcare to be blameworthy; condemn: *His remarks convicted him of a lack of sensitivity.* **3.** To make aware of one's sinfulness or guilt. *—intr.* To return a verdict of guilty in a court: *"We need jurors . . . who will not convict merely because they are suspicious"* (Scott Turow). **—convict** (kŏn′vĭkt′) *n.* *Law.* **1.** A person found or declared guilty of an offense or crime. **2.** A person serving a sentence of imprisonment. **—convict** *adj.* *Archaic.* Found guilty; convicted. [Middle English *convicten*, from Latin *convincere, convict-*. See CONVINCE.]

con·vic·tion (kən-vĭk′shən) *n.* **1.** *Law.* **a.** The judgment of a jury or judge that a person is guilty of a crime as charged. **b.** The state of being found or proved guilty: *evidence that led to the suspect's conviction.* **2.a.** The act or process of convincing. **b.** The state of being convinced. See Synonyms at **certainty. 3.** A fixed or strong belief. See Synonyms at **opinion. —con·vic′tion·al** *adj.*

con·vic·tive (kən-vĭk′tĭv) *adj.* Having power or serving to convince or convict. **—con·vic′tive·ly** *adv.*

con·vince (kən-vĭns′) *tr.v.* **-vinced, -vinc·ing, -vinc·es. 1.** To bring by the use of argument or evidence to firm belief or a course of action. See Synonyms at **persuade. 2.** *Obsolete.* To prove to be wrong or guilty. **3.** *Obsolete.* To conquer; overpower. [Latin *convincere*, to prove wrong : *com-*, intensive pref.; see COM– + *vincere*, to conquer; see **weik-³** in Appendix.] **—con·vince′ment** *n.* **—con·vinc′er** *n.* **—con·vinc′i·ble** *adj.*

USAGE NOTE: According to a traditional rule, one *persuades* someone to act but *convinces* someone of the truth of a statement or proposition: *By convincing me that no good could come of staying, he persuaded me to leave.* If the distinction is accepted, then *convince* should not be used with an infinitive: *He persuaded* (not *convinced*) *me to go.* In an earlier survey, a majority of the Usage Panel held that this distinction should be maintained, but the use of *convince* with an infinitive has become increasingly common even among reputable writers, and it is unlikely that this stricture can be maintained for much longer.

con·vinc·ing (kən-vĭn′sĭng) *adj.* **1.** Serving to convince: *a convincing argument; a convincing manner.* **2.** Believable; plausible: *a convincing story.* See Synonyms at **valid. —con·vinc′ing·ly** *adv.* **—con·vinc′ing·ness** *n.*

con·viv·i·al (kən-vĭv′ē-əl) *adj.* **1.** Fond of feasting, drinking, and good company; sociable. See Synonyms at **social. 2.** Merry; festive: *a convivial atmosphere at the reunion.* [Late Latin *convīviālis*, from Latin *convīvium*, banquet : *com-*, com- + *vīvere*, to live; see **gʷei-** in Appendix.] **—con·viv′i·al′i·ty** (-ăl′ĭ-tē) *n.* **—con·viv′i·al·ly** *adv.*

con·vo·ca·tion (kŏn′və-kā′shən) *n.* *Abbr.* **conv. 1.a.** The act of convoking. **b.** A group of people convoked, especially the members of a college or university community who are assembled for a ceremony. **2.** A clerical assembly of the Anglican Church similar to a synod but assembling only when called. **3.a.** An assembly of the clergy and representative laity of a section of a diocese of the Episcopal Church. **b.** The district represented at such an assembly. **—con′vo·ca′tion·al** *adj.*

con·voke (kən-vōk′) *tr.v.* **-voked, -vok·ing, -vokes.** To cause to assemble in a meeting. See Synonyms at **call.** [French *convoquer,* from Old French, from Latin *convocāre* : *com-,* com- + *vocāre,* to call; see **wekʷ-** in Appendix.] **—con·vok′er** *n.*

con·vo·lute (kŏn′və-lo͞ot′) *adj.* Rolled or coiled together in overlapping whorls, as certain leaves, petals, or shells. **—convolute** *intr. & tr.v.* **-lut·ed, -lut·ing, -lutes.** To coil or fold or cause to coil or fold in overlapping whorls. [Latin *convolūtus,* past participle of *convolvere,* to convolve. See CONVOLVE.] **—con′vo·lute′ly** *adv.*

con·vo·lut·ed (kŏn′və-lo͞o′tĭd) *adj.* **1.** Having numerous overlapping coils or folds: *a convoluted seashell.* **2.** Intricate; complicated: *convoluted legal language; convoluted reasoning.*

con·vo·lu·tion (kŏn′və-lo͞o′shən) *n.* **1.** A form or part that is folded or coiled. **2.** One of the convex folds of the surface of the brain. **—con′vo·lu′tion·al** *adj.*

con·volve (kən-vŏlv′) *v.* **-volved, -volv·ing, -volves.** *—tr.* To roll together; coil up. *—intr.* To form convolutions. [Latin *convolvere* : *com-,* com- + *volvere,* to roll; see **wel-²** in Appendix.]

con·vol·vu·lus (kən-vŏl′vyə-ləs) *n., pl.* **-lus·es** or **-li** (-lī′). Any of various mostly trailing or twining plants of the widespread genus *Convolvulus,* having funnel-shaped flowers and including several weeds and a few grown as ornamentals. [Latin, bindweed, from *convolvere,* to intertwine. See CONVOLVE.]

con·voy (kŏn′voi′) *n.* **1.** The act of accompanying or escorting, especially for protective purposes. **2.** An accompanying and protecting force, as of ships or troops. **3.** A group, as of ships or motor vehicles, traveling together with a protective escort or for safety or convenience. **—convoy** (kŏn′voi′, kən-voi′) *tr.v.* **-voyed, -voy·ing, -voys.** To accompany, especially for protection; escort: *warships convoying merchant vessels across the Atlantic.* [From Middle English *convoyen,* to escort, from Old French *convoier,* variant of *conveier.* See CONVEY.]

con·vul·sant (kən-vŭl′sənt) *adj.* Causing or producing convulsions. **—convulsant** *n.* An agent, such as a drug, that causes convulsions.

con·vulse (kən-vŭls′) *tr.v.* **-vulsed, -vuls·ing, -vuls·es. 1.** To shake or agitate violently: *tremors that convulsed the countryside; when civil war convulsed the nation.* See Synonyms at **agitate. 2.** To affect with irregular and involuntary muscular contractions; throw into convulsions. **3.** To cause to shake with laughter or strong emotion. [Latin *convellere, convuls-,* to pull violently : *com-,* intensive pref.; see COM– + *vellere,* to pull.]

con·vul·sion (kən-vŭl′shən) *n.* **1.** An intense, paroxysmal, involuntary muscular contraction. **2.** An uncontrolled fit, as of laughter. **3.** Violent turmoil: *"The market convulsions of the last few weeks have shaken the world"* (Felix Rohatyn).

con·vul·sive (kən-vŭl′sĭv) *adj.* **1.** Marked by or having the nature of convulsions. **2.** Having or producing convulsions. **—con·vul′sive·ly** *adv.* **—con·vul′sive·ness** *n.*

Con·way (kŏn′wā′). **1.** A city of central Arkansas north-northwest of Little Rock. It is a trade and industrial center in an agricultural region. Population, 20,375. **2.** A community of east-central Florida, a suburb of Orlando. Population, 16,000.

Conway, Thomas. 1735?–1800. Irish-born American Revolutionary general known for his role in the Conway Cabal, a conspiracy to remove George Washington from command of the Continental Army.

♦ **co·ny** (kō′nē, kŭn′ē) *n.* Variant of **coney¹.**

coo (ko͞o) *v.* **cooed, coo·ing, coos.** *—intr.* **1.** To utter the murmuring sound of a dove or pigeon or a sound resembling it. **2.** To talk fondly or amorously in murmurs: *The visitors cooed over the newborn baby.* *—tr.* To express or utter with soft murmuring sounds. [Imitative.] **—coo′er** *n.*

Cooch Be·har (ko͞och′ bə-här′). A former princely state of northeast India. Once a powerful part of Assam, it came under British rule in 1772.

cook (ko͝ok) *v.* **cooked, cook·ing, cooks.** *—tr.* **1.** To prepare (food) for eating by applying heat. **2.** To prepare or treat by heating: *slowly cooked the medicinal mixture.* **3.** *Slang.* To alter or falsify so as to make a more favorable impression; doctor: *disreputable accountants who were paid to cook the firm's books.* *—intr.* **1.** To prepare food for eating by applying heat. **2.** To undergo application of heat especially for the purpose of later ingestion. **3.** *Slang.* To happen, develop, or take place: *What's cooking in town?* **4.** *Slang.* To proceed or perform very well: *The band really got cooking after midnight.* **—cook** *n.* A person who prepares food for eating. ***—phrasal verb.*** **cook up.** *Informal.* To fabricate; concoct: *cook up an excuse.* ***—idiom.*** **cook (one's) goose.** *Slang.* To ruin (one's) chances: *The speeding ticket cooked his goose with his father. Her goose was cooked when she was caught cheating on the test.* [Middle English *coken,* from *coke,* cook, from Old English *cōc,* from Vulgar Latin **cōcus,* from Latin *cocus, coquus,* from *coquere,* to cook. See **pekʷ-** in Appendix.]

Cook (ko͝ok), **Frederick Albert.** 1865–1940. American physician and Arctic explorer who announced that he had reached the North Pole in 1908, a claim that was rejected by the scientific community.

Cook, James. Known as "Captain Cook." 1728–1779. British navigator and explorer who commanded three major voyages of discovery, charting and naming many islands of the Pacific Ocean. He also sailed along the coast of North America as far north as the Bering Strait.

Cook, Mount. Also **A·o·rang·i** (ä′ō-räng′gē) The highest mountain, 3,766.4 m (12,349 ft), of New Zealand, on South Island in the Southern Alps.

cook·book (ko͝ok′bo͝ok′) *n.* A book containing recipes and other information about the preparation of food.

Cooke (ko͝ok), **(Alfred) Alistair.** Born 1908. British-born American journalist and broadcaster, whose books include *Around the World in 50 Years* (1966) and *Alistair Cooke's America* (1973).

Cooke, Jay. 1821–1905. American financier noted for his part in marketing Union bonds to finance the Civil War. The collapse of his bank led to the Panic of 1873.

cook·er (ko͝ok′ər) *n.* **1.** One that cooks, especially a utensil or an appliance for cooking. **2.** A person employed to operate cooking apparatuses in the commercial preparation of food and drink.

cook·er·y (ko͝ok′ə-rē) *n., pl.* **-ies. 1.** The art or practice of preparing food. **2.** A place for cooking.

Cooke·ville (ko͝ok′vĭl′). A city of central Tennessee east of Nashville. It is a farm trade center. Population, 20,535.

cook·ie also **cook·y** (ko͝ok′ē) *n., pl.* **-ies. 1.** A small, usually flat and crisp cake made from sweetened dough. **2.** *Slang.* A person, usually of a specified kind: *a lawyer who was a tough cookie.* [Dutch *koekje,* diminutive of *koek,* cake, from Middle Dutch *koeke.*]

Cook Inlet. An inlet of the Gulf of Alaska in southern Alaska west of the Kenai Peninsula. It is a major fishing ground for salmon and herring and has the largest tidal bore in the United States.

Cook Islands. An island group of the southern Pacific Ocean southeast of Samoa. Probably inhabited by Polynesians more than 1,500 years ago, the islands were first sighted by Capt. James Cook in 1773. They are now self-governing under the sovereignty of New Zealand.

cook-off (ko͝ok′ôf′, -ŏf′) *n.* A cooking competition.

cook·out (ko͝ok′out′) *n.* A meal cooked and served outdoors.

Cook Strait. A narrow channel separating North Island and South Island in New Zealand.

cook·ware (ko͝ok′wâr′) *n.* Cooking utensils.

cook·y (ko͝ok′ē) *n.* Variant of **cookie.**

cool (ko͞ol) *adj.* **cool·er, cool·est. 1.** Neither warm nor very cold; moderately cold: *fresh, cool water; a cool autumn evening.* **2.** Giving or suggesting relief from heat: *a cool breeze; a cool blouse.* **3.** Marked by calm self-control: *a cool negotiator.* **4.** Marked by indifference, disdain, or dislike; unfriendly or unresponsive: *a cool greeting; was cool to the idea of higher taxes.* **5.** Of, relating to, or characteristic of colors, such as blue and green, that produce the impression of coolness. **6.** *Slang.* Excellent; first-rate: *has a cool sports car; had a cool time at the party.* **7.** *Slang.* Entire; full: *worth a cool million.* **—cool** *v.* **cooled, cool·ing, cools.** *—tr.* **1.** To make less warm. **2.** To make less ardent, intense, or zealous: *problems that soon cooled my enthusiasm for the project.* *—intr.* **1.** To become less warm: *took a dip to cool off.* **2.** To become calmer: *needed time for tempers to cool.* **—cool** *n.* **1.** A cool place, part, or time: *the cool of early morning.* **2.** The state or quality of being cool. **3.** *Slang.* Composure; poise: *"Our release marked a victory. The nation had kept its cool"* (Moorhead Kennedy). ***—idioms.*** **cool it.** *Slang.* To calm down; relax. **cool (one's) heels.** *Informal.* To wait or be kept waiting. [Middle English *cole,* from Old English *cōl.* See **gel-** in Appendix.] **—cool′ish** *adj.* **—cool′ly** *adv.* **—cool′ness** *n.*

SYNONYMS: *cool, composed, collected, unruffled, nonchalant, imperturbable, detached.* These adjectives apply to persons, their attitudes, their behavior, or their actions to indicate absence of excitement or discomposure, especially in times of stress. *Cool* usually implies merely a high degree of self-control, though it may also indicate aloofness: *"Keep strong, if possible. In any case, keep cool. Have unlimited patience"* (B.H. Liddell Hart). *"An honest hater is often a better fellow than a cool friend"* (John Stuart Blackie). *Composed* implies a serene, often sedate quality arising from self-discipline: *The performer was composed as she readied herself for her entrance on stage. Collected* suggests self-possessed composure: *The witness remained collected throughout the cross-examination. Unruffled* emphasizes calm despite circumstances that might elicit agitation: *"with contented mind and unruffled spirit"* (Anthony Trollope). *Nonchalant* describes a casual manner that may suggest, sometimes misleadingly, a lack of interest or concern: *He doesn't seem excited; on the contrary, his demeanor is easy and nonchalant. Imperturbable* stresses unshakable calmness considered usually as an inherent trait rather than as a product of self-discipline: *"A man . . ./Cool, and quite English, imperturbable"* (Byron). *Detached* implies aloofness resulting either from lack of active concern or from resistance to emotional involvement: *She may be detached, she may even be unfeeling, but at least she's not hypocritically effusive.* See also Synonyms at **cold.**

cool·ant (ko͞o′lənt) *n.* An agent that produces cooling, especially a fluid that draws off heat by circulating through an engine or by bathing a mechanical part.

cool·er (ko͞o′lər) *n.* **1.** A device, container, or room that cools

ă pat	oi boy
ā pay	ou out
âr care	o͝o took
ä father	o͞o boot
ĕ pet	ŭ cut
ē be	ûr urge
ĭ pit	th thin
ī pie	*th* this
îr pier	hw which
ŏ pot	zh vision
ō toe	ə about, item
ô paw	♦ regionalism

Stress marks: **′** (primary); ′ (secondary), as in **dictionary** (dĭk′shə-nĕr′ē)

or keeps cool. **2.** A cold drink, often a mixture of white wine and juice. **3.** *Slang.* A jail.

Coo·ley's anemia (ko͞o′lēz) *n.* A usually fatal form of thalassemia in which normal hemoglobin is absent, characterized by severe anemia, enlargement of the heart, liver, and spleen, and skeletal deformation. [After Thomas Benton *Cooley* (1871–1945), American physician.]

cool-head·ed (ko͞ol′hĕd′ĭd) *adj.* Not easily excited or flustered.

Coo·lidge (ko͞o′lĭj), **Grace Goodhue.** 1879–1957. First lady of the United States (1923–1929) as the wife of President Calvin Coolidge. She was known for her outgoing manner.

Calvin Coolidge

Coolidge, (John) Calvin. 1872–1933. The 30th President of the United States (1923–1929), who took office after the death of Warren G. Harding. A strong supporter of business, he encouraged speculation that led to a stock market boom in the 1920's, followed by economic collapse.

coo·lie also **coo·ly** (ko͞o′lē) *n., pl.* **-lies.** *Offensive.* An unskilled Asian laborer. [Hindi *kulī.*]

coon (ko͞on) *n.* **1.** *Informal.* A raccoon. **2.** *Offensive Slang.* Used as a disparaging term for a Black person. [Short for RACCOON.]

coon·can (ko͞on′kăn′) or **con·qui·an** (kŏng′kē-ən) *n. Games.* A card game for 2 players using 40 cards that is an early version of rummy. [Alteration of American Spanish *conquián,* probably from Spanish *con quién,* with whom : *con,* with (from Latin *cum;* see **kom** in Appendix) + *quien,* whom (from Latin *quem,* accusative of *quis,* who; see **kʷo-** in Appendix).]

Grace Coolidge

coon·hound (ko͞on′hound′) *n.* Any of various smooth-coated hounds of a breed developed in the southeast United States to hunt raccoons.

Coon Rapids (ko͞on). A city of eastern Minnesota, a suburb of Minneapolis–St. Paul. Population, 35,826.

coon's age (ko͞onz) *n. Slang.* A long time.

coon·skin (ko͞on′skĭn′) *n.* **1.** The pelt of a raccoon. **2.** An article, such as a hat, made of the pelts of raccoons.

coon·tie (ko͞on′tē) *n.* Any of several evergreen species of the genus *Zamia* native to southern Florida, Mexico, and the West Indies, having compound leaves, unisexual cones, and conspicuously thickened underground stems that yield starch resembling arrowroot. Also called *Seminole bread.* [Florida Creek *kuntíi,* arrowroot.]

coop (ko͞op) *n.* **1.** An enclosure or cage, as for poultry or small animals. **2.** *Slang.* **a.** An uncomfortably confined space. **b.** A prison. **—coop** *v.* **cooped, coop·ing, coops.** *—tr.* To confine in or as if in a coop. See Synonyms at **enclose.** *—intr. Informal.* To sleep or shirk in a parked patrol car while on duty. Used of a police officer. ***—idiom.* fly** (or **blow**) **the coop.** To make a getaway; escape. [Middle English *coupe,* possibly from Middle Dutch *kūpe,* basket, tub, from Germanic **kūpōn,* possibly from Latin *cūpa,* cask.]

coop
Chicken coop

co-op (kō′ŏp′, kō-ŏp′) *n.* A cooperative.

coop. *abbr.* Cooperative.

coop·er (ko͞o′pər) *n.* One who makes or repairs wooden barrels, casks, and tubs. [Middle English *couper,* from Middle Dutch *kūper,* from *kūpe,* basket, tub. See COOP.] **—coop′er** *v.* **—coop′er·age** *n.*

Coo·per (ko͞o′pər, ko͝op′ər), **Gary.** 1901–1961. American actor who gained fame for his portrayals of strong, quiet heroes. He won an Academy Award for *Sergeant York* (1941) and *High Noon* (1952).

Cooper, James Fenimore. 1789–1851. American novelist who is best remembered for his novels of frontier life, such as *The Last of the Mohicans* (1826).

Cooper, Peter. 1791–1883. American manufacturer, inventor, and philanthropist who built the first American locomotive and founded Cooper Union (1859) in New York City, which offered free courses in the arts and sciences.

coot
American coot
Fulica americana

co·op·er·ate (kō-ŏp′ə-rāt′) *intr.v.* **-at·ed, -at·ing, -ates. 1.** To work or act together toward a common end or purpose. **2.** To acquiesce willingly; be compliant: *asked the child to cooperate and go to bed.* **3.** To form an association for common, usually economic, benefit: *When buyers cooperate, they can make large wholesale purchases at a discount.* [Late Latin *cooperārī, cooperāt-* : Latin *co-,* co- + *operārī,* to work (from *opus, oper-,* work; see **op-** in Appendix).] **—co·op′er·a′tor** *n.*

co·op·er·a·tion (kō-ŏp′ə-rā′shən) *n.* **1.** The act or practice of cooperating. **2.** The association of persons or businesses for common, usually economic, benefit. **—co·op′er·a′tion·ist** *n.*

co·op·er·a·tive (kō-ŏp′ər-ə-tĭv, -ə-rā′tĭv, -ŏp′rə-) *adj.* **1.** Done in cooperation with others: *a cooperative effort.* **2.** Marked by willingness to cooperate; compliant: *a cooperative patient.* **3.** Of, relating to, or formed as an enterprise or organization jointly owned or managed by those who use its facilities or services: *a cooperative department store; cooperative apartment buildings.* **—cooperative** *n. Abbr.* **coop.** An enterprise or organization owned or managed jointly by those who use its facilities or services. **—co·op′er·a·tive·ly** *adv.* **—co·op′er·a·tive·ness** *n.*

cop²

Coo·per's hawk (ko͞o′pərz, ko͝op′ərz) *n.* A short-winged hawk *(Accipiter cooperii)* widespread throughout North America, having a dark back, a long tail, and a rusty-barred chest. [After William *Cooper* (died 1864), American ornithologist.]

Coo·pers·town (ko͞o′pərz-toun′). A residential village of east-central New York west-southwest of Schenectady. The National Baseball Hall of Fame is here. Population, 2,342.

co-opt (kō-ŏpt′, kō′ŏpt′) *tr.v.* **-opt·ed, -opt·ing, -opts. 1.** To elect as a fellow member of a group. **2.** To appoint summarily. **3.** To take or assume for one's own use; appropriate: *co-opted the criticism by embracing it.* **4.** To neutralize or win over (an independent minority, for example) through assimilation into an established group or culture: *co-opt rebels by giving them positions of authority.* [Latin *cooptāre* : *co-,* co- + *optāre,* to choose.] **—co′-op·ta′tion** *n.* **—co-op′ta·tive** (-tə-tĭv) *adj.* **—co-op′tion** (-ŏp′shən) *n.* **—co-op′tive** *adj.*

co·or·di·nate (kō-ôr′dn-āt′, -ĭt) *n.* **1.** One that is equal in importance, rank, or degree. **2. coordinates.** A set of articles, as of clothing or luggage, designed to match or complement one other, as in style or color. **3.** *Mathematics.* Any of a set of two or more numbers used to determine the position of a point, line, curve, or plane in a space of a given dimension with respect to a system of lines or other fixed reference. **—coordinate** (-ĭt, -āt′) *adj.* **1.** Of equal importance, rank, or degree: *coordinate offices of a business.* **2.** Of or involving coordination. **3.** Of or based on a system of coordinates. **—coordinate** (-āt′) *v.* **-nat·ed, -nat·ing, -nates.** *—tr.* **1.** To place in the same order, class, or rank. **2.** To harmonize in a common action or effort: *coordinating the moving parts of a machine; coordinate the colors of a design.* *—intr.* **1.** To be coordinate: *The generators coordinate so that one is always running.* **2.** To work together harmoniously: *a nursing staff that coordinates smoothly.* **3.** To form a pleasing combination; match: *shoes that coordinate with the rest of the outfit.* [CO– + ORDINATE.] **—co·or′di·nate·ly** (-ĭt-lē) *adv.* **—co·or′di·nate·ness** (-ĭt-nĭs) *n.* **—co·or′di·na′tive** *adj.* **—co·or′di·na′tor** *n.*

coordinate bond *n.* A covalent chemical bond between two atoms that is produced when one atom shares a pair of electrons with another atom lacking such a pair. Also called *coordinate covalent bond.*

coordinate system *n.* A method of representing points in a space of given dimensions by coordinates.

co·or·di·nat·ing conjunction (kō-ôr′dn-ā′tĭng) *n. Grammar.* A conjunction that connects two identically constructed grammatical elements, such as *or* in *They don't know whether they're coming or going.*

co·or·di·na·tion (kō-ôr′dn-ā′shən) *n.* **1. a.** The act of coordinating. **b.** The state of being coordinate; harmonious adjustment or interaction. **2.** *Physiology.* Harmonious functioning of muscles or groups of muscles in the execution of movements. [French, from Medieval Latin *coōrdinātiō, coōrdinātiōn-* : *co-,* co- + Latin *ōrdinātiō,* arrangement (from *ōrdinātus,* past participle of *ōrdināre,* to arrange in order, from *ōrdō,* order; see **ar-** in Appendix).]

coordination compound *n.* A chemical compound formed by joining independent molecules or ions usually to a central metallic atom by coordinate bonds. Also called *coordination complex.*

Coo·sa (ko͞o′sə). A river rising in northwest Georgia and flowing about 460 km (286 mi) southwest through eastern Alabama to join the Tallapoosa River near Montgomery and form the Alabama River.

coot (ko͞ot) *n.* **1.** Any of several dark-gray aquatic birds of the genus *Fulica* of North America and Europe, having a black head and neck, lobed toes, and a white bill. **2.** See **scoter. 3.** *Informal.* A foolish, eccentric, or senile person. [Middle English *coote,* possibly from Middle Dutch *coet.*]

♦ **coot·er** (ko͞o′tər) *n. Lower Southern U.S.* **1.** An edible freshwater turtle of the genus *Chrysemys.* **2.** Any of various turtles or tortoises. See Regional Note at **goober.** [Gullah, of Niger-Congo origin; akin to Mandingo *kuta.*]

coo·tie (ko͞o′tē) *n. Slang.* A body louse. [Probably from Malay *kutu.*]

cop¹ (kŏp) *n. Informal.* A police officer. **—cop** *tr.v.* **copped, cop·ping, cops.** *Slang.* **1.** To take unlawfully or without permission; steal. See Synonyms at **steal. 2. a.** To get hold of; gain or win: *a show that copped four awards; copped a ticket to the game.* **b.** To take or catch: *"copped a quick look at the gentleman in a caramel cashmere sport coat on the right"* (Gail Sheehy). ***—phrasal verb.* cop out.** *Slang.* To avoid fulfilling a commitment or responsibility; renege: *copped out on my friends; copped out by ducking the issue.* ***—idiom.* cop a plea.** *Slang.* To plead guilty to a lesser charge so as to avoid standing trial for a more serious charge. [Short for *copper,* probably from *cop,* variant of *cap,* to catch, from Old French *caper,* from Latin *capere.* See CAPTURE.]

cop² (kŏp) *n.* **1.** A cone-shaped or cylindrical roll of yarn or thread wound on a spindle. **2.** *Chiefly British.* A summit or crest, as of a hill. [Middle English, summit, from Old English.]

cop. *abbr.* Copyright.

Cop. *abbr.* Coptic.

co·pa·cet·ic or **co·pa·set·ic** (kō′pə-sĕt′ĭk) *adj.* Excellent; first-rate: *"You had to be a good judge of what a man was like, and the English was copacetic"* (John O'Hara). [Origin unknown.]

WORD HISTORY: We know very little about the origin of the word *copacetic,* meaning "excellent, first-rate." Is its origin to be found in Italian, in the speech of southern Black people, in the Creole French dialect of Louisiana, or in Hebrew? John O'Hara, who used the word in *Appointment in Samarra,* later wrote that *copacetic* was "a Harlem and gangster corruption of an Italian word." O'Hara went on to say, "I don't know how to spell the Italian, but it's something like copacetti." His uncertainty about how to spell the Italian is paralleled by uncertainty about how to spell *copacetic* itself. *Copacetic* has been recorded with the spellings *copasetic, copasetty, copesetic, copisettic,* and *kopasettee.* The spelling is now more or less fixed, however, as *copacetic* or *copasetic,* even though the origin of the word has not been determined. The Harlem connection mentioned by O'Hara would seem more likely than the Italian, since *copacetic* was used by Black jazz musicians and is said to have been Southern slang in the late 19th century. If *copacetic* is Creole French in origin, it would also have a Southern homeland. According to this explanation, *copacetic* came from the Creole French word *coupersètique,* which meant "able to be coped with," "able to cope with anything and everything," "in good form," and also "having a healthy appetite or passion for life or love." Those who support the Hebrew or Yiddish origin of *copacetic* do not necessarily deny the Southern connections of the word. One explanation has it that Jewish storekeepers used the Hebrew phrase *kol bĕṣedeq,* "all with justice," when asked if things were O.K. Black children who were in the store as customers or employees heard this phrase as *copacetic.* No explanation of the origin of *copacetic,* including the ones discussed here, has won the approval of scholars, as is clearly shown by the etymology of *copacetic* in the first volume of the *Dictionary of American Regional English,* published in 1985: "Etym unknown."

---

co·pai·ba (kō-pī′bə, -pā′-) *n.* A transparent, often yellowish, viscous oleoresin obtained from South American trees of the genus *Copaifera* in the pea family, used in certain varnishes and as a fixative in some perfumes. [Spanish, from Portuguese *copaíba,* from Tupi *cupaiba.*]

co·pal (kō′pəl, -păl′) *n.* Any of several brittle, aromatic, yellow to red resins of recent or fossil origin, obtained from various tropical trees and used in certain varnishes. [Spanish, from Nahuatl *copalli,* resin.]

Co·pán (kō-pän′). A ruined Mayan city of western Honduras that flourished from c. 300 B.C. to A.D. 900. The ruins include the Hieroglyphic Stairway with nearly 2,000 glyphs.

co·par·ce·nar·y (kō-pär′sə-nĕr′ē) *n., pl.* **-ies. 1.** *Law.* Joint inheritance or heirship of property. Also called *parcenary.* **2.** Joint ownership. **—co·par′ce·nar′y** *adj.*

co·par·ce·ner (kō-pär′sə-nər) *n. Law.* One of two or more persons sharing an inheritance; a joint heir. Also called *parcener.*

co-par·ent·ing (kō-pâr′ən-tĭng, -păr′-) *n. Usage Problem.* An arrangement in a divorce or separation by which parents share legal and physical custody of a child or children. See Usage Note at **parent. —co′-par′ent** *n.*

co·part·ner (kō-pärt′nər, kō′pärt′-) *n.* A joint partner, as in a business enterprise; an associate. **—co·part′ner·ship′** *n.*

co·pa·set·ic (kō′pə-sĕt′ĭk) *adj.* Variant of **copacetic.**

cope¹ (kōp) *intr.v.* **coped, cop·ing, copes. 1.** To contend or strive, especially on even terms or with success: *coping with child rearing and a full-time job.* **2.** To contend with difficulties and act to overcome them: *"Facing unprecedented problems, the Federal Reserve of the early 1930s couldn't cope"* (Robert J. Samuelson). [Middle English *copen, coupen,* to strike, from Old French *couper,* from Vulgar Latin **colpāre,* from Late Latin *colpus,* blow, from Latin *colaphus,* from Greek *kolaphos.*] **—cop′er** *n.*

cope² (kōp) *n.* **1.** A long ecclesiastical vestment worn over an alb or surplice. **2.** A covering resembling a cloak or mantle. **3.** A coping. **—cope** *tr.v.* **coped, cop·ing, copes. 1.** To cover or dress in a cope. **2.** To provide with coping: *cope a wall.* [Middle English *cope,* from Old English *-cāp,* from Medieval Latin *cāpa,* cloak, from Late Latin *cappa.*]

co·peck (kō′pĕk) *n.* Variant of **kopeck.**

Co·pen·ha·gen (kō′pən-hā′gən, -hä′-). The capital and largest city of Denmark, in the extreme eastern part of the country on the eastern coast of Sjaelland. It was a trading and fishing center by the 11th century and became the capital in 1443. Population, 482,937.

co·pe·pod (kō′pə-pŏd′) *n.* Any of numerous minute marine and freshwater crustaceans of the subclass Copepoda, having an elongated body and a forked tail. [From New Latin *Copepoda,* order name : Greek *kōpē,* oar; see **kap-** in Appendix + *-poda,* -pod.]

Co·per·ni·can (kō-pûr′nĭ-kən, kə-) *adj.* Of or relating to the theory of Copernicus that the earth rotates daily on its axis and, with the other planets in the solar system, revolves around the sun.

Co·per·ni·cus (kō-pûr′nə-kəs, kə-), **Nicolaus.** 1473–1543. Polish astronomer who advanced the theory that the earth and other planets revolve around the sun, disrupting the Ptolemaic system of astronomy.

cope·stone (kōp′stōn) *n.* A capstone. [COPE² + STONE.]

cop·i·er (kŏp′ē-ər) *n.* **1.** An office machine that makes copies of printed or graphic matter. **2.** One that transcribes or copies: *a copier of ancient manuscripts.*

co·pi·lot (kō′pī′lət) *n.* The second or relief pilot of an aircraft.

cop·ing (kō′pĭng) *n.* The top layer or course of a masonry wall, usually having a slanting upper surface to shed water; a cope. [From COPE².]

coping saw *n.* A light handsaw with a slender blade stretched across a U-shaped frame, used for cutting designs in wood.

co·pi·ous (kō′pē-əs) *adj.* **1.** Yielding or containing plenty; affording ample supply: *a copious harvest.* See Synonyms at **plentiful. 2.** Large in quantity; abundant: *copious rainfall.* **3.** Abounding in matter, thoughts, or words; wordy: *"I found our speech copious without order, and energetic without rules"* (Samuel Johnson). [Middle English, from Latin *cōpiōsus,* from *cōpia,* abundance. See **op-** in Appendix.] **—co′pi·ous·ly** *adv.* **—co′pi·ous·ness** *n.*

co·pla·nar (kō-plā′nər) *adj.* Lying or occurring in the same plane. Used of points, lines, or figures. **—co′pla·nar′i·ty** (kō′plə-năr′ĭ-tē) *n.*

Cop·land (kŏp′lənd), **Aaron.** 1900–1990. American composer whose works include the ballets *Rodeo* (1942) and *Appalachian Spring* (1944), which won a Pulitzer Prize.

Cop·ley (kŏp′lē), **John Singleton.** 1738–1815. American Loyalist painter who did portraits of John Hancock and Paul Revere before departing for England when the American Revolution seemed imminent.

co·pol·y·mer (kō-pŏl′ə-mər) *n.* A polymer of two or more different monomers. **—co·pol′y·mer′ic** (-mĕr′ĭk) *adj.*

co·pol·y·mer·ize (kō-pŏl′ə-mə-rīz′, kō′pə-lĭm′ə-) *v.* **-ized, -iz·ing, -iz·es.** —*tr.* To polymerize (different monomers) together. —*intr.* To react to form a copolymer. **—co·pol′y·mer·i·za′tion** (-mər-ĭ-zā′shən) *n.*

cop-out also **cop·out** (kŏp′out′) *n. Slang.* **1.** A failure to fulfill a commitment or responsibility or to face a difficulty squarely. **2.** A person who fails to fulfill a commitment or responsibility. **3.** An excuse for inaction or evasion.

cop·per¹ (kŏp′ər) *n.* **1.** *Symbol* **Cu** A ductile, malleable, reddish-brown metallic element that is an excellent conductor of heat and electricity and is widely used for electrical wiring, water piping, and corrosion-resistant parts, either pure or in alloys such as brass and bronze. Atomic number 29; atomic weight 63.54; melting point 1,083°C; boiling point 2,595°C; specific gravity 8.96; valence 1, 2. See table at **element. 2.** A coin, usually of small denomination, made of copper or a copper alloy. **3.** *Chiefly British.* A large cooking pot made of copper or often of iron. **4.** Any of various small butterflies of the subfamily Lycaeninae, having predominantly copper-colored wings. **5.** *Color.* A reddish brown. **—copper** *tr.v.* **-pered, -per·ing, -pers. 1.** To coat or finish with a layer of copper. **2.** *Slang.* To bet against, as in faro. [Middle English *coper,* from Old English, from Late Latin *cuprum,* from Latin *Cyprium (aes),* Cyprian (metal), from *Cyprius,* of Cyprus, from Greek *Kuprios,* from *Kupros,* Cyprus.] **—cop′per·y** *adj.*

cop·per² (kŏp′ər) *n. Slang.* A police officer. [From COP¹.]

cop·per·as (kŏp′ər-əs) *n.* See **ferrous sulfate.** [Middle English *coperose,* a metallic sulfate, from Old French, from Medieval Latin *cuperosa,* probably short for **aqua cuprosa,* copper water, from Late Latin *cuprum,* copper. See COPPER¹.]

Cop·per·as Cove (kŏp′ər-əs). A city of central Texas southwest of Waco. It is a trade center in an agricultural area. Population, 19,469.

cop·per·head (kŏp′ər-hĕd′) *n.* **1.** A venomous snake *(Agkistrodon contortrix)* of the eastern and central United States, having a reddish-brown body marked with darker crossbands arranged in an hourglass pattern. **2. Copperhead.** A Northerner who sympathized with the South during the Civil War.

cop·per·leaf (kŏp′ər-lēf′) *n.* Any of various plants of the genus *Acalypha,* especially *A. wilkesiana,* an ornamental shrub of the Pacific Islands widely grown for its decorative, colorful, variously patterned leaves.

Cop·per·mine (kŏp′ər-mīn′). A river of northern Northwest Territories, Canada, flowing about 845 km (525 mi) northward to the Arctic Ocean.

cop·per·plate (kŏp′ər-plāt′) *n.* **1.** A copper printing plate engraved or etched to form a recessed pattern of the matter to be printed. **2.** A print or engraving made by using such a plate.

copper pyrites *n.* See **chalcopyrite.**

Cop·per River (kŏp′ər). A river rising in the Wrangell Mountains of southern Alaska and flowing about 483 km (300 mi) southward to the Gulf of Alaska.

cop·per·smith (kŏp′ər-smĭth′) *n.* **1.** One that works or manufactures objects, especially utensils, in copper. **2.** A brightly colored bird *(Megalaima haemacephala)* of southeast Asia, characterized by its ringing, metallic call.

copper sulfate *n.* A poisonous blue crystalline copper salt, $CuSO_4 \cdot 5H_2O$, used in agriculture, textile dyeing, leather treatment, electroplating, and the manufacture of germicides.

cop·per·ware (kŏp′ər-wâr′) *n.* Articles made of copper.

cop·pice (kŏp′ĭs) *n.* A thicket or grove of small trees or shrubs, especially one maintained by periodic cutting or pruning to encourage suckering, as in the cultivation of cinnamon trees for their bark. [Old French *copeiz.* See COPSE.]

co·pra (kō′prə, kŏp′rə) *n.* The dried white flesh of the coconut from which coconut oil is extracted. [Portuguese, from Malayalam *koppara.*]

copro– *pref.* Excrement; dung: *coprolite.* [From Greek *kopros,* dung. See **kekʷ-** in Appendix.]

cop·ro·la·li·a (kŏp′rə-lā′lē-ə) *n. Psychiatry.* The uncontrolled, often excessive use of obscene or scatological language

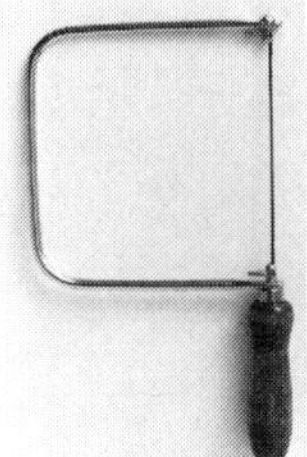

coping saw

John Singleton Copley
Self-portrait

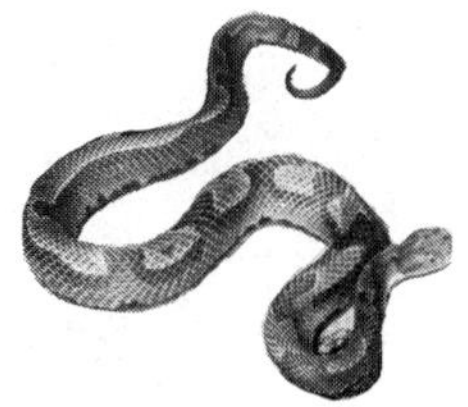

copperhead
Agkistrodon contortrix

ă pat	oi boy
ā pay	ou out
âr care	o͝o took
ä father	o͞o boot
ĕ pet	ŭ cut
ē be	ûr urge
ĭ pit	th thin
ī pie	*th* this
îr pier	hw which
ŏ pot	zh vision
ō toe	ə about, item
ô paw	♦ regionalism

Stress marks: ′ (primary); ′ (secondary), as in **dictionary** (dĭk′shə-nĕr′ē)

that may accompany certain mental disorders, such as schizophrenia or Tourette's syndrome. [COPRO– + Greek *lalia,* babbling (from *lalein,* to talk).]

cop·ro·lite (kŏp′rə-līt′) *n.* Fossilized excrement. **—cop′ro·lit′ic** (-lĭt′ĭk) *adj.*

cop·rol·o·gy (kŏ-prŏl′ə-jē) *n.* Scatology.

cop·roph·a·gous (kŏ-prŏf′ə-gəs) *adj.* Feeding on excrement: *coprophagous beetles.* **—cop·roph′a·gy** (-ə-jē) *n.*

cop·ro·phil·i·a (kŏp′rə-fĭl′ē-ə) *n.* An abnormal, often obsessive interest in excrement, especially the use of feces for sexual excitement. **—cop′ro·phil′i·ac′** (-ē-ăk′) *n.* **—cop′ro·phil′ic** *adj.*

cop·roph·i·lous (kŏ-prŏf′ə-ləs) *adj.* Living or growing on excrement, as certain fungi.

copse (kŏps) *n.* A thicket of small trees or shrubs; a coppice. [Middle English *copys,* from Old French *copeiz,* thicket for cutting, from *coper, couper,* to cut. See COPE[1].]

Copt (kŏpt) *n.* **1.** An Egyptian belonging to or descended from the people of ancient or pre-Islamic Egypt. **2.** A member of the Coptic Church. [French *Copte,* from New Latin *Coptus,* from Arabic *Qubṭ,* Copts, from Coptic *Gyptias,* from Greek *Aiguptios,* an Egyptian, from *Aiguptos,* Egypt, of Egyptian origin.]

Copt. *abbr.* Coptic.

cop·ter (kŏp′tər) *n. Informal.* A helicopter.

Cop·tic (kŏp′tĭk) *n. Abbr.* **Copt., Cop.** The Afro-Asiatic language of the Copts, which survives only as a liturgical language of the Coptic Church. **—Coptic** *adj.* Of or relating to the Copts, the Coptic Church, or the Coptic language.

Coptic Church *n.* The Christian church of Egypt, adhering to the Monophysite doctrine.

cop·u·la (kŏp′yə-lə) *n.* **1.** *Grammar.* A verb, such as a form of *be* or *seem,* that identifies the predicate of a sentence with the subject. Also called *linking verb.* **2.** *Logic.* The word or set of words that serves as a link between the subject and predicate of a proposition. [Latin *cōpula,* link.] **—cop′u·lar** (-lər) *adj.*

cop·u·late (kŏp′yə-lāt′) *intr.v.* **-lat·ed, -lat·ing, -lates.** To engage in coitus or sexual intercourse. **—copulate** (-lĭt) *adj.* Coupled; joined. [Latin *cōpulāre, cōpulāt-,* to join together, from *cōpula,* link.] **—cop′u·la′tion** *n.* **—cop′u·la·to′ry** (-lə-tôr′ē, -tōr′ē) *adj.*

cop·u·la·tive (kŏp′yə-lā′tĭv, -lə-tĭv) *adj.* **1.** *Grammar.* **a.** Serving to connect coordinate words or clauses: *a copulative conjunction.* **b.** Serving as a copula: *a copulative verb.* **2.** Of or relating to copulation. **—copulative** *n. Grammar.* A copulative word or group of words. **—cop′u·la′tive·ly** *adv.*

coral

cop·y (kŏp′ē) *n., pl.* **-ies. 1.** An imitation or reproduction of an original; a duplicate: *a copy of a painting; made two copies of the letter.* **2.** One specimen or example of a printed text or picture: *an autographed copy of a novel.* **3.** *Abbr.* **c., C.** Material, such as a manuscript, that is to be set in type. **4.** The words to be printed or spoken in an advertisement. **5.** Suitable source material for journalism: *Celebrities make good copy.* **—copy** *v.* **-ied, -y·ing, -ies.** *—tr.* **1.** To make a reproduction or copy of. **2.** To follow as a model or pattern; imitate. See Synonyms at **imitate.** *—intr.* **1.** To make a copy or copies. **2.** To admit of being copied: *colored ink that does not copy well.* [Middle English *copie,* from Old French, from Medieval Latin *cōpia,* transcript, from Latin, profusion. See **op-** in Appendix.] **—cop′y·a·ble** *adj.*

cop·y·book (kŏp′ē-bo͝ok′) *n.* An exercise book containing models of penmanship for teaching handwriting. **—copybook** *adj.* Unoriginal; trite: *used copybook phrases in the essay.*

copy boy also **cop·y·boy** (kŏp′ē-boi′) *n.* A boy employed by a newspaper or broadcast news office to carry copy and run errands.

cop·y·cat (kŏp′ē-kăt′) *Informal. n.* One that closely imitates or mimics another. **—copycat** *v.* **-cat·ted, -cat·ting, -cats.** *—intr.* To act as an imitator or mimic. *—tr.* To imitate closely; mimic. **—copycat** *adj.* Closely imitating or following another: *a copycat version of a successful product; a copycat crime.*

copy desk *n.* The desk in a news office where copy is edited and prepared for typesetting or broadcasting.

cop·y·ed·it or **cop·y-ed·it** (kŏp′ē-ĕd′ĭt) *tr.v.* **-it·ed, -it·ing, -its.** To correct and prepare (a manuscript, for example) for typesetting and printing. **—cop′y·ed′i·tor** *n.*

copy girl also **cop·y·girl** (kŏp′ē-gûrl′) *n.* A girl employed by a newspaper or broadcast news office to carry copy and run errands.

coral snake

cop·y·hold·er (kŏp′ē-hōl′dər) *n.* **1.** An assistant who reads manuscript aloud to a proofreader. **2.** A device that holds copy in place, especially for a typesetter.

cop·y·ist (kŏp′ē-ĭst) *n.* One who makes written copies.

copy protection *n. Computer Science.* A means of preventing the illegal or unauthorized copying of a software product, especially a preventive routine that is incorporated into a copyrighted program. **—cop′y-pro·tect′ed** (kŏp′ē-prə-tĕk′tĭd) *adj.*

cop·y·read·er (kŏp′ē-rē′dər) *n.* One who edits and corrects newspaper copy for publication.

cop·y·right (kŏp′ē-rīt′) *n. Abbr.* **c., C., cop.** The legal right granted to an author, a composer, a playwright, a publisher, or a distributor to exclusive publication, production, sale, or distribution of a literary, musical, dramatic, or artistic work. **—copyright** *adj.* **1.** Of or relating to a copyright: *copyright law; a copyright agreement.* **2.** Protected by copyright: *permission to publish copyright material.* **—copyright** *tr.v.* **-right·ed, -right·ing, -rights.** To secure a copyright for. **—cop′y·right′a·ble** *adj.* **—cop′y·right′er** *n.*

cop·y·writ·er (kŏp′ē-rī′tər) *n.* One who writes copy, especially for advertising.

coq au vin (kōk′ ō văN′) *n.* A dish of chicken cooked in red wine. [French : *coq,* chicken + *à,* with + *vin,* wine.]

co·quet (kō-kĕt′) *intr.v.* **-quet·ted, -quet·ting, -quets. 1.** To engage in coquetry; flirt. **2.** To trifle; dally. [French *coqueter,* from *coquet,* flirtatious man, diminutive of *coq,* cock, from Old French *coc,* from Late Latin *coccus.* See COCK[1].]

co·quet·ry (kō′kĭ-trē, kō-kĕt′rē) *n., pl.* **-ries.** Dalliance; flirtation. [French *coquetterie,* from *coquette,* coquette. See COQUETTE.]

co·quette (kō-kĕt′) *n.* A woman who makes teasing sexual or romantic overtures; a flirt. [French, feminine of *coquet,* flirtatious man. See COQUET.] **—co·quet′tish** *adj.* **—co·quet′tish·ly** *adv.* **—co·quet′tish·ness** *n.*

co·quil·la nut (kō-kēl′yə, -kē′yə) *n.* The thick-shelled seed of a Brazilian feather-leaved palm *(Attalea funifera),* polished and used for decorative carving or turning. [Portuguese *coquilho,* diminutive of *côco,* coco. See COCONUT.]

co·quille (kō-kēl′) *n.* A scallop-shaped dish or a scallop shell in which various seafood dishes are browned and served. [French, from Latin *conchȳlia,* pl. of *conchȳlium,* shellfish, from Greek *konkhulion,* diminutive of *konkhos.*]

co·qui·na (kō-kē′nə) *n.* **1.** Any of various small marine clams of the genus *Donax* that are common in the coastal waters of the eastern and southern United States and have variously colored, often striped or banded shells. **2.** A soft, porous limestone, composed essentially of fragments of shells and coral, used as a building material. [Spanish, cockle, probably diminutive of *concha,* shell, from Latin, mussel. See CONCH.]

co·qui·to (kō-kē′tō) *n., pl.* **-tos.** A feather-leaved palm *(Jubaea chilensis)* native to Chile, having a thick trunk from which is obtained a sugary sap used for making wine and a kind of honey, and widely cultivated as an ornamental in warm dry regions. [Spanish, diminutive of *coco,* coco palm, from Portuguese *côco.* See COCONUT.]

cor. *abbr.* **1.** Corner. **2.** *Music.* Cornet. **3.** Coroner. **4.** Corpus. **5.** Correction. **6. a.** Correspondence; correspondent. **b.** Corresponding.

Cor. *abbr. Bible.* Corinthians.

cor·a·cle (kôr′ə-kəl, kŏr′-) *n. Nautical.* A small, rounded boat made of waterproof material stretched over a wicker or wooden frame. [Welsh *corwgl,* from Middle Irish *curach,* from Old Irish.]

cor·a·coid (kôr′ə-koid′, kŏr′-) *n.* **1.** A bony process projecting from the scapula toward the sternum in mammals. **2.** A beak-shaped bone articulating with the scapula and sternum in most lower vertebrates, such as birds and reptiles. **—coracoid** *adj.* Of, relating to, or resembling a coracoid. [New Latin *coracoīdēs,* from Greek *korakoeidēs,* ravenlike : *korax, korak-,* raven + *-oeidēs,* -oid.]

cor·al (kôr′əl, kŏr′-) *n.* **1. a.** A rocklike deposit consisting of the calcareous skeletons secreted by various anthozoans. Coral deposits often accumulate to form reefs or islands in warm seas. **b.** Any of numerous chiefly colonial marine polyps of the class Anthozoa that secrete such calcareous skeletons. **c.** The red-orange, pinkish, or white deposits secreted by corals of the genus *Corallium,* used to make jewelry and ornaments. **d.** An object made of this material. **2.** *Color.* A deep or strong pink to moderate red or reddish orange. **3.** The unfertilized eggs of a female lobster, which turn a reddish color when cooked. **—coral** *adj. Color.* Of a deep or strong pink to moderate red or reddish orange. [Middle English, from Old French, from Latin *corallium,* from Greek *korallion.*]

coral bean *n.* See **coral tree.**

cor·al-bells (kôr′əl-bĕlz′, kŏr′-) *pl.n. (used with a sing. or pl. verb).* A species of alumroot *(Heuchera sanguinea)* native to the southwest United States and Mexico, widely cultivated in gardens for its clusters of small, bell-shaped, red to white flowers.

cor·al·ber·ry (kôr′əl-bĕr′ē, kŏr′-) *n.* **1.** A North American deciduous shrub *(Symphoricarpos orbiculatus)* cultivated for its abundant clusters of coral-red, berrylike fruits. Also called *Indian currant.* **2.** Any of certain eastern Asian evergreen shrubs of the genus *Ardisia,* such as spiceberry, cultivated as a houseplant for its clusters of long-lasting, red, berrylike fruits.

coral fungus *n.* Any of numerous fungi, especially of the family Clavariaceae, whose often brightly colored spore-bearing structures are club-shaped to intricately branched and resemble coral.

Cor·al Ga·bles (kôr′əl gā′bəlz, kŏr′-). A city of southeast Florida on Biscayne Bay southwest of Miami. It is mainly residential. Population, 43,241.

cor·al·line (kôr′ə-lĭn, -līn′, kŏr′-) *adj.* **1.** Of, consisting of, or producing coral. **2.** Resembling coral, especially in color. **—coralline** *n.* **1.** Any of various red algae of the family Corallinaceae whose fronds are covered with calcareous deposits. **2.** Any of various organisms that resemble coral, such as certain bryozoans or hydrozoans. [French *corallin,* from Late Latin *corallīnus,* from Latin *corallium,* coral. See CORAL.]

cor·al·loid (kôr′ə-loid′, kŏr′-) also **cor·al·loid·al** (-loid′l) *adj.* Resembling coral in appearance or form. [Latin *corallium,* coral; see CORAL + –OID.]

coral pink *n. Color.* A moderate to deep yellowish pink.

coral reef *n.* An erosion-resistant marine ridge or mound consisting chiefly of compacted coral together with algal material and biochemically deposited magnesium and calcium carbonates.

cor·al·root (kôr′əl-ro͞ot′, -ro͝ot′, kŏr′-) *n.* Any of several terrestrial, saprophytic, chiefly New World orchids of the genus *Corallorhiza* having yellowish-green to purplish-brown leafless stems and small flowers. [From the corallike appearance of its branched rhizomes.]

Coral Sea. An arm of the southwest Pacific Ocean bounded by New Hebrides, northeast Australia, and southeast New Guinea. It was the scene of a U.S. World War II naval victory in May 1942.

coral snake *n.* Any of various venomous snakes of the genus *Micrurus,* native to tropical America and the southern United States, characteristically having brilliant red, yellow, and black banded markings.

Coral Springs. A city of southeast Florida, a suburb of Fort Lauderdale. Population, 37,349.

coral tree *n.* Any of various mostly deciduous trees or shrubs of the genus *Erythrina* in the pea family, native to and widely cultivated in warm regions, having trifoliolate leaves, showy red or orange flowers, and pods containing often brightly colored seeds. Also called *coral bean.*

coral vine *n.* A climbing woody vine *(Antigonon leptopus)* native to Mexico and widely cultivated in warm regions, having heart-shaped leaves and tendril-bearing clusters of small, red to white flowers.

Co·ran·tijn (kôr′ən-tīn′, kôr′-). See **Courantyne.**

cor·ban (kôr′bən, -băn′) *n.* A sacrifice made to God by the ancient Hebrews at the Temple in Jerusalem. [Middle English, from Late Latin, from Greek *korban,* from Hebrew *qurbān.*]

cor·beil also **cor·beille** (kôr′bəl, kôr-bā′) *n.* A sculptured basket of flowers or fruits used as an architectural ornament. [French *corbeille,* from Late Latin *corbicula,* little basket, diminutive of Latin *corbis,* basket.]

cor·bel (kôr′bəl, -bĕl′) *n.* A bracket of stone, wood, brick, or other building material, projecting from the face of a wall and generally used to support a cornice or an arch. **—corbel** *tr.v.* **-beled, -bel·ing, -bels** also **-belled, -bel·ling, -bels.** To provide with or support by a corbel or corbels. [Middle English, from Old French, diminutive of *corp,* raven (from the similarity of its shape to that of a raven's beak), from Latin *corvus.*]

cor·bel·ing (kôr′bə-lĭng, -bĕl′-) *n.* An overlapping arrangement of bricks or stones in which each course extends farther out from the vertical of the wall than the course below.

Cor·bett (kôr′bət), **James John.** Known as "Gentleman Jim." 1866–1933. American heavyweight boxing champion (1892–1897) who was famed for his courteous manner.

cor·bie gable (kôr′bē) *n.* A gable roof with corbie-steps.

cor·bie-step also **cor·bie·step** (kôr′bē-stĕp′) *n.* One of a series of steps or steplike projections on the top of a gable wall. [Middle English *corbie,* raven, from Old French *corbin,* from Latin *corvīnus,* ravenlike. See CORBINA.]

cor·bi·na (kôr-bē′nə) also **cor·vi·na** (-vē′nə) *n.* **1.** A food and game fish *(Menticirrhus undulatus)* of North American Pacific waters and especially coastal California. **2.** Any of several related marine fishes of the family Sciaenidae. [Spanish *corbina, corvina,* from feminine of *corvino,* ravenlike (from its color), from Latin *corvīnus,* from *corvus,* raven.]

Cor·co·va·do (kôr′kə-vä′dō, kôr′kô-vä′do͞o). A mountain, 704.6 m (2,310 ft) high, of southeast Brazil overlooking Rio de Janeiro. A popular tourist attraction, it has a funicular railroad and is topped by an enormous statue of Christ the Redeemer.

Cor·cy·ra (kôr-sī′rə). See **Corfu.**

cord (kôrd) *n.* **1.** A slender length of flexible material usually made of twisted strands or fibers and used to bind, tie, connect, or support. **2.** An insulated, flexible electric wire fitted with a plug or plugs. **3.** A hangman's rope. **4.** An influence, feeling, or force that binds or restrains; a bond or tie. **5.** Also **chord** *(also* kôrd). *Anatomy.* A long ropelike structure, such as a nerve or tendon: *a spinal cord.* **6. a.** A raised rib on the surface of cloth. **b.** A fabric or cloth with such ribs. **7. cords.** Trousers made of corduroy. **8.** *Abbr.* **cd.** A unit of quantity for cut fuel wood, equal to a stack measuring 4 × 4 × 8 feet or 128 cubic feet (3.62 cubic meters). **—cord** *tr.v.* **cord·ed, cord·ing, cords. 1.** To fasten or bind with a cord. **2.** To furnish with a cord. **3.** To pile (wood) in cords. [Middle English, from Old French *corde,* from Latin *chorda,* from Greek *khordē.* See **gherə-** in Appendix.] **—cord′er** *n.*

cord·age (kôr′dĭj) *n.* **1.** Cords or ropes, especially the ropes in the rigging of a ship. **2.** The amount of wood in an area as measured in cords.

cor·date (kôr′dāt′) *adj.* Having a heart-shaped outline: *a cordate leaf.* [New Latin *cordātus,* from Latin *cor, cord-,* heart. See **kerd-** in Appendix.] **—cor′date′ly** *adv.*

Cor·day (kôr-dā′, kôr′dā), **Charlotte.** 1768–1798. French Revolutionary heroine who was guillotined for the assassination of Jean Paul Marat in 1793.

cord·ed (kôr′dĭd) *adj.* **1.** Tied or bound with cords. **2.** Furnished with or made of cords. **3.** Ribbed or twilled: *a corded bedspread.* **4.** Stacked in cords: *corded firewood.*

cord grass *n.* Any of several perennial grasses of the genus *Spartina,* several of which form colonies in salt marshes and are important as coastal soil binders.

cor·dial (kôr′jəl) *adj.* **1.** Warm and sincere; friendly: *a cordial greeting; cordial relations.* See Synonyms at **gracious. 2.** Strongly felt; fervent: *a cordial abhorrence of waste.* **3.** Serving to invigorate; stimulating. **—cordial** *n.* **1.** A stimulant; a tonic. **2.** A liqueur. [Middle English, of the heart, from Medieval Latin *cordiālis,* from Latin *cor, cord-,* heart. See **kerd-** in Appendix.] **—cor·dial′i·ty** (-jăl′ĭ-tē, -jē-ăl′-, -dē-ăl′-), **cor′dial·ness** *n.* **—cor′dial·ly** *adv.*

cor·di·er·ite (kôr′dē-ə-rīt′) *n.* A dichroic violet-blue to gray mineral silicate of magnesium, aluminum, and sometimes iron. Also called *dichroite.* [French, after Pierre L. *Cordier* (1777–1861), French geologist.]

cor·di·form (kôr′də-fôrm′) *adj.* Heart-shaped. [Latin *cor, cord-,* heart; see **kerd-** in Appendix + –FORM.]

cor·dil·le·ra (kôr′dl-yâr′ə, kôr-dĭl′ər-ə) *n.* An extensive chain of mountains or mountain ranges, especially the principal mountain system of a continent. [Spanish, from *cordilla,* diminutive of *cuerda,* cord, from Latin *chorda.* See CORD.] **—cor′dil·le′ran** (-yâr′ən) *adj.*

Cor·dil·le·ra Cen·tral (kôr′dĭl-yĕr′ə sĕn-träl′, *-thē-yĕ′rä*). **1.** The central of three ranges of the Andes in western Colombia. **2.** A mountain range of central Dominican Republic. **3.** A range of the Andes extending northwest and southeast in north-central Peru. **4.** A range of south-central Puerto Rico.

Cordillera Mé·ri·da (mĕr′ĭ-də, mĕ′rē-*thä*). A mountain range of western Venezuela extending northeast and southwest. Pico Bolívar, 5,005.4 m (16,411 ft), is the highest elevation.

Cordillera Oc·ci·den·tal (ŏk′sĭ-dĕn-täl′, ôk′sē-*thĕn*-). A range of the western Andes with branches in western Colombia and along the Pacific coast of Peru.

Cordillera O·rien·tal (ôr′ē-ĕn-täl′, ô′ryĕn-). A range of the eastern Andes with branches in central Bolivia, western Colombia, and southeast Peru. Its highest elevation is Salcantay, 6,275.4 m (20,575 ft), in Peru.

Cordillera Re·al (rā-äl′). A range of the Andes with branches in western Bolivia and central Ecuador.

Cor·dil·le·ras (kôr′dĭl-yĕr′əz, kôr′*thē*-yĕ′räs). The entire complex of mountain ranges in western North America, Mexico, Central America, and South America, extending from Alaska to Cape Horn.

cord·ite (kôr′dīt′) *n.* A smokeless explosive powder consisting of nitrocellulose, nitroglycerin, and petrolatum that has been dissolved in acetone, dried, and extruded in cords.

cord·less (kôrd′lĭs) *adj.* **1.** Having no cord: *a cordless telephone.* **2.** Using batteries as a source of power: *a cordless electric shaver.* **—cord′less·ly** *adv.*

cor·do·ba (kôr′də-bə, -və) *n.* See table at **currency.** [American Spanish *córdoba,* after Francisco Fernández de *Córdoba* (1475?–1526?), Spanish explorer.]

Cór·do·ba (kôr′də-bə, -və, *-thô*-vä). **1.** A city of north-central Argentina northwest of Buenos Aires. It was founded in 1573. Population, 993,055. **2.** A city of southern Spain on the Guadalquivir River east-northeast of Seville. Probably established by Carthaginians, it was ruled by Romans, Visigoths, and Arabs until 1031. Population, 291,370. **—Cor′do·van** (-vən) *adj. & n.*

cor·don (kôr′dn) *n.* **1.** A line of people, military posts, or ships stationed around an area to enclose or guard it. **2.** A cord or braid worn as a fastening or an ornament. **3.** A ribbon usually worn diagonally across the breast as a badge of honor or a decoration. **4.** *Architecture.* A stringcourse. **5.** *Botany.* A tree or shrub, especially a fruit tree such as an apple or a pear, repeatedly pruned and trained to grow on a support as a single ropelike stem. **—cordon** *tr.v.* **-doned, -don·ing, -dons.** To form a cordon around (an area) so as to prevent movement in or out: *Troops cordoned off the riot zone.* [French, from Old French, diminutive of *corde,* cord. See CORD.]

cor·don bleu (kôr′dôɴ blœ′) *n., pl.* **cor·dons bleus** (kôr′-dôɴ blœ′). A person highly distinguished in a field, especially a master chef. [French : *cordon,* ribbon + *bleu,* blue.]

cor·don sa·ni·taire (kôr-dôɴ′ sä-nē-târ′) *n., pl.* **cor·dons sa·ni·taires** (kôr-dôɴ′ sä-nē-târ′). **1.** A barrier designed to prevent a disease or other undesirable condition from spreading. **2.** A chain of buffer states organized around a nation considered ideologically dangerous or potentially hostile. [French, quarantine line : *cordon,* line + *sanitaire,* sanitary.]

cor·do·van (kôr′də-vən) *n.* A fine leather originally made of goatskin but now more frequently of split horsehide. [Spanish *cordován,* from *Córdova,* Córdoba, Spain.]

cor·du·roy (kôr′də-roi′) *n.* **1.** A durable cut-pile fabric, usually made of cotton, with vertical ribs. **2. corduroys.** Trousers made of corduroy. **3.** A road made of logs laid down crosswise. **—corduroy** *adj.* **1.** Made of a fabric with vertical ribs. **2.** Made of logs laid down crosswise: *a corduroy road.* **—corduroy** *tr.v.* **-royed, -roy·ing, -roys.** To build (a road) of logs laid down crosswise. [Probably from CORD + obsolete *duroy,* a coarse woolen fabric.]

cord·wood (kôrd′wo͝od′) *n.* **1.** Wood cut and piled in cords. **2.** Wood sold by the cord.

core (kôr, kōr) *n.* **1.** The hard or fibrous central part of certain fruits, such as the apple or pear, containing the seeds. **2.** The

corbel

corbie-step

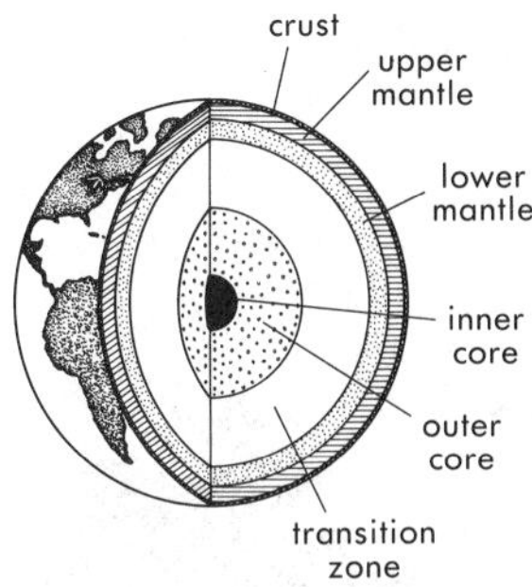

core
Cutaway view of Earth

ă **pat**	oi **boy**
ā **pay**	ou **out**
âr **care**	o͝o **took**
ä **father**	o͞o **boot**
ĕ **pet**	ŭ **cut**
ē **be**	ûr **urge**
ĭ **pit**	th **thin**
ī **pie**	*th* **this**
îr **pier**	hw **which**
ŏ **pot**	zh **vision**
ō **toe**	ə **about, item**
ô **paw**	♦ **regionalism**

Stress marks: ′ (primary); ′ (secondary), as in **dictionary** (dĭk′shə-nĕr′ē)

Corinth Canal
Across the Isthmus of Corinth

central or innermost part: *the hard elastic core of a baseball; a rod with a hollow core.* **3.** The basic or most important part; the essence: *a small core of dedicated supporters; the core of the problem.* See Synonyms at **substance. 4.** A set of subjects or courses that make up a required portion of a curriculum. **5.** *Electricity.* A soft iron rod in a coil or transformer that provides a path for and intensifies the magnetic field produced by the windings. **6. a.** *Computer Science.* A memory, especially one consisting of a series of tiny doughnut-shaped masses of magnetic material. Also called *core memory.* **b.** One of the magnetic doughnut-shaped masses that make up such a memory. Also called *magnetic core.* **7.** The central portion of Earth below the mantle, beginning at a depth of about 2,900 kilometers (1,800 miles) and probably consisting of iron and nickel. It is made up of a liquid outer core and a solid inner core. **8.** A mass of dry sand placed within a mold to provide openings or shape to a casting. **9.** The part of a nuclear reactor where fission occurs. **10.** A cylindrical mass drilled vertically into the earth and removed from it to determine composition or presence of oil or gas. **11.** The base, usually of soft or inferior wood, to which veneer woods are glued. **—core** *tr.v.* **cored, cor·ing, cores.** To remove the core of: *core apples.* [Middle English.]

CORE *abbr.* Congress of Racial Equality.

core dump *n. Computer Science.* A copy of the data stored in the core memory of a computer, usually on a device for external storage.

co·re·lig·ion·ist (kō′rĭ-lĭj′ə-nĭst) *n.* One having the same religion as another.

core memory *n. Computer Science.* See **core** (sense 6a).

cor·e·op·sis (kôr′ē-ŏp′sĭs, kōr-) *n.* Any of various plants of the genus *Coreopsis* in the composite family, especially the North American species, having showy radiate flower heads with yellow or, rarely, purplish flowers. Also called *tickseed.* [New Latin *Coreopsis,* genus name : Greek *koris,* bedbug; see **sker-¹** in Appendix + -OPSIS.]

Corinthian order

co·re·pres·sor (kō′rĭ-prĕs′ər) *n.* A substance that combines with and activates a genetic repressor, thus preventing gene transcription and inhibiting protein synthesis.

cor·er (kôr′ər, kōr′-) *n.* A device for coring apples.

co·re·spon·dent (kō′rĭ-spŏn′dənt) *n. Law.* A person charged with having committed adultery with the defendant in a divorce suit. **—co′re·spon′den·cy** *n.*

Cor·ey (kôr′ē), **Elias James.** Born 1928. American chemist. He won a 1990 Nobel Prize for developing techniques of creating synthetic compounds.

corf (kôrf) *n., pl.* **corves** (kôrvz). *Chiefly British.* A truck, tub, or basket used in a mine. [Middle English, basket, from Middle Dutch *corf* or Middle Low German *korf,* both probably from Latin *corbis.*]

Cor·fu (kôr′fo͞o, -fyo͞o, kôr-fo͞o′) also **Kér·ki·ra** (kĕr′kē-rä′). Formerly **Cor·cy·ra** (kôr-sī′rə). An island of Greece in the Ionian Islands off the northwest coast of the mainland. Settled c. 700 B.C., the island was controlled by Rome, Byzantium, Sicily, Venice, and Great Britain before being ceded to Greece in 1864.

cor·gi (kôr′gē) *n.* A Welsh corgi. [Welsh : *cor,* dwarf + *ci,* dog; see **kwon-** in Appendix.]

co·ri·a (kôr′ē-ə, kōr′-) *n.* Plural of **corium.**

cor·i·a·ceous (kôr′ē-ā′shəs, kŏr′-) *adj.* Of or like leather, especially in texture. [From Late Latin *coriāceus,* from Latin *corium,* leather. See **sker-¹** in Appendix.]

co·ri·an·der (kôr′ē-ăn′dər, kōr′-, kôr′ē-ăn′dər, kōr′-) *n.* **1.** An aromatic annual Eurasian herb *(Coriandrum sativum)* in the parsley family, having parsleylike leaves and umbels of tiny white to pinkish flowers. It is cultivated for its edible fruits, leafy shoots, and roots. **2.** The fresh, young, leafy plantlets of this herb, used in salads and various dishes as a flavoring and garnish. Also called *Chinese parsley, cilantro.* **3.** The seedlike fruit of this plant, used whole or ground as a flavoring for food and as a seasoning, as in curry powder. [Middle English *coriandre,* from Old French, from Latin *coriandrum,* from Greek *koriandron.*]

Cor·inth (kôr′ĭnth, kŏr′-) also **Kó·rin·thos** (kô′rĭn-thôs′). A city of southern Greece in the northeast Peloponnesus on the Gulf of Corinth. It is near the site of the ancient city of **Corinth,** which was founded in Homeric times. Population, 22,658.

Corinth, Gulf of. Formerly **Gulf of Le·pan·to** (lĭ-păn′tō, lĕ′-pän-tô). An inlet of the Ionian Sea between the Peloponnesus and central Greece.

Corinth, Isthmus of. A narrow isthmus connecting central Greece with the Peloponnesus. It lies between the Gulf of Corinth and the Saronic Sea and is crossed by the **Corinth Canal,** constructed from 1881 to 1893.

Co·rin·thi·an (kə-rĭn′thē-ən) *adj.* **1.** Of or relating to ancient Corinth or its people or culture. **2.** *Architecture.* Of or relating to the Corinthian order. **3.** Elegantly or elaborately ornate. **4.** Given to licentious and profligate luxury. **—Corinthian** *n.* **1.** A native or inhabitant of Corinth. **2.** A luxury-loving person; a bon vivant. **3.** A wealthy amateur sportsman, especially an amateur yachtsman. **4. Corinthians** *(used with a sing. verb). Abbr.* **Co, Cor.** *Bible.* See table at **Bible.**

Corinthian order *n. Architecture.* The most ornate of the three classical orders, characterized by a slender fluted column having an ornate bell-shaped capital decorated with acanthus leaves.

Co·ri·o·lis effect (kôr′ē-ō′lĭs, kōr′-) *n.* The observed effect of the Coriolis force, especially the deflection of an object moving above the earth, rightward in the northern hemisphere and leftward in the southern hemisphere.

Coriolis force *n.* An apparent force used mathematically to describe motion, as of aircraft or cloud formations, relative to a noninertial, uniformly rotating frame of reference such as Earth. [After Gaspard G. de *Coriolis* (1792–1843), French mathematician.]

co·ri·um (kôr′ē-əm, kōr′-) *n., pl.* **-ri·a** (-ē-ə). *Anatomy.* See **dermis.** [Latin, skin. See **sker-¹** in Appendix.]

cork (kôrk) *n.* **1.** The lightweight, elastic outer bark of the cork oak, used especially for bottle closures, insulation, floats, and crafts. **2. a.** Something made of cork, especially a bottle stopper. **b.** A bottle stopper made of other material, such as plastic. **3.** A small float used on a fishing line or net to buoy up the line or net or to indicate when a fish bites. **4.** *Botany.* A nonliving, water-resistant protective tissue that is formed on the outside of the cork cambium in the woody stems and roots of many seed plants. In this sense, also called *phellem.* **—cork** *tr.v.* **corked, cork·ing, corks. 1.** To stop or seal with or as if with a cork. **2.** To restrain or check; hold back: *tried to cork my anger.* **3.** To blacken with burnt cork. [Middle English, from Dutch *kurk* or Low German *korck,* both from Spanish *alcorque,* cork-soled shoe, probably from Arabic dialectal *al-qūrq,* from Latin *quercus,* oak. See **perkʷu-** in Appendix.]

Cork (kôrk). A city of southern Ireland near the head of **Cork Harbor,** an inlet of the Atlantic Ocean. Cork was occupied by the Danes in the ninth century and by Oliver Cromwell in 1649. Population, 136,344.

cork·age (kôr′kĭj) *n.* A charge exacted at a restaurant for every bottle of liquor served that was not bought on the premises.

cork·board (kôrk′bôrd′, -bōrd′) *n.* A construction and insulating sheet material made of compressed and baked granules of cork.

cork cambium *n. Botany.* A lateral ring of meristematic tissue found in woody seed plants, producing cork on the outside of the ring and parenchyma on the inside of the ring. Also called *phellogen.*

corked (kôrkt) *adj.* **1.** Sealed with or as if with a cork. **2.** Tainted in flavor by an unsound cork: *corked port.* **3.** Blackened by burnt cork.

cork·er (kôr′kər) *n.* **1.** One that corks bottles, for example. **2.** *Slang.* A remarkable or astounding person or thing.

cork·ing (kôr′kĭng) *Slang. adj.* Splendid; fine: *a corking party.* **—corking** *adv.* Used as an intensive: *a corking good story.* [From CORKER.]

cork oak *n.* A Mediterranean evergreen oak tree *(Quercus suber)* having thick bark that is periodically stripped, yielding commercial cork. Also called *cork tree.*

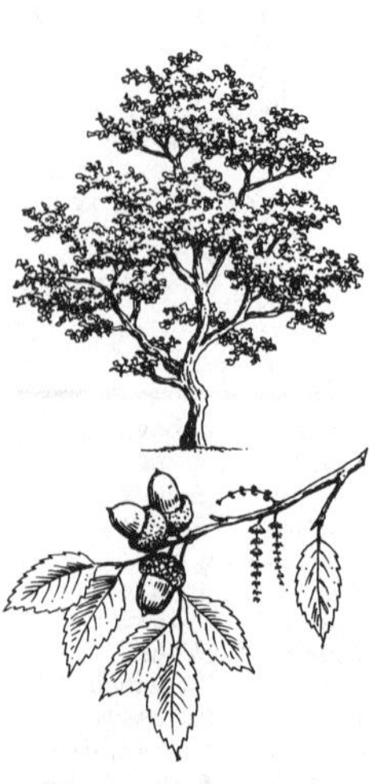

cork oak
Quercus suber

cork·screw (kôrk′skro͞o′) *n.* A device for drawing corks from bottles, consisting of a pointed metal spiral attached to a handle. **—corkscrew** *adj.* Spiral in shape. **—corkscrew** *intr. & tr.v.* **-screwed, -screw·ing, -screws.** To move or cause to move in a spiral or winding course.

cork tree *n.* **1.** See **cork oak. 2.** Any of various deciduous trees of the genus *Phellodendron* native to eastern Asia and cultivated as an ornamental, especially *P. amurense,* having deeply furrowed, thick, corky bark.

cork·wood (kôrk′wo͝od′) *n.* **1.** A deciduous shrub or small tree *(Leitneria floridana)* native to wet regions of the southeast United States and having soft, lightweight wood. **2.** See **balsa** (sense 1). **3.** Any of certain Australian shrubs or small trees of the genus *Duboisia* having leaves used for the commercial extraction of belladonna alkaloids.

cork·y (kôr′kē) *adj.* **-i·er, -i·est. 1.** Of or resembling cork. **2.** *Informal.* Lively; buoyant. **—cork′i·ness** *n.*

corm (kôrm) *n.* A short, thick, solid, food-storing underground stem, sometimes bearing papery scale leaves, as in the crocus or gladiolus. [New Latin *cormus,* from Greek *kormos,* a trimmed tree trunk. See **sker-¹** in Appendix.]

cor·mel (kôr′məl, kôr-mĕl′) *n.* A small young corm produced by a fully developed corm. [CORM + *-el,* diminutive suff. (from Latin *-ellus*).]

cor·mo·rant (kôr′mər-ənt, -mə-rănt′) *n.* **1.** Any of several large, widely distributed marine diving birds of the genus *Phalacrocorax,* having dark plumage, webbed feet, a slender hooked bill, and a distensible pouch. **2.** A greedy, rapacious person. **—cormorant** *adj.* Greedy; rapacious. [Middle English *cormoraunt,* from Old French *cormorant* : *corp,* raven; see CORBEL + *marenc,* of the sea (from Latin *marīnus;* see MARINE).]

corn¹ (kôrn) *n.* **1. a.** Any of numerous cultivated forms of a widely grown, usually tall annual cereal grass *(Zea mays)* bearing grains or kernels on large ears. **b.** The grains or kernels of this plant, used as food for human beings and livestock or for the extraction of an edible oil or starch. **c.** An ear of this plant. Also called *Indian corn, maize.* **2.** *Chiefly British.* Any of various cereal plants or grains, especially the principal crop cultivated in a particular region, such as wheat in England or oats in Scotland. **3. a.** A single grain of a cereal plant. **b.** A seed or fruit of various other plants, such as a peppercorn. **4.** Corn snow. **5.** *Informal.* Corn whiskey. **6.** *Slang.* Something considered trite, dated, melodramatic, or unduly sentimental. **—corn** *v.* **corned, corn·ing, corns.** *—tr.* **1.** To cause to form hard particles; granulate. **2. a.**

To season and preserve with granulated salt. **b.** To preserve (beef, for example) in brine. **3.** To feed (animals) with corn or grain. —*intr.* To form hard particles; become grainy: *"After the snow melts all day, it corns up at night for fine conditions"* (Hatfield MA Valley Advocate). [Middle English, grain, from Old English. See **gr̥-no-** in Appendix.]

corn² (kôrn) *n.* A horny thickening of the skin, usually on or near a toe, resulting from pressure or friction. Also called *clavus.* [Middle English *corne,* from Old French, horn, from Latin *cornū.* See **ker-¹** in Appendix.]

corn·ball (kôrn′bôl′) *Slang. n.* One who behaves in a mawkish or unsophisticated manner. —**cornball** *adj.* Mawkish or unsophisticated; corny: *a kid's cornball humor.* [From *corn ball,* a ball of popcorn and molasses.]

Corn Belt (kôrn). An agricultural region of the central United States primarily in Iowa and Illinois but also including parts of Indiana, Minnesota, South Dakota, Nebraska, Kansas, Missouri, and Ohio.

corn borer *n.* **1.** The larva of a European moth *(Pyrausta nubilalis),* now common in many areas of eastern North America, that feeds on and destroys corn and other plants, including potatoes and beans. Also called *European corn borer.* **2.** Any of various insect larvae similar to the corn borer that infest corn.

corn·braid (kôrn′brād′) *tr.v.* **-braid·ed, -braid·ing, -braids.** To style (hair) in rows of thin braids; cornrow —**corn′braid′** *n.*

corn bread or **corn·bread** (kôrn′brĕd′) *n.* Bread made from cornmeal.

♦**corn cake** or **corn·cake** (kôrn′kāk′) *n. Chiefly Southern U.S.* See **johnnycake.** See Regional Note at **johnnycake.**

corn chip *n.* A thin, crisp piece of food made from cornmeal batter.

corn·cob (kôrn′kŏb′) *n.* **1.** The hard, thick, cylindrical central core on which are borne the grains or kernels of an ear of corn, usually in rows. **2.** A corncob pipe.

corncob pipe *n.* A pipe with a bowl made of a dried, hollowed corncob.

corn cockle *n.* A weedy annual Mediterranean plant *(Agrostemma githago)* having reddish-purple flowers and opposite leaves.

corn·crake (kôrn′krāk′) *n.* A common Eurasian bird *(Crex crex)* with a short bill and brownish-yellow plumage, found in grain fields and meadows.

corn·crib (kôrn′krĭb′) *n.* A structure for storing and drying ears of corn.

♦**corn·dodg·er** (kôrn′dŏj′ər) *n. Chiefly Southern U.S.* A small, round ball of cornmeal, flour, milk, oil, and sugar that is fried in deep fat. Also called ♦*dodger.*

cor·ne·a (kôr′nē-ə) *n.* The transparent, convex, anterior portion of the outer fibrous coat of the eyeball that covers the iris and the pupil and is continuous with the sclera. [Medieval Latin *cornea (tēla),* horny (tissue), from Latin *corneus,* horny, from *cornū,* horn. See **ker-¹** in Appendix.] —**cor′ne·al** (-əl) *adj.*

corn earworm *n.* The large, destructive larva of a moth *(Heliothis zea)* that feeds on corn and many other plants. Also called *bollworm, earworm.*

Cor·neille (kôr-nā′), **Pierre.** 1606–1684. French playwright whose works, including *Le Cid* (c. 1637) and *Horace* (1640), dramatize grand moral themes within elegant verse.

cor·ne·i·tis (kôr′nē-ī′tĭs) *n.* Inflammation of the cornea.

cor·nel (kôr′nəl, -nĕl′) *n.* Any of various plants of the genus *Cornus,* which includes the bunchberry and dogwoods. [Short for German *Kornelbaum* (from Old High German *curnil-*) or from French *cornouille,* both from Medieval Latin *corniola,* from diminutive of Latin *cornus.*]

cor·nel·ian (kôr-nēl′yən) *n.* Variant of **carnelian.**

cornelian cherry *n.* **1.** A deciduous Eurasian shrub or small tree *(Cornus mas)* cultivated for its clusters of early blooming, small yellow flowers and cherrylike, edible, sour fruits. **2.** The fruit of this plant, used for jellies and preserves. [From CORNEL.]

Cor·ne·lius (kôr-nēl′yəs, -nāl′-, -nā′lē-o͝os′), **Peter von.** 1783–1867. German painter known for his frescoes and recognized as a leader of the new school of German art.

Cor·nell (kôr-nĕl′), **Ezra.** 1807–1874. American businessman and philanthropist who helped develop and unify telegraph systems in the United States and founded Cornell University (1865) with Andrew D. White.

Cornell, Katharine. 1893–1974. American actress known for her Broadway performances in *A Bill of Divorcement* (1921) and *The Barretts of Wimpole Street* (1931).

cor·ne·ous (kôr′nē-əs) *adj.* Made of horn or a hornlike substance; horny. [From Latin *corneus,* from *cornū,* horn. See **ker-¹** in Appendix.]

cor·ner (kôr′nər) *n. Abbr.* **cor. 1.a.** The position at which two lines, surfaces, or edges meet and form an angle: *the four corners of a rectangle.* **b.** The area enclosed or bounded by an angle formed in this manner: *sat by myself in the corner; the corner of one's eye.* **2.** The place where two roads or streets join or intersect. **3.a.** *Sports.* Any of the four angles of a boxing or wrestling ring where the ropes are joined. **b.** *Baseball.* Either side of home plate, toward or away from the batter. **4.** A threatening or embarrassing position from which escape is difficult: *got myself into a corner by boasting.* **5.** A remote, secluded, or secret place: *the four corners of the earth; a beautiful little corner of Paris.* **6.** A part or piece made to fit on a corner, as in mounting or for protection. **7.a.** A speculative monopoly of a stock or commodity created by purchasing all or most of the available supply in order to raise its price. **b.** Exclusive possession; monopoly: *"Neither party . . . has a corner on all the good ideas"* (George B. Merry). —**corner** *v.* **-nered, -ner·ing, -ners.** —*tr.* **1.** To furnish with corners. **2.** To place or drive into a corner: *cornered the thieves and captured them.* **3.** To form a corner in (a stock or commodity): *cornered the silver market.* —*intr.* **1.** To come together or be situated on or at a corner. **2.** To turn, as at a corner: *a truck that corners poorly.* —**corner** *adj.* **1.** Located at a street corner: *a corner drugstore.* **2.** Designed for use in a corner: *a corner table.* [Middle English, from Anglo-Norman, from Old French *corne,* corner, horn, from Vulgar Latin **corna,* from Latin *cornua,* pl. of *cornū,* horn, point. See **ker-¹** in Appendix.]

cor·ner·back also **corner back** (kôr′nər-băk′) *n. Football.* Either of two defensive halfbacks stationed a short distance behind the linebackers and relatively near the sidelines.

Cor·ner Brook (kôr′nər). A city of west-central Newfoundland, Canada, on an estuary emptying into the Gulf of St. Lawrence. Population, 24,339.

cor·ner·stone also **corner stone** (kôr′nər-stōn′) *n.* **1.a.** A stone at the corner of a building uniting two intersecting walls; a quoin. **b.** Such a stone, often inscribed, laid at a ceremony marking the origin of a building. **2.** An indispensable and fundamental basis: *the cornerstone of an argument.*

cor·ner·wise (kôr′nər-wīz′) also **cor·ner·ways** (-wāz′) *adv.* **1.** With a corner toward the front. **2.** So as to form a corner. **3.** From corner to corner; diagonally.

cor·net (kôr-nĕt′) *n.* **1.** *Abbr.* **cor.** *Music.* A wind instrument of the trumpet class, having three valves operated by pistons. **2.** (*also* kôr′nĭt). A piece of paper twisted into a cone and used to hold small wares such as candy or nuts. **3.** (*also* kôr′nĭt). A headdress, often cone-shaped, worn by women in the 12th and 13th centuries. [Middle English, from Old French, diminutive of *corn,* horn, from Latin *cornū.* See **ker-¹** in Appendix.]

cor·net-à-pis·tons (kôr-nĕt′ə-pĭs′tənz) *n., pl.* **cor·nets-à-pis·tons** (kôr-nĕts′ə-pĭs′tənz). *Music.* A cornet. [French : *cornet,* horn, trumpet + *à,* with + *pistons,* valves.]

cor·net·ist also **cor·net·tist** (kôr-nĕt′ĭst) *n. Music.* One who plays a cornet.

corn-fed (kôrn′fĕd′) *adj.* **1.** Fed on corn: *corn-fed pigs.* **2.** *Slang.* Healthy and strong, but provincial and unsophisticated.

corn flakes *pl.n.* A crisp, flaky, commercially prepared cold cereal made from coarse cornmeal.

corn·flow·er (kôrn′flou′ər) *n.* An annual Eurasian plant *(Centaurea cyanus)* in the composite family, cultivated and also naturalized in North America and having showy heads of blue, purple, pink, or white flowers. Also called *bachelor's button.* [So called because it is found in cornfields.]

corn·husk (kôrn′hŭsk′) *n.* The leafy husk of an ear of corn.

corn·husk·ing (kôrn′hŭs′kĭng) *n.* **1.** The husking of corn. **2.** A social gathering for husking corn. In this sense, also called *husking bee.* —**corn′husk′er** *n.*

cor·nice (kôr′nĭs) *n.* **1.a.** A horizontal molded projection that crowns or completes a building or wall. **b.** The uppermost part of an entablature. **2.** The molding at the top of the walls of a room, between the walls and ceiling. **3.** An ornamental horizontal molding or frame used to conceal rods, picture hooks, or other devices. —**cornice** *tr.v.* **-niced, -nic·ing, -nic·es.** To supply, decorate, or finish with or as if with a cornice. [Obsolete French, from Italian, possibly from Latin *cornīx, cornīc-,* crow, from its resemblance to a crow's beak (influenced by Greek *korōnis,* curved line, flourish, from *korōnos,* curved. See CROWN).]

cor·ni·cle (kôr′nĭ-kəl) *n.* See **siphuncle** (sense 2). [Latin *corniculum,* little horn. See CORNICULATE.]

cor·nic·u·late (kôr-nĭk′yə-lāt′, -lĭt) *adj.* Having horns or hornlike projections. [Latin *corniculātus,* from *corniculum,* diminutive of *cornū,* horn. See **ker-¹** in Appendix.]

cor·ni·fi·ca·tion (kôr′nə-fĭ-kā′shən) *n.* The conversion of squamous epithelial cells into a keratinized, horny material, such as hair, nails, or feathers. [Latin *cornū,* horn; see **ker-¹** in Appendix + -FICATION.]

cor·ni·fy (kôr′nə-fī′) *intr.v.* **-fied, -fy·ing, -fies.** To undergo cornification.

Cor·nish (kôr′nĭsh) *adj.* Of or relating to Cornwall, its people, or the Cornish language. —**Cornish** *n.* **1.** The Brythonic language of Cornwall, which has been extinct since the late 18th century. **2.** Any of an English breed of domestic fowl often crossbred to produce roasters.

Cor·nish·man (kôr′nĭsh-mən) *n.* A man who is a native or inhabitant of Cornwall, England.

Cor·nish·wom·an (kôr′nĭsh-wo͝om′ən) *n.* A woman who is a native or inhabitant of Cornwall, England.

Corn Law *n.* One of a series of British laws in force before 1846 regulating the grain trade and restricting imports of grain.

corn lily *n.* Any of various bulbous herbs of the genus *Ixia* native to southern Africa and widely cultivated as an ornamental, having grasslike leaves and showy clusters of variously colored flowers.

corn·meal also **corn meal** (kôrn′mēl′) *n.* Meal made from corn, used in a wide variety of foods. Also called *Indian meal.*

cormorant
Double-crested cormorant
Phalacrocorax auritus

cornet
c. 1840 brass
valve cornet

ă pat	oi boy
ā pay	ou out
âr care	o͝o took
ä father	o͞o boot
ĕ pet	ŭ cut
ē be	ûr urge
ĭ pit	th thin
ī pie	*th* this
îr pier	hw which
ŏ pot	zh vision
ō toe	ə about, item
ô paw	♦ regionalism

Stress marks: ′ (primary); ′ (secondary), as in **dictionary** (dĭk′shə-nĕr′ē)

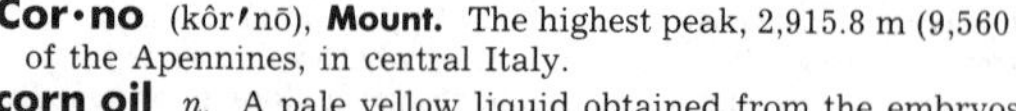

Cor•no (kôr′nō), **Mount.** The highest peak, 2,915.8 m (9,560 ft), of the Apennines, in central Italy.

corn oil *n.* A pale yellow liquid obtained from the embryos of corn grains, used especially as a cooking and salad oil and in the manufacture of margarines.

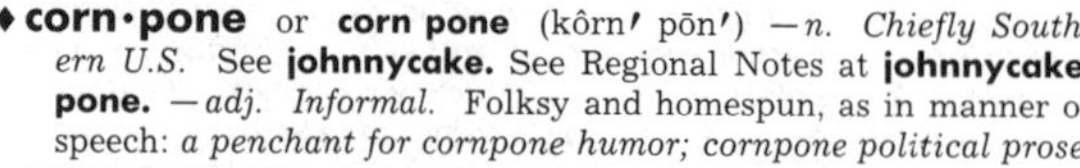

♦**corn•pone** or **corn pone** (kôrn′ pōn′) —*n. Chiefly Southern U.S.* See **johnnycake.** See Regional Notes at **johnnycake, pone.** —*adj. Informal.* Folksy and homespun, as in manner or speech: *a penchant for cornpone humor; cornpone political prose.*

corn poppy *n.* An annual Eurasian plant *(Papaver rhoeas)* naturalized in North America and having showy, usually scarlet flowers.

cornrow

corn•row (kôrn′rō′) *tr.v.* To arrange or style (hair) by dividing into sections and braiding close to the scalp in rows. —**corn′row′** *n.*

corn salad *n.* Any of several plants of the genus *Valerianella,* especially a Eurasian annual *(V. locusta* or *V. olitoria),* having small, white to pale bluish flowers and edible young leaves used in salads or as a potherb. Also called *lamb's lettuce, mache.*

corn silk *n.* The styles and stigmas that appear as a silky tuft or tassel at the tip of an ear of corn, used as a diuretic in herbal medicine.

corn snow *n.* Snow that has melted and refrozen into a rough, granular surface.

corn•stalk also **corn stalk** (kôrn′stôk′) *n.* The stalk or stem of a corn plant.

corn•starch (kôrn′stärch′) *n.* Starch prepared from corn grains, used industrially and as a thickener in cooking.

corn sugar *n.* Dextrose obtained from cornstarch.

corn syrup *n.* A syrup prepared from cornstarch, used in industry and in numerous food products as a sweetener.

cor•nu (kôr′no͞o, -nyo͞o) *n., pl.* **-nu•a** (-no͞o-ə, -nyo͞o-ə). A part or structure, such as a bony protuberance, that resembles a horn. [Latin *cornū,* horn. See **ker-**[1] in Appendix.] —**cor′nu•al** (-əl) *adj.*

cornucopia
Detail of a c. 1770–1780 wall painting at Marmion plantation in Virginia

cor•nu•co•pi•a (kôr′nə-kō′pē-ə, -nyə-) *n.* **1.** A goat's horn overflowing with fruit, flowers, and grain, signifying prosperity. Also called *horn of plenty.* **2.** *Greek Mythology.* The horn of the goat that suckled Zeus, which broke off and became filled with fruit. In folklore, it became full of whatever its owner desired. **3.** A cone-shaped ornament or receptacle. **4.** An overflowing store; an abundance: *a cornucopia of employment opportunities.* [Late Latin *cornūcōpia,* from Latin *cornū cōpiae* : *cornū,* horn; see CORNU + *cōpiae,* genitive of *cōpia,* plenty; see **op-** in Appendix.] —**cor′nu•co′pi•an** *adj.*

cor•nute (kôr-no͞ot′, -nyo͞ot′) also **cor•nut•ed** (-no͞o′tĭd, -nyo͞o′-) *adj.* **1.** Shaped like a horn. **2.** Having horns or horn-shaped processes. [Latin *cornūtus,* from *cornū,* horn. See CORNU.]

Corn•wall (kôrn′wôl′). **1.** A region of extreme southwest England on a peninsula bounded by the Atlantic Ocean and English Channel. Its tin and copper mines were known to ancient Greek traders. **2.** A city of southeast Ontario, Canada, on the St. Lawrence River and the New York border southeast of Ottawa. It is a manufacturing center. Population, 46,144.

Corn•wal•lis (kôrn-wŏl′ĭs, -wô′lĭs), **Charles.** First Marquis and Second Earl Cornwallis. 1738–1805. British military and political leader who commanded forces in North Carolina during the American Revolution. His surrender at Yorktown in 1781 marked the final British defeat.

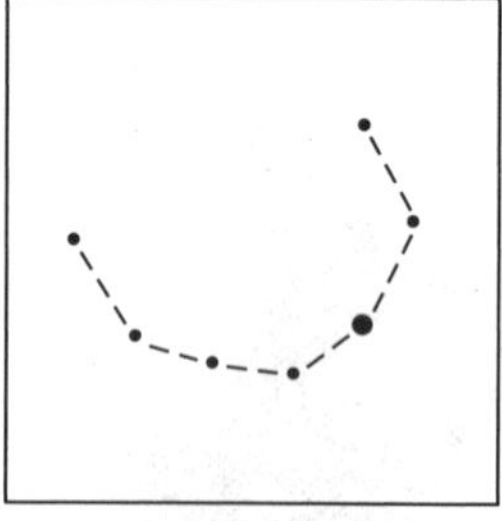

Corona Borealis

corn whiskey *n.* Whiskey distilled from corn.

corn•y (kôr′nē) *adj.* **-i•er, -i•est.** Trite, dated, melodramatic, or mawkishly sentimental. [From CORN[1].] —**corn′i•ly** *adv.* —**corn′i•ness** *n.*

corol. *abbr.* Corollary.

co•rol•la (kə-rŏl′ə, -rō′lə) *n. Botany.* The petals of a flower considered as a group or unit. [Latin, small garland, diminutive of *corōna,* garland. See CORONA.] —**co•rol′late′** (-rŏl′āt′) *adj.*

cor•ol•lar•y (kôr′ə-lĕr-ē, kŏr′-) *n., pl.* **-ies.** *Abbr.* **corol. 1.** A proposition that follows with little or no proof required from one already proven. **2.** A deduction or an inference. **3.** A natural consequence or effect; a result. —**corollary** *adj.* Consequent; resultant. [Middle English *corolarie,* from Latin *corollārium,* money paid for a garland, gratuity, from *corolla,* small garland. See COROLLA.]

Cor•o•man•del Coast (kôr′ə-măn′dl). A region of southeast India bounded by the Bay of Bengal and the Eastern Ghats.

coronation
Coronation of Elizabeth II, Westminster Abbey, June 2, 1953

co•ro•na (kə-rō′nə) *n., pl.* **-nas** or **-nae** (-nē). **1.** *Astronomy.* **a.** A faintly colored luminous ring appearing to surround a celestial body visible through a haze or thin cloud, especially such a ring around the moon or sun, caused by diffraction of light from suspended matter in the intervening medium. Also called *aureole.* **b.** The luminous, irregular envelope of highly ionized gas outside the chromosphere of the sun. **2.** *Architecture.* The projecting top part of a cornice. **3.** A cigar with a long, tapering body and blunt ends. **4.** *Anatomy.* The crownlike upper portion of a bodily part or structure, such as the top of the head. **5.** *Botany.* A crown-shaped, funnel-shaped, or trumpet-shaped outgrowth or appendage of the perianth of certain flowers, such as the daffodil or the spider lily. Also called *crown.* **6.** *Electricity.* A faint glow enveloping the high-field electrode in a corona discharge, often accompanied by streamers directed toward the low-field electrode. [Latin *corōna.* See CROWN.]

Co•ro•na (kə-rō′nə). A city of southern California southwest of Riverside. It is a manufacturing center in a citrus-growing area. Population, 37,791.

Corona Aus•tra•lis (ô-strā′lĭs) *n.* A constellation in the Southern Hemisphere near Telescopium and Sagittarius. Also called *Southern Crown.* [Latin *Corōna austrālis* : *corōna,* crown + *austrālis,* southern.]

Corona Bo•re•al•is (bôr′ē-ăl′ĭs, -ā′lĭs, bōr′ē-) *n.* A constellation in the Northern Hemisphere between Hercules and Boötes. Also called *Northern Crown.* [Latin *Corōna boreālis* : *corōna,* crown + *boreālis,* northern.]

corona discharge *n.* An electrical discharge characterized by a corona and occurring when one of two electrodes in a gas has a shape causing the electric field at its surface to be significantly greater than that between the electrodes.

Cor•o•na•do (kôr′ə-nä′dō, kŏr′-). A city of southern California on a narrow spit of land west of San Diego. It is a popular tourist resort. Population, 18,790.

Co•ro•na•do (kôr′ə-nä′dō, kōr′-, kô′rô-nä′*th*ô), **Francisco Vásquez de.** 1510–1554. Spanish explorer who in his quest for the fabled Seven Cities of Cibola was the first to explore Arizona and New Mexico.

co•ro•nae (kə-rō′nē) *n.* A plural of **corona.**

co•ro•na•graph also **co•ro•no•graph** (kə-rō′nə-grăf′) *n.* A telescope or an attachment for a telescope equipped with a disk that blacks out most of the sun, used to photograph the sun's corona.

cor•o•nal (kôr′ə-nəl, kŏr′-, kə-rō′nəl) *n.* A garland, wreath, or circlet for the head. —**coronal** *adj.* **1.** Of or relating to a corona, especially of the head. **2.** Of, relating to, or having the direction of the coronal suture or of the plane dividing the body into front and back portions. [Middle English, from Latin *corōnālis,* of a crown, from *corōna,* crown. See CROWN.]

coronal suture *n. Anatomy.* The suture extending across the skull between the two parietal bones and the frontal bone.

cor•o•nar•y (kôr′ə-nĕr′ē, kŏr′-) *adj.* **1.** Of, relating to, or being the coronary arteries or coronary veins. **2.** Of or relating to the heart. —**coronary** *n., pl.* **-ies.** A coronary thrombosis. [Latin *corōnārius,* of a crown, from *corōna,* crown. See CROWN.]

coronary artery *n.* Either of two arteries that originate in the aorta and supply blood to the muscular tissue of the heart.

coronary bypass surgery A surgical procedure performed to improve blood supply to the heart by creating new routes for blood flow when one or more of the coronary arteries become obstructed. The surgery involves removing a healthy blood vessel from another part of the body, such as the leg, and grafting it onto the heart to circumvent the blocked artery.

coronary care unit *n. Abbr.* **CCU** A hospital unit that is specially equipped to treat patients with serious heart conditions, such as coronary thrombosis.

coronary occlusion *n.* The partial or complete obstruction of blood flow in a coronary artery, as by a thrombus or the progressive buildup of atherosclerotic plaque.

coronary sinus *n.* A venous sinus that opens into the right atrium of the heart and serves to drain the coronary veins.

coronary thrombosis *n.* Obstruction of a coronary artery by a thrombus, often leading to destruction of heart muscle.

coronary vein *n.* Any one of the veins that drains blood from the muscular tissue of the heart and empties into the coronary sinus.

cor•o•na•tion (kôr′ə-nā′shən, kŏr′-) *n.* The act or ceremony of crowning a sovereign or the sovereign's consort. [Middle English *coronacioun,* from Medieval Latin *corōnātiō, corōnātiōn-,* from Latin *corōnātus,* past participle of *corōnāre,* to crown, from *corōna,* crown. See CROWN.]

cor•o•ner (kôr′ə-nər, kŏr′-) *n. Abbr.* **cor.** A public officer whose primary function is to investigate by inquest any death thought to be of other than natural causes. [Middle English, officer of the crown, from Anglo-Norman *corouner,* from *coroune,* crown, from Latin *corōna.* See CROWN.] —**cor′o•ner•ship′** *n.*

WORD HISTORY: *Coroner* comes from Anglo-Norman *corouner,* a word derived from *coroune,* "crown." *Corouner* was the term used for the royal judicial officer who was called in Latin *custos placitorum coronae,* or "guardian of the crown's pleas." The person holding the office of coroner, a position dating from the 12th century, was charged with keeping local records of legal proceedings in which the crown had jurisdiction. He helped raise money for the crown by funneling the property of executed criminals into the king's treasury. The coroner also investigated any suspicious deaths among the Normans, who as the ruling class wanted to be sure that their deaths were not taken lightly. At one time in England all criminal proceedings were included in the coroner's responsibilities. Over the years these responsibilities decreased markedly, but coroners have continued to display morbid curiosity. In the United States, where there is no longer the crown, a coroner's main duty is the investigation of any sudden, violent, or unexpected death that may not have had a natural cause.

cor•o•net (kôr′ə-nĕt′, kŏr′-) *n.* **1.** A small crown worn by princes and princesses and by other nobles below the rank of sovereign. **2.** A chaplet or headband decorated with gold or jewels. **3.** The upper margin of a horse's hoof. [Middle English *coronette,* from Old French, diminutive of *corone,* crown. See CROWN.]

co·ro·no·graph (kə-rō′nə-grăf′) *n.* Variant of **coronagraph.**

Co·rot (kô-rō′, kə-), **Jean Baptiste Camille.** 1796–1875. French painter noted for his sketches of Italian landscapes.

co·ro·tate (kō-rō′tāt′) *intr.v.* **-tat·ed, -tat·ing, -tates.** To rotate in conjunction with another body. **—co′ro·ta′tion** *n.* **—co′ro·ta′tion·al** *adj.*

corp. *abbr.* Corporation.

cor·poc·ra·cy (kôr-pŏk′rə-sē) *n., pl.* **-cies. 1.** Corporate bureaucracy. **2.** A company characterized by top-heavy, isolated, risk-averse management, excess paperwork, low productivity, poor interdepartmental communication, and lack of imagination, especially in product development and marketing. [CORPO(RATE) + (BUREAU)CRACY.] **—cor′po·crat′ic** (-pə-krăt′ĭk) *adj.*

cor·po·ra (kôr′pər-ə) *n.* Plural of **corpus.**

corpora cal·lo·sa (kə-lō′-sə) *n. Anatomy.* Plural of **corpus callosum.**

cor·po·ral[1] (kôr′pər-əl, kôr′prəl) *adj.* Of or relating to the body. See Synonyms at **bodily.** [Middle English, from Old French, from Latin *corporālis,* from *corpus, corpor-,* body. See **kʷrep-** in Appendix.] **—cor′po·ral′i·ty** (-pə-răl′ĭ-tē) *n.* **—cor′po·ral·ly** *adv.*

cor·po·ral[2] (kôr′pər-əl, kôr′prəl) *n. Abbr.* **Cpl. 1.** A noncommissioned rank in the U.S. Army that is above private first class and below sergeant or in the U.S. Marine Corps that is above lance corporal and below sergeant. **2.** One who holds this rank. [Obsolete French, alteration of *caporal,* from Old Italian *caporale,* from *capo,* head, from Latin *caput.* See **kaput-** in Appendix.]

cor·po·ral[3] (kôr′pər-əl, kôr′prəl) *n. Ecclesiastical.* A white linen cloth on which the consecrated elements are placed during the celebration of the Eucharist. [Middle English, from Old French and from Medieval Latin *corporāle,* both from Latin *corporālis,* of the body (the Eucharistic bread being representative of Christ's body), from *corpus, corpor-,* body. See **kʷrep-** in Appendix.]

corpora lu·te·a (lo͞o′tē-ə) *n.* Plural of **corpus luteum.**

corpora stri·a·ta (strī-ā′tə) *n. Anatomy.* Plural of **corpus striatum.**

cor·po·rate (kôr′pər-ĭt, kôr′prĭt) *adj.* **1.** Formed into a corporation; incorporated. **2.** Of or relating to a corporation: *corporate assets; corporate culture.* **3.** United or combined into one body; collective: *made a corporate effort to finish the job.* **4.** Corporative. [Latin *corporātus,* past participle of *corporāre,* to make into a body, from *corpus,* body. See **kʷrep-** in Appendix.] **—cor′po·rate·ly** *adv.*

cor·po·ra·tion (kôr′pə-rā′shən) *n. Abbr.* **corp. 1.** A body that is granted a charter legally recognizing it as a separate legal entity having its own rights, privileges, and liabilities distinct from those of its members. **2.** Such a body created for purposes of government. Also called *body corporate.* **3.** A group of people combined into or acting as one body.

cor·po·ra·tive (kôr′pər-ə-tĭv, -pə-rā′tĭv) *adj.* **1.** Of, relating to, or associated with a corporation. **2.** Of or relating to a government or political system in which the principal economic functions, such as banking, industry, labor, and government, are organized as corporate entities.

cor·po·ra·tor (kôr′pə-rā′tər) *n.* A member of a corporation.

cor·po·re·al (kôr-pôr′ē-əl, -pōr′-) *adj.* **1.** Of, relating to, or characteristic of the body. See Synonyms at **bodily. 2.** Of a material nature; tangible. [From Latin *corporeus,* from *corpus, corpor-,* body. See **kʷrep-** in Appendix.] **—cor·po′re·al′i·ty** (-al′ĭ-tē), **cor·po′re·al·ness** *n.* **—cor·po′re·al·ly** *adv.*

cor·po·re·i·ty (kôr′pə-rē′ĭ-tē, -rā′-) *n.* The state of being material or corporeal; physical existence.

cor·po·sant (kôr′pə-zănt) *n.* See **Saint Elmo's fire.** [Portuguese and obsolete Spanish *corpo santo,* both from Latin *corpus sanctum,* holy body : *corpus,* body; see **kʷrep-** in Appendix + *sanctus,* holy, past participle of *sancīre,* to consecrate; see **sak-** in Appendix.]

corps (kôr, kōr) *n., pl.* **corps** (kôrz, kōrz). **1.** *Abbr.* **c., C. a.** A separate branch or department of the armed forces having a specialized function. **b.** A tactical unit of ground combat forces between a division and an army commanded by a lieutenant general and composed of two or more divisions and auxiliary service troops. **2.** A body of persons acting together or associated under common direction: *the press corps.* See Synonyms at **band[2].** [French, from Old French, from Latin *corpus,* body. See **kʷrep-** in Appendix.]

corps de bal·let (kôr′ də bă-lā′, kōr′) *n.* The dancers in a ballet troupe who perform as a group. [French : *corps,* corps + *de,* of + *ballet,* ballet.]

corpse (kôrps) *n.* A dead body, especially the dead body of a human being. See Synonyms at **body.** [Middle English *corps,* from Latin *corpus.* See **kʷrep-** in Appendix.]

corps·man (kôr′mən, kōr′-, kôrz′mən, kōrz′-) *n.* **1.** An enlisted person in the armed forces who has been trained to give first aid and basic medical treatment, especially in combat situations. **2.** A member of a government-sponsored group designated as a corps: *Peace Corpsmen.*

cor·pu·lence (kôr′pyə-ləns) *n.* The condition of being excessively fat; obesity. [Middle English, corporality, from Latin *corpulentia,* corpulence, from *corpulentus,* corpulent, from *corpus,* body. See **kʷrep-** in Appendix.]

cor·pu·lent (kôr′pyə-lənt) *adj.* Excessively fat. See Synonyms at **fat. —cor′pu·lent·ly** *adv.*

cor pul·mo·na·le (kôr′ po͝ol′mə-nä′lē, -năl′ē, pŭl′-) *n.* Acute strain or hypertrophy of the right ventricle caused by a disorder of the lungs or of the pulmonary blood vessels. [New Latin : Latin *cor,* heart + New Latin *pulmōnālis,* of the lungs.]

cor·pus (kôr′pəs) *n., pl.* **-po·ra** (-pər-ə). *Abbr.* **cor. 1.** A large collection of writings of a specific kind or on a specific subject. **2.** The principal or capital, as distinguished from the interest or income, as of a fund or estate. **3.** *Anatomy.* **a.** The main part of a bodily structure or organ. **b.** A distinct bodily mass or organ having a specific function. **4.** *Music.* The overall length of a violin. [Middle English, from Latin. See **kʷrep-** in Appendix.]

corpus al·bi·cans (ăl′bĭ-kănz′) *n.* The white fibrous scar tissue in an ovary that results after the involution and regression of the corpus luteum. [New Latin : Latin *corpus,* body + New Latin *albicāns,* whitening.]

corpus cal·lo·sum (kə-lō′səm) *n., pl.* **corpora cal·lo·sa** (kə-lō′sə). *Anatomy.* The arched bridge of nervous tissue that connects the two cerebral hemispheres, allowing communication between the right and left sides of the brain. [New Latin : Latin *corpus,* body + Latin *callōsum,* neuter of *callōsus,* callous.]

Cor·pus Chris·ti[1] (kôr′pəs krĭs′tē). A city of southern Texas on **Corpus Christi Bay,** an arm of the Gulf of Mexico. The city is highly industrialized and has a large shrimp-fishing fleet. Population, 231,999.

Cor·pus Chris·ti[2] (kôr′pəs krĭs′tē) *n. Roman Catholic Church.* **1.** A feast in honor of the Eucharist. **2.** The first Thursday after Trinity Sunday, the day on which this feast is observed. [Middle English, from Medieval Latin, body of Christ : Latin *corpus,* body + Latin *Christī,* genitive of *Christus,* Christ.]

cor·pus·cle (kôr′pə-səl, -pŭs′əl) *n.* **1.a.** An unattached body cell, such as a blood or lymph cell. **b.** A rounded, globular mass of cells, such as the pressure receptor on certain nerve endings. **2.** A discrete particle, such as a photon or an electron. **3.** A minute globular particle. [Latin *corpusculum,* diminutive of *corpus,* body. See **kʷrep-** in Appendix.] **—cor·pus′cu·lar** (kôr-pŭs′kyə-lər) *adj.*

corpus de·lic·ti (dĭ-lĭk′tī′) *n.* **1.** *Law.* The material evidence in a homicide, such as the discovered corpse of a murder victim, showing that a crime has been committed. **2.** A corpse. [New Latin : Latin *corpus,* body + Latin *delictī,* genitive of *delictum,* crime.]

corpus lu·te·um (lo͞o′tē-əm) *n., pl.* **corpora lu·te·a** (lo͞o′tē-ə). A yellow, progesterone-secreting mass of cells that forms from an ovarian follicle after the release of a mature egg. [New Latin : Latin *corpus,* body + Latin *lūteum,* neuter of *lūteus,* yellow.]

corpus stri·a·tum (strī-ā′təm) *n., pl.* **corpora stri·a·ta** (strī-ā′tə). *Anatomy.* Either of two gray and white, striated bodies of nerve fibers located in the lower lateral wall of each cerebral hemisphere. [New Latin : Latin *corpus,* body + Latin *striātum,* neuter of *striātus,* striated.]

corr. *abbr.* **1.** Correction. **2.** Correspondence; correspondent.

cor·rade (kə-rād′) *tr. & intr.v.* **-rad·ed, -rad·ing, -rades.** To erode or be eroded by abrasion. [Latin *corrādere,* to scrape together : *com-,* com- + *rādere,* to scrape; see **rēd-** in Appendix.] **—cor·ra′sion** (-rā′zhən) *n.* **—cor·ra′sive** (-sĭv, -zĭv) *adj.*

cor·ral (kə-răl′) *n.* **1.** An enclosure for confining livestock. **2.** An enclosure formed by a circle of wagons for defense against attack during an encampment. **—corral** *tr.v.* **-ralled, -ral·ling, -rals. 1.** To drive into and hold in a corral. **2.** To arrange (wagons) in a corral. **3.** To take control or possession of. [Spanish, from Vulgar Latin *currāle, enclosure for carts, from Latin *currus,* cart, from *currere,* to run. See **kers-** in Appendix.]

corral

cor·rect (kə-rĕkt′) *v.* **-rect·ed, -rect·ing, -rects.** *—tr.* **1.a.** To remove the errors or mistakes from. **b.** To indicate or mark the errors in. **2.** To punish for the purpose of improving or reforming. **3.** To remove, remedy, or counteract (a malfunction, for example). **4.** To adjust so as to meet a required standard or condition: *correct the wheel alignment on a car.* *—intr.* **1.** To make corrections. **2.** To make adjustments; compensate: *correcting for the effects of air resistance.* **—correct** *adj.* **1.** Free from error or fault; true or accurate. **2.** Conforming to standards; proper: *correct behavior.* [Middle English *correcten,* from Latin *corrigere, corrēct-,* to correct : *com-,* intensive pref.; see COM– + *regere,* to rule; see **reg-** in Appendix.] **—cor·rect′a·ble, cor·rect′i·ble** *adj.* **—cor·rect′ly** *adv.* **—cor·rect′ness** *n.* **—cor·rec′tor** *n.*

SYNONYMS: *correct, rectify, remedy, redress, reform, revise, amend.* These verbs mean to make right what is wrong. *Correct* refers to eliminating faults, errors, or defects: *correct spelling mistakes; correct a misapprehension. Rectify* stresses the idea of bringing something into conformity with a standard of what is right: *The omission of your name from the list will be rectified. I hope I can find a way to rectify your opinion of my behavior. Remedy* involves removing or counteracting something considered a cause of harm or damage: *Nothing has been done to remedy the lack. He took courses to remedy his abysmal ignorance. Redress* refers to setting right something considered immoral or unethical and usually involves making reparation: *The wrong is too great to be redressed. Reform* implies broad change that alters form or character for the better: *"Let us reform our schools, and we shall find little reform needed in our prisons"* (John Ruskin). *"Nothing*

ă pat	oi boy
ā pay	ou out
âr care	o͝o took
ä father	o͞o boot
ĕ pet	ŭ cut
ē be	ûr urge
ĭ pit	th thin
ī pie	*th* this
îr pier	hw which
ŏ pot	zh vision
ō toe	ə about, item
ô paw	♦ regionalism

Stress marks: ′ (primary); ′ (secondary), as in **dictionary** (dĭk′shə-nĕr′ē)

so needs reforming as other people's habits" (Mark Twain). *Revise* suggests change that results from reconsideration: *revise a manuscript; revising the tax laws; revise our judgment of the situation. Amend* implies improvement through alteration or correction: "*Whenever* [the people] *shall grow weary of the existing government, they can exercise their constitutional right of amending it, or their revolutionary right to dismember or overthrow it*" (Abraham Lincoln). See also Synonyms at **punish.**

cor·rec·tion (kə-rĕk′shən) *n. Abbr.* **cor., corr. 1.** The act or process of correcting. **2.** Something offered or substituted for a mistake or fault: *made corrections in the report.* **3.a.** Punishment intended to rehabilitate or improve. **b. corrections.** The treatment of offenders through a system of penal incarceration, rehabilitation, probation, and parole, or the administrative system by which these are effectuated. **4.** An amount or quantity added or subtracted in order to correct. **5.** A decline in stock-market activity or prices following a period of increases. **—cor·rec′tion·al** *adj.*

cor·rec·ti·tude (kə-rĕk′tĭ-to͞od′, -tyo͞od′) *n.* Appropriate manners and behavior; propriety.

cor·rec·tive (kə-rĕk′tĭv) *adj.* Tending or intended to correct. **—corrective** *n.* An agent that corrects. **—cor·rec′tive·ly** *adv.*

Cor·reg·gio (kə-rĕj′ō, -ē-ō′, kô-rĕd′jō), **Antonio Allegri da.** 1494–1534. Italian High Renaissance painter known for his use of chiaroscuro.

Cor·reg·i·dor (kə-rĕg′ĭ-dôr′, -dōr′, kôr-rĕ′hē-*thôr*′). An island of the northern Philippines at the entrance to Manila Bay. Despite a heroic defense, Filipino and U.S. troops were forced to surrender the fortified island to Japan in May 1942. U.S. paratroopers recaptured the island in March 1945.

corsage
Wrist corsage

correl. *abbr.* Correlative.

cor·re·late (kôr′ə-lāt′, kŏr′-) *v.* **-lat·ed, -lat·ing, -lates.** —*tr.* **1.** To put or bring into causal, complementary, parallel, or reciprocal relation. **2.** To establish or demonstrate as having a correlation: *correlated drug abuse and crime.* —*intr.* To be related by a correlation. **—correlate** (-lĭt, -lāt′) *adj.* Related by a correlation, especially having corresponding characteristics. **—correlate** (-lĭt, -lāt′) *n.* Either of two correlate entities; a correlative. [Back-formation from CORRELATION.]

cor·re·la·tion (kôr′ə-lā′shən, kŏr′-) *n.* **1.** A causal, complementary, parallel, or reciprocal relationship, especially a structural, functional, or qualitative correspondence between two comparable entities: *a correlation between drug abuse and crime.* **2.** *Statistics.* The simultaneous change in value of two numerically valued random variables: *the positive correlation between cigarette smoking and the incidence of lung cancer; the negative correlation between age and normal vision.* **3.** An act of correlating or the condition of being correlated. [Medieval Latin *correlātiō, correlātiōn-* : Latin *com-*, com- + Latin *relātiō*, relation, report (from *relātus*, past participle of *referre*, to carry back; see RELATE).] **—cor′re·la′tion·al** *adj.*

correlation coefficient *n.* A measure of the interdependence of two random variables that ranges in value from −1 to +1, indicating perfect negative correlation at −1, absence of correlation at zero, and perfect positive correlation at +1. Also called *coefficient of correlation.*

cor·rel·a·tive (kə-rĕl′ə-tĭv) *adj. Abbr.* **correl. 1.** Related; corresponding. **2.** *Grammar.* Indicating a reciprocal or complementary relationship: *a correlative conjunction.* **—correlative** *n. Abbr.* **correl. 1.** Either of two correlative entities; a correlate. **2.** *Grammar.* A correlative word or expression. **—cor·rel′a·tive·ly** *adv.*

corset

cor·re·spond (kôr′ĭ-spŏnd′, kŏr′-) *intr.v.* **-spond·ed, -spond·ing, -sponds. 1.** To be in agreement, harmony, or conformity. **2.** To be similar or equivalent in character, quantity, origin, structure, or function: *English* navel *corresponds to Greek* omphalos. See Synonyms at **agree. 3.** To communicate by letter, usually over a period of time. [French *correspondre*, from Medieval Latin *correspondēre* : Latin *com-*, com- + *respondēre*, to respond; see RESPOND.]

cor·re·spon·dence (kôr′ĭ-spŏn′dəns, kŏr′-) *n. Abbr.* **cor., corr. 1.** The act, fact, or state of agreeing or conforming. **2.** Similarity or analogy. **3.a.** Communication by the exchange of letters. **b.** The letters written or received. **—correspondence** *adj.* **1.** Of, relating to, or dealing with correspondence: *a correspondence secretary.* **2.** Of, relating to, or constituting instruction by mail: *correspondence courses in French and mathematics.*

correspondence principle *n.* The principle that predictions of quantum theory approach those of classical physics in the limit of large quantum numbers.

correspondence school *n.* A school that offers instruction by mail, sending lessons and examinations to a student.

cor·re·spon·den·cy (kôr′ĭ-spŏn′dən-sē, kŏr′-) *n., pl.* **-cies.** Correspondence.

cor·re·spon·dent (kôr′ĭ-spŏn′dənt, kŏr′-) *n. Abbr.* **cor., corr. 1.** One who communicates by means of letters. **2.** One employed by the print or broadcast media to supply news stories or articles: *a foreign correspondent.* **3.** One that has regular business dealings with another, especially at a distance. **4.** Something that corresponds; a correlative. **—correspondent** *adj.* Corresponding. **—cor′re·spon′dent·ly** *adv.*

cor·re·spond·ing (kôr′ĭ-spŏn′dĭng, kŏr′-) *adj. Abbr.* **cor. 1.** Having the same or nearly the same relationship. **2.** Accompanying another: *a high corporate position and its corresponding problems.* **3.a.** Having been assigned the responsibility of written communications: *a corresponding secretary.* **b.** Participating at a distance from the rest of a group: *a corresponding member of the bar association.* **—cor′re·spond′ing·ly** *adv.*

cor·re·spon·sive (kôr′ĭ-spŏn′sĭv, kŏr′-) *adj.* Jointly responsive. **—cor′re·spon′sive·ly** *adv.*

cor·ri·da (kô-rē′də, -thä) *n.* A bullfight. [Spanish, from past participle of *correr*, to run, from Latin *currere.* See **kers-** in Appendix.]

cor·ri·dor (kôr′ĭ-dər, -dôr′, kŏr′-) *n.* **1.** A narrow hallway, passageway, or gallery, often with rooms or apartments opening onto it. **2.a.** A tract of land forming a passageway, such as one that allows an inland country access to the sea through another country. **b.** A restricted tract of land for the passage of trains. **c.** Restricted airspace for the passage of aircraft. **d.** The restricted path followed by a spacecraft on a particular mission. **3.** A thickly populated strip of land connecting two or more urban areas: *the Boston-Washington corridor.* **—*idiom.* corridors of power.** A place in which powerful leaders work and rule. [French, from Italian *corridore*, from *correre*, to run, from Latin *currere.* See **kers-** in Appendix.]

cor·rie (kôr′ē, kŏr′ē) *n.* A round hollow in a hillside; a cirque. [Scottish Gaelic *coire*, hollow, cauldron, from Old Irish, cauldron, whirlpool.]

Cor·ri·en·tes (kôr′ē-ĕn′tĕs). A city of northeast Argentina on the Paraná River and the Paraguay border. It was founded in 1588. Population, 180,612.

Cor·ri·gan (kôr′ĭ-gən, kŏr′-), **Mairead.** Born 1944. Irish peace activist. She shared the 1976 Nobel Peace Prize for work in Northern Ireland's peace movement.

cor·ri·gen·dum (kôr′ə-jĕn′dəm, kŏr′-) *n., pl.* **-da** (-də). **1.** An error to be corrected, especially a printer's error. **2. corrigenda.** A list of errors in a book along with their corrections. [Latin, neuter gerundive of *corrigere*, to correct. See CORRECT.]

cor·ri·gi·ble (kôr′ĭ-jə-bəl, kŏr′-) *adj.* Capable of being corrected, reformed, or improved. [Middle English, from Old French, from Medieval Latin *corrigibilis*, from Latin *corrigere*, to correct. See CORRECT.] **—cor′ri·gi·bil′i·ty** *n.* **—cor′ri·gi·bly** *adv.*

cor·ri·val (kə-rī′vəl, kō-) *n.* A rival or an opponent. [French, from Latin *corrīvālis* : *com-*, intensive pref.; see COM– + *rīvālis*, rival; see RIVAL.] **—cor·ri′val** *adj.* **—cor·ri′val·ry** (-rē) *n.*

cor·rob·o·rant (kə-rŏb′ər-ənt) *adj. Archaic.* Producing or stimulating physical vigor. Used of a medicine.

cor·rob·o·rate (kə-rŏb′ə-rāt′) *tr.v.* **-rat·ed, -rat·ing, -rates.** To strengthen or support with other evidence; make more certain. See Synonyms at **confirm.** [Latin *corrōborāre, corrōborāt-* : *com-*, com- + *rōborāre*, to strengthen (from *rōbur, rōbor-*, strength; see **reudh-** in Appendix).] **—cor·rob′o·ra′tion** *n.* **—cor·rob′o·ra′tive** (-ə-rā′tĭv, -ər′ə-tĭv) *adj.* **—cor·rob′o·ra′tor** *n.* **—cor·rob′o·ra·to′ry** (-ər-ə-tôr′ē, -tōr′ē) *adj.*

cor·rob·o·ree (kə-rŏb′ə-rē) *n.* **1.** An Australian aboriginal dance festival held at night to celebrate tribal victories or other events. **2.** *Australian.* **a.** A large, noisy celebration. **b.** A great tumult; a disturbance. [From Dharuk (Aboriginal language of southeast Australia) *garaabara.*]

cor·rode (kə-rōd′) *v.* **-rod·ed, -rod·ing, -rodes.** —*tr.* **1.** To destroy a metal or alloy gradually, especially by oxidation or chemical action: *acid corroding metal.* **2.** To impair steadily; deteriorate. "*Doubt and mistrust could creep into our lives, corroding personal and professional relationships*" (Philip Taubman). —*intr.* To be eaten or worn away. [Middle English *corroden*, from Latin *corrōdere*, to gnaw away : *com-*, intensive pref.; see COM– + *rōdere*, to gnaw; see **rēd-** in Appendix.] **—cor·rod′i·ble, cor·ro′si·ble** (-rō′sə-bəl) *adj.*

cor·ro·sion (kə-rō′zhən) *n.* **1.a.** The act or process of corroding. **b.** The condition produced by corroding. **2.** A substance, such as rust, formed by corroding. [Middle English *corosioun*, corrosion of tissue, from Old French *corrosion*, from Medieval Latin *corrōsiō, corrōsiōn-*, the act of gnawing, from Latin *corrōsus*, past participle of *corrōdere*, to gnaw away. See CORRODE.]

cor·ro·sive (kə-rō′sĭv, -zĭv) *adj.* **1.** Having the capability or tendency to cause corrosion: *a corrosive acid.* **2.** Gradually destructive; steadily harmful: *corrosive anxiety; corrosive increases in prices; a corrosive narcotics trade.* **3.** Spitefully sarcastic: *corrosive criticism; corrosive wit.* **—corrosive** *n.* A substance having the capability or tendency to cause corrosion. **—cor·ro′sive·ly** *adv.* **—cor·ro′sive·ness** *n.*

corrosive sublimate *n.* See **mercuric chloride.**

cor·ru·gate (kôr′ə-gāt′, kŏr′-) *v.* **-gat·ed, -gat·ing, -gates.** —*tr.* To shape into folds or parallel and alternating ridges and grooves. —*intr.* To become shaped into such folds or ridges and grooves: "*Now the immense ocean . . . sensed the change. Its surface rippled and corrugated where sweeping cloud shadows touched it*" (John Updike). [Latin *corrūgāre, corrūgāt-*, to wrinkle up : *com-*, com- + *rūgāre*, to wrinkle (from *rūga*, wrinkle).] **—cor′ru·gate′, cor′ru·gat′ed** (-gā′tĭd) *adj.*

corrugated iron *n.* A structural sheet iron, usually galvanized, shaped in parallel furrows and ridges for rigidity.

cor·ru·ga·tion (kôr′ə-gā′shən, kŏr′-) *n.* **1.a.** The act or process of corrugating. **b.** The state of being corrugated. **2.** A groove or ridge on a corrugated surface.

ă pat	oi boy
ā pay	ou out
âr care	o͝o took
ä father	o͞o boot
ĕ pet	ŭ cut
ē be	ûr urge
ĭ pit	th thin
ī pie	*th* this
îr pier	hw which
ŏ pot	zh vision
ō toe	ə about, item
ô paw	♦ regionalism

Stress marks: ′ (primary); ′ (secondary), as in **dictionary** (dĭk′shə-nĕr′ē)

cor·rupt (kə-rŭpt′) *adj.* **1.** Marked by immorality and perversion; depraved. **2.** Venal; dishonest: *a corrupt mayor.* **3.** Containing errors or alterations, as a text: *a corrupt translation.* **4.** *Archaic.* Tainted; putrid. **—corrupt** *v.* **-rupt·ed, -rupt·ing, -rupts.** *—tr.* **1.** To destroy or subvert the honesty or integrity of. **2.** To ruin morally; pervert. **3.** To taint; contaminate. **4.** To cause to become rotten; spoil. **5.** To change the original form of (a text, for example). *—intr.* To become corrupt. [Middle English, from Latin *corruptus,* past participle of *corrumpere,* to destroy : *com-,* intensive pref.; see COM– + *rumpere,* to break; see **reup-** in Appendix.] **—cor·rupt′er, cor·rup′tor** *n.* **—cor·rup′tive** *adj.* **—cor·rupt′ly** *adv.* **—cor·rupt′ness** *n.*

SYNONYMS: *corrupt, debase, debauch, deprave, pervert, vitiate.* The central meaning shared by these verbs is "to ruin utterly in character or quality": *was corrupted by limitless power; debased himself by pleading with the captors; a youth debauched by drugs and drink; indulgence that depraves the moral fiber; perverted her talent by putting it to evil purposes; a proof vitiated by a serious omission.*

cor·rupt·i·ble (kə-rŭp′tə-bəl) *adj.* Capable of being corrupted: *corruptible judges.* **—cor·rupt′i·bil′i·ty, cor·rupt′i·ble·ness** *n.* **—cor·rupt′i·bly** *adv.*

cor·rup·tion (kə-rŭp′shən) *n.* **1.a.** The act or process of corrupting. **b.** The state of being corrupt. **2.** Decay; rot. **3.** *Archaic.* Something that corrupts.

cor·rup·tion·ist (kə-rŭp′shə-nĭst) *n.* One who defends or practices corruption, particularly in politics.

cor·sage (kôr-säzh′, -säj′) *n.* **1.** A small bouquet of flowers worn by a woman at the shoulder or waist or on the wrist. **2.** The bodice or waist of a dress. [Middle English, torso, from Old French, from *cors,* body, from Latin *corpus.* See **k^wrep-** in Appendix.]

cor·sair (kôr′sâr′) *n.* **1.** A pirate, especially along the Barbary Coast. **2.** A swift pirate ship, often operating with official sanction. [French *corsaire,* from Old Provençal *corsari,* from Old Italian *corsaro,* from Medieval Latin *cursārius,* from *cursus,* plunder, from Latin, run, course. See COURSE.]

corse (kôrs) *n.* *Archaic.* A corpse. [Middle English *cors,* from Old French, from Latin *corpus.* See **k^wrep-** in Appendix.]

cor·se·let (kôr′slĭt) *n.* **1.** Also **cors·let.** Body armor, especially a breastplate. **2.** Also **corse·lette** (kôr′sə-lĕt′). An undergarment that is a combination of a light corset and a brassiere. [French, diminutive of Old French *cors,* body. See CORSET.]

cor·set (kôr′sĭt) *n.* **1.** A close-fitting undergarment, often reinforced by stays, worn to support and shape the waistline, hips, and breasts. **2.** A medieval outer garment, especially a laced jacket or bodice. **—corset** *tr.v.* **-set·ed, -set·ing, -sets.** To enclose in or as if in a corset. [Middle English, bodice, from Old French, diminutive of *cors,* body, from Latin *corpus.* See **k^wrep-** in Appendix.]

Cor·si·ca (kôr′sĭ-kə). An Island of France in the Mediterranean Sea north of Sardinia. Napoleon Bonaparte was born on the island, which was ceded to France by Genoa in 1768. **—Cor′si·can** *adj.* & *n.*

Cor·si·ca·na (kôr′sĭ-kăn′ə). A city of northeast Texas south-southeast of Dallas. It is in an oil-producing region. Population, 21,712.

cors·let (kôr′slĭt) *n.* Variant of **corselet** (sense 1).

cor·tege also **cor·tège** (kôr-tĕzh′) *n.* **1.** A train of attendants, as of a distinguished person; a retinue. **2.a.** A ceremonial procession. **b.** A funeral procession. [French *cortège,* from Old Italian *corteggio,* from *corteggiare,* to pay honor, from *corte,* court, from Latin *cohors, cohort-,* throng. See **gher-[1]** in Appendix.]

Cor·tés (kôr-tĕz′, -tĕs′), **Hernando** or **Hernán.** 1485–1547. Spanish explorer and conquistador who conquered Aztec Mexico for Spain.

cor·tex (kôr′tĕks′) *n., pl.* **-ti·ces** (-tĭ-sēz′) or **-tex·es. 1.** *Anatomy.* **a.** The outer layer of an internal organ or body structure, as of the kidney or adrenal gland. **b.** The outer layer of gray matter that covers the surface of the cerebral hemisphere. **2.** *Botany.* The region of tissue in a root or stem lying between the epidermis and the vascular tissue. **3.** An external layer, such as bark or rind. [Latin, bark. See **sker-[1]** in Appendix.]

cortic– *pref.* Variant of **cortico–.**

cor·ti·cal (kôr′tĭ-kəl) *adj.* **1.** Of, relating to, derived from, or consisting of cortex. **2.** Of, relating to, associated with, or depending on the cerebral cortex. **—cor′ti·cal·ly** *adv.*

cor·ti·cate (kôr′tĭ-kĭt, -kāt′) also **cor·ti·cat·ed** (-kāt′ĭd) *adj.* Having a cortex or a similar specialized outer layer.

cor·ti·ces (kôr′tĭ-sēz′) *n.* A plural of **cortex.**

cortico– or **cortic–** *pref.* Cortex: *corticotropin.* [From Latin *cortex, cortic-,* bark, rind. See CORTEX.]

cor·ti·coid (kôr′tĭ-koid′) *n.* A corticosteroid.

cor·tic·o·lous (kôr-tĭk′ə-ləs) *adj.* Growing or living on tree bark, as some lichens and mosses. [CORTI(CO)– + –COLOUS.]

cor·ti·co·spi·nal (kôr′tĭ-kō-spī′nəl) *adj.* Of or relating to the cerebral cortex and the spinal cord.

cor·ti·co·ste·roid (kôr′tĭ-kō-stîr′oid′,-stĕr′-) *n.* Any of the steroid hormones produced by the adrenal cortex or their synthetic equivalents, such as cortisol and aldesterone.

cor·ti·cos·ter·one (kôr′tĭ-kŏs′tə-rōn′) *n.* A corticosteroid, $C_{21}H_{30}O_4$, that functions in the metabolism of carbohydrates and proteins. [CORTICO– + STER(OL) + –ONE.]

cor·ti·co·tro·pin (kôr′tĭ-kō-trō′pən) also **cor·ti·co·tro·phin** (-trō′fĭn) *n.* See **ACTH.** [CORTICO– + –TROP(IC) + –IN.]

cor·tin (kôr′tn) *n.* An adrenal cortex extract that contains a mixture of hormones including cortisone. [CORT(EX) + –IN.]

cor·ti·sol (kôr′tĭ-sôl′, -zôl′, -sōl′, -zōl′) *n.* See **hydrocortisone** (sense 1). [CORTIS(ONE) + –OL[1].]

cortege

cor·ti·sone (kôr′tĭ-sōn′, -zōn′) *n.* A naturally occurring corticosteroid, $C_{21}H_{28}O_5$, that functions primarily in carbohydrate metabolism and is used in the treatment of rheumatoid arthritis, adrenal insufficiency, certain allergies, and gout. [Alteration of CORTICOSTERONE.]

Cort·land[1] (kôrt′lənd). A city of central New York south of Syracuse. It was settled in 1792. Population, 20,138.

Cort·land[2] (kôrt′lənd) *n.* A large, red-skinned cultivated variety of apple. [After *Cortland,* a county of central New York.]

co·run·dum (kə-rŭn′dəm) *n.* An extremely hard mineral, aluminum oxide, Al_2O_3, sometimes containing iron, magnesia, or silica, that occurs in gem varieties such as ruby and sapphire and in a common black, brown, or blue form used chiefly in abrasives. [Tamil *kuruntam.*]

co·rus·cant (kə-rŭs′kənt) *adj.* Giving forth flashes of light; glittering.

cor·us·cate (kôr′ə-skāt′, kŏr′-) *intr.v.* **-cat·ed, -cat·ing, -cates. 1.** To give forth flashes of light; sparkle and glitter: *diamonds coruscating in the candlelight.* **2.** To exhibit sparkling virtuosity: *a flutist whose music coruscated throughout the concert hall.* [Latin *coruscāre, coruscāt-,* to flash.] **—cor′us·ca′tion** *n.*

Hernando Cortés

Cor·val·lis (kôr-văl′ĭs). A city of western Oregon on the Willamette River south-southwest of Salem. It is the seat of Oregon State University (established 1858). Population, 40,960.

cor·vée (kôr-vā′, kôr′vā′) *n.* **1.** Labor exacted by a local authority for little or no pay or instead of taxes and used especially in the maintenance of roads. **2.** A day of unpaid work required of a vassal by his feudal lord. [French *corvée* and Middle English *corve,* both from Old French *corovee,* from Medieval Latin *(opera) corrogāta,* (work) requested, from Latin *corrogāre,* to summon together : *com-,* com- + *rogāre,* to ask; see **reg-** in Appendix.]

corves (kôrvz) *n.* Plural of **corf.**

cor·vette (kôr-vĕt′) *n.* **1.** A fast, lightly armed warship, smaller than a destroyer, often armed for antisubmarine operations. **2.** An obsolete sailing warship, smaller than a frigate, usually armed with one tier of guns. [French, a kind of warship, probably from Middle Dutch *corf,* basket, small ship. See CORF.]

cor·vi·na (kôr-vē′nə) *n.* Variant of **corbina.**

cor·vine (kôr′vīn′, -vĭn) *adj.* Of, resembling, or characteristic of crows. [Latin *corvīnus,* from *corvus,* raven.]

Cor·vus (kôr′vəs) *n.* A constellation in the Southern Hemisphere near Crater and Virgo. Also called *Crow.* [Latin *corvus,* raven.]

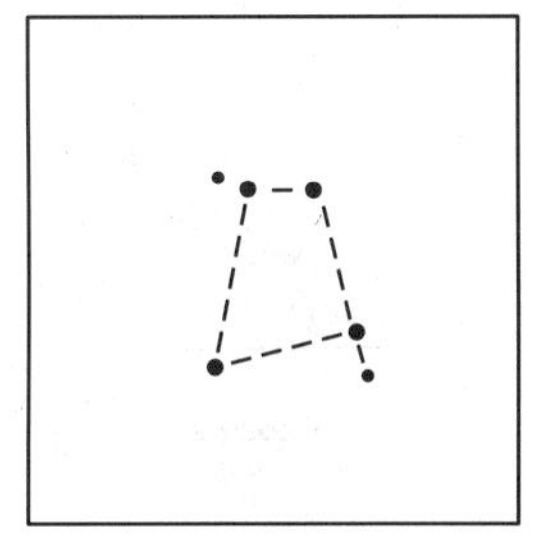
Corvus

Cor·y·bant (kôr′ə-bănt′, kŏr′-) *n., pl.* **-bants** or **-ban·tes** (-băn′tēz′). *Greek Mythology.* A priest of the Phrygian goddess Cybele whose rites were celebrated with music and ecstatic dances. **—Cor′y·ban′tic** *adj.*

co·ryd·a·lis (kə-rĭd′l-ĭs) *n.* Any of various herbs of the genus *Corydalis* native chiefly to northern temperate regions and having finely divided leaves and spurred, often yellow or pinkish flowers. [New Latin *Corydalis,* genus name, from Greek *korudallis,* crested lark (from the shape of the flowers), from *korudos.* See **ker-[1]** in Appendix.]

cor·ymb (kôr′ĭmb, -ĭm, kŏr′-) *n.* *Botany.* A usually flat-topped flower cluster in which the individual flower stalks grow upward from various points of the main stem to approximately the same height. [French *corymbe,* from Latin *corymbus,* bunch of flowers, from Greek *korumbos,* head. See **ker-[1]** in Appendix.] **—cor′ym·bose′** (-ĭm-bōs′), **co·rym′bous** (kə-rĭm′bəs) *adj.* **—cor′ym·bose′ly** *adv.*

co·ry·ne·bac·te·ri·um (kôr′ə-nē-băk-tîr′ē-əm, kə-rĭn′ə-) *n.* Any of various gram-positive, rod-shaped bacteria of the genus *Corynebacterium,* which includes many animal and plant pathogens, such as the causative agent of diphtheria. [New Latin *Corynēbacterium,* genus name : Greek *korunē,* club; see **ker-[1]** in Appendix + BACTERIUM.]

co·ryn·e·form (kə-rĭn′ə-fôrm′) *adj.* Having the shape of a corynebacterium. [CORYNE(BACTERIUM) + –FORM.]

cor·y·phae·us (kôr′ə-fē′əs, kŏr′-) *n., pl.* **-phae·i** (-fē′ī′). **1.** The leader of a Greek chorus. **2.** A leader or spokesperson. [Latin, leader, from Greek *koruphaios,* from *koruphē,* head. See **ker-[1]** in Appendix.]

cor·y·phée (kôr′ə-fā′, kŏr′-) *n.* A ballet dancer who ranks above a member of the corps de ballet and below a soloist and who performs in small ensembles. [French, from Latin *coryphaeus,* leader. See CORYPHAEUS.]

corymb

co·ry·za (kə-rī′zə) *n.* See **cold** (sense 3). [Late Latin *coryza,* from Greek *koruza,* catarrh.]

cos[1] (kôs, kŏs) *n.* See **romaine.** [After *Cos* (Kos).]

cos[2] *abbr.* Cosine.

Cos (kŏs, kôs). See **Kos.**

Co·sa Nos·tra (kō′sə nō′strə) *n.* A crime syndicate active throughout the United States, hierarchic in structure, made up of locally independent families, and believed to have an important relationship with the Sicilian Mafia. [Italian, our concern : *cosa,* thing, affair + *nostra,* feminine of *nostro,* our.]

co·se·cant (kō-sē′kănt′, -kənt) *n. Abbr.* **csc, cosec** *Mathematics.* **1.** The reciprocal of the sine of an angle in a right triangle. **2.** The secant of the complement of a directed angle or arc.

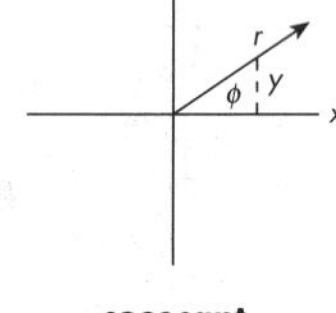

cosecant
cosecant $\phi = \frac{r}{y}$

co·seis·mal (kō-sīz′məl, -sīs′-) also **co·seis·mic** (-mĭk) —*adj.* Relating to or designating a line connecting the points on a map that indicate the places simultaneously affected by an earthquake shock. —*n.* A coseismal line.

Co·sen·za (kō-zĕn′sə, kô-zĕn′tsä). A city of southern Italy southeast of Naples. It has frequently suffered severe earthquake damage. Population, 105,806.

cosh (kŏsh) *Chiefly British. n.* A weighted weapon similar to a blackjack. —**cosh** *tr.v.* **coshed, cosh·ing, cosh·es.** To attack or hit with or as if with this weapon. [Perhaps from Romany *kosh,* stick.]

co·sign (kō-sīn′) *tr.v.* **-signed, -sign·ing, -signs. 1.** To sign (a document) jointly. **2.** To endorse (another's signature), as for a loan. —**co·sign′er** *n.*

co·sig·na·to·ry (kō-sĭg′nə-tôr′ē, -tōr′ē) *adj.* Signed jointly. —**cosignatory** *n., pl.* **-ries.** One who cosigns.

co·sine (kō′sīn′) *n. Abbr.* **cos 1.** In a right triangle, the ratio of the length of the side adjacent to an acute angle to the length of the hypotenuse. **2.** The abscissa at the endpoint of an arc of a unit circle centered at the origin of a Cartesian coordinate system, the arc being of length x and measured counterclockwise from the point (1, 0) if x is positive or clockwise if x is negative.

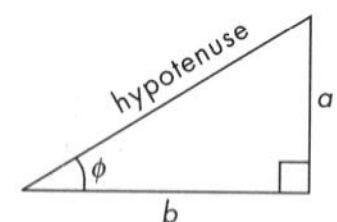

cosine
cosine $\phi = \frac{b}{Hyp}$

cos lettuce *n.* See **romaine.**

cosm– *pref.* Variant of **cosmo–.**

cos·met·ic (kŏz-mĕt′ĭk) *n.* **1.** A preparation, such as powder or a skin cream, designed to beautify the body by direct application. **2.** Something superficial that is used to cover a deficit or defect. —**cosmetic** *adj.* **1.** Serving to beautify the body, especially the face and hair. **2.** Serving to modify or improve the appearance of a physical feature, defect, or irregularity: *cosmetic surgery.* **3.a.** Decorative rather than functional: *cosmetic fenders on cars.* **b.** Lacking depth or significance; superficial: *made a few cosmetic changes when she took over the company.* [French *cosmétique,* from Greek *kosmētikos,* skilled in arranging, from *kosmētos,* well-ordered, from *kosmein,* to arrange, from *kosmos,* order.] —**cos·met′i·cal·ly** *adv.*

cos·me·ti·cian (kŏz′mĭ-tĭsh′ən) *n.* One whose occupation is manufacturing, selling, or applying cosmetics.

cos·met·i·cize (kŏz-mĕt′ĭ-sīz′) *tr.v.* **-cized, -ciz·ing, -ciz·es.** To make superficially attractive or acceptable: *"cosmeticized packages of song and dance for easy audience consumption"* (Saturday Review).

cos·me·tol·o·gy (kŏz′mĭ-tŏl′ə-jē) *n.* The study or art of cosmetics and their use. [French *cosmétologie* : *cosmétique,* cosmetic; see COSMETIC + *-logie,* -logy.] —**cos′me·tol′o·gist** *n.*

cos·mic (kŏz′mĭk) also **cos·mi·cal** (-mĭ-kəl) *adj.* **1.** Of or relating to the universe, especially as distinct from Earth. **2.** Infinitely or inconceivably extended; vast: *"a coming together of heads of government to take up the cosmic business of nations"* (Meg Greenfield). [Greek *kosmikos,* from *kosmos,* universe.] —**cos′mi·cal·ly** *adv.*

cosmic dust *n.* Clouds of fine solid particles of matter in interstellar space.

cosmic noise *n.* Radio-frequency radiation originating outside Earth's atmosphere, such as that originating from sunspots.

cosmic ray *n.* A stream of ionizing radiation of extraterrestrial origin, consisting chiefly of protons, alpha particles, and other atomic nuclei but including some high-energy electrons, that enters the atmosphere, collides with atomic nuclei, and produces secondary radiation, principally pions, muons, electrons, and gamma rays.

cosmo– or **cosm–** *pref.* Universe; world: *cosmology.* [From Greek *kosmos,* order, universe.]

cos·mo·chem·is·try (kŏz′mō-kĕm′ĭ-strē) *n.* The science of the chemical composition of the universe. —**cos′mo·chem′i·cal** (-ĭ-kəl) *adj.*

cos·mo·drome (kŏz′mə-drōm′) *n.* A launch site for spacecraft in the Soviet Union. [Russian *kosmodrom,* blend of *kosmonaut,* cosmonaut; see COSMONAUT, and *-drom,* arena (from Latin *-dromus;* see –DROME).]

cos·mo·gen·ic (kŏz′mə-jĕn′ĭk) *adj.* Produced by cosmic rays. [COSM(IC RAY) + –GENIC.]

cos·mog·o·ny (kŏz-mŏg′ə-nē) *n., pl.* **-nies. 1.** The astrophysical study of the origin and evolution of the universe. **2.** A specific theory or model of the origin and evolution of the universe. —**cos′mo·gon′ic** (-mə-gŏn′ĭk), **cos′mo·gon′i·cal** *adj.* —**cos′mo·gon′i·cal·ly** *adv.* —**cos·mog′o·nist** *n.*

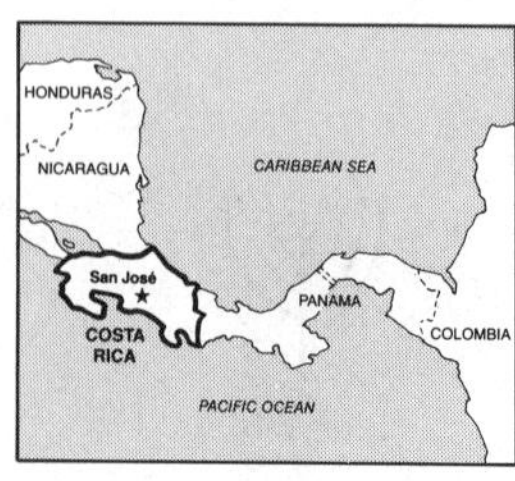

Costa Rica

cos·mog·ra·phy (kŏz-mŏg′rə-fē) *n., pl.* **-phies. 1.** The study of the visible universe that includes geography and astronomy. **2.** A general description or depiction of the world or universe: *"a full-blown cosmography in which Earth is 'the garbage dump of the universe'"* (Mark Muro). —**cos·mog′ra·pher** *n.* —**cos′mo·graph′ic** (-mə-grăf′ĭk), **cos′mo·graph′i·cal** *adj.* —**cos′mo·graph′i·cal·ly** *adv.*

cos·mol·o·gy (kŏz-mŏl′ə-jē) *n., pl.* **-gies. 1.** The study of the physical universe considered as a totality of phenomena in time and space. **2.a.** The astrophysical study of the history, structure, and constituent dynamics of the universe. **b.** A specific theory or model of this structure and these dynamics. —**cos′mo·log′ic** (-mə-lŏj′ĭk), **cos′mo·log′i·cal** *adj.* —**cos′mo·log′i·cal·ly** *adv.* —**cos·mol′o·gist** *n.*

cos·mo·naut (kŏz′mə-nôt′) *n.* A Soviet astronaut. [Russian *kosmonaut* : Greek *kosmos,* universe + Greek *nautēs,* sailor; see **nāu-** in Appendix.]

cos·mop·o·lis (kŏz-mŏp′ə-lĭs) *n.* A large city inhabited by people from many different countries. [COSMO– + Greek *polis,* city; see **pelə-**[3] in Appendix.]

cos·mo·pol·i·tan (kŏz′mə-pŏl′ĭ-tn) *adj.* **1.** Pertinent or common to the whole world: *an issue of cosmopolitan import.* **2.** Having constituent elements from all over the world or from many different parts of the world: *the ancient and cosmopolitan societies of Syria and Egypt.* **3.** So sophisticated as to be at home in all parts of the world or conversant with many spheres of interest: *a cosmopolitan traveler.* **4.** *Ecology.* Growing or occurring in many parts of the world; widely distributed. —**cosmopolitan** *n.* A cosmopolitan person or organism; a cosmopolite. —**cos′mo·pol′i·tan·ism** *n.*

cos·mop·o·lite (kŏz-mŏp′ə-līt′) *n.* **1.** A cosmopolitan person: *a true cosmopolite—a Renaissance man.* **2.** *Ecology.* An organism found in most parts of the world. **3.** See **painted lady.** [Greek *kosmopolitēs* : *kosmos,* world + *politēs,* citizen (from *polis,* city; see **pelə-**[3] in Appendix).] —**cos·mop′o·lit′ism** (-lī-tĭz′əm, -lĭ-tĭz′-) *n.*

cos·mos (kŏz′məs, -mŏs′, -mōs′) *n.* **1.** The universe regarded as an orderly, harmonious whole. **2.** An ordered, harmonious whole. **3.** Harmony and order as distinct from chaos. **4.** *pl.* **cos·mos·es** or **cosmos.** Any of various mostly Mexican herbs of the genus *Cosmos* in the composite family, having radiate flower heads of variously colored flowers and opposite pinnate leaves, especially *C. bipinnatus* and *C. sulphureus,* widely cultivated as garden annuals. [Greek *kosmos.*]

co·spon·sor (kō-spŏn′sər) *tr.v.* **-sored, -sor·ing, -sors.** To function in the capacity of a joint sponsor of: *corporations that cosponsored a marathon.* —**cosponsor** *n.* A joint sponsor: *two senators who were cosponsors of new legislation.* —**co·spon′sor·ship′** *n.*

Cos·sack (kŏs′ăk) *n.* A member of a people of southern European Russia and adjacent parts of Asia, noted as cavalrymen especially during czarist times. [Russian *kazak* and Ukrainian *kozak,* both from South Turkic *qazaq,* adventurer. See KAZAKH.] —**Cos′sack′** *adj.*

cos·set (kŏs′ĭt) *tr.v.* **-set·ed, -set·ing, -sets.** To pamper. —**cosset** *n.* A pet, especially a pet lamb. [Possibly from Anglo-Norman *coscet,* pet lamb, from Middle English *cotsete,* cottage-dweller, from Old English *cotsǣta* : *cot,* cottage + *sǣta, -sǣte,* inhabitant; see **sed-** in Appendix.]

cost (kôst) *n.* **1.** An amount paid or required in payment for a purchase; a price. **2.** The expenditure of something, such as time or labor, necessary for the attainment of a goal. See Synonyms at **price. 3. costs.** *Law.* The charges fixed for litigation, often payable by the losing party. —*attributive.* Often used to modify another noun: *cost consciousness; cost overruns.* —**cost** *v.* **cost, cost·ing, costs.** —*intr.* To require a specified payment, expenditure, effort, or loss: *It costs more to live in the city.* —*tr.* **1.** To have as a price. **2.** To cause to lose, suffer, or sacrifice: *Participating in the strike cost me my job.* **3.** *past tense and past participle* **costed.** To estimate or determine the cost of: *The accountants costed out our expenses.* [Middle English, from Old French, from *coster,* to cost, from Latin *cōnstāre,* to be fixed, cost. See CONSTANT.] —**cost′less** *adj.* —**cost′less·ness** *n.*

cos·ta (kŏs′tə) *n., pl.* **-tae** (-tē). *Biology.* A rib or a riblike part, such as the midrib of a leaf or a thickened anterior vein or margin of an insect's wing. [Latin. See **kost-** in Appendix.] —**cos′tal** *adj.*

Cos·ta Bra·va (kŏs′tə brä′və, kô′stə, kō′-, kôs′tä brä′vä). The northeast coast of Spain, on the Mediterranean Sea from Barcelona to the French border.

cost accountant *n.* An accountant who keeps records of the costs of production and distribution. —**cost accounting** *n.*

Cos·ta del Sol (kŏs′tə dĕl sōl′, kô′stə, kôs′tä *th*ĕl sôl′). The southern coast of Spain northeast of Gibraltar.

cos·tae (kŏs′tē) *n. Biology.* Plural of **costa.**

Cos·ta Me·sa (kŏs′tə mā′sə, kō′stə). A city of southern California south-southwest of Santa Ana. It has an electronics industry. Population, 82,562.

co·star also **co-star** (kō′stär′) —*n.* A starring actor or actress given equal status with another or others in a play or film. —*tr. & intr.v.* **-starred, -star·ring, -stars.** To act or present as a costar.

cos·tard (kŏs′tərd) *n.* **1.** An English variety of large cooking apple. **2.** *Archaic.* The human head. [Middle English, from Old North French, possibly from *coste,* rib (from its ribbed appearance), from Latin *costa.* See **kost-** in Appendix.]

Cos·ta Ri·ca (kŏs′tə rē′kə, kô′stə, kō′-, kôs′tä rē′kä). *Abbr.* **C.R.** A country of Central America between Panama and Nicaragua. Spanish conquest of the area began in 1563, and the country achieved independence in 1821. San José is the capital and the largest city. Population, 2,534,000. —**Cos′ta Ri′can** (rē′kən) *adj. & n.*

cos·tate (kŏs′tāt′, kô′stāt′) *adj.* Having a costa or costae; ribbed.

cost-ef·fec·tive (kôst′ĭ-fĕk′tĭv) *adj.* Economical in terms of the goods or services received for the money spent. **—cost′-ef·fec′tive·ly** *adv.* **—cost′-ef·fec′tive·ness** *n.*

Cos·tel·lo (kŏs-tĕl′ō), **John Aloysius.** 1891–1976. Irish prime minister (1948–1951 and 1954–1957) who took Ireland out of the Commonwealth of Nations (1949).

Costello, Lou. 1908–1959. American comedian. As part of the Abbott and Costello comedy team he made a number of films, including *Buck Privates* (1941) and *Abbott and Costello Meet Frankenstein* (1948).

cos·ter·mon·ger (kŏs′tər-mŭng′gər, -mŏng′-) *n. Chiefly British.* One who sells fruit, vegetables, fish, or other goods from a cart, barrow, or stand in the streets. [Obsolete *costard-monger* : COSTARD + MONGER.]

cos·tive (kŏs′tĭv) *adj.* **1.a.** Suffering from constipation. **b.** Causing constipation. **2.** Slow; sluggish. **3.** Stingy. [Middle English *costif,* from Old French *costeve,* past participle of *costever,* to constipate, from Latin *cōnstīpāre.* See CONSTIPATE.] **—cos′tive·ly** *adv.* **—cos′tive·ness** *n.*

cost·ly (kôst′lē) *adj.* **-li·er, -li·est. 1.** Of high price or value; expensive: *costly jewelry.* **2.** Entailing loss or sacrifice: *a costly war.* **—cost′li·ness** *n.*

cost·mar·y (kôst′mâr′ē) *n., pl.* **-ies.** A Eurasian perennial herb *(Chrysanthemum balsamita)* in the composite family, having aromatic foliage sometimes used for potpourri, tea, or flavoring. [Middle English *costmarie* : *cost,* costmary (from Old English, from Latin *costum,* from Greek *kostos,* from Sanskrit *kuṣṭhaḥ*) + *marie,* Mary, the mother of Jesus.]

cost of living *n.* **1.** The average cost of the basic necessities of life, such as food, shelter, and clothing. **2.** The cost of basic necessities as defined by an accepted standard. **—cost′-of-liv′ing** (kôst′əv-lĭv′ĭng) *adj.*

cost-of-living adjustment *n. Abbr.* **COLA** An adjustment in wages that corresponds with a change in the cost of living.

cost-of-living index *n.* See **consumer price index.**

cost-plus (kôst′plŭs′) *n.* The cost of production plus a fixed rate of profit. **—cost′-plus′** *adj.*

cost-push (kôst′po͝osh′) *n.* Inflation in which increased production costs, as from higher wages, tend to drive prices up.

cos·trel (kŏs′trəl) *n.* A flat, pear-shaped drinking vessel with loops for attachment to the belt of the user. [Middle English, from Old French *costerel,* possibly from *costier,* at the side, from *coste,* rib, from Latin *costa.* See **kost-** in Appendix.]

cos·tume (kŏs′to͞om′, -tyo͞om′) *n.* **1.** A prevalent fashion of dress, including garments, accessories, and hair style. **2.a.** A style of dress characteristic of a particular country, period, or people, often worn in a play or at a masquerade. **b.** An outfit or a disguise worn on Mardi Gras, Halloween, or similar occasions: *Dressed up as a gigantic chicken, she won the prize for the best costume.* **3.** A set of clothes appropriate for a particular occasion or season. *—attributive.* Often used to modify another noun: *a costume ball; a costume play.* **—costume** (kŏ-sto͞om′, -styo͞om′, kŏs′to͞om′, -tyo͞om′) *tr.v.* **-tumed, -tum·ing, -tumes. 1.** To put a costume on; dress. **2.** To design or furnish costumes for. [French, from Italian, style, dress, from Latin *cōnsuētūdō,* custom. See CUSTOM.]

cos·tum·er (kŏs′to͞o′mər, -tyo͞o′-, kŏ-sto͞o′mər, -styo͞o′-) also **cos·tum·i·er** (kŏ-sto͞o′mē-ər, -styo͞o′-, kôs′to͞om-yā′) *n.* One that makes or supplies costumes, as for plays or masquerades.

co·sy (kō′zē) *adj., v. & n.* Variant of **cozy.**

cot¹ (kŏt) *n.* **1.** A narrow bed, especially one made of canvas on a collapsible frame. **2.** *Chiefly British.* A crib. [Hindi *khāṭ,* from Sanskrit *khaṭvā,* from Tamil *kaṭṭu,* to bind, tie.]

WORD HISTORY: People might assume that there is nothing particularly exotic about the history of the word *cot.* However, *cot* happens to be a good example of how words are borrowed from other cultures, becoming so firmly naturalized over time that they lose their émigré flavor. The British first encountered the object denoted by *cot,* a light frame strung with tapes or rope, in India, where their trading stations had been established as early as 1612. The word *cot,* first recorded in English in 1634, comes from *khāṭ,* the Hindi name for the contrivance. During subsequent years, *cot* has been used to denote other types of beds, including in British usage a crib.

cot² (kŏt) *n.* **1.** A small house. **2.** A protective covering or sheath. [Middle English, from Old English.]

co·tan·gent (kō-tăn′jənt) *n. Abbr.* **cot, ctn** *Mathematics.* **1.** The reciprocal of the tangent of an angle in a right triangle. **2.** The tangent of the complement of a directed angle or arc. **—co′-tan·gen′tial** (-jĕn′shəl) *adj.*

cot death *n. Chiefly British.* Sudden infant death syndrome.

cote¹ (kōt) *n.* A small shed or shelter for sheep or birds. [Middle English, from Old English.]

cote² (kōt) *tr.v.* **cot·ed, cot·ing, cotes.** *Obsolete.* To go around by the side of; skirt. [Probably from French *côtoyer,* to skirt, from *côté,* side, from Old French *coste,* rib. See COSTREL.]

Côte d'A·zur (kōt′ də-zo͝or′, dä-zür′). The Mediterranean coast of southeast France. It is known for its fashionable resorts.

co·ten·ant (kō-tĕn′ənt) *n.* One of two or more tenants sharing property. **—co·ten′an·cy** *n.*

co·ter·ie (kō′tə-rē, kō′tə-rē′) *n.* A small, often select group of persons who associate with one another frequently. See Synonyms at **circle.** [French, from Old French, peasant association, from *cotier,* cottager, from **cote,* cottage, possibly of Germanic origin.]

co·ter·mi·nous (kō-tûr′mə-nəs) *adj.* Variant of **conterminous.**

Côte Saint Luc (sānt lo͝ok′, sənt, săN lük′). A city of southern Quebec, Canada, a suburb of Montreal. Population, 27,531.

coth *abbr.* Hyperbolic cotangent.

co·thur·nus (kō-thûr′nəs) *n., pl.* **-ni** (-nī′). **1.** A buskin worn by actors of classical tragedy. **2.** The ancient style of classical tragedy. [Latin, from Greek *kothornos.*]

co·tid·al (kō-tīd′l) *adj.* **1.** Indicating coincidence of high tides or low tides. **2.** Of or relating to a line that passes through each location on a coastal map where tides occur at the same time of day.

co·til·lion also **co·til·lon** (kō-tĭl′yən, kə-) *n.* **1.** A formal ball, especially one at which girls are presented to society. **2.a.** A lively dance, originating in France in the 18th century, having varied, intricate patterns and steps. **b.** A quadrille. **c.** Music for these dances. [French *cotillon,* from Old French, petticoat, diminutive of *cote,* coat. See COAT.]

co·to·ne·as·ter (kə-tō′nē-ăs′tər) *n.* Any of various erect or creeping shrubs of the genus *Cotoneaster* in the rose family, native to Eurasia, having white to pinkish flowers and tiny, red or black applelike fruits, and frequently cultivated for ornament. [New Latin *Cotoneaster,* genus name : Latin *cotōneum,* quince; see QUINCE + Latin *-aster,* partially resembling.]

Co·to·nou (kōt′n-o͞o′). A city of southern Benin on the Gulf of Guinea. The largest city in the country, it is a seaport and commercial center. Population, 215,000.

Co·to·pax·i (kō′tə-păk′sē, kô′tô-pä′hē). An active volcano, 5,900.8 m (19,347 ft) high, in the Andes of central Ecuador.

cot·quean (kŏt′kwēn′) *n. Archaic.* **1.** A coarse or scolding woman. **2.** A man who busies himself with domestic matters traditionally regarded as suitable only for women. [COT² + QUEAN.]

Cots·wold (kŏt′swōld′) *n.* A sheep of a breed distinguished by its long wool, originally developed in the Cotswold Hills.

Cotswold Hills. A range of southwest England extending about 80 km (50 mi) northeast from Bristol and rising to approximately 329 m (1,080 ft).

cot·ta (kŏt′ə) *n., pl.* **cot·tae** (kŏt′ē) or **cot·tas.** A short surplice. [Medieval Latin, of Germanic origin.]

cot·tage (kŏt′ĭj) *n.* **1.** A small, single-storied house, especially in the country. **2.** A small summer house. [Middle English *cotage,* from Anglo-Norman, from Medieval Latin *cotāgium,* of Germanic origin.]

♦ **cottage cheese** *n.* A soft, white cheese made of strained and seasoned curds of skim milk. Also called *Dutch cheese, pot cheese,* ♦ *smearcase.*

Cot·tage Grove (kŏt′ĭj). A city of eastern Minnesota, a residential suburb of St. Paul. Population, 18,994.

cottage industry *n.* **1.** A usually small-scale industry carried on at home or out of the home by family members using their own equipment. **2.** A small, loosely organized, yet flourishing complex of activity or industry: *"The study of Gandhi has become a virtual cottage industry in the last 30 years, producing schools, museums, foundations and more than 400 biographies"* (Jean Strouse).

cot·tag·er (kŏt′ĭ-jər) *n.* One who resides in a cottage.

cottage tulip *n.* A late-blooming type of garden tulip having long stems and egg-shaped, variously colored flowers.

Cott·bus also **Kott·bus** (kŏt′bəs, kôt′bo͞os′). A city of east-central Germany near the Polish border. It developed as a market center in the late 12th century. Population, 120,723.

cot·ter (kŏt′ər) *n.* **1.** A bolt, wedge, key, or pin inserted through a slot in order to hold parts together. **2.** A cotter pin. [Origin unknown.]

cotter pin *n.* A split cotter inserted through holes in two or more pieces and bent at the ends to fasten the pieces together.

Cot·ti·an Alps (kŏt′ē-ən). A range of the Alps between northwest Italy and southeast France. It rises to 3,843.6 m (12,602 ft) at Mount Viso.

cot·ton (kŏt′n) *n.* **1.a.** Any of various shrubby plants of the genus *Gossypium,* having showy flowers and grown for the soft, white, downy fibers surrounding oil-rich seeds. **b.** The fiber of any of these plants, used in making textiles and other products. **c.** Thread or cloth manufactured from the fiber of these plants. **2.** The crop of these plants. **3.** Any of various soft, downy substances produced by other plants, as on the seeds of a cottonwood. *—attributive.* Often used to modify another noun: *cotton shirts; cotton mills.* **—cotton** *intr.v.* **-toned, -ton·ing, -tons.** *Informal.* **1.** To take a liking; attempt to be friendly: *a dog that didn't cotton to strangers; an administration that will cotton up to the most repressive of regimes.* **2.** To come to understand. Often used with *to* or *onto: "The German bosses . . . never cottoned to such changes"* (N.R. Kleinfeld). [Middle English *cotoun,* from Old French *coton,* from Old Italian *cotone,* from Arabic dialectal *qoṭon,* from Arabic *quṭn.*]

Cot·ton (kŏt′n), **Charles.** 1630–1687. English poet and trans-

costume
Halloween costumes

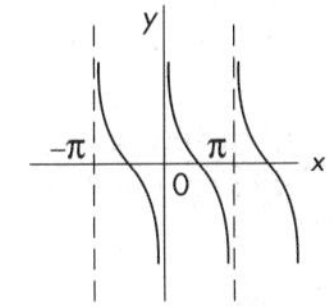

cotangent
Graph of cotangent function: $y = \cot x$

ă pat	oi boy
ā pay	ou out
âr care	o͝o took
ä father	o͞o boot
ĕ pet	ŭ cut
ē be	ûr urge
ĭ pit	th thin
ī pie	*th* this
îr pier	hw which
ŏ pot	zh vision
ō toe	ə about, item
ô paw	♦ regionalism

Stress marks: ′ (primary); ′ (secondary), as in **dictionary** (dĭk′shə-nĕr′ē)

lator known for his poems on country life as well as his translation (1685) of Montaigne's essays.

Cotton, John. 1584–1652. English-born American cleric who was vicar of Saint Botolph's Church in England until he was summoned to court for his Puritanism. He fled to Boston, Massachusetts, where he became a civil and religious leader.

Cotton Belt. An agricultural region of the southeast United States extending through North Carolina, South Carolina, Georgia, Alabama, Mississippi, Tennessee, Arkansas, Louisiana, Texas, and Oklahoma and including small sections of Missouri, Kentucky, Florida, and Virginia.

cotton candy *n.* A light, very sweet candy of threaded sugar, often tinted with food coloring and twirled onto a stick. Also called *spun sugar.*

cotton gin *n.* A machine that separates the seeds, seed hulls, and other small objects from the fibers of cotton.

cotton grass *n.* Any of various perennial grasslike plants of the genus *Eriophorum* native chiefly to wet places in northern temperate and cold regions and bearing at maturity one or more conspicuous tufts of cottony bristles.

cot·ton·mouth (kŏt′n-mouth′) *n.* See **water moccasin** (sense 1). [From the white interior of its mouth.]

cot·ton-pick·ing (kŏt′n-pĭk′ĭng) *adj. Informal.* Used as an intensive: *a cotton-picking fool; out of your cotton-picking mind.*

cot·ton·seed (kŏt′n-sēd′) *n.* The seed of the cotton plant, the source of cottonseed oil.

cottonseed oil *n.* The usually pale yellow oil obtained from cottonseed, used in manufacturing, industry, and cooking.

cotton stainer *n.* Any of various small, flat, red and black bugs of the genus *Dysdercus* that pierce cotton bolls and stain the fibers.

cot·ton·tail (kŏt′n-tāl′) *n.* Any of several North American rabbits of the genus *Sylvilagus,* having grayish or brownish fur and a tail with a fluffy white underside. Also called *wood rabbit.*

cot·ton·weed (kŏt′n-wēd′) *n.* Any of various plants having cottony down, as some species of the genus *Froelichia.*

cot·ton·wood (kŏt′n-wo͝od′) *n.* Any of several North American poplar trees, especially *Populus deltoides,* which has triangular leaves and a tuft of cottony hairs on the seeds.

cottonwood
Eastern cottonwood
Populus deltoides

cotton wool *n.* Cotton in its natural or raw state.

cot·ton·y (kŏt′n-ē) *adj.* **1.** Of or resembling cotton; fluffy. **2.** Covered with fibers resembling cotton; nappy.

co·tur·nix (kə-tûr′nĭks) *n.* A small, stub-tailed Eurasian quail *(Coturnix coturnix)* having sandy, streaked plumage and commonly used in laboratory research. Also called *Japanese quail.* [Latin, quail.]

Co·ty (kō-tē′, kô-), **René.** 1882–1962. French politician and the last president (1953–1959) of the Fourth Republic.

cot·y·le·don (kŏt′l-ēd′n) *n.* **1.** *Botany.* A leaf of the embryo of a seed plant, which, upon germination either remains in the seed or emerges, enlarges, and becomes green. Also called *seed leaf.* **2.** *Anatomy.* One of the lobules constituting the uterine side of the mammalian placenta, consisting mainly of a rounded mass of villi. [Latin, navelwort, from Greek *kotulēdōn,* from *kotulē,* hollow object.] **—cot′y·le′don·al, cot′y·le′do·nous** (-ēd′n-əs) *adj.*

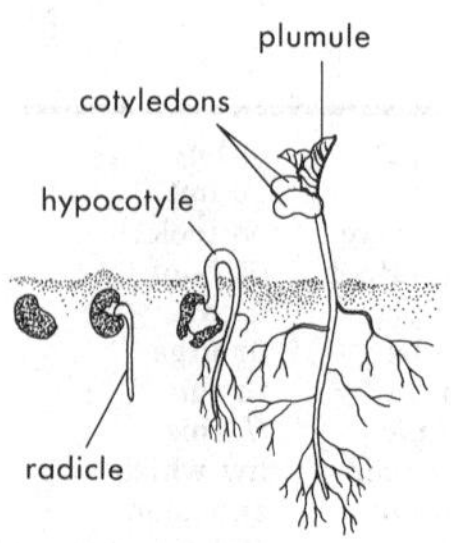

cotyledon

cot·y·loid (kŏt′l-oid′) also **cot·y·loid·al** (kŏt′l-oid′l) *adj.* Shaped like a cup. [Greek *kotuloeidēs* : *kotulē,* hollow object + *-oeidēs,* -oid.]

couch (kouch) *n.* **1.a.** A sofa. **b.** A sofa on which a patient lies while undergoing psychoanalysis or psychiatric treatment. **2.a.** The frame or floor on which grain, usually barley, is spread in malting. **b.** A layer of grain, usually barley, spread to germinate. **3.** A priming coat of paint or varnish used in artistic painting. **—couch** *v.* **couched, couch·ing, couch·es.** *—tr.* **1.** To word in a certain manner; phrase: *couched their protests in diplomatic language.* **2.** To cause (oneself) to lie down, as for rest. **3.** To embroider by laying thread flat on a surface and fastening it by stitches at regular intervals. **4.** To spread (grain) on a couch to germinate, as in malting. **5.** To lower (a spear, for example) to horizontal position, as for an attack. *—intr.* **1.** To lie down; recline, as for rest. **2.** To lie in ambush or concealment; lurk. **3.** To be in a heap or pile, as leaves for decomposition or fermentation. [Middle English *couche,* from Old French, from *couchier,* to lay down, lie down, from Latin *collocāre.* See COLLOCATE.] **—couch′er** *n.*

couch·ant (kou′chənt) *adj. Heraldry.* Lying down with the head raised. [Middle English, from Old French, present participle of *couchier,* to lie down. See COUCH.]

cou·chette (ko͞o-shĕt′) *n.* **1.** A compartment on a European passenger train equipped with four to six berths for sleeping. **2.** A sleeping berth in one of these compartments. [French, diminutive of *couche,* bed, from Old French. See COUCH.]

couch grass *n.* A Eurasian grass *(Agropyron repens)* that has whitish-yellow root stocks and has become a troublesome weed in the New World. Also called *quack grass, witch grass.* [Alteration of QUITCH GRASS.]

couch potato *n. Slang.* A person who spends much time sitting or lying down, usually watching television.

Cou·é (ko͞o-ā′, kwā), **Émile.** 1857–1926. French doctor who popularized a system of psychotherapy based on autosuggestion.

cou·gar (ko͞o′gər) *n.* See **mountain lion.** [French *couguar,* alteration (influenced by *jaguar,* from Portuguese; see JAGUAR) of Portuguese *çuçuarana,* from Tupi *suasuarana* : *suasú,* deer + *rana,* like (from its color).]

cough (kôf, kŏf) *v.* **coughed, cough·ing, coughs.** *—intr.* **1.** To expel air from the lungs suddenly and noisily, often to keep the respiratory passages free of irritating material. **2.** To make a noise similar to noisy expulsion of air from the lungs: *The engine coughed and died.* *—tr.* To expel by coughing: *coughed up phlegm.* **—cough** *n.* **1.** The act of coughing. **2.** An illness marked by frequent coughing. ***—phrasal verb.*** **cough up.** *Slang.* **1.** To hand over or relinquish (money or another possession), often reluctantly. **2.** To confess or disclose: *When he saw that the police might arrest him, he coughed up the details of what he had seen.* [Middle English *coughen,* ultimately of imitative origin.]

cough drop *n.* A small, often medicated and sweetened lozenge taken orally to ease coughing or soothe a sore throat.

Cough·lin (kŏg′lĭn), **Charles Edward.** 1891–1979. Canadian-born American priest and political activist who gained a wide audience through radio broadcasts of his sermons.

cough syrup *n.* A sweetened medicated liquid taken orally to ease coughing.

could (ko͝od) *aux.v.* Past tense of **can**[1]. **1.** Used to indicate ability, possibility, or permission in the past: *I could run faster then. It could be no better at that time. Only men could go to the club in those days.* **2.** Used with hypothetical or conditional force: *If we could help, we would.* **3.** Used to indicate tentativeness or politeness: *I could be wrong. Could you come over here?*

could·est (ko͝od′ĭst) or **couldst** (ko͝odst) *aux.v. Archaic.* A second person singular past tense of **can**[1].

could·n't (ko͝od′nt). Could not.

♦**cou·lee** (ko͞o′lē) *n.* **1.** *Western U.S.* A deep gulch or ravine with sloping sides, often dry in summer. **2.** *Louisiana & Southern Mississippi.* **a.** A stream bed, often dry according to the season. **b.** A small stream, bayou, or canal. **3.** *Upper Midwest.* A valley with hills on either side. **4.a.** A stream of molten lava. **b.** A sheet of solidified lava. [Canadian French *coulée,* from French, flow, from *couler,* to flow, from Latin *cōlāre,* to filter, from *cōlum,* sieve.]

cou·lisse (ko͞o-lēs′) *n.* **1.** A grooved timber in which something slides. **2.a.** One of the side scenes of the stage in a theater. **b.** The space between the side scenes. **c.** A backstage area in a theater. [French, from Old French *(porte) couleice,* sliding door. See PORTCULLIS.]

cou·loir (ko͞ol-wär′) *n.* A deep mountainside gorge or gully, especially in the Swiss Alps. [French, from *couler,* to slide, to flow. See COULEE.]

cou·lomb[1] (ko͞o′lŏm′, -lōm′) *n. Abbr.* **C** The meter-kilogram-second unit of electrical charge equal to the quantity of charge transferred in one second by a steady current of one ampere. See table at **measurement.** [After Charles Augustin de COULOMB.]

cou·lomb[2] (ko͞o′lŏm′, -lōm′) or **cou·lom·bic** (ko͞o-lŏm′bĭk, -lōm′-) *adj.* Of or relating to the Coulomb force.

Cou·lomb (ko͞o′lŏm′, -lōm′, ko͞o-lŏm′, -lôN′), **Charles Augustin de.** 1736–1806. French physicist who pioneered research into magnetism and electricity and formulated Coulomb's law.

Coulomb force *n.* An attractive or repulsive electrostatic force described by Coulomb's law.

Cou·lomb's law (ko͞o′lŏmz′, -lōmz′) *n.* The fundamental law of electrostatics stating that the force between two charged particles is directly proportional to the product of their charges and inversely proportional to the square of the distance between them. [After Charles Augustin de COULOMB.]

cou·lom·e·try (ko͞o-lŏm′ĭ-trē) *n.* An analytical method for determining the amount of a substance released during electrolysis in which the number of coulombs used is measured. [COULO(MB)[1] + -METRY.] **—cou′lo·met′ric** (-lə-mĕt′rĭk) *adj.* **—cou′lo·met′ri·cal·ly** *adv.*

coul·ter (kōl′tər) *n.* A blade or wheel attached to the beam of a plow that makes vertical cuts in the soil in advance of the plowshare. [Middle English *culter,* from Old English *culter* and Old French *coltre,* both from Latin *culter,* knife, plowshare. See **skel-**[1] in Appendix.]

Coul·ter pine (kōl′tər) *n.* A pine tree *(Pinus coulteri)* native to California and Baja California, having bluish-green needles in bundles of three and bearing sharp-scaled cones. [After Thomas *Coulter* (1793–1843), Irish botanist.]

cou·ma·rin (ko͞o′mər-ĭn) *n.* A fragrant crystalline compound, $C_9H_6O_2$, extracted from several plants, such as tonka beans and sweet clover, or produced synthetically and widely used in perfumes. [French *coumarine,* from *coumarou,* tonka bean tree, from Spanish *coumarú,* from Portuguese *cumaru,* from Tupi *cumarú, commaru.*] **—cou′ma·ric** (-mər-ĭk) *adj.*

coun·cil (koun′səl) *n.* **1.a.** An assembly of persons called together for consultation, deliberation, or discussion. **b.** A body of people elected or appointed to serve in an administrative, legislative, or advisory capacity. **c.** An assembly of church officials and theologians convened for regulating matters of doctrine and discipline. **2.** The discussion or deliberation that takes place in such an assembly or body. *—attributive.* Often used to modify another noun: *a council chamber; the council table.* [Middle English *counceil,* from Old French *concile,* from Latin *concilium.* See **kele-**[2] in Appendix.]

USAGE NOTE: *Council, counsel,* and *consul* are never interchangeable as such, though their meanings are related. *Council* and *councilor* refer principally to a deliberative assembly (such as a city council or student council), its work, and its membership. *Counsel* and *counselor* pertain chiefly to advice and guidance in general and to a person (such as a lawyer or camp counselor) who provides it. *Consul* denotes an officer in the foreign service of a country.

Coun•cil Bluffs (koun′səl). A city of southwest Iowa on the Missouri River opposite Omaha, Nebraska. It was settled as Kanesville in 1846 and renamed in 1852. Population, 56,449.

coun•cil•lor (koun′sə-lər, -slər) *n.* Variant of **councilor.**

coun•cil•man (koun′səl-mən) *n.* A man who is a member of a council, especially of the local governing body of a city or town.

council of ministers *n., pl.* **councils of ministers.** A body of advisers to a head of state.

coun•cil•or also **coun•cil•lor** (koun′sə-lər, -slər) *n.* A member of a council, as one convened to advise a governor. See Usage Note at **council.**

coun•cil•wom•an (koun′səl-wo͝om′ən) *n.* A woman who is a member of a council, especially of the local governing body of a city or town.

coun•sel (koun′səl) *n.* **1.** The act of exchanging opinions and ideas; consultation. **2.** Advice or guidance, especially as solicited from a knowledgeable person. See Synonyms at **advice. 3.** A plan of action. **4.** Private, guarded thoughts or opinions: *keep one's own counsel.* **5.** A lawyer or group of lawyers giving legal advice and especially conducting a case in court. See Synonyms at **lawyer.** See Usage Note at **council. —counsel** *v.* **-seled, -sel•ing, -sels** or **-selled, -sel•ling, -sels.** —*tr.* **1.** To give counsel to; advise. See Synonyms at **advise. 2.** To recommend: *counseled care in the negotiations.* —*intr.* To give or take advice. [Middle English *counseil,* from Old French *conseil,* from Latin *cōnsilium;* akin to *cōnsulere,* to take counsel, consult.]

coun•sel•or also **coun•sel•lor** (koun′sə-lər, -slər) *n.* **1.** A person who gives counsel; an adviser. **2.** An attorney, especially a trial lawyer. See Synonyms at **lawyer. 3.** A person who supervises young people at a summer camp. See Usage Note at **council. —coun′se•lor•ship′** *n.*

coun•sel•or-at-law (koun′sə-lər-ət-lô′, -slər-) *n., pl.* **coun•sel•ors-at-law.** An attorney; a counsel.

count¹ (kount) *v.* **count•ed, count•ing, counts.** —*tr.* **1.a.** To name or list (the units of a group or collection) one by one in order to determine a total; number. **b.** To recite numerals in ascending order up to and including: *count three before firing.* **c.** To include in a reckoning; take account of: *ten dogs, counting the puppies.* **2.** *Informal.* **a.** To include by or as if by counting: *Count me in.* **b.** To exclude by or as if by counting: *Count me out.* **3.** To believe or consider to be; deem: *Count yourself lucky.* —*intr.* **1.** To recite or list numbers in order or enumerate items by units or groups: *counted by tens.* **2.a.** To have importance: *You really count with me.* **b.** To have a specified importance or value: *Their opinions count for little. Each basket counts for two points.* **3.** *Music.* To keep time by counting beats. **—count** *n.* **1.** The act of counting or calculating. **2.a.** A number reached by counting. **b.** The totality of specific items in a particular sample: *a white blood cell count.* **3.** *Law.* Any of the separate and distinct charges in an indictment. **4.** *Sports.* The counting from one to ten seconds, during which time a boxer who has been knocked down must rise or be declared the loser. **5.** *Baseball.* The number of balls and strikes that an umpire has called against a batter. ***—phrasal verb.* count on. 1.** To rely on; depend on: *You can count on my help.* **2.** To be confident of; anticipate: *counted on getting a raise.* ***—idiom.* count heads** (or **noses**)**.** To make a count of members, attendees, or participants by or as if by noting bodily presence. [Middle English *counten,* from Old French *conter,* from Latin *computāre,* to calculate : *com-,* com- + *putāre,* to think; see **peu-** in Appendix.]

SYNONYMS: *count, import, matter, signify, weigh.* The central meaning shared by these verbs is "to be of significance or importance": *an opinion that counts for a great deal; actions that import little; decisions that really matter; thoughts that signify much; considerations that do not weigh with her.*

count² (kount) *n. Abbr.* **Ct. 1.** A nobleman in some European countries. **2.** Used as a title for such a nobleman. [Middle English *counte,* from Old French *conte,* from Late Latin *comes, comit-,* occupant of any state office, from Latin, companion. See **ei-** in Appendix.]

count•a•ble (koun′tə-bəl) *adj.* **1.** That can be counted: *countable items; countable sins.* **2.** *Mathematics.* That can be put into a one-to-one correspondence with the positive integers. **—count′a•bil′i•ty** *n.* **—count′a•bly** *adv.*

count•down (kount′doun′) *n.* **1.** The counting backward aloud from an arbitrary starting number to indicate the time remaining before an event or operation, such as the launching of a missile or space vehicle. **2.** The checks and preparations carried out during this activity.

coun•te•nance (koun′tə-nəns) *n.* **1.** Appearance, especially the expression of the face. **2.** The face or facial features. See Synonyms at **face. 3.a.** A look or expression indicative of encouragement or of moral support. **b.** Support or approval. **4.** *Obsolete.* Bearing; demeanor. **—countenance** *tr.v.* **-nanced, -nanc•ing, -nanc•es.** To give or express approval to; condone: *The college administration will not countenance cheating.* [Middle English *contenaunce,* from Old French, from *contenir,* to behave. See CONTAIN.] **—coun′te•nanc•er** *n.*

coun•ter¹ (koun′tər) *adj.* Contrary; opposing: *moves and counter moves on the checkerboard.* **—counter** *n.* **1.** One that is an opposite. **2.** *Sports.* A boxing blow given while receiving or parrying another. **3.** *Sports.* A fencing parry in which one foil follows the other in a circular fashion. **4.** A stiff piece of leather around the heel of a shoe. **5.** *Nautical.* The portion of a ship's stern extending from the water line to the extreme outward swell. **6.** *Printing.* The depression between the raised lines of a typeface. **—counter** *v.* **-tered, -ter•ing, -ters.** —*tr.* **1.** To meet or return (a blow) by another blow. **2.** To move or act in opposition to; oppose. **3.** To offer in response: *countered that she was too busy to be thorough.* —*intr.* To move, act, or respond so as to be in opposition. **—counter** *adv.* **1.** In a contrary manner or direction. **2.** To or toward an opposite or dissimilar course or outcome: *a method running counter to traditional techniques.* [From COUNTER–.]

count•er² (koun′tər) *n.* **1.** *Abbr.* **ctr.** A flat surface on which money is counted, business is transacted, or food is prepared or served. **2.** *Games.* A piece, as of wood or ivory, used for keeping a count or a place. **3.a.** An imitation coin; a token. **b.** A piece of money. [Middle English *countour,* from Anglo-Norman *counteor,* from Medieval Latin *computātōrium,* counting house, from Latin *computāre,* to calculate. See COUNT¹.]

count•er³ (koun′tər) *n.* One that counts, especially an electronic or mechanical device that automatically counts occurrences or repetitions of phenomena or events.

counter– *pref.* **1.** Contrary; opposite; opposing: *counterclaim.* **2.** Corresponding; complementary: *counterfoil.* [Middle English *countre-,* from Old French *contre-,* from Latin *contrā.* See **kom** in Appendix.]

coun•ter•act (koun′tər-ăkt′) *tr.v.* **-act•ed, -act•ing, -acts.** To oppose and mitigate the effects of by contrary action; check. See Synonyms at **neutralize. —coun′ter•ac′tion** *n.* **—coun′ter•ac′tive** *adj.* **—coun′ter•ac′tive•ly** *adv.*

coun•ter•ar•gu•ment (koun′tər-är′gyə-mənt) *n.* **1.** An argument in opposition to another. **2.** Something that undermines an argument or deters someone from action: *The students considered demonstrating for free elections, but their country's secret police provided a powerful counterargument.*

coun•ter•at•tack (koun′tər-ə-tăk′) *n.* A return attack. **—counterattack** (koun′tər-ə-tăk′) *intr. & tr.v.* **-tacked, -tack•ing, -tacks.** To deliver a return attack or make a return attack against.

coun•ter•bal•ance (koun′tər-băl′əns, koun′tər-băl′əns) *n.* **1.** A force or influence equally counteracting another. **2.** A weight that acts to balance another; a counterpoise or counterweight. **—counterbalance** (koun′tər-băl′əns, koun′tər-băl′əns) *tr.v.* **-anced, -anc•ing, -anc•es. 1.** To act as a counteracting force, influence, or weight to; counterpoise. **2.** To oppose with an equal force; offset.

coun•ter•blow (koun′tər-blō′) *n.* A blow delivered in return.

coun•ter•change (koun′tər-chānj′) *tr.v.* **-changed, -chang•ing, -chang•es. 1.** To cause to change places; transpose. **2.** To make checkered; variegate.

coun•ter•charge (koun′tər-chärj′) *n.* A charge in opposition to another charge. **—countercharge** (koun′tər-chärj′) *v.* **-charged, -charg•ing, -charg•es.** —*tr.* To bring a charge against (one's accuser). —*intr.* To make a countercharge.

coun•ter•check (koun′tər-chĕk′) *n.* **1.** Something that serves to check, restrict, or limit something else. **2.** Something that confirms or denies the correctness of a previous check. **—countercheck** (koun′ter-chĕk′) *tr.v.* **-checked, -check•ing, -checks. 1.** To oppose or check by a counteraction. **2.** To check again in order to verify.

counter check *n.* A bank check for the use of customers making a withdrawal.

coun•ter•claim (koun′tər-klām′) *n.* A claim filed in opposition to another claim, especially in a legal action. **—counterclaim** (koun′tər-klām′) *intr. & tr.v.* **-claimed, -claim•ing, -claims.** To plead an opposing claim or make an opposing claim against. **—coun′ter•claim′ant** (-klā′mənt) *n.*

coun•ter•clock•wise (koun′tər-klŏk′wīz′) *adv. & adj. Abbr.* **cckw., ccw.** In a direction opposite to the rotating hands of a clock.

coun•ter•con•di•tion•ing (koun′tər-kən-dĭsh′ə-nĭng) *n. Psychology.* Conditioning intended to replace a negative response to a stimulus with a positive response.

coun•ter•coup (koun′tər-ko͞o′) *n.* A sudden overthrow of a government that gained power by a coup d'état.

coun•ter•cul•ture (koun′tər-kŭl′chər) *n.* A culture, especially of young people, with values or lifestyles in opposition to those of the established culture. **—coun′ter•cul′tur•al** *adj.* **—coun′ter•cul′tur•ist** *n.*

coun•ter•cur•rent (koun′tər-kûr′ənt, -kŭr′-) *n.* A current that flows in an opposite direction to the flow of another current. **—coun′ter•cur′rent** *adj.* **—coun′ter•cur′rent•ly** *adv.*

coun•ter•cy•cli•cal (koun′tər-sĭk′lĭ-kəl, -sī′klĭ-) *adj.* In-

ă pat	oi boy
ā pay	ou out
âr care	o͝o took
ä father	o͞o boot
ĕ pet	ŭ cut
ē be	ûr urge
ĭ pit	th thin
ī pie	*th* this
îr pier	hw which
ŏ pot	zh vision
ō toe	ə about, item
ô paw	♦ regionalism

Stress marks: **′** (primary); ′ (secondary), as in **dictionary** (dĭk′shə-nĕr′ē)

tended to compensate for immoderate developments in a business cycle: *a countercyclical federal aid program.*

coun·ter·dem·on·stra·tion (koun′tər-dĕm′ən-strā′shən) *n.* A demonstration held in opposition to another demonstration. **—coun′ter·dem′on·stra′tor** *n.*

coun·ter·es·pi·o·nage (koun′tər-ĕs′pē-ə-näzh′, -nĭj) *n.* Espionage undertaken to detect and counteract enemy espionage.

coun·ter·ex·am·ple (koun′tər-ĭg-zăm′pəl) *n.* An example that refutes or disproves a hypothesis, proposition, or theorem.

coun·ter·fac·tu·al (koun′tər-făk′cho͞o-əl) *adj.* Running contrary to the facts: *"Cold war historiography vividly illustrates how the selection of the counterfactual question to be asked generally anticipates the desired answer"* (Timothy Garton Ash). **—coun′ter·fac′tu·al** *n.*

coun·ter·feit (koun′tər-fĭt′) *v.* **-feit·ed, -feit·ing, -feits.** —*tr.* **1.** To make a copy of, usually with the intent to defraud; forge: *counterfeits money.* **2.** To make a pretense of; feign: *counterfeited interest in the story.* See Synonyms at **pretend.** —*intr.* **1.** To carry on a deception; dissemble. **2.** To make fraudulent copies of something valuable. **—counterfeit** *adj.* **1.** Made in imitation of what is genuine with the intent to defraud: *a counterfeit dollar bill.* **2.** Simulated; feigned: *a counterfeit illness.* **—counterfeit** *n.* A fraudulent imitation or facsimile. [Middle English *countrefeten,* from *contrefet,* made in imitation, from Old French *contrefait,* past participle of *contrefaire,* to counterfeit : *contre-,* counter- + *faire,* to make (from Latin *facere;* see **dhē-** in Appendix).] **—coun′ter·feit′er** *n.*

coun·ter·foil (koun′tər-foil′) *n.* The part of a check or other commercial paper retained by the issuer as a record of a transaction.

coun·ter·force (koun′tər-fôrs′, -fōrs′) *n.* A contrary or opposing force, especially a military force capable of destroying the nuclear armaments of an enemy. —*attributive.* Often used to modify another noun: *a counterforce strategy; counterforce weapons.*

coun·ter·glow (koun′tər-glō′) *n.* See **gegenschein.**

coun·ter·in·sur·gen·cy (koun′tər-ĭn-sûr′jən-sē) *n.* Political and military strategy or action intended to oppose and forcefully suppress insurgency. **—coun′ter·in·sur′gent** *n.*

coun·ter·in·tel·li·gence (koun′tər-ĭn-tĕl′ə-jəns) *n.* The branch of an intelligence service charged with keeping sensitive information from an enemy, deceiving that enemy, preventing subversion and sabotage, and collecting political and military information.

coun·ter·ir·ri·tant (koun′tər-ĭr′ĭ-tənt) *n.* An agent that induces local inflammation to relieve inflammation in underlying or adjacent tissues. **—counterirritant** *adj.* Of or producing the effect of such an agent. **—coun′ter·ir′ri·ta′tion** (-tā′shən) *n.*

coun·ter·man (koun′tər-măn′, -mən) *n.* A man who tends a counter, as in a diner.

coun·ter·mand (koun′tər-mănd′, koun′tər-mănd′) *tr.v.* **-mand·ed, -mand·ing, -mands. 1.** To cancel or reverse (a previously issued command or order). **2.** To recall by a contrary order: *countermanded the air strikes.* **—countermand** (koun′tər-mănd′) *n.* **1.** An order or command reversing another one. **2.** Cancellation of an order or command. [Middle English *countremaunden,* from Old French *contremander* : *contre-,* counter- + *mander,* to command (from Latin *mandāre;* see **man-**[2] in Appendix).]

coun·ter·march (koun′tər-märch′) *n.* **1.** A march back or in a reverse direction. **2.** A complete reversal of method or conduct. **—countermarch** (koun′tər-märch′) *intr. & tr.v.* **-marched, -march·ing, -march·es.** To execute or cause to execute a countermarch.

coun·ter·mea·sure (koun′tər-mĕzh′ər) *n.* A measure or action taken to counter or offset another one.

coun·ter·mine (koun′tər-mīn′) *v.* **-mined, -min·ing, -mines.** —*tr.* **1.** To frustrate or defeat by secret and opposite measures. **2.** To make or use a countermine against. —*intr.* To make or lay down countermines. **—countermine** (koun′tər-mīn′) *n.* **1.** A tunnel dug to intercept and destroy an enemy's mine. **2.** A plot to frustrate or defeat an attack.

coun·ter·move (koun′tər-mo͞ov′) *n.* A move made in opposition or retaliation to another. **—countermove** (koun′tər-mo͞ov′) *intr.v.* **-moved, -mov·ing, -moves.** To make a move in retaliation or opposition. **—coun′ter·move′ment** *n.*

coun·ter·of·fen·sive (koun′tər-ə-fĕn′sĭv) *n.* A large-scale counterattack by an armed force, intended to stop an enemy offensive.

coun·ter·of·fer (koun′tər-ô′fər, -ŏf′ər) *n.* An offer made in return by one who rejects an unsatisfactory offer.

countersink

coun·ter·pane (koun′tər-pān′) *n.* A cover for a bed; a bedspread. [Alteration of obsolete *counterpoint,* from Middle English *countrepoint,* from Old French *contrepointe,* alteration of *coultepointe,* from Medieval Latin *culcita puncta,* stitched quilt : Latin *culcita,* quilt, mattress; see QUILT + Latin *punctus,* stitched, pricked; see POINT.]

coun·ter·part (koun′tər-pärt′) *n.* **1.a.** One that closely resembles another. **b.** One that has the same functions and characteristics as another; an opposite number: *The foreign minister is the counterpart of the secretary of state.* **2.** A copy or duplicate of a legal paper. **3.a.** One of two parts that fit and complete each other. **b.** One that serves as a complement.

coun·ter·per·son (koun′tər-pûr′sən) *n.* A person who tends a counter, as in a diner.

coun·ter·plan (koun′tər-plăn′) *n.* **1.** A plan intended to counter or oppose another plan. **2.** An alternate plan.

coun·ter·play (koun′tər-plā′) *n. Games.* A threat or offensive position in chess intended to counter an opponent's advantage in another part of the board.

coun·ter·plea (koun′tər-plē′) *n. Law.* A plaintiff's reply to a defendant's plea or counterclaim; an answering plea.

coun·ter·plot (koun′tər-plŏt′) *n.* **1.** A plot or scheme intended to subvert another plot. **2.** See **subplot** (sense 1). **—counterplot** *v.* **-plot·ted, -plot·ting, -plots.** —*intr.* To oppose or subvert one plot with another. —*tr.* To plot against; thwart with a counterplot.

coun·ter·point (koun′tər-point′) *n.* **1.** *Music.* **a.** Melodic material that is added above or below an existing melody. **b.** The technique of combining two or more melodic lines in such a way that they establish a harmonic relationship while retaining their linear individuality. **c.** A composition or piece that incorporates or consists of contrapuntal writing. **2.a.** A contrasting but parallel element, item, or theme. **b.** Use of contrasting elements in a work of art. **—counterpoint** *tr.v.* **-point·ed, -point·ing, -points. 1.** *Music.* To write or arrange (music) in counterpoint. **2.** To set in contrast: *"The complex, clotted computer talk sadly counterpoints the simplistic nature of the characters"* (Rhoda Koenig).

coun·ter·poise (koun′tər-poiz′) *n.* **1.** A counterbalancing weight. **2.** A force or influence that balances or equally counteracts another. **3.** The state of being in equilibrium. **—counterpoise** *tr.v.* **-poised, -pois·ing, -pois·es. 1.** To oppose with an equal weight; counterbalance. **2.** To act against with an equal force or power; offset. [Alteration (influenced by POISE[1]) of Middle English *countrepeis,* from Old French *contrepeis* : *contre-,* counter- + *peis,* weight; see AVOIRDUPOIS.]

coun·ter·pose (koun′tər-pōz′) *tr.v.* **-posed, -pos·ing, -pos·es.** To set in contrast, opposition, or balance.

coun·ter·pro·duc·tive (koun′tər-prə-dŭk′tĭv) *adj.* Tending to hinder rather than serve one's purpose: *"Violation of the court order would be counterproductive"* (Philip H. Lee). **—coun′ter·pro·duc′tive·ly** *adv.*

coun·ter·pro·gram·ming (koun′tər-prō′grăm-ĭng, -grə-mĭng) *n.* The scheduling of television programs so as to attract viewers away from programs broadcast simultaneously on another network.

coun·ter·pro·pos·al (koun′tər-prə-pō′zəl) *n.* A proposal offered to nullify or substitute for a previous one.

coun·ter·punch (koun′tər-pŭnch′) *n.* A countering attack or blow, especially one delivered by a boxer. **—counterpunch** *intr.v.* **-punched, -punch·ing, -punch·es.** To deliver a counterpunch. **—coun′ter·punch′er** *n.*

coun·ter·ref·or·ma·tion (koun′tər-rĕf′ər-mā′shən) *n.* A reformation intended to counter the consequences of a previous reformation.

Coun·ter Reformation (koun′tər) *n.* A reform movement within the Roman Catholic Church that arose in 16th-century Europe in response to the Protestant Reformation.

coun·ter·rev·o·lu·tion (koun′tər-rĕv′ə-lo͞o′shən) *n.* **1.** A revolution whose aim is the deposition and reversal of a political or social system set up by a previous revolution. **2.** A movement to oppose revolutionary tendencies and developments. **—coun′ter·rev′o·lu′tion·ar′y** (-shə-nĕr′ē) *adj. & n.* **—coun′ter·rev′o·lu′tion·ist** *n.*

coun·ter·shad·ing (koun′tər-shā′dĭng) *n.* Protective coloration in an animal or insect, characterized by darker coloring of areas exposed to light and lighter coloring of areas that are normally shaded.

coun·ter·shaft (koun′tər-shăft′) *n.* An intermediate shaft between the powered and driven shafts in a belt drive.

coun·ter·sign (koun′tər-sīn′) *tr.v.* **-signed, -sign·ing, -signs.** To sign (a previously signed document), as for authentication. **—countersign** *n.* **1.** A second or confirming signature, as on a previously signed document. Also called *countersignature.* **2.a.** A secret sign or signal to be given to a sentry in order to obtain passage; a password. **b.** A secret sign or signal given in answer to another.

coun·ter·sig·na·ture (koun′tər-sĭg′nə-chər) *n.* See **countersign** (sense 1).

coun·ter·sink (koun′tər-sĭngk′) *n. Abbr.* **csk. 1.** A hole with the top part enlarged so that the head of a screw or bolt will lie flush with or below the surface. **2.** A tool for making such a hole. **—countersink** *tr.v.* **-sunk** (-sŭngk′), **-sink·ing, -sinks. 1.** To make a countersink on or in. **2.** To drive a screw or bolt into (a countersink).

coun·ter·spy (koun′tər-spī′) *n., pl.* **-spies.** A spy working in opposition to enemy espionage.

coun·ter·stain (koun′tər-stān′) *n.* A stain of a contrasting color used to color the components in a microscopic specimen that are not made visible by the principal stain. **—counterstain** *tr.v.* **-stained, -stain·ing, -stains.** To color (a microscopic specimen) with such a stain.

coun·ter·sue (koun′tər-so͞o′) *tr.v.* **-sued, -su·ing, -sues.** *Law.* To bring proceedings against (a plaintiff) in opposition to a suit brought against oneself. **—coun′ter·suit′** (-so͞ot′) *n.*

coun·ter·sunk (koun′tər-sŭngk′) *v.* Past tense and past participle of **countersink.**

coun·ter·ten·or (koun′tər-tĕn′ər) *n. Music.* **1.** An adult male voice with a range above that of tenor. **2.** A singer having a voice that is within this range. —*attributive.* Often used to modify another noun: *a countertenor part; a countertenor arrangement.*

coun·ter·ter·ror (koun′tər-tĕr′ər) *adj.* Intended to prevent or counteract terrorism: *counterterror measures; counterterror weapons.* **—counterterror** *n.* Action or strategy intended to counteract or suppress terrorism. **—coun′ter·ter′ror·ism** *n.* **—coun′ter·ter′ror·ist** *adj. & n.*

coun·ter·top (koun′tər-tŏp′) *n.* A level surface on a cabinet or display case, as in a kitchen or department store. —*attributive.* Often used to modify another noun: *a countertop appliance; countertop goods on sale.*

coun·ter·trade (koun′tər-trād′) *n.* International barter in which one country agrees to import commodities from another country to which it exports commodities. **—coun′ter·trad′er** *n.*

coun·ter·trans·fer·ence (koun′tər-trăns-fûr′əns, -trăns′fər-) *n.* The surfacing of a psychotherapist's own repressed feelings through identification with the emotions, experiences, or problems of a person undergoing treatment.

coun·ter·vail (koun′tər-vāl′, koun′tər-vāl′) *v.* **-vailed, -vail·ing, -vails.** —*tr.* **1.** To act against with equal force; counteract. **2.** To compensate for; offset. —*intr.* To act against an often detrimental influence or power. [Middle English *countrevaillen,* from Old French *contrevaloir, contrevail-* : *contre-,* counter- + *valoir,* to be worth (from Latin *valēre,* to be strong; see **wal-** in Appendix).]

coun·ter·weigh (koun′tər-wā′) *intr. & tr.v.* **-weighed, -weigh·ing, -weighs.** To counterbalance or cause to counterbalance.

coun·ter·weight (koun′tər-wāt′) *n.* **1.** A weight used as a counterbalance. **2.** A force or influence equally counteracting another. **—coun′ter·weight′ed** (-wā′tĭd) *adj.*

coun·ter·wom·an (koun′tər-wo͝om′ən) *n.* A woman who tends a counter, as in a diner.

count·ess (koun′tĭs) *n.* **1.** A woman holding the title of count or earl. **2.a.** The wife or widow of a count in various European countries. **b.** The wife or widow of an earl in Great Britain. **3.** Used as a title for such a noblewoman. [Middle English *countes,* from Old French *contesse,* feminine of *conte,* count. See COUNT[2].]

count·ing·house also **count·ing house** (koun′tĭng-hous′) *n.* A building, room, or office in which a business firm carries on operations such as accounting and correspondence.

count·less (kount′lĭs) *adj.* Incapable of being counted; innumerable. See Synonyms at **incalculable.** **—count′less·ly** *adv.*

count noun *n.* A noun for an object, such as *chair,* or for an idea, such as *experience,* that speakers of a language identify as referring to a single entity and that can form a plural or occur in a noun phrase construction with an indefinite article, with numerals, or with such terms as *many.*

count palatine *n., pl.* **counts palatine. 1.a.** Any of various noblemen originally exercising certain royal powers within their own domains, especially a count of the Holy Roman Empire having sovereign powers in his own territories. **b.** A feudal lord having sovereign powers over his lands. **2.** The titled proprietor of a county palatine in England or Ireland.

coun·tri·fied also **coun·try·fied** (kŭn′trĭ-fīd′) *adj.* **1.** Resembling or having the characteristics of country life; rural. **2.** Lacking sophistication.

coun·try (kŭn′trē) *n., pl.* **-tries. 1.a.** A nation or state. **b.** The territory of a nation or state; land. **c.** The people of a nation or state; populace: *The whole country will profit from the new economic reforms.* **2.** The land of a person's birth or citizenship: *Foreign travel is restricted in his country.* **3.** A region, territory, or large tract of land distinguishable by features of topography, biology, or culture: *hill country; Bible country.* **4.** A district outside of cities and towns; a rural area: *a vacation in the country.* **5.** *Law.* A jury. **6.** *Informal.* Country music. **—country** *adj.* **1.** Of, relating to, or typical of the country: *a country road; country cooking.* **2.** Of or relating to country music. **—*idiom.* in country.** In Vietnam during the period of U.S. military operations there: *"He'd been in country a month longer than the other four"* (Nelson DeMille). [Middle English *countre,* from Old French *contree,* from Vulgar Latin **(terra) contrāta,* (land) opposite, before, from Latin *contrā,* opposite. See **kom** in Appendix.]

country and western *n. Abbr.* **C & W, C and W** See **country music.**

country club *n.* A suburban club for social and sports activities, usually featuring a golf course.

country cousin *n.* One whose ingenuousness or rustic ways may bemuse or entertain city dwellers.

coun·try-dance (kŭn′trē-dăns′) *n.* A folk dance of English origin in which two lines of dancers face each other.

coun·try·fied (kŭn′trĭ-fīd′) *adj.* Variant of **countrified.**

country gentleman *n.* A man who owns a country estate.

coun·try·man (kŭn′trē-mən) *n.* **1.** A person from one's own country; a compatriot. **2.** A native or inhabitant of a particular country. **3.** A man who lives in the country or has country ways.

country mile *n. Informal.* A very great distance.

country music *n. Music.* Popular music based on the folk style of the southern rural United States or on the music of cowboys in the American West. Also called *country and western.*

coun·try·seat (kŭn′trē-sēt′) *n.* An estate or mansion in the country.

coun·try·side (kŭn′trē-sīd′) *n.* **1.** A rural region. **2.** The inhabitants of a rural region.

country singer *n. Music.* One who sings country music.

coun·try·wide (kŭn′trē-wīd′) *adv. & adj.* Throughout a whole country; nationwide: *launched a fundraising campaign countrywide; a countrywide search.*

coun·try·wom·an (kŭn′trē-wo͝om′ən) *n.* **1.** A woman from one's own country; a compatriot. **2.** A woman from a particular country. **3.** A woman who lives in the country or has country ways.

coun·ty (koun′tē) *n., pl.* **-ties.** *Abbr.* **co, co. 1.** An administrative subdivision of a state in the United States. **2.a.** A territorial division exercising administrative, judicial, and political functions in Great Britain and Ireland. **b.** The territory under the jurisdiction of a count or earl. **3.** The people living in a county. [Middle English *counte,* territorial division, from Old French *conte,* the territory of a count, from Medieval Latin *comitātus,* from Late Latin, the office of count, from Latin, retinue, from *comes, comit-,* companion. See **ei-** in Appendix.] **—coun′ty** *adj.*

county agent *n.* A government employee who serves as a consultant and adviser in a chiefly rural county on such matters as agriculture, education, and home economics.

county fair *n.* A fair usually held every year at the same location in a county, especially for the competitive showing of livestock and farm products.

county palatine *n., pl.* **counties palatine.** The domain of a count palatine in England or Ireland.

county seat *n.* A town or city that is the administrative center of its county.

county town *n. Chiefly British.* A county seat. Also called *shire town.*

coun·ty·wide (koun′tē-wīd′) *adv. & adj.* Throughout a whole county: *found at locations countywide; a countywide war on drugs.*

coup (ko͞o) *n., pl.* **coups** (ko͞oz). **1.** A brilliantly executed stratagem; a masterstroke. **2.** A coup d'état. **3.** Among certain Native American peoples, a feat of bravery performed in battle, especially the touching of an enemy's body without causing injury. **—*idiom.* count coup.** Among certain Native American peoples, to ceremoniously recount one's exploits in battle. [French, stroke, from Old French *colp,* from Late Latin *colpus.* See COPE[1].]

coup de grâce (ko͞o′ də gräs′) *n., pl.* **coups de grâce. 1.** A deathblow delivered to end the misery of a mortally wounded victim. **2.** A finishing stroke or decisive event. [French : *coup,* stroke + *de,* of + *grâce,* mercy.]

coup de main (də măN′) *n., pl.* **coups de main.** A sudden action undertaken to surprise an enemy. [French : *coup,* stroke, blow + *de,* of + *main,* hand.]

coup d'é·tat (dā-tä′) *n., pl.* **coups d'état** or **coup d'états** (-dā-tä′). The sudden overthrow of a government by a usually small group of persons in or previously in positions of authority. [French : *coup,* blow, stroke + *de,* of + *état,* state.]

coup de thé·â·tre (də tā-ä′trə) *n., pl.* **coups de théâtre. 1.** A sudden, dramatic turn of events in a play. **2.** An unexpected and sensational event, especially one that reverses or negates a prevailing situation. [French : *coup,* stroke + *de,* of + *théâtre,* theater.]

coup d'oeil (dœ′yə) *n., pl.* **coups d'oeil.** A quick survey; a glance. [French : *coup,* stroke + *de,* of + *oeil,* eye.]

coupe[1] (ko͞op) *n.* **1.a.** A dessert of ice cream or fruit-flavored ice, garnished and served in a special dessert glass. **b.** The stemmed glass in which a coupe is served. **2.** A shallow, bowl-shaped dessert dish. [French, cup, from Late Latin *cuppa.*]

coupe[2] (ko͞op) *n.* Variant of **coupé** (sense 2).

cou·pé (ko͞o-pā′) *n.* **1.** A closed four-wheel carriage with two seats inside and one outside. **2.** Also **coupe** (ko͞op). A closed two-door automobile. [French, from past participle of *couper,* to cut, from *coup,* blow. See COUP.]

Cou·pe·rin (ko͞o-pə-răN′, ko͞op-răN′), **François.** 1668–1733. French composer who was court organist at Versailles during the reign of Louis XIV.

cou·ple (kŭp′əl) *n.* **1.** Two items of the same kind; a pair. **2.** Something that joins or connects two things together; a link. **3.** *(used with a sing. or pl. verb).* **a.** Two people united, as by betrothal or marriage. **b.** Two people together. **4.** *Informal.* A few; several: *a couple of days.* **5.** *Physics.* A pair of forces of equal magnitude acting in parallel but opposite directions, capable of causing rotation but not translation. **—couple** *v.* **-pled, -pling, -ples.** —*tr.* **1.** To link together; connect: *coupled her refusal with an explanation.* **2.a.** To join as spouses; marry. **b.** To join in sexual union. **3.** *Electricity.* To link (two circuits or currents) as by magnetic induction. —*intr.* **1.** To form pairs; join. **2.** To unite sexually; copulate. **3.** To join chemically. **—couple** *adj. Informal.* Two or few: *"Every couple years the urge strikes, to . . . haul off to a new site"* (Garrison Keillor). [Middle English, from Old French, from Latin *cōpula,* bond, pair.]

SYNONYMS: *couple, pair, brace, yoke.* These nouns denote two individuals of the same kind together. *Couple* does not necessarily

ă pat	oi boy
ā pay	ou out
âr care	o͝o took
ä father	o͞o boot
ĕ pet	ŭ cut
ē be	ûr urge
ĭ pit	th thin
ī pie	*th* this
îr pier	hw which
ŏ pot	zh vision
ō toe	ə about, item
ô paw	♦ regionalism

Stress marks: ′ (primary); ′ (secondary), as in **dictionary** (dĭk′shə-nĕr′ē)

imply more than association: *a square dance performed by four couples.* The term may also mean simply "few": *a couple of minutes; a couple of books. Pair* stresses close association and often reciprocal dependence of things (*a pair of gloves; a pair of pajamas*); sometimes it denotes a single thing with interdependent parts (*a pair of scissors; a pair of spectacles*). *Brace* refers principally to certain animals or game birds (*a brace of hounds; a brace of partridges*), and *yoke* to two joined draft animals (*a yoke of oxen*).

USAGE NOTE: When used to refer to two people who function socially as a unit, as in *a married couple,* the word *couple* may take either a singular or a plural verb, depending on whether the members are considered individually or collectively: *The couple were married last week. Only one couple was unaccounted for.* When a pronoun follows, *they* and *their* are more common than *it* and *its*: *The couple decided to spend their* (less commonly *its*) *vacation in Italy.* Care should be taken that the verb and the pronoun agree in number: *The couple have their* (less commonly *has its*) *primary residence in New York.* • Although the phrase *a couple of* has been well established in English since before the Renaissance, it has been criticized on several grounds. Grammarians used to insist that *a couple of* should be used only to refer to things closely linked to one another and so was improperly used in phrases such as *a couple of years ago.* This objection has not been heard in some time and was never well supported. Modern critics have sometimes maintained that *a couple of* is too inexact to be appropriate in formal writing. But the inexactitude of *a couple of* may serve a useful communicative purpose, suggesting that the writer is indifferent to the precise number of items involved. Thus the sentence *She lives only a couple of miles away* implies not only that the distance is short but that its exact measure is unimportant. Furthermore, *a couple of* is different from *a few* in that it does not imply that the relevant amount is relatively small. One might say admiringly of an exceptional center fielder that *he can throw the ball a couple of hundred feet,* but not, except ironically, *a few hundred feet,* which would suggest that such a throw was unremarkable. The usage should be considered unobjectionable on all levels of style.

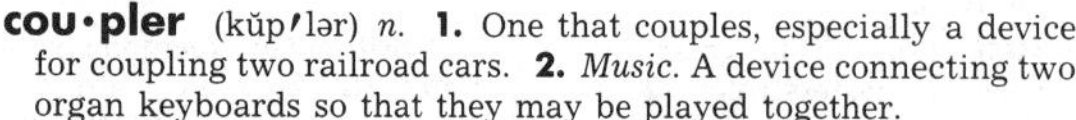

Gustave Courbet

cou•pler (kŭp′lər) *n.* **1.** One that couples, especially a device for coupling two railroad cars. **2.** *Music.* A device connecting two organ keyboards so that they may be played together.

cou•plet (kŭp′lĭt) *n.* **1.** A unit of verse consisting of two successive lines, usually rhyming and having the same meter and often forming a complete thought or syntactic unit. **2.** Two similar things; a pair. [French, from Old French, diminutive of *couple,* couple. See COUPLE.]

cou•pling (kŭp′lĭng) *n.* **1.** The act of forming couples. **2.** The act of uniting sexually. **3.** A device that links or connects. **4.** *Electronics.* Transfer of energy from one circuit to another. **5.** The body part of a four-footed animal that connects the hindquarters to the forequarters.

cou•pon (ko͞o′pŏn′, kyo͞o′-) *n. Abbr.* **cp. 1.** A negotiable certificate attached to a bond that represents a sum of interest due. **2.a.** One of a set of detachable certificates that may be torn off and redeemed as needed: *a food coupon.* **b.** A detachable part, as of a ticket or advertisement, that entitles the bearer to certain benefits, such as a cash refund or a gift. **c.** A certificate accompanying a product that may be redeemed for a cash discount. **d.** A printed form, as in an advertisement, to be used as an order blank or for requesting information or obtaining a discount on merchandise. **3.** A detachable slip calling for periodic payments, as for merchandise bought on an installment plan. [French, from Old French *colpon,* piece cut off, from *colper,* to cut, from *colp,* blow. See COUP.]

WORD HISTORY: A Roman might have had difficulty predicting what would become of the Latin word *colaphus,* which meant "a blow with the fist." In Old French, a language that developed from Latin, Late Latin *colpus,* from Latin *colaphus,* became *colp,* or modern French *coup,* with the same sense. *Coup* has had a rich development in French, gaining numerous senses, participating in numerous phrases, such as *coup d'état* (a term that we have borrowed), and giving rise to many derivatives, including *couper,* "to cut; literally, to divide with a blow or stroke." *Couper* yielded the word *coupon,* "a portion that is cut off," which came to refer to a certificate that was detachable from a principal certificate. The detachable certificate could be exchanged for interest or dividend payments by the holder of the principal certificate. *Coupon* is first recorded in English in 1822 with this sense and then came to apply to forms or tickets, detachable or otherwise, that could be exchanged for various benefits or used to request information.

course
Slalom ski course

cou•pon•ing (ko͞o′pŏn′ĭng, kyo͞o′-) *n.* The sending out or turning in of coupons, especially the regular redemption of a manufacturer's coupon for cash.

cour•age (kûr′ĭj, kŭr′-) *n.* The state or quality of mind or spirit that enables one to face danger, fear, or vicissitudes with self-possession, confidence, and resolution; bravery. [Middle English *corage,* from Old French, from Vulgar Latin **corāticum,* from Latin *cor.* See **kerd-** in Appendix.]

cou•ra•geous (kə-rā′jəs) *adj.* Having or characterized by courage; valiant. See Synonyms at **brave. —cou•ra′geous•ly** *adv.* **—cou•ra′geous•ness** *n.*

cou•rante (ko͞o-ränt′) *n.* **1.** A 17th-century French dance characterized by running and gliding steps to an accompaniment in triple time. **2.** *Music.* The second movement of the classical baroque suite, typically following the allemande. [French, from feminine present participle of *courir,* to run, from Old French *courre,* from Latin *currere.* See **kers-** in Appendix.]

Cour•an•tyne also **Co•ran•tijn** (kōr′ən-tīn′, kôr′-). A river rising in southeast Guyana and flowing about 724 km (450 mi) to the Atlantic Ocean. It forms the Guyana-Suriname border in its lower course.

Cour•bet (ko͞or-bā′, -bĕ′), **Gustave.** 1819–1877. French painter known for his realistic depiction of everyday scenes. His works include *Burial at Ornans* (1850), *Bonjour M. Courbet* (1854), and *The Artist's Studio* (1855).

cour•gette (ko͞or-zhĕt′) *n. Chiefly British.* A zucchini. [French dialectal, diminutive of *courge,* gourd, from Old French *cohourde,* from Latin *cucurbita.*]

cou•ri•er (ko͞or′ē-ər, kûr′-, kŭr′-) *n.* **1.a.** A messenger, especially one on official diplomatic business. **b.** A spy carrying secret information. **2.a.** A personal attendant hired to make arrangements for a journey. **b.** An employee of a travel agency serving as a guide for tourists. [French *courrier,* from Old French, from Old Italian *corriere,* from *correre,* to run, from Latin *currere.* See **kers-** in Appendix.]

cour•lan (ko͞or′lən) *n.* See **limpkin.** [French, perhaps alteration of *courliri,* from Galibi *kurliri.*]

Cour•land also **Kur•land** (ko͞or′lənd). A historical region and former duchy of southern Latvia between the Baltic Sea and the Western Dvina River. It passed to Russia in 1795 and was largely incorporated into Latvia in 1918.

course (kôrs, kōrs) *n.* **1.** Onward movement in a particular direction; progress. **2.** The direction of continuing movement: *took a northern course.* **3.** The route or path taken by something, such as a stream, that moves. See Synonyms at **way. 4.** Movement in time; duration: *in the course of a year.* **5.** *Sports.* A designated area of land or water on which a race is held or a sport played. **6.** A mode of action or behavior: *followed the best course and invested her money.* **7.** A typical or natural manner of proceeding or developing; customary passage: *a fad that ran its course.* **8.** A systematic or orderly succession; a sequence: *a course of medical treatments.* **9.** A continuous layer of building material, such as brick or tile, on a wall or roof of a building. **10.a.** A complete body of prescribed studies constituting a curriculum. **b.** A unit of such a curriculum. **11.** A part of a meal served as a unit at one time. **12.** *Nautical.* The lowest sail on a mast of a square-rigged ship. **13.** A point on the compass, especially the one toward which a ship is sailing. **—course** *v.* **coursed, cours•ing, cours•es.** *—tr.* **1.** To move swiftly through or over; traverse: *ships coursing the seas.* **2.a.** To hunt (game) with hounds. **b.** To set (hounds) to chase game. *—intr.* **1.** To proceed or move swiftly along a specified course: *"Big tears now coursed down her face"* (Iris Murdoch). **2.** To hunt game with hounds. ***—idioms.*** **in due course.** At the proper or right time. **of course. 1.** In the natural or expected order of things; naturally. **2.** Without any doubt; certainly. [Middle English, from Old French *cours,* from Latin *cursus,* from past participle of *currere,* to run. See **kers-** in Appendix.]

cours•er[1] (kôr′sər, kōr′-) *n.* **1.** A dog trained for coursing. **2.** A huntsman.

cours•er[2] (kôr′sər, kōr′-) *n.* A swift horse; a charger.

course•ware (kôrs′wâr′, kōrs′-) *n. Computer Science.* Educational software designed especially for classroom use. [COURSE + (SOFT)WARE.]

cours•ing (kôr′sĭng, kōr′-) *n.* Hunting with dogs trained to chase game by sight instead of scent.

court (kôrt, kōrt) *n. Abbr.* **C., ct. 1.a.** An extent of open ground partially or completely enclosed by walls or buildings; a courtyard. **b.** A short street, especially a wide alley walled by buildings on three sides. **c.** A large open section of a building, often with a glass roof or skylight. **d.** A large building, such as a mansion, standing in a courtyard. **2.a.** The place of residence of a sovereign or dignitary; a royal mansion or palace. **b.** The retinue of a sovereign, including the royal family and personal servants, advisers, and ministers. **c.** A sovereign's governing body, including the council of ministers and state advisers. **d.** A formal meeting or reception presided over by a sovereign. **3.** *Law.* **a.** A person or body of persons whose task is to hear and submit a decision on cases at law. **b.** The building, hall, or room in which such cases are heard and determined. **c.** The regular session of a judicial assembly. **d.** A similar authorized tribunal having military or ecclesiastical jurisdiction. **4.** *Sports.* An open, level area marked with appropriate lines, upon which a game, such as tennis, handball, or basketball, is played. **5.** The body of directors of an organization, especially of a corporation. **6.** A legislative assembly. *—attributive.* Often used to modify another noun: *a court jester; court records.* **—court** *v.* **court•ed, court•ing, courts.** *—tr.* **1.a.** To attempt to gain; seek: *courting wealth and fame.* **b.** To behave so as to invite or incur: *courts disaster by taking drugs.* **2.** To try to gain the love or affections of, especially to seek to marry. **3.** To attempt to gain the favor of by attention or flattery: *a salesperson courting a potential customer.* *—intr.* To pursue a courtship; woo. ***—idiom.*** **pay court to. 1.** To flatter with solicitous overtures in an attempt to obtain something or clear away antagonism. **2.** To seek someone's love; woo. [Middle

English, from Old French *cort,* from Latin *cohors, cohort-,* courtyard, retinue. See **gher-**[1] in Appendix.]

court bouillon (ko͝or, kôr, kōr) *n.* A poaching liquid for fish whose ingredients usually include water, vinegar or wine, diced vegetables, and seasonings. [French : *court,* short + *bouillon,* broth.]

cour·te·ous (kûr′tē-əs) *adj.* Characterized by gracious consideration toward others. See Synonyms at **polite.** [Middle English *corteis,* courtly, from Old French, from *cort,* court. See COURT.] **—cour′te·ous·ly** *adv.* **—cour′te·ous·ness** *n.*

cour·te·san (kôr′tĭ-zən, kōr′-) *n.* A woman who is a prostitute, especially one whose clients are men of rank or wealth. [French *courtisane,* from Old French, from Old Italian *cortigiana,* feminine of *cortigiano,* courtier, from *corte,* court, from Latin *cohors, cohort-.* See **gher-**[1] in Appendix.]

cour·te·sy (kûr′tĭ-sē) *n., pl.* **-sies. 1.a.** Polite behavior. **b.** A polite gesture or remark. **2.a.** Consent or agreement in spite of fact; indulgence: *They call this pond a lake by courtesy only.* **b.** Willingness or generosity in providing something needed: *free advertising through the courtesy of the local newspaper.* **—courtesy** *adj.* **1.** Given or done as a polite gesture: *paid a courtesy visit to the new neighbors.* **2.** Free of charge: *courtesy tickets for the reporters.* [Middle English *courtesie,* from Old French, from *corteis,* courtly. See COURTEOUS.]

courtesy card *n.* A card that confers on its bearer a special right or privilege, as at a supermarket or bank.

courtesy title *n.* **1.** A title of no legal validity that is assumed or granted by custom, such as the academic title *professor* given to any instructor at a college. **2.a.** In Great Britain, the title that the heir of a high-ranking peer customarily uses, consisting of a secondary title accorded to the peer. **b.** In Great Britain, the prefixes *Lord* and *Lady* added to the given names of the younger children of dukes and marquises or *the Honourable* added to the children of viscounts and barons.

court·house (kôrt′hous′, kōrt′-) *n. Abbr.* **c.h., C.H. 1.** *Law.* A building housing judicial courts. **2.a.** A building housing the offices of a county government. **b.** A county seat.

court·i·er (kôr′tē-ər, -tyər, kōr′-) *n.* **1.** An attendant at a sovereign's court. **2.** One who seeks favor, especially by insincere flattery or obsequious behavior. [Middle English *courteour,* from Anglo-Norman, from Old French *cortoier,* to be at a royal court, from *cort,* court. See COURT.]

court·ly (kôrt′lē, kōrt′-) *adj.* **-li·er, -li·est. 1.** Suitable for a royal court; stately: *courtly furniture and pictures.* **2.** Elegant; refined: *courtly manners.* **3.** Flattering in an insincere way; obsequious. **—courtly** *adv.* In a courtly manner; elegantly or politely. **—court′li·ness** *n.*

courtly love *n.* An idealized and often illicit form of love celebrated in the literature of the Middle Ages and the Renaissance in which a knight or courtier devotes himself to a noblewoman who is usually married and feigns indifference to preserve her reputation.

court-mar·tial (kôrt′mär′shəl, kōrt′-) *n., pl.* **courts-mar·tial** (kôrts′-, kōrts′-). *Abbr.* **c.m. 1.** A military or naval court of officers appointed by a commander to try persons for offenses under military law. **2.** A trial by such a military tribunal. **—court-martial** *tr.v.* **-tialed, -tial·ing, -tials** also **-tialled, -tial·ling, -tials.** To try by military tribunal. [From *martial court.*]

court of appeals *n., pl.* **courts of appeals.** *Law.* A court to which appeals are made on points of law resulting from the judgment of a lower court.

court of chancery *n., pl.* **courts of chancery.** *Law.* A court with jurisdiction in equity.

court of claims *n., pl.* **courts of claims.** *Law.* A U.S. federal court that determines claims brought by individuals against the government.

court of common pleas *n., pl.* **courts of common pleas.** *Law.* **1.** A court in some states of the United States having general jurisdiction. **2.** A court in Great Britain that formerly heard civil cases between commoners.

court of domestic relations *n., pl.* **courts of domestic relations.** *Law.* A court having the judicial authority to investigate and decide on cases involving marital and especially parental rights and obligations, including child custody, support, and well-being.

Court of Exchequer (kôrt, kōrt) *n. Law.* A former superior court in Great Britain dealing with matters of revenue, now merged with the King's or Queen's Bench.

court of law *n., pl.* **courts of law.** *Law.* A court that hears cases and makes decisions based on statutes or the common law.

court of record *n., pl.* **courts of record.** *Law.* A court whose proceedings and decisions are kept on permanent record.

Court of Saint James's (sānt jāmz′, jām′zĭz) *n.* The British royal court.

court order *n. Law.* An order issued by a court that requires a person to do or refrain from doing something.

court plaster *n.* Cloth coated with an adhesive substance and used to cover cuts or scratches on the skin. [From its use by ladies at court to make beauty spots.]

Cour·trai (ko͝or-trā′, ko͝or-). See **Kortrijk.**

court reporter *n. Law.* A stenographer who makes a verbatim record and transcription of proceedings, as in a court.

court·room (kôrt′ro͞om′, -ro͝om′, kōrt′-) *n. Law.* A room in which the proceedings of a court are held.

court·ship (kôrt′shĭp′, kōrt′-) *n.* The act, process, or period of courting.

court·side (kôrt′sīd′, kōrt′-) *n. Sports.* The area immediately bordering the official court of play, as in tennis or basketball.

courts-mar·tial (kôrts′mär′shəl, kōrts′-) *n.* Plural of **court-martial.**

court tennis *n. Sports.* A form of tennis played in a large indoor court with a specially marked-out floor and high cement walls off which the ball may be played.

court·yard (kôrt′yärd′, kōrt′-) *n.* An open space surrounded by walls or buildings, adjoining or within a building such as a large house or housing complex.

cous·cous (ko͞os′ko͞os′) *n.* **1.** A pasta of North African origin made of crushed and steamed semolina. **2.** A traditional North African dish consisting of pasta steamed with a meat and vegetable stew. [French, from Arabic *kuskus,* from *kaskasa,* to pulverize.]

cous·in (kŭz′ĭn) *n.* **1.** A child of one's aunt or uncle. Also called *first cousin.* **2.** A relative descended from a common ancestor, such as a grandparent, by two or more steps in a diverging line. **3.** A relative by blood or marriage; a kinsman or kinswoman. **4.** A member of a kindred group or country: *our Canadian cousins.* **5.** Used as a form of address by a sovereign in addressing another sovereign or a high-ranking member of the nobility. [Middle English *cosin,* a relative, from Old French, from Latin *cōnsōbrīnus,* cousin : *com-,* com- + *sōbrīnus,* cousin on the mother's side; see **swesor-** in Appendix.] **—cous′in·hood′** *n.* **—cous′in·ly** *adj.* **—cous′in·ship′** *n.*

Jacques Cousteau

cous·in-ger·man (kŭz′ĭn-jûr′mən) *n., pl.* **cous·ins-ger·man** (kŭz′ĭnz-). A child of one's aunt or uncle; a first cousin.

Cous·teau (ko͞o-stō′), **Jacques Yves.** Born 1910. French underwater explorer, film producer, and author who helped produce the Aqua-Lung (1943).

couth (ko͞oth) *adj.* Marked by or possessing a high degree of sophistication; refined: *"Many picnics manage without this sophistication, but we like to be couth and feel that the delicacies of gracious living enhance the chances"* (John Gould). **—couth** *n.* Refinement; sophistication: *"The man has no couth"* (Los Angeles Times). [Back-formation from UNCOUTH.]

cou·ture (ko͞o-to͝or′, -tür′) *n.* **1.** The business of designing, making, and selling highly fashionable, usually custom-made clothing for women. **2.** Dressmakers and fashion designers considered as a group. **3.** The high-fashion clothing created by designers. [French, sewing, from Old French *cousture,* from Vulgar Latin **cōnsūtūra,* from Latin *cōnsuere, cōnsūt-,* to sew together : *com-,* com- + *suere,* to sew; see **syū-** in Appendix.]

cou·tu·rier (ko͞o-to͝or′ē-ər, -ē-ā′, -tür-yā′) *n.* **1.** An establishment engaged in couture. **2.** One who designs for or owns such an establishment. [French, dressmaker, from Old French *cousturier,* from *cousture,* sewing. See COUTURE.]

cou·tu·rière (ko͞o-to͝or′ē-ər, -ē-âr′, -tür-yĕr′) *n.* A woman who designs for or owns an establishment engaged in couture. [French, dressmaker, seamstress, from Old French *cousturiere,* feminine of *cousturier.* See COUTURIER.]

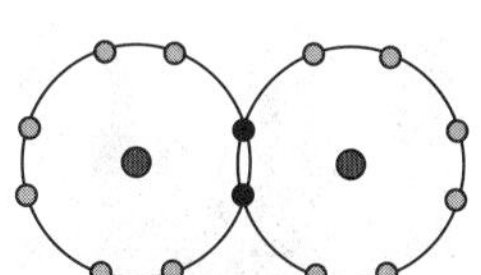

covalent bond

cou·vade (ko͞o-väd′) *n.* A practice in certain cultures in which the husband of a woman in labor takes to his bed as though he were bearing the child. [French, from Old French, from *couver,* to incubate, hatch, from Latin *cubāre,* to lie down on.]

co·va·lence (kō-vā′ləns) *n.* The number of electron pairs an atom can share with other atoms. **—co·va′len·cy** *n.* **—co·va′lent** *adj.* **—co·va′lent·ly** *adv.*

covalent bond *n.* A chemical bond formed by the sharing of one or more electrons, especially pairs of electrons, between atoms.

co·var·i·ance (kō-vâr′ē-əns) *n.* A statistical measure of the variance of two random variables that are observed or measured in the same mean time period. This measure is equal to the product of the deviations of corresponding values of the two variables for their respective means.

co·var·i·ant (kō-vâr′ē-ənt) *adj.* **1.** *Physics.* Expressing, exhibiting, or relating to covariant theory. **2.** *Statistics.* Varying with another variable quantity in a manner that leaves a specified relationship unchanged.

covariant theory *n.* The principle that the laws of physics have the same form regardless of the system of coordinates in which they are expressed.

Co·var·ru·bias (kō′və-ro͞o′bē-əs, kô′vä-ro͞o′byäs), **Miguel.** 1904–1957. Mexican artist and author who is best known for his book and magazine illustrations.

cove[1] (kōv) *n.* **1.** A small sheltered bay in the shoreline of a sea, river, or lake. **2.a.** A recess or small valley in the side of a mountain. **b.** A cave or cavern. **3.** A narrow gap or pass between hills or woods. **4.** *Architecture.* **a.** A concave molding. **b.** A curved surface forming a junction between a ceiling and a wall. In this sense, also called *coving.* **—cove** *tr.v.* **coved, cov·ing, coves.** To make in an inward curving form. [Middle English, chamber, cave, from Old English *cofa.*]

cove[2] (kōv) *n. Chiefly British.* A fellow; a man. [Probably from Romany *kova,* man.]

co·vel·lite (kō-vĕl′īt′, kō′və-līt′) *n.* A lustrous indigo-blue

ă pat	oi boy
ā pay	ou out
âr care	o͝o took
ä father	o͞o boot
ĕ pet	ŭ cut
ē be	ûr urge
ĭ pit	th thin
ī pie	*th* this
îr pier	hw which
ŏ pot	zh vision
ō toe	ə about, item
ô paw	♦ regionalism

Stress marks: ′ (primary); ′ (secondary), as in **dictionary** (dĭk′shə-nĕr′ē)

coveralls

mineral, CuS, an important ore of copper. [After Nicolò *Covelli* (1790–1829), Italian mineralogist.]

cov·en (kŭv′ən, kō′vən) *n.* An assembly of 13 witches. [Perhaps from Middle English *covent,* assembly, convent. See CONVENT.]

cov·e·nant (kŭv′ə-nənt) *n.* **1.** A binding agreement; a compact. See Synonyms at **bargain. 2.** *Law.* **a.** A formal sealed agreement or contract. **b.** A suit to recover damages for violation of such a contract. **3.** In the Bible, God's promise to the human race. **—covenant** *v.* **-nant·ed, -nant·ing, -nants.** *—tr.* To promise by or as if by a covenant. See Synonyms at **promise.** *—intr.* To enter into a covenant. [Middle English, from Old French, from present participle of *convenir,* to agree. See CONVENE.] **—cov′e·nant′al** (-năn′tl) *adj.* **—cov′e·nant′al·ly** *adv.*

cov·e·nant·ee (kŭv′ə-năn-tē′, -nən-) *n.* The party in a covenant to whom the promise is made.

cov·e·nant·er (kŭv′ə-năn′tər) *n.* **1.** One who makes a covenant. **2. Covenanter.** A Scottish Presbyterian who supported either of two agreements, the National Covenant of 1638 or the Solemn League and Covenant of 1643, intended to defend and extend Presbyterianism.

cov·e·nan·tor (kŭv′ə-năn′tər, -nən-, kŭv′ə-năn-tôr′) *n.* The party in a covenant by whom the promise is to be carried out.

covered bridge

Cov·ent Garden (kŭv′ənt, kŏv′-). An area in London long noted for its produce market (established in 1671) and its royal theater (first built in 1731–1732). The market was moved to a site on the Thames River in 1974.

Cov·en·try[1] (kŭv′ĭn-trē). **1.** A city of central England east-southeast of Birmingham. Famous as the home of Lady Godiva in the 11th century, Coventry was severely damaged in air raids during World War II (November 1940). Population, 318,600. **2.** A town of west-central Rhode Island southwest of Providence. It was settled in 1643 and was formerly a noted lacemaking center. Population, 27,065.

Cov·en·try[2] (kŭv′ən-trē) *n.* A state of ostracism or exile: *"It's not that smoke-filled rooms are back; smokers huddle in Coventry these days"* (Flora Lewis). [After COVENTRY[1], England (possibly from the sending of Royalist prisoners there during the English Civil War).]

cov·er (kŭv′ər) *v.* **-ered, -er·ing, -ers.** *—tr.* **1.** To place something upon or over, so as to protect or conceal. **2.** To overlay or spread with something: *cover potatoes with gravy.* **3. a.** To put a cover or covering on. **b.** To wrap up; clothe. **4.** To invest (oneself) with a great deal of something: *covered themselves with glory.* **5. a.** To spread over the surface of: *Dust covered the table. Snow covered the ground.* **b.** To extend over: *a farm covering more than 100 acres.* **6. a.** To copulate with (a female). Used especially of horses. **b.** To sit on in order to hatch. **7.** To hide or screen from view or knowledge; conceal: *covered up his misdemeanors.* **8. a.** To protect or shield from harm, loss, or danger. **b.** To protect by insurance: *took out a new policy that will cover all our camera equipment.* **c.** To compensate or make up for. **9.** To be sufficient to defray, meet, or offset the cost or charge of: *had enough funds to cover her check.* **10.** To make provision for; take into account: *The law does not cover all crimes.* **11.** To deal with; treat of: *The book covers the feminist movement.* **12.** To travel or pass over; traverse: *They covered 60 miles in two days.* **13. a.** To have as one's territory or sphere of work. **b.** To be responsible for reporting the details of (an event or situation): *Two reporters covered the news story.* **14.** To hold within the range and aim of a weapon, such as a firearm. **15.** To protect, as from enemy attack, by occupying a strategic position. **16.** *Sports.* **a.** To be responsible for guarding (an opponent). **b.** To be responsible for defending (a position): *cover left field.* **17.** To match (an opponent's stake) in a wager. **18.** To purchase (stock that one has shorted). **19.** *Games.* To play a higher-ranking card than (the one previously played). **20.** *Obsolete.* To pardon or remit. *—intr.* **1.** To spread over a surface to protect or conceal something: *a paint that covers well.* **2.** To act as a substitute or replacement during someone's absence: *Her assistant covered for her.* **3.** To hide something in order to save someone from censure or punishment: *cover up for a colleague.* **4.** *Games.* To play a higher card than the one previously played. **—cover** *n.* **1.** Something that covers or is laid, placed, or spread over or upon something else, as: **a.** A lid or top. **b.** A binding or enclosure for a book or magazine. **c.** A protective overlay, as for a mattress or furniture. **2. a.** Something that provides shelter. **b.** Strategic protection given by armed units during hostile action: *The battleship approached the combat zone under a cover of fighter planes.* **3. a.** Something, such as vegetation, covering the surface of the ground. **b.** Vegetation, such as underbrush, serving as protective concealment for wild animals. **4. a.** Something, such as darkness, that screens, conceals, or disguises. See Synonyms at **shelter. b.** A false background and identity, especially for a spy. **5.** A table setting for one person: *Covers were laid for ten.* **6.** A cover charge. **7.** An envelope or wrapper for mail. **8.** Funds sufficient to meet an obligation or secure against loss. **9.** One who substitutes for another. ***—idioms.* cover (one's) tracks.** To conceal traces so as to elude pursuers. **cover (the) ground. 1.** To traverse a given distance with satisfying speed. **2.** To deal with or accomplish something in a certain manner: *The history course covered a lot of ground in six weeks.* **take cover.** To seek concealment or protection, as from enemy fire. **under cover. 1.** In an enclosure for mailing. **2.** Being hidden or protected, as by darkness. [Middle English *coveren,* from Old French *covrir,* from Latin *cooperīre,* to cover completely : *co-,* intensive pref.; see CO– + *operīre,* to cover; see **wer-**[4] in Appendix.] **—cov′er·a·ble** *adj.* **—cov′er·er** *n.* **—cov′er·less** *adj.*

covered wagon

cowcatcher

cov·er·age (kŭv′ər-ĭj) *n.* **1.** The extent or degree to which something is observed, analyzed, and reported: *complete news coverage of the election.* **2. a.** Inclusion in an insurance policy or protective plan. **b.** The extent of protection afforded by an insurance policy. **3.** The amount of funds reserved to meet liabilities. **4.** The percentage of persons reached by a medium of communication, such as television or a newspaper.

cov·er·alls (kŭv′ər-ôlz′) *pl.n.* A loose-fitting one-piece work garment worn to protect clothes.

cover boy *n.* An attractive young man whose picture is featured on a magazine cover.

cover charge *n.* A fixed amount added to the bill at a nightclub or restaurant for entertainment or services.

cover crop *n.* A crop, such as winter rye or clover, planted between periods of regular crop production to prevent soil erosion and provide humus or nitrogen.

Cov·er·dale (kŭv′ər-dāl′), **Miles.** 1488–1568. English cleric and scholar who produced the first complete English translation of the Bible (1535).

cov·ered bridge (kŭv′ərd) *n.* A bridge whose roadway is protected by a roof and sides.

covered wagon *n.* A large wagon with an arched canvas top, used especially by American pioneers for prairie travel.

cover girl *n.* An attractive young woman whose picture is featured on a magazine cover.

cover glass *n.* **1.** A small thin piece of glass used to cover a specimen on a microscope slide. Also called *cover slip.* **2.** A protective sheet of glass for a transparency.

cov·er·ing (kŭv′ər-ĭng) *n.* Something that covers, so as to protect or conceal.

covering letter *n.* A letter sent with other documents to explain more fully or provide more information. Also called *cover letter.*

cov·er·let (kŭv′ər-lĭt) also **cov·er·lid** (-lĭd) *n.* A bedspread. [Middle English *coverlite,* from Anglo-Norman *coverelyth* : *covrir,* to cover; see COVER + *lit,* bed (from Latin *lectus;* see **legh-** in Appendix).]

cover letter *n.* See **covering letter.**

cov·er·lid (kŭv′ər-lĭd) *n.* Variant of **coverlet.**

covers *abbr. Mathematics.* Versed cosine.

co·ver·sine (kō-vûr′sīn′) *n. Mathematics.* See **versed cosine.**

cover slip *n.* See **cover glass** (sense 1).

cover story *n.* **1.** A featured story in a magazine that concerns the illustration on the cover. **2.** A false story intended to deceive or mislead: *The spy's cover story required posing as a diplomat.*

cov·ert (kŭv′ərt, kō′vərt, kō-vûrt′) *adj.* **1.** Not openly practiced, avowed, engaged in, accumulated, or shown: *covert military operations; covert funding for the rebels.* See Synonyms at **secret. 2.** Covered or covered over; sheltered. **3.** *Law.* Being married and therefore protected by one's husband. **—covert** *n.* **1.** A covering or cover. **2. a.** A covered place or shelter; hiding place. **b.** Thick underbrush or woodland affording cover for game. **3.** *Zoology.* One of the small feathers covering the bases of the longer feathers of a bird's wings or tail. **4.** A flock of coots. See Synonyms at **flock**[1]. [Middle English, from Old French, from past participle of *covrir,* to cover. See COVER.] **—cov′ert·ly** *adv.* **—cov′ert·ness** *n.*

cov·er·ture (kŭv′ər-chər, -cho͝or′) *n.* **1. a.** A covering; a shelter. **b.** The state of being concealed; disguise. **2.** *Law.* The status of a married woman under common law. [Middle English, from Old French. See COVERT.]

cov·er-up or **cov·er·up** (kŭv′ər-ŭp′) *n.* **1.** An effort or strategy of concealment, especially a planned effort to prevent something potentially scandalous from becoming public. **2.** A loose garment for wear over other clothing, such as a swimsuit or an evening dress.

cov·et (kŭv′ĭt) *v.* **-et·ed, -et·ing, -ets.** *—tr.* **1.** To feel blameworthy desire for (that which is another's). See Synonyms at **envy. 2.** To wish for longingly. See Synonyms at **desire.** *—intr.* To feel immoderate desire for that which is another's. [Middle English *coveiten,* from Old French *coveitier,* from *covitie,* desire, from Latin *cupiditās,* from Latin *cupidus,* desirous, from *cupere,* to desire.] **—cov′et·a·ble** *adj.* **—cov′et·er** *n.* **—cov′et·ing·ly** *adv.*

cov·et·ous (kŭv′ĭ-təs) *adj.* **1.** Excessively and culpably desirous of the possessions of another. See Synonyms at **jealous. 2.** Marked by extreme desire to acquire or possess: *covetous of learning.* **—cov′et·ous·ly** *adv.* **—cov′et·ous·ness** *n.*

cov·ey (kŭv′ē) *n., pl.* **-eys. 1.** A family or small flock of birds, especially partridge or quail. See Synonyms at **flock**[1]. **2.** A small group, as of persons. [Middle English, from Old French *covee,* brood, from feminine past participle of *cover,* to incubate, from Latin *cubāre,* to lie down.]

Co·vi·na (kō-vē′nə). A city of southern California east of Los Angeles. It has a large citrus-processing industry. Population, 33,751.

cov·ing (kō′vĭng) *n.* See **cove**[1] (sense 4).

Cov·ing·ton (kŭv′ĭng-tən). A city of extreme northern Kentucky on the Ohio River opposite Cincinnati. Settled in 1812 on the site of an earlier tavern and ferry landing, it is now heavily industrialized. Population, 49,563.

cow¹ (kou) *n.* **1.** The mature female of cattle of the genus *Bos.* **2.** The mature female of other large animals, such as whales, elephants, or moose. **3.** A domesticated bovine of either sex or any age. ***—idiom.* till the cows come home.** *Informal.* For a long time; indefinitely: *The guests stayed till the cows came home.* [Middle English *cou,* from Old English *cū.* See **gʷou-** in Appendix.] **—cow′y** *adj.*

cow² (kou) *tr.v.* **cowed, cow·ing, cows.** To frighten with threats or a show of force. See Synonyms at **intimidate.** [Probably of Scandinavian origin.] **—cow′ed·ly** (-ĭd-lē) *adv.*

cow·ard (kou′ərd) *n.* One who shows ignoble fear in the face of danger or pain. [Middle English, from Old French *couard,* from *coue,* tail, from Latin *cauda.*] **—cow′ard** *adj.*

Cow·ard (kou′ərd), Sir **Noel Pierce.** 1899–1973. British actor, playwright, and composer especially noted for his witty and worldly comedies, such as *Hay Fever* (1925) and *Private Lives* (1930).

cow·ard·ice (kou′ər-dĭs) *n.* Ignoble fear in the face of danger or pain. [Middle English *cowardise,* from Old French *couardise,* alteration of *couardie,* from *couard,* coward. See COWARD.]

cow·ard·ly (kou′ərd-lē) *adj.* Exhibiting the characteristics of a coward, particularly ignoble fear: *a cowardly surrender.* **—cow′ard·li·ness** *n.* **—cow′ard·ly** *adv.*

cow·bane (kou′bān′) *n.* **1.** A perennial North American herb *(Oxypolis rigidior)* having pinnately compound leaves and umbels of small white flowers. **2.** Any of several related plants, such as the water hemlock.

cow·bell (kou′bĕl′) *n.* A bell hung from a collar around a cow's neck.

cow·ber·ry (kou′bĕr′ē) *n.* **1.** A low, creeping, evergreen shrub *(Vaccinium vitis-idaea),* native to northern parts of North America and Eurasia and having drooping clusters of small white or pinkish flowers. **2.** The edible red berry of this plant, used to make sauces, jams, and preserves. Also called *lingberry, lingonberry, mountain cranberry.*

cow·bird (kou′bûrd′) *n.* Any of various blackbirds of the genus *Molothrus,* especially the common North American species *M. ater,* that lay their eggs in the nests of other birds and are often seen accompanying herds of grazing cattle. [From their habit of staying with cattle.]

♦**cow·boy** (kou′boi′) *n.* **1.** A hired man, especially in the western United States, who tends cattle and performs many of his duties on horseback. Also called ♦*buckaroo,* ♦*cowman,* ♦*cowpoke,* ♦*cowpuncher,* ♦*vaquero,* ♦*waddy.* See Regional Note at **vaquero. 2.** An adventurous hero. **3.** *Slang.* A reckless person, such as a driver, pilot, or manager, who ignores potential risks.

cowboy boot *n.* A high-arched boot with a high Cuban heel and usually ornamental stitching.

cowboy hat *n.* A felt hat having a tall crown and very wide brim. Also called *ten-gallon hat.*

cow·catch·er (kou′kăch′ər, -kĕch′-) *n.* The metal grille or frame projecting from the front of a locomotive and serving to clear the track of obstructions.

cow college *n.* *Informal.* **1.** An agricultural college. **2.** A college or university considered to be provincial and unsophisticated.

cow·er (kou′ər) *intr.v.* **-ered, -er·ing, -ers.** To cringe in fear. [Middle English *couren,* of Scandinavian origin.]

Cowes (kouz). A town on the northern coast of the Isle of Wight off southern England. It is the headquarters of the Royal Yacht Club and the site of annual fashionable regattas. Population, 19,663.

cow·fish (kou′fĭsh′) *n., pl.* **cowfish** or **-fish·es. 1.** Any of various small whales, porpoises, or similar aquatic mammals, especially a whale of the genus *Mesoplodon,* having a pointed snout. **2.** Any of various marine fishes of the family Ostraciidae, especially *Lactophrys quadricornis* of warm Atlantic waters, having hornlike spines over each eye.

cow·girl (kou′gûrl′) *n.* A hired woman, especially in the western United States, who tends cattle and performs many of her duties on horseback.

cow·hand (kou′hănd′) *n.* A cowboy or cowgirl.

cow·herb (kou′ûrb′, -hûrb′) *n.* An annual plant *(Vaccaria pyramidata),* native to Eurasia and naturalized in North America and having clusters of deep-pink flowers.

cow·herd (kou′hûrd′) *n.* One who herds or tends cattle.

cow·hide (kou′hīd′) *n.* **1. a.** The hide of a cow. **b.** The leather made from this hide. **2.** A strong, heavy, flexible whip, usually made of braided leather. **—cowhide** *tr.v.* **-hid·ed, -hid·ing, -hides.** To beat with a strong, heavy, flexible whip.

cowl (koul) *n.* **1. a.** The hood or hooded robe worn especially by a monk. **b.** A draped neckline on a woman's garment. **2.** A hood-shaped covering used to increase the draft of a chimney. **3.** The top portion of the front part of an automobile body, supporting the windshield and dashboard. **4.** The cowling on an aircraft. **—cowl** *tr.v.* **cowled, cowl·ing, cowls.** To cover with or as if with a cowl. [Middle English *coule,* from Old English *cugele,* from Late Latin *cuculla,* from Latin *cucullus,* hood.]

cowled (kould) *adj.* **1.** Wearing or supplied with a cowl; hooded. **2.** Having the shape of a hood.

Cow·ley (kou′lē), **Abraham.** 1618–1667. English metaphysical poet whose works include *Davideis* (1656), an epic on the life of King David.

Cowley, Malcolm. 1898–1989. American writer, editor, and critic whose works include studies of American expatriate writers of the 1920's and commentaries on William Faulkner.

cow·lick (kou′lĭk′) *n.* A projecting tuft of hair on the head that grows in a different direction from the rest of the hair and will not lie flat.

cowl·ing (kou′lĭng) *n.* A removable metal covering for an engine, especially an aircraft engine.

cow·man (kou′mən, -măn′) *n.* **1.** An owner of cattle or a cattle ranch. **2. a.** See **cowboy** (sense 1). **b.** A cowherd.

co·work·er or **co-work·er** (kō′wûr′kər) *n.* One that works with another; a fellow worker.

cow parsnip *n.* Any of several tall, coarse herbs of the genus *Heracleum* in the parsley family, native chiefly to northern temperate regions and having compound umbels of small flowers.

cow·pea (kou′pē′) *n.* **1.** An annual African plant *(Vigna unguiculata)* in the pea family, widely cultivated in warm regions for food, forage, and soil improvement. **2.** An edible seed of this plant. Also called *black-eyed pea, catjang.*

Cow·per (ko͞o′pər, kou′-, ko͝op′ər), **William.** 1731–1800. British poet considered a precursor of romanticism. His best-known work, *The Task* (1785), praises rural life and leisure.

Cow·per's gland (kou′pərz, ko͞o′-) *n.* See **bulbourethral gland.** [After William *Cowper* (1666–1709), English surgeon.]

cow pilot *n.* See **sergeant major** (sense 3).

cow·poke (kou′pōk′) *n.* See **cowboy** (sense 1).

cow pony *n.* A small, agile horse used in herding cattle.

cow·pox (kou′pŏks′) *n.* A mild, contagious skin disease of cattle, usually affecting the udder, that is caused by a virus and characterized by the eruption of a pustular rash. When the virus is transmitted to humans, as by vaccination, it can confer immunity to smallpox. Also called *vaccinia.*

cow·punch·er (kou′pŭn′chər) *n.* See **cowboy** (sense 1).

cow·rie or **cow·ry** (kou′rē) *n., pl.* **-ries.** Any of various tropical marine gastropods of the family Cypraeidae, having glossy, often brightly marked shells, some of which are used as currency in the South Pacific and Africa. [Hindi *kauṛī,* from Sanskrit *kapardikā,* diminutive of *kapardaḥ,* shell, of Dravidian origin.]

co·write (kō-rīt′) *tr.v.* **-wrote** (-rōt′), **-writ·ten** (-rĭt′n), **-writ·ing, -writes.** To write jointly or in collaboration with another author. **—co′writ·er** *n.*

cow·ry (kou′rē) *n.* Variant of **cowrie.**

cow shark *n.* Any of several sharks of the family Hexanchidae of warm and temperate seas.

cow·shed (kou′shed′) *n.* A shed for housing cows.

cow·slip (kou′slĭp′) *n.* **1.** A Eurasian primrose *(Primula veris),* usually having fragrant yellow flowers, widely cultivated as an ornamental, and long used in herbal medicine. **2.** See **marsh marigold. 3.** The Virginia cowslip. [Middle English *cowslyppe,* from Old English *cūslyppe* : *cū,* cow; see **gʷou-** in Appendix + *slypa,* slime; see **sleubh-** in Appendix.]

cow town *n.* A small town in a cattle-raising area.

cox (kŏks) *Nautical. n.* A coxswain. **—cox** *intr. & tr.v.* **coxed, cox·ing, cox·es.** To act as coxswain or serve as coxswain for.

cox·a (kŏk′sə) *n., pl.* **cox·ae** (kŏk′sē′). **1.** *Anatomy.* The hip or hip joint. **2.** *Zoology.* The first segment of the leg of an insect or other arthropod, joining the leg to the body. [Latin, hip.] **—cox′al** *adj.*

cox·al·gi·a (kŏk-săl′jē-ə, -jə) *n.* Pain in or disease of the hip or hip joint. [COX(A) + –ALGIA.] **—cox·al′gic** (-jĭk) *adj.*

cox·comb (kŏks′kōm′) *n.* **1.** A conceited dandy; a fop. **2.** *Obsolete.* A jester's cap; a cockscomb. [Middle English *cokkes comb,* crest of a cock : *cokkes,* genitive of *cok,* cock; see COCK¹ + *comb,* crest; see COMB.]

cox·comb·ry (kŏk′skōm′rē, -skəm-) *n., pl.* **-ries.** Behavior that is characteristic of or appropriate to a coxcomb; foppish conceit.

Cox·ey (kŏk′sē), **Jacob Sechler.** 1854–1951. American businessman and reformer who led a march on Washington, D.C., to protest unemployment and recommended the use of fiat money to finance a work program.

cox·i·tis (kŏk-sī′tĭs) *n.* Inflammation of the hip joint. [COX(A) + –ITIS.]

cox·sack·ie·vi·rus also **Cox·sack·ie virus** (ko͝ok-sä′kē-vī′rəs, kŏk-săk′ē-) *n.* Any of a group of enteroviruses that can cause a disease resembling poliomyelitis but without paralysis. [After *Coxsackie,* a village of east-central New York.]

cox·swain (kŏk′sən, -swān′) *Nautical. n.* **1.** A person who usually steers a ship's boat and has charge of its crew. **2.** A person in a racing shell who usually directs the rest of the crew. **—coxswain** *intr. & tr.v.* **-swained, -swain·ing, -swains.** To act as coxswain or serve as coxswain for. [Middle English *cokswaynne* : *cok,* cockboat; see COCKBOAT + *swain,* servant; see SWAIN.]

coy (koi) *adj.* **coy·er, coy·est. 1.** Tending to avoid people and social situations; reserved. **2.** Affectedly and usually flirtatiously

cowl

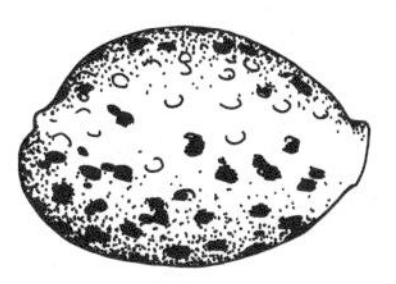

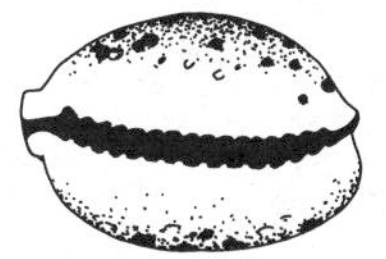

cowrie

coxswain
Coxswain and rower

ă pat	oi boy
ā pay	ou out
âr care	o͝o took
ä father	o͞o boot
ĕ pet	ŭ cut
ē be	ûr urge
ĭ pit	th thin
ī pie	*th* this
îr pier	hw which
ŏ pot	zh vision
ō toe	ə about, item
ô paw	♦ regionalism

Stress marks: ′ (primary); ′ (secondary), as in **dictionary** (dĭk′shə-nĕr′ē)

shy or modest. See Synonyms at **shy**[1]. **3.** Annoyingly unwilling to make a commitment. [Middle English, from Old French *quei, coi,* quiet, still, from Vulgar Latin **quētus,* from Latin *quiētus.* See **kʷeiə-** in Appendix.] **—coy′ly** *adv.* **—coy′ness** *n.*

coy·dog (kī′dôg′, -dŏg′) *n.* The hybrid offspring of a coyote and a feral dog. [COY(OTE) + DOG.]

coy·o·te (kī-ō′tē, kī′ōt′) *n.* **1.** A small, wolflike carnivorous animal *(Canis latrans)* native to western North America and found in many other regions of the continent. Also called *prairie wolf.* **2.** A firefighter who is sent to battle remote, usually very severe forest fires, often for days at a time. [American Spanish, from Nahuatl *cóyotl.*]

coy·o·til·lo (koi′ə-tĭl′ō, -tē′yō, kī′ə-) *n., pl.* **-los.** A poisonous shrub *(Karwinskia humboldtiana)* native to Texas and Mexico, having small greenish flowers and black fruits. [American Spanish, diminutive of *coyote,* coyote. See COYOTE.]

coy·pu (koi′po͞o) *n., pl.* **-pus.** A large aquatic South American rodent *(Myocastor coypus)* having webbed feet and a long tail. Also called *nutria.* [American Spanish *coipú,* from Araucanian *kóypu.*]

coz (kŭz) *n. Informal.* A cousin.

coz·en (kŭz′ən) *v.* **-ened, -en·ing, -ens.** *—tr.* **1.** To mislead by means of a petty trick or fraud; deceive. **2.** To persuade or induce to do something by cajoling or wheedling. **3.** To obtain by deceit or persuasion. *—intr.* To act deceitfully. [Perhaps from Middle English *cosin,* fraud, trickery.] **—coz′en·er** *n.*

coz·en·age (kŭz′ə-nĭj) *n.* **1.** The art or practice of cozening. **2.** An act or example of cozening.

Co·zu·mel (kō′zə-mĕl′, so͞o-). An island off the coast of southeast Mexico near Cancún. It is a growing resort area.

co·zy also **co·sy** (kō′zē) *—adj.* **-zi·er, -zi·est** also **-si·er, -si·est.** **1.** Snug, comfortable, and warm. **2.** Marked by friendly intimacy. See Synonyms at **comfortable. 3.** *Informal.* Marked by close association for devious purposes: *a cozy agreement with the competition.* *—intr.v.* **-zied, -zy·ing, -zies** also **-sied, -sy·ing, -sies.** *Informal.* To try to get on friendly or intimate terms; ingratiate oneself: *"out on the . . . hustings, cozying up to reactionaries and racists alike"* (Chuck Stone). *—n., pl.* **-zies** also **-sies.** A padded or knitted covering placed especially over a teapot to keep the tea hot. [Probably of Scandinavian origin.] **—co′zi·ly** *adv.* **—co′zi·ness** *n.*

cp *abbr.* Candlepower.

cP *abbr.* Centipoise.

CP *abbr.* **1.** Chemically pure. **2.** Or **C.P.** Command post. **3.** Communist Party.

cp. *abbr.* **1.** Compare. **2.** Coupon.

C.P. *abbr.* Cape Province.

CPA also **C.P.A.** *abbr.* Certified public accountant.

cpd. *abbr.* Compound.

CPFF *abbr.* Cost plus fixed fee.

CPI *abbr.* Consumer price index.

cpl *abbr.* **1.** Complete. **2.** *Ecclesiastical.* Complin.

Cpl. *abbr.* Corporal.

cpm or **CPM** *abbr.* **1.** Cost per thousand. **2.** Cycles per minute.

CPO *abbr.* Chief petty officer.

CPOM *abbr.* Master chief petty officer.

CPOS *abbr.* Senior chief petty officer.

CPR *abbr.* Cardiopulmonary resuscitation.

cps *abbr.* **1.** Characters per second. **2.** Cycles per second.

CPS also **C.P.S.** *abbr.* Certified professional secretary.

Cpt. or **CPT** *abbr.* Captain.

CPU *abbr. Computer Science.* Central processing unit.

CQ[1] (sē′kyo͞o′) *n.* Code letters used at the beginning of radio messages intended for all receivers. [Origin unknown.]

CQ[2] *abbr.* Call to quarters.

Cr The symbol for the element **chromium.**

CR *abbr. Psychology.* **1.** Conditioned reflex. **2.** Conditioned response.

cr. *abbr.* **1.** Credit; creditor. **2.** Creek. **3.** Crescendo. **4.** Crown.

C.R. *abbr.* Costa Rica.

crab[1] (krăb) *n.* **1.a.** Any of various predominantly marine crustaceans of the division Brachyura within the order Decapoda, characterized by a broad, flattened cephalothorax covered by a hard carapace with a small abdomen concealed beneath it, short antennae, and five pairs of legs, of which the anterior pair are large and pincerlike. **b.** Any of various similar related crustaceans, such as the hermit crab or the king crab. **c.** A horseshoe crab. **2.a.** A crab louse. **b. crabs.** *Slang.* Infestation by crab lice. **3.** The maneuvering of an aircraft partially into a crosswind to compensate for drift. **4.** A machine for handling or hoisting heavy weights. **—crab** *v.* **crabbed, crab·bing, crabs.** *—intr.* **1.** To hunt or catch crabs. **2.** To scurry sideways in the manner of a crab. **3.** To drift diagonally or sideways. **4.** To direct an aircraft into a crosswind. *—tr.* **1.** To direct (an aircraft) partly into a crosswind to eliminate drift. **2.** To cause to move or scurry sideways. ***—idiom.* catch a crab.** To strike the water with an oar in recovering a stroke or miss it in making one while rowing. [Middle English *crabbe,* from Old English *crabba.* See **gerbh-** in Appendix.] **—crab·ber** *n.*

crab[2] (krăb) *n.* **1.** A crab apple tree or its fruit. **2.** A quarrelsome, ill-tempered person. **—crab** *v.* **crabbed, crab·bing, crabs.** *—intr. Informal.* To find fault; criticize someone or something. *—tr.* **1.** *Informal.* To interfere with and ruin; spoil. **2.** *Informal.* To find fault with; complain about. **3.** To make ill-tempered or sullen. [Middle English *crabbe,* possibly from *crabbe,* crab (shellfish). See CRAB[1].] **—crab′ber** *n.*

Crab (krăb) *n.* See **Cancer.**

crab apple also **crab·ap·ple** (krăb′ăp′əl) *n.* **1.** Any of several deciduous trees of the genus *Malus,* native to North America and Eurasia and having clusters of white, pink, or reddish flowers. **2.** The small, tart fruit of such a tree, sometimes used to make jelly and preserves.

crab·bed (krăb′ĭd) *adj.* **1.** Irritable and perverse in disposition; ill-tempered. **2.** Difficult to understand; complicated. **3.** Difficult to read: *crabbed handwriting.* [Middle English, from *crabbe,* crab (influenced by CRAB[2]). See CRAB[1].] **—crab′bed·ly** *adv.* **—crab′bed·ness** *n.*

crab·by (krăb′ē) *adj.* **-bi·er, -bi·est.** *Informal.* Grouchy; ill-tempered. **—crab′bi·ly** *adv.* **—crab′bi·ness** *n.*

crab cactus *n.* See **Thanksgiving cactus.**

crab·grass or **crab grass** (krăb′grăs′) *n.* Any of certain grasses of the genus *Digitaria,* especially *D. sanguinalis* or *D. ischaemum,* widely naturalized in North America.

crab louse *n.* A sucking louse *(Phthirus pubis)* that generally infests the pubic region and causes severe itching.

crab·meat (krăb′mēt′) *n.* The edible flesh of a crab.

crab's eye (krăbz) *n.* See **rosary pea.**

crab·stick (krăb′stĭk′) *n.* **1.** A stick made of crab apple wood. **2.** A crabby, ill-tempered person.

crab·wise (krăb′wīz′) *adv.* **1.** Sideways. **2.** In a furtive or circumspect manner; indirectly.

crack (krăk) *v.* **cracked, crack·ing, cracks.** *—intr.* **1.** To break or snap apart. **2.** To make a sharp, snapping sound. **3.** To break without complete separation of parts; fissure: *The mirror cracked.* **4.** To change sharply in pitch or timbre, as from hoarseness or emotion. Used of the voice. **5.** To break down; fail: *The defendant's composure finally began to crack.* **6.** To have a mental or physical breakdown: *cracked under the pressure.* **7.** To move or go rapidly: *was cracking along at 70 miles an hour.* **8.** *Chemistry.* To break into simpler molecules by means of heat. *—tr.* **1.** To cause to make a sharp, snapping sound. **2.** To cause to break without complete separation of parts: *cracked the glass.* **3.a.** To break with a sharp, snapping sound. See Synonyms at **break. b.** To crush (corn or wheat, for example) into small pieces. **4.** To strike with a sudden, sharp sound. **5.** *Informal.* **a.** To break open or into: *crack a safe.* **b.** To open up for use or consumption: *crack a book; cracked a beer.* **c.** To break through (an obstacle) in order to win acceptance or acknowledgement: *finally cracked the "men-only" rule at the club.* **6.** To discover the solution to, especially after considerable effort: *crack a code.* **7.** To cause (the voice) to crack. **8.** *Informal.* To tell (a joke), especially on impulse or in an effective manner. **9.** To cause to have a mental or physical breakdown. **10.** To impair or destroy: *Their rude remarks cracked his equanimity.* **11.** To reduce (petroleum) to simpler compounds by cracking. **—crack** *n.* **1.** A sharp, snapping sound, such as the report of a firearm. **2.a.** A partial split or break; a fissure. **b.** A slight, narrow space: *The window was open a crack.* **3.** A sharp, resounding blow. **4.a.** A mental or physical impairment; a defect. **b.** A breaking, harshly dissonant vocal tone or sound, as in hoarseness. **5.** An attempt or try: *gave him a crack at the job; took a crack at photography.* **6.** A witty or sarcastic remark. See Synonyms at **joke. 7.** A moment; an instant: *at the crack of dawn.* **8.** *Slang.* Chemically purified, very potent cocaine in pellet form that is smoked through a glass pipe and is considered highly and rapidly addictive. **—crack** *adj.* Excelling in skill or achievement; first-rate: *a crack shot; a crack tennis player.* ***—phrasal verbs.* crack down.** To act more forcefully to regulate, repress, or restrain: *The police cracked down on speeding.* **crack up.** *Informal.* **1.** To praise highly: *He was simply not the genius he was cracked up to be.* **2.a.** To damage or wreck (a vehicle or vessel): *crack up a plane; crack up a boat.* **b.** To wreck a vehicle in an accident: *cracked up on the expressway.* **3.** To have a mental or physical breakdown. **4.** To experience or cause to experience a great deal of amusement: *really cracked up when I heard that joke.* ***—idiom.* crack the whip.** To behave in a domineering manner; demand hard work and efficiency from those under one's control. [Middle English *craken,* from Old English *cracian.* See **gerə-**[2] in Appendix.]

crack·a·jack (krăk′ə-jăk′) *adj. Slang.* Variant of **crackerjack.**

crack·brain (krăk′brān′) *n.* A foolish or eccentric person. **—crack′brained′** *adj.*

crack·down (krăk′doun′) *n.* An act or example of forceful regulation, repression, or restraint: *a crackdown on crime.*

cracked (krăkt) *adj.* **1.a.** Broken so that fissures appear on the surface: *a cracked mirror.* **b.** Broken into small or coarse pieces: *cracked corn; cracked ice.* **2.** Having a harsh or dissonant tone: *a cracked voice.* **3.** *Informal.* Mentally deranged; crazy.

cracked wheat *n.* Whole wheat grains that have been cut or crushed into smaller pieces.

crack·er (krăk′ər) *n.* **1.** A thin, crisp wafer or biscuit, usually made of unsweetened dough. **2.** One that cracks, especially: **a.** A firecracker. **b.** A small cardboard cylinder covered with decorative paper that holds candy or a party favor and pops when a paper strip is pulled at one or both ends and torn. **c.** The appa-

crab[1]
Lady crab
Ovalipes ocellatus

ă pat	oi boy
ā pay	ou out
âr care	o͝o took
ä father	o͞o boot
ĕ pet	ŭ cut
ē be	ûr urge
ĭ pit	th thin
ī pie	*th* this
îr pier	hw which
ŏ pot	zh vision
ō toe	ə about, item
ô paw	♦ regionalism

Stress marks: ′ (primary); ′ (secondary), as in **dictionary** (dĭk′shə-nĕr′ē)

ratus used in the cracking of petroleum. **d.** One who makes unauthorized use of a computer, especially to tamper with data or programs. **3.** *Offensive.* Used as a disparaging term for a poor white person of the rural, especially southeast United States.

crack·er-bar·rel (krăk′ər-băr′əl) *adj.* Resembling or characteristic of the extended informal discussions carried on by persons habitually assembled at a country store: *cracker-barrel philosophy.* [After the cracker barrels that people supposedly would gather round for conversation in old-time general stores.]

crack·er·jack (krăk′ər-jăk′) also **crack·a·jack** (krăk′ə-) *adj. Slang.* Of excellent quality or ability; fine. [Probably from CRACK, first-rate + JACK.] **—crack′er·jack′, crack′a·jack′** *n.*

Crack·er Jack (krăk′ər). A trademark used for a candied popcorn confection.

crack·ers (krăk′ərz) *adj. Chiefly British.* Insane; mad. [Probably from CRACKER, breakdown.]

crack house *n. Slang.* A heavily fortified and guarded building or apartment, often containing a laboratory where cocaine is converted to crack, in which a drug dealer dispenses crack to customers.

crack·ing (krăk′ĭng) *n. Chemistry.* Thermal decomposition, sometimes with catalysis, of a complex substance, especially the breaking of petroleum molecules into shorter molecules to extract low-boiling fractions such as gasoline. **—cracking** *adj.* Excellent; great: *had a cracking time at the dance.* **—cracking** *adv.* Used as an intensive: *a cracking good show.*

crack·le (krăk′əl) *v.* **-led, -ling, -les.** *—intr.* **1.** To make a succession of slight sharp, snapping noises: *a fire crackling in the wood stove.* **2.** To show liveliness or brilliance: *a book that crackles with humor.* **3.** To become covered with a network of fine cracks; craze. *—tr.* **1.** To crush (paper, for example) with sharp, snapping sounds. **2.** To cause (china, for example) to become covered with a network of fine cracks. **—crackle** *n.* **1.** The act or sound of crackling. **2. a.** A network of fine cracks on the surface of glazed pottery, china, or glassware. **b.** Crackleware. [Frequentative of CRACK.]

crack·le·ware (krăk′əl-wâr′) *n.* Glazed pottery or glassware bearing a decorative surface network of fine cracks.

crack·ling (krăk′lĭng) *n.* **1.** The production of a succession of slight sharp, snapping noises. **2. cracklings.** The crisp bits that remain after rendering fat from meat or frying or roasting the skin, especially of a pig or a goose. [Sense 2, Dutch *krakeling,* from obsolete Dutch *kraeckelingh,* from Middle Dutch *krākelinc,* from *krāken,* to crack. See CRACKNEL.]

crack·ly (krăk′lē) *adj.* **-li·er, -li·est.** Likely to crackle; crisp.

crack·nel (krăk′nəl) *n.* **1.** A hard, crisp biscuit. **2. cracknels.** Crisp bits of fried pork fat; cracklings. [Middle English *crakenele,* alteration of Old French *craquelin,* from Middle Dutch *krākelinc,* small cake, from *krāken,* to crack. See **gerə-²** in Appendix.]

crack·pot (krăk′pŏt′) *n.* An eccentric person, especially one with bizarre ideas. [CRACK(ED) + POT¹, skull (obsolete).]

crack·up or **crack-up** (krăk′ŭp′) *n. Informal.* **1.** A crash, as one involving an airplane or an automobile. **2.** A mental or physical breakdown.

Crac·ow also **Kra·ków** (krăk′ou, krä′kou, -ko͞of). A city of southern Poland on the Vistula River south-southeast of Warsaw. Founded in the eighth century A.D., it was the national capital from 1305 to 1595. Population, 740,300.

-cracy *suff.* Government; rule: *meritocracy.* [French *-cratie,* from Old French, from Late Latin *-cratia,* from Greek *-kratia,* from *kratos,* strength, power. See **kar-** in Appendix.]

cra·dle (krād′l) *n.* **1.** A small low bed for an infant, often furnished with rockers. **2. a.** The earliest period of life: *from the cradle to the grave.* **b.** A place of origin; a birthplace: *the cradle of civilization.* **3. a.** A framework of wood or metal used to support something, such as a ship undergoing construction or repair. **b.** A framework used to protect an injured limb. **4.** A low flat framework that rolls on casters, used by a mechanic working beneath an automobile. Also called *creeper.* **5.** The part of a telephone that contains the connecting switch upon which the receiver and mouthpiece unit is supported. **6. a.** A frame projecting above a scythe, used to catch grain as it is cut so that it can be laid flat. **b.** A scythe equipped with such a frame. **7.** A boxlike device furnished with rockers, used for washing gold-bearing dirt. **—cradle** *v.* **-dled, -dling, -dles.** *—tr.* **1. a.** To place or retain in or as if in a cradle. **b.** To care for or nurture in infancy. **c.** To hold or support protectively: *cradled the cat in his arms.* **2.** To reap (grain) with a cradle. **3.** To place or support (a ship, for example) in a cradle. **4.** To wash (gold-bearing dirt) in a cradle. *—intr. Obsolete.* To lie in or as if in a cradle. [Middle English *cradel,* from Old English.] **—cra′dler** *n.*

cra·dle·board (krād′l-bôrd′, -bōrd′) *n.* A board or frame on which an infant is secured, as by binding or wrapping in a blanket, used by certain Native American peoples as a portable cradle and for carrying an infant on the back.

cradle cap *n.* A form of dermatitis that occurs in infants and is characterized by heavy, yellow, crusted lesions on the scalp.

cra·dle·song (krād′l-sông′, -sŏng′) *n.* A lullaby.

craft (krăft) *n.* **1.** Skill in doing or making something, as in the arts; proficiency. See Synonyms at **art¹**. **2.** Skill in evasion or deception; guile. **3. a.** An occupation or trade requiring manual dexterity or skilled artistry. **b.** The membership of such an occupation or trade; guild. **4.** *pl.* **craft.** A boat, ship, or aircraft. **—craft** *tr.v.* **craft·ed, craft·ing, crafts. 1.** To make by hand. **2.** *Usage Problem.* To make or construct (something) in a manner suggesting great care or ingenuity: *"It was not the Chamber of Commerce that crafted the public policies that have resulted in a $26 billion annual subvention to the farmers"* (William F. Buckley, Jr.). [Middle English, from Old English *cræft.*] **—craft′er** *n.*

USAGE NOTE: *Craft* has been used as a verb since the Old English period and was used in Middle English to refer specifically to the artful construction of a text or discourse. In recent years, *crafted,* the past participle of *craft,* has enjoyed a vogue as a participle referring to well-wrought writing. This may be a sign that the Jamesian conception of the literary muse has begun to yield to a Trollopian conception of literature as a kind of intellectual handicraft; or it may indicate little more than the desperation with which book reviewers seize on any novel adjective. In any event, the usage is more acceptable when applied to literary works than to other sorts of writing, and more acceptable as a participle than as a verb. It was acceptable to 73 percent of the Usage Panel in the phrase *beautifully crafted prose.* By contrast, only 35 percent of the Panel accepted the sentence *The planners crafted their proposal so as to anticipate the objections of local businesses.*

craft beer *n.* A distinctively flavored beer that is brewed and distributed regionally. Also called *craft brew.*

crafts·man (krăfts′mən) *n.* A man who practices a craft with great skill. **—crafts′man·like′** *adj.* **—crafts′man·ly** *adj.* **—crafts′man·ship′** *n.*

crafts·people (krăfts′pē′pəl) *pl.n.* Artisans considered as a group.

crafts·per·son (krăfts′pûr′sən) *n.* A craftsman or a craftswoman.

crafts·wom·an (krăfts′wo͝om′ən) *n.* A woman who practices a craft with great skill.

craft union *n.* A labor union limited in membership to workers engaged in the same craft. Also called *horizontal union.*

craft·work (krăft′wûrk′) *n.* Work made or done by craftspeople. **—craft′work′er** *n.*

craft·y (krăf′tē) *adj.* **-i·er, -i·est. 1.** Skilled in or marked by underhandedness, deviousness, or deception. See Synonyms at **sly. 2.** *Chiefly British.* Skillful; dexterous. [Middle English, from Old English *cræftig,* strong, skillful, from *cræft,* skill.] **—craft′i·ly** *adv.* **—craft′i·ness** *n.*

crag (krăg) *n.* A steeply projecting mass of rock forming part of a rugged cliff or headland. [Middle English, from Welsh *craig* or Scottish Gaelic *creagh.*] **—crag′ged** (krăg′ĭd) *adj.*

crag·gy (krăg′ē) *adj.* **-gi·er, -gi·est. 1.** Having crags: *craggy terrain.* **2.** Rugged and uneven: *a craggy face.* **—crag′gi·ly** *adv.* **—crag′gi·ness** *n.*

Craig (crāg), **Edward Gordon.** 1872–1966. British theatrical producer, director, and designer whose innovative productions and simplified stage designs influenced modern theater.

Crai·gie (krā′gē), Sir **William Alexander.** 1876–1957. British lexicographer and philologist who was joint editor of the *Oxford English Dictionary* (1901–1933).

Cra·io·va (krə-yō′və, krä-yô′vä). A city of southwest Romania west of Bucharest. Built on the site of a Roman settlement, it was destroyed by an earthquake in 1790 and burned by the Turks in 1802. Population, 260,422.

crake (krāk) *n.* Any of several short-billed birds of the family Rallidae, such as the corncrake. [Middle English, crow, probably from Old Norse *krāka.* See **gerə-²** in Appendix.]

cram (krăm) *v.* **crammed, cram·ming, crams.** *—tr.* **1.** To force, press, or squeeze into an insufficient space; stuff. **2.** To fill too tightly. **3. a.** To gorge with food. **b.** To eat quickly and greedily. **4.** *Informal.* To prepare (students) hastily for an impending examination. *—intr.* **1.** To gorge oneself with food. **2.** *Informal.* To study hastily for an impending examination: *was up all night cramming for the history midterm.* **—cram** *n.* **1.** A group that has been crammed together; a crush. **2.** *Informal.* Hasty study for an imminent examination. [Middle English *crammen,* from Old English *crammian.* See **ger-** in Appendix.] **—cram′mer** *n.*

cram·be (krăm′bē) *n.* Any of certain Old World annual plants of the genus *Crambe* in the mustard family, cultivated for their seeds, which yield a useful oil similar to rape oil. [Latin *crambē,* cabbage, from Greek *krambē.*]

cram·bo (krăm′bō) *n., pl.* **-boes** or **-bos. 1.** A word game in which a player or team must find and express a rhyme for a word or line presented by the opposing player or team. **2.** Doggerel. [Obsolete *crambe,* cabbage, from Latin *crambē (repetīta),* (warmed-over) cabbage, said of pedestrian writing, from Greek *krambē.*]

cramp¹ (krămp) *n.* **1.** A sudden, involuntary, spasmodic muscular contraction causing severe pain, often occurring in the leg or shoulder as the result of strain or chill. **2.** A temporary partial paralysis of habitually or excessively used muscles. **3. cramps.** Spasmodic contractions of the uterus, such as those occurring during menstruation or labor, usually causing pain in the abdomen that may radiate to the lower back and thighs. **—cramp** *v.* **cramped, cramp·ing, cramps.** *—tr.* To affect with or as if with a cramp. *—intr.* To suffer from or experience cramps. [Middle English *crampe,* from Old French, of Germanic origin.]

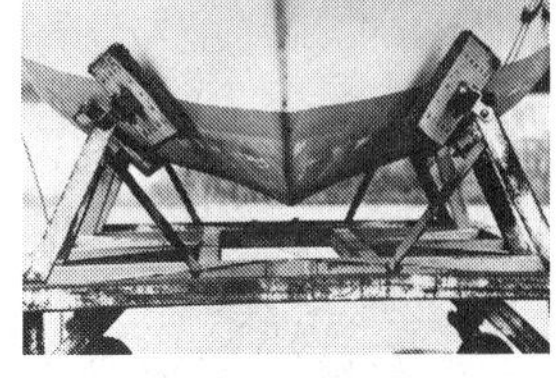

cradle
Top: 17th-century English oak cradle
Bottom: Supporting a boat

cradleboard
1900 photograph by H. Fair on the Colville Reservation, Washington

crag
Quoddy Head State Park, Maine

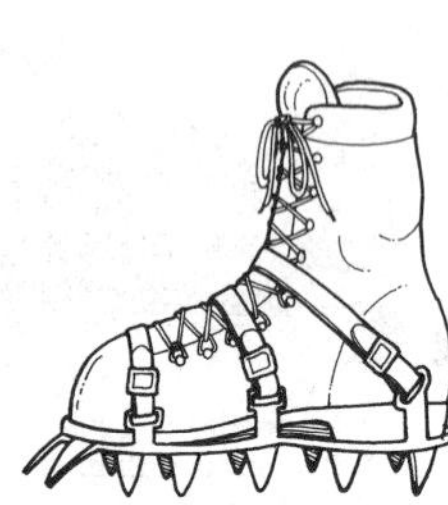
crampon

crane
Top: Black crowned crane
Balearica pavonina
Bottom: Mechanical crane

cramp² (krămp) *n.* **1.** A frame with an adjustable part to hold pieces together; a clamp. **2.** A cramp iron. **3.** A compressing or restraining force, influence, or thing. **4.** A confined position or part. **—cramp** *tr.v.* **cramped, cramp·ing, cramps. 1.** To hold together with a cramp. **2.** To shut in so closely as to restrict the physical freedom of: *were cramped in the tiny cubicle.* **3.a.** To steer (the wheels of a vehicle) to make a turn. **b.** To jam (a wheel) by a short turn. **—cramp** *adj.* **1.** Restricted; narrowed. **2.** Difficult to read or decipher: *cramped handwriting.* **—*idiom.* cramp (one's) style.** To restrict or prevent from free action or expression. [Probably Middle Dutch *crampe,* hook, cramp.]

cramp·fish (krămp′fĭsh′) *n., pl.* **crampfish** or **-fish·es.** See **electric ray.** [From CRAMP¹ (from its ability to give electric shocks).]

cramp iron *n.* A bar, usually of iron, with right-angle bends at both ends, used for permanently holding together stones, timber, and other materials used in building.

cram·pon (krăm′pŏn′, -pən) *n.* **1.** Often **crampons.** A hinged pair of curved iron bars for raising heavy objects, such as stones or timber. **2.** An iron spike attached to the shoe to prevent slipping when walking on ice or climbing. In this sense, also called *climbing iron.* [Middle English, from Old French, of Germanic origin.]

cram school *n.* A school especially in Japan that prepares its students for university entrance examinations by way of an accelerated curriculum.

Cra·nach (krä′näKH), **Lucas.** Known as "the Elder." 1472–1553. German painter and engraver noted for his many portraits and religious works, some of which depict the theological views of his friend Martin Luther.

cran·ber·ry (krăn′bĕr′ē) *n.* **1.** A mat-forming, evergreen shrub *(Vaccinium macrocarpum)* of eastern North America, having pink flowers and tart, red, edible berries. **2.** The berries of this plant, used in sauces, jellies, relishes, and beverages. **3.** Any of several similar or related plants, especially *Vaccinium oxycoccos.* [Partial translation of Low German *Kraanbere* : *Kraan,* crane (from Middle Low German *kran;* see **gerə-²** in Appendix) + *bere,* berry.]

cranberry bush *n.* A North American shrub *(Viburnum trilobum)* having broad clusters of white flowers and scarlet fruit. Also called *cranberry tree, highbush cranberry.*

crane (krān) *n.* **1.a.** Any of various large wading birds of the family Gruidae, having a long neck, long legs, and a long bill. **b.** A similar bird, such as a heron. **2.** A machine for hoisting and moving heavy objects by means of cables attached to a movable boom. **3.** Any of various devices with a swinging arm, as in a fireplace for suspending a pot. **—crane** *v.* **craned, cran·ing, cranes.** —*tr.* **1.** To hoist or move with or as if with a crane. **2.** To strain and stretch (the neck, for example) in order to see better. —*intr.* **1.** To stretch one's neck toward something for a better view. **2.** To be irresolute; hesitate. [Middle English, from Old English *cran.* See **gerə-²** in Appendix.]

Crane (krān), **(Harold) Hart.** 1899–1932. American poet whose works, including *The Bridge* (1930), celebrate America's cultural past, present, and future.

Crane, Stephen. 1871–1900. American writer whose works include *The Red Badge of Courage* (1895) and the short story "The Open Boat" (1898).

crane fly *n.* Any of numerous long-legged, slender-bodied flies of the family Tipulidae, having the general appearance of a large mosquito. Also called *daddy longlegs.*

cranes·bill (krānz′bĭl′) *n.* See **geranium** (sense 1).

Cran·ford (krăn′fərd). A community of northeast New Jersey west of Elizabeth. Mainly residential, it has varied industries. Population, 24,573.

crani– *pref.* Variant of **cranio–.**

cra·ni·a (krā′nē-ə) *n.* A plural of **cranium.**

cra·ni·al (krā′nē-əl) *adj.* Of or relating to the skull or cranium. [From CRANIUM.] **—cra′ni·al·ly** *adv.*

cranial index *n.* The ratio of the maximum breadth to the maximum length of the skull, multiplied by 100.

cranial nerve *n.* Any of several nerves that arise in pairs from the brainstem and reach the periphery through openings in the skull. There are 12 such pairs in mammals, birds, and reptiles and usually 10 pairs in amphibians and fish.

cra·ni·ate (krā′nē-ĭt, -āt′) *adj.* Having a skull or cranium. **—craniate** *n.* An animal or a human being having a skull or cranium.

cra·ni·ec·to·my (krā′nē-ĕk′tə-mē) *n., pl.* **-mies.** Surgical removal of a portion of the cranium.

cranio– or **crani–** *pref.* Cranium: *craniometer.* [From CRANIUM.]

cra·ni·o·cer·e·bral (krā′nē-ō-sĕr′ə-brəl, -sə-rē′brəl) *adj.* Of or relating to both the cranium and the cerebrum.

cra·ni·o·fa·cial (krā′nē-ō-fā′shəl) *adj.* Of or involving both the cranium and the face: *craniofacial surgery.*

cra·ni·ol·o·gy (krā′nē-ŏl′ə-jē) *n.* The scientific study of the characteristics of the skull, such as size and shape, especially in human beings. **—cra′ni·o·log′i·cal** (-ə-lŏj′ĭ-kəl) *adj.* **—cra′ni·o·log′i·cal·ly** *adv.* **—cra′ni·ol′o·gist** *n.*

cra·ni·om·e·ter (krā′nē-ŏm′ĭ-tər) *n.* An instrument or device used to measure the skull. **—cra′ni·o·met′ric** (-ə-mĕt′rĭk), **cra′ni·o·met′ri·cal** *adj.*

cra·ni·om·e·try (krā′nē-ŏm′ĭ-trē) *n.* Measurement of the skull to determine its characteristics as related to sex, race, or body type.

cra·ni·o·sac·ral (krā′nē-ō-săk′rəl, -sā′krəl) *adj.* **1.** Of or associated with both the cranium and the sacrum. **2.** Of or relating to the parasympathetic nervous system.

cra·ni·ot·o·my (krā′nē-ŏt′ə-mē) *n., pl.* **-mies. 1.** Surgical incision into the skull. **2.** The cutting or breaking of the fetal skull to reduce its size for removal when normal delivery is not possible.

cra·ni·um (krā′nē-əm) *n., pl.* **-ni·ums** or **-ni·a** (-nē-ə). **1.** The skull of a vertebrate. **2.** The portion of the skull enclosing the brain; the braincase. [Middle English *craneum,* from Medieval Latin *cranium,* from Greek *kranion.* See **ker-¹** in Appendix.]

crank¹ (krăngk) *n.* **1.** A device for transmitting rotary motion, consisting of a handle or arm attached at right angles to a shaft. **2.** A clever turn of speech; a verbal conceit: *quips and cranks.* **3.** A peculiar or eccentric idea or action. **4.** *Informal.* **a.** A grouchy person. **b.** An eccentric person, especially one who is unduly zealous. **—crank** *v.* **cranked, crank·ing, cranks.** —*tr.* **1.a.** To start or operate (an engine, for example) by turning a handle. **b.** To move or operate (a window, for example) by or as if by turning a handle. **2.** To make into the shape of a crank; bend. **3.** To provide with a handle that is used in turning. —*intr.* **1.** To turn a handle. **2.** To wind in a zigzagging course. **—crank** *adj.* Of, being, or produced by an eccentric person: *a crank letter; a crank phone call.* **—*phrasal verbs.* crank out.** To produce, especially mechanically and rapidly: *cranks out memo after memo.* **crank up. 1.** To cause to start or get started as if by turning a crank: *cranked up a massive publicity campaign.* **2.** To cause to intensify, as in volume or force: *cranks up the sound on the stereo.* [Middle English, from Old English *cranc-,* as in *crancstæf,* weaving implement.]

crank² (krăngk) *adj. Nautical.* Liable to capsize; unstable. [Origin unknown.]

crank·case (krăngk′kās′) *n.* The metal case enclosing the crankshaft and associated parts in a reciprocating engine.

crank·pin also **crank pin** (krăngk′pĭn′) *n.* A bar or cylinder in the arm of a crank to which a reciprocating member or connecting rod is attached.

crank·shaft (krăngk′shăft′) *n.* A shaft that turns or is turned by a crank.

crank·y¹ (krăng′kē) *adj.* **-i·er, -i·est. 1.** Having a bad disposition; peevish. **2.** Having eccentric ways; odd. **3.** Full of bends and turns; crooked: *a cranky mountain road.* **4.** Working unpredictably; erratic: *a cranky old truck.* **5.** Rickety; loose. **—crank′i·ly** *adv.* **—crank′i·ness** *n.*

crank·y² (krăng′kē) *adj.* **-i·er, -i·est.** *Nautical.* Liable to capsize.

Cran·mer (krăn′mər), **Thomas.** 1489–1556. English prelate who as archbishop of Canterbury (1533–1553) was instrumental in the marital machinations of Henry VIII, revised the *Book of Common Prayer* (1552), and instituted other reforms. Under Mary I, a Roman Catholic, he was convicted of heresy and burned at the stake.

cran·ny (krăn′ē) *n., pl.* **-nies.** A small opening, as in a wall or rock face; a crevice. [Middle English *crani,* perhaps alteration of Old French *cren, cran,* notch, from **crener,* to notch.] **—cran′nied** *adj.*

Cran·ston (krăn′stən). A city of east-central Rhode Island south of Providence. It was settled in 1636. Population, 71,992.

crap¹ (krăp) *Vulgar Slang. n.* **1.** Excrement. **2.** An act of defecating. **3.** Worthless nonsense; rubbish. **—crap** *intr.v.* **crapped, crap·ping, craps.** To defecate. [Middle English *crappe,* chaff, from Old French *crappe,* from Medieval Latin *crappa,* perhaps of Germanic origin.]

crap² (krăp) *Games. n.* See **craps. —crap** *v.* **crapped, crap·ping, craps.** To make a losing throw in the game of craps. [Back-formation from CRAPS.]

crape (krāp) *n.* **1.** See **crepe** (sense 1). **2.** A black band worn, as on the sleeve, as a sign of mourning. Also called *crepe.* **—crape** *tr.v.* **craped, crap·ing, crapes.** To cover or drape with or as if with crape. [Alteration of French *crêpe.* See CREPE.]

crape·hang·er (krāp′hăng′ər) *n.* A morose, gloomy, or pessimistic person.

crape jasmine *n.* An evergreen shrub *(Tabernaemontana divaricata)* native to India and cultivated as an ornamental in warm regions for its fragrant white flowers. [From the crinkled lobes of the corolla.]

crape myrtle also **crepe myrtle** *n.* A deciduous shrub *(Lagerstroemia indica)* native to China and widely cultivated in warm regions for its showy clusters of variously colored flowers with crinkled petals.

crap·per (krăp′ər) *n. Vulgar Slang.* A toilet. [From CRAP¹.]

crap·pie (krŏp′ē) *n., pl.* **-pies.** Either of two edible North American sunfishes, the black crappie *(Pomoxis nigromaculatus)* or the white crappie *(P. annularis).* [Canadian French *crapet.*]

craps (krăps) *pl.n. (used with a sing. or pl. verb).* **1.** A gambling game played with two dice in which a first throw of 7 or 11 wins, a first throw of 2, 3, or 12 loses the bet, and a first throw of any other number (a point) must be repeated to win before a 7 is thrown, which loses both the bet and the dice. **2.** A losing throw in this game. Also called *crap.* [Louisiana French, game of hazard, from English *crabs,* lowest throw in hazard, from CRAB[1] or CRAB[2].]

crap·shoot (krăp′sho͞ot′) *n. Slang.* A risky enterprise.

crap·shoot·er (krăp′sho͞o′tər) *n. Games.* One who plays craps.

crap·u·lence (krăp′yə-ləns) *n.* **1.** Sickness caused by excessive eating or drinking. **2.** Excessive indulgence; intemperance. [From CRAPULENT, sick from gluttony, from Late Latin *crāpulentus,* very drunk, from Latin *crāpula,* intoxication, from Greek *kraipalē.*] **—crap′u·lent** *adj.* **—crap′u·lous** *adj.*

crash[1] (krăsh) *v.* **crashed, crash·ing, crash·es.** *—intr.* **1.a.** To break violently or noisily; smash. **b.** To undergo sudden damage or destruction on impact: *Their car crashed into a guardrail. The airplane crashed over the ocean.* **2.** To make a sudden loud noise: *breakers crashing against the rocks.* **3.** To move noisily or so as to cause damage: *went crashing through the woods.* **4.** To fail suddenly, as a market or an economy. **5.** *Slang.* To undergo a period especially of depression as an aftereffect of drug-taking. **6.** *Slang.* **a.** To find temporary lodging or shelter, as for the night. **b.** To go to sleep. *—tr.* **1.** To cause to crash. **2.** To dash to pieces; smash. **3.** *Informal.* To join or enter (a party, for example) without invitation. **—crash** *n.* **1.** A sudden loud noise, as of an object breaking. **2.a.** A smashing to pieces. **b.** A collision, as between two automobiles. See Synonyms at **collision. 3.** A sudden economic or fiscal failure. **4.** *Slang.* Mental depression after drug-taking. **—crash** *adj. Informal.* Of or characterized by an intensive effort to produce or accomplish: *a crash course on income-tax preparation; a crash diet.* **—*idiom.* crash and burn.** *Slang.* **1.** To fail utterly. **2.** To fall asleep from exhaustion. **3.** To wipe out, as in skateboarding. [Middle English *crasschen;* probably akin to *crasen,* to shatter. See CRAZE.] **—crash′er** *n.*

crash[2] (krăsh) *n.* **1.** A coarse, light, unevenly woven fabric of cotton or linen, used for towels and curtains. **2.** Starched reinforced fabric used to strengthen a book binding or the spine of a bound book. [From Russian *krashenina,* colored linen, from *krashenie,* coloring, from *krasit',* to color. See **ker-[3]** in Appendix.]

Crash·aw (krăsh′ô), **Richard.** 1613?–1649. English metaphysical poet best known for his collection of religious verse, *Steps to the Temple* (1646).

crash dive *n.* A rapid dive made by a submarine, especially in an emergency.

crash-dive (krăsh′dīv′) *intr.v.* **-dived** or **-dove** (-dōv′), **-div·ing, -dives.** To undergo a crash dive.

crash helmet *n.* A padded helmet, as one worn by bicyclists, motorcyclists, or aviators, to protect the head in case of accident.

crash·ing (krăsh′ĭng) *adj.* Total; absolute: *a crashing bore.*

crash-land (krăsh′lănd′) *v.* **-land·ed, -land·ing, -lands.** *—tr.* To land (an aircraft or a spacecraft) under emergency conditions, usually with damage to the craft. *—intr.* To land an aircraft or a spacecraft under emergency conditions.

crash landing *n.* An emergency landing by an aircraft or a spacecraft.

crash pad *n.* **1.** Padding inside vehicles, such as automobiles or tanks, for protecting occupants in the event of an accident or sudden stop. **2.** *Slang.* A place affording free and usually temporary lodging: *"the head shops and crash pads of the psychedelic past"* (Wall Street Journal).

crash truck *n.* A truck specially designed and equipped to rescue victims of an air crash. Also called *crash wagon.*

crash·wor·thy (krăsh′wûr′thē) *adj.* Capable of withstanding the effects of a crash: *crashworthy cars.* **—crash′wor′thi·ness** *n.*

crass (krăs) *adj.* **crass·er, crass·est.** So crude and unrefined as to be lacking in discrimination and sensibility. [Latin *crassus,* dense.] **—crass′i·tude′** (-ĭ-to͞od′, -tyo͞od′), **crass′ness** *n.* **—crass′ly** *adv.*

Cras·sus (krăs′əs), **Marcus Licinius.** 115?–53 B.C. Roman politician and general who joined Julius Caesar and Pompey in the first triumvirate to challenge the senate's power (60).

-crat *suff.* A participant in or supporter of a specified form of government: *technocrat.* [French *-crate,* from Greek *-kratēs,* ruler, from *kratos,* strength, power. See -CRACY.]

crate (krāt) *n.* **1.** A container, such as a slatted wooden case, used for storing or shipping. **2.** *Slang.* An old, rickety vehicle, especially a decrepit automobile or aircraft. **—crate** *tr.v.* **crat·ed, crat·ing, crates.** To pack into a container, such as a slatted wooden case. [Latin *crātis,* wickerwork.]

cra·ter (krā′tər) *n.* **1.** A bowl-shaped depression at the mouth of a volcano or geyser. **2.a.** A bowl-shaped depression in a surface made by an explosion or the impact of a body, such as a meteoroid. **b.** A pit; a hollow. **3.** Variant of **krater. —crater** *v.* **-tered, -ter·ing, -ters.** *—tr.* To make craters in: *"The missiles did not . . . crater the airfield"* (Tom Clancy). *—intr.* To form a crater or craters. [Latin *crātēr,* from Greek *kratēr,* mixing vessel. See **kera-** in Appendix.]

Cra·ter (krā′tər) *n.* A constellation in the Southern Hemisphere near Hydra and Corvus. [Latin *crātēr,* mixing bowl, crater.]

Crater Lake. A lake of southwest Oregon in a volcanic crater of the Cascade Range. At 589.3 m (1,932 ft) deep, it is the second-deepest lake in North America.

cra·ter·let (krā′tər-lĭt) *n.* A small crater.

cra·vat (krə-văt′) *n.* A scarf or band of fabric worn around the neck as a tie. [French *cravate,* necktie worn by Croatian mercenaries in the service of France, from *Cravate,* a Croatian, from German dialectal *Krabate,* from Serbo-Croatian *Hrvāt.*]

crave (krāv) *v.* **craved, crav·ing, craves.** *—tr.* **1.** To have an intense desire for. See Synonyms at **desire. 2.** To need urgently; require. **3.** To beg earnestly for; implore. See Synonyms at **beg.** *—intr.* To have an eager or intense desire. [Middle English *craven,* from Old English *crafian,* to beg.] **—crav′er** *n.* **—crav′ing·ly** *adv.*

cra·ven (krā′vən) *adj.* Characterized by abject fear; cowardly. **—craven** *n.* A coward. [Middle English *cravant,* perhaps from Old French *crevant,* present participle of *crever,* to burst, from Latin *crepāre,* to break.] **—cra′ven·ly** *adv.* **—cra′ven·ness** *n.*

crav·ing (krā′vĭng) *n.* A consuming desire; a yearning.

craw (krô) *n.* **1.** The crop of a bird or insect. **2.** The stomach of an animal. **—*idiom.* stick in (one's) craw.** To cause abiding discontent and resentment. [Middle English *crawe.*]

♦ **craw·dad** (krô′dăd′) *n. Chiefly Southern U.S.* See **crayfish** (sense 1). [Probably alteration of CRAWFISH.]

craw·fish (krô′fĭsh′) *n.* Variant of **crayfish. —crawfish** *intr.v.* **-fished, -fish·ing, -fish·es.** *Informal.* To withdraw from an undertaking.

Craw·ford (krô′fərd), **Francis Marion.** 1854–1909. American writer of more than 40 romantic novels, including *The Three Fates* (1892) and *The White Nun* (1909).

Crawford, Joan. 1908–1977. American actress noted for her portrayals of tough-minded, ambitious women in films such as *The Woman* (1939) and *Mildred Pierce* (1945), for which she won an Academy Award.

Crawford, Thomas. 1814–1857. American sculptor and noted exponent of neoclassicism. His works include *Armed Freedom* atop the U.S. Capitol.

crawl[1] (krôl) *intr.v.* **crawled, crawl·ing, crawls. 1.** To move slowly on the hands and knees or by dragging the body along the ground; creep. **2.** To advance slowly, feebly, laboriously, or with frequent stops: *We crawled along until we reached the open road.* **3.** To proceed or act servilely. **4.** To be or feel as if swarming or covered with moving things: *The accident scene was crawling with police officers. My flesh crawled in horror.* See Synonyms at **teem[1]. 5.** To swim the crawl. **—crawl** *n.* **1.** The action of moving slowly on the hands or knees or dragging the body along the ground. **2.** An extremely slow pace: *Traffic was moving at a crawl.* **3.** *Sports.* A rapid swimming stroke consisting of alternating overarm strokes and a flutter kick. **4.** A set of letters or figures that move across, up, or down a movie or television screen, usually giving information, such as film credits or weather alerts. [Middle English *craulen,* from Old Norse *krafla.* See **gerbh-** in Appendix.] **—crawl′ing·ly** *adv.*

crawl[2] (krôl) *n.* A pen in shallow water, as for confining fish or turtles. [Afrikaans *kraal,* enclosure for animals. See KRAAL.]

crawl·er (krô′lər) *n.* **1.** One that crawls, especially an early form of certain insect larvae. **2.** A vehicle, such as a bulldozer, that moves on continuous belts of metal plates.

crawl·space or **crawl space** (krôl′spās) *n.* A low or narrow space, such as one beneath the upper or lower story of a building, that gives workers access to plumbing or wiring equipment.

crawl·y (krô′lē) *adj.* **-i·er, -i·est.** *Informal.* **1.** Creepy. **2.** Feeling as if covered with moving things.

♦ **cray·fish** (krā′fĭsh′) also **craw·fish** (krô′-) *n., pl.* **crayfish** or **-fish·es** also **crawfish** or **-fish·es. 1.** Any of various freshwater crustaceans of the genera *Cambarus* and *Astacus,* resembling a lobster but considerably smaller. Also called ♦*crawdad,* ♦*mudbug.* **2.** See **spiny lobster.** [By folk etymology from Middle English *crevise,* from Old French *crevice,* perhaps from Old High German *krebiz,* edible crustacean. See **gerbh-** in Appendix.]

WORD HISTORY: The crayfish, also known as the crawfish, owes its name to a misunderstanding. The actual source of the word may be the Old High German word *krebiz,* "edible crustacean," or a word related to it. From this Germanic source came Old French *crevice,* which when taken into English became *crevise* (first recorded in a document written in 1311–1312). In Old French and Middle English these words designated the crayfish. People began to pronounce and spell the last part of this word as if it were *fish,* the first *fish* spelling (actually *fysshes*) being recorded in 1555. Because of a variation in Anglo-Norman pronunciation, two forms of the word have come down to Modern English: *crayfish* and *crawfish.*

cray·on (krā′ŏn′, -ən) *n.* **1.** A stick of colored wax, charcoal, or chalk, used for drawing. **2.** A drawing made with one of these sticks. **—crayon** *tr.v.* **-oned, -on·ing, -ons.** To draw, color, or decorate with a stick of colored wax, charcoal, or chalk. [French, diminutive of *craie,* chalk, from Latin *crēta.*] **—cray′on·ist** (-ə-nĭst) *n.*

craze (krāz) *v.* **crazed, craz·ing, craz·es.** *—tr.* **1.** To cause to become mentally deranged or obsessed; make insane. **2.** To produce a network of fine cracks in the surface or glaze of. *—intr.* **1.** To become mentally deranged or obsessed; go insane. **2.** To become covered with fine cracks. **—craze** *n.* **1.** A short-lived popular fashion; a fad. **2.** A fine crack in a surface or glaze. [Middle English *crasen,* to shatter, of Scandinavian origin.]

crater
Lunar crater
Eratosthenes

cravat

ă pat	oi boy
ā pay	ou out
âr care	o͝o took
ä father	o͞o boot
ĕ pet	ŭ cut
ē be	ûr urge
ĭ pit	th thin
ī pie	*th* this
îr pier	hw which
ŏ pot	zh vision
ō toe	ə about, item
ô paw	♦ regionalism

Stress marks: ′ (primary); ′ (secondary), as in **dictionary** (dĭk′shə-nĕr′ē)

creamcups
Platystemon californicus

creamer
19th-century Tiffany silver creamer

credenza

cra·zy (krā′zē) *adj.* **-zi·er, -zi·est. 1.** Affected with madness; insane. **2.** *Informal.* Departing from proportion or moderation, especially: **a.** Possessed by enthusiasm or excitement: *The crowd at the game went crazy.* **b.** Immoderately fond; infatuated: *was crazy about boys.* **c.** Intensely involved or preoccupied: *is crazy about cars and racing.* **d.** Foolish or impractical; senseless: *a crazy scheme for making quick money.* **—crazy** *n., pl.* **-zies.** One who is or appears insane: *"To them she is not a brusque crazy, but 'appropriately passionate'"* (Mary McGrory). **—*idiom.* like crazy.** *Informal.* To an exceeding degree: *They were running around like crazy.* **—cra′zi·ly** *adv.* **—cra′zi·ness** *n.*

crazy bone *n. Informal.* The funny bone.

Cra·zy Horse (krā′zē hôrs′). Real name Tashunca-Uitco. 1849?–1877. Sioux leader who militarily resisted the encroachment of whites in the Black Hills and joined Sitting Bull in the defeat of Gen. George A. Custer at Little Bighorn (1876).

crazy quilt *n.* **1.** A patchwork quilt of pieces of cloth of various shapes, colors, and sizes, arranged haphazardly. **2.** A disorderly mixture; a hodgepodge: *The map was a crazy quilt of districts and precincts.*

cra·zy·weed (krā′zē-wēd′) *n.* See **locoweed.** [From its toxic effect on some animals.]

C-re·ac·tive protein (sē′rē-ăk′tĭv) *n. Abbr.* **CRP** A globulin that appears in the blood in certain acute inflammatory conditions, such as rheumatic fever, bacterial infections, and neoplastic diseases. [*C-(polysaccharide) reactive.*]

creak (krēk) *intr.v.* **creaked, creak·ing, creaks. 1.** To make a grating or squeaking sound. **2.** To move with a creaking sound. **—creak** *n.* A grating or squeaking sound. [Middle English *creken,* croak, complain, of imitative origin.] **—creak′ing·ly** *adv.*

creak·y (krē′kē) *adj.* **-i·er, -i·est. 1.** Tending or likely to creak. **2.** Dilapidated; decrepit. **—creak′i·ly** *adv.* **—creak′i·ness** *n.*

cream (krēm) *n.* **1.a.** The yellowish fatty component of unhomogenized milk that tends to accumulate at the surface. **b.** Any of various substances resembling or containing cream: *hand cream.* **2.** *Color.* A pale yellow to yellowish white. **3.** The choicest part: *the cream of the crop.* **—cream** *v.* **creamed, cream·ing, creams.** *—intr.* **1.** To form cream. **2.** To form foam or froth at the top. *—tr.* **1.** To remove the cream from; skim. **2.** To select or remove the best part from: *Many special schools cream off the highest achievers.* **3.** To beat into a creamy consistency. **4.** To prepare or cook in or with a cream sauce. **5.** To add cream to. **6.** *Slang.* To defeat overwhelmingly: *The home team was creamed last night.* [Middle English *creme,* from Old French *craime* (from Late Latin *crāmum,* of Celtic origin) and from Old French *cresme* (from Latin *chrīsma,* an anointing, from Greek *khrisma,* unguent, from *khriein,* to anoint; see **ghrēi-** in Appendix).] **—cream** *adj.*

cream cheese *n.* A soft white cheese made of cream and milk.

cream-col·ored (krēm′kŭl′ərd) *adj. Color.* Of the color of cream; yellowish-white.

cream·cups (krēm′kŭps′) *pl.n. (used with a sing. or pl. verb).* An annual plant *(Platystemon californicus)* native to the southwest United States and Mexico and cultivated for its showy cream-colored to yellowish flowers.

cream·er (krē′mər) *n.* **1.** A small jug or pitcher for cream. **2.** A machine or device for separating cream from milk. **3.** A refrigerator in which milk is placed to form cream. **4.** A substitute for cream: *a nondairy coffee creamer.*

cream·er·y (krē′mə-rē) *n., pl.* **-ies.** An establishment where dairy products are prepared or sold.

cream of tartar *n.* See **potassium bitartrate.**

cream puff also **cream·puff** (krēm′pŭf′) *n.* **1.** A shell of light pastry filled with whipped cream, custard, or ice cream. **2.** *Slang.* A weakling. **3.** *Slang.* An old, especially secondhand car in very good condition.

cream sauce *n.* A white sauce made by cooking together a mixture of flour and butter with milk or cream.

cream soda *n.* A sweet carbonated drink with a vanilla flavor.

cream·y (krē′mē) *adj.* **-i·er, -i·est.** Rich in or resembling cream. **—cream′i·ly** *adv.* **—cream′i·ness** *n.*

crease (krēs) *n.* **1.** A line made by pressing, folding, or wrinkling. **2.** *Sports.* **a.** A rectangular area marked off in front of the goal in hockey. **b.** One of the lines in cricket marking off the positions of the bowler and batter or the space between two of these lines. **—crease** *v.* **creased, creas·ing, creas·es.** *—tr.* **1.** To make a pressed, folded, or wrinkled line in. **2.** To graze or wound superficially with a bullet. *—intr.* To become wrinkled. [Alteration of *creaste,* perhaps from Middle English *creste,* ridge. See CREST.] **—crease′less** *adj.* **—crease′proof′** *adj.* **—creas′er** *n.* **—creas′y** *adj.*

cre·ate (krē-āt′) *tr.v.* **-at·ed, -at·ing, -ates. 1.** To cause to exist; bring into being. See Synonyms at **found**[1]. **2.** To give rise to; produce: *That remark created a stir.* **3.** To invest with an office or title; appoint. **4.** To produce through artistic or imaginative effort: *create a poem; create a role.* **—create** *adj. Archaic.* Created. [Middle English *createn,* from Latin *creāre, creāt-.* See **ker-**[2] in Appendix.]

cre·a·tine (krē′ə-tēn′, -tĭn) also **cre·a·tin** (-tĭn) *n.* A nitrogenous organic acid, $C_4H_9N_3O_2$, that is found in the muscle tissue of vertebrates mainly in the form of phosphocreatine and supplies energy for muscle contraction. [Greek *kreas,* **kreat-,* flesh; see **kreuə-** in Appendix + -INE[2].]

creatine kinase *n.* An enzyme present in muscle, brain, and other tissues of vertebrates that catalyzes the reversible conversion of ADP and phosphocreatine into ATP and creatine.

creatine phosphate *n.* See **phosphocreatine.**

cre·at·i·nine (krē-ăt′n-ēn′, -ĭn) *n.* A creatine anhydride, $C_4H_7N_3O$, formed by the metabolism of creatine, that is found in muscle tissue and blood and normally excreted in the urine as a metabolic waste. [CREATIN(E) + -INE[2].]

cre·a·tion (krē-ā′shən) *n.* **1.a.** The act of creating. **b.** The fact or state of having been created. **2.** The act of investing with a new office or title. **3.a.** The world and all things in it. **b.** All creatures or a class of creatures. **4. Creation.** *Theology.* The act of God by which the world was brought into existence. Often used with *the.* **5.** An original product of human invention or artistic imagination: *the latest creation in the field of computer design.* **—cre·a′tion·al** *adj.*

cre·a·tion·ism (krē-a′shə-nĭz′əm) *n.* The position that the account of the creation of the universe given at the beginning of the Bible is literally true. **—cre·a′tion·ist** *adj. & n.*

creation science *n.* An effort to give scientific proof for the account of the creation of the universe given at the beginning of the Bible.

cre·a·tive (krē-ā′tĭv) *adj.* **1.** Having the ability or power to create: *Human beings are creative animals.* **2.** Productive; creating. **3.** Marked by originality and expressiveness; imaginative: *creative writing.* **—creative** *n.* One who displays productive originality: *the creatives in the advertising department.* **—cre·a′tive·ly** *adv.* **—cre′a·tiv′i·ty** (-ĭ-tē), **cre·a′tive·ness** *n.*

cre·a·tor (krē-ā′tər) *n.* **1.** One that creates: *the creator of a new television series; a born creator of trouble.* **2. Creator.** God. Used with *the.*

crea·ture (krē′chər) *n.* **1.** Something created. **2.a.** A living being, especially an animal. **b.** A human being. **3.** One dependent on or subservient to another; a tool. **—crea′tur·al** *adj.* **—crea′ture·li·ness** *n.* **—crea′ture·ly** *adj.*

creature comfort *n.* Something that contributes to physical comfort.

crèche (krĕsh) *n.* **1.** A representation of the Nativity, usually with statues or figurines. **2.** A hospital for foundlings. **3.** *Chiefly British.* A day nursery. [French, from Old French *cresche,* crib, of Germanic origin.]

Cré·cy (krĕs′ē, krā-sē′) or **Cré·cy-en-Pon·thieu** (-än-pôn-tyœ′). A town of northern France northwest of Amiens. It was the site of the first decisive battle of the Hundred Years' War (August 26, 1346), in which Edward III of England defeated Philip VI of France.

cre·dence (krēd′ns) *n.* **1.** Acceptance as true or valid; belief. See Synonyms at **belief. 2.** Claim to acceptance; trustworthiness. **3.** Recommendation; credentials: *a letter of credence.* **4.** A small table or shelf for holding the bread, wine, and vessels of the Eucharist when they are not in use at the altar. [Middle English, from Old French, from Medieval Latin *crēdentia,* from Latin *crēdēns, crēdent-,* present participle of *crēdere,* to believe. See **kerd-** in Appendix.]

cre·den·tial (krĭ-dĕn′shəl) *n.* **1.** That which entitles one to confidence, credit, or authority. **2. credentials.** Evidence or testimonials concerning one's right to credit, confidence, or authority: *The new ambassador presented her credentials to the president.* **—credential** *tr.v. Usage Problem.* **-tialed, -tial·ing, -tials.** To supply with credentials: *"trained, professional, credentialed child care"* (Lee Salk). [From Medieval Latin *crēdentiālis,* giving authority, from *crēdentia,* trust. See CREDENCE.]

USAGE NOTE: The participle *credentialed* is well established in reference to certified teachers and some other professions, but its more general use to mean "possessing professional or expert credentials" is still widely considered jargon. The sentence *The board heard testimony from a number of credentialed witnesses* was unacceptable to 85 percent of the Usage Panel.

cre·den·tial·ism (krĭ-dĕn′shə-lĭz′əm) *n.* Overemphasis on diplomas or degrees in giving jobs or conferring social status: *"Neo-liberalism made useful points in its critique of vested interests, of bureaucratic follies* [and] *of credentialism"* (Arthur M. Schlesinger, Jr.).

cre·den·za (krĭ-dĕn′zə) *n.* A buffet, sideboard, or bookcase, especially one without legs. [Italian, from Medieval Latin *crēdentia,* trust (possibly from the practice of placing food and drink on a sideboard to be tasted by a servant before being served to ensure that it contained no poison). See CREDENCE.]

cred·i·bil·i·ty (krĕd′ə-bĭl′ĭ-tē) *n.* **1.** The quality, capability, or power to elicit belief: *"America's credibility must not be squandered, especially by its leaders"* (Henry A. Kissinger). **2.** A capacity for belief: *a story that strained our credibility.*

credibility gap *n.* **1.** Public skepticism about the truth of statements, especially official claims and pronouncements: *"The credibility gap* [is] *the result of a deliberate policy of artificial manipulation of official news"* (Walter Lippmann). **2.** Lack of trustworthiness. **3.** A discrepancy or disparity, especially between words and actions.

cred·i·ble (krĕd′ə-bəl) *adj.* **1.** Capable of being believed; plausible. See Synonyms at **plausible. 2.** Worthy of confidence;

reliable. [Middle English, from Latin *crēdibilis,* from *crēdere,* to believe. See **kerd-** in Appendix.] **—cred′i·ble·ness** *n.* **—cred′i·bly** *adv.*

USAGE NOTE: *Credible* is widely but incorrectly used where *credulous* would be appropriate, as in *He was credible* (should be *credulous*) *enough to believe the manufacturer's claims.*

cred·it (krĕd′ĭt) *n. Abbr.* **cr. 1.** Belief or confidence in the truth of something. See Synonyms at **belief. 2.** A reputation for sound character or quality; standing. **3.** A source of honor or distinction: *She is a credit to her family.* **4.** Approval for an act, ability, or quality; praise: *Why should he get all the credit?* **5.** Influence based on the good opinion or confidence of others. **6.** Often **credits.** An acknowledgment of work done, as in the production of a motion picture or publication: *At the end of the film we stayed to watch the credits.* **7.a.** Official certification or recognition that a student has successfully completed a course of study: *He received full credit for his studies at a previous school.* **b.** A unit of study so certified: *This course carries three credits.* **8.** Reputation for solvency and integrity entitling a person to be trusted in buying or borrowing: *You should have no trouble getting the loan if your credit is good.* **9.a.** An arrangement for deferred payment of a loan or purchase: *a store that offers credit; bought my stereo on credit.* **b.** The terms governing such an arrangement: *low prices and easy credit.* **c.** The time allowed for deferred payment: *an automatic 30-day credit on all orders.* **10.** *Accounting.* **a.** The deduction of a payment made by a debtor from an amount due. **b.** The right-hand side of an account on which such amounts are entered. **c.** An entry or the sum of the entries on this side. **d.** The positive balance or amount remaining in a person's account. **e.** A credit line. **—credit** *tr.v.* **-it·ed, -it·ing, -its. 1.** To believe in; trust: *"She refused steadfastly to credit the reports of his death"* (Agatha Christie). **2.a.** To regard as having performed an action or being endowed with a quality: *had to credit them with good intentions.* **b.** To ascribe to a person; attribute: *credit the invention to him.* See Synonyms at **attribute. 3.** *Accounting.* **a.** To enter as a credit: *credited $500 to her account.* **b.** To make a credit entry in: *credit an account.* **4.** To give or award an educational credit to. **5.** *Archaic.* To bring honor or distinction to. [French, from Old French, from Old Italian *credito,* from Latin *crēditum,* loan, from neuter past participle of *crēdere,* to entrust. See **kerd-** in Appendix.]

cred·it·a·ble (krĕd′ĭ-tə-bəl) *adj.* **1.** Deserving of often limited praise or commendation: *The student made a creditable effort on the essay.* **2.** Worthy of belief: *a creditable story.* **3.** Deserving of commercial credit; creditworthy: *a creditable customer.* **4.** That can be assigned. **—cred′it·a·bil′i·ty, cred′it·a·ble·ness** *n.* **—cred′it·a·bly** *adv.*

credit bureau *n.* An organization to which business firms apply for credit information on prospective customers.

credit card *n.* A card issued by a bank or business authorizing the holder to buy goods or services on credit. Also called *charge card.*

credit hour *n.* A credit in a school or college, usually representing one hour of class per week for one term.

credit line *n.* **1.** A line of copy acknowledging the source or origin of a news dispatch, published article, or other work. **2.** The maximum amount of credit to be extended to a customer. In this sense, also called *line of credit.*

cred·i·tor (krĕd′ĭ-tər) *n. Abbr.* **cr.** One to whom money or its equivalent is owed.

credit rating *n.* An estimate of the amount of credit that can be extended to a company or person without undue risk.

credit union *n.* A cooperative organization that makes loans to its members at low interest rates.

cred·it·wor·thy (krĕd′ĭt-wûr′thē) *adj.* Having an acceptable credit rating. **—cred′it·wor′thi·ness** *n.*

cre·do (krē′dō, krā′-) *n., pl.* **-dos. 1.** A creed. **2. Credo. a.** The Apostles' Creed or the Nicene Creed. **b.** The musical setting for the Apostles' Creed or the Nicene Creed, as in a choral Mass. [Middle English, the Apostles' Creed, from Latin *crēdō,* I believe (the first word of the Apostles' Creed or the Nicene Creed), first person sing. present tense of *crēdere,* to believe. See **kerd-** in Appendix.]

cre·du·li·ty (krĭ-do͞o′lĭ-tē, -dyo͞o′-) *n.* A disposition to believe too readily. [Middle English *credulite,* from Old French, from Latin *crēdulitās,* from *crēdulus,* credulous. See CREDULOUS.]

cred·u·lous (krĕj′ə-ləs) *adj.* **1.** Disposed to believe too readily; gullible. **2.** Arising from or characterized by credulity. See Usage Note at **credible.** [From Latin *crēdulus,* from *crēdere,* to believe. See **kerd-** in Appendix.] **—cred′u·lous·ly** *adv.* **—cred′u·lous·ness** *n.*

Cree (krē) *n., pl.* **Cree** or **Crees. 1.a.** A Native American people inhabiting a large area from eastern Canada west to Alberta and the Great Slave Lake. Formerly located in central Canada, the Cree expanded westward and eastward in the 17th and 18th centuries, the western Cree adopting the Plains Indian life and the eastern Cree retaining their woodland culture. **b.** A member of this people. **2.** The Algonquian language of the Cree.

creed (krēd) *n.* **1.** A formal statement of religious belief; a confession of faith. **2.** A system of belief, principles, or opinions: *laws banning discrimination on the basis of race or creed; an architectural creed that demanded simple lines.* [Middle English *crede,* from Old English *crēda,* from Latin *crēdō,* I believe. See CREDO.] **—creed′al** (krēd′l) *adj.*

♦**creek** (krēk, krĭk) *n. Abbr.* **cr. 1.** A small stream, often a shallow or intermittent tributary to a river. Also called ♦*branch,* ♦*brook,* ♦*kill,* ♦*run.* **2.** A channel or stream running through a salt marsh: *tidal creeks teeming with shore wildlife.* **3.** *Chiefly British.* A small inlet in a shoreline, extending farther inland than a cove. **—*idiom.* up the creek** (or **up the creek without a paddle**). *Informal.* In a difficult, unfortunate, or inextricable position. [Middle English *creke,* probably from Old Norse *kriki,* bend.]

Creek (krēk) *n., pl.* **Creek** or **Creeks. 1.a.** A Native American people formerly inhabiting eastern Alabama, southwest Georgia, and northwest Florida and now located in central Oklahoma and southern Alabama. The Creek were removed to Indian Territory in the 1830's. **b.** A member of this people. **c.** The Muskogean language of the Creek. **2.a.** A Native American confederacy made up of the Creek and various smaller southeast tribes. **b.** A member of this confederacy. Also called *Muskogee.*

creel (krēl) *n.* **1.** A wicker basket, especially one used by anglers for carrying fish. **2.** A frame for holding bobbins or spools in a spinning machine. [Middle English *crel,* from Old French **creille,* latticework, from Latin *crātīcula,* gridiron, diminutive of *crātis,* wickerwork.]

creel

creep (krēp) *intr.v.* **crept** (krĕpt), **creep·ing, creeps. 1.** To move with the body close to the ground, as on hands and knees. **2.a.** To move stealthily or cautiously. **b.** To move or proceed very slowly: *Traffic creeps at that hour.* **3.** *Botany.* **a.** To grow or spread along a surface, rooting at intervals or clinging by means of suckers or tendrils. **b.** To grow horizontally under the ground, as the rhizomes of many plants. **4.** To slip out of place; shift gradually. **5.** To have a tingling sensation, made by or as if by things moving stealthily: *a moan that made my flesh creep.* **—creep** *n.* **1.** The act of creeping; a creeping motion or progress. **2.** *Slang.* An annoyingly unpleasant or repulsive person. **3.** A slow flow of metal when under high temperature or great pressure. **4.** A slow change in a characteristic of electronic equipment, such as a decrease in power with continued usage. **5.** *Geology.* The slow movement of rock debris and soil down a weathered slope. **6. creeps.** *Informal.* A sensation of fear or repugnance, as if things were crawling on one's skin: *That house gives me the creeps.* [Middle English *crepen,* from Old English *crēopan.*]

creep·er (krē′pər) *n.* **1.** One that creeps. **2.** *Botany.* A plant that spreads by means of stems that creep. **3.** See **cradle** (sense 4). **4.** A grappling device for dragging bodies of water, such as lakes or rivers. **5.** A one-piece fitted garment for an infant. **6. creepers.** A metal frame with a spike or spikes, attached to a shoe or boot to prevent slipping, especially on ice.

creep·ing (krē′pĭng) *adj.* Developing gradually over a period of time: *creeping insanity.*

creeping Char·lie (chär′lē) *n.* See **moneywort.**

creeping eruption *n.* A human skin disease caused by hookworm or roundworm larvae burrowing and creeping beneath the skin and characterized by eruptions in the form of progressing reddish lines.

creeping Jen·nie also **creeping Jen·ny** (jĕn′ē) *n.* See **moneywort.**

creep·y (krē′pē) *adj.* **-i·er, -i·est.** *Informal.* **1.** Of or producing a sensation of uneasiness or fear, as of things crawling on one's skin: *a creepy feeling; a creepy story.* **2.** Annoyingly unpleasant: *the creepy kids next door.* **—creep′i·ness** *n.*

creese (krēs) *n.* Variant of **kris.**

cre·mains (krĭ-mānz′) *pl.n.* The ashes that remain after cremation of a corpse. [Blend of CREMATED and REMAINS.]

cre·mate (krē′māt′, krĭ-māt′) *tr.v.* **-mat·ed, -mat·ing, -mates.** To incinerate (a corpse). [Latin *cremāre, cremāt-.* See **ker-**[3] in Appendix.] **—cre·ma′tion** (krĭ-mā′shən) *n.* **—cre′ma′tor** *n.*

cre·ma·to·ri·um (krē′mə-tôr′ē-əm, -tōr′-) *n., pl.* **-to·ri·ums** or **-to·ri·a** (-tôr′ē-ə, -tōr′-). A furnace or establishment for the incineration of corpses.

cre·ma·to·ry (krē′mə-tôr′ē, -tōr′ē, krĕm′ə-) *n., pl.* **-ries.** A crematorium. **—crematory** *adj.* Of or relating to cremation.

crème de ca·cao (krĕm′ də kə-kou′, kə-kā′ō) *n.* A sweet white or brownish liqueur with a chocolate flavor. [French : *crème,* cream + *de,* of + *cacao,* cacao.]

crème de la crème (krĕm′ də lä krĕm′) *n.* **1.** Something superlative. **2.** People of the highest social level. [French : *crème,* cream + *de,* of + *la,* the + *crème,* cream.]

crème de menthe (krĕm də mäɴt′, mĕnth′, mĭnt′) *n.* A sweet green or white liqueur flavored with mint. [French : *crème,* cream + *de,* of + *menthe,* mint.]

crème fraîche (krĕm′ frĕsh′) *n.* Cream that has been slightly fermented and thickened with lactic acid, often used as a topping or an ingredient in sauces. [French : *crème,* cream + *fraîche,* fresh.]

Cre·mer (krē′mər), Sir **William Randal.** 1838–1908. British pacifist who founded the Workmen's Peace Association (1870). He won the 1903 Nobel Peace Prize.

Cre·mo·na (krə-mō′nə, krĕ-mô′nä). A city of northern Italy on the Po River east-southeast of Milan. Originally a Roman colony, it was an independent commune in the Middle Ages until its surrender to Milan in 1334. Population, 80,758.

ă pat	oi boy
ā pay	ou out
âr care	o͝o took
ä father	o͞o boot
ĕ pet	ŭ cut
ē be	ûr urge
ĭ pit	th thin
ī pie	*th* this
îr pier	hw which
ŏ pot	zh vision
ō toe	ə about, item
ô paw	♦ regionalism

Stress marks: **′** (primary); ′ (secondary), as in **dictionary** (dĭk′shə-nĕr′ē)

crenate

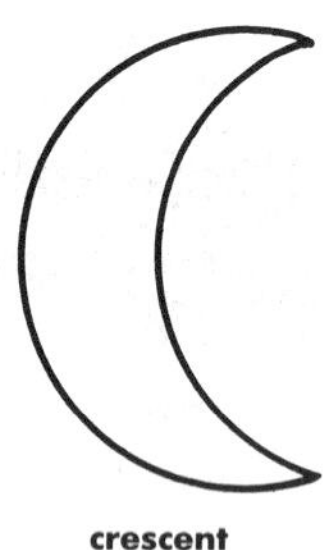
crescent

cre•nate (krē′nāt′) also **cre•nat•ed** (-nā′tĭd) *adj.* Having a margin with low, rounded or scalloped projections: *a crenate leaf.* [New Latin *crēnātus,* from Medieval Latin *crēna,* notch.] **—cre′nate′ly** *adv.*

cre•na•tion (krĭ-nā′shən) *n.* **1.** A rounded projection, as on the margin of a shell. **2.** The condition or state of being crenate. **3.** A process resulting from osmosis in which red blood cells, in a hypertonic solution, undergo shrinkage and acquire a notched or scalloped surface.

cren•a•ture (krĕn′ə-chər, krē′nə-) *n.* A rounded projection; a crenation.

cren•e•lat•ed also **cren•el•lat•ed** (krĕn′ə-lā′tĭd) *adj.* **1.** Having battlements. **2.** Indented; notched: *a crenelated wall.* [Probably from French *créneler,* to furnish with battlements, from Old French *crenel,* crenelation, diminutive of *cren,* notch. See CRANNY.] **—cren′e•la′tion** *n.*

cren•shaw (krĕn′shô′) *n.* A variety of winter melon *(Cucumis melo* var. *inodorus)* having a greenish-yellow rind and sweet, usually salmon-pink flesh. [Origin unknown.]

cren•u•late (krĕn′yə-lĭt, -lāt′) also **cren•u•lat•ed** (-lā′tĭd) *adj.* Having a margin with very small, low, rounded teeth: *a crenulate leaf.* [New Latin *crēnulātus,* from *crēnula,* diminutive of Medieval Latin *crēna,* notch.] **—cren′u•la′tion** *n.*

cre•o•dont (krē′ə-dŏnt′) *n.* Any of various extinct carnivorous mammals of the suborder Creodonta, of the Paleocene Epoch to the Pliocene Epoch. [From New Latin *Creodonta,* suborder name : Greek *kreas,* flesh; see **kreuə-** in Appendix + Greek *odous, odont-,* tooth.]

Cre•ole (krē′ōl′) *n.* **1.** A person of European descent born in the West Indies or Spanish America. **2. a.** A person descended from or culturally related to the original French settlers of the southern United States, especially Louisiana. **b.** The French dialect spoken by these people. **3.** A person descended from or culturally related to the Spanish and Portuguese settlers of the Gulf States. **4.** Often **creole.** A person of mixed Black and European ancestry who speaks a creolized language, especially one based on French or Spanish. **5.** A Black slave born in the Americas as opposed to one brought from Africa. **6. creole.** A creolized language. **7.** Haitian Creole. **—Creole** *adj.* **1.** Of, relating to, or characteristic of the Creoles. **2. creole.** Cooked with a spicy sauce containing tomatoes, onions, and peppers: *shrimp creole; creole cuisine.* [French *créole,* from Spanish *criollo,* person native to a locality, from Portuguese *crioulo,* diminutive of *cria,* person raised in the house, especially a servant, from *criar,* to bring up, from Latin *creāre,* to beget. See **ker-**[2] in Appendix.]

cre•o•lized language (krē′ə-līzd′) *n.* A language derived from a pidgin but more complex in grammar and vocabulary than the ancestral pidgin because it has become the native tongue of a community.

Cre•on (krē′ŏn′) *n.* *Greek Mythology.* The brother of Iocasta and uncle of Antigone who became the king of Thebes after the fall of Oedipus.

cre•o•sol (krē′ə-sôl′, -sŏl′, -sōl′) *n.* A colorless to yellow aromatic liquid, $C_8H_{10}O_2$, that is a constituent of creosote. [CREO-S(OTE) + -OL[1].]

cre•o•sote (krē′ə-sōt′) *n.* **1.** A colorless to yellowish oily liquid containing phenols and creosols, obtained by the destructive distillation of wood tar, especially from the wood of a beech, and formerly used as an expectorant in treating chronic bronchitis. **2.** A yellowish to greenish-brown oily liquid containing phenols and creosols, obtained from coal tar and used as a wood preservative and disinfectant. It can cause severe neurological disturbances if inhaled in strong concentrations. **—creosote** *tr.v.* **-sot•ed, -sot•ing, -sotes.** To treat or paint with creosote. [German *Kreosot* : Greek *kreas,* flesh; see **kreuə-** in Appendix + Greek *sōtēr,* preserver (from *sōzein,* to save; see **teuə-** in Appendix).]

creosote bush *n.* Any of several resinous, aromatic evergreen shrubs of the genus *Larrea,* especially *L. tridentata,* a yellow-flowered plant characteristic of warm deserts in the southwest United States and Mexico.

crepe also **crêpe** (krāp) *n.* **1.** A light, soft, thin fabric of silk, cotton, wool, or another fiber, with a crinkled surface. Also called *crape.* **2.** See **crape** (sense 2). **3.** Crepe paper. **4.** Crepe rubber. **5.** *(also* krĕp). A very thin, small pancake, often stuffed and rolled up. [French *crêpe,* from Old French *crespe,* curly, from Latin *crispus.* See **sker-**[2] in Appendix.]

crêpe de Chine (krāp′ də shēn′) *n., pl.* **crêpes de Chine** (krāp′) also **crêpe de Chines** (shēn′). A silk crepe used for dresses and blouses. [French : *crêpe,* crepe + *de,* of + *Chine,* China.]

crepe myrtle *n.* Variant of **crape myrtle.**

crepe paper *n.* Crinkled tissue paper, resembling the fabric crepe, used for decorations.

crepe rubber *n.* Rubber with a crinkled texture, used especially for shoe soles.

crêpe su•zette (krāp′ so͞o-zĕt′, krĕp′) *n., pl.* **crêpe su•zettes** or **crêpes su•zettes** (krāp′ so͞o-zĕt′, krĕp′). A thin dessert pancake usually rolled with hot orange or tangerine sauce and often served with a flaming brandy or curaçao sauce. [French : *crêpe,* pancake + *Suzette,* Suzy, allegedly after *Suzette* (for Suzanne) Reichenberg (1853–1924), French actress.]

crep•i•tate (krĕp′ĭ-tāt′) *intr.v.* **-tat•ed, -tat•ing, -tates.** To make a crackling or popping sound; crackle. [Latin *crepitāre, crepitāt-,* to crackle, frequentative of *crepāre,* to creak.] **—crep′i•tant** (-tənt) *adj.* **—crep′i•ta′tion** *n.*

crept (krĕpt) *v.* Past tense and past participle of **creep.**

cre•pus•cle (krĭ-pŭs′əl) *n.* Variant of **crepuscule.**

cre•pus•cu•lar (krĭ-pŭs′kyə-lər) *adj.* **1.** Of or like twilight; dim: *"the period's crepuscular charm and a waning of the intense francophilia that used to shape the art market"* (Wall Street Journal). **2.** *Zoology.* Becoming active at twilight or before sunrise, as do bats and certain insects and birds.

cre•pus•cule (krĭ-pŭs′kyo͞ol) also **cre•pus•cle** (-pŭs′əl) *n.* Twilight. [Middle English, from Old French, from Latin *crepusculum,* from *creper,* dark.]

cres•cen•do (krə-shĕn′dō) *n., pl.* **-dos** or **-di** (-dē). **1.** *Abbr.* **cr.** *Music.* **a.** A gradual increase, especially in the volume or intensity of sound in a passage. **b.** A passage played with a gradual increase in volume or intensity. **2. a.** A steady increase in intensity or force: *"insisted* [that] *all paragraphs . . . should be structured as a crescendo rising to a climactic last sentence"* (Henry A. Kissinger). **b.** *Usage Problem.* The climactic point or moment after such a progression: *"The attacks . . . began in December . . . and reached a crescendo during* [the president's] *September visit"* (Foreign Affairs). **—crescendo** *adj.* Gradually increasing in volume, force, or intensity. **—crescendo** *adv.* *Music.* With a crescendo. **—crescendo** *intr.v.* **-doed, -do•ing, -does.** To build up to or reach a point of great intensity, force, or volume: *"The designer-name craze crescendoed in the mid-seventies"* (Bernice Kanner). [Italian, present participle of *crescere,* to increase, from Latin *crēscere.* See **ker-**[2] in Appendix.]

USAGE NOTE: *Crescendo* is sometimes used by reputable speakers and writers to denote a climax or peak, as in noise level, rather than an increase. Although citational evidence over time attests to widespread currency, it is difficult for anyone acquainted with the technical musical sense of *crescendo* to use it to mean "a peak." Such usage, as in *When the guard sank a three-pointer to tie the game, the noise of the crowd reached a crescendo,* was unacceptable to 55 percent of the Usage Panel.

cres•cent (krĕs′ənt) *n.* **1.** The figure of the moon as it appears in its first or last quarter, with concave and convex edges terminating in points. **2.** Something having concave and convex edges terminating in points. **—crescent** *adj.* **1.** Crescent-shaped. **2.** Waxing, as the moon; increasing. [Middle English *cressaunt,* from Anglo-Norman, variant of Old French *creissant,* from present participle of *creistre,* to grow, from Latin *crēscere.* See **ker-**[2] in Appendix.] **—cres•cen′tic** (krə-sĕn′tĭk) *adj.*

cre•sol (krē′sôl′, -sŏl′, -sōl′) *n.* Any of three isomeric phenols, $CH_3C_6H_4OH$, used in resins and as a disinfectant. [Alteration of CREOSOL.]

cress (krĕs) *n.* **1.** An Old World annual plant *(Lepidium sativum)* in the mustard family, cultivated for its edible seedlings and leaves. **2.** Any of several related plants, such as pennycress and watercress. [Middle English *cresse,* from Old English.]

cres•set (krĕs′ĭt) *n.* A metal cup, often suspended on a pole, containing burning oil or pitch and used as a torch. [Middle English, from Old French, alteration of *croisuel,* probably from Vulgar Latin **croceolus,* small lamp.]

Cres•si•da (krĕs′ĭ-də) *n.* A Trojan woman in medieval romances who first returns the love of Troilus but later forsakes him for Diomedes.

crest (krĕst) *n.* **1. a.** A usually ornamental tuft, ridge, or similar projection on the head of a bird or other animal. **b.** An elevated, irregularly toothed ridge on the stigmas of certain flowers. **2. a.** A plume used as decoration on top of a helmet. **b.** A helmet. **3. a.** *Heraldry.* A device placed above the shield on a coat of arms. **b.** A representation of such a device. **4. a.** The top, as of a hill or wave. **b.** The highest or culminating point; the peak: *the crest of a flood; at the crest of her career.* **5.** The ridge on a roof. **—crest** *v.* **crest•ed, crest•ing, crests.** *—tr.* **1.** To decorate or furnish with a crest. **2.** To reach the crest of: *crested the ridge.* *—intr.* **1.** To form into a crest or crests: *waves cresting over the sea wall.* **2.** To reach a crest: *The swollen river crested at 9* P.M. [Middle English *creste,* from Old French, from Latin *crista.* See **sker-**[2] in Appendix.]

crest•ed wheat•grass (krĕs′tĭd hwēt′grăs′, wēt′-) *n.* A Eurasian perennial grass *(Agropyron cristatum)* cultivated for pasture and rangeland in the Great Plains and western North America.

crest•fall•en (krĕst′fô′lən) *adj.* Dispirited and depressed; dejected. **—crest′fall′en•ly** *adv.* **—crest′fall′en•ness** *n.*

crest•ing (krĕs′tĭng) *n.* An ornamental ridge, as on top of a wall or roof.

Cres•tone Needle (krĕs′tōn). A peak, 4,330.1 m (14,197 ft) high, in the Sangre de Cristo Mountains of south-central Colorado.

Crestone Peak. A mountain, 4,359.7 m (14,294 ft) high, in the Sangre de Cristo Mountains of south-central Colorado.

cre•syl (krē′sĭl) *n.* See **tolyl.** [CRESO(L) + -YL.]

cre•syl•ic (krĭ-sĭl′ĭk) *adj.* Of or relating to creosote or cresol. [CRES(OL) + -YL + -IC.]

Cre•ta•ceous (krĭ-tā′shəs) *adj.* **1.** Of, belonging to, or designating the geologic time, system of rocks, and sedimentary deposits of the third and last period of the Mesozoic Era, characterized by the development of flowering plants and the disappearance of dinosaurs. See table at **geologic time. 2. cretaceous.** Of, containing, or resembling chalk. **—Cretaceous** *n.* The Cretaceous Period. [From Latin *crētāceus,* chalky, from *crēta,* chalk, from *Crēta (terra),* Cretan (earth).] **—cre·ta′ceous·ly** *adv.*

Crete (krēt). An island of southeast Greece in the eastern Mediterranean Sea. Its Minoan civilization was one of the earliest in the world and reached the height of its wealth and power c. 1600 B.C. Crete subsequently fell to the Greeks, Romans, Byzantines, Arabs, Venetians, and Ottoman Turks. The islanders proclaimed their union with modern Greece in 1908. **—Cre′tan** *adj. & n.*

cre·tic (krē′-tĭk) *n.* See **amphimacer.** [Latin *Crēticus,* of Crete, Cretic foot, from *Crēta,* Crete.]

cre·tin (krēt′n) *n.* **1.** A person afflicted with cretinism. **2.** *Slang.* An idiot. [French *crétin,* from French dialectal, deformed and mentally retarded person, from Vulgar Latin **christiānus,* Christian, human being, poor fellow, from Latin *Chrīstiānus,* Christian. See CHRISTIAN.] **—cre′tin·oid′** (-oid′) *adj.* **—cre′tin·ous** (-əs) *adj.*

cre·tin·ism (krēt′n-ĭz′əm) *n.* A congenital condition caused by a deficiency of thyroid hormone during prenatal development and characterized in childhood by dwarfed stature, mental retardation, dystrophy of the bones, and a low basal metabolism. Also called *congenital myxedema.*

cre·tonne (krĭ-tŏn′, krē′tŏn′) *n.* A heavy unglazed cotton, linen, or rayon fabric, colorfully printed and used for draperies and slipcovers. [After *Creton,* a village of northwest France.]

Cre·ü·sa (krē-ōō′zə) *n.* *Greek Mythology.* The wife of Aeneas, who was lost while fleeing from Troy but came back as a ghost to warn Aeneas of his future.

Creutz·feldt-Ja·kob disease (kroits′fĕlt-yä′kôp) *n.* A rare, usually fatal disease of the brain, characterized by progressive dementia and gradual loss of muscle control, that occurs most often in middle age and is caused by a slow virus. Also called *Jakob-Creutzfeldt disease.* [After Hans G. *Creutzfeld* (1883–1964) and Alfons M. *Jakob* (1884–1931), German psychiatrists.]

cre·val·le (krĭ-văl′ē) *n.* Any of several marine fishes of the family Carangidae, such as the crevalle jack. [Alteration of CAVALLA.]

crevalle jack *n.* A food and game fish *(Caranx hippos)* of warm seas, having a laterally compressed silvery body.

cre·vasse (krĭ-văs′) *n.* **1.** A deep fissure, as in a glacier; a chasm. **2.** A crack or breach in a dike or levee. **—crevasse** *intr. & tr.v.* **-vassed, -vass·ing, -vass·es.** To develop or cause to develop crevasses. [French, from Old French *crevace,* crevice. See CREVICE.]

Crève·coeur (krĕv-kœr′), **Michel Guillaume Jean de.** Pen name J. Hector Saint John. 1735–1813. French-born American agriculturalist, writer, and diplomat whose *Letters from an American Farmer* (1782), a collection of essays on American life, was read widely in France.

crev·ice (krĕv′ĭs) *n.* A narrow crack or opening; a fissure or cleft. [Middle English, from Old French *crevace,* probably from Vulgar Latin **crepācia,* from **crepa,* from Latin *crepāre,* to crack.] **—crev′iced** *adj.*

crew¹ (krōō) *n.* **1.a.** A group of people working together; a gang: *a crew of stagehands.* **b.** A group of people gathered together temporarily; a crowd. **2.a.** All personnel operating or serving aboard a ship. **b.** All of a ship's personnel except the officers. **c.** All personnel operating or serving aboard an aircraft in flight. **3.a.** *Sports.* A team of rowers, as of a racing shell. **b.** The sport of rowing. **—crew** *intr.v.* **crewed, crew·ing, crews.** To serve as a member of a crew: *crewed for my sister on a sloop; a spacecraft that was crewed by a team of eight people.* [Middle English *creue,* military reinforcement, from Old French *creue,* increase, from feminine past participle of *creistre,* to grow, from Latin *crēscere.* See **ker-²** in Appendix.]

crew² (krōō) *v.* *Chiefly British.* A past tense of **crow².**

crew chief *n.* A noncommissioned air force officer who is in charge of a group of enlisted people, such as maintenance specialists, on the flight line.

crew cut or **crew·cut** (krōō′kŭt′) *n.* A closely cropped haircut. [So called because it was worn by rowers.]

crewed (krōōd) *adj.* Operated by an onboard crew: *a crewed space flight.*

crew·el (krōō′əl) *n.* Loosely twisted worsted yarn used for fancywork and embroidery. [Middle English *crule.*]

crew·el·work (krōō′əl-wûrk′) *n.* Needlework produced with crewel.

crew·mate (krōō′māt′) *n.* A fellow member of a crew, especially of a crew of astronauts.

crew neck *n.* **1.** A round close-fitting neckline. **2.** Often **crew·neck** (krōō′nĕk′). A garment, especially a sweater, with such a neckline. [From the wearing of similarly styled sweaters by rowers.]

crew sock *n.* A warm, usually ribbed sock. [From its use by rowers.]

crib (krĭb) *n.* **1.** A bed with high sides for a young child or baby. **2.a.** A small building, usually with slatted sides, for storing corn. **b.** A rack or trough for fodder; a manger. **c.** A stall for cattle. **3.** A small, crude cottage or room. **4.** A framework to support or strengthen a mine or shaft. **5.** A wicker basket. **6.a.** A petty theft. **b.** Plagiarism. **c.** See **pony** (sense 4). **7.** *Games.* A set of cards made up from discards by each player in cribbage, used by the dealer. **—crib** *v.* **cribbed, crib·bing, cribs.** —*tr.* **1.** To confine in or as if in a crib. **2.** To furnish with a crib. **3.a.** To plagiarize (an idea or answer, for example). **b.** To steal. —*intr.* To plagiarize; cheat. [Middle English, manger, from Old English *cribb.*] **—crib′ber** *n.*

crib·bage (krĭb′ĭj) *n.* *Games.* A card game for from two to four players in which the score is kept by inserting small pegs into holes arranged in rows on a small board. [From CRIB.]

crib-bit·ing (krĭb′bī′tĭng) *n.* An injurious habit of horses in which they bite at the edge of a feed trough or other object and swallow air at the same time.

crib death *n.* See **sudden infant death syndrome.**

crib·ri·form (krĭb′rə-fôrm′) *adj.* Perforated like a sieve. [Latin *crībrum,* sieve; see **krei-** in Appendix + -FORM.]

cri·ce·tid (krī-sē′tĭd, -sĕt′ĭd) *n.* Any of various small rodents of the family Cricetidae, which includes muskrats and gerbils. [From New Latin *Cricetidae,* family name, from *Cricetus,* hamster genus, from Medieval Latin *cricetus,* hamster, perhaps from Old Czech *křeček,* diminutive of *křeč.*] **—cri·ce′tid** *adj.*

Crich·ton (krīt′n), **James.** Known as "the Admirable Crichton." 1560–1582. Scottish adventurer, linguist, and scholar whose intellectual achievements were lauded by Aldus Manutius and Thomas Urquhart. He was killed in a brawl.

crick¹ (krĭk) *n.* A painful cramp or muscle spasm, as in the back or neck. **—crick** *tr.v.* **cricked, crick·ing, cricks.** To cause a painful cramp or muscle spasm in by turning or wrenching. [Middle English *crike.*]

♦**crick²** (krĭk) *n.* *Inland Northern & Western U.S.* Variant of **creek.** See Regional Note at **run.**

Crick (krĭk), **Francis Henry Compton.** Born 1916. British biologist who with James D. Watson proposed a spiral model, the double helix, for the molecular structure of DNA. He shared a 1962 Nobel Prize for advances in the study of genetics.

crick·et¹ (krĭk′ĭt) *n.* Any of various insects of the family Gryllidae, having long antennae and legs adapted for leaping. The males of many species produce a shrill chirping sound by rubbing the front wings together. [Middle English *criket,* from Old French *criquet,* from *criquer,* to click, of imitative origin.]

crick·et² (krĭk′ĭt) *n.* **1.** *Sports.* An outdoor game played with bats, a ball, and wickets by two teams of 11 players each. **2.** Good sportsmanship and fair conduct: *It's not cricket to cheat at cards.* **—cricket** *intr.v.* **-et·ed, -et·ing, -ets.** *Sports.* To play the game of cricket. [Obsolete French *criquet,* piece of wood, from Old French, stick for a bowling game, perhaps from Middle Dutch *cricke,* walking stick.] **—crick′et·er, crick′et·eer′** (-ĭ-tîr′) *n.*

crick·et³ (krĭk′ĭt) *n.* A small wooden footstool. [Origin unknown.]

cri·coid (krī′koid′) *n.* A ring-shaped cartilage of the lower larynx that articulates with the thyroid cartilage and artenoid cartilages. [New Latin *cricoīdēs,* from Greek *krikoeidēs,* ring-shaped : *krikos,* ring; see **sker-²** in Appendix + *-oeidēs,* -oid.]

cri de coeur (krē′ də kœr′) *n., pl.* **cris de coeur** (krē′). An impassioned outcry, as of entreaty or protest. [French : *cri,* cry + *de,* of + *coeur,* heart.]

cried (krīd) *v.* Past tense and past participle of **cry.**

cri·er (krī′ər) *n.* **1.** An official who announces the orders of a court of law. **2.** A town crier. **3.** A hawker.

cries (krīz) *v.* Third person singular present tense of **cry. —cries** *n.* Plural of **cry.**

Crile (krīl), **George Washington.** 1864–1943. American surgeon noted for his research on surgical trauma, shock, and other medical issues.

crim. *abbr.* Criminal.

crim. con. *abbr. Law.* Criminal conversation.

crime (krīm) *n.* **1.** An act committed or omitted in violation of a law forbidding or commanding it and for which punishment is imposed upon conviction. **2.** Unlawful activity: *statistics relating to violent crime.* **3.** A serious offense, especially one in violation of morality. See Synonyms at **offense. 4.** An unjust, senseless, or disgraceful act or condition: *It's a crime to squander our country's natural resources.* [Middle English, from Old French, from Latin *crīmen.* See **krei-** in Appendix.]

Cri·me·a (krī-mē′ə, krĭ-). A region and peninsula of southern Ukraine on the Black Sea and Sea of Azov. In ancient times it was colonized by Greeks and Romans and later overrun by Ostrogoths, Huns, and Mongols. Conquered by the Ottoman Turks in 1475, the area was annexed by Russia in 1783. The peninsula was the scene of the Crimean War (1853–1856), in which a coalition of English, French, and Turkish troops defeated the Russian forces, although Crimea itself did not change hands. **—Cri·me′an** *adj.*

crim·i·nal (krĭm′ə-nəl) *adj. Abbr.* **crim. 1.** Of, involving, or having the nature of crime: *criminal abuse.* **2.** Relating to the administration of penal law. **3.a.** Guilty of crime. **b.** Characteristic of a criminal. **4.** Shameful; disgraceful: *a criminal waste of talent.* **—criminal** *n.* One that has committed or been legally convicted of a crime. [Middle English, from Old French *criminel,* from Late Latin *crīminālis,* from Latin *crīmen, crīmin-,* accusation. See CRIME.] **—crim′i·nal·ly** *adv.*

criminal conversation *n. Abbr.* **crim. con.** *Law.* Adultery.

criminal court *n. Law.* A court empowered to hear and decide on cases involving offenses against criminal law.

crew¹
In a racing shell

cribbage

ă pat	oi boy
ā pay	ou out
âr care	ŏŏ took
ä father	ōō boot
ĕ pet	ŭ cut
ē be	ûr urge
ĭ pit	th thin
ī pie	*th* this
îr pier	hw which
ŏ pot	zh vision
ō toe	ə about, item
ô paw	♦ regionalism

Stress marks: ′ (primary); ′ (secondary), as in **dictionary** (dĭk′shə-nĕr′ē)

crim·i·nal·i·ty (krĭm′ə-năl′ĭ-tē) *n., pl.* **-ties. 1.** The state, quality, or fact of being criminal. **2.** A criminal practice or act.

crim·i·nal·ize (krĭm′ə-nə-līz′) *tr.v.* **-ized, -iz·ing, -iz·es. 1.** To impose a criminal penalty on or for; outlaw. **2.** To treat as a criminal. **—crim′i·nal·i·za′tion** (-nə-lĭ-zā′shən) *n.*

criminal justice *n.* The system of law enforcement, the bar, the judiciary, corrections, and probation that is directly involved in the apprehension, prosecution, defense, sentencing, incarceration, and supervision of those suspected of or charged with criminal offenses. *—attributive.* Often used to modify another noun: *criminal justice issues; criminal justice programs.*

criminal law *n.* Law that deals with crimes and their punishments.

crim·i·nate (krĭm′ə-nāt′) *tr.v.* **-nat·ed, -nat·ing, -nates.** To incriminate. [Latin *crīminārī, crīmināt-,* to accuse, from *crīmen, crīmin-,* accusation. See CRIME.] **—crim′i·na′tion** *n.* **—crim′i·na′tive, crim′i·na·to′ry** (-nə-tôr′ē, -tōr′ē) *adj.* **—crim′i·na′tor** *n.*

crim·i·no·gen·ic (krĭm′ə-nə-jĕn′ĭk) also **crim·o·gen·ic** (krī′mə-) *adj.* Producing or tending to produce crime or criminality: *"Alcohol is the most criminogenic substance in America"* (James B. Jacobs).

crim·i·nol·o·gy (krĭm′ə-nŏl′ə-jē) *n. Abbr.* **criminol.** The scientific study of crime, criminals, criminal behavior, and corrections. [Italian *criminologia,* from Latin *crīmen, crīmin-,* accusation. See CRIME.] **—crim′i·no·log′i·cal** (-nə-lŏj′ĭ-kəl) *adj.* **—crim′i·no·log′i·cal·ly** *adv.* **—crim′i·nol′o·gist** *n.*

crim·o·gen·ic (krī′mə-jĕn′ĭk) *adj.* Variant of **criminogenic.**

crimp[1] (krĭmp) *tr.v.* **crimped, crimp·ing, crimps. 1.** To press or pinch into small, regular folds or ridges: *crimp a pie crust.* **2.** To bend or mold (leather) into shape. **3.** To cause (hair) to form tight curls or waves. **4.** To have a hampering or obstructive effect on: *Supplies of foreign oil were crimped by the embargo.* **—crimp** *n.* **1.** The act of crimping. **2.** Something made by or as if by crimping, as: **a.** Hair that has been tightly curled or waved. **b.** A series of curls, as of wool fibers. **c.** A crease or bend. **3.** An obstructing agent or force: *Rising interest rates put a crimp in new construction.* [Dutch or Low German *krimpen,* from Middle Dutch or Middle Low German.] **—crimp′er** *n.*

crimp[2] (krĭmp) *n.* A person who tricks or coerces men into service as sailors or soldiers. **—crimp** *tr.v.* **crimped, crimp·ing, crimps.** To procure (sailors or soldiers) by trickery or coercion. [Origin unknown.]

crimp·y (krĭm′pē) *adj.* **-i·er, -i·est.** Full of crimps; wavy. **—crimp′i·ness** *n.*

crim·son (krĭm′zən) *n. Color.* A deep to vivid purplish red to vivid red. **—crimson** *tr. & intr.v.* **-soned, -son·ing, -sons.** To make or become deeply or vividly red. [Middle English *cremesin,* from Old Spanish *cremesín,* Old Italian *cremesino* or Medieval Latin *cremesīnus,* all from Arabic *qirmizīy,* from *qirmiz,* kermes insect. See KERMES.] **—crim′son** *adj.*

cringe (krĭnj) *intr.v.* **cringed, cring·ing, cring·es. 1.** To shrink back, as in fear; cower. **2.** To behave in a servile way; fawn. **—cringe** *n.* An act or instance of cringing. [Middle English *crengen,* to bend haughtily, probably ultimately from Old English *cringan,* to give way.]

crin·gle (krĭng′gəl) *n. Nautical.* A small ring or grommet of rope or metal fastened to the edge of a sail. [Low German *kringel,* diminutive of *kring,* ring, from Middle Low German.]

crin·kle (krĭng′kəl) *v.* **-kled, -kling, -kles.** *—intr.* **1.** To form wrinkles or ripples. **2.** To make a soft, crackling sound; rustle. *—tr.* To cause to crinkle. **—crinkle** *n.* A wrinkle, ripple, or fold. [From Middle English *crinkled,* full of turnings.] **—crin′kly** *adj.*

crin·kle·root (krĭng′kəl-ro͞ot′, -ro͝ot′) *n.* A woodland plant *(Cardamine diphylla)* of eastern North America, having fleshy rootstocks, trifoliolate leaves, and clusters of white or pinkish flowers.

crinkleroot
Cardamine diphylla

cri·noid (krī′noid′) *n.* Any of various echinoderms of the class Crinoidea, including the sea lilies and feather stars, that are characterized by a cup-shaped body, feathery radiating arms, and either a stalk or clawlike structure with which they are able to attach to a surface. **—crinoid** *adj.* Of or belonging to the Crinoidea. [From New Latin *Crinoidea,* class name : Greek *krinon,* lily + Greek *-oeidēs,* -oid.]

crin·o·line (krĭn′ə-lĭn) *n.* **1.** A coarse, stiff fabric of cotton or horsehair used especially to line and stiffen hats and garments. **2.** A petticoat made of this fabric. **3.** A hoop skirt. [French, from Italian *crinolino* : *crino,* horsehair (from Latin *crīnis,* hair; see **sker-[2]** in Appendix) + *lino,* flax (from Latin *līnum;* see **līno-** in Appendix).] **—crin′o·line, crin′o·lined** (-lĭnd) *adj.*

cri·num (krī′nəm) *n.* Any of various bulbous plants of the genus *Crinum,* native to warm regions and having strap-shaped leaves and showy umbels of variously colored flowers. Also called *spider lily.* [New Latin *Crinum,* genus name, from Greek *krinon,* lily.]

cri·ol·lo (krē-ō′lō, -ô′yô) *n., pl.* **-los** (-ō′lōz, -ô′yôs). A Spanish American of European, usually Spanish descent. **—criollo** *adj.* **1.** Of or relating to a criollo or criollos. **2.** Indigenous to or characteristic of a Spanish-American country: *criollo cattle; a criollo dish.* [Spanish. See CREOLE.]

cri·o·sphinx (krī′ə-sfĭngks′) *n.* A sphinx with the head of a ram. [Greek *krios,* ram; see **ker-[1]** in Appendix + SPHINX.]

criosphinx

crip·ple (krĭp′əl) *n.* **1.** One that is partially disabled or unable to use a limb or limbs: *cannot race a horse that is a cripple.* **2.** A damaged or defective object or device. **—cripple** *tr.v.* **-pled, -pling, -ples. 1.** To cause to lose the use of a limb or limbs. **2.** To disable, damage, or impair the functioning of: *a strike that crippled the factory.* [Middle English *crepel,* from Old English *crypel.*] **—crip′pler** *n.*

cri·sis (krī′sĭs) *n., pl.* **-ses** (-sēz). **1.a.** A crucial or decisive point or situation; a turning point. **b.** An unstable condition, as in political, social, or economic affairs, involving an impending abrupt or decisive change. **2.** A sudden change in the course of a disease or fever, toward either improvement or deterioration. **3.** An emotionally stressful event or a traumatic change in a person's life. **4.** A point in a story or drama when a conflict reaches its highest tension and must be resolved. *—attributive.* Often used to modify another noun: *crisis intervention; crisis planning.* [Middle English, from Latin, from Greek *krisis,* from *krinein,* to separate. See **krei-** in Appendix.]

SYNONYMS: *crisis, crossroad, exigency, head, juncture, pass.* The central meaning shared by these nouns is "a critical point or state of affairs": *a military crisis; government policy at the crossroad; had failed to predict the health-care exigency; a problem that is coming to a head; negotiations that had reached a crucial juncture; things rapidly coming to a desperate pass.*

crisis center *n.* A center staffed especially by volunteers who give support and advice to people experiencing personal crises.

crisis management *n.* Special measures taken under pressure to solve problems caused by a crisis.

crisp (krĭsp) *adj.* **crisp·er, crisp·est. 1.** Firm but easily broken or crumbled; brittle: *crisp potato chips.* **2.** Pleasingly firm and fresh: *crisp carrot and celery sticks.* **3.a.** Bracing; invigorating: *crisp mountain air.* **b.** Lively; sprightly: *music with a crisp rhythm.* **4.** Conspicuously clean or new: *a crisp dollar bill.* **5.** Marked by clarity, conciseness, and briskness: *a crisp reply.* See Synonyms at **incisive. 6.** Having small curls, waves, or ripples. **—crisp** *tr. & intr.v.* **crisped, crisp·ing, crisps.** To make or become crisp. **—crisp** *n.* **1.** Something crisp or easily crumbled: *The roast was burned to a crisp.* **2.** A dessert of fruit baked with a crumbly topping: *apple crisp.* **3.** *Chiefly British.* A potato chip. [Middle English, curly, from Old English, from Latin *crispus.* See **sker-[2]** in Appendix.] **—crisp′ly** *adv.* **—crisp′ness** *n.*

cris·pate (krĭs′pāt′) also **cris·pat·ed** (-pā′tĭd) *adj.* Curled or ruffled, as the margins of certain leaves. [Latin *crispātus,* past participle of *crispāre,* to curl, from *crispus,* curly. See **sker-[2]** in Appendix.]

cris·pa·tion (krĭs-pā′shən) *n.* **1.a.** The act of crisping or curling. **b.** The state of being crisped or curled. **2.** A slight involuntary muscular contraction, often producing a crawling sensation of the skin.

crisped (krĭspt) *adj. Botany.* Crispate.

crisp·er (krĭs′pər) *n.* One that crisps, especially a compartment in a refrigerator used for storing vegetables and keeping them fresh.

Cris·pin (krĭs′pĭn), Saint. Third century A.D. Roman shoemaker who with his brother Saint **Crispinian** sought to spread Christianity and was martyred.

crisp·y (krĭs′pē) *adj.* **-i·er, -i·est.** Crisp. **—crisp′i·ness** *n.*

cris·sa (krĭs′ə) *n.* Plural of **crissum.**

criss·cross (krĭs′krôs′, -krŏs′) *v.* **-crossed, -cross·ing, -cross·es.** *—tr.* **1.** To mark with crossing lines. **2.** To move back and forth through or over: *crisscrossed the country on a speaking tour.* *—intr.* To move back and forth. **—crisscross** *n.* **1.** A mark or pattern made of crossing lines. **2.** A state of being at conflicting or contrary purposes. **—crisscross** *adj.* Crossing one another or marked by crossings. **—crisscross** *adv.* In a manner or direction that crosses or is marked by crossings. [Alteration of Middle English *Cristcrosse,* mark of a cross, short for *Crist-cross (me speed),* may Christ's cross (give me success).]

cris·sum (krĭs′əm) *n., pl.* **cris·sa** (krĭs′ə). *Zoology.* The feathers or area under the tail of a bird surrounding the cloacal opening. [New Latin, from Latin *crīsāre,* to move the buttocks during intercourse. See **sker-[2]** in Appendix.] **—cris′sal** (-əl) *adj.*

cris·ta (krĭs′tə) *n., pl.* **-tae** (-tē). **1.** *Anatomy.* A crest or ridge, as on the top of a bone. **2.** *Biology.* One of the inward projections or folds of the inner membrane of a mitochondrion. [Latin. See **sker-[2]** in Appendix.]

cris·tate (krĭs′tāt′) also **cris·tat·ed** (-tā′tĭd) *adj.* Having or forming a crest or crista. [Latin *cristātus,* from *crista,* tuft. See **sker-[2]** in Appendix.]

crit. *abbr.* Critic; critical; criticism.

cri·te·ri·on (krī-tîr′ē-ən) *n., pl.* **-te·ri·a** (-tîr′ē-ə) or **-te·ri·ons.** A standard, rule, or test on which a judgment or decision can be based. See Synonyms at **standard.** [Greek *kritērion,* from *kritēs,* judge, from *krinein,* to separate, judge. See **krei-** in Appendix.] **—cri·te′ri·al** (-əl) *adj.*

USAGE NOTE: Like the analogous etymological plurals *agenda* and *data, criteria* is widely used as a singular form. Unlike them, however, it is not yet acceptable in that use.

crit·ic (krĭt′ĭk) *n.* **1.** One who forms and expresses judgments of the merits, faults, value, or truth of a matter. **2.** *Abbr.* **crit.** One who specializes especially professionally in the evaluation and appreciation of literary or artistic works: *a film critic; a dance critic.* **3.** One who tends to make harsh or carping judgments; a faultfinder. [Latin *criticus,* from Greek *kritikos,* able to discern, from *kritēs,* judge, from *krinein,* to separate, judge. See **krei-** in Appendix.]

crit·i·cal (krĭt′ĭ-kəl) *adj. Abbr.* **crit. 1.** Inclined to judge severely and find fault. **2.** Characterized by careful, exact evaluation and judgment: *a critical reading.* **3.** Of, relating to, or characteristic of critics or criticism: *critical acclaim; a critical analysis of Melville's writings.* **4.** Forming or having the nature of a turning point; crucial or decisive: *a critical point in the campaign.* **5.a.** Of or relating to a medical crisis: *an illness at the critical stage.* **b.** Being or relating to a grave physical condition especially of a patient. **6.** Indispensable; essential: *a critical element of the plan; a second income that is critical to the family's well-being.* **7.** Being in or verging on a state of crisis or emergency: *a critical shortage of food.* **8.** Fraught with danger or risk; perilous. **9.** *Mathematics.* Of or relating to a point at which a curve has a maximum, minimum, or point of inflection. **10.** *Chemistry & Physics.* Of or relating to the value of a measurement, such as temperature, at which an abrupt change in a quality, property, or state occurs: *A critical temperature of water is 100°C, its boiling point at standard atmospheric pressure.* **11.** *Physics.* Capable of sustaining a nuclear chain reaction. **—crit′i·cal·ly** *adv.* **—crit′i·cal·ness** *n.*

SYNONYMS: *critical, captious, censorious, faultfinding, hypercritical.* The central meaning shared by these adjectives is "tending or marked by a tendency to find and call attention to errors and flaws": *a critical attitude; a captious pedant; censorious of petty failings; an excessively demanding and faultfinding tutor; hypercritical of colloquial speech.*
ANTONYM: *uncritical.*

critical angle *n.* **1.** *Physics.* The smallest angle of incidence at which a light ray passing from one medium to another less refractive medium can be totally reflected from the boundary between the two. **2.** The angle of attack of an airfoil at which airflow abruptly changes, causing changes in the lift and drag of an aircraft.

crit·i·cal·i·ty (krĭt′ĭ-kăl′ĭ-tē) *n.* **1.** The quality, state, or degree of being of the highest importance: *"The challenge of our future food supply is approaching criticality"* (New York Times). **2.** *Physics.* The point at which a nuclear reaction is self-sustaining.

critical mass *n.* **1.** The smallest mass of a fissionable material that will sustain a nuclear chain reaction at a constant level. **2.** A very important or crucial stage: *"The sudden national uproar over drugs and drug abuse has reached politically critical mass in Washington"* (Tom Morganthau).

critical point *n.* **1.** *Physics.* The temperature and pressure at which the liquid and gaseous phases of a pure stable substance become identical. Also called *critical state.* **2.** *Mathematics.* **a.** A maximum, minimum, or point of inflection of a curve. **b.** A point at which the derivative of a function is zero or infinite.

critical pressure *n.* The least applied pressure required at the critical temperature to liquefy a gas.

critical state *n.* See **critical point** (sense 1).

critical temperature *n.* The temperature above which a gas cannot be liquefied, regardless of the pressure applied.

crit·ic·as·ter (krĭt′ĭ-kăs′tər) *n.* A petty or inferior critic. [CRITIC + Latin *-aster,* pejorative suff.]

crit·i·cism (krĭt′ĭ-sĭz′əm) *n. Abbr.* **crit. 1.** The act of criticizing, especially adversely. **2.** A critical comment or judgment. **3.a.** The art, skill, or profession of making discriminating judgments and evaluations, especially of literary or other artistic works. **b.** A review or article expressing such judgment and evaluation. **4.** Detailed investigation of the origin and history of literary documents, such as the Bible.

crit·i·cize (krĭt′ĭ-sīz′) *v.* **-cized, -ciz·ing, -ciz·es.** *—tr.* **1.** To find fault with: *criticized the decision as unrealistic.* See Usage Note at **critique. 2.** To judge the merits and faults of; analyze and evaluate. *—intr.* To act as a critic. **—crit′i·ciz′a·ble** *adj.* **—crit′i·ciz′er** *n.*

SYNONYMS: *criticize, blame, reprehend, censure, condemn, denounce.* These verbs are compared as they mean to express an unfavorable judgment. *Criticize* can mean merely to evaluate good and bad points without necessarily finding fault: *"To criticize is to appreciate, to appropriate, to take intellectual possession"* (Henry James). Usually, however, the word implies the expression of disapproval: *The reviewer roundly criticized the novel. Blame* emphasizes the finding of fault and the fixing of responsibility: *"People are always blaming their circumstances for what they are"* (George Bernard Shaw). *Reprehend* implies sharp disapproval: *"reprehends students who have protested apartheid"* (New York Times). *Censure* refers to open and strong expression of criticism; often it implies a formal reprimand: *"No man can justly censure or condemn another, because indeed no man truly knows another"* (Thomas Browne). *Condemn* denotes the pronouncement of harshly adverse judgment: *"The wrongs which we seek to condemn and punish have been so calculated, so malignant and so devastating that civilization cannot tolerate their being ignored because it cannot survive their being repeated"* (Robert H. Jackson). *Denounce* implies public proclamation of condemnation or repudiation: *The press denounces clandestine support for the counterrevolution.*

cri·tique (krĭ-tēk′) *n.* **1.** A critical review or commentary, especially one dealing with works of art or literature. **2.** A critical discussion of a specified topic. **3.** The art of criticism. **—critique** *tr.v.* **-tiqued, -tiqu·ing, -tiques.** *Usage Problem.* To review or discuss critically. [French, from Greek *kritikē (tekhnē),* (art of) criticism, from feminine of *kritikos,* critical. See CRITIC.]

USAGE NOTE: *Critique* has been used as a verb meaning "to review or discuss critically" since the 18th century, but lately this usage has gained much wider currency, in part because the verb *criticize,* once neutral between praise and censure, is now mainly used in a negative sense. (One is not likely to say, for example, *She criticized the bill approvingly.*) But this use of *critique* is still regarded by many as pretentious jargon; 69 percent of the Usage Panel rejects the sentence *As mock inquisitors grill him, top aides take notes and critique the answers with the President afterward.* There is no exact synonym, but in most contexts one can usually substitute *go over, review,* or *analyze.*

♦ **crit·ter** (krĭt′ər) *n. Regional.* **1.** A living creature. **2.** A domestic animal, especially a cow, horse, or mule. **3.** A person. [Alteration of CREATURE.]

♦ ***REGIONAL NOTE:*** *Critter,* a pronunciation spelling of *creature,* actually reflects a pronunciation that would have been very familiar to Shakespeare: 16th- and 17th-century English had not yet begun to pronounce the *–ture* suffix with its modern (ch) sound. This archaic pronunciation still exists in regional American *critter* and in Irish *creature,* pronounced (krā′tŭr) and used in the same senses as the American regionalism. The most common meaning of *critter* is "a living creature," whether wild or domestic; it also can mean "a child" when used as a term of sympathetic endearment, or it can mean "an unfortunate person." In old-fashioned regional speech, *critter* and *beast* denoted a large domestic animal. The more restricted senses "a cow," "a horse," or "a mule" are still characteristic of the speech in specific regions of the United States. The use of *critter* among younger speakers almost always carries with it a jocular or informal connotation.

croak (krōk) *n.* A low, hoarse sound, as that characteristic of frogs and crows. **—croak** *v.* **croaked, croak·ing, croaks.** *—tr.* **1.** To utter in a low, hoarse sound. **2.** *Slang.* To kill. *—intr.* **1.a.** To utter a low, hoarse sound. **b.** To speak with a low, hoarse voice. **2.** To mutter discontentedly; grumble. **3.** *Slang.* To die. [From Middle English *croken,* to croak, probably of imitative origin.] **—croak′i·ly** *adv.* **—croak′y** *adj.*

croak·er (krō′kər) *n.* **1.a.** A croaking animal, especially a frog. **b.** A person who grumbles or habitually predicts evil. **2.** Any of various fishes, chiefly of the family Sciaenidae, that make croaking or grunting sounds.

Croat (krōt, krō′ăt′) *n.* **1.** A native or inhabitant of Croatia. **2.** Serbo-Croatian as used in Croatia, distinguished from Serbian primarily by its being written in the Latin alphabet. Also called *Croatian.* [New Latin *Croata,* from Serbo-Croatian *Hrvāt.*]

Cro·a·tia (krō-ā′shə, -shē-ə). A region and former kingdom of southern Europe along the northeast Adriatic coast. It was settled by Croats in the 7th century, became a kingdom in the 10th century, and reached the height of its power in the 11th century before being conquered by Hungary in 1091. After the collapse of the Austro-Hungarian Empire in 1918 the Kingdom of Serbs, Croats, and Slovenes was formed. The region eventually became part of modern-day Yugoslavia.

Cro·a·tian (krō-ā′shən) *n.* See **Croat. —Croatian** *adj.* Of or relating to Croatia or its people, language, or culture.

croc (krŏk) *n. Informal.* A crocodile.

Cro·ce (krō′chĕ), **Benedetto.** 1866–1952. Italian philosopher, historian, and critic noted for a major work of modern idealism, *Philosophy of the Spirit* (1902–1917), and as a staunch opponent of fascism.

cro·ce·in (krō′sē-ĭn) *n.* Any of various red or orange acid azo dyes. [Latin *croceus,* saffron-colored (from *crocus,* saffron) + –IN.]

cro·chet (krō-shā′) *v.* **-cheted** (-shād′), **-chet·ing** (-shā′ĭng), **-chets** (-shāz′). *—intr.* To make a piece of needlework by looping thread with a hooked needle. *—tr.* To make by looping thread with a hooked needle: *crochet a sweater.* **—crochet** *n.* Needlework made by looping thread with a hooked needle. [From French *crocheter,* from Old French *crochet,* hook, diminutive of *croche,* feminine of *croc,* of Germanic origin.]

cro·ci (krō′sī, -kī) *n.* A plural of **crocus.**

cro·cid·o·lite (krō-sĭd′l-īt′) *n.* A fibrous, lavender-blue or greenish mineral, a sodium iron silicate that is used as a commercial form of asbestos. [Greek *krokus, krokis, krokud-, krokid-,* nap on woolen cloth + –LITE.]

crock¹ (krŏk) *n.* **1.a.** An earthenware vessel. **b.** A broken piece of earthenware. **2.** *Slang.* Foolish talk; nonsense: *That story is nothing but a crock.* [Middle English *crokke,* from Old English *crocc.* Sense 2, perhaps from *crock of shit.*]

♦ **crock²** (krŏk) *Regional. n.* Soot. **—crock** *v.* **crocked, crock·**

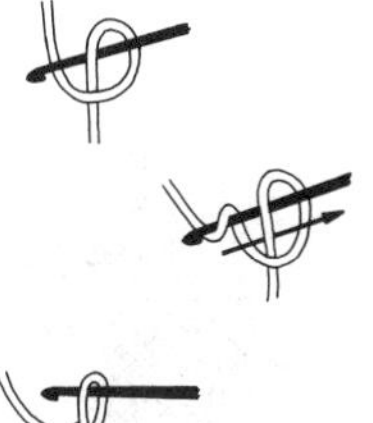

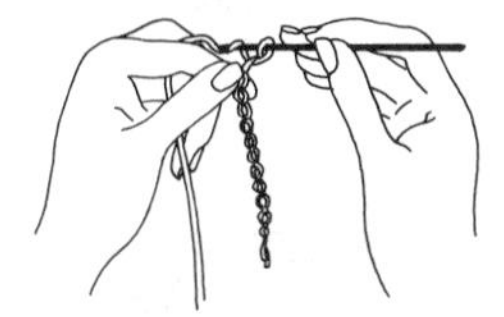

crochet

ă pat	oi boy
ā pay	ou out
âr care	ŏŏ took
ä father	ōō boot
ĕ pet	ŭ cut
ē be	ûr urge
ĭ pit	th thin
ī pie	*th* this
îr pier	hw which
ŏ pot	zh vision
ō toe	ə about, item
ô paw	♦ regionalism

Stress marks: **′** (primary); ′ (secondary), as in **dictionary** (dĭk′shə-nĕr′ē)

ing, crocks. —*tr.* To soil with or as if with crock. —*intr.* To give off soot or color. [Origin unknown.]

crock[3] (krŏk) *Chiefly British. n.* One that is worn-out, decrepit, or impaired; a wreck. —**crock** *v.* **crocked, crock•ing, crocks.** —*intr.* To become weak or disabled. Often used with *up.* —*tr.* To disable; wreck. Often used with *up.* [Origin unknown.]

crocked (krŏkt) *adj. Slang.* Drunk. [Possibly from CROCK[3].]

crock•er•y (krŏk′ə-rē) *n.* Earthenware.

crock•et (krŏk′ĭt) *n. Architecture.* A projecting ornament, usually in the form of a cusp or curling leaf, placed along outer angles of pinnacles and gables. [Middle English *croket,* ornamental curl of hair, hook, from Old North French *croquet,* shepherd's crook, diminutive of *croque,* variant of Old French *croche.* See CROCHET.]

Davy Crockett

Crock•ett (krŏk′ĭt), **David.** Known as "Davy." 1786–1836. American frontiersman and politician who was a U.S. representative from Tennessee (1827–1831 and 1833–1835) and joined the Texas revolutionaries fighting against Mexico. He died at the siege of the Alamo.

Crock-Pot (krŏk′pŏt′). A trademark used for an electric cooker that maintains a low temperature. This trademark often occurs in print in lowercase without a hyphen and occasionally in figurative uses: *"Pressure cookers and crock pots are proven labor savers for beans, stews, meats, and poultry"* (Christian Science Monitor). *"First Super Bowl Sunday, now* WORLD WAR *III; out of the frying pan, into the crock pot"* (Washington Post).

crocodile

croc•o•dile (krŏk′ə-dīl′) *n.* **1.** Any of various large aquatic reptiles, chiefly of the genus *Crocodylus,* native to tropical and subtropical regions and having thick, armorlike skin and long, tapering jaws. **2.** A crocodilian reptile, such as an alligator, a caiman, or a gavial. **3.** Leather made from crocodile skin. [Middle English *cocodril,* from Old French, from Latin *cocodrillus,* variant of *crocodīlus,* from Greek *krokodilos* : *krokē,* pebble + *drilos,* circumcized man, worm.]

WORD HISTORY: The crocodile may owe its name to its resemblance to a much smaller creature, a lizard that lived in the stone walls of Ionia. This lizard's name, *krokodilos,* is thought to be a compound of *krokē,* "pebble, gravel," and *drilos,* which is only attested as meaning "circumcised man" but is assumed to mean "worm" as well. According to Herodotus, Ionians in Egypt noted the resemblance, probably humorously, between basking crocodiles and their own "worm of the stones." The modern form of English *crocodile* represents a return to the Classical Latin spelling *crocodīlus,* Latin having borrowed the word from Greek. But other spellings occurred in Classical Greek and Latin, and one of these Latin spellings, *cocodrillus,* passed into Medieval Latin and Old French (*cocodril*) and then into English, so that our earliest possible use of the word, in a work perhaps composed before 1300, is spelled *cokedrille.* It was not until the 16th century that the word came to have its present spelling. The various spellings met with in the history of *crocodile* reflect the same sort of variations that occurred in the history of *alligator.*

croissant

crocodile bird *n.* A black and white African bird *(Pluvianus aegyptius)* that is related to the plover and feeds on insects that parasitize crocodiles.

Croc•o•dile River (krŏk′ə-dīl′). See **Limpopo.**

crocodile tears *pl.n.* An insincere display of grief; false tears. [From the belief that crocodiles weep either to attract a victim or when eating one.]

croc•o•dil•i•an (krŏk′ə-dĭl′ē-ən, -dĭl′yən) *n.* Any of various reptiles of the order Crocodylia, which includes the alligators, crocodiles, caimans, and gavials. —**crocodilian** *adj.* **1.** Of, relating to, or resembling a crocodile. **2.** Belonging to the order Crocodylia.

Oliver Cromwell

croc•o•ite (krŏk′ō-īt′, krō′kō-) also **croc•oi•site** (krŏk′wə-zīt′) *n.* A rare lead chromate mineral, $PbCrO_4$, that forms brilliant orange crystals. [Alteration of French *crocoise,* from Greek *krokoeis,* saffron-colored, from *krokos,* saffron. See CROCUS.]

♦ **cro•cus** (krō′kəs) *n., pl.* **-cus•es** or **-ci** (-sī, -kī). **1. a.** Any of various perennial Eurasian herbs of the genus *Crocus,* having grasslike leaves and showy, variously colored flowers. **b.** Any of several other plants, such as the autumn crocus. **2.** *Color.* A grayish to light reddish purple. **3.** A dark red powdered variety of iron oxide, Fe_2O_3, used as an abrasive for polishing. **4.** A coarse, loosely woven material like burlap, once used to make sacks for shipping saffron. See Regional Note at **gunnysack.** [Middle English, from Old French, from Latin, from Greek *krokos,* of Semitic origin.]

♦ **crocus sack** *n. South Atlantic U.S.* See **gunnysack.** See Regional Note at **gunnysack.**

Croe•sus[1] (krē′səs). Died c. 546 B.C. Last king of Lydia (560–546) whose kingdom, which had prospered during his reign, fell to the Persians under Cyrus.

Croe•sus[2] (krē′səs) *n.* A very wealthy man. [After CROESUS[1].]

croft (krôft, krŏft) *n. Chiefly British.* **1.** A small enclosed field or pasture near a house. **2.** A small farm, especially a tenant farm. [Middle English, from Old English.]

croft•er (krôf′tər, krŏf′-) *n. Chiefly British.* One who rents and cultivates a croft; a tenant farmer.

crois•sant (krwä-säN′, krə-sänt′) *n.* A rich, crescent-shaped roll of leavened dough or puff pastry. [French, from Old French *creissant, croissant,* crescent. See CRESCENT.]

WORD HISTORY: The words *croissant* and *crescent* illustrate double borrowings, each coming into English from a different form of the same French word. In Latin the word *crēscere,* "to grow," when applied to the moon meant "to wax"; one could have the phrase *lūna crēscēns,* "waxing moon." Old French *croissant,* the equivalent of Latin *crēscēns,* came to mean "the time during which the moon waxes," "the crescent-shaped figure of the moon in its first and last quarters," and "a crescent-shaped object." In Middle English, which adopted *croissant* in its Anglo-Norman form *cressaunt,* the first instance of our English word, recorded in a document dated 1399–1400, meant "a crescent-shaped ornament." *Crescent,* the Modern English descendant of Middle English *cressaunt,* owes its second *c* to Latin *crēscere. Croissant* is not an English development but instead a borrowing of the Modern French descendant of Old French *croissant.* It is first recorded in English in 1899. French *croissant* was used to translate German *Hörnchen,* the name given by the Viennese to this pastry, which was first baked in 1689 to commemorate the raising of the siege of Vienna by the Turks, whose symbol was the crescent.

Croix de Guerre (krwä′ də gâr′) *n.* A French military decoration for bravery in combat. [French : *croix,* cross + *de,* of + *guerre,* war.]

♦ **cro•ker sack** (krō′kər) *n. Lower Southern U.S.* See **gunnysack.** See Regional Note at **gunnysack.** [Alteration of CROCUS SACK.]

Cro-Mag•non (krō-măg′nən, -măn′yən) *n.* An early form of modern human being *(Homo sapiens)* inhabiting Europe in the late Paleolithic Era and characterized by a broad face and tall stature. It is known from skeletal remains first found in the Cro-Magnon cave in southern France. —**Cro-Mag′non** *adj.*

crom•lech (krŏm′lĕk′) *n.* **1.** A prehistoric monument consisting of monoliths encircling a mound. **2.** A dolmen. [Welsh : *crom,* feminine of *crwm,* arched + *llech,* stone.]

cro•mo•lyn sodium (krō′mə-lĭn) *n.* A drug, $C_{23}H_{14}Na_2O_{11}$, usually administered by inhalation and used to prevent certain allergic attacks, especially those associated with asthma or hay fever. [Rearrangement of chemical name *carboxychromon-yloxyhydroxypropane.*]

Cromp•ton (krŏmp′tən), **Samuel.** 1753–1827. British inventor of the spinning mule (1779).

Crom•well (krŏm′wĕl′, -wəl, krŭm′-), **Oliver.** 1599–1658. English military, political, and religious figure who led the Parliamentarian victory in the English Civil War (1642–1649) and called for the execution of Charles I. As lord protector of England (1653–1658) he ruled as a virtual dictator. His son **Richard** (1626–1712) succeeded him briefly as lord protector (1658–1659) before the restoration of the monarchy under Charles II. —**Crom•well′i•an** *adj.*

Cromwell, Thomas. Earl of Essex. 1485?–1540. English politician who proposed the legislation that established the monarch as head of the established church (1534).

crone (krōn) *n.* An ugly, withered old woman; a hag. [Middle English, from Old North French *carogne,* carrion, cantankerous woman, from Vulgar Latin **carōnia,* carrion, from Latin *carō, carn-,* flesh. See **sker-**[1] in Appendix.]

Cro•nin (krō′nĭn), **A(rchibald) J(oseph).** 1896–1981. British physician and writer whose novels include *Hatter's Castle* (1931) and *The Judas Tree* (1961).

Cro•nus (krō′nəs) *n. Greek Mythology.* A Titan who ruled the universe until dethroned by his son Zeus.

cro•ny (krō′nē) *n., pl.* **-nies.** A long-time close friend or companion. [Possibly from Greek *khronios,* long lasting, from *khronos,* time.]

cro•ny•ism (krō′nē-ĭz′əm) *n.* Favoritism shown to old friends without regard for their qualifications, as in political appointments to office.

crook[1] (kro͝ok) *n.* **1.** An implement or tool, such as a bishop's crosier or a shepherd's staff, with a bent or curved part. **2.** A part that is curved or bent like a hook. **3.** A curve or bend; a turn: *a crook in the path.* **4.** *Informal.* One who makes a living by dishonest methods. —**crook** *v.* **crooked, crook•ing, crooks.** —*tr.* To make a crook in; bend. —*intr.* To bend or curve. See Synonyms at **bend**[1]. [Middle English *crok,* from Old Norse *krōkr.*]

crook[2] (kro͝ok) *adj. Australian.* **1.** Out of order; faulty. **2.** Not well; ill. **3.** Of poor quality; inferior. **4.** Not honest; crooked. [From CROOKED or CROOK[1].]

crook•back (kro͝ok′băk′) *n. Obsolete.* See **hunchback** (sense 1). —**crook′backed′** *adj.*

crook•ed (kro͝ok′ĭd) *adj.* **1.** Having or marked by bends, curves, or angles. **2.** *Informal.* Dishonest or unscrupulous; fraudulent. —**crook′ed•ly** *adv.* —**crook′ed•ness** *n.*

crook•er•y (kro͝ok′ə-rē) *n.* Dishonest practices, as in business or politics.

Crookes (kro͝oks), Sir **William.** 1832–1919. British chemist and physicist who discovered thallium (1861), invented the radiometer (1875), and studied cathode rays.

Crookes tube *n.* A low-pressure discharge tube used to study the properties of cathode rays. [After Sir William CROOKES.]

crook•neck (kro͝ok′nĕk′) *n.* Any of several edible varieties of

ă pat	oi boy
ā pay	ou out
âr care	o͝o took
ä father	o͞o boot
ĕ pet	ŭ cut
ē be	ûr urge
ĭ pit	th thin
ī pie	*th* this
îr pier	hw which
ŏ pot	zh vision
ō toe	ə about, item
ô paw	♦ regionalism

Stress marks: ′ (primary); ′ (secondary), as in **dictionary** (dĭk′shə-nĕr′ē)

summer squash having a narrow crooked or curved neck and a yellow rind and flesh.

croon (kro͞on) *v.* **crooned, croon·ing, croons.** —*intr.* **1.** To hum or sing softly. **2.** To sing popular songs in a soft, sentimental manner. **3.** *Scots.* To roar or bellow. —*tr.* To sing softly or in a humming way: *crooning a lullaby.* —**croon** *n.* A soft singing or humming. [Middle English *crounen,* from Middle Dutch *krōnen,* to lament. See **gerə-²** in Appendix.] —**croon′er** *n.*

crop (krŏp) *n.* **1.a.** Cultivated plants or agricultural produce, such as grain, vegetables, or fruit. **b.** The total yield of such produce in a particular season or place. **2.** A group, quantity, or supply appearing at one time: *a crop of new ideas.* **3.** A short haircut. **4.** An earmark on an animal. **5.a.** A short whip used in horseback riding, with a loop serving as a lash. **b.** The stock of a whip. **6.** *Zoology.* **a.** A pouchlike enlargement of a bird's gullet in which food is partially digested or stored for regurgitation to nestlings. **b.** A similar enlargement in the digestive tract of annelids and insects. —**crop** *v.* **cropped, crop·ping, crops.** —*tr.* **1.a.** To cut or bite off the tops or ends of: *crop a hedge; sheep cropping grass.* **b.** To cut (hair, for example) very short. **c.** To clip (an animal's ears, for example). **d.** To trim (a photograph or picture, for example). **2.a.** To harvest: *crop salmon.* **b.** To cause to grow or yield a crop. —*intr.* **1.** To feed on growing grasses and herbage. **2.** To plant, grow, or yield a crop. —***phrasal verb.*** **crop up.** To appear unexpectedly or occasionally: *"one of the many theories that keep cropping up in his story"* (Christopher Lehmann-Haupt). [Middle English, from Old English *cropp,* ear of grain.]

crop-dust·er or **crop duster** (krŏp′dŭst′ər) *n.* **1.** A light airplane equipped for spraying crops with powdered insecticides or fungicides. **2.** The pilot of such an airplane.

crop-dust·ing (krŏp′dŭs′tĭng) *n.* The process of spraying crops with powdered insecticides or fungicides from an airplane. —**crop′-dust′** *v.*

crop-eared (krŏp′îrd′) *adj.* **1.** Having the ears cropped. **2.** Having the hair cut so short that the ears show.

crop·land (krŏp′lănd′) *n.* Land that is fit or used for growing crops.

crop·per¹ (krŏp′ər) *n.* A person who works land in return for a share of the yield; a sharecropper.

crop·per² (krŏp′ər) *n.* **1.** A heavy fall; a tumble. **2.** A disastrous failure; a fiasco. [Perhaps from the phrase *neck and crop,* completely.]

crop rotation *n.* The successive planting of different crops on the same land to improve soil fertility and help control insects and diseases.

cro·quet (krō-kā′) *Games. n.* **1.** An outdoor game in which the players drive wooden balls through a series of wickets using long-handled mallets. **2.** The act of driving away an opponent's croquet ball by hitting one's own ball when the two are in contact. —**croquet** *tr.v.* **-queted** (-kād′), **-quet·ing** (-kā′ĭng), **-quets** (-kāz′). To drive away (an opponent's croquet ball) by hitting one's own ball when the two are in contact. [French dialectal, hockey stick, from Old North French, shepherd's crook, diminutive of *croque.* See CROCKET.]

cro·quette (krō-kĕt′) *n.* A small cake of minced food, such as poultry, vegetables, or fish, that is usually coated with bread crumbs and fried in deep fat. [French, from *croquer,* to crunch.]

cro·qui·gnole (krō′kən-yōl′) *n.* A permanent wave in which the hair is wound around metal rods from the ends of the hair toward the scalp. [French, small, crisp pastry, tap on the head, from *croquer,* to crunch.]

Cros·by (krŏz′bē), **Harry Lillis.** Known as "Bing." 1904–1977. American singer and actor noted for his crooning voice and for roles in many films, including *Going My Way* (1944), for which he won an Academy Award.

cro·sier or **cro·zier** (krō′zhər) *n.* **1.** A staff with a crook or cross at the end, carried by or before an abbot, a bishop, or an archbishop as a symbol of office. **2.** *Botany.* See **fiddlehead** (sense 2). [Middle English *croser,* from Old French *crossier,* staff bearer (influenced by *croisier,* one who bears a cross, from *crois,* cross, from Latin *crux*) from *crosse,* crosier, of Germanic origin.]

cross (krôs, krŏs) *n.* **1.a.** An upright post with a transverse piece near the top, on which condemned persons were executed in ancient times. **b.** *Often* **Cross.** The upright post with a transverse piece upon which Jesus was crucified. **c.** A symbolic representation of the structure on which Jesus was crucified. **d.** A crucifix. **2.** A sign made by tracing the outline of a cross with the right hand upon the forehead and chest as a devotional act. **3.** A trial, affliction, or frustration. See Synonyms at **burden¹**. **4.** A medal, emblem, or insignia in the form of an upright post with a transverse piece near the top of it, or a modification thereto. **5.** A mark or pattern formed by the intersection of two lines, especially such a mark (X) used as a signature. **6.** A pipe fitting with four branches in upright and transverse form, used as a junction for intersecting pipes. **7.** *Biology.* **a.** A plant or animal produced by crossbreeding; a hybrid. **b.** The process of crossbreeding; hybridization. **8.** One that combines the qualities of two other things: *a novel that is a cross between romance and satire.* **9.** *Slang.* A contest whose outcome has been dishonestly prearranged. —**cross** *v.* **crossed, cross·ing, cross·es.** —*tr.* **1.** To go or extend across; pass from one side of to the other: *crossed the room to greet us; a bridge that crosses the bay.* **2.** To carry or conduct across something: *crossed the horses at the ford.* **3.** To extend or pass through or over; intersect: *Elm Street crosses Oak Street.* **4.a.** To delete or eliminate by or as if by drawing a line through: *crossed tasks off her list as she did them.* **b.** To make or put a line across: *Cross your t's.* **5.** To place crosswise one over the other: *cross one's legs.* **6.** To make the sign of the cross upon or over as a sign of devotion. **7.** To encounter in passing: *His path crossed mine.* **8.** *Informal.* **a.** To interfere with; thwart or obstruct: *Don't cross me.* **b.** To ruin completely. Used with *up: Their lack of cooperation crossed up the whole project.* **9.** *Biology.* To crossbreed or cross-fertilize (plants or animals). —*intr.* **1.** To lie or pass across each other; intersect. **2.a.** To move or extend from one side to another: *crossed through Canada en route to Alaska.* **b.** To make a crossing: *crossed into Germany from Switzerland.* **3.** To change from one condition or loyalty to another. Used with *over.* **4.** To meet in or as if in passing: *Our letters must have crossed in the mail.* **5.** *Biology.* To crossbreed or cross-fertilize. —**cross** *adj.* **1.** Lying or passing crosswise; intersecting: *a cross street.* **2.** Contrary or counter; opposing. **3.** Showing ill humor; annoyed. **4.** Involving interchange; reciprocal. **5.** Crossbred; hybrid. —**cross** *adv.* Crosswise. —**cross** *prep.* Across. —***idioms.*** **cross (someone's) palm.** To pay, tip, or bribe. **cross swords.** To quarrel or fight. [Middle English *cros,* from Old English, probably from Old Norse *kross,* from Old Irish *cros,* from Latin *crux.*] —**cross′er** *n.* —**cross′ly** *adv.* —**cross′ness** *n.*

Cross, Wilbur Lucius. 1862–1948. American politician and educator who was editor of the *Yale Review* (1911–1940) and governor of Connecticut (1931–1939).

cross·bar (krôs′bär′, krŏs′-) *n.* A horizontal bar, line, or stripe.

cross·beam (krôs′bēm′, krŏs′-) *n.* A horizontal or transverse beam, especially a structural member resting on two supports.

cross·bill (krôs′bĭl′, krŏs′-) *n.* Any of various finches of the genus *Loxia,* having curved mandibles with narrow tips that cross when the bill is closed.

cross·bones (krôs′bōnz′, krŏs′-) *pl.n.* A representation of two bones placed crosswise, usually under a skull, symbolizing danger or death.

cross·bow (krôs′bō′, krŏs′-) *n.* A weapon consisting of a bow fixed crosswise on a wooden stock, with grooves on the stock to direct the projectile. —**cross′bow′man** *n.*

cross·bred (krôs′brĕd, krŏs′-) *adj.* Produced by the mating of individuals of different breeds, varieties, or species. —**cross′-bred′** *n.*

cross·breed (krôs′brēd′, krŏs′-) *v.* **-bred** (-brĕd′), **-breed·ing, -breeds.** —*tr.* To produce (an organism) by the mating of individuals of different breeds, varieties, or species; hybridize. —*intr.* To mate so as to produce a hybrid; interbreed. —**crossbreed** *n.* An organism produced by mating of individuals of different varieties or breeds.

cross·check (krôs′chĕk′, krŏs′-) *tr.v.* **-checked, -check·ing, -checks.** **1.** To verify by comparing with parallel or supplementary data. **2.** *Sports.* To check illegally in ice hockey by striking an opponent with one's hockey stick held in both hands and lifted off the ice. —**crosscheck** *n.* The act of crosschecking.

cross-coun·try (krôs′kŭn′trē, krŏs′-) *adj.* **1.** *Abbr.* **XC, X-C** Moving or directed across open country rather than following tracks, roads, or runs: *a cross-country race.* **2.** From one side of a country to the opposite side: *a cross-country flight.* —**cross-country** *n. Abbr.* **XC, X-C** *Sports.* A cross-country sport, especially racing or skiing. —**cross′-coun′try** *adv.*

cross-country ski·ing (skē′ĭng) *n. Sports.* The sport of skiing over the countryside rather than on downhill runs.

cross·court (krôs′kôrt′, -kōrt′, krŏs′-) *adv. & adj. Sports.* To or toward the other side of a playing court, especially a basketball or tennis court.

cross cousin *n.* A cousin who is the child of one's mother's brother or one's father's sister.

cross-cul·tur·al (krôs′kŭl′chər-əl, krŏs′-) *adj.* Comparing or dealing with two or more different cultures: *a cross-cultural survey; cross-cultural influences on an artist's work.* —**cross′-cul′tur·al·ly** *adv.*

cross·cur·rent (krôs′kûr′ənt, -kŭr′-, krŏs′-) *n.* **1.** A current flowing across another current. **2.** A conflicting tendency, inclination, or movement: *a crosscurrent of dissent; sociopolitical crosscurrents.*

cross·cut (krôs′kŭt′, krŏs′-) *v.* **-cut, -cut·ting, -cuts.** —*tr.* **1.** To cut or run across or through. **2.** To cut using a crosscut saw. **3.** To interweave (fragments of two or more scenes) in a film. —*intr.* To use the cinematic technique of crosscutting. —**crosscut** *adj.* **1.** Constructed or used for cutting crosswise: *crosscut teeth on a saw* **2.** Cut across or crosswise: *a crosscut slice of beef; a crosscut incision.* —**crosscut** *n.* **1.** A course or cut going crosswise. **2.** A path more direct than the main path; a shortcut. **3.** A level in a mine driven so that it intersects a vein of ore. **4.** A crosscut saw. **5.** An example of the cinematic technique of interweaving fragments of two or more scenes.

crosscut saw *n.* A saw for cutting wood across the grain.

cross·cut·ting (krôs′kŭt′ĭng, krŏs′-) *n.* A technique used especially in filmmaking in which fragments of two or more separate scenes are interwoven.

cross-dress (krôs′drĕs′, krŏs′-) *intr.v.* **-dressed, -dress·ing, -dress·es.** To dress in the clothing characteristic of the opposite sex. —**cross′-dress′er** *n.* —**cross′-dress′ing** *n.*

crop-dusting

crosier
13th-century French crosier head for a bishop's staff, depicting Saint Michael trampling a serpent

crossbow
Soldier, with foot in stirrup, resetting crossbow

cross-country skiing

crosse (krôs, krŏs) *n. Sports.* The stick used in lacrosse. [French, from Old French *crosse,* staff. See CROSIER.]

cross-ex·am·ine (krôs′ĭg-zăm′ĭn, krŏs′-) *v.* **-ined, -in·ing, -ines.** —*tr.* **1.** To question (a person) closely, especially with regard to answers or information given previously. **2.** *Law.* To question (a witness already examined by the opposing side). —*intr.* To question a person closely. —**cross′-ex·am′i·na′tion** *n.* —**cross′-ex·am′in·er** *n.*

cross-eye (krôs′ī′, krŏs′ī′) *n.* A form of strabismus in which one or both eyes deviate toward the nose. —**cross′-eyed′** *adj.*

cross-fer·til·i·za·tion (krôs′fûr′tl-ĭ-zā′shən, krŏs′-) *n.* **1.** *Biology.* Fertilization by the union of gametes from different individuals, sometimes of different varieties or species. Also called *allogamy.* **2.** Mutual exchange, as between dissimilar concepts, cultures, or classifications, that enhances understanding or produces something beneficial. —**cross′-fer′tile** *adj.*

cross-fer·til·ize (krôs′fûr′tl-īz′, krŏs′-) *intr. & tr.v.* **-ized, -iz·ing, -iz·es.** To undergo or cause to undergo cross-fertilization.

cross-file (krôs′fīl′, krŏs′-) *tr. & intr.v.* **-filed, -fil·ing, -files.** To register (someone) or be registered as a candidate in the primaries of more than one political party. —**cross′-fil′er** *n.*

cross·fire (krôs′fīr′, krŏs′-) *n.* **1.** Lines of fire from two or more positions crossing each other at a single point: *soldiers caught in crossfire.* **2.** A confrontational situation in which opposing factions, forces, views, or opinions converge. **3.** Rapid, heated discussion.

Cross-Flo·ri·da Waterway (krôs′flôr′ĭ-də, -flŏr′-, krŏs′-). See Lake **Okeechobee.**

cross-grained (krôs′grānd′, krŏs′-) *adj.* **1.** Having an irregular, transverse, or diagonal grain, as opposed to a parallel grain. **2.** Troublesome to deal with; contrary.

cross hair or **cross·hair** (krôs′hâr′, krŏs′-) *n.* Either of two fine strands of wire crossed in the focus of the eyepiece of an optical instrument and used as a calibration or sighting reference.

cross·hatch (krôs′hăch′, krŏs′-) *tr.v.* **-hatched, -hatch·ing, -hatch·es.** To mark or shade with two or more sets of intersecting parallel lines. —**cross′hatch′** *n.* —**cross′-hatch′ing** *n.*

cross·head (krôs′hĕd′, krŏs′-) *n.* A beam that connects the piston rod to the connecting rod of a reciprocating engine.

cross-in·dex (krôs′ĭn′dĕks′, krŏs′-) *v.* **-dexed, -dex·ing, -dex·es.** —*tr.* **1.** To index (a particular item) under more than one heading. **2.** To furnish (an index in a book, for example) with cross-references. —*intr.* To furnish cross-references.

crosse

cross·ing (krô′sĭng, krŏs′ĭng) *n.* **1.** The act or action of crossing. **2. a.** A place at which roads, lines, or tracks intersect; an intersection. **b.** A place at which a river, railroad, or highway, for example, may be crossed: *a railroad crossing; a pedestrian crossing.* **3.** The intersection of the nave and transept in a cruciform church.

crossing over or **cros·sing-o·ver** (krô′sĭng-ō′vər, krŏs′-ĭng-) *n.* The exchange of genetic material between homologous chromosomes that occurs during meiosis and contributes to genetic variability.

cross-leg·ged (krôs′lĕg′ĭd, -lĕgd′, krŏs′-) *adv. & adj.* **1.** With the legs or ankles crossed and the knees far apart. **2.** With one leg lying over and across the other leg.

cross-link (krôs′lĭngk′, krŏs′-) *tr.v.* **-linked, -link·ing, -links.** To join (adjacent chains of a polymer or protein) by creating covalent bonds. —**cross-link** *n.* A chemical bond or link created by cross-linking.

cross match·ing (măch′ĭng) *n.* The process of determining the compatibility of blood from a donor with that of a recipient before transfusion.

cross-mul·ti·ply (krôs′mŭl′tə-plī′, krŏs′-) *intr.v.* **-plied, -ply·ing, -plies.** To multiply the numerator of one of a pair of fractions by the denominator of the other. —**cross multiplication** *n.*

cros·sop·te·ryg·i·an (krŏ-sŏp′tə-rĭj′ē-ən) *n.* A member of the Crossopterygii, a group of bony fishes with paired, rounded fins that are extinct except for the coelacanths and are regarded as ancestors of amphibians and other terrestrial vertebrates. [From New Latin *Crossopterygia,* subclass name : Greek *krossoi,* fringe (from *krossōtos,* fringed, from *krossai,* projecting stone blocks) + Greek *pterugia,* fins, pl. diminutive of *pterux, pterug-,* wing. See PTERYGOID.] —**cros·sop′te·ryg′i·an** *adj.*

cross·o·ver (krôs′ō′vər, krŏs′-) *n.* **1.** A place at which or the means by which a crossing is made. **2.** A short connecting track by which a train can be transferred from one line to another. **3.** *Genetics.* **a.** Crossing over. **b.** A characteristic resulting from the exchange of genetic material between homologous chromosomes during meiosis. **4.** A registered member of one political party who votes in the primary of the other party. **5. a.** The adaptation of a musical style, as by blending elements of two or more styles or categories, in order to appeal to a wider audience. **b.** A recording designed to appeal to more than one segment or portion of the listening audience. **c.** One that appeals to a wide or diverse audience. —*attributive.* Often used to modify another noun: *the crossover vote in California; a big crossover hit.*

cross·patch (krôs′păch′, krŏs′-) *n.* A peevish, irascible person; a grouch. [CROSS + *patch,* jester.]

cross·piece (krôs′pēs′, krŏs′-) *n.* A transverse or horizontal piece, as of a structure or implement.

cross-pol·li·nate (krôs′pŏl′ə-nāt′, krŏs′-) *tr.v.* **-nat·ed, -nat·ing, -nates.** **1.** To pollinate (a flower) by means of cross-pollination. **2.** To influence or inspire (another), especially in a reciprocal manner.

cross-pol·li·na·tion (krôs′pŏl′ə-nā′shən, krŏs′-) *n.* **1.** The transfer of pollen from an anther of the flower of one plant to a stigma of the flower of another plant. **2.** Influence or inspiration between or among diverse elements: *"Jazz is fundamentally the cross-pollination of individual musicians playing together and against each other in small groups"* (Ralph de Toledano).

cross product *n. Mathematics.* See **vector product.**

cross-pur·pose (krôs′pûr′pəs, krŏs′-) *n.* A usually unintentionally conflicting or contrary purpose. —***idiom.* at cross-purposes.** Having or acting under a misunderstanding of each other's purposes: *We're working at cross-purposes. We're talking at cross-purposes.*

cross-ques·tion (krôs′kwĕs′chən, krŏs′-) *tr.v.* **-tioned, -tion·ing, -tions.** To question closely; cross-examine. —**cross-question** *n.* A question asked during cross-examination.

cross-re·ac·tion (krôs′rē-ăk′shən, krŏs′-) *n.* The reaction between an antigen and an antibody that was generated against a different but similar antigen. —**cross′-re·act′** *v.* —**cross′-re·ac′tive** *adj.* —**cross′-re·ac·tiv′i·ty** *n.*

cross-re·fer (krôs′rĭ-fûr′, krŏs′-) *v.* **-ferred, -fer·ring, -fers.** —*tr.* To refer (a reader) from one part or passage to another. —*intr.* To make a cross-reference.

cross-ref·er·ence (krôs′rĕf′ər-əns, -rĕf′rəns, krŏs′-) *n.* A reference from one part of a book, index, catalogue, or file to another part containing related information. —**cross-reference** *tr.v.* **-enced, -enc·ing, -enc·es.** To provide with cross-references.

cross-re·sis·tance (krôs′rĭ-zĭs′təns, krŏs′-) *n.* Tolerance to a usually toxic substance as a result of exposure to a similarly acting substance: *Some insects develop cross-resistance to insecticides.*

cross·road (krôs′rōd′, krŏs′-) *n.* **1.** A road that intersects another road. **2. crossroads** *(used with a sing. verb).* **a.** A place where two or more roads meet. **b.** A small, usually rural community situated at an intersection of two or more roads. **c.** A place that is centrally located. **d.** A crucial point. See Synonyms at **crisis.**

cross·ruff (krôs′rŭf′, -rŭf′, krŏs′-) *Games. n.* A series of plays in games of the whist family in which partnership hands alternately trump suits led by the other partner. —**crossruff** *v.* **-ruffed, -ruff·ing, -ruffs.** —*intr.* To perform a crossruff or a series of crossruffs. —*tr.* To trump (one's partner's lead or a lead from the dummy) in alternating plays.

cross section also **cross-sec·tion** (krôs′sĕk′shən, krŏs′-) *n.* **1. a.** A section formed by a plane cutting through an object, usually at right angles to an axis. **b.** A piece so cut or a graphic representation of such a piece. **2.** *Physics.* A measure of the probability of an encounter between particles that will result in the occurrence of a particular atomic or nuclear reaction. Also called *collision cross section.* **3.** *Statistics.* A sample meant to be representative of a whole population. **4.** *Informal.* A variety; a diversity. —**cross′-sec′tion·al** (krôs′sĕk′shə-nəl, krŏs′-) *adj.*

USAGE NOTE: Informally, one can speak of a *cross section* of a population even if the group chosen is not statistically representative of the population as a whole. Thus it is possible to say *You meet a cross section of Americans when you travel by interstate bus,* even though it is clear that some types of Americans are likely to be underrepresented among the interstate bus-riding public. When *cross section* is used in reference to the samples used in surveys and other investigations, however, the presumption is usually that the group has been chosen so as to be representative of the larger population. Thus in the sentence *We interviewed a representative cross section of moviegoers,* the phrase *representative cross section* was found to be redundant by 84 percent of the Usage Panel. See Usage Note at **redundancy.**

cross-stitch (krôs′stĭch′, krŏs′-) *n.* **1.** A double stitch forming an X in sewing and embroidery. **2.** Needlework made with X-shaped stitches. —**cross-stitch** *v.* **-stitched, -stitch·ing, -stitch·es.** —*tr.* To make or embroider with X-shaped stitches. —*intr.* To work in the fashion of X-shaped stitches.

cross·talk (krôs′tôk′, krŏs′-) *n.* **1.** *Electronics.* Undesired signals or sounds, as of voices, in a telephone or other communications device as a result of coupling between transmission circuits. **2.** Ancillary, incidental conversation: *crosstalk among members of the panel.*

cross·tie (krôs′tī′, krŏs′-) *n.* A transverse beam or rod serving as a support, especially a beam that connects and supports the rails of a railroad.

cross-tol·er·ance (krôs′tŏl′ər-əns, krŏs′-) *n.* Resistance to the effects of a substance as a result of continued exposure to a different substance having a similar pharmacologic action.

cross-town or **cross·town** (krôs′toun′, krŏs′-) —*adj.* Running, extending, or going across a city or town: *a cross-town street; cross-town traffic.* —*adv.* Across a city or town: *traveling cross-town.*

cross·tree (krôs′trē′, krŏs′-) *n. Nautical.* One of the two horizontal crosspieces at the upper ends of the lower masts in fore-and-aft-rigged vessels, serving to spread the shrouds.

cross vault *n.* A vaulting formed by the intersection of two or more simple vaults. Also called *cross vaulting.*

cross vine *n.* See **bignonia.**

cross•walk (krôs′wôk′, krŏs′-) *n.* A path marked off for pedestrians crossing a street.

cross•way (krôs′wā′, krŏs′-) *n.* A crossroad.

cross•ways (krôs′wāz′, krŏs′-) *adv.* Variant of **crosswise.**

cross•wind (krôs′wĭnd′, krŏs′-) *n.* A wind blowing at right angles to a given direction, as to an aircraft's line of flight.

cross•wise (krôs′wīz′, krŏs′-) also **cross•ways** (-wāz′) —*adv.* So as to be or lie in a cross direction; across: *placed the kindling crosswise to the rest of the wood.* —*adj.* Crossing: *a crosswise piece.*

cross•word puzzle (krôs′wûrd′, krŏs′-) *n.* A puzzle in which an arrangement of numbered squares is to be filled with words running both across and down in answer to correspondingly numbered clues.

crotch (krŏch) *n.* **1.** The angle or region of the angle formed by the junction of two parts or members, such as two branches, limbs, or legs. **2.** The fork of a pole or other support. [Possibly alteration of CRUTCH and partly from *croche,* crook, crosier (from Old French *croche,* hook, shepherd's crook, feminine of *croc,* hook).] —**crotched** (krŏcht) *adj.*

crotch•et (krŏch′ĭt) *n.* **1.** An odd, whimsical, or stubborn notion. **2.** *Music.* See **quarter note. 3.** *Obsolete.* A small hook or hooklike structure. [Middle English *crochet,* from Old French. See CROCHET.]

crotch•et•y (krŏch′ĭ-tē) *adj.* Capriciously stubborn or eccentric; perverse. —**crotch′et•i•ness** *n.*

Croth•ers (krŭ*th*′ərz), **Rachel.** 1878–1958. American playwright, director, and producer whose plays, including *Susan and God* (1937), often concern women's issues.

cro•ton (krōt′n) *n.* **1.** Any of various plants of the genus *Croton,* which includes the sources of cascarilla bark and croton oil. **2.** An Old World tropical evergreen shrub *(Codiaeum variegatum)* widely cultivated as a houseplant for its glossy, multicolored foliage. [New Latin *Croton,* genus name, from Greek *krotōn,* castor oil plant.]

Cro•ton bug (krōt′n) *n.* See **German cockroach.** [After the *Croton* River of southeast New York.]

cro•ton•ic acid (krō-tŏn′ĭk) *n.* An organic acid, $C_4H_6O_2$, used in the preparation of pharmaceuticals and resins. [From New Latin *Croton,* plant genus. See CROTON.]

croton oil *n.* A brownish-yellow oil obtained from the seeds of a tropical Asian shrub or small tree *(Croton tiglium)* and having a cathartic action too violent for human use.

crot•tin (krŏt′n) *n.* **1.** A pungent cheese made of goat's milk and formed into small disks. **2.** A disk of this cheese. [French, from Old French *crotin,* animal dropping, diminutive of *crotte,* dung, probably of Germanic origin.]

crouch (krouch) *v.* **crouched, crouch•ing, crouch•es.** —*intr.* **1.a.** To stoop, especially with the knees bent: *They crouched over the grate with a flashlight, searching for the lost gem.* **b.** To press the entire body close to the ground with the limbs bent: *a cat crouching near its prey.* **2.** To bend servilely or timidly; cringe. —*tr.* To bend (the head or knee, for example) low, as in fear or humility. —**crouch** *n.* The act or posture of bending low or crouching. [Middle English *crouchen,* probably from Old North French **crouchir,* to become bent, variant of Old French *crochir,* from *croche,* hook. See CROCHET.]

croup¹ (kro͞op) *n.* A pathological condition of the larynx, especially in infants and children, that is characterized by respiratory difficulty and a hoarse, brassy cough. [From dialectal *croup,* to croak.] —**croup′ous** (kro͞o′pəs), **croup′y** *adj.*

croup² (kro͞op) *n.* The rump of a beast of burden, especially a horse. [Middle English *croupe,* from Old French, of Germanic origin.]

crou•pi•er (kro͞o′pē-ər, -pē-ā′) *n.* An attendant at a gaming table who collects and pays bets. [French, one who rides behind another on a horse (obsolete), croupier, from *croupe,* rump, croup, from Old French. See CROUP².]

crouse (kro͞os) *adj. Scots.* Lively; vivacious. [Middle English *crous,* fierce, bold, perhaps from Middle Flemish *cruus,* curly, bold.]

Crouse (krous), **Russel.** 1893–1966. American playwright whose works include several collaborations, such as *State of the Union,* for which he shared a Pulitzer Prize (1946), and the musical *Call Me Madam* (1950).

crous•tade (kro͞o-städ′) *n.* A molded or hollowed bowllike crust, as of pastry, rice, or bread, used as a serving container for another food. [French, from Provençal *croustado,* from Latin *crustātus,* past participle of *crustāre,* to encrust, from *crusta,* crust. See CRUST.]

crou•ton (kro͞o′tŏn′, kro͞o-tŏn′) *n.* A small crisp piece of toasted or fried bread. [French *croûton,* diminutive of *croûte,* crust, from Old French *crouste,* from Latin *crusta.* See **kreus-** in Appendix.]

crow¹ (krō) *n.* **1.** Any of several large, glossy, black birds of the genus *Corvus,* having a characteristic raucous call, especially *C. brachyrhynchos* of North America. **2.** A crowbar. —***idiom.* as the crow flies.** In a straight line. [Middle English *croue,* from Old English *crāwe.* See **gerə-²** in Appendix.]

crow² (krō) *intr.v.* **crowed, crow•ing, crows. 1.** To utter the shrill cry characteristic of a cock or rooster. **2.** To exult loudly, as over another's defeat; boast. See Synonyms at **boast¹. 3.** To make a sound expressive of pleasure or well-being, characteristic of an infant. —**crow** *n.* **1.** The shrill cry of a cock. **2.** An inarticulate sound expressive of pleasure or delight. [Middle English *crouen,* from Old English *crāwan.* See **gerə-²** in Appendix.]

Crow¹ (krō) *n., pl.* **Crow** or **Crows. 1.a.** A Native American people formerly inhabiting an area of the northern Great Plains between the Platte and Yellowstone rivers, now located in southeast Montana. The Crow became nomadic buffalo hunters after migrating west from the Missouri River in North Dakota in the 18th century. **b.** A member of this people. **2.** The Siouan language of the Crow. Also called *Absaroke.*

Crow² (krō) *n.* See **Corvus.**

crow•bar (krō′bär′) *n.* A straight bar of iron or steel, with the working end shaped like a chisel and often slightly bent and forked, used as a lever. —**crowbar** *tr.v.* **-barred, -bar•ring, -bars.** To extract, remove, or insert forcibly: "[The newsmagazines] *can crowbar stories in as late as Sunday and still be out on Monday"* (Edwin Diamond). [From the resemblance of its forked end to a crow's foot or beak.]

crow•ber•ry (krō′bĕr′ē) *n.* **1.** A low-growing evergreen shrub *(Empetrum nigrum)* native to cool regions of the Northern Hemisphere and having tiny leaves, small pinkish or purplish flowers, and black, berrylike fruits. **2.** The fruit of this plant.

crow blackbird *n.* See **grackle** (sense 1).

crowd¹ (kroud) *n.* **1.** A large number of persons gathered together; a throng. **2.** The common people; the populace. **3.** A group of people united by a common characteristic, as age, interest, or vocation: *the over-30 crowd.* **4.** A group of people attending a public function; an audience: *The play drew a small but appreciative crowd.* **5.** A large number of things positioned or considered together. —**crowd** *v.* **crowd•ed, crowd•ing, crowds.** —*intr.* **1.** To congregate in a restricted area; throng: *The children crowded around the TV.* **2.** To advance by pressing or shoving: *A bevy of reporters crowded toward the candidate.* —*tr.* **1.** To force by or as if by pressing or shoving: *Police crowded the spectators back to the viewing stand. Urban sprawl crowded the small farmers out of the immediate area.* **2.** To draw or stand near to: *The batter crowded the plate.* **3.** To press, cram, or force tightly together: *crowded the clothes into the closet.* **4.** To fill or occupy to overflowing: *Books crowded the shelves.* **5.** *Informal.* To put pressure on, as to pay a debt. —***idiom.* crowd (on) sail.** *Nautical.* To spread a large amount of sail to increase speed. [From Middle English *crowden,* to crowd, from Old English *crūdan,* to hasten.] —**crowd′er** *n.*

SYNONYMS: *crowd, crush, flock, horde, mob, press, throng.* The central meaning shared by these nouns is "a large group of people gathered close to one another": *a crowd of well-wishers; a crush of autograph seekers; a flock of schoolchildren; a horde of demonstrators; a mob of hard-rock enthusiasts; a press of shoppers; throngs of tourists.*

crowd² (kroud, kro͝od) *n.* **1.** *Music.* An ancient Celtic stringed instrument that was bowed or plucked. Also called *crwth.* **2.** *Chiefly British.* A fiddle. [Middle English *croud,* from Welsh *crwth,* hump, crowd.]

crow•die or **crow•dy** (kro͞o′dē, krō′-, kro͝od′ē) *n., pl.* **-dies.** *Scots.* **1.** A soft cheese made from curds. **2.** Porridge; gruel. [Origin unknown.]

crowd pleas•er also **crowd-pleas•er** or **crowd•pleas•er** (kroud′plē′zər) *n. Informal.* A person, spectacle, work, or idea that appeals to popular taste: *"an ambitious exhibit that is neither an easy crowd pleaser nor a rehash of old ideas, but an original look at German expressionist sculpture"* (Mark Stevens).

crowd-pleas•ing or **crowd•pleas•ing** (kroud′plē′zĭng) *adj. Informal.* Having characteristics that satisfy popular taste: *a crowd-pleasing musical comedy.*

crow•dy (kro͞o′dē, krō′-, kro͝od′ē) *n.* Variant of **crowdie.**

crow•foot (krō′fo͝ot′) *n.* **1.** *pl.* **-foots. a.** Any of numerous plants of the genus *Ranunculus* that have palmately cleft or divided leaves, such as the buttercups. **b.** Any of several other plants having leaves or other parts somewhat resembling a bird's foot. **2.** *pl.* **-feet** (-fēt′) An iron ball with four spikes arranged so that one always points upwards, used to delay the advance of mounted troops and infantry; a caltrop. **3.** *pl.* **-feet.** *Nautical.* A set of small lines passed through holes of a batten or fitting to help support the backbone of an awning.

Crow•ley (krou′lē). A city of southern Louisiana west of Lafayette. It is the trade and shipping center of a rice-growing region. Population, 16,036.

crown (kroun) *n. Abbr.* **cr. 1.** An ornamental circlet or head covering, often made of precious metal set with jewels and worn as a symbol of sovereignty. **2.** Often **Crown. a.** The power, position, or empire of a monarch or of a state governed by constitutional monarchy. **b.** The monarch as head of state. **3.** A distinction or reward for achievement, especially a title signifying championship in a sport. **4.** Something resembling a diadem in shape. **5.a.** A coin stamped with a crown or crowned head on one side. **b.** A silver coin formerly used in Great Britain and worth five shillings. **c.** Any one of several coins, such as the koruna, the krona, or the krone, having a name that means "crown."

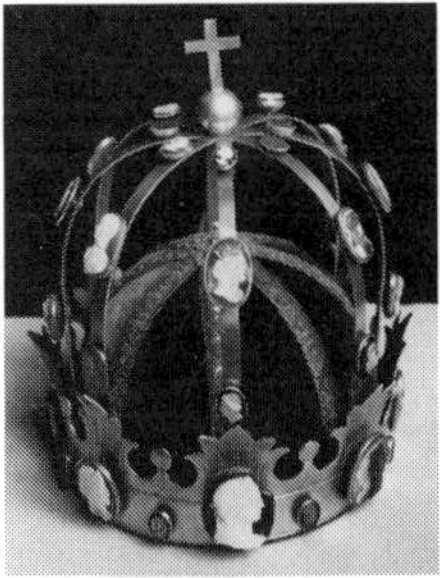

crown

ă pat	oi boy
ā pay	ou out
âr care	o͝o took
ä father	o͞o boot
ĕ pet	ŭ cut
ē be	ûr urge
ĭ pit	th thin
ī pie	*th* this
îr pier	hw which
ŏ pot	zh vision
ō toe	ə about, item
ô paw	♦ regionalism

Stress marks: **′** (primary); ′ (secondary), as in **dictionary** (dĭk′shə-nĕr′ē)

d. See table at **currency.** **6.a.** The top or highest part of the head. **b.** The head itself. **7.** The top or upper part of a hat. **8.** The highest point or summit. **9.** The highest, primary, or most valuable part, attribute, or state: *considered the rare Turkish stamp the crown of their collection.* **10.** *Dentistry.* **a.** The part of a tooth that is covered by enamel and projects beyond the gum line. **b.** An artificial substitute for the natural crown of a tooth. **11.** *Nautical.* The lowest part of an anchor, where the arms are joined to the shank. **12.** *Botany.* **a.** The upper part of a tree, which includes the branches and leaves. **b.** The part of a plant, usually at ground level, where the stem and roots merge. **c.** The persistent, mostly underground base of a perennial herb. **d.** See **corona** (sense 5). **13.** The crest of an animal, especially of a bird. **14.** The portion of a cut gem above the girdle. **—crown** *v.* **crowned, crown·ing, crowns.** *—tr.* **1.** To put a crown or garland on the head of. **2.** To invest with regal power; enthrone. **3.** To confer honor, dignity, or reward upon. **4.** To surmount or be the highest part of. **5.** To form the crown, top, or chief ornament of. **6.** To bring to completion or successful conclusion; consummate: *crowned the event with a lavish reception.* **7.** *Dentistry.* To put a crown on (a tooth). **8.** *Games.* To make (a piece in checkers that has reached the last row) into a king by placing another piece upon it. **9.** *Informal.* To hit on the head. *—intr.* To reach a stage in labor when a large segment of the fetal scalp is visible at the vaginal orifice. Used of a fetus or the head of a fetus. [Middle English *crowne,* from Anglo-Norman *coroune,* from Latin *corōna,* wreath, garland, crown, from Greek *korōnē, korōna,* anything curved, kind of crown, from *korōnos,* curved. See **sker-**[2] in Appendix.]

crown canopy *n.* See **canopy** (sense 5).

crown colony *n.* A British colony in which the government in London has some control of legislation, usually administered by an appointed governor.

crown daisy *n.* See **garland chrysanthemum.**

crown gall *n.* A widespread disease of numerous plants caused by the bacterium *Agrobacterium tumefaciens* and characterized by formation of galls especially at the junction of root and stem.

crown glass *n.* **1.** A soda-lime optical glass that is exceptionally hard and clear, with low refraction and low dispersion. **2.** A form of window glass made by whirling a glass bubble to make a flat circular disk with a lump left in the center by the glass blower's rod.

crow's-nest

crown jewel *n.* **1.a.** A precious stone that is part of a sovereign's regalia. **b. crown jewels.** The jewels, such as those in a crown or scepter, used ceremonially by a sovereign. **2.a.** Something felt to resemble the ceremonial jewels of a sovereign, as in brilliance. **b.** A prized corporate asset, typically a very profitable part of a company sought by another party in a hostile takeover attempt.

crown lens *n.* The crown-glass element in an achromatic lens.

crown-of-thorns (kroun′əv-thôrnz′) *n.* **1.** A trailing or climbing spiny shrub *(Euphorbia milii)* native to Madagascar and cultivated as a houseplant, having showy flower clusters with usually red, petallike bracts. **2.** The Christ's thorn.

Crown Point. **1.** A city of northwest Indiana, a mainly residential suburb of Gary. Population, 16,455. **2.** A village of northeast New York on the western shore of Lake Champlain. It was the site of a French fort captured by the British in 1759 during the French and Indian War. In the American Revolution it was taken by the Green Mountain Boys, retaken by the British in 1777, and abandoned the same year after the defeat at Saratoga. Population, 900.

crown prince *n.* The male heir apparent to a throne.

crown princess *n.* **1.** The female heir apparent to a throne. **2.** The wife of a crown prince.

crown roast *n.* A pork, lamb, or veal roast consisting of the rib sections of two loins placed upright and fastened together in a circle.

crown rot *n.* Any of several mostly fungal diseases of plants characterized by a rotting of the stem near ground level.

crown saw *n.* A cylindrical saw with teeth on the bottom edge of the cylinder, used for cutting round holes.

Crucifixion
The Crucifixion by Nathaniel Currier

crown vetch *n.* A perennial European herb *(Coronilla varia)* in the pea family, grown for forage and erosion control and having clusters of small white or pink flowers and pinnately compound leaves.

crow's-foot (krōz′fo͝ot′) *n., pl.* **-feet** (-fēt′). **1.** Often **crow's-feet.** A lasting wrinkle or wrinkles formed at the outer corner of the eye. **2.** A three-pointed embroidery stitch, especially one in the form of a filled triangle used as finishing, as at the end of a seam.

crow's-nest (krōz′nĕst′) *n.* **1.** *Nautical.* A small lookout platform with a protective railing and windscreen, located near the top of a ship's mast or superstructure. **2.** A similar lookout platform located ashore.

croze (krōz) *n.* A groove inside the end of a barrel or cask into which the head is set. [French *creux,* from Old French *crues,* groove, from Vulgar Latin **crosus,* perhaps of Celtic origin.]

cro·zier (krō′zhər) *n.* Variant of **crosier.**

CRP *abbr.* C-reactive protein.

CRT *abbr.* Cathode-ray tube.

cru (kro͞o) *n., pl.* **crus.** **1.** A vineyard or wine-producing region in France. **2.** A grade or class of wine: *premier cru.* [French, from the past participle of *croître,* to grow, from Old French *creistre.* See CRESCENT.]

cru·ces (kro͞o′sēz) *n.* A plural of **crux.**

cru·cial (kro͞o′shəl) *adj.* **1.a.** Extremely significant or important: *a crucial problem.* **b.** Vital to the resolution of a crisis; decisive: *a crucial election.* See Synonyms at **decisive.** **2.** *Archaic.* Having the form of a cross; cross-shaped. [From New Latin *(instantia) crucis, (experimentum) crucis,* crossroads (case), crossroads (experiment), from Latin *crux, cruc-,* cross. Sense 2, French, from Old French, from Latin *crux, cruc-,* cross.] **—cru′cial·ly** *adv.*

WORD HISTORY: A crucial election is like a signpost because it shows which way the electorate is moving. The metaphor of a signpost, in fact, gives us the sense of the word *crucial,* "of supreme importance, critical." Francis Bacon used the phrase *instantia crucis,* "crucial instance," to refer to something in an experiment that proves one of two hypotheses and disproves the other. Bacon's phrase was based on a sense of the Latin word *crux,* "cross," which had come to mean "a guidepost that gives directions at a place where one road becomes two," and hence was suitable for Bacon's metaphor. Both Robert Boyle, often called the father of modern chemistry, and Isaac Newton used the similar Latin phrase *experimentum crucis,* "crucial experiment." When these phrases were translated into English, they became *crucial instance* and *crucial experiment.*

cru·ci·ate (kro͞o′shē-āt′) *adj.* **1.** Arranged in or forming a cross; cruciform. **2.a.** Overlapping or crossing, as the wings of some insects when at rest. **b.** Shaped like a cross: *the cruciate ligaments of the knee.* [New Latin *cruciātus,* from Latin *crux, cruc-,* cross.] **—cru′ci·ate′ly** *adv.*

cru·ci·ble (kro͞o′sə-bəl) *n.* **1.** A vessel made of a refractory substance such as graphite or porcelain, used for melting and calcining materials at high temperatures. **2.** A severe test, as of patience or belief; a trial. See Synonyms at **trial.** **3.** A place, time, or situation characterized by the confluence of powerful intellectual, social, economic, or political forces: *"Yale is a crucible in American life for the accommodation of intellectual achievement, of wisdom, of refinement, with the democratic ideals of openness, of social justice and of equal opportunity"* (Benno C. Schmidt, Jr.). [Middle English *crusible,* from Medieval Latin *crūcibulum,* night-light, crucible, possibly from Old French *croisuel,* cresset. See CRESSET.]

crucible steel *n.* See **drill steel.**

cru·ci·fer (kro͞o′sə-fər) *n.* **1.** One who bears a cross in a religious procession. **2.** *Botany.* Any of various plants in the mustard family (Cruciferae or Brassicaceae), which includes the alyssum, candytuft, cabbage, radish, broccoli, and many weeds. [Late Latin : *crux, cruc-,* cross + *-fer,* -fer.] **—cru·cif′er·ous** (-sĭf′ər-əs) *adj.*

cru·ci·fix (kro͞o′sə-fĭks′) *n.* **1.** An image or figure of Jesus on the cross. **2.** A cross viewed as a symbol of Jesus's crucifixion. [Middle English, from Old French, from Late Latin *crucifīxus,* from Latin, past participle of *crucifīgere,* crucify. See CRUCIFY.]

cru·ci·fix·ion (kro͞o′sə-fĭk′shən) *n.* **1.a.** The act of crucifying; execution on a cross. **b. Crucifixion.** The crucifying of Jesus on Calvary. Used with *the.* **c.** A representation of Jesus on the cross. **2.** An extremely difficult, painful trial; torturous suffering.

crucifixion thorn *n.* Any of several unrelated shrubs or small trees of desert regions in the southwest United States and Mexico, having tiny, early deciduous leaves and branches and stems resembling a mass of thorns.

cru·ci·form (kro͞o′sə-fôrm′) *adj.* Shaped like a cross; cruciate. [Latin *crux, cruc-,* cross + -FORM.] **—cru′ci·form′** *n.* **—cru′ci·form′ly** *adv.*

cru·ci·fy (kro͞o′sə-fī′) *tr.v.* **-fied, -fy·ing, -fies.** **1.** To put (a person) to death by nailing or binding to a cross. **2.** To mortify or subdue (the flesh). **3.** To subject to cruel treatment; torment: *a candidate who was crucified by the press.* [Middle English *crucifien,* from Old French *crucifier,* alteration of Latin *crucifīgere* : *crux, cruc-,* cross + *fīgere,* to attach; see **dhīgʷ-** in Appendix.] **—cru′ci·fi′er** *n.*

crud (krŭd) *n.* **1.** *Slang.* **a.** A coating or an incrustation of filth or refuse. **b.** Something loathsome, despicable, or worthless. **c.** One who is contemptible or disgusting. **2.** A disease or ailment, imaginary or real, especially one affecting the skin. **3.** *Sports.* Heavy, sticky snow that is unsuitable for skiing. [Middle English *crudde,* possibly from Old English **cruden,* past participle of *crūdan,* to press, drive.]

crud·dy (krŭd′ē) *adj.* **-di·er, -di·est.** *Slang.* Worthless, loathsome, or disgusting. **—crud·di·ness** *n.*

crude (kro͞od) *adj.* **crud·er, crud·est.** **1.** Being in an unrefined or natural state; raw. **2.** Lacking tact, refinement, or taste. **3.a.** Not carefully or completely made; rough. **b.** *Statistics.* In an unanalyzed form; not adjusted to allow for related circumstances or data. **4.** Displaying a lack of knowledge or skill. **5.** Undisguised or unadorned; blunt: *must face the crude truth.* **6.** *Archaic.* Unripe or immature. **—crude** *n.* A substance, especially petroleum, in its unrefined state. [Middle English, from Latin *crūdus.* See **kreuə-** in Appendix.] **—crude′ly** *adv.* **—cru′di·ty** (kro͞o′dĭ-tē), **crude′ness** *n.*

SYNONYMS: *crude, native, raw.* The central meaning shared by these adjectives is "in a natural state and not yet processed for use": *crude rubber; native iron; raw cotton.* See also Synonyms at **rude.**

crude oil *n.* Unrefined petroleum.

cru·di·tés (kro͞o′dĭ-tā′) *pl.n.* Cut raw vegetables, such as carrot sticks and pepper strips, served often with a dip as an appetizer. [French, pl. of *crudité,* indigestibility, from Old French *crudite,* from Latin *crūditās,* indigestion, undigested food, from *crūdus,* raw. See CRUDE.]

cru·el (kro͞o′əl) *adj.* **-el·er, -el·est** or **-el·ler, -el·lest. 1.** Disposed to inflict pain or suffering. **2.** Causing suffering; painful. [Middle English, from Old French, from Latin *crūdēlis.* See **kreuə-** in Appendix.] **—cru′el·ly** *adv.*

SYNONYMS: *cruel, fierce, ferocious, barbarous, inhuman, savage, vicious.* These adjectives mean showing a disposition to inflict violence, pain, or hardship, or to find satisfaction in the suffering of others. *Cruel* implies both disposition to harm and satisfaction in or indifference to suffering: *a cruel tyrant. Fierce* suggests the fearless aggression of a wild animal: *a fierce attack; fierce anger. Ferocious* adds to *fierce* connotations of rabid fury and rampant brutality: *a ferocious attack dog; a ferocious battle for supremacy. Barbarous* suggests harshness and cruelty that befit only primitive human beings: *committed a barbarous crime. Inhuman* means markedly deficient in those qualities such as kindness and sympathy that are proper to a human being: *cruel and inhuman behavior. Savage* implies a lack of the control or moderation expected of a civilized person: *a savage outburst of temper; a savage slap. Vicious* suggests a disposition to malicious, violent, or destructive behavior: *vicious animosity; a vicious anonymous letter; a vicious kick.*

cru·el·ty (kro͞o′əl-tē) *n., pl.* **-ties. 1.** The quality or condition of being cruel. **2.** Something, such as a cruel act or remark, that causes pain or suffering. **3.** *Law.* The infliction of physical or mental distress, especially when considered a determinant in granting a divorce.

cru·et (kro͞o′ĭt) *n.* **1.** A small glass bottle for holding a condiment, such as vinegar or oil, at the table. **2.** A small vessel for holy water or for water or wine used in the consecration of the Eucharist. [Middle English, from Old French, diminutive of *crue,* flask, of Germanic origin.]

Cruik·shank (kro͝ok′shăngk′), **George.** 1792–1878. British caricaturist and illustrator of the works of Charles Dickens and other novelists.

cruise (kro͞oz) *v.* **cruised, cruis·ing, cruis·es.** *—intr.* **1.a.** To sail or travel about, as for pleasure or reconnaissance. **b.** To go or move along, especially in an unhurried or unconcerned fashion: *"A whole cache of babies . . . cruised imperiously in their strollers, propelled by their mothers or by pairs of grandmothers"* (Anne Tyler). **2.** To travel at a constant speed, or at a speed providing maximum operating efficiency for a sustained period. **3.a.** *Informal.* To move leisurely about an area in the hope of discovering something: *taxis cruising for fares.* **b.** *Slang.* To look for a sexual partner, as in a public place. **4.** To inspect a wooded area to determine its lumber yield. *—tr.* **1.** To travel about or journey over. **2.** *Slang.* **a.** To look in (a public area) for a sexual partner. **b.** To seek out and make a sexual overture to. **3.** To inspect in order to determine lumber yield. **—cruise** *n.* The act or an instance of cruising, especially a sea voyage for pleasure. [Dutch *kruisen,* to cross, from Dutch *kruis,* cross, from Middle Dutch *cruce,* from Latin *crux, cruc-,* cross.]

cruise control *n.* **1.** A system in a motor vehicle for maintaining a constant speed. **2.** Maintenance of a constant speed in such a vehicle.

cruise missile *n.* An unmanned aircraft that serves as a self-contained bomb.

cruis·er (kro͞o′zər) *n.* **1.** One of a class of fast warships of medium tonnage with a long cruising radius and less armor and firepower than a battleship. **2.** *Nautical.* A cabin cruiser. **3.** See **squad car.**

cruis·er·weight (kro͞ozər-wāt′) *n.* **1.** *Sports.* A boxer in a subcategory of the heavyweight division, having an upper weight limit set at 190 pounds (86 kilograms). **2.** *Chiefly British.* A light heavyweight boxer. [Possibly after the *cruiser warship,* the second and heaviest warship.]

cruis·ing radius (kro͞o′zĭng) *n.* The maximum distance that a ship or aircraft can travel away from and back to its point of origin without refueling.

♦ **crul·ler** (krŭl′ər) *n.* **1.** A small, usually ring-shaped or twisted cake of sweet dough fried in deep fat. **2.** *Chiefly New England & Pennsylvania.* An unraised doughnut, usually twisted but also shaped into rings or oblongs. [From obsolete Dutch *krulle-koken,* rolled-up cake, from Middle Dutch *crulle-koken,* to curl, from *crulle,* curly.]

crumb (krŭm) *n.* **1.** A very small piece broken from a baked item, such as a cookie, cake, or bread. **2.** A small fragment, scrap, or portion: *eraser crumbs; not a crumb of kindness for you.* **3.** The soft inner portion of bread. **4.** *Slang.* A contemptible, untrustworthy, or loathsome person. **—crumb** *v.* **crumbed, crumb·ing, crumbs.** *—tr.* **1.** To break into very small pieces; crumble. **2.** To cover or prepare with very small pieces of bread. **3.** To brush (a table or cloth) clear of small scraps or fragments of food. *—intr.* To break apart in very small pieces: *a solid cake that won't crumb.* [Middle English *crome,* from Old English *cruma.*]

crum·ble (krŭm′bəl) *v.* **-bled, -bling, -bles.** *—tr.* To break into small fragments or particles. *—intr.* **1.** To fall into small fragments or particles; disintegrate. See Synonyms at **decay. 2.** To give way; collapse: *an ego that crumbles under pressure.* [Alteration (influenced by CRUMB) of Middle English *cremelen,* from Old English **crymelen,* frequentative of *gecrymmian,* to break into crumbs, from *cruma,* crumb.]

crum·bly (krŭm′blē) *adj.* **-bli·er, -bli·est.** Easily crumbled; friable. **—crum′bli·ness** *n.*

crumb·y (krŭm′ē) *adj. Slang.* Variant of **crummy.**

crum·horn (krŭm′hôrn′) *n. Music.* Variant of **krummhorn.**

crum·mie (krŭm′ē) *n. Scots.* A cow, especially one with crooked horns. [From Scots *crumb,* crooked, from Middle English. See CRUMPET.]

crum·my also **crumb·y** (krŭm′ē) *adj.* **-mi·er, -mi·est** also **-i·er, -i·est.** *Slang.* **1.** Miserable or wretched: *a crummy situation in the family.* **2.** Shabby or cheap: *a crummy little rowboat.* [Probably from CRUMB.]

crump (krŭmp) *v.* **crumped, crump·ing, crumps.** *—tr.* **1.** To crush or crunch with the teeth. **2.** To strike heavily with a crunching sound. *—intr.* To make a crunching sound, especially in walking over snow. **—crump** *n.* **1.a.** A crunching sound. **b.** The sound of an exploding shell. **2.** A heavy blow. [Imitative.]

crum·pet (krŭm′pĭt) *n.* A small, flat round of bread, baked on a griddle and usually served toasted. [Possibly from Middle English *crompid (cake),* curled (cake), probably past participle of *crumpen,* to curl up, probably from *crumb, crump,* crooked, from Old English.]

crum·ple (krŭm′pəl) *v.* **-pled, -pling, -ples.** *—tr.* **1.** To crush together or press into wrinkles; rumple. **2.** To cause to fall apart. *—intr.* **1.** To become wrinkled. **2.** To fall apart; collapse: *a regime that finally crumpled.* **—crumple** *n.* An irregular fold, crease, or wrinkle. [Middle English *crumplen,* probably frequentative of *crumpen,* to curl up. See CRUMPET.] **—crum′ply** *adj.*

crunch (krŭnch) *v.* **crunched, crunch·ing, crunch·es.** *—tr.* **1.** To chew with a noisy crackling sound. **2.** To crush, grind, or tread noisily. **3.** *Slang.* To perform operations on; manipulate or process (numerical or mathematical data). *—intr.* **1.** To chew noisily with a crackling sound: *crunching on celery.* **2.** To move with a crushing sound: *crunching through the snow.* **3.** To produce or emit a crushing sound. **—crunch** *n.* **1.** The act or sound of crunching. **2.a.** A decisive confrontation. **b.** A critical moment or situation, especially one that occurs because of a shortage of time or resources: *a year-end crunch; an energy crunch.* **c.** A period of financial difficulty characterized by tight money and unavailability of credit. [Alteration of *craunch,* possibly of imitative origin.] **—crunch′a·ble** *adj.*

crunch·er (crŭnch′ər) *n. Slang.* A finishing or decisive blow.

crunch·y (krŭn′chē) *adj.* **-i·er, -i·est.** Making a crunching or cracking sound, as when chewed; crisp: *crunchy fresh vegetables.*

crup·per (krŭp′ər) *n.* **1.** A leather strap looped under a horse's tail and attached to a harness or saddle to keep it from slipping forward. **2.** The rump of a horse; the croup. [Middle English *crouper,* from Old French *cropiere,* from *croupe,* rump. See CROUP[2].]

cru·ra (kro͝or′ə) *n.* Plural of **crus.**

cru·ral (kro͝or′əl) *adj.* Of or relating to the leg, shank, or thigh. [Latin *crūrālis,* from *crūs, crūr-,* leg.]

crus (kro͞os, krŭs) *n., pl.* **cru·ra** (kro͝or′ə). **1.** The section of the leg or hind limb between the knee and foot; shank. **2.a.** A leglike part. **b.** A body part consisting of elongated masses or diverging bands that resemble legs or roots. [Latin *crūs, crūr-,* leg.]

cru·sade (kro͞o-sād′) *n.* **1.** Often **Crusade.** Any of the military expeditions undertaken by European Christians in the 11th, 12th, and 13th centuries to recover the Holy Land from the Moslems. **2.** A holy war undertaken with papal sanction. **3.** A vigorous concerted movement for a cause or against an abuse. See Synonyms at **campaign. —crusade** *intr.v.* **-sad·ed, -sad·ing, -sades.** To engage in a crusade. [French *croisade* and Spanish *cruzada,* both ultimately from Latin *crux, cruc-,* cross.] **—cru·sad′er** *n.*

cru·sa·do (kro͞o-sä′dō) also **cru·za·do** (-zä′-) *n., pl.* **-does** or **-dos.** An old Portuguese coin of gold or silver having a cross pictured on the reverse. [Portuguese, from past participle of *cruzar,* to mark with a cross, from *cruz,* cross, from Latin *crux, cruc-.*]

cruse (kro͞oz, kro͞os) *n.* A small earthenware container, such as a pot or jar, for holding liquids. [Middle English *crouse,* perhaps from Middle Dutch *cruyse,* pot.]

crush (krŭsh) *v.* **crushed, crush·ing, crush·es.** *—tr.* **1.** To press between opposing bodies so as to break or injure. **2.** To break, pound, or grind (stone or ore, for example) into small fragments or powder. **3.** To put down; subdue: *crushed the rebellion.* **4.** To overwhelm or oppress severely: *spirits that had been crushed by rejection and failure.* **5.** To crumple or rumple: *crushed the freshly ironed shirt.* **6.** To hug, especially with great force. **7.** To press upon, shove, or crowd. **8.** To extract or obtain by pressing or squeezing: *crush juice from a grape.* **9.** *Archaic.* To drink; quaff. *—intr.* **1.** To be or become crushed. **2.** To proceed or move by crowding or pressing. **—crush** *n.* **1.** The act of crush-

cruet
c. 1817 French by Jean Baptiste Claude Odiot (1763–1850)

ă pat	oi boy
ā pay	ou out
âr care	o͝o took
ä father	o͞o boot
ĕ pet	ŭ cut
ē be	ûr urge
ĭ pit	th thin
ī pie	*th* this
îr pier	hw which
ŏ pot	zh vision
ō toe	ə about, item
ô paw	♦ regionalism

Stress marks: **′** (primary); ′ (secondary), as in **dictionary** (dĭk′shə-nĕr′ē)

ing; extreme pressure. **2.** The state of being crushed. **3.** A great crowd: *a crush of spectators.* **4.** A substance prepared by or as if by crushing, especially a fruit drink: *orange crush.* **5.** *Informal.* **a.** A usually temporary infatuation. **b.** The object of such an infatuation. **6.** A decisive or critical moment or situation. **7.** The process of stamping or crushing grapes for wine. [Middle English *crushen,* from Old French *croissir,* of Germanic origin.] **—crush′a·ble** *adj.* **—crush′er** *n.* **—crush′proof′** (-pro͞of′) *adj.*

SYNONYMS: *crush, mash, pulp, smash, squash.* The central meaning shared by these verbs is "to press forcefully so as to reduce to a pulpy mass": *crush rose geranium leaves; mashed the sweet potatoes; pulped raspberries through a sieve; smashing bamboo stems with a hammer; squash an egg under one's foot.* See also Synonyms at **crowd**[1].

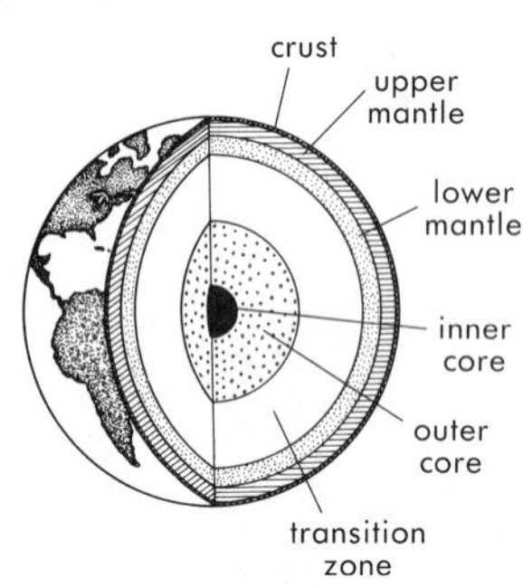

crust
Cutaway view of Earth

crushed (krŭsht) *adj.* Treated so as to have a permanently crinkled or rumpled appearance. Used of a fabric: *crushed velvet; crushed denim.*

crust (krŭst) *n.* **1.a.** The hard outer portion or surface area of bread. **b.** A piece of bread consisting mostly of the hard outer portion. **c.** A piece of bread that has become hard and dry. **2.** A pastry shell, as of a pie or tart. **3.** A hard, crisp covering or surface: *snow with a firm crust.* **4.** A hard deposit formed on the interior of a wine bottle as the wine matures. **5.** *Geology.* **a.** The exterior portion of the earth that lies above the Mohorovičić discontinuity. **b.** The outermost solid layer of a planet or moon. **6.** The hard outer covering or integument of certain plants and animals, such as lichens and crustaceans. **7.** *Pathology.* An outer layer or coating formed by the drying of a bodily exudate such as pus or blood; a scab. **8.** *Informal.* Insolence; audacity; gall. **—crust** *v.* **crust·ed, crust·ing, crusts.** *—tr.* **1.** To cover with a crust. **2.** To form into a crust. *—intr.* **1.** To become covered with a crust. **2.** To harden into a crust. [Middle English *cruste,* from Old French *crouste,* from Latin *crusta.* See **kreus-** in Appendix.] **—crust′less** *adj.*

crus·ta·cean (krŭ-stā′shən) *n.* Any of various predominantly aquatic arthropods of the class Crustacea, including lobsters, crabs, shrimps, and barnacles, characteristically having a segmented body, a chitinous exoskeleton, and paired, jointed limbs. **—crustacean** *adj.* Of or belonging to the Crustacea. [From New Latin *Crustācea,* class name, neuter pl. of *crustāceus,* hard-shelled, from Latin *crusta,* shell. See **kreus-** in Appendix.]

crus·ta·ceous (krŭ-stā′shəs) *adj.* **1.** Having, resembling, or constituting a hard crust or shell. **2.** Crustacean. [Latin *crusta,* shell; see **kreus-** in Appendix + -ACEOUS.]

crust·al (krŭs′təl) *adj.* Of or relating to a crust, especially that of the earth or the moon.

crus·tose (krŭs′tōs′) *adj.* Of or relating to a lichen whose thallus is thin, crusty, and closely adherent to or embedded in the surface on which it grows. [Latin *crustōsus,* crusted, from *crusta,* crust. See **kreus-** in Appendix.]

crust·y (krŭs′tē) *adj.* **-i·er, -i·est.** **1.** Having, resembling, or being a crust. **2.** Seemingly rough and surly in manner. See Synonyms at **gruff.** **—crust′i·ly** *adv.* **—crust′i·ness** *n.*

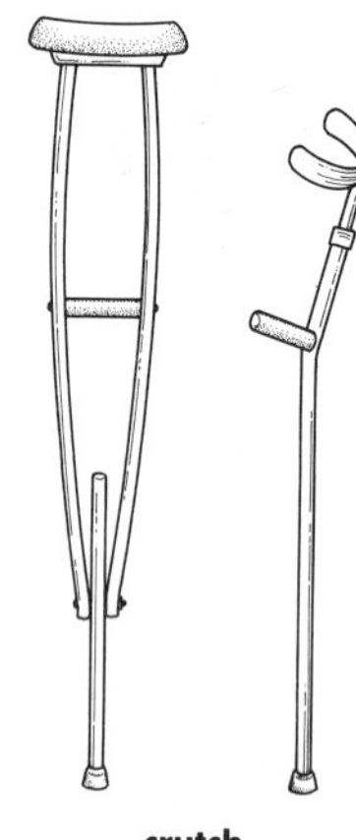
crutch

crutch (krŭch) *n.* **1.** A staff or support used by the physically injured or disabled as an aid in walking, usually designed to fit under the armpit and often used in pairs. **2.** A forked leg rest on a sidesaddle. **3.** A device used for assistance or support; a prop: *a mnemonic crutch.* **4.** The crotch of a person or animal. **5.** A forked device or part. **—crutch** *tr.v.* **crutched, crutch·ing, crutch·es.** To support on or as if on crutches; prop up. [Middle English *crucche,* from Old English *crycc.*]

crux (krŭks, kro͝oks) *n., pl.* **crux·es** or **cru·ces** (kro͞o′sēz). **1.** The basic, central, or critical point or feature: *the crux of the matter; the crux of an argument.* **2.** A puzzling or apparently insoluble problem. [Probably short for Medieval Latin *crux (interpretum),* torment (of interpreters), from Latin *crux,* cross.]

Crux (krŭks, kro͝oks) *n.* See **Southern Cross.**

cru·za·do (kro͞o-zä′dō) *n.* Variant of **crusado.**

Cru·zan (kro͞o-zăn′, kro͞o′zăn) *n.* A native or inhabitant of St. Croix in the U.S. Virgin Islands. [From American Spanish *Santa Cruz,* St. Croix.] **—Cru′zan** *adj.*

cru·zei·ro (kro͞o-zâr′ō, -zā′ro͞o) *n., pl.* **-ros.** See table at **currency.** [Portuguese, from *cruz,* cross (from the figure on the coin), from Latin *crux, cruc-.*]

crwth (kro͞oth) *n. Music.* See **crowd**[2] (sense 1). [Welsh.]

cry (krī) *v.* **cried** (krīd), **cry·ing, cries** (krīz). *—intr.* **1.** To sob or shed tears because of grief, sorrow, or pain; weep. **2.** To call loudly; shout. **3.** To utter a characteristic sound or call. Used of an animal. **4.** To demand or require immediate action or remedy: *grievances crying out for redress.* *—tr.* **1.** To utter loudly; call out. **2.** To proclaim or announce in public: *crying one's wares in the marketplace.* **3.** To bring into a particular condition by weeping: *cry oneself to sleep.* **4.** *Archaic.* To beg for; implore: *cry forgiveness.* **—cry** *n., pl.* **cries** (krīz). **1.** A loud utterance of an emotion, such as fear, anger, or despair. **2.** A loud exclamation; a shout or call. **3.** A fit of weeping: *had a good long cry.* **4.** An urgent entreaty or appeal. **5.** A public or general demand or complaint. **6.** A common view or general report. **7.** An advertising of wares by calling out: *venders' cries at the fish market.* **8.** A rallying call or signal: *a cry to arms.* **9.** A slogan, especially a political one. **10.** The characteristic call or utterance of an animal. **11.a.** The baying of hounds during the chase. **b.** A pack of hounds. **12.** *Obsolete.* Clamor; outcry. **13.** *Obsolete.* A public announcement; a proclamation. ***—phrasal verbs.*** **cry down.** To belittle or disparage. **cry off.** To break or withdraw from a promise, agreement, or undertaking. **cry up.** To praise highly; extol. ***—idioms.*** **cry havoc.** To sound an alarm; warn. **cry (one's) eyes** (or **heart) out.** To weep inconsolably for a long time. **cry on (someone's) shoulder.** To tell one's problems to someone else in an attempt to gain sympathy or consolation. **cry over spilled milk.** To regret in vain what cannot be undone or rectified. **cry wolf.** To raise a false alarm. **in full cry.** In hot pursuit, as hounds hunting. [Middle English *crien,* from Old French *crier,* from Vulgar Latin **critāre,* from Latin *quirītāre,* to cry out.]

SYNONYMS: *cry, weep, wail, keen, whimper, sob, blubber.* These verbs mean to make inarticulate sounds of grief, unhappiness, or pain. *Cry* and *weep* both involve the shedding of tears; *cry* more strongly implies accompanying sound: *"And when he* [William of Orange] *died the little children cried in the streets"* (John Lothrop Motley). *"I weep for what I'm like when I'm alone"* (Theodore Roethke). *Wail* refers primarily to sustained, inarticulate mournful sound: *"The women . . . began to wail together; they mourned with shrill cries"* (Joseph Conrad). *Keen* suggests the wailing associated with lamentation for those who have died: *"It is the wild Irish women keening over their dead"* (George A. Lawrence). *Whimper* refers to low, plaintive broken or repressed cries, as those made by a child: *The condemned prisoner cowered and began to whimper for clemency. Sob* describes weeping or a mixture of broken speech and weeping marked by convulsive breathing or gasping: *"sobbing and crying, and wringing her hands as if her heart would break"* (Laurence Sterne). *Blubber* refers to noisy, unrestrained shedding of tears accompanied by broken or inarticulate speech: *He blubbered like a child who had been spanked.*

cry·ba·by (krī′bā′bē) *n.* A person who cries or complains frequently with little cause.

cry·ing (krī′ĭng) *adj.* Demanding or requiring action or attention: *a crying need.* **—idiom. for crying out loud.** Used to express annoyance or astonishment: *Let's get going, for crying out loud!.*

cry·mo·ther·a·py (krī′mō-thĕr′ə-pē) *n.* See **cryotherapy.** [Greek *krumos,* cold; see **kreus-** in Appendix + THERAPY.]

cryo– *pref.* Cold; freezing: *cryoscopy.* [From Greek *kruos,* icy cold. See **kreus-** in Appendix.]

cry·o·bank (krī′ə-băngk′) *n.* A place of storage that uses very low temperatures to preserve semen or transplantable tissues.

cry·o·bi·ol·o·gy (krī′ō-bī-ŏl′ə-jē) *n.* The study of the effects of very low temperatures on living organisms. **—cry′o·bi′o·log′i·cal** (-bī′ə-lŏj′ĭ-kəl) *adj.* **—cry′o·bi′o·log′i·cal·ly** *adv.* **—cry′o·bi·ol′o·gist** *n.*

cry·o·gen (krī′ə-jən) *n.* A liquid, such as liquid nitrogen, that boils at a temperature below about 110 K (−160°C) and is used to obtain very low temperatures; a refrigerant.

cry·o·gen·ic (krī′ə-jĕn′ĭk) *adj.* **1.** Of or relating to low temperatures. **2.** Requiring or suitable to cryogenic storage. **—cry′o·gen′i·cal·ly** *adv.*

cry·o·gen·ics (krī′ə-jĕn′ĭks) *n. (used with a sing. or pl. verb).* The production of low temperatures or the study of low-temperature phenomena. Also called *cryogeny.*

cry·og·e·ny (krī-ŏj′ə-nē) *n.* See **cryogenics.**

cry·o·lite (krī′ə-līt′) *n.* An uncommon, white, vitreous natural fluoride of aluminum and sodium, Na_3AlF_6, nearly invisible in water in powdered form and used chiefly in the electrolytic recovery of aluminum. Also called *Greenland spar.*

cry·om·e·ter (krī-ŏm′ĭ-tər) *n.* A thermometer capable of measuring very low temperatures.

cry·on·ics (krī-ŏn′ĭks) *n. (used with a sing. verb).* The process of freezing and storing the body of a diseased, recently deceased person to prevent tissue decomposition so that at some future time the person might be brought back to life upon development of new medical cures. [CRY(O)– + *-onics,* as in BIONICS.] **—cry·on′ic** *adj.*

cry·o·phil·ic (krī′ə-fĭl′ĭk) also **cry·oph·i·lous** (krī-ŏf′ə-ləs) *adj.* Having an affinity for or thriving at low temperatures.

cry·o·pre·serve (krī′ō-prĭ-zûrv′) *tr.v.* **-served, -serv·ing, -serves.** To preserve (cells or tissue, for example) by freezing at very low temperatures. **—cry′o·pres′er·va′tion** (-prĕz′ər-vā′shən) *n.*

cry·o·probe (krī′ə-prōb′) *n.* A surgical instrument used to apply extreme cold to tissues during cryosurgery.

cry·o·pro·tec·tant (krī′ō-prə-tĕk′tənt) *n.* A substance, such as glycerol, used to protect cells or tissues from damage during freezing. **—cry′o·pro·tec′tant** *adj.* **—cry′o·pro·tec′tive** *adj.*

cry·o·scope (krī′ə-skōp′) *n.* An instrument used to measure the freezing point of a liquid.

cry·os·co·py (krī-ŏs′kə-pē) *n.* A technique for determining the molecular weight of a solute by dissolving a known quantity of it in a solvent and recording the amount by which the freezing point of the solvent drops. **—cry′o·scop′ic** (-ə-skŏp′ĭk) *adj.*

cry·o·stat (krī′ə-stăt′) *n.* An apparatus used to maintain constant low temperature. **—cry′o·stat′ic** *adj.*

cry·o·sur·ger·y (krī′ō-sûr′jə-rē) *n.* The selective exposure of tissues to extreme cold, often by applying a probe containing liquid nitrogen, to bring about the destruction or elimination of abnormal cells. **—cry′o·sur′geon** (-jən) *n.* **—cry′o·sur′gi·cal** (-jĭ-kəl) *adj.*

cry·o·ther·a·py (krī′ō-thĕr′ə-pē) *n.* The local or general use of low temperatures in medical therapy. Also called *crymotherapy.*

crypt (krĭpt) *n.* **1.** An underground vault or chamber, especially one beneath a church that is used as a burial place. **2.** *Anatomy.* A small pit, recess, or glandular cavity in the body. [Latin *crypta,* from Greek *kruptē,* from feminine of *kruptos,* hidden, from *kruptein,* to hide.]

crypt– *pref.* Variant of **crypto–.**

crypt·aes·the·sia (krĭp′təs-thē′zhə, -zhē-ə) *n. Psychology.* Variant of **cryptesthesia.**

crypt·a·nal·y·sis (krĭp′tə-năl′ĭ-sĭs) *n.* **1.** The analysis and deciphering of cryptographic writings or systems. **2.** Also **crypt·an·a·lyt·ics** (krĭp′tăn-ə-lĭt′ĭks). *(used with a sing. verb).* The study of techniques for deciphering cryptographic writings or systems. [CRYPT(OGRAM) + ANALYSIS.] **—crypt·an′a·lyst** (krĭp-tăn′ə-lĭst) *n.* **—crypt·an′a·lyt′ic** (-lĭt′ĭk) *adj.*

crypt·an·a·lyze (krĭp-tăn′ə-līz′) *tr.v.* **-lyzed, -lyz·ing, -lyz·es.** To decipher or decode.

crypt·es·the·sia or **crypt·aes·the·sia** (krĭp′təs-thē′zhə, -zhē-ə) *n. Psychology.* A mode of paranormal perception, such as clairvoyance.

cryp·tic (krĭp′tĭk) also **cryp·ti·cal** (-tĭ-kəl) *adj.* **1.** Having hidden meaning; mystifying. See Synonyms at **ambiguous. 2.** Secret or occult. **3.** Using code or cipher. **4.** *Biology.* Tending to conceal or camouflage: *cryptic coloring.* [Late Latin *crypticus,* from Greek *kruptikos,* from *kruptos,* hidden, from *kruptein,* to hide.] **—cryp′ti·cal·ly** *adv.* **—cryp′tic·ness** *n.*

cryp·to (krĭp′tō) *n., pl.* **-tos.** One who covertly supports a certain doctrine, group, or party. **—crypto** *adj.* **1.** Secret; covert. **2.** Of, relating to, or employing cryptography. [From CRYPTO–.]

crypto– or **crypt–** *pref.* Hidden; secret: *cryptoclastic.* [From Greek *kruptos,* hidden, from *kruptein,* to hide.]

cryp·to·clas·tic (krĭp′tō-klăs′tĭk) *adj.* Composed of microscopic rock fragments.

cryp·to·coc·co·sis (krĭp′tə-kŏ-kō′sĭs) *n.* A systemic infection caused by the fungus *Cryptococcus neoformans* that can affect any organ of the body but most often occurs in the central nervous system.

cryp·to·coc·cus (krĭp′tə-kŏk′əs) *n.* Any of various yeastlike fungi of the genus *Cryptococcus,* commonly occurring in the soil and including certain pathogenic species, such as the causative agent of cryptococcosis. **—cryp′to·coc′cal** *adj.*

cryp·to·crys·tal·line (krĭp′tō-krĭs′tə-lĭn, -līn′) *adj.* Having a microscopic crystalline structure.

cryp·to·gam (krĭp′tə-găm′) *n. Botany.* A member of a formerly recognized taxonomic group that included all seedless plants, such as mosses, algae, fungi, and ferns. [From New Latin *Cryptogamia,* genus name : CRYPTO– + *-gamia,* -gamy.] **—cryp′to·gam′ic, cryp·tog′a·mous** (-tŏg′ə-məs) *adj.*

cryp·to·gen·ic (krĭp′tə-jĕn′ĭk) also **cryp·tog·e·nous** (krĭp-tŏj′ə-nəs) *adj.* Of obscure or unknown origin. Used of diseases.

cryp·to·gram (krĭp′tə-grăm′) *n.* **1.** A piece of writing in code or cipher. Also called *cryptograph.* **2.** A figure or representation having a secret or occult significance. **—cryp′to·gram′mic** *adj.*

cryp·to·graph (krĭp′tə-grăf′) *n.* **1.** See **cryptogram** (sense 1). **2.** A system of secret or cipher writing; a cipher. **3.a.** A device for translating plain text into cipher. **b.** A device for deciphering codes and ciphers. **—cryptograph** *tr.v.* **-graphed, -graph·ing, -graphs.** To write (a message, for example) in code or cipher.

cryp·tog·ra·pher (krĭp-tŏg′rə-fər) *n.* One who uses, studies, or develops cryptographic systems and writings.

cryp·tog·ra·phy (krĭp-tŏg′rə-fē) *n.* **1.** The process or skill of communicating in or deciphering secret writings or ciphers. **2.** Secret writing. **—cryp′to·graph′ic** (-tə-grăf′ĭk) *adj.* **—cryp′to·graph′i·cal·ly** *adv.*

cryp·tol·o·gy (krĭp-tŏl′ə-jē) *n.* The study of cryptanalysis or cryptography. **—cryp′to·log′ic** (-tə-lŏj′ĭk), **cryp′to·log′i·cal** (-ĭ-kəl) *adj.* **—cryp·tol′o·gist** *n.*

cryp·to·me·ri·a (krĭp′tə-mîr′ē-ə) *n.* See **Japanese cedar.** [New Latin *Cryptomeria,* genus name : CRYPTO– + Greek *meros,* part.]

crypt·or·chism (krĭp-tôr′kĭz′əm) also **crypt·or·chi·dism** (-kĭ-dĭz′əm) *n.* A developmental defect marked by the failure of the testes to descend into the scrotum. [From New Latin *cryptorchidismus* : CRYPT(O)– + *orchis,* testicle (from Greek *orkhis*).] **—crypt·or′chid** *n.*

cryp·to·spo·rid·i·o·sis (krĭp′tō-spə-rĭd′ē-ō′sĭs) *n.* A pathological condition caused by protozoa of the genus *Cryptosporidium* that infects human beings and some animals. [New Latin *Cryptosporidium,* genus name (CRYPTO– + SPOR(O)– + Latin *-idium,* diminutive suff.) + –OSIS.]

cryp·to·zo·ite (krĭp′tə-zō′īt′) *n.* A malarial parasite at the stage of development in which it inhabits bodily tissue before invading the red blood cells. [CRYPTO– + ZO(O)– + –ITE[1].]

cryp·to·zo·ol·o·gy (krĭp′tō-zō-ŏl′ə-jē) *n.* The study of creatures, such as the Sasquatch, whose existence has not been substantiated. **—cryp′to·zo′o·log′i·cal** (-zō′ə-lŏj′ĭ-kəl) *adj.* **—cryp′to·zo·ol′o·gist** *n.*

crys·tal (krĭs′təl) *n.* **1.a.** A homogenous solid formed by a repeating, three-dimensional pattern of atoms, ions, or molecules and having fixed distances between constituent parts. **b.** The unit cell of such a pattern. **2.** A mineral, especially a transparent form of quartz, having a crystalline structure, often characterized by external planar faces. **3.a.** A natural or synthetic crystalline material having piezoelectric or semiconducting properties. **b.** An electronic device, such as an oscillator or a detector, using such a material. **4.a.** A high-quality clear, colorless glass. **b.** An object, especially a vessel or an ornament, made of such glass. **c.** Such objects considered as a group. **5.** A clear glass or plastic protective cover for the face of a watch or clock. **6.** *Slang.* A stimulant drug, usually methamphetamine, in its powdered form. **—crystal** *adj.* Clear or transparent: *a crystal lake; the crystal clarity of their reasoning.* [Middle English *cristal,* from Old French, from Latin *crystallum,* from Greek *krustallos.* See **kreus-** in Appendix.]

Crys·tal (krĭs′təl). A city of eastern Minnesota, a suburb of Minneapolis. Population, 25,543.

crystal ball *n.* **1.** A globe of quartz crystal or glass in which images, especially those believed to portend the future, are supposedly visible to fortune tellers. **2.** A vehicle or technique for making predictions.

crystal clear or **crys·tal-clear** (krĭs′təl-klîr′) *adj.* Absolutely clear; pellucid: *a crystal clear sky; gave me crystal clear directions.*

crystal detector *n.* A rectifying detector used especially in early radio receivers and consisting of a semiconducting crystal in point contact with a fine metal wire.

crystal gaz·ing (gā′zĭng) *n.* **1.** Divination by gazing into a crystal ball. **2.** The making of determinations or predictions using questionable or unscientific means. **—crystal gazer** *n.*

crys·tal·ize (krĭs′tə-līz′) *v.* Variant of **crystallize.**

crystall– *pref.* Variant of **crystallo–.**

Crystal Lake. A city of northeast Illinois north of Elgin. It is in a summer resort area. Population, 18,590.

crystal lattice *n.* A geometric arrangement of the points in space at which the atoms, molecules, or ions of a crystal occur. Also called *space lattice.*

crys·tal·lif·er·ous (krĭs′tə-lĭf′ər-əs) also **crys·tal·lig·er·ous** (-lĭj′-) *adj.* Producing or containing crystals.

crys·tal·line (krĭs′tə-lĭn, -līn′, -lēn′) *adj.* **1.** Being, relating to, or composed of crystal or crystals. **2.** Resembling crystal, as in transparency or distinctness of structure or outline. [Middle English *cristallin,* from Old French, from Latin *crystallinus,* from Greek *krustallinos,* from *krustallos,* crystal. See **kreus-** in Appendix.] **—crys′tal·lin′i·ty** (-lĭn′ĭ-tē) *n.*

crystalline lens *n.* The lens of an eye.

crys·tal·lite (krĭs′tə-līt′) *n.* Any of numerous minute rudimentary, crystalline bodies of unknown composition found in glassy igneous rocks. **—crys′tal·lit′ic** (-lĭt′ĭk) *adj.*

crys·tal·lize also **crys·tal·ize** (krĭs′tə-līz′) *—v.* **-lized, -liz·ing, -liz·es** also **-ized, -iz·ing, -iz·es.** *—tr.* **1.** To cause to form crystals or assume a crystalline structure. **2.** To give a definite, precise, and usually permanent form to: *It only took a week for her to crystallize her design for the decorations.* **3.** To coat with crystals, as of sugar. *—intr.* **1.** To assume a crystalline form. **2.** To take on a definite, precise, and usually permanent form. **—crys′tal·liz′a·ble** *adj.* **—crys′tal·li·za′tion** (-lĭ-zā′shən) *n.* **—crys′tal·liz′er** *n.*

crystal

crystallo– or **crystall–** *pref.* Crystal: *crystallize.* [From Greek *krustallo-,* from *krustallos,* crystal. See **kreus-** in Appendix.]

crys·tal·log·ra·phy (krĭs′tə-lŏg′rə-fē) *n.* The science of crystal structure and phenomena. **—crys′tal·log′ra·pher** *n.* **—crys′tal·lo·graph′ic** (-lə-grăf′ĭk), **crys′tal·lo·graph′i·cal** *adj.* **—crys′tal·lo·graph′i·cal·ly** *adv.*

crys·tal·loid (krĭs′tə-loid′) *n.* **1.** *Chemistry.* A substance that can be crystallized. **2.** *Botany.* Any of various minute crystallike particles consisting of protein and found in certain plant cells, especially oily seeds. **—crystalloid** *adj.* Resembling or having properties of a crystal or crystalloid. **—crys′tal·loi′dal** (-loid′l) *adj.*

crystal pleat *n.* One of a series of very narrow pleats creased in the same direction.

crystal set *n.* An early radio receiver using a crystal detector.

crystal violet *n.* A dye derived from gentian violet that is used as a general biological stain and an acid-base indicator.

Cs The symbol for the element **cesium.**

CS *abbr.* **1.** Capital stock. **2.** Chief of staff. **3.a.** Christian Science. **b.** Christian Scientist. **4.** Civil service. **5.** *Psychology.* Conditioned stimulus.

cs. *abbr.* Case.

C.S.A. *abbr.* Confederate States of America.

csc *abbr. Mathematics.* Cosecant.

CSC *abbr.* Civil Service Commission.

csch *abbr. Mathematics.* Hyperbolic cosecant.

C-sec·tion (sē′sĕk′shən) *n.* A cesarean section.

ă pat	oi boy
ā pay	ou out
âr care	ŏŏ took
ä father	ōō boot
ĕ pet	ŭ cut
ē be	ûr urge
ĭ pit	th thin
ī pie	*th* this
îr pier	hw which
ŏ pot	zh vision
ō toe	ə about, item
ô paw	♦ regionalism

Stress marks: ′ (primary); ′ (secondary), as in **dictionary** (dĭk′shə-nĕr′ē)

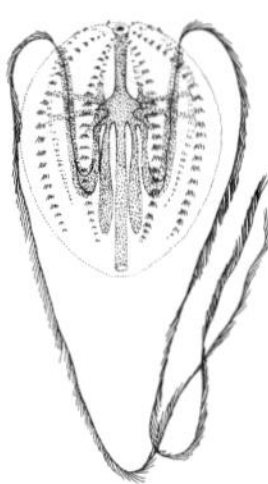
ctenophore

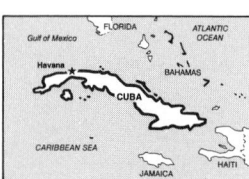

Cuba

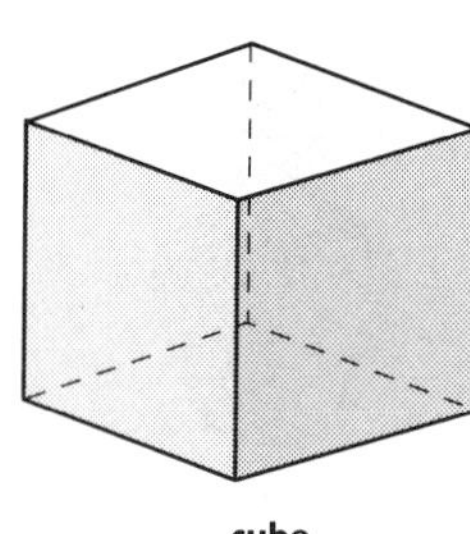
cube

cubicle
Office cubicle

CSF *abbr.* Cerebrospinal fluid.

csk. *abbr.* **1.** Cask. **2.** Countersink.

CST *abbr.* **1.** Or **C.S.T.** Central Standard Time. **2.** Convulsive shock treatment.

c-store or **C-store** (sē′stôr′, -stōr′) *n.* A convenience store.

CT *abbr.* **1.** Computerized tomography. **2.** Connecticut.

ct. *abbr.* **1.** Cent. **2.** Certificate. **3.** Court.

Ct. *abbr.* **1.** Connecticut. **2.** Count (title).

cte·nid·i·um (tĭ-nĭd′ē-əm) *n., pl.* **-i·a** (-ē-ə). *Zoology.* A comblike structure, such as the respiratory apparatus of a mollusk or a row of spines in some insects. [New Latin, from Greek *kteis, kten-,* comb.]

cten·oid (tĕn′oid′, tē′noid′) *adj. Biology.* **1.** Comblike. **2.** Having marginal projections that resemble the teeth of a comb: *a ctenoid fish.* [Greek *ktenoeidēs,* comblike : *kteis, kten-,* comb + *-oeidēs,* -oid.]

cten·o·phore (tĕn′ə-fôr′, -fōr′) *n.* Any of various marine animals of the phylum Ctenophora, having transparent, gelatinous bodies bearing eight rows of comblike cilia used for swimming. Also called *comb jelly.* [From New Latin *Ctenophora,* phylum name : Greek *kteis, kten-,* comb + New Latin *-phora,* from neuter pl. of Greek *-phoros,* -phore.] **—cte·noph′o·ran** (tĭ-nŏf′ər-ən) *adj.*

Ctes·i·phon (tĕs′ə-fŏn′, tē′sə-). An ancient city of central Iraq on the Tigris River southeast of Baghdad. As the residence of Parthian kings it was renowned for its splendor. The Arabs captured and plundered the city in 637.

ctf. *abbr.* Certificate.

ctg. *abbr.* Cartage.

ctge. *abbr.* Cartage.

ctn *abbr. Mathematics.* Cotangent.

ctn. *abbr.* Carton.

ctr. *abbr.* **1.** Center. **2.** Counter.

CT scan (sē′tē′) *n.* See **CAT scan.**

CT scanner *n.* See **CAT scanner.**

Cu The symbol for the element **copper**[1] (sense 1). [Latin *cuprum.*]

cu. or **cu** *abbr.* Cubic.

cua·dril·la (kwä-drē′yə, -drēl′yə) *n., pl.* **-las.** The group of assistants to the matador in a bullfight. [Spanish, diminutive of *cuadra,* square, from Latin *quadra.* See QUADRILLE[1].]

Cuan·za also **Kwan·za** (kwän′zə). A river rising in central Angola and flowing about 965 km (600 mi) generally northwest to the Atlantic Ocean.

cuat·ro (kwä′trō) *n., pl.* **-ros.** *Music.* A small guitarlike instrument of Latin America, usually having four or five pairs of strings. [Spanish, from Latin *quattuor,* four. See QUATRAIN.]

cub (kŭb) *n.* **1.** The young of certain carnivorous animals, such as the bear, wolf, or lion. **2.** A youth, especially one who is inexperienced, awkward, or ill-mannered. **3.** A novice or learner, particularly in newspaper reporting. **4. Cub.** A Cub Scout. [Origin unknown.]

Cu·ba (kyo͞o′bə). An island country in the Caribbean Sea south of Florida. Discovered by Columbus in 1492, it was a Spanish colony until 1898. Fulgencio Batista dominated the government of Cuba from 1933 until 1959, when he was ousted by Fidel Castro. Havana is the capital and the largest city. Population, 9,723,605. **—Cu′ban** *adj. & n.*

cub·age (kyo͞o′bĭj) *n.* Cubic content, volume, or displacement.

Cuban heel *n.* A broad heel of moderate height with a slightly tapered back and straight front, used in shoes and some boots.

♦ **Cuban sandwich** *n. Florida.* See **submarine** (sense 2). See Regional Note at **submarine.**

cu·ba·ture (kyo͞o′bə-cho͝or′, -chər) *n.* **1.** The determination of the cubic contents of a solid. **2.** Cubage. [CUB(E) + (QUADR)ATURE.]

cub·by (kŭb′ē) *n., pl.* **-bies.** A small room; a cubbyhole. [Short for CUBBYHOLE.]

cub·by·hole (kŭb′ē-hōl′) *n.* **1.** A snug or cramped space or room. **2.** A small compartment. **3.** A category, especially an overly restrictive one. [From *cub,* pen, hutch (perhaps from Flemish *cubbe,* from Middle Flemish) + HOLE.]

cube (kyo͞ob) *n.* **1.** *Mathematics.* A regular solid having six congruent square faces. **2. a.** Something having the general shape of a cube: *a cube of sugar.* **b.** A cubicle, used for work or study. **3.** *Mathematics.* The third power of a number or quantity. **4. cubes.** *Slang.* Cubic inches. Used especially of an internal combustion engine. **—cube** *tr.v.* **cubed, cub·ing, cubes. 1.** *Mathematics.* To raise (a quantity or number) to the third power. **2.** To determine the cubic contents of. **3.** To form or cut into cubes; dice. **4.** To tenderize (meat) by cutting the surface in a pattern of squares. [Latin *cubus,* from Greek *kubos.*] **—cub′er** *n.*

cu·bé also **cu·be** (kyo͞o′bā′, kyo͞o-bā′) *n.* Any of several tropical American woody plants of the genus *Lonchocarpus* in the pea family, whose roots are used locally as a fish poison and commercially as a source of rotenone. [American Spanish.]

cu·beb (kyo͞o′bĕb′) *n.* **1.** A tropical southeast Asian shrubby vine *(Piper cubeba)* having spicy, berrylike fruits, heart-shaped leaves, and small flowers in cylindrical spikes. **2.** The dried, unripe, berrylike fruit of this plant, used in perfumery, pharmaceuticals, and commercial flavorings. [Middle English *cubebe,* from Old French, from Medieval Latin *cubēba,* from Arabic *kabābah.*]

cube root *n. Mathematics.* A number whose cube is equal to a given number.

cube steak *n.* A thin slice of beef tenderized by cubing.

cu·bic (kyo͞o′bĭk) *adj.* **1. a.** Having the shape of a cube. **b.** Shaped similar to a cube. **2.** *Abbr.* **c, cu., cu a.** Having three dimensions. **b.** Having a volume equal to a cube whose edge is of a stated length: *a cubic foot.* **3.** *Mathematics.* Of the third power, order, or degree. **4.** Of or relating to a crystalline form that has three equal axes at right angles to each other; isometric. **—cubic** *n. Mathematics.* A cubic expression, curve, or equation. **—cu′bic·ly** *adv.*

cu·bi·cal (kyo͞o′bĭ-kəl) *adj.* **1.** Cubic. **2.** Of or relating to volume. **—cu′bi·cal·ly** *adv.* **—cu′bi·cal·ness** *n.*

cu·bi·cle (kyo͞o′bĭ-kəl) *n.* **1.** A small compartment, as for work or study. **2.** A small sleeping compartment, especially within a dormitory. [Middle English, from Latin *cubiculum,* bed chamber, from *cubāre,* to lie down.]

cubic measure *n.* A unit, such as a cubic foot, or a system of units used to measure volume or capacity.

cubic zirconia *n.* A synthetic gemstone, ZrO_2, used in jewelry as an artificial diamond.

cu·bi·form (kyo͞o′bə-fôrm′) *adj.* Having the shape of a cube.

cub·ism also **Cub·ism** (kyo͞o′bĭz′əm) *n.* A nonobjective school of painting and sculpture developed in Paris in the early 20th century, characterized by the reduction and fragmentation of natural forms into abstract, often geometric structures usually rendered as a set of discrete planes. **—cub′ist** *n.* **—cu·bis′tic** *adj.* **—cu·bis′ti·cal·ly** *adv.*

cu·bit (kyo͞o′bĭt) *n.* An ancient unit of linear measure, originally equal to the length of the forearm from the tip of the middle finger to the elbow, or about 17 to 22 inches (43 to 56 centimeters). [Middle English *cubite,* from Latin *cubitum,* cubit, elbow.]

cu·boid (kyo͞o′boid′) *adj.* Having the approximate shape of a cube. **—cuboid** *n.* **1.** *Anatomy.* A tarsal bone on the outer side of the foot in front of the calcaneus and behind the fourth and fifth metatarsal bones. **2.** *Mathematics.* A rectangular parallelepiped. **—cu·boi′dal** (kyo͞o-boid′l) *adj.*

cuboidal epithelium *n.* Epithelial tissue consisting of one or more cell layers, the most superficial of which is composed of cube-shaped or somewhat prismatic cells.

Cub Scout *n.* A member of the junior division of the Boy Scouts, for boys of ages eight through ten.

cu·chi·fri·to (ko͞o′chĭ-frē′tō) *n.* **-tos.** A small deep-fried cube of pork. [American Spanish : *cuchí,* pig (alteration of Spanish *cochino,* diminutive of *coch,* interj. used to call pigs) + Spanish *frito,* past participle of *freír,* to fry (from Latin *frīgere*).]

Cu·chul·ain (ko͞o-kŭl′ĭn, -KHŬL′-) *n. Mythology.* A hero of ancient Ulster who single-handedly defended it against the rest of Ireland.

cuck·ing stool (kŭk′ĭng) *n.* An instrument of punishment no longer in use, consisting of a chair in which the offender was tied and exposed to public derision or ducked in water. [Middle English *cukking stol,* from *cukken,* to defecate, of Scandinavian origin. See **kakka-** in Appendix.]

cuck·old (kŭk′əld, ko͝ok′-) *n.* A man married to an unfaithful wife. **—cuckold** *tr.v.* **-old·ed, -old·ing, -olds.** To make a cuckold of. [Middle English *cokewald,* from Anglo-Norman **cucuald,* from *cucu,* the cuckoo, from Vulgar Latin **cuccūlus,* from Latin *cucūlus.*]

WORD HISTORY: In our era of more relaxed sexual mores, the allusion to the cuckoo on which the word *cuckold* is based may be little appreciated. The female of some Old World cuckoos lays its eggs in the nests of other birds, leaving them to be cared for by the resident nesters. This parasitic tendency has given the female bird a figurative reputation for unfaithfulness as well. Hence in Old French we find the word *cucuault,* composed of *cocu,* "cuckoo, cuckold," and the pejorative suffix *–ald* and used to designate a husband whose wife has wandered afield like the female cuckoo. An earlier assumed form of the Old French word was borrowed into Middle English by way of Anglo-Norman. Middle English *cokewold,* the ancestor of Modern English *cuckold,* is first recorded in a work written around 1250.

cuck·old·ry (kŭk′əl-drē, ko͝ok′-) *n.* **1.** The state of being a cuckold. **2.** The act of making someone a cuckold.

cuck·oo (ko͞o′ko͞o, ko͝ok′o͞o) *n., pl.* **-oos. 1. a.** A grayish European bird *(Cuculus canorus)* that has a characteristic two-note call and lays its eggs in the nests of birds of other species. **b.** Any of various related birds of the family Cuculidae, having grayish-brown plumage and a slender body. **2.** The call or cry of one of these birds. **3.** *Slang.* A foolish or crazy person. **—cuckoo** *tr.v.* **-ooed, -oo·ing, -oos.** To repeat incessantly, as a cuckoo does its call. **—cuckoo** *adj. Slang.* Lacking in sense; foolish or crazy. [Middle English *cuccu,* of imitative origin.]

cuckoo clock *n.* A wall or shelf clock that announces intervals of time with a sound imitative of a cuckoo's call and often with the simultaneous emergence of a mechanical bird from a small door.

cuck·oo·flow·er (ko͞o′ko͞o-flou′ər, ko͝ok′o͞o-) *n.* **1.** A perennial herb *(Cardamine pratensis)* in the mustard family, native to the northern temperate regions and having pinnate leaves and pink, purple, or sometimes white flowers. Also called *lady's smock.* **2.** See **ragged robin.**

cuck·oo·pint (ko͞o′ko͞o-pīnt′, ko͝ok′o͞o-) *n.* A European plant *(Arum maculatum)* having arrow-shaped leaves, a yellow-green spathe, and scarlet berries. Also called *lords-and-ladies.* [From obsolete *cuckoopintle,* from Middle English *cokkupintel* : *cokku, cuccu,* cuckoo; see CUCKOO + *pintel,* penis (from Old English).]

cuckoo spit *n.* A frothy mass of liquid secreted on plant stems as a protective covering by nymphs of the spittlebug. Also called *frog spit.*

cu·cul·late (kyo͞o′kə-lāt′, kyo͞o-kŭl′āt′) *adj. Botany.* Having the shape of a cowl or hood; hooded: *cucullate sepals.* [Medieval Latin *cucullātus,* from Latin *cucullus,* hood. See COWL.] **—cu′cul·late′ly** *adv.*

cu·cum·ber (kyo͞o′kŭm′bər) *n.* **1.a.** A tendril-bearing, climbing or sprawling annual plant *(Cucumis sativus)* widely cultivated for its edible cylindrical fruit that has a green rind and crisp white flesh. **b.** The fruit of this plant, eaten fresh or pickled. **2.** Any of several related or similar plants, such as the bur cucumber or the squirting cucumber. [Middle English *cucomer,* from Old French *coucombre,* from Latin *cucumis, cucumer-.*]

cucumber mosaic *n.* A viral disease of the cucumber and many other plants, characterized by mottled and curled leaves and misshapen and mottled fruits.

cucumber tree *n.* Any of certain magnolias, especially *Magnolia acuminata,* a deciduous tree of eastern North America, having greenish-yellow flowers and a cucumber-shaped aggregate fruit.

cu·cur·bit (kyo͞o-kûr′bĭt) *n.* **1.** Any of various mostly climbing or trailing plants of the family Cucurbitaceae, which includes the squash, pumpkin, cucumber, gourd, watermelon, and cantaloupe. **2.** A gourd-shaped flask forming the body of an alembic, formerly used in distillation. [Middle English *cucurbite,* from Old French, from Latin *cucurbita,* gourd.]

Cú·cu·ta (ko͞o′kə-tə, -ko͞o-tä′). A city of northeast Colombia near the Venezuelan border. It was rebuilt after a devastating earthquake in 1875. Population, 355,828.

cud (kŭd) *n.* **1.** Food regurgitated from the first stomach to the mouth of a ruminant and chewed again. **2.** Something held in the mouth and chewed, such as a quid of tobacco. [Middle English, from Old English *cudu.*]

Cud·a·hy (kŭd′ə-hē). **1.** A city of southern California southeast of Los Angeles. It is a processing and manufacturing center. Population, 17,984. **2.** A city of southeast Wisconsin, an industrial suburb of Milwaukee on Lake Michigan. Population, 19,547.

cud·bear (kŭd′bâr′) *n.* A purplish-red dye derived from certain lichens. [After *Cuthbert* Gordon, 18th-century Scottish chemist.]

cud·dle (kŭd′l) *v.* **-dled, -dling, -dles.** *—tr.* To fondle in the arms; hug tenderly. See Synonyms at **caress.** *—intr.* To nestle; snuggle. **—cuddle** *n.* The act of cuddling; a hug or embrace. [Origin unknown.] **—cud′dle·some** *adj.* **—cud′dly** *adj.*

cud·dy¹ (kŭd′ē) *n., pl.* **-dies. 1.** *Nautical.* A small cabin or the cook's galley on a ship. **2.** A small room, cupboard, or closet. [Origin unknown.]

cud·dy² (kŭd′ē) *n., pl.* **-dies.** *Scots.* **1.** A donkey. **2.** A fool; a dolt. [Perhaps from *Cuddy,* nickname for *Cuthbert.*]

cudg·el (kŭj′əl) *n.* A short, heavy stick; a club. **—cudgel** *tr.v.* **-eled, -el·ing, -els** or **-elled, -el·ling, -els.** To beat or strike with or as if with a cudgel. [Middle English *cuggel,* from Old English *cycgel.*]

cud·weed (kŭd′wēd′) *n.* **1.** Any of various woolly plants of the genus *Gnaphalium* in the composite family, having small whitish or yellowish flower heads. **2.** Any of several similar and related plants in the genus *Filago.*

cue¹ (kyo͞o) *n.* **1.** *Games.* A long tapered rod with a leather tip used to strike the cue ball in billiards and pool. **2.** *Games.* A long stick with a concave attachment at one end for shoving disks in shuffleboard. **3.** A queue of hair. **4.** A line of waiting people or vehicles; a queue. **—cue** *v.* **cued, cu·ing, cues.** *—tr.* **1.** *Games.* To strike with a cue. **2.** To braid or twist (hair) into a queue. *—intr.* To form a line or queue. [Variant of QUEUE.]

cue² (kyo͞o) *n.* **1.** A signal, such as a word or an action, used to prompt another event in a performance, such as an actor's speech or entrance, a change in lighting, or a sound effect. **2.a.** A reminder or a prompting. **b.** A hint or suggestion. **3.** *Music.* **a.** An extract from the music for another part printed, usually in smaller notes, within a performer's part as a signal to enter after a long rest. **b.** A gesture by a conductor signaling the entrance of a performer or part. **4.** *Psychology.* A stimulus, either consciously or unconsciously perceived, that elicits or signals a type of behavior. **5.** *Archaic.* One's assigned role or function. **6.** *Archaic.* A mood; a disposition. **—cue** *tr.v.* **cued, cu·ing, cues. 1.** To give a cue to; signal or prompt. **2.** To insert or cause to be inserted into the sequence of a performance. ***—phrasal verb.* cue (someone) in.** To give information or instructions to (a latecomer, for example). [Perhaps from *q, qu,* abbreviation of Latin *quandō,* when, used for actors' copies of plays. See **kʷo-** in Appendix.]

cue³ (kyo͞o) *n.* The letter *q.*

cue ball *n. Games.* The white ball that is propelled with the cue in billiards and pool.

cue card *n.* A large card held out of the audience's sight, bearing words or dialogue in large letters as an aid for a speaker or an actor chiefly in television broadcasting.

cued speech (kyo͞od) *n.* A means of communication in which a speaker uses hand signals to clarify ambiguous mouth movements for lip readers.

Cuen·ca (kwĕng′kə, -kä). A city of south-central Ecuador southeast of Guayaquil. Founded in 1557, it is known as "the Marble City" for its fine buildings. Population, 157,213.

Cuer·na·va·ca (kwĕr-nə-vä′kə, -nä-vä′kä). A city of south-central Mexico in the **Cuernavaca Valley** near Mexico City. It is an industrial city and a popular resort. Population, 192,770.

cues·ta (kwĕs′tə) *n.* A ridge with a gentle slope on one side and a cliff on the other. [Spanish, from Latin *costa,* side. See **kost-** in Appendix.]

cuff¹ (kŭf) *n.* **1.a.** A fold used as trimming at the bottom of a sleeve. **b.** A band, often having an opening with a button closure, at the bottom of a sleeve. **2.** The turned-up fold at the bottom of a trouser leg. **3.** The band at the top of a sock. **4.** The part of a glove that extends over the wrist. **5.** A handcuff. **6.** *Medicine.* An inflatable band, usually wrapped around the upper arm, that is used along with a sphygmomanometer in measuring arterial blood pressure. **—cuff** *tr.v.* **cuffed, cuff·ing, cuffs. 1.** To form a cuff or cuffs on. **2.** To put handcuffs on. ***—idioms.* off the cuff.** In an extemporaneous or informal manner. **on the cuff.** On credit. [Middle English *cuffe,* mitten.]

cuff² (kŭf) *tr.v.* **cuffed, cuff·ing, cuffs.** To strike with or as if with the open hand; slap. **—cuff** *n.* A blow or slap with the open hand. [Origin unknown.]

cuff link or **cuff·link** (kŭf′lĭngk′) *n.* A fastening for a shirt cuff, usually consisting of two buttons or buttonlike parts connected with a chain or shank that passes through two slits in the cuff.

Cu·fic (ko͞o′fĭk, kyo͞o′-) *adj.* Variant of **Kufic.**

Cu·ia·bá (ko͞o′yə-bä′). A city of west-central Brazil west of Brasília on the **Cuiabá River,** about 483 km (300 mi) long. The city was founded during the gold rush of the early 18th century. Population, 167,880.

cui bo·no (kwē′ bō′nō) *n.* Utility, advantage, or self-interest considered as the determinant of value or motivation. [Latin : *cui,* to whose, dative of *quī* + *bonō,* dative of *bonum,* advantage.]

cui·rass (kwĭ-răs′) *n.* **1.a.** A piece of armor for protecting the breast and back. **b.** The breastplate alone. **2.** A defense or protection: *"A carefully primped irony, that cuirass of art in the early Eighties, is necessary—a distance so affected as to constitute a hopeless impediment to feeling"* (Robert Hughes). **3.** *Zoology.* A protective covering of bony plates or scales. **—cuirass** *tr.v.* **-rassed, -rass·ing, -rass·es.** To protect with a cuirass. [Middle English *curas,* from Old French *cuirace,* probably alteration (influenced by Old French *cuir,* leather) of Old Provençal *coirassa,* from Late Latin *coriācea (vestis),* leather (garment), feminine of *coriāceus,* from Latin *corium,* hide. See **sker-¹** in Appendix.]

cui·ras·sier (kwîr′ə-sîr′) *n.* A horse soldier in European armies whose equipment included the cuirass. [French, from *cuirasse,* cuirass, from Old French. See CUIRASS.]

Cui·se·naire (kwē′zə-nâr′). A trademark used for a set of colored rods and disks employed in the teaching of mathematics.

cuish (kwĭsh) *n.* Variant of **cuisse.**

Cui·si·nart (kwē′zə-närt′, kwē′zə-närt′). A trademark used for a kind of food processor and its attachments.

cui·sine (kwĭ-zēn′) *n.* **1.** A characteristic manner or style of preparing food: *Spanish cuisine.* **2.** Food; fare. [French, from Old French, from Vulgar Latin **cocīna,* variant of Latin *coquīna,* kitchen, cookery, from *coquere,* to cook. See **pekʷ-** in Appendix.]

cuisine bourgeoise *n.* Simple home cooking, especially as practiced in France. [French : *cuisine,* cooking + *bourgeoise,* middle-class.]

cuisine min·ceur (măɴ-sœr′) *n.* A low-calorie style of French cooking. [French : *cuisine,* cooking + *minceur,* thinness, slimness.]

cuisse (kwĭs) also **cuish** (kwĭsh) *n.* Plate armor worn to protect the front of the thigh. [Middle English *quisse,* probably back-formation from *quisseues,* pl. of *quisseu,* cuisse, from Old French *quisseuz,* pl. of *quissel,* from *quisse,* thigh, from Latin *coxa,* hip.]

cuit·tle (kü′tl) *tr.v.* **-tled, -tling, -tles.** *Scots.* To coax; cajole. [Origin unknown.]

cui-ui (kwē′wē) *n.* A freshwater sucker *(Chasmistes cujus)* found only in Nevada. [Northern Paiute *kuyui.*]

cuke (kyo͞ok) *n. Informal.* A cucumber.

Cul·bert·son (kŭl′bərt-sən), **Ely.** 1891–1955. American contract bridge authority whose dominance of international matches and several books, including *The Contract Bridge Blue Book* (1930), helped popularize the card game.

♦ **culch** or **cultch** (kŭlch) *n.* **1.** A natural bed for oysters, consisting of gravel or crushed shells to which the oyster spawn may adhere. **2.** The spawn of the oyster. **3.** Also **scultch** or **sculch** (skŭlch). *New England.* Clean trash or rubbish, such as string, paper, and cloth: *"We always had a culch box around"* (New Hampshire informant in DARE). **4.** A person or thing not highly regarded. [Perhaps ultimately from Old French *culche,* couch. See COUCH.]

cul-de-sac (kŭl′dĭ-săk′, ko͝ol′-) *n., pl.* **culs-de-sac** (kŭlz′-, ko͝olz′-) or **cul-de-sacs** (kŭl′-). **1.a.** A dead-end street. **b.** An impasse: *"This was the cul-de-sac the year kept driving me to-*

cubism
1910 drawing *Nude Woman* by Pablo Picasso

cuckoo clock

cue ball

ă pat	oi boy
ā pay	ou out
âr care	o͝o took
ä father	o͞o boot
ĕ pet	ŭ cut
ē be	ûr urge
ĭ pit	th thin
ī pie	*th* this
îr pier	hw which
ŏ pot	zh vision
ō toe	ə about, item
ô paw	♦ regionalism

Stress marks: ′ (primary); ′ (secondary), as in **dictionary** (dĭk′shə-nĕr′ē)

culverin
1523 Italian

Culver's root
Veronicastrum virginicum

culvert

ward: men and women would always be at odds" (Philip Weiss). **2.** *Anatomy.* A saclike cavity or tube open only at one end. [French : *cul,* bottom (from Old French, from Latin *cūlus;* see CULET) + *de,* of (from Old French, from Latin *dē;* see DE–) + *sac,* sack (from Old French, from Latin *saccus;* see SACK[1]).]

Cu·le·bra Cut (ko͞o-lā′brə). See **Gaillard Cut.**

Culebra Peak. A mountain, 4,284.3 m (14,047 ft) high, in the Sangre de Cristo Mountains of extreme south-central Colorado.

cu·let (kyo͞o′lĭt, kŭl′ĭt) *n.* **1.** The small flat face at the bottom of a gem cut as a brilliant. **2.** Armor consisting of overlapping plates used to protect the buttocks. [Obsolete French, diminutive of *cul,* rump, from Latin *cūlus.* See **(s)keu-** in Appendix.]

cu·lex (kyo͞o′lĕks′) *n., pl.* **-li·ces** (-lĭ-sēz′). Any of various mosquitoes of the genus *Culex,* which includes the common house mosquito *(C. pipiens).* [Latin, gnat.]

Cu·lia·cán (ko͞ol′yə-kän′). A city of western Mexico west-northwest of Durango on the **Culiacán River,** about 282 km (175 mi) long. The city was founded in 1531 and figured prominently as a departure point for early Spanish expeditions to the north. Population, 304,826.

cu·li·nar·y (kyo͞o′lə-nĕr′ē, kŭl′ə-) *adj.* Of or relating to a kitchen or to cookery. [Latin *culīnārius,* from *culīna,* kitchen. See **pek^w-** in Appendix.]

cull (kŭl) *tr.v.* **culled, cull·ing, culls. 1.** To pick out from others; select. **2.** To gather; collect. **3.** To remove rejected members or parts from (a herd, for example). **—cull** *n.* Something picked out from others, especially something rejected because of inferior quality. [Middle English *cullen,* from Old French *cuillir,* from Latin *colligere.* See COLLECT[1].] **—cull′er** *n.*

Cul·len (kŭl′ən), **Countée.** 1903–1946. American poet whose collections *Colors* (1926) and *Copper Sun* (1927) established him as a leading figure of the Harlem Renaissance.

cul·let (kŭl′ĭt) *n.* Scraps of broken or waste glass gathered for remelting, especially with new material. [Probably alteration of *collet,* neck of glass left on the blowing iron, from French, collar, diminutive of *col,* neck, from Old French, from Latin *collum.* See **k^{w}el-[1]** in Appendix.]

cul·lion (kŭl′yən) *n. Archaic.* A contemptible fellow; a rascal. [Middle English *coilon,* testicle, from Old French *coillon,* from Latin *culleus,* bag.]

cul·lis (kŭl′ĭs) *n.* A gutter or groove in a roof. [Middle English *colis,* from Old French *coleis,* channel, from *coler,* to pour, from Latin *cōlāre,* to filter, from *cōlum,* sieve.]

Cul·lo·den Moor (kə-lŏd′n, -lôd′n). A moor in northern Scotland east of Inverness. It was the site of the final defeat of the Highland Jacobites by English forces (April 16, 1746).

cul·ly (kŭl′ē) *Archaic. n., pl.* **-lies.** A fool or dupe. **—cully** *tr.v.* **-lied, -ly·ing, -lies.** To fool; cheat. [Perhaps from CULLION.]

culm[1] (kŭlm) *n.* The stem of a grass or similar plant. [Latin *culmus,* stalk.]

culm[2] (kŭlm) *n.* **1.** Waste from anthracite coal mines, consisting of fine coal, coal dust, and dirt. **2.a.** Carboniferous shale. **b.** Inferior anthracite coal. [Middle English *colme,* coal dust, perhaps from Old English *col,* coal.]

cul·mi·nant (kŭl′mə-nənt) *adj.* **1.** Being at the highest altitude. **2.** Reaching the highest point or degree; highest.

cul·mi·nate (kŭl′mə-nāt′) *v.* —*intr.* **-nat·ed, -nat·ing, -nates. 1.a.** To reach the highest point or degree; climax: *habitual antagonism that culminated in open hostility.* **b.** To come to completion; end: *Years of waiting culminated in a tearful reunion.* **2.** *Astronomy.* To reach the highest point above an observer's horizon. Used of stars and other celestial bodies. —*tr.* To bring to the point of greatest intensity or to completion; climax: *The ceremony culminated a long week of preparation.* [Late Latin *culmināre, culmināt-,* from Latin *culmen, culmin-,* summit. See **kel-[2]** in Appendix.] **—cul′mi·na′tion** *n.*

cu·lotte (ko͞o-lŏt′, kyo͞o-, ko͞o′lŏt′, kyo͞o′-) *n.* A woman's full trousers cut to resemble a skirt. Often used in the plural. [French, breeches, diminutive of *cul,* rump, from Latin *cūlus.* See **(s)keu-** in Appendix.]

cul·pa·ble (kŭl′pə-bəl) *adj.* Deserving of blame or censure as being wrong, evil, improper, or injurious. See Synonyms at **blameworthy.** [Middle English *coupable,* from Old French, from Latin *culpābilis,* from *culpāre,* to blame, from *culpa,* fault.] **—cul′pa·bil′i·ty** *n.* **—cul′pa·bly** *adv.*

Cul·pep·er (kŭl′pĕp′ər), Lord **Thomas.** 1635–1689. English colonial administrator who served as governor of Virginia (1677–1683).

cul·prit (kŭl′prĭt) *n.* **1.** One charged with an offense or crime. **2.** One guilty of a fault or crime. [Probably from *cul. prit,* abbreviation for Anglo-Norman **culpable: prit d'averrer nostre bille,* guilty: (I am) ready to aver our indictment : *culpable,* guilty (from Latin *culpābilis;* see CULPABLE) + **prit,* ready (variant of *prest,* from Latin *praestō;* see PRESTO).]

WORD HISTORY: According to British legal tradition, the word *culprit* comes from *cul. prit,* an abbreviation of the Anglo-Norman legal phrase *Culpable: prit d'averrer nostre bille.* These words, said by the clerk of the crown in response to a not-guilty plea, meant, "Guilty: I am ready to aver our indictment." After law French went out of official use in the courts, the shortened form *cul. prit* was misinterpreted as a term of address used by the clerk to a prisoner indicted for high treason or felony and pleading "not guilty." *Culprit* is first recorded in such a use in 1678. The term was thereafter taken to mean "the accused," and then, by association with Latin *culpa,* "guilt," it came to mean "a guilty party."

culs-de-sac (kŭlz′dĭ-săk′, ko͝olz′-) *n.* A plural of **cul-de-sac.**

cult (kŭlt) *n.* **1.a.** A religion or religious sect generally considered to be extremist or false, with its followers often living in an unconventional manner under the guidance of an authoritarian, charismatic leader. **b.** The followers of such a religion or sect. **2.** A system or community of religious worship and ritual. **3.** The formal means of expressing religious reverence; religious ceremony and ritual. **4.** A usually nonscientific method or regimen claimed by its originator to have exclusive or exceptional power in curing a particular disease. **5.a.** Obsessive, especially faddish, devotion to or veneration for a person, principle, or thing. **b.** The object of such devotion. **6.** An exclusive group of persons sharing an esoteric, usually artistic or intellectual interest. —*attributive.* Often used to modify another noun: *a cult figure; cult films.* [Latin *cultus,* worship, from past participle of *colere,* to cultivate. See **k^{w}el-[1]** in Appendix.] **—cul′tic, cult′ish** *adj.* **—cult′ism** *n.* **—cult′ist** *n.*

♦ **cultch** (kŭlch) *n.* Variant of **culch.**

cul·ti (kŭl′tī) *n.* A plural of **cultus.**

cul·ti·gen (kŭl′tə-jən) *n.* An organism, especially a cultivated plant, such as a banana, not known to have a wild or uncultivated counterpart. [CULTI(VATED) + –GEN.]

cul·ti·va·ble (kŭl′tə-və-bəl) *adj.* Capable of undergoing cultivation: *cultivable land.* **—cul′ti·va·bil′i·ty** *n.*

cul·ti·var (kŭl′tə-vär′, -vâr′) *n. Abbr.* **cv.** A horticultural race or variety of a plant that has originated and persisted only under cultivation. [CULTI(VATED) + VAR(IETY).]

cul·ti·vate (kŭl′tə-vāt′) *tr.v.* **-vat·ed, -vat·ing, -vates. 1.a.** To improve and prepare (land), as by plowing or fertilizing, for raising crops; till. **b.** To loosen or dig soil around (growing plants). **2.** To grow or tend (a plant or crop). **3.** To promote the growth of (a biological culture). **4.** To nurture; foster. See Synonyms at **nurture. 5.** To form and refine, as by education. **6.** To seek the acquaintance or good will of; make friends with. [Medieval Latin *cultivāre, cultivāt-,* from *cultīvus,* tilled, from Latin *cultus,* past participle of *colere,* to till. See **k^{w}el-[1]** in Appendix.] **—cul′ti·vat′a·ble** *adj.*

cul·ti·vat·ed (kŭl′tə-vā′tĭd) *adj.* **1.** Of or relating to cultivation; produced in cultivation: *a cultivated plant.* **2.** Educated; polished; refined.

cul·ti·va·tion (kŭl′tə-vā′shən) *n.* **1.a.** The act of cultivating. **b.** The state of being cultivated. **2.** Refinement; culture.

cul·ti·va·tor (kŭl′tə-vā′tər) *n.* **1.** One who cultivates: *an inveterate cultivator of beautiful gardens; a cultivator of valuable corporate contacts.* **2.** An implement or a machine for loosening the soil and destroying weeds around growing plants.

cul·trate (kŭl′trāt′) also **cul·trat·ed** (-trā′tĭd) *adj.* Sharp-edged and pointed; knifelike: *cultrate leaves.* [Latin *cultrātus,* from *culter, cultr-,* knife. See **skel-[1]** in Appendix.]

cul·tur·al (kŭl′chər-əl) *adj.* Of or relating to culture or cultivation. **—cul′tur·al·ly** *adv.*

cultural anthropology *n.* The scientific study of the development of human cultures based on archaeological, ethnologic, ethnographic, linguistic, social, and psychological data and methods of analysis.

Cul·tur·al Revolution (kŭl′chər-əl) *n.* A comprehensive reform movement in China, initiated by Mao Zedong in 1965 to eliminate counterrevolutionary elements in the country's institutions and leadership. It was characterized by political zealotry, purges of intellectuals, and social and economic chaos.

cul·tu·ra·ti (kŭl′chə-rä′tē) *pl.n.* People interested in culture and cultural activities. [CULTUR(E) + (LITER)ATI.]

cul·ture (kŭl′chər) *n.* **1.a.** The totality of socially transmitted behavior patterns, arts, beliefs, institutions, and all other products of human work and thought. **b.** These patterns, traits, and products considered as the expression of a particular period, class, community, or population: *Edwardian culture; Japanese culture; the culture of poverty.* **c.** These patterns, traits, and products considered with respect to a particular category, such as a field, subject, or mode of expression: *religious culture in the Middle Ages; musical culture; oral culture.* **2.** Intellectual and artistic activity, and the works produced by it. **3.a.** Development of the intellect through training or education. **b.** Enlightenment resulting from such training or education. **4.** A high degree of taste and refinement formed by aesthetic and intellectual training. **5.** Special training and development: *voice culture for singers and actors.* **6.** The cultivation of soil; tillage. **7.** The breeding of animals or growing of plants, especially to produce improved stock. **8.** *Biology.* **a.** The growing of microorganisms, tissue cells, or other living matter in a specially prepared nutrient medium. **b.** Such a growth or colony, as of bacteria. **—culture** *tr.v.* **-tured, -tur·ing, -tures. 1.** To cultivate. **2.a.** To grow (microorganisms or other living matter) in a specially prepared nutrient medium. **b.** To use (a substance) as a medium for culture: *culture milk.* [Middle English, cultivation, from Old French, from Latin *cultūra,* from *cultus,* past participle of *colere.* See CULTIVATE.]

cul·tured (kŭl′chərd) *adj.* **1.** Educated, polished, and refined; cultivated. **2.** Produced under artificial and controlled conditions: *cultured pearls.*

ă pat	oi boy
ā pay	ou out
âr care	o͝o took
ä father	o͞o boot
ĕ pet	ŭ cut
ē be	ûr urge
ĭ pit	th thin
ī pie	*th* this
îr pier	hw which
ŏ pot	zh vision
ō toe	ə about, item
ô paw	♦ regionalism

Stress marks: ′ (primary); ′ (secondary), as in **dictionary** (dĭk′shə-nĕr′ē)

culture medium *n.* A liquid or gelatinous substance containing nutrients in which microorganisms or tissues are cultivated for scientific purposes.

culture shock *n.* A condition of confusion and anxiety affecting a person suddenly exposed to an alien culture or milieu.

cul·tus (kŭl′təs) *n., pl.* **-tus·es** or **-ti** (-tī). A cult, especially a religious one. [Latin, veneration. See CULT.]

cul·ver (kŭl′vər) *n.* A dove or a pigeon. [Middle English, from Old English *culufre,* from Vulgar Latin **columbra,* from Latin *columbula,* diminutive of *columba,* dove.]

Cul·ver City (kŭl′vər). A city of southern California, a residential suburb of Los Angeles. Its motion-picture industry dates to c. 1915. Population, 38,139.

cul·ver·in (kŭl′vər-ĭn) *n.* **1.** An early, crudely made musket. **2.** A long heavy cannon used in the 16th and 17th centuries. [Middle English, from Old French *coulevrine,* from *couleuvre,* snake, from Latin *colubra,* feminine of *coluber.*]

Cul·ver's root (kŭl′vərz) *n.* **1.** A perennial herb *(Veronicastrum virginicum)* native to eastern North America, having whorled leaves and small white or pinkish flowers in slender spikes. **2.** The rootstock of this plant, formerly used in medicine as a cathartic and an emetic. [After *Culver,* 18th-century American physician.]

cul·vert (kŭl′vərt) *n.* **1.** A sewer or drain crossing under a road or embankment. **2. a.** The part of a road or embankment that passes over such a sewer or drain. **b.** The channel or conduit for such a sewer or drain. [Origin unknown.]

cum (ko͝om, kŭm) *prep.* Together with; plus. Often used in combination: *our attic-cum-studio.* [Latin. See **kom** in Appendix.]

cum. *abbr.* Cumulative.

Cu·mae (kyo͞o′mē). An ancient city and Greek colony of south-central Italy near present-day Naples. Founded c. 750 B.C., it is the earliest-known Greek settlement in Italy. Cumae adopted Roman culture after the second century B.C. and gradually declined as neighboring cities rose to power.

Cu·ma·ná (ko͞o′mä-nä′). A city of northeast Venezuela on the Caribbean Sea east of Caracas. It was founded in 1521 to exploit nearby pearl fisheries. Population, 173,000.

cum·ber (kŭm′bər) *tr.v.* **-bered, -ber·ing, -bers. 1.** To weigh down; burden: *was cumbered with many duties.* **2.** To hamper or hinder, as by being in the way: *was cumbered with a long poncho.* **3.** To litter; clutter up: *Weeds cumbered the garden paths.* **4.** *Archaic.* To bother; distress. **—cumber** *n.* A hindrance; an encumbrance. [Middle English *cumbren,* to annoy, from Old French *combrer,* from *combre,* hindrance, from Vulgar Latin **comboros,* of Celtic origin.] **—cum′ber·er** *n.*

Cum·ber·land (kŭm′bər-lənd). A city of northwest Maryland in the Panhandle on the Potomac River and the West Virginia border. It is a shipping center for a coal-mining area. Population, 25,933.

Cumberland Gap. A natural passage through the Cumberland Plateau near the junction of the Kentucky, Virginia, and Tennessee borders. It was discovered in 1750 and used by Daniel Boone in 1775 as a strategic point along his Wilderness Road, the principal route of westward migration for the next half century.

Cumberland Plateau or **Cumberland Mountains.** The southwest section of the Appalachian Mountains, extending northeast to southwest from southern West Virginia through Virginia, Kentucky, and Tennessee into northern Alabama.

Cumberland River. A river rising in southeast Kentucky and flowing about 1,105 km (687 mi) in a winding course southwest into northern Tennessee then northwest to the Ohio River near Paducah in southwest Kentucky.

cum·ber·some (kŭm′bər-səm) *adj.* **1.** Difficult to handle because of weight or bulk. See Synonyms at **heavy. 2.** Troublesome or onerous. **—cum′ber·some·ly** *adv.*

Cum·bri·a (kŭm′brē-ə). An ancient Celtic kingdom of northwest England. The southern part came under Anglo-Saxon control c. 944; the northern portion passed to Scotland in 1018. **—Cum′bri·an** *adj. & n.*

cum·brous (kŭm′brəs) *adj.* Cumbersome. [Middle English, from *cumbren,* to annoy. See CUMBER.] **—cum′brous·ly** *adv.* **—cum′brous·ness** *n.*

cum·in (kŭm′ĭn, ko͞o′mĭn, kyo͞o′-) *n.* **1. a.** An annual Mediterranean herb *(Cuminum cyminum)* in the parsley family, having finely divided leaves and clusters of small white or pink flowers. **b.** The seedlike fruit of this plant used for seasoning, as in curry and chili powders. **2.** Black cumin. [Middle English, from Old French, from Latin *cumīnum,* from Greek *kuminon,* probably of Semitic origin.]

cum lau·de (ko͝om lou′də, lou′dē, kŭm lô′dē) *adv. & adj.* With honor. Used to express academic distinction: *graduated cum laude; 25 cum laude graduates.* [Probably Medieval Latin *cum laudē* : Latin *cum,* with + Latin *laudē,* ablative of *laus,* praise.]

cum·mer·bund (kŭm′ər-bŭnd′) *n.* A broad sash, especially one that is pleated lengthwise and worn as an article of formal dress, as with a dinner jacket. [Hindi *kamarband,* from Persian : *kamar,* waist + *band,* band; see BUND[1].]

Cum·mings (kŭm′ĭngz), **Edward Estlin.** Usually styled e. e. cummings. 1894–1962. American writer. Best known for his lyrical and typographically eccentric poetry, he also wrote *The Enormous Room* (1922), an account of his imprisonment in France during World War I.

cum·quat (kŭm′kwŏt′) *n.* Variant of **kumquat.**

cum·shaw (kŭm′shô′) *n.* A tip; a gratuity. [Pidgin English, from Chinese (Amoy) *gamsia,* an expression of thanks.]

cumul– *pref.* Variant of **cumulo–.**

cu·mu·late (kyo͞om′yə-lāt′) *v.* **-lat·ed, -lat·ing, -lates.** *—tr.* **1.** To gather in a heap; accumulate. **2.** To combine into one unit; merge. *—intr.* To become massed. **—cumulate** *adj.* Having cumulated or having been cumulated; heaped up or amassed. [Latin *cumulāre, cumulāt-,* from *cumulus,* heap. See **keuə-** in Appendix.] **—cu′mu·la′tion** *n.*

cummerbund

cu·mu·la·tive (kyo͞om′yə-lā′tĭv, -yə-lə-tĭv) *adj. Abbr.* **cum. 1.** Increasing or enlarging by successive addition. **2.** Acquired by or resulting from accumulation. **3.** Of or relating to interest or a dividend that is added to the next payment if not paid when due. **4.** *Law.* **a.** Supporting the same point as earlier evidence: *cumulative evidence.* **b.** Imposed with greater severity upon a repeat offender: *cumulative punishment.* **c.** Following successively; consecutive: *cumulative sentences.* **5.** *Statistics.* **a.** Of or relating to the sum of the frequencies of experimentally determined values of a random variable that are less than or equal to a specified value. **b.** Of or relating to experimental error that increases in magnitude with each successive measurement. **—cu′mu·la′tive·ly** *adv.* **—cu′mu·la′tive·ness** *n.*

cumulative voting *n.* A system of voting in which each voter is given as many votes as there are positions to be filled and allowed to cast those votes for one candidate or distribute them in any way among the candidates.

cu·mu·li (kyo͞om′yə-lī′) *n.* Plural of **cumulus.**

cumuli– *pref.* Variant of **cumulo–.**

cu·mu·li·form (kyo͞om′yə-lə-fôrm′) *adj.* Having the shape of a cumulus.

cumulo– or **cumuli–** or **cumul–** *pref.* Cumulus: *cumulonimbus.* [From CUMULUS.]

cu·mu·lo·nim·bus (kyo͞om′yə-lō-nĭm′bəs) *n., pl.* **-bus·es** or **-bi** (-bī). An extremely dense, vertically developed cumulus with a relatively hazy outline and a glaciated top extending to great heights, usually producing heavy rains, thunderstorms, or hailstorms.

cumulonimbus

cu·mu·lous (kyo͞o′myə-ləs) *adj.* Resembling a pile or mound; heaped up.

cu·mu·lus (kyo͞om′yə-ləs) *n., pl.* **-li** (-lī′). **1.** A dense, white, fluffy, flat-based cloud with a multiple rounded top and a well-defined outline, usually formed by the ascent of thermally unstable air masses. **2.** A pile, mound, or heap. [Latin, heap. See **keuə-** in Appendix.]

Cu·nax·a (kyo͞o-năk′sə). An ancient town of Babylonia northwest of Babylon. It was the site of a battle (401 B.C.) in which Artaxerxes II of Persia defeated his brother Cyrus the Younger, leading to the Retreat of the Ten Thousand described by Xenophon in his *Anabasis.*

cunc·ta·tion (kŭngk-tā′shən) *n.* Procrastination; delay. [Latin *cūnctātiō, cūnctātiōn-,* from *cūnctātus,* past participle of *cūnctārī,* to delay. See **konk-** in Appendix.] **—cunc′ta′tive** (kŭngk′tā′tĭv, -tə-tĭv) *adj.* **—cunc′ta′tor** *n.*

cu·ne·al (kyo͞o′nē-əl) *adj.* Wedge-shaped. [New Latin *cuneālis,* from Latin *cuneus,* wedge.]

cu·ne·ate (kyo͞o′nē-ĭt, -āt′) *adj. Botany.* Wedge-shaped. Used especially to describe a leaf or petal base that is narrowly triangular. [Latin *cuneātus,* past participle of *cuneāre,* to make wedge-shaped, from *cuneus,* wedge.] **—cu′ne·ate′ly** *adv.*

cumulus

cu·ne·i·form (kyo͞o′nē-ə-fôrm′, kyo͞o-nē′-) *adj.* **1.** Wedge-shaped. **2. a.** Being a character or characters formed by the arrangement of small wedge-shaped elements and used in ancient Sumerian, Akkadian, Assyrian, Babylonian, and Persian writing. **b.** Relating to, composed in, or using such characters. **3.** *Anatomy.* Of, relating to, or being a wedge-shaped bone or cartilage. **—cuneiform** *n.* **1.** Writing typified by the use of characters formed by the arrangement of small wedge-shaped elements. **2.** *Anatomy.* A wedge-shaped bone, especially one of three such bones in the tarsus of the foot. [Probably from French *cunéiforme,* from Latin *cuneus,* wedge.]

Cu·ne·ne also **Ku·ne·ne** (ko͞o-nā′nə). A river rising in west-central Angola and flowing about 1,207 km (750 mi) south and west to the Atlantic Ocean. It forms the Angola-Namibia border in its lower course.

cun·ner (kŭn′ər) *n.* A small fish *(Tautogolabrus adspersus)* of North American Atlantic waters that is common along the shore of the eastern United States. [Origin unknown.]

cun·ni·lin·gus (kŭn′ə-lĭng′gəs) *n.* Oral stimulation of the clitoris or vulva. [New Latin, from Latin, he who licks the vulva : *cunnus,* vulva; see **(s)keu-** in Appendix + *lingere,* to lick; see **leigh-** in Appendix.] **—cun′ni·lin′gual** *adj.*

cuneiform

cun·ning (kŭn′ĭng) *adj.* **1.** Marked by or given to artful subtlety and deceptiveness. See Synonyms at **sly. 2.** Executed with or exhibiting ingenuity. **3.** Delicately pleasing; pretty or cute: *a cunning little pet.* **—cunning** *n.* **1.** Skill in deception; guile. **2.** Skill or adeptness in execution or performance; dexterity. [Middle English, present participle of *connen,* to know, from Old English *cunnan.* See **gnō-** in Appendix.] **—cun′ning·ly** *adv.* **—cun′ning·ness** *n.*

Cun·ning·ham (kŭn′ĭng-hăm′), **Merce.** Born c. 1922. American dancer and choreographer of avant-garde works, including *Squaregame* (1976).

cunt (kŭnt) *n. Obscene.* **1.** The female genital organs. **2.** Sexual intercourse with a woman. **3. a.** Used as a disparaging term for a woman. **b.** Used as a disparaging term for a person one dislikes or finds extremely disagreeable. [Middle English *cunte.*]

cup (kŭp) *n.* **1. a.** A small, open container, usually with a flat bottom and a handle, used for drinking. **b.** Such a container and its contents. **2.** *Abbr.* **c., C.** A unit of capacity or volume equal to 16 tablespoons or 8 fluid ounces (237 milliliters). See table at **measurement. 3.** The bowl of a drinking vessel. **4.** The chalice or the wine used in the celebration of the Eucharist. **5.** A decorative cup-shaped vessel awarded as a prize or trophy. **6.** *Sports.* A golf hole or the metal container inside a hole. **7.** Either of the two parts of a brassiere that fit over the breasts. **8.** An athletic supporter having a protective reinforcement of rigid plastic or metal. **9.** A sweetened, flavored, usually chilled beverage, especially one made with wine: *claret cup.* **10.** A dish served in a cup-shaped vessel: *fruit cup.* **11. a.** A cuplike object. **b.** *Biology.* A cuplike structure or organ. **12.** A lot or portion to be suffered or enjoyed. **—cup** *tr.v.* **cupped, cup·ping, cups. 1.** To place in or as in a cup. **2.** To shape like a cup: *cup one's hand.* **3.** To subject to the therapeutic procedure of cupping. ***—idioms.*** **cup of tea. 1.** Something that one excels in or enjoys: *Opera is not my cup of tea.* **2.** A matter to be reckoned or dealt with: *Recreational sport is relaxing. Professional sport is another cup of tea altogether.* **in (one's) cups.** Intoxicated; drunk. [Middle English *cuppe,* from Old English, from Late Latin *cuppa,* drinking vessel, perhaps variant of Latin *cūpa,* tub, cask.]

cup-and-sau·cer plant (kŭp′ən-sô′sər) *n.* A tendril-bearing Mexican vine *(Cobaea scandens)* cultivated for its showy flowers. Also called *Mexican ivy vine.*

cup·bear·er (kŭp′bâr′ər) *n.* One who fills and distributes cups of wine, as in a royal household.

cup·board (kŭb′ərd) *n.* A closet or cabinet, usually with shelves for storing food, crockery, and utensils.

cup·cake (kŭp′kāk′) *n.* A small cake baked in a cup-shaped container.

cupid

cu·pel (kyo͞o′pəl, kyo͞o-pĕl′) *n.* **1.** A porous cup, often made of bone ash, used in assaying to separate precious metals from base elements such as lead. **2.** The bottom or receptacle in a silver-refining furnace. **—cupel** *tr.v.* **-peled, -pel·ing, -pels** or **-pelled, -pel·ling, -pels.** To assay or separate from base metals in a cupel. [French *coupelle,* from Old French, diminutive of *coupe,* cup, from Late Latin *cuppa,* drinking vessel.] **—cu′pel·ler, cu′pel·er** *n.*

cu·pel·la·tion (kyo͞o′pə-lā′shən) *n.* A refining process for nonoxidizing metals, such as silver and gold, in which a metallic mixture is oxidized at high temperatures and base metals are separated by absorption into the walls of a cupel.

Cu·per·ti·no (ko͞o′pər-tē′nō, kyo͞o′-). A city of western California west of San Jose. It has an electronics industry. Population, 34,265.

cup·flow·er (kŭp′flou′ər) *n.* Any of various South American plants of the genus *Nierembergia,* cultivated as annual bedding plants for their showy purple or sometimes white flowers.

cup·ful (kŭp′fo͝ol′) *n., pl.* **-fuls. 1.** The amount that a cup can hold. **2.** A measure of capacity equal to one cup.

cup fungus *n.* Any of various ascomycetous fungi, especially of the family Pezizaceae, characterized by a spore-bearing structure that is often stalkless and cup-shaped or disk-shaped.

cupola

Cu·pid (kyo͞o′pĭd) *n.* **1.** *Roman Mythology.* The god of love; the son of Venus. **2. cupid.** A representation of Cupid as a naked, cherubic boy usually having wings and holding a bow and arrow, used as a symbol of love. [Middle English *Cupide,* from Old French, from Latin *cupīdō,* desire, Cupid, from *cupere,* to desire.]

cu·pid·i·ty (kyo͞o-pĭd′ĭ-tē) *n.* Excessive desire, especially for wealth; covetousness or avarice. [Middle English *cupidite,* from Old French, from Latin *cupiditās,* from *cupidus,* desiring, from *cupere,* to desire.]

Cu·pid's bow (kyo͞o′pĭdz bō′) *n., pl.* **Cupid's bows.** An archery bow that curves inward at the center and usually outward at the ends.

cu·pid's-dart (kyo͞o′pĭdz-därt′) *n., pl.* **cupid's-darts.** A perennial Mediterranean herb *(Catananche caerulea)* in the composite family, cultivated for its long-stalked flower heads with showy, usually blue ray flowers.

cu·po·la (kyo͞o′pə-lə) *n.* **1.** *Architecture.* **a.** A domed roof or ceiling. **b.** A small structure surmounting a roof. **2.** A cylindrical shaft type of blast furnace used for remelting metals, usually iron, before casting. **3.** A small rounded and domed structure, as for observation, on a tracked, armored vehicle. [Italian, from Late Latin *cūpula,* diminutive of Latin *cūpa,* tub.]

cup·pa (kŭp′ə) *n. Chiefly British.* A cup of tea. [Short for *cuppa tea,* alteration of *cup of tea.*]

cup·ping (kŭp′ĭng) *n.* A treatment in which evacuated glass cups are applied to intact or scarified skin in order to draw blood toward or through the surface. It was used for disorders associated with an excess of blood, one of the four humors of medieval physiology.

cup plant *n.* A coarse perennial herb *(Silphium perfoliatum)* in the composite family, native to the central and southeast United States and having showy radiate flower heads of yellow flowers and opposite leaves whose bases fuse to form a cup around the stem.

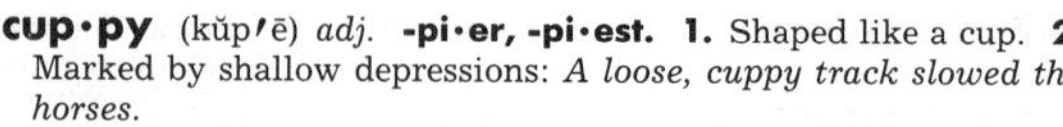

cup·py (kŭp′ē) *adj.* **-pi·er, -pi·est. 1.** Shaped like a cup. **2.** Marked by shallow depressions: *A loose, cuppy track slowed the horses.*

cupr– *pref.* Variant of **cupro–.**

cu·pre·ous (ko͞o′prē-əs, kyo͞o′-) *adj.* Of, resembling, or containing copper; coppery. [From Late Latin *cūpreus,* from *cūprum,* copper. See COPPER[1].]

cupri– *pref.* Variant of **cupro–.**

cu·pric (ko͞o′prĭk, kyo͞o′-) *adj.* Of or containing divalent copper.

cu·prif·er·ous (ko͞o-prĭf′ər-əs, kyo͞o-) *adj.* Containing copper.

cu·prite (ko͞o′prīt′, kyo͞o′-) *n.* A natural red secondary ore of copper, essentially Cu_2O, that forms as a result of weathering.

cupro– or **cupri–** or **cupr–** *pref.* Copper: *cupriferous.* [From Late Latin *cūprum,* copper. See COPPER[1].]

cu·pro·nick·el (ko͞o′prō-nĭk′əl, kyo͞o′-) *n.* An alloy of copper that contains 10 to 30 percent nickel.

cu·prous (ko͞o′prəs, kyo͞o′-) *adj.* Of, relating to, or containing univalent copper.

cu·pu·late (kyo͞o′pyə-lāt′, -lĭt) also **cu·pu·lar** (-lər) *adj.* **1.** Resembling a small cup; cup-shaped. **2.** Having or bearing a cupule.

cu·pule (kyo͞o′pyo͞ol) *n. Biology.* A small cup-shaped structure or organ, such as the cup at the base of an acorn or one of the suckers on the feet of certain flies. [Late Latin *cūpula,* little cask, diminutive of Latin *cūpa,* tub.]

cur (kûr) *n.* **1.** A dog considered to be inferior or undesirable; a mongrel. **2.** A base or cowardly person. [Middle English *curre,* perhaps of Scandinavian origin. See **gerə-**[2] in Appendix.]

cur. *abbr.* **1.** Currency. **2.** Current.

cur·a·ble (kyo͝or′ə-bəl) *adj.* Being such that curing or healing is possible: *curable diseases.* **—cur′a·bil′i·ty, cur′a·ble·ness** *n.* **—cur′a·bly** *adv.*

cu·ra·çao (kyo͝or′ə-sō′, -sou′, ko͝or′-) also **cu·ra·çoa** (-sō′ə) *n.* A liqueur flavored with the peel of the sour orange. [After CURAÇAO.]

Cu·ra·çao (ko͝or′ə-sou′, -sō′, kyo͝or′-, ko͝or′ə-sou′, -sō′, kyo͝or′-). An island of the Netherlands Antilles in the southern Caribbean Sea off the northwest coast of Venezuela. It was discovered in 1499 and settled by the Spanish in 1527. The Dutch gained control in 1634, although the British held the island during the Napoleonic Wars (1807–1815).

cu·ra·cy (kyo͝or′ə-sē) *n., pl.* **-cies.** The office, duties, or term of office of a curate. [CURA(TE)[1] + -CY.]

cu·ra·re also **cu·ra·ri** (ko͞o-rä′rē, kyo͞o-) *n.* **1.** A dark resinous extract obtained from several tropical American woody plants, especially *Chondrodendron tomentosum* or certain species of *Strychnos,* used as an arrow poison by some Indian peoples of South America. **2.** A purified preparation or alkaloid obtained from *Chondrodendron tomentosum,* used in medicine and surgery to relax skeletal muscles. **3.** A plant yielding curare. [Portuguese or Spanish *curaré,* both of Cariban and Tupian origin.]

cu·ra·rize (ko͞o-rä′rīz′, kyo͞o-) *tr.v.* **-rized, -riz·ing, -riz·es. 1.** To poison with curare. **2.** To treat with curare so as to relax the skeletal muscles. **—cu·ra′ri·za′tion** (-rĭ-zā′shən) *n.*

cu·ras·sow (ko͝or′ə-sō′, kyo͝or′-) *n.* Any of several long-tailed, crested South and Central American game birds of the family Cracidae, related to the pheasants and domestic fowl. [Alteration of CURAÇAO.]

cu·rate[1] (kyo͝or′ĭt) *n.* **1.** A cleric, especially one who has charge of a parish. **2.** A cleric who assists a rector or vicar. [Middle English *curat,* from Medieval Latin *cūrātus,* from Late Latin *cūra,* spiritual charge, from Latin, care. See CURE.]

cu·rate[2] (kyo͝or′āt′) *tr.v. Usage Problem.* To act as curator of; organize and oversee. [Back-formation from CURATOR.]

USAGE NOTE: The verb *curate* is widely used in art circles to mean "arrange or supervise (an exhibition of art)," as in *She has curated two exhibitions for the Modern Museum.* This usage is rejected by 81 percent of the Usage Panel.

cu·ra·tive (kyo͝or′ə-tĭv) *adj.* **1.** Serving or tending to cure. **2.** Of or relating to the cure of disease. **—curative** *n.* Something that cures; a remedy. [Middle English, from Old French *curatif,* from Medieval Latin *cūrātīvus,* from Latin *cūrātus,* past participle of *cūrāre,* to cure, from *cūra,* care. See CURE.] **—cu′ra·tive·ly** *adv.* **—cu′ra·tive·ness** *n.*

cu·ra·tor (kyo͞o-rā′tər, kyo͝or′ə-tər) *n.* One that manages or oversees, as the administrative director of a museum collection or a library. [Middle English *curatour,* legal guardian, from Old French *curateur,* from Latin *cūrātor,* overseer, from *cūrāre,* to take care of. See CURATIVE.] **—cu′ra·to′ri·al** (kyo͝or′ə-tôr′ē-əl, -tōr′-) *adj.* **—cu·ra′tor·ship′** *n.*

curb (kûrb) *n.* **1.** A concrete border or row of joined stones forming part of a gutter along the edge of a street. **2.** An enclosing framework, such as that around a skylight. **3.** A raised margin along an edge used to confine or strengthen. **4.** Something that checks or restrains: *High interest rates put a curb on spending.* **5.** A chain or strap that passes under a horse's lower jaw and serves in conjunction with the bit to restrain the horse. **—curb** *tr.v.* **curbed, curb·ing, curbs. 1.** To check, restrain, or control as if with a curb; rein in. See Synonyms at **restrain. 2.** To lead (a dog)

ă pat	oi boy
ā pay	ou out
âr care	o͝o took
ä father	o͞o boot
ĕ pet	ŭ cut
ē be	ûr urge
ĭ pit	th thin
ī pie	*th* this
îr pier	hw which
ŏ pot	zh vision
ō toe	ə about, item
ô paw	♦ regionalism

Stress marks: ′ (primary); ′ (secondary), as in **dictionary** (dĭk′shə-nĕr′ē)

off the sidewalk into the gutter so that it can excrete waste matter. **3.** To furnish with a curb. [Blend of Middle English, curved piece of wood (from Old French *corbe,* curved object, from *corbe,* curved, from Latin *curvus*) and Middle English *corbe,* horse strap (from *corben,* to bow down, halt, from Old French *corber,* to bow down, from Latin *curvāre,* from *curvus,* curved, bent; see **sker-**[2] in Appendix).]

curb bit *n.* A horse's bit to which a curb is attached.

curb cut *n.* A small ramp built into the curb of a sidewalk to ease passage to the street, especially for bicyclists, pedestrians with baby carriages, and physically disabled people.

curb·ing (kûr′bĭng) *n.* **1.** The material used to construct a curb. **2.** A row of curbstones; a curb.

curb roof *n.* A roof having two slopes on each side, as a gambrel roof or a mansard roof.

curb service *n.* Service or attendance, especially from a restaurant, provided to customers remaining in their parked vehicles.

curb·side (kûrb′sīd′) *n.* **1.** The side of a pavement or street that is bordered by a curb. **2.** A sidewalk. **—curbside** *adj.* Located, operating, or occurring at or along the sidewalk or curb: *curbside trash collection.*

curb·stone (kûrb′stōn′) *n.* A stone or row of stones that constitutes a curb. **—curbstone** *adj.* Untrained or unsophisticated; amateurish: *a curbstone commentator.*

cur·cu·li·o (kər-kyo͞o′lē-ō′) *n., pl.* **-os.** See **snout beetle.** [Latin *curculiō,* a kind of weevil.]

cur·cu·ma (kûr′kyə-mə) *n.* Any of various tropical Asian plants of the genus *Curcuma,* which includes turmeric. [New Latin *Curcuma,* genus name, from Arabic *kurkum,* saffron.]

curd (kûrd) *n.* **1.** The part of milk that coagulates when the milk sours or is treated with enzymes. Curd is used to make cheese. **2.** A coagulated liquid that resembles milk curd. **—curd** *intr. & tr.v.* **curd·ed, curd·ing, curds.** To form or cause to form into curd; curdle. [Middle English, variant of *crud.*] **—curd′y** *adj.*

curd cheese *n. Chiefly British.* Cottage cheese.

cur·dle (kûr′dl) *v.* **-dled, -dling, -dles.** *—intr.* **1.a.** To change into curd. See Synonyms at **coagulate. b.** To become congealed as if by having changed into curd: *The blood in my veins curdled at the horrific sight.* **2.** To go bad or become spoiled. *—tr.* To cause to change into or as if into curd. [Frequentative of CURD.]

cure (kyo͝or) *n.* **1.** Restoration of health; recovery from disease. **2.** A method or course of medical treatment used to restore health. **3.** An agent, such as a drug, that restores health; a remedy. **4.** Something that corrects or relieves a harmful or disturbing situation: *The cats proved to be a good cure for our mouse problem.* **5.** *Ecclesiastical.* Spiritual charge or care, as of a priest for a congregation. **6.** The office or duties of a curate. **7.** The act or process of preserving a product. **—cure** *v.* **cured, cur·ing, cures.** *—tr.* **1.** To restore to health. **2.** To effect a recovery from: *cure a cold.* **3.** To remove or remedy (something harmful or disturbing): *cure an evil.* **4.** To preserve (meat, for example), as by salting, smoking, or aging. **5.** To prepare, preserve, or finish (a substance) by a chemical or physical process. **6.** To vulcanize (rubber). *—intr.* **1.** To effect a cure or recovery: *a medicine that cures.* **2.** To be prepared, preserved, or finished by a chemical or physical process: *hams curing in the smokehouse.* [Middle English, from Old French, medical treatment, from Latin *cūra,* from Old Latin *coisa-.*] **—cur′er** *n.* **—cure′less** *adj.*

SYNONYMS: *cure, heal, remedy.* The central meaning shared by these verbs is "to set right an undesirable or unhealthy condition": *cure an ailing economy; heal a wounded spirit; remedy a structural defect.*

cu·ré (kyo͞o-rā′, kyo͝or′ā′) *n.* A parish priest. [French, from Old French, from Medieval Latin *cūrātus.* See CURATE[1].]

cure-all (kyo͝or′ôl′) *n.* A remedy that cures all diseases or evils; a panacea.

cu·ret (kyo͞o-rĕt′) *n.* Variant of **curette.**

cu·ret·tage (kyo͝or′ĭ-täzh′) *n.* The removal of tissue or growths from a body cavity, such as the uterus, by scraping with a curette. Also called *curettement.*

cu·rette also **cu·ret** (kyo͞o-rĕt′) *n.* A surgical instrument shaped like a scoop or spoon, used to remove tissue or growths from a body cavity. [French, from Old French, from *curer,* to cure, from Latin *cūrāre,* to take care of, from *cūra,* care. See CURE.]

cu·rette·ment (kyo͞o-rĕt′mənt) *n.* See **curettage.**

cur·few (kûr′fyo͞o) *n.* **1.** A regulation requiring certain or all people to leave the streets or be at home at a prescribed hour. **2.a.** The time at which such a restriction begins or is in effect: *a 10 P.M. curfew for all residents.* **b.** The signal, such as a bell, announcing the beginning of this restriction. [Middle English *curfew,* from Old French *cuevrefeu* : *covrir,* to cover; see COVER + *feu,* fire (from Latin *focus,* hearth).]

cu·ri·a (ko͝or′ē-ə, kyo͝or′-) *n., pl.* **cu·ri·ae** (ko͝or′ē-ē′, kyo͝or′-). **1.a.** One of the ten primitive subdivisions of a tribe in early Rome, consisting of ten gentes. **b.** The assembly place of such a subdivision. **2.a.** The Roman senate or any of the various buildings in which it met in republican Rome. **b.** The place of assembly of high councils in various Italian cities under Roman administration. **3.** The ensemble of central administrative and governmental services in imperial Rome. **4.** Often **Curia.** *Roman Catholic Church.* The central administration governing the Church. **5.a.** A medieval assembly or council. **b.** A medieval royal court of justice. [Latin, council, curia. See **wī-ro-** in Appendix.] **—cu′ri·al** *adj.*

cu·rie (kyo͝or′ē, kyo͞o-rē′) *n.* A unit of radioactivity, equal to the amount of a radioactive isotope that decays at the rate of 3.7 $\times 10^{10}$ disintegrations per second. [After Marie CURIE.]

Cu·rie (kyo͝or′ē, kyo͞o-rē′, kü-), **Eve Denise.** Born 1904. French pianist, writer, and editor best known for *Madame Curie* (1937), a biography of her mother, Marie Curie.

Curie also **Cu·rie-Jo·liot** (kyo͝or′ē-zhô-lyō′, kyo͞o-rē′-, kü-), **Irène.** See Irène **Joliot-Curie.**

Curie, Marie. Originally Manja Skłodowska. 1867–1934. Polish-born French chemist. She shared a 1903 Nobel Prize with her husband, **Pierre Curie** (1859–1906), and Henri Becquerel for fundamental research on radioactivity. In 1911 she won a second Nobel Prize for her discovery and study of radium and polonium.

Curie point *n.* A transition temperature marking a change in the magnetic or ferroelectric properties of a substance, especially the change from ferromagnetism to paramagnetism. Also called *Curie temperature.* [After Pierre CURIE.]

cu·ri·o (kyo͝or′ē-ō′) *n., pl.* **-os.** A curious or unusual object of art or piece of bric-a-brac. [Short for CURIOSITY.]

cu·ri·o·sa (kyo͝or′ē-ō′sə, -zə) *pl.n.* Books or other writings dealing with unusual, especially pornographic, topics. [New Latin, neuter pl. of Latin *cūriōsus,* inquisitive. See CURIOUS.]

cu·ri·os·i·ty (kyo͝or′ē-ŏs′ĭ-tē) *n., pl.* **-ties. 1.** A desire to know or learn. **2.** A desire to know about people or things that do not concern one; nosiness. **3.** An object that arouses interest, as by being novel or extraordinary: *kept the carved bone and displayed it as a curiosity.* **4.** A strange or odd aspect. **5.** *Archaic.* Fastidiousness. [Middle English *curiosite,* from Old French, from Latin *cūriōsitās,* from *cūriōsus,* inquisitive. See CURIOUS.]

cu·ri·ous (kyo͝or′ē-əs) *adj.* **1.** Eager to learn more: *curious investigators; a trap door that made me curious.* **2.** Unduly inquisitive; prying. **3.** Arousing interest because of novelty or strangeness: *a curious fact.* **4.** *Archaic.* **a.** Accomplished with skill or ingenuity. **b.** Extremely careful; scrupulous. [Middle English, from Old French *curios,* from Latin *cūriōsus,* careful, inquisitive, from *cūra,* care. See CURE.] **—cu′ri·ous·ly** *adv.* **—cu′ri·ous·ness** *n.*

SYNONYMS: *curious, inquisitive, snoopy, nosy.* These adjectives apply to persons who show a marked desire for information or knowledge. *Curious* most often implies an avid desire to know or learn, though it can suggest an undue interest in the affairs of others: *A curious child is a teacher's delight. Inquisitive* frequently suggests excessive curiosity and the asking of many questions: *"Remember, no revolvers. The police are, I believe, proverbially inquisitive"* (Lord Dunsany). Both *snoopy* and *nosy* imply an unworthy motive. *Snoopy* suggests underhanded prying: *The snoopy neighbor watched our activities all day. Nosy* implies impertinent curiosity likened to that of an animal using its nose to examine or probe: *I watched him flip through the letters on my desk in his nosy way.* See also Synonyms at **strange.**

Cu·ri·ti·ba (ko͝or′ĭ-tē′bə). A city of southeast Brazil southwest of São Paulo. It was founded in 1654 but did not grow rapidly until the late 19th and early 20th centuries when German, Italian, and Slavic immigrants began to develop the surrounding area. Population, 1,024,975.

cu·ri·um (kyo͝or′ē-əm) *n. Symbol* **Cm** A silvery, metallic synthetic radioactive transuranic element. Its longest lived isotope is Cm 247 with a half-life of 16.4 million years. Atomic number 96; melting point (estimated) 1,350°C; valence 3. See table at **element.** [After Marie CURIE and Pierre CURIE.]

curl (kûrl) *v.* **curled, curl·ing, curls.** *—tr.* **1.** To twist (the hair, for example) into ringlets or coils. **2.** To form into a coiled or spiral shape: *curled the ends of the ribbon.* **3.** To decorate with coiled or spiral shapes. **4.** To raise and turn under (the upper lip), as in snarling or showing scorn. *—intr.* **1.** To form ringlets or coils. **2.** To assume a spiral or curved shape. **3.** To move in a curve or spiral: *The wave curled over the surfer.* **4.** *Sports.* To engage in curling. **—curl** *n.* **1.** Something with a spiral or coiled shape. **2.** A coil or ringlet of hair. **3.** A treatment in which the hair is curled. **4.a.** The act of curling: *the curl of a meandering river.* **b.** The state of being curled. **5.** *Sports.* A weightlifting exercise using one or two hands, in which a barbell held at the thigh or to the side of the body is raised to the chest or shoulder and then lowered without moving the upper arms, shoulders, or back. **6.** Any of various plant diseases in which the leaves roll up. ***—phrasal verb.*** **curl up.** To assume a position with the legs drawn up: *The child curled up in an armchair to read.* [Middle English *crullen, curlen,* from *crulle,* curly, perhaps of Middle Low German origin.]

curl·er (kûr′lər) *n.* **1.** One that curls, as a device on which hair is wound for curling. **2.** *Sports.* A player of curling.

cur·lew (kûrl′yo͞o, kûr′lo͞o) *n.* Any of several brownish, long-legged shore birds of the genus *Numenius,* having long, slender, downward-curving bills. [Middle English *curleu,* from Old French *courlieu,* perhaps of imitative origin.]

Cur·ley (kûr′lē), **James Michael.** 1874–1958. American politician who as mayor of Boston (1914–1918, 1922–1926, 1930–

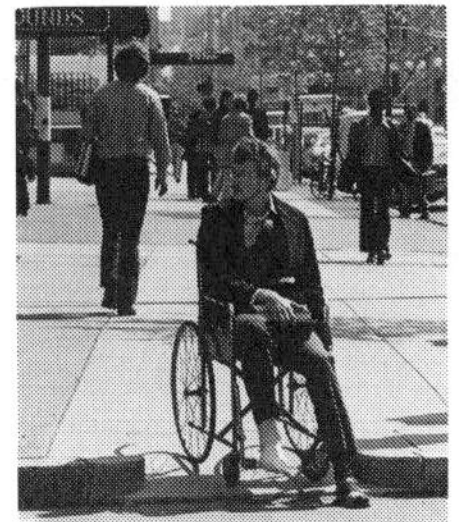
curb cut

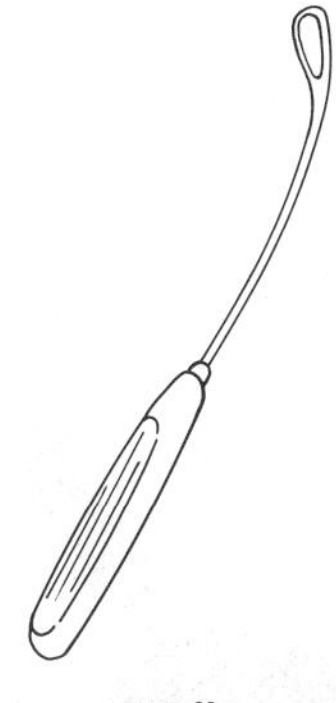
curette

Marie Curie

Pierre Curie

1934, and 1946–1950) and governor of Massachusetts (1935–1937) was known for his colorful leadership of Boston's Democratic political machine.

curl·i·cue also **curl·y·cue** (kûr′lĭ-kyo͞o′) *n.* A fancy twist or curl, such as a flourish made with a pen. [CURLY + CUE[1], tail and possibly CUE[3].] **—curl′i·cued** *adj.*

curl·ing (kûr′lĭng) *n. Sports.* A game originating in Scotland in which two four-person teams slide heavy, oblate stones toward the center of a circle at either end of a length of ice.

curling iron *n.* A rod-shaped metal implement used when heated to curl the hair.

curl paper *n.* A piece of soft paper on which a lock of hair is rolled up for curling.

curl·y (kûr′lē) *adj.* **-i·er, -i·est. 1.** Having curls. **2.** Having the tendency to curl. **3.** Having a wavy grain: *curly maple wood.* **—curl′i·ly** *adv.* **—curl′i·ness** *n.*

curl·y·cue (kûr′lĭ-kyo͞o′) *n.* Variant of **curlicue.**

curly top *n.* A viral disease of many plants, such as beets, beans, and tomatoes, characterized by curled leaves and stunted growth.

cur·mudg·eon (kər-mŭj′ən) *n.* An ill-tempered person full of resentment and stubborn notions. [Origin unknown.] **—cur·mudg′eon·ly** *adj.* **—cur·mudg′eon·ry** *n.*

WORD HISTORY: The etymology of the word *curmudgeon* has eluded us for at least two centuries, although some lexicographers have thought the solution was at hand, one to his embarrassment. When Samuel Johnson stated in his famous dictionary of 1755 that *curmugeon* "is a vicious manner of pronouncing *cœur méchant,* Fr. an unknown correspondent," he was giving credit to an anonymous writer for the statement that *curmudgeon* came from French *cœur,* "heart," and *méchant,* "evil." Another lexicographer, John Ash, following in Johnson's tracks though none too carefully, gave the etymology a bit differently in his dictionary of 1775: "from the French *cœur* unknown, and *mechant* a correspondent"; thus misinterpreting Johnson's attribution as a gloss for the French. Although its origin is unknown, *curmudgeon* has been around for some time, being first recorded in a work published in 1577.

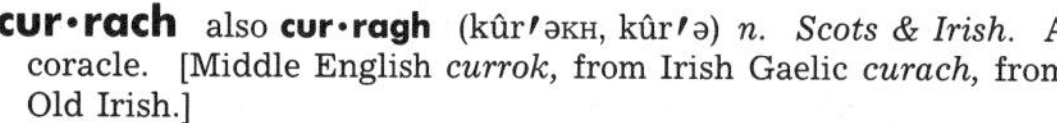

currycomb

cur·rach also **cur·ragh** (kûr′əкн, kûr′ə) *n. Scots & Irish.* A coracle. [Middle English *currok,* from Irish Gaelic *curach,* from Old Irish.]

cur·rant (kûr′ənt, kŭr′-) *n.* **1.** Any of various deciduous, spineless shrubs of the genus *Ribes,* native chiefly to the Northern Hemisphere and having flowers in racemes and edible, variously colored berries. **2.** The fruits of any of these plants, used for jams, jellies, desserts, or beverages. **3.** A small, seedless raisin of the Mediterranean region, used chiefly in baking. **4.** Any of several other plants or their fruit. [From Middle English *(raysons of) coraunte,* (raisins of) Corinth, currants, from Anglo-Norman *(raisins de) Corauntz,* from Latin *Corinthus,* from Greek *Korinthos.*]

cur·ren·cy (kûr′ən-sē, kŭr′-) *n., pl.* **-cies.** *Abbr.* **cur. 1.** Money in any form when in actual use as a medium of exchange, especially circulating paper money. **2.** Transmission from person to person as a medium of exchange; circulation: *coins now in currency.* **3.** General acceptance or use; prevalence: *the currency of a slang term.* [From Middle English *curraunt,* in circulation. See CURRENT.]

cur·rent (kûr′ənt, kŭr′-) *adj.* **1.** *Abbr.* **cur. a.** Belonging to the present time: *current events; current leaders.* **b.** Being in progress now: *current negotiations.* **2.** Passing from one to another; circulating: *current bills and coins.* **3.** Prevalent, especially at the present time: *current fashions.* See Synonyms at **prevailing. 4.** Running; flowing. **—current** *n.* **1.** A steady, smooth onward movement: *a current of air from a fan; a current of spoken words.* See Synonyms at **flow. 2.** The part of a body of liquid or gas that has a continuous onward movement: *rowed out into the river's swift current.* **3.** A general tendency, movement, or course. See Synonyms at **tendency. 4.** *Symbol* **i, I** *Electricity.* **a.** A flow of electric charge. **b.** The amount of electric charge flowing past a specified circuit point per unit time. [Middle English *curraunt,* from Old French *corant,* present participle of *courre,* to run, from Latin *currere.* See **kers-** in Appendix.] **—cur′rent·ly** *adv.* **—cur′rent·ness** *n.*

current assets *pl.n.* Cash or assets convertible into cash at short notice.

current density *n.* **1.** *Symbol* **j, J** *Electricity.* The ratio of the magnitude of current flowing in a conductor to the cross-sectional area perpendicular to the current flow. **2.** *Physics.* The number of subatomic particles per unit time crossing a unit area in a designated plane perpendicular to the direction of movement of the particles.

current ratio *n.* The arithmetic ratio of current assets to liabilities.

cur·ri·cle (kûr′ĭ-kəl) *n.* A light, open, two-wheeled carriage, drawn by two horses abreast. [From Latin *curriculum,* course, racing chariot, from *currere,* to run. See CURRENT.]

cur·ric·u·lum (kə-rĭk′yə-ləm) *n., pl.* **-la** (-lə) or **-lums. 1.** All the courses of study offered by an educational institution. **2.** A group of related courses, often in a special field of study: *the engineering curriculum.* —*attributive.* Often used to modify another noun: *curriculum development; curriculum enhancements.* [Latin, course, from *currere,* to run. See CURRENT.] **—cur·ric′u·lar** (-lər) *adj.*

cur·ric·u·lum vi·tae (kə-rĭk′yə-ləm vī′tē, vē′tī, kə-rĭk′o͞o-lo͝om wē′tī′) *n., pl.* **cur·ric·u·la vi·tae** (-lə). *Abbr.* **CV** A summary of one's education, professional history, and job qualifications, as for a prospective employer. [Latin, the race of life : *curriculum,* course + *vitae,* genitive of *vita,* life.]

cur·rie (kûr′ē, kŭr′ē) *n.* Variant of **curry[2].**

cur·ri·er (kûr′ē-ər, kŭr′-) *n.* One that prepares tanned hides for use. [Middle English *curreiour,* from Old French, from Latin *coriārius,* from *corium,* leather. See **sker-[1]** in Appendix.]

Cur·ri·er (kûr′ē-ər, kŭr′-), **Nathaniel.** 1813–1888. American lithographer who with his business partner James Merritt Ives produced more than 7,000 different prints illustrating American life and tradition, each signed "Currier & Ives."

cur·ri·er·y (kûr′ē-ə-rē, kŭr′-) *n., pl.* **-ies.** The trade, work, or shop of a currier.

cur·rish (kûr′ĭsh) *adj.* Snarling and bad-tempered. **—cur′rish·ly** *adv.*

cur·ry[1] (kûr′ē, kŭr′ē) *tr.v.* **-ried, -ry·ing, -ries. 1.** To groom (a horse) with a currycomb. **2.** To prepare (tanned hides) for use, as by soaking or coloring. **—*idiom.* curry favor.** To seek or gain favor by fawning or flattery. [Middle English *curreien,* from Anglo-Norman *curreier,* to arrange, curry, from Vulgar Latin **conrēdāre* : Latin *com-,* com- + Vulgar Latin **-rēdāre,* to make ready (of Germanic origin; see **reidh-** in Appendix).]

cur·ry[2] also **cur·rie** (kûr′ē, kŭr′ē) —*n., pl.* **-ries. 1.** Curry powder. **2.** A heavily spiced sauce or relish made with curry powder and eaten with rice, meat, fish, or other food. **3.** A dish seasoned with curry powder. —*tr.v.* **-ried, -ry·ing, -ries.** To season (food) with curry. [Tamil *kaṟi.*]

Cur·ry (kûr′ē, kŭr′ē), **John Steuart.** 1897–1946. American painter noted for his vigorous depictions of the rural American scene, such as *Tornado over Kansas* (1929).

cur·ry·comb (kûr′ē-kōm′, kŭr′-) *n.* A comb with metal teeth, used for grooming horses. **—currycomb** *tr.v.* **-combed, -comb·ing, -combs.** To groom with a currycomb.

curry powder *n.* A blended, pungent condiment prepared from cumin, coriander, turmeric, and other spices.

curse (kûrs) *n.* **1. a.** An appeal or prayer for evil or misfortune to befall someone or something. **b.** The evil or misfortune that comes in or as if in response to such an appeal: *bewailed the curse of ill health.* **2.** One that is accursed. **3.** A source or cause of evil; a scourge: *"Selfishness is the greatest curse of the human race"* (William Ewart Gladstone). **4.** A profane word or phrase; a swearword. **5.** *Ecclesiastical.* A censure, ban, or anathema. **6.** *Slang.* Menstruation. Used with *the.* **—curse** *v.* **cursed** or **curst** (kûrst), **curs·ing, curs·es.** —*tr.* **1.** To invoke evil or misfortune upon; damn. **2.** To swear at. **3.** To bring evil upon; afflict: *was cursed with crippling arthritis.* **4.** *Ecclesiastical.* To put under a ban or an anathema; excommunicate. —*intr.* To utter curses; swear. [Middle English, from Old English *curs.*] **—curs′er** *n.*

curs·ed (kûr′sĭd, kûrst) also **curst** (kûrst) *adj.* So wicked and detestable as to deserve to be cursed. **—curs′ed·ly** *adv.* **—curs′ed·ness** *n.*

cur·sive (kûr′sĭv) *adj.* Having the successive letters joined together: *cursive writing; a cursive style of type.* **—cursive** *n.* **1.** A cursive character or letter. **2.** A manuscript written in cursive characters. **3.** *Printing.* A type style that imitates handwriting. [French *(écriture) cursive,* cursive (handwriting), from Medieval Latin *(scripta) cursīva,* from Latin *cursus,* past participle of *currere,* to run. See **kers-** in Appendix.] **—cur′sive·ly** *adv.* **—cur′sive·ness** *n.*

cur·sor (kûr′sər) *n. Computer Science.* A bright, usually blinking, movable indicator on a display, marking the position at which a character can be entered, corrected, or deleted. [Middle English, runner, from Latin, from *cursus,* past participle of *currere,* to run. See **kers-** in Appendix.]

cur·so·ri·al (kûr-sôr′ē-əl, -sōr′-) *adj.* Adapted to or specialized for running: *cursorial birds; cursorial legs.* [From Late Latin *cursōrius,* of running. See CURSORY.]

cur·so·ry (kûr′sə-rē) *adj.* Performed with haste and scant attention to detail: *a cursory glance at the headlines.* See Synonyms at **superficial.** [Late Latin *cursōrius,* of running, from Latin *cursor, cursōr-,* runner. See CURSOR.] **—cur′so·ri·ly** *adv.* **—cur′so·ri·ness** *n.*

curst (kûrst) *v.* A past tense and a past participle of **curse.** **—curst** *adj.* Variant of **cursed.**

curt (kûrt) *adj.* **curt·er, curt·est. 1.** Rudely brief or abrupt, as in speech or manner. See Synonyms at **gruff. 2.** Using few words; terse. **3.** Having been shortened. [Middle English, short, brief, from Anglo-Norman, from Latin *curtus.* See **sker-[1]** in Appendix.] **—curt′ly** *adv.* **—curt′ness** *n.*

cur·tail (kər-tāl′) *tr.v.* **-tailed, -tail·ing, -tails.** To cut short; abbreviate. See Synonyms at **shorten.** [Middle English *curtailen,* to restrict, probably blend of Old French *courtauld,* docked; see CURTAL, and Middle English *taillen,* to cut (from Old French *tailler;* see TAILOR).] **—cur·tail′er** *n.* **—cur·tail′ment** *n.*

cur·tain (kûr′tn) *n.* **1.** Material that hangs in a window or other opening as a decoration, shade, or screen. **2.** Something that functions as or resembles a screen, cover, or barrier: *the curtain of mist before the mountain; a heavy curtain of artillery fire.* **3. a.** The movable screen or drape in a theater or hall that separates the stage from the auditorium or that serves as a backdrop. **b.** The rising or opening of a theater curtain at the beginning of a performance or an act. **c.** Curtain time. **d.** The fall or closing of a theater curtain at the end of a performance or an act. **e.** The concluding line, speech, or scene of a play or an act. **4.** The part of a rampart or parapet connecting two bastions or gates. **5.** *Architecture.* An enclosing wall connecting two towers or similar structures. **6. curtains.** *Slang.* **a.** The end. **b.** Absolute ruin: *"If the employee doesn't shape up, it's curtains"* (Business Week). **c.** Death. **—curtain** *tr.v.* **-tained, -tain·ing, -tains. 1.** To provide (something) with or as if with a curtain. **2.** To shut off (something) with or as if with a curtain. [Middle English *cortine,* from Old French, from Late Latin *cōrtīna,* from Latin *cōrs, cōrt-,* variant of *cohors,* court. See COURT.]

curtain call *n.* The appearance of performers or a performer at the end of a performance in response to applause.

curtain lecture *n.* A private reprimand given to a husband by his wife. [So called because it was originally given in a curtained bed.]

curtain rais·er (rā′zər) *n.* **1.** A short play or skit presented before the principal dramatic production. **2.** A preliminary event.

curtain speech *n.* A talk given in front of the curtain at the conclusion of a theatrical performance.

curtain time *n.* The time at which a theatrical performance begins or is scheduled to begin.

cur·tal (kûr′tl) *n. Archaic.* **1.** An animal with a docked tail. **2.** Something cut short or docked. **—curtal** *adj. Obsolete.* Cut short or docked. [Obsolete French *courtault,* from Old French, from *court,* short, from Latin *curtus.* See **sker-**[1] in Appendix.]

curtal ax *n. Archaic.* A cutlass. [By folk etymology from earlier *coutelace, curtelace,* cutlass, from Old French *coutelas.* See CUTLASS.]

cur·tate (kûr′tāt′) *adj.* Having been shortened; abbreviated. [Latin *curtātus,* past participle of *curtāre,* to shorten, from *curtus,* cut short. See CURT.]

cur·te·sy (kûr′tĭ-sē) *n., pl.* **-sies.** *Law.* The life tenure that by common law is held by a man over the property of his deceased wife if children with rights of inheritance were born during the marriage. [Middle English *curtesie.* See COURTESY.]

cur·ti·lage (kûr′tl-ĭj) *n. Law.* The enclosed area immediately surrounding a house or dwelling. [Middle English, from Old French *courtillage,* from *courtil,* diminutive of *cort,* court. See COURT.]

Cur·tis (kûr′tĭs), **Benjamin Robbins.** 1809–1874. American jurist who served as an associate justice of the U.S. Supreme Court (1851–1857). He resigned in protest after the Dred Scott decision.

Curtis, Charles. 1860–1936. Vice President of the United States (1929–1933) under Herbert Hoover.

Cur·tiss (kûr′tĭs), **Glenn Hammond.** 1878–1930. American aviation pioneer who developed the first airplane to complete a one-kilometer flight (1908), the first seaplane (1911), and the aileron (1911).

curt·sy or **curt·sey** (kûrt′sē) *—n., pl.* **-sies** or **-seys.** A gesture of respect or reverence made chiefly by women by bending the knees with one foot forward and lowering the body. *—intr.v.* **-sied, -sy·ing, -sies** or **-seyed, -sey·ing, -seys.** To make a curtsy. [Variant of COURTESY.]

cu·rule (kyo͝or′o͞ol′) *adj.* Privileged to sit in a curule chair; of superior rank. [Latin *curūlis,* of a curule chair, from *currus,* chariot, from *currere,* to run. See **kers-** in Appendix.]

curule chair *n.* A seat with heavy curved legs and no back, reserved for the use of the highest officials in ancient Rome. Also called *curule seat.*

cur·va·ceous (kûr-vā′shəs) *adj.* Having the curves of a full or voluptuous figure. **—cur·va′ceous·ly** *adv.* **—cur·va′ceous·ness** *n.*

cur·va·ture (kûr′və-cho͝or′, -chər) *n.* **1.** The act of curving or the state of being curved. **2.** *Mathematics.* **a.** The ratio of the change in the angle of a tangent that moves over a given arc to the length of the arc. **b.** The limit of this ratio as the length of the arc approaches zero. **c.** The reciprocal of the radius of a circle. **3.** *Medicine.* A curving or bending, especially an abnormal one: *curvature of the spine.* [Middle English, from Latin *curvātūra,* from *curvātus,* past participle of *curvāre,* to bend, from *curvus,* curved. See **sker-**[2] in Appendix.]

curve (kûrv) *n.* **1.a.** A line that deviates from straightness in a smooth, continuous fashion. **b.** A surface that deviates from planarity in a smooth, continuous fashion. **c.** Something characterized by such a line or surface, especially a rounded line or contour of the human body. **2.** A relatively smooth bend in a road or other course. **3.a.** A line representing data on a graph. **b.** A trend derived from or as if from such a graph. **4.** A graphic representation showing the relative performance of individuals as measured against each other, used especially as a method of grading students in which the assignment of grades is based on predetermined proportions of students. **5.** *Mathematics.* **a.** The graph of a function on a coordinate plane. **b.** The intersection of two surfaces in three dimensions. **6.** *Baseball.* A curve ball. **7.** *Slang.* A trick or deception. **—curve** *v.* **curved, curv·ing, curves.** *—intr.* To move in or take the shape of a curve: *The path curves around the lake.* *—tr.* **1.** To cause to curve. See Synonyms at **bend**[1]. **2.** *Baseball.* To pitch a curve ball to. **3.** To grade (students, for example) on a curve. [From Middle English, curved, from Latin *curvus.* See **sker-**[2] in Appendix.] **—curv′ed·ness** *n.* **—curv′y** *adj.*

curve ball or **curve·ball** (kûrv′bôl′) *n. Baseball.* A pitched ball that veers or breaks to the left when thrown with the right hand and to the right when thrown with the left hand. ***—idiom.*** **pitch** (or **throw**) **(someone) a curve ball.** *Slang.* **1.** To mislead; deceive. **2.** To cause to be surprised, especially unpleasantly so.

cur·vet (kûr-vĕt′) *n.* A light leap by a horse, in which both hind legs leave the ground just before the forelegs are set down. **—curvet** *v.* **-vet·ted, -vet·ting, -vets** or **-vet·ed, -vet·ing, -vets.** *—intr.* **1.** To leap in a curvet. **2.** To prance; frolic. *—tr.* To cause to leap in a curvet. [Italian *corvetta,* from Old Italian, from Old French *courbette,* from *courber,* to curve, from Latin *curvāre,* from *curvus,* curved. See **sker-**[2] in Appendix.]

cur·vi·lin·e·ar (kûr′və-lĭn′ē-ər) also **cur·vi·lin·e·al** (-əl) *adj.* Formed, bounded, or characterized by curved lines. [Latin *curvus,* curved; see CURVE + LINEAR.] **—cur′vi·lin′e·ar′i·ty** (-ē-ăr′ĭ-tē) *n.* **—cur′vi·lin′e·ar·ly** *adv.*

Cur·zon (kûr′zən), **George Nathaniel.** First Marquis Curzon of Kedleston. 1859–1925. British politician who served as viceroy and governor-general of India (1898–1905) and as secretary of state for foreign affairs (1919–1924).

Cus·co (ko͞o′skō). See **Cuzco.**

cus·cus (kŭs′kəs) *n.* Any of several nocturnal marsupials of the genus *Phalanger* of New Guinea, Australia, and adjacent islands, having large eyes, small ears, a pointed snout, and a long, prehensile tail. [New Latin, probably from a New Guinean word.]

cu·sec (kyo͞o′sĕk′) *n.* A volumetric unit for measuring the flow of liquids, equal to one cubic foot per second. [CU(BIC) + SEC(OND)[1].]

Cush[1] (kŭsh, ko͝osh). In the Old Testament, the oldest son of Ham.

Cush[2] also **Kush** (kŭsh, ko͝osh). **1.** An ancient region of northeast Africa where the biblical descendants of Cush settled. It is often identified with Ethiopia. **2.** An ancient kingdom of Nubia in northern Sudan. It flourished from the 11th century B.C. to the 4th century A.D., when its capital fell to the Ethiopians.

cu·shaw (kə-shô′, ko͞o′shô′) *n.* Any of several kinds of winter squash *(Cucurbita mixta)* having a curved neck. [Origin unknown.]

Cush·ing (ko͝osh′ĭng), **Caleb.** 1800–1879. American lawyer, politician, and diplomat who as special envoy to China (1843–1845) negotiated a treaty that opened five Chinese ports to American trade.

Cushing, Harvey Williams. 1869–1939. American neurologist noted for his study of the brain and the pituitary gland.

Cushing, William. 1732–1810. American jurist who served as an associate justice of the U.S. Supreme Court (1789–1810).

Cush·ing's disease (ko͝osh′ĭngz) *n.* The form of Cushing's syndrome involving the pituitary gland. [After Harvey Williams CUSHING.]

Cushing's syndrome *n.* A syndrome caused by an increased production of ACTH from a tumor of the adrenal cortex or of the anterior lobe of the pituitary gland, or by excessive intake of glucocorticoids. It is characterized by obesity and weakening of the muscles. [After Harvey Williams CUSHING.]

cush·ion (ko͝osh′ən) *n.* **1.** A pad or pillow with a soft filling, used for resting, reclining, or kneeling. **2.** Something resilient used as a rest, support, or shock absorber. **3.** A mat placed or attached beneath carpeting to provide softness and increase durability. **4.** A padlike body part. **5.** *Games.* The rim bordering the playing surface of a billiard table. **6.** A pillow used in lacemaking. **7.** Something that mitigates or relieves an adverse effect: *extra funds serving as a cushion against future inflation.* **—cushion** *tr.v.* **-ioned, -ion·ing, -ions. 1.** To provide with a cushion: *cushion a bench.* **2.** To place or seat on a cushion. **3.** To cover or hide (something) with or as if with a cushion. **4.** To protect from impacts or other disturbing effects: *an automobile suspension that cushions the ride.* **5.** To mitigate the effects of; absorb the shock of: *cushion a blow.* [Middle English *cushin,* from Old French *coussin,* from Vulgar Latin **coxīnum,* from Latin *coxa,* hip.] **—cush′ion·y** *adj.*

Cush·it·ic (ko͝o-shĭt′ĭk) *n.* A branch of the Afro-Asiatic language family spoken in Somalia, Ethiopia, and northern Kenya and including Beja, Orono, and Somali. **—Cush·it′ic** *adj.*

cush·y (ko͝osh′ē) *adj.* **-i·er, -i·est.** *Informal.* Making few demands; comfortable: *a cushy job.* [Origin unknown.] **—cush′i·ly** *adv.* **—cush′i·ness** *n.*

WORD HISTORY: Since *cushy* has such an informal, breezy, American ring, it is difficult to believe that it is an import, as some etymologists claim. Members of the British army in India are supposed to have picked up the Anglo-Indian version of the Hindi word *k̲h̲ūsh,* meaning "pleasant," to which the suffix *-y,* as in *empty* and *sexy,* was added, thus forming a new English word. *Cushy,* however, is actually first recorded in a letter from the European battlefront during World War I. This fact, in conjunction with our inability to find an Anglo-Indian source, casts some doubt on the Hindi or Anglo-Indian origin of *cushy.* Two other possibilities are that *cushy* is a shortening of *cushion* with the *-y*

ă pat	oi boy
ā pay	ou out
âr care	o͝o took
ä father	o͞o boot
ĕ pet	ŭ cut
ē be	ûr urge
ĭ pit	th thin
ī pie	*th* this
îr pier	hw which
ŏ pot	zh vision
ō toe	ə about, item
ô paw	♦ regionalism

Stress marks: **′** (primary); ′ (secondary), as in **dictionary** (dĭk′shə-nĕr′ē)

CURRENCY TABLE: LISTED BY COUNTRY

COUNTRY	BASIC UNIT	SUBUNIT
Afghanistan	afghani	100 puls
Albania	lek	100 qindarka
Algeria	dinar	100 centimes
Andorra	peseta	100 centimos
Angola	kwanza	100 lwei
Argentina	austral	100 centavos
Australia	dollar	100 cents
Austria	schilling	100 groschen
Bahamas	dollar	100 cents
Bahrain	dinar	1000 fils
Bangladesh	taka	100 paisas
Barbados	dollar	100 cents
Belgium	franc	100 centimes
Belize	dollar	100 cents
Benin	franc	100 centimes
Bhutan	ngultrum	100 chetrums
Bolivia	boliviano	100 centavos
Botswana	pula	100 thebe
Brazil	cruzeiro	100 centavos
Brunei	dollar	100 cents
Bulgaria	lev	100 stotinki
Burkina Faso	franc	100 centimes
Burma	kyat	100 pyas
Burundi	franc	100 centimes
Cambodia	riel	100 sen
Cameroon	franc	100 centimes
Canada	dollar	100 cents
Cape Verde	escudo	100 centavos
Cayman Islands	dollar	100 cents
Central African Republic	franc	100 centimes
Chad	franc	100 centimes
Chile	peso	100 centesimos
China	yuan	10 jiao
Colombia	peso	100 centavos
Comoros	franc	100 centimes
Congo	franc	100 centimes
Costa Rica	colon	100 centimos
Cuba	peso	100 centavos
Cyprus	pound	100 cents
Czechoslovakia	koruna	100 halers
Denmark	krone	100 öre
Djibouti	franc	100 centimes
Dominica	dollar	100 cents
Dominican Republic	peso	100 centavos
Ecuador	sucre	100 centavos
Egypt	pound	100 piasters
El Salvador	colon	100 centavos
Equatorial Guinea	ekpwele	
Ethiopia	birr	100 cents
Fiji	dollar	100 cents
Finland	markka	100 penni
France	franc	100 centimes
Gabon	franc	100 centimes
Gambia	dalasi	100 butut
Germany	deutsche mark	100 pfennigs
Ghana	cedi	100 pesewa
Greece	drachma	100 lepta
Grenada	dollar	100 cents
Guatemala	quetzal	100 centavos
Guinea	franc	100 centimes
Guinea-Bissau	peso	100 centavos
Guyana	dollar	100 cents
Haiti	gourde	100 centimes
Honduras	lempira	100 centavos
Hong Kong	dollar	100 cents
Hungary	forint	100 fillér
Iceland	krona	100 aurar
India	rupee	100 paise
Indonesia	rupiah	100 sen
Iran	rial	100 dinars
Iraq	dinar	1000 fils
Ireland	pound	100 pence
Israel	shekel	100 agorot
Italy	lira	100 centesimi
Ivory Coast	franc	100 centimes
Jamaica	dollar	100 cents
Japan	yen	100 sen
Jordan	dinar	1000 fils
Kenya	shilling	100 cents
Kiribati	dollar	100 cents
Kuwait	dinar	1000 fils
Laos	kip	100 at
Lebanon	pound	100 piasters
Lesotho	loti	100 lisente
Liberia	dollar	100 cents
Libya	dinar	100 dirhams
Liechtenstein	franc	100 centimes
Luxembourg	franc	100 centimes
Macao	pataca	100 avos
Madagascar	franc	100 centimes
Malawi	kwacha	100 tambala
Malaysia	ringgit	100 sen
Maldives	rufiyaa	100 larees
Mali	franc	100 centimes
Malta	lira	100 cents
Mauritania	ouguiya	5 khoums
Mauritius	rupee	100 cents
Mexico	peso	100 centavos
Monaco	franc	100 centimes
Mongolia	tugrik	100 mongo
Morocco	dirham	100 centimes
Mozambique	metical	100 centavos
Namibia	rand	100 cents
Nauru	dollar	100 cents
Nepal	rupee	100 paisas
Netherlands	guilder	100 cents
Netherlands Antilles	guilder	100 cents
New Zealand	dollar	100 cents
Nicaragua	cordoba	100 centavos
Niger	franc	100 centimes
Nigeria	naira	100 kobos
North Korea	won	100 chon
Norway	krone	100 öre
Oman	riyal-omani	1000 baiza
Pakistan	rupee	100 paisas
Panama	balboa	100 centesimos
Papua New Guinea	kina	100 toea
Paraguay	guarani	100 centimos
Peru	inti	
Philippines	peso	100 centavos
Poland	zloty	100 groszy
Portugal	escudo	100 centavos
Qatar	riyal	100 dirhams
Romania	leu	100 bani
Rwanda	franc	100 centimes
Saint Lucia	dollar	100 cents
Saint Vincent and the Grenadines	dollar	100 cents
San Marino	lira	100 centesimi
São Tomé and Príncipe	dobra	100 centavos
Saudi Arabia	riyal	20 qurush
Senegal	franc	100 centimes
Seychelles	rupee	100 cents
Sierra Leone	leone	100 cents
Singapore	dollar	100 cents
Solomon Islands	dollar	100 cents
Somalia	shilling	100 cents
South Africa	rand	100 cents
South Korea	won	100 chon
Spain	peseta	100 centimos
Sri Lanka	rupee	100 cents
Sudan	pound	100 piasters
Suriname	guilder	100 cents
Swaziland	lilangeni	100 cents
Sweden	krona	100 öre
Switzerland	franc	100 centimes
Syria	pound	100 piasters
Taiwan	dollar	100 cents
Tanzania	shilling	100 cents
Thailand	baht	100 satang
Togo	franc	100 centimes
Tonga	pa'anga	100 seniti
Trinidad and Tobago	dollar	100 cents
Tunisia	dinar	1000 millimes
Turkey	lira	100 kurus
Tuvalu	dollar	100 cents
Uganda	shilling	100 cents
Union of Soviet Socialist Republics	ruble	100 kopecks
United Arab Emirates	dirham	1000 fils
United Kingdom	pound	100 pence
United States	dollar	100 cents
Uruguay	peso	100 centesimos
Vanuatu	vatu	100 centimes
Vatican City	lira	100 centesimi
Venezuela	bolivar	100 centimos
Vietnam	dong	10 hao
Western Samoa	tala	100 sene
Yemen	dinar	100 fils
Yugoslavia	dinar	100 para
Zaire	zaire	100 makuta
Zambia	kwacha	100 ngwee
Zimbabwe	dollar	100 cents

CURRENCY TABLE: LISTED BY BASIC UNIT (BOLD) AND SUBUNIT

UNIT	COUNTRY
afghani	Afghanistan
agora	Israel
at	Laos
aurar	(pl. of *eyrir*)
austral	Argentina
avo	Macao
baht	Thailand
baiza	Oman
balboa	Panama
ban	Romania
birr	Ethiopia
bolivar	Venezuela
boliviano	Bolivia
butut	Gambia
cedi	Ghana
cent	Australia
	Bahamas
	Barbados
	Belize
	Brunei
	Canada
	Cayman Islands
	Cyprus
	Dominica
	Ethiopia
	Fiji
	Grenada
	Guyana
	Hong Kong
	Jamaica
	Kenya
	Kiribati
	Liberia
	Malta
	Mauritius
	Namibia
	Nauru
	Netherlands
	Netherlands Antilles
	New Zealand
	Saint Lucia
	Saint Vincent and the Grenadines
	Seychelles
	Sierra Leone
	Singapore
	Solomon Islands
	Somalia
	South Africa
	Sri Lanka
	Suriname
	Swaziland
	Taiwan
	Tanzania
	Trinidad and Tobago
	Tuvalu
	Uganda
	United States
	Zimbabwe
centavo	Argentina
	Bolivia
	Brazil
	Cape Verde
	Colombia
	Cuba
	Dominican Republic
	Ecuador
	El Salvador
	Guatemala
	Guinea-Bissau
	Honduras
	Mexico
	Mozambique
	Nicaragua
	Philippines
	Portugal
	São Tomé and Príncipe
centesimo	Chile
	Italy
	Panama
	San Marino
	Vatican City
centime	Algeria
	Belgium
	Benin
	Burkina Faso
	Burundi
	Cameroon
	Central African Republic
	Chad
	Comoros
	Congo
	Djibouti
	France
	Gabon
	Guinea
	Haiti
	Ivory Coast
	Liechtenstein
	Luxembourg
	Madagascar
	Mali
	Monaco
	Morocco
	Niger
	Rwanda
	Senegal
	Switzerland
	Togo
	Vanuatu
centimo	Andorra
	Costa Rica
	Paraguay
	Spain
	Venezuela
chetrum	Bhutan
chon	North Korea
	South Korea
colon	Costa Rica
	El Salvador
cordoba	Nicaragua
cruzeiro	Brazil
dalasi	Gambia
deutsche mark	Germany
dinar	Algeria
	Bahrain
	Iraq
	Jordan
	Kuwait
	Libya
	Tunisia
	Yemen
	Yugoslavia
dinar	Iran
dirham	Morocco
	United Arab Emirates
dirham	Libya
	Qatar
dobra	São Tomé and Príncipe
dollar	Australia
	Bahamas
	Barbados
	Belize
	Brunei
	Canada
	Cayman Islands
	Dominica
	Fiji
	Grenada
	Guyana
	Hong Kong
	Jamaica
	Kiribati
	Liberia
	Nauru
	New Zealand
	Saint Lucia
	Saint Vincent and the Grenadines
	Singapore
	Solomon Islands
	Taiwan
	Trinidad and Tobago
	Tuvalu
	United States
	Zimbabwe
dong	Vietnam
drachma	Greece
ekpwele	Equatorial Guinea
escudo	Cape Verde
	Portugal
eyrir	Iceland
fillér	Hungary
fils	Bahrain
	Iraq
	Jordan
	Kuwait
	United Arab Emirates
	Yemen
forint	Hungary
franc	Belgium
	Benin
	Burkina Faso
	Burundi
	Cameroon
	Central African Republic
	Chad
	Comoros
	Congo
	Djibouti
	France
	Gabon
	Guinea
	Ivory Coast
	Liechtenstein
	Luxembourg
	Madagascar
	Mali
	Monaco
	Niger
	Rwanda
	Senegal
	Switzerland
	Togo
gourde	Haiti
groschen	Austria
grosz	Poland
guarani	Paraguay
guilder	Netherlands
	Netherlands Antilles
	Suriname
haler	Czechoslovakia
hao	Vietnam
inti	Peru
jiao	China
khoum	Mauritania
kina	Papua New Guinea
kip	Laos
kobo	Nigeria
kopeck	U.S.S.R.
koruna	Czechoslovakia
krona	Iceland
	Sweden
krone	Denmark
	Norway
kurus	Turkey
kwacha	Malawi
	Zambia
kwanza	Angola
kyat	Burma
laree	Maldives
lek	Albania
lempira	Honduras
leone	Sierra Leone
lepton	Greece
leu	Romania
lev	Bulgaria
likuta	Zaire
lilangeni	Swaziland
lira	Italy
	Malta
	San Marino
	Turkey
	Vatican City
lisente	(pl. of *sente*)
loti	Lesotho
lwei	Angola
makuta	(pl. of *likuta*)
markka	Finland
metical	Mozambique
millime	Tunisia
mongo	Mongolia
naira	Nigeria
ngultrum	Bhutan
ngwee	Zambia
öre	Denmark
	Norway
	Sweden
ouguiya	Mauritania
pa'anga	Tonga
paisa	Bangladesh
	India
	Nepal
	Pakistan
para	Yugoslavia
pataca	Macao
penni	Finland
penny	Ireland
	United Kingdom
peseta	Andorra
	Spain
pesewa	Ghana
peso	Chile
	Colombia
	Cuba
	Dominican Republic
	Guinea-Bissau
	Mexico
	Philippines
	Uruguay
pfennig	Germany
piaster	Egypt
	Lebanon
	Sudan
	Syria
pound	Cyprus
	Egypt
	Ireland
	Lebanon
	Sudan
	Syria
	United Kingdom
pul	Afghanistan
pula	Botswana
pya	Burma
qindarka	Albania
quetzal	Guatemala
qurush	Saudi Arabia
rand	Namibia
	South Africa
rial	Iran
riel	Cambodia
ringgit	Malaysia
riyal	Qatar
	Saudi Arabia
riyal-omani	Oman
ruble	U.S.S.R.
rufiyaa	Maldives
rupee	India
	Mauritius
	Nepal
	Pakistan
	Seychelles
	Sri Lanka
rupiah	Indonesia
satang	Thailand
schilling	Austria
sen	Cambodia
	Indonesia
	Japan
	Malaysia
sene	Western Samoa
seniti	Tonga
sente	Lesotho
shekel	Israel
shilling	Kenya
	Somalia
	Tanzania
	Uganda
stotinka	Bulgaria
sucre	Ecuador
taka	Bangladesh
tala	Western Samoa
tambala	Malawi
thebe	Botswana
toea	Papua New Guinea
tugrik	Mongolia
vatu	Vanuatu
won	North Korea
	South Korea
yen	Japan
yuan	China
zaire	Zaire
zloty	Poland

suffix or that it is a borrowing of French *couchée,* "lying down; a bed."

cusk (kŭsk) *n., pl.* **cusk** or **cusks. 1.** A food fish *(Brosme brosme)* of North Atlantic coastal waters that is related to the cod. **2.** See **burbot.** [Probably alteration of *tusk,* a kind of codfish, perhaps from Norwegian dialectal *tusk,* variant of Norwegian *torsk, tosk,* from Old Norse *thorskr.* See **ters-** in Appendix.]

cusk eel *n.* Any of several bottom-dwelling, eellike, chiefly marine fishes of the family Ophidiidae.

cusp (kŭsp) *n.* **1.** A point or pointed end. **2.** *Anatomy.* **a.** A pointed or rounded projection on the chewing surface of a tooth. **b.** A triangular fold or flap of a heart valve. **3.** *Mathematics.* A point at which a curve crosses itself and at which the two tangents to the curve coincide. **4.** *Architecture.* The point of intersection of two ornamental arcs or curves, such as the inner points of a trefoil. **5.** *Astronomy.* Either point of a crescent moon. **6.** A transitional point or time, as between two astrological signs. [Latin *cuspis,* point.]

cus·pate (kŭs′pāt′) also **cus·pat·ed** (-pā′tĭd) *adj.* **1.** Having a cusp. **2.** Shaped like a cusp.

cus·pid (kŭs′pĭd) *n.* See **canine** (sense 2). [From Latin *cuspis, cuspid-,* point.]

cus·pi·date (kŭs′pĭ-dāt′) also **cus·pi·dat·ed** (-dā′tĭd) *adj.* **1.** Having a cusp. **2.** *Biology.* Terminating in or tipped with a sharp, firm point: *a cuspidate leaf apex.* [Latin *cuspidātus,* past participle of *cuspidāre,* to make pointed, from *cuspis, cuspid-,* point.]

cus·pi·da·tion (kŭs′pĭ-dā′shən) *n. Architecture.* Decoration with cusps.

cus·pi·dor (kŭs′pĭ-dôr′, -dōr′) *n.* A spittoon. [Portuguese, from *cuspir,* to spit, from Latin *cōnspuere,* to spit upon : *com-,* intensive pref.; see COM– + *spuere,* to spit.]

George Armstrong Custer
Photographed by Mathew Brady

cuss (kŭs) *Informal. intr. & tr.v.* **cussed, cuss·ing, cuss·es.** To curse or curse at. **—cuss** *n.* **1.** A curse. **2.** An odd or perverse creature. [Alteration of CURSE.]

cuss·ed (kŭs′ĭd) *adj. Informal.* **1.** Perverse; stubborn. **2.** Cursed. **—cuss′ed·ly** *adv.* **—cuss′ed·ness** *n.*

cus·tard (kŭs′tərd) *n.* A dish consisting of milk, eggs, flavoring, and sometimes sugar, boiled or baked until set. [Middle English *crustade, custard,* a pie with a crust, probably from Old Provençal *croustado.* See CROUSTADE.] **—cus′tard·y** *adj.*

custard apple *n.* **1.** Any of several tropical American trees of the genus *Annona,* especially *A. reticulata,* having large, nearly heart-shaped edible fruits with white to yellowish flesh. **2.** The fruit of any of these trees. Also called *bullock's heart.* [So called because its pulp resembles custard.]

Cus·ter (kŭs′tər), **George Armstrong.** 1839–1876. American soldier. A brigadier general at age 23, he was killed and his troops annihilated by Sioux and Cheyenne warriors led by Sitting Bull and Crazy Horse at Little Bighorn.

cus·to·di·al (kŭ-stō′dē-əl) *adj.* **1.** Of or relating to the work of guarding or maintaining: *the custodial duties of a security guard.* **2.a.** Having custody, especially of a child: *"children whose custodial parent has remarried"* (American Demographics). **b.** Of or relating to child custody: *custodial households.* **3.** Marked by care and supervision rather than efforts to cure: *custodial treatment of terminal patients.*

cus·to·di·an (kŭ-stō′dē-ən) *n.* **1.** One that has charge of something; a caretaker: *the custodian of a minor child's estate; the custodian of an absentee landlord's property.* **2.** A janitor: *worked nights as custodian of a high school.* **—cus·to′di·an·ship′** *n.*

cus·to·dy (kŭs′tə-dē) *n., pl.* **-dies. 1.** The act or right of guarding, especially such a right granted by a court: *an adult who was given custody of the child.* **2.** Care, supervision, and control exerted by one in charge. See Synonyms at **care. 3.** The state of being detained or held under guard, especially by the police: *took the robbery suspect into custody.* [Middle English *custodie,* from Latin *custōdia,* from *custōs, custōd-,* guard.]

cus·tom (kŭs′təm) *n.* **1.** A practice followed by people of a particular group or region. **2.** A habitual practice of a person: *my custom of reading a little before sleep.* See Synonyms at **habit. 3.** *Law.* A common tradition or usage so long established that it has the force or validity of law. **4.a.** Habitual patronage, as of a store. **b.** Habitual customers; patrons. **5. customs.** *(used with a sing. verb).* **a.** A duty or tax imposed on imported and, less commonly, exported goods. **b.** The governmental agency authorized to collect these duties. **c.** The procedure for inspecting goods and baggage entering a country. **6.** Tribute, service, or rent paid by a feudal tenant to a lord. **—custom** *adj.* **1.** Made to order. **2.** Specializing in the making or selling of made-to-order goods: *a custom tailor.* [Middle English *custume,* from Old French *costume,* from Latin *cōnsuētūdō, cōnsuētūdin-,* from *cōnsuētus,* past participle of *cōnsuēscere,* to accustom : *com-,* intensive pref.; see COM– + *suēscere,* to become accustomed; see **s(w)e-** in Appendix.]

cus·tom·a·ble (kŭs′tə-mə-bəl) *adj.* Subject to tariffs: *customable imports.*

cus·tom·ar·y (kŭs′tə-mĕr′ē) *adj.* **1.** Commonly practiced, used, or encountered; usual. See Synonyms at **usual. 2.** Based on custom or tradition rather than written law or contract. **—cus′tom·ar′i·ly** (-mâr′ə-lē) *adv.* **—cus′tom·ar′i·ness** *n.*

cus·tom-built (kŭs′təm-bĭlt′) *adj.* Built according to the specifications of the buyer.

cus·tom·er (kŭs′tə-mər) *n.* **1.** One that buys goods or services. **2.** *Informal.* An individual with whom one must deal: *a tough customer.*

cus·tom·house (kŭs′təm-hous′) also **cus·toms·house** (-təmz-) *n. Abbr.* **c.h., C.H.** A governmental building or office where customs are collected and ships are cleared for entering or leaving the country.

cus·tom·ize (kŭs′tə-mīz′) *tr.v.* **-ized, -iz·ing, -iz·es.** To make or alter to individual or personal specifications: *customize a van.* **—cus′tom·i·za′tion** (-ĭ-zā′shən) *n.* **—cus′tom·iz′er** *n.*

cus·tom-made (kŭs′təm-mād′) *adj.* Made according to the specifications of an individual purchaser.

cus·toms·house (kŭs′təmz-hous′) *n.* Variant of **customhouse.**

customs union *n.* An international association organized to eliminate customs restrictions on goods exchanged between member nations and to establish a uniform tariff policy toward nonmember nations.

♦ **cut** (kŭt) *v.* **cut, cut·ting, cuts.** *—tr.* **1.** To penetrate with a sharp edge; strike a narrow opening in. **2.** To separate into parts with or as if with a sharp-edged instrument; sever: *cut cloth with scissors.* **3.** To sever the edges or ends of; shorten: *cut one's hair.* **4.** To reap; harvest: *cut grain.* **5.** To fell by sawing; hew. **6.** To have (a new tooth) grow through the gums. **7.** To form or shape by severing or incising: *a doll that was cut from paper.* **8.a.** To form by penetrating, probing, or digging: *cut a trench.* **b.** To exhibit the appearance or give the impression of: *cuts a fine figure on the dance floor.* **9.** To separate from a main body; detach: *cut a limb from a tree.* **10.** To discharge from a group or number: *had to cut three players from the team.* **11.** To pass through or across; cross: *a sailboat cutting the water.* **12.** *Games.* To divide (a deck of cards) into two parts, as in completing a shuffle or in exposing a card at random. **13.** To reduce the size, extent, or duration of; curtail or shorten: *cut a payroll; cut a budget; cut the cooking time in half.* **14.** To lessen the strength of; dilute: *cut whiskey with distilled water.* **15.** To dissolve by breaking down the fat of: *Soap cuts grease.* **16.** To injure the feelings of; hurt keenly. **17.** To refuse to speak to or recognize; snub: *She cut me dead at the party.* **18.** To fail to attend purposely: *cut a class.* **19.** *Informal.* To cease; stop: *cut the noise; cut an engine.* **20.** *Sports.* To strike (a ball) so that it spins in a reverse direction. **21.a.** To perform: *cut a caper.* **b.** To make out and issue: *cut a check to cover travel expenses.* **22.** *Slang.* To be able to manage; handle successfully: *He couldn't cut the long hours anymore.* **23.** To stop filming (a movie scene). **24.a.** To record a performance on (a phonograph record or other medium). **b.** To make a recording of. **25.** To edit (film or recording tape). *—intr.* **1.** To make an incision or a separation: *Cut along the dotted line.* **2.** To allow incision or severing: *Butter cuts easily.* **3.** To function as a sharp-edged instrument. **4.** To grow through the gums. Used of teeth. **5.** To penetrate injuriously. **6.** To change direction abruptly: *Cut to the left at the next intersection.* **7.** To go directly and often hastily: *cut across a field.* **8.** *Games.* To divide a pack of cards into two parts, especially in order to make a chance decision or selection. **9.** To make an abrupt change of image or sound, as in filming: *cut from one shot to another.* **—cut** *n.* **1.** The act of cutting. **2.** The result of cutting, especially an opening or wound made by a sharp edge. **3.** A part that has been cut from a main body: *a cut of beef; a cut of cloth.* **4.** A passage made by digging or probing. **5.** The elimination or removal of a part: *a cut in a speech.* **6.** A reduction: *a cut in salary.* **7.** The style in which a garment is cut: *a suit of traditional cut.* **8.** *Informal.* A portion of profits or earnings; a share. **9.** A wounding remark; an insult. **10.** An unexcused absence, as from school or a class. **11.** A step in a scale of value or quality; degree: *a cut above the average.* **12.** *Printing.* **a.** An engraved block or plate. **b.** A print made from such a block. **13.** *Sports.* A stroke that causes a ball to spin in a reverse direction. **14.** *Baseball.* A swing of a bat. **15.** *Games.* The act of dividing a deck of cards into two parts, as before dealing. **16.** One of the objects used in drawing lots. **17.** An abrupt change of image or sound, as between shots in a film. **18.** A movie at a given stage in its editing: *approved the final cut for distribution.* **19.** A single selection of music from a recording, especially a phonograph recording. ***—phrasal verbs.* cut back. 1.** To shorten by cutting; prune. **2.** To reduce or decrease: *cut back production.* **cut down. 1.** To kill or strike down. **2.** To alter by removing extra or additional fittings: *cut down a car for racing.* **3.** To reduce the amount taken or used: *cutting down on one's intake of rich foods.* **cut in. 1.** To move into a line of people or things out of turn. **2.** To interrupt: *During the debate my opponent kept cutting in.* **3.** To interrupt a dancing couple in order to dance with one of them. **4.** To connect or become connected into an electrical circuit. **5.** To mix in with or as if with cutting motions: *Measure out the flour and use a pair of knives to cut the shortening in.* **6.** To include, especially among those profiting. **cut off. 1.** To separate from others; isolate. **2.** To stop suddenly; discontinue. **3.** To shut off; bar. **4.** To interrupt the course or passage of: *The infielder cut off the throw to the plate.* **5.** To interrupt or break the line of communication of: *The telephone operator cut us off.* **6.** To disinherit: *cut their heirs off without a cent.* **cut out. 1.** To remove by or as if by cutting. **2.** To form or shape by or as if by cutting. **3.** To take the place of; supplant. **4.** To suit or fit by nature: *I'm not cut out to be a hero.* **5.** To assign beforehand or by necessity; pre-

ă pat	oi boy
ā pay	ou out
âr care	o͝o took
ä father	o͞o boot
ĕ pet	ŭ cut
ē be	ûr urge
ĭ pit	th thin
ī pie	*th* this
îr pier	hw which
ŏ pot	zh vision
ō toe	ə about, item
ô paw	♦ regionalism

Stress marks: **′** (primary); ′ (secondary), as in **dictionary** (dĭk′shə-nĕr′ē)

determine: *We've got our work cut out for us.* **6.** To deprive: *felt cut out of all the fun.* **7.** To stop; cease. **8.** *Informal.* To depart hastily. **9.** *Chiefly Southern U.S.* To turn off (a light or television set). **cut up.** *Informal.* **1.** To behave in a playful, comic, or boisterous way; clown. **2.** To criticize severely. —***idioms.*** **cut a fat hog.** *Texas.* To take on more than one is able to accomplish: *"Boy, has he cut a fat hog, as they say down home"* (Hughes Rudd). **cut corners.** To do something in the easiest or most inexpensive way. **cut down to size.** To deflate the self-importance of. **cut loose.** To speak or act without restraint: *cut loose with a string of curses.* **cut no ice.** To make no effect or impression: *Your objections will cut no ice with management.* **cut (one's) losses.** To withdraw from a losing situation. **cut (one's) teeth on.** To learn or do as a beginner or at the start of one's career. **cut short.** To stop before the end; abbreviate. [Middle English *cutten.*] —**cut′ta·ble** *adj.*

cut-and-dried (kŭt′n-drīd′) also **cut-and-dry** (-drī′) *adj.* **1.** Prepared and arranged in advance; settled. **2.** Ordinary; routine: *cut-and-dried dialogue.*

cu·ta·ne·ous (kyo͞o-tā′nē-əs) *adj.* Of, relating to, or affecting the skin. [From New Latin *cutāneus,* back-formation from Late Latin *intercutāneus* and *subcutāneus,* both from Latin *cutis,* skin. See **(s)keu-** in Appendix.] —**cu·ta′ne·ous·ly** *adv.*

cut·a·way (kŭt′ə-wā′) *n.* **1.** A man's formal daytime coat, with front edges sloping diagonally from the waist and forming tails at the back. **2.** A brief shot that interrupts the visual continuity of the main action of a film, often to depict related matter or supposedly concurrent action. **3.** A model or diagram of an object with part of the outer layer removed so as to reveal the interior. **4.** *Sports.* A back dive in which the diver turns in the air so as to face the board before entering the water.

cut·back (kŭt′băk′) *n.* **1.** A decrease; a curtailment: *"The political effects of food cutbacks could be devastating"* (New York Times). **2.** A sharp reversal of direction, as of a ball carrier in football.

cutch (kŭch) *n.* See **catechu** (sense 1). [Malay *kachu,* of Dravidian origin.]

cute (kyo͞ot) *adj.* **cut·er, cut·est. 1.** Delightfully pretty or dainty. **2.** Obviously contrived to charm; precious: "[He] *mugs so ferociously he kills the humor—it's an insufferably cute performance"* (David Ansen). **3.** Shrewd; clever. [Short for ACUTE.] —**cute′ly** *adv.* —**cute′ness** *n.*

WORD HISTORY: *Cute* is a good example of how a shortened form of a word can take on a life of its own, developing a sense that dissociates it from the longer word from which it was derived. *Cute* was originally a shortened form of *acute* in the sense "keenly perceptive or discerning, shrewd." In this sense *cute* is first recorded in a dictionary published in 1731. Probably *cute* came to be used as a term of approbation for things demonstrating acuteness, and so it went on to develop its own sense of "attractive, fetching," first recorded with reference to "gals" in 1838.

cu·tes (kyo͞o′tēz) *n. Anatomy.* A plural of **cutis.**

cute·sy (kyo͞ot′sē) *adj.* **-si·er, -si·est.** *Informal.* Deliberately or affectedly cute; precious: *a cutesy boutique for children's fashions.* —**cute′si·ness** *n.*

cut·ey (kyo͞o′tē) *n. Informal.* Variant of **cutie.**

cut flower *n.* Any of various showy flowers used in fresh arrangements.

cut glass *n.* Glassware shaped or decorated by cutting instruments or abrasive wheels. —**cut′-glass′** (kŭt′glăs′) *adj.*

cut·grass also **cut grass** (kŭt′grăs′) *n.* **1.** Any of several grasses of the genus *Leersia,* found mostly along marshes, ponds, and streams and having leaves with very rough margins. **2.** Any of several other grasses with rough margins.

cu·ti·cle (kyo͞o′tĭ-kəl) *n.* **1.** The outermost layer of the skin of vertebrates; epidermis. **2.** The strip of hardened skin at the base and sides of a fingernail or toenail. **3.** Dead or cornified epidermis. **4.** *Zoology.* The noncellular, hardened or membranous protective covering of many invertebrates, such as the transparent membrane that covers annelids. **5.** *Botany.* The layer of cutin covering the epidermis of the aerial parts of plants. [Latin *cutīcula,* diminutive of *cutis,* skin. See **(s)keu-** in Appendix.] —**cu·tic′u·lar** (-tĭk′yə-lər) *adj.*

cut·ie also **cut·ey** (kyo͞o′tē) *n., pl.* **-ies** also **-eys.** *Informal.* A cute person.

cu·tin (kyo͞ot′n) *n. Botany.* A waxlike, water-repellent material present in the walls of some plant cells and forming the cuticle, which covers the epidermis. [Latin *cutis,* skin; see **(s)keu-** in Appendix + –IN.]

cu·tin·ize (kyo͞ot′n-īz′) *v.* **-ized, -iz·ing, -iz·es.** —*tr.* To coat or impregnate with cutin. —*intr.* To become coated or impregnated with cutin. —**cu′tin·i·za′tion** (-ĭ-zā′shən) *n.*

cu·tis (kyo͞o′tĭs) *n., pl.* **-tes** (-tēz) or **-tis·es.** *Anatomy.* See **dermis.** [Latin, skin. See **(s)keu-** in Appendix.]

cut·lass also **cut·las** (kŭt′ləs) *n.* **1.** A short heavy sword with a curved single-edged blade, once used as a weapon by sailors. **2.** *Caribbean.* A machete. [French *coutelas,* from Old French *coutelasse,* probably augmentative of *coutel,* knife, from Latin *cultellus,* diminutive of *culter,* knife. See **skel-**[1] in Appendix.]

cutlass fish *n.* Any of several marine fishes of the genus *Trichiurus,* having a long, ribbonlike body and a pointed tail.

cut·ler (kŭt′lər) *n.* One who makes, repairs, or sells knives or other cutting instruments. [Middle English *cuteler,* from Old French *coutelier,* from *coutel,* knife. See CUTLASS.]

Cut·ler (kŭt′lər), **Manasseh.** 1742–1823. American cleric, botanist, and pioneer noted for his study of New England flora and as a central figure in the settlement of the Ohio River valley.

Cutler Ridge. A community of extreme southeast Florida on Biscayne Bay south-southwest of Miami. Population, 20,886.

cut·ler·y (kŭt′lə-rē) *n.* **1.** Cutting instruments and tools. **2.** Utensils such as knives, forks, and spoons used as tableware. **3.** The occupation of a cutler. [Middle Engish *cutellerie,* from Old French *coutelerie,* from *coutel,* knife. See CUTLASS.]

cut·let (kŭt′lĭt) *n.* **1.** A thin slice of meat, usually veal or lamb, cut from the leg or ribs. **2.** A patty of chopped meat or fish, usually coated with bread crumbs and fried; a flat croquette. [French *côtelette,* from Old French *costelette,* diminutive of *coste,* rib, from Latin *costa.* See **kost-** in Appendix.]

cut·off also **cut-off** (kŭt′ôf′, -ŏf′) —*n.* **1.** A designated limit or point of termination. **2.** A shortcut or bypass. **3.** A new channel cut by a river across the neck of an oxbow. **4.** The act or an instance of cutting off: *a cutoff of funds; an electricity cutoff.* **5.** *Baseball.* The interception by an infielder of a throw to home plate from the outfield. **6.** A device that cuts off a flow of fluid. **7.** *Music.* A conductor's signal indicating a stop or break in playing or singing. **8. cutoffs.** Pants, such as blue jeans, made into shorts by cutting off part of the legs. —*adj.* **1.** Designating a limit or point of termination: *a cutoff date for applications.* **2.** *Baseball.* Serving to intercept or relay a throw to home plate from the outfield: *the cutoff man.*

cutaway

cut·out (kŭt′out′) *n.* **1.** Something cut out or intended to be cut out from something else. **2.** *Electricity.* A device that interrupts, bypasses, or disconnects a circuit or circuit element. **3.** A recording that is no longer current and whose remaining stock is sold at a discounted price. **4.** *Slang.* A mutually trusted intermediary who handles communications between espionage agents.

cut·o·ver (kŭt′ō′vər) *adj.* Cleared of trees, especially those that bear valuable lumber.

cut·purse (kŭt′pûrs′) *n.* A pickpocket.

cut-rate (kŭt′rāt′) *adj.* Sold or on sale at a reduced price: *cut-rate goods.*

Cut·tack (kŭt′ək). A city of eastern India southwest of Calcutta. Founded in the tenth century, it was long noted for gold and silver filigree work. Population, 269,950.

cut·ter (kût′ər) *n.* **1.** One that cuts, especially in tailoring. **2.** A device or machine that cuts. **3.** *Nautical.* **a.** A single-masted, fore-and-aft-rigged sailing vessel with two or more headsails and a mast set somewhat farther aft than that of a sloop. **b.** A ship's boat, powered by a motor or oars and used for transporting stores or passengers. **4.** A small, lightly armed boat used by the Coast Guard. **5.** A small sleigh, usually seating one person and drawn by a single horse.

cut·throat (kŭt′thrōt′) *n.* **1.** A murderer, especially one who cuts throats. **2.** An unprincipled, ruthless person. **3.** A cutthroat trout. —**cutthroat** *adj.* **1.** Cruel; murderous. **2.** Relentless or merciless in competition: *a cutthroat business.* **3.** *Sports & Games.* Being a form of a game in which each of three or more players acts and scores individually: *cutthroat handball; cutthroat bridge.*

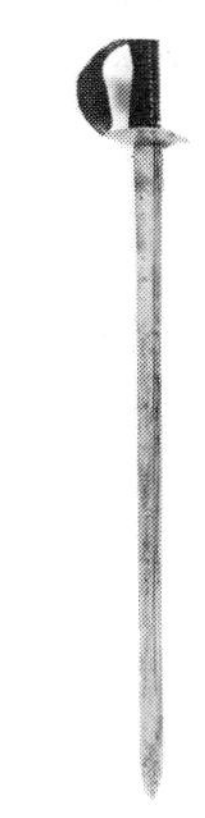
cutlass

cutthroat trout *n.* A large trout *(Salmo clarkii)* found in western North American waters that resembles the rainbow trout and is distinguished by red or orange markings on the lower jaw.

cut time *n. Music.* Duple or quadruple meter with the half note being the unit of time.

cut·ting (kŭt′ĭng) *adj.* **1.** Capable of or designed for incising, shearing, or severing: *a cutting tool.* **2.** Sharply penetrating; piercing: *a cutting wind.* **3.** Injuring or capable of injuring the feelings of others: *a cutting remark.* See Synonyms at **incisive.** —**cutting** *n.* **1.** A part cut off from a main body. **2.** A part, such as a stem, leaf, or root, removed from a plant to propagate a new plant, as through rooting or grafting. **3.** An excavation made through high ground in a construction project. **4.** The editing of film or recording tape. **5.** *Chiefly British.* A clipping, as from a newspaper. —**cut′ting·ly** *adv.*

cutting edge *n.* **1.** An effective quality or element. **2.** The position of greatest advancement or importance; the forefront: *"California is on the cutting edge of trends that spread nationwide"* (Carl Ingram).

cut·tle·bone (kŭt′l-bōn′) *n.* The calcareous internal shell of a cuttlefish, used as a dietary supplement for cage birds or ground into powder for use as a polishing agent. [Middle English : Middle English *codel, cutil,* cuttlefish; see CUTTLEFISH + BONE.]

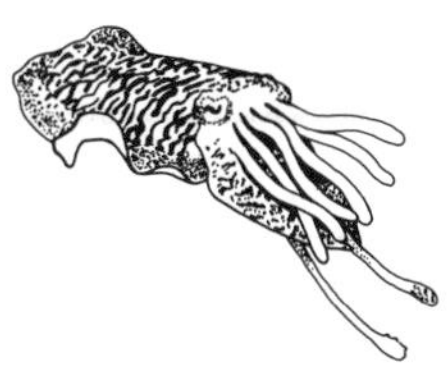
cuttlefish

cut·tle·fish (kŭt′l-fĭsh′) *n., pl.* **cuttlefish** or **-fish·es.** Any of various squidlike cephalopod marine mollusks of the genus *Sepia* that have ten arms and a calcareous internal shell and eject a dark, inky fluid when in danger. [Probably Middle English *codel, cutil,* cuttlefish (from Old English *cudele*) + FISH.]

cut·up (kŭt′ŭp′) *n. Informal.* A mischievous person; a prankster.

cut·wa·ter (kŭt′wô′tər, -wŏt′ər) *n.* **1.** *Nautical.* The forward part of a ship's prow. **2.** The wedge-shaped end of a bridge pier, designed to divide the current and break up ice floes.

cut·work (kŭt′wûrk′) *n.* Openwork embroidery in which the ground fabric is cut away from the design.

cut·worm (kŭt′wûrm′) *n.* The larva of various moths of the family Noctuidae that feed on and destroy a wide variety of plants. [So called because many species eat through stems of plants.]

cu·vette (kyo͞o-vĕt′) *n.* A small, transparent, often tubular laboratory vessel. [French, diminutive of *cuve,* tub, from Latin *cūpa.*]

Cu·vier (kyo͞o′vē-ā′, ko͞ov-yā′, kü-vyā′), Baron **Georges Léopold Chrétien Frédéric Dagobert.** 1769–1832. French naturalist who is considered the founder of comparative anatomy and vertebrate paleontology.

Cuy·a·ho·ga Falls (kī′ə-hō′gə, kə-hō′-, -hô′-, -hä′-). A city of northeast Ohio on the **Cuyahoga River,** about 129 km (80 mi) long. The city is a residential and industrial suburb of Akron. Population, 43,890.

Cuz·co also **Cus·co** (ko͞o′skō). A city of southern Peru in the Andes east-southeast of Lima. It was built on the plundered site of an ancient city supposedly founded in the 11th century by Manco Capac, the first ruler of the Incas. As the capital of a vast and prosperous empire, it was known as "the City of the Sun." Population, 89,563.

CV *abbr.* **1.** Cardiovascular. **2.** Curriculum vitae.

cv. *abbr.* Cultivar.

C.V. *abbr.* Cape Verde.

CVA *abbr.* Cerebrovascular accident.

cvt. *abbr.* Convertible.

cw or **CW** *abbr.* Continuous wave.

cw. *abbr.* Clockwise.

cwm (ko͞om) *n.* See **cirque.** [Welsh, valley.]

CWO *abbr.* Chief warrant officer.

c.w.o. *abbr.* Cash with order.

cwt. or **cwt** *abbr.* Hundredweight.

CY *abbr.* Calendar year.

–cy *suff.* **1.** State; condition; quality: *bankruptcy.* **2.** Rank; office: *baronetcy.* [Middle English *-cie,* from Old French *-cie, -tie,* from Latin *-cia, -tia* and Greek *-kia, -keia, -tia, -teia.*]

cy·an (sī′ăn′, -ən) *n. Color.* A greenish blue, considered a primary color in printing and photography. [Greek *kuanos,* dark blue.]

Cybele

cyan– *pref.* Variant of **cyano–.**

cy·an·am·ide also **cy·an·am·id** (sī-ăn′ə-mĭd) *n.* **1.** A caustic acidic crystalline compound, NHCNH, prepared by treating calcium cyanamide with sulfuric acid. **2.** Calcium cyanamide.

cy·a·nate (sī′ə-nāt′, -nət) *n.* A salt or ester of cyanic acid.

cy·an·ic (sī-ăn′ĭk) *adj.* **1.** Relating to or containing cyanogen. **2.** *Color.* Of a blue or bluish hue.

cyanic acid *n.* A poisonous, unstable, highly volatile organic acid, HOCN, used to prepare cyanates.

cy·a·nide (sī′ə-nīd′) also **cy·a·nid** (-nĭd) *n.* Any of various salts or esters of hydrogen cyanide containing a CN group, especially the extremely poisonous compounds potassium cyanide and sodium cyanide. **—cyanide** *tr.v.* **-nid·ed, -nid·ing, -nides. 1.** To treat (a metal surface) with cyanide to produce a hard surface. **2.** To treat (an ore) with cyanide to extract gold or silver.

cyanide process *n.* A process of extracting gold or silver from ores by treating them with a solution of sodium cyanide or calcium cyanide.

cy·a·nine (sī′ə-nēn′, -nĭn) *n.* Any of various blue dyes, used to sensitize photographic emulsions to a greater range of light.

cy·a·nite (sī′ə-nīt′) *n.* Variant of **kyanite.**

cyano– or **cyan–** *pref.* **1.** Blue: *cyanotype.* **2. a.** Cyanogen: *cyanic.* **b.** Cyanide: *cyanogenesis.* [Greek *kuano-,* from *kuanos,* dark blue.]

cy·a·no·ac·ry·late (sī′ə-nō-ăk′rə-lāt′, sī-ăn′ō-) *n.* An adhesive substance with an acrylate base that is used in industry and medicine.

cy·a·no·bac·te·ri·um (sī′ə-nō-băk-tîr′ē-əm, sī-ăn′ō-) *n.* A photosynthetic bacterium of the class Coccogoneae or Hormogoneae, generally blue-green in color and in some species capable of nitrogen fixation. Cyanobacteria were once thought to be algae. Also called *blue-green alga.*

cy·a·no·co·bal·a·min (sī′ə-nō′kō-băl′ə-mĭn, sī-ăn′ō-) *n.* See **vitamin B_{12}.**

cy·an·o·gen (sī-ăn′ə-jən) *n.* **1.** A colorless, flammable, pungent, highly poisonous gas, C_2N_2, used as a rocket propellant, an insecticide, and a chemical weapon. **2.** A univalent radical, CN, found in simple and complex cyanide compounds.

cy·a·no·gen·e·sis (sī′ə-nō-jĕn′ĭ-sĭs, sī-ăn′ō-) *n.* Generation of cyanide. **—cy′a·no·ge·net′ic** (-jə-nĕt′ĭk), **cy′a·no·gen′ic** (-jĕn′ĭk) *adj.*

cy·a·no·hy·drin (sī′ə-nō-hī′drĭn, sī-ăn′ō-) *n.* Any of several compounds that contain both the CN and OH radicals. [CYANO– + HYDR(O)– + –IN.]

cy·a·nosed (sī′ə-nōzd′, -nōsd′) *adj.* Afflicted with cyanosis. [From CYANOSIS.]

cy·a·no·sis (sī′ə-nō′sĭs) *n.* A bluish discoloration of the skin and mucous membranes resulting from inadequate oxygenation of the blood. **—cy′a·not′ic** (-nŏt′ĭk) *adj.*

cy·an·o·type (sī-ăn′ə-tīp′) *n.* See **blueprint** (sense 1).

cy·a·nu·ric acid (sī′ə-no͝or′ĭk, -nyo͝or′-) *n.* A white crystalline acid, $C_3N_3(OH)_3$, that decomposes with heating to form cyanic acid.

ă pat	oi boy
ā pay	ou out
âr care	o͝o took
ä father	o͞o boot
ĕ pet	ŭ cut
ē be	ûr urge
ĭ pit	th thin
ī pie	*th* this
îr pier	hw which
ŏ pot	zh vision
ō toe	ə about, item
ô paw	♦ regionalism

Stress marks: ′ (primary); ′ (secondary), as in **dictionary** (dĭk′shə-nĕr′ē)

cy·ath·i·um (sī-ăth′ē-əm) *n.* An inflorescence consisting of a cuplike cluster of modified leaves enclosing a female flower and several male flowers, as in the poinsettia. [New Latin, from Greek *kuathion,* diminutive of *kuathos,* ladle.]

Cyb·e·le (sĭb′ə-lē) *n. Greek Mythology.* The Phrygian goddess of nature of ancient Asia Minor.

cy·ber·nate (sī′bər-nāt′) *tr.v.* **-nat·ed, -nat·ing, -nates.** To control (an industrial process) by computer. [CYBERN(ETICS) + –ATE[1].] **—cy′ber·na′tion** *n.*

cy·ber·net·ics (sī′bər-nĕt′ĭks) *n. (used with a sing. verb).* The theoretical study of communication and control processes in biological, mechanical, and electronic systems, especially the comparison of these processes in biological and artificial systems. [From Greek *kubernētēs,* governor, from *kubernan,* to govern.] **—cy′ber·net′ic** *adj.* **—cy′ber·net′i·cal·ly** *adv.* **—cy′ber·net′i·cist, cy′ber·ne·ti′cian** (-nĭ-tĭsh′ən) *n.*

cy·borg (sī′bôrg′) *n.* A human being who has certain physiological processes aided or controlled by mechanical or electronic devices. [CYB(ERNETIC) + ORG(ANISM).]

cy·cad (sī′kăd′, -kəd) *n.* Any of various palmlike gymnospermous cone-bearing evergreen plants of the division Cycadophyta, native to warm regions and having large pinnately compound leaves. [New Latin *Cycas, Cycad-,* genus name, from Greek *kukas,* erroneous reading of *koïkas,* accusative pl. of *koïx,* a kind of palm tree, perhaps of Egyptian origin.]

cycl– *pref.* Variant of **cyclo–.**

Cyc·la·des (sĭk′lə-dēz′) also **Ki·klá·dhes** (kē-klä′thĕs). A group of islands of southeast Greece in the southern Aegean Sea. The name was used in ancient times for the islands surrounding the small island of Delos.

cy·cla·mate (sī′klə-māt′, sĭk′lə-) *n.* A salt of cyclamic acid formerly used as an artificial sweetener, especially: **a.** Sodium cyclamate. **b.** Calcium cyclamate. [CYCLAM(IC ACID) + –ATE[2].]

cy·cla·men (sī′klə-mən, sĭk′lə-) *n.* Any of various plants of the genus *Cyclamen,* especially a Mediterranean species *(C. persicum)* widely cultivated as a houseplant, having decorative leaves and showy, variously colored flowers with reflexed petals. [New Latin, genus name, from Latin *cyclamīnos,* from Greek *kuklaminos,* probably from *kuklos,* circle, wheel (perhaps from its bulbous roots). See CYCLE.]

cyc·la·mic acid (sĭk′lə-mĭk′, sĭk′lə-) *n.* A crystalline acid, $C_6H_{13}NO_3S$, used to produce cyclamates. [Short for *cycl(ohexylsulf)amic acid.*]

cy·clase (sī′klās′, -klāz′) *n.* An enzyme that acts as a catalyst in the cyclization of a compound. [CYCL(IC) + –ASE.]

cy·cle (sī′kəl) *n.* **1.** An interval of time during which a characteristic, often regularly repeated event or sequence of events occurs: *Sunspots increase and decrease in intensity in an 11-year cycle.* **2. a.** A single complete execution of a periodically repeated phenomenon: *A year constitutes a cycle of the seasons.* **b.** A periodically repeated sequence of events: *the cycle of birth, growth, and death; a cycle of reprisal and retaliation.* **3.** The orbit of a celestial body. **4.** A long period of time; an age. **5. a.** The aggregate of traditional poems or stories organized around a central theme or hero: *the Arthurian cycle.* **b.** A series of poems or songs on the same theme: *Schubert's song cycles.* **6.** A bicycle, motorcycle, or similar vehicle. **7.** *Botany.* A circular or whorled arrangement of flower parts such as those of petals or sepals. **—cycle** *v.* **-cled, -cling, -cles.** —*intr.* **1.** To occur in or pass through a cycle. **2.** To move in or as if in a circle. **3.** To ride a bicycle, motorcycle, or similar vehicle. —*tr.* To use in or put through a cycle: *cycled the heavily soiled laundry twice; cycling the recruits through eight weeks of basic training.* [Middle English, from Late Latin *cyclus,* from Greek *kuklos,* circle. See **kʷel-**[1] in Appendix.] **—cy′cler** *n.*

cy·clic (sī′klĭk, sĭk′lĭk) or **cy·cli·cal** (sī′klĭ-kəl, sĭk′lĭ-kəl) *adj.* **1. a.** Of, relating to, or characterized by cycles: *a cyclic pattern of weather changes.* **b.** Recurring or moving in cycles: *cyclical history.* **2.** *Chemistry.* Of or relating to compounds having atoms arranged in a ring or closed-chain structure. **3.** *Botany.* **a.** Having parts arranged in a whorl. **b.** Forming a whorl. **—cy′cli·cal′i·ty** (sĭk′lə-kăl′ĭ-tē, sī′klə-) *n.* **—cy′cli·cal·ly** *adv.*

cyclic AMP *n.* A cyclic nucleotide of adenosine that acts at the cellular level as a regulator of various metabolic processes.

cyclic GMP *n.* A cyclic nucleotide of guanosine thought to act at the cellular level as a regulator of various metabolic processes, possibly as an antagonist to cyclic AMP.

cy·clist (sī′klĭst) *n.* One who rides or races a bicycle, motorcycle, or similar vehicle.

cy·cli·za·tion (sī′klĭ-zā′shən, sĭk′lĭ-) *n.* The formation of one or more rings in a hydrocarbon.

cyclo– or **cycl–** *pref.* **1.** Circle; cycle: *cyclorama.* **2.** A cyclic compound: *cyclohexane.* [Greek *kuklo-,* from *kuklos,* circle. See **kʷel-**[1] in Appendix.]

cy·clo·al·kane (sī′klō-ăl′kān) *n.* An alicyclic hydrocarbon with a saturated ring. Also called *cycloparaffin.*

cy·clo·hex·ane (sī′klō-hĕk′sān′) *n.* An extremely flammable, colorless, mobile liquid, C_6H_{12}, obtained from petroleum and benzene and used in the manufacture of nylon and as a solvent, a paint, and a varnish remover.

cy·clo·hex·i·mide (sī′klō-hĕk′sə-mīd′, -mĭd) *n.* A colorless crystalline compound, $C_{15}H_{23}NO_4$, that is used as an agricultural fungicide.

cy·cloid (sī′kloid′) *adj.* **1.** Resembling a circle. **2.** *Zoology.* **a.** Thin, rounded, and smooth-edged; disklike. Used of fish scales. **b.** Having or composed of such scales. **3.** *Psychiatry.* Afflicted with or relating to cyclothymia. **—cycloid** *n.* **1.** *Mathematics.* The curve traced by a point on the circumference of a circle that rolls on a straight line. **2.** *Zoology.* A fish having cycloid scales. [French *cycloïde,* from Greek *kukloeidēs,* circular : *kuklos,* circle; see **kʷel-¹** in Appendix + *-oeidēs,* -oid.] **—cy·cloi′dal** (-kloid′l) *adj.*

cy·clom·e·ter (sī-klŏm′ĭ-tər) *n.* **1.** An instrument that records the revolutions of a wheel to indicate distance traveled. **2.** An instrument that measures circular arcs. **—cy′clo·met′ric** (-klə-mĕt′rĭk) *adj.* **—cy·clom′e·try** *n.*

cy·clone (sī′klōn′) *n.* **1.** *Meteorology.* An atmospheric system characterized by the rapid, inward circulation of air masses about a low-pressure center, usually accompanied by stormy, often destructive, weather. Cyclones circulate counterclockwise in the Northern Hemisphere and clockwise in the Southern Hemisphere. **2.** A violent, rotating windstorm. **3.** Any of various devices using centrifugal force to separate materials. [From Greek *kuklōn,* present participle of *kukloun,* to rotate, from *kuklos,* circle. See **kʷel-¹** in Appendix.] **—cy·clon′ic** (-klŏn′ĭk), **cy·clon′i·cal** *adj.*

cyclone cellar *n.* An underground shelter in or adjacent to a house, used for protection from severe windstorms. Also called *storm cellar.*

cy·clo·pae·di·a (sī′klə-pē′dē-ə) *n.* Variant of **cyclopedia.**

cy·clo·par·af·fin (sī′klō-păr′ə-fĭn) *n.* See **cycloalkane.**

cy·clo·pe·an (sī′klə-pē′ən, sī-klō′pē-) *adj.* **1.** Often **Cyclopean.** Relating to or suggestive of a Cyclops: *a great Cyclopean monocle.* **2.** Of or constituting a primitive style of masonry characterized by the use of massive stones of irregular shape and size.

cy·clo·pe·di·a also **cy·clo·pae·di·a** (sī′klə-pē′dē-ə) *n.* An encyclopedia. [Short for ENCYCLOPEDIA.] **—cy′clo·pe′dic** (-dĭk) *adj.* **—cy′clo·pe′dist** (-dĭst) *n.*

cy·clo·pen·tane (sī′klə-pĕn′tān′, sĭk′lə-) *n.* A colorless, flammable, liquid cycloalkane, C_5H_{10}, derived from petroleum and used as a solvent and motor fuel.

Cy·clo·pes (sī-klō′pēz) *n.* *Greek Mythology.* Plural of **Cyclops.**

cy·clo·phos·pha·mide (sī′klə-fŏs′fə-mīd′) *n.* A highly toxic, immunosuppressive, antineoplastic drug, $C_7H_{15}Cl_2N_2P$, used in the treatment of Hodgkin's disease, lymphoma, and certain leukemias.

cy·clo·ple·gia (sī′klə-plē′jə) *n.* Paralysis of the ciliary muscles of the eye, resulting in the loss of visual accomodation.

cy·clo·pro·pane (sī′klə-prō′pān′) *n.* A highly flammable, explosive, colorless gas, C_3H_6, sometimes used as an anesthetic.

Cy·clops (sī′klŏps) *n., pl.* **Cy·clo·pes** (sī-klō′pēz). *Greek Mythology.* **1.** Any of the three one-eyed Titans who forged thunderbolts for Zeus. **2.** Any of a race of one-eyed giants, reputedly descended from these Titans, inhabiting the island of Sicily. [Latin, from Greek *Kuklōps* : *kuklos,* circle; see CYCLE + *ōps,* eye; see MYOPIA.]

cy·clo·ram·a (sī′klə-răm′ə, -rä′mə) *n.* **1.** A large composite picture placed on the interior walls of a cylindrical room so as to appear in natural perspective to a spectator standing in the center of the room. **2.** A large curtain or wall, usually concave, hung or placed at the rear of a stage. [CYCL(O)– + (PAN)ORAMA.] **—cy′clo·ram′ic** *adj.*

cy·clo·ser·ine (sī′klō-sĕr′ēn) *n.* An antibiotic effective against a wide range of bacteria, used especially in the treatment of tuberculosis and infections of the urinary tract.

cy·clo·sis (sī-klō′sĭs) *n., pl.* **-ses** (-sēz). The streaming rotary motion of protoplasm within certain cells and one-celled organisms. [New Latin, from Greek *kuklōsis,* a surrounding, from *kukloun,* to surround, from *kuklos,* circle. See **kʷel-¹** in Appendix.]

cy·clo·spor·ine (sī′klə-spôr′ēn, -ĭn, -spōr′-) also **cy·clo·spor·in** (-ĭn) *n.* An immunosuppressive drug obtained from certain soil fungi, used mainly to prevent the rejection of transplanted organs.

cy·clo·stome (sī′klə-stōm′) *n.* Any of various primitive eellike vertebrates of the class Agnatha, such as a lamprey, lacking jaws and true teeth and having a circular, sucking mouth. [From New Latin *Cyclostomī* and *Cyclostomata,* class names : CYCLO– + Greek *stoma, stomat-,* mouth.] **—cy·clos′to·mate′** (sī-klŏs′tə-māt′, -mĭt), **cy′clo·stom′a·tous** (sī′klə-stŏm′ə-təs, -stō′mə-) *adj.*

cy·clo·thyme (sī′klə-thīm′) *n.* A person afflicted with cyclothymia.

cy·clo·thy·mi·a (sī′klə-thī′mē-ə) *n.* *Psychiatry.* A mild affective disorder characterized by alternating periods of elation and depression. **—cy′clo·thy′mic** (-mĭk) *adj. & n.*

cy·clo·tron (sī′klə-trŏn′) *n.* A circular particle accelerator in which charged subatomic particles generated at a central source are accelerated spirally outward in a plane perpendicular to a fixed magnetic field by an alternating electric field. A cyclotron is capable of generating particle energies between a few million and several tens of millions of electron volts.

cy·der (sī′dər) *n.* *Chiefly British.* Variant of **cider.**

cyg·net (sĭg′nĭt) *n.* A young swan. [Middle English *cignet,* from Anglo-Norman, diminutive of Old French *cygne,* swan, from Latin *cygnus,* from Greek *kuknos.*]

Cyg·nus (sĭg′nəs) *n.* A constellation in the Northern Hemisphere near Lacerta and Lyra, containing the star Deneb. Also called *Northern Cross, Swan.* [Latin *cygnus,* swan. See CYGNET.]

cyl·in·der (sĭl′ən-dər) *n. Abbr.* **cyl. 1.** *Mathematics.* **a.** The surface generated by a straight line intersecting and moving along a closed plane curve, the directrix, while remaining parallel to a fixed straight line that is not on or parallel to the plane of the directrix. **b.** The portion of such a surface bounded by two parallel planes and the regions of the planes bounded by the surface. **c.** A solid bounded by two parallel planes and such a surface, especially such a surface having a circle as its directrix. **2.** A cylindrical container or object. **3.** *Engineering.* **a.** The chamber in which a piston of a reciprocating engine moves. **b.** The chamber of a pump from which fluid is expelled by a piston. **4.** The rotating chamber of a revolver that holds the cartridges. **5.** Any of several rotating parts in a printing press, especially one that carries the paper. **6.** *Archaeology.* A cylindrical stone or clay object with an engraved design or inscription. [Latin *cylindrus,* from Greek *kulindros,* from *kulindein,* to roll.]

cylinder head *n.* The closed, often detachable, end of a cylinder in an internal-combustion engine.

cy·lin·dri·cal (sə-lĭn′drĭ-kəl) also **cy·lin·dric** (-drĭk) *adj.* **1.** Of, relating to, or having the shape of a cylinder, especially of a circular cylinder. **2.** *Mathematics.* Of or relating to the coordinate system, or to any of three coordinates in it, formed by two polar coordinates in a plane and a rectangular coordinate measured perpendicularly from the plane. **—cy·lin′dri·cal′i·ty** (-kăl′ĭ-tē) *n.* **—cy·lin′dri·cal·ly** *adv.*

cyl·in·droid (sĭl′ən-droid′) *n.* *Mathematics.* A cylindrical surface or solid all of whose sections perpendicular to the elements are elliptical. **—cylindroid** *adj.* Resembling a cylinder.

cy·ma (sī′mə) *n.* *Architecture.* A molding for a cornice, having a partly concave and partly convex curve in profile, used especially in classical architecture. Also called *cymatium.* [Greek *kuma,* wave, cyma, from *kuein,* to swell. See **keuə-** in Appendix.]

cy·ma·tium (sī-mā′shəm, -shē-əm) *n., pl.* **-tia** (-shə, -shē-ə). *Architecture.* **1.** See **cyma. 2.** The topmost molding of a classical cornice. [Latin, from Greek *kumation,* diminutive of *kuma,* cyma. See CYMA.]

cym·bal (sĭm′bəl) *n.* *Music.* A percussion instrument consisting of a concave brass plate that makes a loud clashing tone when hit with a drumstick or when used in pairs. [Middle English, from Old English and from Old French *cymbale,* both from Latin *cymbalum,* from Greek *kumbalon,* from *kumbē,* bowl.] **—cym′bal·eer′** (sĭm′bə-lîr′), **cym′bal·er**, **cym′bal·ist** *n.*

cym·bid·i·um (sĭm-bĭd′ē-əm) *n.* Any of various epiphytic orchids of the genus *Cymbidium,* native to tropical Asia and Australia and extensively hybridized and cultivated for their elongate clusters of showy blooms. [New Latin *Cymbidium,* genus name, from Latin *cymba,* boat, from Greek *kumbē.*]

cyme (sīm) *n.* *Botany.* A usually flat-topped or convex flower cluster in which the main axis and each branch end in a flower that opens before the flowers below or to the side of it. [Latin *cȳma,* young cabbage sprout, from Greek *kuma.* See CYMA.] **—cy·mif′er·ous** (sī-mĭf′ər-əs) *adj.*

cy·mene (sī′mēn′) *n.* Any of three colorless isomeric liquid hydrocarbons, $C_{10}H_{14}$, obtained chiefly from the essential oils of cumin and thyme and used in the manufacture of synthetic resins. [French *cymène,* from Greek *kuminon,* cumin, probably of Semitic origin.]

cym·ling (sĭm′lĭng) also **cym·lin** (-lĭn) *n.* A greenish-white, flat, round squash with a scalloped edge. [Alteration of SIMNEL.]

cy·mo·gene (sī′mə-jēn′) *n.* A flammable gaseous fraction of petroleum, consisting chiefly of butane. [CYM(ENE) + –GENE.]

cy·moid (sī′moid′) *adj.* **1.** *Architecture.* Resembling a cyma. **2.** *Botany.* Resembling a cyme.

cy·mo·phane (sī′mə-fān′) *n.* A variety of chrysoberyl having a shimmering luster and microscopic, needlelike inclusions that reflect a streak of light. [French : Greek *kuma,* wave, cyma; see CYMA + Greek *-phanēs,* appearing; see –PHANE.]

cy·mose (sī′mōs′) also **cy·mous** (-məs) *adj.* **1.** Relating to or resembling a cyme; determinate. **2.** Bearing a cyme or cymes. [CYM(E) + –OSE[1].] **—cy′mose′ly** *adv.*

Cym·ric (kĭm′rĭk, sĭm′-) *adj.* Of or relating to the Cymry. **—Cymric** *n.* See **Welsh** (sense 2).

Cym·ry (kĭm′rē, sĭm′-) *n.* (*used with a pl. verb*). **1.** The Brythonic Celts of Wales, Cornwall, and Brittany. **2.** The Welsh. [Welsh, pl. of *Cymro,* the Welsh people, Wales, from British Celtic **kombrogos,* fellow countryman. See **merg-** in Appendix.]

Cyn·e·wulf (kĭn′ə-wo͝olf′) or **Cyn·wulf** (kĭn′wo͝olf′). fl. c. 900. Anglo-Saxon poet whose extant works are *Juliana, Elene, The Ascension,* and *The Fates of the Apostles.*

cyn·ic (sĭn′ĭk) *n.* **1.** A person who believes all people are motivated by selfishness. **2. Cynic.** A member of a sect of ancient Greek philosophers who believed virtue to be the only good and self-control to be the only means of achieving virtue. **—cynic** *adj.* **1.** Cynical. **2. Cynic.** Of or relating to the Cynics or their beliefs. [Latin *cynicus,* Cynic philosopher, from Greek *kunikos,* from *kuōn, kun-,* dog. See **kwon-** in Appendix.]

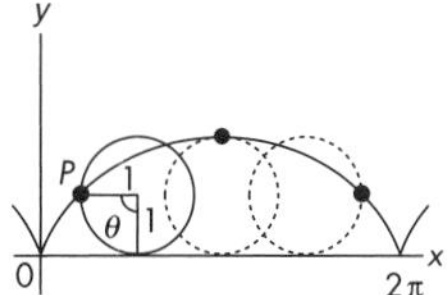

cycloid
Coordinates of *P:*
$x = \phi - \sin \phi$
$y = 1 - \cos \phi$

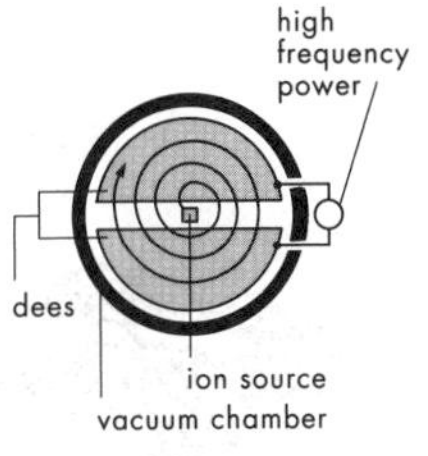

cyclotron

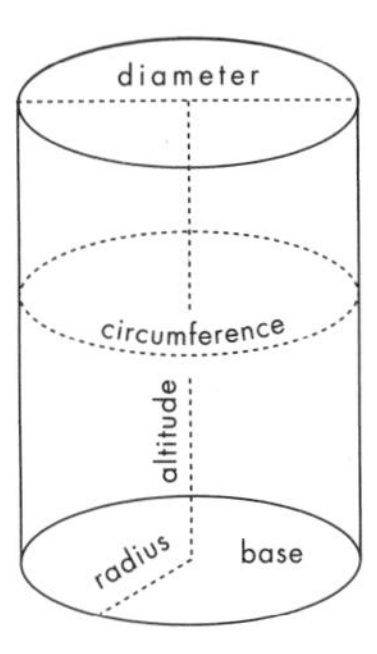

cylinder

cymbal
Pair of cymbals

WORD HISTORY: A cynic may be pardoned for thinking that this is a dog's life. The Greek word *kunikos,* from which *cynic* comes, was originally an adjective meaning "doglike," from *kuōn,* "dog." The word was most likely applied to the Cynic philosophers because of the nickname *kuōn* given to Diogenes of Sinope, the prototypical Cynic. He is said to have performed such actions as barking in public, urinating on the leg of a table, and masturbating on the street. The first use of the word recorded in English, in a work published from 1547 to 1564, is in the plural for members of this philosophical sect. In 1596 we find the first instance of *cynic* meaning "faultfinder," a sense that was to develop into our modern sense. The meaning "faultfinder" came naturally from the behavior of countless Cynics who in their pursuit of virtue pointed out the flaws in others. Such faultfinding could lead quite naturally to the belief associated with cynics of today that selfishness determines human behavior.

cyn·i·cal (sĭn′ĭ-kəl) *adj.* **1.** Scornful of the motives, virtue, or integrity of others: *a cynical distrust of friendly strangers; a cynical view of the average voter's intelligence.* **2.** Expressing or exhibiting scorn and bitter mockery: *cynical laughter.* **—cyn′i·cal·ly** *adv.* **—cyn′i·cal·ness** *n.*

cyn·i·cism (sĭn′ĭ-sĭz′əm) *n.* **1.** A scornful, bitterly mocking attitude or quality: *the public cynicism aroused by governmental scandals.* **2.** A scornful, bitterly mocking comment or act. **3. Cynicism.** The beliefs of the ancient Cynics.

Cyn·os·ceph·a·lae (sĭn′ə-sĕf′ə-lē, sī′nə-). Two hills of southeast Thessaly in northeast Greece. The Theban general Pelopidas was killed in battle here (364 B.C.).

cypress

cy·no·sure (sī′nə-sho͝or′, sĭn′ə-) *n.* **1.** An object that serves as a focal point of attention and admiration. **2.** Something that serves to guide. [French, Ursa Minor (which contains the guiding star Polaris), from Latin *cynosūra,* from Greek *kunosoura,* dog's tail, Ursa Minor : *kuōn, kun-,* dog; see **kwon-** in Appendix + *oura,* tail; see **ors-** in Appendix.] **—cy′no·sur′al** *adj.*

Cyn·wulf (kĭn′wo͝olf′). See **Cynewulf.**

CYO *abbr.* Catholic Youth Organization.

cy·pher (sī′fər) *n.* & *v.* Variant of **cipher.**

cy pres (sē′ prā′) *n.* The legal doctrine that allows a court freedom in interpreting the terms of a will or gift if carrying out the terms literally would be impracticable or illegal. At the same time, the general intent of the testator or donor is supposed to be observed as closely as possible. [Middle English, from Anglo-Norman : *cy* (from Latin *sīc,* so; see SIC[1]) + *pres* (from Late Latin *pressē,* close to, from Latin *pressus,* past participle of *premere,* to press closely; see PRESS[1]).]

cy·press (sī′prĭs) *n.* **1.a.** Any of various evergreen trees or shrubs of the genus *Cupressus,* native to Eurasia and North America and having opposite, scalelike leaves and globose, woody cones. **b.** Any of several similar or related coniferous trees, such as the bald cypress. **c.** The wood of any of these trees. **2.** Cypress branches used as a symbol of mourning. [Middle English *cipres,* from Old French, from Late Latin *cypressus,* probably blend of Latin *cupressus* and *cyparissus* (from Greek *kuparissos*).]

Cy·press (sī′prĭs). A city of southern California, a suburb of Long Beach. Population, 40,391.

cypress spurge *n.* A perennial European ornamental plant *(Euphorbia cyparissias)* having numerous narrow leaves and flower clusters with petaloid bracts.

cypress vine *n.* An annual twining tropical American vine *(Ipomoea quamoclit)* naturalized in warm regions, having pinnately cut leaves and showy, usually scarlet flowers.

Cyprus

Cyp·ri·an (sĭp′rē-ən) *adj.* **1.** Of or relating to Cyprus; Cypriot. **2.a.** Of or relating to the ancient worship of Aphrodite on Cyprus. **b.** Licentious; wanton. **—Cyprian** *n.* **1.** See **Cypriot** (sense 1). **2.** Also **cyprian. a.** A wanton person. **b.** A prostitute.

Cyprian, Saint. Died A.D. 258. Christian prelate and martyr who led Christians in North Africa during persecution by the Roman emperors Decius and Valerian.

cyp·ri·nid (sĭp′rə-nĭd) *n.* Any of numerous often small freshwater fishes of the family Cyprinidae, which includes the minnows, carps, and shiners. **—cyprinid** *adj.* Of, relating to, or belonging to the family Cyprinidae. [From New Latin *Cyprīnidae,* family name, from *Cyprīnus,* type genus, from Latin *cyprīnus,* carp, from Greek *kuprinos.*]

cy·prin·o·dont (sĭ-prĭn′ə-dŏnt′, -prī′nə-) *n.* Any of various small, soft-finned fishes of the family Cyprinodontidae, which includes the killifishes, topminnows, and many species popular in home aquariums. **—cyprinodont** *adj.* Of, relating to, or belonging to the family Cyprinodontidae. [Latin *cyprīnus,* carp (from Greek *kuprinos*) + -ODONT.]

cyp·ri·noid (sĭp′rə-noid′, sĭ-prī′-) *adj.* Of, relating to, or resembling a carp or other cyprinid fish. **—cyprinoid** *n.* A cyprinoid fish. [From New Latin *Cyprīnoidēa,* suborder name, from *Cyprīnus,* genus name. See CYPRINID.]

Cyp·ri·ot (sĭp′rē-ət, -ŏt′) also **Cyp·ri·ote** (-ōt′, -ət) *—n.* **1.** A native or inhabitant of Cyprus. Also called *Cyprian.* **2.** The ancient or modern Greek dialect of Cyprus. *—adj.* **1.** Of or relating to Cyprus or its people or culture. **2.** Of or relating to Cypriot Greek as used on Cyprus. [French *cypriote,* from Greek *Kupriōtēs,* from *Kupros,* Cyprus.]

cyp·ri·pe·di·um (sĭp′rĭ-pē′dē-əm) *n.* Any of various orchids of the genus *Cypripedium,* such as the lady's slipper. [New Latin *Cypripedium,* genus name : Late Latin *Cypris,* Venus (from Greek *Kupris,* Aphrodite, from *Kupros,* Cyprus, legendary birthplace of Aphrodite) + New Latin *-pedium* (alteration of Greek *pedilon,* sandal; see **ped-** in Appendix).]

cy·pro·hep·ta·dine (sī′prō-hĕp′tə-dēn′) *n.* An antihistamine, $C_{21}H_{21}N$, used to relieve the symptoms of various allergic reactions, such as itching and skin rash. [CY(CLIC) + PRO(PYL) + HEPTA– + (PIPERI)DINE.]

cy·prot·er·one (sī-prŏt′ə-rōn′) *n.* A synthetic steroid that inhibits the secretion of androgens. [CY(CLO)– + PRO(GES)TERONE.]

Cy·prus (sī′prəs). An island country in the eastern Mediterranean Sea south of Turkey. Site of an ancient Neolithic culture, the island was settled by Phoenicians c. 800 B.C. and thereafter fell successively to the Assyrians, Egyptians, Persians, Macedonian Greeks, Egyptians again, and finally Romans (58 B.C.) The Byzantines controlled it from A.D. 395 until 1191, when it was captured by Richard I of England during the Third Crusade. Venice annexed it in 1489, Turkey conquered it in 1571, and Great Britain proclaimed its sovereignty in 1914. Cyprus became independent in 1960. Nicosia is the capital and the largest city. Population, 642,731.

cyp·se·la (sĭp′sə-lə) *n., pl.* **-lae** (-lē′). An achene fruit derived from an inferior ovary, characteristic of plants in the composite family. [New Latin, from Greek *kupselē,* hollow vessel.]

Cy·ra·no de Ber·ge·rac (sîr′ə-nō də bûr′zhə-răk′, bĕr′-), **Savinien de.** 1619–1655. French satirist and duelist whose works include the spirited drama *The Pedant Imitated* (1654).

Cyr·e·na·ic (sîr′ə-nā′ĭk, sī′rə-) *adj.* **1.** Of or relating to Cyrenaica or Cyrene. **2.** Of or advocating the doctrines of Aristippus of Cyrene, who argued that pleasure is the only good in life. **—Cyrenaic** *n.* **1.** A native or inhabitant of Cyrenaica or Cyrene. **2.** A disciple of the Cyrenaic school of philosophy.

Cyr·e·na·i·ca (sîr′ə-nā′ĭ-kə, sī′rə-). An ancient region of northeast Libya bordering on the Mediterranean Sea. It was colonized by the Greeks in the seventh century B.C. and became a Roman province in the first century B.C.

Cy·re·ne (sī-rē′nē). An ancient Greek city of Cyrenaica. Founded c. 630 B.C., it was noted as an intellectual center with distinguished schools of medicine and philosophy.

Cyr·il (sîr′əl), Saint. 827–869. Christian missionary and theologian who with his brother Saint Methodius (826–885) worked in Moravia, translating the Scriptures into Old Church Slavonic.

Cy·ril·lic (sə-rĭl′ĭk) *adj.* Of, relating to, or constituting the old Slavic alphabet ascribed to Saint Cyril, at present used in modified form for Russian, Bulgarian, certain other Slavic languages, and other languages of the Soviet Union.

Cy·rus (sī′rəs). Known as "the Younger." 424?–401 B.C. Persian prince who led a mammoth force of Greeks against his brother Artaxerxes II. The retreat that followed his defeat and death are described in Xenophon's *Anabasis.*

Cyrus II. Known as "Cyrus the Great." 600?–529? B.C. King of Persia (550–529) and founder of the Persian Empire who conquered Lydia and Babylon. Tolerant in religious matters, he allowed the worship of native gods and permitted the exiled Jews to return to Jerusalem (537).

cyst (sĭst) *n.* **1.** *Pathology.* An abnormal membranous sac containing a gaseous, liquid, or semisolid substance. **2.** *Anatomy.* A sac or vesicle in the body. **3.** *Biology.* A small capsulelike sac that encloses certain organisms in their dormant or larval stage. **4.** *Botany.* A thick-walled resting spore, as in certain algae or fungi. [New Latin *cystis,* from Greek *kustis,* bladder. See **kwes-** in Appendix.]

cyst– *pref.* Variant of **cysto–.**

cys·tec·to·my (sĭ-stĕk′tə-mē) *n., pl.* **-mies. 1.** Surgical removal of a cyst. **2.a.** Surgical removal of the gallbladder. **b.** Surgical removal of all or part of the urinary bladder.

cys·te·ine (sĭs′tə-ēn′, -ĭn, -tē-) *n.* An amino acid, $C_3H_7O_2NS$, derived from cystine and found in most proteins. [CYST(INE) + –EIN.]

cys·tic (sĭs′tĭk) *adj.* **1.** Of, relating to, or having the characteristic of a cyst. **2.** Having or containing cysts or a cyst. **3.** Enclosed in a cyst. **4.** *Anatomy.* Of, relating to, or involving the gallbladder or urinary bladder.

cystic duct *n.* The duct that conveys bile from the gallbladder to the common bile duct.

cys·ti·cer·ci (sĭs′tĭ-sûr′sī′) *n.* Plural of **cysticercus.**

cys·ti·cer·coid (sĭs′tĭ-sûr′koid) *n.* The larval stage of certain tapeworms, resembling a cysticercus but having the scolex completely filling the enclosing cyst. [CYSTICERC(US) + –OID.]

cys·ti·cer·co·sis (sĭs′tĭ-sər-kō′sĭs) *n.* The condition of being infested with cysticerci. [CYSTICERC(US) + –OSIS.]

cys·ti·cer·cus (sĭs′tĭ-sûr′kəs) *n., pl.* **-ci** (-sī′). The larval stage of many tapeworms, consisting of a single invaginated scolex enclosed in a fluid-filled cyst. [New Latin : Greek *kustis,* cyst; see CYST + Greek *kerkos,* tail.]

cystic fibrosis *n. Abbr.* **CF** A hereditary disease of the exocrine glands, usually developing during early childhood and affecting mainly the pancreas, respiratory system, and sweat glands. It is characterized by the production of abnormally viscous mucus by the affected glands, usually resulting in chronic respiratory infections and impaired pancreatic function. Also called *mucoviscidosis.*

cys·tine (sĭs′tēn′) *n.* A white crystalline amino acid, $C_6H_{12}N_2O_4S_2$, found in many proteins, especially keratin. [From its discovery in bladder stones.]

cys·ti·tis (sĭ-stī′tĭs) *n.* Inflammation of the urinary bladder.

cysto– or **cyst–** *pref.* Bladder; cyst; sac: *cystocele.* [From New Latin *cystis,* bladder, from Greek *kustis.* See **kwes-** in Appendix.]

cys·to·cele (sĭs′tə-sēl′) *n.* Herniation of the urinary bladder through the wall of the vagina.

cys·toid (sĭs′toid′) *adj.* Formed like or resembling a cyst. **—cystoid** *n.* A cystoid structure.

cys·to·lith (sĭs′tə-lĭth′) *n.* **1.** *Botany.* A mineral concretion, usually of calcium carbonate, occurring in the epidermal cells of certain plants, such as figs. **2.** See **urinary calculus.**

cys·to·scope (sĭs′tə-skōp′) *n.* A tubular instrument equipped with a light and used to examine the interior of the urinary bladder and ureter. **—cys′to·scop′ic** (-skŏp′ĭk) *adj.* **—cys·tos′co·py** (sĭ-stŏs′kə-pē) *n.*

cys·tos·to·my (sĭ-stŏs′tə-mē) *n., pl.* **-mies.** The surgical formation of an opening into the urinary bladder.

cyt– *pref.* Variant of **cyto–.**

–cyte *suff.* Cell: *leukocyte.* [New Latin *-cyta,* from Greek *kutos,* hollow vessel. See **(s)keu-** in Appendix.]

Cy·the·ra (sĭ-thîr′ə, sĭth′ər-ə) also **Kí·thi·ra** (kē′thē-rä′). An island of southern Greece in the Mediterranean Sea south of the Peloponnesus. Southernmost of the Ionian Islands, it was the chief center for the worship of Aphrodite.

Cyth·e·re·a (sĭth′ə-rē′ə) *n. Greek Mythology.* See **Aphrodite.**

cy·ti·dine (sī′tĭ-dēn′) *n.* A white, crystalline nucleoside, $C_9H_{13}N_3O_5$, composed of one molecule each of cytosine and ribose. [CYT(O)– + –ID(E) + –INE^2.]

cyto– or **cyt–** *pref.* Cell: *cytoplasm.* [From Greek *kutos,* hollow vessel. See **(s)keu-** in Appendix.]

cy·to·chem·is·try (sī′tō-kĕm′ĭ-strē) *n.* The branch of biochemistry that deals with the study of the chemical composition and activity of cells. **—cy′to·chem′i·cal** (-kĕm′ĭ-kəl) *adj.*

cy·to·chrome (sī′tə-krōm′) *n.* Any of a class of iron-containing proteins important in cell respiration as catalysts of oxidation-reduction reactions.

cytochrome oxidase *n.* An oxidizing enzyme containing iron and a porphyrin, found in mitochondria and important in cell respiration as an agent of electron transfer from certain cytochrome molecules to oxygen molecules.

cy·to·gen·e·sis (sī′tō-jĕn′ĭ-sĭs) *n.* The formation, development, and variation of cells. Also called *cytogeny.*

cy·to·ge·net·ics (sī′tō-jə-nĕt′ĭks) *n. (used with a sing. verb).* The branch of biology that deals with heredity and the cellular components, particularly chromosomes, associated with heredity. **—cy′to·ge·net′ic, cy′to·ge·net′i·cal** *adj.* **—cy′to·ge·net′i·cal·ly** *adv.* **—cy′to·ge·net′i·cist** (-sĭst) *n.*

cy·tog·e·ny (sī-tŏj′ə-nē) *n.* See **cytogenesis.**

cy·to·ki·ne·sis (sī′tō-kĭ-nē′sĭs, -kī-) *n.* The division of the cytoplasm of a cell following the division of the nucleus. **—cy′to·ki·net′ic** (-nĕt′ĭk) *adj.*

cy·to·ki·nin (sī′tə-kī′nĭn) *n.* Any of a class of plant hormones that promote cell division and growth and delay the senescence of leaves.

cy·tol·o·gy (sī-tŏl′ə-jē) *n. Abbr.* **cytol.** The branch of biology that deals with the formation, structure, and function of cells. **—cy′to·log′ic** (-tə-lŏj′ĭk), **cy′to·log′i·cal** *adj.* **—cy·tol′o·gist** *n.*

cy·tol·y·sin (sī-tŏl′ĭ-sĭn) *n.* A substance, such as an antibody, capable of dissolving or destroying cells. [CYTOLYS(IS) + –IN.]

cy·tol·y·sis (sī-tŏl′ĭ-sĭs) *n.* The dissolution or destruction of a cell. **—cy′to·lyt′ic** (sī′tə-lĭt′ĭk) *adj.*

cy·to·me·gal·ic (sī′tō-mĭ-găl′ĭk) *adj.* Of, relating to, or characterized by greatly enlarged cells.

cy·to·meg·a·lo·vi·rus (sī′tə-mĕg′ə-lō-vī′rəs) *n. Abbr.* **CMV** Any of a group of herpes viruses that attack and enlarge epithelial cells. Such viruses also cause a disease of infants characterized by circulatory dysfunction and microcephaly.

cy·to·mem·brane (sī′tə-mĕm′brān) *n.* See **cell membrane.**

cy·to·path·ic (sī′tə-păth′ĭk) *adj.* Of or relating to degeneration or disease of cells.

cy·to·path·o·gen·ic (sī′tə-păth′ə-jĕn′ĭk) *adj.* Of, relating to, or producing pathological changes in cells. **—cy′to·path′o·ge·nic′i·ty** (-jə-nĭs′ĭ-tē) *n.*

cy·to·phil·ic (sī′tə-fĭl′ĭk) *adj.* Having an affinity for cells.

cy·to·pho·tom·e·ter (sī′tō-fō-tŏm′ĭ-tər) *n.* An instrument used to identify and locate the chemical compounds within a cell by measuring the intensity of light passing through stained sections of the cytoplasm.

cy·to·pho·tom·e·try (sī′tə-fō-tŏm′ĭ-trē) *n.* The study of cells and chemical compounds within cells by means of a cytophotometer. **—cy′to·pho′to·met′ric** (-tə-mĕt′rĭk) *adj.* **—cy′to·pho′to·met′ri·cal·ly** *adv.*

cy·to·plasm (sī′tə-plăz′əm) *n.* The protoplasm outside the nucleus of a cell. **—cy′to·plas′mic** (-plăz′mĭk) *adj.* **—cy′to·plas′mi·cal·ly** *adv.*

cy·to·plast (sī′tə-plăst′) *n.* The intact cytoplasm of a single cell. **—cy′to·plas′tic** (-plăs′tĭk) *adj.*

cy·to·sine (sī′tə-sēn′) *n.* A pyrimidine base, $C_4H_5N_3O$, that is an essential constituent of RNA and DNA. [CYT(O)– + (RIB)OS(E) + –INE^2.]

cy·to·skel·e·ton (sī′tə-skĕl′ĭtn) *n.* The internal framework of a cell, composed largely of actin filaments and microtubules.

cy·to·sol (sī′tə-sôl′, -sŏl′) *n.* The fluid component of cytoplasm, excluding organelles and the insoluble, usually suspended, cytoplasmic components. [CYTO– + SOL(UTION).]

cy·to·sta·sis (sī′tə-stā′sĭs, -stăs′ĭs) *n.* Arrest of cellular growth and multiplication.

cy·to·sta·tic (sī′tə-stăt′ĭk) *adj.* Inhibiting or suppressing cellular growth and multiplication. **—cytostatic** *n.* A cytostatic agent. **—cy′to·stat′i·cal·ly** *adv.*

cy·to·tax·on·o·my (sī′tō-tăk-sŏn′ə-mē) *n. Biology.* The classification of organisms based on cellular structure and function, especially on the structure and number of chromosomes. **—cy′to·tax′o·nom′ic** (-tăk′sə-nŏm′ĭk) *adj.* **—cy′to·tax·on′o·mist** *n.*

cy·to·tech·nol·o·gist (sī′tə-tĕk-nŏl′ə-jĭst) *n.* A technician trained in medical examination and identification of cellular abnormalities. **—cy′to·tech·nol′o·gy** *n.*

cy·to·tox·ic (sī′tə-tŏk′sĭk) *adj.* Of, relating to, or producing a toxic effect on cells. **—cy′to·tox·ic′i·ty** (-tŏk-sĭs′ĭ-tē) *n.*

cytotoxic T cell *n.* See **killer cell.**

cy·to·tox·in (sī′tə-tŏk′sĭn) *n.* A substance having a specific toxic effect on certain cells.

CZ or **C.Z.** *abbr.* Canal Zone.

czar (zär, tsär) *n.* **1.** Also **tsar** or **tzar** (zär, tsär). A male monarch or emperor, especially one of the emperors who ruled Russia until the revolution of 1917. **2.** A person having great power; an autocrat: *"the square-jawed, ruddy complacency of Jack Farrell, the czar of the Fifteenth Street police station"* (Ernest Hemingway). **3.** *Informal.* An appointed official having special powers to regulate or supervise an activity: *a racetrack czar; an energy czar.* [Russian *tsar′,* from Old Russian *tsĭsarĭ,* emperor, king, from Old Church Slavonic *tsěsarĭ,* from Gothic *kaisar,* from Greek *kaisar,* from Latin *Caesar,* emperor. See CAESAR.] **—czar′dom** *n.*

USAGE NOTE: The word *czar* can also be spelled *tsar. Czar* is the most common form in American usage and virtually the only one employed in the extended senses "any tyrant" or informally, "one in authority." But *tsar* is preferred by most scholars of Slavic studies as a more accurate transliteration of the Russian and is often found in scholarly writing with reference to one of the Russian emperors.

czar·das (chär′däsh′) *n.* **1.** An intricate Hungarian dance characterized by variations in tempo. **2.** Music for this dance. [Hungarian *csárdás,* from *csárda,* wayside tavern, from Serbo-Croatian *čardāk,* watchtower, from Turkish *çardak,* hut, trellis, from Persian *chār ṭāq,* from *chahār ṭāq,* four-cornered vault : *chahār,* four (from Old Iranian *cathwārō;* see **kʷetwer-** in Appendix) + *ṭāq,* vault.]

czar·e·vitch (zär′ə-vĭch′, tsär′-) *n.* The eldest son of a Russian czar. [Russian *tsarevich* : *tsar′,* czar; see CZAR + *-evich,* masculine patronymic suff.]

cza·rev·na (zä-rĕv′nə, tsä-) *n.* **1.** The daughter of a Russian czar. **2.** The wife of a czarevitch. [Russian *tsarevna* : *tsar′,* czar; see CZAR + *-evna,* feminine patronymic suff.]

cza·ri·na (zä-rē′nə, tsä-) *n.* The wife of a Russian czar. [Alteration (perhaps influenced by Latin *rēgīna,* queen) of Russian *tsaritsa* : *tsar′,* czar; see CZAR + *-itza,* feminine suff.]

czar·ism (zär′ĭz′əm, tsär′-) *n.* The system of government in Russia under the czars. **—czar′ist** *adj. & n.*

cza·rit·za (zä-rĭt′sə, tsä-rēt′-) *n.* An empress of Russia. [Russian *tsaritsa* : *tsar′,* czar; see CZAR + *-itza,* feminine suff.]

Czech (chĕk) *n.* **1.** A native or inhabitant of Czechoslovakia, especially a Bohemian, Moravian, or Silesian. **2.** The Slavic language of the Czechs. [Polish, from Czech *Čech.*] **—Czech** *adj.*

Czech·o·slo·va·ki·a (chĕk′ə-slə-vä′kē-ə, -ō-slō-). *Abbr.* **Czech.** A country of central Europe. It was formed in 1918 from Czech-speaking and Slovak-speaking territories of the Austro-Hungarian Empire, although disparate ethnic elements led to internal conflicts before World War II. Communist forces gained control of the country after the war and wielded almost total power until late 1989. Prague is the capital and the largest city. Population, 15,479,642. **—Czech′o·slo′vak, Czech′o·slo·va′ki·an** *adj. & n.*

Czer·ny (chĕr′nē), **Karl.** 1791–1857. Austrian pianist and composer. A student of Beethoven and the teacher of Liszt, he wrote piano exercises, such as *School of the Left Hand,* which remain in wide use.

Czę·sto·cho·wa (chĕn′stə-kō′və, chĕɴ′stô-hô′vä). A city of southern Poland north of Katowice. It is heavily industrialized. Population, 246,600.

Czechoslovakia

ă pat	oi boy
ā pay	ou out
âr care	ŏŏ took
ä father	ōō boot
ĕ pet	ŭ cut
ē be	ûr urge
ĭ pit	th thin
ī pie	*th* this
îr pier	hw which
ŏ pot	zh vision
ō toe	ə about, item
ô paw	♦ regionalism

Stress marks: ′ (primary); ′ (secondary), as in **dictionary** (dĭk′shə-nĕr′ē)

Dd

Phoenician
The fourth letter of the Phoenician alphabet stood for the sound of *d* in *dāleth,* "door."

Early Greek
It was adopted by the Greeks, whose name for it, *delta,* still describes objects that have a triangular shape.

Roman
Rounding off one of the angles produced the form used in classical Roman inscriptions.

d[1] or **D** (dē) *n., pl.* **d's** or **D's.** **1.** The fourth letter of the modern English alphabet. **2.** Any of the speech sounds represented by the letter *d.* **3.** The fourth in a series. **4.** *Music.* **a.** The second tone in the scale of C major or the fourth tone in the relative minor scale. **b.** A key or scale in which D is the tonic. **c.** A written or printed note representing this tone. **d.** A string, key, or pipe tuned to the pitch of this tone. **5. D.** The lowest passing grade given to a student in a school or college. **6.** Something shaped like the letter D.

d[2] *abbr.* **1.** Day. **2.** Deuteron. **3.** *Physics.* Down quark.

D[1] **1.** The symbol for the isotope deuterium. **2.** Also **d.** The symbol for the Roman numeral 500.

D[2] also **D.** *abbr.* Democrat; democratic.

d. *abbr.* **1.** Dam (zoology). **2.** Date. **3.** Daughter. **4.** Also **D.** Deputy. **5.** Died. **6.** Also **D.** Dose. **7.** Also **D.** Drachma. **8.** *Chiefly British.* Penny (1/12 of a shilling).

D. *abbr.* **1.** Department. **2.** Deus. **3.** Diopter. **4.** Doctor (in academic degrees). **5.** Don (title). **6.** Duchess. **7.** Duke.

'd **1.** Had: *He'd already left.* **2.** Would; should: *I'd rather walk than drive.* **3.** Did: *Who'd you ask?*

DA[1] (dē′ā′) *n.* See **ducktail.** [Abbreviation of *duck's ass.*]

DA[2] *abbr.* **1.** Delayed action. **2.** Deposit account. **3.** Also **D.A.** Don't answer.

Da. *abbr.* Danish.

D.A. *abbr.* **1.** Also **DA.** *Law.* District attorney. **2.** Doctor of Arts.

dab[1] (dăb) *v.* **dabbed, dab·bing, dabs.** —*tr.* **1.** To apply with short, poking strokes: *dabbed some paint on the worn spots.* **2.** To cover lightly with or as if with a moist substance. **3.** To strike or hit lightly. —*intr.* To tap gently; pat. —**dab** *n.* **1.** A small amount: *a dab of jelly.* **2.** A quick, light pat. [Middle English *dabben,* to strike.]

dab[2] (dăb) *n.* Any of various flatfishes, chiefly of the genera *Limanda* and *Hippoglossoides,* related to and resembling the flounders. [Middle English *dabbe.*]

dab[3] (dăb) *n.* *Chiefly British.* A dab hand. [Origin unknown.]

dab·ber (dăb′ər) *n.* A cushioned pad used by printers and engravers to apply ink.

dab·ble (dăb′əl) *v.* **-bled, -bling, -bles.** —*tr.* To splash or spatter with or as if with a liquid: *"The moon hung over the harbor dabbling the waves with gold"* (Katherine Mansfield). —*intr.* **1.** To splash liquid gently and playfully. **2.** To undertake something superficially or without serious intent. **3.** To bob forward and under in shallow water so as to feed off the bottom. [Possibly from Dutch *dabbelen,* frequentative of *dabben,* to strike, tap.]

dab·bler (dăb′lər) *n.* One who engages in an activity superficially or without serious intent. See Synonyms at **amateur.**

dab·bling duck (dăb′lĭng) *n.* Any of various ducks, chiefly of the genus *Anas,* including the mallards, teals, and shovelers, that feed by dabbling in shallow water and are favored as game birds.

dab·chick (dăb′chĭk′) *n.* Any of various small grebes of the genus *Podiceps.* [Alteration of *dobchick* : Middle English *doppe,* diving bird (from Old English *-doppe;* see DIDAPPER) + CHICK.]

dab hand *n.* A person skilled in a particular activity; an expert: *a dab hand at gardening.*

Dą·bro·wa Gór·ni·cza (dôm-brô′və go͝or-nē′chə). A city of southern Poland northeast of Katowice. It has been a coal-mining center since the 1790's. Population, 136,800.

da ca·po (dä kä′pō) *adv.* *Abbr.* **D.C.** *Music.* From the beginning. Used as a direction to repeat a passage. [Italian : *da,* from + *capo,* head.]

Dac·ca also **Dha·ka** (dăk′ə, dä′kə). The capital and largest city of Bangladesh, in the east-central part of the country. It was the Mogul capital of Bengal in the 17th century and came under British rule in 1765. After India achieved independence in 1947, Dacca was made the capital of East Pakistan, which became Bangladesh in 1971. Population, 1,850,000.

dace (dās) *n., pl.* **dace** or **dac·es.** Any of various small freshwater fishes of the family Cyprinidae, which also includes carps and minnows. [Middle English *dace, darce,* from Old French *dars,* from Late Latin *darsus,* possibly of Celtic origin.]

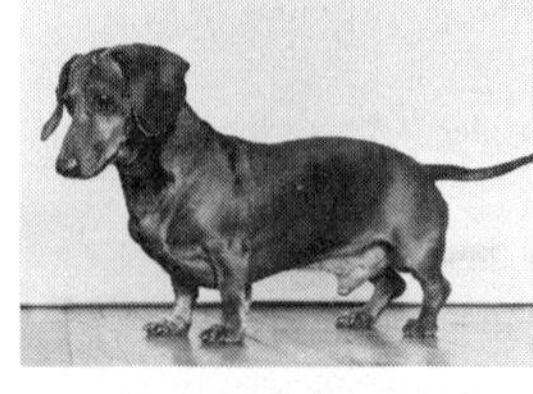

dachshund
Shorthaired dachshund

da·cha (dä′chə) *n.* A Russian country house or villa. [Russian, gift, land, country house. See **dō-** in Appendix.]

Da·chau (dä′kou′, -KHOU′). A city of southeast Germany north-northwest of Munich. It was the site of a Nazi concentration camp built in 1935 and captured by the Allies in April 1945. Population, 33,141.

dachs·hund (däks′ho͝ont′, dăk′sənt) *n.* A small dog of a breed developed in Germany for hunting badgers and having a long body, a usually short-haired brown or black and brown coat, drooping ears, and very short legs. [German : *Dachs,* badger (from Middle High German *dahs,* from Old High German; see **teks-** in Appendix) + *Hund,* dog (from Middle High German *hunt,* from Old High German; see **kwon-** in Appendix).]

Da·ci·a (dā′shē-ə, -shə). An ancient region and Roman province corresponding roughly to present-day Romania. Inhabited before the Christian era by a people of Thracian stock with an advanced material culture, the region was abandoned to the Goths after A.D. 270. —**Da′ci·an** *adj. & n.*

da·coit also **da·koit** (də-koit′) *n.* **1.** A member of any of the robber bands of India and Burma who formerly lived in the hills and attacked in armed gangs, usually on horseback. **2.** A member of a robber gang in modern India and Burma. [Hindi *ḍakait.*]

da·coit·y (də-koi′tē) *n.* Robbery by a band or gang of dacoits. [Hindi *ḍakaitī,* from *ḍakait,* dacoit.]

dac·quoise (dă-kwŏz′) *n.* A cake made of ground almond or hazelnut meringue layers with fruit or variously flavored cream fillings between the layers. [French, from feminine of *dacquois,* of Dax, a town of southwest France.]

Da·cron (dā′krŏn′, dăk′rŏn′). A trademark used for a synthetic polyester fabric or the fiber from which it is made.

dac·ti·no·my·cin (dăk′tə-nō-mī′sĭn) *n.* An antibiotic of the actinomycin group, $C_{62}H_{86}N_{12}O_{16}$, isolated from bacteria and used as an antineoplastic agent in the treatment of certain cancers. Also called *actinomycin D.* [*d-* (abbr. of DEXTROROTATORY) + ACTINOMYCIN.]

dac·tyl (dăk′təl) *n.* **1.** A metrical foot consisting of one accented syllable followed by two unaccented or of one long syllable followed by two short, as in *flattery.* **2.** A finger, toe, or similar part or structure; a digit. [Middle English *dactil,* from Latin *dactylus,* from Greek *daktulos,* finger, dactyl.] —**dac·tyl′ic** (-tĭl′ĭk) *adj. & n.* —**dac·tyl′i·cal·ly** *adv.*

dactylo– or **dactyl–** *pref.* Finger; toe; digit: *dactylogram.* [From Greek *daktulos,* finger.]

dac·tyl·o·gram (dăk-tĭl′ə-grăm′) *n.* A fingerprint.

dac·ty·log·ra·phy (dăk′tə-lŏg′rə-fē) *n.* The study of fingerprints as a method of identification. —**dac′ty·lo·graph′ic** (-lō-grăf′ĭk) *adj.*

dac·ty·lol·o·gy (dăk′tə-lŏl′ə-jē) *n.* The use of the fingers and hands to communicate and convey ideas, as in the manual alphabet used by hearing-impaired and speech-impaired people.

dad (dăd) *n.* *Informal.* A father. [Probably of baby-talk origin.]

Da·da or **da·da** (dä′dä) *n.* A European artistic and literary movement (1916–1923) that flouted conventional aesthetic and cultural values by producing works marked by nonsense, travesty, and incongruity. [French *dada,* hobbyhorse, Dada, of baby-talk origin.] —**Da′da·ism** *n.* —**Da′da·ist** *adj. & n.* —**Da′da·is′tic** *adj.*

dad·dy (dăd′ē) *n., pl.* **-dies.** *Informal.* A father. —**dad′dy·ish** *adj.*

daddy long·legs (lông′lĕgz′, lŏng′-) *n., pl.* **daddy longlegs.** **1.** Any of various arachnids of the order Phalangida, with a small, rounded body and long, slender legs. Also called *harvestman.* **2.** See **crane fly.**

dad·gum (dăd′gŭm′) *adj.* *Chiefly Southern U.S.* Used as an intensive to express mild annoyance. See Regional Note at **damned.** [Alteration of GODDAMN.]

da·do (dā′dō) *n., pl.* **-does.** **1.** *Architecture.* The section of a pedestal between base and surbase. **2.** The lower portion of the wall of a room, decorated differently from the upper section, as with panels. **3.a.** A rectangular groove cut into a board so that a like piece may be fitted into it. **b.** The groove so cut. **—dado** *tr.v.* **-doed, -do·ing, -does. 1.** To furnish with a dado. **2.a.** To cut a dado in. **b.** To fit into a dado. [Italian, from Latin *datum,* neuter past participle of *dare,* to give. See **dō-** in Appendix.]

dae·dal (dēd′l) *adj.* **1.** Ingenious and complex in design or function; intricate. **2.** Finely or skillfully made or employed; artistic. [Latin *daedalus,* from Greek *daidalos.*]

Dae·da·lus (dĕd′l-əs) *n. Greek Mythology.* A legendary artist and inventor, builder of the Labyrinth. **—Dae·da′li·an, Dae·da′le·an** (dĭ-dā′lē-ən, -dāl′yən) *adj.*

dae·mon (dē′mən) *n.* Variant of **demon** (senses 4, 5).

dae·mon·ic (dĭ-mŏn′ĭk) *adj.* Variant of **demonic.**

daf·fo·dil (dăf′ə-dĭl) *n.* **1.a.** A bulbous plant *(Narcissus pseudonarcissus)* having showy, usually yellow flowers with a trumpet-shaped central crown. **b.** The flower of this plant. **2.** *Color.* A brilliant to vivid yellow. [Alteration of Middle English *affodil,* from Latin *asphodelus,* asphodel. See ASPHODEL.]

daf·fy (dăf′ē) *adj.* **-fi·er, -fi·est.** *Informal.* **1.** Silly; foolish. **2.** Crazy. [From obsolete *daff,* fool, from Middle English *daffe*; probably akin to *dafte,* foolish. See DAFT.] **—daf′fi·ly** *adv.* **—daf′fi·ness** *n.*

daft (dăft) *adj.* **daft·er, daft·est. 1.** Mad; crazy. **2.** Foolish; stupid. **3.** *Scots.* Frolicsome. [Middle English *dafte,* foolish, from Old English *gedæfte,* meek.] **—daft′ly** *adv.* **—daft′ness** *n.*

dag¹ (dăg) *n.* **1.** A lock of matted or dung-coated wool. **2.** A hanging end or shred. [Middle English *dagge,* shred.]

dag² *abbr.* Decagram.

Da·gan (dä′gän′) *n. Mythology.* The Babylonian god of the earth.

DAGC *abbr. Electronics.* Delayed automatic gain control.

Da·ges·tan (dä′gĭ-stän, də-gyĭ-). A region of southwest Russia bordering on the Caspian Sea. Settled in the first millennium B.C., it was ceded to Russia by Persia in 1813.

dag·ga (dăg′ə) *n. South African.* Indian hemp used as a narcotic; cannabis. [Afrikaans, from Khoikoin *dachab.*]

dag·ger (dăg′ər) *n.* **1.** A short pointed weapon with sharp edges. **2.** Something that agonizes, torments, or wounds. **3.** *Printing.* **a.** See **obelisk** (sense 2). **b.** A double dagger. ***—idiom.* look daggers at.** To glare at angrily or hatefully. [Middle English *daggere,* alteration of Old French *dague,* from Old Provençal *dague* or Old Italian *daga,* both perhaps from Vulgar Latin **dāca (ēnsis),* Dacian (knife), from feminine of Latin *Dācus.*]

dagger fern *n.* See **Christmas fern.**

da·go also **Da·go** (dā′gō) *n., pl.* **-gos** or **-goes.** *Offensive Slang.* Used as a disparaging term for an Italian, a Spaniard, or a Portuguese. [Alteration of Spanish *Diego,* a given name, from Latin *Jacōbus,* Jacob.]

Da·gon (dā′gŏn′) *n. Mythology.* The chief god of the ancient Philistines and later the Phoenicians, represented as half-man and half-fish.

Da·guerre (də-gâr′, dä-gĕr′), **Louis Jacques Mandé.** 1789–1851. French artist and inventor of the daguerreotype process for obtaining positive photographic prints.

da·guerre·o·type (də-gâr′ə-tīp′) *n.* **1.** An early photographic process with the image made on a light-sensitive silver-coated metallic plate. **2.** A photograph made by this process. **—daguerreotype** *tr.v.* **-typed, -typ·ing, -types.** To make a daguerreotype of. [French, after Louis Jacques Mandé DAGUERRE.] **—da·guerre′o·typ′er** *n.* **—da·guerre′o·typ′y** *n.*

dag·wood also **Dag·wood** (dăg′wo͝od′) *n.* A multilayered sandwich with a variety of fillings. [After *Dagwood* Bumstead, a character who made such sandwiches in the comic strip *Blondie* by Murat Bernard ("Chic") Young (1901–1973).]

dah (dä) *n.* The spoken representation of a dash in Morse code. [Imitative.]

da·ha·be·ah also **da·ha·bee·yah** or **da·ha·bi·ah** (dä′hə-bē′ə) *n. Nautical.* A houseboat having sails and sometimes an engine, used on the Nile. [Arabic *ḏahabīya,* from *ḏahabī,* golden, the Golden One, name of the gilded barge of the Moslem rulers of Egypt, from *ḏahab,* gold.]

dahl (däl) *n.* **1.** See **cajan pea. 2.** A thick creamy East Indian stew made with lentils, onions, and various spices. [Hindi *dāl,* dahl seed, from Sanskrit *dalaḥ, dalam,* piece split off, from *dalati,* he splits.]

dahl·ia (dăl′yə, däl′-, dāl′-) *n.* **1.** Any of several plants of the genus *Dahlia* native to the mountains of Mexico, Central America, and Colombia, having tuberous roots and showy, rayed, variously colored flower heads. **2.** The flower head of one of these plants. [New Latin *Dahlia,* genus name, after Anders *Dahl* (1751–1787), Swedish botanist.]

Da·ho·mey (də-hō′mē, dä-ô-mā′). See **Benin** (sense 2). **—Da·ho′me·an** (də-hō′mē-ən), **Da·ho′man** (-mən) *adj. & n.*

da·hoon (də-ho͞on′) *n.* A small tree *(Ilex cassine)* of the southeast United States, having red or sometimes orange to yellow fruit and leathery, dark green leaves. Also called *cassina.* [Origin unknown.]

Dai (dī) *n. & adj.* Variant of **Tai.**

dai·kon (dī′kŏn′, -kən) *n.* A white radish *(Raphanus sativus* var. *longipinnatus)* of Japan, having a long root that is eaten raw, pickled, or cooked. Also called *Chinese radish, Japanese radish, Oriental radish.* [Japanese : *dai,* big + *kon,* root.]

dai·ly (dā′lē) *adj.* **1.** Of or occurring during the day. **2.** Happening or done every day: *the physician's daily rounds.* **3.** Computed or assessed for each day: *a daily record.* **4.** Everyday: *casual clothes only for daily use.* **—daily** *adv.* **1.** Every day: *Exercise daily.* **2.** Once a day: *Wind the clock daily.* **—daily** *n., pl.* **-lies. 1.** A newspaper published every day or every weekday. **2. dailies.** The first unedited print of movie film usually viewed after a day's shooting; the rushes. [Middle English *dayly,* from Old English *dæglīc,* from *dæg,* day. See DAY.] **—dai′li·ness, dai′ly·ness** *n.*

daily double *n. Sports & Games.* A bet won by choosing both winners of two specified races on one day, as in horse racing.

dai·mi·o or **dai·my·o** (dī′mē-ō′, dīm′yō′) *n., pl.* **daimio** or **-mi·os** also **daimyo** or **-my·os.** A feudal lord of Japan who was a large landowner. [Japanese *daimyō* : *dai,* great (from Chinese *dà*) + *myō,* name (from Chinese *míng*).]

Daim·ler (dīm′lər), **Gottlieb.** 1834–1900. German engineer and pioneer automobile manufacturer who produced the first high-speed internal-combustion engine (1885).

dai·mon (dī′mōn′) *n.* Variant of **demon** (senses 4, 5).

dai·my·o (dī′mē-ō′, dīm′yō′) *n.* Variant of **daimio.**

dain·ty (dān′tē) *adj.* **-ti·er, -ti·est. 1.** Delicately beautiful or charming; exquisite: *"No dainty rhymes or sentimental love verses for you, terrible year"* (Walt Whitman). **2.** Delicious or choice. See Synonyms at **delicate. 3.** Of refined taste; discriminating. **4.** Overly fastidious; squeamish. **—dainty** *n., pl.* **-ties.** Something delicious; a delicacy. [Middle English *deinte,* excellent, from *deinte,* excellence, from Old French *deintie,* from Latin *dignitās,* from *dignus,* worthy. See **dek-** in Appendix.] **—dain′ti·ly** *adv.* **—dain′ti·ness** *n.*

dai·qui·ri (dī′kə-rē, dăk′ə-) *n., pl.* **-ris.** An iced cocktail of rum, lime or lemon juice, and sugar. [After *Daiquirí,* a village of eastern Cuba.]

Dai·ren (dī′rĕn′). See **Dalian.**

dair·y (dâr′ē) *n., pl.* **-ies. 1.** A commercial establishment for processing or selling milk and milk products. **2.** A place where milk and cream are stored and processed. **3.** A dairy farm. **4.** The dairy business; dairying. **—dairy** *adj.* **1.** Of, for, or relating to milk or milk products: *the dairy section at the grocery store.* **2.** Of or relating to dairying. **3.** *Judaism.* Of, relating to, or intended for the consumption or preparation of milk or milk products exclusively, as dictated by dietary law. [Middle English *daierie,* from Anglo-Norman : Middle English *daie,* dairymaid (from Old English *dǣge,* bread kneader; see **dheigh-** in Appendix) + *-erie,* place (from Old French; see -ERY).]

dairy cattle *pl.n.* Cows bred and raised for milk rather than meat.

dair·y·er (dâr′ē-ər) *n.* One who owns or manages a dairy or works in one.

dairy farm *n.* A farm for producing milk and milk products.

dair·y·ing (dâr′ē-ĭng) *n.* The business of owning and operating a dairy or a dairy farm.

dair·y·maid (dâr′ē-mād′) *n.* A woman or girl who works in a dairy.

dair·y·man (dâr′ē-mən) *n.* **1.** A man who owns or manages a dairy. **2.** A man who works in a dairy.

dair·y·wom·an (dâr′ē-wo͝om′ən) *n.* **1.** A woman who owns or manages a dairy. **2.** A woman who works in a dairy.

da·is (dā′ĭs, dī′-, dās) *n.* A raised platform, as in a lecture hall, for speakers or honored guests. [Middle English *deis,* from Anglo-Norman, platform, from Late Latin *discus,* table, from Latin, discus, quoit. See DISK.]

dai·shi·ki (dī-shē′kē) *n.* Variant of **dashiki.**

dai·sy (dā′zē) *n., pl.* **-sies. 1.** Any of several plants of the composite family, especially a widely naturalized Eurasian plant *(Chrysanthemum leucanthemum)* having flower heads with a yellow center and white rays. Also called *oxeye daisy, white daisy.* **2.** A low-growing European plant *(Bellis perennis)* having flower heads with pink or white rays. Also called *English daisy.* **3.** The flower head of any of these plants. **4.** *Slang.* One that is deemed excellent or notable. [Middle English *daisie,* from Old English *dæges ēage* : *dæges,* genitive of *dæg,* day; see **agh-** in Appendix + *ēage,* eye; see **okʷ-** in Appendix.]

daisy chain *n.* **1.** A garland made of daisies joined together in or as if in a long chain. **2.** Something, such as a series of connected events, activities, or experiences, likened to a garland: *"It's a vast daisy chain of status, stretching from the first toddler group to the entry-level position at an investment banking house"* (James Traub).

daisy fleabane *n.* An eastern North American weed *(Erigeron annuus)* naturalized in Europe, having rayed, white to bluish flower heads grouped in corymblike panicles.

daisy wheel *n.* A printing device used especially in the printing machines attached to computers and word processors and consisting of printing characters fixed at the ends of spokes on a wheel.

Da·kar (də-kär′, dăk′är′). The capital and largest city of Senegal, in the western part of the country on the Atlantic Ocean. It grew around a French fort built in 1857 and was the capital of French West Africa from 1904 to 1959. Population, 1,341,000.

Da·kin (dā′kĭn), **Henry Drysdale.** 1880–1952. British bio-

Dada
Bicycle Wheel, 1951,
by Marcel Duchamp
Metal wheel, 25½" diameter, mounted on painted wood stool, 23¾" high; overall 50½" × 16⅝" × 25½"
The Museum of Modern Art, New York. The Sidney and Harriett Janis Collection.

daffodil
Narcissus pseudonarcissus

dagger
Fifth-century B.C. Achaemenian

ă pat	oi boy
ā pay	ou out
âr care	o͝o took
ä father	o͞o boot
ĕ pet	ŭ cut
ē be	ûr urge
ĭ pit	th thin
ī pie	*th* this
îr pier	hw which
ŏ pot	zh vision
ō toe	ə about, item
ô paw	♦ regionalism

Stress marks: ′ (primary); ′ (secondary), as in **dictionary** (dĭk′shə-nĕr′ē)

Salvador Dali
Photographed in 1936 aboard the S.S. *Normandie*

Dalmatian

dalmatic
1570 Dutch clerical dalmatic

dam [1]
Tennessee Valley Authority's Norris Dam on the Clinch River

chemist noted for his research on enzymes and antiseptics.

Da·kin's solution (dā′kĭnz) *n.* A dilute aqueous solution of sodium hypochlorite used in cleansing wounds. [After Henry Drysdale DAKIN.]

da·koit (də-koit′) *n.* Variant of **dacoit.**

Da·ko·ta (də-kō′tə) *n., pl.* **Dakota** or **-tas. 1.a.** Any of the Sioux peoples, especially any of the peoples of the Santee branch. **b.** A member of a Sioux people, especially a Santee. **2.** The Siouan language of the Dakota. **—Da·ko′tan** *adj. & n.*

Da·ko·tas (də-kō′təz). The Dakota Territory or (after 1889) the states of North Dakota and South Dakota.

Dakota Territory. A territory of the north-central United States organized in 1861 and divided into the states of North Dakota and South Dakota in 1889. The territory included much of present-day Montana until 1864 and Wyoming until 1868.

dal *abbr.* Decaliter.

Da·la·dier (də-lä′dē-ā′, dä-lä-dyā′), **Édouard.** 1884–1970. French statesman who signed the Munich Pact with Adolf Hitler in September 1938.

Da·lai La·ma (dä′lī lä′mə) *n.* The traditional governmental ruler and highest priest of the Lamaist religion in Tibet and Mongolia. [Tibetan : Mongolian *dalai,* ocean + Tibetan *bla-ma,* monk (so called because he is known as the ocean of compassion).]

dal·a·pon (dăl′ə-pŏn′) *n.* An organic acid, $C_3H_4Cl_2O_2$, used as a herbicide that selectively kills grasses and other monocotyledons. [Probably D(I)–[1] + AL(PH)A + P(ROPI)ON(IC ACID).]

da·la·si (dä-lä′sē) *n., pl.* **dalasi.** See table at **currency.** [Mandingo, possibly ultimately from English *dollars.* See DOLLAR.]

dale (dāl) *n.* A valley: *galloped over hill and dale.* [Middle English, from Old English *dæl.*]

Dale (dāl), Sir **Henry Hallett.** 1875–1968. British physiologist. He shared a 1936 Nobel Prize for work on the chemical transmission of nerve impulses.

Dale, Sir **Thomas.** Died 1619. English-born naval commander and colonial administrator noted for his strict rule of Virginia from 1611 to 1616.

Dale City. A community of northeast Virginia southwest of Alexandria. It is mainly residential. Population, 23,000.

da·leth (dä′lĭd, -lĕt, -lĕth) *n.* The fourth letter of the Hebrew alphabet. See table at **alphabet.** [Hebrew *dāleth,* from *dālt,* door.]

Da·ley (dā′lē), **Richard Joseph.** 1902–1976. American politician who dominated Chicago politics during his years as mayor (1955–1976).

Dal·hou·sie (dăl-ho͞o′zē, -hou′-), Tenth Earl and First Marquis of. Title of James Andrew Broun Ramsay. 1812–1860. British colonial administrator in India whose term as governor-general (1847–1856) was marked by acquisition of territory and development of communication and transportation lines.

Da·li (dä′lē), **Salvador.** 1904–1989. Spanish surrealist artist known for his flamboyant personal style and his disquieting interpretation of fantastic images in meticulously rendered canvases. Among his most famous works is *Persistence of Memory* (1931), a desolate landscape inhabited by limp, melting watches. **—Da′li·esque′** (-ĕsk′) *adj.*

Dal·ian (däl′yän′) also **Ta·lien** (tä′lyĕn′). Formerly **Dai·ren** (dī′rĕn′). A city of northeast China on the Liaodong Peninsula and the Bo Hai. A major seaport, it was opened to foreign commerce in 1901 and occupied by the Japanese during the Russo-Japanese War (1904–1905). Dalian and Lüshun form the conurbation of Lüda. Population, 1,380,000.

Dal·las (dăl′əs). A city of northeast Texas on the Trinity River east of Fort Worth. It was founded by French settlers in 1841 and became a cotton market in the 1870's. Population, 904,078.

Dallas, George Mifflin. 1792–1864. Vice President of the United States (1845–1849) under James K. Polk. He also served as minister to Russia (1837–1839) and Great Britain (1856–1861).

dalles (dălz) *pl.n.* The rapids of a river that runs between the steep precipices of a gorge or narrow valley. [French, pl. of *dalle,* gutter, from Old French, from Old Norse *dæla.*]

Dalles (dălz), **The.** A city of northern Oregon on the Columbia River east of Portland. An important stop on the Oregon Trail in the 1800's, it is now a busy inland port. Population, 10,800.

dal·li·ance (dăl′ē-əns) *n.* **1.** Frivolous spending of time; dawdling. **2.** Playful flirtation.

Dal·lis grass (dăl′ĭs) *n.* A tall, South American perennial grass *(Paspalum dilatatum)* grown for pasturage in the southern United States. [Probably alteration of DALLAS, Texas.]

Dall sheep (dôl) or **Dall's sheep** (dôlz) *n.* A stocky wild sheep *(Ovis dalli)* of the mountainous regions of northwest North America, ranging from white to nearly black and having curved, yellowish horns. [After William Healey *Dall* (1845–1927), American naturalist.]

dal·ly (dăl′ē) *v.* **-lied, -ly·ing, -lies.** *—intr.* **1.** To play amorously; flirt: *"Sylvester dallied about Lena until he began to make mistakes in his work"* (Willa Cather). See Synonyms at **flirt. 2.** To trifle; toy. **3.** To waste time; dawdle. *—tr.* To waste (time). [Middle English *dalien,* from Old French *dalier.*] **—dal′li·er** *n.* **—dal′ly·ing·ly** *adv.*

Dal·mane (dăl′mān). A trademark used for a hypnotic drug prescribed for insomnia.

Dal·ma·ti·a (dăl-mā′shə). A historical region of western Yugoslavia on the Adriatic Sea. Subdued by the Romans in the 1st century B.C., it was divided between the kingdoms of Serbia and Croatia in the 10th century and held by numerous powers after the 15th century.

Dal·ma·tian (dăl-mā′shən) *n.* **1.** A native or inhabitant of Dalmatia. **2.** Also **dalmatian.** A dog of a breed believed to have originated in Dalmatia, having a short, smooth white coat covered with black or dark brown spots. In this sense, also called *carriage dog, coach dog.* **—Dalmatian** *adj.* Of or relating to Dalmatia or its inhabitants or culture.

dal·mat·ic (dăl-măt′ĭk) *n.* **1.** The wide-sleeved garment worn over the alb by a deacon, cardinal, bishop, or abbot at the celebration of Mass. **2.** A wide-sleeved garment worn by an English monarch at his or her coronation. [Middle English *dalmatik,* from Old French *dalmatique,* from Medieval Latin *dalmatica (vestis),* Dalmatian (garment) (originally made of white wool from Dalmatia), from Latin *dalmaticus,* of Dalmatia.]

dal se·gno (däl sān′yō) *adv. Abbr.* **d.s., D.S.** *Music.* From a place marked by the sign § to a designated point. Used as a direction to repeat a passage. [Italian : *da,* from + *il,* the + *segno,* sign.]

dal·ton (dôl′tən) *n.* See **atomic mass unit.** [After John DALTON.]

Dal·ton (dôl′tən). A city of northwest Georgia southeast of Chattanooga, Tennessee. It is an industrial center in an agricultural region. Population, 20,939.

Dalton, Hugh. Baron Dalton of Forest and Frith. 1887–1962. British politician who as Chancellor of the Exchequer (1945–1947) oversaw the nationalization of the Bank of England.

Dalton, John. 1766–1844. British chemist whose pioneer work on the properties of gases led to his formulation of the atomic theory. He also studied his own condition of colorblindness.

Dalton, Robert. 1867–1892. American outlaw noted for his exploits as a horse thief, train robber, and leader of the Dalton gang, which included his two brothers.

dal·ton·ism also **Dal·ton·ism** (dôl′tə-nĭz′əm) *n.* An inherited defect in perception of red and green; red-green colorblindness. [After John DALTON.] **—dal·to′ni·an** (-tō′nē-ən), **dal·ton′ic** (-tŏn′ĭk) *adj.*

Da·ly (dā′lē), **(John) Augustin.** 1839–1899. American playwright and theatrical manager best known for melodramas such as *Under the Gaslight* (1867).

Daly City. A city of western California, a suburb of San Francisco. It was settled in 1906 by refugees from the San Francisco earthquake. Population, 78,519.

dam[1] (dăm) *n.* **1.a.** A barrier constructed across a waterway to control the flow or raise the level of water. **b.** A body of water controlled by such a barrier. **2.** A barrier against the passage of liquid or loose material, as a rubber sheet used in dentistry to isolate one or more teeth from the rest of the mouth. **3.** An obstruction; a hindrance. **—dam** *tr.v.* **dammed, dam·ming, dams. 1.** To hold back or confine by means of a dam. **2.** To close up; obstruct: *He tried to dam his grief.* See Synonyms at **hinder**[1]. [Middle English, probably from Old English *damm.] **—dam′mer** *n.*

dam[2] (dăm) *n.* **1.** *Abbr.* **d.** A female parent. Used of a four-legged animal. **2.** *Archaic.* A mother. [Middle English *dam, dame,* lady, mother. See DAME.]

dam[3] *abbr.* Decameter.

dam·age (dăm′ĭj) *n.* **1.** Impairment of the usefulness or value of person or property; harm. **2. damages.** *Law.* Money ordered to be paid as compensation for injury or loss. **3.** *Informal.* Cost; price. **—damage** *v.* **-aged, -ag·ing, -ag·es.** *—tr.* To cause damage to. See Synonyms at **injure.** *—intr.* To suffer or be susceptible to damage. [Middle English, from Old French : *dam,* loss (from Latin *damnum*) + *-age,* -age.] **—dam′age·a·bil′i·ty** *n.* **—dam′age·a·ble** *adj.* **—dam′ag·ing·ly** *adv.*

damage control *n.* An effort to minimize or curtail damage or loss.

Da·man (də-män′). A region of northwest India on the eastern shore of the Gulf of Cambay. A Portuguese colony after the 16th century, it was annexed by India in 1961.

Da·man·hur (dăm′ən-ho͝or′, dä′män-ho͝or′). A city of northeast Egypt on the Nile River delta northwest of Cairo. In ancient times it was known as Hermopolis Parva. Population, 221,500.

dam·ar (dăm′ər) *n.* Variant of **dammar.**

dam·as·cene (dăm′ə-sēn′, dăm′ə-sēn′) *tr.v.* **-cened, -cen·ing, -cenes.** To decorate (metal) with wavy patterns of inlay or etching. **—damascene** *n.* Metalwork decorated with wavy patterns of inlay or etching. **—damascene** *adj.* **1.** Of or relating to damascening. **2.** Of or relating to damask. [French *damasquiner,* from *damasquin,* of Damascus, from Latin *Damascēnus,* from Greek *Damaskēnos,* from *Damaskos,* Damascus.] **—dam′a·scen′er** *n.*

Da·mas·cus (də-măs′kəs). The capital and largest city of Syria, in the southwest part of the country. Inhabited since prehistoric times, the city became a thriving commercial center under the Romans and was a Saracen stronghold during the Crusades. Population, 1,259,000. **—Dam′a·scene′** (dăm′ə-sēn′) *adj. & n.*

Damascus steel *n.* An early form of steel having wavy markings, developed in Near Eastern countries and used chiefly in sword blades.

dam·ask (dăm′əsk) *n.* **1.** A rich patterned fabric of cotton, linen, silk, or wool. **2.** A fine, twilled table linen. **3.** Damascus steel. **4.** The wavy pattern on Damascus steel. **—damask** *tr.v.* **-asked, -ask·ing, -asks. 1.** To damascene. **2.** To decorate or weave with rich patterns. [Middle English, Damascus, damask, from Latin *Damascus,* from Greek *Damaskos.*] **—dam′ask** *adj.*

damask rose *n.* A rose *(Rosa damascena)* native to Asia that has fragrant red or pink flowers and is used as a source of attar. [From Middle English *Damask,* Damascus. See DAMASK.]

damask steel *n.* Damascus steel.

dame (dām) *n.* **1.** Used formerly as a courtesy title for a woman in authority or a mistress of a household. **2. a.** A married woman; a matron. **b.** An elderly woman. **3.** *Slang.* A woman. **4.** *Chiefly British.* **a.** A woman holding a nonhereditary title conferred by a sovereign in recognition of personal merit or service to the country. **b.** The wife or widow of a knight. **c.** Used as the title for such a woman. [Middle English, from Old French, from Latin *domina,* feminine of *dominus,* lord, master. See **dem-** in Appendix.]

dame's rocket (dāmz) *n., pl.* **dame's rockets.** A European plant *(Hesperis matronalis)* having clusters of fragrant purple to white flowers. Also called *dame's violet.*

Da·mien de Veus·ter (dā′mē-ən də vyo͞o′stər, dä-myăN′ də vœ-stĕr′), **Joseph.** Known as "Father Damien." 1840–1889. Belgian Roman Catholic missionary who ministered to the leper colony on Molokai (1873–1889), where he contracted leprosy and died.

Dam·i·et·ta (dăm′ē-ĕt′ə) also **Dum·yat** (do͝om-yät′). A city of northeast Egypt on the Nile River delta north-northeast of Cairo. It was conquered by Crusaders in 1219. Population, 118,100.

da·min·o·zide (də-mĭn′ə-zīd′) *n.* A chemical plant growth regulator, $C_6H_{12}N_2O_3$, used commercially on apples to retard growth, enhance color, and increase storage life. [D(IMETHYL) + AMINO- + (HYDRA)Z(INE) + -IDE.]

dam·mar or **dam·ar** also **dam·mer** (dăm′ər) *n.* Any of various hard resins obtained from trees of the genera *Shorea, Balanocarpus,* and *Hopea,* native to southeast Asia and the Malay Archipelago and used in varnishes and lacquers. [Malay *damar,* resin.]

dam·mit (dăm′ĭt) *interj.* Used to express anger, irritation, contempt, or disappointment. [Alteration of *damn it.*]

damn (dăm) *v.* **damned, damn·ing, damns.** *—tr.* **1.** To pronounce an adverse judgment upon. See Synonyms at **condemn. 2.** To bring about the failure of; ruin. **3.** To condemn as harmful, illegal, or immoral: *a cleric who damned gambling and strong drink.* **4.** *Theology.* To condemn to everlasting punishment or a similar fate; doom. **5.** To swear at. *—intr.* To swear; curse. **—damn** *interj.* Used to express anger, irritation, contempt, or disappointment. **—damn** *n.* **1.** The saying of "damn" as a curse. **2.** *Informal.* The least valuable bit; a jot: *not worth a damn.* **—damn** *adv. & adj.* Damned. ***—idiom.* damn well.** Without any doubt; positively: *I am damn well going to file charges against him.* [Middle English *dampnen,* from Old French *dampner,* from Latin *damnāre,* to condemn, inflict loss upon, from *damnum,* loss.] **—damn′ing·ly** *adv.*

dam·na·ble (dăm′nə-bəl) *adj.* Deserving condemnation; odious. **—dam′na·ble·ness** *n.* **—dam′na·bly** *adv.*

♦**dam·na·tion** (dăm-nā′shən) *n.* **1.** The act of damning or the condition of being damned. **2.** *Theology.* **a.** Condemnation to everlasting punishment; doom. **b.** Everlasting punishment. **3.** Failure or ruination incurred by adverse criticism. **—damnation** *interj.* Used to express anger or annoyance. See Regional Note at **tarnation.**

dam·na·to·ry (dăm′nə-tôr′ē, -tōr′ē) *adj.* Threatening with or expressing condemnation; damning.

♦**damned** (dămd) *adj.* **damned·er** (dăm′dər), **damned·est** (dăm′dĭst). **1.** Condemned, especially to eternal punishment. **2.** *Informal.* Deserving condemnation; detestable: *this damned weather.* **3.** Used as an intensive: *a damned fool.* **—damned** *adv.* **damneder, damnedest.** Used as an intensive: *a damned poor excuse.* **—damned** *n.* *Theology.* Souls doomed to eternal punishment.

♦ ***REGIONAL NOTE:*** There are many regional variants, mostly euphemisms, for *damned,* both as an oath and as a mild intensive. Southern exclamations and intensives tend to begin with *dad-,* a euphemism for "god"—hence *dadblamed, dadblasted, dadburn,* and *dadgum. Dadgum* can be combined with *it* in the interjection *dadgummit.* Another such euphemism is the better known *doggone,* probably originally Southern but now widespread. Like *dadgum, doggone* is used as a mild intensive: *"The best doggone deals in Alabama"* (billboard in Montgomery). *Doggone* likewise appears in phrasal interjections: *Doggonit, I dropped my hammer.* A common regional variant of *damned* is *durn,* also euphemistic and relatively mild, as in this snatch of Baltimore dialogue: *"If that's not just the weirdest durn thing I ever laid eyes on"* (Anne Tyler).

damned·est (dăm′dĭst) *adj.* Superlative of **damned. —damnedest** *n.* All that is possible; the utmost: *did my damnedest to deliver the term paper on time.*

Dam·o·cles (dăm′ə-klēz′). fl. fourth century B.C. Greek courtier to Dionysius the Elder, tyrant of Syracuse, who according to legend was forced to sit at a banquet table under a sword suspended by a single hair to demonstrate the precariousness of a king's fortunes.

dam·oi·selle (dăm′ə-zĕl′) *n.* *Archaic.* Variant of **damosel.**

Da·mon (dā′mən) *n.* A legendary figure who, out of devotion, pledged his life as a guarantee that his condemned friend Pythias would return to face execution. Both were subsequently pardoned.

dam·o·sel also **dam·oi·selle** or **dam·o·zel** (dăm′ə-zĕl′) *n.* *Archaic.* A young woman; a damsel. [Middle English *damoisele,* from Old French *damoiselle,* damsel. See DAMSEL.]

damp (dămp) *adj.* **damp·er, damp·est. 1.** Slightly wet. See Synonyms at **wet. 2.** *Archaic.* Dejected. **—damp** *n.* **1.** Moisture in the air; humidity. **2.** Foul or poisonous gas that sometimes pollutes the air in coal mines. **3.** Lowness of spirits; depression. **4.** A restraint or check; a discouragement. **—damp** *tr.v.* **damped, damp·ing, damps. 1.** To make damp or moist; moisten. **2.** To extinguish (a fire, for example) by cutting off air. **3.** To restrain or check; discourage. **4.** *Music.* To provide (the strings of a keyboard instrument) with dampers as a means of reducing the dynamic level. **5.** *Physics.* To decrease the amplitude of (a wave). ***—phrasal verb.* damp off.** *Botany.* To be affected by damping off. [Middle English, poison gas, perhaps from Middle Dutch, vapor.] **—damp′ish** *adj.* **—damp′ly** *adv.* **—damp′ness** *n.*

damp·en (dăm′pən) *v.* **-ened, -en·ing, -ens.** *—tr.* **1.** To make damp. **2.** To deaden, restrain, or depress: *"trade moves . . . aimed at dampening protectionist pressures in Congress"* (Christian Science Monitor). **3.** To soundproof. *—intr.* To become damp. **—damp′en·er** *n.*

damp·er (dăm′pər) *n.* **1.** One that deadens, restrains, or depresses: *Rain put a damper on our picnic plans.* **2.** An adjustable plate, as in the flue of a furnace or stove, for controlling the draft. **3.** *Music.* **a.** A device in various keyboard instruments for deadening the vibrations of the strings. **b.** A mute for various brass instruments. **4.** A device that eliminates or progressively diminishes vibrations or oscillations, as of a magnetic needle.

Father Damien

Dam·pi·er (dăm′pē-ər), **William.** 1652–1715. English buccaneer and navigator who described his circumnavigation of the globe in *A New Voyage Round the World* (1697) and later explored the South Seas.

damp·ing (dăm′pĭng) *n.* The capacity built into a mechanical or electrical device to prevent excessive correction and the resulting instability or oscillatory conditions.

damping off *n.* *Botany.* A disease of seedlings that is caused by fungi and results in wilting and death.

Dam·rosch (dăm′rŏsh), **Leopold.** 1832–1885. German-born American musician who was the first to conduct Wagnerian opera at New York's Metropolitan Opera House. His son **Walter Johannes Damrosch** (1862–1950) continued the tradition, introducing Wagner's works throughout the United States.

dam·sel (dăm′zəl) *n.* A young woman or girl; a maiden. [Middle English *damisele,* from Old French *dameisele, damoiselle,* from Vulgar Latin **dominicella,* diminutive of *domina,* lady. See DAME.]

dam·sel·fish (dăm′zəl-fĭsh′) *n., pl.* **damselfish** or **-fish·es.** Any of various small tropical marine fishes of the family Pomacentridae, having laterally compressed, usually brightly colored bodies. Also called *demoiselle.*

dam·sel·fly (dăm′zəl-flī′) *n.* Any of various often brightly colored, predatory insects having a long slender body and elongated wings that fold together when the insect is at rest. Also called *demoiselle, devil's darning needle.*

dam·son (dăm′zən, -sən) *n.* **1.** A Eurasian plum tree *(Prunus insititia)* cultivated since ancient times for its edible fruit. Also called *bullace plum.* **2.** The oval, bluish-black, juicy plum of this tree. [Middle English *damson, damacene,* from Latin *(prūnum) Damascēnum,* (plum) of Damascus, from *Damascēnus.* See DAMASCENE.]

dan also **Dan** (dän, dăn) *n.* **1.** *Sports.* **a.** Any of 12 levels of proficiency at the grade of black belt in martial arts such as judo and karate. **b.** One who has achieved such a level. **2.** *Games.* An expert or expert level in shogi and other such games. [Japanese.]

Dan¹ (dăn). In the Old Testament, a son of Jacob and the forebear of one of the tribes of Israel.

Dan² (dăn) *n.* *Archaic.* Used formerly as a title of honor for respected men, such as clerics and poets. [Middle English, from Old French, from Medieval Latin *Domnus,* from Latin *dominus,* master, lord. See **dem-** in Appendix.]

Dan. *abbr.* **1.** *Bible.* Daniel. **2.** Danish.

Da·na (dā′nə), **Charles Anderson.** 1819–1897. American newspaperman who as owner-editor of the *New York Sun* (after 1868) promoted a lively, readable style and stressed human-interest stories.

Dana, James Dwight. 1813–1895. American scientist whose textbooks established him as the foremost geologist of his time.

Dana, Richard Henry. 1815–1882. American lawyer and writer best known for his *Two Years Before the Mast* (1840), an account of his voyage from Boston to California around Cape Horn.

Dan·a·e also **Dan·a·ë** (dăn′ə-ē′) *n.* *Greek Mythology.* The daughter of Eurydice and Acrisius and mother of Perseus who was imprisoned by her father in a bronze chamber.

Da·na·i·des also **Da·na·ï·des** (də-nā′ĭ-dēz′) *pl.n.* *Greek Mythology.* The daughters of Danaus, who at their father's command murdered their bridegrooms on their wedding night and

ă **pat**	oi **boy**
ā **pay**	ou **out**
âr **care**	o͝o **took**
ä **father**	o͞o **boot**
ĕ **pet**	ŭ **cut**
ē **be**	ûr **urge**
ĭ **pit**	th **thin**
ī **pie**	*th* **this**
îr **pier**	hw **which**
ŏ **pot**	zh **vision**
ō **toe**	ə **about, item**
ô **paw**	♦ **regionalism**

Stress marks: **′** (primary); **′** (secondary), as in **dictionary** (dĭk′shə-nĕr′ē)

were condemned in Hades to pour water eternally into a leaky vessel.

Dan·a·kil (dăn′ə-kĭl′, də-nä′kēl). A desert region of northeast Ethiopia and northern Djibouti bordering on the Red Sea. It is part of the Great Rift Valley.

Da Nang or **Da·nang** (də năng′, dä′ näng′). Formerly **Tou·rane** (to͞o-rän′). A city of central Vietnam on the South China Sea. It was the site of an important U.S. military base during the Vietnam War. Population, 318,655.

Dan·a·us also **Dan·a·üs** (dăn′ē-əs) *n.* *Greek Mythology.* A king of Argos, father of the Danaides.

Dan·bur·y (dăn′bĕr′ē, -bə-rē). A city of southwest Connecticut northwest of Bridgeport. Settled in 1685, it was largely destroyed by the British in 1777 during the American Revolution. Population, 60,470.

dance (dăns) *v.* **danced, danc·ing, danc·es.** —*intr.* **1.** To move rhythmically usually to music, using prescribed or improvised steps and gestures. **2. a.** To leap or skip about excitedly. **b.** To appear to flash or twinkle: *eyes that danced with merriment.* **c.** *Informal.* To appear to skip about; vacillate: *danced around the issue.* **3.** To bob up and down. —*tr.* **1.** To engage in or perform (a dance). **2.** To cause to dance. **3.** To bring to a particular state or condition by dancing: *My partner danced me to exhaustion.* —**dance** *n.* **1.** A series of rhythmical motions and steps, usually to music. **2.** The art of dancing: "[They] *have both offered as a definition of dance: a spiritual activity in physical form*" (Susan Sontag). **3.** A party or gathering of people for dancing; a ball. **4.** One round or turn of dancing: *May I have this dance?* **5.** A musical or rhythmical accompaniment composed or played for dancing. **6.** The act or an instance of dancing. [Middle English *dauncen,* from Old French *danser,* perhaps of Germanic origin.] —**danc′er** *n.* —**danc′ing·ly** *adv.*

dandelion
Taraxacum officinale

dance·a·ble (dăn′sə-bəl) *adj.* Suitable for dancing: *a danceable melody.* —**dance′a·bil′i·ty** *n.*

dance·go·er (dăns′gō′ər) *n.* One who frequently attends dance performances. —**dance′go′ing** *adj.* & *n.*

dance hall or **dance·hall** (dăns′hôl′) *n.* A building or part of a building with facilities for dancing.

dan·cer·ly (dăn′sər-lē) *adj.* Having or displaying the movements, skills, or knowledge of a dancer or the dance: *"impressionistic doodles, symphonic splashes and dancerly flourishes"* (Los Angeles Times).

dance·wear (dăns′wâr′) *n.* Clothing such as leotards and warmup suits that are worn for dance practice and exercising.

danc·y also **danc·ey** (dăn′sē) *adj.* **-i·er, -i·est.** *Informal.* Suitable for or inviting dancing; danceable: *dancy music.*

D and C *n.* Dilation and curettage.

dan·de·li·on (dăn′dl-ī′ən) *n.* **1.** A Eurasian plant *(Taraxacum officinale)* of the composite family having many-rayed yellow flower heads and deeply notched basal leaves. Widely naturalized as a weed in North America, it is used in salads and to make wine. **2.** Any of several similar or related plants. **3.** *Color.* A brilliant to vivid yellow. [Middle English *dent-de-lioun,* from Old French *dentdelion,* from Medieval Latin *dēns leōnis,* lion's tooth (from its sharply indented leaves) : Latin *dēns, dent-,* tooth; see **dent-** in Appendix + Latin *leōnis,* genitive of *leō,* lion; see LION.]

WORD HISTORY: *Dentdelioun,* the Middle English form of *dandelion,* makes it easy to see that our word is a borrowing of Old French *dentdelion,* literally, "tooth of the lion," referring to the sharply indented leaves of the plant. Modern French *dent-de-lion,* unlike Modern English *dandelion,* reveals to anyone who knows French what the components of the word are. The English spelling, on the other hand, reflects the pronunciation of the Old French word at the time it was borrowed into English. For example, the *t* in *dentdelion* probably disappeared early in Old French, having been absorbed into the related sound of the *d.* The earliest recorded instance of the word occurs in a herbal written in 1373, but we find an instance of *dandelion* used in a proper name (Willelmus Dawndelyon) in a document dated 1363.

dan·der¹ (dăn′dər) *n.* *Informal.* Temper or anger: *What got their dander up?* [Perhaps alteration of *dunder,* fermented cane juice used in rum-making, fermentation, possibly alteration of Spanish *redundar,* to overflow, from Latin *redundāre.* See REDUNDANT.]

dan·der² (dăn′dər) *n.* Scurf from the coat or feathers of various animals, often of an allergenic nature. [Alteration of DANDRUFF.]

Dandie Dinmont

Dan·die Din·mont (dăn′dē dĭn′mŏnt′) *n.* A small terrier of a breed developed in the border counties of England and Scotland and having a rough grayish or brownish coat, a long body, drooping ears, and short legs. [After *Dandie Dinmont,* the owner of two such dogs in *Guy Mannering,* a novel by Sir Walter Scott.]

dan·di·fy (dăn′də-fī′) *tr.v.* **-fied, -fy·ing, -fies.** To dress as or cause to resemble a dandy. —**dan′di·fi·ca′tion** (-fĭ-kā′shən) *n.*

♦ **dan·dle** (dăn′dl) *tr.v.* **-dled, -dling, -dles. 1.** To move (a small child) up and down on the knees or in the arms in a playful way: *"Somebody who was dandled on Queen Victoria's knee must appear an old fogy"* (Edward, Duke of Windsor). **2.** To pamper or pet. —**dandle** *n.* *Narragansett Bay.* See **seesaw** (sense 1). See Regional Note at **teeter-totter.** [Origin unknown.]

♦ **dandle board** *n.* *Narragansett Bay.* See **seesaw** (sense 1). See Regional Note at **teeter-totter.**

Dan·dong (dăn′dông′) also **Tan·tung** (tän′to͝ong′) or **An·tung** (än′to͝ong′). A city of northeast China on the Yalu River opposite North Korea. It is a seaport and manufacturing center. Population, 400,000.

dan·druff (dăn′drəf) *n.* A scaly scurf formed on and shed from the scalp, sometimes caused by seborrhea. [*dand-,* of unknown origin + dialectal *hurf,* scurf (from Old Norse *hrufa,* crust, scab).] —**dan′druff·y** *adj.*

dan·dy (dăn′dē) *n., pl.* **-dies. 1.** A man who affects extreme elegance in clothes and manners; a fop. **2.** *Informal.* Something very good or agreeable. **3.** *Nautical.* See **yawl** (sense 1). —**dandy** *adj.* **-di·er, -di·est. 1.** Suggestive of or attired like a dandy; foppish. **2.** *Informal.* Fine; good. [Perhaps short for *jack-a-dandy,* fop.] —**dan′dy·ish** *adj.* —**dan′dy·ish·ly** *adv.* —**dan′dy·ism** *n.*

dandy fever *n.* See **dengue.** [Alteration of DENGUE.]

dandy roll *n.* A cylinder of wire gauze pressed on moist pulp before it starts through the rollers of a papermaking device and resulting in the production of a watermark. Also called *dandy roller.*

Dane (dān) *n.* **1.** A native or inhabitant of Denmark. **2.** A person of Danish ancestry. [Middle English *Dan,* from Old Norse *Danr.*]

Dane·geld (dān′gĕld′) also **Dane·gelt** (-gĕlt′) *n.* A tax levied in England from the 10th to the 12th century to finance protection against Danish invasion. [Middle English : *Dane,* genitive pl. of *Dan,* Dane; see DANE + *geld,* tribute (from Old English *geld, gield,* payment).]

Dane·law also **Dane·lagh** (dān′lô′) *n.* **1.** The body of law established by the Danish invaders and settlers in northeast England in the ninth and tenth centuries. **2.** The sections of England under the jurisdiction of this law. [Middle English *Denelage,* from Old English *Dena lagu* : *Dena,* genitive of *Dene,* the Danes + *lagu,* law; see LAW.]

dang (dăng) *n., adv., & adj.* Damn. [Alteration of DAMN.]

dan·ger (dān′jər) *n.* **1.** Exposure or vulnerability to harm or risk. **2.** A source or an instance of risk or peril. **3.** *Obsolete.* Power, especially power to harm. [Middle English *daunger,* power, dominion, peril, from Old French *dangier,* from Vulgar Latin **dominiārium,* authority, power, from Latin *dominium,* sovereignty, from *dominus,* lord, master. See **dem-** in Appendix.]

dan·ger·ous (dān′jər-əs) *adj.* **1.** Involving or filled with danger; perilous. **2.** Being able or likely to do harm. —**dan′ger·ous·ly** *adv.* —**dan′ger·ous·ness** *n.*

dan·gle (dăng′gəl) *v.* **-gled, -gling, -gles.** —*intr.* **1.** To hang loosely and swing or sway to and fro. **2.** To be a hanger-on. —*tr.* **1.** To cause to hang loosely or swing. **2.** To cause (one's expectations or hopes) to hang uncertainly or remain unresolved. —**dangle** *n.* **1.** The act or an instance of dangling. **2.** Something dangled. [Perhaps from Danish *dangle* or Swedish *dangla.*] —**dan′gler** *n.* —**dan′gly** *adj.*

dan·gle·ber·ry (dăng′gəl-bĕr′ē) *n.* A deciduous shrub *(Gaylussacia frondosa)* of the eastern United States, having dark blue fruits. Also called *dwarf huckleberry.* [Probably alteration of *tangleberry.*]

dan·gling participle (dăng′glĭng) *n.* *Grammar.* A participle, usually in a subordinate clause, that lacks a clear grammatical relation with the subject of the sentence, such as *approaching* in the sentence *Approaching New York, the skyline came into view.*

Dan·iel (dăn′yəl) *n.* *Bible.* **1.** In the Old Testament, a Hebrew prophet of the sixth century B.C. **2.** *Abbr.* **Dan., Dn** See table at **Bible.** [Hebrew *Dānī'ēl,* God is my judge.]

Daniel, Peter Vivian. 1784–1860. American jurist who served as an associate justice of the U.S. Supreme Court (1841–1860).

Daniel, Samuel. 1562?–1619. English writer whose works include *The Civil Wars* (1595–1609), a poetic account of the Wars of the Roses.

Dan·iels (dăn′yəlz), **Josephus.** 1862–1948. American journalist who served as secretary of the navy (1913–1921) and ambassador to Mexico (1933–1941).

da·ni·o (dā′nē-ō′) *n., pl.* **-os.** Any of various small, often brightly colored freshwater fishes of the genera *Danio* and *Brachydanio,* native to Asia and popular as aquarium fish. [New Latin *Danio,* genus name.]

Dan·ish (dā′nĭsh) *adj.* *Abbr.* **Dan., Da.** Of or relating to Denmark, the Danes, their language, or their culture. —**Danish** *n.* **1.** *Abbr.* **Dan., Da.** The North Germanic language of the Danes. **2.** *pl.* **Danish** or **-ish·es.** A Danish pastry. [Middle English, alteration (influenced by Old Norse *Danr,* Dane) of *Denish,* from Old English *Denisc,* from *Dene,* the Danes.]

Danish pastry *n.* A sweet, buttery pastry made with raised dough.

Dan·ite (dăn′īt′) *n.* *Bible.* In the Old Testament, a descendant of Dan. —**Danite** *adj.* Of or relating to the Hebrew tribe descended from Dan.

dank (dăngk) *adj.* **dank·er, dank·est.** Disagreeably damp or humid. See Synonyms at **wet.** [Middle English, probably of Scandinavian origin.] —**dank′ly** *adv.* —**dank′ness** *n.*

D'An·nun·zio (dän-no͞on′tsyō), **Gabriele.** 1863–1938. Ital-

ă pat	oi boy
ā pay	ou out
âr care	o͝o took
ä father	o͞o boot
ĕ pet	ŭ cut
ē be	ûr urge
ĭ pit	th thin
ī pie	*th* this
îr pier	hw which
ŏ pot	zh vision
ō toe	ə about, item
ô paw	♦ regionalism

Stress marks: ′ (primary); ′ (secondary), as in **dictionary** (dĭk′shə-nĕr′ē)

ian writer best known for his passionate, free-spirited heroes and his support of Benito Mussolini's fascist regime.

Da·no-Nor·we·gian (dā′-nō-nôr-wē′jən) *n.* An official literary form of Norwegian based on written Danish. Also called *Bokmål, Riksmål.*

dan·seur (däɴ-sœr′) *n., pl.* **-seurs** (-sœr′). A man who is a ballet dancer. [French, from Old French, from *danser,* to dance. See DANCE.]

dan·seuse (däɴ-sœz′) *n., pl.* **-seuses** (-sœz′). A woman who is a ballet dancer. [French, feminine of *danseur,* danseur. See DANSEUR.]

Dan·te A·li·ghie·ri (dän′tā ä′lē-gyĕ′rē, dăn′tē). 1265–1321. Italian poet whose masterpiece, *The Divine Comedy* (completed 1321), details his visionary progress through Hell and Purgatory, escorted by Virgil, and through Heaven, guided by his lifelong idealized love Beatrice. **—Dan′te·an** *adj. & n.* **—Dan·tesque′** (dăn-tĕsk′, dăn-) *adj.*

Dan·ton (däɴ-tôɴ′), **Georges Jacques.** 1759–1794. French Revolutionary leader who took part in the storming of the Bastille (1789) and supported the execution of Louis XVI (1793) but was guillotined for his opposition to the Reign of Terror.

Da·nu (dä′no͞o) *n. Mythology.* The mother of the Irish gods, and the goddess of death.

Dan·ube (dăn′yo͞ob). A river of south-central Europe rising in southwest Germany and flowing about 2,848 km (1,770 mi) southeast through Austria, Hungary, Yugoslavia, and Romania to the Black Sea. It has been a major trade route since the Middle Ages. **—Dan·u′bi·an** *adj.*

Dan·vers (dăn′vərz). A town of northeast Massachusetts north-northeast of Boston. It was settled in the 1630's and set off from Salem in 1752. Population, 24,100.

Dan·ville (dăn′vĭl′). **1.** A city of western California, a suburb of Oakland. Population, 26,446. **2.** A city of eastern Illinois east-northeast of Decatur. It is a commercial center in an agricultural region. Population, 38,985. **3.** An independent city of southern Virginia on the Dan River near the North Carolina border. Founded in 1793, it was the last capital of the Confederacy in 1865. Population, 45,642.

Dan·zig (dăn′sĭg, dän′tsĭk). See Gdańsk.

Danzig Free City. A former state (1919–1939) on the Gulf of Gdańsk surrounding and including the city of Gdańsk.

dap (dăp) *intr.v.* **dapped, dap·ping, daps. 1.** To fish by letting a baited hook fall gently onto the water. **2.** To dip lightly or quickly into water, as a bird does. **3.** To skip or bounce, especially over the surface of water. [Probably alteration of DAB[1].]

daph·ne (dăf′nē) *n.* Any of several Eurasian shrubs of the genus *Daphne* often cultivated for their glossy evergreen foliage and clusters of small, bell-shaped flowers. [Latin, laurel, from Greek *daphnē.*]

Daph·ne (dăf′nē) *n. Greek Mythology.* A nymph who metamorphosed into a laurel tree as a means of escaping from Apollo.

daph·ni·a (dăf′nē-ə) *n., pl.* **daphnia.** Any of various water fleas of the genus *Daphnia,* some species of which are commonly used as food for aquarium fish. [New Latin *Daphnia,* genus name, perhaps from Latin *Daphnē,* Daphne.]

Daph·nis (daf′nĭs) *n. Greek Mythology.* A Sicilian shepherd and son of Hermes who was famed as a musician and reputed to be the inventor of pastoral poetry.

Da Pon·te (də pŏn′tē, dä pôn′tĕ), **Lorenzo.** 1749–1838. Italian-born American poet and educator who wrote librettos for Mozart's *Marriage of Figaro* (1786), *Don Giovanni* (1787), and *Così fan Tutte* (1790).

dap·per (dăp′ər) *adj.* **1.a.** Neatly dressed; trim. **b.** Very stylish in dress. **2.** Lively and alert. [Middle English *daper,* elegant, probably from Middle Dutch *dapper,* quick, strong.] **—dap′per·ly** *adv.* **—dap′per·ness** *n.*

dap·ple (dăp′əl) *n.* **1.a.** Mottled or spotted marking, as on a horse's coat. **b.** An individual spot. **2.** An animal with a mottled or spotted skin or coat. **—dapple** *tr.v.* **-pled, -pling, -ples.** To mark or mottle with spots. [Back-formation from DAPPLED.] **—dap′ple** *adj.*

dap·pled (dăp′əld) *adj.* Spotted; mottled. [Middle English, probably from Old Norse *depill,* spot, splash, diminutive of *dapi,* pool.]

dap·ple-gray (dăp′əl-grā′) *adj.* Gray with a mottled pattern of darker gray markings. **—dapple-gray** *n.* A horse having a coat of mottled gray. [Middle English *dappel-grai,* probably alteration (influenced by DAPPLED) of **appel-grai,* apple-gray, from Old Norse *apalgrār* : *apall-,* apple + *grār,* gray.]

dap·sone (dăp′sōn′, -zōn′) *n.* An antibacterial drug, $C_{12}H_{12}N_2O_2S$, used primarily to treat leprosy and some forms of dermatitis. [D(I)-¹ + A(MINO)- + (DI)P(HENYL) + S(ULF)ONE.]

DAR *abbr.* **1.** Damage assessment routine. **2.** Daughters of the American Revolution.

Dar·by and Joan (där′bē; jōn) *n.* An elderly married couple who live a placid, harmonious life together and are seldom seen apart. [Probably after *Darby and Joan,* a couple in an 18th-century English ballad.]

Dard (därd) also **Dar·dic** (där′dĭk) *n.* A group of Indic languages spoken in the upper Indus River valley.

Dar·dan (där′dn) or **Dar·da·ni·an** (där-dā′nē-ən) *n. Archaic.* A Trojan. [After *Dardanus,* the mythical founder of Troy.] **—Dar′dan** *adj.*

Dar·da·nelles (där′dn-ĕlz′). Formerly **Hel·les·pont** (hĕl′ĭ-spŏnt′). A strait connecting the Aegean Sea with the Sea of Marmara. In ancient times it was the scene of the legendary exploits of Hero and Leander.

Dar·da·nus (där′dn-əs) *n. Greek Mythology.* The founder of Troy.

Dar·dic (där′dĭk) *n.* Variant of **Dard.**

dare (dâr) *v.* **dared, dar·ing, dares.** —*tr.* **1.** To have the courage required for: *The gymnast dared a breathtakingly difficult move.* **2.** To challenge (someone) to do something requiring boldness: *They dared me to dive off the high board.* **3.** To confront or oppose boldly; defy. See Synonyms at **defy.** —*intr.* To be courageous or bold enough to do or try something: *Go ahead and dive if you dare.* —*aux.* To be courageous or bold enough to: *I dare not say. How dare she go?* **—dare** *n.* An act of daring; a challenge. [Middle English *daren,* from Old English *dearr,* first and third person sing. present indicative of *durran,* to venture, dare. See **dhers-** in Appendix.] **—dar′er** *n.*

USAGE NOTE: Depending on its sense, the verb *dare* sometimes behaves like an auxiliary verb (such as *can* or *may*) and sometimes like a main verb (such as *want* or *try*). When used as an auxiliary verb, *dare* does not agree with its subject: *Let him say that if he dare.* It also does not combine with *do* in questions, negations, or certain other constructions: *Dare we tell her the truth? I dare not mention their names.* Finally, it does not take *to* before the complement verb that follows it: *If you dare breathe a word about it I'll never speak to you again.* When used as a main verb, *dare* does agree with its subject (*If he dares to show up at her house I'll be surprised*), and it does combine with *do* (*Did anyone dare to admit it?*). It may optionally take *to* before the verb following it: *No one dares* (or *dares to*) *speak freely about the political situation.* The auxiliary forms are used primarily in present tense questions, negations, imperatives, and conditional clauses. These forms differ subtly in meaning from the main verb forms in that they emphasize the attitude or involvement of the speaker while the main verb forms present a more objective situation. Thus *How dare she take the exam without ever once coming to class?* expresses indignation at the student's action, whereas *How did she dare to take the exam without ever once coming to class?* is a genuine request for information. When *dare* is used as a transitive verb meaning "challenge," only main verb forms are possible and *to* is required: *Anyone who dares* (not *dare*) *him to attempt* (not just *attempt*) *it will be sorry.*

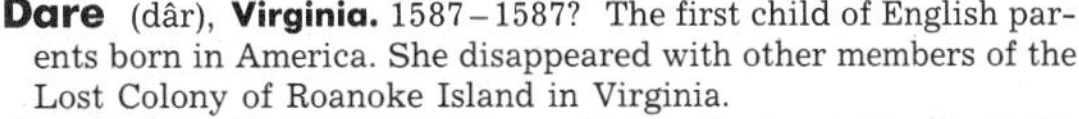

Dare (dâr), **Virginia.** 1587–1587? The first child of English parents born in America. She disappeared with other members of the Lost Colony of Roanoke Island in Virginia.

dare·dev·il (dâr′dĕv′əl) *n.* One who is recklessly bold. **—daredevil** *adj.* Recklessly bold. See Synonyms at **adventurous.** **—dare′dev′il·ry, dare′dev′il·try** (-trē) *n.*

dare·say (dâr′sā′) *intr. & tr.v.* To think very likely or almost certain; suppose. Used in the first person singular present tense: *Will they be late? Yes, I daresay. I daresay you're wrong.*

Dar es Sa·laam (där′ ĕs sə-läm′). The de facto capital and largest city of Tanzania, in the eastern part of the country on an arm of the Indian Ocean. It was founded in 1862 by the sultan of Zanzibar. The name means "haven of peace." Population, 757,346.

Dar·fur (där-fo͝or′). A region and former sultanate of western Sudan. Occupied since prehistoric times, the area fell to the Egyptians in 1874 and later to the British, who incorporated it into their holdings in the Sudan.

Dar·i·en (dâr′ē-ĕn′, dâr′-, dăr′ē-ən, dâr′-). A town of southwest Connecticut northwest of Stamford. Settled c. 1641, it is mainly residential. Population, 18,892.

Da·ri·én (dâr′ē-ĕn′, där-yĕn′). A region of eastern Panama on the **Gulf of Darién,** a wide bay of the Caribbean Sea between eastern Panama and northwest Colombia. In 1513 Vasco Núñez de Balboa led an expedition across the **Isthmus of Darién** (now the Isthmus of Panama) and became the first European to view the Pacific Ocean from the New World.

dar·ing (dâr′ĭng) *adj.* Willing to take or seek out risks; bold and venturesome. See Synonyms at **adventurous.** **—daring** *n.* Audacious bravery; boldness. **—dar′ing·ly** *adv.* **—dar′ing·ness** *n.*

Da·rí·o (dä-rē′ō), **Rubén.** 1867–1916. Nicaraguan poet who is considered the father of modern Spanish poetry. His works include *Cantos de Vida y Esperanza* (1905).

dar·i·ole (dăr′ē-ōl′) *n.* **1.** A small cooking mold. **2.** A dish, as of vegetables, fish, custard, or pastry, that is cooked and served in a small mold. [Middle English *dariol,* from Old French *dariole,* a small, filled pastry, alteration of dialectal *doriole,* from *dorer,* to gild. See DORY[2].]

Da·ri·us I (də-rī′əs). Known as "Darius the Great." 550?–486 B.C. King of Persia (521–486) who expanded the empire, organized a highly efficient administrative system, and invaded Greece, only to be defeated at the Battle of Marathon in 490.

Darius III. Died 330 B.C. King of Persia (336–330) who was defeated in several battles by Alexander the Great. His murder by a Bactrian satrap effectively ended the Persian Empire.

Dar·jee·ling¹ (där-jē′lĭng). A town of northeast India in the lower Himalaya Mountains on the Sikkim border. At an altitude of 2,287.5 m (7,500 ft), it is a popular tourist center with com-

Daphne

dapple-gray

daredevil
Evel Knievel at the Los Angeles Coliseum, 1973

Darius I
Fifth-century B.C. low relief from Persepolis, widely recognized as Darius the Great

manding views of Mount Kanchenjunga and Mount Everest. Population, 57,603.

Dar·jee·ling² (där-jē′lĭng) *n.* A fine variety of black tea grown especially in the northern part of India.

dark (därk) *adj.* **dark·er, dark·est.** *Abbr.* **dk.** **1.a.** Lacking or having very little light: *a dark corner.* **b.** Lacking brightness: *a dark day.* **2.** Reflecting only a small fraction of incident light. **3.** Of a shade tending toward black in comparison with other shades. Used of a color. **4.** Having a complexion that is not fair; swarthy. **5.** Characterized by gloom; dismal: *took a dark view of the consequences.* **6.** Sullen or threatening: *a dark scowl.* **7.** Difficult to understand; obscure: *stories that are large in scope and dark in substance.* **8.** Concealed or secret; mysterious: *"the dark mysteries of Africa and the fabled wonders of the East"* (W. Bruce Lincoln). **9.** Lacking enlightenment, knowledge, or culture: *a dark age in the history of education.* **10.** Exhibiting or stemming from evil characteristics or forces; sinister: *"churned up dark undercurrents of ethnic and religious hostility"* (Peter Maas). **11.** Having richness or depth: *a dark, melancholy vocal tone.* **12.** Not giving performances; closed: *The movie theater is dark on Mondays.* **—dark** *n.* **1.** Absence of light. **2.** A place having little or no light. **3.** Night; nightfall: *home before dark.* **4.** A deep hue or color. **—*idiom.* in the dark.** **1.** In secret: *decisions made in the dark.* **2.** In a state of ignorance; uninformed: *kept me in the dark about their plans.* [Middle English *derk,* from Old English *deorc.*] **—dark′ish** *adj.* **—dark′ly** *adv.* **—dark′ness** *n.*

SYNONYMS: *dark, dim, murky, dusky, obscure, opaque, shady, shadowy.* These adjectives indicate the absence of light or clarity. *Dark,* the most widely applicable, can refer to insufficiency of illumination for seeing: *"Under the earth, in the flat, dark air, the wet, gloomy rock gave quarter grudgingly"* (Jimmy Breslin). The word can also denote deepness of shade or color (*dark brown*), absence of cheer (*a dark, somber mood*), or lack of rectitude: *"It* [gold] *serves what life requires,/But dreadful too, the dark Assassin hires"* (Alexander Pope). *Dim* suggests lack of clarity of outline, as of physical entities or mental processes such as recollection: *"life and the memory of it cramped,/dim, on a piece of Bristol board"* (Elizabeth Bishop); it can also apply to a source of light to indicate insufficiency: *"storied Windows richly dight,/Casting a dim religious light"* (John Milton). *Murky* implies darkness, often extreme, such as that produced by smoke or fog: *"an atmosphere murky with sand"* (Willa Cather). *"The path was altogether indiscernible in the murky darkness which surrounded them"* (Sir Walter Scott). Figuratively it can imply dark vagueness: *"the narrow crevice of one good deed in a murky life of guilt"* (Charles Dickens). *Dusky* applies principally to the dimness that is characteristic of diminishing light, as at twilight: *"The dusky night rides down the sky,/And ushers in the morn"* (Henry Fielding); it often refers to deepness of shade of a color: *"A dusky blush rose to her cheek"* (Edith Wharton). *Obscure* usually means unclear to the mind or senses (*an obscure communiqué requiring clarification*), but it can refer to physical darkness (*the obscure rooms of a shuttered mansion*). *Opaque* means not admitting penetration by light (*opaque rock crystals*); figuratively it applies to something that is unintelligible: *"Nixon confined himself to opaque philosophical statements that indicated he was not ready for a discussion of basic assumptions"* (Henry A. Kissinger). *Shady* refers literally to what is sheltered from light, especially sunlight (*a shady grove of catalpas*) or figuratively to what is of questionable honesty (*shady business deals*). *Shadowy* also implies obstructed light (*a shadowy avenue through thick foliage*) but may suggest shifting illumination and indistinctness: "[He] *retreated from the limelight to the shadowy fringe of music history"* (Charles Sherman). The word can refer to something that seems to lack substance and is mysterious and possibly sinister: *a shadowy figure in a black Homburg traversing the fogbound park.*

Clarence Darrow

dark adaptation *n.* The physical and chemical adjustments of the eye, including dilation of the pupil and increased activity of rods in the retina, that make vision possible in relative darkness. **—dark′-a·dapt′** (därk′ə-dăpt′) *v.* **—dark′-a·dapt′ed** (därk′ə-dăp′tĭd) *adj.*

Dark Age *n.* **1.** An era of repression and unenlightenment: *The war plunged the country into a Dark Age.* **2. Dark Ages. a.** The period from about A.D. 476 to about the year 1000. **b.** The entire period from the end of classical civilization to the revival of learning in the West; the Middle Ages.

Dark Continent. A former name for Africa, so used because its hinterland was largely unexplored and therefore mysterious until the 19th century. Henry M. Stanley was probably the first to use the term in his 1878 account *Through the Dark Continent.*

dark·en (där′kən) *v.* **-ened, -en·ing, -ens.** *—tr.* **1.a.** To make dark or darker. **b.** To give a darker hue to. **2.** To fill with sadness; make gloomy. **3.** To render vague or uncertain; obscure: *The sudden drop in stock prices darkened the future for investors.* **4.** To tarnish or stain: *a scandal that darkened the family's good name.* *—intr.* To become dark or darker. **—dark′en·er** *n.*

dark-field microscope (därk′fēld′) *n.* A microscope in which an object is illuminated only from the sides so that it appears bright against a dark background.

dark horse *n.* **1.** One who achieves unexpected support and success as a political candidate, typically during a party's convention. **2.** A little-known, unexpectedly successful entrant, as in a horserace.

dark lantern *n.* A lantern whose light can be blocked, as by a sliding panel.

dar·kle (där′kəl) *v.* **-kled, -kling, -kles.** *—intr.* **1.** To appear darkly or indistinctly. **2.a.** To grow dark. **b.** To become gloomy. *—tr.* To make dark or indistinct: *"the dramatist . . . whose province it is to darkle and obscure"* (London National Observer). [Back-formation from DARKLING.]

dar·kling (där′klĭng) *adv.* In the dark. **—darkling** *adj.* **1.** Occurring or enacted in the dark. **2.** Dark; dim. **—darkling** *n.* The dark: *"She carried some rugs for me through the shrubbery in the darkling"* (H.G. Wells).

darkling beetle *n.* A beetle of the family Tenebrionidae, having a brown or black body and feeding on decaying vegetation, living plants, or stored grain. It is found in a variety of habitats, including deserts. Also called *tenebrionid.*

dark reaction *n.* The second stage of photosynthesis, not requiring light to occur, and during which energy released from ATP drives the production of organic molecules from carbon dioxide.

dark·room (därk′ro͞om′, -ro͝om′) *n.* A room in which photographic materials are processed, either in complete darkness or with a safelight.

dark·some (därk′səm) *adj.* Dark and somber.

dark star *n.* A star that is normally obscured or too faint for direct visual observation, especially the component of an eclipsing binary star detectable by spectral analysis or in the eclipse of the bright component.

Dar·lan (där-läN′), **Jean Louis Xavier François.** 1881–1942. French admiral. A leading member of Marshal Pétain's Vichy government, he was nevertheless instrumental in persuading French territories in northern and western Africa to side with the Allies after 1942.

dar·ling (där′lĭng) *n.* **1.** A dearly beloved person. **2.** One that is greatly liked or preferred; a favorite: *"the pride and vanity of the rich, the darlings of fate"* (Mario Puzo). **—darling** *adj.* **1.** Dearly beloved. **2.** Regarded with special favor; favorite: *"Metaphysics and poetry . . . are my darling studies"* (Samuel Taylor Coleridge). **3.** *Informal.* Charming or amusing: *a darling hat.* [Middle English *dereling,* from Old English *dēorling* : *dēore,* dear + *-ling,* diminutive suff.; see -LING¹.]

Dar·ling Range (där′lĭng). An upland region of southwest Australia extending along the Pacific coast north and south of Perth.

Darling River. A river rising in the Great Dividing Range of southeast Australia and flowing about 2,739 km (1,702 mi) generally southwest to the Murray River. It is the longest river in Australia but has a sporadic flow.

Dar·ling·ton (där′lĭng-tən). A borough of northeast England south of Newcastle. It is a railroad center. Population, 97,800.

Darm·stadt (därm′stăt, -shtät′). A city of southwest Germany southeast of Frankfurt. It was chartered in 1330. Population, 134,718.

darn¹ (därn) *v.* **darned, darn·ing, darns.** *—tr.* To mend (a garment, for example) by weaving thread or yarn across a gap or hole. *—intr.* To repair a hole, as in a garment, by weaving thread or yarn across it. **—darn** *n.* A hole repaired by weaving thread or yarn across it: *a sock full of darns.* [French dialectal *darner,* perhaps from Norman French *darne,* piece, from Breton *darn.*] **—darn′er** *n.*

darn² (därn) *interj.* Used to express dissatisfaction or annoyance. **—darn** *adv. & adj.* Damn. **—darn** *tr. & intr.v.* **darned, darn·ing, darns.** To damn. [Alteration of DAMN.]

♦ **dar·na·tion** (där-nā′shən) *n. & interj.* Damnation. See Regional Note at **tarnation.**

darned (därnd) *adj.* Damned.

darned·est or **darnd·est** (därn′dĭst) *n.* The most possible: *I did my darnedest to finish on time.*

dar·nel (där′nəl) *n.* Any of several Eurasian grasses of the genus *Lolium,* especially *L. temulentum* or *L. perenne.* Also called *rye grass.* [Middle English.]

♦ **darn·ing needle** (där′nĭng) *n.* **1.** A long, large-eyed needle used in darning. **2.** *Upper Northern U.S.* See **dragonfly.** See Regional Note at **dragonfly.**

Darn·ley (därn′lē), Lord. Title of Henry Stewart or Stuart. 1545–1567. Scottish nobleman and second husband (1565–1567) of Mary Queen of Scots. He plotted to kill David Rizzio, Mary's secretary, in 1566 and was himself murdered the following year, possibly at the urging of Mary's lover, the Earl of Bothwell.

Dar·row (dăr′ō), **Clarence Seward.** 1857–1938. American lawyer known for his highly publicized defense of so-called lost causes, such as the Leopold-Loeb murder case (1924) and the Scopes evolution trial (1925).

dart (därt) *n.* **1.a.** A slender, pointed missile, often having tail fins, thrown by hand, shot from a blowgun, or expelled by an exploding bomb. **b.** An object likened to a slender, pointed missile either in shape, use, or effect. **2.** The stinger of an insect. **3. darts.** *(used with a sing. or pl. verb). Games.* A game in which small, slender, pointed missiles are thrown at a target. **4.** A sudden, rapid movement. **5.** A tapered tuck sewn to adjust the fit of a garment. **—dart** *v.* **dart·ed, dart·ing, darts.** *—intr.* To move suddenly and rapidly: *The dog darted across the street.* *—tr.* **1.** To thrust or throw suddenly and rapidly. **2.** To cause to move swiftly and abruptly: *The squirrel darted its head from side to side* *before scampering up the tree.* [Middle English, from Old French, of Germanic origin.]

dart·er (där′tər) *n.* **1.** One that moves suddenly and rapidly. **2.** See **anhinga. 3.** Any of various small, often brilliantly colored freshwater fishes of the family Percidae, closely related to the perches and found in eastern North America.

Dart·ford (därt′fərd). A municipal borough of southeast England east-southeast of London. The Peasants' Revolt led by Wat Tyler began here in June 1381. Population, 77,900.

Dart·moor (därt′mo͝or′, -môr′, -mōr′). An upland region of southwest England noted for its bare granite tors and remains of numerous Bronze Age settlements.

Dart·mouth (därt′məth). **1.** A city of southern Nova Scotia, Canada, on an inlet of the Atlantic Ocean opposite Halifax. It was founded by the British in the 1750's. Population, 62,277. **2.** A town of southeast Massachusetts on Buzzards Bay southwest of New Bedford. Formerly a shipbuilding center, it is now a tourist resort. Population, 23,966.

Dar·von (där′vŏn). A trademark used for propoxyphene hydrochloride.

Dar·win (där′wĭn). A city of northern Australia on **Port Darwin,** an inlet of the Timor Sea. It was founded as Palmerston in 1869 and renamed in 1911. Population, 65,200.

Darwin, Charles Robert. 1809–1882. British naturalist who revolutionized the study of biology with his theory of evolution based on natural selection. His most famous works include *Origin of Species* (1859) and *The Descent of Man* (1871). **—Dar·win′i·an** *adj. & n.*

Darwin, Erasmus. 1731–1802. British physician, scientist, reformer, and poet whose *Zoonomia* (1794–1796) anticipated the evolutionary theories of his grandson Charles.

Dar·win·ism (där′wĭ-nĭz′əm) *n.* A theory of biological evolution developed by Charles Darwin and others, stating that all species of organisms arise and develop through the natural selection of small, inherited variations that increase the individual's ability to compete, survive, and reproduce. Also called *Darwinian theory.* **—Dar′win·ist** *n.* **—Dar′win·is′tic** *adj.*

DASD *abbr. Computer Science.* Direct access storage device.

dash¹ (dăsh) *v.* **dashed, dash·ing, dash·es.** *—tr.* **1.** To break or smash by striking violently. **2.** To hurl, knock, or thrust with sudden violence. **3.** To splash; bespatter. **4.** To perform or complete hastily: *dash off a letter; dash down a glass of juice.* **5. a.** To add an enlivening or altering element to. **b.** To affect by adding another element or ingredient to: *ice cream that was dashed with rum.* **6. a.** To destroy or wreck: *Our dreams were dashed.* See Synonyms at **blast. b.** To confound; abash. *—intr.* **1.** To strike violently; smash. **2.** To move with haste; rush: *dashed to the door.* **—dash** *n.* **1.** A swift, violent blow or stroke: *knocked the books to the floor with an impatient dash of his hand.* **2. a.** A splash. **b.** A small amount of an added ingredient: *a dash of sherry.* **3.** A quick stroke, as with a pencil or brush. **4.** A sudden movement; a rush: *made a dash for the exit.* **5.** *Sports.* A footrace, usually less than a quarter-mile long, run at top speed from the outset. **6.** A spirited quality in action or style; verve. See Synonyms at **vigor. 7.** A punctuation mark (—) used in writing and printing. **8.** In Morse and similar codes, the long sound or signal used in combination with the dot and silent intervals to represent letters or numbers. **9.** A dashboard. [Middle English *dashen,* probably of Scandinavian origin; akin to Danish *daske,* to beat.]

dash² (dăsh) *tr.v.* **dashed, dash·ing, dash·es.** To damn. [Alteration of DAMN.]

dash·board (dăsh′bôrd′, -bōrd′) *n.* A panel under the windshield of a vehicle, containing indicator dials, compartments, and sometimes control instruments.

da·sheen (dă-shēn′) *n.* See **taro.** [Origin unknown.]

dash·er (dăsh′ər) *n.* One that dashes, especially the plunger of an ice-cream freezer.

da·shi (dä′shē) *n.* A clear soup stock, usually with a fish or vegetable base. [Japanese, broth.]

da·shi·ki (də-shē′kē) also **dai·shi·ki** (dī-) *n., pl.* **-kis.** A loose, brightly colored African garment. [Yoruba *danṣiki.*]

dash·ing (dăsh′ĭng) *adj.* **1.** Audacious and gallant; spirited. **2.** Marked by showy elegance; splendid: *a dashing coat.* See Synonyms at **fashionable. —dash′ing·ly** *adv.*

dash·pot (dăsh′pŏt′) *n.* A device consisting of a piston that moves within a cylinder containing oil, used to dampen and control motion.

Dasht-e-Ka·vir (dăsht′ē-kə-vîr′, dăsht′ē-kä-vîr′). A salt desert of north-central Iran southeast of the Elburz Mountains.

Dasht-e-Lut (dăsht′ē-lo͞ot′). A sand and stone desert of eastern Iran extending southward from the Dasht-e-Kavir.

das·sie (dăs′ē) *n.* See **hyrax.** [Afrikaans, diminutive of *das,* badger, from Middle Dutch. See **teks-** in Appendix.]

das·tard (dăs′tərd) *n.* A sneaking, malicious coward. [Middle English, probably alteration of Old Norse *dæstr,* exhausted, from past participle of *dæsa,* to languish, decay.]

das·tard·ly (dăs′tərd-lē) *adj.* Cowardly and malicious; base. **—das′tard·li·ness** *n.*

das·y·ure (dăs′ē-yo͝or′) *n.* Any of various often carnivorous marsupials of the family Dasyuridae of Australia, Tasmania, and adjacent islands, including marsupial mice and rats, native cats, the Tasmanian devil, and the Tasmanian wolf. [New Latin *Dasyurus,* genus name : Greek *dasus,* hairy + *oura,* tail; see **ors-** in Appendix.]

dat. *abbr.* Dative.

da·ta (dā′tə, dăt′ə, dä′tə) *pl.n. (used with a sing. or pl. verb).* **1.** Factual information, especially information organized for analysis or used to reason or make decisions. **2.** *Computer Science.* Numerical or other information represented in a form suitable for processing by computer. **3.** Values derived from scientific experiments. **4.** Plural of **datum** (sense 1). *—attributive.* Often used to modify another noun: *data communications; data updates.* [Latin, pl. of *datum.* See DATUM.]

USAGE NOTE: Data originated as the plural of Latin *datum,* "something given," and many maintain that it must still be treated as a plural form. The *New York Times,* for example, adheres to the traditional rule in this headline: *"Data Are Elusive on the Homeless."* But while *data* comes from a Latin plural form, the practice of treating *data* as a plural in English often does not correspond to its meaning, given an understanding of what counts as data in modern research. We know, for example, what "data on the homeless" would consist of—surveys, case histories, statistical analyses, and so forth—but it would be a vain exercise to try to sort all of these out into sets of individual facts, each of them a "datum" on the homeless. (Does a case history count as a single datum, or as a collection of them? Is a correlation between rates of homelessness and unemployment itself a datum, or is it an abstraction over a number of data?) Since scientists and researchers think of data as a singular mass entity like information, it is entirely natural that they should have come to talk about it as such and that others should defer to their practice. Sixty percent of the Usage Panel accepts the use of *data* with a singular verb and pronoun in the sentence *Once the data is in, we can begin to analyze it.* A still larger number, 77 percent, accepts the sentence *We have very little data on the efficacy of such programs,* where the singularity of *data* is implicit in the use of the quantifier *very little* (contrast the oddness of *We have very little facts on the efficacy of such programs*).

Charles Darwin

data bank or **da·ta·bank** (dā′tə-băngk′, dăt′ə-) *n. Computer Science.* **1.** See **database. 2.** An organization chiefly concerned with building, maintaining, and using a data bank.

da·ta·base also **data base** (dā′tə-bās′, dăt′ə-) *Computer Science. n.* A collection of data arranged for ease and speed of search and retrieval. Also called *data bank.* **—database** *tr.v.* **-based, -bas·ing, -bas·es.** To put (data) into a database.

data carrier *n. Computer Science.* A medium, such as magnetic tape, that is selected to record and often transport or communicate data.

data did·dling (dĭd′lĭng) *n. Slang.* Computer crime involving the illegal manipulation of data before or during input.

data processing *n. Abbr.* **DP** *Computer Science.* **1.** Conversion of data into a form that can be processed by computer. **2.** The storing or processing of data by a computer. **—da′ta-pro′cess′ing** (dā′tə-prŏs′ĕs′ĭng, -prō′sĕs′-, dăt′ə-) *adj.*

data processor *n.* **1.** *Computer Science.* A device, such as a calculator or computer, that performs operations on data. **2.** A person who processes data.

data set *n. Abbr.* **DS** *Computer Science.* **1.** An electronic device that provides an interface in the transmission of data to a remote station. **2.** A collection of related data records on a computer-readable medium, such as a disk. **3.** See **modem.**

date¹ (dāt) *n. Abbr.* **d. 1. a.** Time stated in terms of the day, month, and year. **b.** A statement of calendar time, as on a document. **2.** A specified day of a month. **3.** A particular point or period of time at which something happened or existed, or is expected to happen. **4.** The time during which something lasts; duration. **5.** The time or historical period to which something belongs: *artifacts of a later date.* **6. a.** An appointment, especially an engagement to go out socially with a member of the opposite sex. See Synonyms at **engagement. b.** A person's companion on such an outing. **7.** An engagement for a performance: *has four singing dates this month.* **—date** *v.* **dat·ed, dat·ing, dates.** *—tr.* **1.** To mark or supply with a date: *date a letter.* **2.** To determine the date of: *date a fossil.* **3.** To betray the age of: *Pictures of old cars date the book.* **4.** To go on a date with. *—intr.* **1.** To have origin in a particular time in the past: *This statue dates from 500 B.C.* **2.** To become old-fashioned. **3.** To go on dates. [Middle English, from Old French, from Medieval Latin *data,* from Latin *data (Romae),* issued (at Rome) (on a certain day), feminine past participle of *dare,* to give. See **dō-** in Appendix.] **—dat′a·ble, date′a·ble** *adj.* **—dat′er** *n.*

date² (dāt) *n.* **1.** The sweet, edible, oblong or oval fruit of the date palm, containing a narrow, hard seed. **2.** A date palm. [Middle English, from Old French, from Old Provençal *datil,* from Latin *dactylus,* from Greek *daktulos,* date, finger (from its shape).]

dat·ed (dā′tĭd) *adj.* **1.** Marked with or displaying a date. **2.** Old-fashioned. **—dat′ed·ly** *adv.* **—dat′ed·ness** *n.*

date·less (dāt′lĭs) *adj.* **1.** Having no date whatsoever. **2.** So ancient that no date can be determined. **3.** Having no limits in time; timeless.

date·line (dāt′līn′) *n.* A phrase at the beginning of a newspaper or magazine article that gives the date and place of its origin. **—date′line′** *v.*

date line *n.* The International Date Line.

ă pat	oi boy
ā pay	ou out
âr care	o͝o took
ä father	o͞o boot
ĕ pet	ŭ cut
ē be	ûr urge
ĭ pit	th thin
ī pie	*th* this
îr pier	hw which
ŏ pot	zh vision
ō toe	ə about, item
ô paw	♦ regionalism

Stress marks: ′ (primary); ′ (secondary), as in **dictionary** (dĭk′shə-nĕr′ē)

datura

date palm *n.* A palm tree *(Phoenix dactylifera)* of western Asia and northern Africa and cultivated also in California, having featherlike leaves and bearing clusters of dates.

date rape *n.* Rape perpetrated by the victim's social escort.

dat·ing bar (dā′tĭng) *n.* See **singles bar.**

da·tive (dā′tĭv) *Grammar. adj. Abbr.* **dat.** Of, relating to, or being the grammatical case that in some Indo-European languages, such as Latin and Russian, as well as in some non-Indo-European languages, marks the recipient of action and is used with prepositions or other function words corresponding in meaning to English *to* and *for.* **—dative** *n.* **1.** The dative case. **2.** A word or form in the dative case. [Middle English *datif,* from Latin *(cāsus) datīvus,* (case) of giving (translation of Greek *dotikē (ptōsis)*) from *datus,* past participle of *dare,* to give. See **dō-** in Appendix.] **—da′tive·ly** *adv.*

Da·tong (dä′tông′) also **Ta·tung** (tä′to͝ong′). A city of northeast China west of Beijing. It is an important industrial and railroad center. Population, 688,200.

da·tum (dā′təm, dăt′əm, dä′təm) *n.* **1.** *pl.* **-ta** (-tə). A fact or proposition used to draw a conclusion or make a decision. See Usage Note at **data. 2.** *pl.* **-tums.** A point, line, or surface used as a reference, as in surveying, mapping, or geology. [Latin, something given, from neuter past participle of *dare,* to give. See **dō-** in Appendix.]

da·tu·ra (də-to͝or′ə, -tyo͝or′ə) *n.* Any of several plants of the genus *Datura,* having large trumpet-shaped flowers up to 25 centimeters (10 inches) long and usually prickly fruits. The leaves and seeds yield alkaloids with narcotic properties. Also called *thorn apple.* [New Latin *Datura,* genus name, from Hindi *dhatūrā,* from Sanskrit *dhattūrā,* thorn-apple.]

daub (dôb) *v.* **daubed, daub·ing, daubs.** *—tr.* **1.** To cover or smear with a soft, adhesive substance, such as plaster, grease, or mud. **2.** To apply paint to with hasty or crude strokes. *—intr.* To apply paint or coloring with crude, unskillful strokes. **—daub** *n.* **1.** The act or a stroke of daubing. **2.** A soft, adhesive coating material, such as plaster, grease, or mud. **3.** Matter daubed on; a smear. **4.** A crude, amateurish painting or picture. [Middle English *dauben,* from Old French *dauber,* from Latin *dēalbāre,* to whitewash : *dē-,* intensive pref.; see DE– + *albus,* white; see **albho-** in Appendix.] **—daub′er·y** (dô′bə-rē) *n.*

Dau·bi·gny (dō-bē-nyē′), **Charles François.** 1817–1878. French landscape painter best known for his sensitive portrayal of light, which influenced the later impressionists.

Dau·det (dō-dā′), **Alphonse.** 1840–1897. French writer of the naturalist school whose stories of life in his native Provence include *Lettres de mon Moulin* (1869).

Daudet, Léon. 1867–1942. French writer known for his highly charged political essays and numerous volumes of memoirs.

Dau·gav·pils (dou′gəf-pĭlz′, -gäf-pēlz′). A city of southeast Latvia southeast of Riga. Founded in the 13th century, it was held by Lithuania and Poland before being ceded to Russia in 1771. Population, 124,000.

Bette Davis
Photographed in the mid 1950's

daugh·ter (dô′tər) *n. Abbr.* **d. 1.** One's female child. **2.** A female descendant. **3.** A woman considered as if in a relationship of child to parent: *a daughter of the nation.* **4.** One personified or regarded as a female descendant: *"Culturally Japan is a daughter of Chinese civilization"* (Edwin O. Reischauer). **5.** *Physics.* The immediate product of the radioactive decay of an element. **—daughter** *adj.* Possessing the characteristics of a daughter; having the relationship of a daughter. [Middle English *doughter,* from Old English *dohtor.* See **dhughəter-** in Appendix.] **—daugh′ter·ly** *adj.*

daughter cell *n. Biology.* Either of the two identical cells that form when a cell divides.

daugh·ter-in-law (dô′tər-ĭn-lô′) *n., pl.* **daugh·ters-in-law** (dô′tərz-). The wife of one's son.

Dau·mier (dō-myā′), **Honoré.** 1808–1879. French artist best known for his bitterly satirical lithographs of scenes from bourgeois society.

daunt (dônt, dänt) *tr.v.* **daunt·ed, daunt·ing, daunts.** To abate the courage of; discourage. See Synonyms at **dismay.** [Middle English *daunten,* from Old French *danter,* from Latin *domitāre,* frequentative of *domāre,* to tame. See **demə-** in Appendix.] **—daunt′er** *n.* **—daunt′ing·ly** *adv.*

daunt·less (dônt′lĭs, dänt′-) *adj.* Incapable of being intimidated or discouraged; fearless. See Synonyms at **brave. —daunt′less·ly** *adv.* **—daunt′less·ness** *n.*

davit

dau·phin (dô′fĭn) *n.* **1.** The eldest son of the king of France from 1349 to 1830. **2.** Used as a title for such a nobleman. [Middle English, from Old French, title of the lords of Dauphiné, from *Dalphin, Dalfin,* a surname, from *dalfin,* dolphin (from the device on the family's coat of arms). See DOLPHIN.]

dau·phine (dô-fēn′) *n.* The wife of a dauphin. [French, feminine of *dauphin.* See DAUPHIN.]

Dau·phi·né (dō-fē-nā′). A historical region and former province of southeast France bordering on Italy. After 1349 it became an appanage controlled by the eldest son of the king of France.

DAV *abbr.* Disabled American Veterans.

Da·vao (dä′vou′). A city of southeast Mindanao, Philippines, on **Davao Gulf,** an inlet of the Pacific Ocean. Davao is a major port and commercial center. Population, 270,600.

Dav·e·nant or **D'Av·e·nant** (dăv′ə-nənt, dăv′nənt), Sir **William.** 1606–1668. English playwright whose works include *The Wits* (performed 1633) and *The Siege of Rhodes* (1656), one of the earliest known dramas to combine words and music.

dav·en·port (dăv′ən-pôrt′, -pōrt′) *n.* **1.** A large sofa, often convertible into a bed. **2.** A small desk. [From *davenport,* a small writing desk (obsolete), probably from the name of the manufacturer.]

Dav·en·port (dăv′ĭn-pôrt′, -pōrt′). A city of eastern Iowa on the Mississippi River opposite Moline and Rock Island, Illinois. It grew rapidly after the first railroad bridge across the Mississippi was completed in 1856. Population, 103,264.

Davenport, John. 1597–1670. English Puritan who fled to America in 1637 and helped found a colony at New Haven, Connecticut.

Da·vid (dā′vĭd). Died c. 962 B.C. The second king of Judah and Israel. According to the Old Testament, he slew the Philistine giant Goliath and succeeded Saul as king. He is the reputed author of many of the Psalms.

David, Saint. c. 520–600. Patron saint of Wales. His shrine at St. David's in southwest Wales was an important place of pilgrimage during the Middle Ages.

David I. 1082?–1153. King of Scotland (1124–1153) who transformed Scotland into a feudalistic society.

Da·vid (dä′vət), **Gerard.** 1460?–1523. Dutch painter of religious subjects who is regarded as one of the most important Flemish primitives.

Da·vid (dä-vēd′), **Jacques Louis.** 1748–1825. French painter known for his classicism and his commitment to the ideals of the French Revolution. His works include *The Oath of the Horatii* (1785) and *The Death of Marat* (1793).

Da·vid·son (dā′vĭd-sən), **Jo(seph).** 1883–1952. American sculptor best remembered for his vigorous portrait busts of Woodrow Wilson and Albert Einstein, among others.

Da·vie (dā′vē). A town of southeast Florida southwest of Fort Lauderdale. It is in a citrus-growing area. Population, 20,877.

Da·vies (dā′vēz), **Arthur Bowen.** 1862–1928. American painter who was the chief organizer of the revolutionary Armory Show in 1913.

Dá·vi·la y Pa·di·lla (dä′və-lə ē pä-dē′ə, dä′vē-lä ē pä-*thē′*yä), **Agustín.** Known as "Chronicler of the Indies." 1562–1604. Mexican prelate and historian who wrote a mammoth study of the Spanish colonial era in Mexico and Florida.

da Vin·ci (də vĭn′chē, dä), **Leonardo.** See **Leonardo da Vinci.**

Da·vis (dā′vĭs). A city of central California west of Sacramento. A branch of the University of California (established 1908) is here. Population, 36,640.

Davis, Alexander Jackson. 1803–1892. American architect noted for his Greek revival edifices, such as the Patent Office in Washington, D.C. (1832), and the state capitols of Indiana (1835) and North Carolina (1837).

Davis, Benjamin Oliver. 1877–1970. American cavalry officer who was the first Black general in the U.S. Army (1940–1948). His son **Benjamin Oliver Davis, Jr.** (born 1912), was the first Black general in the U.S. Air Force (1954–1970).

Davis, Bette. 1908–1989. American actress who won an Academy Award for *Dangerous* (1935) and *Jezebel* (1938).

Davis, David. 1815–1886. American jurist who served as an associate justice of the U.S. Supreme Court (1862–1877).

Davis, Dwight Filley. 1879–1945. American tennis player and donor (1900) of the Davis Cup for the annual international team tennis competition.

Davis, Jefferson. 1808–1889. American soldier and president of the Confederacy (1861–1865). He was captured by Union soldiers in 1865 and imprisoned for two years, and although he was indicted for treason (1866), he was never prosecuted.

Davis, John. See John **Davys.**

Davis, John William. 1873–1955. American politician and diplomat who ran unsuccessfully for President against Calvin Coolidge in 1924.

Davis, Miles Dewey, Jr. 1926–1991. American jazz musician acclaimed for his warm, often muted trumpet style.

Davis, Rebecca Blaine Harding. 1831–1910. American writer whose early works, such as the novel *Margaret Howth* (1862), are among the first examples of American realism.

Davis, Richard Harding. 1864–1916. American writer whose vivid coverage of the Spanish-American, Boer, and Russo-Japanese wars established him as the leading correspondent of his day.

Davis, Stuart. 1894–1964. American artist who often incorporated jazz tempos into his vibrant canvases. In the 1920's he was strongly influenced by cubism.

Davis Strait. A strait of the northern Alantic Ocean between southeast Baffin Island and southwest Greenland.

dav·it (dăv′ĭt, dā′vĭt) *n. Nautical.* Any of various types of small cranes that project over the side of a ship and are used to hoist boats, anchors, and cargo. [Middle English *daviot,* from Norman French *daviot,* diminutive of *Davi,* David.]

Da·vy (dā′vē), Sir **Humphry.** 1778–1829. British chemist who was a pioneer of electrochemistry, using its methods to isolate sodium and potassium (1807) and barium, boron, calcium, and magnesium (1808).

Davy Jones (jōnz′) *n.* The bottom of the sea, as personified in songs and stories. [Origin unknown.]

Davy Jones's locker (jōn′zĭz, jōnz) *n.* The bottom of the sea, especially as the grave of all who perish at sea.

Da·vys also **Da·vis** (dā′vĭs), **John.** 1550?–1605. English navigator who explored the Arctic while searching for the Northwest Passage and later sailed to the South Seas.

daw (dô) *n.* A jackdaw. [Middle English *dawe,* from Old English **dāwe.*]

daw·dle (dôd′l) *v.* **-dled, -dling, -dles.** —*intr.* **1.** To take more time than necessary: *dawdled through breakfast.* **2.** To move aimlessly or lackadaisically: *dawdling on the way to work.* —*tr.* To waste (time) by idling: *dawdling the hours away.* [Perhaps alteration of dialectal *daddle,* to diddle.] **—daw′dler** *n.* **—daw′dling·ly** *adv.*

Dawes (dôz), **Charles Gates.** 1865–1951. Vice President of the United States (1925–1929) under Calvin Coolidge. He shared the 1925 Nobel Peace Prize for proposing the Dawes Plan to reduce Germany's World War I reparations.

Dawes, William. 1745–1799. American patriot who rode with Paul Revere on April 18, 1775, to warn of the British advance on Lexington and Concord, Massachusetts.

dawn (dôn) *n.* **1.** The time each morning at which daylight first begins. **2.** A first appearance; a beginning: *the dawn of history.* See Synonyms at **beginning.** **—dawn** *intr.v.* **dawned, dawn·ing, dawns. 1.** To begin to become light in the morning. **2.** To begin to appear or develop; emerge. **3.** To begin to be perceived or understood: *Realization of the danger soon dawned on us.* [From Middle English *daunen,* to dawn, probably a back-formation from *dauning,* daybreak, alteration of *dauing,* from Old English *dagung,* from *dagian,* to dawn. See **agh-** in Appendix.]

dawn redwood *n.* A cone-bearing Chinese tree *(Metasequoia glyptostroboides)* related to the redwood, having deciduous, flat, opposite leaves and small, globular cones. It is now commonly cultivated in the United States.

Daw·son (dô′sən). A town of western Yukon Territory, Canada, at the confluence of the Yukon and Klondike rivers. A boom town during the Klondike gold rush of the late 1890's, it was the territorial capital from 1898 to 1951. Population, 697.

Dawson, Sir **John William.** 1820–1899. Canadian geologist and anti-Darwinist who was an authority on fossils.

Dawson Creek. A city of eastern British Columbia, Canada, near the Alberta border. It is the southern terminus of the Alaska Highway. Population, 11,373.

day (dā) *n. Abbr.* **d 1.** The period of light between dawn and nightfall; the interval from sunrise to sunset. **2.a.** The 24-hour period during which Earth completes one rotation on its axis. **b.** The period during which a celestial body makes a similar rotation. **3.** One of the numbered 24-hour periods into which a week, month, or year is divided. **4.** The portion of a 24-hour period that is devoted to work, school, or business: *an eight-hour day; a sale that lasted for three days.* **5.** A 24-hour period or a portion of it that is reserved for a certain activity: *a day of rest.* **6.a.** A specific, characteristic period in one's lifetime: *That writer has had his day. In grandmother's day, skirts were long.* **b.** A period of opportunity: *Every defendant is entitled to a day in court.* **7.** A period of time in history; an era: *We studied the tactics used in Napoleon's day. The day of computer science is well upon us.* **—day** *adj.* **1.** Of or relating to the day. **2.** Working during the day: *the day nurse.* **3.** Occurring before nightfall: *a day hike.* **—*idioms.* day after day.** For many days; continuously. **day in, day out.** Every day without fail; continuously. [Middle English *dai, day,* from Old English *dæg.* See **agh-** in Appendix.]

Day (dā), **Benjamin Henry.** 1810–1889. American printer and journalist who founded the first penny newspaper, the *New York Sun* (1833). His son **Benjamin** (1838–1916) invented the Ben Day process for shading printed illustrations.

Day, Clarence Shepard, Jr. 1874–1935. American writer best known for his autobiographical *Life with Father* (1935) and *Life with Mother* (published 1937).

Day, Dorothy. 1897–1980. American journalist and reformer who cofounded the *Catholic Worker* in 1933 to promote pacifism and social justice.

Day or **Daye** (dā), **Stephen.** 1594?–1668. English-born colonist who was the first printer in New England. His *Bay Psalm Book* appeared in 1640.

Day, William Rufus. 1849–1923. American jurist who served as an associate justice of the U.S. Supreme Court (1903–1922).

Day·ak (dā′ăk′) or **Dy·ak** (dī′-) *n., pl.* **Dayak** or **-aks** also **Dyak** or **-aks. 1.** A member of any of various Indonesian peoples inhabiting Borneo. **2.** The language of the Dayak.

Da·yan (dä-yän′), **Moshe.** 1915–1981. Israeli military leader and politician who directed the 1956 Sinai campaign and the 1967 Six-Day War.

day bed or **day·bed** (dā′bĕd′) *n.* A couch or sofa that is convertible into a bed.

day·book (dā′bo͝ok′) *n. Abbr.* **DB, D.B. 1.** A book in which daily transactions are recorded. **2.** A diary.

day·break (dā′brāk′) *n.* The beginning of day; dawn.

day camp *n.* A children's camp providing recreation and meals during the day but no overnight facilities.

day·care or **day care** (dā′kâr′) *n.* Provision of daytime training, supervision, recreation, and often medical services for children of preschool age, for the disabled, or for the elderly. —*attributive.* Often used to modify another noun: *daycare providers; day care centers.*

day·dream (dā′drēm′) *n.* A dreamlike musing or fantasy while awake, especially of the fulfillment of wishes or hopes. **—daydream** *intr.v.* **-dreamed** or **-dreamt** (-drĕmt′), **-dream·ing, -dreams.** To have dreamlike musings or fantasies while awake. **—day′dream′er** *n.*

Daye (dā), **Stephen.** See Stephen **Day.**

day·flow·er (dā′flou′ər) *n.* Any of various plants of the genus *Commelina* having blue or purplish flowers that wilt quickly.

day·fly (dā′flī′) *n.* See **mayfly.**

Day-Glo (dā′glō′). A trademark used for fluorescent coloring agents and materials. This trademark sometimes occurs in print in figurative contexts and in lowercase: *"It was during that Day-Glo decade when the world finally found the path to McLuhan's door"* (New York Times). *"The troupe's staging . . . follows Alice's fantasy romp through day-glo daisies, past a smiling Cheshire cat"* (Los Angeles Times).

day·hop (dā′hŏp′) *n. Informal.* **1.** A trip that can be made in one day's time: *It was just a dayhop from New York City to the Berkshires for skiing.* **2.** A day student at a boarding school, college, or university.

day labor *n.* Labor that is hired and paid by the day. **—day laborer** *n.*

day letter *n.* A telegram sent during the day.

Day Lew·is (lo͞o′ĭs), **Cecil.** 1904–1972. Irish-born poet and critic who became poet laureate in 1968 and wrote detective novels under the pen name Nicholas Blake.

day·light (dā′līt′) *n.* **1.** The light of day; sunlight. **2.a.** Daybreak. **b.** Daytime. **3.** Exposure to public notice: *corrupt business practices that were finally brought into the daylight.* **4.** Understanding or insight into what was formerly obscure: *finally began to see daylight concerning the root of the problem.* **5. daylights.** *Slang.* One's wits: *"His adventurism had scared the daylights out of them"* (Frederick Forsyth).

day·light-sav·ing time (dā′līt-sā′vĭng) *n. Abbr.* **DST, D.S.T.** Time during which clocks are set one hour or more ahead of standard time to provide more daylight at the end of the working day during late spring, summer, and early fall.

day lily or **day·lil·y** (dā′lĭl′ē) *n.* Any of several perennial Eurasian herbs of the genus *Hemerocallis* in the lily family, having often grasslike leaves and yellow, orange, or purplish lilylike flowers. Also called *hemerocallis.*

day·long (dā′lông′, -lŏng′) *adj.* Lasting through the whole day. **—daylong** *adv.* Through the day; all day.

day nursery *n.* A facility for the supervision of preschool children, especially during the hours that their parents are at work.

Day of Atonement *n.* See **Yom Kippur.** [Translation of Hebrew *yôm kippûr.*]

Day of Judgment *n.* See **Judgment Day** (sense 1).

day one *n. Informal.* The very beginning; the first day: *worked hard on the project from day one.*

day·pack (dā′păk′) *n.* A rather small, lightweight backpack for carrying articles such as books.

day room *n.* A recreation room, especially one found in a barracks on a military installation.

day sail·er (sā′lər) *n. Nautical.* A small sailboat for day trips.

day school *n.* **1.** A private school for pupils living at home. **2.** A school that holds classes during the day.

day shift or **day·shift** (dā′shĭft′) *n.* **1.** A group of employees working during the day in a factory or business. **2.** The period of time for such work.

day·side (dā′sīd′) *n.* **1.** Office employees and other personnel who work days. **2.** The side of a planet facing the sun. **—day′side′** *adj.*

days of grace (dāz) *pl.n.* Extra days, usually three, allowed for payment of a note or bill after it has come due. [Translation of Latin *diēs gratiae.*]

day·star (dā′stär′) *n.* **1.** The morning star. **2.** The sun.

day student *n.* A student at a school or university who does not reside in the facilities provided by the institution.

day·time (dā′tīm′) *n.* The time between sunrise and sunset. **—daytime** *adj.* Occurring in or appropriate for use during the day: *daytime tasks; daytime clothes.*

day-to-day (dā′tə-dā′) *adj.* **1.** Occurring on a routine or daily basis: *the day-to-day movements of the stock market.* **2.** Subsisting one day at a time with little regard for the future: *lived a day-to-day existence.*

Day·ton (dāt′n). A city of southwest Ohio north-northeast of Cincinnati. Now a manufacturing center, it was the home of Orville and Wilbur Wright. Population, 193,444.

Day·to·na Beach (dā-tō′nə). A city of northeast Florida on the Atlantic coast north-northeast of Orlando. Automobile speed trials and races have been held on its hard, white beach since the early 1900's. Population, 54,176.

day-trip·per (dā′trĭp′ər) *n.* One who takes a trip during the day without an overnight stop.

day·wear (dā′wâr′) *n.* Attire that is appropriate for use during the day.

daze (dāz) *tr.v.* **dazed, daz·ing, daz·es. 1.** To stun, as with a heavy blow or shock; stupefy. **2.** To dazzle, as with strong light.

Moshe Dayan

day lily

ă pat	oi boy
ā pay	ou out
âr care	o͝o took
ä father	o͞o boot
ĕ pet	ŭ cut
ē be	ûr urge
ĭ pit	th thin
ī pie	*th* this
îr pier	hw which
ŏ pot	zh vision
ō toe	ə about, item
ô paw	♦ regionalism

Stress marks: **′** (primary); ′ (secondary), as in **dictionary** (dĭk′shə-nĕr′ē)

—daze *n.* A stunned or bewildered condition. [Middle English *dasen,* of Scandinavian origin; akin to Old Norse *dasask,* to become weary, reflexive of **dasa,* to tire out.]

SYNONYMS: *daze, bemuse, benumb, stun, stupefy.* The central meaning shared by these verbs is "to dull or paralyze the mental capacities with or as if with a shock": *dazed by the defeat; bemused by the senator's resignation; a boring performance that benumbed the audience; stunned by their sudden death; a display that stupefied all onlookers.*

daz·zle (dăz′əl) *v.* **-zled, -zling, -zles.** *—tr.* **1.** To dim the vision of, especially to blind with intense light. **2.** To amaze, overwhelm, or bewilder with spectacular display: *a figure skater who dazzled the audience with virtuosic jumps.* *—intr.* **1.** To become blinded. **2.** To inspire admiration or wonder. **—dazzle** *n.* The act of dazzling or the state of being dazzled. [Frequentative of DAZE.] **—daz′zler** *n.* **—daz′zling·ly** *adv.*

dB *abbr.* Decibel.

DB or **D.B.** *abbr.* Daybook.

d.b.a. *abbr.* Doing business as.

D.B.A. *abbr.* Doctor of Business Administration.

D.B.E. *abbr.* Dame Commander of the British Empire.

d.b.h. *abbr.* Diameter at breast height.

D.Bib. *abbr.* Douay Bible.

dble. *abbr.* Double.

dc or **DC** *abbr.* Direct current.

DC or **D.C.** *abbr.* District of Columbia.

D.C. *abbr.* **1.** *Music.* Da capo. **2.** Doctor of Chiropractic.

D.C.L. *abbr.* **1.** Doctor of Canon Law. **2.** Doctor of Civil Law.

DCM or **D.C.M.** *abbr.* Distinguished Conduct Medal.

dd. *abbr.* Delivered.

D.D. *abbr.* **1.** Demand draft. **2.** Dishonorable discharge. **3.** *Latin.* Divinitatis Doctor (Doctor of Divinity).

D-day
Soldiers landing in Normandy, France, June 6, 1944

D-day (dē′dā′) *n.* The unnamed day on which an operation or offensive is to be launched, especially June 6, 1944, the day on which the Allied forces invaded France during World War II. [*D* (abbr. of DESIGNATED) + DAY.]

D.D.S. *abbr.* **1.** Doctor of Dental Science. **2.** Doctor of Dental Surgery.

DDT (dē′dē-tē′) *n.* A colorless contact insecticide, $C_{14}H_9Cl_5$, toxic to human beings and animals when swallowed or absorbed through the skin. It has been banned in the United States for most uses since 1972. [D(ICHLORO)D(IPHENYL)T(RICHLOROETHANE).]

DE *abbr.* Delaware.

de– *pref.* **1.** Do or make the opposite of; reverse: *decriminalize.* **2.** Remove or remove from: *delouse; deoxygenate.* **3.** Out of: *deplane; defenestration.* **4.** Reduce; degrade: *declass.* **5.** Derived from: *deverbative.* [Middle English *de-,* from Old French *de-* or *des-;* Old French *de-,* from Latin *dē-,* from, off, apart, away, down, out, completely (from *dē;* see **de-** in Appendix) or from Old French *des-,* out, off, apart, away, completely (from Latin *dis-,* dis-, and Latin *dē-*).]

de·ac·ces·sion (dē′ăk-sĕsh′ən) *v.* **-sioned, -sion·ing, -sions.** *—tr.* To remove and sell (a work of art) from a museum's collection, especially in order to purchase other works of art: *"He also denied that . . . friends of the museum were permitted to buy . . . pieces that were deaccessioned"* (New York Times). *—intr.* To remove a work of art from a museum's collection and sell it. **—de′ac·ces′sion** *n.*

de·a·cid·i·fy (dē′ə-sĭd′ə-fī′) *tr.v.* **-fied, -fy·ing, -fies.** To remove the acid from or reduce the acid content of. **—de′a·cid′i·fi·ca′tion** (-fĭ-kā′shən) *n.*

dea·con (dē′kən) *n.* **1.** A cleric ranking just below a priest in the Anglican, Eastern Orthodox, and Roman Catholic churches. **2.** A Protestant layperson who assists the minister in various functions. **3.** Used as a title prefixed to the surname of such a person: *Deacon Brown.* [Middle English *deken,* from Old English *dīacon,* from Late Latin *diāconus,* from Greek *diakonos,* attendant.]

dea·con·ess (dē′kə-nĭs) *n.* **1.** A Protestant woman who assists the minister in various functions. **2.** Used as a title prefixed to the surname of such a woman: *Deaconess Brown.*

dea·con·ry (dē′kən-rē) *n., pl.* **-ries. 1.** The office or position of a deacon. **2.** Deacons considered as a group.

dead bolt
Lock and extended bolt

de·ac·ti·vate (dē-ăk′tə-vāt′) *tr.v.* **-vat·ed, -vat·ing, -vates. 1.** To render inactive or ineffective. **2.** To inhibit, block, or disrupt the action of (an enzyme or other biological agent). **3.** To remove from active military status. **—de·ac′ti·va′tion** *n.* **—de·ac′ti·va′tor** *n.*

dead (dĕd) *adj.* **dead·er, dead·est. 1.** Having lost life; no longer alive. **2.** Marked for certain death; doomed: *was marked as a dead man by the assassin.* **3. a.** Having the physical appearance of death: *a dead pallor.* **b.** Lacking feeling or sensitivity; numb or unresponsive: *Passersby were dead to our pleas for help.* **c.** Weary and worn-out; exhausted. **4. a.** Not having the capacity to live; inanimate or inert. **b.** Not having the capacity to produce or sustain life; barren: *dead soil.* **5. a.** No longer in existence, use, or operation. **b.** No longer having significance or relevance. **c.** Physically inactive; dormant: *a dead volcano.* **6. a.** Not commercially productive; idle: *dead capital.* **b.** Not circulating or running; stagnant: *dead water; dead air.* **7. a.** Devoid of human or vehicular activity; quiet: *a dead town.* **b.** Lacking all animation, excitement, or activity; dull: *The party being dead, we left early.* **8.** Having no resonance. Used of sounds: *"One characteristic of compact discs we all can hear is dead sound. It may be pure but it has no life"* (Musical Heritage Review). **9.** Having grown cold; having been extinguished: *dead coals; a dead flame.* **10.** Lacking elasticity or bounce: *That tennis ball is dead.* **11.** Out of operation because of a fault or breakdown: *The motor is dead.* **12. a.** Sudden; abrupt: *a dead stop.* **b.** Complete; utter: *dead silence.* **c.** Exact; unerring. **13.** *Sports.* Out of play. Used of a ball. **14. a.** Lacking connection to a source of electric current. **b.** Drained of electric charge; discharged: *a dead battery.* **—dead** *n.* **1.** One who has died: *respect for the dead.* **2.** The period exhibiting the greatest degree of intensity: *the dead of winter; the dead of night.* **—dead** *adv.* **1.** Absolutely; altogether: *You can be dead sure of my innocence.* **2.** Directly; exactly: *There's a gas station dead ahead.* **3.** Suddenly: *She stopped dead on the stairway.* ***—idioms.*** **dead and buried.** No longer in use or under consideration: *All past animosities are dead and buried now.* **dead in the water.** Unable to function or move: *The crippled ship was dead in the water. With no leadership, the project was dead in the water.* **dead to rights.** In the very act of making an error or committing a crime: *The police caught the thief dead to rights with my silverware.* [Middle English *ded,* from Old English *dēad.* See **dheu-**[2] in Appendix.] **—dead′ness** *n.*

SYNONYMS: *dead, deceased, departed, extinct, lifeless, inanimate.* These adjectives all mean without life. *Dead,* which has the widest use, applies in general to whatever once had — but no longer has — physical life (*a dead man; a dead leaf*), function (*The battery is dead*), or force or currency (*a dead issue; a dead language*). *Deceased* — like *departed,* which is a euphemistic term — refers only to nonliving human beings: *attended a memorial service for a recently deceased friend; "shedding funereal tears over his departed dog"* (Ben Jonson). *Extinct* can refer to what has no living successors (*The dodo is extinct*) or to what is extinguished or inactive (*an extinct volcano*). *Lifeless* applies to what no longer has physical life (*a lifeless body*), to what does not support life (*a lifeless planet*), and to what lacks animation, spirit, or brightness (*a lifeless performance of the sonata; lifeless colors*). *Inanimate* is most often limited to what has never had physical life: *"He then fell, like an inanimate log, to the earth"* (James Fenimore Cooper).

dead air *n.* An unintended interruption in a broadcast during which there is no sound.

dead-air space (dĕd′âr′) *n.* An unventilated space.

dead·beat[1] (dĕd′bēt′) *n.* *Slang.* **1.** One who does not pay one's debts. **2.** A lazy person; a loafer.

dead·beat[2] (dĕd′bĕt′) *adj.* Having an indicator that stops without oscillation.

dead bolt also **dead·bolt** (dĕd′bōlt′) *n.* A bolt on a lock that is moved by turning the key or knob without activation of a spring.

dead center *n.* The point at the end of each stroke of a moving crank and connecting rod at which the two lie in the same straight line and the turning force applied by the connecting rod is zero. Also called *dead point.*

dead duck *n.* *Slang.* One doomed to failure or to death.

dead·en (dĕd′n) *v.* **-ened, -en·ing, -ens.** *—tr.* **1.** To render less intense, sensitive, or vigorous: *a medication to deaden the pain; wall tiles that deaden the sound from the rehearsal studio.* **2.** To make soundproof. **3.** To make less colorful or brilliant. *—intr.* **1.** To become dead. **2.** To lose vigor, brilliance, or liveliness. **—dead′en·er** *n.*

dead end *n.* **1.** An end of a passage, such as a street or pipe, that affords no exit. **2.** A point beyond which no movement or progress can be made; an impasse.

dead-end (dĕd′ĕnd′) *adj.* **1.** Having no exit. **2.** Permitting no opportunity for advancement: *a dead-end job.* **3.** *Informal.* Tough and rowdy: *a dead-end gang.* **—dead-end** *intr.v.* **-end·ed, -end·ing, -ends.** To terminate with no exit or possibility of advancement: *The road dead-ends at the lake. That job dead-ends at the end of the year.*

dead·en·ing (dĕd′n-ĭng) *n.* Material used for soundproofing.

dead·eye (dĕd′ī′) *n.* **1.** *Nautical.* A flat hardwood disk with a grooved perimeter, pierced by three holes through which the lanyards are passed, used to fasten the shrouds. **2.** *Slang.* An expert shooter: *a deadeye with the rifle.*

dead·fall (dĕd′fôl′) *n.* **1.** A trap for large animals in which a heavy weight is arranged to fall on and kill or disable the prey. **2.** A mass of fallen timber and tangled brush.

dead hand *n.* **1.** The ever-present, oppressive influence of past events. **2.** Mortmain. [Middle English *dede hond,* translation of Old French *mortemain* or Medieval Latin *manus mortua,* mortmain.]

dead·head (dĕd′hĕd′) *Informal. n.* **1.** A person who uses a free ticket for admittance, accommodation, or entertainment. **2.** A vehicle, such as an aircraft, that transports no passengers or freight during a trip. **3.** A person regarded as dull-witted or sluggish. **4.** A partially submerged log or trunk. *—tr.* **-head·ed, -head·ing, -heads. 1.** To pilot or drive (a vehicle) carrying no passengers or freight. **2.** To pull (dead or dying blossoms) off a flower. *—intr.* To bypass a senior employee in order to promote a more junior employee. —**deadhead** *adv.* Without passengers or freight; empty.

dead heat *n. Sports.* A race in which two or more contestants compete evenly or finish at the same time.

dead letter *n.* **1.** An unclaimed or undelivered letter that after a period of time is destroyed or returned to the sender by the postal service. **2.** A law, directive, or factor still formally in effect but no longer valid or enforced.

dead lift *n. Sports.* A weightlifting event in which the weight is lifted from the floor to the level of the hips and then lowered by controlled effort to the floor.

dead•light (dĕd′līt′) *n.* **1.** *Nautical.* **a.** A strong shutter or plate fastened over a ship's porthole or cabin window in stormy weather. **b.** A thick window set in a ship's side or deck. **2.** A skylight constructed so that it cannot be opened.

dead•line (dĕd′līn′) *n.* **1.** A time limit, as for payment of a debt or completion of an assignment. **2.** A boundary line in a prison that prisoners can cross only at the risk of being shot. —**deadline** *tr.v.* **-lined, -lin•ing, -lines.** To govern by setting a time limit: *"He was never going to be deadlined by a day, or even a month"* (New Yorker).

dead load *n.* The fixed weight of a structure or piece of equipment, such as a bridge on its supports. Also called *dead weight.*

dead•lock (dĕd′lŏk′) *n.* A standstill resulting from the opposition of two unrelenting forces or factions. —**deadlock** *tr. & intr.v.* **-locked, -lock•ing, -locks.** To bring or come to a standstill.

dead•ly (dĕd′lē) *adj.* **-li•er, -li•est.** **1.** Causing or tending to cause death: *deadly weapons; a deadly spill of radioactive waste products.* See Synonyms at **fatal. 2.** Suggestive of death: *a deadly pallor.* **3.** Aiming or wanting to kill; implacable: *deadly enemies.* **4.a.** Destructive in effect: *gave the film a deadly review.* **b.** Tending to take away vitality, effectiveness, or force: *the deadly habit of procrastination.* **5.** Absolute; utter: *deadly concentration.* **6.** Extreme or terrible: *worked under deadly strain.* **7.** Extremely accurate; unerring: *She is a deadly shot with the bow.* **8.** Dull, tedious, and boring: *a deadly prose style.* —**deadly** *adv.* **1.** So as to suggest death. **2.** To an extreme: *deadly serious.* —**dead′li•ness** *n.*

deadly nightshade *n.* **1.** See **belladonna** (sense 1). **2.** See **bittersweet nightshade.**

deadly sin *n.* One of the seven sins—anger, covetousness, envy, gluttony, lust, pride, and sloth—that are supposed to be fatal to one's spiritual development and progress.

dead-man's float (dĕd′mănz′) *n. Sports.* A prone floating position in swimming in which the swimmer's arms are extended straight forward above the head and the legs are held together.

dead march *n. Music.* A slow, solemn funeral march.

dead nettle *n.* Any of several weedy plants of the genus *Lamium,* native to Eurasia and northern Africa and having clusters of small, usually purplish flowers with two lips. [So called because it looks like a nettle but does not sting.]

dead-on (dĕd′ôn′, -ŏn′) *adj. Informal.* Precisely accurate and to the point: *"She avoids big scenes . . . preferring to rely on small gestures and dead-on dialogue"* (Peter S. Prescott).

dead•pan (dĕd′păn′) *n.* **1.** A blank, expressionless face. **2.** A person, especially a performer, who has or assumes a blank expression. —**deadpan** *adj.* Impassively matter-of-fact, as in style, behavior, or expression: *deadpan delivery of the joke.* —**deadpan** *adv.* With a blank, expressionless face. —**deadpan** *v.* **-panned, -pan•ning, -pans.** —*tr.* To express in an impassive, matter-of-fact way. —*intr.* To express oneself in an impassive, matter-of-fact way.

dead point *n.* See **dead center.**

dead reckoning *n.* **1.** *Abbr.* **DR** A method of estimating the position of an aircraft or a ship without astronomical observations, as by applying to a previously determined position the course and distance traveled since. **2.** Predictive calculation based on inference; guesswork. [Possibly alteration of *ded.,* abbr. of *deduced,* from *deduce,* to trace from the beginning. See DEDUCE.]

Dead Sea (dĕd). A salt lake, about 397 m (1,300 ft) below sea level, between Israel and Jordan. It is one of the saltiest bodies of water known and is the lowest point on the earth.

dead spot *n.* A zone within the range of a radio transmitter where little or no radio signal can be received.

dead weight *n.* **1.** The unrelieved weight of a heavy, motionless mass. **2.** An oppressive burden or difficulty. **3.** *Abbr.* **DW** See **dead load.**

dead•wood (dĕd′wo͝od′) *n.* **1.** Dead branches or wood on a tree. **2.** One that is burdensome or superfluous. **3.** *Nautical.* The vertical planking between the keel of a vessel and the sternpost, serving as a reinforcement.

deaf (dĕf) *adj.* **deaf•er, deaf•est.** **1.** Partially or completely lacking in the sense of hearing. **2. Deaf.** Of or relating to the Deaf or their culture. **3.** Unwilling or refusing to listen; heedless: *was deaf to our objections.* —**deaf** *n. (used with a pl. verb).* **1.** Deaf people considered as a group. **2. Deaf.** The community of deaf people who use American Sign Language as a primary means of communication. [Middle English *def, deef,* from Old English *dēaf.*] —**deaf′ly** *adv.* —**deaf′ness** *n.*

USAGE NOTE: Some writers have lately introduced a distinction between the lowercase noun *deaf,* which is used to refer simply to people with extensive hearing disorders, and the capitalized noun *Deaf,* which refers to the culture and community that has grown up around the use of American Sign Language as a primary means of communication.

deaf•en (dĕf′ən) *v.* **-ened, -en•ing, -ens.** —*tr.* **1.** To make deaf, especially momentarily by a loud noise. **2.** To make soundproof. —*intr.* To cause permanent or momentary deafness. —**deaf′en•ing•ly** *adv.*

deaf-mute also **deaf mute** (dĕf′myo͞ot′) *Offensive.*—*n.* A person who can neither hear nor speak. —*adj.* (dĕf-myo͞ot′). Unable to speak or hear.

deal¹ (dēl) *v.* **dealt** (dĕlt), **deal•ing, deals.** —*tr.* **1.** To give out as a share or portion; apportion. **2.** To distribute among several recipients. See Synonyms at **distribute. 3.** To sell: *deal prescriptions; deal cocaine.* **4.** To administer; deliver: *dealt him a blow to the stomach.* **5.** *Games.* **a.** To distribute (playing cards) among players. **b.** To give (a specific card) to a player while so distributing. —*intr.* **1.** To be occupied or concerned; treat: *a book that deals with the Middle Ages.* **2.** To behave in a specified way toward another or others; have transactions: *deal honestly with competitors.* **3.** To take action with respect to someone or something: *The committee will deal with this complaint.* See Synonyms at **treat. 4.** To do business; trade: *dealing in diamonds.* **5.** *Games.* To distribute playing cards. —**deal** *n.* **1.** The act or a round of apportioning or distributing. **2.** *Games.* **a.** Distribution of playing cards. **b.** The cards so distributed; a hand. **c.** The right or turn of a player to distribute the cards. **d.** The playing of one hand. **3.** An indefinite quantity, extent, or degree: *has a great deal of experience.* **4.** An agreement often arranged secretly, as in business or politics. **5.a.** A business transaction. **b.** An agreement, especially one that is mutually beneficial. See Synonyms at **bargain. 6.** *Informal.* A sale favorable especially to the buyer; a bargain. **7.** *Informal.* Treatment received: *a raw deal; a fair deal.* [Middle English *delen,* from Old English *dǣlan,* to divide, share. See **dail-** in Appendix.]

deal² (dēl) *n.* **1.a.** A fir or pine board cut to standard dimensions. **b.** Such boards or planks considered as a group. **2.** Fir or pine wood. [Middle English *dele,* from Middle Dutch and Middle Low German *dele,* plank.]

de•a•late (dē-ā′lāt′) or **de•a•lat•ed** (-lā′tĭd) —*adj.* Having lost the wings. Used of ants, termites, and other insects that shed their wings after a mating flight. —*n.* A dealate insect. —**de′a•la′tion** *n.*

de•al•co•hol•ize (dē-ăl′kə-hô-līz′) *tr.v.* **-ized, -iz•ing, -izes.** To remove some or all of the alcohol from (beverages): *dealcoholized the white wine.* —**de•al′co•hol′i•za′tion** (-hô′lĭ-zā′shən, -hŏl′ĭ-) *n.*

deal•er (dē′lər) *n. Abbr.* **dlr. 1.** One that is engaged in buying and selling: *a used-car dealer; a drug dealer.* **2.** *Games.* The one who distributes cards.

deal•er•ship (dē′lər-shĭp′) *n.* A franchise to sell specified items in a certain area.

deal•fish (dēl′fĭsh′) *n., pl.* **dealfish** or **-fish•es.** An Atlantic ribbonfish *(Trachipterus arcticus)* having a compressed, tapering, silvery body that can attain a length of 2.6 meters (8½ feet). [From DEAL².]

de•a•lign•ment (dē′ə-līn′mənt) *n.* A movement among voters toward nonpartisanship, resulting in a weakening of party structure.

deal•ing (dē′lĭng) *n.* **1. dealings.** Transactions or relations with others, usually in business. **2.** Method or manner of conduct in relation to others; treatment: *honest dealing.*

deal•mak•er (dēl′mā′kər) *n.* One that makes deals, as in business, finance, or politics. —**deal′mak′ing** (-mā′kĭng) *n.*

dealt (dĕlt) *v.* Past tense and past participle of **deal¹.**

de•am•i•nase (dē-ăm′ə-nās′, -nāz′) *n.* Any of a class of enzymes that catalyze the hydrolysis of compounds containing the amino group NH_2.

de•am•i•nate (dē-ăm′ə-nāt′) *tr.v.* **-nat•ed, -nat•ing, -nates.** To remove an amino group, NH_2, from (an organic compound). —**de•am′i•na′tion** *n.*

de•am•i•nize (dē-ăm′ə-nīz′) *tr.v.* **-nized, -niz•ing, -niz•es.** To deaminate. —**de•am′i•ni•za′tion** (-nĭ-zā′shən) *n.*

dean (dēn) *n.* **1.a.** An administrative officer in charge of a college, faculty, or division in a university. **b.** An officer of a college or high school who counsels students and supervises the enforcement of rules. **2.** *Ecclesiastical.* The head of the chapter of canons governing a cathedral or collegiate church. **3.** *Roman Catholic Church.* A priest appointed to oversee a group of parishes within a diocese. **4.** The senior member of a body or group: *the dean of the Washington diplomatic corps.* [Middle English *deen,* from Old French *deien,* from Late Latin *decānus,* chief of ten, from Greek *dekanos,* from *deka,* ten. See **dekm̥** in Appendix.] —**dean′ship′** *n.*

Dean (dēn), **James Byron.** 1931–1955. American actor whose moody, rebellious persona in films such as *East of Eden* and *Rebel Without a Cause* (both 1955) made him a cult figure. He died in an automobile accident.

Deane (dēn), **Silas.** 1737–1789. American diplomat who per-

James Dean

ă pat	oi boy
ā pay	ou out
âr care	o͝o took
ä father	o͞o boot
ĕ pet	ŭ cut
ē be	ûr urge
ĭ pit	th thin
ī pie	*th* this
îr pier	hw which
ŏ pot	zh vision
ō toe	ə about, item
ô paw	♦ regionalism

Stress marks: ′ (primary); ′ (secondary), as in **dictionary** (dĭk′shə-nĕr′ē)

suaded France to supply commercial and military aid to the Revolutionary cause.

dean·er·y (dē′nə-rē) *n., pl.* **-ies.** The office, jurisdiction, or official residence of an ecclesiastical dean.

dean's list (dēnz) *n., pl.* **deans' lists.** A list of students in a high school, college, or university who have attained high academic rank.

dear[1] (dîr) *adj.* **dear·er, dear·est. 1.a.** Loved and cherished: *my dearest friend.* **b.** Greatly valued; precious: *lost everything dear to them.* **2.** Highly esteemed or regarded. Used in direct address, especially in salutations: *Dear Lee Dawson.* **3.a.** High-priced; expensive. **b.** Charging high prices. **4.** Earnest; ardent: *"This good man was a dear lover and constant practicer of angling"* (Izaak Walton). **5.** *Obsolete.* Noble; worthy. **—dear** *n.* **1.** One that is greatly loved. **2.** An endearing, lovable, or kind person. **—dear** *adv.* **1.** With fondness; affectionately. **2.** At a high cost: *sold their wares dear.* **—dear** *interj.* Used as a polite exclamation, chiefly of surprise or distress: *oh dear; dear me.* [Middle English *dere,* from Old English *dēore.*] **—dear′ly** *adv.* **—dear′ness** *n.*

dear[2] (dîr) *adj.* Severe; grievous; sore: *our dearest need.* [Middle English *dere,* from Old English *dēor.*]

Dear·born (dîr′bôrn′, -bərn). A city of southeast Michigan west of Detroit. Greenfield Village, the restored birthplace of Henry Ford, is here. Population, 90,660.

Dearborn, Henry. 1751–1829. American soldier and politician who fought in the American Revolution and later represented Maine in the U.S. Congress (1793–1797).

death cup
Amanita phalloides

Dearborn Heights. A city of southeast Michigan, a suburb of Detroit. Population, 67,706.

Dear John (dîr) *n.* A letter, as to a serviceman, requesting a divorce or ending a personal relationship.

dearth (dûrth) *n.* **1.** A scarce supply; a lack. **2.** Shortage of food; famine. [Middle English *derthe,* from Old English **dēorthu,* costliness, from *dēore,* costly. See DEAR[1].]

death (dĕth) *n.* **1.** The act of dying; termination of life. **2.** The state of being dead. **3.** The cause of dying: *Drugs were the death of him.* **4.** A manner of dying: *a heroine's death.* **5.** Often **Death.** A personification of the destroyer of life, usually represented as a skeleton holding a scythe. **6.a.** Bloodshed; murder. **b.** Execution. **7.** *Christian Science.* The product of human belief of life in matter. **8.** *Law.* Civil death. **9.** The termination or extinction of something: *the death of imperialism.* **—*idioms.* at death's door.** Near to death; gravely ill or injured. **be the death of (someone).** To distress or irritate (someone) to an intolerable degree. **put to death.** To execute. **to death.** To an intolerable degree; extremely: *worried to death.* [Middle English *deeth,* from Old English *dēath.* See **dheu-**[2] in Appendix.]

death angel *n. Botany.* See **death cup.**

death·bed (dĕth′bĕd′) *n.* **1.** The bed on which a person dies. **2.** The last hours before death. *—attributive.* Often used to modify another noun: *a deathbed confession; deathbed pallor.* **—*idiom.* on one's deathbed.** Close to death.

death benefit *n.* Insurance money payable to a deceased person's stipulated beneficiary.

death·blow (dĕth′blō′) *n.* **1.** A stroke or blow that causes death. **2.** A destructive event or occurrence: *dealt a deathblow to our hopes.*

death camas also **death camass** *n.* Any of several plants of the genus *Zigadenus* of western North America, having grasslike leaves and clusters of usually greenish-white flowers. All parts of the plant are poisonous to livestock.

death cup *n.* A poisonous, usually white mushroom *(Amanita phalloides)* having a prominent cup-shaped base. Also called *death angel, death cap.*

death mask

death duty *n. Chiefly British.* A tax on inherited property; an inheritance tax.

death house *n.* See **death row.**

death instinct *n. Psychiatry.* **1.** A primitive impulse for destruction, decay, and death, manifested by a turning away from pleasure, postulated by Sigmund Freud as coexisting with and opposing the life instinct. Also called *Thanatos.* **2.** Death wish.

death·less (dĕth′lĭs) *adj.* Not subject to termination or death; immortal: *deathless renown.* **—death′less·ly** *adv.* **—death′less·ness** *n.*

death·ly (dĕth′lē) *adj.* **1.** Of, resembling, or characteristic of death: *a deathly silence.* **2.** Causing death; fatal. **—deathly** *adv.* **1.** In the manner of death. **2.** Extremely; very: *The night was deathly cold.*

death mask *n.* A cast of a person's face taken after death.

death penalty *n.* A sentence of punishment by execution.

death point *n.* An environmental limit, as of temperature or radiation, beyond which a specified life form cannot survive: *the thermal death point of bacteria.*

death qualify *tr.v. Law.* To excuse (opponents of the death penalty) from serving on a jury. **—death qualification** *n.*

death rate *n.* The ratio of total deaths to total population in a specified community or area over a specified period of time. The death rate is often expressed as the number of deaths per 1,000 of the population per year. Also called *fatality rate.*

death rattle *n.* A gurgling or rattling sound sometimes made in the throat of a dying person, caused by loss of the cough reflex and passage of the breath through accumulating mucus.

death row (rō) *n.* The part of a prison for housing inmates who have received the death penalty. Also called *death house.*

death seat *n. Informal.* The passenger seat next to the driver of an automotive vehicle. [Australian, so called because this seat is said to be the most dangerous one in the event of an accident.]

death's-head (dĕths′hĕd′) *n.* The human skull as a symbol of mortality or death.

deaths·man (dĕths′mən) *n. Archaic.* An executioner.

death tax *n.* **1.** See **inheritance tax. 2.** See **estate tax.**

death·trap (dĕth′trăp′) *n.* **1.** An unsafe building or other structure. **2.** A perilous circumstance or situation.

Death Valley. An arid desert basin of eastern California and western Nevada. It includes the lowest point, 86 m (282 ft) below sea level, in the Western Hemisphere.

death warrant *n.* **1.** *Law.* An official order authorizing a person's execution. **2.** Something that destroys hope or expectation; a deathblow.

death·watch (dĕth′wŏch′) *n.* **1.** A vigil kept beside a dying or dead person. **2.** One who guards a condemned person before execution. **3.** A deathwatch beetle.

deathwatch beetle *n.* Any one of several beetles of the family Anobiidae, especially *Xestobium rufovillosum,* whose head makes a clicking sound as it burrows into wood or wooden structures. The sound was superstitiously regarded as a portent of death.

death wish *n.* **1.** *Psychiatry.* **a.** A desire for self-destruction, often accompanied by feelings of depression, hopelessness, and self-reproach. **b.** The desire, often unconscious, for the death of another person, such as a parent, toward whom one has unconscious hostility. **2.** A suicidal urge thought to drive certain people to put themselves consistently into dangerous situations. [Translation of German *Todeswunsch.*]

de·at·tri·bu·tion (dē′ă-trə-byo͞o′shən) *n.* A downgrading in the attribution of a work of art.

Deau·ville (dō′vĭl, dō-vēl′). A city of northwest France on the English Channel. It is a fashionable resort with a noted racecourse. Population, 4,682.

deb (dĕb) *n. Informal.* A debutante.

deb. *abbr.* Debenture.

de·ba·cle (dĭ-bä′kəl, -băk′əl) *n.* **1.** A sudden, disastrous collapse, downfall, or defeat; a rout. **2.** A total, often ludicrous failure. **3.** The breaking up of ice in a river. **4.** A violent flood. [French *débâcle,* from *débâcler,* to unbar, from Old French *desbacler* : *des-,* de- + *bacler,* to bar (from Vulgar Latin **bacculāre,* from Latin *baculum,* rod; see **bak-** in Appendix).]

De Ba·key (də bā′kē), **Michael Ellis.** Born 1908. American heart surgeon who implanted the first totally artificial heart in a human being (1966).

de·bar (dē-bär′) *tr.v.* **-barred, -bar·ring, -bars. 1.** To exclude or shut out; bar. **2.** To forbid, hinder, or prevent. [Middle English *debarren,* from Old French *desbarer,* to unbar : *des-,* de- + *barer,* to bar (from *barre,* bar; see BAR[1]).] **—de·bar′ment** *n.*

de·bark (dĭ-bärk′) *v.* **-barked, -bark·ing, -barks.** *—tr.* To unload, as from a ship or an airplane. *—intr.* To disembark. [French *débarquer* : *dé-,* from (from Old French *de-;* see DE–) + *barque,* ship (from Old French; see BARK[3]).] **—de′bar·ka′tion** (dē′bär-kā′shən) *n.*

de·base (dĭ-bās′) *tr.v.* **-based, -bas·ing, -bas·es.** To lower in character, quality, or value; degrade. See Synonyms at **adulterate, corrupt, degrade.** [DE– + BASE[2].] **—de·base′ment** *n.* **—de·bas′er** *n.*

de·bat·a·ble (dĭ-bā′tə-bəl) *adj.* **1.** Being such that formal argument or discussion is possible. **2.** Open to dispute; questionable. **3.** In dispute, as land or territory claimed by more than one country. **—de·bat′a·bly** *adv.*

de·bate (dĭ-bāt′) *v.* **-bat·ed, -bat·ing, -bates.** *—intr.* **1.** To consider something; deliberate. **2.** To engage in argument by discussing opposing points. **3.** To engage in a formal discussion or argument. See Synonyms at **discuss. 4.** *Obsolete.* To fight or quarrel. *—tr.* **1.** To deliberate on; consider. **2.** To dispute or argue about. **3.** To discuss or argue (a question, for example) formally. **4.** *Obsolete.* To fight or argue for or over. **—debate** *n.* **1.** A discussion involving opposing points; an argument. **2.** Deliberation; consideration: *passed the motion with little debate.* **3.** A formal contest of argumentation in which two opposing teams defend and attack a given proposition. **4.** *Obsolete.* Conflict; strife. [Middle English *debaten,* from Old French *debatre* : *de-,* de- + *battre,* to beat; see BATTER[1].] **—de·bate′ment** *n.* **—de·bat′er** *n.*

de·bauch (dĭ-bôch′) *v.* **-bauched, -bauch·ing, -bauch·es.** *—tr.* **1.a.** To corrupt morally. **b.** To lead away from excellence or virtue. **2.** To reduce the value, quality, or excellence of; debase. See Synonyms at **corrupt. 3.** *Archaic.* To cause to forsake allegiance. *—intr.* To indulge in dissipation. **—debauch** *n.* **1.** The act or a period of debauchery. **2.** An orgy. [French *débaucher,* from Old French *desbauchier,* to lead astray, roughhew timber : *des-,* de- + *bauch,* beam, of Germanic origin.] **—de·bauch′ed·ly** (-bô′chĭd-lē) *adv.* **—de·bauch′er** *n.*

de·bauch·ee (dĭ-bô′chē′, dĕb′ə-shē′, -shā′) *n.* A person who habitually indulges in debauchery or dissipation; a libertine.

de·bauch·er·y (dĭ-bô′chə-rē) *n., pl.* **-ies. 1.a.** Extreme indulgence in sensual pleasures; dissipation. **b. debaucheries.** Orgies. **2.** *Archaic.* Seduction from morality, allegiance, or duty.

de·ben·ture (dĭ-bĕn′chər) *n. Abbr.* **deb. 1.** A certificate or voucher acknowledging a debt. **2.** An unsecured bond issued by a civil or governmental corporation or agency and backed only by the credit standing of the issuer. **3.** A customhouse certificate providing for the payment of a drawback. [Middle English *debentur,* from Latin *dēbentur,* they are due (probably the first word appearing on certificates of indebtedness), third person pl. passive of *dēbēre,* to owe. See **ghabh-** in Appendix.]

de·bil·i·tate (dĭ-bĭl′ĭ-tāt′) *tr.v.* **-tat·ed, -tat·ing, -tates.** To sap the strength or energy of; enervate. [Latin *dēbilitāre, dēbilitāt-,* from *dēbilis,* weak. See **bel-** in Appendix.] **—de·bil′i·ta′tion** *n.* **—de·bil′i·ta′tive** *adj.*

de·bil·i·tat·ed (dĭ-bĭl′ĭ-tā′tĭd) *adj.* Showing impairment of energy or strength; enfeebled. See Synonyms at **weak.**

de·bil·i·ty (dĭ-bĭl′ĭ-tē) *n., pl.* **-ties.** The state of being weak or feeble; infirmity. [Middle English *debilite,* from Old French, from Latin *dēbilitās,* from *dēbilis,* weak. See **bel-** in Appendix.]

deb·it (dĕb′ĭt) *n.* **1.** An item of debt as recorded in an account. **2. a.** An entry of a sum in the debit or left-hand side of an account. **b.** The sum of such entries. **3.** The left-hand side of an account or accounting ledger where bookkeeping entries are made. **4.** A drawback; a detriment. **—debit** *tr.v.* **-it·ed, -it·ing, -its. 1.** To enter (a sum) on the left-hand side of an account or accounting ledger. **2.** To charge with a debit: *The bank debited my account for the overdrawn check.* [Middle English *debite,* from Latin *dēbitum,* debt. See DEBT.]

deb·o·nair also **deb·o·naire** (dĕb′ə-nâr′) *adj.* **1.** Suave; urbane. **2.** Affable; genial. **3.** Carefree and gay; jaunty. [Middle English *debonaire,* gracious, kindly, from Old French, from *de bon aire,* of good lineage or disposition : *de,* of (from Latin *dē;* see DE–) + *bon, bonne,* good (from Latin *bonus;* see **deu-²** in Appendix) + *aire,* nest, family; see AERIE.] **—deb′o·nair′ly** *adv.* **—deb′o·nair′ness** *n.*

de·bone (dē-bōn′) *tr.v.* **-boned, -bon·ing, -bones.** To remove the bones from: *debone a chicken breast.*

Deb·o·rah (dĕb′ər-ə, dĕb′rə). In the Old Testament, a judge and prophet who aided the Israelites in their victory over the Canaanites.

de·bouch (dĭ-bouch′, -bo͞osh′) *v.* **-bouched, -bouch·ing, -bouch·es.** *—intr.* **1.** To march from a narrow or confined area into the open. **2.** To emerge; issue: *a river into which a large stream debouches.* *—tr.* To cause to emerge or issue. [French *déboucher* : *dé-,* out of (from Old French *des-;* see DE–) + *bouche,* mouth (from Latin *bucca,* cheek, mouth).]

de·bouch·ment (dĭ-bouch′mənt, -bo͞osh′-) *n.* **1.** The act or an instance of marching from a narrow, confined area into the open. **2.** A debouchure.

de·bou·chure (dĭ-bo͞o′sho͝or′) *n.* An opening or mouth, as of a river or stream.

De·bre·cen (dĕb′rĭt-sĕn′, -rĕ-tsĕn′). A city of eastern Hungary near the Romanian border east of Budapest. First known in the 13th century, it was the provisional capital from 1944 to 1945. Population, 208,891.

dé·bride·ment (dā′brēd-mäɴ′, dĭ-brēd′mənt) *n.* Surgical excision of dead, devitalized, or contaminated tissue and removal of foreign matter from a wound. [French, from *débrider,* to débride, from Old French *desbrider,* to open up, unbridle : *des-,* de- + *bride,* bridle (probably from Middle High German *brīdel,* rein).] **—dé·bride′** *v.*

de·brief (dē-brēf′) *tr.v.* **-briefed, -brief·ing, -briefs. 1.** To question to obtain knowledge or intelligence gathered especially on a military mission. **2.** To instruct (a government agent, for example) not to reveal classified or secret information after employment has ceased.

de·brief·ing (dē-brē′fĭng) *n.* **1.** The act or process of debriefing or of being debriefed. **2.** The information imparted during the process of being debriefed.

de·bris also **dé·bris** (də-brē′, dā-, dā′brē′) *n.* **1. a.** The scattered remains of something broken or destroyed; rubble or wreckage. **b.** Carelessly discarded refuse; litter. **2.** *Geology.* An accumulation of relatively large rock fragments: *glacial debris.* **3.** *Biology.* The fragmented remains of dead or damaged cells or tissue. [French *débris,* from Old French *debrisier,* to break to pieces : *de-,* intensive pref.; see DE– + *brisier,* to break (from Vulgar Latin **brīsāre,* to press grapes, probably of Celtic origin).]

Debs (dĕbz), **Eugene Victor.** 1855–1926. American labor organizer and socialist leader who ran unsuccessfully for President five times between 1900 and 1920.

debt (dĕt) *n.* **1.** Something owed, such as money, goods, or services. **2. a.** An obligation or liability to pay or render something to someone else. **b.** The condition of owing: *a young family always in debt.* **3.** An offense requiring forgiveness or reparation; a trespass. [Middle English *dette,* from Old French, from Vulgar Latin **dēbita,* pl. of Latin *dēbitum,* debt, neuter past participle of *dēbēre,* to owe. See **ghabh-** in Appendix.] **—debt′less** *adj.*

debt·or (dĕt′ər) *n.* **1.** *Abbr.* **dr.** One that owes something to another. **2.** One who is guilty of a trespass or sin; a sinner. [Middle English *dettour,* from Old French *dettor,* from Latin *dēbitor,* from *dēbitus,* past participle of *dēbēre,* to owe. See DEBT.]

de·bug (dē-bŭg′) *tr.v.* **-bugged, -bug·ging, -bugs. 1.** To remove a hidden electronic device, such as a microphone, from: *debug a conference room.* **2.** To make (a hidden microphone, for example) ineffective. **3.** To search for and eliminate malfunctioning elements or errors in: *debug a spacecraft before launch; debug a computer program.* **4.** To remove insects from, as with a pesticide. **—de·bug′ger** *n.*

de·bunk (dē-bŭngk′) *tr.v.* **-bunked, -bunk·ing, -bunks.** To expose or ridicule the falseness, sham, or exaggerated claims of: *debunk a supposed miracle drug.* **—de·bunk′er** *n.*

WORD HISTORY: One can readily see that *debunk* is constructed from the prefix *de–,* meaning "to remove," and the word *bunk.* But what is the origin of the word *bunk,* denoting the nonsense that is to be removed? *Bunk* came from a place where much bunk has originated, the United States Congress. During the 16th Congress (1819–1821) Felix Walker, a representative from western North Carolina whose district included Buncombe County, continued on with a dull speech in the face of protests by his colleagues. Walker replied he had felt obligated "to make a speech for Buncombe." Such a masterful symbol for empty talk could not be ignored by the speakers of the language, and *Buncombe,* actually spelled *Bunkum* in its first recorded appearance in 1828 and later shortened to *bunk,* became synonymous with *claptrap.* The response to all this bunk seems to have been delayed, for *debunk* is not recorded until 1923.

De·bus·sy (də-byo͞o′sē, dĕb′yo͞o-sē′, də-bü-sē′), **Claude Achille.** 1862–1918. French composer who is considered the first exponent of musical impressionism. His works include the tone poem *L'Après-midi d'un Faune* (1894).

Claude Debussy

de·but also **dé·but** (dā-byo͞o′, dā′byo͞o′) *—n.* **1.** A first public appearance, as of a performer. **2.** The formal presentation of a young woman to society. **3.** The beginning of a course of action: *the debut of a new foreign policy.* *—tr. & intr.v.* **-buted** (-byo͞od′), **-but·ing** (-byo͞o′ĭng), **-buts** (-byo͞oz′). *Usage Problem.* To present in or make a debut. [French *début,* from *débuter,* to give the first stroke in a game, begin : *dé-,* from, away (from Old French *de-;* see DE–) + *but,* goal, target (from Old French *butte;* see BUTT³).]

USAGE NOTE: *Debut* is widely used as a verb, both intransitively (*Her new series will debut next March on network television*) and transitively (*The network will debut her new series next March*). These usages are well established in connection with entertainment and the performing arts but are not entirely acceptable when used of other sorts of introductions, as of products (*The company will debut the new six-cylinder convertible next fall*) or publications (*The national edition of the newspaper debuted last summer*), probably because of the association of the form with the language of show-business publicity.

deb·u·tante (dĕb′yo͞o-tänt′, dā′byo͞o-) *n.* A young woman making a formal debut into society. [French *débutante,* feminine present participle of *débuter,* to begin. See DEBUT.]

De·bye (də-bī′), **Peter Joseph Wilhelm.** 1884–1966. Dutch-born American physicist. He won a 1936 Nobel Prize for his investigations on dipole movements and on diffraction of x-rays and electrons in gases.

dec. *abbr.* **1.** Deceased. **2.** Declaration. **3.** Declension. **4.** Declination. **5.** Decorated. **6.** Decorative. **7.** Decrease. **8.** *Music.* Decrescendo.

Dec. or **Dec** *abbr.* December.

deca– or **dec–** also **deka–** or **dek–** *pref.* Ten: *decane.* [Greek *deka-,* from *deka,* ten. See **dekm̥** in Appendix.]

dec·ade (dĕk′ād′, dĕ-kād′) *n.* **1.** A period of ten years. **2.** A group or series of ten. [Middle English, a group of ten, from Old French, from Late Latin *decas, decad-,* from Greek *dekas,* from *deka,* ten. See **dekm̥** in Appendix.]

dec·ade·long (dĕk′ād-lông′, -lŏng′, də-kād′-) *adj.* Lasting a decade: *a decadelong national research effort.*

dec·a·dence (dĕk′ə-dəns, dĭ-kād′ns) *n.* **1.** A process, condition, or period of deterioration or decline, as in morals or art; decay. **2.** Often **Decadence.** A literary movement especially of late 19th-century France and England characterized by refined aestheticism, artifice, and the quest for new sensations. [French *décadence,* from Old French *decadence,* from Medieval Latin *dēcadentia,* a decaying, declining, from Vulgar Latin **dēcadere,* to decay; see DECAY.]

dec·a·den·cy (dĕk′ə-dən-sē, dĭ-kād′n-) *n.* Decadence.

dec·a·dent (dĕk′ə-dənt, dĭ-kād′nt) *adj.* **1.** Being in a state of decline or decay. **2.** Marked by or providing unrestrained gratification; self-indulgent. **3.** Often **Decadent.** Of or relating to literary Decadence. **—decadent** *n.* **1.** A person in a condition or process of mental or moral decay. **2.** Often **Decadent.** A member of the Decadence movement. [French *décadent,* back-formation from *décadence,* decadence. See DECADENCE.] **—dec′a·dent·ly** *adv.*

de·caf (dē′kăf′) *n. Informal.* Decaffeinated coffee. **—de′caf′** *adj.*

de·caf·fein·at·ed (dē-kăf′ə-nā′tĭd, -kăf′ē-ə-) *adj.* Having the caffeine removed: *decaffeinated coffee; decaffeinated soft drinks.* **—de·caf′fein·ate′** *v.* **—de·caf′fein·a′tion** *n.*

dec·a·gon (dĕk′ə-gŏn′) *n.* A polygon with ten angles and ten sides. [Medieval Latin *decagōnum,* from Greek *dekagōnon* : *deka,*

ă pat	oi boy
ā pay	ou out
âr care	o͝o took
ä father	o͞o boot
ĕ pet	ŭ cut
ē be	ûr urge
ĭ pit	th thin
ī pie	*th* this
îr pier	hw which
ŏ pot	zh vision
ō toe	ə about, item
ô paw	♦ regionalism

Stress marks: **′** (primary); ′ (secondary), as in **dictionary** (dĭk′shə-nĕr′ē)

ten; see **dekm̥** in Appendix + *-gōnon,* -gon.] **—de·cag′o·nal** (dĭ-kăg′ə-nəl) *adj.* **—de·cag′o·nal·ly** *adv.*

dec·a·gram or **dek·a·gram** (dĕk′ə-grăm′) *n. Abbr.* **dag, dkg** A metric unit of mass equal to 10 grams.

dec·a·he·dron (dĕk′ə-hē′drən) *n., pl.* **-drons** or **-dra** (-drə). A polyhedron with ten faces. **—dec′a·he′dral** *adj.*

de·cal (dē′kăl′, dĭ-kăl′) *n.* **1.** A picture or design transferred by decalcomania. **2.** A decorative sticker.

de·cal·ci·fy (dē-kăl′sə-fī′) *v.* **-fied, -fy·ing, -fies.** *—tr.* To remove calcium or calcium compounds from (bones or teeth, for example). *—intr.* To lose calcium or calcium compounds. **—de·cal′ci·fi·ca′tion** (-fĭ-kā′shən) *n.* **—de·cal′ci·fi′er** *n.*

de·cal·co·ma·ni·a (dē-kăl′kə-mā′nē-ə, -măn′yə) *n.* **1.** The process of transferring pictures or designs printed on specially prepared paper to materials such as glass or metal. **2.** A decal. [French *décalcomanie* : from *décalquer,* to transfer a tracing (*de-,* from, from Latin *dē-;* see DE– + *calquer,* to trace; see CALQUE) + *manie,* craze (from its popularity in the 19th century) (from Latin *mania,* madness; see MANIA).]

de·ca·les·cence (dē′kə-lĕs′əns) *n.* A sudden slowing in the rate of temperature increase in a metal being heated, caused by endothermic structural changes and resulting in a darkening of the metal. [From DE– + Latin *calēscere,* to become warm, inchoative of *calēre,* to be warm; see **kelə-¹** in Appendix.] **—de′ca·les′cent** *adj.*

dec·a·li·ter or **dek·a·li·ter** (dĕk′ə-lē′tər) *n. Abbr.* **dal, dkl** A metric unit of volume equal to 10 liters.

Dec·a·logue or **Dec·a·log** (dĕk′ə-lôg′, -lŏg′) *n.* **1.** *Bible.* The Ten Commandments. **2.** A fundamental set of rules having authoritative weight. [Middle English *decalog,* from Late Latin *decalogus,* from Greek *dekalogos* : *deka,* ten; see **dekm̥** in Appendix + *logos,* word, pronouncement; see **leg-** in Appendix.]

dec·a·me·ter or **dek·a·me·ter** (dĕk′ə-mē′tər) *n. Abbr.* **dam, dkm** A metric unit of length equal to 10 meters.

dec·a·met·ric (dĕk′ə-mĕt′rĭk) *adj.* Of, relating to, or being a radio wave of wavelength between one and ten decameters.

de·camp (dĭ-kămp′) *intr.v.* **-camped, -camp·ing, -camps. 1.** To depart secretly or suddenly. **2.** To depart from a camp or camping ground. [French *décamper,* from Old French *descamper,* to strike camp : *des-,* de- + *camper,* to camp (from *camp,* camp; see CAMP¹).] **—de·camp′ment** *n.*

dec·ane (dĕk′ān′) *n.* Any of various liquid isomers, $C_{10}H_{22}$, of the methane series.

dec·a·no·ic acid (dĕk′ə-nō′ĭk) *n.* See **capric acid.**

de·cant (dĭ-kănt′) *tr.v.* **-cant·ed, -cant·ing, -cants. 1.** To pour off (wine, for example) without disturbing the sediment. **2.** To pour from one container into another. [Medieval Latin *dēcanthāre* : Latin *dē-,* de- + Latin *canthus,* rim of a wheel or vessel (of Celtic origin).] **—de′can·ta′tion** (dē′kăn-tā′shən) *n.*

de·cant·er (dĭ-kăn′tər) *n.* A vessel used for decanting, especially a decorative bottle used for serving wine.

de·cap·i·tate (dĭ-kăp′ĭ-tāt′) *tr.v.* **-tat·ed, -tat·ing, -tates.** To cut off the head of; behead. [Late Latin *dēcapitāre, dēcapitāt-* : Latin *dē-,* de- + Latin *caput, capit-,* head; see **kaput-** in Appendix.] **—de·cap′i·ta′tion** *n.* **—de·cap′i·ta′tor** *n.*

dec·a·pod (dĕk′ə-pŏd′) *n.* **1.** A crustacean of the order Decapoda, such as a crab, lobster, or shrimp, characteristically having ten legs, each joined to a segment of the thorax. **2.** A cephalopod mollusk, such as a squid or cuttlefish, having ten armlike tentacles. **—decapod** *adj.* Of or relating to the Decapoda or a decapod. [From New Latin *Decapoda,* order name : DECA– + *-poda,* -pod.] **—de·cap′o·dal** (dĭ-kăp′ə-dəl), **de·cap′o·dan** (-dən), **de·cap′o·dous** (-dəs) *adj.*

De·cap·o·lis (dĭ-kăp′ə-lĭs). A confederacy in northeast Palestine of ten Roman-controlled cities settled by Greeks. It was formed after 63 B.C. and dominated by Damascus.

de·car·bon·ate (dē-kär′bə-nāt′) *tr.v.* **-at·ed, -at·ing, -ates.** To remove carbon dioxide or carbonic acid from. **—de·car′bon·a′tion** *n.*

de·car·bon·ize (dē-kär′bə-nīz′) *tr.v.* **-ized, -iz·ing, -iz·es.** To remove carbon from; decarburize. **—de·car′bon·i·za′tion** (-bə-nĭ-zā′shən) *n.* **—de·car′bon·iz′er** *n.*

de·car·box·yl·ase (dē′kär-bŏk′sə-lās′, -lāz′) *n.* Any of various enzymes that hydrolize the carboxyl radical.

de·car·box·yl·a·tion (dē′kär-bŏk′sə-lā′shən) *n.* Removal of a carboxyl group from a chemical compound, usually with hydrogen replacing it.

de·car·bu·rize (dē-kär′bə-rīz′, -byə-) *tr.v.* **-rized, -riz·ing, -riz·es.** To decarbonize. **—de·car′bu·ri·za′tion** (-rĭ-zā′shən) *n.*

dec·are (dĕk′âr′, -är′) *n.* A metric unit of area equal to 10 ares.

dec·a·syl·la·ble (dĕk′ə-sĭl′ə-bəl) *n.* A line of verse having ten syllables. **—dec′a·syl·lab′ic** (-sə-lăb′ĭk) *adj.*

de·cath·lete (dĭ-kăth′lēt) *n. Sports.* An athlete who participates in a decathlon.

de·cath·lon (dĭ-kăth′lən, -lŏn′) *n. Sports.* An athletic contest in which each contestant participates in the following ten track and field events: the 100-meter, 400-meter, and 1,500-meter runs; the 110-meter high hurdle; the discus and javelin throws; the shot-put; the pole vault; the high jump; and the long jump. [DECA– + (PENTA)THLON.]

De·ca·tur (dĭ-kā′tər). **1.** A city of northern Alabama on the Tennessee River north of Birmingham. Most of the original city was destroyed during the Civil War. Population, 42,002. **2.** A city of northwest Georgia, a residential suburb of Atlanta. Population, 18,404. **3.** A city of central Illinois east of Springfield. Abraham Lincoln practiced law here. Population, 94,081.

Decatur, Stephen. 1779–1820. American naval officer known for his heroic deeds in the Tripolitan War, the War of 1812, and skirmishes against the Barbary pirates.

de·cay (dĭ-kā′) *v.* **-cayed, -cay·ing, -cays.** *—intr.* **1.** *Biology.* To break down into component parts; rot. **2.** *Physics.* To disintegrate or diminish by radioactive decay. **3.** *Electronics.* To decrease gradually in magnitude. Used of voltage or current. **4.** *Aerospace.* To decrease in orbit. Used of an artificial satellite. **5.** To fall into ruin: *a civilization that had begun to decay.* **6.** *Pathology.* To decline in health or vigor; waste away. **7.** To decline from a state of normality, excellence, or prosperity; deteriorate. *—tr.* To cause to decay. **—decay** *n.* **1.a.** The destruction or decomposition of organic matter as a result of bacterial or fungal action; rot. **b.** Rotted matter. **2.** *Physics.* Radioactive decay. **3.** *Aerospace.* The decrease in orbital altitude of an artificial satellite as a result of conditions such as atmospheric drag. **4.** A gradual deterioration to an inferior state: *tooth decay; urban decay.* **5.** A falling into ruin. [Middle English *decayen,* from Old French *decair,* from Vulgar Latin **dēcadere* : Latin *dē-,* de- + Latin *cadere,* to fall; see **kad-** in Appendix.] **—de·cay′er** *n.*

SYNONYMS: *decay, rot, putrefy, spoil, crumble, molder, disintegrate, decompose.* These verbs all refer to gradual change resulting in destruction or dissolution. *Decay* denotes a falling away from soundness; it may imply a stage in deterioration short of complete destruction: *Dentists advise their patients to brush and floss regularly to prevent their teeth from decaying. Rot* is sometimes synonymous with *decay* (*wood that had rotted*), but it often, like *putrefy,* stresses a stage of deterioration marked by offensiveness to the sense of smell: *Animal flesh that rots is attractive to vultures. The intact carcass of the prehistoric animal was prevented from putrefying by the arctic cold. Spoil* usually refers to the process by which perishable substances, especially food, become unfit for use or consumption: *I put the veal scallops into the refrigerator before they could spoil. Crumble* implies the physical breakdown of a substance into small fragments or particles: *We saw the remains of an ancient church that had crumbled to ruins.* To *molder* is to crumble to dust: *Her grandmother's shawl had moldered away in the trunk. Disintegrate* refers to complete breakdown into component parts and implies the destruction of usefulness or integrity: *The sandstone façade had disintegrated from long exposure to the elements. Decompose,* largely restricted to the breakdown of substances into their chemical components, also connotes rotting and putrefying, both literally and figuratively: *"trivial personalities decomposing in the eternity of print"* (Virginia Woolf).

Dec·can (dĕk′ən). A plateau of south-central India between the Eastern Ghats and the Western Ghats. The name is also used for the entire Indian peninsula south of the Narmada River.

decd. *abbr.* Deceased.

de·cease (dĭ-sēs′) *intr.v.* **-ceased, -ceas·ing, -ceas·es.** To die. **—decease** *n.* The act of dying; death. [Middle English *decesen,* from *deces,* death, from Old French, from Latin *dēcessus,* departure, death, from past participle of *dēcēdere,* to depart, die : *dē-,* de- + *cēdere,* to go; see **ked-** in Appendix.]

de·ceased (dĭ-sēst′) *adj. Abbr.* **dec., decd.** No longer living; dead. See Synonyms at **dead. —deceased** *n., pl.* **deceased.** A dead person.

de·ce·dent (dĭ-sēd′nt) *n. Law.* A dead person. [Latin *dēcēdēns, dēcēdent-,* present participle of *dēcēdere,* to depart, die. See DECEASE.]

de·ceit (dĭ-sēt′) *n.* **1.** The act or practice of deceiving; deception. **2.** A stratagem; a trick. **3.** The quality of being deceitful; falseness. [Middle English *deceite,* from Old French, from past participle of *deceveir,* to deceive. See DECEIVE.]

de·ceit·ful (dĭ-sēt′fəl) *adj.* **1.** Given to cheating or deceiving. **2.** Deliberately misleading; deceptive. See Synonyms at **dishonest. —de·ceit′ful·ly** *adv.* **—de·ceit′ful·ness** *n.*

de·ceive (dĭ-sēv′) *v.* **-ceived, -ceiv·ing, -ceives.** *—tr.* **1.** To cause to believe what is not true; mislead. **2.** *Archaic.* To catch by guile; ensnare. *—intr.* To practice deceit. [Middle English *deceiven,* from Old French *deceveir,* from Vulgar Latin **dēcipēre,* from Latin *dēcipere,* to ensnare, deceive : *dē-,* de- + *capere,* to seize; see **kap-** in Appendix.] **—de·ceiv′a·ble** *adj.* **—de·ceiv′er** *n.* **—de·ceiv′ing·ly** *adv.*

SYNONYMS: *deceive, betray, mislead, beguile, delude, dupe, hoodwink, bamboozle, double-cross.* These verbs mean to lead another into error, danger, or a disadvantageous position, for the most part by underhand means. *Deceive* involves the deliberate concealment or the misrepresentation of the truth: *"There is a moment of difficulty and danger at which flattery and falsehood can no longer deceive"* (Letters of Junius). *Betray* implies faithlessness or treachery: *"When you betray somebody else, you also betray yourself"* (Isaac Bashevis Singer). *Mislead* means to lead in the wrong direction or into error of thought or action: *"My manhood, long misled by wandering fires,/Followed false lights"* (John Dryden). *Beguile* suggests deceiving or misleading by means of pleasant or alluring methods: *They beguiled unwary investors with tales of overnight fortunes.* To *delude* is to mislead to the point where a person is unable to tell truth from falsehood or to form sound judgments: *The government deluded the public about the dangers of low-level radiation. Dupe* means to delude by playing upon another's susceptibilities or naiveté: *Gullible shoppers are easily duped by unscrupulous advertisers. Hoodwink* refers to deluding by trickery: *It is difficult to hoodwink a smart lawyer. Bamboozle* less formally means to delude by the use of such tactics as hoaxing, befuddling, or artful persuasion: *"Perhaps if I wanted to be understood or to understand I would bamboozle myself into belief, but I am a reporter"* (Graham Greene). *Double-cross* implies the betrayal of a confidence or the willful breaking of a pledge: *New members of the party felt they had been double-crossed by the old guard.*

---

de·cel·er·ate (dē-sĕl′ə-rāt′) *v.* **-at·ed, -at·ing, -ates.** —*tr.* **1.** To decrease the velocity of. **2.** To slow down the rate of advancement of: *measures intended to decelerate the arms buildup.* —*intr.* To decrease in velocity. [DE– + (AC)CELERATE.] **—de·cel′er·a′tion** *n.* **—de·cel′er·a′tor** *n.*

De·cem·ber (dĭ-sĕm′bər) *n. Abbr.* **Dec., Dec** The 12th month of the year in the Gregorian calendar. See table at **calendar.** [Middle English *decembre,* from Old French, from Latin *December,* the tenth month of the Roman year, probably from **decemmembris,* from **decem-mēnsris* : *decem,* ten; see **dekm̥** in Appendix + *mēnsis,* month; see MENSES.]

De·cem·brist (dĭ-sĕm′brĭst) *n.* A participant in the unsuccessful conspiracy to overthrow Czar Nicholas I of Russia in December 1825.

de·cem·vir (dĭ-sĕm′vər) *n., pl.* **-virs** or **-vi·ri** (-və-rī′). **1.** One of a body of ten Roman magistrates, especially a member of one of two such bodies appointed in 451 and 450 B.C. to draw up a code of laws. **2.** One of an authoritative body of ten. [Middle English, from Latin, sing. of *decemvirī,* commission of ten men : *decem,* ten; see **dekm̥** in Appendix + *virī,* pl. of *vir,* man; see **wī-ro-** in Appendix.] **—de·cem′vi·ral** *adj.* **—de·cem′vi·rate** (-vər-ĭt, -və-rāt′) *n.*

de·cen·cy (dē′sən-sē) *n., pl.* **-cies. 1.** The state or quality of being decent; propriety. **2.** Conformity to prevailing standards of propriety or modesty. **3. decencies. a.** Social or moral proprieties. **b.** Surroundings or services deemed necessary for an acceptable standard of living.

de·cen·na·ry (dĭ-sĕn′ə-rē) *adj.* Of or relating to a ten-year period. **—decennary** *n., pl.* **-ries.** A period of ten years; a decade. [From Latin *decennis,* lasting for ten years. See DECENNIUM.]

de·cen·ni·a (dĭ-sĕn′ē-ə) *n.* A plural of **decennium.**

de·cen·ni·al (dĭ-sĕn′ē-əl) *adj.* **1.** Relating to or lasting for ten years. **2.** Occurring every ten years. **—decennial** *n.* A tenth anniversary. [From Latin *decennium,* a period of ten years. See DECENNIUM.] **—de·cen′ni·al·ly** *adv.*

de·cen·ni·um (dĭ-sĕn′ē-əm) *n., pl.* **-cen·ni·ums** or **-cen·ni·a** (-sĕn′ē-ə). A period of ten years; a decade. [Latin, from *decennis,* lasting for ten years : *decem,* ten; see **dekm̥** in Appendix + *annus,* year; see **at-** in Appendix.]

de·cent (dē′sənt) *adj.* **1.** Characterized by conformity to recognized standards of propriety or morality. **2.** Free from indelicacy; modest. **3.** Meeting accepted standards; adequate: *a decent salary.* **4. a.** Morally upright; respectable. **b.** Kind or obliging: *very decent of them to lend you money.* **5.** *Informal.* Properly or modestly dressed. [Latin *decēns, decent-,* present participle of *decēre,* to be fitting. See **dek-** in Appendix.] **—de′cent·ly** *adv.* **—de′cent·ness** *n.*

de·cen·tral·ize (dē-sĕn′trə-līz′) *v.* **-ized, -iz·ing, -iz·es.** —*tr.* **1.** To distribute the administrative functions or powers of (a central authority) among several local authorities. **2. a.** To bring about the redistribution of (an urban population and industry) to suburban areas. **b.** To cause to withdraw or disperse from a center of concentration: *decentralize a university complex.* —*intr.* To undergo redistribution or dispersal away from a central location or authority. **—de·cen′tral·i·za′tion** (-trə-lĭ-zā′shən) *n.* **—de·cen′tral·i·za′tion·ist** *n.*

de·cep·tion (dĭ-sĕp′shən) *n.* **1.** The use of deceit. **2.** The fact or state of being deceived. **3.** A ruse; a trick. [Middle English *decepcioun,* from Old French *deception,* from Late Latin *dēceptiō, dēceptiōn-,* from Latin *dēceptus,* past participle of *dēcipere,* to deceive. See DECEIVE.]

de·cep·tive (dĭ-sĕp′tĭv) *adj.* Deceptive or tending to deceive. See Synonyms at **misleading. —de·cep′tive·ness** *n.*

de·cep·tive·ly (dĭ-sĕp′tĭv-lē) *adv.* In a deceptive or deceiving manner; so as to deceive.

USAGE NOTE: There appears to be a great deal of confusion about the sense of *deceptively* when it is used to modify an adjective. Does the sentence *The proof is deceptively simple* mean that the proof is simpler or more difficult than it appears? The Usage Panel was asked to choose among paraphrases for the sentence *The pool is deceptively shallow:* 50 percent said that it means "The pool is shallower than it appears"; 32 percent said that it means "The pool is deeper than it appears"; and 18 percent found it ambiguous. Thus the writer who used such a sentence in a warning notice could expect that at least half the public would either misinterpret the message or would be uncertain as to which sense was intended. Where the context does not make the meaning clear, a substitute should be used, as *The pool is shallower than it looks* or *The proof is simple, despite appearances.*

---

de·cer·e·brate (dē-sĕr′ə-brāt′) *tr.v.* **-brat·ed, -brat·ing, -brates.** To eliminate cerebral brain function in (an animal) by removing the cerebrum, cutting across the brain stem, or severing certain arteries in the brain stem, as for purposes of experimentation. **—decerebrate** (*also* -brĭt) *adj.* **1.** Deprived of cerebral function, as by having the cerebrum removed. **2.** Resulting from or as if from decerebration: *decerebrate rigidity; decerebrate movements.* **3.** Lacking intelligence or reason. **—decerebrate** (*also* -brĭt) *n.* A decerebrate animal or person. **—de·cer′e·bra′tion** *n.*

de·cer·ti·fy (dē-sûr′tə-fī′) *tr.v.* **-fied, -fy·ing, -fies.** To revoke the certification of: *voted to decertify the union.* **—de·cer′ti·fi·ca′tion** (dē-sûr′tə-fĭ-kā′shən, dē′sər-) *n.*

deci– *pref.* One tenth (10): *deciliter.* [French *déci-,* from Latin *decimus,* tenth, from *decem,* ten. See **dekm̥** in Appendix.]

dec·i·are (dĕs′ē-âr′, -är′) *n.* One-tenth (10) of an are.

dec·i·bel (dĕs′ə-bəl, -bĕl′) *n. Abbr.* **dB** A unit used to express relative difference in power or intensity, usually between two acoustic or electric signals, equal to ten times the common logarithm of the ratio of the two levels. [DECI– + BEL.]

de·cide (dĭ-sīd′) *v.* **-cid·ed, -cid·ing, -cides.** —*tr.* **1.** To settle conclusively all contention or uncertainty about: *decide a case; decided the dispute in favor of the workers.* **2.** To influence or determine the outcome of: *A few votes decided the election.* **3.** To cause to make or reach a decision. —*intr.* **1.** To pronounce a judgment; announce a verdict. **2.** To make up one's mind. [Middle English *deciden,* from Old French *decider,* from Latin *dēcīdere,* to cut off, decide : *dē-,* de- + *caedere,* to cut; see **kae-id-** in Appendix.] **—de·cid·a·bil′i·ty** *n.* **—de·cid′a·ble** *adj.* **—de·cid′er** *n.*

SYNONYMS: *decide, determine, settle, rule, conclude, resolve.* These verbs are compared as they mean to make or cause to make a decision. *Decide* is the least specific: *"If two laws conflict with each other, the courts must decide on the operation of each"* (John Marshall). *Her parents' pleas decided her against dropping out of college. Determine* often involves somewhat narrower issues: *A jury will determine whether the charges are true or false. Settle* stresses finality of decision: *"The lama waved a hand to show that the matter was finally settled in his mind"* (Rudyard Kipling). *Rule* implies that the decision is handed down by someone in authority: *The faculty committee ruled that changes in the curriculum should be implemented. Conclude* suggests that a decision, opinion, or judgment has been arrived at after careful consideration: *She concluded that it would be better to ignore the criticism. Resolve* stresses the exercise of choice in making a firm decision: *I resolved to lose weight. We resolved that nothing they said could induce us to trust them.*

---

de·cid·ed (dĭ-sī′dĭd) *adj.* **1.** Without doubt or question; definite: *a decided success.* **2.** Free from hesitation or vacillation; resolute. **—de·cid′ed·ly** *adv.* **—de·cid′ed·ness** *n.*

de·cid·ing (dĭ-sī′dĭng) *adj.* Determining or able to determine an outcome: *the deciding factor; the deciding vote.*

de·cid·u·a (dĭ-sĭj′o͞o-ə) *n., pl.* **-u·as** or **-u·ae** (-o͞o-ē′). A mucous membrane lining the uterus, modified during pregnancy and shed at parturition or during menstruation. [New Latin *(membrāna) dēcidua,* (membrane) that falls off, from Latin *dēciduus,* falling off. See DECIDUOUS.] **—de·cid′u·al** *adj.*

de·cid·u·ate (dĭ-sĭj′o͞o-ĭt) *adj.* **1.** Characterized by or having a decidua: *a deciduate mammal.* **2.** Characterized by shedding.

de·cid·u·ous (dĭ-sĭj′o͞o-əs) *adj.* **1.** Falling off or shed at a specific season or stage of growth: *deciduous antlers; deciduous leaves; deciduous teeth.* **2.** Shedding or losing foliage at the end of the growing season: *deciduous trees.* **3.** Not lasting; ephemeral. [From Latin *dēciduus,* from *dēcidere,* to fall off : *dē-,* de- + *cadere,* to fall; see **kad-** in Appendix.] **—de·cid′u·ous·ly** *adv.* **—de·cid′u·ous·ness** *n.*

dec·i·gram (dĕs′ĭ-grăm′) *n. Abbr.* **dg** A metric unit of mass or weight equal to one-tenth (10) of a gram.

dec·ile (dĕs′īl′, -əl) *n. Statistics.* **1.** Any one of the numbers or values in a series dividing the distribution of the individuals in the series into ten groups of equal frequency. **2.** Any one of the ten groups. [DEC(I)– + –ILE[2].]

dec·i·li·ter (dĕs′ə-lē′tər) *n. Abbr.* **dl** A metric unit of volume equal to one-tenth (10) of a liter.

de·cil·lion (dĭ-sĭl′yən) *n.* **1.** The cardinal number equal to 10^{33}. **2.** *Chiefly British.* The cardinal number equal to 10^{60}. [Latin *decem,* ten; see DECI– + (M)ILLION.] **—de·cil′lion** *adj. & pron.*

de·cil·lionth (dĭ-sĭl′yənth) *n.* **1.** The ordinal number matching the number decillion in a series. **2.** One of a decillion equal parts. **—de·cil′lionth** *adv. & adj.*

dec·i·mal (dĕs′ə-məl) *n. Mathematics.* **1.** A linear array of integers that represents a fraction, every decimal place indicating a multiple of a negative power of 10. For example, the decimal 0.1 = 1/10, 0.12 = 12/100, 0.003 = 3/1000. Also called *decimal fraction.* **2.** A number written using the base 10. **—decimal** *adj.* **1.** Expressed or expressible as a decimal. **2. a.** Based on 10. **b.** Numbered or ordered by groups of 10. [Medieval Latin *decimālis,* of tenths or tithes, from Latin *decima,* a tenth part or tithe, from

ă pat	oi boy
ā pay	ou out
âr care	o͝o took
ä father	o͞o boot
ĕ pet	ŭ cut
ē be	ûr urge
ĭ pit	th thin
ī pie	*th* this
îr pier	hw which
ŏ pot	zh vision
ō toe	ə about, item
ô paw	♦ regionalism

Stress marks: ′ (primary); ′ (secondary), as in **dictionary** (dĭk′shə-nĕr′ē)

decem, ten. See **dekm̥** in Appendix.] **—dec′i·mal·ly** *adv.*

dec·i·mal·ize (dĕs′ə-mə-līz′) *tr.v.* **-ized, -iz·ing, -iz·es.** *Mathematics.* To change to a decimal system. **—dec′i·mal·i·za′tion** (-mə-lĭ-zā′shən) *n.*

decimal place *n. Mathematics.* The position of a digit to the right of a decimal point, usually identified by successive ascending ordinal numbers with the digit immediately to the right of the decimal point being first: *a figure accurate to the third decimal place.*

decimal point *n. Mathematics.* A dot written in a decimal number to indicate where the place values change from positive to negative powers of 10.

decimal system *n. Mathematics.* **1.** A number system based on units of 10. **2.** A system of measurement in which all derived units are multiples of 10 of the fundamental units.

dec·i·mate (dĕs′ə-māt′) *tr.v.* **-mat·ed, -mat·ing, -mates.** **1.** To destroy or kill a large part of (a group). **2.** *Usage Problem.* **a.** To inflict great destruction or damage on: *The fawns decimated my sister's rose bushes.* **b.** To reduce markedly in amount: *a profligate heir who decimated his trust fund.* **3.** To select by lot and kill one in every ten of. [Latin *decimāre, decimāt-,* to punish every tenth person, from *decimus,* tenth, from *decem,* ten. See **dekm̥** in Appendix.] **—dec′i·ma′tion** *n.*

USAGE NOTE: *Decimate* originally referred to the killing of every tenth person, a punishment used in the Roman army for mutinous legions. Today this meaning is commonly extended to include the killing of any large proportion of a group. Sixty-six percent of the Usage Panel accepts this extension in the sentence *The Jewish population of Germany was decimated by the war,* even though it is common knowledge that the number of Jews killed was much greater than a tenth of the original population. However, when the meaning is further extended to include large-scale destruction other than killing, as in *The supply of fresh produce was decimated by the accident at Chernobyl,* the usage is accepted by only 26 percent of the Panel.

WORD HISTORY: *Decimate* comes from the Latin word *decimāre,* which meant "to punish every tenth man chosen by lot, as in a mutinous military unit," *decimāre* being derived from *decimus,* "tenth." Our word *decimate* is first recorded in this sense in 1600 in *A Treatise of Ireland,* written by John Dymmok: "All . . . were by a martiall courte condemned to dye, which sentence was yet mittigated by the Lord Lieutenants mercy by which they were onely decimated by lott." *Decimate* then passed beyond the military context and came to be used rhetorically or loosely with reference to more than a tenth. Charlotte Brontë, for example, stated in a letter of 1848 that "Typhus fever decimated the school periodically," although typhus fever certainly did not always kill exactly a tenth of the school's population.

dec·i·me·ter (dĕs′ə-mē′tər) *n. Abbr.* **dm** A metric unit of length equal to one-tenth (10) of a meter.

de·ci·pher (dĭ-sī′fər) *tr.v.* **-phered, -pher·ing, -phers.** **1.** To read or interpret (ambiguous, obscure, or illegible matter). See Synonyms at **solve. 2.** To convert from a code or cipher to plain text; decode. **—de·ci′pher·a·ble** *adj.* **—de·ci′pher·er** *n.* **—de·ci′pher·ment** *n.*

de·ci·sion (dĭ-sĭzh′ən) *n.* **1.** The passing of judgment on an issue under consideration. **2.** The act of reaching a conclusion or making up one's mind. **3.** A conclusion or judgment reached or pronounced; a verdict. **4.** Firmness of character or action; determination. **5.** *Sports.* A victory in boxing won on points when no knockout has occurred. **—decision** *tr.v.* **-sioned, -sion·ing, -sions.** *Sports.* To achieve a victory over, as in boxing: *He decisioned his opponent in the third round of the match.* [Middle English *decisioun,* from Old French *decision,* from Latin *dēcīsiō, dēcīsiōn-,* curtailment, settlement, from *dēcīdere,* to cut off, decide. See DECIDE.] **—de·ci′sion·al** *adj.*

SYNONYMS: *decision, conclusion, determination.* The central meaning shared by these nouns is "a position, an opinion, or a judgment reached after consideration": *a decision unfavorable to the opposition; came to the conclusion not to proceed; satisfied with the panel's determination.*

de·ci·sion-mak·er (dĭ-sĭzh′ən-mā′kər) *n.* One that makes decisions, especially one in a position of authority or power.

de·ci·sion-mak·ing (dĭ-sĭzh′ən-mā′kĭng) *n.* The making of decisions, especially by persons in positions of authority or power: *"No one can doubt the need for Presidential decision-making when split-second questions of nuclear war or peace may be involved"* (New York Times). **—de·ci′sion-mak′ing** *adj.*

de·ci·sive (dĭ-sī′sĭv) *adj.* **1.** Having the power to decide; conclusive. **2.** Characterized by decision and firmness; resolute. **3.** Beyond doubt; unmistakable: *a decisive defeat.* **—de·ci′sive·ly** *adv.* **—de·ci′sive·ness** *n.*

SYNONYMS: *decisive, conclusive, crucial, definitive, determinative.* The central meaning shared by these adjectives is "determining or having the power to determine an outcome": *the decisive vote; a conclusive reason; crucial experiments; a definitive verdict; the determinative battle.*
ANTONYM: *indecisive.*

De·cius (dē′shəs, -shē-əs). A.D. 201–251. Emperor of Rome (249–251) who was proclaimed emperor by his soldiers against his will. His reign was marked by severe persecution of Christians.

deck[1] (dĕk) *n. Abbr.* **dk. 1.** *Nautical.* A platform extending horizontally from one side of a ship to the other. **2. a.** A platform or surface likened to a ship's deck. **b.** A roofless, floored area, typically with low sides, that adjoins a house. **c.** The roadway of a bridge or an elevated freeway. **3. a.** A pack of playing cards. **b.** *Computer Science.* A group of data processing cards. **4.** A tape deck. **5.** *Slang.* A packet of narcotics. **—deck** *tr.v.* **decked, deck·ing, decks. 1.** To furnish with or as if with a deck. **2.** *Slang.* To knock down with force: *He decked his sparring partner.* **—*idioms.* clear the deck.** *Informal.* To prepare for action. **hit the deck.** *Slang.* **1.** To get out of bed. **2.** To fall or drop to a prone position. **3.** To prepare for action. **on deck. 1.** On hand; present. **2.** *Sports.* Waiting to take one's turn, especially as a batter in baseball. [Middle English *dekke,* from Middle Dutch *dec,* roof, covering. See **(s)teg-** in Appendix.]

deck[2] (dĕk) *tr.v.* **decked, deck·ing, decks. 1.** To clothe with finery; adorn. Often used with *out: We were all decked out for the party.* **2.** To decorate: *decked the halls for the holidays.* [Dutch *dekken,* to cover, from Middle Dutch *decken.* See **(s)teg-** in Appendix.]

deck chair *n.* A folding chair that usually has arms and a leg rest.

deck·er (dĕk′ər) *n.* Something having a deck or an indicated number of levels, stories, or tiers. Often used in combination: *a three-decker apartment house; double-decker buses.*

deck hand *n. Nautical.* A member of a ship's crew who performs manual labor.

deck·house (dĕk′hous′) *n. Nautical.* A superstructure on the upper deck of a ship.

deck·le (dĕk′əl) *n.* **1.** A frame used in making paper by hand to form paper pulp into sheets of a desired size. **2.** A deckle edge. [German *Deckel,* from *Decke,* cover, from *decken,* to cover, from Middle High German, from Old High German *decchen.* See **(s)teg-** in Appendix.]

deckle edge *n.* The rough edge of handmade paper formed in a deckle. Also called *featheredge.* **—deck′le-edged′** (dĕk′əl-ĕjd′) *adj.*

deck tennis *n. Sports.* A game in which a small ring is tossed back and forth over a net.

decl. *abbr.* Declension.

de·claim (dĭ-klām′) *v.* **-claimed, -claim·ing, -claims.** *—intr.* **1.** To deliver a formal recitation, especially as an exercise in rhetoric or elocution. **2.** To speak loudly and vehemently; inveigh. *—tr.* To utter or recite with rhetorical effect. [Middle English *declamen,* from Latin *dēclāmāre* : *dē-,* intensive pref.; see DE– + *clāmāre,* to cry out; see **kelə-[2]** in Appendix.] **—de·claim′er** *n.*

dec·la·ma·tion (dĕk′lə-mā′shən) *n.* **1.** A recitation delivered as an exercise in rhetoric or elocution. **2. a.** Vehement oratory. **b.** A speech marked by strong feeling; a tirade. [Middle English *declamacioun,* from Latin *dēclāmātiō, dēclāmātiōn-,* from *dēclāmātus,* past participle of *dēclāmāre,* to declaim. See DECLAIM.]

de·clam·a·to·ry (dĭ-klăm′ə-tôr′ē, -tōr′ē) *adj.* **1.** Having the quality of a declamation. **2.** Pretentiously rhetorical; bombastic.

de·clar·ant (dĭ-klâr′ənt) *n.* One that makes a declaration, especially a person who has signed a declaration of intent to become a U.S. citizen.

dec·la·ra·tion (dĕk′lə-rā′shən) *n. Abbr.* **dec. 1.** An explicit, formal announcement, either oral or written. **2.** The act or process of declaring. **3.** A statement of taxable goods or of properties subject to duty. **4.** *Law.* **a.** A formal statement by a plaintiff specifying the facts and circumstances constituting his or her cause of action. **b.** An unsworn statement of facts that is admissible as evidence. **5.** *Games.* A bid, especially the final bid of a hand in certain card games.

de·clar·a·tive (dĭ-klâr′ə-tĭv, -klăr′-) *adj.* Serving to declare or state. **—de·clar′a·tive·ly** *adv.*

de·clar·a·to·ry (dĭ-klâr′ə-tôr′ē, -tōr′ē) *adj.* **1.** Declarative. **2.** *Law.* **a.** Setting forth that which is the law. **b.** Explaining a legal interpretation or right.

de·clare (dĭ-klâr′) *v.* **-clared, -clar·ing, -clares.** *—tr.* **1.** To make known formally or officially. See Synonyms at **announce. 2.** To state emphatically or authoritatively; affirm. **3.** To reveal or make manifest; show. **4.** To make a full statement of (dutiable goods, for example). **5.** *Games.* To designate (a trump suit or no-trump) with the final bid of a hand in bridge. *—intr.* **1.** To make a declaration. **2.** To proclaim one's support, choice, opinion, or resolution. See Synonyms at **assert. —*idiom.* declare war. 1.** To state formally the intention to carry on armed hostilities against. **2.** To state one's intent to suppress or eradicate: *declared war on drug dealing in the neighborhood.* [Middle English *declaren,* from Old French *declarer,* from Latin *dēclārāre* : *dē-,* intensive pref.; see DE– + *clārāre,* to make clear (from *clārus,* clear; see **kelə-[2]** in Appendix).] **—de·clar′a·ble** *adj.* **—de·clar′er** *n.*

de·class (dē-klăs′) *tr.v.* **-classed, -class·ing, -class·es.** To lower in class or status.

dé·clas·sé (dā′klă-sā′) *adj.* **1.** Lowered in class, rank, or social position. **2.** Lacking high station or birth; of inferior social status. [French, past participle of *déclasser,* to lower in class :

dé-, down (from Latin *dē-;* see DE–) + *classe,* class; see CLASS.]

de·clas·si·fy (dē-klăs′ə-fī′) *tr.v.* **-fied, -fy·ing, -fies.** To remove official security classification from (a document). **—de·clas′si·fi′a·ble** *adj.* **—de·clas′si·fi·ca′tion** (-fĭ-kā′shən) *n.*

de·claw (dē-klô′) *tr.v.* **-clawed, -claw·ing, -claws. 1.** To remove the claws from: *declaw a cat.* **2.** To strip of power, potency, or strength; make harmless or less threatening.

de·clen·sion (dĭ-klĕn′shən) *n. Abbr.* **dec., decl. 1.** *Linguistics.* **a.** In certain languages, the inflection of nouns, pronouns, and adjectives in categories such as case, number, and gender. **b.** A class of words of one language with the same or a similar system of inflections, such as the first declension in Latin. **2.** A descending slope; a descent. **3.** A decline or decrease; deterioration: *"States and empires have their periods of declension"* (Laurence Sterne). **4.** A deviation, as from a standard or practice. [Middle English *declenson,* from Old French *declinaison,* from Latin *dēclīnātiō, dēclīnātiōn-,* grammatical declension, declination. See DECLINATION.] **—de·clen′sion·al** *adj.*

dec·li·na·tion (dĕk′lə-nā′shən) *n. Abbr.* **dec. 1.** A sloping or bending downward. **2.** A falling off, especially from prosperity or vigor; a decline. **3.** A deviation, as from a specific direction or standard. **4.** A refusal to accept. **5.** Magnetic declination. **6.** *Astronomy.* The angular distance to a point on a celestial object, measured north or south from the celestial equator. [Middle English *declinacioun,* from Old French *declination,* from Latin *dēclīnātiō, dēclīnātiōn-,* from *dēclīnātus,* past participle of *dēclīnāre,* to turn away. See DECLINE.] **—dec′li·na′tion·al** *adj.*

de·cline (dĭ-klīn′) *v.* **-clined, -clin·ing, -clines.** —*intr.* **1.** To express polite refusal. **2. a.** To slope downward; descend. **b.** To bend downward; droop. **3.** To degrade or lower oneself; condescend. **4.** To deteriorate gradually; fail. **5. a.** To sink, as the setting sun. **b.** To draw to a gradual close; wane. —*tr.* **1.** To refuse politely: *I declined their offer of help.* See Synonyms at **refuse**[1]. **2.** To cause to slope or bend downward. **3.** *Grammar.* To inflect (a noun, a pronoun, or an adjective) for number and case. **—decline** *n.* **1.** The process or result of declining, especially a gradual deterioration. **2.** A downward movement. **3.** The period when something approaches an end. **4.** A downward slope; a declivity. **5.** A disease that gradually weakens or wastes the body. [Middle English *declinen,* from Old French *decliner,* from Latin *dēclīnāre,* to turn away, bend downward, change the form of a word : *dē-,* de- + *-clīnāre,* to lean, bend; see **klei-** in Appendix.] **—de·clin′a·ble** *adj.* **—de·clin′er** *n.*

de·cliv·i·tous (dĭ-klĭv′ĭ-təs) *adj.* Rather steep.

de·cliv·i·ty (dĭ-klĭv′ĭ-tē) *n., pl.* **-ties.** A downward slope, as of a hill. [Latin *dēclīvitās,* from *dēclīvis,* sloping down : *dē-,* de- + *clīvus,* slope; see **klei-** in Appendix.]

dec·o (dĕk′ō) *n.* Art deco.

de·coct (dĭ-kŏkt′) *tr.v.* **-coct·ed, -coct·ing, -cocts. 1.** To extract the flavor of by boiling. **2.** To make concentrated; boil down. [Middle English *decocten,* to boil, from Latin *dēcoquere, dēcoct-,* to boil down or away : *dē-,* de- + *coquere,* to boil, to cook; see **pek**ʷ**-** in Appendix.] **—de·coc′tion** *n.*

de·code (dē-kōd′) *tr.v.* **-cod·ed, -cod·ing, -codes.** To convert from code into plain text. **—de·cod′er** *n.*

de·col·late[1] (dĭ-kŏl′āt′) *tr.v.* **-lat·ed, -lat·ing, -lates.** To behead. [Latin *dēcollāre, dēcollāt-* : *dē-,* de- + *collum,* neck; see **k**ʷ**el-**[1] in Appendix.] **—de′col·la′tion** *n.*

de·col·late[2] (dĕk′ə-lāt′, dē-kō′-) *tr.v.* **-lat·ed, -lat·ing, -lates.** To separate the copies of (a multiple-copy computer printout, for example). **—de′col·la′tor** *n.*

de·col·lec·tiv·ize (dē′kə-lĕk′tə-vīz′) *tr.v.* **-ized, -iz·ing, -iz·es.** To free from collective control. **—de′col·lec·ti·vi·za′tion** (-vĭ-zā′shən) *n.*

dé·colle·tage (dā′kôl-täzh′) *n.* **1.** A low neckline on a woman's garment, especially a dress. **2.** A dress with a low neckline in front. [French, from *décolleté,* having a low neckline. See DÉCOLLETÉ.]

dé·colle·té (dā′kôl-tā′) *adj.* **1.** Cut low at the neckline: *a décolleté dress.* **2.** Wearing a garment that is low-cut or strapless. [French, past participle of *décolleter,* to lower a neckline, uncover the neck : *dé-,* off (from Latin *dē-;* see DE–) + *collet,* collar (from Old French, diminutive of *col,* neck, collar, from Latin *collum,* neck; see **k**ʷ**el-**[1] in Appendix).]

de·col·o·nize (dē-kŏl′ə-nīz′) *tr.v.* **-nized, -niz·ing, -niz·es.** To free (a colony) from dependent status. **—de·col′o·ni·za′tion** (-nĭ-zā′shən) *n.*

de·col·or·ant (dē-kŭl′ər-ənt) *n.* A bleaching agent.

de·col·or·ize (dē-kŭl′ə-rīz′) *tr.v.* **-ized, -iz·ing, -iz·es.** To remove the color from. **—de·col′or·i·za′tion** (-kŭl′ər-ĭ-zā′shən) *n.* **—de·col′or·iz′er** *n.*

de·com·mis·sion (dē′kə-mĭsh′ən) *tr.v.* **-sioned, -sion·ing, -sions.** To withdraw (a ship, for example) from active service.

de·com·pen·sa·tion (dē′kŏm-pən-sā′shən) *n.* Failure of the heart to maintain adequate blood circulation, marked by labored breathing, engorged blood vessels, and edema. **—de·com′pen·sate′** *v.*

de·com·pose (dē′kəm-pōz′) *v.* **-posed, -pos·ing, -pos·es.** —*tr.* **1.** To separate into components or basic elements. **2.** To cause to rot. —*intr.* **1.** To become broken down into components; disintegrate. **2.** To decay; putrefy. See Synonyms at **decay.** **—de′com·pos′a·bil′i·ty** *n.* **—de′com·pos′a·ble** *adj.*

de·com·pos·er (dē′kəm-pō′zər) *n. Ecology.* An organism, often a bacterium or fungus, that feeds on and breaks down dead plant or animal matter, thus making organic nutrients available to the ecosystem.

de·com·po·si·tion (dē-kŏm′pə-zĭsh′ən) *n.* **1.** The act or result of decomposing; disintegration. **2. a.** *Chemistry.* Separation into constituents by chemical reaction. **b.** *Biology.* Breakdown or decay of organic materials. **—de·com′po·si′tion·al** *adj.*

de·com·pound[1] (dē-kŏm′pound′, dē′kəm-pound′) *adj.* **1.** Compounded or consisting of things or parts that are already compound. **2.** *Botany.* Having or consisting of divisions that are themselves once or several times compound; bipinnate: *a decompound leaf.*

de·com·pound[2] (dē′kəm-pound′) *tr.v.* **-pound·ed, -pound·ing, -pounds.** To decompose.

de·com·press (dē′kəm-prĕs′) *v.* **-pressed, -press·ing, -press·es.** —*tr.* **1.** To relieve of pressure or compression. **2.** To bring (a person exposed to conditions of increased pressure) gradually back to normal atmospheric pressure. —*intr.* **1.** To adjust to normal atmospheric conditions after being exposed to increased pressure. **2.** *Informal.* To relax: *decompressed after 12 hours of driving.*

de·com·pres·sion (dē′kəm-prĕsh′ən) *n.* **1.** The act or process of decompressing. **2.** A surgical procedure used to relieve pressure on an organ or part, such as the abdomen, cranium, or spinal cord.

decompression chamber *n.* A compartment in which atmospheric pressure can be gradually raised or lowered, used especially in readjusting divers or underwater workers to normal atmospheric pressure or in treating decompression sickness.

decompression sickness *n.* A disorder, seen especially in deep-sea divers or in caisson and tunnel workers, caused by the formation of nitrogen bubbles in the blood following a rapid drop in pressure and characterized by severe pains in the joints and chest, skin irritation, cramps, and paralysis. Also called *caisson disease.*

de·con·cen·trate (dē-kŏn′sən-trāt′) *tr.v.* **-trat·ed, -trat·ing, -trates.** To decentralize. **—de′con·cen·tra′tion** *n.*

de·con·di·tion (dē′kən-dĭsh′ən) *v.* **-tioned, -tion·ing, -tions.** —*tr.* **1.** *Psychology.* To cause (a conditioned response, such as a phobia) to become extinct. **2.** To cause to decline from a condition of physical fitness, as through a prolonged period of inactivity or, in astronauts, through weightlessness in space. —*intr.* To lose physical fitness.

de·con·gest (dē′kən-jĕst′) *tr.v.* **-gest·ed, -gest·ing, -gests.** To relieve the congestion of (sinuses, for example). **—de′con·ges′tion** (-jĕs′chən) *n.* **—de′con·ges′tive** *adj.*

de·con·ges·tant (dē′kən-jĕs′tənt) *n.* A medication or treatment that breaks up congestion, as of the sinuses, by reducing swelling. **—decongestant** *adj.* Capable of relieving congestion.

de·con·se·crate (dē-kŏn′sĭ-krāt′) *tr.v.* **-crat·ed, -crat·ing, -crates.** To make (a church, synagogue, or temple, for example) no longer consecrated.

de·con·struct (dē′kən-strŭkt′) *tr.v.* **-struct·ed, -struct·ing, -structs.** To write about or analyze (a literary text, for example), following the tenets of deconstruction.

de·con·struc·tion (dē′kən-strŭk′shən) *n.* A philosophical movement and theory of literary criticism that questions traditional assumptions about certainty, identity, and truth, asserts that words can only refer to other words, and attempts to demonstrate how statements about any text subvert their own meanings: *"In deconstruction, the critic claims there is no meaning to be found in the actual text, but only in the various, often mutually irreconcilable, 'virtual texts' constructed by readers in their search for meaning"* (Rebecca Goldstein). **—de′con·struc′tion·ism** *n.* **—de′con·struc′tion·ist** *n. & adj.*

de·con·tam·i·nate (dē′kən-tăm′ə-nāt′) *tr.v.* **-nat·ed, -nat·ing, -nates. 1.** To eliminate contamination in. **2.** To make safe by eliminating poisonous or otherwise harmful substances, such as noxious chemicals or radioactive material. **—de′con·tam′i·nant** (-nənt) *n.* **—de′con·tam′i·na′tion** *n.* **—de′con·tam′i·na′tor** *n.*

de·con·trol (dē′kən-trōl′) *tr.v.* **-trolled, -trol·ling, -trols.** To stop control of, especially by the government: *decontrolled oil and natural-gas prices.* **—de′con·trol′** *n.*

dé·cor or **de·cor** (dā′kôr′, dā-kôr′) *n.* **1. a.** Decoration. **b.** A decorative style or scheme, as of a room. **2.** A stage setting; scenery. [French, from *décorer,* to decorate, from Latin *decorāre,* to beautify. See DECORATE.]

dec·o·rate (dĕk′ə-rāt′) *tr.v.* **-rat·ed, -rat·ing, -rates. 1.** To furnish, provide, or adorn with something ornamental; embellish. **2.** To confer a medal or other honor on: *was decorated for bravery.* [From Middle English *decorat,* made beautiful, from Latin *decorātus,* past participle of *decorāre,* to beautify, from *decus, decor-,* honor, ornament. See **dek-** in Appendix.]

dec·o·ra·tion (dĕk′ə-rā′shən) *n.* **1.** The act, process, technique, or art of decorating. **2.** Something used to decorate. **3.** An emblem of honor, such as a medal or badge.

Dec·o·ra·tion Day (dĕk′ə-rā′shən) *n.* See **Memorial Day.**

dec·o·ra·tive (dĕk′ər-ə-tĭv, -ə-rā′-) *adj. Abbr.* **dec.** Serving to decorate or embellish; ornamental. **—dec′o·ra·tive·ly** *adv.* **—dec′o·ra·tive·ness** *n.*

dec·o·ra·tor (dĕk′ə-rā′tər) *n.* One that decorates, especially

ă pat	oi boy
ā pay	ou out
âr care	ŏŏ took
ä father	ōō boot
ĕ pet	ŭ cut
ē be	ûr urge
ĭ pit	th thin
ī pie	*th* this
îr pier	hw which
ŏ pot	zh vision
ō toe	ə about, item
ô paw	♦ regionalism

Stress marks: ′ (primary); ′ (secondary), as in **dictionary** (dĭk′shə-nĕr′ē)

an interior decorator. **—decorator** *adj.* Appropriate for interior decoration: *decorator colors.*

dec·o·rous (dĕk′ər-əs, dĭ-kôr′əs, -kōr′-) *adj.* Characterized by or exhibiting decorum; proper: *decorous behavior.* [From Latin *decōrus,* becoming, handsome, from *decor,* seemliness, beauty. See **dek-** in Appendix.] **—dec′o·rous·ly** *adv.* **—dec′o·rous·ness** *n.*

de·cor·ti·cate (dē-kôr′tĭ-kāt′) *tr.v.* **-cat·ed, -cat·ing, -cates. 1.** To remove the bark, husk, or outer layer from; peel. **2.** To remove the surface layer, membrane, or fibrous cover of (an organ or a structure). [Latin *dēcorticāre, dēcorticāt-* : *dē-,* de- + *cortex, cortic-,* bark, rind; see **sker-**[1] in Appendix.] **—de·cor′ti·ca′tion** *n.* **—de·cor′ti·ca′tor** *n.*

de·co·rum (dĭ-kôr′əm, -kōr′-) *n.* **1.** Appropriateness of behavior or conduct; propriety. **2.** The conventions of polite behavior. See Synonyms at **etiquette. 3.** The appropriateness of an element of an artistic or literary work, such as style or tone, to its particular circumstance or to the composition as a whole. [Latin *decōrum,* from *decōrus,* becoming, handsome. See DECOROUS.]

de·cou·page also **dé·cou·page** (dā′ko͞o-päzh′) *n.* **1.** The technique of decorating a surface with cutouts, as of paper. **2.** A creation produced by this technique. [French *découpage,* from *découper,* to cut up or out, from Old French *descolper* : *des-,* de- + *colper,* to cut (from *colp,* stroke; see COUP).]

de·cou·ple (dē-kŭp′əl) *tr.v.* **-pled, -pling, -ples. 1.** *Electronics.* To reduce or eliminate the coupling of (one circuit or part to another). **2.** *Physics.* To decrease or eliminate airborne shock waves from (an explosion) by having it take place underground. **3.** To separate or detach: *"There's not the slightest possibility that America would be decoupled from Europe by the pursuit of this vital initiative"* (Caspar W. Weinberger). **—de·cou′pler** *n.*

de·coy (dē′koi′, dĭ-koi′) *n.* **1.a.** A living or artificial bird or other animal used to entice game into a trap or within shooting range. **b.** An enclosed place, such as a pond, into which wildfowl are lured for capture. **2.** A means used to mislead or lead into danger. **—decoy** (dĭ-koi′) *tr.v.* **-coyed, -coy·ing, -coys.** To lure or entrap by or as if by a decoy. See Synonyms at **lure.** [Possibly from Dutch *de kooi,* the cage : *de,* the (from Middle Dutch; see **to-** in Appendix) + *kooi,* cage (from Middle Dutch *côie,* from Latin *cavea*).] **—de·coy′er** *n.*

de·crease (dĭ-krēs′) *intr. & tr.v.* **-creased, -creas·ing, -creas·es.** To grow or cause to grow gradually less or smaller, as in number, amount, or intensity. **—decrease** (dē′krēs′) *n. Abbr.* **dec. 1.** The act or process of decreasing. **2.** The amount by which something decreases. [Middle English *decresen,* from Old French *decreistre, decreiss-,* from Latin *dēcrēscere* : *dē-,* de- + *crēscere,* to grow; see **ker-**[2] in Appendix.] **—de·creas′ing·ly** *adv.*

SYNONYMS: *decrease, lessen, reduce, dwindle, abate, diminish, subside.* These verbs mean to become or cause to become smaller or less. *Decrease* and *lessen,* interchangeable in most contexts, refer to steady or gradual diminution: *Traffic decreases on holidays. Lack of success decreases confidence. Use your seat belt to lessen the danger of injury in an accident. His appetite lessens as his illness progresses. Reduce* emphasizes bringing down, as in size, degree, or intensity: *The workers reduced their wage demands. Dwindle* suggests decreasing bit by bit to a vanishing point: *Their savings dwindled away. Abate* stresses a decrease in amount or intensity and suggests a reduction of excess: *Toward evening the fire began to abate. Nothing can abate the force of that argument. Diminish* implies taking away or removal: *An occasional outburst didn't diminish my respect for her. The warden's authority diminished after the revolt. Subside* implies a falling away to a more normal level: *The wild enthusiasm the team's victory aroused did not subside.*

decoy

de·cree (dĭ-krē′) *n.* **1.** An authoritative order having the force of law. **2.** *Law.* The judgment of a court of equity, admiralty, probate, or divorce. **3.** *Roman Catholic Church.* **a.** A doctrinal or disciplinary act of an ecumenical council. **b.** An administrative act applying or interpreting articles of canon law. **—decree** *v.* **-creed, -cree·ing, -crees.** *—tr.* To ordain, establish, or decide by decree. See Synonyms at **dictate.** *—intr.* To issue a decree. [Middle English *decre,* from Old French *decret,* from Latin *dēcrētum,* principle, decision, from neuter past participle of *dēcernere,* to decide : *dē-,* de- + *cernere,* to sift; see **krei-** in Appendix.] **—de·cree′a·ble** *adj.* **—de·cre′er** *n.*

dec·re·ment (dĕk′rə-mənt) *n.* **1.** The act or process of decreasing or becoming gradually less. **2.** The amount lost by gradual diminution or waste. **3.** *Mathematics.* The amount by which a variable is decreased; a negative increment. [Latin *dēcrēmentum,* from *dēcrēscere,* to decrease. See DECREASE.] **—dec′re·men′tal** (-mĕn′tl) *adj.*

de·cre·o·li·za·tion (dē-krē′ə-lĭ-zā′shən) *n.* The loss of creole features in an original creole language as the result of contact with a major international language that was one of its ancestors.

de·crep·it (dĭ-krĕp′ĭt) *adj.* Weakened, worn out, impaired, or broken down by old age, illness, or hard use. See Synonyms at **weak.** [Middle English, from Old French, from Latin *dēcrepitus,* worn out, feeble : *dē-,* de- + *crepitus,* past participle of *crepāre,* to burst, crack.] **—de·crep′it·ly** *adv.*

de·crep·i·tate (dĭ-krĕp′ĭ-tāt′) *v.* **-tat·ed, -tat·ing, -tates.** *—tr.* To roast or calcine (crystals or salts) until they emit a crackling sound or until crackling stops. *—intr.* To make a crackling sound when roasted. [New Latin *dēcrepitāre, dēcrepitāt-* : Latin *dē-,* de- + Latin *crepitāre,* to crackle, frequentative of *crepāre,* to burst, crack.] **—de·crep′i·ta′tion** *n.*

de·crep·i·tude (dĭ-krĕp′ĭ-to͞od′, -tyo͞od′) *n.* The quality or condition of being weakened, worn out, impaired, or broken down by old age, illness, or hard use.

de·cre·scen·do (dā′krə-shĕn′dō, dē′-) *Music. adv. & adj. Abbr.* **dec.** With gradually diminishing force or loudness. Used chiefly as a direction. **—decrescendo** *n., pl.* **-dos.** *Abbr.* **dec. 1.** A gradual decrease in force or loudness. **2.** A decrescendo passage. [Italian, gerund of *decrescere,* to decrease, from Latin *dēcrēscere.* See DECREASE.]

de·cres·cent (dĭ-krĕs′ənt) *adj.* Becoming gradually less; waning. [Latin *dēcrēscēns, dēcrēscent-,* present participle of *dēcrēscere,* to decrease. See DECREASE.]

de·cre·tal (dĭ-krēt′l) *n. Roman Catholic Church.* A decree, especially a papal letter giving a decision on a point or question of canon law. [Middle English, from Old French *decretale,* from Late Latin *dēcrētālis,* fixed by decree, from Latin *dēcrētum,* principle, decision. See DECREE.]

de·cre·tive (dĭ-krē′tĭv) *adj.* Decretory.

dec·re·to·ry (dĕk′rĭ-tôr′ē, -tōr′ē, dĭ-krē′tə-rē) *adj.* Of, relating to, or having the force of a decree.

de·crim·i·nal·ize (dē-krĭm′ə-nə-līz′) *tr.v.* **-ized, -iz·ing, -iz·es.** To reduce or abolish criminal penalties for: *decriminalize the use of marijuana.* **—de·crim′i·nal·i·za′tion** (-nə-lĭ-zā′shən) *n.*

de·cry (dĭ-krī′) *tr.v.* **-cried, -cry·ing, -cries. 1.** To condemn openly. **2.** To depreciate (currency, for example) by official proclamation or by rumor. [French *décrier,* from Old French *descrier* : *des-,* de- + *crier,* to cry; see CRY.] **—de·cri′er** *n.*

SYNONYMS: *decry, disparage, depreciate, derogate, belittle, minimize, downgrade.* These verbs mean to think, write, or speak of as being of little value or importance. *Decry* implies open denunciation or condemnation: *A staunch materialist, he decries economy. Disparage* often implies the communication of a low opinion by indirection: *Some critics disparage psychoanalysis as being a pseudoscience.* To *depreciate* is to assign a lower than customary value to someone or something: *Some musicologists depreciate Liszt's compositions. Derogate* implies a detraction that impairs: *People often derogate what they don't understand. Belittle* and *minimize* mean to make less important, but *minimize* strongly implies the minimum level: *belittled the child's attempts to draw; trying to minimize the accomplishment.* To *downgrade* is to minimize in importance or estimation: *Her rival downgraded the painting, calling it decorative but superficial.*

de·crypt (dē-krĭpt′) *tr.v.* **-crypt·ed, -crypt·ing, -crypts. 1.** To decipher. **2.** To decode. **—decrypt** (dē′krĭpt′) *n.* A deciphered or decoded message. [DE– + *-crypt* (from CRYPTOGRAM).] **—de·cryp′tion** *n.*

de·cu·bi·tus ulcer (dĭ-kyo͞o′bĭ-təs) *n.* See **bedsore.** [Medieval Latin *dēcubitus,* lying down, being bedridden, from past participle of Latin *dēcumbere,* to lie down. See DECUMBENT.]

de·cum·bent (dĭ-kŭm′bənt) *adj.* **1.** Lying down; reclining. **2.** *Botany.* Lying or growing on the ground but with erect or rising tips: *decumbent stems.* [Latin *dēcumbēns, dēcumbent-,* present participle of *dēcumbere,* to lie down : *dē-,* de- + *-cumbere,* to lie down.] **—de·cum′bence** (-bəns), **de·cum′ben·cy** (-bən-sē) *n.*

dec·u·ple (dĕk′yə-pəl) *adj.* **1.** Ten times as great; tenfold. **2.** In groups of ten. [Middle English, from Old French, from Late Latin *decuplus* : Latin *decem,* ten; see **dekm̥** in Appendix + Latin *-plus,* -fold; see **pel-**[2] in Appendix.]

de·cur·rent (dĭ-kûr′ənt, -kŭr′-) *adj. Botany.* Having the leaf base extending down the stem below the insertion: *decurrent leaves.* [Middle English, from Latin *dēcurrēns, dēcurrent-,* present participle of *dēcurrere,* to run down : *dē-,* de- + *currere,* to run; see **kers-** in Appendix.] **—de·cur′rent·ly** *adv.*

de·cus·sate (dĭ-kŭs′āt′, dĕk′ə-sāt′) *tr. & intr.v.* **-sat·ed, -sat·ing, -sates.** To cross or become crossed so as to form an X; intersect. **—decussate** *adj.* **1.** Intersected or crossed in the form of an X. **2.** *Botany.* Arranged on a stem in opposite pairs at right angles to those above or below, resulting in four vertical rows: *decussate leaves.* [Latin *decussāre, decussāt-,* from *decussis,* the number ten, intersection of two lines (from the Romans' use of X for the numeral 10), a ten-as coin : *decem,* ten; see **dekm̥** in Appendix + *assis,* as (coin).] **—de·cus′sate′ly** *adv.*

dec·us·sa·tion (dĕk′ə-sā′shən, dē′kə-) *n.* **1.** A crossing in the shape of an X. **2.** *Anatomy.* An X-shaped crossing, especially of nerves or bands of nerve fibers, connecting corresponding parts on opposite sides of the brain or spinal cord.

D.Ed. *abbr.* Doctor of Education.

de·dans (də-däN′) *n., pl.* **dedans** (-däN′, -dänz′). *Sports.* **1.** A screened gallery for spectators at the service end of a court-tennis court. **2.** The spectators at a court-tennis match. [French, from *dedans,* inside, from Old French *dedenz* : *de,* of, from (from Latin *dē;* see DE–) + *denz,* within (from Late Latin *deintus,* from within : Latin *dē* + Latin *intus,* within; see **en** in Appendix).]

Ded·ham (dĕd′əm). A town of eastern Massachusetts, a mainly residential suburb of Boston on the Charles River. Population, 25,298.

ded·i·cate (dĕd′ĭ-kāt′) *tr.v.* **-cat·ed, -cat·ing, -cates. 1.** To set apart for a deity or for religious purposes; consecrate. **2.** To set apart for a special use: *dedicated their money to scientific research.* **3.** To commit (oneself) to a particular course of thought or action: *dedicated ourselves to starting our own business.* See Synonyms at **devote. 4.** To address or inscribe (a literary work, for example) to another as a mark of respect or affection. **5.a.** To open (a building, for example) to public use. **b.** To show to the public for the first time: *dedicate a monument.* [Middle English *dedicaten,* from Latin *dēdicāre, dēdicāt-* : *dē-,* de- + *dicāre,* to proclaim; see **deik-** in Appendix.] **—ded′i·ca′tor** *n.*

ded·i·cat·ed (dĕd′ĭ-kā′tĭd) *adj.* **1.** Wholly committed to a particular course of thought or action; devoted: *a dedicated musician.* **2.** Designed for a particular use or function: *"The satellite beams the information down to Earth, where it is sent through dedicated telephone wires to the Space Telescope Science Institute"* (Boston Globe). **—ded′i·cat′ed·ly** (-kā′tĭd-lē) *adv.*

ded·i·ca·tee (dĕd′ĭ-kā-tē′) *n.* One to whom something, such as a literary work, is dedicated.

ded·i·ca·tion (dĕd′ĭ-kā′shən) *n.* **1.** The act of dedicating or the state of being dedicated. **2.** A note prefixed to a literary, artistic, or musical composition dedicating it to someone in token of affection or esteem. **3.** A rite or ceremony of dedicating. **4.** Selfless devotion: *served the public with dedication and integrity.* **—ded′i·ca′tive, ded′i·ca·to′ry** (-kə-tôr′ē, -tōr′ē) *adj.*

de·dif·fer·en·ti·a·tion (dē′dĭf-ə-rĕn′shē-ā′shən) *n. Biology.* Regression of a specialized cell or tissue to a simpler, more embryonic, unspecialized form. Dedifferentiation may occur before the regeneration of appendages in plants and certain animals and in the development of some cancers. **—de′dif·fer·en′ti·ate′** *v.*

de·duce (dĭ-do͞os′, -dyo͞os′) *tr.v.* **-duced, -duc·ing, -duc·es. 1.** To reach (a conclusion) by reasoning. **2.** To infer from a general principle; reason deductively. **3.** To trace the origin or derivation of. [Middle English *deducen,* from Latin *dēdūcere,* to lead away or down : *dē-,* de- + *dūcere,* to lead; see **deuk-** in Appendix.] **—de·duc′i·ble** *adj.*

de·duct (dĭ-dŭkt′) *v.* **-duct·ed, -duct·ing, -ducts.** *—tr.* **1.** To take away (a quantity) from another; subtract. **2.** To derive by deduction; deduce. *—intr.* To take away a desirable part: *Poor plumbing deducts from the value of the house.* [Middle English *deducten,* from Latin *dēdūcere, dēduct-,* to lead away or down. See DEDUCE.]

de·duct·i·ble (dĭ-dŭk′tə-bəl) *adj.* That can be deducted, especially with respect to income taxes: *deductible expenses.* **—deductible** *n.* **1.** Something, such as an expense, that can be deducted, as for income-tax purposes. **2.** A clause in an insurance policy that exempts the insurer from paying an initial specified amount in the event that the insured sustains a loss. **—de·duct′i·bil′i·ty** *n.*

de·duc·tion (dĭ-dŭk′shən) *n.* **1.** The act of deducting; subtraction. **2.** An amount that is or may be deducted: *tax deductions.* **3.** The drawing of a conclusion by reasoning; the act of deducing. **4.** *Logic.* **a.** The process of reasoning in which a conclusion follows necessarily from the stated premises; inference by reasoning from the general to the specific. **b.** A conclusion reached by this process.

de·duc·tive (dĭ-dŭk′tĭv) *adj.* **1.** Of or based on deduction. **2.** Involving or using deduction in reasoning. **—de·duc′tive·ly** *adv.*

dee (dē) *n.* The letter *d.*

Dee (dē). **1.** A river rising in the Cairngorm Mountains of eastern Scotland and flowing about 145 km (90 mi) eastward to the North Sea through an artificial channel at Aberdeen. It is known for its scenic beauty and salmon fisheries. **2.** A river of northern Wales and western England flowing about 113 km (70 mi) partially along the Welsh-English border to the Irish Sea.

deed (dēd) *n.* **1.** Something that is carried out; an act or action. **2.** A usually praiseworthy act; a feat or exploit. **3.** Action or performance in general: *Deeds, not words, matter most.* **4.** *Law.* A document sealed as an instrument of bond, contract, or conveyance, especially relating to property. **—deed** *tr.v.* **deed·ed, deed·ing, deeds.** To transfer by means of a deed: *deeded the property to the children.* [Middle English *dede,* from Old English *dǣd.* See **dhē-** in Appendix.]

dee·jay (dē′jā′) *n. Informal.* A disc jockey. [From the abbr. *D.J.*]

deem (dēm) *v.* **deemed, deem·ing, deems.** *—tr.* **1.** To have as an opinion; judge: *deemed it was time for a change.* **2.** To regard as; consider: *deemed the results unsatisfactory.* See Usage Note at **as**[1]. *—intr.* To have an opinion; think. See Synonyms at **consider.** [Middle English *demen,* from Old English *dēman.* See **dhē-** in Appendix.]

de-em·pha·size (dē-ĕm′fə-sīz′) *tr.v.* **-sized, -siz·ing, -siz·es.** To decrease the emphasis on; minimize the importance of. **—de-em′pha·sis** (-sĭs) *n.*

deep (dēp) *adj.* **deep·er, deep·est. 1.a.** Extending far downward below a surface: *a deep hole in the river ice.* **b.** Extending far inward from an outer surface: *a deep cut.* **c.** Extending far backward from front to rear: *a deep walk-in refrigerator.* **d.** Extending far from side to side from a center: *a deep yard surrounding the house.* **e.** Far distant down or in: *deep in the woods.* **f.** Coming from or penetrating to a depth: *a deep sigh.* **g.** *Sports.* Located or taking place near the outer boundaries of the area of play: *deep left field.* **2.** Extending a specific distance in a given direction: *snow four feet deep.* **3.** Far distant in time or space: *deep in the past.* **4.a.** Difficult to penetrate or understand; recondite: *a deep metaphysical theory.* **b.** Of a mysterious or obscure nature: *a deep secret; ancient and deep tribal rites.* **c.** Very learned or intellectual; wise: *a deep philosopher.* **d.** Exhibiting great cunning or craft: *deep political machinations.* **5.a.** Of a grave or extreme nature: *deep trouble; deepest deceit.* **b.** Very absorbed or involved: *deep in thought; deep in financial difficulties.* **c.** Profound in quality or feeling: *a deep trance; deep devotion.* **6.** Rich and intense in shade. Used of a color: *a deep red.* **7.** Low in pitch; resonant: *a deep voice.* **8.** Covered or surrounded to a designated degree. Often used in combination: *waist-deep in the water; ankle-deep in snow.* **9.** Large in quantity or size; big: *deep cuts in the budget.* **—deep** *adv.* **1.** To a great depth; deeply: *dig deep; feelings that run deep.* **2.** Well along in time; late: *worked deep into the night.* **3.** *Sports.* Close to the outer boundaries of the area of play: *played deep for the first three innings; ran deep into their opponents' territory.* **—deep** *n.* **1.a.** A deep place in land or in a body of water: *drowned in the deep of the river.* **b.** A vast, immeasurable extent: *the deep of outer space.* **2.** The extent of encompassing time or space; firmament. **3.** The most intense or extreme part: *the deep of night.* **4.** The ocean. **5.** *Nautical.* A distance estimated in fathoms between successive marks on a sounding line. ***—idioms.*** **deep down.** At bottom; basically: *Deep down, she was still a rebel.* **in deep water.** In difficulty. [Middle English *dep,* from Old English *dēop.* See **dheub-** in Appendix.] **—deep′ly** *adv.* **—deep′ness** *n.*

SYNONYMS: *deep, abysmal, profound.* The central meaning shared by these adjectives is "extending far downward or inward from a surface": *a deep lake; falling from a cliff through abysmal space; a profound glacial chasm.*
ANTONYM: *shallow.*

deep-dish (dēp′dĭsh′) *adj.* Made or used in a deep baking dish: *a deep-dish apple pie; deep-dish recipes.*

deep·en (dē′pən) *tr. & intr.v.* **-ened, -en·ing, -ens.** To make or become deep or deeper.

deep fat *n.* Hot fat or oil for deep-frying food.

deep freeze *n.* A condition of being held in temporary suspension or inactivity.

deep-freeze (dēp′frēz′) *tr.v.* **-froze** (-frōz′), **-fro·zen** (-frō′zən), **-freez·ing, -freez·es. 1.** To quick-freeze. **2.** To store in a frozen condition. **3.** To suspend or defer indefinitely: *"American long-term obligations . . . which have been deep-frozen since the early 1950s"* (Paul Kennedy).

Deep·freeze (dēp′frēz′). A trademark used for a refrigerator designed to freeze food for long periods.

deep freezer *n.* A freezer for the quick-freezing and long-term storage of food.

deep-froze (dēp′frōz′) *v.* Past tense of **deep-freeze.**

deep-fro·zen (dēp′frō′zən) *v.* Past participle of **deep-freeze.**

deep-fry (dēp′frī′) *tr.v.* **-fried, -fry·ing, -fries.** To fry by immersing in a deep utensil of fat or oil: *deep-fry doughnuts; deep-fried the chicken wings.*

deep fryer *n.* A utensil for deep-frying food.

deep pocket *n.* A source of substantial wealth or financial support. Often used in the plural: *"Japanese investors . . . have all but pulled out of the market—and there's no deep pocket outside Japan to take their place"* (Larry Martz).

Deep River (dēp). A river rising in north-central North Carolina and flowing about 201 km (125 mi) southeast and east to join the Haw River and form the Cape Fear River.

deep-root·ed (dēp′ro͞o′tĭd, -ro͝ot′ĭd) *adj.* Firmly implanted; well-established: *deep-rooted prejudices.*

deep-sea (dēp′sē′) *adj.* Of, relating to, or taking place in the deeper parts of the sea: *deep-sea exploration.*

deep-seat·ed (dēp′sē′tĭd) *adj.* **1.** Being so far below the surface as to be unsusceptible to superficial examination, study, or treatment: *a deep-seated infection.* **2.** Deeply rooted; ingrained: *deep-seated ideological differences.*

deep-set (dēp′sĕt′) *adj.* **1.** Deeply set or placed: *deep-set eyes.* **2.** Deep-seated: *deep-set hatred.*

deep six *n. Slang.* **1.** Burial at sea. **2.** Disposal or rejection of something: *gave all our plans the deep six.* [American slang, a grave, referring to the conventional depth of a grave (six feet).]

deep-six (dēp′sĭks′) *tr.v.* **-sixed, -six·ing, -six·es.** *Slang.* **1.** To toss overboard. **2.** To toss out; get rid of: *deep-sixed the incriminating papers.*

Deep South. A region of the southeast United States, usually comprising the states of Alabama, Georgia, Louisiana, Mississippi, and South Carolina.

deep space *n.* The regions beyond the gravitational influence of Earth encompassing interplanetary, interstellar, and intergalactic space.

deep structure *n. Linguistics.* An abstract underlying structure that determines the actual form of a sentence.

deep-wa·ter (dēp′wô′tər, -wŏt′ər) *adj.* Of, relating to, or carried on in waters of a relatively great depth: *a deep-water port; deep-water drilling for oil.*

deer (dîr) *n., pl.* **deer.** Any of various hoofed ruminant mam-

deer
Mule deer buck
Odocoileus hemionus

ă **pat**	oi **boy**
ā **pay**	ou **out**
âr **care**	o͝o **took**
ä **father**	o͞o **boot**
ĕ **pet**	ŭ **cut**
ē **be**	ûr **urge**
ĭ **pit**	th **thin**
ī **pie**	*th* **this**
îr **pier**	hw **which**
ŏ **pot**	zh **vision**
ō **toe**	ə **about, item**
ô **paw**	♦ **regionalism**

Stress marks: ′ (primary); ′ (secondary), as in **dictionary** (dĭk′shə-nĕr′ē)

mals of the family Cervidae, characteristically having deciduous antlers borne chiefly by the males. The deer family also includes the elk, moose, caribou, and reindeer. [Middle English *der,* beast, from Old English *dēor.*]

WORD HISTORY: In various Middle English texts one finds a fish, an ant, or a fox called a *der,* the Middle English ancestor of our word *deer.* In its Old English form *dēor,* our word referred to any animal, including members of the deer family, and continued to do so in Middle English, although it took on the specific sense "a deer." By the end of the Middle English period, around 1500, the general sense had all but disappeared. *Deer* is a commonly cited example of a semantic process called specialization, by which the range of meaning of a word is narrowed or restricted. When Shakespeare uses the expression "mice and rats, and such small deer" for Edgar's diet in *King Lear,* probably written in 1605, we are not sure whether *deer* has the general or the specific sense.

Deere (dîr), **John.** 1804–1886. American industrialist who pioneered the manufacture of plows especially suited to working prairie soil.

Deer·field (dîr′fēld′). A village of northeast Illinois, a residential suburb of Chicago. Population, 17,430.

Deerfield Beach. A city of southeast Florida on the Atlantic Ocean north of Fort Lauderdale. It is in a truck-farming area. Population, 39,193.

deer fly

deer fly or **deer·fly** (dîr′flī′) *n.* Any of various stout-bodied, blood-sucking flies of the genus *Chrysops,* closely related to the horseflies but smaller and having spotted or banded wings.

deer grass *n.* See **meadow beauty.**

deer·hound (dîr′hound′) *n.* A dog of an old breed developed in Scotland, related to and resembling the greyhound but taller and larger and having a wiry coat. It was originally bred for hunting deer. Also called *Scottish deerhound.*

deer mouse *n.* A North American mouse *(Peromyscus maniculatus)* having white feet and underparts, and a long, bicolored tail.

Deer Park (dîr). A city of southeast Texas east of Houston. It is an industrial center in a truck-farming area. Population, 22,648.

deer·skin (dîr′skĭn′) *n.* **1.** Leather made from the hide of a deer. **2.** A garment made from deerskin.

deer·stalk·er (dîr′stô′kər) *n.* A tight-fitting hat with visors in the front and back, originally worn by hunters.

deer·yard (dîr′yärd′) *n.* A place where deer gather for wintering.

de-es·ca·late or **de·es·ca·late** (dē-ĕs′kə-lāt′) *—v.* **-lat·ed, -lat·ing, -lates.** *—tr.* To decrease the size, scope, or intensity of (a war, for example). *—intr.* To decrease or diminish in size, scope, or intensity: *The birth rate has begun to de-escalate.* **—de-es′ca·la′tion** *n.* **—de-es′ca·la·tor′y** (-lə-tôr′ē, -tōr′ē) *adj.*

deet (dēt) *n.* A colorless, oily liquid, $C_{12}H_{17}NO$, that has a mild odor and is used as an insect repellent. [From *d.t.,* abbr. of DIETHYL TOLUAMIDE.]

def. *abbr.* **1.** Defective. **2.** Defendant. **3.** Defense. **4.** Deferred. **5.** *Grammar.* Definite. **6.** Definition.

de·face (dĭ-fās′) *tr.v.* **-faced, -fac·ing, -fac·es. 1.** To mar or spoil the appearance or surface of; disfigure. **2.** To impair the usefulness, value, or influence of. **3.** *Obsolete.* To obliterate; destroy. [Middle English *defacen,* from Old French *desfacier* : *des-,* de- + *face,* face; see FACE.] **—de·face′a·ble** *adj.* **—de·face′ment** *n.* **—de·fac′er** *n.*

de fac·to (dĭ făk′tō, dā) *adv.* In reality or fact; actually. **—de facto** *adj.* **1.** Actual: *de facto segregation.* **2.** Actually exercising power though not legally or officially established: *a de facto government.* [Latin : *dē,* from, according to + *factō,* ablative of *factum,* fact.]

de·fal·cate (dĭ-făl′kāt′, -fôl′-, dĕf′əl-) *intr.v.* **-cat·ed, -cat·ing, -cates.** To misuse funds; embezzle. [Medieval Latin *dēfalcāre, dēfalcāt-,* to mow, deduct : Latin *dē-,* de- + Latin *falx, falc-,* sickle.] **—de′fal·ca′tion** (dē′făl-kā′shən, -fôl-, dĕf′əl-) *n.* **—de·fal′ca′tor** *n.*

def·a·ma·tion (dĕf′ə-mā′shən) *n.* The act of defaming; calumny. **—de·fam′a·to′ry** (dĭ-făm′ə-tôr′ē, -tōr′ē) *adj.*

de·fame (dĭ-fām′) *tr.v.* **-famed, -fam·ing, -fames. 1.** To damage the reputation, character, or good name of by slander or libel. See Synonyms at **malign. 2.** *Archaic.* To disgrace. [Middle English *defamen,* from Old French *defamer,* from Medieval Latin *dēfāmāre,* alteration of Latin *diffāmāre,* to spread news of, slander : *dis-,* abroad, apart; see DIS– + *fāma,* rumor, reputation; see **bhā-**[2] in Appendix.] **—de·fam′er** *n.*

de·fang (dē-făng′) *tr.v.* **-fanged, -fang·ing, -fangs. 1.** To remove the fangs of (a snake, for example). **2.** To undermine the strength or power of; make ineffectual: *an attempt to defang the opposition.*

de·fat (dē-făt′) *tr.v.* **-fat·ted, -fat·ting, -fats.** To remove fat from: *had to defat the chicken stock.*

de·fault (dĭ-fôlt′) *n.* **1.** Failure to perform a task or fulfill an obligation, especially failure to meet a financial obligation: *in default on a loan.* **2.** *Law.* Failure to make a required court appearance. **3.** The failure of one or more competitors or teams to participate in a contest: *won the championship by default.* **4.** *Computer Science.* A particular value for a variable that is assigned automatically by an operating system and remains in effect unless canceled or overridden by the operator. **—default** *v.* **-fault·ed, -fault·ing, -faults.** *—intr.* **1.a.** To fail to do what is required. **b.** To fail to pay money when it is due. **2.** *Law.* **a.** To fail to appear in court when summoned. **b.** To lose a case by not appearing. **3.** To fail to take part in or complete a scheduled contest. *—tr.* **1.** To fail to perform or pay. **2.** *Law.* To lose (a case) by failing to appear in court. **3.** To fail to take part in or complete (a contest, for example). ***—idiom.* in default of.** Through the failure, absence, or lack of. [Middle English *defaute,* from Old French, from past participle of *defaillir,* to fail, grow weak : *de-,* intensive pref.; see DE– + *faillir;* see FAIL.] **—de·fault′er** *n.*

de·fea·sance (dĭ-fē′zəns) *n.* **1.** A rendering void; an annulment. **2.a.** The voiding of a contract or deed. **b.** A clause within a contract or deed providing for annulment. [Middle English *defesaunce,* from Anglo-Norman, from Old French *defesance,* from *defesant,* present participle of *desfaire,* to destroy. See DEFEAT.]

de·fea·si·ble (dĭ-fē′zə-bəl) *adj.* Capable of being annulled or invalidated: *a defeasible claim to an estate.* **—de·fea′si·bil′i·ty, de·fea′si·ble·ness** *n.*

de·feat (dĭ-fēt′) *tr.v.* **-feat·ed, -feat·ing, -feats. 1.** To win victory over; beat. **2.** To prevent the success of; thwart: *Internal strife defeats the purpose of teamwork.* **3.** *Law.* To make void; annul. **—defeat** *n.* **1.** The act of defeating or state of being defeated. **2.** Failure to win. **3.** A coming to naught; frustration: *the defeat of a lifelong dream.* **4.** *Law.* The act of making null and void. [Middle English *defeten,* from *defet,* disfigured, from Old French *desfait,* past participle of *desfaire,* to destroy, from Medieval Latin *disfacere,* to destroy, mutilate, undo : Latin *dis-,* dis- + Latin *facere,* to do; see **dhē-** in Appendix.] **—de·feat′er** *n.*

SYNONYMS: *defeat, conquer, vanquish, beat, rout, subdue, subjugate, overcome.* These verbs mean to get the better of an adversary. *Defeat* is the most general: *"Whether we defeat the enemy in one battle, or by degrees, the consequences will be the same"* (Thomas Paine). *Conquer* suggests decisive and often wide-scale victory: *"A conquering army on the border will not be halted by the power of eloquence"* (Otto von Bismarck). *Vanquish* emphasizes total mastery: *The forces of Napoleon were vanquished at Waterloo. Beat,* less formal, is often the equivalent of *defeat,* though *beat* may convey greater emphasis: *"To win battles . . . you beat the soul . . . of the enemy man"* (George S. Patton). *Rout* implies complete victory followed by the disorderly flight of the defeated force: *An entire division was routed during the first hours of the war. Subdue* suggests mastery and control achieved by overpowering: *"It cost* [the Romans] *two great wars, and three great battles, to subdue that little kingdom* [Macedonia]*"* (Adam Smith). *Subjugate* more strongly implies reducing an opponent to submission: *"The last foreigner to subjugate England was a Norman duke in the Middle Ages named William"* (Stanley Meisler). To *overcome* is to prevail over, often by persevering: *overcome an enemy; overcome temptation; overcome a physical handicap.*

de·feat·ism (dĭ-fē′tĭz′əm) *n.* Acceptance of or resignation to the prospect of defeat. **—de·feat′ist** *adj. & n.*

def·e·cate (dĕf′ĭ-kāt′) *v.* **-cat·ed, -cat·ing, -cates.** *—intr.* To void feces from the bowels. *—tr.* To remove (impurities, as in a chemical solution); clarify. [Latin *dēfaecāre,* to clean the dregs from : *dē-,* de- + *faex, faec-,* dregs.] **—def′e·ca′tion** *n.* **—def′e·ca′tor** *n.*

de·fect (dē′fĕkt′, dĭ-fĕkt′) *n.* **1.** The lack of something necessary or desirable for completion or perfection; deficiency: *a visual defect.* **2.** An imperfection that causes inadequacy or failure; a shortcoming. See Synonyms at **blemish. —defect** (dĭ-fĕkt′) *intr.v.* **-fect·ed, -fect·ing, -fects. 1.** To disown allegiance to one's country and take up residence in another: *a Soviet citizen who defected to Israel.* **2.** To abandon a position or an association, often to join an opposing group: *defected from the party over the issue of free trade.* [Middle English, from Latin *dēfectus,* failure, want, from past participle of *dēficere,* to desert, be wanting : *dē-,* de- + *facere,* to do; see **dhē-** in Appendix.] **—de·fec′tion** *n.* **—de·fec′tor** *n.*

de·fec·tive (dĭ-fĕk′tĭv) *adj. Abbr.* **def. 1.a.** Having a defect; faulty: *a defective appliance.* **b.** Marked by subnormal structure, function, intelligence, or behavior: *defective speech.* **2.** *Grammar.* Lacking one or more of the inflected forms normal for a particular category of word, as the verb *may* in English. **—defective** *n.* *Offensive.* One that is physically or mentally deficient. **—de·fec′tive·ly** *adv.* **—de·fec′tive·ness** *n.*

de·fem·i·nize (dē-fĕm′ə-nīz′) *tr.v.* **-nized, -niz·ing, -niz·es.** To divest of feminine traits, qualities, or characteristics.

de·fence (dĭ-fĕns′) *n. & v. Chiefly British.* Variant of **defense.**

de·fend (dĭ-fĕnd′) *v.* **-fend·ed, -fend·ing, -fends.** *—tr.* **1.** To make or keep safe from danger, attack, or harm. **2.** To support or maintain, as by argument or action; justify. **3.** *Law.* **a.** To represent (a defendant) in a civil or criminal action. **b.** To attempt to disprove or invalidate (an action or a claim). *—intr.* To make a defense. [Middle English *defenden,* from Old French *defendre,* from Latin *dēfendere,* to ward off. See **g**ʷ**hen-** in Appendix.] **—de·fend′a·ble** *adj.* **—de·fend′er** *n.*

SYNONYMS: *defend, protect, guard, preserve, shield, safeguard.* These verbs mean to make or keep safe from danger, attack, or harm. *Defend* implies the taking of measures to repel an attack: *defending the island against invasion; tried to defend his reputation.* *Protect* often suggests providing a cover to repel discomfort, injury, or attack: *bought a dog to protect the children from unfriendly strangers; wore sunglasses to protect my eyes; has to learn to protect herself.* *Guard* suggests keeping watch: *police guarding the entrance to the embassy; guarded the house against intruders.* To *preserve* is to take measures to maintain something in safety: *fighting to preserve freedom; ecologists working to preserve our natural resources.* *Shield* suggests protection likened to a piece of defensive armor interposed between the threat and the threatened: *His lawyers tried to shield him from the angry reporters.* *Safeguard* stresses protection against potential or less imminent danger and often implies preventive action: *The Bill of Rights safeguards our individual liberties.*

de·fen·dant (dĭ-fĕn′dənt) *n. Abbr.* **def., dft.** *Law.* The party against which an action is brought.

de·fen·es·trate (dē-fĕn′ĭ-strāt′) *tr.v.* **-trat·ed, -trat·ing, -trates.** To throw out of a window. [Back-formation from DEFENESTRATION.]

de·fen·es·tra·tion (dē-fĕn′ĭ-strā′shən) *n.* An act of throwing someone or something out of a window. [From DE– + Latin *fenestra,* window.]

de·fense (dĭ-fĕns′) *n. Abbr.* **def.** **1.** The act of defending against attack, danger, or injury. **2.** A means or method of defending or protecting. **3.** An argument in support or justification of something. See Synonyms at **apology. 4.** *Law.* **a.** The action of the defendant in opposition to complaints against him or her. **b.** The defendant and his or her legal counsel. **5.** The science or art of defending oneself; self-defense. **6.** *Sports.* The team or those players on the team attempting to stop the opposition from scoring. **7.** The military, governmental, and industrial complex, especially as it authorizes and manages weaponry production. **—defense** *tr.v.* **-fensed, -fens·ing, -fens·es.** *Sports.* To attempt to stop (the opposition) from scoring. [Middle English, from Old French, from Latin *dēfēnsa,* from feminine past participle of *dēfendere,* to ward off. See DEFEND.] **—de·fense′less** *adj.* **—de·fense′less·ly** *adv.* **—de·fense′less·ness** *n.*

de·fense·man (dĭ-fĕns′mən, -măn′) *n. Sports.* A team member, as in hockey, who plays a defensive zone or position.

defense mechanism *n.* **1.** *Biology.* A physiological reaction of an organism used in self-protection, as against infection. **2.** *Psychology.* Any of a variety of mental devices, usually unconscious, that an individual may use to protect the ego from shame, anxiety, conflict, loss of self-esteem, or other unacceptable feelings or thoughts. Defense mechanisms, commonly used in coping with problems, include behaviors such as repression, projection, denial, and rationalization.

de·fen·si·ble (dĭ-fĕn′sə-bəl) *adj.* Capable of being defended, protected, or justified: *defensible arguments.* **—de·fen′si·bil′i·ty, de·fen′si·ble·ness** *n.* **—de·fen′si·bly** *adv.*

de·fen·sive (dĭ-fĕn′sĭv) *adj.* **1.** Intended or appropriate for defending; protective. **2. a.** Intended to withstand or deter aggression or attack: *a defensive weapons system; defensive behavior.* **b.** *Sports.* Of or relating to the effort to prevent an opponent from gaining points in a game or an athletic contest. **3.** Of or relating to defense. **4.** *Psychology.* Constantly protecting oneself from criticism, exposure of one's shortcomings, or other real or perceived threats to the ego. **—defensive** *n.* **1.** A means of defense. **2.** An attitude or position of defense. **—*idiom.* on the defensive.** Prepared to withstand or counter aggression or attack. **—de·fen′sive·ly** *adv.* **—de·fen′sive·ness** *n.*

de·fer[1] (dĭ-fûr′) *v.* **-ferred, -fer·ring, -fers.** *—tr.* **1.** To put off; postpone. **2.** To postpone the induction of (one eligible for the military draft). *—intr.* To procrastinate. [Middle English *differren,* to postpone, differ. See DIFFER.] **—de·fer′ra·ble** *adj.* **—de·fer′rer** *n.*

SYNONYMS: *defer, postpone, shelve, stay, suspend.* The central meaning shared by these verbs is "to put off until a later time": *deferred paying the bills; postponing our trip; shelved the issue; stay an execution; suspending train service.*

de·fer[2] (dĭ-fûr′) *v.* **-ferred, -fer·ring, -fers.** *—intr.* To submit to the opinion, wishes, or decision of another through respect or in recognition of his or her authority, knowledge, or judgment. See Synonyms at **yield.** *—tr.* To commit or entrust to another. [Middle English *deferen,* from Old French *deferer,* from Latin *dēferre,* to carry away, refer to : *dē-,* de- + *ferre,* to carry; see **bher-**[1] in Appendix.] **—de·fer′rer** *n.*

def·er·ence (dĕf′ər-əns, dĕf′rəns) *n.* **1.** Submission or courteous yielding to the opinion, wishes, or judgment of another. **2.** Courteous respect. See Synonyms at **honor.**

def·er·ent[1] (dĕf′ər-ənt, dĕf′rənt) *adj.* Showing deference; deferential.

def·er·ent[2] (dĕf′ər-ənt, dĕf′rənt) *adj.* **1.** *Anatomy.* Carrying down or away. Used of a duct or vessel. **2.** Serving or adapted to carry or transport. [Middle English *defferent,* from Latin *dēferēns, dēferent-,* present participle of *dēferre,* to carry away. See DEFER[2].]

def·er·en·tial (dĕf′ə-rĕn′shəl) *adj.* Marked by or exhibiting deference. **—def′er·en′tial·ly** *adv.*

de·fer·ment (dĭ-fûr′mənt) *n.* **1.** The act or an instance of delaying or putting off. **2.** Officially sanctioned postponement of compulsory military service.

de·fer·ral (dĭ-fûr′əl) *n.* Deferment.

de·ferred (dĭ-fûrd′) *adj. Abbr.* **def.** **1.** Postponed or delayed: *deferred gratification; deferred military draft.* **2.** Withheld until a future date: *deferred benefits; a deferred payment.*

de·fer·ves·cence (dē′fər-vĕs′əns) *n. Medicine.* Abatement of a fever. [From Latin *dēfervēscēns, dēfervēscent-,* present participle of *dēfervēscere,* to stop boiling, cool off : *dē-,* de- + *fervēscere,* to grow hot, inchoative of *fervēre,* to be hot, boil; see **bhreu-** in Appendix.] **—de′fer·vesce′** (-vĕs′) *v.* **—de′fer·ves′cent** *adj.*

de·fi·ance (dĭ-fī′əns) *n.* **1.** The act or an example of defying; bold resistance to an opposing force or authority. **2.** Intentionally contemptuous behavior or attitude; readiness to contend or resist. **—*idiom.* in defiance of.** In spite of; contrary to: *went on strike in defiance of union policy.* [Middle English *defiaunce,* from Old French *desfiance,* from *desfier,* to defy. See DEFY.]

De·fi·ance (dĭ-fī′əns). A city of northwest Ohio southwest of Toledo. Fort Defiance was built on the site by Anthony Wayne in 1794. Population, 16,810.

de·fi·ant (dĭ-fī′ənt) *adj.* Marked by defiance; boldly resisting. **—de·fi′ant·ly** *adv.*

de·fib·ril·late (dē-fĭb′rə-lāt′, -fī′brə-) *tr.v.* **-lat·ed, -lat·ing, -lates.** To stop the fibrillation of (a heart) and restore normal contractions through the use of drugs or an electric shock. **—de·fib′ril·la′tion** *n.* **—de·fib′ril·la′tive** *adj.* **—de·fib′ril·la·to′ry** (-lə-tôr′ē, -tōr′ē) *adj.*

de·fib·ril·la·tor (dē-fĭb′rə-lā′tər, -fī′brə-) *n.* An electrical device used to counteract fibrillation of the heart muscle and restore normal heartbeat by applying a brief electric shock.

de·fi·cien·cy (dĭ-fĭsh′ən-sē) *n., pl.* **-cies. 1.** The quality or condition of being deficient; incompleteness or inadequacy. **2.** A lack or shortage, especially of something essential to health; an insufficiency: *a nutritional deficiency.*

deficiency disease *n.* A disease, such as rickets or scurvy, that is caused by a dietary deficiency of specific nutrients, especially a vitamin or mineral. The disease may stem from insufficient intake, digestion, absorption, or utilization of a nutrient.

de·fi·cient (dĭ-fĭsh′ənt) *adj.* **1.** Lacking an essential quality or element: *deficient in common sense.* **2.** Inadequate in amount or degree; insufficient: *a deficient education.* [Latin *dēficiēns, dēficient-,* present participle of *dēficere,* to fail, be wanting. See DEFECT.] **—de·fi′cient** *n.* **—de·fi′cient·ly** *adv.*

def·i·cit (dĕf′ĭ-sĭt) *n.* **1. a.** Inadequacy or insufficiency: *a deficit in grain production.* **b.** A deficiency or impairment in mental or physical functioning. **c.** An unfavorable condition or position; a disadvantage: *rallied from a three-game deficit to win the playoffs.* **2. a.** The amount by which a sum of money falls short of the required or expected amount; a shortage: *large budget deficits.* **b.** A business loss. [French *déficit,* from Latin *dēficit,* it is lacking, third person sing. present tense of *dēficere,* to fail, be lacking. See DEFECT.]

deficit spending *n.* The spending of public funds obtained by borrowing rather than by taxation.

de·fi·er (dĭ-fī′ər) *n.* One that defies: *a staunch defier of tradition.*

def·i·lade (dĕf′ə-lād′, -läd′) *tr.v.* **-lad·ed, -lad·ing, -lades.** To arrange (fortifications) in such a way as to give protection from enfilading and other fire. **—defilade** *n.* **1.** The act or procedure of defilading. **2.** A fortified position offering protection from enfilading and other fire. [DE– + (EN)FILADE.]

de·file[1] (dĭ-fīl′) *tr.v.* **-filed, -fil·ing, -files. 1.** To make filthy or dirty; pollute: *defile a river with sewage.* **2.** To debase the pureness or excellence of; corrupt: *a country landscape that was defiled by urban sprawl.* **3.** To profane or sully (a good name, for example). **4.** To make unclean or unfit for ceremonial use; desecrate: *defile a temple.* **5.** To violate the chastity of. [Middle English *defilen,* alteration (influenced by *filen,* from Old English *fȳlan;* see **pū-** in Appendix) of *defoulen,* to trample on, abuse, pollute, from Old French *defouler,* to trample, full cloth : *de-,* de- + *fouler,* to trample, beat down; see FULL[2].] **—de·file′ment** *n.* **—de·fil′er** *n.* **—de·fil′ing·ly** *adv.*

de·file[2] (dĭ-fīl′) *intr.v.* **-filed, -fil·ing, -files.** To march in single file or in files or columns. **—defile** *n.* **1.** A narrow gorge or pass that restricts lateral movement, as of troops. **2.** A march in a line. [French *défiler* : *dé-,* away, off (from Old French *de-;* see DE–) + *file,* line, file (from Old French *filer,* to spin thread, march in line; see FILE[1]). N., from French *défilé,* from past participle of *défiler.*]

de·fine (dĭ-fīn′) *v.* **-fined, -fin·ing, -fines.** *—tr.* **1. a.** To state the precise meaning of (a word or sense of a word, for example). **b.** To describe the nature or basic qualities of; explain: *define the properties of a new drug; a study that defines people according to their median incomes.* **2. a.** To delineate the outline or form of: *gentle hills that were defined against the sky.* **b.** To specify distinctly: *define the weapons to be used in limited warfare.* **3.** To serve to distinguish; characterize: *"portraits that defined the style of an epoch"* (Gloria Vanderbilt). *—intr.* To make or write a definition. [Middle English *definen, diffinen,* from Old French *definir, diffiner,* from Latin *dēfīnīre,* to limit, determine : *dē-,* intensive pref.; see DE– + *fīnis,* boundary, limit.] **—de·fin′a·bil′i·ty** *n.* **—de·fin′a·ble** *adj.* **—de·fin′a·bly** *adv.* **—de·fine′ment** *n.* **—de·fin′er** *n.*

ă pat	oi boy
ā pay	ou out
âr care	ŏŏ took
ä father	ōō boot
ĕ pet	ŭ cut
ē be	ûr urge
ĭ pit	th thin
ī pie	*th* this
îr pier	hw which
ŏ pot	zh vision
ō toe	ə about, item
ô paw	♦ regionalism

Stress marks: ′ (primary); ′ (secondary), as in **dictionary** (dĭk′shə-nĕr′ē)

de·fin·i·en·dum (dĭ-fĭn′ē-ĕn′dəm) *n., pl.* **-da** (-də). A word or expression that is being defined. [Latin *dēfīniendum,* neuter gerundive of *dēfīnīre,* to define. See DEFINE.]

de·fin·i·ens (dĭ-fĭn′ē-ĕnz′) *n., pl.* **-en·ti·a** (-ĕn′shē-ə, -shə). The word or words serving to define another word or expression, as in a dictionary entry. [Latin *dēfīniēns,* present participle of *dēfīnīre,* to define. See DEFINE.]

def·i·nite (dĕf′ə-nĭt) *adj.* **1.** Having distinct limits: *definite restrictions on the sale of alcoholic beverages.* **2.** Indisputable; certain: *a definite victory.* **3.** Clearly defined; explicitly precise: *a definite statement of the terms of the will.* See Synonyms at **explicit. 4.** *Abbr.* **def.** *Grammar.* Limiting or particularizing. **5.** *Botany.* **a.** Of a specified number not exceeding 20, as certain floral organs, especially stamens. **b.** Cymose; determinate. [Middle English *diffinite,* defined, from Latin *dēfīnītus,* past participle of *dēfīnīre,* to define. See DEFINE.] **—def′i·nite·ly** *adv.* **—def′i·nite·ness** *n.*

USAGE NOTE: *Definite* and *definitive* both apply to what is precisely defined or explicitly set forth. But *definitive* generally refers specifically to a judgment or description that serves as a standard or reference point for others, as in *the definitive decision of the court* (which sets forth a final resolution of a judicial matter) or *the definitive biography of Nelson* (i.e., the biography that sets the standard against which all other accounts of Nelson's life must be measured).

definite article *n. Grammar.* A member of the class of determiners that restrict or particularize a noun. In English, *the* is the definite article.

definite integral *n. Mathematics.* An integral that is calculated between two specified limits, usually expressed in the form $\int_b^a f(x)dx$. The result of performing the integral is a number that represents the area under the curve of $f(x)$ between the limits and the x-axis.

def·i·ni·tion (dĕf′ə-nĭsh′ən) *n. Abbr.* **def. 1. a.** A statement conveying fundamental character. **b.** A statement of the meaning of a word, phrase, or term, as in a dictionary entry. **2.** The act or process of stating a precise meaning or significance; formulation of a meaning. **3. a.** The act of making clear and distinct: *a definition of one's intentions.* **b.** The state of being closely outlined or determined: *"With the drizzle, the trees in the little clearing had lost definition"* (Anthony Hyde). **c.** A determination of outline, extent, or limits: *the definition of a President's authority.* **4. a.** The clarity of detail in an optically produced image, such as a photograph, effected by a combination of resolution and contrast. **b.** The degree of clarity with which a televised image or broadcast signal is received. [Middle English *diffinicioun,* from Old French *definition,* from Latin *dēfīnītiō-, dēfīnītiōn-,* from *dēfīnītus,* past participle of *dēfīnīre,* to define. See DEFINE.] **—def′i·ni′tion·al** *adj.*

de·fin·i·tive (dĭ-fĭn′ĭ-tĭv) *adj.* **1.** Precisely defined or explicit. **2.** Supplying or being a final settlement or decision; conclusive. See Synonyms at **decisive. 3.** Authoritative and complete: *a definitive biography.* See Usage Note at **definite. 4.** *Biology.* Fully formed or developed, as an organ or structure. **—definitive** *n. Grammar.* A word that defines or limits, such as the definite article or a demonstrative pronoun. **—de·fin′i·tive·ly** *adv.* **—de·fin′i·tive·ness** *n.*

definitive host *n.* The host organism in or on which a parasite reaches reproductive maturity.

de·fin·i·tude (dĭ-fĭn′ĭ-to͞od′, -tyo͞od′) *n.* The quality of being definite or exact; precision.

def·la·grate (dĕf′lə-grāt′) *intr. & tr.v.* **-grat·ed, -grat·ing, -grates.** To burn or cause to burn with intense heat and light. [Latin *dēflagrāre, dēflagrāt-* : *dē-,* intensive pref.; see DE– + *flagrāre,* to blaze; see **bhel-**[1] in Appendix.] **—def′la·gra′tion** *n.*

de·flate (dĭ-flāt′) *v.* **-flat·ed, -flat·ing, -flates.** *—tr.* **1. a.** To release contained air or gas from. **b.** To collapse by releasing contained air or gas. **2.** To reduce or lessen the size or importance of: *Losing the contest deflated my ego.* **3.** *Economics.* **a.** To reduce the amount or availability of (currency or credit), effecting a decline in prices. **b.** To produce deflation in (an economy). *—intr.* To be or become deflated: *The balloon deflated slowly.* [DE– + (IN)FLATE.] **—de·fla′tor** *n.*

de·fla·tion (dĭ-flā′shən) *n.* **1.** The act of deflating or the condition of being deflated. **2.** *Economics.* A persistent decrease in the level of consumer prices or a persistent increase in the purchasing power of money because of a reduction in available currency and credit. **—de·fla′tion·ar′y** (-shə-nĕr′ē) *adj.* **—de·fla′tion·ist** *n.*

de·flect (dĭ-flĕkt′) *intr. & tr.v.* **-flect·ed, -flect·ing, -flects.** To turn aside or cause to turn aside; bend or deviate. [Latin *dēflectere* : *dē-,* de- + *flectere,* to bend.] **—de·flect′a·ble** *adj.* **—de·flec′tive** *adj.* **—de·flec′tor** *n.*

de·flec·tion (dĭ-flĕk′shən) *n.* **1.** The act of deflecting or the condition of being deflected. **2.** Deviation or a specified amount of deviation. **3.** The deviation of an indicator of a measuring instrument from zero or from its normal position. **4.** The movement of a structure or structural part as a result of stress.

de·flexed (dĭ-flĕkst′, dē′flĕkst′) *adj. Botany.* Bent or turned abruptly downward at a sharp angle: *deflexed petals.* [From Latin *dēflexus,* past participle of *dēflectere,* to bend. See DEFLECT.]

de·flex·ion (dĭ-flĕk′shən) *n. Chiefly British.* Variant of **deflection.**

def·lo·ra·tion (dĕf′lə-rā′shən) *n.* **1.** The act of deflowering. **2.** Rupture of the hymen, typically in sexual intercourse. [Middle English *defloracioun,* from Late Latin *dēflōrātiō, dēflōrātiōn-,* from *dēflōrātus,* past participle of *dēflōrāre,* to deflower. See DEFLOWER.]

de·flow·er (dē-flou′ər) *tr.v.* **-ered, -er·ing, -ers. 1.** To take away the virginity of (a woman). **2.** To destroy the innocence, integrity, or beauty of; ravage. [Middle English *deflouren,* from Old French *defflourer,* from Late Latin *dēflōrāre* : Latin *dē-,* de- + Latin *flōs, flōr-,* flower; see **bhel-**[3] in Appendix.] **—de·flow′er·er** *n.*

de·foam (dē-fōm′) *tr.v.* **-foamed, -foam·ing, -foams. 1.** To remove foam from. **2.** To prevent the formation of foam on.

de·fo·cus (dē-fō′kəs) *tr.v.* **-cused, -cus·ing, -cus·es** or **-cussed, -cus·sing, -cus·ses.** To cause (a beam or a lens) to deviate from accurate focus. **—defocus** *n.* The act or result of causing a lens to deviate from accurate focus.

De·foe (dĭ-fō′), **Daniel.** 1660–1731. British writer whose most famous novel, *Robinson Crusoe* (1719), was inspired by the exploits of a Scottish sailor and castaway, Alexander Selkirk.

de·fog (dē-fôg′, -fŏg′) *tr.v.* **-fogged, -fog·ging, -fogs.** To remove condensed water vapor from: *defog a windshield.* **—de·fog′ger** *n.*

de·fo·li·ant (dē-fō′lē-ənt) *n.* A chemical sprayed or dusted on plants to cause the leaves to fall off.

de·fo·li·ate (dē-fō′lē-āt′) *v.* **-at·ed, -at·ing, -ates.** *—tr.* **1.** To deprive (a plant, tree, or forest) of leaves. **2.** To cause the leaves of (a plant, tree, or forest) to fall off, especially by the use of chemicals. *—intr.* To lose foliage. [Late Latin *dēfoliāre, dēfoliāt-* : Latin *dē-,* de- + Latin *folium,* leaf; see **bhel-**[3] in Appendix.] **—de·fo′li·ate** (-ĭt) *adj.* **—de·fo′li·a′tion** *n.* **—de·fo′li·a′tor** *n.*

de·force (dē-fôrs′, -fōrs′) *tr.v.* **-forced, -forc·ing, -forc·es.** *Law.* To withhold (something) by force from the rightful owner. [Middle English *deforcen,* from Anglo-Norman *deforcer,* from Old French *desforcier* : *des-,* de- + *forcier,* to force (from Vulgar Latin **fortiāre,* from Latin *fortis,* strong; see **bhergh-**[2] in Appendix).] **—de·force′ment** *n.*

de·for·est (dē-fôr′ĭst, -fŏr′-) *tr.v.* **-est·ed, -est·ing, -ests.** To cut down and clear away the trees or forests from. **—de·for′es·ta′tion** (-ĭ-stā′shən) *n.* **—de·for′est·er** *n.*

De For·est (dĭ fôr′ĭst, fŏr′-), **Lee.** Known as "the Father of Radio." 1873–1961. American electrical engineer who patented the triode electron tube (1907) that made possible the amplification and detection of radio waves.

de·form (dĭ-fôrm′) *v.* **-formed, -form·ing, -forms.** *—tr.* **1.** To spoil the natural form of; misshape: *a body that had been deformed by disease.* **2.** To spoil the beauty or appearance of; disfigure. **3.** *Physics.* To alter the shape of by pressure or stress. *—intr.* To become deformed. See Synonyms at **distort.** [Middle English *deformen,* from Old French *deformer,* from Latin *dēfōrmāre* : *dē-,* de- + *forma,* form.] **—de·form′a·bil′i·ty** *n.* **—de·form′a·ble** *adj.*

de·for·ma·tion (dē′fôr-mā′shən, dĕf′ər-) *n.* **1. a.** The act or process of deforming. **b.** The condition of being deformed. **2.** An alteration of form for the worse. **3.** *Physics.* **a.** An alteration of shape by pressure or stress. **b.** The shape that results from such an alteration.

de·formed (dĭ-fôrmd′) *adj.* Distorted in form; misshapen.

de·for·mi·ty (dĭ-fôr′mĭ-tē) *n., pl.* **-ties. 1.** The state of being deformed. **2.** A bodily malformation, distortion, or disfigurement. **3.** A deformed person or thing. **4.** Gross ugliness or distortion.

de·fraud (dĭ-frôd′) *tr.v.* **-fraud·ed, -fraud·ing, -frauds.** To take something from by fraud; swindle: *defrauded the immigrants by selling them worthless land deeds.* [Middle English *defrauden,* from Old French *defrauder,* from Latin *dēfraudāre* : *dē-,* de- + *fraudāre,* to cheat (from *fraus, fraud-,* fraud).] **—de′fraud·a′tion** (dē′frô-dā′shən) *n.* **—de·fraud′er** *n.*

de·fray (dĭ-frā′) *tr.v.* **-frayed, -fray·ing, -frays.** To undertake the payment of (costs or expenses); pay. [French *défrayer,* from Old French *desfrayer* : *des-,* de- + **frai,* expense (from Latin *frāctum,* from neuter past participle of *frangere,* to break; see **bhreg-** in Appendix).] **—de·fray′a·ble** *adj.* **—de·fray′al** *n.*

de·frock (dē-frŏk′) *tr.v.* **-frocked, -frock·ing, -frocks.** To unfrock.

de·frost (dē-frôst′, -frŏst′) *v.* **-frost·ed, -frost·ing, -frosts.** *—tr.* **1.** To remove ice or frost from. **2.** To cause to thaw. *—intr.* To become thawed.

de·frost·er (dē-frô′stər, -frŏs′tər) *n.* **1.** A heating device designed to remove frost or prevent its formation. **2.** A device designed to thaw frozen goods.

deft (dĕft) *adj.* **deft·er, deft·est.** Quick and skillful; adroit. See Synonyms at **dexterous.** [Middle English, gentle, humble, variant of *dafte,* foolish. See DAFT.] **—deft′ly** *adv.* **—deft′ness** *n.*

de·fu·el (dē-fyo͞o′əl) *tr.v.* **-eled, -el·ing, -els** also **-elled, -el·ling, -els.** To remove the fuel from: *defuel a rocket.*

de·funct (dĭ-fŭngkt′) *adj.* Having ceased to exist or live: *a defunct political organization.* [Latin *dēfūnctus,* past participle of *dēfungī,* to finish : *dē-,* de- + *fungī,* to perform.] **—de·func′tive** *adj.* **—de·funct′ness** *n.*

de·fund (dē-fŭnd′) *tr.v.* **-fund·ed, -fund·ing, -funds.** To stop the flow of funds to: *defund a federal program.*

de·fuse (dē-fyo͞oz′) *tr.v.* **-fused, -fus·ing, -fus·es. 1.** To remove the fuse from (an explosive device). **2.** To make less dangerous, tense, or hostile: *a diplomatic move that defused the international crisis.*

de·fy (dĭ-fī′) *tr.v.* **-fied, -fy·ing, -fies. 1.a.** To oppose or resist with boldness and assurance: *defied the blockade by sailing straight through it.* **b.** To refuse to submit to or cooperate with: *defied the court order by leaving the country; played his trumpet past midnight, defying the neighbors.* **2.** To be unaffected by; resist or withstand: *"So the plague defied all medicines"* (Daniel Defoe). **3.** To challenge or dare (someone) to do something: *She defied her accusers to prove their charges.* [Middle English *defien,* from Old French *desfier,* from Vulgar Latin **disfīdāre* : Latin *dis-,* dis- + Latin *fīdus,* faithful; see **bheidh-** in Appendix.]

SYNONYMS: *defy, beard, brave, challenge, dare, face, front.* The central meaning shared by these verbs is "to confront boldly and courageously": *an innovator defying tradition; bearded the power of the king; braving all criticism; challenged the opposition to produce proof; daring him to deny the statement; faced her accusers; front death with dignity.*

deg or **deg.** *abbr.* Degree.

dé·ga·gé (dā′gä-zhā′) *adj.* Free and relaxed in manner; casual. [French, past participle of *dégager,* to disengage, from Old French *desgagier* : *des-,* de- + *gage,* pledge (of Germanic origin).]

de·gas (dē-găs′) *tr.v.* **-gassed, -gas·sing, -gas·ses** or **-gas·es.** To remove gas from.

De·gas (də-gä′), **(Hilaire Germain) Edgar.** 1834–1917. French painter and sculptor noted especially for his fluid studies of ballet dancers.

de Gaulle (də gōl′, gôl′), **Charles André Joseph Marie.** 1890–1970. French general and politician. During World War II he gained enormous popularity as the leader of Free French forces in exile. Later, after years of self-imposed retirement, he emerged as the first president (1959–1969) of the Fifth Republic and led the country through its turbulent withdrawal from Algeria.

Charles de Gaulle

de·gauss (dē-gous′) *tr.v.* **-gaussed, -gauss·ing, -gauss·es. 1.** To neutralize the magnetic field of (a ship, for example). **2.** To erase information from (a magnetic disk or other storage device). [DE– + GAUSS.] **—de·gauss′er** *n.*

de·gen·er·a·cy (dĭ-jĕn′ər-ə-sē) *n., pl.* **-cies. 1.** The process of degenerating. **2.** The state of being degenerate. **3.** Corrupt, vulgar, vicious behavior, especially sexual perversion. **4.** *Genetics.* The presence in a genetic code of multiple codons for the same amino acid.

de·gen·er·ate (dĭ-jĕn′ər-ĭt) *adj.* **1.** Having declined, as in function or nature, from a former or original state: *a degenerate form of an ancient folk art.* **2.** Having fallen to an inferior or undesirable state, especially in mental or moral qualities. **3.** *Physics.* Taking on several discrete values or existing in two or more quantum states: *degenerate energy levels.* **4.** *Physics.* Characterized by great density and consisting of atoms stripped of electrons: *degenerate matter.* **5.** *Medicine.* Characterized by degeneration, as of tissue, a cell, or an organ. **6.** *Biology.* Having lost one or more highly developed functions, characteristics, or structures through evolution: *a degenerate life form.* **7.** *Genetics.* **a.** Coding for the same amino acid as another codon. **b.** Having more than one codon specify the same amino acid. Used of a genetic code. **—degenerate** *n.* **1.** A depraved, corrupt, or vicious person. **2.** A person lacking or having progressively lost normative biological or psychological characteristics. **—degenerate** (-ə-rāt′) *intr.v.* **-at·ed, -at·ing, -ates. 1.** To fall below a normal or desirable state, especially functionally or morally; deteriorate: *old water pipes that are degenerating with age; a dispute that degenerated into a brawl.* **2.** To decline in quality: *The quality of his writing degenerated as he continued to drink.* **3.** To undergo degeneration. [Latin *dēgenerātus,* past participle of *dēgenerāre,* to depart from one's own kind, deteriorate : *dē-,* de- + *genus, gener-,* race; see **genə-** in Appendix.] **—de·gen′er·ate·ly** *adv.* **—de·gen′er·ate·ness** *n.*

de·gen·er·a·tion (dĭ-jĕn′ə-rā′shən) *n.* **1.** The process of degenerating. **2.** The state of being degenerate. **3.** *Medicine.* Gradual deterioration of specific tissues, cells, or organs with corresponding impairment or loss of function, caused by injury, disease, or aging. **4.** *Biology.* The evolutionary decline or loss of a function, characteristic, or structure in an organism or a species. **5.** *Electronics.* Loss of or gain in power in an amplifier caused by unintentional negative feedback.

de·gen·er·a·tive (dĭ-jĕn′ər-ə-tĭv) *adj.* Of, relating to, causing, or characterized by degeneration: *a degenerative disease.*

degenerative joint disease *n.* See **osteoarthritis.**

de·glam·or·ize (dē-glăm′ə-rīz′) *tr.v.* **-ized, -iz·ing, -iz·es.** To make less glamorous: *"pressing the entertainment industry to deglamorize the use of drugs in films"* (Larry Martz).

de·glaze (dē-glāz′) *tr.v.* **-glazed, -glaz·ing, -glaz·es. 1.** To remove the glaze from (pottery, for example). **2.** To dissolve the remaining bits of sautéed or roasted food in (a pan or pot) by adding a liquid and heating.

de·glu·ti·nate (dĭ-glo͞ot′n-āt′) *tr.v.* **-nat·ed, -nat·ing, -nates.** To extract the gluten from (wheat flour, for example). [Latin *dēglūtināre, dēglūtināt-* : *dē-,* de- + *glūten, glutin-,* glue.] **—de·glu′ti·na′tion** *n.*

de·glu·ti·tion (dē′glo͞o-tĭsh′ən) *n.* The act or process of swallowing. [French *déglutition,* from *déglutir,* to swallow, from Latin *dēglūtīre* : *dē-,* de- + *glūtīre,* to gulp.] **—de·glu′ti·to′ry** (-tĭ-tôr′ē, -tōr′ē) *adj.*

de·grad·a·ble (dĭ-grā′də-bəl) *adj.* That can be chemically degraded: *degradable plastic wastes; degradable paper products.* **—de·grad′a·bil′i·ty** *n.*

deg·ra·da·tion (dĕg′rə-dā′shən) *n.* **1.** The act or process of degrading. **2.** The state of being degraded; degeneration. **3.** A decline to a lower condition, quality, or level. **4.** *Geology.* A general lowering of the earth's surface by erosion or weathering. **5.** *Chemistry.* Decomposition of a compound by stages, exhibiting well-defined intermediate products. **6.** *Computer Science.* The state in which a computer operates when some of its memory or peripherals are not available.

de·grade (dĭ-grād′) *tr.v.* **-grad·ed, -grad·ing, -grades. 1.** To reduce in grade, rank, or status; demote. **2.** To lower in dignity; dishonor or disgrace: *a scandal that degraded the participants.* **3.** To lower in moral or intellectual character; debase. **4.** To reduce in worth or value: *degrade a currency.* **5.** To impair in physical structure or function. **6.** *Geology.* To lower or wear by erosion or weathering. **7.** To cause (an organic compound) to undergo degradation. [Middle English *degraden,* from Old French *degrader,* from Late Latin *dēgradāre* : Latin *dē-,* de- + Latin *gradus,* step; see **ghredh-** in Appendix.] **—de·grad′er** *n.*

SYNONYMS: *degrade, abase, debase, demean, humble, humiliate.* These verbs mean to deprive of self-esteem or self-worth. *Degrade* implies reduction to a state of shame or disgrace: *"Charity degrades those who receive it and hardens those who dispense it"* (George Sand). *Abase* refers principally to loss of rank or prestige: *refused to abase herself by asking for an invitation. Debase* implies reduction in quality or value: *"debasing the moral currency"* (George Eliot). *Demean* suggests lowering in social position: *"It puts him where he can make the advances without demeaning himself"* (William Dean Howells). *Humble* can refer to lowering in rank or, more often, to driving out undue pride: *He dreamed of humbling his opponent.* To *humiliate* is to subject to loss of self-respect or dignity: *a defeat that humiliated both army and nation.* See also Synonyms at **demote.**

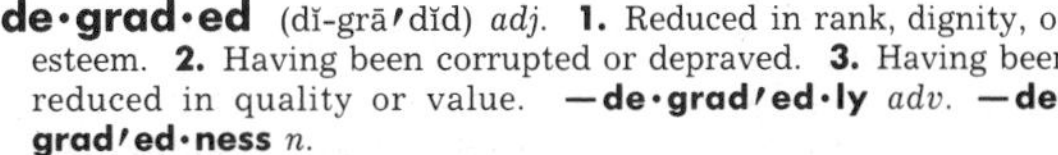

de·grad·ed (dĭ-grā′dĭd) *adj.* **1.** Reduced in rank, dignity, or esteem. **2.** Having been corrupted or depraved. **3.** Having been reduced in quality or value. **—de·grad′ed·ly** *adv.* **—de·grad′ed·ness** *n.*

de·grad·ing (dĭ-grā′dĭng) *adj.* Tending or intended to degrade: *"There is nothing so degrading as the constant anxiety about one's means of livelihood"* (W. Somerset Maugham). **—de·grad′ing·ly** *adv.*

de·gran·u·la·tion (dē-grăn′yə-lā′shən) *n.* The process of losing granules.

de·grease (dē-grēs′, -grēz′) *tr.v.* **-greased, -greas·ing, -greas·es.** To remove grease from: *degrease machinery; degrease chicken stock.* **—de·greas′er** *n.*

de·gree (dĭ-grē′) *n.* **1.** One of a series of steps in a process, course, or progression; a stage: *rose by degrees from clerk to manager of the store.* **2.** A step in a direct hereditary line of descent or ascent: *First cousins are two degrees from their common ancestor.* **3.** Relative social or official rank, dignity, or position. **4.** Relative intensity or amount, as of a quality or an attribute: *a high degree of accuracy.* **5.** The extent or measure of a state of being, an action, or a relation: *modernized their facilities to a large degree.* **6.** *Abbr.* **deg, deg.** A unit division of a temperature scale. **7.** *Mathematics.* A planar unit of angular measure equal in magnitude to ¹⁄₃₆₀ of a complete revolution. **8.** A unit of latitude or longitude, equal to ¹⁄₃₆₀ of a great circle. **9.** *Mathematics.* **a.** The greatest sum of the exponents of the variables in a term of a polynomial or polynomial equation. **b.** The exponent of the derivative of highest order in a differential equation in standard form. **10.a.** An academic title given by a college or university to a student who has completed a course of study: *received the Bachelor of Arts degree at commencement.* **b.** A similar title conferred as an honorary distinction. **11.** *Law.* A division or classification of a specific crime according to its seriousness: *murder in the second degree.* **12.** A classification of the severity of an injury, especially a burn: *a third-degree burn.* **13.** *Grammar.* One of the forms used in the comparison of adjectives and adverbs. For example, *sweet* is the positive degree, *sweeter* the comparative degree, and *sweetest* the superlative degree of the adjective *sweet.* **14.** *Music.* **a.** One of the seven notes of a diatonic scale. **b.** A space or line of the staff. **—*idioms.* by degrees.** Little by little; gradually. **to a degree.** To a small extent; in a limited way. [Middle English *degre,* from Old French, from Vulgar Latin **dēgradus* : Latin *dē-,* de- + Latin *gradus,* step; see **ghredh-** in Appendix.]

de·greed (dĭ-grēd′) *adj.* Having or requiring an academic degree: *a degreed biologist; a degreed profession.*

de·gree-day (dĭ-grē′dā′) *n.* A unit of measurement equal to a difference of one degree between the mean outdoor temperature on a certain day and a reference temperature, used in estimating the energy needs for heating or cooling a building.

degree of freedom *n., pl.* **degrees of freedom. 1.** *Statistics.* Any of the unrestricted, independent random variables that constitute a statistic. **2.** *Physics.* **a.** Any of the minimum num-

ă pat	oi boy
ā pay	ou out
âr care	o͝o took
ä father	o͞o boot
ĕ pet	ŭ cut
ē be	ûr urge
ĭ pit	th thin
ī pie	*th* this
îr pier	hw which
ŏ pot	zh vision
ō toe	ə about, item
ô paw	♦ regionalism

Stress marks: ′ (primary); ′ (secondary), as in **dictionary** (dĭk′shə-nĕr′ē)

ber of coordinates required to specify completely the motion of a mechanical system. **b.** Any of the independent thermodynamic variables, such as pressure, temperature, or composition, required to specify a system with a given number of phases and components.

de·gres·sion (dĭ-grĕsh′ən, dē-) *n.* A descent by stages or steps. [Middle English, from Medieval Latin *dēgressiō, dēgressiōn-,* descent, from Latin *dēgressus,* past participle of *dēgredī,* to step down : *dē-,* de- + *gradī,* to step; see **ghredh-** in Appendix.] **—de·gres′sive** *adj.*

de·gust (dĭ-gŭst′, dē-) *tr.v.* **-gust·ed, -gust·ing, -gusts.** To taste with relish; savor. [Latin *dēgustāre* : *dē-,* de- + *gustāre,* to taste; see **geus-** in Appendix.] **—de′gus·ta′tion** (dē′gŭ-stā′shən) *n.*

de Ha·vil·land (də hăv′ə-lənd), **Olivia.** Born 1916. British-born American actress who portrayed Melanie in *Gone With the Wind* (1939) and won an Academy Award for *To Each His Own* (1946) and *The Heiress* (1949).

Olivia de Havilland
Photographed in 1977

de·hire (dē-hīr′) *tr.v.* **-hired, -hir·ing, -hires.** *Slang.* To lay off or otherwise terminate (an employee): "[When] *top executives . . . are dehired, headhunters get nervous. It's not the way they like to see new business develop*" (Forbes).

de·hisce (dĭ-hĭs′) *intr.v.* **-hisced, -hisc·ing, -hisc·es. 1.** *Botany.* To open at definite places, discharging seeds, pollen, or other contents, as the ripe capsules or pods of some plants. **2.** *Medicine.* To rupture or break open, as a surgical wound. [Latin *dehīscere* : *dē-,* de- + *hīscere,* to split, inchoative of *hiāre,* to be open.]

de·his·cence (dē-hĭs′əns) *n.* **1.** *Botany.* An opening at definite places at maturity to release or expose the contents, such as seeds from a fruit or pollen from an anther. **2.** *Medicine.* A splitting open or a rupture, as of a surgical wound or of an organ or a structure to discharge its contents. **—de·his′cent** *adj.*

de·horn (dē-hôrn′) *tr.v.* **-horned, -horn·ing, -horns. 1.** To remove the horns from. **2.** To prevent growth in the horns of (cattle, for example), as by cauterization.

Deh·ra Dun (dā′rə do͞on′). A city of northern India north-northeast of Delhi. It is a trade center and has a forestry college. Population, 211,416.

de·hu·man·ize (dē-hyo͞o′mə-nīz′) *tr.v.* **-ized, -iz·ing, -iz·es. 1.** To deprive of human qualities such as individuality, compassion, or civility: *slaves who had been dehumanized by their abysmal condition.* **2.** To render mechanical and routine. **—de·hu′man·i·za′tion** (-mə-nĭ-zā′shən) *n.*

de·hu·mid·i·fy (dē′hyo͞o-mĭd′ə-fī′) *tr.v.* **-fied, -fy·ing, -fies.** To remove atmospheric moisture from. **—de′hu·mid′i·fi·ca′tion** (-fĭ-kā′shən) *n.* **—de′hu·mid′i·fi′er** *n.*

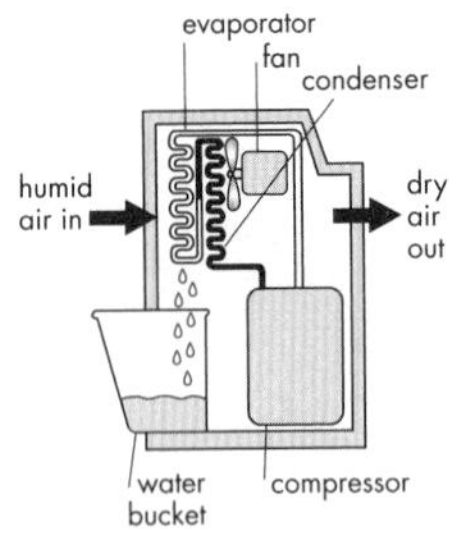

dehumidify

de·hy·dra·tase (dē-hī′drə-tās′, -tāz′) *n.* *Biochemistry.* An enzyme that catalyzes the removal of oxygen and hydrogen from organic compounds in the form of water.

de·hy·drate (dē-hī′drāt′) *v.* **-drat·ed, -drat·ing, -drates.** *—tr.* **1.** To remove water from; make anhydrous. **2.** To preserve by removing water from (vegetables, for example). See Synonyms at **dry.** *—intr.* To lose water or moisture; become dry. **—de·hy′dra′tor** *n.*

de·hy·dra·tion (dē′hī-drā′shən) *n.* **1.** The process of removing water from a substance or compound. **2.** Excessive loss of water from the body or from an organ or a body part, as from illness or fluid deprivation.

de·hy·dra·tor (dē-hī′drā′tər) *n.* **1.** A substance, such as sulfuric acid, that removes water. **2.** A container or an engineered system designed to remove water from substances such as absorbents or food.

de·hy·dro·chlo·rin·ase (dē-hī′drə-klôr′ə-nās′, -nāz′, -klōr′-) *n.* *Biochemistry.* An enzyme that catalyzes the removal of hydrogen and chlorine from a chlorinated hydrocarbon.

de·hy·dro·chlo·rin·ate (dē-hī′drə-klôr′ə-nāt′, -klōr′-) *tr.v.* **-at·ed, -at·ing, -ates.** *Biochemistry.* To remove hydrogen and chlorine or hydrogen chloride from (a compound). **—de·hy′dro·chlo′ri·na′tion** *n.*

de·hy·dro·gen·ase (dē′hī-drŏj′ə-nās′, -nāz′, dē-hī′drə-jə-) *n.* *Biochemistry.* An enzyme that catalyzes the removal and transfer of hydrogen from a substrate in an oxidation-reduction reaction.

de·hy·dro·gen·ate (dē′hī-drŏj′ə-nāt′, dē-hī′drə-jə-) *tr.v.* **-at·ed, -at·ing, -ates.** *Chemistry.* To remove hydrogen from. **—de·hy′dro·gen·a′tion** *n.*

de·hy·dro·gen·ize (dē′hī-drŏj′ə-nīz′, dē-hī′drə-jə-) *tr.v.* **-ized, -iz·ing, -iz·es.** *Chemistry.* To dehydrogenate. **—de·hy′dro·gen·i·za′tion** (-ə-nĭ-zā′shən) *n.*

de·hyp·no·tize (dē-hĭp′nə-tīz′) *tr.v.* **-tized, -tiz·ing, -tiz·es.** To arouse from a hypnotic state.

de·ice (dē-īs′) *tr.v.* **-iced, -ic·ing, -ic·es.** To make or keep free of ice; melt ice from: *deiced the plane's wings before takeoff.*

de·ic·er (dē-ī′sər) *n.* **1.** A device used on an aircraft to keep the wings and propeller free from ice or to remove ice after it has formed. **2.** A compound, such as ethylene glycol, used to prevent the formation of ice, as on windshields.

deic·tic (dīk′tĭk) *adj.* **1.** *Logic.* Directly proving by argument. **2.** *Linguistics.* Serving to point out or specify, as the demonstrative pronoun *this.* [Greek *deiktikos,* from *deiktos,* able to show directly, from *deiknunai,* to show. See **deik-** in Appendix.] **—deic′ti·cal·ly** *adv.*

de·if·ic (dē-ĭf′ĭk) *adj.* **1.** Making or tending to make divine. **2.** Of or characterized by divine or godlike nature. [Late Latin *deificus* : Latin *deus,* god; see **deiw-** in Appendix + Latin *-ficus,* -fic.]

de·i·fi·ca·tion (dē′ə-fĭ-kā′shən) *n.* **1.a.** The act or process of deifying. **b.** The condition of being deified. **2.** One that embodies the qualities of a god.

de·i·fy (dē′ə-fī′) *tr.v.* **-fied, -fy·ing, -fies. 1.** To make a god of; raise to the condition of a god. **2.** To worship or revere as a god: *deify a leader.* **3.** To idealize; exalt: *deifying success.* [Middle English *deifien,* from Old French *deifier,* from Late Latin *deificāre,* from *deificus,* deific. See DEIFIC.] **—de′i·fi′er** *n.*

deign (dān) *v.* **deigned, deign·ing, deigns.** *—intr.* To think it appropriate to one's dignity; condescend: *wouldn't deign to greet the servant who opened the door.* See Synonyms at **stoop**[1]. *—tr.* To condescend to give or grant; vouchsafe. "*Nor would we deign him burial of his men*" (Shakespeare). [Middle English *deinen,* from Old French *deignier,* to regard as worthy, from Latin *dignārī,* from *dignus,* worthy. See **dek-** in Appendix.]

deil (dēl) *n.* *Scots.* **1.** The devil; Satan. **2.** A mischievous person; an imp. [Scots, from Middle English *dele,* variant of *devel.* See DEVIL.]

Dei·mos (dē′mōs, dā′-, dī′mŏs) *n.* The satellite of Mars that is second in distance from the planet. [Greek, one of the sons of Ares, from *deimos,* fear, terror.]

de·in·dus·tri·al·ize (dē′ĭn-dŭs′trē-ə-līz′) *v.* **-ized, -iz·ing, -iz·es.** *—tr.* **1.** To cause (a nation or an area) to lose industrial capability or strength: *felt that America was being deindustrialized by foreign competition.* **2.** To deprive (a defeated country) of its industrial infrastructure and potential: *After World War I the Allies attempted to deindustrialize Germany.* *—intr.* To undergo or suffer loss of industrial infrastructure and potential. **—de′in·dus′tri·al·i·za′tion** (-ə-lĭ-zā′shən) *n.*

de·in·sti·tu·tion·al·ize (dē-ĭn′stĭ-to͞o′shə-nə-līz′, -tyo͞o′-) *tr.v.* **-ized, -iz·ing, -iz·es. 1.** To remove the status of an institution from. **2.** To release (a mental health patient, for example) from an institution for placement and care in the community. **—de·in′sti·tu′tion·al·i·za′tion** (-shə-nə-lĭ-zā′shən) *n.*

de·i·on·ize (dē-ī′ə-nīz′) *tr.v.* **-ized, -iz·ing, -iz·es.** To remove ions from (a solution) using an ion-exchange process. **—de·i′on·iz′er** *n.*

Deir·dre (dîr′drə, -drē) *n.* A legendary princess of Ulster who eloped with her lover, Naoise, to escape marriage to King Conchobar. After the king murdered Naoise, she killed herself.

de·ism (dē′ĭz′əm) *n.* The belief, based solely on reason, in a God who created the universe and then abandoned it, assuming no control over life, exerting no influence on natural phenomena, and giving no supernatural revelation. [French *déisme,* from Latin *deus,* god. See **deiw-** in Appendix.] **—de′ist** *n.* **—de·is′tic** *adj.* **—de·is′ti·cal·ly** *adv.*

de·i·ty (dē′ĭ-tē) *n., pl.* **-ties. 1.** A god or goddess. **2.a.** The essential nature or condition of being a god; divinity. **b. Deity.** God. Used with *the.* [Middle English *deite,* from Old French, from Late Latin *deitās,* divine nature, from Latin *deus,* god. See **deiw-** in Appendix.]

dé·jà vu (dā′zhä vü′) *n.* **1.** *Psychology.* The illusion of having already experienced something actually being experienced for the first time. **2.a.** An impression of having seen or experienced something before: *Old-timers watched the stock-market crash with a distinct sense of déjà vu.* **b.** Dull familiarity; monotony: *the déjà vu of the tabloid headlines.* [French : *déjà,* already + *vu,* seen.]

de·ject (dĭ-jĕkt′) *tr.v.* **-ject·ed, -ject·ing, -jects.** To lower the spirits of; dishearten. [Middle English *dejecten,* from Latin *dēicere, dēiect-,* to cast down : *dē-,* de- + *iacere,* to throw; see **yē-** in Appendix.]

de·ject·ed (dĭ-jĕk′tĭd) *adj.* Being in low spirits; depressed. See Synonyms at **depressed. —de·ject′ed·ly** *adv.* **—de·ject′ed·ness** *n.*

de·jec·tion (dĭ-jĕk′shən) *n.* **1.** The state of being dejected; low spirits. **2.** *Medicine.* **a.** Evacuation of the bowels; defecation. **b.** Excrement.

de ju·re (dē jo͝or′ē, dā yo͝or′ā) *adv. & adj.* *Law.* According to law; by right. [Latin *dē iūre* : *dē,* from + *iūre,* ablative of *iūs,* law.]

dek– or **deka–** *pref.* Variants of **deca–.**

dek·a·gram (dĕk′ə-grăm′) *n.* *Abbr.* **dkg** Variant of **decagram.**

De Kalb (dĭ kălb′). A city of northern Illinois south-southeast of Rockford. It is a manufacturing center in a farming region. Population, 33,099.

dek·a·li·ter (dĕk′ə-lē′tər) *n.* *Abbr.* **dkl** Variant of **decaliter.**

dek·a·me·ter (dĕk′ə-mē′tər) *n.* *Abbr.* **dkm** Variant of **decameter.**

deke (dēk) *Sports.* *tr.v.* **deked, dek·ing, dekes.** To deceive (an opponent) in ice hockey by a fake: *deked the goalie with a move from left to right.* **—deke** *n.* A fake, intended to deceive a member of an opposing team. [Short for DECOY.]

Dek·ker (dĕk′ər), **Thomas.** 1572–1632. English playwright whose comedy *The Shoemaker's Holiday* (1600) is notable for its vivid portrayal of daily life in London.

de Koo·ning (dĭ ko͞o′nĭng), **Willem.** Born 1904. Dutch-born American painter and leader of the abstract expressionist school.

In the 1950's he produced a monumental series entitled *Woman,* characterized by unrestrained color and a violent treatment of subject matter. His wife, **Elaine Fried de Kooning** (1920–1989), painted in a variety of styles, often devoting numerous works to a single theme, as in her drawings and portraits of John F. Kennedy.

del. *abbr.* **1.** Delegate; delegation. **2.** Delete.

Del. *abbr.* Delaware.

De·la·croix (də-lä-krwä′), **(Ferdinand Victor) Eugène.** 1798–1863. French romantic painter known for his vast, dramatic canvases and exuberant use of color, as in *The Massacre of Chios* (1824) and *Liberty Leading the People* (1831).

Del·a·go·a Bay (dĕl′ə-gō′ə). An inlet of the Indian Ocean in southern Mozambique. The bay was discovered by the Portuguese in 1502 and explored after 1544. Portugal's claim to the area was upheld in 1875 after a dispute with Great Britain.

de la Mare (də lə mâr′, dĕl′ə-mâr′), **Walter John.** 1873–1956. British writer whose delight in the fantasy world of childhood is reflected in his poems and novels, such as *Early One Morning* (1935).

de·lam·i·nate (dē-lăm′ə-nāt′) *intr.v.* **-nat·ed, -nat·ing, -nates.** To split into thin layers.

de·lam·i·na·tion (dē-lăm′ə-nā′shən) *n.* **1.** The act of splitting or separating a laminate into layers. **2.** *Embryology.* The splitting of the blastoderm into two layers of cells to form a gastrula.

De·land (də-lănd′), **Margaret.** 1857–1945. American writer whose works, many of them set in her native Pennsylvania, include *The Awakening of Helen Richie* (1906) and its sequel, *The Iron Woman* (1911).

De·la·ney (də-lā′nē), **Shelagh.** Born 1930. British playwright best known for *A Taste of Honey* (1958).

De·la·no (də-lā′nō). A city of south-central California in the San Joaquin Valley north-northwest of Bakersfield. It is a processing and shipping center. Population, 16,491.

De·lan·y (də-lā′nē), **Martin Robinson.** 1812–1885. American physician and social reformer who founded and edited the *North Star* (1847–1849) with Frederick Douglass.

de la Roche (də lə rōch′, rôsh′), **Mazo.** 1885–1961. Canadian writer known for her series of 16 novels, including *Jalna* (1927), featuring the Whiteoak family of Ontario.

De·la·roche (də-lä-rōsh′, -rôsh′), **Hippolyte Paul.** 1797–1856. French portrait and mural painter whose eclectic works combined elements of the classical and romantic schools.

De·la·vigne (də-lä-vēn′yə), **(Jean François) Casimir.** 1793–1843. French writer known for his dramas and for his satiric elegies *Les Messéniennes* (1818).

Del·a·ware¹ (dĕl′ə-wâr′) *n., pl.* **Delaware** or **-wares. 1.a.** A group of closely related Native American peoples formerly inhabiting the Delaware and Hudson river valleys and the area between, with present-day populations in Oklahoma, Kansas, Wisconsin, and Ontario. The Delaware formed a variety of political alliances in their westward migration after losing their lands to white settlement in the 17th and 18th centuries. **b.** A member of a Delaware people. Also called *Lenape, Lenni Lenape.* **2.** One or both of the Algonquian languages of the Delaware. **—Del′a·war′e·an** *adj.*

Del·a·ware² (dĕl′ə-wâr′). **1.** *Abbr.* **DE, Del.** A state of the eastern United States on the Atlantic Ocean. It was admitted as the first of the original Thirteen Colonies in 1787. Settled by the Dutch in 1631 and by Swedes in 1638, the region passed to England in 1664. It was part of William Penn's Pennsylvania grant from 1682 until 1776. Dover is the capital and Wilmington the largest city. Population, 594,317. **2.** A city of central Ohio north of Columbus. Rutherford B. Hayes was born here. Population, 18,780.

Del·a·ware³ (dĕl′ə-wâr′) *n.* A variety of grape having sweet, light red fruit. [After DELAWARE².]

Delaware Bay. An estuary of the Delaware River emptying into the Atlantic Ocean between eastern Delaware and southern New Jersey.

Delaware River. A river rising in the Catskill Mountains of southeast New York and flowing about 451 km (280 mi) generally southward along the New York–Pennsylvania border and the Pennsylvania–New Jersey border to northern Delaware, where it enters Delaware Bay. The Dutch explorers named it the South River to distinguish it from the North River, an estuary of the Hudson River.

De La Warr (dĕl′ə wâr′, wər), Baron. Title of Thomas West. 1577–1618. English-born American colonial administrator chosen as the first governor of the Virginia Company colony. He arrived at Jamestown in 1610 in time to prevent the colonists from deserting the settlement.

de·lay (dĭ-lā′) *v.* **-layed, -lay·ing, -lays.** —*tr.* **1.** To postpone until a later time; defer. **2.** To cause to be later or slower than expected or desired: *Heavy traffic delayed us.* —*intr.* To act or move slowly; put off an action or a decision. **—delay** *n.* **1.** The act of delaying; postponement: *responded without delay.* **2.** The condition of being delayed; detainment. **3.** The period of time during which one is delayed. **4.** The interval of time between two events. [Middle English *delaien,* from Anglo-Norman *delaier,* from Old French *deslaier* : *des-,* de- + *laier,* to leave, of Germanic origin. See **leip-** in Appendix.] **—de·lay′er** *n.*

SYNONYMS: *delay, slow, retard, detain.* These verbs mean to cause to be later or slower than expected or desired. To *delay* is to cause to be behind schedule: *The bus was delayed by a cloudburst. Slow* implies a decrease in speed, often deliberate: *A sprained ankle slowed my pace. The driver slowed the car before coming to a full stop.* To *retard* is to slow and delay or impede progress, action, or accomplishment: *"the increasing hatred, which retarded the execution of his great designs"* (Edward Gibbon). *Detain* stresses being held back and prevented from proceeding: *She was detained by an unexpected visitor.*

Del·brück (dĕl′bro͝ok′, -brük′), **Max.** 1906–1981. German-born American biologist. He shared a 1969 Nobel Prize for investigating the mechanism of viral infection in living cells.

Del City (dĕl). A city of central Oklahoma, a residential suburb of Oklahoma City. Population, 28,523.

de·le (dē′lē) *Printing. n.* A sign indicating that something is to be removed from typeset matter. **—dele** *tr.v.* **-led, -le·ing, -les. 1.** To remove, especially from written or typeset matter; delete. **2.** To mark with a sign indicating deletion. [Latin *dēle,* third person sing. imperative of *dēlēre,* to delete.]

de·lec·ta·ble (dĭ-lĕk′tə-bəl) *adj.* **1.** Greatly pleasing; delightful. **2.** Greatly pleasing to the taste; delicious. See Synonyms at **delicious. —delectable** *n.* Something delightful or delicious: *a feast of home-cooked delectables.* [Middle English, from Old French, from Latin *dēlectābilis,* from *dēlectāre,* to please. See DELIGHT.] **—de·lec′ta·bil′i·ty, de·lec′ta·ble·ness** *n.* **—de·lec′ta·bly** *adv.*

de·lec·ta·tion (dē′lĕk-tā′shən) *n.* **1.** Delight. **2.** Enjoyment; pleasure. See Synonyms at **pleasure.** [Middle English *delectacioun,* from Old French, from Latin *dēlectātiō, dēlectātiōn-,* from *dēlectus,* past participle of *dēlectāre,* to please. See DELIGHT.]

De·led·da (dĕ-lĕd′dä), **Grazia.** 1875–1936. Italian writer many of whose novels and short stories reflect her Sardinian background. She won the 1926 Nobel Prize for literature.

del·e·ga·cy (dĕl′ĭ-gə-sē) *n., pl.* **-cies. 1.** The act of delegating or state of being delegated. **2.** The authority, office, or position of a delegate. **3.** A body of delegates; a delegation.

de·le·gal·ize (dē-lē′gə-līz′) *tr.v.* **-ized, -iz·ing, -iz·es.** To revoke the legality of: *After two years the state legislature delegalized gambling.* **—de·le′gal·i·za′tion** (-gə-lĭ-zā′shən) *n.*

del·e·gate (dĕl′ĭ-gāt′, -gĭt) *n. Abbr.* **del. 1.** A person authorized to act as representative for another; a deputy or an agent. **2.** A representative to a conference or convention. **3.** A member of a House of Delegates, the lower house of the Maryland, Virginia, or West Virginia legislature. **4.** An elected or appointed representative of a U.S. territory in the House of Representatives who is entitled to speak but not vote. **—delegate** (-gāt′) *tr.v.* **-gat·ed, -gat·ing, -gates. 1.** To authorize and send (another person) as one's representative. **2.** To commit or entrust to another: *delegate a task to a subordinate.* **3.** *Law.* To appoint (one's debtor) as a debtor to one's creditor in place of oneself. [Middle English *delegat,* from Medieval Latin *dēlēgātus,* from past participle of *dēlēgāre,* to dispatch : *dē-,* de- + *lēgāre,* to send; see **leg-** in Appendix.] **—del′e·ga′tor** *n.*

del·e·ga·tion (dĕl′ĭ-gā′shən) *n.* **1.a.** The act of delegating. **b.** The condition of being delegated. **2.** *Abbr.* **del.** A person or group of persons officially elected or appointed to represent another or others.

de·le·git·i·mize (dē′lə-jĭt′ə-mīz′) *tr.v.* **-mized, -miz·ing, -miz·es.** To revoke the legal or legitimate status of: *an attempt to delegitimize the Vichy government; delegitimized the dictator in the eyes of the world.* **—de′le·git′i·mi·za′tion** (-mĭ-zā′shən) *n.*

de Les·seps (də lĕs′əps, lĕ-sĕps′), Vicomte **Ferdinand Marie.** See Ferdinand Marie de **Lesseps.**

de·lete (dĭ-lēt′) *tr.v.* **-let·ed, -let·ing, -letes.** *Abbr.* **del.** To remove by striking out or canceling: *deleted some unnecessary words in the first draft.* See Synonyms at **erase.** [Latin *dēlēre, dēlēt-,* to wipe out.]

del·e·te·ri·ous (dĕl′ĭ-tîr′ē-əs) *adj.* Having a harmful effect; injurious. [From Greek *dēlētērios,* from *dēlētēr,* destroyer, from *dēleisthai,* to harm.] **—del′e·te′ri·ous·ly** *adv.* **—del′e·te′ri·ous·ness** *n.*

de·le·tion (dĭ-lē′shən) *n.* **1.** The act of deleting; removal by striking out. **2.** Material, such as a word or passage, that has been removed from a body of written or printed matter. **3.** *Genetics.* The loss, as through mutation, of one or more nucleotides from a chromosome.

delft (dĕlft) *n.* **1.** A style of glazed earthenware, usually blue and white, originally made in Delft, Netherlands. **2.** Pottery made in this style.

Delft (dĕlft). A city of southwest Netherlands southeast of The Hague. Fine pottery has been produced here since the 16th century. Population, 86,733.

Del·hi (dĕl′ē). A city of north-central India on the Jumna River. Important since ancient times, the old city was rebuilt by Shah Jahan in the 17th century with high stone walls enclosing the Red Fort that contained the imperial Mogul palace. The new part of Delhi became the capital of British India in 1912 and of independent India in 1947. Population, 4,884,234.

del·i (dĕl′ē) *n., pl.* **-is.** *Informal.* A delicatessen. —*attributive.* Often used to modify another noun: *deli food; a deli restaurant.*

Eugène Delacroix

delft
Early 18th-century Rosh Hashanah plate

ă pat	oi boy
ā pay	ou out
âr care	o͝o took
ä father	o͞o boot
ĕ pet	ŭ cut
ē be	ûr urge
ĭ pit	th thin
ī pie	*th* this
îr pier	hw which
ŏ pot	zh vision
ō toe	ə about, item
ô paw	♦ regionalism

Stress marks: ′ (primary); ′ (secondary), as in **dictionary** (dĭk′shə-nĕr′ē)

de·lib·er·ate (dĭ-lĭb′ər-ĭt) *adj.* **1.** Done with or marked by full consciousness of the nature and effects; intentional: *mistook the oversight for a deliberate insult.* **2.** Arising from or marked by careful consideration: *a deliberate decision.* See Synonyms at **voluntary. 3.** Unhurried in action, movement, or manner, as if trying to avoid error: *moved at a deliberate pace.* See Synonyms at **slow. —deliberate** (-ə-rāt′) *v.* **-at·ed, -at·ing, -ates.** *—intr.* **1.** To think carefully and often slowly, as about a choice to be made. **2.** To consult with another or others in a process of reaching a decision. *—tr.* To consider (a matter) carefully and often slowly, as by weighing alternatives. See Synonyms at **ponder.** [Latin *dēlīberātus,* past participle of *dēlīberāre,* to consider, weigh : *dē-,* de- + *lībrāre,* to balance (from *lībra,* a balance, scales).] **—de·lib′er·ate·ly** *adv.* **—de·lib′er·ate·ness** *n.*

de·lib·er·a·tion (dĭ-lĭb′ə-rā′shən) *n.* **1.** The act or process of deliberating. **2. deliberations.** Discussion and consideration of all sides of an issue: *the deliberations of a jury.* **3.** Thoughtfulness in decision or action. **4.** Leisureliness in motion or manner: *The girl stacked the blocks with deliberation.*

de·lib·er·a·tive (dĭ-lĭb′ə-rā′tĭv, -ər-ə-tĭv) *adj.* **1.** Assembled or organized for deliberation or debate: *a deliberative legislature.* **2.** Characterized by or for use in deliberation or debate. **—de·lib′er·a′tive·ly** *adv.* **—de·lib′er·a′tive·ness** *n.*

De·libes (də-lēb′), **(Clément Philibert) Léo.** 1836–1891. French composer of melodic orchestral works, such as the ballets *Coppélia* (1870) and *Sylvia* (1876).

del·i·ca·cy (dĕl′ĭ-kə-sē) *n., pl.* **-cies. 1.** The quality of being delicate. **2.** Something pleasing and appealing, especially a choice food. **3.** Fineness of appearance, construction, or execution; elegance: *brushwork of great delicacy.* **4.** Frailty of bodily constitution or health. **5.** Sensitivity of perception, discrimination, or taste; refinement. **6. a.** Sensitivity to the feelings of others; tact: *phrased the apology with delicacy.* **b.** Sensitivity to what is proper; propriety. **c.** Undue sensitivity to or concern with what may be considered offensive or improper; squeamishness: *scenes that might offend a viewer's delicacy.* **7.** The need for tact in treatment or handling: *a topic of some delicacy.* **8.** Sensitivity to very small changes; precision: *the delicacy of a set of scales.* [Middle English *delicacie,* from *delicat,* delicate. See DELICATE.]

del·i·cate (dĕl′ĭ-kĭt) *adj.* **1.** Pleasing to the senses, especially in a subtle way: *a delicate flavor; a delicate violin passage.* **2.** Exquisitely fine or dainty: *delicate china.* **3.** Frail in constitution or health. **4.** Easily broken or damaged: *a kite too delicate to fly.* **5.** Marked by sensitivity of discrimination: *a critic's delicate perception.* **6. a.** Considerate of the feelings of others. **b.** Concerned with propriety. **c.** Squeamish or fastidious. **7.** Requiring tactful treatment: *a delicate situation.* **8.** Fine or soft in touch or skill: *a surgeon's delicate touch.* **9.** Measuring, indicating, or responding to very small changes; precise: *a delicate set of scales.* **10.** Very subtle in difference or distinction. [Middle English *delicat* and French *délicat,* both from Latin *dēlicātus,* pleasing.] **—del′i·cate·ly** *adv.* **—del′i·cate·ness** *n.*

dells
On the Arkansas River at Independence Pass, Colorado

SYNONYMS: *delicate, choice, dainty, elegant, exquisite, fine.* The central meaning shared by these adjectives is "appealing to refined taste": *a delicate flavor; choice exotic flowers; a dainty dish; elegant handwriting; an exquisite wine; the finest embroidery.* See also Synonyms at **fragile.**

del·i·ca·tes·sen (dĕl′ĭ-kə-tĕs′ən) *n.* **1.** A shop that sells cooked or prepared foods ready for serving. **2.** Ready-to-serve foods such as cheeses, cold cooked meats, and salads. *—attributive.* Often used to modify another noun: *delicatessen food; delicatessen counters.* [German *Delikatessen,* from pl. of *Delikatesse,* delicacy, from French *délicatesse,* from Italian *delicatezza,* from *delicato,* delicate, dainty, from Latin *dēlicātus,* pleasing.]

de·li·cious (dĭ-lĭsh′əs) *adj.* **1.** Highly pleasing or agreeable to the senses, especially of taste or smell. **2.** Very pleasant; delightful: *a delicious revenge.* [Middle English, from Anglo-Norman, from Late Latin *dēliciōsus,* pleasing, from Latin *dēlicia,* pleasure, from *dēlicere,* to allure. See DELIGHT.] **—de·li′cious·ly** *adv.* **—de·li′cious·ness** *n.*

SYNONYMS: *delicious, ambrosial, delectable, luscious, scrumptious, toothsome, yummy.* The central meaning shared by these adjectives is "extremely pleasing to the sense of taste": *a delicious pâté; ambrosial smoked salmon; delectable raspberries; luscious chocolate bonbons; a scrumptious peach; a toothsome apple; yummy fudge.*

De·li·cious (dĭ-lĭsh′əs) *n.* A variety of sweet apple whose flesh is often streaked with yellow and red.

de·lict (dĭ-lĭkt′) *n. Law.* A legal offense; a misdemeanor. [Latin *dēlictum,* from neuter past participle of *dēlinquere,* to offend. See DELINQUENT.]

de·light (dĭ-līt′) *n.* **1.** Great pleasure; joy. See Synonyms at **pleasure. 2.** Something that gives great pleasure or enjoyment. **—delight** *v.* **-light·ed, -light·ing, -lights.** *—intr.* **1.** To take great pleasure or joy: *delights in taking long walks.* **2.** To give great pleasure or joy: *an old movie that still delights.* *—tr.* To please greatly. See Synonyms at **please.** [Middle English *delit,* from Old French, a pleasure, from *delitier,* to please, charm, from Latin *dēlectāre,* frequentative of *dēlicere,* to allure : *dē-,* de- + *lacere,* to entice.]

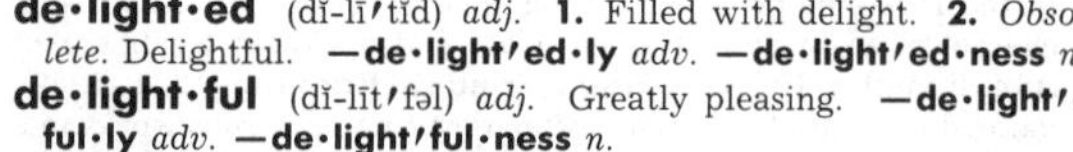

de·light·ed (dĭ-lī′tĭd) *adj.* **1.** Filled with delight. **2.** *Obsolete.* Delightful. **—de·light′ed·ly** *adv.* **—de·light′ed·ness** *n.*

de·light·ful (dĭ-līt′fəl) *adj.* Greatly pleasing. **—de·light′ful·ly** *adv.* **—de·light′ful·ness** *n.*

de·light·some (dĭ-līt′səm) *adj.* Delightful. **—de·light′some·ly** *adv.* **—de·light′some·ness** *n.*

De·li·lah (də-lī′lə). In the Old Testament, a mistress of Samson who betrayed him to the Philistines by having his hair shorn while he slept, thus depriving him of his strength.

de·lim·it (dĭ-lĭm′ĭt) also **de·lim·i·tate** (-ĭ-tāt′) *tr.v.* **-it·ed, -it·ing, -its** also **-tat·ed, -tat·ing, -tates.** To establish the limits or boundaries of; demarcate. [French *délimiter,* from Latin *dēlīmitāre* : *dē-,* de- + *līmitāre,* to limit (from *līmes, līmit-,* boundary line).] **—de·lim′i·ta′tion** *n.* **—de·lim′i·ta′tive** *adj.*

de·lim·it·er (dĭ-lĭm′ĭ-tər) *n. Computer Science.* A character marking the beginning or end of a unit of data.

de·lin·e·ate (dĭ-lĭn′ē-āt′) *tr.v.* **-at·ed, -at·ing, -ates. 1.** To draw or trace the outline of; sketch out. **2.** To represent pictorially; depict. **3.** To depict in words or gestures; describe. See Synonyms at **represent.** [Latin *dēlīneāre, dēlīneāt-* : *dē-,* de- + *līnea,* line, thread; see LINE [1].] **—de·lin′e·a′tion** *n.* **—de·lin′e·a′tive** *adj.* **—de·lin′e·a′tor** *n.*

de·lin·quen·cy (dĭ-lĭng′kwən-sē, -lĭn′-) *n., pl.* **-cies. 1.** Juvenile delinquency. **2.** Failure to do what law or duty requires. **3.** An offense or a misdemeanor; a misdeed. **4.** A debt or other financial obligation on which payment is overdue. **—delinquency** *adj.* Of or relating to juvenile delinquency: *delinquency problems.*

de·lin·quent (dĭ-lĭng′kwənt, -lĭn′-) *adj.* **1.** Failing to do what law or duty requires. **2.** Overdue in payment: *a delinquent account.* **—delinquent** *n.* **1.** A juvenile delinquent. **2.** A person who neglects or fails to do what law or duty requires. [Latin *dēlinquēns, dēlinquent-,* present participle of *dēlinquere,* to offend : *dē-,* de- + *linquere,* to leave, abandon; see **leikʷ-** in Appendix.] **—de·lin′quent·ly** *adv.*

del·i·quesce (dĕl′ĭ-kwĕs′) *intr.v.* **-quesced, -quesc·ing, -quesc·es. 1. a.** To melt away. **b.** To disappear as if by melting. **2.** *Chemistry.* To dissolve and become liquid by absorbing moisture from the air. See Synonyms at **melt. 3.** *Botany.* **a.** To branch out into numerous subdivisions that lack a main axis, as the stem of an elm. **b.** To become fluid or soft on maturing, as certain fungi. [Latin *dēliquēscere* : *dē-,* de- + *liquēscere,* to melt, inchoative of *liquēre,* to be liquid.] **—del′i·ques′cence** *n.* **—del′i·ques′cent** *adj.*

de·lir·i·a (dĭ-lîr′ē-ə) *n.* A plural of **delirium.**

de·lir·i·ous (dĭ-lîr′ē-əs) *adj.* **1.** Of, suffering from, or characteristic of delirium. **2.** Marked by uncontrolled excitement or emotion; ecstatic: *delirious joy; a crowd of delirious baseball fans.* **—de·lir′i·ous·ly** *adv.* **—de·lir′i·ous·ness** *n.*

de·lir·i·um (dĭ-lîr′ē-əm) *n., pl.* **-i·ums** or **-i·a** (-ē-ə). **1.** A temporary state of mental confusion and clouded consciousness resulting from high fever, intoxication, shock, or other causes. It is characterized by anxiety, disorientation, hallucinations, delusions, trembling, and incoherent speech. **2.** A state of uncontrolled excitement or emotion: *sports fans in delirium after their team's victory.* [Latin *dēlīrium,* from *dēlīrāre,* to be deranged : *dē-,* de- + *līra,* furrow; see **leis-** [1] in Appendix.] **—de·lir′i·ant** *adj.*

delirium tre·mens (trē′mənz) *n.* An acute, sometimes fatal episode of delirium usually caused by withdrawal or abstinence from alcohol following habitual, excessive drinking. It also may occur during an episode of heavy alcohol consumption. [New Latin *dēlīrium tremēns* : Latin *dēlīrium,* delirium + Latin *tremēns,* trembling.]

de·list (dē-lĭst′) *tr.v.* **-list·ed, -list·ing, -lists.** To remove from a list, especially from a list of securities that may be traded on a stock exchange: *delisted the stock.*

De·lius (dē′lē-əs, dēl′yəs), **Frederick.** 1862–1934. British composer who spent most of his life in France. His work, influenced by Edvard Grieg, combines romanticism and impressionism.

de·liv·er (dĭ-lĭv′ər) *v.* **-ered, -er·ing, -ers.** *—tr.* **1.** To bring or transport to the proper place or recipient; distribute: *deliver groceries; deliver the mail.* **2.** To surrender (someone or something) to another; hand over: *delivered the criminal to the police.* **3.** To secure (something promised or desired), as for a candidate or political party: *campaign workers who delivered the ward for the mayor.* **4.** To throw or hurl: *The pitcher delivered the ball.* **5.** To strike (a blow). **6.** To express in words; declare or utter: *deliver a lecture.* **7. a.** To give birth to: *She delivered a baby boy this morning.* **b.** To assist (a woman) in giving birth: *The doctor delivered her of twins.* **c.** To assist or aid in the birth of: *The midwife delivered the baby.* **8.** To give forth or produce: *The oil well delivered only 50 barrels a day.* **9.** To set free, as from misery, peril, or evil: *deliver a captive from slavery.* See Synonyms at **save** [1]. *—intr.* **1.** To produce or achieve what is desired or expected; make good: *The senator delivered on her pledge. He is a manager who just can't seem to deliver.* **2.** To give birth: *She expects to deliver in late August.* ***—idiom.* deliver (oneself) of.** To pronounce; utter: *Before leaving I delivered myself of a few choice comments.* [Middle English *deliveren,* from Old French *delivrer,* from Late Latin *dēlīberāre* : Latin *dē-,* de- + *līberāre,* to free (from *līber,* free; see **leudh-** in Appendix).] **—de·liv′er·a·bil′i·ty** *n.* **—de·liv′er·a·ble** *adj.* **—de·liv′er·er** *n.*

de·liv·er·ance (dĭ-lĭv′ər-əns, -lĭv′rəns) *n.* **1.** The act of delivering or the condition of being delivered. **2.** Rescue from bondage or danger. **3.** A publicly expressed opinion or judgment, such as the verdict of a jury.

de·liv·er·y (dĭ-lĭv′ə-rē, -lĭv′rē) *n., pl.* **-ies.** *Abbr.* **dely., dlvy., dy. 1.a.** The act of conveying or delivering. **b.** Something delivered, as a shipment or package. **2.a.** The act of transferring to another. **b.** *Law.* A formal act of transferring ownership of property to another: *delivery of a deed.* **3.** The act of giving up; surrender. **4.** The act or manner of throwing or discharging. **5.** The act of giving birth; parturition. **6.a.** Utterance or enunciation: *The historic speech required but two minutes in delivery.* **b.** The act or manner of speaking or singing: *a folk singer's casual delivery.* **7.** The act of releasing or rescuing.

delivery room *n.* **1.** A room or an area in a hospital that is equipped for delivering babies. **2.** A room or an area set aside for making or receiving deliveries, as for circulating books in a library.

delivery system *n.* **1.** A means or procedure for providing a product or service to the public: *the health care delivery system.* **2.** A means, technology, or device for administering drugs to a patient. **3.** The technology for conveying nuclear weapons to their targets.

dell (dĕl) *n.* A small, secluded, wooded valley. [Middle English *del,* from Old English *dell.*]

del·la Rob·bia (dĕl′ə rō′bē-ə, dĕl′lä rôb′byä), **Luca.** 1400?–1482. Italian sculptor noted for his works of enameled terra cotta, for which he perfected a special glazing made of tin, antimony, and other substances. His nephew **Andrea** (1435–1525) and Andrea's son **Giovanni** (1469–1529) successively took over his workshop, one of the most important of the Florentine Renaissance.

dells (dĕlz) *pl.n.* The rapids of a river. [Alteration (influenced by DELL) of DALLES.]

Del·mar·va Peninsula (dĕl-mär′və). A peninsula of the eastern United States separating Chesapeake Bay from Delaware Bay and the Atlantic Ocean. It includes all of Delaware and parts of eastern Maryland and Virginia.

Del·mon·i·co (dĕl-mŏn′ĭ-kō′), **Lorenzo.** 1813–1881. Swiss-born American restaurateur who popularized European cuisine in New York City and is largely credited with establishing the restaurant as an institution in American cities.

Delmonico steak *n.* A small, often boned steak from the front section of the short loin of beef. Also called *club steak.* [After Lorenzo DELMONICO.]

de·lo·cal·ize (dē-lō′kə-līz′) *tr.v.* **-ized, -iz·ing, -iz·es. 1.** To remove from a native or usual locality. **2.** To broaden the range or scope of. **—de·lo′cal·i·za′tion** (-kə-lĭ-zā′shən) *n.*

De·lorme or **de l'Orme** (də-lôrm′), **Philibert.** 1515?–1570. French royal architect who directed the construction at Fontainebleau and built the Tuileries for Catherine de Médicis.

De·los (dē′lŏs′, dĕl′ōs). An island of southeast Greece in the southern Aegean Sea. It is the smallest of the Cyclades Islands and was traditionally considered sacred to Apollo.

de·louse (dē-lous′) *tr.v.* **-loused, -lous·ing, -lous·es.** To rid (a person or an animal) of lice by physical or chemical means.

Del·phi (dĕl′fī′). An ancient town of central Greece near Mount Parnassus. Dating to at least the seventh century B.C., it was the seat of a famous oracle of Apollo.

Del·phic (dĕl′fĭk) also **Del·phi·an** (-fē-ən) *adj.* **1.** *Greek Mythology.* Of or relating to Delphi or to the oracle of Apollo at Delphi. **2.** Obscurely prophetic; oracular: *made a great deal of Delphic pronouncements.* **—Del′phi·cal·ly** *adv.*

del·phin·i·um (dĕl-fĭn′ē-əm) *n.* A plant of the genus *Delphinium,* especially any of several tall cultivated varieties having palmate leaves and long racemes of showy, variously colored spurred flowers. Also called *larkspur.* [New Latin *Delphinium,* genus name, from Greek *delphinion,* larkspur, diminutive of *delphis, delphin-,* dolphin (from the shape of the nectary).]

Del·phi·nus (dĕl-fī′nəs) *n.* A constellation in the Northern Hemisphere near Pegasus and Aquila. [Latin *delphīnus,* dolphin. See DOLPHIN.]

Del·ray Beach (dĕl′rā′). A city of southeast Florida on the Atlantic Ocean north of Boca Raton. Settled in 1901, it is a tourist resort. Population, 34,325.

Del Ri·o (dĕl rē′ō). A city of southwest Texas on the Rio Grande west of San Antonio. Founded in 1868, it is a market and shipping center in an agricultural region. Population, 30,034.

del·ta (dĕl′tə) *n.* **1.** The fourth letter of the Greek alphabet. See table at **alphabet. 2.** An object shaped like a triangle. **3.a.** A usually triangular alluvial deposit at the mouth of a river. **b.** A similar deposit at the mouth of a tidal inlet, caused by tidal currents. **4.** *Mathematics.* A finite increment in a variable. [Middle English, from Latin, from Greek; akin to Hebrew *delet,* door, from Phoenician *dalt.*] **—del·ta′ic** (-tā′ĭk), **del′tic** (-tĭk) *adj.*

WORD HISTORY: A Δ sits at the mouth of many rivers. The Greeks, noticing the resemblance between the island formed by sediment at the mouth of a river such as the Nile and the triangular shape of their letter delta, gave the name *delta* to such an island. English borrowed this sense from Greek, although the word *delta* appeared first in English as the name of the letter, in a work written possibly around 1200. The sense "alluvial deposit" is not recorded until 1555, when *delta* is used with reference to the Nile River delta.

delta ray *n.* An electron ejected from matter by ionizing radiation.

delta wave *n.* A slow brain wave, having a frequency of fewer than six cycles per second, that emanates from the forward portion of the brain and is associated with deep sleep in normal adults. Also called *delta rhythm.*

delta wing *n.* An aircraft with swept-back wings that give it the appearance of an isosceles triangle.

del·ti·ol·o·gy (dĕl′tē-ŏl′ə-jē) *n.* The collection and study of postcards. [From Greek *deltion,* diminutive of *deltos,* writing tablet, letter.]

del·toid (dĕl′toid′) *n.* A thick, triangular muscle covering the shoulder joint, used to raise the arm from the side. **—deltoid** *adj.* **1.** Triangular. **2.** Of or relating to the deltoid. [New Latin *deltoidēs,* from Greek *deltoeidēs,* triangular : *delta,* delta; see DELTA + *-oeidēs,* -oid.]

de·lude (dĭ-lo͞od′) *tr.v.* **-lud·ed, -lud·ing, -ludes. 1.** To deceive the mind or judgment of: *fraudulent ads that delude consumers into sending in money.* See Synonyms at **deceive. 2.** *Obsolete.* To elude or evade. **3.** *Obsolete.* To frustrate the hopes or plans of. [Middle English *deluden,* from Latin *dēlūdere* : *dē-,* de- + *lūdere,* to play; see **leid-** in Appendix.] **—de·lud′er** *n.* **—de·lud′ing·ly** *adv.*

del·uge (dĕl′yo͞oj) *n.* **1.a.** A great flood. **b.** A heavy downpour. **2.** Something that overwhelms as if by a great flood: *a deluge of fan mail.* **3. Deluge.** *Bible.* In the Old Testament, the great flood that occurred in the time of Noah. **—deluge** *tr.v.* **-uged, -ug·ing, -ug·es. 1.** To overrun with water; inundate. **2.** To overwhelm with a large number or amount; swamp: *The press secretary was deluged with requests for information.* [From Middle English, flood, from Old French, from Latin *dīluvium,* from *dīluere,* to wash away : *dis-,* apart; see DIS– + *-luere,* to wash; see **leu(ə)-** in Appendix.]

de·lu·sion (dĭ-lo͞o′zhən) *n.* **1.a.** The act or process of deluding. **b.** The state of being deluded. **2.** A false belief or opinion: *labored under the delusion that success was at hand.* **3.** *Psychiatry.* A false belief strongly held in spite of invalidating evidence, especially as a symptom of mental illness: *delusions of persecution.* [Middle English *delusioun,* from Latin *dēlūsiō, dēlūsiōn-,* from *dēlūsus,* past participle of *dēlūdere,* to delude. See DELUDE.] **—de·lu′sion·al** *adj.*

de·lu·sive (dĭ-lo͞o′sĭv) *adj.* **1.** Tending to delude. See Synonyms at **misleading. 2.** Having the nature of a delusion; false: *a delusive faith in a wonder drug.* **—de·lu′sive·ly** *adv.* **—de·lu′sive·ness** *n.*

de·lu·so·ry (dĭ-lo͞o′sə-rē, -zə-) *adj.* Tending to deceive; delusive. See Synonyms at **misleading.**

de luxe also **de·luxe** (dĭ-lŭks′, -lo͝oks′) *—adj.* Particularly elegant and luxurious; sumptuous: *a de luxe automobile; deluxe accommodations.* *—adv.* In an elegant and luxurious manner; sumptuously: *traveling de luxe.* [French : *de,* of + *luxe,* luxury.]

delve (dĕlv) *v.* **delved, delv·ing, delves.** *—intr.* **1.** To search deeply and laboriously: *delved into the court records.* **2.** To dig the ground, as with a spade. *—tr.* *Archaic.* To dig (ground) with a spade. [Middle English *delven,* to dig, from Old English *delfan.*] **—delv′er** *n.*

dely. *abbr.* Delivery.

dem. *abbr.* **1.** *Grammar.* Demonstrative. **2.** Demurrage.

Dem. *abbr.* Democrat; Democratic.

de·mag·net·ize (dē-măg′nĭ-tīz′) *tr.v.* **-ized, -iz·ing, -iz·es. a.** To remove magnetic properties from. **b.** To erase (a magnetic storage device). **—de·mag′net·i·za′tion** (-nĭ-tĭ-zā′shən) *n.* **—de·mag′net·iz′er** *n.*

dem·a·gog·ic (dĕm′ə-gŏj′ĭk, -gŏg′-, -gō′jĭk) also **dem·a·gog·i·cal** (-gŏj′ĭ-kəl, -gŏg′-, -gō′jĭ-kəl) *adj.* Of, relating to, or characteristic of a demagogue. **—dem′a·gog′i·cal·ly** *adv.*

dem·a·gog·ism (dĕm′ə-gô′gĭz-əm, -gŏg′ĭz-) *n.* Demagoguery.

dem·a·gogue (dĕm′ə-gôg′, -gŏg′) *n.* **1.** A leader who obtains power by means of impassioned appeals to the emotions and prejudices of the populace. **2.** A leader of the common people in ancient times. [Greek *dēmagōgos,* popular leader : *dēmos,* people; see **dā-** in Appendix + *agōgos,* leading (from *agein,* to lead; see **ag-** in Appendix).]

dem·a·gogu·er·y (dĕm′ə-gô′gə-rē, -gŏg′ə-) *n.* The practices or rhetoric of a demagogue.

dem·a·gog·y (dĕm′ə-gŏj′ē, -gô′jē, -gŏg′ē, -gō′jē) *n.* The character or practices of a demagogue; demagoguery.

de·mand (dĭ-mănd′) *v.* **-mand·ed, -mand·ing, -mands.** *—tr.* **1.** To ask for urgently or peremptorily: *demand an investigation into the murder; demanding that he leave immediately; demanded to speak to the manager.* **2.** To claim as just or due: *demand repayment of a loan.* **3.** To ask to be informed of: *I demand a reason for this interruption.* **4.** To require as useful, just, proper, or necessary; call for: *a gem that demands a fine setting.* **5.** *Law.* **a.** To summon to court. **b.** To claim formally; lay legal claim to. *—intr.* To make a demand. **—demand** *n.* **1.** The act of demanding. **2.** Something demanded: *granted the employees' demands.* **3.** An urgent requirement or need: *the heavy demands of her job; the emotional demands of his marriage; an increased ox-*

delphinium
Spring larkspur
Delphinium tricorne

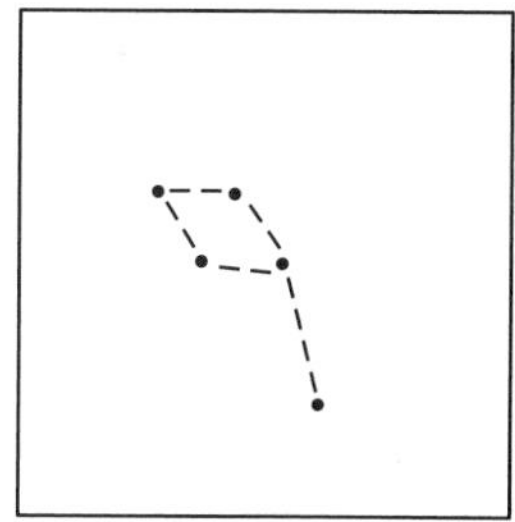

Delphinus

ă pat	oi boy
ā pay	ou out
âr care	o͝o took
ä father	o͞o boot
ĕ pet	ŭ cut
ē be	ûr urge
ĭ pit	th thin
ī pie	*th* this
îr pier	hw which
ŏ pot	zh vision
ō toe	ə about, item
ô paw	♦ regionalism

Stress marks: ′ (primary); ′ (secondary), as in **dictionary** (dĭk′shə-nĕr′ē)

ygen demand. **4.** The state of being sought after: *in great demand as a speaker.* **5.** *Economics.* **a.** The desire to possess a commodity or make use of a service, combined with the ability to purchase it. **b.** The amount of a commodity or service that people are ready to buy for a given price: *Supply should rise to meet demand.* **6.** *Computer Science.* A coding technique in which a command to read or write is initiated as the need for a new block of data occurs, thus eliminating the need to store data. **7.** *Law.* A formal claim. **8.** *Archaic.* An emphatic question or inquiry. ***—idiom.*** **on demand. 1.** When presented for payment: *a note payable on demand.* **2.** When needed or asked for: *fed the baby on demand.* [Middle English *demanden,* from Old French *demander,* to charge with doing, and from Medieval Latin *dēmandāre,* to demand, both from Latin, to entrust : *dē-,* de- + *mandāre,* to entrust; see **man-**[2] in Appendix.] **—de·mand′a·ble** *adj.* **—de·mand′er** *n.*

SYNONYMS: *demand, claim, exact, require.* The central meaning shared by these verbs is "to ask for urgently or insistently": *demanding better working conditions; claiming repayment of a debt; exacted obedience from the child; tax payments required by law.*

de·mand·ant (dĭ-măn′dənt) *n. Archaic.* A plaintiff.

demand deposit *n.* A bank deposit that can be withdrawn without advance notice.

demand draft *n. Abbr.* **D.D.** See **sight draft.**

de·mand·ing (dĭ-măn′dĭng) *adj.* Requiring much effort or attention: *exhausted by a demanding job.* See Synonyms at **burdensome.** **—de·mand′ing·ly** *adv.*

demand loan *n. Abbr.* **D/L** See **call loan.**

demand note *n.* A bill or draft payable in lawful money upon presentation or demand.

de·mand-pull (dĭ-mănd′po͝ol′) *n.* Increased demand for a limited supply of goods and services, tending to cause consumer prices to increase. **—de·mand′-pull′** *adj.*

de·man·toid (dĭ-măn′toid′) *n.* A transparent, green variety of garnet used as a gem. [German, from *Demant,* diamond, from Middle High German *diemant,* from Old French *diamant.* See DIAMOND.]

de·mar·cate (dĭ-mär′kāt′, dē′mär-kāt′) *tr.v.* **-cat·ed, -cat·ing, -cates. 1.** To set the boundaries of; delimit. **2.** To separate clearly as if by boundaries; distinguish: *demarcate categories.* [Back-formation from DEMARCATION.] **—de·mar′ca′tor** *n.*

de·mar·ca·tion also **de·mar·ka·tion** (dē′mär-kā′shən) *n.* **1.** The setting or marking of boundaries or limits. **2.** A separation; a distinction: *a line of demarcation between two rock strata.* [Spanish *demarcación,* from *demarcar,* to mark boundaries : *de-,* off (from Latin *dē-;* see DE–) + *marcar,* to mark (from Italian *marcare,* from Old Italian, of Germanic origin; see **merg-** in Appendix).]

dé·marche (dā-märsh′) *n.* **1.** A course of action; a maneuver. **2.** A diplomatic representation or protest. **3.** A statement or protest addressed by citizens to public authorities. [French, from Old French *demarche,* gait, from *demarchier,* to march : *de-,* de- + *marchier,* to march (probably of Germanic origin; see MARCH[1]).]

de·mar·ka·tion (dē′mär-kā′shən) *n.* Variant of **demarcation.**

de·ma·te·ri·al·ize (dē′mə-tîr′ē-ə-līz′) *tr. & intr.v.* **-ized, -iz·ing, -iz·es.** To deprive of or lose apparent physical substance; make or become immaterial: *Mirrors have the effect of dematerializing a wall. The dry ice seemed to dematerialize as it sublimated.* **—de′ma·te′ri·al·i·za′tion** (-ə-lĭ-zā′shən) *n.*

deme (dēm) *n.* **1.** One of the townships of ancient Attica. **2.** *Ecology.* A local, usually stable population of interbreeding organisms of the same kind or species. [Greek *dēmos,* people, land. See **dā-** in Appendix.]

de·mean[1] (dĭ-mēn′) *tr.v.* **-meaned, -mean·ing, -means.** To conduct or behave (oneself) in a particular manner: *demeaned themselves well in class.* [Middle English *demeinen,* to govern, from Old French *demener* : *de-,* de- + *mener,* to conduct (from Latin *mināre,* to drive (animals), from *minārī,* to threaten, from *minae,* threats; see **men-**[2] in Appendix).]

de·mean[2] (dĭ-mēn′) *tr.v.* **-meaned, -mean·ing, -means. 1.** To debase, as in dignity or social standing: *professionals who feel demeaned by unskilled work.* **2.** To humble (oneself). See Synonyms at **degrade.** [DE– + MEAN[2].] **—de·mean′ing·ly** *adv.*

de·mean·or (dĭ-mē′nər) *n.* The way in which a person behaves; deportment. See Synonyms at **bearing.**

de·ment (dĭ-mĕnt′) *tr.v.* **-ment·ed, -ment·ing, -ments.** To make insane. [Late Latin *dēmentāre,* from Latin *dēmēns, dēment-,* senseless : *dē-,* de- + *mēns,* mind; see **men-**[1] in Appendix.]

de·ment·ed (dĭ-mĕn′tĭd) *adj.* **1.** Mentally ill; insane. **2.** Suffering from dementia. **—de·ment′ed·ly** *adv.* **—de·ment′ed·ness** *n.*

de·men·tia (dĭ-mĕn′shə) *n.* **1.** Deterioration of intellectual faculties, such as memory, concentration, and judgment, resulting from an organic disease or a disorder of the brain. It is often accompanied by emotional disturbance and personality changes. **2.** Madness; insanity. See Synonyms at **insanity.** [Latin *dēmentia,* madness, from *dēmēns, dēment-,* senseless. See DEMENT.] **—de·men′tial** *adj.*

dementia prae·cox (prē′kŏks′) *n.* Schizophrenia. No longer in scientific use. [New Latin : *dēmentia,* dementia + Latin *praecox,* premature.]

de·mer·it (dĭ-mĕr′ĭt) *n.* **1.a.** A quality or characteristic deserving of blame or censure; a fault. **b.** Absence of merit. **2.** A mark made against one's record for a fault or for misconduct. [Middle English *demerite,* offense, from Old French *desmerite,* from Latin *dēmeritum,* from neuter past participle of *dēmerēre,* to deserve : *dē-,* de- + *merēre,* to earn; see MERIT.] **—de·mer′i·to′ri·ous** (-tôr′ē-əs, -tōr′-) *adj.* **—de·mer′i·to′ri·ous·ly** *adv.*

Dem·er·ol (dĕm′ə-rôl′, -rŏl′, -rōl′). A trademark used for a medicinal preparation of meperidine.

de·mer·sal (dĭ-mûr′səl) *adj.* **1.** Dwelling at or near the bottom of a body of water: *a demersal fish.* **2.** Sinking to or deposited near the bottom of a body of water: *demersal fish eggs.* [From Latin *dēmersus,* past participle of *dēmergere,* to sink : *dē-,* de- + *mergere,* to sink.]

de·mesne (dĭ-mān′, -mēn′) *n.* **1.** *Law.* Possession and use of one's own land. **2.** Manorial land retained for the private use of a feudal lord. **3.** The grounds belonging to a mansion or country house. **4.** An extensive piece of landed property; an estate. **5.** A district; a territory. **6.** A realm; a domain. [Middle English *demeine, *demesne,* from Anglo-Norman, from Old French *demaine.* See DOMAIN.]

De·me·ter (dĭ-mē′tər) *n. Greek Mythology.* The goddess of the harvest, daughter of Rhea and Cronus and mother of Persephone. [Greek *Dēmētēr.* See **māter-** in Appendix.]

dem·e·ton (dĕm′ĭ-tŏn′) *n.* Either of two pale-yellow, highly toxic organophosphorous liquids, $C_6H_{15}O_3PS_2$ or $C_6H_{15}O_4PS_2$, used as systemic insecticides. [Blend of *diethyl,* containing two ethyls (DI–[1] + ETHYL), MERCAPTAN and *thionate,* salt or ester of a thionic acid (THION– + –ATE[2]).]

demi– *pref.* **1.** Half: *demirelief.* **2.** To some degree; part; partly: *demigod.* [Middle English *demi,* a half of a measure or unit, from Old French, from Medieval Latin *dīmedius,* from Latin *dīmidius,* divided in half : *dis-,* dis- + *medius,* half; see MEDIUM.]

dem·i·god (dĕm′ē-gŏd′) *n.* **1.** *Mythology.* **a.** A male being, often the offspring of a god and a mortal, who has some but not all of the powers of a god. **b.** An inferior deity; a minor god. **c.** A deified man. **2.** A person who is highly honored or revered.

dem·i·god·dess (dĕm′ē-gŏd′ĭs) *n.* **1.** A female being, often the offspring of a god and a mortal, who has some but not all of the powers of a goddess. **2.** A deified woman.

dem·i·john (dĕm′ē-jŏn′) *n.* A large, narrow-necked bottle made of glass or earthenware, usually encased in wickerwork. [Probably alteration of French *dame-Jeanne* : *dame,* lady; see DAME + *Jeanne,* personal name.]

demijohn

de·mil·i·ta·rize (dē-mĭl′ĭ-tə-rīz′) *tr.v.* **-rized, -riz·ing, -riz·es. 1.** To eliminate the military character of. **2.** To prohibit military forces or installations in: *demilitarize a buffer zone between hostile countries.* **3.** To replace military control of with civilian control. **—de·mil′i·ta·ri·za′tion** (-tər-ĭ-zā′shən) *n.*

de·mil·i·ta·rized zone (dē-mĭl′ĭ-tə-rīzd′) *n. Abbr.* **DMZ** An area from which military forces, operations, and installations are prohibited.

De Mille (də mĭl′), **Agnes George.** Born 1905. American choreographer who introduced innovative dance to a wide public audience with her choreography for *Oklahoma!* (1943), *Carousel* (1945), and other musicals.

De Mille, Cecil Blount. 1881–1959. American filmmaker known for his spectacular epic productions, including *The Ten Commandments* (1923 and 1956).

dem·i·mon·daine (dĕm′ē-mŏn-dān′, -mŏn′dān′) *n.* A woman belonging to the demimonde. [French, from *demi-monde,* demimonde. See DEMIMONDE.]

dem·i·monde (dĕm′ē-mŏnd′) *n.* **1.a.** A class of women kept by wealthy lovers or protectors. **b.** Women prostitutes considered as a group. **2.** A group whose respectability is dubious or whose success is marginal: *the literary demimonde of ghost writers, hacks, and publicists.* In this sense, also called *demiworld.* [French : *demi-,* demi- + *monde,* world (from Latin *mundus*).]

de·min·er·al·i·za·tion (dē-mĭn′ər-ə-lĭ-zā′shən) *n.* **1.** The act or process of removing minerals or mineral salts from a liquid, such as water. **2.** The loss, deprivation, or removal of minerals or mineral salts from the body, especially through disease, as the loss of calcium from bones or teeth.

de·min·er·al·ize (dē-mĭn′ər-ə-līz′) *tr.v.* **-ized, -iz·ing, -iz·es.** To remove minerals or mineral salts from (a liquid). **—de·min′er·al·i′zer** *n.*

dem·i·re·lief (dĕm′ē-rĭ-lēf′) *n.* See **half relief.**

dem·i·rep (dĕm′ē-rĕp′) *n.* A person of doubtful reputation or respectability. [DEMI– + REP(UTATION).]

de·mise (dĭ-mīz′) *n.* **1.a.** Death. **b.** The end of existence or activity; termination: *the demise of the streetcar.* **2.** *Law.* Transfer of an estate by lease or will. **3.** The transfer of a ruler's authority by death or abdication. **—demise** *v.* **-mised, -mis·ing, -mis·es.** *—tr.* **1.** *Law.* To transfer (an estate) by will or lease. **2.** To transfer (sovereignty) by abdication or will. *—intr.* **1.** *Law.* To be transferred by will or descent: *The land demised to a charitable institution.* **2.** To die. [Middle English, transfer of property, from Old French *dimis,* past participle of *demettre,* to release. See DEMIT.] **—de·mis′a·ble** *adj.*

dem·i·sem·i·qua·ver (dĕm′ē-sĕm′ē-kwā′vər) *n. Chiefly British.* A thirty-second note.

de·mis·sion (dĭ-mĭsh′ən) *n.* Relinquishment of an office or

ă pat	oi boy
ā pay	ou out
âr care	o͝o took
ä father	o͞o boot
ĕ pet	ŭ cut
ē be	ûr urge
ĭ pit	th thin
ī pie	*th* this
îr pier	hw which
ŏ pot	zh vision
ō toe	ə about, item
ô paw	♦ regionalism

Stress marks: **′** (primary); ′ (secondary), as in **dictionary** (dĭk′shə-nĕr′ē)

function. [Middle English *dimissioun,* from Anglo-Norman, from Latin *dīmissiō, dīmissiōn-,* dismissal, from *dīmissus,* past participle of *dīmittere,* to release. See DEMIT.]

de·mit (dĭ-mĭt′) *v.* **-mit·ted, -mit·ting, -mits.** —*tr.* **1.** To relinquish (an office or function). **2.** *Archaic.* To dismiss. —*intr.* To give up an office or position; resign. [Middle English *dimitten,* to release, from Old French *demettre,* from Latin *dīmittere* : *dis-,* away; see DIS– + *mittere,* to send.]

dem·i·tasse (dĕm′ē-tăs′, -täs′) *n.* **1.** A small cup of strong black coffee or espresso. **2.** The small cup used to serve this drink. [French : *demi-,* demi- + *tasse,* cup (from Old French, from Arabic *ṭašt,* basin, from Persian).]

dem·i·urge (dĕm′ē-ûrj′) *n.* **1.** A powerful creative force or personality. **2.** A public magistrate in some ancient Greek states. **3. Demiurge.** A deity in Gnosticism, Manicheeism, and other religions who creates the material world and is sometimes viewed as the originator of evil. **4. Demiurge.** A Platonic deity who orders or fashions the material world out of chaos. [Late Latin *dēmiurgus,* from Greek *dēmiourgos,* artisan : *dēmios,* public (from *dēmos,* people; see **dā-** in Appendix) + *ergos,* worker (from *ergon,* work; see **werg-** in Appendix).] —**dem′i·ur′geous** (-ûr′jəs), **dem′i·ur′gic** (-jĭk) , **dem′i·ur′gi·cal** (-jĭ-kəl) *adj.* —**dem′i·ur′gi·cal·ly** *adv.*

dem·i·world (dĕm′ē-wûrld′) *n.* See **demimonde** (sense 2).

dem·o (dĕm′ō) *n., pl.* **-os.** *Informal.* **1.a.** A demonstration, as of a product or service. **b.** A brief tape or recording used to illustrate the qualities of a musician or other performer. **2.** A product, such as an automobile, used for demonstration and often sold later at a discount. —**dem′o** *v.*

de·mob (dē-mŏb′) *Chiefly British. tr.v.* **-mobbed, -mob·bing, -mobs.** To demobilize (armed forces). —**demob** *n.* Demobilization of armed forces.

de·mo·bil·ize (dē-mō′bə-līz′) *tr.v.* **-ized, -iz·ing, -iz·es.** **1.** To discharge from military service or use. **2.** To disband (troops). —**de·mo′bil·i·za′tion** (-bə-lĭ-zā′shən) *n.*

de·moc·ra·cy (dĭ-mŏk′rə-sē) *n., pl.* **-cies. 1.** Government by the people, exercised either directly or through elected representatives. **2.** A political or social unit that has such a government. **3.** The common people, considered as the primary source of political power. **4.** Majority rule. **5.** The principles of social equality and respect for the individual within a community. [French *démocratie,* from Late Latin *dēmocratia,* from Greek *dēmokratia* : *dēmos,* people; see **dā-** in Appendix + *-kratia,* -cracy.]

dem·o·crat (dĕm′ə-krăt′) *n.* **1.** An advocate of democracy. **2. Democrat.** *Abbr.* **Dem., D, D.** A member of the Democratic Party. [French *démocrate,* back-formation from *démocratie,* democracy. See DEMOCRACY.]

Democrat, Mount. A peak, 4,315.1 m (14,148 ft) high, of central Colorado in the Park Range of the Rocky Mountains.

dem·o·crat·ic (dĕm′ə-krăt′ĭk) *adj.* **1.** Of, characterized by, or advocating democracy: *democratic government; a democratic union.* **2.** Of or for the people in general; popular: *a democratic movement; democratic art forms.* **3.** Believing in or practicing social equality: *"a proper democratic scorn for bloated dukes and lords"* (George du Maurier). **4. Democratic.** *Abbr.* **Dem., D, D.** Of, relating to, or characteristic of the Democratic Party. —**dem′o·crat′i·cal·ly** *adv.*

Democratic Party *n.* One of the two major political parties in the United States, owing its origin to a split in the Democratic-Republican Party under Andrew Jackson in 1828.

Dem·o·crat·ic-Re·pub·li·can Party (dĕm′ə-krăt′ĭk-rĭ-pŭb′lĭ-kən) *n.* A political party in the United States that was opposed to the Federalist Party and was founded by Thomas Jefferson in 1792 and dissolved in 1828.

de·moc·ra·tize (dĭ-mŏk′rə-tīz′) *tr.v.* **-tized, -tiz·ing, -tiz·es.** To make democratic. —**de·moc′ra·ti·za′tion** (-tĭ-zā′shən) *n.*

De·moc·ri·tus (dĭ-mŏk′rĭ-təs). Known as "the Laughing Philosopher." 460?–370? B.C. Greek philosopher who developed an atomist theory of the universe and espoused the doctrine that pleasure, along with self-control, is the goal of human life.

dé·mo·dé (dā′mō-dā′) *adj.* No longer in fashion; outmoded. [French, past participle of *démoder,* to outmode : *dé-,* out (from Old French *de-;* see DE–) + *mode,* fashion; see MODE.]

de·mod·u·late (dē-mŏj′ə-lāt′, -mŏd′yə-) *tr.v.* **-lat·ed, -lat·ing, -lates.** To extract (information) from a modulated carrier wave. —**de·mod′u·la′tor** *n.*

de·mod·u·la·tion (dē-mŏj′ə-lā′shən) *n.* The conversion of a modulated carrier wave into a current equivalent to the original signal. Also called *detection.*

De·mo·gor·gon (dē′mə-gôr′gən, dē′mə-gôr′-) *n. Mythology.* A terrifying ancient deity or demon of the underworld.

dem·o·graph·ic (dĕm′ə-grăf′ĭk, dē′mə-) also **dem·o·graph·i·cal** (-ĭ-kəl) *adj.* Of or relating to demography. —**dem′o·graph′i·cal·ly** *adv.*

dem·o·graph·ics (dĕm′ə-grăf′ĭks, dē′mə-) *n. (used with a pl. verb).* The characteristics of human populations and population segments, especially when used to identify consumer markets: *The demographics of the Southwest indicate a growing population of older consumers.*

de·mog·ra·phy (dĭ-mŏg′rə-fē) *n.* The study of the characteristics of human populations, such as size, growth, density, distribution, and vital statistics. [French *démographie* : Greek *dēmos,* people; see **dā-** in Appendix + French *-graphie,* writing (from Greek *-graphia,* -graphy).] —**de·mog′ra·pher** *n.*

dem·oi·selle (dĕm′wə-zĕl′) *n.* **1.** A young woman. **2.** A demoiselle crane. **3.** See **damselfly. 4.** See **damselfish.** [French, damsel, from Old French *dameisele.* See DAMSEL.]

demoiselle crane *n.* A small crane *(Anthropoides virgo)* of Asia, northern Africa, and Europe, having gray and black plumage, long black breast feathers, and white plumes at the side of the head.

de·mol·ish (dĭ-mŏl′ĭsh) *tr.v.* **-ished, -ish·ing, -ish·es. 1.** To tear down completely; raze. **2.** To do away with completely; put an end to. **3.** To damage (someone's reputation, for example) severely. See Synonyms at **ruin.** [French *démolir, démoliss-,* from Latin *dēmōlīrī* : *dē-,* de- + *mōlīrī,* to build (from *mōlēs,* mass).]

dem·o·li·tion (dĕm′ə-lĭsh′ən, dē′mə-) *n.* **1.** The act or process of wrecking or destroying, especially destruction by explosives. **2. demolitions.** Explosives, especially when designed or used as weapons. [French *démolition,* from Latin *dēmōlītiō, dēmōlītiōn-,* from *dēmōlīrī,* to demolish. See DEMOLISH.] —**dem′o·li′tion·ist** *n.*

demolition derby *n. Sports.* A contest in which drivers crash old cars into each other until only one is left running.

de·mon (dē′mən) *n.* **1.** An evil supernatural being; a devil. **2.** A persistently tormenting person, force, or passion: *the demon of drug addiction.* **3.** One who is extremely zealous, skillful, or diligent: *worked away like a demon; a real demon at math.* **4.** Also **dae·mon** or **dai·mon** (dī′mōn′). *Greek Mythology.* An inferior deity, such as a deified hero. **5.** Also **dae·mon** or **dai·mon** (dī′mōn′). An attendant spirit; a genius. [Middle English, from Late Latin *daemōn,* from Latin, spirit, from Greek *daimōn,* divine power. See **dā-** in Appendix.]

demon. *abbr. Grammar.* Demonstrative.

de·mon·e·tize (dē-mŏn′ĭ-tīz′, -mŭn′-) *tr.v.* **-tized, -tiz·ing, -tiz·es. 1.** To divest (a coin, for example) of monetary value. **2.** To stop using (a metal) as a monetary standard. [French *démonétiser* : *dé-,* away from (from Old French *de-;* see DE–) + Latin *monēta,* coin; see MONEY.] —**de·mon′e·ti·za′tion** (-tĭ-zā′shən) *n.*

de·mo·ni·ac (dĭ-mō′nē-ăk′) also **de·mo·ni·a·cal** (dē′mə-nī′ə-kəl) —*adj.* **1.** Possessed, produced, or influenced by a demon: *demoniac creatures.* **2.** Of, resembling, or suggestive of a devil; fiendish: *demoniac energy; a demoniacal fit.* —*n.* One who is or seems to be possessed by a demon. [Middle English *demoniak,* from Late Latin *daemoniacus,* from Greek **daimoniakos,* from *daimonios,* of a spirit, from *daimōn,* divine power. See DEMON.] —**de′mo·ni′a·cal·ly** *adv.*

de·mon·ic also **dae·mon·ic** (dĭ-mŏn′ĭk) *adj.* **1.** Befitting a demon; fiendish. **2.** Motivated by a spiritual force or genius; inspired. —**de·mon′i·cal·ly** *adv.*

de·mon·ize (dē′mə-nīz′) *tr.v.* **-ized, -iz·ing, -iz·es. 1.** To turn into or as if into a demon. **2.** To possess by or as if by a demon. **3.** To represent as evil or diabolic: *wartime propaganda that demonizes the enemy.* —**de′mon·i·za′tion** (-mə-nĭ-zā′shən) *n.*

de·mon·ol·o·gy (dē′mə-nŏl′ə-jē) *n.* **1.** The study of demons. **2.** Belief in or worship of demons. **3.** A list or catalog of one's enemies: *"As the years passed* [the magazine's] *demonology expanded to include Bolsheviks, radicals, Franklin D. Roosevelt, the New Deal, Government work programs or aid programs of any kind"* (Maggie Nichols). —**de′mon·o·log′ic** (-ə-lŏj′ĭk), **de′mon·o·log′i·cal** (-ĭ-kəl) *adj.* —**de′mon·ol′o·gist** *n.*

de·mon·stra·ble (dĭ-mŏn′strə-bəl) *adj.* **1.** Capable of being demonstrated or proved: *demonstrable truths.* **2.** Obvious or apparent: *demonstrable lies.* —**de·mon′stra·bil′i·ty, de·mon′stra·ble·ness** *n.* —**de·mon′stra·bly** *adv.*

dem·on·strate (dĕm′ən-strāt′) *v.* **-strat·ed, -strat·ing, -strates.** —*tr.* **1.** To show clearly and deliberately; manifest: *demonstrated her skill as a gymnast; demonstrate affection by hugging.* **2.** To show to be true by reasoning or adducing evidence; prove: *demonstrate a proposition.* **3.** To present by experiments, examples, or practical application; explain and illustrate: *demonstrated the laws of physics with laboratory equipment.* **4.** To show the use of (an article) to a prospective buyer: *The salesperson plugged in and demonstrated the vacuum cleaner.* —*intr.* **1.** To give a demonstration: *described the dance step, then took a partner and demonstrated.* **2.** To participate in a public display of opinion: *demonstrated against tax hikes.* [Latin *dēmōnstrāre, dēmōnstrāt-* : *dē-,* completely; see DE– + *mōnstrāre,* to show (from *mōnstrum,* divine portent, from *monēre,* to warn; see **men-**[1] in Appendix).]

dem·on·stra·tion (dĕm′ən-strā′shən) *n.* **1.** The act of showing or making evident. **2.** Conclusive evidence; proof. **3.** An illustration or explanation, as of a theory or product, by exemplification or practical application. **4.** A manifestation, as of one's feelings. **5.** A public display of group opinion, as by a rally or march: *peace demonstrations.*

de·mon·stra·tive (dĭ-mŏn′strə-tĭv) *adj.* **1.** Serving to manifest or prove. **2.** Involving or characterized by demonstration. **3.** Given to or marked by the open expression of emotion: *an affectionate and demonstrative family.* **4.** *Abbr.* **demon., dem.** *Grammar.* Specifying or singling out the person or thing referred to: *the demonstrative pronouns* these *and* that. —**demonstrative** *n. Abbr.* **demon., dem.** *Grammar.* A demonstrative pronoun or

demitasse

demoiselle crane
Anthropoides virgo

demolition
Scollay Square, Boston, in the early 1960's

adjective. **—de·mon′stra·tive·ly** *adv.* **—de·mon′stra·tive·ness** *n.*

dem·on·stra·tor (dĕm′ən-strā′tər) *n.* **1.** One that demonstrates, such as a participant in a public display of opinion. **2.** An article or product used in a demonstration.

de·mor·al·ize (dĭ-môr′ə-līz′, -mŏr′-) *tr.v.* **-ized, -iz·ing, -iz·es. 1.** To undermine the confidence or morale of; dishearten: *an inconsistent policy that demoralized the staff.* **2.** To put into disorder; confuse. **3.** To debase the morals of; corrupt. **—de·mor′al·i·za′tion** (-ə-lĭ-zā′shən) *n.* **—de·mor′al·iz′er** *n.*

De Mor·gan (dĭ môr′gən), **Augustus.** 1806–1871. British mathematician and logician who wrote important works on calculus and with George Boole laid the foundation for modern symbolic logic.

de·mos (dē′mŏs′) *n.* **1.** The common people; the populace. **2.** The common people of an ancient Greek state. [Greek *dēmos,* district, people. See **dā-** in Appendix.]

De·mos·the·nes (dĭ-mŏs′thə-nēz′). 384–322 B.C. Greek orator whose reputation is based mainly on his *Philippics,* a series of orations exhorting the citizens of Athens to rise up against Philip II of Macedon.

de·mote (dĭ-mōt′) *tr.v.* **-mot·ed, -mot·ing, -motes.** To reduce in grade, rank, or status. [DE– + (PRO)MOTE.] **—de·mo′tion** *n.*

SYNONYMS: *demote, break, bust, degrade, downgrade, reduce.* The central meaning shared by these verbs is "to lower in grade, rank, or status": *was demoted from captain to lieutenant; a noncommissioned officer broken to the ranks; a detective who was busted to uniformed traffic patrol for insubordination; a supervisor degraded to an assistant; a popular author downgraded by critical opinion to a genre writer; a captain who was reduced from command of a battleship to administrative duty ashore.*
ANTONYM: *promote.*

de·mot·ic (dĭ-mŏt′ĭk) *adj.* **1.** Of or relating to the common people; popular: *demotic speech; demotic entertainments.* **2.** Of, relating to, or written in the simplified form of ancient Egyptian hieratic writing. **3. Demotic.** Of or relating to a form of modern Greek based on colloquial use. **—demotic** *n.* Demotic Greek. [Greek *dēmotikos,* from *dēmotēs,* a commoner, from *dēmos,* people. See **dā-** in Appendix.]

de·mount (dē-mount′) *tr.v.* **-mount·ed, -mount·ing, -mounts.** To remove (a motor, for example) from a position on a mounting or other support. **—de·mount′a·ble** *adj.*

Demp·sey (dĕmp′sē), **William Harrison.** Known as "Jack." Called "the Manassa Mauler." 1895–1983. American prizefighter who won the world heavyweight title in 1919 but lost it to Gene Tunney in 1926.

de·mul·cent (dĭ-mŭl′sənt) *adj.* Serving to soothe or soften. **—demulcent** *n.* A soothing, usually mucilaginous or oily substance, such as glycerin or lanolin, used especially to relieve pain in inflamed or irritated mucous membranes. [Latin *dēmulcēns, dēmulcent-,* present participle of *dēmulcēre,* to soften : *dē-,* de- + *mulcēre,* to stroke.]

de·mur (dĭ-mûr′) *intr.v.* **-murred, -mur·ring, -murs. 1.** To voice opposition; object: *demurred at the suggestion.* See Synonyms at **object. 2.** *Law.* To enter a demurrer. **3.** To delay. **—demur** *n.* **1.** The act of demurring. **2.** An objection. **3.** A delay. [Middle English *demuren,* to delay, from Anglo-Norman *demurer,* from Latin *dēmorārī* : *dē-,* de- + *morārī,* to delay (from *mora,* delay).] **—de·mur′ra·ble** *adj.*

de·mure (dĭ-myo͝or′) *adj.* **-mur·er, -mur·est. 1.** Modest and reserved in manner or behavior. **2.** Affectedly shy, modest, or reserved. See Synonyms at **shy**[1]. [Middle English, probably from Anglo-Norman *demure* (influenced by Old French *mur, meur,* mature, serious, from Latin *mātūrus;* see MATURE), past participle of *demurer,* to delay, wait. See DEMUR.] **—de·mure′ly** *adv.* **—de·mure′ness** *n.*

de·mur·rage (dĭ-mûr′ĭj, -mŭr′-) *n. Abbr.* **dem. 1.** Detention of a ship, freight car, or other cargo conveyance during loading or unloading beyond the scheduled time of departure. **2.** Compensation paid for such detention.

de·mur·ral (dĭ-mûr′əl, -mŭr′-) *n.* The act of demurring, especially a mild, polite, or considered expression of opposition.

de·mur·rer (dĭ-mûr′ər, -mŭr′-) *n.* **1.** One that demurs; an objector. **2.** An objection. **3.** *Law.* A method of objecting that admits the facts of the opponent's argument but denies that they sustain the pleading based upon them.

De·muth (dĭ-mo͞oth′), **Charles.** 1883–1935. American painter known for his still-life watercolors. He was one of the first artists to use the geometric shapes of modern technology in his work.

de·my (dĭ-mī′) *n., pl.* **-mies.** Any of several standard sizes of paper, especially paper measuring 16 by 21 inches. [Alteration of DEMI–.]

de·my·e·lin·ate (dē-mī′ə-lə-nāt′) *tr.v.* **-at·ed, -at·ing, -ates.** To destroy or remove the myelin sheath of (a nerve fiber), as through disease. **—de·my′e·lin·a′tion** *n.*

de·mys·ti·fy (dē-mĭs′tə-fī′) *tr.v.* **-fied, -fy·ing, -fies.** To make less mysterious; clarify: *an autobiography that demystified the career of an eminent physician.* **—de·mys′ti·fi·ca′tion** (-fĭ-kā′shən) *n.* **—de·mys′ti·fi′er** *n.*

de·my·thol·o·gize (dē′mĭ-thŏl′ə-jīz′) *tr.v.* **-gized, -giz·ing, -giz·es. 1.** To rid of mythological elements in order to discover the underlying meaning: *demythologize biblical legends.* **2.** To remove the mysterious or mythical aspects from: *"providing an antiheroic age with heroes suitably demythologized, yet also grand"* (John Simon). **—de′my·thol′o·gi·za′tion** (-jĭ-zā′shən) *n.* **—de′my·thol′o·giz′er** *n.*

den (dĕn) *n.* **1.** The shelter or retreat of a wild animal; a lair. **2.** A cave or hollow used as a refuge or hiding place. **3.** A hidden or squalid dwelling place: *a den of thieves.* **4.** A secluded room for study or relaxation. **5.** A unit of about eight to ten Cub Scouts. **—den** *intr.v.* **denned, den·ning, dens.** To inhabit or hide in a den. [Middle English, from Old English *denn.*]

Den. *abbr.* Denmark.

De·na·li (də-nä′lē). See Mount **McKinley.**

de·nar·i·us (dĭ-nâr′ē-əs) *n., pl.* **-i·i** (-ē-ī′). **1.** An ancient Roman silver coin. **2.** An ancient Roman gold coin valued at 25 silver denarii. [Middle English, from Latin *dēnārius.* See DENARY.]

den·a·ry (dĕn′ə-rē) *adj.* **1.** Tenfold. **2.** Divided or counted by tens; decimal. [Latin *dēnārius,* from *dēnī,* by tens. See **dekm̥** in Appendix.]

de·na·tion·al·ize (dē-năsh′ə-nə-līz′) *tr.v.* **-ized, -iz·ing, -iz·es. 1.** To deprive of national rights or characteristics. **2.** To transfer (an industry, for example) from governmental to private ownership. **—de·na′tion·al·i·za′tion** (-shə-nə-lĭ-zā′shən) *n.*

de·nat·u·ral·ize (dē-năch′ər-ə-līz′) *tr.v.* **-ized, -iz·ing, -iz·es. 1.** To make unnatural. **2.** To deprive of the rights of citizenship. **—de·nat′u·ral·i·za′tion** (-ər-ə-lĭ-zā′shən) *n.*

de·na·ture (dē-nā′chər) *tr.v.* **-tured, -tur·ing, -tures. 1.** To change the nature or natural qualities of. **2.** To render unfit to eat or drink without destroying usefulness in other applications, especially to add methanol to (ethyl alcohol). **3.** *Biochemistry.* To alter the structure of (a protein), as with heat, alkali, or acid, so that some of its original properties, especially its biological activity, are diminished or eliminated. **4.** *Physics.* To add nonfissionable matter to (fissionable material) so as to prevent use in an atomic weapon. **—de·na′tur·ant** *n.* **—de·na′tur·a′tion** *n.*

de·na·tured alcohol (dē-nā′chərd) *n.* Ethyl alcohol to which a poisonous substance, such as acetone or methanol, has been added to make it unfit for consumption.

dendr– or **dendri–** *pref.* Variants of **dendro–.**

den·dri·form (dĕn′drə-fôrm′) *adj.* Shaped like or having the form of a tree.

den·drite (dĕn′drīt′) *n.* **1.a.** A mineral crystallizing in another mineral in the form of a branching or treelike mark. **b.** A rock or mineral bearing such a mark or marks. **2.** A branched protoplasmic extension of a nerve cell that conducts impulses from adjacent cells inward toward the cell body. A single nerve may possess many dendrites. In this sense, also called *dendron.*

den·drit·ic (dĕn-drĭt′ĭk) also **den·drit·i·cal** (-ĭ-kəl) *adj.* **1.** Of, relating to, or resembling a dendrite. **2.** Dendriform. **—den·drit′i·cal·ly** *adv.*

dendro– or **dendri–** or **dendr–** *pref.* Tree; treelike: *dendrochronology.* [From Greek *dendron,* tree. See **deru-** in Appendix.]

den·dro·bi·um (dĕn-drō′bē-əm) *n.* Any of numerous species of the orchid genus *Dendrobium* native to tropical or subtropical Asia, Australia, and the islands of the Pacific Ocean. [New Latin, genus name : DENDRO– + Greek *bios,* life; see **g**ʷ**ei-** in Appendix.]

den·dro·chro·nol·o·gy (dĕn′drō-krə-nŏl′ə-jē) *n.* The study of climate changes and past events by comparing the successive annual growth rings of trees or old timber. **—den′dro·chron′o·log′i·cal** (-krŏn′ə-lŏj′ĭ-kəl) *adj.* **—den′dro·chron′o·log′i·cal·ly** *adv.* **—den′dro·chro·nol′o·gist** *n.*

den·droid (dĕn′droid′) also **den·droid·al** (dĕn-droid′l) *adj.* Shaped like a tree.

den·drol·o·gy (dĕn-drŏl′ə-jē) *n.* The botanical study of trees and other woody plants. **—den′dro·log′ic** (-drə-lŏj′ĭk), **den′dro·log′i·cal** *adj.* **—den·drol′o·gist** *n.*

den·dron (dĕn′drŏn′) *n.* See **dendrite** (sense 2). [Greek, tree. See **deru-** in Appendix.]

dene (dēn) *n. Chiefly British.* A sandy tract or dune by the seashore. [Possibly East Frisian *düne,* a sand dune; akin to DUNE.]

De·neb (dĕn′ĕb′) *n.* The brightest star in the constellation Cygnus, approximately 1,630 light-years from Earth. [Arabic *ḏanab,* tail.]

De·neb·o·la (də-nĕb′ə-lə) *n.* A star in the constellation Leo, approximately 43 light-years from Earth. [From Arabic *ḏanab al-'asad,* tail of the lion.]

den·e·ga·tion (dĕn′ĭ-gā′shən) *n.* A denial. [French *dénégation,* from Latin *dēnegātiō, dēnegātiōn-,* from *dēnegātus,* past participle of *dēnegāre,* to deny. See DENY.]

de·ner·vate (dē-nûr′vāt′) *tr.v.* **-va·ted, -va·ting, -vates.** *Medicine.* To deprive (an organ or body part) of a nerve supply, as by surgically removing or cutting a nerve or by blocking a nerve connection with drugs. **—de′ner·va′tion** *n.*

den·gue (dĕng′gē, -gā) *n.* An acute, infectious tropical disease caused by an arbovirus transmitted by mosquitoes, and characterized by high fever, rash, headache, and severe muscle and joint pain. Also called *breakbone fever, dandy fever, dengue fever.* [Spanish, alteration (influenced by *dengue,* affectation) of Swahili *ki-dinga.*]

Deng Xiao·ping (dŭng′ shou′pĭng′, dœng′ shyou′pĭng′) also **Teng Hsiao-ping** (tŭng′ shyou′pĭng′, dœng′). Born 1904. Chinese Communist leader who was twice purged from the Communist Party (1967 and 1976) and twice rehabilitated (1973 and 1977) before gaining supreme power in China. He officially retired as head of state in November 1989.

de·ni·a·ble (dĭ-nī′ə-bəl) *adj.* **1.** Possible to contradict or declare untrue: *deniable accusations.* **2.** Being such that plausible disavowal or disclaimer is possible: *"Covert action was deniable; a Pentagon program would not be"* (Bob Woodward). **—de·ni′a·bil′i·ty** *n.* **—de·ni′a·bly** *adv.*

de·ni·al (dĭ-nī′əl) *n.* **1.** A refusal to comply with or satisfy a request. **2.a.** A refusal to grant the truth of a statement or allegation; a contradiction. **b.** *Law.* The opposing by a defendant of an allegation of the plaintiff. **3.a.** A refusal to accept or believe something, such as a doctrine or belief. **b.** *Psychology.* An unconscious defense mechanism characterized by refusal to acknowledge painful realities, thoughts, or feelings. **4.** The act of disowning or disavowing; repudiation. **5.** Abstinence; self-denial. [From DENY.]

de·ni·er[1] (dĭ-nī′ər) *n.* One that denies: *a denier of harsh realities.*

den·ier[2] (dən-yā′) *n.* **1.** (*also* dĕn′yər). A unit of fineness for rayon, nylon, and silk fibers, based on a standard mass per length of 1 gram per 9,000 meters of yarn. **2.** (*also* də-nîr′). **a.** A small coin of varying composition and value current in western Europe from the eighth century until the French Revolution. **b.** *Archaic.* A small, trifling sum. [Middle English *denere,* a coin, from Old French *dener,* from Latin *dēnārius.* See DENARIUS.]

den·i·grate (dĕn′ĭ-grāt′) *tr.v.* **-grat·ed, -grat·ing, -grates. 1.** To attack the character or reputation of; speak ill of; defame. **2.** To disparage; belittle: *The critics have denigrated our efforts.* [Latin *dēnigrāre, dēnigrāt-,* to blacken, defame : *dē-,* de- + *niger, nigr-,* black.] **—den′i·gra′tion** *n.* **—den′i·gra′tor** *n.*

den·im (dĕn′ĭm) *n.* **1.a.** A coarse twilled cloth, usually cotton, used for jeans, overalls, and work uniforms. **b. denims.** Trousers or another garment made of this cloth. **2.** A similar but finer fabric used in draperies and upholstery. [French *(serge) de Nîmes,* (serge) of Nîmes, after NÎMES, France.]

De·nis or **De·nys** (dĕn′ĭs, də-nē′), Saint. Third century A.D. Patron saint of France. Sent to minister to the Gauls as the first bishop of Paris, he suffered martyrdom by decapitation.

Den·i·son (dĕn′ĭ-sən). A city of northern Texas near the Oklahoma border north-northeast of Dallas. It was founded as a railroad junction on the site of a stagecoach station. Population, 23,884.

de·ni·tri·fy (dē-nī′trə-fī′) *tr.v.* **-fied, -fy·ing, -fies. 1.** To remove nitrogen or nitrogen groups from (a compound). **2.** To reduce (nitrates or nitrites) to nitrogen-containing gases, as by bacterial action on soil. **—de·ni′tri·fi·ca′tion** (-fĭ-kā′shən) *n.*

den·i·zen (dĕn′ĭ-zən) *n.* **1.** An inhabitant; a resident: *denizens of Monte Carlo.* **2.** One that frequents a particular place: *a bar and its denizens.* **3.** *Ecology.* An animal or a plant naturalized in a region. **4.** *Chiefly British.* A foreigner who is granted rights of residence and sometimes of citizenship. **—denizen** *tr.v.* **-zened, -zen·ing, -zens.** *Chiefly British.* To make a denizen of; grant rights of residence to. [Middle English *denisein,* from Anglo-Norman *denzein,* from *deinz,* within, from Late Latin *dēintus,* from within. See DEDANS.] **—den′i·zen·a′tion** *n.*

Den·mark (dĕn′märk′). *Abbr.* **Den.** A country of northern Europe on Jutland and adjacent islands. It was unified in the 10th century by the Viking king Harold Bluetooth (died 985), who converted the people to Christianity. Denmark controlled England briefly in the 11th century and was united with Sweden until 1523 and with Norway until 1814. Copenhagen is the capital and the largest city. Population, 5,112,130.

Denmark Strait. A channel between Greenland and Iceland connecting the Arctic Ocean with the northern Atlantic Ocean.

den mother *n.* A woman who supervises a den of Cub Scouts.

denom. *abbr.* Denomination.

de·nom·i·nate (dĭ-nŏm′ə-nāt′) *tr.v.* **-nat·ed, -nat·ing, -nates. 1.** To issue or express in terms of a given monetary unit: *securities that are denominated in dollars or yen.* **2.** To give a name to; designate. **—denominate** (-ə-nĭt) *adj.* Of or relating to a quantity as a multiple of a unit: 12 *in* 12 pounds *is denominate.* [Latin *dēnōmināre, dēnōmināt-* : *dē-,* de- + *nōmināre,* to name (from *nōmen,* name; see **nō-men-** in Appendix).] **—de·nom′i·na·ble** (-nə-bəl) *adj.*

de·nom·i·na·tion (dĭ-nŏm′ə-nā′shən) *n. Abbr.* **denom. 1.** A large group of religious congregations united under a common faith and name and organized under a single administrative and legal hierarchy. **2.** One of a series of kinds, values, or sizes, as in a system of currency or weights: *Cash registers have compartments for bills of different denominations. The stamps come in 25¢ and 45¢ denominations.* **3.** A name or designation, especially for a class or group. See Synonyms at **name. —de·nom′i·na′tion·al** *adj.* **—de·nom′i·na′tion·al·ly** *adv.*

de·nom·i·na·tion·al·ism (dĭ-nŏm′ə-nā′shə-nə-lĭz′əm) *n.* **1.** The tendency to separate into religious denominations. **2.** Advocacy of separation into religious denominations. **3.** Strict adherence to a denomination; sectarianism. **—de·nom′i·na′tion·al·ist** *n.*

de·nom·i·na·tive (dĭ-nŏm′ə-nā′tĭv, -nə-tĭv) *adj.* **1.** Giving or constituting a name; naming. **2.** Formed from a noun or an adjective. **—denominative** *n.* A word, especially a verb, that is derived from a noun or an adjective.

de·nom·i·na·tor (dĭ-nŏm′ə-nā′tər) *n.* **1.** *Mathematics.* The expression written below the line in a common fraction that indicates the number of parts into which one whole is divided. **2.** A common trait or characteristic. **3.** An average level or standard: *The success of the film demonstrates the denominator of public taste.*

de·no·ta·tion (dē′nō-tā′shən) *n.* **1.** The act of denoting; indication. **2.** Something, such as a sign or symbol, that denotes. **3.** Something signified or referred to; a particular meaning of a symbol. **4.** The most specific or direct meaning of a word, in contrast to its figurative or associated meanings.

de·no·ta·tive (dĭ-nō′tə-tĭv, dē′nō-tā′-) *adj.* **1.** Denoting or naming; designative. **2.** Specific or direct: *denotative and connotative meanings.* **—de·no′ta·tive·ly** *adv.*

de·note (dĭ-nōt′) *tr.v.* **-not·ed, -not·ing, -notes. 1.** To mark; indicate: *a frown that denoted increasing impatience.* **2.** To serve as a symbol or name for the meaning of; signify: *A flashing yellow light denotes caution.* **3.** To signify directly; refer to specifically: See Synonyms at **mean**[1]. [French *dénoter,* from Latin *dēnotāre* : *dē-,* de- + *notāre,* to mark; see CONNOTE.] **—de·not′a·ble** *adj.* **—de·no′tive** *adj.*

USAGE NOTE: *Denote* means "to mark" or "to signify directly"; *connote* means "to suggest or convey to the mind what is not explicit." In speaking of words or expressions, *denote* describes the relation between the expression and the thing it conventionally names, whereas *connote* describes the relation between the word and the images or associations it evokes. Thus, the word *Christmas* denotes the holiday celebrated on December 25 and connotes turkey, mistletoe, and chestnuts roasting on an open fire.

Deng Xiaoping

de·noue·ment also **dé·noue·ment** (dā′no͞o-mäɴ′) *n.* **1.a.** The final resolution or clarification of a dramatic or narrative plot. **b.** The events following the climax of a drama or novel in which such a resolution or clarification takes place. **2.** The outcome of a sequence of events; the end result. [French *dénouement,* from Old French *desnouement,* an untying, from *desnouer,* to undo : *des-,* de- + *nouer,* to tie (from Latin *nōdāre,* from *nōdus,* knot; see **ned-** in Appendix).]

de·nounce (dĭ-nouns′) *tr.v.* **-nounced, -nounc·ing, -nounc·es. 1.** To condemn openly as being evil or reprehensible. See Synonyms at **criticize. 2.** To accuse formally. **3.** To give formal announcement of the ending of (a treaty). [Middle English *denouncen,* to proclaim, from Anglo-Norman *denuncier* and Medieval Latin *dēnūntiāre,* both from Latin : *dē-,* de- + *nūntiāre,* to announce (from *nūntius,* messenger; see **neu-** in Appendix).] **—de·nounce′ment** *n.* **—de·nounc′er** *n.*

dense (dĕns) *adj.* **dens·er, dens·est. 1.a.** Having relatively high density. **b.** Crowded closely together; compact: *a dense population.* **2.** Hard to penetrate; thick: *a dense jungle.* **3.a.** Permitting little light to pass through, because of compactness of matter: *dense glass; a dense fog.* **b.** Opaque, with good contrast between light and dark areas. Used of a photographic negative. **4.** Difficult to understand because of complexity or obscurity: *a dense novel.* **5.** Slow to apprehend; thickheaded. See Synonyms at **stupid.** [Latin *dēnsus.*] **—dense′ly** *adv.* **—dense′ness** *n.*

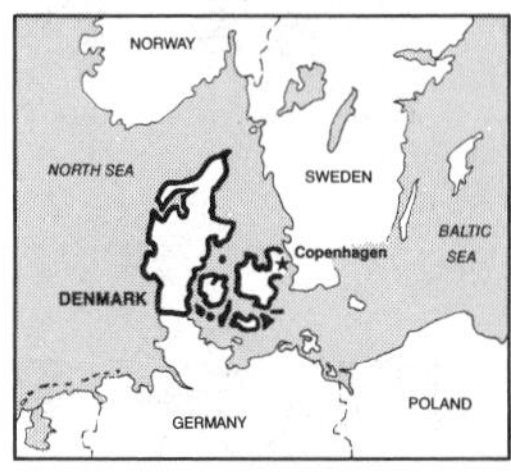

Denmark

den·sim·e·ter (dĕn-sĭm′ĭ-tər) *n.* An instrument used to measure density or specific gravity. Also called *densitometer.* [Latin *dēnsus,* dense + -METER.] **—den′si·met′ric** (-sə-mĕt′rĭk) *adj.*

den·si·tom·e·ter (dĕn′sĭ-tŏm′ĭ-tər) *n.* **1.** An apparatus for measuring the optical density of a material, such as a photographic negative. **2.** See **densimeter.** [DENSIT(Y) + -METER.] **—den′si·tom′e·try** (-ĭ-trē) *n.*

den·si·ty (dĕn′sĭ-tē) *n., pl.* **-ties. 1.** The quality or condition of being dense. **2.a.** The quantity of something per unit measure, especially per unit length, area, or volume. **b.** The mass per unit volume of a substance under specified conditions of pressure and temperature. **3.** *Computer Science.* The number of units of useful information contained within a linear dimension. **4.** The number of individuals, such as inhabitants or housing units, per unit of area. **5.** The degree of optical opacity of a medium or material, as of a photographic negative. **6.** Thickness of consistency; impenetrability. **7.** Complexity of structure or content. **8.** Stupidity; dullness.

dent[1] (dĕnt) *n.* **1.** A depression in a surface made by pressure or a blow: *a dent in the side of a car.* **2.** *Informal.* A significant, usually diminishing effect or impression: *The loss put a dent in the team's confidence.* **3.** *Informal.* Meaningful progress; headway: *at least made a dent in the work.* **—dent** *v.* **dent·ed, dent·ing, dents.** *—tr.* To make a dent in. *—intr.* To become dented: *a fender that dents easily.* [Middle English *dent,* variant of *dint,* blow, from Old English *dynt.*]

dent[2] (dĕnt) *n.* See **tooth** (sense 3). [French. See DENTIST.]

dent. *abbr.* Dental; dentist; dentistry.

dent- *pref.* Variant of **denti-.**

den·tal (dĕn′tl) *adj.* **1.** *Abbr.* **dent.** Of, relating to, or for the teeth: *dental caps.* **2.** *Abbr.* **dent.** Of, relating to, or intended for dentistry: *dental work; dental bills.* **3.** *Linguistics.* Articulated with the tip of the tongue near or against the upper front teeth: *the English dental consonants* t *and* d. **—dental** *n.* *Linguistics.*

ă pat	oi boy
ā pay	ou out
âr care	o͝o took
ä father	o͞o boot
ĕ pet	ŭ cut
ē be	ûr urge
ĭ pit	th thin
ī pie	*th* this
îr pier	hw which
ŏ pot	zh vision
ō toe	ə about, item
ô paw	♦ regionalism

Stress marks: ′ (primary); ′ (secondary), as in **dictionary** (dĭk′shə-nĕr′ē)

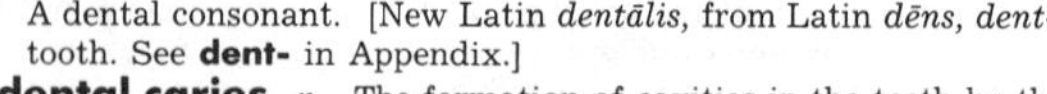

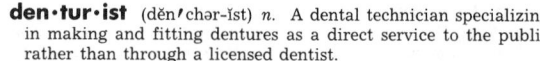

A dental consonant. [New Latin *dentālis,* from Latin *dēns, dent-,* tooth. See **dent-** in Appendix.]

dental caries *n.* The formation of cavities in the teeth by the action of bacteria; tooth decay.

dental floss *n.* A waxed or unwaxed thread used to remove food particles and plaque from the teeth.

dental hygiene *n.* **1.** The practice of keeping the mouth, teeth, and gums clean and healthy to prevent disease, as by regular brushing and flossing and visits to a dentist. **2.** The state of one's oral health, resulting from this practice or its neglect. Also called *oral hygiene.*

dentate

dental hygienist *n.* A person trained and licensed to provide preventive dental services, such as cleaning the teeth and taking x-rays, usually in conjunction with a dentist.

den·ta·li·a (dĕn-tā′lē-ə) *n.* A plural of **dentalium.**

dental implant *n.* A tooth, usually artificial, that is anchored in the gums or jawbone to replace a missing tooth.

den·ta·li·um (dĕn-tā′lē-əm) *n., pl.* **-li·a** (-lē-ə) or **-li·ums.** Any of various tooth shells of the genus *Dentalium.* [New Latin *Dentālium,* genus name, from *dentālis,* toothy. See DENTAL.]

dental plate *n.* See **denture** (sense 1).

dental technician *n.* One who makes dental appliances and restorative devices, such as bridges or dentures, to the specifications of a dentist.

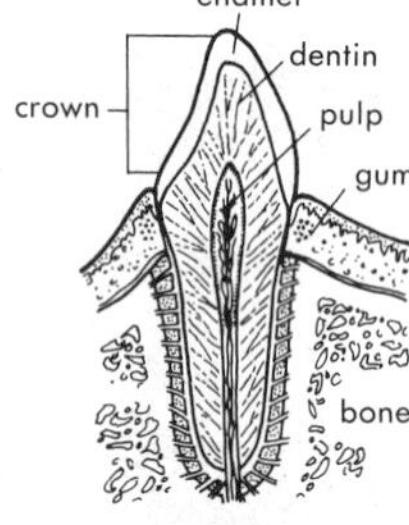

dentin

den·tate (dĕn′tāt′) *adj.* Edged with toothlike projections; toothed: *dentate leaves.* [Latin *dentātus,* from *dēns, dent-,* tooth. See **dent-** in Appendix.] **—den′tate′ly** *adv.*

den·ta·tion (dĕn-tā′shən) *n.* **1.** The condition of being dentate. **2.** A toothlike part or projection.

dent corn *n.* A tall-growing variety of corn *(Zea mays* var. *indentata)* having yellow or white kernels that are indented at the tip.

denti– or **dent–** *pref.* **1.** Tooth: *dentoid.* **2.** Dental: *dentilabial.* [From Latin *dēns, dent-,* tooth. See **dent-** in Appendix.]

den·ti·cle (dĕn′tĭ-kəl) *n.* A small tooth or toothlike projection. [Middle English, from Latin *denticulus,* diminutive of *dēns, dent-,* tooth. See **dent-** in Appendix.] **—den·tic′u·lar** *adj.*

den·tic·u·late (dĕn-tĭk′yə-lĭt) also **den·tic·u·lat·ed** (-lā′tĭd) *adj.* **1.** Finely toothed or notched; minutely dentate: *denticulate leaves; denticulate fish scales.* **2.** *Architecture.* Having dentils. [Latin *denticulātus,* from *denticulus,* denticle. See DENTICLE.] **—den·tic′u·late·ly** *adv.* **—den·tic′u·la′tion** *n.*

den·ti·form (dĕn′tə-fôrm′) *adj.* Shaped like a tooth: *dentiform crystals.*

den·ti·frice (dĕn′tə-frĭs′) *n.* A substance, such as a paste or powder, for cleaning the teeth. [French, from Old French, from Latin *dentifricium* : *denti-,* denti- + *fricāre,* to rub.]

den·tig·er·ous (dĕn-tĭj′ər-əs) *adj.* Having or furnished with teeth. [DENTI– + Latin *gerere,* to bear.]

den·til (dĕn′tĭl) *n.* *Architecture.* One of a series of small rectangular blocks forming a molding or projecting beneath a cornice. [Obsolete French *dentille,* from Old French, diminutive of *dent,* tooth. See DENTIST.]

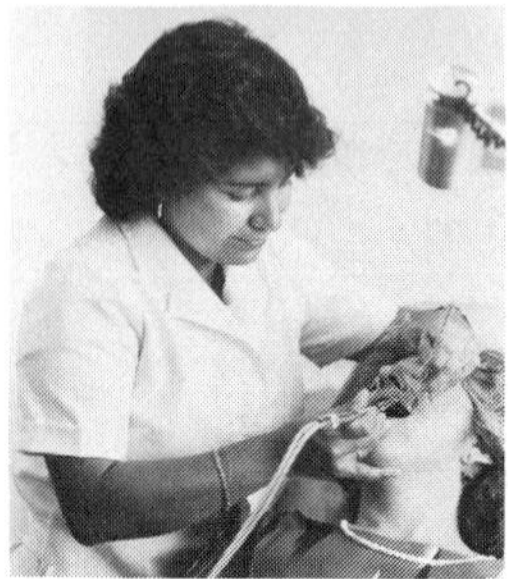

dentist

den·tin (dĕn′tĭn) or **den·tine** (-tēn′) *n.* The main, calcareous part of a tooth, beneath the enamel and surrounding the pulp chamber and root canals. **—den·tin′al** (dĕn-tē′nəl, dĕn′tə-) *adj.*

den·tist (dĕn′tĭst) *n.* *Abbr.* **dent.** A person who is trained and licensed to practice dentistry. [French *dentiste,* from *dent,* tooth, from Old French, from Latin *dēns, dent-.* See **dent-** in Appendix.]

WORD HISTORY: "*Dentist* figures [appears] now in our newspapers, and may do well enough for a French puffer [a writer of inflated advertisements]; but we fancy Rutter is content with being called a *tooth-drawer.*" In this quotation from the September 15, 1759, issue of the *Edinburgh Chronicle* we see *dentist* in its infancy as an English word, trailing evidence of its French origin. If we had formed a word in English like *dentist,* which comes from the French word *dent,* "tooth," we would have *toothist,* a word that does not exist. But *toothist* and *tooth-drawer* lack the elegance of the French borrowing *dentist,* an elegance that is shared by other borrowings from French during the past four centuries, such as *ballet, champagne, coquette, coterie,* and *negligee.*

den·tist·ry (dĕn′tĭ-strē) *n.* *Abbr.* **dent.** The science concerned with the diagnosis, prevention, and treatment of diseases of the teeth, gums, and related structures of the mouth and including the repair or replacement of defective teeth.

den·ti·tion (dĕn-tĭsh′ən) *n.* **1.** *Zoology.* The type, number, and arrangement of a set of teeth. **2.** The process of growing new teeth; teething. [Latin *dentītiō, dentītiōn-,* from *dentītus,* past participle of *dentīre,* to teethe, from *dēns, dent-,* tooth. See DENTIST.]

Denver boot

den·toid (dĕn′toid′) *adj.* Having the form of a tooth; toothlike.

Den·ton (dĕn′tən). A city of northeast Texas north-northwest of Dallas. It is a trade and agricultural center. Population, 48,063.

den·tu·lous (dĕn′chə-ləs) *adj.* Possessing teeth; toothed. [Back-formation from EDENTULOUS, toothless.]

den·ture (dĕn′chər) *n.* **1.** A partial or complete set of artificial teeth for either the upper or lower jaw. Also called *dental plate.* **2.** Often **dentures.** A complete set of removable artificial teeth for both jaws. [French, from Old French, from *dent,* tooth. See DENTIST.]

den·tur·ist (dĕn′chər-ĭst) *n.* A dental technician specializing in making and fitting dentures as a direct service to the public rather than through a licensed dentist.

de·nu·cle·ar·ize (dē-nōō′klē-ə-rīz′, -nyōō′-) *v.* **-ized, -iz·ing, -iz·es.** *—tr.* To remove or ban nuclear weapons from: *a proposal to denuclearize Europe.* *—intr.* To reduce or eliminate a store of nuclear weapons. **—de·nu′cle·ar·i·za′tion** (-ər-ĭ-zā′shən) *n.*

de·nu·date (dĭ-nōō′dāt′, -nyōō′-) *tr.v.* **-dat·ed, -dat·ing, -dates.** To denude. **—denudate** *adj.* Bare; denuded. [Latin *dēnūdāre, dēnūdāt-.* See DENUDE.]

de·nude (dĭ-nōōd′, -nyōōd′) *tr.v.* **-nud·ed, -nud·ing, -nudes.** **1.** To divest of covering; make bare. See Synonyms at **strip**[1]. **2.** *Geology.* To expose (rock strata) by erosion. [Latin *dēnūdāre* : *dē-,* de- + *nūdāre,* to make bare (from *nūdus,* nude; see **nog^{w}-** in Appendix).] **—de′nu·da′tion** (dē′nōō-dā′shən, -nyōō-, dĕn′yōō-) *n.*

de·nu·mer·a·ble (dĭ-nōō′mər-ə-bəl, -nyōō′-) *adj.* Capable of being put into one-to-one correspondence with the positive integers; countable. [From *denumerate,* to count, from Late Latin *dēnumerāre, dēnumerāt-,* alteration of Latin *dīnumerāre* : *dī-, dis-,* dis- + *numerāre,* to number; see NUMERATE.] **—de·nu′mer·a·bil′i·ty** *n.* **—de·nu′mer·a·bly** *adv.*

de·nun·ci·a·tion (dĭ-nŭn′sē-ā′shən, -shē-) *n.* **1.** The act or an instance of denouncing, especially a public condemnation or censure. **2.** The act of accusing another of a crime before a public prosecutor. [Middle English *denunciacioun,* from Latin *dēnuntiātiō, dēnuntiātiōn-,* from *dēnuntiātus,* past participle of *dēnuntiāre,* to announce. See DENOUNCE.] **—de·nun′ci·a′tive** (-ā′tĭv, -ə-tĭv), **de·nun′ci·a·to′ry** (-ə-tôr′ē, -tōr′ē) *adj.*

Den·ver (dĕn′vər). The capital and largest city of Colorado, in the north-central part of the state on the South Platte River. It was settled by gold prospectors in 1858 and became territorial capital in 1867. Population, 492,365.

Denver boot *n.* A device locked to the wheel of a parked vehicle to keep it from being driven, used especially to force settlement of outstanding traffic violations. [After DENVER, one of the first cities to use it.]

de·ny (dĭ-nī′) *tr.v.* **-nied, -ny·ing, -nies.** **1.** To declare untrue; contradict. **2.** To refuse to believe; reject. **3.** To refuse to recognize or acknowledge; disavow. **4.a.** To decline to grant or allow; refuse: *deny the student's request; denied the prisoner food or water.* **b.** To give a refusal to; turn down or away: *The protesters were determined not to be denied.* **c.** To restrain (oneself) especially from indulgence in pleasures. [Middle English *denien,* from Old French *denier,* from Latin *dēnegāre* : *dē-,* de- + *negāre,* to say no; see **ne** in Appendix.]

SYNONYMS: *deny, contradict, contravene, disaffirm, gainsay, negate, negative, traverse.* The central meaning shared by these verbs is "to refuse to admit the existence, truth, or value of": *denied the rumor; contradicted the statement; contravene a conclusion; disaffirm a suggestion; trying to gainsay the evidence; negate reality; negatived the allegations; traverse an indictment.*
ANTONYM: *affirm.*

De·nys (dĕn′ĭs, də-nē′), Saint. See Saint **Denis.**

de·o·dar (dē′ə-där′) or **de·o·dar·a** (-där′ə) *n.* A tall cedar *(Cedrus deodara)* native to the Himalaya Mountains and having drooping branches and dark bluish-green leaves. It is an important timber tree in India. [Hindi *deodār,* from Sanskrit *devadāru* : *deva-,* divine; see **deiw-** in Appendix + *dāru,* wood; see **deru-** in Appendix.]

de·o·dor·ant (dē-ō′dər-ənt) *n.* **1.** A substance applied to the skin to mask or suppress body odors. **2.** A substance released into the air to counteract unwanted odors. **—deodorant** *adj.* Capable of masking or neutralizing odors.

de·o·dor·ize (dē-ō′də-rīz′) *tr.v.* **-ized, -iz·ing, -iz·es.** **1.** To mask or neutralize the odor of. **2.** To make more acceptable, as by elimination or suppression of an offensive aspect: *"Tighter regulation and the entrance of big developers . . . have helped deodorize the industry, but it is still plagued by undercapitalized and even fraudulent developers"* (Forbes). **—de·o′dor·i·za′tion** (-dər-ĭ-zā′shən) *n.* **—de·o′dor·iz′er** *n.*

de·on·tol·o·gy (dē′ŏn-tŏl′ə-jē) *n.* The theory or study of moral obligation; ethics. [Greek *deon, deont-,* obligation, necessity (from neuter present participle of *dein,* to need, lack; see **deu-**[1] in Appendix) + –LOGY.] **—de·on′to·log′i·cal** (-tə-lŏj′ĭ-kəl) *adj.* **—de′on·tol′o·gist** *n.*

de·or·bit (dē-ôr′bĭt) *intr. & tr.v.* **-bit·ed, -bit·ing, -bits.** To go or cause to go out of orbit. **—deorbit** *n.* The act or process of going out of orbit.

de·ox·i·dize (dē-ŏk′sĭ-dīz′) *tr.v.* **-dized, -diz·ing, -diz·es.** To remove oxygen from (a compound); reduce. **—de·ox′i·di·za′tion** (-dĭ-zā′shən) *n.* **—de·ox′i·diz′er** *n.*

deoxy– *pref.* Denoting a molecule containing less oxygen than another to which it is closely related: *deoxycorticosterone.*

de·ox·y·cor·ti·co·ster·one (dē-ŏk′sē-kôr′tĭ-kŏs′tə-rōn′) *n.* A steroid hormone, $C_{21}H_{30}O_3$, secreted by the adrenal cortex or produced synthetically and used to treat adrenal insufficiency.

de·ox·y·gen·ate (dē-ŏk′sə-jə-nāt′) *tr.v.* **-at·ed, -at·ing, -ates.** To remove dissolved oxygen from (a liquid, such as water). **—de·ox′y·gen·a′tion** *n.*

de·ox·y·ri·bo·nu·cle·ase (dē-ok′sē-rī′bō-no͞o′klē-ās′, -āz′, -nyo͞o′-) *n.* DNase.

de·ox·y·ri·bo·nu·cle·ic acid (dē-ŏk′sē-rī′bō-no͞o-klē′-ĭk, -klā′-, -nyo͞o-) *n.* DNA.

de·ox·y·ri·bo·nu·cle·o·tide (dē-ŏk′sē-rī′bō-no͞o′-klē-ə-tīd′, -nyo͞o′-) *n.* A nucleotide containing deoxyribose that is a constituent of DNA. [DEOXYRIBO(SE) + NUCLEOTIDE.]

de·ox·y·ri·bose (dē-ŏk′sē-rī′bōs′) *n.* A sugar, $C_5H_{10}O_4$, that is a constituent of DNA.

dep. *abbr.* **1.** Department. **2.** Departure. **3.** Dependency. **4.** Deponent. **5.** Deposed. **6.** Deposit. **7.** Depot. **8.** Deputy.

de·part (dĭ-pärt′) *v.* **-part·ed, -part·ing, -parts.** —*intr.* **1.** To go away; leave. **2.** To die. **3.** To vary, as from a regular course; deviate: *depart from custom.* See Synonyms at **swerve.** —*tr.* To go away from; leave. [Middle English *departen,* from Old French *departir,* to split, divide : *de-,* de- + *partir,* to divide (from Latin *partīre,* from *pars, part-,* part; see PART).]

de·part·ed (dĭ-pär′tĭd) *adj.* **1.** Bygone; past: *relics from a departed era.* **2.** Dead. See Synonyms at **dead.** —**departed** *n.* **1.** A dead person, especially one who has died recently: *The family of the departed remained after the funeral service.* **2.** Dead persons considered as a group; the dead.

de·part·ment (dĭ-pärt′mənt) *n. Abbr.* **dept., dpt., dep., D. 1.** A distinct, usually specialized division of a large organization, especially: **a.** A principal administrative division of a government: *the fire department; the department of public works.* **b.** A division of a business specializing in a particular product or service: *the personnel department.* **c.** A division of a school or college dealing with a particular field of knowledge: *the physics department.* **2. Department.** One of the principal executive divisions of the federal government of the United States, headed by a cabinet officer. **3.** A section of a department store selling a particular line of merchandise: *the home furnishings department.* **4.** An administrative district in France. **5.** *Informal.* An area of particular knowledge or responsibility; a specialty: *Getting the kids to bed is my department.* [French *département,* from Old French, separation, from *departir,* to divide. See DEPART.] —**de′part·men′tal** (dē′pärt-mĕn′tl) *adj.* —**de′part·men′tal·ly** *adv.*

de·part·men·tal·ize (dē′pärt-mĕn′tl-īz′) *tr.v.* **-ized, -iz·ing, -iz·es.** To organize into departments. —**de′part·men′tal·i·za′tion** (-ĭ-zā′shən) *n.*

department store *n.* A large retail store offering a variety of merchandise and services and organized in separate departments.

de·par·ture (dĭ-pär′chər) *n. Abbr.* **dep. 1.** The act of leaving. **2.** A starting out, as on a trip or a new course of action. **3.** A divergence or deviation, as from an established rule, plan, or procedure: *ordered curry as a departure from his usual bland diet.* **4.** *Nautical.* The distance sailed due east or west by a ship on its course. —*attributive.* Often used to modify another noun: *a departure lounge; departure dates.*

de·pau·pe·rate (də-pô′pər-ĭt) *adj.* **1.** Arrested in growth or development; stunted. **2.** Severely diminished; impoverished: *"But there were no pleasures in Australia. How could my friend admire so paleontologically depauperate a place?"* (Jake Page). [Middle English *depauperat,* from Medieval Latin *dēpauperātus,* past participle of *dēpauperāre,* to make poor : Latin *dē-,* de- + *pauper,* poor; see PAUPER.] —**de·pau′pe·ra′tion** *n.*

de·pend (dĭ-pĕnd′) *intr.v.* **-pend·ed, -pend·ing, -pends. 1.** To rely, especially for support or maintenance: *Children must depend on their parents.* **2.** To place trust or confidence: *You can depend on his honesty.* See Synonyms at **rely. 3.** To be determined, conditioned, or contingent: *a grade depending on the results of the final exam.* **4.** To have a dependence: *began to depend more and more on drugs.* **5.** To be pending or undecided, as in a court or legislature. **6.** To hang down: *"And ever-living Lamps depend in Rows"* (Alexander Pope). [Middle English *dependen,* to hang down, from Old French *dependre,* from Latin *dēpendēre* : *dē-,* de- + *pendēre,* to hang; see **(s)pen-** in Appendix.]

USAGE NOTE: *Depend,* indicating condition or contingency, is always followed by *on* or *upon,* as in *It depends on who is in charge.* Omission of the preposition is typical of casual speech.

de·pend·a·ble (dĭ-pĕn′də-bəl) *adj.* Trustworthy. See Synonyms at **reliable.** —**de·pend′a·bil′i·ty, de·pend′a·ble·ness** *n.* —**de·pend′a·bly** *adv.*

de·pend·ance (dĭ-pĕn′dəns) *n.* Variant of **dependence.**

de·pend·an·cy (dĭ-pĕn′dən-sē) *n.* Variant of **dependency.**

de·pend·ant (dĭ-pĕn′dənt) *n.* Variant of **dependent.**

de·pend·ence also **de·pend·ance** (dĭ-pĕn′dəns) *n.* **1.** The state of being dependent, as for support. **2. a.** Subordination to someone or something needed or greatly desired. **b.** Trust; reliance. See Synonyms at **trust. 3.** The state of being determined, influenced, or controlled by something else. **4.** A compulsive or chronic need; an addiction: *an alcohol dependence.*

de·pend·en·cy also **de·pend·an·cy** (dĭ-pĕn′dən-sē) *n., pl.* **-cies. 1.** Dependence. **2.** Something dependent or subordinate. **3.** *Abbr.* **dep.** A territory under the jurisdiction of a state of which it does not form an integral part.

de·pend·ent (dĭ-pĕn′dənt) *adj.* **1.** Contingent on another. **2.** Subordinate. **3.** Relying on or requiring the aid of another for support: *dependent children.* **4.** Hanging down. —**dependent** *n.* also **de·pend·ant.** One who relies on another especially for financial support. —**de·pend′ent·ly** *adv.*

SYNONYMS: *dependent, conditional, contingent, relative, subject.* The central meaning shared by these adjectives is "determined or to be determined by something else": *a water supply dependent on adequate rainfall; conditional acceptance of the apology; assistance contingent on continuing need; the importance of a discovery as relative to its usefulness; promotion subject to merit.*
ANTONYM: *independent.*

dependent clause *n. Grammar.* A clause that cannot stand alone as a full sentence and functions as a noun, adjective, or adverb within a sentence. Also called *subordinate clause.*

dependent variable *n.* **1.** *Mathematics.* A mathematical variable whose value is determined by the value assumed by an independent variable. **2.** *Statistics.* The observed variable in an experiment or study whose changes are determined by the presence or degree of one or more independent variables.

de·per·son·al·i·za·tion (dē-pûr′sə-nə-lĭ-zā′shən) *n.* **1. a.** The act of depersonalizing. **b.** The state of being depersonalized. **2.** *Psychology.* A state in which the normal sense of personal identity and reality is lost, characterized by feelings that one's actions and speech cannot be controlled.

de·per·son·al·ize (dē-pûr′sə-nə-līz′) *tr.v.* **-ized, -iz·ing, -iz·es. 1.** To deprive of individual character or a sense of personal identity: *a large corporation that depersonalizes its employees.* **2.** To render impersonal: *depersonalize an interview.*

De·pew (dĭ-pyo͞o′). A village of western New York, an industrial suburb of Buffalo. Population, 19,819.

de·pict (dĭ-pĭkt′) *tr.v.* **-pict·ed, -pict·ing, -picts. 1.** To represent in a picture or sculpture. **2.** To represent in words; describe. See Synonyms at **represent.** [Middle English *depicten,* from Latin *dēpingere, dēpict-* : *dē-,* de- + *pingere,* to picture; see **peig-** in Appendix.] —**de·pic′tion** *n.*

de·pig·men·ta·tion (dē-pĭg′mən-tā′shən, -mĕn-) *n.* Loss or removal of normal pigmentation.

dep·i·late (dĕp′ə-lāt′) *tr.v.* **-lat·ed, -lat·ing, -lates.** To remove hair from (the body). [Latin *dēpilāre, dēpilāt-* : *dē-,* de- + *pilāre,* to deprive of hair (from *pilus,* hair).] —**dep′i·la′tion** *n.* —**dep′i·la′tor** *n.*

de·pil·a·to·ry (dĭ-pĭl′ə-tôr′ē, -tōr′ē) *adj.* Having the capability to remove hair. —**depilatory** *n., pl.* **-ries.** A preparation in the form of a liquid or cream that is used to remove unwanted hair from the body.

de·plane (dē-plān′) *intr.v.* **-planed, -plan·ing, -planes.** To disembark from an airplane.

de·plete (dĭ-plēt′) *tr.v.* **-plet·ed, -plet·ing, -pletes.** To decrease the fullness of; use up or empty out. [Latin *dēplēre, dēplēt-,* to empty : *dē-,* de- + *plēre,* to fill; see **pelə-**[1] in Appendix.] —**de·plet′a·ble** *adj.*

SYNONYMS: *deplete, drain, exhaust, impoverish, enervate.* These verbs all mean to weaken severely by removing something essential. *Deplete* refers to using up gradually and only hints at harmful consequences: *I always replenish my food supply before it is depleted. Drain* suggests reduction by gradual drawing off and is stronger in implying harm: *War often drains a nation's economy. Exhaust* stresses reduction to a point of no further usefulness: *"The resources of civilization are not yet exhausted"* (William Ewart Gladstone). *Impoverish* refers to severe reduction of resources or qualities essential to adequate functioning: *"His death has eclipsed the gaiety of nations, and impoverished the public stock of harmless pleasure"* (Samuel Johnson). *Enervate* refers to weakening or destruction of vitality or strength: *Idleness enervates the will to succeed.*

de·ple·tion (dĭ-plē′shən) *n.* **1.** The act or process of depleting. **2.** The state of being depleted; exhaustion. **3.** The gradual use or consumption of a resource, especially a natural resource.

de·plor·a·ble (dĭ-plôr′ə-bəl, -plōr′-) *adj.* **1.** Worthy of severe condemnation or reproach: *a deplorable act of violence.* **2.** Lamentable; woeful: *My finances were in a deplorable state of neglect.* **3.** Wretched; bad: *deplorable housing conditions in the inner city.* —**de·plor′a·ble·ness, de·plor′a·bil′i·ty** *n.* —**de·plor′a·bly** *adv.*

de·plore (dĭ-plôr′, -plōr′) *tr.v.* **-plored, -plor·ing, -plores. 1.** To feel or express strong disapproval of; condemn: *"Somehow we had to master events, not simply deplore them"* (Henry A. Kissinger). **2.** To express sorrow or grief over. **3.** To regret; bemoan. [French *déplorer,* lament, regret, from Latin *dēplōrāre* : *dē-,* de- + *plōrāre,* to wail.]

de·ploy (dĭ-ploi′) *v.* **-ployed, -ploy·ing, -ploys.** —*tr.* **1. a.** To position (troops) in readiness for combat, as along a front or line. **b.** To bring (forces or material) into action. **c.** To base (a weapons system) in the field. **2.** To distribute (persons or forces) systematically or strategically. **3.** To put into use or action: *"Samuel Beckett's friends suspected that he was a genius, yet no one knew . . . how his abilities would be deployed"* (Richard Ellmann). —*intr.* To be or become deployed. [French *déployer,* from Old French *despleier,* from Latin *displicāre,* to scatter : *dis-,* dis- + *plicāre,* to fold; see **plek-** in Appendix.] —**de·ploy′a·**

deodar
Cedrus deodara

ă pat	oi boy
ā pay	ou out
âr care	o͝o took
ä father	o͞o boot
ĕ pet	ŭ cut
ē be	ûr urge
ĭ pit	th thin
ī pie	*th* this
îr pier	hw which
ŏ pot	zh vision
ō toe	ə about, item
ô paw	♦ regionalism

Stress marks: **′** (primary); ′ (secondary), as in **dictionary** (dĭk′shə-nĕr′ē)

bil′i·ty *n.* **—de·ploy′a·ble** *adj.* **—de·ploy′er** *n.* **—de·ploy′ment** *n.*

de·plume (dē-plo͞om′) *tr.v.* **-plumed, -plum·ing, -plumes.** To pluck the feathers from. [Middle English *deplumen,* from Old French *deplumer,* from Medieval Latin *dēplūmāre* : Latin *dē-,* de- + Latin *plūma,* feather.] **—de′plu·ma′tion** *n.*

de·po·lar·ize (dē-pō′lə-rīz′) *tr.v.* **-ized, -iz·ing, -iz·es. 1.** To partially or completely eliminate or counteract the polarization of. **2.** To demagnetize. **—de·po′lar·i·za′tion** (-lər-ĭ-zā′shən) *n.*

de·po·lit·i·cize (dē′pə-lĭt′ĭ-sīz′) *tr.v.* **-cized, -ciz·ing, -ciz·es.** To remove the political aspect from; remove from political influence or control: *depoliticize the administration of justice.* **—de′po·lit′i·ci·za′tion** (-sĭ-zā′shən) *n.*

de·pol·lute (dē′pə-lo͞ot′) *tr.v.* **-lut·ed, -lut·ing, -lutes.** To remove the pollution from: *depollute a river.*

de·pone (dĭ-pōn′) *v.* **-poned, -pon·ing, -pones.** *Law. —tr.* To testify or declare under oath. *—intr.* To give testimony. [Middle English *deponen,* from Medieval Latin *dēpōnere,* from Latin, to put down : *dē-,* de- + *pōnere,* to put; see **apo-** in Appendix.]

de·po·nent (dĭ-pō′nənt) *adj. Abbr.* **dep., dpt.** *Grammar.* Being a verb of active meaning but passive or middle form, as certain Latin and Greek verbs. **—deponent** *n. Abbr.* **dep., dpt. 1.** *Grammar.* A deponent verb. **2.** *Law.* One who testifies under oath, especially in writing. [Middle English, from Latin *dēpōnēns, dēpōnent-,* present participle of *dēpōnere,* to put down. See DEPONE.]

de·pop·u·late (dē-pŏp′yə-lāt′) *tr.v.* **-lat·ed, -lat·ing, -lates.** To reduce sharply the population of, as by disease, war, or forcible relocation. [Latin *dēpopulārī, dēpopulāt-,* to lay waste : *dē-,* de- + *populārī,* to ravage (from *populus,* people, throng).] **—de·pop′u·la′tion** *n.* **—de·pop′u·la′tor** *n.*

de·port (dĭ-pôrt′, -pōrt′) *tr.v.* **-port·ed, -port·ing, -ports. 1.** To expel from a country. See Synonyms at **banish. 2.** To behave or conduct (oneself) in a given manner; comport. [French *déporter,* to banish, from Latin *dēportāre,* to carry away : *dē-,* de- + *portāre,* to carry; see **per-**[2] in Appendix. Sense 2, Middle English, from Old French *deporter,* to behave, from Latin *dēportāre.*]

de·port·a·ble (dĭ-pôr′tə-bəl, -pōr′-) *adj.* **1.** Subject to deportation: *a deportable alien.* **2.** Punishable by deportation: *a deportable offense.*

de·por·ta·tion (dē′pôr-tā′shən, -pōr-) *n.* **1.** The act or an instance of deporting. **2.** Expulsion of an undesirable alien from a country.

de·port·ee (dē′pôr-tē′, -pōr-) *n.* A deported person.

de·port·ment (dĭ-pôrt′mənt, -pōrt′-) *n.* A manner of personal conduct; behavior. See Synonyms at **behavior.**

de·pos·al (dĭ-pō′zəl) *n.* The act or an instance of deposing from office.

de·pose (dĭ-pōz′) *v.* **-posed, -pos·ing, -pos·es.** *—tr.* **1.a.** To remove from office or power. **b.** To dethrone. **2.** *Law.* **a.** To state or affirm in a deposition or by affidavit. **b.** To take a deposition from: *Investigators will depose the witness behind closed doors.* **3.** To put or lay down; deposit. *—intr. Law.* To give a deposition; testify. [Middle English *deposen,* from Old French *deposer,* alteration (influenced by *poser,* to put; see POSE[1]) of Latin *dēpōnere,* to put down. See DEPONE.] **—de·pos′a·ble** *adj.*

de·pos·it (dĭ-pŏz′ĭt) *v.* **-it·ed, -it·ing, -its.** *—tr.* **1.** To put or set down; place. **2.** To lay down or leave behind by a natural process: *layers of sediment that were deposited on the ocean floor; glaciers that deposited their debris as they melted.* **3.a.** To give over or entrust for safekeeping. **b.** To put (money) in a bank or financial account. **4.** To give as partial payment or security. *—intr.* To become deposited; settle. **—deposit** *n. Abbr.* **dep. 1.** Something, such as money, that is entrusted for safekeeping, as in a bank. **2.** The condition of being deposited: *funds on deposit with a broker.* **3.** A partial or initial payment of a cost or debt: *left a $100 deposit toward the purchase of a stereo system.* **4.** A sum of money given as security for an item acquired for temporary use. **5.** A depository. **6.** Something deposited, especially by a natural process, as: **a.** *Geology.* A concentration of mineral matter or sediment in a layer, vein, or pocket: *iron ore deposits; rich deposits of oil and natural gas.* **b.** *Physiology.* An accumulation of organic or inorganic material, such as a lipid or mineral, in a body tissue, structure, or fluid. **c.** A sediment or precipitate that has settled out of a solution. **7.** A coating or crust left on a surface, as by evaporation or electrolysis. [Latin *dēpōnere, dēposit-* : *dē-,* de- + *pōnere,* to put; see **apo-** in Appendix.] **—de·pos′i·tor** *n.*

de·pos·i·tar·y (dĭ-pŏz′ĭ-tĕr′ē) *n.* **-ies. 1.** One entrusted with something for preservation or safekeeping. **2.** A depository.

dep·o·si·tion (dĕp′ə-zĭsh′ən) *n.* **1.** The act of deposing, as from high office. **2.** The act of depositing, especially the laying down of matter by a natural process. **3.** Something deposited; a deposit. **4.** *Law.* Testimony under oath, especially a statement by a witness that is written down or recorded for use in court at a later date. **5. Deposition.** The removal of Jesus from the cross. **—dep′o·si′tion·al** *adj.*

de·pos·i·to·ry (dĭ-pŏz′ĭ-tôr′ē, -tōr′ē) *n., pl.* **-ries. 1.** A place where something is deposited, as for storage or safekeeping; a repository. **2.** A trustee; a depositary.

de·pot (dē′pō, dĕp′ō) *n. Abbr.* **dep. 1.** A railroad or bus station. **2.** A warehouse or storehouse. **3.a.** A storage installation for military equipment and supplies. **b.** A station for assembling military recruits and forwarding them to active units. [French *dépôt,* from Old French *depost,* from Latin *dēpositum,* something deposited, from neuter past participle of *dēpōnere,* to put down, deposit. See DEPOSIT.]

depot
Train depot in Black Butte, California, 1926

de·prave (dĭ-prāv′) *tr.v.* **-praved, -prav·ing, -praves.** To debase, especially morally; corrupt. See Synonyms at **corrupt.** [Middle English *depraven,* to corrupt, from Old French *depraver,* from Latin *dēprāvāre* : *dē-,* de- + *prāvus,* crooked.] **—dep′ra·va′tion** (dĕp′rə-vā′shən) *n.* **—de·prav′er** *n.*

de·praved (dĭ-prāvd′) *adj.* Morally corrupt; perverted. **—de·prav′ed·ly** (-prā′vĭd-lē, -prāvd′lē) *adv.*

de·prav·i·ty (dĭ-prăv′ĭ-tē) *n., pl.* **-ties. 1.** Moral corruption or degradation. **2.** A depraved act or condition.

dep·re·cate (dĕp′rĭ-kāt′) *tr.v.* **-cat·ed, -cat·ing, -cates. 1.** To express disapproval of; deplore. **2.** To belittle; depreciate. [Latin *dēprecārī, dēprecāt-,* to ward off by prayer : *dē-,* de- + *precārī,* to pray; see **prek-** in Appendix.] **—dep′re·cat′ing·ly** *adv.* **—dep′re·ca′tion** *n.* **—dep′re·ca′tor** *n.*

USAGE NOTE: The first and fully accepted meaning of *deprecate* is "to express disapproval of." But the word has steadily encroached on the meaning of *depreciate.* It is now used, almost to the exclusion of *depreciate,* in the sense "to belittle or mildly disparage," as in *He deprecated his own contribution.* In an earlier survey, this newer sense was approved by a majority of the Usage Panel.

dep·re·ca·to·ry (dĕp′rĭ-kə-tôr′ē, -tōr′ē) also **dep·re·ca·tive** (-kā′tĭv) *adj.* **1.** Expressing disapproval or criticism. **2.** Mildly disparaging or uncomplimentary, especially of oneself. **—dep′re·ca·to′ri·ly** *adv.*

de·pre·cia·ble (dĭ-prē′shə-bəl) *adj.* That can be depreciated in value: *depreciable assets.*

de·pre·ci·ate (dĭ-prē′shē-āt′) *v.* **-at·ed, -at·ing, -ates.** *—tr.* **1.** To lessen the price or value of. **2.** To think or speak of as being of little worth; belittle. See Synonyms at **decry.** See Usage Note at **deprecate.** *—intr.* To diminish in price or value. [Medieval Latin *dēpreciāre, dēpreciāt-,* alteration of Latin *dēpretiāre* : *dē-,* de- + *pretium,* price; see **per-**[5] in Appendix.] **—de·pre′ci·a′tor** *n.*

de·pre·ci·a·tion (dĭ-prē′shē-ā′shən) *n.* **1.** A decrease or loss in value, as because of age, wear, or market conditions. **2.** *Accounting.* An allowance made for a loss in value of property. **3.** Reduction in the purchasing value of money. **4.** An instance of disparaging or belittlement.

de·pre·cia·to·ry (dĭ-prē′shə-tôr′ē, -tōr′ē) also **de·pre·cia·tive** (-shə-tĭv, -shē-ā′tĭv) *adj.* **1.** Diminishing in value. **2.** Disparaging; belittling.

dep·re·date (dĕp′rĭ-dāt′) *v.* **-dat·ed, -dat·ing, -dates.** *—tr.* To ransack; plunder. *—intr.* To engage in plundering. [Late Latin *dēpraedārī, dēpraedāt-* : Latin *dē-,* de- + Latin *praedārī,* to plunder (from *praeda,* booty; see **ghend-** in Appendix).] **—dep′re·da′tor** *n.* **—de·pred′a·to′ry** (dĭ-prĕd′ə-tôr′ē, -tōr′ē, dĕp′rĭ-də-) *adj.*

dep·re·da·tion (dĕp′rĭ-dā′shən) *n.* **1.** A predatory attack; a raid. **2.** Damage or loss; ravage: "[Carnegie Hall has] *withstood the wear and tear of enthusiastic music lovers and the normal depredations of time*" (Mechanical Engineering).

de·press (dĭ-prĕs′) *tr.v.* **-pressed, -press·ing, -press·es. 1.** To lower in spirits; deject. **2.a.** To cause to drop or sink; lower: *The drought depressed the water level in the reservoirs.* **b.** To press down: *Depress the space bar on a typewriter.* **3.** To lessen the activity or force of; weaken: *feared that rising inflation would further depress the economy.* **4.** To lower prices in (a stock market). [Middle English *depressen,* to push down, from Old French *depresser,* from Latin *dēprimere, dēpress-* : *dē-,* de- + *premere,* to press; see **per-**[4] in Appendix.] **—de·press′i·ble** *adj.*

de·pres·sant (dĭ-prĕs′ənt) *adj.* Tending to lower the rate of vital physiological activities. **—depressant** *n.* An agent, especially a drug, that decreases the rate of vital physiological activities.

de·pressed (dĭ-prĕst′) *adj.* **1.** Low in spirits; dejected. **2.** Suffering from psychological depression. **3.** Sunk below the surrounding region: *the depressed center of a crater.* **4.** Lower in amount, degree, or position: *Oil reserves were at depressed levels because of increasing industrial demands.* **5.a.** Sluggish in growth or activity: *a depressed sector of the economy.* **b.** Suffering from social and economic hardship: *a depressed region.* **6.** *Botany.* Flattened downward, as if pressed from above. **7.** *Zoology.* Flattened along the dorsal and ventral surfaces.

SYNONYMS: *depressed, blue, dejected, dispirited, downcast, downhearted.* The central meaning shared by these adjectives is "affected or marked by low spirits": *depressed by the loss of his job; lonely and blue in a strange city; is dejected but trying to look cheerful; a dispirited and resigned expression on her face; looked downcast after his defeat; a card welcomed by the downhearted patient.*

de·press·ing (dĭ-prĕs′ĭng) *adj.* **1.** Causing especially emotional depression. **2.** Dismal; dreary: *a week of rainy, depressing weather.* **—de·press′ing·ly** *adv.*

de·pres·sion (dĭ-prĕsh′ən) *n.* **1.a.** The act of depressing. **b.** The condition of being depressed. **2.** An area that is sunk below its surroundings; a hollow. **3.** The condition of feeling sad or despondent. **4.** *Psychology.* A psychotic or neurotic condition characterized by an inability to concentrate, insomnia, and feelings of extreme sadness, dejection, and hopelessness. **5.a.** A reduction in activity or force. **b.** A reduction in physiological vigor or activity: *a depression in respiration.* **c.** A lowering in amount, degree, or position. **6.** *Economics.* A period of drastic decline in a national or international economy, characterized by decreasing business activity, falling prices, and unemployment. **7.** *Meteorology.* A region of low barometric pressure. **8.** The angular distance below the horizontal plane through the point of observation. **9.** *Astronomy.* The angular distance of a celestial body below the horizon.

De·pres·sion glass (dĭ-prĕsh′ən) *n.* Glassware of many colors and patterns produced in large quantities during the 1920's and 1930's. [After the Great *Depression,* a period of severe economic hardship during the 1930's.]

de·pres·sive (dĭ-prĕs′ĭv) *adj.* **1.** Tending to depress or lower. **2.** Depressing; gloomy: *"Americans entertained the depressive thought that they had ceased to be themselves"* (Lance Morrow). **3.** Of or relating to psychological depression. **—depressive** *n.* A person suffering from psychological depression. **—de·pres′sive·ly** *adv.* **—de·pres′sive·ness** *n.*

de·pres·sor (dĭ-prĕs′ər) *n.* **1.** Something that depresses or is used to depress. **2.** An instrument used to depress a part: *a tongue depressor.* **3.** Any of various muscles that serve to draw down a part of the body.

depressor nerve *n.* A nerve that when stimulated acts to lower arterial blood pressure.

de·pres·sur·ize (dē-prĕsh′ə-rīz′) *tr.v.* **-ized, -iz·ing, -iz·es.** To reduce the pressure of air or gas within (a chamber or vehicle, for example). **—de·pres′sur·i·za′tion** (-prĕsh′ər-ĭ-zā′shən) *n.*

de·priv·al (dĭ-prī′vəl) *n.* Deprivation.

dep·ri·va·tion (dĕp′rə-vā′shən) *n.* **1.a.** The act or an instance of depriving; loss. **b.** The condition of being deprived; privation. **2.** A removal of rank or office.

de·prive (dĭ-prīv′) *tr.v.* **-prived, -priv·ing, -prives. 1.** To take something away from: *The court ruling deprived us of any share in the inheritance.* **2.** To keep from possessing or enjoying; deny: *They were deprived of a normal childhood by the war.* **3.** To remove from office. [Middle English *depriven,* from Old French *depriver,* from Medieval Latin *dēprīvāre* : Latin *dē-,* de- + Latin *prīvāre,* to rob (from *prīvus,* alone, without; see **per**[1] in Appendix).] **—de·priv′a·ble** *adj.*

de·prived (dĭ-prīvd′) *adj.* **1.** Marked by deprivation, especially of economic or social necessities. **2.** Lacking in advantage, opportunity, or experience: *"Preschool is designed to give children from educationally deprived households an early boost"* (Jeff Brody).

de·pro·gram (dē-prō′grăm′, -grəm) *tr.v.* **-grammed, -gram·ming, -grams** or **-gramed, -gram·ing, -grams.** To counteract or try to counteract the effect of an indoctrination, especially a religious or cult indoctrination. **—de·pro′gram′mer** *n.*

dept. *abbr.* **1.** Department. **2.** Deputy.

depth (dĕpth) *n.* **1.** The condition or quality of being deep. **2.a.** The extent, measurement, or dimension downward, backward, or inward: *dove to a depth of 30 feet; shelves with enough depth to store the large boxes.* **b.** The measurement or sense of distance from an observation point, such as linear perspective in painting. **3.** Often **depths.** A deep part or place: *the ocean depths; in the depths of the forest.* **4.a.** The most profound or intense part or stage: *the depth of despair; an experience that touched the depths of tragedy.* **b.** Intensity; force: *had not realized the depth of their feelings for one another.* **5.** The severest or worst part: *in the depth of an economic depression.* **6.** A low point, level, or degree: *Production has fallen to new depths.* **7.** Intellectual complexity or penetration; profundity: *a novel of great depth.* **8.** The range of one's understanding or competence: *I am out of my depth when it comes to cooking.* **9.** Strength held in reserve, especially a supply of skilled or capable replacements: *a team with depth at every position.* **10.** The degree of richness or intensity: *depth of color.* **11.** Lowness in pitch. **12.** Complete detail; thoroughness: *the depth of her research; an interview conducted in great depth.* [Middle English *depthe,* from *dep,* deep. See DEEP.]

depth charge *n.* A charge designed for detonation at a preset depth under water, used especially against submarines. Also called *depth bomb.*

depth finder *n.* An instrument used to measure the depth of water, especially by radar or ultrasound.

depth perception *n.* The ability to perceive spatial relationships, especially distances between objects, in three dimensions.

depth psychology *n.* **1.** Psychology of the unconscious mind. **2.** Psychoanalysis.

depth sounder *n.* An ultrasonic instrument used to measure the depth of water under a ship.

dep·u·rate (dĕp′yə-rāt′) *tr. & intr.v.* **-rat·ed, -rat·ing, -rates.** To cleanse or purify or become cleansed or purified. [Medieval Latin *dēpūrāre, dēpūrāt-* : Latin *dē-,* de- + *pūrus,* pure; see **peuə-** in Appendix.] **—dep′u·ra′tion** *n.* **—dep′u·ra′tor** *n.*

dep·u·ta·tion (dĕp′yə-tā′shən) *n.* **1.** A person or group appointed to represent another or others; a delegation. **2.a.** The act of deputing. **b.** The state of being deputed.

de·pute (dĭ-pyōōt′) *tr.v.* **-put·ed, -put·ing, -putes. 1.** To appoint or authorize as an agent or a representative. **2.** To assign (authority or duties) to another; delegate. [Middle English *deputen,* from Old French *deputer,* from Late Latin *dēputāre,* to allot, from Latin, to consider : *dē-,* de- + *putāre,* to ponder; see **peuə-** in Appendix.]

dep·u·tize (dĕp′yə-tīz′) *tr. & intr.v.* **-tized, -tiz·ing, -tiz·es.** To appoint or serve as a deputy. **—dep′u·ti·za′tion** (-tĭ-zā′shən) *n.*

dep·u·ty (dĕp′yə-tē) *n., pl.* **-ties.** *Abbr.* **dep., dept., d., D. 1.** A person appointed or empowered to act for another. **2.** An assistant exercising full authority in the absence of his or her superior and equal authority in emergencies: *a deputy to the sheriff.* **3.** A representative in a legislative body in certain countries. [Middle English *depute,* from Old French, from past participle of *deputer,* to depute. See DEPUTE.]

De Quin·cey (dĭ kwĭn′sē, -zē), **Thomas.** 1785–1859. British writer best known for his autobiographical *Confessions of an English Opium Eater* (1821).

der. *abbr.* **1.** Derivation. **2.** Derivative.

de·rac·i·nate (də-răs′ə-nāt′) *tr.v.* **-nat·ed, -nat·ing, -nates. 1.** To pull out by the roots; uproot. **2.** To displace from one's native or accustomed environment. [From French *déraciner,* from Old French *desraciner* : *des-,* de- + *racine,* root (from Late Latin *rādīcīna,* from Latin *rādīx;* see **wrād-** in Appendix).] **—de·rac′i·na′tion** *n.*

de·rail (dē-rāl′) *intr. & tr.v.* **-railed, -rail·ing, -rails. 1.** To run or cause to run off the rails. **2.** To come or bring to a sudden halt: *a campaign derailed by lack of funds; a policy that derailed under the new administration.* [French *dérailler* : *dé-,* off (from Old French *de-;* see DE–) + *rail,* rail (from English; see RAIL[1]).] **—de·rail′ment** *n.*

de·rail·leur (dĭ-rā′lər) *n.* A device for shifting gears on a bicycle by moving the chain between sprocket wheels of different sizes. [French *dérailleur,* from *dérailler,* to derail. See DERAIL.]

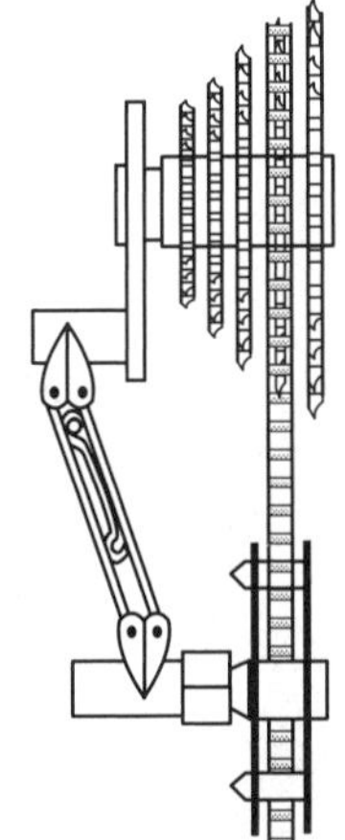

derailleur

De·rain (də-răN′), **André.** 1880–1954. French artist who was one of the original fauvists but eventually adopted a more conservative style.

de·range (dĭ-rānj′) *tr.v.* **-ranged, -rang·ing, -rang·es. 1.** To disturb the order or arrangement of. **2.** To upset the normal condition or functioning of. **3.** To disturb mentally; make insane. [French *déranger,* from Old French *desrengier* : *des-,* de- + *reng,* line (of Germanic origin; see **sker-**[2] in Appendix).] **—de·range′ment** *n.*

der·by (dûr′bē; *British* där′bē) *n., pl.* **-bies. 1.** *Sports.* Any of various annual horse races, especially for three-year-olds. **2.** *Sports.* A formal race usually having an open field of contestants: *a motorcycle derby.* **3.** A stiff felt hat with a round crown and a narrow, curved brim. [After Edward Stanley, 12th Earl of *Derby* (1752–1834), founder of the English Derby.]

derby

Der·by (där′bē). A city of central England west of Nottingham. Settled by the Romans, it is a trade and manufacturing center with a pottery industry dating from the 18th century. Population, 216,500.

de·rec·og·nize (dē-rĕk′əg-nīz′) *tr.v.* **-nized, -niz·ing, -niz·es.** To rescind formal, especially diplomatic recognition of: *a proposal to derecognize the outlaw terrorist state.* **—de·rec′og·ni′tion** (-nĭsh′ən) *n.*

de·reg·u·late (dē-rĕg′yə-lāt′) *tr.v.* **-lat·ed, -lat·ing, -lates.** To free from regulation, especially to remove government regulations from: *deregulate the airline industry.* **—de·reg′u·la′tion** *n.* **—de·reg′u·la′tor** *n.* **—de·reg′u·la·to′ry** (-lə-tôr′ē, -tōr′ē) *adj.*

der·e·lict (dĕr′ə-lĭkt′) *adj.* **1.** Deserted by an owner or keeper; abandoned. **2.** Run-down; dilapidated. **3.** Neglectful of duty or obligation; remiss. See Synonyms at **negligent. —derelict** *n.* **1.** Abandoned property, especially a ship abandoned at sea. **2.** A homeless or jobless person; a vagrant. **3.** *Law.* Land left dry by a permanent recession of the water line. [Latin *dērelictus,* past participle of *dērelinquere,* to abandon : *dē-,* de- + *relinquere,* to leave behind; see RELINQUISH.]

der·e·lic·tion (dĕr′ə-lĭk′shən) *n.* **1.** Willful neglect, as of duty or principle. **2.a.** The act of abandoning; abandonment. **b.** A state of abandonment or neglect. **3.** *Law.* **a.** A gaining of land by the permanent recession of the water line. **b.** The land so gained.

de·re·press (dē′rĭ-prĕs′) *tr.v.* **-pressed, -press·ing, -press·es.** To induce the operation of (a gene) by deactivating the repressor. **—de′re·pres′sion** (-prĕsh′ən) *n.*

de·rib (dē-rĭb′) *tr.v.* **-ribbed, -rib·bing, -ribs.** To remove the ribs from before preparing as part of a meal: *deribbed the green peppers.*

de·ride (dĭ-rīd′) *tr.v.* **-rid·ed, -rid·ing, -rides.** To speak of or treat with contemptuous mirth. See Synonyms at **ridicule.** [Latin *dērīdēre* : *dē-,* de- + *rīdēre,* to laugh at.] **—de·rid′er** *n.* **—de·rid′ing·ly** *adv.*

de ri·gueur (də rē-gœr′) *adj.* Required by the current fashion

ă pat	oi boy
ā pay	ou out
âr care	ŏŏ took
ä father	ōō boot
ĕ pet	ŭ cut
ē be	ûr urge
ĭ pit	th thin
ī pie	*th* this
îr pier	hw which
ŏ pot	zh vision
ō toe	ə about, item
ô paw	♦ regionalism

Stress marks: ′ (primary); ′ (secondary), as in **dictionary** (dĭk′shə-nĕr′ē)

or custom; socially obligatory. [French : *de*, of + *rigueur*, rigor, strictness.]

de·ri·sion (dĭ-rĭzh′ən) *n.* **1.a.** Contemptuous or jeering laughter; ridicule. **b.** A state of being derided: *The proposal was held in derision by members of the board.* **2.** An object of ridicule; a laughingstock. [Middle English *derisioun*, from Anglo-Norman, from Late Latin *dērīsiō*, *dērīsiōn-*, from Latin *dērīsus*, past participle of *dērīdēre*, to deride. See DERIDE.]

de·ri·sive (dĭ-rī′sĭv, -zĭv, -rĭs′ĭv, -rĭz′-) *adj.* Mocking; jeering. **—de·ri′sive·ly** *adv.* **—de·ri′sive·ness** *n.*

de·ri·so·ry (dĭ-rī′sə-rē, -zə-) *adj.* **1.** Expressing derision; derisive. **2.** Laughable; ridiculous: *a contribution so small as to be derisory.*

deriv. *abbr.* **1.** Derivation. **2.** Derivative.

der·i·vate (dĕr′ə-vāt′) *adj.* Derivative.

der·i·va·tion (dĕr′ə-vā′shən) *n. Abbr.* **der., deriv. 1.** The act or process of deriving. **2.** The state or fact of being derived; originating: *a custom of recent derivation.* **3.** Something derived; a derivative. **4.** The form or source from which something is derived; an origin. **5.** The historical origin and development of a word; an etymology. **6.** *Linguistics.* **a.** The process by which words are formed from existing words or bases by adding affixes, as *singer* from *sing* or *undo* from *do*, by changing the shape of the word or base, as *song* from *sing*, or by adding an affix and changing the pronunciation of the word or base, as *electricity* from *electric.* **b.** A linguistic description of the process of word formation. **7.** *Logic & Mathematics.* A logical or mathematical process indicating through a sequence of statements that a result such as a theorem or a formula necessarily follows from the initial assumptions. **—der′i·va′tion·al** *adj.*

derrick
For hole-boring equipment

de·riv·a·tive (dĭ-rĭv′ə-tĭv) *adj.* **1.** Resulting from or employing derivation: *a derivative word; a derivative process.* **2.** Copied or adapted from others: *a highly derivative prose style.* **—derivative** *n. Abbr.* **deriv., der. 1.** Something derived. **2.** *Linguistics.* A word formed from another by derivation, such as *electricity* from *electric.* **3.** *Mathematics.* **a.** The limiting value of the ratio of the change in a function to the corresponding change in its independent variable. **b.** The instantaneous rate of change of a function with respect to its variable. **c.** The slope of a graph of an equation at a given point. Also called *differential coefficient, fluxion.* **4.** *Chemistry.* A compound derived from another and containing essential elements of the parent substance. **—de·riv′a·tive·ly** *adv.* **—de·riv′a·tive·ness** *n.*

de·rive (dĭ-rīv′) *v.* **-rived, -riv·ing, -rives.** *—tr.* **1.** To obtain or receive from a source. **2.** To arrive at by reasoning; deduce or infer: *derive a conclusion from facts.* **3.** To trace the origin or development of (a word). **4.** *Chemistry.* To produce or obtain (a compound) from another substance by chemical reaction. *—intr.* To issue from a source; originate. See Synonyms at **stem**[1]. [Middle English *deriven*, to be derived from, from Old French *deriver*, from Latin *dērīvāre*, to derive, draw off : *dē-*, de- + *rīvus*, stream; see **rei-** in Appendix.] **—de·riv′a·ble** *adj.* **—de·riv′er** *n.*

derm– *pref.* Variant of **derma–.**

–derm *suff.* Skin; covering: *blastoderm.* [From Greek *derma*, skin (possibly influenced by French *-derme*). See **der-** in Appendix.]

der·ma[1] (dûr′mə) *n.* See **dermis.** [Greek, skin. See **der-** in Appendix.]

dervish

der·ma[2] (dûr′mə) *n.* Beef casing stuffed with a seasoned mixture of matzo meal or flour, onion, and suet, prepared by boiling, then roasting. Also called *kishke, stuffed derma.* [Possibly Yiddish *gederem*, intestines, from Middle High German *darm*, intestine, from Old High German. See **terə-**[1] in Appendix.]

derma– or **derm–** or **dermo–** *pref.* Skin: *dermal.* [From Greek *derma*, skin. See DERMA[1].]

–derma *suff.* Skin; skin disease: *scleroderma.* [New Latin, from Greek *derma*, skin. See **der-** in Appendix.]

der·ma·bra·sion (dûr′mə-brā′zhən) *n.* A surgical procedure designed to remove skin imperfections, such as scars, by abrading the surface of the skin with fine sandpaper or wire brushes.

der·mal (dûr′məl) also **der·mic** (-mĭk) *adj.* Of or relating to the skin or dermis.

der·map·ter·an (dər-măp′tər-ən) *n.* Any of various insects of the order Dermaptera, including the earwigs, having an elongated, flattened body equipped with a pair of pincerlike appendages at the posterior end. **—dermapteran** *adj.* Of or belonging to the order Dermaptera. [From New Latin *Dermaptera*, order name : Greek *derma-*, derma- + Greek *ptera*, pl. of *pteron*, wing; see –PTER.]

dermat– *pref.* Variant of **dermato–.**

der·ma·ti·tis (dûr′mə-tī′tĭs) *n.* Inflammation of the skin.

dermato– or **dermat–** *pref.* Skin: *dermatophyte.* [Greek *derma*, *dermat-*, skin. See **der-** in Appendix.]

der·mat·o·gen (dûr-măt′ə-jən) *n. Botany.* The outer layer of apical meristem, from which the epidermis is formed. Also called *protoderm.*

der·ma·toid (dûr′mə-toid′) also **der·moid** (-moid′) *adj.* Resembling skin; skinlike.

der·ma·tol·o·gy (dûr′mə-tŏl′ə-jē) *n.* The branch of medicine that is concerned with the physiology and pathology of the skin. **—der′ma·to·log′i·cal** (-tə-lŏj′ĭ-kəl), **der′ma·to·log′ic** *adj.* **—der′ma·tol′o·gist** *n.*

der·ma·tome (dûr′mə-tōm′) *n.* **1.** *Anatomy.* An area of skin innervated by sensory fibers from a single spinal nerve. **2.** *Medicine.* An instrument used in cutting thin slices of the skin, as for skin grafts. **3.** *Embryology.* The part of a mesodermal somite from which the dermis develops. [DERMA[1] + –TOME.]

der·mat·o·phyte (dûr-măt′ə-fīt′, dûr′mə-tə-) *n.* Any of various fungi that can cause parasitic skin infections. **—der·mat′o·phyt′ic** (-fĭt′ĭk) *adj.*

der·ma·to·phy·to·sis (dûr′mə-tō′fī-tō′sĭs) *n.* A fungal infection of the skin, especially athlete's foot.

der·ma·to·plas·ty (dûr′mə-tō-plăs′tē) *n.* The use of skin grafts in plastic surgery to correct defects or replace skin destroyed by injury or disease.

der·ma·to·sis (dûr′mə-tō′sĭs) *n., pl.* **-ses** (-sēz). *Pathology.* A skin disease, especially one that is not accompanied by inflammation.

–dermatous *suff.* Having a specified kind of skin: *sclerodermatous.* [Greek *derma*, *dermat-*, skin; see DERMATO– + –OUS.]

der·mic (dûr′mĭk) *adj.* Variant of **dermal.**

der·mis (dûr′mĭs) *n.* The sensitive connective tissue layer of the skin located below the epidermis, containing nerve endings, sweat and sebaceous glands, and blood and lymph vessels. Also called *corium, cutis, derma.* [New Latin, back-formation from *epidermis.* See EPIDERMIS.]

dermo– *pref.* Variant of **derma–.**

der·moid (dûr′moid′) *adj.* Variant of **dermatoid.**

der·nier cri (dĕr′nyā krē′) *n.* The latest thing; the newest fashion. [French : *dernier*, last, latest + *cri*, cry.]

der·o·gate (dĕr′ə-gāt′) *v.* **-gat·ed, -gat·ing, -gates.** *—intr.* **1.** To take away; detract: *an error that will derogate from your reputation.* **2.** To deviate from a standard or expectation; go astray. *—tr.* To disparage; belittle. See Synonyms at **decry.** [Middle English *derogaten*, from Latin *dērogāre*, *dērogāt-* : *dē-*, de- + *rogāre*, to ask; see **reg-** in Appendix.] **—der′o·ga′tion** *n.*

de·rog·a·tive (dĭ-rŏg′ə-tĭv, dĕr′ə-gā′-) *adj.* **1.** Tending to derogate; detractive. **2.** Disparaging; derogatory. **—de·rog′a·tive·ly** *adv.*

de·rog·a·to·ry (dĭ-rŏg′ə-tôr′ē, -tōr′ē) *adj.* **1.** Disparaging; belittling: *a derogatory comment.* **2.** Tending to detract or diminish. **—de·rog′a·to′ri·ly** *adv.* **—de·rog′a·to′ri·ness** *n.*

der·rick (dĕr′ĭk) *n.* **1.** A machine for hoisting and moving heavy objects, consisting of a movable boom equipped with cables and pulleys and connected to the base of an upright stationary beam. **2.** A tall framework over a drilled hole, especially an oil well, used to support boring equipment or hoist and lower lengths of pipe. [Obsolete *derick*, hangman, gallows, after *Derick*, 16th-century English hangman.]

der·ri·ère also **der·ri·ere** (dĕr′ē-âr′) *n.* The buttocks; the rear. [French, behind, from Old French *deriere*, in back of, from Vulgar Latin **dē retrō* : Latin *dē*, from, of; see DE– + Latin *retrō*, back; see RETRO–.]

der·ring-do (dĕr′ĭng-do͞o′) *n.* Daring or reckless action. [Middle English, from *durring don*, daring to do : *durring*, present participle of *durren*, to dare (from Old English *durran*; see DARE) + *don*, to do; see DO[1].]

der·rin·ger (dĕr′ĭn-jər) *n.* A short-barreled pistol that has a large bore and is small enough to be carried in a pocket. [After Henry *Deringer* (1786–1868), American gunsmith.]

der·ris (dĕr′ĭs) *n.* Any of various usually woody vines of the genus *Derris* of tropical Asia, whose roots yield the insecticide rotenone. [New Latin, genus name, from Greek, covering. See **der-** in Appendix.]

Der·ry (dĕr′ē). See **Londonderry.**

der·vish (dûr′vĭsh) *n.* **1.** A member of any of various Moslem ascetic orders, some of which perform whirling dances and vigorous chanting as acts of ecstatic devotion. **2.** One that possesses abundant, often frenzied energy: "[She] *is a dervish of unfocused energy, an accident about to happen*" (Jane Gross). [Turkish *derviş*, mendicant, from Persian *darvēsh.*]

WORD HISTORY: The word *dervish* calls to mind the phrases *howling dervish* and *whirling dervish.* Certainly there are dervishes whose religious exercises include making loud howling noises or whirling rapidly so as to bring about a dizzy, mystical state. But a dervish is really the Moslem equivalent of a monk or friar, the Persian word *darvēsh*, the ultimate source of *dervish*, meaning "religious mendicant." The word is first recorded in English in 1585.

Der·zha·vin (dĕr-zhä′vĭn, dyĭr-), **Gavriil Romanovish.** 1743–1816. Russian lyric poet regarded as the greatest national poet before Pushkin.

DES (dē′ē-ĕs′) *n.* A synthetic nonsteroidal substance, $C_{18}H_{20}O_2$, having estrogenic properties and once used to treat menstrual disorders. It is no longer prescribed because of the incidence of certain vaginal cancers in the daughters of women so treated. [D(I)E(THYL)S(TILBESTROL).]

de·sa·cral·ize (dē-sā′krə-līz′, -săk′rə-) *tr.v.* **-ized, -iz·ing, -iz·es.** To divest of sacred or religious significance.

de·sal·i·nate (dē-săl′ə-nāt′) *tr.v.* **-nat·ed, -nat·ing, -nates.** To desalinize. **—de·sal′i·na′tion** *n.* **—de·sal′i·na′tor** *n.*

de·sal·i·nize (dē-săl′ə-nīz′) *tr.v.* **-nized, -niz·ing, -niz·es.**

To remove salts and other chemicals from (sea water or soil, for example). **—de·sal′i·ni·za′tion** (-nĭ-zā′shən) *n.*

de·salt (dē-sôlt′) *tr.v.* **-salt·ed, -salt·ing, -salts.** To desalinize.

De·sargues (dā-zärg′), **Gérard.** 1591–1661. French army officer and mathematician regarded as one of the founders of modern geometry.

des·cant (dĕs′kănt′) *n.* **1.** Also **dis·cant** (dĭs′-). *Music.* **a.** An ornamental melody or counterpoint sung or played above a theme. **b.** The highest part sung in part music. **2.** A discussion or discourse on a theme. **—descant** (dĕs′kănt′, dĕ-skănt′) *intr.v.* **-cant·ed, -cant·ing, -cants. 1.** To comment at length; discourse: *"He used to descant critically on the dishes which had been at table"* (James Boswell). **2.** Also **dis·cant** (dĭs′kănt′, dĭ-skănt′). *Music.* **a.** To sing or play a descant. **b.** To sing melodiously. [Middle English, from Anglo-Norman *descaunt,* from Medieval Latin *discantus,* a refrain : Latin *dis-,* dis- + Latin *cantus,* song, from past participle of *canere,* to sing. See **kan-** in Appendix.] **—des′cant′er** *n.*

Des·cartes (dā-kärt′), **René.** 1596–1650. French mathematician and philosopher. Considered the father of analytic geometry, he formulated the Cartesian system of coordinates. His philosophy is based on the rationalistic premise "I think, therefore I am."

de·scend (dĭ-sĕnd′) *v.* **-scend·ed, -scend·ing, -scends.** —*intr.* **1.** To move from a higher to a lower place; come or go down. **2.** To slope, extend, or incline downward: *"A rough path descended like a steep stair into the plain"* (J.R.R. Tolkien). **3. a.** To come from an ancestor or ancestry: *She was descended from a pioneer family.* **b.** To come down from a source; derive: *a tradition descending from colonial days.* **c.** To pass by inheritance: *The house has descended through four generations.* **4.** To lower oneself; stoop: *"She, the conqueror, had descended to the level of the conquered"* (James Bryce). **5.** To proceed or progress downward, as in rank, pitch, or scale: *titles listed in descending order of importance; notes that descended to the lower register.* **6.** To arrive or attack in a sudden or an overwhelming manner: *summer tourists descending on the seashore village.* —*tr.* **1. a.** To move from a higher to a lower part of; go down. **b.** To get down from: *"People descended the minibus that shuttled guests to the nearby . . . beach"* (Howard Kaplan). **2.** To extend or proceed downward along: *a road that descended the mountain in sharp curves.* [Middle English *descenden,* from Old French *descendre,* from Latin *dēscendere* : *dē-,* de- + *scandere,* to climb; see **skand-** in Appendix.] **—de·scend′i·ble, de·scend′a·ble** *adj.*

de·scen·dant (dĭ-sĕn′dənt) *n.* **1.** A person, an animal, or a plant whose descent can be traced to a particular individual or group. **2.** Something derived from a prototype or earlier form: *Today's bicycles are descendants of the earlier velocipede.* **—descendant** *adj.* Variant of **descendent.**

de·scen·dent also **de·scen·dant** (dĭ-sĕn′dənt) *adj.* **1.** Moving downward; descending. **2.** Proceeding by descent from an ancestor.

de·scend·er (dĭ-sĕn′dər) *n.* **1.** One that descends. **2.** *Printing.* **a.** The part of the lowercase letters, such as *g, p,* and *q,* that extends below the other lowercase letters. **b.** A letter with such a part.

de·scent (dĭ-sĕnt′) *n.* **1.** The act or an instance of descending. **2.** A way down. **3.** A downward incline or passage; a slope. **4. a.** Hereditary derivation; lineage: *a person of African descent.* **b.** One generation of a specific lineage. **5. a.** The fact or process of coming down or being derived from a source: *a paper tracing the descent of the novel from old picaresque tales.* **b.** Development in form or structure during transmission from an original source. **6.** *Law.* Transference of property by inheritance. **7.** A lowering or decline, as in status or level: *Her career went into a rapid descent after the charges of misconduct.* **8.** A sudden visit or attack; an onslaught. [Middle English, from Old French, from *descendre,* to descend. See DESCEND.]

Des·chutes (dā-sho͞ot′, də-sho͞ots′). A river rising in the Cascade Range of west-central Oregon and flowing about 402 km (250 mi) generally north to the Columbia River near The Dalles.

de·scram·ble (dē-skrăm′bəl) *tr.v.* **-bled, -bling, -bles.** To unscramble (a coded message or signal, for example).

de·scram·bler (dē-skrăm′blər) *n.* An electronic device that decodes a scrambled transmission into a signal that is intelligible to the receiving apparatus.

de·scribe (dĭ-skrīb′) *tr.v.* **-scribed, -scrib·ing, -scribes. 1.** To give an account of in speech or writing. **2.** To convey an idea or impression of; characterize: *She described her childhood as a time of wonder and discovery.* **3.** To represent pictorially; depict: *Goya's etchings describe the horrors of war in grotesque detail.* **4.** To trace the form or outline of: *describe a circle with a compass.* [Middle English *describen,* from Latin *dēscrībere,* to write down : *dē-,* de- + *scrībere,* to write; see **skrībh-** in Appendix.] **—de·scrib′a·ble** *adj.* **—de·scrib′er** *n.*

SYNONYMS: *describe, narrate, recite, recount, rehearse, relate, report.* The central meaning shared by these verbs is "to tell the facts, details, or particulars of something verbally or in writing": *described the accident; narrated their experiences in the Far East; an explorer reciting her adventures; a mercenary recounting his exploits; parents rehearsing the dangers the children faced; related the day's events; came back and reported what she had seen.*

de·scrip·tion (dĭ-skrĭp′shən) *n.* **1.** The act, process, or technique of describing. **2.** A statement or an account describing something: *published a description of her travels; gave a vivid description of the game.* **3.** A pictorial representation: *Monet's ethereal descriptions of haystacks and water lilies.* **4.** A kind or sort: *cars of every size and description.* [Middle English *descripcioun,* from Anglo-Norman, from Latin *dēscrīptiō, dēscrīptiōn-,* from *dēscrīptus,* past participle of *dēscrībere,* to write down. See DESCRIBE.]

de·scrip·tive (dĭ-skrĭp′tĭv) *adj.* **1.** Involving or characterized by description; serving to describe. **2.** Concerned with classification or description: *a descriptive science.* **3.** *Grammar.* **a.** Expressing an attribute of the modified noun, as *green* in *green grass.* Used of an adjective or adjectival clause. **b.** Nonrestrictive. **—de·scrip′tive·ly** *adv.* **—de·scrip′tive·ness** *n.*

descriptive clause *n. Grammar.* A nonrestrictive clause.

descriptive linguistics *n.* The study of a language or languages at a specific stage of development, with emphasis on constructing a complete grammar rather than on historical development or comparison with other languages.

de·scrip·tor (dĭ-skrĭp′tər) *n. Computer Science.* A word, a phrase, or an alphanumeric character used to identify an item in an information storage and retrieval system. [Late Latin, describer, from Latin *dēscrībere, dēscript-,* to describe. See DESCRIBE.]

de·scry (dĭ-skrī′) *tr.v.* **-scried, -scry·ing, -scries. 1.** To catch sight of (something difficult to discern). See Synonyms at **see[1]**. **2.** To discover by careful observation or scrutiny; detect: *descried a message of hope in her words.* [Middle English *descrien,* from Old French *descrier,* to call, cry out. See DECRY.] **—de·scri′er** *n.*

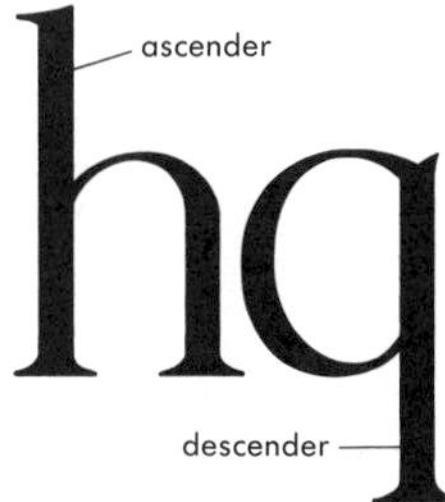

descender

des·e·crate (dĕs′ĭ-krāt′) *tr.v.* **-crat·ed, -crat·ing, -crates.** To violate the sacredness of; profane. [DE– + (CON)SECRATE.] **—des′e·crat′er, des′e·cra′tor** *n.* **—des′e·cra′tion** *n.*

de·seg·re·gate (dē-sĕg′rĭ-gāt′) *v.* **-gat·ed, -gat·ing, -gates.** —*tr.* **1.** To abolish or eliminate segregation in. **2.** To open (a school or workplace, for example) to members of all races or ethnic groups, especially by force of law. —*intr.* To become open to members of all races or ethnic groups. **—de·seg′re·ga′tion** *n.* **—de·seg′re·ga′tion·ist** *n.*

de·sen·si·tize (dē-sĕn′sĭ-tīz′) *tr.v.* **-tized, -tiz·ing, -tiz·es. 1.** To render insensitive or less sensitive. **2.** *Immunology.* To make (an individual) nonreactive or insensitive to an antigen. **3.** To make emotionally insensitive or unresponsive, as by long exposure or repeated shocks: *"The successive assassinations and attempts, not just on Presidential figures but on Martin Luther King Jr. and others, have desensitized us"* (Anthony Lewis). **4.** To make (a photographic film or substance) less sensitive to light. **—de·sen′si·ti·za′tion** (-tĭ-zā′shən) *n.* **—de·sen′si·tiz′er** *n.*

Des·er·et (dĕz′ə-rĕt′). An area proposed by the Mormons in 1849 as an independent state or a state of the Union. Deseret would have included much of the southwest United States, with a capital at Salt Lake City. Congress refused to recognize the provisional state and created the Utah Territory in 1850.

desert[1]

des·ert[1] (dĕz′ərt) *n.* **1.** A barren or desolate area, especially: **a.** A dry, often sandy region of little rainfall, extreme temperatures, and sparse vegetation. **b.** A region of permanent cold that is largely or entirely devoid of life. **c.** An apparently lifeless area of water. **2.** An empty or forsaken place; a wasteland: *a cultural desert.* **3.** *Archaic.* A wild, uncultivated, and uninhabited region. **—desert** *adj.* **1.** Of, relating to, characteristic of, or inhabiting a desert: *desert fauna.* **2.** Barren and uninhabited; desolate: *a desert island.* [Middle English, from Old French, from Late Latin *dēsertum,* from neuter past participle of *dēserere,* to desert. See DESERT[3].]

de·sert[2] (dĭ-zûrt′) *n.* **1.** Often **deserts.** Something that is deserved or merited, especially a punishment: *They got their just deserts when the scheme was finally uncovered.* **2.** The state or fact of deserving reward or punishment. [Middle English, from Old French *deserte,* from feminine past participle of *deservir,* to deserve. See DESERVE.]

WORD HISTORY: When Shakespeare says in Sonnet 72, "Unless you would devise some virtuous lie,/To do more for me than mine own desert," he is using the word *desert* in the sense of "worthiness; deserving," a word that is perhaps most familiar to us in the plural, meaning "something that is deserved," as in the phrase *just deserts.* This word goes back to the Latin word *dēservīre,* "to devote oneself to the service of," which in Vulgar Latin came to mean "to merit by service." *Dēservīre* is made up of *dē–,* meaning "thoroughly," and *servīre,* "to serve." Knowing this, we can distinguish this *desert* from *desert,* "a wasteland," and *desert,* "to abandon," both of which go back to Latin *dēserere,* "to forsake, leave uninhabited," which is made up of *dē–,* expressing the notion of undoing, and the verb *serere,* "to link together." We can also distinguish all three *deserts* from *dessert,* "a sweet course at the end of a meal," which is from the French word *desservir,* "to clear the table." *Desservir* is made up of *des–,* expressing the notion of reversal, and *servir* (from Latin *servīre*), "to serve," hence, "to unserve" or "to clear the table."

de·sert[3] (dĭ-zûrt′) *v.* **-sert·ed, -sert·ing, -serts.** —*tr.* **1.** To leave empty or alone; abandon. **2.** To withdraw from, especially in spite of a responsibility or duty; forsake: *deserted her friend in a time of need.* **3.** To abandon (a military post, for example) in

ă pat	oi boy
ā pay	ou out
âr care	o͝o took
ä father	o͞o boot
ĕ pet	ŭ cut
ē be	ûr urge
ĭ pit	th thin
ī pie	*th* this
îr pier	hw which
ŏ pot	zh vision
ō toe	ə about, item
ô paw	♦ regionalism

Stress marks: ′ (primary); ′ (secondary), as in **dictionary** (dĭk′shə-nĕr′ē)

violation of orders or an oath. —*intr.* To forsake one's duty or post, especially to be absent without leave from the armed forces with no intention of returning. [French *déserter*, from Late Latin *dēsertāre*, from Latin *dēserere, dēsert-*, to abandon : *dē-*, de- + *serere*, to join; see **ser-**[2] in Appendix.] —**de·sert′er** *n.*

de·sert·i·fi·ca·tion (dĭ-zûr′tə-fĭ-kā′shən) *n.* The transformation of arable or habitable land to desert, as by a change in climate or destructive land use.

de·ser·tion (dĭ-zûr′shən) *n.* **1.a.** The act or an instance of deserting. **b.** The state of being deserted. **2.** *Law.* Willful abandonment of one's spouse or children or both without their consent and with the intention of forsaking all legal obligations to them.

de·serve (dĭ-zûrv′) *v.* **-served, -serv·ing, -serves.** —*tr.* To be worthy of; merit. See Synonyms at **earn**[1]. —*intr.* To be worthy or deserving. [Middle English *deserven*, from Old French *deservir*, from Latin *dēservīre*, to serve zealously : *dē-*, intensive pref.; see DE– + *servīre*, to serve; see SERVE.]

de·served (dĭ-zûrvd′) *adj.* Merited or earned: *a richly deserved punishment.* —**de·serv′ed·ly** (-zûr′vĭd-lē) *adv.* —**de·serv′ed·ness** *n.*

de·serv·ing (dĭ-zûr′vĭng) *adj.* Worthy, as of reward, praise, or aid. —**deserving** *n.* Merit; worthiness. —**de·serv′ing·ly** *adv.*

de Se·ver·sky (də sə-vĕr′skē), **Alexander Procofieff.** 1894–1974. Russian-born American aeronautical engineer who invented various airplane devices, including a bombsight used by the U.S. military.

de·sex (dē-sĕks′) *tr.v.* **-sexed, -sex·ing, -sex·es.** To remove part or all of the reproductive organs of; neuter.

de·sex·u·al·ize (dē-sĕk′sho͞o-ə-līz′) *tr.v.* **-ized, -iz·ing, -iz·es.** **1.** To take away the sexual quality of. **2.** To desex. —**de·sex′u·al·i·za′tion** (-ə-lĭ-zā′shən) *n.*

des·ha·bille (dĕs′ə-bēl′, -bē′) *n.* Variant of **dishabille.**

De Si·ca (də sē′kə), **Vittorio.** 1901–1974. Italian filmmaker whose *Bicycle Thief* (1948) and *Umberto D* (1952) are considered classics of postwar realism.

des·ic·cant (dĕs′ĭ-kənt) *n.* A substance, such as calcium oxide or silica gel, that has a high affinity for water and is used as a drying agent. [From Latin *dēsiccāns, dēsiccant-*, present participle of *dēsiccāre*, to desiccate. See DESICCATE.] —**des′ic·cant** *adj.*

des·ic·cate (dĕs′ĭ-kāt′) *v.* **-cat·ed, -cat·ing, -cates.** —*tr.* **1.** To dry out thoroughly. **2.** To preserve (foods) by removing the moisture. See Synonyms at **dry. 3.** To make dry, dull, or lifeless. —*intr.* To become dry; dry out. —**desiccate** (*also* -kĭt) *adj.* Lacking spirit or animation; arid: *"There was only the sun-bruised and desiccate feeling in his mind"* (J.R. Salamanca). [Latin *dēsiccāre, dēsiccāt-* : *dē-*, de- + *siccāre*, to dry up (from *siccus*, dry).] —**des′ic·ca′tion** *n.* —**des′ic·ca′tive** *adj.* —**des′ic·ca′tor** *n.*

de·sid·er·a·ta (dĭ-sĭd′ə-rä′tə, -rā′-) *n.* Plural of **desideratum.**

de·sid·er·ate (dĭ-sĭd′ə-rāt′) *tr.v.* **-at·ed, -at·ing, -ates.** To wish to have or see happen. [Latin *dēsīderāre, dēsīderāt-*, to desire. See DESIRE.] —**de·sid′er·a′tion** *n.*

de·sid·er·a·tive (dĭ-sĭd′ər-ə-tĭv, -ə-rā′-, -zĭd′-) *adj.* **1.** Of, relating to, or expressing desire. **2.** *Grammar.* Designating a clause, a sentence, or in some languages an inflected verb form that expresses desire.

de·sid·er·a·tum (dĭ-sĭd′ə-rä′təm, -rā′-) *n., pl.* **-ta** (-tə). Something considered necessary or highly desirable: *"The point is not that the artist has 'penetrated the character' of his sitter, that commonplace desideratum of portraiture"* (Robert Hughes). [Latin *dēsīderātum*, from neuter past participle of *dēsīderāre*, to desire. See DESIRE.]

design

de·sign (dĭ-zīn′) *v.* **-signed, -sign·ing, -signs.** —*tr.* **1.a.** To conceive or fashion in the mind; invent: *design a good excuse for not attending the conference.* **b.** To formulate a plan for; devise: *designed a marketing strategy for the new product.* **2.** To plan out in systematic, usually graphic form: *design a building; design a computer program.* **3.** To create or contrive for a particular purpose or effect: *a game designed to appeal to all ages.* **4.** To have as a goal or purpose; intend. **5.** To create or execute in an artistic or highly skilled manner. —*intr.* **1.** To make or execute plans. **2.** To have a goal or purpose in mind. **3.** To create designs. —**design** *n.* **1.a.** A drawing or sketch. **b.** A graphic representation, especially a detailed plan for construction or manufacture. **2.** The purposeful or inventive arrangement of parts or details: *the aerodynamic design of an automobile; furniture of simple but elegant design.* **3.** The art or practice of designing or making designs. **4.** Something designed, especially a decorative or an artistic work. **5.** An ornamental pattern. See Synonyms at **figure. 6.** A basic scheme or pattern that affects and controls function or development: *the overall design of an epic poem.* **7.** A plan; a project. See Synonyms at **plan. 8.a.** A reasoned purpose; an intent: *It was her design to set up practice on her own as soon as she was qualified.* **b.** Deliberate intention: *He became a photographer more by accident than by design.* **9.** Often **designs.** A secretive plot or scheme: *He has designs on my job.* [Middle English *designen*, from Latin *dēsignāre*, to designate. See DESIGNATE.] —**de·sign′a·ble** *adj.*

des·ig·nate (dĕz′ĭg-nāt′) *tr.v.* **-nat·ed, -nat·ing, -nates.** **1.** To indicate or specify; point out. **2.** To give a name or title to; characterize. **3.** To select and set aside for a duty, an office, or a purpose. See Synonyms at **allocate, appoint.** —**designate** (-nĭt) *adj.* Appointed but not yet installed in office: *the commissioner designate.* [Latin *dēsignāre, dēsignāt-* : *dē-*, de- + *signāre*, to mark (from *signum*, sign; see **sekʷ-**[1] in Appendix).] —**des′ig·na′tive, des′ig·na·to′ry** (-nə-tôr′ē, -tōr′ē) *adj.* —**des′ig·na′tor** *n.*

des·ig·nat·ed hitter (dĕz′ĭg-nā′tĭd) *n. Abbr.* **DH, dh** *Baseball.* A player designated at the start of a game to bat instead of the pitcher in the lineup.

des·ig·na·tion (dĕz′ĭg-nā′shən) *n.* **1.** The act of designating; a marking or pointing out. **2.** Nomination or appointment. **3.** A distinguishing name or title. See Synonyms at **name.**

des·ig·nee (dĕz′ĭg-nē′) *n.* A person who has been designated.

de·sign·er (dĭ-zī′nər) *n.* One that produces designs: *a book designer; a dress designer.* —**designer** *adj.* **1.** Bearing the name, signature, or identifying pattern of a specific designer: *designer clothing.* **2.** Conceived or created by a designer.

designer drug *n.* A drug with properties and effects similar to a known hallucinogen or narcotic but having a slightly altered chemical structure, especially such a drug created in order to evade restrictions against illegal substances.

de·sign·ing (dĭ-zī′nĭng) *adj.* **1.** Conniving; crafty. **2.** Showing or exercising forethought. —**de·sign′ing·ly** *adv.*

de·si·pra·mine (dĭ-zĭp′rə-mēn, dĕz′ə-prăm′ĭn) *n.* A tricyclic antidepressant, $C_{18}H_{22}N_2$, used in the treatment of psychological depression. [*desmethyl* (*des-*, variant of DE– + METHYL) + (IM)IPRAMINE.]

de·sir·a·ble (dĭ-zīr′ə-bəl) *adj.* **1.** Worth having or seeking, as by being useful, advantageous, or pleasing: *a desirable job in the film industry; a home computer with many desirable features.* **2.** Worth doing or achieving; advisable: *a desirable reform; a desirable outcome.* **3.** Arousing desire, especially sexual desire. —**desirable** *n.* A desirable person or thing. —**de·sir′a·bil′i·ty, de·sir′a·ble·ness** *n.* —**de·sir′a·bly** *adv.*

de·sire (dĭ-zīr′) *tr.v.* **-sired, -sir·ing, -sires.** **1.** To wish or long for; want. **2.** To express a wish for; request. —**desire** *n.* **1.** A wish or longing. **2.** A request or petition. **3.** The object of longing: *My greatest desire is to go back home.* **4.** Sexual appetite; passion. [Middle English *desiren*, from Old French *desirer*, from Latin *dēsīderāre* : *dē-*, de- + *sīdus, sīder-*, star.] —**de·sir′er** *n.*

SYNONYMS: *desire, covet, crave, want, wish.* The central meaning shared by these verbs is "to have a strong longing for": *desire peace; coveted the new convertible; craving fame and fortune; wanted a drink of water; got all she wished.*

de·sir·ous (dĭ-zīr′əs) *adj.* Having or expressing desire; desiring: *Both sides were desirous of finding a quick solution to the problem.* —**de·sir′ous·ly** *adv.* —**de·sir′ous·ness** *n.*

de·sist (dĭ-sĭst′, -zĭst′) *intr.v.* **-sist·ed, -sist·ing, -sists.** To cease doing something; forbear. See Synonyms at **stop.** [Middle English *desisten*, from Old French *desister*, from Latin *dēsistere* : *dē-*, de- + *sistere*, to bring to a standstill; see **stā-** in Appendix.]

desk (dĕsk) *n.* **1.** A piece of furniture typically having a flat or sloping top for writing and often drawers or compartments. **2.** A table, counter, or booth at which specified services or functions are performed: *an information desk; a reception desk.* **3.** A department of a large organization in charge of a specified operation: *a newspaper's city desk.* **4.** A lectern. **5.** *Music.* A music stand in an orchestra. [Middle English *deske*, from Medieval Latin *desca*, table, from Old Italian *desco*, from Latin *discus*, quoit. See DISK.]

de·skill (dē-skĭl′) *tr.v.* **-skilled, -skill·ing, -skills.** **1.** To eliminate the need for skilled labor in (an industry), especially by the introduction of high technology. **2.** To downgrade (a job or an occupation) from a skilled to a semiskilled or unskilled position.

desk·man (dĕsk′măn′, -mən) *n.* A man who works at a desk, especially a newspaper writer.

desk·top (dĕsk′tŏp′) *n.* The top of a desk. —**desktop** *adj.* **1.** Designed for use on a desk or table: *a desktop telephone.* **2.** Small enough to fit conveniently in an individual workspace: *a desktop computer.*

desktop publishing *n. Computer Science.* The design and production of publications, such as newsletters, trade journals, or brochures, using microcomputers with graphics capability.

des·man (dĕs′mən) *n., pl.* **-mans.** Either of two aquatic, insectivorous, molelike mammals, *Desmana moschata* of eastern Europe and western Asia or *Galemys pyrenaicus* of southwest Europe, having dense, brownish fur, a long snout, and a flattened, scaly tail. [Short for Swedish *desmanråtta*, muskrat : *desman*, musk (from Middle Low German *desem*, from Medieval Latin *bisamum*, of Semitic origin; akin to Hebrew *beśem*, odor) + *råtta*, rat (akin to Old English *ræt*).]

De Smet (də smĕt′), **Pierre Jean.** 1801–1873. Belgian-born missionary in America who built mission stations in the Columbia River valley during the 1840's and later succeeded in arranging a temporary truce with the Sioux in the Bighorn River valley (1868).

des·mid (dĕs′mĭd) *n.* Any of various green, unicellular freshwater algae of the family Desmidiaceae, often forming chainlike colonies. [From New Latin *Desmidiaceae*, family name, from *Desmidium*, type genus, from Greek *desmos*, bond, from *dein*, to bind.]

Des Moines (dĭ moin′). The capital and largest city of Iowa, in the south-central part of the state on the Des Moines River. Fort Des Moines was built on the site in 1843, and the surrounding settlement became a city in 1851. It was chosen as state capital in 1857. Population, 191,003.

Des Moines River. A river rising in southwest Minnesota and flowing about 861 km (535 mi) southeastward across Iowa to the Mississippi River.

Des·mou·lins (dā-mo͞o-lăɴ′), **(Lucie Simplice) Camille (Benoît).** 1760–1794. French journalist and revolutionary who along with Danton urged moderation during the Reign of Terror. She was arrested and guillotined after a mock trial.

Des·na (də-snä′, dyə-). A river rising east of Smolensk in western Russia and flowing about 885 km (550 mi) generally south to the Dnieper River above Kiev in the Ukraine.

des·o·late (dĕs′ə-lĭt, dĕz′-) *adj.* **1.a.** Devoid of inhabitants; deserted: *"streets which were usually so thronged now grown desolate"* (Daniel Defoe). **b.** Barren; lifeless: *the rocky, desolate surface of the moon.* **2.** Rendered unfit for habitation or use: *the desolate cities of war-torn Europe.* **3.** Dreary; dismal. **4.** Bereft of friends or hope; sad and forlorn. See Synonyms at **sad.** **—desolate** (-lāt′) *tr.v.* **-lat·ed, -lat·ing, -lates. 1.** To rid or deprive of inhabitants. **2.** To lay waste; devastate: *"Here we have no wars to desolate our fields"* (Michel Guillaume Jean de Crèvecoeur). **3.** To forsake; abandon. **4.** To make lonely, forlorn, or wretched. [Middle English, from Latin *dēsōlātus,* past participle of *dēsōlāre,* to abandon : *dē-,* de- + *sōlus,* alone; see **s(w)e-** in Appendix.] **—des′o·late·ly** *adv.* **—des′o·late·ness** *n.* **—des′o·lat′er, des′o·la′tor** *n.*

des·o·la·tion (dĕs′ə-lā′shən, dĕz′-) *n.* **1.** The act or an instance of desolating. **2.** The state of being desolate. **3.** Devastation; ruin: *a drought that brought desolation to the region.* **4.a.** The state of being abandoned or forsaken; loneliness: *a sense of utter desolation following the death of his parents.* **b.** Wretchedness; misery.

de·sorb (dē-sôrb′, -zôrb′) *tr.v.* **-sorbed, -sorb·ing, -sorbs.** To remove (an absorbed or adsorbed substance) from. **—de·sorp′tion** (-sôrp′shən, -zôrp′-) *n.*

de So·to (dĭ sō′tō, dē sô′tô), **Hernando** or **Fernando.** 1496?–1542. Spanish explorer who landed in Florida in 1539 with 600 men and set out to search for the fabled riches of the north. For the next three years he explored much of southern North America, crossing the Mississippi River in 1541.

de·spair (dĭ-spâr′) *intr.v.* **-spaired, -spair·ing, -spairs. 1.** To lose all hope: *despaired of reaching shore safely.* **2.** To be overcome by a sense of futility or defeat. **—despair** *n.* **1.** Complete loss of hope. **2.** One despaired of or causing despair: *unmotivated students that are the despair of their teachers.* [Middle English *despeiren,* from Old French *desperer,* from Latin *dēspērāre* : *dē-,* de- + *spērāre,* to hope; see **spē-** in Appendix. N., from Middle English *despeir,* from Anglo-Norman, from Old French *desperer,* to despair.]

SYNONYMS: *despair, hopelessness, desperation, despondency, discouragement.* These nouns denote loss of hope. *Despair* and *hopelessness* stress the utter absence of hope and often imply a sense of powerlessness or resignation: *When the bank repossessed the house, their depression turned to despair. A spirit of hopelessness pervaded the refugee camp. Desperation* is despair that drives a person to take risky, often reckless action: *"The mass of men lead lives of quiet desperation"* (Henry David Thoreau). *Despondency* emphasizes depression of spirit resulting from cessation of hope and a belief that continued efforts will fail: *Her despondency arises from her inability to find employment. Discouragement* denotes loss of confidence or courage in the face of obstacles but is the weakest of these terms: *The farmer experienced moments of discouragement over the failure of his crops.*

de·spair·ing (dĭ-spâr′ĭng) *adj.* Characterized by or resulting from despair; hopeless. See Synonyms at **despondent.** **—de·spair′ing·ly** *adv.*

des·patch (dĭ-spăch′) *v.* & *n.* Variant of **dispatch.**

des·per·a·do (dĕs′pə-rä′dō, -rā′-) *n., pl.* **-does** or **-dos.** A bold or desperate outlaw, especially of the American frontier. [Probably from Spanish *desperado, desesperado,* desperate person, from past participle of *desesperar,* to despair, from Latin *dēspērāre.* See DESPAIR.]

des·per·ate (dĕs′pər-ĭt) *adj.* **1.** Having lost all hope; despairing. **2.** Marked by, arising from, or showing despair: *the desperate look of hunger; a desperate cry for help.* **3.** Reckless or violent because of despair: *a desperate criminal.* **4.** Undertaken out of extreme urgency or as a last resort: *a desperate attempt to save the family business.* **5.** Nearly hopeless; critical: *a desperate illness; a desperate situation.* **6.** Suffering or driven by great need or distress: *desperate for recognition.* **7.** Extremely intense: *felt a desperate urge to tell the truth.* [Middle English *desperat,* from Latin *dēspērātus,* past participle of *dēspērāre,* to despair. See DESPAIR.] **—des′per·ate·ly** *adv.* **—des′per·ate·ness** *n.*

des·per·a·tion (dĕs′pə-rā′shən) *n.* **1.** The condition of being desperate. See Synonyms at **despair.** **2.** Recklessness arising from despair.

des·pi·ca·ble (dĕs′pĭ-kə-bəl, dĭ-spĭk′ə-) *adj.* Deserving of contempt or scorn; vile. [Late Latin *dēspicābilis,* from Latin *dēspicārī,* to despise. See **spek-** in Appendix.] **—des′pi·ca·ble·ness** *n.* **—des′pi·ca·bly** *adv.*

de·spise (dĭ-spīz′) *tr.v.* **-spised, -spis·ing, -spis·es. 1.** To regard with contempt or scorn: *despised all cowards and flatterers.* **2.** To dislike intensely; loathe: *despised the frigid weather in January.* **3.** To regard as unworthy of one's interest or concern: *despised any thought of their own safety.* [Middle English *despisen,* from Old French *despire, despis-,* from Latin *dēspicere* : *dē-,* de- + *specere,* to look; see **spek-** in Appendix.] **—de·spis′al** (-spī′zəl) *n.* **—de·spis′er** *n.*

SYNONYMS: *despise, contemn, disdain, scorn, scout.* The central meaning shared by these verbs is "to regard with utter contempt": *despises incompetence; contemned the actions of the dictator; disdained my suggestion; scorns sentimentality; scouted simplistic explanations.*
ANTONYM: *esteem.*

de·spite (dĭ-spīt′) *prep.* In spite of; notwithstanding: *won the game despite overwhelming odds.* **—despite** *n.* **1.** Contemptuous defiance or disregard. **2.** Spite; malice: *"He died soon after . . . of pure despite and vexation"* (Sir Walter Scott). [Short for *in despite of,* from Middle English *despit,* spite, from Old French, from Latin *dēspectus,* from past participle of *dēspicere,* to despise. See DESPISE.]

de·spite·ful (dĭ-spīt′fəl) *adj.* Full of malice; spiteful. **—de·spite′ful·ly** *adv.* **—de·spite′ful·ness** *n.*

de·spit·e·ous (dĭ-spĭt′ē-əs) *adj. Archaic.* Despiteful. **—de·spit′e·ous·ly** *adv.*

Des Plaines (dĕs plānz′). A city of northeast Illinois, a suburb of Chicago on the Des Plaines River. Population, 53,568.

Des Plaines River. A river rising in southeast Wisconsin and flowing about 241 km (150 mi) generally southward to the Kankakee River in northeast Illinois.

de·spoil (dĭ-spoil′) *tr.v.* **-spoiled, -spoil·ing, -spoils. 1.** To sack; plunder. **2.** To deprive of something valuable by force; rob: *a region despoiled of its scenic beauty by unchecked development.* [Middle English *despoilen,* from Old French *despoillier,* from Latin *dēspoliāre* : *dē-,* de- + *spoliāre,* to plunder (from *spolium,* booty).] **—de·spoil′er** *n.* **—de·spoil′ment** *n.*

de·spo·li·a·tion (dĭ-spō′lē-ā′shən) *n.* The act of despoiling or the condition of being despoiled. [Late Latin *dēspoliātiō, dēspoliātiōn-,* from Latin *dēspoliātus,* past participle of *dēspoliāre,* to despoil. See DESPOIL.]

de·spond (dĭ-spŏnd′) *intr.v.* **-spond·ed, -spond·ing, -sponds.** To become disheartened or discouraged. **—despond** *n.* Despondency: *"The outward show of fight masked a spreading inner despond at the White House"* (Newsweek). [Latin *dēspondēre,* to give up : *dē-,* de- + *spondēre,* to promise; see **spend-** in Appendix.] **—de·spond′ing·ly** *adv.*

de·spon·dence (dĭ-spŏn′dəns) *n.* Despondency.

de·spon·den·cy (dĭ-spŏn′dən-sē) *n.* Depression of spirits from loss of hope, confidence, or courage; dejection. See Synonyms at **despair.**

de·spon·dent (dĭ-spŏn′dənt) *adj.* Feeling or expressing despondency; dejected. **—de·spon′dent·ly** *adv.*

SYNONYMS: *despondent, despairing, forlorn, hopeless.* The central meaning shared by these adjectives is "being without or almost without hope": *despondent about the failure of the enterprise; took a despairing view of world politics; a forlorn cause; a hopeless case.*
ANTONYM: *hopeful.*

des·pot (dĕs′pət) *n.* **1.** A ruler with absolute power. **2.** A person who wields power oppressively; a tyrant. **3.a.** A Byzantine emperor or prince. **b.** An Eastern Orthodox bishop or patriarch. [French *despote,* from Medieval Latin *despota,* from Greek *despotēs,* master. See **dem-** in Appendix.] **—des·pot′ic** (dĭ-spŏt′ĭk) *adj.* **—des·pot′i·cal·ly** *adv.*

des·pot·ism (dĕs′pə-tĭz′əm) *n.* **1.** Rule by or as if by a despot; absolute power or authority. **2.** The actions of a despot; tyranny. **3.a.** A government or political system in which the ruler exercises absolute power: *"Kerensky has a place in history, of a brief interlude between despotisms"* (William Safire). **b.** A state so ruled.

des·qua·mate (dĕs′kwə-māt′) *intr.v.* **-mat·ed, -mat·ing, -mates.** To shed, peel, or come off in scales. Used of skin. [Latin *dēsquāmāre, dēsquāmāt-* : *dē-,* de- + *squāma,* scale.] **—des′qua·ma′tion** *n.*

Des·sa·lines (dĕ-sä-lēn′), **Jean Jacques.** 1758?–1806. African-born emperor of Haiti (1804–1806) who defeated the French (1803) to gain the island's independence.

Des·sau (dĕs′ou). A city of east-central Germany north of Leipzig. It was the site of the Bauhaus school headed by Walter Gropius from 1925 to 1932. Population, 103,738.

des·sert (dĭ-zûrt′) *n.* **1.** A usually sweet course or dish, as of fruit, ice cream, or pastry, served at the end of a meal. **2.** *Chiefly British.* Fresh fruit, nuts, or sweetmeats served after the sweet course of a dinner. [French, from Old French *desservir,* to clear the table : *des-,* de- + *servir,* to serve; see SERVE.]

des·sert·spoon (dĭ-zûrt′spo͞on′) *n.* A spoon intermediate in size between a tablespoon and a teaspoon, used for eating dessert. **—des·sert′spoon′ful** (-fo͝ol) *n.*

Hernando de Soto

ă pat	oi boy
ā pay	ou out
âr care	o͝o took
ä father	o͞o boot
ĕ pet	ŭ cut
ē be	ûr urge
ĭ pit	th thin
ī pie	*th* this
îr pier	hw which
ŏ pot	zh vision
ō toe	ə about, item
ô paw	♦ regionalism

Stress marks: **′** (primary); ′ (secondary), as in **dictionary** (dĭk′shə-nĕr′ē)

dessert wine *n.* A usually sweet wine, such as Sauternes, served with or after dessert.

de·sta·bi·lize (dē-stā′bə-līz′) *tr.v.* **-lized, -liz·ing, -liz·es. 1.** To upset the stability or smooth functioning of: *a policy that threatens to destabilize the economy; a new weapon that threatens to destabilize nuclear deterrence.* **2.** To undermine the power of (a government or leader) by subversive or terrorist acts. **—de·sta′bi·li·za′tion** (-lĭ-zā′shən) *n.*

de·stain (dē-stān′) *tr.v.* **-stained, -stain·ing, -stains.** To remove stain from (a specimen) to aid in microscopic study.

de·sta·lin·i·za·tion (dē-stä′lĭ-nĭ-zā′shən) *n.* The process of discrediting and eliminating the political policies, methods, and personal image of Joseph Stalin.

de·ster·i·lize (dē-stĕr′ə-līz′) *tr.v.* **-lized, -liz·ing, -liz·es.** To release (gold) from an inactive status and return it to use as a backing for credit and new currency.

de Stijl (də stīl′, stāl′) *n.* A school of art originating in the Netherlands in 1917 and characterized by the use of rectangular shapes and primary colors. [Dutch : *de,* the + *stijl,* style.]

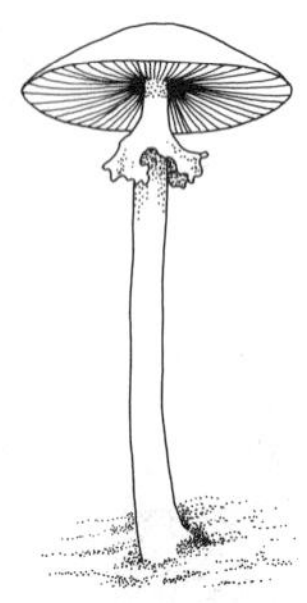

destroying angel

des·ti·na·tion (dĕs′tə-nā′shən) *n.* **1.** The place to which one is going or directed. **2.** The ultimate purpose for which something is created or intended. **3.** *Archaic.* An act of appointing or setting aside for a specific purpose.

des·tine (dĕs′tĭn) *tr.v.* **-tined, -tin·ing, -tines. 1.** To determine beforehand; preordain: *a foolish scheme destined to fail; a film destined to become a classic.* **2.** To assign for a specific end, use, or purpose: *money destined to pay for their child's education.* **3.** To direct toward a given destination: *a flight destined for Tokyo.* [Middle English *destinen,* from Old French *destiner,* from Latin *dēstināre,* to determine. See **stā-** in Appendix.]

des·ti·ny (dĕs′tə-nē) *n., pl.* **-nies. 1.** The inevitable or necessary fate to which a particular person or thing is destined; one's lot. See Synonyms at **fate. 2.** A predetermined course of events considered as something beyond human power or control: *"Marriage and hanging go by destiny"* (Robert Burton). **3.** The power or agency thought to predetermine events; fate: *Destiny brought them together.* [Middle English *destine,* from Old French *destinee,* from feminine past participle of *destiner,* to destine. See DESTINE.]

des·ti·tute (dĕs′tĭ-to͞ot′, -tyo͞ot′) *adj.* **1.** Utterly lacking; devoid: *Young recruits destitute of any experience.* **2.** Lacking resources or the means of subsistence; completely impoverished. See Synonyms at **poor.** [Middle English, from Latin *dēstitūtus,* past participle of *dēstituere,* to abandon : *dē-,* de- + *statuere,* to set; see **stā-** in Appendix.] **—des′ti·tute′ness** *n.*

des·ti·tu·tion (dĕs′tĭ-to͞o′shən, -tyo͞o′-) *n.* **1.** Extreme want of resources or the means of subsistence; complete poverty. **2.** A deprivation or lack; a deficiency.

des·tri·er (dĕs′trē-ər, dĭ-strîr′) *n. Archaic.* A war horse. [Middle English *destrer,* from Anglo-Norman, from Vulgar Latin **dextrārius,* right-hand, from Latin *dexter,* right.]

de·stroy (dĭ-stroi′) *v.* **-stroyed, -stroy·ing, -stroys.** —*tr.* **1.** To ruin completely; spoil: *The ancient manuscripts were destroyed by fire.* **2.** To tear down or break up; demolish. See Synonyms at **ruin. 3.** To do away with; put an end to: *"In crowded populations, poverty destroys the possibility of cleanliness"* (George Bernard Shaw). **4.** To kill: *destroy a rabid dog.* **5.** To subdue or defeat completely; crush: *The rebel forces were destroyed in battle.* **6.** To render useless or ineffective: *destroyed the testimony of the prosecution's chief witness.* —*intr.* To be destructive; cause destruction: *"Too much money destroys as surely as too little"* (John Simon). [Middle English *destroien,* from Old French *destruire,* from Vulgar Latin **dēstrūgere,* from Latin *dēstruere* : *dē-,* de- + *struere,* to pile up; see **ster-²** in Appendix.]

de·stroy·er (dĭ-stroi′ər) *n.* **1.** One that destroys: *a destroyer of family unity; a destroyer of our environment.* **2.** A small, fast, highly maneuverable warship armed with guns, torpedoes, depth charges, and guided missiles.

destroyer escort *n.* A warship, usually smaller than a destroyer, used in antisubmarine action.

de·stroy·ing angel (dĭ-stroi′ĭng) *n.* Any of several poisonous mushrooms of the genus *Amanita.*

de·struct (dĭ-strŭkt′, dē′strŭkt′) *n.* The intentional, usually remote-controlled destruction of a space vehicle, rocket, or missile after launching, as for defective performance or reasons of safety. **—destruct** *v.* **-struct·ed, -struct·ing, -structs.** —*tr.* To destroy intentionally (a rocket or missile) after launch. —*intr.* To self-destruct. [Back-formation from DESTRUCTION.]

de·struc·ti·ble (dĭ-strŭk′tə-bəl) *adj.* Breakable or easily destroyed: *destructible glassware.* **—de·struc′ti·bil′i·ty, de·struc′ti·ble·ness** *n.*

de·struc·tion (dĭ-strŭk′shən) *n.* **1.a.** The act of destroying. **b.** The condition of having been destroyed. **2.** The cause or means of destroying: *weapons that could prove to be the destruction of humankind.* [Middle English, from Old French, from Latin *dēstructiō, dēstructiōn-,* from *dēstructus,* past participle of *dēstruere,* to destroy. See DESTROY.]

de·struc·tion·ist (dĭ-strŭk′shə-nĭst) *n.* One who believes in or advocates destruction, especially of existing social institutions.

de·struc·tive (dĭ-strŭk′tĭv) *adj.* **1.** Causing or wreaking destruction; ruinous: *a destructive act; a policy that is destructive to the economy.* **2.** Designed or tending to disprove or discredit: *destructive criticism.* **—de·struc′tive·ly** *adv.* **—de·struc′tive·ness, de′struc·tiv′i·ty** (dē′strŭk-tĭv′ĭ-tē) *n.*

destructive distillation *n.* A process by which organic substances such as wood, coal, and oil shale are decomposed by heat in the absence of air and distilled to produce useful products such as coke, charcoal, oils, and gases.

de·struc·tor (dĭ-strŭk′tər) *n.* **1.** An incinerator for refuse. **2.** An explosive, usually remote-controlled device for effecting a destruct.

des·ue·tude (dĕs′wĭ-to͞od′, -tyo͞od′) *n.* A state of disuse or inactivity. [French *désuétude,* from Latin *dēsuētūdō,* from *dēsuētus,* past participle of *dēsuēscere,* to put out of use : *dē-,* de- + *suēscere,* to become accustomed; see **s(w)e-** in Appendix.]

de·sul·fur·ize (dē-sŭl′fə-rīz′) *tr.v.* **-ized, -iz·ing, -iz·es.** To eliminate sulfur from (petroleum, for example). **—de·sul′fur·i·za′tion** (-fər-ĭ-zā′shən) *n.*

des·ul·to·ry (dĕs′əl-tôr′ē, -tōr′ē, dĕz′-) *adj.* **1.** Moving or jumping from one thing to another; disconnected: *a desultory speech.* **2.** Occurring haphazardly; random. See Synonyms at **chance.** [Latin *dēsultōrius,* leaping, from *dēsultor,* a leaper, from *dēsilīre, dēsult-,* to leap down : *dē-,* de- + *salīre,* to jump; see **sel-** in Appendix.] **—des′ul·to′ri·ly** *adv.* **—des′ul·to′ri·ness** *n.*

det. *abbr.* **1.** Detachment. **2.** Detail.

de·tach (dĭ-tăch′) *tr.v.* **-tached, -tach·ing, -tach·es. 1.** To separate or unfasten; disconnect: *detach a check from the checkbook; detach burs from one's coat.* **2.** To remove from association or union with something: *detach a calf from its mother; detached herself from the group.* **3.** To send (troops or ships, for example) on a special mission. [French *détacher,* from Old French *destachier* : *des-,* de- + *attachier,* to attach; see ATTACH.] **—de·tach′a·bil′i·ty** *n.* **—de·tach′a·ble** *adj.* **—de·tach′a·bly** *adv.*

de·tached (dĭ-tăcht′) *adj.* **1.** Separated; disconnected: *a detached part; a detached plug.* **2.** Standing apart from others; separate: *a house with a detached garage.* **3.** Marked by an absence of emotional involvement and an aloof, impersonal objectivity. See Synonyms at **cool, indifferent. —de·tach′ed·ly** (-tăch′ĭd-lē, -tăcht′lē) *adv.* **—de·tach′ed·ness** *n.*

de·tach·ment (dĭ-tăch′mənt) *n.* **1.** The act or process of disconnecting or detaching; separation. **2.** The state of being separate or detached. **3.** Indifference to or remoteness from the concerns of others; aloofness: *preserved a chilly detachment in his relations with the family.* **4.** Absence of prejudice or bias; disinterest: *strove to maintain her professional detachment in the case.* **5.a.** The dispatch of a military unit, such as troops or ships, from a larger body for a special duty or mission. **b.** *Abbr.* **det.** The unit so dispatched. **c.** *Abbr.* **det.** A permanent unit, usually smaller than a platoon, organized for special duties.

de·tail (dĭ-tāl′, dē′tāl′) *n. Abbr.* **det. 1.** An individual part or item; a particular. See Synonyms at **item. 2.** Particulars considered individually and in relation to a whole: *careful attention to detail.* **3.** A minor or an inconsequential item or aspect; a minutia: *skipped the details to get to the main point.* **4.** A minute or thorough treatment or account: *went into detail about his travels.* **5.a.** A discrete part or portion of a work, such as a painting, building, or decorative object, especially when considered in isolation. **b.** A representation of such a part or portion: *a detail of a Rembrandt portrait illustrating the technique of chiaroscuro.* **6.a.** A small elaborated element of a work of art, craft, or design. **b.** Such elements considered together: *the intricate detail of a rococo altarpiece.* **c.** The rendering of artistic detail: *the fine detail of the painter's brushwork.* **7.a.** The selection of one or more troops for a particular duty, usually a fatigue duty. **b.** The personnel so selected. **c.** The duty assigned: *garbage detail.* **—detail** (dĭ-tāl′) *tr.v.* **-tailed, -tail·ing, -tails. 1.** To report or relate minutely or in particulars. **2.** To name or state explicitly: *detailed the charges against the defendant.* **3.** To provide with artistic or decorative detail: *detailed the quilt with colorful appliqué.* **4.** To select and dispatch for a particular duty. **—*idiom.* in detail.** With attention to particulars; thoroughly or meticulously: *explained her proposal in detail.* [French *détail,* from Old French *detail,* a piece cut off, from *detaillir,* to cut up : *de-,* de- + *tailler,* to cut; see TAILOR.] **—de·tail′er** *n.*

de·tailed (dĭ-tāld′, dē′tāld′) *adj.* Characterized by abundant use of detail or thoroughness of treatment: *a detailed report on the state of the economy.*

SYNONYMS: *detailed, circumstantial, minute, particular.* The central meaning shared by these adjectives is "marked by attention to detail": *a detailed account of the trip; a circumstantial narrative; an exact and minute report; a faithful and particular description.*

detail man *n.* A representative of a manufacturer of drugs or medical supplies who calls on doctors, pharmacists, and other professional distributors to promote new drugs and supplies.

de·tain (dĭ-tān′) *tr.v.* **-tained, -tain·ing, -tains. 1.** To keep from proceeding; delay or retard. See Synonyms at **delay. 2.** To keep in custody or temporary confinement: *The police detained several suspects for questioning. The disruptive students were detained after school until their parents had been notified.* **3.** *Obsolete.* To retain or withhold (payment or property, for example). [Middle English *deteinen,* from Old French *detenir,* from Vulgar Latin **dētenīre,* from Latin *dētinēre* : *dē-,* de- + *tenēre,* to hold; see **ten-** in Appendix.] **—de·tain′ment** *n.*

de·tain·ee (dē′tā-nē′, dĭ-tā′-) *n.* A person held in custody or confinement: *a political detainee.*

de·tain·er (dĭ-tā′nər) *n. Law.* **1.** A withholding from the rightful owner of property that has lawfully come into the possession of the current holder. **2.** The detention of a person, especially in custody. **3.** A writ authorizing the further detention of a person in custody, pending further action.

de·tect (dĭ-tĕkt′) *tr.v.* **-tect·ed, -tect·ing, -tects. 1.** To discover or ascertain the existence, presence, or fact of. **2.** To discern the true nature or character of: *detected malice behind the smile.* **3.** *Electronics.* To demodulate. [Middle English *detecten,* from Latin *dētegere, dētect-,* to uncover : *dē-,* de- + *tegere,* to cover; see **(s)teg-** in Appendix.] **—de·tect′a·ble, de·tect′i·ble** *adj.* **—de·tect′er** *n.*

de·tec·tion (dĭ-tĕk′shən) *n.* **1.** The act or process of detecting; discovery: *detection of a crime; detection of radiation from a distant galaxy.* **2.** See **demodulation.**

de·tec·tive (dĭ-tĕk′tĭv) *n.* A person, usually a member of a police force, who investigates crimes and obtains evidence or information. **—detective** *adj.* **1.** Of or relating to detectives or their work: *detective novels.* **2.** Suited for or used in detection.

WORD HISTORY: The first detective may have come into existence before the word itself. C. Auguste Dupin, Edgar Allan Poe's hero in "The Murders in the Rue Morgue," which is considered the world's first real detective story, was introduced to the world in 1841. Nine years later we find the first recorded instance of the word *detective,* although the phrases *detective police* and *detective policeman,* from which it was shortened, are recorded first in 1843. Hence, Dupin precedes all recorded instances of *detective,* just as he precedes all other detectives.

de·tec·tor (dĭ-tĕk′tər) *n.* One that detects, especially a mechanical, electrical, or chemical device that automatically identifies and records or registers a stimulus, such as an environmental change in pressure or temperature, an electric signal, or radiation from a radioactive material.

de·tent (dĭ-tĕnt′) *n.* A catch or lever that locks the movement of one part of a mechanism. [French *détente,* a loosening, from Old French *destente,* from feminine past participle of *destendre,* to release : *des-,* de- + *tendre,* to stretch (from Latin *tendere;* see **ten-** in Appendix).]

dé·tente (dā-tänt′, -täɴt′) *n.* **1.** A relaxing or easing, as of tension between rivals. **2.** A policy toward a rival nation or bloc characterized by increased diplomatic, commercial, and cultural contact and a desire to reduce tensions, as through negotiation or talks. [French. See DETENT.] **—dé·tent′ist** *n.*

de·ten·tion (dĭ-tĕn′shən) *n.* **1.a.** The act of detaining. **b.** The state of being detained, especially a period of temporary custody while awaiting trial. **2.** A forced or punitive delay. [Middle English *detencioun,* act of withholding, from Anglo-Norman, from Latin *dētentiō, dētentiōn-,* from *dētentus,* past participle of *dētinēre,* to detain. See DETAIN.]

detention home *n.* A place where juvenile offenders are held in custody, especially for a temporary period while awaiting court action on their cases.

de·ter (dĭ-tûr′) *v.* **-terred, -ter·ring, -ters.** *—tr.* To prevent or discourage from acting, as by means of fear or doubt: *"Does negotiated disarmament deter war?"* (Edward Teller). See Synonyms at **dissuade.** *—intr.* To prevent or discourage the occurrence of an action, as by means of fear or doubt: *"It's this edge that gives nuclear weapons their power to deter"* (Thomas Powers). [Latin *dēterrēre* : *dē-,* de- + *terrēre,* to frighten.] **—de·ter′ment** *n.* **—de·ter′ra·ble** *adj.* **—de·ter′rer** *n.*

de·terge (dĭ-tûrj′) *tr.v.* **-terged, -terg·ing, -terg·es.** To wash or wipe off (a wound, for example); cleanse. [French *déterger,* from Latin *dētergēre* : *dē-,* de- + *tergēre,* to wipe.]

de·ter·gence (dĭtûr′jəns) *n.* Detergency.

de·ter·gen·cy (dĭ-tûr′jən-sē) *n.* The power or quality of cleansing.

de·ter·gent (dĭ-tûr′jənt) *n.* A cleansing substance that acts similarly to soap but is made from chemical compounds rather than fats and lye. **—detergent** *adj.* Having cleansing power.

de·te·ri·o·rate (dĭ-tîr′ē-ə-rāt′) *v.* **-rat·ed, -rat·ing, -rates.** *—tr.* To diminish or impair in quality, character, or value: *Time and neglect had deteriorated the property.* *—intr.* **1.** To grow worse; degenerate: *The weather deteriorated overnight. His health had deteriorated while he was in prison.* **2.** To weaken or disintegrate; decay: *The nation's highways are deteriorating at a rapid pace.* [Late Latin *dēteriōrāre, dēteriōrāt-,* from Latin *dēterior,* worse. See **de-** in Appendix.] **—de·te′ri·o·ra′tion** *n.* **—de·te′ri·o·ra′tive** *adj.*

de·ter·min·a·ble (dĭ-tûr′mə-nə-bəl) *adj.* **1.** Capable of being determined, limited, or fixed: *determinable velocities.* **2.** *Law.* Capable of being settled or decided: *matters determinable by common law.* **—de·ter′min·a·ble·ness** *n.* **—de·ter′min·a·bly** *adv.*

de·ter·mi·na·cy (dĭ-tûr′mə-nə-sē) *n.* **1.** The quality or condition of being determinate. **2.** The condition of being determined or characterized.

de·ter·mi·nant (dĭ-tûr′mə-nənt) *adj.* Determinative. **—determinant** *n.* **1.** An influencing or determining element or factor: *"Education is the second most important determinant of recreational participation"* (John P. Robinson). **2.** *Mathematics.* A square matrix of numbers or other elements having a value determined by a rule of combination for the elements and used especially in solving certain classes of simultaneous equations. **3.** *Immunology.* The portion of an immunogenic molecule with which an antibody or lymphocyte reacts.

de·ter·mi·nate (dĭ-tûr′mə-nĭt) *adj.* **1.** Precisely limited or defined; definite: *a determinate number; a determinate distance.* **2.** Conclusively settled; final. **3.** Firm in purpose; resolute. **4.** *Botany.* **a.** Terminating in a flower and blooming in a sequence beginning with the uppermost or central flower; cymose: *a determinate inflorescence.* **b.** Not continuing indefinitely at the tip of an axis: *determinate growth.* [Middle English, from Latin *dētermināatus,* past participle of *dēterminiāre,* to determine. See DETERMINE.] **—de·ter′mi·nate·ly** *adv.* **—de·ter′mi·nate·ness** *n.*

de·ter·mi·nat·er (dĭ-tûr′mə-nā′tər) *n.* A determiner.

de·ter·mi·na·tion (dĭ-tûr′mə-nā′shən) *n.* **1.a.** The act of making or arriving at a decision. See Synonyms at **decision. b.** The decision reached. **2.a.** Firmness of purpose; resolve: *approached the task with determination and energy.* **b.** A fixed intention or resolution: *returned to school with a determination to finish.* **3.a.** The settling of a question or case by an authoritative decision or pronouncement, especially by a judicial body: *The choice of a foster home was left to the determination of the court.* **b.** The decision or pronouncement made. **4.a.** The ascertaining or fixing of the quantity, quality, position, or character of something: *a determination of the ship's longitude; a determination of the mass of the universe.* **b.** The result of such ascertaining. **5.** A fixed movement or tendency toward an object or end. **6.** *Logic.* **a.** The defining of a concept through its constituent elements. **b.** The qualification of a concept or proposition to render it more definite or specific.

de·ter·mi·na·tive (dĭ-tûr′mə-nā′tĭv, -nə-) *adj.* Tending, able, or serving to determine. See Synonyms at **decisive. —determinative** *n.* A determining factor. **—de·ter′mi·na′tive·ly** *adv.* **—de·ter′mi·na′tive·ness** *n.*

detector

de·ter·mine (dĭ-tûr′mĭn) *v.* **-mined, -min·ing, -mines.** *—tr.* **1.a.** To decide or settle (a dispute, for example) conclusively and authoritatively. **b.** To end or decide, as by judicial action. **2.** To establish or ascertain definitely, as after consideration, investigation, or calculation. See Synonyms at **discover. 3.** To cause (someone) to come to a conclusion or resolution. **4.** To be the cause of; regulate: *Demand determines production.* **5.** To give direction to: *The management committee determines departmental policy.* **6.** To limit in scope or extent. **7.** *Mathematics.* To fix or define the position, form, or configuration of. **8.** *Logic.* To explain or limit by adding differences. **9.** *Law.* To put an end to; terminate. *—intr.* **1.** To reach a decision; resolve. See Synonyms at **decide. 2.** *Law.* To come to an end. [Middle English *determinen,* from Old French *determiner,* from Latin *dēterminiāre,* to limit : *dē-,* de- + *terminus,* boundary.]

de·ter·mined (dĭ-tûr′mĭnd) *adj.* **1.** Marked by or showing determination; resolute: *was engaged in a protracted struggle with a determined enemy.* **2.** Decided or resolved. **—de·ter′mined·ly** *adv.* **—de·ter′mined·ness** *n.*

de·ter·min·er (dĭ-tûr′mə-nər) *n.* **1.** One that determines. **2.** *Grammar.* A word belonging to a group of noun modifiers, which include articles, demonstratives, possessive adjectives, and words such as *any, both,* or *whose,* and occupying the first position in a noun phrase or the second or third position after another determiner.

de·ter·min·ism (dĭ-tûr′mə-nĭz′əm) *n.* The philosophical doctrine that every event, act, and decision is the inevitable consequence of antecedents that are independent of the human will. **—de·ter′min·ist** *n.* **—de·ter′min·is′tic** *adj.* **—de·ter′min·is′ti·cal·ly** *adv.*

de·ter·rence (dĭ-tûr′əns, -tŭr′-) *n.* **1.** The act or a means of deterring. **2.** Measures taken by a state or an alliance of states to prevent hostile action by another state.

de·ter·rent (dĭ-tûr′ənt, -tŭr′-) *adj.* Tending to deter: *deterrent weapons.* **—deterrent** *n.* **1.** Something that deters: *a deterrent to theft.* **2.** A retaliatory means of discouraging enemy attack: *a nuclear deterrent.*

de·ter·sive (dĭ-tûr′sĭv, -zĭv) *adj.* Detergent. [French *détersif,* from Latin *dētersus,* past participle of *dētergēre,* to deterge. See DETERGE.] **—de·ter′sive** *n.*

de·test (dĭ-tĕst′) *tr.v.* **-test·ed, -test·ing, -tests.** To dislike intensely; abhor. [French *détester,* from Latin *dētestārī,* to curse : *dē-,* de- + *testārī,* to invoke (from *testis,* witness; see **trei-** in Appendix).] **—de·test′er** *n.*

de·test·a·ble (dĭ-tĕs′tə-bəl) *adj.* Inspiring or deserving abhorrence or scorn. See Synonyms at **hateful. —de·test′a·bil′i·ty, de·test′a·ble·ness** *n.* **—de·test′a·bly** *adv.*

de·tes·ta·tion (dē′tĕ-stā′shən) *n.* **1.** Strong dislike or hatred; abhorrence. **2.** One that is detested.

de·thatch (dē-thăch′) *v.* **-thatched, -thatch·ing, -thatch·es.** *—tr.* To remove (dead grass) from a lawn. *—intr.* To remove dead grass from a lawn. **—de·thatch′er** *n.*

de·throne (dē-thrōn′) *tr.v.* **-throned, -thron·ing, -thrones. 1.** To remove from the throne; depose. **2.** To remove from a prominent or powerful position. **—de·throne′ment** *n.*

det·i·nue (dĕt′n-o͞o′, -yo͞o′) *n. Law.* **1.a.** An action to recover possession or the value of property wrongfully detained. **b.** The writ authorizing such action. **2.** The act of unlawfully detaining personal property. [Middle English *detenue,* from Old

ă pat	oi boy
ā pay	ou out
âr care	o͝o took
ä father	o͞o boot
ĕ pet	ŭ cut
ē be	ûr urge
ĭ pit	th thin
ī pie	*th* this
îr pier	hw which
ŏ pot	zh vision
ō toe	ə about, item
ô paw	♦ regionalism

Stress marks: ′ (primary); ′ (secondary), as in **dictionary** (dĭk′shə-nĕr′ē)

French, detention, from past participle of *detenir,* to detain. See DETAIN.]

det·o·na·ble (dĕt′n-ə-bəl) *adj.* That can be detonated: *detonable warheads; detonable bombs.*

det·o·nate (dĕt′n-āt′) *intr. & tr.v.* **-nat·ed, -nat·ing, -nates.** To explode or cause to explode. [Latin *dētonāre, dētonāt-,* to thunder down : *dē-,* de- + *tonāre,* to thunder; see **(s)tenə-** in Appendix.] **—det′o·nat′a·ble** *adj.*

det·o·na·tion (dĕt′n-ā′shən) *n.* **1.** The act of exploding. **2.** An explosion.

det·o·na·tor (dĕt′n-ā′tər) *n.* **1.** A device, such as a fuse or percussion cap, used to set off an explosive charge. **2.** An explosive.

de·tour (dē′to͝or′, dĭ-to͝or′) *n.* **1.** A roundabout way or course, especially a road used temporarily instead of a main route. **2.** A deviation from a direct course of action. **—detour** *intr. & tr.v.* **-toured, -tour·ing, -tours.** To go or cause to go by a roundabout way. [French *détour,* from Old French *destor,* from *destorner,* to turn away : *des-,* de- + *torner,* to turn; see TURN.]

de·tox (dē-tŏks′) *Informal. tr.v.* **-toxed, -tox·ing, -tox·es.** To subject to detoxification. **—detox** (dē′tŏks′) *n.* A section of a hospital or clinic in which patients are detoxified. [Short for DETOXIFY.]

de·tox·i·cate (dē-tŏk′sĭ-kāt′) *tr.v.* **-cat·ed, -cat·ing, -cates.** To detoxify.

de·tox·i·fi·ca·tion (dē-tŏk′sə-fĭ-kā′shən) *n.* **1.** The process of detoxifying. **2.** The state or condition of being detoxified. **3.** *Physiology.* The metabolic process by which the toxic qualities of a poison or toxin are reduced by the body. **4.** A medically supervised treatment program for alcohol or drug addiction designed to purge the body of intoxicating or addictive substances. Such a program is used as a first step in overcoming physiological or psychological addiction.

de·tox·i·fy (dē-tŏk′sə-fī′) *tr.v.* **-fied, -fy·ing, -fies. 1.** To counteract or destroy the toxic properties of. **2.** To remove the effects of poison from. **3.** To treat (an individual) for alcohol or drug dependence, usually under a medically supervised program designed to rid the body of intoxicating or addictive substances. [DE– + TOXI(C) + –FY.]

de·tract (dĭ-trăkt′) *v.* **-tract·ed, -tract·ing, -tracts.** —*tr.* **1.** To draw or take away; divert: *They could detract little from so solid an argument.* **2.** *Archaic.* To speak ill of; belittle. —*intr.* **1.** To undergo reduction in value, importance, or quality; become reduced, as in effect. Often used with *from: testimony that only detracts from the strength of the plaintiff's case.* **2.** To divert or draw away qualities or a quality essential to the value, importance, or effect of something: *a decorating scheme that detracts but does not enhance.* [Middle English *detracten,* from Latin *dētrahere, dētract-,* to remove : *dē-,* de- + *trahere,* to pull. Sense 2, from Latin *dētrāctāre,* frequentative of *dētrahere,* to take away.] **—de·trac′tor** *n.*

de·trac·tion (dĭ-trăk′shən) *n.* **1.** The act of detracting or taking away. **2.** A derogatory or damaging comment on a person's character or reputation; disparagement: *The candidate responded sharply to the long list of detractions concocted by his opponent.* **—de·trac′tive** *adj.* **—de·trac′tive·ly** *adv.*

de·train (dē-trān′) *intr. & tr.v.* **-trained, -train·ing, -trains.** To leave or cause to leave a railroad train. **—de·train′ment** *n.*

de·trib·al·ize (dē-trī′bə-līz′) *tr.v.* **-ized, -iz·ing, -iz·es.** To cause to lose tribal membership and customs. **—de·trib′al·i·za′tion** (-trī′bə-lĭ-zā′shən) *n.*

det·ri·ment (dĕt′rə-mənt) *n.* **1.** Damage, harm, or loss: *took a long leave of absence without detriment to her career.* See Synonyms at **disadvantage. 2.** Something that causes damage, harm, or loss: *Smoking is now considered a detriment to good health.* [Middle English, from Old French, from Latin *dētrīmentum,* from *dētrītus,* past participle of *dēterere,* to lessen, wear down : *dē-,* de- + *terere,* to rub; see **terə-**[1] in Appendix.]

det·ri·men·tal (dĕt′rə-mĕn′tl) *adj.* Causing damage or harm; injurious. **—det′ri·men′tal·ly** *adv.*

de·tri·tion (dĭ-trĭsh′ən) *n.* The act of wearing away by friction: *beach pebbles worn smooth by detrition.* [Medieval Latin *dētrītiō, dētrītiōn-,* from Latin *dētrītus,* past participle of *dēterere,* to lessen, rub away. See DETRIMENT.]

de·tri·tus (dĭ-trī′təs) *n., pl.* **detritus. 1.** Loose fragments or grains that have been worn away from rock. **2. a.** Disintegrated or eroded matter: *the detritus of past civilizations.* **b.** Accumulated material; debris: *"Poems, engravings, press releases—he eagerly scrutinizes the detritus of fame"* (Carlin Romano). [French *détritus,* from Latin *dētrītus,* from past participle of *dēterere,* to lessen, wear away. See DETRIMENT.] **—de·tri′tal** (-trīt′l) *adj.*

De·troit (dĭ-troit′). A city of southeast Michigan opposite Windsor, Ontario, on the **Detroit River,** about 51 km (32 mi) long. Founded by French settlers in 1701, Detroit became known as "the automobile capital of the world" in the early 20th century. Population, 1,203,399.

de trop (də trō′) *adj.* Too much or too many; excessive or superfluous: *In retrospect the elaborate preparations seemed de trop.* [French : *de,* in, of + *trop,* excess.]

de·tu·mes·cence (dē′to͞o-mĕs′əns, -tyo͞o-) *n.* Reduction or lessening of a swelling, especially the restoration of a swollen organ or part to normal size. [From Latin *dētumēscere,* to subside : *dē-,* de- + *tumēscere,* to swell, inchoative of *tumēre;* see **teuə-** in Appendix.] **—de′tu·mes′cent** *adj.*

Deu·ca·li·on (do͞o-kā′lē-ən, dyo͞o-) *n. Greek Mythology.* A son of Prometheus who with his wife, Pyrrha, built an ark and floated in it to survive the deluge sent by Zeus. The couple became the ancestors of the renewed human race.

deuce[1] (do͞os, dyo͞os) *n.* **1.** *Games.* **a.** A playing card having two spots or the side of a die bearing two pips. **b.** A cast of dice totaling two. **2.** *Sports.* A tied score in tennis in which each player or side has 40 points, or 5 or more games, and one player or side must win 2 successive points to win the game, or 2 successive games to win the set. **—deuce** *tr.v.* **deuced, deuc·ing, deuc·es.** *Sports.* To make the score of (a tennis game or set) deuce. [Middle English *deus,* from Old French, two, from Latin *duōs,* masculine accusative of *duo.* See **dwo-** in Appendix.]

deuce[2] (do͞os, dyo͞os) *Informal. n.* **1.** The devil: *"Love is a bodily infirmity . . . which breaks out the deuce knows how or why"* (Thackeray). **2.** An outstanding example, especially of something difficult or bad: *had a deuce of a time getting out of town; a deuce of a family row.* **3.** A severe reprimand or expression of anger: *got the deuce for being late.* **4.** *Informal.* Used as an intensive: *What the deuce were they thinking of?* [Probably from Low German *duus,* a throw of two in dice games, bad luck, ultimately from Latin *duo,* two. See DEUCE[1].]

deuc·ed (do͞o′sĭd, dyo͞o′-) *adj. Informal.* Darned; confounded. [From DEUCE[2].]

deuc·es wild (do͞o′sĭz, dyo͞o′-) *n. Games.* A variation of certain card games, such as poker, in which each deuce may represent any card the holder chooses.

De·us (dā′əs) *n. Abbr.* **D.** God. [Middle English, from Latin. See **deiw-** in Appendix.]

deus ex ma·chi·na (ĕks mä′kə-nə, -nä′, măk′ə-nə) *n.* **1.** In Greek and Roman drama, a god lowered by stage machinery to resolve a plot or extricate the protagonist from a difficult situation. **2.** An unexpected, artificial, or improbable character, device, or event introduced suddenly in a work of fiction or drama to resolve a situation or untangle a plot. **3.** A person or event that provides a sudden and unexpected solution to a difficulty. [New Latin *deus ex machinā* : *deus,* god + *ex,* from + *machina,* machine (translation of Greek *theos apo mēkhanēs*).]

De·us Ra·mos (dĕ′o͞osh rä′mo͞osh), **João de.** 1830–1896. Portuguese poet regarded as the foremost of his time. He is best remembered for his love poems.

Deut. *abbr. Bible.* Deuteronomy.

deut– *pref.* Variant of **deuto–.**

deuter– *pref.* Variant of **deutero–.**

deu·ter·ag·o·nist (do͞o′tə-răg′ə-nĭst, dyo͞o-) *n.* The character second in importance to the protagonist in classical Greek drama. [Greek *deuteragōnistēs,* an actor of second-class parts : *deuteros,* second; see **deu-**[1] in Appendix + *agōnistēs,* actor; see PROTAGONIST.]

deu·ter·a·no·pi·a (do͞o′tər-ə-nō′pē-ə, dyo͞o′-) *n.* A form of colorblindness characterized by insensitivity to green. [DEUTER(O)– + AN– + –OPIA, so called because green is considered the second of the primary colors.] **—deu′ter·a·nope′** (-nōp′) *n.* **—deu′ter·a·nop′ic** (-nŏp′ĭk, -nō′pĭk) *adj.*

deu·ter·ate (do͞o′tə-rāt′, dyo͞o′-) *tr.v.* **-at·ed, -at·ing, -ates.** To introduce deuterium into (a chemical compound). [DEUTER(IUM) + –ATE[1].] **—deu′te·ra′tion** *n.*

deu·te·ri·um (do͞o-tîr′ē-əm, dyo͞o-) *n.* An isotope of hydrogen with one proton and one neutron in the nucleus having an atomic weight of 2.014. [DEUTER(O)– + –IUM.]

deuterium oxide *n.* An isotopic form of water with composition D_2O, isolated for use as a moderator in certain nuclear reactors.

deutero– or **deuter–** *pref.* Second; secondary: *deuterocanonical.* [Greek *deuteros,* second, secondary. See **deu-**[1] in Appendix.]

deu·ter·o·ca·non·i·cal (do͞o′tə-rō′kə-nŏn′ĭ-kəl, dyo͞o′-) *adj. Bible.* Of, relating to, or being a second canon, especially that consisting of sections of the Old and New Testaments not included in the original Roman Catholic canon but accepted by theologians in 1548 at the Council of Trent.

deu·ter·og·a·my (do͞o′tə-rŏg′ə-mē, dyo͞o′-) *n.* See **digamy.**

deu·ter·on (do͞o′tə-rŏn′, dyo͞o′-) *n. Abbr.* **d** The nucleus of a deuterium atom, consisting of a proton and a neutron, regarded as a subatomic particle with unit positive charge. [DEUTER(IUM) + –ON[1].]

Deu·ter·on·o·my (do͞o′tə-rŏn′ə-mē, dyo͞o′-) *n. Abbr.* **Deut., Dt.** *Bible.* See table at **Bible.** [Late Latin *deuteronomium,* from Greek *deuteronomion,* a second law (from *(to) deuteronomion (touto),* Septuagint mistranslation of Hebrew *mišnê hattôrâ hazzō't,* a copy of this law) : *deuteros,* second; see **deu-**[1] in Appendix + *nomos,* law; see **nem-** in Appendix.] **—Deu′ter·o·nom′ic** (-tər-ə-nŏm′ĭk) *adj.*

deuto– or **deut–** *pref.* Second; secondary: *deutoplasm.* [Alteration of DEUTERO–.]

deu·to·plasm (do͞o′tə-plăz′əm, dyo͞o′-) *n.* The nutritive substances or yolk in the cytoplasm of an ovum or other cell. **—deu′to·plas′mic** *adj.*

deut·sche mark also **deut·sche·mark** (doi′chə-märk′) *n.*

Abbr. **DM** See table at **currency.** [German : *deutsch*, German + *Mark*, mark.]

deut•zi•a (do͞ot′sē-ə, dyo͞ot′-) *n.* Any of various shrubs of the genus *Deutzia*, cultivated for their clusters of white or pinkish flowers. [After Jan van der *Deutz*, 18th-century Dutch patron of botany.]

dev. *abbr.* Deviation.

De Va•le•ra (dĕv′ə-lĕr′ə, -lîr′ə), **Eamon.** 1882–1975. American-born Irish political leader who fought in the 1916 Easter Rebellion and was president of Sinn Fein (1918–1926) before becoming three-time prime minister of the Irish Free State and the first president of the Republic of Ireland (1959–1973).

De Val•ois (də văl′wä), Dame **Ninette.** Originally Edris Stannus. Born 1898. Irish-born British dancer and choreographer who danced with the Ballets Russes from 1926 to 1929 and then returned to London, where she later founded the Sadler's Wells Ballet, which became the Royal Ballet at Covent Garden (1956).

de•val•ue (dē-văl′yo͞o) also **de•val•u•ate** (-văl′yo͞o-āt′) *v.* **-ued, -u•ing, -ues** also **-at•ed, -at•ing, -ates.** —*tr.* **1.** To lessen or cancel the value of. **2.** To lower the exchange value of (a currency) by lowering its gold equivalency. —*intr.* To lower the exchange value of a currency by lowering its gold equivalency. —**de•val′u•a′tion** *n.*

De•va•na•ga•ri (dā′və-nä′gə-rē) *n.* The alphabet in which Sanskrit and many modern Indian languages are written. [Sanskrit *devanāgarī* : *deva-*, divine; see **deiw-** in Appendix + *nāgarī*, feminine of *nāgara-*, of a town (from *nagaram*, town, probably of Dravidian origin).]

dev•as•tate (dĕv′ə-stāt′) *tr.v.* **-tat•ed, -tat•ing, -tates. 1.** To lay waste; destroy. **2.** To overwhelm; confound; stun: *was devastated by the rude remark.* [Latin *dēvāstāre, dēvāstāt-* : *dē-*, de- + *vāstāre*, to lay waste (from *vāstus*, empty, desolate; see **eu-**[2] in Appendix).] —**dev′as•tat′ing•ly** *adv.* —**dev′as•ta′tion** *n.* —**dev′as•ta′tor** *n.*

de•vel•op (dĭ-vĕl′əp) *v.* **-oped, -op•ing, -ops.** —*tr.* **1.** To bring from latency to or toward fulfillment: *an instructor who develops the capabilities of each student.* **2. a.** To expand or enlarge: *developed a national corporation into a worldwide business.* **b.** To aid in the growth of; strengthen: *exercises that develop muscles.* **c.** To improve the quality of; refine: *develops his recipes to perfection; an extra year of study to develop virtuosic technique.* **3. a.** To cause to become more complex or intricate; add detail and fullness to; elaborate: *began with a good premise but developed it without imagination.* **b.** *Music.* To elaborate (a theme) with rhythmic and harmonic variations. **4. a.** To bring into being gradually: *develop a new cottage industry.* **b.** To set forth or clarify by degrees: *developed her thesis in a series of articles.* **5. a.** To come to have gradually; acquire: *develop a taste for opera; develop a friendship.* **b.** To become affected with; contract; *developed a rash; developed agoraphobia.* **6.** To cause gradually to acquire a specific role, function, or form, as: **a.** To influence the behavior of toward a specific end: *an investigator who develops witnesses through flattery and intimidation.* **b.** To cause (a tract of land) to serve a particular purpose: *developed the site as a community of condominiums.* **c.** To make available and effective to fulfill a particular end or need: *develop the state's water resources to serve a growing population.* **d.** To convert or transform: *developed the play into a movie.* **7.** *Games.* To move (a chess piece) to or toward a more strategic position. **8. a.** To process (a photosensitive material), especially with chemicals, in order to render a recorded image visible. **b.** To render (an image) visible by this means. —*intr.* **1. a.** To grow by degrees into a more advanced or mature state: *With hard work, she developed into a great writer.* See Synonyms at **mature. b.** To increase or expand. **c.** To improve; advance: *Their skill developed until it rivaled their teacher's.* **2.** To come gradually into existence or activity: *Tension developed between students and faculty.* **3.** To come gradually to light; be disclosed: *reports the news as it develops.* **4.** *Biology.* **a.** To progress from earlier to later stages of a life cycle: *Caterpillars develop into butterflies.* **b.** To progress from earlier to later or from simpler to more complex stages of evolution. [French *développer*, from Old French *desveloper* : *des-*, dis- + *voloper*, to wrap (possibly of Celtic origin).] —**de•vel′op•a•ble** *adj.*

de•vel•oped (dĭ-vĕl′əpt) *adj.* Advanced in industrial capability, technological sophistication, and economic productivity: *traveled through the least developed areas of the world.*

de•vel•op•er (dĭ-vĕl′ə-pər) *n.* **1.** One that develops: *a developer of hidden talent.* **2.** A person who develops real estate, epecially by preparing a site for residential or commercial use. **3.** A chemical used to render visible the image recorded on a photosensitive surface.

de•vel•op•ing (dĭ-vĕl′ə-pĭng) *adj.* Having a relatively low level of industrial capability, technological sophistication, and economic productivity: *studied the economies of developing nations.*

de•vel•op•ment (dĭ-vĕl′əp-mənt) *n.* **1.** The act of developing. **2.** The state of being developed. **3.** A significant event, occurrence, or change. **4.** A group of dwellings built by the same contractor. **5.** Determination of the best techniques for applying a new device or process to production of goods or services. **6.** *Music.* **a.** Elaboration of a theme with rhythmic and harmonic variations. **b.** The part of a movement in sonata form in which the theme is elaborated and explored. —**de•vel′op•men′tal** (-mĕn′tl) *adj.* —**de•vel′op•men′tal•ly** *adv.*

SYNONYMS: *development, evolution, progress.* The central meaning shared by these nouns is "a progression from a simpler or lower to a more advanced, mature, or complex form or stage": *the development of an aptitude into an accomplishment; the evolution of a plant from a seed; attempts made to foster social progress.*

developmental disability *n.* A mental or physical incapacity, such as cerebral palsy, arising before adulthood and usually lasting throughout life.

developmental psychology *n.* The branch of psychology concerned with the study of behavioral changes in an individual from birth until death.

dé•vel•op•pé (də-vĕl′ə-pā′) *n.* A ballet movement in which one leg is raised to the knee of the supporting leg and fully extended. [French, from past participle of *développer*, to develop. See DEVELOP.]

De•ven•ter (dā′vən-tər). A city of east-central Netherlands on the Ijssel River east-northeast of Utrecht. A member of the Hanseatic League, it was a noted center of piety and learning during the Middle Ages. Population, 64,823.

de•ver•bal *n.* See **deverbative.**

de•verb•a•tive (dē-vûr′bə-tĭv) *Grammar. adj.* **1.** Formed from a verb, such as the noun *worker* derived from the verb *work.* **2.** Used in derivation from a verb, such as the suffix *-er* in *teacher.* —**deverbative** *n.* A deverbative word or element. Also called *deverbal.*

Dev•er•eux (dĕv′ə-ro͞o′), **Robert.** Second Earl of Essex. 1566–1601. English nobleman and favorite of Elizabeth I. He was executed for treason after taking part in an uprising of the people of London.

de•vest (dĭ-vĕst′) *tr.v.* **-vest•ed, -vest•ing, -vests. 1.** *Law.* To take away (a right or possession, for example). **2.** *Archaic.* **a.** To remove the clothing or covering of. **b.** To deprive of a title, right, or item of property. [Obsolete French *desvestir*, to undress, from Medieval Latin *disvestīre* : Latin *dis-*, dis- + Latin *vestis*, garment; see **wes-**[2] in Appendix.]

De•vi (dā′vē) *n. Hinduism.* A mother goddess having various manifestations and roles, especially that of consort to Shiva. [Sanskrit *devī*, feminine of *devaḥ*, god. See **deiw-** in Appendix.]

de•vi•ant (dē′vē-ənt) *adj.* Differing from a norm or from the accepted standards of a society. —**deviant** *n.* One that differs from a norm, especially a person whose behavior and attitudes differ from accepted social standards. [Middle English *deviaunt*, from Late Latin *dēviāns, dēviant-*, present participle of *dēviāre*, to deviate. See DEVIATE.] —**de′vi•ance, de′vi•an•cy** *n.*

de•vi•ate (dē′vē-āt′) *v.* **-at•ed, -at•ing, -ates.** —*intr.* **1.** To turn aside from a course or way. **2.** To depart, as from a norm, a purpose, or a subject; stray. See Synonyms at **swerve.** —*tr.* To cause to turn aside or differ. —**deviate** (-ĭt) *n.* A deviant. [Late Latin *dēviāre, dēviāt-* : Latin *dē-*, de- + Latin *via*, road; see **wegh-** in Appendix.] —**de′vi•a′tor** *n.* —**de′vi•a•to′ry** (-ə-tôr′ē, -tōr′ē) *adj.*

de•vi•a•tion (dē′vē-ā′shən) *n. Abbr.* **dev. 1.** The act of deviating or turning aside. **2.** An abnormality; a departure: *"Vice was a deviation from our nature"* (Henry Fielding). **3.** Deviant behavior or attitudes. **4.** Divergence from an accepted political policy or party line. **5.** Deflection of a compass needle caused by local magnetic influence, especially on a ship. **6.** *Statistics.* The difference, especially the absolute difference, between one number in a set and the mean of the set. —**de′vi•a′tion•ism** *n.* —**de′vi•a′tion•ist** *adj. & n.*

SYNONYMS: *deviation, aberration, divergence.* The central meaning shared by these nouns is "a departure from what is prescribed or expected": *tolerates no deviation from the rules; regretted the aberrations of her early life; the divergence of two cultures.*

de•vice (dĭ-vīs′) *n.* **1.** A contrivance or an invention serving a particular purpose, especially a machine used to perform one or more relatively simple tasks. **2. a.** A technique or means. **b.** A plan or scheme, especially a malign one. **3.** A literary contrivance, such as parallelism or personification, used to achieve a particular effect. **4.** A decorative design, figure, or pattern, as one used in embroidery. See Synonyms at **figure. 5.** A graphic symbol or motto, especially in heraldry. **6.** *Archaic.* The act, state, or power of devising. —***idiom.* leave to (one's) own devices.** To allow to do as one pleases: *left the child to her own devices for an hour in the afternoon.* [Middle English, from Old French *devis*, division, wish and Old French *devise*, design, both from Latin *dīvīsus, dīvīsa*, past participle of *dīvidere*, to divide, separate.]

dev•il (dĕv′əl) *n.* **1.** Often **Devil.** *Theology.* In many religions, the major personified spirit of evil, ruler of Hell, and foe of God. Used with *the.* **2.** A subordinate evil spirit; a demon. **3.** A wicked or malevolent person. **4.** A person: *a handsome devil; the poor devil.* **5.** An energetic, mischievous, daring, or clever person. **6.** *Printing.* A printer's devil. **7.** A device or machine, especially one having teeth or spikes and used for tearing. **8.** An outstanding example, especially of something difficult or bad: *has a devil of a temper.* **9.** A severe reprimand or expression of anger: *gave me the devil for cutting class.* **10.** *Informal.* Used as an intensive: *Who the devil do you think you are?* **11.** *Christian Science.* The

ă pat	oi boy
ā pay	ou out
âr care	o͝o took
ä father	o͞o boot
ĕ pet	ŭ cut
ē be	ûr urge
ĭ pit	th thin
ī pie	*th* this
îr pier	hw which
ŏ pot	zh vision
ō toe	ə about, item
ô paw	♦ regionalism

Stress marks: **′** (primary); ′ (secondary), as in **dictionary** (dĭk′shə-nĕr′ē)

opposite of Truth; error. **—devil** *tr.v.* **-iled, -il·ing, -ils** or **-illed, -il·ling, -ils. 1.** To season (food) heavily. **2.** To annoy, torment, or harass. **3.** To tear up (cloth or rags) in a toothed machine. **—*idioms.* between the devil and the deep blue sea.** Between two equally unacceptable choices. **give the devil his due.** To give credit to a disagreeable or malevolent person. **go to the devil. 1.** To be unsuccessful; fail. **2.** To become depraved. **3.** Used in the imperative to express anger or impatience. **play the devil with.** To upset or ruin. **the devil take the hindmost.** Let each person follow self-interest, leaving others to fare as they may. **the devil to pay.** Trouble to be faced as a result of an action: *There'll be the devil to pay if you allow the piglets inside the house.* [Middle English *devel,* from Old English *dēofol,* from Latin *diabolus,* from Late Greek *diabolos,* from Greek, slanderer, from *diaballein,* to slander : *dia-,* dia- + *ballein,* to hurl; see **gʷelə-** in Appendix.]

dev·il·fish (dĕv′əl-fĭsh′) *n., pl.* **devilfish** or **-fish·es. 1.** See **manta** (sense 2). **2.** See **octopus** (sense 1). **3.** See **gray whale.**

dev·il·ish (dĕv′ə-lĭsh) *adj.* **1.** Of, resembling, or characteristic of a devil, as: **a.** Malicious; evil. **b.** Mischievous, teasing, or annoying. **2.** Excessive; extreme: *devilish heat.* **—devilish** *adv.* Extremely; very. **—dev′il·ish·ly** *adv.* **—dev′il·ish·ness** *n.*

dev·il·kin (dĕv′əl-kĭn) *n.* A little devil; an imp.

dev·il-may-care (dĕv′əl-mā-kâr′) *adj.* **1.** Heedless of caution; reckless. **2.** Jovial and rakish in manner.

dev·il·ment (dĕv′əl-mənt) *n.* Devilish behavior; mischief.

dev·il·ry (dĕv′əl-rē) *n.* Variant of **deviltry.**

dev·il's advocate (dĕv′əlz) *n.* **1.** One who argues against a cause or position, not as a committed opponent but simply for the sake of argument or to determine the validity of the cause or position. **2.** *Roman Catholic Church.* An official appointed to present arguments against a proposed canonization or beatification.

devil's bit *n.* See **blazing star** (sense 1).

devil's club *n.* A spiny shrub *(Oplopanax horridus)* of western North America, having greenish-white flowers and scarlet fruit clustered in umbels.

♦**devil's darning needle** *n.* **1.** *Upper Northern U.S.* See **dragonfly.** See Regional Note at **dragonfly. 2.** See **damselfly.**

devil's food cake *n.* A rich chocolate cake.

Dev·il's Island (dĕv′ĭlz). An island in the Caribbean Sea off French Guiana. A French penal colony after the 1850's, it was used mainly for political prisoners, including Alfred Dreyfus (sequestered 1894–1899).

devil's paintbrush *n.* See **orange hawkweed.**

devil's walking stick *n.* See **Hercules' club** (sense 1).

dev·il·try (dĕv′əl-trē) or **dev·il·ry** (-əl-rē) *n., pl.* **-tries** or **-ries. 1.** Reckless mischief. **2.** Extreme cruelty; wickedness. **3.** Evil magic; witchcraft. **4.** An act of mischief, cruelty, or witchcraft. [Alteration of DEVILRY.]

devilwood
Osmanthus americanus

dev·il·wood (dĕv′əl-wo͝od′) *n.* A tree *(Osmanthus americanus)* of the southeast United States, having fragrant greenish flowers, hard wood, and whitish bark. Also called *wild olive.*

De Vin·ne (də vĭn′ē), **Theodore Low.** 1828–1914. American printer who did much to advance fine typography through his workmanship and his writings, including *The Practice of Typography* (1900–1904).

de·vi·ous (dē′vē-əs) *adj.* **1.** Not straightforward; shifty: *a devious character.* **2.** Departing from the correct or accepted way; erring: *achieved success by devious means.* **3.** Deviating from the straight or direct course; roundabout: *a devious route.* **4.** Away from a main road or course; distant or removed. [From Latin *dēvius,* out-of-the-way : *dē-,* de- + *via,* road; see **wegh-** in Appendix.] **—de′vi·ous·ly** *adv.* **—de′vi·ous·ness** *n.*

de·vise (dĭ-vīz′) *tr.v.* **-vised, -vis·ing, -vis·es. 1.** To form, plan, or arrange in the mind; design or contrive: *devised a new system for handling mail orders.* **2.** *Law.* To transmit or give (real property) by will. **3.** *Archaic.* To suppose; imagine. **—devise** *n. Law.* **1. a.** The act of transmitting or giving real property by will. **b.** The property or lands so transmitted or given. **2.** A will or clause in a will transmitting or giving real property. [Middle English *devisen,* from Old French *deviser,* from Vulgar Latin **dēvīsāre,* from Latin **dīvīsāre,* frequentative of *dīvidere,* to divide.] **—de·vis′a·ble** *adj.* **—de·vis′er** *n.*

de·vi·see (dĭ-vī′zē′, dĕv′ĭ-zē′) *n. Law.* One to whom a devise is made.

de·vi·sor (dĭ-vī′zər, dĕv′ĭ-zôr′) *n. Law.* One that makes a devise.

de·vi·tal·ize (dē-vīt′l-īz′) *tr.v.* **-ized, -iz·ing, -iz·es.** To diminish or destroy the strength or vitality of. **—de·vit′al·i·za′tion** (-ĭ-zā′shən) *n.*

de·vit·ri·fy (dē-vĭt′rə-fī′) *tr.v.* **-fied, -fy·ing, -fies.** To cause (a glassy material) to become crystalline and brittle. **—de·vit′ri·fi′a·ble** *adj.* **—de·vit′ri·fi·ca′tion** (-fĭ-kā′shən) *n.*

de·vo·cal·ize (dē-vō′kə-līz′) *tr.v.* **-ized, -iz·ing, -iz·es.** *Linguistics.* To devoice. **—de·vo′cal·i·za′tion** (-kə-lĭ-zā′shən) *n.*

de·voice (dē-vois′) *tr.v.* **-voiced, -voic·ing, -voic·es.** *Linguistics.* To pronounce (a normally voiced sound) without vibration of the vocal chords so as to make it wholly or partly voiceless.

de·void (dĭ-void′) *adj.* Completely lacking; destitute or empty: *a novel devoid of wit and inventiveness.* [Middle English, past participle of *devoiden,* to remove, eliminate, from Old French *desvoidier* : *des-,* de- + *voidier,* to empty (from *voide,* empty; see VOID).]

de·voir (dəv-wär′, dĕv′wär′) *n.* **1.** Often **devoirs.** An act or expression of respect or courtesy; civility: *pay one's devoirs.* **2.** Duty or responsibility. [Middle English, duty, from Old French, from *devoir,* to owe, from Latin *dēbēre.* See **ghabh-** in Appendix.]

de·vol·a·til·ize (dē-vŏl′ə-tl-īz′) *tr.v.* **-ized, -iz·ing, -iz·es.** To remove volatile material from: *devolatilize coal.* **—de·vol′a·til·i·za′tion** (-ĭ-zā′shən) *n.*

dev·o·lu·tion (dĕv′ə-lo͞o′shən, dē′və-) *n.* **1.** A passing down or descent through successive stages of time or a process. **2.** Transference, as of rights, or qualities, to a successor. **3.** Delegation of authority or duties to a subordinate or substitute. **4.** A transfer of powers from a central government to local units. **5.** *Biology.* Degeneration. [Late Latin *dēvolūtiō, dēvolūtiōn-,* from Latin *dēvolūtus,* past participle of *dēvolvere,* to roll down, fall to. See DEVOLVE.] **—dev′o·lu′tion·ar′y** (-shə-nĕr′ē) *adj.* **—dev′o·lu′tion·ist** *n.*

de·volve (dĭ-vŏlv′) *v.* **-volved, -volv·ing, -volves.** *—tr.* **1.** To pass on or delegate to another: *The senator devolved the duties of office upon a group of aides.* **2.** *Archaic.* To cause to roll onward or downward. *—intr.* **1.** To be passed on or transferred to another: *The burden of proof devolved upon the defendant. The estate devolved to an unlikely heir.* **2.** *Archaic.* To roll onward or downward. [Middle English *devolven,* to transfer, from Old French *devolver,* to confer, ascribe, from Latin *dēvolvere,* to roll down, fall to : *dē-,* de- + *volvere,* to roll; see **wel-**[2] in Appendix.] **—de·volve′ment** *n.*

Dev·on[1] (dĕv′ən). A region of southwest England bordering on the English Channel. Occupied in Paleolithic times, it became part of Wessex in the eighth century.

Dev·on[2] (dĕv′ən) *n.* Any of a breed of reddish cattle originally developed in the English county of Devon and raised primarily for beef.

De·vo·ni·an (dĭ-vō′nē-ən) *adj.* Of, belonging to, or designating the geologic time, system of rocks, or sedimentary deposits of the fourth period of the Paleozoic Era, after the Silurian and before the Mississippian or Carboniferous Period, and characterized by the appearance of forests and amphibians. See table at **geologic time. —Devonian** *n.* The Devonian Period or its system of deposits. [After *Devon,* a county of southwest England.]

Devon Island. An island of northeast Northwest Territories, Canada, between Baffin and Ellesmere islands.

Dev·on·shire cream (dĕv′ən-shîr′, -shər) *n.* See **clotted cream.** [After *Devonshire,* or Devon, a county of southwest England.]

de·vote (dĭ-vōt′) *tr.v.* **-vot·ed, -vot·ing, -votes. 1.** To give or apply (one's time, attention, or self) entirely to a particular activity, pursuit, cause, or person. **2.** To set apart for a specific purpose or use: *land devoted to mining.* **3.** To set apart by or as if by a vow or solemn act; consecrate: *a temple devoted to Apollo.* [Latin *dēvovēre, dēvōt-,* to vow : *dē-,* de- + *vovēre,* to vow.] **—de·vote′ment** *n.*

SYNONYMS: *devote, dedicate, consecrate, pledge.* These verbs are compared as they mean "to give to a particular end and especially to a higher purpose." *Devote* implies faithfulness and loyalty: *Nurses devote themselves to the care of the sick. Dedicate* connotes a solemn, often formal commitment: *"To such a task we can dedicate our lives and our fortunes, everything that we are and everything that we have"* (Woodrow Wilson). *Consecrate* suggests sacred commitment: *His entire life is consecrated to science.* To *pledge* is to back a personal commitment by a solemn promise: *"I pledge you, I pledge myself, to a new deal for the American people"* (Franklin D. Roosevelt).

de·vot·ed (dĭ-vō′tĭd) *adj.* **1.** Feeling or displaying strong affection or attachment; ardent: *a devoted friend.* **2.** Having been consecrated; dedicated. **—de·vot′ed·ly** *adv.* **—de·vot′ed·ness** *n.*

dev·o·tee (dĕv′ə-tē′, -tā′) *n.* **1.** One who is ardently devoted to something; an enthusiast or advocate: *a devotee of sports.* **2.** An ardent or fanatical adherent of a religion. See Synonyms at **votary.**

de·vo·tion (dĭ-vō′shən) *n.* **1.** Ardent, often selfless affection and dedication, as to a person. See Synonyms at **love. 2.** Religious ardor or zeal; piety. **3.** Often **devotions. a.** An act of religious observance or prayer, especially when private. **b. devotions.** Prayers or religious texts: *a book of devotions.* **4.** The act of devoting or the state of being devoted.

de·vo·tion·al (dĭ-vō′shə-nəl) *adj.* Of, relating to, expressive of, or used in devotion, especially of a religious nature. **—devotional** *n.* A short religious service. **—de·vo′tion·al·ly** *adv.*

de·vour (dĭ-vour′) *tr.v.* **-voured, -vour·ing, -vours. 1.** To eat up greedily. See Synonyms at **eat. 2.** To destroy, consume, or waste: *Flames devoured the structure in minutes.* **3.** To take in eagerly: *devour a novel.* **4.** To prey upon voraciously: *was devoured by jealousy.* [Middle English *devouren,* from Old French *devourer,* from Latin *dēvorāre* : *dē-,* de- + *vorāre,* to swallow.] **—de·vour′er** *n.* **—de·vour′ing·ly** *adv.*

de·vout (dĭ-vout′) *adj.* **-er, -est. 1.** Devoted to religion or to the fulfillment of religious obligations. See Synonyms at **religious. 2.** Displaying reverence or piety. **3.** Sincere; earnest: *devout wishes for their success.* [Middle English, from Old French, from Latin *dēvōtus,* past participle of *dēvovēre,* to vow. See DEVOTE.] —**de·vout′ly** *adv.* —**de·vout′ness** *n.*

De Vries (də vrēs′), **Hugo.** 1848–1935. Dutch botanist who studied evolution by observing mutations rather than natural selection. He was an early proponent of the works of Gregor Mendel.

dew (do͞o, dyo͞o) *n.* **1.** Water droplets condensed from the air, usually at night, onto cool surfaces. **2.** Something moist, fresh, pure, or renewing: *"The timely dew of sleep/. . . inclines/Our eyelids"* (John Milton). **3.** Moisture, as in the form of tears or perspiration, that appears in small drops. —**dew** *tr.v.* **dewed, dew·ing, dews.** To wet with or as if with dew. [Middle English *deu,* from Old English *dēaw.* See **dheu-**[1] in Appendix.]

DEW *abbr.* Distant early warning.

de·wan (dĭ-wän′) *n.* Any of various government officials in India, especially a regional prime minister. [Hindi *dīvān,* from Persian, account book.]

Dew·ar (do͞o′ər, dyo͞o′-), Sir **James.** 1842–1923. Scottish-born chemist and physicist who studied the liquefaction of gases and the properties of matter at very low temperatures and invented cordite (1889) with Sir Frederick Abel.

Dewar flask *n.* An insulated container used especially to store liquefied gases, having a double wall with a vacuum between the walls and silvered surfaces facing the vacuum. [After Sir James DEWAR.]

de·wat·er (dē-wô′tər, -wŏt′ər) *tr.v.* **-ered, -er·ing, -ers.** To remove water from (a waste product or streambed, for example).

dew·ber·ry (do͞o′bĕr′ē, dyo͞o′-) *n.* **1.** Any of several trailing forms of the blackberry, such as *Rubus hispidus* of North America and *R. caesius* of Europe. **2.** The fruit of any of these plants.

dew·claw (do͞o′klô′, dyo͞o′-) *n.* A vestigial digit or claw not reaching the ground and found on the feet of certain mammals. [Origin unknown, perhaps from alteration of TOE.] —**dew′-clawed′** *adj.*

dew·drop (do͞o′drŏp′, dyo͞o′-) *n.* A drop of dew.

Dew·ey (do͞o′ē, dyo͞o′ē), **George.** 1837–1917. American naval officer known for his victory at Manila Bay (May 1, 1898) in the Spanish-American War.

Dewey, John. 1859–1952. American philosopher and educator who was a leading exponent of philosophical pragmatism and rejected traditional methods of teaching by rote in favor of a broad-based system of practical experience.

Dewey, Melvil. 1851–1931. American librarian and founder of the decimal system of classification (1876).

Dewey, Thomas Edmund. 1902–1971. American politician who was the Republican nominee for President in 1944 and 1948. In the latter election he was unexpectedly beaten by Harry S. Truman's whistle-stop campaign.

Dewey decimal classification *n.* A system used in libraries for organizing nonfiction publications into subject categories corresponding to three-digit numerals, with further specification expressed by numerals following a decimal point. [After Melvil DEWEY.]

dew·fall (do͞o′fôl′, dyo͞o′-) *n.* **1.** The formation of dew. **2.** The time of evening when dew begins to form.

De Witt (də wĭt′, vĭt′), **Jan.** 1625–1672. Dutch politician. He and his brother **Cornelius** (1623–1672) were murdered by an angry mob for their opposition to William of Orange.

dew·lap (do͞o′lăp′, dyo͞o′-) *n.* **1.** A fold of loose skin hanging from the neck of certain animals. **2.** A pendulous part similar to this, such as the wattle of a bird. [Middle English *dewlappe* : *dew,* origin unknown + *lappe,* fold; see LAP[2].]

DEW line (do͞o, dyo͞o) *n.* A line of radar stations near the 70th parallel across the North American continent, maintained by the United States and Canada and intended to give advance warning of approaching enemy aircraft and missiles. [*D(istant) E(arly) W(arning).*]

de·worm (dē-wûrm′) *tr.v.* **-wormed, -worm·ing, -worms.** To cure (an animal) of worms; worm. —**de·worm′er** *n.*

dew point *n. Abbr.* **DP** The temperature at which air becomes saturated and produces dew.

dew-worm also **dew worm** (do͞o′wûrm′, dyo͞o′-) *n.* An earthworm found on or near the surface of the ground and used as fishing bait.

dew·y (do͞o′ē, dyo͞o′ē) *adj.* **-i·er, -i·est. 1.** Moist with or as if with dew: *dewy grass in early morning.* **2.** Accompanied by dew: *a dewy morning.* **3.** Suggestive of the freshness or purity of dew, as in innocence or naiveté: *never gave up the dewy outlook of youth.* —**dew′i·ly** *adv.* —**dew′i·ness** *n.*

dew·y-eyed (do͞o′ē-īd′, dyo͞o′-) *adj.* Innocent; naive.

dex (dĕks) *n. Slang.* Dextroamphetamine.

dex·a·meth·a·sone (dĕk′sə-mĕth′ə-sōn′, -zōn′) *n.* A synthetic glucocorticoid used primarily in the treatment of inflammatory disorders. [*Dexa(myl),* a dextroamphetamine compound + METH(YL) + (CORTI)SONE.]

Dex·e·drine (dĕk′sĭ-drĭn, -drēn′). A trademark used for dextroamphetamine.

dex·ie (dĕk′sē) *n. Slang.* A pill or tablet containing dextroamphetamine.

dex·ter (dĕk′stər) *adj.* **1.** Of or located on the right side. **2.** *Heraldry.* Situated on or being the side of a shield on the wearer's right and the observer's left. **3.** *Obsolete.* Auspicious; favorable. [Latin.]

dex·ter·i·ty (dĕk-stĕr′ĭ-tē) *n.* **1.** Skill and grace in physical movement, especially in the use of the hands; adroitness. **2.** Mental skill or adroitness; cleverness. [French *dextérité,* from Latin *dexteritās,* from *dexter,* skillful.]

dex·ter·ous (dĕk′stər-əs, -strəs) also **dex·trous** (-strəs) *adj.* **1.** Skillful in the use of the hands. **2.** Having mental skill or adroitness. **3.** Done with dexterity. [From Latin *dexter,* skillful.] —**dex′ter·ous·ly** *adv.* —**dex′ter·ous·ness** *n.*

SYNONYMS: *dexterous, deft, adroit, handy, nimble.* These adjectives refer to skill and ease in performance. *Dexterous* implies physical or mental agility: *dexterous fingers. "This study* [of law] *renders men acute, inquisitive, dexterous, prompt in attack, ready in defense, full of resources"* (Edmund Burke). *Deft* suggests quickness, sureness, neatness, and lightness of touch: *decorated the cake with a few deft strokes; defused the hostility with a deft turn of phrase. Adroit* implies ease and natural skill, especially in dealing with challenging situations: *an adroit skier; an adroit negotiator. Handy* suggests a more modest aptitude, principally in manual work: *handy with a saw and hammer. Nimble* stresses quickness and lightness in physical or mental performance: *nimble feet; nimble wits.*

dextr– *pref.* Variant of **dextro–.**

dex·tral (dĕk′strəl) *adj.* **1.** Of, relating to, or located on the right side; right. **2.** Right-handed. **3.** *Zoology.* Of or relating to a gastropod shell that coils clockwise and has its aperture to the right when facing the observer with the apex upward. —**dex·tral′i·ty** (dĕk-străl′ĭ-tē) *n.* —**dex′tral·ly** *adv.*

dex·tran (dĕk′străn′, -strən) *n.* Any of a group of long-chain polymers of glucose with various molecular weights that are used in confections, in lacquers, as food additives, and as plasma volume expanders. [DEXTR(OSE) + –AN[2].]

dex·trin (dĕk′strĭn) also **dex·trine** (dĕk′strĭn, -strēn′) *n.* Any of various soluble polysaccharides obtained from starch by the application of heat or acids and used mainly as adhesives and thickening agents.

dex·tro (dĕk′strō) *adj.* Dextrorotatory.

dextro– or **dextr–** *pref.* **1.** On or to the right; right: *dextrorotation.* **2.** Dextrorotatory: *dextrose.* [Latin, from *dexter,* on the right side.]

dex·tro·am·phet·a·mine (dĕk′strō-ăm-fĕt′ə-mēn′, -mĭn) *n.* A white crystalline compound, $C_9H_{13}N$, that is the dextrorotatory isomer of amphetamine and is used in the form of its phosphate or sulfate salt as a central nervous system stimulant.

dex·tro·glu·cose (dĕk′strə-glo͞o′kōs′) *n.* See **dextrose.**

dex·tro·ro·ta·tion (dĕk′strə-rō-tā′shən) *n.* A turning to the right. Used especially of the plane of polarization of light.

dex·tro·ro·ta·to·ry (dĕk′strə-rō′tə-tôr′ē, -tōr′ē) also **dex·tro·ro·ta·ry** (-rō′tə-rē) *adj.* Turning or rotating the plane of polarization of light to the right or clockwise: *a dextrorotatory solution.*

dex·trorse (dĕk′strôrs′) *adj. Botany.* Growing upward in a spiral that turns from left to right: *a dextrorse vine.* [Latin *dextrōrsus,* from *dextrōvorsus,* turning toward the right : *dexter,* right + *versus,* past participle of *vertere,* to turn; see **wer-**[2] in Appendix.] —**dex′trorse′ly** *adv.*

dex·trose (dĕk′strōs′) *n.* The dextrorotatory form of glucose, $C_6H_{12}O_6 \cdot H_2O$, found naturally in animal and plant tissue and derived synthetically from starch. Also called *dextroglucose.*

dex·trous (dĕk′strəs) *adj.* Variant of **dexterous.**

dey (dā) *n.* **1.** Used formerly as the title of the governor of Algiers before the French conquest in 1830. **2.** Used formerly as the title for rulers of the states of Tunis and Tripoli. [French, from Turkish *dayı,* maternal uncle.]

Dezh·nev (dĕzh′nəf, dĕzh′nē-ôf′, dĭzh-nyôf′), **Cape.** Also **East Cape.** A cape of extreme northeast Russia on the Bering Strait opposite Alaska.

DF *abbr.* Distance finder.

D.F. *abbr.* Defender of the Faith.

D.F.A. *abbr.* Doctor of Fine Arts.

DFC or **D.F.C.** *abbr.* Distinguished Flying Cross.

dft. *abbr.* **1.** Defendant. **2.** Draft.

dg *abbr.* Decigram.

DH or **dh** *abbr. Baseball.* Designated hitter.

D.H. *abbr.* Doctor of Humanities.

Dha·ka (dăk′ə, dä′kə). See **Dacca.**

dhar·ma (där′mə, dûr′-) *n.* **1.** *Hinduism & Buddhism.* **a.** The principle or law that orders the universe. **b.** Individual conduct in conformity with this principle. **c.** The essential function or nature of a thing. **2.** *Hinduism.* Individual obligation with respect to caste, social custom, civil law, and sacred law. **3.** *Buddhism.* **a.** The body of teachings expounded by the Buddha. **b.** Knowledge of or duty to undertake conduct set forth by the Buddha as a way to enlightenment. **c.** One of the basic, minute elements from which all things are made. [Sanskrit, statute, law. See **dher-** in Appendix.] —**dhar′mic** *adj.*

dhar·na (där′nə, dûr′-) also **dhur·na** (dûr′nə) *n.* A fast conducted at the door of an offender, especially a debtor, in India as a means of obtaining compliance with a demand for justice, such as payment of a debt. [Hindi *dharnā,* from Prakrit *dharaṇa.* See **dher-** in Appendix.]

Thomas Dewey

ă pat	oi boy
ā pay	ou out
âr care	o͝o took
ä father	o͞o boot
ĕ pet	ŭ cut
ē be	ûr urge
ĭ pit	th thin
ī pie	*th* this
îr pier	hw which
ŏ pot	zh vision
ō toe	ə about, item
ô paw	♦ regionalism

Stress marks: ′ (primary); ′ (secondary), as in **dictionary** (dĭk′shə-nĕr′ē)

Dhau·la·gi·ri (dou′lə-gîr′ē). A peak, 8,177.1 m (26,810 ft) high, in the Himalaya Mountains of west-central Nepal. It was first scaled in 1960.

Dhe·gi·ha (dā′jē-hä′) *n., pl.* **Dhegiha** or **-has. 1.** A branch of the Siouan linguistic family comprising the Omaha, Ponca, Osage, Kansa, and Quapaw languages. **2.a.** The peoples speaking Dhegiha. **b.** A member of any of these peoples.

D.H.L. *abbr.* **1.** Doctor of Hebrew Letters. **2.** Doctor of Hebrew Literature.

dhole (dōl) *n.* A wild Asian dog *(Cuon alpinus)* having reddish fur and usually hunting with a pack. [Perhaps from Kanarese *tōla,* wolf.]

dho·ti (dō′tē) also **dhoo·tie** (do͞o′-) *n., pl.* **-tis** also **-ties. 1.** A loincloth worn by Hindu men in India. **2.** The cotton fabric used for such loincloths. [Hindi *dhotī.*]

dhow (dou) *n. Nautical.* A lateen-rigged ship used especially by Arabs along the coasts of the Indian Ocean. [Arabic *dāw.*]

dhow
On the Nile River

Dhu'l-Hij·jah (do͞ol-hĭj′ä) *n.* The 12th month of the year in the Moslem calendar. See table at **calendar.** [Arabic *ḏū-l-ḥijjah* : *ḏū,* the one + *al,* of + *ḥijja,* pilgrimage.]

Dhu'l-Qa·'dah (do͞ol-kä′dä) *n.* The 11th month of the year in the Moslem calendar. See table at **calendar.** [Arabic *ḏū-l-qa'dah* : *ḏū,* the one + *al,* of + *qa'da,* sitting.]

dhur·na (dûr′nə) *n.* Variant of **dharna.**

dhur·rie (dûr′ē) *n.* A flat-woven cotton rug made in India. [Hindi *darī.*]

Di The symbol for **didymium** (sense 1).

DI *abbr.* Drill instructor.

di–[1] *pref.* **1.** Two; twice; double: *dichromatic.* **2.** Containing two atoms, radicals, or groups: *dichloride.* [Greek. See **dwo-** in Appendix.]

di–[2] *pref.* Variant of **dia–.**

dia. *abbr.* Diameter.

dia– or **di–** *pref.* **1.** Through: *diachronic.* **2.** Across: *diatropism.* [Greek, from *dia,* through.]

di·a·base (dī′ə-bās′) *n.* A dark-gray to black, fine-textured igneous rock composed mainly of feldspar and pyroxene and used for monuments and as crushed stone. [French, partly from Greek *diabasis,* a crossing over (from *diabainein,* to pass through or over; see DIABETES) and partly from *diabase (dia-,* two, alteration of *di-,* from Greek *di-;* see DI–[1] + *base,* basis, from Old French; see BASE[1]).]

di·a·be·tes (dī′ə-bē′tĭs, -tēz) *n.* Any of several metabolic disorders marked by excessive discharge of urine and persistent thirst, especially one of the two types of diabetes mellitus. [Middle English *diabete,* from Medieval Latin *diabētēs,* from Latin, from Greek, siphon, diabetes, from *diabainein,* to cross over, straddle : *dia-,* dia- + *bainein,* to go; see **g^wā-** in Appendix.]

WORD HISTORY: Diabetes is named for one of its distressing symptoms. The disease was known to the Greeks as *diabētēs,* a word derived from the verb *diabainein,* made up of the prefix *dia–,* "across, apart," and the word *bainein,* "to walk, stand." The verb *diabeinein* meant "to stride, walk, or stand with legs asunder"; hence, its derivative *diabētēs* meant "one that straddles," or specifically "a compass, siphon." The sense "siphon" gave rise to the use of *diabētēs* as the name for a disease involving the discharge of excessive amounts of urine. *Diabetes* is first recorded in English, in the form *diabete,* in a medical text written around 1425.

diabetes in·sip·i·dus (ĭn-sĭp′ĭ-dəs) *n.* A chronic metabolic disorder characterized by intense thirst and excessive urination, caused by a deficiency of the pituitary hormone vasopressin. [New Latin *diabētēs īnsipidus* : Latin *diabētēs,* diabetes + Latin *īnsipidus,* insipid.]

diabetes mel·li·tus (mə-lī′təs, mĕl′ĭ-) *n.* **1.** A severe, chronic form of diabetes caused by insufficient production of insulin and resulting in abnormal metabolism of carbohydrates, fats, and proteins. The disease, which typically appears in childhood or adolescence, is characterized by increased sugar levels in the blood and urine, excessive thirst, frequent urination, acidosis, and wasting. Also called *insulin-dependent diabetes.* **2.** A mild form of diabetes that typically appears first in adulthood and is exacerbated by obesity and an inactive lifestyle. This disease often has no symptoms, is usually diagnosed by tests that indicate glucose intolerance, and is treated with changes in diet and an exercise regimen. Also called *non-insulin-dependent diabetes.* [New Latin *diabētēs mellītus* : Latin *diabētēs,* diabetes + Latin *mellītus,* honey-sweet.]

di·a·bet·ic (dī′ə-bĕt′ĭk) *adj.* **1.** Of, relating to, having, or resulting from diabetes: *diabetic patients; a diabetic coma.* **2.** Intended for use by a person with diabetes: *diabetic candy.* **—diabetic** *n.* A person who has diabetes.

di·ab·le (dē-ä′blə) *adj.* Flavored with hot spices: *sauce diable.* [French *(à la) diable,* from *diable,* devil, from Old French. See DIABLERIE.]

di·a·ble·rie (dē-ä′blə-rē, -äb′lə-) *n.* **1.** Sorcery; witchcraft. **2.** Representation of devils or demons, as in paintings or fiction. **3.** Devilish conduct; deviltry. [French, from Old French, from *diable,* devil, from Latin *diabolus.* See DEVIL.]

di·ab·lo (dē-ä′blō) *adj.* Diable. [Alteration (influenced by Spanish *diablo,* devil, from Latin *diabolus;* see DEVIL) of DIABLE.]

di·a·bol·i·cal (dī′ə-bŏl′ĭ-kəl) also **di·a·bol·ic** (-ĭk) *adj.* **1.** Of, concerning, or characteristic of the devil; satanic. **2.** Appropriate to a devil, especially in degree of wickedness or cruelty. [From Middle English *deabolik,* from Old French *diabolique,* from Late Latin *diabolicus,* from Latin *diabolus,* devil. See DEVIL.] **—di′a·bol′i·cal·ly** *adv.* **—di′a·bol′i·cal·ness** *n.*

di·ab·o·lism (dī-ăb′ə-lĭz′əm) *n.* **1.** Dealings with or worship of the devil or demons; sorcery. **2.** Devilish conduct or character. **—di·ab′o·list** *n.*

di·ab·o·lize (dī-ăb′ə-līz′) *tr.v.* **-lized, -liz·ing, -liz·es. 1.** To cause to be devilish or diabolical. **2.** To represent as diabolical.

di·a·ce·tyl·mor·phine (dī′ə-sēt′l-môr′fēn′, dī-ăs′ĭ-tl-) *n.* See **heroin.** [DI–[1] + ACETYL + MORPHINE.]

di·a·chron·ic (dī′ə-krŏn′ĭk) *adj.* Of or concerned with phenomena, especially of language, as they change through time. [From DIA– + Greek *khronos,* time.] **—di′a·chron′i·cal·ly** *adv.*

di·ach·ro·ny (dī-ăk′rə-nē) *n.* **1.** Diachronic or historical arrangement or analysis, especially of language. **2.** Change, as in language, occurring over time. [DIACHRON(IC) + –Y[2].]

di·ac·o·nal (dī-ăk′ə-nəl) *adj.* Of or concerning a deacon or the diaconate. [Late Latin *diācōnālis,* from *diāconus,* deacon. See DEACON.]

di·ac·o·nate (dī-ăk′ə-nĭt, -nāt′) *n.* **1.** The rank, office, or tenure of a deacon. **2.** Deacons considered as a group. [Late Latin *diāconātus,* from *diāconus,* deacon. See DEACON.]

di·a·crit·ic (dī′ə-krĭt′ĭk) *adj.* **1.** Diacritical. **2.** *Medicine.* Diagnostic or distinctive. **—diacritic** *n.* A mark, such as the cedilla of *façade* or the acute accents of *résumé,* added to a letter to indicate a special phonetic value or distinguish words that are otherwise graphically identical. [Greek *diakritikos,* distinguishing, from *diakritos,* distinguished, from *diakrinein,* to distinguish : *dia-,* apart; see DIA– + *krinein,* to separate; see **krei-** in Appendix.]

di·a·crit·i·cal (dī′ə-krĭt′ĭ-kəl) *adj.* **1.** Marking a distinction; distinguishing. **2.** Able to discriminate or distinguish: *a mind of great diacritical power.* **3.** Serving as a diacritic. [From DIACRITIC.] **—di′a·crit′i·cal·ly** *adv.*

Dí·a de la Ra·za (dē′ä də lä rä′ sä, *thĕ* lä) *n.* October 12, celebrated as a holiday in Spain, Latin America, and Hispanic regions and territories of the United States to commemorate the discovery in 1492 of the New World by Christopher Columbus.

di·a·del·phous (dī′ə-dĕl′fəs) *adj. Botany.* Having the filaments of a flower united into two groups: *diadelphous stamens.*

di·a·dem (dī′ə-dĕm′, -dəm) *n.* **1.** A crown worn as a sign of royalty. **2.** Royal power or dignity. **—diadem** *tr.v.* **-demed, -dem·ing, -dems.** To adorn with or as if with a diadem. [Middle English *diademe,* from Old French, from Latin *diadēma,* from Greek, band, from *diadein,* to bind around : *dia-,* dia- + *dein, dē-,* to bind.]

di·aer·e·sis (dī-ĕr′ĭ-sĭs) *n.* Variant of **dieresis.**

diag. *abbr.* **1.** Diagonal. **2.** Diagram.

di·a·gen·e·sis (dī′ə-jĕn′ĭ-sĭs) *n.* The process of chemical and physical change in deposited sediment during its conversion to rock. **—di′a·ge·net′ic** (-jə-nĕt′ĭk) *adj.*

di·a·ge·ot·ro·pism (dī′ə-jē-ŏt′rə-pĭz′əm) *n. Botany.* The tendency of growing parts, such as roots, to become oriented at right angles to the direction of gravitational force. **—di′a·ge′o·trop′ic** (-ə-trŏp′ĭk, -trō′pĭk) *adj.*

Dia·ghi·lev (dē-ä′gə-lĕf′, dyä′gĭ-lĭf), **Sergei Pavlovich.** 1872–1929. Russian ballet impresario whose Ballets Russes company, founded in Paris in 1909, featured the extraordinary talents of, among others, the dancers Nijinsky and Pavlova, the choreographers Fokine and Massine, the composers Ravel and Stravinsky, and the artists Léger and Picasso.

di·ag·nose (dī′əg-nōs′, -nōz′) *v.* **-nosed, -nos·ing, -nos·es.** *—tr.* To distinguish or identify (a disease, for example) by diagnosis. *—intr.* To make a diagnosis. [Back-formation from DIAGNOSIS.] **—di′ag·nos′a·ble** *adj.*

di·ag·no·sis (dī′əg-nō′sĭs) *n., pl.* **-ses** (-sēz). **1.** *Medicine.* **a.** The act or process of identifying or determining the nature and cause of a disease or injury through evaluation of patient history, examination, and review of laboratory data. **b.** The opinion derived from such an evaluation. **2.a.** A critical analysis of the nature of something. **b.** The conclusion reached by such analysis. **3.** *Biology.* A brief description of the distinguishing characteristics of an organism, as for taxonomic classification. [Greek *diagnōsis,* discernment, from *diagignōskein,* to distinguish : *dia-,* apart; see DIA– + *gignōskein, gnō-,* to come to know, discern; see **gnō-** in Appendix.]

di·ag·nos·tic (dī′əg-nŏs′tĭk) *adj.* **1.** Of, relating to, or used in a diagnosis. **2.** Serving to identify a particular disease; characteristic. **—diagnostic** *n.* **1.** Often **diagnostics** *(used with a sing. verb).* The art or practice of medical diagnosis. **2.** A symptom or a distinguishing feature serving as supporting evidence in a diagnosis. **3.** An instrument or a technique used in medical diagnosis. [Greek *diagnōstikos,* able to distinguish, from *diagnōstos,* distinguished, from *diagignōskein,* to distinguish. See DIAGNOSIS.] **—di′ag·nos′ti·cal·ly** *adv.*

di·ag·nos·ti·cian (dī′əg-nŏ-stĭsh′ən) *n.* A person who diagnoses, especially a physician specializing in medical diagnostics.

di·ag·o·nal (dī-ăg′ə-nəl) *adj. Abbr.* **diag. 1.** *Mathematics.* **a.** Joining two nonadjacent vertices of a polygon. **b.** Joining two vertices of a polyhedron not in the same face. **2.** Having a slanted or oblique direction. **3.** Having oblique lines or markings. **—diagonal** *n.* **1.** *Abbr.* **diag.** *Mathematics.* A diagonal line or plane. **2.** Something, such as a row, course, or part, that is arranged obliquely. **3.** A fabric woven with diagonal lines. [Latin *diagōnālis,* from Greek *diagōnios,* from angle to angle : *dia-,* dia- + *gōnia,* angle, corner; see **genu-**[1] in Appendix.] **—di·ag′o·nal·ly** *adv.*

di·a·gram (dī′ə-grăm′) *n. Abbr.* **diag. 1.** A plan, sketch, drawing, or outline designed to demonstrate or explain how something works or to clarify the relationship between the parts of a whole. **2.** *Mathematics.* A graphic representation of an algebraic or geometric relationship. **3.** A chart or graph. **—diagram** *tr.v.* **-grammed, -gram·ming, -grams** or **-gramed, -gram·ing, -grams.** To indicate or represent by or as if by a diagram. [Latin *diagramma,* figure, from Greek, a figure worked out by lines, plan, from *diagraphein,* to mark out, delineate : *dia-,* dia- + *graphein,* to write; see **gerbh-** in Appendix.] **—di′a·gram′ma·ble** *adj.* **—di′a·gram·mat′ic** (-grə-măt′ĭk), **di′a·gram·mat′i·cal** *adj.* **—di′a·gram·mat′i·cal·ly** *adv.*

di·a·ki·ne·sis (dī′ə-kə-nē′sĭs, -kī-) *n., pl.* **-ses** (-sēz). *Genetics.* The final stage of the prophase in meiosis, characterized by shortening and thickening of the paired chromosomes, formation of the spindle fibers, disappearance of the nucleolus, and degeneration of the nuclear membrane. **—di′a·ki·net′ic** (-nĕt′ĭk) *adj.*

di·al (dī′əl) *n.* **1.** A graduated surface or face on which a measurement, such as speed, is indicated by a moving needle or pointer. **2. a.** The face of a clock. **b.** A sundial. **3. a.** The panel or face on a radio or television receiver on which the frequencies or channels are indicated. **b.** A movable control knob or other device on a radio or television receiver used to change the frequency. **4.** A rotatable disk on a telephone with numbers and letters, used to signal the number to which a call is made. **—dial** *v.* **-aled, -al·ing, -als** or **-alled, -al·ling, -als.** *—tr.* **1.** To measure with or as if with a dial. **2.** To point to, indicate, or register by means of a dial. **3.** To control or select by means of a dial. **4.** To call (a party) on a telephone. *—intr.* To use a dial, as on a telephone. [Middle English, sundial, clock, from Old French *dyal,* from Medieval Latin *diāle,* from *diālis,* daily, from Latin *diēs,* day. See **deiw-** in Appendix.] **—di′al·er** *n.*

dial. *abbr.* **1. a.** Dialect. **b.** Dialectal. **2. a.** Dialectic. **b.** Dialectical. **3.** Dialogue.

di·a·lect (dī′ə-lĕkt′) *n. Abbr.* **dial. 1. a.** A regional variety of a language distinguished by pronunciation, grammar, or vocabulary, especially a variety of speech differing from the standard literary language or speech pattern of the culture in which it exists: *Cockney is a dialect of English.* **b.** A variety of language that with other varieties constitutes a single language of which no single variety is standard: *the dialects of Ancient Greek.* **2.** The language peculiar to an occupational group or a particular social class; jargon: *the dialect of science.* **3.** The manner or style of expressing oneself in language or the arts. **4.** A language considered as part of a larger family of languages or a linguistic branch: *Spanish and French are Romance dialects.* [French *dialecte,* from Old French, from Latin *dialectus,* form of speech, from Greek *dialektos,* speech, from *dialegesthai,* to discourse, use a dialect : *dia-,* between, over; see DIA– + *legesthai,* middle voice of *legein,* to speak; see **leg-** in Appendix.] **—di′a·lec′tal** *adj.* **—di′a·lec′tal·ly** *adv.*

SYNONYMS: *dialect, vernacular, jargon, cant, argot, lingo, patois.* These nouns denote forms of language that vary from the standard. *Dialect* applies to the vocabulary, grammar, and pronunciation characteristic of a specific geographic area or locality. The *vernacular* is the everyday language spoken by a people as distinguished from the literary language. *Jargon* is the specialized language used by a social or occupational group but not understood by the general public. *Cant* now usually refers to the specialized vocabulary of a group or trade and is often marked by the use of stock phrases. *Argot* applies especially to the language of the underworld or, by extension, to that of any specific group. *Lingo* is applied, often humorously or contemptuously, to language that is unfamiliar or so specialized that it is difficult to understand. *Patois* refers especially to a regional dialect without a literary tradition or to a creole.

dialect atlas *n.* See **linguistic atlas.**

dialect geography *n.* See **linguistic geography.**

di·a·lec·tic (dī′ə-lĕk′tĭk) *n. Abbr.* **dial. 1.** The art or practice of arriving at the truth by the exchange of logical arguments. **2. a.** The process especially associated with Hegel of arriving at the truth by stating a thesis, developing a contradictory antithesis, and combining and resolving them into a coherent synthesis. **b.** Hegel's critical method for the investigation of this process. **3. a.** Often **dialectics** *(used with a sing. or pl. verb).* The Marxian process of change through the conflict of opposing forces, whereby a given contradiction is characterized by a primary and a secondary aspect, the secondary succumbing to the primary, which is then transformed into an aspect of a new contradiction. **b.** The Marxian critique of this process. **4. dialectics.** *(used with a sing. verb).* A method of argument or exposition that systematically weighs contradictory facts or ideas with a view to the resolution of their real or apparent contradictions. **5.** The contradiction between two conflicting forces viewed as the determining factor in their continuing interaction. [Middle English *dialetik,* from Old French *dialetique,* from Latin *dialectica,* logic, from Greek *dialektikē (tekhnē),* (art of) debate, from *dialektos,* speech, conversation. See DIALECT.] **—di′a·lec′ti·cal, di′a·lec′tic** *adj.* **—di′a·lec′ti·cal·ly** *adv.*

dialectical materialism *n.* The Marxian interpretation of reality that views matter as the sole subject of change and all change as the product of a constant conflict between opposites arising from the internal contradictions inherent in all events, ideas, and movements.

di·a·lec·ti·cian (dī′ə-lĕk-tĭsh′ən) *n.* **1.** One who specializes in the study of dialects. **2.** One who practices or is skilled in dialectic.

di·a·lec·tol·o·gy (dī′ə-lĕk-tŏl′ə-jē) *n.* The study of dialects. **—di′a·lec′to·log′i·cal** (-tə-lŏj′ĭ-kəl) *adj.* **—di′a·lec′to·log′i·cal·ly** *adv.* **—di′a·lec·tol′o·gist** *n.*

di·a·log (dī′ə-lôg′, -lŏg′) *n. & v.* Variant of **dialogue.**

di·a·log·ic (dī′ə-lŏj′ĭk) also **di·a·log·i·cal** (-ĭ-kəl) *adj.* Of, relating to, or written in dialogue. **—di′a·log′i·cal·ly** *adv.*

di·al·o·gist (dī-ăl′ə-jĭst, dī′ə-lô′gĭst, -lŏg′ĭst) *n.* **1.** A writer of dialogue. **2.** One who speaks in a dialogue. **—di′a·lo·gis′tic** (dī′ə-lə-jĭs′tĭk), **di′a·lo·gis′ti·cal** *adj.*

di·a·logue or **di·a·log** (dī′ə-lôg′, -lŏg′) *—n. Abbr.* **dial. 1.** A conversation between two or more people. **2. a.** Conversation between characters in a drama or narrative. **b.** The lines or passages in a script that are intended to be spoken. **3.** A literary work written in the form of a conversation: *the dialogues of Plato.* **4.** *Music.* A composition or passage for two or more parts, suggestive of conversational interplay. **5.** An exchange of ideas or opinions: *achieving constructive dialogue with all political elements.* *—v.* **-logued, -logu·ing, -logues** or **-loged, -log·ing, -logs.** *—tr.* To express as or in a dialogue. *—intr.* **1.** To converse in a dialogue. **2.** *Usage Problem.* To engage in an informal exchange of views. [Middle English *dialog,* from Old French *dialogue,* from Latin *dialogus,* from Greek *dialogos,* conversation, from *dialegesthai,* to discuss. See DIALECT.] **—di′a·log′uer** *n.*

USAGE NOTE: In recent years the verb sense of *dialogue* meaning "to engage in an informal exchange of views" has been revived, particularly with reference to communication between parties in institutional or political contexts. Although Shakespeare, Coleridge, and Carlyle used it, this usage today is widely regarded as jargon or bureaucratese. For example, 98 percent of the Usage Panel rejects the sentence *Critics have charged that the department was remiss in not trying to dialogue with representatives of the community before hiring the new officers.*

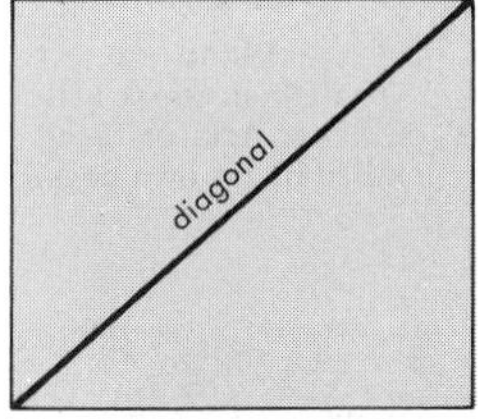

diagonal

dial tone *n.* A low, steady tone in a telephone receiver indicating that a number may be dialed.

di·al·y·sis (dī-ăl′ĭ-sĭs) *n., pl.* **-ses** (-sēz′). **1.** The separation of smaller molecules from larger molecules or of dissolved substances from colloidal particles in a solution by selective diffusion through a semipermeable membrane. **2.** Hemodialysis. [Greek *dialusis,* separating, dissolution, from *dialuein,* to break up, dissolve : *dia-,* apart; see DIA– + *luein,* to loosen; see **leu-** in Appendix.] **—di′a·lyt′ic** (-ə-lĭt′ĭk) *adj.* **—di′a·lyt′i·cal·ly** *adv.*

di·a·lyze (dī′ə-līz′) *tr. & intr.v.* **-lyzed, -lyz·ing, -lyz·es.** To subject to or undergo dialysis. [Back-formation from DIALYSIS.] **—di′a·lyz′a·bil′i·ty** *n.* **—di′a·lyz′a·ble** *adj.*

di·a·lyz·er (dī′ə-lī′zər) *n.* A machine equipped with a semipermeable membrane and used for performing dialysis.

diam. *abbr.* Diameter.

di·a·mag·net (dī′ə-măg′nĭt) *n.* A diamagnetic substance. [From DIAMAGNETIC.]

di·a·mag·net·ic (dī′ə-măg-nĕt′ĭk) *adj.* Of or relating to a substance that is repelled by a magnet. **—di′a·mag′ne·tism** (-nĭ-tĭz′əm) *n.*

di·a·man·te or **di·a·man·té** (dē′ə-män-tā′) *n.* **1.** A small, glittering ornament, such as a rhinestone or a sequin, applied to fabric or a garment. **2.** Fabric that has been covered with many of these ornaments. [French *diamanté,* decorated with diamonds, from *diamant,* diamond. See DIAMOND.]

Di·a·man·ti·na (dī′ə-mən-tē′nə). A river, about 901 km (560 mi) long, of east-central Australia flowing generally southwest as a tributary of the Warburton River.

diamond
Aerial view of a baseball diamond

di·am·e·ter (dī-ăm′ĭ-tər) *n.* **1.** *Abbr.* **dia., diam.** *Mathematics.* **a.** A straight line segment passing through the center of a figure, especially of a circle or sphere, and terminating at the periphery. **b.** The length of such a segment. **2.** Thickness or width. [Middle English *diametre,* from Old French, from Latin *diametrus,* from Greek *diametros* : *dia-,* dia- + *metron,* measure; see **mē-**[2] in Appendix.] **—di·am′e·tral** (-trəl) *adj.*

di·a·met·ri·cal (dī′ə-mĕt′rĭ-kəl) also **di·a·met·ric** (-rĭk) *adj.* **1.** Of, relating to, or along a diameter. **2.** Exactly opposite; contrary. **—di′a·met′ri·cal·ly** *adv.*

di·am·ine (dī-ăm′ēn′, -ĭn, dī′ə-mēn′, -mĭn) *n.* Any of various chemical compounds containing two amino groups, especially hydrazine.

di·a·mond (dī′ə-mənd, dī′mənd) *n.* **1.** An extremely hard, highly refractive crystalline form of carbon that is usually colorless and is used as a gemstone and in abrasives, cutting tools, and

ă pat	oi boy
ā pay	ou out
âr care	o͝o took
ä father	o͞o boot
ĕ pet	ŭ cut
ē be	ûr urge
ĭ pit	th thin
ī pie	*th* this
îr pier	hw which
ŏ pot	zh vision
ō toe	ə about, item
ô paw	♦ regionalism

Stress marks: **′** (primary); ′ (secondary), as in **dictionary** (dĭk′shə-nĕr′ē)

Diamond Head
Diamond Head (*background*) and Waikiki (*foreground*)

Diana
Detail from Greek bell krater of Actaeon being killed by his own dogs

Diana
Princess of Wales

Diane de Poitiers

other applications. **2.** A figure with four equal sides forming two inner obtuse angles and two inner acute angles; a rhombus or lozenge. **3.** *Games.* **a.** A red, lozenge-shaped figure on certain playing cards. **b.** A playing card with this figure. **c. diamonds.** *(used with a sing. or pl. verb).* The suit of cards represented by this figure. **4.** *Baseball.* **a.** An infield. **b.** The whole playing field. —*attributive.* Often used to modify another noun: *a diamond bracelet; diamond jewelry.* —**diamond** *tr.v.* **-mond·ed, -mond·ing, -monds.** To adorn with or as if with diamonds. [Middle English *diamaunt,* from Old French *diamant,* from Medieval Latin *diamas, diamant-,* alteration of Latin *adamas.* See ADAMANT.]

di·a·mond·back moth (dī′ə-mənd-băk′, dī′mənd-) *n.* One of several small moths of the family Plutellidae having brightly patterned front wings that reveal light diamond-shaped spots when folded.

diamondback rattlesnake *n.* Either of two large venomous rattlesnakes *(Crotalus adamanteus* or *C. atrox)* found in the southern and western United States and in Mexico and having diamond-shaped markings on the back.

diamondback terrapin *n.* One of several turtles of the genus *Malaclemys* of the southern Atlantic and Gulf coasts of the United States, having edible flesh and a carapace with diamond-shaped ridged or knobbed markings.

Di·a·mond Head (dī′ə-mənd, dī′mənd). A promontory, 232.1 m (761 ft) high, on the southeast coast of Oahu, Hawaii.

di·a·mond·if·er·ous (dī′ə-mən-dĭf′ər-əs, dī′mən-) *adj.* Bearing or yielding diamonds.

diamond in the rough *n., pl.* **diamonds in the rough.** One having exceptionally good qualities or the potential for greatness but lacking polish and refinement.

Di·an·a (dī-ăn′ə) *n. Roman Mythology.* The virgin goddess of hunting and childbirth, traditionally associated with the moon and identified with the Greek Artemis. [Middle English, from Latin *Diāna.* See **deiw-** in Appendix.]

Diana, Princess of Wales. Title of Lady Diana Frances Spencer. Born 1961. Consort (since 1981) of Charles, Prince of Wales, heir to the British throne.

di·an·drous (dī-ăn′drəs) *adj. Botany.* Having two stamens, as in the flowers of the sage.

Di·ane de Poi·tiers (dē-än′ də pwä-tyā′) Duchesse de Valentinois. 1499–1566. French noblewoman and mistress of Henry II. Her influence, lasting throughout his reign (1547–1559), overshadowed that of his wife, Catherine de Médicis.

di·an·thus (dī-ăn′thəs) *n.* A plant of the genus *Dianthus,* which includes carnations and pinks. [New Latin *Dianthus,* genus name, probably alteration (influenced by DI–[1]) of Greek *diosanthos,* carnation : *Dios-,* of Zeus; see DIOSCURI + *anthos,* flower.]

di·a·pa·son (dī′ə-pā′zən, -sən) *n. Music.* **1.** A full, rich outpouring of harmonious sound. **2.** The entire range of an instrument or voice. **3.** Either of the two principal stops on a pipe organ that form the tonal basis for the entire scale of the instrument. **4.** The interval and the consonance of an octave. **5.** A standard indication of pitch. **6.** A tuning fork. [Middle English *diapasoun,* from Latin *diapāsōn,* the whole octave, from Greek *(dia) pasōn (khordōn),* (through) all (the notes), feminine genitive pl. of *pas.* See **pant-** in Appendix.]

di·a·pause (dī′ə-pôz′) *n. Zoology.* A period during which growth or development is suspended and physiological activity is diminished, as in certain insects in response to adverse environmental conditions. [Greek *diapausis,* pause, from *diapauein,* to pause : *dia-,* between; see DIA– + *pauein,* to stop.]

di·a·pe·de·sis (dī′ə-pĭ-dē′sĭs) *n., pl.* **-ses** (-sēz). The movement or passage of blood cells, especially white blood cells, through intact capillary walls into surrounding body tissue. [Greek *diapēdēsis,* transudation, from *diapēdan,* to ooze through : *dia-,* dia- + *pēdan,* to leap, throb; see **ped-** in Appendix.] —**di′a·pe·det′ic** (-dĕt′ĭk) *adj.*

di·a·per (dī′ə-pər, dī′pər) *n.* **1.a.** A folded piece of absorbent material, such as paper or cloth, that is placed between a baby's legs and fastened at the waist to contain excretions. **b.** A similar piece of material, worn by incontinent adults. **2.a.** A white cotton or linen fabric patterned with small, duplicative diamond-shaped figures. **b.** A piece of such cloth. **c.** Such a pattern. —**diaper** *tr.v.* **-pered, -per·ing, -pers. 1.** To put a diaper on. **2.** To weave or decorate in a diamond-shaped pattern. [Middle English, a patterned fabric, from Old French *diapre, diaspre,* from Medieval Latin *diasprum,* a white silken material, from Medieval Greek *diaspros,* pure white : *dia-,* intensive pref.; see DIA– + *aspros,* white (probably from Latin *asper,* rough).]

di·aph·a·nous (dī-ăf′ə-nəs) *adj.* **1.** Of such fine texture as to be transparent or translucent: *diaphanous tulle.* **2.** Characterized by delicacy of form. See Synonyms at **airy. 3.** Vague or insubstantial: *diaphanous dreams of glory.* [From Medieval Latin *diaphanus,* transparent, from Greek *diaphanēs,* from *diaphainein,* to be transparent : *dia-,* dia- + *phainein, phan-,* to show; see **bhā-**[1] in Appendix.] —**di′a·pha·ne′i·ty** (dī′ə-fə-nē′ĭ-tē), **di·aph′a·nous·ness** *n.* —**di·aph′a·nous·ly** *adv.*

di·a·pho·re·sis (dī′ə-fə-rē′sĭs, dī-ăf′ə-) *n.* Perspiration, especially when copious and medically induced. [Late Latin *diaphorēsis,* from Greek, from *diaphorein,* to disperse : *dia-,* dia- + *phorein,* to convey, frequentative of *pherein,* to carry; see **bher-**[1] in Appendix.]

di·a·pho·ret·ic (dī′ə-fə-rĕt′ĭk, dī-ăf′ə-) *adj.* Producing or increasing perspiration. —**diaphoretic** *n.* A medicine or other agent that produces perspiration. [DIAPHOR(ESIS) + –ETIC.]

di·a·phragm (dī′ə-frăm′) *n.* **1.** *Anatomy.* A muscular membranous partition separating the abdominal and thoracic cavities and functioning in respiration. Also called *midriff.* **2.** A membranous part that divides or separates. **3.** A thin disk, especially in a microphone or telephone receiver, that vibrates in response to sound waves to produce electric signals, or that vibrates in response to electric signals to produce sound waves. **4.** A contraceptive device consisting of a thin flexible disk, usually made of rubber, that is designed to cover the uterine cervix to prevent the entry of sperm during sexual intercourse. **5.** A disk having a fixed or variable opening used to restrict the amount of light traversing a lens or optical system. [Middle English *diafragma,* from Late Latin *diaphragma,* midriff, from Greek, partition, from *diaphrassein,* to barricade : *dia-,* intensive pref.; see DIA– + *phrassein, phrag-,* to enclose.] —**di′a·phrag·mat′ic** (-frăg-măt′ĭk) *adj.* —**di′a·phrag·mat′i·cal·ly** *adv.*

di·aph·y·sis (dī-ăf′ĭ-sĭs) *n., pl.* **-ses** (-sēz′). *Anatomy.* The shaft of a long bone. [Greek *diaphusis,* spinous process of the tibia, from *diaphuesthai,* to grow between : *dia-,* dia- + *phuesthai,* to grow, middle voice of *phuein;* see **bheuə-** in Appendix.] —**di′a·phys′i·al, di′a·phys′e·al** (dī′ə-fĭz′ē-əl) *adj.*

di·a·pir (dī′ə-pîr′) *n.* An anticlinal fold in which a mobile core, such as salt or gypsum, has pierced through the more brittle overlying rock. [French, from Greek *diapeirein,* to push through : *dia-,* dia- + *peirein,* to pierce; see **per-**[2] in Appendix.] —**di′a·pir′ic** *adj.*

di·a·poph·y·sis (dī′ə-pŏf′ĭ-sĭs) *n., pl.* **-ses** (-sēz′). *Anatomy.* The superior or articular surface of the transverse process of a vertebra. [DI(A)– + APOPHYSIS.] —**di·ap′o·phys′i·al** (-ăp′ə-fĭz′ē-əl) *adj.*

di·ar·chy also **dy·ar·chy** (dī′är′kē) *n., pl.* **-chies.** Government by two joint rulers.

di·a·rist (dī′ə-rĭst) *n.* A person who keeps a diary.

di·ar·rhe·a also **di·ar·rhoe·a** (dī′ə-rē′ə) *n.* Excessive and frequent evacuation of watery feces, usually indicating gastrointestinal distress or disorder. [Middle English *diaria,* from Medieval Latin, from Late Latin *diarrhoea,* from Greek *diarrhoia,* from *diarrhein,* to flow through : *dia-,* dia- + *rhein,* to flow, run; see **sreu-** in Appendix.] —**di′ar·rhe′al, di′ar·rhe′ic** (-ĭk) , **di′ar·rhet′ic** (-rĕt′ĭk) *adj.*

di·ar·thro·sis (dī′är-thrō′sĭs) *n., pl.* **-ses** (-sēz). Any of several types of bone articulation permitting free motion in a joint, as that of the shoulder or hip. [Greek *diarthrōsis,* from *diarthroun,* to articulate : *dia-,* between; see DIA– + *arthroun,* to fasten by a joint (from *arthron,* joint; see **ar-** in Appendix).] —**di′ar·thro′di·al** (-dē-əl) *adj.*

di·a·ry (dī′ə-rē) *n., pl.* **-ries. 1.** A daily record, especially a personal record of events, experiences, and observations; a journal. **2.** A book for use in keeping a personal record, as of experiences. [Latin *diārium,* daily allowance, daily journal, from *diēs,* day. See **deiw-** in Appendix.]

Di·as (dē′əs, -əsh), **Bartolomeu.** 1450?–1500. Portuguese navigator who was the first to round the Cape of Good Hope. Because of storms he did not actually sight it until the return leg of his voyage (May 1488).

Di·as·po·ra (dī-ăs′pər-ə) *n.* **1.** The dispersion of Jews outside of Israel from the sixth century B.C., when the Jews were exiled to Babylonia, until the present time. **2.** Often **diaspora.** The body of Jews or Jewish communities outside Palestine or modern Israel. **3. diaspora.** A dispersion of an originally homogeneous people. **4. diaspora.** A dispersion of an originally homogeneous entity, such as a language or a culture: *"the diaspora of English into several mutually incomprehensible languages"* (Randolph Quirk). [Greek *diaspora,* dispersion, from *diaspeirein,* to spread about : *dia-,* apart; see DIA– + *speirein,* to sow, scatter; see **sper-** in Appendix.]

di·a·spore (dī′ə-spôr′, -spōr′) *n.* **1.** A white, pearly hydrous aluminum oxide, AlO(OH), found in bauxite, corundum, and dolomite and used as a refractory and abrasive. **2.** *Botany.* See **disseminule.** [From Greek *diaspora,* dispersion, scattering. See DIASPORA.]

di·a·stase (dī′ə-stās′, -stāz′) *n.* An amylase or a mixture of amylases that converts starch to maltose, found in certain germinating grains such as malt. [French, from Greek *diastasis,* separation. See DIASTASIS.] —**di′a·sta′sic** (-stā′sĭk, -zĭk) *adj.*

di·as·ta·sis (dī-ăs′tə-sĭs) *n., pl.* **-ses** (-sēz′). **1.** *Pathology.* Separation of normally joined parts, such as the separation of adjacent bones without fracture or of certain abdominal muscles during pregnancy. **2.** *Physiology.* The last stage of diastole in the heart, occurring just before contraction and during which little additional blood enters the ventricle. [Greek, separation, from *diistanai,* to separate : *dia-,* apart; see DIA– + *histanai,* to cause to stand; see **stā-** in Appendix.] —**di′a·stat′ic** (dī′ə-stăt′ĭk) *adj.*

di·a·ste·ma (dī′ə-stē′mə) *n., pl.* **-ma·ta** (-mə-tə). A gap or space between two teeth. [Late Latin, interval, from Greek *diastēma,* from *diastēnai,* to separate, second aorist of *diistanai.* See DIASTASIS.] —**di′a·ste·mat′ic** (-stə-măt′ĭk) *adj.*

di·as·to·le (dī-ăs′tə-lē) *n.* **1.** *Physiology.* The normal rhythmically occurring relaxation and dilatation of the heart chambers, especially the ventricles, during which they fill with blood. **2.** The lengthening of a normally short syllable in Greek and Latin

ă pat	oi boy
ā pay	ou out
âr care	ŏŏ took
ä father	ōō boot
ĕ pet	ŭ cut
ē be	ûr urge
ĭ pit	th thin
ī pie	*th* this
îr pier	hw which
ŏ pot	zh vision
ō toe	ə about, item
ô paw	♦ regionalism

Stress marks: ′ (primary); ′ (secondary), as in **dictionary** (dĭk′shə-nĕr′ē)

verse. [Greek *diastolē,* dilation, separation, from *diastellein,* to expand : *dia-,* apart; see DIA– + *stellein,* to place, send; see **stel-** in Appendix.] **—di'a·stol'ic** (dī'ə-stŏl'ĭk) *adj.*

di·as·tro·phism (dī-ăs'trə-fĭz'əm) *n.* The process of deformation by which the major features of the earth's crust, including continents, mountains, ocean beds, folds, and faults, are formed. [From Greek *diastrophē,* distortion, from *diastrephein,* to distort : *dia-,* apart; see DIA– + *strephein,* to twist; see **streb(h)-** in Appendix.] **—di'a·stroph'ic** (dī'ə-strŏf'ĭk, -strō'fĭk) *adj.*

di·a·tes·sa·ron (dī'ə-tĕs'ər-ən) *n.* The four Gospels combined into a single narrative. [Middle English, interval of a fourth, from Latin *diatessarōn,* made of four (ingredients), from Greek *dia tessarōn,* out of four : *dia-,* according to; see DIA– + *tessarōn,* genitive of *tessares,* four; see **kʷetwer-** in Appendix.]

di·a·ther·my (dī'ə-thûr'mē) *n.* The therapeutic generation of local heat in body tissues by high-frequency electromagnetic currents. **—di'a·ther'mic** (-mĭk) *adj.*

di·ath·e·sis (dī-ăth'ĭ-sĭs) *n., pl.* **-ses** (-sēz'). A hereditary predisposition of the body to a disease, a group of diseases, an allergy, or another disorder. [Greek, disposition, condition, from *diatithenai,* to dispose : *dia-,* dia- + *tithenai,* to place, set; see **dhē-** in Appendix.] **—di'a·thet'ic** (dī'ə-thĕt'ĭk) *adj.*

di·a·tom (dī'ə-tŏm') *n. Botany.* Any of various microscopic one-celled or colonial algae of the class Bacillariophyceae, having cell walls of silica consisting of two interlocking symmetrical valves. [New Latin *diatoma,* from Greek *diatomos,* cut in half, from *diatemnein,* to cut in half : *dia-,* dia- + *temnein,* to cut; see **tem-** in Appendix.]

di·a·to·ma·ceous (dī'ə-tə-mā'shəs, dī-ăt'ə-) *adj.* Consisting of diatoms or their skeletons.

diatomaceous earth *n.* A light-colored porous rock composed of the shells of diatoms.

di·a·tom·ic (dī'ə-tŏm'ĭk) *adj.* Made up of two atoms: *a diatomic molecule.*

di·at·o·mite (dī-ăt'ə-mīt') *n.* A fine, powdered diatomaceous earth used in industry as a filler, a filtering agent, an absorbent, a clarifier, and an insulator. Also called *kieselguhr.*

di·a·ton·ic (dī'ə-tŏn'ĭk) *adj. Music.* Of or using only the eight tones of a standard major or minor scale without chromatic deviations. [Late Latin *diatonicus,* from Greek *diatonikos* : *dia-,* dia- + *tonos,* tone; see TONE.] **—di'a·ton'i·cal·ly** *adv.* **—di'a·ton'i·cism** (-ĭ-sĭz'əm) *n.*

di·a·tribe (dī'ə-trīb') *n.* A bitter, abusive denunciation. [Latin *diatriba,* learned discourse, from Greek *diatribē,* pastime, lecture, from *diatribein,* to consume, wear away : *dia-,* intensive pref.; see DIA– + *tribein,* to rub; see **terə-**[1] in Appendix.]

WORD HISTORY: Listening to a lengthy diatribe may seem like a waste of time, an attitude for which there is some etymological justification. The Greek word *diatribē,* the ultimate source of our word, is derived from the verb *diatribein,* made up of the prefix *dia–,* "completely," and *tribein,* "to rub," "to wear away, spend, or waste time," "to be busy." The verb *diatribein* meant "to rub hard," "to spend or waste time," and the noun *diatribē* meant "wearing away of time, amusement, serious occupation, study," as well as "discourse, short ethical treatise or lecture, debate, argument." It is the serious occupation of time in discourse, lecture, and debate that gave us the first use of *diatribe* recorded in English (1581), in the now archaic sense "discourse, critical dissertation." The critical element of this kind of diatribe must often have been uppermost, explaining the origin of the current sense of *diatribe,* "a bitter criticism."

di·at·ro·pism (dī-ăt'rə-pĭz'əm) *n.* The tendency of certain plants or their parts to arrange themselves at right angles to a stimulus. **—di'a·trop'ic** (dī'ə-trŏp'ĭk, -trō'pĭk) *adj.*

Dí·az (dē'äs, -äz), **(José de la Cruz) Porfirio.** 1830–1915. Mexican soldier and politician who became president after a coup in 1876 and governed the country until 1911 (except for the years 1880–1884).

Dí·az del Cas·til·lo (dē'äth *th*ĕl kä-stēl'yô), **Bernal.** 1492?–1581. Spanish soldier and historian whose eyewitness account of the conquest of Mexico (1519–1521) remains a classic depiction of the 16th-century conquistadors.

Dí·az de Vi·var (dē'äth *th*ĕ vē-vär'), **Rodrigo.** See the **Cid.**

di·az·e·pam (dī-ăz'ə-păm') *n.* A tranquilizer, $C_{16}H_{13}ClN_2O$, used in the treatment of anxiety and tension and as a sedative, a muscle relaxant, and an anticonvulsant. [DIAZ(O) + EP(OXIDE) + AM(MONIA).]

di·a·zine (dī'ə-zēn', dī-ăz'ĭn) *n.* A compound containing a benzene ring in which two of the carbon atoms have been replaced by nitrogen atoms, especially any of three isomers having the composition $C_4H_4N_2$. [DI–[1] + AZ(O)– + –INE[2].]

di·az·i·non (dī-ăz'ə-nŏn') *n.* A dark amber liquid, $C_{12}H_{21}N_2O_3PS$, used as an insecticide. [DIAZ(O) + –IN(E)[2] + –ON[3].]

di·az·o (dī-ăz'ō) *adj.* Relating to or containing a pair of bonded nitrogen atoms, one of which is also bonded to an aromatic hydrocarbon.

di·a·zo·ni·um (dī'ə-zō'nē-əm) *n.* The univalent cation RN_2, in which R is an aromatic hydrocarbon. [DIAZ(O) + (AMM)ONIUM.]

di·ba·sic (dī-bā'sĭk) *adj.* **1.** Containing two replaceable hydrogen atoms. **2.** Or or relating to salts or acids forming salts with two atoms of a univalent metal.

dib·ber (dĭb'ər) *n.* A dibble. [Alteration of DIBBLE.]

dib·ble (dĭb'əl) *n.* A pointed gardening implement used to make holes in soil, especially for planting bulbs or seedlings. **—dibble** *tr.v.* **-bled, -bling, -bles. 1.** To make holes in (soil) with a pointed implement. **2.** To plant by means of a pointed implement. [Middle English *dibbel.*] **—dib'bler** *n.*

di·bran·chi·ate (dī-brăng'kē-ĭt) *n.* A member of the order Dibranchiata, a classification formerly used for the two-gilled cephalopods, which include the octopuses, cuttlefish, and squids. **—dibranchiate** *adj.* Of or belonging to the order Dibranchiata. [From New Latin *Dibranchiata,* order name : DI–[1] + Greek *brankhia,* gills.]

di·bro·mide (dī-brō'mīd', -mĭd) *n.* A chemical compound containing two bromine atoms bound to another element or radical.

dibs (dĭbz) *pl.n. Slang.* **1.** A claim; rights: *I have dibs on that last piece of pie.* **2.** Money, especially in small amounts. [Short for *dibstones,* counters used in a game, probably from obsolete *dib,* to tap.]

di·car·box·yl·ic (dī-kär'bŏk-sĭl'ĭk) *adj.* Containing two carboxyl groups per molecule.

di·cast (dī'kăst', dĭk'ăst') *n.* One of the 6,000 citizens chosen each year in ancient Athens to sit in the law courts, with functions resembling those of a judge and juror. [Greek *dikastēs,* judge, from *dikazein,* to judge, from *dikē,* right, custom. See **deik-** in Appendix.] **—di·cas'tic** *adj.*

dice (dīs) *n.* **1.** *Games.* Plural of **die**[2] (sense 3). **2.** *pl.* **dice** also **dices** A small cube, as of food. **—dice** *v.* **diced, dic·ing, dic·es.** *—intr. Games.* To play or gamble with dice. *—tr.* **1.** *Games.* To win or lose (money) by gambling with dice. **2.** To cut (food) into small cubes. **3.** To decorate with dicelike figures. [Pl. of DIE[2].]

di·cen·tra (dī-sĕn'trə) *n.* A plant of the genus *Dicentra,* which includes the bleeding heart and Dutchman's breeches. [New Latin *Dicentra,* genus name : DI–[1] + Greek *kentron,* point (from *kentein,* to prick; see **kent-** in Appendix).]

di·ceph·a·lous (dī-sĕf'ə-ləs) *adj.* Having two heads.

dic·er (dī'sər) *n.* A device used for dicing food.

dic·ey (dī'sē) *adj.* **-i·er, -i·est.** Involving or fraught with danger or risk: *"an extremely dicey future on a brave new world of liquid nitrogen, tar, and smog"* (New Yorker). [From DICE.]

dich– *pref.* Variant of **dicho–.**

di·cha·si·um (dī-kā'zē-əm, -zhē-əm, -zhəm) *n., pl.* **-si·a** (-zē-ə, -zhē-ə, -zhə). *Botany.* A cyme having two lateral flowers or branches originating from opposite points beneath a terminal flower. [New Latin, from Greek *dikhasis,* division, from *dikhazein,* to divide in two, from *dikha,* in two. See **dwo-** in Appendix.] **—di·cha'si·al** (-zē-əl, -zhē-əl, -zhəl) *adj.* **—di·cha'si·al·ly** *adv.*

di·chlo·ride (dī-klôr'īd', -klōr'-) *n.* A chemical compound containing two chlorine atoms bound to another element or radical. Also called *bichloride.*

di·chlo·ro·di·phen·yl·tri·chlo·ro·eth·ane (dī-klôr'ō-dī-fĕn'əl-trī-klôr'ō-ĕth'ān', -klōr'-, -fē'nəl-, dī-klōr'-) *n.* DDT.

di·chlor·vos (dī-klôr'vŏs', -vəs, -klōr'-) *n.* A nonpersistent organophosphorous pesticide, $C_4H_7O_4Cl_2P$, of low toxicity to human beings. [DI–[1] + CHLOR(O)– + V(INYL) + (PH)OS(PHATE).]

dicho– or **dich–** *pref.* In two; into two parts: *dichogamous.* [Greek *dikho-,* from *dikha,* in two. See **dwo-** in Appendix.]

di·chog·a·mous (dī-kŏg'ə-məs) *adj. Botany.* Having pistils and stamens that mature at different times, thus promoting cross-pollination rather than self-pollination. **—di·chog'a·my** (-mē) *n.*

di·chon·dra (dī-kŏn'drə) *n.* A small creeping herb *(Dichondra micrantha)* commercially cultivated as a substitute for lawn grass. [New Latin, genus name : DI–[1] + Greek *khondros,* granule; see CHONDRO–.]

di·chot·o·mize (dī-kŏt'ə-mīz') *v.* **-mized, -miz·ing, -miz·es.** *—tr.* To separate into two parts or classifications. *—intr.* To be or become divided into parts or branches; fork. **—di·chot'o·mist** (-mĭst) *n.* **—di·chot'o·mi·za'tion** (-mĭ-zā'shən) *n.*

di·chot·o·mous (dī-kŏt'ə-məs) *adj.* **1.** Divided or dividing into two parts or classifications. **2.** Characterized by dichotomy. **—di·chot'o·mous·ly** *adv.* **—di·chot'o·mous·ness** *n.*

di·chot·o·my (dī-kŏt'ə-mē) *n., pl.* **-mies. 1.** Division into two usually contradictory parts or opinions: *"the dichotomy of the one and the many"* (Louis Auchincloss). **2.** *Astronomy.* The phase of the moon, Mercury, or Venus when half of the disk is illuminated. **3.** *Botany.* Branching characterized by successive forking into two approximately equal divisions. [Greek *dikhotomia,* from *dikhotomos,* divided in two : *dikho-,* dicho- + *temnein,* to cut; see **tem-** in Appendix.]

di·chro·ic (dī-krō'ĭk) *adj.* **1.** Manifesting dichroism. **2.** *Pathology.* Dichromatic. [From Greek *dikhroos,* bicolored : *di-,* two; see DI–[1] + *khrōs,* color, skin.]

di·chro·ism (dī'krō-ĭz'əm) *n. Chemistry.* **1.** The property possessed by some solutions of showing different colors at different concentrations. **2.** The property possessed by some crystals of exhibiting two different colors when viewed along different axes.

di·chro·ite (dī-krō'īt') *n.* See **cordierite.** [DICHRO(IC) + –ITE[1].]

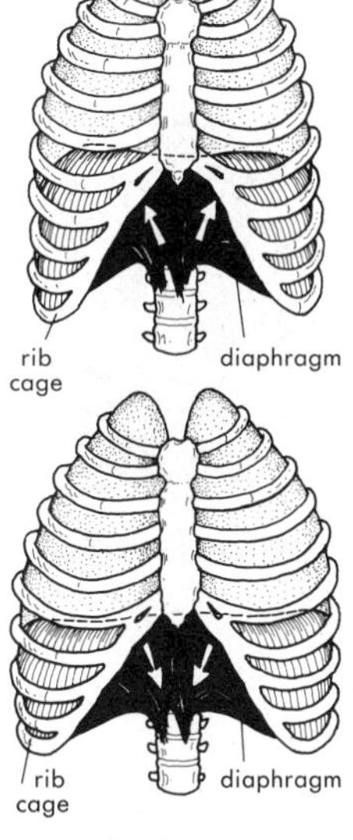

diaphragm
Top: Exhalation
Bottom: Inhalation

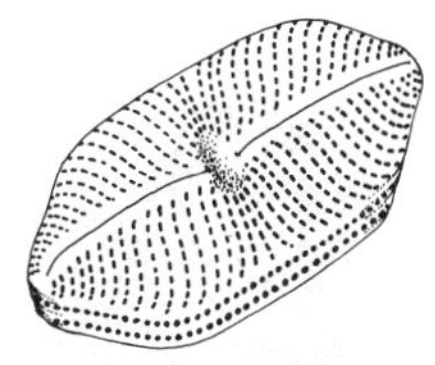
diatom

dibble

di·chro·mate (dī-krō′māt′, dī′krō-) *n.* A compound containing the divalent negative ion, Cr_2O_7, usually having a characteristic orange-red color. Also called *bichromate.*

di·chro·mat·ic (dī′krō-măt′ĭk) *adj.* **1.** Possessing or exhibiting two colors. **2.** *Zoology.* Having two distinct color phases not associated with season, sex, or age, as do certain species of birds. **3.** *Pathology.* Of or relating to dichromatism.

di·chro·ma·tism (dī-krō′mə-tĭz′əm) also **di·chro·mism** (-mĭz′əm) *n.* **1.** The quality or condition of being dichromatic. **2.** *Pathology.* A form of colorblindness in which only two of the three fundamental colors can be distinguished due to a lack of one of the cone pigments.

di·chro·mic (dī-krō′mĭk) *adj.* **1.** *Pathology.* Dichromatic. **2.** *Chemistry.* Containing two chromium atoms per molecule.

dichromic acid *n.* An acid, $H_2Cr_2O_7$, known only in solution.

di·chro·mism (dī-krō′mĭz′əm) *n.* Variant of **dichromatism.**

dick[1] (dĭk) *n. Slang.* A detective. [Shortening and alteration of DETECTIVE.]

dick[2] (dĭk) *n.* **1.** *Chiefly British.* A fellow; a guy. **2.** *Vulgar Slang.* A penis. [From *Dick,* nickname for *Richard.*]

Dick (dĭk), **George Frederick.** 1881–1967. American medical researcher who teamed with his wife, **Gladys Henry Dick** (1881–1963), to isolate the germ that causes scarlet fever. They developed a serum for the disease (1923) and the Dick test for susceptibility (1924).

dick·cis·sel (dĭk-sĭs′əl, dĭk′sĭs′-) *n.* A sparrowlike bird *(Spiza americana)* native to southern Ontario and the central United States, of which the male has a yellow breast marked with a small black bib on the throat. [Imitative of its song.]

dick·ens (dĭk′ənz) *n. Informal.* **1.** A severe reprimand or expression of anger: *gave me the dickens for being late.* **2.** Used as an intensive: *What in the dickens is that?* [Perhaps from the name *Dickens,* from diminutive of *Dick.* See DICK[2].]

Charles Dickens

Dick·ens (dĭk′ĭnz), **Charles John Huffam.** Pen name Boz. 1812–1870. British writer known for his tales of Victorian life and times. Immensely popular both then and now, his works include *The Pickwick Papers* (1836–1837), *Oliver Twist* (1837–1838), and *David Copperfield* (1849–1850). **—Dick·en′si·an** (dĭ-kĕn′zē-ən) *adj.*

dick·er (dĭk′ər) *intr.v.* **-ered, -er·ing, -ers.** To bargain; barter. **—dicker** *n.* The act or process of bargaining. [Probably from *dicker,* a quantity of ten, ten hides, from Middle English *diker,* perhaps from Old English **dicor,* from Latin *decuria,* set of ten, from *decem,* ten. See **dekm̥** in Appendix.]

WORD HISTORY: Perhaps a desire to see history repeat itself has been at work in the case of an etymology suggested for the verb *dicker,* first recorded in 1802 with reference to horse trading and the haggling that accompanies it. In a work published in 1848 James Fenimore Cooper used the word with reference to frontier trade. This use would support a connection with the noun *dicker,* which denotes a quantity of ten and was a common unit used in trading hides or furs. If the verb *dicker* originated in the fur trade, a parallel would exist with the noun *dicker.* The noun may have come into the Germanic languages and hence to English by way of trade or tribute in furs between the Germanic peoples and the Roman Empire, with the Germanic word coming from the Latin word *decuria,* "a group of ten men," which in Late Latin was used as a measure of skins. The difficulty with this parallel is that no existing evidence proves conclusively the derivation of the verb *dicker* from the noun *dicker.*

dick·ey also **dick·ie** or **dick·y** (dĭk′ē) *n., pl.* **-eys** also **-ies. 1.a.** A woman's blouse front worn under a suit jacket or low-necked garment. **b.** A man's detachable shirt front. **c.** A collar for a shirt. **d.** A child's bib or pinafore. **2.** A donkey. **3.** A small bird. **4.a.** The driver's seat on a carriage. **b.** A rear seat for servants on a carriage. [From diminutive of *Dick,* nickname for *Richard.*]

Dick·ey (dĭk′ē), **James Lafayette.** Born 1923. American writer, especially of poetry, although he is perhaps best known for his novel *Deliverance* (1970).

Emily Dickinson
Only known extant photograph, taken at age 16

Dick·in·son, Emily Elizabeth (dĭk′ĭn-sən). 1830–1886. American poet who was virtually a recluse at her home in Amherst, Massachusetts, where she wrote more than a thousand verses infused with emotional depth and subtlety. The first volume of her poetry was not published until 1890.

Dickinson, John. 1732–1808. American Revolutionary politician and pamphleteer who became the leading conservative voice of opposition to Great Britain through his *Letters from a Farmer in Pennsylvania* (1767–1768).

Dick test *n.* A skin test used to determine immunity or susceptibility to scarlet fever. [After George Frederick DICK and Gladys Henry DICK.]

dick·y[1] (dĭk′ē) *n.* Variant of **dickey.**

dick·y[2] (dĭk′ē) *adj. Informal.* Impaired; faulty; weak: *"'I've got this dicky heart,' he'd say to the fool"* (John le Carré). [Origin unknown.]

di·cli·nous (dī-klī′nəs) *adj. Botany.* Having stamens and pistils in separate flowers: *a diclinous plant.* [DI-[1] + Greek *klinē,* bed, couch; see **klei-** in Appendix + -OUS.] **—di′cli′ny** (dī′klī′nē) *n.*

di·co·fol (dī-kō′fôl, -fōl, -fōl) *n.* A pesticide, $C_{14}H_9Cl_5O$, containing a small percentage of DDT and used primarily to control mites on crops. [Origin unknown.]

di·cot·y·le·don (dī′kŏt′l-ēd′n) also **di·cot** (dī′kŏt′) *n.* A flowering plant with two cotyledons that usually appear at germination. **—di′cot′y·le′don·ous** (-lēd′n-əs) *adj.*

di·cro·tism (dī′krə-tĭz′əm) *n.* A condition in which the pulse is felt as two beats per single heartbeat. [From Greek *dikrotos,* double-beating : *di-,* two; see DI-[1] + *krotos,* rattling noise.] **—di·crot′ic** (-krŏt′ĭk) *adj.*

dict. *abbr.* **1.** Dictation. **2.** Dictionary.

dic·ta (dĭk′tə) *n.* A plural of **dictum.**

Dic·ta·phone (dĭk′tə-fōn′). A trademark used for an apparatus that records and reproduces dictation for transcription. This trademark sometimes occurs in print in lowercase: *"the master himself, alone and hunched over his dictaphone far into the night"* (New Republic). *"There's a dictaphone in the lab, so we're talking as we work"* (Chicago Tribune).

dic·tate (dĭk′tāt′, dĭk-tāt′) *v.* **-tat·ed, -tat·ing, -tates.** *—tr.* **1.** To say or read aloud to be recorded or written by another: *dictate a letter.* **2.a.** To prescribe with authority; impose: *dictated the rules of the game.* **b.** To control or command: *"Foreign leaders were . . . dictated by their own circumstances, bound by the universal imperatives of politics"* (Doris Kearns Goodwin). *—intr.* **1.** To say or read aloud material to be recorded or written by another: *dictated for an hour before leaving for the day.* **2.** To issue orders or commands. **—dictate** (dĭk′tāt′) *n.* **1.** A directive; a command. **2.** A guiding principle: *followed the dictates of my conscience.* [Latin *dictāre, dictāt-,* frequentative of *dīcere,* to say. See **deik-** in Appendix.]

SYNONYMS: *dictate, decree, impose, ordain, prescribe.* The central meaning shared by these verbs is "to set forth expressly and authoritatively": *victors dictating the terms of surrender; confiscation of alien property decreed by the legislature; impose obedience; a separation seemingly ordained by fate; taxes prescribed by law.*

dic·ta·tion (dĭk-tā′shən) *n. Abbr.* **dict. 1.a.** The act or process of dictating material to another for transcription. **b.** The material so dictated. **2.** An authoritative command or order.

dic·ta·tor (dĭk′tā′tər, dĭk-tā′-) *n.* **1.a.** An absolute ruler. **b.** A tyrant; a despot. **2.** An ancient Roman magistrate appointed temporarily to deal with an immediate crisis or emergency. **3.** One who dictates: *These initials are those of the dictator of the letter.*

dic·ta·to·ri·al (dĭk′tə-tôr′ē-əl, -tōr′-) *adj.* **1.** Tending to dictate; domineering. **2.** Of, relating to, or characteristic of a dictator or dictatorship; autocratic. **—dic′ta·to′ri·al·ly** *adv.* **—dic′ta·to′ri·al·ness** *n.*

SYNONYMS: *dictatorial, authoritarian, dogmatic, doctrinaire, imperious, overbearing.* These adjectives mean asserting or tending to assert one's authority or to impose one's will on other persons. *Dictatorial* stresses the inclination to exercise authority in the highhanded, peremptory manner characteristic of a dictator: *The hostess indicated where the guests were to sit in her usual dictatorial manner. Authoritarian* implies the expectation of unquestioning obedience: *the timid, compliant child of authoritarian parents. Dogmatic* suggests the imposing of one's will or opinion as though these were beyond challenge: *"When people are least sure, they are often most dogmatic"* (John Kenneth Galbraith). *Doctrinaire* implies the imposition of one's theories, beliefs, or doctrines: *"They didn't know the facts . . . and I don't think it would've mattered in the slightest if they had. Very doctrinaire"* (George V. Higgins). *Imperious* suggests the arrogant manner of one accustomed to commanding: *She dismissed my opinion with an imperious wave of her hand. Overbearing* implies a tendency to be oppressively or rudely domineering: *His behavior toward the waiter was insufferably overbearing.*

dic·ta·tor·ship (dĭk-tā′tər-shĭp′, dĭk′tā′-) *n.* **1.** The office or tenure of a dictator. **2.** A state or government under dictatorial rule. **3.** Absolute or despotic control or power.

dic·tion (dĭk′shən) *n.* **1.** Choice and use of words in speech or writing. **2.** Degree of clarity and distinctness of pronunciation in speech or singing; enunciation. [Middle English *diccion,* a saying, word, from Old French, from Latin *dictiō, dictiōn-,* rhetorical delivery, from *dictus,* past participle of *dīcere,* to say, speak. See **deik-** in Appendix.] **—dic′tion·al** *adj.* **—dic′tion·al·ly** *adv.*

SYNONYMS: *diction, wording, vocabulary, phraseology, phrasing.* These nouns denote choice of words and the way in which they are used. *Diction* is the selection and arrangement of words in relation to effective expression: *very poor diction in the essay; a new poetic diction. Wording* stresses style or manner of expression: *writing in which the wording takes on a regional flavor. Vocabulary* is the aggregate of words a person understands or uses: *the general vocabulary of an educated native speaker of English. Phraseology* and *phrasing* include vocabulary, characteristic style, and the way in which words are grouped: *the abstruse phraseology of physics; a composition marked by elegant phrasing.*

dic·tion·ar·y (dĭk′shə-nĕr′ē) *n., pl.* **-ies.** *Abbr.* **dict. 1.** A reference book containing an alphabetical list of words, with information given for each word, usually including meaning, pronunciation, and etymology. **2.** A book listing the words of a language with translations into another language. **3.** A book listing words or other linguistic items in a particular category or subject with specialized information about them: *a medical dictionary.* **4.** *Computer Science.* **a.** A list of words stored in machine-readable form for reference as by spelling-checking software. **b.** An electronic spelling checker. [Medieval Latin *dictiōnārium,* from Latin *dictiō, dictiōn-,* diction. See DICTION.]

dic•tum (dĭk′təm) *n., pl.* **-ta** (-tə) or **-tums. 1.** An authoritative, often formal, pronouncement: *"He cites Augustine's dictum that 'If you understand it, it is not God' "* (Joseph Sobran). **2.** *Law.* See **obiter dictum** (sense 1). [Latin, from neuter past participle of *dīcere,* to say. See **deik-** in Appendix.]

dic•ty•o•some (dĭk′tē-ə-sōm′) *n. Botany.* The Golgi apparatus in plant cells. [Greek *diktuon,* net (from *dikein,* to throw; see **deik-** in Appendix) + –SOME[3].]

did (dĭd) *v.* Past tense of **do[1].**

di•dact (dī′dăkt′) *n.* A didactic person. [Back-formation from DIDACTIC.]

di•dac•tic (dī-dăk′tĭk) also **di•dac•ti•cal** (-tĭ-kəl) *adj.* **1.** Intended to instruct. **2.** Morally instructive. **3.** Inclined to teach or moralize excessively. [Greek *didaktikos,* skillful in teaching, from *didaktos,* taught, from *didaskein, didak-,* to teach, educate.] **—di•dac′ti•cal•ly** *adv.* **—di•dac′ti•cism** (-tĭ-sĭz′əm) *n.*

di•dac•tics (dī-dăk′tĭks) *n. (used with a sing. or pl. verb).* Instruction; teaching; pedagogy.

di•dap•per (dī′dăp′ər) *n.* A small grebe, such as the dabchick. [Middle English *didopper,* alteration of *divedap* : from Old English *dūfedoppa,* pelican : *dūfan,* to dive; see DIVE[1] + *-doppa,* a kind of bird.]

did•dle[1] (dĭd′l) *v.* **-dled, -dling, -dles. —diddle** *tr.v.* **1.** *Slang.* To cheat; swindle: *"The Swiss have special laws for people who diddle hotels"* (John le Carré). **2.** *Computer Science.* To fabricate, change, or otherwise manipulate (data) illegally. [Perhaps akin to Old English *dydrian,* to deceive, or from variant of dialectal *doodle,* fool, simpleton; akin to Low German *dudeldopp.*] **—did′dler** *n.*

did•dle[2] (dĭd′l) *v.* **-dled, -dling, -dles.** *—tr.* **1.** To jerk up and down or back and forth. **2.** *Vulgar Slang.* **a.** To have intercourse with (a woman). **b.** To practice masturbation upon. *—intr.* **1.** To shake rapidly; jiggle. **2.** *Slang.* To play with: *The children diddled with the knobs on the television all afternoon.* **3.** *Slang.* To waste time: *diddled around all morning.* [Probably alteration of dialectal *didder,* to quiver, tremble, from Middle English *dideren,* variant of *daderen, doderen,* perhaps from Low German.]

did•dly (dĭd′lē) *n. Slang.* A small or worthless amount: *His advice wasn't worth diddly to me.* [Short for *diddlyshit.* See DIDDLYSQUAT.]

did•dly•squat (dĭd′lē-skwŏt′) *n. Slang.* Diddly. [Alteration of *diddlyshit* : *diddly* (alteration of DOODLE) + SHIT.]

Di•de•rot (dē′də-rō′, dē-drō′), **Denis.** 1713–1784. French philosopher and writer whose supreme accomplishment was his work on the *Encyclopédie* (1751–1772), which epitomized the spirit of Enlightenment thought.

did•n't (dĭd′nt). Did not.

di•do (dī′dō) *n., pl.* **-dos** or **-does.** A mischievous prank or antic; a caper. [Origin unknown.]

Di•do (dī′dō) *n. Roman Mythology.* The founder and queen of Carthage, who fell in love with Aeneas and killed herself when he abandoned her.

Did•rik•son (dĭd′rik-sən), **Mildred Ella.** In full Mildred Ella Didrikson Zaharias. Known as "Babe." 1914–1956. American athlete who excelled in basketball, baseball, and track, winning two gold medals at the 1932 Summer Olympics. She later took up golf and won the U.S. (1946) and British (1947) amateur titles and the U.S. Open (1948, 1950, and 1954).

didst (dĭdst) *v. Archaic.* Second person singular past tense of **do[1].**

di•dym•i•um (dī-dĭm′ē-əm) *n.* **1.** *Symbol* **Di** A metallic mixture, once considered an element, composed of neodymium and praseodymium. **2.** A mixture of rare-earth elements and oxides used chiefly in manufacturing and coloring various forms of glass. [From Greek *didumos,* twin, double. See **dwo-** in Appendix.]

did•y•mous (dĭd′ə-məs) *adj.* Arranged or occurring in pairs; twin. [From Greek *didumos,* twin. See **dwo-** in Appendix.]

di•dyn•a•mous (dī-dĭn′ə-məs) *adj. Botany.* Having four stamens in two pairs of unequal length. [From New Latin *Didynamia,* former class name : DI–[1] + Greek *dunamis,* power; see DYNAMIC.]

die[1] (dī) *intr.v.* **died, dy•ing** (dī′ĭng), **dies. 1.** To cease living; become dead; expire. **2.** To cease existing, especially by degrees; fade: *The sunlight died in the west.* **3.** To experience an agony or suffering suggestive of that of death: *nearly died of embarrassment.* **4.** *Informal.* To desire something greatly: *I am dying for a box of chocolates. She was dying to see the exhibit.* **5. a.** To cease operation; stop: *If your vehicle dies, stay with it.* **b.** To be destroyed, as in combat: *could see the remains of two aircraft that had died in the attack.* **—*phrasal verbs.* die back.** *Botany.* To be affected by dieback. **die down.** To lose strength; subside: *The winds died down.* **die off.** To undergo a sudden, sharp decline in population: *Rabbits were dying off in that county.* **die out.** To cease living completely; become extinct: *tribes and tribal customs that died out centuries ago.* **—*idiom.* die hard. 1.** To take a long time in passing out of existence: *racial prejudices that die hard.* **2.** To resist against overwhelming, hopeless odds: *radicalism that dies hard.* [Middle English *dien,* probably from Old Norse *deyja.* See **dheu-[2]** in Appendix.]

die[2] (dī) *n., pl.* **dies** or **dice** (dīs). **1.** *pl.* **dies.** A device used for cutting out, forming, or stamping material, especially: **a.** An engraved metal piece used for impressing a design onto a softer metal, as in coining money. **b.** One of several component pieces that are fitted into a diestock to cut threads on screws or bolts. **c.** A part on a machine that punches shaped holes in, cuts, or forms sheet metal, cardboard, or other stock. **d.** A metal block containing small conical holes through which plastic, metal, or other ductile material is extruded or drawn. **2.** *pl.* **dies.** *Architecture.* The dado of a pedestal, especially when cube-shaped. **3.** *pl.* **dice.** *Games.* **a.** A small cube marked on each side with from one to six dots, usually used in pairs in gambling and in various other games. **b. dice.** *(used with a sing. verb).* A game of chance using dice. **—die** *tr.v.* **died, die•ing, dies.** To cut, form, or stamp with or as if with a die. **—*idioms.* load the dice. 1.** To make an outcome highly probable; predetermine a result: *"These factors merely load the dice, upping the odds that a household will fall into a certain . . . income distribution"* (Thomas G. Exter). **2.** To put another at a distinct disadvantage, as through prior maneuver: *The dice were loaded against the defendant before the trial.* **no dice. 1.** Of no use; futile. **2.** Used as a refusal to a request. **the die is cast.** The decision has been made and is irrevocable. [Middle English *de,* gaming die, from Old French, from Latin *datum,* from neuter past participle of *dare,* to give. See **dō-** in Appendix.]

die•back (dī′băk′) *n. Botany.* The gradual dying of plant shoots, starting at the tips, as a result of various diseases or climatic conditions.

di•e•cious (dī-ē′shəs) *adj. Botany.* Variant of **dioecious.**

Die•fen•ba•ker (dē′fən-bā′kər), **John George.** 1895–1979. Canadian politician who served as prime minister (1957–1963).

dief•fen•bach•i•a (dē′fən-bä′kē-ə, -băk′ē-ə) *n.* Any of several plants of the genus *Dieffenbachia* native to tropical America, having stout, jointed stems and large, variegated leaves and widely cultivated as an indoor plant. Also called *dumb cane, dumb plant.* [New Latin, genus name, after Ernst *Dieffenbach* (1811–1855), German naturalist.]

die-hard also **die•hard** (dī′härd′) *—adj.* Stubbornly resisting change or clinging to a seemingly hopeless or outdated cause. *—n.* One who stubbornly resists change or tenaciously adheres to a seemingly hopeless or outdated cause: *rebel die-hards who refused to surrender.* **—die′-hard′ism** *n.*

diel•drin (dēl′drĭn) *n.* A chlorinated hydrocarbon, $C_{12}H_8Cl_6O$, used as an insecticide and in mothproofing. [From *Diel(s-A)ld(e)r (reaction),* after Otto Paul Hermann DIELS and Kurt ALDER.]

di•e•lec•tric (dī′ĭ-lĕk′trĭk) *n.* A nonconductor of electricity, especially a substance with electrical conductivity less than a millionth (10^{-6}) of a siemens. [DI(A)– + ELECTRIC.] **—di′e•lec′tric** *adj.* **—di′e•lec′tri•cal•ly** *adv.*

dielectric constant *n. Physics.* See **permittivity.**

dielectric heating *n.* The heating of electrically nonconducting materials by a rapidly varying electromagnetic field.

Diels (dēlz, dēls), **Otto Paul Hermann.** 1876–1954. German chemist. He shared a 1950 Nobel Prize for discoveries concerning the structure of organic matter.

Di•em (dē-ĕm′, dyĕm), **Ngo Dinh.** 1901–1963. Vietnamese political leader who became president of South Vietnam in 1954. He was assassinated in a military coup d'état.

Dien Bien Phu (dyĕn′ byĕn′ fo͞o′). A town of northwest Vietnam near the Laos border. The French military base here fell to Vietminh troops on May 7, 1954, after a 56-day siege, leading to the end of France's involvement in Indochina.

di•en•ceph•a•lon (dī′ĕn-sĕf′ə-lŏn′, -lən) *n.* The posterior part of the forebrain that connects the mesencephalon with the cerebral hemispheres, encloses the third ventricle, and contains the thalamus and hypothalamus. Also called *betweenbrain, interbrain, thalamencephalon.* [DI(A)– + ENCEPHALON.] **—di•en•ce•phal′ic** (-sə-făl′ĭk) *adj.*

die-off (dī′ôf′, -ŏf′) *n.* The elimination of a species, population, or community of plants or animals as a result of natural causes.

Di•eppe (dē-ĕp′, dyĕp). A city of northeast France on the English Channel north of Rouen. It is a port for channel steamers and a beach resort. Allied forces led a disastrous commando attack on the city (August 19, 1942) to test the strength of German defenses. Population, 35,957.

di•er•e•sis or **di•aer•e•sis** (dī-ĕr′ĭ-sĭs) *n., pl.* **-ses** (-sēz′). **1.** *Linguistics.* **a.** A mark (¨) placed over the second of two adjacent vowels to indicate that they are to be pronounced as separate sounds rather than a diphthong, as in *naïve.* **b.** A mark (¨) placed over a vowel, such as the final vowel in *Brontë,* to indicate that the vowel is not silent. **2.** *Poetry.* A break or pause in a line of verse that occurs when the end of a word and the end of a metric foot coincide. [Late Latin *diaeresis,* from Greek *diairesis,* from *diairein,* to divide : *dia-,* apart; see DIA– + *hairein,* to take.]

die•sel (dē′zəl, -səl) *n.* **1.** A diesel engine. **2.** A vehicle powered by a diesel engine.

Die•sel (dē′zəl), **Rudolf.** 1858–1913. German engineer who devised and patented (1892) an internal-combustion engine.

Babe Didrikson

ă pat	oi boy
ā pay	ou out
âr care	o͝o took
ä father	o͞o boot
ĕ pet	ŭ cut
ē be	ûr urge
ĭ pit	th thin
ī pie	*th* this
îr pier	hw which
ŏ pot	zh vision
ō toe	ə about, item
ô paw	♦ regionalism

Stress marks: ′ (primary); ′ (secondary), as in **dictionary** (dĭk′shə-nĕr′ē)

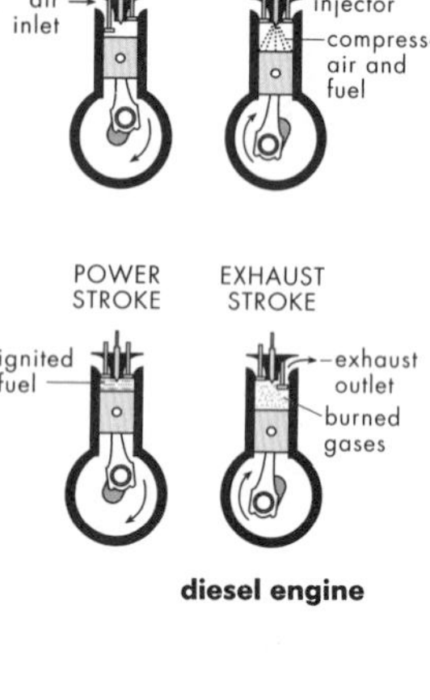

diesel engine

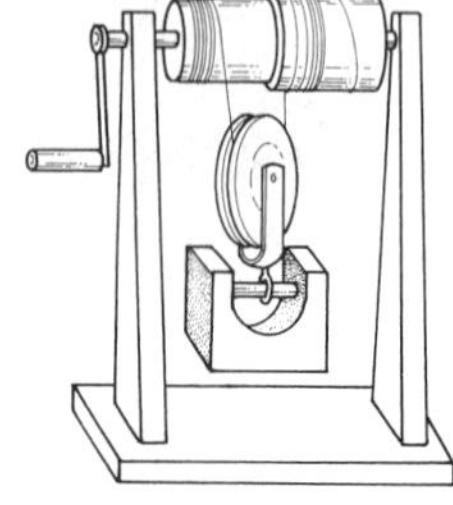
differential windlass

ă pat	oi boy
ā pay	ou out
âr care	ŏŏ took
ä father	ōō boot
ĕ pet	ŭ cut
ē be	ûr urge
ĭ pit	th thin
ī pie	*th* this
îr pier	hw which
ŏ pot	zh vision
ō toe	ə about, item
ô paw	♦ regionalism

Stress marks: **ʹ** (primary); ʹ (secondary), as in **dictionary** (dĭkʹshə-nĕrʹē)

diesel engine *n.* An internal-combustion engine that uses the heat of highly compressed air to ignite a spray of fuel introduced after the start of the compression stroke. [After Rudolf DIESEL.]

die•sink•er (dīʹsĭngʹkər) *n.* One that makes or engraves metal dies for stamping or shaping. **—dieʹsinkʹing** *n.*

Di•es I•rae (dēʹās îrʹāʹ) *n.* A medieval Latin hymn describing Judgment Day, used in some masses for the dead. [Medieval Latin *Diēs īrae,* day of wrath (the first words of the hymn) : Latin *diēs,* day + Latin *īrae,* genitive of *īra,* wrath.]

di•e•sis (dīʹĭ-sĭs) *n., pl.* **-ses** (-sēzʹ). *Printing.* See **double dagger.** [Medieval Latin, semitone (which was indicated by a double dagger), from Latin, quarter tone, from Greek *diesis,* a letting through, from *diienai,* to send through : *dia-,* dia- + *hienai,* to send; see **yē-** in Appendix.]

die•stock (dīʹstŏkʹ) *n.* An apparatus for holding the dies that cut threads on screws, bolts, pipes, or rods.

di•es•trus (dī-ĕsʹtrəs) also **di•es•trum** (-trəm) *n.* The sexually inactive period of the estrous cycle. [DI(A)– + ESTRUS.] **—di•esʹtrous** *adj.*

di•et¹ (dīʹĭt) *n.* **1.** The usual food and drink of a person or animal. **2.** A regulated selection of foods, especially as prescribed for medical reasons. **3.** Something used, enjoyed, or provided regularly: *subsisted on a diet of detective novels during his vacation.* **—diet** *v.* **-et•ed, -et•ing, -ets.** *—intr.* To eat and drink according to a regulated system, especially so as to lose weight or control a medical condition. *—tr.* To regulate or prescribe food and drink for. [Middle English *diete,* from Old French, from Latin *diaeta,* way of living, diet, from Greek *diaita.*] **—diʹet•er** *n.*

di•et² (dīʹĭt) *n.* **1.** A national or local legislative assembly in certain countries, such as Japan. **2.** A formal general assembly of the princes or estates of the Holy Roman Empire. [Middle English *diete,* day's journey, day for meeting, assembly, from Medieval Latin *diēta,* alteration (influenced by Latin *diēs,* day; see **deiw-** in Appendix) of Latin *diaeta,* daily routine. See DIET¹.]

di•e•tar•y (dīʹĭ-tĕrʹē) *adj.* Of or relating to diet. **—dietary** *n., pl.* **-ies. 1.** A system or regimen of dieting. **2.** A regulated daily food allowance. **—diʹe•tarʹi•ly** (-târʹə-lē) *adv.*

dietary law *n. Judaism.* The body of regulations prescribing the kinds and combinations of food that may be eaten.

di•e•tet•ic (dīʹĭ-tĕtʹĭk) *adj.* **1.** Of or relating to diet or its regulation. **2.** Specially prepared or processed for restrictive diets. [Late Latin *diaetēticus,* from Greek *diaitētikos,* from *diaita,* diet.] **—diʹe•tetʹi•cal•ly** *adv.*

di•e•tet•ics (dīʹĭ-tĕtʹĭks) *n. (used with a sing. verb).* The study of nutrition as it relates to health. Also called *sitology.*

di•eth•yl•car•bam•a•zine citrate (dī-ĕthʹəl-kär-bămʹə-zēnʹ) *n.* An anthelmintic agent, $C_{16}H_{29}O_8N_3$, used especially in the treatment of ascariasis and filariasis. [DI–¹ + ETHYL + CARBAM(IC ACID) + (PIPER)AZINE.]

di•eth•yl ether (dī-ĕthʹəl) *n.* See **ether** (sense 2).

di•eth•yl•stil•bes•trol (dī-ĕthʹəl-stĭl-bĕsʹtrôlʹ, -trōlʹ, -trŏlʹ) *n.* DES.

diethyl tol•u•am•ide (tŏlʹyōō-ămʹīdʹ, -ĭd) *n.* Deet. [DI–¹ + ETHYL + TOLU(ENE) + AMIDE.]

di•e•ti•tian or **di•e•ti•cian** (dīʹĭ-tĭshʹən) *n.* A person specializing in dietetics. [DIET¹ + *-itian* (alteration of –ICIAN).]

Die•trich (dēʹtrĭk, -trĭKH), **Marlene.** Born 1901. German-born American actress and singer whose first internationally famous role was the sultry-voiced temptress in *The Blue Angel* (1930).

dif. *abbr.* Difference.

diff. *abbr.* Difference.

dif•fer (dĭfʹər) *intr.v.* **-fered, -fer•ing, -fers. 1.** To be dissimilar or unlike in nature, quality, amount, or form: *Ambition differs from greed.* **2.** To be of a different opinion; disagree: *The critic differed with the author on several facts.* **3.** *Obsolete.* To quarrel; dispute. [Middle English *differren,* from Old French *differer,* from Latin *differre,* to differ, delay : *dis-,* apart; see DIS– + *ferre,* to carry; see **bher-¹** in Appendix.]

SYNONYMS: *differ, disagree, vary.* The central meaning shared by these verbs is "to be unlike or dissimilar": *Birds differ from mammals. The testimony of the two witnesses disagreed on significant points. People vary in intelligence.*
ANTONYM: *agree.*

dif•fer•ence (dĭfʹər-əns, dĭfʹrəns) *n. Abbr.* **dif., diff. 1.** The quality or condition of being unlike or dissimilar. **2.a.** An instance of disparity or unlikeness. **b.** A degree or amount by which things differ. **c.** A specific point or element that distinguishes one thing from another. **3.** A noticeable change or effect: *Exercise has made a difference in her health.* **4.a.** A disagreement or controversy. **b.** A cause of a disagreement or controversy. **5.** Discrimination in taste or choice; distinction. **6.** *Mathematics.* **a.** The amount by which one quantity is greater or less than another. **b.** The amount that remains after one quantity is subtracted from another. **7.** *Archaic.* A distinct mark or peculiarity. **—difference** *tr.v.* **-enced, -enc•ing, -enc•es.** To distinguish or differentiate.

SYNONYMS: *difference, dissimilarity, unlikeness, divergence, variation, distinction, discrepancy.* These nouns refer to a lack of correspondence or agreement. *Difference* is the most general: *differences in color and size; a difference of opinion. Dissimilarity* is difference between things otherwise alike or capable of close comparison: *a striking dissimilarity between the personalities of the sisters. Unlikeness* usually implies greater and more obvious difference: *more likeness than unlikeness among children of that age. Divergence* suggests an often gradually increasing difference between things originally similar: *points of divergence between British and American English. Variation* is difference between things of the same class or species; often it refers to modification of something original, prescribed, or typical: *variations in temperature; a variation in shape. Distinction* often means a difference in detail between like or related things, determinable only by close inspection: *the distinction in meaning between "good" and "excellent." A discrepancy* is a difference between things that should correspond or match, as a conflict in two accounts of an incident: *a discrepancy between what was promised and what was done.*

dif•fer•ent (dĭfʹər-ənt, dĭfʹrənt) *adj.* **1.** Unlike in form, quality, amount, or nature; dissimilar: *took different approaches to the problem.* **2.** Distinct or separate: *That's a different issue altogether.* **3.** Various or assorted: *interviewed different members of the community.* **4.** Differing from all others; unusual: *a different point of view.* [Middle English, from Old French, from Latin *differēns, different-,* present participle of *differre,* to differ. See DIFFER.] **—difʹfer•ent•ly** *adv.* **—difʹfer•ent•ness** *n.*

USAGE NOTE: *Different from* and *different than* are both common in British and American English. Critics since the 18th century have singled out *different than* as incorrect, though it is well attested in the works of reputable writers. Where the comparison is drawn directly between two persons or things, *from* is usually the safer choice: *My book is different from* (not *than*) *yours.* But *different than* is more acceptably used, particularly in American usage, where the object of comparison is expressed by a full clause: *The campus is different than it was 20 years ago* (or *The campus is different from how it was 20 years ago*). As a result, a simple noun phrase following *different than* is often construed as elliptical for a clause, which allows for a subtle distinction in meaning between the two constructions. *How different this seems from Paris* suggests that the object of comparison is the city of Paris itself, whereas *How different this seems than Paris* suggests that the object of comparison is something like "the way things were in Paris" or "what happened in Paris." • The construction *different to* is chiefly British.

dif•fer•en•ti•a (dĭfʹə-rĕnʹshē-ə, -shə) *n., pl.* **-ti•ae** (-shē-ēʹ). An attribute that distinguishes one entity from another, especially an attribute that distinguishes one species from others of the same genus. [Latin, difference, from *differēns, different-,* present participle of *differre,* to differ. See DIFFER.]

dif•fer•en•tia•ble (dĭfʹə-rĕnʹshə-bəl, -shē-ə-) *adj.* **1.** That can be differentiated: *differentiable species.* **2.** *Mathematics.* Possessing a derivative. **—difʹfer•enʹtia•bilʹi•ty** *n.*

dif•fer•en•ti•ae (dĭfʹə-rĕnʹshē-ēʹ) *n.* Plural of **differentia.**

dif•fer•en•tial (dĭfʹə-rĕnʹshəl) *adj.* **1.** Of, relating to, or showing a difference. **2.** Constituting or making a difference; distinctive. **3.** Dependent on or making use of a specific difference or distinction. **4.** *Mathematics.* Of or relating to differentiation. **5.** Involving differences in speed or direction of motion. **—differential** *n.* **1.** *Mathematics.* **a.** An infinitesimal increment in a variable. **b.** The product of the derivative of a function containing one variable multiplied by the increment of the independent variable. **2.** Differential gear. **3.** A difference in wage rate or in price. **—difʹfer•enʹtial•ly** *adv.*

differential analyzer *n. Computer Science.* A mechanical or electronic analog computer used to solve especially complicated differential equations.

differential calculus *n. Mathematics.* **1.** The mathematics of the variation of a function with respect to changes in independent variables. **2.** The study of slopes of curves, accelerations, maxima, and minima by means of derivatives and differentials.

differential coefficient *n. Mathematics.* See **derivative** (sense 3).

differential equation *n. Mathematics.* An equation that expresses a relationship between functions and their derivatives.

differential gear *n.* An arrangement of gears in an epicyclic train permitting the rotation of two shafts at different speeds, used on the rear axle of automotive vehicles to allow different rates of wheel rotation on curves.

differential rate *n.* **1.** A difference in wage rate paid for the same work performed under differing conditions. **2.a.** A difference in the transportation rate or the number of vehicles per unit time to the same destination over different routes, so as to equalize traffic. **b.** A difference in rates over the same route owing to differences in the commodities being transported.

differential windlass *n.* A hoisting device that has two drums of different sizes on the same axis. A line wound on the larger and unwound from the smaller provides extra lifting power. Also called *Chinese windlass.*

dif•fer•en•ti•ate (dĭfʹə-rĕnʹshē-ātʹ) *v.* **-at•ed, -at•ing, -ates.** *—tr.* **1.** To constitute the distinction between: *subspecies that are differentiated by the markings on their wings.* **2.** To perceive or show the difference in or between; discriminate. **3.** To make different by alteration or modification. **4.** *Mathematics.* To calculate the derivative or differential of (a function). *—intr.*

1. To become distinct or specialized; acquire a different character. **2.** To make distinctions; discriminate. **3.** *Biology.* To undergo a progressive, developmental change to a more specialized form or function. Used especially of embryonic cells or tissues. **—dif′fer·en′ti·a′tion** *n.*

dif·fi·cult (dĭf′ĭ-kŭlt′, -kəlt) *adj.* **1.** Hard to do or accomplish; demanding considerable effort or skill; arduous: *"To entertain is far more difficult than to enlighten"* (Anthony Burgess). See Synonyms at **hard. 2.** Hard to endure; trying: *fell upon difficult times.* **3.** Hard to comprehend or solve: *a difficult puzzle.* **4.** Hard to please, satisfy, or manage: *a difficult child.* **5.** Hard to persuade or convince; stubborn. [Middle English, back-formation from *difficulte,* difficulty. See DIFFICULTY.] **—dif′fi·cult′ly** *adv.*

dif·fi·cul·ty (dĭf′ĭ-kŭl′tē, -kəl-) *n., pl.* **-ties. 1.** The condition or quality of being difficult: *the difficulty of a task.* **2.** Something not easily done, accomplished, comprehended, or solved. **3.** Often **difficulties.** A troublesome or embarrassing state of affairs, especially of financial affairs. **4.** A laborious effort; a struggle; trouble: *had difficulty walking; completed the test with difficulty.* **5.** A disagreement or dispute. **6.** Reluctance or an objection; unwillingness. [Middle English *difficulte,* from Old French *dificulte,* from Latin *difficultās,* from *difficilis,* difficult : *dis-,* dis- + *facilis,* easy; see **dhē-** in Appendix.]

SYNONYMS: *difficulty, hardship, rigor, vicissitude.* The central meaning shared by these nouns is "something that requires great effort to overcome": *grappling with financial difficulties; a life of hardship; undergoing the rigors of prison; withstood the vicissitudes of an army career.*

dif·fi·dence (dĭf′ĭ-dəns, -dĕns′) *n.* The quality or state of being diffident; timidity or shyness.

dif·fi·dent (dĭf′ĭ-dənt, -dĕnt′) *adj.* **1.** Lacking or marked by a lack of self-confidence; shy and timid. See Synonyms at **shy**[1]. **2.** Reserved in manner. [Middle English, from Latin *diffīdēns, diffīdent-,* present participle of *diffīdere,* to mistrust : *dis-,* dis- + *fīdere,* to trust; see **bheidh-** in Appendix.] **—dif′fi·dent·ly** *adv.*

dif·fract (dĭ-frăkt′) *intr. & tr.v.* **-fract·ed, -fract·ing, -fracts.** To undergo or cause to undergo diffraction. [Back-formation from DIFFRACTION.] **—dif·frac′tive** *adj.* **—dif·frac′tive·ly** *adv.* **—dif·frac′tive·ness** *n.*

dif·frac·tion (dĭ-frăk′shən) *n.* Change in the directions and intensities of a group of waves after passing by an obstacle or through an aperture. [New Latin *diffrāctiō, diffrāctiōn-,* from Latin *diffrāctus,* past participle of *diffringere* : *dis-,* apart; see DIS– + *frangere,* to break; see **bhreg-** in Appendix.]

diffraction grating *n.* A usually glass or polished metal surface having a large number of very fine parallel grooves or slits cut in the surface and used to produce optical spectra by diffraction of reflected or transmitted light.

dif·fuse (dĭ-fyo͞oz′) *v.* **-fused, -fus·ing, -fus·es.** *—tr.* **1.** To pour out and cause to spread freely. **2.** To spread about or scatter; disseminate. **3.** To make less brilliant; soften. *—intr.* **1.** To become widely dispersed; spread out. **2.** *Physics.* To undergo diffusion. **—diffuse** (dĭ-fyo͞os′) *adj.* **1.** Widely spread or scattered; not concentrated. **2.** Characterized by verbosity; wordy. See Synonyms at **wordy.** [From Middle English, dispersed, from Anglo-Norman *diffus,* from Latin *diffūsus,* past participle of *diffundere,* to spread : *dis-,* out, apart; see DIS– + *fundere,* to pour; see **gheu-** in Appendix.] **—dif·fuse′ly** (-fyo͞os′lē) *adv.* **—dif·fuse′ness** (-fyo͞os′nĭs) *n.*

dif·fus·er (dĭ-fyo͞o′zər) *n.* **1.** One that diffuses, as: **a.** A light fixture, such as a frosted globe, that spreads light evenly. **b.** A medium that scatters light, used in photography to soften shadows. **c.** A device, such as a cone or baffle, placed in front of a loudspeaker diaphragm to diffuse the sound waves. **2.** A flow passage in a wind tunnel that decelerates a stream of gas or liquid from a high to a low velocity.

dif·fus·i·ble (dĭ-fyo͞o′zə-bəl) *adj.* Capable of diffusing or of undergoing diffusion: *diffusible dyes.* **—dif·fus′i·bly** *adv.*

dif·fu·sion (dĭ-fyo͞o′zhən) *n.* **1.** The process of diffusing or the condition of being diffused. **2.** Needless profusion of words; prolixity. **3.** *Physics.* **a.** The scattering of incident light by reflection from a rough surface. **b.** The transmission of light through a translucent material. **c.** The spontaneous intermingling of the particles of two or more substances as a result of random thermal motion. **—dif·fu′sion·al** *adj.*

dif·fu·sive (dĭ-fyo͞o′sĭv, -zĭv) *adj.* Characterized by diffusion. **—dif·fu′sive·ly** *adv.* **—dif·fu′sive·ness** *n.*

dig (dĭg) *v.* **dug** (dŭg), **dig·ging, digs.** *—tr.* **1.** To break up, turn over, or remove (earth or sand, for example), as with a shovel, a spade, or the hands. **2.** To make or form by removing earth or other material: *dug my way out of the snow.* **3.** To obtain or unearth by digging: *dig coal; a dog digging bones.* **4.** To learn or discover by careful research or investigation: *dug up the evidence; dug out the real facts.* **5.** To force down and into something; thrust: *dug his foot in the ground.* **6.** To poke or prod: *dug me in the ribs.* **7.** *Slang.* **a.** To understand fully: *Do you dig what I mean?* **b.** To like, enjoy, or appreciate: *"They really dig our music and, daddy, I dig swinging for them"* (Louis Armstrong). **c.** To take notice of: *Dig that wild outfit.* *—intr.* **1.** To loosen, turn over, or remove earth or other material. **2.** To make one's way by or as if by pushing aside or removing material: *dug through the files.* **3.** *Slang.* To have understanding: *Do you dig?* **—dig** *n.* **1.** A poke or thrust: *a sharp dig in the ribs.* **2.** A sarcastic, taunting remark; a gibe. **3.** An archaeological excavation. **4. digs.** *Chiefly British.* Lodgings. **—*phrasal verb.* dig in. 1.** To dig trenches for protection. **2.** To hold on stubbornly, as to a position; entrench oneself. **3. a.** To begin to work intensively. **b.** To begin to eat heartily. [Middle English *diggen;* perhaps akin to Old French *digue,* dike, trench. See **dhīgʷ-** in Appendix. V., tr., sense 7 and intr., sense 3, perhaps influenced by Wolof *degg,* to hear, find out, understand, or Irish Gaelic *tuigim,* I understand; see TWIG[2].]

dig. *abbr.* Digest.

di·gam·ma (dī-găm′ə) *n.* A letter occurring in certain early forms of Greek and transliterated in English as *w.* [Latin, from Greek : *di-,* two; see DI–[1] + *gamma,* gamma; see GAMMA.]

dig·a·my (dĭg′ə-mē) *n.* Remarriage after the death or divorce of one's first husband or wife. Also called *deuterogamy.* **—dig′a·mous** (-məs) *adj.*

di·gas·tric (dī-găs′trĭk) *Anatomy. adj.* Having two fleshy ends connected by a thinner tendinous portion. Used of certain muscles. **—digastric** *n.* A muscle of the lower jaw that elevates the hyoid bone and assists in lowering the jaw.

di·gest (dī-jĕst′, dĭ-) *v.* **-gest·ed, -gest·ing, -gests.** *—tr.* **1.** *Physiology.* To convert (food) into simpler chemical compounds that can be absorbed and assimilated by the body, as by chemical and muscular action in the alimentary canal. **2.** To absorb or assimilate mentally. **3. a.** To organize into a systematic arrangement, usually by summarizing or classifying. **b.** To condense or abridge (a written work). **4.** To endure or bear patiently. **5.** *Chemistry.* To soften or disintegrate by means of chemical action, heat, or moisture. *—intr.* **1.** *Physiology.* **a.** To become assimilated into the body. **b.** To assimilate food substances. **2.** *Chemistry.* To undergo exposure to heat, liquids, or chemical agents. **—digest** (dī′jĕst′) *n.* **1.** *Abbr.* **dig.** A collection of previously published material, such as articles, essays, or reports, usually in edited or condensed form. **2.** *Law.* A systematic arrangement of statutes or court decisions. **3.** A periodical containing literary abridgments or other condensed works. **4. Digest.** See **pandect** (sense 3). [Middle English *digesten,* from Latin *dīgerere, dīgest-,* to separate, arrange : *dī-, dis-,* apart; see DIS– + *gerere,* to carry. N., from Latin *dīgesta,* neuter pl. of *dīgestus,* past participle of *dīgerere,* to separate.]

dig
Archaeological dig in Iraq

di·gest·er (dĭ-jĕs′tər, dī-) *n.* **1.** One that makes a digest. **2.** *Chemistry.* A vessel in which substances are softened or decomposed, usually for further processing.

di·gest·i·ble (dī-jĕs′tə-bəl, dĭ-) *adj.* Readily or easily digested: *digestible meals.* **—di·gest′i·bil′i·ty, di·gest′i·ble·ness** *n.* **—di·gest′i·bly** *adv.*

di·ges·tion (dī-jĕs′chən, dĭ-) *n.* **1.** *Physiology.* **a.** The process by which food is converted into substances that can be absorbed and assimilated by the body. It is accomplished in the alimentary canal by the mechanical and enzymatic breakdown of foods into simpler chemical compounds. **b.** The result of this process. **c.** The ability to digest food. **2.** The process of decomposing organic matter in sewage by bacteria. **3.** Assimilation of ideas or information; understanding.

di·ges·tive (dī-jĕs′tĭv, dĭ-) *adj.* **1.** Relating to or aiding digestion. **2.** Functioning to digest food. **—digestive** *n.* A substance that aids digestion. **—di·ges′tive·ly** *adv.* **—di·ges′tive·ness** *n.*

digestive gland *n.* A gland, such as the liver or pancreas, that secretes into the alimentary canal substances necessary for digestion.

digestive system *n.* The alimentary canal and digestive glands regarded as an integrated system responsible for the ingestion, digestion, and absorption of food.

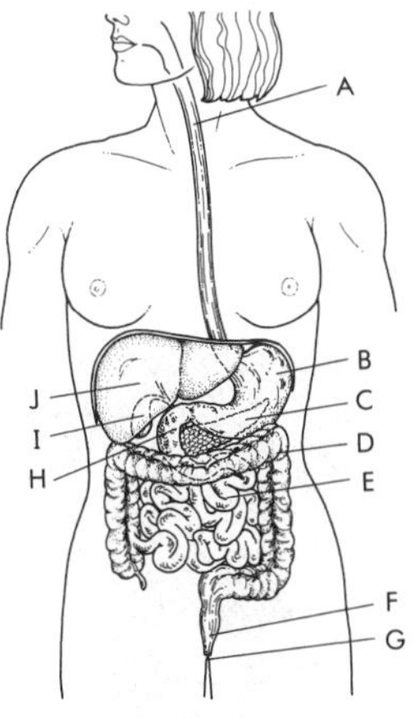

digestive system
A. Esophagus
B. Stomach
C. Pancreas
D. Large intestine
E. Small intestine
F. Rectum
G. Anus
H. Duodenum
I. Gallbladder
J. Liver

digestive tract *n.* See **alimentary canal.**

dig·ger (dĭg′ər) *n.* **1. a.** One that digs: *a digger of gardens; a digger for information; a digger of bones.* **b.** A tool or machine used for digging or excavating. **2.** *Informal.* A soldier from New Zealand or Australia in World War I.

digger wasp *n.* Any of various wasps of the family Sphecidae that burrow into the ground to build their nests and that paralyze their prey by stinging.

dig·gings (dĭg′ĭngz) *pl.n.* **1.** An excavation site, as for digging ore. **2.** Materials that have been excavated. **3.** *Chiefly British.* Rooms; lodgings.

dight (dīt) *tr.v.* **dight** or **dight·ed, dight·ing, dights.** *Archaic.* To dress; adorn. [Middle English *dighten,* from Old English *dihtan,* to arrange, from Latin *dictāre,* to dictate. See DICTATE.]

dig·it (dĭj′ĭt) *n.* **1. a.** A human finger or toe. **b.** A corresponding part in other vertebrates. **2.** A unit of length derived from the breadth of a finger and equal to about ¾ of an inch (2.0 centimeters). **3. a.** One of the ten Arabic number symbols, 0 through 9. **b.** Such a symbol used in a system of numeration. [Middle English, from Latin *digitus,* finger, toe. See **deik-** in Appendix.]

dig·i·tal (dĭj′ĭ-tl) *adj.* **1.** Of, relating to, or resembling a digit, especially a finger. **2.** Operated or done with the fingers: *a digital switch.* **3.** Having digits. **4.** Expressed in digits, especially for use by a computer. **5.** Using or giving a reading in digits: *a digital clock.* **—digital** *n.* A key played with the finger, as on a piano. **—dig′i·tal·ly** *adv.*

digital computer *n.* *Computer Science.* A computer that performs calculations and logical operations with quantities represented as digits, usually in the binary number system.

dig·i·tal·in (dĭj′ĭ-tăl′ĭn) *n.* **1.** A white crystalline glycoside, $C_{36}H_{56}O_{14}$, that is obtained from the seeds of the common foxglove. **2.** One of several mixtures of digitalis glycosides that are extracted from the leaves or seeds of the common foxglove. [DIGITAL(IS) + –IN.]

dig·i·tal·is (dĭj′ĭ-tăl′ĭs) *n.* **1.** A plant of the genus *Digitalis,* which includes the foxgloves. **2.** A drug prepared from the seeds and dried leaves of this plant, used in medicine as a cardiac stimulant. [Latin *digitālis,* of a finger (from the finger-shaped corollas of foxglove), from *digitus,* finger. See DIGIT.]

WORD HISTORY: The name of the plant genus *Digitalis,* whose member the foxglove provides an important drug used to treat heart disease, is associated with another part of the body, the finger. In *Digitalis,* which comes from the Latin word *digitālis,* meaning "relating to a finger," we recognize *digit,* which derives from Latin *digitus,* "finger, toe." In Modern Latin the genus name was chosen because the German name for the foxglove is *Fingerhut,* "thimble," or literally "finger hat." The second part of our word *foxglove* also refers to the similarity of the foxglove blossoms to the fingers of a glove. *Digitalis* is first recorded in English in a work published in 1664.

dig·i·tal·ize (dĭj′ĭ-tl-īz′) *tr.v.* **-ized, -iz·ing, -iz·es. 1.** To administer digitalis in a dosage sufficient to achieve the maximum therapeutic effect without producing toxic symptoms. **2.** To digitize. **—dig′i·tal·i·za′tion** (-ĭ-zā′shən) *n.*

digital recording *n.* **1.** A method of recording in which portions of sound waves are converted into numbers and stored for later reproduction. **2.** A record, tape, or disk that is recorded using this process.

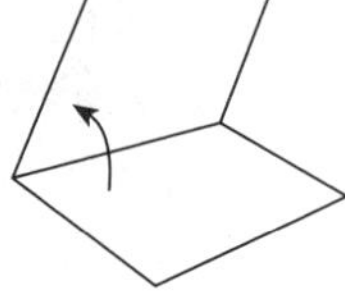
dihedral angle

dig·i·tate (dĭj′ĭ-tāt′) also **dig·i·tat·ed** (-tā′tĭd) *adj.* **1.** Having digits or fingerlike projections. **2.** *Botany.* Having distinct parts arising from a common point or center; palmate. **—dig′i·tate′ly** *adv.*

dig·i·ta·tion (dĭj′ĭ-tā′shən) *n.* **1.** Division into fingerlike parts. **2.** A fingerlike part or process.

dig·i·ti·grade (dĭj′ĭ-tĭ-grād′) *adj.* Relating to an animal, such as a horse, cat, or dog, whose weight is borne on the toes. [French : Latin *digitus,* toe; see DIGIT + Latin *gradus,* step; see GRADE.]

dig·i·tize (dĭj′ĭ-tīz′) *tr.v.* **-tized, -tiz·ing, -tiz·es.** To put (data, for example) into digital form. **—dig′i·ti·za′tion** (-tĭ-zā′shən) *n.* **—dig′i·tiz′er** *n.*

dig·i·tox·in (dĭj′ĭ-tŏk′sĭn) *n.* A highly active glycoside, $C_{41}H_{64}O_{13}$, derived from digitalis and prescribed in the treatment of certain cardiac conditions. [DIGI(TALIS) + TOXIN.]

dig·los·si·a (dī-glŏs′ē-ə, glô′sē-ə) *n.* A sociolinguistic situation in which complementary social functions are distributed between two different varieties of a language, a prestigious, formal, or high variety and a common, colloquial, or low variety, as in Italian, German, or Scottish English. [From Greek *diglōssos,* speaking two languages : *di-,* two; see DI–¹ + *glōssa,* tongue, language.]

di·glyc·er·ide (dī-glĭs′ə-rīd′) *n.* An ester of two fatty acids and glycerol.

dik-dik

dig·ni·fied (dĭg′nə-fīd′) *adj.* Having or expressing dignity. **—dig′ni·fied′ly** (-fīd′lē, -fī′ĭd-lē) *adv.*

dig·ni·fy (dĭg′nə-fī′) *tr.v.* **-fied, -fy·ing, -fies. 1.** To confer dignity or honor on; give distinction to: *dignified him with a title.* **2.** To raise the status of (something unworthy or lowly); make honorable: *would not dignify the insulting question with a response.* [Middle English *dignifien,* from Old French *dignifier,* from Late Latin *dignificāre* : Latin *dignus,* worthy; see **dek-** in Appendix + Latin *-ficāre,* -fy.]

dig·ni·tar·y (dĭg′nĭ-tĕr′ē) *n., pl.* **-ies.** A person of high rank or position.

dig·ni·ty (dĭg′nĭ-tē) *n., pl.* **-ties. 1.** The quality or state of being worthy of esteem or respect. **2.** Inherent nobility and worth: *the dignity of honest labor.* **3.a.** Poise and self-respect. **b.** Stateliness and formality in manner and appearance. **4.** The respect and honor associated with an important position. **5.** A high office or rank. **6. dignities.** The ceremonial symbols and observances attached to high office. **7.** *Archaic.* A dignitary. [Middle English *dignite,* from Old French, from Latin *dignitās,* from *dignus,* worthy. See **dek-** in Appendix.]

dig·ox·in (dĭj-ŏk′sĭn) *n.* A cardiac glycoside, $C_{41}H_{64}O_{14}$, obtained from the leaves of a foxglove, *Digitalis lanata,* with pharmacological effects similar to digitalis. [DIG(ITALIS) + (T)OXIN.]

di·graph (dī′grăf′) *n.* **1.** A pair of letters representing a single speech sound, such as the *ph* in *pheasant* or the *ea* in *beat.* **2.** A single character consisting of two letters run together and representing a single sound, such as Old English *æ.* **—di·graph′ic** (dī-grăf′ĭk) *adj.*

di·gress (dī-grĕs′, dĭ-) *intr.v.* **-gressed, -gress·ing, -gress·es.** To turn aside, especially from the main subject in writing or speaking; stray. See Synonyms at **swerve.** [Latin *dīgredī, dīgress-* : *dī-, dis-,* apart; see DIS– + *gradī,* to go; see **ghredh-** in Appendix.]

di·gres·sion (dī-grĕsh′ən, dĭ-) *n.* **1.** The act of digressing. **2.** An instance of digressing, especially a written or spoken passage that has no bearing on the main subject. **—di·gres′sion·al** *adj.*

di·gres·sive (dī-grĕs′ĭv, dĭ-) *adj.* Marked by digressions; rambling. **—di·gres′sive·ly** *adv.* **—di·gres′sive·ness** *n.*

di·he·dral (dī-hē′drəl) *adj.* *Mathematics.* **1.** Formed by or having two plane faces; two-sided. **2.** Relating to, having, or forming a dihedral angle. **—dihedral** *n.* **1.** *Mathematics.* A dihedral angle. **2.** *Aeronautics.* The upward or downward inclination of an aircraft wing from true horizontal.

dihedral angle *n.* **1.** *Mathematics.* The angle formed by two intersecting planes. **2.** *Aeronautics.* The dihedral of an aircraft wing.

di·hy·brid (dī-hī′brĭd) *n.* *Genetics.* The hybrid of parents that differ at only two gene loci, for which each parent is homozygous with different alleles.

di·hy·dric (dī-hī′drĭk) *adj.* Containing two hydroxyl radicals.

di·hy·drox·y·phen·yl·al·a·nine (dī′hī-drŏk′sē-fĕn′əl-ăl′ə-nēn′, -fē′nəl-) *n.* Dopa.

Di·jon (dē-zhôN′). A city of eastern France north of Lyons. It is an industrial center and a transportation hub noted for its foodstuffs, including mustard and cassis. Population, 140,942.

di·kar·y·on (dī-kăr′ē-ŏn′, -ən) *n.* The state in certain fungi in which each compartment of a hypha contains two nuclei, each derived from a different parent. [DI–¹ + Greek *karuon,* nut, kernel; see KARYO–.]

dik-dik (dĭk′dĭk′) *n.* Any of several very small African antelopes of the genus *Madoqua.* [Perhaps of East African origin.]

dike¹ also **dyke** (dīk) *—n.* **1.a.** An embankment of earth and rock built to prevent floods. **b.** *Chiefly British.* A low wall, often of sod, dividing or enclosing lands. **2.** A barrier blocking a passage, especially for protection. **3.** A raised causeway. **4.** A ditch; a channel. **5.** *Geology.* A long mass of igneous rock that cuts across the structure of adjacent rock. *—tr.v.* **diked, dik·ing, dikes** also **dyked, dyk·ing, dykes. 1.** To protect, enclose, or provide with a dike. **2.** To drain with dikes or ditches. [Middle English, from Old English *dīc,* trench; see **dhīgʷ-** in Appendix, and from Old Norse *dīki,* ditch.] **—dik′er** *n.*

dike² (dīk) *n.* *Offensive Slang.* Variant of **dyke².**

dik·tat (dĭk-tät′) *n.* **1.** A harsh, unilaterally imposed settlement with a defeated party. **2.** An authoritative or dogmatic statement or decree. [German, from Latin *dictātum,* from neuter past participle of *dictāre,* to dictate. See DICTATE.]

dil. *abbr.* Dilute.

Di·lan·tin (dī-lăn′tĭn). A trademark used for phenytoin.

di·lap·i·date (dĭ-lăp′ĭ-dāt′) *tr. & intr.v.* **-dat·ed, -dat·ing, -dates. 1.** To bring or fall into a state of partial ruin, decay, or disrepair. **2.** *Archaic.* To squander; waste. [Latin *dīlapidāre, dīlapidāt-,* to demolish, destroy : *dis-,* apart; see DIS– + *lapidāre,* to throw stones (from *lapis, lapid-,* stone; see LAPIDARIAN).] **—di·lap′i·da′tion** *n.*

di·lap·i·dat·ed (dĭ-lăp′ĭ-dā′tĭd) *adj.* Having fallen into a state of disrepair or deterioration, as through neglect; broken-down and shabby.

di·la·tan·cy (dī-lāt′n-sē, dĭ-) *n., pl.* **-cies. 1.** The increase in volume of a granular substance when its shape is changed, because of greater distance between its particles. **2.** The phenomenon whereby a viscous substance solidifies under pressure.

di·la·tant (dī-lāt′nt, dĭ-) *adj.* **1.** Tending to dilate; dilating. **2.** Exhibiting dilatancy. **—dilatant** *n.* A dilator.

dil·a·ta·tion (dĭl′ə-tā′shən, dī′lə-) *n.* **1.a.** The act or process of expanding; dilation. **b.** The condition of being expanded or stretched. **c.** A dilated formation or part. **2.** *Medicine.* The condition of being abnormally enlarged or dilated, as of an organ, an orifice, or a tubular structure: *dilatation of the stomach.* Also called *dilation.* **3.** Lengthy explanation or elaboration of a subject in writing or speech. **—dil′a·ta′tion·al** *adj.*

dilatation and curettage *n.* Dilation and curettage.

dil·a·ta·tor (dĭl′ə-tā′tər, dī′lə-) *n.* A dilator.

di·late (dī-lāt′, dī′lāt′) *v.* **-lat·ed, -lat·ing, -lates.** *—tr.* To make wider or larger; cause to expand. *—intr.* **1.** To become wider or larger; expand. **2.** To speak or write at great length on a subject; expatiate. [Middle English *dilaten,* from Old French *dilater,* from Latin *dīlātāre,* to enlarge : *dis-,* apart; see DIS– + *lātus,* wide.] **—di·lat′a·bil′i·ty** *n.* **—di·lat′a·ble** *adj.* **—di·lat′a·bly** *adv.* **—di·la′tive** *adj.*

di·lat·ed (dī-lā′tĭd, dī′lā′-) *adj.* **1.** Having been widened; expanded. **2.** Distended. **—di·lat′ed·ness** *n.*

di·la·tion (dī-lā′shən, dĭ-) *n.* **1.** The act of expanding or the state of being expanded. **2.** *Medicine.* See **dilatation** (sense 2).

dilation and curettage *n.* A surgical procedure in which the cervix is expanded using a dilator and the uterine lining scraped with a curette, performed for the diagnosis and treatment of various uterine conditions.

dil·a·tom·e·ter (dĭl′ə-tŏm′ĭ-tər, dī′lə-) *n.* An instrument used to measure thermal expansion and dilation in solids and liquids. [DILATE + –METER.] **—dil′a·to·met′ric** (-tə-mĕt′rĭk) *adj.* **—dil′a·tom′e·try** *n.*

di·la·tor (dī-lā′tər, dī′lā′-, dĭ-lā′-) *n.* **1.** A muscle that dilates a body part, such as a blood vessel or the pupil of the eye. **2.** An instrument that dilates a body part, such as a cavity, canal, or orifice.

dil·a·to·ry (dĭl′ə-tôr′ē, -tōr′ē) *adj.* **1.** Intended to delay. **2.** Tending to postpone or delay: *dilatory in his work habits.* See Synonyms at **slow.** [Middle English *dilatorie,* from Latin *dīlātōrius,* from *dīlātor,* delayer, from *dīlātus,* past participle of *differre,* to delay : *dis-*, apart; see DIS– + *lātus,* carried; see **tele-** in Appendix.] **—dil′a·to′ri·ly** *adv.* **—dil′a·to′ri·ness** *n.*

dil·do also **dil·doe** (dĭl′dō) *n., pl.* **-dos** also **-does.** An object used as a substitute for an erect penis. [Origin unknown.]

di·lem·ma (dĭ-lĕm′ə) *n.* **1.** A situation that requires a choice between options that are or seem equally unfavorable or mutually exclusive. **2.** *Usage Problem.* A problem that seems to defy a satisfactory solution. **3.** *Logic.* An argument that presents an antagonist with a choice of two or more alternatives, each of which contradicts the original contention and is conclusive. [Late Latin, from Greek *dilēmma,* ambiguous proposition : *di-,* two; see DI–[1] + *lēmma,* proposition; see LEMMA[1].] **—dil′em·mat′ic** (dĭl′ə-măt′ĭk) *adj.*

USAGE NOTE: In its primary sense *dilemma* denotes a situation in which a choice must be made between alternative courses of action or argument. Although citational evidence attests to widespread use of the term meaning simply "problem" or "predicament" and involving no issue of choice, 74 percent of the Usage Panel rejected the sentence *Juvenile drug abuse is the great dilemma of the 1980's.* • It is sometimes claimed that because the *di–* in *dilemma* comes from a Greek prefix meaning "two," the word should be used only when exactly two choices are involved. But 64 percent of the Usage Panel accepts its use for choices among three or more options in the example *Ph.D. students who haven't completed their dissertations by the time their fellowships expire face a difficult dilemma: whether to take out loans to support themselves, to try to work part-time at both a job and their research, or to give up on the degree entirely.*

dil·et·tante (dĭl′ĭ-tänt′, dĭl′ĭ-tänt′, -tän′tē, -tănt′, -tăn′tē) *n., pl.* **-tantes** also **-tan·ti** (-tän′tē, -tăn′-). **1.** A dabbler in an art or a field of knowledge. See Synonyms at **amateur. 2.** A lover of the fine arts; a connoisseur. **—dilettante** *adj.* Superficial; amateurish. [Italian, lover of the arts, from present participle of *dilettare,* to delight, from Latin *dēlectāre.* See DELIGHT.] **—dil′et·tan′tish** *adj.* **—dil′et·tan′tism** *n.*

dil·i·gence[1] (dĭl′ə-jəns) *n.* **1.** Earnest and persistent application to an undertaking; steady effort; assiduity. **2.** Attentive care; heedfulness.

dil·i·gence[2] (dĭl′ə-jəns, dē′lē-zhäns′) *n.* A large stagecoach. [French, from *(carrosse de) diligence,* speed (coach), from Old French, diligence, dispatch, from Latin *dīligentia,* from *dīligēns, dīligent-,* diligent. See DILIGENT.]

dil·i·gent (dĭl′ə-jənt) *adj.* Marked by persevering, painstaking effort. See Synonyms at **busy.** [Middle English, from Old French, from Latin *dīligēns, dīligent-,* present participle of *dīligere,* to esteem, love : *dī-, dis-,* apart; see DIS– + *legere,* to choose; see **leg-** in Appendix.] **—dil′i·gent·ly** *adv.*

dill (dĭl) *n.* **1.** An aromatic herb *(Anethum graveolens)* native to Eurasia, having finely dissected leaves and small yellow flowers clustered in umbels. **2.** The leaves or seeds of this plant, used as a seasoning. [Middle English *dile,* from Old English.]

Dil·lin·ger (dĭl′ĭn-jər), **John.** 1902–1934. American gangster who was declared Public Enemy Number One by the F.B.I. in 1933 for his role in a string of bank robberies and at least three murders. He died in a gun battle with F.B.I. agents in front of the Biograph Theater in Chicago.

dill pickle *n.* A pickled cucumber flavored with dill.

dil·ly (dĭl′ē) *n., pl.* **-lies.** *Slang.* One that is remarkable or extraordinary, as in size or quality: *had a dilly of a fight.* [Obsolete *dilly,* delightful, alteration of DELIGHTFUL.]

dil·ly-dal·ly (dĭl′ē-dăl′ē) *intr.v.* **-lied, -lying, -lies.** To waste time, especially in indecision; dawdle or vacillate. [Reduplication of DALLY.] **—dil′ly-dal′li·er** *n.*

dil·u·ent (dĭl′yo͞o-ənt) *adj.* Serving to dilute. **—diluent** *n. Chemistry.* An inert substance used to dilute. [Latin *dīluēns, dīluent-,* present participle of *dīluere,* to dilute. See DILUTE.]

di·lute (dĭ-lo͞ot′, dī-) *tr.v.* **-lut·ed, -lut·ing, -lutes. 1.** To make thinner or less concentrated by adding a liquid such as water. **2.** To lessen the force, strength, purity, or brilliance of, especially by admixture. **—dilute** *adj. Abbr.* **dil.** Weakened; diluted. [Latin *dīluere, dīlūt-* : *dī-, dis-,* apart, away; see DIS– + *-luere,* to wash (from *lavere;* see **leu(ə)-** in Appendix).] **—di·lut′er, di·lut′or** *n.* **—di·lu′tive** *adj.*

di·lu·tion (dĭ-lo͞o′shən, dī-) *n.* **1.a.** The process of making weaker or less concentrated. **b.** A dilute or weakened condition. **2.** A diluted substance. **3.** A decrease in the equity position of a share of stock because of the issuance of additional shares.

di·lu·vi·al (dĭ-lo͞o′vē-əl) also **di·lu·vi·an** (-ən) *adj.* Of, relating to, or produced by a flood. [Late Latin *dīluviālis,* from Latin *dīluvium,* flood, from *dīluere,* to wash away. See DILUTE.]

dim (dĭm) *adj.* **dim·mer, dim·mest. 1.a.** Lacking in brightness: *a dim room.* **b.** Emitting only a small amount of light; faint: *a dim lightbulb.* **2.** Lacking luster; dull and subdued. **3.a.** Faintly outlined; indistinct: *a dim figure in the distance.* **b.** Obscure to the mind or the senses: *a dim recollection of the accident.* **4.** Lacking sharpness or clarity of understanding or perception. See Synonyms at **dark. 5.** Lacking keenness or vigor. **6.** Negative, unfavorable, or disapproving: *took a dim view of their prospects.* **—dim** *tr. & intr.v.* **dimmed, dim·ming, dims.** To make or become dim. **—dim** *n.* **1.a.** A parking light on a motor vehicle. **b.** Low beam. **2.** *Archaic.* Dusk. [Middle English, from Old English.] **—dim′ly** *adv.* **—dim′ness** *n.*

dim. *abbr.* **1.** Dimension. **2.** Diminished. **3.** *Music.* Diminuendo. **4.** Diminutive.

Di·Mag·gio (də-mä′zhē-ō, -măj′ē-ō), **Joseph Paul.** Known as "Jolting Joe" and "the Yankee Clipper." Born 1914. American baseball player. A center fielder for the New York Yankees (1936–1951), he is considered the best all-around player ever at that position. In 1941 he hit safely in 56 consecutive games.

dime (dīm) *n.* **1.** A coin of the United States or Canada worth ten cents. **2.** *Slang.* A dime bag. ***—idioms.* a dime a dozen.** Overly abundant; commonplace. **on a dime.** Within a narrowly defined area: *a sports car that stops on a dime.* [Middle English, tenth part, from Old French *disme,* from Latin *decima (pars),* tenth (part), from *decem,* ten. See **dekm̥** in Appendix.]

dime bag *n. Slang.* A specified amount of an unlawful drug, packaged and sold for a fixed price.

di·men·hy·dri·nate (dī′mĕn-hī′drə-nāt′) *n.* An antihistamine, $C_{24}H_{28}ClN_5O_3$, used to treat motion sickness and allergic disorders. [DIME(THYL) + (AMI)N(E) + *hydrinate* (HYDR(AM)IN(E) + –ATE[2]).]

dime novel *n.* A melodramatic novel of romance or adventure, usually in paperback. [After the *Dime Book Series,* published by Erastus Flavel Beadle.] **—dime novelist** *n.*

di·men·sion (dĭ-mĕn′shən, dī-) *n. Abbr.* **dim. 1.** A measure of spatial extent, especially width, height, or length. **2.** Often **dimensions.** Extent or magnitude; scope: *a problem of alarming dimensions.* **3.** Aspect; element: *"He's a good newsman, and he has that extra dimension"* (William S. Paley). **4.** *Mathematics.* **a.** One of the least number of independent coordinates required to specify uniquely a point in space or in space and time. **b.** The range of such a coordinate. **5.** *Physics.* A physical property, such as mass, length, time, or a combination thereof, regarded as a fundamental measure or as one of a set of fundamental measures of a physical quantity: *Velocity has the dimensions of length divided by time.* **—dimension** *tr.v.* **-sioned, -sion·ing, -sions. 1.** To cut or shape to specified dimensions. **2.** To mark with specified dimensions. [Middle English *dimensioun,* from Latin *dīmēnsiō, dīmēnsiōn-,* extent, from *dīmēnsus,* past participle of *dīmētīrī,* to measure out : *dis-,* dis- + *mētīrī,* to measure; see **mē-**[2] in Appendix.] **—di·men′sion·al** *adj.* **—di·men′sion·al′i·ty** (-shə-năl′ĭ-tē) *n.* **—di·men′sion·al·ly** *adv.* **—di·men′sion·less** *adj.*

di·mer (dī′mər) *n.* **1.** A molecule consisting of two identical simpler molecules. **2.** A chemical compound consisting of such molecules. [DI–[1] + (POLY)MER.] **—di·mer′ic** (dī-mĕr′ĭk) *adj.*

di·mer·cap·rol (dī′mər-kăp′rôl, -rōl, -rŏl) *n.* A colorless, oily, viscous liquid, $C_3H_8OS_2$, used as an antidote for poisoning caused by lewisite, organic arsenic compounds, and heavy metals including mercury and gold. Also called *British anti-lewisite.* [DI–[1] + MERCAP(TAN) + (P)R(OPANE) + –OL(E).]

dim·er·ous (dĭm′ər-əs) *adj.* **1.** Consisting of two parts or segments, as the tarsus in certain insects. **2.** *Botany.* Having flower parts, such as petals, sepals, and stamens, in sets of two. **—dim′er·ism** *n.*

dime store *n.* See **five-and-ten.**

dim·e·ter (dĭm′ĭ-tər) *n.* A line of verse consisting of two metrical feet. [Late Latin, from Greek *dimetros,* having two meters : *di-,* two; see DI–[1] + *metron,* meter; see METER[1].]

di·meth·o·ate (dī-mĕth′ō-āt′) *n.* A crystalline compound, $C_5H_{12}NO_3PS_2$, used as an insecticide. [Probably DIMETH(YL) + (THI)O– + –ATE[2].]

di·meth·yl (dī-mĕth′əl) *n.* An organic compound, especially ethane, containing two methyl groups.

di·meth·yl·ni·tros·a·mine (dī-mĕth′əl-nī-trō′sə-mēn′, -nī′trō-săm′ĭn) *n.* A carcinogenic nitrosamine, $C_2H_6N_2O$, that occurs in tobacco smoke and certain foods.

di·meth·yl·sulf·ox·ide (dī-mĕth′əl-sŭl-fŏk′sīd′) *n.* DMSO.

dimin. *abbr.* **1.** *Music.* Diminuendo. **2.** Diminutive.

di·min·ish (dĭ-mĭn′ĭsh) *v.* **-ished, -ish·ing, -ish·es.** *—tr.* **1.a.** To make smaller or less or to cause to appear so. **b.** To detract from the authority, reputation, or prestige of. **2.** To cause to taper. **3.** *Music.* To reduce (a perfect or minor interval) by a semitone. *—intr.* **1.** To become smaller or less. See Synonyms at **decrease. 2.** To taper. [Middle English *diminishen,* blend of *diminuen,* to lessen (from Old French *diminuer,* from Latin *dīminuere,* variant of *dēminuere* : *dē-,* de- + *minuere,* to lessen) and *minishen,* to reduce (from Old French *minuiser,* from Vulgar Latin **minūtiāre,* from Latin *minūtia,* smallness, from *minūtus,* small, from past participle of *minuere,* to lessen; see **mei-**[2] in Appendix).] **—di·min′ish·a·ble** *adj.* **—di·min′ish·ment** *n.*

di·min·ished capacity (dĭ-mĭn′ĭsht) *n. Law.* Lack of ability to achieve the state of mind necessary for the commission of a particular crime.

di·min·ish·ing returns (dĭ-mĭn′ĭ-shĭng) *pl.n.* A yield rate that after a certain point fails to increase proportionately to additional outlays of capital or investments of time and labor.

di·min·u·en·do (dĭ-mĭn′yo͞o-ĕn′dō) *n., adv., & adj. Abbr.* **dim., dimin.** *Music.* Decrescendo. [Italian, present participle of *diminuire,* to diminish, from Latin *dīminuere.* See DIMINISH.]

dim·i·nu·tion (dĭm′ə-no͞o′shən, -nyo͞o′-) *n.* **1.a.** The act or process of diminishing; a lessening or reduction. **b.** The resulting reduction; decrease. **2.** *Music.* Repetition of a theme in notes one-quarter or one-half the duration of the original. [Middle English *diminucioun,* from Old French *diminution,* from Latin *dīminūtiō,*

dill
Anethum graveolens

Joe DiMaggio

ă pat	oi boy
ā pay	ou out
âr care	o͝o took
ä father	o͞o boot
ĕ pet	ŭ cut
ē be	ûr urge
ĭ pit	th thin
ī pie	*th* this
îr pier	hw which
ŏ pot	zh vision
ō toe	ə about, item
ô paw	♦ regionalism

Stress marks: ′ (primary); ′ (secondary), as in **dictionary** (dĭk′shə-nĕr′ē)

dīminūtiōn-, from *dīminūtus*, past participle of *dīminuere*. See DIMINISH.] **—dim′i·nu′tion·al** *adj.*

di·min·u·tive (dĭ-mĭn′yə-tĭv) *adj. Abbr.* **dim., dimin. 1.** Extremely small in size; tiny. See Synonyms at **small. 2.** *Grammar.* Of or being a suffix that indicates smallness, youth, familiarity, affection, or contempt, as *-let* in *booklet, -kin* in *lambkin,* or *-et* in *nymphet.* **—diminutive** *n.* **1.** *Grammar.* A diminutive suffix, word, or name. **2.** A very small person or thing. [Middle English *diminutif,* from Old French, from Latin *dīminūtīvus,* from *dīminūtus,* present participle of *dīminuere.* See DIMINISH.] **—di·min′u·tive·ly** *adv.* **—di·min′u·tive·ness** *n.*

dim·i·ty (dĭm′ĭ-tē) *n., pl.* **-ties.** A sheer, crisp cotton fabric with raised woven stripes or checks, used chiefly for curtains and dresses. [Middle English *demyt,* from Medieval Latin *dimitum,* from Greek *dimiton,* from neuter of *dimitos,* double-threaded : *di-,* two; see DI–[1] + *mitos,* thread.]

dim·mer (dĭm′ər) *n.* **1.** A rheostat or other device used to vary the intensity of an electric light. **2.a.** A parking light on a motor vehicle. **b.** Low beam.

di·mor·phic (dī-môr′fĭk) also **di·mor·phous** (-fəs) *adj.* Existing or occurring in two distinct forms; exhibiting dimorphism: *a dimorphic crystal; dimorphic organisms.*

di·mor·phism (dī-môr′fĭz′əm) *n.* **1.** *Biology.* The existence within a species of two distinct forms that differ in one or more characteristics, such as coloration, size, or shape. **2.** *Botany.* The occurrence of two distinct forms of the same parts in one plant, as in the juvenile and adult leaves of ivy. **3.** *Chemistry & Physics.* Dimorphic crystallization.

di·mor·phous (dī-môr′fəs) *adj.* Variant of **dimorphic.**

dim-out (dĭm′out′) *n.* **1.** Restricted use of lights at night, as to make a city less visible from the air in wartime. **2.** The semi-darkness resulting from restricted use of lights at night.

dinghy

dim·ple (dĭm′pəl) *n.* **1.** A small natural indentation in the flesh on a part of the human body, especially in the cheek or on the chin. **2.** A slight depression or indentation in a surface. **—dimple** *v.* **-pled, -pling, -ples.** *—intr.* To form dimples by smiling. *—tr.* To produce dimples in. [Middle English *dimpel,* from Old English **dympel.*] **—dim′ply** *adj.*

dim sum (dĭm′ so͝om′, sŭm′) *n.* A traditional Chinese cuisine in which small portions of a variety of foods, including an assortment of steamed or fried dumplings, are served in succession. [Chinese (Cantonese) *dim sem,* from Chinese (Mandarin) *diǎn xīn,* light refreshments : *diǎn,* spot, drop + *xīn,* heart, center.]

dim·wit (dĭm′wĭt′) *n. Slang.* A stupid person. **—dim′wit′ted** *adj.* **—dim′wit′ted·ly** *adv.* **—dim′wit′ted·ness** *n.*

dingo
Canis dingo

din (dĭn) *n.* A jumble of loud, usually discordant sounds. See Synonyms at **noise. —din** *v.* **dinned, din·ning, dins.** *—tr.* **1.** To stun with deafening noise. **2.** To instill by wearying repetition: *dinned the Latin conjugations into the student's heads.* *—intr.* To make a loud noise. [Middle English *dine,* from Old English *dyne.*]

di·nar (dĭ-när′, dē′när′) *n. Abbr.* **din. 1.** See table at **currency. 2.** Any of several units of gold and silver currency formerly used in the Middle East. [Arabic *dīnār,* from Late Greek *dēnarion,* from Latin *dēnārius.* See DENARIUS.]

Di·nar·ic Alps (dĭ-năr′ĭk). A range of western Yugoslavia extending about 644 km (400 mi) along the eastern coast of the Adriatic Sea. The partially submerged western part of the system forms numerous islands along the coastline.

dine (dīn) *v.* **dined, din·ing, dines.** *—intr.* To have dinner. *—tr.* To give dinner to; entertain at dinner: *wined and dined the visiting senators.* [Middle English *dinen,* from Old French *diner, disner,* from Vulgar Latin **disiūnāre,* from **disiēiūnāre* : Latin *dis-,* dis- + Latin *iēiūnium,* fast.]

din·er (dī′nər) *n.* **1.** One that dines: *midnight diners enjoying the meal after the theater.* **2.** See **dining car. 3.** A small, usually inexpensive restaurant with a long counter and booths and housed in a building designed to resemble a dining car.

Di·ne·sen (dē′nĭ-sən, dĭn′ĭ-), **Isak.** Pen name of Baroness Karen Blixen. 1885–1962. Danish writer who lived in Kenya from 1914 to 1933 and is best known for her sensitive memoir *Out of Africa* (1937).

di·nette (dī-nĕt′) *n.* **1.** A nook or alcove located in or near a kitchen and used for informal meals. **2.** The table and chairs used to furnish such an area. [DINE + –ETTE.]

ding[1] (dĭng) *v.* **dinged, ding·ing, dings.** *—intr.* **1.** To ring; clang. **2.** To speak persistently and repetitiously. *—tr.* **1.** To cause to clang, as by striking. **2.** To instill with constant repetition: *dinged advice into my head.* **—ding** *n.* A ringing sound. [Partly imitative and partly alteration of DIN.]

ding[2] (dĭng) *n. Informal.* A small dent or nick, as in the body of a car. [From *ding,* to strike, beat on (from Middle English *dingen;* akin to Old Norse *dengja*) and from DING[1].] **—ding** *v.*

ding-a-ling (dĭng′ə-lĭng) *n. Slang.* A scatterbrained or eccentric person.

ding·bat (dĭng′băt′) *n.* **1.** *Slang.* An empty-headed or silly person. **2.** An object, such as a brick or stone, used as a missile. **3.** *Slang.* An unspecified gadget or other small article, especially one whose name is unknown or forgotten. **4.** *Printing.* A typographical ornament or symbol. [Origin unknown.]

ding-dong (dĭng′dông′, -dŏng′) *n.* **1.** The peal of a bell. **2.** *Slang.* An empty-headed person; a fool. **—ding-dong** *intr.v.* **-donged, -dong·ing, -dongs.** To ring; jingle. **—ding-dong** *adj.* Characterized by a hammering exchange, as of blows: *a ding-dong fight.* [Imitative.]

din·ghy (dĭng′ē) *n., pl.* **-ghies.** *Nautical.* **1.** A small open boat carried as a tender, lifeboat, or pleasure craft on a larger boat. **2.** A small rowboat. **3.** An inflatable rubber life raft. [Hindi *ḍiṅgī,* diminutive of *ḍeṅgā,* boat.]

din·gle (dĭng′gəl) *n.* A small, wooded valley; a dell. [Middle English, dell, hollow.]

Ding Ling (dĭng′ lĭng′). 1904–1986. Chinese writer known for her novels, stories, and plays that explore the evolving role of women in Communist China.

din·go (dĭng′gō) *n., pl.* **-goes.** A wild dog *(Canis dingo)* of Australia, having a reddish-brown or yellowish-brown coat. [Dharuk (Aboriginal language of southeast Australia) *diŋgu.*]

din·gus (dĭng′əs) *n. Slang.* An article whose name is unknown or forgotten. [Dutch *dinges,* probably from German, genitive of *Ding,* thing, from Old High German.]

din·gy (dĭn′jē) *adj.* **-gi·er, -gi·est. 1.** Darkened with smoke and grime; dirty or discolored. **2.** Shabby, drab, or squalid. [Possibly from Middle English *dinge,* dung, variant of *dung.* See DUNG.] **—din′gi·ly** *adv.* **—din′gi·ness** *n.*

din·ing car (dī′nĭng) *n.* A railroad car in which meals are served. Also called *diner.*

dining room *n. Abbr.* **DR** A room, as in a house or hotel, in which meals are eaten.

di·ni·tro·ben·zene (dī-nī′trō-bĕn′zēn′, -bĕn-zēn′) *n.* Any of three isomeric compounds, $C_6H_4(NO_2)_2$, made from a mixture of nitric acid, sulfuric acid, and heated benzene and used in celluloid manufacture, in dyes, and in organic synthesis.

dink (dĭngk) *n. Sports.* A drop shot. [Perhaps alteration of DINKY.]

DINK or **dink** (dĭnk) *n.* A two-career couple with no children. [*D(ual) I(ncome) N(o) K(ids).*]

din·key also **din·ky** (dĭng′kē) *n., pl.* **-keys** also **-kies.** A small locomotive used in a railroad yard, as for shunting. [From DINKY.]

din·kum (dĭn′kəm) *Australian. adj.* Genuine; real. **—dinkum** *adv.* Honestly; truly. [From English dialectal and Australian, work.]

din·ky (dĭng′kē) *adj.* **-ki·er, -ki·est.** *Informal.* **1.** Of small size or consequence; insignificant. **2.** Of poor quality; shabby. **—dinky** *n.* Variant of **dinkey.** [Probably from Scots *dink,* neat, trim.]

din·ner (dĭn′ər) *n.* **1.a.** The chief meal of the day, eaten in the evening or at midday. **b.** A banquet or formal meal in honor of a person or an event. **c.** The food prepared for either of these meals. **2.** A full-course meal served at a fixed price; table d'hôte. *—attributive.* Often used to modify another noun: *dinner dishes; dinner music; dinner attire.* [Middle English *diner,* morning meal, from Old French *disner, diner,* to dine, morning meal. See DINE.]

WORD HISTORY: Eating foods such as pizza and ice cream for breakfast may be justified by the fact that in Middle English *dinner* meant "breakfast," as did the Old French word *disner,* or *diner,* which was the source of our word. The Old French word came from the Vulgar Latin word **disiūnāre,* meaning "to break one's fast; that is, to eat one's first meal," a notion also contained in our word *breakfast.* The Vulgar Latin word was derived from an earlier word, **disiēiūnāre,* the Latin elements of which are *dis–,* denoting reversal, and *iēiūnium,* "fast." Middle English *diner* not only meant "breakfast" but, echoing usage of the Old French word *diner,* more commonly meant "the first big meal of the day, usually eaten between 9 A.M. and noon." Customs change, however, and over the years we have let the chief meal become the last meal of the day, by which time we have broken our fast more than once.

dinner jacket *n.* See **tuxedo** (sense 1).

dinner theater *n.* A restaurant that presents a play during or after dinner.

din·ner·time (dĭn′ər-tīm′) *n.* The time during which dinner is normally eaten.

din·ner·ware (dĭn′ər-wâr′) *n.* **1.** The plates, serving bowls, platters, and other tableware used in serving a meal. **2.** A set of dishes.

di·no·flag·el·late (dī′nō-flăj′ə-lĭt, -lāt′, -flə-jĕl′ĭt) *n.* Any of numerous minute, chiefly marine protozoans of the order Dinoflagellata, characteristically having two flagella and a cellulose covering and forming one of the chief constituents of plankton. They include bioluminescent forms and forms that produce red tide. [From New Latin *Dinoflagellata,* class name : Greek *dinos,* eddy (from *dinein,* to whirl) + Latin *flagellum,* flagellum; see FLAGELLUM.]

di·no·saur (dī′nə-sôr′) *n.* **1.** Any of various extinct, often gigantic, carnivorous or herbivorous reptiles of the orders Saurischia and Ornithischia that were chiefly terrestrial and existed during the Mesozoic era. **2.** A relic of the past: *"living dinosaurs of the world of vegetation"* (John Olmsted). **3.** One that is hopelessly outmoded or unwieldy: *"The old, big-city teaching hospital is a dinosaur"* (Peggy Breault). [Greek *deinos,* monstrous + Greek *sauros,* lizard.] **—di′no·sau′ric** (-sôr′ĭk) *adj.*

di·no·sau·ri·an (dī′nə-sôr′ē-ən) *adj.* Of, relating to, or characteristic of a dinosaur. **—dinosaurian** *n.* A dinosaur.

di·no·there (dī′nə-thîr′) *n.* Any of various extinct elephantlike mammals of the genus *Dinotherium* that existed during the Miocene, Pliocene, and Pleistocene epochs. [From New Latin *Dinotherium,* genus name : Greek *deinos,* monstrous + Greek *thērion,* diminutive of *thēr,* beast; see **ghwer-** in Appendix.]

dint (dĭnt) *n.* **1.** Force or effort; power: *succeeded by dint of hard work.* **2.** A dent. **—dint** *tr.v.* **dint·ed, dint·ing, dints. 1.** To put a dent in. **2.** To impress or drive in forcibly. [Middle English. See DENT[1].]

di·nu·cle·o·tide (dī-no͞o′klē-ə-tīd′, -nyo͞o′-) *n.* A nucleotide molecule that consists of a combination of two nucleotide units.

Din·wid·die (dĭn-wĭd′ē, dĭn′wĭd-ē), **Robert.** 1693–1770. Scottish-born British colonial administrator in Virginia. As lieutenant governor of the colony (1751–1758) he attempted unsuccessfully to secure the frontier regions against the encroachments of the French.

di·oc·e·san (dī-ŏs′ĭ-sən) *adj.* Of or relating to a diocese. **—diocesan** *n.* The bishop of a diocese.

di·o·cese (dī′ə-sĭs, -sēs′, -sēz′) *n.* The district or churches under the jurisdiction of a bishop; a bishopric. [Middle English *diocise,* from Old French, from Late Latin *diocēsis,* from Latin *dioecēsis,* jurisdiction, from Greek *dioikēsis,* administration, from *dioikein,* to keep house, administer : *dia-,* intensive pref.; see DIA– + *oikein, oikē-,* to inhabit (from *oikos,* house; see **weik-**[1] in Appendix).]

Di·o·cle·tian (dī′ə-klē′shən). Originally Gaius Aurelius Valerius Diocletianus. A.D. 245?–313? Emperor of Rome (284–305) who divided the empire into east and west (286) in an attempt to rule the territory more effectively. His desire to revive the old religion of Rome led to the last major persecution of the Christians (303).

di·ode (dī′ōd′) *n.* **1.** An electronic device that restricts current flow chiefly to one direction. **2.** An electron tube having a cathode and an anode. **3.** A two-terminal semiconductor device used chiefly as a rectifier.

di·oe·cious also **di·e·cious** (dī-ē′shəs) *adj. Botany.* **1.** Having the male and female reproductive organs borne on separate individuals of the same species. **2.** Marked by species in which the male and female reproductive organs occur on different individuals; sexually distinct. [From New Latin *Dioecia,* former class name : DI–[1] + Greek *oikia,* a dwelling; see **weik-**[1] in Appendix.] **—di·oe′cious·ly** *adv.* **—di·oe′cism** (-sĭz′əm) *n.*

Di·og·e·nes (dī-ŏj′ə-nēz′). Died c. 320 B.C. Greek philosopher who founded the Cynic school of philosophy, stressing self-control and the pursuit of virtue. He is said to have once wandered through the streets of Athens with a lantern, searching for an honest man.

di·oi·cous (dī-oi′kəs) *adj. Botany.* Having sex organs on separate plants; unisexual. Used of mosses and related plants. [From New Latin *dioecus* : DI–[1] + Greek *oikos,* house; see **weik-**[1] in Appendix.]

Di·o·mede Islands (dī′ə-mēd′). Two rocky islands in the Bering Strait between Alaska and Siberia. **Little Diomede** belongs to the United States; **Big Diomede,** to Russia. The islands were named by Vitus Bering in 1728.

Di·o·me·des (dī′ə-mē′dēz) *n. Greek Mythology.* One of the Greek heroes of the Trojan War.

Di·o·ne (dī-ō′nē) *n.* **1.** *Greek Mythology.* The mother of Aphrodite by Zeus. **2.** The satellite of Saturn that is 11th in distance from the planet. [Greek *Diōnē,* from *Dios,* genitive of *Zeus,* Zeus. See **deiw-** in Appendix.]

Dione B *n.* The satellite of Saturn that is 12th in distance from the planet.

Di·o·nys·i·a (dī′ə-nĭz′ē-ə, -nĭzh′ē-ə, -nĭs′ē-ə) *pl.n.* Ancient Greek festivals held seasonally, chiefly at Athens, in honor of Dionysus, especially those held in the fall and connected with the development of early Greek drama. [Latin *Dionȳsia,* from Greek *(ta) Dionusia (hiera),* (festivities) of Dionysus, neuter pl. of *Dionusios.* See DIONYSIAN.]

Di·o·nys·i·ac (dī′ə-nĭs′ē-ăk′) *adj.* **1.a.** *Greek Mythology.* Of or relating to Dionysus. **b.** Of or relating to the Dionysia. **2.** Often **dionysiac.** Ecstatic or wild; Dionysian. [Latin *Dionȳsiacus,* from Greek *Dionusiakos,* from *Dionusios.* See DIONYSIAN.]

Di·o·nys·i·an (dī′ə-nĭsh′ən, -nĭzh′ən, -nĭs′ē-ən) *adj.* **1.** *Greek Mythology.* **a.** Of or relating to Dionysus. **b.** Of or devoted to the worship of Dionysus. **2.** Often **dionysian.** Of an ecstatic, orgiastic, or irrational nature; frenzied or undisciplined: *"remained the nearest to the instinctual, the irrational in music, and thus to the Dionysian spirit in art"* (Musco Carner). **3.** Often **dionysian.** In the philosophy of Nietzsche, of or displaying creative-intuitive power as opposed to critical-rational power. [From Latin *Dionȳsius,* from Greek *Dionusios,* from *Dionusos,* Dionysus.]

Di·o·ny·si·us (dī-ə-nĭsh′ē-əs, -nĭsh′əs, -nī′sē-əs). Known as "the Elder." 430?–367 B.C. Tyrant of Syracuse (405–367) noted for his campaigns against the Carthaginians in Sicily. His son **Dionysius** (395?–343?), known as "the Younger," succeeded him as tyrant in 367 and was exiled in 343 for his despotic rule.

Dionysius Ex·ig·u·us (ĕg-zĭg′yo͞o-əs, ĕk-sĭg′-). A.D. 500?–560? Scythian monk and scholar who introduced the method of reckoning the Christian era from the birth of Christ.

Dionysius of Hal·i·car·nas·sus (hăl′ĭ-kär-năs′əs). First century B.C. Greek historian whose 20-volume history of Rome, of which 10 volumes are extant, is a valuable source for early Roman history.

Dionysius Thrax (thrăks). fl. 100 B.C. Greek grammarian who taught at Rhodes and Rome and wrote an influential synthesis of Greek grammar, the *Art of Grammar.*

Di·o·ny·sus (dī′ə-nī′səs, -nē′-) *n. Greek & Roman Mythology.* The god of wine and of an orgiastic religion celebrating the power and fertility of nature. Also called *Bacchus.* [Latin *Dionȳsus,* from Greek *Dionusos.*]

di·o·phan·tine analysis (dī′ə-făn′tīn′, -tĭn) *n.* A method for determining integral solutions of certain algebraic equations. [After *Diophantus,* third-century A.D. Greek mathematician.]

di·op·side (dī-ŏp′sīd′) *n.* A light green, monoclinic pyroxene mineral, $CaMgSi_2O_6$, used as a gemstone and refractory. [French : *di-,* two (from Greek; see DI–[1]) + Greek *opsis,* –opsis.]

di·op·ter (dī-ŏp′tər) *n. Abbr.* **D.** A unit of measurement of the refractive power of lenses equal to the reciprocal of the focal length measured in meters. [Obsolete *diopter,* an instrument for measuring angles, from Latin *dioptra,* from Greek : *dia-,* dia- + *optos,* visible; see **okʷ-** in Appendix.] **—di·op′tral** (-trəl) *adj.*

di·op·tom·e·ter (dī′ŏp-tŏm′ĭ-tər) *n.* An instrument used for measuring ocular refraction. [DI(A)– + OPT(IC) + –METER.] **—di′op·tom′e·try** *n.*

di·op·tric (dī-ŏp′trĭk) also **di·op·tri·cal** (-trĭ-kəl) *adj.* **1.** Of or relating to dioptrics. **2.** Relating to optical refraction; refractive. [From Greek *dioptrikos,* of a diopter, from *dioptra,* diopter. See DIOPTER.]

di·op·trics (dī-ŏp′trĭks) *n. (used with a sing. verb).* The study of the refraction of light. [From DIOPTRIC.]

Di·or (dē-ôr′), **Christian.** 1905–1957. French fashion designer noted for his New Look of 1947 that emphasized narrow shoulders, tight waists, and long, full skirts.

di·o·ram·a (dī′ə-răm′ə, -rä′mə) *n.* **1.** A three-dimensional miniature or life-size scene in which figures, stuffed wildlife, or other objects are arranged in a naturalistic setting against a painted background. **2.** A scene reproduced on cloth transparencies with various lights shining through the cloths to produce changes in effect, intended for viewing at a distance through an aperture. [French, blend of *dia-,* through (from Greek; see DIA–) and *panorama,* panorama (from English; see PANORAMA).] **—di′o·ram′ic** (-răm′ĭk) *adj.*

di·o·rite (dī′ə-rīt′) *n.* Any of various dark, granite-textured, crystalline rocks rich in plagioclase and having little quartz. [French, from Greek *diorizein,* to distinguish : *dia-,* apart, between; see DIA– + *horizein,* to divide, limit; see HORIZON.] **—di′o·rit′ic** (-rĭt′ĭk) *adj.*

Di·os·cu·ri (dī-ŏs′kyə-rī′, dī′ə-skyo͝or′ī) *pl.n. Greek Mythology.* Castor and Pollux, the twin sons of Leda and brothers of Helen and Clytemnestra, who were transformed by Zeus into the constellation Gemini. [Greek *Dioskouroi* : *Dios,* genitive of *Zeus,* Zeus; see **deiw-** in Appendix + *kouroi,* pl. of *kouros,* boy; see **ker-**[2] in Appendix.]

di·ox·ane (dī-ŏk′sān′) *n.* A flammable, potentially explosive, colorless liquid, $C_4H_8O_2$, used as a solvent for fats, greases, and resins and in various products including paints, lacquers, glues, cosmetics, and fumigants.

di·ox·ide (dī-ŏk′sīd) *n.* A compound with two oxygen atoms per molecule.

di·ox·in (dī-ŏk′sĭn) *n.* Any of several carcinogenic or teratogenic heterocyclic hydrocarbons that occur as impurities in petroleum-derived herbicides. [DI–[1] + OX(O)– + –IN.]

dip (dĭp) *v.* **dipped, dip·ping, dips.** *—tr.* **1.** To plunge briefly into a liquid, as in order to wet, coat, or saturate. **2.** To color or dye by immersing: *dip Easter eggs.* **3.** To immerse (a sheep or other animal) in a disinfectant solution. **4.** To form (a candle) by repeatedly immersing a wick in melted wax or tallow. **5.** To galvanize or plate (metal) by immersion. **6.** To scoop up by plunging the hand or a receptacle below the surface, as of a liquid; ladle: *dip water out of a bucket.* **7.** To lower and raise (a flag) in salute. **8.** To lower or drop (something) suddenly: *dipped my head to avoid the branch.* *—intr.* **1.** To plunge into water or other liquid and come out quickly. **2.** To plunge the hand or a receptacle into liquid or a container, especially so as to take something up or out: *I dipped into my pocket for some coins.* **3.** To make inroads into funds: *We dipped into our savings.* **4.** To drop down or sink out of sight suddenly: *The sun dipped below the horizon.* **5.** To drop suddenly before climbing. Used of an aircraft. **6.** To slope downward; decline: *The road dipped.* **7.** To decline slightly and usually temporarily: *Sales dipped after Christmas.* **8.** *Geology.* To lie at an angle to the horizontal plane, as a rock stratum or vein. **9.a.** To read here and there at random; browse: *dipping into Chaucer.* **b.** To investigate a subject superficially; dabble: *dipped into psychology.* **—dip** *n.* **1.** A brief plunge or immersion, especially a quick swim. **2.** A liquid into which something is dipped, as for dyeing or disinfecting. **3.** A savory creamy mixture into which crackers, raw vegetables, or other foods may be dipped. **4.** An amount taken up by dipping. **5.** A container for dipping. **6.** A candle made by repeated dipping in tallow or wax. **7.** A downward slope; a decline. **8.** A sharp downward course; a drop: *a dip in prices.* **9.** *Geology.* The downward inclination of a rock stratum or vein in reference to the plane of the horizon. **10.** Magnetic dip. **11.** A hollow or depression. **12.** *Sports.* A gymnastic exercise on the parallel bars in which the body is lowered by bending the elbows until the chin reaches the level of the bars and then

Dionysus
Detail from a Roman sarcophagus

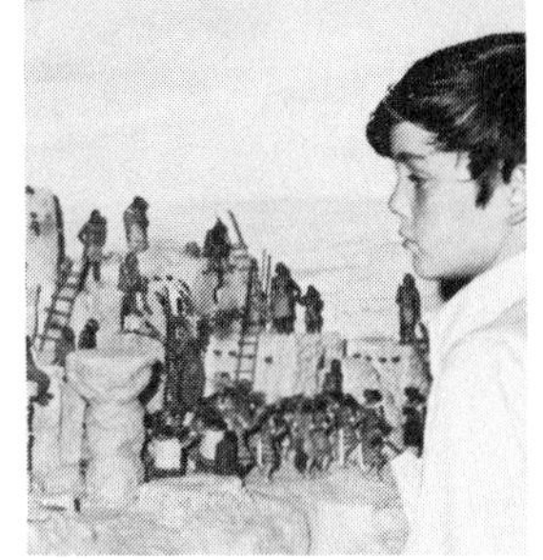

diorama
Hopi village

ă pat	oi boy
ā pay	ou out
âr care	o͝o took
ä father	o͞o boot
ĕ pet	ŭ cut
ē be	ûr urge
ĭ pit	th thin
ī pie	*th* this
îr pier	hw which
ŏ pot	zh vision
ō toe	ə about, item
ô paw	♦ regionalism

Stress marks: ′ (primary); ′ (secondary), as in **dictionary** (dĭk′shə-nĕr′ē)

is raised by straightening the arms. **13.** *Slang.* A pickpocket. **14.** *Slang.* A foolish or stupid person. [Middle English *dippen,* from Old English *dyppan.* See **dheub-** in Appendix.]

SYNONYMS: *dip, douse, duck, dunk, immerse, souse, submerge.* The central meaning shared by these verbs is "to plunge briefly into a liquid": *dipped a doughnut into his coffee; doused her head in the shower; playmates ducking each other in the pool; dunked the dirty shirt into soapsuds; immersed the tomatoes in boiling water; managed to avoid falling and being soused in the puddle; tents and trailers submerged by the deluge.*

dip. *abbr.* Diploma.

di·pep·ti·dase (dī-pĕp′tĭ-dās′, -dāz′) *n.* An enzyme that hydrolyzes dipeptides into their constituent amino acids.

di·pep·tide (dī-pĕp′tīd′) *n.* A peptide that, on hydrolysis, yields two amino acid molecules.

di·pet·al·ous (dī-pĕt′l-əs) *adj.* Having two petals.

di·phase (dī′fāz′) also **di·pha·sic** (dī-fā′zĭk) *adj.* Having two phases.

di·phen·yl (dī-fĕn′əl, -fē′nəl) *n.* See **biphenyl.**

di·phen·yl·a·mine (dī-fĕn′əl-ə-mēn′, -ăm′ĭn, -fē′nəl-) *n.* A colorless crystalline compound, $(C_6H_5)_2NH$, used as a stabilizer for plastics and in the manufacture of dyes, explosives, pesticides, and pharmaceuticals.

di·phen·yl·a·mine·chlo·ro·ar·sine (dī-fĕn′əl-ə-mēn′klôr′ō-är-sēn′, -är′sēn′, -ăm′ĭn-, -klōr′-, -fē′nəl-) *n.* See **phenarsazine chloride.**

di·phen·yl·hy·dan·to·in (dī-fĕn′əl-hī-dăn′tō-ĭn, -fē′-nəl-) *n.* See **phenytoin.** [DIPHENYL + *hydantoin* (HYD(ROGEN) + (ALL)ANTO(IS) + –IN).]

di·phen·yl·ke·tone (dī-fĕn′əl-kē′tōn, -fē′nəl-) *n.* See **benzophenone.**

di·phos·gene (dī-fŏz′jēn′) *n.* A colorless liquid, $ClCO_2CCl_3$, used in organic synthesis. Its vapor was used as a poison gas in World War I.

di·phos·phate (dī-fŏs′fāt′) *n.* An ester of phosphoric acid containing two phosphate groups.

di·phos·pho·gly·cer·ic acid (dī-fŏs′fō-glĭ-sĕr′ĭk) *n.* A diphosphate of glyceric acid that is an important intermediate in various metabolic processes, such as photosynthesis, glycolysis, and fermentation.

diph·the·ri·a (dĭf-thîr′ē-ə, dĭp-) *n.* An acute infectious disease caused by the bacillus *Corynebacterium diphtheriae,* characterized by the production of a systemic toxin and the formation of a false membrane on the lining of the mucous membrane of the throat and other respiratory passages, causing difficulty in breathing, high fever, and weakness. The toxin is particularly harmful to the tissues of the heart and central nervous system. [New Latin *diphthēria,* from French *diphthérie,* from Greek *diphthera,* piece of hide, leather.] **—diph′the·rit′ic** (-thə-rĭt′ĭk), **diph·ther′ic** (-thĕr′ĭk), **diph·the′ri·al** *adj.*

diph·thong (dĭf′thông′, -thŏng′, dĭp′-) *n. Linguistics.* A complex speech sound or glide that begins with one vowel and gradually changes to another vowel within the same syllable, as (oi) in *boil* or (ī) in *fine.* [Middle English *diptonge,* from Old French *diptongue,* from Late Latin *dipthongus,* from Greek *diphthongos* : *di-,* two; see DI–[1] + *phthongos,* sound.] **—diph·thon′gal** *adj.*

diph·thong·ize (dĭf′thông-īz′, -thŏng-, dĭp′-) *tr. & intr.v.* **-ized, -iz·ing, -iz·es.** *Linguistics.* To pronounce as or become a diphthong. **—diph′thong·i·za′tion** (-ĭ-zā′shən) *n.*

diph·y·cer·cal (dĭf′ĭ-sûr′kəl) *adj.* Having a tail fin in which the vertebral column extends to the tip, with symmetrical upper and lower parts. [Greek *diphuēs,* double; see DIPHYODONT + *kerkos,* tail + –AL[1].] **—diph·y·cer′cy** (-sûr′sē) *n.*

di·phy·let·ic (dī′fī-lĕt′ĭk) *adj.* Descended from two ancestral lines or individuals.

di·phyl·lous (dī-fĭl′əs) *adj. Botany.* Having two leaves.

di·phy·o·dont (dī-fī′ə-dŏnt′) *adj.* Having two successive sets of teeth, deciduous and permanent. [From Greek *diphuēs,* double (*di-,* two; see DI–[1]) + *phuein,* to grow; see **bheuə-** in Appendix + –ODONT.]

dipl. *abbr.* Diplomat; diplomatic.

dipl– *pref.* Variant of **diplo–.**

di·ple·gia (dī-plē′jə, -jē-ə) *n.* Paralysis of corresponding parts on both sides of the body.

di·plex (dī′plĕks′) *adj.* Capable of simultaneous transmission or reception of two messages in the same radio channel. [DI–[1] + (DU)PLEX.]

di·plex·er (dī′plĕk-sər) *n.* A coupling device that permits two radio transmitters to share the same antenna.

diplo– or **dipl–** *pref.* **1.** Double: *diplococcus.* **2.** Having double the basic number of chromosomes; diploid: *diplont.* [From Greek, from *diploos,* double. See **dwo-** in Appendix.]

dip·lo·blas·tic (dĭp′lō-blăs′tĭk) *adj.* Derived from two embryonic germ layers, the ectoderm and the endoderm. Used of lower invertebrates, such as sponges and coelenterates.

dip·lo·coc·cus (dĭp′lō-kŏk′əs) *n., pl.* **-coc·ci** (-kŏk′sī′, -kŏk′ī′). Any of various paired spherical bacteria, including those of the genus *Diplococcus,* some of which are pathogenic. **—dip′lo·coc′cal** (-kŏk′əl), **dip′lo·coc′cic** (-kŏk′sĭk, -kŏk′ĭk) *adj.*

di·plod·o·cus (dĭ-plŏd′ə-kəs, dī-) *n.* A very large herbivorous dinosaur of the genus *Diplodocus* that existed during the Jurassic period. [New Latin *Diplodocus,* genus name : Greek *diplo-,* diplo- + Greek *dokos,* beam; see **dek-** in Appendix.]

dip·lo·e (dĭp′lō-ē′) *n.* The spongy, porous, bony tissue between the hard outer and inner bone layers of the cranium. [New Latin *diploē,* from Greek, a fold, doubling, from feminine of *diploos,* twofold. See **dwo-** in Appendix.] **—dip′lo·ic** (-lō-ĭk) *adj.*

dip·loid (dĭp′loid′) *adj.* **1.** Double or twofold. **2.** *Genetics.* Having two sets of chromosomes: *diploid somatic cells.* **—diploid** *n. Genetics.* An organism having diploid cells. [Greek *diplous,* double; see **dwo-** in Appendix + –OID.]

dip·loi·dy (dĭp′loi′dē) *n.* The state of being diploid.

di·plo·ma (dĭ-plō′mə) *n. Abbr.* **dip. 1.** A document issued by an educational institution, such as a university, testifying that the recipient has earned a degree or has successfully completed a particular course of study. **2.** A certificate conferring a privilege or honor. **3.** An official document or charter. [Latin *diplōma,* letter of introduction, from Greek, document, folded paper, from *diploos,* double. See **dwo-** in Appendix.]

di·plo·ma·cy (dĭ-plō′mə-sē) *n.* **1.** The art or practice of conducting international relations, as in negotiating alliances, treaties, and agreements. **2.** Tact and skill in dealing with people. See Synonyms at **tact.**

dip·lo·mat (dĭp′lə-măt′) *n.* **1.** *Abbr.* **dipl.** One, such as an ambassador, who has been appointed to represent a government in its relations with other governments. **2.** One who uses skill and tact in dealing with others. [French *diplomate,* back-formation from *diplomatique,* diplomatic. See DIPLOMATIC.]

dip·lo·mate (dĭp′lə-māt′) *n.* One who has received a diploma, especially a physician certified as a specialist by a board of examiners.

dip·lo·mat·ic (dĭp′lə-măt′ĭk) *adj.* **1.** *Abbr.* **dipl.** Of, relating to, or involving diplomacy or diplomats. **2.** Using or marked by tact and sensitivity in dealing with others. See Synonyms at **suave. 3. a.** Of or relating to diplomatics. **b.** Being an exact copy of the original: *a diplomatic edition.* [French *diplomatique,* from New Latin *diplōmaticus,* from Latin *diplōma, diplōmat-,* letter of introduction. See DIPLOMA.] **—dip′lo·mat′i·cal·ly** *adv.*

diplomatic corps *n.* The body of diplomatic personnel in residence at a nation's capital.

diplomatic immunity *n.* The exemption from taxation and ordinary processes of law afforded to diplomatic personnel in a foreign country.

dip·lo·mat·ics (dĭp′lə-măt′ĭks) *n.* (*used with a sing. verb*). The branch of paleography that deals with the study of old official documents and determines their age and authenticity.

di·plo·ma·tist (dĭ-plō′mə-tĭst) *n.* A diplomat.

dip·lont (dĭp′lŏnt′) *n.* An organism having somatic cells with the diploid number of chromosomes. **—dip·lont′ic** (-lŏn′tik) *adj.*

dip·lo·pi·a (dĭ-plō′pē-ə) *n.* See **double vision. —dip·lo′pic** (-plō′pĭk, dĭ-plŏp′ĭk) *adj.*

dip·lo·pod (dĭp′lə-pŏd′) *n.* See **millipede. —dip·lop′o·dous** (-lŏp′ə-dəs) *adj.*

dip·lo·sis (dĭ-plō′sĭs) *n.* The formation during fertilization of the diploid number of chromosomes by the fusion of the nuclei of two haploid gametes. [New Latin *diplōsis,* from Greek, a doubling, from *diploun,* to double, from *diploos,* double. See DIPLO–.]

dip·no·an (dĭp′nō-ən) *n.* Any of various fishes of the group Dipnoi, which includes the lungfishes, characterized by modified lungs that enable them to breathe atmospheric air. **—dipnoan** *adj.* Of or belonging to the Dipnoi. [From New Latin *Dipnoi,* order name, from Greek, pl. of *dipnoos,* having two apertures for breathing : *di-,* two; see DI–[1] + *-pnoos,* breathing (from *pnoē,* breath, from *pnein,* to breathe; see **pneu-** in Appendix).]

dip·o·dy (dĭp′ə-dē) *n., pl.* **-dies.** A prosodic unit consisting of two feet. [Late Latin *dipodia,* from Greek, from *dipous,* two-footed : *di-,* two; see DI–[1] + *pous, pod-,* foot; see –POD.]

di·pole (dī′pōl′) *n.* **1.** *Physics.* A pair of electric charges or magnetic poles, of equal magnitude but of opposite sign or polarity, separated by a small distance. **2.** *Electronics.* An antenna, usually fed from the center, consisting of two equal rods extending outward in a straight line. **—di·pol′ar** *adj.*

dipole moment *n.* **1.** The product of either charge in an electric dipole with the distance separating them. **2.** The product of the strength of either pole in a magnetic dipole with the distance separating them.

dip·per (dĭp′ər) *n.* **1.** One that dips, especially a container for taking up water. **2.** One of several small birds of the genus *Cinclus* that dive into swift-moving streams and feed along the bottom. In this sense, also called *water ouzel.*

Dip·per (dĭp′ər) *n.* **1.** The Big Dipper. **2.** The Little Dipper.

dip·py (dĭp′ē) *adj.* **-pi·er, -pi·est.** *Slang.* Not sensible; foolish. [Origin unknown.]

di·pro·pel·lant (dī′prə-pĕl′ənt) *n.* See **bipropellant.**

di·prot·ic (dī-prŏt′ĭk) *adj.* Having two hydrogen ions to donate to bases in an acid-base reaction. [DI–[1] + PROT(ON) + –IC.]

dip·so·ma·ni·a (dĭp′sə-mā′nē-ə, -mān′yə) *n.* An insatiable, often periodic craving for alcoholic beverages. [Greek *dipsa*, thirst + –MANIA.] **—dip′so·ma′ni·ac** (-ăk′) *adj. & n.* **—dip′-so·ma·ni′a·cal** (-mə-nī′ə-kəl) *adj.*

dip·stick (dĭp′stĭk′) *n.* A graduated rod for measuring the depth or amount of liquid in a container, as of oil in a crankcase.

dip·ter·an (dĭp′tər-ən) also **dip·ter·on** (-tə-rŏn′) *—n.* A dipterous insect. *—adj.* Of or belonging to the order Diptera; dipterous.

dip·ter·ous (dĭp′tər-əs) *adj.* **1.** Of, relating to, or belonging to the Diptera, a large order of insects that includes the true flies and mosquitoes, characterized by a single pair of membranous wings and a pair of club-shaped balancing organs. **2.** Having two wings, as certain insects, or winglike appendages, as certain fruits and seeds: *the dipterous fruit of the maple.* [From New Latin *Diptera*, order name, from Greek *dipteros*, having two wings : *di-*, two; see DI–[1] + *pteron*, wing; see –PTER.]

dip·tych (dĭp′tĭk) *n.* **1.** An ancient writing tablet having two leaves hinged together. **2.** A work consisting of two painted or carved panels that are hinged together. [Late Latin *diptycha*, from Greek *diptukha*, from neuter pl. of *diptukhos*, folded double : *di-*, two; see DI–[1] + *ptukhē*, fold (from *ptussein*, *ptukh-*, to fold).]

di·pyr·id·a·mole (dī-pĭr′ĭ-də-mōl′, -pə-rĭd′ə-) *n.* A drug, $C_{24}H_{40}N_8O_4$, that acts as a coronary vasodilator and is used, for example, in the long-term treatment of angina pectoris. [DI–[1] + PYRID(INE) + –AM(INE) + –OLE.]

di·quat (dī′kwăt′) *n.* A strong, nonpersistent, yellow, crystalline herbicide, $C_{12}H_{12}Br_2N_2$, used to control water weeds. [DI–[1] + QUAT(ERNARY).]

dir. *abbr.* Director.

Di·rac (dĭ-răk′), **Paul Adrien Maurice.** 1902–1984. British mathematician and physicist. He shared a 1933 Nobel Prize for new formulations of the atomic theory.

dire (dīr) *adj.* **dir·er, dir·est. 1.** Warning of or having dreadful or terrible consequences; calamitous: *a dire economic forecast; dire threats.* **2.** Urgent; desperate: *in dire need; dire poverty.* [Latin *dīrus*, fearsome, terrible; akin to Greek *deinos*.] **—dire′ly** *adv.* **—dire′ness** *n.*

di·rect (dĭ-rĕkt′, dī-) *v.* **-rect·ed, -rect·ing, -rects.** *—tr.* **1.** To manage or conduct the affairs of; regulate. **2.** To have or take charge of; control. **3.** To give authoritative instructions to: *directed the student to answer.* **4.** To cause to move toward a goal; aim. See Synonyms at **aim. 5.** To show or indicate the way for: *directed us to the airport.* **6.** To cause to move in or follow a straight course: *directed their fire at the target.* **7.** To indicate the intended recipient on (a letter, for example). **8.** To address or adapt (remarks, for example) to a specific person, audience, or purpose. **9. a.** To give guidance and instruction to (actors or musicians, for example) in the rehearsal and performance of a work. **b.** To supervise the performance of. *—intr.* **1.** To give commands or directions. **2.** To conduct a performance or rehearsal. **—direct** *adj.* **1.** Proceeding without interruption in a straight course or line; not deviating or swerving: *a direct route.* **2.** Straightforward and candid; frank: *a direct response.* **3.** Having no intervening persons, conditions, or agencies; immediate: *direct contact; direct sunlight.* **4.** Effected by action of the voters, rather than through elected representatives or delegates: *direct elections.* **5.** Being of unbroken descent; lineal: *a direct descendant of the monarch.* **6.** Consisting of the exact words of the writer or speaker: *a direct quotation.* **7.** Lacking compromising or mitigating elements; absolute: *direct opposites.* **8.** *Mathematics.* Varying in the same manner as another quantity, especially increasing if another quantity increases or decreasing if it decreases. **9.** *Astronomy.* Designating west-to-east motion of a planet in the same direction as the sun's movement against the stars. **—direct** *adv.* Straight; directly. [Middle English *directen*, from Latin *dīrigere*, *dīrēct-*, to give direction to : *dī-*, *dis-*, apart; see DIS– + *regere*, to guide; see **reg-** in Appendix.]

direct access storage device *n. Abbr.* **DASD** *Computer Science.* A type of storage device, such as a magnetic disk, in which bits of data are stored at precise locations, enabling the computer to retrieve information directly without having to scan a series of records.

direct action *n.* The strategic use of immediately effective acts, such as strikes, demonstrations, or sabotage, to achieve a political or social end.

di·rect-ac·tion (dĭ-rĕkt′ăk′shən, dī-) *adj.* Operating without intermediate ingredients, components, stages, or processes.

direct current *n. Abbr.* **dc, DC** An electric current flowing in one direction only.

di·rect·ed angle (dĭ-rĕk′tĭd, dī-) *n. Mathematics.* An angle having an indicated positive sense.

directed distance *n. Mathematics.* A segment of a line having an indicated positive sense.

di·rec·tion (dĭ-rĕk′shən, dī-) *n.* **1.** The act or function of directing. **2.** Management, supervision, or guidance of an action or operation. **3.** The art or action of musical or theatrical directing. **4.** *Music.* A word or phrase in a score indicating how a passage is to be played or sung. **5.** Often **directions.** An instruction or series of instructions for doing or finding something. **6.** An authoritative indication; an order or a command. **7. a.** The distance-independent relationship between two points in space that specifies the angular position of either with respect to the other; the relationship by which the alignment or orientation of any position with respect to any other position is established. **b.** A position to which motion or another position is referred. **c.** A line leading to a place or point. **d.** The line or course along which a person or thing moves. **8.** The statement in degrees of the angle measured between due north and a given line or course on a compass. **9.** A course or area of development; a tendency toward a particular end or goal: *charting a new direction for the company.* [Middle English, arrangement, from Latin *dīrēctiō*, *dīrēctiōn-*, from *dīrēctus*, past participle of *dīrigere*, to direct. See DIRECT.] **—di·rec′tion·less** *adj.*

di·rec·tion·al (dĭ-rĕk′shə-nəl, dī-) *adj.* **1.** Of or indicating direction: *an automobile's directional lights.* **2.** *Electronics.* Capable of receiving or sending signals in one direction only. **3.** Relating to guidance in effort, behavior, or thought: *directional training.* **4.** Serving to point the future direction, as of fashion: *"A directional group of sweater knit colors are winter pastels"* (Women's Wear Daily). **—directional** *n.* A directional signal. **—di·rec′tion·al′i·ty** (-shə-năl′ĭ-tē) *n.*

directional antenna *n.* An antenna that receives or sends signals most effectively in a particular direction.

directional signal *n.* One of two lights on the front and rear of an automotive vehicle that flash to indicate the direction of a turn. Also called *turn signal.*

direction finder *n.* A device for determining the source of a transmitted signal, consisting mainly of a radio receiver and a coiled rotating antenna.

di·rec·tive (dĭ-rĕk′tĭv, dī-) *n.* An order or instruction, especially one issued by a central authority. **—directive** *adj.* Serving to direct, indicate, or guide.

♦ **di·rect·ly** (dĭ-rĕkt′lē, dī-) *adv.* **1.** In a direct line or manner; straight: *The road runs directly north.* **2.** Without anyone or anything intervening: *directly responsible.* **3.** Exactly or totally: *directly opposite.* **4.** At once; instantly: *Leave directly.* **5.** Candidly; frankly: *answered very directly.* **6.** *Chiefly Southern U.S.* In a little while; shortly: *He'll be coming directly.* **—directly** *conj. Chiefly British.* As soon as.

direct mail *n.* Advertising circulars or other printed matter sent directly through the mail to prospective customers or contributors. **—di·rect′-mail′** (dĭ-rĕkt′māl′, dī-) *adj.* **—direct mailer** *n.*

direct object *n. Grammar.* In English and some other languages, the word or phrase in a sentence referring to the person or thing receiving the action of a transitive verb. For example, in *mail the letter* and *call him, letter* and *him* are direct objects.

di·rec·tor (dĭ-rĕk′tər, dī-) *n. Abbr.* **dir. 1.** One that supervises, controls, or manages. **2.** A member of a group of persons chosen to control or govern the affairs of an institution or a corporation. **3.** A person who supervises the creative aspects of a dramatic production or film and instructs the actors and crew. **4.** *Music.* The conductor of an orchestra or a chorus. **5.** An electronic device that continually calculates and displays information used for firing weapons at moving targets, such as missiles or aircraft. **—di·rec′tor·ship′** *n.*

di·rec·tor·ate (dĭ-rĕk′tər-ĭt, dī-) *n.* **1.** The office or position of a director. **2.** A board of directors, as of a corporation. **3.** The entire staff of a bureau or department.

di·rec·to·ri·al (dĭ-rĕk′tôr′ē-əl, -tōr′-, dī-) *adj.* **1.** Of or relating to a director or directorate. **2.** Serving to direct; directive. **—di·rec′to′ri·al·ly** *adv.*

di·rec·tor's chair (dĭ-rĕk′tərz, dī-) *n.* A light, folding armchair having a plastic, wooden, or metal frame and a back and seat usually made of canvas. [From its use by motion picture directors on the set.]

di·rec·to·ry (dĭ-rĕk′tə-rē, dī-) *n., pl.* **-ries. 1.** A book containing an alphabetical or classified listing of names, addresses, and other data, such as telephone numbers, of specific persons, groups, or firms. **2.** *Computer Science.* **a.** A listing of the files contained in a storage device, such as a magnetic disk. **b.** A description of the various characteristics of a file, such as the layout of the fields in it. **3.** A book of rules or directions. **4.** A group or body of directors. **—directory** *adj.* Serving to direct.

direct primary *n.* A preliminary election in which a party's candidates for public office are nominated by direct vote of the people.

di·rec·trix (dĭ-rĕk′trĭks, dī-) *n., pl.* **di·rec·trix·es** or **di·rec·tri·ces** (dī′rĕk-trī′sēz). **1.** *Mathematics.* The fixed curve traversed by a generatrix in generating a conic section or a cylinder. **2.** The median line in the trajectory of fire of an artillery piece.

direct tax *n.* A tax, such as an income or a property tax, levied directly on the taxpayer.

dire·ful (dīr′fəl) *adj.* **1.** Inspiring dread; terrible. **2.** Foreshadowing evil or disaster; ominous. **—dire′ful·ly** *adv.* **—dire′ful·ness** *n.*

dire wolf *n.* A large wolflike mammal *(Canis dirus)* that inhabited North America during the Pleistocene epoch.

dirge (dûrj) *n.* **1.** *Music.* **a.** A funeral hymn or lament. **b.** A slow, mournful musical composition. **2.** A mournful or elegiac poem or other literary work. **3.** *Roman Catholicism.* The Office for the Dead. [Middle English, an antiphon at Matins in the Office for the Dead, from Medieval Latin *dīrige Domine*, direct, O Lord (the opening words of the antiphon), imperative of *dīrigere*, to direct. See DIRECT.] **—dirge′ful** *adj.*

ă pat	oi boy
ā pay	ou out
âr care	ŏŏ took
ä father	ōō boot
ĕ pet	ŭ cut
ē be	ûr urge
ĭ pit	th thin
ī pie	*th* this
îr pier	hw which
ŏ pot	zh vision
ō toe	ə about, item
ô paw	♦ regionalism

Stress marks: **′** (primary); ′ (secondary), as in **dictionary** (dĭk′shə-nĕr′ē)

WORD HISTORY: The history of the word *dirge* illustrates how a word with neutral connotations, such as *direct,* can become emotionally charged because of a specialized use. The Latin word *dīrige* is a form of the verb *dīrigere,* "to direct, guide," that is used in uttering commands. In the Office for the Dead *dīrige* is the first word in the antiphon for the first nocturn of matins. The complete opening words of this antiphon are *"Dirige, Domine, Deus meus, in conspectu tuo viam meam,"* "Direct, O Lord, my God, my way in thy sight." The part of the Office for the Dead that begins with this antiphon was named *Dīrige* in Ecclesiastical Latin, a use of *dirige* as an English word that is first recorded in a work possibly written before 1200. *Dirige* was then extended to refer to the chanting or reading of the Office for the Dead as part of a funeral or memorial service. In Middle English the word was shortened to *dirge,* although it was pronounced as two syllables. After the Middle Ages the word took on its more general senses of "a funeral hymn or lament" and "a mournful poem or musical composition" and developed its one-syllable pronunciation.

dir•ham (də-răm′) *n.* See table at **currency.** [Arabic, from Greek *drakhmē,* drachma.]

dir•i•gi•ble (dĭr′ə-jə-bəl, də-rĭj′ə-bəl) *n.* See **airship.** [Latin *dīrigere,* to direct; see DIRECT + -IBLE.]

dirk (dûrk) *n.* A dagger. **—dirk** *tr.v.* **dirked, dirk•ing, dirks.** To stab with a dirk. [Scots *durk.*]

Dirk•sen (dûrk′sən), **Everett McKinley.** 1896–1969. American politician who represented Illinois in the U.S. Congress (1933–1969) and was known for his flamboyant oratory.

dirndl

dirn•dl (dûrn′dl) *n.* **1.** A full-skirted dress with a tight bodice, low neck, and short, full sleeves. **2.** A full skirt with a gathered waistband. [German, short for *Dirndlkleid* : German dialectal *Dirndl,* diminutive of *Dirne,* girl (from Old High German *diorna*) + *Kleid,* dress.]

dirt (dûrt) *n.* **1.** Earth or soil. **2.a.** A filthy or soiling substance, such as mud or dust. **b.** Excrement. **3.** A squalid or filthy condition. **4.** One that is mean, contemptible, or vile. **5.a.** Obscene language or subject matter. **b.** Malicious or scandalous gossip. **c.** Information that embarrasses or accuses. **6.** Unethical behavior or practice; corruption. **7.** Material, such as gravel or slag, from which metal is extracted in mining. [Middle English, variant of *drit,* excrement, filth, mud, from Old Norse.]

dirt bike *n.* A motorbike or bicycle designed for use on rough surfaces, such as dirt roads or trails.

dirt-cheap (dûrt′chēp′) *adv. & adj.* Very cheap: *bought the property dirt-cheap; a dirt-cheap piece of property.*

♦**dirt dauber** *n. Chiefly Southern U.S.* See **potter wasp.**

dirt farmer *n. Informal.* A farmer who does all the work on his or her property. **—dirt farming** *n.*

dirt-poor (dûrt′po͝or′) *adj.* Lacking most of the necessities of life.

dirt•y (dûr′tē) *adj.* **-i•er, -i•est. 1.a.** Soiled, as with dirt; unclean. **b.** Spreading dirt; polluting: *The air near the foundry was always dirty.* **c.** Apt to soil with dirt or grime: *a dirty job at the garage.* **2.** Squalid or filthy; run-down: *dirty slums.* **3.a.** Obscene or indecent: *dirty movies; a dirty joke.* **b.** Malicious or scandalous: *a dirty lie.* **4.a.** Unethical or corrupt; sordid: *dirty politics.* **b.** Not sportsmanlike: *dirty players; a dirty fighter.* **c.** Acquired by illicit or improper means: *dirty money.* **d.** *Slang.* Possessing or using illegal drugs. **5.a.** Unpleasant or distasteful; thankless: *Laying off workers is the dirty part of this job.* **b.** Extremely unfortunate or regrettable: *a dirty shame.* **6.** Expressing disapproval or hostility: *gave us a dirty look.* **7.** Not bright and clear in color; somewhat dull or drab. Often used in combination: *dirty-blonde hair; dirty-green walls.* **8.** Producing a very great amount of long-lived radioactive fallout. Used of nuclear weapons. **9.** Stormy: *dirty weather.* **—dirty** *v.* **-ied, -y•ing, -ies.** *—tr.* **1.** To make soiled. **2.** To stain or tarnish with dishonor. *—intr.* To become soiled. **—dirt′i•ly** *adv.* **—dirt′i•ness** *n.*

dirt bike

SYNONYMS: *dirty, filthy, foul, nasty, squalid, grimy.* These adjectives apply to what is unclean, impure, or unkempt. *Dirty,* the most general, describes what is covered or stained with dirt: *dirty clothes; dirty feet; dirty sidewalks.* Something that is *filthy* is disgustingly dirty: *filthy rags; a room as filthy as a pigsty. Foul* suggests gross offensiveness, particularly to the sense of smell: *a foul exudation; a foul pond. Nasty* can refer to what is unpleasant because of the presence of dirt (*Scrubbing bathrooms is a nasty job*) but is often applied to what is merely annoying or unpleasant (*nasty ideas; a nasty trick*). *Squalid* suggests dirtiness, wretchedness, and sordidness: *lived in a squalid apartment. Grimy* describes something whose surface is smudged with dirt such as grime or soot: *grimy hands.*

dirty linen *n. Informal.* Personal affairs that could cause embarrassment or distress if made public. Also called *dirty laundry.*

dirty old man *n. Informal.* A middle-aged or elderly man with lewd or lecherous inclinations.

dirty pool *n. Slang.* Unjust or dishonest conduct. [From POOL[2].]

♦**dirty rice** *n. Southern Louisiana.* A side dish of white rice cooked with chicken livers and gizzards and seasoned with herbs and spices.

dirty tricks *pl.n. Informal.* **1.** Covert intelligence operations designed to disrupt the economy or upset the political situation in another country. **2.** Unethical behavior in politics, especially acts undertaken to destroy the credibility or reputation of an opponent. **3.** Commercial espionage. **—dirty trickster** *n.*

dirty word *n.* A word, an expression, or a concept that is inappropriate or offensive from a particular point of view.

dis. *abbr.* **1.** Discharge. **2.** Discount. **3.** Distance. **4.** Distant.

dis– *pref.* **1.** Not: *dissimilar.* **2.a.** Absence of: *disinterest.* **b.** Opposite of: *disfavor.* **3.** Undo; do the opposite of: *disarrange.* **4.a.** Deprive of: *disfranchise.* **b.** Remove: *disbud.* **5.** Free from: *disintoxicate.* **6.** Used as an intensive: *disannul.* [Middle English, from Old French *des-,* from Latin *dis-, dī-,* from *dis,* apart, asunder.]

dis•a•bil•i•ty (dĭs′ə-bĭl′ĭ-tē) *n., pl.* **-ties. 1.a.** The condition of being disabled; incapacity. **b.** The period of such a condition: *never received a penny during her disability.* **2.** A disadvantage or deficiency, especially a physical or mental impairment that prevents or restricts normal achievement. **3.** Something that hinders or incapacitates. **4.** *Law.* A legal incapacity or disqualification.

dis•a•ble (dĭs-ā′bəl) *tr.v.* **-bled, -bling, -bles. 1.** To deprive of capability or effectiveness, especially to impair the physical abilities of. **2.** *Law.* To render legally disqualified. **3.** *Computer Science.* To suppress (an interrupt feature). **—dis•a′ble•ment** *n.* **—dis•a′bling** *adj.* **—dis•a′bling•ly** *adv.*

dis•a•bled (dĭs-ā′bəld) *adj.* **1.** Inoperative: *a disabled vehicle.* **2.** Impaired, as in physical functioning: *a disabled veteran; disabled children.* **—disabled** *n.* Physically impaired people considered as a group. Often used with *the*: *"I have a terrible responsibility now. I'm . . . representing the disabled. That feeling fills me with pride"* (Christopher Nolan). See Usage Note at **handicapped.**

dis•a•buse (dĭs′ə-byo͞oz′) *tr.v.* **-bused, -bus•ing, -bus•es.** To free from a falsehood or misconception: *I must disabuse you of your feelings of grandeur.* [French *désabuser* : *dés-,* dis- + *abuser,* to delude (from Old French, to misuse; see ABUSE).]

di•sac•cha•ri•dase (dī-săk′ər-ĭ-dās′, -dāz′) *n.* An enzyme, such as invertase or lactase, that catalyzes the hydrolysis of disaccharides to monosaccharides.

di•sac•cha•ride (dī-săk′ə-rīd′) *n.* Any of a class of carbohydrates, including lactose and sucrose, that yield two monosaccharides upon hydrolysis.

dis•ac•cord (dĭs′ə-kôrd′) *n.* Lack of harmony; disagreement. **—disaccord** *intr.v.* **-cord•ed, -cord•ing, -cords.** To disagree. [From Middle English *disaccorden,* to disagree, from Old French *desacorder* : *des-,* dis- + *acorder,* to agree; see ACCORD.]

dis•ac•cus•tom (dĭs′ə-kŭs′təm) *tr.v.* **-tomed, -tom•ing, -toms.** To render (a person) unaccustomed to something to which the person has been previously accustomed; cause to break a habit. [Middle English *disacustome,* from Old French *desacostumer* : *des-,* dis- + *acostumer,* to accustom; see ACCUSTOM.]

dis•ad•van•tage (dĭs′əd-văn′tĭj) *n.* **1.** An unfavorable condition or circumstance. **2.** Something that places one in an unfavorable condition or circumstance. **3.** Damage or loss, especially to reputation or finances; detriment. **—disadvantage** *tr.v.* **-taged, -tag•ing, -tag•es.** To put at a disadvantage; hinder or harm. [Middle English *disavauntage,* from Old French *desavantage* : *des-,* dis- + *avantage,* advantage; see ADVANTAGE.]

SYNONYMS: *disadvantage, detriment, drawback, handicap.* The central meaning shared by these nouns is "a condition, circumstance, or characteristic unfavorable to success": *poor health, a disadvantage to an athlete; is free to do as she wishes without detriment; responsibilities that are a drawback to our pleasure; illiteracy, a serious handicap in life.*
ANTONYM: *advantage.*

dis•ad•van•taged (dĭs′əd-văn′tĭjd) *adj.* **1.** Deprived of some of the basic necessities or advantages of life, such as adequate housing, medical care, or educational facilities. **2.** Being at a disadvantage, especially with respect to competitive or opposing elements or forces: *"We can't have . . . disadvantaged conventional forces on one hand and strategic nuclear forces on the other"* (Bernard Rogers). **—disadvantaged** *n. (used with a pl. verb).* Deprived people considered as a group. **—dis′ad•van′taged•ness** *n.*

dis•ad•van•ta•geous (dĭs-ăd′vən-tā′jəs, dĭs′ăd-vən-) *adj.* Detrimental; unfavorable. **—dis•ad′van•ta′geous•ly** *adv.* **—dis•ad′van•ta′geous•ness** *n.*

dis•af•fect (dĭs′ə-fĕkt′) *tr.v.* **-fect•ed, -fect•ing, -fects.** To cause to lose affection or loyalty. See Synonyms at **estrange.** **—dis′af•fec′tion** *n.*

dis•af•fect•ed (dĭs′ə-fĕk′tĭd) *adj.* Resentful and rebellious, especially against authority. **—dis′af•fect′ed•ly** *adv.*

dis•af•fil•i•ate (dĭs′ə-fĭl′ē-āt′) *v.* **-at•ed, -at•ing, -ates.** *—tr.* To remove from association. *—intr.* To end an affiliation. **—dis′af•fil′i•a′tion** *n.*

dis•af•firm (dĭs′ə-fûrm′) *tr.v.* **-firmed, -firm•ing, -firms. 1.** To deny or contradict. See Synonyms at **deny. 2.** *Law.* To repudiate. **—dis′af•fir′mance** (dĭs′ə-fûr′məns), **dis•af′fir•ma′tion** (dĭs-ăf′ər-mā′shən) *n.*

dis•ag•gre•gate (dĭs-ăg′rĭ-gāt′) *v.* **-gat•ed, -gat•ing, -gates.** *—tr.* To divide into constituent parts. *—intr.* To break up or break apart. **—dis·ag′gre·ga′tion** (-grə-gā′shən) *n.* **—dis·ag′gre·ga′tive** *adj.*

dis·a·gree (dĭs′ə-grē′) *intr.v.* **-greed, -gree·ing, -grees. 1.** To fail to correspond: *our figures disagree.* See Synonyms at **differ. 2.a.** To have a differing opinion: *She disagrees with him on everything. They say it will rain, but I disagree.* **b.** To dispute or quarrel. **3.** To cause adverse effects: *Caffeine disagrees with me.* [Middle English *disagreen,* from Old French *desagreer* : *des-,* dis- + *agreer,* to agree; see AGREE.]

dis·a·gree·a·ble (dĭs′ə-grē′ə-bəl) *adj.* **1.** Not to one's liking; unpleasant or offensive. **2.** Having a quarrelsome, bad-tempered manner. **—dis′a·gree′a·ble·ness** *n.* **—dis′a·gree′a·bly** *adv.*

dis·a·gree·ment (dĭs′ə-grē′mənt) *n.* **1.** A failure or refusal to agree. **2.** A disparity; an inconsistency. **3.a.** A conflict or difference of opinion. **b.** A quarrel.

dis·al·low (dĭs′ə-lou′) *tr.v.* **-lowed, -low·ing, -lows. 1.** To refuse to allow: "[The government] *disallowed his aging and dying parents any reunion with their only child"* (John Simon). **2.** To reject as invalid, untrue, or improper. [Middle English *disallowen,* from Old French *desalouer,* to reprimand : *des-,* dis- + *alouer,* to approve; see ALLOW.] **—dis′al·low′a·ble** *adj.* **—dis′al·low′ance** *n.*

dis·am·big·u·ate (dĭs′ăm-bĭg′yo͞o-āt′) *tr.v.* **-at·ed, -at·ing, -ates.** To establish a single grammatical or semantic interpretation for. **—dis′am·big′u·a′tion** *n.*

dis·an·nul (dĭs′ə-nŭl′) *tr.v.* **-nulled, -null·ing, -nuls.** To annul or cancel. **—dis′an·nul′ment** *n.*

dis·ap·pear (dĭs′ə-pîr′) *intr.v.* **-peared, -pear·ing, -pears. 1.** To pass out of sight; vanish. **2.** To cease to exist. **—dis′ap·pear′ance** *n.*

SYNONYMS: *disappear, evanesce, evaporate, fade, vanish.* The central meaning shared by these verbs is "to pass out of sight or existence": *a skyscraper disappearing in the fog; time seeming to evanesce; courage evaporating; hopes fading away; memories vanishing slowly but surely.*
ANTONYM: *appear.*

dis·ap·point (dĭs′ə-point′) *v.* **-point·ed, -point·ing, -points.** *—tr.* **1.** To fail to satisfy the hope, desire, or expectation of. **2.** To frustrate or thwart. *—intr.* To cause disappointment. [Middle English *disappointen,* from Old French *desapointier,* to remove from office : *des-,* dis- + *apointer,* to appoint; see APPOINT.]

dis·ap·point·ed (dĭs′ə-poin′tĭd) *adj.* Thwarted in hope, desire, or expectation. **—dis′ap·point′ed·ly** *adv.*

dis·ap·point·ing (dĭs′ə-poin′tĭng) *adj.* Not up to expectations: *finished the marathon in a disappointing 12th place.* **—dis′ap·point′ing·ly** *adv.*

dis·ap·point·ment (dĭs′ə-point′mənt) *n.* **1.a.** The act of disappointing. **b.** The condition or feeling of being disappointed. **2.** One that disappoints.

dis·ap·pro·ba·tion (dĭs-ăp′rə-bā′shən) *n.* Moral disapproval; condemnation.

dis·ap·prov·al (dĭs′ə-pro͞o′vəl) *n.* The act of disapproving; condemnation or censure.

dis·ap·prove (dĭs′ə-pro͞ov′) *v.* **-proved, -prov·ing, -proves.** *—tr.* **1.** To have an unfavorable opinion of; condemn. **2.** To refuse to approve; reject. *—intr.* To have an unfavorable opinion: *disapproves of drinking.* **—dis′ap·prov′er** *n.* **—dis′ap·prov′ing·ly** *adv.*

dis·arm (dĭs-ärm′) *v.* **-armed, -arm·ing, -arms.** *—tr.* **1.a.** To divest of a weapon or weapons. **b.** To deprive of the means of attack or defense; render harmless. *"Have the courage to appear poor, and you disarm poverty of its sharpest sting"* (Washington Irving). **2.a.** To overcome or allay the suspicion, hostility, or antagonism of. **b.** To win the confidence of. *—intr.* **1.** To lay down arms. **2.** To reduce or abolish armed forces. [Middle English *disarmen,* from Old French *desarmer* : *des-,* dis- + *armer,* to arm (from Latin *armāre,* from *arma,* weapons; see **ar-** in Appendix).] **—dis·arm′er** *n.*

dis·ar·ma·ment (dĭs-är′mə-mənt) *n.* **1.** The act of laying down arms, especially the reduction or abolition of a nation's military forces and armaments. **2.** The condition of being disarmed.

dis·arm·ing (dĭs-är′mĭng) *adj.* Tending to allay suspicion or hostility; winning favor or confidence: *a disarming smile.* **—dis·arm′ing·ly** *adv.*

dis·ar·range (dĭs′ə-rānj′) *tr.v.* **-ranged, -rang·ing, -rang·es.** To upset the proper arrangement or order of. **—dis′ar·range′ment** *n.*

dis·ar·ray (dĭs′ə-rā′) *n.* **1.** A state of disorder; confusion. **2.** Disorderly dress. **—disarray** *tr.v.* **-rayed, -ray·ing, -rays. 1.** To throw into confusion; upset. **2.** To undress.

dis·ar·tic·u·late (dĭs′är-tĭk′yə-lāt′) *v.* **-lat·ed, -lat·ing, -lates.** *—tr.* To separate at the joints; disjoint. *—intr.* To become disjointed. **—dis′ar·tic′u·la′tion** *n.* **—dis′ar·tic′u·la′tor** *n.*

dis·as·sem·ble (dĭs′ə-sĕm′bəl) *v.* **-bled, -bling, -bles.** *—tr.* To take apart: *disassemble a toaster.* *—intr.* **1.** To come apart: *The unit disassembles easily.* **2.** To break up in random fashion: *The spectators began to disassemble.* **—dis′as·sem′bly** *n.*

dis·as·so·ci·ate (dĭs′ə-sō′shē-āt′, -sē-) *tr.v.* **-at·ed, -at·ing, -ates.** To remove from association; dissociate. **—dis′as·so′ci·a′tion** *n.*

dis·as·ter (dĭ-zăs′tər, -săs′-) *n.* **1.a.** An occurrence causing widespread destruction and distress; a catastrophe. **b.** A grave misfortune. **2.** *Informal.* A total failure: *The dinner party was a disaster.* **3.** *Obsolete.* An evil influence of a star or planet. [French *désastre,* from Italian *disastro* : *dis-,* pejorative pref. (from Latin *dis-;* see DIS–) + *astro,* star (from Latin *astrum,* from Greek *astron;* see **ster-**[3] in Appendix).]

SYNONYMS: *disaster, calamity, catastrophe, cataclysm.* These nouns refer to an event having fatal or ruinous results. *Disaster* generally implies great destruction, hardship, or loss of life: *"A nuclear disaster, spread by winds and waters and fear, could well engulf the great and the small, the rich and the poor, the committed and the uncommitted alike"* (John F. Kennedy). *Calamity* emphasizes distress, grief, or the sense of loss: *"the heaviest calamity in English history, the breach with America"* (James George Frazer). *Catastrophe* especially stresses the sense of a tragic final outcome: *"The unleashed power of the atom has changed everything save our modes of thinking, and we thus drift toward unparalleled catastrophes"* (Albert Einstein). A *cataclysm* is a violent upheaval that brings about a fundamental change: *old aristocratic institutions destroyed by the revolutionary cataclysm.*

disaster area *n.* An area that officially qualifies for emergency governmental aid as a result of a catastrophe, such as an earthquake or a flood.

dis·as·trous (dĭ-zăs′trəs, -săs′-) *adj.* **1.** Accompanied by or causing distress or disaster; calamitous. **2.** Extremely bad; terrible: *a disastrous report card.* **—dis·as′trous·ly** *adv.* **—dis·as′trous·ness** *n.*

dis·a·vow (dĭs′ə-vou′) *tr.v.* **-vowed, -vow·ing, -vows.** To disclaim knowledge of, responsibility for, or association with. [Middle English *disavowen,* from Old French *desavouer* : *des-,* dis- + *avouer,* to avow; see AVOW.] **—dis′a·vow′a·ble** *adj.* **—dis′a·vow′al** *n.*

dis·band (dĭs-bănd′) *v.* **-band·ed, -band·ing, -bands.** *—tr.* To dissolve the organization of (a corporation, for example). *—intr.* To cease to function as an organization; disperse. [Obsolete French *desbander,* to separate someone from a troop : *des-,* dis- + Old French *band,* troop; see BAND[2].] **—dis·band′ment** *n.*

dis·bar (dĭs-bär′) *tr.v.* **-barred, -bar·ring, -bars.** *Law.* To expel (an attorney) from the practice of law by official action or procedure. **—dis·bar′ment** *n.*

dis·be·lief (dĭs′bĭ-lēf′) *n.* Refusal or reluctance to believe.

dis·be·lieve (dĭs′bĭ-lēv′) *v.* **-lieved, -liev·ing, -lieves.** *—tr.* To refuse to believe in; reject. *—intr.* To withhold or reject belief. **—dis′be·liev′er** *n.* **—dis′be·liev′ing·ly** *adv.*

dis·branch (dĭs-brănch′) *tr.v.* **-branched, -branch·ing, -branch·es. 1.** To cut or break a branch from (a tree). **2.** To remove (a limb or branch) from a tree.

dis·bud (dĭs-bŭd′) *tr.v.* **-bud·ded, -bud·ding, -buds. 1.** To remove buds from (a plant) to promote better blooms from the remaining buds or control the shape of the plant. **2.a.** To prevent the growth of newly developing horns on (livestock). **b.** To remove such horns from (livestock).

dis·bur·den (dĭs-bûr′dn) *v.* **-dened, -den·ing, -dens.** *—tr.* **1.a.** To relieve (a pack animal, for example) of a burden. **b.** To free of a burden or trouble: *disburden one's mind.* **2.** To unload: *disburdened the goods in the shipping room.* *—intr.* To unload a burden. **—dis·bur′den·ment** *n.*

dis·bur·sal (dĭs-bûr′səl) *n.* Disbursement.

dis·burse (dĭs-bûrs′) *tr.v.* **-bursed, -burs·ing, -burs·es.** To pay out, as from a fund; expend. See Synonyms at **spend.** [Obsolete French *desbourser,* from Old French *desborser* : *des-,* dis- + *borse,* purse (from Late Latin *bursa,* purse; see BURSA).] **—dis·burs′a·ble** *adj.* **—dis·burs′er** *n.*

dis·burse·ment (dĭs-bûrs′mənt) *n.* **1.** The act or process of disbursing. **2.** Money paid out; expenditure.

disc (dĭsk) *n. & v.* Variant of **disk.**

disc. *abbr.* Discount.

disc– *pref.* Variant of **disco–.**

dis·calced (dĭs-kălst′) *adj.* Barefoot or wearing sandals. Used of certain religious orders. [From Latin *discalceātus* : *dis-,* dis- + *calceātus,* shod (from *calceus,* shoe, from *calx, calc-,* heel).]

dis·cant (dĭs′kănt′) *Music. n.* Variant of **descant** (sense 1). **—discant** (dĭs′kănt′, dĭ-skănt′) *v.* Variant of **descant** (sense 2).

dis·card (dĭ-skärd′) *v.* **-card·ed, -card·ing, -cards.** *—tr.* **1.** To throw away; reject. **2.** *Games.* **a.** To throw out (a playing card) from one's hand. **b.** To play (a card other than a trump) from a suit different from that of the card led. *—intr. Games.* To discard a playing card. **—discard** (dĭs′kärd′) *n.* **1.** *Games.* **a.** The act of discarding in a card game. **b.** A discarded playing card. **2.** One that is discarded or rejected. **—dis·card′a·ble** *adj.* **—dis·card′er** *n.*

dis·car·nate (dĭs-kär′nĭt, -nāt′) *adj.* Having no material body or form: *a discarnate spirit.* [DIS– + (IN)CARNATE.] **—dis·car′nate** *n.*

disc brake also **disk brake** *n.* A brake in which the friction is caused by a set of pads that press against a rotating disk.

dis·cern (dĭ-sûrn′, -zûrn′) *v.* **-cerned, -cern·ing, -cerns.** *—tr.* **1.** To perceive with the eyes or intellect; detect. **2.** To

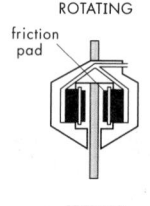

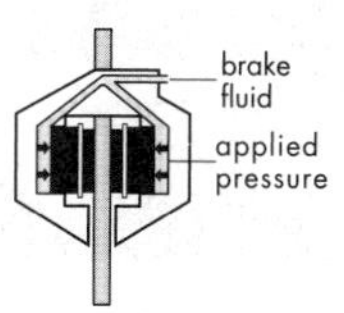

disc brake

ă pat	oi boy
ā pay	ou out
âr care	o͝o took
ä father	o͞o boot
ĕ pet	ŭ cut
ē be	ûr urge
ĭ pit	th thin
ī pie	*th* this
îr pier	hw which
ŏ pot	zh vision
ō toe	ə about, item
ô paw	♦ regionalism

Stress marks: **′** (primary); ′ (secondary), as in **dictionary** (dĭk′shə-nĕr′ē)

recognize or comprehend mentally. **3.** To perceive or recognize as being different or distinct; distinguish. See Synonyms at **see**[1]. —*intr.* To perceive differences. [Middle English *discernen,* from Old French *discerner,* from Latin *discernere,* to separate : *dis-,* apart; see DIS– + *cernere,* to perceive; see **krei-** in Appendix.] —**dis·cern′er** *n.*

dis·cern·i·ble (dĭ-sûr′nə-bəl, -zûr′-) *adj.* Perceptible, as by the faculty of vision or the intellect. See Synonyms at **perceptible.** —**dis·cern′·i·bly** *adv.*

dis·cern·ing (dĭ-sûr′nĭng, -zûr′-) *adj.* Exhibiting keen insight and good judgment; perceptive. —**dis·cern′ing·ly** *adv.*

dis·cern·ment (dĭ-sûrn′mənt, -zûrn′-) *n.* **1.** The act or process of exhibiting keen insight and good judgment. **2.** Keenness of insight and judgment.

dis·charge (dĭs-chärj′) *v.* **-charged, -charg·ing, -charg·es.** *Abbr.* **dis.** —*tr.* **1. a.** To relieve of a burden or of contents; unload. **b.** To unload or empty (contents). **2. a.** To release, as from confinement, care, or duty: *discharge a patient; discharge a soldier.* **b.** To let go; empty out: *a train discharging commuters.* **c.** To pour forth; emit: *a vent discharging steam.* **d.** To shoot: *discharge a pistol.* **3.** To remove from office or employment. See Synonyms at **dismiss. 4.** To perform the obligations or demands of (an office, duty, or task). See Synonyms at **perform. 5.** To comply with the terms of (a debt or promise, for example). **6.** *Law.* **a.** To acquit completely: *discharged the defendant.* **b.** To set aside; annul: *discharge a court order.* **7.** To remove (color) from cloth, as by chemical bleaching. **8.** *Electricity.* To cause the release of stored energy or electric charge from (a battery, for example). **9.** *Architecture.* **a.** To apportion (weight) evenly, as over a door. **b.** To relieve (a part) of excess weight by distribution of pressure. —*intr. Abbr.* **dis. 1.** To get rid of a burden, load, or weight. **2. a.** To go off; fire: *The musket discharged loudly.* **b.** To pour forth, emit, or release contents. **c.** To become blurred, as a color or dye; run. **3.** To undergo the release of stored energy or electric charge. —**discharge** (dĭs′chärj′, dĭs-chärj′) *n. Abbr.* **dis. 1.** The act of removing a load or burden. **2.** The act of shooting or firing a projectile or weapon. **3. a.** A flowing out or pouring forth; emission; secretion: *a discharge of pus.* **b.** The amount or rate of emission or ejection. **c.** Something that is discharged, released, emitted, or excreted: *a watery discharge.* **4.** The act or an instance of removing an obligation, a burden, or a responsibility. **5. a.** Fulfillment of the terms of something, such as a debt or promise. **b.** Performance, as of an office or a duty. **6. a.** Dismissal or release from employment, service, care, or confinement. **b.** An official document certifying such release, especially from military service. **7.** *Law.* An annulment or acquittal; dismissal, as of a court order. **8.** *Electricity.* **a.** Release of stored energy in a capacitor by the flow of current between its terminals. **b.** Conversion of chemical energy to electric energy in a storage battery. **c.** A flow of electricity in a dielectric, especially in a rarefied gas. **d.** Elimination of net electric charge from a charged body. [Middle English *dischargen,* from Old French *deschargier,* from Late Latin *discarricāre* : Latin *dis-,* dis- + Late Latin *carricāre,* to load; see CHARGE.] —**dis·charge′a·ble** *adj.* —**dis′-charg·ee′** *n.* —**dis·charg′er** *n.*

disc jockey

discharge lamp *n.* A lamp that generates light by means of an internal electrical discharge between electrodes in a gas.

discharge tube *n.* A closed insulating vessel containing a gas at low pressure through which an electric current flows when sufficient voltage is applied to its electrodes.

disc harrow *n.* Variant of **disk harrow.**

disci– *pref.* Variant of **disco–.**

dis·ci·form (dĭs′ə-fôrm′, dĭs′kə-) *adj.* Flat and rounded in shape; discoid: *disciform fungi.*

dis·ci·ple (dĭ-sī′pəl) *n.* **1. a.** One who embraces and assists in spreading the teachings of another. **b.** An active adherent, as of a movement or philosophy. **2.** Often **Disciple.** One of the 12 original followers of Jesus. **3. Disciple.** A member of the Disciples of Christ. [Middle English, from Old English *discipul* and from Old French *desciple,* both from Latin *discipulus,* pupil, from *discere,* to learn. See **dek-** in Appendix.] —**dis·ci′ple·ship′** *n.*

Dis·ci·ples of Christ (dĭ-sī′pəlz) *pl.n.* *(used with a sing. or pl. verb).* A Christian denomination founded in 1809 that accepts the Bible as the only rule of Christian faith and practice, rejects denominational creeds, and practices baptism by immersion.

dis·ci·plin·a·ble (dĭs′ə-plĭn′ə-bəl, dĭs′ə-plĭn′-) *adj.* **1.** Deserving of or subject to discipline: *a disciplinable misdeed.* **2.** Responsive to training; easily taught.

dis·ci·pli·nar·i·an (dĭs′ə-plə-nâr′ē-ən) *n.* One that enforces or believes in strict discipline. —**disciplinarian** *adj.* Disciplinary.

dis·ci·pli·nar·y (dĭs′ə-plə-nĕr′ē) *adj.* **1.** Of, relating to, or used for discipline: *disciplinary training; disciplinary measures.* **2.** Of or relating to a specific field of academic study. —**dis′-ci·pli·nar′i·ly** (-nâr′ə-lē) *adv.* —**dis′ci·pli·nar′i·ty** (-nâr′-ĭ-tē, -năr′-) *n.*

dis·ci·pline (dĭs′ə-plĭn) *n.* **1.** Training expected to produce a specific character or pattern of behavior, especially training that produces moral or mental improvement. **2.** Controlled behavior resulting from disciplinary training; self-control. **3. a.** Control obtained by enforcing compliance or order. **b.** A systematic method to obtain obedience: *a military discipline.* **c.** A state of order based on submission to rules and authority: *a teacher who demanded discipline in the classroom.* **4.** Punishment intended to correct or train. **5.** A set of rules or methods, as those regulating the practice of a church or monastic order. **6.** A branch of knowledge or teaching. —**discipline** *tr.v.* **-plined, -plin·ing, -plines. 1.** To train by instruction and practice, especially to teach self-control to. **2.** To teach to obey rules or accept authority. See Synonyms at **teach. 3.** To punish in order to gain control or enforce obedience. See Synonyms at **punish. 4.** To impose order on: *needed to discipline their study habits.* [Middle English, from Old French *descepline,* from Latin *disciplīna,* from *discipulus,* pupil. See DISCIPLE.] —**dis′ci·pli·nal** (-plə-nəl) *adj.* —**dis′ci·plin′er** *n.*

dis·ci·plined (dĭs′ə-plĭnd) *adj.* Possessing or indicative of discipline: *a dancer's disciplined body; a disciplined set of work habits.*

disc jockey also **disk jockey** *n. Abbr.* **DJ** An announcer who presents and comments on popular recorded music, especially on the radio.

dis·claim (dĭs-klām′) *v.* **-claimed, -claim·ing, -claims.** —*tr.* **1.** To deny or renounce any claim to or connection with; disown. **2.** To deny the validity of; repudiate. **3.** *Law.* To renounce one's right or claim to. —*intr. Law.* To renounce a right or claim. [Middle English *disclaimen,* from Anglo-Norman *desclaimer* : *des-,* dis- + *claimer,* to claim (from Latin *clāmāre,* to cry out; see CLAIM).]

dis·claim·er (dĭs-klā′mər) *n.* **1.** A repudiation or denial of responsibility or connection. **2.** *Law.* A renunciation of one's right or claim. [Middle English, denial of a feudal claim, from Anglo-Norman *desclaimer,* to disclaim, denial of a feudal claim. See DISCLAIM.]

dis·cla·ma·tion (dĭs′klə-mā′shən) *n.* The act or an instance of disavowing; renunciation. [Probably from Anglo-Norman *desclaimer, disclamer,* to disclaim. See DISCLAIM.]

dis·cli·max (dĭs-klī′măks′) *n. Ecology.* A climax community that has been disturbed by various influences, especially by human beings and domestic animals, such as a grassland community that has been altered to desert by overgrazing.

dis·close (dĭ-sklōz′) *tr.v.* **-closed, -clos·ing, -clos·es. 1.** To expose to view, as by removing a cover; uncover. **2.** To make known (something heretofore kept secret). See Synonyms at **reveal**[1]. [Middle English *disclosen,* from Old French *desclore, desclos-* : *des-,* dis- + *clore,* to close (from Latin *claudere*).] —**dis·clos′a·ble** *adj.* —**dis·clos′er** *n.*

dis·clos·ing agent (dĭ-sklō′zĭng) *n.* A dye used in dentistry as a diagnostic aid, applied to the teeth to reveal the presence of dental plaque. Also called *disclosing solution.*

dis·clo·sure (dĭ-sklō′zhər) *n.* **1.** The act or process of revealing or uncovering. **2.** Something uncovered; a revelation.

dis·co (dĭs′kō) *n., pl.* **-cos. 1.** A discotheque. **2. a.** *Music.* Popular dance music characterized by strong repetitive bass rhythms. **b.** A style of dancing done especially to disco music. —**disco** *intr.v.* **-coed, -co·ing, -cos.** To dance to disco music. [Short for DISCOTHEQUE.] —**dis′co** *adj.*

disco– or **disc–** also **disci–** *pref.* **1.** Disk: *discoid.* **2.** Phonograph record: *discophile.* [Latin, from Greek *disko-,* from *diskos,* disk. See DISK.]

dis·cog·ra·phy (dĭ-skŏg′rə-fē) *n., pl.* **-phies. 1.** The study and cataloguing of phonograph records. **2.** A comprehensive list of the recordings made by a particular performer or of a particular composer's works. .—**dis·cog′ra·pher** *n.* —**dis′co·graph′i·cal** (dĭs′kə-grăf′ĭ-kəl), **dis′co·graph′ic** (-grăf′ĭk) *adj.*

dis·coid (dĭs′koid′) also **dis·coi·dal** (dĭ-skoid′l) *adj.* **1.** Having a flat, circular form; disk-shaped. **2.** Related to or having a disk. **3.** *Botany.* Having disk flowers only. Used of a composite flower head. —**dis′coid′** *n.*

dis·col·or (dĭs-kŭl′ər) *v.* **-ored, -or·ing, -ors.** —*tr.* To alter or spoil the color of; stain. —*intr.* To become altered or spoiled in color. [Middle English *discolouren,* from Old French *discolerer* : *des-,* dis- + *colourer,* to color (from Latin *colōrāre,* from *color,* color; see COLOR).]

dis·col·or·a·tion (dĭs-kŭl′ə-rā′shən) *n.* **1. a.** The act of discoloring. **b.** The condition of being discolored. **2.** A discolored spot, smudge, or area; a stain.

dis·com·bob·u·late (dĭs′kəm-bŏb′yə-lāt′) *tr.v.* **-lat·ed, -lat·ing, -lates.** To throw into a state of confusion. See Synonyms at **confuse.** [Perhaps alteration of DISCOMPOSE.] —**dis′-com·bob′u·la′tion** *n.*

dis·com·fit (dĭs-kŭm′fĭt) *tr.v.* **-fit·ed, -fit·ing, -fits. 1.** To make uneasy or perplexed; disconcert. See Synonyms at **embarrass. 2.** To thwart the plans of; frustrate. **3.** *Archaic.* To defeat in battle; vanquish. —**discomfit** *n.* Discomfiture. [Middle English *discomfiten,* from Old French *desconfit,* past participle of *desconfire, descumfire,* to defeat : *des-,* dis- + *confire,* to make (from Latin *cōnficere,* to prepare; see COMFIT).]

USAGE NOTE: It is true that *discomfit* originally meant "to defeat, frustrate," and that its newer use meaning "to embarrass, disconcert," probably arose in part through confusion with *discomfort.* But the newer sense is now the most common use of the verb in all varieties of writing and should be considered entirely standard.

dis·com·fi·ture (dĭs-kŭm′fĭ-chŏŏr′, -chər) *n.* **1.** Frustration or disappointment. **2.** Lack of ease; perplexity and embarrassment. **3.** *Archaic.* Defeat.

dis·com·fort (dĭs-kŭm′fərt) *n.* **1.** Mental or bodily distress. **2.** Something that disturbs one's comfort; annoyance. **—discomfort** *tr.v.* **-fort·ed, -fort·ing, -forts.** To make uncomfortable; distress. See Usage Note at **discomfit.** [Middle English, from Old French *desconfort,* from *desconforter,* to discourage : *des-,* dis- + *conforter,* to strengthen; see COMFORT.] **—dis·com′fort·a·ble** (-kŭm′fər-tə-bəl, -kŭmf′tə-bəl) *adj.* **—dis·com′fort·ing·ly** *adv.*

dis·com·mend (dĭs′kə-mĕnd′) *tr.v.* **-mend·ed, -mend·ing, -mends. 1.** To show or voice disapproval of. **2.** To cause to come into disfavor or ill regard. **—dis′com·mend′a·ble** *adj.*

dis·com·mode (dĭs′kə-mōd′) *tr.v.* **-mod·ed, -mod·ing, -modes.** To put to inconvenience; trouble. [DIS– + *commode,* to suit (from Latin *commodāre,* from *commodus,* convenient; see COMMODIOUS).]

dis·com·pose (dĭs′kəm-pōz′) *tr.v.* **-posed, -pos·ing, -pos·es. 1.** To disturb the composure or calm of; perturb. **2.** To put into a state of disorder. **—dis′com·pos′ed·ly** (-pō′zĭd-lē) *adv.* **—dis′com·pos′ing·ly** *adv.*

dis·com·po·sure (dĭs′kəm-pō′zhər) *n.* Absence of composure.

dis·con·cert (dĭs′kən-sûrt′) *tr.v.* **-cert·ed, -cert·ing, -certs. 1.** To upset the self-possession of; ruffle. See Synonyms at **embarrass. 2.** To frustrate (plans, for example) by throwing into disorder; disarrange. [Obsolete French *disconcerter,* from Old French *desconcerter* : *des-,* dis- + *concerter,* to bring into agreement (from Old Italian *concertare*).] **—dis′con·cert′ing·ly** *adv.*

dis·con·form·i·ty (dĭs′kən-fôr′mĭ-tē) *n., pl.* **-ties. 1.** *Geology.* A type of unconformity in which the rock layers are parallel. **2.** Refusal or failure to conform; nonconformity.

dis·con·nect (dĭs′kə-nĕkt′) *v.* **-nect·ed, -nect·ing, -nects.** *—tr.* **1.** To sever or interrupt the connection of or between: *disconnected the hose.* **2.** *Electricity.* To shut off the current in (an appliance) by removing its connection to a power source. *—intr.* To sever or interrupt a connection. **—dis′con·nec′tion** *n.*

dis·con·nect·ed (dĭs′kə-nĕk′tĭd) *adj.* **1.** Not connected; separate or detached. **2.** Marked by unrelated parts; incoherent: *described the accident in a disconnected way.* **—dis′con·nect′ed·ly** *adv.* **—dis′con·nect′ed·ness** *n.*

dis·con·so·late (dĭs-kŏn′sə-lĭt) *adj.* **1.** Seeming beyond consolation; extremely dejected: *disconsolate at the loss of the dog.* **2.** Cheerless; gloomy: *a disconsolate winter landscape.* [Middle English, from Medieval Latin *discōnsōlātus* : Latin *dis-,* dis- + *cōnsōlātus,* past participle of *cōnsōlārī,* to console; see CONSOLE[1].] **—dis·con′so·late·ly** *adv.* **—dis·con′so·late·ness, dis·con′so·la′tion** (-kŏn′sə-lā′shən) *n.*

dis·con·tent (dĭs′kən-tĕnt′) *n.* **1.a.** Absence of contentment; dissatisfaction. **b.** A restless longing for better circumstances. **2.** One who is discontented. **—discontent** *adj.* Discontented. **—discontent** *tr.v.* **-tent·ed, -tent·ing, -tents.** To make discontented. **—dis′con·tent′ment** *n.*

dis·con·tent·ed (dĭs′kən-tĕn′tĭd) *adj.* Restlessly unhappy; malcontent. **—dis′con·tent′ed·ly** *adv.* **—dis′con·tent′ed·ness** *n.*

dis·con·tin·u·ance (dĭs′kən-tĭn′yo͞o-əns) *n.* **1.** The act or an instance of discontinuing or the condition of being discontinued; cessation. **2.** *Law.* Termination of an action by the plaintiff.

dis·con·tin·u·a·tion (dĭs′kən-tĭn′yo͞o-ā′shən) *n.* A cessation; a discontinuance.

dis·con·tin·ue (dĭs′kən-tĭn′yo͞o) *v.* **-ued, -u·ing, -ues.** *—tr.* **1.** To put a stop to; terminate. **2.** To cease trying to accomplish or continue; abandon. **3.** *Law.* To terminate (an action) by discontinuance. *—intr.* To come to an end. See Synonyms at **stop.** [Middle English *discontinuen,* from Old French *descontinuer,* from Medieval Latin *discontinuāre* : Latin *dis-,* dis- + Latin *continuāre,* to continue; see CONTINUE.]

dis·con·ti·nu·i·ty (dĭs-kŏn′tə-no͞o′ĭ-tē, -nyo͞o′-) *n., pl.* **-ties. 1.** Lack of continuity, logical sequence, or cohesion. **2.** A break or gap. **3.** *Geology.* A surface at which seismic wave velocities change. **4.** *Mathematics.* **a.** A point at which a function is defined but is not continuous. **b.** A point at which a function is undefined.

dis·con·tin·u·ous (dĭs′kən-tĭn′yo͞o-əs) *adj.* **1.a.** Marked by breaks or interruptions; intermittent: *discontinuous applause.* **b.** Consisting of distinct or unconnected elements, such as the physical features of a landscape. **c.** Being without sequential order or coherent form. **2.** *Mathematics.* Possessing one or more discontinuities, as a function. **—dis′con·tin′u·ous·ly** *adv.* **—dis′con·tin′u·ous·ness** *n.*

discontinuous variation *n. Biology.* Variation within a population in which few or no intermediate phenotypes fall between the extremes.

dis·co·phile (dĭs′kə-fīl′) *n.* A collector of or specialist in phonograph records.

dis·cord (dĭs′kôrd′) *n.* **1.a.** Lack of agreement among persons, groups, or things. **b.** Tension or strife resulting from a lack of agreement; dissension. **2.** A confused or harsh sound or mingling of sounds. **3.** *Music.* Inharmonious combination of simultaneously sounded tones; dissonance. **—discord** (dĭ-skôrd′, dĭs′kôrd′) *intr.v.* **-cord·ed, -cord·ing, -cords.** To fail to agree or harmonize; clash. [Middle English, from Old French *descorde,* from Latin *discordia,* from *discors, discord-,* disagreeing : *dis-,* apart; see DIS– + *cor,* heart; see **kerd-** in Appendix.]

SYNONYMS: *discord, strife, contention, dissension, conflict, clash, variance.* These nouns are compared as they mean a state of disagreement and disharmony. *Discord* is a lack of harmony often marked by bickering and antipathy: *family discord. Strife* usually implies a struggle, often destructive, between rivals or factions: *a measure intended to end party strife. Contention* in this sense is largely limited to dispute in the form of heated debate or quarreling: *Political discussions often give rise to lively contention. Dissension* implies difference of opinion that disrupts unity within a group: *Dissension is rampant among the members of the committee. Conflict* suggests antagonism of ideas or interests that often results in hostility or divisiveness: *conflict between smoking and nonsmoking factions. Clash* implies sharp conflict involving irreconcilable ideas or interests: *had to exercise all her tact to prevent clashes between the two opinionated guests. Variance* usually suggests discrepancy or incompatibility: *His actions are often at variance with his principles.*

dis·cord·ance (dĭ-skôr′dns) *n.* **1.** The state or an instance of disagreement; discord. **2.** *Genetics.* The presence of a given genetic trait in only one member of a pair of identical twins.

dis·cor·dant (dĭ-skôr′dnt) *adj.* **1.** Not being in accord; conflicting. See Synonyms at **inconsistent. 2.** Disagreeable in sound; harsh or dissonant. **—dis·cor′dan·cy** *n.* **—dis·cor′dant·ly** *adv.*

Dis·cor·di·a (dĭ-skôr′dē-ə) *n. Roman Mythology.* The goddess of strife, identified with the Greek Eris. [Latin, from *discordia,* discord. See DISCORD.]

dis·co·theque also **dis·co·thèque** (dĭs′kə-tĕk′, dĭs′kə-tĕk′) *n.* A nightclub that features dancing to recorded or sometimes live music and often has showy decor and elaborate lighting. [French, record library, discothèque, from Italian *discoteca,* record library : *disco,* disk, record (from Latin *discus,* quoit; see DISCUS) + *biblioteca,* library (from Latin *bibliothēca;* see BIBLIOTHECA).]

dis·count (dĭs′kount′, dĭs-kount′) *v.* **-count·ed, -count·ing, -counts.** *Abbr.* **dis., disc.** *—tr.* **1.** To deduct or subtract from a cost or price. **2.a.** To purchase or sell (a bill, note, or other commercial paper) at a reduction equal to the amount of interest that will accumulate before it matures. **b.** To lend money on (a commercial paper not immediately payable) after deducting the interest. **3.a.** To sell or offer for sale at a reduced price. **b.** To reduce in quantity or value. **4.a.** To leave out of account as being untrustworthy or exaggerated; disregard: *discount a rumor.* **b.** To underestimate the significance or effectiveness of; minimize: *took care not to discount his wife's accomplishments.* **c.** To regard with doubt or disbelief. **5.** To anticipate and make allowance for; reckon with in advance. *—intr.* To lend money after deduction of interest. **—discount** (dĭs′kount′) *n.* **1.** A reduction from the full or standard amount of a price or debt. **2.** The interest deducted prior to purchasing, selling, or lending a commercial paper; the discount rate. **3.** The act or an instance of discounting a bill of exchange, note, or other commercial paper. *—attributive.* Often used to modify another noun: *a discount market; discount merchandise.* [Alteration (influenced by DIS– and COUNT[1]) of French *décompter,* from Old French *desconter* : *des-,* away; see DIS– + *conter,* to count; see COUNT[1].] **—dis′count′a·ble** *adj.*

discount broker *n.* **1.** An agent who discounts a bill, note, or other commercial paper. **2.** A broker or brokerage house that gives a discount on commission fees. **—discount brokerage** *n.*

dis·coun·te·nance (dĭs-koun′tə-nəns) *tr.v.* **-nanced, -nanc·ing, -nanc·es. 1.** To view or treat with disfavor. **2.** To put out of countenance; disconcert. **—discountenance** *n.* Disfavor or disapproval.

dis·count·er (dĭs-koun′tər) *n.* **1.** One that discounts, as a person who runs a discount store or business. **2.** See **discount store.**

discount house *n.* See **discount store.**

discount rate *n.* **1.** The interest deducted in advance in purchasing, selling, or lending a commercial paper. **2.** The interest rate charged by the Federal Reserve Bank on loans to its member banks.

discount store *n.* A store that sells merchandise, especially consumer goods, at a discount from the manufacturer's suggested retail price. Also called *discounter, discount house.*

dis·cour·age (dĭ-skûr′ĭj, -skŭr′-) *tr.v.* **-aged, -ag·ing, -ag·es. 1.** To deprive of confidence, hope, or spirit. **2.** To hamper by discouraging; deter. **3.** To try to prevent by expressing disapproval or raising objections. [Middle English *discoragen,* from Old French *descoragier* : *des-,* dis- + *corage,* courage; see COURAGE.] **—dis·cour′age·a·ble** *adj.* **—dis·cour′ag·er** *n.* **—dis·cour′ag·ing·ly** *adv.*

SYNONYMS: *discourage, dishearten, dispirit.* The central meaning shared by these verbs is "to make less hopeful or enthusiastic": *discouraged by the magnitude of the problem; lack of interest that disheartened the instructor; a failure that dispirited the team.* See also Synonyms at **dissuade.**
ANTONYM: *encourage.*

dis·cour·age·ment (dĭ-skûr′ĭj-mənt, -skŭr′-) *n.* **1.a.** The

ă pat	oi boy
ā pay	ou out
âr care	o͝o took
ä father	o͞o boot
ĕ pet	ŭ cut
ē be	ûr urge
ĭ pit	th thin
ī pie	*th* this
îr pier	hw which
ŏ pot	zh vision
ō toe	ə about, item
ô paw	♦ regionalism

Stress marks: ′ (primary); ′ (secondary), as in **dictionary** (dĭk′shə-nĕr′ē)

act of discouraging. **b.** The condition of being discouraged. See Synonyms at **despair.** **2.** Something that discourages.

dis·course (dĭs′kôrs′, -kōrs′) *n.* **1.** Verbal expression in speech or writing. **2.** Verbal exchange; conversation. **3.** A formal, lengthy discussion of a subject, either written or spoken. **4.** *Archaic.* The process or power of reasoning. **—discourse** (dĭ-skôrs′, -skōrs′) *v.* **-coursed, -cours·ing, -cours·es.** *—intr.* **1.** To speak or write formally and at length. See Synonyms at **speak.** **2.** To engage in conversation or discussion; converse. *—tr. Archaic.* To narrate or discuss. [Middle English *discours,* process of reasoning, from Medieval Latin *discursus,* from Latin, a running about, from past participle of *discurrere,* to run about : *dis-,* apart; see DIS– + *currere,* to run; see **kers-** in Appendix.] **—dis·cours′er** *n.*

dis·cour·te·ous (dĭs-kûr′tē-əs) *adj.* Exhibiting no courtesy; rude. **—dis·cour′te·ous·ly** *adv.* **—dis·cour′te·ous·ness** *n.*

dis·cour·te·sy (dĭs-kûr′tĭ-sē) *n., pl.* **-sies. 1.** Lack of courtesy; rudeness. **2.** A rude act or statement.

dis·cov·er (dĭ-skŭv′ər) *tr.v.* **-ered, -er·ing, -ers. 1.** To obtain knowledge of, as through observation or study. **2.** To be the first to find, learn of, or observe. **3.** *Archaic.* To reveal or expose. [Middle English *discoveren,* to reveal, from Old French *descovrir,* from Late Latin *discooperīre* : *dis-,* dis- + *cooperīre,* to cover; see COVER.] **—dis·cov′er·a·ble** *adj.* **—dis·cov′er·er** *n.*

SYNONYMS: *discover, ascertain, determine, learn.* The central meaning shared by these verbs is "to gain knowledge or awareness of something not known before": *discovered that the world is round; ascertaining the facts; tried to determine the date of delivery; learned that her friend had married.*

dis·cov·er·y (dĭ-skŭv′ə-rē) *n., pl.* **-ies. 1.** The act or an instance of discovering. **2.** Something discovered. **3.** *Law.* Data or documents that a party to a legal action is compelled to disclose to another party either before or during a proceeding.

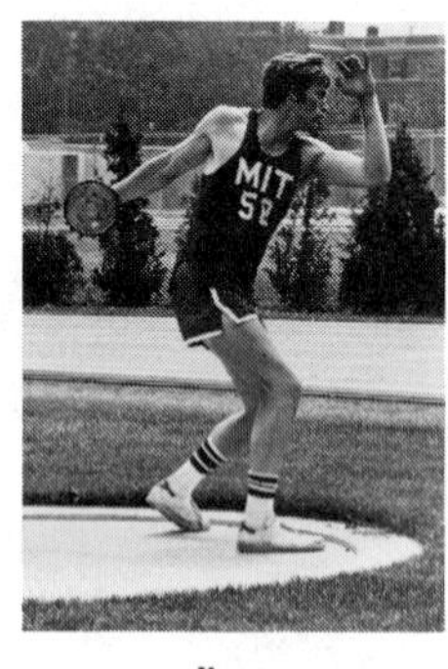

discus
Preparing to throw a discus

dis·cred·it (dĭs-krĕd′ĭt) *tr.v.* **-it·ed, -it·ing, -its. 1.** To damage in reputation; disgrace. **2.** To cause to be doubted or distrusted. **3.** To refuse to believe. **—discredit** *n.* **1.** Loss of or damage to one's reputation. See Synonyms at **disgrace. 2.** Lack or loss of trust or belief; doubt. **3.** Something damaging to one's reputation or stature.

dis·cred·it·a·ble (dĭs-krĕd′ĭ-tə-bəl) *adj.* Harmful to one's reputation; blameworthy: *discreditable behavior.* **—dis·cred′it·a·bly** *adv.*

dis·creet (dĭ-skrēt′) *adj.* **1.** Marked by, exercising, or showing prudence and wise self-restraint in speech and behavior; circumspect. **2.** Free from ostentation or pretension; modest. [Middle English, from Old French *discret,* from Medieval Latin *discrētus,* from Latin, past participle of *discernere,* separate, to discern. See DISCERN.] **—dis·creet′ly** *adv.* **—dis·creet′ness** *n.*

dis·crep·ance (dĭ-skrĕp′əns) *n.* Discrepancy.

dis·crep·an·cy (dĭ-skrĕp′ən-sē) *n., pl.* **-cies. 1.** Divergence or disagreement, as between facts. **2.** An instance of divergence or disagreement. See Synonyms at **difference.**

dis·crep·ant (dĭ-skrĕp′ənt) *adj.* Marked by discrepancy; disagreeing. See Synonyms at **inconsistent.** [Middle English *discrepaunt,* from Latin *discrepāns, discrepant-,* present participle of *discrepāre,* to disagree : *dis-,* apart; see DIS– + *crepāre,* to rattle.] **—dis·crep′ant·ly** *adv.*

dis·crete (dĭ-skrēt′) *adj.* **1.** Constituting a separate thing; distinct. **2.** Consisting of unconnected distinct parts. See Synonyms at **distinct. 3.** *Mathematics.* Defined for a finite set of values; not continuous. [Middle English, from Old French, from Latin *discrētus,* past participle of *discernere,* to separate. See DISCREET.] **—dis·crete′ly** *adv.* **—dis·crete′ness** *n.*

discrete variable *n. Mathematics.* A variable that assumes only whole number values.

dis·cre·tion (dĭ-skrĕsh′ən) *n.* **1.** The quality of being discreet; circumspection. See Synonyms at **prudence. 2.** Ability or power to decide responsibly. **3.** Freedom to act or judge on one's own: *All the decisions were left to our discretion.* **—dis·cre′tion·al** *adj.* **—dis·cre′tion·al·ly** *adv.*

dis·cre·tion·ar·y (dĭ-skrĕsh′ə-nĕr′ē) *adj.* **1.** Left to or regulated by one's own discretion or judgment. **2.** Available for use as needed or desired: *a discretionary fund.* **—dis·cre′tion·ar′i·ly** (-nâr′ə-lē) *adv.*

discretionary account *n.* A stock or commodity account in which an agent is free to trade without prior consultation with the customer.

discretionary income *n.* Individual income that is not allocated for necessary items such as food and shelter.

dis·cret·i·za·tion (dĭ-skrē′tĭ-zā′shən) *n. Mathematics.* The act of making mathematically discrete.

dis·crim·i·na·bil·i·ty (dĭ-skrĭm′ə-nə-bĭl′ĭ-tē) *n.* **1.** The quality of being discriminable. **2.** The capacity or power to discriminate.

dis·crim·i·na·ble (dĭs-krĭm′ə-nə-bəl) *adj.* That can be discriminated; distinguishable: *discriminable faults; a skyline that was discriminable even through smog.* **—dis·crim′i·na·bly** *adv.*

dis·crim·i·nant (dĭ-skrĭm′ə-nənt) *n. Mathematics.* An expression used to distinguish or separate other expressions in a quantity or an equation.

discriminant function *n. Statistics.* A function of a set of variables used to classify an object or event.

dis·crim·i·nate (dĭ-skrĭm′ə-nāt′) *v.* **-nat·ed, -nat·ing, -nates.** *—intr.* **1.a.** To make a clear distinction; distinguish: *discriminate among the options available.* **b.** To make sensible decisions; judge wisely. **2.** To make distinctions on the basis of class or category without regard to individual merit; show preference or prejudice: *was accused of discriminating against women; discriminated in favor of his cronies.* *—tr.* **1.** To perceive the distinguishing features of; recognize as distinct: *discriminate right from wrong.* **2.** To distinguish by noting differences; differentiate: *unable to discriminate colors.* [Latin *discrīmināre, discrīmināt-,* from *discrīmen, discrīmin-,* distinction. See **krei-** in Appendix.] **—dis·crim′i·nate** (-nĭt) *adj.* **—dis·crim′i·nate·ly** *adv.*

dis·crim·i·nat·ing (dĭ-skrĭm′ə-nā′tĭng) *adj.* **1.a.** Able to recognize or draw fine distinctions; perceptive. **b.** Showing careful judgment or fine taste: *a discriminating collector of rare books; a dish for the discriminating palate.* **2.** Separating into distinct parts or components; analytical. **3.** Serving to distinguish; distinctive: *a discriminating characteristic.* **4.** Marked by or showing bias; discriminatory. **—dis·crim′i·nat′ing·ly** *adv.*

dis·crim·i·na·tion (dĭ-skrĭm′ə-nā′shən) *n.* **1.** The act of discriminating. **2.** The ability or power to see or make fine distinctions; discernment. **3.** Treatment or consideration based on class or category rather than individual merit; partiality or prejudice: *"It's necessary to eliminate all forms of sexual discrimination"* (Jimmy Carter). See Usage Note at **bias.** **—dis·crim′i·na′tion·al** *adj.*

dis·crim·i·na·tive (dĭ-skrĭm′ə-nā′tĭv, -nə-tĭv) *adj.* **1.** Drawing distinctions. **2.** Marked by or showing prejudice: *discriminative hiring practices.* **—dis·crim′i·na′tive·ly** *adv.*

dis·crim·i·na·tor (dĭ-skrĭm′ə-nā′tər) *n.* **1.** One that discriminates. **2.** *Electronics.* A device that converts a property of an input signal, such as frequency or phase, into an amplitude variation, depending on how the signal differs from a standard or reference signal.

dis·crim·i·na·to·ry (dĭ-skrĭm′ə-nə-tôr′ē, -tōr′ē) *adj.* **1.** Marked by or showing prejudice; biased. **2.** Making distinctions. **—dis·crim′i·na·to′ri·ly** *adv.*

dis·cur·sive (dĭ-skûr′sĭv) *adj.* **1.** Covering a wide field of subjects; rambling. **2.** Proceeding to a conclusion through reason rather than intuition. [Medieval Latin *discursīvus,* from Latin *discursus,* running about. See DISCOURSE.] **—dis·cur′sive·ly** *adv.* **—dis·cur′sive·ness** *n.*

dis·cus (dĭs′kəs) *n., pl.* **-cus·es. 1.** *Sports.* **a.** A disk, typically wooden or plastic with a metal rim, that is thrown for distance in athletic competitions. **b.** A track and field event in which a discus is thrown. **2.** A small, brilliantly colored South American freshwater fish *(Symphysodon discus)* that has a disk-shaped body and is popular in home aquariums. **3.** Something resembling a flat, circular plate; a disk. **4.** *Botany.* See **disk** (sense 5). [Latin. See DISK.]

dis·cuss (dĭ-skŭs′) *tr.v.* **-cussed, -cuss·ing, -cuss·es. 1.** To speak with others about; talk over. **2.** To examine or consider (a subject) in speech or writing. [Middle English *discussen,* to examine, from Anglo-Norman *discusser,* from Latin *discussus,* past participle of *discutere,* to break up : *dis-,* apart; see DIS– + *quatere,* to shake; see **kwēt-** in Appendix.] **—dis·cuss′a·ble, dis·cuss′i·ble** *adj.* **—dis·cuss′er** *n.*

SYNONYMS: *discuss, argue, debate, dispute, contend.* These verbs mean to talk with others in an effort to reach agreement, to ascertain truth, or to convince. *Discuss* involves close examination of a subject with interchange of opinions: *"Men are never so likely to settle a question rightly as when they discuss it freely"* (Macaulay). *Argue* emphasizes the presentation of facts and reasons in support of a position opposed by others: *"There is no good in arguing with the inevitable"* (James Russell Lowell). *Debate* involves formal, often public argument: *The candidates agreed to debate the campaign issues face to face. Dispute* implies differences of opinion and usually sharp argument: *members of the legislature disputing over increases in the military budget.* To *contend* is to strive in debate or controversy: *"Letting a hundred flowers blossom and a hundred schools of thought contend is the policy"* (Mao Zedong).

dis·cuss·ant (dĭ-skŭs′ənt) *n.* A participant in a formal discussion.

dis·cus·sion (dĭ-skŭsh′ən) *n.* **1.** Consideration of a subject by a group; an earnest conversation. **2.** A formal discourse on a topic; an exposition.

dis·dain (dĭs-dān′) *tr.v.* **-dained, -dain·ing, -dains. 1.** To regard or treat with haughty contempt; despise. See Synonyms at **despise. 2.** To consider or reject as beneath oneself. **—disdain** *n.* A feeling or show of contempt and aloofness; scorn. [Middle English *disdeinen,* from Old French *desdeignier,* from Vulgar Latin **disdignāre,* from Latin *dēdignārī* : *dē-,* de- + *dignārī,* to deem worthy (from *dignus,* worthy; see **dek-** in Appendix).]

dis·dain·ful (dĭs-dān′fəl) *adj.* Expressive of disdain; scornful and contemptuous. See Synonyms at **proud.** **—dis·dain′ful·ly** *adv.* **—dis·dain′ful·ness** *n.*

dis·ease (dĭ-zēz′) *n.* **1.** A pathological condition of a part, an organ, or a system of an organism resulting from various causes, such as infection, genetic defect, or environmental stress, and characterized by an identifiable group of signs or symptoms. **2.** A condition or tendency, as of society, regarded as abnormal and harmful. **3.** *Obsolete.* Lack of ease; trouble. [Middle English *disese,* from Old French : *des-,* dis- + *aise,* ease; see EASE.]

dis·eased (dĭ-zēzd′) *adj.* **1.** Affected with disease. **2.** Unsound or disordered.

dis·em·bark (dĭs′ĕm-bärk′) *v.* **-barked, -bark·ing, -barks.** —*intr.* **1.** To go ashore from a ship. **2.** To leave a vehicle or aircraft. —*tr.* To take ashore from a ship. [Probably obsolete French *desembarquer* : *des-,* dis- + *embarquer,* to embark; see EMBARK.] **—dis·em′bar·ka′tion** *n.*

dis·em·bar·rass (dĭs′ĕm-băr′əs) *tr.v.* **-rassed, -rass·ing, -rass·es.** To free from something bothersome or encumbering; relieve. **—dis′em·bar′rass·ment** *n.*

dis·em·bod·y (dĭs′ĕm-bŏd′ē) *tr.v.* **-ied, -y·ing, -ies. 1.** To free (the soul or spirit) from the body. **2.** To divest of material existence or substance. **—dis′em·bod′i·ment** *n.*

dis·em·bogue (dĭs′ĕm-bōg′) *v.* **-bogued, -bogu·ing, -bogues.** —*intr.* To flow out or empty, as water from a channel: *"the river whose dirty waters disembogue into the harbor"* (John Updike). —*tr.* To discharge or pour forth (water, for example). [From Spanish *desemboque,* mouth of a river, from *desembocar,* to flow out : *des-,* reversal (from Latin *dis-;* see DIS–) + *embocar,* to put into the mouth (*en-,* in, from Latin *in-;* see IN–[2] + *boca,* mouth, from Latin *bucca,* cheek).] **—dis′em·bogue′ment** *n.*

dis·em·bow·el (dĭs′ĕm-bou′əl) *tr.v.* **-eled, -el·ing, -els** or **-elled, -el·ling, -els. 1.** To remove the entrails from. **2.** To deprive of meaning or substance. **—dis′em·bow′el·ment** *n.*

dis·em·ploy (dĭs′ĕm-ploi′) *tr.v.* **-ployed, -ploy·ing, -ploys.** To deprive of employment. **—dis′em·ploy′ment** *n.*

dis·em·pow·er (dĭs′ĕm-pou′ər) *tr.v.* **-ered, -er·ing, -ers.** To deprive of power or influence. **—dis′em·pow′er·ment** *n.*

dis·en·a·ble (dĭs′ĕ-nā′bəl) *tr.v.* **-bled, -bling, -bles.** To make unable or incapable; prevent.

dis·en·chant (dĭs′ĕn-chănt′) *tr.v.* **-chant·ed, -chant·ing, -chants.** To free from illusion or false belief; undeceive. [Obsolete French *desenchanter,* from Old French, to break a spell : *des-,* dis- + *enchanter,* to enchant; see ENCHANT.] **—dis′en·chant′er** *n.* **—dis′en·chant′ing·ly** *adv.* **—dis′en·chant′ment** *n.*

dis·en·cum·ber (dĭs′ĕn-kŭm′bər) *tr.v.* **-bered, -ber·ing, -bers.** To relieve of burdens or hardships. [Obsolete French *desencombrer,* from Old French : *des-,* dis- + *encombrer,* to encumber; see ENCUMBER.] **—dis′en·cum′ber·ment** *n.*

dis·en·dow (dĭs′ĕn-dou′) *tr.v.* **-dowed, -dow·ing, -dows.** To deprive of financial endowment: *disendow a college.* **—dis′en·dow′er** *n.* **—dis′en·dow′ment** *n.*

dis·en·fran·chise (dĭs′ĕn-frăn′chīz′) *tr.v.* **-chised, -chis·ing, -chis·es.** To disfranchise. **—dis′en·fran′chise′ment** (-chīz′mənt, -chĭz-) *n.*

dis·en·gage (dĭs′ĕn-gāj′) *v.* **-gaged, -gag·ing, -gag·es.** —*tr.* **1.** To release from something that holds fast, connects, or entangles. See Synonyms at **extricate. 2.** To release (oneself) from an engagement, pledge, or obligation. —*intr.* To free or detach oneself; withdraw. **—dis′en·gage′ment** *n.*

dis·en·tail (dĭs′ĕn-tāl′) *tr.v.* **-tailed, -tail·ing, -tails.** *Law.* To release (an estate) from entail. **—dis′en·tail′ment** *n.*

dis·en·tan·gle (dĭs′ĕn-tăng′gəl) *v.* **-gled, -gling, -gles.** —*tr.* **1.** To extricate from entanglement or involvement; free. See Synonyms at **extricate. 2.** To clear up or resolve (a plot, for example); unravel. —*intr.* To become free of entanglement. **—dis′en·tan′gle·ment** *n.*

dis·en·thrall (dĭs′ĕn-thrôl′) *tr.v.* **-thralled, -thrall·ing, -thralls.** To free from a controlling force or influence.

dis·en·tomb (dĭs′ĕn-to͞om′) *tr.v.* **-tombed, -tomb·ing, -tombs.** To remove from or as if from a tomb.

dis·en·twine (dĭs′ĕn-twīn′) *tr. & intr.v.* **-twined, -twin·ing, -twines.** To untwine or become untwined.

dis·e·quil·i·brate (dĭs′ĭ-kwĭl′ə-brāt′) *tr.v.* **-brat·ed, -brat·ing, -brates.** To upset the equilibrium of (the economy, for example); unbalance. **—dis′e·quil′·i·bra′tion** *n.*

dis·e·qui·lib·ri·um (dĭs-ē′kwə-lĭb′rē-əm, -ĕk′wə-) *n.* Loss or lack of stability or equilibrium.

dis·es·tab·lish (dĭs′ĭ-stăb′lĭsh) *tr.v.* **-lished, -lish·ing, -lish·es. 1.** To alter the status of (something established by authority or general acceptance). **2.** To deprive (a church) of official governmental support. **—dis′es·tab′lish·ment** *n.*

dis·es·tab·lish·men·tar·i·an (dĭs′ĭ-stăb′lĭsh-mən-târ′ē-ən) *n.* Often **Disestablishmentarian.** An opponent of an established order, especially one who opposes state support of an established church. **—dis′es·tab′lish·men·tar′i·an** *adj.*

dis·es·teem (dĭs′ĭ-stēm′) *tr.v.* **-teemed, -teem·ing, -teems.** To hold in disfavor. **—disesteem** *n.* Lack of esteem; disfavor.

di·seur (dē-zûr′, -zœr′) *n.* A man who is a skilled and usually professional performer of monologues. [French, from Old French, from *dire, dis-,* to say, from Latin *dīcere.* See DICTION.]

di·seuse (dē-zœz′, də-) *n.* A woman who is a skilled and usually professional performer of monologues. [French, feminine of *diseur,* monologuist. See DISEUR.]

dis·fa·vor (dĭs-fā′vər) *n.* **1.** Unfavorable opinion or regard; disapproval. **2.** The condition of being regarded with disapproval. **—disfavor** *tr.v.* **-vored, -vor·ing, -vors.** To view or treat with dislike or disapproval.

dis·fea·ture (dĭs-fē′chər) *tr.v.* **-tured, -tur·ing, -tures.** To disfigure: *a face disfeatured by a deep scar.* **—dis·fea′ture·ment** *n.*

dis·fig·ure (dĭs-fĭg′yər) *tr.v.* **-ured, -ur·ing, -ures.** To mar or spoil the appearance or shape of; deform. [Middle English *disfiguren,* from Old French *desfigurer* : *des-,* dis- + *figure,* figure (from Latin *figūra,* shape; see **dheigh-** in Appendix).] **—dis·fig′u·ra′tion, dis·fig′ure·ment** *n.* **—dis·fig′ur·er** *n.*

dis·fran·chise (dĭs-frăn′chīz′) *tr.v.* **-chised, -chis·ing, -chis·es. 1.** To deprive of a privilege, an immunity, or a right of citizenship, especially the right to vote; disenfranchise. **2.** To deprive (a corporation) of a privilege or franchise. **—dis·fran′chise′ment** (-chīz′mənt, -chĭz-) *n.*

dis·frock (dĭs-frŏk′) *tr.v.* **-frocked, -frock·ing, -frocks.** To unfrock.

dis·func·tion (dĭs-fŭngk′shən) *n.* Variant of **dysfunction.**

dis·gorge (dĭs-gôrj′) *v.* **-gorged, -gorg·ing, -gorg·es.** —*tr.* **1.** To bring up and expel from the throat or stomach; vomit. **2.** To discharge violently; spew. **3.** To surrender (stolen goods or money, for example) unwillingly. —*intr.* To discharge or pour forth contents. [Middle English *disgorgen,* from Old French *desgorger* : *des-,* dis- + *gorger,* to pack (from *gorge,* throat; see GORGE).] **—dis·gorge′ment** *n.*

dis·grace (dĭs-grās′) *n.* **1.** Loss of honor, respect, or reputation; shame. **2.** The condition of being strongly and generally disapproved. **3.** One that brings disfavor or discredit: *Your handwriting is a disgrace.* **—disgrace** *tr.v.* **-graced, -grac·ing, -grac·es. 1.** To bring shame or dishonor on: *disgraced the entire community.* **2.** To deprive of favor or good repute; treat with disfavor: *The family was disgraced by the scandal.* [French *disgrâce,* from Italian *disgrazia* : *dis-,* not (from Latin; see DIS–) + *grazia,* favor (from Latin *grātia,* from *grātus,* pleasing; see **gʷerə-**[2] in Appendix).] **—dis·grac′er** *n.*

SYNONYMS: *disgrace, dishonor, shame, infamy, ignominy, odium, obloquy, opprobrium, disrepute, discredit.* These nouns denote the condition of being held in low regard. *Disgrace* implies strong disfavor or ostracism: *"Between the possibility of being hanged in all innocence, and the certainty of a public and merited disgrace, no gentleman of spirit could long hesitate"* (Robert Louis Stevenson). *Dishonor* means loss of esteem, respect, or good reputation previously enjoyed: *To fail while trying hard is no dishonor. Shame* suggests mortifying loss of status, such as that which might result from the commission of a moral offense: *"only the deep sense of some deathless shame"* (John Webster). *Infamy* is public disgrace or shameful notoriety: *"December 7, 1941—a date which will live in infamy"* (Franklin D. Roosevelt). *Ignominy* implies public contempt: *suffered the ignominy of being sent to prison. Odium* adds to *disgrace* the sense of being the object of general dislike or detestation: *"It was his lot to taste the bitterness of popular odium"* (Nathaniel Hawthorne). *Obloquy* implies being subjected to abuse and vilification: *"his long public life, so singularly checkered with good and evil, with glory and obloquy"* (Macaulay). *Opprobrium* is the condition of being harshly condemned: *"The name* [was] *a by-word of scorn and opprobrium throughout the city"* (Washington Irving). *Disrepute* involves lack or loss of a good name: *Because of the scandal the school has fallen into disrepute. Discredit* implies loss of esteem resulting from personal misconduct: *Your actions will bring discredit to your name.*

dis·grace·ful (dĭs-grās′fəl) *adj.* Bringing or warranting disgrace; shameful. **—dis·grace′ful·ly** *adv.* **—dis·grace′ful·ness** *n.*

dis·grun·tle (dĭs-grŭn′tl) *tr.v.* **-tled, -tling, -tles.** To make discontented. [DIS– + *gruntle,* to grumble (from Middle English *gruntelen,* frequentative of *grunten,* to grunt; see GRUNT).] **—dis·grun′tle·ment** *n.*

dis·guise (dĭs-gīz′) *tr.v.* **-guised, -guis·ing, -guis·es. 1.a.** To modify the manner or appearance of in order to prevent recognition. **b.** To furnish with a disguise. **2.** To conceal or obscure by dissemblance or false show; misrepresent: *disguise one's true intentions.* **—disguise** *n.* **1.a.** The act or an instance of disguising. **b.** The condition of being disguised. **2.** Clothes or accessories worn to conceal one's true identity. **3.a.** Appearance that misrepresents the true character of something: *a blessing in disguise.* **b.** A pretense or misrepresentation: *His repeated references to his dangerous hobbies were only a disguise to cover up his insecurity.* [Middle English *disguisen,* from Old French *desguiser* : *des-,* dis- + *guise,* manner; see GUISE.] **—dis·guis′ed·ly** (-gī′zĭd-lē) *adv.* **—dis·guise′ment** *n.* **—dis·guis′er** *n.*

SYNONYMS: *disguise, camouflage, cloak, dissemble, dissimulate, mask.* The central meaning shared by these verbs is "to change or modify so as to conceal the true identity or character of": *disguised her interest with nonchalance; trying to camouflage their impatience; cloaked his anxiety with a smile; dissembling ill will with false solicitude; couldn't dissimulate her vanity; ambition that is masked as altruism.*

dis·gust (dĭs-gŭst′) *tr.v.* **-gust·ed, -gust·ing, -gusts. 1.** To excite nausea or loathing in; sicken. **2.** To offend the taste or

ă pat	oi boy
ā pay	ou out
âr care	o͝o took
ä father	o͞o boot
ĕ pet	ŭ cut
ē be	ûr urge
ĭ pit	th thin
ī pie	*th* this
îr pier	hw which
ŏ pot	zh vision
ō toe	ə about, item
ô paw	♦ regionalism

Stress marks: **′** (primary); ′ (secondary), as in **dictionary** (dĭk′shə-nĕr′ē)

moral sense of; repel. —**disgust** *n.* Profound aversion or repugnance excited by something offensive. [French *dégoûter,* from Old French *desgouster,* to lose one's appetite : *des-,* dis- + *gouster,* to eat, taste (from Latin *gustāre;* see **geus-** in Appendix).]

SYNONYMS: *disgust, nauseate, repel, revolt, sicken.* The central meaning shared by these verbs is "to offend the senses or feelings of": *a stench that disgusted us; hypocrisy that nauseated me; was repelled by such ruthlessness; brutality that revolts the sensibilities of civilized people; a fetid odor that sickened the hospital workers.*

dis·gust·ed (dĭs-gŭs′tĭd) *adj.* Filled with disgust or irritated impatience. —**dis·gust′ed·ly** *adv.*

dis·gust·ful (dĭs-gŭst′fəl) *adj.* **1.** Causing disgust; repugnant. **2.** Full of or marked by disgust. —**dis·gust′ful·ly** *adv.*

dis·gust·ing (dĭs-gŭs′tĭng) *adj.* Arousing disgust; repugnant. See Synonyms at **offensive.** —**dis·gust′ing·ly** *adv.*

dish (dĭsh) *n.* **1.a.** An open, generally shallow concave container for holding or serving food. **b. dishes.** The containers and often the utensils used when eating: *took out the dishes and silverware; washed the dishes.* **c.** A shallow concave container used for purposes other than eating: *an evaporating dish.* **2.** The amount that a dish can hold. **3.a.** The food served or contained in a dish: *a dish of ice cream.* **b.** A particular variety or preparation of food: *Chowder is a good dish for a cold winter evening.* **4.a.** A depression similar to that in a shallow concave container for food. **b.** The degree of concavity in such a depression. **5.** *Electronics.* A dish antenna. **6.** *Slang.* A good-looking person, especially an attractive woman. —**dish** *v.* **dished, dish·ing, dish·es.** —*tr.* **1.** To serve (food) in or as if in a dish: *dished up the potatoes.* **2.** To present: *dished up an excellent entertainment.* **3.** To hollow out; make concave. **4.** *Chiefly British.* To foil or cheat; ruin. —*intr. Informal.* To talk idly, especially to gossip. —***phrasal verb.*** **dish out.** To give out; dispense freely: *likes to dish out advice.* [Middle English, from Old English *disc,* from Latin *discus.* See DISK.]

dish antenna

dis·ha·bille (dĭs′ə-bēl′, -bē′) also **des·ha·bille** (dĕs′-) *n.* **1.** The state of being partially or very casually dressed. **2.** Casual or lounging attire. **3.** An intentionally careless manner. [French *déshabillé,* from past participle of *déshabiller,* to undress : *des-,* dis- + *habiller,* to clothe; see HABILIMENT.]

dish antenna *n. Electronics.* A microwave transmitter or receiver consisting of a concave parabolic reflector.

dis·har·mo·ni·ous (dĭs′här-mō′nē-əs) *adj.* Lacking in harmony. —**dis′har·mo′ni·ous·ly** *adv.*

dis·har·mo·nize (dĭs-här′mə-nīz′) *tr.v.* **-nized, -niz·ing, -niz·es.** To make disharmonious.

dis·har·mo·ny (dĭs-här′mə-nē) *n.* Lack of harmony; discord.

dish·cloth (dĭsh′klôth′, -klŏth′) *n.* A cloth for washing dishes. Also called *dishrag.*

dishcloth gourd *n.* See **loofa** (sense 2).

dis·heart·en (dĭs-här′tn) *tr.v.* **-ened, -en·ing, -ens.** To shake or destroy the courage or resolution of; dispirit. See Synonyms at **discourage.** —**dis·heart′en·ing·ly** *adv.* —**dis·heart′en·ment** *n.*

dished (dĭsht) *adj.* **1.** Concave. **2.** Slanting toward one another at the bottom. Used of a pair of wheels.

di·shev·el (dĭ-shĕv′əl) *tr.v.* **-eled, -el·ing, -els** or **-elled, -el·ling, -els. 1.a.** To loosen and let fall (hair or clothing) in disarray. **b.** To disarrange the hair or clothing of. **2.** To throw into disorder. [Back-formation from DISHEVELED.] —**di·shev′el·ment** *n.*

di·shev·eled or **di·shev·elled** (dĭ-shĕv′əld) *adj.* **1.** Being in loose disarray; unkempt, as hair or clothing. **2.** Marked by disorder; untidy: *a disheveled pile of books on the library table.* [Middle English *discheveled,* from Old French *deschevele,* past participle of *descheveler,* to disarrange the hair : *des-,* apart; see DIS– + *chevel,* hair (from Latin *capillus*).]

dis·hon·est (dĭs-ŏn′ĭst) *adj.* **1.** Disposed to lie, cheat, defraud, or deceive. **2.** Resulting from or marked by a lack of honesty. [Middle English *dishoneste,* dishonorable, from Old French *deshoneste,* probably from Medieval Latin **dishonestus* : Latin *dis-,* dis- + Latin *honestus,* honorable; see HONEST.] —**dis·hon′est·ly** *adv.*

SYNONYMS: *dishonest, lying, untruthful, deceitful, mendacious.* These adjectives mean lacking honesty or truthfulness. *Dishonest* is the least specific: *a dishonest answer; a dishonest car dealer; dishonest profits. Lying* conveys a blunt accusation of untruth: *Inconsistencies in his testimony made it obvious that he was a lying witness. Untruthful* is a softer but closely related term; it suggests both lack of veracity and divergence from fact: *made an untruthful statement. As experiments are completed the hypothesis seems increasingly untruthful. Deceitful* implies misleading by falsehood or by concealment of the truth: *deceitful advertising; a deceitful person. Mendacious,* a more formal equivalent of *lying,* suggests a chronic inclination toward untruth when it is applied to persons: *submitted a mendacious insurance claim. Even when she is not being overtly mendacious, she tinkers with the truth.*

dis·hon·es·ty (dĭs-ŏn′ĭ-stē) *n.* **-ties. 1.** Lack of honesty or integrity; improbity. **2.** A dishonest act or statement.

ă pat	oi boy
ā pay	ou out
âr care	o͝o took
ä father	o͞o boot
ĕ pet	ŭ cut
ē be	ûr urge
ĭ pit	th thin
ī pie	*th* this
îr pier	hw which
ŏ pot	zh vision
ō toe	ə about, item
ô paw	♦ regionalism

Stress marks: **′** (primary); ′ (secondary), as in **dictionary** (dĭk′shə-nĕr′ē)

dis·hon·or (dĭs-ŏn′ər) *n.* **1.** Loss of honor, respect, or reputation. See Synonyms at **disgrace. 2.** The condition of having lost honor or good repute. **3.** A cause of loss of honor: *had become a dishonor to the club.* **4.** Failure to pay or refusal to accept a note, a bill, or another commercial obligation. —**dishonor** *tr.v.* **-ored, -or·ing, -ors. 1.** To bring shame or disgrace upon. **2.** To treat in a disrespectful or demeaning manner. **3.** To fail or refuse to accept or pay (a note, bill, or check, for example). [Middle English *dishonour,* from Old French *deshonor* : *des-,* dis- + *honor,* honor; see HONOR.] —**dis·hon′or·er** *n.*

dis·hon·or·a·ble (dĭs-ŏn′ər-ə-bəl) *adj.* **1.** Characterized by or causing dishonor or discredit. **2.** Lacking integrity; unprincipled. —**dis·hon′or·a·ble·ness** *n.* —**dis·hon′or·a·bly** *adv.*

dishonorable discharge *n. Abbr.* **D.D.** Discharge from the armed forces for a grave offense, such as cowardice, murder, sabotage, or espionage.

dish·pan (dĭsh′păn′) *n.* A flat-bottomed basin for washing dishes.

dishpan hands *pl.n. (used with a sing. or pl. verb).* A rough, dry, scaly condition of the hands typically caused by sensitivity to or excessive use of household detergents or cleaning agents.

dish·rag (dĭsh′răg′) *n.* See **dishcloth.**

dish·tow·el (dĭsh′tou′əl) *n.* A towel for drying dishes.

dish·ware (dĭsh′wâr′) *n.* Dishes, as of glass, plastic, or china, used in serving food.

dish·wash·er (dĭsh′wŏsh′ər, -wô′shər) *n.* **1.** A person who washes dishes, especially one hired to wash dishes in a restaurant. **2.** A machine for washing dishes.

dish·wash·ing (dĭsh′wŏsh′ĭng, -wô′shĭng) *n.* The act or process of washing dishes. —**dishwashing** *adj.* Of, relating to, or used for washing dishes: *a dishwashing liquid.*

dish·wa·ter (dĭsh′wô′tər, -wŏt′ər) *n.* Water in which dishes are to be or have been washed.

dish·y (dĭsh′ē) *adj.* **-i·er, -i·est.** *Chiefly British.* Good-looking; attractive.

dis·il·lu·sion (dĭs′ĭ-lo͞o′zhən) *tr.v.* **-sioned, -sion·ing, -sions.** To free or deprive of illusion. —**disillusion** *n.* **1.** The act of disenchanting. **2.** The condition or fact of being disenchanted. —**dis′il·lu′sion·ment** *n.* —**dis′il·lu′sive** (-sĭv, -zĭv) *adj.*

dis·in·cen·tive (dĭs′ĭn-sĕn′tĭv) *n.* Something that prevents or discourages action; a deterrent.

dis·in·cli·na·tion (dĭs-ĭn′klə-nā′shən) *n.* A lack of inclination; a mild aversion or reluctance.

dis·in·cline (dĭs′ĭn-klīn′) *v.* **-clined, -clin·ing, -clines.** —*tr.* To make reluctant or averse. —*intr.* To be unwilling.

dis·in·clined (dĭs′ĭn-klīnd′) *adj.* Unwilling or reluctant: *They were usually disinclined to socialize.*

dis·in·cor·po·rate (dĭs′ĭn-kôr′pə-rāt′) *tr. & intr.v.* **-rat·ed, -rat·ing, -rates.** To remove or become removed from the status of a corporation. —**dis′in·cor′po·ra′tion** *n.*

dis·in·fect (dĭs′ĭn-fĕkt′) *tr.v.* **-fect·ed, -fect·ing, -fects.** To cleanse so as to destroy or prevent the growth of disease-carrying microorganisms: *disinfect a wound.* —**dis′in·fec′tion** *n.*

dis·in·fec·tant (dĭs′ĭn-fĕk′tənt) *n.* An agent, such as heat, radiation, or a chemical, that disinfects by destroying, neutralizing, or inhibiting the growth of disease-carrying microorganisms. —**disinfectant** *adj.* Serving to disinfect.

dis·in·fest (dĭs′ĭn-fĕst′) *tr.v.* **-fest·ed, -fest·ing, -fests.** To rid of vermin. —**dis·in′fes·ta′tion** (-fĕ-stā′shən) *n.*

dis·in·fes·tant (dĭs′ĭn-fĕs′tənt) *n.* An agent that eradicates an infestation, as of vermin.

dis·in·fla·tion (dĭs′ĭn-flā′shən) *n.* Downward movement of inflated prices to a more normal level. —**dis′in·fla′tion·ar′y** (-shə-nĕr′ē) *adj.*

dis·in·form (dĭs′ĭn-fôrm′) *tr.v.* **-formed, -form·ing, -forms.** To give disinformation to. [Back-formation from DISINFORMATION.] —**dis′in·form′er, dis′in·form′ant** *n.*

dis·in·for·ma·tion (dĭs-ĭn′fər-mā′shən) *n.* **1.** Deliberately misleading information announced publicly or leaked by a government or especially by an intelligence agency in order to influence public opinion or the government in another nation: *"He would be the unconscious channel for a piece of disinformation aimed at another country's intelligence service"* (Ken Follett). **2.** Dissemination of such misleading information. —*attributive.* Often used to modify another noun: *disinformation operations; disinformation experts.* [Possibly translation of Russian *dezinformatsiya.*]

dis·in·gen·u·ous (dĭs′ĭn-jĕn′yo͞o-əs) *adj.* Not straightforward or candid; crafty: *"an ambitious, disingenuous, philistine, and hypocritical operator, who . . . exemplified . . . the most disagreeable traits of his time"* (David Cannadine). —**dis′in·gen′u·ous·ly** *adv.* —**dis′in·gen′u·ous·ness** *n.*

dis·in·her·it (dĭs′ĭn-hĕr′ĭt) *tr.v.* **-it·ed, -it·ing, -its. 1.** To exclude from inheritance or the right to inherit. **2.** To deprive of a natural or an established right or privilege. —**dis′in·her′i·tance** *n.*

dis·in·hib·it (dĭs′ĭn-hĭb′ĭt) *tr.v.* **-it·ed, -it·ing, -its.** To free from inhibitions.

dis·in·hi·bi·tion (dĭs′ĭn-hə-bĭsh′ən, -ĭn-ə-, dĭs-ĭn′-) *n.* **1.** A loss of inhibition, as through the influence of drugs or alcohol. **2.** *Psychology.* A temporary loss of an inhibition caused by an unrelated stimulus, such as a loud noise. In conditioning experiments, disinhibition may result in the revival of a suppressed conditioned response.

dis·in·te·grate (dĭs-ĭn′tĭ-grāt′) *v.* **-grat·ed, -grat·ing, -grates.** —*intr.* **1.** To become reduced to components, fragments, or particles. **2.** *Physics & Chemistry.* To decompose, decay, or undergo a nuclear transformation. —*tr.* To cause to disintegrate. See Synonyms at **decay. —dis·in′te·gra′tive** *adj.* **—dis·in′te·gra′tor** *n.*

dis·in·te·gra·tion (dĭs-ĭn′tĭ-grā′shən) *n.* **1.** The act or process of disintegrating. **2.** The state of being disintegrated. **3.** *Physics & Chemistry.* The natural or induced transformation of an atomic nucleus from a more massive to a less massive configuration by the emission of particles or radiation.

dis·in·ter (dĭs′ĭn-tûr′) *tr.v.* **-terred, -ter·ring, -ters. 1.** To dig up or remove from a grave or tomb; exhume. **2.** To bring to public notice; disclose. **—dis′in·ter′ment** *n.*

dis·in·ter·est (dĭs-ĭn′tər-ĭst, -ĭn′trĭst) *n.* **1.** Freedom from selfish bias or self-interest; impartiality. **2.** Lack of interest.

dis·in·ter·est·ed (dĭs-ĭn′trĭ-stĭd, -ĭn′tə-rĕs′tĭd) *adj.* **1.** Free of bias and self-interest; impartial: *"disinterested scientific opinion on fluorides in the water supply"* (Ellen R. Shell). **2.a.** Not interested; indifferent: *"disinterested in all efforts to find a peaceful solution"* (C.L. Sulzberger). **b.** Having lost interest. **—dis·in′ter·est·ed·ly** *adv.* **—dis·in′ter·est·ed·ness** *n.*

USAGE NOTE: Despite critical disapproval, *disinterested* has come to be widely used by many educated writers to mean "uninterested" or "having lost interest," as in *Since she discovered skiing, she is disinterested in her schoolwork* (a sense it had at an earlier stage of English, but which had in the interim become outmoded). Many maintain that the word can legitimately be used only in its sense of "having no stake in (an outcome or issue)," as in *Since the judge stands to profit from the sale of the company, she cannot be considered a disinterested party in the dispute.* In our most recent survey, 89 percent of the Usage Panel rejected the sentence *His unwillingness to give five minutes of his time proves that he is disinterested in finding a solution to the problem,* a proportion that is not significantly different from the 93 percent who disapproved of the same usage in an earlier survey.

dis·in·ter·me·di·a·tion (dĭs-ĭn′tər-mē′dē-ā′shən) *n.* Withdrawal of funds from intermediary financial institutions, such as banks and savings and loan associations, in order to invest in instruments yielding a higher return.

dis·in·tox·i·cate (dĭs′ĭn-tŏk′sĭ-kāt′) *tr.v.* **-cat·ed, -cat·ing, -cates.** To free from the effects of intoxication or from dependence on intoxicating agents. **—dis′in·tox′i·ca′tion** *n.*

dis·in·vent (dĭs′ĭn-vĕnt′) *tr.v.* **-vent·ed, -vent·ing, -vents.** To rescind the invention or existence of: *"The atomic bomb . . . cannot be disinvented"* (Patrick J. Buchanan). **—dis′in·ven′tion** *n.*

dis·in·vest·ment (dĭs′ĭn-vĕst′mənt) *n.* Withdrawal of capital investment from a company or country.

dis·in·vite (dĭs′ĭn-vīt′) *tr.v.* **-vit·ed, -vit·ing, -vites.** To rescind an invitation to: *disinvited our friends for dinner because of an emergency.* **—dis·in·vi·ta′tion** (-vĭ-tā′shən) *n.*

dis·join (dĭs-join′) *v.* **-joined, -join·ing, -joins.** —*tr.* To undo the joining of; separate. —*intr.* To become separated. [Middle English *disjoinen,* from Old French *desjoindre,* from Latin *disiungere* : *dis-,* dis- + *iungere,* to join; see JOIN.]

dis·joint (dĭs-joint′) *v.* **-joint·ed, -joint·ing, -joints.** —*tr.* **1.** To put out of joint; dislocate. **2.** To take apart at the joints. **3.** To destroy the coherence or connections of. **4.** To separate; disjoin. —*intr.* **1.** To come apart at the joints. **2.** To become dislocated. **—disjoint** *adj. Mathematics.* Having no elements in common. Used of sets. [Middle English *disjointen,* to destroy, ultimately from Old French *desjoint,* past participle of *desjoindre,* to disjoin. See DISJOIN.]

dis·joint·ed (dĭs-join′tĭd) *adj.* **1.** Separated at the joints. **2.** Out of joint; dislocated. **3.** Lacking order or coherence: *disjointed sentences.* **—dis·joint′ed·ly** *adv.* **—dis·joint′ed·ness** *n.*

dis·junct (dĭs-jŭngkt′) *adj.* **1.** Characterized by separation. **2.** *Music.* Relating to progression by intervals larger than major seconds. **3.** *Zoology.* Having deep constrictions separating the head, thorax, and abdomen, as in insects. [Middle English *disjuncte,* from Latin *disiūnctus,* past participle of *disiungere,* to disjoin. See DISJOIN.]

dis·junc·tion (dĭs-jŭngk′shən) *n.* **1.** The act of disjoining or the condition of being disjointed. **2.** *Logic.* A proposition that presents two or more alternative terms, with the assertion that only one is true. **3.** *Genetics.* The separation of homologous chromosomes during meiosis.

dis·junc·tive (dĭs-jŭngk′tĭv) *adj.* **1.** Serving to separate or divide. **2.** *Grammar.* Serving to establish a relationship of contrast or opposition. The conjunction *but* in the phrase *poor but comfortable* is disjunctive. **3.** *Logic.* **a.** Of a proposition that presents two or more alternative terms. **b.** Of a syllogism that contains a disjunction as one premise. **—disjunctive** *n. Grammar.* A disjunctive conjunction. **—dis·junc′tive·ly** *adv.*

dis·junc·ture (dĭs-jŭngk′chər) *n.* Disjunction; disunion; separation.

disk also **disc** (dĭsk) —*n.* **1.** A thin, flat, circular object or plate. **2.** Something resembling such an object: *The moon's disk was reflected in the pond.* **3.a.** The disk used in a disc brake. **b.** A disk used on a disk harrow. **4.** A round, flattened, platelike structure in an animal, such as an intervertebral disk. **5.** *Botany.* The enlarged area bearing numerous tiny flowers, as in the flower head of composite plants, such as the daisy. Also called *discus.* **6.a.** A phonograph record. **b.** An optical disk, especially a compact disk. **c.** *Computer Science.* A magnetic disk. **7.** A circular grid in a phototypesetting machine. —*tr.v.* **disked, disk·ing, disks** also **disced, disc·ing, discs. 1.** To work (soil) with a disk harrow. **2.** To make (a recording) on a phonograph record. [Latin *discus,* quoit, from Greek *diskos,* from *dikein,* to throw. See **deik-** in Appendix.]

disk brake *n.* Variant of **disc brake.**

disk drive *n. Computer Science.* A device that reads data stored on a magnetic or optical disk and writes data onto the disk for storage.

disk·ette (dĭ-skĕt′) *n. Computer Science.* See **floppy disk.**

disk flower *n.* Any of the tiny tubular flowers in the central portion of the flower head of certain composite plants, such as the daisy.

disk harrow or **disc harrow** *n.* A harrow equipped with a series of disks set on edge or at an angle on one or more axles.

disk jockey *n.* Variant of **disc jockey.**

disk operating system *n.* DOS.

disk pack *n.* A computer storage device consisting of several magnetic disks that can be used and stored as a unit.

disk sander *n.* An electric sander that uses a revolving abrasive disk.

disk wheel *n.* A spokeless wheel in which a disk joins the hub to the rim.

dis·like (dĭs-līk′) *tr.v.* **-liked, -lik·ing, -likes.** To regard with distaste or aversion. **—dislike** *n.* An attitude or a feeling of distaste or aversion. **—dis·lik′a·ble** *adj.*

dis·lo·cate (dĭs′lō-kāt′, dĭs-lō′kāt) *tr.v.* **-cat·ed, -cat·ing, -cates. 1.** To put out of usual or proper place, position, or relationship. **2.** To displace (a body part), especially to displace a bone from its normal position. **3.** To throw into confusion or disorder; disrupt: *a continuing drought that dislocated the state's economy.* [Medieval Latin *dislocāre, dislocāt-* : *dis-,* dis- + Latin *locāre,* to place (from *locus,* place).]

dis·lo·ca·tion (dĭs′lō-kā′shən) *n.* **1.** The act or process of dislocating or the state of having been dislocated: *"the severe emotional dislocation experienced by millions of immigrants . . . who were forced to separate themselves forever from the . . . circle of people and places on which they had depended"* (Doris Kearns Goodwin). **2.** Displacement of a body part, especially the temporary displacement of a bone from its normal position. **3.** An imperfection in the crystal structure of a metal or other solid resulting from an absence of an atom or atoms in one or more layers of a crystal. **4.** *Geology.* See **displacement** (sense 4).

disk harrow

dis·lodge (dĭs-lŏj′) *v.* **-lodged, -lodg·ing, -lodg·es.** —*tr.* To remove or force out from a position or dwelling previously occupied. —*intr.* To move or go from a dwelling or former position. [Middle English *disloggen,* from Old French *deslogier* : *des-,* dis- + *logier,* to lodge (from *loge,* shed, of Germanic origin).] **—dis·lodge′ment, dis·lodg′ment** *n.*

dis·loy·al (dĭs-loi′əl) *adj.* Lacking loyalty. See Synonyms at **faithless.** [Middle English *disloial, from Old French *desloial* : *des-,* dis- + *loial,* loyal; see LOYAL.] **—dis·loy′al·ly** *adv.*

dis·loy·al·ty (dĭs-loi′əl-tē) *n., pl.* **-ties. 1.** The quality of being disloyal; faithlessness. **2.** A disloyal act.

♦**dis·mal** (dĭz′məl) *adj.* **1.** Causing gloom or depression; dreary: *dismal weather; took a dismal view of the economy.* **2.** Characterized by ineptitude, dullness, or a lack of merit: *a dismal book; a dismal performance on the cello.* **3.** *Obsolete.* Dreadful; disastrous. **—dismal** *n. Chiefly South Atlantic U.S.* See **pocosin.** See Regional Note at **pocosin.** [Middle English, unlucky days, unlucky, from Anglo-Norman, unlucky days, from Medieval Latin *diēs malī* : Latin *diēs,* day; see **deiw-** in Appendix + Latin *malī,* pl. of *malus,* evil; see **mel-**[3] in Appendix.] **—dis′mal·ly** *adv.* **—dis′mal·ness** *n.*

Dis·mal Swamp (dĭz′məl). A swampy region of southeast Virginia and northeast North Carolina. The heavily forested area has been greatly reduced by drainage.

dis·man·tle (dĭs-măn′tl) *tr.v.* **-tled, -tling, -tles. 1.a.** To take apart; disassemble; tear down. **b.** To put an end to in a gradual systematic way: *dismantling the cumbersome regulations for interstate trucking.* **2.** To strip of furnishings or equipment: *dismantled the house before knocking it down.* **3.** To strip of covering or clothing. [Obsolete French *desmanteler,* to raze fortifications round a town, from Old French : *des-,* dis- + *emmanteler,* to cover with a coat, shelter (ultimately from *mantel,* cloak; see MANTLE).] **—dis·man′tle·ment** *n.*

dis·mast (dĭs-măst′) *tr.v.* **-mast·ed, -mast·ing, -masts.** *Nautical.* To remove or break off the mast of.

dis·may (dĭs-mā′) *tr.v.* **-mayed, -may·ing, -mays. 1.** To destroy the courage or resolution of by exciting dread or apprehension. **2.** To cause to lose enthusiasm; disillusion: *was dismayed to learn that her favorite dancer used drugs.* **3.** To upset or alarm. **—dismay** *n.* A sudden or complete loss of courage in the face of trouble or danger. [Middle English *dismaien,* from Anglo-Norman *desmaiier : probably *de-,* intensive pref.; see DE– + Old French *esmaier,* to frighten (from Vulgar Latin *exmagāre,

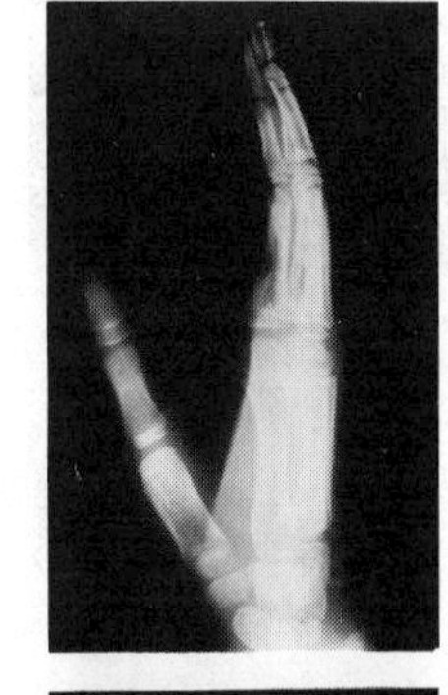

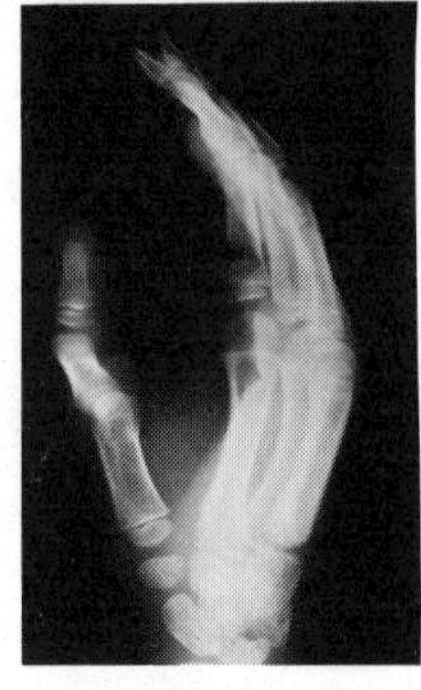

dislocate
Top: X-ray of a normal hand
Bottom: X-ray showing dislocated thumb

to deprive of power : Latin *ex-*, ex- + Germanic **magan*, to be able to; see **magh-** in Appendix).] —**dis·may′ing·ly** *adv.*

SYNONYMS: *dismay, appall, daunt, horrify, shake.* These verbs mean to deprive a person of courage or the power to act as a result of fear or anxiety. *Dismay* is the least specific: *The news of plummeting stock prices dismayed speculators. Appall* implies a sense of helplessness caused by an awareness of the enormity of something: *"for as this appalling ocean surrounds the verdant land"* (Herman Melville). *Daunt* suggests an abatement of courage: *"captains courageous, whom death could not daunt"* (Anonymous ballad). *Horrify* implies dread, shock, or revulsion: *horrified by the possibility of nuclear war.* To *shake* is to dismay profoundly: *"A little swift brutality shook him to the very soul"* (John Galsworthy). See also Synonyms at **fear.**

dis·mem·ber (dĭs-mĕm′bər) *tr.v.* **-bered, -ber·ing, -bers. 1.** To cut, tear, or pull off the limbs of. **2.** To divide into pieces. [Middle English *dismembren*, from Old French *desmembrer*, from Vulgar Latin **dismembrāre* : Latin *dis-*, dis- + Latin *membrum*, limb; see MEMBER.] —**dis·mem′ber·ment** *n.*

dis·miss (dĭs-mĭs′) *tr.v.* **-missed, -miss·ing, -miss·es. 1.** To end the employment or service of; discharge. **2.** To direct or allow to leave: *dismissed troops after the inspection; dismissed the student after reprimanding him.* **3. a.** To stop considering; rid one's mind of; dispel: *dismissed all thoughts of running for office.* **b.** To refuse to accept or recognize; reject: *dismissed the claim as highly improbable.* **4.** *Law.* To put (a claim or action) out of court without further hearing. **5.** *Sports.* To put out (a batter) in cricket. [Middle English *dismissen*, from Medieval Latin *dismittere, dismiss-*, variant of Latin *dīmittere* : *dī-*, *dis-*, apart; see DIS– + *mittere*, to send.] —**dis·miss′i·ble** *adj.* —**dis·mis′sion** (-mĭsh′ən) *n.*

SYNONYMS: *dismiss, boot, bounce, can, cashier, discharge, drop, fire, sack.* The central meaning shared by these verbs is "to terminate the employment of": *was dismissed for insubordination; was booted for being habitually tardy; afraid of being bounced for union activities; wasn't canned because his father-in-law owns the business; will be cashiered from the army; resort workers discharged at the end of the season; was dropped for incompetence; was fired on the spot for insolence; a reporter sacked for revealing a confidential source.* See also Synonyms at **eject.**

dis·miss·al (dĭs-mĭs′əl) *n.* **1. a.** The act of dismissing. **b.** The condition of being dismissed. **2.** An order or notice of discharge.

dis·mis·sive (dĭs-mĭs′ĭv) *adj.* **1.** Serving to dismiss. **2.** Showing indifference or disregard: *a dismissive shrug.*

dis·mount (dĭs-mount′) *v.* **-mount·ed, -mount·ing, -mounts.** —*intr.* To get off or down, as from a horse or vehicle. —*tr.* **1.** To remove from a support, setting, or mounting. **2.** To unseat or throw off, as from a horse. **3.** To disassemble (a mechanism, for example). —**dismount** (dĭs′mount′) *n.* **1.** The act or manner of dismounting, especially from a horse. **2.** *Sports.* A move in gymnastics whereby the gymnast gets off an apparatus or completes a floor exercise, typically landing on both feet. [Probably alteration of obsolete French *desmonter*, to unseat : *des-*, dis- + *monter*, to mount; see MOUNT[1].] —**dis·mount′a·ble** *adj.*

Walt Disney

Dis·ney (dĭz′nē), **Walter Elias.** Known as "Walt." 1901–1966. American animator, showman, and film producer. Noted for his creation of the cartoon characters Mickey Mouse and Donald Duck, he produced the first animated film with sound, *Steamboat Willie* (1928), and the first full-length animated feature, *Snow White* (1938).

dis·o·be·di·ence (dĭs′ə-bē′dē-əns) *n.* Refusal or failure to obey. —**dis′o·be′di·ent** *adj.* —**dis′o·be′di·ent·ly** *adv.*

dis·o·bey (dĭs′ə-bā′) *v.* **-beyed, -bey·ing, -beys.** —*intr.* To refuse or fail to follow an order or a rule. —*tr.* To refuse or fail to obey (an order or a rule). [Middle English *disobeien*, from Old French *desobeir*, from Vulgar Latin **disobedīre* : Latin *dis-*, dis- + Latin *oboedīre*, to obey; see OBEY.] —**dis′o·bey′er** *n.*

dis·o·blige (dĭs′ə-blīj′) *tr.v.* **-bliged, -blig·ing, -blig·es. 1.** To refuse or neglect to act in accord with the wishes of. **2.** To inconvenience. **3.** To give offense to; affront. —**dis′o·blig′ing·ly** *adv.*

dis·or·der (dĭs-ôr′dər) *n.* **1.** A lack of order or regular arrangement; confusion. **2.** A breach of civic order or peace; a public disturbance. **3.** An ailment that affects the function of mind or body: *eating disorders and substance abuse.* —**disorder** *tr.v.* **-dered, -der·ing, -ders. 1.** To throw into confusion or disarray. **2.** To disturb the normal physical or mental health of; derange.

dis·or·dered (dĭs-ôr′dərd) *adj.* **1.** Being in a condition of confusion or disarray. **2.** Physically or mentally ill. —**dis·or′dered·ly** *adv.* —**dis·or′dered·ness** *n.*

dis·or·der·ly (dĭs-ôr′dər-lē) *adj.* **1.** Lacking regular or logical order or arrangement: *a disorderly pile of clothes.* **2.** Undisciplined; unruly: *disorderly youths.* **3.** *Law.* Disturbing the public peace or decorum. —**dis·or′der·li·ness** *n.*

disorderly conduct *n.* *Law.* An offense involving disturbance of the public peace and decency.

dis·or·gan·ize (dĭs-ôr′gə-nīz′) *tr.v.* **-ized, -iz·ing, -iz·es.** To destroy the organization, systematic arrangement, or unity of. —**dis·or′gan·i·za′tion** (-gə-nĭ-zā′shən) *n.*

dis·o·ri·ent (dĭs-ôr′ē-ĕnt′, -ōr′-) *tr.v.* **-ent·ed, -ent·ing, -ents.** To cause (a person, for example) to experience disorientation.

dis·o·ri·en·ta·tion (dĭs-ôr′ē-ĕn-tā′shən) *n.* **1.** Loss of one's sense of direction, position, or relationship with one's surroundings. **2.** Intellectual or moral confusion. **3.** *Psychology.* A temporary or permanent state of confusion regarding place, time, or personal identity.

dis·own (dĭs-ōn′) *tr.v.* **-owned, -own·ing, -owns.** To refuse to acknowledge or accept as one's own; repudiate.

disp. *abbr.* Dispensary.

dis·par·age (dĭ-spăr′ĭj) *tr.v.* **-aged, -ag·ing, -ag·es. 1.** To speak of in a slighting way; belittle. See Synonyms at **decry. 2.** To reduce in esteem or rank. [Middle English *disparagen*, to degrade, from Old French *desparager* : *des-*, dis- + *parage*, high birth (from *per*, peer; see PEER[2]).] —**dis·par′age·ment** *n.* —**dis·par′ag·er** *n.* —**dis·par′ag·ing·ly** *adv.*

dis·pa·rate (dĭs′pər-ĭt, dĭ-spăr′ĭt) *adj.* Fundamentally distinct or different in kind; entirely dissimilar. [Latin *disparātus*, past participle of *disparāre*, to separate : *dis-*, apart; see DIS– + *parāre*, to prepare; see **perə-**[1] in Appendix.] —**dis′pa·rate·ly** *adv.* —**dis′pa·rate·ness** *n.*

dis·par·i·ty (dĭ-spăr′ĭ-tē) *n.*, *pl.* **-ties. 1.** The condition or fact of being unequal, as in age, rank, or degree; difference: *"narrow the economic disparities among regions and industries"* (Courtenay Slater). **2.** Unlikeness; incongruity. [French *disparité*, from Old French *desparite*, from Late Latin *disparitās* : Latin *dis-*, dis- + Late Latin *paritās*, equality; see PARITY[1].]

dis·par·lure (dĭs′pär-lo͝or′) *n.* **1.** A pheromone, $C_{19}H_{38}O$, produced by female gypsy moths. **2.** A synthetic substance used to attract male gypsy moths to traps. [New Latin *(Porthetria) dispār*, gypsy moth (from *dispār* : *dis-*, dis- + *pār*, equal; see PAR) + LURE.]

dis·pas·sion (dĭs-păsh′ən) *n.* Freedom from passion, bias, or emotion; objectivity.

dis·pas·sion·ate (dĭs-păsh′ə-nĭt) *adj.* Devoid of or unaffected by passion, emotion, or bias. See Synonyms at **fair**[1]. —**dis·pas′sion·ate·ly** *adv.* —**dis·pas′sion·ate·ness** *n.*

dis·patch also **des·patch** (dĭ-spăch′) —*tr.v.* **-patched, -patch·ing, -patch·es. 1.** To relegate to a specific destination or send on specific business. See Synonyms at **send**[1]. **2. a.** To complete, transact, or dispose of promptly. **b.** To eat up (food); finish off (a dish or meal). **3.** To put to death summarily. —*n.* **1.** The act of sending off, as to a specific destination. **2.** The act of putting to death. **3.** Speed in performance or movement. See Synonyms at **haste. 4.** (*also* dĭs′păch′). **a.** A written message, particularly an official communication, sent with speed. **b.** An important message sent by a diplomat or an officer in the armed forces. **5.** (*also* dĭs′păch′). A news item sent to a news organization, as by a correspondent. **6.** An organization or a conveyance for delivering goods. [Spanish *despachar* or Italian *dispacciare*, both probably ultimately from Old Provençal *empachar*, to impede, from Vulgar Latin **impāctāre*, frequentative of Latin *impingere*, dash against. See IMPINGE.]

dis·patch·er (dĭs-păch′ər) *n.* One that dispatches, as: **a.** One that sends out trains, buses, trucks, or cars according to a schedule. **b.** *Computer Science.* A routine that controls the order in which input and output devices obtain access to the processing system.

dis·pel (dĭ-spĕl′) *tr.v.* **-pelled, -pel·ling, -pels. 1.** To rid one's mind of: *managed to dispel my doubts.* **2.** To drive away or off by or as if by scattering. See Synonyms at **scatter.** [Middle English *dispellen*, from Latin *dispellere* : *dis-*, apart; see DIS– + *pellere*, to drive; see **pel-**[5] in Appendix.]

dis·pen·sa·ble (dĭ-spĕn′sə-bəl) *adj.* **1.** Not essential; unimportant: *dispensable items of personal property.* **2.** Capable of being dispensed, administered, or distributed: *dispensable drugs.* **3.** Subject to dispensation, as a vow or church law. —**dis·pen′sa·bil′i·ty, dis·pen′sa·ble·ness** *n.*

dis·pen·sa·ry (dĭ-spĕn′sə-rē) *n.*, *pl.* **-ries.** *Abbr.* **disp. 1.** An office in a hospital, school, or other institution from which medical supplies, preparations, and treatments are dispensed. **2.** A public institution that dispenses medicines or medical aid.

dis·pen·sa·tion (dĭs′pən-sā′shən, -pĕn-) *n.* **1. a.** The act of dispensing. **b.** Something dispensed. **c.** A specific arrangement or system by which something is dispensed. **2.** An exemption or a release from an obligation or a rule, granted by or as if by an authority. **3. a.** An exemption from a church law, a vow, or another similar obligation granted in a particular case by an ecclesiastical authority. **b.** The document containing this exemption. **4.** *Theology.* **a.** The divine ordering of worldly affairs. **b.** A religious system or code of commands considered to have been divinely revealed or appointed. —**dis′pen·sa′tion·al** *adj.*

dis·pen·sa·to·ry (dĭ-spĕn′sə-tôr′ē, -tōr′ē) *n.*, *pl.* **-ries.** A book in which the contents, preparation, and uses of medicines are described; a pharmacopoeia.

dis·pense (dĭ-spĕns′) *v.* **-pensed, -pens·ing, -pens·es.** —*tr.* **1.** To deal out in parts or portions; distribute. See Synonyms at **distribute. 2.** To prepare and give out (medicines). **3.** To administer (laws, for example). **4.** To exempt or release, as from a duty or religious obligation. —*intr.* To grant a dispensation or an exemption. —***phrasal verb.*** **dispense with. 1.** To manage without; forgo. **2.** To get rid of; do away with: *a country that has dispensed with tariff barriers.* [Middle English *dispensen*, from Old French *dispenser*, from Latin *dispēnsāre*, to distribute, frequentative of *dispendere,* to weigh out : *dis-,* out; see DIS– + *pendere,* to weigh; see **(s)pen-** in Appendix.]

dis·pens·er (dĭ-spĕn′sər) *n.* One that dispenses or gives out, especially a machine or container that allows the contents to be removed and used in convenient or prescribed amounts.

dis·peo·ple (dĭs-pē′pəl) *tr.v.* **-pled, -pling, -ples.** To depopulate.

dis·per·sal (dĭ-spûr′səl) *n.* The act or process of dispersing or the condition of being dispersed; distribution.

dis·perse (dĭ-spûrs′) *v.* **-persed, -pers·ing, -pers·es.** —*tr.* **1.a.** To drive off or scatter in different directions: *The police dispersed the crowd.* **b.** To strew or distribute widely: *The airplane dispersed the leaflets over the city.* **2.** To cause to vanish or disappear. See Synonyms at **scatter. 3.** To disseminate (knowledge, for example). **4.** To separate (light) into spectral rays. **5.** To distribute (particles) evenly throughout a medium. —*intr.* **1.** To move in different directions; scatter. **2.** To vanish; dissipate: *The storm clouds had dispersed by noon.* [Middle English *dispersen,* from Old French *disperser,* from Latin *dispergere, dispers-,* to disperse : *dis-,* apart; see DIS– + *spargere,* to scatter.] **—dis·per′sant** *n.* **—dis·pers′ed·ly** (-spûr′sĭd-lē) *adv.* **—dis·pers′er** *n.* **—dis·pers′i·ble** *adj.*

disperse phase *n.* The particles or droplets in a disperse system that are dispersed throughout a medium.

disperse system *n. Chemistry.* A system, such as a colloid, consisting of a disperse phase in a dispersion medium. Also called *dispersion.*

dis·per·sion (dĭ-spûr′zhən, -shən) *n.* **1.a.** The act or process of dispersing. **b.** The state of being dispersed. **2.** *Statistics.* The degree of scatter of data, usually about an average value, such as the median. **3.** *Physics.* **a.** Separation of a complex wave into its component parts according to a given characteristic, such as frequency or wavelength. **b.** Separation of visible light into colors by refraction or diffraction. **4.** *Chemistry.* See **disperse system.**

dispersion medium *n.* The continuous medium, such as a gas, liquid, or solid, in which a disperse phase is distributed.

dis·per·sive (dĭ-spûr′sĭv, -zĭv) *adj.* **1.** Tending to become dispersed. **2.** Tending to produce dispersion. **—dis·per′sive·ly** *adv.* **—dis·per′sive·ness** *n.*

dis·pir·it (dĭ-spĭr′ĭt) *tr.v.* **-it·ed, -it·ing, -its.** To lower in or deprive of spirit; dishearten. See Synonyms at **discourage.** [DI(S)– + SPIRIT.]

dis·pir·it·ed (dĭ-spĭr′ĭ-tĭd) *adj.* Affected or marked by low spirits; dejected. See Synonyms at **depressed. —dis·pir′it·ed·ly** *adv.*

dis·place (dĭs-plās′) *tr.v.* **-placed, -plac·ing, -plac·es. 1.** To move or shift from the usual place or position, especially to force to leave a homeland: *millions of refugees who were displaced by the war.* **2.** To take the place of; supplant. **3.** To discharge from an office or position. **—dis·place′a·ble** *adj.* **—dis·plac′er** *n.*

dis·placed homemaker (dĭs-plāst′) *n.* A woman who, after managing a household for years, is forced by financial necessity to find a wage-paying job.

displaced person *n. Abbr.* **DP, D.P.** One who has been driven from one's homeland by war or internal upheaval.

dis·place·ment (dĭs-plās′mənt) *n.* **1.a.** The act of displacing. **b.** The condition of having been displaced. **2.** *Chemistry.* A reaction in which an atom, a radical, or a molecule replaces another in a compound. **3.** *Physics.* **a.** The weight or volume of a fluid displaced by a floating body, used especially as a measurement of the weight or bulk of ships. **b.** A vector or the magnitude of a vector from the initial position to a subsequent position assumed by a body. **4.** *Geology.* **a.** The relative movement between the two sides of a fault. **b.** The distance between the two sides of a fault. Also called *dislocation.* **5.** *Psychiatry.* A defense mechanism in which there is an unconscious shift of emotions, affect, or desires from the original object to a more acceptable or immediate substitute.

displacement ton *n. Nautical.* A unit for measuring the displacement of a ship afloat, equivalent to one long ton or about one cubic meter of salt water.

dis·play (dĭ-splā′) *v.* **-played, -play·ing, -plays.** —*tr.* **1.a.** To present or hold up to view. **b.** *Computer Science.* To provide (information or graphics) on a screen. **2.** To give evidence of; manifest. **3.** To exhibit ostentatiously; show off. **4.** To be endowed with an identifiable form or character: *a shrub that displays hardiness.* **5.** To express, as by gestures or bodily posture: *a smirk that displayed contempt.* **6.** To spread out; unfurl: *The peacock displayed its fan.* —*intr. Computer Science.* To provide information or graphics on a screen: *a personal computer that displays and prints.* **—display** *n.* **1.a.** The act of displaying. **b.** A public exhibition. **c.** Objects or merchandise set out for viewing by the public. **2.** A demonstration or manifestation: *a display of temper.* **3.a.** *Biology.* A specialized pattern of behavior used to communicate visually, such as the presentation of colors or plumage by male birds as part of courtship or intimidation. **b.** An instance of such behavior. **4.** Ostentatious exhibition. **5.** An advertisement or headline designed to catch the eye. **6.a.** *Computer Science.* A device that gives information in a visual form, as on a screen. **b.** A visual representation of information. —*attributive.* Often used to modify another noun: *a display cabinet; picked display type for the new advertising campaign.* [Middle English *displayen,* from Anglo-Norman *despleier,* from Medieval Latin *displicāre,* to unfold, from Latin, to scatter : *dis-,* apart; see DIS– + *plicāre,* to fold; see **plek-** in Appendix.]

SYNONYMS: *display, array, panoply, parade, pomp.* The central meaning shared by these nouns is "an impressive or ostentatious exhibition": *a tasteless display of wealth; an array of diamond rings in a showcase; a panoply of alpine peaks; a parade of knowledge and virtue; the pomp of a coronation ceremony.* See also Synonyms at **show.**

dis·please (dĭs-plēz′) *v.* **-pleased, -pleas·ing, -pleas·es.** —*tr.* To cause annoyance or vexation to. —*intr.* To cause annoyance or displeasure. [Middle English *displesen,* from Old French *desplaire, desplais-,* from Vulgar Latin **displacēre,* from Latin *displicēre* : Latin *dis-,* dis- + Latin *placēre,* to please; see PLEASE.] **—dis·pleas′ing·ly** *adv.*

dis·pleas·ure (dĭs-plĕzh′ər) *n.* **1.** The condition or fact of being displeased; dissatisfaction. **2.** Discomfort, uneasiness, or pain. **3.** *Archaic.* An injurious offense. [Middle English *displesure,* from Old French *desplaisir* : *des-,* dis- + *plaisir,* pleasure; see PLEASURE.]

dis·plode (dĭ-splōd′) *tr. & intr.v.* **-plod·ed, -plod·ing, -plodes.** *Archaic.* To explode. [Latin *displōdere* : *dis-,* dis- + *plaudere,* to clap, beat.]

dis·port (dĭ-spôrt′, -spōrt′) *v.* **-port·ed, -port·ing, -ports.** —*intr.* To amuse oneself in a light, frolicsome manner. —*tr.* **1.** To amuse (oneself) in a light, frolicsome manner. **2.** To display. **—disport** *n.* Frolicsome diversion. [Middle English *disporten,* from Old French *desporter,* to divert : *des-,* apart; see DIS– + *porter,* to carry (from Latin *portāre;* see PORT[5]).]

dis·pos·a·ble (dĭ-spō′zə-bəl) *adj.* **1.** Designed to be disposed of after use: *disposable diapers; disposable razors.* **2.a.** Remaining to a person after taxes have been deducted: *disposable income.* **b.** Free for use; available: *Every disposal piece of equipment was sent to the fire.* **—disposable** *n.* An article, such as a paper diaper or hypodermic syringe, that can be disposed of after one use. **—dis·pos′a·bil′i·ty** *n.*

dis·pos·al (dĭ-spō′zəl) *n.* **1.** A particular order, distribution, or placement: *a pleasing disposal of plants and lawn.* **2.** A particular method of attending to or settling matters. **3.** Transference by gift or sale. **4.** The act or process of getting rid of something. **5.** An electric device installed below a sink that grinds garbage so it can be flushed away. **6.** The liberty or power to dispose of: *funds at our disposal.*

dis·pose (dĭ-spōz′) *v.* **-posed, -pos·ing, -pos·es.** —*tr.* **1.** To place or set in a particular order; arrange. **2.** To put (business affairs, for example) into correct, definitive, or conclusive form. **3.** To put into a willing or receptive frame of mind; incline. See Synonyms at **incline.** —*intr.* To settle or decide a matter. **—dispose** *n. Obsolete.* **1.** Disposal. **2.** Disposition; demeanor. ***—phrasal verb.*** **dispose of. 1.** To attend to; settle: *disposed of the problem quickly.* **2.** To transfer or part with, as by giving or selling. **3.** To get rid of; throw out. **4.** To kill or destroy: *a despot who disposed of all his enemies, real or imagined.* [Middle English *disposen,* from Old French *disposer,* alteration (influenced by *poser,* to put, place; see POSE[1]) : of Latin *dispōnere,* to arrange : *dis-,* apart; see DIS– + *pōnere,* to put; see **apo-** in Appendix.] **—dis·pos′er** *n.*

dis·po·si·tion (dĭs′pə-zĭsh′ən) *n.* **1.** One's usual mood; temperament: *a sweet disposition.* **2.a.** A habitual inclination; a tendency: *a disposition to disagree.* **b.** A physical property or tendency: *a swelling with a disposition to rupture.* **3.** Arrangement, positioning, or distribution: *a cheerful disposition of colors and textures; a convoy oriented into a north-south disposition.* **4.** A final settlement: *disposition of the deceased's property.* **5.** An act of disposing of; a bestowal or transfer to another. **6.a.** The power or liberty to control, direct, or dispose. **b.** Management; control. [Middle English *disposicioun,* from Old French *disposition,* from Latin *dispositiō, dispositiōn-,* from *dispositus,* past participle of *dispōnere,* to dispose. See DISPOSE.]

SYNONYMS: *disposition, temperament, character, personality, nature.* These nouns refer to the combination of qualities that identify a person. *Disposition* is approximately equivalent to prevailing frame of mind or spirit: *"A patronizing disposition always has its meaner side"* (George Eliot). *Temperament* applies broadly to the sum of physical, emotional, and intellectual characteristics that affect or determine a person's actions and reactions: *"Her highly strung temperament made her uncertain . . . capricious . . . enchanting"* (George Bernard Shaw). *Character* especially emphasizes moral and ethical qualities: *"Education has for its object the formation of character"* (Herbert Spencer). *Personality* is the sum of distinctive traits that give a person individuality: *"The meeting of two personalities is like the contact of two chemical substances: if there is any reaction, both are transformed"* (Carl Jung). *Nature* denotes native or inherent qualities: *"It is my habit,—I hope I may say, my nature,—to believe the best of people"* (George W. Curtis).

dis·pos·sess (dĭs′pə-zĕs′) *tr.v.* **-sessed, -sess·ing, -sess·es.** To deprive (another) of the possession or occupancy of something, such as real property. **—dis′pos·ses′sion** (-zĕsh′ən) *n.* **—dis′pos·ses′sor** *n.* **—dis′pos·ses′so·ry** (-zĕs′ə-rē) *adj.*

dis·pos·sessed (dĭs′pə-zĕst′) *adj.* **1.** Deprived of posses-

ă **pat**	oi **boy**
ā **pay**	ou **out**
âr **care**	o͝o **took**
ä **father**	o͞o **boot**
ĕ **pet**	ŭ **cut**
ē **be**	ûr **urge**
ĭ **pit**	th **thin**
ī **pie**	*th* **this**
îr **pier**	hw **which**
ŏ **pot**	zh **vision**
ō **toe**	ə **about, item**
ô **paw**	♦ **regionalism**

Stress marks: **′** (primary); ′ (secondary), as in **dictionary** (dĭk′shə-nĕr′ē)

sion. **2.** Spiritually impoverished or alienated. **—dis′pos·sessed′** *n.*

dis·praise (dĭs-prāz′) *tr.v.* **-praised, -prais·ing, -prais·es.** To express disapproval of; censure. **—dispraise** *n.* Disapproval; censure. [Middle English *dispreisen,* from Old French *despreisier,* variant of *desprisier,* from Late Latin *dēpretiāre.* See DEPRECIATE.] **—dis·prais′er** *n.* **—dis·prais′ing·ly** *adv.*

dis·prize (dĭs-prīz′) *tr.v.* **-prized, -priz·ing, -priz·es.** *Archaic.* To disdain or undervalue; scorn. [Middle English *disprisen,* from Old French *desprisier.* See DISPRAISE.]

dis·proof (dĭs-pro͞of′) *n.* **1.** The act of refuting or disproving. **2.** Evidence that refutes or disproves.

dis·pro·por·tion (dĭs′prə-pôr′shən, -pōr′-) *n.* **1.** Absence of proportion, symmetry, or proper relation: *the disproportion between the gravity of geopolitical events and the time available to deal with them.* **2.** An instance of a disproportionate relation. **—disproportion** *tr.v.* **-tioned, -tion·ing, -tions.** To make disproportionate.

dis·pro·por·tion·al (dĭs′prə-pôr′shə-nəl, -pōr′-) *adj.* Disproportionate. **—dis′pro·por′tion·al·ly** *adv.*

dis·pro·por·tion·ate (dĭs′prə-pôr′shə-nĭt, -pōr′-) *adj.* Out of proportion, as in size, shape, or amount. **—dis′pro·por′tion·ate·ly** *adv.* **—dis′pro·por′tion·ate·ness** *n.*

dis·prove (dĭs-pro͞ov′) *tr.v.* **-proved, -prov·ing, -proves.** To prove to be false, invalid, or in error; refute. [Middle English *disproven,* from Old French *desprover* : *des-,* dis- + *prover,* to prove; see PROVE.] **—dis·prov′a·ble** *adj.* **—dis·prov′al** *n.*

dis·put·a·ble (dĭ-spyo͞o′tə-bəl, dĭs′pyə-) *adj.* Open to dispute; debatable: *disputable testimony.* **—dis·put′a·bil′i·ty** *n.* **—dis·put′a·bly** *adv.*

dis·pu·tant (dĭ-spyo͞ot′nt, dĭs′pyə-tənt) *adj.* Engaged in dispute or argument. **—disputant** *n.* One engaged in a dispute.

dis·pu·ta·tion (dĭs′pyə-tā′shən) *n.* **1.** The act of disputing; debate. **2.** An academic exercise consisting of a formal debate or an oral defense of a thesis.

dis·pu·ta·tious (dĭs′pyə-tā′shəs) *adj.* Inclined to dispute. See Synonyms at **argumentative.** **—dis′pu·ta′tious·ly** *adv.* **—dis′pu·ta′tious·ness** *n.*

dis·pute (dĭ-spyo͞ot′) *v.* **-put·ed, -put·ing, -putes.** *—tr.* **1.** To argue about; debate. **2.** To question the truth or validity of; doubt: *Her friends disputed her intentions.* **3.** To strive to win (a prize, for example); contest for: *Our team disputed the visitors' claim to the championship.* **4.** To strive against; resist: *disputed the actions of his competitors.* *—intr.* **1.** To engage in discussion or argument; debate. See Synonyms at **discuss.** **2.** To quarrel angrily. **—dispute** *n.* **1.** A verbal controversy; a debate. **2.** An angry altercation; a quarrel. See Synonyms at **argument.** [Middle English *disputen,* from Old French *desputer,* from Latin *disputāre,* to examine : *dis-,* apart; see DIS– + *putāre,* to reckon; see **peu-** in Appendix.] **—dis·put′er** *n.*

dis·qual·i·fi·ca·tion (dĭs-kwŏl′ə-fĭ-kā′shən) *n.* **1.** The act of disqualifying or the condition of having been disqualified. **2.** Something that disqualifies: *illness as a disqualification for enlistment in the army.*

dis·qual·i·fy (dĭs-kwŏl′ə-fī′) *tr.v.* **-fied, -fy·ing, -fies. 1.a.** To render unqualified or unfit. **b.** To declare unqualified or ineligible. **2.** To deprive of legal rights, powers, or privileges.

dis·qui·et (dĭs-kwī′ĭt) *tr.v.* **-et·ed, -et·ing, -ets.** To deprive of peace or rest; trouble. **—disquiet** *n.* Absence of peace or rest; anxiety. **—disquiet** *adj.* *Archaic.* Uneasy; restless. **—dis·qui′et·ing·ly** *adv.* **—dis·qui′et·ly** *adv.* **—dis·qui′et·ness** *n.*

dis·qui·e·tude (dĭs-kwī′ĭ-to͞od′, -tyo͞od′) *n.* Worried unease; anxiety: *a state of brooding disquietude.*

dis·qui·si·tion (dĭs′kwĭ-zĭsh′ən) *n.* A formal discourse on a subject, often in writing. [Latin *disquīsītiō, disquīsītiōn-,* investigation, from *disquīsītus,* past participle of *disquīrere,* to investigate : *dis-,* dis- + *quaerere,* to search for.]

Benjamin Disraeli

Dis·rae·li (dĭz-rā′lē), **Benjamin.** First Earl of Beaconsfield. Known as "Dizzy." 1804–1881. British politician who served as prime minister (1868 and 1874–1880) and was instrumental in extending the power and scope of the British Empire.

dis·rate (dĭs-rāt′) *tr.v.* **-rat·ed, -rat·ing, -rates.** To reduce in rank or rating; demote.

dis·re·gard (dĭs′rĭ-gärd′) *tr.v.* **-gard·ed, -gard·ing, -gards. 1.** To pay no attention or heed to; ignore. **2.** To treat without proper respect or attentiveness. **—disregard** *n.* Lack of thoughtful attention or due regard. **—dis′re·gard′er** *n.* **—dis′re·gard′ful** *adj.*

dis·rel·ish (dĭs-rĕl′ĭsh) *tr.v.* **-ished, -ish·ing, -ish·es.** To have distaste for; dislike. **—disrelish** *n.* Distaste; aversion.

dis·re·mem·ber (dĭs′rĭ-mĕm′bər) *v.* **-bered, -ber·ing, -bers.** *Informal.* *—tr.* To fail to remember. *—intr.* To forget.

dis·re·pair (dĭs′rĭ-pâr′) *n.* The condition of being in need of repair: *a house in disrepair.*

dis·rep·u·ta·ble (dĭs-rĕp′yə-tə-bəl) *adj.* Lacking respectability, as in character, behavior, or appearance. **—dis·rep′u·ta·bil′i·ty, dis·rep′u·ta·ble·ness** *n.* **—dis·rep′u·ta·bly** *adv.*

dis·re·pute (dĭs′rĭ-pyo͞ot′) *n.* Damage to or loss of reputation. See Synonyms at **disgrace.**

dis·re·spect (dĭs′rĭ-spĕkt′) *n.* Lack of respect, esteem, or courteous regard. **—disrespect** *tr.v.* **-spect·ed, -spect·ing, -spects.** To show a lack of respect for: *disrespected her elders; disrespected the law.*

dis·re·spect·a·ble (dĭs′rĭ-spĕk′tə-bəl) *adj.* Unworthy of respect. **—dis′re·spect′a·bil′i·ty** *n.*

dis·re·spect·ful (dĭs′rĭ-spĕkt′fəl) *adj.* Having or exhibiting a lack of respect; rude and discourteous. **—dis′re·spect′ful·ly** *adv.* **—dis′re·spect′ful·ness** *n.*

dis·robe (dĭs-rōb′) *v.* **-robed, -rob·ing, -robes.** *—tr.* To remove the clothing or covering from. *—intr.* To undress oneself. **—dis·rob′er** *n.*

dis·rupt (dĭs-rŭpt′) *tr.v.* **-rupt·ed, -rupt·ing, -rupts. 1.** To throw into confusion or disorder: *Protesters disrupted the candidate's speech.* **2.** To interrupt or impede the progress, movement, or procedure of: *Our efforts in the garden were disrupted by an early frost.* **3.** To break or burst; rupture. [Latin *disrumpere, disrupt-,* to break apart : *dis-,* dis- + *rumpere,* to break apart; see **reup-** in Appendix.] **—dis·rupt′er, dis·rup′tor** *n.* **—dis·rup′tion** *n.*

dis·rup·tive (dĭs-rŭp′tĭv) *adj.* Relating to, causing, or produced by disruption. **—dis·rup′tive·ly** *adv.*

diss. *abbr.* Dissertation.

dis·sat·is·fac·tion (dĭs-săt′ĭs-făk′shən) *n.* **1.** The condition or feeling of being displeased or unsatisfied; discontent. **2.** A cause of discontent.

dis·sat·is·fac·to·ry (dĭs-săt′ĭs-făk′tə-rē) *adj.* Unsatisfactory.

dis·sat·is·fied (dĭs-săt′ĭs-fīd′) *adj.* Feeling or exhibiting a lack of contentment or satisfaction. **—dis·sat′is·fied′ly** *adv.*

dis·sat·is·fy (dĭs-săt′ĭs-fī′) *tr.v.* **-fied, -fy·ing, -fies.** To fail to satisfy; disappoint.

dissd. *abbr.* Dissolved.

dis·seat (dĭs-sēt′) *tr.v.* **-seat·ed, -seat·ing, -seats.** *Archaic.* To unseat.

dis·sect (dĭ-sĕkt′, dī-, dī′sĕkt′) *tr.v.* **-sect·ed, -sect·ing, -sects. 1.** To cut apart or separate (tissue), especially for anatomical study. **2.** To examine, analyze, or criticize in minute detail: *dissected the plan afterward to learn why it had failed.* See Synonyms at **analyze.** [Latin *dissecāre, dissect-,* to cut apart : *dis-,* dis- + *secāre,* to cut up; see **sek-** in Appendix.] **—dis·sec′ti·ble** *adj.* **—dis·sec′tor** *n.*

dis·sect·ed (dĭ-sĕk′tĭd, dī-) *adj.* **1.** *Botany.* Divided into many deep, narrow segments: *dissected leaves.* **2.** *Geology.* Cut by irregular valleys and hills.

dis·sec·tion (dĭ-sĕk′shən, dī-) *n.* **1.** The act or an instance of dissecting. **2.** Something that has been dissected, such as a tissue specimen under study. **3.** A detailed examination or analysis.

dis·seise (dĭs-sēz′) *v.* *Law.* Variant of **disseize.**

dis·sei·sin (dĭs-sē′zĭn) *n.* *Law.* Variant of **disseizin.**

dis·seize also **dis·seise** (dĭs-sēz′) *tr.v.* **-seized, -seiz·ing, -seiz·es** also **-seised, -seis·ing, -seis·es.** *Law.* To dispossess unlawfully of real property; oust. [Middle English *disseisen,* from Anglo-Norman *disseisir,* variant of Old French *dessaisir* : *des-,* dis- + *saisir,* to seize; see SEIZE.]

dis·sei·zin also **dis·sei·sin** (dĭs-sē′zĭn) *n.* *Law.* Wrongful dispossession of one in the possession of real property. [Middle English *disseisine,* from Anglo-Norman, variant of Old French *dessaisine* : *des-,* dis- + *seisine,* seisin; see SEISIN.]

dis·sem·ble (dĭ-sĕm′bəl) *v.* **-bled, -bling, -bles.** *—tr.* **1.** To disguise or conceal behind a false appearance. See Synonyms at **disguise.** **2.** To make a false show of; feign. *—intr.* To disguise or conceal one's real nature, motives, or feelings behind a false appearance. [Middle English *dissemblen,* from Old French *dessembler,* to be different : *des-,* dis- + *sembler,* to appear, seem; see SEMBLABLE.] **—dis·sem′blance** *n.* **—dis·sem′bler** *n.* **—dis·sem′bling·ly** *adv.*

dis·sem·i·nate (dĭ-sĕm′ə-nāt′) *v.* **-nat·ed, -nat·ing, -nates.** *—tr.* **1.** To scatter widely, as in sowing seed. **2.** To spread abroad; promulgate: *disseminate information.* *—intr.* To become diffused; spread. [Latin *dissēmināre, dissēmināt-* : *dis-,* dis- + *sēmināre,* to sow (from *sēmen, sēmin-,* seed; see **sē-** in Appendix).] **—dis·sem′i·na′tion** *n.* **—dis·sem′i·na′tor** *n.*

dis·sem·i·nat·ed (dĭ-sĕm′ə-nā′tĭd) *adj.* Spread over a large area of a body, a tissue, or an organ.

dis·sem·i·nule (dĭ-sĕm′ə-nyo͞ol′) *n.* A reproductive plant part, such as a seed, fruit, or spore, that is modified for dispersal. Also called *diaspore.* [DISSEMIN(ATE) + –ULE.]

dis·sen·sion (dĭ-sĕn′shən) *n.* Difference of opinion; disagreement. See Synonyms at **discord.** [Middle English *dissencioun,* from Old French *dissension,* from Latin *dissēnsiō, dissēnsiōn-,* from *dissēnsus,* past participle of *dissentīre,* to dissent. See DISSENT.]

dis·sent (dĭ-sĕnt′) *intr.v.* **-sent·ed, -sent·ing, -sents. 1.** To differ in opinion or feeling; disagree. **2.** To withhold assent or approval. **—dissent** *n.* **1.** Difference of opinion or feeling; disagreement. **2.** The refusal to conform to the authority or doctrine of an established church; nonconformity. **3.** *Law.* A justice's refusal to concur with the opinion of a majority, as on a higher court. In this sense, also called *dissenting opinion.* [Middle English *dissenten,* from Latin *dissentīre* : *dis-,* dis- + *sentīre,* to feel; see **sent-** in Appendix.] **—dis·sent′ing·ly** *adv.*

dis·sent·er (dĭ-sĕn′tər) *n.* **1.** One who dissents: *political dissenters.* **2.** Often **Dissenter.** One who refuses to accept the doctrines or usages of an established or a national church, especially a Protestant who dissents from the Church of England.

dis·sen·tient (dĭ-sĕn′shənt) *adj.* Dissenting, especially from the sentiment or policies of a majority. **—dissentient** *n.* A dissenter. **—dis·sen′tience** *n.*

dis·sent·ing opinion (dĭ-sĕn′tĭng) *n. Law.* See **dissent** (sense 3).

dis·sep·i·ment (dĭ-sĕp′ə-mənt) *n. Botany.* A partition dividing an organ, such as an ovary or a fruit, into chambers. [Latin *dissaepīmentum,* partition, from *dissaepīre,* to divide : *dis-,* dis- + *saepīre,* hedge off (from *saepēs,* hedge).] **—dis·sep′i·men′tal** (-mĕn′tl) *adj.*

dis·ser·tate (dĭs′ər-tāt′) also **dis·sert** (dĭ-sûrt′) *intr.v.* **-tat·ed, -tat·ing, -tates** also **-sert·ed, -sert·ing, -serts.** To discourse formally. [Latin *dissertāre, dissertāt-,* frequentative of *disserere,* to discuss : *dis-,* dis- + *serere,* to connect; see **ser-**[2] in Appendix.] **—dis′ser·ta′tor** *n.*

dis·ser·ta·tion (dĭs′ər-tā′shən) *n. Abbr.* **diss.** A lengthy, formal treatise, especially one written by a candidate for the doctoral degree at a university; a thesis.

dis·serve (dĭs-sûrv′) *tr.v.* **-served, -serv·ing, -serves.** To treat badly; harm.

dis·serv·ice (dĭs-sûr′vĭs) *n.* A harmful action; an injury.

dis·sev·er (dĭ-sĕv′ər) *v.* **-ered, -er·ing, -ers.** *—tr.* **1.** To separate; sever. **2.** To divide into parts; break up. *—intr.* To become separated or disunited. [Middle English *disseveren,* from Old French *dessevrer,* from Late Latin *dissēparāre* : Latin *dis-,* dis- + Latin *sēparāre,* to separate; see SEPARATE.] **—dis·sev′er·ance, dis·sev′er·ment** *n.*

dis·si·dence (dĭs′ĭ-dəns) *n.* Disagreement, as of opinion or belief; dissent.

dis·si·dent (dĭs′ĭ-dənt) *adj.* Disagreeing, as in opinion or belief. **—dissident** *n.* One who disagrees; a dissenter. [Latin *dissidēns, dissident-,* present participle of *dissidēre,* to disagree : *dis-,* apart; see DIS– + *sedēre,* to sit; see **sed-** in Appendix.]

dis·sil·i·ent (dĭ-sĭl′ē-ənt) *adj. Botany.* Bursting apart, as some seed pods when ripe. [Latin *dissiliēns, dissilient-,* present participle of *dissilīre,* to fly apart : *dis-,* apart; see DIS– + *salīre,* to leap; see **sel-** in Appendix.]

dis·sim·i·lar (dĭ-sĭm′ə-lər) *adj.* Unlike; different. **—dis·sim′i·lar·ly** *adv.*

dis·sim·i·lar·i·ty (dĭ-sĭm′ə-lăr′ĭ-tē) *n., pl.* **-ties. 1.** The quality of being distinct or unlike; difference. **2.** A point of distinction or difference. See Synonyms at **difference.**

dis·sim·i·late (dĭ-sĭm′ə-lāt′) *v.* **-lat·ed, -lat·ing, -lates.** *—tr.* **1.** To make unlike or dissimilar. **2.** *Linguistics.* To cause to undergo dissimilation. *—intr.* **1.** To become unlike or dissimilar. **2.** *Linguistics.* To undergo dissimilation. [DIS– + (AS)SIMILATE.]

dis·sim·i·la·tion (dĭ-sĭm′ə-lā′shən) *n.* **1.** The act or process of making or becoming dissimilar. **2.** *Linguistics.* The process by which one of two similar or identical sounds in a word becomes less like the other, such as the *l* in English *marble* (from French *marbre*).

dis·si·mil·i·tude (dĭs′ə-mĭl′ĭ-to͞od′, -tyo͞od′) *n.* Lack of resemblance; dissimilarity. [Middle English, from Latin *dissimilitūdō,* from *dissimilis,* different : *dis-,* dis- + *similis,* like; see SIMILAR.]

dis·sim·u·late (dĭ-sĭm′yə-lāt′) *v.* **-lat·ed, -lat·ing, -lates.** *—tr.* To disguise (one's intentions, for example) under a feigned appearance. See Synonyms at **disguise.** *—intr.* To conceal one's true feelings or intentions. [Middle English *dissimulaten,* from Latin *dissimulāre, dissimulāt-* : *dis-,* dis- + *simulāre,* to simulate; see SIMULATE.] **—dis·sim′u·la′tion** *n.* **—dis·sim′u·la′tive** *adj.* **—dis·sim′u·la′tor** *n.*

dis·si·pate (dĭs′ə-pāt′) *v.* **-pat·ed, -pat·ing, -pates.** *—tr.* **1.** To drive away; disperse. **2.** To attenuate to or almost to the point of disappearing: *The wind finally dissipated the smoke.* See Synonyms at **scatter. 3.a.** To spend or expend intemperately or wastefully; squander. **b.** To use up, especially recklessly; exhaust: *dissipated their energy.* See Synonyms at **waste. 4.** To cause to lose (energy, such as heat) irreversibly. *—intr.* **1.** To vanish by dispersion: *The dark clouds finally dissipated.* **2.** To indulge in the intemperate pursuit of pleasure. [Middle English *dissipaten,* from Latin *dissipāre, dissipāt-.*] **—dis′si·pat′er, dis′si·pa′tor** *n.* **—dis′si·pa′tive** *adj.*

dis·si·pat·ed (dĭs′ə-pā′tĭd) *adj.* **1.** Intemperate in the pursuit of pleasure; dissolute. **2.** Wasted or squandered. **3.** Irreversibly lost. Used of energy. **—dis′si·pat′ed·ly** *adv.* **—dis′si·pat′ed·ness** *n.*

dis·si·pa·tion (dĭs′ə-pā′shən) *n.* **1.** The act of dissipating or the condition of having been dissipated. **2.** Wasteful expenditure or consumption. **3.** Dissolute indulgence in sensual pleasure; intemperance. **4.** An amusement; a diversion.

dis·so·cia·ble (dĭ-sō′shə-bəl, -shē-ə-bəl) *adj.* That can be dissociated; separable: *To many, drugs and crime are not dissociable.* **—dis·so′cia·bil′i·ty, dis·so′cia·ble·ness** *n.* **—dis·so′cia·bly** *adv.*

dis·so·ci·ate (dĭ-sō′shē-āt′, -sē-) *v.* **-at·ed, -at·ing, -ates.** *—tr.* **1.** To remove from association; separate: *"Marx never dissociated man from his social environment"* (Sidney Hook). **2.** *Chemistry.* To cause to undergo dissociation. *—intr.* **1.** To cease associating; part. **2.** *Biology.* To mutate or change morphologically, often reversibly. **3.** *Chemistry.* To undergo dissociation. [Latin *dissociāre, dissociāt-* : *dis-,* dis- + *sociāre,* to unite (from *socius,* companion; see **sek^{w}-**[1] in Appendix).] **—dis·so′ci·a′tive** *adj.*

dis·so·ci·a·tion (dĭ-sō′sē-ā′shən, -shē-) *n.* **1.** The act of dissociating or the condition of having been dissociated. **2.** *Chemistry.* **a.** The chemical process by means of which a change in physical condition, as in pressure or temperature, or the action of a solvent causes a molecule to split into simpler groups of atoms, single atoms, or ions. **b.** The separation of an electrolyte into ions of opposite charge. **3.** *Biology.* The process by which some microbes differentiate or mutate. **4.** *Psychiatry.* Separation of a group of related psychological activities into autonomously functioning units, as in the generation of multiple personalities.

dis·sol·u·ble (dĭ-sŏl′yə-bəl) *adj.* That can be dissolved: *dissoluble airborne pollutants brought back to the earth as rain.* [Latin *dissolūbilis,* from *dissolūtus,* past participle of *dissolvere,* to dissolve. See DISSOLVE.] **—dis′sol·u·bil′i·ty, dis·sol′u·ble·ness** *n.*

dis·so·lute (dĭs′ə-lo͞ot′) *adj.* Lacking moral restraint; indulging in sensual pleasures or vices. [Middle English, from Latin *dissolūtus,* past participle of *dissolvere,* to dissolve. See DISSOLVE.] **—dis′so·lute′ly** *adv.* **—dis′so·lute′ness** *n.*

dis·so·lu·tion (dĭs′ə-lo͞o′shən) *n.* **1.** Decomposition into fragments or parts; disintegration. **2.** Indulgence in sensual pleasures; debauchery. **3.** Termination or extinction by disintegration or dispersion: *The dissolution of the empire was remarkably swift.* **4.** Extinction of life; death. **5.** Annulment or termination of a formal or legal bond, tie, or contract. **6.** Formal dismissal of an assembly or legislature. **7.** Reduction to a liquid form; liquefaction. **—dis′so·lu′tive** *adj.*

dis·solve (dĭ-zŏlv′) *v.* **-solved, -solv·ing, -solves.** *—tr.* **1.** To cause to pass into solution: *dissolve salt in water.* **2.** To reduce (solid matter) to liquid form; melt. **3.** To cause to disappear or vanish; dispel. **4.** To break into component parts; disintegrate. **5.** To bring to an end by or as if by breaking up; terminate. **6.** To dismiss (a legislative body, for example): *dissolved parliament and called for new elections.* **7.** To cause to break down emotionally or psychologically; upset. **8.** To cause to lose definition; blur; confuse: *"Morality has finally been dissolved in pity"* (Leslie Fiedler). **9.** *Law.* To annul; abrogate. *—intr.* **1.** To pass into solution. **2.** To become liquid; melt. **3.** To break up or disperse. **4.** To become disintegrated; disappear. **5.** To be overcome emotionally or psychologically: *I dissolved into helpless laughter.* **6.** To lose clarity or definition; fade away. **7.** To shift scenes in a motion-picture film or videotape by having one scene fade out while the next scene appears behind it and grows clearer as the first one dims. **—dissolve** *n.* A scene transition in a motion-picture film or videotape made by fading out one scene while the next scene grows clearer. Also called *lap dissolve.* [Middle English *dissolven,* from Latin *dissolvere* : *dis-,* dis- + *solvere,* to release; see **leu-** in Appendix.] **—dis·solv′a·ble** *adj.* **—dis·solv′er** *n.*

dis·sol·vent (dĭ-zŏl′vənt) *adj.* Capable of dissolving a substance; solvent. **—dissolvent** *n.* A solvent.

dis·so·nance (dĭs′ə-nəns) *n.* **1.** A harsh, disagreeable combination of sounds; discord. **2.** Lack of agreement, consistency, or harmony; conflict. **3.** *Music.* A combination of tones conventionally considered to suggest unrelieved tension and require resolution.

dis·so·nan·cy (dĭs′ə-nən-sē) *n., pl.* **-cies.** Dissonance.

dis·so·nant (dĭs′ə-nənt) *adj.* **1.** Harsh and inharmonious in sound; discordant. **2.** Being at variance; disagreeing. **3.** *Music.* Constituting or producing a dissonance. [Middle English *dissonaunt,* from Old French *dissonant,* from Latin *dissonāns, dissonant-,* present participle of *dissonāre,* to be dissonant : *dis-,* apart; see DIS– + *sonāre,* to sound; see **swen-** in Appendix.] **—dis′so·nant·ly** *adv.*

dis·suade (dĭ-swād′) *tr.v.* **-suad·ed, -suad·ing, -suades.** To deter (a person) from a course of action or a purpose by persuasion or exhortation: *dissuaded my friend from pursuing such a rash scheme.* [Latin *dissuādēre* : *dis-,* dis- + *suādēre,* to advise; see **swād-** in Appendix.] **—dis·suad′er** *n.*

SYNONYMS: *dissuade, deter, discourage.* The central meaning shared by these verbs is "to persuade someone not to do something": *tried to dissuade the general from taking disciplinary action; couldn't be deterred from smoking; discouraged her from accepting the offer.*
ANTONYM: *persuade.*

dis·sua·sion (dĭ-swā′zhən) *n.* The act or an instance of dissuading. [Middle English, from Old French, from Latin *dissuāsiō, dissuāsiōn-,* from *dissuāsus,* past participle of *dissuādēre,* to dissuade. See DISSUADE.] **—dis·sua′sive** *adj.* **—dis·sua′sive·ly** *adv.* **—dis·sua′sive·ness** *n.*

dis·syl·la·ble (dĭ′sĭl′ə-bəl, dĭ-sĭl′-, dī-) *n.* Variant of **disyllable.**

dis·sym·me·try (dĭs-sĭm′ĭ-trē) *n., pl.* **-tries.** Lack of symmetry. **—dis′sym·met′ric** (dĭs′sĭ-mĕt′rĭk), **dis′sym·met′ri·cal** (-rĭ-kəl) *adj.* **—dis′sym·met′ri·cal·ly** *adv.*

dist. *abbr.* **1.** Distance; distant. **2.** District.

dis·taff (dĭs′tăf′) *n.* **1.a.** A staff that holds on its cleft end the unspun flax, wool, or tow from which thread is drawn in spinning by hand. **b.** An attachment for a spinning wheel that serves this purpose. **2.** Work and concerns traditionally considered impor-

distaff
Distaff highlighted in oval

ă pat	oi boy
ā pay	ou out
âr care	o͝o took
ä father	o͞o boot
ĕ pet	ŭ cut
ē be	ûr urge
ĭ pit	th thin
ī pie	*th* this
îr pier	hw which
ŏ pot	zh vision
ō toe	ə about, item
ô paw	♦ regionalism

Stress marks: **′** (primary); ′ (secondary), as in **dictionary** (dĭk′shə-nĕr′ē)

tant to women. **3.** Women considered as a group. [Middle English *distaf,* from Old English *distæf* : *dis-,* bunch of flax + *stæf,* staff.]

distaff side *n.* The female line or maternal branch of a family. [From the idea that spinning is women's work.]

dis·tal (dĭs′təl) *adj.* **1.** Anatomically located far from a point of reference, such as an origin or a point of attachment. **2.** Situated farthest from the middle and front of the jaw, as a tooth or tooth surface. [DIST(ANT) + –AL[1].] **—dis′tal·ly** *adv.*

dis·tance (dĭs′təns) *n. Abbr.* **dist., dis. 1.** The extent of space between two objects or places; an intervening space. **2.** The fact or condition of being apart in space; remoteness. **3.** *Mathematics.* The length or numerical value of a straight line or curve. **4.a.** The extent of space between points on a measured course. **b.** The length of a race, especially of a horserace. **5.a.** A point or an area that is far away: *"Telephone poles stretched way into a distance I couldn't quite see"* (Leigh Allison Wilson). **b.** A depiction of a point or an area that is far away. **6.** A stretch of space without designation of limit; an expanse: *a land of few hills and great distances.* **7.** The extent of time between two events; an intervening period. **8.** A point removed in time: *At a distance of 11 years, the details of the crime were clouded in his mind.* **9.** The period or length of a contest: *The challenger had never attempted the distance of 12 rounds.* **10.** An amount of progress: *The curriculum committee is a distance from where it was two months ago.* **11.** Difference or disagreement: *The candidates could not be at a greater distance on this issue.* **12.** Chillness of manner; aloofness. **—distance** *tr.v.* **-tanced, -tanc·ing, -tanc·es. 1.** To place or keep at or as if at a distance: *"To understand Russian strategy . . . it is necessary for us to distance ourselves from our own myths and to enter into theirs"* (Freeman J. Dyson). **2.** To cause to appear at a distance. **3.** To leave far behind; outrun.

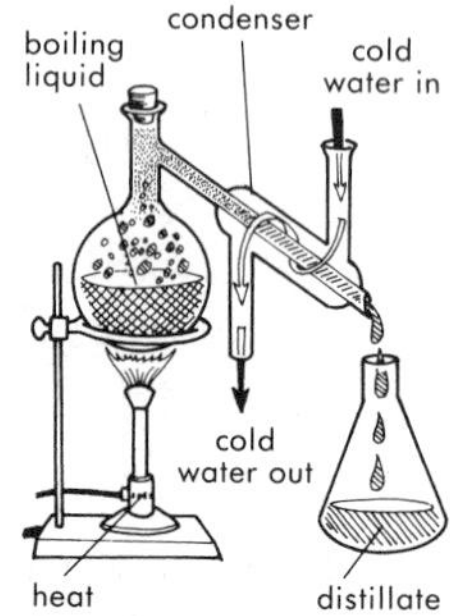

distillation
Simple distillation

dis·tant (dĭs′tənt) *adj. Abbr.* **dist., dis. 1.a.** Separate or apart in space. **b.** Far removed; remote: *distant lands.* **2.** Coming from or going to a distance: *a distant sound; a distant telephone call.* **3.** Far removed or apart in time: *the distant past; distant events.* **4.** Far apart in relationship: *a distant cousin.* **5.** Minimally similar: *a distant likeness.* **6.** Far removed mentally: *distant thoughts.* **7.** Aloof or chilly: *a distant smile.* [Middle English *distaunt,* from Old French, from Latin *distāns, distant-,* present participle of *distāre,* to be remote : *dis-,* apart; see DIS– + *stāre,* to stand; see **stā-** in Appendix.] **—dis′tant·ly** *adv.*

SYNONYMS: *distant, far, far-off, faraway, remote, removed.* These adjectives mean apart from others in space, time, or relationship. *Distant* can indicate a specific separation (*a house a mile distant from town*), or it can indicate an indefinite but sizable interval (*heard the sound of distant traffic*). *Far* applies to what is a great distance off: *"We be come from a far country"* (Joshua 9:6). *"He seems so near, and yet so far"* (Tennyson). *Far-off* and *faraway* imply an even greater distance than *far: troops landing on far-off shores; faraway mountains and lakes. Remote* not only means faraway but suggests isolation from the speaker's locality or point in time: *remote stars; a remote outpost of civilization; the remote past. Removed* implies distinct separation between two entities in place, time, kind, or character: *a civilization ten centuries removed from modern times; a hideaway far removed from towns and cities.*

dis·taste (dĭs-tāst′) *n.* Dislike or aversion. **—distaste** *tr.v.* **-tast·ed, -tast·ing, -tastes.** *Archaic.* **1.** To feel repugnance for; dislike. **2.** To offend; displease.

dis·taste·ful (dĭs-tāst′fəl) *adj.* **1.a.** Unpleasant; disagreeable: *found cocktail parties distasteful.* **b.** Objectionable; offensive: *used distasteful language.* **2.** Expressing aversion or dislike: *shot me a distasteful glance.* **—dis·taste′ful·ly** *adv.* **—dis·taste′ful·ness** *n.*

Dist. Atty. *abbr. Law.* District attorney.

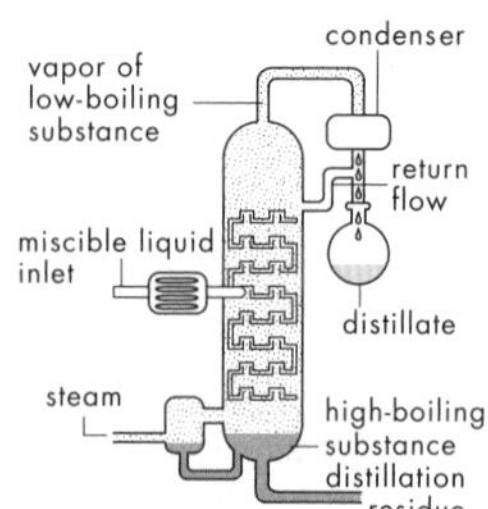

distillation column

dis·tem·per¹ (dĭs-tĕm′pər) *n.* **1.a.** An infectious viral disease occurring in dogs, characterized by loss of appetite, a catarrhal discharge from the eyes and nose, vomiting, fever, lethargy, partial paralysis caused by destruction of myelinated nerve tissue, and sometimes death. Also called *canine distemper.* **b.** A similar viral disease of cats characterized by fever, vomiting, diarrhea leading to dehydration, and sometimes death. Also called *feline distemper, panleukopenia.* **c.** Any of various similar mammalian diseases. **2.** An illness or a disease; an ailment: *"He died . . . of a broken heart, a distemper which kills many more than is generally imagined"* (Henry Fielding). **3.** Ill humor; testiness. **4.** Disorder or disturbance, especially of a social or political nature. **—distemper** *tr.v.* **-pered, -per·ing, -pers. 1.** To put out of order. **2.** *Archaic.* To unsettle; derange. [From Middle English *distemperen,* to upset the balance of the humors, from Old French *destemprer,* to disturb, from Late Latin *distemperāre* : Latin *dis-,* dis- + Latin *temperāre,* to mix properly.]

dis·tem·per² (dĭs-tĕm′pər) *n.* **1.a.** A process of painting in which pigments are mixed with water and a glue-size or casein binder, used for flat wall decoration or scenic and poster painting. **b.** The paint used in this process. **2.** A painting made by this process. **—distemper** *tr.v.* **-pered, -per·ing, -pers. 1.** To mix (powdered pigments or colors) with water and size. **2.** To paint (a work) in distemper. [Middle English *distemperen,* to dilute. See DISTEMPER[1].]

dis·tend (dĭ-stĕnd′) *v.* **-tend·ed, -tend·ing, -tends.** *—intr.* To swell out or expand from or as if from internal pressure. *—tr.* **1.** To cause to expand by or as if by internal pressure; dilate. **2.** To extend. [Middle English *distenden,* from Latin *distendere* : *dis-,* dis- + *tendere,* to stretch; see **ten-** in Appendix.]

dis·ten·si·ble (dĭ-stĕn′sə-bəl) *adj.* That can be distended: *a fish with a distensible stomach.* **—dis·ten′si·bil′i·ty** *n.*

dis·ten·tion also **dis·ten·sion** (dĭ-stĕn′shən) *n.* The act of distending or the state of being distended. [Middle English *distensioun,* from Old French, from Latin *distēnsiō, distēnsiōn-,* alteration of *distentiō,* from *distentus,* past participle of *distendere,* to distend. See DISTEND.]

dis·tich (dĭs′tĭk) *n., pl.* **-tichs. 1.** A unit of verse consisting of two lines, especially as used in Greek and Latin elegiac poetry. **2.** A rhyming couplet. [Latin *distichon,* from Greek *distikhon,* from neuter of *distikhos,* having two rows or verses : *di-,* two; see DI–[1] + *stikhos,* line of verse; see **steigh-** in Appendix.]

dis·ti·chous (dĭs′tĭ-kəs) *adj. Botany.* Arranged in two vertical rows on opposite sides of an axis: *distichous leaves.* [From Latin *distichus,* having two rows, from Greek *distikhos.* See DISTICH.] **—dis′ti·chous·ly** *adv.*

dis·till also **dis·til** (dĭ-stĭl′) *—v.* **-tilled, -till·ing, -tills** also **-tilled, -til·ling, -tils.** *—tr.* **1.** To subject (a substance) to distillation. **2.** To separate (a distillate) by distillation. **3.** To increase the concentration of, separate, or purify by or as if by distillation. **4.** To separate or extract the essential elements of: *distill the crucial points of the book.* **5.** To exude or give off (matter) in drops or small quantities. *—intr.* **1.** To undergo or be produced by distillation. **2.** To fall or exude in drops or small quantities. [Middle English *distillen,* from Old French *distiller,* from Latin *distillāre,* variant of *dēstillāre,* to trickle : *dē-,* de- + *stillāre,* to drip (from *stilla,* drop).] **—dis·till′a·ble** *adj.*

dis·til·late (dĭs′tə-lāt′, -lĭt, dĭ-stĭl′ĭt) *n.* **1.** A liquid condensed from vapor in distillation. **2.** A purified form; an essence: *"Finally the President knows the most crucial things about every facet of reality, the pristine distillate of the world's critical information"* (Peregrine Worsthorne).

dis·til·la·tion (dĭs′tə-lā′shən) *n.* **1.** The evaporation and subsequent collection of a liquid by condensation as a means of purification: *the distillation of water.* **2.** The extraction of the volatile components of a mixture by the condensation and collection of the vapors that are produced as the mixture is heated: *petroleum distillation.* **3.** A distillate.

distillation column *n.* A tall metal cylinder internally fitted with perforated horizontal plates used to promote separation of miscible liquids ascending in the cylinder as vapor.

dis·till·er (dĭ-stĭl′ər) *n.* **1.** One that distills, as a condenser. **2.** One that makes alcoholic liquors by the process of distillation.

dis·till·er·y (dĭ-stĭl′ə-rē) *n., pl.* **-ies.** An establishment for distilling, especially for distilling alcoholic liquors.

dis·tinct (dĭ-stĭngkt′) *adj.* **1.** Readily distinguishable from all others; discrete: *on two distinct occasions.* **2.** Easily perceived by the senses or intellect; clear: *a distinct flavor.* **3.** Clearly defined; unquestionable: *at a distinct disadvantage.* **4.** Very likely; probable: *There is a distinct possibility that she won't come.* **5.** Notable: *a distinct honor and high privilege.* [Middle English, past participle of *distincten,* to distinguish, discern, from Old French *destincter,* from Latin *distīnctus,* past participle of *distinguere,* to distinguish. See DISTINGUISH.] **—dis·tinct′ly** *adv.* **—dis·tinct′ness** *n.*

SYNONYMS: *distinct, discrete, separate, several.* The central meaning shared by these adjectives is "distinguished from others in nature or qualities": *six distinct colors; a government with three discrete divisions; a problem consisting of two separate issues; performed the several steps of the process.* See also Synonyms at **apparent.**

USAGE NOTE: A thing is *distinct* if it is sharply distinguished from other things; a property or attribute is *distinctive* if it enables us to distinguish one thing from another. *The warbler is not a distinct species* means that the warbler is not a clearly defined type of bird. *The warbler has a distinctive song* means that the warbler's song enables us to distinguish the warbler from other birds.

dis·tinc·tion (dĭ-stĭngk′shən) *n.* **1.** The act of distinguishing; differentiation. **2.** The condition or fact of being dissimilar or distinct; difference: *"the crucial distinction between education and indoctrination"* (A. Bartlett Giamatti). See Synonyms at **difference. 3.** A distinguishing factor, attribute, or characteristic. **4.a.** Excellence or eminence, as of performance, character, or reputation: *a diplomat of distinction.* **b.** A special feature or quality conferring superiority. **5.** Recognition of achievement or superiority; honor: *graduated with distinction.*

dis·tinc·tive (dĭ-stĭngk′tĭv) *adj.* **1.** Serving to identify; distinguishing: *distinctive tribal tattoos.* See Usage Note at **distinct. 2.** Characteristic or typical: *"Jerusalem has a distinctive Middle East flavor"* (Curtis Wilkie). **3.** *Linguistics.* Phonemically relevant and capable of conveying a difference in meaning, as nasalization in the initial sound of *mat* versus *bat.* **—dis·tinc′tive·ly** *adv.* **—dis·tinc′tive·ness** *n.*

dis·tin·gué (dēs′tăng-gā′, dĭs′-, dĭ-stăng′gā) *adj.* Distinguished in manner or bearing. [French, past participle of *distinguer,* to distinguish, from Old French. See DISTINGUISH.]

dis·tin·guish (dĭ-stĭng′gwĭsh) *v.* **-guished, -guish·ing, -guish·es.** *—tr.* **1.** To perceive as being different or distinct. **2.**

To perceive distinctly; discern: *distinguished the masts of ships on the horizon.* **3.** To make noticeable or different; set apart. **4.** To cause (oneself) to be eminent or recognized: *They have distinguished themselves as dedicated social workers.* —*intr.* To perceive or indicate differences; discriminate: *distinguish between right and wrong.* [Alteration of obsolete *distingue,* from Middle English *distinguen,* from Old French *distinguer,* from Latin *distinguere,* to separate. See **steig-** in Appendix.] —**dis·tin′guish·a·ble** *adj.* —**dis·tin′guish·a·bly** *adv.*

dis·tin·guished (dĭ-stĭng′gwĭsht) *adj.* **1.** Characterized by excellence or distinction; eminent. **2.** Dignified in conduct or appearance.

Dis·tin·guished Conduct Medal (dĭ-stĭng′gwĭsht) *n.* *Abbr.* **DCM, D.C.M.** A British military decoration for distinguished conduct in the field.

Distinguished Flying Cross *n.* *Abbr.* **DFC, D.F.C.** **1.** A U.S. military decoration awarded for heroism or extraordinary achievement in aerial combat. **2.** A British military decoration awarded to officers of the Royal Air Force for extraordinary achievement.

Distinguished Service Cross *n.* *Abbr.* **DSC, D.S.C.** **1.** A U.S. Army decoration awarded for exceptional heroism in combat. **2.** A British military decoration awarded to officers of the Royal Navy for gallantry in action.

Distinguished Service Medal *n.* *Abbr.* **DSM, D.S.M.** **1.** A U.S. military decoration awarded for distinguished performance in a duty of great responsibility. **2.** A British military decoration awarded to noncommissioned officers and men in the Royal Navy and Royal Marines for distinguished conduct in war.

Distinguished Service Order *n.* *Abbr.* **DSO, D.S.O.** A British military decoration for gallantry in action.

dis·tort (dĭ-stôrt′) *tr.v.* **-tort·ed, -tort·ing, -torts.** **1.** To twist out of a proper or natural relation of parts; misshape. **2.** To give a false or misleading account of; misrepresent. **3.** To cause to work in a twisted or disorderly manner; pervert. [Latin *distorquēre, distort-* : *dis-,* apart; see DIS– + *torquēre,* to twist; see **terk**ʷ**-** in Appendix.] —**dis·tort′er** *n.*

SYNONYMS: *distort, twist, deform, contort, warp.* These verbs mean to change and spoil the form or character of something. To *distort* is to alter in shape, as by torsion or wrenching; the term also applies to verbal or pictorial misrepresentation and to alteration or perversion of the meaning of something: *"The human understanding is like a false mirror, which, receiving rays irregularly, distorts and discolors the nature of things by mingling its own nature with it"* (Francis Bacon). *Twist* applies to distortion of form or meaning: *a mouth twisted with pain. He accused me of twisting his words to mean what I wanted them to. Deform* refers to change that disfigures and often implies the loss of desirable qualities such as beauty: *Great erosion deformed the landscape. "The earlier part of his discourse was deformed by pedantic divisions and subdivisions"* (Macaulay). *Contort* implies violent change that produces unnatural or grotesque effects: *a face contorted with rage; a contorted line of reasoning. Warp* can refer to a turning or twisting from a flat or straight form (*floorboards that had warped over the years*). It also can imply the bending or turning of something from a true course or direction: *Prejudice warps the judgment.*

dis·tor·tion (dĭ-stôr′shən) *n.* **1. a.** The act or an instance of distorting. **b.** The condition of being distorted. **2.** A statement that twists fact; a misrepresentation. **3.** A change in the shape of an image resulting from imperfections in an optical system, such as a lens. **4.** *Electronics.* **a.** An undesired change in the waveform of a signal. **b.** A consequence of such a change, especially a lack of fidelity in reception or reproduction. **5.** *Psychology.* The modification of unconscious impulses into forms acceptable by conscious or dreaming perception. —**dis·tor′tion·al, dis·tor′tion·ar′y** *adj.*

dis·tor·tive (dĭ-stôr′tĭv) *adj.* Serving to distort: *harsh and distortive peaks in the recorded music; a robust fortissimo without distortive vibration.*

distr. *abbr.* **1.** Distribution. **2.** Distributor.

dis·tract (dĭ-străkt′) *tr.v.* **-tract·ed, -tract·ing, -tracts.** **1.** To cause to turn away from the original focus of attention or interest; divert. **2.** To pull in conflicting emotional directions; unsettle. [Middle English *distracten,* from Latin *distrahere, distrāct-,* to pull away : *dis-,* apart; see DIS– + *trahere,* to draw.] —**dis·tract′ing·ly** *adv.* —**dis·trac′tive** *adj.*

dis·tract·ed (dĭ-străk′tĭd) *adj.* **1.** Having the attention diverted. **2.** Suffering conflicting emotions; distraught. —**dis·tract′ed·ly** *adv.*

dis·tract·er also **dis·trac·tor** (dĭ-străk′tər) *n.* One of the incorrect answers presented as a choice in a multiple-choice test.

dis·trac·tion (dĭ-străk′shən) *n.* **1.** The act of distracting or the condition of being distracted. **2.** Something, especially an amusement, that distracts. **3.** Extreme mental or emotional disturbance; obsession: *loved the puppy to distraction.*

dis·trac·tor (dĭ-străk′tər) *n.* Variant of **distracter.**

dis·train (dĭ-strān′) *v.* **-trained, -train·ing, -trains.** *Law.* —*tr.* **1.** To seize and hold (property) to compel payment or reparation, as of debts. **2.** To seize the property of (a person) in order to compel payment of debts; distress. —*intr.* To levy a distress. [Middle English *distreinen,* from Old French *destreindre, destreign-,* from Medieval Latin *distringere, districnt-,* from Latin, to hinder : *dis-,* apart; see DIS– + *stringere,* to draw tight; see **streig-** in Appendix.] —**dis·train′a·ble** *adj.* —**dis·train′ment** *n.* —**dis·trai′nor, dis·train′er** *n.*

dis·train·ee (dĭs′trā-nē′) *n.* *Law.* One that has been distrained.

dis·traint (dĭ-strānt′) *n.* *Law.* The act or process of distraining; distress. [From DISTRAIN.]

dis·trait (dĭ-strā′) *adj.* Inattentive or preoccupied, especially because of anxiety: *"When she did not occupy her accustomed chair at the seminar, Freud felt uneasy and distrait"* (Times Literary Supplement). [Middle English, from Old French, past participle of *distraire,* to distract, from Latin *distrahere.* See DISTRACT.]

dis·traught (dĭ-strôt′) *adj.* **1.** Deeply agitated, as from emotional conflict. See Synonyms at **abstracted. 2.** Mad; insane. [Middle English, alteration of *distract,* past participle of *distracten,* to distract. See DISTRACT.]

dis·tress (dĭ-strĕs′) *tr.v.* **-tressed, -tress·ing, -tress·es.** **1.** To cause strain, anxiety, or suffering to. See Synonyms at **trouble. 2.** *Law.* To hold the property of (a person) against the payment of debts. **3.** To mar or otherwise treat (an object or a fabric, for example) to give the appearance of an antique or of heavy prior use: *"There are the fakes—new rugs which have been intentionally distressed for an older look"* (Hatfield MA Valley Advocate). **4.** *Archaic.* To constrain or overcome by harassment. —**distress** *n.* **1.** Anxiety or mental suffering. **2. a.** Severe strain resulting from exhaustion or an accident. **b.** Acute physical discomfort. **c.** Physical deterioration, as of a highway, caused by hard use over time: *pavement distress.* **3.** The condition of being in need of immediate assistance: *a motorist in distress.* **4.** *Law.* **a.** The act of distraining or seizing to compel payment. **b.** The goods thus seized. —*attributive.* Often used to modify another noun: *distress merchandise; a distress sale.* [Middle English *distressen,* from Old French *destresser,* from *destresse,* constraint, from Vulgar Latin **districtia,* from Latin *districtus,* past participle of *distringere,* to hinder. See DISTRAIN.] —**dis·tress′ing·ly** *adv.*

dis·tressed (dĭ-strĕst′) *adj.* **1.** Suffering distress: *the distressed parents of wayward youths.* **2.** Damaged or previously used: *distressed merchandise.* **3.** Having been foreclosed and offered for sale, usually at a price below market value: *distressed real estate.* **4.** Intentionally marred or faded to convey an antique or a used look: *distressed furniture; distressed denim.*

dis·tress·ful (dĭ-strĕs′fəl) *adj.* Causing or experiencing distress. —**dis·tress′ful·ly** *adv.* —**dis·tress′ful·ness** *n.*

distress signal *n.* An international signal used by a distressed ship or aircraft to request help, as by radio broadcasts, flags, or flares.

dis·trib·u·tar·y (dĭ-strĭb′yə-tĕr′ē) *n., pl.* **-ies.** A branch of a river that flows away from the main stream.

dis·trib·ute (dĭ-strĭb′yo͞ot) *v.* **-ut·ed, -ut·ing, -utes.** —*tr.* **1.** To divide and dispense in portions. **2. a.** To supply (goods) to retailers. **b.** To deliver or pass out: *distributing handbills on the street.* **3. a.** To spread or diffuse over an area; scatter: *distribute grass seed over the lawn.* **b.** To apportion so as to be evenly spread throughout a given area: *180 pounds of muscle that were well distributed over his 6-foot frame.* **4.** To separate into categories; classify. **5.** *Logic.* To use (a term) so as to include all individuals or entities of a given class. —*intr.* *Mathematics.* To be distributive. [Middle English *distributen,* from Latin *distribuere, distribūt-* : *dis-,* apart; see DIS– + *tribuere,* to give; see TRIBUTE.]

distortion

SYNONYMS: *distribute, divide, dispense, dole, deal, ration.* These verbs mean to give out in portions or shares. *Distribute* is the least specific: *In the 19th century the government distributed land to settlers willing to cultivate it. Divide* implies giving out portions, often equal, on the basis of a plan or purpose: *The estate will be divided among the heirs. Dispense* stresses the careful determination of portions, often according to measurement or weight: *dispensing medication; dispensed tax dollars judiciously; dispense advice and sympathy. Dole,* often followed by *out,* implies careful, usually sparing measurement of portions; it can refer to the distribution of charity (*surplus milk and cheese doled out to the needy*) but more often suggests lack of generosity: *The professor seldom doled out praise, and even when he did it was with reluctance. Deal* implies orderly, equitable distribution, often piece by piece: *dealt out one hamburger each to the children. Ration* refers to equitable division of scarce items, often necessities, in accordance with a system that limits individual portions: *ration fuel in wartime; rationing water during the drought.*

dis·tri·bu·tion (dĭs′trə-byo͞o′shən) *n.* *Abbr.* **distr.** **1.** The act of distributing or the condition of being distributed; apportionment. **2.** Something distributed; an allotment. **3.** The act of dispersing or the condition of being dispersed; diffusion. **4. a.** The geographic occurrence or range of an organism. **b.** The geographic occurrence or range of a custom, a usage, or another feature. **5.** Division into categories; classification. **6.** The process of marketing and supplying goods, especially to retailers. **7.** A spatial or temporal array of objects or events: *the distribution of theaters on Broadway.* **8.** *Law.* The division of an estate or property among rightful heirs. **9.** *Statistics.* A set of numbers collected from a well-defined universe of possible measurements

ă pat	oi boy
ā pay	ou out
âr care	o͝o took
ä father	o͞o boot
ĕ pet	ŭ cut
ē be	ûr urge
ĭ pit	th thin
ī pie	*th* this
îr pier	hw which
ŏ pot	zh vision
ō toe	ə about, item
ô paw	♦ regionalism

Stress marks: **′** (primary); ′ (secondary), as in **dictionary** (dĭk′shə-nĕr′ē)

arising from a property or relationship under study. **—dis′tri·bu′tion·al** *adj.*

dis·trib·u·tive (dĭ-strĭb′yə-tĭv) *adj.* **1.a.** Of, relating to, or involving distribution. **b.** Serving to distribute. **2.** *Mathematics.* Of or relating to a rule that the same product results in multiplication when performed on a set of numbers as when performed on members of the set individually. If $a \times (b + c) = a \times b + a \times c$, then $\times$ is distributive over $+$. **3.** *Grammar.* Referring to each individual or entity of a group separately rather than collectively, as *every* in the sentence *Every employee attended the meeting.* **—distributive** *n.* A distributive word or term. **—dis·trib′u·tive·ly** *adv.* **—dis·trib′u·tive·ness** *n.*

distributive education *n.* A program in which students receive both classroom instruction and on-the-job training.

dis·trib·u·tor (dĭ-strĭb′yə-tər) *n. Abbr.* **distr.** **1.** One that distributes, especially a device that applies electric current in proper sequence to the spark plugs of an engine. **2.** One that markets or sells merchandise, especially a wholesaler. **—dis·trib′u·tor·ship′** *n.*

dis·trict (dĭs′trĭkt) *n. Abbr.* **dist.** **1.** A division of an area, as for administrative purposes. **2.** A region or locality marked by a distinguishing feature: *went to the lake district for their vacation.* See Synonyms at **area.** **—district** *tr.v.* **-trict·ed, -trict·ing, -tricts.** To mark off or divide into districts. [French, from Old French, from Medieval Latin *districtus,* from Latin, past participle of *distringere,* to hinder. See DISTRAIN.] **—dis′trict·wide′** *adv. & adj.*

district attorney *n. Abbr.* **D.A., DA, Dist. Atty.** *Law.* The prosecuting officer of a judicial district.

district court *n. Law.* **1.** A U.S. federal trial court serving a judicial district. **2.** A state court of general jurisdiction in some states.

Dis·trict of Co·lum·bi·a (dĭs′trĭkt′; kə-lŭm′bē-ə). *Abbr.* **DC, D.C.** A federal district of the eastern United States on the Potomac River between Virginia and Maryland. Coextensive with the city of Washington, it was established by congressional acts of 1790 and 1791 on a site selected by George Washington.

dis·trust (dĭs-trŭst′) *n.* Lack of trust or confidence. **—distrust** *tr.v.* **-trust·ed, -trust·ing, -trusts.** To have no confidence in.

dis·trust·ful (dĭs-trŭst′fəl) *adj.* Feeling or showing doubt. **—dis·trust′ful·ly** *adv.* **—dis·trust′ful·ness** *n.*

dis·turb (dĭ-stûrb′) *tr.v.* **-turbed, -turb·ing, -turbs.** **1.** To break up or destroy the tranquillity or settled state of: *"Subterranean fires and deep unrest disturb the whole area"* (Rachel Carson). **2.** To trouble emotionally or mentally; upset. **3.a.** To interfere with; interrupt: *noise that disturbed my sleep.* **b.** To intrude on; inconvenience: *Constant calls disturbed her work.* **4.** To put out of order; disarrange. [Middle English *distourben,* from Old French *destourber,* from Latin *disturbāre* : Latin *dis-,* dis- + Latin *turbāre,* to agitate (from *turba,* confusion, probably from Greek *turbē*).] **—dis·turb′er** *n.* **—dis·turb′ing·ly** *adv.*

dis·tur·bance (dĭ-stûr′bəns) *n.* **1.a.** The act of disturbing. **b.** The condition of being disturbed: *"The forest . . . is in various stages of disturbance. Only the biggest trees . . . have been left standing"* (Alex Shoumatoff). **2.** Something that disturbs, as a commotion, scuffle, or public tumult. **3.** Mental or emotional unbalance or disorder. **4.** A variation in normal wind conditions. **5.** *Geology.* Folding or faulting that affects a relatively large area.

di·sul·fide (dī-sŭl′fīd′) *n.* A chemical compound containing two sulfur atoms combined with other elements or radicals. Also called *bisulfide.*

di·sul·fo·ton (dī-sŭl′fə-tŏn′) *n.* A pale yellow, highly toxic systemic insecticide, $C_8H_{19}O_2PS_3$, used for some vegetables and flowers. [*di(ethyl),* containing two ethyls (DI–^{1} + ETHYL) + SULFO– + probably *t(hi)on(ate),* salt or ester of a thionic acid (THION– + –ATE^2).]

dis·un·ion (dĭs-yo͞on′yən) *n.* **1.** The state of being disunited; separation. **2.** Lack of unity; discord.

dis·un·ion·ist (dĭs-yo͞on′yə-nĭst) *n.* An advocate of disunion, especially a secessionist during the U.S. Civil War.

dis·u·nite (dĭs′yo͞o-nīt′) *tr. & intr.v.* **-nit·ed, -nit·ing, -nites.** To separate or become separate.

dis·u·ni·ty (dĭs-yo͞o′nĭ-tē) *n., pl.* **-ties.** Lack of unity.

dis·use (dĭs-yo͞os′) *n.* The state of not being used or of being no longer in use.

dis·u·til·i·ty (dĭs′yo͞o-tĭl′ĭ-tē) *n.* The state or fact of being useless or counterproductive.

dis·val·ue (dĭs-văl′yo͞o) *tr.v.* **-ued, -u·ing, -ues.** **1.** To regard as of little or no value. **2.** *Archaic.* To disparage. **—disvalue** *n.* **1.** A negative value of something. **2.** *Obsolete.* Disesteem.

di·syl·la·ble also **dis·syl·la·ble** (dī′sĭl′ə-bəl, dĭ-sĭl′-, dī-) *n. Linguistics.* A word with two syllables. **—di′syl·lab′ic** (dī′sĭ-lăb′ĭk, dĭs′sĭ-) *adj.*

dit (dĭt) *n.* The spoken representation of the dot in radio and telegraph code. [Imitative.]

ditch (dĭch) *n.* A long narrow trench or furrow dug in the ground, as for irrigation, drainage, or a boundary line. **—ditch** *v.* **ditched, ditch·ing, ditch·es.** —*tr.* **1.** To dig or make a long narrow trench or furrow in. **2.** To surround with a long narrow trench or furrow. **3.a.** To drive (a vehicle) into a long narrow trench, as one beside a road. **b.** To derail (a train). **4.** *Slang.* **a.** To get rid of; discard: *ditched the old yard furniture.* **b.** To get away from (a person, especially a companion). **c.** To skip (class or school). **5.** To crash-land (an aircraft) on water. —*intr.* **1.** To dig a ditch. **2.** To crash-land in water. Used of an aircraft or a pilot. [Middle English *dich,* from Old English *dīc.* See **dhīgʷ-** in Appendix.]

dith·er (dĭth′ər) *n.* A state of indecisive agitation. **—dither** *intr.v.* **-ered, -er·ing, -ers.** To be nervously irresolute in acting or doing. [Alteration of *didder,* from Middle English *didderen,* to tremble.]

dith·y·ramb (dĭth′ĭ-răm′, -rămb′) *n.* **1.** A frenzied, impassioned choric hymn and dance of ancient Greece in honor of Dionysus. **2.** An irregular poetic expression suggestive of the ancient Greek dithyramb. **3.** A wildly enthusiastic speech or piece of writing. [Latin *dīthyrambus,* from Greek *dithurambos.*] **—dith′y·ramb′ic** *adj.*

Dit·mars (dĭt′märz′), **Raymond Lee.** 1876–1942. American naturalist and writer who was a noted authority on reptiles.

dit·sy also **dit·zy** (dĭt′sē) *adj.* **-si·er, -si·est** also **-zi·er, -zi·est.** *Slang.* Eccentrically scatterbrained or inane: *"Needless to say, this ditsy crew succeeds in spite of itself"* (David Ansen). [Perhaps blend of DOTTY + DIZZY.]

dit·ta·ny (dĭt′n-ē) *n., pl.* **-nies.** **1.** An aromatic woolly plant *(Origanum dictamnus)* native to Crete, formerly believed to have magical powers. **2.** See **stone mint.** **3.** See **gas plant.** [Middle English *ditaine,* from Old French *ditan,* from Latin *dictamnus,* from Greek *diktamnon,* perhaps after Mount *Diktē* (Dhíkti), a peak in eastern Crete.]

dit·to (dĭt′ō) *n., pl.* **-tos.** *Abbr.* **do.** **1.** The same as stated above or before. **2.** A duplicate; a copy. **3.** A pair of small marks (″) used to indicate that the word, phrase, or figure given above is to be repeated. **—ditto** *adv.* As before. **—ditto** *tr.v.* **-toed, -to·ing, -tos.** To duplicate (a document, for example). [Italian dialectal, past participle of Italian *dire,* to say, from Latin *dīcere.* See **deik-** in Appendix.]

WORD HISTORY: *Ditto,* which at first glance seems a handy and insignificant sort of word, actually has a Roman past, for it comes from *dictus,* "having been said," the past participle of the verb *dīcere,* "to say." In Italian *dīcere* became *dire* and *dictus* became *detto,* or in the Tuscan dialect *ditto.* Italian *detto* or *ditto* meant what *said* does in English, as in the locution "the said story." Thus in a construction such as *December 22* the word *detto* or *ditto* could be used by itself instead of the month name at the next mention of a date in the same month, for example, *26 detto.* The first recorded use (1625) of *ditto* occurs in English in such a construction. The sense "copy" is an English development, first recorded in 1818. *Ditto* has even become a trademark for a duplicating machine, something that has not happened to *said* yet.

dit·ty (dĭt′ē) *n., pl.* **-ties.** A simple song. [Middle English *dite,* a literary composition, from Old French *dite,* from Latin *dictātum,* thing dictated, from past participle of *dictāre,* to dictate, frequentative of *dīcere,* to say. See **deik-** in Appendix.]

ditty bag *n.* A bag used by armed forces personnel to carry small items such as sewing implements. [Origin unknown.]

dit·zy (dĭt′sē) *adj. Slang.* Variant of **ditsy.**

Di·u (dē′o͞o). An island of western India northwest of Bombay. A Portuguese possession after 1535, Diu was invaded by India in 1961 and annexed the following year.

di·u·re·sis (dī′ə-rē′sĭs) *n.* Excessive discharge of urine. [New Latin, from Late Latin *diūrēticus,* diuretic. See DIURETIC.]

di·u·ret·ic (dī′ə-rĕt′ĭk) *adj.* Tending to increase the discharge of urine. **—diuretic** *n.* A substance or drug that tends to increase the discharge of urine. [Middle English *diuretik,* from Old French *diuretique,* from Late Latin *diūrēticus,* from Greek *diourētikos,* from *diourein,* to pass urine : *dia-,* dia- + *ourein,* to urinate.] **—di′u·ret′ic·al·ly** *adv.*

di·ur·nal (dī-ûr′nəl) *adj.* **1.** Relating to or occurring in a 24-hour period; daily. **2.** Occurring or active during the daytime rather than at night: *diurnal animals.* **3.** *Botany.* Opening during daylight hours and closing at night. **—diurnal** *n.* **1.** A book containing all the offices for the daily canonical hours of prayer except matins. **2.** *Archaic.* **a.** A diary or journal. **b.** A daily newspaper. [Middle English, from Late Latin *diurnālis,* from Latin *diurnus,* from *diēs,* day. See **deiw-** in Appendix.] **—di·ur′nal·ly** *adv.*

di·u·ron (dĭ′ə-rŏn′) *n.* A white, crystalline solid, $C_9H_{10}Cl_2N_2O$, used as an agricultural herbicide. [DI–^{1} + UR(EA) + –ON^3.]

div. *abbr.* **1.** Divergence; divergency. **2.** Diversion. **3.** Divided; division. **4.** Dividend. **5.** Divorced.

di·va (dē′və) *n., pl.* **-vas** or **-ve** (-vā). *Music.* An operatic prima donna. [Italian, from Latin *dīva,* goddess, feminine of *dīvus,* god. See **deiw-** in Appendix.]

di·va·gate (dī′və-gāt′, dĭv′ə-) *intr.v.* **-gat·ed, -gat·ing, -gates.** **1.** To wander or drift about. **2.** To ramble; digress. [Late Latin *dīvagārī, dīvagāt-* : Latin *dī-, dis-,* apart; see DIS– + Latin *vagārī,* to wander (from *vagus,* wandering).] **—di′va·ga′tion** *n.*

di·va·lent (dī-vā′lənt) *adj.* Having a valence of 2.

di·van (dĭ-văn′) *n.* **1.** (*also* dī′văn′). A long backless sofa, especially one set with pillows against a wall. **2.** (*also* dĭ-vän′, dī-văn′). **a.** A counting room, tribunal, or public audience room in Moslem countries. **b.** The seat used by an administrator when holding audience. **c.** A government bureau or council chamber. **3.** (*also* dĭ-vän′, dĭ-văn′). A coffeehouse or smoking room. **4.** (*also* dĭ-vän′, dĭ-văn′). A book of poems, especially one written in Arabic or Persian by a single author. [French, from Turkish, from Persian *dīvān,* place of assembly, roster, probably from Old Iranian *dipivahanam, document house : Old Persian *dipī-,* writing, document (from Akkadian *tuppu,* tablet, letter, from Sumerian *dub,* to write) + Old Persian *vahanam,* house; see **wes-**[1] in Appendix.]

di•var•i•cate (dī-văr′ĭ-kāt′, dĭ-) *intr.v.* **-cat•ed, -cat•ing, -cates.** To diverge at a wide angle; spread apart. **—divaricate** (dī-văr′ə-kĭt, -kāt′, dĭ-) *adj.* **1.** *Biology.* Branching or spreading widely from a point or axis, as branches or on an insect's wings; diverging. **2.** Relating to a separation of two bones normally adjacent or attached but not located in a joint; distatic. [Latin *dī-vāricāre, dīvāricāt-* : *dī, dis-,* dis- + *vāricāre,* to straddle (from *vārus,* bent).] **—di•var′i•cate′ly** *adv.*

di•var•i•ca•tion (dī-văr′ĭ-kā′shən, dĭ-) *n.* **1.** The act of divaricating. **2.** The point at which branching occurs. **3.** A divergence of opinion.

dive[1] (dīv) *v.* **dived** or **dove** (dōv), **dived, div•ing, dives.** *—intr.* **1.a.** To plunge, especially headfirst, into water. **b.** To execute a dive in athletic competition. **c.** To participate in the sport of competitive diving. **2.a.** To go toward the bottom of a body of water; submerge. **b.** To engage in the activity of scuba diving. **c.** To submerge under power. Used of a submarine. **3.a.** To fall head down through the air. **b.** To descend nose down at an acceleration usually exceeding that of free fall. Used of an airplane. **c.** To engage in the sport of skydiving. **4.** To drop sharply and rapidly; plummet: *Stock prices dove 100 points in a single day of trading.* **5.a.** To rush headlong and vanish into: *dive into a crowd.* **b.** To plunge one's hand into. **6.** To lunge: *dove for the loose ball.* **7.** To plunge into an activity or enterprise with vigor and gusto. *—tr.* To cause (an aircraft, for example) to dive. **—dive** *n.* **1.a.** A plunge into water, especially done headfirst and in a way established for athletic competition. **b.** The act or an instance of submerging, as of a submarine or a skin diver. **c.** A nearly vertical descent at an accelerated speed through the air. **d.** A quick, pronounced drop. **2.** *Slang.* A disreputable or rundown bar or nightclub. **3.** A knockout feigned by prearrangement between prizefighters: *The challenger took a dive.* **4.a.** A lunge or a headlong jump: *made a dive to catch the falling teacup.* **b.** *Football.* An offensive play in which the carrier of the ball plunges into the opposing line in order to gain short yardage. [Middle English *diven,* from Old English *dȳfan,* to dip, and from *dūfan,* to sink; see **dheub-** in Appendix.]

USAGE NOTE: Either *dove* or *dived* is acceptable as the past tense of *dive. Dived* is actually the earlier form, and the emergence of *dove* may appear anomalous in light of the general tendencies of change in English verb forms. Old English had two classes of verbs: strong verbs, whose past tense was indicated by a change in their vowel (a process that survives in such present-day English verbs as *drive/drove* or *fling/flung*); and weak verbs, whose past was formed with a suffix related to *-ed* in Modern English (as in present-day English *live/lived* and *move/moved*). Since the Old English period, many verbs have changed from the strong pattern to the weak one; for example, the past tense of *help,* formerly *healp,* became *helped,* and the past tense of *step,* formerly *stop,* became *stepped.* Over the years, in fact, the weak pattern has become so prevalent that we use the term *regular* to refer to verbs that form their past tense by suffixation of *-ed.* However, there have occasionally been changes in the other direction: the past tense of *wear,* now *wore,* was once *werede;* that of *spit,* now *spat,* was once *spitede;* and the development of *dove* is an additional example of the small group of verbs that have swum against the historical tide.

di•ve[2] (dē′vā) *n. Music.* A plural of **diva.**

dive-bomb (dīv′bŏm′) *tr.v.* **-bombed, -bomb•ing, -bombs.** To bomb from an airplane at the end of a steep dive toward the target. **—dive′-bomb′er** *n.*

dive brake *n.* A flap that can be extended on an aircraft to increase drag and reduce the speed of descent.

div•er (dī′vər) *n.* **1.** One that dives: *a high diver who excelled in performing the jackknife.* **2.** One that works under water, especially one equipped with breathing apparatus and weighted clothing. **3.** Any of several diving water birds, especially the loon.

di•verge (dĭ-vûrj′, dī-) *v.* **-verged, -verg•ing, -verg•es.** *—intr.* **1.** To go or extend in different directions from a common point; branch out. **2.** To differ, as in opinion or manner. **3.** To depart from a set course or norm; deviate. See Synonyms at **swerve. 4.** *Mathematics.* To fail to approach a limit, as an infinite sequence. *—tr.* To cause (light rays, for example) to diverge; deflect. [Latin *dīvergere* : Latin *dis-,* apart; see DIS– + Latin *vergere,* to bend; see **wer-**[2] in Appendix.]

di•ver•gence (dĭ-vûr′jəns, dī-) *n. Abbr.* **div. 1.a.** The act of diverging. **b.** The state of being divergent. **c.** The degree by which things diverge. **2.** *Physiology.* A turning of both eyes outward from a common point or of one eye when the other is fixed. **3.** Departure from a norm; deviation. **4.** Difference, as of opinion. See Synonyms at **deviation, difference. 5.** *Biology.* The evolutionary tendency or process by which animals or plants that are descended from a common ancestor evolve into different forms when living under different conditions. **6.** *Mathematics.* The property or manner of diverging; failure to approach a limit. **7.** A meteorological condition characterized by the uniform expansion in volume of a mass of air over a region, usually accompanied by fair dry weather.

di•ver•gen•cy (dĭ-vûr′jən-sē) *n., pl.* **-cies.** *Abbr.* **div.** Divergence.

di•ver•gent (dĭ-vûr′jənt, dī-) *adj.* **1.** Drawing apart from a common point; diverging. **2.** Departing from convention. **3.** Differing from another: *a divergent opinion.* **4.** *Mathematics.* Failing to approach a limit; not convergent. **—di•ver′gent•ly** *adv.*

di•vers (dī′vərz) *adj.* Various; several; sundry. [Middle English. See DIVERSE.]

di•verse (dĭ-vûrs′, dī-, dī′vûrs′) *adj.* **1.** Differing one from another. **2.** Made up of distinct characteristics, qualities, or elements: *"Prague . . . offers visitors a series of excursions into a rich and diverse past"* (Olivier Bernier). [Middle English *divers,* from Old French *divers,* from Latin *dīversus,* past participle of *dīvertere,* to divert. See DIVERT.] **—di•verse′ly** *adv.* **—di•verse′ness** *n.*

di•ver•si•form (dĭ-vûr′sə-fôrm′, dī-) *adj.* Having different forms; variform.

di•ver•si•fy (dĭ-vûr′sə-fī′, dī-) *v.* **-fied, -fy•ing, -fies.** *—tr.* **1.a.** To give variety to; vary: *diversify a menu.* **b.** To extend (business activities) into disparate fields. **2.** To distribute (investments) among different companies or securities in order to limit losses in the event of a fall in a particular market or industry. *—intr.* To spread out activities or investments, especially in business. [Middle English *diversifien,* from Old French *diversifier,* from Medieval Latin *dīversificāre* : Latin *dīversus;* see DIVERSE + Latin *-ficāre,* -fy.] **—di•ver′si•fi•ca′tion** (-fĭ-kā′shən) *n.*

di•ver•sion (dĭ-vûr′zhən, -shən, dī-) *n. Abbr.* **div. 1.** The act or an instance of diverting or turning aside; deviation. **2.** Something that distracts the mind and relaxes or entertains. **3.** A maneuver that draws the attention of an opponent away from a planned point of action, especially as part of military strategy. [Late Latin *dīversiō, dīversiōn-,* act of turning aside, from Latin *dīversus,* past participle of *dīvertere,* to divert. See DIVERT.] **—di•ver′sion•ar′y** *adj.*

di•ver•sion•ist (dĭ-vûr′zhə-nĭst, -shə-, dī-) *n.* One engaged in diversionary, disruptive, or subversive activities.

di•ver•si•ty (dĭ-vûr′sĭ-tē, dī-) *n., pl.* **-ties. 1.a.** The fact or quality of being diverse; difference. **b.** A point or respect in which things differ. **2.** Variety or multiformity: *"Charles Darwin saw in the diversity of species the principles of evolution that operated to generate the species: variation, competition and selection"* (Scientific American).

di•vert (dĭ-vûrt′, dī-) *v.* **-vert•ed, -vert•ing, -verts.** *—tr.* **1.** To turn aside from a course or direction: *Traffic was diverted around the scene of the accident.* **2.** To distract: *My attention was diverted by an argument between motorists.* **3.** To entertain by distracting the attention from worrisome thoughts or cares; amuse. See Synonyms at **amuse.** *—intr.* To turn aside. [Middle English *diverten,* from Old French *divertir,* from Latin *dīvertere* : *dī-, dis-,* aside; see DIS– + *vertere,* to turn; see **wer-**[2] in Appendix.] **—di•vert′er** *n.* **—di•vert′ing•ly** *adv.*

di•ver•tic•u•la (dī′vûr-tĭk′yə-lə) *n.* Plural of **diverticulum.**

di•ver•tic•u•li•tis (dī′vûr-tĭk′yə-lī′tĭs) *n.* Inflammation of a diverticulum or of diverticula in the intestinal tract, causing fecal stagnation and pain.

di•ver•tic•u•lo•sis (dī′vûr-tĭk′yə-lō′sĭs) *n.* A condition marked by the presence of numerous diverticula in the colon.

di•ver•tic•u•lum (dī′vûr-tĭk′yə-ləm) *n., pl.* **-la** (-lə). A pouch or sac branching out from a hollow organ or structure, such as the intestine. [New Latin, from Latin *dēverticulum,* by-path, from *dēvertere,* to turn aside : *dē-,* de- + *vertere,* to turn; see DIVERT.] **—di′ver•tic′u•lar** *adj.*

di•ver•ti•men•to (dĭ-vĕr′tə-mĕn′tō) *n., pl.* **-tos -ti** (-tē). *Music.* A chiefly 18th-century form of instrumental chamber music having several short movements. Also called *divertissement.* [Italian, from *divertire,* to divert, from Old French *divertir.* See DIVERT.]

di•ver•tisse•ment (də-vûr′tĭs-mənt, dē-vĕr-tēs-mäɴ′) *n.* **1.** A short performance, typically a ballet, that is presented as an interlude in an opera or a play. **2.** *Music.* See **divertimento. 3.** A diversion; an amusement. [French, from *divertir,* to divert, from Old French. See DIVERT.]

Di•ves (dī′vēz′) *n.* A man of great wealth. [Middle English, from Latin *dīves.* See **deiw-** in Appendix.]

di•vest (dĭ-vĕst′, dī-) *tr.v.* **-vest•ed, -vest•ing, -vests. 1.** To strip, as of clothes. **2.a.** To deprive, as of rights or property; dispossess. See Synonyms at **strip**[1]. **b.** To free of; rid: *"Most secretive of men, let him at last divest himself of secrets, both his and ours"* (Brendan Gill). **3.** To sell off or otherwise dispose of (a subsidiary company or an investment). **4.** *Law.* To devest. [Alteration (influenced by Medieval Latin *dīvestīre,* to undress; see DIVESTITURE) of DEVEST.] **—di•vest′ment** *n.*

di•ves•ti•ture (dĭ-vĕs′tĭ-chər, -cho͝or′, dī-) *n.* **1.** An act of divesting. **2.** The sale, liquidation, or spinoff of a corporate division or subsidiary. [From Medieval Latin *dīvestītus,* past participle of *dīvestīre,* to undress, variant of *disvestīre* : Latin *dis-,* dis- + Latin *vestīre,* to dress; see VESTMENT.]

diver
Scuba diver

ă **pat**	oi **boy**
ā **pay**	ou **out**
âr **care**	o͝o **took**
ä **father**	o͞o **boot**
ĕ **pet**	ŭ **cut**
ē **be**	ûr **urge**
ĭ **pit**	th **thin**
ī **pie**	*th* **this**
îr **pier**	hw **which**
ŏ **pot**	zh **vision**
ō **toe**	ə **about, item**
ô **paw**	♦ **regionalism**

Stress marks: ′ (primary); ′ (secondary), as in **dictionary** (dĭk′shə-nĕr′ē)

di·vide (dĭ-vīd′) *v.* **-vid·ed, -vid·ing, -vides.** —*tr.* **1.a.** To separate into parts, sections, groups, or branches. See Synonyms at **separate. b.** To sector into units of measurement; graduate. **c.** To separate and group according to kind; classify. **2.a.** To separate into opposing factions; disunite: *"They want not to divide either the Revolution or the Church but to be an integral part of both"* (Conor Cruise O'Brien). **b.** To cause (members of a parliament) to vote by separating into groups, as pro and con. **3.** To separate from something else; cut off: *divided the boys from the girls for gym class.* **4.** To apportion among a number. See Synonyms at **distribute. 5.** *Mathematics.* **a.** To subject to the process of division. **b.** To be an exact divisor of. —*intr.* **1.a.** To become separated into parts. **b.** To branch out, as a river. **c.** To form into factions; take sides. **d.** To vote by dividing. **2.** *Mathematics.* To perform the operation of division. **3.** *Biology.* To undergo cell division. **—divide** *n.* **1.** A dividing point or line: *"would clearly tip the court . . . across a dangerous constitutional divide"* (Laurence H. Tribe). **2.** A ridge of land; a watershed. [Middle English *dividen,* from Latin *dīvidere* : *dī-, dis-,* dis- + *-videre,* to separate.] **—di·vid′a·ble** *adj.*

di·vid·ed (dĭ-vī′dĭd) *adj. Abbr.* **div. 1.** Separated into parts or pieces. **2.** Being in a state of disagreement or disunity: *a divided nation.* **3.** Moved by conflicting interests, emotions, or activities: *divided loyalties.* **4.** Separated by distance: *a child divided from her familiar surroundings.* **5.** Having the lanes for opposing traffic separated: *divided highways.* **6.** *Botany.* Having indentations extending to the midrib or base and forming distinct lobes: *divided leaves.*

divi-divi
Caesalpinia coriaria

div·i·dend (dĭv′ĭ-dĕnd′) *n. Abbr.* **div. 1.** *Mathematics.* A quantity to be divided. **2.a.** A share of profits received by a stockholder or by a policyholder in a mutual insurance society. **b.** A payment pro rata to a creditor of a person adjudged bankrupt. **3.a.** A share of a surplus; a bonus. **b.** An unexpected gain, benefit, or advantage. [Alteration (influenced by French *dividende,* dividend) of Middle English *divident,* from Latin *dīvidēns, dīvident-,* present participle of *dīvidere,* to divide. See DIVIDE.]

di·vid·er (dĭ-vī′dər) *n.* **1.a.** One that divides, especially a screen or other partition. **b.** *Chiefly British.* A highway median strip. **2.** A device resembling a compass, used for dividing lines and transferring measurements.

div·i-div·i (dĭv′ē-dĭv′ē) *n., pl.* **-is. 1.** A small tree *(Caesalpinia coriaria)* of the West Indies and South America, having compound leaves and long pods. **2.** Tannin extracted from the pods of this tree. [Spanish *dividivi,* probably of Cariban or Arawakan origin.]

div·i·na·tion (dĭv′ə-nā′shən) *n.* **1.** The art or act of foretelling future events or revealing occult knowledge by means of augury or an alleged supernatural agency. **2.** An inspired guess or presentiment. **3.** Something that has been divined. **—di·vin′a·to′ry** (dĭ-vĭn′ə-tôr′ē, -tōr′ē) *adj.*

di·vine (dĭ-vīn′) *adj.* **-vin·er, -vin·est. 1.a.** Having the nature of or being a deity. **b.** Of, relating to, emanating from, or being the expression of a deity: *sought divine guidance through meditation.* **c.** Being in the service or worship of a deity; sacred. **2.** Superhuman; godlike. **3.a.** Supremely good or beautiful; magnificent: *a divine performance of the concerto.* **b.** Extremely pleasant; delightful: *had a divine time at the ball.* **4.** Heavenly; perfect. **—divine** *n.* **1.** A cleric. **2.** A theologian. **—divine** *v.* **-vined, -vin·ing, -vines.** —*tr.* **1.** To foretell through or as if through the art of divination. See Synonyms at **foretell. 2.a.** To know by inspiration, intuition, or reflection. **b.** To guess. **3.** To locate (underground water or minerals) with a divining rod; douse. —*intr.* **1.** To practice divination. **2.** To guess. [Middle English, from Old French *devine,* from Latin *dīvīnus,* divine, foreseeing, from *dīvus,* god. See **deiw-** in Appendix. V., Middle English *divinen,* from Old French *deviner,* from Latin *dīvīnāre,* from *dīvīnus,* foreseeing.] **—di·vine′ly** *adv.* **—di·vine′ness** *n.* **—di·vin′er** *n.*

divining rod

Di·vine Liturgy (dĭ-vīn′) *n.* The Eastern Orthodox Eucharistic rite.

Divine Office *n.* The office of the breviary.

divine right *n.* The doctrine that monarchs derive their right to rule directly from God and are accountable only to God.

div·ing beetle (dī′vĭng) *n.* Any of various predatory aquatic beetles of the family Dytiscidae.

diving bell *n.* A large vessel for underwater work, open on the bottom and supplied with air under pressure.

diving board *n. Sports.* A flexible board from which a dive may be executed, secured at one end and projecting over water at the other. Also called *springboard.*

diving reflex *n.* A reflexive response to diving in many aquatic mammals and birds, characterized by physiological changes that decrease oxygen consumption, such as slowed heart rate and decreased blood flow to the abdominal organs and muscles, until breathing resumes. Though less pronounced, the reflex also occurs in certain nonaquatic animals, including human beings, upon submersion in water.

diving suit *n.* A heavy waterproof garment with a detachable air-fed helmet, used for underwater work.

di·vin·ing rod (dĭ-vī′nĭng) *n.* A forked branch or stick that is believed to indicate subterranean water or minerals by bending downward when held over a source.

di·vin·i·ty (dĭ-vĭn′ĭ-tē) *n., pl.* **-ties. 1.** The state or quality of being divine. **2.a. Divinity.** The godhead; God. Used with *the.* **b.** A deity, such as a god or goddess. **3.** Godlike character. **4.** Theology. **5.** A soft white candy, usually containing nuts.

di·vis·i·ble (dĭ-vĭz′ə-bəl) *adj.* Capable of being divided, especially with no remainder: *15 is divisible by 3 and 5.* **—di·vis′i·bil′i·ty, di·vis′i·ble·ness** *n.* **—di·vis′i·bly** *adv.*

di·vi·sion (dĭ-vĭzh′ən) *n. Abbr.* **div. 1.a.** The act or process of dividing. **b.** The state of having been divided. **2.** The proportional distribution of a quantity or entity. **3.** Something, such as a boundary or partition, that serves to divide or keep separate. **4.** One of the parts, sections, or groups into which something is divided. **5.a.** An area of government or corporate activity organized as an administrative or functional unit. **b.** A territorial section marked off for political or governmental purposes. **6.a.** An administrative and tactical military unit that is smaller than a corps but is self-contained and equipped for prolonged combat activity. **b.** A group of several ships of similar type forming a tactical unit under a single command in the U.S. Navy. **c.** A unit of the U.S. Air Force larger than a wing and smaller than an air force. **7.** *Botany.* The highest taxonomic category, consisting of one or more related classes, and corresponding approximately to a phylum in zoological classification. See table at **taxonomy. 8.** A category created for purposes of competition, as in boxing. **9.a.** Variance of opinion; disagreement. **b.** A splitting into factions; disunion. **10.** The physical separation and regrouping of members of a parliament according to their stand on an issue put to vote. **11.** *Mathematics.* The operation of determining how many times one quantity is contained in another; the inverse of multiplication. **12.** *Biology.* Cell division. **13.** A type of propagation characteristic of plants that spread by means of newly formed parts such as bulbs, suckers, or rhizomes. [Middle English *divisioun,* from Old French *division,* from Latin *dīvīsiō, dīvīsiōn-,* from *dīvīsus,* past participle of *dīvidere,* to divide. See DIVIDE.] **—di·vi′sion·al** *adj.*

di·vi·sion·ism (də-vĭzh′ə-nĭz′əm) *n.* A branch of neoimpressionism in which colors are divided into their components and mechanically arranged so that the eye organizes the shape. **—di·vi′sion·ist** *n.*

division sign *n. Mathematics.* **1.** The symbol (÷) placed between two quantities written on a single line to indicate the division of the first by the second. **2.** The symbol (/) placed between two quantities written horizontally, as in 2/3, or the symbol (—) placed between two quantities written vertically, as in $\frac{2}{3}$, to indicate a fraction.

di·vi·sive (dĭ-vī′sĭv) *adj.* Creating dissension or discord. **—di·vi′sive·ly** *adv.* **—di·vi′sive·ness** *n.*

di·vi·sor (dĭ-vī′zər) *n. Mathematics.* The quantity by which another quantity, the dividend, is to be divided.

di·vorce (dĭ-vôrs′, -vōrs′) *n.* **1.** The legal dissolution of a marriage. **2.** A complete or radical severance of closely connected things. **—divorce** *v.* **-vorced, -vorc·ing, -vorc·es.** —*tr.* **1.** To dissolve the marriage bond between. **2.** To end marriage with (one's spouse) by way of legal divorce. **3.** To cut off; separate or disunite: *an idea that was completely divorced from reality.* See Synonyms at **separate.** —*intr.* To obtain a divorce. [Middle English, from Old French, from Latin *dīvortium,* from *dīvortere,* to divert, variant of *dīvertere.* See DIVERT.]

di·vor·cé (dĭ-vôr-sā′, -sē′, -vōr-, -vôr′sā′, -sē′, -vōr′-) *n.* A divorced man. [French, masculine past participle of *divorcer,* to divorce, from Old French, from *divorce,* divorce. See DIVORCE.]

di·vor·cée (dĭ-vôr-sā′, -sē′, -vōr-, -vôr′sā′, -sē′, -vōr′-) *n.* A divorced woman. [French, feminine past participle of *divorcer,* to divorce, from Old French, from *divorce,* divorce. See DIVORCE.]

di·vorce·ment (dĭ-vôrs′mənt, -vōrs′-) *n.* Complete separation.

div·ot (dĭv′ət) *n.* **1.** *Sports.* A piece of turf torn up by a golf club in striking a ball. **2.** *Scots.* A thin square of turf or sod used for roofing. [Scots, a turf.]

di·vulge (dĭ-vŭlj′) *tr.v.* **-vulged, -vulg·ing, -vulg·es. 1.** To make known (something private or secret). See Synonyms at **reveal. 2.** *Archaic.* To proclaim publicly. [Middle English *divulgen,* from Old French *divulguer,* from Latin *dīvulgāre,* to publish : *dī-, dis-,* among; see DIS– + *vulgāre,* to spread among the multitude (from *vulgus,* common people).] **—di·vul′gence** *n.* **—di·vulg′er** *n.*

div·vy (dĭv′ē) *Slang. tr.v.* **-vied, -vy·ing, -vies.** To divide: *divvied up the loot.* **—divvy** *n., pl.* **-vies.** A share or portion. [Shortening and alteration of DIVIDEND.]

Dix (dĭks), **Dorothea Lynde.** 1802–1887. American philanthropist, reformer, and educator who was a pioneer in the movement for specialized treatment of the mentally ill.

Dix, Dorothy. See Elizabeth Meriwether **Gilmer.**

Dix·ie[1] (dĭk′sē). A region of the southern and eastern United States, usually comprising the states that joined the Confederacy during the Civil War. The term was popularized in the minstrel song "Dixie's Land," written by Daniel D. Emmett (1815–1904) in 1859.

Dix·ie[2] (dĭk′sē) *n.* Any one of several songs bearing this name, popular as Confederate war songs. ***—idiom.* whistle Dixie.** *Slang.* To engage in unrealistically rosy fantasizing: *"If you think mass transportation is going to replace the automobile I think you're whistling Dixie"* (Henry Ford II). [After DIXIE[1].]

Dix·ie·crat (dĭk′sē-krăt′) *n.* A member of a dissenting group of Democrats in the South who formed the States' Rights Party in 1948. [DIXIE[1] + (DEMO)CRAT.] **—Dix′ie·crat′ic** *adj.*

ă pat	oi boy
ā pay	ou out
âr care	ŏŏ took
ä father	ōō boot
ĕ pet	ŭ cut
ē be	ûr urge
ĭ pit	th thin
ī pie	*th* this
îr pier	hw which
ŏ pot	zh vision
ō toe	ə about, item
ô paw	♦ regionalism

Stress marks: **′** (primary); ′ (secondary), as in **dictionary** (dĭk′shə-nĕr′ē)

Dix·ie·land (dĭk′sē-lănd′) *n. Music.* A style of instrumental jazz associated with New Orleans and characterized by a relatively fast two-beat rhythm and by group and solo improvisations.

Di·yar·ba·kir (dĭ-yär′bə-kîr′, dē-yär′bŭk-ər). A city of southeast Turkey on the Tigris River. It was a Roman colony called Amida from A.D. 230 to 363 and was finally captured by the Ottoman Turks in 1515. Population, 235,617.

di·zen (dī′zən, dĭz′ən) *tr.v.* **-zened, -zen·ing, -zens.** *Archaic.* To deck out in fine clothes and ornaments; bedizen. [Possibly Middle Dutch *disen,* to prepare a distaff with flax for spinning, from Middle Low German *dise, disene,* bunch of flax.] **—di′zen·ment** *n.*

di·zy·got·ic (dī′zī-gŏt′ĭk) or **di·zy·gous** (dī-zī′gəs) *adj.* Derived from two separately fertilized eggs. Used especially of fraternal twins.

diz·zy (dĭz′ē) *adj.* **-zi·er, -zi·est. 1.** Having a whirling sensation and a tendency to fall. See Synonyms at **giddy. 2.** Bewildered or confused. **3.a.** Producing or tending to produce giddiness: *a dizzy height.* **b.** Caused by giddiness; reeling. **4.** Characterized by impulsive haste; very rapid: *"The American language had begun its dizzy onward march before the Revolution"* (H.L. Mencken). **5.** *Slang.* Scatterbrained or silly. **—dizzy** *tr.v.* **-zied, -zy·ing, -zies. 1.** To make dizzy. **2.** To confuse or bewilder. [Middle English *dusie, disi,* from Old English *dysig,* foolish.] **—diz′zi·ly** *adv.* **—diz′zi·ness** *n.* **—diz′zy·ing·ly** *adv.*

dj *abbr.* Dust jacket.

DJ *abbr.* Disc jockey.

D.J. *abbr.* **1.** *Law.* District judge. **2.** *Latin.* Doctor Juris (Doctor of Law).

Dja·kar·ta (jə-kär′tə). See **Jakarta.**

djel·la·ba or **djel·la·bah** also **jel·la·ba** (jə-lä′bə) or **ga·la·bi·a** (-bē-ə) *n.* A long, loose, hooded garment with full sleeves, worn especially in Moslem countries. [French, from Arabic *jallābīyah,* from *jallāb,* attractive.]

Dji·bou·ti (jĭ-bo͞o′tē). **1.** Formerly **A·fars and Is·sas** (ə-färs′; ī′səs). A country of eastern Africa on the Gulf of Aden. A French colony from 1896 until 1946 and a territory thereafter, it became independent in 1977. Population, 226,000. **2.** The capital and largest city of Djibouti, in the southeast part of the country on an inlet of the Gulf of Aden. Population, 120,000.

Dji·las (jĭl′äs), **Milovan.** Born 1911. Yugoslavian writer and politician who was a prominent member of Tito's resistance movement during World War II and later held high government and Communist Party positions before his dismissal in 1954 for criticizing the regime.

djin·ni or **djin·ny** (jĭn′ē, jĭ-nē′) *n.* Variant of **jinni.**

Djok·ja·kar·ta (jŏk′yə-kär′tə). See **Jogjakarta.**

dk. *abbr.* **1.** Dark. **2.** Deck. **3.** Dock.

dkg *abbr.* Dekagram.

dkl *abbr.* Dekaliter.

dkm *abbr.* Dekameter.

dl *abbr.* Deciliter.

D/L *abbr.* Demand loan.

D layer *n.* The lowest layer of the ionosphere, existing only during the day.

D.Lit. or **D.Litt.** *abbr. Latin.* Doctor Litterarum (Doctor of Letters; Doctor of Literature).

DLO *abbr.* Dead letter office.

dlr. *abbr.* Dealer.

D.L.S. *abbr.* Doctor of Library Science.

dm *abbr.* Decimeter.

DM *abbr.* **1.** Data management. **2.** Deutsche mark.

D.M.A. *abbr.* Doctor of Musical Arts.

D.M.D. *abbr. Latin.* Dentariae Medicinae Doctor (Doctor of Dental Medicine).

D.M.L. *abbr.* Doctor of Modern Languages.

DMSO (dē′ĕm-ĕs-ō′) *n.* A colorless hygroscopic liquid, $(CH_3)_2SO$, obtained from lignin, used as an industrial solvent and in medicine as a penetrant to convey medications into the tissues. [D(I)M(ETHYL)S(ULF)O(XIDE).]

DMZ *abbr.* Demilitarized zone.

Dn *abbr. Bible.* Daniel.

dn. *abbr.* Down.

DNA (dē′ĕn-ā′) *n.* A nucleic acid that carries the genetic information in the cell and is capable of self-replication and synthesis of RNA. DNA consists of two long chains of nucleotides twisted into a double helix and joined by hydrogen bonds between the complementary bases adenine and thymine or cytosine and guanine. The sequence of nucleotides determines individual hereditary characteristics. [D(EOXYRIBO)N(UCLEIC) A(CID).]

DNAase (dē′ĕn-ā′ās) *n.* Variant of **DNase.**

DNA polymerase *n.* An enzyme that catalyzes the replication and repair of DNA by using single-stranded DNA as a template.

DNase also **DNAse** (dē-ĕn′ās) also **DNAase** (dē′ĕn-ā′ās) *n.* An enzyme that catalyzes the hydrolysis of DNA. [DN(A) + -ASE.]

DNA virus *n.* A virus that possesses a genome composed of DNA.

Dne·pro·dzer·zhinsk (nĕp′rō-dər-zhĭnsk′, dnyĭ′prə-dzĭr-zhĭnsk′). A city of east-central Ukraine on the Dnieper River south-southwest of Kharkov. It is a port and major industrial center. Population, 271,000.

Dne·pro·pe·trovsk (nĕp′rō-pə-trôfsk′, dnyĭ′prə-pyĭ-trôfsk′). A city of east-central Ukraine on the Dnieper River south-southwest of Kharkov. Founded in 1787 on the site of a Cossack village, it has a huge iron and steel industry. Population, 1,153,000.

Dnie·per (nē′pər, dnyĕ′pər). A river rising near Smolensk in west-central Russia and flowing about 2,285 km (1,420 mi) southward through Belorussia and the Ukraine to the Black Sea. It has been a commercial waterway since the ninth century.

Dnies·ter (nē′stər, dnyĕ′stər). A river rising in western Ukraine and flowing about 1,368 km (850 mi) generally southeast through eastern Moldavia then back into the Ukraine, where it empties into the Black Sea near Odessa.

♦**do**[1] (do͞o) *v.* **did** (dĭd), **done** (dŭn), **do·ing, does** (dŭz). *—tr.* **1.a.** To perform or execute: *do one's assigned task; do a series of business deals.* **b.** To fulfill the requirements of: *did my duty at all times.* **c.** To carry out; commit: *a crime that had been done on purpose.* **2.a.** To produce, especially by creative effort: *do a play on Broadway.* **b.** To play the part or role of in a creative production: *did Elizabeth I in the film.* **c.** To mimic: *"doing the Southern voice, improvising it inventively as he goes along"* (William H. Pritchard). **3.a.** To bring about; effect: *Crying won't do any good now.* **b.** To render; give: *do equal justice to the opposing sides; do honor to one's family.* **4.** To put forth; exert: *Do the best you can.* **5.a.** To attend to in such a way as to take care of or put in order: *did the bedrooms before the guests arrived.* **b.** To prepare for further use especially by washing: *did the dishes.* **6.a.** To set or style (the hair). **b.** To apply cosmetics to: *did her face.* **7.** To have as an occupation or a profession: *Have you decided what you will do after graduate school?* **8.** To work out by studying: *do a homework assignment.* **9.** *Informal.* **a.** To travel (a specified distance): *do a mile in four minutes.* **b.** To make a tour of; visit: "[He] *did 15 countries of Western Europe in only a few days"* (R.W. Apple, Jr.). **10.a.** To be sufficient in meeting the needs of; serve: *This room will do us very nicely.* **b.** *Informal.* To serve (a prison term). **11.** *Slang.* To cheat; swindle: *do a relative out of an inheritance.* **12.** *Slang.* To take (drugs) illegally: *"If you do drugs you are going to be in continual trouble"* (Jimmy Breslin). *—intr.* **1.** To behave or conduct oneself; act: *Do as I say and you won't get into trouble.* **2.a.** To get along; fare: *students who do well at school.* **b.** To carry on; manage: *We can very easily do without your interference.* **c.** To make good use of something because of need: *I could do with a nice hot bath.* **3.a.** To serve a specified purpose: *This coat will do for another season.* **b.** To be proper or fitting: *Such behavior just won't do.* **4.** To take place; happen: *What's doing in London this time of year?* **5.** Used as a substitute for an antecedent verb: *worked as hard as everyone else did.* **6.** Used after another verb for emphasis: *Run quickly, do!* *—aux.* **1.** Used with the infinitive without *to* in questions, negative statements, and inverted phrases: *Do you understand? I did not sleep well. Little did we know what was in store for us.* **2.** Used as a means of emphasis: *I do want to be sure. Do be still!* **—do** *n., pl.* **do's** or **dos. 1.** A statement of what should be done: *a list of the do's and don'ts of management.* **2.** *Informal.* An entertainment; a party: *attended a big do at the embassy.* **3.** *Regional.* A commotion. **4.** *Chiefly British.* A swindle; a cheat. **5.** *Archaic.* Duty; deed. **—*phrasal verbs.* do by.** To behave with respect to; deal with: *The children have done well by their aged parents.* **do for.** To care or provide for; take care of. **do in.** *Slang.* **1.** To tire completely; exhaust: *The marathon did me in.* **2.** To kill. **3.** To ruin utterly: *Huge losses on the stock market did many investors in.* **do up. 1.** To adorn or dress lavishly: *The children were all done up in matching outfits.* **2.** To wrap and tie (a package). **3.** To fasten: *do up the buttons on a dress.* **do without.** To manage in spite of a lack or absence: *There was no television on the island, but we soon learned to do without.* **—*idioms.* do a disappearing act.** *Informal.* To vanish. **do away with. 1.** To make an end of; eliminate. **2.** To destroy; kill. **do (one) proud.** To act or perform in a way that gives cause for pride. **do (one's) bit.** To make an individual contribution toward an overall effort. **do (one's) own thing.** *Slang.* To do what one does best or finds most enjoyable: *"I get paid to try cases and to do my thing on trial"* (Bruce Cutler). **do or die.** To exert supreme effort. [Middle English *don,* from Old English *dōn.* See **dhē-** in Appendix.]

do[2] (dō) *n. Music.* The first tone of the diatonic scale in solfeggio. [Italian, more singable replacement of *ut.* See GAMUT.]

do. *abbr.* Ditto.

D.O. *abbr.* **1.** Doctor of Optometry. **2.** Doctor of Osteopathy.

DOA *abbr.* Dead on arrival.

do·a·ble (do͞o′ə-bəl) *adj.* Possible to do: *a program that is tough but doable.*

DOB *abbr.* Date of birth.

dob·bin (dŏb′ĭn) *n.* A horse, especially a working farm horse. [From *Dobbin,* alteration of *Robin,* nickname for *Robert.*]

dob·by (dŏb′ē) *n., pl.* **-bies. 1.** A mechanical part in a loom that controls the harnesses so as to permit weaving of small geometric figures. **2.a.** A small geometric figure woven into fabric. **b.** A fabric with such figures. [Perhaps from *Dobbie,* diminutive of *Dob,* alteration of *Rob,* nickname for *Robert.*]

Do·ber·man pin·scher (dō′bər-mən pĭn′shər) *n.* A medium-sized to large dog of a breed originating in Germany, having short hair and a smooth, usually dark brown or black coat.

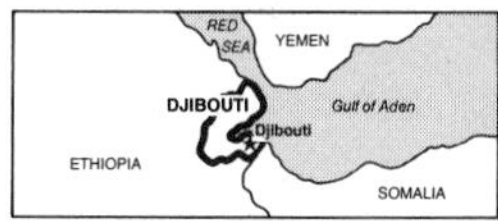

Djibouti

DNA

Doberman pinscher

[German *Dobermann* (after Ludwig *Dobermann,* 19th-century German dog breeder) + German *Pinscher,* terrier (probably from PINCH, from the cropping of its ears and tail).]

WORD HISTORY: The word *Doberman* in *Doberman pinscher* comes from the last name of the German breeder Ludwig Dobermann, who is thought to have developed this breed in the latter half of the 19th century. He crossed a number of breeds, including a type of German terrier called a *Pinscher.* The name *Doberman pinscher* thus reminds us of one of its ancestors and of the person without whom the breed would possibly not exist. The dog's name is first recorded in English in 1917 in the *Policeman's Monthly.*

Do·bie (dō′bē), **James Frank.** 1888–1964. American historian best known for his works on the history and folklore of the Southwest, including *The Longhorns* (1941).

do·bra (dō′brə) *n.* See table at **currency.** [Portuguese, ultimately from Latin *duplus,* double. See DUPLE.]

Do·bro (dō′brō). A trademark used for stringed musical instruments, specifically guitars and banjos.

dob·son (dŏb′sən) *n.* See **hellgrammite.** [Probably from the name *Dobson.*]

dob·son·fly (dŏb′sən-flī′) *n.* An insect *(Corydalus cornutus)* having four large, many-veined wings and in the male long, pincerlike mandibles.

dobsonfly
Corydalus cornutus

doc (dŏk) *n. Informal.* A physician, dentist, or veterinarian. [Short for DOCTOR.]

doc. *abbr.* Document.

do·cent (dō′sənt, dō-sĕnt′) *n.* **1.** A teacher or lecturer at some universities who is not a regular faculty member. **2.** A lecturer or tour guide in a museum or cathedral. [Obsolete German, from Latin *docēns, docent-,* present participle of *docēre,* to teach. See **dek-** in Appendix.]

Do·ce·tism (dō-sē′tĭz′əm, dō′sə-tĭz′əm) *n.* An opinion especially associated with the Gnostics that Jesus had no human body and only appeared to have died on the cross. [Probably from Late Greek *Dokētai,* espousers of Docetism, from Greek *dokein,* to seem. See **dek-** in Appendix.] **—Do·ce′tist** *n.*

doc·ile (dŏs′əl, -īl′) *adj.* **1.** Ready and willing to be taught; teachable. **2.** Yielding to supervision, direction, or management; tractable. See Synonyms at **obedient.** [Latin *docilis,* from *docēre,* to teach. See **dek-** in Appendix.] **—doc′ile·ly** *adv.* **—do·cil′i·ty** (dŏ-sĭl′ĭ-tē, dō-) *n.*

dock¹ (dŏk) *n. Abbr.* **dk. 1.** The area of water between two piers or alongside a pier that receives a ship for loading, unloading, or repairs. **2.** A pier; a wharf. **3.** Often **docks.** A group of piers on a commercial waterfront that serve as a general landing area for ships or boats. **4.** A platform at which trucks or trains load or unload cargo. **—dock** *v.* **docked, dock·ing, docks.** *—tr.* **1.** To maneuver (a vessel or vehicle) into or next to a dock. **2.** *Aerospace.* To couple (two or more spacecraft, for example) in space. *—intr.* To move or come into a dock. [Dutch *dok,* from Middle Dutch *doc,* from *dūken,* to go under water, dive.]

dock¹

dock² (dŏk) *n.* **1.** The solid or fleshy part of an animal's tail. **2.** The tail of an animal after it has been bobbed or clipped. **—dock** *tr.v.* **docked, dock·ing, docks. 1.** To clip short or cut off (an animal's tail, for example). **2.** To deprive of a benefit or a part of one's wages, especially as a punishment: *The company docks its employees for unauthorized absences.* **3.** To withhold or deduct a part from (one's salary or wages). [Middle English *dok.*]

dock³ (dŏk) *n.* An enclosed place where the defendant stands or sits in a court of law. ***—idiom.* in the dock.** On trial or under intense scrutiny. [Obsolete Flemish *docke,* cage.]

dock⁴ (dŏk) *n.* See **sorrel¹** (sense 1). [Middle English, from Old English *docce.*]

dock·age (dŏk′ĭj) *n.* **1.** A charge for docking privileges. **2.** Facilities for docking vessels. **3.** The docking of ships.

dock·er¹ (dŏk′ər) *n.* A dockworker; a longshoreman.

dock·er² (dŏk′ər) *n.* One that docks something, such as the tail of an animal.

dock·et (dŏk′ĭt) *n.* **1.** *Law.* **a.** A calendar of the cases awaiting action in a court. **b.** A brief entry of the court proceedings in a legal case. **c.** The book containing such entries. **2.** A summary or other brief statement of the contents of a document; an abstract. **3.** A list of things to be done; an agenda. **4.** A label or ticket affixed to a package listing the contents or directions for assembling or operating. **—docket** *tr.v.* **-et·ed, -et·ing, -ets. 1.** *Law.* To enter in a court calendar or in a record of court proceedings. **2.** To provide with a brief identifying statement. **3.** To label or ticket (a parcel). [Middle English *doggett,* summary, digest.]

dock·hand (dŏk′hănd′) *n.* A dockworker; a longshoreman.

dock·mack·ie (dŏk′măk′ē) *n.* A shrub *(Viburnum acerifolium)* of eastern North America, having clusters of white flowers. Also called *possum haw.* [Probably from American Dutch, perhaps of Mahican origin.]

dock·o·min·i·um (dŏk′ə-mĭn′ē-əm) *n., pl.* **-ums. 1.** A dockside community of privately owned boats moored in slips that are purchased for year-round living. **2.** A slip in such a community. [DOCK¹ + (COND)OMINIUM.]

dock·side (dŏk′sīd′) *n.* The area adjacent to a boating dock.

dock·work·er (dŏk′wûr′kər) *n.* A dockhand.

dock·yard (dŏk′yärd′) *n.* **1.** An area, often bordering a body of water, with facilities for building, repairing, or dry-docking ships. **2.** *Chiefly British.* A navy yard.

doc·tor (dŏk′tər) *n.* **1.** A person, especially a physician, dentist, or veterinarian, trained in the healing arts and licensed to practice. **2.a.** A person who has earned the highest academic degree awarded by a college or university in a specified discipline. **b.** A person awarded an honorary degree by a college or university. **3.** *Abbr.* **Dr.** Used as a title and form of address for a person holding the degree of doctor. **4.** *Roman Catholic Church.* An eminent theologian. **5.** A rig or device contrived for remedying an emergency situation or for doing a special task. **6.** Any of several brightly colored artificial flies used in fly fishing. **—doctor** *v.* **-tored, -tor·ing, -tors.** *—tr.* **1.** *Informal.* To give medical treatment to: "[He] *does more than practice medicine. He doctors people. There's a difference"* (Charles Kuralt). **2.** To repair, especially in a makeshift manner; rig. **3.a.** To falsify or change in such a way as to make favorable to oneself: *doctored the evidence.* **b.** To add ingredients so as to improve or conceal the taste, appearance, or quality of: *doctor the soup with a dash of sherry.* See Synonyms at **adulterate. c.** To alter or modify for a specific end: *doctored my standard speech for the small-town audience.* *—intr. Informal.* To practice medicine. [Middle English, an expert, authority, from Old French *docteur,* from Latin *doctor,* teacher, from *docēre,* to teach. See **dek-** in Appendix.] **—doc′tor·al** *adj.* **—doc′tor·ly** *adj.*

doc·tor·ate (dŏk′tər-ĭt) *n.* The degree or status of a doctor as conferred by a university.

doc·tri·naire (dŏk′trə-nâr′) *n.* A person inflexibly attached to a practice or theory without regard to its practicality. **—doctrinaire** *adj.* Of, relating to, or characteristic of a person inflexibly attached to a practice or theory. See Synonyms at **dictatorial.** [French, from *doctrine,* doctrine, from Old French. See DOCTRINE.] **—doc′tri·nair′ism** *n.* **—doc′tri·nar′i·an** *n.*

doc·tri·nal (dŏk′trə-nəl) *adj.* Characterized by, belonging to, or concerning doctrine. **—doc′tri·nal·ly** *adv.*

doc·trine (dŏk′trĭn) *n.* **1.** A principle or body of principles presented for acceptance or belief, as by a religious, political, scientific, or philosophic group; dogma. **2.** A rule or principle of law, especially when established by precedent. **3.** A statement of official government policy, especially in foreign affairs and military strategy. **4.** *Archaic.* Something taught; a teaching. [Middle English, from Old French, from Latin *doctrīna,* from *doctor,* teacher, from *docēre,* to teach. See **dek-** in Appendix.]

SYNONYMS: *doctrine, dogma, tenet.* The central meaning shared by these nouns is "a principle taught, advanced, or accepted, as by a group of philosophers": *the legal doctrine of due process; church dogma; experimentation, one of the tenets of the physical sciences.*

doc·u·dra·ma (dŏk′yə-drä′mə, -drăm′ə) *n.* A television or movie dramatization of events based on fact. [DOCU(MENTARY) + DRAMA.] **—doc′u·dra·mat′ic** (-drə-măt′ĭk) *adj.*

doc·u·ment (dŏk′yə-mənt) *n. Abbr.* **doc. 1.a.** A written or printed paper that bears the original, official, or legal form of something and can be used to furnish decisive evidence or information. **b.** Something, such as a recording or a photograph, that can be used to furnish evidence or information. **c.** A writing that contains information. **2.** Something, especially a material substance such as a coin bearing a revealing symbol or mark, that serves as proof or evidence. **—document** (-mĕnt′) *tr.v.* **-ment·ed, -ment·ing, -ments. 1.** To furnish with a document or documents. **2.** To support (an assertion or a claim, for example) with evidence or decisive information. **3.** To support (statements in a book, for example) with written references or citations; annotate. [Middle English, precept, from Old French, from Latin *documentum,* example, proof, from *docēre,* to teach. See **dek-** in Appendix.] **—doc′u·men′tal** (-mĕn′tl) *adj.* **—doc′u·ment′er** *n.*

doc·u·ment·a·ble (dŏk′yə-mĕn′tə-bəl) *adj.* Being such that documenting is possible: *a fact, easily documentable; a documentable case of theft.*

doc·u·ment·al·ist (dŏk′yə-mĕn′tl-ĭst′) *n.* A specialist in documentation.

doc·u·men·tar·i·an (-mĕn-târ′ē-ən, -mən-) also **doc·u·men·ta·rist** (dŏk′yə-mĕn′tər-ĭst) *n.* One that makes documentaries or a documentary.

doc·u·men·ta·ry (dŏk′yə-mĕn′tə-rē) *adj.* **1.** Consisting of, concerning, or based on documents. **2.** Presenting facts objectively without editorializing or inserting fictional matter, as in a book or film. **—documentary** *n., pl.* **-ries.** A work, such as a film or television program, presenting political, social, or historical subject matter in a factual and informative manner and often consisting of actual news films or interviews accompanied by narration.

doc·u·men·ta·tion (dŏk′yə-mĕn-tā′shən) *n.* **1.a.** The act or an instance of the supplying of documents or supporting references or records. **b.** The documents or references so supplied. **2.** The collation, synopsizing, and coding of printed material for future reference. **3.** *Computer Science.* The organized collection of records that describe the structure, purpose, operation, maintenance, and data requirements for a computer program.

doc·u·tain·ment (dŏk′yə-tān′mənt) *n.* See **infotainment.** [DOCU(MENTARY) + (ENTER)TAINMENT.]

DOD *abbr.* Department of Defense.

dod·der¹ (dŏd′ər) *intr.v.* **-dered, -der·ing, -ders. 1.** To

ă pat	oi boy
ā pay	ou out
âr care	ŏŏ took
ä father	ōō boot
ĕ pet	ŭ cut
ē be	ûr urge
ĭ pit	th thin
ī pie	*th* this
îr pier	hw which
ŏ pot	zh vision
ō toe	ə about, item
ô paw	♦ regionalism

Stress marks: **′** (primary); ′ (secondary), as in **dictionary** (dĭk′shə-nĕr′ē)

shake or tremble, as from old age; totter. **2.** To progress in a feeble, unsteady manner. [Alteration of Middle English *daderen.*] **—dod′der·er** *n.*

dod·der² (dŏd′ər) *n.* Any of various leafless, annual parasitic herbs of the genus *Cuscuta* that lack chlorophyll and have slender, twining, yellow or reddish stems and small whitish flowers. [Middle English *doder,* possibly from Middle Dutch, yolk of an egg (from the yellow color of the blossom of one species of this plant).]

dod·dered (dŏd′ərd) *adj.* **1.** *Botany.* Lacking the top branches as a result of age or decay. **2.** Infirm; feeble. [Probably alteration of *dodded,* past participle of dialectal *dod,* to lop off, from Middle English *dodden,* perhaps from *dodde,* a measure of grain.]

dod·der·ing (dŏd′ər-ĭng) *adj.* Infirm, feeble, and often senile.

do·dec·a·gon (dō-dĕk′ə-gŏn′) *n.* A polygon with 12 sides. [Greek *dōdekagōnon* : *dōdeka,* twelve (*duo,* two; see **dwo-** in Appendix + *deka,* ten; see **dekm̥** in Appendix) + *-gōnon,* -gon.] **—do′de·cag′o·nal** (dō′dĕ-kăg′ə-nəl) *adj.*

do·dec·a·he·dron (dō′dĕk-ə-hē′drən) *n., pl.* **-drons** or **-dra** (-drə). A polyhedron with 12 faces. [Greek *dōdekaedron* : *dōdeka,* twelve; see DODECAGON + *-edron,* -hedron.] **—do′dec·a·he′dral** *adj.*

Do·dec·a·nese (dō-dĕk′ə-nēz′, -nēs′). An island group of southeast Greece in the Aegean Sea between Turkey and Crete. The name means "12 islands," although there are also several islets. The islands were held by Turkey from 1522 until 1912.

do·dec·a·phon·ic (dō′dĕk-ə-fŏn′ĭk) *adj. Music.* Relating to, composed in, or consisting of twelve-tone music. [Greek *dōdeka,* twelve; see DODECAGON + PHON(O)–, tone, pitch + –IC.] **—do·dec′a·phon·ist** (dō-dĕk′ə-fə-nĭst, dō′də-kăf′ə-) *n.* **—do·dec′a·phon′y** (dō-dĕk′ə-fō′nē, dō′də-kăf′ə-), **do·dec′a·phon·ism** *n.*

dodge (dŏj) *v.* **dodged, dodg·ing, dodg·es.** *—tr.* **1.** To avoid (a blow, for example) by moving or shifting quickly aside. **2.** To evade (an obligation, for example) by cunning, trickery, or deceit: *kept dodging the reporter's questions.* **3.** To blunt or reduce the intensity of (a section of a photograph) by shading during the printing process. *—intr.* **1.** To move aside or in a given direction by shifting or twisting suddenly: *The child dodged through the crowd.* **2.** To practice trickery or cunning; prevaricate. **—dodge** *n.* **1.** The act of dodging. **2.** An ingenious expedient intended to evade or trick. See Synonyms at **artifice.** [Origin unknown.]

Dodge (dŏj), **Grenville Mellen.** 1831–1916. American civil engineer and politician noted for his efforts to expand railroad lines in the West and Southwest.

Dodge, Mary Elizabeth Mapes. 1831–1905. American editor and writer best known for her children's classic *Hans Brinker, or the Silver Skates* (1865).

dodge ball *n. Games.* A game in which players outside a circle try to eliminate players on the inside by hitting them with an inflated ball.

Dodge City. A city of southwest Kansas on the Arkansas River west of Wichita. Laid out on the Santa Fe Trail in 1872, it soon became a wild and rowdy cow town whose residents included such legendary figures as Wyatt Earp and Bat Masterson. Population, 18,001.

♦**dodg·er** (dŏj′ər) *n.* **1.** One that dodges or evades: *a skilled dodger of reporters' questions.* **2.** A shifty, dishonest person; a trickster. **3.** A small printed handbill. **4.** *Chiefly Southern U.S.* See **corndodger.**

Dodg·son (dŏj′sən), **Charles Lutwidge.** Pen name Lewis Carroll. 1832–1898. British mathematician and writer. His stories about Alice, invented to amuse the young daughter of a friend, appear in the classics *Alice's Adventures in Wonderland* (1865) and *Through the Looking-Glass* (1872).

dodg·y (dŏj′ē) *adj.* **-i·er, -i·est.** *Chiefly British.* **1.** Evasive; shifty. **2.** Unsound, unstable, and unreliable. **3.** So risky as to require very deft handling.

do·do (dō′dō) *n., pl.* **-does** or **-dos. 1.** A large, clumsy, flightless bird *(Raphus cucullatus),* formerly of the island of Mauritius in the Indian Ocean, that has been extinct since the late 17th century. **2.** *Informal.* One whose dress, lifestyle, and ideas are hopelessly passé. **3.** *Informal.* A stupid person; an idiot. [Portuguese *dodó,* alteration of obsolete Dutch *dodors* : Dutch *dot,* tuft of feathers + obsolete Dutch *ors,* tail (from Middle Dutch *ærs;* see **ors-** in Appendix).]

Do·do·ma (dō′də-mä, -dō-). The official capital of Tanzania, in the central part of the country. Population, 46,000.

Do·do·na (də-dō′nə). An ancient city of northwest Greece. It was a center of Pelasgian worship dedicated to Zeus.

doe (dō) *n., pl.* **doe** or **does. 1.** The female of a deer or related animal. **2.** The female of various mammals, such as the hare, goat, or kangaroo. [Middle English *do,* from Old English *dā.*]

Doe·nitz also **Dö·nitz** (dœ′nĭts), **Karl.** 1891–1980. German naval officer who was chief naval commander during World War II and briefly headed the German government after the death of Adolf Hitler (1945).

do·er (do͞o′ər) *n.* **1.** One who does something: *a doer of evil deeds.* **2.** A particularly active, energetic person: *a real doer in party politics.*

does (dŭz) *v.* Third person singular present tense of **do¹.**

doe·skin (dō′skĭn′) *n.* **1.a.** The skin of a doe, deer, or goat. **b.** Leather made from this skin, used especially for gloves. **2.** A fine, soft, smooth woolen fabric. **3.** A densely napped finish for certain woolen fabrics, such as flannel.

does·n't (dŭz′ənt). Does not.

do·est (do͞o′ĭst) *v. Archaic.* A second person singular present tense of **do¹.**

do·eth (do͞o′əth) *v. Archaic.* A third person singular present tense of **do¹.**

doff (dôf, dŏf) *tr.v.* **doffed, doff·ing, doffs. 1.** To take off; remove: *doff one's clothes.* **2.** To tip or remove (one's hat) in salutation. **3.** To put aside; discard. [Middle English *doffen,* from *don off,* to do off : *don,* to do; see DO¹ + *off,* off; see OFF.]

dog (dôg, dŏg) *n.* **1.** A domesticated carnivorous mammal *(Canis familiaris)* related to the foxes and wolves and raised in a wide variety of breeds. **2.** Any of various carnivorous mammals of the family Canidae, such as the dingo. **3.** A male animal of the family Canidae, especially of the fox or a domesticated breed. **4.** Any of various other animals, such as the prairie dog. **5.** *Informal.* **a.** A person: *You won, you lucky dog.* **b.** A person regarded as contemptible: *You stole my watch, you dog.* **6.** *Slang.* **a.** A person regarded as unattractive or uninteresting. **b.** A hopelessly inferior product or creation: *"The President had read the speech to some of his friends and they told him it was a dog"* (John P. Roche). **7. dogs.** *Slang.* The feet. **8.** See **andiron. 9.** *Slang.* A hot dog; a wiener. **10.** Any of various hooked or U-shaped metallic devices used for gripping or holding heavy objects. **11.** *Astronomy.* A sun dog. **—dog** *adv.* Totally; completely. Often used in combination: *dog-tired.* **—dog** *tr.v.* **dogged, dog·ging, dogs. 1.** To track or trail persistently: *"A stranger then is still dogging us"* (Arthur Conan Doyle). **2.** To hold or fasten with a mechanical device: *"Watertight doors and hatches were dropped into place and dogged down to give the ship full watertight integrity"* (Tom Clancy). **—*idioms.* dog it.** *Slang.* To fail to expend the required effort to do or accomplish something. **go to the dogs.** To go to ruin; degenerate. **put on the dog.** *Informal.* To make an ostentatious display of elegance, wealth, or culture. [Middle English *dogge,* from Old English *docga.*]

dog-and-po·ny show (dôg′ən-pō′nē, dŏg′-) *n. Slang.* An elaborate presentation orchestrated to gain approval, as for a policy or product. [From the razzle-dazzle of trained animal acts at circuses.]

dog·bane (dôg′bān′, dŏg′-) *n.* Any of several plants of the genus *Apocynum,* having milky juice and bell-shaped white or pink flowers.

dog·ber·ry (dôg′bĕr′ē, dŏg′-) *n.* **1.** A wild gooseberry *(Ribes cynosbati)* of eastern North America, bearing large, prickly berries. **2.** A wild mountain ash *(Pyrus decora)* of eastern North America. **3.** The fruit of either of these plants.

dog biscuit *n.* A hard cracker for dogs.

dog·cart (dôg′kärt′, dŏg′-) *n.* **1.** A vehicle drawn by one horse and accommodating two persons seated back to back. **2.** A small cart pulled by dogs.

dog·catch·er (dôg′kăch′ər, dŏg′-) *n.* A dog officer.

dog chew *n.* A leather object intended as a chewing toy for dogs.

dog collar *n.* **1.** A collar for a dog. **2.** *Informal.* A clerical collar. **3.** A choker: *a duchess resplendent in ermine robes, a tiara, and a diamond dog collar.*

dog days *pl.n.* **1.** The hot, sultry period of summer between early July and early September. **2.** A period of stagnation. [Translation of Late Latin *diēs canīculārēs,* Dog Star days (so called because the Dog Star (Sirius) rises and sets with the sun during this time) : Latin *diēs,* days + Late Latin *canīculāris,* of the Dog Star.]

doge (dōj) *n.* The elected chief magistrate of the former republics of Venice and Genoa. [Italian dialectal, from Latin *dux, duc-,* leader, from *dūcere,* to lead. See **deuk-** in Appendix.]

dog-ear (dôg′îr′, dŏg′-) *n.* A turned-down corner of a page in a book. **—dog-ear** *tr.v.* **-eared, -ear·ing, -ears. 1.** To turn down the corner of (the page of a book). **2.** To make worn or shabby from overuse. **—dog′-eared′** *adj.*

dog-eat-dog (dôg′ēt-dôg′, dŏg′ēt-dŏg′) *adj.* Ruthlessly acquisitive or competitive: *a dog-eat-dog society.*

dog·face (dôg′fās′, dŏg′-) *n. Slang.* A U.S. Army foot soldier, especially in World War II.

dog fennel *n.* **1.** A strong-smelling European weed *(Anthemis cotula)* naturalized in North America. **2.** A weedy plant *(Eupatorium capillifolium)* of the southeast United States, having pinnately divided leaves and long clusters of greenish flowers.

dog·fight (dôg′fīt′, dŏg′-) *n.* **1.a.** A violent fight between or as if between dogs. **b.** An illegal, organized fight betwen dogs, arranged for spectator entertainment and betting. **2.** An aerial battle between fighter planes. **—dog′fight′er** *n.*

dog·fight·ing (dôg′fī′tĭng, dŏg′-) *n.* An illegal, organized activity in which dogs are fought for spectator entertainment and betting.

dog·fish (dôg′fĭsh′, dŏg′-) *n., pl.* **dogfish** or **-fish·es. 1.** Any of various small sharks, chiefly of the family Squalidae, of Atlantic and Pacific coastal waters. Also called *grayfish.* **2.** See **bowfin.**

dog·ged (dô′gĭd, dŏg′ĭd) *adj.* Stubbornly persevering; tenacious. See Synonyms at **obstinate. —dog′ged·ly** *adv.* **—dog′ged·ness** *n.*

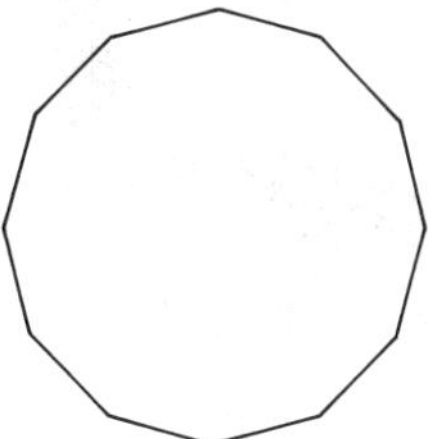
dodecagon

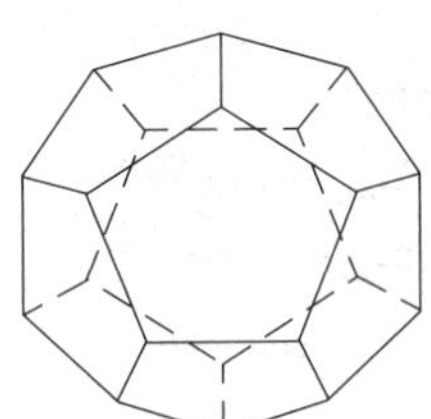
dodecahedron

Charles Dodgson
"Lewis Carroll"

dodo
Raphus cucullatus

Dog·ger Bank (dôʹgər, dŏgʹər). An extensive sandbank of the central North Sea between Great Britain and Denmark. It is a major breeding ground for fish.

dog·ger·el (dôʹgər-əl, dŏgʹər-) also **dog·grel** (dôgʹrəl, dŏgʹ-) *n.* Crudely or irregularly fashioned verse, often of a humorous or burlesque nature. [From Middle English, poor, worthless, from *dogge,* dog. See DOG.] **—dogʹger·el** *adj.*

dog·gie (dôʹgē, dŏgʹē) *n. & adj.* Variant of **doggy.**

doggie bag *n.* Variant of **doggy bag.**

dog·gish (dôʹgĭsh, dŏgʹĭsh) *adj.* **1.** Relating to or suggestive of a dog. **2.** Surly; gruff. **3.** *Informal.* Showily stylish. **—dogʹgish·ly** *adv.* **—dogʹgish·ness** *n.*

dog·go (dôʹgō, dŏgʹō) *adv. Informal.* In concealment: *" 'You'd better lie doggo,' I advised her out of my own nervousness"* (John M. Myers). [Probably from DOG.]

♦**dog·gone** (dôgʹgônʹ, -gŏnʹ, dŏgʹ-) *Informal. tr. & intr.v.* To damn. **—doggone** *interj., n., adv., & adj.* Damn. See Regional Note at **damned.** [Alteration of Scots *dagone,* from *dag on (it)* : *dag,* confound (probably alteration of *goddamn*) + ON.]

dog·grel (dôgʹrəl, dŏgʹ-) *n.* Variant of **doggerel.**

dogsled

dog·gy or **dog·gie** (dôʹgē, dŏgʹē) *—n., pl.* **-gies.** A dog, especially a small one. *—adj.* **-gi·er, -gi·est.** Of or suggestive of a dog; doggish.

doggy bag or **doggie bag** *n.* A bag for leftover food that a customer of a restaurant may take home after a meal. [From the assumption that such food would be given to the customer's dog.]

♦**dog·hanged** (dôgʹhăngd, dŏgʹ-) *adj. Chiefly Southern U.S.* Hangdog. See Regional Note at **everwhere.**

dog·house (dôgʹhousʹ, dŏgʹ-) *n.* A small shelter for a dog. *—idiom.* **in the doghouse.** *Slang.* In great disfavor or trouble.

♦**do·gie** also **do·gy** (dōʹgē) *n., pl.* **-gies.** *Western U.S.* A stray or motherless calf. [Origin unknown.]

♦***REGIONAL NOTE:*** In the language of the American West, a motherless calf is known as a *dogie.* In *Western Words* Ramon F. Adams gives one possible etymology for *dogie,* whose origin is unknown. During the 1880's, when a series of harsh winters left large numbers of orphaned calves, the little calves, weaned too early, were unable to digest coarse range grass, and their swollen bellies "very much resembled a batch of sourdough carried in a sack." Such a calf was referred to as *dough-guts.* The term, altered to *dogie* according to Adams, "has been used ever since throughout cattleland to refer to a pot-gutted orphan calf." Another possibility is that *dogie* is an alteration of Spanish *dogal,* "lariat."

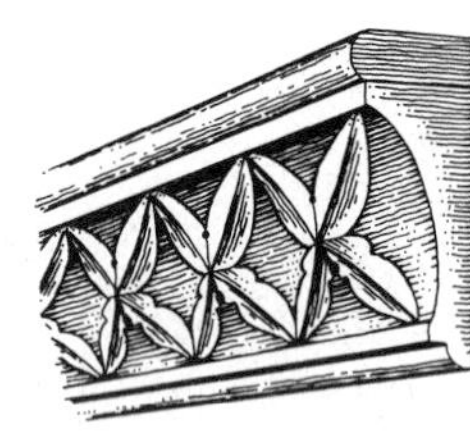
dogtooth

dog in the manger *n., pl.* **dogs in the manger.** One who prevents others from enjoying what one has no use for oneself. [From a fable in which a dog prevented an ox from eating hay he did not want himself.]

♦**dog iron** *n. Upper Southern U.S.* See **andiron.** [(FIRE)DOG + (AND)IRON.]

dog·leg (dôgʹlĕgʹ, dŏgʹ-) *n.* **1.a.** Something that has a sharp bend, especially a road or route that bends abruptly. **b.** A sharp bend or turn: *Make a dogleg at the fire station and continue south.* **2.** *Sports.* A golf hole in which the fairway is abruptly angled. **—dogleg** *intr.v.* **-legged, -leg·ging, -legs.** To make a sharp bend or turn: *The street doglegs to the left.* **—dogʹlegʹged** (-lĕgʹĭd, -lĕgdʹ) *adj.*

dog·ma (dôgʹmə, dŏgʹ-) *n., pl.* **-mas** or **-ma·ta** (-mə-tə). **1.** *Theology.* A doctrine or a corpus of doctrines relating to matters such as morality and faith, set forth in an authoritative manner by a church. **2.** An authoritative principle, belief, or statement of ideas or opinion, especially one considered to be absolutely true. See Synonyms at **doctrine. 3.** A principle or belief or a group of them: *"The dogmas of the quiet past are inadequate to the stormy present"* (Abraham Lincoln). [Latin, from Greek, opinion, belief, from *dokein,* to seem, think. See **dek-** in Appendix.]

dogwood
Cornus florida

dog·mat·ic (dôg-mătʹĭk, dŏg-) *adj.* **1.** Relating to, characteristic of, or resulting from dogma. **2.** Characterized by an authoritative, arrogant assertion of unproved or unprovable principles. See Synonyms at **dictatorial.** [Late Latin *dogmaticus,* from Greek *dogmatikos,* from *dogma, dogmat-,* belief. See DOGMA.] **—dog·matʹi·cal·ly** *adv.*

dog·mat·ics (dôg-mătʹĭks, dŏg-) *n. (used with a sing. verb).* The study of religious dogmas, especially those of a Christian church.

dog·ma·tism (dôgʹmə-tĭzʹəm, dŏgʹ-) *n.* Arrogant, stubborn assertion of opinion or belief.

dog·ma·tist (dôgʹmə-tĭst, dŏgʹ-) *n.* **1.** An arrogantly assertive person. **2.** One who expresses or sets forth dogma.

dog·ma·tize (dôgʹmə-tīzʹ, dŏgʹ-) *v.* **-tized, -tiz·ing, -tiz·es.** *—intr.* To express oneself dogmatically in writing or speech. *—tr.* To proclaim as dogma. **—dogʹma·ti·zaʹtion** (-tĭ-zāʹshən) *n.*

doily

dog·nap (dôgʹnăpʹ, dŏgʹ-) *tr.v.* **-napped, -nap·ping, -naps** or **-naped, -nap·ing, -naps.** To steal (a dog), especially for the purpose of selling it to a research laboratory. [DOG + (KID)NAP.] **—dogʹnapʹper** *n.*

dog officer *n.* One appointed or elected to impound stray dogs.

do-good (do͞oʹgo͝odʹ) *adj.* Naively idealistic in the support of philanthropic or humanitarian causes. **—doʹ-goodʹism** *n.*

do-good·er (do͞oʹgo͝odʹər) *n.* A naive idealist who supports philanthropic or humanitarian causes or reforms.

do-good·ing (do͞oʹgo͝odʹĭng) *adj.* Of or characteristic of a naive philanthropist or humanitarian: *"his do-gooding mother"* (John Updike). **—doʹ-goodʹing** *n.*

dog paddle *n. Sports.* A prone swimming stroke in which the arms and legs remain submerged and each limb paddles in alternation.

Dog·rib (dôgʹrĭbʹ, dŏgʹ-) *n., pl.* **Dogrib** or **-ribs. 1.a.** A Native American people inhabiting an area between the Great Bear and Great Slave lakes in the Northwest Territories of Canada. **b.** A member of this people. **2.** The Athabaskan language of this people. [Translation of Cree *atimospikay.*]

dog rose *n.* A prickly wild rose *(Rosa canina)* native to Europe and naturalized in eastern North America, having fragrant pink or white flowers.

dogs·bod·y (dôgzʹbŏdʹē, dŏgzʹ-) *n. Chiefly British.* One who does menial work; a drudge. [British slang, naval rations (obsolete), midshipman.]

dog's chance (dôgz, dŏgz) *n. Slang.* A very slim chance.

dog·sled or **dog sled** (dôgʹslĕdʹ, dŏgʹ-) *n.* A sled pulled by one or more dogs. **—dogʹsledʹ** *v.* **—dogʹsledʹder** *n.* **—dogʹsledʹding** *n.*

dog's life *n. Slang.* A miserably unhappy existence.

dog's mercury *n.* A creeping, ill-smelling Old World weed *(Mercurialis perennis)* having small greenish flowers.

Dog Star (dôg, dŏg) *n.* **1.** See **Sirius. 2.** See **Procyon.** [The brightest star in the constellation Canis Major, the Big Dog.]

dog tag *n.* **1.** A metal identification disk attached to a dog's collar. **2.** A metal identification tag worn on a chain around the neck by members of the armed forces.

dog·tooth (dôgʹto͞othʹ, dŏgʹ-) *n.* **1.** A canine tooth; an eyetooth. **2.** *Architecture.* A medieval ornament consisting of four leaflike projections radiating from a raised center.

dogtooth violet *n.* Any of several plants of the genus *Erythronium,* having leaves with reddish blotches and nodding, colorful, solitary, lilylike flowers on leafless stems. Also called *adder's-tongue, trout lily.*

♦**dog·trot** (dôgʹtrŏtʹ, dŏgʹ-) *n.* **1.** A steady trot like that of a dog. **2.** *Chiefly Southern U.S.* A roofed passage between two parts of a structure. **—dogtrot** *intr.v.* **-trot·ted, -trot·ting, -trots.** To move at a steady trot.

dog·watch (dôgʹwŏchʹ, dŏgʹ-) *n.* **1.** *Nautical.* Either of two short periods of watch duty, from 4 to 6 P.M. or 6 to 8 P.M. **2.** A late night shift. [Probably from *dog-sleep,* a light or interrupted sleep.]

dog·wood (dôgʹwo͝odʹ, dŏgʹ-) *n.* **1.** A tree *(Cornus florida)* of eastern North America, having small greenish flowers surrounded by four large, showy white or pink bracts that resemble petals. **2.** Any of several trees or shrubs of the genus *Cornus.* Also called *flowering dogwood.*

♦**do·gy** (dōʹgē) *n. Western U.S.* Variant of **dogie.**

Do·ha (dōʹhə, -hä). The capital of Qatar, on the Persian Gulf. It was a tiny village before oil production began in 1949. Population, 190,000.

doi·ly (doiʹlē) *n., pl.* **-lies. 1.** A small ornamental mat, usually of lace or linen. **2.** A small table napkin. [After *Doily* or *Doyly,* 18th-century London draper.]

do·ing (do͞oʹĭng) *n.* **1.** Performance of an act: *a job not worth the doing.* **2. doings. a.** Activities that go on every day: *"A motley crew they are, their doings as dark as they are ludicrous"* (John Simon). **b.** Social events and activities.

do-it-your·self (do͞oʹĭt-yər-sĕlfʹ) *adj.* Of, relating to, or designed to be done by an amateur or as a hobby: *do-it-yourself home repairs; a do-it-yourself sailboat kit.* **—doʹ-it-your·selfʹer** *n.*

do·jo (dōʹjō) *n.* A school for training in Japanese arts of self-defense, such as judo and karate. [Japanese *dōjō.*]

dol. *abbr.* **1.** Dollar. **2.** *Music.* Dolce.

do·lab·ri·form (dō-lăbʹrə-fôrmʹ) also **do·lab·rate** (-rātʹ) *adj. Biology.* Having the shape of the head of an ax. [Latin *dolābra,* pickax (from *dolāre,* to hew) + -FORM.]

Dol·by (dōlʹbē). A trademark used for an electronic device that eliminates noise from recorded sound and audio signals.

dol·ce (dōlʹchāʹ) *Music. adv. & adj. Abbr.* **dol.** Gently and sweetly. Used chiefly as a direction. [From Italian, sweet, from Latin *dulcis.*]

dolce vi·ta (vēʹtə, -tä) *n.* A luxurious, self-indulgent way of life. [Italian : *dolce,* sweet + *vita,* life.]

dol·drums (dōlʹdrəmzʹ, dôlʹ-, dŏlʹ-) *pl.n. (used with a sing. or pl. verb).* **1.a.** A period of stagnation or slump. **b.** A period of depression or unhappy listlessness. **2.a.** A region of the ocean near the equator, characterized by calms, light winds, or squalls. **b.** The weather conditions characteristic of these regions of the ocean. [Alteration (influenced by TANTRUM) of obsolete *doldrum,* dullard, from Middle English *dold,* past participle of *dullen,* to dull, from *dul,* dull. See DULL.]

dole¹ (dōl) *n.* **1.** Charitable dispensation of goods, especially money, food, or clothing. **2.** A share of money, food, or clothing that has been charitably given. **3.** *Chiefly British.* The distribution by the government of relief payments to the unemployed; welfare. **4.** *Archaic.* One's fate. **—dole** *tr.v.* **doled, dol·ing,**

doles. **1.** To dispense as charity. **2.** To give out in small portions; distribute sparingly. See Synonyms at **distribute.** —*idiom.* **on the dole.** Receiving regular relief payments from or as if from the government. [Middle English *dol,* part, share, from Old English *dāl.* See **dail-** in Appendix.]

dole² (dōl) *n. Archaic.* Sorrow; grief; dolor. [Middle English *dol,* from Old French *dol, deul,* from Late Latin *dolus,* from Latin *dolēre,* to feel pain, grieve.]

dole·ful (dōl′fəl) *adj.* **1.** Filled with or expressing grief; mournful. See Synonyms at **sad. 2.** Causing grief: *a doleful loss.* —**dole′ful·ly** *adv.* —**dole′ful·ness** *n.*

dol·er·ite (dŏl′ə-rīt′) *n. Chiefly British.* A dark, fine-grained igneous rock; diabase. [French *dolérite,* from Greek *doleros,* deceitful (from its easily being mistaken for diorite), from *dolos,* trick. See **del-²** in Appendix.] —**dol′er·it′ic** (ə-rĭt′ĭk) *adj.*

dol·i·cho·ce·phal·ic (dŏl′ĭ-kō-sə-făl′ĭk) also **dol·i·cho·ceph·a·lous** (-sĕf′ə-ləs) *adj.* Having a relatively long head with a cephalic index below 76. [Greek *dolikhos,* long; see **del-¹** in Appendix + -CEPHALIC.] —**dol′i·cho·ceph′a·lism** (-sĕf′ə-lĭz′əm), **dol′i·cho·ceph′a·ly** (-sĕf′ə-lē) *n.*

dol·i·cho·cra·ni·al (dŏl′ə-kō-krā′nē-əl) also **dol·i·cho·cra·nic** (-nĭk) *adj.* Having a relatively long skull with a cranial index of 74.9 or less. [Greek *dolikhos,* long; see **del-¹** in Appendix + CRANIAL.] —**dol′i·cho·cra′ny** *n.*

do-lit·tle (do͞o′lĭt′l) *n. Informal.* A lazy person.

doll (dŏl) *n.* **1.** A child's usually small toy representing a human being. **2.** A pretty child. **3.** *Slang.* **a.** An attractive person. **b.** A woman. **c.** A sweetheart or darling. **d.** A helpful or obliging person. —*phrasal verb.* **doll up.** *Slang.* **1.** To dress oneself smartly and often ostentatiously, especially for a special occasion. **2.** To add embellishing details to in order to make much more attractive. [From *Doll,* nickname for *Dorothy.*]

WORD HISTORY: The word *doll* has come up in the world, at least if *up* means moving from the backstairs to the nursery. *Doll* and *Dolly* were originally nicknames for *Dorothy. Doll,* along with other names like *Jill* and *Nan,* took on the generic sense of "a mistress," so we have Shakespeare's Doll Tearsheet and Ben Jonson's Doll Common. This association probably caused the name *Dorothy* to go out of use temporarily, about the time near the beginning of the 18th century when we find *doll* first recorded for a child's toy. *Doll* came to refer to larger beings again, however, for in the latter part of the 18th century it was once more applied to women, this time to pretty, empty-headed women. *Doll* has gone on to more general applications, and a man can be a doll as well.

dol·lar (dŏl′ər) *n. Abbr.* **dol. 1.** See table at **currency. 2.** A coin or note worth one dollar. [Low German *Daler,* taler, from German *Taler,* short for *Joachimstaler,* after *Joachimstal* (Jáchymov), a town of northeast Czechoslovakia where similar coins were first minted.]

dol·lar-a-year (dŏl′ər-ə-yîr′) *adj.* Of, relating to, or being an official, an employee, or a consultant who receives token payment for services rendered: *a dollar-a-year senator.*

dollar cost averaging *n.* Periodic investment of a fixed dollar amount.

dollar day *n.* A day on which a store offers its merchandise on sale for one dollar or at greatly reduced prices.

Dol·lard des Or·meaux or **Dol·lard-des-Or·meaux** (dō-yär′dā-zôr-mō′). A town of southern Quebec, Canada, a residential suburb of Montreal. Population, 39,940.

dollar diplomacy *n.* **1.** A policy aimed at furthering the interests of the United States abroad by encouraging the investment of U.S. capital in foreign countries. **2.** A policy intended to safeguard a nation's foreign investments.

dol·lar·fish (dŏl′ər-fĭsh′) *n., pl.* **dollarfish** or **-fish·es.** See **moonfish** (sense 1).

dollar sign *n.* The symbol ($) for a dollar when placed before a numeral.

Doll·fuss (dôl′fo͝os′), **Engelbert.** 1892–1934. Austrian politician who as chancellor (1932–1934) established an authoritarian, one-party state. He was assassinated by Austrian Nazis.

doll·house (dŏl′hous′) *n.* **1.** A small model house used as a children's toy or to display miniature dolls and furniture. **2.** A house so small that it is likened to a toy house.

dol·lop (dŏl′əp) *n.* **1.** A large lump or portion of a solid matter: *a dollop of ice cream.* **2.** A small quantity or splash of a liquid: *a dollop of whiskey.* **3.** A modicum; a bit: *not a dollop of truth to the story.* [Earlier tuft, clump; perhaps akin to Norwegian *dolp,* lump.]

dol·ly (dŏl′ē) *n., pl.* **-lies. 1.** *Informal.* A child's doll. **2. a.** A hand truck or low mobile platform that rolls on casters, used for transporting heavy loads. **b.** Such a platform as used by one working underneath a motor vehicle. **3.** A wheeled apparatus used to transport a movie or television camera about a set. **4.** A small locomotive, as for use in a railroad yard or on a construction site. **5.** A wooden implement for stirring clothes in a washtub. **6.** A tool used to hold one end of a rivet while the opposite end is being hammered to form a head. **7.** A small piece of wood or metal placed on the head of a pile to prevent damage to the pile while it is being driven. —**dolly** *intr.v.* **-lied, -ly·ing, -lies.** To move the wheeled apparatus on which a movie or television camera is mounted toward or away from the scene of action.

Dol·ly Var·den (dŏl′ē vär′dn) *n.* A colorfully spotted trout *(Salvelinus malma)* of northwest North America and eastern Asia. [After *Dolly Varden,* a character known for her colorful costume in the novel *Barnaby Rudge* by Charles Dickens.]

dol·ma (dŏl′mə, -mä) *n., pl.* **dol·mas** or **dol·ma·des** (dŏl-mä′dĕs). A grape leaf stuffed and cooked with ingredients such as ground beef, minced lamb, herbs, or rice. [Turkish, filling.]

dol·man (dŏl′mən) *n.* A woman's garment having capelike arm pieces. [French, from German, from Magyar *dolmany,* from Turkish *dōlămān,* robe, from *dolamak,* to wind.]

dolman sleeve *n.* A full sleeve that is very wide at the armhole and narrow at the wrist.

dol·men (dŏl′mən, dŏl′-) *n.* A prehistoric megalithic structure consisting of two or more upright stones with a capstone, typically forming a chamber. [French, from Breton **taolvean* : **taol,* alteration (influenced by *taol,* table, from Latin *tabula*) of *tol,* key + *men,* stone; see MENHIR.]

dol·o·mite (dō′lə-mīt′, dŏl′ə-) *n.* **1.** A white or light-colored mineral, essentially $CaMg(CO_3)_2$, used in fertilizer, as a furnace refractory, and as a construction and ceramic material. **2.** A magnesia-rich sedimentary rock resembling limestone. [French, after Déodat de *Dolomieu* (1750–1801), French geologist.] —**dol′o·mit′ic** (-mĭt′ĭk) *adj.* —**dol′o·mit′i·za′tion** (-mĭt′ĭ-zā′shən) *n.* —**dol′o·mit·ize′** (-mĭ-tīz′) *v.*

Do·lo·mite Alps (dō′lə-mīt′, dŏl′ə-). A range of the eastern Alps in northeast Italy rising to 3,344.3 m (10,965 ft). The dolomitic limestone peaks of the range are famous for their vivid coloring at sunrise and sunset.

do·lor (dō′lər) *n.* Sorrow; grief. [Middle English *dolour,* from Old French, from Latin *dolor,* pain, from *dolēre,* to suffer, feel pain.]

do·lo·ro·so (dō′lə-rō′sō) *Music. adv.* With a mournful or plaintive tempo or quality. Used chiefly as a direction. —**doloroso** *adj.* Mournful; plaintive. [Italian, from Latin *dolōrōsus,* dolorous. See DOLOROUS.]

do·lor·ous (dō′lər-əs, dŏl′ə-) *adj.* Marked by or exhibiting sorrow, grief, or pain. [Middle English, from Old French *doloros,* from Late Latin *dolōrōsus,* from *dolor,* dolor. See DOLOR.] —**do′lor·ous·ly** *adv.* —**do′lor·ous·ness** *n.*

do·lour (dō′lər) *n. Chiefly British.* Variant of **dolor.**

dol·phin (dŏl′fĭn, dôl′-) *n.* **1.** Any of various marine cetacean mammals, such as the bottle-nosed dolphin, of the family Delphinidae, related to the whales but generally smaller and having a beaklike snout. **2.** Either of two marine game fishes *(Coryphaena hippurus* or *C. equisetis)* having iridescent coloring. [Middle English, from Old French *daulfin,* blend of *daufin* and Old Provençal *dalfin,* both from Medieval Latin **dalfinus,* from Latin *delphinus,* from Greek *delphis, delfin-,* from *delphus,* womb (from its shape).]

dolphin striker *n. Nautical.* A small vertical spar under the bowsprit of a sailboat that extends and helps support the martingale.

dolt (dōlt) *n.* A person regarded as stupid. [Middle English *dulte,* from past participle of *dullen,* to dull, from *dul,* dull. See DULL.] —**dolt′ish** *adj.* —**dolt′ish·ly** *adv.* —**dolt′ish·ness** *n.*

Dol·ton (dōl′tən). A village of northern Illinois south of Chicago. It is a manufacturing center in a truck-farming area. Population, 24,766.

Dom (dŏm; *Portuguese* dōN) *n.* **1.** Used formerly as a title for men of Portuguese and Brazilian royalty, aristocracy, and hierarchy, preceding the given name. **2.** *Roman Catholic Church.* Used as a title before the names of Benedictine and Carthusian monks in major or minor orders. [Portuguese, from Latin *dominus,* lord, master. See **dem-** in Appendix.]

dom. *abbr.* **1.** Domestic. **2.** Dominant. **3.** Dominion.

Dom. *abbr. Roman Catholic Church.* Dominican.

D.O.M. *abbr. Latin.* Deo Optimo Maximo (to God, the best and the greatest).

-dom *suff.* **1.** State; condition: *stardom.* **2. a.** Domain; position; rank: *dukedom.* **b.** Those that collectively have a specified position, office, or character: *officialdom.* [Middle English, from Old English *-dōm.* See **dhē-** in Appendix.]

do·main (dō-mān′) *n.* **1.** A territory over which rule or control is exercised. **2.** A sphere of activity, concern, or function; a field: *the domain of history.* See Synonyms at **field. 3.** *Physics.* Any of numerous contiguous regions in a ferromagnetic material in which the direction of spontaneous magnetization is uniform and different from that in neighboring regions. **4.** *Law.* **a.** The land of one with paramount title and absolute ownership. **b.** Public domain. **5.** *Mathematics.* **a.** The set of all possible values of an independent variable of a function. **b.** An open connected set that contains at least one point. [French *domaine,* blend of Old French *demaine* (from Late Latin *dominicum*) and Latin *dominium,* property, both from *dominus,* lord. See **dem-** in Appendix.]

dome (dōm) *n.* **1. a.** A hemispherical roof or vault. **b.** A structure or other object resembling such a hemispherical roof or vault. **2.** *Slang.* The human head. **3.** *Chemistry.* A form of crystal with two similarly inclined faces that meet at an edge parallel to the horizontal axis. **4.** *Archaic.* A large, stately building. —**dome** *v.* **domed, dom·ing, domes.** —*tr.* **1.** To cover with or as if with a hemispherical roof or vault. **2.** To shape like such a roof or vault. —*intr.* To rise or swell into the shape of a hemispherical roof or vault. [From French *dôme,* dome, cathedral (from Italian *duomo,*

dollhouse

dolphin

dome
Top: Florence Cathedral, Italy
Bottom: Onion-shaped domes on a building in the Kremlin, Moscow

ă pat	oi boy
ā pay	ou out
âr care	o͝o took
ä father	o͞o boot
ĕ pet	ŭ cut
ē be	ûr urge
ĭ pit	th thin
ī pie	*th* this
îr pier	hw which
ŏ pot	zh vision
ō toe	ə about, item
ô paw	♦ regionalism

Stress marks: **′** (primary); ′ (secondary), as in **dictionary** (dĭk′shə-nĕr′ē)

cathedral, from Latin *domus,* house; see **dem-** in Appendix) and from French *dôme,* roof (from Provençal *doma,* from Greek *dōma,* house; see **dem-** in Appendix).]

Domes·day Book (do͞omz′dā′, dōmz′-) also **Dooms·day Book** (do͞omz′-) *n.* The written record of a census and survey of English landowners and their property made by order of William the Conqueror in 1085–1086. [From Middle English *domesday,* doomsday. See DOOMSDAY.]

do·mes·tic (də-mĕs′tĭk) *adj. Abbr.* **dom. 1.** Of or relating to the family or household: *domestic chores.* **2.** Fond of home life and household affairs. **3.** Tame or domesticated. Used of animals. **4.** Of or relating to a country's internal affairs: *domestic issues such as tax rates and highway construction.* **5.** Produced in or indigenous to a particular country: *domestic oil; domestic wine.* **—domestic** *n. Abbr.* **dom. 1.** A household servant. **2.a.** Cotton cloth. **b.** Often **domestics.** Household linens. **3.** A product or substance discovered in, developed in, or exported from a particular country. [Middle English, from Old French *domestique,* from Latin *domesticus,* from *domus,* house. See **dem-** in Appendix.] **—do·mes′ti·cal·ly** *adv.*

do·mes·ti·cate (də-mĕs′tĭ-kāt′) *tr.v.* **-cat·ed, -cat·ing, -cates. 1.** To cause to feel comfortable at home. **2.** To adopt or make fit for domestic use or life. **3.a.** To train or adapt (an animal or a plant) to live in a human environment and be of use to human beings. **b.** To introduce and accustom (an animal or a plant) into another region; naturalize. **4.** To bring down to the level of the ordinary person. **—do·mes′ti·ca′tion** *n.*

do·mes·tic·i·ty (dō′mĕ-stĭs′ĭ-tē) *n., pl.* **-ties. 1.** The quality or condition of being domestic. **2.** Home life or devotion to it. **3. domesticities.** Household affairs.

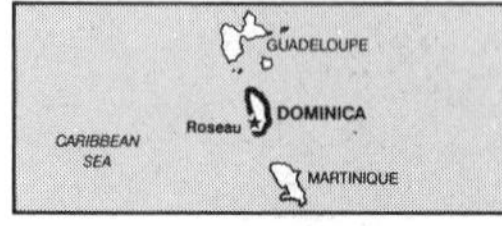

Dominica

do·mes·ti·cize (də-mĕs′tĭ-sīz′) *tr.v.* **-cized, -ciz·ing, -ciz·es.** To domesticate.

domestic partner *n.* A person with whom one cohabits in a sexual relationship.

domestic prelate *n. Roman Catholic Church.* A priest who is an honorary member of the papal household.

domestic relations court *n. Law.* In certain U.S. states, a court with jurisdiction over family disputes, especially those involving the custody, support, and welfare of children.

do·mi·cal (dō′mĭ-kəl, dŏm′ĭ-) *adj.* Shaped like or having a dome. [DOM(E) + (CON)ICAL.] **—do′mi·cal·ly** *adv.*

dom·i·cile (dŏm′ĭ-sīl′, -səl, dō′mĭ-) *n.* **1.** A residence; a home. **2.** One's legal residence. **—domicile** *v.* **-ciled, -cil·ing, -ciles.** *—tr.* **1.** To establish (oneself or another person) in a residence. **2.** To provide with often temporary lodging. *—intr.* To reside; dwell. [Middle English *domicilie,* from Old French *domicile,* from Latin *domicilium,* from *domus,* house. See **dem-** in Appendix.] **—dom′i·cil′i·ar′y** (-sĭl′ē-ĕr′ē) *adj.*

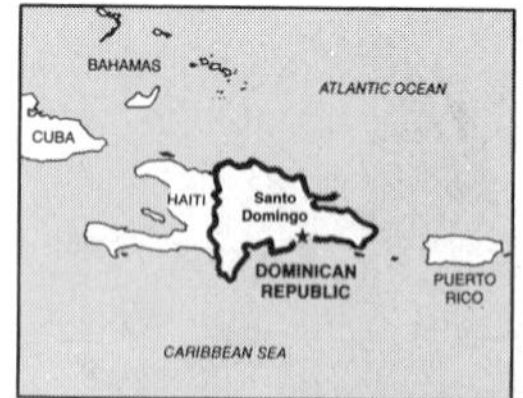

Dominican Republic

dom·i·nance (dŏm′ə-nəns) *n.* The condition or fact of being dominant.

dom·i·nant (dŏm′ə-nənt) *adj. Abbr.* **dom. 1.** Exercising the most influence or control. **2.** Most prominent, as in position; ascendant. **3.** *Genetics.* Of, relating to, or being an allele that produces the same phenotypic effect whether inherited with a homozygous or heterozygous allele. **4.** *Ecology.* Of, relating to, or being a species that is most characteristic of an ecological community and usually determines the presence, abundance, and type of other species. **5.** *Music.* Relating to or based on the fifth tone of a diatonic scale. **—dominant** *n. Abbr.* **dom. 1.** *Genetics.* A dominant allele or trait. **2.** *Ecology.* A dominant species. **3.** *Music.* The fifth tone of a diatonic scale. [Middle English *dominaunt,* from Old French, from Latin *domināns, dominant-,* present participle of *dominārī,* to dominate. See DOMINATE.] **—dom′i·nant·ly** *adv.*

domino [1]

SYNONYMS: *dominant, predominant, preponderant, paramount, preeminent.* These adjectives mean surpassing all others in power, influence, or position. *Dominant* applies to what exercises principal control or authority or is unmistakably ascendant: *The Soviet Union is the dominant nation of Eastern Europe. Predominant* is often nearly identical with *dominant* but more often implies being uppermost at a particular time or for the time being: *"Egrets, gulls and small mammals are the predominant wildlife on the island these days"* (Dan McCoubrey). *Preponderant* implies superiority as the result of outweighing or outnumbering all others: *"No big modern war has been won without preponderant sea power"* (Samuel Eliot Morison). *Paramount* means first in importance, rank, or regard: *"My paramount object in this struggle is to save the Union"* (Abraham Lincoln). *Preeminent* especially suggests generally recognized supremacy: *He is the preeminent tenor of the modern era.*

Fats Domino

dom·i·nate (dŏm′ə-nāt′) *v.* **-nat·ed, -nat·ing, -nates.** *—tr.* **1.** To control, govern, or rule by superior authority or power: *Successful leaders dominate events rather than react to them.* **2.** To exert a supreme, guiding influence on or over: *Ambition dominated their lives.* **3.** To enjoy a commanding, controlling position in: *a drug company that dominates the tranquilizer market.* **4.** To overlook from a height: *a view from the cliffside chalet that dominates the valley.* *—intr.* **1.** To have or exert strong authority or mastery. **2.** To be situated in or occupy a position that is more elevated or decidedly superior to others. [Latin *dominārī, domināt-,* to rule, from *dominus,* lord. See **dem-** in Appendix.] **—dom′i·na′tive** *adj.* **—dom′i·na′tor** *n.*

dom·i·na·tion (dŏm′ə-nā′shən) *n.* **1.a.** Mastery or supremacy over another or others. **b.** The exercise of such mastery or supremacy. **2. dominations.** *Theology.* The fourth of the nine orders of angels. In this sense, also called *dominions.*

dom·i·na·trix (dŏm′ə-nā′trĭks) *n., pl.* **-na·trix·es** or **-na·tri·ces** (-nā′trĭ-sēz′, -nə-trī′sēz). **1.** A woman who acts out the role of the dominating partner in a sadomasochistic relationship. **2.** A woman regarded as overbearing. [DOMINA(TE) + -TRIX.]

dom·i·neer (dŏm′ə-nîr′) *v.* **-neered, -neer·ing, -neers.** *—tr.* To rule over or control arbitrarily or arrogantly; tyrannize. *—intr.* To exercise arbitrary or arrogant rule or control. [Dutch *domineren,* from French *dominer,* from Latin *dominārī,* to dominate. See DOMINATE.]

dom·i·neer·ing (dŏm′ə-nîr′ĭng) *adj.* Tending to domineer; overbearing. **—dom′i·neer′ing·ly** *adv.*

Dom·i·nic (dŏm′ə-nĭk), Saint. 1170?–1221. Spanish-born priest who preached against the Albigensian heresy and founded the Dominican order of friars (1216).

Dom·i·ni·ca (dŏm′ə-nē′kə, də-mĭn′ĭ-kə). An island country of the eastern Caribbean between Guadeloupe and Martinique. Discovered by Christopher Columbus in 1493, the island became a British colony in the early 1800's and gained its independence in 1978. Roseau is the capital. Population, 77,000. **—Dom′i·ni′can** *adj. & n.*

do·min·i·cal (də-mĭn′ĭ-kəl) *adj. Ecclesiastical.* **1.** Of or associated with Jesus as the Lord. **2.** Relating to Sunday as the Lord's day. [Late Latin *dominicālis,* from Latin *dominicus,* of a lord, from *dominus,* lord. See **dem-** in Appendix.]

Do·min·i·can [1] (də-mĭn′ĭ-kən) *adj.* Of or relating to the Dominican Republic or its people or culture. **—Dominican** *n.* **1.** A native or inhabitant of the Dominican Republic. **2.** A person of Dominican ancestry.

Do·min·i·can [2] (də-mĭn′ĭ-kən) *n. Abbr.* **Dom.** *Roman Catholic Church.* A member of an order of preaching friars established in 1216 by Saint Dominic. **—Do·min′i·can** *adj.*

Dominican Republic. A country of the West Indies on the eastern part of the island of Hispaniola. The country became independent from Haiti in 1844 but has had a turbulent history, including many years of dictatorship under Rafael Trujillo Molina (1930–1961). Santo Domingo is the capital and the largest city. Population, 5,674,977.

Dom·i·nick (dŏm′ə-nĭk) *n.* Variant of **Dominique.**

dom·i·nie (dŏm′ə-nē′, dō′mə-) *n. Scots.* **1.** A cleric. **2.** A schoolmaster. [Obsolete *domine,* clergyman, from Latin, vocative of *dominus,* lord. See **dem-** in Appendix.]

do·min·ion (də-mĭn′yən) *n. Abbr.* **dom. 1.** Control or the exercise of control; sovereignty: *"The devil . . . has their souls in his possession, and under his dominion"* (Jonathan Edwards). **2.** A territory or sphere of influence or control; a realm. **3.** Often **Dominion.** One of the self-governing nations within the British Commonwealth. **4. dominions.** *Theology.* See **domination** (sense 2). [Middle English *dominioun,* from Old French *dominion,* from Medieval Latin *dominiō, dominion-,* from Latin *dominium,* property, from *dominus,* lord. See **dem-** in Appendix.]

Dominion Day *n.* July 1, observed in Canada in commemoration of the formation of the Dominion in 1867.

Dom·i·nique (dŏm′ə-nēk′, dŏm′ə-nĭk) also **Dom·i·nick** (dŏm′ə-nĭk) *n.* One of a breed of American domestic fowl having gray, barred plumage, yellow legs, and a rose-colored comb. [After DOMINICA.]

dom·i·no [1] (dŏm′ə-nō′) *n., pl.* **-noes** or **-nos. 1.** *Games.* **a.** A small, rectangular, wood or plastic block, the face of which is divided into halves, each half being blank or marked by one to six dots resembling those on dice. **b. dominoes** or **dominos** *(used with a sing. or pl. verb).* A game played with a set of these small blocks, generally 28 in number. **2.** A country expected to react politically to events as predicted by the domino theory: *"The dominos did indeed fall in Indochina"* (Arthur M. Schlesinger, Jr.). [French, probably from *domino,* mask, perhaps because of the resemblance between the eyeholes and the spots on some of the tiles. See DOMINO [2].]

dom·i·no [2] (dŏm′ə-nō′) *n., pl.* **-noes** or **-nos. 1.a.** A costume consisting of a hooded robe worn with an eye mask at a masquerade. **b.** The mask so worn. **2.** One wearing this costume. [French, probably from Latin *(benedīcāmus) dominō,* (let us praise) the Lord, from *dominus,* lord. See **dem-** in Appendix.]

Dom·i·no (dŏm′ə-nō′), **Fats.** Originally Antoine Domino. Born 1928. American singer, pianist, and songwriter whose popular rhythm and blues songs of the early 1950's include *Ain't It A Shame* and *Blue Monday.*

domino effect *n.* A cumulative effect produced when one event sets off a chain of similar events: *the domino effect of increasing the speed limit in one of several contiguous states.* [So called from the fact that a row of dominoes stood on end will fall in succession if the first one is knocked over.]

domino theory *n.* **1.** A theory that if one nation comes under Communist control, then neighboring nations will also come under Communist control. **2.** A theory that one event will set off a train of similar events.

Do·mi·tian (də-mĭsh′ən). A.D. 51–96. Emperor of Rome (81–96) who completed the conquest of Britain. After 89 his government became dictatorial, leading to a reign of terror. Domitian was assassinated by a freedman in connivance with his empress and officers of the court.

Dom·ré·my-la-Pu·celle (dôɴ-rā-mē-lä-pü-sĕl′). A village of northeast France on the Meuse River east of Troyes. Joan of Arc was born here.

don¹ (dŏn) *n.* **1. Don.** *Abbr.* **D.** Used as a courtesy title before the name of a man in a Spanish-speaking area. **2.** *Chiefly British.* **a.** A head, tutor, or fellow at a college of Oxford or Cambridge. **b.** A college or university professor. **3.** The leader of an organized-crime family. **4.** *Archaic.* An important personage. [Spanish dialectal and Italian, both from Latin *dominus,* lord. See **dem-** in Appendix.]

don² (dŏn) *tr.v.* **donned, don·ning, dons. 1.** To put on (clothing). **2.** To assume or take on: *donned the air of the injured party.* [Middle English, contraction of *do on,* to put on. See DO¹.]

Do·ña (dō′nyä) *n.* Used as a courtesy title before the name of a woman in a Spanish-speaking area. [Spanish, from Latin *domina,* feminine of *dominus,* lord. See DON¹.]

do·nate (dō′nāt′, dō-nāt′) *tr.v.* **-nat·ed, -nat·ing, -nates.** To present as a gift to a fund or cause; contribute. [Back-formation from DONATION.] **—do′na·tor** *n.*

Don·a·tel·lo (dŏn′ə-tĕl′ō, dô′nä-tĕl′lô). 1386?–1466. Italian sculptor renowned as a pioneer of the Renaissance style with his natural, lifelike figures, such as the bronze statue *David.*

do·na·tion (dō-nā′shən) *n.* **1.** The act of giving to a fund or cause. **2.** A gift or grant; a contribution. [Middle English *donacioun,* gift, benefice, from Old French, from Latin *dōnātiō, dōnātiōn-,* from *dōnātus,* past participle of *dōnāre,* to give, from *dōnum,* gift. See **dō-** in Appendix.]

Don·a·tist (dŏn′ə-tĭst, dō′nə-) *n.* A member of a rigorist, schismatic Christian sect, strongly opposed by Saint Augustine, that arose in North Africa in the fourth century A.D. and believed in sanctity as requisite for church membership and administration of all sacraments. [Medieval Latin *Donatista,* after *Donatus,* fourth-century A.D. ecclesiastic and rival claimant of the bishopric of Carthage.] **—Don′a·tism** *n.*

don·a·tive (dō′nə-tĭv, dŏn′ə-) *n.* A special donation. **—donative** *adj.* Marked by, constituting, or subject to donation. [Latin *dōnātīvum,* from neuter of *dōnātīvus,* of a donation, from *dōnātus,* past participle of *dōnāre,* to give. See DONATION.]

Don·bas (dŏn′bäs). See **Donets Basin.**

Don·cas·ter (dŏng′kə-stər). A borough of north-central England northeast of Sheffield. A manufacturing center, it is the site of a famous annual horse race, the St. Leger. Population, 81,900.

done (dŭn) *v.* Past participle of **do¹. —done** *adj.* **1.** Having been carried out or accomplished; finished: *a done deed.* **2.** Cooked adequately. **3.** Socially acceptable: *Spitting on the street is just not done in polite society.* **4.** *Informal.* Totally worn out; exhausted. **—*idiom.* done for.** *Informal.* Doomed to death or destruction. **—done′ness** *n.*

do·nee (dō-nē′) *n.* The recipient of a gift. [DON(OR) + -EE¹.]

Do·nets (də-nĕts′, dŭ-nyĕts′). A river rising in western Russia and flowing about 1,046 km (650 mi) through the eastern Ukraine to join the Don River.

Donets Basin also **Don·bas** (dŏn′bäs). A major industrial region of eastern Ukraine and southeast Russia north of the Sea of Azov and west of the Donets River. Developed after the 1870's, it is one of the densest industrial concentrations in the world.

Do·netsk (də-nĕtsk′, dŭ-nyĕts′). A city of eastern Ukraine east-southeast of Kiev. Founded c. 1870, it is the leading industrial center of the region. Population, 1,073,000.

dong¹ (dông, dŏng) *n.* See table at **currency.** [Vietnamese, from Chinese *tóng,* copper coin.]

dong² (dông, dŏng) *n.* *Vulgar Slang.* A penis. [Origin unknown.]

Dö·nitz (dœ′nĭts), **Karl.** See Karl **Doenitz.**

Don·i·zet·ti (dŏn′ĭ-zĕt′ē, dô′nē-dzĕt′tē), **Gaetano.** 1797–1848. Italian composer of some 75 operas, including *Lucia di Lammermoor* (1835).

don·jon (dŏn′jən, dŭn′-) *n.* The fortified main tower of a castle; a keep. [Variant of DUNGEON.]

Don Juan (dŏn wŏn′, hwŏn′, jo͞o′ən) *n.* **1.** A libertine; a profligate. **2.** A man who is an obsessive seducer of women. [After *Don Juan,* legendary 14th-century Spanish nobleman and libertine.]

don·key (dŏng′kē, dŭng′-, dông′-) *n., pl.* **-keys. 1.** The domesticated ass *(Equus asinus).* **2.** *Slang.* An obstinate person. **3.** *Slang.* A stupid person. [Perhaps from the name *Duncan* or of imitative origin.]

donkey engine *n.* **1.** A small auxiliary steam engine used for hoisting or pumping, especially aboard ship. **2.** A small locomotive.

don·key's tail (dŏng′kēz, dŭng′-, dông′-) *n.* See **burro's tail.**

don·key·work (dŏng′kē-wûrk′, dŭng′-, dông′-) *n.* *Slang.* Hard physical labor.

Don·na (dŏn′ə, dôn′nä) *n.* Used as a courtesy title before the name of a woman in an Italian-speaking area. [Italian, from Latin *domina.* See DOÑA.]

Donne (dŭn), **John.** 1572–1631. English metaphysical poet and divine who served as chaplain to James I and dean of Saint Paul's Cathedral (after 1621). His works include *Divine Poems* (1607).

don·née (dŏ-nā′, dô-) *n.* **1.** A set of literary or artistic principles or assumptions on which a creative work is based: *"He worked outward from the donnée toward the expression of some general theme or idea"* (Hugh Honour). **2.** A set of notions, facts, or conditions that governs and shapes an act or a way of life: *"His heart, his mind, his body, composed the donnée of his life"* (Louis Auchincloss). [French, from feminine past participle of *donner,* to give, from Old French, from Latin *dōnāre.* See DONATE.]

Don·ner Pass (dŏn′ər). A pass, 2,162.1 m (7,089 ft) high, in the Sierra Nevada of eastern California near Lake Tahoe. It is named after the Donner Party of westward migrants whose survivors supposedly practiced cannibalism after being trapped in a snowstorm near here in October 1846.

don·nish (dŏn′ĭsh) *adj.* Of, relating to, or held to be characteristic of a university don; bookish or pedantic. See Synonyms at **pedantic.**

don·ny·brook (dŏn′ē-bro͝ok′) *n.* An uproar; a free-for-all. See Synonyms at **brawl.** [After *Donnybrook* fair, held annually in Donnybrook, a suburb of Dublin, Ireland, and noted for its brawls.]

do·nor (dō′nər) *n.* **1.** One that contributes something, such as money, to a cause or fund. **2.** *Medicine.* One from whom blood, tissue, or an organ is taken for use in a transfusion or transplant. **3.** *Electronics.* An element introduced into a semiconductor with a negative valence greater than that of the pure semiconductor. [Middle English, from Anglo-Norman *donour,* from Latin *dōnātor,* from *dōnāre,* to give. See DONATION.]

donor card *n.* A card, usually carried on one's person, authorizing the use of one's bodily organs for transplantation in the event of one's death.

do-no·thing (do͞o′nŭth′ĭng) *Informal. adj.* Offering no initiative for change, especially in politics. **—do-nothing** *n.* An idle or lazy person. **—do′-no′thing·ism** *n.*

Don·o·van (dŏn′ə-vən), **William Joseph.** Known as "Wild Bill." 1883–1959. American army officer and public official who founded and directed (1942–1945) the Office of Strategic Services, an intelligence-gathering agency that was a forerunner of the CIA.

donkey
Equus asinus

Don Qui·xo·te (dŏn′ kē-hō′tē, kwĭk′sət) *n.* An impractical idealist bent on righting incorrigible wrongs. [After *Don Quixote,* hero of a satirical chivalric romance by Miguel de Cervantes.]

Don River (dŏn). A river of western Russia flowing about 1,963 km (1,220 mi) generally south then west into the northeast Sea of Azov.

don't (dōnt). **1.** Do not. **2.** *Non-Standard.* Does not. **—don't** *n., pl.* **don'ts** (dōnts). A statement of what should not be done: *a list of the do's and don'ts.*

do·nut (dō′nŭt′, -nət) *n.* Variant of **doughnut.**

doo·dad (do͞o′dăd′) *n.* *Informal.* An unnamed or nameless gadget or trinket.

doo·dle (do͞od′l) *v.* **-dled, -dling, -dles.** *—intr.* **1.** To scribble aimlessly, especially when preoccupied. **2.** To kill time. *—tr.* To draw (figures) while preoccupied. **—doodle** *n.* A figure, design, or scribble drawn or written absent-mindedly. [English dialectal, to fritter away time, perhaps from *doodle,* fool. See DOODLEBUG.]

WORD HISTORY: One might wonder what, if any, connection exists among *Yankee Doodle,* a *doodlebug,* and the *doodle* that one draws when one is bored or abstracted. The word *doodle* in the latter two uses may come from a Low German word meaning "fool." "Fool," the first (and now probably obsolete) sense of the word *doodle* to be recorded in English (1628), would seem naturally to have been used in *Yankee Doodle,* the name of a tune composed in 1755 to mock the American colonists. However, the origin of *Doodle* in this expression is unknown; it may be from *tootle,* because the piece was apparently composed originally for flute or fife. In the case of *doodlebug,* it is thought that *doodle,* meaning "simpleton," is the first part of the insect name. The sense "absent-minded scrawl" may come directly from the sense "fool" or from a British dialectal verb, meaning "to cheat, fritter time away," that was derived from the noun sense "fool."

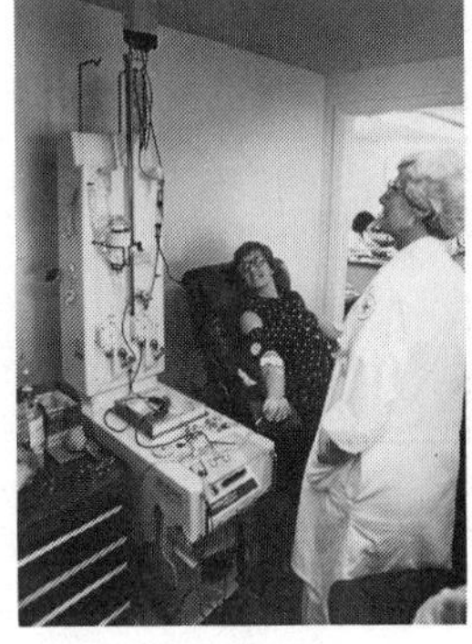

donor
An apheresis donor

doo·dle·bug (do͞od′l-bŭg′) *n.* **1.** See **ant lion** (sense 2). **2.** A divining rod. [Perhaps dialectal *doodle,* fool, simpleton (from Low German *dudel-*) + BUG.]

doo-doo (do͞o′do͞o′) *n.* *Slang.* Fecal matter or something likened to it. [Of baby-talk origin.]

doo·hick·ey (do͞o′hĭk′ē) *n., pl.* **-eys.** *Informal.* An unnamed gadget or trinket. [Perhaps DOO(DAD) + HICKEY.]

Doo·lit·tle (do͞o′lĭt′l), **Hilda.** Pen name H.D. 1886–1961. American poet whose imagist verse was published in works such as *Sea Garden* (1916) and *Helen in Egypt* (1961).

Doolittle, James Harold. Known as "Jimmy." Born 1896. American army officer and aviator who commanded daring bombing raids of Tokyo and other Japanese cities in April 1942.

doom (do͞om) *n.* **1.** A decision or judgment, especially an official condemnation to a severe penalty. **2.** Fate, especially a tragic or ruinous one. **3.** Inevitable destruction or ruin. **4.** Judgment Day. **5.** A statute or ordinance, especially one in force in Anglo-Saxon England. **—doom** *tr.v.* **doomed, doom·ing, dooms. 1.** To condemn to ruination or death. See Synonyms at **condemn. 2.**

ă pat	oi boy
ā pay	ou out
âr care	o͝o took
ä father	o͞o boot
ĕ pet	ŭ cut
ē be	ûr urge
ĭ pit	th thin
ī pie	*th* this
îr pier	hw which
ŏ pot	zh vision
ō toe	ə about, item
ô paw	♦ regionalism

Stress marks: **′** (primary); ′ (secondary), as in **dictionary** (dĭk′shə-nĕr′ē)

To destine to an unhappy end. [Middle English *dom*, from Old English *dōm*, judgment. See **dhē-** in Appendix.]

doom palm *n.* A palm *(Hyphaene thebaica)* native to the Nile Valley of northeast Africa and having oblong or ovoid fruits the size of an orange with a distinctive aroma and taste. Also called *doum, gingerbread palm.* [Probably from Arabic dialectal *dōm.*]

doom•say•er (do͞om′sā′ər) *n.* One who predicts calamity at every opportunity.

dooms•day (do͞omz′dā′) *n.* Judgment Day. [Middle English *domesday*, from Old English *dōmes dæg* : *dōm*, judgment; see DOOM + *dæg*, day; see DAY.]

Dooms•day Book (do͞omz′dā′) *n.* Variant of **Domesday Book.**

door (dôr, dōr) *n.* **1.a.** A movable structure used to close off an entrance, typically consisting of a panel that swings on hinges or that slides or rotates. **b.** A similar part on a piece of furniture or a vehicle. **2.** A doorway. **3.** The room or building to which a door belongs: *They live three doors down the hall.* **4.** A means of approach or access: *looking for the door to success.* —*attributive.* Often used to modify another noun: *a door chain; a door handle.* **—door** *tr.v.* **doored, door•ing, doors. 1.** *Slang.* To strike (a passing bicyclist, for example) by suddenly opening a vehicular door. **2.** To serve as a doorman or doorwoman of (a nightclub, for example). —***idioms.*** **at (one's) door.** Within one's sphere of accountability. **close** (or **shut) the door on.** To refuse to allow for the possibility of: *The secretary of state closed the door on future negotiations.* **leave the door open.** To allow for the possibility of: *Let's leave the door open for future stylistic changes.* **show (someone) the door.** *Informal.* **1.** To eject (someone) from the premises. **2.** To terminate the employment of; fire. [Middle English *dor*, from Old English *duru, dor.* See **dhwer-** in Appendix.] **—door′less** *adj.*

doornail

door•bell (dôr′bĕl′, dōr′-) *n.* A bell, chime, or buzzer outside a door that is rung to announce the presence of a visitor or caller.

door•jamb (dôr′jăm′, dōr′-) *n.* Either of the two vertical pieces framing a doorway and supporting the lintel. Also called *doorpost.*

door•keep•er (dôr′kē′pər, dōr′-) *n.* One who is employed to guard an entrance or gateway.

door•knob (dôr′nŏb′, dōr′-) *n.* A knob-shaped handle for opening and closing a door.

door•man (dôr′măn′, -mən, dōr′-) *n.* A man employed to attend the entrance of a hotel, an apartment house, or other building.

door•mat (dôr′măt′, dōr′-) *n.* **1.** A mat placed before a doorway for wiping the shoes. **2.** *Slang.* One who submits meekly to domination or mistreatment by others.

door•nail (dôr′nāl′, dōr′-) *n.* A large-headed nail. —***idiom.*** **dead as a doornail.** Undoubtedly dead.

door opener *n.* **1.** An electromechanical or electronic device for automatically opening a door, as one to a garage. **2.** *Informal.* An effective means of gaining success or seizing an opportunity.

Door Peninsula (dôr). A peninsula of eastern Wisconsin between Green Bay and Lake Michigan.

door•post (dôr′pōst′, dōr′-) *n.* See **doorjamb.**

door prize *n.* A prize awarded by lottery to the holder of a ticket purchased at or before a function.

door•sill (dôr′sĭl′, dōr′-) *n.* The threshold of a doorway.

door•step (dôr′stĕp′, dōr′-) *n.* A step leading to a door.

door•stop (dôr′stŏp′, dōr′-) *n.* **1.** A wedge inserted beneath a door to hold it open at a desired position. **2.** A weight or spring that prevents a door from slamming. **3.** A rubber-tipped projection attached to a wall to protect it from the impact of an opening door.

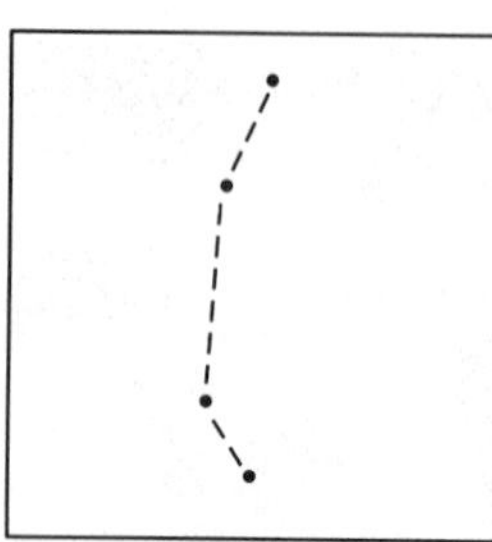

Dorado

door•way (dôr′wā′, dōr′-) *n.* The entranceway to a room, building, or passage.

door•wom•an (dôr′wo͝om′ən, dōr′-) *n.* A woman employed to attend the entrance of a hotel, an apartment house, or another building.

door•yard (dôr′yärd′, dōr′-) *n.* The yard in front of the door of a house.

doo-wop or **doo•wop** (do͞o′wŏp′) *n.* *Music.* A style of music popularized in the 1950's and characterized by words and nonsense syllables sung in harmony by small groups against a stylized rhythmic melody. [Imitative.] **—doo′-wop′** *adj.*

doo•zy or **doo•zie** (do͞o′zē) *n., pl.* **-zies.** *Slang.* Something extraordinary or bizarre: *"Among the delicious names taken by, or given to, minor political parties in the United States . . . are these doozies: Quids, Locofocos, Barnburners, Coodies, Hunkies, Bucktails"* (Saturday Review). [Possibly blend of DAISY and *Duesenberg*, a luxury car of the late twenties and thirties.]

do•pa (dō′pə) *n.* An amino acid, $C_9H_{11}NO_4$, formed in the liver from tyrosine and converted to dopamine in the brain. [*d(i-hydr)o(xy)p(henyl)a(lanine).*]

do•pa•mine (dō′pə-mēn′) *n.* A monoamine neurotransmitter formed in the brain by the decarboxylation of dopa and essential to the normal functioning of the central nervous system. A reduction in its concentration within the brain is associated with Parkinson's disease. [DOP(A) + AMINE.]

dop•ant (dō′pənt) *n.* *Electronics.* A substance, such as boron, added in small amounts to a pure semiconductor material to alter its conductive properties for use in transistors and diodes. [DOP(E) + -ANT.]

♦dope (dōp) *n.* **1.** *Informal.* **a.** A narcotic, especially an addictive narcotic. **b.** Narcotics considered as a group. **c.** An illicit drug, especially marijuana. **2.** A narcotic preparation used to stimulate a racehorse. **3.** *Informal.* A person regarded as stupid. **4.** *Informal.* Factual information, especially of a private nature. **5.** *Chemistry.* An absorbent or adsorbent material used in certain manufacturing processes, such as the nitroglycerin used in making dynamite. **6.** A type of lacquer formerly used to protect, waterproof, and tauten the cloth surfaces of airplane wings. **7.** *Chiefly Southern U.S.* See **cola**[1]. **8.** *Lower Northern U.S.* Syrup or sweet sauce poured on ice cream. **—dope** *v.* **doped, dop•ing, dopes.** —*tr.* **1.** *Informal.* **a.** To administer a narcotic to: *was doped up for the operation.* **b.** To add a narcotic to: *They doped his drink before robbing him.* **2.** *Informal.* To figure out (a puzzle, for example). **3.** *Informal.* To make a rough plan of: *doped out our proposal on scratch paper.* **4.** *Electronics.* To treat (a semiconductor) with a dopant. —*intr.* *Informal.* To take narcotics. [Dutch *doop*, sauce, from *doopen*, to dip.] **—dop′er** *n.*

♦ *REGIONAL NOTE:* Before it came to mean "a narcotic or narcotics considered as a group," *dope* was borrowed into English from the Dutch word *doop*, "sauce." Throughout the 19th century it meant "gravy." In the lower northern United States, from Pennsylvania westward to Missouri, *dope* still means "a sauce of sorts"; it is now the term for a topping for ice cream, such as syrup or a chocolate or fruit sauce. In the South, on the other hand, *dope* means "a cola-flavored soft drink." The term might be related to the northern usage as a reference to the sweet syrup base of a cola drink. However, folk wisdom has it that *dope* recalls the inclusion of minute amounts of cocaine in the original recipe for Coca-Cola, which was named after this exotic ingredient.

dope sheet *n.* *Slang.* A scratch sheet.

dope•ster (dōp′stər) *n.* One that analyzes and forecasts future events, as in sports or politics.

dop•ey also **dop•y** (dō′pē) *adj.* **dop•i•er, dop•i•est.** *Slang.* **1.** Dazed or lethargic, as if drugged. **2.** Stupid; doltish: *a dopey kid.* **3.** Silly; foolish: *a dopey answer.*

dop•pel•gäng•er or **dop•pel•gang•er** (dŏp′əl-găng′ər, dôp′əl-gĕng′ər) *n.* A ghostly double of a living person, especially one that haunts its fleshly counterpart. [German, a double : *doppel*, double (from French *double;* see DOUBLE) + *Gänger*, goer (from *Gang*, a going, from Middle High German *ganc*, from Old High German).]

Dop•pler (dŏp′lər) *adj.* Of, relating to, or using the Doppler effect or Doppler radar.

Doppler, Christian Johann. 1803–1853. Austrian physicist and mathematician who first enunciated the principle known as the Doppler effect in 1842.

Doppler effect *n.* *Physics.* An apparent change in the frequency of waves, as of sound or light, occurring when the source and observer are in motion relative to each other, with the frequency increasing when the source and observer approach each other and decreasing when they move apart. [After Christian Johann DOPPLER.]

Doppler radar *n.* Radar that uses the Doppler effect to measure velocity.

dop•y (dō′pē) *adj.* *Slang.* Variant of **dopey.**

Dor. *abbr.* Doric.

Do•ra•do (də-rä′dō) *n.* A constellation of the Southern Hemisphere near Reticulum and Pictor, containing a great portion of the large Magellanic Cloud. [Spanish, dolphin (fish), from Late Latin *deaurātus*, past participle of *deaurāre*, to gild. See DORY[2].]

dor•bee•tle (dôr′bēt′l) *n.* A European dung beetle *(Geotrupes stercorarius)* that flies with a droning sound. [Obsolete *dor*, a buzzing bee or beetle (from Middle English *dorre*, from Old English *dora*) + BEETLE[1].]

Dor•ches•ter (dôr′chĕs′tər, -chĭ-stər). A municipal borough of southern England west of Poole. An agricultural market, it was the model for Casterbridge in Thomas Hardy's novels. Population, 14,049.

Dor•dogne (dôr-dōn′, -dôn′yə). A river rising in the Auvergne Mountains of south-central France and flowing about 483 km (300 mi) southwest to join the Garonne River north of Bordeaux and form the Gironde estuary.

Dor•drecht (dôr′drĕkt′, -drĕκʜt′) also **Dort** (dôrt). A city of southwest Netherlands on the Meuse River southeast of Rotterdam. Founded in the 11th century, it is a railroad junction and river port. Population, 107,475.

Do•ré (dô-rā′), **(Paul) Gustave.** 1832–1883. French artist best known for his imaginative drawings and lithographs in editions of Balzac's *Droll Stories* (1856) and Cervantes's *Don Quixote* (1863).

Do•ri•an (dôr′ē-ən, dōr′-) *n.* One of a Hellenic people that invaded Greece around 1100 B.C. and remained culturally and linguistically distinct within the Greek world. [Latin *Dōriānus*, from *Dōrius*, from Greek *Dōrios*, from *Dōris*, Doris.] **—Do′ri•an** *adj.*

Dor•ic (dôr′ĭk, dŏr′-) *n.* *Abbr.* **Dor.** A dialect of ancient Greek spoken in the Peloponnesus, Crete, certain of the Aegean Islands, Sicily, and southern Italy. **—Doric** *adj.* *Abbr.* **Dor. 1.** Of, relat-

ă pat	oi boy
ā pay	ou out
âr care	o͝o took
ä father	o͞o boot
ĕ pet	ŭ cut
ē be	ûr urge
ĭ pit	th thin
ī pie	*th* this
îr pier	hw which
ŏ pot	zh vision
ō toe	ə about, item
ô paw	♦ regionalism

Stress marks: ′ (primary); ′ (secondary), as in **dictionary** (dĭk′shə-nĕr′ē)

ing to, characteristic of, or designating Doric. **2.** In the style of or designating the Doric order. [Latin *Dōricus,* from Greek *Dōrikos,* from *Dōris,* Doris.]

Doric order *n.* The oldest and simplest of the three orders of classical Greek architecture, characterized by heavy, fluted columns with plain, saucer-shaped capitals and no base.

Dor·is (dôr′ĭs, dōr′-, dŏr′-). An ancient region of central Greece. It was the traditional homeland of the Dorians.

Dor·king (dôr′kĭng) *n.* A heavy-bodied domestic fowl having five toes on each foot and raised chiefly for table use. [After *Dorking,* an urban district of southern England.]

dorm (dôrm) *n. Informal.* A dormitory.

dor·mant (dôr′mənt) *adj.* **1.** Lying asleep or as if asleep; inactive. **2.** Latent but capable of being activated: *"a harrowing experience which . . . lay dormant but still menacing"* (Charles Jackson). **3.** Temporarily quiescent: *a dormant volcano.* See Synonyms at **inactive, latent. 4.** In a condition of biological rest or inactivity characterized by cessation of growth or development and the suspension of many metabolic processes. [Middle English, from Old French, from present participle of *dormir,* to sleep, from Latin *dormīre.*] **—dor′man·cy** *n.*

dor·mer (dôr′mər) *n.* **1.** A window set vertically into a small gable projecting from a sloping roof. **2.** The gable holding such a window. [Obsolete French *dormeor,* sleeping room, from *dormir,* to sleep. See DORMANT.]

dor·mie (dôr′mē) *adj. Sports.* Variant of **dormy.**

dor·min (dôr′mĭn) *n.* Abscisic acid. [DORM(ANCY) + –IN.]

dor·mi·to·ry (dôr′mĭ-tôr′ē, -tōr′ē) *n., pl.* **-ries. 1.** A room providing sleeping quarters for a number of persons. **2.** A building for housing a number of persons, as at a school or resort. **3.** A residential community whose inhabitants commute to a nearby metropolis for employment and recreation. [Latin *dormītōrium,* from *dormītōrius,* of sleep, from *dormītus,* past participle of *dormīre,* to sleep.]

dor·mouse (dôr′mous′) *n.* Any of various small, squirrellike Old World rodents of the family Gliridae. [Middle English, probably alteration (influenced by *mouse;* see MOUSE) of Anglo-Norman *dormeus,* inclined to sleep, hibernating, from Old French *dormir,* to sleep. See DORMANT.]

dor·my also **dor·mie** (dôr′mē) *adj. Sports.* Ahead of an opponent in a golf match by as many strokes as there are holes remaining to be played. [Origin unknown.]

dor·nick[1] (dôr′nĭk) *n.* A coarse damask. [Middle English, after *Doornik* (Tournai), a city of southwest Belgium.]

♦**dor·nick[2]** (dôr′nĭk) *n. Lower Northern U.S.* A stone small enough to throw from a field being cleared. [Probably from Irish Gaelic *dornóg,* a small round stone.]

♦ ***REGIONAL NOTE:*** The word *dornick* is used from Pennsylvania westward to Illinois. It probably comes from Irish Gaelic *dornóg,* "a small round stone." However, it is not clear which group of Gaelic-speaking Irish immigrants brought the word with them. Craig M. Carver, author of *American Regional Dialects,* thinks it unlikely that *dornick* came over with the large numbers of Irish immigrants after the famine of 1846–1847 since the word was apparently well established in Missouri and Arkansas by the middle of the 19th century. Carver attributes the introduction of the term to the Scotch-Irish Protestants from Northern Ireland who emigrated to America in the 18th century. *Dornick* must have been one of the "few purely Irish terms" in the otherwise English and Scots lexicon of the Scotch-Irish.

do·ron·i·cum (də-rŏn′ĭ-kəm) *n.* A plant of the genus *Doronicum,* which includes the leopard's bane. [New Latin, from Arabic *dorūnaj,* from Persian *darūnak.*]

Dorr (dôr), **Thomas Wilson.** 1805–1854. American politician and reformer who led Dorr's Rebellion (1842), a campaign to change Rhode Island's antiquated suffrage laws.

dors– *pref.* Variant of **dorso–.**

dor·sa (dôr′sə) *n. Anatomy.* Plural of **dorsum.**

dor·sad (dôr′săd′) *adv. Anatomy.* In the direction of the back; dorsally.

dor·sal (dôr′səl) *adj.* **1.** *Anatomy.* Of, toward, on, in, or near the back or upper surface of an organ, a part, or an organism. **2.** *Botany.* Of or on the outer surface, underside, or back of an organ. [Middle English, from Late Latin *dorsālis,* from Latin *dorsuālis,* from *dorsum,* back.] **—dor′sal·ly** *adv.*

dorsal fin *n.* The main fin located on the back of fishes and certain marine mammals.

dorsal root *n.* The more posterior of the two nerve fiber bundles of a spinal nerve that carries sensory information to the central nervous system.

Dor·set (dôr′sĭt). A region of southwest England on the English Channel. Part of the Anglo-Saxon kingdom of Wessex, it was used as the setting for many of Thomas Hardy's novels.

Dorset Horn *n.* A domestic sheep of a breed having large horns and medium-length wool. [After DORSET, England.]

Dor·sey (dôr′sē), **Tommy.** 1905–1956. American band leader. He and his brother **Jimmy** (1904–1957) were known for their swing bands that were particularly popular in the 1930's and 1940's.

dorsi– *pref.* Variant of **dorso–.**

dor·si·ven·tral (dôr′sĭ-vĕn′trəl) or **dor·so·ven·tral** (-sō-) *adj.* **1.** *Botany.* Flattened and having distinct upper and lower surfaces, as most leaves do. **2.** *Biology.* Extending from a dorsal to a ventral surface: *dorsiventral muscles.* **—dor′si·ven′tral·ly** *adv.*

dorso– or **dorsi–** or **dors–** *pref.* **1.** Back: *dorsad.* **2.** Dorsal: *dorsoventral.* [From Latin *dorsum,* back.]

dor·so·lat·er·al (dôr′sō-lăt′ər-əl) *adj.* Of or involving both the back and the side. **—dor′so·lat′er·al·ly** *adv.*

dor·so·ven·tral (dôr′sō-vĕn′trəl) *adj. Botany & Biology.* Variant of **dorsiventral.**

dor·sum (dôr′səm) *n., pl.* **-sa** (-sə). *Anatomy.* **1.** The back. **2.** The upper, outer surface of an organ, an appendage, or a part: *the dorsum of the foot.* [Latin, back.]

Dort (dôrt). See **Dordrecht.**

Dort·mund (dôrt′mənd, -mo͝ont′). A city of west-central Germany north-northeast of Cologne. First mentioned c. 885, it flourished from the 13th to the 17th century as a member of the Hanseatic League. Population, 579,697.

Dor·val (dôr-văl′). A town of southern Quebec, Canada, a residential suburb of Montreal on the southern shore of Montreal Island. Population, 17,722.

do·ry[1] (dôr′ē, dōr′ē) *n., pl.* **-ries.** *Nautical.* A small, narrow, flat-bottomed fishing boat with high sides and a sharp prow. [Origin unknown.]

do·ry[2] (dôr′ē, dōr′ē) *n., pl.* **-ries. 1.** John Dory. **2.** See **walleye** (sense 3). [Middle English *dorre,* from Old French *doree,* from feminine past participle of *dorer,* to gild, from Late Latin *deaurāre* : Latin *de-,* de- + Latin *aurum,* gold.]

DOS (dŏs, dôs) *n. Computer Science.* An operating system that resides on a disk. [D(ISK) O(PERATING) S(YSTEM).]

dos·age (dō′sĭj) *n.* **1.a.** Administration of a therapeutic agent in prescribed amounts. **b.** Determination of the amount to be so administered. **c.** The amount so administered. **2.** Addition of an ingredient to a substance in a specific amount, especially to wine.

dose (dōs) *n. Abbr.* **d., D. 1.** *Medicine.* **a.** A specified quantity of a therapeutic agent, such as a drug or medicine, prescribed to be taken at one time or at stated intervals. **b.** The amount of radiation administered as therapy to a given site. **2.** An ingredient added, especially to wine, to impart flavor or strength. **3.** *Informal.* An amount, especially of something unpleasant, to which one is subjected: *a dose of hard luck.* **4.** *Slang.* A venereal infection. **—dose** *tr.v.* **dosed, dos·ing, dos·es. 1.** To give (someone) a dose, as of medicine. **2.** To give or prescribe (medicine) in specified amounts. [French, from Late Latin *dosis,* from Greek *dosis,* something given, from *didonai,* to give. See **dō-** in Appendix.] **—dos′er** *n.*

do-si-do (dō′sē-dō′) *n., pl.* **-dos. 1.** A movement in square dancing in which two dancers approach each other and circle back to back, then return to their original positions. **2.** The call given to signal such a movement. [Alteration of French *dos à dos,* back to back, from *dos,* back, from Old French. See DOSSIER.]

do·sim·e·ter (dō-sĭm′ĭ-tər) *n.* An instrument that measures and indicates the amount of x-rays or radiation absorbed in a given period. [DOS(E) + –METER.]

do·sim·e·try (dō-sĭm′ĭ-trē) *n. Medicine.* The accurate measurement of doses, especially of radiation. [DOS(E) + –METRY.] **—do·si·met′ric** (-sə-mĕt′rĭk) *adj.*

Dos Pas·sos (dōs păs′ōs), **John Roderigo.** 1896–1970. American writer whose works, such as the trilogy *U.S.A.* (1930–1936), combine narrative, stream of consciousness, biography, and newspaper quotations to depict American life.

doss (dŏs) *Chiefly British. n.* A crude or makeshift bed. **—doss** *intr.v.* **dossed, doss·ing, doss·es.** To go to bed; sleep. [Perhaps alteration of *dorse,* back, from Latin *dorsum.*]

dos·sal also **dos·sel** (dŏs′əl) *n.* An ornamental hanging of rich fabric, as behind an altar. [Medieval Latin *dossāle,* from neuter of *dossālis,* dorsal, from Late Latin *dorsālis.* See DORSAL.]

dos·si·er (dŏs′ē-ā′, dô′sē-ā′) *n.* A collection of papers giving detailed information about a particular person or subject. [French, from Old French, bundle of papers labeled on the back, from *dos,* back, from Latin *dorsum.*]

dost (dŭst) *v. Archaic.* A second person singular present tense of **do[1]**.

Dos·to·yev·sky or **Dos·to·ev·ski** (dŏs′tə-yef′skē, -toi-, dŭs-), **Feodor Mikhailovich.** 1821–1881. Russian writer whose works combine religious mysticism with profound psychological insight. His four great novels are *Crime and Punishment* (1866), *The Idiot* (1868–1869), *The Possessed* (1871), and *The Brothers Karamazov* (1879–1880). **—Dos′to·yev′ski·an** *adj.*

dot[1] (dŏt) *n.* **1.a.** A tiny round mark made by or as if by a pointed instrument; a spot. **b.** Such a mark used in orthography, as above an *i.* **2.** A tiny amount. **3.** In Morse and similar codes, the short sound or signal used in combination with the dash and silent intervals to represent letters, numbers, or punctuation. **4.** *Mathematics.* **a.** A decimal point. **b.** A symbol of multiplication. **5.** *Music.* A mark after a note indicating an increase in time value by half. **—dot** *v.* **dot·ted, dot·ting, dots.** —*tr.* **1.** To mark with a dot. **2.** To form or make with dots. **3.** To cover with or as if with dots: *"Campfires, like red, peculiar blossoms, dotted the night"* (Stephen Crane). —*intr.* To make a dot. **—*idiom.* on. (**or **at) the dot.** Exactly at the appointed time; punctual or punctually: *arrived at nine o'clock on the dot.* [Middle English **dot,* from Old English *dott,* head of a boil.] **—dot′ter** *n.*

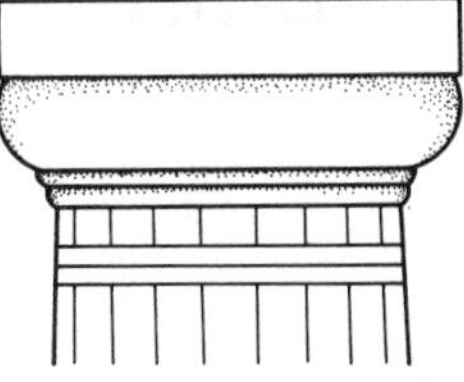

Doric order

dormer

dory[1]
Oil painting of
a Cape Ann dory
by Albert S. Bigelow

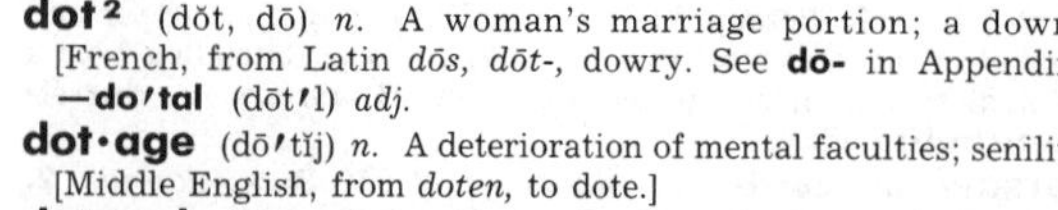

dot[2] (dŏt, dō) *n.* A woman's marriage portion; a dowry. [French, from Latin *dōs, dōt-,* dowry. See **dō-** in Appendix.] **—do′tal** (dōt′l) *adj.*

dot·age (dō′tĭj) *n.* A deterioration of mental faculties; senility. [Middle English, from *doten,* to dote.]

dot·ard (dō′tərd) *n.* A person who is in his or her dotage. [Middle English, from *doten,* to dote.]

dote (dōt) *intr.v.* **dot·ed, dot·ing, dotes.** To show excessive love or fondness: *parents who dote on their only child.* See Synonyms at **like[1].** [Middle English *doten.*] **—dot′er** *n.*

double bass

doth (dŭth) *v. Archaic.* A third person singular present tense of **do[1].**

Do·than (dō′thən). A city of southeast Alabama near the Florida border. Settled in 1885, it is a trading center for a large agricultural area. Population, 48,750.

dot matrix *n. Computer Science.* A dense grid of dots or pins used to form alphanumeric characters or designs, as by some computer printers and visual display units.

dot product *n. Mathematics.* See **scalar product.** [From the use of a dot to indicate the function, as in $x \cdot y$.]

dot·ted swiss (dŏt′ĭd) *n.* A crisp cotton fabric, embellished with woven, flocked, or embroidered dots.

dot·tle (dŏt′l) *n.* The plug of tobacco ash left in the bowl of a pipe after it has been smoked. [From DOT[1], lump (obsolete).]

dot·ty (dŏt′ē) *adj.* **-ti·er, -ti·est. 1.a.** Mentally unbalanced; crazy. **b.** Amusingly eccentric or unconventional. **c.** Ridiculous or absurd: *a dotty scheme.* **2.** Having a feeble or unsteady gait; shaky. **3.** Obsessively infatuated or enamored. [Probably alteration of Scots *dottle,* silly, from Middle English *doten,* to dote.] **—dot′ti·ly** *adv.* **—dot′ti·ness** *n.*

Dou or **Douw** (dou), **Gerard** or **Gerrit.** 1613–1675. Dutch genre painter whose works, such as *Woman with Dropsy,* are brighter and more detailed than those of his mentor, Rembrandt.

Dou·ai (do͞o-ā′). Formerly **Dou·ay** (do͞o-ā′). A town of northern France northeast of Amiens. Under the patronage of Philip II of Spain a Roman Catholic college for English priests was established here and produced the first English translation of the Old Testament in the early 1600's. Population, 42,576.

Dou·a·la also **Du·a·la** (do͞o-ä′lä). The largest city of Cameroon, in the southwest part of the country on the Bight of Biafra. It is the country's chief port. Population, 841,000.

Dou·ay (do͞o-ā′). See **Douai.**

double-decker
Tour bus in Victoria, Canada

Dou·ay Bible (do͞o′ā, do͞o-ā′) *n. Abbr.* **D.Bib.** An English translation of the Latin Vulgate Bible by Roman Catholic scholars. Also called *Douay Version.* [After DOUAI, France.]

dou·ble (dŭb′əl) *adj. Abbr.* **dble. 1.** Twice as much in size, strength, number, or amount: *a double dose.* **2.** Composed of two like parts: *double doors.* **3.** Composed of two unlike parts; dual: *a double meaning; a double role for an actor.* **4.** Accommodating or designed for two: *a double bed; a double room.* **5.** Characterized by duplicity; deceitful: *speak with a double tongue.* **6.** *Botany.* Having many more than the usual number of petals, usually in a crowded or an overlapping arrangement: *a double chrysanthemum.* **—double** *n. Abbr.* **dble. 1.** Something increased twofold. **2.** One that closely resembles another; a duplicate. **3.a.** An actor's understudy. **b.** An actor who takes the place of another actor in scenes requiring special skills or preparations: *a stunt double; a body double.* **4.** An apparition; a wraith. **5.a.** A sharp turn in a direction of movement; a reversal. **b.** A sharp, often devious change in position or argument; a shift. **6. doubles.** *Sports.* A form of a game, such as tennis or handball, having two players on each side. **7.** *Baseball.* See **two-base hit. 8.** *Games.* **a.** A bid in bridge indicating strength to one's partner; a request for a bid. **b.** A bid doubling one's opponent's bid in bridge, thus increasing the penalty for failure to fulfill the contract. **c.** A hand justifying such a bid. **—double** *v.* **-bled, -bling, -bles.** *—tr.* **1.** To make twice as great. **2.** To be twice as much as: *doubled the score of his opponent.* **3.** To fold in two. **4.** To clench (one's fist). **5.** To duplicate; repeat. **6.** To turn (an enemy spy) into a double agent. **7.** *Baseball.* **a.** To cause the scoring of (a run) by hitting a two-base hit. **b.** To advance or score (a runner) by hitting a two-base hit. **8.** *Baseball.* To put out (a runner) as the second part of a double play. **9.** *Games.* To challenge (an opponent's bid) with a double in bridge. **10.** *Music.* To duplicate (another part or voice) an octave higher or lower or in unison. **11.** *Nautical.* To sail around: *double a cape.* *—intr.* **1.** To be increased twofold: *The debt soon doubled.* **2.** To turn sharply or all the way around; reverse one's course: *had to double back to touch the missed base.* **3.** To serve in an additional capacity: *a frying pan that doubles as a pie tin; a conductor who doubles as a pianist.* **4.** To replace an actor in the actor's absence or in a certain scene. **5.** *Baseball.* To hit a two-base hit. **6.** *Games.* To announce a double in bridge. **—double** *adv.* **1.** To twice the amount or extent; doubly: *paid double for the customized car.* **2.** Two together; in pairs: *sleeping double.* **3.** In two: *bent double.* ***—phrasal verb.*** **double up. 1.** To bend suddenly, as in pain or laughter. **2.** To share accommodations meant for one person. ***—idiom.*** **on** (or **at**) **the double. 1.** Immediately. **2.** In double time. [Middle English, from Old French, from Latin *duplus.* See **dwo-** in Appendix.] **—dou′ble·ness** *n.*

double dutch

double agent *n.* A person pretending to work as a spy for one government while actually working as a spy for another government.

double bar *n. Music.* A double vertical or heavy black line drawn through a staff to indicate the end of any of the main sections of a composition.

dou·ble-bar·reled (dŭb′əl-băr′əld) *adj.* **1.** Having two barrels mounted side by side: *a double-barreled shotgun.* **2.** Serving two purposes; twofold.

double bass (bās) *n. Music.* The largest bowed stringed instrument in the modern orchestra, also used frequently in jazz ensembles, especially played pizzicato. The double bass, usually considered a member of the violin family, is tuned in fourths and has the sloping shoulders and flat back characteristic of the viols. It has a deep range beginning about three octaves below middle C. Also called *bass fiddle, bass viol, bull fiddle, contrabass, string bass.*

double bassoon *n.* See **contrabassoon.**

double bind *n.* **1.** A psychological impasse created when contradictory demands are made of an individual, such as a child or an employee, so that no matter which directive is followed, the response will be construed as incorrect. **2.** A situation in which a person must choose between equally unsatisfactory alternatives; a punishing and inescapable dilemma.

double blind *n.* A testing procedure, designed to eliminate biased results, in which the identity of those receiving a test treatment is concealed from both administrators and subjects until after the study is completed. **—dou′ble-blind′** (dŭb′əl-blīnd′) *adj.*

double boiler *n.* A cooking utensil consisting of two nested pans, designed to allow slow, even cooking or heating of food in the upper pan by the action of water boiling in the lower.

double bond *n.* A covalent bond in which two electron pairs are shared between two atoms.

dou·ble-breast·ed (dŭb′əl-brĕs′tĭd) *adj.* **1.** Fastened by lapping one edge of the front of a garment well over the other and usually having a double row of buttons with a single row of buttonholes. Used especially of a coat or jacket. **2.** Having a double-breasted coat: *a double-breasted suit.*

double check *n.* A careful reinspection or reexamination to assure accuracy or proper condition; verification.

dou·ble-check (dŭb′əl-chĕk′) *v.* **-checked, -check·ing, -checks.** *—tr.* To inspect or examine again; verify: *double-checked the fuel gauge before taking off.* *—intr.* To make a double check.

double chin *n.* A fold of fatty flesh beneath the chin.

double coconut *n.* See **coco-de-mer.**

dou·ble-cross (dŭb′əl-krôs′, -krŏs′) *tr.v.* **-crossed, -cross·ing, -cross·es.** To betray by acting in contradiction to a prior agreement. See Synonyms at **deceive. —double-cross** *n.* **1.** Often **double cross.** An act of betraying an ally, a friend, or an associate. **2. double cross.** *Genetics.* A cross in which each parent is the product of a single cross, represented as AB × CD, where A, B, C, and D are inbred lines. **—dou′ble-cross′er** *n.*

double dagger *n. Printing.* A reference mark (‡) used in printing and writing. Also called *diesis.*

double date *n.* A date in which two couples participate. **—dou′ble-date′** (dŭb′əl-dāt′) *v.*

Dou·ble·day (dŭb′əl-dā′), **Abner.** 1819–1893. American army officer traditionally considered the inventor of baseball, although a game similar to baseball predates him.

dou·ble-deal·ing (dŭb′əl-dē′lĭng) *adj.* Duplicitous or deceitful; treacherous. **—double-dealing** *n.* Duplicity or deceit; treachery. **—dou′ble-deal′er** *n.*

dou·ble-deck·er (dŭb′əl-dĕk′ər) *n.* One, such as a vehicle, structure, or sandwich, that has two decks, floors, or layers.

double decomposition *n.* A chemical reaction between two compounds in which the first and second parts of one reactant are united, respectively, with the second and first parts of the other reactant.

dou·ble-dig·it (dŭb′əl-dĭj′ĭt) *adj.* Being between 10 and 99 percent: *double-digit inflation.*

double dip·ping (dĭp′ĭng) *n.* The practice of drawing two incomes from the government, usually by holding a government job and receiving a pension, as for prior military service. **—double dipper** *n.*

double dribble *n. Basketball.* An illegal dribble in which a player uses both hands simultaneously to dribble the ball or begins to dribble the ball a second time after having come to a complete stop.

double dutch also **double Dutch** (dŭch) *n.* A game of jump rope in which players jump over two ropes swung in a crisscross formation by two turners.

dou·ble-edged (dŭb′əl-ĕjd′) *adj.* **1.** Having two cutting edges: *a double-edged blade.* **2.a.** Effective or capable of being interpreted in two ways: *double-edged praise.* **b.** Having a dual purpose: *combat troops with a double-edged mission.*

dou·ble-en·ten·dre (dŭb′əl-än-tän′drə, do͞o-blän-tän′drə) *n.* **1.** A word or phrase having a double meaning, especially when the second meaning is risqué. **2.** The use of such a word or phrase; ambiguity. [Obsolete French : *double,* double + *entendre,* meaning, interpretation.]

double entry *n.* A method of bookkeeping in which a transaction is entered both as a debit to one account and a credit to another account, so that the totals of debits and credits are equal.

dou·ble-faced (dŭb′əl-fāst′) *adj.* **1.** Having two faces or aspects. **2.** Usable on both sides: *double-faced fabric.* **3.** Duplicitous; hypocritical.

double feature *n.* A movie program consisting of two full-length films.

double fertilization *n.* The union in flowering plants of two sperm nuclei. One sperm nucleus unites with the egg to form the diploid zygote, from which the embryo develops, and the other unites with two polar nuclei to form the triploid, primary endosperm nucleus.

dou·ble-head·er also **dou·ble·head·er** (dŭb′əl-hĕd′ər) *n.* **1.** *Sports.* Two games or events held in succession on the same program, especially in baseball. **2.** A train pulled by two locomotives.

double helix *n.* The coiled structure of double-stranded DNA in which strands linked by hydrogen bonds form a spiral configuration.

dou·ble-hung window (dŭb′əl-hŭng′) *n.* A window having two sashes that slide up and down.

double indemnity *n.* A clause in an insurance policy that provides for payment of double the face value of the contract in case of accidental death.

double jeopardy *n. Law.* The act of putting a person through a second trial for an offense for which he or she has already been prosecuted or convicted.

dou·ble-joint·ed (dŭb′əl-join′tĭd) *adj.* Having unusually flexible joints, especially of the limbs or fingers.

double knit also **dou·ble-knit** (dŭb′əl-nĭt′) *n.* A jerseylike fabric knitted on a machine equipped with two sets of needles so that a double thickness of fabric is produced in which the two sides of the fabric are interlocked. **—dou′ble-knit′** *adj.*

double negative *n. Grammar.* A construction that employs two negatives, especially to express a single negation.

USAGE NOTE: Double or multiple negatives are acceptably used when they combine to form an affirmative: *He cannot just do nothing* (that is, "he must do something"). An affirmative meaning is also assigned when *not* is used together with an adjective or adverb that begins with a negative prefix such as *in–* or *un–*, as in *a not infrequent visitor, a not unwisely chosen plan.* In these expressions the double negative conveys a weaker affirmative than would be conveyed by the positive adjective or adverb by itself; for example, *a not infrequent visitor* may visit less frequently than *a frequent visitor.* • A double (or more accurately, multiple) negative is considered unacceptable when it is used to convey or reinforce a negative meaning, as in *He didn't say nothing* (meaning in Standard English "he said nothing" or "he didn't say anything"). Such constructions—common usage in many other languages—were once wholly acceptable in English as well, so that Chaucer could say of the Friar, *"Ther nas no man nowher so vertuous"*; and Shakespeare could allow Viola to say of her heart, *"Nor never none/Shall mistress of it be, save I alone."* But in the 18th century the view was advanced that, as one grammarian put it, "two Negatives in English destroy one another, or are equivalent to an Affirmative"; and today this view is accepted as dogma by all but those few scholars who are aware of just how pliable such logic can be. • The restriction on multiple negatives extends to the combination of negatives with adverbs such as *hardly* and *scarcely;* therefore it is regarded as incorrect to say *I couldn't hardly do it* or *It scarcely needs no oil.* These adverbs are "negatives" not in the sense that they express logical negation but rather in the sense that they derive their meaning by reference to the negative case; thus, *hardly* means "almost not at all." Multiple negatives continue to be widely used in a number of nonstandard varieties of English and are quite often used by speakers of all backgrounds and educational levels when they want to strike a colloquial or popular note, as in *We don't need no badges* or *You don't go nowhere 'til you clean up that room!* But constructions like these are considered marks of ignorance or illiteracy when they appear in formal speech or in writing. • The canonical stricture on the use of double negatives to convey emphasis is suspended when the second negative appears in a separate clause, as in *I will not surrender, not today, not ever* or *He does not seek money, no more than he seeks fame.* Commas must be used to separate the negative phrases in these examples. The sentence *He does not seek money no more than he seeks fame* is unacceptable, whereas the equivalent sentence with *any* requires no comma: *He does not seek money any more than he seeks fame.* See Usage Notes at **hardly, scarcely.**

dou·ble-park (dŭb′əl-pärk′) *tr. & intr.v.* **-parked, -park·ing, -parks.** To park alongside another vehicle already parked parallel to the curb. **—dou′ble-park′er** *n.*

double play *n. Abbr.* **DP** *Baseball.* A play in which two players are put out.

double pneumonia *n.* Pneumonia affecting both lungs.

dou·ble-quick (dŭb′əl-kwĭk′) *adj.* Very quick; rapid. **—double-quick** *n.* A marching cadence; double time. **—double-quick** *intr. & tr.v.* **-quicked, -quick·ing, -quicks.** To double-time.

dou·bler (dŭb′lər) *n.* A device that doubles the frequency or voltage of an input signal.

double reed *n. Music.* **1.** A pair of joined reeds that vibrate together to produce sound in certain wind instruments, such as bassoons and oboes. **2.** An instrument in which sound is produced by a pair of joined reeds. **—dou′ble-reed′** *adj.*

double refraction *n.* See **birefringence.**

double rhyme *n.* A two-syllable feminine rhyme, as in *regal/eagle* or *attic/dramatic.*

double salt *n.* A salt, such as alum, that ionizes in solution as if it were two separate salts but forms a single substance upon crystallization.

dou·ble-space (dŭb′əl-spās′) *intr. & tr.v.* **-spaced, -spac·ing, -spac·es.** To type so that there is a full space between lines.

dou·ble·speak (dŭb′əl-spēk′) *n.* See **double talk** (sense 2).

double standard *n.* A set of principles permitting greater opportunity or liberty to one than to another, especially the granting of greater sexual freedom to men than to women.

double star *n.* See **binary star.**

dou·blet (dŭb′lĭt) *n.* **1.** A close-fitting jacket, with or without sleeves, worn by European men between the 15th and 17th centuries. **2. a.** A pair of similar or identical things. **b.** A member of such a pair. **c.** *Physics.* A multiplet with two members. **3.** *Linguistics.* One of two words derived from the same historical source by different routes of transmission, such as *skirt* from Scandinavian and *shirt* from English. **4. doublets.** *Games.* A throw of two dice in which the same number of dots appears on the upper face of each. [Middle English, from Old French, diminutive of *double,* double. See DOUBLE.]

doublet
c.1565 portrait of Robert Dudley, First Earl of Leicester, by Steven van der Meulen (fl. 1543–1563)

double take *n.* A delayed reaction to an unusual remark or circumstance, often used as a comic device.

double talk *n.* **1.** Meaningless speech that consists of nonsense syllables mixed with intelligible words; gibberish. **2.** Deliberately ambiguous or evasive language. In this sense, also called *doublespeak.*

dou·ble-team (dŭb′əl-tēm′) *tr.v.* **-teamed, -team·ing, -teams.** *Sports.* To guard or cover (an offensive player) with two defensive players simultaneously.

dou·ble·think (dŭb′əl-thĭngk′) *n.* Thought marked by the acceptance of gross contradictions and falsehoods, especially when used as a technique of self-indoctrination: *"Doublethink . . . is a vast system of mental cheating"* (George Orwell).

double time *n. Abbr.* **d.t. 1.** A marching pace of 180 three-foot steps per minute. **2.** *Music.* Duple time. **3.** A rate of pay, as for overtime work, that is twice the regular rate.

dou·ble-time (dŭb′əl-tīm′) *intr. & tr.v.* **-timed, -tim·ing, -times.** To move or cause to move at double time: *The troops double-timed to the mess hall. The sergeant double-timed the platoon.*

dou·ble·ton (dŭb′əl-tən) *n. Games.* A pair of cards that are the only ones of their suit in a hand dealt to a player. [DOUBLE + SINGLE(TON).]

dou·ble-tongue (dŭb′əl-tŭng′) *intr.v.* **-tongued, -tongu·ing, -tongues.** *Music.* To play a rapidly repeated series of notes on a wind instrument by placing the tongue alternately between the positions for *t* and *k.*

dou·ble·tree (dŭb′əl-trē′) *n.* A crossbar on a wagon or carriage to which two whiffletrees are attached for harnessing two animals abreast.

dou·ble-u (dŭb′əl-yo͞o′) *n.* The letter *w.*

double vision *n.* A disorder of vision in which a single object appears double. Also called *diplopia.*

dou·ble·wide (dŭb′əl-wīd′) *n.* Two mobile homes, each 24 feet in width, bolted together as a single unit and used as a permanent residence. **—dou′ble·wide′** *adj.*

dou·ble·word also **double word** (dŭb′əl-wûrd′) *n. Computer Science.* Two computer words considered as a single storage entity.

dou·bloon (dŭ-blo͞on′) *n.* A gold coin formerly used in Spain and Spanish America. [Spanish *doblón,* augmentative of *dobla,* Spanish coin, from Latin *dupla,* feminine of *duplus,* double. See **dwo-** in Appendix.]

dou·bly (dŭb′lē) *adv.* **1.** To a double degree; twice: *doubly protected; made doubly certain.* **2.** In a twofold manner.

Doubs (do͞o). A river rising in the Jura Mountains of eastern France and flowing about 434 km (270 mi) northeast to and along the French-Swiss border, into Switzerland, then back into France, where it meanders in a generally southwest course to the Saône River.

doubt (dout) *v.* **doubt·ed, doubt·ing, doubts.** —*tr.* **1.** To be undecided or skeptical about: *began to doubt some accepted doctrines.* **2.** To tend to disbelieve; distrust: *doubts politicians when they make sweeping statements.* **3.** To regard as unlikely: *I doubt that we'll arrive on time.* **4.** *Archaic.* To suspect; fear. —*intr.* To be undecided or skeptical. **—doubt** *n.* **1.** A lack of certainty that often leads to irresolution. See Synonyms at **uncertainty. 2.** A lack of trust. **3.** A point about which one is uncertain or skeptical: *reassured me by answering my doubts.* **4.** The condition of being unsettled or unresolved: *an outcome still in doubt.* **—*idioms.* beyond** (or **without**) **doubt.** Without question; certainly; definitely. **no doubt. 1.** Certainly. **2.** Probably. [Middle English *douten,* from Old French *douter,* from Latin *dubitāre,* to waver. See **dwo-** in Appendix.] **—doubt′er** *n.*

USAGE NOTE: *Doubt* and *doubtful* may be followed by clauses introduced by *that, whether,* or *if.* The choice among these three is partly guided by the intended meaning of the sentence but is not

ă pat	oi boy
ā pay	ou out
âr care	o͝o took
ä father	o͞o boot
ĕ pet	ŭ cut
ē be	ûr urge
ĭ pit	th thin
ī pie	*th* this
îr pier	hw which
ŏ pot	zh vision
ō toe	ə about, item
ô paw	♦ regionalism

Stress marks: ′ (primary); ′ (secondary), as in **dictionary** (dĭk′shə-nĕr′ē)

cast in stone. *Whether* normally introduces an indirect question and is therefore the traditional choice when the subject is in a state of genuine uncertainty about alternative possibilities: *Sue has studied so much philosophy this year that she's begun to doubt whether she exists. At one time it was doubtful whether the company could recover from its financial difficulties, but the government loan seems to have helped.* On the other hand, *that* is the choice when *doubt* is being used as an understated way of expressing disbelief: *I doubt that we've seen the last of* that *problem* (with the meaning "I think we haven't seen the last . . . "). *That* is also the usual choice when the truth of the clause following *doubt* is assumed, as in negative sentences and questions. Thus *I never doubted for a minute that I would be rescued* implies "I was certain that I would be rescued." By the same token, *Do you doubt that you will be paid?* seems to pose a rhetorical question ("Surely you believe that you will be paid"), whereas *Do you doubt whether you will be paid?* may express a genuine request for information and might be followed by *because if you do, you should make the client post a bond.* In other cases, however, this distinction between *whether* and *that* is not always observed, and *that* is frequently used as a substitute for *whether. If* may also be used as a substitute for *whether* but is more informal in tone. • In informal speech the clause following *doubt* is sometimes introduced with *but: I don't doubt but* (or *but what*) *he will come.* Reputable precedent exists for this construction, as in *"I do not doubt but England is at present as polite a Nation as any in the World"* (Richard Steele), but modern critics sometimes object to its use in formal writing. See Usage Notes at **but, if.**

Frederick Douglass

doubt·ful (dout′fəl) *adj.* **1.** Subject to or causing doubt: *a doubtful claim; doubtful prospects.* **2.** Experiencing or showing doubt: *Doubtful that the cord would hold, we strengthened it.* **3.** Of uncertain outcome; undecided. **4.** Raising doubts as to legitimacy, honesty, or respectability; suspicious: *the candidate's doubtful past.* See Usage Note at **doubt.** **—doubt′ful·ly** *adv.* **—doubt′ful·ness** *n.*

SYNONYMS: *doubtful, dubious, questionable.* These adjectives express a degree of uncertainty or reservation about someone or something. *Doubtful* suggests pronounced lack of certainty: *It is doubtful whether she will be admitted to graduate school. He is an author of doubtful reputation. Dubious* expresses uncertainty less directly and less forcefully; often it suggests hesitancy, suspicion, or mistrust: *dubious about agreeing to go; a painting of dubious value. Questionable* can mean merely open to question (*Whether this is true is questionable*); often, however, it implies dubious morality, respectability, or propriety: *questionable dealings; a questionable stockbroker.*

doubt·ing Thom·as (dou′tĭng tŏm′əs) *n.* One who is habitually doubtful. [After Saint THOMAS, who doubted Jesus's resurrection until he had proof of it.]

doubt·less (dout′lĭs) *adv.* **1.** Certainly: *The wind was doubtless a factor.* **2.** Presumably; probably: *as you doubtless already know.* **—doubtless** *adj.* Certain; assured. **—doubt′less·ly** *adv.*

dou·ceur (do͞o-sûr′, -sœr′) *n.* Money given as a tip, gratuity, or bribe. [French, from Late Latin *dulcor,* sweetness, from Latin *dulcis,* sweet.]

douche (do͞osh) *n.* **1.a.** A stream of water, often containing medicinal or cleansing agents, that is applied to a body part or cavity for hygienic or therapeutic purposes. **b.** A stream of air applied in a similar way. **2.** The application of a douche. **3.** An instrument for applying a douche. **—douche** *v.* **douched, douch·ing, douch·es.** *—tr.* To cleanse or treat by means of a douche. *—intr.* To cleanse or treat oneself with a douche. [French, shower, from Italian *doccia,* conduit, back-formation from *doccione,* pipe, from Latin *ductiō, ductiōn-,* act of leading, from *ductus,* past participle of *dūcere,* to lead. See **deuk-** in Appendix.]

dough (dō) *n.* **1.a.** A soft, thick mixture of dry ingredients, such as flour or meal, and liquid, such as water, that is kneaded, shaped, and baked, especially as bread or pastry. **b.** A pasty mass similar to this mixture. **2.** *Slang.* Money. [Middle English *dogh,* from Old English *dāg.* See **dheigh-** in Appendix.]

dough·boy (dō′boi′) *n.* **1.** A piece of bread dough that is rolled thin and fried in deep fat. **2.** An American infantryman in World War I. [Sense 2, perhaps from the large buttons on American uniforms of the 1860's, said to resemble doughboys (sense 1).]

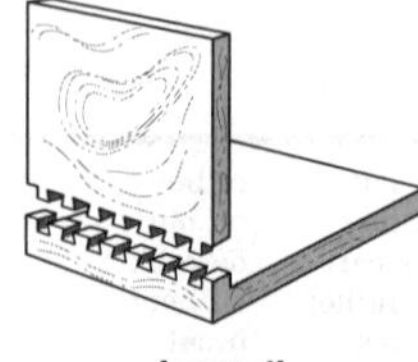
dovetail

dough·face (dō′fās) *n.* A Northerner who sided with the South in the U.S. Civil War, especially a member of Congress who supported slavery.

♦**dough·nut** also **do·nut** (dō′nŭt′, -nət) *n.* **1.** A small ring-shaped cake made of rich, light dough that is fried in deep fat. Also called ♦*olicook.* **2.** Something whose form is reminiscent of a ring-shaped cake. **3.** A fast, tight 360° turn made in a motor vehicle or motorized boat.

dough·ty (dou′tē) *adj.* **-ti·er, -ti·est.** Marked by stouthearted courage. See Synonyms at **brave.** [Middle English, from Old English *dohtig.* See **dheugh-** in Appendix.] **—dough′ti·ly** *adv.* **—dough′ti·ness** *n.*

Dough·ty (dou′tē), **Charles Montagu.** 1843–1926. British writer best known for *Travels in Arabia Deserta* (1888).

dough·y (dō′ē) *adj.* **-i·er, -i·est.** Having the consistency or appearance of dough. **—dough′i·ness** *n.*

Doug·las (dŭg′ləs). A municipal borough of southeast Isle of Man, England, on the Irish Sea. It is a popular seaside resort and the most important city on the island. Population, 20,368.

Douglas, Stephen Arnold. Called "the Little Giant." 1813–1861. American politician who served as U.S. representative (1843–1847) and senator (1847–1861) from Illinois. He proposed legislation that allowed individual territories to determine whether they would allow slavery (1854) and in the senatorial campaign of 1858 engaged Abraham Lincoln in a famous series of debates.

Douglas, William Orville. 1898–1980. American jurist who served as an associate justice of the U.S. Supreme Court (1939–1975).

Douglas fir *n.* A tall evergreen timber tree *(Pseudotsuga menziesii* formerly *P. taxifolia)* of northwest North America, having short needles and egg-shaped cones. [After David *Douglas* (1798–1834), Scottish botanist who traveled in North America.]

Doug·las-Home (dŭg′ləs-hyo͞om′), Sir **Alexander Frederick.** Born 1903. British politician who served as prime minister (1963–1964). He renounced his peerage in order to take office.

Doug·lass (dŭg′ləs), **Frederick.** 1817–1895. American abolitionist and journalist who escaped from slavery (1838) and became an influential lecturer in the North and abroad. He wrote *Narrative of the Life of Frederick Douglass* (1845) and cofounded and edited the *North Star* (1847–1860), an abolitionist newspaper.

Dou·kho·bor (do͞o′kə-bôr′) *n.* Variant of **Dukhobor.**

doum (do͞om) *n.* See **doom palm.** [French, probably from Arabic dialectal *dūm.*]

dour (do͝or, dour) *adj.* **dour·er, dour·est. 1.** Marked by sternness or harshness; forbidding: *a dour, self-sacrificing life.* **2.** Silently ill-humored; gloomy: *the proverbially dour New England Puritan.* See Synonyms at **glum. 3.** Sternly obstinate; unyielding: *a dour determination.* [Middle English, possibly from Middle Irish *dúr,* probably from Latin *dūrus,* hard. See **deru-** in Appendix.] **—dour′ly** *adv.* **—dour′ness** *n.*

dou·ra or **dou·rah** (do͝or′ə) *n.* Variants of **durra.**

dou·rine (do͞o-rēn′) *n. Veterinary Medicine.* A contagious disease of horses, asses, and mules caused by the protozoan parasite *Trypanosoma equiperdum,* which is transmitted during copulation. [French, from Arabic *darina,* to be dirty.]

Dou·ro (dôr′o͞o, dō′ro͞o) also **Due·ro** (dwĕr′ō). A river rising in north-central Spain and flowing about 772 km (480 mi) westward then southwestward along the Spanish-Portuguese border.

douse[1] also **dowse** (dous) *—v.* **doused, dous·ing, dous·es** also **dowsed, dows·ing, dows·es.** *—tr.* **1.** To plunge into liquid; immerse. See Synonyms at **dip. 2.** To wet thoroughly; drench. **3.** To put out (a light or fire); extinguish. *—intr.* To become thoroughly wet. *—n.* A thorough drenching. [From obsolete *douse,* to strike.] **—dous′er** *n.*

douse[2] (douz) *v.* Variant of **dowse**[1]**.**

Douw (dou), **Gerard.** See Gerard **Dou.**

dove[1] (dŭv) *n.* **1.** Any of various widely distributed birds of the family Columbidae, which includes the pigeons, having a small head and a characteristic cooing call. **2.** A gentle, innocent person. **3.** A person who advocates peace, conciliation, or negotiation in preference to confrontation or armed conflict. [Middle English *douve,* from Old English **dūfe.*] **—dov′ish** *adj.* **—dov′ish·ness** *n.*

♦**dove**[2] (dōv) *v.* A past tense of **dive**[1]. See Usage Note at **dive**[1]. See Regional Note at **wake**[1]**.**

Dove (dŭv) *n.* See **Columba.**

dove·cote (dŭv′kōt′, -kŏt′) also **dove·cot** (-kŏt′) *n.* A compartmental structure, often raised on a pole, for housing domesticated pigeons.

dove·kie also **dove·key** (dŭv′kē) *n.* A small black-and-white sea bird *(Alle alle)* of the Arctic and northern Atlantic oceans, having a short bill and a stout body. Also called *little auk.* [Diminutive of DOVE[1].]

Do·ver (dō′vər). **1.** A municipal borough of southeast England on the Strait of Dover opposite Calais, France. Site of a Roman lighthouse, it has been a strategic port since medieval times. The chalk cliffs rising above the city have caves and tunnels originally used by smugglers. Population, 33,700. **2.** The capital of Delaware, in the central part of the state. Founded in 1683 on orders from William Penn, it became capital in 1777. Population, 23,507. **3.** A city of southeast New Hampshire northwest of Portsmouth. It was the first permanent settlement in New Hampshire (c. 1623). Population, 22,377.

Dover, Strait of. A narrow channel at the eastern end of the English Channel between southeast England and northern France.

Do·ver's powder (dō′vərz) *n.* A powdered drug containing ipecac and opium, formerly used to relieve pain and induce perspiration. [After Thomas *Dover* (1660–1742), British physician.]

dove·tail (dŭv′tāl′) *n.* **1.** A fan-shaped tenon that forms a tight interlocking joint when fitted into a corresponding mortise. **2.** A joint formed by interlocking one or more such tenons and mortises. **—dovetail** *v.* **-tailed, -tail·ing, -tails.** *—tr.* **1.** To cut into or join by means of dovetails. **2.** To connect or combine precisely or harmoniously. *—intr.* **1.** To be joined together by means of dovetails. **2.** To combine or interlock into a unified whole: *The nurses' schedules dovetailed, so that one was always on duty.*

Dow (dou), **Charles Henry.** 1851–1902. American economist and publisher who with Edward D. Jones (1856–1920) established

Dow Jones & Company (1882), a publisher of financial bulletins. In 1889 he founded the *Wall Street Journal.*

dow·a·ger (dou′ə-jər) *n.* **1.** A widow who holds a title or property derived from her deceased husband. **2.** An elderly woman of high social station. [Obsolete French *douagière,* from *douage,* dower, from *douer,* to endow, from Latin *dōtāre,* from *dōs, dōt-,* dowry. See **dō-** in Appendix.]

dow·a·ger's hump (dou′ə-jərz) *n.* An abnormal curvature of the spine that is primarily manifested as a rounded hump in the upper back. Typically affecting older women, the curvature is a result of collapse of the spinal column, caused by osteoporosis.

Dow·den (doud′n), **Edward.** 1843–1913. Irish editor, writer, and critic noted for his works on Shakespeare.

dow·dy (dou′dē) *adj.* **-di·er, -di·est. 1.** Lacking stylishness or neatness; shabby: *a dowdy gray outfit.* **2.** Old-fashioned; antiquated. **—dowdy** *n., pl.* **-dies.** A dowdy person; a frump. [From Middle English *doude,* immoral, unattractive, or shabbily dressed woman.] **—dow′di·ly** *adv.* **—dow′di·ness** *n.* **—dow′dy·ish** *adj.*

dow·el (dou′əl) *n.* **1.** A usually round pin that fits tightly into a corresponding hole to fasten or align two adjacent pieces. **2.** A piece of wood driven into a wall to act as an anchor for nails. **—dowel** *tr.v.* **-eled, -el·ing, -els** also **-elled, -el·ling, -els. 1.** To fasten or align with dowels: *table legs that are doweled into the top.* **2.** To equip with dowels. [Middle English *doule,* part of a wheel, perhaps from Middle Low German *dovel,* plug, or from Old French *doele,* barrel stave (diminutive of *douve,* from Late Latin *doga,* vessel, from Greek *dokhē,* receptacle; see SYNECDOCHE).]

dow·er (dou′ər) *n.* **1.** The part or interest of a deceased man's real estate allotted by law to his widow for her lifetime. Also called *dowry.* **2.** See **dowry** (sense 1). **3.** A natural endowment or gift; a dowry. **—dower** *tr.v.* **-ered, -er·ing, -ers.** To give a dower to; endow. [Middle English *douere,* from Old French *douaire,* from Medieval Latin *dōtārium,* from Latin *dōs, dōt-,* dowry. See **dō-** in Appendix.]

dow·itch·er (dou′ĭ-chər) *n.* Either of two shore birds *(Limnodromus griseus* or *L. scolopaceus)* of northern regions, having brownish plumage and a long, straight bill. [Perhaps from Mohawk *tawistawis,* snipe.]

Dow Jones Averages. A trademark used for an index of the relative price of selected industrial, transportation, and utility stocks based on a formula developed and periodically revised by Dow Jones & Company, Inc.

down[1] (doun) *adv. Abbr.* **dn. 1.a.** From a higher to a lower place or position: *hiked down from the peak.* **b.** Toward, to, or on the ground, floor, or bottom: *tripped and fell down.* **2.** In or into a sitting or reclining position: *knelt down; lying down.* **3.** Toward or in the south; southward: *flew down to Florida.* **4.a.** Away from a place considered central or a center of activity, such as a city or town: *down on the farm; sent down to work at the firm's regional office.* **b.** Away from the present place. **5.** To a specific location or source: *tracking a rumor down.* **6.** Toward or at a low or lower point on a scale: *from the biggest down to the smallest.* **7.a.** To or in a quiescent or subdued state: *calmed down.* **b.** In or into an inactive or inoperative state: *The generators went down at midnight.* **8.** To or at a lower intensity. **9.** To or into a lower or inferior condition, as of subjection, defeat, or disgrace. **10.** To an extreme degree; heavily: *worn down by worry.* **11.** Seriously or vigorously: *get down to the project at hand.* **12.** From earlier times or people: *tradition handed down from one generation to the next.* **13.** To a reduced or concentrated form: *pared the term paper down to five pages.* **14.** In writing; on paper: *wrote the statement down.* **15.** In partial payment at the time of purchase: *put ten dollars down on the necklace.* **16.** Into or toward a secure position: *nailed down the boards; bolted the furniture down.* **—down** *adj. Abbr.* **dn. 1.a.** Moving or directed downward: *a down elevator.* **b.** Low or lower: *Stock prices were down today.* **c.** Reduced; diminished: *The wind is down.* **2.** Afflicted; sick: *She's down with a bad cold.* **3.** Malfunctioning or not operating, especially temporarily: *The computer is down.* **4.** Low in spirits; depressed: *feeling down today.* **5.a.** *Sports & Games.* Trailing an opponent: *a team down 20 points in the last quarter; down two pawns in the endgame.* **b.** *Football.* Not in play: *The ball is down on the 50-yard line.* **c.** *Baseball.* Retired; out: *two down in the last of the ninth.* **6.** Completed; done: *three down, two to go.* **7.** Learned or known perfectly: *had the algebra problems down.* **—down** *prep.* **1.** In a descending direction along, upon, into, or through: *rolled down the hill; floating down the river; went down cellar.* **2.** Along the course of: *walking down the street.* **3.** In or at: *The cans are stored down cellar.* **—down** *n. Abbr.* **dn. 1.** A downward movement; descent. **2.** *Football.* Any of a series of four plays during which a team must advance at least ten yards to retain possession of the ball. **—down** *v.* **downed, down·ing, downs.** *—tr.* **1.** To bring, put, strike, or throw down: *downed his opponent in the first round.* **2.** To swallow hastily; gulp: *downed the glass of water.* **3.** *Football.* To put (the ball) out of play by touching it to the ground. *—intr.* To go or come down; descend. ***—idioms.* down in** (or **at**) **the mouth.** Discouraged; sad; dejected. **down on.** *Informal.* Hostile or negative toward; ill-disposed to: *was down on jogging after his injury.* **down on (one's) luck.** Afflicted by misfortune. [Middle English *doun,* from Old English *-dūne-,* as in *ofdūne,* downwards, from *dūne,* dative of *dūn,* hill. See **dhū-no-** in Appendix.]

down[2] (doun) *n.* **1.** Fine, soft, fluffy feathers forming the first plumage of a young bird and underlying the contour feathers in certain adult birds. **2.** *Botany.* A covering of soft, short hairs, as on some leaves or fruit. **3.** A soft, silky, or feathery substance, such as the first growth of a human beard. [Middle English *doun,* from Old Norse *dūnn.*]

down[3] (doun) *n.* **1.** Often **downs.** An expanse of rolling, grassy, treeless upland used for grazing. **2.** Often **Down.** Any of several breeds of sheep having short wool, originally bred in the Downs of southern England. [Middle English *doune,* from Old English *dūn.* See **dhū-no-** in Appendix.]

down-and-out or **down and out** (doun′ənd-out′, -ən-) *—adj.* **1.** Lacking funds, resources, or prospects; destitute. **2.** Incapacitated; prostrate. **—**Also **down-and-out·er** (-ou′tər) *n.* One who is down-and-out.

down-at-heel (doun′ət-hēl′) or **down-at-the-heel** (-ət-thə-) *adj.* **1.** Worn out from long use or neglect; dilapidated. **2.** Shabbily dressed because of poverty; seedy.

down·beat (doun′bēt′) *n.* **1.** *Music.* The downward stroke made by a conductor to indicate the first beat of a measure. **2.** *Informal.* A period of stagnation or inactivity. **—downbeat** *adj.* Cheerless; pessimistic.

down-bow or **down·bow** (doun′bō′) *n. Music.* A stroke made by drawing a bow from handle to tip across the strings of a violin or other bowed instrument.

down·burst (doun′bûrst′) *n.* An extremely powerful downward air current from a cumulonimbus cloud, typically associated with thunderstorm activity.

down·cast (doun′kăst′) *adj.* **1.** Directed downward: *a downcast glance.* **2.** Low in spirits; depressed. See Synonyms at **depressed.**

down·court (doun-kôrt′, -kōrt′) *adv. & adj. Sports.* To, into, or in the far end of the court, especially in basketball.

down·draft (doun′drăft′) *n.* **1.** A strong downward current of air. **2.** A downward trend; downturn: *The business hit a downdraft.*

Down East also **down East** (doun ēst′). New England, especially Maine. **—Down East′er, down-East′er** (down-ē′stər) *n.* **—Down East′ern** *adj.*

down·er (dou′nər) *n. Slang.* **1.** A depressant or sedative drug, such as a barbiturate or tranquilizer. **2.** A depressing experience or predicament.

Dow·ners Grove (dou′nərz). A village of northeast Illinois, a manufacturing suburb of Chicago. Population, 42,572.

Dow·ney (dou′nē). A city of southern California, a residential and industrial suburb of Los Angeles. Population, 82,602.

down·fall (doun′fôl′) *n.* **1.a.** A sudden loss of wealth, rank, reputation, or happiness; ruin. **b.** A cause of sudden ruin. **2.** A fall of rain or snow, especially a heavy or unexpected one.

down·fall·en (doun′fô′lən) *adj.* Fallen, as from high position; ruined.

down·field (doun′-fēld′) *adv. & adj. Sports.* To, into, or in the defensive team's end of the field.

down·grade (doun′grād′) *n.* **1.** A descending slope, as in a road. **2.** A turn or trend downward. **3.** A decline, as in fortune, status, or condition: *a neighborhood on the downgrade.* **—downgrade** *tr.v.* **-grad·ed, -grad·ing, -grades. 1.** To lower the status or salary of. **2.** To minimize the importance, value, or reputation of. See Synonyms at **decry, demote.**

down·haul (doun′hôl′) *n. Nautical.* A rope or set of ropes for hauling down or securing a sail or spar.

down·heart·ed (doun′här′tĭd) *adj.* Low in spirit; depressed. See Synonyms at **depressed. —down′heart′ed·ly** *adv.* **—down′heart′ed·ness** *n.*

down·hill (doun′hĭl′) *adv.* **1.** Down the slope of a hill. **2.** Toward a lower or worse condition: *The alcoholic's health went downhill fast.* **—downhill** (doun′hĭl′) *adj.* **1.** Sloping downward; descending. **2.** *Sports.* Of, relating to, or constituting skiing down a slope: *a downhill racer.* **—downhill** *n.* **1.** A downhill skiing race. **2.** A downward gradient; a descending slope.

down-home (doun′hōm′) *adj.* Of, relating to, or reminiscent of a simple, wholesome, unpretentious lifestyle, especially that associated with the rural southern United States.

Down·ing (dou′nĭng), **Andrew Jackson.** 1815–1852. American landscape architect and horticulturist who wrote the classic *A Treatise on Landscape Gardening* (1841) and designed the grounds of the White House and the U.S. Capitol.

Downing Street[1]**.** A thoroughfare of Westminster in London, England, off Whitehall. No. 10 Downing Street is the official residence of the first lord of the Treasury, who is usually but not necessarily the prime minister of Great Britain. Nearly all prime ministers have lived at No. 10 since the time of Robert Walpole in the early 1700's.

Downing Street[2] *n.* The British government.

down·link (doun′lĭngk′) *n.* A transmission path for the communication of signals and data from a communications satellite or other space vehicle to the earth and back. **—down′link′** *v.*

down·load (doun′lōd′) *v.* **-load·ed, -load·ing, -loads.** *—tr.* **1.** To unload: *download cargo from a transport aircraft.* **2.** *Computer Science.* To transfer (data or programs) from a central computer to a peripheral computer or device. *—intr. Computer Science.* To transfer data or programs to a peripheral computer or device.

down-mar·ket also **down·mar·ket** (doun′mär′kĭt) *adj.*

ă pat	oi boy
ā pay	ou out
âr care	o͝o took
ä father	o͞o boot
ĕ pet	ŭ cut
ē be	ûr urge
ĭ pit	th thin
ī pie	*th* this
îr pier	hw which
ŏ pot	zh vision
ō toe	ə about, item
ô paw	♦ regionalism

Stress marks: **′** (primary); ′ (secondary), as in **dictionary** (dĭk′shə-nĕr′ē)

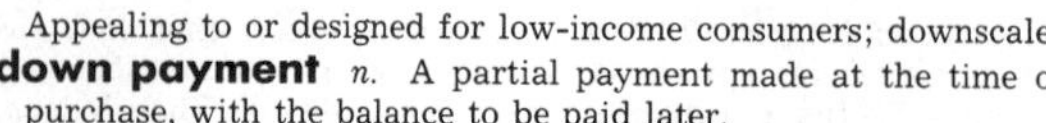

downspout

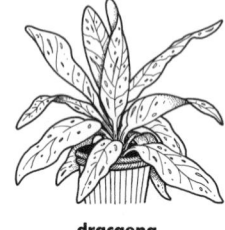

dracaena

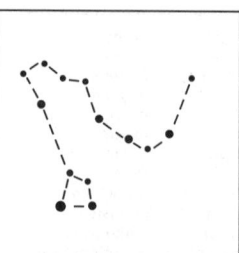

Draco[2]

Appealing to or designed for low-income consumers; downscale.

down payment *n.* A partial payment made at the time of purchase, with the balance to be paid later.

down·play (doun′plā′) *tr.v.* **-played, -play·ing, -plays.** To minimize the significance of; play down: *downplayed the bad news.*

down·pour (doun′pôr′, -pōr′) *n.* A heavy fall of rain.

down quark *n. Abbr.* **d** A quark with a charge of −⅓, a mass about 607 times that of the electron, and a downward spin. It is a component of protons and neutrons. See table at **subatomic particle.**

down·range (doun′rānj′) *adv. & adj.* In a direction away from the launch site and along the flight line of a missile test range: *landed a thousand miles downrange; the downrange target area.*

down·rig·ger (doun′rĭg′ər) *n. Nautical.* A trolling rig that consists of a weighted cable attached below the boat to a fishing line, used to troll live bait at or near the floor of a body of water and eliminating the need for a weight on the fishing line.

down·right (doun′rīt′) *adj.* **1.** Thoroughgoing; unequivocal: *a downright lie.* **2.** Forthright; candid. **—downright** *adv.* Thoroughly; absolutely.

down·riv·er (doun′rĭv′ər) *adv. & adj.* Toward or near the mouth of a river; in the direction of the current: *swam downriver; a downriver canoe race.*

Downs (dounz). Two roughly parallel ranges of chalk hills in southeast England. The **North Downs** extend about 161 km (100 mi) from west to east; the **South Downs,** about 105 km (65 mi).

down·scale (doun′skāl′) *adj.* Of, for, or relating to low-income consumers: *mass-produced downscale versions of high-priced fashions.* **—downscale** *tr. & intr.v.* **-scaled, -scal·ing, -scales.** To reduce in scale; scale down.

down·shift (doun′shĭft′) *intr.v.* **-shift·ed, -shift·ing, -shifts.** To shift a motor vehicle into a lower gear. **—down′shift′** *n.*

down·side (doun′sīd′) *n.* **1.** The lower side or portion. **2.** A disadvantageous aspect: *an option with a downside as well as benefits.* **3.** A downward tendency, as in the price of a stock.

down·size (doun′sīz′) *tr.v.* **-sized, -siz·ing, -siz·es.** To make in a smaller size: *cars that were downsized during the gasoline-conscious 1970's; a corporation that downsized its personnel in response to a poor economy.*

down·slide (doun′slīd′) *n.* A downward course; a decline: *"a growing concern among . . . board leaders about whether the economy could be headed for a downslide"* (Andrée Brooks).

down·spin (doun′spĭn′) *n.* An extremely swift, acute downturn, as in market activity.

down·spout (doun′spout′) *n.* A vertical pipe for carrying rainwater down from a roof gutter.

Down's syndrome (dounz) *n.* Variant of **Down syndrome.**

down·stage (doun′stāj′) *adv.* Toward, at, or on the front part of a stage. **—downstage** (doun′stāj′) *adj.* Of or relating to the front part of a stage. **—downstage** (doun′stāj′) *n.* The front half of a stage.

down·stairs (doun′stârz′) *adv.* **1.** Down the stairs: *raced my friend downstairs.* **2.** To or on a lower floor: *went downstairs to answer the front door.* **—downstairs** (doun′stârz′) also **down·stair** (-stâr′) *adj.* Located on a lower or main floor. **—downstairs** (doun′stârz′) *n. (used with a sing. verb).* The lower or main floor.

down·state (doun′stāt′) *n.* The southerly section of a state in the United States. **—downstate** *adv. & adj.* To, from, or in the southerly section of a state. **—down′stat′er** *n.*

down·stream (doun′strēm′) *adj.* In the direction of a stream's current. **—downstream** (doun′strēm′) *adv.* Down a stream.

down·swing (doun′swĭng′) *n.* **1.** A swing downward, as of a golf club. **2.** A decline, as of a business.

Down syndrome (doun) or **Down's syndrome** (dounz) *n.* A congenital disorder, caused by the presence of an extra 21st chromosome, in which the affected person has mild to moderate mental retardation, short stature, and a flattened facial profile. Also called *trisomy 21.* [After John L.H. *Down* (1828–1896), British physician.]

down·tick (doun′tĭk′) *n.* **1.** A decrease, especially a small or incremental one. **2.** A transaction in a stock market security below the price of the previous transaction.

down·time (doun′tīm′) *n.* The period of time when something, such as a factory or a piece of machinery, is not in operation, especially as the result of a malfunction.

down-to-earth (doun′tōō-ûrth′, -tə-) *adj.* Realistic; sensible.

down·town (doun′toun′) *n.* The lower part or the business center of a city or town. **—downtown** (doun′toun′) *adv.* To, toward, or in the lower part or the business center of a city or town. **—downtown** (doun′toun′) *adj.* Of, relating to, or located downtown.

down·trend (doun′trĕnd′) *n.* A downward trend; a downturn. **—down′trend′** *v.*

down·trod·den (doun′trŏd′n) *adj.* Oppressed; tyrannized.

down·turn (doun′tûrn′) *n.* A tendency downward, especially in business or economic activity.

down under *adv. Informal.* To or in Australia or New Zealand.

down·ward (doun′wərd) *adv. & adj.* **1.** From a higher to a lower place, point, level, or condition: *floating downward; a downward trend.* **2.** From a prior source or earlier time: *passed downward through the ages.* **—down′ward·ly** *adv.* **—down′wards** *adv.*

down·wind (doun′wĭnd′) *adv.* In the direction in which the wind blows. **—down′wind′** *adj.*

down·y (dou′nē) *adj.* **-i·er, -i·est.** **1.** Made of or covered with down. **2.a.** Resembling down: *downy white clouds.* **b.** Quietly soothing; soft.

downy mildew *n.* A disease of plants caused by fungi of the order Peronosporales and characterized by gray, velvety patches of spores on the lower surfaces of leaves.

downy woodpecker *n.* A black and white North American woodpecker *(Picoides pubescens)* having a solid white back and a small bill.

down·zone (doun′zōn′) *v.* **-zoned, -zon·ing, -zones.** *—tr.* To reduce (density of housing or permitted expansion of construction) in a designated neighborhood: *proposed to downzone residential areas near the shore.* *—intr.* To reduce the permitted density of housing or the degree of proposed new construction in a designated neighborhood: *the city's complex plan to downzone.*

dow·ry (dou′rē) *n., pl.* **-ries.** **1.** Money or property brought by a bride to her husband at marriage. Also called *dower.* **2.** A sum of money required of a postulant at a convent. **3.** A natural endowment or gift; a talent. **4.** *Archaic.* See **dower** (sense 1). [Middle English *douerie,* from Anglo-Norman *douarie,* from Medieval Latin *dōtārium, dōārium, dōāria,* dower. See DOWER.]

dowse[1] also **douse** (douz) *intr.v.* **dowsed, dows·ing, dows·es** also **doused, dous·ing, dous·es.** To use a divining rod to search for underground water or minerals. [Origin unknown.]

dowse[2] (dous) *v. & n.* Variant of **douse[1].**

dows·er (dou′zər) *n.* **1.** A person who uses a divining rod to search for underground water or minerals. **2.** A divining rod.

Dow·son (dou′sən), **Ernest Christopher.** 1867–1900. British Decadent poet best known for his refrain "I have been faithful to thee, Cynara, in my fashion."

Dow theory *n.* A theory of stock market forecasting based on price movements of selected industrial and transportation stocks. [After Charles Henry DOW.]

dox·ol·o·gy (dŏk-sŏl′ə-jē) *n., pl.* **-gies.** An expression of praise to God, especially a short hymn sung as part of a Christian worship service. [Medieval Latin *doxologia,* from Greek, praise : *doxa,* glory, honor (from *dokein,* to seem; see **dek-** in Appendix) + *-logia,* -logy.] **—dox′o·log′i·cal** (dŏk′sə-lŏj′ĭ-kəl) *adj.* **—dox′o·log′i·cal·ly** *adv.*

dox·o·ru·bi·cin (dŏk′sə-rōō′bĭ-sĭn) *n.* An antibiotic obtained from the bacterium *Streptomyces peuceticus,* used as an anticancer drug. [D(E)OX(Y)– + Latin *ruber,* red; see RUBRIC + –(MY)CIN.]

dox·y (dŏk′sē) *n., pl.* **-ies.** *Slang.* **1.** A loose woman; a prostitute. **2.** A paramour. [Perhaps from obsolete Dutch *docke,* doll.]

dox·y·cy·cline (dŏk′sĭ-sī′klēn′, -klīn) *n.* A broad-spectrum antibiotic, $C_{22}H_{24}N_2O_8$, derived from tetracycline. [DE– + OXY– + (TETRA)CYCLINE.]

doy·en (doi-ĕn′, doi′ən, dwä-yăN′) *n.* A man who is the eldest or senior member of a group. [Probably French, from Old French *doien,* from Late Latin *decānus,* chief of ten. See DEAN.]

doy·enne (doi-ĕn′, dwä-yĕn′) *n.* A woman who is the eldest or senior member of a group. [French, feminine of *doyen,* senior member. See DOYEN.]

Doyle (doil), Sir **Arthur Conan.** 1859–1930. British writer known chiefly for a series of stories featuring the brilliant detective Sherlock Holmes, including *The Hound of the Baskervilles* (1902).

D'Oy·ly Carte (doi′lē kärt′), **Richard.** See Richard D'Oyly **Carte.**

doz. *abbr.* Dozen.

doze (dōz) *v.* **dozed, doz·ing, doz·es.** *—intr.* To sleep lightly and intermittently. *—tr.* To spend (time) dozing or as if dozing: *dozed the summer away.* **—doze** *n.* A short, light sleep. ***—phrasal verb.* doze off.** To fall into a light sleep. [Probably of Scandinavian origin.] **—doz′er** *n.*

doz·en (dŭz′ən) *n. Abbr.* **doz., dz.** **1.** *pl.* **dozen.** A set of 12. **2. dozens.** An indefinite, large number: *dozens of errands to run.* **—dozen** *adj.* Twelve. [Middle English *dozeine,* from Old French *dozaine,* from *doze,* twelve, ultimately from Latin *duodecim* : *duo,* two; see **dwo-** in Appendix + *decem,* ten; see **dekm̥** in Appendix.] **—doz′enth** (-ənth) *adj.*

do·zy (dō′zē) *adj.* **-zi·er, -zi·est.** Half asleep; drowsy. **—doz′i·ly** *adv.* **—do′zi·ness** *n.*

DP *abbr.* **1.** *Computer Science.* Data processing. **2.** Dew point. **3.** Also **D.P.** Displaced person. **4.** *Baseball.* Double play.

D.Ph. *abbr.* Doctor of Philosophy.

D.Phil. *abbr.* Doctor of Philosophy.

DPT *abbr.* Diptheria, pertussis, tetanus.

dpt. *abbr.* **1.** Department. **2.** Deponent.

dr *abbr.* Dram.

DR *abbr.* **1.** Dead reckoning. **2.** Dining room.

dr. *abbr.* Debtor.

Dr. *abbr.* **1.** Doctor. **2.** Drive.

drab[1] (drăb) *adj.* **drab·ber, drab·best. 1.** *Color.* **a.** Of a dull light brown. **b.** Of a light olive brown or khaki color. **2.** Faded and dull in appearance. **3.** Dull or commonplace in character; dreary: *a drab personality.* See Synonyms at **dull.** —**drab** *n.* **1.** *Color.* A moderate to grayish or light grayish yellowish brown or light olive brown. **2.** Cloth of a light dull brown or grayish brown or unbleached natural color, especially a heavy woolen or cotton fabric. [Alteration of obsolete French *drap,* cloth, from Old French. See DRAPE.] —**drab′ly** *adv.* —**drab′ness** *n.*

drab[2] (drăb) *n.* **1.** A slattern. **2.** A prostitute. —**drab** *intr.v.* **drabbed, drab·bing, drabs.** To consort with prostitutes: *"Even amid his drabbing, he himself retained some virginal airs"* (Stanislaus Joyce). [Possibly of Celtic origin; akin to Scottish Gaelic *dràbag,* Irish Gaelic *drabóg,* slattern, or Dutch *drab,* dregs.]

drab[3] (drăb) *n.* A negligible amount: *finished the work in dribs and drabs.* [Probably alteration of DRIB.]

drab·ble (drăb′əl) *tr. & intr.v.* **-bled, -bling, -bles.** To make or become wet and soiled by dragging; draggle. [Middle English *drabelen.*]

dra·cae·na (drə-sē′nə) *n.* Any of several tropical plants of the genera *Dracaena* and *Cordyline,* some species of which are cultivated as house plants for their decorative foliage. [Late Latin, female dragon, from Greek *drakaina,* feminine of *drakōn,* serpent. See DRAGON.]

drachm (drăm) *n.* **1.** A dram. **2.** A drachma.

drach·ma (drăk′mə) *n., pl.* **-mas** or **-mae** (-mē). *Abbr.* **d., D. 1.** See table at **currency. 2.** An ancient Greek silver coin. **3.** One of several modern units of weight, especially the dram. [Latin, from Greek *drakhmē,* from *drassesthai, drakh-,* to grasp.]

Dra·co[1] (drā′kō). Seventh century B.C. Athenian politician who codified the laws of Athens (c. 621). Lauded for its impartiality, his code was unpopular for its severity. —**Dra·co′ni·an** *adj.*

Dra·co[2] (drā′kō) *n.* A constellation in the polar region of the Northern Hemisphere near Cepheus and Ursa Major. Also called *Dragon.* [Latin *dracō,* dragon. See DRAGON.]

dra·co·ni·an (drā-kō′nē-ən, drə-) *adj.* Exceedingly harsh; very severe: *a draconian legal code; draconian budget cuts.* [After DRACO[1].]

dra·con·ic[1] (drā-kŏn′ĭk) *adj.* Of or suggestive of a dragon. [From Latin *dracō, dracōn-,* dragon. See DRAGON.]

dra·con·ic[2] (drā-kŏn′ĭk, drə-) *adj.* Draconian. —**dra·con′i·cal·ly** *adv.*

Dra·cut (drā′kət). A town of northeast Massachusetts on the Merrimack River near the New Hampshire border. It was settled in 1664. Population, 21,249.

draft (drăft) *n. Abbr.* **dft. 1.** A current of air in an enclosed area. **2.** A device that regulates the flow or circulation of air. **3.a.** The act of pulling loads; traction. **b.** Something that is pulled or drawn; a load. **c.** A team of animals used to pull loads. **4.** *Nautical.* The depth of a vessel's keel below the water line, especially when loaded: *a river vessel of shallow draft.* **5.** A heavy demand on resources. **6.** A written order directing the payment of money from an account or fund. **7.a.** A gulp, a swallow, or an inhalation. **b.** The amount taken in by a single act of drinking or inhaling. **c.** A measured portion; a dose. **8.a.** The drawing of a liquid, as from a cask or keg. **b.** An amount drawn: *ordered two drafts of ale.* **9.a.** The process or method of selecting one or more individuals from a group, as for a service or duty: *a candidate who did not pursue the nomination, but accepted a draft by the party convention.* **b.** Compulsory enrollment in the armed forces; conscription. **c.** A body of a people selected or conscripted. **10.** *Sports.* A system in which the exclusive rights to new players are distributed among professional teams. **11.a.** The act of drawing in a fishnet. **b.** The quantity of fish caught. **12.a.** A preliminary outline of a plan, document, or picture: *the first draft of a report.* **b.** A representation of something to be constructed. **13.** A narrow line chiseled on a stone to guide a stonecutter in leveling its surface. **14.** A slight taper given a die to facilitate the removal of a casting. **15.** An allowance made for loss in weight of merchandise. —**draft** *v.* **draft·ed, draft·ing, drafts.** —*tr.* **1.** To select from a group for some usually compulsory service: *drafted into the army.* **2.** To draw up a preliminary version of or plan for. **3.** To create by thinking and writing; compose: *draft a speech.* —*intr.* To drive close behind another vehicle to take advantage of the reduced air pressure in its wake. —**draft** *adj.* **1.** Suited for or used for drawing heavy loads: *oxen and other draft animals.* **2.** Drawn from a cask or tap: *draft beer.* —***idiom.*** **on draft.** Drawn from a large container, such as a keg. [Middle English *draught,* act of drawing or pulling, from Old English **dreaht;* akin to *dragan,* to draw.]

draft board *n.* A local board of civilians in charge of the selection of persons for compulsory military service.

draft·ee (drăf-tē′) *n.* One who is drafted, especially for military service.

draft·er (drăf′tər) *n.* One that drafts, especially a person who drafts plans or designs or a person who composes a document.

draft·ing (drăf′tĭng) *n.* The systematic representation and dimensional specification of mechanical and architectural structures.

drafts·man (drăfts′mən) *n.* **1.** A man who draws plans or designs, as of structures to be built. **2.** A man who draws, especially an artist. —**drafts′man·ship′** *n.*

drafts·per·son (drăfts′pûr′sən) *n.* A drafter.

drafts·wom·an (drăfts′wo͝om′ən) *n.* **1.** A woman who draws plans or designs, as of structures to be built. **2.** A woman who draws, especially an artist.

draft·y (drăf′tē) *adj.* **-i·er, -i·est.** Having or exposed to drafts of air. —**draft′i·ly** *adv.* —**draft′i·ness** *n.*

drag (drăg) *v.* **dragged, drag·ging, drags.** —*tr.* **1.** To pull along with difficulty or effort; haul: *dragged the heavy box out of the way.* See Synonyms at **pull. 2.** To cause to trail along a surface, especially the ground. **3.** To move or bring by force or with great effort: *had to drag me to the dentist; dragged the truth out of the reluctant witness.* **4.a.** To search or sweep the bottom of (a body of water), as with a grappling hook or dragnet. **b.** To bring up or catch by such means. **5.** To prolong tediously: *dragged the story out.* **6.** *Baseball.* To hit (a bunt) while taking the first steps toward first base. —*intr.* **1.** To trail along the ground: *The dog's leash dragged on the sidewalk.* **2.** To move slowly or with effort. **3.** To lag behind. **4.** To pass or proceed slowly, tediously, or laboriously: *The time dragged as we waited.* **5.** To search or dredge the bottom of a body of water: *dragging for the sunken craft.* **6.** To take part in or as if in a drag race. **7.** To draw on a cigarette, pipe, or cigar. —**drag** *n.* **1.** The act of dragging. **2.** Something, such as a harrow or an implement for spreading manure, that is dragged along the ground. **3.** A device, such as a grappling hook, that is used for dragging under water. **4.** A heavy sledge or cart for hauling loads. **5.** A large four-horse coach with seats inside and on top. **6.** Something, such as a sea anchor or a brake on a fishing reel, that retards motion. **7.** One that impedes or slows progress; a drawback or burden: *the drag of taxation on economic growth.* **8.** The degree of resistance involved in dragging or hauling. **9.** The retarding force exerted on a moving body by a fluid medium such as air or water. **10.** A slow, laborious motion or movement. **11.a.** The scent or trail of a fox or another animal. **b.** Something that provides an artificial scent. **12.** *Slang.* One that is obnoxiously tiresome: *The evening was a real drag.* **13.** A puff on a cigarette, pipe, or cigar. **14.** *Slang.* A street or road: *the town's main drag.* **15.** The clothing characteristic of one sex when worn by a member of the opposite sex: *an actor in drag.* —***idiom.*** **drag (one's) feet** (or **heels).** To act or work with intentional slowness; delay: *"The bureaucracy has been known to drag its feet in implementing directives with which it disagrees"* (Henry A. Kissinger). [Middle English *draggen,* from Old Norse *draga* or variant of Middle English *drawen;* see DRAW.]

drag bunt *n. Baseball.* A bunt executed while taking the first steps toward first base.

dra·gée (drä-zhā′) *n.* A small, often medicated candy. [French, from Old French *dragie.* See DREDGE[2].]

drag·ger (drăg′ər) *n.* One that drags, especially a vessel using nets dragged along the bottom to catch fish.

drag·gle (drăg′əl) *v.* **-gled, -gling, -gles.** —*tr.* To make wet and dirty by dragging on the ground. —*intr.* **1.** To become wet and muddy by being dragged. **2.** To follow slowly; straggle. [Probably frequentative of DRAG.]

drag·gy (drăg′ē) *adj.* **-gi·er, -gi·est. 1.** Dull and listless. **2.** *Slang.* Very tiresome.

drag·lift (drăg′lĭft′) *n. Sports.* A ski lift, such as a rope tow, a T-bar, or a J-bar, that pulls skiers up a slope.

drag·line (drăg′līn′) *n.* **1.** A line used for dragging. **2.** A kind of dredging machine.

drag link *n.* A link for transmitting rotary motion between cranks on two parallel but slightly offset shafts, such as the rod connecting the lever of the steering gear to the steering arm in an automobile.

drag·net (drăg′nĕt′) *n.* **1.** A system of coordinated procedures for apprehending criminal suspects or other wanted persons. **2.a.** A net for trawling; a trawl. **b.** A net for catching small game.

drag·o·man (drăg′ə-mən) *n., pl.* **-mans** or **-men.** An interpreter or guide in countries where Arabic, Turkish, or Persian is spoken. [Middle English *dragman,* from Old French *drugeman,* from Medieval Latin *dragumannus,* from Medieval Greek *dragoumanos,* from Arabic *tarjumān,* from Aramaic *tūrgemānā,* from Akkadian *targumānu,* interpreter.]

drag·on (drăg′ən) *n.* **1.** A mythical monster traditionally represented as a gigantic reptile having a lion's claws, the tail of a serpent, wings, and a scaly skin. **2.a.** A fiercely vigilant or intractable person. **b.** Something very formidable or dangerous. **3.** Any of various lizards, such as the Komodo dragon or the flying lizard. **4.** *Archaic.* A large snake or serpent. [Middle English, from Old French, from Latin *dracō, dracōn-,* large serpent, from Greek *drakōn,* perhaps from *derkesthai,* to look.]

Drag·on (drăg′ən) *n.* See **Draco**[2].

drag·on·et (drăg′ə-nĭt) *n.* Any of various small, often brightly colored marine fishes of the family Callionymidae, having a slender body and a flattened head. [Middle English, young dragon, from Old French, diminutive of *dragon,* dragon. See DRAGON.]

♦**drag·on·fly** (drăg′ən-flī′) *n., pl.* **-flies.** Any of various large insects of the order Odonata or suborder Anisoptera, having a long slender body and two pairs of narrow, net-veined wings that are usually held outstretched while the insect is at rest. Also

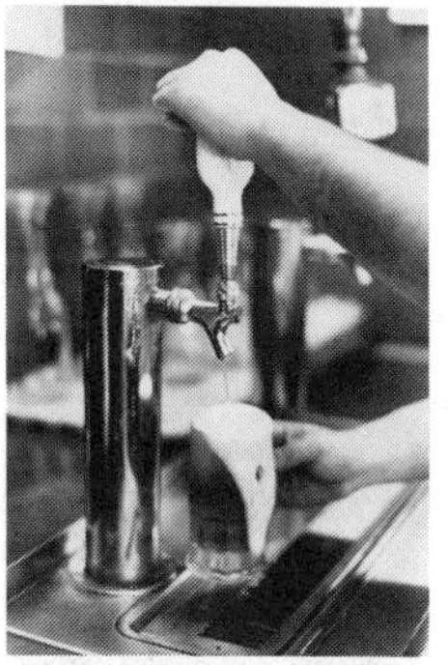

draft
Top: Hauling logs
Bottom: Draft beer

dragonfly

ă pat	oi boy
ā pay	ou out
âr care	o͝o took
ä father	o͞o boot
ĕ pet	ŭ cut
ē be	ûr urge
ĭ pit	th thin
ī pie	*th* this
îr pier	hw which
ŏ pot	zh vision
ō toe	ə about, item
ô paw	♦ regionalism

Stress marks: **′** (primary); ′ (secondary), as in **dictionary** (dĭk′shə-nĕr′ē)

called ♦*darning needle,* ♦*devil's darning needle,* ♦*ear sewer,* ♦*mosquito hawk,* ♦*skeeter hawk,* ♦*snake doctor,* ♦*snake feeder,* ♦*spindle.*

♦***REGIONAL NOTE:*** Regional terms for the dragonfly are numerous, providing good evidence for dialect boundaries in the United States. The greatest variety of terms is to be found in the South, where the most widespread term is *snake doctor* (a name based on a folk belief that dragonflies take care of snakes). The Midland equivalent is *snake feeder.* Speakers from the Lower South, on the other hand, are more likely to refer to the same insect as a *mosquito hawk* or, in the South Atlantic states, a *skeeter hawk.* The imagery outside the South alludes more to the insect's shape than to its behavior or diet: Upper Northern speakers call it a *darning needle* or a *devil's darning needle;* those in Coastal New Jersey, a *spindle;* and Northern Californians, an *ear sewer.*

dragon tree
Dracaena draco

drag·on·head (drăg′ən-hĕd′) *n.* Any of several plants of the genera *Dracocephalum* and *Physostegia,* having terminal spikes of rose-pink or purplish flowers.

drag·on·root (drăg′ən-ro͞ot′, -ro͝ot′) *n.* See **green dragon.**

drag·on's blood (drăg′ənz) *n.* **1.** A red, resinous substance obtained from the fruit of a climbing palm *(Daemonorops draco)* of tropical Asia, formerly used in the manufacture of varnishes and lacquers. **2.** Any of several resins similar to this substance.

dragon's mouth *n.* See **swamp pink.**

dragon tree *n.* A tree *(Dracaena draco)* of the Canary Islands, having a thick trunk, clusters of sword-shaped leaves, and orange fruit.

dra·goon (drə-go͞on′, dră-) *n.* A heavily armed trooper in some European armies of the 17th and 18th centuries. **—dragoon** *tr.v.* **-gooned, -goon·ing, -goons. 1.** To subjugate or persecute by the imposition of troops. **2.** To compel by violent measures or threats; coerce. [French *dragon,* carbine, dragoon, from Old French *dragon,* dragon. See DRAGON.]

drag queen *n. Offensive Slang.* A man, especially a performer, who dresses as a woman.

drag race *n.* A race between two cars to determine which can accelerate faster from a standstill. [From DRAG, an automobile (slang).] **—drag racer** *n.* **—drag racing** *n.*

drag·ster (drăg′stər) *n.* **1.** An automobile specially built or modified for drag racing. **2.** A person who races such an automobile.

drag strip *n.* A short, straight course or track for drag racing.

Sir Francis Drake

drain (drān) *v.* **drained, drain·ing, drains.** *—tr.* **1.** To draw off (a liquid) by a gradual process: *drained water from the sink.* **2.a.** To cause liquid to go out from; empty: *drained the bathtub; drain the pond.* **b.** To draw off the surface water of: *The Mississippi River drains a vast area.* **3.** To drink all the contents of: *drained the cup.* **4.a.** To deplete gradually, especially to the point of complete exhaustion. See Synonyms at **deplete. b.** To fatigue or spend emotionally or physically: *The day's events completely drained me of all strength.* *—intr.* **1.** To flow off or out: *Gasoline drained slowly from the tilted can.* **2.** To become empty by the drawing off of liquid: *watched the tub slowly drain.* **3.** To discharge surface or excess water: *The Niagara River drains into Lake Ontario. When flooded, the swamp drains northward.* **4.** To become gradually depleted; dwindle: *felt his enthusiasm draining.* **—drain** *n.* **1.** A pipe or channel by which liquid is drawn off. **2.** *Medicine.* A device, such as a tube, inserted into the opening of a wound or body cavity to facilitate discharge of fluid or purulent material. **3.** The act or process of draining. **4.a.** A gradual outflow or loss; consumption or depletion: *the drain of young talent by emigration.* **b.** Something that causes a gradual loss: *interruptions that are a drain on my patience.* **—*idiom.* down the drain.** To or into the condition of being wasted or lost: *All of our best laid plans are down the drain.* [Middle English *dreinen,* to strain, drain, from Old English *drēahnian.*] **—drain′a·ble** *adj.* **—drain′er** *n.*

drain·age (drā′nĭj) *n.* **1.** The action or a method of draining. **2.** A system of drains. **3.** Something that is drained off. **4.** *Medicine.* The removal of fluid or purulent material from a wound or body cavity.

drainage basin *n.* An area drained by a river system.

drain·pipe (drān′pīp′) *n.* A pipe for carrying off water or sewage.

drake[1] (drāk) *n.* A male duck. [Middle English.]

drake[2] (drāk) *n.* A mayfly used as fishing bait. Also called *drake fly.* [Middle English, dragon, from Old English *draca,* from West Germanic **drako,* from Latin *dracō.* See DRAGON.]

Drake (drāk), Sir **Francis.** 1540?–1596. English naval hero and explorer who was the first Englishman to circumnavigate the world (1577–1580) and was vice admiral of the fleet that destroyed the Spanish Armada (1588).

drake fly *n.* See **drake**[2].

Dra·kens·burg Mountains (drä′kənz-bûrg′). A range of eastern South Africa, Lesotho, and Swaziland rising to 3,484.6 m (11,425 ft).

Drake Passage. A strait between Cape Horn and Antarctica. It connects the southern Atlantic and Pacific oceans.

dram (drăm) *n.* **1.** *Abbr.* **dr a.** A unit of weight in the U.S. Customary System equal to 1/16 of an ounce or 27.34 grains (1.77 grams). **b.** A unit of apothecary weight equal to 1/8 of an ounce or 60 grains (3.89 grams). See table at **measurement. 2.a.** A small draft: *took a dram of brandy.* **b.** A small amount; a bit: *not a dram of compassion.* [Middle English *dragme,* a drachma, a unit of weight, from Old French, from Late Latin *dragma,* from Latin *drachma.* See DRACHMA.]

dram. *abbr.* Dramatic; dramatist.

dra·ma (drä′mə, drăm′ə) *n.* **1.a.** A prose or verse composition, especially one telling a serious story, that is intended for representation by actors impersonating the characters and performing the dialogue and action. **b.** A serious narrative work or program for television, radio, or the cinema. **2.** Theatrical plays of a particular kind or period: *Elizabethan drama.* **3.** The art or practice of writing or producing dramatic works. **4.** A situation or succession of events in real life having the dramatic progression or emotional effect characteristic of a play: *the drama of the prisoner's escape and recapture.* **5.** The quality or condition of being dramatic: *a summit meeting full of drama.* [Late Latin *drāma, drāmat-,* from Greek, from *dran,* to do, perform.]

Dram·a·mine (drăm′ə-mēn′). A trademark used for dimenhydrinate.

dra·mat·ic (drə-măt′ĭk) *adj.* **1.** *Abbr.* **dram.** Of or relating to drama or the theater. **2.** Characterized by or expressive of the action or emotion associated with drama or the theatre: *a dramatic rescue at sea.* **3.** Arresting or forceful in appearance or effect: *a dramatic sunset.* **4.** *Music.* Having a powerful, expressive singing voice: *a dramatic tenor.* [Late Latin *drāmaticus,* from Greek *dramatikos,* from *drama, dramat-,* drama. See DRAMA.] **—dra·mat′i·cal·ly** *adv.*

SYNONYMS: *dramatic, histrionic, melodramatic, stagy, theatrical.* The central meaning shared by these adjectives is "suggestive of acting or of an emotional and often affected stage performance": *made a dramatic entrance in a swirling cape; a histrionic gesture; struck an attitude of melodramatic despair; stagy heroics; assumed a theatrical pose.*

dramatic irony *n.* The dramatic effect achieved by leading an audience to understand an incongruity between a situation and the accompanying speeches, while the characters in the play remain unaware of the incongruity.

dramatic monologue *n.* A literary, usually verse composition in which a speaker reveals his or her character, often in relation to a critical situation or event, in a monologue addressed to the reader or to a presumed listener.

dra·mat·ics (drə-măt′ĭks) *n. (used with a sing. or pl. verb).* **1.** The art or practice of acting and stagecraft. **2.** Dramatic or stagy behavior: *Cut the dramatics and get to the point.*

dram·a·tis per·so·nae (drăm′ə-tĭs pər-sō′nē, drä′mə-tĭs pər-sō′nī′) *pl.n.* **1.** The characters in a play or story. **2.** A list of the characters in a play or story. [Latin *drāmatis,* genitive of *drāma,* drama + *persōnae,* pl. of *persona,* character.]

dram·a·tist (drăm′ə-tĭst, drä′mə-) *n. Abbr.* **dram.** One who writes plays; a playwright.

dram·a·ti·za·tion (drăm′ə-tĭ-zā′shən, drä′mə-) *n.* **1.** The act or art of dramatizing: *the dramatization of a novel.* **2.** A work adapted for dramatic presentation: *a dramatization by actors of actual recorded events.*

dram·a·tize (drăm′ə-tīz′, drä′mə-) *v.* **-tized, -tiz·ing, -tiz·es.** *—tr.* **1.** To adapt (a literary work) for dramatic presentation, as in a theater or on television or radio. **2.** To present or view in a dramatic or melodramatic way. *—intr.* **1.** To be adaptable to dramatic form. **2.** To indulge in self-dramatization.

dram·a·turge (drăm′ə-tûrj′, drä′mə-) *n.* A writer or adapter of plays; a playwright. [French, from Greek *dramatourgos* : *drama, dramat-,* drama; see DRAMA + *ergon,* work; see **werg-** in Appendix.]

dram·a·tur·gy (drăm′ə-tûr′jē, drä′mə-) *n.* The art of the theater, especially the writing of plays. **—dram′a·tur′gic, dram′a·tur′gi·cal** *adj.*

drank (drăngk) *v.* Past tense of **drink.**

dr ap *abbr.* Apothecaries' dram.

drape (drāp) *v.* **draped, drap·ing, drapes.** *—tr.* **1.** To cover, dress, or hang with or as if with cloth in loose folds: *draped the coffin with a flag; a robe that draped her figure.* See Synonyms at **clothe. 2.** To arrange or let fall in loose folds: *draping the banner from the balcony.* **3.** To hang or rest limply: *draped my legs over the chair.* *—intr.* To fall or hang in loose folds: *arranged the cloth to drape over the table legs.* **—drape** *n.* **1.** A drapery; a curtain. **2.** A cloth arranged over a patient's body during a medical examination or treatment or during surgery, designed to provide a sterile field around the area being examined or treated or around the operative incision. **3.** The way in which cloth falls or hangs: *adjusted the drape of the gown.* [Middle English *drapen,* to weave, from Old French *draper,* from *drap,* cloth, from Late Latin *drappus.*]

drap·er (drā′pər) *n. Chiefly British.* A dealer in cloth or clothing and dry goods. [Middle English, weaver or seller of cloth, from Old French *drapier,* from *drap,* cloth. See DRAPE.]

Dra·per (drā′pər), **Henry.** 1837–1882. American astronomer who was the first to photograph a stellar spectrum (1872) and a nebula (1880).

drap·er·y (drā′pə-rē) *n., pl.* **-ies. 1.** Cloth or clothing gracefully arranged in loose folds. **2.** A piece or pieces of heavy fabric

ă pat	oi boy
ā pay	ou out
âr care	o͝o took
ä father	o͞o boot
ĕ pet	ŭ cut
ē be	ûr urge
ĭ pit	th thin
ī pie	*th* this
îr pier	hw which
ŏ pot	zh vision
ō toe	ə about, item
ô paw	♦ regionalism

Stress marks: ′ (primary); ′ (secondary), as in **dictionary** (dĭk′shə-nĕr′ē)

hanging straight in loose folds, used as a curtain. **3.** Cloth; fabric. **4.** *Chiefly British.* The business of a draper.

dras·tic (drăs′tĭk) *adj.* **1.** Severe or radical in nature; extreme: *the drastic measure of amputating the entire leg; drastic social change brought about by the French Revolution.* **2.** Taking effect violently or rapidly: *a drastic emetic.* [Greek *drastikos,* active, from *drastos,* to be done, from *dran,* to do.] **—dras′ti·cal·ly** *adv.*

drat (drăt) *interj.* Used to express annoyance. [Short for *God rot.*]

drat·ted (drăt′ĭd) *adj.* Damned; confounded.

Drau (drou). See **Drava.**

draught (drăft) *n., v., & adj. Chiefly British.* Variant of **draft.**

draughts (drăfts, dräfts) *n. (used with a sing. or pl. verb). Chiefly British.* The game of checkers. [Middle English *draughtes,* pl. of *draught,* act of pulling, move at chess. See DRAFT.]

Dra·va or **Dra·ve** (drä′və) also **Drau** (drou). A river rising in the Carnic Alps of southern Austria and flowing about 724 km (450 mi) eastward into and across northern Yugoslavia to the Danube River.

dr avdp *abbr.* Avoirdupois dram.

Dra·ve (drä′və). See **Drava.**

Dra·vid·i·an (drə-vĭd′ē-ən) *n.* **1.** A large family of languages spoken especially in southern India and northern Sri Lanka that includes Tamil, Telugu, Malayalam, and Kannada. **2.** A member of any of the peoples that speak one of the Dravidian languages, especially a member of one of the pre-Indo-European peoples of southern India. [From Sanskrit *drāviḍaḥ,* a Dravidian.] **—Dra·vid′i·an, Dra·vid′ic** (-vĭd′ĭk) *adj.*

♦**draw** (drô) *v.* **drew** (dro͞o), **drawn** (drôn), **draw·ing, draws.** *—tr.* **1.a.** To cause to move after or toward one by applying continuous force; drag: *drew the chair closer to the table; a team of horses drawing a wagon.* See Synonyms at **pull. b.** To cause to move in a given direction or to a given position, as by leading: *The teacher drew the children into the room to see the decorations.* **c.** To move or pull so as to cover or uncover something: *draw the curtains.* **2.** To cause to flow forth: *a pump drawing water; a blow that drew blood.* **3.** To suck or take in (air, for example); inhale. **4.** To require (a specified depth of water) for floating: *a boat drawing 18 inches.* **5.** To take or pull out: *drew a gun from beneath the counter; drew out a fat wallet.* **6.** To extract or take from for one's own use: *drew strength from their religious faith.* **7.** To eviscerate; disembowel. **8.a.** To cause to come by attracting; attract: *afraid the casino will draw undesirable elements to the town.* **b.** To select or take in from a given group, type, or region: *draw clients from all levels of society.* **9.** To bring to a certain condition or action; lead: *drawn to despair; drew them to resign.* **10.** To bring on oneself as a result; provoke: *drew enemy fire.* **11.** To evoke as a response; elicit: *a performance that drew jeers from the audience.* **12.** To earn; gain: *deposits that draw interest at a rate of 5 percent.* **13.a.** To withdraw (money). **b.** To use (a check, for example) when paying. **c.** To receive on a regular basis or at a specified time: *draw a pension.* **14.** To take or receive by chance: *draw lots.* **15.** *Games.* **a.** To take (cards) from a dealer or central stack. **b.** To force (a card) to be played. **16.** To end or leave (a contest) tied or undecided. **17.** To hit or strike (a ball) so as to give it backspin. **18.** To pull back the string of (a bow). **19.** To distort the shape of. **20.** To stretch taut. **21.a.** To flatten, stretch, or mold (metal) by hammering or die stamping. **b.** To shape or elongate (a wire, for example) by pulling through dies. **22.a.** To inscribe (a line or lines) with a pencil or other marking implement. **b.** To make a likeness of on a surface, using mostly lines; depict with lines: *drew a map of the area; drawing landscapes and still lifes.* **c.** To portray in writing or speech; depict with words: *draws moving scenes of ghetto life.* **23.** To formulate or devise from evidence or data at hand: *draw a comparison.* **24.** To compose or write out in legal format: *draw a deed.* *—intr.* **1.** To proceed or move steadily: *a ship drawing near the shore.* **2.** To attract customers or spectators: *The new play is drawing well.* **3.** To cause a flow of liquid: *The patient's veins don't draw easily.* **4.** To cause suppuration. **5.** To take in a draft of air: *The flue isn't drawing.* **6.** To steep in or as if in the manner of tea. **7.** To pull out a weapon for use. **8.** To use or call upon part of a fund or supply: *drawing on an account; drew from the experience of fellow workers.* **9.** To contract or tighten: *material that draws when it dries.* **10.** To conclude a contest without either side winning; tie: *The chess players drew in 32 moves.* **11.** To make a likeness with lines on a surface; sketch. **—draw** *n.* **1.a.** An act of drawing. **b.** The result of drawing. **2.** Something drawn, especially a lot, card, or cards drawn at random. **3.** An inhalation, especially through a pipe or other smoking implement. **4.** Something that attracts interest, customers, or spectators: *a singer who is a popular draw.* **5.** The movable part of a drawbridge. **6.** A special advantage; an edge: *have the draw on one's enemies.* **7.** A contest ending without either side winning. **8.** A small natural depression that water drains into; a shallow gully. **9.** *Games.* A draw shot. **—*phrasal verbs.* draw away.** To move ahead of competitors. **draw back.** To retreat. **draw down.** To deplete by consuming or spending: *drew down our food reserves.* **draw on.** To approach: *as evening draws on.* **draw out. 1.** To prolong; protract. **2.** To induce to speak freely: *managed to draw the shy child out.* **draw up. 1.** To compose or write in a set form; write out: *draw up a contract; draw up a list.* **2.** To bring (troops, for example) into order. **3.** To bring or come to a halt. **4.** To bring (oneself) into an erect posture, often as an expression of dignity or indignation. **5.** *Chiefly Southern U.S.* To shrink when washed. Used of clothes. **—*idioms.* draw a blank.** To fail to find or remember something. **draw and quarter. 1.** To execute (a prisoner) by tying each limb to a horse and driving the horses in different directions. **2.** To disembowel and dismember after hanging. **3.** *Informal.* To punish severely: *The teenager was drawn and quartered for wrecking the family's only car.* **draw straws.** To decide by a lottery with straws of unequal lengths. [Middle English *drauen,* from Old English *dragan.*]

draw·back (drô′băk′) *n.* **1.** A disadvantage or inconvenience. See Synonyms at **disadvantage. 2.** A refund or remittance, such as a discount on duties or taxes for goods destined for reexport.

draw·bar (drô′bär′) *n.* **1.** A bar across the rear of a tractor for hitching machinery. **2.** A railroad coupler.

draw·bridge (drô′brĭj′) *n.* A bridge that can be raised or drawn aside either to prevent access or to permit passage beneath it.

draw·down (drô′doun′) *n.* **1.** The act, process, or result of depleting: *the drawdown of oil supplies; a drawdown of investment capital.* **2.** A lowering of the water level in a reservoir or other body of water.

draw·ee (drô′ē′) *n.* The party on which an order for the payment of money is drawn.

draw·er (drô′ər) *n.* **1.** One that draws, especially one that draws an order for the payment of money. **2.** (*also* drôr). A boxlike compartment in furniture that can be pulled out and pushed in. **3. drawers** (drôrz). Underpants.

draw·ing (drô′ĭng) *n.* **1.** The act or an instance of drawing. **2.a.** The art of representing objects or forms on a surface chiefly by means of lines. **b.** A work produced by this art.

drawing card *n.* An attraction drawing large audiences.

drawing pin *n. Chiefly British.* A thumbtack.

drawing room *n.* **1.** A large room in which guests are entertained. **2.** A ceremonial reception. **3.** A large private room on a railroad sleeping car. [Akin to *withdrawing room.*]

draw·knife (drô′nīf′) *n.* A knife with a handle at each end of the blade, used with a drawing motion to shave a surface. Also called *drawshave.*

drawl (drôl) *v.* **drawled, drawl·ing, drawls.** *—intr.* To speak with lengthened or drawn-out vowels. *—tr.* To utter with lengthened or drawn-out vowels: *"We-e-ell," the clerk drawled.* **—drawl** *n.* The speech or manner of speaking of one who drawls: *a Southern drawl.* [Probably from Low German *drauelen,* to loiter, delay.] **—drawl′er** *n.*

drawn (drôn) *v.* Past participle of **draw. —drawn** *adj.* Haggard, as from fatigue or ill health: *a wan, drawn face.*

drawn butter *n.* Melted butter, often seasoned and used as a sauce. [*drawn,* past participle of DRAW, to bring to a proper consistency (obsolete).]

draw poker *n. Games.* Poker in which each player is dealt five cards face down and may then discard and get replacements for a specified number of cards after the first round of betting.

draw·shave (drô′shāv′) *n.* See **drawknife.**

draw shot *n. Games.* A billiards shot in which the cue ball is struck below center so that it draws back from the object ball after impact.

draw·string (drô′strĭng′) *n.* A cord or ribbon run through a hem or casing and pulled to tighten or close an opening.

draw·tube (drô′to͞ob′, -tyo͞ob′) *n.* A tube that slides within another tube, as in a small hand telescope.

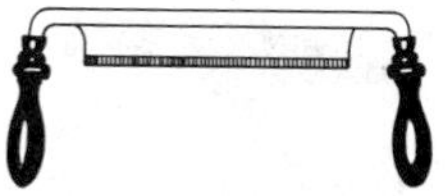
drawknife

dray (drā) *n.* A low, heavy cart without sides, used for haulage. **—dray** *tr.v.* **drayed, dray·ing, drays.** To haul by means of a low, heavy sideless cart. [Middle English *draie,* sledge, cart, from Old English *dragan,* to draw.]

dray·age (drā′ĭj) *n.* **1.** Transport by dray. **2.** A charge for transport by dray.

dray·man (drā′mən) *n.* A driver of a dray.

Dray·ton (drāt′n), **Michael.** 1563–1631. English poet who produced a wide range of works, including sonnets, dramas, satires, and eclogues, such as those in *Idea, The Shepherd's Garland* (1593).

Drayton Plains. A community of southeast Michigan, a suburb of Pontiac. Population, 18,000.

dread (drĕd) *v.* **dread·ed, dread·ing, dreads.** *—tr.* **1.** To be in terror of. **2.** To anticipate with alarm, distaste, or reluctance: *dreaded the long drive home.* **3.** *Archaic.* To hold in awe or reverence. *—intr.* To be very afraid. **—dread** *n.* **1.** Profound fear; terror. **2.** Fearful or distasteful anticipation. See Synonyms at **fear. 3.** An object of fear, awe, or reverence. **4.** *Archaic.* Awe; reverence. **—dread** *adj.* **1.** Causing terror or fear: *a dread disease.* **2.** Inspiring awe: *the dread presence of the headmaster.* [Middle English *dreden,* short for *adreden,* from Old English *adrǣdan,* from *ondrǣdan,* to advise against, fear : *ond-, and-,* against; see UN−[2] + *rǣdan,* to advise; see REDE.]

dread·ful (drĕd′fəl) *adj.* **1.** Inspiring dread; terrible. **2.** Extremely unpleasant; distasteful or shocking: *dreadful manners; this dreadful heat.* **—dread′ful·ly** *adv.* **—dread′ful·ness** *n.*

dread·locks (drĕd′lŏks′) *pl.n.* Long, thin braids or natural locks of hair densely radiating from the scalp, in a style popularized by Rastafarians. **—dread′locked′** *adj.*

dread·nought (drĕd′nôt′) *n.* A heavily armed battleship.

dreadnought
U.S.S. *Alabama*

dream (drēm) *n.* **1.** A series of images, ideas, emotions, and sensations occurring involuntarily in the mind during certain stages of sleep. **2.** A daydream; a reverie. **3.** A state of abstraction; a trance. **4.** A wild fancy or hope. **5.** A condition or achievement that is longed for; an aspiration: *a dream of owning their own business.* **6.** One that is exceptionally gratifying, excellent, or beautiful: *Our new car runs like a dream.* **—dream** *v.* **dreamed** or **dreamt** (drĕmt), **dream·ing, dreams.** *—intr.* **1.** To experience a dream in sleep: *dreamed of meeting an old friend.* **2.** To daydream. **3.** To have a deep aspiration: *dreaming of a world at peace.* **4.** To regard something as feasible or practical: *I wouldn't dream of trick skiing on icy slopes.* *—tr.* **1.** To experience a dream of while asleep: *Did it storm last night, or did I dream it?* **2.** To conceive of; imagine. **3.** To pass (time) idly or in reverie. ***—phrasal verb.*** **dream up.** To invent; concoct: *dreamed up a plan to corner the market.* [Middle English *drem,* from Old English *drēam,* joy, music; akin to Old Saxon *drōm,* mirth, dream.]

dream·er (drē′mər) *n.* **1.** One that dreams. **2. a.** A visionary. **b.** An idealist. **3.** A habitually impractical person.

dream·land (drēm′lănd′) *n.* **1.** An ideal or imaginary land. **2.** A state of sleep.

dream·scape (drēm′skāp′) *n.* A dreamlike scene or picture having surreal qualities.

dreamt (drĕmt) *v.* A past tense and a past participle of **dream.**

dream·time also **Dream·time** (drēm′tīm′) *n.* The time of the creation of the world in the mythology of the Australian aborigines: *"Aboriginal myths tell of the legendary totemic beings who wandered across the country in the Dreamtime . . . singing the world into existence"* (Bruce Chatwin).

dream vision *n.* A narrative poem, especially in medieval literature, in which the main character falls asleep and experiences events having allegorical, didactic, or moral significance.

dream·y (drē′mē) *adj.* **-i·er, -i·est. 1.** Resembling a dream; ethereal or vague. **2.** Given to daydreams or reverie. **3.** Soothing and serene. **4.** *Informal.* Inspiring delight; wonderful. **—dream′i·ly** *adv.* **—dream′i·ness** *n.*

drear (drîr) *adj.* Dreary.

drea·ry (drîr′ē) *adj.* **-ri·er, -ri·est. 1.** Dismal; bleak. **2.** Boring; dull: *dreary tasks.* [Middle English *dreri,* bloody, frightened, sad, from Old English *drēorig,* bloody, sad, from *drēor,* gore. See **dhreu-** in Appendix.] **—drea′ri·ly** *adv.* **—drea′ri·ness** *n.*

dreck (drĕk) *n. Slang.* Trash, especially inferior merchandise. [German *Dreck,* from Middle High German *drëc.* See **sker-**[3] in Appendix.] **—dreck′y** *adj.*

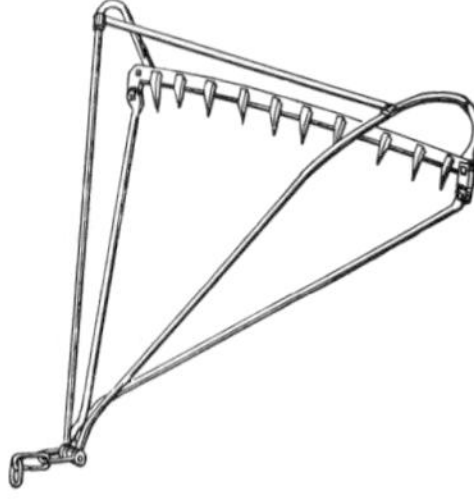

dredge[1]
Oyster dredge

dredge[1] (drĕj) *n.* **1.** Any of various machines equipped with scooping or suction devices and used to deepen harbors and waterways and in underwater mining. **2.** *Nautical.* A boat or barge equipped with a dredge. **3.** An implement consisting of a net on a frame, used for gathering shellfish. **—dredge** *v.* **dredged, dredg·ing, dredg·es.** *—tr.* **1.** To clean, deepen, or widen with a dredge. **2.** To bring up with a dredge: *dredged up the silt.* **3.** To come up with; unearth: *dredged up bitter memories.* *—intr.* To use a dredge: *dredging for alluvial gold.* [Middle English *dreg-,* in *dreg-boat,* boat for dredging; akin to Old English *dragan,* to draw.]

dredge[2] (drĕj) *tr.v.* **dredged, dredg·ing, dredg·es.** To coat (food) by sprinkling with a powder, such as flour or sugar. [From obsolete *dredge,* a sweetmeat, from Middle English *dragge,* from Old French *dragie,* alteration of Latin *tragēmata,* confectionary, from Greek *tragēmata,* pl. of *tragēma,* sweetmeat. See **terə-**[1] in Appendix.]

dredg·er[1] (drĕj′ər) *n.* **1.** A dredging machine. **2.** *Nautical.* A barge or boat equipped with a dredge.

dredg·er[2] (drĕj′ər) *n.* A container with a perforated lid used for coating food with a powder, such as flour or sugar.

D region *n.* The region of the ionosphere about 40 to 65 kilometers (25 to 40 miles) above the earth.

dreg (drĕg) *n.* **1.** The sediment in a liquid; lees. Often used in the plural. **2.** The basest or least desirable portion. Often used in the plural: *the dregs of humanity.* **3.** A small amount; a residue. [Middle English *dreg,* from Old Norse *dregg.*]

dreidel

drei·del also **drei·dl** (drād′l) *n.* A toy similar to a spinning top used in games of chance played by children and adults at Hanukkah. [Yiddish *dreydl,* from *dreyen,* to turn, from Middle High German *drǣjen,* from Old High German *drāen.*]

Drei·ser (drī′sər, -zər), **Theodore Herman Albert.** 1871–1945. American writer and editor whose naturalistic novels, such as *Sister Carrie* (1900) and *An American Tragedy* (1925), portray life as a struggle against ungovernable forces.

drench (drĕnch) *tr.v.* **drenched, drench·ing, drench·es. 1.** To wet through and through; soak. **2.** To administer a large oral dose of liquid medicine to (an animal). **3.** To provide with something in great abundance; surfeit: *just drenched in money.* **—drench** *n.* **1.** The act of wetting or becoming wet through and through. **2.** A large dose of liquid medicine, especially one administered to an animal by pouring down the throat. [Middle English *drenchen,* to drown, from Old English *drencan,* to give to drink, drown. See **dhreg-** in Appendix.] **—drench′er** *n.*

Dres·den (drĕz′dən). A city of east-central Germany on the Elbe River east-southeast of Leipzig. An industrial and cultural center, it was severely damaged in bombing raids during World War II. Its china industry was moved to Meissen in the early 18th century. Population, 522,532.

Dresden china *n.* Meissen porcelain. [After DRESDEN.]

dress (drĕs) *v.* **dressed, dress·ing, dress·es.** *—tr.* **1. a.** To put clothes on; clothe. **b.** To furnish with clothing. **2.** To decorate or adorn: *dress a Christmas tree.* **3.** To arrange a display in: *dress a store window.* **4.** To arrange (troops) in ranks; align. **5.** To apply medication, bandages, or other therapeutic materials to (a wound). **6.** To arrange and groom (the hair), as by styling, combing, or washing. **7.** To groom (an animal); curry. **8.** To cultivate (land or plants). **9.** To clean (fish or fowl) for cooking or sale. **10.** To trim and finish the surface of: *dress a plank.* *—intr.* **1.** To put on clothes. **2.** To wear clothes of a certain kind or style: *dresses casually.* **3.** To wear formal clothes: *dress for dinner.* **4.** To get into proper alignment with others: *The troops dressed on the squad leader.* **—dress** *n.* **1.** Clothing; apparel. **2.** A style of clothing: *folk dancers in peasant dress.* **3.** A one-piece outer garment for women or girls. **4.** Outer covering or appearance; guise: *an ancient ritual in modern dress.* **—dress** *adj.* **1.** Suitable for formal occasions: *dress shoes.* **2.** Requiring formal clothes: *a dress dinner.* ***—phrasal verbs.*** **dress down. 1.** To scold; reprimand: *I was dressed down by the teacher for lateness.* **2.** To wear informal clothes, befitting an occasion or location: *I dressed down for such a casual occasion.* **dress up.** To wear formal or fancy clothes: *They dressed up and went to the prom.* ***—idiom.*** **dress ship.** *Nautical.* To display the ensign, signal flags, and bunting on a ship. [Middle English *dressen,* to arrange, put on clothing, from Old French *drecier,* to arrange, from Vulgar Latin **dīrectiāre,* from Latin *dīrectus,* past participle of *dīrigere,* to direct. See DIRECT.]

WORD HISTORY: A dress is such a common article of modern attire that it is difficult to imagine that the word *dress* at one time did not refer to such a thing. The earliest sense of *dress,* recorded in a work written before 1450, was "speech, talk." The relationship of our modern sense to this early sense is explained by the fact that the noun *dress* comes from the verb *dress,* which goes back through Old French *drecier,* "to arrange," and the assumed Vulgar Latin *dīrectiāre* to Latin *dīrectus,* a form of the verb *dīrigere,* "to direct." In accordance with its etymology the verb *dress* has meant or still means "to place," "to arrange," and "to put in order." The sense "to clothe" is related to the notion of putting in order, specifically in regard to clothing. This verb sense then gave rise to the noun sense "personal attire" as well as to the important garment sense, which has made the fortune of many a fashion designer. The earliest noun sense, "speech," comes from a verb sense having to do with addressing or directing words to other people.

dres·sage (drə-säzh′, drĕ-) *n. Sports.* The guiding of a horse through a series of complex maneuvers by slight movements of the rider's hands, legs, and weight. [French, preparation, training, dressage, from *dresser,* to set up, arrange, train, from Old French *drecier,* to set up, arrange. See DRESS.]

dress circle *n.* A section of seats in a theater or opera house, usually the first tier above the orchestra.

dress code *n.* A set of rules, as in a school, indicating the approved manner of dress: *"the company's white-shirt black-tie dress code"* (David Pauly).

dress·er[1] (drĕs′ər) *n.* **1.** One that dresses: *a careful dresser.* **2.** A wardrobe assistant, as for an actor.

dress·er[2] (drĕs′ər) *n.* **1.** A low chest of drawers often supporting a mirror and typically used for holding clothes and personal items. **2.** A cupboard or set of shelves for dishes or kitchen utensils. [Middle English *dressour,* table for preparing food, from Old French *dreceur,* from *drecier,* to set up, arrange. See DRESS.]

dress·ing (drĕs′ĭng) *n.* **1.** A therapeutic or protective material applied to a wound. **2.** A sauce for certain dishes, such as salads. **3.** A stuffing, as for poultry or fish. **4.** Manure or other fertilizing material for soil.

dress·ing-down (drĕs′ĭng-doun′) *n.* A severe scolding.

dressing gown *n.* A robe worn for lounging or before dressing.

dressing room *n.* A room, as in a theater, for changing costumes or clothes and applying makeup.

dressing table *n.* A low table with a mirror at which one sits while applying makeup. Also called *vanity.*

dress·mak·er (drĕs′mā′kər) *n.* One that makes women's clothing, especially dresses. **—dress′mak′ing** *n.*

dress rehearsal *n.* A full, uninterrupted rehearsal of a play with costumes and stage properties.

dress·y (drĕs′ē) *adj.* **-i·er, -i·est. 1.** Showy or elegant in dress or appearance. **2.** Smart; stylish. **—dress′i·ness** *n.*

drew (dro͞o) *v.* Past tense of **draw.**

Drew (dro͞o). Family of American actors, including **John** (1827–1862), his wife, **Louisa** (1820–1897), and their son **John** (1853–1927).

Drew, Daniel. 1797–1879. American financier who as a director of the Erie Railroad manipulated stock prices to his own advantage and with James Fisk and Jay Gould engaged Cornelius Vanderbilt in a bitter stock-market struggle (1866–1868) for control of the railroad.

Drex·el Hill (drĕk′səl). A community of southeast Pennsylvania, a residential suburb of Philadelphia. Population, 29,600.

Drey·fus (drīʹfəs, drā-), **Alfred.** 1859–1935. French army officer of Jewish descent who was convicted of treason (1894), sentenced to life imprisonment, and ultimately acquitted when the evidence against him was shown to have been forged.

drib (drĭb) *n.* A negligible amount: *finished the work in dribs and drabs.* [Perhaps from DRIBLET.]

drib·ble (drĭbʹəl) *v.* **-bled, -bling, -bles.** —*intr.* **1.** To flow or fall in drops or an unsteady stream; trickle. **2.** To let saliva drip from the mouth; drool. **3.** *Sports.* **a.** To move a ball or puck with repeated light bounces or kicks. **b.** To advance by dribbling: *dribbled down the court.* —*tr.* **1.** To let flow or fall in drops or an unsteady stream. **2.** *Sports.* **a.** To move (a ball or puck) by repeated light bounces or kicks, as in basketball or soccer. **b.** To hit (a baseball, for example) so that it bounces slowly. —**dribble** *n.* **1.** A weak, unsteady stream; a trickle. **2.** A small quantity; a bit. **3.** *Sports.* The act of dribbling a ball. [Frequentative of obsolete *drib,* alteration of DRIP.] —**dribʹbler** *n.*

drib·let (drĭbʹlĭt) *n.* **1.** A tiny falling drop of liquid. **2.** A small amount or portion. [From obsolete *drib,* to fall in drops, alteration of DRIP.]

dried (drīd) *v.* Past tense and past participle of **dry.**

dri·er[1] also **dry·er** (drīʹər) *n.* **1.** One that dries. **2.** A substance added to paint, varnish, or ink to speed drying.

dri·er[2] (drīʹər) *adj.* A comparative of **dry.**

dries (drīz) *v.* Third person singular present tense of **dry.**

dri·est (drīʹĭst) *adj.* A superlative of **dry.**

♦**drift** (drĭft) *v.* **drift·ed, drift·ing, drifts.** —*intr.* **1.** To be carried along by currents of air or water: *a balloon drifting eastward; as the wreckage drifted toward shore.* **2.** To proceed or move unhurriedly and smoothly: *drifting among the party guests.* **3.** To move leisurely or sporadically from place to place, especially without purpose or regular employment: *a day laborer, drifting from town to town.* **4.a.** To wander from a set course or point of attention; stray. **b.** To vary from or oscillate randomly about a fixed setting, position, or mode of operation. **5.** To be piled up in banks or heaps by the force of a current: *snow drifting to five feet.* —*tr.* **1.** To cause to be carried in a current: *drifting the logs downstream.* **2.** To pile up in banks or heaps: *Wind drifted the loose straw against the barn.* **3.** *Western U.S.* To drive (livestock) slowly or far afield, especially for grazing. —**drift** *n.* **1.** The act or condition of drifting. **2.** Something moving along in a current of air or water. **3.** A bank or pile, as of sand or snow, heaped up by currents of air or water. **4.** *Geology.* Rock debris transported and deposited by or from ice, especially by or from a glacier. **5.a.** A general trend or tendency, as of opinion. See Synonyms at **tendency. b.** General meaning or purport; tenor: *caught the drift of the conversation.* **6.a.** A gradual change in position. **b.** A gradual deviation from an original course, model, method, or intention. **c.** Variation or random oscillation about a fixed setting, position, or mode of behavior. **7.** A gradual change in the output of a circuit or amplifier. **8.** The rate of flow of a water current. **9.a.** A tool for ramming or driving something down. **b.** A tapered steel pin for enlarging and aligning holes. **10.a.** A horizontal or nearly horizontal passageway in a mine running through or parallel to a vein. **b.** A secondary mine passageway between two main shafts or tunnels. **11.** A drove or herd, especially of swine. See Synonyms at **flock[1].** [From Middle English, drove, herd, act of driving. See **dhreibh-** in Appendix.] —**driftʹy** *adj.*

drift·age (drĭfʹtĭj) *n.* **1.** Deviation from a set course caused by drifting. **2.** Matter that has been carried along or deposited by air or water currents.

drift·er (drĭfʹtər) *n.* One that drifts, especially a person who moves aimlessly from place to place or from job to job.

drift net *n.* A large fishing net buoyed up by floats that is carried along with the current or tide.

drift·wood (drĭftʹwo͝odʹ) *n.* Wood floating in or washed up by the water.

drill[1] (drĭl) *n.* **1.a.** An implement with cutting edges or a pointed end for boring holes in hard materials, usually by a rotating abrasion or repeated blows; a bit. **b.** The hand-operated or hand-powered holder for this implement. **c.** A loud, harsh noise made by or as if by a powered tool of this kind. **2.a.** Disciplined, repetitious exercise as a means of teaching and perfecting a skill or procedure. **b.** A task or exercise for teaching a skill or procedure by repetition: *conducted an air-raid drill; a drill for learning the multiplication tables.* **3.** The training of soldiers in marching and the manual of arms. **4.** Any of various marine gastropod mollusks, chiefly of the genus *Urosalpinx,* that bore holes into the shells of bivalve mollusks. *U. cinera* is destructive to oysters. —**drill** *v.* **drilled, drill·ing, drills.** —*tr.* **1.a.** To make a hole in (a hard material) with a drill: *a bit for drilling masonry.* **b.** To make (a hole) with or as if with a drill: *drills holes in trees with its chisellike bill.* **2.** To strike or hit sharply: *The batter drilled a single through the infield.* **3.a.** To instruct thoroughly by repetition in a skill or procedure: *drill pupils in grammar.* **b.** To infuse knowledge of or skill in by repetitious instruction. See Synonyms at **practice, teach. 4.** To train (soldiers) in marching and the manual of arms. —*intr.* **1.** To make a hole with or as if with a drill. **2.** To perform a training exercise. [Obsolete Dutch *dril,* from *drillen,* to bore, from Middle Dutch *drillen.* See **terə-[1]** in Appendix.] —**drillʹer** *n.*

drill[2] (drĭl) *n.* **1.** A shallow trench or furrow in which seeds are planted. **2.** A row of planted seeds. **3.** A machine or implement for planting seeds in holes or furrows. —**drill** *tr.v.* **drilled, drill·ing, drills. 1.** To sow (seeds) in rows. **2.** To plant (a field) in drills. [Perhaps from *drill,* rill, from Middle English *drille,* sip.]

drill[3] (drĭl) *n.* Durable cotton or linen twill of varying weights, generally used for work clothes. [Short for *drilling,* alteration of German *Drillich,* from Middle High German *drilich,* from Old High German *drilīh,* alteration of Latin *trilīx, trilīc-,* triple-twilled. See TRELLIS.]

drill[4] (drĭl) *n.* A baboon *(Papio leucophaeus)* of western Africa, related to and resembling the mandrill. [Possibly of West African origin.]

drill instructor *n. Abbr.* **DI** A noncommissioned officer who instructs recruits in military drill and discipline.

drill·mas·ter (drĭlʹmăsʹtər) *n.* **1.** A drill instructor. **2.** An instructor given to extremely rigorous training.

drill press *n.* A powered vertical drilling machine in which the drill is pressed to the work automatically or by a hand lever.

drill steel *n.* A high-grade steel used in tools and dies that is made by fusing low-carbon steel with charcoal or cast iron. Formerly prepared in a graphite crucible, it is now produced in an electric furnace. Also called *crucible steel.*

drill·stock (drĭlʹstŏkʹ) *n.* The part of a drilling tool or machine that holds the shank of a drill or bit.

Drin (drēn). A river, about 282 km (175 mi) long, of Albania flowing north and west to the Adriatic Sea.

Dri·na (drēʹnə, -nä). A river, about 459 km (285 mi) long, of central Yugoslavia flowing generally north to the Sava River.

drink (drĭngk) *v.* **drank** (drăngk), **drunk** (drŭngk), **drink·ing, drinks.** —*tr.* **1.** To take into the mouth and swallow (a liquid). **2.** To swallow the liquid contents of (a vessel): *drank a cup of tea.* **3.** To take in or soak up; absorb: *drank the fresh air; spongy earth that drank up the rain.* **4.** To take in eagerly through the senses or intellect: *drank in the beauty of the day.* **5.a.** To give or make (a toast). **b.** To toast (a person or an occasion, for example): *We'll drink your health.* **6.** To bring to a specific state by drinking alcoholic liquors: *drank our sorrows away.* —*intr.* **1.** To swallow liquid: *drank noisily; drink from a goblet.* **2.** To imbibe alcoholic liquors: *They only drink socially.* **3.** To salute a person or an occasion with a toast: *We will drink to your continued success.* —**drink** *n.* **1.** A liquid that is fit for drinking; a beverage. **2.** An amount of liquid swallowed: *took a long drink from the fountain.* **3.** An alcoholic beverage, such as a cocktail or highball. **4.** Excessive or habitual indulgence in alcoholic liquor. **5.** *Slang.* A body of water; the sea: *The hatch cover slid off the boat and into the drink.* [Middle English *drinken,* from Old English *drincan.* See **dhreg-** in Appendix.]

drink·a·ble (drĭngʹkə-bəl) *adj.* Suitable or fit for drinking; potable: *drinkable water.* —**drinkable** *n.* A beverage. —**drinkʹa·bilʹi·ty** *n.*

drink·er (drĭngʹkər) *n.* **1.** One that drinks. **2.** One who drinks alcoholic liquors, especially habitually or excessively: *a hard drinker.*

drink·ing fountain (drĭngʹkĭng) *n.* A device equipped with a nozzle that when activated provides a stream of drinking water for public use.

drip (drĭp) *v.* **dripped, drip·ping, drips.** —*intr.* **1.** To fall in drops: *Water is dripping from that leaky faucet.* **2.** To shed drops: *an umbrella that is dripping all over the floor.* **3.** To ooze or be saturated with or as if with liquid: *"His playing drips with exaggerated rubato and unorthodox tempi"* (Annalyn Swan). —*tr.* To let fall in or as if in drops: *a brush dripping paint; a speech that dripped invective.* —**drip** *n.* **1.** The process of forming and falling in drops. **2.a.** Liquid or moisture that falls in drops. **b.** A slight intermittent flow or leak: *fixed the drip in the faucet.* **3.** The sound made by liquid falling in drops: *listened to the steady drip of the rain.* **4.** A projection on a cornice or sill that protects the area below from rainwater. **5.** *Slang.* A tiresome or annoying person. [Middle English *drippen.* See **dhreu-** in Appendix.]

drip coffee *n.* Coffee made by pouring boiling water through a perforated container holding ground coffee into a pot that is fitted underneath.

drip-dry (drĭpʹdrīʹ) *adj.* Made of a fabric that will not wrinkle when hung dripping wet for drying. —**drip-dry** *intr.v.* **-dried, -dry·ing, -dries.** To dry with no wrinkles when hung dripping wet.

drip feed *n.* **1.** Administration of blood, plasma, saline, or sugar solutions, usually intravenously, a drop at a time. **2.a.** The device or tubes by which such a substance is administered. **b.** The substance administered. —**dripʹ-feedʹ** (drĭpʹfēdʹ) *v.*

drip·less (drĭpʹlĭs) *adj.* Made or designed to prevent dripping: *a dripless faucet; a dripless paint roller.*

♦**drip pan** *n.* A pan for catching the drippings from roasting meat. Also called ♦*bakersheet.*

drip·ping (drĭpʹĭng) *n.* **1.** The act or sound of something falling in drops. **2.** Often **drippings.** The fat and juices exuded from roasting meat, often used in making gravy.

drip·py (drĭpʹē) *adj.* **-pi·er, -pi·est. 1.** Characterized by dripping; drizzly: *a drippy, wet day.* **2.** *Slang.* **a.** Tiresome or annoying. **b.** Mawkishly sentimental: *a drippy love scene.* —**dripʹpi·ly** *adv.* —**dripʹpi·ness** *n.*

drip·stone (drĭpʹstōnʹ) *n.* **1.** A protective drip made of stone, as on a cornice over a door or window. Also called *hoodmold.* **2.** Calcium carbonate in the form of stalactites or stalagmites.

drive (drīv) *v.* **drove** (drōv), **driv·en** (drĭvʹən), **driv·ing,**

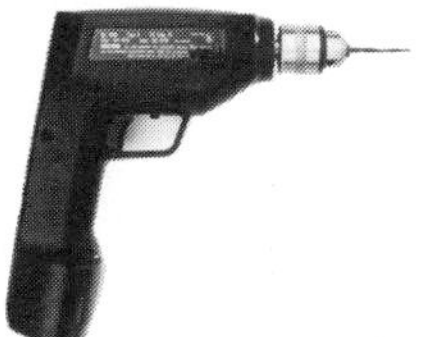

drill[1]
Hand-held electric drill

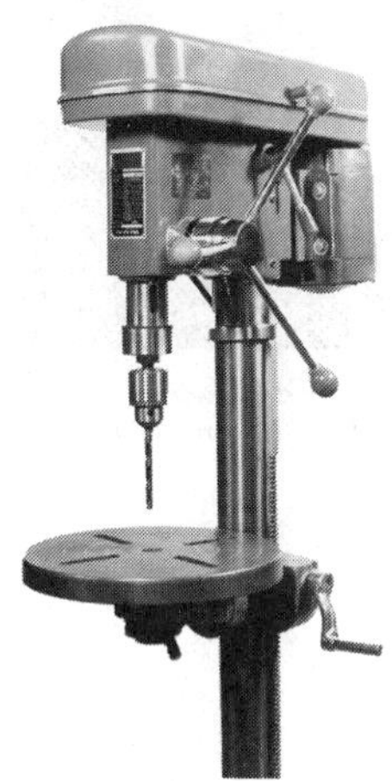

drill press

drinking fountain

ă pat	oi boy
ā pay	ou out
âr care	o͝o took
ä father	o͞o boot
ĕ pet	ŭ cut
ē be	ûr urge
ĭ pit	th thin
ī pie	*th* this
îr pier	hw which
ŏ pot	zh vision
ō toe	ə about, item
ô paw	♦ regionalism

Stress marks: ʹ (primary); ʹ (secondary), as in **dictionary** (dĭkʹshə-nĕrʹē)

drives. —*tr.* **1.** To push, propel, or press onward forcibly; urge forward: *drove the horses into the corral.* **2.** To repulse forcefully; put to flight: *drove the attackers away; drove out any thought of failure.* **3.** To guide, control, or direct (a vehicle). **4. a.** To convey or transport in a vehicle: *drove the children to school.* **b.** To traverse in a vehicle: *drive the freeways to work.* **5.** To supply the motive force or power to and cause to function: *Steam drives the engine.* **6.** To compel or force to work, often excessively: *"Every serious dancer is driven by notions of perfection—perfect expressiveness, perfect technique"* (Susan Sontag). **7.** To force into or from a particular act or state: *Indecision drives me crazy.* **8.** To force to go through or penetrate: *drove the stake into the ground.* **9.** To create or produce by penetrating forcibly: *The nail drove a hole in the tire.* **10.** To carry through vigorously to a conclusion: *drove home his point.* **11. a.** *Sports.* To throw, strike, or cast (a ball, for example) hard or rapidly. **b.** *Basketball.* To move with the ball directly through: *drove the lane and scored.* **c.** *Baseball.* To cause (a run) to be scored. **12. a.** To chase (game) into the open or into traps or nets. **b.** To search (an area) for game in such a manner. —*intr.* **1.** To move along or advance quickly as if pushed by an impelling force. **2.** To rush, dash, or advance violently against an obstruction: *The wind drove into my face.* **3.** To operate a vehicle, such as a car. **4.** To go or be transported in a vehicle: *drove to the supermarket.* **5. a.** *Sports.* To hit, throw, or impel a ball or other missile forcibly. **b.** *Basketball.* To move directly to the basket with the ball. **6.** To make an effort to reach or achieve an objective; aim. —**drive** *n.* **1.** The act of driving. **2.** A trip or journey in a vehicle. **3.** *Abbr.* **Dr.** A road for automobiles and other vehicles. **4. a.** The means or apparatus for transmitting motion or power to a machine or from one machine part to another. **b.** The means by which automotive power is applied to a roadway: *four-wheel drive.* **c.** The means or apparatus for controlling and directing an automobile: *right-hand drive.* **5.** *Computer Science.* A device that reads data from and writes data onto a storage medium, such as a floppy disk. **6.** A strong organized effort to accomplish a purpose. See Synonyms at **campaign. 7.** Energy, push, or aggressiveness. **8.** *Psychology.* A strong motivating tendency or instinct, especially of sexual or aggressive origin, that prompts activity toward a particular end. **9.** A massive, sustained military offensive. **10. a.** *Sports.* The act of hitting, knocking, or thrusting a ball very swiftly. **b.** *Sports.* The stroke or thrust by which a ball is driven. **c.** *Basketball.* The act of moving with the ball directly to the basket. **11. a.** A rounding up and driving of cattle to new pastures or to market. **b.** A gathering and driving of logs down a river. **c.** The cattle or logs thus driven. —***phrasal verb.* drive at.** To mean to do or say: *I don't understand what you're driving at.* [Middle English *driven,* from Old English *drīfan.* See **dhreibh-** in Appendix.] —**driv′a·bil′i·ty** *n.* —**driv′a·ble** *adj.*

dromedary
Camelus dromedarius

drive-in (drīv′ĭn′) *n.* An establishment designed to permit customers to remain in their motor vehicles while being accommodated. —**drive′-in′** *adj.*

driv·el (drĭv′əl) *v.* **-eled, -el·ing, -els** or **-elled, -el·ling, -els.** —*intr.* **1.** To slobber; drool. **2.** To flow like spittle or saliva. **3.** To talk stupidly or childishly. —*tr.* **1.** To allow to flow from the mouth. **2.** To say (something) stupidly. —**drivel** *n.* **1.** Saliva flowing from the mouth. **2.** Stupid or senseless talk. [Middle English *drevelen,* from Old English *dreflian.*] —**driv′el·er** *n.*

drive·line (drīv′līn′) *n.* The components of an automotive vehicle that connect the transmission with the driving axles and include the universal joint and drive shaft. Also called *drive train.*

driv·en (drĭv′ən) *v.* Past participle of **drive.** —**driven** *adj.* **1.** Piled up or carried along by a current: *driven snow.* **2.** Motivated by or having a compulsive quality or need: *a driven person.*

driv·er (drī′vər) *n.* **1.** One that drives, as the operator of a motor vehicle. **2.** A tool, such as a screwdriver or hammer, that is used for imparting forceful pressure on another object. **3.** A machine part that transmits motion or power to another part. **4.** A golf club with a wide head and a long shaft, used for making long shots from the tee. **5.** *Nautical.* A jib-headed spanker.

driver ant *n.* See **army ant.**

driv·er's seat (drī′vərz) *n.* A position of control or authority.

drive shaft also **drive·shaft** (drīv′shăft′) *n.* A rotating shaft that transmits mechanical power from a motor or an engine to a point or region of application.

drive time *n.* **1.** The time of day during which commuters go to and from work: *interesting radio programming during drive time.* **2.** The time it takes to drive a specified distance or route: *a drive time of 11 hours between Kansas City and Denver.*

drive train *n.* See **driveline.**

drive-up (drīv′ŭp′) *adj.* Designed to permit customers to remain in their motor vehicles while being accommodated: *a drive-up window at the bank.* —**drive′-up′** *n.*

drive·way (drīv′wā′) *n.* A private road that connects a house, a garage, or another building with the street.

driv·ing (drī′vĭng) *adj.* **1.** Transmitting power or motion. **2.** Violent, intense, or forceful: *a driving rain.* **3.** Energetic or active: *a driving personality.* —**driv′ing·ly** *adv.*

driz·zle (drĭz′əl) *v.* **-zled, -zling, -zles.** —*intr.* To rain gently in fine, mistlike drops. —*tr.* **1.** To let fall in fine drops or particles: *drizzled melted butter over the asparagus.* **2.** To moisten with fine drops: *drizzled the asparagus with melted butter.* —**drizzle** *n.* A fine, gentle, misty rain. [Perhaps from Middle English *drisning,* fall of dew, from Old English *-drysnian,* in *gedrysnian,* to pass away, vanish. See **dhreu-** in Appendix.] —**driz′zly** *adj.*

Dro·ghe·da (drô′ĭ-də, drŏ′hĭ-). A municipal borough of eastern Ireland on the Boyne River. Oliver Cromwell stormed the town in 1649 and massacred the inhabitants. Population, 23,247.

drogue (drōg) *n.* **1.** *Nautical.* See **sea anchor. 2.** A drogue parachute. **3.** A funnel-shaped or cone-shaped device towed behind an aircraft as a target. **4.** A funnel-shaped device at the end of the hose of a tanker aircraft, used as a stabilizer and receptacle for the probe of a receiving aircraft, as in refueling. [Perhaps alteration of DRAG.]

drogue parachute *n.* **1.** A parachute used to stabilize or decelerate a fast-moving object, especially a small parachute used to slow down a reentering spacecraft or satellite prior to deployment of the main parachute. **2.** A small parachute used to pull a main parachute from its storage pack.

droit (droit, drwä) *n.* *Law.* **1.** A legal right. **2.** Something to which one has legal right. [Middle English, a fee allowed by law, from Old French, right, from Late Latin *dīrectum,* from neuter of Latin *dīrectus,* straight. See DIRECT.]

droll (drōl) *adj.* **droll·er, droll·est.** Amusingly odd or whimsically comical. —**droll** *n.* *Archaic.* A buffoon. [French *drôle,* buffoon, droll, from Old French *drolle,* bon vivant, possibly from Middle Dutch *drol,* goblin.] —**droll′ness** *n.* —**drol′ly** *adv.*

droll·er·y (drō′lə-rē) *n., pl.* **-ies. 1.** A comical or whimsical quality. **2.** A comical or whimsical way of acting, talking, or behaving. **3. a.** The act of joking; clowning. **b.** Something, such as a story, that is comical or whimsical.

–drome *suff.* **1.** Racecourse: *hippodrome.* **2.** Field; arena: *airdrome.* **3.** Running: *palindrome.* [Latin *-dromos,* from Greek *dromos,* racecourse.]

drom·e·dar·y (drŏm′ĭ-dĕr′ē, drŭm′-) *n., pl.* **-ies.** The one-humped domesticated camel *(Camelus dromedarius),* widely used as a beast of burden in northern Africa and western Asia. Also called *Arabian camel.* [Middle English *dromedarie,* from Old French *dromedaire,* from Late Latin *dromedārius,* from Latin *dromas, dromad-,* from Greek, running.]

drom·ond (drŏm′ənd, drŭm′-) *n.* *Nautical.* A large medieval sailing galley. [Middle English, from Anglo-Norman *dromund,* from Late Latin *dromō, dromōn-,* a kind of ship, from Late Greek *dromōn,* from Greek *dromos,* race.]

–dromous *suff.* Running; moving: *catadromous.* [From New Latin *-dromus,* from Greek *-dromos,* from *dromos,* act of running.]

drone[1] (drōn) *n.* **1.** A male bee, especially a honeybee, that is characteristically stingless, performs no work, and produces no honey. Its only function is to mate with the queen bee. **2.** An idle person who lives off others; a loafer. **3.** A pilotless aircraft operated by remote control. [Middle English, from Old English *drān.*]

drone[2] (drōn) *v.* **droned, dron·ing, drones.** —*intr.* **1.** To make a continuous low dull humming sound: *"Somewhere an electric fan droned without end"* (William Styron). **2.** To speak in a monotonous tone: *The lecturer droned on for hours.* **3.** To pass or act in a monotonous way. —*tr.* To utter in a monotonous low tone: *"The mosquitoes droned their angry chant"* (W. Somerset Maugham). —**drone** *n.* **1.** A continuous low humming or buzzing sound. **2.** *Music.* **a.** Any of the pipes of a bagpipe tuned to produce a single tone. **b.** A single sustained tone. [Probably from DRONE[1] (from the bee's humming sound).]

drool (dro͞ol) *v.* **drooled, drool·ing, drools.** —*intr.* **1.** To let saliva run from the mouth; drivel. **2.** *Informal.* To make an extravagant show of appreciation or desire. **3.** *Informal.* To talk nonsense. —*tr.* To let run from the mouth. —**drool** *n.* **1.** Saliva. **2.** *Informal.* Senseless talk; drivel. [Perhaps alteration of DRIVEL.]

droop (dro͞op) *v.* **drooped, droop·ing, droops.** —*intr.* **1.** To bend or hang downward: *"His mouth drooped sadly, pulled down, no doubt, by the plump weight of his jowls"* (Gore Vidal). **2.** To bend or sag gradually: *flowers drooping in the midday heat.* **3.** To sag in dejection or exhaustion: *drooped from lack of sleep.* —*tr.* To let bend or hang down: *"He drooped his body over the rail"* (Norman Mailer). —**droop** *n.* The act or condition of drooping. [Middle English *droupen,* from Old Norse *drūpa.* See **dhreu-** in Appendix.] —**droop′i·ly, droop′ing·ly** *adv.* —**droop′y** *adj.*

droop nose *n.* An aircraft nose section that can be inclined downward to increase runway visibility on takeoff and landing. Also called *droop snoot.*

♦ **drop** (drŏp) *n.* **1.** The smallest quantity of liquid heavy enough to fall in a spherical mass. See table at **measurement. 2.** A small quantity of a substance. **3. drops.** Liquid medicine administered in drops. **4.** A trace or hint: *not a drop of pity.* **5. a.** Something shaped or hanging like a drop. **b.** A small globular piece of hard candy. **6.** The act of falling; descent. **7.** A swift decline or decrease, as in quality, quantity, or intensity. **8. a.** The vertical distance from a higher to a lower level. **b.** The distance through which something falls or drops. **9.** A sheer incline, such as the face of a cliff. **10. a.** A descent by parachute. **b.** Personnel and equipment landed by means of parachute. **11.** Something, such as a trap door on a gallows, that is arranged to fall or be lowered. **12.** A drop curtain. **13.** A slot through which something is deposited in a receptacle. **14.** A central place or establishment where something, such as mail, is brought and subsequently distributed. **15. a.** A predetermined location for the deposit and subsequent removal of secret communications or illicit goods, such as drugs. **b.** The act of depositing such communications or materials. **16.** *Electronics.* A connection made available for an input or output unit on a transmission line. **—drop** *v.* **dropped, drop·ping, drops.** *—intr.* **1.** To fall in drops. **2.** To fall from a higher to a lower place or position. **3.** To become less, as in number, intensity, or volume. **4.** To descend from one level to another. **5.** To fall or sink into a state of exhaustion or death. **6.** To pass or slip into a specified state or condition: *dropped into a doze.* **7.** *Sports.* To fall or roll into a basket or hole. Used of a ball. *—tr.* **1.** To let fall by releasing hold of. **2.** To let fall in drops. **3.** To cause to become less; reduce: *drop the rate of production.* **4.** To cause to fall, as by hitting or shooting. **5.** *Sports.* To hurl or strike (a ball) into a basket or hole. **6.** To give birth to. Used of animals. **7.** To say or offer casually: *drop a hint.* **8.** To write at one's leisure: *drop me a note.* **9.** To cease consideration or treatment of: *dropped the matter altogether.* **10.** To terminate an association or a relationship with. See Synonyms at **dismiss. 11.** To leave unfinished: *drop everything and help.* **12.** To leave out (a letter, for example) in speaking or writing. **13.** To leave or set down at a particular place; unload. **14.** To parachute. **15.** To lower the level of (the voice). **16.** To lose (a game or contest, for example). **17.** *Slang.* To take, as a drug, by mouth: *drop acid.* **18.** *New England.* To poach (an egg). ***—phrasal verbs.* drop behind.** To fall behind: *dropped behind the rest of the class during her long illness.* **drop by.** To stop in for a short visit. **drop off. 1.** To fall asleep. **2.** To decrease: *Sales dropped off in the fourth quarter.* **drop out. 1.** To withdraw from participation, as in a game, club, or school. **2.** To withdraw from established society, especially because of disillusion with conventional values. ***—idiom.* get** (or **have**) **the drop on.** To achieve a distinct advantage over. [Middle English *droppe,* from Old English *dropa.* See **dhreu-** in Appendix.]

drop cloth *n.* A sheet, as of cloth or plastic, for protection against spills or dripping, used especially by painters.

drop curtain *n.* **1.** An unframed curtain that is lowered to a stage from the flies, often serving as background scenery. **2.** A theater curtain that is lowered or raised vertically rather than drawn to the side.

drop-dead (drŏp′dĕd′) *adj. Slang.* Very impressive; spectacular: *"a special video of the best-dressed women making drop-dead, knockout entrances at parties and fashion shows in Paris and New York"* (André Leon Talley).

drop·forge (drŏp′fôrj′, -fōrj′) *tr.v.* **-forged, -forg·ing, -forg·es.** To forge or stamp (a metal) between dies by the force of a falling weight such as a drop hammer.

drop hammer *n.* A machine consisting of an anvil or base aligned with a hammer that is raised and then dropped on molten metal, used to forge or stamp the metal resting on the anvil.

drop-in (drŏp′ĭn′) *n.* **1.** One who casually drops in, as to visit or obtain an appointment. **2.** An informal social event.

drop kick *n. Football.* A kick made by dropping the ball to the ground and kicking it just as it starts to rebound. **—drop′-kick′** (drŏp′kĭk′) *v.*

drop leaf *n.* A hinged wing on a table that can be folded down when not in use.

drop·let (drŏp′lĭt) *n.* A tiny drop.

droplet infection *n.* An infection transmitted from one individual to another by droplets of moisture expelled from the upper respiratory tract through sneezing or coughing.

drop letter *n.* A letter that is mailed and delivered from the same post office.

drop·light (drŏp′līt′) *n.* A hanging lamp that can be lowered and raised on its cord.

drop-off (drŏp′ôf′, -ŏf′) *n.* **1.** A steep or abrupt downward slope. **2.** A noticeable decrease: *a drop-off in attendance.*

drop·out (drŏp′out′) *n.* **1.a.** One who quits school. **b.** One who has withdrawn from a given social group or environment. **2.** *Computer Science.* **a.** A segment of magnetic tape on which expected information is absent. **b.** The failure to read a bit of stored information.

drop·per (drŏp′ər) *n.* One that drops, especially a small tube with a suction bulb at one end for drawing in a liquid and releasing it in drops.

drop·ping (drŏp′ĭng) *n.* **1.** Something dropped. **2. droppings.** The excrement of animals.

drop shot *n. Sports.* A shot in various racquet games in which a ball or shuttlecock drops quickly after crossing the net or hitting the wall.

drop·sy (drŏp′sē) *n.* Edema. No longer in scientific use. [Middle English *dropesie,* short for *idropesie,* from Old French *ydropisie,* from Medieval Latin *ydrōpisia,* from Latin *hydrōpisis,* from Greek *hudrōpiasis,* from *hudrōps,* dropsy, a dropsical person, from *hudōr,* water. See **wed-[1]** in Appendix.] **—drop′si·cal** (-sĭ-kəl) *adj.* **—drop′si·cal·ly** *adv.*

drop·wort (drŏp′wôrt′, -wûrt′) *n.* A Eurasian plant *(Filipendula vulgaris,* formerly *F. hexapetala)* having finely divided leaflets and clusters of small white flowers.

dros·er·a (drŏs′ər-ə) *n.* See **sundew.** [Greek, feminine of *droseros,* dewy, from *drosos,* dew.]

drosh·ky (drŏsh′kē) also **dros·ky** (drŏs′-) *n., pl.* **-kies** also **-kys.** An open four-wheeled horse-drawn carriage formerly used in Russia and Poland. [Russian *drozhki,* diminutive of *drogi,* wagon, plural of *droga,* shaft of a wagon.]

dro·soph·i·la (drō-sŏf′ə-lə, drə-) *n.* Any of various small fruit flies of the genus *Drosophila,* especially *D. melanogaster,* used extensively in genetic research. [New Latin *Drosophila,* genus name : Greek *drosos,* dew + New Latin *-phila,* pl. of *-philus,* -phile; see -PHILE.]

dross (drŏs, drôs) *n.* **1.** A waste product or an impurity, especially an oxide, formed on the surface of molten metal. **2.** Worthless, commonplace, or trivial matter: *"He was wide-awake and his mind worked clearly, purged of all dross"* (Vladimir Nabokov). [Middle English *dros,* from Old English *drōs,* dregs.] **—dross′y** *adj.*

drought (drout) also **drouth** (drouth) *n.* **1.** A long period of abnormally low rainfall, especially one that adversely affects growing or living conditions. **2.** A prolonged dearth or shortage. [Middle English, from Old English *drūgoth.*] **—drought′y** *adj.*

drove[1] (drōv) *v.* Past tense of **drive.**

drove[2] (drōv) *n.* **1.** A flock or herd being driven in a body. **2.a.** A large mass of people moving or acting as a body. **b.** A large body of like things. See Synonyms at **flock[1]. 3.a.** A stonemason's broad-edged chisel used for rough hewing. **b.** A stone surface dressed with such a chisel. [Middle English, from Old English *drāf,* from *drīfan,* to drive. See **dhreibh-** in Appendix.]

drov·er (drō′vər) *n.* One that drives cattle or sheep.

drown (droun) *v.* **drowned, drown·ing, drowns.** *—tr.* **1.** To kill by submerging and suffocating in water or another liquid. **2.** To drench thoroughly or cover with or as if with a liquid. **3.** To deaden one's awareness of; blot out: *people who drowned their troubles in drink.* **4.** To muffle or mask (a sound) by a louder sound: *screams that were drowned out by the passing train.* *—intr.* To die by suffocating in water or another liquid. [Middle English *drounen,* probably of Scandinavian origin. See **dhreg-** in Appendix.]

drowse (drouz) *v.* **drowsed, drows·ing, drows·es.** *—intr.* To be half-asleep: *drowsed in the warm sun.* *—tr.* **1.** To make drowsy: *"drowsed with the fume of poppies"* (John Keats). **2.** To pass (time) by drowsing. **—drowse** *n.* The condition of being sleepy. [Perhaps ultimately from Old English *drūsian,* to sink, be sluggish. See **dhreu-** in Appendix.]

drows·y (drou′zē) *adj.* **-i·er, -i·est. 1.** Dull with sleepiness; sluggish. **2.** Produced or characterized by sleepiness. **3.** Inducing sleepiness; soporific. **—drows′i·ly** *adv.* **—drows′i·ness** *n.*

dr t *abbr.* Troy dram.

drub (drŭb) *v.* **drubbed, drub·bing, drubs.** *—tr.* **1.** To thrash with a stick. **2.** To instill forcefully: *drubbed the lesson into my head.* **3.a.** To defeat emphatically. **b.** To berate harshly. **4.** To stamp (the feet). *—intr.* **1.** To beat the ground; stamp. **2.** To pound; throb. **—drub** *n.* A blow with a heavy instrument, such as a stick. [Perhaps Arabic *ḍaraba,* to beat.] **—drub′ber** *n.*

drub·bing (drŭb′ĭng) *n.* **1.** A severe thrashing. **2.** A total defeat.

drudge[1] (drŭj) *n.* A person who does tedious, menial, or unpleasant work. **—drudge** *intr.v.* **drudged, drudg·ing, drudg·es.** To do tedious, unpleasant, or menial work. [From Middle English *druggen,* to labor; akin to Old English *drēogan,* to work, suffer.] **—drudg′er** *n.* **—drudg′ing·ly** *adv.*

♦**drudge[2]** (drŭj) *n. & v. Chesapeake Bay.* Variant of **dredge[1].**

♦***REGIONAL NOTE:*** "Out here on the Chesapeake, they call it 'drudging for arsters,'" says Charles Kuralt in his book *On the Road with Charles Kuralt.* The Standard English verb *dredge* is pronounced with a centralized vowel by Chesapeake Bay oyster fishermen, yielding *drudge. Drudge* in turn has been picked up by city dwellers on the Delmarva Peninsula; a survey of some young people from Baltimore revealed that they did not even know that there was a Standard English verb *dredge.* Kuralt gives the regional pronunciation a whimsical folk etymology with the standard meaning of *drudge,* "to do tedious, menial, or unpleasant work," observing, "Whatever you do for a living, it's not as hard as 'drudging for arsters.'"

drudg·er·y (drŭj′ə-rē) *n., pl.* **-ies.** Tedious, menial, or unpleasant work. See Synonyms at **work.**

drudge·work (drŭj′wûrk′) *n.* Drudgery: *"This account . . . of decades of drudgework amid others' possessions is drudgework for the reader as well"* (New Yorker).

drug (drŭg) *n.* **1.a.** A substance used in the diagnosis, treatment, or prevention of a disease or as a component of a medication. **b.** Such a substance as recognized or defined by the U.S. Food, Drug, and Cosmetic Act. **2.** A chemical substance, such as a narcotic or hallucinogen, that affects the central nervous system, causing changes in behavior and often addiction. **3.** *Obsolete.* A chemical or dye. **—drug** *tr.v.* **drugged, drug·ging, drugs. 1.** To administer a drug to. **2.** To poison or mix (food or drink) with a drug. **3.** To stupefy or dull with or as if with a drug: *drugged with sleep.* [Middle English *drogge,* from Old French *drogue,* drug, perhaps from Middle Dutch *droge (vate),* dry (cases), pl. of *drog,* dry.]

drug·get (drŭg′ĭt) *n.* **1.a.** A heavy felted fabric of wool or wool and cotton, used as a floor covering. **b.** A coarse rug of this fabric, made in India. **2.** A fabric woven wholly or partly of wool, formerly used for clothing. [French *droguet,* probably from *drogue,* drug, worthless object. See DRUG.]

drop leaf
Mid to late 18th-century American drop leaf table

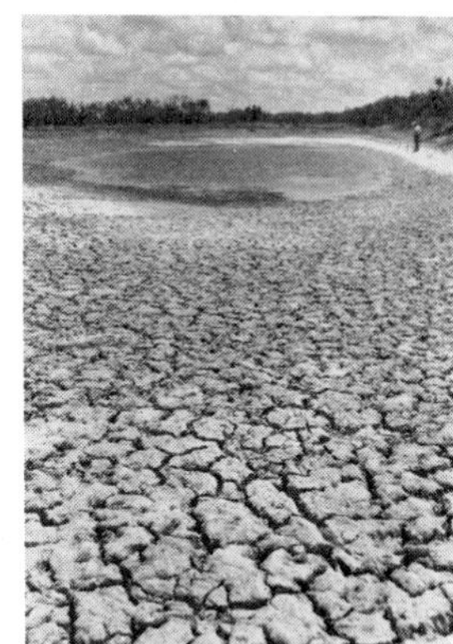

drought

ă pat	oi boy
ā pay	ou out
âr care	ŏŏ took
ä father	ōō boot
ĕ pet	ŭ cut
ē be	ûr urge
ĭ pit	th thin
ī pie	*th* this
îr pier	hw which
ŏ pot	zh vision
ō toe	ə about, item
ô paw	♦ regionalism

Stress marks: ′ (primary); ′ (secondary), as in **dictionary** (dĭk′shə-nĕr′ē)

drug·gie also **drug·gy** (drŭg′ē) *n., pl.* **-gies.** *Slang.* One that takes or is addicted to drugs: *"They're like druggies, but without drugs; they're drugged on their own apathy"* (Pauline Kael).

drug·gist (drŭg′ĭst) *n.* **1.** A pharmacist. **2.** One who sells drugs.

drug·gy[1] (drŭg′ē) *Slang. adj.* **-gi·er, -gi·est.** Of or relating to drugs: *"boozy, druggy confessions"* (Vincent Canby).

drug·gy[2] (drŭg′ē) *n.* Variant of **druggie.**

drug·o·la (drŭg-ō′lə) *n. Slang.* Bribery with payment or kickbacks made by using illegal drugs as the medium of exchange. [DRUG + (PAY)OLA.]

drug·store also **drug store** (drŭg′stôr′, -stōr′) *n.* A store where prescriptions are filled and drugs and other articles are sold.

dru·id also **Dru·id** (dro͞o′ĭd) *n.* A member of an order of priests in ancient Gaul and Britain who appear in Welsh and Irish legend as prophets and sorcerers. [From Latin *druidēs,* druids, of Celtic origin. See **deru-** in Appendix.] **—dru·id′ic** (dro͞o-ĭd′ĭk), **dru·id′i·cal** (-ĭ-kəl) *adj.* **—dru′id·ism** *n.*

drum (drŭm) *n.* **1.** *Music.* **a.** A percussion instrument consisting of a hollow cylinder or hemisphere with a membrane stretched tightly over one or both ends, played by beating with the hands or sticks. **b.** A sound produced by this instrument. **2.** Something resembling a drum in shape or structure, especially a barrellike metal container or a metal cylinder wound with cable, wire, or heavy rope. **3.** Any of various marine and freshwater fishes of the family Sciaenidae that make a drumming sound. **4.** *Anatomy.* The eardrum. **—drum** *v.* **drummed, drum·ming, drums.** *—intr.* **1.** To play a drum or drums. **2.** To thump or tap rhythmically or continually: *nervously drummed on the table.* **3.** To produce a booming, reverberating sound by beating the wings, as certain birds do. *—tr.* **1.** To perform (a piece or tune) on or as if on a drum. **2.** To summon by or as if by beating a drum. **3.** To make known to or force upon (a person) by constant repetition: *drummed the answers into my head.* **4.** To expel or dismiss in disgrace: *was drummed out of the army.* **—*phrasal verb.* drum up. 1.** To bring about by continuous, persistent effort: *drum up new business.* **2.** To devise; invent: *drummed up an alibi.* [Middle English *drom,* from Middle Dutch *tromme,* probably of imitative origin.]

drum·beat (drŭm′bēt′) *n.* **1.** The sound produced by beating a drum. **2.** A cause supported ardently and vehemently.

drum·beat·er (drŭm′bē′tər) *n.* One that supports a cause, especially vehemently. **—drum′beat′ing** *n.*

drum·ette (drŭm-ĕt′) *n.* The small fleshy part of a chicken wing, often fried and served as an appetizer.

drum·fire (drŭm′fīr′) *n.* **1.** Heavy, continuous gunfire: *a barrage of drumfire.* **2.** Something likened to continuous gunfire: *a drumfire of criticism.*

drum·head (drŭm′hĕd′) *n.* **1.** *Music.* The membrane stretched over the open end of a drum. **2.** *Nautical.* The circular top part of a capstan, used to hold bars for turning.

drumhead court-martial *n.* A court-martial held for the summary trial of an offense committed during military operations. [So called because it was sometimes held around a drumhead.]

drum·lin (drŭm′lĭn) *n.* An elongated hill or ridge of glacial drift. [From *drum,* ridge, from Irish Gaelic *druim,* back, ridge, from Old Irish.]

drum major *n.* A man who leads a marching band or drum corps, often twirling a baton.

drum majorette *n.* A woman who leads a marching band or drum corps, often twirling a baton. See Usage Note at **-ette.**

drum memory *n. Computer Science.* A memory device consisting of a rotating metal cylinder with a magnetizable coating on its outer surface, usually used as a nonprogrammable random-access memory.

drum·mer (drŭm′ər) *n. Music.* One who plays a drum, as in a band.

Drum·mond·ville (drŭm′ənd-vĭl′). A city of southern Quebec, Canada, northeast of Montreal. It is an industrial center. Population, 27,374.

drum printer *n.* A line printer in which a revolving cylinder acts as the printing element.

drum·stick (drŭm′stĭk′) *n.* **1.** *Music.* A stick for beating a drum. **2.** The lower part of the leg of a cooked fowl.

drunk (drŭngk) *v.* Past participle of **drink. —drunk** *adj. Usage Problem.* **1.a.** Intoxicated with alcoholic liquor to the point of impairment of physical and mental faculties. **b.** Caused or influenced by intoxication. **2.** Overcome by strong feeling or emotion: *drunk with power.* **—drunk** *n.* **1.** A drunkard. **2.** A bout of drinking.

USAGE NOTE: As an adjective the form *drunk* is used predicatively while the form *drunken* is now used only attributively: *He was drunk last night. A drunken man at the table beside us ruined our evening.* In most contexts the attributive use of *drunk* is considered unacceptable in formal style. But the phrases *drunk driver* and *drunk driving* are supported not only by common usage but also, in many jurisdictions, by a legal distinction between the expressions *drunk driver* (a driver whose alcohol level exceeds the legal limit) and *drunken driver* (a driver who is inebriated).

drunk·ard (drŭng′kərd) *n.* One who is habitually drunk.

drunk·en (drŭng′kən) *adj. Usage Problem.* **1.** Delirious with or as if with strong drink; intoxicated. **2.** Habitually drunk. **3.** Of, involving, or occurring during intoxication: *a drunken brawl.* See Usage Note at **drunk. —drunk′en·ly** *adv.* **—drunk′en·ness** *n.*

dru·pa·ceous (dro͞o-pā′shəs) *adj.* **1.** Resembling, relating to, or consisting of a drupe: *drupaceous fruit.* **2.** Producing drupes: *a drupaceous tree.*

drupe (dro͞op) *n.* A fleshy fruit, such as a peach, plum, or cherry, usually having a single hard stone that encloses a seed. Also called *stone fruit.* [Latin *drūpa, druppa,* overripe olive, from Greek, olive, possibly an alteration of *drupepēs,* ripened on the tree : *dru-,* tree; see **deru-** in Appendix + *peptein, pep-,* ripe; see **pek**^{w}**-** in Appendix.]

drupe·let (dro͞op′lĭt) *n.* A small drupe, such as one of the many subdivisions of a raspberry or blackberry.

druse (dro͞oz) *n.* A crust of tiny crystals lining a rock cavity, usually composed of the same minerals that occur in the rock. [German *Druse,* weathered ore, probably from Middle High German *druos,* gland, tumor.]

Druse (dro͞oz) *n.* Variant of **Druze.**

Dru·sus (dro͞o′səs), **Nero Claudius.** Known as "Drusus Senior." 38–9 B.C. Roman general who sought to impose Roman rule on the Germanic tribes.

druth·ers (drŭ*th*′ərz) *pl.n. Informal.* A choice or preference: *"Given their druthers, these hell-for-leather free marketeers might sell the post office"* (George F. Will). [Alteration of the phrase *'d rather,* from *would rather.*]

Druze also **Druse** (dro͞oz) *n.* A member of a Syrian people following a religion marked by monotheism and a belief in al-Hakim (985–1021), an Ismaili caliph, as the embodiment of God. [Arabic *Durūz,* pl. of *durzī,* a Druse, after Ismail al-*Darazi* (died c. 1019), Moslem religious leader.]

dry (drī) *adj.* **dri·er, dri·est** or **dry·er, dry·est. 1.** Free from liquid or moisture: *changed to dry clothes.* **2.** Having or characterized by little or no rain: *a dry climate.* **3.** Marked by the absence of natural or normal moisture: *a dry month.* **4.** Not under water: *dry land.* **5.** Having all the water or liquid drained away, evaporated, or exhausted: *a dry river.* **6.** No longer yielding liquid, especially milk: *a dry cow.* **7.** Lacking a mucous or watery discharge: *a dry cough.* **8.** Not shedding tears: *dry sobs.* **9.** Needing or desiring drink; thirsty: *a dry mouth.* **10.** No longer wet: *The paint is dry.* **11.** Of or relating to solid rather than liquid substances or commodities: *dry weight.* **12.** Not sweet as a result of the decomposition of sugar during fermentation. Used of wines. **13.** Having a large proportion of strong liquor to other ingredients: *a dry martini.* **14.** Eaten or served without butter, gravy, or other garnish: *dry toast; dry meat.* **15.** Having no adornment or coloration; plain: *the dry facts.* **16.** Devoid of bias or personal concern: *presented us with a dry critique.* **17.a.** Lacking tenderness, warmth, or involvement; severe: *The actor gave a dry reading of the lines.* **b.** Matter-of-fact or indifferent in manner: *rattled off the facts in a dry mechanical tone.* **18.** Wearisome; dull: *a dry lecture filled with trivial details.* **19.** Humorous or sarcastic in a shrewd, impersonal way: *dry wit.* **20.** Prohibiting or opposed to the sale or consumption of alcoholic beverages: *a dry county.* **21.** Unproductive of the expected results: *a mind dry of new ideas.* **22.** Constructed without mortar or cement: *dry masonry.* **—dry** *v.* **dried** (drīd), **dry·ing, dries** (drīz). *—tr.* **1.** To remove the moisture from; make dry: *laundry dried by the sun.* **2.** To preserve (meat or other foods, for example) by extracting the moisture. *—intr.* To become dry: *The sheets dried quickly in the sun.* **—dry** *n., pl.* **drys.** *Informal.* A prohibitionist. **—*phrasal verbs.* dry out.** *Informal.* To undergo a cure for alcoholism. **dry up. 1.** To make or become unproductive, especially to do so gradually. **2.** *Informal.* To stop talking. [Middle English *drie,* from Old English *drȳge.*] **—dry′ly, dri′ly** *adv.* **—dry′ness** *n.*

SYNONYMS: *dry, dehydrate, desiccate, parch.* The central meaning shared by these verbs is "to remove the moisture from": *drying the dishes; add water to dehydrated eggs; a factory where coconut meat is shredded and desiccated; land parched by the sun.* See also Synonyms at **sour.**
ANTONYM: *moisten.*

dry·ad (drī′əd, -ăd′) *n. Greek Mythology.* A divinity presiding over forests and trees; a wood nymph. [Middle English *Driad,* from Latin *Dryas, Dryad-,* from Greek *Druas,* from *drus,* tree. See **deru-** in Appendix.] **—dry·ad′ic** (-ăd′ĭk) *adj.*

dry·as·dust (drī′əz-dŭst′) *n.* A dull, pedantic speaker or writer. [After Dr. Jonas *Dryasdust,* a fictitious character to whom Sir Walter Scott dedicated some of his novels.] **—dry′as·dust′** *adj.*

dry cell *n.* A voltage-generating cell having an electrolyte in the form of moist paste. [So called because its contents cannot spill.]

dry-clean (drī′klēn′) *tr.v.* **-cleaned, -clean·ing, -cleans.** To clean (clothing or fabrics) with chemical solvents that have little or no water. **—dry cleaner** *n.* **—dry clean′ing** (klē′nĭng) *n.*

Dry·den (drīd′n), **John.** 1631–1700. English writer and poet laureate (after 1668). The outstanding literary figure of the Restoration, he wrote critical essays, poems, such as *Absalom and Achitophel* (1681), and dramas, including *All for Love* (1678).

dry dock *n. Nautical.* A large dock in the form of a basin from which the water can be emptied, used for building or repairing a ship below its water line.

dry-dock (drīʹdŏkʹ) *tr. & intr.v.* **-docked, -dock·ing, -docks.** *Nautical.* To place in or go into a dry dock.

dry·er (drīʹər) *n.* **1.** An appliance that removes moisture by heating or another process: *a clothes dryer; a hair dryer.* **2.** Variant of **drier**[1].

dry farm·ing (färʹmĭng) *n.* A type of farming practiced in arid areas without irrigation by planting drought-resistant crops and maintaining a fine surface tilth or mulch that protects the natural moisture of the soil from evaporation. **—dry farm** *n.* **—dryʹ-farmʹ** (drīʹfärmʹ) *v.* **—dry farmer** *n.*

dry fly *n.* An artificial fly used in fishing that floats on the surface of the water when cast.

dry gangrene *n.* Gangrene that develops as a result of arterial obstruction and is characterized by mummification of the dead tissue and absence of bacterial decomposition.

dry goods *pl.n.* Textiles, clothing, and related articles of trade. Also called *soft goods.*

dry hole *n.* An unsuccessful venture, especially an exploratory oil well that produces no oil.

dry ice *n.* Solid carbon dioxide that sublimates at −78.5°C (−110°F) and is used primarily as a coolant.

dry·ing oil (drīʹĭng) *n.* An organic oil, such as linseed oil, used as a binder in paints and varnishes. It dries into a tough elastic layer when applied in a thin film and exposed to air.

dry kiln *n.* A heated chamber in which cut lumber is dried and seasoned.

dry measure *n.* A system of units for measuring dry commodities such as grains, fruits, and vegetables.

dry mop *n.* See **dust mop.**

dry nurse *n.* A nurse employed to care for but not breast-feed an infant. **—dryʹ-nurseʹ** (drīʹnûrsʹ) *v.*

dry·o·pith·e·cine (drīʹō-pĭthʹĭ-sēnʹ) *n.* An extinct ape of the genus *Dryopithecus,* known from Old World fossil remains of the Miocene and Pliocene epochs and believed to be an ancestor of the anthropoid apes and human beings. **—dryopithecine** *adj.* Of or belonging to the genus *Dryopithecus.* [From New Latin *Dryopithēcus,* genus name : Greek *drus,* oak; see **deru-** in Appendix + Greek *pithēkos,* ape.]

dry point *n.* **1.** A technique of intaglio engraving in which a hard steel needle is used to incise lines in a metal, usually copper plate, with the rough burr at the sides of the incised lines often retained to produce a velvety black tone in the print. **2.** An engraving or print made using this technique.

dry rot *n.* **1.** A fungous disease that causes timber to become brittle and crumble into powder. **2.** A plant disease in which the plant tissue remains relatively dry while fungi invade and ultimately decay bulbs, fruits, or woody tissues.

dry run *n.* **1.** A trial exercise; a rehearsal. **2.** A test exercise in combat skills without the use of live ammunition.

dry-salt·er (drīʹsôlʹtər) *n. Chiefly British.* A dealer in chemical products and dyes. **—dryʹsaltʹer·y** *n.*

dry socket *n.* A painful inflamed condition at the site of extraction of a tooth that occurs when a blood clot fails to form properly or is dislodged.

Dry Tor·tu·gas (drī tôr-tōōʹgəz). An island group of southern Florida west of Key West. Famed for their marine life, the islands were named *Tortugas* ("turtles") by the Spanish explorer Juan Ponce de León in 1513.

dry wall or **dry·wall** (drīʹwôlʹ) *n.* **1.a.** Plasterboard. **b.** A wall or ceiling constructed of a prefabricated material, such as plasterboard or paneling. **2.** A wall constructed from rocks that are not cemented together.

dry wash *n.* Laundry that has been washed and dried but not ironed.

dry well also **dry·well** (drīʹwĕlʹ) *n.* A subterranean chamber near a building, having stones or gravel inside and used to collect rainwater runoff from the roof of the building as a means of avoiding soil erosion.

DS *abbr. Computer Science.* Data set.

d.s. *abbr.* **1.** Also **D.S.** *Music.* Dal segno. **2.** *Business.* Days after sight. **3.** Document signed.

DSC or **D.S.C.** *abbr.* Distinguished Service Cross.

DSM or **D.S.M.** *abbr.* Distinguished Service Medal.

DSO or **D.S.O.** *abbr.* Distinguished Service Order.

d.s.p. *abbr. Latin.* Decessit sine prole (died without issue).

DST or **D.S.T.** *abbr.* Daylight-saving time.

DT or **D.T.** *abbr.* Daylight time.

Dt. *abbr. Bible.* Deuteronomy.

d.t. *abbr.* Double time.

D.T. *abbr.* Doctor of Theology.

D.T.'s or **d.t.'s** (dēʹtēzʹ) *n. (used with a sing. or pl. verb).* Delirium tremens.

Du. *abbr.* **1.** Duke. **2.** Dutch.

du·ad (dōōʹădʹ, dyōōʹ-) *n.* A unit of two objects; a pair. [Greek *duas, duad-,* two, from *duo.* See **dwo-** in Appendix.]

du·al (dōōʹəl, dyōōʹ-) *adj.* **1.** Composed of two usually like or complementary parts; double: *dual controls for pilot and copilot; a car with dual exhaust pipes.* **2.** Having a double character or purpose: *a belief in the dual nature of reality.* **3.** *Grammar.* Of, relating to, or being a number category that indicates two persons or things, as in Greek, Sanskrit, and Old English. **—dual** *n. Grammar.* **1.** The dual number. **2.** An inflected form of a noun, adjective, pronoun, or verb used with two items or people. [Latin *duālis,* from *duo,* two. See **dwo-** in Appendix.] **—duʹal·ly** *adv.*

Du·a·la (dōō-äʹlə). See **Douala.**

du·al·ism (dōōʹə-lĭzʹəm, dyōōʹ-) *n.* **1.** The condition of being double; duality. **2.** *Philosophy.* The view that the world consists of or is explicable as two fundamental entities, such as mind and matter. **3.** *Psychology.* The view that the mind and body function separately, without interchange. **4.** *Theology.* **a.** The concept that the world is ruled by the antagonistic forces of good and evil. **b.** The concept that human beings have two basic natures, the physical and the spiritual. **—duʹal·ist** *n.* **—duʹal·isʹtic** *adj.* **—duʹal·isʹti·cal·ly** *adv.*

du·al·i·ty (dōō-ălʹĭ-tē, dyōō-) *n.* The quality or character of being twofold; dichotomy.

du·al-pur·pose (dōōʹəl-pûrʹpəs, dyōōʹ-) *adj.* Designed for or serving two purposes: *dual-purpose technologies for commercial and military applications.*

Duar·te (dwärʹtē). A city of southern California east of Pasadena. It is mainly residential with varied light industries. Population, 16,766.

dub[1] (dŭb) *tr.v.* **dubbed, dub·bing, dubs. 1.** To tap lightly on the shoulder by way of conferring knighthood. **2.** To honor with a new title or description. **3.** To give a name to facetiously or playfully; nickname. **4.** To strike, cut, or rub (timber or leather, for example) so as to make even or smooth. **5.** To dress (a fowl). **6.** To execute (a golf stroke, for example) poorly. **—dub** *n.* An awkward person or player; a bungler. [Middle English *dubben,* from Old English *dubbian,* perhaps from Old French *aduber.*]

dub[2] (dŭb) *v.* **dubbed, dub·bing, dubs.** —*tr.* **1.** To thrust at; poke. **2.** To beat (a drum). —*intr.* **1.** To make a thrust. **2.** To beat on a drum. **—dub** *n.* **1.** The act of dubbing. **2.** A drumbeat. [Perhaps from Low German *dubben,* to hit, strike.]

dub[3] (dŭb) *tr.v.* **dubbed, dub·bing, dubs. 1.a.** To transfer (recorded material) onto a new recording medium. **b.** To copy (a record or tape). **2.** To insert a new sound track, often a synchronized translation of the original dialogue, into (a film). **3.** To add (sound) into a film or tape: *dub in strings behind the vocal.* **—dub** *n.* **1.** The new sounds added by dubbing. **2.** A dubbed copy of a tape or record. [Short for DOUBLE.] **—dubʹber** *n.*

dub[4] (dŭb) *n. Scots.* A puddle or small pool. [Origin unknown.]

Du·bai (dōō-bīʹ). A city and sheikdom of eastern United Arab Emirates on the Persian Gulf. Oil was discovered here in the 1960's. Population, 265,702.

Du Bar·ry (dōō bărʹē, dyōō-, dü bä-rēʹ), Comtesse. Title of Marie Jeanne Bécu. 1743–1793. French courtier and influential mistress of Louis XV. She was guillotined for crimes against the state by a Revolutionary tribunal.

Du·bawnt (dōō-bôntʹ). A river, about 933 km (580 mi) long, of southeast Northwest Territories, Canada, flowing through **Dubawnt Lake** and into Baker Lake.

dub·bin (dŭbʹĭn) also **dub·bing** (-ĭng) *n.* An application of tallow and oil for dressing leather. [From DUB[1].]

Dub·ček (dōōbʹchĕk, dōōpʹ-), **Alexander.** Born 1921. Czechoslovakian politician. As first secretary of the Communist Party (1968) he introduced reforms and pursued an independent foreign policy. In August 1968 Soviet authorities sent tanks into Prague and arrested Dubček, who was forced to resign.

du Bel·lay (dōō bə-lāʹ, dü bĕ-lāʹ), **Joachim.** See Joachim du **Bellay.**

du·bi·e·ty (dōō-bīʹĭ-tē, dyōō-) *n., pl.* **-ties. 1.** A feeling of doubt that often results in wavering. See Synonyms at **uncertainty. 2.** A matter of doubt. [Late Latin *dubietās,* from Latin *dubius,* doubtful. See DUBIOUS.]

Du·bin·sky (dōō-bĭnʹskē), **David.** 1892–1982. Russian-born American labor leader who was president of the International Ladies' Garment Workers Union (1932–1966).

du·bi·ous (dōōʹbē-əs, dyōōʹ-) *adj.* **1.** Fraught with uncertainty or doubt; undecided. **2.** Arousing doubt; doubtful: *a dubious distinction.* **3.** Of questionable character: *dubious profits.* See Synonyms at **doubtful.** [From Latin *dubius.* See **dwo-** in Appendix.] **—duʹbi·ous·ly** *adv.* **—duʹbi·ous·ness** *n.*

du·bi·ta·ble (dōōʹbĭ-tə-bəl, dyōōʹ-) *adj.* Subject to doubt or question; uncertain. [Latin *dubitābilis,* from *dubitāre,* to doubt. See DOUBT.] **—duʹbi·ta·bly** *adv.*

Dub·lin (dŭbʹlĭn). **1.** The capital and largest city of Ireland, in the east-central part of the country on the Irish Sea. A Danish stronghold until 1014, Dublin was the scene of the Black Monday massacre of English residents in 1209 and the bloody Easter Rebellion of April 24, 1916. The Sinn Fein movement began here in the early 20th century. Population, 525,882. **2.** A city of central Georgia east-southeast of Macon. It is a commercial center in a lumbering area. Population, 16,083. **—Dubʹlin·er** *n.*

Du Bois (dōō boisʹ), **William Edward Burghardt.** 1868–1963. American civil rights leader who cofounded the NAACP, edited journals, such as *Crisis* (1910–1932), and wrote books, including *Color and Democracy* (1945), that promoted the concerns of Black Americans and Africans.

dry dock
U.S.S. *Iowa* in dry dock

Madame du Barry

W.E.B. Du Bois

ă pat	oi boy
ā pay	ou out
âr care	ŏŏ took
ä father	ōō boot
ĕ pet	ŭ cut
ē be	ûr urge
ĭ pit	th thin
ī pie	*th* this
îr pier	hw which
ŏ pot	zh vision
ō toe	ə about, item
ô paw	♦ regionalism

Stress marks: ʹ (primary); ʹ (secondary), as in **dictionary** (dĭkʹshə-nĕrʹē)

Du·bon·net (do͞o′bə-nā′, dyo͞o′-). A trademark used for apéritif wines.

Du·bos (do͞o-bôs′, -bō′, dü-), **René Jules.** 1901–1982. French-born American bacteriologist noted for his research on natural antibiotics, tuberculosis, and environmental factors in disease.

Du·brov·nik (do͞o′brôv-nĭk′). Formerly **Ra·gu·sa** (rə-go͞o′zə, rä-go͞o′zä). A city of southwest Yugoslavia on a promontory jutting into the Adriatic Sea. A popular tourist resort, it was a center of Serbo-Croatian culture and literature in medieval times. Population, 31,106.

Du·buf·fet (do͞o-bə-fā′, dü-bü-fĕ′), **Jean.** Born 1901. French artist who developed *art brut,* "raw art," to express the vitality and immediacy absent from some academic art.

Du·buque (də-byo͞ok′). A city of eastern Iowa on the Mississippi River opposite the Illinois-Wisconsin border. It was first settled permanently in 1833 and is the oldest city in the state. Population, 62,321.

du·cal (do͞o′kəl, dyo͞o′-) *adj.* Of or relating to a duke or dukedom: *a ducal estate.* [Middle English, from Old French, from Late Latin *ducālis,* from Latin *dux, duc-,* leader. See DUKE.] **—du′cal·ly** *adv.*

duc·at (dŭk′ət) *n.* **1.** Any of various gold coins formerly used in certain European countries. **2.** *Slang.* **a.** A piece of money. **b.** An admission ticket. [Middle English, from Old French, from Old Italian *ducato,* from Medieval Latin *ducātus,* duchy (a word used on one of the early ducats). See DUCHY.]

du·ce (do͞o′chā) *n.* A leader or commander; a chief. [Italian, from Latin *dux, duc-.* See DUKE.]

Du·champ (do͞o-shäɴ′, dü), **Marcel.** 1887–1968. French-born modernist artist and a leader of the Dada movement in New York City who was the first to exhibit commonplace objects as art. His paintings include *Nude Descending a Staircase* (1912).

Du·chenne's muscular dystrophy (do͞o-shĕnz′) *n.* The most common form of muscular dystrophy, in which fat and fibrous tissue infiltrate muscle tissue, causing eventual weakening of the respiratory muscles and the myocardium. The disease, which almost exclusively affects males, begins in early childhood and usually causes death before adulthood. [After Guillaume B.A. *Duchenne* (1806–1875), French physician.]

duch·ess (dŭch′ĭs) *n. Abbr.* **D. 1.** The wife or widow of a duke. **2.** A woman holding title to a duchy in her own right. **3.** Used as the title for such a noblewoman. [Middle English *duchesse,* from Old French, from Medieval Latin *ducissa,* from Latin *dux, duc-,* leader. See DUKE.]

duch·y (dŭch′ē) *n., pl.* **-ies.** The territory ruled by a duke or duchess; a dukedom. [Middle English *duchie,* from Old French *duche,* from Medieval Latin *ducātus,* from Latin *dux, duc-,* leader. See DUKE.]

duck[1]

duck[1] (dŭk) *n.* **1.** Any of various wild or domesticated swimming birds of the family Anatidae, characteristically having a broad, flat bill, short legs, and webbed feet. **2.** A female duck. **3.** The flesh of a duck used as food. **4.** *Slang.* A person, especially one thought of as peculiar. **5.** Often **ducks** *(used with a sing. verb). Chiefly British.* A dear. [Middle English *doke,* from Old English *dūce,* possibly from **dūcan,* to dive. See DUCK[2].]

duck[2] (dŭk) *v.* **ducked, duck·ing, ducks.** *—tr.* **1.** To lower quickly, especially so as to avoid something. **2.** To evade; dodge: *duck responsibility; ducked the reporter's question.* **3.** To push suddenly under water. See Synonyms at **dip. 4.** *Games.* To deliberately play a card that is lower than (an opponent's card). *—intr.* **1.** To lower the head or body. **2.** To move swiftly, especially so as to escape being seen: *ducked behind a bush.* **3.** To submerge the head or body briefly in water. **4.** To evade a responsibility or obligation. Often used with *out: duck out on one's family.* **5.** *Games.* To lose a trick by deliberately playing lower than one's opponent. **—duck** *n.* **1.** A quick lowering of the head or body. **2.** A plunge into water. [Middle English *douken,* to dive, possibly from Old English **dūcan;* akin to Middle Low German and Middle Dutch *dūken.*] **—duck′er** *n.*

duck[3] (dŭk) *n.* **1.** A durable, closely woven heavy cotton or linen fabric. **2. ducks.** Clothing made of duck, especially white trousers. [Dutch *doek,* cloth, from Middle Dutch *doec.*]

duck[4] (dŭk) *n.* **1.** An amphibious military truck used during World War II. **2.** An amphibious truck used in emergencies, as to evacuate flood victims. [Alteration (influenced by DUCK[1]) of *DUKW,* its code designation.]

duck·bill (dŭk′bĭl′) *n.* See **platypus.**

duck-billed platypus (dŭk′bĭld′) *n.* See **platypus.**

duck blind *n.* A shelter, often camouflaged with reeds and grasses, for concealing duck hunters.

duck·board (dŭk′bôrd′, -bōrd′) *n.* A board or boardwalk laid across wet or muddy ground or flooring.

duck hawk *n.* See **peregrine falcon.**

ducking stool

duck·ing stool (dŭk′ĭng) *n.* A device formerly used in Europe and New England for punishment, consisting of a chair in which an offender was tied and ducked into water.

duck·ling (dŭk′lĭng) *n.* A young duck.

duck·pin (dŭk′pĭn′) *n. Sports.* **1.** A bowling pin that is shorter and squatter than a tenpin. **2. duckpins** *(used with a sing. verb).* A bowling game played with such pins and a small ball. [From its squat appearance.]

ducks and drakes (dŭks) *n. Games.* The game of skipping flat stones along the surface of water. ***—idiom.* make ducks and drakes of** (or **play ducks and drakes with**). To squander; waste.

duck soup *n. Slang.* An easily accomplished task or assignment.

duck·tail (dŭk′tāl′) *n.* A hairstyle in which the hair is swept back at the sides to meet in an upturned point in back. Also called *DA.*

duck·weed (dŭk′wēd′) *n.* Any of various small, free-floating, stemless aquatic flowering plants of the genus *Lemna.*

duck·y (dŭk′ē) *adj.* **-i·er, -i·est.** *Slang.* Excellent; fine.

Du·com·mun (dü-kô-mœɴ′), **Élie.** 1833–1906. Swiss journalist who organized the International Bureau of Peace in Bern (1891). He shared the 1902 Nobel Peace Prize.

duct (dŭkt) *n.* **1.** An often enclosed passage or channel for conveying a substance, especially a liquid or gas. **2.** *Anatomy.* A tubular bodily canal or passage, especially one for carrying a glandular secretion: *a tear duct.* **3.** A tube or pipe for enclosing electrical cables or wires. **—duct** *tr.v.* **duct·ed, duct·ing, ducts. 1.** To channel through a duct: *duct the moist air away.* **2.** To supply with ducts. [Latin *ductus,* act of leading, from past participle of *dūcere,* to lead. See **deuk-** in Appendix.] **—duct′al** *adj.* **—duct′less** *adj.*

duc·tile (dŭk′təl, -tīl′) *adj.* **1.** Easily drawn into wire or hammered thin: *ductile metals.* **2.** Easily molded or shaped. See Synonyms at **malleable. 3.** Capable of being readily persuaded or influenced; tractable. [Middle English *ductil,* from Old French, from Latin *ductilis,* from *ductus,* past participle of *dūcere,* to lead. See **deuk-** in Appendix.] **—duc·til′i·ty** (-tĭl′ĭ-tē), **duc′ti·li·bil′i·ty** (-lə-bĭl′ĭ-tē) *n.*

duct·ing (dŭk′tĭng) *n.* **1.** A duct or system of ducts. **2.** Material for making ducts.

duct·less gland (dŭkt′lĭs) *n.* See **endocrine gland.**

duct·ule (dŭk′to͞ol′) *n.* A small duct.

duct·work (dŭkt′wûrk′) *n.* A group or system of ducts: *installed new ductwork in the building.*

dud (dŭd) *n.* **1.** A bomb, shell, or explosive round that fails to detonate. **2.** *Informal.* One that is disappointingly ineffective or unsuccessful. **3. duds.** *Informal.* **a.** Clothing. **b.** Personal belongings. [Middle English *dudde,* a cloak.]

dude (do͞od, dyo͞od) *n.* **1.** *Informal.* An Easterner or city person who vacations on a ranch in the West. **2.** *Informal.* A man who is very fancy or sharp in dress and demeanor. **3.** *Slang.* A fellow; a chap. **—dude** *tr.v.* **dud·ed, dud·ing, dudes.** *Slang.* To dress elaborately or flamboyantly: *got all duded up for the show.* [Origin unknown.]

du·deen (do͞o-dēn′) *n.* A short-stemmed clay pipe. [Irish Gaelic *dúidín,* diminutive of *dúd,* stump, pipe.]

dude ranch *n.* A resort patterned after a Western ranch, featuring camping, horseback riding, and other outdoor activities.

dudg·eon[1] (dŭj′ən) *n.* A sullen, angry, or indignant humor: *"Slamming the door in Meg's face, Aunt March drove off in high dudgeon"* (Louisa May Alcott). [Origin unknown.]

dudg·eon[2] (dŭj′ən) *n.* **1.** *Obsolete.* A kind of wood used in making knife handles. **2.** *Archaic.* **a.** A dagger with a hilt made of this wood. **b.** The hilt of a dagger. [Middle English *dogeon,* possibly from Anglo-Norman.]

Dud·ley (dŭd′lē). A borough of west-central England west-northwest of Birmingham. It had thriving iron, coal, and limestone industries until the 1870's. Population, 300,700.

Dudley, Robert. First Earl of Leicester. 1532?–1588. English courtier, politician, and favorite of Elizabeth I. Pardoned for his involvement in the plot to secure the throne for Lady Jane Grey (1553), he sought the hand of Elizabeth, who refused him, partly because his wife, Amy Robsart, had died (1560) under suspicious circumstances.

Dudley, Thomas. 1576–1653. English colonial administrator in America who served as governor of Massachusetts Bay Colony (1634, 1640, 1645, and 1650) and as one of Harvard College's first overseers.

due (do͞o, dyo͞o) *adj.* **1.** Payable immediately or on demand. **2.** Owed as a debt; owing: *the amount still due.* **3.** In accord with right, convention, or courtesy; appropriate: *due esteem; all due respect.* **4.** Meeting special requirements; sufficient: *We have due cause to honor them.* **5.** Expected or scheduled, especially appointed to arrive: *Their plane is due in 15 minutes.* **6.a.** Anticipated; looked for: *a long due promotion.* **b.** Expecting or ready for something as part of a normal course or sequence: *We're due for some rain. This batter is due for another hit.* **7.** *Usage Problem.* Capable of being attributed. See Usage Note at **due to. —due** *n.* **1.** Something owed or deserved: *You finally received your due.* **2. dues.** A charge or fee for membership, as in a club or organization. **—due** *adv.* **1.** Straight; directly: *Go due west.* **2.** *Archaic.* Duly. [Middle English, from Old French *deu,* past participle of *devoir,* to owe, from Latin *dēbēre.* See **ghabh-** in Appendix.]

due bill *n.* A written acknowledgment of indebtedness to a particular party but not payable to the party's order or transferable by endorsement.

du·el (do͞o′əl, dyo͞o′-) *n.* **1.** A prearranged, formal combat between two persons, usually fought to settle a point of honor. **2.** A struggle for domination between two contending persons, groups, or ideas. **—duel** *v.* **-eled, -el·ing, -els** or **-elled, -el·ling, -els.** *—tr.* **1.** To engage (another) in or as if in formal combat. **2.**

To oppose actively and forcefully. —*intr.* To engage in or as if in formal combat. [Middle English *duelle,* from Medieval Latin *duellum,* from Latin, war, variant of *bellum.*] —**du′el·er, du′el·ist** *n.*

du·en·de (do͞o-ĕn′dā′) *n.* The ability to attract others through personal magnetism and charm. [Spanish dialectal, charm, from Spanish, ghost.]

due process *n. Law.* An established course for judicial proceedings or other governmental activities designed to safeguard the legal rights of the individual.

Due·ro (dwĕr′ō). See **Douro.**

du·et (do͞o-ĕt′, dyo͞o-) *n.* **1.** *Music.* **a.** A composition for two voices or instruments. **b.** The two performers of such a composition. **2.** A pair. [Italian *duetto,* diminutive of *duo,* from Latin, two. See **dwo-** in Appendix.]

due to *prep.* Because of.

USAGE NOTE: *Due to* has been widely used for many years as a compound preposition like *owing to,* but some critics have insisted that the adjectival status of *due* must be retained. According to this view, it is incorrect to say *The concert was canceled due to the rain,* as opposed to the acceptable *The cancellation of the concert was due to the rain,* where *due* continues to function as an adjective modifying *cancellation.*

Du·fay (do͞o-fā′, dü-), **Guillaume.** 1400?–1474. Flemish composer regarded as the first great composer of the Renaissance. He is particularly known for his Mass compositions.

duff¹ (dŭf) *n.* A stiff flour pudding boiled in a cloth bag or steamed. [Dialectal variation of DOUGH.]

duff² (dŭf) *n.* **1.** Decaying leaves and branches covering a forest floor. **2.** Fine coal; slack. [Origin unknown.]

duff³ (dŭf) *n. Slang.* The buttocks. [Origin unknown.]

duf·fel or **duf·fle** (dŭf′əl) *n.* **1.** A blanket fabric made of low-grade woolen cloth with a nap on both sides. **2.** Clothing and other personal gear carried by a camper. [Dutch, after *Duffel,* a town of northern Belgium.]

duffel bag *n.* Variant of **duffle bag.**

duffel coat *n.* Variant of **duffle coat.**

duff·er (dŭf′ər) *n.* **1.** *Informal.* **a.** An incompetent or dull-witted person. **b.** A casual or mediocre player of a sport, especially golf. **2.** *Slang.* A peddler of cheap merchandise. **3.** *Slang.* Something worthless or useless. [Origin unknown.]

duf·fle (dŭf′əl) *n.* Variant of **duffel.**

duffle bag or **duffel bag** *n.* A large cylindrical cloth bag of canvas or duck for carrying personal belongings.

duffle coat or **duffel coat** *n.* A warm, usually hooded coat made of duffel or a similar material and fastened with toggles.

Du·fy (do͞o-fē′, dü-), **Raoul.** 1877–1953. French painter noted for his brightly colored scenes of racing and the seaside and for the panel *La Fée Électricité* (1937).

dug¹ (dŭg) *n.* An udder, breast, or teat of a female animal. [Origin unknown.]

dug² (dŭg) *v.* Past tense and past participle of **dig.**

du·gong (do͞o′gŏng′, -gông′) *n.* A herbivorous marine mammal *(Dugong dugon),* native to tropical coastal waters of the Indian Ocean, Red Sea, and southwest Pacific Ocean and having flipperlike forelimbs and a deeply notched tail fin. [New Latin *Dugong,* genus name, possibly from Malay *duyong.*]

dug·out (dŭg′out′) *n.* **1.** A boat or canoe made of a hollowed-out log. **2.** A pit dug into the ground or on a hillside and used as a shelter. **3.** *Baseball.* Either of two usually sunken shelters at the side of a field where the players stay while not on the field.

Du·ha·mel (do͞o′ə-mĕl′, dyo͞o′-, dü-ä-), **Georges.** 1884–1966. French writer and physician noted for his romans-fleuves, including the five-volume *Life and Adventures of Salavin* (1920–1932).

dui·ker (dī′kər) *n.* Any of various small African antelopes of the genera *Cephalopus* or *Sylvicapra,* having short, backward-pointing horns. [Afrikaans, from Dutch *duiken,* to dive, from Middle Dutch *dūken.*]

Duis·burg (do͞os′bûrg′, do͞oz′-, düs′bo͝ork′). A city of west-central Germany at the confluence of the Rhine and Ruhr rivers. It is a major inland port and a steel-producing center. Population, 522,829.

duke (do͞ok, dyo͞ok) *n. Abbr.* **D., Du.** **1.** A nobleman with the highest hereditary rank, especially a man of the highest grade of the peerage in Great Britain. **2.** A sovereign prince who rules an independent duchy in some European countries. **3.** Used as the title for such a nobleman. **4.** Often **dukes.** *Slang.* A fist: *Put up your dukes!* **5.** *Botany.* A type of cherry intermediate between a sweet and a sour cherry. —**duke** *intr.v.* **duked, duk·ing, dukes.** To fight, especially with fists: *duking it out.* [Middle English, from Old French *duc,* from Latin *dux, duc-,* leader, from *dūcere,* to lead. See **deuk-** in Appendix. N., sense 4, short for *Duke of Yorks,* rhyming slang for *forks,* fingers.]

duke·dom (do͞ok′dəm, dyo͞ok′-) *n.* **1.** A duchy. **2.** The office, rank, or title of a duke.

Du·kho·bor also **Dou·kho·bor** (do͞o′kə-bôr′) *n.* A member of an 18th-century Russian Christian group, many of whom migrated to Canada in the 1890's to escape persecution for their views, which included rejection of ecclesiastical and state authority. [Russian *Dukhobor* : *dukh,* spirit, Holy Ghost + *-bor,* fighter (from *borot'sya,* to fight).]

Dul·bec·co (dŭl-bĕk′ō), **Renato.** Born 1914. Italian-born American virologist. He shared a 1975 Nobel Prize for research on the interaction of tumor viruses and genetic material.

dul·cet (dŭl′sĭt) *adj.* **1.a.** Pleasing to the ear; melodious. **b.** Having a soothing, agreeable quality. **2.** *Archaic.* Sweet to the taste. [Alteration (influenced by Latin *dulcis*) of Middle English *doucet,* from Old French, diminutive of *douce,* feminine of *doux,* sweet, from Latin *dulcis.*] —**dul′cet·ly** *adv.*

dul·ci·fy (dŭl′sə-fī′) *tr.v.* **-fied, -fy·ing, -fies.** **1.** To make agreeable or gentle; mollify. **2.** To sweeten. [Late Latin *dulcificāre,* to sweeten : Latin *dulcis,* sweet + *-ficāre,* -fy.] —**dul′ci·fi·ca′tion** (-fĭ-kā′shən) *n.*

dul·ci·mer (dŭl′sə-mər) *n. Music.* An instrument with wire strings of graduated lengths stretched over a sound box, played by striking with two padded hammers or by plucking. [Alteration (influenced by Latin *dulcis,* sweet) of Middle English *doucemer,* from Old French *doulcemer, doulcemele,* probably from Latin *dulce melos,* sweet song : *dulce,* neuter of *dulcis,* sweet + *melos,* song (from Greek *melos*).]

dulcimer

dull (dŭl) *adj.* **dull·er, dull·est.** **1.** Intellectually weak or obtuse; stupid. **2.** Lacking responsiveness or alertness; insensitive. **3.** Dispirited; depressed. **4.** Not brisk or rapid; sluggish: *Business is dull.* **5.** Not having a sharp edge or point; blunt: *a dull knife.* **6.** Not intensely or keenly felt: *a dull ache.* **7.** Arousing no interest or curiosity; boring: *a dull play.* **8.** Not bright or vivid. Used of a color: *a dull brown.* **9.** Cloudy or overcast: *a dull sky.* **10.** Not clear or resonant: *a dull thud.* —**dull** *tr. & intr.v.* **dulled, dull·ing, dulls.** To make or become dull. [Middle English *dul;* akin to Old English *dol.*] —**dull′ish** *adj.* —**dull′ness, dul′ness** *n.* —**dul′ly** *adv.*

SYNONYMS: *dull, colorless, drab, humdrum, lackluster, pedestrian, stodgy, uninspired.* The central meaning shared by these adjectives is "lacking in liveliness, charm, or surprise": *a competent but dull performance of the role; a colorless and unimaginative person; a drab and boring job; a humdrum conversation; a lackluster life; a pedestrian movie plot; a stodgy dinner party; an uninspired lecture.* See also Synonyms at **stupid.**
ANTONYM: *lively.*

dull·ard (dŭl′ərd) *n.* A person regarded as mentally dull; a dolt.

Dul·les (dŭl′ĭs), **Allen Welsh.** 1893–1969. American public official. Director of the C.I.A. (1953–1961), he resigned after the failed invasion of the Bay of Pigs.

Dulles, John Foster. 1888–1959. American diplomat and politician who as U.S. secretary of state (1953–1959) pursued a policy of opposition to the U.S.S.R. largely through military and economic aid to American allies.

dulls·ville (dŭlz′vĭl′) *n. Slang.* A dull place, thing, or condition: *"You're on the down escalator to doubt, dullsville, and despair"* (James Wolcott).

dulse (dŭls) *n.* An edible red alga *(Palmaria palmata)* that grows on rocky shores on both sides of the northern Atlantic Ocean. [Scots Gaelic *duileasg,* from Old Irish *duilesc.*]

Du·luth (də-lo͞oth′). A city of northeast Minnesota on Lake Superior opposite Superior, Wisconsin. Permanent settlement began here in the 1850's. The city's fine harbor accommodates oceangoing vessels. Population, 92,811.

du·ly (do͞o′lē, dyo͞o′-) *adv.* **1.** In a proper manner: *a duly appointed official.* **2.** At the expected time. [Middle English *duely,* from *due,* due. See DUE.]

du·ma (do͞o′mə) *n.* A Russian national parliament during czarist times. [Russian, of Germanic origin. See **dhē-** in Appendix.]

Du·mas (do͞o-mä′, dyo͞o-, dü-), **Alexandre.** Known as "Dumas *père.*" 1802–1870. French writer of swashbuckling historical romances, such as *The Count of Monte Cristo* and *The Three Musketeers* (both 1844). His son **Alexandre** (1824–1895), known as "Dumas *fils,*" was a dramatist whose works include *La Dame aux Camélias (1852).*

Daphne du Maurier

du Mau·ri·er (do͞o môr′ē-ā′, dyo͞o, dü mô-ryā′), Dame **Daphne.** 1907–1989. British writer noted for her melodramatic novels, including *Rebecca* (1938).

du Maurier, George Louis Palmella Busson. 1834–1896. British illustrator and writer known for his caricatures in *Punch,* his illustrations of the works of William Makepeace Thackeray among others, and his novels, such as *Trilby* (1894).

dumb (dŭm) *adj.* **dumb·er, dumb·est.** **1.a.** Lacking the power of speech. Used of animals and inanimate objects. **b.** *Offensive.* Incapable of using speech; mute. Used of human beings. **2.** Temporarily speechless, as with shock or fear: *I was dumb with disbelief.* **3.** Unwilling to speak; taciturn. **4.** Not expressed or articulated in sounds or words: *dumb resentment.* **5.** *Nautical.* Not self-propelling. **6.** Conspicuously unintelligent; stupid: *dumb officials; a dumb decision.* **7.** Unintentional; haphazard: *dumb luck.* **8.** *Computer Science.* Incapable of processing data: *a dumb terminal.* —**dumb** *tr.v.* **dumbed, dumb·ing, dumbs.** To make silent or dumb. —***phrasal verb.*** **dumb down** (or **up**). *Slang.* To rewrite for a less intelligent audience. [Middle English, from Old English.] —**dumb′ly** *adv.* —**dumb′ness** *n.*

SYNONYMS: *dumb, inarticulate, mute, speechless.* The central meaning shared by these adjectives is "lacking the faculty of speech or the power to speak": *dumb with fear; inarticulate with*

ă pat	oi boy
ā pay	ou out
âr care	o͝o took
ä father	o͞o boot
ĕ pet	ŭ cut
ē be	ûr urge
ĭ pit	th thin
ī pie	*th* this
îr pier	hw which
ŏ pot	zh vision
ō toe	ə about, item
ô paw	♦ regionalism

Stress marks: ′ (primary); ′ (secondary), as in **dictionary** (dĭk′shə-nĕr′ē)

rage; mute with astonishment; speechless with horror. See also Synonyms at **stupid.**

dumbwaiter

dumb·bell (dŭm′bĕl′) *n.* **1.** A weight consisting of a short bar with a metal ball or disk at each end that is lifted for muscular development and exercise. **2.** *Slang.* A person regarded as stupid. [From an apparatus similar to that used in ringing a church bell, but without the bell, used for practice or physical exercise.]

dumb cane *n.* See **dieffenbachia.** [So called because its leaves contain a substance that swells the throat when eaten.]

dumb·found also **dum·found** (dŭm′found′) *tr.v.* **-found·ed, -found·ing, -founds.** To fill with astonishment and perplexity; confound. See Synonyms at **surprise.** [DUMB + (CON)FOUND.]

dum·bo (dŭm′bō) *n., pl.* **-bos.** *Slang.* A person regarded as stupid.

dumb plant *n.* See **dieffenbachia.** [See DUMB CANE.]

dumb show *n.* **1.** A part of a play, especially in medieval and Renaissance drama, that is enacted without speaking. **2.** Communication or acting by means of expressive gestures; pantomime.

dumb·struck (dŭm′strŭk′) *adj.* So shocked or astonished as to be rendered speechless.

dumb·wait·er (dŭm′wā′tər) *n.* **1.** A small elevator used to convey food or other goods from one floor of a building to another. **2.** A portable serving stand or table.

dum-dum (dŭm′dŭm′) *n. Slang.* A person regarded as stupid. [Reduplication and alteration of DUMB.]

dum·dum bullet (dum′dum′) *n.* A hollow-point small-arms bullet designed to expand upon impact, inflicting a gaping wound. [After *Dum Dum,* a town of northeast India.]

dum·found (dŭm′found′) *v.* Variant of **dumbfound.**

Dum·fries (dŭm-frēs′). A burgh of southern Scotland south-southwest of Edinburgh. Robert Burns is buried here. Population, 31,800.

dumm·kopf (do͝om′kôf′, -kôpf′, dŭm′-) *n.* A person regarded as stupid. [German : *dumm,* dumb (from Middle High German *tump, tumb,* from Old High German *tumb*) + *kopf,* head (from Middle High German, cup, cranium, from Old High German, cup, from Late Latin *cuppa*).]

dum·my (dŭm′ē) *n., pl.* **-mies. 1.** An imitation of a real or original object, intended to be used as a practical substitute. **2. a.** A mannequin used in displaying clothes. **b.** A figure of a person or an animal manipulated by a ventriloquist. **c.** A stuffed or pasteboard figure used as a target. **d.** *Football.* A heavy stuffed cylindrical bag used for blocking and tackling practice. **3.** A person regarded as stupid. **4.** A silent or taciturn person. **5.** A person or an agency secretly in the service of another. **6.** *Printing.* **a.** One of a set of model pages with text and illustrations pasted into place to direct the printer. Also called *dummy page.* **b.** A set of bound blank pages used as a model to show the size and general appearance of a book being published. **7.** *Games.* **a.** The partner in bridge who exposes his or her hand to be played by the declarer. **b.** The hand thus exposed. **8.** *Computer Science.* A character or other piece of information entered into a computer only to meet prescribed conditions, such as word length, and having no effect on operations. **—dummy** *adj.* **1.** Simulating or replacing something but lacking its function: *a dummy pocket.* **2.** Serving as a front or cover for another: *a dummy corporation.* **3.** *Games.* Played with a dummy. **4.** *Computer Science.* Entered or provided only to meet prescribed conditions: *a dummy variable.* **—dummy** *tr.v.* **-mied, -my·ing, -mies.** *Printing.* To make a model of (a publication or page). ***—phrasal verb.*** **dummy up.** *Slang.* To keep silence; clam up. [From DUMB.]

dummy
Young performer with a ventriloquist's dummy

Du·mont (do͞o′mŏnt′, dyo͞o′-). A borough of northeast New Jersey, a residential suburb of Hackensack. It was settled by the Dutch in 1677. Population, 18,334.

du·mor·ti·er·ite (do͞o-môr′tē-ə-rīt′, dyo͞o-) *n.* A glassy pink, green, violet, or blue aluminum borosilicate mineral, $Al_8BSi_3O_{19}OH$, used in spark-plug ceramics and as imitation lapis lazuli. [French, after Eugène *Dumortier,* 19th-century French paleontologist.]

dump (dŭmp) *v.* **dumped, dump·ing, dumps.** —*tr.* **1.** To release or throw down in a large mass. **2. a.** To empty (material) out of a container or vehicle: *dumped the load of stones.* **b.** To empty out (a container or vehicle), as by overturning or tilting. **3. a.** To get rid of; discard: *a fine for dumping trash on public land; dumped the extra gear overboard.* **b.** *Informal.* To discard or reject unceremoniously: *dump an old friend.* **4.** To place (goods or stock, for example) on the market in large quantities and at a low price. **5.** *Computer Science.* To transfer (data stored internally in a computer) from one place to another, as from a memory to a printout, without processing. **6.** *Slang.* To knock down; beat. —*intr.* **1.** To fall or drop abruptly. **2.** To discharge cargo or contents; unload. **3.** *Slang.* To criticize another severely: *was always dumping on me.* **—dump** *n.* **1.** A place where refuse is dumped. **2.** A storage place for goods or supplies; a depot: *an ammunition dump.* **3.** An unordered accumulation; a pile. **4.** *Computer Science.* An instance or the result of dumping stored data. **5.** *Slang.* A poorly maintained or disreputable place. [Middle English *dumpen, dompen,* to fall suddenly, drop, of Scandinavian origin.] **—dump′er** *n.*

dump truck

dump·ling (dŭmp′lĭng) *n.* **1.** A small ball of dough cooked with stew or soup. **2.** Sweetened dough wrapped around fruit, such as an apple, baked and served as a dessert. **3.** *Informal.* A short, chubby creature. [Origin unknown.]

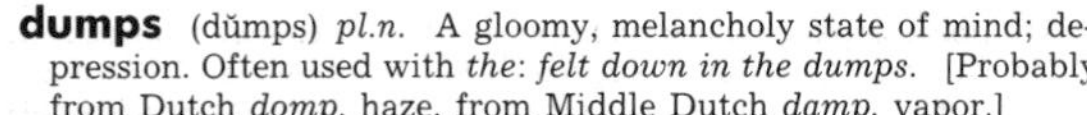

dumps (dŭmps) *pl.n.* A gloomy, melancholy state of mind; depression. Often used with *the: felt down in the dumps.* [Probably from Dutch *domp,* haze, from Middle Dutch *damp,* vapor.]

dump·site (dŭmp′sīt′) *n.* The location of a dump, especially a garbage dump.

Dump·ster (dŭmp′stər). A trademark used for containers designed for receiving, transporting, and dumping waste materials. This trademark often occurs in print in lowercase: "[He] *testified that he had seen the motorcycle parked for a number of days next to a trash dumpster"* (Legal Times). "[The street is] *lined with low-cost apartment buildings and strewn with blue dumpsters"* (Chicago Tribune).

dump truck *n.* A heavy-duty truck having a bed that tilts backward to dump loose material.

dump·y[1] (dŭm′pē) *adj.* **-i·er, -i·est.** Short and stout; squat. [Probably from *dump,* lump.] **—dump′i·ly** *adv.* **—dump′i·ness** *n.*

dum·py[2] (dŭm′pē) *adj.* **-i·er, -i·est.** Resembling a dump, as in shabbiness; disreputable: *"The place had a dark and dumpy look"* (Washington Post).

dumpy level *n.* A surveyor's instrument having a short telescope fixed rigidly to a horizontally rotating table.

Dum·yat (do͞om-yät′). See **Damietta.**

dun[1] (dŭn) *tr.v.* **dunned, dun·ning, duns.** To importune (a debtor) for payment: *a dunning letter.* **—dun** *n.* **1.** One that duns. **2.** An importunate demand for payment. [Origin unknown.]

dun[2] (dŭn) *n.* **1.** *Color.* An almost neutral brownish gray to dull grayish brown. **2.** A fishing fly having this color. **3.** A horse of this color. [Middle English, from Old English *dunn,* perhaps of Celtic origin.]

Du·nant (do͞o-näN′, dü-), **Jean Henri.** 1828–1910. Swiss philanthropist who founded the International Red Cross (1864). He shared the 1901 Nobel Peace Prize.

Dun·bar (dŭn′bär), **Paul Laurence.** 1872–1906. American writer primarily noted for his poetry, which reflects Black American life and dialect.

Dun·bar (dŭn-bär′), **William.** 1460?–1520? Scottish poet known for his allegorical works, such as *The Thrissill and the Rois* (1503), and an elegy on bygone poets, *Lament of the Makaris* (c. 1508).

Dun·can (dŭng′kən). A city of southern Oklahoma south-southwest of Oklahoma City. It is the center of an oil-producing region. Population, 22,517.

Duncan, Isadora. 1878–1927. American dancer whose use of simple costumes and free movement greatly influenced modern dance.

Dun·can·ville (dŭng′kən-vĭl′). A city of northeast Texas, a residential suburb of Dallas. Population, 27,781.

dunce (dŭns) *n.* A person regarded as stupid. [After John DUNS SCOTUS, whose writings and philosophy were ridiculed in the 16th century.]

dunce cap also **dunce's cap** (dŭn′sĭz) *n.* A cone-shaped paper cap, formerly placed on the head of a slow or lazy pupil. Also called *fool's cap.*

Dun·das (dŭn′dəs). A town of southeast Ontario, Canada, a manufacturing suburb of Hamilton. Population, 19,586.

Dun·dee (dŭn-dē′). A burgh of east-central Scotland on the northern bank of the Firth of Tay. It was a stronghold of the Covenanters in the religious wars of the Scottish Reformation. Population, 185,616.

dun·der·head (dŭn′dər-hĕd′) *n.* A dunce. [Perhaps Dutch *donder,* thunder (from Middle Dutch *doner;* see **(s)tene-** in Appendix) + HEAD.]

dun·drear·ies (dŭn-drîr′ēz) *pl.n.* Long sideburns worn with a clean-shaven chin. [After Lord *Dundreary,* a character in the play *Our American Cousin* by Tom Taylor.]

dune (do͞on, dyo͞on) *n.* A hill or ridge of wind-blown sand. [French, from Old French, from Middle Dutch *dūne.* See **dhū-no-** in Appendix.]

dune buggy *n.* A recreational vehicle having oversize tires designed for use on sand dunes or beaches, especially a light vehicle with a modified engine mounted on an open chassis. Also called *beach buggy.*

Dun·e·din (dŭn-ēd′n). **1.** A city of southeast South Island, New Zealand. A major port, it was settled by Scottish Presbyterians in 1848. Population, 74,500. **2.** A city of west-central Florida on the Gulf of Mexico west of Tampa. It is a popular winter resort. Population, 30,203.

Dun·ferm·line (dŭn-fûrm′lĭn). A burgh of east-central Scotland northwest of Edinburgh. It was long a favorite residence of Scottish kings. Population, 53,800.

dung (dŭng) *n.* **1. a.** The excrement of animals. **b.** Manure. **2.** Something foul or abhorrent. **—dung** *tr.v.* **dunged, dung·ing, dungs.** To fertilize (land) with manure. [Middle English, from Old English.] **—dung′y** *adj.*

dun·ga·ree (dŭng′gə-rē′) *n.* **1.** A sturdy, often blue denim fabric. **2. dungarees.** Trousers or overalls made of sturdy denim fabric. [Hindi *dungrī.*]

dung beetle *n.* Any of various beetles of the family Scarabaeidae that form balls of dung on which they feed and in which they lay their eggs.

Dun·ge·ness crab (dŭn′jə-nĕs′, -nĭs) *n.* An edible crab *(Cancer magister)* common along the Pacific coast from Alaska to northern California. [After *Dungeness,* a town of northwest Washington.]

dun·geon (dŭn′jən) *n.* **1.** A dark, often underground chamber or cell used to confine prisoners. **2.** A donjon. [Middle English *donjon,* castle keep, dungeon, from Old French, keep, probably from Medieval Latin *domniō,* the lord's tower, from Latin *dominus,* master. See **dem-** in Appendix.]

WORD HISTORY: The word *dungeon* may have gone down in the world quite literally, if one etymology of the word is correct. *Dungeon* may go back to a Vulgar Latin word, *domniō,* meaning "the lord's tower," which came from Latin *dominus,* "master." In Middle English, in which our word is first recorded in a work composed around the beginning of the 14th century, it meant "a fortress, castle," and "the keep of a castle" as well as "a prison cell underneath the keep of the castle." *Dungeon* can still mean "keep," although the usual spelling for this sense is *donjon,* but the meaning most usually associated with it is certainly not elevated. It is also possible that *dungeon* goes back to a Germanic word related to our word *dung.* This assumed Germanic word would have meant "an underground house constructed of dung." If this etymology is correct, the word *dungeon* has ended up where it began.

dung·hill (dŭng′hĭl′) *n.* **1.** A heap of animal excrement. **2.** A foul, degraded condition or place.

du·nite (do͞o′nīt′, dŭn′īt′) *n.* A dense igneous rock that consists mainly of olivine and is a source of magnesium. [After Mount *Dun* in northern South Island, New Zealand.] **—du·nit′ic** (do͞o-nĭt′ĭk, də-) *adj.*

dunk (dŭngk) *v.* **dunked, dunk·ing, dunks.** *—tr.* **1.** To plunge into liquid; immerse. See Synonyms at **dip. 2.** To dip (food) into a liquid before eating it. **3.** *Basketball.* To slam (a ball) through the basket from above. *—intr.* **1.** To submerge oneself briefly in water. **2.** *Basketball.* To slam a ball through the basket from above. **—dunk** *n.* **1.** The act or an instance of dunking. **2.** *Basketball.* A dunk shot. [Pennsylvania Dutch *dunke,* from Middle High German *dunken,* from Old High German *dunkōn.*] **—dunk′er** *n.*

Dunk·er (dŭng′kər) also **Dun·kard** (-kərd) *n.* A member of the German Baptist Brethren, a group of German-American Baptists opposed to military service and the taking of legal oaths. [Pennsylvania Dutch, from *dunke,* to dunk (from the practice of baptism by immersion). See DUNK.]

Dun·kirk[1] (dŭn′kûrk′). Also **Dun·kerque** (dœn-kĕrk′). A city of northern France on the North Sea. In World War II more than 330,000 Allied troops were evacuated from its beaches in the face of enemy fire (May–June 1940). Population, 73,120.

Dun·kirk[2] (dŭn′kûrk′) *n.* **1.** A desperate retreat. **2.** A condition in which a desperate last effort is the only alternative to total defeat. [After DUNKIRK[1].]

dunk shot *n. Basketball.* A shot made by jumping and slamming the ball down through the basket. Also called *stuff shot.*

Dun Laoghai·re (dŭn lâr′ə). A borough of east-central Ireland on the Irish Sea southeast of Dublin. It is a yachting center. Population, 54,496.

dun·lin (dŭn′lĭn) *n.* A rust-brown and white sandpiper *(Calidris alpina)* native to northern regions of North America, Europe, and Asia. [DUN[2] + –LIN(G)[1].]

Dun·more (dŭn′môr′, -mōr′). A borough of northeast Pennsylvania, an industrial suburb of Scranton. Population, 16,781.

Dun·more (dŭn-môr′, -mōr′), Fourth Earl of. Title of John Murray. 1732–1809. British colonial governor of Virginia (1771–1776) who opposed the independence of the colonies and was forced to return to England.

dun·nage (dŭn′ĭj) *n.* **1.** Loose packing material used to protect a ship's cargo from damage during transport. **2.** Personal baggage. [Middle English *dennage,* from Middle Dutch *denne,* flooring of a ship.]

Dunne (dŭn), **Finley Peter.** 1867–1936. American humorist and journalist known for his books featuring Mr. Dooley, an Irish saloonkeeper who comments satirically on current events.

Duns Sco·tus (dŭnz skō′təs), **John.** Known as "the Subtle Doctor." 1265?–1308. Scottish Franciscan monk and theologian who wrote *On the First Principal* and disputed Thomas Aquinas's harmony of faith and reason.

Dun·stan (dŭn′stən), Saint. 924–988. English prelate. As bishop of Winchester (957) and archbishop of Canterbury (959–978) he attempted to integrate the Danes and the English as a nation.

du·o (do͞o′ō, dyo͞o′ō) *n., pl.* **-os. 1.** *Music.* **a.** A duet. **b.** Two performers singing or playing together. **2.** Two people in close association: *a duo of negotiators.* [Italian, from Latin, two. See **dwo-** in Appendix.]

duo– *pref.* Two: *duopsony.* [Latin, from *duo,* two. See **dwo-** in Appendix.]

du·o·dec·i·mal (do͞o′ə-dĕs′ə-məl, dyo͞o′-) *adj.* **1.** Of, relating to, or based on the number 12: *the duodecimal number system.* **2.** Of or relating to twelfths. **—duodecimal** *n.* A twelfth. [From Latin *duodecimus,* twelfth, from *duodecim,* twelve : *duo,* two; see **dwo-** in Appendix + *decem,* ten; see **dekm** in Appendix.]

du·o·dec·i·mo (do͞o′ə-dĕs′ə-mō′, dyo͞o′-) *n., pl.* **-mos.** *Printing.* **1.** The size (5 by 7¾ inches) of book pages formed by folding single sheets from a printing press into 12 leaves each. Also called *twelvemo.* **2.** A book composed of pages of this size. [Latin *(in) duodecimō,* (in) a twelfth, ablative of *duodecimus,* twelfth. See DUODECIMAL.]

du·o·de·num (do͞o′ə-dē′nəm, dyo͞o′-, do͞o-ŏd′n-əm, dyo͞o-) *n., pl.* **du·od·e·na** (do͞o′ə-dē′nə, dyo͞o′-, do͞o-ŏd′n-ə, dyo͞o-) or **du·o·de·nums.** The beginning portion of the small intestine, starting at the lower end of the stomach and extending to the jejunum. [Middle English, from Medieval Latin, short for *intestīnum duodēnum digitōrum,* intestine of twelve fingers (in length), from Latin *duodēnum,* genitive pl. of *duodēnī,* twelve each, from *duodecim,* twelve. See DUODECIMAL.] **—du′o·de′nal** (do͞o′ə-dē′nəl, dyo͞o′-, do͞o-ŏd′n-əl, dyo͞o-) *adj.*

du·o·logue (do͞o′ə-lôg′, -lŏg′, dyo͞o′-) *n.* A dialogue or conversation between two persons: *"a reasonably well-constructed duologue for two experienced performers"* (Noel Coward).

duo·mo (dwō′mō) *n., pl.* **-mos.** A cathedral, especially one in Italy. [Italian. See DOME.]

du·op·o·ly (do͞o-ŏp′ə-lē, dyo͞o-) *n.* An economic or political condition in which power is concentrated in two persons or groups. [DUO– + (MONO)POLY.]

du·op·so·ny (do͞o-ŏp′sə-nē, dyo͞o-) *n., pl.* **-nies.** A stock-market condition wherein two rival buyers exert a controlling influence on numerous sellers. [DUO– + Greek *opsōnia,* purchasing of provisions (from *opsōnein,* to buy food : *opson,* cooked food + *ōnē,* buying, from *ōneisthai,* to buy; see **wes-[3]** in Appendix).]

dup. *abbr.* Duplicate.

dupe (do͞op, dyo͞op) *n.* **1.** An easily deceived person. **2.** A person who functions as the tool of another person or power. **—dupe** *tr.v.* **duped, dup·ing, dupes.** To deceive (an unwary person). See Synonyms at **deceive.** [French, from Old French, probably alteration of *huppe,* hoopoe (from the bird's stupid appearance). See HOOPOE.] **—dup′a·bil′i·ty** *n.* **—dup′a·ble** *adj.*

dup·er·y (do͞o′pə-rē, dyo͞o′-) *n., pl.* **-ies.** The act of duping or the condition of having been duped.

du·ple (do͞o′pəl, dyo͞o′-) *adj.* **1.** Consisting of two; double. **2.** *Music.* Consisting of two or a multiple of two beats to the measure. [Latin *duplus.* See **dwo-** in Appendix.]

Du·ples·sis-Mor·nay (do͞o-plĕ-sē′ môr-nā′, dü-). See Philippe de **Mornay.**

du·plex (do͞o′plĕks′, dyo͞o′-) *adj.* **1.** Twofold; double. **2.** Relating to or being a single assembly of machinery having two identical units that are capable of operating simultaneously or independently. **3.** *Electronics.* Of or relating to a communications mode, as in a telephone system, that provides simultaneous transmission and reception in both directions. **—duplex** *n.* **1.** A house divided into two living units or residences, usually having separate entrances. **2.** A duplex apartment. [Latin. See **dwo-** in Appendix.] **—du·plex′i·ty** (-plĕk′sĭ-tē) *n.*

duplex apartment *n.* An apartment having rooms on two adjoining floors connected by an inner staircase.

du·pli·cate (do͞o′plĭ-kĭt, dyo͞o′-) *adj. Abbr.* **dup. 1.** Identically copied from an original. **2.** Existing or growing in two corresponding parts; double. **3.** *Games.* Denoting a manner of play in cards in which partnerships or teams play the same deals and compare scores at the end: *duplicate bridge.* **—duplicate** *n. Abbr.* **dup. 1.** An identical copy; a facsimile. **2.** One that corresponds exactly to another, especially an original. **3.** *Games.* A card game in which partnerships or teams play the same deals and compare scores at the end. **—duplicate** (-kāt′) *v.* **-cat·ed, -cat·ing, -cates.** *—tr.* **1.** To make an exact copy of. **2.** To make twofold; double. **3.** To make or perform again; repeat: *a hard feat to duplicate.* *—intr.* To become duplicate. [Middle English, from Latin *duplicātus,* past participle of *duplicāre,* to double, from *duplex, duplic-,* twofold. See **dwo-** in Appendix.] **—du′pli·ca·ble, du′pli·cat′a·ble** (-kā′tə-bəl) *adj.* **—du′pli·cate·ly** *adv.* **—du′pli·ca′tive** *adj.* **—du′pli·ca·to′ry** (-kĭ-tôr′ē, -tōr′ē) *adj.*

du·pli·ca·tion (do͞o′plĭ-kā′shən, dyo͞o′-) *n.* **1.a.** The act or procedure of duplicating. **b.** The condition of being duplicated. **2.** A duplicate; a replica. **3.** *Genetics.* **a.** The occurrence of a repeated section of genetic material in a chromosome. **b.** The formation of such a duplication.

du·pli·ca·tor (do͞o′plĭ-kā′tər, dyo͞o′-) *n.* A machine, such as a mimeograph, that reproduces printed or written material.

du·plic·i·tous (do͞o-plĭs′ĭ-təs, dyo͞o-) *adj.* Given to or marked by deliberate deceptiveness in behavior or speech. **—du·plic′i·tous·ly** *adv.* **—du·plic′i·tous·ness** *n.*

du·plic·i·ty (do͞o-plĭs′ĭ-tē, dyo͞o-) *n., pl.* **-ties. 1.a.** Deliberate deceptiveness in behavior or speech. **b.** An instance of deliberate deceptiveness; double-dealing. **2.** The quality or state of being twofold or double. [Middle English *duplicite,* from Old French, from Late Latin *duplicitās,* doubleness, from Latin *duplex, duplic-,* twofold. See **dwo-** in Appendix.]

Du Pont de Ne·mours (do͞o pŏnt′ də nə-mo͝or′, dü pôN′), **Pierre Samuel.** 1739–1817. French-born economist and politician who took part in negotiations after the American Revolution (1783) and in the acquisition of the Louisiana Territory (1803). His son **Éleuthère Irénée** (1771–1834) established a gunpowder works in Delaware (1802) that developed into the chemical firm of E.I. Du Pont de Nemours and Company.

du Pré (do͞o prā′, dyo͞o), **Jacqueline.** 1945–1987. British cellist

Isadora Duncan

dune buggy

dunk shot

ă pat	oi boy
ā pay	ou out
âr care	o͝o took
ä father	o͞o boot
ĕ pet	ŭ cut
ē be	ûr urge
ĭ pit	th thin
ī pie	*th* this
îr pier	hw which
ŏ pot	zh vision
ō toe	ə about, item
ô paw	♦ regionalism

Stress marks: **′** (primary); ′ (secondary), as in **dictionary** (dĭk′shə-nĕr′ē)

considered among the world's best until multiple sclerosis cut short her career.

Du·que de Ca·xi·as (do͝o′kē də kə-shē′əs, do͝o′kĭ dĭ kä-shē′äs). A city of southeast Brazil, a commercial and residential suburb of Rio de Janeiro on Guanabara Bay. Population, 306,243.

du·ra·ble (do͝or′ə-bəl, dyo͝or′-) *adj.* **1.** Capable of withstanding wear and tear or decay: *a durable fabric.* **2.** Lasting; stable: *a durable friendship.* **3.** *Economics.* Not depleted or consumed by use: *durable goods.* **—durable** *n. Economics.* A manufactured product, such as an automobile or a household appliance, that can be used over a relatively long period without being depleted or consumed. Often used in the plural. [Middle English, from Old French, from Latin *dūrābilis,* from *dūrāre,* to last. See **deuə-** in Appendix.] **—du′ra·bil′i·ty, du′ra·ble·ness** *n.* **—du′ra·bly** *adv.*

durable press *n.* See **permanent press.**

du·ral (do͝or′əl, dyo͝or′-) *adj.* Of or relating to the dura mater.

du·ral·u·min (do͞o-răl′yə-mĭn, dyo͞o-) *n.* An alloy of aluminum that contains copper, manganese, magnesium, iron, and silicon and is resistant to corrosion by acids and sea water. [Originally a trademark.]

Jimmy Durante

du·ra ma·ter (do͝or′ə mā′tər, mä-, dyo͝or′ə) *n.* The tough fibrous membrane covering the brain and the spinal cord and lining the inner surface of the skull. It is the outermost of the three meninges that surround the brain and spinal cord. [Middle English, from Medieval Latin *dūra mater (cerebri),* hard mother (of the brain), dura mater (translation of Arabic *'umm ad-dimāġ aṣ-ṣāfīqah,* the dense mother of the brain) : Latin *dūra,* feminine of *dūrus,* hard; see DURAMEN + Latin *mater,* mother; see MATER.]

du·ra·men (do͞o-rā′mən, dyo͞o-) *n. Botany.* See **heartwood.** [Latin *dūrāmen,* hard growth of a vine, from *dūrāre,* to harden, from *dūrus,* hard. See **deru-** in Appendix.]

du·rance (do͝or′əns, dyo͝or′-) *n.* Confinement or restraint by force; imprisonment: *"There should be a durance vile for justices who use an argument as weak as the one the majority used"* (George F. Will). [Middle English *duraunce,* duration, from Old French *durance,* from *durer,* to last, from Latin *dūrāre.* See **deuə-** in Appendix.]

Du·rand (də-rănd′), **Asher Brown.** 1796–1886. American artist and a founder of the Hudson River School known for his paintings of the Hudson River and the Catskill Mountains.

Albrecht Dürer

Du·ran·go (do͞o-răng′gō). A city of north-central Mexico north-northwest of Guadalajara. Founded as a mining town c. 1560, it was an important political and religious center during the early history of northern Mexico. Population, 257,915.

Du·rant, (də-rănt′), **William James.** Known as "Will." 1885–1981. American historian who wrote *The Story of Civilization* (1935–1975), an 11-volume history of the world on which his wife **Ariel** (1898–1981) collaborated.

Du·ran·te (də-răn′tē), **Jimmy.** 1893–1980. American comedian remembered for his hoarse voice, ample nose, and time-worn hat. He appeared in a number of films and Broadway shows, including *Red, Hot, and Blue* (1936).

du·ra·tion (do͞o-rā′shən, dyo͞o-) *n.* **1.** Continuance or persistence in time. **2.** A period of existence or persistence: *sat quietly through the duration of the speech.* [Middle English *duracioun,* from Old French *duration,* from Medieval Latin *dūrātiō, dūrātiōn-,* from Latin *dūrātus,* past participle of *dūrāre,* to last. See **deuə-** in Appendix.]

Dur·ban (dûr′bən). A city of eastern South Africa on **Durban Bay,** an inlet of the Indian Ocean. First visited by Vasco da Gama in 1497, the site was settled after the arrival of the British in 1824. Durban is a major seaport and year-round resort. Population, 677,760.

dur·bar (dûr′bär′) *n.* **1.** A state reception formerly given by Indian princes for a British sovereign or one given for an Indian prince by his subjects. **2.** The court of an Indian prince. [Urdu *darbār,* audience hall, court, from Persian : *dar,* indoors (from Middle Persian, door, from Old Persian *duvara-*; see **dhwer-** in Appendix) + *bār,* audience hall (from East Iranian **dwāra-,* courtyard; see **dhwer-** in Appendix).]

Dü·ren (do͝or′ən, dür′-). A city of west-central Germany southwest of Cologne. It was a center of Carolingian culture. Population, 84,631.

Dü·rer (do͝or′ər, dyo͝or′-, dü′rər), **Albrecht.** 1471–1528. German painter and engraver who incorporated the classicism of the Italian Renaissance into northern European art.

du·ress (do͞o-rĕs′, dyo͞o-) *n.* **1.** Constraint by threat; coercion: *confessed under duress.* **2.** *Law.* **a.** Coercion illegally applied. **b.** Forcible confinement. [Middle English *duresse,* harshness, compulsion, from Old French *durece,* hardness, from Latin *dūritia,* from *dūrus,* hard. See **deru-** in Appendix.]

Dur·ga·pur (do͝or′gə-po͝or′, -gä-). A city of northeast India northwest of Calcutta. Its steel plant, completed in 1962, was built with British aid. Population, 311,798.

Dur·ham¹ (dûr′əm). A city of north-central North Carolina east of Greensboro. Settled c. 1750, it is the seat of Duke University (founded 1838). Population, 100,538.

Dur·ham² (dûr′əm) *n.* See **shorthorn.** [After *Durham,* a county of northern England.]

du·ri·an (do͝or′ē-ən, -än′, dyo͝or′-) *n.* **1.** A tree *(Durio zibethinus)* of southeast Asia, bearing edible fruit. **2.** The fruit of this plant, having a hard, prickly rind and soft pulp with an offensive odor but a pleasant taste. [Malay *dūrīan,* from *dūrī,* thorn.]

dur·ing (do͝or′ĭng, dyo͝or′-) *prep.* **1.** Throughout the course or duration of: *suffered food shortages during the war.* **2.** At some time in: *was born during a blizzard.* [Middle English, from present participle of *duren,* to last, from Old French *durer,* from Latin *dūrāre.* See **deuə-** in Appendix.]

Durk·heim (dûrk′hīm, dür-kĕm′), **Émile.** 1858–1917. French social scientist and a founder of sociology who is known for his study of social values and alienation. His important works include *The Rules of Sociological Method* (1895).

dur·mast (dûr′măst′) *n.* A European oak *(Quercus petraea)* having tough, elastic wood. [Perhaps alteration of *dun mast* : DUN² + MAST².]

♦ **durn** (dûrn) *Chiefly Southern U.S. interj., adv., adj., & v.* Variant of **darn².** See Regional Note at **damned.**

du·roc also **Du·roc** (do͝or′ŏk′, dyo͝or′-) *n.* A large red hog of a breed developed during the 19th century in the United States. Also called *Duroc-Jersey.* [After *Duroc,* a horse owned by the developer of the breed.]

Du·ro·cher (də-rō′chər, -shər), **Leo Ernest.** 1906–1991. American baseball player and manager remembered for his toughness and his dictum "Nice guys finish last."

Du·roc-Jer·sey (do͝or′ŏk-jûr′zē, dyo͝or′-) *n.* See **duroc.**

dur·ra also **dou·ra** or **dou·rah** (do͝or′ə) *n.* A cereal grain *(Sorghum bicolor)* of Asia and northern Africa, much cultivated in dry regions. Also called *Egyptian corn.* [Arabic *ḏurah,* grain.]

Dur·rell (dûr′əl), **Lawrence George.** 1912–1990. British writer of Irish descent whose best-known work is *The Alexandria Quartet* (1957–1960), a series of novels treating the same characters from different perspectives.

Dür·ren·matt (do͝or′ən-mät′, dyo͝or′-, dür′-), **Friedrich.** Born 1921. Swiss writer known for his absurdist novels and plays, such as *The Visit* (1956).

Dur·rës (do͝or′əs). A city of western Albania on the Adriatic Sea. Founded as a Greek colony c. 625 B.C., it is the country's chief seaport. Population, 72,400.

durst (dûrst) *v. Archaic.* A past tense and a past participle of **dare.**

du·rum (do͝or′əm, dyo͝or′-, dûr′-, dŭr′-) *n.* A hardy wheat *(Triticum turgidum,* formerly *T. durum)* used chiefly in making pasta. [From Latin *dūrum,* neuter of *dūrus,* hard. See **deru-** in Appendix.]

Dur·yea (do͝or′yā, -ē-ā′), **Charles Edgar.** 1861–1938. American inventor and automobile manufacturer. With his brother **James Frank Duryea** (1869–1967) he built one of the first American automobiles (1893).

Du·se (do͞o′zĕ), **Eleonora.** 1859?–1924. Italian actress who was highly acclaimed as a heroine in the plays of Gabriele D'Annunzio and Henrik Ibsen.

Du·shan·be (do͞o-shăm′bə, -shäm′-, -shŭn-byĕ′). The capital of Tadzhikistan, in the western part of the region. It is a major industrial and commercial center in a rich agricultural area. Population, 552,000.

dusk (dŭsk) *n.* The darker stage of twilight, especially in the evening. **—dusk** *adj.* Tending to darkness; dusky. **—dusk** *intr. & tr.v.* **dusked, dusk·ing, dusks.** To become or make dark or dusky. [From Middle English, dark, alteration of Old English *dox.*]

dusk·y (dŭs′kē) *adj.* **-i·er, -i·est. 1.** Characterized by little or inadequate light; shadowy. **2.** Rather dark in color. See Synonyms at **dark. —dusk′i·ly** *adv.* **—dusk′i·ness** *n.*

dusky grouse *n.* See **blue grouse.**

Düs·sel·dorf (do͞os′əl-dôrf′, düs′-). A city of west-central Germany on the Rhine River north-northwest of Cologne. Chartered in 1288, it has been a leading industrial center since the 1870's. Population, 565,843.

dust (dŭst) *n.* **1.** Fine, dry particles of matter. **2.** A cloud of fine, dry particles. **3.** Particles of matter regarded as the result of disintegration: *fabric that had fallen to dust over the centuries.* **4. a.** Earth, especially when regarded as the substance of the grave: *"ashes to ashes, dust to dust"* (Book of Common Prayer). **b.** The surface of the ground. **5.** A debased or despised condition. **6.** Something of no worth. **7.** *Chiefly British.* Rubbish readied for disposal. **8.** Confusion; agitation; commotion: *won't go back in until the dust settles.* **—dust** *v.* **dust·ed, dust·ing, dusts.** *—tr.* **1.** To remove dust from by wiping, brushing, or beating: *dust the furniture.* **2.** To sprinkle with a powdery substance: *dusted the cookies with sugar; dust crops with fertilizer.* **3.** To apply or strew in fine particles: *dusted talcum powder on my feet.* **4.** *Baseball.* To deliver a pitch so close to (the batter) as to make the batter back away. *—intr.* **1.** To clean by removing dust. **2.** To cover itself with such particulate matter. Used of a bird. ***—phrasal verb.* dust off.** To restore to use: *dusted off last year's winter coat.* ***—idioms.* in the dust.** Far behind, as in a race or competition: *a marketing strategy that left our competitors in the dust.* **make the dust fly.** To go about a task with great energy and speed. [Middle English, from Old English *dūst.*]

dust·bin (dŭst′bĭn′) *n. Chiefly British.* A can or barrel for refuse.

dust bowl *n.* A region reduced to aridity by drought and dust storms.

dust catcher *n. Informal.* A little-used decorative object or piece of furniture.

ă pat	oi boy
ā pay	ou out
âr care	o͝o took
ä father	o͞o boot
ĕ pet	ŭ cut
ē be	ûr urge
ĭ pit	th thin
ī pie	*th* this
îr pier	hw which
ŏ pot	zh vision
ō toe	ə about, item
ô paw	♦ regionalism

Stress marks: ′ (primary); ′ (secondary), as in **dictionary** (dĭk′shə-nĕr′ē)

dust cover *n.* **1.** A removable or hinged plastic cover used to protect a piece of equipment, such as a turntable or printer. **2.** See **dust jacket** (sense 1).

dust devil *n.* A small whirlwind, usually of short duration, that swirls dust, debris, and sand to great heights.

dust·er (dŭs′tər) *n.* **1.** One that dusts, especially: **a.** A cloth or brush used to remove dust. **b.** A device for sifting or scattering a powdered substance. **2.** A smock worn to protect one's clothing from dust. **3.** A woman's loose dress-length housecoat.

dust·ing (dŭs′tĭng) *n.* **1.** A light sprinkling: *sidewalks covered with a dusting of new snow.* **2.** *Slang.* A beating or defeat: *gave the bully a good dusting.*

dusting powder *n.* A fine powder, such as talcum powder, used on the skin.

dust jacket *n.* *Abbr.* **dj 1.** A removable paper cover used to protect the binding of a book. Also called *dust cover.* **2.** A cardboard sleeve in which a phonograph record is packaged.

dust mop *n.* A mop, usually of soft or fluffy material, that is used dry to remove dust from floors. Also called *dry mop.*

dust-off or **dust·off** (dŭst′ôf′, -ŏf′) *n.* *Slang.* Medevac.

dust·pan (dŭst′păn′) *n.* A short-handled pan or scoop into which dust is swept.

dust ruffle *n.* A gathered or pleated strip of cloth reaching from the bottom of a mattress or box spring to the floor.

dust storm *n.* A severe windstorm that sweeps clouds of dust across an extensive area, especially in an arid region.

dust·up (dŭst′ŭp′) *n.* *Slang.* A row; a dispute.

dust·y (dŭs′tē) *adj.* **-i·er, -i·est. 1.** Covered or filled with dust. **2.** Consisting of or resembling dust; powdery. **3.** Tinged with gray. **4.** Timeworn; stale: *the dusty precepts of a bygone era.* **—dust′i·ly** *adv.* **—dust′i·ness** *n.*

dusty miller *n.* Any of various plants of the genera *Artemisia, Centaurea, Chrysanthemum, Lychnis,* and *Senecio,* having leaves and stems covered with dustlike down.

Dutch (dŭch) *adj.* *Abbr.* **D., Du. 1.a.** Of or relating to the Netherlands or its people or culture. **b.** Of or relating to the Dutch language. **2.** *Archaic.* **a.** German. **b.** Of or relating to any of the Germanic peoples or languages. **3.** Of or relating to the Pennsylvania Dutch. **—Dutch** *n.* **1.a.** The people of the Netherlands. **b.** *Archaic.* A Germanic people. **c.** The Pennsylvania Dutch. **2.a.** The official West Germanic language of the Netherlands. **b.** *Archaic.* One or more of the West Germanic languages of Germany, Switzerland, and the Low Countries. **c.** See **Pennsylvania Dutch** (sense 2). **3.** *Slang.* Anger or temper. ***—idioms.*** **go Dutch.** To pay one's own expenses on a date or outing. **in Dutch.** In disfavor or trouble. [Middle English *Duch,* German, Dutch, from Middle Dutch *Duutsch.* See **teutā-** in Appendix.]

Dutch cheese *n.* See **cottage cheese.**

Dutch clover *n.* See **white clover.**

Dutch courage *n.* *Informal.* Courage acquired from drinking liquor.

Dutch door *n.* A door divided in two horizontally so that either part can be left open or closed.

Dutch East In·dies (ĭn′dēz). See **Indonesia.**

Dutch elm disease *n.* A disease of elm trees caused by the fungus *Ceratocystis ulmi,* characterized by brown streaks in the wood and resulting in eventual death of the trees.

Dutch Gui·a·na (gē-ăn′ə, -ä′nə, gī-). See **Suriname.**

Dutch hoe *n.* See **scuffle**[2]**.**

♦ **Dutch·man** (dŭch′mən) *n.* **1.a.** A man who is a native or inhabitant of the Netherlands. **b.** A man of Dutch ancestry. **2.a.** *Archaic.* A member of any of the Germanic peoples of central or northern Europe. **b.** *Regional.* A person of German ancestry. **3. dutchman.** Something used to conceal faulty construction.

Dutch·man's breeches (dŭch′mənz) *pl.n.* *(used with a sing. or pl. verb).* A woodland plant *(Dicentra cucullaria)* of eastern North America, having finely divided leaves and yellowish-white flowers with two spurs.

Dutchman's pipe *n.* See **pipe vine.**

Dutch metal *n.* An alloy of 80 percent copper and 20 percent zinc used to make low-priced jewelery and in thin sheets as an inexpensive imitation of gold leaf.

Dutch oven *n.* **1.** A large, heavy pot or kettle, usually of cast iron and with a tight lid, used for slow cooking. **2.** A metal utensil open on one side and equipped with shelves, placed before an open fire for baking or roasting food. **3.** A wall oven in which food is baked by means of preheated brick walls.

Dutch treat *n.* An outing, as for dinner or a movie, in which all persons pay their own expenses.

Dutch uncle *n.* A stern, candid critic or adviser.

Dutch West In·dies (ĭn′dēz). See **Netherlands Antilles.**

Dutch·wom·an (dŭch′wo͝om′ən) *n.* **1.** A woman who is a native or inhabitant of the Netherlands. **2.** A woman of Dutch ancestry.

du·te·ous (do͞o′tē-əs, dyo͞o′-) *adj.* Obedient or dutiful. [From DUTY.] **—du′te·ous·ly** *adv.*

du·ti·a·ble (do͞o′tē-ə-bəl, dyo͞o′-) *adj.* Subject to import tax.

du·ti·ful (do͞o′tĭ-fəl, dyo͞o′-) *adj.* **1.** Careful to fulfill obligations. **2.** Expressing or filled with a sense of obligation. **—du′ti·ful·ly** *adv.* **—du′ti·ful·ness** *n.*

Du·tra (do͞o′trə), **Eurico Gaspar.** 1885–1974. Brazilian military and political leader who directed a coup d'état against Getulio Vargas in 1945 and subsequently served as president (1946–1951).

du·ty (do͞o′tē, dyo͞o′-) *n., pl.* **-ties. 1.** An act or a course of action that is required of one by position, social custom, law, or religion: *Do your duty to your country.* **2.a.** Moral obligation: *acting out of duty.* **b.** The compulsion felt to meet such obligation. See Synonyms at **obligation. 3.** A service, function, or task assigned to one, especially in the armed forces: *hazardous duty.* **4.** Function or work; service: *jury duty.* See Synonyms at **function. 5.** *Abbr.* **dy.** A tax charged by a government, especially on imports. **6.** *Abbr.* **dy. a.** The work performed by a machine under specified conditions. **b.** A measure of efficiency expressed as the amount of work done per unit of energy used. **7.** The total volume of water required to irrigate a given area in order to cultivate a specific crop until harvest. ***—idiom.*** **duty bound.** Obliged: *You are duty bound to help your little sister and brother.* [Middle English *duete,* from Anglo-Norman, from *due,* variant of Old French *deu,* due. See DUE.]

du·ty-free (do͞o′tē-frē′, dyo͞o′-) *adj.* **1.** Exempt from customs duties: *duty-free merchandise.* **2.** Of, relating to, or being a region or establishment in which imported goods are exempt from customs duties: *a duty-free port; a duty-free shop.* **—du′ty-free′** *adv.*

du·um·vir (do͞o-ŭm′vər, dyo͞o-) *n.* A member of a duumvirate. [Latin : *duum,* genitive pl. of *duo,* two; see DUO + *vir,* man; see **wī-ro-** in Appendix.]

du·um·vi·rate (do͞o-ŭm′vər-ĭt, dyo͞o-) *n.* **1.** Any of various two-man executive boards in the Roman Republic. **2.** A regime or partnership of two persons.

Du·va·lier (do͞o′väl-yā′, dü-), **François.** Known as "Papa Doc." 1907–1971. Haitian dictator. Elected president in 1957, he declared himself president for life in 1964 and ruled in an authoritarian manner until his death. His son **Jean-Claude** (born 1951), known as "Baby Doc," succeeded him in 1971 but fled the country in 1986 after widespread civil unrest.

Du·vall (do͞o-väl′), **Gabriel.** 1752–1844. American jurist who served as an associate justice of the U.S. Supreme Court (1811–1835).

du·vet (do͞o-vā′, dyo͞o-) *n.* A quilt, usually with a washable cover, that may be used in place of a bedspread and top sheet. [French, down, from Old French, alteration of *dumet,* diminutive of *dum, dun,* from Old Norse *dūnn.*]

du·ve·tyn also **du·ve·tyne** (do͞o′və-tēn′, dyo͞o′-, do͞o′və-tēn′, dyo͞o′-) *n.* A soft, short-napped fabric with a twill weave, made of wool, cotton, rayon, or silk. [French *duvetine,* from *duvet,* down. See DUVET.]

du Vi·gneaud (do͞o vēn′yō, dyo͞o), **Vincent.** 1901–1978. American biochemist. He won a 1955 Nobel Prize for his work on pituitary hormones.

D.V. *abbr.* **1.** *Latin.* Deo volente (God willing). **2.** *Bible.* Douay Version.

Dvi·na (dvē-nä′). **1.** Also **Northern Dvina.** A river, about 748 km (465 mi) long, of north-west Russia flowing north and north-east into **Dvina Bay,** an arm of the White Sea. **2.** Also **Western Dvina.** A river rising in west-central Russia and flowing generally westward about 1,022 km (635 mi) through Belorussia and Latvia to the Gulf of Riga.

D.V.M. *abbr.* Doctor of Veterinary Medicine.

Dvo·rak (dvôr′ăk) *adj.* Of, relating to, or designating a configuration of typewriter or computer keyboard keys arranged to increase the speed and ease of typing, the home row of keys being for the characters A, O, E, U, I, D, H, T, N, and S. [After August *Dvorak* (1894–1975), American educator.]

Dvoř·ák (dvôr′zhäk, -zhăk), **Anton** or **Antonín.** 1841–1904. Czechoslovakian composer whose works, such as *Slavic Dances* (1878), often incorporate folk music. His final symphony, *From the New World* (1893), was composed while he was director of the National Conservatory in New York City (1892–1895).

DW *abbr.* **1.** Dead weight. **2.** Distilled water.

D/W *abbr.* *Law.* Dock warrant.

dwarf (dwôrf) *n., pl.* **dwarfs** or **dwarves** (dwôrvz). **1.a.** An abnormally small person, often having limbs and features not properly proportioned or formed. **b.** An atypically small animal or plant. **2.** A small creature resembling a human being, often ugly, appearing in legends and fairy tales. **3.** A dwarf star. *—attributive.* Often used to modify another noun: *a dwarf tree; dwarf shrubbery.* **—dwarf** *v.* **dwarfed, dwarf·ing, dwarfs.** *—tr.* **1.** To check the natural growth or development of; stunt: *"The oaks were dwarfed from lack of moisture"* (John Steinbeck). **2.** To cause to appear small by comparison: *"Together these two big men dwarfed the tiny Broadway office"* (Saul Bellow). *—intr.* To become stunted or grow smaller. [Middle English *dwerf,* from Old English *dweorh.*] **—dwarf′ish** *adj.* **—dwarf′ish·ness** *n.*

dwarf cornel *n.* A herbaceous plant *(Cornus canadensis)* of northern North America, having creeping rhizomes, scarlet fruit, and inconspicuous greenish flowers surrounded by four white, petallike bracts. Also called *bunchberry.*

dwarf huckleberry *n.* See **dangleberry.**

dwarf·ism (dwôr′fĭz′əm) *n.* A pathological condition of arrested growth having various causes. Also called *nanism.*

dwarf shoot *n.* A lateral branch that is much smaller than the main one, as in the cedar, larch, and ginkgo.

dust storm
Near Boise City, Oklahoma, in the mid 1930's

Dutchman's breeches
Dicentra cucullaria

Dutch oven

"Papa Doc" Duvalier

Mary Dyer
Bronze statue by
Sylvia Shaw Judson
(1897–1978)

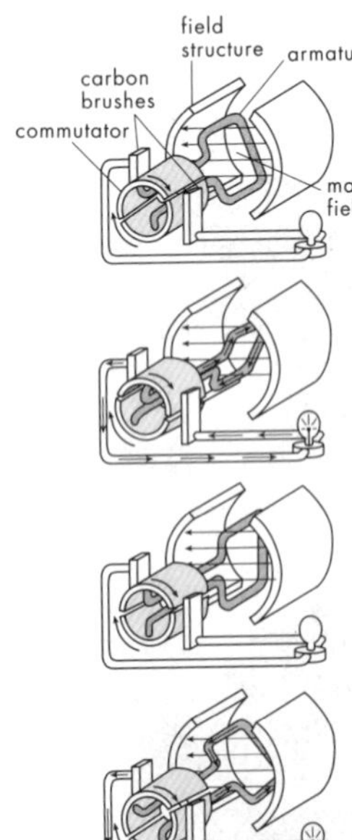

dynamo

dwarf star *n.* A star, such as the sun, having relatively low mass, small size, and average or below average luminosity.

dwarves (dwôrvz) *n.* A plural of **dwarf.**

dweeb (dwēb) *n. Slang.* **1.** A subservient person; a flunky. **2.** A despised person. [Origin unknown.]

dwell (dwĕl) *intr.v.* **dwelt** (dwĕlt) or **dwelled, dwell·ing, dwells. 1.** To live as a resident; reside. **2.** To exist in a given place or state: *dwell in joy.* **3.a.** To fasten one's attention: *kept dwelling on what went wrong.* See Synonyms at **brood. b.** To speak or write at length; expatiate: *dwelt on the need to trim the budget.* **4.** *Computer Science.* A programmed time delay of variable duration. [Middle English *dwellen,* from Old English *dwellan,* to mislead.] **—dwell′er** *n.*

dwell·ing (dwĕl′ĭng) *n.* A place to live in; an abode.

dwelt (dwĕlt) *v.* A past tense and a past participle of **dwell.**

DWI *abbr.* Driving while intoxicated.

Dwight (dwīt), **Timothy.** 1752–1817. American clergyman, author, and educator who was a leading supporter of Federalism and served as president of Yale University (1795–1817).

dwin·dle (dwĭn′dl) *v.* **-dled, -dling, -dles.** *—intr.* To become gradually less until little remains. *—tr.* To cause to dwindle. See Synonyms at **decrease.** [Frequentative of Middle English *dwinen,* to waste away, from Old English *dwīnan,* to shrink. See **dheu-**[2] in Appendix.]

dwt. *abbr.* Pennyweight.

Dy The symbol for the element **dysprosium.**

dy. *abbr.* **1.** Delivery. **2.** Duty.

dy·ad (dī′ăd′, -əd) *n.* **1.** Two individuals or units regarded as a pair: *the mother-daughter dyad.* **2.** *Biology.* One pair of homologous chromosomes resulting from the division of a tetrad during meiosis. **3.** *Chemistry.* A divalent atom or radical. **4.** *Mathematics.* An operator represented as a pair of vectors juxtaposed without multiplication. **—dyad** *adj.* Made up of two units. [From Greek *duas, duad-,* from *duo,* two. See **dwo-** in Appendix.]

dy·ad·ic (dī-ăd′ĭk) *adj.* **1.** Twofold. **2.** Of or relating to a dyad. **—dyadic** *n. Mathematics.* The direct product ($\boldsymbol{B \cdot C}$) $\boldsymbol{AD}$ of two dyads $\boldsymbol{AB}$ and $\boldsymbol{CD}$.

Dy·ak (dī′ăk′) *n.* Variant of **Dayak.**

dy·ar·chy (dī′är′kē) *n.* Variant of **diarchy.**

dyb·buk (dĭb′ŏŏk, dē-bŏŏk′) *n., pl.* **dyb·buks** or **dyb·buk·im** (dĭ-bŏŏk′ĭm, dē′bōō-kēm′). In Jewish folklore, the wandering soul of a dead person that enters the body of a living person and controls his or her behavior. [Yiddish *dibek,* from Hebrew *dibbūq,* probably from *dābaq,* to cling.]

dye (dī) *n.* **1.** A substance used to color materials. Also called *dyestuff.* **2.** A color imparted by dyeing. **—dye** *v.* **dyed, dye·ing, dyes.** *—tr.* To color (a material), especially by soaking in a coloring solution. *—intr.* To take on or impart color. ***—idiom.* of the deepest dye.** Of the most extreme sort. [Middle English *deie,* from Old English *dēag, dēah.*] **—dy′er** *n.*

dyed-in-the-wool (dīd′ĭn-*th*ə-wŏŏl′) *adj.* **1.** Thoroughgoing; out-and-out: *a dyed-in-the-wool populist.* **2.** Dyed before being woven into cloth.

Dy·er, (dī′ər), **Mary.** Died 1660. English-born American Quaker martyr who was twice banished from Boston because of her beliefs. She was hanged after returning to the city a second time.

dy·er's broom (dī′ərz) *n.* See **dyer's greenweed.**

dy·er's greenweed (dī′ərz) *n.* A small Eurasian shrub *(Genista tinctoria)* having clusters of yellow flowers that yield a dye. Also called *dyer's broom, woadwaxen, woodwaxen.*

dyer's rocket *n.* A European plant *(Reseda luteola)* having long spikes of small, yellowish-green flowers and yielding a yellow dye. Also called *weld.*

dy·er's-weed (dī′ərz-wēd′) *n.* Any of various plants yielding coloring matter used as dye.

dye·stuff (dī′stŭf′) *n.* See **dye** (sense 1).

dye·wood (dī′wŏŏd′) *n.* A wood used as a dyestuff.

dy·ing (dī′ĭng) *v.* Present participle of **die**[1]. **—dying** *adj.* **1.** About to die: *dying patients.* **2.** Drawing to an end; declining: *in the dying hours of the legislative session.* **3.** Done or uttered just before death: *a dying request.*

dyke[1] (dīk) *n. & v.* Variant of **dike**[1].

dyke[2] (dīk) also **dike** *n. Offensive Slang.* Used as a disparaging term for a lesbian. [Origin unknown.]

Dy·lan (dĭl′ən), **Bob.** Born 1941. American musician who drew on blues, country and western, and folk music to create distinctive protest music in the 1960's. His song "Blowin' in the Wind" became an anthem of the civil rights movement.

dyn *abbr. Physics.* Dyne.

dy·nam·ic (dī-năm′ĭk) also **dy·nam·i·cal** (-ĭ-kəl) *adj.* **1.a.** Of or relating to energy or to objects in motion. **b.** Of or relating to the study of dynamics. **2.** Characterized by continuous change, activity, or progress: *a dynamic market.* **3.** Marked by intensity and vigor; forceful. See Synonyms at **active. 4.** Of or relating to variation of intensity, as in musical sound. **—dynamic** *n.* **1.** An interactive system or process, especially one involving competing or conflicting forces: *"the story of a malign dynamic between white prejudice and black autonomy"* (Edmund S. Morgan). **2.** A force, especially political, social, or psychological: *the main dynamic behind the revolution.* [French *dynamique,* ultimately from Greek *dunamikos,* powerful, from *dunamis,* power, from *dunasthai,* to be able. See **deu-**[2] in Appendix.] **—dy·nam′i·cal·ly** *adv.*

dynamic headroom *n. Electronics.* The capacity of an amplifier to reproduce unusually strong signals without distortion.

dy·nam·ics (dī-năm′ĭks) *n.* **1.a.** *(used with a sing. verb).* The branch of mechanics that is concerned with the effects of forces on the motion of a body or system of bodies, especially of forces that do not originate within the system itself. Also called *kinetics.* **b.** *(used with a pl. verb).* The forces and motions that characterize a system: *The dynamics of ocean waves are complex.* **2.** *(used with a pl. verb).* The social, intellectual, or moral forces that produce activity and change in a given sphere: *The dynamics of international trade have influenced our business decisions on this matter.* **3.** *(used with a pl. verb).* Variation in force or intensity, especially in musical sound: *"The conductor tended to overpower her with aggressive dynamics"* (Thor Eckert, Jr.). **4.** *(used with a sing. verb).* Psychodynamics.

dy·na·mism (dī′nə-mĭz′əm) *n.* **1.** Any of various theories or philosophical systems that explain the universe in terms of force or energy. **2.** A process or mechanism responsible for the development or motion of a system. **3.** Continuous change, activity, or progress; vigor. [French *dynamisme,* from Greek *dunamis,* power. See DYNAMIC.] **—dy′na·mist** *n.* **—dy′na·mis′tic** *adj.*

dy·na·mite (dī′nə-mīt′) *n.* **1.** Any of a class of powerful explosives composed of nitroglycerin or ammonium nitrate dispersed in an absorbent medium with a combustible dope, such as wood pulp, and an antacid, such as calcium carbonate, used in blasting and mining. **2.** *Slang.* **a.** Something exceptionally exciting or wonderful. **b.** Something exceptionally dangerous: *These allegations are political dynamite.* **—dynamite** *tr.v.* **-mit·ed, -mit·ing, -mites. 1.** To blow up, shatter, or otherwise destroy with or as if with dynamite. **2.** To charge with dynamite. **—dynamite** *adj. Slang.* Outstanding; superb: *a dynamite performance; a dynamite outfit.* [Swedish *dynamit,* from Greek *dunamis,* power. See DYNAMIC.] **—dy′na·mit′er** *n.*

WORD HISTORY: The same man who gave us dynamite gave us the Nobel Peace Prize, an irony that was surely not lost on the pacifistic Alfred Nobel himself. It is perhaps less well known that Nobel also contributed the word *dynamite.* Coined in Swedish in the form *dynamit,* the word was taken from Greek *dunamis,* "power," and the Swedish suffix *–it,* which corresponds to our suffix *–ite* used in various scientific fields. Greek *dunamis* also gave us words such as *dynamic* and *dynamo* and itself probably goes back to the verb *dunasthai,* "to be able," from which comes *dynasty.*

dy·na·mo (dī′nə-mō′) *n., pl.* **-mos. 1.** A generator, especially one for producing direct current. **2.** An extremely energetic and forceful person: *a vice president who was the real dynamo of the corporation.* [Short for *dynamoelectric machine.*]

dy·na·mo·e·lec·tric (dī′nə-mō′ĭ-lĕk′trĭk) **dy·na·mo·e·lec·tri·cal** (-trĭ-kəl) *adj.* Of or relating to the conversion of mechanical energy to electrical energy or vice versa. [Greek *dunamis,* power; see DYNAMIC + ELECTRIC.]

dy·na·mom·e·ter (dī′nə-mŏm′ĭ-tər) *n.* Any of several instruments used to measure mechanical power. [French *dynamomètre* : Greek *dunamis,* power; see DYNAMIC + *-mètre,* -meter.] **—dy′na·mo·met′ric** (-mō-mĕt′rĭk), **dy′na·mo·met′ri·cal** (-rĭ-kəl) *adj.* **—dy′na·mom′e·try** *n.*

dy·na·mo·tor (dī′nə-mō′tər) *n.* A rotating electric machine with two armatures, used to convert alternating current to direct current. [Greek *dunamis,* power; see DYNAMIC + MOTOR.]

dy·nast (dī′năst′, -nəst) *n.* A ruler, especially a hereditary one. [Latin *dynastēs,* from Greek *dunastēs,* lord, from *dunasthai,* to be able. See **deu-**[2] in Appendix.]

dy·nas·ty (dī′nə-stē) *n., pl.* **-ties. 1.** A succession of rulers from the same family or line. **2.** A family or group that maintains power for several generations: *a political dynasty controlling the state.* [Middle English *dynastie,* from Old French, from Late Latin *dynastīa,* lordship, from Greek *dunasteia,* from *dunastēs,* lord. See DYNAST.] **—dy·nas′tic** (dī-năs′tĭk) *adj.* **—dy·nas′ti·cal·ly** *adv.*

dy·na·tron (dī′nə-trŏn′) *n. Electronics.* A tetrode with grid and plate potentials so arranged that plate current decreases when plate potential increases. [Greek *dunamis,* power; see DYNAMIC + –TRON.]

dyne (dīn) *n. Abbr.* **dyn** A centimeter-gram-second unit of force, equal to the force required to impart an acceleration of one centimeter per second per second to a mass of one gram. [From Greek *dunamis,* power. See DYNAMIC.]

Dy·nel (dī-nĕl′). A trademark used for a copolymer of vinyl chloride and acrylonitrile employed in making fire-resistant, insect-resistant, easily dyed textile fiber.

dy·node (dī′nōd′) *n.* An electrode used in certain electron tubes to provide secondary emission. [Greek *dunamis,* power; see DYNAMIC + –ODE.]

dys– *pref.* **1.** Abnormal: *dysplasia.* **2.a.** Impaired: *dysgraphia.* **b.** Difficult: *dysphonia.* **3.** Bad: *dyslogistic.* [Latin *dys-,* bad, from Greek *dus-.* See **dus-** in Appendix.]

dys·cal·cu·li·a (dĭs′kăl-kyōō′lē-ə) *n.* Impairment of the ability to solve mathematical problems, usually resulting from brain dysfunction. [DYS– + CALCUL(ATE) + –IA[1].]

dys·cra·sia (dĭs-krā′zhə, -zhē-ə) *n.* An abnormal bodily condition, especially of the blood. [Medieval Latin, bad mixture, disease, from Greek *duskrasia* : *dus-*, dys- + *krasis,* mixing; see **kerə-** in Appendix.]

dys·en·ter·y (dĭs′ən-tĕr′ē) *n.* An inflammatory disorder of the lower intestinal tract, usually caused by a bacterial, parasitic, or protozoan infection and resulting in pain, fever, and severe diarrhea, often accompanied by the passage of blood and mucus. [Middle English *dissenterie,* from Old French, from Latin *dysenteria,* from Greek *dusenteria* : *dus-,* dys- + *enteron,* intestine; see **en** in Appendix.] **—dys′en·ter′ic** *adj.*

dys·func·tion also **dis·func·tion** (dĭs-fŭngk′shən) *n.* Abnormal or impaired functioning, especially of a bodily system or organ. **—dys·func′tion·al** *adj.*

dys·gen·e·sis (dĭs-jĕn′ĭ-sĭs) *n.* Defective or abnormal development of an organ, especially of the gonads.

dys·gen·ic (dĭs-jĕn′ĭk) *adj.* Relating to or causing the deterioration of hereditary qualities in offspring.

dys·gen·ics (dĭs-jĕn′ĭks) *n. (used with a sing. verb).* The biological study of the factors producing degeneration in offspring, especially of a particular race or species.

dys·graph·ia (dĭs-grăf′ē-ə) *n.* Impairment of the ability to write, usually caused by brain dysfunction or disease. [New Latin : DYS– + Greek *-graphia,* -graphy.] **—dys·graph′ic** *adj.*

dys·ki·ne·sia (dĭs′kə-nē′zhə, -kī-) *n.* An impairment in the ability to control movements, characterized by spasmodic or repetitive motions or lack of coordination.

dys·lex·i·a (dĭs-lĕk′sē-ə) *n.* A learning disorder marked by impairment of the ability to recognize and comprehend written words. [New Latin : DYS– + Greek *lexis,* speech (from *legein,* to speak; see **leg-** in Appendix).] **—dys·lec′tic** (-lĕk′tĭk) *n.*

dys·lex·ic (dĭs-lĕk′sĭk) *n.* A person who is affected by dyslexia. **—dyslexic** *adj.* Of or relating to dyslexia.

dys·lo·gis·tic (dĭs′lə-jĭs′tĭk) *adj.* Conveying censure. [DYS– + (EU)LOGISTIC.] **—dys′lo·gis′ti·cal·ly** *adv.*

dys·men·or·rhe·a also **dys·men·or·rhoe·a** (dĭs-mĕn′ə-rē′ə) *n.* Painful menstruation. [New Latin : DYS– + Greek *mēn,* month; see **mē-²** in Appendix + –RRHEA.] **—dys·men′or·rhe′al** (-rē′əl), **dys·men′or·rhe′ic** (-rē′ĭk) *adj.*

dys·pep·sia (dĭs-pĕp′shə, -sē-ə) *n.* Disturbed digestion; indigestion. [Latin, from Greek *duspepsia* : *dus-,* dys- + *-pepsia,* digestion; see **pekʷ-** in Appendix.]

dys·pep·tic (dĭs-pĕp′tĭk) *adj.* **1.** Relating to or having dyspepsia. **2.** Of or displaying a morose disposition. **—dyspeptic** *n.* One affected by dyspepsia. **—dys·pep′ti·cal·ly** *adv.*

dys·pha·gia (dĭs-fā′jə, -jē-ə) *n.* Difficulty in swallowing. **—dys·phag′ic** (-făj′ĭk) *adj.*

dys·pha·sia (dĭs-fā′zhə, -zhē-ə) *n.* Impairment of speech and verbal comprehension, especially when associated with brain injury. **—dys·pha′sic** (-zĭk) *adj. & n.*

dys·pho·ni·a (dĭs-fō′nē-ə) *n.* Difficulty in speaking, usually evidenced by hoarseness. [New Latin : DYS– + Greek *-phōnia,* -phony.] **—dys·phon′ic** (-fŏn′ĭk) *adj.*

dys·pho·ri·a (dĭs-fôr′ē-ə, -fōr′-) *n.* An emotional state characterized by anxiety, depression, and restlessness. [New Latin, from Greek *dusphoria,* distress, from *dusphoros,* hard to bear : *dus-,* dys- + *-phoros,* -phorous.] **—dys·phor′ic** (-fôr′ĭk, -fŏr′-) *adj.*

dys·pla·sia (dĭs-plā′zhə, -zhē-ə) *n.* Abnormal development or growth of tissues, organs, or cells. **—dys·plas′tic** (-plăs′tĭk) *adj.*

dysp·ne·a (dĭsp-nē′ə) *n.* Difficulty in breathing, often associated with lung or heart disease and resulting in shortness of breath. Also called *air hunger.* [Latin *dyspnoea,* from Greek *duspnoia* : *dus-,* dys- + *pnoia,* breathing; see **pneu-** in Appendix.] **—dysp·ne′ic** (-nē′ĭk) *adj.*

dys·pro·si·um (dĭs-prō′zē-əm, -zhē-əm) *n. Symbol* **Dy** A soft, silvery rare-earth element used in nuclear research. Atomic number 66; atomic weight 162.50; melting point 1,407°C; boiling point 2,600°C; specific gravity 8.536; valence 3. See table at **element.** [New Latin, from Greek *dusprositos,* difficult to approach : *dus-,* dys- + *prositos,* approachable (from *prosienai,* to approach : *pros-,* toward + *ienai, i-,* to go; see **ei-** in Appendix).]

dys·rhyth·mi·a (dĭs-rĭ*th*′mē-ə) *n.* An abnormality in an otherwise normal rhythmic pattern, as of brain waves being recorded by an electroencephalograph. [New Latin : DYS– + Latin *rythmus,* rhythm; see RHYTHM.]

dys·tel·e·ol·o·gy (dĭs-tĕl′ē-ŏl′ə-jē, -tē′lē-) *n.* **1.** The doctrine of purposelessness in nature. **2.** Purposelessness in natural structures, as manifested by the existence of vestigial or nonfunctional organs or parts. **—dys·tel′e·o·log′i·cal** (-ə-lŏj′ĭ-kəl) *adj.* **—dys·tel′e·ol′o·gist** *n.*

dys·to·pi·a (dĭs-tō′pē-ə) *n.* **1.** An imaginary place or state in which the condition of life is extremely bad, as from deprivation, oppression, or terror. **2.** A work describing such a place or state: *"dystopias such as* Brave New World*"* (Times Literary Supplement). [DYS– + (U)TOPIA.]

dys·to·pi·an (dĭs-tō′pē-ən) *adj.* **1.** Of or relating to a dystopia. **2.** Dire; grim: *"AIDS is one of the dystopian harbingers of the global village"* (Susan Sontag).

dys·tro·phi·a (dĭ-strō′fē-ə) *n.* Variant of **dystrophy.**

dys·troph·ic (dĭ-strŏf′ĭk, -strō′fĭk) *adj.* **1.** *Medicine.* Of, relating to, or afflicted with dystrophy. **2.** *Ecology.* Having brownish acidic waters, a high concentration of humic matter, and a small plant population. Used of a lake or pond. **—dys′tro·phi·ca′tion** (dĭs′trə-fĭ-kā′shən) *n.*

dys·tro·phy (dĭs′trə-fē) also **dys·tro·phi·a** (dĭ-strō′fē-ə) *n.* **1.** A degenerative disorder caused by inadequate or defective nutrition. **2.** Any of several disorders, especially muscular dystrophy, in which the muscles weaken and atrophy. **3.** *Ecology.* The condition of being dystrophic.

dys·u·ri·a (dĭs-yo͝or′ē-ə) *n.* Painful or difficult urination. [Middle English *dissure, dissuria,* from Old French *dissure,* from Medieval Latin *dissuria,* from Late Latin *dysūria,* from Greek *dusouria* : *dus-,* dys- + *-ouria,* -uria.] **—dys·u′ric** (-yo͝or′ĭk) *adj.*

dz. *abbr.* Dozen.

Dzer·shinsk (dər-zhĭnsk′, dzĭr-). A city of west-central Russia on the Oka River west of Kazan. It is an industrial center. Population, 274,000.

Dzham·bul (jäm-bo͞ol′). A city of south-central Kazakhstan near the Kirghiz border. Founded in the seventh century, it was ruled by Turks in the eighth and ninth centuries and passed to Russia in 1864. Population, 303,000.

Dzun·gar·i·a (dzo͝ong-gâr′ē-ə, zo͝ong-). A vast historical region of northwest China. It was a Mongol kingdom from the 11th to the 14th century and was conquered by the Chinese in the 1750's.

ă pat	oi boy
ā pay	ou out
âr care	o͝o took
ä father	o͞o boot
ĕ pet	ŭ cut
ē be	ûr urge
ĭ pit	th thin
ī pie	*th* this
îr pier	hw which
ŏ pot	zh vision
ō toe	ə about, item
ô paw	♦ regionalism

Stress marks: **′** (primary); ′ (secondary), as in **dictionary** (dĭk′shə-nĕr′ē)

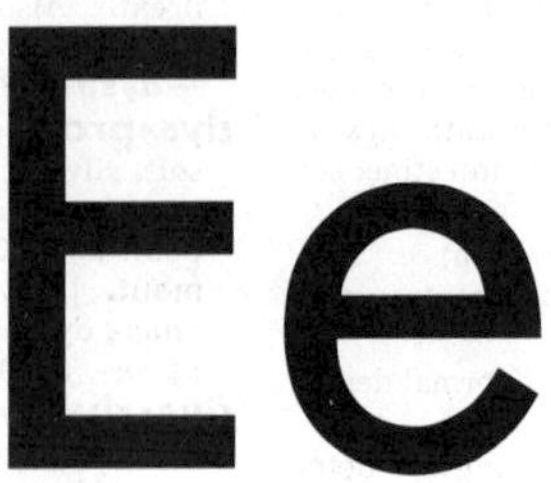

Phoenician
In the Phoenician alphabet this letter stood for a Semitic consonantal sound *h*.

Early Greek
Because this sound was lacking in their own language, the Greeks applied it instead to the vowel *e* (specifically "simple e," that is, short *e*, *e psilon*).

Roman
It retained this value in the Roman script and into modern times.

e[1] or **E** (ē) *n., pl.* **e's** or **E's.** **1.** The fifth letter of the modern English alphabet. **2.** Any of the speech sounds represented by the letter *e*. **3.** The fifth in a series. **4.** *Music.* **a.** The third tone in the scale of C major or the fifth tone in the relative minor scale. **b.** A key or scale in which E is the tonic. **c.** A written or printed note representing this tone. **d.** A string, key, or pipe tuned to the pitch of this tone. **5. E.** A grade that indicates excellence in achievement or quality. **6. e.** *Mathematics.* The base of the natural system of logarithms, having a numerical value of approximately 2.7183.

e[2] *abbr.* **1.** Electron. **2.** Or **e.** *Baseball.* Error.

E *abbr.* **1.** Or **E. e, e.** East. **2.** Or **E.** English.

e. or **E.** *abbr.* Engineer; engineering.

E. *abbr.* Earl.

each (ēch) *adj. Abbr.* **ea.** Being one of two or more considered individually; every: *Each person cast a vote. My technique improved with each lesson.* **—each** *pron.* Every one of a group considered individually; each one. **—each** *adv.* For or to each one; apiece: *ten cents each.* [Middle English *ech,* from Old English *ǣlc.* See **līk-** in Appendix.]

USAGE NOTE: The traditional rule holds that when the subject of a sentence begins with *each,* it is grammatically singular, and the verb and following pronouns must be singular as well: *Each of the suites has* (not *have*) *its* (not *their*) *own private entrance* (not *entrances*). When *each* follows a plural subject, however, the verb and subsequent pronouns remain in the plural: *The suites each have their own private entrances* (not *has its own private entrance*). An exception is made when *each* follows the verb with a first-person plural subject: one may say either *We boys have each our own room* or *We boys have each his own room,* though the latter form is somewhat stilted in modern use. • The expression *each and every* is likewise followed by a singular verb and singular pronoun in formal style: *Each and every driver knows* (not *know*) *what his or her* (not *their*) *job is to be.* See Usage Note at **every, he[1].**

each other *pron.* Each the other. Used to indicate that a relationship or an action is reciprocal among the members of the set referred to by the antecedent: *The boys like each other.*

USAGE NOTE: It is often maintained that *each other* should be used to denote a reciprocal relation between two entities, with *one another* reserved for more than two: thus *The twins dislike each other* but *The triplets dislike one another.* Sixty-four percent of the Usage Panel says that they follow this rule in their own writing. But it should be pointed out that many reputable writers from Johnson onward have ignored the rule and that the use of *each other* for more than two, or of *one another* for two, cannot be considered incorrect. In particular, there are contexts in which *each other* and *one another* are subtly different in meaning. When speaking of an ordered series of events or stages, *one another* is the preferred form. Thus the sentence *The waiters followed one another into the room* was preferred by 73 percent of the Usage Panel to the sentence *The waiters followed each other into the room.* • *Each other* should not be used as the subject of a clause in writing. Instead of *We always know what each other is thinking,* one should write *Each of us knows what the other is thinking.* • The possessive forms of *each other* and *one another* are written *each other's* and *one another's: The boys wore each other's* (not *each others'*) *coats. They had forgotten one another's* (not *one anothers'*) *names.*

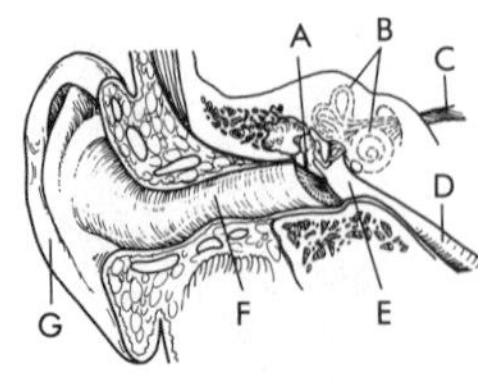

ear
A. Eardrum
B. Inner ear
C. Auditory nerve
D. Eustachian tube
E. Middle ear
F. Ear canal
G. Auricle

Eads (ēdz), **James Buchanan.** 1820–1887. American engineer who produced ironclad steamships, bridged the Mississippi River at St. Louis (1874), and improved the navigability of the mouth of the Mississippi.

Ea·gan (ē′gən). A city of eastern Minnesota, a suburb of Minneapolis–St. Paul. Population, 20,700.

ea·ger[1] (ē′gər) *adj.* **-ger·er, -ger·est. 1.** Having or showing keen interest, intense desire, or impatient expectancy. See Usage Note at **anxious. 2.** *Obsolete.* Tart; sharp; cutting. [Middle English *eger,* sour, sharp, impetuous, from Anglo-Norman *egre,* from Latin *ācer.* See **ak-** in Appendix.] **—ea′ger·ly** *adv.* **—ea′ger·ness** *n.*

SYNONYMS: *eager, avid, keen, agog.* These adjectives mean animated by or showing great interest or desire. *Eager* suggests intensity of interest and impatient desire: *eager to travel abroad; eager to learn. Avid* implies ardent desire and unbounded craving: *has an avid ambition to succeed; an avid sports fan. Keen* suggests acuteness or intensity of interest or emotional drive: *takes keen pleasure in music. Agog* implies a state of heightened anticipation: *The prospect of Christmas left the children agog.*

ea·ger[2] (ē′gər, ā′-) *n.* Variant of **eagre.**

eager beaver *n. Informal.* One that is exceptionally, often excessively industrious or zealous: *"The eager beavers of industry seldom reach their potential, much less rise to the top"* (Newsweek). **—ea′ger-bea′ver** (ē′gər-bē′vər) *adj.*

ea·gle (ē′gəl) *n.* **1.** Any of various large diurnal birds of prey of the family Accipitridae, including members of the genera *Aquila* and *Haliaeetus,* characterized by a powerful hooked bill, keen vision, long broad wings, and strong, soaring flight. **2.** A representation of an eagle used as an emblem or insignia. **3.** A gold coin formerly used in the United States, stamped with an eagle on the reverse side and having a face value of ten dollars. **4.** *Sports.* A golf score of two strokes under par on a hole. **—eagle** *v.* **-gled, -gling, -gles.** *Sports.* —*tr.* To shoot (a hole in golf) in two strokes under par. —*intr.* To score an eagle in golf. [Middle English *egle,* from Anglo-Norman, from Old Provençal *aigla,* from Latin *aquila.*]

ea·gle-eyed (ē′gəl-īd′) *adj.* **1.** Having keen eyesight. **2.** Showing close attention to detail; perceptive: *an eagle-eyed accountant who monitored every expense.*

eagle owl *n.* A large Eurasian owl *(Bubo bubo)* having brownish plumage and prominent ear tufts.

Ea·gle Pass (ē′gəl). A city of southwest Texas west-southwest of San Antonio. It was a way station on the route to California during the gold rush of 1848–1849. Population, 21,407.

eagle ray *n.* Any of numerous rays of the family Myliobatididae, found worldwide in tropical and subtropical shallow seas and noted for their massive jaws and large winglike pectoral fins, which they flap for propulsion.

Eagle Scout *n.* One who has achieved the highest rank in the Boy Scouts.

ea·glet (ē′glĭt) *n.* A young eagle.

ea·gre also **ea·ger** (ē′gər, ā′gər) *n.* See **bore[3].** [Origin unknown.]

Ea·kins (ā′kĭnz), **Thomas.** 1844–1916. American painter known for highly realistic works, such as *Max Schmitt in a Single Scull* (1871).

eal·dor·man (ôl′dər-mən) *n.* The chief magistrate of a district in Anglo-Saxon England. [Old English. See ALDERMAN.]

Eames (ēmz), **Charles.** 1907–1978. American designer noted for an innovative series of chairs made of molded plywood.

Eames chair *n.* A functional chair, originally of molded plywood, with seat and back pieces shaped to the contours of the human body. [After Charles EAMES.]

ear[1] (îr) *n.* **1.** *Anatomy.* **a.** The vertebrate organ of hearing, responsible for maintaining equilibrium as well as sensing sound and divided in mammals into the external ear, the middle ear, and the inner ear. **b.** The part of this organ that is externally visible. **2.** An invertebrate organ analogous to the mammalian ear. **3.** The sense of hearing: *a sound that grates on the ear.* **4.** Sensitivity or receptiveness to sound, especially: **a.** Sharpness or refinement of hearing: *a singer with a good ear for harmony.* **b.** The ability to retain and reproduce a passage of music: *plays the piano by ear.* **c.** Responsiveness to the sounds or forms of spoken language: *a writer with a good ear for dialogue; has an ear for foreign languages.* **5.** Sympathetic or favorable attention: "[The President] *wavers between the two positions, depending on who last had his ear"* (Joseph C. Harsch). **6.** Something resembling the external ear in position or shape, especially: **a.** A flexible tuft of feathers located above the eyes of certain birds, such as owls, that functions in visual communication but not in hearing. Also called *ear tuft.* **b.** A projecting handle, as on a vase or pitcher. **7.** A small box in the upper corner of the page in a newspaper or periodical that contains a printed notice, such as promotional material or weather information. **8. ears.** *Informal.* Headphones. **—*idioms.* all ears.** *Informal.* Acutely attentive: *If you want to tell your story, we're all ears.* **give** (or **lend**) **an ear.** To pay close attention; listen attentively. **have** (or **keep**) **an ear to the ground.** To be on the watch for new trends or information. **in one ear and out the other.** Without any influence or effect; unheeded: *Since his mind was already made up, my arguments went in one ear and out the other.* **on its** (or **someone's**) **ear.** In a state of amazement, excitement, or uproar: *a controversial film that set the entertainment world on its ear.* **play it by ear.** *Informal.* To act according to the circumstances; improvise: *"He plays his negotiations by ear, going into them with no clear or fixed plan"* (George F. Kennan). **up to (one's) ears.** *Informal.* Deeply involved or committed: *I'm up to my ears in work.* [Middle English *ere,* from Old English *ēare.* See **ous-** in Appendix.]

ear[2] (îr) *n.* The seed-bearing spike of a cereal plant, such as corn. **—ear** *intr.v.* **eared, ear·ing, ears.** To form or grow ears. [Middle English *ere,* from Old English *ēar.* See **ak-** in Appendix.]

ear·ache (îr′āk′) *n.* Pain in the ear; otalgia.

♦ **ear·bob** (îr′bŏb′) *n.* *Chiefly Southern U.S.* See **earring.**

ear canal *n.* The narrow, tubelike passage through which sound enters the ear. Also called *external auditory canal.*

ear candy *n.* *Informal.* A light, often short piece of music considered to be pleasing.

ear·drop (îr′drŏp′) *n.* **1.** An earring, especially one with a pendant. **2. eardrops.** Liquid medicine administered into the ear.

ear·drum (îr′drŭm′) *n.* *Anatomy.* The thin, semitransparent, oval-shaped membrane that separates the middle ear from the external ear. Also called *tympanic membrane, tympanum.*

eared (îrd) *adj.* **1.** Having ears or earlike projections. **2.** Having a specified kind or number of ears. Often used in combination: *a lop-eared puppy.*

eared seal *n.* Any of various seals of the family Otariidae, which includes the sea lions and fur seals, characterized by external ears, oarlike front flippers, and hind flippers that can be turned forward for walking on land.

ear·flap (îr′flăp′) *n.* A flap attached to a cap that may be turned down to cover the ears. Also called *earlap.*

ear·ful (îr′fo͝ol′) *n.* **1.** An abundant or excessive amount of something heard, such as talk or music. **2.** Gossip, especially of an intimate or scandalous nature. **3.** A scolding or reprimand.

Ear·hart (âr′härt′), **Amelia.** 1897?–1937. American aviator who was the first woman to fly solo across the Atlantic Ocean (1932) and from Hawaii to California (1935). While attempting to fly around the world, she crashed in the Pacific Ocean (1937).

ear·ing (îr′ĭng) *n.* *Nautical.* A short line attaching an upper corner of a sail to the yard. [Perhaps from EAR[1].]

earl (ûrl) *n.* *Abbr.* **E. 1.** A British nobleman next in rank above a viscount and below a marquis, corresponding to a count in continental Europe. **2.** Used as a title for such a nobleman. [Middle English *erl,* nobleman of high rank, from Old English *eorl.*]

ear·lap (îr′lăp′) *n.* See **earflap.**

earl·dom (ûrl′dəm) *n.* **1.** The rank or title of an earl. **2.** The territory of an earl.

ear·less seal (îr′lĭs) *n.* Any of various seals of the family Phocidae, which includes the hair seals, characterized by short fore flippers, reduced hind flippers specialized for swimming, and the absence of external ears. Also called *true seal.*

ear·lobe also **ear lobe** (îr′lōb′) *n.* The soft, fleshy, pendulous lower part of the external ear.

ear·ly (ûr′lē) *adj.* **-li·er, -li·est. 1.** Of or occurring near the beginning of a given series, period of time, or course of events: *in the early morning; scored two runs in the early innings.* **2.a.** Of or belonging to a previous or remote period of time: *the early inhabitants of the British Isles.* **b.** Of or belonging to an initial stage of development: *an early form of life; an early computer.* **3.** Occurring, developing, or appearing before the expected or usual time: *an early spring; an early retirement.* **4.** Maturing or developing relatively soon: *an early variety of tomato.* **5.** Occurring in the near future: *Observers predicted an early end to the negotiations.* **—early** *adv.* **-lier, -liest. 1.** Near the beginning of a given series, period of time, or course of events: *departed early in the day; scored important victories early in the campaign.* **2.** At or during a remote or initial period: *decided very early to go into medicine.* **3.** Before the expected or usual time: *arrived at the meeting a few minutes early.* **4.** Soon in relation to others of its kind: *a rose that was cultivated to bloom early.* [Middle English *erli,* from Old English *ǣrlīce* : *ǣr,* before; see **ayer-** in Appendix + *-līce,* adv. suff.; see –LY[2].] **—ear′li·ness** *n.*

Ear·ly (ûr′lē), **Jubal Anderson.** 1816–1894. American Confederate general whose forces threatened Washington, D.C. (1864) but were ultimately defeated by Union troops.

early bird *n.* *Informal.* **1.** A person who arises early in the morning. **2.** One that arrives or takes place early or before others. [From the expression "The early bird catches the worm".] **—ear′ly-bird′** (ûr′lē-bûrd′) *adj.*

early on *adv.* At an early stage or point: *"Early on,* [he] *found that being honest and being funny were almost the same thing"* (Maureen Orth).

early warning radar *n.* Radar based at the boundary of a defended area to detect incoming enemy missiles or aircraft in time to allow deployment of a countermeasure.

early warning system *n.* **1.** A network of sensing devices, such as satellites or radar, for detecting an enemy attack in time to take defensive or counteroffensive measures. **2.** A system or procedure designed to warn of a potential or an impending problem.

ear·mark (îr′märk′) *n.* **1.** An identifying feature or characteristic: *a novel with all the earmarks of success.* **2.** An identifying mark on the ear of a domestic animal. **—earmark** *tr.v.* **-marked, -mark·ing, -marks. 1.** To reserve or set aside for a particular purpose. See Synonyms at **allocate. 2.** To place an identifying or distinctive mark on. **3.** To mark the ear of (a domestic animal) for identification.

ear·muff (îr′mŭf′) *n.* Either of a pair of ear coverings often attached to an adjustable headband and worn to protect the ears especially against the cold.

earn[1] (ûrn) *tr.v.* **earned, earn·ing, earns. 1.** To gain especially for the performance of service, labor, or work: *earned money by mowing lawns.* **2.** To acquire or deserve as a result of effort or action: *She earned a reputation as a hard worker.* **3.** To yield as return or profit: *a savings account that earns interest on deposited funds.* **—*idiom.* earn (one's) spurs.** To gain a position through hard work and the accumulation of experience, often in the face of difficulties: *a diplomat who had earned his spurs as the prime minister's personal assistant.* [Middle English *ernen,* from Old English *earnian.*] **—earn′er** *n.*

SYNONYMS: *earn, deserve, merit, rate, win.* The central meaning shared by these verbs is "to gain as a result of one's behavior or effort": *earns a large salary; deserves our congratulations; a suggestion that merits consideration; an event that didn't even rate a mention in the news; a candidate who won wide support.*

earn[2] (ûrn) *intr.v.* **earned, earn·ing, earns.** *Obsolete.* To yearn. [Middle English *ernen,* variant of *yernen.* See YEARN.]

earned run (ûrnd) *n.* *Baseball.* A run scored without the aid of an error, used in computing earned run averages.

earned run average *n.* *Abbr.* **ERA** *Baseball.* A measure of a pitcher's performance obtained by dividing the total of earned runs allowed by the total of innings pitched and multiplying by nine.

ear·nest[1] (ûr′nĭst) *adj.* **1.** Marked by or showing deep sincerity or seriousness: *an earnest gesture of good will.* **2.** Of an important or weighty nature; grave. See Synonyms at **serious. —*idiom.* in earnest. 1.** With a purposeful or sincere intent: *settled down to study in earnest for the examination.* **2.** Serious; determined: *"Both sides are deeply in earnest, with passions that approximate those of civil war"* (Conor Cruise O'Brien). [Middle English *ernest,* from Old English *eornoste.* See **er-[1]** in Appendix.] **—ear′nest·ly** *adv.* **—ear′nest·ness** *n.*

ear·nest[2] (ûr′nĭst) *n.* **1.** Money paid in advance as part payment to bind a contract or bargain. **2.** A token of something to come; a promise or an assurance. [Middle English *ernest,* variant of *ernes,* alteration of Old French *erres,* pl. of *erre,* pledge, from Latin *arra,* alteration of *arrabō,* from Greek *arrabōn,* earnest-money, from Hebrew *'ērābôn,* from *'ārab,* to pledge.]

earn·ings (ûr′nĭngz) *pl.n.* **1.** Salary or wages. **2.a.** Business profits. **b.** Gains from investments.

Earp (ûrp), **Wyatt.** 1848–1929. American frontier law officer involved in the famous gunfight at the O.K. Corral in Tombstone, Arizona (1881).

ear·phone (îr′fōn′) *n.* A device that converts electric signals, as from a telephone, stereo, or radio receiver, to audible sound and fits over or in the ear. Also called *earpiece.*

ear·piece (îr′pēs′) *n.* **1.** A part, as of a telephone receiver or hearing aid, that fits in or is held next to the ear. **2.** See **earphone. 3.** Either of the two parts of an eyeglasses frame that extend over or around the ear.

ear·plug (îr′plŭg′) *n.* **1.** An object made of a soft, pliable material, such as cotton or rubber, and fitted into the ear canal to block the entry of water or sound. **2.** An earphone, especially one that fits into the ear.

♦ **ear·ring** (îr′rĭng, îr′ĭng) *n.* An ornament worn on or pendent from the ear, especially the earlobe. Also called ♦*earbob.*

ear rot *n.* Any of various fungus diseases of corn characterized by decay and molding of the ears.

♦ **ear sew·er** (sō′ər) *n.* *Northern California.* See **dragonfly.** See Regional Note at **dragonfly.**

ear shell *n.* **1.** See **abalone. 2.** The shell of the abalone. [From its shape.]

ear·shot (îr′shŏt′) *n.* The range within which sound can be heard by the unaided ear; hearing distance: *listened until the parade was out of earshot.*

ear·split·ting (îr′splĭt′ĭng) *adj.* Loud and shrill enough to hurt the ears. See Synonyms at **loud.**

earth (ûrth) *n.* **1.a.** The land surface of the world. **b.** The softer, friable part of land; soil, especially productive soil. **2.** Often **Earth.** The third planet from the sun, having a sidereal period

Amelia Earhart

earmuff
Pair of earmuffs

Wyatt Earp
Photographed in 1883

earring

ă pat	oi boy
ā pay	ou out
âr care	o͝o took
ä father	o͞o boot
ĕ pet	ŭ cut
ē be	ûr urge
ĭ pit	th thin
ī pie	*th* this
îr pier	hw which
ŏ pot	zh vision
ō toe	ə about, item
ô paw	♦ regionalism

Stress marks: ′ (primary); ′ (secondary), as in **dictionary** (dĭk′shə-nĕr′ē)

earthquake
Searching for survivors in Mexico City after the September 19, 1985, earthquake

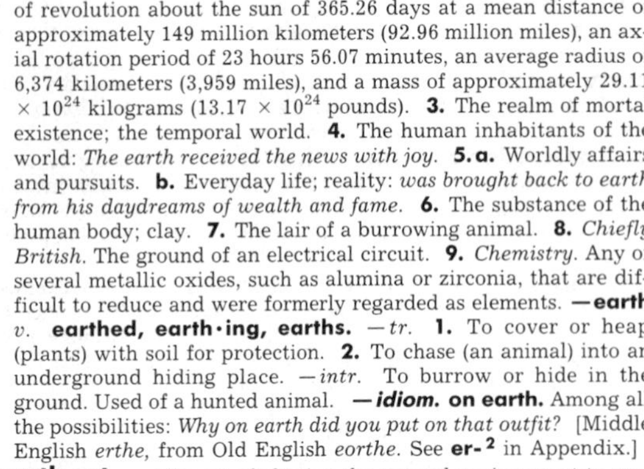

of revolution about the sun of 365.26 days at a mean distance of approximately 149 million kilometers (92.96 million miles), an axial rotation period of 23 hours 56.07 minutes, an average radius of 6,374 kilometers (3,959 miles), and a mass of approximately 29.11 × 10^{24} kilograms (13.17 × 10^{24} pounds). **3.** The realm of mortal existence; the temporal world. **4.** The human inhabitants of the world: *The earth received the news with joy.* **5.a.** Worldly affairs and pursuits. **b.** Everyday life; reality: *was brought back to earth from his daydreams of wealth and fame.* **6.** The substance of the human body; clay. **7.** The lair of a burrowing animal. **8.** *Chiefly British.* The ground of an electrical circuit. **9.** *Chemistry.* Any of several metallic oxides, such as alumina or zirconia, that are difficult to reduce and were formerly regarded as elements. **—earth** *v.* **earthed, earth·ing, earths.** —*tr.* **1.** To cover or heap (plants) with soil for protection. **2.** To chase (an animal) into an underground hiding place. —*intr.* To burrow or hide in the ground. Used of a hunted animal. **—*idiom.* on earth.** Among all the possibilities: *Why on earth did you put on that outfit?* [Middle English *erthe,* from Old English *eorthe.* See **er-**[2] in Appendix.]

earth art *n.* The art of altering the natural environment to create earthworks.

earth·born (ûrth′bôrn′) *adj.* **1.a.** Springing from or born on the earth. **b.** Human; mortal: *earthborn existence.* **2.** Of or connected with earthly life: *earthborn pleasures.*

earth·bound also **earth-bound** (ûrth′bound′) *adj.* **1.** Fastened in or to the soil: *earthbound roots.* **2.a.** Attached or confined to the earth or to earthly concerns: *an earthbound existence.* **b.** Unimaginative; ordinary. **3.** Headed for the earth: *an earthbound meteor.*

earth·en (ûr′thən, -*th*ən) *adj.* **1.** Made of earth or clay: *an earthen fortification; an earthen pot.* **2.** Earthly; worldly.

earth·en·ware (ûr′thən-wâr′, -*th*ən-) *n.* Pottery made from a porous clay that is fired at relatively low temperatures. Faience, delft, and majolica are examples of earthenware.

earthworm

earth·light (ûrth′līt′) *n.* See **earthshine.**

earth·ling (ûrth′lĭng) *n.* **1.** One, especially a human being, that inhabits the planet Earth. **2.** A person devoted to the world; a worldling.

earth·ly (ûrth′lē) *adj.* **1.** Of, relating to, or characteristic of this earth. **2.a.** Terrestrial; not heavenly or divine: *earthly existence.* **b.** Worldly: *earthly delights; one's earthly possessions.* **3.** Conceivable; possible: *no earthly meaning whatever.* **—earth′li·ness** *n.*

earth·man (ûrth′măn′) *n.* A human inhabitant of the planet Earth; an earthling.

earth mother *n.* **1.** A goddess or female spirit representing the earth as the giver of life; a fertility goddess. **2.** A woman combining maternal and sensual qualities.

earth·mov·er (ûrth′mo͞o′vər) *n.* A machine, such as a bulldozer or backhoe, that is used for digging or pushing earth. **—earth′mov′ing** *adj.*

earth·nut (ûrth′nŭt′) *n.* **1.a.** A Eurasian and northern African plant *(Conopodium denudatum)* having tuberous roots that are edible when roasted. **b.** The tuber of this plant. **2.** Any of various other plants, such as the peanut, similar to the earthnut.

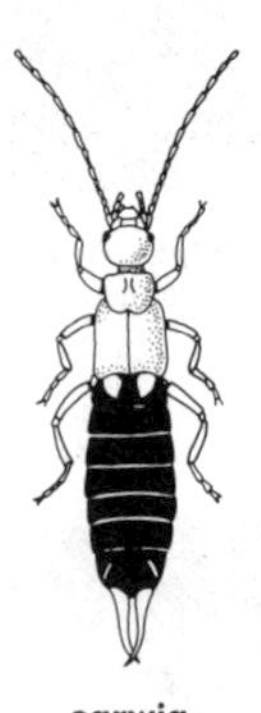

earwig

earth·quake (ûrth′kwāk′) *n.* A sudden movement of the earth's crust caused by the release of stress accumulated along geologic faults or by volcanic activity. Also called *seism, temblor.*

earth·rise (ûrth′rīz′) *n.* The rising of the earth above the horizon as seen from the moon.

earth science *n.* Any of several essentially geologic sciences that are concerned with the origin, structure, and physical phenomena of the earth.

earth·shak·ing (ûrth′shā′kĭng) *adj.* Of great consequence or importance. **—earth′shak′ing·ly** *adv.*

earth·shine (ûrth′shīn′) *n.* The sunlight reflected from the earth's surface that illuminates part of the moon not directly lighted by the sun. Also called *earthlight.*

earth smoke *n. Botany.* See **fumitory.** [Translation of Medieval Latin *fūmus terrae.* See FUMITORY.]

earth·star (ûrth′stär′) *n.* A fungus of the genus *Geastrum,* related to and resembling the puffballs and having an outer covering that splits open in a starlike form.

easel

earth station *n.* An on-ground terminal linked to a spacecraft or satellite by an antenna and associated electronic equipment for the purpose of transmitting or receiving messages, tracking, or control.

earth tone *n.* Any of various rich, warm tones of brown.

earth·ward (ûrth′wərd) *adv. & adj.* To or toward the earth. **—earth′wards** *adv.*

earth·work (ûrth′wûrk′) *n.* **1.** An earthen embankment, especially one used as a fortification. See Synonyms at **bulwark.** **2.** *Engineering.* Excavation and embankment of earth. **3.** A work of art made by altering an area of land or a natural geographic feature, especially on a large scale.

earth·worm (ûrth′wûrm′) *n.* Any of various terrestrial annelid worms of the class Oligochaeta, especially those of the family Lumbricidae, that burrow into and help aerate and enrich soil.

earth·y (ûr′thē) *adj.* **-i·er, -i·est.** **1.** Of, relating to, consisting of, or resembling earth: *an earthy smell.* **2.** Relating to or characteristic of this world; worldly. **3.** Crude or off-color; indecent: *an earthy joke.* **4.** Hearty or uninhibited; natural: *an earthy enjoyment of life.* **—earth′i·ly** *adv.* **—earth′i·ness** *n.*

ear trumpet *n.* A horn-shaped device formerly used to direct sound into the ear of a hearing-impaired person.

ear tuft *n.* See **ear**[1] (sense 6a).

ear·wax (îr′wăks′) *n.* The yellowish, waxlike secretion of certain glands lining the canal of the external ear. Also called *cerumen.*

ear·wig (îr′wĭg′) *n.* Any of various elongate insects of the order Dermaptera, having a pair of pincerlike appendages protruding from the rear of the abdomen. **—earwig** *tr.v.* **-wigged, -wig·ging, -wigs.** To attempt to influence by persistent confidential argument or talk. [Middle English *erwig,* from Old English *ēarwicga* : *ēare,* ear; see EAR[1] + *wicga,* insect; see **wegh-** in Appendix.]

WORD HISTORY: In an Anglo-Norman text written around the beginning of the 15th century we are told that elephants guard their ears diligently against flies and earwigs. Elephants have good cause to protect themselves against these insects if, as folklore has it, earwigs go through the ear into the head. The earwig, however, prefers to dine on things such as flowers, fruit, and small insects rather than brain tissue. Folklore is responsible, though, for the insect's name, which was formed in Old English from *ēare,* the Old English source of our word *ear,* and *wicga,* "insect," a word presumably related to our word *wiggle.*

ear·worm (îr′wûrm′) *n.* See **corn earworm.**

ease (ēz) *n.* **1.** The condition of being comfortable or relieved. **2.a.** Freedom from pain, worry, or agitation: *Her mind was at ease knowing that the children were safe.* **b.** Freedom from constraint or embarrassment; naturalness. See Synonyms at **rest**[1]. **3.a.** Freedom from difficulty, hardship, or effort: *rose through the ranks with apparent ease.* **b.** Readiness or dexterity in performance; facility: *She practiced until she could play the sonata with ease.* **4.** Freedom from financial difficulty; affluence: *a life of luxury and ease.* **5.** A state of rest, relaxation, or leisure: *He took his ease by the swimming pool.* **—ease** *v.* **eased, eas·ing, eas·es.** —*tr.* **1.** To free from pain, worry, or agitation: *He eased his conscience by returning the stolen money.* **2.a.** To lessen the discomfort or pain of: *She shifted position so as to ease her back.* **b.** To alleviate; assuage: *prescribed a drug to ease the pain.* **3.** To give respite from: *eased the burden on her staff by hiring temporary help.* **4.** To slacken the strain, pressure, or tension of; loosen: *ease off a cable.* **5.** To reduce the difficulty or trouble of: *ease credit terms; eased the entrance requirements.* **6.** To move or maneuver slowly and carefully: *eased the car into a narrow space; eased the director out of office.* —*intr.* **1.** To lessen, as in discomfort, pressure, or stress: *pain that never eased.* **2.** To move or proceed with little effort: *eased through life doing as little as possible.* **—*idiom.* at ease.** **1.** In a relaxed position, especially standing silently at rest with the right foot stationary: *put the soldiers at ease while waiting for inspection.* **2.** Used as a command for troops to assume a relaxed position. [Middle English *ese,* from Old French *aise,* perhaps from Latin *adiacēns,* lying near. See ADJACENT.]

ease·ful (ēz′fəl) *adj.* Affording or characterized by comfort and peace; restful. **—ease′ful·ly** *adv.* **—ease′ful·ness** *n.*

ea·sel (ē′zəl) *n.* An upright frame for displaying or supporting something, such as an artist's canvas. [Dutch *ezel,* ass, from Middle Dutch *esel,* from Latin *asellus,* diminutive of *asinus.*]

WORD HISTORY: "A painter's ass" is not a phrase that immediately brings to mind an accessory to the artist's profession. But *easel* comes to us from the Dutch word *ezel,* meaning "an ass, one of several hoofed mammals of the genus *Equus.*" The Dutch word was eventually extended to mean "an upright frame for displaying or supporting something, such as an artist's canvas," in the same way that the English word *horse* has come to mean "a piece of gymnastic equipment with an upholstered body used especially for vaulting." Developments such as these illustrate the playfulness present in language when its speakers use similarities perceived between two objects in order to name one of them. This kind of naming can involve a dash of wit, as is probably the case with the Dutch word *ezel.* It is certainly the case with the name for a bank of outdoor seats for spectators. When sitting in the open air in a stadium, one is exposed to the sun just as linens are when they are bleached on a clothesline; thus, *bleachers.*

ease·ment (ēz′mənt) *n.* **1.** The act of easing or the condition of being eased. **2.** Something that affords ease or comfort. **3.** *Law.* A right, such as a right of way, afforded a person to make limited use of another's real property.

eas·i·ly (ē′zə-lē) *adv.* **1.** In an easy manner; with ease. **2.** Without question; certainly: *easily the best play this season.* **3.** In all likelihood; well: *a mistake that could easily have ended in disaster.*

east (ēst) *n. Abbr.* **E, E., e, e.** **1.a.** The cardinal point on the mariner's compass 90° clockwise from due north and directly opposite west. **b.** The direction of the earth's axial rotation. **2.** An area or a region lying in the east. **3.** Often **East.** **a.** The eastern part of the earth, especially eastern Asia. **b.** The eastern part of a region or country. **4.** Often **East.** **a.** The region of the United States east of the Allegheny Mountains and north of the Mason-Dixon Line. **b.** The former Communist bloc of countries in Asia and Eastern Europe. **—east** *adj. Abbr.* **E, E., e, e.** **1.** To, toward, of, facing, or in the east. **2.** Originating in or coming from the east: *a cool east wind.* —**east** *adv. Abbr.* **E, E., e, e.** In, from, or toward the east. [Middle English *est,* from Old English *ēast.* See **aus-** in Appendix.]

East An·gli·a (ăng′glē-ə). A region and Anglo-Saxon kingdom of eastern England. Settled by Angles in the late fifth century A.D., it was a powerful kingdom by the late sixth century but became a dependency of Mercia for long periods after 650. The Danes controlled the region from 886 to 917, after which it became an English earldom.

East A·sia (ā′zhə, ā′shə). A region of Asia coextensive with the Far East. —**East A′sian** *adj. & n.*

East Ber·lin (bûr-lĭn′). See **Berlin.** —**East Ber·lin′er** *n.*

East Bes·kids (bĕs′kĭdz, bĕs-kēdz′). See **Beskids.**

east·bound (ēst′bound′) *adj.* Going toward the east.

East·bourne (ēst′bôrn′, -bōrn′). A borough of southeast England on the English Channel south-southeast of London. It is a popular resort. Population, 77,300.

East Bruns·wick (brŭnz′wĭk). A community of central New Jersey south of New Brunswick. Population, 37,711.

east by north *n. Abbr.* **EbN** The direction or point on the mariner's compass halfway between due east and east-northeast, or 78°45′ east of due north. —**east by north** *adv. & adj. Abbr.* **EbN** Toward or from east by north.

east by south *n. Abbr.* **EbS** The direction or point on the mariner's compass halfway between due east and east-southeast, or 101°15′ east of due north. —**east by south** *adv. & adj. Abbr.* **EbS** Toward or from east by south.

East Cape. See Cape **Dezhnev.**

East·ches·ter (ēst′chĕs′tər). A community of southeast New York, a residential suburb of New York City. Population, 22,600.

East Chi·ca·go (shĭ-kä′gō, -kô′-). A city of northwest Indiana on Lake Michigan in the Calumet region south-southeast of Chicago, Illinois. It is an industrial center. Population, 39,786.

East Chi·na Sea (chī′nə). An arm of the western Pacific Ocean bounded by China, South Korea, Taiwan, and the Ryukyu and Kyushu islands. It has rich fishing grounds.

East Cleve·land (klēv′lənd). A city of northeast Ohio, a residential suburb of Cleveland. Population, 36,957.

East Coast. A region of the eastern United States along the Atlantic coastline, especially the urban corridor from Boston to Washington, D.C.

East De·troit (dĭ-troit′). A city of southeast Michigan, a residential suburb of Detroit. Population, 38,280.

East End. A section of eastern London north of the Thames River. It was long a densely populated working-class and immigrant area centered around the docks and warehouses.

Eas·ter (ē′stər) *n.* **1.** A Christian feast commemorating the Resurrection of Jesus. **2.** The day on which this feast is observed, the first Sunday following the full moon that occurs on or next after March 21. **3.** Eastertide. [Middle English *ester,* from Old English *ēastre.* See **aus-** in Appendix.]

Easter cactus *n.* A branching cactus *(Rhipsalidopsis gaertneri)* having terminal clusters of large, scarlet flowers and arching, flattened branches. [So called because it blooms in the spring.]

Easter egg *n.* A dyed or decorated egg, traditionally associated with Easter.

Easter Island. Known locally as **Ra·pa Nu·i** (rä′pə no͞o′ē). An island of Chile in the southern Pacific Ocean about 3,701 km (2,300 mi) west of the mainland. Discovered by Dutch explorers on Easter Day, 1722, the island is famous for its hieroglyphic tablets and colossal heads carved from volcanic rock.

Easter lily *n.* Any of various lilies, especially *Lilium longiflorum* var. *eximium,* having large, white, trumpet-shaped flowers that bloom in the spring and are displayed during the Easter season. Also called *Bermuda lily.*

east·er·ly (ē′stər-lē) *adj.* **1.** Situated toward the east. **2.** Coming or being from the east: *easterly winds.* —**easterly** *n., pl.* **-lies.** A storm or wind coming from the east. —**east′er·ly** *adv.*

Easter Monday *n.* The Monday following Easter, observed as a holiday in some countries and North Carolina.

east·ern (ē′stərn) *adj.* **1.** Situated in, toward, or facing the east. **2.** Coming from the east: *eastern breezes.* **3.** Native to or growing in the east. **4.** Often **Eastern.** Of, relating to, or characteristic of eastern regions or the East. **5. Eastern. a.** Of or relating to the Eastern Church. **b.** Of or relating to the Eastern Orthodox Church. [Middle English *estern,* from Old English *ēasterne.* See **aus-** in Appendix.] —**east′ern·ness′** *n.*

eastern camass *n.* A bulbous plant *(Camassia scilloides)* native to the eastern United States, having white, blue, or violet flowers and bright yellow anthers. Also called *indigo squill, wild hyacinth.*

Eastern Church *n.* **1.** The church of the Byzantine Empire, including the patriarchates of Constantinople, Antioch, Alexandria, and Jerusalem. **2.** The Eastern Orthodox Church. **3.** Often **Eastern church.** A Uniat church.

Eastern Empire. The Byzantine Empire.

east·ern·er also **East·ern·er** (ē′stər-nər) *n.* A native or inhabitant of the east, especially the eastern United States.

Eastern Eu·rope (yo͝or′əp). The countries of eastern Europe, especially those allied with the U.S.S.R. in the Warsaw Pact from 1955 to 1991.

Eastern Ghats (gôts). See **Ghats.**

Eastern Hemisphere. The half of the earth comprising Europe, Africa, Asia, and Australia.

Eastern High·lands (hī′ləndz). See **Great Dividing Range.**

east·ern·most (ē′stərn-mōst′) *adj.* Farthest east.

Eastern Orthodox Church *n.* The body of modern churches, including among others the Greek and Russian Orthodox, that is derived from the church of the Byzantine Empire, adheres to the Byzantine rite, and acknowledges the honorary primacy of the patriarch of Constantinople.

Eastern Shore. A region of Maryland and Virginia east of Chesapeake Bay.

Eastern Shoshone *n.* See **Shoshone** (sense 1c).

Eastern Sioux *n.* See **Santee[1].**

Eastern Standard Time *n. Abbr.* **EST, E.S.T.** Standard time in the fifth time zone west of Greenwich, England, reckoned at 75° west and used, for example, in the eastern part of North America. Also called *Eastern Time.*

Eas·ter·tide (ē′stər-tīd′) *n.* The Easter season, extending from Easter to Ascension Day, Whitsunday, or Trinity Sunday.

East Fri·sian Islands (frĭzh′ən, frē′zhən). See **Frisian Islands.**

East Germanic *n.* The subdivision of the Germanic languages that includes Gothic.

East Ger·ma·ny (jûr′mə-nē). A former country of northern Europe on the Baltic Sea, formed in 1949 from the zone of Germany occupied by Soviet troops after World War II and reunified with West Germany in 1990. —**East Ger′man** *adj. & n.*

East Hart·ford (härt′fərd). A town of north-central Connecticut on the Connecticut River opposite Hartford. It was settled c. 1640. Population, 52,563.

East Ha·ven (hā′vən). A town of southern Connecticut on Long Island Sound east of New Haven. It is a residential community and summer resort. Population, 25,028.

East In·dies (ĭn′dēz). Indonesia. The term is sometimes used to refer to all of Southeast Asia. Historically, it referred chiefly to India. —**East In′di·an** *adj. & n.*

east·ing (ē′stĭng) *n.* **1.** The difference in longitude between two positions as a result of movement to the east. **2.** Progress toward the east.

East·lake (ēst′lāk′). A city of northeast Ohio, a residential suburb of Cleveland on Lake Erie. Population, 22,104.

East Lan·sing (lăn′sĭng). A city of south-central Michigan, a residential suburb of Lansing. It is the seat of Michigan State University (founded 1855). Population, 51,392.

East·leigh (ēst′lē). A municipal borough of southern England north-northeast of Southampton. Its industries include railroad shops. Population, 92,400.

East Liv·er·pool (lĭv′ər-po͞ol′). A city of eastern Ohio on the West Virginia border south of Youngstown. It has been a ceramics center since the 1830's. Population, 16,687.

East·main (ēst′mān′). A river rising in central Quebec, Canada, and flowing about 821 km (510 mi) eastward to James Bay.

East·man (ēst′mən), **George.** 1854–1932. American inventor and industrialist who invented a dry-plate process of photographic film development, flexible film, a box camera, and a process for color photography.

Eastman, Max Forrester. 1883–1969. American writer and editor of *The Masses* (1913–1918) and *The Liberator* (1919–1922).

East Mo·line (mō-lēn′). A city of northwest Illinois, a residential and industrial suburb of Moline on the Mississippi River. Population, 20,907.

east-north·east (ēst′nôrth′ēst′) *n. Abbr.* **ENE** The direction or point on the mariner's compass halfway between due east and northeast, or 67°30′ east of due north. —**east-northeast** *adj. Abbr.* **ENE** To, toward, of, facing, or in the east-northeast. —**east-northeast** *adv. Abbr.* **ENE** In, from, or toward the east-northeast.

East·on (ē′stən). **1.** A town of southeast Massachusetts southwest of Brockton. It was settled in 1694. Population, 16,623. **2.** A city of eastern Pennsylvania north of Philadelphia. Founded in 1751, it was formerly a coal-receiving port. Population, 26,027.

East Or·ange (ôr′ĭnj, ŏr′-). A city of northeast New Jersey, a residential suburb of Newark. Population, 77,690.

East Pak·i·stan (păk′ĭ-stăn′, pä′kĭ-stän′). A former region of southern Asia on the Bay of Bengal. Originally part of Bengal, it was held by Pakistan from 1947 to 1971, when it achieved independence as Bangladesh.

East Pal·o Al·to (păl′ō ăl′tō). A community of western California on San Francisco Bay southeast of San Mateo. It is mainly residential. Population, 18,191.

East Pe·or·i·a (pē-ôr′ē-ə, -ōr′-). A city of north-central Illinois, a manufacturing suburb of Peoria on the Illinois River. Population, 22,385.

East Point. A city of northwest Georgia, an industrial suburb of Atlanta. Population, 37,486.

East Prov·i·dence (prŏv′ĭ-dəns). A city of eastern Rhode Island, an industrial suburb of Providence. Population, 50,980.

East Prus·sia (prŭsh′ə). A historical region and former province of Prussia on the Baltic Sea. From 1919 to 1939 it was separated from Germany by the Polish Corridor. After 1945 the area was divided between Poland and the U.S.S.R.

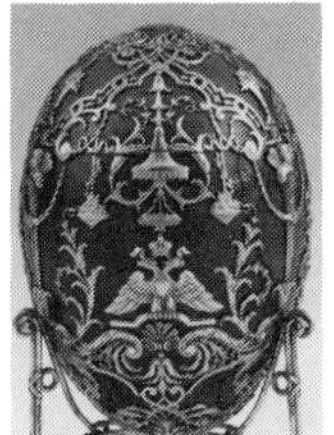

Easter egg
c. 1912 jeweled lapis lazuli and gold Easter egg by Peter Carl Fabergé

Easter Island

Easter lily

George Eastman

ă pat	oi boy
ā pay	ou out
âr care	o͝o took
ä father	o͞o boot
ĕ pet	ŭ cut
ē be	ûr urge
ĭ pit	th thin
ī pie	*th* this
îr pier	hw which
ŏ pot	zh vision
ō toe	ə about, item
ô paw	♦ regionalism

Stress marks: ′ (primary); ′ (secondary), as in **dictionary** (dĭk′shə-nĕr′ē)

East Ridge. A city of southeast Tennessee, a suburb of Chattanooga on the Georgia border. Population, 21,236.

East River. A narrow tidal strait connecting Upper New York Bay with Long Island Sound and separating the boroughs of Manhattan and the Bronx from Brooklyn and Queens.

East Saint Lou·is (sānt lo͞o′ĭs). A city of southwest Illinois on the Mississippi River opposite St. Louis, Missouri. It is a railroad center with varied industries. Population, 55,200.

East Si·ber·i·an Sea (sī-bîr′ē-ən). An arm of the Arctic Ocean from Wrangel Island to the New Siberian Islands.

East Side. A section of New York City on Manhattan Island east of Fifth Avenue. The northern part, approximately between 57th Street and 96th Street, is also known as the **Upper East Side** and includes many fashionable shops and residences. The **Lower East Side,** south of 14th Street, was long a home to immigrants from eastern Europe.

east-south·east (ēst′south′ēst′) *n. Abbr.* **ESE** The direction or point on the mariner's compass halfway between due east and southeast, or 112°30′ east of due north. **—east-southeast** *adj. Abbr.* **ESE** To, toward, of, facing, or in the east-southeast. **—east-southeast** *adv. Abbr.* **ESE** In, from, or toward the east-southeast.

east·ward (ēst′wərd) *adv. & adj.* Toward, to, or in the east. **—eastward** *n.* An eastward direction, point, or region. **—east′ward·ly** *adv. & adj.* **—east′wards** *adv.*

eaves

eas·y (ē′zē) *adj.* **-i·er, -i·est. 1.** Capable of being accomplished or acquired with ease; posing no difficulty: *an easy victory; an easy problem.* **2.** Requiring or exhibiting little effort or endeavor; undemanding: *took the easy way out of her problems; wasn't satisfied with easy answers.* **3.** Free from worry, anxiety, trouble, or pain: *My mind was easy, knowing that I had done my best.* **4.a.** Affording comfort or relief; soothing: *soft light that was easy on the eyes.* **b.** Prosperous; well-off: *easy living; easy circumstances.* **5.** Causing little hardship or distress: *an easy penalty; a habit that isn't easy to give up.* **6.** Socially at ease: *an easy, good-natured manner.* **7.a.** Relaxed in attitude; easygoing: *an easy disposition.* **b.** Not strict or severe; lenient: *an easy teacher; easy standards.* **8.** Readily exploited, imposed on, or tricked: *an easy mark; an easy victim.* **9.a.** Not hurried or forced; moderate: *an easy pace; an easy walk around the block.* **b.** Light; gentle: *an easy tap on the shoulder.* **10.** Not steep or abrupt; gradual: *an easy climb.* **11.** *Economics.* **a.** Less in demand and therefore readily obtainable: *Commodities are easier this quarter.* **b.** Plentiful and therefore at low interest rates: *easy money.* **12.** Promiscuous; loose. **—easy** *adv.* **1.** Without haste or agitation: *Relax and take it easy for a while.* **2.** With little effort; easily: *success that came too easy.* **3.** In a restrained or moderate manner: *Go easy on the butter.* **4.** Without much hardship or cost: *got off easy with only a small fine.* **—*idiom.* easy as pie.** *Informal.* Capable of being accomplished or done with no difficulty. [Middle English *esi,* from Old French *aaisie,* past participle of *aaisier,* to put at ease : *a-,* to (from Latin *ad-,* ad-) + *aise,* ease; see EASE.] **—eas′i·ness** *n.*

SYNONYMS: *easy, simple, facile, effortless, smooth, light.* These adjectives mean requiring little effort or posing little if any difficulty. *Easy* applies both to tasks that require little effort and to persons who are not demanding: *"The diagnosis of disease is often easy, often difficult, and often impossible"* (Peter M. Latham). *Not wanting to be called an easy marker, the teacher graded the essays severely. Simple* implies lack of complexity that facilitates understanding or performance: *a simple game; a simple problem; "the faculty . . . of reducing his thought on any subject to the simplest and plainest terms possible"* (Baron Charnwood). *Facile* stresses readiness and fluency (*a facile speaker*); often, though, the word has unfavorable connotations, as of lack of care, glibness or insincerity, or superficiality: *The explanation is too facile for such a complex phenomenon. Effortless* refers to performance in which the application of great strength or skill makes the execution seem easy: *a skater performing an effortless double axel; wrote effortless prose. Smooth* suggests freedom from hindrances or difficulties that impede progress: *The path of the bill through the legislature was smooth and orderly. Light* refers to tasks or impositions that involve no taxing burdens or responsibilities: *light duties; light taxes.*

ecce homo

easy chair *n.* A large, comfortable, well-upholstered chair.

eas·y·go·ing also **eas·y-go·ing** (ē′zē-gō′ĭng) *adj.* **1.a.** Living without undue worry or concern; calm. **b.** Lax or negligent; careless. **c.** Relaxed or informal in attitude or standards: *an easygoing teacher who allowed extra time for assignments.* **2.** Not rigorous, demanding, or stressful: *an easygoing life as a part-time consultant.* **3.** Leisurely; unhurried: *an easygoing pace.*

easy lis·ten·ing (lĭs′ə-nĭng) *n. Music.* Light or popular compositions with broad appeal, usually having a prominent melody and a quiet or blended arrangement.

easy street *n. Informal.* A condition of financial security or independence.

eat (ēt) *v.* **ate** (āt), **eat·en** (ēt′n), **eat·ing, eats.** *—tr.* **1.a.** To take into the body by the mouth for digestion or absorption. **b.** To include habitually or by preference in one's diet: *a bird that eats insects, fruit, and seeds; stopped eating red meat on advice from her doctor.* **2.** To consume, ravage, or destroy by or as if by ingesting: *"Covering news in the field eats money"* (George F. Will). **3.** To erode or corrode: *waves that ate away the beach; an acid that eats the surface of a machine part.* **4.** To produce by or as if by eating: *Moths ate holes in our sweaters.* **5.** *Slang.* To absorb the cost or expense of: *"You can eat your loss and switch the remaining money to other investment portfolios"* (Marlys Harris). **6.** *Informal.* To bother or annoy: *What's eating him? —intr.* **1.a.** To consume food. **b.** To have or take a meal. **2.** To exercise a consuming or eroding effect: *a drill that ate away at the rock; exorbitant expenses that were eating into profits.* **3.** To cause persistent annoyance or distress: *"How long will it be before the frustration eats at you?"* (Howard Kaplan). **—*phrasal verb.* eat up.** *Slang.* To receive or enjoy enthusiastically or avidly: *She really eats up the constant publicity.* **—*idioms.* eat crow.** To be forced to accept a humiliating defeat. **eat (one's) heart out. 1.** To feel bitter anguish or grief. **2.** To be consumed by jealousy. **eat (one's) words.** To retract something that one has said. **eat out of (someone's) hand.** To be manipulated or dominated by another. **eat (someone) alive.** *Slang.* To overwhelm or defeat thoroughly: *an inexperienced manager who was eaten alive in a competitive corporate environment.* [Middle English *eten,* from Old English *etan.* See **ed-** in Appendix.] **—eat′er** *n.*

SYNONYMS: *eat, consume, devour, ingest.* The central meaning shared by these verbs is "to take food into the body by the mouth": *ate a hearty dinner; greedily consumed the sandwich; hyenas devouring their prey; whales ingesting krill.*

eat·a·ble (ē′tə-bəl) *adj.* Fit to be eaten; edible: *an eatable meal.* **—eatable** *n.* **1.** Something fit to be eaten. **2. eatables.** Food.

eat·en (ēt′n) *v.* Past participle of **eat.**

eat·er·y (ē′tə-rē) *n., pl.* **-ies.** *Informal.* A restaurant.

eat·ing (ē′tĭng) *adj.* **1.** Suitable for being eaten, especially without cooking: *good eating apples.* **2.** Used in the ingestion of food, as at the table: *eating utensils.*

eating disorder *n.* A potentially life-threatening neurotic condition, such as anorexia nervosa or bulimia, usually seen in young women.

eats (ēts) *pl.n. Slang.* Food, especially snacks.

Eau Claire (ō klâr′). A city of west-central Wisconsin at the mouth of the **Eau Clair River,** about 113 km (70 mi) long. Founded in the 1840's, the city grew as the center of a lumbering region. Population, 51,509.

eau de co·logne (ō′ də kə-lōn′) *n., pl.* **eaux de cologne** (ō′, ōz′). See **cologne.** [French *eau-de-cologne.* See COLOGNE.]

eau de vie (ō′ də vē′) *n., pl.* **eaux de vie** (ō′, ōz′). Brandy. [French *eau-de-vie* : *eau,* water + *de,* of + *vie,* life.]

eaves (ēvz) *pl.n.* The projecting overhang at the lower edge of a roof. [Middle English *eves,* from Old English *efes.* See **upo** in Appendix.]

eaves·drop (ēvz′drŏp′) *intr.v.* **-dropped, -drop·ping, -drops.** To listen secretly to the private conversation of others. [Probably back-formation from *eavesdropper,* one who eavesdrops, from Middle English *evesdropper,* from *evesdrop,* place where water falls from the eaves, from Old English *yfes drype.* See **upo** in Appendix.] **—eaves′drop′per** *n.*

♦ **eaves spout** *n. New England & Northern U.S.* See **gutter** (sense 2). See Regional Note at **gutter.**

♦ **eaves trough** *n. Northern U.S.* See **gutter** (sense 2). See Regional Note at **gutter.**

E·ban (ē′bən), **Abba.** Born 1915. South African-born Israeli politician who served as Israel's first permanent delegate to the United Nations (1949–1959) and foreign minister (1966–1974).

ebb (ĕb) *n.* **1.** Ebb tide. **2.** A period of decline or diminution: *"Insistence upon rules of conduct marks the ebb of religious fervor"* (Alfred North Whitehead). **—ebb** *intr.v.* **ebbed, ebb·ing, ebbs. 1.** To fall back from the flood stage. **2.** To fall away or back; decline or recede. See Synonyms at **recede.** [Middle English *ebbe,* from Old English *ebba.* See **apo-** in Appendix.]

ebb tide *n.* The receding or outgoing tide; the period between high water and the succeeding low water.

EBCDIC (ĕb′sē-dĭk) *n. Computer Science.* A standard code that uses 8 bits to represent each of up to 256 alphanumeric characters. [*E(xtended) B(inary) C(oded) D(ecimal) I(nterchange) C(ode).*]

Eb·la (ĕb′lə, ē′blə). An ancient city of southwest Asia near the site of present-day Aleppo, Syria. The cuneiform Ebla Tablets, discovered from 1974 to 1975, describe a thriving third-millennium B.C. civilization centered around the city.

Eb·la·ite (ĕb′lə-īt′, ē′blə-) *n.* The Semitic language of ancient Ebla.

Eb·lis (ĕb′lĭs) *n. Mythology.* The principal evil spirit or devil of Islamic mythology.

EbN *abbr.* East by north.

eb·on (ĕb′ən) *adj.* **1.** Made of ebony. **2.** Black in color. **—ebon** *n.* Ebony. [Middle English *eban,* ebony wood, from Old French, from Latin *ebenus,* ebony tree, from Greek *ebenos.* See EBONY.]

eb·on·ite (ĕb′ə-nīt′) *n.* A relatively inelastic rubber, made by vulcanization with a large amount of sulfur and used as an electrical insulating material.

eb·on·ize (ĕb′ə-nīz′) *tr.v.* **-ized, -iz·ing, -iz·es.** To stain black like ebony.

eb·on·y (ĕb′ə-nē) *n., pl.* **-ies. 1.** A tropical tree *(Diospyros* *ebenum)* of southern Asia, having hard, dark-colored heartwood. **2.** The wood of this tree, used in cabinetwork and for piano keys. **3.** The color black; ebon. **—ebony** *adj.* **1.** Made of or suggesting ebony. **2.** Black in color. [Probably from Middle English *hebenyf,* ebony wood, from alteration of Late Latin *ebeninus,* of ebony, from Greek *ebeninos,* from *ebenos,* ebony tree, from Egyptian *h-b-ny.*]

e·brac·te·ate (ē-brăk′tē-āt′) *adj.* *Botany.* Having no bracts. [New Latin *ēbracteātus* : Latin *ē-, ex-,* ex- + Latin *bractea,* gold leaf, bract.]

Eb·ro (ē′brō, ĕb′rō, ĕ′vrô). A river rising in the Cantabrian Mountains of northern Spain and flowing about 925 km (575 mi) to the Mediterranean Sea southwest of Barcelona.

EbS *abbr.* East by south.

e·bul·lience (ĭ-bo͝ol′yəns, ĭ-bŭl′-) *n.* Zestful enthusiasm.

e·bul·lien·cy (ĭ-bo͝ol′yən-sē, ĭ-bŭl′-) *n.* Ebullience.

e·bul·lient (ĭ-bo͝ol′yənt, ĭ-bŭl′-) *adj.* **1.** Zestfully enthusiastic. **2.** Boiling or seeming to boil; bubbling. [Latin *ēbulliēns, ēbullient-,* present participle of *ēbullīre,* to bubble up : *ē-, ex-,* up, out; see EX– + *bullīre,* to bubble, boil.] **—e·bul′lient·ly** *adv.*

eb·ul·li·tion (ĕb′ə-lĭsh′ən) *n.* **1.** The state or process of boiling. **2.** A sudden, violent outpouring, as of emotion: *"did not . . . give way to any ebullitions of private grief"* (Thackeray). [Middle English *ebullitiun,* from Late Latin *ēbullītiō, ēbullītiōn-,* from Latin *ēbullītus,* past participle of *ēbullīre,* to bubble up. See EBULLIENT.]

e·bur·na·tion (ē′bər-nā′shən, ĕb′ər-) *n.* Degeneration of bone into a hard, ivorylike mass, as that which occurs at the articular surfaces of bones in osteoarthritis. [From Latin *eburnus,* ivory, from *ebur.* See IVORY.]

EBV *abbr.* Epstein-Barr virus.

Ec. *abbr.* Ecuador.

E·ca·te·pec de Mo·re·los (ā-kä′tə-pĕk′ də mô-rĕl′əs, ĕ-kä′tä-pĕk′ dĕ mô-rĕl′ôs). A city of central Mexico near Mexico City. An industrial center, it occupies the site of an Aztec kingdom established in the 12th century. Population, 741,821.

Ec·ba·ta·na (ĕk-băt′n-ə). A city of ancient Media on the site of present-day Hamadan in western Iran. It was captured by Cyrus the Great in 549 B.C. and plundered by Alexander, Seleucus I, and Antiochus III.

ec·ce ho·mo (ĕk′sē hō′mō, ĕk′ĕ) *n.* A depiction of Jesus wearing the crown of thorns. [Late Latin *ecce homō,* behold the man : Latin *ecce,* behold + Latin *homō,* man.]

ec·cen·tric (ĭk-sĕn′trĭk, ĕk-) *adj.* **1.** Departing from a recognized, conventional, or established norm or pattern. See Synonyms at **strange. 2.** Deviating from a circular form or path, as in an elliptical orbit. **3.a.** Not situated at or in the geometric center. **b.** Having the axis located elsewhere than at the geometric center. **—eccentric** *n.* **1.** One that deviates markedly from an established norm, especially a person of odd or unconventional behavior. **2.** *Physics.* A disk or wheel having its axis of revolution displaced from its center so that it is capable of imparting reciprocating motion. [Middle English *eccentrik,* planetary orbit of which the earth is not at the center, from Medieval Latin *eccentricus,* not having the same center, from Greek *ekkentros* : *ek-,* out of; see ECTO– + *kentron,* center (from *kentein,* to prick; see **kent-** in Appendix).] **—ec·cen′tri·cal·ly** *adv.*

ec·cen·tric·i·ty (ĕk′sĕn-trĭs′ĭ-tē) *n., pl.* **-ties. 1.a.** The quality of being eccentric. **b.** Deviation from the normal, expected, or established. **2.** An example or instance of eccentric behavior. **3.** *Physics.* The distance between the center of an eccentric and its axis. **4.** *Mathematics.* The ratio of the distance of any point on a conic section from a focus to its distance from the corresponding directrix. This ratio is constant for any particular conic section.

SYNONYMS: *eccentricity, idiosyncrasy, quirk.* These nouns refer to peculiarity of behavior. *Eccentricity* implies divergence from the usual or customary: *"England is the paradise of individuality, eccentricity, heresy, anomalies, hobbies, and humors"* (George Santayana). *Idiosyncrasy* more often refers to such divergency viewed as being peculiar to the temperament of an individualist and serving as an identifying trait: *The use of lowercase letters for capital letters was one of the idiosyncrasies of the poet e.e. cummings. Quirk,* a milder term, merely suggests an odd trait or mannerism: *"Every man had his own quirks and twists"* (Harriet Beecher Stowe).

ec·chy·mo·sis (ĕk′ĭ-mō′sĭs) *n.* The passage of blood from ruptured blood vessels into subcutaneous tissue, marked by a purple discoloration of the skin. [New Latin, from Greek *ekkhumōsis,* extravasation, from *ekkhumousthai,* to extravasate : *ek-,* out; see ECTO– + *khumos,* juice; see **gheu-** in Appendix.] **—ec′chy·mot′ic** (-mŏt′ĭk) *adj.*

eccl. *abbr.* Ecclesiastic; ecclesiastical.

Ec·cles (ĕk′əlz), Sir **John Carew.** Born 1903. Australian physiologist. He shared a 1963 Nobel Prize for research on nerve cells.

Eccles. *abbr.* **1.** *Bible.* Ecclesiastes. **2. eccles.** Ecclesiastic; ecclesiastical.

ec·cle·si·a (ĭ-klē′zhē-ə, -zē-ə) *n., pl.* **-si·ae** (-zhē-ē′, -zē-ē′). **1.** The political assembly of citizens of an ancient Greek state. **2.** A church or congregation. [Latin *ecclēsia,* from Greek *ekklēsia,* from *ekkalein,* to summon forth : *ek-,* out; see ECTO– + *kalein, klē-,* to call; see **kelə-²** in Appendix.]

Ec·cle·si·as·tes (ĭ-klē′zē-ăs′tēz′) *n.* *(used with a sing. verb). Abbr.* **Eccles.** *Bible.* See table at **Bible.** [Late Latin *Ecclēsiastēs,* from Greek *Ekklēsiastēs,* preacher (translation of Hebrew *Qoholeth*), from *ekklēsiastēs,* a member of the ecclesia, from *ekklēsia,* ecclesia. See ECCLESIA.]

ec·cle·si·as·tic (ĭ-klē′zē-ăs′tĭk) *adj. Abbr.* **eccl., eccles.** Ecclesiastical. **—ecclesiastic** *n. Abbr.* **eccl., eccles.** A minister or priest; a cleric. [Late Latin *ecclēsiasticus,* from Greek *ekklēsiastikos,* from *ekklēsiastēs,* a member of the ecclesia. See ECCLESIASTES.]

ec·cle·si·as·ti·cal (ĭ-klē′zē-ăs′tĭ-kəl) *adj. Abbr.* **eccl., eccles. 1.** Of or relating to a church, especially as an organized institution. **2.** Appropriate to a church or to use in a church: *ecclesiastical architecture; ecclesiastical robes.* **—ec·cle′si·as′ti·cal·ly** *adv.*

ec·cle·si·as·ti·cism (ĭ-klē′zē-ăs′tə-sĭz′əm) *n.* **1.** Ecclesiastical principles, practices, and activities. **2.** Excessive adherence to ecclesiastical principles and forms.

Ec·cle·si·as·ti·cus (ĭ-klē′zē-ăs′tĭ-kəs) *n.* *Bible.* See table at **Bible.**

ec·cle·si·ol·o·gy (ĭ-klē′zē-ŏl′ə-jē) *n.* **1.** The branch of theology that is concerned with the nature, constitution, and functions of a church. **2.** The study of ecclesiastical architecture and ornamentation. [ECCLESI(A) + –LOGY.] **—ec·cle′si·o·log′i·cal** (-ə-lŏj′ĭ-kəl) *adj.*

ec·crine (ĕk′rĭn, -rīn′, -rēn′) *adj.* **1.** Relating to an eccrine gland or its secretion, especially sweat. **2.** Exocrine. [From Greek *ekkrinein,* to secrete : *ek-,* out; see ECTO– + *krinein,* to separate; see **krei-** in Appendix.]

eccrine gland *n.* Any of the numerous small sweat glands distributed over the body's surface that produce a clear aqueous secretion devoid of cytoplasmic constituents and important in regulating body temperature.

ECCS *abbr.* *Physics.* Emergency core cooling system.

ec·dys·i·ast (ĕk-dĭz′ē-ăst′, -əst) *n.* A striptease artist. [From ECDYSIS.]

ec·dy·sis (ĕk′dĭ-sĭs) *n., pl.* **-ses** (-sēz′). The shedding of an outer integument or layer of skin, as by insects, crustaceans, and snakes; molting. [Greek *ekdusis,* a stripping off, from *ekduein,* to take off : *ek-,* out, off; see ECTO– + *duein,* to put on.]

ec·dy·sone (ĕk′də-sōn′) *n.* A steroid hormone produced by insects and crustaceans that promotes growth and controls molting. [ECDYS(IS) + (HORM)ONE.]

e·ce·sis (ĭ-sē′sĭs) *n.* The successful establishment of a plant or animal species in a habitat. [From Greek *oikēsis,* inhabitation, from *oikein,* to dwell, from *oikos,* house. See **weik-¹** in Appendix.]

ECG *abbr.* **1.** Electrocardiogram. **2.** Electrocardiograph.

ec·hard (ĕk′härd′) *n.* *Ecology.* Soil water not available for absorption by plants. [From Greek *ekhein,* to hold back; see **segh-** in Appendix + *ardein,* to irrigate.]

E·che·ga·ray y Ei·za·guir·re (ā′chə-gə-rī′ ē ā′sə-gîr′ā, -gwîr′ā, ĕ′chĕ-gä-rī′ ē ā′thä-gē′rĕ), **José.** 1832–1916. Spanish mathematician, politician, and playwright who shared the 1904 Nobel Prize for literature.

ech·e·lon (ĕsh′ə-lŏn′) *n.* **1.a.** A formation of troops in which each unit is positioned successively to the left or right of the rear unit to form an oblique or steplike line. **b.** A flight formation or arrangement of craft in this manner. **c.** A similar formation of groups, units, or individuals. **2.** A subdivision of a military or naval force: *a command echelon.* **3.** A level of responsibility or authority in a hierarchy; a rank: *a job in the lower echelon of the corporation.* **—echelon** *tr. & intr.v.* **-loned, -lon·ing, -lons.** To arrange or take place in an echelon. [French *échelon,* from Old French *eschelon,* rung of a ladder, from *eschiele,* ladder, from Late Latin *scāla,* from Latin *scālae,* steps. See **skand-** in Appendix.]

echelon grating *n.* A diffraction grating made of parallel glass plates, each of which extends slightly beyond the next, used to examine extremely fine structures.

ech·e·ve·ri·a (ĕch′ə-və-rē′ə) *n.* Any of numerous tropical American plants of the genus *Echeveria,* having thick, succulent leaves often clustered in a showy rosette. [New Latin *Echeveria,* genus name, after Atanasio *Echeverría,* 19th-century Mexican botanical illustrator.]

e·chid·na (ĭ-kĭd′nə) *n.* Any of several nocturnal, burrowing, egg-laying mammals of the genera *Tachyglossus* and *Zaglossus* of Australia, Tasmania, and New Guinea, having a spiny coat, slender snout, and an extensible sticky tongue used for catching insects. Also called *spiny anteater.* [Latin, adder, viper, from Greek *ekhidna,* from *ekhis.*]

echin– *pref.* Variant of **echino–.**

ech·i·nate (ĕk′ə-nāt′) *adj.* Bearing or covered with spines or bristles; prickly.

e·chi·ni (ĭ-kī′nī′) *n.* Plural of **echinus.**

echino– or **echin–** *pref.* **1.** Spiny; prickly: *echinate.* **2.** Echinoderm: *echinoid.* [From Latin *echīnus,* sea urchin. See ECHINUS.]

e·chi·no·coc·ci (ĭ-kī′nə-kŏk′sī′, -kŏk′ī′) *n.* Plural of **echinococcus.**

e·chi·no·coc·co·sis (ĭ-kī′nə-kə-kō′sĭs) *n., pl.* **-ses** (-sēz). Infestation with echinococci. [ECHINOCOCC(US) + –OSIS.]

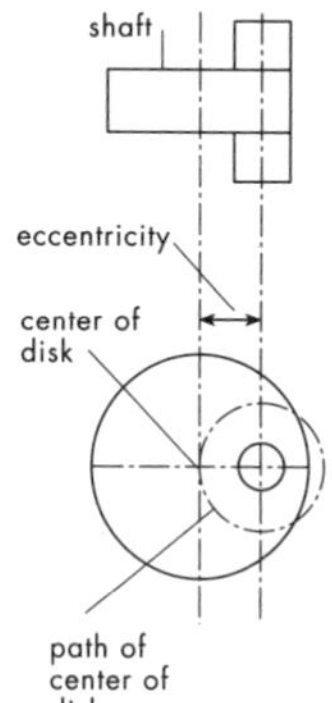

eccentric

echeveria
Echeveria pulvinata

echidna
Tachyglossus aculeatus

ă pat	oi boy
ā pay	ou out
âr care	o͝o took
ä father	o͞o boot
ĕ pet	ŭ cut
ē be	ûr urge
ĭ pit	th thin
ī pie	*th* this
îr pier	hw which
ŏ pot	zh vision
ō toe	ə about, item
ô paw	♦ regionalism

Stress marks: **′** (primary); ′ (secondary), as in **dictionary** (dĭk′shə-nĕr′ē)

e·chi·no·coc·cus (ĭ-kī′nə-kŏk′əs) *n., pl.* **-coc·ci** (-kŏk′sī′, -kŏk′ī′). Any of several parasitic tapeworms of the genus *Echinococcus,* the larvae of which infect mammals and form large, spherical cysts in the liver or lungs, causing serious or fatal disease. [New Latin *Echinococcus,* genus name : ECHINO– + –COCCUS.]

e·chi·no·derm (ĭ-kī′nə-dûrm′) *n.* Any of numerous radially symmetrical marine invertebrates of the phylum Echinodermata, which includes the starfishes, sea urchins, and sea cucumbers, having an internal calcareous skeleton and often covered with spines. **—e·chi′no·der′mal, e·chi′no·der′ma·tous** (-dûr′mə-təs) *adj.*

e·chi·noid (ĭ-kī′noid′) *n.* An echinoderm of the class Echinoidea, which includes the sand dollars and sea urchins.

e·chi·nus (ĭ-kī′nəs) *n., pl.* **-ni** (-nī′). **1.** A sea urchin of the genus *Echinus.* **2.** *Architecture.* A convex molding just below the abacus of a Doric capital. [Latin *echīnus,* sea urchin, from Greek *ekhinos,* sea urchin, hedgehog, from *ekhis,* adder, viper.]

ech·o (ĕk′ō) *n., pl.* **-oes. 1.a.** Repetition of a sound by reflection of sound waves from a surface. **b.** The sound produced in this manner. **2.** A repetition or an imitation: *a fashion that is an echo of an earlier style.* **3.** A remnant or vestige: *found echoes of past civilizations while examining artifacts in the Middle East.* **4.** One who imitates another, as in opinions, speech, or dress. **5.** A sympathetic response: *Their demand for justice found an echo in communities across the nation.* **6.** A consequence or repercussion: *Her resignation had echoes throughout the department.* **7.** Repetition of certain sounds or syllables in poetry, as in echo verse. **8.** *Music.* Soft repetition of a note or phrase. **9.** *Electronics.* A reflected wave received by a radio or radar. **—echo** *v.* **-oed, -o·ing, -oes.** *—tr.* **1.** To repeat (a sound) by the reflection of sound waves from a surface. **2.** To repeat or imitate: *followers echoing the cries of their leader; events that echoed a previous incident in history.* *—intr.* **1.** To be repeated by or as if by an echo: *The shout echoed off the wall. The speaker's words echoed in her mind.* **2.** To resound with or as if with an echo; reverberate: *rooms echoing with laughter.* [Middle English, from Old French, from Latin *ēchō,* from Greek *ēkhō.*] **—ech′o·er** *n.* **—ech′o·ey** *adj.*

SYNONYMS: *echo, reecho, reflect, resound, reverberate.* The central meaning shared by these verbs is "to send back the sound of": *a cry echoed by the canyon; a cathedral roof reechoing joyous hymns; caves that reflect the noise of footsteps; cliffs resounding the thunder of the ocean; blasting reverberated by quarry walls.*

WORD HISTORY: One might think that our word *echo* is from the name of the nymph Echo, whom Greek mythology associates with echoes. According to one version of her story, she was torn to pieces by shepherds driven to this act by the god Pan, who was hopelessly in love with her. Pieces of Echo hidden in the ground still respond to Pan's frenzied cries, producing the phenomena known as echoes. A second version of her tale has it that Echo, as a penalty for distracting Hera from observing Zeus's infidelities, lost all power of speech, except the ability to reply. This defect lost her the love of Narcissus, which caused Echo to pine away until only her voice was left. The hapless nymph, however, cannot even claim credit for echoes because the Greek word *ēkhō,* the source of English *echo,* existed with our common noun sense before any mention of Echo is found. Our word *echo* is first recorded in Middle English in a work composed in 1340.

Ech·o (ĕk′ō) *n. Greek Mythology.* A nymph whose unrequited love for Narcissus caused her to pine away until nothing but her voice remained.

ech·o·car·di·o·gram (ĕk′ō-kär′dē-ə-grăm′) *n.* A visual record produced by an echocardiograph.

ech·o·car·di·o·graph (ĕk′ō-kär′dē-ə-grăf′) *n.* An instrument that in a painless and noninvasive manner employs the differential transmission and reflection of ultrasonic waves to visualize structural and functional abnormalities of the heart. **—ech′o·car′di·o·graph′ic** *adj.* **—ech′o·car′di·og′ra·phy** (-ŏg′rə-fē) *n.*

echo chamber *n.* A room or enclosure with acoustically reflective walls used in broadcasting and recording to produce echoes or similar sound effects.

echo check *n. Computer Science.* An error control technique in which the receiving terminal or computer returns the transmitted data to verify correct reception.

ech·o·en·ceph·a·lo·gram (ĕk′ō-ĕn-sĕf′ə-lə-grăm′, -ə-lō-) *n.* A visual record produced by an echoencephalograph.

ech·o·en·ceph·a·lo·graph (ĕk′ō-ĕn-sĕf′ə-lə-grăf′, -ə-lō-) *n.* An instrument that in a painless and noninvasive manner uses the differential transmission and reflection of ultrasonic waves to create a detailed visual image of the brain. **—ech′o·en·ceph′a·lo·graph′ic** *adj.* **—ech′o·en·ceph′a·log′ra·phy** (-lŏg′rə-fē) *n.*

ech·o·gram (ĕk′ō-grăm′) *n.* See **sonogram.**

e·chog·ra·phy (ĕ-kŏg′rə-fē) *n.* See **ultrasonography.**

e·cho·ic (ĕ-kō′ĭk) *adj.* **1.** Of or resembling an echo. **2.** Imitative of natural sounds; onomatopoeic: *an echoic word.*

ech·o·la·li·a (ĕk′ō-lā′lē-ə) *n.* **1.** *Psychiatry.* The immediate and involuntary repetition of words or phrases just spoken by others, often a symptom of autism or some types of schizophrenia. **2.** An infant's repetition of the sounds made by others, a normal occurrence in childhood development. [ECHO + Greek *lalia,* talk (from *lalos,* talkative).] **—ech′o·la′lic** (-lĭk) *adj.*

ech·o·lo·ca·tion (ĕk′ō-lō-kā′shən) *n.* **1.** A sensory system in certain animals, such as bats and dolphins, in which usually high-pitched sounds are emitted and their echoes interpreted to determine the direction and distance of objects. **2.** *Electronics.* A process for determining the location of objects by emitting sound waves and analyzing the waves reflected back to the sender by the object. Also called *echo ranging.* **—ech′o·lo·cate′** *v.*

echo sounder *n.* A device for measuring depth of water by sending pressure waves down from the surface and recording the time until the echo returns from the bottom.

echo verse *n.* Verse in which the final words or syllables of a line or stanza are repeated as a response, often with an ironic effect.

ech·o·vi·rus (ĕk′ō-vī′rəs) *n., pl.* **-rus·es.** *Microbiology.* Any of a number of retroviruses of the family Picornaviridae, inhabiting the gastrointestinal tract and associated with various diseases, such as viral meningitis, mild respiratory infections, and severe diarrhea in newborns. [*e(nteric) c(ytopathogenic) h(uman) o(rphan) virus.*]

Eck (ĕk), **Johann.** 1486–1543. German Roman Catholic theologian who opposed the reforms of Martin Luther and procured from Rome the papal bull that declared Luther a heretic (1520).

Eck·hart also **Eck·art** or **Eck·ardt** (ĕk′härt′, -ärt′), **Johannes.** Known as "Meister Eckhart." 1260?–1327? German theologian regarded as the founder of mysticism in Germany.

ECL *abbr. Computer Science.* Emitter-coupled logic.

é·clair (ā-klâr′, ā′klâr′) *n.* An elongated pastry filled with custard or whipped cream and usually iced with chocolate. [French, from Old French *esclair,* lightning, from *esclairier,* to light up, from Vulgar Latin **exclāriāre,* from Latin *exclārāre* : *ex-,* intensive pref.; see EX– + *clārus,* clear; see **kelə-**[2] in Appendix.]

é·clair·cisse·ment (ā-klâr-sēs-mäN′) *n.* A clarification; an enlightenment. [French, from Old French *esclarcir, esclarciss-,* to clarify, from Vulgar Latin **exclāricīre,* variant of **exclāriāre.* See ÉCLAIR.]

e·clamp·si·a (ĭ-klămp′sē-ə) *n.* Coma and convulsions during or immediately after pregnancy, characterized by edema, hypertension, and proteinuria. [New Latin, from Greek *eklampsis,* a shining forth, from *eklampein,* to shine forth : *ek-,* out; see ECTO– + *lampein,* to shine.] **—e·clamp′tic** (-tĭk) *adj.*

é·clat (ā-klä′, ā′klä′) *n.* **1.** Great brilliance, as of performance or achievement. **2.** Conspicuous success. **3.** Great acclamation or applause. **4.** *Archaic.* Notoriety; scandal. [French, brilliance, from Old French *esclat,* splinter, from *esclater,* to burst out, splinter, probably of Germanic origin.]

e·clec·tic (ĭ-klĕk′tĭk) *adj.* **1.** Selecting or employing individual elements from a variety of sources, systems, or styles: *an eclectic taste in music; an eclectic approach to managing the economy.* **2.** Made up of or combining elements from a variety of sources: *"a popular bar patronized by an eclectic collection of artists, writers, secretaries and aging soldiers on reserve duty"* (Curtis Wilkie). **—eclectic** *n.* One that follows an eclectic method. [Greek *eklektikos,* selective, from *eklektos,* selected, from *eklegein,* to select : *ek-,* out; see ECTO– + *legein,* to gather; see **leg-** in Appendix.] **—e·clec′ti·cal·ly** *adv.*

e·clec·ti·cism (ĭ-klĕk′tə-sĭz′əm) *n.* An eclectic system or method.

e·clipse (ĭ-klĭps′) *n.* **1.a.** The partial or complete obscuring, relative to a designated observer, of one celestial body by another. **b.** The period of time during which such an obscuration occurs. **2.** A temporary or permanent dimming or cutting off of light. **3.a.** A fall into obscurity or disuse; a decline: *"A composer . . . often goes into eclipse after his death and never regains popularity"* (Time). **b.** A disgraceful or humiliating end; a downfall: *Revelations of wrongdoing helped bring about the eclipse of the governor's career.* **—eclipse** *tr.v.* **e·clipsed, e·clips·ing, e·clips·es. 1.a.** To cause an eclipse of. **b.** To obscure; darken. **2.a.** To obscure or diminish in importance, fame, or reputation. **b.** To surpass; outshine: *an outstanding performance that eclipsed the previous record.* [Middle English, from Old French, from Latin *eclīpsis,* from Greek *ekleipsis,* from *ekleipein,* to fail to appear : *ek-,* out; see ECTO– + *leipein,* to leave; see **leikʷ-** in Appendix.]

eclipse plumage *n.* Dull or colorless plumage that certain birds, such as male ducks, acquire at the end of the breeding season.

e·clips·ing binary (ĭ-klĭp′sĭng) *n.* A binary star whose components pass in front of each other, thereby causing a regular eclipse of one of the stars. Also called *eclipsing variable star.*

e·clip·tic (ĭ-klĭp′tĭk) *n.* **1.** The intersection plane of the earth's orbit with the celestial sphere, along which the sun appears to move as viewed from the earth. **2.** A great circle inscribed on a terrestrial globe inclined at an approximate angle of 23°27′ to the equator and representing the apparent motion of the sun in relation to the earth during a year. [Middle English *ecliptik,* from Medieval Latin *(līnea) eclīptica,* ecliptic (line), from Latin *eclīpticus,* of an eclipse, from Greek *ekleiptikos,* from *ekleipein,* to fail to appear. See ECLIPSE.]

ec·logue (ĕk′lôg′, -lŏg′) *n.* A pastoral poem, usually in the form of a dialogue between shepherds. [Middle English *eclog,* from Latin *ecloga,* from Greek *eklogē,* selection, from *eklegein,* to select. See ECLECTIC.]

e·clo·sion (ĭ-klō′zhən) *n.* The emergence of an adult insect from a pupal case or an insect larva from an egg. [French *éclosion,* from *éclore,* to open, from Old French, from Vulgar Latin *exclaudere, to shut out : Latin *ex-*, ex- + Latin *claudere,* to shut.]

ECM *abbr.* European Common Market.

eco– *pref.* Ecology; ecological: *ecosystem.* [From ECOLOGY.]

ec·o·ca·tas·tro·phe (ĕk′ō-kə-tăs′trə-fē, ē′kō-) *n.* A large-scale disruption of the balance of nature, usually as a result of human intervention.

ec·o·cide (ĕk′ō-sīd′, ē′kō-) *n.* Heedless or deliberate destruction of the natural environment, as by pollutants or an act of war.

ec·o·freak (ĕk′ō-frēk′, ē′kō-) *n. Slang.* An environmentalist considered to be overly zealous.

ecol. *abbr.* **1.** Ecology. **2.** Ecological.

E. co·li (ē kō′lī) *n.* A bacillus *(Escherichia coli)* normally found in the human gastrointestinal tract and existing as numerous strains, some of which are responsible for diarrheal diseases. Other strains have been used experimentally in molecular biology. [New Latin *Escherichia coli* : after Theodor *Escherich* (1857–1911), German physician + Latin *colī,* genitive of *colon;* see COLON[2].]

e·col·o·gy (ĭ-kŏl′ə-jē) *n., pl.* **-gies.** *Abbr.* **ecol. 1.a.** The science of the relationships between organisms and their environments. Also called *bionomics.* **b.** The relationship between organisms and their environment. **2.** The branch of sociology that is concerned with studying the relationships between human groups and their physical and social environments. Also called *human ecology.* **3.** The study of the detrimental effects of modern civilization on the environment, with a view toward prevention or reversal through conservation. Also called *human ecology.* [German *Ökologie* : Greek *oikos,* house; see **weik-**[1] in Appendix + German *-logie,* study (from Greek *-logia,* -logy).] **—ec′o·log′i·cal** (ĕk′ə-lŏj′ĭ-kəl, ē′kə-), **ec′o·log′ic** (-ĭk) *adj.* **—ec′o·log′i·cal·ly** *adv.* **—e·col′o·gist** *n.*

econ. *abbr.* Economics; economist; economy.

e·con·o·met·rics (ĭ-kŏn′ə-mĕt′rĭks) *n. (used with a sing. verb).* Application of mathematical and statistical techniques to economics in the study of problems, the analysis of data, and the development and testing of theories and models. [ECONO(MICS) + –METRICS.] **—e·con′o·met′ric, e·con′o·met′ri·cal** *adj.* **—e·con′o·met′ri·cal·ly** *adv.* **—e·con′o·me·tri′cian** (-mĭ-trĭsh′ən), **e·con′o·met′rist** *n.*

ec·o·nom·ic (ĕk′ə-nŏm′ĭk, ē′kə-) *adj.* **1.a.** Of or relating to the production, development, and management of material wealth, as of a country, household, or business enterprise. **b.** Of or relating to an economy: *a period of sustained economic growth.* **2.** Of or relating to the science of economics: *new economic theories regarding the effects of deficit spending.* **3.** Of or relating to the practical necessities of life; material: *wrote the book primarily for economic reasons.* **4.a.** Financially rewarding; economical: *It was no longer economic to keep the manufacturing facilities open.* **b.** Efficient; economical: *an economic use of home heating oil.*

ec·o·nom·i·cal (ĕk′ə-nŏm′ĭ-kəl, ē′kə-) *adj.* **1.** Prudent and thrifty in management; not wasteful or extravagant. See Synonyms at **sparing. 2.** Intended to save money, as by efficient operation or elimination of unnecessary features; economic: *a modern, economical heating system; an economical approach to control of corporate growth.* **—ec′o·nom′i·cal·ly** *adv.*

economic rent *n.* See **rent**[1] (sense 3).

ec·o·nom·ics (ĕk′ə-nŏm′ĭks, ē′kə-) *n. Abbr.* **econ. 1.** *(used with a sing. verb).* The social science that deals with the production, distribution, and consumption of goods and services and with the theory and management of economies or economic systems. **2.** *(used with a sing. or pl. verb).* Economic matters, especially relevant financial considerations: *"Economics are slowly killing the family farm"* (Christian Science Monitor).

e·con·o·mist (ĭ-kŏn′ə-mĭst) *n. Abbr.* **econ. 1.** A specialist in economics. **2.** *Archaic.* An economical person.

e·con·o·mize (ĭ-kŏn′ə-mīz′) *v.* **-mized, -miz·ing, -miz·es.** *—intr.* **1.** To practice economy, as by avoiding waste or reducing expenditures. **2.** To make economical use of something: *"The best that can be said for this method is that it economizes on thought"* (Christopher Hitchens). *—tr.* To use or manage with thrift: *the need to economize scarce resources.* **—e·con′o·miz′er** *n.*

e·con·o·my (ĭ-kŏn′ə-mē) *n., pl.* **-mies.** *Abbr.* **econ. 1.a.** Careful, thrifty management of resources, such as money, materials, or labor: *learned to practice economy in making out the household budget.* **b.** An example or result of such management; a saving. **2.a.** The system or range of economic activity in a country, region, or community: *Effects of inflation were felt at every level of the economy.* **b.** A specific type of economic system: *an industrial economy; a planned economy.* **3.** An orderly, functional arrangement of parts; an organized system: *"the sense that there is a moral economy in the world, that good is rewarded and evil is punished"* (George F. Will). **4.** Efficient, sparing, or conservative use: *wrote with an economy of language; a well-organized group that worked with an economy of effort.* **5.** Economy class. **6.** *Theology.* The method of God's government of and activity within the world. **—economy** *adj.* Economical or inexpensive to buy or use: *an economy car; an economy motel.* [Middle English *yconomye,* management of a household, from Latin *oeconomia,* from Greek *oikonomia,* from *oikonomos,* one who manages a household : *oikos,* house; see **weik-**[1] in Appendix + *nemein,* to allot, manage; see **nem-** in Appendix.]

WORD HISTORY: Managing an economy has at least an etymological justification. The word *economy* can probably be traced back to the Greek word *oikonomos,* "one who manages a household," derived from *oikos,* "house," and *nemein,* "to manage." From *oikonomos* was derived *oikonomia,* which had not only the sense "management of a houseold or family" but also senses such as "thrift," "direction," "administration," "arrangement," and "public revenue of a state." The first recorded sense of our word *economy,* found in a work possibly composed in 1440, is "the management of economic affairs," in this case, of a monastery. *Economy* is later recorded in other senses shared by *oikonomia* in Greek, including "thrift" and "administration." What is probably our most frequently used current sense, "the economic system of a country or an area," seems not to have developed until the 19th or 20th century.

economy class *n.* The least expensive class of accommodations, especially on an airplane.

ec·o·phys·i·ol·o·gy (ĕk′ō-fĭz′ē-ŏl′ə-jē, ē′kō-) *n.* The study of the interrelationship between an organisms's physical functioning and its environment.

é·cor·ché (ā′kôr-shā′) *n.* An anatomical representation of the body or a part of the body with the skin removed so as to display the musculature. [French, from past participle of *écorcher,* to flay, from Latin *excorticāre* : *ex-*, off, away; see EX– + *cortex, cortic-*, bark, skin; see CORTEX.]

ec·o·spe·cies (ĕk′ō-spē′shēz, -sēz, ē′kō-) *n., pl.* **ecospecies.** A taxonomic species considered in terms of its ecological characteristics and usually including several interbreeding ecotypes.

ec·o·sphere (ĕk′ō-sfîr′, ē′kō-) *n.* The regions of the universe, especially on the earth, that are capable of supporting life; the biosphere.

ec·o·sys·tem (ĕk′ō-sĭs′təm, ē′kō-) *n.* An ecological community together with its environment, functioning as a unit.

ec·o·tone (ĕk′ə-tōn′, ē′kə-) *n.* A transitional zone between two communities containing the characteristic species of each. [ECO– + Greek *tonos,* tension, tone; see TONE.]

ec·o·type (ĕk′ə-tīp′, ē′kə-) *n.* The smallest taxonomic subdivision of an ecospecies, consisting of populations adapted to a particular set of environmental conditions. The populations are infertile with other ecotypes of the same ecospecies. **—ec′o·typ′ic** (-tĭp′ĭk) *adj.*

ec·ru (ĕk′ro͞o, ā′kro͞o) *n. Color.* A grayish to pale yellow or light grayish-yellowish brown. [French *écru,* raw, unbleached, from Old French *escru* : *es-*, intensive pref. (from Latin *ex-*; see EX–) + *cru,* raw (from Latin *crūdus;* see **kreuə-** in Appendix).]

ec·sta·sy (ĕk′stə-sē) *n., pl.* **-sies. 1.** Intense joy or delight. **2.** A state of emotion so intense that one is carried beyond rational thought and self-control: *an ecstasy of rage.* **3.** The trance, frenzy, or rapture associated with mystic or prophetic exaltation. [Middle English *extasie,* from Old French, from Late Latin *extasis,* terror, from Greek *ekstasis,* astonishment, distraction, from *existanai,* to displace, derange : *ex-*, out of; see EXO– + *histanai,* to place; see **stā-** in Appendix.]

SYNONYMS: *ecstasy, rapture, transport, exaltation.* These nouns all refer to a state of elated bliss. In its original sense *ecstasy* denoted a trancelike condition marked by loss of orientation toward rational experience and by concentration on a single emotion; now it usually means intense delight: *"To burn always with this hard, gemlike flame, to maintain this ecstasy, is success in life"* (Walter Pater). *Rapture* originally meant a being caught up in an emotional state, typically involuntary and uncontrollable. In current usage *rapture,* like *ecstasy,* simply means great joy: *"Oliver would sit . . . listening to the sweet music, in a perfect rapture"* (Charles Dickens). *Transport* is the state of being carried away by strong emotion: *"Surprised by joy—impatient as the Wind/I turned to share the transport"* (William Wordsworth). *Exaltation* is a feeling or condition of elevated, often excessively passionate emotion: *"There are men in the world who derive as stern an exaltation from the proximity of disaster and ruin, as others from success"* (Winston S. Churchill).

ec·stat·ic (ĕk-stăt′ĭk) *adj.* **1.** Marked by or expressing ecstasy. **2.** Being in a state of ecstasy; enraptured. [French *extatique,* from Greek *ekstatikos,* from *ekstasis,* distraction. See ECSTASY.] **—ec·stat′i·cal·ly** *adv.*

ECT *abbr.* Electroconvulsive therapy.

ecto– *pref.* Outer; external: *ectoparasite.* [Greek *ekto-*, from *ektos,* outside, from *ek, ek-*, out. See **eghs** in Appendix.]

ec·to·com·men·sal (ĕk′tə-kə-mĕn′səl) *n.* A commensal organism that lives on the outer body surface of another organism.

ec·to·derm (ĕk′tə-dûrm′) *n.* **1.** The outermost of the three primary germ layers of an embryo, from which the epidermis, nervous tissue, and, in vertebrates, sense organs develop. **2.** The outer layer of a diploblastic animal, such as a jellyfish. **—ec′to·der′mal, ec′to·der′mic** *adj.*

ec·tog·e·nous (ĕk-tŏj′ə-nəs) also **ec·to·gen·ic** (ĕk′tə-jĕn′ĭk) *adj.* Able to live and develop outside a host, as certain pathogenic microorganisms do.

ec·to·mere (ĕk′tə-mîr′) *n.* Any of the blastomeres from which the ectoderm develops. **—ec′to·mer′ic** (-mîr′ĭk, -mĕr′-) *adj.*

ec·to·morph (ĕk′tə-môrf′) *n.* An individual having a lean,

ă pat	oi boy
ā pay	ou out
âr care	o͝o took
ä father	o͞o boot
ĕ pet	ŭ cut
ē be	ûr urge
ĭ pit	th thin
ī pie	*th* this
îr pier	hw which
ŏ pot	zh vision
ō toe	ə about, item
ô paw	♦ regionalism

Stress marks: ′ (primary); ′ (secondary), as in **dictionary** (dĭk′shə-nĕr′ē)

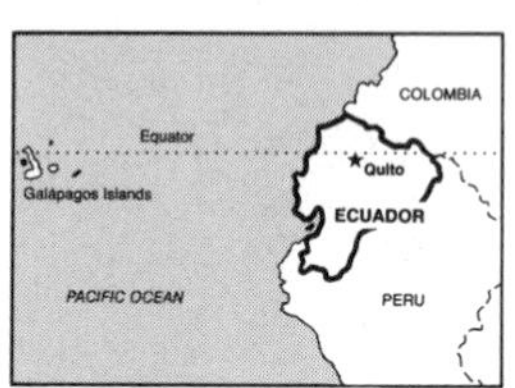

Ecuador

Mary Baker Eddy

edelweiss
Leontopodium alpinum

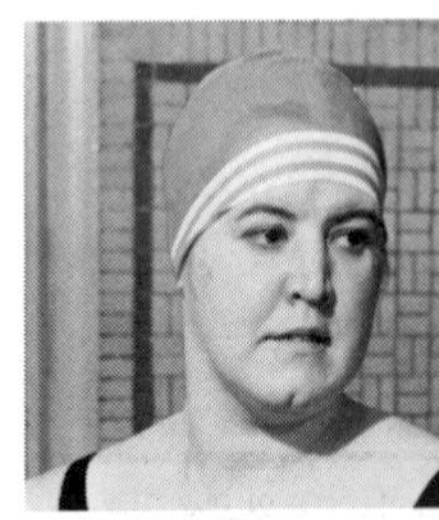

Gertrude Ederle

slightly muscular body build in which tissues derived from the embryonic ectoderm predominate. [ECTO(DERM) + –MORPH.]

ec·to·mor·phic (ĕk′tə-môr′fĭk) *adj.* Of or relating to an ectomorph. [ECTO(DERM) + –MORPHIC.] **—ec′to·mor′phy** *n.*

-ectomy *suff.* Surgical removal: *tonsillectomy.* [New Latin *-ectomia* : Greek *ek-*, out; see ECTO– + *-tomia*, -tomy.]

ec·to·par·a·site (ĕk′tə-păr′ə-sīt′) *n.* A parasite, such as a flea, that lives on the exterior of another organism. **—ec′to·par′a·sit′ic** (-sĭt′ĭk) *adj.* **—ec′to·par′a·sit′ism** *n.*

ec·to·pi·a (ĕk-tō′pē-ə) *n.* An abnormal location or position of an organ or a body part, occurring congenitally or as the result of injury. [New Latin, from Greek *ektopos,* away from a place : *ek-*, away from, out of; see ECTO– + *topos,* place.] **—ec·top′ic** (-tŏp′ĭk) *adj.*

ectopic pregnancy *n.* Implantation and subsequent development of a fertilized ovum outside the uterus, as in a fallopian tube.

ec·to·plasm (ĕk′tə-plăz′əm) *n.* **1.** *Biology.* The outer portion of the continuous phase of cytoplasm of a cell, sometimes distinguishable as a somewhat rigid, gelled layer beneath the cell membrane. **2.a.** The visible substance believed to emanate from the body of a spiritualistic medium during communication with the dead. **b.** An immaterial or ethereal substance, especially the transparent corporeal presence of a spirit or ghost. **3.** *Informal.* An image projected onto a movie screen. **—ec′to·plas′mic** *adj.*

ec·to·sarc (ĕk′tə-särk′) *n.* The ectoplasm of certain protozoans, such as the amoeba. [ECTO– + Greek *sarx, sarc-*, flesh.]

ec·to·therm (ĕk′tə-thûrm′) *n.* An organism that regulates its body temperature largely by exchanging heat with its surroundings; a poikilotherm.

ec·to·ther·mic (ĕk′tə-thûr′mĭk) also **ec·to·ther·mal** (ĕk′tə-thûr′məl) or **ec·to·ther·mous** (-məs) *adj.* Of or relating to an organism that regulates its body temperature largely by exchanging heat with its surroundings; cold-blooded.

é·cu (ā-kyo͞o′) *n., pl.* **é·cus** (ā-kyo͞o′). Any of various old French coins, especially a silver five-franc piece. [French, from Old French *escu,* from Latin *scūtum,* shield (from the shield stamped on the coin). See **skei-** in Appendix.]

Ec·ua·dor (ĕk′wə-dôr′). *Abbr.* **Ec., Ecua.** A country of northwest South America on the Pacific Ocean. First occupied by the Spanish in 1534, the area achieved independence in 1830. Quito is the capital and Guayaquil the largest city. Population, 8,050,630. **—Ec′ua·dor′i·an** *adj. & n.*

ec·u·men·i·cal (ĕk′yə-mĕn′ĭ-kəl) also **ec·u·men·ic** (-mĕn′ĭk) *adj.* **1.** Of worldwide scope or applicability; universal. **2.a.** Of or relating to the worldwide Christian church. **b.** Concerned with establishing or promoting unity among churches or religions. [From Late Latin *oecūmenicus,* from Greek *oikoumenikos,* from *(hē) oikoumenē (gē),* (the) inhabited (world), feminine present passive participle of *oikein,* to inhabit, from *oikos,* house. See **weik-**[1] in Appendix.] **—ec′u·men′i·cal** *n.* **—ec′u·men′i·cal·ism** *n.* **—ec′u·men′i·cal·ly** *adv.*

ecumenical patriarch *n.* The patriarch of Constantinople, the highest ecclesiastical official of the Eastern Orthodox Church.

ec·u·men·i·cism (ĕk′yə-mĕn′ĭ-sĭz′əm) *n.* Ecumenism. **—ec′u·men′i·cist** *n.*

ec·u·me·nism (ĕk′yə-mə-nĭz′əm, ĭ-kyo͞o′-) *n.* **1.** A movement promoting unity among Christian churches or denominations. **2.** A movement promoting worldwide unity among religions through greater cooperation and improved understanding. **—ec′u·men′ist** *n.*

ec·ze·ma (ĕk′sə-mə, ĕg′zə-, ĭg-zē′-) *n.* A noncontagious inflammation of the skin, characterized chiefly by redness, itching, and the outbreak of lesions that may discharge serous matter and become encrusted and scaly. [New Latin, from Greek *ekzema,* from *ekzein,* to break out, boil over : *ek-*, out; see ECTO– + *zein,* to boil; see **yes-** in Appendix.] **—ec·zem′a·tous** (ĕg-zĕm′ə-təs, -zē′mə-təs, ĭg-) *adj.*

ed. *abbr.* **1.** Edition; editor. **2.** Education.

E.D. *abbr.* Election district.

-ed[1] *suff.* Used to form the past tense of regular verbs: *tasted.* [Middle English *-ede,* from Old English *-ade, -ede, -ode.*]

-ed[2] *suff.* Used to form the past participle of regular verbs: *absorbed.* [Middle English, from Old English *-ad, -ed, -od.*]

-ed[3] *suff.* Having; characterized by; resembling: *blackhearted.* [Middle English *-ede, -de,* from Old English *-ed, -od.*]

e·da·cious (ĭ-dā′shəs) *adj.* Characterized by voracity; devouring. [From Latin *edāx, edāc-*, from *edere,* to eat. See **ed-** in Appendix.] **—e·dac′i·ty** (ĭ-dăs′ĭ-tē) *n.*

E·dam[1] (ē′dəm, ē′dăm′, ā-däm′). A town of western Netherlands on the Ijsselmeer. Chartered in 1357, it has a famous cheese market. Population, 24,019.

E·dam[2] (ē′dəm, ē′dăm′) *n.* A mild, yellow Dutch cheese, pressed into balls and usually covered with red wax. [After EDAM[1].]

e·daph·ic (ĭ-dăf′ĭk) *adj.* **1.** Of or relating to soil, especially as it affects living organisms. **2.** Influenced by the soil rather than by the climate. [From Greek *edaphos,* ground, soil. See **sed-** in Appendix.]

edaphic climax *n.* A climax community determined by soil factors, such as alkalinity, salinity, or drainage, rather than by climatic or physiographic characteristics.

Ed·da (ĕd′ə) *n.* **1.** A collection of Old Norse poems, called the Elder or Poetic Edda, assembled in the early 13th century. **2.** A manual of Icelandic poetry, called the Younger or Prose Edda, written by Snorri Sturluson. [Old Norse.] **—Ed′dic** *adj.*

Ed·ding·ton (ĕd′ĭng-tən), Sir **Arthur Stanley.** 1882–1944. British mathematician, astronomer, and physicist who was an early exponent of the theory of relativity.

ed·do (ĕd′ō) *n., pl.* **-does.** See **taro.** [Of Niger-Congo origin; akin to Akan (Fante) *edwo,* yam.]

ed·dy (ĕd′ē) *n., pl.* **-dies. 1.** A current, as of water or air, moving contrary to the direction of the main current, especially in a circular motion. **2.** A drift or tendency that is counter to or separate from a main current, as of opinion, tradition, or history. **—eddy** *v.* **-died, -dy·ing, -dies.** —*intr.* To move in or as if in an eddy. See Synonyms at **turn.** —*tr.* To cause to move in or as if in an eddy. [Middle English *ydy,* probably of Scandinavian origin; akin to Old Norse *idha.*]

Ed·dy (ĕd′ē), **Mary (Morse) Baker.** 1821–1910. American religious leader who founded Christian Science (1879), the tenets of which she explained in *Science and Health* (1875).

Ed·dy·stone Rocks (ĕd′ĭ-stən). A rocky islet of southwest England in the English Channel south of Plymouth. It has been the site of a strategic lighthouse since the 1690's.

e·del·weiss (ā′dəl-vīs′, -wīs′) *n.* An alpine plant *(Leontopodium alpinum),* native to Europe and having leaves covered with whitish down and small flower heads surrounded by conspicuous whitish bracts. [German : *edel,* noble (from Middle High German *edele,* from Old High German *edili*) + *weiss,* white (from Middle High German *wīz,* from Old High German *wīz, hwīz;* see **kweit-** in Appendix).]

e·de·ma also **oe·de·ma** (ĭ-dē′mə) *n., pl.* **-mas** or **-ma·ta** (-mə-tə). **1.** *Pathology.* An excessive accumulation of serous fluid in tissue spaces or a body cavity. **2.** *Botany.* Extended swelling in plant organs caused primarily by an excessive accumulation of water. [Middle English *ydema,* from Greek *oidēma,* a swelling, from *oidein,* to swell.] **—e·dem′a·tous** (ĭ-dĕm′ə-təs) *adj.*

E·den[1] (ēd′n) *n.* **1.** *Bible.* The garden that was the first home of Adam and Eve. Also called *Garden of Eden.* **2.** A delightful place; a paradise. **3.** A state of innocence, bliss, or ultimate happiness. [Middle English, from Late Latin, from Greek *Ēdēn,* from Hebrew *'Ēden,* from *'ēden,* delight.] **—E·den′ic** (ē-dĕn′ĭk) *adj.*

E·den[2] (ēd′n). A city of northern North Carolina near the Virginia border north of Greensboro. It is a processing and shipping center in an agricultural area. Population, 15,672.

Eden, Sir **(Robert) Anthony.** First Earl of Avon. 1897–1977. British politician who as foreign minister (1935–1938, 1940–1945, and 1951–1955) was instrumental in the founding of the United Nations (1945) and as prime minister (1955–1957) supported the 1956 Anglo-French invasion of Egypt.

Eden Prairie. A city of eastern Minnesota, a residential suburb of Minneapolis. Population, 16,263.

e·den·tate (ē-dĕn′tāt′) *Biology. adj.* **1.** Lacking teeth. **2.** Of or belonging to the order Edentata, which includes mammals having few or no teeth, such as anteaters, armadillos, and sloths. **—edentate** *n.* A member of the Edentata. [Latin *ēdentātus,* past participle of *ēdentāre,* to knock out the teeth : *ē-, ex-*, ex- + *dēns, dent-*, tooth; see **dent-** in Appendix.]

e·den·tu·lous (ē-dĕn′chə-ləs) *adj. Biology.* Having no teeth; toothless. [From Latin *ēdentulus* : *ē-, ex-*, ex- + *dēns, dent-*, tooth; see **dent-** in Appendix.]

E·der (ā′dər). A river rising in central Germany and flowing about 177 km (110 mi) generally eastward to the Fulda River.

E·der·le (ā′dər-lē), **Gertrude Caroline.** Born 1906. American swimmer who in 1926 became the first woman to swim the English Channel, doing so in 14 hours and 31 minutes.

E·des·sa (ĭ-dĕs′ə). An ancient city of Mesopotamia on the site of present-day Urfa in southeast Turkey. A major Christian center after the third century A.D., it fell to the Arabs in 639 and was captured by Crusaders in 1097.

edge (ĕj) *n.* **1.a.** A thin, sharpened side, as of the blade of a cutting instrument. **b.** The degree of sharpness of a cutting blade. **c.** A penetrating, incisive quality: *"His simplicity sets off the satire, and gives it a finer edge"* (William Hazlitt). **2.** Keenness, as of desire or enjoyment; zest: *The brisk walk gave an edge to my appetite.* **3.a.** The line of intersection of two surfaces: *the edge of a brick; the rounded edges of the table.* **b.** A rim or brink: *the edge of a cliff.* **4.a.** The area or part away from the middle; an extremity: *lifted the edge of the carpet.* **b.** A dividing line; a border: *a house on the edge of town.* See Synonyms at **border. c.** A point of transition: *on the edge of war.* **5.** A margin of superiority; an advantage: *a slight edge over the opposition.* See Synonyms at **advantage. —edge** *v.* **edged, edg·ing, edg·es.** —*tr.* **1.a.** To give an edge to (a blade); sharpen. **b.** *Sports.* To tilt (a ski or both skis) in such a way that an edge or both edges bite into the snow. **2.a.** To put a border or edge on: *edged the quilt with fanciful embroidery.* **b.** To act as or be an edge of: *flowers that edged the garden path.* **3.** To advance or push slightly or gradually: *The dog edged the ball toward the child with its nose.* **4.** To trim or shape the edge of: *edge a lawn.* —*intr.* To move gradually or hesitantly: *The child edged toward the door.* **—*phrasal verb.* edge out.** To surpass or beat by a small margin: *The downhill racer edged her opponent out on the middle stretch.* **—*idioms.* on edge.** Highly tense or nervous; irritable. **on the edge. 1.** In a precarious position. **2.** In a state of keen excitement, as from danger or risk: *"the excitement of combat, of living on the edge"* (Nelson DeMille). [Middle English *egge,* from Old English *ecg.* See **ak-** in Appendix.] **—edge′less** *adj.*

edge effect *n. Ecology.* The occurrence of greater species diversity and biological density in an ecotone than in any of the adjacent ecological communities.

edg·er (ĕj′ər) *n.* One that edges, such as a tool for trimming the edge of a lawn.

edge tool *n.* A tool, such as a chisel, that has a cutting edge.

edge·wise (ĕj′wīz′) also **edge·ways** (-wāz′) *adv.* **1.** With the edge foremost. **2.** On, by, with, or toward the edge.

Edge·wood (ĕj′wo͝od′). A community of northeast Maryland on an inlet of Chesapeake Bay northeast of Baltimore. A U.S. Army arsenal is nearby. Population, 19,455.

Edge·worth (ĕj′wûrth′), **Maria.** 1767–1849. British writer noted for her realistic novels, such as *Castle Rackrent* (1800), which broke away from the prevalent Gothic style.

edg·ing (ĕj′ĭng) *n.* Something that forms or serves as an edge or a border.

edg·y (ĕj′ē) *adj.* **-i·er, -i·est. 1.** Nervous or irritable: *The performers were edgy as they waited for the show to begin.* **2.** Having a sharp or biting edge: *an edgy wit.* **—edg′i·ly** *adv.* **—edg′i·ness** *n.*

edh also **eth** (ĕth) *n.* **1.** A letter (ð) appearing in Old English, Old Saxon, Old Norse, and modern Icelandic to represent an interdental fricative. **2.** The symbol in the International Phonetic Alphabet representing the interdental voiced fricative, as in *the* or *with.* [Icelandic *edh.*]

ed·i·ble (ĕd′ə-bəl) *adj.* Fit to be eaten: *edible roots; an edible mushroom.* **—edible** *n.* Something fit to be eaten; food. [Late Latin *edibilis,* from Latin *edere,* to eat. See **ed-** in Appendix.] **—ed′i·bil′i·ty, ed′i·ble·ness** *n.*

edible canna *n.* **1.** A South American and West Indian plant *(Canna edulis)* having large red flowers and edible tubers. Also called *achira, Queensland arrowroot.* **2.** The tubers of this plant.

e·dict (ē′dĭkt′) *n.* **1.** A decree or proclamation issued by an authority and having the force of law. **2.** A formal pronouncement or command. [Latin *ēdictum,* from neuter past participle of *ēdīcere,* to declare : *ē-, ex-,* ex- + *dīcere,* to speak; see **deik-** in Appendix.]

ed·i·fi·ca·tion (ĕd′ə-fĭ-kā′shən) *n.* Intellectual, moral, or spiritual improvement; enlightenment.

ed·i·fice (ĕd′ə-fĭs) *n.* **1.** A building, especially one of imposing appearance or size. See Synonyms at **building. 2.** An elaborate conceptual structure: *observations that provided the foundation for the edifice of evolutionary theory.* [Middle English, from Old French, from Latin *aedificium,* from *aedificāre,* to build : *aedis,* a building + *-ficāre,* -fy.]

ed·i·fy (ĕd′ə-fī′) *tr.v.* **-fied, -fy·ing, -fies.** To instruct especially so as to encourage intellectual, moral, or spiritual improvement. [Middle English *edifien,* from Old French *edifier,* from Late Latin *aedificāre,* to instruct spiritually, from Latin, to build. See EDIFICE.] **—ed′i·fi′er** *n.*

E·di·na (ĭ-dī′nə). A city of eastern Minnesota, a residential suburb of Minneapolis. Population, 46,073.

Ed·in·burg (ĕd′n-bûrg′). A city of southern Texas near the Mexican border west-northwest of Brownsville. It is a processing center in an agricultural region. Population, 24,075.

Ed·in·burgh (ĕd′n-bûr′ə, -bŭr′ə, -brə). The capital of Scotland, in the eastern part of the country on the Firth of Forth. Once known as "Auld Reekie" for the thick clouds of smoke that hung over its low-lying areas, the picturesque city is a brewing center, a popular tourist attraction, and the site of an annual international festival of the arts. Population, 446,361.

Edinburgh, Duke of. See Prince **Philip.**

E·dir·ne (ĕ-dîr′nĕ). Formerly **A·dri·a·no·ple** (ā′drē-ə-nō′pəl). A city of northwest Turkey northwest of Istanbul. It was founded c. A.D. 125 by the Roman emperor Hadrian on the site of an earlier Thracian town. Population, 71,914.

Ed·i·son (ĕd′ĭ-sən). A community of central New Jersey northeast of New Brunswick. Population, 70,193.

Edison, Thomas Alva. 1847–1931. American inventor who patented more than a thousand inventions, among them the microphone (1877), the phonograph (1878), and an incandescent lamp (1879).

ed·it (ĕd′ĭt) *tr.v.* **-it·ed, -it·ing, -its. 1.a.** To prepare (written material) for publication or presentation, as by correcting, revising, or adapting. **b.** To prepare an edition of for publication: *edit a collection of short stories.* **c.** To modify or adapt so as to make suitable or acceptable: *edited her remarks for presentation to a younger audience.* **2.** To supervise the publication of (a newspaper or magazine, for example). **3.** To assemble the components of (a film or sound track, for example), as by cutting and splicing. **4.** To eliminate; delete: *edited the best scene out.* **—edit** *n.* An act or instance of editing: *made several last-minute edits for reasons of space.* [Partly back-formation from EDITOR and partly from French *éditer,* to publish (from Latin *ēditus,* past participle of *ēdere;* see EDITION).]

WORD HISTORY: The word *edit* is often cited as an example of back-formation. In other words, *edit* is not the source of *editor,* as *dive* is of *diver,* the expected derivational pattern; rather, the reverse is the case. *Edit* in the sense "to prepare for publication," first recorded in 1793, comes from *editor,* first recorded in 1712 in the sense "one who edits." There is more to the story, however. *Edit* also partly comes from the French word *éditer,* "to publish, edit," first recorded in 1784. In the case of *edit,* two processes, borrowing and back-formation, have thus occurred either independently or together, perhaps one person taking *edit* from French originally, another from *editor,* and yet a third from both.

edit. *abbr.* Edition; editor.

e·di·tion (ĭ-dĭsh′ən) *n. Abbr.* **ed., edit. 1.a.** The entire number of copies of a publication issued at one time or from a single set of type. **b.** A single copy from this group. **c.** The form in which a publication is issued: *a paperback edition of a novel; an annotated edition of Shakespeare.* **d.** A version of an earlier publication having substantial changes or additions: *a newly revised edition of a standard reference work.* **2.** All the copies of a specified issue of a newspaper: *the morning edition; the Sunday edition.* **3.** A broadcast of a radio or television news program: *Thursday's edition of the six o'clock news.* **4.a.** The entire number of like or identical items issued or produced as a set: *a limited edition of early jazz recordings; a signed edition of a group of lithographs.* **b.** Any of the various or successive forms in which something is offered or presented: *this year's edition of fall fashions from Paris.* **5.** One that closely resembles an original; a version: *The boy was a smaller edition of his father.* [Middle English *edicion,* version, translation, from Latin *ēditiō, ēditiōn-,* publication, production, from *ēditus,* past participle of *ēdere,* to publish, produce : *ē-, ex-,* ex- + *dare,* to give; see **dō-** in Appendix.]

ed·i·tor (ĕd′ĭ-tər) *n. Abbr.* **ed., edit. 1.** One who edits, especially as an occupation. **2.** One who writes editorials. **3.** A device for editing film, consisting basically of a splicer and viewer. **4.** *Computer Science.* A program or set of instructions used to edit text or data files. [Late Latin *ēditor,* publisher, from Latin *ēditus,* past participle of *ēdere,* to publish. See EDITION.]

ed·i·to·ri·al (ĕd′ĭ-tôr′ē-əl, -tōr′-) *n.* **1.** An article in a publication expressing the opinion of its editors or publishers. **2.** A commentary on television or radio expressing the opinion of the station or network. **—editorial** *adj.* **1.** Of or relating to an editor or editing: *an editorial position with a publishing company; an editorial policy prohibiting the use of unnamed sources.* **2.** Of or resembling an editorial, especially in expressing an opinion: *an editorial comment.* **—ed′i·to′ri·al·ly** *adv.*

ed·i·to·ri·al·ist (ĕd′ĭ-tôr′ē-ə-lĭst, -tōr′-) *n.* One who writes or presents editorials.

ed·i·to·ri·al·ize (ĕd′ĭ-tôr′ē-ə-līz′, -tōr′-) *intr.v.* **-ized, -iz·ing, -iz·es. 1.** To express an opinion in or as if in an editorial. **2.** To present an opinion in the guise of an objective report. **—ed′i·to′ri·al·i·za′tion** (-ə-lĭ-zā′shən) *n.* **—ed′i·to′ri·al·i′zer** *n.*

editor in chief *n., pl.* **editors in chief.** The editor having final responsibility for the operations and policies of a publication.

ed·i·tor·ship (ĕd′ĭ-tər-shĭp′) *n.* The position, functions, or guidance of an editor.

Ed.M. *abbr. Latin.* Educationis Magister (Master of Education).

Ed·mond (ĕd′mənd). A city of central Oklahoma north of Oklahoma City. It is a trade center in an oil-producing area. Population, 34,637.

Ed·monds (ĕd′məndz). A city of northwest Washington on Puget Sound north of Seattle. It was settled in 1866. Population, 27,679.

Ed·mon·ton (ĕd′mən-tən). The capital and largest city of Alberta, Canada, in the central part of the province north of Calgary. It was founded in 1795 as a fort and trading post of the Hudson's Bay Company. Population, 532,246.

Ed·mund I (ĕd′mənd). 921–946. King of the English (939–946) who drove the Danes from Northumbria and secured peace with Scotland.

Edmund II. Known as "Edmund Ironside." 993?–1016. King of the English (1016) who partitioned the kingdom in a settlement with Canute and died only weeks later.

E·do (ĕd′ō). See **Tokyo.**

E·dom (ē′dəm). An ancient country of Palestine between the Dead Sea and the Gulf of Aqaba. According to the Old Testament, the original inhabitants were descendants of Esau.

E·dom·ite (ē′də-mīt′) *n.* A member of a Semitic people inhabiting Edom in ancient times. **—E′dom·it′ish** *adj.*

EDP *abbr. Computer Science.* Electronic data processing.

EDT or **E.D.T.** *abbr.* Eastern Daylight Time.

EDTA (ē′dē-tē-ā′) *n.* A crystalline acid, $C_{10}H_{16}N_2O_8$, that acts as a strong chelating agent. The sodium salt of EDTA is used as an antidote for metal poisoning, an anticoagulant, and an ingredient in a variety of industrial reagents. [*e(thylene)d(iamine)t(etraacetic) a(cid).*]

educ. *abbr.* Education; educational.

ed·u·ca·ble (ĕj′ə-kə-bəl) *adj.* Capable of being educated or taught: *educable youngsters.* **—ed′u·ca·bil′i·ty** *n.*

ed·u·cate (ĕj′ə-kāt′) *v.* **-cat·ed, -cat·ing, -cates.** —*tr.* **1.** To develop the innate capacities of, especially by schooling or instruction. See Synonyms at **teach. 2.** To provide with knowledge or training in a particular area or for a particular purpose: *decided to educate herself in foreign languages; entered a seminary to be educated for the priesthood.* **3.a.** To provide with information; inform: *a campaign that educated the public about the*

Thomas Edison
Photographed in 1893

ă pat	oi boy
ā pay	ou out
âr care	o͝o took
ä father	o͞o boot
ĕ pet	ŭ cut
ē be	ûr urge
ĭ pit	th thin
ī pie	*th* this
îr pier	hw which
ŏ pot	zh vision
ō toe	ə about, item
ô paw	♦ regionalism

Stress marks: ′ (primary); ′ (secondary), as in **dictionary** (dĭk′shə-nĕr′ē)

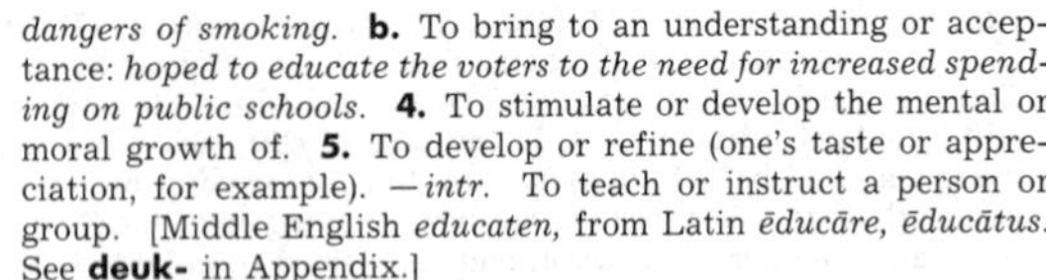
dangers of smoking. **b.** To bring to an understanding or acceptance: *hoped to educate the voters to the need for increased spending on public schools.* **4.** To stimulate or develop the mental or moral growth of. **5.** To develop or refine (one's taste or appreciation, for example). —*intr.* To teach or instruct a person or group. [Middle English *educaten,* from Latin *ēducāre, ēducātus.* See **deuk-** in Appendix.]

Edward VII
Photographed in 1902

ed·u·cat·ed (ĕj′ə-kā′tĭd) *adj.* **1.** Having an education, especially one above the average. **2.a.** Showing evidence of schooling, training, or experience. **b.** Having or exhibiting cultivation; cultured: *an educated manner.* **3.** Based on a certain amount of experience or factual knowledge: *an educated guess.*

ed·u·ca·tion (ĕj′ə-kā′shən) *n. Abbr.* **ed., educ. 1.** The act or process of educating or being educated. **2.** The knowledge or skill obtained or developed by a learning process. **3.** A program of instruction of a specified kind or level: *driver education; a college education.* **4.** The field of study that is concerned with the pedagogy of teaching and learning. **5.** An instructive or enlightening experience: *Her work in the inner city was a real education.*

ed·u·ca·tion·al (ĕj′ə-kā′shə-nəl) *adj. Abbr.* **educ. 1.** Of or relating to education. **2.** Serving to educate; instructive: *an educational film.* **—ed′u·ca′tion·al·ly** *adv.*

ed·u·ca·tion·al·ist (ĕj′ə-kā′shə-nə-lĭst) *n.* Variant of **educationist.**

educational psychology *n.* The branch of psychology that is concerned with the development of effective teaching techniques, the assessment of student aptitudes and progress, and the selection of students for specialized programs of study, such as those for the learning-disabled or the gifted.

educational television *n. Abbr.* **ETV 1.** See **public television. 2.** An often closed-circuit video system that provides instructional material.

ed·u·ca·tion·ist (ĕj′ə-kā′shə-nĭst) also **ed·u·ca·tion·al·ist** (-shə-nə-lĭst) *n.* A specialist in the theory of education.

ed·u·ca·tive (ĕj′ə-kā′tĭv) *adj.* Educational.

ed·u·ca·tor (ĕj′ə-kā′tər) *n.* **1.** One trained in teaching; a teacher. **2.a.** A specialist in the theory and practice of education. **b.** An administrator of a school or an educational institution.

Edward VIII
Photographed while Duke of Windsor

e·duce (ĭ-do͞os′, ĭ-dyo͞os′) *tr.v.* **e·duced, e·duc·ing, e·duc·es. 1.** To draw or bring out; elicit. See Synonyms at **evoke. 2.** To assume or work out from given facts; deduce. [Middle English *educen,* to direct the flow of, from Latin *ēdūcere* : *ē-, ex-,* ex- + *dūcere,* to lead; see **deuk-** in Appendix.] **—e·duc′i·ble** *adj.* **—e·duc′tion** (ĭ-dŭk′shən) *n.*

Ed·ward[1] (ĕd′wərd). Known as "the Confessor." 1003?–1066. King of the English (1042–1066) whose reign was marked by political conflict between Norman and English groups.

Ed·ward[2] (ĕd′wərd) Prince of Wales. Known as "the Black Prince." 1330–1376. English soldier during the Hundred Years' War. The eldest son of Edward III, he fought at Crécy (1346) and Poitiers (1356).

Edward I. 1239–1307. King of England (1272–1307) who conquered Wales and warred with Scotland. His Model Parliament of 1295 is sometimes considered England's first full parliament.

Edward II. 1284–1327. King of England (1307–1327) who was defeated at Bannockburn by the Scots (1314). Captured (1326) and deposed (1327) during the rebellion of Roger de Mortimer, he was imprisoned in Berkeley Castle and murdered.

Edward III. 1312–1377. King of England (1327–1377) whose reign was marked by the beginning of the Hundred Years' War, epidemics of the Black Death, and the emergence of the Commons as a powerful arm of Parliament.

Edward IV. 1442–1483. King of England (1461–1470 and 1471–1483) who was crowned after leading the Yorkists to victory in the Wars of the Roses. In 1470 he was dethroned in a rebellion but won back the crown in a battle at Tewkesbury (1471).

Edward V. 1470–1483. King of England (1483) who was crowned at the age of 13 on the death of his father, Edward IV, and was immediately confined in the Tower of London, where he and his younger brother were murdered, possibly by their uncle the Duke of Gloucester, later Richard III, or by Henry VII.

Edward VI. 1537–1553. King of England and Ireland (1547–1553). The son of Henry VIII and Jane Seymour, he died of tuberculosis.

Edward VII. 1841–1910. King of Great Britain and Ireland (1901–1910) who was known for his elegant, sporting style.

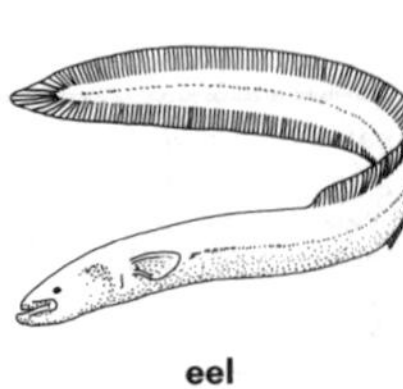
eel

Edward VIII. Later known as Duke of Windsor. 1894–1972. King of Great Britain and Ireland (1936) who precipitated a constitutional crisis by his determination to marry Wallis Warfield Simpson, an American divorcée. He abdicated, married (1937), and spent much of the rest of his life in France.

Edward, Lake. A lake in the Great Rift Valley of central Africa on the Zaire-Uganda border.

Ed·ward·i·an (ĕd-wôr′dē-ən, -wär′-) *adj.* Of, relating to, or characteristic of the reign of Edward VII of England.

Ed·wards (ĕd′wərdz), **Jonathan.** 1703–1758. American theologian and philosopher whose original sermons and writings stimulated the Great Awakening, a period of renewed American interest in religion.

Ed·win (ĕd′wĭn). 585?–633. King of Northumbria (617–633) who ruled as far north as Edinburgh and was converted to Christianity (627).

e.e. *abbr.* Errors excepted.

E.E. *abbr.* **1.** Electrical engineer. **2.** Electrical engineering.

-ee[1] *suff.* **1.a.** One that receives or benefits from a specified action: *addressee.* **b.** One that possesses a specified thing: *mortgagee.* **2.** One that performs a specified action: *absentee.* [Middle English, from Anglo-Norman *-e, -ee,* past participle suff., from Latin *-ātus.* See -ATE[1].]

USAGE NOTE: Reflecting its origins in the French passive participle ending *-é* (feminine *-ée*), the suffix *-ee* was first used in English to refer to indirect objects and then direct objects of transitive verbs, particularly in legal contexts (as in *donee, lessee,* or *trustee*) and military and political jargon (*draftee, trainee,* or *nominee*). Beginning around the mid-19th century, primarily in American English, it was often extended to denote the agent or subject of an intransitive verb; for example, *standee, returnee,* or *attendee.* Although the pattern is very common and a number of these coinages, such as *honoree, deportee,* and *escapee,* have become widely accepted, in general they retain an informal character as jocular nonce words.

-ee[2] *suff.* **1.a.** One resembling: *goatee.* **b.** A particular, especially a diminutive kind of: *bootee.* **2.** One connected with: *bargee.* [Variant of -Y[1].]

EEC *abbr.* European Economic Community.

EEG *abbr.* **1.** Electroencephalogram. **2.** Electroencephalograph.

eel (ēl) *n., pl.* **eel** or **eels. 1.** Any of various long, snakelike, scaleless marine or freshwater fishes of the order Anguilliformes or Apodes, especially *Anguilla rostrata* of eastern North America or *A. anguilla* of Europe, that lack pelvic fins and characteristically migrate from fresh water to salt water to spawn. **2.** Any of several similar fishes, such as the lamprey and electric eel. [Middle English *ele,* from Old English *ǣl.*]

eel·grass (ēl′grăs′) *n.* Any of several submersed aquatic plants of the genus *Vallisneria.* Also called *tape grass, wild celery.*

eel·pout (ēl′pout′) *n., pl.* **eelpout** or **-pouts. 1.** Any of various bottom-dwelling marine fishes of the family Zoarcidae, having an elongated body and a large head. **2.** See **burbot.**

eel·worm (ēl′wûrm′) *n.* Any of various often parasitic nematode worms, such as the vinegar eel.

e'en[1] (ēn) *n.* Evening.

e'en[2] (ēn) *adv.* Even.

EEO *abbr.* Equal employment opportunity.

-eer *suff.* One associated with, concerned with, or engaged in: *balladeer.* [French *-ier,* from Old French, from Latin *-ārius,* -ary.]

e'er (âr) *adv.* Ever.

ee·rie or **ee·ry** (îr′ē) *adj.* **-ri·er, -ri·est. 1.a.** Inspiring inexplicable fear, dread, or uneasiness; strange and frightening. **b.** Suggestive of the supernatural; mysterious. See Synonyms at **weird. 2.** *Scots.* Frightened or intimidated by superstition. [Middle English *eri,* fearful, from Old English *earg,* cowardly.] **—ee′ri·ly** *adv.* **—ee′ri·ness** *n.*

ef (ĕf) *n.* The letter *f.*

eff. *abbr.* Efficiency.

ef·face (ĭ-fās′) *tr.v.* **-faced, -fac·ing, -fac·es. 1.** To rub or wipe out; erase. **2.** To make indistinct as if by rubbing: *"Five years' absence had done nothing to efface the people's memory of his firmness"* (Alan Moorehead). See Synonyms at **erase. 3.** To conduct (oneself) inconspicuously: *"When the two women went out together, Anna deliberately effaced herself and played to the dramatic Molly"* (Doris Lessing). [Middle English *effacen,* from French *effacer,* from Old French *esfacier* : *es-,* out (from Latin *ex-,* ex-) + *face,* face (from Latin *faciēs;* see **dhē-** in Appendix).] **—ef·face′a·ble** *adj.* **—ef·face′ment** *n.* **—ef·fac′er** *n.*

ef·fect (ĭ-fĕkt′) *n.* **1.** Something brought about by a cause or an agent; a result. **2.** The power to produce an outcome or achieve a result; influence: *The drug had an immediate effect on the pain. The government's action had no effect on the trade imbalance.* **3.** A scientific law, hypothesis, or phenomenon: *the photovoltaic effect.* **4.** Advantage; avail: *used her words to great effect in influencing the jury.* **5.** The condition of being in full force or execution: *a new regulation that goes into effect tomorrow.* **6.a.** Something that produces a specific impression or supports a general design or intention: *The lighting effects emphasized the harsh atmosphere of the drama.* **b.** A particular impression: *large windows that gave an effect of spaciousness.* **c.** Production of a desired impression: *spent lavishly on dinner just for effect.* **7.** The basic or general meaning; import: *He said he was greatly worried, or words to that effect.* **8. effects.** Movable belongings; goods. **—effect** *tr.v.* **-fect·ed, -fect·ing, -fects. 1.** To bring into existence. **2.** To produce as a result. **3.** To bring about. See Usage Note at **affect**[1]. ***—idiom.* in effect.** In essence; to all purposes: *testimony that in effect contradicted her earlier statement.* [Middle English, from Old French, from Latin *effectus,* past participle of *efficere,* to accomplish : *ex-,* ex- + *facere,* to make; see **dhē-** in Appendix.] **—ef·fect′er** *n.* **—ef·fect′i·ble** *adj.*

SYNONYMS: *effect, consequence, result, outcome, upshot, sequel.* These nouns denote something, such as an occurrence, a situation, or a condition, that is brought about by a cause. An *effect* is produced by the action of an agent or a cause and follows it in time: *"Every cause produces more than one effect"* (Herbert Spencer). A *consequence* also follows a cause and is traceable to it, but the relationship between them is less sharply definable: *"Servitude is at once the consequence of his crime and the punishment of his* *guilt"* (John P. Curran). A *result* is an effect, or the last in a series of effects, that is viewed as the end product of the operation of the cause: *"Judging from the results I have seen . . . I cannot say . . . that I agree with you"* (William H. Mallock). An *outcome* is a result but more strongly than *result* implies finality and may suggest the operation of a cause over a relatively long period: *If you had refused, the outcome would probably not have been very different.* An *upshot* is a decisive result, often of the nature of a climax: *"The upshot of the matter . . . was that she showed both of them the door"* (Robert Louis Stevenson). A *sequel* is a consequence that ensues after a lapse of time: *"Our dreams are the sequel of our waking knowledge"* (Ralph Waldo Emerson). See also Synonyms at **perform.**

ef·fec·tive (ĭ-fĕk′tĭv) *adj.* **1.a.** Having an intended or expected effect. **b.** Producing a strong impression or response; striking: *gave an effective performance as Othello.* **2.** Operative; in effect: *The law is effective immediately.* **3.** Existing in fact; actual: *a decline in the effective demand.* **4.** Prepared for use or action, especially in warfare. **—effective** *n.* A soldier or a piece of military equipment that is ready for combat: *"The 'company' was no more than two platoons of effectives"* (Tom Clancy). **—ef·fec′tive·ness, ef′fec·tiv′i·ty** *n.*

SYNONYMS: *effective, effectual, efficacious, efficient.* The central meaning shared by these adjectives is "producing or capable of producing a desired effect": *an effective reprimand; an effectual complaint; an efficacious remedy; the efficient cause of the revolution.*
ANTONYM: *ineffective.*

ef·fec·tive·ly (ĭ-fĕk′tĭv-lē) *adv.* **1.** In an effective way. **2.** For all practical purposes; in effect: *Though a few rebels still held out, the fighting was effectively ended.*

ef·fec·tor (ĭ-fĕk′tər) *n.* **1.** A muscle, a gland, or an organ capable of responding to a stimulus, especially a nerve impulse. **2.** A nerve ending that carries impulses to a muscle, a gland, or an organ and activates muscle contraction or glandular secretion. **3.** *Biochemistry.* A small molecule that when bound to the allosteric site of an enzyme causes either a decrease or an increase in the activity of the enzyme. **4.** *Computer Science.* A device used to produce a desired change in an object in response to input.

ef·fec·tu·al (ĭ-fĕk′cho͞o-əl) *adj.* Producing or sufficient to produce a desired effect; fully adequate. See Synonyms at **effective.** [Middle English *effectuel,* from Old French, from Late Latin *effectuālis,* from Latin *effectus.* See EFFECT.] **—ef·fec′tu·al′i·ty** (-ăl′ĭ-tē), **ef·fec′tu·al·ness** *n.* **—ef·fec′tu·al·ly** *adv.*

ef·fec·tu·ate (ĭ-fĕk′cho͞o-āt′) *tr.v.* **-at·ed, -at·ing, -ates.** To bring about; effect. [Medieval Latin *effectuāre, effectuāt-,* from Latin *effectus,* an effect. See EFFECT.] **—ef·fec′tu·a′tion** *n.*

ef·fem·i·na·cy (ĭ-fĕm′ə-nə-sē) *n.* The quality or condition of being effeminate.

ef·fem·i·nate (ĭ-fĕm′ə-nĭt) *adj.* **1.** Having qualities or characteristics more often associated with women than men. See Synonyms at **feminine. 2.** Characterized by weakness and excessive refinement. [Middle English *effeminat,* from Latin *effēminātus,* past participle of *effēmināre,* to make feminine : *ex-,* ex- + *fēmina,* woman; see **dhē(i)-** in Appendix.] **—ef·fem′i·nate** *n.* **—ef·fem′i·nate·ly** *adv.* **—ef·fem′i·nate·ness** *n.*

ef·fen·di (ĭ-fĕn′dē) *n., pl.* **-dis. 1.** Used as a title of respect for men in Turkey, equivalent to *sir.* **2.** An educated or respected man in the Near East. [Turkish *efendi,* from Medieval Greek *aphentēs,* master, alteration of Greek *authentēs.* See AUTHENTIC.]

ef·fer·ent (ĕf′ər-ənt) *adj.* **1.** Directed away from a central organ or section. **2.** Carrying impulses from the central nervous system to an effector. **—efferent** *n.* An efferent organ or body part, such as a blood vessel. [From Latin *efferēns, efferent-,* present participle of *efferre,* to carry off : *ex-,* ex- + *ferre,* to carry; see **bher-**[1] in Appendix.] **—ef′fer·ent·ly** *adv.*

ef·fer·vesce (ĕf′ər-vĕs′) *intr.v.* **-vesced, -vesc·ing, -vesc·es. 1.** To emit small bubbles of gas, as a carbonated or fermenting liquid. **2.** To escape from a liquid as bubbles. **3.** To show high spirits or excitement. [Latin *effervēscere* : *ex-,* up, out; see EX– + *fervēscere,* to start boiling, inchoative of *fervēre,* to boil; see **bhreu-** in Appendix.] **—ef′fer·ves′cence, ef′fer·ves′cen·cy** *n.* **—ef′fer·ves′cent** *adj.* **—ef′fer·ves′cent·ly** *adv.*

ef·fete (ĭ-fēt′) *adj.* **1.** Depleted of vitality, force, or effectiveness; exhausted: *the final, effete period of the baroque style.* **2.** Marked by self-indulgence, triviality, or decadence: *an effete group of self-professed intellectuals.* **3.** Overrefined; effeminate. **4.** No longer productive; infertile. [Latin *effētus,* worn out, exhausted : *ex-,* ex- + *fētus,* bearing young, pregnant; see **dhē(i)-** in Appendix.] **—ef·fete′ly** *adv.* **—ef·fete′ness** *n.*

WORD HISTORY: The fact that *effete* has come to mean "effeminate" marks a return to its etymological roots. *Effete* came into English from the Latin word *effētus,* made up of *ex–,* "out," and the adjective *fētus,* "having recently given birth," which is related to the noun *fētus,* "offspring," a word we have borrowed as well. Latin *effētus* was used of plants that had borne fruit or of animals that had borne young, but *effētus* could also mean "worn out with bearing young, exhausted, feeble." The English word *effete,* whose earliest appearance is recorded in 1621, was first used in senses similar or identical to senses of Latin *effētus;* however, in the last two centuries or so the senses "characterized by weakness or decadence" and "overrefined, effeminate," have appeared. Both *effeminate* and *effete* go back to the same Indo-European root, *dhē(i)–,* meaning "to suck." In *effeminate* we see the development from a form of the root meaning literally "she who suckles"; in *effete,* the development from a form of the root that refers to the baby who sucks milk from the mother.

ef·fi·ca·cious (ĕf′ĭ-kā′shəs) *adj.* Producing or capable of producing a desired effect. See Synonyms at **effective.** [From Latin *efficāx, efficāc-,* from *efficere,* to effect. See EFFECT.] **—ef′fi·ca′cious·ly** *adv.* **—ef′fi·ca′cious·ness** *n.*

ef·fi·ca·cy (ĕf′ĭ-kə-sē) *n.* Power or capacity to produce a desired effect; effectiveness. [Latin *efficācia,* from *efficāx, efficāc-,* efficacious. See EFFICACIOUS.]

ef·fi·cien·cy (ĭ-fĭsh′ən-sē) *n., pl.* **-cies.** *Abbr.* **eff. 1.a.** The quality or property of being efficient. **b.** The degree to which this quality is exercised: *The program was implemented with great efficiency and speed.* **2.a.** The ratio of the effective or useful output to the total input in any system. **b.** The ratio of the energy delivered by a machine to the energy supplied for its operation. **3.** An efficiency apartment.

efficiency apartment *n.* A small, usually furnished apartment with a private bathroom and kitchenette.

efficiency expert *n.* A specialist who seeks to increase the productivity of a business or an industry by improving the efficiency of its operations.

ef·fi·cient (ĭ-fĭsh′ənt) *adj.* **1.** Acting directly to produce an effect: *an efficient cause.* See Synonyms at **effective. 2.a.** Acting or producing effectively with a minimum of waste, expense, or unnecessary effort. **b.** Exhibiting a high ratio of output to input. [Middle English, from Old French, from Latin *efficiēns, efficient-,* present participle of *efficere,* to effect. See EFFECT.] **—ef·fi′cient·ly** *adv.*

ef·fi·gy (ĕf′ə-jē) *n., pl.* **-gies. 1.** A crude figure or dummy representing a hated person or group. **2.** A likeness or image, especially of a person. ***—idiom.* in effigy.** Symbolically, especially in the form of an effigy: *The deposed dictator was burned in effigy by the crowd.* [French *effigie,* from Latin *effigiēs,* likeness, from *effingere,* to portray : *ex-,* ex- + *fingere,* to shape; see **dheigh-** in Appendix.]

ef·flo·resce (ĕf′lə-rĕs′) *intr.v.* **-resced, -resc·ing, -resc·es. 1.** To blossom; bloom. **2.** *Chemistry.* **a.** To become a powder by losing water of crystallization, as when a hydrated crystal is exposed to air. **b.** To become covered with a powdery deposit. [Latin *efflōrēscere* : *ex-,* ex- + *flōrēscere,* inchoative of *flōrēre,* to blossom (from *flōs, flōr-,* flower; see **bhel-**[3] in Appendix).]

ef·flo·res·cence (ĕf′lə-rĕs′əns) *n.* **1.** *Botany.* A state or time of flowering; anthesis. **2.a.** A gradual process of unfolding or developing. **b.** The highest point; the culmination. See Synonyms at **bloom**[1]. **3.** *Chemistry.* **a.** The deposit that results from the process of efflorescing. Also called *bloom.* **b.** The process of efflorescing. **c.** A growth of salt crystals on a surface caused by evaporation of salt-laden water. **4.** *Pathology.* Redness, a rash, or an eruption on the skin. **—ef′flo·res′cent** *adj.*

ef·flu·ence (ĕf′lo͞o-əns) *n.* **1.** The act or an instance of flowing out. **2.** Something that flows out or forth; an emanation: *"tremendous emotional effluences that affected blocks of people at a time, causing them to walk faster"* (Coleman Dowell).

ef·flu·ent (ĕf′lo͞o-ənt) *adj.* Flowing out or forth. **—effluent** *n.* Something that flows out or forth, especially: **a.** A stream flowing out of a body of water. **b.** An outflow from a sewer or sewage system. **c.** A discharge of liquid waste, as from a factory or nuclear plant. [Middle English, from Latin *effluēns, effluent-,* present participle of *effluere,* to flow out : *ex-,* ex- + *fluere,* to flow; see **bhleu-** in Appendix.]

ef·flu·vi·um (ĭ-flo͞o′vē-əm) *n., pl.* **-vi·a** (-vē-ə) or **-vi·ums. 1.** A usually invisible emanation or exhalation, as of vapor or gas. **2.a.** A byproduct or residue; waste. **b.** The odorous fumes given off by waste or decaying matter. **3.** An impalpable emanation; an aura. [Latin, from *effluere,* to flow out. See EFFLUENT.] **—ef·flu′vi·al** *adj.*

ef·flux (ĕf′lŭks′) *n.* **1.** A flowing outward. **2.** Something that flows out or forth; an effluence. **3.** A passing or an expiration, as of time. [From Latin *effluxus,* past participle of *effluere,* to flow out. See EFFLUENT.] **—ef·flux′ion** (ĭ-flŭk′shən) *n.*

ef·fort (ĕf′ərt) *n.* **1.** The use of physical or mental energy to do something; exertion. **2.** A difficult exertion of the strength or will: *It was an effort to get up.* **3.** A usually earnest attempt: *Make an effort to arrive promptly.* **4.** Something done or produced through exertion: *a play that was his finest effort.* **5.** *Physics.* Force applied against inertia. [Middle English, from Old French *esfort,* from *esforcier,* to force, exert, from Medieval Latin *exfortiāre* : Latin *ex-,* ex- + Latin *fortis,* strong; see **bhergh-**[2] in Appendix.] **—ef′fort·ful** *adj.* **—ef′fort·ful·ly** *adv.*

SYNONYMS: *effort, exertion, endeavor, application, pains, trouble.* These nouns refer to the expenditure of physical or mental energy to accomplish something. *Effort* applies to an attempt, great or small, to do something; where it is not qualified, the term usually implies a substantial expenditure of time, strength, or faculties: *"What is written without effort is in general read without pleasure"* (Samuel Johnson). *Exertion* implies the exercise of vigorous effort: *"England has saved herself by her exertions"* (William Pitt the Younger). *Endeavor* suggests earnest striving to

ă pat	oi boy
ā pay	ou out
âr care	o͝o took
ä father	o͞o boot
ĕ pet	ŭ cut
ē be	ûr urge
ĭ pit	th thin
ī pie	*th* this
îr pier	hw which
ŏ pot	zh vision
ō toe	ə about, item
ô paw	♦ regionalism

Stress marks: **′** (primary); ′ (secondary), as in **dictionary** (dĭk′shə-nĕr′ē)

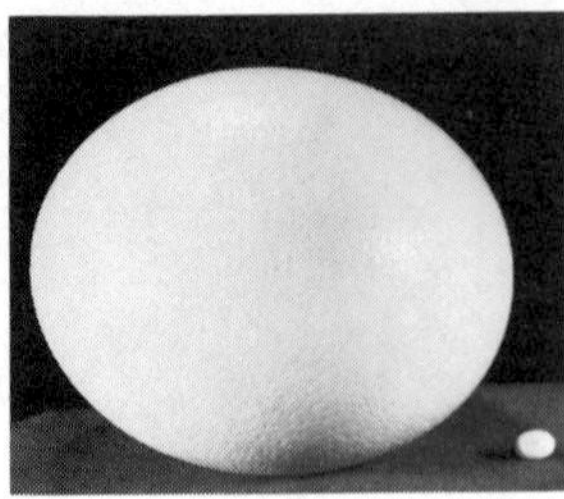

egg[1]
Ostrich egg (*left*) and hummingbird egg (*right*)

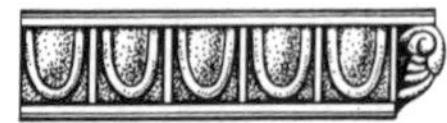

egg-and-dart

eggplant
Solanum melongena

Egypt

achieve a serious goal: *"There must be positive endeavors to preserve peace"* (Franklin D. Roosevelt). *Application* connotes diligence, persistence, and hard work: *He succeeded in his studies by dint of steadfast application. Pains* implies attentive or laborious effort: *"Genius is an infinite capacity for taking pains"* (Jane Ellice Hopkins). *Trouble* refers to effort that causes inconvenience or bother: *Many people watch the news on television to save themselves the trouble of reading the newspaper.*

ef·fort·less (ĕf′ərt-lĭs) *adj.* Calling for, requiring, or showing little or no effort. See Synonyms at **easy.** **—ef′fort·less·ly** *adv.* **—ef′fort·less·ness** *n.*

ef·front·er·y (ĭ-frŭn′tə-rē) *n., pl.* **-ies.** Brazen boldness; presumptuousness. See Synonyms at **temerity.** [French *effronterie,* from *effronté,* shameless, from Old French *esfronte,* possibly from Late Latin *effrōns, effront-* : *ex-,* ex- + *frōns, front-,* front, forehead.]

ef·ful·gence (ĭ-fo͝ol′jəns, ĭ-fŭl′-) *n.* A brilliant radiance.

ef·ful·gent (ĭ-fo͝ol′jənt, ĭ-fŭl′-) *adj.* Shining brilliantly; resplendent. See Synonyms at **bright.** [Latin *effulgēns, effulgent-,* present participle of *effulgēre,* to shine out : *ex-,* ex- + *fulgēre,* to shine; see **bhel-**[1] in Appendix.]

ef·fuse (ĭ-fyo͞os′) *adj. Botany.* Spreading out loosely. **—effuse** (ĭ-fyo͞oz′) *v.* **-fused, -fus·ing, -fus·es.** *—tr.* **1.** To pour out (a liquid). **2.** To radiate; diffuse. *—intr.* **1.** To spread or flow out. **2.** To ooze forth; exude. [Latin *effūsus,* past participle of *effundere,* to pour out : *ex-,* ex- + *fundere,* to pour; see **gheu-** in Appendix.]

ef·fu·sion (ĭ-fyo͞o′zhən) *n.* **1.a.** The act or an instance of effusing. **b.** Liquid or other matter poured forth. **2.** An unrestrained outpouring of feeling, as in speech or writing: *"the devout effusions of sacred eloquence"* (Edmund Burke). **3.** *Pathology.* **a.** The seeping of serous, purulent, or bloody fluid into a body cavity or tissue. **b.** The effused fluid.

ef·fu·sive (ĭ-fyo͞o′sĭv) *adj.* **1.** Unrestrained or excessive in emotional expression; gushy: *an effusive manner.* **2.** Profuse; overflowing: *effusive praise.* **—ef·fu′sive·ly** *adv.* **—ef·fu′sive·ness** *n.*

Ef·ik (ĕf′ĭk) *n., pl.* **Efik** or **-iks.** **1.** A member of a people inhabiting southern Nigeria. **2.** The Niger-Congo language of the Efik people, closely related to Ibibio. **—Ef′ik** *adj.*

EFM *abbr.* Electronic fetal monitor.

eft (ĕft) *n.* An immature newt, especially the reddish-orange terrestrial form of a North American species, *Notophthalmus viridescens.* [Middle English *evete,* from Old English *efeta.*]

EFTS *abbr.* Electronic funds transfer system.

eft·soons (ĕft-so͞onz′) *adv. Archaic.* **1.** Soon afterward; presently. **2.** Once again. [From Middle English *eftsone,* from Old English *eftsōna* : *eft,* again; see **apo-** in Appendix + *sōna,* soon.]

e.g. *abbr.* Exempli gratia.

e·gad (ĭ-găd′) or **e·gads** (ĭ-gădz′) *interj.* Used as a mild exclamation. [Alteration of *oh God.*]

Eg·a·di Islands (ĕg′ə-dē) also **Ae·ga·de·an Isles** (ē-gā′dē-ən) or **Ae·ga·tes** (-tēz). An island group of southwest Italy in the Mediterranean Sea west of Sicily. A Roman naval victory over the Carthaginians, achieved in a battle fought in the waters off the islands in 241 B.C., ended the First Punic War.

e·gal·i·tar·i·an (ĭ-găl′ĭ-târ′ē-ən) *adj.* Affirming, promoting, or characterized by belief in equal political, economic, social, and civil rights for all people. [From French *égalitaire,* from *égalité,* equality, from Latin *aequālitās,* from *aequālis,* equal. See EQUAL.] **—e·gal′i·tar′i·an** *n.* **—e·gal′i·tar′i·an·ism** *n.*

Eg·bert (ĕg′bərt). Died 839. West Saxon king (802–839) who became the first overlord of all the English peoples (829).

EGD *abbr.* Electrogasdynamics.

E·ge·ri·a (ĭ-jîr′ē-ə) *n.* A woman adviser or counselor. [After *Egeria,* Roman nymph or goddess and adviser to Numa Pompilius, a legendary Roman king.]

e·gest (ē-jĕst′) *tr.v.* **e·gest·ed, e·gest·ing, e·gests.** To discharge or excrete from the body. [Latin *ēgerere, ēgest-,* to carry out : *ē-, ex-,* ex- + *gerere,* to carry.] **—e·ges′tion** *n.* **—e·ges′tive** *adj.*

e·ges·ta (ē-jĕs′tə) *pl.n.* Egested matter, especially excrement. [Latin, neuter pl. of *ēgestus,* past participle of *ēgerere,* to carry out. See EGEST.]

EGF *abbr.* Epidermal Growth Factor.

egg[1] (ĕg) *n.* **1.a.** A female gamete; an ovum. Also called *egg cell.* **b.** The round or oval female reproductive body of various animals, including birds, reptiles, amphibians, fishes, and insects, consisting usually of an embryo surrounded by nutrient material and a protective covering. **c.** The oval, thin-shelled reproductive body of a bird, especially that of a hen, used as food. **2.** Something having the ovoid shape of an egg. **3.** *Slang.* A fellow; a person: *He's a good egg.* **—egg** *tr.v.* **egged, egg·ing, eggs. 1.** To cover with beaten egg, as in cooking. **2.** *Slang.* To throw eggs at. ***—idioms.*** **put** (or **have**) **all (one's) eggs in one basket.** *Informal.* To risk everything on a single venture. **egg on (one's) face.** *Informal.* Embarrassment; humiliation: *If you do that, you'll end up with egg on your face.* [Middle English *egge,* bird's egg, from Old Norse *egg.* See **awi-** in Appendix.] **—egg′less** *adj.* **—egg′y** *adj.*

egg[2] (ĕg) *tr.v.* **egged, egg·ing, eggs.** To encourage or incite to action: *The racing fans egged their favorites on. My friends just egged me to drive faster.* [Middle English *eggen,* from Old Norse *eggja.* See **ak-** in Appendix.]

egg-and-dart (ĕg′ən-därt′) *n.* A decorative molding consisting of a series of egg-shaped figures alternating with dart-shaped, anchor-shaped, or tongue-shaped figures.

eg·gar (ĕg′ər) *n.* Variant of **egger.**

egg·beat·er (ĕg′bē′tər) *n.* A hand-held kitchen utensil with rotating blades for beating, whipping, or mixing.

egg case *n.* **1.** A protective capsule of certain animals, such as insects and mollusks, that contains eggs; an ootheca. **2.** See **egg sac.**

egg cell *n.* See **egg**[1] (sense 1a).

egg cream *n.* A drink made of milk, syrup, and soda water. [Probably from its foamy, egg-whitelike head.]

egg·cup (ĕg′kŭp′) *n.* A cup for holding a usually soft-boiled egg.

eg·ger also **eg·gar** (ĕg′ər) *n.* Any of various moths of the family Lasiocampidae, whose larvae often construct tentlike webs among the branches of trees. [From the shape of its cocoon.]

egg·fruit (ĕg′fro͞ot′) *n. Botany.* See **canistel.**

egg·head (ĕg′hĕd′) *n. Informal.* An intellectual; a highbrow.

egg·head·ed (ĕg′hĕd′ĭd) *adj. Informal.* Befitting or having the qualities of an intellectual. **—egg′head′ed·ness** *n.*

Eg·gle·ston (ĕg′əl-stən), **Edward.** 1837–1902. American writer known for his realistic but sentimental novels, such as *The Hoosier Schoolmaster* (1871).

egg·nog (ĕg′nŏg′) *n.* A drink consisting of milk or cream, sugar, and eggs beaten together and often mixed with an alcoholic liquor such as rum or brandy. [EGG[1] + *nog,* ale.]

egg·plant (ĕg′plănt′) *n.* **1.a.** An Indian plant *(Solanum melongena* var. *esculenta)* cultivated for its large edible, ovoid, glossy, usually purple-skinned fruit. **b.** The fruit of this plant. Also called *aubergine, melongene.* **2.** *Color.* A blackish purple.

egg roll *n.* A usually deep-fried cylindrical casing of thin egg dough, filled with minced vegetables and often bits of seafood or meat. Also called *spring roll.*

egg sac *n.* The silken pouch in which many spiders deposit their eggs. Also called *egg case.*

eggs Ben·e·dict (ĕgz′ bĕn′ĭ-dĭkt′) *pl.n. (used with a sing. or pl. verb).* A dish consisting of toasted halves of English muffin topped with broiled ham, poached eggs, and hollandaise sauce. [Probably from the name *Benedict.*]

egg·shell (ĕg′shĕl′) *n.* **1.** The thin, brittle, exterior covering of the egg of a bird or reptile. **2.** *Color.* A pale yellow to yellowish white. **—egg′shell′** *adj.*

egg timer *n.* A small hourglass running three to five minutes, used for timing the boiling of eggs.

egg tooth *n.* A hard, toothlike projection from the beak of embryonic birds, or from the upper jaw of embryonic reptiles, that is used to cut the egg membrane and shell upon hatching and that later falls off.

egg white *n.* The albumen of an egg, used especially in cooking.

e·gis (ē′jĭs) *n.* Variant of **aegis.**

eg·lan·tine (ĕg′lən-tīn′, -tēn′) *n.* See **sweetbrier.** [Middle English *eglentin,* from Old French *eglantine,* diminutive of *aiglent,* from Vulgar Latin **aculentum,* from neuter of **aculentus,* spiny, from Latin *aculeus,* spine, from *acus,* needle. See **ak-** in Appendix.]

e·go (ē′gō, ĕg′ō) *n., pl.* **e·gos. 1.** The self, especially as distinct from the world and other selves. **2.** In psychoanalysis, the division of the psyche that is conscious, most immediately controls thought and behavior, and is most in touch with external reality. **3.a.** An exaggerated sense of self-importance; conceit. **b.** Appropriate pride in oneself; self-esteem. [New Latin, from Latin, I. See **eg** in Appendix.]

e·go·cen·tric (ē′gō-sĕn′trĭk, ĕg′ō-) *adj.* **1.** Holding the view that the ego is the center, object, and norm of all experience. **2.a.** Confined in attitude or interest to one's own needs or affairs. **b.** Caring only about oneself; selfish. **3.** *Philosophy.* **a.** Viewed or perceived from one's own mind as a center. **b.** Taking one's own self as the starting point in a philosophical system. **—e′go·cen′tric** *n.* **—e′go·cen′tric·al·ly** *adv.* **—e′go·cen·tric′i·ty** (-trĭs′ĭ-tē) *n.* **—e′go·cen′trism** *n.*

ego ideal *n.* In psychoanalysis, the part of one's ego that contains an idealized self based on those people, especially parents and peers, one admires and wishes to emulate.

e·go·ism (ē′gō-ĭz′əm, ĕg′ō-) *n.* **1.a.** The ethical doctrine that morality has its foundations in self-interest. **b.** The ethical belief that self-interest is the just and proper motive for all human conduct. **2.** Excessive preoccupation with one's own well-being and interests, usually accompanied by an inflated sense of self-importance. **3.** Egotism; conceit. See Synonyms at **conceit.**

e·go·ist (ē′gō-ĭst, ĕg′ō-) *n.* **1.** One devoted to one's own interests and advancement; an egocentric person. **2.** An egotist. **3.** An adherent of egoism. **—e′go·is′tic, e′go·is′ti·cal** *adj.* **—e′go·is′ti·cal·ly** *adv.*

e·go·ma·ni·a (ē′gō-mā′nē-ə, -mān′yə, ĕg′ō-) *n.* Obsessive preoccupation with the self. **—e′go·ma′ni·ac′** (-nē-ăk′) *n.* **—e′·go·ma·ni′a·cal** (-mə-nī′ə-kəl) *adj.* **—e′go·ma·ni′a·cal·ly** *adv.*

e·go·tism (ē′gə-tĭz′əm, ĕg′ə-) *n.* **1.** The tendency to speak or

ă pat	oi boy
ā pay	ou out
âr care	o͝o took
ä father	o͞o boot
ĕ pet	ŭ cut
ē be	ûr urge
ĭ pit	th thin
ī pie	*th* this
îr pier	hw which
ŏ pot	zh vision
ō toe	ə about, item
ô paw	♦ regionalism

Stress marks: ′ (primary); ′ (secondary), as in **dictionary** (dĭk′shə-nĕr′ē)

write of oneself excessively and boastfully. **2.** An inflated sense of one's own importance; conceit. See Synonyms at **conceit.** [EGO + *-tism,* as in NEPOTISM.]

e·go·tist (ē′gə-tĭst, ĕg′ə-) *n.* **1.** A conceited, boastful person. **2.** A selfish, self-centered person. **—e′go·tis′tic, e′go·tis′ti·cal** *adj.* **—e′go·tis′ti·cal·ly** *adv.*

ego trip *n. Slang.* An act, an experience, or a course of behavior that gratifies the ego.

e·go-trip (ē′gō-trĭp′, ĕg′ō-) *intr.v.* **-tripped, -trip·ping, -trips.** *Slang.* To act in an egotistic or conceited manner. **—e′go-trip′per** *n.*

e·gre·gious (ĭ-grē′jəs, -jē-əs) *adj.* Conspicuously bad or offensive. See Synonyms at **flagrant.** [From Latin *ēgregius,* outstanding : *ē-, ex-,* ex- + *grex, greg-,* herd; see **ger-** in Appendix.] **—e·gre′gious·ly** *adv.* **—e·gre′gious·ness** *n.*

e·gress (ē′grĕs′) *n.* **1.** The act of coming or going out; emergence. **2.** The right of going out: *refugees who were denied egress.* **3.** A path or opening for going out; an exit. **4.** *Astronomy.* The emergence of a celestial body from eclipse or occultation. **—egress** *intr.v.* **e·gressed, e·gress·ing, e·gress·es.** To go out; emerge. [Latin *ēgressus,* from past participle of *ēgredī,* to go out : *ē-, ex-,* ex- + *gradī,* to go; see **ghredh-** in Appendix.]

e·gres·sion (ĭ-grĕsh′ən) *n.* The act or process of emerging; egress.

e·gret (ē′grĭt, ĕg′rĭt) *n.* Any of several usually white herons of the genera *Bubulcus, Casmerodius, Egretta,* and related genera, characteristically having long, showy, drooping plumes during the breeding season. [Middle English, from Old French *aigrette,* from Old Provençal *aigreta,* from *aigron,* heron, of Germanic origin.]

E·gypt (ē′jĭpt). Formerly (1958–1961) **United Ar·ab Republic** (ăr′əb). A country of northeast Africa on the Mediterranean Sea. In ancient times it was a flourishing kingdom and one of the earliest known civilizations, producing magnificent structures and delicate works of art. After the seventh century B.C. the kingdom declined, falling to various conquerors ranging from the Assyrians, Greeks, and Romans to the Turks, French, and British. It became an independent state in 1922. Cairo is the capital and the largest city. Population, 48,503,000.

E·gyp·tian (ĭ-jĭp′shən) *n.* **1.** A native or inhabitant of Egypt. **2.** The now extinct Afro-Asiatic language of the ancient Egyptians. **—Egyptian** *adj.* **1.** Of or relating to Egypt or its people. **2.** Of or relating to the language of the ancient Egyptians.

Egyptian clover *n.* See **berseem.**

Egyptian corn *n.* See **durra.**

Egyptian cotton *n.* A long-staple, fine cotton grown chiefly in northern Africa.

Egyptian millet *n.* See **Johnson grass.**

Egyptian mongoose *n.* See **ichneumon** (sense 1).

Egyptian paper rush *n.* See **papyrus** (sense 1).

E·gyp·tol·o·gy (ē′jĭp-tŏl′ə-jē) *n.* The study of the culture and artifacts of the ancient Egyptian civilization. **—E·gyp′to·log′i·cal** (ĭ-jĭp′tə-lŏj′ĭ-kəl) *adj.* **—E′gyp·tol′o·gist** *n.*

eh (ā, ĕ) *interj.* Used in asking a question or in seeking repetition or confirmation of a statement.

EHF *abbr.* Extremely high frequency.

EHP *abbr.* **1.** Effective horsepower. **2.** Electric horsepower.

Eh·ren·burg (ĕr′ən-bo͝org′, ĕr′yĭn-bo͝ork′), **Ilya Grigorievich.** 1891–1967. Russian writer whose novels include *The Storm* (1948) and *The Thaw* (1954).

Ehr·lich (âr′lĭkh), **Paul.** 1854–1915. German bacteriologist. He shared a 1908 Nobel Prize for discoveries in immunology.

EHV *abbr.* Extra-high voltage.

Eich·mann (īk′mən, īkh′-, īkh-män′), **Adolf.** 1906–1962. German Nazi official who as head of the Gestapo's Jewish section (1939–1945) was chiefly responsible for the murder of millions of Jews during World War II.

ei·der (ī′dər) *n.* Any of several large sea ducks, especially of the genus *Somateria* of northern regions, having soft, commercially valuable down and predominantly black and white plumage in the male. [Ultimately from Old Norse *ædhar,* genitive of *ædhr.*]

ei·der·down also **eider down** (ī′dər-doun′) *n.* **1.** The down of the eider duck, used as stuffing for quilts and pillows. **2.** A quilt stuffed with the down of the eider duck. **3.** A warm, napped fabric.

eider duck *n.* The eider.

ei·det·ic (ī-dĕt′ĭk) *adj.* Of, relating to, or marked by extraordinarily detailed and vivid recall of visual images. [German *eidetisch,* from Greek *eidos,* form. See **weid-** in Appendix.] **—ei·det′i·cal·ly** *adv.*

ei·do·lon (ī-dō′lən) *n., pl.* **-lons** or **-la** (-lə). **1.** A phantom; an apparition. **2.** An image of an ideal. [Greek *eidōlon,* from *eidos,* form. See **weid-** in Appendix.]

Eif·fel (ī′fəl, ĭ-fĕl′), **Alexandre Gustave.** 1832–1923. French engineer who designed the Eiffel Tower for the Paris Exhibition of 1889. The tower is located on the southern bank of the Seine River and is 300 meters (984 feet) high.

Ei·gen (ī′gən), **Manfred.** Born 1927. German chemist. He shared a 1967 Nobel Prize for research on high-speed chemical reactions.

eight (āt) *n.* **1.** The cardinal number equal to 7 + 1. **2.** The eighth in a set or sequence. **3.** Something having eight parts, units, or members, especially: **a.** *Sports.* An eight-oared racing shell. **b.** An eight-cylinder engine or motor vehicle. [Middle English *eighte,* from Old English *eahta.* See **oktō(u)** in Appendix.] **—eight** *adj. & pron.*

eight ball *n. Games.* A black pool ball that bears the number eight and that may put a player at a disadvantage. **—*idiom.* behind the eight ball.** *Slang.* In an unfavorable or uncomfortable position.

eight·een (ā-tēn′) *n.* **1.** The cardinal number equal to 17 + 1. **2.** The 18th in a set or sequence. [Middle English *eightetene,* from Old English *eahtatēne.* See **oktō(u)** in Appendix.] **—eight·een′** *adj. & pron.*

eight·een·mo (ā-tēn′mō) *n., pl.* **-mos.** *Printing.* See **octodecimo.** [From *18mo,* abbr. of OCTODECIMO.]

eight·eenth (ā-tēnth′) *n.* **1.** The ordinal number matching the number 18 in a series. **2.** One of 18 equal parts. **—eight·eenth′** *adv. & adj.*

eight·een-wheel·er (ā′tēn-hwē′lər, -wē′-) or **18-wheel·er** *n. Informal.* A combination of a tractor and a semitrailer; a tractor-trailer rig.

eighth (ātth, āth) *n.* **1.** The ordinal number matching the number eight in a series. **2.** One of eight equal parts. [Middle English *eighthe,* from Old English *eahtotha,* from *eahta,* eight. See **oktō(u)** in Appendix.] **—eighth** *adv. & adj.*

eighth note *n. Music.* A note having one-eighth the time value of a whole note.

eight·i·eth (ā′tē-ĭth) *n.* **1.** The ordinal number matching the number 80 in a series. **2.** One of 80 equal parts. **—eight′i·eth** *adv. & adj.*

eight·pen·ny nail (āt′pĕn′ē) *n.* A nail 2½ inches (6.4 centimeters) long. [From the former price per hundred.]

eight·vo (āt′vō′) *n., pl.* **-vos.** *Printing.* See **octavo.** [From *8vo,* abbr. of OCTAVO.]

eight·y (ā′tē) *n., pl.* **-ies. 1.** The cardinal number equal to 8 × 10. **2. eighties. a.** Often **Eighties.** The decade from 80 to 89 in a century. **b.** A decade or the numbers from 80 to 89: *They were still active in their eighties. Before noon, the temperature shot into the eighties.* [Middle English *eighti,* from Old English *eahtatig.* See **oktō(u)** in Appendix.] **—eight′y** *adj. & pron.*

eight·y-six or **86** (ā′tē-sĭks′) *tr.v.* **eight·y-sixed, eight·y-six·ing, eight·y-six·es** or **86·ed, 86·ing, 86·es.** *Slang.* **1.** To refuse to serve (an unwelcome customer) at a bar or restaurant. **2. a.** To throw out; eject. **b.** To throw away; discard. [Perhaps after Chumley's bar and restaurant at *86* Bedford Street in Greenwich Village, New York City.]

-ein *suff.* A chemical compound related to a specified compound with a similar name ending in *-in* or *-ine: phthalein.* [Alteration of –IN.]

Eind·ho·ven (īnt′hō′vən). A city of southern Netherlands southeast of Rotterdam. Chartered in 1232, it was a major Allied objective in World War II. Population, 192,854.

ein·korn (īn′kôrn′) *n.* A one-seeded wheat *(Triticum monococcum)* grown in arid regions. It was used as fodder during the Stone Age. [German : *ein,* one (from Old High German; see **oi-no-** in Appendix) + *Korn,* grain (from Old High German; see **grə-no-** in Appendix).]

Ein·stein (īn′stīn′), **Albert.** 1879–1955. German-born American theoretical physicist whose special and general theories of relativity revolutionized modern thought on the nature of space and time and formed a theoretical base for the exploitation of atomic energy. He won a 1921 Nobel Prize for his explanation of the photoelectric effect.

ein·stein·i·um (īn-stī′nē-əm) *n. Symbol* **Es** A synthetic transuranic element first produced by neutron irradiation of uranium in a thermonuclear explosion and now usually produced in the laboratory by irradiating plutonium and other elements. Its longest-lived isotope is Es 254 with a half-life of 276 days. Atomic number 99; melting point 860°C. See table at **element.** [After Albert EINSTEIN.]

Eir·e (âr′ə, ī′rə, âr′ē, ī′rē). See **Ireland²**.

Ei·sen·how·er (ī′zən-hou′ər), **Dwight David.** Known as "Ike." 1890–1969. American general and the 34th President of the United States (1953–1961). As supreme commander of the Allied Expeditionary Force (1943–1945) he launched the invasion of Normandy (June 6, 1944) and oversaw the final defeat of Germany (1945). His presidency was marked by an end to the Korean War (1953), domestic racial problems, cold war with the Soviet Union, and a break in diplomatic relations with Cuba (1961).

Eisenhower, Mamie Geneva Doud. Born 1896. First Lady of the United States (1953–1961) as the wife of President Dwight D. Eisenhower. She worked tirelessly to fulfill the growing number of commitments demanded of a First Lady.

Ei·sen·staedt (ī′zən-stät′), **Alfred.** Born 1898. German-born American photographer who pioneered photojournalism with his unposed documentary photographs.

Ei·sen·stein (ī′zən-stīn′, ā′zyĭn-shtān′), **Sergei Mikhailovich.** 1898–1948. Soviet filmmaker considered among the most influential directors in the history of motion pictures. His films include *Potemkin* (1925) and *Alexander Nevsky* (1938).

eis·tedd·fod (ā-stĕth′vŏd, ī-stĕth′-) *n., pl.* **eis·tedd·fods** or **eis·tedd·fod·au** (ā′stĕth-vŏd′ī, ī′stĕth-). An annual competitive festival of Welsh poets and musicians. [Welsh : *eistedd,* sitting; see **sed-** in Appendix + *bod,* to be; see **bheuə-** in Appendix.]

ei·ther (ē′thər, ī′thər) *pron.* The one or the other: *Which movie*

Alexandre Eiffel

Albert Einstein

Dwight D. Eisenhower
Photographed in 1956

Mamie Eisenhower

do you want to see? Either will be fine. **—either** *conj.* Used before the first of two or more coordinates or clauses linked by *or*: *Either we go now or we remain here forever.* **—either** *adj.* **1.** Any one of two; one or the other: *Wear either coat.* **2.** One and the other; each: *rings on either hand.* **—either** *adv.* Likewise; also. Used as an intensive following negative statements: *If you don't order a dessert, I won't either.* [Middle English, from Old English *ǣther, ǣghwæther.* See **kʷo-** in Appendix.]

USAGE NOTE: The traditional rule holds that *either* should be used only to refer to one of two items and that *any* is required when more than two items are involved: *Any* (not *either*) *of the three opposition candidates still in the race would make a better president than the incumbent.* But reputable writers have often violated this rule, and in any case it applies only to the use of *either* as a pronoun or an adjective. When *either* is used as a conjunction no paraphrase with *any* is available, and so *either* is unexceptionable even when it applies to more than two clauses: *Either the union will make a counteroffer or the original bid will be refused by the board or the deal will go ahead as scheduled.* • In *either . . . or* constructions, the two conjunctions should be followed by parallel elements. The following is regarded as incorrect: *You may either have the ring or the bracelet* (properly, *You may have either the ring or the bracelet*). The following is also incorrect: *She can take either the examination offered to all applicants or ask for a personal interview* (properly, *She can either take . . .*). • When used as a pronoun, *either* is singular and takes a singular verb: *The two left-wing parties disagree with each other more than either does* (not *do*) *with the right.* When followed by *of* and a plural noun, *either* is often used with a plural verb: *Either of the parties have enough support to form a government.* But this usage is widely regarded as incorrect; in an earlier survey it was rejected by 92 percent of the Usage Panel. • When all the elements in an *either . . . or* construction (or a *neither . . . nor* construction) used as the subject of a sentence are singular, the verb is singular: *Either Eve or Herb* has been *invited.* Analogously, when all the elements in the *either . . . or* construction are plural, the verb is plural too: *Either the Clarks or the Kays* have been *invited.* When the construction mixes singular and plural elements, however, there is some confusion as to which form the verb should take. It has sometimes been suggested that the verb should agree with whichever noun phrase is closest to it; thus one would write *Either Eve or the Kays* have been *invited,* but *Either the Kays or Eve* has been *invited.* This pattern is accepted by 54 percent of the Usage Panel. Others have maintained that the construction is fundamentally inconsistent whichever number is assigned to the verb and that such sentences should be rewritten accordingly. As Wilson Follett put it: "This [construction] is defensible, but a workmanlike writer may put his pride in not writing sentences that need defending." See Usage Notes at **every, neither, or¹.**

eland
Common eland
Taurotragus oryx

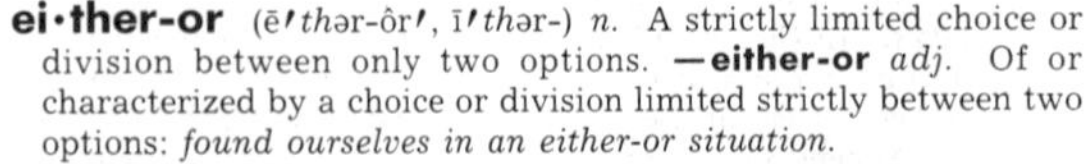

ei·ther-or (ē′*th*ər-ôr′, ī′*th*ər-) *n.* A strictly limited choice or division between only two options. **—either-or** *adj.* Of or characterized by a choice or division limited strictly between two options: *found ourselves in an either-or situation.*

e·jac·u·late (ĭ-jăk′yə-lāt′) *v.* **-lat·ed, -lat·ing, -lates.** —*tr.* **1.** To eject or discharge abruptly, especially to discharge (semen) in orgasm. **2.** To utter suddenly and passionately; exclaim. —*intr.* To eject semen. **—ejaculate** (ĭ-jăk′yə-lĭt) *n.* Semen ejaculated in orgasm. [Latin *ēiaculārī, ēiaculāt-* : *ē-, ex-,* ex- + *iaculārī,* to throw (from *iaculum,* dart; see **yē-** in Appendix).] **—e·jac′u·la′tor** *n.*

e·jac·u·la·tion (ĭ-jăk′yə-lā′shən) *n.* **1.a.** The act of ejaculating. **b.** An abrupt discharge of fluid, especially of seminal fluid. **2.** A sudden, short exclamation, especially a brief, pious utterance or prayer.

e·jac·u·la·to·ry (ĭ-jăk′yə-lə-tôr′ē, -tōr′ē) *adj.* **1.** Of or relating to physiological ejaculation. **2.** Relating to or constituting a sudden, brief utterance; exclamatory.

e·ject (ĭ-jĕkt′) *v.* **e·ject·ed, e·ject·ing, e·jects.** —*tr.* **1.** To throw out forcefully; expel. **2.a.** To compel to leave: *The patron of the bar was ejected for creating a disturbance.* **b.** To evict: *tenants who were ejected for violations of their lease.* —*intr.* To make an emergency exit from an aircraft by deployment of an ejection seat or capsule. [Middle English *ejecten,* from Latin *ēicere, ēiect-* : *ē-, ex-,* ex- + *iacere,* to throw; see **yē-** in Appendix.] **—e·ject′a·ble** *adj.* **—e·jec′tive** *adj.*

SYNONYMS: *eject, expel, evict, dismiss, oust.* These verbs mean to put out by force. To *eject* is to throw or cast out from within: *The fire ejected yellow flames into the night sky. The heckler was ejected from the auditorium for creating a disturbance. Expel* means to drive out or away; it implies permanent removal: *expelled the invaders from the country; expel a student from a university. Evict* most commonly refers to the expulsion of persons from property, as for failing to live up to the terms of a lease, by legal process: *evicted the tenants to convert the building into condominiums. Dismiss* refers to putting someone or something out of one's mind (*trying to dismiss his fears*) or, in law, to refusing to give something, such as an appeal or a complaint, further consideration (*dismissed the case for lack of evidence*). *Oust* is applied chiefly to the removing of persons from a position, such as a political office, by means lawful or otherwise: *There were no grounds for ousting the prime minister.*

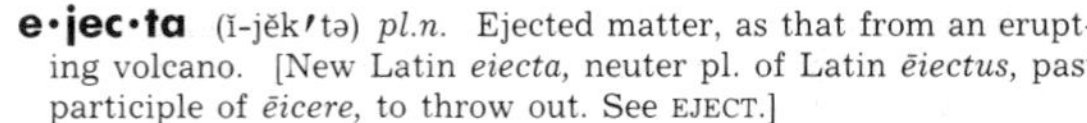

e·jec·ta (ĭ-jĕk′tə) *pl.n.* Ejected matter, as that from an erupting volcano. [New Latin *eiecta,* neuter pl. of Latin *ēiectus,* past participle of *ēicere,* to throw out. See EJECT.]

e·jec·tion (ĭ-jĕk′shən) *n.* **1.** The act of ejecting or the condition of being ejected. **2.** Ejected matter.

ejection capsule *n.* A cockpit, usually fitted with survival gear, designed to eject the occupant clear of an aircraft during an in-flight emergency.

ejection seat *n.* A seat fitted with an explosive charge and designed to eject the occupant clear of an aircraft during an in-flight emergency.

e·ject·ment (ĭ-jĕkt′mənt) *n.* **1.** The act or an instance of ejecting; dispossession. **2.** *Law.* An action to regain possession of real estate held by another.

e·jec·tor (ĭ-jĕk′tər) *n.* **1.** One that ejects, especially a device in a gun that ejects the empty shell after each firing. **2.** A device using a jet of water, air, or steam to withdraw a fluid or gas from a space.

eke¹ (ēk) *tr.v.* **eked, ek·ing, ekes. 1.** To supplement with great effort: *eked out an income by working two jobs.* **2.** To get with great effort or strain: *eke a bare existence from farming in an arid area.* **3.** To make (a supply) last by practicing strict economy. [Middle English *eken,* to increase, from Old English *ēcan.* See **aug-** in Appendix.]

eke² (ēk) *adv. Archaic.* Also. [Middle English, from Old English *ēc.*]

EKG *abbr.* **1.** Electrocardiogram. **2.** Electrocardiograph.

e·kis·tics (ĭ-kĭs′tĭks) *n. (used with a sing. verb).* The science of human settlements, including city or community planning and design. [Ultimately from Greek *oikistikos,* of settlements, from *oikistēs,* colonizer, founder, from *oikizein,* to settle, from *oikos,* house. See ECONOMY.] **—e·kis′tic, e·kis′ti·cal** *adj.* **—ek′is·ti′cian** (ĕk′ĭ-stĭsh′ən) *n.*

ek·pwe·le (ĕk-pwā′lē, -lā) *n.* See table at **currency.**

el¹ also **ell** (ĕl) *n.* The letter *l.*

el² (ĕl) *n. Informal.* An elevated railway.

el. *abbr.* Elevation.

e·lab·o·rate (ĭ-lăb′ər-ĭt) *adj.* **1.** Planned or executed with painstaking attention to numerous parts or details. **2.** Intricate and rich in detail. **—elaborate** (ĭ-lăb′ə-rāt′) *v.* **-rat·ed, -rat·ing, -rates.** —*tr.* **1.** To work out with care and detail; develop thoroughly. **2.** To produce by effort; create. —*intr.* **1.** To become elaborate. **2.** To express at greater length or in greater detail: *asked me to elaborate on my proposal.* [Latin *ēlabōrātus,* past participle of *ēlabōrāre,* to work out : *ē-, ex-,* intensive pref.; see EX– + *labōrāre,* to work (from *labōr,* work).] **—e·lab′o·rate·ly** *adv.* **—e·lab′o·rate·ness** *n.* **—e·lab′o·ra′tion** *n.* **—e·lab′o·ra′tor** *n.*

SYNONYMS: *elaborate, complicated, intricate.* The central meaning shared by these adjectives is "marked by complexity of detail": *an elaborate lace pattern; the eye, a complicated organ; an intricate problem.*
ANTONYM: *simple.*

El·a·gab·a·lus (ĕl′ə-găb′ə-ləs). See **Heliogabalus.**

E·laine (ĭ-lān′) *n.* **1.** In Arthurian legend, a woman who died of unrequited love of Lancelot. **2.** In Arthurian legend, the mother of Galahad by Lancelot.

El Al·a·mein (ĕl ăl′ə-mān′, ä′lə-) also **Al Al·a·mayn** (ăl ăl′ə-mān′, ä′lə-). A town of northern Egypt on the Mediterranean Sea. In a decisive battle of World War II British forces defeated Rommel's German troops here in November 1942.

E·lam (ē′ləm) also **Su·si·a·na** (so͞o′zē-ä′nə, -ăn′ə). An ancient country of southwest Asia in present-day southwest Iran. It was established east of the Tigris River before 3000 B.C. and was known for its warlike people.

E·la·mite (ē′lə-mīt′) *n.* **1.** A native or inhabitant of Elam. **2.** The language of the ancient Elamites, of no known linguistic affiliation.

é·lan (ā-läɴ′, ā-län′) *n.* **1.** Enthusiastic vigor and liveliness. **2.** Distinctive style or flair. [French, from Old French *eslan,* rush, from *eslancer,* to hurl : *es-,* out (from Latin *ex-*; see EX–) + *lancer,* to throw (from Late Latin *lanceāre,* to throw a lance, from Latin *lancea,* lance).]

e·land (ē′lənd) *n., pl.* **eland** also **e·lands.** Either of two large African antelopes *(Taurotragus oryx* or *T. derbianus)* having a light brown or grayish coat and spirally twisted horns. [Afrikaans, from Dutch, elk, from obsolete German *Elend,* of Baltic origin; akin to Lithuanian *élnias,* deer.]

élan vi·tal (vē-täl′) *n.* The vital force hypothesized by Henri Bergson as a source of efficient causation and evolution in nature. Also called *life force.* [French : *élan,* ardor + *vital,* vital.]

el·a·pid (ĕl′ə-pĭd) *n.* Any of several venomous snakes of the family Elapidae, which includes the cobras, mambas, and coral snakes. **—elapid** *adj.* Of or belonging to the family Elapidae. [From New Latin *Elapidae,* family name, from Medieval Greek *elaps, elap-,* fish, variant of Greek *ellops.*]

e·lapse (ĭ-lăps′) *intr.v.* **e·lapsed, e·laps·ing, e·laps·es.** To slip by; pass: *Weeks elapsed before we could start renovating.* **—elapse** *n.* Passage; lapse: *met again after an elapse of many years.* [Latin *ēlābī, ēlāps-* : *ē, ex-,* ex- + *lābī,* to slip.]

e·lapsed time (ĭ-lăpst′) *n.* *Abbr.* **ET** The measured duration of an event.

E·la·ra (ē′lər-ə) *n.* The seventh largest moon of Jupiter and the 13th in distance from the planet. [Greek, mother by Zeus of the giant Tityus.]

e·las·mo·branch (ĭ-lăz′mə-brăngk′) *n.* Any of numerous fishes of the class Chondrichthyes, characterized by a cartilaginous skeleton and placoid scales and including the sharks, rays, and skates. **—elasmobranch** *adj.* Of or belonging to the class Chondrichthyes. [From New Latin *Elasmobranchii,* former subclass name : Greek *elasmos,* metal beaten out (from *elaunein, elas-,* to beat) + Late Latin *branchia,* gill (from Latin *branchiae,* gills, from Greek *brankhia*).]

e·las·tase (ĭ-lăs′tās, -tāz) *n.* An enzyme found especially in pancreatic juice that catalyzes the hydrolysis of elastin.

e·las·tic (ĭ-lăs′tĭk) *adj.* **1.a.** Easily resuming original shape after being stretched or expanded; flexible. See Synonyms at **flexible. b.** Springy; rebounding. **2.** *Physics.* Returning to or capable of returning to an initial form or state after deformation. **3.** Quick to recover, as from disappointment: *an elastic spirit.* **4.** Capable of adapting to change or a variety of circumstances. **—elastic** *n.* **1.a.** A flexible, stretchable fabric made with interwoven strands of rubber or an imitative synthetic fiber. **b.** An object made of this fabric. **2.** A rubber band. [New Latin *elasticus,* from Late Greek *elastos,* beaten, ductile, variant of Greek *elatos,* from *elaunein,* to beat out.] **—e·las′ti·cal·ly** *adv.*

elastic collision *n.* *Physics.* A collision of particles in which the total kinetic energy of the particles is conserved.

elastic fiber *n.* A thick, yellow connective-tissue fiber composed principally of elastin and characterized by great elasticity.

e·las·tic·i·ty (ĭ-lă-stĭs′ĭ-tē, ē′lă-) *n.* **1.** The condition or property of being elastic; flexibility. **2.** *Physics.* **a.** The property of returning to an initial form or state following deformation. **b.** The degree to which this property is exhibited.

e·las·ti·cized (ĭ-lăs′tĭ-sīzd′) *adj.* Made with strands or inserts of elastic: *slacks with an elasticized waistband.*

elastic tissue *n.* A type of connective tissue consisting mainly of elastic fibers and found in the walls of arteries, in the dermis of the skin, and in certain ligaments and tendons.

e·las·tin (ĭ-lăs′tĭn) *n.* A protein similar to collagen that is the principal structural component of elastic fibers. [ELAST(IC) + -IN.]

e·las·to·mer (ĭ-lăs′tə-mər) *n.* Any of various polymers having the elastic properties of natural rubber. [ELAST(IC) + -MER(E).] **—e·las′to·mer′ic** (-mĕr′ĭk) *adj.*

e·late (ĭ-lāt′) *tr.v.* **e·lat·ed, e·lat·ing, e·lates.** To make proud or joyful: *Her success elated the family.* **—elate** *adj.* Elated. [From Latin *ēlātus,* past participle of *efferre,* to bring out, exalt : *ē-, ex-,* ex- + *lātus,* brought; see **tela-** in Appendix.] **—e·la′tion** *n.*

e·lat·ed (ĭ-lā′tĭd) *adj.* Exultantly proud and joyful. **—e·lat′ed·ly** *adv.* **—e·lat′ed·ness** *n.*

el·a·ter (ĕl′ə-tər) *n.* **1.** An elaterid beetle. **2.** *Botany.* A tiny elongated structure that forces the dispersal of spores by the absorption of moisture. It is either a band attached to the spore, as in horsetails, or a filament occurring among the spores, as in liverworts. [Greek *elatēr,* driver, from *elaunein,* to drive.]

e·lat·er·id (ĭ-lăt′ər-ĭd) *n.* Any of numerous beetles of the family Elateridae, which includes the click beetles. **—elaterid** *adj.* Of or belonging to the family Elateridae. [From New Latin *Elatēridae,* family name, from Greek *elatēr,* driver. See ELATER.]

e·lat·er·ite (ĭ-lăt′ə-rīt′) *n.* A brown-to-black, soft, elastic hydrocarbon resin. [ELATER, elasticity (obsolete) + -ITE[1].]

El·a·vil (ĕl′ə-vĭl). A trademark used for a preparation of amitriptyline, an antidepressant drug.

E layer *n.* A region of the ionosphere, occurring from about 90 to 150 kilometers (55 to 95 miles) above Earth and influencing long-distance communications by strongly reflecting radio waves in the range from one to three megahertz. Also called *E region, Heaviside layer, Kennelly-Heaviside layer.*

El·ba (ĕl′bə). An island of Italy in the Tyrrhenian Sea between Corsica and the mainland. Napoleon Bonaparte spent his first period of exile here (May 1814–February 1815).

El·be (ĕl′bə, ĕlb). A river of Czechoslovakia and Germany flowing about 1,167 km (725 mi) to the North Sea. It has been a major waterway since Roman times.

El·bert (ĕl′bərt), **Mount.** A peak, 4,402.1 m (14,433 ft) high, in the Sawatch Range of central Colorado. It is the highest elevation in the range and also the highest of the U.S. Rocky Mountains.

el·bow (ĕl′bō′) *n.* **1.a.** The joint or bend of the arm between the forearm and the upper arm. **b.** The bony outer projection of this joint. **2.** A joint, as of a bird or quadruped, corresponding to the human elbow. **3.** Something having a bend or an angle similar to an elbow, especially: **a.** A length of pipe with a sharp bend in it. **b.** A sharp bend in a river or road. **—elbow** *v.* **-bowed, -bow·ing, -bows.** *—tr.* **1.a.** To push or jostle (another or others) with the elbow. **b.** To shove (another or others) aside with the elbow. **2.** To open up (a means of passage, for example) by or as if by use of the elbow: *She elbowed her way through the crowd.* *—intr.* **1.** To make one's way by pushing with the elbow. **2.** To turn at an angle; bend: *The lane elbows to the left.* ***—idioms.*** **at (one's) elbow.** Close at hand; nearby. **out at the elbows. 1.** Poorly dressed. **2.** Lacking money. [Middle English *elbowe,* from Old English *elnboga.* See **el-** in Appendix.]

el·bow-bend·er (ĕl′bō-bĕn′dər) *n.* *Slang.* One who habitually indulges in the drinking of alcoholic beverages. **—el′bow-bend′ing** (-bĕn′dĭng) *adj.* & *n.*

elbow grease *n.* *Informal.* Strenuous physical labor and effort.

el·bow·room (ĕl′bō-ro͞om′, -ro͝om′) *n.* **1.** Room to move around or work freely. **2.** Ample scope: *elbowroom to experiment.* See Synonyms at **room.**

El·brus (ĕl-bro͞os′), **Mount.** A peak, 5,645.6 m (18,510 ft) high, in the Caucasus Mountains of northwest Georgia. It is the highest elevation in the range.

El·burz Mountains (ĕl-bo͝orz′). A range of northern Iran rising to 5,774.9 m (18,934 ft).

El Ca·jon (kə-hōn′). A city of southern California, an industrial and residential suburb of San Diego. Population, 73,892.

El Cap·i·tan (kăp′ĭ-tăn′). A peak, 2,308.5 m (7,569 ft) high, in the Sierra Nevada of central California. Its dramatic exposed monolith rises some 1,098 m (3,600 ft).

El Cen·tro (sĕn′trō). A city of southern California in the Imperial Valley near the Mexican border. It is a shipping point for fruits and vegetables. Population, 23,996.

El Cer·ri·to (sə-rē′tō). A city of western California on San Francisco Bay north of Oakland. It is mainly residential. Population, 22,731.

El·che (ĕl′chĕ). A city of southeast Spain southwest of Alicante. An ancient Roman colony, it was held by the Moors from the 8th to the 13th century. Population, 144,600.

eld·er¹ (ĕl′dər) *adj.* **1.** Greater than another in age or seniority. **2.** Superior to another or others, as in rank. **—elder** *n.* **1.** An older person. **2.** An older, influential member of a family, tribe, or community. **3.** One of the governing officers of a church, often having pastoral or teaching functions. **4.** *Mormon Church.* A member of the higher order of priesthood. [Middle English *eldre,* from Old English *eldra.* See **al-²** in Appendix.] **—el′der·ship′** *n.*

USAGE NOTE: *Elder* and *eldest* generally apply to persons, unlike *older* and *oldest,* which also apply to things. *Elder* and *eldest* are used principally with reference to seniority: *elder sister; elder statesman; John the Elder.*

el·der² (ĕl′dər) *n.* Any of various shrubs or small trees of the genus *Sambucus,* having clusters of small white flowers and red or purplish-black berrylike fruit. [Middle English *eldre,* from Old English *ellærn.*]

el·der·ber·ry (ĕl′dər-bĕr′ē) *n.* **1.** The small, edible, purplish-black fruit of the common American elder *(Sambucus canadensis),* sometimes used to make wine or preserves. **2.** A shrub or tree that bears elderberries.

eld·er·care (ĕl′dər-kâr′) *n.* Social and medical programs and facilities intended for the care and maintenance of the aged. *—attributive.* Often used to modify another noun: *eldercare issues; eldercare resources.*

eld·er·ly (ĕl′dər-lē) *adj.* **1.** Being past middle age and approaching old age; rather old. **2.** Of, relating to, or characteristic of older persons or life in later years. **—elderly** *n.* **1.** *pl.* **-lies.** An elderly person. **2.** *(used with a pl. verb).* Older people considered as a group. Often used with *the*: *special recreational programs for the elderly.* **—el′der·li·ness** *n.*

SYNONYMS: *elderly, old, aged, venerable, superannuated.* These adjectives are compared as they mean far along in years or life. One who is *elderly* is between middle age and old age: *Elderly residents of the city could still recall the construction of the first skyscraper. Old* implies advanced years: *"an old man's eagle mind"* (William Butler Yeats). *"There are so few who can grow old with a good grace"* (Richard Steele). *Aged* emphasizes old age and usually suggests infirmity: *The Western world has yet to respect the aged members of its society as the Japanese do.* One who is *venerable* commands respect by virtue of dignity and age: *"a venerable-looking man, with white hair and beard and a face of great sagacity"* (Samuel Butler). *Superannuated* applies to one who has reached the age of retirement and has been pensioned (*a superannuated civil servant*); the term can also refer to one too old for use, work, or service: *"He left the house . . . for the support of twelve superannuated wool carders"* (Anthony Trollope).

elder statesman *n.* A prominent, highly experienced older person, especially a retired official acting as an unofficial adviser.

eld·est (ĕl′dĭst) *adj.* Greatest in age or seniority. See Usage Note at **elder¹.** [Middle English, from Old English *eldesta.* See **al-²** in Appendix.]

eldest hand *n.* *Games.* The player first to receive cards dealt.

El Di·en·te Peak (dē-ĕn′tē). A mountain, 4,318.5 m (14,159 ft) high, in the Rocky Mountains of southwest Colorado.

El Do·ra·do¹ (də-rä′dō). **1.** A vaguely defined historical region and city of the New World, often thought to be in northern South America. Fabled for its great wealth of gold and precious jewels, it was eagerly sought after by 16th- and 17th-century explorers, including Sir Walter Raleigh. **2.** A city of southern Arkansas near the Louisiana border south-southwest of Little Rock. Oil was discovered nearby in 1921. Population, 25,270.

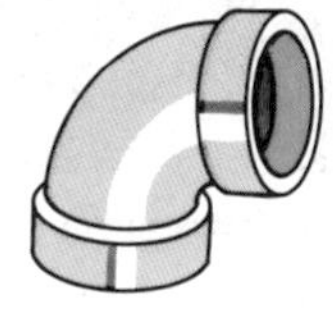

elbow

ă pat	oi boy
ā pay	ou out
âr care	o͝o took
ä father	o͞o boot
ĕ pet	ŭ cut
ē be	ûr urge
ĭ pit	th thin
ī pie	*th* this
îr pier	hw which
ŏ pot	zh vision
ō toe	ə about, item
ô paw	♦ regionalism

Stress marks: ′ (primary); ′ (secondary), as in **dictionary** (dĭk′shə-nĕr′ē)

Eleanor of Aquitaine
The Embarkation for the Second Crusade, early 15th-century miniature from *Grandes Chroniques de France*

electric guitar

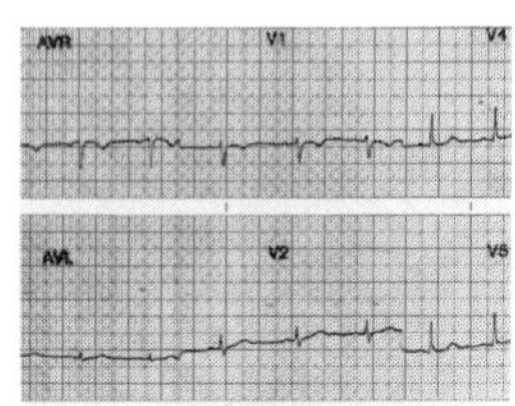

electrocardiogram
Normal reading

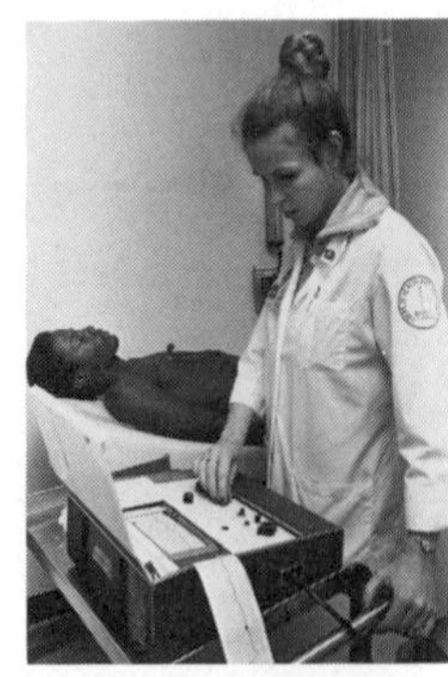
electrocardiograph
Nurse monitoring an electrocardiograph

El Do·ra·do² (də-rä′dō) *n.* A place of fabulous wealth or inordinately great opportunity. [After EL DORADO¹.]

el·dritch (ĕl′drĭch) *adj.* Strange or unearthly; eerie. [Perhaps Middle English *elriche : Old English *el-,* strange, other; see **al-¹** in Appendix + Old English *rīce,* realm; see **reg-** in Appendix.]

E·le·a (ē′lē-ə) also **Ve·li·a** (vē′lē-ə). An ancient Greek colony of southern Italy near the Gulf of Salerno. Reputedly founded by Xenophanes, it was the center of the Eleatic school of philosophy.

El·ea·nor of Aq·ui·taine (ĕl′ə-nər, -nôr′; ăk′wĭ-tān′). 1122?–1204. Queen of France (1137–1152) and England (1152–1204). Her marriage to Louis VII of France was annulled in 1152, and shortly afterward she married Henry II of England.

Eleanor of Cas·tile (kə-stēl′). 1246?–1290. Queen of England (1274–1290) as the wife of Edward I, whom she accompanied on a crusade (1270–1273).

El·e·at·ic (ĕl′ē-ăt′ĭk) *adj. Philosophy.* Of or characteristic of the school of philosophy founded by Xenophanes and Parmenides and holding the belief that immutable being is the only knowable reality and that change is the subject of mere opinion. [Latin *Eleāticus,* from Greek *Eleatikos,* from ELEA.] **—El′e·a′tic** *n.* **—El′e·at′i·cism** (-ĭ-sĭz′əm) *n.*

elec. *abbr.* **1.** Electric; electrical. **2.** Electrician. **3.** Electricity.

el·e·cam·pane (ĕl′ĭ-kăm-pān′) *n.* A tall, coarse plant *(Inula helenium)* native to central Asia, having rayed yellow flower heads. The roots are used medicinally. [Middle English *elecampana* : Old English *elene* (from Medieval Latin *enula,* from Latin *inula,* from Greek *helenion;* see **wel-²** in Appendix) + Medieval Latin *campāna,* of the field (from Latin *campānea,* feminine of *campāneus,* from *campus,* field).]

e·lect (ĭ-lĕkt′) *v.* **e·lect·ed, e·lect·ing, e·lects.** *—tr.* **1.** To select by vote for an office or for membership. **2.** To pick out; select: *elect an art course.* See Synonyms at **choose. 3.** To decide, especially by preference: *elected to take the summer off.* **4.** *Theology.* To select by divine will for salvation. *—intr.* To make a choice or selection. **—elect** *adj.* **1.** Chosen deliberately; singled out. **2.a.** Elected but not yet installed. Often used in combination: *the governor-elect.* **b.** Chosen for marriage. Often used in combination: *the bride-elect.* **3.** *Theology.* Selected by divine will for salvation. **—elect** *n.* **1.** One that is chosen or selected. **2.** *Theology.* One selected by divine will for salvation. **3.** *(used with a pl. verb).* An exclusive group of people. Used with *the*: *one of the elect who have power inside the government.* [Middle English *electen,* from Latin *ēligere, ēlēct-,* to select : *ē-, ex-,* ex- + *legere,* to choose; see **leg-** in Appendix.]

e·lect·a·ble (ĭ-lĕk′tə-bəl) *adj.* Fit or able to be elected, especially to public office: *an electable candidate.* **—e·lect′a·bil′i·ty** *n.*

e·lec·tion (ĭ-lĕk′shən) *n.* **1.a.** The act or power of electing. **b.** The fact of being elected. **2.** The right or ability to make a choice. See Synonyms at **choice. 3.** *Theology.* Predestined salvation, especially as conceived by Calvinists.

E·lec·tion Day (ĭ-lĕk′shən) *n.* A day set by law for the election of public officials.

e·lec·tion·eer (ĭ-lĕk′shə-nîr′) *intr.v.* **-eered, -eer·ing, -eers.** To work actively for a candidate or political party. **—e·lec′tion·eer′er** *n.*

e·lec·tive (ĭ-lĕk′tĭv) *adj.* **1.** Of or relating to a selection by vote. **2.** Filled or obtained by election: *elective office.* **3.** Having the power or authority to elect; electoral. **4.** Permitting or involving a choice; optional: *elective surgery.* **—elective** *n.* An optional academic course or subject. **—e·lec′tive·ly** *adv.* **—e·lec′tive·ness** *n.*

e·lec·tor (ĭ-lĕk′tər) *n.* **1.** A qualified voter in an election. **2.** A member of the Electoral College of the United States. **3.** One of the German princes of the Holy Roman Empire entitled to elect the emperor.

e·lec·tor·al (ĭ-lĕk′tər-əl) *adj.* **1.** Of, relating to, or composed of electors. **2.** Of or relating to election. **—e·lec′tor·al·ly** *adv.*

E·lec·tor·al College (ĭ-lĕk′tər-əl) *n.* A body of electors chosen to elect the President and Vice President of the United States.

e·lec·tor·ate (ĭ-lĕk′tər-ĭt) *n.* **1.** A body of qualified voters. **2.** The territory of an elector of the Holy Roman Empire.

electr– *pref.* Variant of **electro–.**

E·lec·tra (ĭ-lĕk′trə) *n. Greek Mythology.* A daughter of Clytemnestra and Agamemnon who with her brother Orestes avenged the murder of Agamemnon by killing their mother and her lover, Aegisthus.

Electra complex *n.* In psychoanalysis, a daughter's unconscious libidinal desire for her father.

e·lec·tret (ĭ-lĕk′trĭt) *n.* A solid dielectric that exhibits persistent dielectric polarization. [ELECTR(ICITY) + (MAGN)ET.]

e·lec·tric (ĭ-lĕk′trĭk) *adj.* **1.** Also **e·lec·tri·cal** (-trĭ-kəl). *Abbr.* **elec.** Of, relating to, or operated by electricity: *electric current; an electrical appliance.* **2.a.** Emotionally exciting; thrilling: *gave an electric reading of the play.* **b.** Exceptionally tense; highly charged with emotion: *an atmosphere electric with suspicion.* **—electric** *n.* An electrically powered machine or vehicle: *The lawn mower is an electric.* [New Latin *ēlectricus,* deriving from amber, as by rubbing, from Latin *ēlectrum,* amber, from Greek *ēlektron.*] **—e·lec′tri·cal·ly** *adv.*

electrical engineering *n. Abbr.* **E.E.** The branch of engineering that deals with the technology of electricity, especially the design and application of circuitry and equipment for power generation and distribution, machine control, and communications. **—electrical engineer** *n.*

electrical storm *n.* A thunderstorm.

electric arc *n. Electricity.* An arc.

electric chair *n.* **1.** A chair used in the electrocution of a prisoner sentenced to death by law. **2.** Execution by means of electrocution. **3.** The sentence of death by electrocution.

electric eel *n.* A long, eellike freshwater fish *(Electrophorus electricus)* of northern South America, having organs capable of producing a powerful electric discharge.

electric eye *n.* See **photoelectric cell.**

electric field *n.* A region of space characterized by the existence of a force generated by electric charge.

electric guitar *n. Music.* A guitar that transmits tones to an amplifier by means of an electronic pickup placed under the strings.

e·lec·tri·cian (ĭ-lĕk-trĭsh′ən, ē′lĕk-) *n. Abbr.* **elec.** One whose occupation is the installation, maintenance, repair, or operation of electric equipment and circuitry.

electric intensity *n.* The ratio of the electrostatic force exerted on a body to the charge on the body.

e·lec·tric·i·ty (ĭ-lĕk-trĭs′ĭ-tē, ē′lĕk-) *n. Abbr.* **elec. 1.a.** The physical phenomena arising from the behavior of electrons and protons that is caused by the attraction of particles with opposite charges and the repulsion of particles with the same charge. **b.** The physical science of such phenomena. **2.** Electric current used or regarded as a source of power. **3.** Intense, contagious emotional excitement. *—attributive.* Often used to modify another noun: *electricity bills; electricity costs.*

electric light *n.* **1.** A light that uses electricity to produce illumination. Also called *electric lamp.* **2.** Illumination produced electrically.

electric moment *n.* The dipole moment of an electric dipole.

electric motor *n.* A motor powered by electricity.

electric ray *n.* Any of various tropical or subtropical marine fishes of the family Torpedinidae, having a rounded body and a pair of organs capable of producing an electric discharge, which is used to stun or kill prey. Also called *crampfish, numbfish, torpedo.*

electric razor *n.* A shaver powered by electricity.

e·lec·tri·fy (ĭ-lĕk′trə-fī′) *tr.v.* **-fied, -fy·ing, -fies. 1.** To produce electric charge on or in (a conductor). **2.a.** To wire or equip (a building, for example) for the use of electric power. **b.** To provide with electric power. **c.** *Music.* To amplify (music) by electronic means. **3.** To thrill, startle greatly, or shock: *a powerful performance that electrified the audience.* [ELECTRI(C) + –FY.] **—e·lec′tri·fi′a·ble** *adj.* **—e·lec′tri·fi·ca′tion** (-fĭ-kā′shən) *n.* **—e·lec′tri·fi′er** *n.* **—e·lec′tri·fy′ing·ly** *adv.*

electro– or **electr–** *pref.* **1.a.** Electricity: *electromagnet* **b.** Electric; electrically: *electrocute.* **2.** Electrolysis: *electrodeposit.* **3.** Electron: *electronegative.* [New Latin *ēlectro-,* from Latin *ēlectrum,* amber, from Greek *ēlektron.*]

e·lec·tro·a·cous·tics (ĭ-lĕk′trō-ə-ko͞o′stĭks) *n. (used with a sing. verb).* The science that deals with the interaction or interconversion of electric and acoustic phenomena. **—e·lec′tro·a·cous′tic** *adj.* **—e·lec′tro·a·cous′tic·al·ly** *adv.*

e·lec·tro·a·nal·y·sis (ĭ-lĕk′trō-ə-năl′ĭ-sĭs) *n., pl.* **-ses** (-sēz′). Chemical analysis using electrolytic techniques. **—e·lec′tro·an′a·lyt′ic** (-ăn′ə-lĭt′ĭk), **e·lec′tro·an′a·lyt′i·cal** *adj.*

e·lec·tro·car·di·o·gram (ĭ-lĕk′trō-kär′dē-ə-grăm′) *n. Abbr.* **ECG, EKG** The curve traced by an electrocardiograph. Also called *cardiogram.*

e·lec·tro·car·di·o·graph (ĭ-lĕk′trō-kär′dē-ə-grăf′) *n. Abbr.* **ECG, EKG** An instrument used in the detection and diagnosis of heart abnormalities that measures electrical potentials on the body surface and generates a record of the electrical currents associated with heart muscle activity. Also called *cardiograph.* **—e·lec′tro·car′di·o·graph′ic** (-grăf′ĭk) *adj.* **—e·lec′tro·car′di·o·graph′i·cal·ly** *adv.* **—e·lec′tro·car′di·og′ra·phy** (-kär′dē-ŏg′rə-fē) *n.*

e·lec·tro·chem·i·cal cell (ĭ-lĕk′trō-kĕm′ĭ-kəl) *n.* See **cell** (sense 5a).

e·lec·tro·chem·is·try (ĭ-lĕk′trō-kĕm′ĭ-strē) *n.* The science of the interaction or interconversion of electric and chemical phenomena. **—e·lec′tro·chem′i·cal·ly** *adv.* **—e·lec′tro·chem′ist** *n.*

e·lec·tro·co·ag·u·la·tion (ĭ-lĕk′trō-kō-ăg′yə-lā′shən) *n. Medicine.* Therapeutic use of a high-frequency electric current to bring about the coagulation and destruction of tissue.

e·lec·tro·con·vul·sive therapy (ĭ-lĕk′trō-kən-vŭl′sĭv) *n. Abbr.* **ECT** Administration of electric current to the brain through electrodes placed on the head in order to induce unconsciousness and brief convulsions, used in the treatment of certain mental disorders, especially acute depression. Also called *electroshock, electroshock therapy.*

e·lec·tro·cute (ĭ-lĕk′trə-kyo͞ot′) *tr.v.* **-cut·ed, -cut·ing, -cutes. 1.** To kill with electricity: *a worker who was electrocuted by a high-tension wire.* **2.** To execute (a condemned prisoner) by means of electricity. [ELECTRO– + (EXE)CUTE.] **—e·lec′tro·cu′tion** (-kyo͞o′shən) *n.*

e·lec·trode (ĭ-lĕk′trōd′) *n.* **1.** A solid electric conductor through which an electric current enters or leaves an electrolytic cell or other medium. **2.** A collector or emitter of electric charge or of electric-charge carriers, as in a semiconducting device.

e·lec·tro·de·pos·it (ĭ-lĕk′trō-dĭ-pŏz′ĭt) *tr.v.* **-it·ed, -it·ing, -its.** To deposit (a dissolved or suspended substance) on an electrode by electrolysis. **—electrodeposit** *n.* The substance so deposited. **—e·lec′tro·dep′o·si′tion** (-dĕp′ə-zĭsh′ən, -dē′-pə-) *n.*

e·lec·tro·der·mal (ĭ-lĕk′trō-dûr′məl) *adj.* Of or relating to the electrical properties of the skin.

e·lec·tro·di·al·y·sis (ĭ-lĕk′trō-dī-ăl′ĭ-sĭs) *n., pl.* **-ses** (-sēz′). Dialysis at a rate increased by the application of an electric potential across the dialysis membrane, used especially to remove electrolytes from a colloidal suspension.

e·lec·tro·dy·nam·ics (ĭ-lĕk′trō-dī-năm′ĭks) *n.* *(used with a sing. verb).* The physics of the relationship between electric current and magnetic or mechanical phenomena. **—e·lec′tro·dy·nam′ic** *adj.*

e·lec·tro·dy·na·mom·e·ter (ĭ-lĕk′trō-dī′nə-mŏm′ĭ-tər) *n.* An instrument that measures electric current by indicating the level of magnetic attraction or repulsion between a fixed and a movable coil, one of which carries the current to be measured.

e·lec·tro·en·ceph·a·lo·gram (ĭ-lĕk′trō-ĕn-sĕf′ə-lə-grăm′) *n. Abbr.* **EEG** A graphic record of the electrical activity of the brain as recorded by an electroencephalograph. Also called *encephalogram.*

e·lec·tro·en·ceph·a·lo·graph (ĭ-lĕk′trō-ĕn-sĕf′ə-lə-grăf′) *n. Abbr.* **EEG** An instrument that measures electrical potentials on the scalp and generates a record of the electrical activity of the brain. Also called *encephalograph.* **—e·lec′tro·en·ceph′a·lo·graph′ic** *adj.* **—e·lec′tro·en·ceph′a·log′ra·phy** (-lŏg′rə-fē) *n.*

e·lec·tro·form (ĭ-lĕk′trə-fôrm′) *tr.v.* **-formed, -form·ing, -forms.** To produce or reproduce (an object) by electrodeposition on a mold.

e·lec·tro·gas·dy·nam·ics (ĭ-lĕk′trə-găs′dī-năm′ĭks) *n.* *(used with a sing. verb). Abbr.* **EGD** Generation of electrical energy based on the conversion of the kinetic energy contained in a high-pressure, ionized, moving combustion gas. **—e·lec′tro·gas′dy·nam′ic** *adj.*

e·lec·tro·gen·e·sis (ĭ-lĕk′trə-jĕn′ĭ-sĭs) *n.* Production of electrical impulses in living organisms or tissues. **—e·lec′tro·gen′ic** *adj.*

e·lec·tro·graph (ĭ-lĕk′trə-grăf′) *n.* **1.** An electrically produced graph or tracing. **2.** Equipment used to produce such a graph or tracing in facsimile transmission.

e·lec·tro·hy·drau·lic (ĭ-lĕk′trō-hī-drô′lĭk) *adj.* Of, relating to, or involving a combination of electric and hydraulic mechanisms. **—e·lec′tro·hy·drau′li·cal·ly** *adv.*

e·lec·tro·kin·et·ics (ĭ-lĕk′trō-kĭ-nĕt′ĭks) *n.* *(used with a sing. verb).* The electrodynamics of heating effects and current distribution in electric networks.

e·lec·trol·o·gist (ĭ-lĕk-trŏl′ə-jĭst, ē′lĕk-) *n.* One who removes body hair by means of an electric current.

e·lec·tro·lu·mi·nes·cence (ĭ-lĕk′trō-lo͞o′mə-nĕs′əns) *n.* **1.** Direct conversion of electric energy to light by a solid phosphor subjected to an alternating electric field. **2.** Emission of light caused by electric discharge in a gas. **—e·lec′tro·lu′mi·nes′cent** *adj.*

e·lec·trol·y·sis (ĭ-lĕk-trŏl′ĭ-sĭs, ē′lĕk-) *n.* **1.** Chemical change, especially decomposition, produced in an electrolyte by an electric current. **2.** Destruction of living tissue, especially of hair roots, by means of an electric current applied with a needle-shaped electrode.

e·lec·tro·lyte (ĭ-lĕk′trə-līt′) *n.* **1.** A chemical compound that ionizes when dissolved or molten to produce an electrically conductive medium. **2.** *Physiology.* Any of various ions, such as sodium, potassium, or chloride, required by cells to regulate the electric charge and flow of water molecules across the cell membrane.

e·lec·tro·lyt·ic (ĭ-lĕk′trə-lĭt′ĭk) *adj.* **1.a.** Of or relating to electrolysis. **b.** Produced by electrolysis. **2.** Of or relating to electrolytes. **—e·lec′tro·lyt′i·cal·ly** *adv.*

electrolytic cell *n.* **1.** A cell containing an electrolyte through which an externally generated electric current is passed by a system of electrodes in order to produce an electrochemical reaction. **2.** A cell containing an electrolyte in which an electrochemical reaction produces an electromotive force.

e·lec·tro·lyze (ĭ-lĕk′trə-līz′) *tr.v.* **-lyzed, -lyz·ing, -lyz·es.** To cause to decompose by electrolysis.

e·lec·tro·mag·net (ĭ-lĕk′trō-măg′nĭt) *n.* A magnet consisting essentially of a coil of insulated wire wrapped around a soft iron core that is magnetized only when current flows through the wire.

e·lec·tro·mag·net·ic (ĭ-lĕk′trō-măg-nĕt′ĭk) *adj. Abbr.* **EM** Of or exhibiting electromagnetism. **—e·lec′tro·mag·net′i·cal·ly** *adv.*

electromagnetic field *n.* The field of force associated with electric charge in motion, having both electric and magnetic components and containing a definite amount of electromagnetic energy.

electromagnetic pulse *n. Abbr.* **EMP** The pulse of intense electromagnetic radiation generated by a nuclear explosion high above Earth.

electromagnetic spectrum *n.* The entire range of radiation extending in frequency from approximately 10^{23} hertz to 0 hertz or, in corresponding wavelengths, from 10^{-13} centimeter to infinity and including, in order of decreasing frequency, cosmic-ray photons, gamma rays, x-rays, ultraviolet radiation, visible light, infrared radiation, microwaves, and radio waves.

electromagnetic unit *n. Abbr.* **emu** Any of various systems of units for electricity and magnetism based on a system of equations in which the permeability of free space is taken as unity and by means of which the abampere is defined as the fundamental unit of current.

electromagnetic wave *n.* A wave of energy having a frequency within the electromagnetic spectrum and propagated as a periodic disturbance of the electromagnetic field when an electric charge oscillates or accelerates.

e·lec·tro·mag·net·ism (ĭ-lĕk′trō-măg′nĭ-tĭz′əm) *n.* **1.** Magnetism produced by electric charge in motion. **2.** The physics of electricity and magnetism.

e·lec·tro·mech·an·i·cal (ĭ-lĕk′trō-mə-kăn′ĭ-kəl) *adj.* Relating to a mechanical device or system that is actuated or controlled by electricity.

e·lec·tro·met·al·lur·gy (ĭ-lĕk′trō-mĕt′l-ûr′jē) *n.* The use of electric and electrolytic processes to purify metals or reduce metallic compounds to metals. **—e·lec′tro·met′al·lur′gi·cal** *adj.*

e·lec·trom·e·ter (ĭ-lĕk′trŏm′ĭ-tər, ē′lĕk-) *n.* An instrument for measuring voltage.

e·lec·tro·mo·tive (ĭ-lĕk′trō-mō′tĭv) *adj.* Of, relating to, or producing electric current.

electromotive force *n. Abbr.* **emf, EMF** The energy per unit charge that is converted reversibly from chemical, mechanical, or other forms of energy into electrical energy in a battery or dynamo.

e·lec·tro·my·o·gram (ĕ-lĕk′trō-mī′ō-grăm′) *n. Abbr.* **EMG** A graphic record of the electrical activity of a muscle as recorded by an electromyograph.

e·lec·tro·my·o·graph (ĭ-lĕk-trō-mī′ə-graf′) *n.* An instrument used in the diagnosis of neuromuscular disorders that produces an audio or visual record of the electrical activity of a skeletal muscle by means of an electrode inserted into the muscle or placed on the skin. **—e·lec′tro·my′o·graph′ic** *adj.* **—e·lec′tro·my′o·graph′i·cal·ly** *adv.* **—e·lec′tro·my·og′ra·phy** (-mī-ŏg′rə-fē) *n.*

e·lec·tron (ĭ-lĕk′trŏn′) *n. Abbr.* **e** A stable subatomic particle in the lepton family having a rest mass of 9.1066×10^{-28} gram and a unit negative electric charge of approximately 1.602×10^{-19} coulomb. See table at **subatomic particle.** [ELECTR(IC) + -ON[1].]

e·lec·tro·neg·a·tive (ĭ-lĕk′trō-nĕg′ə-tĭv) *adj.* **1.** Having a negative electric charge. **2.** Tending to attract electrons to form a chemical bond. **3.** Capable of acting as a negative electrode.

electron gun *n.* The electrode, especially in a cathode-ray tube, that produces a beam of accelerated electrons.

electron hole *n. Physics.* See **hole** (sense 9).

e·lec·tron·ic (ĭ-lĕk-trŏn′ĭk, ē′lĕk-) *adj.* **1.** Of or relating to electrons. **2.** Of, relating to, based on, operated by, or otherwise involving the controlled conduction of electrons or other charge carriers, especially in a vacuum, gas, or semiconducting material. **3.** Of or relating to electronics. **—e·lec′tron′i·cal·ly** *adv.*

electronic fetal monitor *n. Abbr.* **EFM** An electronic device used during labor to monitor fetal heartbeat and maternal uterine contractions.

electronic flash *n.* A portable flash lamp for photography that uses a capacitor as a power source.

electronic mail *n. Computer Science.* Messages sent and received electronically via telecommunication links, as between microcomputers or terminals. Also called *E-mail.*

electronic music *n. Music.* Music produced or altered by electronic means, as by a tape recorder or synthesizer.

e·lec·tron·ics (ĭ-lĕk′trŏn′ĭks, ē′lĕk-) *n.* **1.** *(used with a sing. verb).* The science and technology of electronic phenomena. **2.** *(used with a pl. verb).* Electronic devices and systems: *The electronics aboard the new aircraft are very sophisticated.*

electronic stylus *n. Computer Science.* See **light pen.**

electron lens *n.* Any of various devices that use an electric or a magnetic field to focus a beam of electrons.

electron micrograph *n.* A micrograph made by an electron microscope.

electron microscope *n. Abbr.* **EM** Any of a class of microscopes that use electrons rather than visible light to produce magnified images, especially of objects having dimensions smaller than the wavelengths of visible light, with linear magnification approaching or exceeding a million (10^6).

electron microscopy *n.* Microscopy involving use of an electron microscope. **—electron microscopist** *n.*

electron multiplier *n.* A vacuum tube in which a single electron produces a large number of secondary electrons by collision with an anode, the process generally being repeated through a number of stages to achieve great amplification of current.

electron neutrino *n.* A stable elementary particle in the lep-

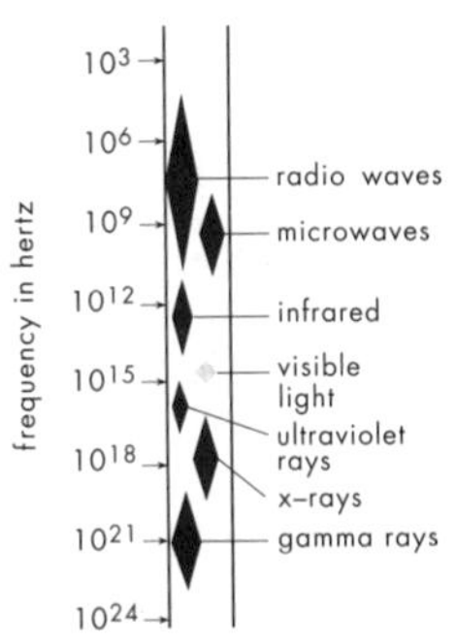

electromagnetic spectrum

ă pat	oi boy
ā pay	ou out
âr care	o͝o took
ä father	o͞o boot
ĕ pet	ŭ cut
ē be	ûr urge
ĭ pit	th thin
ī pie	*th* this
îr pier	hw which
ŏ pot	zh vision
ō toe	ə about, item
ô paw	♦ regionalism

Stress marks: ′ (primary); ′ (secondary), as in **dictionary** (dĭk′shə-nĕr′ē)

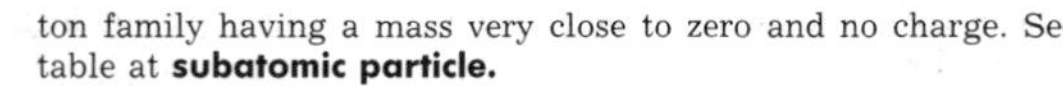

ton family having a mass very close to zero and no charge. See table at **subatomic particle.**

electron optics *n. (used with a sing. verb).* The science of the control of electron motion by electron lenses in systems or under conditions analogous to those involving or affecting visible light.

electron pair *n.* **1.** Two electrons functioning or regarded as functioning in concert, especially two electrons that form a nonpolar covalent bond between atoms. **2.** The combination of an electron and a positron as produced by a high-energy photon.

electron transport *n. Biochemistry.* The successive passage of electrons from one cytochrome or flavoprotein to another by a series of oxidation-reduction reactions during the aerobic production of ATP, with the electrons originating from an oxidizable substrate and ultimately being passed to molecular oxygen. The oxidation-reduction reactions generate the energy required for the production of ATP.

electron tube *n.* A sealed enclosure, either highly evacuated or containing a controlled quantity of gas, in which electrons can be made sufficiently mobile to act as the principal carriers of current between at least one pair of electrodes.

electron volt *n. Abbr.* **eV** A unit of energy equal to the energy gained by an electron falling through a potential difference of one volt, about 1.602×10^{-19} joule. See table at **measurement.**

e·lec·tro·phile (ĭ-lĕk′trə-fīl′) *n.* A chemical compound or group that is attracted to electrons and tends to accept electrons.

e·lec·tro·pho·rese (ĭ-lĕk′trō-fə-rēs′) *tr.v.* **-resed, -res·ing, -res·es.** To subject to electrophoresis. [Back-formation from ELECTROPHORESIS.]

electrostatic generator

e·lec·tro·pho·re·sis (ĭ-lĕk′trō-fə-rē′sĭs) *n.* **1.** The migration of charged colloidal particles or molecules through a solution under the influence of an applied electric field usually provided by immersed electrodes. Also called *cataphoresis.* **2.** A method of separating substances, especially proteins, and analyzing molecular structure based on the rate of movement of each component in a colloidal suspension while under the influence of an electric field. **—e·lec′tro·pho·ret′ic** (-rĕt′ĭk) *adj.*

e·lec·tro·pho·ret·o·gram (ĭ-lĕk′trō-fə-rĕt′ə-grăm′) *n.* A record of the results of an electrophoresis, such as a filter paper on which the components of a mixture are deposited as they migrate under the influence of an electric field. [ELECTROPHORET(IC) + -GRAM.]

e·lec·troph·o·rus (ĭ-lĕk′trŏf′ər-əs, ē′lĕk-) *n., pl.* **-o·ri** (-ə-rī′, -ə-rē′). An apparatus for generating static electricity, consisting of a hard rubber disk that is given a negative charge by friction and a metal plate that is given a net positive charge by induction when in contact with the disk. [New Latin : ELECTRO- + Greek *-phoros,* -phorous.]

e·lec·tro·phys·i·ol·o·gy (ĭ-lĕk′trō-fĭz′ē-ŏl′ə-jē) *n.* **1.** The branch of physiology that studies the relationship between electric phenomena and bodily processes. **2.** The electric activity associated with a bodily part or function. **—e·lec′tro·phys′i·o·log′ic** (-ə-lŏj′ĭk), **e·lec′tro·phys′i·o·log′i·cal** (-ĭ-kəl) *adj.* **—e·lec′tro·phys′i·o·log′i·cal·ly** *adv.* **—e·lec′tro·phys′i·ol′o·gist** *n.*

e·lec·tro·plate (ĭ-lĕk′trə-plāt′) *tr.v.* **-plat·ed, -plat·ing, -plates.** To coat or cover with a thin layer of metal by electrodeposition.

e·lec·tro·pos·i·tive (ĭ-lĕk′trō-pŏz′ĭ-tĭv) *adj.* **1.** Having a positive electric charge. **2.** Capable of acting as a positive electrode. **3.** Tending to release electrons to form a chemical bond.

e·lec·tro·re·cep·tor (ĭ-lĕk′trō-rĭ-sĕp′tər) *n.* Any of a series of sensory organs in certain fish, such as sharks, skates, and electric eels, that detect electric fields and are located on the head and along the lateral line. **—e·lec′tro·re·cep′tion** *n.*

e·lec·tro·scope (ĭ-lĕk′trə-skōp′) *n.* An instrument used to detect the presence, sign, and in some configurations the magnitude of an electric charge by the mutual attraction or repulsion of metal foils or pith balls. **—e·lec′tro·scop′ic** (-skŏp′ĭk) *adj.*

e·lec·tro·shock (ĭ-lĕk′trō-shŏk′) *n.* See **electroconvulsive therapy. —electroshock** *tr.v.* **-shocked, -shock·ing, -shocks.** To administer electroconvulsive therapy to.

electroshock therapy *n.* See **electroconvulsive therapy.**

e·lec·tro·stat·ic (ĭ-lĕk′trō-stăt′ĭk) *adj.* **1.a.** Of or relating to electric charges at rest. **b.** Produced or caused by such charges. **2.** Of or relating to electrostatics. **—e·lec′tro·stat′i·cal·ly** *adv.*

electrostatic generator *n.* Any of various devices, including the electrophorus, the Wimshurst machine, and especially the Van de Graaff generator, that generate high voltages by accumulating large quantities of electric charge.

electrostatic precipitation *n.* The removal of very fine particles suspended in a gas by electrostatic charging and subsequent precipitation onto a collector in a strong electric field.

electrostatic printing *n.* A process for printing or copying in which electrostatic forces form the image in powder or ink directly on the surface to be printed. **—electrostatic printer** *n.*

e·lec·tro·stat·ics (ĭ-lĕk′trō-stăt′ĭks) *n. (used with a sing. verb).* The physics of electrostatic phenomena.

electrostatic unit *n. Abbr.* **esu** Any unit of electricity or magnetism in the centimeter-gram-second system based on the forces of interaction between electric charges.

e·lec·tro·sur·ger·y (ĭ-lĕk′trō-sûr′jə-rē) *n.* The surgical use of high-frequency electric current for cutting or destroying tissue, as in cauterization. **—e·lec′tro·sur′gi·cal** (-jĭ-kəl) *adj.* **—e·lec′tro·sur′gi·cal·ly** *adv.*

e·lec·tro·ther·a·peu·tics (ĭ-lĕk′trō-thĕr′ə-pyo͞o′tĭks) *n. (used with a sing. verb).* See **electrotherapy.**

e·lec·tro·ther·a·py (ĭ-lĕk′trō-thĕr′ə-pē) *n., pl.* **-pies.** Medical therapy using electric currents. Also called *electrotherapeutics.*

e·lec·tro·ther·mal (ĭ-lĕk′trō-thûr′məl) *adj.* **1.** Of, relating to, or involving both electricity and heat. **2.** Of or relating to the production of heat by electricity. **—e·lec′tro·ther′mal·ly** *adv.*

e·lec·trot·o·nus (ĭ-lĕk′trŏt′n-əs, ē′lĕk-) *n.* Alteration in excitability and conductivity of a nerve or muscle during the passage of an electric current through it. **—e·lec′tro·ton′ic** (-trə-tŏn′ĭk) *adj.*

e·lec·tro·type (ĭ-lĕk′trə-tīp′) *n.* **1.** A metal plate used in letterpress printing, made by electroplating a lead or plastic mold of the page to be printed. **2.** The process of making an electrotype. **—e·lec′tro·type′** *v.* **—e·lec′tro·typ′er** *n.* **—e·lec′tro·typ′ic** (-trō-tĭp′ĭk) *adj.*

e·lec·tro·va·lence (ĭ-lĕk′trō-vā′ləns) *n.* **1.** Valence characterized by the transfer of electrons from atoms of one element to atoms of another during the formation of an ionic bond between the atoms. **2.** The number of electric charges lost or gained by an atom in such a transfer. **—e·lec′tro·va′lent** *adj.*

e·lec·tro·va·len·cy (ĭ-lĕk′tro-vā′lən-sē) *n.* Electrovalence.

electrovalent bond *n.* See **ionic bond.**

e·lec·trum (ĭ-lĕk′trəm) *n.* An alloy of silver and gold. [Middle English, from Latin, amber, from Greek *ēlektron.*]

e·lec·tu·ar·y (ĭ-lĕk′cho͞o-ĕr′ē) *n., pl.* **-ies.** A drug mixed with sugar and water or honey into a pasty mass suitable for oral administration. [Middle English *electuarie,* from Late Latin *ēlēctuārium,* probably alteration of Greek *ekleikton,* from *ekleikhein,* to lick up : *ek-,* out; see **eghs** in Appendix + *leikhein,* to lick; see **leigh-** in Appendix.]

el·ee·mos·y·nar·y (ĕl′ə-mŏs′ə-nĕr′ē, ĕl′ē-ə-) *adj.* **1.** Of, relating to, or dependent on charity. **2.** Contributed as an act of charity; gratuitous. See Synonyms at **benevolent.** [Medieval Latin *eleēmosynārius,* from Late Latin *eleēmosyna,* alms. See ALMS.]

el·e·gance (ĕl′ĭ-gəns) *n.* **1.a.** Refinement, grace, and beauty in movement, appearance, or manners. **b.** Tasteful opulence in form, decoration, or presentation. **2.a.** Restraint and grace of style. **b.** Scientific exactness and precision. **3.** Something elegant.

SYNONYMS: *elegance, grace, polish, urbanity.* The central meaning shared by these nouns is "refined and tasteful beauty of manner, form, or style": *a woman of unstudied elegance; walks with unconscious grace; comported herself with dignity and polish; tact and urbanity, the marks of a true diplomat.*
ANTONYM: *inelegance.*

el·e·gan·cy (ĕl′ĭ-gən-sē) *n., pl.* **-cies.** Elegance or an instance of it.

el·e·gant (ĕl′ĭ-gənt) *adj.* Characterized by or exhibiting refined, tasteful beauty of manner, form, or style. See Synonyms at **delicate.** [Middle English, from Old French, from Latin *ēlegāns, ēlegant-,* present participle of **ēlegāre,* variant of *ēligere,* to select. See ELECT.] **—el′e·gant·ly** *adv.*

el·e·gi·ac (ĕl′ə-jī′ək, ĭ-lē′jē-ăk′) *adj.* **1.** Of, relating to, or involving elegy or mourning or expressing sorrow for that which is irrecoverably past: *an elegiac lament for youthful ideals.* **2.** Of or composed in elegiac couplets. [Late Latin *elegīacus,* from Greek *elegeiakos,* from *elegeia,* elegy. See ELEGY.] **—el′·e·gi′ac** *n.* **—el′e·gi′a·cal** *adj.* **—el′e·gi′a·cal·ly** *adv.*

elegiac couplet *n.* A unit of verse in Greek and Roman prosody consisting of a line of dactylic hexameter followed by a line of dactylic pentameter.

elegiac stanza *n.* A four-line stanza in iambic pentameter rhyming on alternate lines. Also called *heroic quatrain.*

el·e·gist (ĕl′ə-jĭst) *n.* The creator of an elegy.

e·le·git (ĭ-lē′jĭt) *n. Law.* A writ of execution against a debtor by which the debtor's property or goods are delivered to the plaintiff until the debtor can settle the debt. [Medieval Latin *ēlēgit,* from Latin, one has chosen (the first word of a phrase frequently used in the writ), third person sing. perfect tense of *ēligere,* to choose. See ELECT.]

el·e·gize (ĕl′ə-jīz′) *v.* **-gized, -giz·ing, -giz·es.** *—intr.* To compose an elegy. *—tr.* To compose an elegy upon or for.

el·e·gy (ĕl′ə-jē) *n., pl.* **-gies. 1.** A poem composed in elegiac couplets. **2.a.** A poem or song composed especially as a lament for a deceased person. **b.** Something resembling such a poem or song. **3.** *Music.* A composition that is melancholy or pensive in tone. [French *élégie,* from Latin *elegīa,* from Greek *elegeia,* from pl. of *elegeion,* elegiac distich, from *elegos,* song, mournful song.]

elem. *abbr.* Elementary.

el·e·ment (ĕl′ə-mənt) *n.* **1.** A fundamental, essential, or irreducible constituent of a composite entity. **2. elements.** The basic assumptions or principles of a subject. **3.** *Mathematics.* **a.** A member of a set. **b.** A point, line, or plane. **c.** A part of a geometric configuration, such as an angle in a triangle. **d.** The generatrix of a geometric figure. **e.** Any of the terms in the rectangular array of terms that constitute a matrix or determinant. **4.**

ă pat	oi boy
ā pay	ou out
âr care	o͝o took
ä father	o͞o boot
ĕ pet	ŭ cut
ē be	ûr urge
ĭ pit	th thin
ī pie	*th* this
îr pier	hw which
ŏ pot	zh vision
ō toe	ə about, item
ô paw	♦ regionalism

Stress marks: ′ (primary); ′ (secondary), as in **dictionary** (dĭk′shə-nĕr′ē)

Chemistry & Physics. A substance composed of atoms having an identical number of protons in each nucleus. Elements cannot be reduced to simpler substances by normal chemical means. **5.** One of four substances, earth, air, fire, or water, formerly regarded as a fundamental constituent of the universe. **6.** *Electricity.* The resistance wire in an electrical appliance such as a heater or an oven. **7. elements.** The forces that constitute the weather, especially severe or inclement weather: *outside paint that had been damaged by the elements.* **8.** An environment naturally suited to or associated with an individual: *He is in his element when traveling. The business world is her element.* **9.** A distinct group within a larger community: *the dissident element on campus.* **10. elements.** The bread and wine of the Eucharist. [Middle English, from Old French, from Latin *elementum.*]

SYNONYMS: *element, component, constituent, factor, ingredient.* The central meaning shared by these nouns is "one of the individual parts of which a composite entity is made up": *the grammatical elements of a sentence; jealousy, a component of his character; melody and harmony, two of the constituents of a musical composition; ambition as a key factor in her success; humor, an effective ingredient of a speech.*

element 104 *n.* An artificially produced radioactive element with atomic number 104 whose isotopes have mass numbers of 257, 259, 260, and 261 with half lives respectively of 0.5, 3, 0.1, and 70 seconds.

element 105 *n.* An artificially produced radioactive element with atomic number 105 whose isotopes have mass numbers of 260, 261, and 262, with half lives respectively of 1.6, 2, and 40 seconds.

el·e·men·tal (ĕl′ə-mĕn′tl) *adj.* **1.** Of, relating to, or being an element. **2.a.** Fundamental or essential; basic. **b.** Of or relating to fundamentals; elementary. **c.** Constituting an integral part; inborn. **3.** Of such character as to resemble a force of nature in power or effect: *elemental violence.* **—el′e·men′tal** *n.* **—el′e·men′tal·ly** *adv.*

el·e·men·ta·ry (ĕl′ə-mĕn′tə-rē, -trē) *adj. Abbr.* **elem. 1.** Of, relating to, or constituting the basic, essential, or fundamental part: *an elementary need for love and nurturing.* **2.** Of, relating to, or involving the fundamental or simplest aspects of a subject: *an elementary problem in statistics.* **3.** Of or relating to an elementary school or elementary education: *the elementary grades; elementary teachers.* **—el′e·men·ta′ri·ly** (-tĕr′ə-lē) *adv.* **—el′e·men′ta·ri·ness** *n.*

elementary particle *n.* Any of the subatomic particles that compose matter and energy, especially one hypothesized or regarded as an irreducible constituent of matter. Also called *fundamental particle.* See table at **subatomic particle.**

elementary school *n.* **1.** A school usually for the first six or eight grades. **2.** The first six to eight years of a child's formal education. Also called *grade school, grammar school, primary school.*

el·e·mi (el′ə-mē) *n., pl.* **-mis.** Any of various oily resins derived from certain tropical trees, especially *Canarium luzonicum* of the Philippines, and used in making varnishes and inks. [From New Latin *elimi,* probably from Arabic *elemī,* variant of *al-lamīy,* the elemi.]

el·e·phant (ĕl′ə-fənt) *n.* **1.** Either of two very large herbivorous mammals, *Elephas maximus* of south-central Asia or *Loxodonta africana* of Africa, having thick, almost hairless skin, a long, flexible, prehensile trunk, upper incisors forming long, curved tusks of ivory, and, in the African species, large, fan-shaped ears. **2.** Any of various extinct or living animals related to either of these two animals. [Middle English *elefaunt,* from Old French *olifant,* from Vulgar Latin **olifantus,* from Latin *elephantus,* from Greek *elephas, elephant-.*]

elephant folio *n. Printing.* A book or publication of the largest size, often about 60 centimeters (2 feet) in height.

el·e·phan·ti·a·sis (ĕl′ə-fən-tī′ə-sĭs) *n.* Chronic, often extreme enlargement and hardening of cutaneous and subcutaneous tissue, especially of the legs and external genitals, resulting from lymphatic obstruction and usually caused by infestation of the lymph glands and vessels with a filarial worm. [Latin, from Greek : *elephas, elephant-,* elephant + *-iasis,* -iasis.]

el·e·phan·tine (ĕl′ə-făn′tēn′, -tīn′, ĕl′ə-fən-) *adj.* **1.** Of or relating to an elephant. **2.a.** Enormous in size or strength. **b.** Ponderously clumsy.

El·e·phan·ti·ne (ĕl′ə-făn-tī′nē). An island of southeast Egypt in the Nile River below the First Cataract. In ancient times it was a military post guarding the southern frontier of Egypt.

elephant seal *n.* Either of two large seals, *Mirounga angustirostris* mainly of Pacific coastal waters of California or *M. leonina* of coastal waters of the Southern Hemisphere, the males of which have an inflatable, trunklike proboscis. Also called *sea elephant.*

el·e·phant's foot (ĕl′ə-fənts) *n., pl.* **elephant's foots. 1.** An African species of yam *(Dioscorea elephantipes)* having unusual clusters of tubers that grow above the ground. **2.** Any of several plants of the genus *Elephantopus* in the composite family, having small purplish flowers grouped in discoid flower heads.

Eleusinian mysteries *pl.n.* The ancient religious rites celebrated at Eleusis in honor of Demeter. [From Latin *Eleusīnius,* of Eleusis, from Greek *Eleusinios,* from *Eleusis, Eleusin-,* Eleusis.]

E·leu·sis (ĭ-lo͞o′sĭs). An ancient city of eastern Greece near Athens, site of the Eleusinian mysteries. **—El′eu·sin′i·an** (ĕl′yo͞o-sĭn′ē-ən) *adj. & n.*

elev. *abbr.* Elevation.

el·e·vate (ĕl′ə-vāt′) *tr.v.* **-vat·ed, -vat·ing, -vates. 1.** To move (something) to a higher place or position from a lower one; lift. **2.** To increase the amplitude, intensity, or volume of. **3.** To promote to a higher rank. **4.** To raise to a higher moral, cultural, or intellectual level. **5.** To lift the spirits of; elate. See Synonyms at **lift.** [Middle English *elevaten,* from Latin *ēlevāre, ēlevāt-* : *ē-, ex-,* up; see EX– + *levāre,* to raise; see **leg^wh-** in Appendix.]

el·e·vat·ed (ĕl′ə-vā′tĭd) *adj.* **1.a.** Raised especially above the ground: *an elevated platform.* See Synonyms at **high. b.** Increased in amount or degree: *an elevated temperature.* **2.a.** Morally or intellectually superior. **b.** Formal; lofty: *an elevated prose style.* **3.** Elated in feeling or mood; high-spirited. **—elevated** *n.* An elevated railway.

elevated railway *n.* A railway that operates on a raised structure in order to permit passage of vehicles or pedestrians beneath it.

el·e·va·tion (ĕl′ə-vā′shən) *n. Abbr.* **el., elev. 1.a.** The act or an instance of elevating. **b.** The condition of being elevated. **2.** An elevated place or position. **3.** The height to which something is elevated above a point of reference such as the ground. **4.** Loftiness of thought or feeling. **5.** A scale drawing of the side, front, or rear of a structure. **6.** The height of a thing above a reference level; altitude. **7.a.** The ability to achieve height in a jump, as in ballet. **b.** The degree of height reached when such a jump is executed.

SYNONYMS: *elevation, altitude, height.* The central meaning shared by these nouns is "the distance of something above a point of reference such as the horizon": *a city at an elevation of 3,000 feet above sea level; a blimp flying at an altitude of one mile; a boy who grew to a height of six feet.*

el·e·va·tor (ĕl′ə-vā′tər) *n.* **1.a.** A platform or an enclosure raised and lowered in a vertical shaft to transport people or freight. **b.** The enclosure or platform with its operating equipment, motor, cables, and accessories. **2.** A movable control surface, usually attached to the horizontal stabilizer of an aircraft, that is used to produce motion up or down. **3.** A mechanism, often with buckets or scoops attached to a conveyor, used for hoisting materials. **4.** A granary equipped with devices for hoisting and discharging grain.

e·lev·en (ĭ-lĕv′ən) *n.* **1.** The cardinal number equal to 10 + 1. **2.** The 11th in a set or sequence. **3.** Something with 11 parts or members, especially a football team. [Middle English *elleven,* from Old English *endleofan.* See **oi-no-** in Appendix.] **—e·lev′en** *adj. & pron.*

e·lev·ens·es (ĭ-lĕv′ən-zəs) *pl.n. Chiefly British.* Tea or coffee taken at midmorning and often accompanied by a snack.

e·lev·enth (ĭ-lĕv′ənth) *n.* **1.** The ordinal number matching the number 11 in a series. **2.** One of 11 equal parts. **—e·lev′enth** *adv. & adj.*

eleventh hour *n.* The latest possible time: *turned in the report at the eleventh hour.*

el·e·von (ĕl′ə-vŏn′) *n.* A control surface on an airplane that combines the functions of an elevator and an aileron. [ELEV(ATOR) + (AILER)ON.]

elf (ĕlf) *n., pl.* **elves** (ĕlvz). **1.** A small, often mischievous creature considered to have magical powers. **2.a.** A lively, mischievous child. **b.** A usually sprightly or mischievous or sometimes spiteful person. [Middle English, from Old English *ælf.* See **albho-** in Appendix.]

ELF *abbr.* Extremely low frequency.

El Fer·rol (fə-rôl′, fĕ-). A city of northwest Spain on the Atlantic Ocean. An important naval station since the 18th century, it was occupied by the British and then the French in the early 1800's. Population, 90,410.

elf·in (ĕl′fĭn) *adj.* **1.a.** Relating to or suggestive of an elf. **b.** Made, done, or produced by an elf. **2.** Small and sprightly; mischievous. **3.** Having a magical quality or charm; fairylike: *moved across the dimly lit stage with elfin grace.* [Probably from Middle English *elvene,* pl. of *elve,* elf, from Old English *-elfen,* as in *wuduelfen,* dryad. See **albho-** in Appendix.]

elf·ish (ĕl′fĭsh) also **elv·ish** (ĕl′vĭsh) *adj.* **1.** Of or relating to elves. **2.** Prankish; mischievous. **—elf′ish·ly** *adv.* **—elf′ish·ness** *n.*

elf·lock (ĕlf′lŏk′) *n.* A lock of hair tangled as if by elves. Often used in the plural.

El·gar (ĕl′gär′, -gər), Sir **Edward.** 1857–1934. British composer whose orchestral works include *Enigma Variations* (1896) and five *Pomp and Circumstance* marches (1901–1930).

El·gin (ĕl′jĭn). A city of northeast Illinois on the Fox River west-northwest of Chicago. It is a trade and industrial center. Population, 63,981.

El·gon (ĕl′gŏn′), **Mount.** An extinct volcano, 4,324.3 m (14,178 ft) high, on the Kenya-Uganda border.

El Grec·o (grĕk′ō). See El **Greco.**

el·hi (ĕl′hī′) *adj. Informal.* Of, relating to, involving, or designed for use in grades 1 to 12. [EL(EMENTARY) + HI(GH SCHOOL).]

elephant
Top: African elephant
Loxodonta africana
Bottom: Indian elephant
Elephas maximus

elevated railway
Boston's MBTA Orange Line, c. 1980

PERIODIC TABLE OF THE ELEMENTS

1	atomic number
H	symbol
Hydrogen	
1.00797	atomic weight (or **mass number** of most stable isotope if in parentheses)

The periodic table arranges the chemical elements in two ways. The first is by **atomic number**, starting with hydrogen (atomic number = 1) in the upper left-hand corner and continuing in ascending order from left to right. The second is by the number of electrons in the outermost **shell**. Elements having the same number of electrons in the outermost shell are placed in the same column. Since the number of electrons in the outermost shell in large part determines the chemical nature of an element, elements in the same column have similar chemical properties.

This arrangement of the elements was devised by **Dmitri Mendeleev** in 1869, before all the elements were yet known. To maintain the overall logic of the table, Mendeleev allowed space for undiscovered elements whose existence he predicted.

The table has since been filled in, most recently by the addition of Element 104 and Element 105. The solid lines around these elements indicate that they have been isolated experimentally although not officially named. Broken lines around elements 106–109 indicate that these elements, though not yet isolated, are known to exist.

The **lanthanide** series (elements 57–71) and the **actinide** series (elements 89–103) do not conform to the **periodic law** and are therefore placed below the main body of the table.

	GROUP 1a	GROUP 2a	GROUP 3b	GROUP 4b	GROUP 5b	GROUP 6b	GROUP 7b	GROUP 8	GROUP 8
PERIOD 1	1 **H** Hydrogen 1.00797								
PERIOD 2	3 **Li** Lithium 6.939	4 **Be** Beryllium 9.0122							
PERIOD 3	11 **Na** Sodium 22.9898	12 **Mg** Magnesium 24.312							
PERIOD 4	19 **K** Potassium 39.102	20 **Ca** Calcium 40.08	21 **Sc** Scandium 44.956	22 **Ti** Titanium 47.90	23 **V** Vanadium 50.942	24 **Cr** Chromium 51.996	25 **Mn** Manganese 54.9380	26 **Fe** Iron 55.847	27 **Co** Cobalt 58.9332
PERIOD 5	37 **Rb** Rubidium 85.47	38 **Sr** Strontium 87.62	39 **Y** Yttrium 88.905	40 **Zr** Zirconium 91.22	41 **Nb** Niobium 92.906	42 **Mo** Molyb-denum 95.94	43 **Tc** Technetium (99)	44 **Ru** Ruthenium 101.07	45 **Rh** Rhodium 102.905
PERIOD 6	55 **Cs** Cesium 132.905	56 **Ba** Barium 137.34	57-71* Lanthanides	72 **Hf** Hafnium 178.49	73 **Ta** Tantalum 180.948	74 **W** Tungsten 183.85	75 **Re** Rhenium 186.2	76 **Os** Osmium 190.2	77 **Ir** Iridium 192.2
PERIOD 7	87 **Fr** Francium (223)	88 **Ra** Radium (226)	89-103** Actinides	104	105	106	107	108	109

*LANTHANIDES	57 **La** Lanthanum 138.91	58 **Ce** Cerium 140.12	59 **Pr** Praseo-dymium 140.907	60 **Nd** Neodym-ium 144.24	61 **Pm** Prome-thium (145)	62 **Sm** Samarium 150.35	63 **Eu** Europium 151.96
**ACTINIDES	89 **Ac** Actinium (227)	90 **Th** Thorium 232.038	91 **Pa** Protac-tinium (231)	92 **U** Uranium 238.03	93 **Np** Neptunium (237)	94 **Pu** Plutonium (244)	95 **Am** Americium (243)

TABLE OF THE ELEMENTS

ELEMENT	SYMBOL	ATOMIC NUMBER	ELEMENT	SYMBOL	ATOMIC NUMBER	ELEMENT	SYMBOL	ATOMIC NUMBER	ELEMENT	SYMBOL	ATOMIC NUMBER
Actinium	Ac	89	Cadmium	Cd	48	Element 104	–	104	Holmium	Ho	67
Aluminum	Al	13	Calcium	Ca	20	Element 105	–	105	Hydrogen	H	1
Americium	Am	95	Californium	Cf	98	Erbium	Er	68	Indium	In	49
Antimony	Sb	51	Carbon	C	6	Europium	Eu	63	Iodine	I	53
Argon	Ar	18	Cerium	Ce	58	Fermium	Fm	100	Iridium	Ir	77
Arsenic	As	33	Cesium	Cs	55	Fluorine	F	9	Iron	Fe	26
Astatine	At	85	Chlorine	Cl	17	Francium	Fr	87	Krypton	Kr	36
Barium	Ba	56	Chromium	Cr	24	Gadolinium	Gd	64	Lanthanum	La	57
Berkelium	Bk	97	Cobalt	Co	27	Gallium	Ga	31	Lawrencium	Lr	103
Beryllium	Be	4	Copper	Cu	29	Germanium	Ge	32	Lead	Pb	82
Bismuth	Bi	83	Curium	Cm	96	Gold	Au	79	Lithium	Li	3
Boron	B	5	Dysprosium	Dy	66	Hafnium	Hf	72	Lutetium	Lu	71
Bromine	Br	35	Einsteinium	Es	99	Helium	He	2	Magnesium	Mg	12

GROUP 8	GROUP 1b	GROUP 2b	GROUP 3a	GROUP 4a	GROUP 5a	GROUP 6a	GROUP 7a	GROUP 0
								2 **He** Helium 4.0026
			5 **B** Boron 10.811	6 **C** Carbon 12.01115	7 **N** Nitrogen 14.0067	8 **O** Oxygen 15.9994	9 **F** Fluorine 18.9984	10 **Ne** Neon 20.183
			13 **Al** Aluminum 26.9815	14 **Si** Silicon 28.086	15 **P** Phos-phorus 30.9738	16 **S** Sulfur 32.064	17 **Cl** Chlorine 35.453	18 **Ar** Argon 39.948
28 **Ni** Nickel 58.71	29 **Cu** Copper 63.546	30 **Zn** Zinc 65.37	31 **Ga** Gallium 69.72	32 **Ge** Germanium 72.59	33 **As** Arsenic 74.9216	34 **Se** Selenium 78.96	35 **Br** Bromine 79.904	36 **Kr** Krypton 83.80
46 **Pd** Palladium 106.4	47 **Ag** Silver 107.868	48 **Cd** Cadmium 112.40	49 **In** Indium 114.82	50 **Sn** Tin 118.69	51 **Sb** Antimony 121.75	52 **Te** Tellurium 127.60	53 **I** Iodine 126.9044	54 **Xe** Xenon 131.30
78 **Pt** Platinum 195.09	79 **Au** Gold 196.967	80 **Hg** Mercury 200.59	81 **Tl** Thallium 204.37	82 **Pb** Lead 207.19	83 **Bi** Bismuth 208.980	84 **Po** Polonium (210)	85 **At** Astatine (210)	86 **Rn** Radon (222)

64 **Gd** Gadolinium 157.25	65 **Tb** Terbium 158.924	66 **Dy** Dysprosium 162.50	67 **Ho** Holmium 164.930	68 **Er** Erbium 167.26	69 **Tm** Thulium 168.934	70 **Yb** Ytterbium 173.04	71 **Lu** Lutetium 174.97
96 **Cm** Curium (247)	97 **Bk** Berkelium (247)	98 **Cf** Californium (251)	99 **Es** Einsteinium (254)	100 **Fm** Fermium (257)	101 **Md** Mende-levium (256)	102 **No** Nobelium (255)	103 **Lr** Lawren-cium (257)

ELEMENT	SYMBOL	ATOMIC NUMBER
Manganese	Mn	25
Medelevium	Md	101
Mercury	Hg	80
Molybdenum	Mo	42
Neodymium	Nd	60
Neon	Ne	10
Neptunium	Np	93
Nickel	Ni	28
Niobium	Nb	41
Nitrogen	N	7
Nobelium	No	102
Osmium	Os	76
Oxygen	O	8

ELEMENT	SYMBOL	ATOMIC NUMBER
Palladium	Pd	46
Phosphorus	P	15
Platinum	Pt	78
Plutonium	Pu	94
Polonium	Po	84
Potassium	K	19
Praseodymium	Pr	59
Promethium	Pm	61
Protactinium	Pa	91
Radium	Ra	88
Radon	Rn	86
Rhenium	Re	75
Rhodium	Rh	45

ELEMENT	SYMBOL	ATOMIC NUMBER
Rubidium	Rb	37
Ruthenium	Ru	44
Samarium	Sm	62
Scandium	Sc	21
Selenium	Se	34
Silicon	Si	14
Silver	Ag	47
Sodium	Na	11
Strontium	Sr	38
Sulfur	S	16
Tantalum	Ta	73
Technetium	Tc	43
Tellurium	Te	52

ELEMENT	SYMBOL	ATOMIC NUMBER
Terbium	Tb	65
Thallium	Tl	81
Thorium	Th	90
Thulium	Tm	69
Tin	Sn	50
Titanium	Ti	22
Tungsten	W	74
Uranium	U	92
Vanadium	V	23
Xenon	Xe	54
Ytterbium	Yb	70
Yttrium	Y	39
Zinc	Zn	30
Zirconium	Zr	40

George Eliot

Elizabeth I
c. 1588 portrait by an anonymous artist

Elizabeth II
1957 photograph by Antony Armstrong Jones (Lord Snowdon)

Duke Ellington

E·li (ē′lī). In the Old Testament, a judge of Israel who was the teacher of Samuel.

e·lic·it (ĭ-lĭs′ĭt) *tr.v.* **-it·ed, -it·ing, -its. 1.a.** To bring or draw out (something latent); educe. **b.** To arrive at (a truth, for example) by logic. **2.** To call forth (a reaction, for example). See Synonyms at **evoke.** [Latin *ēlicere, ēlicit-* : *ē-, ex-*, ex- + *lacere*, to entice.] **—e·lic′i·ta′tion** *n.* **—e·lic′i·tor** *n.*

e·lide (ĭ-līd′) *tr.v.* **e·lid·ed, e·lid·ing, e·lides. 1.a.** To omit or slur over (a syllable, for example) in pronunciation. **b.** To strike out (something written). **2.a.** To eliminate or leave out of consideration. **b.** To cut short; abridge. [Latin *ēlīdere*, to strike out : *ē-, ex-*, ex- + *laedere*, to strike.]

el·i·gi·ble (ĕl′ĭ-jə-bəl) *adj.* **1.** Qualified or entitled to be chosen: *eligible to run for office; eligible for retirement.* **2.** Desirable and worthy of choice, especially for marriage: *an eligible bachelor.* **3.** *Football.* Allowed under the rules to catch a forward pass: *an eligible receiver.* [Middle English, from Old French, from Late Latin *ēligibilis*, from Latin *ēligere*, to select. See ELECT.] **—el′i·gi·bil′i·ty** *n.* **—el′·i·gi·ble** *n.* **—el′i·gi·bly** *adv.*

E·li·jah (ĭ-lī′jə). Ninth century B.C. Hebrew prophet. According to Scripture, he did not die but was carried skyward in a chariot of fire.

e·lim·i·nate (ĭ-lĭm′ə-nāt′) *tr.v.* **-nat·ed, -nat·ing, -nates. 1.** To get rid of; remove: *an effort to eliminate capital punishment; eliminated his enemies.* **2.a.** To leave out or omit from consideration; reject. **b.** To remove from consideration by defeating, as in a contest. **3.** *Mathematics.* To remove (an unknown quantity) by combining equations. **4.** *Physiology.* To excrete (bodily wastes). [Latin *ēlīmināre, ēlīmināt-*, to banish : *ē-, ex-*, ex- + *līmen, līmin-*, threshold.] **—e·lim′i·na′tion** *n.* **—e·lim′i·na′tive, e·lim′i·na·to′ry** (-nə-tôr′ē, -tōr′ē) *adj.* **—e·lim′i·na′tor** *n.*

SYNONYMS: *eliminate, eradicate, liquidate, purge.* The central meaning shared by these verbs is "to wipe out someone or something undesirable, especially by using drastic methods such as banishment or execution": *eliminated all political opposition; eradicate guerrilla activity; liquidating traitors; purged all the imprisoned dissidents.*

El·i·ot (ĕl′ē-ət), **Charles William.** 1834–1926. American educator and editor who was president of Harvard University (1869–1909) and edited the *Harvard Classics* (1909–1910), a 50-volume selection of world literature.

Eliot, George. Pen name of Mary Ann Evans. 1819–1880. British writer whose novels, all in the 19th-century realist tradition, include *Adam Bede* (1859), *Silas Marner* (1861), and her masterpiece, *Middlemarch* (1871–1872).

Eliot, John. 1604–1690. English missionary in America who contributed to *The Bay Psalm Book* (1640), the first book printed in New England.

Eliot, T(homas) S(tearns). 1888–1965. American-born British critic and writer whose poems "The Love Song of J. Alfred Prufrock" (1915) and *The Waste Land* (1922) established him as a major literary figure. He won the 1948 Nobel Prize for literature.

E·lis (ē′lĭs). A region and city of ancient Greece in the western Peloponnesus. The plain of Olympia, in the southern part of the area, was the site of the original Olympic games.

ELISA (ĭ-lī′zə, -sə) *n.* A sensitive immunoassay that uses an enzyme linked to an antibody or antigen as a marker for the detection of a specific protein, especially an antigen or antibody. It is often used as a diagnostic test to determine exposure to a particular infectious agent, such as the AIDS virus, by identifying antibodies present in a blood sample. [*e(nzyme)-l(inked) i(mmunoad)s(orbent) a(ssay).*]

E·lis·a·beth·ville (ĭ-lĭz′ə-bəth-vĭl′). See **Lubumbashi.**

E·li·sha (ĭ-lī′shə). Ninth century B.C. In the Old Testament, a Hebrew prophet who was chosen by Elijah to be his successor.

e·li·sion (ĭ-lĭzh′ən) *n.* **1.a.** *Linguistics.* Omission of a final or initial sound in pronunciation. **b.** Omission of an unstressed vowel or syllable, as in scanning a verse. **2.** The act or an instance of omitting something. [Latin *ēlīsiō, ēlīsiōn-*, from *ēlīsus*, past participle of *ēlīdere*, to strike out. See ELIDE.]

e·lite or **é·lite** (ĭ-lēt′, ā-lēt′) *n., pl.* **elite** or **e·lites. 1.a.** A group or class of persons or a member of such a group or class, enjoying superior intellectual, social, or economic status: *"In addition to notions of social equality there was much emphasis on the role of elites and of heroes within them"* (Times Literary Supplement). **b.** The best or most skilled members of a group: *the football team's elite.* **2.** A size of type on a typewriter, equal to 12 characters per linear inch. [French *élite*, from Old French *eslite*, from feminine past participle of *eslire*, to choose, from Latin *ēligere.* See ELECT.] **—e·lite′** *adj.*

e·lit·ism or **é·lit·ism** (ĭ-lē′tĭz′əm, ā-lē-) *n.* **1.** The belief that certain persons or members of certain classes or groups deserve favored treatment by virtue of their perceived superiority, as in intellect, social status, or financial resources. **2.a.** The sense of entitlement enjoyed by such a group or class. **b.** Control, rule, or domination by such a group or class. **—e·lit′ist** *adj. & n.*

e·lix·ir (ĭ-lĭk′sər) *n.* **1.** A sweetened aromatic solution of alcohol and water, serving as a vehicle for medicine. **2.a.** See **philosophers' stone. b.** A substance believed to maintain life indefinitely. Also called *elixir of life.* **c.** A substance or medicine believed to have the power to cure all ills. **3.** An underlying principle. [Middle English, a substance of transmutative properties, from Old French *elissir*, from Medieval Latin *elixir*, from Arabic *al-'iksīr* : *al*, the + *iksīr*, elixir (probably from Greek *xērion*, desiccative powder, from *xēros*, dry).]

E·liz·a·beth[1] (ĭ-lĭz′ə-bəth). In the New Testament, the mother of John the Baptist and a kinswoman of Mary.

Elizabeth[2]**.** 1843–1916. Queen of Romania (1881–1916) and poet who wrote under the pseudonym Carmen Sylva.

Elizabeth[3]**.** Born 1900. Queen of Great Britain and Northern Ireland (1936–1952) as the wife of George VI.

Elizabeth[4]**.** A city of northeast New Jersey south of Newark. Settled as Elizabethtown in 1664, it was the capital of New Jersey until 1686. Population, 106,201.

Elizabeth I. 1533–1603. Queen of England and Ireland (1558–1603) who succeeded the Catholic Mary I and reestablished Protestantism in England. Her reign was marked by the execution of Mary Queen of Scots (1587), the defeat of the Spanish Armada (1588), and domestic prosperity and literary achievement.

Elizabeth II. Born 1926. Queen of Great Britain and Northern Ireland (since 1952) who ascended to the throne on the death of her father, George VI.

E·liz·a·be·than (ĭ-lĭz′ə-bē′thən, -bĕth′ən) *adj. Abbr.* **Eliz.** Of, relating to, or characteristic of Elizabeth I of England or her reign. **—E·liz′a·be′than** *n.*

Elizabethan sonnet *n.* See **Shakespearean sonnet.**

Elizabeth Pe·trov·na (pə-trôv′nə). 1709–1762. Empress of Russia (1741–1762) whose reign saw a return to the political spirit of her father, Peter I, and was marked by cultural development and Russian involvement in the War of the Austrian Succession (1740–1748) and the Seven Years' War (1756–1763).

elk (ĕlk) *n., pl.* **elk** or **elks. 1.** See **wapiti. 2.** The moose. **3.** A light, pliant leather of horsehide or calfskin, tanned and finished to resemble elk hide. [Middle English, probably alteration of Old English *eolh.*]

Elk Grove Village (ĕlk). A village of northeast Illinois, an industrial suburb of Chicago. Population, 28,907.

Elk·hart (ĕl′kärt′, ĕlk′härt′). A city of northern Indiana east of South Bend. It was settled in 1824. Population, 41,305.

elk·hound (ĕlk′hound′) *n.* The Norwegian elkhound.

Elk Mountains. A range of the Rocky Mountains in west-central Colorado rising to 4,350.8 m (14,265 ft) at Castle Peak.

ell[1] (ĕl) *n.* **1.** A wing of a building at right angles to the main structure. **2.** A right-angled bend in a pipe or conduit; an elbow. [From its resemblance to the shape of the capital letter L, or short for ELBOW.]

ell[2] (ĕl) *n.* An English linear measure equal to 45 inches (114 centimeters). [Middle English, from Old English *eln*, the length from the elbow to the middle finger's tip, ell. See **el-** in Appendix.]

ell[3] (ĕl) *n.* Variant of **el**[1]**.**

el·lag·ic acid (ĭ-lăj′ĭk) *n.* A yellow crystalline compound, $C_{14}H_6O_8$, that is obtained from tannins and used as a hemostatic. [French *ellagique*, from *ellag*, backward spelling of *galle*, plant gall, from Latin *galla.*]

Elles·mere Island (ĕlz′mîr′). An island of northern Northwest Territories, Canada, in the Arctic Ocean separated from Greenland by a narrow passage.

Ellesmere Port. A municipal borough of northwest England on the Mersey River south-southeast of Liverpool. It has oil refineries and various light industries. Population, 82,500.

El·lice Islands (ĕl′ĭs). See **Tuvalu.**

El·ling·ton (ĕl′ĭng-tən), **Edward Kennedy.** Known as "Duke." 1899–1974. American jazz composer, pianist, and bandleader whose compositions include "Mood Indigo" (1930).

El·li·ot Lake (ĕl′ē-ət). A community of south-central Ontario, Canada, west-southwest of Sudbury. Population, 16,723.

el·lipse (ĭ-lĭps′) *n.* **1.** A plane curve, especially: **a.** A conic section whose plane is not parallel to the axis, base, or generatrix of the intersected cone. **b.** The locus of points for which the sum of the distances from each point to two fixed points is equal. **2.** Ellipsis. [French, from Latin *ellīpsis*, from Greek *elleipsis*, from *elleipein*, to fall short (from the relationship between the line joining the vertices of a conic and the line through the focus and parallel to the directrix of a conic). See ELLIPSIS.]

el·lip·sis (ĭ-lĭp′sĭs) *n., pl.* **-ses** (-sēz). **1.a.** The omission of a word or phrase necessary for a complete syntactical construction but not necessary for understanding. **b.** An example of such omission. **2.** A mark or series of marks (. . . or * * * , for example) used in writing or printing to indicate an omission, especially of letters or words. [Latin *ellīpsis*, from Greek *elleipsis*, from *elleipein*, to fall short : *en-*, in; see EN–[2] + *leipein*, to leave; see **leikʷ-** in Appendix.]

el·lip·soid (ĭ-lĭp′soid′) *n.* A geometric surface, all of whose plane sections are either ellipses or circles. **—el·lip′soid′, el′lip·soid′al** (-soid′l) *adj.*

el·lip·tic (ĭ-lĭp′tĭk) or **el·lip·ti·cal** (-tĭ-kəl) *adj.* **1.** Of, relating to, or having the shape of an ellipse. **2.** Containing or characterized by ellipsis. **3.a.** Of or relating to extreme economy of oral or written expression. **b.** Marked by deliberate obscurity of style or expression. [New Latin *ellīpticus*, from Greek *elleiptikos*, defective, from *elleipsis*, a falling short, ellipsis, from *elleipein*, to fall short. See ELLIPSIS.] **—el·lip′ti·cal·ly** *adv.*

el·lip·tic·i·ty (ĭ-lĭp′-tĭs′ĭ-tē) *n.* **1.** Deviation from perfect circular or spherical form toward elliptic or ellipsoidal form. **2.** The degree of this deviation.

El·lis (ĕl′ĭs), **Alexander John.** 1814–1890. British philologist and mathematician noted for his scientific study of phonetics.

Ellis, (Henry) Havelock. 1859–1939. British psychologist and writer known for his pioneering works on sexuality, such as *Studies in the Psychology of Sex* (seven volumes, 1897–1928).

Ellis Island. An island of Upper New York Bay southwest of Manhattan. It was the chief immigration station of the United States from 1892 to 1943.

El·li·son (ĕl′ĭ-sən), **Ralph Waldo.** Born 1914. American writer whose novel *Invisible Man* (1952) is a naturalistic depiction of a young Black man's struggle against American society.

Ells·worth (ĕlz′wûrth′), **Lincoln.** 1880–1951. American explorer who took part in several polar expeditions, including a 1935 flight across the Antarctic.

Ellsworth, Oliver. 1745–1807. American jurist and politician. A U.S. senator from Connecticut (1789–1796), he worked on the legislation that created the federal court system (1789) and later served as the chief justice of the U.S. Supreme Court (1796–1800).

Ellsworth Land. A high plateau of western Antarctica south of the Antarctic Peninsula. It includes the **Ellsworth Mountains,** rising to 5,142.3 m (16,860 ft) at Vinson Massif.

elm (ĕlm) *n.* **1.** Any of various deciduous trees of the genus *Ulmus,* characteristically having arching or curving branches and serrate leaves with asymmetrical bases. Elms are widely planted as shade trees. **2.** The wood of one of these trees. [Middle English, from Old English.]

El·man (ĕl′mən), **Mischa.** 1891–1967. Russian-born American violinist regarded as one of the foremost violinists of his time.

El Man·su·ra (măn-so͝or′ə). A city of northern Egypt on a branch of the Nile River. It is a commercial and industrial center. Population, 328,700.

elm bark beetle *n.* Either of two bark beetles *(Scolytus multistriatus* or *Hylurgopinus rufipes)* that transmit the fungus causing Dutch elm disease.

Elm·hurst (ĕlm′hûrst′). A city of northeast Illinois, a residential and industrial suburb of Chicago. Population, 44,276.

El·mi·ra (ĕl-mī′rə). A city of southern New York near the Pennsylvania border west of Binghamton. Mark Twain is buried here. Population, 35,327.

El Mis·ti (mē′stē). A dormant volcano, 5,825.8 m (19,101 ft) high, in the Cordillera Occidental of southern Peru. It has long figured in Peruvian legends and poetry.

El Mon·te (mŏn′tē). A city of southern California east of Los Angeles. It is an industrial center in an area noted for its walnut groves. Population, 79,494.

Elm·wood Park (ĕlm′wo͝od′). **1.** A village of northeast Illinois, a residential suburb of Chicago. Population, 24,016. **2.** A borough of northeast New Jersey southeast of Paterson. It was originally called East Paterson. Population, 18,377.

El Ni·ño (nēn′yō) *n. Oceanography.* A warming of the ocean surface off the western coast of South America that occurs every 4 to 12 years when upwelling of cold, nutrient-rich water does not occur. It causes plankton and fish to die and affects weather over much of the Pacific Ocean. [American Spanish, from Spanish, the Christ child (from the association between the onset of the warming and Christmastide) : *el,* the (from Latin *ille;* see **al-**[1] in Appendix) + *niño,* child (from Old Spanish *ninno,* from Vulgar Latin **ninnus*).]

El O·beid (ō-bād′). See **Al Ubayyid.**

el·o·cu·tion (ĕl′ə-kyo͞o′shən) *n.* **1.** The art of public speaking in which gesture, vocal production, and delivery are emphasized. **2.** A style or manner of speaking, especially in public. [Middle English *elocucion,* from Latin *ēlocūtiō, ēlocūtiōn-,* from *ēlocūtus,* past participle of *ēloquī,* to speak out : *ē-, ex-,* ex- + *loquī,* to speak; see **tolkʷ-** in Appendix.] **—el′o·cu′tion·ar′y** (-shə-nĕr′ē) *adj.* **—el′o·cu′tion·ist** *n.*

e·lo·de·a (ĭ-lō′dē-ə) *n.* Any of various small, submersed herbs of the genus *Elodea,* having grasslike leaves. [New Latin *Elodea,* genus name, from Greek *helōdēs,* marshy, from *helos,* marsh.]

e·loign (ĭ-loin′) *tr.v.* **e·loigned, e·loign·ing, e·loigns.** *Archaic.* **1.** To remove or carry away to a distance, especially so as to conceal. **2.** To take (oneself) to a distance. [Middle English *elongen,* from Old French *esloigner* : *es-,* from (from Latin *ex-;* see EX–) + *loing,* far (from Latin *longē,* distant, from *longus,* long; see **del-**[1] in Appendix).]

e·lon·gate (ĭ-lông′gāt′, ĭ-lŏng′-) *tr. & intr.v.* **-gat·ed, -gat·ing, -gates.** To make or grow longer. **—elongate** or **elongated** *adj.* **1.** Made longer; extended. **2.** Having more length than width; slender. [Late Latin *ēlongāre, ēlongāt-* : Latin *ē-, ex-,* ex- + Latin *longē,* distant; see ELOIGN.]

e·lon·ga·tion (ĭ-lông′-gā′shən, ĭ-lŏng′-, ē′lông-, ē′lŏng-) *n.* **1.** The act of elongating or the condition of being elongated. **2.** Something that elongates; an extension. **3.** The angular distance between two celestial bodies as seen from Earth.

e·lope (ĭ-lōp′) *intr.v.* **e·loped, e·lop·ing, e·lopes.** **1.** To run away with a lover, especially with the intention of getting married. **2.** To run away; abscond. [Perhaps Anglo-Norman *aloper,* to run away from one's husband with a lover, from Middle Dutch *ontlopen,* to run away : *ont-,* away from, along; see **ant-** in Appendix + *lopen,* to run.] **—e·lope′ment** *n.* **—e·lop′er** *n.*

el·o·quence (ĕl′ə-kwəns) *n.* **1.a.** Persuasive, powerful discourse. **b.** The skill or power of using such discourse. **2.** The quality of persuasive, powerful expression.

el·o·quent (ĕl′ə-kwənt) *adj.* **1.** Characterized by persuasive, powerful discourse: *an eloquent speaker; an eloquent sermon.* **2.** Vividly or movingly expressive: *a look eloquent with compassion.* See Synonyms at **expressive.** [Middle English, from Old French, from Latin *ēloquēns, ēloquent-,* present participle of *ēloquī,* to speak out. See ELOCUTION.] **—el′o·quent·ly** *adv.* **—el′o·quent·ness** *n.*

El Pas·o (păs′ō). A city of extreme western Texas on the Rio Grande opposite Ciudad Juárez, Mexico. The surrounding area was first settled by Spanish missionaries, soldiers, and traders in the 17th century. Population, 425,259.

El Sal·va·dor (săl′və-dôr′, säl′vä-*th*ôr′). A country of Central America bordering on the Pacific Ocean. Discovered in 1523, the region became independent from Spain in 1821. San Salvador is the capital and the largest city. Population, 4,949,000. **—El Sal′va·dor′i·an** (săl′və-dôr′ē-ən, -dōr′-) *adj. & n.*

else (ĕls) *adj.* **1.** Other; different: *Ask somebody else.* **2.** Additional; more: *Would you like anything else?* **—else** *adv.* **1.** In a different or an additional time, place, or manner: *I have always done it this way and I do not know how else it could be done. Where else would you like to go besides San Francisco?* **2.** If not; otherwise: *Be careful, or else you will make a mistake.* ***—idiom.*** **or else.** Regardless of any extenuating circumstances: *Be there on time or else!* [Middle English *elles,* from Old English. See **al-**[1] in Appendix.]

USAGE NOTE: *Else* is often used redundantly in combination with prepositions such as *but, except,* and *besides: No one else but Sam saw the accident* (omit *else*). • When a pronoun is followed by *else,* the possessive form is generally written thus: *someone else's* (not *someone's else*). Both *who else's* and *whose else* are in use, but not *whose else's: Who else's book could it have been? Whose else could it have been?* See Usage Notes at **who, whose.**

else·where (ĕls′hwâr′, -wâr′) *adv.* In or to a different or another place: *has property at the shore and elsewhere.*

El·si·nore (ĕl′sə-nôr′, -nōr′). See **Helsingør.**

ELSS *abbr. Aerospace.* Extravehicular life support system.

El To·ro (tôr′ō). A community of southern California southeast of Santa Ana. It is mainly residential. Population, 38,153.

el·u·ant (ĕl′yo͞o-ənt) *n.* A substance used as a solvent in the process of elution. [From Latin *ēluēns, ēluent-,* present participle of *ēluere,* to wash out. See ELUTE.]

el·u·ate (ĕl′yo͞o-ĭt, -āt′) *n.* The solution of solvent and dissolved matter resulting from elution. [Latin *ēluere,* to wash out; see ELUTE + –ATE[1].]

e·lu·ci·date (ĭ-lo͞o′sĭ-dāt′) *v.* **-dat·ed, -dat·ing, -dates.** *—tr.* To make clear or plain, especially by explanation; clarify. *—intr.* To give an explanation that serves to clarify. See Synonyms at **explain.** [Late Latin *ēlūcidāre, ēlūcidāt-* : *ē-, ex-,* intensive pref.; see EX– + Latin *lūcidus,* bright (from *lūcēre,* to shine; see **leuk-** in Appendix).] **—e·lu′ci·da′tion** *n.* **—e·lu′ci·da′tive** *adj.* **—e·lu′ci·da′tor** *n.*

e·lude (ĭ-lo͞od′) *tr.v.* **e·lud·ed, e·lud·ing, e·ludes.** **1.** To evade or escape from, as by daring, cleverness, or skill: *The suspect continues to elude the police.* **2.** To escape the understanding or grasp of: *a metaphor that eluded them.* See Synonyms at **escape.** [Latin *ēlūdere* : *ē-, ex-,* ex- + *lūdere,* to play (from *lūdus,* play; see **leid-** in Appendix).]

E·lul (ĕl′o͞ol, ĕ-lo͞ol′) *n.* The 12th month of the year in the Jewish calendar. See table at **calendar.** [Hebrew *'Elūl,* from Akkadian *ulūlu, elūlu,* the month Ululu (August/September).]

e·lu·sive (ĭ-lo͞o′sĭv, -zĭv) *adj.* **1.** Tending to elude capture, perception, comprehension, or memory: *"an invisible cabal of conspirators, each more elusive than the archterrorist* [himself]*"* (David Kline). **2.** Difficult to define or describe: *"Failures are more finely etched in our minds than triumphs, and success is an elusive, if not mythic, goal in our demanding society"* (Hugh Drummond). [From Latin *ēlūsus,* past participle of *ēlūdere,* to elude. See ELUDE.] **—e·lu′sive·ly** *adv.* **—e·lu′sive·ness** *n.*

e·lute (ĭ-lo͞ot′) *tr.v.* **e·lut·ed, e·lut·ing, e·lutes.** To extract (one material) from another, usually by means of a solvent. [From Latin *ēluere, ēlūt-,* to wash out : *ē-, ex-,* ex- + *lavere,* to wash; see **leu(ə)-** in Appendix.] **—e·lu′tion** *n.*

e·lu·tri·ate (ĭ-lo͞o′trē-āt′) *tr.v.* **-at·ed, -at·ing, -ates.** **1.** To purify, separate, or remove (ore, for example) by washing, decanting, and settling. **2.** To wash away the lighter or finer particles of (soil, for example). [Latin *elutriāre, elutriāt-* (from **elutrium,* vat, bath, from Greek **elutrion,* diminutive of *elutron,* sheath, tank; see ELYTRON) or *ēlūtriāre* (from **ēlūtor,* one who washes, from *ēluere,* to wash out; see ELUTE).] **—e·lu′tri·a′tion** *n.*

e·lu·vi·ate (ĭ-lo͞o′vē-āt′) *intr.v.* **-at·ed, -at·ing, -ates.** To undergo eluviation.

e·lu·vi·a·tion (ĭ-lo͞o′vē-ā′shən) *n.* The lateral or downward movement of dissolved or suspended material within soil when rainfall exceeds evaporation. [ELUVI(UM) + –ATION.]

e·lu·vi·um (ĭ-lo͞o′vē-əm) *n.* Residual deposits of soil, dust, and rock particles produced by the action of the wind. [New Latin *ēluvium,* from Latin *ēluere,* to wash out. See ELUTE.] **—e·lu′vi·al** (-əl) *adj.*

el·ver (ĕl′vər) *n.* See **glass eel.** [Alteration of *eelfare,* a brood

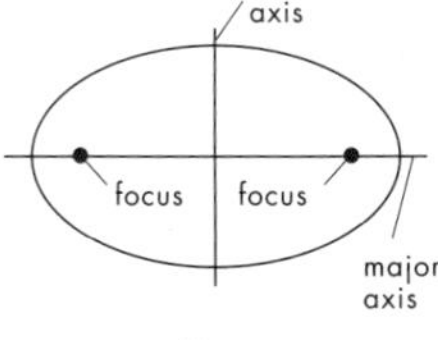

ellipse

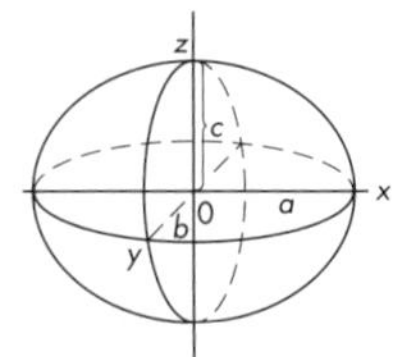

ellipsoid

$$\frac{x^2}{a^2} + \frac{y^2}{b^2} - \frac{z^2}{c^2} = 1$$

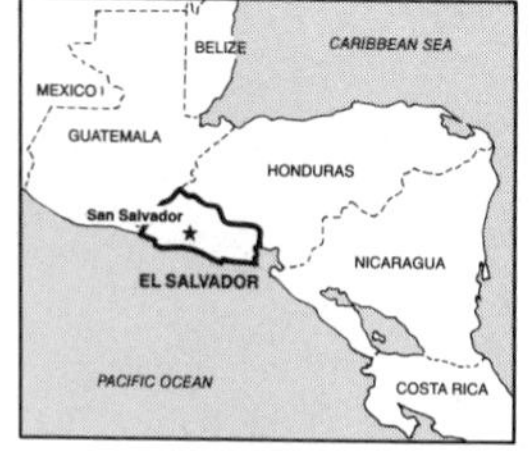

El Salvador

ă pat	oi boy
ā pay	ou out
âr care	o͝o took
ä father	o͞o boot
ĕ pet	ŭ cut
ē be	ûr urge
ĭ pit	th thin
ī pie	*th* this
îr pier	hw which
ŏ pot	zh vision
ō toe	ə about, item
ô paw	♦ regionalism

Stress marks: ′ (primary); ′ (secondary), as in **dictionary** (dĭk′shə-nĕr′ē)

of young eels, the passage of young eels up a river : EEL + FARE, journey (obsolete).]

elves (ĕlvz) *n.* Plural of **elf.**

elv·ish (ĕl′vĭsh) *adj.* Variant of **elfish.**

E·ly (ē′lē), **Isle of.** A region of east-central England with extensive drained fens. The name *Isle* comes from the high ground amid the fens; *Ely* probably refers to the eels formerly found in the fens. The city of **Ely** (population, 10,268) is noted for its cathedral, dating from the 11th century.

E·ly·ri·a (ĭ-lîr′ē-ə). A city of northern Ohio west-southwest of Cleveland. Settled in 1817, it is an industrial center. Population, 57,538.

E·ly·sian (ĭ-lĭzh′ən) *adj.* **1.** *Greek Mythology.* Of or relating to Elysium. **2.** Blissful; delightful.

Elysian Fields *pl.n. Greek Mythology.* The abode of the blessed after death.

E·ly·si·um (ĭ-lĭz′ē-əm, ĭ-lĭzh′-) *n.* **1.** *Greek Mythology.* The Elysian Fields. **2.** A place or condition of ideal happiness. [Latin *Ēlysium,* from Greek *Ēlusion (pedion),* Elysian (fields).]

El·y·tis (ĕl′ē-tēs′), **Odysseus.** Born 1911. Greek poet. He won the 1979 Nobel Prize for literature.

el·y·tron (ĕl′ĭ-trŏn′) *n., pl.* **-tra** (-trə). Either of the leathery or chitinous forewings of a beetle or a related insect, serving to encase the thin, membranous hind wings used in flight. Also called *wing case.* [New Latin, from Greek *elutron,* sheath. See **wel-²** in Appendix.] **—el′y·troid′** (-troid′) *adj.*

em (ĕm) *n.* **1.** The letter *m.* **2.** *Abbr.* **m, M** *Printing.* **a.** The width of a square or nearly square piece of type, used as a unit of measure for matter set in that size of type. **b.** Such a measure for 12-point type; a pica.

EM *abbr.* **1.** Electromagnetic. **2.** Electron microscope. **3.** Enlisted man.

E.M. *abbr.* Engineer of Mines.

em–¹ *pref.* Variant of **en–¹.**

em–² *pref.* Variant of **en–².**

'em (əm) *pron. Informal.* Them. [From Middle English *hem,* from Old English *him, heom,* dative and accusative pl. of *hē,* he. See HE¹.]

e·ma·ci·ate (ĭ-mā′shē-āt′) *tr. & intr.v.* **-at·ed, -at·ing, -ates.** To make or become extremely thin, especially as a result of starvation. [Latin *ēmaciāre, ēmaciāt-* : *ē-, ex-,* intensive pref.; see EX– + *maciāre,* to make thin (from *macer,* thin; see **māk-** in Appendix).] **—e·ma′ci·a′tion** *n.*

E-mail (ē′māl′) *n. Computer Science.* See **electronic mail.**

em·a·lan·ge·ni (ĕm′ə-läng-gĕn′ē) *n.* Plural of **lilangeni.**

em·a·nate (ĕm′ə-nāt′) *intr. & tr.v.* **-nat·ed, -nat·ing, -nates.** To come or send forth, as from a source: *light that emanated from a lamp; a stove that emanated a steady heat.* See Synonyms at **stem¹.** [Latin *ēmānāre, ēmānāt-,* to flow out : *ē-, ex-,* ex- + *mānāre,* to flow.] **—em′a·na′tive** *adj.*

em·a·na·tion (ĕm′ə-nā′shən) *n.* **1.** The act or an instance of emanating. **2. a.** Something that issues from a source; an emission. **b.** *Chemistry.* Any of several radioactive gases that are isotopes of radon and are products of radioactive decay. **—em′a·na′tion·al** *adj.*

e·man·ci·pate (ĭ-măn′sə-pāt′) *tr.v.* **-pat·ed, -pat·ing, -pates.** **1.** To free from bondage, oppression, or restraint; liberate. **2.** *Law.* To release (a child) from the control of parents or a guardian. [Latin *ēmancipāre, ēmancipāt-* : *ē-, ex-,* ex- + *mancipium,* ownership (from *manceps,* purchaser; see **man-²** in Appendix).] **—e·man′ci·pa′tive, e·man′ci·pa·to′ry** (-pə-tôr′ē, -tōr′ē) *adj.* **—e·man′ci·pa′tor** *n.*

e·man·ci·pa·tion (ĭ-măn′sə-pā′shən) *n.* **1.** The act or an instance of emancipating. **2.** The state of being emancipated.

e·mar·gi·nate (ĭ-mär′jə-nĭt, -nāt′) *adj.* Having a shallow notch at the tip, as in some petals and leaves. [Latin *ēmarginātus,* past participle of *ēmargināre,* to take the edge away : *ē-, ex-,* ex- + *margō, margin-,* margin; see **merg-** in Appendix.] **—e·mar′gi·na′tion** (-nā′shən) *n.*

e·mas·cu·late (ĭ-măs′kyə-lāt′) *tr.v.* **-lat·ed, -lat·ing, -lates.** **1.** To castrate. **2.** To deprive of strength or vigor; weaken. **—emasculate** (-lĭt) *adj.* Deprived of virility, strength, or vigor. [Latin *ēmasculāre, ēmasculāt-* : *ē-, ex-,* ex- + *masculus,* male, diminutive of *mās,* male, man.] **—e·mas′cu·la′tion** *n.* **—e·mas′cu·la′tive, e·mas′cu·la·to′ry** (-lə-tôr′ē, -tōr′ē) *adj.* **—e·mas′cu·la′tor** *n.*

em·balm (ĕm-bäm′) *tr.v.* **-balmed, -balm·ing, -balms.** **1.** To treat (a corpse) with preservatives in order to prevent decay. **2.** To protect from change or oblivion; preserve or fix: *"A precedent embalms a principle"* (Benjamin Disraeli). **3.** To impart fragrance to; perfume. [Middle English *embaumen,* from Old French *embasmer* : *en-,* in; see EN–¹ + *basme,* balm; see BALM.] **—em·balm′er** *n.* **—em·balm′ment** *n.*

em·bank (ĕm-băngk′) *tr.v.* **-banked, -bank·ing, -banks.** To confine, support, or protect with an embankment.

em·bank·ment (ĕm-băngk′mənt) *n.* **1.** The act of embanking. **2.** A mound of earth or stone built to hold back water or to support a roadway.

em·bar·go (ĕm-bär′gō) *n., pl.* **-goes.** **1.** A government order prohibiting the movement of merchant ships into or out of its ports. **2.** A prohibition by a government on certain or all trade with a foreign nation: *an embargo on the sale of computers to unfriendly nations.* **3.** A prohibition; a ban: *an embargo on criticism.* **—embargo** *tr.v.* **-goed, -go·ing, -goes.** To impose an embargo on. [Spanish, from *embargar,* to impede, from Vulgar Latin **imbarricāre,* to barricade : Latin *in-,* in; see EN–¹ + Vulgar Latin **barricāre,* to barricade (from **barrīca,* barrel, barrier, from **barra,* bar, barrier).]

WORD HISTORY: Could an embargo on alcoholic beverages be related to a bar other than in the obvious way? The words *embargo* and *bar* are related, albeit distantly. *Embargo* comes to us from Spanish, where it was derived from the verb *embargar,* "to arrest, impede." This verb came from the Vulgar Latin word **imbarricāre,* made up of the Latin prefix *in–,* "in, into," and the assumed Vulgar Latin form **barricāre,* derived from Vulgar Latin **barrīca,* "barrier." **Barrīca,* in turn, was derived from Vulgar Latin **barra,* "bar, barrier," the ultimate source of our word *bar. Imbarricāre* meant essentially "to impede with a barrier." Our word *bar* is first recorded in English with the sense "barrier," eventually developing the sense "a counter for serving drinks."

em·bark (ĕm-bärk′) *v.* **-barked, -bark·ing, -barks.** *—tr.* **1.** To cause to board a vessel or aircraft: *stopped to embark passengers.* **2.** To enlist (a person or persons) or invest (capital) in an enterprise. *—intr.* **1.** To go aboard a vessel or aircraft, as at the start of a journey. **2.** To set out on a venture; commence: *embark on a world tour.* [French *embarquer* : *en-,* in; see EN–¹ + *barque,* ship; see BARK³.] **—em′bar·ka′tion, em·bark′ment** *n.*

em·bar·rass (ĕm-băr′əs) *tr.v.* **-rassed, -rass·ing, -rass·es.** **1.** To cause to feel self-conscious or ill at ease; disconcert: *Meeting adults embarrassed the shy child.* **2.** To involve in or hamper with financial difficulties. **3.** To hinder with obstacles or difficulties; impede. **4.** To complicate. [French *embarrasser,* to encumber, hamper, from Spanish *embarazar,* from Italian *imbarazzare,* from *imbarazzo,* obstacle, obstruction, from *imbarrare,* to block, bar : *in-,* in (from Latin; see EN–¹) + Vulgar Latin **barra,* bar.] **—em·bar′rassed·ly** *adv.* **—em·bar′rass·ing·ly** *adv.*

SYNONYMS: *embarrass, abash, chagrin, discomfit, disconcert, faze, rattle.* The central meaning shared by these verbs is "to cause someone to feel self-conscious and uneasy": *was embarrassed by her child's tantrum; felt abashed at the extravagant praise; will be chagrined if his confident prediction fails; was discomfited by the sudden personal question; is disconcerted by sarcastic remarks; refuses to be fazed by your objections; isn't easily rattled before an audience.*

em·bar·rass·ment (ĕm-băr′əs-mənt) *n.* **1.** The act or an instance of embarrassing. **2.** The state of being embarrassed. **3.** A source or cause of being embarrassed. **4.** An overabundance: *an embarrassment of choices at a buffet dinner; an embarrassment of riches.*

em·bas·sage (ĕm′bə-sĭj) *n. Archaic.* An embassy. [Middle English *ambassage,* office or function of an ambassador, possibly variant of *ambassade,* from Old French *ambassade, ambaxade,* from Old Spanish *ambaxada* or Old Provençal *ambaissada,* both from Medieval Latin *ambactiāta,* from *ambactia,* from Latin *ambactus,* servant. See **ag-** in Appendix.]

em·bas·sy (ĕm′bə-sē) *n., pl.* **-sies.** **1.** A building containing the offices of an ambassador and staff. **2.** The position, function, or assignment of an ambassador. **3.** A mission to a foreign government headed by an ambassador. **4.** A staff of diplomatic representatives headed by an ambassador. [Variant of *ambassy,* office or function of an ambassador, from obsolete French *ambassée,* from Medieval Latin *ambactiāta.* See EMBASSAGE.]

em·bat·tle (ĕm-băt′l) *tr.v.* **-tled, -tling, -tles.** **1.** To prepare for battle; array. **2.** To furnish with battlements for defense. [Middle English *embataillen,* from Old French *embataillier* : *en-,* in; see EN–¹ + *batailler,* to battle (from *bataille,* battle; see BATTLE).]

em·bat·tled (ĕm-băt′ld) *adj.* **1.** Prepared or fortified for battle or engaged in battle: *embattled troops; an embattled city.* **2.** Beset with attackers, criticism, or controversy: *an embattled legislative minority; an embattled governor.*

em·bat·tle·ment (ĕm-băt′l-mənt, ĭm-) *n.* See **battlement.**

em·bay (ĕm-bā′) *tr.v.* **-bayed, -bay·ing, -bays.** To put, shelter, or detain in a bay.

em·bay·ment (ĕm-bā′mənt) *n.* **1.** A bay or baylike shape. **2.** The formation of a bay.

em·bed (ĕm-bĕd′) also **im·bed** (ĭm-) *v.* **-bed·ded, -bed·ding, -beds.** *—tr.* **1.** To fix firmly in a surrounding mass: *embed a post in concrete; fossils embedded in shale.* **2.** To enclose snugly or firmly. **3.** To cause to be an integral part of a surrounding whole. **4.** *Biology.* To enclose (a specimen) in a supporting material before sectioning for microscopic examination. *—intr.* To become embedded: *The harpoon struck but did not embed.* **—em·bed′ment** *n.*

em·bel·lish (ĕm-bĕl′ĭsh) *tr.v.* **-lished, -lish·ing, -lish·es.** **1.** To make beautiful, as by ornamentation; decorate. **2.** To add ornamental or fictitious details to: *a fanciful account that embellishes the true story.* [Middle English *embelishen,* from Old French *embellir, embelliss-* : *en-,* causative pref.; see EN–¹ + *bel,* beautiful (from Latin *bellus;* see **deu-²** in Appendix).] **—em·bel′lish·er** *n.*

em·bel·lish·ment (ĕm-bĕl′ĭsh-mənt) *n.* **1.** The act of embellishing or the state of being embellished. **2.** Something that embellishes; a decoration. **3.** *Music.* A note that embellishes a melody.

em•ber (ĕm′bər) *n.* **1.** A small, glowing piece of coal or wood, as in a dying fire. **2. embers.** The smoldering coal or ash of a dying fire. [Middle English *embre,* from Old English *ǣmerge.*]

Em•ber Day (ĕm′bər) *n.* A day reserved for prayer and fasting by some Christian churches, observed on the Wednesday, Friday, and Saturday after the first Sunday of Lent, after Whitsunday, after September 14, and after December 13. [Middle English *ymer daye,* from Old English *ymbrendæg* : *ymbryne,* recurrence, course of time (*ymbe,* around; see **ambhi** in Appendix + *ryne,* a running; see **rei-** in Appendix) + *dæg,* day; see DAY.]

em•bez•zle (ĕm-bĕz′əl) *tr.v.* **-zled, -zling, -zles.** To take (money, for example) for one's own use in violation of a trust. [Middle English *embesilen,* from Anglo-Norman *enbesiler* : Old French *en-,* intensive pref.; see EN–[1] + Old French *besillier,* to ravage.] **—em•bez′zle•ment** *n.* **—em•bez′zler** *n.*

em•bit•ter (ĕm-bĭt′ər) *tr.v.* **-tered, -ter•ing, -ters. 1.** To make bitter in flavor. **2.** To arouse bitter feelings in: *was embittered by years of unrewarded labor.* **—em•bit′ter•ment** *n.*

em•blaze[1] (ĕm-blāz′) *tr.v.* **-blazed, -blaz•ing, -blaz•es. 1.** To set on fire. **2.** To cause to glow; light up.

em•blaze[2] (ĕm-blāz′) *tr.v.* **-blazed, -blaz•ing, -blaz•es.** *Archaic.* **1.** To emblazon. **2.** To decorate lavishly.

em•bla•zon (ĕm-blā′zən) *tr.v.* **-zoned, -zon•ing, -zons. 1.a.** To adorn (a surface) richly with prominent markings: *emblazon a doorway with a coat of arms.* **b.** To inscribe (a prominent marking) on a surface: *emblazon a cross on a banner.* **2.** To make resplendent with brilliant colors. **3.** To make illustrious; celebrate: *emblazoning a heroine's deeds in song.* **—em•bla′zon•er** *n.* **—em•bla′zon•ment** *n.*

em•bla•zon•ry (ĕm-blā′zən-rē) *n., pl.* **-ries. 1.** The act or art of emblazoning. **2.** Colorful or prominent decoration, especially heraldic decoration.

em•blem (ĕm′bləm) *n.* **1.** An object or a representation that functions as a symbol. See Synonyms at **symbol. 2.** A distinctive badge, design, or device: *trucks marked with the company emblem; the emblem of the air force.* **3.** An allegorical picture usually inscribed with a verse or motto presenting a moral lesson. [Middle English, pictorial fable, from Latin *emblēma,* raised ornament, from Greek, embossed design, from *emballein,* to insert, set in : *en-,* in; see EN–[2] + *ballein,* to throw; see **gʷele-** in Appendix.]

em•blem•at•ic (ĕm′blə-măt′ĭk) or **em•blem•at•i•cal** (-ĭ-kəl) *adj.* Of, relating to, or serving as an emblem; symbolic. [French *emblématique,* from Medieval Latin *emblēmaticus,* of an emblem, from Latin *emblēma, emblēmat-,* emblem. See EMBLEM.] **—em′blem•at′i•cal•ly** *adv.*

em•blem•a•tize (ĕm-blĕm′ə-tīz′) also **em•blem•ize** (ĕm′blə-mīz′) *tr.v.* **-tized, -tiz•ing, -tiz•es** also **-ized, -iz•ing, -iz•es.** To represent with or as if with an emblem; symbolize.

em•ble•ments (ĕm′blə-mənts) *pl.n. Law.* The crops or products of the land legally belonging to a tenant. [From Middle English *emblaiment,* from Old French *emblaement,* from *emblaer,* to sow with grain, from Medieval Latin *imblādāre* : Latin *in-,* in; see EN–[1] + Medieval Latin *blādum, blādium,* grain (of Germanic origin; see **bhel-[3]** in Appendix).]

em•blem•ize (ĕm′blə-mīz′) *v.* Variant of **emblematize.**

em•bod•i•ment (ĕm-bŏd′ē-mənt, ĭm-) *n.* **1.** The act of embodying or the state of being embodied. **2.** One that embodies: *"The flag is the embodiment, not of sentiment, but of history"* (Woodrow Wilson).

em•bod•y (ĕm-bŏd′ē) *tr.v.* **-bod•ied, -bod•y•ing, -bod•ies. 1.** To give a bodily form to; incarnate. **2.** To represent in bodily or material form: *"As John Adams embodied the old style, Andrew Jackson embodied the new"* (Richard Hofstadter). **3.** To make part of a system or whole; incorporate: *laws that embody a people's values.*

em•bold•en (ĕm-bōl′dən) *tr.v.* **-ened, -en•ing, -ens.** To foster boldness or courage in; encourage. See Synonyms at **encourage.**

em•bo•lec•to•my (ĕm′bə-lĕk′tə-mē) *n., pl.* **-mies.** Surgical removal of an embolus. [EMBOL(US) + –ECTOMY.]

em•bo•li (ĕm′bə-lī′) *n.* Plural of **embolus.**

em•bol•ic (ĕm-bŏl′ĭk) *adj.* **1.** *Pathology.* Of, relating to, or caused by an embolus or an embolism. **2.** *Embryology.* Of or relating to emboly.

em•bo•lism (ĕm′bə-lĭz′əm) *n.* **1.** Obstruction or occlusion of a blood vessel by an embolus. **2.** An embolus. [Middle English *embolisme,* insertion of one or more days in a calendar, from Late Latin *embolismus,* from Greek *embolismos,* from *emballein,* to insert. See EMBLEM.] **—em′bo•lis′mic** *adj.*

em•bo•lus (ĕm′bə-ləs) *n., pl.* **-li** (-lī′). A mass, such as an air bubble, a detached blood clot, or a foreign body, that travels through the bloodstream and lodges so as to obstruct or occlude a blood vessel. [Latin, piston of a pump, from Greek *embolos,* stopper, plug, from *emballein,* to insert. See EMBLEM.]

em•bo•ly (ĕm′bə-lē) *n., pl.* **-lies.** *Embryology.* The formation of a gastrula from a blastula by invagination. [Greek *embolē,* insertion, from *emballein,* to insert. See EMBLEM.]

em•bon•point (äN′bôN-pwăN′) *n.* The condition of being plump; stoutness. [French, from *en bon point,* in good condition : *en,* in (from Latin *in, in-;* see EN–[1]) + *bon,* good (from Old French; see BOON[2]) + *point,* situation, condition; see POINT.]

em•bos•om (ĕm-bo͝oz′əm, -bo͞o′zəm) *tr.v.* **-omed, -om•ing, -oms. 1.** To enclose protectively; envelop. **2.** *Archaic.* To clasp to or hold in the bosom.

em•boss (ĕm-bôs′, -bŏs′) *tr.v.* **-bossed, -boss•ing, -boss•es. 1.** To mold or carve in relief: *emboss a design on a coin.* **2.** To decorate with or as if with a raised design: *emboss leather.* **3.** To adorn; decorate. **4.** To cover with many protuberances; stud: *"The whole buoy was embossed with barnacles"* (Herman Melville). [Middle English *embosen,* from Old French *embocer* : *en-,* in; see EN–[1] + *boce,* knob.] **—em•boss′er** *n.*

em•boss•ment (ĕm-bôs′mənt, -bŏs′-) *n.* **1.** The act or process of embossing or the condition of being embossed. **2.** Embossed ornamentation. **3.** The distance between the nondeformed part of a document surface and a specified point on a printed character in optical character recognition.

em•bou•chure (äm′bo͞o-sho͝or′) *n.* **1.** The mouth of a river. **2.** *Music.* **a.** The mouthpiece of a wind instrument. **b.** The manner in which the lips and tongue are applied to such a mouthpiece. [French, from *emboucher,* to put or go into the mouth, from Old French : *en-,* in; see EN–[1] + *bouche,* mouth (from Latin *bucca,* cheek).]

em•bour•geoise•ment (ĕm-bo͝or′zhwäz-mənt, -mänt′) *n.* Conversion to bourgeois values, loyalties, or tastes: *"The Soviet party, despite a new appearance of embourgeoisement, remained tightly faithful to Soviet discipline"* (New York Times). [French, from *bourgeois,* bourgeois. See BOURGEOIS.]

em•bowed (ĕm-bōd′) *adj.* **1.** Bent or curved like a bow. **2.** *Architecture.* **a.** Having an arch or arches. **b.** Protruding in an outward curve so as to form a recess within.

em•bow•el (ĕm-bou′əl) *tr.v.* **-eled, -el•ing, -els** or **-elled, -el•ling, -els. 1.** To disembowel. **2.** *Obsolete.* To enclose. [Obsolete French *emboueler* : *en-,* intensive pref.; see EN–[1] + Old French *boeler* (from *boel, bouele,* entrails; see BOWEL). Sense 2 : EN–[1] + BOWEL.]

em•bow•er (ĕm-bou′ər) *tr.v.* **-ered, -er•ing, -ers.** To enclose in or as if in a bower.

em•brace (ĕm-brās′) *v.* **-braced, -brac•ing, -brac•es.** —*tr.* **1.** To clasp or hold close with the arms, usually as an expression of affection. **2.a.** To surround; enclose: *We allowed the warm water to embrace us.* **b.** To twine around: *a trellis that was embraced by vines.* **3.** To include as part of something broader. See Synonyms at **include. 4.** To take up willingly or eagerly: *embrace a social cause.* **5.** To avail oneself of: *"I only regret, in my chilled age, certain occasions and possibilities I didn't embrace"* (Henry James). —*intr.* To join in an embrace. **—embrace** *n.* **1.** An act of holding close with the arms, usually as an expression of affection; a hug. **2.** An enclosure or encirclement: *caught in the jungle's embrace.* **3.** Eager acceptance: *your embrace of Catholicism.* [Middle English *embracen,* from Old French *embracer* : *en-,* in; see EN–[1] + *brace,* the two arms; see BRACE.] **—em•brace′a•ble** *adj.* **—em•brace′ment** *n.*

em•brace•or or **em•brac•er** (ĕm-brā′sər) *n. Law.* One guilty of attempting to influence a court illegally. [Middle English *imbrasour,* from Anglo-Norman *embraceor,* probably from *embracer,* to embrace, incite, influence a court by illegal means, from Old French. See EMBRACE.]

em•brac•er[1] (ĕm-brā′sər) *n.* One that embraces: *an embracer of novel ideas.*

em•brac•er[2] (ĕm-brā′sər) *n. Law.* Variant of **embraceor.**

em•brac•er•y (ĕm-brā′sə-rē) *n., pl.* **-ies.** *Law.* An attempt to corrupt a jury, as with bribery. [Middle English *embracerie,* from *embracen,* to influence a jury by illegal means, to embrace. See EMBRACE.]

em•branch•ment (ĕm-brănch′mənt) *n.* **1.** A branching out, as of a mountain range or river. **2.** A branch or ramification.

em•bran•gle (ĕm-brăng′gəl) *tr.v.* **-gled, -gling, -gles.** To entangle; embroil. [EN–[1] + dialectal *brangle,* to shake, waver, confuse (variant of *branle, brandle,* from French *branler,* from Old French *brandeler,* perhaps from *brand,* sword; see BRANDISH).] **—em•bran′gle•ment** *n.*

em•bra•sure (ĕm-brā′zhər) *n.* **1.** An opening in a thick wall for a door or window, especially one with sides angled so that the opening is larger on the inside of the wall than on the outside. **2.** A flared opening for a gun in a wall or parapet. [French, from *embraser,* to widen an opening.] **—em•bra′sured** *adj.*

em•brit•tle (ĕm-brĭt′l) *tr. & intr.v.* **-tled, -tling, -tles.** To make or become brittle. **—em•brit′tle•ment** *n.*

em•bro•cate (ĕm′brə-kāt′) *tr.v.* **-cat•ed, -cat•ing, -cates.** To moisten and rub (a part of the body) with a liniment or lotion. [Medieval Latin *embrocāre, embrocāt-,* from Late Latin *embrocha,* lotion, from Greek *embrokhē,* from *embrekhein,* to foment : *en-,* in; see EN–[2] + *brekhein,* to wet.]

em•bro•ca•tion (ĕm′brə-kā′shən) *n.* **1.** The act or process of moistening and rubbing a part of the body with a liniment or lotion. **2.** A liniment or lotion.

em•broi•der (ĕm-broi′dər) *v.* **-dered, -der•ing, -ders.** —*tr.* **1.** To ornament with needlework: *embroider a pillow cover.* **2.** To make by means of needlework: *embroider a design on a bedspread.* **3.** To add embellishments or fanciful details to: *embroider the truth.* —*intr.* **1.** To make needlework. **2.** To add embellishments or fanciful details. [Middle English *embrouderen,* partly from *embrouden* (from *brouden, broiden,* braided, embroi-

emblem
International medical alert emblem

ă pat	oi boy
ā pay	ou out
âr care	o͝o took
ä father	o͞o boot
ĕ pet	ŭ cut
ē be	ûr urge
ĭ pit	th thin
ī pie	*th* this
îr pier	hw which
ŏ pot	zh vision
ō toe	ə about, item
ô paw	♦ regionalism

Stress marks: ′ (primary); ′ (secondary), as in **dictionary** (dĭk′shə-nĕr′ē)

dered, from Old English *brogden,* past participle of *bregdan,* to weave; see BRAID) and partly from Old French *embroder* (*en-,* intensive pref.; see EN–[1] + *broder, brosder,* to embroider, of Germanic origin).] —**em·broi′der·er** *n.*

em·broi·der·y (ĕm-broi′də-rē) *n., pl.* **-ies. 1.** The act or art of embroidering. **2.** Ornamentation of fabric with needlework. **3.** A piece of embroidered fabric. **4.** Embellishment with fanciful details.

em·broil (ĕm-broil′) *tr.v.* **-broiled, -broil·ing, -broils. 1.** To involve in argument, contention, or hostile actions: *"Avoid . . . any step that may embroil us with Great Britain"* (Alexander Hamilton). **2.** To throw into confusion or disorder; entangle. [French *embrouiller* : *en-,* intensive pref.; see EN–[1] + *brouiller,* to confuse (from Old French; see BROIL[2]).] —**em·broil′ment** *n.*

em·brown (ĕm-broun′) *tr.v.* **-browned, -brown·ing, -browns. 1.** To make brown or dusky. **2.** To darken.

em·brue (ĕm-bro͞o′) *v.* Variant of **imbrue.**

em·bry·ec·to·my (ĕm′brē-ĕk′tə-mē) *n., pl.* **-mies.** Surgical removal of an embryo, especially one implanted outside of the uterus.

em·bry·o (ĕm′brē-ō′) *n., pl.* **-os. 1.a.** An organism in its early stages of development, especially before it has reached a distinctively recognizable form. **b.** An organism at any time before full development, birth, or hatching. **2.a.** The fertilized egg of a vertebrate animal following cleavage. **b.** In human beings, the prefetal product of conception from implantation through the eighth week of development. **3.** *Botany.* The minute, rudimentary plant contained within a seed or an archegonium. **4.** A rudimentary or beginning stage: *"To its founding fathers, the European* [Economic] *Community was the embryo of the United States of Europe"* (Economist). [Medieval Latin *embryō,* from Greek *embruon* : *en-,* in; see EN–[2] + *bruein,* to be full to bursting.]

embroidery
Crewelwork

em·bry·o·gen·e·sis (ĕm′brē-ō-jĕn′ĭ-sĭs) also **em·bry·og·e·ny** (-ŏj′ə-nē) *n.* The development and growth of an embryo. —**em′bry·o·gen′ic** (-jĕn′ĭk), **em′bry·o·ge·net′ic** (-ō-jə-nĕt′ĭk) *adj.*

em·bry·oid (ĕm′brē-oid′) *n.* A minute plant or animal form that resembles an embryo. —**embryoid** *adj.* Resembling an embryo.

em·bry·ol·o·gy (ĕm′brē-ŏl′ə-jē) *n.* **1.** The branch of biology that deals with the formation, early growth, and development of living organisms. **2.** The embryonic structure or development of a particular organism. —**em′bry·o·log′ic** (-ə-lŏj′ĭk), **em′bry·o·log′i·cal** *adj.* —**em′bry·o·log′i·cal·ly** *adv.* —**em′bry·ol′o·gist** *n.*

em·bry·on·ic (ĕm′brē-ŏn′ĭk) also **em·bry·on·al** (ĕm′brē-ə-nəl) *adj.* **1.** Of, relating to, or being an embryo. **2.** Also **em·bry·ot·ic** (-ŏt′ĭk). Rudimentary; incipient: *an embryonic nation, not yet self-governing.* —**em′bry·on′ic·al·ly** *adv.*

embryonic disk *n.* **1.** A platelike mass of cells in the blastocyst from which a mammalian embryo develops. Also called *embryonic shield.* **2.** See **germinal disk.**

embryonic membrane *n.* Any of the membranous structures associated with or surrounding a developing vertebrate embryo, including the amnion, chorion, allantois, and yolk sac.

embryonic shield *n.* See **embryonic disk** (sense 1).

em·bry·op·a·thy (ĕm′brē-ŏp′ə-thē) *n., pl.* **-thies.** A developmental disorder in an embryo.

embryo sac *n.* The female gametophyte of a seed plant, within which the embryo develops.

em·bry·ot·ic (ĕm′brē-ŏt′ĭk) *adj.* Variant of **embryonic** (sense 2).

em·cee (ĕm′sē′) *n.* A master of ceremonies. —**emcee** *v.* **-ceed, -cee·ing, -cees.** —*tr.* To serve as master of ceremonies of: *emcee a variety show.* —*intr.* To act as master of ceremonies. [Pronunciation of *M.C.,* abbr. of *master of ceremonies.*]

–eme *suff.* A distinctive unit of linguistic structure: *semanteme.* [French *-ème,* from *phonème,* phoneme. See PHONEME.]

e·mend (ĭ-mĕnd′) *tr.v.* **e·mend·ed, e·mend·ing, e·mends.** To improve by critical editing: *emend a faulty text.* [Middle English *emenden,* from Latin *ēmendāre* : *ē-, ex-,* ex- + *mendum,* defect, fault.] —**e·mend′er** *n.*

e·men·date (ē′mĕn-dāt′, ĭ-mĕn′-) *tr.v.* **-dat·ed, -dat·ing, -dates.** To make textual corrections in. [Latin *ēmendāre, ēmendāt-,* to emend. See EMEND.] —**e′men·da′tor** (-dā′tər) *n.* —**e·men′da·to′ry** (ĭ-mĕn′də-tôr′ē, -tōr′ē) *adj.*

e·men·da·tion (ĭ-mĕn′dā′shən, ē′mĕn-) *n.* **1.** The act of emending. **2.** An alteration intended to improve: *textual emendations made by the editor.*

emer. *abbr.* Emerita; emeritus.

em·er·ald (ĕm′ər-əld, ĕm′rəld) *n.* **1.** A brilliant green to grass-green transparent variety of beryl, used as a gemstone. **2.** *Color.* A strong yellowish green. —**emerald** *adj. Color.* Of a strong yellowish green. [Middle English *emeraude,* from Old French, from Medieval Latin *esmeralda, esmeraldus,* from Latin *smaragdus,* from Greek *smaragdos.*]

e·merge (ĭ-mûrj′) *intr.v.* **e·merged, e·merg·ing, e·merg·es. 1.** To rise from or as if from immersion: *Sea mammals must emerge periodically to breathe.* **2.** To come forth from obscurity: *new leaders who may emerge.* **3.** To become evident: *The truth emerged at the inquest.* **4.** To come into existence. See Synonyms at **appear.** [Latin *ēmergere* : *ē-, ex-,* ex- + *mergere,* to immerse.]

e·mer·gence (ĭ-mûr′jəns) *n.* **1.** The act or process of emerging. **2.** *Botany.* A superficial outgrowth of plant tissue, such as the prickle of a rose.

e·mer·gen·cy (ĭ-mûr′jən-sē) *n., pl.* **-cies. 1.** A serious situation or occurrence that happens unexpectedly and demands immediate action. **2.** A condition of urgent need for action or assistance: *a state of emergency; a voice full of emergency.* —**emergency** *adj.* For use during emergencies: *emergency food rations.*

emergency brake *n.* A separate brake system in a vehicle for use in case of failure of the regular brakes and commonly used as a parking brake. Also called *hand brake.*

emergency medical technician *n. Abbr.* **EMT** A person trained and certified to appraise and initiate the administration of emergency care for victims of trauma or acute illness before or during transportation of the victims to a health care facility via ambulance or aircraft.

emergency medicine *n.* The branch of medicine that deals with evaluation and initial treatment of medical conditions caused by trauma or sudden illness.

emergency room *n. Abbr.* **ER** The section of a health care facility intended to provide rapid treatment for victims of sudden illness or trauma.

e·mer·gent (ĭ-mûr′jənt) *adj.* **1.a.** Coming into view, existence, or notice: *emergent spring shoots; an emergent political leader.* **b.** Emerging: *emergent nations.* **2.** Rising above a surrounding medium, especially a fluid. **3.** Demanding prompt action; urgent. **4.** Occurring as a consequence; resultant. —**emergent** *n.* One that is coming into view or existence: *"The giant redwoods . . . outstrip the emergents of the rain forest, which rarely reach two hundred feet"* (Catherine Caulfield).

emergent evolution *n.* A theory holding that completely new types of organisms and characteristics appear at certain stages of the evolutionary process, usually as a result of an unpredictable rearrangement of the preexisting elements.

e·merg·ing (ĭ-mûr′jĭng) *adj.* Newly formed or just coming into prominence; emergent: *emerging markets; the emerging states of Africa.*

e·mer·i·ta (ĭ-mĕr′ĭ-tə) *adj. Abbr.* **emer.** Retired but retaining an honorary title corresponding to that held immediately before retirement. Used of a woman: *a professor emerita.* —**emerita** *n., pl.* **-tae** (-tē′) or **-tas.** A woman who is retired but retains an honorary title corresponding to that held immediately before retirement. [Latin *ēmerita,* feminine of *ēmeritus.* See EMERITUS.]

e·mer·i·tus (ĭ-mĕr′ĭ-təs) *adj. Abbr.* **emer.** Retired but retaining an honorary title corresponding to that held immediately before retirement: *a professor emeritus.* —**emeritus** *n., pl.* **-ti** (-tī′). One who is retired but retains an honorary title corresponding to that held immediately before retirement. [Latin *ēmeritus,* past participle of *ēmerērī,* to earn by service : *ē-, ex-,* from; see EX– + *merērī,* to deserve, earn; see **(s)mer-**[2] in Appendix.]

e·mersed (ĭ-mûrst′) *adj. Botany.* Rising above the surface of water: *emersed aquatic plants.* [From Latin *ēmersus.* See EMERSION.]

e·mer·sion (ĭ-mûr′zhən, -shən) *n.* The act of emerging; emergence. [From Latin *ēmersus,* past participle of *ēmergere,* to emerge. See EMERGE.]

Em·er·son (ĕm′ər-sən), **Ralph Waldo.** 1803–1882. American writer, philosopher, and central figure of American transcendentalism. His poems, orations, and essays are regarded as landmarks in the development of American thought and literary expression. —**Em′er·so′ni·an** (-sō′nē-ən) *adj.*

em·er·y (ĕm′ə-rē, ĕm′rē) *n.* A fine-grained impure corundum used for grinding and polishing. [Middle English, from Old French *emeri, emeril,* from Late Latin *smericulum,* from Greek *smiris.*]

emery board *n.* A nail file consisting of a strip of cardboard coated with powdered emery.

em·e·sis (ĕm′ĭ-sĭs) *n., pl.* **-ses** (-sēz′). The act of vomiting. [Greek, from *emein,* to vomit. See **wemə-** in Appendix.]

e·met·ic (ĭ-mĕt′ĭk) *adj.* Causing vomiting. —**emetic** *n.* An agent that causes vomiting. [Latin *emetica,* feminine of *emeticus,* provoking vomiting, from Greek *emetikos,* from *emetos,* vomiting, from *emein,* to vomit. See **wemə-** in Appendix.] —**e·met′i·cal·ly** *adv.*

em·e·tine (ĕm′ĭ-tēn′) *n.* A bitter-tasting crystalline alkaloid, $C_{29}H_{40}N_2O_4$, derived from ipecac root and used in the treatment of amebiasis and as an emetic. [French *émétine,* from *émétique,* emetic, from Latin *emeticus.* See EMETIC.]

emf or **EMF** *abbr.* Electromotive force.

EMG *abbr.* Electromyogram.

–emia or **–hemia, –aemia** or **–haemia** *suff.* Blood: *leukemia.* [New Latin, from Greek *-aimia,* from *haima,* blood. See HEMO–.]

em·i·grant (ĕm′ĭ-grənt) *n.* One that emigrates. —**emigrant** *adj.* Of or relating to emigrants or the act of emigrating.

em·i·grate (ĕm′ĭ-grāt′) *intr.v.* **-grat·ed, -grat·ing, -grates.** To leave one country or region to settle in another. See Usage Note at **migrate.** [Latin *ēmigrāre, ēmigrāt-* : *ē-, ex-,* ex- + *migrāre,* to move; see **mei-**[1] in Appendix.] —**em′i·gra′tion** (ĕm′ĭ-grā′shən) *n.*

é·mi·gré (ĕm′ĭ-grā′) *n.* One who has left a native country, especially for political reasons. [French, from past participle of *émigrer,* to emigrate, from Latin *ēmigrāre.* See EMIGRATE.]

E·mi·lia-Ro·ma·gna (ĕ-mēl′yə-rō-mä′nyä). A region of northern Italy bordering on the Adriatic Sea. Named for the Aemilian Way, a Roman road laid out in 187 B.C. that connected Piacenza with Rimini, the area became part of the kingdom of Italy in 1861.

em·i·nence (ĕm′ə-nəns) *n.* **1.** A position of great distinction or superiority: *rose to eminence as a surgeon.* **2.** A rise of ground; a hill. **3.a.** A person of high station or great achievements. **b.** Also **Eminence.** *Roman Catholic Church.* Used with *His* or *Your* as a title and form of address for a cardinal.

é·mi·nence grise (ā-mē-näns grēz′) *n., pl.* **é·mi·nence grises** (ā-mē-näns grēz′). A powerful adviser or decision-maker who operates secretly or unofficially. Also called *gray eminence.* [French, the power behind the throne : *éminence,* power + *gris,* gray, shadowy.]

em·i·nen·cy (ĕm′ə-nən-sē) *n., pl.* **-cies.** Eminence.

em·i·nent (ĕm′ə-nənt) *adj.* **1.** Towering or standing out above others; prominent: *an eminent peak.* **2.** Of high rank, station, or quality; noteworthy: *eminent members of the community.* **3.** Outstanding, as in character or performance; distinguished: *an eminent historian.* See Synonyms at **noted.** [Middle English, from Latin *ēminēns, ēminent-,* present participle of *ēminēre,* to stand out : *ē-, ex-,* ex- + *-minēre,* to jut out; see **men-**[2] in Appendix.] **—em′i·nent·ly** *adv.*

eminent domain *n. Law.* The right of a government to appropriate private property for public use, usually with compensation to the owner.

e·mir (ĭ-mîr′, ā-mîr′) also **a·mir** (ə-mîr′, ā-mîr′) *n.* A prince, chieftain, or governor, especially in the Middle East. [French *émir,* from Arabic *'amīr,* commander, from *'amara,* to command.]

e·mir·ate (ĭ-mîr′ĭt, -āt′) *n.* **1.** The office of an emir. **2.** The nation or territory ruled by an emir.

em·is·sar·y (ĕm′ĭ-sĕr′ē) *n., pl.* **-ies.** An agent sent on a mission to represent or advance the interests of another. [Latin *ēmissārius,* from *ēmissus,* past participle of *ēmittere,* to send out. See EMIT.]

e·mis·sion (ĭ-mĭsh′ən) *n.* **1.** The act or an instance of emitting. **2.** Something emitted. **3.** A substance discharged into the air, especially by an internal combustion engine. [Latin *ēmissiō, ēmissiōn-,* a sending out, from *ēmissus,* past participle of *ēmittere,* to send out. See EMIT.]

emission nebula *n.* A nebula that absorbs ultraviolet radiation from stars and reemits it as visible light.

emission spectrum *n.* The spectrum of bright lines, bands, or continuous radiation characteristic of and determined by a specific emitting substance subjected to a specific kind of excitation.

e·mis·sive (ĭ-mĭs′ĭv) *adj.* Having the power or tendency to emit matter or energy; emitting.

em·is·siv·i·ty (ĕm′ĭ-sĭv′ĭ-tē) *n.* The ratio of the radiation emitted by a surface to the radiation emitted by a blackbody at the same temperature.

e·mit (ĭ-mĭt′) *tr.v.* **e·mit·ted, e·mit·ting, e·mits. 1.** To give or send out matter or energy: *isotopes that emit radioactive particles; a stove emitting heat.* **2.a.** To give out as sound; utter: *"She emitted her small strange laugh"* (Edith Wharton). **b.** To voice; express: *emit an opinion.* **3.** To issue with authority, especially to put (currency) into circulation. [Latin *ēmittere,* to send out : *ē-, ex-,* ex- + *mittere,* to send.] **—e·mit′ter** *n.*

em·men·a·gogue (ĭ-mĕn′ə-gôg′, -gŏg′) *n.* A drug or an agent that induces or hastens menstrual flow. [Greek *emmēna,* the menses (from neuter pl. of *emmēnos,* monthly : *en-,* in; see EN–[2] + *mēn,* month; see **mē-**[2] in Appendix) + –AGOGUE.]

em·mer (ĕm′ər) *n.* A Eurasian wheat *(Triticum dicoccum)* first cultivated by the Babylonians and now widely grown as a cereal grain and as livestock feed. Also called *starch wheat, two-grained spelt.* [German, from Old High German *amaro.*]

em·met (ĕm′ĭt) *n. Archaic.* An ant. [Middle English *emete,* from Old English *ǣmete.*]

em·me·tro·pi·a (ĕm′ĭ-trō′pē-ə) *n.* The condition of the normal eye when parallel rays are focused exactly on the retina and vision is perfect. [Greek *emmetros,* well-proportioned, fitting (*en,* in; see EN–[2] + *metron,* measure; see METER[2]) + –OPIA.] **—em′me·trop′ic** (-trŏp′ĭk, -trō′pĭk) *adj.*

Em·my (ĕm′ē) *n., pl.* **-mys.** A statuette awarded annually by the Academy of Television Arts and Sciences for outstanding achievement in television. [Possibly alteration (influenced by the name *Emmy,* diminutive of *Emma*) of *immy,* alteration of *image orthicon.*]

em·o·din (ĕm′ə-dĭn′) *n.* An orange crystalline compound, $C_{14}H_4O_2(OH)_3CH_3$, obtained from rhubarb and other plants and used as a laxative. [New Latin *ēmōdi,* a species of rhubarb (from Greek *Ēmōdos,* the Himalayas) + –IN.]

e·mol·lient (ĭ-mŏl′yənt) *adj.* **1.** Softening and soothing, especially to the skin. **2.** Making less harsh or abrasive; mollifying: *the emollient approach of a diplomatic mediator.* **—emollient** *n.* **1.** An agent that softens or soothes the skin. **2.** An agent that assuages or mollifies. [Latin *ēmolliēns, ēmollient-,* present participle of *ēmollīre,* to soften : *ē-, ex-,* intensive pref.; see EX– + *mollīre,* to soften (from *mollis,* soft; see **mel-**[1] in Appendix).]

e·mol·u·ment (ĭ-mŏl′yə-mənt) *n.* Payment for an office or employment; compensation. [Middle English, from Latin *ēmolumentum,* gain, originally a miller's fee for grinding grain, from *ēmolere,* to grind out : *ē-, ex-,* ex- + *molere,* to grind; see **melə-** in Appendix.]

e·mote (ĭ-mōt′) *intr.v.* **e·mot·ed, e·mot·ing, e·motes.** To express emotion, especially in an excessive or theatrical manner: *"The more she emotes, the less he listens, and the less he listens, the more strident and emotive she becomes"* (Maggie Scarf). [Back-formation from EMOTION.] **—e·mot′er** *n.*

e·mo·tion (ĭ-mō′shən) *n.* **1.** An intense mental state that arises subjectively rather than through conscious effort and is often accompanied by physiological changes; a strong feeling: *the emotions of joy, sorrow, reverence, hate, and love.* **2.** A state of mental agitation or disturbance: *spoke unsteadily in a voice that betrayed his emotion.* See Synonyms at **feeling. 3.** The part of the consciousness that involves feeling; sensibility: *"The very essence of literature is the war between emotion and intellect"* (Isaac Bashevis Singer). [French *émotion,* from Old French *esmovoir,* to excite, from Vulgar Latin **exmovēre* : Latin *ex-,* ex- + Latin *movēre,* to move; see **meuə-** in Appendix.]

e·mo·tion·al (ĭ-mō′shə-nəl) *adj.* **1.** Of or relating to emotion: *an emotional illness; emotional crises.* **2.** Readily affected with or stirred by emotion: *an emotional person who often weeps.* **3.** Arousing or intended to arouse the emotions: *an emotional appeal.* **4.** Marked by or exhibiting emotion: *an emotional farewell.* **—e·mo′tion·al′i·ty** (-shə-năl′ĭ-tē) *n.* **—e·mo′tion·al·ly** *adv.*

e·mo·tion·al·ism (ĭ-mō′shə-nə-lĭz′əm) *n.* **1.** An inclination to rely on or place too much value on emotion. **2.** Undue display of emotion.

e·mo·tion·al·ist (ĭ-mō′shə-nə-lĭst) *n.* **1.** One whose conduct, thought, or rhetoric is governed by emotion rather than reason, often as a matter of policy. **2.** An excessively emotional person. **—e·mo′tion·al·is′tic** *adj.*

e·mo·tion·al·ize (ĭ-mō′shə-nə-līz′) *tr.v.* **-ized, -iz·ing, -iz·es.** To impart an emotional quality to.

e·mo·tion·less (ĭ-mō′shən-lĭs) *adj.* Devoid of emotion; impassive. **—e·mo′tion·less·ness** *n.*

e·mo·tive (ĭ-mō′tĭv) *adj.* **1.** Of or relating to emotion: *the emotive aspect of symbols.* **2.** Characterized by, expressing, or exciting emotion: *an emotive trial lawyer; the emotive issue of nuclear disarmament.* **—e·mo′tive·ly** *adv.* **—e·mo′tive·ness, e′mo·tiv′i·ty** (ē′mō-tĭv′ĭ-tē) *n.*

EMP *abbr.* Electromagnetic pulse.

emp. *abbr.* Emperor; empire; empress.

em·pale (ĕm-pāl′) *v.* Variant of **impale.**

em·pa·na·da (ĕm′pə-nä′də, -pä-nä′thä) *n.* A Spanish or Latin-American turnover with a flaky crust and a spicy or sweet filling. [Spanish, from past participle of *empanar,* to coat with breadcrumbs : *en-,* in (from Latin *in-;* see EN–[1]) + *pan,* bread; see PANADA.]

em·pan·el (ĕm-păn′əl) *v. Law.* Variant of **impanel.**

em·pa·thet·ic (ĕm′pə-thĕt′ĭk) *adj.* Empathic. **—em′pa·thet′i·cal·ly** *adv.*

em·path·ic (ĕm-păth′ĭk) *adj.* Of, relating to, or characterized by empathy.

em·pa·thize (ĕm′pə-thīz′) *intr.v.* **-thized, -thiz·ing, -thiz·es.** To feel or experience empathy: *empathized with the striking miners.* **—em′pa·thiz′er** *n.*

em·pa·thy (ĕm′pə-thē) *n.* **1.** Identification with and understanding of another's situation, feelings, and motives. See Synonyms at **pity. 2.** The attribution of one's own feelings to an object. [EN–[2] + –PATHY (translation of German *Einfühlung*).]

Em·ped·o·cles (ĕm-pĕd′ə-klēz′). Fifth century B.C. Greek philosopher who believed that all matter is composed of elemental particles of fire, water, earth, and air.

em·pen·nage (ĕm′pə-nĭj) *n.* The tail of an airplane. [French, feathers on an arrow, empennage, from *empenner,* to feather an arrow : *en-,* in; see EN–[1] + *penne,* feather (from Latin *penna;* see **pet-** in Appendix).]

em·per·or (ĕm′pər-ər) *n.* **1.** *Abbr.* **emp.** The male ruler of an empire. **2.a.** The emperor butterfly. **b.** The emperor moth. [Middle English *emperour,* from Old French *empereor,* from Latin *imperātor,* from *imperāre,* to command : *in-,* in; see EN–[1] + *parāre,* to prepare; see **perə-**[1] in Appendix.] **—em′per·or·ship′** *n.*

emperor butterfly *n.* Any of several brightly colored butterflies of the family Nymphalidae, such as *Asterocampa clyton,* having orange-tawny wings with dark markings.

emperor moth *n.* Any of several moths of the family Saturnidae, especially *Saturnia pavonia* of Eurasia, having distinctively patterned wings.

emperor penguin *n.* A large penguin *(Aptenodytes forsteri)* of Antarctic regions, having yellow-orange patches on the neck.

em·per·y (ĕm′pə-rē) *n., pl.* **-ies.** Absolute dominion or jurisdiction; sovereignty. [Middle English *emperie,* from Old French, from Latin *imperium.* See EMPIRE.]

em·pha·sis (ĕm′fə-sĭs) *n., pl.* **-ses** (-sēz′). **1.** Special forcefulness of expression that gives importance to something singled out; stress: *a lecture on housekeeping with emphasis on neatness; paused for emphasis, then announced the winner's name.* **2.** Special attention or effort directed toward something: *a small-town newspaper's emphasis on local affairs.* **3.** Prominence given to a syllable, word, or words, as by raising the voice or printing in italic type. [Latin, from Greek, from *emphainein,* to exhibit, dis-

ă pat	oi boy
ā pay	ou out
âr care	ŏŏ took
ä father	ōō boot
ĕ pet	ŭ cut
ē be	ûr urge
ĭ pit	th thin
ī pie	*th* this
îr pier	hw which
ŏ pot	zh vision
ō toe	ə about, item
ô paw	♦ regionalism

Stress marks: ′ (primary); ′ (secondary), as in **dictionary** (dĭk′shə-nĕr′ē)

play : *en-*, in; see EN–[2] + *phainein,* to show; see **bhā-**[1] in Appendix.]

SYNONYMS: *emphasis, accent, stress.* The central meaning shared by these nouns is "special weight placed on something considered important": *laid a strong emphasis on the study of foreign languages; opposition to nuclear power plants, with the accent on total elimination; lay heavy stress on law and order.*

em·pha·size (ĕm′fə-sīz′) *tr.v.* **-sized, -siz·ing, -siz·es.** To give emphasis to; stress. [From EMPHASIS.]

em·phat·ic (ĕm-făt′ĭk) *adj.* **1.** Expressed or performed with emphasis: *responded with an emphatic "no."* **2.** Forceful and definite in expression or action. **3.** Standing out in a striking and clearly defined way. [Medieval Latin *emphaticus,* from Greek *emphatikos,* from *emphainein,* to exhibit, display. See EMPHASIS.] **—em·phat′i·cal·ly** *adv.*

em·phy·se·ma (ĕm′fĭ-sē′mə, -zē′-) *n.* **1.** A pathological condition of the lungs marked by an abnormal increase in the size of the air spaces, resulting in labored breathing and an increased susceptibility to infection. It can be caused by irreversible expansion of the alveoli or by the destruction of alveolar walls. **2.** An abnormal distention of body tissues caused by retention of air. [Greek *emphusēma,* inflation, from *emphusan,* to blow in : *en-,* in; see EN–[2] + *phūsān,* to blow (from *phusa,* bellows, bladder).] **—em′phy·sem′a·tous** (-sĕm′ə-təs, -sē′mə-, -zĕm′ə-, -zē′mə-) *adj.* **—em′phy·se′mic** *adj. & n.*

em·pire (ĕm′pīr′) *n.* **1.** *Abbr.* **emp. a.** A political unit having an extensive territory or comprising a number of territories or nations and ruled by a single supreme authority. **b.** The territory included in such a unit. **2.** An extensive enterprise under a unified authority: *a publishing empire.* **3.** Imperial or imperialistic sovereignty, domination, or control: *"There is a growing sense that the course of empire is shifting toward the . . . Asians"* (James Traub). [Middle English, from Old French, from Latin *imperium,* from *imperāre,* to command. See EMPEROR.]

Em·pire (ŏm-pîr′, ĕm′pīr′) *adj.* Of, relating to, or characteristic of a neoclassic style, as in clothing or the decorative arts, prevalent in France during the first part of the 19th century. [After the First *Empire* of France (1804–1815).]

Empire
Top: Detail of *Comtesse Daru,* 1810, by Jacques Louis David
Bottom: c. 1810 American couch by Samuel McIntire (1757–1811)

em·pir·ic (ĕm-pîr′ĭk) *n.* **1.** One who is guided by practical experience rather than precepts or theory. **2.** An unqualified or dishonest practitioner; a charlatan. [Latin *empiricus,* from Greek *empeirikos,* experienced, from *empeiros,* skilled : *en-,* in; see EN–[2] + *peiran,* to try (from *peira,* try, attempt; see **per-**[3] in Appendix).]

em·pir·i·cal (ĕm-pîr′ĭ-kəl) *adj.* **1.a.** Relying on or derived from observation or experiment: *empirical results that supported the hypothesis.* **b.** Verifiable or provable by means of observation or experiment: *empirical laws.* **2.** Guided by practical experience and not theory, especially in medicine. **—em·pir′i·cal·ly** *adv.*

empirical formula *n.* A chemical formula that indicates the relative proportions of the elements in a molecule rather than the actual number of atoms of the elements.

em·pir·i·cism (ĕm-pîr′ĭ-sĭz′əm) *n.* **1.** The view that experience, especially of the senses, is the only source of knowledge. **2.a.** Employment of empirical methods, as in science. **b.** An empirical conclusion. **3.** The practice of medicine that disregards scientific theory and relies solely on practical experience. **—em·pir′i·cist** *n.*

em·place (ĕm-plās′) *tr.v.* **-placed, -plac·ing, -plac·es.** To put into place or position: *emplace a fortification on the hilltop.*

em·place·ment (ĕm-plās′mənt) *n.* **1.** A prepared position, such as a mounting or silo, for a military weapon. **2.** The act of putting into a certain position; placement. **3.** Position; location. [French, from obsolete *emplacer,* to place in position : *en-,* in; see EN–[1] + Old French *place,* open space; see PLACE.]

em·plane (ĕm-plān′) *v.* Variant of **enplane.**

em·ploy (ĕm-ploi′) *tr.v.* **-ployed, -ploy·ing, -ploys. 1.a.** To engage the services of; put to work: *agreed to employ the job applicant.* **b.** To provide with gainful work: *factories that employ thousands.* **2.** To put to use or service. See Synonyms at **use. 3.** To devote (time, for example) to an activity or purpose: *employed much time and energy to the hobby.* **—employ** *n.* **1.** The state of being employed: *in the employ of the city.* **2.** *Archaic.* Occupation. [Middle English *emploien,* from Old French *emploier,* from Latin *implicāre,* to involve : *in-,* in; see EN–[1] + *plicāre,* to fold; see **plek-** in Appendix.] **—em·ploy′a·bil′i·ty** *n.* **—em·ploy′a·ble** *adj.* **—em·ploy′er** *n.*

em·ploy·ee also **em·ploy·e** (ĕm-ploi′ē, ĭm-, ĕm′ploi-ē′) *n.* A person who works for another in return for financial or other compensation. *—attributive.* Often used to modify another noun: *employee benefits; employee unions; employee relations.*

em·ploy·ment (ĕm-ploi′mənt) *n.* **1.a.** The act of employing. **b.** The state of being employed. **2.** The work in which one is engaged; occupation. **3.** An activity to which one devotes time. **4.** The percentage or number of people gainfully employed: *"a vicious spiral of rising prices under full employment"* (William Henry Beveridge). *—attributive.* Often used to modify another noun: *employment opportunities; employment counselors.*

employment agency *n.* An agency that finds jobs for people seeking them and finds people to fill particular jobs.

em·poi·son (ĕm-poi′zən) *tr.v.* **-soned, -son·ing, -sons. 1.** To fill with venom; embitter. **2.** *Archaic.* To poison.

em·po·ri·a (ĕm-pôr′ē-ə, -pōr′-) *n.* A plural of **emporium.**

ă pat	oi boy
ā pay	ou out
âr care	o͝o took
ä father	o͞o boot
ĕ pet	ŭ cut
ē be	ûr urge
ĭ pit	th thin
ī pie	*th* this
îr pier	hw which
ŏ pot	zh vision
ō toe	ə about, item
ô paw	♦ regionalism

Stress marks: **′** (primary); ′ (secondary), as in **dictionary** (dĭk′shə-nĕr′ē)

Em·po·ri·a (ĕm-pôr′ē-ə, -pōr′-). A city of east-central Kansas southwest of Topeka. Founded in 1856, it was the home of the noted newspaper editor William Allen White from 1895 to 1944. Population, 25,287.

em·po·ri·um (ĕm-pôr′ē-əm, -pōr′-) *n., pl.* **-po·ri·ums** or **-po·ri·a** (-pôr′ē-ə, -pōr′-). **1.** A place where various goods are bought and sold; a marketplace. **2.** A large retail store or place of business: *a furniture emporium.* [Latin, from Greek *emporion,* from *emporos,* traveler, merchant : *en-,* in; see EN–[2] + *poros,* journey; see **per-**[2] in Appendix.]

em·pow·er (ĕm-pou′ər) *tr.v.* **-ered, -er·ing, -ers.** To invest with power, especially legal power or official authority. See Synonyms at **authorize. —em·pow′er·ment** *n.*

em·press (ĕm′prĭs) *n.* *Abbr.* **emp. 1.** The woman ruler of an empire. **2.** The wife or widow of an emperor. [Middle English *emperesse,* from Old French, feminine of *empereor,* emperor. See EMPEROR.]

em·presse·ment (äN′prĕs-mäN′) *n.* Effusive cordiality. [French, from *s'empresser,* to be eager : *en-,* in; see EN–[1] + *presser,* to press (from Old French; see PRESS[1]).]

em·prise (ĕm-prīz′) *n.* **1.** A chivalrous or adventurous undertaking. **2.** Chivalrous daring or prowess. [Middle English, from Old French, from feminine past participle of *emprendre,* to undertake, from Vulgar Latin **imprendere* : Latin *in-,* in; see EN–[1] + Latin *prendere,* to take, grasp; see **ghend-** in Appendix.]

emp·ty (ĕmp′tē) *adj.* **-ti·er, -ti·est. 1.a.** Holding or containing nothing. **b.** *Mathematics.* Having no elements or members; null: *an empty set.* **2.** Having no occupants or inhabitants; vacant: *an empty chair; empty desert.* **3.** Lacking force or power: *an empty threat.* **4.** Lacking purpose or substance; meaningless: *an empty life.* **5.** Not put to use; idle: *empty hours.* **6.** Needing nourishment; hungry: *"More fierce and more inexorable far/Than empty tigers or the roaring sea"* (Shakespeare). **7.** Devoid; destitute: *empty of pity.* **—empty** *v.* **-tied, -ty·ing, -ties.** *—tr.* **1.** To remove the contents of: *emptied the dishwasher.* **2.** To transfer or pour off completely: *empty the ashes into a pail.* **3.** To unburden; relieve: *empty oneself of doubt.* *—intr.* **1.** To become empty: *The theater emptied after the performance.* **2.** To discharge its contents: *The river empties into a bay.* **—empty** *n., pl.* **-ties.** *Informal.* An empty container. [Middle English, from Old English *ǣmtig,* vacant, unoccupied, from *ǣmetta,* leisure. See **med-** in Appendix.] **—emp′ti·ly** *adv.* **—emp′ti·ness** *n.*

SYNONYMS: *empty, vacant, blank, void, vacuous, bare, barren.* These adjectives describe what contains nothing and inferentially lacks what it could or should have. *Empty* applies to what is without contents or substance: *an empty box; an empty room; empty promises. Vacant* refers to what is without an occupant or incumbent: *The auditorium is full of vacant seats. The chairmanship is vacant.* Figuratively the word refers to the absence of intelligent meaning or thought: *a vacant stare; a vacant mind. Blank* stresses the absence of something, especially on a surface, that would convey meaning or content: *blank pages; a blank expression. Void* applies to what is free from or completely destitute of discernible content: *space void of matter; gibberish void of all meaning. Vacuous* describes what is as devoid of substance as a vacuum is: *a vacuous smile; led a vacuous life.* Something that is *bare* lacks surface covering (*trees standing bare in November; a bare head*) or detail (*just the bare facts*); the word also denotes the condition of being stripped of contents or furnishings: *The closet is bare. Barren* stresses lack of productivity in both literal and figurative applications: *barren land; writing barren of insight.* See also Synonyms at **vain.**

WORD HISTORY: In Old English *Ic eom ǣmtig* could mean "I am empty," "I am unoccupied," or "I am unmarried." The sense "unoccupied, at leisure," which did not survive Old English, points to the derivation of *ǣmtig* from the Old English word *ǣmetta,* "leisure, rest." The word *ǣmetta* may in turn go back to the Germanic root *mōt–,* meaning "ability, leisure." In any case, Old English *ǣmtig* also meant "vacant," a sense that was destined to take over the meaning of the word. *Empty,* the Modern English descendant of Old English *ǣmtig,* has come to have the sense "idle," so that one can speak of empty leisure.

emp·ty-hand·ed (ĕmp′tē-hăn′dĭd) *adj.* **1.** Bearing nothing. **2.** Having received or gained nothing.

emp·ty-head·ed (ĕmp′tē-hĕd′ĭd) *adj.* Lacking sense or discretion; scatterbrained.

empty nester *n.* *Informal.* A parent whose children have matured and left home.

Emp·ty Quar·ter (ĕmp′tē kwôr′tər). See **Rub al Khali.**

em·pur·ple (ĕm-pûr′pəl) *tr. & intr.v.* **-pled, -pling, -ples.** To make or become purple.

em·py·e·ma (ĕm′pī-ē′mə) *n., pl.* **-ma·ta** (-mə-tə). The presence of pus in a body cavity, especially the pleural cavity. [Medieval Latin *empyēma,* from Greek *empuēma,* from *empuein,* to suppurate. See **pū-** in Appendix.] **—em′py·e′mic** *adj.*

em·pyr·e·al (ĕm′pī-rē′əl, ĕm-pîr′ē-əl) *adj.* **1.** Empyrean. **2.** Of the sky; celestial. **3.** Elevated; sublime. [Middle English *emperiall,* from Medieval Latin *empyreus,* from Greek *empurios,* fiery : *en-,* in; see EN–[2] + *pur,* fire; see **pūr-** in Appendix.]

em·py·re·an (ĕm′pī-rē′ən, ĕm-pîr′ē-ən) *n.* **1.a.** The highest reaches of heaven, believed by the ancients to be a realm of pure fire or light. **b.** The abode of God and the angels; paradise. **2.**

The sky. **—empyrean** *adj.* Of or relating to the empyrean of ancient belief. [From Medieval Latin *empȳreum,* from *empȳreus,* empyreal. See EMPYREAL.]

Ems (ĕmz, ĕms). A river of northwest Germany flowing about 335 km (208 mi) to the North Sea at the Netherlands border.

EMS *abbr.* Electrical muscle stimulation.

EMT *abbr.* Emergency medical technician.

e•mu[1] (ē′myo͞o) *n.* A large, flightless Australian bird *(Dromiceius novaehollandiae)* related to and resembling the ostrich and the cassowary. [Portuguese *ema,* rhea.]

emu[2] *abbr.* Electromagnetic unit.

em•u•late (ĕm′yə-lāt′) *tr.v.* **-lat•ed, -lat•ing, -lates. 1.** To strive to equal or excel, especially through imitation: *an older pupil whose accomplishments and style I emulated.* **2.** To compete with successfully; approach or attain equality with. See Synonyms at **rival. 3.** *Computer Science.* To imitate the function of (another system), as by modifications to hardware or software that allow the imitating system to accept the same data, execute the same programs, and achieve the same results as the imitated system. **—emulate** (-lĭt) *adj. Obsolete.* Ambitious; emulous. [Latin *aemulārī, aemulāt-,* from *aemulus,* emulous.] **—em′u•la′tive** *adj.* **—em′u•la′tive•ly** *adv.* **—em′u•la′tor** *n.*

em•u•la•tion (ĕm′yə-lā′shən) *n.* **1.** Effort or ambition to equal or surpass another. **2.** Imitation of another. **3.** *Computer Science.* The process or technique of emulating. **4.** *Obsolete.* Jealous rivalry.

em•u•lous (ĕm′yə-ləs) *adj.* **1.** Eager or ambitious to equal or surpass another. **2.** Characterized or prompted by a spirit of rivalry. **3.** *Obsolete.* Covetous of power or honor; envious. [From Latin *aemulus.*] **—em′u•lous•ly** *adv.* **—em′u•lous•ness** *n.*

e•mul•si•ble (ĭ-mŭl′sə-bəl) *adj.* That can be emulsified: *an emulsible oil.*

e•mul•si•fy (ĭ-mŭl′sə-fī′) *tr.v.* **-fied, -fy•ing, -fies.** To make into an emulsion. [EMULSI(ON) + -FY.] **—e•mul′si•fi•ca′tion** (-fĭ-kā′shən) *n.* **—e•mul′si•fi′er** *n.*

e•mul•sion (ĭ-mŭl′shən) *n.* **1.** A suspension of small globules of one liquid in a second liquid with which the first will not mix: *an emulsion of oil in vinegar.* **2.** A photosensitive coating, usually of silver halide grains in a thin gelatin layer, on photographic film, paper, or glass. [New Latin *ēmulsiō, ēmulsiōn-,* from Latin *ēmulsus,* past participle of *ēmulgēre,* to milk out : *ē-, ex-,* ex- + *mulgēre,* to milk; see **melg-** in Appendix.] **—e•mul′sive** *adj.*

e•munc•to•ry (ĭ-mŭngk′tə-rē) *adj.* Serving to carry waste out of the body; excretory. **—emunctory** *n., pl.* **-ries.** An organ or duct that removes or carries waste from the body. [Middle English *emunctorie,* from Medieval Latin *ēmunctōrius,* from Latin *ēmunctus,* past participle of *ēmungere,* to blow one's nose : *ē-, ex-,* intensive pref.; see EX- + *mungere,* to blow one's nose.]

en (ĕn) *n.* **1.** The letter *n.* **2.** *Abbr.* **n, N** *Printing.* A space equal to half the width of an em.

en-[1] or **em-** or **in-** *pref.* **1.a.** To put into or onto: *encapsulate.* **b.** To go into or onto: *enplane.* **2.** To cover or provide with: *enrobe.* **3.** To cause to be: *endear.* **4.** Thoroughly. Used often as an intensive: *entangle.* [Middle English, from Old French, from Latin *in-,* in. See **en** in Appendix.]

en-[2] or **em-** *pref.* In; into; within: *enzootic.* [Middle English, from Latin, from Greek. See **en** in Appendix.]

-en[1] *suff.* **1.a.** To cause to be: *cheapen.* **b.** To become: *redden.* **2.a.** To cause to have: *hearten.* **b.** To come to have: *lengthen.* [Middle English *-enen, -nen,* from Old English *-nian.*]

-en[2] *suff.* Made of; resembling: *earthen.* [Middle English, from Old English.]

en•a•ble (ĕ-nā′bəl) *tr.v.* **-bled, -bling, -bles. 1.a.** To supply with the means, knowledge, or opportunity; make able: *a hole in the fence that enabled us to watch; techniques that enable surgeons to open and repair the heart.* **b.** To make feasible or possible: *funds that will enable construction of new schools.* **2.** To give legal power, capacity, or sanction to: *a law enabling the new federal agency.* **3.** To make operational; activate: *enabled the computer's modem; enable a nuclear warhead.* **—en•a′bler** *n.*

en•act (ĕn-ăkt′) *tr.v.* **-act•ed, -act•ing, -acts. 1.** To make into law: *Congress enacted a tax reform bill.* **2.** To act (something) out, as on a stage: *enacted the part of the parent.* **—en•act′a•ble** *adj.* **—en•ac′tor** *n.*

en•act•ment (ĕn-ăkt′mənt) *n.* **1.a.** The act of enacting. **b.** The state of being enacted. **2.** Something that has been enacted: *"Dance itself is the enactment of an energy which must seem . . . untrammeled, effortless, masterful"* (Susan Sontag).

e•nam•el (ĭ-năm′əl) *n.* **1.** A vitreous, usually opaque, protective or decorative coating baked on metal, glass, or ceramic ware. **2.** An object having such a coating, as in a piece of cloisonné. **3.** A coating that dries to a hard, glossy finish: *nail enamel.* **4.** A paint that dries to a hard, glossy finish. **5.** *Anatomy.* The hard, calcareous substance covering the exposed portion of a tooth. **—enamel** *tr.v.* **-eled, -el•ing, -els** or **-elled, -el•ling, -els. 1.** To coat, inlay, or decorate with enamel. **2.** To give a glossy or brilliant surface to. **3.** To adorn with a brightly colored surface. [From Middle English *enamelen,* to put on enamel, from Anglo-Norman *enamailler* : *en-,* on (from Old French; see EN-[1]) + *amail,* enamel (from Old French *esmail,* of Germanic origin; see **mel-**[1] in Appendix).] **—e•nam′el•er, e•nam′el•ist** *n.*

e•nam•el•ware (ĭ-năm′əl-wâr′) *n.* Ware that is coated with enamel.

en•a•mine (ĕn′ə-mēn′, ĭ-năm′ēn) *n.* An amine that contains the double bond linkage -C=C-N-R. [*en-,* chemically unsaturated (from -ENE) + -AMINE.]

en•am•or (ĭ-năm′ər) *tr.v.* **-ored, -or•ing, -ors.** To inspire with love; captivate: *was enamored of the beautiful dancer; were enamored with the charming island.* [Middle English *enamouren,* from Old French *enamourer* : *en-,* causative pref.; see EN-[1] + *amour,* love; see AMOUR.]

en•am•our (ĭ-năm′ər) *v. Chiefly British.* Variant of **enamor.**

en•an•ti•o•mer (ĭ-năn′tē-ə-mər) *n.* See **enantiomorph.** [Greek *enantios,* opposite; see **ant-** in Appendix + -MER(E).] **—en•an′ti•o•mer′ic** (-mĕr′ĭk) *adj.*

en•an•ti•o•morph (ĕ-năn′tē-ə-môrf′) *n.* Either of a pair of crystals, molecules, or compounds that are mirror images of each other but are not identical. Also called *enantiomer.* [Greek *enantios,* opposite; see **ant-** in Appendix + -MORPH.] **—en•an′ti•o•mor′phic, en•an′ti•o•mor′phous** *adj.* **—en•an′ti•o•morph′ism** *n.*

en•ar•thro•sis (ĕn′är-thrō′sĭs) *n., pl.* **-ses** (-sēz). *Anatomy.* See **ball-and-socket joint** (sense 1). [Greek *enarthrōsis,* from *enarthros,* jointed : *en-,* in; see EN-[2] + *arthron,* joint; see **ar-** in Appendix.]

e•nate (ĭ-nāt′, ē′nāt′) *adj.* **1.** Growing outward. **2.** Also **e•nat•ic** (ĭ-năt′ĭk). Related on the mother's side. **—enate** *n.* A relative on one's mother's side. [Latin *ēnātus,* past participle of *ēnāscī,* to issue forth : *ē-, ex-,* ex- + *nāscī,* to be born; see **gene-** in Appendix.]

e•na•tion (ē-nā′shən) *n. Botany.* An outgrowth on the surface of an organ.

en bloc (äɴ blôk′, ĕn blŏk′) *adv.* As a unit; all together: *"I have been drawing our attention to the public and private qualities of the several arts lest they be treated en bloc"* (William H. Gass). [French : *en,* in + *bloc,* lump, bloc.]

en bro•chette (äɴ′ brô-shĕt′) *adv.* On a skewer: *lamb en brochette.* [French : *en,* on + *brochette,* stick, skewer.]

enc. *abbr.* **1.** Enclosed. **2.** Enclosure.

en•cage (ĕn-kāj′) *tr.v.* **-caged, -cag•ing, -cag•es.** To confine in or as if in a cage.

en•camp (ĕn-kămp′) *v.* **-camped, -camp•ing, -camps.** *—intr.* To set up camp or live in a camp. *—tr.* To provide quarters for in a camp: *encamp migrant workers near the fields.*

en•camp•ment (ĕn-kămp′mənt) *n.* **1.a.** The act of encamping. **b.** The state of being encamped. **2.** A camp; a campsite.

en•cap•su•lant (ĕn-kăp′sə-lənt) *n.* A material used for encapsulating.

en•cap•su•late (ĕn-kăp′sə-lāt′) also **in•cap•su•late** (ĭn-) *—v.* **-lat•ed, -lat•ing, -lates.** *—tr.* **1.** To encase in or as if in a capsule. **2.** To express in a brief summary; epitomize: *headlines that encapsulate the news.* *—intr.* To become encapsulated. **—en•cap′su•la′tion** *n.* **—en•cap′su•la′tor** *n.*

en•cap•su•lat•ed (ĕn-kăp′sə-lā′təd) *adj.* Enclosed by a protective coating or membrane: *an encapsulated bacterium.*

en•cap•sule (ĕn-kăp′səl, -so͞ol) *tr.v.* **-suled, -sul•ing, -sules.** To encapsulate.

en•case (ĕn-kās′) also **in•case** (ĭn-) *tr.v.* **-cased, -cas•ing, -cas•es.** To enclose in or as if in a case. **—en•case′ment** *n.*

en•caus•tic (ĕn-kô′stĭk) *n.* **1.** A paint consisting of pigment mixed with beeswax and fixed with heat after its application. **2.** The art of painting with this substance. **3.** A painting produced with the use of this substance. [Latin *encausticus,* from Greek *enkaustikos,* from *enkaiein,* to paint in encaustic : *en-,* in; see EN-[2] + *kaiein,* to burn.]

-ence *suff.* **1.** State or condition: *dependence.* **2.** Action: *emergence.* [Middle English, from Latin *-entia* (from *-ēns,* -ent) and from Old French *-ance,* -ance.]

en•ceinte[1] (ĕn-sănt′, än-sănt′) *adj.* Carrying an unborn child; pregnant. [French, from Old French, possibly from Medieval Latin *incincta,* without a girdle (*in-,* not; see IN-[1] + Latin *cincta,* feminine past participle of *cingere,* to gird; see **kenk-** in Appendix), by folk etymology from Latin *inciēns,* pregnant. See **keue-** in Appendix.]

en•ceinte[2] (ĕn-sănt′, än-sănt′, äɴ-săɴt′) *n.* **1.** An encircling fortification around a fort, castle, or town. **2.** A structure or an area protected by an encircling fortification. [French, from Late Latin *incincta,* from feminine past participle of *incingere,* to surround closely : Latin *in-,* in; see IN-[2] + Latin *cingere,* to gird; see **kenk-** in Appendix.]

En•cel•a•dus (ĕn-sĕl′ə-dəs) *n.* **1.** *Greek Mythology.* A giant who was defeated in battle and buried under Mount Etna by Athena. **2.** The satellite of Saturn that is seventh in distance from the planet. [Latin, from Greek *Enkelados.*]

encephal- *pref.* Variant of **encephalo-.**

en•ceph•a•la (ĕn-sĕf′ə-lə) *n.* Plural of **encephalon.**

en•ce•phal•ic (ĕn′sə-făl′ĭk) *adj.* **1.** Of or relating to the brain. **2.** Located within the cranial cavity.

en•ceph•a•li•tis (ĕn-sĕf′ə-lī′tĭs) *n.* Inflammation of the brain. **—en•ceph′a•lit′ic** (-lĭt′ĭk) *adj.*

encephalitis le•thar•gi•ca (lə-thär′jĭ-kə) *n.* A viral epidemic encephalitis marked by apathy, paralysis of the extrinsic eye muscle, and extreme muscular weakness. It occurred in various parts of the world between 1915 and 1926. Also called *sleep-*

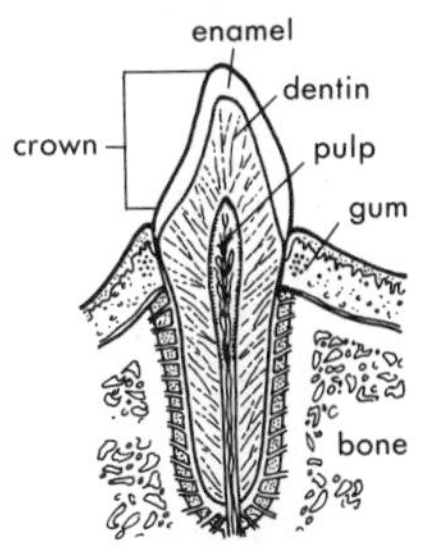

enamel
Top: Russian enameled spoon
Bottom: Cross section of an incisor

encaustic
Late third- to early fourth-century Egyptian encaustic on wood panel portrait

enceinte[2]
Tower of London

ing sickness, sleepy sickness. [New Latin *encephalitis lēthargica* : ENCEPHALITIS + Latin *lēthargicus,* sleepy.]

encephalo– or **encephal–** *pref.* Brain: *encephalitis.* [New Latin, from Greek *(muelos) enkephalos,* (marrow) in the head : *en-,* in; see EN–[2] + *kephalē,* head; see **ghebh-el-** in Appendix.]

en·ceph·a·lo·gram (ĕn-sĕf′ə-lə-grăm′, -ə-lō-) *n.* **1.** An x-ray picture of the brain taken by encephalography. Also called *encephalograph.* **2.** See **electroencephalogram.**

en·ceph·a·lo·graph (ĕn-sĕf′ə-lə-grăf′, -ə-lō-) *n.* **1.** See **encephalogram** (sense 1). **2.** See **electroencephalograph.**

en·ceph·a·log·ra·phy (ĕn-sĕf′ə-lŏg′rə-fē) *n., pl.* **-phies.** Radiographic examination of the brain in which some of the cerebrospinal fluid is replaced with air or another gas that acts as a contrasting medium. **—en·ceph′a·lo·graph′ic** (-ə-lə-grăf′ĭk, -ə-lō-) *adj.* **—en·ceph′a·lo·graph′i·cal·ly** *adv.*

en·ceph·a·lo·ma (ĕn-sĕf′ə-lō′mə) *n., pl.* **-mas** or **-ma·ta** (-mə-tə). A tumor of the brain.

en·ceph·a·lo·my·e·li·tis (ĕn-sĕf′ə-lō-mī′ə-lī′tĭs) *n.* Inflammation of the brain and spinal cord.

en·ceph·a·lon (ĕn-sĕf′ə-lŏn′) *n., pl.* **-la** (-lə). The brain of a vertebrate. [Greek *enkephalon,* neuter of *enkephalos,* in the head. See ENCEPHALO–.] **—en·ceph′a·lous** *adj.*

en·ceph·a·lop·a·thy (ĕn-sĕf′ə-lŏp′ə-thē) *n., pl.* **-thies.** Any of various diseases of the brain. **—en·ceph′a·lo·path′ic** (-lə-păth′ĭk) *adj.*

en·chain (ĕn-chān′) *tr.v.* **-chained, -chain·ing, -chains.** To bind with or as if with chains. **—en·chain′ment** *n.*

en·chant (ĕn-chănt′) *tr.v.* **-chant·ed, -chant·ing, -chants. 1.** To cast a spell over; bewitch. **2.** To attract and delight; entrance. See Synonyms at **charm.** [Middle English *enchanten,* from Old French *enchanter,* from Latin *incantāre,* to utter an incantation, cast a spell : *in-,* against; see EN–[1] + *cantāre,* to sing, frequentative of *canere;* see **kan-** in Appendix.]

en·chant·er (ĕn-chăn′tər) *n.* **1.** One that delights or fascinates. **2.** A sorcerer or magician.

en·chant·ing (ĕn-chăn′tĭng) *adj.* Having the power to enchant; charming: *enchanting music.* **—en·chant′ing·ly** *adv.*

en·chant·ment (ĕn-chănt′mənt) *n.* **1.a.** The act of enchanting. **b.** The state of being enchanted. **2.** Something that enchants.

en·chant·ress (ĕn-chăn′trĭs) *n.* **1.** A woman of great charm or fascination. **2.** A woman who practices magic; a sorceress.

en·chase (ĕn-chās′) *tr.v.* **-chased, -chas·ing, -chas·es. 1.** To set (a gem, for example). **2.** To set with or as if with gems: *enchase a brooch.* **3.** To decorate or ornament by inlaying or engraving. [Middle English, to engrave, from Old French *enchasser,* to set gems : *en-,* in; see EN–[1] + *chasse,* case (from Latin *capsa,* box).]

en·chi·la·da (ĕn′chə-lä′də) *n.* A tortilla rolled and stuffed usually with a mixture containing meat or cheese and served with a sauce spiced with chili. [American Spanish : *en-,* in (from Latin *in-;* see EN–[1]) + *chile,* chili pepper; see CHILI.]

en·chi·rid·i·on (ĕn′kī-rĭd′ē-ən) *n., pl.* **-i·ons** or **-i·a** (-ē-ə). A handbook; a manual. [Late Latin *enchīridion,* from Greek *enkheiridion* : *en-,* in; see EN–[2] + *kheir,* hand; see **ghesor-** in Appendix + *-idion,* diminutive suff.]

–enchyma *suff.* Cellular tissue: *chlorenchyma.* [From PARENCHYMA.]

en·ci·na (ĕn-sē′nə) *n.* See **live oak.** [Spanish, holm oak, from Late Latin *īlicīna,* from Latin *īlex, īlic-.*]

en·ci·pher (ĕn-sī′fər) *tr.v.* **-phered, -pher·ing, -phers.** To put (a message, for example) into cipher. **—en·ci′pher·er** *n.* **—en·ci′pher·ment** *n.*

en·cir·cle (ĕn-sûr′kəl) *tr.v.* **-cled, -cling, -cles. 1.** To form a circle around; surround. See Synonyms at **surround. 2.** To move or go around completely: *a sash that encircled her waist.* **—en·cir′cle·ment** *n.*

encl. *abbr.* **1.** Enclosed. **2.** Enclosure.

en·clasp (ĕn-klăsp′) also **in·clasp** (ĭn-) *tr.v.* **-clasped, -clasp·ing, -clasps.** To hold in a clasp; embrace.

en·clave (ĕn′klāv′, ŏn′-) *n.* **1.** A country or part of a country lying wholly within the boundaries of another. **2.** A distinctly bounded area enclosed within a larger unit: *ethnic enclaves in a large city.* [French, from Old French *enclaver,* to enclose, from Vulgar Latin **inclāvāre* : Latin *in-,* in; see EN–[1] + Latin *clāvis,* key.]

en·clit·ic (ĕn-klĭt′ĭk) *Linguistics. n.* A word or particle that has no independent accent and forms an accentual and sometimes also graphemic unit with the preceding word. In *Give 'em the works,* the pronoun *'em* is an enclitic. **—enclitic** *adj.* Forming an accentual unit with the preceding word, and thus having no independent accent. [Late Latin *encliticus,* from Greek *enklitikos,* from *enklinein,* to lean on : *en-,* on, in; see EN–[2] + *klinein,* to lean; see **klei-** in Appendix.]

en·close (ĕn-klōz′) also **in·close** (ĭn-) *tr.v.* **-closed, -clos·ing, -clos·es. 1.** To surround on all sides; close in. **2.** To fence in so as to prevent common use: *enclosed the pasture.* **3.** To contain, especially so as to envelop or shelter: *"Every one of those darkly clustered houses encloses its own secret"* (Charles Dickens). **4.** To insert into the same envelope or package: *enclose a check with the order.* [Middle English *enclosen,* from Old French *enclos,* past participle of *enclore,* from Latin *inclūdere,* to enclose. See INCLUDE.]

SYNONYMS: *enclose, cage, coop, fence, hem, pen, wall.* The central meaning shared by these verbs is "to surround and confine within a limited area": *cattle enclosed in feedlots; was caged in the office all afternoon; was cooped up in a studio apartment; a garden fenced in by shrubbery; a battalion hemmed in by enemy troops; ships penned up in the harbor during a blockade; prisoners who were walled in.*

en·clo·sure (ĕn-klō′zhər) *n.* **1.a.** The act of enclosing. **b.** The state of being enclosed. **2.** *Abbr.* **enc., encl.** Something enclosed: *a business letter with a supplemental enclosure.* **3.** Something that encloses.

en·code (ĕn-kōd′) *tr.v.* **-cod·ed, -cod·ing, -codes. 1.** To put (a message, for example) into code. **2.** *Computer Science.* To convert (a character, routine, or program) into machine language. **—en·cod′er** *n.*

en·co·mi·a (ĕn-kō′mē-ə) *n.* A plural of **encomium.**

en·co·mi·ast (ĕn-kō′mē-ăst′, -əst) *n.* A person who delivers or writes an encomium; a eulogist. [Greek *enkōmiastēs,* from *enkōmiazein,* to praise, from *enkōmion,* encomium. See ENCOMIUM.] **—en·co′mi·as′tic** (-ăs′tĭk), **en·co′mi·as′ti·cal** (-tĭ-kəl) *adj.*

en·co·mi·um (ĕn-kō′mē-əm) *n., pl.* **-mi·ums** or **-mi·a** (-mē-ə). **1.** Warm, glowing praise. **2.** A formal expression of praise; a tribute. [Latin *encōmium,* from Greek *enkōmion (epos),* (speech) praising a victor, from *enkōmios,* of the victory procession : *en-,* in; see EN–[2] + *kōmos,* celebration.]

en·com·pass (ĕn-kŭm′pəs) *tr.v.* **-passed, -pass·ing, -pass·es. 1.** To form a circle or ring around; surround. See Synonyms at **surround. 2.** To enclose; envelop. **3.** To constitute or include: *a survey that encompassed a wide range of participants.* **4.** To accomplish; achieve. **—en·com′pass·ment** *n.*

en·core (ŏn′kôr′, -kōr′) *n.* **1.** A demand by an audience for an additional performance, usually expressed by applause. **2.** An additional performance in response to the demand of an audience. **—encore** *tr.v.* **-cored, -cor·ing, -cores.** To demand an encore of. **—encore** *interj.* Used to demand an additional performance. [French, still, yet, again, probably from Vulgar Latin **hinc ad hōram,* from that to this hour : Latin *hinc,* from here (from *hic,* this) + Latin *ad,* to; see AD– + Latin *hōram,* accusative of *hōra,* hour; see HOUR.]

en·coun·ter (ĕn-koun′tər) *n.* **1.** A meeting, especially one that is unplanned, unexpected, or brief: *a chance encounter in the park.* **2.a.** A hostile or adversarial confrontation; a contest: *a tense naval encounter.* **b.** An often violent meeting; a clash. **—encounter** *v.* **-tered, -ter·ing, -ters.** *—tr.* **1.** To meet, especially unexpectedly; come upon: *encountered an old friend on the street.* **2.** To confront in battle or contention. **3.** To come up against: *encounter numerous obstacles.* *—intr.* To meet, especially unexpectedly. [Middle English *encountre,* from Old French, from *encontrer,* to meet, from Late Latin *incontrāre* : Latin *in-,* in; see EN–[1] + Latin *contrā,* against; see **kom** in Appendix.]

encounter group *n.* A typically unstructured psychotherapy group in which the participants seek to increase their sensitivity, responsiveness, and emotional expressiveness, as by freely verbalizing and responding to intimate emotions.

en·cour·age (ĕn-kûr′ĭj, -kŭr′-) *tr.v.* **-aged, -ag·ing, -ag·es. 1.** To inspire with hope, courage, or confidence; hearten. **2.** To give support to; foster: *policies designed to encourage private investment.* **3.** To stimulate; spur: *burning the field to encourage new plant growth.* [Middle English *encouragen,* from Old French *encoragier* : *en-,* causative pref.; see EN–[1] + *corage,* courage; see COURAGE.] **—en·cour′ag·er** *n.*

SYNONYMS: *encourage, animate, cheer, embolden, hearten, inspirit.* The central meaning shared by these verbs is "to impart courage, inspiration, and resolution to": *encouraged the student to enter the competition; played patriotic music to animate the troops; a visitor cheering the patient with his presence; was emboldened to sing for the guests; praise that heartened us; a half-time pep talk that inspirited the weary team.*
ANTONYM: *discourage.*

en·cour·age·ment (ĕn-kûr′ĭj-mənt, -kŭr′-) *n.* **1.** The act of encouraging. **2.** The state of being encouraged. **3.** One that encourages.

en·cour·ag·ing (ĕn-kûr′ə-jĭng, -kŭr′-) *adj.* Giving courage, confidence, or hope: *an encouraging advance in medical research.* **—en·cour′ag·ing·ly** *adv.*

en·croach (ĕn-krōch′) *intr.v.* **-croached, -croach·ing, -croach·es. 1.** To take another's possessions or rights gradually or stealthily: *encroach on a neighbor's land.* **2.** To advance beyond proper or former limits: *desert encroaching upon grassland.* [Middle English *encrochen,* to seize illegally, from Old French *encrochier,* to seize : *en-,* in; see EN–[1] + *croc,* hook (of Germanic origin).] **—en·croach′er** *n.* **—en·croach′ment** *n.*

en·crust (ĕn-krŭst′) also **in·crust** (ĭn-) *tr.v.* **-crust·ed, -crust·ing, -crusts.** To cover or surmount with or as if with a crust: *a scepter that is encrusted with diamonds; legalities that were encrusted with tradition.* [Possibly from French *incruster,* from Latin *incrustāre* : *in-,* on; see EN–[1] + *crusta,* crust; see **kreus-** in Appendix.]

en·crust·a·tion (ĕn′krŭs-tā′shən) *n.* Variant of **incrustation.**

en·crypt (ĕn-krĭpt) *tr.v.* **-crypt·ed, -crypt·ing, -crypts. 1.** To put into code or cipher. **2.** *Computer Science.* To scramble access codes to (computerized information) so as to prevent unauthorized access. [EN–[1] + (DE)CRYPT.] **—en·cryp′tion** *n.*

en·cum·ber (ĕn-kŭm′bər) *tr.v.* **-bered, -ber·ing, -bers. 1.** To put a heavy load on; burden: *a hiker who was encumbered with a heavy pack; a life that has always been encumbered with responsibilities.* **2.** To hinder or impede the action or performance of: *restrictions that encumber police work.* **3.** To burden with legal or financial obligations: *an estate that is encumbered with debts.* [Middle English *encombren,* from Old French *encombrer,* to block up : *en-,* in; see EN–[1] + *combre,* hindrance (from Gaulish **comboros*).]

en·cum·brance (ĕn-kŭm′brəns) *n.* **1.** One that encumbers; a burden or impediment. **2.** *Law.* A lien or claim on property.

en·cum·branc·er (ĕn-kŭm′brən-sər) *n.* *Law.* One that holds an encumbrance.

ency. *abbr.* Encyclopedia.

–ency *suff.* Condition or quality: *complacency.* [Middle English, variant of *-ence,* -ence.]

encyc. *abbr.* Encyclopedia.

encycl. *abbr.* Encyclopedia.

en·cyc·li·cal (ĕn-sĭk′lĭ-kəl) *adj.* Intended for general or wide circulation. **—encyclical** *n.* *Roman Catholic Church.* A papal letter addressed to the bishops of the Church or to the hierarchy of a particular country. [From Late Latin *encyclicus,* circular, from Greek *enkuklios* : *en-,* in; see EN–[2] + *kuklos,* circle; see **kʷel-**[1] in Appendix.]

en·cy·clo·pe·di·a (ĕn-sī′klə-pē′dē-ə) *n.* *Abbr.* **encyc., encycl., ency.** A comprehensive reference work containing articles on a wide range of subjects or on numerous aspects of a particular field, usually arranged alphabetically. [Medieval Latin *encyclopaedia,* general education course, from alteration of Greek *enkuklios paideia,* general education : *enkuklios,* circular, general; see ENCYCLICAL + *paideia,* education (from *pais, paid-,* child; see **pau-** in Appendix).]

WORD HISTORY: The word *encyclopedia,* which to us usually means a large set of books, descends from a phrase that involved coming to grips with the contents of such books. The Greek phrase is *enkuklios paideia,* made up of *enkuklios,* "cyclical, periodic, ordinary," and *paideia,* "education," and meaning "general education, literally the arts and sciences that a person should study to be liberally educated." Copyists of Latin manuscripts took this phrase to be the Greek word *enkuklopaedia,* with the same meaning, and this spurious Greek word became the New Latin word *encyclopaedia,* coming into English with the sense "general course of instruction," first recorded in 1531. In New Latin the word was chosen as the title of a reference work covering all knowledge. The first such use in English is recorded in 1644.

en·cy·clo·pe·dic (ĕn-sī′klə-pē′dĭk) *adj.* **1.** Of, relating to, or characteristic of an encyclopedia. **2.** Embracing many subjects; comprehensive: *"an ignorance almost as encyclopedic as his erudition"* (William James). **—en·cy′clo·pe′di·cal·ly** *adv.*

en·cy·clo·pe·dism (ĕn-sī′klə-pē′dĭz′əm) *n.* Encyclopedic learning.

en·cy·clo·pe·dist (ĕn-sī′klə-pē′dĭst) *n.* **1.** A person who writes for or compiles an encyclopedia. **2. Encyclopedist.** One of the writers of the French *Encyclopédie* (1751–1772), including its editors, Diderot and d'Alembert.

en·cyst (ĕn-sĭst′) *v.* **-cyst·ed, -cyst·ing, -cysts.** *—tr.* To enclose in or as if in a cyst. *—intr.* To take the form of or become enclosed in a cyst. **—en·cyst′ment, en′cys·ta′tion** *n.*

end (ĕnd) *n.* **1.** Either extremity of something that has length: *the end of the pier.* **2.** The outside or extreme edge or physical limit; a boundary: *the end of town.* **3.** The point in time when an action, an event, or a phenomenon ceases or is completed; the conclusion: *the end of the day.* **4.** A result; an outcome. **5.** Something toward which one strives; a goal. See Synonyms at **intention. 6.** The termination of life or existence; death: *"A man awaits his end/Dreading and hoping all"* (William Butler Yeats). **7.** The ultimate extent; the very limit: *the end of one's patience.* **8.** *Slang.* The very best; the ultimate: *This pizza's the end.* **9.** A remainder; a remnant. **10. a.** A share of a responsibility or obligation: *your end of the bargain.* **b.** A particular area of responsibility: *in charge of the business end of the campaign.* **11.** *Football.* **a.** Either of the players in the outermost position on the line of scrimmage. **b.** The position played by such a player. **—end** *v.* **end·ed, end·ing, ends.** *—tr.* **1.** To bring to a conclusion. **2.** To form the last or concluding part of: *the song that ended the performance.* **3.** To destroy: *ended our hopes.* *—intr.* **1.** To come to a finish; cease. **2.** To die. **—*idioms.* in the end.** Eventually; ultimately: *All will turn out well in the end.* **no end.** A great deal: *She had no end of stories to tell.* [Middle English *ende,* from Old English. See **ant-** in Appendix.]

end– *pref.* Variant of **endo–.**

en·da·moe·ba or **en·da·me·ba** (ĕn′də-mē′bə) *n.* Variant of **entamoeba.**

en·dan·ger (ĕn-dān′jər) *tr.v.* **-gered, -ger·ing, -gers.** To expose to harm or danger; imperil. **—en·dan′ger·ment** *n.*

SYNONYMS: *endanger, hazard, imperil, jeopardize, risk.* The central meaning shared by these verbs is "to subject to danger, loss, or destruction": *driving that endangers passengers' lives; hazarded his well-being by constant smoking; a forest imperiled by acid rain; strikes that jeopardized the future of the business; risking her financial security by buying speculative stocks.*

en·dan·gered (ĕn-dān′jərd) *adj.* Faced with the danger of extinction: *an endangered species; an endangered culture.*

end·arch (ĕn′därk′) *adj.* *Botany.* Of or relating to a xylem whose early development is toward the center. [END(O)– + Greek *arkhē,* beginning (from *arkhein,* to begin, rule).]

end·ar·te·rec·to·my (ĕn′där-tə-rĕk′tə-mē) *n., pl.* **-mies.** Surgical excision of the inner lining of an artery that is clogged with atherosclerotic buildup. [New Latin *endartērium,* inner lining of an artery (ENDO– + *artērium,* from Latin *artēria;* see ARTERY) + –ECTOMY.]

end·ar·te·ri·tis (ĕn′där-tə-rī′tĭs) *n.* Inflammation of the inner lining of an artery. [New Latin *endartērium,* inner lining of an artery; see ENDARTERECTOMY + –ITIS.]

end·brain (ĕnd′brān′) *n.* See **telencephalon.**

en·dear (ĕn-dîr′) *tr.v.* **-deared, -dear·ing, -dears.** To make beloved or very sympathetic: *a couple whose kindness endeared them to friends.*

en·dear·ing (ĕn-dîr′ĭng) *adj.* Inspiring affection or warm sympathy: *the endearing charm of a little child.* **—en·dear′ing·ly** *adv.*

en·dear·ment (ĕn-dîr′mənt) *n.* **1.** The act of endearing. **2.** An expression of affection, such as a caress.

en·deav·or (ĕn-dĕv′ər) *n.* **1.** A conscientious or concerted effort toward an end; an earnest attempt. **2.** Purposeful or industrious activity; enterprise. See Synonyms at **effort. —endeavor** *v.* **-ored, -or·ing, -ors.** *—tr.* To attempt (fulfillment of a responsibility or an obligation, for example) by employment or expenditure of effort: *endeavored to improve the quality of life in the inner city.* *—intr.* To work with a set or specified goal or purpose. [Middle English *endevour,* from *endeveren,* to make an effort, from *(putten) in dever,* (to put oneself) in duty, make it one's duty : *in,* in; see IN[1] + *dever,* duty (from Old French *deveir, devoir,* duty; see DEVOIR).] **—en·deav′or·er** *n.*

en·deav·our (ĕn-dĕv′ər) *n. & v.* *Chiefly British.* Variant of **endeavor.**

En·de·cott also **En·di·cott** (ĕn′dĭ-kət, -kŏt′), **John.** 1588?–1665. English-born American colonial administrator who was a founder of the Massachusetts Bay Colony.

en·dem·ic (ĕn-dĕm′ĭk) *adj.* **1.** Prevalent in or peculiar to a particular locality, region, or people: *diseases endemic to the tropics.* See Synonyms at **native. 2.** *Ecology.* Native to or confined to a certain region. **—endemic** *n.* *Ecology.* An endemic plant or animal. [From Greek *endēmos* : *en-,* in; see EN–[2] + *dēmos,* people; see **dā-** in Appendix.] **—en·dem′i·cal·ly** *adv.* **—en·dem′ism** *n.*

En·der·by Land (ĕn′dər-bē). A region of Antarctica between Queen Maud Land and Wilkes Land. First explored in 1831 and 1832, it is claimed by Australia.

end·er·gon·ic (ĕn′dər-gŏn′ĭk) *adj.* Requiring energy: *an endergonic chemical reaction.* [END(O)– + Greek *ergon,* work; see **werg-** in Appendix + –IC.]

en·der·mic (ĕn-dûr′mĭk) *adj.* Acting medicinally by absorption through the skin. **—en·der′mi·cal·ly** *adv.*

En·ders (ĕn′dərz), **John Franklin.** 1897–1985. American bacteriologist. He shared a 1954 Nobel Prize for work on the cultivation of the polio virus.

end·game also **end game** (ĕnd′gām′) *n.* *Games.* **1.** The final stage of a chess game after most of the pieces have been removed from the board. **2.** The final stage of an extended process or course of events: *the diplomatic endgame that led to the treaty.*

En·di·cott (ĕn′dĭ-kət, -kŏt′), **John.** See John **Endecott.**

end·ing (ĕn′dĭng) *n.* **1.** A conclusion or termination. **2.** A concluding part; a finale: *a happy ending.* **3.** *Grammar.* The final morpheme added to a word base to make an inflectional form, such as *-ed* in *walked.*

en·dive (ĕn′dīv′, ŏn′dēv′) *n.* **1.** An Indian plant *(Cichorium endivia)* cultivated for its crown of crisp, succulent leaves used in salads. Also called *frisée.* **2.** A variety of the common chicory *Cichorium intybus* cultivated to produce a narrow, pointed cluster of whitish leaves used in salads. Also called *witloof.* [Middle English, from Old French, from Medieval Latin *endivia,* from Medieval Greek *entubia,* pl. diminutive of Greek *entubon,* perhaps from Egyptian *tybi,* January (because the plant grows in this month).]

endive
Top: Curly endive
Bottom: Belgian endive

end leaf *n.* See **endpaper.**

end·less (ĕnd′lĭs) *adj.* **1.** Being or seeming to be without an end or a limit; boundless: *an endless universe; an endless conversation.* **2.** Formed with the ends joined; continuous: *an endless chain.* **—end′less·ly** *adv.* **—end′less·ness** *n.*

end line *n.* *Sports.* A line perpendicular to the sidelines that marks an end boundary of a playing field or court.

end·long (ĕnd′lông′, -lŏng′) *adv.* *Archaic.* Lengthwise.

end man *n.* **1.** The person at the end of a line or row. **2.** The man in a minstrel show who sits at one end of the company and engages in banter with the interlocutor.

end matter *n.* See **back matter.**

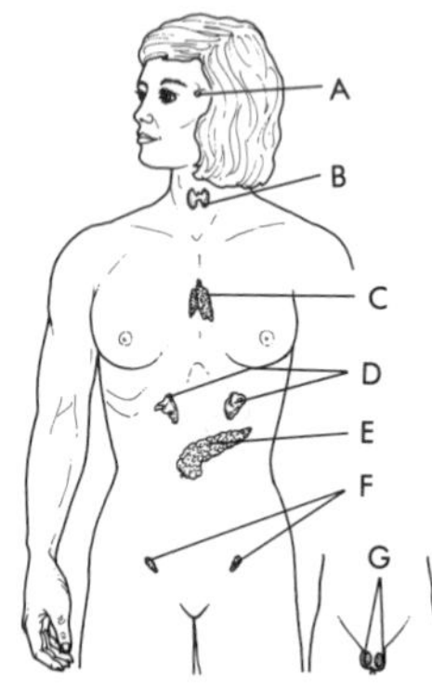

endocrine gland
A. Pituitary gland
B. Thyroid
C. Thymus
D. Adrenal glands
E. Pancreas
F. Ovaries
G. Testes

end·most (ĕnd′mōst′) *adj.* Being at or closest to the end; last.

end·note (ĕnd′nōt′) *n.* A note placed at the end of an article, a chapter, or a book that comments on or cites a reference for a designated part of the text.

endo– or **end–** *pref.* Inside; within: *endometrium.* [Greek, from *endo,* within. See **en** in Appendix.]

en·do·bi·ot·ic (ĕn′də-bī-ŏt′ĭk) *adj.* Living as a parasite or symbiont within the tissues of a host.

en·do·car·di·tis (ĕn′dō-kär-dī′tĭs) *n.* Inflammation of the endocardium. [ENDOCARD(IUM) + –ITIS.] **—en′do·car·dit′ic** (-dĭt′ĭk) *adj.*

en·do·car·di·um (ĕn′dō-kär′dē-əm) *n., pl.* **-di·a** (-dē-ə). The thin serous membrane, composed of endothelial tissue, that lines the interior of the heart. [New Latin : ENDO– + Greek *kardia,* heart; see **kerd-** in Appendix.] **—en′do·car′di·al** *adj.*

en·do·carp (ĕn′də-kärp′) *n.* The hard inner layer of the pericarp of many fruits, such as the pit or stone of a cherry, a peach, or an olive. **—en′do·car′pal** *adj.*

en·do·cra·ni·um (ĕn′dō-krā′nē-əm) *n., pl.* **-ni·a** (-nē-ə). **1.** The outermost layer of the dura mater. **2.** The inner surface of the skull.

en·do·crine (ĕn′də-krĭn, -krēn′, -krīn′) *adj.* **1.** Secreting internally. **2.** Of or relating to endocrine glands or the hormones secreted by them. **—endocrine** *n.* **1.** The secretion of an endocrine gland; a hormone. **2.** An endocrine gland. [French : Greek *endo-,* endo- + Greek *krinein,* to separate; see **krei-** in Appendix.]

endocrine gland *n.* Any of various glands, such as the thyroid, adrenal, or pituitary, having hormonal secretions that pass directly into the bloodstream. Also called *ductless gland.*

en·do·cri·nol·o·gy (ĕn′də-krə-nŏl′ə-jē) *n.* The study of the glands and hormones of the body and their related disorders. **—en′do·cri′no·log′ic** (-krĭn′ə-lŏj′ĭk), **en′do·crin′o·log′i·cal** *adj.* **—en′do·cri·nol′o·gist** *n.*

en·do·cy·to·sis (ĕn′dō-sī-tō′sĭs) *n.* A process of cellular ingestion by which the plasma membrane folds inward to bring substances into the cell. **—en′do·cyt′ic** (-sĭt′ĭk), **en′do·cy·tot′ic** (-sī-tŏt′ĭk) *adj.* **—en′do·cy·tose′** (-tōs′) *v.*

en·do·derm (ĕn′də-dûrm′) also **en·to·derm** (ĕn′tə-) *n.* The innermost of the three primary germ layers of an animal embryo, developing into the gastrointestinal tract, the lungs, and associated structures. Also called *hypoblast.* **—en′do·der′mal** *adj.*

en·do·der·mis (ĕn′də-dûr′mĭs) *n. Botany.* The innermost layer of the cortex that forms a sheath around the vascular tissue of roots and some stems. [ENDO– + (EPI)DERMIS.]

en·do·don·tia (ĕn′dō-dŏn′shə, -shē-ə) *n.* Endodontics.

en·do·don·tics (ĕn′dō-dŏn′tĭks) *n. (used with a sing. verb).* The branch of dentistry that deals with diseases of the tooth root, dental pulp, and surrounding tissue. [ENDO– + (ORTHO)DONTICS.] **—en′do·don′tic** *adj.* **—en′do·don′tist** *n.*

en·do·en·zyme (ĕn′dō-ĕn′zīm′) *n.* An enzyme that acts on or is retained within the cell producing it.

en·do·er·gic (ĕn′dō-ûr′jĭk) *adj. Chemistry.* Endothermic. [ENDO– + Greek *ergon,* work; see **werg-** in Appendix + –IC.]

en·dog·a·my (ĕn-dŏg′ə-mē) *n.* **1.** *Anthropology.* Marriage within a particular group in accordance with custom or law. **2.** *Botany.* Fertilization resulting from pollination among flowers of the same plant. **3.** *Biology.* Reproduction by the fusion of gametes of similar ancestry. **—en·dog′a·mous** *adj.*

en·dog·e·nous (ĕn-dŏj′ə-nəs) *adj.* **1.** Produced or growing from within. **2.** *Biology.* Originating or produced within an organism, a tissue, or a cell: *endogenous secretions.* **—en·dog′e·nous·ly** *adv.* **—en·dog′e·ny** *n.*

en·do·lymph (ĕn′də-lĭmf′) *n.* The fluid in the membranous labyrinth of the inner ear. **—en′do·lym·phat′ic** (-lĭm-făt′ĭk) *adj.*

en·do·me·tri·a (ĕn′dō-mē′trē-ə) *n.* Plural of **endometrium.**

en·do·me·tri·o·sis (ĕn′dō-mē′trē-ō′sĭs) *n.* A condition, usually resulting in pain and dysmenorrhea, that is characterized by the abnormal occurrence of functional endometrial tissue outside the uterus.

en·do·me·tri·um (ĕn′dō-mē′trē-əm) *n., pl.* **-tri·a** (-trē-ə). The glandular mucous membrane that lines the uterus. [New Latin : ENDO– + Greek *mētra,* uterus; see METRO–.] **—en′do·me′tri·al** *adj.*

en·do·mi·to·sis (ĕn′dō-mī-tō′sĭs) *n.* A process by which chromosomes replicate without the division of the cell nucleus. **—en′do·mi·tot′ic** (-tŏt′ĭk) *adj.*

en·do·morph (ĕn′də-môrf′) *n.* **1.** A mineral enclosed within another mineral, such as rutile or tourmaline in quartz. **2.** *Physiology.* An individual characterized by relative prominence of the abdomen and other soft body parts developed from the embryonic endodermal layer. [ENDO(DERM) + –MORPH.]

en·do·mor·phic (ĕn′də-môr′fĭk) *adj.* **a.** Of or relating to an endomorph. **b.** Created through endomorphism. [ENDO(DERM) + –MORPHIC.] **—en′do·mor′phy** *n.*

en·do·morph·ism (ĕn′də-môr′fĭz′əm) *n.* **1.** *Geology.* A change within an intrusive igneous rock caused by the assimilation of portions of the surrounding rock. **2.** A homomorphism that maps a mathematical set into itself.

en·do·nu·cle·ase (ĕn′dō-nōō′klē-ās′, -āz′, -nyōō′-) *n.* Any of a group of enzymes that catalyze the hydrolysis of bonds between nucleic acids in the interior of a DNA or an RNA sequence.

en·do·par·a·site (ĕn′dō-păr′ə-sīt′) *n.* A parasite, such as a tapeworm, that lives within another organism. **—en′do·par·a·sit′ic** (-sĭt′ĭk) *adj.* **—en′do·par′a·sit·ism** (-sĭ-tĭz′əm) *n.*

en·do·pep·ti·dase (ĕn′dō-pĕp′tĭ-dās′, -dāz′) *n.* Any of a large group of enzymes that catalyze the hydrolysis of peptide bonds in the interior of a polypeptide chain or protein molecule.

en·do·phyte (ĕn′də-fīt′) *n.* A plant, such as a fungus, growing within another plant. **—en′do·phyt′ic** (-dō-fĭt′ĭk) *adj.*

en·do·plasm (ĕn′də-plăz′əm) *n.* A central, less viscous portion of the cytoplasm that is distinguishable in certain cells, especially motile cells. **—en′do·plas′mic** *adj.*

endoplasmic reticulum *n.* A membrane network within the cytoplasm of cells involved in the synthesis, modification, and transport of cellular materials.

end organ *n.* The encapsulated termination of a sensory nerve.

en·dor·phin (ĕn-dôr′fĭn) *n.* Any of a group of peptide hormones that bind to opiate receptors and are found mainly in the brain. Endorphins reduce the sensation of pain and affect emotions. [ENDO(GENOUS) + (MO)RPHIN(E).]

en·dorse (ĕn-dôrs′) also **in·dorse** (ĭn-) *tr.v.* **-dorsed, -dors·ing, -dors·es. 1.** To write one's signature on the back of (a check, for example) as evidence of the legal transfer of its ownership, especially in return for the cash or credit indicated on its face. **2.** To place (one's signature), as on a contract, to indicate approval of its contents or terms. **3.** To acknowledge (receipt of payment) by signing a bill, draft, or other instrument. **4.** To give approval of or support to, especially by public statement; sanction: *endorse a political candidate.* See Synonyms at **approve.** [Middle English *endosen,* from Anglo-Norman *endosser,* from Medieval Latin *indorsāre* : Latin *in-,* upon, in; see EN–[1] + Latin *dorsum,* back.] **—en·dors′a·ble** *adj.* **—en·dors′er, en·dor′sor** *n.*

en·dor·see (ĕn′dôr-sē′) *n.* One to whom ownership of a negotiable document is transferred by endorsement.

en·dorse·ment (ĕn-dôrs′mənt) *n.* **1.** The act of endorsing: *The athlete was highly paid to do endorsements of products.* **2.** Something, such as a signature or voucher, that endorses or validates. **3.** Approbation; sanction; support: *The candidates competed for the union's endorsement.* **4.** An amendment to a contract, such as an insurance policy, by which the original terms are changed.

endorsement in blank *n., pl.* **endorsements in blank.** See **blank endorsement.**

en·do·scope (ĕn′də-skōp′) *n.* An instrument for examining visually the interior of a bodily canal or a hollow organ such as the colon, bladder, or stomach. **—en′do·scop′ic** (-skŏp′ĭk) *adj.* **—en′do·scop′ic·al·ly** *adv.* **—en·dos′co·py** (ĕn-dŏs′kə-pē) *n.*

en·do·skel·e·ton (ĕn′dō-skĕl′ĭ-tn) *n.* An internal supporting skeleton, derived from the mesoderm, that is characteristic of vertebrates and certain invertebrates. **—en′do·skel′e·tal** (-ĭ-tl) *adj.*

en·dos·mo·sis (ĕn′dŏz-mō′sĭs, -dŏs-) *n.* The inward flow of a fluid through a permeable membrane toward a fluid of greater concentration. **—en′dos·mot′ic** (-mŏt′ĭk) *adj.* **—en′dos·mot′i·cal·ly** *adv.*

en·do·sperm (ĕn′də-spûrm′) *n.* The nutritive tissue within seeds of flowering plants, surrounding and absorbed by the embryo.

en·do·spore (ĕn′də-spôr′, -spōr′) *n.* **1.** A small asexual spore, as that formed by some bacteria. **2.** The inner layer of the wall of a spore.

en·do·spo·ri·um (ĕn′də-spôr′ē-əm, -spōr′-) *n., pl.* **-spo·ri·a** (-spôr′ē-ə, -spōr′-). **1.** An endospore. **2.** See **intine.**

en·dos·te·um (ĕn-dŏs′tē-əm) *n., pl.* **-te·a** (-tē-ə). The thin layer of cells lining the medullary cavity of a bone. [New Latin : END(O)– + Greek *osteon,* bone; see **ost-** in Appendix.] **—en·dos′te·al** *adj.*

en·do·sul·fan (ĕn′də-sŭl′fən) *n.* A highly toxic crystalline insecticide, $C_9H_6Cl_6O_3S$, used in the control of crop insects and mites. [END(RIN) + –O– + SULF(O)– + –AN[2].]

en·do·the·ci·um (ĕn′dō-thē′sē-əm, -shē-əm) *n., pl.* **-ci·a** (-sē-ə, -shē-ə). *Botany.* The inner tissue of an anther or a moss capsule. [New Latin : ENDO– + Greek *thēkion,* diminutive of *thēkē,* chest, receptacle; see **dhē-** in Appendix.]

en·do·the·li·a (ĕn′dō-thē′lē-ə) *n.* Plural of **endothelium.**

en·do·the·li·o·ma (ĕn′dō-thē′lē-ō′mə) *n., pl.* **-ma·ta** (-mə-tə) or **-mas.** Any of various neoplasms derived from endothelium.

en·do·the·li·um (ĕn′dō-thē′lē-əm) *n., pl.* **-li·a** (-lē-ə). A thin layer of flat epithelial cells that lines serous cavities, lymph vessels, and blood vessels. [New Latin : ENDO– + Greek *thēlē,* nipple; see **dhē(i)-** in Appendix.] **—en′do·the′li·al, en′do·the′li·oid′** *adj.*

en·do·therm (ĕn′də-thûrm′) *n.* An organism that generates heat to maintain its body temperature, typically above the temperature of its surroundings; a homeotherm.

en·do·ther·mic (ĕn′dō-thûr′mĭk) also **en·do·ther·mal** (-məl) *adj.* **1.** *Chemistry.* Characterized by or causing the absorption of heat; endoergic. **2.** *Biology.* Of or relating to an organism that generates heat to maintain its body temperature, typically above the temperature of its surroundings; warm-blooded. **—en′do·ther′my** *n.*

en·do·tox·in (ĕn′dō-tŏk′sən) *n.* A toxin produced by certain bacteria and released upon destruction of the bacterial cell. **—en′do·tox′ic** *adj.*

en·do·tra·che·al (ĕn′də-trā′kē-əl) *adj.* Within or passing through the trachea: *an endotracheal tube.*

en·dow (ĕn-dou′) *tr.v.* **-dowed, -dow·ing, -dows. 1.** To provide with property, income, or a source of income. **2.a.** To equip or supply with a talent or quality: *Nature endowed her with a beautiful singing voice.* **b.** To imagine as having a usually favorable trait or quality: *endowed the family pet with human intelligence.* **3.** *Obsolete.* To provide with a dower. [Middle English *endowen,* from Anglo-Norman *endouer* : Old French *en–,* intensive pref.; see EN–[1] + Old French *douer,* to provide with a dowry (from Latin *dōtāre,* from *dōs, dōt-,* dowry; see **dō-** in Appendix).]

en·dow·ment (ĕn-dou′mənt) *n.* **1.** The act of endowing. **2.** Funds or property donated to an institution, an individual, or a group as a source of income. **3.** A natural gift, ability, or quality.

end·pa·per also **end paper** (ĕnd′pā′pər) *n.* Either of two folded sheets of heavy paper having one half pasted to the inside front or back cover of a book and the other half pasted to the base of the first or last page. Also called *end leaf.*

end·pin (ĕnd′pĭn′) *n. Music.* The thin, usually adjustable leg of a cello or double bass.

end plate *n. Physiology.* The area of synaptic contact between a motor nerve and a muscle fiber.

end·play (ĕnd′plā′) *Games. n.* A play in bridge that forces an opponent to lead and results in the opponents' losing one or more tricks that they would have won had they not been leading. **—endplay** *tr.v.* **-played, -play·ing, -plays.** To force (a bridge opponent) to lead disadvantageously.

end·point or **end point** also **end-point** (ĕnd′point′) *n.* **1.** Either of two points marking the end of a line segment. **2.** *Chemistry.* The point in a titration at which no more titrant should be added. It is determined, for example, by a color change in an indicator or by the appearance of a precipitate. **3.** A tip or point of termination.

end product *n.* The result of a completed series of processes or changes.

end-ran (ĕnd′răn′) *v.* Past tense and past participle of **end-run.**

en·drin (ĕn′drĭn) *n.* A highly toxic chlorinated hydrocarbon, $C_{12}H_8OCl_6$, used as an insecticide. [EN(DO)– + (DIEL)DRIN.]

end run *n.* **1.** *Football.* A play in which the ball carrier attempts to run around one end of the defensive line. **2.** *Informal.* A maneuver in which impediments are bypassed, often by deceit or trickery: *made an end run around the departmental finance officer in order to increase the budget.*

end-run (ĕnd′rŭn′) *tr.v.* **-ran** (-răn′), **-run·ning, -runs.** *Informal.* To bypass (an impediment) often by deceit or trickery: *"The plan to end-run the regular Senate committee ran into instant resistance from some of their new Republican chairmen"* (Peter Goldman).

end-stopped (ĕnd′stŏpt′) *adj.* Ending in a syntactic and rhythmic pause. Used of a line of verse or a couplet.

Ends·ville also **ends·ville** (ĕndz′vĭl′) *n. Slang.* **1.** The greatest, best, or most exciting condition, state, or thing. **2.** An undesirable, usually isolated location, as the end of a road.

end table *n.* A small table, usually placed at either end of a couch or beside a chair.

en·due (ĕn-do͞o′, -dyo͞o′) also **in·due** (ĭn-) *tr.v.* **-dued, -du·ing, -dues. 1.** To provide with a quality or trait; endow: *"Endue her plenteously with heavenly gifts"* (Book of Common Prayer). **2.** To put on (a piece of clothing). [Middle English *enduen,* from Old French *enduire,* to lead in, induct (influenced by Middle English *endowen,* to endow; see ENDOW), from Latin *indūcere;* see INDUCE. Sense 2, Middle English *induen,* to clothe, from Latin *induere,* to put on. See **eu-**[1] in Appendix.]

en·dur·a·ble (ĕn-do͝or′ə-bəl, -dyo͝or′-) *adj.* Possible to be endured; tolerable: *endurable pain.* **—en·dur′a·bly** *adv.*

en·dur·ance (ĕn-do͝or′əns, -dyo͝or′-) *n.* **1.** The act, quality, or power of withstanding hardship or stress: *A marathon tests a runner's endurance.* **2.** The state or fact of persevering: *Through hard work and endurance, we will complete this project.* **3.** Continuing existence; duration. *—attributive.* Often used to modify another noun: *endurance events; endurance swimmers.*

en·dure (ĕn-do͝or′, -dyo͝or′) *v.* **-dured, -dur·ing, -dures.** *—tr.* **1.** To carry on through, despite hardships; undergo: *endure an Arctic winter.* **2.** To bear with tolerance: *"We seek the truth, and will endure the consequences"* (Charles Seymour). See Synonyms at **bear**[1]. *—intr.* **1.** To continue in existence; last: *buildings that have endured for centuries.* **2.** To suffer patiently without yielding. [Middle English *enduren,* from Old French *endurer,* from Latin *indūrāre,* to make hard : *in-,* against, into; see EN–[1] + *dūrus,* hard; see **deru-** in Appendix.]

en·dur·ing (ĕn-do͝or′ĭng, -dyo͝or′-) *adj.* **1.** Lasting; continuing; durable: *a novel of enduring interest.* **2.** Long-suffering; patient. **—en·dur′ing·ly** *adv.* **—en·dur′ing·ness** *n.*

en·dur·o (ĕn-do͝or′ō, -dyo͝or′ō) *n., pl.* **-os.** *Sports.* A race, as of motorcycles or runners, that tests endurance. [Shortening and alteration of ENDURANCE.]

end use also **end-use** (ĕnd′yo͞os′) *n.* The ultimate application for which a product has been designed. **—end′-use′** *adj.*

end user also **end-us·er** (ĕnd′yo͞o′zər) *n.* The ultimate consumer of a product, especially the one for whom the product has been designed.

end·wise (ĕnd′wīz′) also **end·ways** (-wāz′) *adv.* **1.** On end; upright. **2.** With the end foremost. **3.** Lengthwise. **4.** End to end.

En·dym·i·on (ĕn-dĭm′ē-ən) *n. Greek Mythology.* A handsome young man who was loved by a moon goddess and whose youth was preserved by eternal sleep.

end zone *n. Football.* The area at either end of the playing field between the goal line and the end line.

ENE *abbr.* East-northeast.

-ene *suff.* An unsaturated organic compound, especially one containing a double bond between carbon atoms: *ethylene.* [From Greek *-ēnē,* feminine adj. suff.]

en·e·ma (ĕn′ə-mə) *n., pl.* **-mas. 1.** The injection of liquid into the rectum through the anus for cleansing, for stimulating evacuation of the bowels, or for other therapeutic or diagnostic purposes. **2.** The fluid so injected. [Late Latin, from Greek, from *enienai,* to send in, inject : *en-,* in; see EN–[2] + *hienai,* to send; see **yē-** in Appendix.]

en·e·my (ĕn′ə-mē) *n., pl.* **-mies. 1.** One who feels hatred toward, intends injury to, or opposes the interests of another; a foe. **2.a.** A hostile power or force, such as a nation. **b.** A member or unit of such a force. **3.** A group of foes or hostile forces. See Usage Note at **collective noun. 4.** Something destructive or injurious in its effects: *"Art hath an enemy called Ignorance"* (Ben Jonson). **—enemy** *adj.* Of, relating to, or being a hostile power or force. [Middle English *enemi,* from Old French, from Latin *inimīcus* : *in-,* not; see IN–[1] + *amīcus,* friend.]

SYNONYMS: *enemy, foe, opponent.* The central meaning shared by these nouns is "one who is hostile to or opposes the purposes or interests of another": *was betrayed by his enemies; a foe of fascism; a political opponent.*

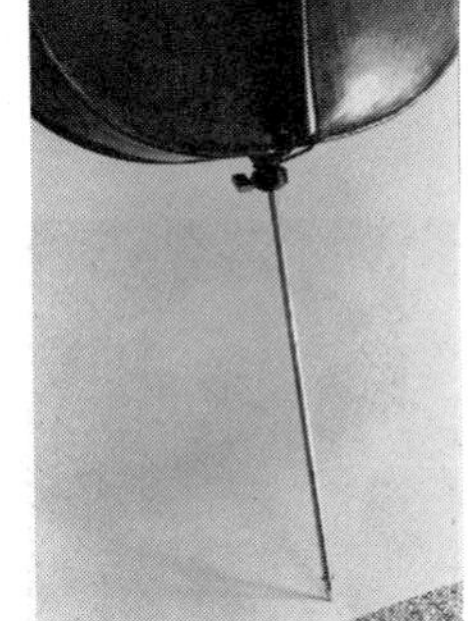

endpin

en·er·get·ic (ĕn′ər-jĕt′ĭk) *adj.* **1.** Possessing, exerting, or displaying energy. See Synonyms at **active. 2.** Of or relating to energy. [Greek *energētikos,* from *energein,* to be active, from *energos,* active. See ENERGY.] **—en′er·get′i·cal·ly** *adv.*

en·er·get·ics (ĕn′ər-jĕt′ĭks) *n.* (*used with a sing. verb*). **1.** The study of the flow and transformation of energy. **2.** The flow and transformation of energy within a particular system.

en·er·gize (ĕn′ər-jīz′) *v.* **-gized, -giz·ing, -giz·es.** *—tr.* **1.** To give energy to; activate or invigorate: *"His childhood—father in . . . prison, factory work as a boy—both haunted and energized him, and he wrote on a grand scale and worked his way free"* (Frank Conroy). **2.** To supply with an electric current; connect to a source of electricity. *—intr.* To release or put out energy. **—en′er·giz′er** *n.*

en·er·gy (ĕn′ər-jē) *n., pl.* **-gies. 1.** The capacity for work or vigorous activity; vigor; power. See Synonyms at **strength. 2.a.** Exertion of vigor or power: *a project requiring a great deal of time and energy.* **b.** Vitality and intensity of expression: *a speech delivered with energy and emotion.* **3.a.** Usable heat or power: *Each year Americans consume a high percentage of the world's energy.* **b.** A source of usable power, such as petroleum or coal. **4.** *Physics.* The capacity of a physical system to do work. *—attributive.* Often used to modify another noun: *energy conservation; energy efficiency; an energy czar.* [French *énergie,* from Late Latin *energīa,* from Greek *energeia,* from *energos,* active : *en-,* in, at; see EN–[2] + *ergon,* work; see **werg-** in Appendix.]

energy audit *n.* An evaluation of energy consumption, as in a home or business, to determine ways in which energy can be conserved.

energy density *n.* The energy per unit volume of a region of space.

energy efficiency ratio *n.* A measure of the relative efficiency of a heating or cooling appliance, such as an air conditioner, that is equal to the unit's output in BTU's per hour divided by its consumption of energy, measured in watts.

energy level *n.* **1.** The energy characteristic of a stationary state of a physical system, especially a quantum mechanical system. **2.** The stationary state of a quantum mechanical system.

en·er·vate (ĕn′ər-vāt′) *tr.v.* **-vat·ed, -vat·ing, -vates. 1.** To weaken or destroy the strength or vitality of: *"the luxury which enervates and destroys nations"* (Henry David Thoreau). See Synonyms at **deplete. 2.** *Medicine.* To remove a nerve or part of a nerve. **—enervate** (ĭ-nûr′vĭt) *adj.* Deprived of strength; debilitated. [Latin *ēnervāre, ēnervāt-* : *ē-, ex-,* ex- + *nervus,* sinew; see **(s)neeu-** in Appendix.] **—en′er·va′tion** *n.* **—en′er·va′tive** *adj.* **—en′er·va′tor** *n.*

E·nes·co (ə-nĕs′kō, ĕ-nĕs′-), **Georges.** 1881–1955. Romanian-born violinist and composer whose works include the opera *Oedipus* (1936) and three symphonies.

en·face (ĕn-fās′) *tr.v.* **-faced, -fac·ing, -fac·es.** To write on the face of (a check, for example). **—en·face′ment** *n.*

en·fant ter·ri·ble (äɴ-fäɴ′ tĕ-rē′blə) **en·fants ter·ri·bles** (äɴ-fäɴ′ tĕ-rē′blə) *n.* One whose startlingly unconventional be-

ă pat	oi boy
ā pay	ou out
âr care	o͝o took
ä father	o͞o boot
ĕ pet	ŭ cut
ē be	ûr urge
ĭ pit	th thin
ī pie	*th* this
îr pier	hw which
ŏ pot	zh vision
ō toe	ə about, item
ô paw	♦ regionalism

Stress marks: **′** (primary); ′ (secondary), as in **dictionary** (dĭk′shə-nĕr′ē)

havior, work, or ideas are a source of embarrassment or dismay to others: *The radical painter was the enfant terrible of the art establishment.* [French : *enfant,* child + *terrible,* frightful.]

en·fee·ble (ĕn-fē′bəl) *tr.v.* **-bled, -bling, -bles.** To deprive of strength; make feeble. **—en·fee′ble·ment** *n.*

en·feoff (ĕn-fēf′, -fĕf′) *tr.v.* **-feoffed, -feoff·ing, -feoffs.** To invest with a feudal estate or fee. [Middle English *enfeffen,* from Anglo-Norman *enfeoffer* : Old French *en-,* causative pref.; see EN–[1] + Old French *fief,* fief; see FEE.] **—en·feoff′ment** *n.*

en·fet·ter (ĕn-fĕt′ər, ĭn-) *tr.v.* **-tered, -ter·ing, -ters.** To bind in fetters; enchain.

En·field (ĕn′fēld′). A town of northern Connecticut near the Massachusetts border. It was settled c. 1680 as part of Massachusetts and annexed by Connecticut in 1749. Population, 42,695.

Enfield rifle *n.* Any of several rifles of varying calibers formerly used by British and American troops, especially the .30 or .303 caliber, bolt-action, breechloading model. [After *Enfield,* a borough of London in southeast England.]

en·fi·lade (ĕn′fə-lād′, -läd′) *n.* **1.** Gunfire directed along the length of a target, such as a column of troops. **2.** A target vulnerable to sweeping gunfire. **—enfilade** *tr.v.* **-lad·ed, -lad·ing, -lades.** To rake with gunfire. [French, series, string, row, from *enfiler,* to string together, run through, from Old French : *en-,* in, on; see EN–[1] + *fil,* thread (from Latin *fīlum;* see **g**ʷ**hī-** in Appendix).]

en·fleu·rage (ŏn′flə-räzh′, -räj′) *n.* A process in making perfume in which odorless fats or oils absorb the fragrance of fresh flowers. [French, from *enfleurer,* to saturate with the perfume of flowers : *en-,* causative pref.; see EN–[1] + *fleur,* flower (from Old French *flour,* from Latin *flōs, flōr-;* see **bhel-**[3] in Appendix).]

Friedrich Engels

en·flur·ane (ĕn-flo͝or′ān′) *n.* A nonflammable liquid, $C_3H_2ClF_5O$, used as an anesthetic. [EN–[1] + (TRI–) + FLU(O)R(O)– + (ETH)ANE.]

en·fold (ĕn-fōld′) *tr.v.* **-fold·ed, -fold·ing, -folds. 1.** To cover with or as if with folds; envelop. **2.** To hold within limits; enclose. **3.** To embrace. **—en·fold′er** *n.*

en·force (ĕn-fôrs′, -fōrs′) *tr.v.* **-forced, -forc·ing, -forc·es. 1.** To compel observance of or obedience to: *enforce a regulation.* **2.** To impose (a kind of behavior, for example); compel: *enforce military discipline.* **3.** To give force to; reinforce: *"enforces its plea with a description of the pains of hell"* (Albert C. Baugh). [Middle English *enforcen,* from Old French *enforcier,* to exert force, compel, and from *enforcir,* to strengthen : *en-,* causative pref.; see EN–[1] + *force,* strength; see FORCE.] **—en·force′a·bil′i·ty** *n.* **—en·force′a·ble** *adj.* **—en·force′ment** *n.* **—en·forc′er** *n.*

SYNONYMS: *enforce, implement, invoke.* The central meaning shared by these verbs is "to cause to be applied or carried out": *enforced the rules; implementing the terms of the agreement; invoke emergency powers.*

en·fran·chise (ĕn-frăn′chīz′) *tr.v.* **-chised, -chis·ing, -chis·es. 1.** To bestow a franchise on. **2.** To endow with the rights of citizenship, especially the right to vote. **3.** To free, as from bondage. [Middle English *enfraunchisen,* from Old French *enfranchir, enfranchiss-,* to set free : *en-,* intensive pref.; see EN–[1] + *franchir* (from *franc,* free; see FRANK[1]).] **—en·fran′chise′ment** *n.*

eng. *abbr.* **1.** Engine. **2.** Engineer. **3.** Engineering.

Eng. *abbr.* **1.** England. **2.** English.

En·ga·dine (ĕng′gə-dēn′). A valley of the Inn River in eastern Switzerland, divided into the **Upper Engadine** in the southwest and the **Lower Engadine** in the northeast.

en·gage (ĕn-gāj′) *v.* **-gaged, -gag·ing, -gag·es.** —*tr.* **1.** To obtain or contract for the services of; employ: *engage a carpenter.* **2.** To arrange for the use of; reserve: *engage a room.* See Synonyms at **book. 3.** To pledge or promise, especially to marry. **4.** To attract and hold the attention of; engross: *a hobby that engaged her for hours at a time.* **5.** To win over or attract: *His smile engages everyone he meets.* **6.** To draw into; involve: *engage a shy person in conversation.* **7.** To require the use of; occupy: *Studying engages most of a serious student's time.* **8.** To enter or bring into conflict with: *We have engaged the enemy.* **9.** To interlock or cause to interlock; mesh: *engage the automobile's clutch.* **10.** To give or take as security. —*intr.* **1.** To involve oneself or become occupied; participate: *engage in conversation.* **2.** To assume an obligation; agree. See Synonyms at **promise. 3.** To enter into conflict or battle: *The armies engaged at dawn.* **4.** To become meshed or interlocked: *The gears engaged.* [Middle English *engagen,* to pledge something as security for repayment of debt, from Old French *engagier* : *en-,* in; see EN–[1] + *gage,* pledge, of Germanic origin.] **—en·gag′er** *n.*

en·ga·gé (ĕn′gä-zhā′) *adj.* Actively committed, as to a political cause. [French, past participle of *engager,* to engage, from Old French *engagier,* to pledge. See ENGAGE.]

en·gaged (ĕn-gājd′) *adj.* **1.** Employed, occupied, or busy. **2.** Committed, as to a cause. **3.** Pledged to marry; betrothed: *an engaged couple.* **4.** Involved in conflict or battle. **5.** Being in gear; meshed. **6.** Partly imbedded, built into, or attached to another part, as columns on a wall.

en·gage·ment (ĕn-gāj′mənt) *n.* **1.** The act of engaging or the state of being engaged. **2.** Betrothal. **3.** Something that serves to engage; a pledge. **4.** A promise or agreement to be at a particular place at a particular time. **5. a.** Employment, especially for a specified time. **b.** A specific, often limited, period of employment. **6.** A hostile encounter; a battle. **7.** The condition of being in gear.

SYNONYMS: *engagement, appointment, assignation, date, rendezvous, tryst.* The central meaning shared by these nouns is "a commitment to appear at a certain time and place": *a business engagement; a dental appointment; a secret assignation; a date to play tennis; a rendezvous of allied troops at the border; a lovers' tryst.*

en·gag·ing (ĕn-gā′jĭng) *adj.* Charming; attractive: *an engaging smile.* **—en·gag′ing·ly** *adv.*

en garde (äɴ gärd′) *interj.* Used to warn a fencer to assume the position preparatory to a match. [French : *en,* on + *garde,* guard.]

en·gar·land (ĕn-gär′lənd) *tr.v.* **-land·ed, -land·ing, -lands.** To encircle or deck with or as if with a garland.

En·gels (ĕng′əlz, -əls), **Friedrich.** 1820–1895. German socialist theorist and writer who met Karl Marx in Paris in 1844 and collaborated with him on *The Communist Manifesto* (1848).

en·gen·der (ĕn-jĕn′dər) *v.* **-dered, -der·ing, -ders.** —*tr.* **1.** To bring into existence; give rise to: *"Every cloud engenders not a storm"* (Shakespeare). **2.** To procreate; propagate. —*intr.* To come into existence; originate. [Middle English *engendren,* from Old French *engendrer,* from Latin *ingenerāre* : *in-,* in; see EN–[1] + *generāre,* to produce; see GENERATE.] **—en·gen′der·er** *n.*

en·gine (ĕn′jĭn) *n. Abbr.* **eng. 1. a.** A machine that converts energy into mechanical force or motion. **b.** Such a machine distinguished from an electric, spring-driven, or hydraulic motor by its use of a fuel. **2. a.** A mechanical appliance, instrument, or tool: *engines of war.* **b.** An agent, an instrument, or a means of accomplishment. **3.** A locomotive. **4.** A fire engine. **—engine** *tr.v.* **-gined, -gin·ing, -gines.** To equip with an engine or engines. [Middle English *engin,* skill, machine, from Old French, innate ability, from Latin *ingenium.* See **gene-** in Appendix.]

engine block *n.* The cast metal block containing the cylinders of an internal-combustion engine.

en·gi·neer (ĕn′jə-nîr′) *n. Abbr.* **e., E., eng., engr. 1.** One who is trained or professionally engaged in a branch of engineering. **2.** One who operates an engine. **3.** One who skillfully or shrewdly manages an enterprise. **—engineer** *tr.v.* **-neered, -neer·ing, -neers. 1.** To plan, construct, or manage as an engineer. **2.** To alter or produce by methods of genetic engineering: *"Researchers . . . compared insulin manufactured by bacteria genetically engineered with recombinant DNA techniques to the commercial insulin obtained from swine or cattle"* (Fusion). **3.** To plan, manage, and put through by skillful acts or contrivance; maneuver. [Middle English *enginour,* from Old French *engigneor,* from Medieval Latin *ingeniātor,* contriver, from *ingeniāre,* to contrive, from Latin *ingenium,* ability. See ENGINE.]

en·gi·neer·ing (ĕn′jə-nîr′ĭng) *n. Abbr.* **e., E., eng. 1. a.** The application of scientific and mathematical principles to practical ends such as the design, manufacture, and operation of efficient and economical structures, machines, processes, and systems. **b.** The profession of or the work performed by an engineer. **2.** Skillful maneuvering or direction: *geopolitical engineering; social engineering.*

en·gird (ĕn-gûrd′) *tr.v.* **-girt** (-gûrt′), **-gird·ing, -girds.** *Archaic.* To encircle.

en·gir·dle (ĕn-gûr′dl) *tr.v.* **-dled, -dling, -dles.** To encircle or surround with or as if with a girdle.

en·girt (ĕn-gûrt′) *v.* Past tense and past participle of **engird.**

en·gla·cial (ĕn-glā′shəl) *adj.* Located or occurring within a glacier.

Eng·land (ĭng′glənd). *Abbr.* **Eng.** A division of the United Kingdom, the southern part of the island of Great Britain. Originally settled by Celtic peoples, it was subsequently conquered by Romans, Angles, Saxons, Jutes, Danes, and Normans. Acts of union joined England with Wales in 1536, with Scotland in 1707 to create the political entity of Great Britain, and with Ireland in 1801 to form the United Kingdom. London is the capital and the largest city of both England and the United Kingdom. Population, 46,220,955.

En·gle·wood (ĕng′gəl-wo͝od′). **1.** A city of north-central Colorado, a residential and industrial suburb of Denver on the South Platte River. Population, 30,021. **2.** A city of northeast New Jersey east of Paterson. Settled by the Dutch in the 17th century, it is a residential suburb of New York City. Population, 23,701.

Eng·lish (ĭng′glĭsh) *adj.* **1.** Of, relating to, or characteristic of England or its people or culture. **2.** Of or relating to the English language. **—English** *n. Abbr.* **E, E., Eng. 1.** The people of England. **2. a.** The West Germanic language of England, the United States, and other countries that are or have been under English influence or control. **b.** The English language of a particular time, region, person, or group of persons: *American English.* **3.** A translation into or an equivalent in the English language. **4.** A course or individual class in the study of English language, literature, or composition. **5.** Often **english.** *Sports & Games.* The spin given to a ball by striking it on one side or releasing it with a sharp twist. **—English** *tr.v.* **-lished, -lish·ing, -lish·es. 1.** To translate into English. **2.** To adapt into English; Anglicize.

ă pat	oi boy
ā pay	ou out
âr care	o͝o took
ä father	o͞o boot
ĕ pet	ŭ cut
ē be	ûr urge
ĭ pit	th thin
ī pie	*th* this
îr pier	hw which
ŏ pot	zh vision
ō toe	ə about, item
ô paw	♦ regionalism

Stress marks: ′ (primary); ′ (secondary), as in **dictionary** (dĭk′shə-nĕr′ē)

[Middle English, from Old English *Englisc,* from *Engle,* the Angles.] **—Eng′lish·ness** *n.*

English bulldog *n.* A short-haired, stocky dog; a bulldog.

English Channel. An arm of the Atlantic Ocean between western France and southern England. It opens into the North Sea and is traversed by a train-ferry service.

English daisy *n.* See **daisy** (sense 2).

English foxhound *n.* Any of a breed of medium-sized hunting dog originating in England and having straight legs and a smooth, black and white or tan and white coat.

English horn *n. Music.* A double-reed woodwind instrument similar to but larger than the oboe and pitched lower by a fifth.

Eng·lish·man (ĭng′glĭsh-mən) *n.* **1.** A man who is a native or inhabitant of England. **2.** A man of English descent.

English muffin *n.* A flat round muffin made from yeast dough that has been baked on a griddle and is usually split and toasted before being eaten.

English plantain *n.* See **ribgrass.**

English saddle *n.* A lightweight, hornless saddle with a steel cantle and pommel, a padded leather seat, and full side flaps usually set forward.

English setter *n.* Any of a breed of medium-sized dog developed in England and having a long, silky white coat usually with black or brownish markings.

English sheepdog *n.* An Old English sheepdog.

English sonnet *n.* See **Shakespearean sonnet.**

English sparrow *n.* See **house sparrow.**

English springer spaniel *n.* Any of a breed of medium-sized hunting dog originating in England and having a silky, liver and white or black and white coat.

English toy spaniel *n.* Any of a breed of spaniel having a round head, a short turned-up nose, a thick wavy coat, and a mane around its neck.

English walnut *n.* **1.** A Eurasian tree *(Juglans regia)* cultivated in southern Europe and California for its valuable wood and its large, edible nuts. **2.** The nut of this tree.

Eng·lish·wom·an (ĭng′glĭsh-wo͝om′ən) *n.* **1.** A woman who is a native or inhabitant of England. **2.** A woman of English descent.

en·glut (ĕn-glŭt′) *tr.v.* **-glut·ted, -glut·ting, -gluts.** To gulp down; swallow greedily. [Anglo-Norman *englutir,* from Late Latin *inglūtīre* : Latin *in-,* intensive pref.; see IN–^{2} + Latin *gluttīre,* to swallow.]

en·gorge (ĕn-gôrj′) *v.* **-gorged, -gorg·ing, -gorg·es.** —*tr.* **1.** To devour greedily. **2.** To gorge; glut. **3.** To fill to excess, as with blood or other fluid. —*intr.* To feed ravenously. [French *engorger,* from Old French *engorgier* : *en-,* in; see EN–^{1} + *gorge,* throat; see GORGE.] **—en·gorge′ment** *n.*

engr. *abbr.* **1.** Engineer. **2.a.** Engraved. **b.** Engraver. **c.** Engraving.

en·graft (ĕn-grăft′) *tr.v.* **-graft·ed, -graft·ing, -grafts. 1.** To graft (a scion) onto or into another plant. **2.** To plant firmly; establish. **—en·graft′ment** *n.*

en·grailed (ĕn-grāld′) *adj.* **1.** Indented along the edge with small curves. **2.** Having an edge or a margin formed by a series of raised dots: *engrailed silver coins.* [Middle English *engreled,* from Old French *engresle,* past participle of *engresler,* to engrail : *en-,* causative pref.; see EN–^{1} + *gresle,* slender, tapered (from Latin *gracilis*).]

en·grain (ĕn-grān′) *tr.v.* **-grained, -grain·ing, -grains.** To ingrain. [Middle English *engreinen,* to dye with cochineal or kermes, from Old French *engrainer* : *en-,* causative pref.; see EN–^{1} + *graine,* grain; see GRAIN.]

en·gram (ĕn′grăm′) *n.* A physical alteration thought to occur in living neural tissue in response to stimuli, posited as an explanation for memory.

en·grave (ĕn-grāv′) *tr.v.* **-graved, -grav·ing, -graves. 1.** To carve, cut, or etch into a material: *engraved the champion's name on the trophy.* **2.** To carve, cut, or etch a design or letters into: *engraved the silver watch with my monogram.* **3.a.** To carve, cut, or etch into a block or surface used for printing. **b.** To print from a block or plate made by such a process. **4.** To impress deeply as if by carving or etching: *The experience was engraved into his memory.* **—en·grav′er** *n.*

en·grav·ing (ĕn-grā′vĭng) *n. Abbr.* **engr. 1.** The art or technique of one that engraves. **2.** A design or text engraved on a surface. **3.** An engraved surface for printing. **4.** A print made from an engraved plate or block.

en·gross (ĕn-grōs′) *tr.v.* **-grossed, -gross·ing, -gross·es. 1.** To occupy exclusively; absorb: *A great novel engrosses the reader.* See Synonyms at **monopolize. 2.** To acquire most or all of (a commodity); monopolize (a market). **3.a.** To write or transcribe in a large, clear hand. **b.** To write or print the final draft of (an official document). [Middle English *engrossen,* to collect in large quantity, monopolize, from Old French *engrossier,* from *en gros,* in large quantity : *en,* in (from Latin *in;* see IN–^{2}) + *gros,* large; see GROSS. Sense 3, from Middle English *engrossen,* to make a finished copy of a legal document, from Anglo-Norman *engrosser,* from Medieval Latin *ingrossāre* : Latin *in-,* in; see EN–^{1} + *grossa,* a copy in a large hand (from Late Latin *grossus,* thick).] **—en·gross′er** *n.*

en·gross·ing (ĕn-grō′sĭng) *adj.* Occupying one's complete attention; wholly absorbing: *listened to an engrossing symphony.* **—en·gross′ing·ly** *adv.*

en·gross·ment (ĕn-grōs′mənt) *n.* The act of engrossing or the state of being engrossed.

en·gulf (ĕn-gŭlf′) *tr.v.* **-gulfed, -gulf·ing, -gulfs.** To swallow up or overwhelm by or as if by overflowing and enclosing: *The spring tide engulfed the beach houses.* **—en·gulf′ment** *n.*

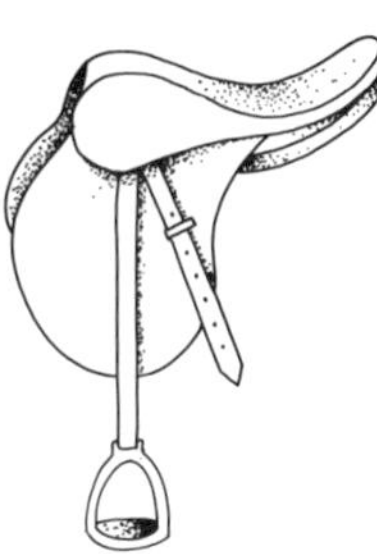

English saddle

en·hance (ĕn-hăns′) *tr.v.* **-hanced, -hanc·ing, -hanc·es.** To make greater, as in value, beauty, or reputation; augment: *"She had a sweetness to her face, a warmth that was enhanced by luminous dark eyes"* (Gioia Diliberto). [Middle English *enhauncen,* from Anglo-Norman *enhauncer,* variant of Old French *enhaucier,* from Vulgar Latin **inaltiāre,* from Late Latin *inaltāre* : Latin *in-,* causative pref.; see EN–^{1} + *altus,* high; see **al-**^{2} in Appendix.] **—en·hance′ment** *n.* **—en·hanc′er** *n.* **—en·hanc′ive** *adj.*

en·har·mon·ic (ĕn′här-mŏn′ĭk) *adj. Music.* Of, relating to, or involving tones that are identical in pitch but are written differently according to the key in which they occur. [Late Latin *enharmonicus,* from Greek *enarmonios* : *en-,* in; see EN–^{2} + *harmonia,* harmony; see HARMONY.] **—en′har·mon′i·cal·ly** *adv.*

E·nid (ē′nĭd). A city of north-central Oklahoma north-northwest of Oklahoma City. It is a trade center. Population, 50,363.

e·nig·ma (ĭ-nĭg′mə) *n.* **1.** One that is puzzling, ambiguous, or inexplicable. **2.** A perplexing speech or text; a riddle. [Latin *aenigma,* from Greek *ainigma,* from *ainissesthai, ainig-,* to speak in riddles, from *ainos,* fable.]

en·ig·mat·ic (ĕn′ĭg-măt′ĭk) or **en·ig·mat·i·cal** (-ĭ-kəl) *adj.* Of or resembling an enigma; puzzling: *a professor's enigmatic grading system.* See Synonyms at **ambiguous.** [Greek *ainigmatikos,* from *ainigma, ainigmat-,* riddle. See ENIGMA.] **—en′ig·mat′i·cal·ly** *adv.*

en·isle (ĕn-īl′) *tr.v.* **-isled, -isl·ing, -isles. 1.** To make into an island. **2.** To set apart from others; isolate.

En·i·we·tok (ĕn′ə-wē′tŏk′, ə-nē′wĭ-). An atoll in the Ralik Chain of the Marshall Islands in the west-central Pacific Ocean. It was the site of U.S. atomic tests from 1948 to 1954.

en·jamb·ment or **en·jambe·ment** (ĕn-jăm′mənt, -jămb′) *n.* The continuation of a syntactic unit from one line or couplet of a poem to the next with no pause. [French *enjambement,* from Old French *enjamber,* to straddle : *en-,* causative pref.; see EN–^{1} + *jambe,* leg; see JAMB.]

en·join (ĕn-join′) *tr.v.* **-joined, -join·ing, -joins. 1.** To direct or impose with authority and emphasis. **2.** To prohibit or forbid. See Synonyms at **forbid.** [Middle English *enjoinen,* from Old French *enjoindre,* from Latin *iniungere* : *in-,* causative pref.; see EN–^{1} + *iungere,* to join; see **yeug-** in Appendix.] **—en·join′er** *n.* **—en·join′ment** *n.*

English setter

en·joy (ĕn-joi′) *v.* **-joyed, -joy·ing, -joys.** —*tr.* **1.** To receive pleasure or satisfaction from. See Synonyms at **like**^{1}. **2.** To have the use or benefit of: *enjoys good health.* —*intr.* To have a pleasurable or satisfactory time. [Middle English *enjoien,* from Old French *enjoir* : *en-,* intensive pref.; see EN–^{1} + *joir,* to rejoice (from Latin *gaudēre;* see **gāu-** in Appendix).] **—en·joy′a·ble** *adj.* **—en·joy′a·bly** *adv.* **—en·joy′er** *n.*

en·joy·ment (ĕn-joi′mənt) *n.* **1.** The act or state of enjoying. See Synonyms at **pleasure. 2.** Use or possession of something beneficial or pleasurable. **3.** Something that gives pleasure: *Classical music was her chief enjoyment.*

en·keph·a·lin (ĕn-kĕf′ə-lĭn) *n.* Either of two closely related pentapeptides having opiate qualities and occurring in the brain, spinal cord, and other parts of the body. [Greek *enkephalos,* in the head (*en-,* in; see **en** in Appendix + *kephalē,* head; see **ghebh-el-** in Appendix) + –IN.]

en·kin·dle (ĕn-kĭn′dl) *v.* **-dled, -dling, -dles.** —*tr.* **1.** To set afire; light. **2.** To incite; arouse. **3.** To make luminous and glowing. —*intr.* To catch fire. **—en·kin′dler** *n.*

enl. *abbr.* **1.** Enlarged. **2.** Enlisted.

en·lace (ĕn-lās′) also **in·lace** (ĭn-) *tr.v.* **-laced, -lac·ing, -lac·es. 1.** To wrap or wind about with or as if with a lace or laces; encircle. **2.** To interlace; entwine. **—en·lace′ment** *n.*

en·large (ĕn-lärj′) *v.* **-larged, -larg·ing, -larg·es.** —*tr.* **1.** To make larger; add to. **2.** To give greater scope to; expand. See Synonyms at **increase.** —*intr.* **1.** To become larger; grow. **2.** To speak or write at greater length or in greater detail; elaborate: *enlarged upon the plan.* [Middle English *enlargen,* from Old French *enlargier* : *en-,* causative pref.; see EN–^{1} + *large,* large; see LARGE.] **—en·larg′er** *n.*

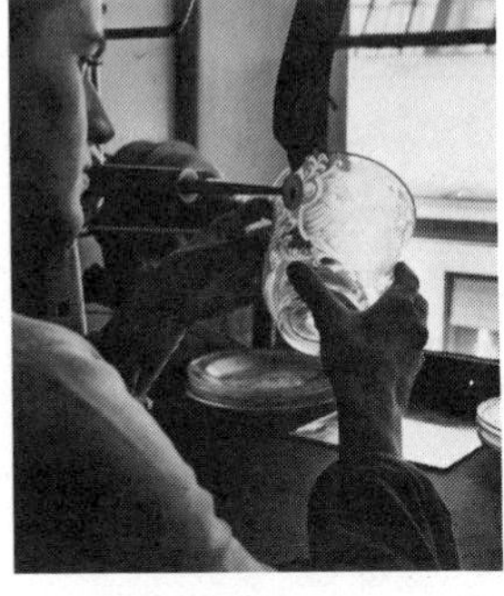

engraving

en·large·ment (ĕn-lärj′mənt) *n.* **1.** An act of enlarging or the state of being enlarged. **2.** Something that enlarges; an addition. **3.** Something that has been enlarged, especially a photographic reproduction or a copy larger than the original print or negative.

en·light·en (ĕn-līt′n) *tr.v.* **-ened, -en·ing, -ens. 1.** To give spiritual or intellectual insight to: *"Enlighten the people generally, and tyranny and oppression of body and mind will vanish like evil spirits at the dawn of day"* (Thomas Jefferson). **2.** To give information to; inform or instruct. **—en·light′en·er** *n.*

en·light·en·ment (ĕn-līt′n-mənt) *n.* **1.a.** The act or a means of enlightening. **b.** The state of being enlightened. **2. Enlightenment.** A philosophical movement of the 18th century that emphasized the use of reason to scrutinize previously accepted doctrines and traditions and that brought about many humanitarian reforms. Used with *the.* **3.** *Buddhism.* A blessed state in which the individual transcends desire and suffering and attains Nirvana.

en·list (ĕn-lĭst′) *v.* **-list·ed, -list·ing, -lists.** —*tr.* **1.** To engage (persons or a person) for service in the armed forces. **2.** To engage the support or cooperation of. —*intr.* **1.** To enter the armed forces. **2.** To participate actively in a cause or an enterprise. **—en·list′ment** *n.*

en·list·ed man (ĕn-lĭs′tĭd) *n. Abbr.* **EM** A male member of the armed forces who ranks below a commissioned officer or warrant officer.

enlisted person *n.* A member of the armed forces who ranks below a commissioned officer or warrant officer.

enlisted woman *n. Abbr.* **EW** A woman member of the armed forces who ranks below a commissioned officer or warrant officer.

en·list·ee (ĕn-lĭs′tē′) *n.* A person who enlists or is enlisted for service in the armed forces.

en·liv·en (ĕn-lī′vən) *tr.v.* **-ened, -en·ing, -ens.** To make lively or spirited; animate. **—en·liv′en·er** *n.* **—en·liv′en·ment** *n.*

en masse (ŏn măs′) *adv.* In one group or body; all together: *The peace activists marched en masse to the capitol.* [French : *en,* in + *masse,* mass.]

en·mesh (ĕn-mĕsh′) also **im·mesh** (ĭm-) *tr.v.* **-meshed, -mesh·ing, -mesh·es.** To entangle, involve, or catch in or as if in a mesh. See Synonyms at **catch. —en·mesh′ment** *n.*

en·mi·ty (ĕn′mĭ-tē) *n., pl.* **-ties.** Deep-seated, often mutual hatred. [Middle English *enemite,* from Old French *enemistie,* from Vulgar Latin **inimīcitās,* from Latin *inimīcus,* enemy. See ENEMY.]

SYNONYMS: *enmity, hostility, antagonism, animosity, rancor, antipathy, animus.* These nouns refer to the feeling or expression of deep-seated ill will. *Enmity* is hatred such as might be felt for an enemy: *The wartime enmity of the two nations subsided into mutual distrust when peace finally came. Hostility* implies the clear expression of enmity, as in the form of belligerent attitudes or violent acts: *"If we could read the secret history of our enemies, we should find in each man's life sorrow and suffering enough to disarm all hostility"* (Henry Wadsworth Longfellow). *Antagonism* is hostility that quickly results in active resistance, opposition, or contentiousness: *antagonism between the liberal and conservative elements of the party. Animosity* is angry ill will that often triggers the taking of rancorous or punitive action: *tried to overcome his animosity toward governmental control. Rancor* suggests the harboring of hatred and resentment typically traceable to past grievances that have led to a desire for revenge: *parting without rancor. Antipathy* is deep-seated aversion or repugnance: *a deep antipathy to social pretension. Animus* is ill will of a distinctively personal nature, often based on one's prejudices or temperament: *an inexplicable animus against intellectuals.*

en·ne·ad (ĕn′ē-ăd′) *n.* A group or set of nine. [Greek *enneas, ennead-,* from *ennea,* nine. See **newn̥** in Appendix.]

en·no·ble (ĕn-nō′bəl) *tr.v.* **-bled, -bling, -bles. 1.** To make noble: *"that chastity of honor . . . which ennobled whatever it touched, and under which vice itself lost half its evil"* (Edmund Burke). **2.** To confer nobility upon: *ennoble a prime minister for distinguished service.* [Middle English **ennoblen,* from Old French *ennoblir* : *en-,* causative pref.; see EN–[1] + *noble,* noble; see NOBLE.] **—en·no′ble·ment** *n.* **—en·no′bler** *n.*

en·nui (ŏn-wē′, ŏn′wē) *n.* Listlessness and dissatisfaction resulting from lack of interest; boredom: *"The servants relieved their ennui with gambling and gossip about their masters"* (John Barth). See Synonyms at **boredom.** [French, from Old French *enui,* from *ennuier,* to annoy, bore, from Vulgar Latin **inodiāre,* from Latin *in odiō (esse),* (to be) odious : *in,* in; see IN–[2] + *odiō,* ablative of *odium,* hate; see **od-** in Appendix.]

WORD HISTORY: Were they alive today, users of Classical Latin might be surprised to find that centuries later a phrase of theirs would still survive, although in the form of a single word. The phrase *mihi in odiō est* (literally translated as "to me in a condition of dislike or hatred is"), meaning "I hate or dislike," gave rise to the Vulgar Latin verb **inodiāre,* "to make odious," the source of Modern French *ennuyer,* "to annoy, bore." In the Old French period a noun meaning "worry, boredom," came from the verb *ennuier.* This noun in its Modern French form *ennui* was borrowed into English in the sense "boredom," the English word being first recorded in 1732. People may have needed a word for boredom in the polite, cultivated world of the 18th century, but at an earlier period, around 1275, we had already borrowed the French verb *ennuier,* the source of our word *annoy.* One of the earliest instances of *annoy* in English is, in fact, used in the sense "to bore an audience."

e·no·ki (ē-nŏk′ē) *n.* Enokidake.

e·no·ki·da·ke (ĭ-nō′kē-dä′kē) *n.* A widely cultivated mushroom *(Flammulina velutipes)* native to North America and eastern Asia, having a pinlike appearance that superficially resembles the bean sprout. Also called *golden needles.* [Japanese : *enoki,* Chinese nettle tree + *take,* bamboo, mushroom.]

e·nol (ē′nôl′, ē′nōl′) *n.* An organic compound containing a hydroxyl group bonded to a carbon atom, which in turn is doubly bonded to another carbon atom. [From –EN(E) + –OL[1].] **—e·nol′ic** (ē-nŏl′ĭk) *adj.*

e·no·lase (ē′nə-lās′, -lāz′) *n.* An enzyme present in muscle tissue that acts in carbohydrate metabolism.

e·nol·o·gy also **oe·nol·o·gy** (ē-nŏl′ə-jē) *n.* The study of wine and the making of wine; viticulture. [Greek *oinos,* wine + –LOGY.] **—e′no·log′i·cal** (ē′nə-lŏj′ĭ-kəl) *adj.* **—e·nol′o·gist** *n.*

e·nor·mi·ty (ĭ-nôr′mĭ-tē) *n., pl.* **-ties. 1.** The quality of passing all moral bounds; excessive wickedness or outrageousness. **2.** A monstrous offense or evil; an outrage. **3.** *Usage Problem.* Great size; immensity: *"Beyond that,* [Russia's] *sheer enormity offered a defense against invaders that no European nation enjoyed"* (W. Bruce Lincoln). [French *énormité,* from Old French, from Latin *ēnormitās,* from *ēnormis,* unusual, enormous. See ENORMOUS.]

USAGE NOTE: *Enormity* is frequently used to refer simply to the property of being enormous, but many would prefer that *enormousness* (or a synonym such as *immensity*) be used for this general sense and that *enormity* be reserved for a property that evokes a negative moral judgment: *Not until the war ended and journalists were able to enter Cambodia did the world really become aware of the enormity of Pol Pot's oppression.* Fifty-nine percent of the Usage Panel rejects the use of *enormity* in the more general sense in the sentence *At that point the engineers sat down to design an entirely new viaduct, apparently undaunted by the enormity of their task.* This distinction between *enormity* and *enormousness* has not always existed historically, but nowadays many observe it. Writers who ignore it in phrases such as *the enormity of her inheritance* may find their words an unintended source of amusement.

e·nor·mous (ĭ-nôr′məs) *adj.* **1.** Very great in size, extent, number, or degree. **2.** *Archaic.* Very wicked; heinous. [From Latin *ēnormis,* unusual, huge : *ē-, ex-,* ex- + *norma,* norm; see **gnō-** in Appendix. Sense 2, from Middle English *enormious,* from Latin *ēnormis,* monstrous.] **—e·nor′mous·ly** *adv.* **—e·nor′mous·ness** *n.*

SYNONYMS: *enormous, immense, huge, gigantic, colossal, mammoth, tremendous, stupendous, gargantuan, vast.* These adjectives describe what is extraordinarily large. *Enormous* suggests a marked excess beyond the norm in size, amount, or degree: *an enormous boulder; enormous expenses. Immense* refers to boundless or immeasurable size or extent: *an immense crowd of people; immense pleasure. Huge* especially implies greatness of size or capacity: *a huge wave; a huge success. Gigantic* refers to size likened to that of a giant: *a gigantic redwood tree; a gigantic disappointment. Colossal* suggests a hugeness that elicits awe or taxes belief: *colossal crumbling ruins of an ancient temple; has a colossal nerve. Mammoth* is applied to something of clumsy or unwieldy hugeness: *a mammoth ship; a mammoth multinational corporation. Tremendous* suggests awe-inspiring or fearsome size: *a tremendous monument 100 feet high; ate a tremendous meal. Stupendous* implies size that astounds or defies description: *an undertaking of stupendous difficulty. "The whole thing was a stupendous, incomprehensible farce"* (W. Somerset Maugham). *Gargantuan* especially stresses greatness of capacity, as for food or pleasure: *a gargantuan appetite. Vast* refers to greatness of extent, size, area, or scope: *"All the land was shrouded in one vast forest"* (Theodore Roosevelt). *"Of creatures, how few vast as the whale"* (Herman Melville).

e·nough (ĭ-nŭf′) *adj.* Sufficient to meet a need or satisfy a desire; adequate: *enough work to keep us all busy.* See Synonyms at **sufficient. —enough** *pron.* An adequate number or quantity: *"The Gods above should give,/They have enough and we do poorly live"* (Henry David Thoreau). **—enough** *adv.* **1.** To a satisfactory amount or degree; sufficiently: *Is the fish cooked enough?* **2.** Very; fully; quite: *We were glad enough to leave.* **3.** Tolerably; rather: *She sang well enough, but the show was a failure.* **—enough** *interj.* Used to express impatience or exasperation: *You've been practicing the violin all afternoon. Enough!* [Middle English *enogh,* from Old English *genōg.* See **nek-**[2] in Appendix.]

e·nounce (ĭ-nouns′) *tr.v.* **e·nounced, e·nounc·ing, e·nounc·es. 1.** To declare formally; state. **2.** To pronounce clearly; enunciate. [From French *énoncer,* from Latin *ēnūntiāre,* to speak out. See ENUNCIATE.] **—e·nounce′ment** *n.*

e·now (ĭ-nou′) *adj. & adv. Archaic.* Enough. [Middle English, variant of *enogh.* See ENOUGH.]

en pas·sant (äN′ pä-säN′) *adv.* **1.** In passing; by the way; incidentally. **2.** *Games.* Used in reference to a move in chess in which a pawn that has just completed an initial advance to its fourth rank is captured by an opponent pawn as if it had only moved to its third rank. [French : *en,* in + *passant,* passing.]

en·phy·tot·ic (ĕn′fī-tŏt′ĭk) *adj.* Of or relating to a plant disease that causes a relatively constant amount of damage each year. [EN–[2] + –PHYT(E) + –OTIC.] **—en′phy·tot′ic** *n.*

en·plane (ĕn-plān′) also **em·plane** (ĕm-) *intr.v.* **-planed, -plan·ing, -planes.** To board an airplane.

en prise (än′ prēz′, äN) *adj. Games.* Exposed to possible capture. Used of a chess piece. [French : *en,* in + *prise,* grip, grasp.]

en·quire (ĕn-kwīr′) *v.* Variant of **inquire.**

en·quir·y (ĕn-kwīr′ē, ĕn′kwə-rē) *n., pl.* **-ies.** Variant of **inquiry.**

en·rage (ĕn-rāj′) *tr.v.* **-raged, -rag·ing, -rag·es.** To put into a rage; infuriate. [Middle English **enragen,* from Old French *enrager* : *en-,* causative pref.; see EN–[1] + *rage,* rage; see RAGE.] **—en·rage′ment** *n.*

en rap·port (äɴ′ rə-pôr′, -pōr′, rä-) *adj.* Being in agreement; harmonious. [French : *en,* in + *rapport,* agreement.]

en·rapt (ĕn-răpt′) *adj.* Filled with or transported by delight; enraptured.

en·rap·ture (ĕn-răp′chər) *tr.v.* **-tured, -tur·ing, -tures.** To fill with rapture or delight. **—en·rap′ture·ment** *n.*

SYNONYMS: *enrapture, entrance, ravish, thrill, transport.* The central meaning shared by these verbs is "to have a powerful, agreeable, and often overwhelming emotional effect on someone": *enraptured by the music; a view of the Alps that entranced us; a painting that ravished the eye; thrilled by their success; transported with joy.*

en·rich (ĕn-rĭch′) *tr.v.* **-riched, -rich·ing, -rich·es. 1.** To make rich or richer. **2.** To make fuller, more meaningful, or more rewarding: *An appreciation of art will enrich your life.* **3.** To add fertilizer to. **4.** To add nutrients to: *The dairy enriched its milk with vitamin D.* **5.** To add to the beauty or character of; adorn: *"Glittering tears enriched her eyes"* (Arnold Bennett). **6.** *Physics.* To increase the amount of one or more radioactive isotopes in (a material, especially a nuclear fuel). [Middle English *enrichen,* from Old French *enrichier* : *en-,* causative pref.; see EN–[1] + *riche,* rich; see RICH.] **—en·rich′er** *n.*

en·rich·ment (ĕn-rĭch′mənt) *n.* **1.** The act of enriching or the state of being enriched. **2.** Something that enriches.

en·robe (ĕn-rōb′) *tr.v.* **-robed, -rob·ing, -robes.** To dress in or as if in a robe.

en·roll also **en·rol** (ĕn-rōl′) *v.* **-rolled, -roll·ing, -rolls** also **-rols.** *—tr.* **1.** To enter or register in a roll, list, or record: *enrolled the child in kindergarten; enroll the minutes of the meeting.* **2.** To roll or wrap up. **3.** To write or print a final copy of; engross. *—intr.* To place one's name on a roll or register; sign up: *We enrolled in the army.* [Middle English *enrollen,* from Old French *enroller* : *en-,* in; see EN–[1] + *rolle,* roll (from Latin *rotula,* little wheel; see ROLL).] **—en·roll·ee′** *n.*

en·roll·ment also **en·rol·ment** (ĕn-rōl′mənt) *n.* **1.a.** The act or process of enrolling. **b.** The state of being enrolled. **2.** The number enrolled: *The class has an enrollment of 27 students.* **3.** A record or an entry.

en·root (ĕn-rōōt′, -rŏŏt′) *tr.v.* **-root·ed, -root·ing, -roots.** To establish firmly by or as if by roots; implant.

en route (ŏn rōōt′, ĕn) *adv. & adj.* On or along the way: *We are en route to the museum. The restaurant was en route.* [French : *en,* on + *route,* route.]

ENS or **Ens.** *abbr.* Ensign.

en·san·guine (ĕn-săng′gwĭn) *tr.v.* **-guined, -guin·ing, -guines.** To cover or stain with or as if with blood.

En·sche·da (ĕn′skə-dä′, -sᴋʜə-). A city of eastern Netherlands near the German border. It is a textile center. Population, 144,938.

en·sconce (ĕn-skŏns′) *tr.v.* **-sconced, -sconc·ing, -sconc·es. 1.** To settle (oneself) securely or comfortably: *She ensconced herself in an armchair.* **2.** To place or conceal in a secure place. [EN–[1] + SCONCE[1].]

en·sem·ble (ŏn-sŏm′bəl) *n.* **1.** A unit or group of complementary parts that contribute to a single effect, especially: **a.** A coordinated outfit or costume. **b.** A group of supporting musicians, singers, dancers, or actors who perform together. **2.** *Music.* **a.** A work for two or more vocalists or instrumentalists. **b.** The vocalists or instrumentalists who perform such a work. [French, from Old French, together, from Late Latin *insimul,* at the same time : *in-,* intensive pref.; see IN–[2] + *simul,* at the same time; see **sem-**[1] in Appendix.]

En·se·na·da (ĕn′sə-nä′də). A city of northwest Mexico on the Pacific Ocean. It is a popular resort. Population, 120,483.

en·shrine (ĕn-shrīn′) also **in·shrine** (ĭn-) *tr.v.* **-shrined, -shrin·ing, -shrines. 1.** To enclose in or as if in a shrine. **2.** To cherish as sacred. **—en·shrine′ment** *n.*

en·shroud (ĕn-shroud′) *tr.v.* **-shroud·ed, -shroud·ing, -shrouds.** To cover with or as if with a shroud: *Clouds enshrouded the summit.*

en·si·form (ĕn′sə-fôrm′) *adj.* Shaped like a sword, as the leaf of an iris. [Latin *ēnsis,* sword + –FORM.]

en·sign (ĕn′sən, -sīn′) *n.* **1.** A national flag displayed on ships and aircraft, often with the special insignia of a branch or unit of the armed forces. **2.** A standard or banner, as of a military unit. **3.** *Archaic.* A standard-bearer. **4.** (ĕn′sən). *Abbr.* **ENS, Ens. a.** A commissioned rank in the U.S. Navy or Coast Guard that is below lieutenant junior grade. **b.** One who holds this rank. **5.a.** A badge of office or power; an emblem: *"I want the seals of power and place,/The ensigns of command,/Charged by the people's unbought grace,/To rule my native land"* (John Quincy Adams). **b.** A sign; a token. [Middle English *ensigne,* from Old French *enseigne,* from Latin *īnsignia,* insignia. See INSIGNIA.]

en·si·lage (ĕn′sə-lĭj) *n.* **1.** The process of storing and fermenting green fodder in a silo. **2.** Fodder preserved in a silo; silage. **—ensilage** *tr.v.* **-laged, -lag·ing, -lag·es.** To ensile. [French, from *ensiler,* to ensile. See ENSILE.]

en·sile (ĕn-sīl′) *tr.v.* **-siled, -sil·ing, -siles.** To store (fodder) in a silo for preservation. [French *ensiler,* from Spanish *ensilar* : *en-,* in (from Latin *in-*; see EN–[1]) + *silo,* silo; see SILO.]

en·slave (ĕn-slāv′) *tr.v.* **-slaved, -slav·ing, -slaves.** To make into or as if into a slave. **—en·slave′ment** *n.* **—en·slav′er** *n.*

en·snare (ĕn-snâr′) also **in·snare** (ĭn-) *tr.v.* **-snared, -snar·ing, -snares.** To take or catch in or as if in a snare. See Synonyms at **catch. —en·snare′ment** *n.* **—en·snar′er** *n.*

en·snarl (ĕn-snärl′) *tr.v.* **-snarled, -snarl·ing, -snarls.** To entangle in or as if in a snarl: *"The Senate has contrived to ensnarl several major proposals in two legislative tangles"* (New York Times).

En·sor (ĕn′sôr), **James.** 1860–1949. Belgian painter whose works, such as *Entry of Christ into Brussels* (1888), influenced surrealism and often feature nightmarish, masked faces.

en·soul (ĕn-sōl′) also **in·soul** (ĭn-) *tr.v.* **-souled, -soul·ing, -souls. 1.** To endow with a soul. **2.** To place, receive, or cherish in the soul.

en·sphere (ĕn-sfîr′) also **in·sphere** (ĭn-) *tr.v.* **-sphered, -spher·ing, -spheres.** To enclose in or as if in a sphere.

en·sta·tite (ĕn′stə-tīt′) *n.* A glassy, usually yellowish gray variety of orthorhombic pyroxene having a magnesium silicate base, mainly $MgSiO_3$, usually found embedded in igneous rocks and meteorites. [Greek *enstatēs,* adversary (because of its refractory quality) : *en-,* in, at, near; see EN–[2] + *-statēs,* one that stands; see **stā-** in Appendix + –ITE[1].]

en·sue (ĕn-sōō′) *intr.v.* **-sued, -su·ing, -sues. 1.** To follow as a consequence or result. See Synonyms at **follow. 2.** To take place subsequently. [Middle English *ensuen,* from Old French *ensuivre, ensu-,* from Vulgar Latin **īnsequere,* from Latin *īnsequī,* to follow closely : *in-,* intensive pref.; see EN–[1] + *sequī,* to follow; see **sekʷ-**[1] in Appendix.]

en suite (äɴ swēt′) *adv. & adj.* In or as part of a series or set: *a room and its furniture that were decorated en suite; en suite decorations.* [French : *en,* in + *suite,* a following, sequence.]

en·sure (ĕn-shŏŏr′) *tr.v.* **-sured, -sur·ing, -sures.** To make sure or certain; insure: *Our precautions ensured our safety.* See Usage Note at **assure.** [Middle English *ensuren,* from Anglo-Norman *enseurer* : Old French *en-,* causative pref.; see EN–[1] + Old French *seur,* secure, variant of *sur;* see SURE.]

ENT *abbr.* *Medicine.* Ear, nose, and throat.

ent– *pref.* Variant of **ento–.**

–ent *suff.* **1.a.** Performing, promoting, or causing a specified action: *absorbent.* **b.** Being in a specified state or condition: *bivalent.* **2.** One that performs, promotes, or causes a specified action: *referent.* [Middle English, from Old French, from Latin *-ēns, -ent-,* present participle suff.]

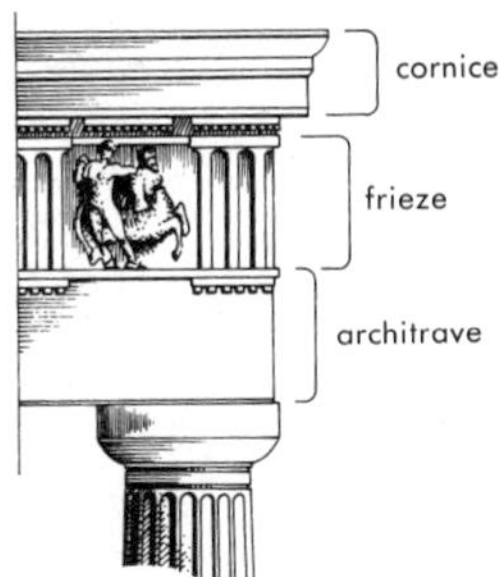

entablature

en·tab·la·ture (ĕn-tăb′lə-chŏŏr′) *n.* The upper section of a classical building, resting on the columns and constituting the architrave, frieze, and cornice. [Obsolete French, from Italian *intavolatura,* from *intavolare,* to put on a table : *in-,* in, on (from Latin; see EN–[1]) + *tavola,* table (from Latin *tabula,* board).]

en·ta·ble·ment (ĕn-tā′bəl-mənt) *n.* A platform above the base and the dado of a pedestal. [French, from Old French : *en-,* in, on; see EN–[1] + *table,* table; see TABLE + *-ment,* -ment.]

en·tail (ĕn-tāl′, ĭn-) *tr.v.* **-tailed, -tail·ing, -tails. 1.** To have, impose, or require as a necessary accompaniment or consequence: *an investment that entailed high risk.* **2.** To limit the inheritance of (property) to a specified succession of heirs. **3.** To bestow or impose on a person or a specified succession of heirs. **—entail** *n.* **1.a.** The act of entailing, especially property. **b.** The state of being entailed. **2.** An entailed estate. **3.** A predetermined order of succession, as to an estate or to an office. **4.** Something transmitted as if by unalterable inheritance. [Middle English *entaillen,* to limit inheritance to specific heirs : *en-,* intensive pref.; see EN–[1] + *taille,* tail; see TAIL[2].] **—en·tail′ment** *n.*

en·ta·moe·ba or **en·ta·me·ba** (ĕn′tə-mē′bə) also **en·da·moe·ba** or **en·da·me·ba** (ĕn′də-) *n., pl.* **-bas** or **-bae** (-bē). Any of several parasitic amoebas of the genus *Entamoeba,* especially *E. histolytica,* causing dysentery and ulceration of the colon and liver. [New Latin *Entamoeba,* genus name : ENT(O)– + AMOEBA.]

en·tan·gle (ĕn-tăng′gəl) *tr.v.* **-gled, -gling, -gles. 1.** To twist together or entwine into a confusing mass; snarl. **2.** To complicate; confuse. **3.** To involve in or as if in a tangle. See Synonyms at **catch. —en·tan′gle·ment** *n.* **—en·tan′gler** *n.*

En·teb·be (ĕn-tĕb′ə, -tĕb′ē). A town of southern Uganda on Lake Victoria. At its airport in 1976 Israeli commando forces rescued most of the hostages held aboard an Air France plane by Palestinian hijackers. Population, 21,289.

en·tel·e·chy (ĕn-tĕl′ĭ-kē) *n., pl.* **-chies. 1.** In the philosophy of Aristotle, the condition of a thing whose essence is fully realized; actuality. **2.** In some philosophical systems, a vital force that directs an organism toward self-fulfillment. [Late Latin *entelechīa,* from Greek *entelekheia* : *entelēs,* complete (*en-,* in; see EN–[2] + *telos,* completion; see **kʷel-**[1] in Appendix) + *ekhein,* to have; see **segh-** in Appendix.]

en·tente (ŏn-tŏnt′) *n.* **1.** An agreement between two or more governments or powers for cooperative action or policy: *"the economic entente between the Soviet Union and western Europe"*

ă pat	oi boy
ā pay	ou out
âr care	ŏŏ took
ä father	ōō boot
ĕ pet	ŭ cut
ē be	ûr urge
ĭ pit	th thin
ī pie	*th* this
îr pier	hw which
ŏ pot	zh vision
ō toe	ə about, item
ô paw	♦ regionalism

Stress marks: **′** (primary); ′ (secondary), as in **dictionary** (dĭk′shə-nĕr′ē)

(Robert W. Tucker). **2.** The parties to such an agreement. [French, from Old French, intent, from feminine past participle of *entendre,* to understand, intend. See INTEND.]

en·ter (ĕn′tər) *v.* **-tered, -ter·ing, -ters.** —*tr.* **1.** To come or go into: *The train entered the tunnel.* **2.** To penetrate; pierce: *The bullet entered the victim's skull.* **3.** To introduce; insert: *She entered the probe into the patient's artery.* **4.a.** To become a participant, member, or part of; join: *too old to enter the army; entered the discussion at a crucial moment.* **b.** To gain admission to (a school, for example). **5.** To cause to become a participant, member, or part of; enroll: *entered the children in private school; entered dahlias in a flower show.* **6.** To embark on; begin: *With Sputnik, the Soviet Union entered the space age.* **7.** To make a beginning in; take up: *entered medicine.* **8.** To write or put in: *We entered our names in the guest book; enters the data into the computer.* **9.** To place formally on record; submit: *enter a plea of innocence; enter a complaint.* **10.** To go to or occupy in order to claim possession of (land). **11.** To report (a ship or cargo) to customs. —*intr.* **1.** To come or go in; make an entry: *As the President entered, the band played "Hail to the Chief."* **2.** To effect penetration. **3.** To become a member or participant. —***phrasal verbs.* enter into. 1.** To participate in; take an active role or interest in: *enter into politics; enter into negotiations.* **2.** To become party to (a contract): *The nations entered into a new agreement.* **3.** To become a component of; form a part of: *Financial matters entered into the discussion.* **4.** To consider; investigate: *The report entered into the effect of high interest rates on the market.* **enter on** (or **upon**). **1.** To set out on; begin: *We enter on a new era in our history. They entered upon the most dangerous part of the journey.* **2.** To begin considering; take up: *After discussing the budget deficit, they entered on the problem of raising taxes.* **3.** To take possession of: *She entered upon the estate of her uncle.* [Middle English *entren,* from Old French *entrer,* from Latin *intrāre,* from *intrā,* inside. See **en** in Appendix.]

enter– *pref.* Variant of **entero–.**

en·ter·ic (ĕn-tĕr′ĭk) also **en·ter·al** (ĕn′tər-əl) *adj.* Of, relating to, or being within the intestine.

enteric fever *n.* See **typhoid fever.**

en·ter·i·tis (ĕn′tə-rī′tĭs) *n.* Inflammation of the intestinal tract, especially of the small intestine.

entero– or **enter–** *pref.* Intestine: *enteritis.* [New Latin, from Greek *enteron,* intestine. See **en** in Appendix.]

en·ter·o·bac·ter·i·um (ĕn′tə-rō-băk-tîr′ē-əm) *n., pl.* **-i·a** (-ē-ə). Any of various gram-negative rod-shaped bacteria of the family Enterobacteriaceae that includes some pathogens of plants and animals, such as the colon bacillus and salmonella.

en·ter·o·bi·a·sis (ĕn′tə-rō-bī′ə-sĭs) *n.* Infestation of the intestine with pinworms. [New Latin *Enterobius,* pinworm genus (ENTERO– + Greek *bios,* life; see BIO–) + –IASIS.]

en·ter·o·coc·cus (ĕn′tə-rō-kŏk′əs) *n., pl.* **-coc·ci** (-kŏk′sī′, -kŏk′ī′). A usually nonpathogenic streptococcus that inhabits the intestine. **—en′ter·o·coc′cal** *adj.*

en·ter·o·coele (ĕn′tə-rō-sēl′) *n. Embryology.* The coelom formed from a pocketlike outgrowth of the wall of the archenteron, especially in echinoderms and chordates.

en·ter·o·co·li·tis (ĕn′tə-rō-kō-lī′tĭs, -kə-) *n.* Inflammation of both the small intestine and the colon.

en·ter·o·gas·trone (ĕn′tə-rō-găs′trōn′) *n.* A hormone released by the upper intestinal mucosa that inhibits gastric motility and secretion. [ENTERO– + GASTR(O)– + (HORM)ONE.]

en·ter·o·hep·a·ti·tis (ĕn′tə-rō-hĕp′ə-tī′tĭs) *n.* See **blackhead** (sense 2).

en·ter·o·ki·nase (ĕn′tə-rō-kī′nās′, -nāz′, -kĭn′ās′, -āz′) *n.* An enzyme secreted by the upper intestinal mucosa that converts the inactive trypsinogen to the digestive enzyme trypsin.

en·ter·on (ĕn′tə-rŏn′) *n.* The alimentary canal; the intestines. [Greek. See **en** in Appendix.]

en·ter·o·path·o·gen·ic (ĕn′tə-rō-păth′ə-jĕn′ĭk) *adj.* Capable of causing disease in the intestinal tract. **—en′ter·o·path′o·gen** *n.*

en·ter·op·a·thy (ĕn′tə-rŏp′ə-thē) *n., pl.* **-thies.** A disease of the intestinal tract.

en·ter·os·to·my (ĕn′tə-rŏs′tə-mē) *n., pl.* **-mies.** A surgical procedure by which an opening is formed in the intestine through the abdominal wall. **—en′ter·os′to·mal** *adj.*

en·ter·ot·o·my (ĕn′tə-rŏt′ə-mē) *n., pl.* **-mies.** Surgical incision into the intestine.

en·ter·o·tox·in (ĕn′tə-rō-tŏk′sĭn) *n.* A toxin produced by bacteria that is specific for intestinal cells and causes the vomiting and diarrhea associated with food poisoning.

en·ter·o·vi·rus (ĕn′tə-rō-vī′rəs) *n., pl.* **-rus·es.** Any of a subgroup of picornaviruses, including polioviruses, coxsackieviruses, and echoviruses, that infect the gastrointestinal tract and often spread to other areas of the body, especially the nervous system. **—en′ter·o·vi′ral** *adj.*

en·ter·prise (ĕn′tər-prīz′) *n.* **1.** An undertaking, especially one of some scope, complication, and risk. **2.** A business organization. **3.** Industrious, systematic activity, especially when directed toward profit: *Private enterprise is basic to capitalism.* **4.** Willingness to undertake new ventures; initiative: *"Through want of enterprise and faith men are where they are, buying and selling, and spending their lives like serfs"* (Henry David Thoreau). [Middle English, from Old French *entreprise,* from past participle of *entreprendre,* to undertake : *entre-,* between (from Latin *inter-;* see INTER–) + *prendre,* to take (from Latin *prendere;* see **ghend-** in Appendix).] **—en′ter·pris′er** *n.*

En·ter·prise (ĕn′tər-prīz′). A city of southeast Alabama south-southeast of Montgomery. It is a processing and manufacturing center. Population, 18,033.

enterprise zone *n.* An impoverished area in which businesses are exempt from certain taxes and are given other economic advantages as an inducement to locate there and employ residents.

en·ter·pris·ing (ĕn′tər-prī′zĭng) *adj.* Showing initiative and willingness to undertake new projects: *The enterprising children opened a lemonade stand.* **—en′ter·pris′ing·ly** *adv.*

en·ter·tain (ĕn′tər-tān′) *v.* **-tained, -tain·ing, -tains.** —*tr.* **1.** To hold the attention of with something amusing or diverting. See Synonyms at **amuse. 2.** To extend hospitality toward: *entertain friends at dinner.* **3.a.** To consider; contemplate: *entertain an idea.* **b.** To hold in mind; harbor: *entertained few illusions.* **4.** *Archaic.* To continue with; maintain. **a.** *Obsolete.* To take into one's service; hire. **b.** To give admittance to; receive. —*intr.* **1.** To show hospitality to guests. **2.** To provide entertainment. [Middle English *entertinen,* to maintain, from Old French *entretenir,* from Medieval Latin *intertenēre* : Latin *inter,* among; see INTER– + Latin *tenēre,* to hold; see **ten-** in Appendix.] **—en′ter·tain′er** *n.*

en·ter·tain·ing (ĕn′tər-tā′nĭng) *adj.* Agreeably diverting; amusing: *The children staged an entertaining puppet show.* **—en′ter·tain′ing·ly** *adv.*

en·ter·tain·ment (ĕn′tər-tān′mənt) *n.* **1.** The act of entertaining. **2.** The art or field of entertaining. **3.** Something that amuses, pleases, or diverts, especially a performance or show. **4.** The pleasure afforded by being entertained; amusement: *The comedian performed for our entertainment.* **5.** *Archaic.* Maintenance; support. **6.** *Obsolete.* Employment.

en·thal·py (ĕn′thăl′pē, ĕn-thăl′-) *n., pl.* **-pies.** *Symbol* **H** A thermodynamic function of a system, equivalent to the sum of the internal energy of the system plus the product of its volume multiplied by the pressure exerted on it by its surroundings. [Greek *enthalpein,* to heat in (*en-,* in; see EN–[2] + *thalpein,* to heat) + –Y[2].]

en·thrall (ĕn-thrôl′) also **in·thrall** (ĭn-) *tr.v.* **-thralled, -thrall·ing, -thralls. 1.** To hold spellbound; captivate: *The magic show enthralled the audience.* **2.** To enslave. [Middle English, to put in bondage : *en-,* causative pref.; see EN–[1] + *thrall,* slave; see THRALL.] **—en·thrall′ing·ly** *adv.* **—en·thrall′ment** *n.*

en·throne (ĕn-thrōn′) also **in·throne** (ĭn-) *tr.v.* **-throned, -thron·ing, -thrones. 1.a.** To seat on a throne. **b.** To invest with sovereign power or with the authority of high office. **2.** To raise to a lofty position; exalt. **—en·throne′ment** *n.*

en·thuse (ĕn-thōōz′) *v.* **-thused, -thus·ing, -thus·es.** *Usage Problem.* —*tr.* To cause to become enthusiastic. —*intr.* To show or express enthusiasm: *"Princess Anne . . . enthused over Sarah Ferguson—'a very, very nice girl'"* (Georgina Howell). [Back-formation from ENTHUSIASM.]

USAGE NOTE: The verb *enthuse* is not well accepted; its use in the sentence *The majority leader enthused over his party's gains* was rejected by 76 percent of the Usage Panel in an earlier survey. This lack of acceptance of *enthuse* is often attributed to its status as a back-formation: such words often meet with disapproval on their first appearance and only gradually become accepted over time. But other back-formations such as *diagnose* (a back-formation from *diagnosis* that was first recorded in 1861) and *donate* (first cited in 1785 as a back-formation from *donation*) are considered unimpeachable English words. This situation suggests that in truth the continued lack of acceptance of *enthuse,* first recorded in 1827, may have less to do with doubts about its lineage than with shortcomings in its character. Unlike *enthusiasm,* which denotes an internal emotional state, *enthuse* denotes either the external expression of emotion, as in *She enthused over attending the Oscar ceremonies,* or the inducement of enthusiasm by an external source, as in *He was so enthused about the miracle diet pills that he agreed to do a testimonial for their television ad.* It is possible that a distaste for this emphasis on external emotional display and manipulation is for some people the source of an unease that manifests itself in a distaste for the word itself. See Usage Note at **intuit.**

en·thu·si·asm (ĕn-thōō′zē-ăz′əm) *n.* **1.** Great excitement for or interest in a subject or cause. **2.** A source or cause of great excitement or interest. **3.** *Archaic.* **a.** Ecstasy arising from supposed possession by a god. **b.** Religious fanaticism. [Late Latin *enthūsiasmus,* from Greek *enthousiasmos,* from *enthousiazein,* to be inspired by a god, from *entheos,* possessed : *en-,* in; see EN–[2] + *theos,* god; see **dhēs-** in Appendix.]

WORD HISTORY: When the English philosopher Henry More stated in a work published in 1660 that "If ever Christianity be exterminated, it will be by Enthusiasme," he clearly used the word differently from the way we do now. He was also using a meaning that differed from the first sense, "possession by a god," recorded in English (1603). *Enthusiasm* and this sense of the word go back to the Greek word *enthousiasmos,* which ultimately comes from the adjective *entheos,* "having the god within," formed from *en–,* "in, within," and *theos,* "god." Henry More in 1660 was referring to belief, either mistaken or unsupported by evidence, in one's own inspiration by the Christian God. *Enthusiasm,* as now most frequently used, has become secularized and at times weakened, so that one can speak of an enthusiasm for fast cars.

---

en·thu·si·ast (ĕn-tho͞o′zē-ăst′) *n.* **1.** One who is filled with enthusiasm; one who is ardently absorbed in an interest or pursuit: *a baseball enthusiast.* **2.** A zealot; a fanatic. See Synonyms at **fanatic.** [Greek *enthousiastēs,* possessed person, from *enthousiazein,* to be inspired. See ENTHUSIASM.]

en·thu·si·as·tic (ĕn-tho͞o′zē-ăs′tĭk) *adj.* Having or demonstrating enthusiasm. **—en·thu′si·as′ti·cal·ly** *adv.*

en·thy·meme (ĕn′thə-mēm′) *n. Logic.* A syllogism in which one of the premises or the conclusion is not stated explicitly. [Latin *enthȳmēma,* from Greek *enthumēma,* a rhetorical argument, from *enthumeisthai,* to consider : *en-,* in; see EN–² + *thumos,* mind.]

en·tice (ĕn-tīs′) *tr.v.* **-ticed, -tic·ing, -tic·es.** To attract by arousing hope or desire; lure: *The promise of higher pay enticed me into the new job.* See Synonyms at **lure.** [Middle English *enticen,* from Old French *enticier,* to instigate, possibly from Vulgar Latin **intītiāre,* to set afire : Latin *in-,* in; see EN–¹ + Latin *tītiō,* firebrand.] **—en·tic′er** *n.* **—en·tic′ing·ly** *adv.*

en·tire (ĕn-tīr′) *adj.* **1.** Having no part excluded or left out; whole: *I read the entire book.* See Synonyms at **whole. 2.** With no reservations or limitations; complete: *gave us his entire attention.* **3.** All in one piece; intact. **4.** Of one piece; continuous. **5.** Not castrated. **6.** *Botany.* Not having an indented margin: *an entire leaf.* **7.** Unmixed or unalloyed; pure or homogenous. **—entire** *n.* **1.** The whole; the entirety. **2.** An uncastrated horse; a stallion. [Middle English, from Old French *entier,* from Latin *integrum,* neuter of *integer.* See **tag-** in Appendix.]

en·tire·ly (ĕn-tīr′lē) *adv.* **1.** Wholly; completely: *entirely satisfied with the meal.* **2.** Solely or exclusively: *He was entirely to blame.*

en·tire·ty (ĕn-tī′rĭ-tē, -tīr′tē) *n., pl.* **-ties. 1.** The state of being entire or complete; wholeness: *To appreciate the sonata, one must hear it in its entirety.* **2.** The entire amount or extent; the whole: *"We rarely remember the entirety of the plot"* (Anthony Burgess).

en·ti·tle (ĕn-tīt′l) *tr.v.* **-tled, -tling, -tles. 1.** To give a name or title to. **2.** To furnish with a right or claim to something: *The coupon entitles the bearer to a 25 percent savings. Every citizen is entitled to equal protection under the law.* [Middle English *entitlen,* from Old French *entiteler,* from Medieval Latin *intitulāre* : Latin *in-,* provide with; see EN–¹ + Latin *titulus,* title.] **—en·ti′tle·ment** *n.*

entitlement program *n.* A government program that guarantees and provides benefits to a particular group: *"cut back on the cost-of-living increases in such entitlement programs as Social Security, civil-service retirement pay, and veterans' pensions"* (Elizabeth Drew).

en·ti·ty (ĕn′tĭ-tē) *n., pl.* **-ties. 1.** Something that exists as a particular and discrete unit: *Persons and corporations are equivalent entities under the law.* **2.** The fact of existence; being. **3.** The existence of something considered apart from its properties. [Medieval Latin *entitās,* from Latin *ēns, ent-,* present participle of *esse,* to be. See **es-** in Appendix.]

ento– or **ent–** *pref.* Inside; within: *entozoan.* [New Latin, from Greek *entos,* within. See **en** in Appendix.]

en·to·blast (ĕn′tə-blăst′) *n.* Any of the blastomeres of an embryo from which the endoderm develops.

en·to·derm (ĕn′tə-dûrm′) *n.* Variant of **endoderm.**

en·toil (ĕn-toil′) *tr.v.* **-toiled, -toil·ing, -toils.** *Archaic.* To ensnare; entrap.

entom. *abbr.* Entomology.

en·tomb (ĕn-to͞om′) *tr.v.* **-tombed, -tomb·ing, -tombs. 1.** To place in or as if in a tomb or grave. **2.** To serve as a tomb for. **—en·tomb′ment** *n.*

entomo– *pref.* Insect: *entomology.* [French, from Greek *entomon,* insect, from neuter of *entomos,* cut in two (from its segmented body), from *entemnein,* to cut up : *en-,* in; see EN–² + *temnein,* to cut; see **tem-** in Appendix.]

en·to·mol·o·gy (ĕn′tə-mŏl′ə-jē) *n. Abbr.* **entom., entomol.** The scientific study of insects. **—en′to·mo·log′ic** (-mə-lŏj′ĭk), **en′to·mo·log′i·cal** (-ĭ-kəl) *adj.* **—en′to·mo·log′i·cal·ly** *adv.* **—en′to·mol′o·gist** *n.*

en·to·moph·a·gous (ĕn′tə-mŏf′ə-gəs) *adj.* Feeding on insects; insectivorous.

en·to·moph·i·lous (ĕn′tə-mŏf′ə-ləs) *adj. Botany.* Pollinated by insects. **—en′to·moph′i·ly** *n.*

en·to·mos·tra·can (ĕn′tə-mŏs′trə-kən) *n.* Any of various small crustaceans formerly constituting the subclass Entomostraca. [From New Latin *Entomostraca,* former subclass name : ENTOM(O)– + Greek *ostraka,* pl. of *ostrakon,* shell; see OSTRACOD.]

en·tou·rage (ŏn′to͞o-räzh′) *n.* **1.** A group of attendants or associates; a retinue. **2.** One's environment or surroundings. [French, from *entourer,* to surround, from Old French *entour,* surroundings : *en-,* in; see EN–¹ + *tour,* circuit; see TOUR.]

en·to·zo·an (ĕn′tə-zō′ən) *n., pl.* **-zo·a** (-zō′ə). Any of various animals, such as tapeworms, that live within other animals, usually as parasites. **—en′to·zo′ic** *adj.*

en·tr'acte (ŏn′trăkt′, äɴ-träkt′) *n.* **1.a.** The interval between two acts of a theatrical performance. **b.** Another performance, as of music or dance, provided between two acts of a theatrical performance. **2.** An interval likened to the one occurring between two acts of a drama. [French : *entre,* between (from Latin *inter;* see INTER–) + *acte,* act (from Old French; see ACT).]

en·trails (ĕn′trālz′, -trəlz) *pl.n.* **1.** The internal organs, especially the intestines; viscera. **2.** Internal parts: *"sidewalk repair shops, where the entrails of bicycles and cars and motorcycles are spread, mechanics poring over them"* (Alan Cowell). [From Middle English *entraille,* from Old French, from Medieval Latin *intrālia,* alteration of Latin *interānea,* from neuter pl. of *interāneus,* internal, from *inter,* within. See **en** in Appendix.]

en·train¹ (ĕn-trān′) *tr.v.* **-trained, -train·ing, -trains. 1.** To pull or draw along after itself. **2.** *Chemistry.* To carry (suspended particles, for example) along in a current. [French *entrainer,* from Old French : *en-,* in; see EN–¹ + *trainer,* to drag; see TRAIN.] **—en·train′er** *n.* **—en·train′ment** *n.*

en·train² (ĕn-trān′) *v.* **-trained, -train·ing, -trains.** —*intr.* To go aboard a train. —*tr.* To put aboard a train.

en·trance¹ (ĕn′trəns) *n.* **1.** The act or an instance of entering. **2.** A means or point by which to enter. **3.** Permission or power to enter; admission: *gained entrance to medical school.* **4.** The point, as in a musical score, at which a performer is to begin. **5.** The first entry of an actor into a scene. [Middle English *entraunce,* right to enter, from Old French, from *entrer,* to enter. See ENTER.]

en·trance² (ĕn-trăns′) *tr.v.* **-tranced, -tranc·ing, -tranc·es. 1.** To put into a trance. **2.** To fill with delight, wonder, or enchantment: *a child who was entranced by a fairy tale.* See Synonyms at **charm, enrapture. —en·trance′ment** *n.* **—en·tranc′ing·ly** *adv.*

en·trance·way (ĕn′trəns-wā′) *n.* An entryway.

en·trant (ĕn′trənt) *n.* One that enters, especially one that enters a competition. [French, from present participle of *entrer,* to enter, from Old French. See ENTER.]

en·trap (ĕn-trăp′) *tr.v.* **-trapped, -trap·ping, -traps. 1.** To catch in or as if in a trap. **2.a.** To lure into danger, difficulty, or a compromising situation. See Synonyms at **catch. b.** To lure into performing a previously or otherwise uncontemplated illegal act. [French *entraper,* from Old French : *en-,* in; see EN–¹ + *trape,* trap (of Germanic origin).] **—en·trap′ment** *n.*

en·treat (ĕn-trēt′) also **in·treat** (ĭn-) —*v.* **-treat·ed, -treat·ing, -treats.** —*tr.* **1.** To make an earnest request of. **2.** To ask for earnestly; petition for. **3.** *Archaic.* To deal with; treat. —*intr.* To make an earnest request or petition; plead. See Synonyms at **beg.** [Middle English *entreten,* from Anglo-Norman *entreter* : *en-,* causative pref.; see EN–¹ + *treter,* to treat; see TREAT.] **—en·treat′ing·ly** *adv.* **—en·treat′ment** *n.*

en·treat·y (ĕn-trē′tē) *n., pl.* **-ies.** An earnest request or petition; a plea.

en·tre·chat (ŏn′trə-shä′) *n.* A jump in ballet during which the dancer crosses the legs a number of times, alternately back and forth. [French, earlier *entrechas,* alteration (influenced by *entre,* between, and *chasse,* chase, from Old French *chacier,* to chase; see CHASE¹) of Italian *(capriola) intrecciata,* intricate (caper), feminine past participle of *intrecciare,* to intertwine : *in-,* in (from Latin; see IN–²) + *treccia,* tress; see TRESS.]

en·tre·côte (äɴ′trə-kōt′) *n.* A cut of steak taken from between the ribs. [French : *entre,* between (from Latin *inter;* see INTER–) + *côte,* rib (from Latin *costa;* see COSTA).]

en·trée or **en·tree** (ŏn′trā, ŏn-trā′) *n.* **1.a.** The main dish of a meal. **b.** A dish served in formal dining immediately before the main course or between two principal courses. **2.a.** The act of entering. **b.** The power, permission, or liberty to enter; admittance. [French, from Old French. See ENTRY.]

en·tre·mets (ŏn′trə-mā′, -mĕ′) *n., pl.* **-mets** (-māz′, -mĕ′). A side dish, such as a relish or dessert, served in addition to the principal course. [Middle English *entremetes,* from Old French *entremes, entremets* : *entre,* between (from Latin *inter;* see INTER–) + *mes, mets,* dish; see MESS.]

en·trench (ĕn-trĕnch′) also **in·trench** (ĭn-) *v.* **-trenched, -trench·ing, -trench·es.** —*tr.* **1.** To provide with a trench, especially for the purpose of fortifying or defending. **2.** To fix firmly or securely: *arguments that only entrench you more firmly in error.* —*intr.* **1.** To dig or occupy a trench. **2.** To encroach, infringe, or trespass. **—en·trench′ment** *n.*

en·tre·pôt (ŏn′trə-pō′) *n.* **1.** A place where goods are stored or deposited and from which they are distributed. **2.** A trading or market center. [French, from *entreposer,* to store : *entre,* in, among (from Latin *inter-;* see INTER–) + *poser,* to place (from Old French; see POSE¹).]

en·tre·pre·neur (ŏn′trə-prə-nûr′, -no͝or′) *n.* A person who organizes, operates, and assumes the risk for a business venture. [French, from Old French, from *entreprendre,* to undertake. See ENTERPRISE.] **—en′tre·pre·neur′i·al** *adj.* **—en′tre·pre·neur′i·al·ism, en′tre·pre·neur′ism** *n.* **—en′tre·pre·neur′ship′** *n.*

en·tre·sol (ĕn′tər-sŏl′, ĕn′trə-, ŏn-trə-sôl′) *n.* The floor just above the ground floor of a building; a mezzanine. [French : *entre-,* between (from Latin *inter-;* see INTER–) + *sol,* floor (from Latin *solum*).]

en·tro·py (ĕn′trə-pē) *n., pl.* **-pies. 1.** *Symbol* **S** For a closed thermodynamic system, a quantitative measure of the amount of

ă pat	oi boy
ā pay	ou out
âr care	o͝o took
ä father	o͞o boot
ĕ pet	ŭ cut
ē be	ûr urge
ĭ pit	th thin
ī pie	*th* this
îr pier	hw which
ŏ pot	zh vision
ō toe	ə about, item
ô paw	♦ regionalism

Stress marks: **′** (primary); ′ (secondary), as in **dictionary** (dĭk′shə-nĕr′ē)

thermal energy not available to do work. **2.** A measure of the disorder or randomness in a closed system. **3.** A measure of the loss of information in a transmitted message. **4.** A hypothetical tendency for all matter and energy in the universe to evolve toward a state of inert uniformity. **5.** Inevitable and steady deterioration of a system or society. [German *Entropie* : Greek *en-*, in; see EN–[2] + Greek *tropē*, transformation; see **trep-** in Appendix.] **—en·tro′pic** (ĕn-trō′pĭk, -trŏp′ĭk) *adj.* **—en·tro′pi·cal·ly** *adv.*

en·trust (ĕn-trŭst′) also **in·trust** (ĭn-) *tr.v.* **-trust·ed, -trust·ing, -trusts. 1.** To give over (something) to another for care, protection, or performance: *"He still has the aura of the priest to whom you would entrust your darkest secrets"* (James Carroll). **2.** To give as a trust to (someone): *entrusted his aides with the task.* See Synonyms at **commit.**

en·try (ĕn′trē) *n., pl.* **-tries. 1.a.** The act or an instance of entering. **b.** The privilege or right of entering. **2.** A means or place by which to enter. **3.a.** The inclusion or insertion of an item, as in a record: *made an entry in the ledger.* **b.** An item entered in this way: *a diary full of interesting entries.* **4.a.** An entry word, as in a dictionary; a headword. **b.** A headword along with its related text. **5.** One entered in a competition: *The magazine received 400 entries for its poetry contest.* [Middle English *entre,* from Old French *entree,* from feminine past participle of *entrer,* to enter. See ENTER.]

en·try-lev·el (ĕn′trē-lĕv′əl) *adj.* Appropriate for or accessible to one who is inexperienced in a field or new to a market: *an entry-level job in advertising; an entry-level computer.*

en·try·way (ĕn′trē-wā′) *n.* A passage or opening by which to enter.

entry word *n.* See **headword** (sense 1).

en·twine (ĕn-twīn′) also **in·twine** (ĭn-) *v.* **-twined, -twin·ing, -twines.** *—tr.* To twine around or together: *The ivy entwined the column.* *—intr.* To twine or twist together. **—en·twine′ment** *n.*

en·twist (ĕn-twĭst′) also **in·twist** (ĭn-) *tr.v.* **-twist·ed, -twist·ing, -twists.** To twist together; entwine.

e·nu·cle·ate (ĭ-nōō′klē-āt′, ĭ-nyōō′-) *tr.v.* **-at·ed, -at·ing, -ates. 1.** *Medicine.* To remove (a tumor or an eye, for example) whole from an enveloping cover or sac. **2.** *Biology.* To remove the nucleus of. **3.** *Archaic.* To explain; elucidate. **—enucleate** (-ĭt, -āt′) *adj. Biology.* Lacking a nucleus. [Latin *ēnucleāre, ēnucleāt-*, to take out the kernel : *ē-, ex-*, ex- + *nucleus,* kernel; see NUCLEUS.] **—e·nu′cle·a′tion** *n.* **—e·nu′cle·a′tor** *n.*

E·nu·gu (ā-nōō′gōō). A city of southeast Nigeria east of the Niger River. It developed as a coal-mining center in the early 1900's. Population, 222,600.

e·nu·mer·a·ble (ĭ-nōō′mər-ə-bəl, ĭ-nyōō′-) *adj.* Denumerable.

e·nu·mer·ate (ĭ-nōō′mə-rāt′, ĭ-nyōō′-) *tr.v.* **-at·ed, -at·ing, -ates. 1.** To count off or name one by one; list: *A spokesperson enumerated the strikers' demands.* **2.** To determine the number of; count. [Latin *ēnumerāre, ēnumerāt-*, to count out : *ē-, ex-*, ex- + *numerus,* number; see **nem-** in Appendix.] **—e·nu′mer·a′tion** *n.* **—e·nu′mer·a′tive** (-mə-rā′tĭv, -mər-ə) *adj.* **—e·nu′mer·a′tor** *n.*

e·nun·ci·ate (ĭ-nŭn′sē-āt′) *v.* **-at·ed, -at·ing, -ates.** *—tr.* **1.** To pronounce; articulate. **2.** To state or set forth precisely or systematically: *enunciate a doctrine.* **3.** To announce; proclaim. *—intr.* To make articulate sounds. [Latin *ēnūntiāre, ēnūntiāt-* : *ē-, ex-*, ex- + *nūntiāre,* to announce (from *nūntius,* messenger; see **neu-** in Appendix).] **—e·nun′ci·a·ble** (-ə-bəl) *adj.* **—e·nun′ci·a′tion** *n.* **—e·nun′ci·a′tive** (-sē-ā′tĭv, -sē-ə-tĭv) *adj.* **—e·nun′ci·a′tive·ly** *adv.* **—e·nun′ci·a′tor** *n.*

en·ure (ĭn-yŏŏr′) *v.* Variant of **inure.**

en·u·re·sis (ĕn′yə-rē′sĭs) *n.* The uncontrolled or involuntary discharge of urine. [New Latin, from Greek *enourein,* to urinate in : *en-*, in; see EN–[2] + *ourein,* to urinate.] **—en′u·ret′ic** (-rĕt′ĭk) *adj.*

en·vel·op (ĕn-vĕl′əp) *tr.v.* **-oped, -op·ing, -ops. 1.** To enclose or encase completely with or as if with a covering: *"Accompanying the darkness, a stillness envelops the city"* (Curtis Wilkie). **2.** To attack (an enemy's flank). [Middle English *envolupen,* to be involved in, from Old French *envoluper, envoloper* : *en-*, in; see EN–[1] + *voloper,* to wrap up.] **—en·vel′op·er** *n.* **—en·vel′op·ment** *n.*

en·ve·lope (ĕn′və-lōp′, ŏn′-) *n.* **1.** A flat, folded paper container, especially for a letter. **2.** Something that envelops; a wrapping. **3.** *Biology.* An enclosing structure or cover, such as a membrane or the outer coat of a virus. **4.** The bag containing the gas in a balloon or an airship. **5.** The set of limitations within which a technological system, especially an aircraft, can perform safely and effectively. **6.** The coma of a comet. **7.** *Mathematics.* A curve or surface that is tangent to every one of a family of curves or surfaces. ***—idiom.* push the envelope.** To increase the operating capabilities of a technological system. [French *enveloppe,* from *envelopper,* to envelop, from Old French *envoloper.* See ENVELOP.]

en·ven·om (ĕn-vĕn′əm) *tr.v.* **-omed, -om·ing, -oms. 1.** To make poisonous or noxious. **2.** To embitter. [Middle English *envenimen,* to poison, from Old French *envenimer* : *en-*, cover with; see EN–[1] + *venim,* venom; see VENOM.]

en·vi·a·ble (ĕn′vē-ə-bəl) *adj.* So desirable as to arouse envy: *"the enviable English quality of being able to be mute without unrest"* (Henry James). **—en′vi·a·bly** *adv.*

en·vi·ous (ĕn′vē-əs) *adj.* **1.** Feeling, expressing, or characterized by envy: *"At times he regarded the wounded soldiers in an envious way. . . . He wished that he, too, had a wound, a red badge of courage"* (Stephen Crane). See Synonyms at **jealous. 2.** *Archaic.* Eager to emulate; emulous. **—en′vi·ous·ly** *adv.* **—en′vi·ous·ness** *n.*

en·vi·ron (ĕn-vī′rən, -vī′ərn) *tr.v.* **-roned, -ron·ing, -rons.** To encircle; surround. See Synonyms at **surround.** [Middle English *envirounen,* from Old French *environner,* from *environ,* round about : *en-*, in; see EN–[1] + *viron,* circle (from *virer,* to turn; see VEER[1]).]

en·vi·ron·ment (ĕn-vī′rən-mənt, -vī′ərn-) *n.* **1.** The circumstances or conditions that surround one; surroundings. **2.** The totality of circumstances surrounding an organism or a group of organisms, especially: **a.** The combination of external physical conditions that affect and influence the growth, development, and survival of organisms: *"We shall never understand the natural environment until we see it as a living organism"* (Paul Brooks). **b.** The complex of social and cultural conditions affecting the nature of an individual or a community. **3.** An artistic or theatrical work that surrounds or involves the audience.

en·vi·ron·men·tal (ĕn-vī′rən-mĕn′tl, -vī′ərn) *adj.* **1.** Of, relating to, or associated with the environment. **2.** Relating to or being concerned with the ecological impact of altering the environment. **3.** *Medicine.* Of or relating to potentially harmful factors originating in the environment: *environmental illness.* **—en·vi′ron·men′tal·ly** *adv.*

en·vi·ron·men·tal·ism (ĕn-vī′rən-mĕn′tl-ĭz′əm, -vī′ərn-) *n.* **1.** Advocacy for or work toward protecting the environment from destruction or pollution. **2.** The theory that environment rather than heredity is the primary influence on intellectual growth and cultural development. **—en·vi′ron·men′tal·ist** *n.*

en·vi·rons (ĕn-vī′rənz, -vī′ərnz) *pl.n.* **1.** A surrounding area, especially of a city. **2.** Surroundings; environment. [French, from Old French, pl. of *environ,* circuit, from *environ,* round about. See ENVIRON.]

en·vis·age (ĕn-vĭz′ĭj) *tr.v.* **-aged, -ag·ing, -ag·es. 1.** To conceive an image or a picture of, especially as a future possibility: *envisaged a world at peace.* **2.** To consider or regard in a certain way. [French *envisager* : Old French *en-*, in; see EN–[1] + Old French *visage,* face; see VISAGE.]

en·vi·sion (ĕn-vĭzh′ən) *tr.v.* **-sioned, -sion·ing, -sions.** To picture in the mind; imagine.

en·voi (ĕn′voi′, ŏn′-) *n.* Variant of **envoy[2].**

en·voy[1] (ĕn′voi′, ŏn′-) *n.* **1.** A representative of a government who is sent on a special diplomatic mission. **2.** A minister plenipotentiary assigned to a foreign embassy, ranking next below the ambassador. **3.** A messenger; an agent. [French *envoyé,* messenger, from past participle of *envoyer,* to send, from Old French *envoier,* from Late Latin *inviāre,* to be on the way : Latin *in-*, in, on; see EN–[1] + Latin *via,* way; see **wegh-** in Appendix.]

en·voy[2] also **en·voi** (ĕn′voi′, ŏn′-) *n.* **1.** A short closing stanza in certain verse forms, such as the ballade or sestina, dedicating the poem to a patron or summarizing its main ideas. **2.** The concluding portion of a prose work or a play. [Middle English *envoie,* from Old French, a sending away, conclusion, from *envoier,* to send. See ENVOY[1].]

en·vy (ĕn′vē) *n., pl.* **-vies. 1.a.** A feeling of discontent and resentment aroused by and in conjunction with desire for the possessions or qualities of another. **b.** The object of such feeling: *Their new pool made them the envy of their neighbors.* **2.** *Obsolete.* Malevolence. **—envy** *tr.v.* **-vied, -vy·ing, -vies. 1.** To feel envy toward. **2.** To regard with envy. [Middle English *envie,* from Old French, from Latin *invidia,* from *invidus,* envious, from *invidēre,* to look at with envy : *in-*, in, on; see EN–[1] + *vidēre,* to see; see **weid-** in Appendix. V., from Middle English *envien,* from Old French *envier,* from Latin *invidēre.*] **—en′vi·er** *n.* **—en′vy·ing·ly** *adv.*

SYNONYMS: *envy, begrudge, covet.* These verbs mean to feel resentful or painful desire for another's advantages or possessions. *Envy* is wider in range than the others since it combines discontent, resentment, and desire: *"When I peruse the conquered fame of heroes and the victories of mighty generals, I do not envy the generals"* (Walt Whitman). *Begrudge* stresses ill will and reluctance to acknowledge another's right or claim: *Why begrudge him his success? Covet* stresses desire, especially a secret longing, for something to which one has no right: *"as thorough an Englishman as ever coveted his neighbor's goods"* (Charles Kingsley).

en·wind (ĕn-wīnd′) also **in·wind** (ĭn-) *tr.v.* **-wound** (-wound′), **-wind·ing, -winds.** To wind around or about.

en·womb (ĕn-wōōm′) *tr.v.* **-wombed, -womb·ing, -wombs.** To enclose in or as if in a womb.

en·wound (ĕn-wound′) *v.* Past tense and past participle of **enwind.**

en·wrap (ĕn-răp′) also **in·wrap** (ĭn-) *tr.v.* **-wrapped, -wrap·ping, -wraps. 1.a.** To wrap up; enclose. **b.** To envelop. **2.** To absorb completely; engross: *I was enwrapped by the fascinating tale.*

en·wreathe (ĕn-rēth′) also **in·wreathe** (ĭn-) *tr.v.*

ă pat	oi boy
ā pay	ou out
âr care	ŏŏ took
ä father	ōō boot
ĕ pet	ŭ cut
ē be	ûr urge
ĭ pit	th thin
ī pie	*th* this
îr pier	hw which
ŏ pot	zh vision
ō toe	ə about, item
ô paw	♦ regionalism

Stress marks: **′** (primary); ′ (secondary), as in **dictionary** (dĭk′shə-nĕr′ē)

-wreathed, -wreath·ing, -wreathes. To surround with or as if with a wreath.

en·zo·ot·ic (ĕn′zō-ŏt′ĭk) *adj.* Affecting or peculiar to animals of a specific geographic area. Used of a disease. **—enzootic** *n.* An enzootic disease. [EN–[2] + ZO(O)– + –OTIC.]

en·zyme (ĕn′zīm) *n.* Any of numerous proteins or conjugated proteins produced by living organisms and functioning as biochemical catalysts. [German *Enzym,* from Medieval Greek *enzumos,* leavened : Greek *en-,* in; see EN–[2] + Greek *zumē,* leaven, yeast.] **—en′zy·mat′ic** (-zə-măt′ĭk), **en·zy′mic** (-zī′mĭk, -zĭm′ĭk) *adj.* **—en′zy·mat′i·cal·ly, en·zy′mi·cal·ly** *adv.*

en·zy·mol·o·gy (ĕn′zə-mŏl′ə-jē) *n.* The branch of science that deals with the biochemical nature and activity of enzymes. **—en′zy·mol′o·gist** *n.*

EO *abbr.* Executive order.

e.o. *abbr. Latin.* Ex officio (by virtue of office).

eo– *pref.* Most primitive; earliest: *eohippus.* [From Greek *ēōs,* dawn. See **aus-** in Appendix.]

E·o·cene (ē′ə-sēn′) *adj.* Of, relating to, or designating the geologic time, rock series, sedimentary deposits, and fossils of the second oldest of the five major epochs of the Tertiary Period, extending from the end of the Paleocene to the beginning of the Oligocene, and characterized by the rise of mammals. See table at **geologic time. —Eocene** *n.* **1.** The Eocene Epoch. **2.** The deposits of the Eocene Epoch.

e·o·hip·pus (ē′ō-hĭp′əs) *n.* A small, herbivorous, extinct mammal of the genus *Hyracotherium* (or *Eohippus*) from the Eocene Epoch of the western United States, having four-toed front feet and three-toed hind feet and related ancestrally to the horse. [New Latin : EO– + Greek *hippos,* horse; see **ekwo-** in Appendix.]

e·o·li·an also **ae·o·li·an** (ē-ō′lē-ən, ē-ōl′yən) *adj.* Relating to, caused by, or carried by the wind. [From AEOLUS.]

e·o·lith (ē′ə-lĭth′) *n.* A crude stone artifact, such as a flint.

E·o·lith·ic (ē′ə-lĭth′ĭk) *adj.* Of or relating to the postulated earliest period of human culture preceding the Lower Paleolithic.

E·o·lus (ē-ō′ləs), **Mount.** A peak, 4,295.3 m (14,083 ft) high, in the San Juan Mountains of southwest Colorado.

e.o.m. *abbr.* End of month.

e·on also **ae·on** (ē′ŏn′, ē′ən) *n.* **1.** An indefinitely long period of time; an age. **2.** The longest division of geologic time, containing two or more eras. [Late Latin *aeōn,* from Greek *aiōn.* See **aiw-** in Appendix.]

e·o·ni·an also **ae·o·ni·an** (ē-ō′nē-ən) *adj.* Of, relating to, or constituting an eon.

E·os (ē′ŏs′) *n. Greek Mythology.* The goddess of the dawn. [Greek *Ēōs,* from *ēōs,* dawn. See **aus-** in Appendix.]

e·o·sin (ē′ə-sən) *n.* **1.** A red crystalline powder, $C_{20}H_8O_5Br_4$, used in textile dyeing and ink manufacturing and in coloring gasoline. **2.** The red sodium or potassium salt of this powder, used in biology to stain cells. [Greek *ēōs,* dawn (from its color); see **aus-** in Appendix + –IN.]

e·o·sin·o·phil (ē′ə-sĭn′ə-fĭl′) also **e·o·sin·o·phile** (-fīl′) *n.* **1.** A type of white blood cell found in vertebrate blood, containing cytoplasmic granules that are easily stained by eosin or other acid dyes. **2.** A microorganism, cell, or histological element easily stained by eosin or other acid dyes. **—e′o·sin′o·phil′, e′o·sin′o·phil′ic, e′o·si·noph′i·lous** (ē′ō-sĭ-nŏf′ə-ləs) *adj.*

e·o·sin·o·phil·i·a (ē′ə-sĭn′ə-fĭl′ē-ə) *n.* An increase in the number of eosinophils in the blood.

–eous *suff.* Having the nature of; resembling: *gaseous.* [Middle English, from Old French *-eux, -eus* (from Latin *-ōsus*) and from Latin *-eus.*]

Ep *abbr. Bible.* Ephesians.

EP *abbr.* **1.** European plan. **2.** Extended play.

ep– *pref.* Variant of **epi–.**

EPA *abbr.* Environmental Protection Agency.

e·pact (ē′păkt′) *n.* The period of time necessary to bring the solar calendar into harmony with the lunar calendar. [French *épacte,* from Late Latin *epacta,* from Greek *epaktē (hēmera),* intercalary (day), feminine of *epaktos,* brought in, inserted, from *epagein,* to bring in, introduce : *ep-, epi-,* epi- + *agein,* to lead; see **ag-** in Appendix.]

E·pam·i·non·das (ĭ-păm′ə-nŏn′dəs). 418?–362 B.C. Theban general and politician who defeated Spartan forces at Leuctra (371), thereby ending Sparta's military dominance.

ep·ar·chy (ĕp′är′kē) *n., pl.* **-chies.** A diocese of an Eastern Orthodox Church. [Greek *eparkhia,* provincial government, from *eparkhein,* to rule over : *ep-, epi-,* epi- + *arkhein,* to rule.]

ep·au·let also **ep·au·lette** (ĕp′ə-lĕt′, ĕp′ə-lĕt′) *n.* A shoulder ornament, especially a fringed strap worn on military uniforms. [French *épaulette,* diminutive of *épaule,* shoulder, from Old French *espaule,* from Late Latin *spatula,* shoulder blade. See ESPALIER.]

é·pée also **e·pee** (ā-pā′, ĕp′ā) *n.* **1.** A fencing sword with a bowl-shaped guard and a long, narrow, fluted blade that has no cutting edge and tapers to a blunted point. **2.** The art or sport of fencing with this sword. [French, from Old French *espee,* from Latin *spatha,* broad double-edged sword. See SPATULA.] **—é·pée′ist** *n.*

ep·ei·rog·e·ny (ĕp′ī-rŏj′ə-nē) *n., pl.* **-nies.** Uplift or depression of the earth's crust, affecting large areas of land or ocean bottom. [Greek *ēpeiros,* continent + –GENY.] **—e·pei′ro·gen′ic** (ĭ-pī′rō-jĕn′ĭk) *adj.* **—e·pei′ro·gen′i·cal·ly** *adv.*

e·pen·the·sis (ĭ-pĕn′thĭ-sĭs) *n., pl.* **-ses** (-sēz′). *Linguistics.* The insertion of a sound in the middle of a word, as in Middle English *thunder* from Old English *thunor.* [Late Latin, from Greek, from *epentithenai,* to insert : *ep-, epi-,* epi- + *en-,* in; see EN–[2] + *tithenai,* to place; see **dhē-** in Appendix.] **—ep′en·thet′ic** (ĕp′ĭn-thĕt′ĭk) *adj.*

e·pergne (ĭ-pûrn′, ā-pârn′) *n.* A large table centerpiece consisting of a frame with extended arms or branches supporting holders, as for flowers, fruit, or sweetmeats. [Perhaps alteration of French *épargne,* a saving, from *épargner,* to save, from Old French *espargnier,* of Germanic origin.]

eohippus

ep·ex·e·ge·sis (ĕp-ĕk′sə-jē′sĭs) *n.* Additional explanation or explanatory material. [Greek *epexēgēsis,* from *epexēgeisthai,* to explain in detail : *ep-, epi-,* epi- + *exēgeisthai,* to explain; see EXEGESIS.] **—ep·ex′e·get′ic** (-jĕt′ĭk), **ep·ex′e·get′i·cal** *adj.* **—ep·ex′e·get′i·cal·ly** *adv.*

Eph. *abbr. Bible.* Ephesians.

e·phah also **e·pha** (ē′fə, ĕf′ä) *n.* An ancient Hebrew unit of dry measure, equal to 1/10 homer or about one bushel (35 liters). [Hebrew *'êpâ,* probably from Egyptian *'pt.*]

e·phebe (ĕf′ēb′, ĭ-fēb′) also **e·phe·bus** (ĭ-fē′bəs) *n., pl.* **e·phebes** also **e·phe·bi** (ĭ-fē′bī). A youth between 18 and 20 years of age in ancient Greece. [Latin *ephēbus,* from Greek *ephēbos* : *ep-, epi-,* epi- + *hēbē,* early manhood.] **—e·phe′bic** *adj.*

e·phed·rine (ĭ-fĕd′rĭn, ĕf′ĭ-drēn′) *n.* A white, odorless, powdered or crystalline alkaloid, $C_{10}H_{15}NO$, isolated from shrubs of the genus *Ephedra* or made synthetically. It is used in the treatment of allergies and asthma. [Latin *ephedra,* horsetail (from Greek *ephedros,* sitting upon : *ep-, epi-,* epi- + *hedra,* seat; see **sed-** in Appendix) + –INE[2].]

e·phem·er·a (ĭ-fĕm′ər-ə) *n.* A plural of **ephemeron.**

e·phem·er·al (ĭ-fĕm′ər-əl) *adj.* **1.** Lasting for a markedly brief time: *"There remain some truths too ephemeral to be captured in the cold pages of a court transcript or . . . opinion"* (Irving R. Kaufman). **2.** Living or lasting only for a day, as certain plants or insects do. See Synonyms at **transient. —ephemeral** *n.* A markedly short-lived thing. [From Greek *ephēmeros* : *ep-, epi-,* epi- + *hēmera,* day.] **—e·phem′er·al′i·ty, e·phem′er·al·ness** *n.* **—e·phem′er·al·ly** *adv.*

epaulet

e·phem·er·id (ĭ-fĕm′ər-ĭd) *n.* An insect of the order Ephemeroptera; a mayfly. [From New Latin *Ephemeridae,* former order name, from Greek *ephēmeron,* mayfly. See EPHEMERON.]

e·phem·er·is (ĭ-fĕm′ər-ĭs) *n., pl.* **eph·e·mer·i·des** (ĕf′ə-mĕr′ə-dēz′). A table giving the coordinates of a celestial body at a number of specific times during a given period. [Late Latin *ephēmeris,* from Greek, diary, from *ephēmeros,* daily. See EPHEMERAL.]

ephemeris time *n.* A highly accurate astronomical system for the measurement of time based on the period of Earth's orbit, but in practice relying on lunar observations and an accurate lunar ephemeris.

e·phem·er·on (ĭ-fĕm′ə-rŏn′) *n., pl.* **-er·a** (-ər-ə) or **-er·ons. 1.** A short-lived thing. **2. ephemera.** Printed matter of passing interest. [Greek *ephēmeron,* mayfly, from neuter of *ephēmeros,* daily, short-lived. See EPHEMERAL.]

E·phe·sian (ĭ-fē′zhən) *n.* **1.** A native or inhabitant of ancient Ephesus. **2. Ephesians.** *(used with a sing. verb). Abbr.* **Eph., Ep** *Bible.* See table at **Bible. —Ephesian** *adj.* Of or relating to ancient Ephesus or its people, language, or culture. [From Latin *Ephesiī,* inhabitants of Ephesus, from Greek *Ephesioi,* from *Ephesos,* Ephesus.]

Eph·e·sus (ĕf′ĭ-səs). An ancient city of Greek Asia Minor in present-day western Turkey. Its temple, dedicated to Artemis, was one of the Seven Wonders of the World.

eph·od (ĕf′ŏd′, ē′fŏd′) *n.* A vestment worn by ancient Hebrew priests. [Middle English, from Late Latin, from Hebrew *'ēpôd.*]

eph·or (ĕf′ôr′, -ər) *n., pl.* **-ors** or **-o·ri** (-ə-rī′). One of a body of five elected magistrates exercising a supervisory power over the kings of Sparta. [Latin *ephorus,* from Greek *ephoros,* from *ephoran,* to oversee : *ep-, epi-,* epi- + *horan,* to see; see **wer-**[3] in Appendix.]

epi– or **ep–** *pref.* **1.** On; upon: *epiphyte.* **2.** Over; above: *epicenter.* **3.** Around: *epicarp.* **4.** Close to; near: *epicalyx.* **5.** Besides: *epiphenomenon.* **6.** After: *epilogue.* [Greek, from *epi,* upon. See **epi** in Appendix.]

ep·i·blast (ĕp′ə-blăst′) *n. Embryology.* The outer layer of a blastula that gives rise to the ectoderm after gastrulation. **—ep′i·blast′ic** *adj.*

e·pib·o·ly (ĭ-pĭb′ə-lē) *n. Embryology.* The growth of a rapidly dividing group of cells around a more slowly dividing group of cells, as in the formation of a gastrula. [Greek *epibolē,* a throwing or laying on, from *epiballein,* to throw on : *epi-* + *ballein,* to throw; see **g[w]ele-** in Appendix.] **—ep′i·bol′ic** (ĕp′ə-bŏl′ĭk) *adj.*

ep·ic (ĕp′ĭk) *n.* **1.** An extended narrative poem in elevated or dignified language, celebrating the feats of a legendary or traditional hero. **2.** A literary or dramatic composition that resembles an extended, narrative poem celebrating heroic feats. **3.** A series of events considered appropriate to an epic: *the epic of the Old West.* **—epic** *adj.* **1.** Of, constituting, having to do with, or suggestive of a literary epic: *an epic poem.* **2.** Surpassing the usual

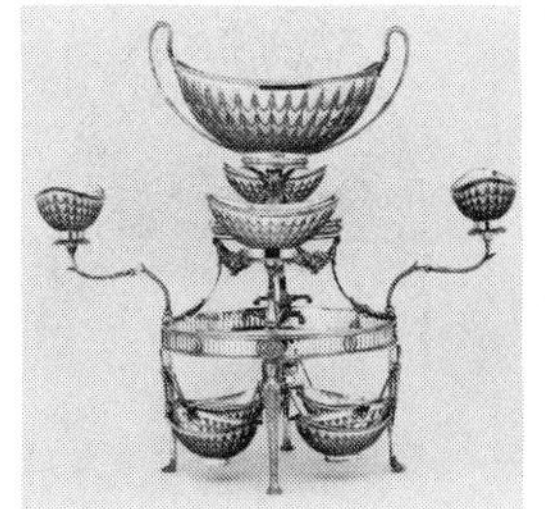
epergne
1757 English by William Cripps

or ordinary, particularly in scope or size: *"A vast musical panorama ... it requires an epic musical understanding to do it justice"* (Tim Page). **3.** Heroic and impressive in quality: *"Here in the courtroom ... there was more of that epic atmosphere, the extra amperage of a special moment"* (Scott Turow). [From Latin *epicus,* from Greek *epikos,* from *epos,* song. See **wekʷ-** in Appendix.]

ep·i·ca·lyx (ĕp′ĭ-kā′lĭks, -kăl′ĭks) *n., pl.* **-ca·lyx·es** or **-ca·ly·ces** (-kā′lĭ-sēz′, -kăl′ĭ-). A series of bracts subtending and resembling a calyx, as in the carnation and hibiscus.

ep·i·can·thic fold (ĕp′ĭ-kăn′thĭk) *n.* A fold of skin of the upper eyelid that partially covers the inner corner of the eye. Also called *epicanthus.*

ep·i·can·thus (ĕp′ĭ-kăn′thəs) *n., pl.* **-thi** (-thī, -thē). See **epicanthic fold.** [New Latin : EPI– + CANTHUS.]

ep·i·car·di·um (ĕp′ĭ-kär′dē-əm) *n., pl.* **-di·a** (-dē-ə). The inner layer of the pericardium that is in actual contact with the surface of the heart. [New Latin : EPI– + Greek *kardia,* heart; see **kerd-** in Appendix.] **—ep′i·car′di·al** *adj.*

ep·i·carp (ĕp′ĭ-kärp′) *n. Botany.* See **exocarp.**

ep·i·cene (ĕp′ĭ-sēn′) *adj.* **1.** Belonging to or having the characteristics of both the male and the female: *an epicene statue.* **2.** Effeminate; unmanly. **3.** Sexless; neuter. **4.** *Linguistics.* Having only one form of the noun for both the male and the female. **—epicene** *n.* **1.** One that is epicene. **2.** *Linguistics.* An epicene word. [Middle English, having only one form of the noun for either gender, from Latin *epicoenus,* from Greek *epikoinos,* in common : *epi-,* epi- + *koinos,* common; see **kom** in Appendix.] **—ep′i·cen′ism** *n.*

ep·i·cen·ter (ĕp′ĭ-sĕn′tər) *n.* **1.** The point of the earth's surface directly above the focus of an earthquake. **2.** A focal point: *at the epicenter of the international crisis.* **—ep′i·cen′tral** *adj.*

ep·i·chlo·ro·hy·drin (ĕp′ĭ-klôr′ə-hī′drĭn, -klōr′-) *n.* A colorless liquid, C_3H_5OCl, used as a solvent in making resins.

ep·i·con·dyle (ĕp′ĭ-kŏn′dīl, -dl) *n.* A rounded projection at the end of a bone, located on or above a condyle and usually serving as a place of attachment for ligaments and tendons.

ep·i·cot·yl (ĕp′ĭ-kŏt′l) *n.* The stem of a seedling or an embryo located between the cotyledons and the first true leaves. [EPI– + COTYL(EDON).]

ep·i·crit·ic (ĕp′ĭ-krĭt′ĭk) *adj.* Of or relating to sensory nerve fibers that enable the perception of slight differences in the intensity of stimuli, especially touch or temperature. [Greek *epikritikos,* decisive, from *epikritēs,* decider, from *epikrinein,* to decide : *epi-,* epi- + *krinein,* to judge; see **krei-** in Appendix.]

epic simile *n.* An extended simile elaborated in great detail. Also called *Homeric simile.*

Ep·ic·te·tus (ĕp′ĭk-tē′təs). A.D. 55?–135? Greek Stoic philosopher who believed that one should act in life as one would at a banquet, by taking a polite portion of all that is offered.

ep·i·cure (ĕp′ĭ-kyo͝or′) *n.* **1.** A person with refined taste especially in food and wine. **2.** A person devoted to sensuous pleasure and luxurious living. See Usage Note at **gourmet.** [Middle English, an Epicurean, from Medieval Latin *epicūrus,* from Latin *Epicūrus,* Epicurus, from Greek *Epikouros.*]

ep·i·cu·re·an (ĕp′ĭ-kyo͞o-rē′ən, -kyo͝or′ē-) *adj.* **1.** Devoted to the pursuit of pleasure; fond of good food, comfort, and ease. **2.** Suited to the tastes of an epicure: *an epicurean repast.* See Synonyms at **sensuous. 3. Epicurean.** Of or relating to Epicurus or Epicureanism. **—epicurean** *n.* **1.** A devotee to sensuous and luxurious living; an epicure. **2. Epicurean.** A follower of Epicurus. [Middle English *Epicurien,* from *Epicure.* See EPICURE.]

Ep·i·cu·re·an·ism (ĕp′ĭ-kyo͞o-rē′ə-nĭz′əm, -kyo͝or′ē-) *n.* A philosophy advanced by Epicurus that considered happiness, or the avoidance of pain and emotional disturbance, to be the highest good.

ep·i·cur·ism (ĕp′ĭ-kyo͞o-rĭz′əm, ĕp′ĭ-kyo͝or′ĭz-əm) *n.* The beliefs, tastes, or lifestyle of an epicure.

Ep·i·cu·rus (ĕp′ĭ-kyo͝or′əs). 341?–270 B.C. Greek philosopher who founded his school of Epicureanism in Athens c. 306.

ep·i·cu·ti·cle (ĕp′ĭ-kyo͞o′tĭ-kəl) *n.* The outermost layer of cuticle of an arthropod exoskeleton, composed mostly of wax.

ep·i·cy·cle (ĕp′ĭ-sī′kəl) *n.* **1.** In Ptolemaic cosmology, a small circle, the center of which moves on the circumference of a larger circle at whose center is Earth and the circumference of which describes the orbit of one of the planets around Earth. **2.** *Mathematics.* A circle whose circumference rolls along the circumference of a fixed circle, thereby generating an epicycloid or a hypocycloid. [Middle English *epicicle,* from Late Latin *epicyclus,* from Greek *epikuklos* : *epi-,* epi- + *kuklos,* circle; see **kʷel-**[1] in Appendix.] **—ep′i·cy′clic** (-sī′klĭk, -sĭk′lĭk) *adj.*

epicyclic train *n.* A system of gears in which at least one rotating gear revolves about another.

ep·i·cy·cloid (ĕp′ĭ-sī′kloid′) *n.* The curve described by a point on the circumference of a circle as the circle rolls on the outside of the circumference of a second, fixed circle. **—ep′i·cy·cloid′al** (-kloid′l) *adj.*

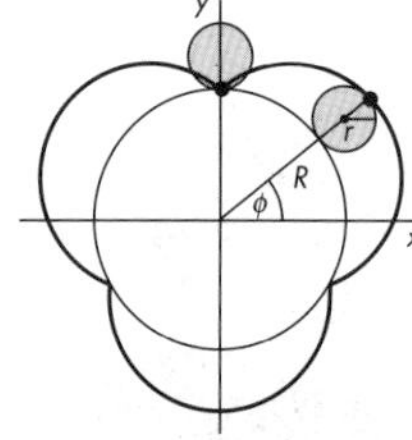

epicycloid

Ep·i·dau·rus (ĕp′ĭ-dôr′əs). An ancient city of Greece on the northeast coast of the Peloponnesus. Its temple of Asclepius, the Greek god of medicine, was renowned for its sculpture.

ep·i·dem·ic (ĕp′ĭ-dĕm′ĭk) also **ep·i·dem·i·cal** (-ĭ-kəl) —*adj.* **1.** Spreading rapidly and extensively by infection and affecting many individuals in an area or a population at the same time: *an epidemic outbreak of influenza.* **2.** Widely prevalent: *epidemic discontent.* —*n.* **1.** An outbreak of a contagious disease that spreads rapidly and widely. **2.** A rapid spread, growth, or development: *an unemployment epidemic.* [French *épidémique,* from *épidémie,* an epidemic, from Old French *espydymie,* from Medieval Latin *epidēmia,* from Greek, prevalence of an epidemic disease, from *epidēmos,* prevalent : *epi-,* epi- + *dēmos,* people; see **dā-** in Appendix.] **—ep′i·dem′i·cal·ly** *adv.*

ep·i·de·mi·ol·o·gy (ĕp′ĭ-dē′mē-ŏl′ə-jē, -dĕm′ē-) *n.* The branch of medicine that deals with the study of the causes, distribution, and control of disease in populations. [Medieval Latin *epidēmia,* an epidemic; see EPIDEMIC + –LOGY.] **—ep′i·de′mi·o·log′ic** (-ə-lŏj′ĭk), **ep′i·de′mi·o·log′i·cal** (-ĭ-kəl) *adj.* **—ep′i·de′mi·o·log′i·cal·ly** *adv.* **—ep′i·de′mi·ol′o·gist** *n.*

ep·i·der·mis (ĕp′ĭ-dûr′mĭs) *n.* **1.** The outer, protective, nonvascular layer of the skin of vertebrates, covering the dermis. **2.** An integument or outer layer of various invertebrates. **3.** The outermost layer of cells covering the leaves and young parts of a plant. [Late Latin, from Greek : *epi-,* epi- + *derma,* skin; see **der-** in Appendix.] **—ep′i·der′mal** (-məl), **ep′i·der′mic** *adj.*

ep·i·der·moid (ĕp′ĭ-dûr′moid′) *adj.* Composed of or resembling epidermal tissue: *epidermoid carcinoma.*

ep·i·di·a·scope (ĕp′ĭ-dī′ə-skōp′) *n.* A machine for projecting the images of opaque objects or transparencies on a screen. [EPI– + DIA– + –SCOPE.]

ep·i·did·y·mis (ĕp′ĭ-dĭd′ə-mĭs) *n., pl.* **-mi·des** (-mĭ-dēz′). *Anatomy.* A long, narrow convoluted tube, part of the spermatic duct system, that lies on the posterior aspect of each testicle, connecting it to the vas deferens. [Greek *epididumis* : *epi-,* epi- + *didumoi,* twins, testicles, pl. of *didumos,* double; see **dwo-** in Appendix.] **—ep′i·did′y·mal** *adj.*

ep·i·dote (ĕp′ĭ-dōt′) *n.* A lustrous yellow, green, or black mineral $Ca_2(Al, Fe)_3(SiO_4)_3OH$, commonly found in metamorphic rock. [French *épidote,* from Greek *epididonai,* to give in addition, increase (from the shape of its crystalline structure) : *epi-,* epi- + *didonai,* to give; see **dō-** in Appendix.] **—ep′i·dot′ic** (-dŏt′ĭk) *adj.*

ep·i·du·ral (ĕp′ĭ-do͝or′əl, -dyo͝or′-) *adj.* Located on or over the dura mater. **—epidural** *n.* An injection into the epidural space of the spine.

epidural anesthesia *n.* Anesthesia produced by the injection of a local anesthetic into the epidural space of the lumbar or sacral region of the spine, inducing regional anesthesia from the abdomen or pelvis downward and used especially to control pain during childbirth.

ep·i·gas·tri·um (ĕp′ĭ-găs′trē-əm) *n., pl.* **-tri·a** (-trē-ə). The upper middle region of the abdomen. [New Latin, from Greek *epigastrion* : *epi-,* epi- + *gastrion,* diminutive of *gastēr,* belly, stomach.] **—ep′i·gas′tric** (-trĭk) *adj.*

ep·i·ge·al (ĕp′ə-jē′əl) also **ep·i·ge·an** (-ən) or **ep·i·ge·ous** (-əs) *adj.* **1.** *Biology.* Living or occurring on or near the surface of the ground. **2.** *Botany.* Of or relating to the emergence of cotyledons above the surface of the ground after germination. [From Greek *epigeios,* on the earth : *epi-,* epi- + *gē,* earth.]

ep·i·gene (ĕp′ə-jēn′) *adj.* Formed, originating, or occurring on or just below the surface of the earth. [French *épigène,* from Greek *epigenēs,* growing after : *epi-,* epi- + *-genēs,* -born; see **gene-** in Appendix.]

ep·i·gen·e·sis (ĕp′ə-jĕn′ĭ-sĭs) *n.* **1.** *Biology.* The theory that an individual is developed by successive differentiation of an unstructured egg rather than by a simple enlarging of a preformed entity. **2.** *Geology.* Change in the mineral content of a rock because of outside influences. **—ep′i·ge·net′ic** (-jə-nĕt′ĭk) *adj.*

e·pig·e·nous (ĭ-pĭj′ə-nəs) *adj. Botany.* Developing or growing on an upper surface, as fungi on leaves.

ep·i·ge·ous (ĕp′ə-jē′əs) *adj. Biology & Botany.* Variant of **epigeal.**

ep·i·glot·tis (ĕp′ĭ-glŏt′ĭs) *n., pl.* **-glot·tis·es** or **-glot·ti·des** (-glŏt′ĭ-dēz′). The thin elastic cartilaginous structure located at the root of the tongue that folds over the glottis to prevent food and liquid from entering the trachea during the act of swallowing. [Greek *epiglōttis* : *epi-,* epi- + *glōttis,* glottis; see GLOTTIS.] **—ep′i·glot′tal** (-glŏt′l), **ep′i·glot′tic** (-glŏt′ĭk) *adj.*

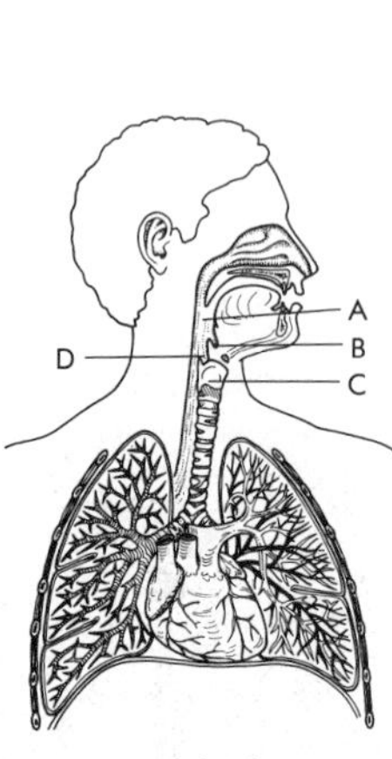

epiglottis
A. Throat
B. Epiglottis
C. Larynx
D. Esophagus

ep·i·gone (ĕp′ĭ-gōn′) *n.* A second-rate imitator or follower, especially of an artist or a philosopher. [French *épigone,* sing. of *épigones,* from Greek *Epigonoi,* sons of the seven heroes against Thebes, from pl. of *epigonos,* born after : *epi-,* epi- + *gonos,* child, seed; see **genə-** in Appendix.] **—ep′i·gon′ic** (-gŏn′ĭk) *adj.* **—e·pig′on·ism** (ĭ-pĭg′ə-nĭz′əm) *n.*

ep·i·gram (ĕp′ĭ-grăm′) *n.* **1.** A short, witty poem expressing a single thought or observation. **2.** A concise, clever, often paradoxical statement. See Synonyms at **saying. 3.** Epigrammatic discourse or expression. [Middle English, from Old French *epigramme,* from Latin *epigramma,* from Greek, from *epigraphein,* to mark the surface, inscribe : *epi-,* epi- + *graphein,* to write; see **gerbh-** in Appendix.]

ep·i·gram·mat·ic (ĕp′ĭ-grə-măt′ĭk) also **ep·i·gram·mat·i·cal** (-ĭ-kəl) *adj.* **1.** Of or having the nature of an epigram. **2.** Containing or given to the use of epigrams. [From *epigrammatical,* from Latin *epigrammaticus,* from Greek **epigrammatikos,* from *epigramma, epigrammat-,* epigram. See EPIGRAM.] **—ep′i·gram·mat′i·cal·ly** *adv.*

ep·i·gram·ma·tism (ĕp′ĭ-grăm′ə-tĭz′əm) *n.* Literary style marked by the use of epigrams. **—ep′i·gram′ma·tist** *n.*

ep·i·gram·ma·tize (ĕp′ĭ-grăm′ə-tīz′) *v.* **-tized, -tiz·ing, -tiz·es.** *—tr.* To express in an epigram. *—intr.* To create an epigram.

ep·i·graph (ĕp′ĭ-grăf′) *n.* **1.** An inscription, as on a statue or building. **2.** A motto or quotation, as at the beginning of a literary composition, setting forth a theme. [Greek *epigraphē,* from *epigraphein,* to write on. See EPIGRAM.] **—ep′i·graph′ic, ep′i·graph′i·cal** *adj.* **—ep′i·graph′i·cal·ly** *adv.*

e·pig·ra·phy (ĭ-pĭg′rə-fē) *n.* **1.** Inscriptions considered as a group. **2.a.** The study of inscriptions. **b.** Decipherment, as of ancient inscriptions. **—e·pig′ra·pher, e·pig′ra·phist** *n.*

e·pig·y·nous (ĭ-pĭj′ə-nəs) *adj.* Having floral parts attached to or near the summit of the ovary, as in the flower of the apple, cucumber, or daffodil. **—e·pig′y·ny** (-nē) *n.*

ep·i·lep·sy (ĕp′ə-lĕp′sē) *n., pl.* **-sies.** Any of various neurological disorders characterized by sudden, recurring attacks of motor, sensory, or psychic malfunction with or without loss of consciousness or convulsive seizures. [French *épilepsie,* from Latin *epilēpsia,* from Greek *epilēpsis,* from *epilambanein,* to lay hold of : *epi-,* epi- + *lambanein, lēp-,* to seize.]

ep·i·lep·tic (ĕp′ə-lĕp′tĭk) *adj.* **1.** Affected with epilepsy. **2.** Of or associated with epilepsy. **—epileptic** *n.* One who has epilepsy. [French *épileptique,* from Late Latin *epilēpticus,* from Greek *epilēptikos,* from *epilēpsis,* epilepsy. See EPILEPSY.]

ep·i·lep·to·gen·ic (ĕp′ə-lĕp′tə-jĕn′ĭk) *adj.* Having the capacity to induce epilepsy.

ep·i·lep·toid (ĕp′ə-lĕp′toid′) *adj.* Resembling epilepsy or any of its symptoms. [EPILEPT(IC) + -OID.]

ep·i·logue also **ep·i·log** (ĕp′ə-lôg′, -lŏg′) *n.* **1.a.** A short poem or speech spoken directly to the audience following the conclusion of a play. **b.** The performer who delivers such a short poem or speech. **2.** A short addition or concluding section at the end of a literary work, often dealing with the future of its characters. In this sense, also called *afterword.* [Middle English *epiloge,* from Old French *epilogue,* from Latin *epilogus,* from Greek *epilogos,* conclusion of a speech : *epi-,* epi- + *logos,* word, speech; see **leg-** in Appendix.]

Ep·i·me·the·us (ĕp′ə-mē′thē-əs, -thyo͞os) *n.* The satellite of Saturn that is fifth in distance from the planet. [Latin *Epimētheus,* son of Iapetus and Pandora and brother of Prometheus, from Greek.]

ep·i·mys·i·um (ĕp′ə-mĭz′ē-əm, -mĭzh′ē-) *n., pl.* **-mys·i·a** (-mĭz′ē-ə, -mĭzh′-). The external sheath of connective tissue surrounding a muscle. [New Latin : EPI- + Greek *mūs,* muscle; see **mūs-** in Appendix.]

ep·i·nas·ty (ĕp′ə-năs′tē) *n., pl.* **-ties.** A downward bending of leaves or other plant parts, resulting from excessive growth of the upper side. **—ep′i·nas′tic** (-tĭk) *adj.*

ep·i·neph·rine also **ep·i·neph·rin** (ĕp′ə-nĕf′rĭn) *n.* **1.** A hormone secreted by the adrenal medulla that is released into the bloodstream in response to physical or mental stress, as from fear or injury. It initiates many bodily responses, including the stimulation of heart action and an increase in blood pressure, metabolic rate, and blood glucose concentration. Also called *adrenaline.* **2.** A white to brownish crystalline compound, $C_9H_{13}NO_3$, isolated from the adrenal glands of certain mammals or synthesized and used in medicine as a heart stimulant, vasoconstrictor, and bronchial relaxant. [EPI- + NEPHR(O)- + -INE[2].]

ep·i·neu·ri·um (ĕp′ə-no͝or′ē-əm, -nyo͝or′-) *n., pl.* **-neu·ri·a** (-no͝or′ē-ə, -nyo͝or′-). The thick sheath of connective tissue surrounding a nerve trunk. [New Latin : EPI- + Greek *neuron,* nerve, tendon; see NEURON.] **—ep′i·neu′ri·al** *adj.*

ep·i·pe·lag·ic (ĕp′ə-pə-lăj′ĭk) *adj.* Of or relating to the part of the oceanic zone into which enough sunlight enters for photosynthesis to take place.

e·pi·pet·al·ous (ĕp′ə-pĕt′l-əs) *adj. Botany.* Borne on or attached to the petals or corolla, as the stamens of the petunia.

e·piph·a·ny (ĭ-pĭf′ə-nē) *n., pl.* **-nies. 1. Epiphany. a.** A Christian feast celebrating the manifestation of the divine nature of Jesus to the Gentiles as represented by the Magi. **b.** January 6, on which this feast is traditionally observed. **2.** A revelatory manifestation of a divine being. **3.a.** A sudden manifestation of the essence or meaning of something. **b.** A comprehension or perception of reality by means of a sudden intuitive realization: *"I experienced an epiphany, a spiritual flash that would change the way I viewed myself"* (Frank Maier). [Middle English *epiphanie,* from Old French, from Late Latin *epiphania,* from Greek *epiphaneia,* manifestation, from *epiphainesthai,* to appear : *epi-,* forth; see EPI- + *phainein, phan-,* to show; see **bhā-**[1] in Appendix.]

ep·i·phe·nom·e·nal·ism (ĕp′ə-fĭ-nŏm′ə-nə-lĭz′əm) *n. Philosophy.* The doctrine holding that mental activities are simply epiphenomena of the neural processes of the brain.

ep·i·phe·nom·e·non (ĕp′ə-fĭ-nŏm′ə-nŏn′) *n., pl.* **-na** (-nə). **1.** A secondary phenomenon that results from and accompanies another: *"Exploitation of one social class or ethnic group by another* [is] *an epiphenomenon of real differences in power between social groups"* (Harper's). **2.** *Pathology.* An additional condition or symptom in the course of a disease, not necessarily connected with the disease. **—ep′i·phe·nom′e·nal** *adj.* **—ep′i·phe·nom′e·nal·ly** *adv.*

e·piph·y·sis (ĭ-pĭf′ĭ-sĭs) *n., pl.* **-ses** (-sēz′). **1.** The end of a long bone that is originally separated from the main bone by a layer of cartilage but that later becomes united to the main bone through ossification. **2.** See **pineal gland.** [Greek *epiphusis,* an excrescence : *epi-,* epi- + *phusis,* growth; see **bheuə-** in Appendix.] **—ep′i·phys′i·al** (ĕp′ə-fĭz′ē-əl), **ep′i·phys′e·al** *adj.*

ep·i·phyte (ĕp′ə-fīt′) *n.* A plant, such as a tropical orchid or a staghorn fern, that grows on another plant upon which it depends for mechanical support but not for nutrients. Also called *aerophyte, air plant.* **—ep′i·phyt′ic** (-fĭt′ĭk), **ep′i·phyt′i·cal** *adj.* **—ep′i·phyt′i·cal·ly** *adv.*

ep·i·phy·tot·ic (ĕp′ə-fī-tŏt′ĭk) *adj.* Of, relating to, or characterized by a sudden or abnormally destructive outbreak of a plant disease, usually over an extended geographic area. **—ep′i·phy·tot′ic** *n.*

E·pi·rus (ĭ-pī′rəs). An ancient country on the Ionian Sea in present-day northwest Greece and southern Albania. It flourished in the 3rd century B.C. and was later a Roman province.

Epis. *abbr.* **1.** Episcopal; Episcopalian. **2.** *Bible.* Epistle.

Episc. *abbr.* Episcopal; Episcopalian.

e·pis·co·pa·cy (ĭ-pĭs′kə-pə-sē) *n., pl.* **-cies. 1.** See **episcopate** (sense 3). **2.** A system of church government in which bishops are the chief clerics. [From EPISCOPATE.]

e·pis·co·pal (ĭ-pĭs′kə-pəl) *adj. Abbr.* **Epis., Episc. 1.** Of or relating to a bishop. **2.** Of, relating to, or involving church government by bishops. **3. Episcopal.** Of or relating to the Episcopal Church. [Middle English, from Late Latin *episcopālis,* from *episcopus,* bishop, from Greek *episkopos,* overseer : *epi-,* epi- + *skopos,* watcher; see **spek-** in Appendix.] **—e·pis′co·pal·ly** *adv.*

Episcopal Church *n.* The church in the United States that is in communion with the see of Canterbury.

E·pis·co·pa·lian (ĭ-pĭs′kə-pā′lē-ən, -pāl′yən) *adj. Abbr.* **Epis., Episc. 1.** Of, relating to, or belonging to the Episcopal Church. **2. episcopalian.** Of or advocating church government by bishops. **—E·pis′co·pa′lian** *n.*

e·pis·co·pate (ĭ-pĭs′kə-pĭt, -pāt′) *n.* **1.** The position, term, or office of a bishop. **2.** The area of jurisdiction of a bishop; a diocese. **3.** Bishops considered as a group. In this sense, also called *episcopacy.* [Late Latin *episcopātus,* from *episcopus,* bishop. See EPISCOPAL.]

ep·i·si·ot·o·my (ĭ-pē′zē-ŏt′ə-mē) *n., pl.* **-mies.** Surgical incision of the perineum during childbirth to facilitate delivery. [Greek *epision,* pubic region + -TOMY.]

ep·i·sode (ĕp′ĭ-sōd′) *n.* **1.a.** An incident or event that is part of a progression or a larger sequence: *"South Africa may remain one of history's most tragic episodes"* (Bayard Rustin). **b.** One of a series of related events in the course of a continuous account. See Synonyms at **occurrence. 2.** A portion of a narrative that relates an event or a series of connected events and forms a coherent story in itself; an incident: *an episode in a picaresque novel.* **3.** A separate part of a serialized work, such as a novel or play. **4.** A section of a classic Greek tragedy that occurs between two choric songs. **5.** *Music.* A passage between statements of a main subject or theme, as in a rondo or fugue. [French *épisode,* from Greek *epeisodion,* parenthetic narrative, from neuter of *epeisodios,* coming in besides : *epi-,* epi- + *eisodios,* entering (*eis,* into; see **en** in Appendix + *hodos,* way, journey).]

ep·i·sod·ic (ĕp′ĭ-sŏd′ĭk) also **ep·i·sod·i·cal** (-ĭ-kəl) *adj.* **1.** Relating to or resembling an episode. **2.** Composed of a series of episodes: *an episodic novel.* **3.** Limited to the duration of an episode; temporary. **—ep′i·sod′i·cal·ly** *adv.*

ep·i·some (ĕp′ĭ-sōm′) *n.* A genetic particle of certain cells, especially bacterial cells, that can exist either autonomously in the cytoplasm or as part of a chromosome. **—ep′i·so′mal** *adj.* **—ep·i·so′mal·ly** *adv.*

Epist. *abbr. Bible.* Epistle.

e·pis·ta·sis (ĭ-pĭs′tə-sĭs) *n., pl.* **-ses** (-sēz′). **1.** *Genetics.* An interaction between nonallelic genes, especially an interaction in which one gene suppresses the expression of another. **2.** *Medicine.* A film that forms over the surface of a urine specimen. **3.** *Medicine.* The suppression of a bodily discharge or secretion. [Greek, stoppage, from *epistanai,* to stop, check : *ep-, epi-,* epi- + *histanai,* to place; see **stā-** in Appendix.] **—ep′i·stat′ic** (ĕp′ĭ-stăt′ĭk) *adj.*

ep·i·stax·is (ĕp′ĭ-stăk′sĭs) *n., pl.* **-stax·es** (-stăk′sēz′). A nosebleed. [Greek, from *epistazein,* to bleed from the nose : *epi-,* epi- + *stazein, stag-,* to drip.]

ep·i·ste·mic (ĕp′ĭ-stē′mĭk) *adj.* Of, relating to, or involving knowledge; cognitive. [From Greek *epistēmē,* knowledge. See EPISTEMOLOGY.] **—ep′i·ste′mi·cal·ly** *adv.*

e·pis·te·mol·o·gy (ĭ-pĭs′tə-mŏl′ə-jē) *n.* The branch of philosophy that studies the nature of knowledge, its presuppositions and foundations, and its extent and validity. [Greek *epistēmē,* knowledge (from *epistasthai,* to understand : *epi-,* epi- + *histanai, stē-,* to place, determine; see **stā-** in Appendix) + -LOGY.] **—e·pis′te·mo·log′i·cal** (-mə-lŏj′ĭ-kəl) *adj.* **—e·pis′te·mo·log′i·cal·ly** *adv.* **—e·pis′te·mol′o·gist** *n.*

e·pis·tle (ĭ-pĭs′əl) *n.* **1.** A letter, especially a formal one. See Synonyms at **letter. 2.** A literary composition in the form of a letter. **3. Epistle.** *Abbr.* **Epis., Epist.** *Bible.* **a.** One of the letters included as a book in the New Testament. **b.** An excerpt from one of these letters, read as part of a religious service. [Middle English *epistel,* from Old French *epistle,* from Latin *epistola,* from

ă pat	oi boy
ā pay	ou out
âr care	o͝o took
ä father	o͞o boot
ĕ pet	ŭ cut
ē be	ûr urge
ĭ pit	th thin
ī pie	*th* this
îr pier	hw which
ŏ pot	zh vision
ō toe	ə about, item
ô paw	♦ regionalism

Stress marks: ′ (primary); ′ (secondary), as in **dictionary** (dĭk′shə-nĕr′ē)

Greek *epistolē,* from *epistellein,* to send a message to : *epi-,* epi- + *stellein,* to send; see **stel-** in Appendix.]

e·pis·tler (ĭ-pĭs′lər) *n.* One who writes an epistle.

epistle side also **Epistle Side** *n.* **1.** In the traditional orientation of some Christian churches, the south side of a chancel or sanctuary when the altar or Eucharistic table faces east. **2.** In some Christian churches, the side of a chancel or sanctuary on the congregation's right.

e·pis·to·lar·y (ĭ-pĭs′tə-lĕr′ē) *adj.* **1.** Of or associated with letters or the writing of letters. **2.** Being in the form of a letter: *epistolary exchanges.* **3.** Carried on by or composed of letters: *an epistolary friendship.* [From Latin *epistolāris,* from *epistola,* epistle. See EPISTLE.]

ep·i·style (ĕp′ĭ-stīl′) *n.* See **architrave** (sense 1). [Latin *epistȳlium,* from Greek *epistulion* : *epi-,* epi- + *stulion,* diminutive of *stulos,* pillar; see **stā-** in Appendix.]

ep·i·taph (ĕp′ĭ-tăf′) *n.* **1.** An inscription on a tombstone in memory of the one buried there. **2.** A brief literary piece commemorating a deceased person. [Middle English, from Old French *epitaphe,* from Latin *epitaphium,* from Greek *epitaphion,* from neuter of *epitaphios,* funerary : *epi-,* epi- + *taphos,* tomb.] **—ep′i·taph′ic** *adj.*

e·pit·a·sis (ĭ-pĭt′ə-sĭs) *n., pl.* **-ses** (-sēz′). The middle part of a play that develops the action leading to the catastrophe. [Greek, stretching, intensity, from *epiteinein,* to stretch, intensify : *epi-,* epi- + *teinein,* to stretch; see **ten-** in Appendix.]

ep·i·tax·y (ĕp′ĭ-tăk′sē) *n., pl.* **-ies.** The growth of the crystals of one mineral on the crystal face of another mineral, such that the crystalline substrates of both minerals have the same structural orientation.

ep·i·tha·la·mi·um (ĕp′ə-thə-lā′mē-əm) or **ep·i·tha·la·mi·on** (-ən) *n., pl.* **-mi·ums** or **-mi·a** (-mē-ə). A lyric ode in honor of a bride and bridegroom. [Latin, from Greek *epithalamion,* from neuter of *epithalamios,* of a wedding : *epi-,* epi- + *thalamos,* bridal chamber; see THALAMUS.]

ep·i·the·li·a (ĕp′ə-thē′lē-ə) *n.* A plural of **epithelium.**

ep·i·the·li·al·ize (ĕp′ə-thē′lē-ə-līz′) or **ep·i·the·lize** (-thē′līz) *v.* **-ized, -iz·ing, -iz·es** or **-lized, -liz·ing, -liz·es.** *—tr.* To cover (a wound, for example) with epithelial tissue. *—intr.* To become covered with epithelial tissue. **—ep′i·the′li·al·i·za′tion** (-ə-lĭ-zā′shən) *n.*

ep·i·the·li·oid (ĕp′ə-thē′lē-oid′) *adj.* Resembling epithelium.

ep·i·the·li·o·ma (ĕp′ə-thē′lē-ō′mə) *n., pl.* **-ma·ta** (-mə-tə) or **-mas.** A benign or malignant tumor derived from epithelium. **—ep′i·the′li·om′a·tous** (-ŏm′ə-təs) *adj.*

ep·i·the·li·um (ĕp′ə-thē′lē-əm) *n., pl.* **-li·ums** or **-li·a** (-lē-ə). Membranous tissue composed of one or more layers of cells separated by very little intercellular substance and forming the covering of most internal and external surfaces of the body and its organs. [New Latin : EPI– + Greek *thēlē,* nipple; see **dhē(i)-** in Appendix.] **—ep′i·the′li·al** *adj.*

ep·i·the·lize (ĕp′ə-thē′līz) *v.* Variant of **epithelialize. —ep′i·the′li·za′tion** (-lĭ-zā′shən) *n.*

ep·i·thet (ĕp′ə-thĕt′) *n.* **1.a.** A term used to characterize a person or thing, such as *rosy-fingered* in *rosy-fingered dawn* or *the Great* in *Catherine the Great.* **b.** A term used as a descriptive substitute for the name or title of a person, such as *The Great Emancipator* for Abraham Lincoln. **2.** An abusive or contemptuous word or phrase. **3.** *Biology.* A word in the scientific name of an animal or a plant following the name of the genus and denoting a species, variety, or other division of the genus, as *sativa* in *Lactuca sativa.* [Latin *epitheton,* from Greek, neuter of *epithetos,* added, attributed, from *epitithenai,* to add to : *epi-,* epi- + *tithenai,* to place; see **dhē-** in Appendix.] **—ep′i·thet′ic, ep′i·thet′i·cal** *adj.*

USAGE NOTE: Strictly speaking, an epithet need not be derogatory, but the term is commonly used as a simple synonym for "term of abuse" or "slur," as in the sentence *There is no place for racial epithets in a police officer's vocabulary.* This usage is accepted by 80 percent of the Usage Panel.

e·pit·o·me (ĭ-pĭt′ə-mē) *n.* **1.** A representative or an example of a class or type: *"He is seen . . . as the epitome of the hawkish, right-of-center intellectual"* (Paul Kennedy). **2.** A brief summary, as of a book or an article; an abstract. [Latin *epitomē,* a summary, from Greek, an abridgment, from *epitemnein,* to cut short : *epi-,* epi- + *temnein,* to cut; see **tem-** in Appendix.]

e·pit·o·mize (ĭ-pĭt′ə-mīz′) *tr.v.* **-mized, -miz·ing, -miz·es. 1.** To make an epitome of; sum up. **2.** To be a typical example of: *behavior that epitomizes selfishness.*

ep·i·zo·ic (ĕp′ĭ-zō′ĭk) *adj.* Living or growing on the external surface of an animal. **—ep′i·zo′ism** *n.*

ep·i·zo·on (ĕp′ĭ-zō′ŏn, -ən) *n., pl.* **-zo·a** (-zō′ə). An epizoic organism.

ep·i·zo·ot·ic (ĕp′ĭ-zō-ŏt′ĭk) *adj.* Affecting a large number of animals at the same time within a particular region or geographic area. Used of a disease. **—epizootic** *n.* An epizootic disease. [EPI– + ZO(O)– + –OTIC.] **—ep′i·zo·ot′i·cal·ly** *adv.*

ep·och (ĕp′ək, ē′pŏk′) *n.* **1.a.** A particular period of history, especially one considered remarkable or noteworthy. **b.** A notable event that marks the beginning of such a period. See Synonyms at **period. 2.** A unit of geologic time that is a division of a period. **3.** *Astronomy.* An instant in time that is arbitrarily selected as a point of reference. [Medieval Latin *epocha,* measure of time, from Greek *epokhē,* a point in time. See **segh-** in Appendix.]

ep·och·al (ĕp′ə-kəl, -ŏk′əl) *adj.* **1.** Of, relating to, or characteristic of an epoch. **2.a.** Highly significant or important; momentous: *epochal decisions made by Roosevelt and Churchill.* **b.** Without parallel: *epochal stupidity.*

ep·och-mak·ing (ĕp′ək-mā′kĭng, ē′pŏk-) *adj.* So significant and momentous as to characterize the beginning of a period: *the President's epoch-making trip to China; epoch-making new technologies; an epoch-making architectural work.*

ep·ode (ĕp′ōd′) *n.* **1.** A lyric poem characterized by couplets formed by a long line followed by a shorter one. **2.** The third division of the triad of a Pindaric ode, having a different or contrasting form from that of the strophe and antistrophe. **3.** The part of a choral ode in classical Greek drama following the strophe and antistrophe and sung while the chorus is standing still. [Latin *epōdos,* a type of lyric poem, from Greek *epōidos,* sung after, from *epaidein,* to sing after : *epi-,* epi- + *aidein,* to sing; see **wed-**[2] in Appendix.]

ep·o·nym (ĕp′ə-nĭm′) *n.* **1.** A person whose name is or is thought to be the source of the name of something, such as a city, country, or era. For example, *Romulus* is the eponym of *Rome.* **2.** *Medicine.* A name of a drug, structure, or disease based on or derived from the name of a person. [French *éponyme,* from Greek *epōnumos,* named after : *epi-,* epi- + *onoma, onuma,* name; see **nō-men-** in Appendix.] **—ep′o·nym′ic** *adj.*

e·pon·y·mous (ĭ-pŏn′ə-məs) *adj.* Of, relating to, or constituting an eponym. [From Greek *epōnumos.* See EPONYM.]

e·pon·y·my (ĭ-pŏn′ə-mē) *n.* Derivation of a name of a city, a country, an era, an institution, or other place or thing from that of a person.

ep·o·pee (ĕp′ə-pē′) *n.* **1.** Epic poetry, especially as a literary genre. **2.** An epic poem. [French *épopée,* from Greek *epopoiia* : *epos,* song, word; see **wek^w-** in Appendix + *poiein,* to make; see **k^{w}ei-**[2] in Appendix.]

ep·os (ĕp′ŏs′) *n.* **1.** A number of poems, not formally united, that treat an epic theme. **2.** An epic. [Latin, from Greek. See **wek^w-** in Appendix.]

ep·ox·ide (ĕ-pŏk′sīd, ĭ-pŏk′-) *n.* **1.** A ring-shaped chemical structure consisting of an oxygen atom bonded to two other atoms, usually of carbon, that are already bonded to each other. **2.** A compound containing such a structure. Also called *epoxy.*

ep·ox·y (ĭ-pŏk′sē) *n., pl.* **-ies. 1.** Any of various usually thermosetting resins capable of forming tight cross-linked polymer structures characterized by toughness, strong adhesion, and low shrinkage, used especially in surface coatings and adhesives. **2.** See **epoxide.** *—attributive.* Often used to modify another noun: *epoxy glues; epoxy resins.* **—epoxy** *tr.v.* **-ied, -y·ing, -ies.** To fasten together with epoxy. [EP(I)– + OXY(GEN).]

Ep·ping Forest (ĕp′ĭng). A former royal hunting preserve of southeast England northeast of London. It is now a public park.

EPROM (ē′prŏm′) *n. Computer Science.* A programmable read-only memory that can be erased by exposure to ultraviolet light and then reprogrammed. [*e(rasable-) p(rogrammable) r(ead) o(nly) m(emory).*]

ep·si·lon (ĕp′sə-lŏn′, -lən) *n.* The fifth letter of the Greek alphabet. See table at **alphabet.** [Greek *e psilon,* simple e, from neuter of *psilos,* simple.]

Ep·som and Ew·ell (ĕp′səm; yōō′əl). A municipal borough of southeast England near London. The Derby is run annually at Epsom Downs racetrack. Epsom salts were originally produced at the mineral springs nearby. Population, 69,000.

Epsom salts *pl.n. (used with a sing. verb).* Hydrated magnesium sulfate, $MgSO_4{\cdot}7H_2O$, used as a cathartic and as an agent to reduce inflammation. [After *Epsom,* former name of Epsom and Ewell, England.]

Jacob Epstein

Ep·stein (ĕp′stīn′), Sir **Jacob.** 1880–1959. American-born British sculptor who is noted for his busts and his massive, controversial works, such as the marble *Venus* (1917).

Ep·stein-Barr virus (ĕp′stīn-bär′) *n. Abbr.* **EBV** A herpesvirus that is the causative agent of infectious mononucleosis. It is also associated with various types of human cancers. [After Michael A. *Epstein* and Y.M. *Barr,* 20th-century British virologists.]

eq. *abbr.* **1.** Equal. **2.** Equation. **3.** Equivalent.

E.Q. *abbr.* Educational quotient.

eq·ua·ble (ĕk′wə-bəl, ē′kwə-) *adj.* **1.a.** Unvarying; steady. **b.** Free from extremes. **2.** Not easily disturbed; serene: *an equable temper.* See Synonyms at **steady.** [Latin *aequābilis,* from *aequāre,* to make even, from *aequus,* even, level.] **—eq′ua·bil′i·ty, eq′ua·ble·ness** *n.* **—eq′ua·bly** *adv.*

e·qual (ē′kwəl) *adj. Abbr.* **eq. 1.** Having the same quantity, measure, or value as another. **2.** *Mathematics.* Being the same or identical to in value. **3.a.** Having the same privileges, status, or rights: *equal before the law.* **b.** Being the same for all members of a group: *gave every player an equal chance to win.* **4.a.** Having the requisite qualities, such as strength or ability, for a task or situation: *"Elizabeth found herself quite equal to the scene"* (Jane Austen). **b.** Adequate in extent, amount, or degree. **5.** Impartial; just; equitable. **6.** Tranquil; equable. **7.** Showing or having no variance in proportion, structure, or appearance. **—equal** *n.*

ă pat	oi boy
ā pay	ou out
âr care	ŏŏ took
ä father	ōō boot
ĕ pet	ŭ cut
ē be	ûr urge
ĭ pit	th thin
ī pie	*th* this
îr pier	hw which
ŏ pot	zh vision
ō toe	ə about, item
ô paw	♦ regionalism

Stress marks: ′ (primary); ′ (secondary), as in **dictionary** (dĭk′shə-nĕr′ē)

Abbr. **eq.** One that is equal to another: *Are men and women equals in physical strength?* **—equal** *tr.v.* **e·qualed, e·qual·ing, e·quals** or **e·qualled, e·qual·ling, e·quals. 1.** To be equal to, especially in value. **2.** To do, make, or produce something equal to: *equaled the world record in the mile run.* [Middle English, from Latin *aequālis,* from *aequus,* even, level.] **—e′qual·ly** *adv.*

USAGE NOTE: It has been argued that *equal* is an absolute term — two quantities either are or are not equal — and hence cannot be qualified as to degree. Therefore one cannot logically speak of *a more equal allocation of resources among the departments.* However, this usage was accepted by 71 percent of the Usage Panel in an earlier survey. What is more, objection to the usage betrays a widespread but questionable assumption that it is in mathematics and logic that we find the model of accuracy most appropriate to the everyday use of language, a supposition that also underlies traditional grammatical discussions of words such as *unique, parallel,* and *center.* According to this account, the "precise" or "literal" meaning of *equal* is realized in the use of the equal sign in an arithmetic expression such as 5 + 2 = 7; and the ordinary-language uses of the term, though they may be permissible, represent "loose" or "imprecise" extensions of that sense. But in fact the mathematical concept of equality is a poor model for using the word *equal* to describe relations between things in the world. As applied to such things, statements of equality are always relative to an implicit standard of tolerance. When someone says *The two boards are of equal length,* we assume that the equality is reckoned to some order of approximation determined by the context; if we did not, we would be required always to use *nearly equal* when speaking of the dimensions of physical objects. What is more, we often want to predicate equality of things that do not admit of quantitative measurement, as when we say *The college draft was introduced in an effort to make the teams in the National Football League as equal as possible,* or *The candidates for the job should all be given equal consideration.* In all such cases, equality is naturally a gradient notion and so is amenable to modification in degree. This much is evident from the existence of the word *unequal.* The prefix *un–* attaches only to gradient adjectives: we say *unmanly* but not *unmale;* and the word *uneven* can be applied to a surface (whose evenness may be a matter of degree) but not to a number (whose evenness is an either-or affair). • The adverb *equally* is generally regarded as redundant when used in combination with *as,* and the following examples employing *equally as* were termed unacceptable by 63 percent of the Usage Panel in an earlier survey: *Experience is equally as valuable as theory. Equally as important is the desire to learn.* In the first example, delete *equally;* in the second, delete *as.* The solution to this usage problem usually involves using *as* alone when a comparison is explicit and *equally* alone when it is not. See Usage Notes at **as[1], center, parallel, perfect, unique.**

e·qual·i·tar·i·an (ĭ-kwŏl′ĭ-târ′ē-ən) *adj.* Egalitarian. **—e·qual′i·tar′i·an·ism** *n.*

e·qual·i·ty (ĭ-kwŏl′ĭ-tē) *n., pl.* **-ties. 1.** The state or quality of being equal. **2.** *Mathematics.* A statement, usually an equation, that one thing equals another. [Middle English *equalite,* from Old French, from Latin *aequālitās,* from *aequālis,* equal. See EQUAL.]

e·qual·ize (ē′kwə-līz′) *v.* **-ized, -iz·ing, -iz·es.** *—tr.* **1.** To make equal: *equalized the responsibilities of the staff members.* **2.** To make uniform. *—intr.* To constitute or induce equality, equilibrium, or balance. **—e′qual·i·za′tion** (ē′kwə-lĭ-zā′shən) *n.*

e·qual·iz·er (ē′kwə-lī′zər) *n.* **1.** One that equalizes, as: **a.** A device for equalizing pressure or strain. **b.** A tone control system designed to compensate for frequency distortion in audio systems. **2.** *Slang.* A weapon, such as a firearm or switchblade.

equal opportunity *n.* Absence of discrimination, as in the workplace, based on race, color, age, gender, national origin, religion, or mental or physical disability.

equal sign *n.* The symbol (=) used to indicate logical or mathematical equality.

equal temperament *n. Music.* Modification of the intervals of just intonation in the tuning of instruments of fixed intonation to permit the modulation of harmony.

e·qua·nim·i·ty (ē′kwə-nĭm′ĭ-tē, ĕk′wə-) *n.* The quality of being calm and even-tempered; composure. [Latin *aequanimitās,* from *aequanimus,* even-tempered, impartial : *aequus,* even + *animus,* mind; see **anə-** in Appendix.]

SYNONYMS: *equanimity, composure, sang-froid, serenity.* These nouns denote the state of a person who is calm and not easily agitated emotionally. *Equanimity* implies mental balance and evenness of temperament, often as a characteristic state: *"And the third* [personal ideal] *has been to cultivate such a measure of equanimity as would enable me to bear success with humility, the affection of my friends without pride"* (William Osler). *Composure* is calmness that suggests the exercise of self-control: *She maintained her composure, though with difficulty, throughout the trial. Sang-froid* is coolness, especially in trying circumstances: *"Let what will be said or done, preserve your sang-froid immovably"* (Thomas Jefferson). *Serenity* is tranquil composure that suggests imperviousness to agitation or turmoil: *"He was always a cool man; nothing could disturb his serenity"* (Mark Twain).

e·quate (ĭ-kwāt′) *v.* **e·quat·ed, e·quat·ing, e·quates.** *—tr.* **1.** To make equal or equivalent. **2.** To reduce to a standard or an average; equalize. **3.** To consider, treat, or depict as equal or equivalent: *equates inexperience with youth.* *—intr.* To be or seem to be equal; correspond. [Middle English *equaten,* from Latin *aequāre, aequāt-,* to make equal, from *aequus,* even.]

e·qua·tion (ĭ-kwā′zhən, -shən) *n. Abbr.* **eq. 1.** The act or process of equating or of being equated. **2.** The state of being equal. **3.** *Mathematics.* A statement asserting the equality of two expressions, usually written as a linear array of symbols that are separated into left and right sides and joined by an equal sign. **4.** *Chemistry.* A representation of a chemical reaction, usually written as a linear array in which the symbols and quantities of the reactants are separated from those of the products by an equal sign, an arrow, or a set of opposing arrows. **5.** A complex of variable elements or factors: *"The world was full of equations . . . there must be an answer for everything, if only you knew how to set forth the questions"* (Anne Tyler). **—e·qua′tion·al** *adj.* **—e·qua′tion·al·ly** *adv.*

e·qua·tor (ĭ-kwā′tər) *n.* **1.a.** The imaginary great circle around the earth's surface, equidistant from the poles and perpendicular to the earth's axis of rotation. It divides the earth into the Northern Hemisphere and the Southern Hemisphere. **b.** A similar great circle drawn on the surface of a celestial body at right angles to the axis of rotation. **2.** The celestial equator. **3.** A circle that divides a sphere or other surface into congruent parts. [Middle English, from Medieval Latin *aequātor (diēī et noctis),* equalizer (of day and night), from *aequāre,* to equalize. See EQUATE.]

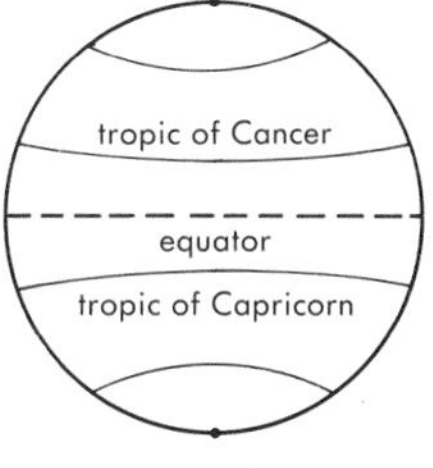

equator

e·qua·to·ri·al (ē′kwə-tôr′ē-əl, -tōr′-, ĕk′wə-) *adj.* **1.a.** Of, relating to, or resembling the earth's equator. **b.** Relating to conditions that exist at the earth's equator: *equatorial heat.* **2.** Having or constituting a support with two perpendicular axes, one of which is parallel to the earth's rotational axis. **—equatorial** *n.* An equatorial telescope. **—e′qua·to′ri·al·ly** *adv.*

equatorial current *n.* One of the surface currents drifting westward through the oceans at the equator.

E·qua·to·ri·al Guin·ea (ē′kwə-tôr′ē-əl gĭn′ē, -tōr′-, ĕk′wə-). A country of west-central Africa including islands in the Gulf of Guinea. It gained independence from Spain in 1968. Malabo is the capital and the largest city. Population, 300,000.

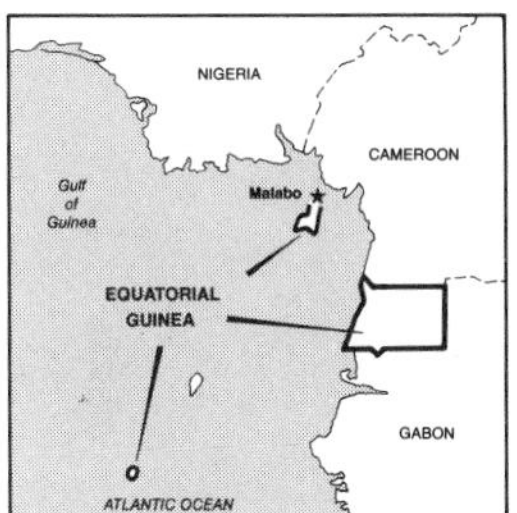

Equatorial Guinea

equatorial plate *n.* The plane located midway between the poles of a dividing cell during the metaphase stage of mitosis or meiosis. It is formed from the migration of the chromosomes to the center of the spindle.

equatorial telescope *n.* An astronomical telescope that keeps a star in view by revolving about an axis that is parallel to the earth's axis of rotation.

eq·uer·ry (ĕk′wə-rē) *n., pl.* **-ries. 1.** A personal attendant to the British royal household. **2.** An officer charged with supervision of the horses belonging to a royal or noble household. [French *écurie,* stable, from Old French *escurie,* from *escuier,* squire. See SQUIRE.]

e·ques·tri·an (ĭ-kwĕs′trē-ən) *adj.* **1.** Of or relating to horseback riding or horseback riders. **2.** Depicted or represented on horseback: *an equestrian statue of a famous monarch.* **—equestrian** *n.* One who rides a horse or performs on horseback. [From Latin *equester, equestr-,* from *eques,* horseman, from *equus,* horse. See **ekwo-** in Appendix.] **—e·ques′tri·an·ism** *n.* **—e·ques′tri·an·ship** *n.*

e·ques·tri·enne (ĭ-kwĕs′trē-ĕn′) *n.* A woman who rides a horse or performs on horseback. [EQUESTR(IAN) + *-ienne* (from French, feminine of *-ien,* -ian).]

equi– *pref.* Equal; equally: *equiangular.* [Middle English, from Latin *aequi-,* from *aequus,* equal.]

equestrian

e·qui·an·gu·lar (ē′kwē-ăng′gyə-lər, ĕk′wē-) *adj.* Having all angles equal.

e·qui·dis·tant (ē′kwĭ-dĭs′tənt, ĕk′wĭ-) *adj.* Equally distant. **—e′qui·dis′tance** (-təns) *n.* **—e′qui·dis′tant·ly** *adv.*

e·qui·lat·er·al (ē′kwə-lăt′ər-əl, ĕk′wə-) *adj.* Having all sides or faces equal. **—equilateral** *n.* **1.** A side exactly equal to others. **2.** A geometric figure having all sides equal. **—e′qui·lat′er·al·ly** *adv.*

e·qui·lat·er·al·ism (ē′kwə-lăt′ər-ə-lĭz′əm, ĕk′wə-) *n.* A political theory holding that since the United States and the Soviet Union are equal in strength, Europe should distance itself equally, and as far as possible, from both. **—e′qui·lat′er·al·ist** *adj. & n.*

e·quil·i·brate (ĭ-kwĭl′ə-brāt′) *v.* **-brat·ed, -brat·ing, -brates.** *—intr.* To be in or bring about equilibrium. *—tr.* To maintain in or bring into equilibrium. **—e·quil′i·bra′tion** *n.*

e·quil·i·bra·tor (ĭ-kwĭl′ə-brā′tər) *n.* A device that brings about and helps maintain equilibrium. **—e·quil′i·bra·to′ry** (-brə-tôr′ē, -tōr′ē) *adj.*

e·quil·i·brist (ĭ-kwĭl′ə-brĭst) *n.* A person who performs feats of balance, such as tightrope walking. [French *équilibriste,* from *équilibre,* equilibrium, from Latin *aequilībrium.* See EQUILIBRIUM.] **—e·quil′i·bris′tic** *adj.*

e·qui·lib·ri·um (ē′kwə-lĭb′rē-əm, ĕk′wə-) *n., pl.* **-ri·ums** or **-ri·a** (-rē-ə). **1.** A condition in which all acting influences are canceled by others, resulting in a stable, balanced, or unchanging system. See Synonyms at **balance.** **2.** Mental or emotional balance; poise. **3.** *Physics.* The state of a body or physical system at rest or in unaccelerated motion in which the resultant of all forces acting on it is zero and the sum of all torques about any axis is zero. **4.** *Chemistry.* The state of a chemical reaction in which its forward and reverse reactions occur at equal rates so that the concentration of the reactants and products does not change with time. [Latin *aequilībrium* : *aequi-*, equi- + *lībra*, balance.]

e·qui·mo·lar (ē′kwə-mō′lər, ĕk′wə-) *adj. Chemistry.* Having an equal number of moles.

e·quine (ē′kwīn′, ĕk′wīn′) *adj.* **1.** Of, relating to, or characteristic of a horse. **2.** Of or belonging to the family Equidae, which includes the horses, asses, and zebras. [Latin *equīnus*, from *equus*, horse. See **ekwo-** in Appendix.] **—e′quine′** *n.*

e·qui·noc·tial (ē′kwə-nŏk′shəl, ĕk′wə-) *adj.* **1.** Relating to an equinox. **2.** Relating to the celestial equator. **—equinoctial** *n.* **1.** A violent storm of wind and rain occurring at or near the time of the equinox. **2.** See **celestial equator.** [Middle English *equinoxial*, from Old French, from Latin *aequinoctiālis*, from *aequinoctium*, equinox. See EQUINOX.]

equinoctial circle *n.* See **celestial equator.**

e·qui·nox (ē′kwə-nŏks′, ĕk′wə-) *n.* **1.** Either of two points on the celestial sphere at which the ecliptic intersects the celestial equator. **2.** Either of the two times during a year when the sun crosses the celestial equator and when the length of day and night are approximately equal; the vernal equinox or the autumnal equinox. [Middle English, from Old French *equinoxe*, from Medieval Latin *aequinoxium*, from Latin *aequinoctium* : *aequi-*, equi- + *nox*, *noct-*, night; see **nekʷ-t-** in Appendix.]

e·quip (ĭ-kwĭp′) *tr.v.* **e·quipped, e·quip·ping, e·quips. 1.a.** To supply with necessities such as tools or provisions. **b.** To furnish with the qualities necessary for performance: *an education that will equip you to handle such problems.* See Synonyms at **furnish. 2.** To dress up. [French *équiper*, from Old French *esquiper*, of Germanic origin; akin to Old Norse *skipa* (from *skip*, ship).]

equip. *abbr.* Equipment.

eq·ui·page (ĕk′wə-pĭj) *n.* **1.** Equipment or furnishings. **2.a.** A horse-drawn carriage with attendants. **b.** The carriage itself. **3.** *Archaic.* A retinue, as of a noble or royal personage. **4.** *Archaic.* **a.** A set of small household articles, such as a dinner or tea service. **b.** A collection of small articles for personal use. [French *équipage*, from *équiper*, to equip. See EQUIP.]

e·quip·ment (ĭ-kwĭp′mənt) *n. Abbr.* **equip. 1.** The act of equipping or the state of being equipped. **2.** Something with which a person, an organization, or a thing is equipped. **3.** The rolling stock especially of a transportation system. **4.** The qualities or traits that make up the mental and emotional resources of an individual.

SYNONYMS: *equipment, apparatus, gear, materiel, outfit, paraphernalia, rig, tackle.* The central meaning shared by these nouns is "the materials needed for a purpose such as a task or a journey": *hiking equipment; laboratory apparatus; skiing gear; naval materiel; an explorer's outfit; sports paraphernalia; a climber's rig; fishing tackle.*

e·qui·poise (ē′kwə-poiz′, ĕk′wə-) *n.* **1.** Equality in distribution, as of weight, relationship, or emotional forces; equilibrium. See Synonyms at **balance. 2.** A counterbalance.

e·qui·pol·lent (ē′kwə-pŏl′ənt, ĕk′wə-) *adj.* **1.** Equal in force, power, effectiveness, or significance. **2.** *Logic.* Validly derived from each other; deducible. **3.** Equivalent. **—equipollent** *n.* An equivalent. [Middle English, from Old French, from Latin *aequipollēns*, *aequipollent-* : *aequi-*, equi- + *pollēns*, present participle of *pollēre*, to be powerful.] **—e′qui·pol′lence** *n.* **—e′qui·pol′lent·ly** *adv.*

e·qui·pon·der·ance (ē′kwə-pŏn′dər-əns, ĕk′wə-) *n.* Equality of weight; equipoise. [From *equiponderant*, from Medieval Latin *aequiponderāns*, *aequiponderant-*, present participle of *aequiponderāre*, to weigh the same. See EQUIPONDERATE.] **—e′qui·pon′der·ant** *adj.*

e·qui·pon·der·ate (ē′kwə-pŏn′də-rāt′, ĕk′wə-) *tr.v.* **-at·ed, -at·ing, -ates. 1.** To counterbalance. **2.** To give equal balance or weight to. [Medieval Latin *aequiponderāre*, *aequiponderāt-* : Latin *aequi-*, equi- + Latin *ponderāre*, to weigh; see **(s)pen-** in Appendix.]

e·qui·po·ten·tial (ē′kwə-pə-tĕn′shəl, ĕk′wə-) *adj.* **1.** Having equal potential. **2.** *Physics.* Having the same electric potential at every point.

e·qui·prob·a·ble (ē′kwə-prŏb′ə-bəl, ĕk′wə-) *adj.* Having equal mathematical or logical probability.

eq·ui·se·tum (ĕk′wə-sē′təm) *n., pl.* **-tums** or **-ta** (-tə). See **horsetail.** [Latin *equisaetum*, horsetail : *equus*, horse; see **ekwo-** in Appendix + *saeta*, bristle, stiff hair.]

eq·ui·ta·ble (ĕk′wĭ-tə-bəl) *adj.* Marked by or having equity; just and impartial. See Synonyms at **fair¹.** [French *équitable*, from Old French, from *equite*, equity. See EQUITY.] **—eq′ui·ta·ble·ness** *n.* **—eq′ui·ta·bly** *adv.*

eq·ui·tant (ĕk′wĭ-tənt) *adj.* Overlapping at the base to form a flat, fanlike arrangement in two ranks, as the leaves of some irises. [Latin *equitāns*, *equitant-*, present participle of *equitāre*, to ride horseback, from *eques*, *equit-*, horseman, from *equus*, horse. See **ekwo-** in Appendix.]

eq·ui·ta·tion (ĕk′wĭ-tā′shən) *n.* The art and practice of riding a horse. [Latin *equitātiō*, *equitātiōn-*, from *equitāre*, to ride horseback. See EQUITANT.]

eq·ui·ty (ĕk′wĭ-tē) *n., pl.* **-ties. 1.** The state, quality, or ideal of being just, impartial, and fair. **2.** Something that is just, impartial, and fair. **3.** *Law.* **a.** Justice applied in circumstances covered by law yet influenced by principles of ethics and fairness. **b.** A system of jurisprudence supplementing and serving to modify the rigor of common law. **c.** An equitable right or claim. **d.** Equity of redemption. **4.** The residual value of a business or property beyond any mortgage thereon and liability therein. **5.a.** The market value of securities less any debt incurred. **b.** Common stock and preferred stock. **6.** Funds provided to a business by the sale of stock. [Middle English *equite*, from Old French, from Latin *aequitās*, from *aequus*, even, fair.]

equity of redemption *n. Law.* The right of one who has mortgaged property to redeem that property upon payment of the sum due within a reasonable amount of time after the due date.

equity stock *n.* Common stock and preferred stock.

equiv. *abbr.* Equivalence; equivalency; equivalent.

e·quiv·a·lence (ĭ-kwĭv′ə-ləns) *n. Abbr.* **equiv. 1.** The state or condition of being equivalent; equality. **2.** *Mathematics.* An equivalence relation.

equivalence relation *n. Mathematics.* A reflexive, symmetrical, and transitive relationship between elements of a set that establishes any two elements in the set as equivalent or nonequivalent.

e·quiv·a·len·cy (ĭ-kwĭv′ə-lən-sē) *n., pl.* **-cies.** *Abbr.* **equiv.** Equivalence.

e·quiv·a·lent (ĭ-kwĭv′ə-lənt) *adj. Abbr.* **equiv., eq. 1.a.** Equal, as in value, force, or meaning. **b.** Having similar or identical effects. **2.** Being essentially equal, all things considered: *a wish that was equivalent to a command.* **3.** *Mathematics.* **a.** Capable of being put into a one-to-one relationship. Used of two sets. **b.** Having virtually identical or corresponding parts. **4.** *Chemistry.* Having the same ability to combine. **—equivalent** *n. Abbr.* **equiv., eq. 1.** Something that is essentially equal to another: *"Prejudicing vital foreign policy considerations in order to rescue individuals finds its domestic equivalent in the inflated awards paid to . . . accident and malpractice victims"* (Moorhead Kennedy). **2.** *Chemistry.* Equivalent weight. [Middle English, from Late Latin *aequivalēns*, *aequivalent-*, present participle of *aequivalēre*, to have equal force : *aequi-*, equi- + *valēre*, to be strong; see **wal-** in Appendix.] **—e·quiv′a·lent·ly** *adv.*

equivalent weight *n. Chemistry.* The weight of a substance that will combine with or replace one mole of hydrogen or one-half mole of oxygen. The equivalent weight is equal to the atomic weight divided by the valence.

e·quiv·o·cal (ĭ-kwĭv′ə-kəl) *adj.* **1.** Open to two or more interpretations and often intended to mislead; ambiguous. See Synonyms at **ambiguous. 2.** Of uncertain significance. **3.** Of a doubtful or uncertain nature. [From Late Latin *aequivocus* : Latin *aequi-*, equi- + Latin *vōx*, *vōc-*, voice; see **wekʷ-** in Appendix.] **—e·quiv′o·cal′i·ty** (-kăl′ĭ-tē), **e·quiv′o·cal·ness** *n.* **—e·quiv′o·cal·ly** *adv.*

e·quiv·o·cate (ĭ-kwĭv′ə-kāt′) *intr.v.* **-cat·ed, -cat·ing, -cates. 1.** To use equivocal language intentionally. **2.** To avoid making an explicit statement. See Synonyms at **lie².** [Middle English *equivocaten*, from Medieval Latin *aequivocāre*, *aequivocāt-*, from Late Latin *aequivocus*, equivocal. See EQUIVOCAL.] **—e·quiv′o·ca′tor** *n.*

e·quiv·o·ca·tion (ĭ-kwĭv′ə-kā′shən) *n.* **1.** The use of equivocal language. **2.** An equivocal statement or expression.

eq·ui·voque also **eq·ui·voke** (ĕk′wə-vōk′, ē′kwə-) *n.* **1.** An equivocal word, phrase, or expression. **2.** A pun. **3.** A double meaning. [French *équivoque*, from Late Latin *aequivocus*, ambiguous. See EQUIVOCAL.]

Er The symbol for the element **erbium.**

ER *abbr.* Emergency room.

-er¹ *suff.* **1.a.** One that performs a specified action: *swimmer.* **b.** One that undergoes or is capable of undergoing a specified action: *broiler.* **c.** One that has: *ten-pounder.* **d.** One associated or involved with: *banker.* **2.a.** Native or resident of: *New Yorker.* **b.** One that is: *foreigner.* [Middle English, partly from Old English *-ere* (from Germanic **-ārjaz*), partly from Anglo-French *-er* (from Old French *-ier*, from Latin *-ārius*, -ary), and partly from Old French *-ere*, *-eor*; see -OR¹.]

-er² *suff.* Used to form the comparative degree of adjectives and adverbs: *darker; faster.* [Middle English, from Old English *-re*, *-ra*.]

e·ra (îr′ə, ĕr′ə) *n.* **1.** A period of time as reckoned from a specific date serving as the basis of its chronological system. **2.a.** A period of time characterized by particular circumstances, events, or personages: *the Colonial era of U.S. history; the Kennedy era.* **b.** A point that marks the beginning of such a period of time. See Synonyms at **period. 3.** The longest division of geologic time, made up of one or more periods. [Late Latin *aera*, from Latin, counters, pl. of *aes*, *aer-*, bronze coin. See **ayes-** in Appendix.]

ERA *abbr.* **1.** *Baseball.* Earned run average. **2.** Equal Rights Amendment.

e·rad·i·cate (ĭ-răd′ĭ-kāt′) *tr.v.* **-cat·ed, -cat·ing, -cates. 1.**

To tear up by the roots. **2.** To get rid of as if by tearing up by the roots: *Their goal was to eradicate poverty.* See Synonyms at **abolish, eliminate.** [Middle English *eradicaten,* from Latin *ērādīcāre, ērādīcāt-* : *ē-, ex-,* ex- + *rādīx, rādīc-,* root; see **wrād-** in Appendix.] **—e·rad′i·ca·ble** (-kə-bəl) *adj.* **—e·rad′i·ca′tion** *n.* **—e·rad′i·ca′tive** *adj.* **—e·rad′i·ca′tor** *n.*

e·rase (ĭ-rās′) *tr.v.* **e·rased, e·ras·ing, e·ras·es. 1.a.** To remove (something written, for example) by rubbing, wiping, or scraping. **b.** To remove (recorded material) from a magnetic tape or other storage medium: *erased a file from the diskette.* **c.** To remove recorded material from (a magnetic tape or disk, for example): *erased the videocassette.* **2.** To remove all traces of. **3.** To remove or destroy as if by wiping out: *had to erase all thoughts of failure from his mind.* [Latin *ērādere, ērās-,* to scratch out : *ē-, ex-,* ex- + *rādere,* to scrape; see **rēd-** in Appendix.] **—e·ras′a·bil′i·ty** *n.* **—e·ras′a·ble** *adj.*

SYNONYMS: *erase, expunge, efface, delete, cancel.* These verbs mean to remove or invalidate something, especially something recorded as by having been written down. To *erase* is to wipe or rub out, literally or figuratively: *erased the equation from the blackboard. Unconsciousness erased the details of the accident from her memory. Expunge* implies thoroughgoing removal that leaves no trace: *expunged their names from the list. Efface* also refers to the removal of every trace: *effacing graffiti from subway cars; tried to efface prejudice from his mind. Delete* is used principally in the sense of removing matter from a manuscript: *The expletives were deleted from the transcript. Cancel* refers to invalidating by or as if by drawing lines through something written or by indicating that the force or effect of something has been terminated: *a postage stamp that had been canceled; cancel vows; cancel a debt.*

e·ras·er (ĭ-rā′sər) *n.* An implement, such as a piece of rubber or a pad of felt, used for erasing.

E·ras·mus (ĭ-răz′məs), **Desiderius.** 1466?–1536. Dutch Renaissance scholar and Roman Catholic theologian who sought to revive classical texts from antiquity and restore simple Christian faith based on Scripture. His works include *The Praise of Folly* (1509).

E·ras·tus (ĭ-răs′təs), **Thomas.** 1524–1583. Swiss Protestant theologian and philosopher who opposed Calvinism and the use of excommunication as a punishment.

e·ra·sure (ĭ-rā′shər) *n.* **1.** The act or an instance of erasing. **2.** The state of being erased: *"The powerful images of his work . . . punishment, mutilation, erasure"* (Joyce Carol Oates).

Er·a·to (ĕr′ə-tō′) *n. Greek Mythology.* The Muse of lyric poetry and mime.

E·ra·tos·the·nes (ĕr′ə-tŏs′thə-nēz′). Third century B.C. Greek mathematician, astronomer, and geographer who devised a map of the world and estimated the circumference of the earth and the distance to the moon and the sun.

Er·bil (îr′bĭl, ĕr′-). See **Irbil.**

er·bi·um (ûr′bē-əm) *n. Symbol* **Er** A soft, malleable, silvery rare-earth element, used in metallurgy and nuclear research and to color glass and porcelain. Atomic number 68; atomic weight 167.26; melting point 1,497°C; boiling point 2,900°C; specific gravity 9.051; valence 3. See table at **element.** [After *Ytterby,* a town in Sweden.]

ere (âr) *prep.* Previous to; before. **—ere** *conj.* Rather than; before. [Middle English *er,* from Old English *ǣr.* See **ayer-** in Appendix.]

Er·e·bus (ĕr′ə-bəs) *n. Greek Mythology.* The dark region of the underworld through which the dead must pass before they reach Hades.

Erebus, Mount. A volcanic peak, 3,796.6 m (12,448 ft) high, on Ross Island in Antarctica.

e·rect (ĭ-rĕkt′) *adj.* **1.** Being in a vertical, upright position: *an erect lily stalk; an erect posture.* **2.** Vertical. **3.** Being in a stiff, rigid physiological condition. **4.** *Archaic.* Wide-awake; alert. **—erect** *tr.v.* **e·rect·ed, e·rect·ing, e·rects. 1.** To construct by assembling: *erect a skyscraper.* **2.** To raise to a rigid or upright condition. **3.** To fix in an upright position. **4.** To set up; establish: *erect a dynasty.* **5.** *Mathematics.* To construct (a perpendicular, for example) from or on a given base. [Middle English, from Latin *ērēctus,* past participle of *ērigere,* to set up : *ē-, ex-,* ex- + *regere,* to guide; see **reg-** in Appendix.] **—e·rect′a·ble** *adj.* **—e·rect′ly** *adv.* **—e·rect′ness** *n.*

e·rec·tile (ĭ-rĕk′təl, -tīl′) *adj.* **1.** Capable of being raised to an upright position. **2.** *Anatomy.* Of or relating to tissue that is capable of filling with blood and becoming rigid. **—e·rec·til′i·ty** (-tĭl′ĭ-tē) *n.*

e·rec·tion (ĭ-rĕk′shən) *n.* **1.** The act of erecting. **2.** Something erected; a construction. **3.** *Physiology.* **a.** The firm and enlarged condition of a body organ or part when the erectile tissue surrounding it becomes filled with blood, especially such a condition of the penis or clitoris. **b.** The process of filling with blood.

e·rec·tor (ĭ-rĕk′tər) *n.* **1.** One that erects: *an erector of skyscrapers.* **2.** *Anatomy.* A muscle that causes or maintains the erection of a body part.

E region *n.* See **E layer.**

ere·long (âr-lông′, -lŏng′) *adv.* Before long; soon.

er·e·mite (âr′ə-mīt′) *n.* A recluse or hermit, especially a religious recluse. [Middle English, from Late Latin *erēmīta.* See HERMIT.] **—er′e·mit′ic** (-mĭt′ĭk), **er′e·mit′i·cal** *adj.*

er·e·mur·us (ĕr′ə-myo͝or′əs) *n.* Any of several Asiatic plants of the genus *Eremurus* in the lily family, having a tall cluster of colorful bell-shaped flowers. [New Latin *Eremurus,* genus name : Greek *erēmos,* solitary + Greek *oura,* tail; see **ors-** in Appendix.]

ere·now (âr-nou′) *adv.* Before now; heretofore.

e·rep·sin (ĭ-rĕp′sən) *n.* An enzyme complex found in intestinal and pancreatic juices that functions in the breakdown of polypeptides into amino acids. [Latin *ēripere,* to snatch away (*ē-, ex-,* ex- + *rapere,* to seize; see **rep-** in Appendix) + (P)EPSIN.]

er·e·thism (ĕr′ə-thĭz′əm) *n.* Abnormal irritability or sensitivity of an organ or a body part to stimulation. [French *éréthisme,* from Greek *erethisma,* a provocation, from *erethizein,* to irritate.] **—er′e·this′mic** (-mĭk) *adj.*

E·re·van (yĕ′rĭ-vän′). See **Yerevan.**

ere·while (âr-hwīl′, -wīl′) also **ere·whiles** (-hwīlz′, -wīlz′) *adv. Archaic.* Some time ago; heretofore.

Er·furt (ĕr′fərt, -fo͝ort′). A city of central Germany southwest of Leipzig. Site of an episcopal see founded by Saint Boniface in the eighth century, it was later a free imperial city and a member of the Hanseatic League. Population, 214,231.

erg (ûrg) *n.* The centimeter-gram-second unit of energy or work equal to the work done by a force of one dyne acting over a distance of one centimeter. [From Greek *ergon,* work. See **werg-** in Appendix.]

er·go (ûr′gō, âr′-) *conj.* Consequently; therefore. **—ergo** *adv.* Consequently; hence. [Latin *ergō.* See **reg-** in Appendix.]

er·go·cal·cif·er·ol (ûr′gō-kăl-sĭf′ə-rôl′, -rŏl′, -rōl′) *n.* See **vitamin D_2.** [ERGO(T) + CALCIFEROL.]

er·go·graph (ûr′gə-grăf′) *n.* A device for measuring the work capacity of a muscle or group of muscles during contraction. [Greek *ergon,* work; see **werg-** in Appendix + -GRAPH.] **—er′go·graph′ic** *adj.*

er·gom·e·ter (ûr-gŏm′ĭ-tər) *n.* An instrument for measuring the amount of work done by a muscle or group of muscles. [Greek *ergon,* work; see **werg-** in Appendix + -METER.] **—er′go·met′ric** (ûr′gə-mĕt′rĭk) *adj.*

er·go·nom·ics (ûr′gə-nŏm′ĭks) *n.* **1.** *(used with a sing. verb).* The applied science of equipment design, as for the workplace, intended to maximize productivity by reducing operator fatigue and discomfort. Also called *biotechnology, human engineering, human factors engineering.* **2.** *(used with a pl. verb).* Design factors, as for the workplace, intended to maximize productivity by minimizing operator fatigue and discomfort: *The ergonomics of the new office were felt to be optimal.* [Greek *ergon,* work; see **werg-** in Appendix + (ECO)NOMICS.] **—er′go·nom′ic, er′go·no·met′ric** (-nə-mĕt′rĭk) *adj.* **—er′go·nom′i·cal·ly** *adv.* **—er·gon′o·mist** (ûr-gŏn′ə-mĭst) *n.*

er·gos·ter·ol (ûr-gŏs′tə-rôl′, -rōl′, -rŏl′) *n.* A crystalline sterol, $C_{28}H_{43}OH$, synthesized by yeast from sugars or derived from ergot and converted to vitamin D_2 when exposed to ultraviolet radiation. [ERGO(T) + STEROL.]

er·got (ûr′gət, -gŏt′) *n.* **1.** A fungus *(Claviceps purpurea)* that infects various cereal plants and forms compact black masses of branching filaments that replace many of the grains of the host plant. **2.** The disease caused by such a fungus. **3.** The dried sclerotia of ergot, usually obtained from rye seed and used as a source of several medicinally important alkaloids and as the basic source of lysergic acid. [French, from Old French *argot,* cock's spur (from its shape).] **—er·got′ic** *adj.*

er·got·a·mine (ûr-gŏt′ə-mēn′, -mĭn) *n.* A crystalline alkaloid, $C_{33}H_{35}N_5O_5$, derived from ergot that induces vasoconstriction and is used especially in treating migraine.

er·got·ism (ûr′gə-tĭz′əm) *n.* Poisoning caused by consuming ergot-infected grain or grain products, or from excessive use of drugs containing ergot.

Er·gun He (ĕr′go͞on′ hĕ′, œr′gün hə′). See **Argun River.**

Er·ic·son also **Er·ics·son** (ĕr′ĭk-sən), **Leif.** fl. c. 1000. Norwegian navigator who, according to Norse sagas, was blown off course during a voyage from Norway to Greenland and thereby discovered and named Vinland.

Er·ics·son (ĕr′ĭk-sən), **John.** 1803–1889. American engineer and inventor who built the first ironclad warship, the *Monitor* (1862), which engaged the Confederate *Merrimack* in a famous naval battle of the Civil War (March 9, 1862).

Ericsson, Leif. See Leif **Ericson.**

Er·ic the Red (ĕr′ĭk). Tenth century. Norwegian navigator who explored and named Greenland and founded its first settlement (c. 985).

E·rid·a·nus (ĭ-rĭd′n-əs) *n.* A constellation in the Southern Hemisphere near Fornax and Cetus. [Greek *Eridanos,* mythical river associated with the myth of Phaeton.]

E·rie¹ (îr′ē) *n., pl.* **Erie** or **E·ries. 1.a.** A Native American people formerly inhabiting the southern shore of Lake Erie in northern Ohio, northwest Pennsylvania, and western New York. The Erie ceased to exist as a people after being defeated by the Iroquois in the mid-17th century. **b.** A member of this people. **2.** The Iroquoian language of the Erie.

E·rie² (îr′ē). A city of northwest Pennsylvania on Lake Erie southwest of Buffalo, New York. A port of entry, it was laid out in 1795 on the site of Fort Presque Isle, built by the French in 1753. Population, 119,123.

Erasmus

ă pat	oi boy
ā pay	ou out
âr care	o͝o took
ä father	o͞o boot
ĕ pet	ŭ cut
ē be	ûr urge
ĭ pit	th thin
ī pie	*th* this
îr pier	hw which
ŏ pot	zh vision
ō toe	ə about, item
ô paw	♦ regionalism

Stress marks: ′ (primary); ′ (secondary), as in **dictionary** (dĭk′shə-nĕr′ē)

Erlenmeyer flask

Max Ernst
Photographed in 1941

eruption
Paricutin volcano, Mexico, 1943

ă pat	oi boy
ā pay	ou out
âr care	o͝o took
ä father	o͞o boot
ĕ pet	ŭ cut
ē be	ûr urge
ĭ pit	th thin
ī pie	*th* this
îr pier	hw which
ŏ pot	zh vision
ō toe	ə about, item
ô paw	♦ regionalism

Stress marks: **ʹ** (primary); ʹ (secondary), as in **dictionary** (dĭkʹshə-nĕrʹē)

Erie, Lake. One of the Great Lakes, bounded by southern Ontario, western New York, northwest Pennsylvania, northern Ohio, and southeast Michigan. It is linked with the Hudson River by the New York State Barge Canal.

Erie Canal. An artificial waterway extending about 579 km (360 mi) across central New York from Albany to Buffalo. Constructed from 1817 to 1825 and enlarged numerous times after 1835, it is now part of the New York State Barge Canal.

E·rig·e·na (ĭ-rĭjʹə-nə), **John Scotus.** 810?–877? Irish-born theologian and philosopher who sought to reconcile Neo-Platonism and Christian belief in his principal work, *On the Division of Nature* (862–866).

Er·ik·son (ĕrʹĭk-sən), **Erik Homburger.** Born 1902. German-born American psychoanalyst whose works include *Childhood and Society* (1950).

Er·in (ĕrʹĭn). A poetic name for Ireland.

E·rin·y·es (ĭ-rĭnʹē-ēzʹ) *pl.n. Greek Mythology.* The Furies.

E·ris (îrʹĭs, ĕrʹ-) *n. Greek Mythology.* The goddess of discord.

e·ris·tic (ĭ-rĭsʹtĭk) also **e·ris·ti·cal** (-tĭ-kəl) *—adj.* Given to or characterized by disputatious, often specious argument. *—n.* **1.** One given to or expert in dispute or argument. **2.** The art or practice of disputation and polemics. [Greek *eristikos,* from *erizein,* to wrangle, quarrel, from *eris, erid-,* strife.]

Er·i·tre·a (ĕrʹĭ-trēʹə). A region of northern Ethiopia bordering on the Red Sea. It was proclaimed an Italian colony in 1890 and became part of Ethiopia in 1952. **—Erʹi·treʹan** *adj. & n.*

E·ri·van (yĕʹrĭ-vänʹ). See **Yerevan.**

Er·lang·en (ĕrʹläng'ən). A city of south-central Germany north-northeast of Nuremberg. Chartered in 1398, it passed to Bavaria in 1810. Population, 100,523.

Er·len·mey·er flask (ûrʹlən-mīʹər, ärʹ-) *n.* A conical laboratory flask with a narrow neck and flat, broad bottom. [After Richard August Carl Emil *Erlenmeyer* (1825–1909), German chemist.]

er·mine (ûrʹmĭn) *n.* **1.** A weasel *(Mustela erminea)* of northern regions, having a black-tipped tail and dark brown fur that in winter changes to white. **2.** The commercially valuable white fur of this animal. [Middle English *ermin,* from Old French *ermine,* possibly of Germanic origin or from Medieval Latin *(mūs) Armenius,* Armenian (mouse).]

Er·na·ku·lum (ĕr-näʹkə-ləm). A city of southwest India on the Malabar Coast west of Madurai. It has a Jewish sector that may date to the second or third century A.D. Population, 213,811.

erne also **ern** (ûrn) *n.* Any of several sea eagles, especially *Haliaeetus albicilla,* of Europe. [Middle English *ern,* eagle, from Old English *earn.* See **or-** in Appendix.]

Ernst (ĕrnst), **Max.** 1891–1976. German-born artist and a founder of Dada and surrealism. Noted for his use of frottage and collage, he explored the subconscious through his stylistically varied works, such as *Old Man, Woman, and Flower* (1923).

e·rode (ĭ-rōdʹ) *v.* **e·rod·ed, e·rod·ing, e·rodes.** *—tr.* **1.** To wear (something) away by or as if by abrasion: *Waves eroded the shore.* **2.** To eat into; corrode. **3.** To make or form by wearing away: *The river eroded a deep valley.* **4.** To cause to diminish, deteriorate, or disappear as if by eating into or wearing away: *"Long enduring peace often erodes popular resolution"* (C.L. Sulzberger). *—intr.* To become worn or eaten away: *The cliffs have eroded over the centuries. Public confidence in the administration eroded.* [Latin *ērōdere,* to gnaw off, eat away : *ē-, ex-,* ex- + *rōdere,* to gnaw; see **rēd-** in Appendix.] **—e·rodʹi·bilʹi·ty** *n.* **—e·rodʹi·ble** *adj.*

e·rog·e·nous (ĭ-rŏjʹə-nəs) *adj.* **1.** Responsive or sensitive to sexual stimulation: *erogenous zones.* **2.** Arousing sexual desire. [Greek *erōs,* sexual love + –GENOUS.]

Er·os (ĕrʹŏsʹ, îrʹ-) *n.* **1.** *Greek Mythology.* The god of love, son of Aphrodite. **2.** *Psychiatry.* **a.** The sum of all instincts for self-preservation. **b.** Sexual drive; libido. **3.** Often **eros.** Creative, often sexual yearning, love, or desire: *"The new playful eros means that impulses and modes from other spheres enter the relations between men and women"* (Herbert Gold). [Latin *Erōs,* from Greek, from *erōs,* sexual love.]

e·rose (ĭ-rōsʹ) *adj.* Irregularly notched, toothed, or indented: *erose leaves.* [From Latin *ērōsus,* past participle of *ērōdere,* to gnaw off. See ERODE.] **—e·roseʹly** *adv.*

e·ro·sion (ĭ-rōʹzhən) *n.* **1.** The process of eroding or the condition of being eroded: *erosion of the beach; progressive erosion of confidence in our legal system; erosion of the value of the dollar abroad.* **2.** The group of natural processes, including weathering, dissolution, abrasion, corrosion, and transportation, by which material is worn away from the earth's surface. [Latin *ērōsiō, ērōsiōn-,* an eating away, from *ērōsus,* eaten away. See EROSE.] **—e·roʹsion·al** *adj.* **—e·roʹsion·al·ly** *adv.*

e·ro·sive (ĭ-rōʹsĭv) *adj.* Causing erosion: *the erosive effect of waves on the shoreline.* **—e·roʹsive·ness, e·ro'sivʹi·ty** *n.*

e·rot·ic (ĭ-rŏtʹĭk) *adj.* **1.** Of or concerning sexual love and desire; amatory. **2.** Tending to arouse sexual desire. **3.** Dominated by sexual love or desire. [Greek *erōtikos,* from *erōs, erōt-,* sexual love.] **—e·rotʹic** *n.* **—e·rotʹi·cal·ly** *adv.*

e·rot·i·ca (ĭ-rŏtʹĭ-kə) *pl.n. (used with a sing. or pl. verb).* Literature or art intended to arouse sexual desire. [Greek *erōtika,* from neuter pl. of *erōtikos,* erotic. See EROTIC.]

e·rot·i·cism (ĭ-rŏtʹĭ-sĭzʹəm) *n.* **1.** An erotic quality or theme. **2.** Sexual excitement. **3.** Abnormally persistent sexual excitement. **—e·rotʹi·cist** *n.*

e·rot·i·cize (ĭ-rŏtʹĭ-sīzʹ) *tr.v.* **-cized, -ciz·ing, -ciz·es.** To make erotic. **—e·rotʹi·ci·zaʹtion** (-sĭ-zāʹshən) *n.*

er·o·tism (ĕrʹə-tĭzʹəm) *n.* Eroticism.

er·o·tize (ĕrʹə-tīzʹ) *tr.v.* **-tized, -tiz·ing, -tiz·es.** To imbue with erotic feeling or import.

e·ro·to·ma·ni·a (ĭ-rōʹtə-māʹnē-ə, ĭ-rŏtʹə-) *n.* Excessive sexual desire. [Greek *erōtomania* : *erōs, erōt-,* sexual love + *-mania,* -mania.]

err (ûr, ĕr) *intr.v.* **erred, err·ing, errs. 1.** To make an error or a mistake. **2.** To violate accepted moral standards; sin. **3.** *Archaic.* To stray. [Middle English *erren,* from Old French *errer,* from Latin *errāre,* to wander. See **ers-** in Appendix.]

USAGE NOTE: The pronunciation (ûr) for the word *err* is traditional, but the pronunciation (ĕr) has gained ground in recent years, perhaps owing to influence from *errant* and *error,* and must now be regarded as an acceptable variant. The Usage Panel was split on the matter: 56 percent preferred (ûr), 34 percent preferred (ĕr), and 10 percent accepted both pronunciations.

er·ran·cy (ĕrʹən-sē) *n., pl.* **-cies.** The state of erring or an instance of it.

er·rand (ĕrʹənd) *n.* **1.a.** A short trip taken to perform a specified task, usually for another. **b.** The purpose or object of such a trip: *Your errand was to mail the letter.* **2.** *Archaic.* **a.** A mission; an embassy. **b.** An oral message that has been entrusted to one. [Middle English *erand,* from Old English *ǣrend.*]

er·rant (ĕrʹənt) *adj.* **1.** Roving, especially in search of adventure: *knights errant.* **2.** Straying from the proper course or standards: *errant youngsters.* **3.a.** Wandering outside the established limits: *errant lambs.* **b.** Aimless or irregular in motion: *an errant afternoon breeze.* [Middle English *erraunt,* from Anglo-Norman, partly from Old French *errer,* to travel about (from Vulgar Latin **iterāre,* from Latin *iter,* journey; see **ei-** in Appendix) and partly from Old French *errer,* to err; see ERR.] **—erʹrant** *n.* **—erʹrant·ly** *adv.*

er·rant·ry (ĕrʹən-trē) *n.* The condition of traveling or roving about, especially in search of adventure.

er·ra·ta (ĭ-räʹtə, ĭ-rāʹ-) *n.* Plural of **erratum.**

er·rat·ic (ĭ-răt'ĭk) *adj.* **1.** Having no fixed or regular course; wandering. **2.** Lacking consistency, regularity, or uniformity. **3.** Deviating from the customary course in conduct or opinion; eccentric: *erratic behavior.* [Middle English *erratik,* from Old French *erratique,* from Latin *errāticus,* from *errāre,* to wander. See **ers-** in Appendix.] **—er·ratʹi·cal·ly** *adv.* **—er·ratʹi·cism** (-ĭ-sĭzʹəm) *n.*

er·ra·tum (ĭ-räʹtəm, ĭ-rāʹ-) *n., pl.* **-ta** (-tə). An error in printing or writing, especially such an error noted in a list of corrections and bound into a book. [Latin *errātum,* from neuter past participle of *errāre,* to stray. See **ers-** in Appendix.]

er·rhine (ĕrʹīnʹ) *adj.* Promoting or inducing nasal discharge. **—errhine** *n.* A medication that promotes or induces such discharge. [New Latin *errhinum,* an errhine medicine, from Greek *errinon* : *en-,* in; see EN–² + *rhis, rhin-,* nose.]

Er Rif (ĕr rĭfʹ). A hilly region along the coast of northern Morocco. The Berber peoples of the area were subdued by French and Spanish forces (1925–1926).

er·ro·ne·ous (ĭ-rōʹnē-əs) *adj.* Containing or derived from error; mistaken: *erroneous conclusions.* [Middle English, from Latin *errōneus,* from *errō, errōn-,* a vagabond, from *errāre,* to err, wander. See **ers-** in Appendix.] **—er·roʹne·ous·ly** *adv.* **—er·roʹne·ous·ness** *n.*

er·ror (ĕrʹər) *n.* **1.** An act, an assertion, or a belief that unintentionally deviates from what is correct, right, or true. **2.** The condition of having incorrect or false knowledge. **3.** The act or an instance of deviating from an accepted code of behavior. **4.** A mistake. **5.** *Mathematics.* The difference between a computed or measured value and a true or theoretically correct value. **6.** *Abbr.* **e, e.** *Baseball.* A defensive fielding or throwing misplay by a player when a play normally should have resulted in an out or prevented an advance by a base runner. [Middle English *errour,* from Old French, from Latin *error,* from *errāre,* to err. See **ers-** in Appendix.] **—erʹror·less** *adj.*

SYNONYMS: *error, mistake, oversight.* These nouns refer to what is not in accord with truth, accuracy, or propriety. *Error* indicates departure from the correct path; it often implies deviation from what is morally or ethically right or proper: *"Irrationally held truths may be more harmful than reasoned errors"* (Thomas H. Huxley). *"There is no error so monstrous that it fails to find defenders among the ablest men"* (Lord Acton). *Mistake* often implies misunderstanding or misinterpretation and is usually weaker than *error* in imputing blame or censure: *"Nothing is easy in war. Mistakes are always paid for in casualties"* (Dwight D. Eisenhower). *Oversight* refers to an inadvertent omission or error that results from inattention: *Through a regrettable oversight I failed to send you an invitation.* See also Synonyms at **offense.**

er·satz (ĕrʹzätsʹ, ĕr-zätsʹ) *adj.* Being an imitation or a substitute, usually an inferior one; artificial: *ersatz coffee made mostly of chicory.* See Synonyms at **artificial.** [German, replacement, from *ersetzen,* to replace, from Old High German *irsezzan* : *ir-,* out; see **ud-** in Appendix + *sezzan,* to set; see **sed-** in Appendix.] **—er′satz′** *n.*

Erse (ûrs) *n.* **1.** See **Irish Gaelic. 2.** See **Scottish Gaelic.** [Middle English *Ersch, Erisch,* Irish, from Old English *Iras,* the Irish. See IRISH.] **—Erse** *adj.*

erst (ûrst) *adv. Archaic.* Erstwhile. [Middle English *erest,* from Old English *ǣrest.* See **ayer-** in Appendix.]

erst•while (ûrst′hwīl′, -wīl′) *adv.* In the past; at a former time; formerly. **—erstwhile** *adj.* Former: *our erstwhile companions.*

e•ru•cic acid (ĭ-ro͞o′sĭk) *n.* A fatty acid, $CH_3(CH_2)_7CH{:}CH(CH_2)_{11}CO_2H$, making up 40 to 50 percent of the total fatty acid in rapeseed, wallflower seed, and mustard seed. [From New Latin *Ērūca,* rocket, cabbage, from Latin *ērūca.*]

e•ruct (ĭ-rŭkt′) *tr. & intr.v.* **e•ruct•ed, e•ruct•ing, e•ructs.** To belch. [Latin *ēructāre* : *ē-, ex-,* ex- + *ructāre,* to belch; see **reug-** in Appendix.]

e•ruc•ta•tion (ĭ-rŭk-tā′shən, ē′rŭk-) *n.* The act or an instance of belching. **—e•ruc′ta•tive** (ĭ-rŭk′tə-tĭv) *adj.*

er•u•dite (ĕr′yə-dīt′, ĕr′ə-) *adj.* Characterized by erudition; learned. See Synonyms at **learned.** [Middle English *erudit,* from Latin *ērudītus,* past participle of *ērudīre,* to instruct : *ē-, ex-,* ex- + *rudis,* rough, untaught; see RUDE.] **—er′u•dite′ly** *adv.* **—er′u•dite′ness** *n.*

WORD HISTORY: One might like to be *erudite* but hesitate to be *rude.* This preference is supported by the etymological relationship between *erudite* and *rude. Erudite* comes from the Latin adjective *ērudītus,* "well-instructed, learned," from the past participle of the verb *ērudīre,* "to educate, train." The verb is in turn formed from the prefix *ex–,* "out, out of," and the adjective *rudis,* "untaught, untrained," the source of our word *rude.* The English word *erudite* is first recorded in a work possibly written before 1425 with the senses "instructed, learned." *Erudite* meaning "learned" is supposed to have become rare except in sarcastic use, at least during the latter part of the 19th century, but the word now seems to have been restored to favor.

er•u•di•tion (ĕr′yə-dĭsh′ən, ĕr′ə-) *n.* Deep, extensive learning. See Synonyms at **knowledge.**

e•rum•pent (ĭ-rŭm′pənt) *adj.* Bursting through or as if through a surface or covering. [Latin *ērumpēns, ērumpent-,* present participle of *ērumpere,* to burst out. See ERUPT.]

e•rupt (ĭ-rŭpt′) *v.* **e•rupt•ed, e•rupt•ing, e•rupts.** *—intr.* **1.** To emerge violently from restraint or limits; explode: *My neighbor erupted in anger over the noise.* **2.** To become violently active: *The volcano erupted after years of dormancy.* **3.** To force out or release something, such as steam, with violence or suddenness. **4.a.** To break through the gums in developing. Used of teeth. **b.** To appear on the skin. Used of a rash or blemish. *—tr.* To force out violently. [Latin *ērumpere, ērupt-* : *ē-, ex-,* ex- + *rumpere,* to break; see **reup-** in Appendix.] **—e•rup′tive** *adj.* **—e•rup′tive•ly** *adv.*

e•rup•tion (ĭ-rŭp′shən) *n.* **1.a.** The act or process of erupting. **b.** An instance of erupting. **2.** A sudden, often violent outburst. **3.a.** An appearance of a rash or blemish on the skin. **b.** Such a rash or blemish. **4.** The emergence of a tooth through the gums.

Er•ving (ûr′vĭng), **Julius Winfield.** Known as "Dr. J." Born 1950. American basketball player. A forward for the Philadelphia 76ers (1976–1987), he was known for his electrifying dunk shot and consistent all-around play.

–ery or **–ry** *suff.* **1.** A place for: *bakery.* **2.** A collection or class: *finery.* **3.** A state or condition: *slavery.* **4.** Act; practice: *bribery.* **5.** Characteristics or qualities of: *snobbery.* [Middle English *-erie,* from Old French : *-er,* agent suff. (partly from *-ier;* see –ER[1], and partly from *-ere, -eor;* see –OR[1]) + *-ie,* noun suff.; see –Y[2].]

Er•y•man•thos or **Er•y•man•thus** (ĕr′ə-măn′thəs, -thŏs, ĕ-rē′măn-thôs′). A mountain range of southern Greece in the northwest Peloponnesus. The tallest peak is **Mount Erymanthos,** about 2,225 m (7,295 ft) high. In Greek legend, the range was the haunt of the ferocious Erymanthian boar, which was ultimately slain by Hercules. **—Er′y•man′thi•an** *adj.*

e•ryn•go (ĭ-rĭng′gō) *n., pl.* **-goes.** Any of several plants of the genus *Eryngium* having spiny leaves and dense clusters of small bluish flowers. [Alteration of Latin *ēryngion,* sea holly, from Greek *ērungion,* diminutive of *ērungos.*]

er•y•sip•e•las (ĕr′ĭ-sĭp′ə-ləs, ĭr′-) *n.* An acute disease of the skin and subcutaneous tissue caused by a species of hemolytic streptococcus and marked by localized inflammation and fever. Also called *Saint Anthony's fire.* [Middle English *erisipila,* from Latin *erysipelas,* from Greek *erusipelas* : *erusi-,* red; see **reudh-** in Appendix + *-pelas,* skin; see **pel-**[3] in Appendix.] **—er′y•si•pel′a•tous** (-sĭ-pĕl′ə-təs) *adj.*

er•y•sip•e•loid (ĕr′ĭ-sĭp′ə-loid′, ĭr′ə-) *n.* An infectious disease of the skin that is contracted by handling fish or meat infected with the bacterium *Erysipelothrix rhusiopathiae* and characterized by red lesions on the hands. [ERYSIPEL(AS) + –OID.]

er•y•the•ma (ĕr′ə-thē′mə) *n.* Redness of the skin caused by dilatation and congestion of the capillaries, often a sign of inflammation or infection. [Greek *eruthēma,* from *eruthainein,* to redden, be red, from *eruthros,* red. See **reudh-** in Appendix.] **—er′y•them′a•tous** (-thĕm′ə-təs, -thē′mə-), **er′y•the•mat′ic** (-măt′ĭk) , **er′y•the′mic** *adj.*

er•y•thor•bic acid (ĕr′ə-thôr′bĭk) *n.* An optical isomer of ascorbic acid used as an antioxidant. [ERYTH(RO)– + (ASC)ORBIC ACID.]

erythr– *pref.* Variant of **erythro–.**

er•y•thrism (ĕr′ə-thrĭz′əm) *n.* Unusual red pigmentation, as of hair or plumage. **—er′y•thris′mal** (-thrĭz′məl) *adj.*

er•y•thrite (ĕr′ə-thrīt′) *n. Geology.* A reddish secondary cobalt mineral, $CO_3(AsO_4)_2{\cdot}8H_2O$, found in veins bearing cobalt and arsenic and used in coloring glass.

erythro– or **erythr–** *pref.* **1.** Red: *erythrocyte.* **2.** Erythrocyte: *erythropoiesis.* [From Greek *eruthros,* red. See **reudh-** in Appendix.]

e•ryth•ro•blast (ĭ-rĭth′rə-blăst′) *n.* Any of the nucleated cells normally found only in bone marrow that develop into erythrocytes. **—e•ryth′ro•blas′tic** *adj.*

e•ryth•ro•blas•to•sis (ĭ-rĭth′rō-blă-stō′sĭs) *n., pl.* **-ses** (-sēz). The abnormal presence of erythroblasts in the blood.

erythroblastosis fe•tal•is (fĭ-tăl′ĭs) *n.* A severe hemolytic disease of a fetus or newborn infant caused by the production of maternal antibodies against the fetal red blood cells, usually involving Rh incompatibility between the mother and fetus. [New Latin, fetal erythroblastosis.]

e•ryth•ro•cyte (ĭ-rĭth′rə-sīt′) *n.* See **red blood cell. —e•ryth′ro•cyt′ic** (-sĭt′ĭk) *adj.*

e•ryth•ro•cy•tom•e•ter (ĭ-rĭth′rə-sī-tŏm′ĭ-tər) *n.* A device for counting the number of red blood cells in a blood sample.

e•ryth•ro•my•cin (ĭ-rĭth′rə-mī′sĭn) *n.* An antibiotic obtained from a strain of the actinomycete *Streptomyces erythreus,* effective against many gram-positive bacteria and some gram-negative bacteria.

e•ryth•ro•poi•e•sis (ĭ-rĭth′rō-poi-ē′sĭs) *n.* The formation or production of red blood cells. **—e•ryth′ro•poi•et′ic** (-ĕt′ĭk) *adj.*

e•ryth•ro•poi•e•tin (ĭ-rĭth′rō-poi-ē′tĭn) *n.* A glycoprotein hormone that stimulates the production of red blood cells by bone marrow. Produced mainly by the kidneys, the hormone is released in response to decreased levels of oxygen in body tissue. [ERYTHROPOIET(IC) + –IN.]

Erz•ge•bir•ge (ĕrts′gə-bîr′gə). A mountain range extending about 153 km (95 mi) along the border of Germany and Czechoslovakia. It rises to 1,244.4 m (4,080 ft).

Er•zu•rum (ĕr′zə-ro͝om′). A city of eastern Turkey east of Ankara. It was known in the fifth century A.D. as an important Byzantine frontier post. Population, 190,241.

Es The symbol for the element **einsteinium.**

–es¹ *suff.* Variant of **–s¹.**

–es² *suff.* Variant of **–s².**

Es•a•ki (ĭ-sä′kē), **Leo.** Born 1925. Japanese-born physicist. He shared a 1973 Nobel Prize for theoretical advances in the field of solid-state electronics.

E•sau (ē′sô). In the Old Testament, the eldest son of Isaac and Rebecca who sold his birthright to his twin brother, Jacob, for a mess of pottage.

Es•bjerg (ĕs′bē-ĕrg′, -byĕr′). A city of southwest Denmark on the North Sea. It is a commercial and industrial center with major fisheries. Population, 80,534.

es•ca•drille (ĕs′kə-drĭl′, -drē′) *n.* A unit of a European air command, as in France during World War I, typically containing six aircraft. [French, from Spanish *escuadrilla,* diminutive of *escuadra,* squadron, from *escuadrar,* to square off, from Vulgar Latin **exquadrāre.* See SQUARE.]

es•ca•lade (ĕs′kə-lăd′, -läd′) *n.* The act of scaling a fortified wall or rampart. [French, from Italian *scalata,* ultimately from Late Latin *scāla,* from Latin *scālae,* steps. See **skand-** in Appendix.] **—es′ca•lade′** *v.* **—es′ca•lad′er** *n.*

es•ca•late (ĕs′kə-lāt′) *v.* **-lat•ed, -lat•ing, -lates.** *—tr.* To increase, enlarge, or intensify: *escalated the hostilities in the Persian Gulf. —intr.* To increase in intensity or extent: *"a deepening long-term impasse that is certain to escalate"* (Stewart L. Udall). [Back-formation from ESCALATOR.] **—es′ca•la′tion** *n.* **—es′ca•la•to′ry** (-lə-tôr′ē, -tōr′ē) *adj.*

es•ca•la•tor (ĕs′kə-lā′tər) *n.* **1.** A moving stairway consisting of steps attached to a continuously circulating belt. **2.** An escalator clause. [Originally a trademark.]

escalator clause *n.* A provision in a contract stipulating an increase or a decrease, as in wages, benefits, or prices, under certain conditions, such as changes in the cost of living.

es•cal•lop (ĭ-skŏl′əp, ĭ-skăl′-) *n. & v.* Variant of **scallop.** [Middle English *escalop,* from Old French *escalope.* See SCALLOP.]

es•ca•pade (ĕs′kə-pād′) *n.* An adventurous, unconventional act or undertaking. [French, a trick, an escape, from Old French, from Old Spanish *escapada* (from *escapar,* to escape) or from Old Italian *scappata* (from *scappare,* to escape), both from Vulgar Latin **excappāre,* to escape. See ESCAPE.]

es•cape (ĭ-skāp′) *v.* **-caped, -cap•ing, -capes.** *—intr.* **1.** To break loose from confinement; get free. **2.** To issue from confinement or an enclosure; leak or seep out: *Gas was escaping.* **3.** To avoid capture, danger, or harm: *Ten prisoners had escaped.* **4.** *Botany.* To grow beyond a cultivated area. *—tr.* **1.** To succeed in avoiding. **2.** To break loose from; get free of. **3.** To elude the memory or comprehension of: *Her name escapes me. The book's significance escaped him.* **4.** To issue involuntarily from: *A sigh*

Julius Erving

Leo Esaki
Photographed in 1973

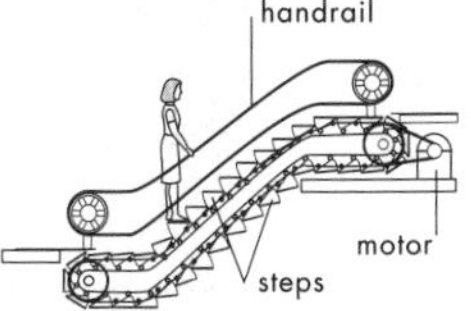

escalator
Top: Escalators in a mall
Bottom: Cutaway view

escapement

escaped my lips. **—escape** *n.* **1.** The act or an instance of escaping. **2.** A means of escaping. **3.** A means of obtaining temporary freedom from worry, care, or unpleasantness: *Television is my escape from worry.* **4.** A gradual effusion from an enclosure; a leakage. **5.** *Botany.* A plant that has become established away from the area of cultivation. **6.** *Computer Science.* A key used especially to interrupt a command, exit a program, or change levels within a program. [Middle English *escapen,* from Old North French *escaper,* from Vulgar Latin **excappāre,* to get out of one's cape, get away : Latin *ex-,* ex- + Medieval Latin *cappa,* cloak.] **—es·cap′a·ble** *adj.* **—es·cap′er** *n.*

SYNONYMS: *escape, avoid, shun, eschew, evade, elude.* These verbs mean to get or stay away from persons or things. *Escape* can mean to get free, as from confinement, or to remain untouched or unaffected by something unwanted: *"Let no guilty man escape, if it can be avoided"* (Ulysses S. Grant). *"It is curious . . . what shifts we make to escape thinking"* (James Russell Lowell). *Avoid* always involves an effort to keep away from what is considered to be a source of danger or difficulty: *avoiding strenuous exercise; avoided committing herself. Shun* refers to deliberately keeping clear of what is unwelcome or undesirable: *"Family friends . . . she shunned like the plague"* (John Galsworthy). *Eschew* involves staying clear of something because to do otherwise would be unwise or morally wrong: *"Eschew evil, and do good"* (Book of Common Prayer). *Evade* implies adroit maneuvering and sometimes implies dishonesty or irresponsibility: *evading capture; tried to evade jury duty.* To *elude* is to get away from artfully: *elude a blow; eluded his pursuers.*

USAGE NOTE: Traditionally, *escape* is used with *from* when it means "break loose" and with a direct object when it means "avoid." Thus we might say *The forger escaped from prison by hiding in a laundry truck,* but *The forger escaped prison when he turned in his accomplices in order to get a suspended sentence.* In recent years, however, *escape* has been used with a direct object in the sense "break free of": *The craft will acquire sufficient velocity to escape the sun's gravitational attraction.* This usage is well established and should be regarded as standard.

escritoire
Late 18th-century French

escape clause *n.* A clause in a contract that specifies the conditions under which the promisor is relieved of liability for failure to meet the terms of the contract.

es·cap·ee (ĭ-skā′pē′, ĕs′kā-) *n.* One that has escaped, especially an escaped prisoner. See Usage Note at **-ee**[1].

es·cape·ment (ĭ-skāp′mənt) *n.* **1.** A mechanism consisting in general of an escape wheel and an anchor, used especially in timepieces to control movement of the wheel and to provide periodic energy impulses to a pendulum or balance. **2.** A mechanism, as in a typewriter, that controls the lateral movement of the carriage. **3. a.** An escape. **b.** A means or way of escape.

escape velocity *n.* The minimum velocity that a body must attain to overcome the gravitational attraction of another body, such as the earth.

escape wheel *n.* The rotating notched wheel periodically engaged and disengaged by the anchor in an escapement.

es·cap·ism (ĭ-skā′pĭz′əm) *n.* The tendency to escape from daily reality or routine by indulging in daydreaming, fantasy, or entertainment.

es·cap·ist (ĭ-skā′pĭst) *adj.* Indulging in or characterized by escapism. **—es·cap′ist** *n.*

es·cap·ol·o·gy (ĕs′kā-pŏl′ə-jē) *n.* The art, skill, or practice of escaping. **—es′cap·ol′o·gist** *n.*

es·car·got (ĕs′kär-gō′) *n., pl.* **-gots** (-gō′). An edible snail, especially one prepared as an appetizer or entrée. [French, from Old French, from Old Provençal *escaragol.*]

es·ca·role (ĕs′kə-rōl′) *n.* A variety of endive *(Cichorium endivia)* having leaves with irregular, frilled edges and often used in salads. [French, from Old French *scariole,* from Late Latin *ēscāriola,* chicory, from Latin *ēscārius,* of food, from *ēsca,* food, from *edere,* to eat. See **ed-** in Appendix.]

es·carp (ĭ-skärp′) *n.* **1.** A steep slope or cliff; an escarpment. **2.** The inner wall of a ditch or trench dug around a fortification. **—escarp** *tr.v.* **-carped, -carp·ing, -carps. 1.** To cause to form a steep slope. **2.** To furnish with an escarp. [French *escarpe,* from Italian *scarpa.* See SCARP.]

es·carp·ment (ĭ-skärp′mənt) *n.* **1.** A steep slope or long cliff that results from erosion or faulting and separates two relatively level areas of differing elevations. **2.** A steep slope in front of a fortification.

-escence *suff.* State; process. Used to form nouns from adjectives in *-escent* or verbs in *-esce*: *fluorescence.* [French, from Old French, from Latin *-ēscentia,* from *-ēscēns, -ēscent-,* -escent.]

-escent *suff.* **1.** Beginning to be; becoming: *juvenescent.* **2.** Characterized by; resembling: *opalescent.* [French, from Old French, from Latin *-ēscēns, -ēscent-,* present participle suff. of inchoative verbs in *-ēscere.*]

esch·a·lot (ĕsh′ə-lŏt′) *n.* See **shallot.** [Obsolete French *eschallotte.* See SHALLOT.]

es·char (ĕs′kär′) *n.* A dry scab or slough formed on the skin as a result of a burn or by the action of a corrosive or caustic substance. [Middle English *escare,* from Old French. See SCAR[1].]

es·cha·rot·ic (ĕs′kə-rŏt′ĭk) *adj.* Producing an eschar. **—escharotic** *n.* A caustic or corrosive substance or drug.

es·cha·tol·o·gy (ĕs′kə-tŏl′ə-jē) *n.* **1.** The branch of theology that is concerned with the end of the world or of humankind. **2.** A belief or a doctrine concerning the ultimate or final things, such as death, the destiny of humanity, or the Last Judgment. [Greek *eskhatos,* last; see **eghs** in Appendix + -LOGY.] **—es·chat′o·log′i·cal** (ĭ-skăt′l-ŏj′ĭ-kəl, ĕs′kə-tə-lŏj′-) *adj.* **—es·chat′o·log′i·cal·ly** *adv.* **—es′cha·tol′o·gist** *n.*

es·cheat (ĭs-chēt′) *n.* **1.** Reversion of land held under feudal tenure to the manor in the absence of legal heirs or claimants. **2.** *Law.* **a.** Reversion of property to the state in the absence of legal heirs or claimants. **b.** Property that has reverted to the state when no legal heirs or claimants exist. **—escheat** *intr. & tr.v.* **-cheat·ed, -cheat·ing, -cheats.** *Law.* To revert or cause to revert by escheat. [Middle English *eschete,* from Old French (from *escheoir,* to fall out) and from Anglo-Latin *escheta,* both from Vulgar Latin **excadēre,* to fall out : Latin *ex-,* ex- + Latin *cadere,* to fall; see **kad-** in Appendix.] **—es·cheat′a·ble** *adj.*

es·cheat·age (ĭs-chē′tĭj) *n. Law.* The right of the state to acquire property by escheat.

es·chew (ĕs-cho͞o′) *tr.v.* **-chewed, -chew·ing, -chews.** To avoid; shun. See Synonyms at **escape.** [Middle English *escheuen,* from Old French *eschivir,* of Germanic origin; akin to SHY[1].] **—es·chew′al** (-əl) *n.*

Es·cof·fier (ĕs-kô-fyā′), **Auguste.** 1846–1935. French chef of grand hotels, such as the Savoy and Carlton in London. He wrote several cookery books, including *Le Guide Culinaire* (1903).

es·co·lar (ĕs′kə-lär′) *n., pl.* **escolar** or **-lars.** Any of several slender fishes of the family Gempylidae, especially *Lepidocybium flavobrunneum,* of warm marine waters. [Spanish, student (from the spectacle-like rings around its eyes), from Late Latin *scholāris,* of a school. See SCHOLAR.]

Es·con·di·do (ĕs′kən-dē′dō). A city of southern California north of San Diego. It is in an area that specializes in grapes and citrus fruit. Population, 64,355.

Es·co·ri·al (ĕ-skôr′ē-əl, ĕ-skōr′-, ĕs′kô-rē-äl′). A monastery and palace of central Spain near Madrid. Built from 1563 to 1584, it was commissioned by Philip II to commemorate a victory over the French.

es·cort (ĕs′kôrt′) *n.* **1. a.** One or more persons accompanying another to guide, protect, or show honor. **b.** A man who is the companion of a woman, especially on a social occasion. **2. a.** One or more vehicles accompanying another vehicle to guide, protect, or honor its passengers. **b.** One or more warships or planes used to defend or protect other craft from enemy attack. **3.** The state of being accompanied by a person or protective guard. **—escort** (ĭ-skôrt′, ĕ-skôrt′, ĕs′kôrt′) *tr.v.* **-cort·ed, -cort·ing, -corts.** To accompany as an escort. See Synonyms at **accompany.** [French *escorte,* from Italian *scorta,* from *scorgere,* to guide, from Vulgar Latin **excorrigere* : Latin *ex-,* ex- + Latin *corrigere,* to set right; see CORRECT.]

es·cri·toire (ĕs′krĭ-twär′) *n.* **1.** A writing table; a desk. **2.** A desk with a top section for books. [Obsolete French, from Old French *escriptoire,* study, from Medieval Latin *scriptōrium.* See SCRIPTORIUM.]

es·crow (ĕs′krō′, ĕ-skrō′) *n.* Money, property, a deed, or a bond put into the custody of a third party for delivery to a grantee only after the fulfillment of the conditions specified. **—escrow** *tr.v.* **-crowed, -crow·ing, -crows.** To place in escrow. ***—idiom.* in escrow.** In trust as an escrow. [Anglo-Norman *escrowe,* variant of Old French *escroe,* scroll. See SCROLL.]

es·cu·do (ĭ-sko͞o′dō) *n., pl.* **-dos.** See table at **currency.** [Portuguese and Spanish, shield, escudo, from Latin *scūtum,* shield. See **skei-** in Appendix.]

es·cu·lent (ĕs′kyə-lənt) *adj.* Suitable for eating; edible. [Latin *ēsculentus,* from *ēsca,* food, from *edere,* to eat. See **ed-** in Appendix.] **—es′cu·lent** *n.*

es·cutch·eon (ĭ-skŭch′ən) *n.* **1.** *Heraldry.* A shield or shield-shaped emblem bearing a coat of arms. **2.** An ornamental or protective plate, as for a keyhole. **3.** *Nautical.* The plate on the stern of a ship inscribed with the ship's name. ***—idiom.* a blot on (one's) escutcheon.** Dishonor to one's reputation. [Middle English *escochon,* from Anglo-Norman *escuchon,* from Vulgar Latin **scūtiō, scūtiōn-,* from Latin *scūtum,* shield. See **skei-** in Appendix.] **—es·cutch′eoned** *adj.*

Es·dra·e·lon (ĕs′drā-ē′lŏn, -drə-, ĕz′-), **Plain of.** A fertile plain of northern Israel extending from the coastal lowlands near Mount Carmel to the Jordan River valley.

Es·dras (ĕz′drəs) *n. Bible.* Either of two books of the Septuagint corresponding to the Hebrew books of Ezra and Nehemiah.

ESE *abbr.* East-southeast.

-ese *suff.* **1.** Of, relating to, characteristic of, or originating in a specified place: *Vietnamese.* **2.** Native or inhabitant of: *Taiwanese.* **3. a.** Language or dialect of: *Chinese.* **b.** Literary style or diction of: *journalese.* [Middle English, from Italian *-ese,* from Latin *-ēnsis,* originating in.]

E·se·nin (yĭ-sā′nyĭn, -syĕ′-), **Sergei Aleksandrov.** See Sergei Aleksandrov **Yesenin.**

es·er·ine (ĕs′ə-rēn′) *n.* See **physostigmine.** [New Latin : Efik *esere,* Calabar bean + -INE[2].]

Es·fa·han (ĕs′fə-hän′). See **Isfahan.**

Esk. *abbr.* Eskimo.

es·ker (ĕs′kər) *n.* A long, narrow ridge of coarse gravel deposited by a stream flowing in or under a decaying glacial ice sheet. Also called *os.* [Irish Gaelic *eiscir,* from Old Irish *escir.*]

Es·kils·tu·na (ĕs′kĭl-styo͞o′nə, -nä). A city of southeast Sweden west of Stockholm. It was chartered in 1659. Population, 88,664.

Es·ki·mo (ĕs′kə-mō′) *n., pl.* **Eskimo** or **-mos.** *Abbr.* **Esk. 1.a.** A group of peoples inhabiting the Arctic coastal regions of North America and parts of Greenland and northeast Siberia. The Eskimo are generally considered a Native American people in Alaska and Canada. **b.** A member of any of these peoples. See Usage Note at **Native American. 2.** Any of the languages of the Eskimo peoples. [French *Esquimaux,* possibly from Spanish *esquimao, esquimal,* from Montagnais *ayashkimew,* Micmac.] **—Es′ki·mo′an** *adj.*

Eskimo dog *n.* A large dog of a breed used in Arctic regions for pulling sleds and having a thick coat and a plumed tail.

Es·ki·şe·hir (ĕs′kĭ-shə-hîr′). A city of west-central Turkey west of Ankara. An industrial center, it has hot mineral springs and Phrygian ruins nearby. Population, 309,341.

ESL *abbr.* English as a second language.

ESOP (ē′sŏp) *n.* A plan under which the employees of a company or corporation acquire its capital stock. [*E(mployee) S(tock-)O(wnership) P(lan).*]

e·soph·a·gus also **oe·soph·a·gus** (ĭ-sŏf′ə-gəs) *n., pl.* **-gi** (-jī′, -gī′). The muscular, membranous tube for the passage of food from the pharynx to the stomach; the gullet. [Middle English *isophagus,* from Medieval Latin, from Greek *oisophagos.*] **—e·soph′a·ge′al** (-jē′əl) *adj.*

es·o·ter·ic (ĕs′ə-tĕr′ĭk) *adj.* **1.a.** Intended for or understood by only a particular group: *an esoteric cult.* See Synonyms at **mysterious. b.** Of or relating to that which is known by a restricted number of people. **2.a.** Confined to a small group: *esoteric interests.* **b.** Not publicly disclosed; confidential. [Greek *esōterikos,* from *esōterō,* comparative of *esō,* within. See **en** in Appendix.] **—es′o·ter′i·cal·ly** *adv.*

es·o·ter·i·ca (ĕs′ə-tĕr′ĭ-kə) *pl.n. (used with a sing. or pl. verb).* Esoteric matters or items. [Greek, from neuter pl. of *esōterikos,* esoteric. See ESOTERIC.]

es·o·ter·i·cism (ĕs′ə-tĕr′ĭ-sĭz′əm) *n.* **1.** Esoteric teachings or practices. **2.** The quality or condition of being esoteric.

ESP (ē′ĕs-pē′) *n.* Communication or perception by means other than the physical senses. [*e(xtra)s(ensory) p(erception).*]

esp. *abbr.* Especially.

es·pa·drille (ĕs′pə-drĭl′) *n.* A shoe usually having a fabric upper part and a sole made of a flexible material, such as rope or rubber. [French, from Provençal *espardilho,* diminutive of *espart,* esparto, from Latin *spartum.* See ESPARTO.]

es·pal·ier (ĭ-spăl′yər, -yā′) *n.* **1.** A tree or shrub that is trained to grow in a flat plane against a wall, often in a symmetrical pattern. **2.** A trellis or other framework on which an espalier is grown. **—espalier** *tr.v.* **-iered, -ier·ing, -iers. 1.** To train as or on an espalier. **2.** To provide with an espalier. [French, from Italian *spalliera,* shoulder support, from *spalla,* shoulder, from Late Latin *spatula,* shoulder blade, from Latin. See SPATULA.]

es·par·to (ĭ-spär′tō) *n., pl.* **-tos.** A tough, wiry grass *(Stipa tenacissima)* of northern Africa, yielding a fiber used in making paper and as cordage. [Spanish, from Latin *spartum,* from Greek *sparton,* rope.]

es·pe·cial (ĭ-spĕsh′əl) *adj.* **1.** Of special importance or significance; exceptional: *an occasion of especial joy.* **2.** Relating to or directed toward a particular person, group, or purpose: *called his father with especial birthday wishes; gave especial attention to the decorations.* **3.** Peculiar to the individual; characteristic: *She has an especial fondness for mushrooms.* [Middle English, from Old French, from Latin *speciālis,* of a kind, from *speciēs,* species. See **spek-** in Appendix.]

es·pe·cial·ly (ĕ-spĕsh′ə-lē, ĭ-spĕsh′-) *adv. Abbr.* **esp.** To an extent or degree deserving of special emphasis; particularly.

es·per·ance (ĕs′pər-əns) *n. Obsolete.* Hope. [Middle English *esperaunce,* from Old French, from Vulgar Latin **spērantia,* from Latin *spērāns, spērant-,* present participle of *spērāre,* to hope. See **spē-** in Appendix.]

Es·pe·ran·to (ĕs′pə-răn′tō, -rän′-) *n.* An artificial international language with a vocabulary based on word roots common to many European languages and a regularized system of inflection. [After Dr. *Esperanto,* "one who hopes," pseudonym of Ludwik Lejzer Zamenhof (1859–1917), Polish philologist.] **—Es′pe·ran′tist** *adj. & n.*

es·pi·al (ĭ-spī′əl) *n.* **1.** The act of watching or observing; observation. **2.** A taking notice of something; a discovery. **3.** The fact of being seen or noticed. [Middle English *espiaille,* from Old French, from *espier,* to watch. See ESPY.]

es·pi·o·nage (ĕs′pē-ə-näzh′, -nĭj) *n.* The act or practice of spying or of using spies to obtain secret information, as about another government or a business competitor. [French *espionnage,* from *espionner,* to spy, from Old French *espion,* spy, from Old Italian *spione,* of Germanic origin. See **spek-** in Appendix.]

Es·pí·ri·tu San·to (ĕ-spîr′ĭ-to͞o sän′tō). An island of the New Hebrides in the southern Pacific Ocean. In World War II it was the site of U.S. military bases after March 1942.

es·pla·nade (ĕs′plə-näd′, -nād′) *n.* A flat, open stretch of pavement or grass, especially one designed as a promenade along a shore. [French, from Italian *spianata,* from *spianare,* to level, from Latin *explānāre,* to make plain. See EXPLAIN.]

Es·poo (ĕs′pō, -pô). A town of southern Finland, a suburb of Helsinki. Population, 152,929.

es·pous·al (ĭ-spou′zəl, -səl) *n.* **1.a.** A betrothal. **b.** A wedding ceremony. **2.** Adoption of an idea or a cause. [Middle English *espousaille,* from sing. of Old French *espousailles,* betrothal, from Latin *spōnsālia,* from neuter pl. of *spōnsālis,* of a betrothal, from *spōnsus,* spouse. See SPOUSE.]

es·pouse (ĭ-spouz′) *tr.v.* **-poused, -pous·ing, -pous·es. 1.a.** To take in marriage; marry. **b.** To give (a woman) in marriage. **2.** To give one's loyalty or support to (a cause, for example); adopt. [Middle English *espousen,* from Old French *espouser,* from Latin *spōnsāre,* from *spondēre, spōns-,* to betroth. See **spend-** in Appendix.] **—es·pous′er** *n.*

es·pres·so (ĭ-sprĕs′ō, ĕ-sprĕs′ō) also **ex·pres·so** (ĭk-sprĕs′ō, ĕk-) *n., pl.* **-sos.** A strong coffee brewed by forcing steam under pressure through darkly roasted, powdered coffee beans. [Italian *(caffè) espresso,* espresso (coffee), past participle of *esprimere,* to press out, from Latin *exprimere* : *ex-,* ex- + *premere,* to press; see PRESS[1].]

es·prit (ĕ-sprē′) *n.* **1.** Liveliness of mind or spirit; sprightliness. **2.** Esprit de corps. See Synonyms at **morale.** [French, from Latin *spīritus,* spirit. See SPIRIT.]

esprit de corps (də kôr′) *n.* A common spirit of comradeship, enthusiasm, and devotion to a cause among the members of a group. See Synonyms at **morale.** [French : *esprit,* spirit + *de,* of + *corps,* group, body.]

es·py (ĭ-spī′) *tr.v.* **-pied, -py·ing, -pies.** To catch sight of (something distant, partially hidden, or obscure); glimpse. See Synonyms at **see[1].** [Middle English *espien,* from Old French *espier,* to watch, of Germanic origin. See **spek-** in Appendix.]

Esq. *abbr.* Esquire (title).

-esque *suff.* In the manner of; resembling: *Lincolnesque.* [French, from Italian *-esco,* from Vulgar Latin **-iscus,* of Germanic origin.]

Es·qui·line (ĕs′kwə-līn′, -lĭn). One of the seven hills of ancient Rome. Nero's Golden House and Trajan's *Thermae,* or hot baths, were in the area. **—Es′qui·line′** *adj.*

Es·qui·mau (ĕs′kə-mō′) *n., pl.* **Esquimau** or **-maux** (-mōz′). An Eskimo. [French, sing. of *Esquimaux,* Eskimo. See ESKIMO.]

es·quire (ĕs′kwīr′, ĭ-skwīr′) *n.* **1.** A male belonging to the gentry in England and ranking directly below a knight. **2. Esquire.** *Abbr.* **Esq.** Used as an honorific usually in its abbreviated form, especially after the name of an attorney or a consular officer: *Jane Doe, Esq.; John Doe, Esq.* **3.** In medieval times, a candidate for knighthood who served a knight as an attendant and a shield bearer. **4.** *Archaic.* An English country gentleman; a squire. [Middle English *esquier,* from Old French *escuier,* from Late Latin *scūtārius,* shield bearer, from Latin *scūtum,* shield. See **skei-** in Appendix.]

ESR *abbr.* Electron spin resonance.

ess (ĕs) *n.* The letter *s.*

-ess *suff.* Female: *lioness.* [Middle English *-esse,* from Old French, from Late Latin *-issa,* from Greek.]

USAGE NOTE: Critics have argued that sexist connotations are implicit in the use of the feminine suffix *-ess,* as found in words such as *ambassadress, sculptress, waitress, stewardess, hostess, actress,* and many others, in that the suffix implies that the denoted roles differ as performed by women and men. In some cases, as with the word *temptress,* there may be some legitimacy to such an implication of difference; and for this reason the acceptability of the suffix may depend on the individual word. In the case of most occupational terms, the suffix is widely felt to be inappropriate. Thus 65 percent of the Usage Panel rejects *sculptress* in the sentence *Georgia O'Keeffe is not as well-known as a sculptress as she is as a painter;* similarly 75 percent rejects *ambassadress* in the sentence *When the ambassadress arrives, please show her directly to my office.* With certain occupations, however, differentiation based on gender may be legitimate: acting, for example, is an occupation in which the parts one can play may in fact depend on one's sex. Thus 92 percent accepts *actress* in *There are not very many good parts available for older actresses,* though it should be noted that many women prefer to be called *actors.* In the case of most social roles, gender is felt to make a legitimate difference, and the suffix is accepted. Thus 87 percent of the Panel accepts *hostess* in the sentence *Mary Ann is such a charming hostess that her parties always go off smoothly;* similarly, 67 percent accepts *seductress* in the sentence *Mata Hari used her ability as a seductress to spy for the Germans.* When the same word may be used in different senses, one social and the other not, the acceptability of the suffix varies accordingly. Thus 93 percent accepts *heiress* in the sentence *His only hope now is to marry an heiress,* while only 34 percent accepts *heiress* in its metaphorical use to mean "successor," as in *His daughter and political heiress has returned to her country in triumph.* See Usage Note at **man.**

es·say (ĕs′ā′, ĕ-sā′) *n.* **1.** (ĕs′ā′). **a.** A short literary composition on a single subject, usually presenting the personal view of the author. **b.** Something resembling such a composition: *a photojournalistic essay.* **2.** A testing or trial of the value or nature of a thing: *an essay of the students' capabilities.* **3.** An initial attempt or endeavor, especially a tentative attempt. **—essay** (ĕ-sā′, ĕs′ā′) *tr.v.* **-sayed, -say·ing, -says. 1.** To make an at-

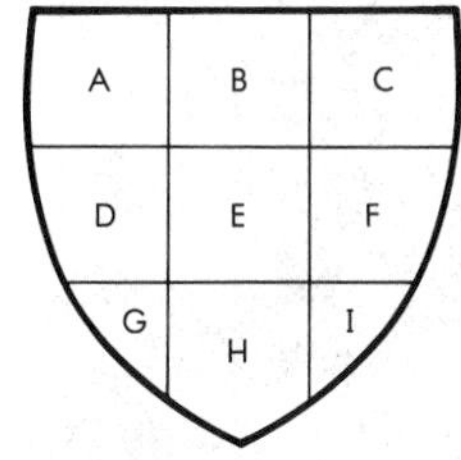

escutcheon
A. Dexter chief
B. Center chief
C. Sinister chief
D. Dexter flank
E. Fess point
F. Sinister flank
G. Dexter base
H. Center base
I. Sinister base

ă pat	oi boy
ā pay	ou out
âr care	o͝o took
ä father	o͞o boot
ĕ pet	ŭ cut
ē be	ûr urge
ĭ pit	th thin
ī pie	*th* this
îr pier	hw which
ŏ pot	zh vision
ō toe	ə about, item
ô paw	♦ regionalism

Stress marks: ′ (primary); ′ (secondary), as in **dictionary** (dĭk′shə-nĕr′ē)

tempt at; try. **2.** To subject to a test. [Middle English *essayen,* to try, from Old French *essaier,* from Vulgar Latin **exagiāre,* to weigh out, from Late Latin *exagium,* a weighing : Latin *ex-,* ex- + Latin *agere,* to drive; see **ag-** in Appendix.] **—es·say′er** *n.*

es·say·ist (ĕs′ā′ĭst) *n.* A writer of essays.

es·say·is·tic (ĕs′ā-ĭs′tĭk) *adj.* **1.** Of or relating to an essay or a writer of essays. **2.** Resembling an essay in nature or quality.

essay question *n.* A test question that calls for a written answer of a specified length, especially a short essay.

Es·sen (ĕs′ən). A city of west-central Germany near the confluence of the Ruhr and Rhine rivers north of Cologne. Founded in the ninth century, it is a major iron and steel center. Population, 625,705.

es·sence (ĕs′əns) *n.* **1.** The intrinsic or indispensable properties that serve to characterize or identify something. **2.** The most important ingredient; the crucial element. **3.** The inherent, unchanging nature of a thing or class of things. **4.a.** An extract that has the fundamental properties of a substance in concentrated form. **b.** Such an extract in a solution of alcohol. **c.** A perfume or scent. **5.** One that has or shows an abundance of a quality as if highly concentrated: *a neighbor who is the essence of hospitality.* **6.** Something that exists, especially a spiritual or incorporeal entity. **—*idioms.* in essence.** By nature; essentially: *He is in essence a reclusive sort.* **of the essence.** Of the greatest importance; crucial: *Time is of the essence.* [Middle English *essencia* and French *essence,* both from Latin *essentia,* from **essēns,* **essent-,* present participle of *esse,* to be (translation of Greek *ousia,* from present participle of *einai,* to be). See **es-** in Appendix.]

Es·sene (ĕs′ēn′, ĭ-sēn′) *n.* A member of an ascetic Jewish sect that existed in ancient Palestine from the second century B.C. to the second century A.D. **—Es·se′ni·an** (ĕ-sē′nē-ən), **Es·sen′ic** (ĕ-sĕn′ĭk) *adj.* **—Es·se′nism** *n.*

es·sen·tial (ĭ-sĕn′shəl) *adj.* **1.** Constituting or being part of the essence of something; inherent. **2.** Basic or indispensable; necessary: *essential ingredients.* See Synonyms at **indispensable. 3.** *Medicine.* Of, relating to, or being a dysfunctional condition or a disease whose cause is unknown: *essential hypertension.* **4.** *Biochemistry.* Being a substance that is required for normal functioning but cannot be synthesized by the body and therefore must be included in the diet. **—essential** *n.* **1.** Something fundamental. **2.** Something necessary or indispensable. **—es·sen′ti·al′i·ty** (-shē-ăl′ĭ-tē), **es·sen′tial·ness** *n.* **—es·sen′tial·ly** *adv.*

Esther
Esther Confounding Haman,
from an engraving
by Gustave Doré

essential oil *n.* A volatile oil, usually having the characteristic odor or flavor of the plant from which it is obtained, used to make perfumes and flavorings.

Es·se·qui·bo (ĕs′ĭ-kwē′bō). A river rising on the Brazilian border of southern Guyana and flowing about 965 km (600 mi) generally northward to the Atlantic Ocean.

Es·sex (ĕs′ĭks). **1.** A historical region and Anglo-Saxon kingdom of southeast England. Probably settled by Saxons in the early sixth century, the kingdom was long dominated by Mercia and later by Wessex before and after its inclusion in the Danelaw territories from 886 to 917. **2.** A community of northeast Maryland, a manufacturing suburb of Baltimore. Population, 39,614.

Essex, Second Earl of. See Robert **Devereux.**

Ess·ling·en (ĕs′lĭng-ən). A city of southwest Germany on the Neckar River southeast of Stuttgart. Founded in the 8th century, it was a free imperial city from the 13th century until 1802. Population, 86,996.

es·so·nite (ĕs′ə-nīt′) also **hes·so·nite** (hĕs′-) *n.* A brown or yellowish-brown variety of garnet. Also called *cinnamon stone.* [French, from Greek *hēssōn,* inferior (from its being softer than true hyacinth), comparative of *ēka, hēka,* slightly.]

EST or **E.S.T.** *abbr.* Eastern Standard Time.

est. *abbr.* **1.** Established. **2.** *Law.* Estate. **3.** Estimate.

Est. *abbr.* *Bible.* Esther.

-est[1] *suff.* Used to form the superlative degree of adjectives and adverbs: *greatest; earliest.* [Middle English, from Old English *-est, -ast, -ost.*]

-est[2] or **-st** *suff.* Used to form the archaic second person singular of English verbs: *comest.* [Middle English, from Old English *-est, -ast.*]

es·tab·lish (ĭ-stăb′lĭsh) *tr.v.* **-lished, -lish·ing, -lish·es. 1.a.** To set up; found. See Synonyms at **found**[1]. **b.** To bring about; generate: *establish goodwill in the neighborhood.* **2.a.** To place or settle in a secure position or condition; install: *They established me in my own business.* **b.** To make firm or secure. **3.** To cause to be recognized and accepted: *a discovery that established his reputation.* **4.** To introduce and put (a law, for example) into force. **5.** To prove the validity or truth of: *The defense attorneys established the innocence of the accused.* **6.** To make a state institution of (a church). [Middle English *establishen,* from Old French *establir, establiss-,* from Latin *stabilīre,* from *stabilis,* firm. See **stā-** in Appendix.] **—es·tab′lish·er** *n.*

es·tab·lished church (ĭ-stăb′lĭsht) *n.* A church that a government officially recognizes as a national institution and to which it accords support.

es·tab·lish·ment (ĭ-stăb′lĭsh-mənt) *n.* **1.a.** The act of establishing. **b.** The condition or fact of being established. **2.** Something established, as: **a.** An arranged order or system, especially a legal code. **b.** A permanent civil, political, or military organization. **c.** An established church. **d.** A place of residence or business with its possessions and staff. **e.** A public or private institution, such as a hospital or school. **3.** Often **Establishment.** An established social order, as: **a.** A group of people holding most of the power and influence in a government or society. Often used with *the.* **b.** A controlling group in a given field of activity. Often used with *the.*

es·tab·lish·men·tar·i·an (ĭ-stăb′lĭsh-mən-târ′ē-ən) *adj.* Of, relating to, or supporting the political or social establishment. **—es·tab′lish·men·tar′i·an** *n.* **—es·tab′lish·men·tar′i·an·ism** *n.*

es·ta·mi·net (ĕ-stä′mē-nā′) *n.* A small café. [French, probably from Walloon *staminé,* cowshed, from *stamō,* hitching post.]

es·tan·cia (ĕ-stän′syä) *n.* A large estate or cattle ranch in Spanish America. [Spanish, room, enclosure, country estate, from Vulgar Latin **stantia,* something standing, from Latin *stāns, stant-,* present participle of *stāre,* to stand. See **stā-** in Appendix.]

es·tate (ĭ-stāt′) *n.* **1.** A landed property, usually of considerable size. **2.** The whole of one's possessions, especially all the property and debts left by one at death. **3.** *Abbr.* **est.** *Law.* The nature and extent of an owner's rights with respect to land or other property. **4.** *Chiefly British.* A housing development. **5.** The situation or circumstances of one's life: *A child's estate gives way to the adult's estate.* **6.** Social position or rank, especially of high order. **7.** A major social class, such as the nobility, the commons, or the clergy, formerly possessing distinct political rights. **8.** *Archaic.* Display of wealth or power; pomp. [Middle English *estat,* condition, from Old French. See STATE.]

Es·tates-Gen·er·al (ĭ-stāts′jĕn′ər-əl) *pl.n.* See **States-General.** [Translation of French *états généraux.*]

estate tax *n.* A tax imposed on the right to transfer property by inheritance and assessed on the net value of a decedent's estate before distribution to the heirs. Also called *death tax.*

Es·te (ĕs′tā). Italian noble family that prospered from the late 10th to the early 19th century and exerted great influence on Renaissance literature.

Es·te·ban E·che·ver·rí·a (ĕ-stĕ′bän ĕ′chĕ-və-rē′ə, -vĕ-rē′ä, -vän). A city of eastern Argentina, a suburb of Buenos Aires. Population, 183,908.

es·teem (ĭ-stēm′) *tr.v.* **-teemed, -teem·ing, -teems. 1.** To regard with respect; prize. See Synonyms at **appreciate. 2.** To regard as; consider: *esteemed it an honor to help them.* **—esteem** *n.* **1.** Favorable regard. See Synonyms at **regard. 2.** *Archaic.* Judgment; opinion. [Middle English *estemen,* to appraise, from Old French *estimer,* from Latin *aestimāre.*]

es·ter (ĕs′tər) *n.* Any of a class of organic compounds corresponding to the inorganic salts and formed from an organic acid and an alcohol. [German, short for *Essigäther* : *Essig,* vinegar (from Middle High German *ezzich,* from Old High German *ezzīh,* from Latin *acētum;* see **ak-** in Appendix) + *Äther,* ether (from Latin *aethēr;* see ETHER).]

es·ter·ase (ĕs′tə-rās′, -rāz′) *n.* Any of various enzymes that catalyze the hydrolysis of an ester.

Es·ter·ha·zy (ĕs′tər-hä′zē), **(Marie Charles) Ferdinand Walsin.** 1847–1923. French army officer who confessed (1899) to forging the evidence against Alfred Dreyfus, who had been wrongly convicted of espionage (1894).

es·ter·i·fi·ca·tion (ĕ-stĕr′ə-fĭ-kā′shən) *n.* A chemical reaction resulting in the formation of at least one ester product.

es·ter·i·fy (ĕ-stĕr′ə-fī′) *intr. & tr.v.* **-fied, -fy·ing, -fies.** To change or cause to change to an ester.

Es·ther (ĕs′tər) *n.* *Bible.* **1.** In the Old Testament, the Jewish queen of Persia who saved her people from massacre. **2.** *Abbr.* **Est., Esth.** See table at **Bible.** [Hebrew *Estēr,* from Persian *sitareh,* star. See **ster-**[3] in Appendix.]

es·the·sia (ĕs-thē′zhə) *n.* Variant of **aesthesia.**

es·the·si·om·e·ter (ĕs-thē′zē-ŏm′ĭ-tər) *n.* An instrument used to measure tactile sensitivity. [ESTHESI(A) + -METER.]

es·thete (ĕs′thēt) *n.* Variant of **aesthete.**

es·thet·ic (ĕs-thĕt′ĭk) *adj. & n.* Variant of **aesthetic.**

es·the·ti·cian (ĕs′thĭ-tĭsh′ən) *n.* Variant of **aesthetician.**

es·thet·i·cism (ĕs-thĕt′ĭ-sĭz′əm) *n.* Variant of **aestheticism.**

es·thet·i·cize (ĕs-thĕt′ə-sīz′) *v.* Variant of **aestheticize.**

es·thet·ics (ĕs-thĕt′ĭks) *n.* Variant of **aesthetics.**

Es·tienne (ĕs-tyĕn′) or **É·tienne** (ĕ-tyĕn′). French family of printers, including **Henri** (1460?–1520), who established the family business in Paris (c. 1505); his son **Robert** (1503–1559), who published Latin (1523) and Greek (1550) New Testaments and a Latin dictionary (1532); and his grandson **Henri** (1528–1598), who published a Greek dictionary (1572).

es·ti·ma·ble (ĕs′tə-mə-bəl) *adj.* **1.** Possible to estimate: *estimable assets; an estimable distance.* **2.** Deserving of esteem; admirable: *an estimable young professor.* [Middle English, from Old French, from Latin *aestimābilis,* from *aestimāre,* to value.] **—es′ti·ma·ble·ness** *n.* **—es′ti·ma·bly** *adv.*

es·ti·mate (ĕs′tə-māt′) *tr.v.* **-mat·ed, -mat·ing, -mates. 1.** To calculate approximately (the amount, extent, magnitude, position, or value of something). **2.** To form an opinion about; evaluate: *"While an author is yet living we estimate his powers by his worst performance"* (Samuel Johnson). **—estimate** (-mĭt) *n.* *Abbr.* **est. 1.** The act of evaluating or appraising. **2.** A tentative evaluation or rough calculation, as of worth, quantity, or size. **3.** A statement of the approximate cost of work to be done, such as a building project or car repairs. **5.** A judgment based on one's impressions; an opinion. [Latin *aestimāre, aestimāt-.*] **—es′ti·ma′tive** *adj.* **—es′ti·ma′tor** *n.*

SYNONYMS: *estimate, appraise, assess, assay, evaluate, rate.* These verbs mean to form a judgment of worth or significance. *Estimate* usually implies a subjective and somewhat inexact judgment: *difficult to estimate the possible results in advance; could only estimate the size of the crowd. Appraise* stresses expert judgment: *appraised the furniture and works of art before distributing them to the heirs. Assess* implies authoritative judgment in setting a monetary value on something as a basis for taxation: *assessing an apartment on the amount for which it is likely to be rented. Assay* refers to careful examination, especially to chemical analysis of an ore to determine its quality, fineness, or purity: *cut a minute piece off the ingot to assay it.* In extended senses *appraise, assess,* and *assay* can refer to any critical analysis or appraisal: *appraised his character and found him wanting; assessing the impact of higher taxes on lower-income households; has no method for assaying merit. Evaluate* implies considered judgment in ascertaining value: *evaluating a student's thesis for content and organization; used projective tests to evaluate her aptitudes. Rate* involves determining the rank or grade of someone or something in relation to others: *Will history rate Picasso above Renoir?*

es·ti·ma·tion (ĕs′tə-mā′shən) *n.* **1.a.** The act or an instance of estimating. **b.** The amount, extent, position, size, or value reached in an estimate. **2.** An opinion or a judgment. **3.** Favorable regard; esteem.

es·ti·val also **aes·ti·val** (ĕs′tə-vəl) *adj.* Of, relating to, or appearing in summer. [Middle English, from Old French, from Latin *aestīvālis,* from *aestīvus,* from *aestās,* summer.]

es·ti·vate also **aes·ti·vate** (ĕs′tə-vāt′) *intr.v.* **-vat·ed, -vat·ing, -vates. 1.** To spend the summer, as at a special place. **2.** *Zoology.* To pass the summer in a dormant or torpid state. [Latin *aestīvāre, aestīvāt-,* from *aestīvus,* estival. See ESTIVAL.]

es·ti·va·tion also **aes·ti·va·tion** (ĕs′tə-vā′shən) *n.* **1.** The act of spending or passing the summer. **2.** *Zoology.* A state of dormancy or torpor during the summer. **3.** *Botany.* The arrangement of flower parts in the bud.

Es·to·ni·a (ĕ-stō′nē-ə). A country of northwest Europe, the northernmost of the Baltic States. Settled before the first century A.D., it was divided many times and held by the Danes, German Livonian Knights, Swedes, and Russians. Estonia was incorporated into the U.S.S.R. as a constituent republic in 1940 and gained its independence in 1991. Tallinn is the capital. Population, 1,530,000.

Es·to·ni·an (ĕ-stō′nē-ən) *adj.* Of or relating to Estonia or its people, language, or culture. **—Estonian** *n.* **1.** A native or inhabitant of Estonia. **2.** The Finno-Ugric language of Estonia.

es·top (ĕ-stŏp′) *tr.v.* **-topped, -top·ping, -tops. 1.** *Law.* To impede or prohibit by estoppel. **2.** *Archaic.* To stop up. [Middle English *estoppen,* from Anglo-Norman *estopper,* from Vulgar Latin **stuppāre,* to stop up. See STOP.] **—es·top′page** (ĕ-stŏp′ĭj) *n.*

es·top·pel (ĕ-stŏp′əl) *n. Law.* A bar preventing one from making an allegation or a denial that contradicts what one has previously stated as the truth. [Obsolete French *estouppail,* from Old French *estouper,* to stop up, from Vulgar Latin **stuppāre.* See STOP.]

Es·tour·nelles de Con·stant (ĕ-stōōr-nĕl′ də kôN-stäN′), Baron **Constant de Rebecque d′.** 1852–1924. French diplomat and pacifist who worked for international peace through the Hague Court of Arbitration. He shared the 1908 Nobel Peace Prize.

es·tra·di·ol (ĕs′trə-dī′ôl′, -ōl′, -ŏl′) *n.* An estrogenic hormone, $C_{18}H_{24}O_2$, produced by the ovaries and used in treating estrogen deficiency. [ESTR(US) + DI–¹ + –OL¹.]

es·tra·gon (ĕs′trə-gŏn′) *n.* Tarragon. [French, probably alteration of *targon,* from Medieval Latin *tragonia, tarchon.* See TARRAGON.]

es·tral (ĕs′trəl) *adj.* Estrous.

estral cycle *n.* The estrous cycle.

es·trange (ĭ-strānj′) *tr.v.* **-tranged, -trang·ing, -trang·es. 1.** To make hostile, unsympathetic, or indifferent; alienate. **2.** To remove from an accustomed place or set of associations. [Middle English *estraungen,* from Old French *estrangier,* from Latin *extrāneāre,* to treat as a stranger, disown, from *extrāneus,* foreign. See STRANGE.] **—es·trange′ment** *n.* **—es·trang′er** *n.*

SYNONYMS: *estrange, alienate, disaffect.* These verbs refer to disruption of a bond of love, friendship, or loyalty. *Estrange* and *alienate* are often used with reference to two persons, such as a husband and wife, whose harmonious relationship has been replaced by hostility or indifference: *Political disagreements led to quarrels that finally estranged the two friends. His persistent antagonism caused his wife to be alienated from him. Disaffect* usually implies discontent, ill will, and disloyalty within the membership of a group: *Colonists were disaffected by the autocratic actions of the royal governor.*

es·tray (ĭ-strā′) *Archaic. n.* A stray. **—estray** *intr.v.* **-trayed, -tray·ing, -trays.** To stray. [Middle English *astrai,* from Anglo-Norman *estray,* from *estraier,* to stray, from Old French. See STRAY.]

Es·tre·ma·du·ra (ĕs′trə-mə-dōōr′ə, ĕs′trä-mä-*thōō*′rä). **1.** A historical region and former province of western Portugal surrounding Lisbon. **2.** A historical region of west-central Spain bordering on Portugal. Reconquered from the Moors in the 12th and 13th centuries, it was frequently a battlefield in the Spanish territorial wars with Portugal and in the Peninsular War fought between France and Great Britain (1808–1814).

es·tri·ol (ĕs′trī-ôl′, -ōl′, -ŏl′, ĕ-strī′-) *n.* An estrogenic hormone, $C_{18}H_{24}O_3$, found in the urine during pregnancy. Also called *theelol.* [ES(TRUS) + TRI– + –OL¹.]

es·tro·gen also **oes·tro·gen** (ĕs′trə-jən) *n.* Any of several steroid hormones produced chiefly by the ovaries and responsible for promoting estrus and the development and maintenance of female secondary sex characteristics. [ESTR(US) + –GEN.] **—es′tro·gen′ic** (-jĕn′ĭk) *adj.* **—es′tro·gen′i·cal·ly** *adv.*

es·trone (ĕs′trōn′) *n.* An estrogenic hormone, $C_{18}H_{22}O_2$, used primarily in the treatment of estrogen deficiency. Also called *theelin.* [ESTR(US) + –ONE.]

es·trous (ĕs′trəs) *adj.* Of, relating to, or being in estrus.

estrous cycle *n.* The recurrent set of physiological and behavioral changes that take place from one period of estrus to another.

es·trus also **oes·trus** (ĕs′trəs) *n.* The periodic state of sexual excitement in the female of most mammals, excluding human beings, that immediately precedes ovulation and during which the female is most receptive to mating; heat. [New Latin, from Latin *oestrus,* frenzy, gadfly, from Greek *oistros.* See **eis-** in Appendix.]

es·tu·a·rine (ĕs′chōō-ə-rīn′, -rēn′) *adj.* Of, relating to, or found in an estuary.

es·tu·ar·y (ĕs′chōō-ĕr′ē) *n., pl.* **-ies. 1.** The part of the wide lower course of a river where its current is met by the tides. **2.** An arm of the sea that extends inland to meet the mouth of a river. [Latin *aestuārium,* from *aestus,* tide, surge, heat.] **—es′tu·ar′i·al** (-âr′ē-əl) *adj.*

esu *abbr.* Electrostatic unit.

e·su·ri·ent (ĭ-sŏŏr′ē-ənt, ĭ-zŏŏr′-) *adj.* Hungry; greedy. [Latin *ēsuriēns, ēsurient-,* present participle of *ēsurīre,* desiderative of *edere,* to eat. See **ed-** in Appendix.] **—e·su′ri·ence** (-əns), **e·su′ri·en·cy** (-ən-sē) *n.* **—e·su′ri·ent·ly** *adv.*

ESV *abbr.* Earth satellite vehicle.

ET *abbr.* **1.** Or **E.T.** Eastern Time. **2.** Elapsed time.

–et *suff.* **1.** Small: *falconet.* **2.** Something worn on: *labret.* [Middle English, from Old French, from Vulgar Latin **-ittum.*]

e·ta (ā′tə, ē′tə) *n.* The seventh letter of the Greek alphabet. See table at **alphabet.** [Greek *ēta,* of Phoenician origin; akin to Hebrew *ḥēt,* heth.]

ETA or **e.t.a.** *abbr.* Estimated time of arrival.

é·ta·gère also **e·ta·gere** (ā′tä-zhâr′) *n.* A piece of furniture with open shelves for small ornaments. [French, from Old French *estagiere,* scaffold, from *estage,* floor. See STAGE.]

et al. *abbr. Latin.* Et alii (and others).

et·a·mine (ĕt′ə-mēn′) *n.* A soft, lightweight, loosely woven cotton or worsted fabric. [French, from Old French *estamine,* from Latin *stāminea,* from feminine of *stāmineus,* made of threads, from *stāmen,* thread. See **stā-** in Appendix.]

eta particle *n.* A neutral elementary particle that has a mass 1,074 times that of an electron.

et cet·er·a (ĕt sĕt′ər-ə, sĕt′rə). *Abbr.* **etc.** And other unspecified things of the same class; and so forth. **—et·cet·er·a** *n.* **1.** A number of unspecified persons or things. **2. etceteras.** Additional odds and ends; extras. [Latin : *et,* and + *cētera,* the rest, neuter pl. of *cēterus;* see **ko-** in Appendix.]

etch (ĕch) *v.* **etched, etch·ing, etch·es.** *—tr.* **1.a.** To cut into the surface of (glass, for example) by the action of acid. **b.** To make or create by this method: *etch a design on glass.* **2.** To impress, delineate, or imprint clearly: *a landscape that is forever etched in my memory; trees that were etched against the winter sky.* *—intr.* To engage in etching. [Dutch *etsen,* from German *ätzen,* from Middle High German *etzen,* from Old High German *ezzen,* to eat. See **ed-** in Appendix.] **—etch′er** *n.*

etch·ing (ĕch′ĭng) *n.* **1.** The art of preparing etched plates, especially metal plates, from which designs and pictures are printed. **2.** A design etched on a plate. **3.** An impression made from an etched plate.

ETD or **e.t.d.** *abbr.* Estimated time of departure.

e·ter·nal (ĭ-tûr′nəl) *adj.* **1.** Being without beginning or end; existing outside of time. See Synonyms at **infinite. 2.** Continuing without interruption; perpetual. **3.** Forever true or changeless: *eternal truths.* **4.** Seemingly endless; interminable. See Synonyms at **ageless, continual. 5.** Of or relating to spiritual communion with God, especially in the afterlife. **—eternal** *n.* **1.** Something timeless, uninterrupted, or endless. **2. Eternal.** God. Used with *the.* [Middle English, from Old French, from Late Latin *aeternālis,* from Latin *aeternus.* See **aiw-** in Appendix.] **—e′ter·nal′i·ty** (ē′tər-năl′ĭ-tē), **e·ter′nal·ness** *n.* **—e·ter′nal·ly** *adv.*

e·ter·nal·ize (ĭ-tûr′nə-līz′) *tr.v.* **-ized, -iz·ing, -iz·es.** To eternize.

e·terne (ĭ-tûrn′) *adj. Archaic.* Eternal. [Middle English, from Old French, from Latin *aeternus.* See ETERNAL.]

e·ter·ni·ty (ĭ-tûr′nĭ-tē) *n., pl.* **-ties. 1.** Time without begin-

Estonia

étagère
Mid 19th-century American

ă pat	oi boy
ā pay	ou out
âr care	ŏŏ took
ä father	ōō boot
ĕ pet	ŭ cut
ē be	ûr urge
ĭ pit	th thin
ī pie	*th* this
îr pier	hw which
ŏ pot	zh vision
ō toe	ə about, item
ô paw	♦ regionalism

Stress marks: ′ (primary); ′ (secondary), as in **dictionary** (dĭk′shə-nĕr′ē)

ning or end; infinite time. **2.** The state or quality of being eternal. **3.a.** The timeless state following death. **b.** The afterlife; immortality. **4.** A very long or seemingly endless time: *waited for an eternity.* [Middle English *eternite,* from Old French, from Latin *aeternitās,* from *aeternus,* eternal. See ETERNAL.]

e·ter·nize (ĭ-tûr′nīz′) *tr.v.* **-nized, -niz·ing, -niz·es. 1.a.** To make eternal. **b.** To protract for an indefinite period. **2.** To make perpetually famous; immortalize. [French *éterniser,* from Old French *eterne,* eternal. See ETERNE.] **—e·ter′ni·za′tion** (-nĭ-zā′shən) *n.*

e·te·sian (ĭ-tē′zhən) *adj.* Occurring annually. Used of the prevailing northerly summer winds of the Mediterranean. [From Latin *etēsius,* from Greek *etēsios,* from *etos,* year. See **wet-**[2] in Appendix.] **—e·te′sian** *n.*

eth (ĕth) *n.* Variant of **edh.**

Eth. *abbr.* Ethiopia.

-eth[1] or **-th** *suff.* Used to form the archaic third person singular present indicative of verbs: *leadeth.* [Middle English, from Old English *-eth, -ath.*]

-eth[2] *suff.* Variant of **-th**[3].

eth·a·cryn·ic acid (ĕth′ə-krĭn′ĭk) *n.* A diuretic compound, $C_{13}H_{12}Cl_2O_4$, used in the treatment of severe edema. [ETH(YL) + AC(ETIC) + (BUTY)R(IC) + -Y(L) + (PHE)N(OL) + -IC.]

eth·am·bu·tol (ĕ-thăm′byə-tôl′, -tō′, -tŏl′) *n.* An antibacterial drug, $C_{10}H_{24}N_2O_2$, used in combination with other drugs in the treatment of pulmonary tuberculosis. [ETH(YLENE) + AM(INE) + BUT(AN)OL.]

eth·a·mine (ĕth′ə-mēn′, ĕth-ăm′ēn′) *n.* See **ethylamine.**

eth·ane (ĕth′ān′) *n.* A colorless, odorless gaseous alkane, C_2H_6, that occurs as a constituent of natural gas and is used as a fuel and a refrigerant. [ETH(YL) + -ANE.]

eth·a·nol (ĕth′ə-nôl′, -nōl′, -nŏl′) *n.* See **alcohol** (sense 1). [ETHAN(E) + -OL[1].]

eth·a·nol·a·mine (ĕth′ə-nŏl′ə-mēn′, -nō′lə-) *n.* A colorless liquid, $NH_2(CH_2)_2ON$, used in the purification of petroleum, as a solvent in dry cleaning, and as an ingredient in paints and pharmaceuticals.

Eth·el·bert (ĕth′əl-bûrt′). 552?–616. Anglo-Saxon king who ruled all of Britain south of the Humber, was converted to Christianity by Saint Augustine (597), and codified English law (604).

Eth·el·red II also **Aeth·el·red II** (ĕth′əl-rĕd′). Called "Ethelred the Unready." 968?–1016. King of the English (978–1016) whose reign was a series of ultimately unsuccessful struggles against Danish invasion.

eth·ene (ĕth′ēn′) *n.* See **ethylene.** [ETH(YL) + -ENE.]

e·ther (ē′thər) *n.* **1.** Any of a class of organic compounds in which two hydrocarbon groups are linked by an oxygen atom. **2.** A volatile, highly flammable liquid, $C_2H_5OC_2H_5$, derived from the distillation of ethyl alcohol with sulfuric acid and widely used as a reagent, a solvent, and an anesthetic. Also called *diethyl ether, ethyl ether.* **3.** The regions of space beyond the earth's atmosphere; the heavens. **4.** The element believed in ancient and medieval civilizations to fill all space above the sphere of the moon and to compose the stars and planets. **5.** *Physics.* An all-pervading, infinitely elastic, massless medium formerly postulated as the medium of propagation of electromagnetic waves. [Middle English, upper air, from Latin *aethēr,* from Greek *aithēr.*] **—e·ther′ic** (ĭ-thĕr′ĭk, ĭ-thîr′-) *adj.*

e·the·re·al (ĭ-thîr′ē-əl) *adj.* **1.** Characterized by lightness and insubstantiality; intangible. **2.** Highly refined; delicate. See Synonyms at **airy. 3.a.** Of the celestial spheres; heavenly. **b.** Not of this world; spiritual. **4.** *Chemistry.* Of or relating to ether. [From Latin *aetherius,* from Greek *aitherios,* from *aithēr,* upper air.] **—e·the′re·al′i·ty** (-ăl′ĭ-tē), **e·the′re·al·ness** *n.* **—e·the′re·al·ly** *adv.*

e·the·re·al·ize (ĭ-thîr′ē-ə-līz′) *tr. & intr.v.* **-ized, -iz·ing, -iz·es.** To make or become ethereal. **—e·the′re·al·i·za′tion** (-ə-lĭ-zā′shən) *n.*

Eth·er·ege (ĕth′ər-ĭj, ĕth′rĭj), Sir **George.** 1635?–1692? English playwright of the Restoration whose comedic works gave rise to the comedy of manners as a dramatic form.

e·ther·i·fy (ĭ-thĕr′ə-fī′) *tr.v.* **-fied, -fy·ing, -fies.** To convert (an alcohol) into an ether. **—e·ther′i·fi·ca′tion** (-fĭ-kā′shən) *n.*

e·ther·ize (ē′thə-rīz′) *tr.v.* **-ized, -iz·ing, -iz·es. 1.** To subject to the fumes of ether; anesthetize. **2.** To etherify. **—e′ther·i·za′tion** (ē′thər-ĭ-zā′shən) *n.* **—e′ther·iz′er** *n.*

eth·ic (ĕth′ĭk) *n.* **1.a.** A set of principles of right conduct. **b.** A theory or a system of moral values: *"An ethic of service is at war with a craving for gain"* (Gregg Easterbrook). **2. ethics.** *(used with a sing. verb).* The study of the general nature of morals and of the specific moral choices to be made by a person; moral philosophy. **3. ethics.** *(used with a sing. or pl. verb).* The rules or standards governing the conduct of a person or the members of a profession: *medical ethics.* [Middle English *ethik,* from Old French *ethique* (from Late Latin *ēthica,* from Greek *ēthika,* ethics) and from Latin *ēthicē* (from Greek *ēthikē*), both from Greek *ēthikos,* ethical, from *ēthos,* character. See **s(w)e-** in Appendix.]

eth·i·cal (ĕth′ĭ-kəl) *adj.* **1.** Of, relating to, or dealing with ethics. **2.** Being in accordance with the accepted principles of right and wrong that govern the conduct of a profession. See Synonyms at **moral. 3.** Of or relating to a drug dispensed solely on the prescription of a physician. **—ethical** *n.* An ethical drug. **—eth′i·cal·ly** *adv.* **—eth′i·cal·ness, eth′i·cal′i·ty** (-kăl′ĭ-tē) *n.*

eth·i·cist (ĕth′ĭ-sĭst) also **e·thi·cian** (ĕ-thĭsh′ən) *n.* A specialist in ethics.

eth·i·on (ĕth′ē-ŏn′) *n.* A highly toxic, liquid organophosphate pesticide, $C_9H_{22}O_4P_2S_3$. [ETH(YL) + (TH)ION-.]

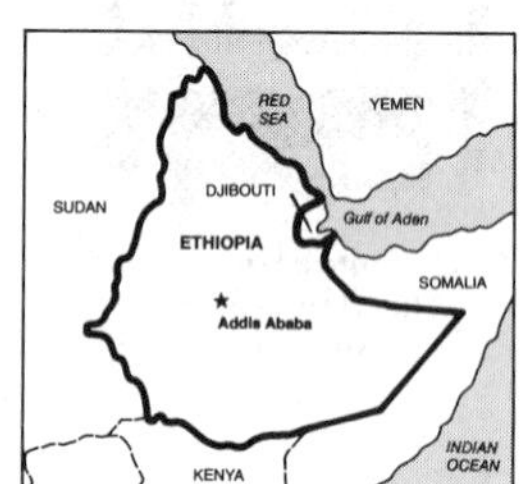

Ethiopia

E·thi·o·pi·a (ē′thē-ō′pē-ə). Formerly **Ab·ys·sin·i·a** (ăb′ĭ-sĭn′ē-ə). *Abbr.* **Eth.** A country of northeast Africa. An ancient kingdom converted to Christianity in the 4th century A.D., the area was in turmoil after the rise of Islam in the 7th century and later (17th–18th century) was beset by ruinous civil wars. It became independent in 1896 but was held by Italy from 1935 to 1941. Addis Ababa is the capital and the largest city. Population, 32,775,000.

E·thi·o·pi·an (ē′thē-ō′pē-ən) *adj.* **1.** Of or relating to Ethiopia or its peoples or cultures. **2.** Of or relating to the zoogeographic region that includes Africa and most of Arabia. **—Ethiopian** *n.* A native or inhabitant of Ethiopia.

E·thi·op·ic (ē′thē-ŏp′ĭk, -ō′pĭk) *n.* The Afro-Asiatic language of ancient Ethiopia that is still used as a liturgical language in the Christian Church in Ethiopia. **—Ethiopic** *adj.* **1.** Of or relating to Ethiopic. **2.** Ethiopian.

eth·moid (ĕth′moid′) also **eth·moid·al** (ĕth-moid′l) *—adj.* Of, relating to, or being a light spongy bone located between the orbits, forming part of the walls and septum of the superior nasal cavity, and containing numerous perforations for the passage of the fibers of the olfactory nerves. *—n.* The ethmoid bone. [French *ethmoïde,* from Greek *ēthmoeidēs,* sievelike : *ēthmos,* strainer (from *ēthein,* to sift) + *-eidēs, -oeidēs,* -oid.]

eth·narch (ĕth′närk′) *n.* The ruler of a province or a people. [Greek *ethnarkhēs* : *ethnos,* nation; see ETHNIC + *-arkhēs,* -arch.] **—eth′nar′chy** *n.*

eth·nic (ĕth′nĭk) *adj.* **1.a.** Of or relating to sizable groups of people sharing a common and distinctive racial, national, religious, linguistic, or cultural heritage. **b.** Being a member of a particular ethnic group. **c.** Of, relating to, or distinctive of members of such a group: *ethnic restaurants; ethnic art.* **2.** Relating to a people not Christian or Jewish; heathen. **—ethnic** *n.* A member of a particular ethnic group, especially one who maintains the language or customs of the group. [Middle English, heathen, from Late Latin *ethnicus,* from Greek *ethnikos,* from *ethnos,* people, nation. See **s(w)e-** in Appendix.]

WORD HISTORY: When in a Middle English text written before 1400 it is said that a part of a temple fell down and "mad a gret distruccione of ethnykis," one wonders why ethnics were singled out for death. The word *ethnic* in this context, however, means "gentile," coming as it does from the Greek adjective *ethnikos,* meaning "national, foreign, gentile." The adjective is derived from the noun *ethnos,* "people, nation, foreign people," that in the plural phrase *ta ethnē* meant "foreign nations." In translating the Hebrew Bible into Greek, this phrase was used for Hebrew *gōyīm,* "gentiles"; hence the sense of the noun in the Middle English quotation. The noun *ethnic* in this sense or the related sense "heathen" is not recorded after 1728, although the related adjective sense is still used. But probably under the influence of other words going back to Greek *ethnos,* such as *ethnography* and *ethnology,* the adjective *ethnic* broadened in meaning in the 19th century. After this broadening the noun sense "a member of a particular ethnic group," first recorded in 1945, came into existence.

eth·ni·cal (ĕth′nĭ-kəl) *adj.* **1.** Ethnic. **2.** Of or relating to ethnology. **—eth′ni·cal·ly** *adv.*

eth·nic·i·ty (ĕth-nĭs′ĭ-tē) *n.* Ethnic character, background, or affiliation.

ethno- *pref.* Race; people: *ethnology.* [Greek, from *ethnos,* people. See **s(w)e-** in Appendix.]

eth·no·bot·a·ny (ĕth′nō-bŏt′n-ē) *n.* **1.** The plant lore and agricultural customs of a people. **2.** The study of such lore and customs. **—eth′no·bo·tan′i·cal** (-bə-tăn′ĭ-kəl) *adj.* **—eth′no·bo·tan′i·cal·ly** *adv.* **—eth′no·bot′a·nist** *n.*

eth·no·cen·trism (ĕth′nō-sĕn′trĭz′əm) *n.* **1.** Belief in the superiority of one's own ethnic group. **2.** Overriding concern with race. **—eth′no·cen′tric** (-trĭk) *adj.* **—eth′no·cen′tri·cal·ly** *adv.* **—eth′no·cen·tric′i·ty** (-sĕn-trĭs′ĭ-tē) *n.*

eth·nog·ra·phy (ĕth-nŏg′rə-fē) *n.* **1.** The branch of anthropology that deals with the scientific description of specific human cultures. **2.** Ethnology. **—eth·nog′ra·pher** *n.* **—eth′no·graph′ic** (ĕth′nə-grăf′ĭk), **eth′no·graph′i·cal** *adj.* **—eth′no·graph′i·cal·ly** *adv.*

eth·no·his·to·ry (ĕth′nō-hĭs′tə-rē) *n.* The scientific study of the development of human cultures, as through systematic analysis of archaeological findings. **—eth′no·his·to′ri·an** (-hĭ-stôr′ē-ən, -stōr′-, stŏr′-) *n.* **—eth′no·his·to′ric** (-hĭ-stôr′ĭk, -stŏr′-), **eth′no·his·to′ri·cal** *adj.*

eth·nol·o·gy (ĕth-nŏl′ə-jē) *n. Abbr.* **ethnol. 1.** The science that analyzes and compares human cultures, as in social structure, language, religion, and technology; cultural anthropology. **2.** The branch of anthropology that deals with the origin, distribution, and characteristics of the races of humankind. **—eth′no·log′ic** (ĕth′nə-lŏj′ĭk), **eth′no·log′i·cal** *adj.* **—eth′no·log′i·cal·ly** *adv.* **—eth·nol′o·gist** *n.*

eth·no·meth·od·ol·o·gy (ĕth′nō-mĕth′ə-dŏl′ə-jē) *n.*

The branch of sociology that deals with the codes and conventions that underlie everyday social interactions and activities. **—eth′no·meth′od·ol′o·gist** *n.*

eth·no·mu·si·col·o·gy (ĕth′nō-myo͞o′zĭ-kŏl′ə-jē) *n.* **1.** The study of music that is distinct from the European classical tradition. **2.** The comparative study of music of different cultures. **—eth′no·mu′si·co·log′i·cal** (-kə-lŏj′ĭ-kəl) *adj.* **—eth′no·mu′si·col′o·gist** *n.*

e·tho·gram (ē′thə-grăm′) *n.* A pictorial catalogue of the behavioral patterns of an organism or a species. [ETHO(LOGY) + -GRAM.]

e·thol·o·gy (ĭ-thŏl′ə-jē, ē-thŏl′-) *n.* **1.** The scientific study of animal behavior, especially as it occurs in a natural environment. **2.** The study of human ethos and its formation. [French *éthologie,* from Latin *ēthologia,* art of depicting character, from Greek : *ēthos,* character; see ETHOS + *-logia,* -logy.] **—eth′o·log′i·cal** (ĕth′ə-lŏj′ĭ-kəl) *adj.* **—e·thol′o·gist** *n.*

e·thos (ē′thŏs′) *n.* The disposition, character, or fundamental values peculiar to a specific person, people, culture, or movement: *"They cultivated a subversive alternative ethos"* (Anthony Burgess). [Greek *ēthos,* character. See **s(w)e-** in Appendix.]

eth·ox·yl (ĭ-thŏk′səl) also **eth·ox·y** (ĭ-thŏk′sē) *n.* The univalent radical C_2H_5O. [ETH(YL) + OX(O)- + -YL.]

eth·yl (ĕth′əl) *n.* A univalent organic radical, C_2H_5. [ETH(ER) + -YL.] **—eth·yl′ic** (ĕ-thĭl′ĭk) *adj.*

ethyl acetate *n.* A colorless, volatile, flammable liquid, $CH_3COOC_2H_5$, used in perfumes, flavorings, lacquers, pharmaceuticals, and rayon and as a general solvent.

ethyl alcohol *n.* See **alcohol** (sense 1).

eth·yl·a·mine (ĕth′ə-lə-mēn′, -lăm′ən) *n.* A colorless, volatile liquid, $C_2H_5NH_2$, used in petroleum refining and detergents and in organic synthesis. Also called *ethamine.*

eth·yl·ate (ĕth′ə-lāt′) *tr.v.* **-at·ed, -at·ing, -ates.** To introduce the ethyl group into (a compound). **—eth′yl·a′tion** *n.*

ethyl chloride *n.* A chemical compound, C_2H_5Cl, a gas at ordinary temperatures and a colorless, volatile, flammable liquid when compressed, used as a solvent, as a refrigerant, and in the manufacture of tetraethyl lead.

eth·yl·ene (ĕth′ə-lēn′) *n.* A colorless, flammable gas, C_2H_4, derived from natural gas and petroleum and used as a source of many organic compounds, in welding and cutting metals, to color citrus fruits, and as an anesthetic. Also called *ethene.* **—eth′yl·e′nic** (-ə-lē′nĭk, -lĕn′ĭk) *adj.*

ethylene glycol *n.* A colorless, syrupy alcohol, $HOCH_2CH_2OH$, used as an antifreeze in cooling and heating systems.

ethyl ether *n.* See **ether** (sense 2).

ethyl mercaptan *n.* A colorless, organic liquid, C_2H_5SH, that has a strong odor and is added to odorless fuel and fuel systems as a warning agent.

-etic *suff.* Used to form adjectives usually from nouns ending in *-esis,* as in *aphaeretic* from *aphaeresis.* [Latin *-ēticus,* from Greek *-ētikos,* from *-etos,* verbal adj. ending.]

É·tienne (ĕ-tyĕn′). See **Estienne.**

e·ti·o·late (ē′tē-ə-lāt′) *v.* **-lat·ed, -lat·ing, -lates.** *—tr.* **1.** *Botany.* To cause (a plant) to develop without chlorophyll by preventing exposure to sunlight. **2.a.** To cause to appear pale and sickly: *a face that was etiolated from years in prison.* **b.** To make weak by stunting the growth or development of. *—intr. Botany.* To become blanched or whitened, as when grown without sunlight. [French *étioler,* from Norman French *étieuler,* to grow into haulm, from *éteule,* stalk, from Old French *esteule,* from Vulgar Latin **stupula,* from Latin *stipula.*] **—e′ti·o·la′tion** *n.*

e·ti·ol·o·gy also **ae·ti·ol·o·gy** (ē′tē-ŏl′ə-jē) *n., pl.* **-gies.** **1.a.** The study of causes or origins. **b.** The branch of medicine that deals with the causes or origins of disease. **2.a.** Assignment of a cause, an origin, or a reason for something. **b.** The cause or origin of a disease or disorder as determined by medical diagnosis. [Late Latin *aetiologia,* from Greek *aitiologia* : *aitia,* cause + *-logia,* -logy.] **—e′ti·o·log′ic** (-ə-lŏj′ĭk), **e′ti·o·log′i·cal** *adj.* **—e′ti·o·log′i·cal·ly** *adv.* **—e′ti·ol′o·gist** *n.*

et·i·quette (ĕt′ĭ-kĕt′, -kĭt) *n.* The practices and forms prescribed by social convention or by authority. [French, from Old French *estiquet,* label. See TICKET.]

SYNONYMS: *etiquette, propriety, protocol, decorum.* These nouns refer to codes governing correct behavior. *Etiquette* and the plural form *proprieties* denote the forms of conduct prescribed in polite society: *"Man is . . . a slave . . . to etiquette"* (Frederick W. Robertson). *Even when she was angry, she observed the proprieties. Protocol* refers to the official etiquette observed in affairs of state: *The visiting prime minister, dispensing with protocol, exchanged informal reminiscences with her neighbor at the table.* The word now often denotes simply a code of correct conduct: *Graduation exercises had to be consistent with academic protocol. Decorum* and the singular form *propriety* denote conformity with established standards of manners or behavior: *"One hour of life, crowded to the full with glorious action . . . is worth whole years of those mean observances of paltry decorum"* (Sir Walter Scott). *"He was afraid that, from some obscure motive of propriety . . . she would bring Janet with her"* (Arnold Bennett).

Et·na also **Aet·na** (ĕt′nə). **Mount.** An active volcano, 3,325.1 m (10,902 ft) high, of eastern Sicily. Its first known eruption occurred in 475 B.C.

ETO *abbr.* European theater of operations.

E·ton (ēt′n). An urban district of southeast-central England on the Thames River opposite Windsor. Its college, the largest and most famous of England's public schools, was founded by Henry VI in 1440. Population, 3,523.

Eton collar *n.* A broad white collar worn over the lapels of a jacket. [After *Eton* College, England.]

Eton jacket *n.* A waist-length black jacket that has wide lapels and is cut square at the hips. [After *Eton* College, England.]

é·touf·fée (ā′to͞o-fā′) *n., pl.* **-fées** (-fā′). A spicy Cajun stew of vegetables and seafood, especially crayfish. [Louisiana French, from French *(à l')étouffée,* stewed, alteration (influenced by *étouffer,* to smother, from Old French *estouffer;* see STIFLE[1]) of *étuvée,* past participle of *étuver,* to stew, from Old French *estuver.* See STEW[1].]

E·tru·ri·a (ĭ-tro͝or′ē-ə). An ancient country of west-central Italy in present-day Tuscany and parts of Umbria. It was the center of the Etruscan civilization, which spread throughout much of Italy before being supplanted by Rome in the third century B.C. **—E·tru′ri·an** *adj. & n.*

E·trus·can (ĭ-trŭs′kən) *adj.* Of or relating to ancient Etruria or its people, language, or culture. **—Etruscan** *n.* **1.** A native or inhabitant of Etruria. **2.** The extinct language of the Etruscans, of unknown linguistic affiliation.

et seq. *abbr. Latin.* Et sequens (and the following one or ones).

-ette *suff.* **1.** Small; diminutive: *kitchenette.* **2.** Female: *usherette.* **3.** An imitation or inferior kind of cloth: *leatherette.* [Middle English, from Old French, feminine of *-et,* -et.]

USAGE NOTE: The adaptation of the French diminutive suffix *-ette* to mean "female," as in *usherette* or *drum majorette,* was attacked on etymological grounds long before people realized that it might also involve socially questionable presuppositions. Historically, *-ette* is the feminine form of a French diminutive suffix that occurs in borrowings such as *banquet, tablet,* and *clarinet* (and in its feminine form, in words such as *cigarette* and *chemisette*). In the past hundred years, *-ette* has become fairly productive as an English diminutive in words denoting inanimates, as in *novelette, kitchenette, luncheonette,* and *laundrette,* but its use to form nouns denoting women is a separate development, most likely derived from the French use of *-ette* to form feminine versions of masculine personal names, as in *Paulette, Georgette, Jeanette,* and *Antoinette.* In this sense, the suffix was first applied to an English common noun in *suffragette,* which served as the model for a number of words that referred to women who occupied positions once reserved for men, as in *farmerette, sailorette,* and *chaufferette.* Among these only *usherette* and *drum majorette* have survived, but the pattern is still widely used to coin the names of women's social groups and auxiliaries, as well as in formations such as *bachelorette,* which enjoyed a vogue not long ago as an attempt to create a feminine counterpart for *bachelor.* In each case, the use of what is essentially a diminutive or pet name suffix to refer to women betrays a patronizing attitude. See Usage Note at **brunette.**

e·tude (ā′to͞od′, -tyo͞od′) *n. Music.* **1.** A piece composed for the development of a specific point of technique. **2.** A composition featuring a point of technique but performed because of its artistic merit. [French *étude,* from Old French *estudie,* study. See STUDY.]

é·tui (ā-twē′) *n., pl.* **é·tuis** (ā-twēz′). A small, usually ornamental case for holding articles such as needles. [French, from Old French *estui,* prison, from *estuier,* to guard, from Vulgar Latin **estudiāre,* to treat carefully, from Latin *studium,* study. See STUDY.]

et ux. *abbr. Latin.* Et uxor (and wife).

ETV *abbr.* Educational television.

etym. *abbr.* Etymological; etymology.

et·y·ma (ĕt′ə-mə) *n.* A plural of **etymon.**

et·y·mo·log·i·cal (ĕt′ə-mə-lŏj′ĭ-kəl) also **et·y·mo·log·ic** (-lŏj′ĭk) *adj. Abbr.* **etym., etymol.** Of or relating to etymology or based on the principles of etymology. **—et′y·mo·log′i·cal·ly** *adv.*

et·y·mol·o·gist (ĕt′ə-mŏl′ə-jĭst) *n.* A specialist in etymology.

et·y·mol·o·gize (ĕt′ə-mŏl′ə-jīz′) *v.* **-gized, -giz·ing, -giz·es.** *—tr.* To trace and state the etymology of. *—intr.* To give or suggest the etymology of a word.

et·y·mol·o·gy (ĕt′ə-mŏl′ə-jē) *n., pl.* **-gies.** *Abbr.* **etym., etymol.** **1.** The origin and historical development of a linguistic form as shown by determining its basic elements, earliest known use, and changes in form and meaning, tracing its transmission from one language to another, identifying its cognates in other languages, and reconstructing its ancestral form where possible. **2.** The branch of linguistics that deals with etymologies. [Middle English *etimologie,* from Old French *ethimologie,* from Medieval Latin *ethimologia,* from Latin *etymologia,* from Greek *etumologia* : *etumon,* true sense of a word; see ETYMON + *-logia,* -logy.]

et·y·mon (ĕt′ə-mŏn′) *n., pl.* **-mons** or **-ma** (-mə). **1.** An earlier form of a word in the same language or in an ancestor language. For example, Indo-European **duwo* and Old English

ă pat	oi boy
ā pay	ou out
âr care	o͝o took
ä father	o͞o boot
ĕ pet	ŭ cut
ē be	ûr urge
ĭ pit	th thin
ī pie	*th* this
îr pier	hw which
ŏ pot	zh vision
ō toe	ə about, item
ô paw	♦ regionalism

Stress marks: ′ (primary); ′ (secondary), as in **dictionary** (dĭk′shə-nĕr′ē)

eucalyptus

twā are etymons of Modern English *two.* **2.** A word or morpheme from which compounds and derivatives are formed. **3.** A foreign word from which a particular loanword is derived. For example, Latin *duo,* "two," is an etymon of English *duodecimal.* [Latin, from Greek *etumon,* true sense of a word, from *etumos,* true.]

Et·zel (ĕt′səl) *n.* The second husband of Kriemhild in the *Nibelungenlied.*

Eu The symbol for the element **europium.**

eu– *pref.* **1.** Good; well; true: *euplastic.* **2.** A derivative of a specified substance: *eucaine.* [Middle English, from Latin, from Greek. See **(e)su-** in Appendix.]

Eu·boe·a (yo͞o-bē′ə) also **Ev·voia** (ĕv′yä). An island of central Greece in the Aegean Sea east of the mainland. It was settled by Ionian and Thracian colonists and was later controlled by Athens, Rome, Byzantium, Venice, and Turkey before becoming part of Greece in 1830.

eu·caine (yo͞o′kān′) *n.* A crystalline substance, $C_{15}H_{21}NO_2$, used as a local anesthetic, substituting for cocaine, in veterinary medicine.

eu·ca·lyp·tol (yo͞o′kə-lĭp′tôl′, -tōl′, -tŏl′) also **eu·ca·lyp·tole** (-tōl′) *n.* A colorless oily liquid, $C_{10}H_{18}O$, derived from eucalyptus and used in pharmaceuticals, flavoring, and perfumery. Also called *cineole.*

eu·ca·lyp·tus (yo͞o′kə-lĭp′təs) *n., pl.* **-tus·es** or **-ti** (-tī′). Any of numerous tall trees of the genus *Eucalyptus,* native to Australia and having aromatic leaves that yield an oil used medicinally and wood valued as timber. [New Latin *Eucalyptus,* genus name : Greek *eu-,* eu- + Greek *kaluptos,* covered (from *kaluptein,* to cover; see **kel-**[1] in Appendix).]

eu·car·y·ote (yo͞o-kăr′ē-ōt′, -ē-ət) *n.* Variant of **eukaryote.**

Eu·cha·rist (yo͞o′kər-ĭst) *n.* **1.a.** A sacrament and the central act of worship in many Christian churches, which was instituted at the Last Supper and in which bread and wine are consecrated and consumed in remembrance of Jesus's death; Communion. **b.** The consecrated elements of this rite; Communion. **2.** *Christian Science.* Spiritual communion with God. [Middle English *eukarist,* from Old French *eucariste,* from Late Latin *eucharistia,* from Greek *eukharistia,* from *eukharistos,* grateful, thankful : *eu-,* eu- + *kharizesthai,* to show favor (from *kharis,* grace; see **gher-**[2] in Appendix).] **—Eu′cha·ris′tic, Eu′cha·ris′ti·cal** *adj.*

eu·chre (yo͞o′kər) *n. Games.* **1.** A card game played usually with the highest 32 cards, in which each player is dealt 5 cards and the player making the trump is required to take at least 3 tricks to win. **2.** The act of euchring an opponent. **—euchre** *tr.v.* **-chred, -chring, -chres. 1.** *Games.* To prevent (an opponent) from taking 3 tricks in euchre. **2.** To deceive by sly or underhand means; cheat: *euchred us out of our life savings.* [Origin unknown.]

eu·chro·ma·tin (yo͞o-krō′mə-tĭn′) *n.* Chromosomal material that is genetically active and stains lightly with basic dyes. **—eu′chro·mat′ic** (yo͞o′krō-măt′ĭk) *adj.*

Euck·en (oi′kən), **Rudolf Christoph.** 1846–1926. German philosopher who viewed philosophy as a means of transforming life and as an active rather than a purely intellectual pursuit. He won the 1908 Nobel Prize for literature.

Eu·clid[1] (yo͞o′klĭd). Third century B.C. Greek mathematician who applied the deductive principles of logic to geometry, thereby deriving statements from clearly defined axioms.

Eu·clid[2] (yo͞o′klĭd). A city of northeast Ohio, a manufacturing suburb of Cleveland on Lake Erie. Population, 59,999.

Eu·clid·e·an also **Eu·clid·i·an** (yo͞o-klĭd′ē-ən) *adj.* Of or relating to Euclid's geometric principles.

eu·de·mon also **eu·dae·mon** (yo͞o-dē′mən) *n.* A good or benevolent spirit.

eu·de·mon·ism also **eu·dae·mon·ism** (yo͞o-dē′mə-nĭz′əm) *n.* A system of ethics that evaluates actions in terms of their capacity to produce happiness. **—eu·de′mo·nist** *n.* **—eu·de′mon·is′tic, eu·de′mon·is′ti·cal** *adj.*

Eu·gene (yo͞o-jēn′). A city of western Oregon on the Willamette River south of Salem. It is the seat of the University of Oregon (founded 1872). Population, 105,624.

Eu·gene (yo͞o-jēn′, yo͞o′jēn′, œ-zhĕn′), Prince of Savoy. 1663–1736. Austrian general in service to the Holy Roman Empire during the War of the Spanish Succession (1701–1714).

eu·gen·ic (yo͞o-jĕn′ĭk) *adj.* **1.** Of or relating to eugenics. **2.** Relating or adapted to the production of good or improved offspring. **—eu·gen′i·cal·ly** *adv.*

eu·gen·i·cist (yo͞o-jĕn′ĭ-sĭst) also **eu·gen·ist** (yo͞o′jə-nĭst) *n.* An advocate of or a specialist in eugenics.

eu·gen·ics (yo͞o-jĕn′ĭks) *n.* (*used with a sing. verb*). The study of hereditary improvement of the human race by controlled selective breeding.

Eugénie
After a portrait by Franz Winterhalter (1805–1873)

Eu·gé·nie (yo͞o-jē′nē, œ-zhā-nē′). 1826–1920. Empress of France (1853–1871) as the wife of Napoleon III. She acted as regent during the emperor's absences and is believed to have had an influence on events that led to the Franco-Prussian War of 1870.

eu·gen·ist (yo͞o′jə-nĭst) *n.* Variant of **eugenicist.**

eu·ge·nol (yo͞o′jə-nôl′, -nōl′, -nŏl′) *n.* A colorless aromatic liquid $C_{10}H_{12}O_2$, made from clove oil and used as a dental analgesic and in perfumery. [New Latin *Eugenia,* genus of the clove plant (after EUGENE, Prince of Savoy) + –OL(E).]

eu·gle·na (yo͞o-glē′nə) *n.* Any of various minute single-celled freshwater organisms of the genus *Euglena,* characterized by the presence of chlorophyll, a reddish eyespot, and a single anterior flagellum. [New Latin : Greek *eu-,* eu- + Greek *glēnē,* eyeball.]

eu·glob·u·lin (yo͞o-glŏb′yə-lĭn) *n.* A simple protein that is soluble in dilute salt solutions and insoluble in distilled water.

eu·he·mer·ism (yo͞o-hē′mə-rĭz′əm, -hĕm′ə-) *n.* A theory attributing the origin of the gods to the deification of historical heroes. [After *Euhemerus,* fourth-century B.C. Greek philosopher.] **—eu·he′mer·ist** *n.* **—eu·he′mer·is′tic** *adj.* **—eu·he′mer·is′ti·cal·ly** *adv.*

eu·he·mer·ize (yo͞o-hē′mə-rīz′, -hĕm′ə-) *tr.v.* **-ized, -iz·ing, -iz·es.** To explain or interpret euhemeristically.

eu·kar·y·ote also **eu·car·y·ote** (yo͞o-kăr′ē-ōt, -ē-ət) *n.* A single-celled or multicellular organism whose cells contain a distinct membrane-bound nucleus. [EU– + Greek *karuōtos,* having nuts (from *karuon,* nut; see **kar-** in Appendix).] **—eu·kar′y·ot′ic** (-ŏt′ĭk) *adj.*

eu·la·chon (yo͞o′lə-kŏn′) *n., pl.* **eulachon** or **-chons.** See **candlefish.** [Chinook Jargon *vlákān.*]

Eu·ler (oi′lər), **Leonhard.** 1707–1783. Swiss mathematician noted for his full development of integral calculus.

Eu·less (yo͞o′lĭs). A city of northeast Texas, a suburb of Fort Worth. Population, 24,002.

eu·lo·gize (yo͞o′lə-jīz′) *tr.v.* **-gized, -giz·ing, -giz·es.** To praise highly in speech or writing. **—eu′lo·gist** (-jĭst), **eu′lo·giz′er** *n.*

eu·lo·gy (yo͞o′lə-jē) *n., pl.* **-gies. 1.** A laudatory speech or written tribute, especially one praising someone who has died. **2.** High praise or commendation. [Middle English *euloge,* from Medieval Latin *eulogium,* from Greek *eulogia,* praise : *eu-,* eu- + *-logia,* -logy.] **—eu′lo·gis′tic** (-jĭs′tĭk) *adj.* **—eu′lo·gis′ti·cal·ly** *adv.*

Eu·men·i·des (yo͞o-mĕn′ĭ-dēz′) *pl.n. Greek Mythology.* The Furies.

eu·nuch (yo͞o′nək) *n.* **1.** A castrated man employed as a harem attendant or as a functionary in certain Asian courts. **2.** A man or boy whose testes are nonfunctioning or have been removed. [Middle English *eunuk,* from Latin *eunūchus,* from Greek *eunoukhos* : *eunē,* bed + *-okhos,* keeping (from *ekhein,* to keep; see **segh-** in Appendix).] **—eu′nuch·ism** *n.*

WORD HISTORY: The word *eunuch* does not derive, as one might think, from the operation that produced a eunuch but rather from one of his functions. *Eunuch* goes back to the Greek word *eunoukhos,* "a castrated person employed to take charge of the women of a harem and act as chamberlain." The Greek word is derived from *eunē,* "bed," and *ekhein,* "to keep." A eunuch, of course, was ideally suited to guard the bedchamber of women.

eu·on·y·mus (yo͞o-ŏn′ə-məs) *n.* Any of various trees, shrubs, or vines of the genus *Euonymus,* cultivated for their decorative foliage or fruits. [Latin *euōnymus,* a kind of tree growing in Lesbos, from Greek *euōnumos,* of good name : *eu-,* eu- + *onuma,* name; see **nō-men-** in Appendix.]

eu·pat·rid (yo͞o-păt′rĭd, yo͞o′pə-trĭd) *n., pl.* **-ri·dae** (-rĭ-dē′) or **-rids.** A member of the hereditary aristocracy of ancient Athens. [Greek *eupatridēs* : *eu-,* eu- + *patēr, patr-,* father; see **pəter-** in Appendix + *-idēs,* patronymic suff.] **—eu·pat′rid** *adj.*

eu·pep·si·a (yo͞o-pĕp′sē-ə, -shə) *n.* Good digestion. [Greek, from *eupeptos,* eupeptic. See EUPEPTIC.]

eu·pep·tic (yo͞o-pĕp′tĭk) *adj.* **1.a.** Relating to or having good digestion. **b.** Conducive to digestion. **2.** Cheerful; happy. [From Greek *eupeptos* : *eu-,* eu- + *peptein,* to digest; see **pekʷ-** in Appendix.] **—eu·pep′ti·cal·ly** *adv.*

eu·phe·mism (yo͞o′fə-mĭz′əm) *n.* The act or an example of substituting a mild, indirect, or vague term for one considered harsh, blunt, or offensive: *"Euphemisms such as 'slumber room' . . . abound in the funeral business"* (Jessica Mitford). [Greek *euphēmismos,* from *euphēmizein,* to use auspicious words, from *euphēmia,* use of auspicious words : *eu-,* eu- + *phēmē,* speech; see **bhā-**[2] in Appendix.] **—eu′phe·mist** *n.* **—eu′phe·mis′tic** (-mĭs′tĭk) *adj.* **—eu′phe·mis′ti·cal·ly** *adv.*

eu·phe·mize (yo͞o′fə-mīz′) *v.* **-mized, -miz·ing, -miz·es.** —*tr.* To speak of or refer to by means of a euphemism. —*intr.* To use euphemisms. **—eu′phe·miz′er** *n.*

eu·phen·ics (yo͞o-fĕn′ĭks) *n.* (*used with a sing. verb*). The study or practice of phenotypic improvement of human beings after birth. [Blend of EU(GEN)ICS and PHEN(OTYPE).] **—eu·phen′ic** *adj.*

eu·pho·ni·ous (yo͞o-fō′nē-əs) *adj.* Pleasing or agreeable to the ear. **—eu·pho′ni·ous·ly** *adv.* **—eu·pho′ni·ous·ness** *n.*

eu·pho·ni·um (yo͞o-fō′nē-əm) *n. Music.* A brass wind instrument similar to the tuba but having a somewhat higher pitch and a mellower sound. [From Greek *euphōnos,* sweet-voiced. See EUPHONY.]

eu·pho·nize (yo͞o′fə-nīz′) *tr.v.* **-nized, -niz·ing, -niz·es.** To make pleasing in sound.

eu·pho·ny (yo͞o′fə-nē) *n., pl.* **-nies.** Agreeable sound, especially in the phonetic quality of words. [French *euphonie,* from Late Latin *euphōnia,* from Greek, from *euphōnos,* sweet-voiced : *eu-,* eu- + *phōnē,* sound; see **bhā-**[2] in Appendix.] **—eu·phon′ic** (yo͞o-fŏn′ĭk) *adj.* **—eu·phon′i·cal·ly** *adv.*

eu·phor·bi·a (yo͞o-fôr′bē-ə) *n.* A plant of the genus *Euphorbia,* which includes the spurges. [Middle English *euforbia,* from

Latin *euphorbea,* after *Euphorbus,* first-century A.D. Greek physician.]

eu·pho·ri·a (yo͞o-fôr′ē-ə, -fōr′-) *n.* A feeling of great happiness or well-being. [New Latin, from Greek, from *euphoros,* healthy : *eu-,* eu- + *pherein,* to bear; see **bher-**[1] in Appendix.] **—eu·phor′ic** (-fôr′ĭk, -fŏr′-) *adj.* **—eu·phor′i·cal·ly** *adv.*

eu·phor·i·ant (yo͞o-fôr′ē-ənt, -fōr′-) *n.* A drug that tends to produce euphoria. **—eu·phor′i·ant** *adj.*

eu·phot·ic (yo͞o-fŏt′ĭk) *adj.* Of, relating to, or being the uppermost layer of a body of water that receives sufficient light for photosynthesis and the growth of green plants.

Eu·phra·tes (yo͞o-frā′tēz). A river of southwest Asia flowing about 2,735 km (1,700 mi) from central Turkey through Syria and into Iraq, where it joins the Tigris River to form the Shatt al Arab.

Eu·phros·y·ne (yo͞o-frŏs′ə-nē) *n. Greek Mythology.* One of the three Graces.

eu·phu·ism (yo͞o′fyo͞o-ĭz′əm) *n.* **1.** An affectedly elegant literary style of the late 16th and early 17th centuries, characterized by elaborate alliteration, antitheses, and similes. **2.** Affected elegance of language. [After *Euphues,* a character in *Euphues, the Anatomy of Wit* and *Euphues and his England* by John Lyly, from Greek *euphuēs,* shapely : *eu-,* eu- + *phuein,* to grow, bring forth; see **bheue-** in Appendix.] **—eu′phu·ist** *n.* **—eu′phu·is′tic, eu′phu·is′ti·cal** *adj.* **—eu′phu·is′ti·cal·ly** *adv.*

eu·plas·tic (yo͞o-plăs′tĭk) *adj.* Readily transformed into tissue, as in the healing of a wound.

eu·ploid (yo͞o′ploid′) *adj.* Having a chromosome number that is an exact multiple of the haploid number for the species. **—euploid** *n.* An organism having a euploid chromosome number. **—eu′ploi′dy** *n.*

eup·ne·a (yo͞op-nē′ə) *n.* Normal, unlabored breathing. [New Latin, from Greek *eupnoia,* from *eupnoos,* breathing well : *eu-,* eu- + *pnein,* to breathe; see **pneu-** in Appendix.] **—eup·ne′ic** *adj.* **—eup·ne′i·cal·ly** *adv.*

Eur. *abbr.* Europe; European.

Eur·a·sia (yo͞o-rā′zhə). The land mass comprising the continents of Europe and Asia.

Eur·a·sian (yo͞o-rā′zhən) *adj.* **1.** Of or relating to Eurasia. **2.** Of mixed European and Asian descent. **—Eurasian** *n.* A person of mixed European and Asian descent.

EURATOM *abbr.* European Atomic Energy Community.

eu·re·ka (yo͞o-rē′kə) *interj.* Used to express triumph upon finding or discovering something. [Greek *heurēka,* I have found (it) (supposedly exclaimed by Archimedes upon discovering how to measure the volume of an irregular solid and thereby determine the purity of a gold object), first person perfect of *heuriskein,* to find.]

Eu·re·ka (yo͞o-rē′kə). A city of northwest California on Humboldt Bay, an arm of the Pacific Ocean. Lumbering, fishing, and tourism are important to its economy. Population, 24,153.

eu·rhyth·mics (yo͞o-rĭth′mĭks) *n. (used with a sing. verb).* Variant of **eurythmics.**

eu·rhyth·my (yo͞o-rĭth′mē) *n.* Variant of **eurythmy.**

Eu·rip·i·des (yo͞o-rĭp′ĭ-dēz′). 480?–406 B.C. Greek dramatist who ranks with Sophocles and Aeschylus as the greatest classical tragedians. He wrote more than 90 tragedies, although only 18, including *Medea, Hippolytus,* and *The Trojan Women,* survive in complete form. **—Eu·rip′i·de′an** *adj.*

eu·ri·pus (yo͞o-rī′pəs) *n., pl.* **-pi** (-pī′). A sea channel characterized by turbulent and unpredictable currents. [Latin, from Greek *euripos* : *eu-,* eu- + *rhipē,* rush (from *riptein,* to throw).]

Euro– *pref.* Europe; European: *Eurocommunism.*

Eu·ro·bond (yo͝or′ō-bŏnd′) *n.* A bond of a U.S. corporation issued in Europe.

Eu·ro·cen·tric (yo͝or′ō-sĕn′trĭk) also **Eu·ro·po·cen·tric** (yo͞o-rō′pə-) *adj.* Centered or focused on Europe and the Europeans: *"The . . . current revivals of classical architecture cannot be dissociated from attempts in other fields to assert the preeminence of Eurocentric Western culture"* (Hugh Honour). **—Eu·ro·cen′trism** *n.*

Eu·ro·com·mu·nism (yo͝or′ō-kŏm′yə-nĭz′əm) *n.* The communism of certain western European Communist parties that support democratic political procedures and claim to be independent from the Soviet government. **—Eu′ro·com′mu·nist** *adj. & n.*

Eu·ro·crat (yo͝or′ə-krăt′) *n.* An administrative official at the headquarters of the Common Market. **—Eu′ro·crat′ic** *adj.*

Eu·ro·cur·ren·cy (yo͝or′ō-kûr′ən-sē, -kŭr′-) *n., pl.* **-cies.** Funds deposited in a bank when those funds are denominated in a currency differing from the bank's own domestic currency.

Eu·ro·dol·lar (yo͝or′ō-dŏl′ər) *n.* A U.S. dollar on deposit with a bank abroad, especially in Europe.

Eu·ro·mar·ket (yo͝or′ō-mär′kĭt) *n.* **1.** The money market in Eurocurrency or Eurobonds. **2.** The Common Market.

Eu·ro·pa (yo͞o-rō′pə) *n.* **1.** *Greek Mythology.* A Phoenician princess abducted to Crete by Zeus, who had assumed the form of a white bull, and by him the mother of Minos, Rhadamanthus, and Sarpedon. **2.** One of the four brightest satellites of Jupiter and the seventh in distance from the planet. It was originally sighted by Galileo. [Latin *Eurōpa,* from Greek *Eurōpē.*]

Eu·rope (yo͝or′əp). *Abbr.* **Eur.** The sixth-largest continent, extending west from the Dardanelles, Black Sea, and Ural Mountains. It is technically a vast peninsula of the Eurasian land mass.

Eu·ro·pe·an (yo͝or′ə-pē′ən) *n. Abbr.* **Eur. 1.** A native or inhabitant of Europe. **2.** A person of European descent. **—European** *adj. Abbr.* **Eur.** Of or relating to Europe or its peoples, languages, or cultures.

European corn borer *n.* See **corn borer** (sense 1).

European Economic Community. *Abbr.* **EEC.** See **Common Market.**

Eu·ro·pe·an·ize (yo͝or′ə-pē′ə-nīz′) *tr.v.* **-ized, -iz·ing, -iz·es.** To make European. **—Eu′ro·pe′an·i·za′tion** (-ə-nĭ-zā′shən) *n.*

European plan *n. Abbr.* **EP** A hotel plan in which the rates include only the charges for a room and not for meals.

European U.S.S.R. A historical region of the U.S.S.R. west of the Ural Mountains and the Caspian Sea.

eu·ro·pi·um (yo͞o-rō′pē-əm) *n. Symbol* **Eu** A silvery-white, soft, rare-earth element occurring in monazite and bastnaesite and used to dope lasers and to absorb neutrons in research. Atomic number 63; atomic weight 151.96; melting point 826°C; boiling point 1,439°C; specific gravity 5.259; valence 2, 3. See table at **element.** [After EUROPE.]

Eu·ro·po·cen·tric (yo͞o-rō′pə-sĕn′trĭk) *adj.* Variant of **Eurocentric.**

Eu·rus (yo͝or′əs) *n. Greek Mythology.* The god of the east or southeast wind.

eury– *pref.* Wide; broad: *eurythermal.* [From Greek *eurus,* wide.]

Eu·ry·a·le (yo͞o-rī′ə-lē) *n. Greek Mythology.* A Gorgon; sister of Medusa and Stheno.

eu·ry·bath·ic (yo͝or′ə-băth′ĭk) *adj.* Capable of living in a wide range of water depths. Used of an aquatic organism. **—eu′ry·bath′** *n.*

Eu·ryd·i·ce (yo͞o-rĭd′ĭ-sē) *n. Greek Mythology.* The wife of Orpheus, whom he failed to rescue from Hades when he looked back at her and so violated the command of Pluto on their journey back to the upper world of the living.

eu·ry·ha·line (yo͝or′ə-hā′līn′, -hăl′-īn′) *adj.* Capable of tolerating a wide range of salt water concentrations. Used of an aquatic organism.

eu·ryph·a·gous (yo͞o-rĭf′ə-gəs) *adj. Ecology.* Feeding on a wide variety of foods.

eu·ryp·ter·id (yo͞o-rĭp′tər-ĭd) *n.* Any of various large, segmented aquatic arthropods of the order Eurypterida that existed from the Ordovician Period to the Permian Period. [From New Latin *Eurypterida,* order name, from pl. of *Eurypterus,* genus name : EURY– + Greek *pteron,* wing; see –PTER.]

eu·ry·ther·mal (yo͝or′ə-thûr′məl) also **eu·ry·ther·mic** (-mĭk) or **eu·ry·ther·mous** (-məs) *adj.* Adaptable to a wide range of temperatures. Used of an organism. **—eu′ry·therm′** *n.*

eu·ryth·mics also **eu·rhyth·mics** (yo͞o-rĭth′mĭks) *n. (used with a sing. verb).* The art of interpreting musical compositions by rhythmical, free-style bodily movement. **—eu·ryth′mic** *adj.*

eu·ryth·my also **eu·rhyth·my** (yo͞o-rĭth′mē) *n.* **1.** Harmony of proportion in architecture. **2.** A system of rhythmical body movements performed to a recitation of verse or prose. [Latin *eurythmia,* from Greek *eeuruthmia,* from *euruthmos,* rhythmic, well-proportioned : *eu-,* eu- + *rhuthmos,* proportion; see RHYTHM.]

eu·ry·top·ic (yo͝or′ĭ-tŏp′ĭk) *adj.* Able to adapt to a wide range of environmental conditions; widely distributed. Used of a plant or an animal. [Greek *eurus,* wide + Greek *topos,* place + –IC.] **—eu′ry·to·pic′i·ty** (-tō-pĭs′ĭ-tē) *n.*

Eu·se·bi·us of Cae·sa·re·a (yo͞o-sē′bē-əs; sē′zə-rē′ə, sĕs′ə-, sĕz′ə-). A.D. 260?–340? Palestinian theologian whose *Ecclesiastical History,* written in Greek, is a record of the chief events in the Christian Church until the year 324.

eu·sta·chian tube or **Eu·sta·chian tube** (yo͞o-stā′shən, -shē-ən, -kē-ən) *n. Anatomy.* A slender tube that connects the tympanic cavity with the nasal part of the pharynx and serves to equalize air pressure on either side of the eardrum. [After Bartolommeo EUSTACHIO.]

Eu·sta·chi·o (yo͞o-stä′kē-ō, ĕ′o͞o-stä′kyô), **Bartolommeo.** 1520–1574. Italian anatomist. A founder of modern anatomy, he is noted for his descriptions of the human ear and heart.

eu·sta·sy (yo͞o′stə-sē) *n., pl.* **-sies.** A worldwide change in sea level. [From *eustatic,* of eustasy : EU– + STAT(O)– + –IC.] **—eu·stat′ic** (-stăt′ĭk) *adj.*

eu·stele (yo͞o′stēl, yo͞o-stē′lē) *n. Botany.* The central cylinder in which the primary vascular tissue is arranged around a pith, as in most seed plants.

eu·tec·tic (yo͞o-tĕk′tĭk) *adj.* **1.** Of, relating to, or formed at the lowest possible temperature of solidification for any mixture of specified constituents. Used especially of an alloy whose melting point is lower than that of any other alloy composed of the same constituents in different proportions. **2.** Exhibiting the constitution or properties of such a solid. **—eutectic** *n.* **1.** A eutectic mixture, solution, or alloy. **2.** The eutectic temperature. [From Greek *eutēktos,* easily melted : *eu-,* eu- + *tēktos,* melted (from *tēkein,* to melt).]

Eu·ter·pe (yo͞o-tûr′pē) *n. Greek Mythology.* The Muse of lyric poetry and music.

eu·tha·na·sia (yo͞o′thə-nā′zhə, -zhē-ə) *n.* The act or practice of ending the life of an individual suffering from a terminal

Europa
Detail of *Rape of Europa*
by Francesco Albani
(1578–1660)

ă pat	oi boy
ā pay	ou out
âr care	o͝o took
ä father	o͞o boot
ĕ pet	ŭ cut
ē be	ûr urge
ĭ pit	th thin
ī pie	*th* this
îr pier	hw which
ŏ pot	zh vision
ō toe	ə about, item
ô paw	♦ regionalism

Stress marks: ′ (primary); ′ (secondary), as in **dictionary** (dĭk′shə-nĕr′ē)

illness or an incurable condition, as by lethal injection or the suspension of extraordinary medical treatment. [Greek, a good death : *eu-*, eu- + *thanatos*, death.]

eu·than·ize (yo͞o′thə-nīz′) also **eu·than·a·tize** (yo͞o-thăn′ə-tīz′) *tr.v.* **-ized, -iz·ing, -iz·es** also **-a·tized, -a·tiz·ing, -a·tiz·es.** To subject to euthanasia.

eu·then·ics (yo͞o-thĕn′ĭks) *n.* (*used with a sing. verb*). The study of the improvement of human functioning and well-being by improvement of living conditions. [From Greek *euthenein*, to flourish.] **—eu·then′ist** *n.*

eu·ther·i·an (yo͞o-thîr′ē-ən) *adj.* Of or belonging to the infraclass Eutheria, a division of mammals to which all the placental mammals belong. [From New Latin *Eutheria*, infraclass name : Greek *eu-*, eu- + *thēria*, pl. of *thērion*, wild animal; see TREACLE.] **—eu·ther′i·an** *n.*

eu·troph·ic (yo͞o-trŏf′ĭk, -trō′fĭk) *adj. Ecology.* Having waters rich in mineral and organic nutrients that promote a proliferation of plant life, especially algae, which reduces the dissolved oxygen content and often causes the extinction of other organisms. Used of a lake or pond. [From Greek *eutrophos*, well-nourished : *eu-*, eu- + *trephein*, to nourish.] **—eu·troph′i·ca′tion** *n.* **—eu′tro·phy** (yo͞o′trə-fē) *n.*

eux·e·nite (yo͞ok′sə-nīt′) *n.* A lustrous, blackish-brown rare-earth mineral consisting primarily of cerium, erbium, titanium, uranium, and yttrium. [Greek *euxenos*, kind to strangers (from its unusual composition) (*eu-*, eu- + *xenos*, stranger; see **ghos-ti-** in Appendix) + -ITE[1].]

eV *abbr.* Electron volt.

EVA *abbr.* Extravehicular activity.

e·vac·u·ant (ĭ-văk′yo͞o-ənt) *adj.* Causing evacuation, especially of the bowels; purgative. **—evacuant** *n.* A purgative.

e·vac·u·ate (ĭ-văk′yo͞o-āt′) *v.* **-at·ed, -at·ing, -ates.** *—tr.* **1.a.** To empty or remove the contents of. **b.** To create a vacuum in. **2.** To excrete or discharge (waste matter), especially from the bowels. **3.a.** To relinquish military possession or occupation of (a town, for example). **b.** To withdraw or send away (troops or inhabitants) from a threatened area. **4.** To withdraw or depart from; vacate. *—intr.* **1.** To withdraw from or vacate a place or area, especially as a protective measure. **2.** To excrete waste matter from the body. [Middle English *evacuaten*, from Latin *ēvacuāre*, *ēvacuāt-*, to empty out : *ē-*, *ex-*, ex- + *vacuus*, empty (from *vacāre*, to be empty; see **eu-**[2] in Appendix).] **—e·vac′u·a′tive** *adj.* **—e·vac′u·a′tor** *n.*

e·vac·u·a·tion (ĭ-văk′yo͞o-ā′shən) *n.* **1.** The act of evacuating or the condition of being evacuated. **2.** *Physiology.* **a.** Discharge of waste materials from the excretory passages of the body, especially from the bowels. **b.** The material so discharged.

e·vac·u·ee (ĭ-văk′yo͞o-ē′) *n.* A person evacuated from a dangerous area.

e·vade (ĭ-văd′) *v.* **e·vad·ed, e·vad·ing, e·vades.** *—tr.* **1.** To escape or avoid by cleverness or deceit: *evade arrest.* **2.a.** To avoid fulfilling, answering, or performing: *evade responsibility.* See Synonyms at **escape. b.** To fail to make payment of (taxes). **3.** To avoid giving a direct answer to. **4.** To baffle or elude: *The accident evades explanation.* *—intr.* **1.** To practice evasion. **2.** To use cleverness or deceit in avoiding or escaping. [French *évader*, from Latin *ēvādere* : *ē-*, *ex-*, ex- + *vādere*, to go.] **—e·vad′a·ble, e·vad′i·ble** *adj.* **—e·vad′er** *n.*

e·vag·i·nate (ĭ-văj′ə-nāt′) *tr.v.* **-nat·ed, -nat·ing, -nates.** To cause (a body part) to turn inside out by eversion of an inner surface. [Latin *ēvāgināre*, *ēvāgināt-*, to unsheath : *ē-*, *ex-*, ex- + *vāgīna*, sheath.] **—e·vag′i·na′tion** *n.*

e·val·u·ate (ĭ-văl′yo͞o-āt′) *tr.v.* **-at·ed, -at·ing, -ates. 1.** To ascertain or fix the value or worth of. **2.** To examine and judge carefully; appraise. See Synonyms at **estimate. 3.** *Mathematics.* To calculate the numerical value of; express numerically. [Back-formation from *evaluation*, from French *évaluation*, from Old French, from *evaluer*, to evaluate : *e-*, out (from Latin *ē-*, *ex-*; see EX–) + *value*, value; see VALUE.] **—e·val′u·a′tion** *n.* **—e·val′u·a·tive** *adj.* **—e·val′u·a·tor** *n.*

evan. *abbr.* Evangelical; evangelist.

ev·a·nesce (ĕv′ə-nĕs′) *intr.v.* **-nesced, -nesc·ing, -nesc·es.** To dissipate or disappear like vapor. See Synonyms at **disappear.** [Latin *ēvānēscere*, to vanish : *ē-*, *ex-*, ex- + *vānēscere*, to disappear (from *vānus*, empty; see **eu-**[2] in Appendix).] **—ev′a·nes′cence** *n.*

ev·a·nes·cent (ĕv′ə-nĕs′ənt) *adj.* Vanishing or likely to vanish like vapor. See Synonyms at **transient. —ev′a·nes′cent·ly** *adv.*

evang. *abbr.* Evangelical; evangelist.

e·van·gel (ĭ-văn′jəl) *n.* **1.** The Christian gospel. **2.** An evangelist. [Middle English *evaungel*, from Late Latin *ēvangelium*, from Greek *euangelion*, good news, from *euangelos*, bringing good news : *eu-*, eu- + *angelos*, messenger.]

e·van·gel·i·cal (ē′văn-jĕl′ĭ-kəl, ĕv′ən-) also **e·van·gel·ic** (-jĕl′ĭk) *—adj. Abbr.* **evan., evang. 1.** Of, relating to, or in accordance with the Christian gospel, especially one of the four gospel books of the New Testament. **2. Evangelical.** Of, relating to, or being a Protestant church that founds its teaching on the gospel. **3. Evangelical.** Of, relating to, or being a Christian church believing in the sole authority and inerrancy of the Bible, in salvation only through regeneration, and in a spiritually transformed personal life. **4. Evangelical. a.** Of or relating to the Lutheran churches in Germany and Switzerland. **b.** Of or relating to all Protestant churches in Germany. **5.** Of or relating to the group in the Church of England that stresses personal conversion and salvation by faith. **6.** Characterized by ardent or crusading enthusiasm; zealous: *an evangelical liberal.* *—n.* **Evangelical.** A member of an evangelical church or party. **—e′van·gel′i·cal·ly** *adv.*

e·van·gel·i·cal·ism (ē′văn-jĕl′ĭ-kə-lĭz′əm, ĕv′ən-) *n.* **1.** Often **Evangelicalism.** Evangelical beliefs or doctrines. **2.** Adherence to a church or party professing evangelical beliefs or doctrines.

e·van·gel·ism (ĭ-văn′jə-lĭz′əm) *n.* **1.** Zealous preaching and dissemination of the gospel, as through missionary work. **2.** Militant zeal for a cause. **—e·van′gel·is′tic** (-jə-lĭs′tĭk) *adj.* **—e·van′gel·is′ti·cal·ly** *adv.*

e·van·gel·ist (ĭ-văn′jə-lĭst) *n. Abbr.* **evan., evang. 1.** Often **Evangelist.** Any one of the authors of the four New Testament gospel books: Matthew, Mark, Luke, or John. **2.** One who practices evangelism, especially a Protestant preacher or missionary.

e·van·gel·ize (ĭ-văn′jə-līz′) *v.* **-ized, -iz·ing, -iz·es.** *—tr.* **1.** To preach the gospel to. **2.** To convert to Christianity. *—intr.* To preach the gospel. **—e·van′gel·i·za′tion** (-jə-lĭ-zā′shən) *n.* **—e·van′gel·iz′er** *n.*

Ev·ans (ĕv′ənz), Sir **Arthur John.** 1851–1941. British archaeologist who unearthed in Crete remnants of a Bronze Age civilization that he named Minoan, after the legendary King Minos.

Evans, Herbert McLean. 1882–1971. American anatomist who isolated four pituitary hormones and discovered vitamin E (1922).

Evans, Mary Ann. See George **Eliot.**

Evans, Mount. A peak, 4,350.5 m (14,264 ft) high, of north-central Colorado in the Front Range of the Rocky Mountains.

Evans, Walker. 1903–1975. American photographer noted for his studies of architecture and for his images of the rural South during the 1930's.

Ev·ans·ton (ĕv′ən-stən). A city of northeast Illinois on Lake Michigan north of Chicago. Mainly residential, it is the seat of Northwestern University (chartered 1851). Population, 73,706.

Ev·ans·ville (ĕv′ənz-vĭl′). A city of extreme southwest Indiana on the Ohio River and the Kentucky border. It is the shipping center for a coal, oil, and farm region. Population, 130,496.

evap. *abbr.* Evaporate.

e·vap·o·ra·ble (ĭ-văp′ər-ə-bəl) *adj.* That can evaporate or undergo evaporation: *evaporable liquids.* **—e·vap′o·ra·bil′i·ty** *n.*

e·vap·o·rate (ĭ-văp′ə-rāt′) *v.* **-rat·ed, -rat·ing, -rates.** *Abbr.* **evap.** *—tr.* **1.a.** To convert or change into a vapor. **b.** To draw off in the form of vapor. **2.** To draw moisture from, as by heating, leaving only the dry solid portion. **3.** To deposit (a metal) on a substrate by vacuum sublimation. *—intr.* **1.a.** To change into vapor. **b.** To pass off in or as vapor. **2.** To produce vapor. **3.** To disappear; vanish: *Our fears at last evaporated.* See Synonyms at **disappear.** [Middle English *evaporaten*, from Latin *ēvapōrāre*, *ēvapōrāt-* : *ē-*, *ex-*, ex- + *vapor*, steam.] **—e·vap′o·ra′tion** *n.* **—e·vap′o·ra′tive** *adj.* **—e·vap′o·ra′tive·ly** *adv.* **—e·vap′o·ra·tiv′i·ty** (-ərə-tĭv′ĭ-tē) *n.* **—e·vap′o·ra′tor** *n.*

e·vap·o·rat·ed milk (ĭ-văp′ə-rā′tĭd) *n.* Concentrated, unsweetened milk made by evaporating some of the water from whole milk.

e·vap·o·rite (ĭ-văp′ə-rīt′) *n.* A sedimentary deposit that results from the evaporation of seawater. [EVAPOR(ATION) + -ITE[1].] **—e·vap′o·rit′ic** (-rĭt′ĭk) *adj.*

e·va·sion (ĭ-vā′zhən) *n.* **1.** The act or an instance of evading. **2.** A means of evading; a subterfuge. [Middle English *evasioun*, from Old French *evasion*, from Late Latin *ēvāsiō*, *ēvāsiōn-*, from Latin *ēvāsus*, past participle of *ēvādere*, to evade. See EVADE.]

e·va·sive (ĭ-vā′sĭv) *adj.* **1.** Inclined or intended to evade: *took evasive action.* **2.** Intentionally vague or ambiguous: *an evasive statement.* **—e·va′sive·ly** *adv.* **—e·va′sive·ness** *n.*

eve (ēv) *n.* **1.** The evening or day preceding a special day, such as a holiday. **2.** The period immediately preceding a certain event: *the eve of war.* **3.** Evening. [Middle English *eve*, variant of *even*. See EVEN[2].]

Eve (ēv). In the Old Testament, the first woman and the wife of Adam.

e·vec·tion (ĭ-vĕk′shən) *n.* Solar perturbation of the lunar orbit. [Latin *ēvectiō*, *ēvectiōn-*, a going up, from *ēvectus*, past participle of *ēvehere*, to raise up : *ē-*, *ex-*, up from; see EX– + *vehere*, to carry; see **wegh-** in Appendix.] **—e·vec′tion·al** *adj.*

Eve·lyn (ēv′lĭn, ĕv′-), **John.** 1620–1706. English writer whose *Diary*, published in 1818, is a valuable record of his times.

e·ven¹ (ē′vən) *adj.* **1.a.** Having a horizontal surface; flat: *an even floor.* **b.** Having no irregularities, roughness, or indentations; smooth. See Synonyms at **level. c.** Being in the same plane or line; parallel: *The picture is even with the window.* **2.a.** Having no variations or fluctuations; uniform: *the even rhythm of his breathing.* See Synonyms at **steady. b.** Of uniform distribution: *an even application of varnish.* **c.** Placid; calm: *an even temperament.* **3.a.** Equal or identical in degree, extent, or amount: *Use even amounts of butter and sugar.* **b.** Equally matched or balanced: *an even fight.* **c.** Just; fair: *an even bargain.* **d.** Having nothing due on either side; square: *If we each take half, then we'll be even.* **e.** Having exacted full revenge. **4.** Having equal probability; as likely as not: *an even chance of winning.* **5.** *Sports.* **a.**

ă pat · ā pay · âr care · ä father · ĕ pet · ē be · ĭ pit · ī pie · îr pier · ŏ pot · ō toe · ô paw · oi boy · ou out · o͝o took · o͞o boot · ŭ cut · ûr urge · th thin · *th* this · hw which · zh vision · ə about, item · ♦ regionalism

Stress marks: ′ (primary); ′ (secondary), as in **dictionary** (dĭk′shə-nĕr′ē)

Having an equal score: *The teams are even at halftime.* **b.** Being equal for each opponent. Used of a score. **6.** *Mathematics.* **a.** Exactly divisible by 2. **b.** Characterized or indicated by a number exactly divisible by 2. **7. a.** Having an even number in a series. **b.** Having an even number of members. **8.** Having an exact amount, extent, or number; precise: *an even pound; an even foot.* **—even** *adv.* **1. a.** To a greater degree or extent. Used as an intensive with comparative adjectives and adverbs: *Looked sick and felt even worse.* **b.** Indeed; moreover. Used as an intensive: *He was depressed, even suicidal. Even a child knows better.* **c.** Used as an intensive to indicate something that is unexpected: *declined even to consider the idea.* **2.** At the same time as; already; just: *Even as we watched, the building collapsed.* **3.** To a degree that extends; fully: *loyal even unto death.* **4.** Exactly; precisely: *It was even as he said: the jewel was gone.* **—even** *tr. & intr.v.* **e·vened, e·ven·ing, e·vens.** To make or become even. ***—idiom.* on an even keel.** In a stable or unimpaired state: *"There was good reason to keep relations with Washington on an even keel"* (Helen Kitchen). [Middle English, from Old English *efen.*] **—e′ven·er** *n.* **—e′ven·ly** *adv.* **—e′ven·ness** *n.*

e·ven² (ē′vən) *n. Archaic.* Evening. [Middle English, from Old English *ǣfen.*]

e·ven·fall (ē′vən-fôl′) *n.* The beginning of evening; twilight.

e·ven·hand·ed (ē′vən-hăn′dĭd) *adj.* Showing no partiality; fair. **—e′ven·hand′ed·ly** *adv.* **—e′ven·hand′ed·ness** *n.*

♦ **eve·ning** (ēv′nĭng) *n. Abbr.* **evg. 1.** The period of decreasing daylight between afternoon and night. **2.** The period between sunset or the evening meal and bedtime: *a quiet evening at home.* **3.** A later period or time: *in the evening of one's life.* **4.** *Chiefly Southern U.S.* Middle to late afternoon. [Middle English, from Old English *ǣfnung,* from *ǣfnian,* to become evening, from *ǣfen,* evening.]

evening dress *n.* **1.** Clothing worn for evening social events. Also called *evening clothes.* **2.** See **evening gown.**

evening gown *n.* A woman's formal dress. Also called *evening dress.*

Eve·ning Prayer (ēv′nĭng prâr) *n.* A daily evening service in the Anglican Church. Also called *evensong.*

evening primrose *n.* Any of various North American plants of the genus *Oenothera,* characteristically having four-petaled yellow flowers that open in the evening. Also called *sundrops.*

evening star *n.* A planet, especially Venus or Mercury, that crosses the local meridian before midnight and is prominent in the west shortly after sunset.

evening stock *n.* A Eurasian plant *(Matthiola longipetala)* having fragrant purple flowers that bloom at night.

evening trumpet flower *n.* See **Carolina jasmine.**

eve·ning·wear (ēv′nĭng-wâr′) *n.* Evening attire and accessories for women.

E·ven·ki (ĭ-wĕng′kē, ĭ-vĕng′-) also **E·wen·ki** (ĭ-wĕng′kē) *n., pl.* **Evenki** or **-kis** also **Ewenki** or **-kis. 1.** A member of a people inhabiting a large area of eastern Siberia in the Soviet Union and northern Nei Monggol (Inner Mongolia) in China. **2.** The Tungusic language of the Evenki. Also called *Tungus.* [Russian, Evenki people, from Evenki *əwənkī.*]

e·ven-pin·nate (ē′vən-pĭn′āt) *adj. Botany.* Of or relating to a compound leaf not terminating in a leaflet.

e·ven·song (ē′vən-sông′, -sŏng′) *n.* **1.** See **Evening Prayer. 2.** *Roman Catholic Church.* A service that includes the office of Vespers. **3.** A song sung in the evening. **4.** *Archaic.* Evening.

e·ven-ste·ven (ē′vən-stē′vən) *adj. Informal.* **1.** Having nothing due or owed on either side: *an even-steven transaction.* **2.** Having an equal score, as in a game or contest. [EVEN¹ + the personal name *Steven,* used as rhyming slang.]

e·vent (ĭ-vĕnt′) *n.* **1. a.** Something that takes place; an occurrence. **b.** A significant occurrence or happening. See Synonyms at **occurrence. c.** A social gathering or activity. **2.** The final result; the outcome. **3.** *Sports.* A contest or an item in a sports program. **4.** *Physics.* A phenomenon or occurrence located at a single point in space-time, regarded as the fundamental observational entity in relativity theory. ***—idioms.* at all events.** In any case. **in any event.** In any case. **in the event.** If it should happen; in case. [Latin *ēventus,* from past participle of *ēvenīre,* to happen : *ē-, ex-,* ex- + *venīre,* to come; see **gʷā-** in Appendix.] **—e·vent′less** *adj.*

e·ven-tem·pered (ē′vən-tĕm′pərd) *adj.* Easygoing; calm.

e·vent·ful (ĭ-vĕnt′fəl) *adj.* **1.** Full of events: *an eventful week.* **2.** Important; momentous: *an eventful decision.* **—e·vent′ful·ly** *adv.* **—e·vent′ful·ness** *n.*

e·ven·tide (ē′vən-tīd′) *n.* Evening. [Middle English, from Old English *ǣfentīd* : *ǣfen,* evening + *tīd,* time; see **dā-** in Appendix.]

event planner *n.* A usually professional planner of parties or social events, as for corporate or government officials.

e·ven·tu·al (ĭ-vĕn′cho͞o-əl) *adj.* **1.** Occurring at an unspecified time in the future; ultimate: *his eventual failure.* See Synonyms at **last¹. 2.** *Archaic.* Dependent on circumstance; contingent. [French *éventuel,* from Latin *ēventus,* outcome. See EVENT.]

e·ven·tu·al·i·ty (ĭ-vĕn′cho͞o-ăl′ĭ-tē) *n., pl.* **-ties.** Something that may occur; a possibility.

e·ven·tu·al·ly (ĭ-vĕn′cho͞o-ə-lē) *adv.* At an unspecified future time: *eventually rose to the position of vice president.*

e·ven·tu·ate (ĭ-vĕn′cho͞o-āt′) *intr.v.* **-at·ed, -at·ing, -ates.** To result ultimately: *The epidemic eventuated in the deaths of thousands.*

ev·er (ĕv′ər) *adv.* **1.** At all times; always: *ever hoping to strike it rich.* **2. a.** At any time: *Have you ever been to Europe?* **b.** In any way; at all: *How did they ever manage?* See Usage Note at **rarely. 3.** To a great extent or degree. Used for emphasis often with *so: He was ever so sorry. Was she ever mad!* ***—idioms.* ever and again** (or **anon**). Now and then; occasionally. **for ever and a day.** Always; forever. [Middle English, from Old English *ǣfre.* See **aiw-** in Appendix.]

ev·er·bear·ing (ĕv′ər-bâr′ĭng) *adj.* Producing continuously, as a tree or shrub.

ev·er·bloom·ing (ĕv′ər-blo͞o′mĭng) *adj.* Blooming throughout the growing season.

Ev·er·est (ĕv′ər-ĭst, ĕv′rĭst), **Mount.** A mountain, 8,853.5 m (29,028 ft) high, of the central Himalaya Mountains on the border of Tibet and Nepal. The highest elevation in the world, it was first scaled in 1953 by members of an expedition including Sir Edmund Hillary and Tenzing Norgay.

Ev·er·ett (ĕv′ər-ĭt, ĕv′rĭt). **1.** A city of eastern Massachusetts, an industrial suburb of Boston. Population, 37,195. **2.** A city of northwest Washington on Puget Sound north of Seattle. It has lumbering, paper, and aircraft industries. Population, 54,413.

Everett, Edward. 1794–1865. American clergyman, orator, educator, and diplomat whose many offices included U.S. representative from Massachusetts (1825–1835), minister to Great Britain (1841–1845), and secretary of state (1852–1853).

ev·er·glade (ĕv′ər-glād′) *n.* A tract of marshland, usually under water and covered in places with tall grass. [After the EVERGLADES.]

Ev·er·glades (ĕv′ər-glādz′). A subtropical swamp area of southern Florida including **Everglades National Park.** It is noted for its wildlife, especially crocodiles, alligators, and egrets.

ev·er·green (ĕv′ər-grēn′) *adj.* **1.** Having foliage that persists and remains green throughout the year. **2.** Perenially fresh or interesting; enduring. **—evergreen** *n.* **1.** A tree, shrub, or plant having foliage that persists and remains green throughout the year. **2. evergreens.** Twigs or branches of evergreen plants used as decoration. **3.** Something that remains perennially fresh, interesting, or well liked.

Ev·er·green Park (ĕv′ər-grēn′). A village of northeast Illinois, a residential suburb of Chicago. Population, 22,260.

ev·er·last·ing (ĕv′ər-lăs′tĭng) *adj.* **1.** Lasting forever; eternal. **2. a.** Continuing indefinitely or for a long period of time. **b.** Persisting too long; tedious: *everlasting complaints.* **—everlasting** *n.* **1. Everlasting.** God. Used with *the.* **2.** Eternal duration; eternity. **3.** Any of various plants, such as the strawflower or one of the genus *Anaphalis,* that retain form and color long after they are dry. **—ev′er·last′ing·ly** *adv.* **—ev′er·last′ing·ness** *n.*

ev·er·more (ĕv′ər-môr′, -mōr′) *adv.* **1.** Forever; always. **2.** In a future time.

Ev·ers (ĕv′ərz), **Medgar Wiley.** 1925–1963. American civil rights worker in Mississippi who was killed by a sniper. His work was continued by his brother **Charles** (born 1923).

e·ver·sion (ĭ-vûr′zhən, -shən) *n.* **1. a.** The act of turning inside out. **b.** The condition of being turned inside out. **2.** The condition of being turned outward. [Middle English *eversioun,* from Old French *eversion,* from Latin *ēversiō, ēversiōn-,* from *ēversus,* past participle of *ēvertere,* to overturn. See EVERT.] **—e·ver′si·ble** (-sə-bəl) *adj.*

e·vert (ĭ-vûrt′) *tr.v.* **e·vert·ed, e·vert·ing, e·verts.** To turn inside out or outward. [Back-formation from Middle English *everted,* turned upside down, from Latin *ēvertus,* past participle of *ēvertere,* to overturn : *ē-, ex-,* ex- + *vertere,* to turn; see **wer-²** in Appendix.]

Ev·ert (ĕv′ərt), **Christine Marie.** Born 1954. American tennis player who won women's singles titles at the U.S. Open (1975–1978, 1980, and 1982) and Wimbledon (1974, 1976, and 1981).

♦ **ev·er·where** (ĕv′ər-hwâr′, -wâr′) *adv. Chiefly Southern U.S.* **1.** Everywhere. **2.** Wherever.

♦ ***REGIONAL NOTE:*** Inversion—the reversal of the two halves of a compound word—is a common process in Southern dialects. It affects a number of indefinite pronouns (*whichever, whatever, whoever*) ending in *-ever,* yielding *everwhich, everwhat,* and *everwho.* The commonly occurring *everwhere* can be an example of inversion when it means "wherever" but illustrates elision of an unstressed syllable in its meaning "everywhere." Other examples of Southern inversion cited by Craig M. Carver in *American Regional Dialects* are *peckerwood, hoppergrass, doll-baby, tie-tongued, doghanged* (meaning "hangdog"), and *right-out* ("outright").

♦ **ev·er·which** (ĕv′ər-hwĭch′, -wĭch′) *pron. Chiefly Southern U.S.* Whichever. See Regional Note at **everwhere.**

eve·ry (ĕv′rē) *adj.* **1. a.** Constituting each and all members of a group without exception. **b.** Being all possible: *had every chance of winning, but lost.* **2.** Being each of a specified succession of objects or intervals: *every third seat; every two hours.* **3.** The highest degree or expression of: *showed us every attention; had every hope of succeeding.* ***—idioms.* every bit.** *Informal.* In all ways; equally: *He is every bit as mean as she is.* **every now and then** (or **again**). From time to time; occasionally. **every**

Everglades
Spanish moss hanging from bald cypress trees

Chris Evert
Playing at the French Open tournament, 1986

once in a while. From time to time; occasionally. **every other.** Each alternate: *She went to visit her aunt every other week.* **every so often.** At intervals; occasionally. **every which way.** *Informal.* **1.** In every direction. **2.** In complete disorder. [Middle English *everi, everich,* from Old English *ǣfre ǣlc* : *ǣfre,* ever; see **aiw-** in Appendix + *ǣlc,* each; see **līk-** in Appendix.]

USAGE NOTE: *Every* is representative of a large class of English words and expressions that are singular in form but felt to be plural in sense. The class includes, for example, noun phrases introduced by *every, any,* and certain uses of *some.* These expressions invariably take a singular verb; we say *Every car has* (not *have*) *been tested. Anyone is* (not *are*) *liable to fall ill.* But when a sentence contains a pronoun whose antecedent is introduced by *every,* grammar and sense pull in different directions. The grammar of these expressions requires a singular pronoun, as in *Every car must have its brakes tested,* but people persist in using the plural pronoun, as in *Every car must have their brakes tested.* Although the latter pattern is common in the speech of all groups, it is still widely regarded as grammatically incorrect in writing. • The effort to adhere to the grammatical rule leads to various complications, however. The first is grammatical. When a pronoun refers to a phrase containing *every* or *any* that falls within a different independent clause, the pronoun cannot be singular. Thus it is simply not English to say *Every man left; he took his raincoat with him.* Nor can one say *No one could be seen, could he?* Writers unwilling to use plural forms in these examples must find another way of expressing their meaning, either by rephrasing the sentence so as to get the pronoun into the same clause (as in *Every man left, taking his raincoat with him*) or by substituting another word for *every* or *any* (as in *All the men left; they took their raincoats with them.*) • The second complication is political. When a phrase introduced by *every* or *any* refers to a group containing both men and women, what shall be the gender of the singular pronoun? This matter is discussed in the Usage Note at *he.* See Usage Notes at **all, any, each, either, he[1], neither, none.**

eve·ry·bod·y (ĕv′rē-bŏd′ē, -bŭd′ē) *pron.* Every person; everyone.

eve·ry·day (ĕv′rē-dā′) *adj.* **1.** Appropriate for ordinary days or routine occasions: *a suit for everyday wear.* **2.** Commonplace; ordinary: *everyday worries.* **—everyday** *n.* The ordinary or routine day or occasion: *"It was not an isolated, violent episode. It had become part of the everyday"* (Sherry Turkle). **—eve′ry·day′ness** *n.*

Eve·ry·man or **eve·ry·man** (ĕv′rē-măn′) *n.* An ordinary person, representative of the human race.

every man jack *n. Informal.* Every single person of a group.

eve·ry·one (ĕv′rē-wŭn′) *pron.* Every person; everybody. See Usage Note at **every, he[1].**

eve·ry·place (ĕv′rē-plās′) *adv. Informal.* Everywhere.

USAGE NOTE: The forms *everyplace* (or *every place*), *anyplace* (or *any place*), *someplace* (or *some place*), and *no place* are widely used in speech and informal writing as equivalents for *everywhere, anywhere, somewhere,* and *nowhere.* Though these usages are not incorrect, they should be avoided in formal writing. But when the two-word expressions *every place, any place, some place,* and *no place* are used to mean "every (any, some, no) spot or location," they are entirely appropriate at all levels of style. The distinction between the two meanings is often subtle, but acceptability can often be gauged by seeing whether an expression with *-where* can be substituted. Thus in the sentence *She has taken extensive photographs of every place she's ever lived in,* substitution of *everywhere* would make no sense, and one can conclude that the sentence would be inappropriate in formal writing.

eve·ry·thing (ĕv′rē-thĭng′) *pron.* **1. a.** All things or all of a group of things. **b.** All relevant matters: *told each other everything.* **2.** The most important fact or consideration: *In business, timing is everything.*

eve·ry·where (ĕv′rē-hwâr′, -wâr′) *adv.* In any or every place; in all places. See Usage Note at **everyplace.**

Eve·ry·wom·an or **eve·ry·wom·an** (ĕv′rē-wo͝om′ən) *n.* An ordinary woman, representative of all women.

evg. *abbr.* Evening.

e·vict (ĭ-vĭkt′) *tr.v.* **e·vict·ed, e·vict·ing, e·victs. 1.** To put out (a tenant, for example) by legal process; expel. **2.** To force out; eject. See Synonyms at **eject. 3.** *Law.* To recover (property, for example) by a superior claim or legal process. [Middle English *evicten,* from Latin *ēvincere, ēvict-,* to vanquish : *ē-, ex-,* intensive pref.; see EX– + *vincere,* to defeat; see **weik-[3]** in Appendix.] **—e·vict·ee′** (ĭ-vĭk-tē′, ĭ-vĭk′tē) *n.* **—e·vic′tion** *n.* **—e·vic′tor** *n.*

ev·i·dence (ĕv′ĭ-dəns) *n.* **1.** A thing or things helpful in forming a conclusion or judgment: *The broken window was evidence that a burglary had taken place. Scientists weigh the evidence for and against a hypothesis.* **2.** Something indicative; an outward sign: *evidence of grief on a mourner's face.* **3.** *Law.* The documentary or oral statements and the material objects admissible as testimony in a court of law. **—evidence** *tr.v.* **-denced, -denc·ing, -denc·es. 1.** To indicate clearly; exemplify or prove. **2.** To support by testimony; attest. **—*idiom.* in evidence. 1.** Plainly visible; to be seen: *It was early, and few pedestrians were in evidence on the city streets.* **2.** *Law.* As legal evidence: *submitted the photograph in evidence.* [Middle English, from Old French, from Late Latin *ēvidentia,* from Latin *ēvidēns, ēvident-,* obvious. See EVIDENT.]

ev·i·dent (ĕv′ĭ-dənt) *adj.* Easily seen or understood; obvious. See Synonyms at **apparent.** [Middle English, from Old French, from Latin *ēvidēns, ēvident-* : *ē-, ex-,* ex- + *vidēns,* present participle of *vidēre,* to see; see **weid-** in Appendix.]

ev·i·den·tial (ĕv′ĭ-dĕn′shəl) *adj. Law.* Of, providing, or constituting evidence. **—ev′i·den′tial·ly** *adv.*

ev·i·den·tia·ry (ĕv′ĭ-dĕn′shə-rē, -shē-ĕr′ē) *adj. Law.* **1.** Of evidence; evidential. **2.** For the presentation or determination of evidence: *an evidentiary hearing.*

ev·i·dent·ly (ĕv′ĭ-dənt-lē, ĕv′ĭ-dĕnt′lē) *adv.* **1.** Obviously; clearly. **2.** According to the evidence available: *The stranger approached the microphone, evidently intending to speak.*

e·vil (ē′vəl) *adj.* **e·vil·er, e·vil·est. 1.** Morally bad or wrong; wicked: *an evil tyrant.* See Synonyms at **bad[1]. 2.** Causing ruin, injury, or pain; harmful: *the evil effects of a poor diet.* **3.** Characterized by or indicating future misfortune; ominous: *evil omens.* **4.** Bad or blameworthy by report; infamous: *an evil reputation.* **5.** Characterized by anger or spite; malicious: *an evil temper.* **—evil** *n.* **1.** The quality of being morally bad or wrong; wickedness. **2.** That which causes harm, misfortune, or destruction: *a leader's power to do both good and evil.* **3.** An evil force, power, or personification. **4.** Something that is a cause or source of suffering, injury, or destruction: *the social evils of poverty and injustice.* **—evil** *adv. Archaic.* In an evil manner. [Middle English, from Old English *yfel.* See **wep-** in Appendix.] **—e′vil·ly** *adv.* **—e′vil·ness** *n.*

e·vil·do·er (ē′vəl-do͞o′ər) *n.* One that performs evil acts. **—e′vil·do′ing** *n.*

evil eye *n.* **1.** A look or stare believed to cause injury or misfortune to others. **2.** The presumed power to cause injury or misfortune to others by magic or supernatural means.

e·vil-mind·ed (ē′vəl-mīn′dĭd) *adj.* Having evil thoughts, opinions, or intentions. **—e′vil-mind′ed·ly** *adv.* **—e′vil-mind′ed·ness** *n.*

e·vince (ĭ-vĭns′) *tr.v.* **e·vinced, e·vinc·ing, e·vinc·es.** To show or demonstrate clearly; manifest: *evince distaste by grimacing.* [Latin *ēvincere,* to prevail, prove. See EVICT.] **—e·vinc′i·ble** *adj.*

e·vis·cer·ate (ĭ-vĭs′ə-rāt′) *v.* **-at·ed, -at·ing, -ates.** *—tr.* **1.** To remove the entrails of; disembowel. **2.** To take away a vital or essential part of: *a compromise that eviscerated the proposed bill.* **3.** *Medicine.* **a.** To remove the contents of (an organ). **b.** To remove an organ, such as an eye, from (a patient). *—intr. Medicine.* To protrude through a wound or surgical incision. [Latin *ēviscerāre, ēviscerāt-* : *ē-, ex-,* ex- + *viscera,* internal organs; see VISCERA.] **—e·vis′cer·a′tion** *n.*

ev·i·ta·ble (ĕv′ĭ-tə-bəl) *adj.* Possible to avoid; avoidable. [Latin *ēvītābilis,* from *ēvītāre,* to shun : *ex-,* ex- + *vītāre,* to avoid.]

ev·o·ca·tion (ĕv′ə-kā′shən ē′və-) *n.* **1.** The act of evoking. **2.** Creation anew through the power of the memory or imagination. **—ev′o·ca′tor** *n.*

e·voc·a·tive (ĭ-vŏk′ə-tĭv) *adj.* Tending or having the power to evoke. **—e·voc′a·tive·ly** *adv.* **—e·voc′a·tive·ness** *n.*

e·voke (ĭ-vōk′) *tr.v.* **e·voked, e·vok·ing, e·vokes. 1.** To summon or call forth: *actions that evoked our mistrust.* **2.** To call to mind by naming, citing, or suggesting: *songs that evoke old memories.* **3.** To create anew, especially by means of the imagination: *a novel that evokes the Depression in accurate detail.* [Latin *ēvocāre* : *ē-, ex-,* ex- + *vocāre,* to call; see **wek^{w}-** in Appendix.] **—ev′o·ca·ble** (ĕv′ə-kə-bəl, ĭ-vō′kə-) *adj.*

SYNONYMS: *evoke, educe, elicit.* The central meaning shared by these verbs is "to draw forth or bring out something latent, hidden, or unexpressed": *evoke laughter; couldn't educe significance from the event; trying to elicit the truth.*

ev·o·lute (ĕv′ə-lo͞ot′, ē′və-) *n. Mathematics.* The locus of the centers of curvature of a given curve. [From Latin *ēvolūtus,* past participle of *ēvolvere,* to unroll. See EVOLVE.]

ev·o·lu·tion (ĕv′ə-lo͞o′shən, ē′və-) *n.* **1.** A gradual process in which something changes into a different and usually more complex or better form. See Synonyms at **development. 2. a.** The process of developing. **b.** Gradual development. **3.** *Biology.* **a.** The theory that groups of organisms change with passage of time, mainly as a result of natural selection, so that descendants differ morphologically and physiologically from their ancestors. **b.** The historical development of a related group of organisms; phylogeny. **4.** A movement that is part of a set of ordered movements. **5.** *Mathematics.* The extraction of a root of a quantity. [Latin *ēvolūtiō, ēvolūtiōn-,* from *ēvolūtus,* past participle of *ēvolvere,* to unroll. See EVOLVE.] **—ev′o·lu′tion·al, ev′o·lu′tion·ar′y** (-shə-nĕr′ē) *adj.* **—ev′o·lu′tion·ar′i·ly** *adv.*

ev·o·lu·tion·ism (ĕv′ə-lo͞o′shə-nĭz′əm, ē′və-) *n.* **1.** A theory of biological evolution, especially that formulated by Charles Darwin. **2.** Advocacy of or belief in biological evolution. **—ev′o·lu′tion·ist** *n.*

e·volve (ĭ-vŏlv′) *v.* **e·volved, e·volv·ing, e·volves.** *—tr.* **1. a.** To develop or achieve gradually: *evolve a style of one's own.* **b.** To work (something) out; devise: *"the schemes he evolved to line his purse"* (S.J. Perelman). **2.** *Biology.* To develop (a characteristic) by evolutionary processes. **3.** To give off; emit. —*intr.* **1.** To undergo gradual change; develop: *an amateur acting group that evolved into a theatrical company.* **2.** *Biology.* To develop or arise through evolutionary processes. [Latin *ēvolvere,* to unroll : *ē-, ex-,* ex- + *volvere,* to roll; see **wel-**[2] in Appendix.] —**e·volv′a·ble** *adj.* —**e·volve′ment** *n.*

e·vul·sion (ĭ-vŭl′shən) *n.* A forcible extraction. [Latin *ēvolsiō, ēvolsiōn-,* from *ēvulsus,* past participle of *ēvellere,* to pull out : *ē-, ex-,* ex- + *vellere,* to pull.]

Ev·voia (ĕv′yä). See **Euboea.**

ev·zone (ev′zōn′) *n.* An infantryman of a special corps of the Greek army. [Modern Greek *euzōnos,* from Greek, well-girded, dressed for exercise : *eu-,* well; see EU– + *zōnē,* girdle.]

EW *abbr.* Enlisted woman.

ewe (yo͞o) *n.* A female sheep, especially when full-grown. [Middle English, from Old English *ēwe, eōwu.* See **owi-** in Appendix.]

E·we (ā′wā′, ā′vā′) *n., pl.* **Ewe** or **E·wes. 1.** A member of a people inhabiting southeast Ghana, southern Togo, and southern Benin. **2.** The Gbe language of the Ewe people.

Ew·ell (yo͞o′əl), **Richard Stoddert.** 1817–1872. American Confederate general who took part in the battles of Gettysburg (1863) and the Wilderness (1864).

ewe-neck (yo͞o′nĕk′) *n.* A defect in a horse or dog in which the neck is thin and has a concave arch. —**ewe′-necked′** *adj.*

E·wen·ki (ĭ-wĕng′kē) *n.* Variant of **Evenki.**

ew·er (yo͞o′ər) *n.* A pitcher, especially a decorative one with a base, an oval body, and a flaring spout. [Middle English *euer,* from Anglo-Norman, from Vulgar Latin **aquāria,* from Latin *aquārius,* of water, from *aqua,* water. See **akʷ-ā-** in Appendix.]

Ew·ing (yo͞o′ĭng). A community of west-central New Jersey north-northwest of Trenton. It is mainly residential. Population, 34,842.

ex[1] (ĕks) *prep.* **1.** Not including; without: *a stock price ex dividend.* **2.** *Abbr.* **x.** *Business.* Free of any transport or handling charges incurred before removal from a given location: *bought the goods ex warehouse.* **3.** From, but not having graduated with, the class of: *a Columbia alumnus, ex '70.* [Latin. See **eghs** in Appendix.]

ex[2] (ĕks) *n.* The letter *x.*

ex[3] (ĕks) *n. Slang.* A former spouse or partner. [From EX–.]

Ex or **Ex.** *abbr. Bible.* Exodus.

ex. *abbr.* **1.** Examination. **2.** Example. **3.** Except; exception. **4.** Exchange. **5.** Executive. **6.** Express. **7.** Extra.

ex– *pref.* **1.** Outside; out of; away from: *exodontia.* **2.** Not; without: *excaudate.* **3.** Former: *ex-president.* [Middle English, from Old French, from Latin. See **eghs** in Appendix.]

ex·ac·er·bate (ĭg-zăs′ər-bāt′) *tr.v.* **-bat·ed, -bat·ing, -bates.** To increase the severity, violence, or bitterness of; aggravate: *a speech that exacerbated racial tensions; a heavy rainfall that exacerbated the flood problems.* [Latin *exacerbāre, exacerbāt-* : *ex-,* intensive pref.; see EX– + *acerbāre,* to make harsh (from *acerbus,* harsh; see **ak-** in Appendix).] —**ex·ac′er·ba′tion** *n.*

ex·act (ĭg-zăkt′) *adj.* **1.** Strictly and completely in accord with fact; not deviating from truth or reality: *an exact account; an exact replica; your exact words.* **2.** Characterized by accurate measurements or inferences with small margins of error; not approximate: *an exact figure; an exact science.* **3.** Characterized by strict adherence to standards or rules: *an exact speaker.* —**exact** *tr.v.* **-act·ed, -act·ing, -acts. 1.** To force the payment or yielding of; extort: *exact tribute from a conquered people.* **2.** To demand and obtain by or as if by force or authority: *a harsh leader who exacts obedience.* See Synonyms at **demand.** [Latin *exāctus,* past participle of *exigere,* to weigh out, demand : *ex-,* ex- + *agere,* to weigh; see **ag-** in Appendix.] —**ex·act′a·ble** *adj.* —**ex·act′ness** *n.* —**ex·ac′tor, ex·act′er** *n.*

ex·act·a (ĭg-zăk′tə) *n. Sports & Games.* A method of betting, as on a horserace, in which the bettor must correctly pick those finishing in the first and second places in precisely that sequence. Also called *perfecta.* [From American Spanish *quiniela exacta,* exact quiniela (a game of chance), from Spanish *exacta,* feminine of *exacto,* from Latin *exāctus.* See EXACT.]

ex·act·ing (ĭg-zăk′tĭng) *adj.* **1.** Making severe demands; rigorous: *an exacting instructor.* **2.** Requiring great care, effort, or attention: *an exacting task.* See Synonyms at **burdensome.** —**ex·act′ing·ly** *adv.* —**ex·act′ing·ness** *n.*

ex·ac·tion (ĭg-zăk′shən) *n.* **1.a.** The act of exacting. **b.** Excessive or unjust demand; extortion. **2.** Something exacted.

ex·ac·ti·tude (ĭg-zăk′tĭ-to͞od, -tyo͞od′) *n.* The state or quality of being exact.

ex·act·ly (ĭg-zăkt′lē) *adv.* **1.** In an exact manner; accurately. **2.** In all respects; just: *Do exactly as you please.* **3.** As you say. Used to indicate agreement.

ex·ag·ger·ate (ĭg-zăj′ə-rāt′) *v.* **-at·ed, -at·ing, -ates.** —*tr.* **1.** To represent as greater than is actually the case; overstate: *exaggerate the size of the enemy force; exaggerated his own role in the episode.* **2.** To enlarge or increase to an abnormal degree: *thick lenses that exaggerated the size of her eyes.* —*intr.* To make overstatements. [Latin *exaggerāre, exaggerāt-,* to heap up, magnify : *ex-,* intensive pref.; see EX– + *aggerāre,* to pile up (from *agger,* pile, from *aggerere,* to bring to : *ad-,* ad- + *gerere,* to bring).] —**ex·ag′ger·at′ed·ly** *adv.* —**ex·ag′ger·a′tion** *n.* —**ex·ag′ger·a′tive, ex·ag′ger·a·to′ry** (-ə-tôr′ē, -tōr′ē) *adj.* —**ex·ag′ger·a′tor** *n.*

SYNONYMS: *exaggerate, inflate, magnify, overstate.* The central meaning shared by these verbs is "to represent something as being larger or greater than it actually is": *exaggerated the size of the fish he had caught; inflated her own importance; magnifying his part in their success; overstated their income on the mortgage application.*
ANTONYM: *minimize.*

ex·alt (ĭg-zôlt′) *tr.v.* **-alt·ed, -alt·ing, -alts. 1.** To raise in rank, character, or status; elevate: *exalted the shepherd to the rank of grand vizier.* **2.** To glorify, praise, or honor. **3.** To increase the effect or intensity of; heighten: *works of art that exalt the imagination.* **4.** *Obsolete.* To fill with sublime emotion; elate. [Middle English *exalten,* from Latin *exaltāre* : *ex-,* up, away; see EX– + *altus,* high; see **al-**[2] in Appendix.] —**ex·alt′er** *n.*

ex·al·ta·tion (ĕg′zôl-tā′shən) *n.* **1.** The act of exalting or the condition of being exalted. **2.** A state or feeling of intense, often excessive exhilaration or well-being. See Synonyms at **ecstasy. 3.** A flight of larks. See Synonyms at **flock**[1]**.**

ex·alt·ed (ĭg-zôl′tĭd) *adj.* **1.** Elevated in rank, character, or status. **2.** Lofty; sublime; noble: *an exalted dedication to liberty.* **3.** Exaggerated; inflated: *He has an exalted sense of his importance to the project.* —**ex·alt′ed·ly** *adv.* —**ex·alt′ed·ness** *n.*

ex·am (ĭg-zăm′) *n.* An examination; a test.

ex·a·men (ĭg-zā′mən) *n.* An examination; an investigation. [Latin *exāmen,* a weighing out. See EXAMINE.]

ex·am·i·nant (ĭg-zăm′ə-nənt) *n.* **1.** One who examines. **2.** One who is examined; an examinee.

ex·am·i·na·tion (ĭg-zăm′ə-nā′shən) *n. Abbr.* **ex. 1.** The act of examining or the state of being examined. **2.** A set of questions or exercises testing knowledge or skill. **3.** A formal interrogation: *examination of the witness.* —**ex·am′i·na′tion·al** *adj.*

ex·am·ine (ĭg-zăm′ĭn) *tr.v.* **-ined, -in·ing, -ines. 1.a.** To observe carefully or critically; inspect: *examined the room for clues.* **b.** To study or analyze: *examine a tissue sample under a microscope; examine the structure of a novel; examine one's own motives.* **2.** To test or check the condition or health of: *examine a patient.* **3.** To determine the qualifications, aptitude, or skills of by means of questions or exercises. **4.** To question formally, as to elicit facts or information; interrogate: *examine a witness under oath.* See Synonyms at **ask.** [Middle English *examinen,* from Old French *examiner,* from Latin *exāmināre,* from *exāmen,* a weighing out, from *exigere,* to weigh out. See EXACT.] —**ex·am′in·a·ble** *adj.* —**ex·am′in·er** *n.*

WORD HISTORY: A student who is being examined might prefer at times to deal with a swarm of bees rather than be weighed in the balance once again. The history of the word *examine* involves both phenomena. *Examine,* first recorded in English in a work composed before 1338, goes back to the Latin word *exāmināre,* which in turn is derived from *exāmen,* meaning both "a swarm of bees" and "the apparatus or process of weighing, balance." *Exāmen* has these senses because it is formed from the prefix *ex–,* "out of," and the root **ag–,* "to drive, force." The semantic possibilities of this combination are shown by the senses of the related verb *exigere,* which meant "to drive out," "to exact payment," "to demand," and "to inquire after or into." The verb *exāmināre* derived from *exāmen* has the sense "to swarm" as well as the senses "to weigh, balance," and "to consider critically."

ex·am·in·ee (ĭg-zăm′ə-nē′) *n.* One that is examined.

ex·am·ple (ĭg-zăm′pəl) *n. Abbr.* **ex. 1.** One that is representative of a group as a whole: *the squirrel, an example of a rodent; introduced each new word with examples of its use.* **2.** One serving as a pattern of a specific kind: *set a good example by arriving on time.* **3.** A similar case that constitutes a model or precedent: *a unique episode, without example in maritime history.* **4.a.** A punishment given as a warning or deterrent. **b.** One that has been given such a punishment: *made an example of the offender.* **5.** A problem or exercise used to illustrate a principle or method. —***idiom.* for example.** As an illustrative instance: *Wear something simple; for example, a skirt and blouse.* [Middle English, from Old French *example, essaumple,* from Latin *exemplum,* from *eximere,* to take out : *ex-,* ex- + *emere,* to take; see **em-** in Appendix.]

SYNONYMS: *example, instance, case, illustration, sample, specimen.* Each of these nouns refers to what is representative of or serves to explain a larger group or class. An *example* represents, usually typically, something of which it is a part and thereby demonstrates the character of the whole: *"Of the despotism to which unrestrained military power leads we have plenty of examples from Alexander to Mao"* (Samuel Eliot Morison). An *instance* is an example that is cited to prove or invalidate a contention or to illustrate a point: *an instance of flagrant corruption.* A *case* is an action, an occurrence, or a condition that constitutes a specific instance of something being discussed, decided, or treated: *a typical case of child neglect; very few cases of diphtheria.* An *illustration* is an example that clarifies or explains: *provided an illustration of the word in context; gave an illustration of her courage.* A *sample* is an actual part of something larger, presented as ev-

ewer
Mid 13th-century Persian engraved brass ewer

ă pat	oi boy
ā pay	ou out
âr care	o͝o took
ä father	o͞o boot
ĕ pet	ŭ cut
ē be	ûr urge
ĭ pit	th thin
ī pie	*th* this
îr pier	hw which
ŏ pot	zh vision
ō toe	ə about, item
ô paw	♦ regionalism

Stress marks: ′ (primary); ′ (secondary), as in **dictionary** (dĭk′shə-nĕr′ē)

idence of the quality or nature of the whole: *distributing samples of a new detergent; gave us a sample of her temper. Specimen* is sometimes synonymous with *sample,* but it often denotes an individual, representative member of a group or class: *This poem is a fair specimen of his work.* See also Synonyms at **ideal.**

ex·an·the·ma (ĕg′zăn-thē′mə) also **ex·an·them** (ĭg-zăn′-thəm) *n., pl.* **-them·a·ta** (-thĕm′ə-tə) or **-the·mas** also **-thems.** *Medicine.* **1.** A skin eruption accompanying certain infectious diseases. **2.** A disease, such as measles or scarlet fever, accompanied by a skin eruption. [Late Latin *exanthēma,* from Greek, eruption, from *exanthein,* to burst forth : *ex-,* ex- + *anthein,* to blossom (from *anthos,* flower).] **—ex·an′the·mat′ic** (ĭg-zăn′-thə-măt′ĭk), **ex′an·them′a·tous** (ĕg′zăn-thĕm′ə-təs) *adj.*

ex·arch¹ (ĕk′särk′) *n.* **1.** A bishop in the Eastern Orthodox Church ranking immediately below a patriarch. **2.** The ruler of a province in the Byzantine Empire. [Late Latin *exarchus,* an overseer, from Greek *exarkhos,* from *exarkhein,* to lead : *ex-,* ex- + *arkhein,* to rule.] **—ex·arch′al** *adj.* **—ex′ar′chate** (ĕk′sär′-kāt), **ex′ar′chy** (-kē) *n.*

ex·arch² (ĕk′särk′) *adj. Botany.* Of or relating to a xylem whose early development is away from the center and toward the periphery. [EX(O)– + Greek *arkhē,* beginning (from *arkhein,* to rule, begin).] **—ex′arch′** *n.*

ex·as·per·ate (ĭg-zăs′pə-rāt′) *tr.v.* **-at·ed, -at·ing, -ates. 1.** To make very angry or impatient; annoy greatly. **2.** To increase the gravity or intensity of: *"a scene . . . that exasperates his rose fever and makes him sneeze"* (Samuel Beckett). [Latin *exasperāre, exasperāt-* : *ex-,* intensive pref.; see EX– + *asperāre,* to make rough (from *asper,* rough).] **—ex·as′per·at′ed·ly** *adv.* **—ex·as′per·at′er** *n.* **—ex·as′per·at′ing·ly** *adv.*

ex·as·per·a·tion (ĭg-zăs′pə-rā′shən) *n.* **1.** The act or an instance of exasperating. **2.** The state of being exasperated; frustrated annoyance.

exc. *abbr.* **1.** Excellent. **2.** Except; exception.

Exc. *abbr.* Excellency.

Ex·cal·i·bur (ĕk-skăl′ə-bər) *n.* In Arthurian legend, the sword belonging to King Arthur. [Middle English, alteration (perhaps influenced by Latin *chalybs,* steel) of Medieval Latin *Caliburnus,* from Middle Welsh *Caletuwlch* or Middle Irish *Caladbolg,* a legendary sword.]

ex ca·the·dra (ĕks′ kə-thē′drə) *adv. & adj.* With the authority derived from one's office or position: *the pope speaking ex cathedra; ex cathedra determinations.* [Latin *ex cathedrā* : *ex,* from + *cathedrā,* ablative of *cathedra,* chair.]

ex·cau·date (ĕk-skô′dāt′) *adj.* Without a tail; tailless.

ex·ca·vate (ĕk′skə-vāt′) *v.* **-vat·ed, -vat·ing, -vates.** *—tr.* **1.** To make a hole in; hollow out: *excavate an ore-rich hillside.* **2.** To form by hollowing out. **3.** To remove by digging or scooping out. **4.** To expose or uncover by or as if by digging: *excavate an archaeological site.* *—intr.* To engage in digging, hollowing out, or removing. [Latin *excavāre, excavāt-,* to hollow out : *ex-,* ex- + *cavāre,* to hollow (from *cavus,* hollow; see **keuə-** in Appendix).]

ex·ca·va·tion (ĕk′skə-vā′shən) *n.* **1.** The act or process of excavating. **2.** A hole formed by excavating.

ex·ca·va·tor (ĕk′skə-vā′tər) *n.* One that excavates, especially a backhoe.

ex·ceed (ĭk-sēd′) *tr.v.* **-ceed·ed, -ceed·ing, -ceeds. 1.** To be greater than; surpass. **2.** To go beyond the limits of: *exceeded their authority.* See Synonyms at **excel.** [Middle English *exceden,* from Old French *exceder,* from Latin *excēdere* : *ex-,* ex- + *cēdere,* to go; see **ked-** in Appendix.]

ex·ceed·ing (ĭk-sē′dĭng) *adj.* Extreme; extraordinary: *a night of exceeding darkness.* **—exceeding** *adv. Archaic.* Exceedingly.

ex·ceed·ing·ly (ĭk-sē′dĭng-lē) *adv.* To an advanced or unusual degree; extremely.

ex·cel (ĭk-sĕl′) *v.* **-celled, -cel·ling, -cels.** *—tr.* To do or be better than; surpass. *—intr.* To show superiority; surpass others. [Middle English *excellen,* from Latin *excellere.* See **kel-²** in Appendix.]

SYNONYMS: *excel, surpass, exceed, transcend, outdo, outstrip.* These verbs mean to be or go beyond a limit or standard. To *excel* is to be preeminent (*excels at figure skating*) or to be or perform at a level higher than that of another or others (*excelled her father as a lawyer*). To *surpass* another is to be superior in performance, quality, or degree: *is surpassed by few as a debater; happiness that surpassed description. Exceed* can refer to being superior, as in quality (*an invention that exceeds all others in ingenuity*), to being greater than another, as in degree or quantity (*a salary exceeding 50 thousand dollars a year*), and to going beyond a proper limit (*exceed one's authority; exceed a speed limit*). *Transcend* often implies the attainment of a level so high that comparison is hardly possible: *Great art transcends mere rules of composition.* To *outdo* is to excel in doing or performing: *didn't want to be outdone in generosity. Outstrip* is often interchangeable with *outdo* but strongly suggests leaving another behind, as in a contest: *It is a case of the student outstripping the teacher.*

ex·cel·lence (ĕk′sə-ləns) *n.* **1.** The state, quality, or condition of excelling; superiority. **2.** Something in which one excels. **3. Excellence.** Excellency.

Ex·cel·len·cy (ĕk′sə-lən-sē) *n., pl.* **-cies.** *Abbr.* **Exc.** Used with *His, Her,* or *Your* as a title and form of address for certain high officials, such as viceroys, ambassadors, and governors.

ex·cel·lent (ĕk′sə-lənt) *adj.* **1.** *Abbr.* **exc.** Of the highest or finest quality; exceptionally good of its kind. **2.** *Archaic.* Superior. [Middle English, from Old French, from Latin *excellēns, excellent-,* present participle of *excellere,* to excel. See EXCEL.] **—ex′cel·lent·ly** *adv.*

ex·cel·si·or (ĭk-sĕl′sē-ər) *n.* Slender, curved wood shavings used especially for packing. [Originally a trade name.]

ex·cept (ĭk-sĕpt′) *prep. Abbr.* **ex., exc.** With the exclusion of; other than; but: *everyone except me.* **—except** *conj.* **1.** If it were not for the fact that; only: *I would buy the suit, except that it costs too much.* **2.** Otherwise than: *They didn't open their mouths except to complain.* **3.** Unless. **—except** *v.* **-cept·ed, -cept·ing, -cepts.** *—tr.* To leave out; exclude: *An admission fee is charged, but children are excepted.* *—intr.* To object: *Counsel excepted to the court's ruling.* [Middle English, from Latin *exceptus,* past participle of *excipere,* to exclude : *ex-,* ex- + *capere,* to take; see **kap-** in Appendix.]

USAGE NOTE: *Except* in the sense of "with the exclusion of" or "other than" is generally construed as a preposition, not a conjunction. A personal pronoun that follows *except* is therefore in the objective case: *No one except me knew it. Every member of the original cast was signed except her.*

ex·cept·ing (ĭk-sĕp′tĭng) *prep.* With the exception of. **—excepting** *conj.* Except.

ex·cep·tion (ĭk-sĕp′shən) *n. Abbr.* **ex., exc. 1.** The act of excepting or the condition of being excepted; exclusion. **2.** One that is excepted, especially a case that does not conform to a rule or generalization. **3.** An objection or a criticism: *opinions that are open to exception.* **4.** *Law.* A formal objection taken in the course of an action or a proceeding.

ex·cep·tion·a·ble (ĭk-sĕp′shə-nə-bəl) *adj.* Open or liable to objection or debate; objectionable or debatable. **—ex·cep′tion·a·bil′i·ty** *n.* **—ex·cep′tion·a·bly** *adv.*

USAGE NOTE: *Exceptionable* and *exceptional* are not interchangeable. Only *exceptionable* is equivalent to "objectionable" or "debatable"; *exceptional* is equivalent to "uncommon" or "extraordinary."

ex·cep·tion·al (ĭk-sĕp′shə-nəl) *adj.* **1.** Being an exception; uncommon. **2.** Well above average; extraordinary: *an exceptional memory.* See Usage Note at **exceptionable. 3.** Deviating widely from a norm, as of physical or mental ability: *special educational provisions for exceptional children.* **—ex·cep′tion·al′i·ty, ex·cep′tion·al·ness** *n.* **—ex·cep′tion·al·ly** (-shə-năl′ĭ-tē) *adv.*

ex·cep·tive (ĭk-sĕp′tĭv) *adj.* **1.** Of, being, or containing an exception. **2.** *Archaic.* Captious; faultfinding.

ex·cerpt (ĕk′sûrpt′) *n.* A passage or segment taken from a longer work, such as a literary or musical composition, a document, or a film. **—excerpt** (ĭk-sûrpt′) *tr.v.* **-cerpt·ed, -cerpt·ing, -cerpts. 1.** To select or use (a passage or segment from a longer work). **2.** To select or use material from (a longer work). [From Middle English, excerpted, from Latin *excerptus,* past participle of *excerpere,* to pick out : *ex-,* ex- + *carpere,* to pluck; see **kerp-** in Appendix.]

ex·cess (ĭk-sĕs′, ĕk′sĕs′) *n.* **1.** The state of exceeding what is normal or sufficient: *rains that filled the reservoirs to excess.* **2.** An amount or quantity beyond what is normal or sufficient; a surplus. **3.** The amount or degree by which one quantity exceeds another: *Profit is the excess of sales over costs.* **4.** Intemperance; overindulgence: *drank to excess.* **5.** A behavior or an action that exceeds proper or lawful bounds: *tried to avoid engaging in emotional excesses such as hysteria and fits of temper.* **—excess** *adj.* Being more than is usual, required, or permitted: *skimming off the excess fat.* See Synonyms at **superfluous. —excess** *tr.v.* **-cessed, -cess·ing, -cess·es.** To eliminate the job or position of. ***—idiom.* in excess of.** Greater than; more than: *unit sales in excess of 20 million.* [Middle English, from Old French, from Latin *excessus,* past participle of *excēdere,* to exceed. See EXCEED.]

ex·ces·sive (ĭk-sĕs′ĭv) *adj.* Exceeding a normal, usual, reasonable, or proper limit. **—ex·ces′sive·ly** *adv.* **—ex·ces′sive·ness** *n.*

SYNONYMS: *excessive, exorbitant, extravagant, immoderate, inordinate, extreme, unreasonable.* These adjectives mean exceeding a normal, usual, reasonable, or proper limit. *Excessive* describes a quantity, an amount, or a degree that is more than what is justifiable, tolerable, or desirable: *excessive speed; excessive drinking. Exorbitant* usually refers to a quantity or degree that far exceeds what is customary or fair: *exorbitant interest rates; an exorbitant price. Extravagant* sometimes specifies excessive or unwise expenditure of money (*extravagant gifts*); often it implies unbridled divergence from the bounds of reason or sound judgment (*extravagant claims; extravagant praise*). *Immoderate* denotes lack of due moderation: *immoderate expenses; immoderate enthusiasm. Inordinate* implies an overstepping of bounds imposed by authority or dictated by good sense: *inordinate vanity; inordinate demands. Extreme* suggests the utmost degree of excessiveness: *extreme joy; extreme danger; extreme opinions. Unreasonable* applies to what exceeds reasonable limits: *charged an unreasonable rent; made an unreasonable request.*

exch. *abbr.* **1.** Exchange. **2.** Also **Exch.** Exchequer.

ex·change (ĭks-chānj′) *v.* **-changed, -chang·ing, -chang·es.** —*tr.* **1.** To give in return for something received; trade: *exchange dollars for francs; exchanging labor for room and board.* **2.** To give and receive reciprocally; interchange: *exchange gifts; exchange ideas.* **3.** To give up for a substitute: *exchange a position in the private sector for a post in government.* **4.** To turn in for replacement: *exchange defective merchandise at a store.* —*intr.* **1.** To give something in return for something received; make an exchange. **2.** To be received in exchange: *At that time the British pound exchanged for $2.80.* —**exchange** *n.* *Abbr.* **exch., ex. 1.** The act or an instance of exchanging: *a prisoner exchange; an exchange of greetings.* **2.** One that is exchanged. **3.** A place where things are exchanged, especially a center where securities or commodities are bought and sold: *a stock exchange.* **4.** A telephone exchange. **5. a.** A system of payments using instruments, such as negotiable drafts, instead of money. **b.** The fee or percentage charged for participating in such a system of payment. **6.** A bill of exchange. **7.** A rate of exchange. **8.** The amount of difference in the actual value of two or more currencies or between values of the same currency at two or more places. [Middle English *eschaungen,* from Anglo-Norman *eschaungier,* from Vulgar Latin **excambiāre* : Latin *ex-,* ex- + Late Latin *cambīre,* to exchange, barter; see CHANGE.] —**ex·change′a·ble** *adj.*

exchange rate *n.* A rate of exchange.

ex·cheq·uer (ĕks′chĕk′ər, ĭks-chĕk′ər) *n.* **1. Exchequer.** The British governmental department charged with the collection and management of the national revenue. **2. Exchequer.** In Great Britain, the Court of Exchequer. **3.** *Abbr.* **exch., Exch.** A treasury, as of a nation or an organization. **4.** Financial resources; funds. [Alteration of Middle English *escheker,* from Old French *eschequier,* counting table, chessboard, from *eschec,* check. See CHECK.]

ex·ci·mer (ĕk′sə-mər) *n.* A diatomic molecule existing in an energy level above the ground state. [EXC(ITED) + (D)IMER.]

ex·cip·i·ent (ĭk-sĭp′ē-ənt) *n.* An inert substance used as a diluent or vehicle for a drug. [Latin *excipiēns, excipient-,* present participle of *excipere,* to take out, exclude. See EXCEPT.]

ex·cis·a·ble (ĭk-sī′zə-bəl) *adj.* Subject to an excise: *excisable commodities.*

ex·cise[1] (ĕk′sīz′) *n.* **1.** An internal tax imposed on the production, sale, or consumption of a commodity or the use of a service within a country: *excises on tobacco, liquor, and long-distance telephone calls.* **2.** A licensing charge or a fee levied for certain privileges. —**excise** *tr.v.* **-cised, -cis·ing, -cis·es.** To levy an excise on. [Middle Dutch *excijs,* alteration (influenced by Latin *excīsus,* past participle of *excīdere,* to cut out; see EXCISE[2]) of *accijs,* tax, probably from Old French *acceis,* partly from Vulgar Latin **accēnsum* (Latin *ad-,* ad- + Latin *cēnsus,* tax; see CENSUS) and partly from Old French *assise,* legislative ordinance; see ASSIZE.]

ex·cise[2] (ĭk-sīz′) *tr.v.* **-cised, -cis·ing, -cis·es.** To remove by or as if by cutting: *excised the tumor; excised two scenes from the film.* [Latin *excīdere, excīs-* : *ex-,* ex- + *caedere,* to cut; see **kae-id-** in Appendix.] —**ex·ci′sion** (-sĭzh′ən) *n.*

ex·cit·a·ble (ĭk-sī′tə-bəl) *adj.* **1.** Easily excited. **2.** Capable of responding to stimuli. —**ex·cit′a·bil′i·ty, ex·cit′a·ble·ness** *n.* —**ex·cit′a·bly** *adv.*

ex·ci·tant (ĭk-sīt′nt) *adj.* Tending to excite; stimulating. —**excitant** *n.* An agent or stimulus that excites; a stimulant.

ex·ci·ta·tion (ĕk′sī-tā′shən) *n.* **1.** The act or process of exciting or an instance of it. **2.** The state or condition of being excited. **3.** *Physiology.* The activity produced in an organ, a tissue, or a part, such as a nerve cell, as a result of stimulation.

ex·ci·ta·tive (ĭk-sī′tə-tĭv) or **ex·ci·ta·to·ry** (-sī′tə-tôr′ē, -tōr′ē) *adj.* Causing or tending to cause excitation.

ex·cite (ĭk-sīt′) *tr.v.* **-cit·ed, -cit·ing, -cites. 1.** To stir to activity. **2.** To call forth (a reaction or emotion, for example); elicit: *odd noises that excited our curiosity.* **3.** To arouse strong feeling in: *speakers who know how to excite a crowd.* See Synonyms at **provoke. 4.** *Physiology.* To produce increased activity or response in (an organ, a tissue, or a part); stimulate. **5.** *Physics.* **a.** To increase the energy of. **b.** To raise (an atom, for example) to a higher energy level. [Middle English *exciten,* from Latin *excitāre,* frequentative of *excīēre* : *ex-,* ex- + *ciēre,* to set in motion; see **kei-**[2] in Appendix.]

ex·cit·ed (ĭk-sī′tĭd) *adj.* **1.** Being in a state of excitement; emotionally aroused; stirred. **2.** *Physics.* Being at an energy level higher than the ground state. —**ex·cit′ed·ly** *adv.*

ex·cite·ment (ĭk-sīt′mənt) *n.* **1. a.** The act or an instance of exciting. **b.** The condition of being excited. **2.** Activity; agitation. **3.** Something that excites: *the dancing tigers and other circus excitements.*

ex·cit·er (ĭk-sī′tər) *n.* **1.** One that excites: *an exciter of animosity.* **2.** An auxiliary generator used to provide field current for a larger generator or alternator. **3.** *Electronics.* An oscillator for generating the carrier frequency of a transmitter.

ex·cit·ing (ĭk-sī′tĭng) *adj.* Creating or producing excitement: *an exciting adventure story.* —**ex·cit′ing·ly** *adv.*

ex·ci·ton (ĕk′sĭ-tŏn′, -sī-) *n.* *Physics.* An electrically neutral excited state of an insulator or semiconductor, often regarded as a bound state of an electron and a hole. [EXCIT(ATION) + -ON[1].]

ex·ci·ton·ics (ĕk′sĭ-tŏn′ĭks, -sī-) *n.* *(used with a sing. verb). Physics.* The study of excitons and their behavior in semiconductors and dielectrics.

ex·ci·tor (ĭk-sī′tər) *n.* A nerve whose stimulation induces an increase in activity of the part it supplies.

excl. *abbr.* **1.** Exclamation. **2.** Exclusive.

ex·claim (ĭk-sklām′) *v.* **-claimed, -claim·ing, -claims.** —*intr.* To cry out suddenly or vehemently, as from surprise or emotion: *The children exclaimed with excitement.* —*tr.* To express or utter (something) suddenly or vehemently: *exclaimed her surprise.* [French *exclamer,* from Latin *exclāmāre* : *ex-,* ex- + *clāmāre,* to call; see **kelə-**[2] in Appendix.] —**ex·claim′er** *n.*

ex·cla·ma·tion (ĕk′sklə-mā′shən) *n.* **1.** An abrupt, forceful utterance: *an exclamation of delight.* **2.** An outcry, as of protest. **3.** *Abbr.* **excl.** *Grammar.* An interjection.

exclamation point *n.* A punctuation mark (!) used after an exclamation. Also called *exclamation mark.*

ex·clam·a·tory (ĭk-sklăm′ə-tôr′ē, -tōr′ē) *adj.* Constituting, containing, relating to, or using exclamation.

ex·clave (ĕk′sklāv′) *n.* A part of a country that is isolated from the main part and is surrounded by foreign territory. [EX- + (EN)CLAVE.]

ex·clude (ĭk-sklōōd′) *tr.v.* **-clud·ed, -clud·ing, -cludes. 1.** To prevent from entering; keep out; bar: *a jar sealed to exclude outside air; an immigration policy that excludes undesirables.* **2.** To prevent from being included, considered, or accepted; reject: *The court excluded the improperly obtained evidence.* **3.** To put out; expel. [Middle English *excluden,* from Latin *exclūdere* : *ex-,* ex- + *claudere,* to shut.] —**ex·clud′a·bil′i·ty** *n.* —**ex·clud′a·ble, ex·clud′i·ble** *adj. & n.* —**ex·clud′er** *n.*

ex·clu·sion (ĭk-sklōō′zhən) *n.* **1.** The act or practice of excluding. **2.** The condition or fact of being excluded. [Middle English *exclusioun,* from Latin *exclūsiō, exclūsiōn-,* from *exclūsus,* past participle of *exclūdere,* to shut. See EXCLUDE.] —**ex·clu′sion·ar′y** (-zhə-nĕr′ē) *adj.*

exclusionary rule *n.* *Law.* A rule that forbids the use of illegally obtained evidence in a criminal trial.

ex·clu·sion·ist (ĭk-sklōō′zhə-nĭst) *n.* One that advocates the exclusion of another or others, as from having or exercising a right or privilege. —**ex·clu′sion·ism** *n.* —**ex·clu′sion·ist, ex·clu′sion·is′tic** *adj.*

exclusion principle *n.* The principle that two particles of a given type, such as electrons, protons, or neutrons, cannot simultaneously occupy a particular quantum state. Also called *Pauli exclusion principle.*

ex·clu·sive (ĭk-sklōō′sĭv) *adj.* *Abbr.* **excl. 1.** Excluding or tending to exclude: *exclusive barriers.* **2.** Not divided or shared with others: *exclusive publishing rights.* **3.** Not accompanied by others; single or sole: *your exclusive function.* **4.** Complete; undivided: *gained their exclusive attention.* **5.** Excluding some or most, as from membership or participation: *an exclusive club.* **6.** Catering to a wealthy clientele; expensive: *exclusive shops.* —**exclusive** *n.* **1.** A news item initially released to only one publication or broadcaster. **2.** An exclusive right or privilege, as to market a product. —**ex·clu′sive·ly** *adv.* —**ex·clu′sive·ness, ex′clu·siv′i·ty** (ĕk′sklōō-sĭv′ĭ-tē) *n.*

exclusive of *prep.* Not including or considering: *bought the house, exclusive of the outbuildings.*

ex·cog·i·tate (ĭk-skŏj′ĭ-tāt′) *tr.v.* **-tat·ed, -tat·ing, -tates.** To consider or think (something) out carefully and thoroughly. [Latin *excōgitāre, excōgitāt-,* to find out by thinking : *ex-,* ex- + *cōgitāre,* to think; see COGITATE.] —**ex·cog′i·ta′tion** *n.* —**ex·cog′i·ta′tive** *adj.*

ex·com·mu·ni·ca·ble (ĕks′kə-myōō′nĭ-kə-bəl) *adj.* Meriting, liable to, or punishable by excommunication: *excommunicable behavior.*

ex·com·mu·ni·cate (ĕks′kə-myōō′nĭ-kāt′) *tr.v.* **-cat·ed, -cat·ing, -cates. 1.** To deprive of the right of church membership by ecclesiastical authority. **2.** To exclude by or as if by decree from membership or participation in a group. —**excommunicate** (-kĭt) *n.* A person who has been excommunicated. —**excommunicate** (-kĭt, -kāt′) *adj.* Having been excommunicated. [Middle English *excommunicaten,* from Late Latin *excommūnicāre, excommūnicāt-* : Latin *ex-,* ex- + Latin *commūnicāre,* to share (from *commūnis,* common; see COMMON).] —**ex′com·mu′ni·ca′tive** (-kā′tĭv, -kə-), **ex′com·mu′ni·ca·to′ry** (-kə-tôr′ē, -tōr′ē) *adj.* —**ex′com·mu′ni·ca′-tor** *n.*

ex·com·mu·ni·ca·tion (ĕks′kə-myōō′nĭ-kā′shən) *n.* **1.** The act of excommunicating. **2.** The state of being excommunicated. **3.** A formal ecclesiastical censure that deprives a person of the right to belong to a church.

ex·co·ri·ate (ĭk-skôr′ē-āt′, -skōr′-) *tr.v.* **-at·ed, -at·ing, -ates. 1.** To tear or wear off the skin of; abrade. See Synonyms at **chafe. 2.** To censure strongly; denounce: *an editorial that excoriated the administration.* [Middle English *excoriaten,* from Latin *excoriāre, excoriāt-* : *ex-,* ex- + *corium,* skin; see **sker-**[1] in Appendix.] —**ex·co′ri·a′tion** *n.* —**ex·co′ri·a′-tor** *n.*

ex·cre·ment (ĕk′skrə-mənt) *n.* Waste material, especially fecal matter, that is expelled from the body after digestion. [Latin *excrēmentum,* from *excrētus,* past participle of *excernere,* to ex-

ă pat	oi boy
ā pay	ou out
âr care	ŏŏ took
ä father	ōō boot
ĕ pet	ŭ cut
ē be	ûr urge
ĭ pit	th thin
ī pie	*th* this
îr pier	hw which
ŏ pot	zh vision
ō toe	ə about, item
ô paw	♦ regionalism

Stress marks: ′ (primary); ′ (secondary), as in **dictionary** (dĭk′shə-nĕr′ē)

crete. See EXCRETE.] **—ex′cre·ment′al** (-mĕn′tl) *adj.* **—ex′cre·men·ti′tious** (-mĕn-tĭsh′əs) *adj.*

ex·cres·cence (ĭk-skrĕs′əns) *n.* **1.** An abnormal outgrowth or enlargement, such as a wart. **2.** A normal outgrowth, such as a fingernail or a beard. **3.** A usually unwanted or unncessary accretion: *"Independent agencies were an excrescence on the Constitution"* (Los Angeles Times). [Middle English, from Latin *excrēscentia,* from neuter pl. of *excrēscēns, excrēscent-,* present participle of *excrēscere,* to grow out : *ex-,* ex- + *crēscere,* to grow; see **ker-²** in Appendix.]

ex·cres·cen·cy (ĭk-skrĕs′ən-sē) *n., pl.* **-cies. 1.** The state or condition of being excrescent. **2.** An excrescence.

ex·cres·cent (ĭk-skrĕs′ənt) *adj.* **1.** Growing out abnormally, excessively, or superfluously. **2.** *Linguistics.* Of or relating to epenthesis; epenthetic. **—ex·cres′cent·ly** *adv.*

ex·cre·ta (ĭk-skrē′tə) *pl.n.* Waste matter, such as sweat, urine, or feces, discharged from the body. [Latin *excrēta,* from neuter pl. past participle of *excernere,* to excrete. See EXCRETE.] **—ex·cre′tal** *adj.*

ex·crete (ĭk-skrēt′) *tr.v.* **-cret·ed, -cret·ing, -cretes.** To separate and discharge (waste matter) from the blood, tissues, or organs. [Latin *excernere, excrēt-* : *ex-,* ex- + *cernere,* to separate; see **krei-** in Appendix.]

ex·cre·tion (ĭk-skrē′shən) *n.* **1.** The act or process of discharging waste matter from the blood, tissues, or organs. **2.** The matter, such as urine or sweat, that is so excreted.

ex·cre·to·ry (ĕk′skrĭ-tôr′ē, -tōr′ē) *adj.* Of, relating to, or used in excretion: *excretory organs.*

ex·cru·ci·ate (ĭk-skrōō′shē-āt′) *tr.v.* **-at·ed, -at·ing, -ates. 1.** To inflict severe pain on; torture. **2.** To inflict great mental distress on. See Synonyms at **afflict.** [Latin *excruciāre, excruciāt-* : *ex-,* intensive pref.; see EX– + *cruciāre,* to crucify, torture (from *crux, cruc-,* cross; see CROSS).] **—ex·cru′ci·a′tion** *n.*

ex·cru·ci·at·ing (ĭk-skrōō′shē-ā′tĭng) *adj.* **1.** Intensely painful; agonizing. **2.** Very intense or extreme: *wrote with excruciating precision.* **—ex·cru′ci·at′ing·ly** *adv.*

ex·cul·pate (ĕk′skəl-pāt′, ĭk-skŭl′-) *tr.v.* **-pat·ed, -pat·ing, -pates.** To clear of guilt or blame. [Medieval Latin *exculpāre, exculpāt-* : Latin *ex-,* ex- + *culpa,* guilt.] **—ex·cul′pa·ble** (ĭk-skŭl′pə-bəl) *adj.* **—ex′cul·pa′tion** *n.*

ex·cul·pa·to·ry (ĭk-skŭl′pə-tôr′ē, -tōr′ē) *adj.* Acting or tending to exculpate.

ex·cur·rent (ĭk-skûr′ənt, -skŭr′-) *adj.* **1. a.** Running or flowing in an outward direction. **b.** Marked by an outward flow of current. **2.** *Botany.* **a.** Having a single, undivided trunk with lateral branches, as in spruce trees. **b.** Extending beyond the apex of a leaf, as a midrib or vein. [Latin *excurrēns, excurrent-,* present participle of *excurrere,* to run out. See EXCURSION.]

ex·cur·sion (ĭk-skûr′zhən) *n.* **1.** A usually short journey made for pleasure; an outing. **2.** A round trip on a passenger vehicle at a special low fare. **3.** A group taking a short pleasure trip together. **4.** A diversion or deviation from a main topic; a digression. **5.** *Physics.* **a.** A movement from and back to a mean position or axis in an oscillating or alternating motion. **b.** The distance traversed in such a movement. [Latin *excursiō, excursiōn-,* from *excursus,* past participle of *excurrere,* to run out : *ex-,* ex- + *currere,* to run; see **kers-** in Appendix.]

ex·cur·sion·ist (ĭk-skûr′zhə-nĭst) *n.* A person who goes on an excursion.

ex·cur·sive (ĭk-skûr′sĭv) *adj.* Of, given to, characterized by, or having the nature of digression. **—ex·cur′sive·ly** *adv.* **—ex·cur′sive·ness** *n.*

ex·cur·sus (ĭk-skûr′səs) *n., pl.* **-sus·es. 1.** A lengthy, appended exposition of a topic or point. **2.** A digression. [Latin, from past participle of *excurrere,* to run out. See EXCURSION.]

ex·cus·a·to·ry (ĭk-skyōō′zə-tôr′ē, -tōr′ē) *adj.* Tending or serving to excuse.

ex·cuse (ĭk-skyōōz′) *tr.v.* **-cused, -cus·ing, -cus·es. 1. a.** To explain (a fault or an offense) in the hope of being forgiven or understood: *He arrived late and excused his tardiness in a flimsy manner.* **b.** To seek to remove the blame from: *She excused herself for being late.* **2. a.** To grant pardon to; forgive: *We quickly excused the latecomer.* **b.** To make allowance for; overlook: *Readers must excuse the author's youth and inexperience.* See Synonyms at **forgive. 3.** To serve as justification for: *Brilliance does not excuse bad manners.* **4.** To free, as from an obligation or duty; exempt: *In my state, physicians and lawyers are excused from jury duty.* **5.** To give permission to leave; release: *The child ate quickly and asked to be excused.* **—excuse** (ĭk-skyōōs′) *n.* **1.** An explanation offered to justify or obtain forgiveness. **2.** A reason or grounds for excusing: *Ignorance is no excuse for breaking the law.* **3.** The act of excusing. **4.** A note explaining an absence. **5.** *Informal.* An inferior example: *a poor excuse for a poet; a sorry excuse for a car.* [Middle English *excusen,* from Old French *excuser,* from Latin *excūsāre* : *ex-,* ex- + *causa,* accusation; see CAUSE.] **—ex·cus′a·ble** *adj.* **—ex·cus′a·ble·ness** *n.* **—ex·cus′a·bly** *adv.* **—ex·cus′er** *n.*

ex·ec (ĭg-zĕk′) *n. Informal.* **1.** An executive. **2.** The executive officer of a unit of the armed forces.

exec. *abbr.* Executor.

ex·e·cra·ble (ĕk′sĭ-krə-bəl) *adj.* **1.** Deserving of execration; hateful. **2.** Extremely inferior; very bad: *an execrable meal.* [Middle English, from Latin *execrābilis,* from *execrārī, exsecrārī,* to execrate. See EXECRATE.] **—ex′e·cra·ble·ness** *n.* **—ex′e·cra·bly** *adv.*

ex·e·crate (ĕk′sĭ-krāt′) *tr.v.* **-crat·ed, -crat·ing, -crates. 1.** To declare to be hateful or abhorrent; denounce. **2.** To feel loathing for; abhor. **3.** *Archaic.* To invoke a curse on. [Latin *execrārī, execrāt-* : *ex-,* ex- + *sacrāre,* to consecrate (from *sacer,* sacred; see **sak-** in Appendix).] **—ex′e·cra′tive** *adj.* **—ex′e·cra′tor** *n.* **—ex′e·cra·to′ry** (-krə-tôr′ē, -tōr′ē) *adj.*

ex·e·cra·tion (ĕk′sĭ-krā′shən) *n.* **1.** The act of cursing. **2.** A curse. **3.** Something that is cursed or loathed.

ex·ec·u·tant (ĭg-zĕk′yə-tənt) *n.* One who performs or carries out, especially a skilled performer: *The dancer is the choreographer's executant.*

ex·e·cute (ĕk′sĭ-kyōōt′) *tr.v.* **-cut·ed, -cut·ing, -cutes. 1.** To put into effect; carry out: *a government that executes the decisions of the ruling party.* **2.** To perform; do: *execute a U-turn.* See Synonyms at **perform. 3.** To create (a work of art, for example) in accordance with a prescribed design. **4.** To make valid, as by signing: *execute a deed.* **5.** To perform or carry out what is required by: *execute the terms of a will.* **6.** To put to death, especially by carrying out a lawful sentence. **7.** *Computer Science.* To run (a program or an instruction). [Middle English *executen,* from Old French *executer,* from Medieval Latin *execūtāre,* from Latin *execūtor,* executor, from *execūtus,* past participle of *exequī, exsequī* : *ex-,* ex- + *sequī,* to follow; see **sek^w-¹** in Appendix.] **—ex′e·cut′a·ble** *adj.* **—ex′e·cut′er** *n.*

ex·e·cu·tion (ĕk′sĭ-kyōō′shən) *n.* **1. a.** The act of executing something. **b.** The state of being executed. **2.** The manner, style, or result of performance: *The plan was sound; its execution, faulty.* **3.** The act or an instance of putting to death or being put to death as a lawful penalty. **4.** *Law.* **a.** The carrying into effect of a court judgment. **b.** A writ empowering an officer to enforce a judgment. **c.** Validation of a legal document by the performance of all necessary formalities. **5.** *Archaic.* Effective, punitive, or destructive action.

ex·e·cu·tion·er (ĕk′sĭ-kyōō′shə-nər) *n.* One who executes, especially one who puts a condemned person to death.

execution time *n. Computer Science.* The time required for a computer to decode and perform a compiled instruction.

ex·ec·u·tive (ĭg-zĕk′yə-tĭv) *n. Abbr.* **ex. 1.** A person or group having administrative or managerial authority in an organization. **2.** The chief officer of a government, state, or political division. **3.** The branch of government charged with putting into effect a country's laws and the administering of its functions. **4.** *Computer Science.* A set of coded instructions designed to process and control other coded instructions. **—executive** *adj. Abbr.* **ex. 1.** Of, relating to, capable of, or suited for carrying out or executing: *an advisory body lacking executive powers.* **2.** Having, characterized by, or relating to administrative or managerial authority: *the executive director of a drama troupe; executive experience and skills.* **3.** Of or relating to the branch of government charged with the execution and administration of the nation's laws. [Middle English, to be carried out, from Old French *exécutif,* from *executer,* to carry out. See EXECUTE.]

executive agreement *n.* An agreement made between the executive branch of the U.S. government and a foreign government without ratification by the Senate.

executive council *n.* **1.** A council that advises or assists a political executive. **2.** A council having the highest executive power or authority.

executive officer *n.* **1. a.** The officer second in command of a military unit smaller than a division. **b.** The officer second in command of a naval unit. **2.** A person holding executive power in an organization.

executive order *n. Abbr.* **EO** See **regulation** (sense 3).

executive privilege *n.* The principle that members of the executive branch of government cannot legally be forced to disclose their confidential communications when such disclosure would adversely affect the operations or procedures of the executive branch.

executive routine *n. Computer Science.* A set of coded instructions designed to use a digital computer to develop or control other routines.

executive secretary *n.* A secretary having administrative duties and responsibilities.

executive session *n.* A session, as of a legislature or committee, often closed to the public, in which executive business is transacted.

ex·ec·u·tor (ĭg-zĕk′yə-tər, ĕk′sĭ-kyōō′tər) *n. Abbr.* **exec., exr. 1.** A person who carries out or performs something. **2.** *Law.* A person who is appointed by a testator to execute the testator's will. **—ex·ec′u·to′ri·al** (-tôr′ē-əl, -tōr′-) *adj.* **—ex·ec′u·tor·ship′** *n.*

ex·ec·u·to·ry (ĭg-zĕk′yə-tôr′ē, -tōr′ē) *adj.* **1.** Of or relating to execution or administration; executive. **2.** In effect; operative. **3.** *Law.* Intended to go into effect or having the potential of becoming effective at a future time; contingent.

ex·ec·u·trix (ĭg-zĕk′yə-trĭks′) *n., pl.* **-trix·es** or **-tri·ces** (-trī′sēz′). *Abbr.* **exrx.** *Law.* A woman who is appointed by a testator to execute the testator's will.

ex·e·dra (ĕk′sĭ-drə, ĭk-sē′-) *n.* **1.** A usually curved outdoor bench with a high back. **2.** An often semicircular portico with seats that was used in ancient Greece and Rome as a place for discussions. [Latin, from Greek : *ex-*, ex- + *hedra,* seat; see **sed-** in Appendix.]

ex·e·ge·sis (ĕk′sə-jē′sĭs) *n., pl.* **-ses** (-sēz). Critical explanation or analysis, especially of a text. [Greek *exēgēsis,* from *exēgeisthai,* to interpret : *ex-*, ex- + *hēgeisthai,* to lead; see **sāg-** in Appendix.]

ex·e·gete (ĕk′sə-jēt′) also **ex·e·ge·tist** (ĕk′sə-jĕt′ĭst) *n.* A person skilled in exegesis. [Greek *exēgētēs,* from *exēgeisthai,* to interpret. See EXEGESIS.]

ex·e·get·ic (ĕk′sə-jĕt′ĭk) also **ex·e·get·i·cal** (-ĭ-kəl) *adj.* Of or relating to exegesis; critically explanatory. **—ex′e·get′i·cal·ly** *adv.*

ex·e·ge·tist (ĕk′sə-jĕt′ĭst) *n.* Variant of **exegete.**

ex·em·pla (ĭg-zĕm′plə) *n.* Plural of **exemplum.**

ex·em·plar (ĭg-zĕm′plär′, -plər) *n.* **1.** One that is worthy of imitation; a model. See Synonyms at **ideal. 2.** One that is typical or representative; an example. **3.** An ideal that serves as a pattern; an archetype. **4.** A copy, as of a book. [Middle English *exemplere,* from Late Latin *exemplārium,* from Latin *exemplum,* example. See EXAMPLE.]

ex·em·pla·ry (ĭg-zĕm′plə-rē) *adj.* **1.** Worthy of imitation; commendable: *exemplary behavior.* **2.** Serving as a model. **3.** Serving as an illustration; typical. **4.** Serving as a warning; admonitory. [From Middle English *exaumplarie, exemplere,* an exemplar. See EXEMPLAR.] **—ex′em·plar′i·ly** (ĕg′zəm-plâr′ə-lē) *adv.* **—ex·em′pla·ri·ness, ex′em·plar′i·ty** (ĕg′zəm-plăr′ĭ-tē) *n.*

ex·em·pli·fi·ca·tion (ĭg-zĕm′plə-fĭ-kā′shən) *n.* **1.** The act of exemplifying. **2.** One that exemplifies; an example. **3.** *Law.* An officially certified copy of a document.

ex·em·pli·fy (ĭg-zĕm′plə-fī′) *tr.v.* **-fied, -fy·ing, -fies. 1.a.** To illustrate by example: *exemplify an argument.* **b.** To serve as an example of: *scenes that exemplify the film director's style.* **2.** *Law.* To make a certified copy of (a document). [Middle English *exemplifien,* from Old French *exemplifier,* from Medieval Latin *exemplificāre* : Latin *exemplum,* example; see EXAMPLE + Latin *-ficāre,* -fy.] **—ex·em′pli·fi′a·ble** *adj.* **—ex·em′pli·fi′er** *n.*

ex·em·pli gra·ti·a (ĭg-zĕm′plē grā′shē-ə, ĕk-sĕm′plē grä′tē-ä′) *adv. Abbr.* **e.g.** For example. [Latin *exemplī grātiā,* for the sake of example : *exemplī,* genitive of *exemplum,* example + *grātiā,* ablative of *grātia,* favor.]

ex·em·plum (ĭg-zĕm′pləm) *n., pl.* **-pla** (-plə). **1.** An example. **2.** A brief story used to make a point in an argument or to illustrate a moral truth. [Latin. See EXAMPLE.]

ex·empt (ĭg-zĕmpt′) *tr.v.* **-empt·ed, -empt·ing, -empts. 1.** To free from an obligation, a duty, or a liability to which others are subject: *exempting the disabled from military service.* **2.** *Obsolete.* To set apart; isolate. **—exempt** *adj.* **1.** Freed from an obligation, a duty, or a liability to which others are subject; excused: *persons exempt from jury duty; income exempt from taxation; a beauty somehow exempt from the aging process.* **2.** *Obsolete.* Set apart; isolated. **—exempt** *n.* One who is exempted from an obligation, a duty, or a liability. [Middle English *exempten,* from Old French *exempter,* from *exempt,* exempt, from Latin *exemptus,* past participle of *eximere,* to take out. See EXAMPLE.] **—ex·empt′i·ble** *adj.*

ex·emp·tion (ĭg-zĕmp′shən) *n.* **1.** The act or an instance of exempting. **2.** The state of being exempt; immunity. **3.** One that is exempted, especially an amount of income that is exempted from taxation.

ex·en·ter·ate (ĭg-zĕn′tə-rāt′) *tr.v.* **-at·ed, -at·ing, -ates. 1.** To disembowel; eviscerate. **2.** *Medicine.* To remove the contents of (an organ). [Latin *exenterāre, exenterāt-,* to disembowel : *ex-*, ex- + Greek *enteron,* entrails; see **en** in Appendix.] **—ex·en′ter·a′tion** *n.*

ex·er·cise (ĕk′sər-sīz′) *n.* **1.** An act of employing or putting into play; use: *the free exercise of intellect; the exercise of an option.* **2.** The discharge of a duty, function, or office. **3.** Activity that requires physical or mental exertion, especially when performed to develop or maintain fitness: *took an hour of vigorous daily exercise at a gym.* **4.** A task, problem, or other effort performed to develop or maintain fitness or increase skill: *a piano exercise; a memory exercise.* **5. exercises.** A program that includes speeches, presentations, and other ceremonial activities performed before an audience: *graduation exercises.* **—exercise** *v.* **-cised, -cis·ing, -cis·es.** *—tr.* **1.** To put into play or operation; employ: *Proceed, but exercise caution.* **2.** To bring to bear; exert: *"The desire to be re-elected exercises a strong brake on independent courage"* (John F. Kennedy). **3.a.** To subject to practice or exertion in order to train, strengthen, or develop: *exercise the back muscles; exercise the memory.* **b.** To put through exercises: *exercise a platoon.* See Synonyms at **practice. 4.** To carry out the functions of; execute: *exercise the role of disciplinarian.* **5.a.** To absorb the attentions of, especially by worry or anxiety. **b.** To stir to anger or alarm; upset: *an injustice that exercised the whole community.* *—intr.* To take exercise. [Middle English, from Old French *exercice,* from Latin *exercitium,* from *exercitus,* past participle of *exercēre,* to exercise : *ex-*, ex- + *arcēre,* to restrain.] **—ex′er·cis′a·ble** *adj.*

exercise bicycle *n.* A stationary piece of fitness equipment having a saddle seat, handlebars, and pedals that can be adjusted to a desired degree of tension, pedaled chiefly to strengthen the user's cardiovascular system. Also called *stationary bicycle.*

exercise book *n.* A booklet for use by students, usually containing problems or exercises and blank space for writing answers or practicing a lesson.

ex·er·cis·er (ĕk′sər-sī′zər) *n.* **1.** One that exercises: *an exerciser of racehorses.* **2.** A device for exercising the body.

ex·er·ci·ta·tion (ĭg-zûr′sĭ-tā′shən) *n.* The act or an instance of exercising. [Middle English *exercitacioun,* from Latin *exercitātiō, exercitātiōn-,* from *exercitāre,* frequentative of *exercēre,* to exercise. See EXERCISE.]

Ex·er·cy·cle A trademark used for a brand of exercise bicycle. This trademark often occurs in print in lowercase: *"all sorts of weight equipment, rowing machines, exercycles"* (Chicago Tribune).

ex·er·gon·ic (ĕk′sər-gŏn′ĭk) *adj.* Releasing energy. [EX(O)– + Greek *ergon,* work; see **werg-** in Appendix + –IC.]

ex·ergue (ĕk′sûrg′, ĕg′zûrg′) *n.* A space on the reverse of a coin or medal, usually below the central design and often giving the date and place of engraving. [French, from New Latin *exergum* : Greek *ex-*, ex- + Greek *ergon,* work; see **werg-** in Appendix.]

ex·ert (ĭg-zûrt′) *tr.v.* **-ert·ed, -ert·ing, -erts. 1.** To put to use or effect; put forth: *exerted all my strength to move the box.* **2.** To bring to bear; exercise: *exert influence.* **3.** To put (oneself) to strenuous effort: *exerted ourselves mightily during the campaign to raise funds.* [Latin *exserere, exsert-,* to put forth, stretch out : *ex-*, ex- + *serere,* to join; see **ser-**[2] in Appendix.]

ex·er·tion (ĭg-zûr′shən) *n.* The act or an instance of exerting, especially a strenuous effort. See Synonyms at **effort.**

Ex·e·ter (ĕk′sĭ-tər). A borough of southwest England northeast of Plymouth. It has been important since Roman times because of its strategic location. Population, 99,200.

ex·e·unt (ĕk′sē-ənt, -o͝ont′). Used as a stage direction to indicate that two or more performers leave the stage. [Latin, third person pl. of *exīre,* to go out. See EXIT.]

ex·fo·li·ate (ĕks-fō′lē-āt′) *v.* **-at·ed, -at·ing, -ates.** *—tr.* **1.** To remove (a layer of bark or skin, for example) in flakes or scales; peel. **2.** To cast off in scales, flakes, or splinters. *—intr.* To come off or separate into flakes, scales, or layers. [Latin *exfoliāre, exfoliāt-,* to strip of leaves : *ex-*, ex- + *folium,* leaf; see **bhel-**[3] in Appendix.] **—ex·fo′li·a′tion** *n.* **—ex·fo′li·a′tive** *adj.* **—ex·fo′li·a′tor** *n.*

ex·ha·lant also **ex·ha·lent** (ĕks-hā′lənt, ĕk-sā′-) *—adj.* Functioning in exhalation. *—n.* An organ, such as the siphon of a clam, that is used for exhalation.

ex·ha·la·tion (ĕks′hə-lā′shən, ĕk′sə-) *n.* **1.** The act or an instance of exhaling. **2.** Something, such as air or vapor, that is exhaled.

ex·hale (ĕks-hāl′, ĕk-sāl′) *v.* **-haled, -hal·ing, -hales.** *—intr.* **1.a.** To breathe out. **b.** To emit air or vapor. **2.** To be given off or emitted. *—tr.* **1.** To blow (something) forth or breathe (something) out. **2.** To give off; emit: *chimneys exhaling dense smoke.* [Middle English *exalen,* from Latin *exhālāre* : *ex-*, ex- + *hālāre,* to breathe.]

ex·ha·lent (ĕks-hā′lənt, ĕk-sā′-) *adj. & n.* Variant of **exhalant.**

ex·haust (ĭg-zôst′) *v.* **-haust·ed, -haust·ing, -hausts.** *—tr.* **1.** To wear out completely. See Synonyms at **tire**[1]. **2.** To drain of resources or properties; deplete: *tobacco crops that exhausted the soil.* See Synonyms at **deplete. 3.** To use up completely: *exhausted our funds before the month was out.* **4.** To treat completely; cover thoroughly: *exhaust a topic.* **5.** To draw out the contents of; drain: *exhaust a tank gradually.* **6.** To let out or draw off: *exhaust vaporous wastes through a pipe.* *—intr.* To escape or pass out: *Steam exhausts through this valve.* **—exhaust** *n.* **1.a.** The escape or release of vaporous waste material, as from an engine. **b.** The fumes or gases so released. **2.** A duct or pipe through which waste material is emitted. **3.** An apparatus for drawing out noxious air or waste material by means of a partial vacuum. [Latin *exhaurīre, exhaust-* : *ex-*, ex- + *haurīre,* to draw.] **—ex·haust′ed·ly** *adv.* **—ex·haust′er** *n.* **—ex·haust′i·bil′i·ty** *n.* **—ex·haust′i·ble** *adj.* **—ex·haust′ing·ly** *adv.*

ex·haus·tion (ĭg-zôs′chən) *n.* **1.** The act or an instance of exhausting. **2.** The state of being exhausted; extreme fatigue: *The runner collapsed from exhaustion.*

ex·haus·tive (ĭg-zô′stĭv) *adj.* **1.** Treating all parts or aspects without omission; thorough: *an exhaustive study.* **2.** Tending to exhaust. **—ex·haus′tive·ly** *adv.* **—ex·haus′tive·ness** *n.* **—ex′haus·tiv′i·ty** *n.*

ex·haust·less (ĭg-zôst′lĭs) *adj.* Impossible to exhaust; inexhaustible. **—ex·haust′less·ly** *adv.* **—ex·haust′less·ness** *n.*

exhaust pipe *n.* See **tailpipe.**

exhaust trail *n.* A condensation trail that is visible when water vapor in aircraft exhaust mixes with the air in the vehicle's wake and saturates it.

ex·hib·it (ĭg-zĭb′ĭt, ĕg-) *v.* **-it·ed, -it·ing, -its.** *—tr.* **1.** To show outwardly; display: *exhibited pleasure by smiling.* **2.a.** To present for others to see: *rolled up his sleeve to exhibit the scar.* **b.** To present in a public exhibition or contest: *exhibited her paintings at a gallery.* See Synonyms at **show. 3.** To give evidence or an instance of; demonstrate: *young musicians eager to exhibit their talent; a plant that exhibits dimorphism.* **4.** *Law.* **a.** To submit (evidence or documents) in a court. **b.** To present or introduce officially. *—intr.* To put something on public display. **—exhibit** *n.* **1.** The act or an instance of exhibiting. **2.** Some-

ă **pat**	oi **boy**
ā **pay**	ou **out**
âr **care**	o͝o **took**
ä **father**	o͞o **boot**
ĕ **pet**	ŭ **cut**
ē **be**	ûr **urge**
ĭ **pit**	th **thin**
ī **pie**	*th* **this**
îr **pier**	hw **which**
ŏ **pot**	zh **vision**
ō **toe**	ə **about, item**
ô **paw**	♦ **regionalism**

Stress marks: **′** (primary); ′ (secondary), as in **dictionary** (dĭk′shə-nĕr′ē)

thing exhibited: *studied the dinosaur exhibits at the museum.* **3.** A public showing; an exhibition: *spent the afternoon at the space exhibit.* **4.** *Law.* Something, such as a document, formally introduced as evidence in court. [Middle English *exhibiten,* from Latin *exhibēre, exhibit-* : *ex-,* ex- + *habēre,* to hold; see **ghabh-** in Appendix.] **—ex·hib'i·tor, ex·hib'it·er** *n.* **—ex·hib'i·to'ry** (-ĭ-tôr'ē, -tōr'ē) *adj.*

ex·hi·bi·tion (ĕk'sə-bĭsh'ən) *n.* **1.** The act or an instance of exhibiting. **2.** Something exhibited; an exhibit. **3.** A large-scale public showing, as of art objects or industrial or agricultural products. **4.** *Chiefly British.* A grant given to a scholar by a school or university.

ex·hi·bi·tion·ism (ĕk'sə-bĭsh'ə-nĭz'əm) *n.* **1.** The act or practice of deliberately behaving so as to attract attention. **2.** *Psychiatry.* A psychosexual disorder marked by the compulsive exposure of the genitalia in public. **—ex'hi·bi'tion·ist** *n.* **—ex'hi·bi'tion·is'tic** *adj.*

ex·hib·i·tive (ĭg-zĭb'ĭ-tĭv) *adj.* Tending to exhibit: *bird behavior exhibitive of the nest-building instinct.* **—ex·hib'i·tive·ly** *adv.*

ex·hil·a·rant (ĭg-zĭl'ər-ənt) *adj.* Serving to exhilarate; exhilarating. **—exhilarant** *n.* Something that exhilarates or stimulates.

ex·hil·a·rate (ĭg-zĭl'ə-rāt') *tr.v.* **-rat·ed, -rat·ing, -rates. 1.** To cause to feel happily refreshed and energetic; elate: *We were exhilarated by the cool, pine-scented air.* **2.** To invigorate; stimulate: *bold designs that exhilarate the viewer's imagination.* [Latin *exhilarāre, exhilarāt-* : *ex-,* intensive pref.; see EX– + *hilarāre,* to make cheerful (from *hilaris, hilarus,* cheerful, from Greek *hilaros*).] **—ex·hil'a·ra'tive** *adj.* **—ex·hil'a·ra'tor** *n.*

ex·hil·a·rat·ing (ĭg-zĭl'ə-rā'tĭng) *adj.* Causing exhilaration; invigorating. **—ex·hil'a·rat'ing·ly** *adv.*

ex·hil·a·ra·tion (ĭg-zĭl'ə-rā'shən) *n.* The state of being stimulated, refreshed, or elated: *"Few Yosemite visitors ever see snow avalanches and fewer still know the exhilaration of riding on them"* (John Muir).

ex·hort (ĭg-zôrt') *v.* **-hort·ed, -hort·ing, -horts.** *—tr.* To urge by strong, often stirring argument, admonition, advice, or appeal: *exhorted the troops to hold the line.* See Synonyms at **urge.** *—intr.* To make urgent appeal. [Middle English *exhorten,* from Latin *exhortārī* : *ex-,* intensive pref.; see EX– + *hortārī,* to encourage; see **gher-**[2] in Appendix.] **—ex·hort'er** *n.*

ex·hor·ta·tion (ĕg'zôr-tā'shən, ĕk'sôr-) *n.* **1.** The act or an instance of exhorting. **2.** A speech or discourse that encourages, incites, or earnestly advises.

ex·hor·ta·tive (ĭg-zôr'tə-tĭv) also **ex·hor·ta·to·ry** (-tôr'ē, -tōr'ē) *adj.* Acting or intended to encourage, incite, or advise.

ex·hume (ĭg-zo͞om', -zyo͞om', ĭk-syo͞om', ĕks-hyo͞om') *tr.v.* **-humed, -hum·ing, -humes. 1.** To remove from a grave; disinter. **2.** To bring to light, especially after a period of obscurity. [French *exhumer,* from Medieval Latin *exhumāre* : Latin *ex-,* ex- + Latin *humus,* ground; see **dhghem-** in Appendix.] **—ex'hu·ma'tion** (ĕg'zyo͞o-mā'shən, ĕks'hyo͞o-) *n.* **—ex·hum'er** *n.*

ex·i·gence (ĕk'sə-jəns) *n.* Exigency.

ex·i·gen·cy (ĕk'sə-jən-sē, ĭg-zĭj'ən-) *n., pl.* **-cies. 1.** The state or quality of requiring much effort or immediate action. **2.** A pressing or urgent situation. See Synonyms at **crisis. 3.** Often **exigencies.** Urgent requirements; pressing needs. See Synonyms at **need.**

ex·i·gent (ĕk'sə-jənt) *adj.* **1.** Requiring immediate action or remedy. See Synonyms at **urgent. 2.** Requiring much effort or expense; demanding. [Latin *exigēns, exigent-,* present participle of *exigere,* to demand. See EXACT.] **—ex'i·gent·ly** *adv.*

ex·i·gu·i·ty (ĕk'sĭ-gyo͞o'ĭ-tē) *n.* The quality or condition of being scanty or meager.

ex·ig·u·ous (ĭg-zĭg'yo͞o-əs, ĭk-sĭg'-) *adj.* Extremely scanty; meager. [From Latin *exiguus,* from *exigere,* to measure out, demand. See EXACT.] **—ex·ig'u·ous·ly** *adv.* **—ex·ig'u·ous·ness** *n.*

ex·ile (ĕg'zīl', ĕk'sīl') *n.* **1. a.** Enforced removal from one's native country. **b.** Self-imposed absence from one's country. **2.** The condition or a period of living away from one's native country. **3.** One who lives away from one's native country, whether because of expulsion or voluntary absence. **—exile** *tr.v.* **-iled, -il·ing, -iles.** To send into exile. See Synonyms at **banish.** [Middle English *exil,* from Old French, from Latin *exilium,* from *exul, exsul,* exiled person, wanderer.] **—ex·il'ic** (ĭg-zĭl'ĭk, ĭk-sĭl'-), **ex·il'ian** (ĭg-zĭl'yən, -zĭl'ē-ən, ĭk-sĭl'yən, -sĭl'ē-ən) *adj.*

ex·ine (ĕk'sēn', -sīn') *n.* *Botany.* The outer layer of the wall of a spore or pollen grain. Also called *exosporium.* [EX(O)– + Greek *is, in-,* tendon; see **wei-** in Appendix.]

ex·ist (ĭg-zĭst') *intr.v.* **-ist·ed, -ist·ing, -ists. 1.** To have actual being; be real. **2.** To have life; live. See Synonyms at **be. 3.** To live at a minimal level; subsist: *barely enough income on which to exist.* **4.** To continue to be; persist: *old customs that still exist in rural areas.* **5.** To be present under certain circumstances or in a specified place; occur: *"Wealth and poverty exist in every demographic category"* (Thomas G. Exter). [Latin *existere, exsistere,* to come forth, be manifest : *ex-,* ex- + *sistere,* to stand; see **stā-** in Appendix.]

ex·is·tence (ĭg-zĭs'təns) *n.* **1.** The fact or state of existing; being. **2.** The fact or state of continued being; life: *our brief existence on earth.* **3. a.** All that exists: *sang the beauty of all existence.* **b.** A thing that exists; an entity. **4.** A mode or manner of existing: *scratched out a meager existence.* **5.** Specific presence; occurrence. *The Geiger counter indicated the existence of radioactivity.*

SYNONYMS: *existence, actuality, being.* The central meaning shared by these nouns is "the fact or state of existing": *laws in existence for centuries; a fantasy that progressed from possibility to actuality; a point of view gradually coming into being.*
ANTONYM: *nonexistence.*

ex·is·tent (ĭg-zĭs'tənt) *adj.* **1.** Having life or being; existing. See Synonyms at **real**[1]. **2.** Occurring or present at the moment; current. **—existent** *n.* One that exists.

ex·is·ten·tial (ĕg'zĭ-stĕn'shəl, ĕk'sĭ-) *adj.* **1.** Of, relating to, or dealing with existence. **2.** Based on experience; empirical. **3.** Of or as conceived by existentialism or existentialists: *an existential moment of choice.* **—ex'is·ten'tial·ly** *adv.*

ex·is·ten·tial·ism (ĕg'zĭ-stĕn'shə-lĭz'əm, ĕk'sĭ-) *n.* *Philosophy.* A philosophy that emphasizes the uniqueness and isolation of the individual experience in a hostile or indifferent universe, regards human existence as unexplainable, and stresses freedom of choice and responsibility for the consequences of one's acts. **—ex'is·ten'tial·ist** *adj. & n.*

ex·it (ĕg'zĭt, ĕk'sĭt) *n.* **1.** The act of going away or out. **2.** A passage or way out: *an emergency exit in a theater; took the second exit on the throughway.* **3.** The departure of a performer from the stage. **4.** Death. **5.** A computer programming technique for ending a repeated cycle of operations. **—exit** *v.* **-it·ed, -it·ing, -its.** *—intr.* To make one's exit; depart. *—tr.* To go out of; leave: *exited the plane through a rear door.* **—exit.** Used as a stage direction for a specified actor to leave the stage. [From Latin, third person sing. of *exīre,* to go out : *ex-,* ex- + *īre,* to go; see **ei-** in Appendix. N., sense 2, from Latin *exitus,* from past participle of *exīre,* to go out.]

exit poll *n.* A poll taken of a sample of voters as they leave a polling place, used especially to predict the outcome of an election or determine the opinions and characteristics of the candidates' supporters.

ex li·bris (ĕks lī'brĭs, lē'-) *n., pl.* **ex libris.** See **bookplate.** [Latin *ex librīs,* from the books : *ex,* from + *librīs,* ablative pl. of *liber,* book.]

ex ni·hi·lo (ĕks nē'ə-lō', nī'-, nĭ'-) *adv. & adj.* Out of nothing. [Latin *ex nihilō* : *ex,* out of + *nihilō,* ablative of *nihil, nihilum,* nothing.]

exo– *pref.* Outside; external: *exoskeleton.* [From Greek *exō,* outside, from *ex,* out of. See **eghs** in Appendix.]

ex·o·bi·ol·o·gy (ĕk'sō-bī-ŏl'ə-jē) *n.* The branch of biology that deals with the search for extraterrestrial life and the effects of extraterrestrial surroundings on living organisms. Also called *astrobiology, space biology.* **—ex'o·bi'o·log'i·cal** (-ə-lŏj'ĭ-kəl) *adj.* **—ex'o·bi·ol'o·gist** *n.*

ex·o·carp (ĕk'sō-kärp') *n.* *Botany.* The outermost layer of the fruit wall. Also called *epicarp.*

ex·o·crine (ĕk'sə-krĭn, -krēn, -krīn') *adj.* **1.** Secreting externally, directly or through a duct: *exocrine cells.* **2.** Of, relating to, or produced by an exocrine gland. [EXO– + Greek *krinein,* to separate; see **krei-** in Appendix.]

exocrine gland *n.* *Physiology.* An externally secreting gland, such as a salivary gland or sweat gland that releases its secretions directly or through a duct.

ex·o·cy·clic (ĕk'sō-sī'klĭk, -sĭk'lĭk) *adj.* External to a chemical ring structure: *an exocyclic double bond.*

ex·o·cy·to·sis (ĕk'sō-sī-tō'sĭs) *n., pl.* **-ses** (-sēz'). *Biology.* A process of cellular secretion or excretion in which substances contained in vesicles are discharged from the cell by fusion of the vesicular membrane with the outer cell membrane. **—ex'o·cy·tose'** (-tōs') *v.* **—ex'o·cy·tot'ic** (-tŏt'ĭk) *adj.*

Exod. *abbr. Bible.* Exodus.

ex·o·don·tia (ĕk'sə-dŏn'shə, -shē-ə) *n.* Exodontics.

ex·o·don·tics (ĕk'sə-dŏn'tĭks) *n. (used with a sing. verb).* The dental specialty that deals with extraction of teeth. **—ex'o·don'tist** *n.*

ex·o·dus (ĕk'sə-dəs) *n.* **1.** A departure of a large number of people. **2. Exodus. a.** The departure of the Israelites from Egypt. **b.** *Abbr.* **Ex, Ex., Exod.** *Bible.* See table at **Bible.** [Late Latin, from Greek *exodos* : *ex-,* out; see EXO– + *hodos,* way, journey.]

ex·o·en·zyme (ĕk'sō-ĕn'zīm') *n.* An enzyme, such as a digestive enzyme, that functions outside the cell from which it originates.

ex·o·er·gic (ĕk'sō-ûr'jĭk) *adj.* Exothermic. [EXO– + Greek *ergon,* work; see **werg-** in Appendix + –IC.]

ex of·fi·ci·o (ĕks' ə-fĭsh'ē-ō') *adv. & adj.* By virtue of office or position. [Latin *ex officiō* : *ex,* from + *officiō,* ablative of *officium,* office.]

ex·og·a·my (ĕk-sŏg'ə-mē) *n., pl* **-mies. 1.** The custom of marrying outside the tribe, family, clan, or other social unit. **2.** *Biology.* The fusion of two gametes that are not closely related. **—ex'o·gam'ic** (ĕk'sə-găm'ĭk), **ex·og'a·mous** (ĕk-sŏg'ə-məs) *adj.*

ex·og·e·nous (ĕk-sŏj'ə-nəs) *adj.* **1.** *Biology.* Derived or developed from outside the body; originating externally. **2.** *Botany.*

Characterized by the addition of layers of woody tissue. **3.** *Medicine.* Having a cause external to the body. Used of diseases. [French *exogène* : Greek *exō-*, outside; see EXO– + French *-gène*, -gen.] **—ex·og′e·nous·ly** *adv.*

ex·on (ĕk′sŏn) *n. Genetics.* A nucleotide sequence in DNA that carries the code for the final messenger RNA molecule and thus defines the amino acid sequence during protein synthesis. [*ex(pressed)* + –ON[1].] **—ex·on′ic** *adj.*

ex·on·er·ate (ĭg-zŏn′ə-rāt′) *tr.v.* **-at·ed, -at·ing, -ates. 1.** To free from blame. **2.** To free from a responsibility, obligation, or task. [Middle English *exoneraten*, from Latin *exonerāre, exonerāt-*, to free from a burden : *ex-*, ex- + *onus, oner-*, burden.] **—ex·on′er·a′tion** *n.* **—ex·on′er·a′tive** *adj.*

ex·o·nu·cle·ase (ĕk′sō-no͞o′klē-ās′, -āz′, -nyo͞o′-) *n.* Any of a group of enzymes that catalyze the hydrolysis of single nucleotides from the end of a DNA or RNA chain.

ex·o·pep·ti·dase (ĕk′sō-pĕp′tĭ-dās′, -dāz′) *n.* Any of a group of enzymes that catalyze the hydrolysis of single amino acids from the end of a polypeptide chain.

ex·oph·thal·mic goiter (ĕk′səf-thăl′mĭk) *n.* See **Graves′ disease.**

ex·oph·thal·mos also **ex·oph·thal·mus** (ĕk′səf-thăl′məs) *n.* Abnormal protrusion of the eyeball. [New Latin *exophthalmus*, from Greek *exophthalmos*, with prominent eyes : *ex-*, ex- + *ophthalmos*, eye; see **okʷ-** in Appendix.] **—ex′oph·thal′mic** *adj.*

ex·or·bi·tance (ĭg-zôr′bĭ-təns) *n.* **1.** Excessiveness, as of price or amount. **2.** Behavior or an action that exceeds what is right or proper.

ex·or·bi·tant (ĭg-zôr′bĭ-tənt) *adj.* Exceeding all bounds, as of custom or fairness: *exorbitant prices.* See Synonyms at **excessive.** [Middle English, aberrant, flagrant, from Old French, excessive, extreme, from Late Latin *exorbitāns, exorbitant-*, present participle of *exorbitāre*, to deviate : *ex-*, ex- + *orbita*, path, track; see ORBIT.] **—ex·or′bi·tant·ly** *adv.*

ex·or·cise (ĕk′sôr-sīz′, -sər-) *tr.v.* **-cised, -cis·ing, -cis·es. 1.** To expel (an evil spirit) by or as if by incantation, command, or prayer. **2.** To free from evil spirits or malign influences. [Middle English *exorcisen*, from Late Latin *exorcizāre*, from Greek *exorkizein* : *ex-*, ex- + *horkizein*, to make one swear (from *horkos*, oath).] **—ex′or·cis′er** *n.*

WORD HISTORY: An oath is to be found at the etymological heart of *exorcise*, a term going back to the Greek word *exorkizein*, meaning "to swear in," "to take an oath by," "to conjure," and "to exorcise." *Exorkizein* in turn is formed from the prefix *ex–*, "thoroughly," and the verb *horkizein*, "to make one swear, administer an oath to," derived from *horkos*, "oath." Our word *exorcise* is first recorded in English in a work composed possibly before the beginning of the 15th century, and in this use *exorcise* means "to call up or conjure spirits" rather than "to drive out spirits," a sense first recorded in 1546.

ex·or·cism (ĕk′sôr-sĭz′əm, -sər-) *n.* **1.** The act, practice, or ceremony of exorcising. **2.** A formula used in exorcising. **—ex′or·cist** *n.*

ex·or·di·um (ĭg-zôr′dē-əm, ĭk-sôr′-) *n., pl.* **-di·ums** or **-di·a** (-dē-ə). A beginning or introductory part, especially of a speech or treatise. [Latin, from *exōrdīrī*, to begin : *ex-*, intensive pref.; see EX– + *ōrdīrī*, to begin; see **ar-** in Appendix.] **—ex·or′di·al** *adj.*

ex·o·skel·e·ton (ĕk′sō-skĕl′ĭ-tn) *n.* A hard outer structure, such as the shell of a crustacean, that provides protection or support for an organism. **—ex′o·skel′e·tal** (-ĭ-tl) *adj.*

ex·os·mo·sis (ĕk′sŏz-mō′sĭs, -sŏs-) *n.* The passage of a fluid through a semipermeable membrane toward a solution of lower concentration, especially the passage of water through a cell membrane into the surrounding medium. [EX(O)– + OSMOSIS.] **—ex′os·mot′ic** (-mŏt′ĭk) *adj.*

ex·o·sphere (ĕk′sō-sfîr′) *n.* **1.** The outermost region of a planet's atmosphere. **2.** The outermost layer of Earth's atmosphere, lying above the thermosphere and extending thousands of kilometers into space, from which molecules having sufficient velocity can escape Earth's gravitation. **—ex′o·spher′ic** (-sfîr′ĭk, -sfĕr′-) *adj.*

ex·o·spore (ĕk′sō-spôr′, -spōr′) *n. Botany.* The outermost layer of a spore in some algae and fungi.

ex·o·spor·i·um (ĕk′sō-spôr′ē-əm, -spōr′-) *n., pl.* **-i·a** (-ē-ə). *Botany.* See **exine.** [New Latin : EXO– + *spora*, spore; see SPORE.]

ex·os·to·sis (ĕk′sŏ-stō′sĭs) *n., pl.* **-ses** (-sēz). A bony growth on the surface of a bone or tooth. [Greek *exostōsis* : *ex-*, out of; see EXO– + *osteon*, bone; see **ost-** in Appendix + *-ōsis*, -osis.]

ex·o·ter·ic (ĕk′sə-tĕr′ĭk) *adj.* **1.** Not confined to an inner circle of disciples or initiates. **2.** Comprehensible to or suited to the public; popular. **3.** Of or relating to the outside; external. [Latin *exōtericus*, external, from Greek *exōterikos*, from *exōterō*, comparative of *exō*, outside, from *ex*, out. See **eghs** in Appendix.] **—ex′o·ter′i·cal·ly** *adv.*

ex·o·ther·mic (ĕk′sō-thûr′mĭk) also **ex·o·ther·mal** (-məl) *adj.* Releasing heat: *an exothermic reaction.* **—ex′o·ther′mi·cal·ly** *adv.*

ex·ot·ic (ĭg-zŏt′ĭk) *adj.* **1.** From another part of the world; foreign: *exotic tropical plants in a greenhouse.* See Synonyms at **foreign. 2.** Intriguingly unusual or different; excitingly strange: *exotic costumes from the Far East.* See Synonyms at **fantastic. 3.** Of or involving striptease: *an exotic dancer.* **—exotic** *n.* **1.** One that is exotic. **2.** A striptease performer. [Latin *exōticus*, from Greek *exōtikos*, from *exō*, outside, from *ex*, out. See **eghs** in Appendix.] **—ex·ot′i·cal·ly** *adv.* **—ex·ot′ic·ness** *n.*

ex·ot·i·ca (ĭg-zŏt′ĭ-kə) *pl.n.* Things that are curiously unusual or excitingly strange: *such gustatory exotica as killer bee honey and fresh catnip sauce.* [Latin *exōtica*, from neuter pl. of *exōticus*, exotic. See EXOTIC.]

ex·ot·i·cism (ĭg-zŏt′ĭ-sĭz′əm) *n.* The quality or condition of being exotic.

ex·o·tox·in (ĕk′sō-tŏk′sĭn) *n.* A poisonous substance secreted by a microorganism and released into the medium in which it grows.

exp *abbr. Mathematics.* Exponent; exponential.

exp. *abbr.* **1.** Expenses. **2.** Experiment; experimental. **3.** Expiration. **4.** Export. **5.** Express.

ex·pand (ĭk-spănd′) *v.* **-pand·ed, -pand·ing, -pands.** *—tr.* **1.** To increase the size, volume, quantity, or scope of; enlarge: *expanded her store by adding a second room.* See Synonyms at **increase. 2.** To express at length or in detail; enlarge on: *expanded his remarks afterward.* **3.** To open (something) up or out; spread out: *The bird expanded its wings and flew off.* **4.** *Mathematics.* To write (a quantity) as a sum of terms in an extended form. *—intr.* **1.** To become greater in size, volume, quantity, or scope: *Air expands when heated. This critic's influence is expanding.* **2.** To speak or write at length or in detail: *expand on a favorite topic.* **3.** To open up or out; unfold: *The chair expands to form a day bed.* **4.** To feel expansive. [Middle English *expanden*, to spread out, from Latin *expandere* : *ex-*, ex- + *pandere*, to spread; see **petə-** in Appendix.] **—ex·pand′a·ble** *adj.* **—ex·pand′er** *n.*

ex·pand·ing universe theory (ĭk-spăn′dĭng) *n.* **1.** The cosmological theory holding that the universe is expanding, based on the interpretation of the color shift in the spectra of all the galaxies as being the result of the Doppler effect and indicating that all galaxies are moving away from one another. **2.** The cosmogonical theory holding that a violent eruption from a point source led to the formation of elementary particles, the subsequent formation of hydrogen and helium, and the dispersion of the galaxies that developed from these elements.

ex·pan·dor (ĭk-spăn′dər) *n.* A transducer designed for a given range of input voltages that produces a larger range of output voltages.

ex·panse (ĭk-spăns′) *n.* **1.** A wide and open extent, as of surface, land, or sky. **2. a.** Expansion. **b.** The distance or amount of expansion. [Latin *expānsum*, from neuter past participle of *expandere*, to spread out. See EXPAND.]

ex·pan·si·ble (ĭk-spăn′sə-bəl) *adj.* That can expand or be expanded: *an expansible antenna.* **—ex·pan′si·bil′i·ty** *n.*

ex·pan·sile (ĭk-spăn′səl, -sīl′) *adj.* Of, relating to, or capable of expansion.

ex·pan·sion (ĭk-spăn′shən) *n.* **1. a.** The act or process of expanding: *the new nation's expansion westward.* **b.** The state of being expanded. **2. a.** An expanded part: *an expansion of a river.* **b.** A product of expanding: *a book that is an expansion of the author's Ph.D. thesis.* **3.** The extent or amount by which something has expanded. **4.** Increase in the dimensions of a body. **5.** *Mathematics.* **a.** A quantity written in an extended form, as a sum of terms or a continued product. **b.** The process of obtaining this form. **6.** An expanse. **7.** A period of increased economic or business activity.

ex·pan·sion·ar·y (ĭk-spăn′shə-nĕr′ē) *adj.* Tending toward or causing expansion: *the empire's expansionary policies in Asia.*

expansion bolt *n.* A bolt having an attachment that expands as the bolt is driven into a surface.

ex·pan·sion·ism (ĭk-spăn′shə-nĭz′əm) *n.* A nation's practice or policy of territorial or economic expansion. **—ex·pan′sion·ist** *adj. & n.*

ex·pan·sive (ĭk-spăn′sĭv) *adj.* **1.** Capable of expanding or tending to expand. **2.** Broad in size or extent; comprehensive: *expansive police powers.* **3.** Disposed to be open, communicative, and generous: *Wine made the guest expansive.* **4.** Grand in scale: *an expansive lifestyle.* **5.** *Psychiatry.* Marked by euphoria and delusions of grandeur. **—ex·pan′sive·ly** *adv.* **—ex·pan′sive·ness, ex′pan·siv′i·ty** (ĕk′spăn-sĭv′ĭ-tē) *n.*

ex par·te (ĕks pär′tē) *adv. & adj.* **1.** *Law.* From or on one side only, with the other side absent or unrepresented: *testified ex parte; an ex parte hearing.* **2.** From a one-sided or strongly biased point of view. [Latin : *ex*, from + *parte*, ablative of *pars*, part, side.]

ex·pa·ti·ate (ĭk-spā′shē-āt′) *intr.v.* **-at·ed, -at·ing, -ates. 1.** To speak or write at length: *expatiated on the subject until everyone was bored.* **2.** To wander freely. [Latin *expatiārī, expatiāt-* : *ex-*, ex- + *spatiārī*, to spread (from *spatium*, space).] **—ex·pa′ti·a′tion** *n.*

ex·pa·tri·ate (ĕk-spā′trē-āt′) *v.* **-at·ed, -at·ing, -ates.** *—tr.* **1.** To send into exile. See Synonyms at **banish. 2.** To remove (oneself) from residence in one's native land. *—intr.* **1.** To give up residence in one's homeland. **2.** To renounce alle-

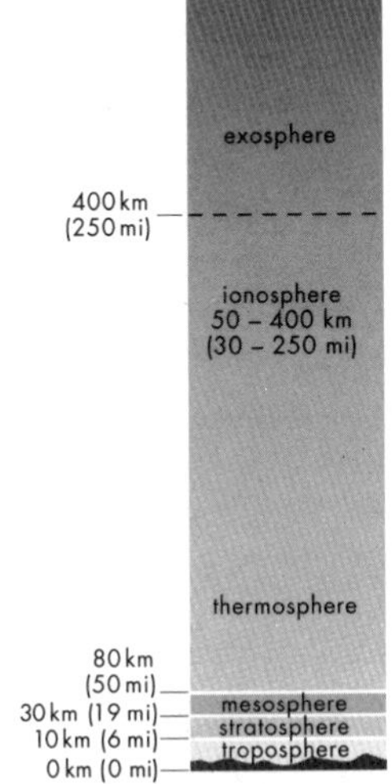

exosphere

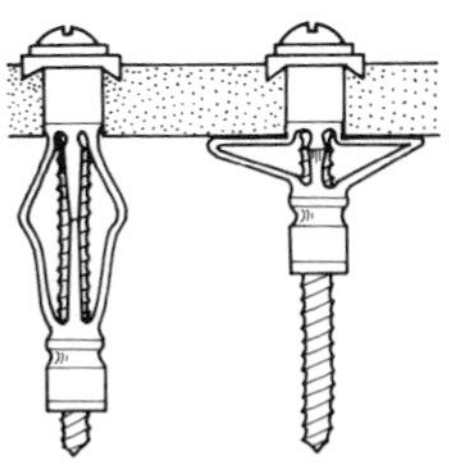
expansion bolt

ă pat ā pay âr care ä father ĕ pet ē be ĭ pit ī pie îr pier ŏ pot ō toe ô paw oi boy ou out o͝o took o͞o boot ŭ cut ûr urge th thin *th* this hw which zh vision ə about, item ♦ regionalism

Stress marks: **′** (primary); ′ (secondary), as in **dictionary** (dĭk′shə-nĕr′ē)

giance to one's homeland. **—expatriate** (-ĭt, -āt′) *n.* **1.** One who has taken up residence in a foreign country. **2.** One who has renounced one's native land. **—expatriate** (-ĭt, -āt′) *adj.* Residing in a foreign country; expatriated. [Medieval Latin *expatriāre, expatriāt-* : Latin *ex-*, ex- + Latin *patria,* native land (from *patrius,* paternal, from *pater,* father; see **pəter-** in Appendix).] **—ex·pa′tri·a′tion** *n.*

ex·pect (ĭk-spĕkt′) *v.* **-pect·ed, -pect·ing, -pects.** *—tr.* **1.a.** To look forward to the probable occurrence or appearance of: *expecting a telephone call; expects rain on Sunday.* **b.** To consider likely or certain: *expect to see them soon.* See Usage Note at **anticipate. 2.** To consider reasonable or due: *We expect an apology.* **3.** To consider obligatory; require: *The school expects its pupils to be on time.* **4.** *Informal.* To presume; suppose. *—intr.* **1.** To look forward to the birth of one's child. Used in progressive tenses: *His sister is expecting in May.* **2.** To be pregnant. Used in progressive tenses: *My wife is expecting again.* [Latin *exspectāre* : *ex-*, ex- + *spectāre,* to look at, frequentative of *specere,* to see; see **spek-** in Appendix.] **—ex·pect′a·ble** *adj.* **—ex·pect′a·bly** *adv.* **—ex·pect′ed·ly** *adv.* **—ex·pect′ed·ness** *n.*

SYNONYMS: *expect, anticipate, hope, await.* These verbs are related in various ways to the idea of looking ahead to something in the future. To *expect* is to look forward to the likely occurrence or appearance of someone or something: *You can expect us for lunch. "We should not expect something for nothing—but we all do and call it Hope"* (Edgar W. Howe). *Anticipate* is sometimes used as a synonym of *expect,* but usually it involves more than expectation. Sometimes it refers to taking advance action, as to forestall or prevent the occurrence of something expected or to meet a wish or request before it is articulated: *anticipated the attack and locked the gates; anticipating her desires.* The term can also refer to having a foretaste of something expected before its occurrence: *anticipate trouble.* To *hope* is to look forward with desire and usually with a measure of confidence in the likelihood of gaining what is desired: *I hope to see you soon. Hope for the best, but expect the worst.* To *await* is to wait in expectation of; it implies certainty: *eagerly awaiting your letter.*

ex·pec·tance (ĭk-spĕk′təns) *n.* Expectancy.

ex·pec·tan·cy (ĭk-spĕk′tən-sē) *n., pl.* **-cies. 1.** The act or state of expecting; expectation: *Tense with expectancy, I waited for my name to be called.* **2.** The state of being expected. **3.** Something expected. **4.** An expected amount calculated on the basis of actuarial data: *a life expectancy of 70 years.* In this sense, also called *expectation.*

ex·pec·tant (ĭk-spĕk′tənt) *adj.* **1.** Having or marked by expectation: *an expectant look; an expectant hush.* **2.** Pregnant: *expectant mothers.* **—ex·pec′tant** *n.* **—ex·pec′tant·ly** *adv.*

ex·pec·ta·tion (ĕk′spĕk-tā′shən) *n.* **1.a.** The act of expecting. **b.** Eager anticipation: *eyes shining with expectation.* **2.** The state of being expected. **3.a.** Something expected: *a result that was beyond my wildest expectation.* **b. expectations.** Prospects, especially of success or gain. **4.** *Statistics.* **a.** The expected value of a random variable. **b.** The mean of a random variable. **5.** See **expectancy** (sense 4). **—ex′pec·ta′tion·al** *adj.*

ex·pec·ta·tive (ĭk-spĕk′tə-tĭv) *adj.* Of, relating to, or characterized by expectation.

ex·pect·ed value (ĭk-spĕk′tĭd) *n.* **1.** The sum of all possible values for a random variable, each value multiplied by its probability of occurrence. **2.** The integral of the probability density function and a continuous random variable over its range of values.

ex·pec·to·rant (ĭk-spĕk′tər-ənt) *adj.* Promoting or facilitating the secretion or expulsion of phlegm, mucus, or other matter from the respiratory tract. **—expectorant** *n.* An expectorant medicine.

ex·pec·to·rate (ĭk-spĕk′tə-rāt′) *v.* **-rat·ed, -rat·ing, -rates.** *—tr.* **1.** To eject from the mouth; spit. **2.** To cough up and eject by spitting. *—intr.* **1.** To spit. **2.** To clear out the chest and lungs by coughing up and spitting out matter. [Latin *expectorāre, expectorāt-,* to drive from the chest : *ex-*, ex- + *pectus, pector-,* chest.] **—ex·pec′to·ra′tion** *n.*

ex·pe·di·ence (ĭk-spē′dē-əns) *n.* Expediency.

ex·pe·di·en·cy (ĭk-spē′dē-ən-sē) *n., pl.* **-cies. 1.** Appropriateness to the purpose at hand; fitness. **2.** Adherence to self-serving means: *an ambitious politician, guided by expediency rather than principle.* **3.** A means; an expedient. **4.** *Obsolete.* Speed; haste.

ex·pe·di·ent (ĭk-spē′dē-ənt) *adj.* **1.** Appropriate to a purpose. **2.a.** Serving to promote one's interest: *was merciful only when mercy was expedient.* **b.** Based on or marked by a concern for self-interest rather than principle; self-interested. **3.** *Obsolete.* Speedy; expeditious. **—expedient** *n.* **1.** Something that is a means to an end. **2.** Something contrived or used to meet an urgent need. See Synonyms at **makeshift.** [Middle English, from Latin *expediēns, expedient-,* present participle of *expedīre,* to make ready. See EXPEDITE.] **—ex·pe′di·ent·ly** *adv.*

ex·pe·di·en·tial (ĭk-spē′dē-ĕn′shəl) *adj.* Of, relating to, or concerned with what is expedient. **—ex·pe′di·en′tial·ly** *adv.*

ex·pe·dite (ĕk′spĭ-dīt′) *tr.v.* **-dit·ed, -dit·ing, -dites. 1.** To speed up the progress of; facilitate. **2.** To perform quickly and efficiently: *could be trusted to expedite the matter.* **3.** To issue officially; dispatch. [Latin *expedīre, expedīt-,* to free from entanglements, make ready. See **ped-** in Appendix.] **—ex′pe·dit′er, ex′pe·di′tor** *n.*

ex·pe·di·tion (ĕk′spĭ-dĭsh′ən) *n.* **1.a.** A journey undertaken by a group of people with a definite objective: *an expedition against the enemy stronghold; a scientific expedition to the South Pole.* **b.** The group undertaking such a journey. **2.** Speed in performance; promptness. See Synonyms at **haste.** [Middle English *expedicioun,* military campaign, from Old French *expedition,* from Latin *expedītiō, expedītiōn-,* from *expedītus,* past participle of *expedīre,* to make ready. See EXPEDITE.]

ex·pe·di·tion·ar·y (ĕk′spĭ-dĭsh′ə-nĕr′ē) *adj.* **1.** Relating to or constituting an expedition. **2.** Sent on or designed for military operations abroad: *the French expeditionary force in Indochina.*

ex·pe·di·tious (ĕk′spĭ-dĭsh′əs) *adj.* Acting or done with speed and efficiency. See Synonyms at **fast**[1]. **—ex′pe·di′tious·ly** *adv.* **—ex′pe·di′tious·ness** *n.*

ex·pel (ĭk-spĕl′) *tr.v.* **-pelled, -pel·ling, -pels. 1.** To force or drive out: *expel an invader.* **2.** To discharge from or as if from a receptacle: *expelled a sigh of relief.* **3.** To force to leave; deprive of membership: *expelled the student from college for cheating.* See Synonyms at **eject.** [Middle English *expellen,* from Latin *expellere* : *ex-*, ex- + *pellere,* to drive; see **pel-**[5] in Appendix.] **—ex·pel′la·ble** *adj.* **—ex·pel′ler** *n.*

ex·pel·lant also **ex·pel·lent** (ĭk-spĕl′ənt) *adj.* Expelling or tending to expel.

ex·pel·lee (ĕk′spĕl-ē′) *n.* One who is expelled.

ex·pel·lent (ĭk-spĕl′ənt) *adj.* Variant of **expellant.**

ex·pend (ĭk-spĕnd′) *tr.v.* **-pend·ed, -pend·ing, -pends. 1.** To lay out; spend: *expending tax revenues on government operations.* See Synonyms at **spend. 2.** To use up; consume: *"Every effort seemed to expend her spirit's force"* (George Meredith). [Middle English *expenden,* from Latin *expendere,* to pay out : *ex-*, ex- + *pendere,* to weigh; see **(s)pen-** in Appendix.]

ex·pend·a·ble (ĭk-spĕn′də-bəl) *adj.* **1.** Subject to use or consumption: *an expendable source.* **2.** Not worth salvaging or reusing: *expendable rocket boosters.* **3.** Not strictly necessary; dispensable: *an expendable budget item; expendable personnel.* **4.** Open to sacrifice in the interests of gaining an objective, especially a military one: *expendable civilian targets.* **—expendable** *n.* Something expendable.

ex·pen·di·ture (ĭk-spĕn′də-chər) *n.* **1.** The act or process of expending; outlay. **2.a.** An amount expended. **b.** An expense. [Medieval Latin *expenditus,* past participle of *expendere,* to expend; see EXPEND + —URE.]

ex·pense (ĭk-spĕns′) *n.* **1.a.** Something spent to attain a goal or accomplish a purpose: *an expense of time and energy on the project.* **b.** A loss for the sake of something gained; a sacrifice: *achieved speed at the expense of accuracy.* See Synonyms at **price. 2.** An expenditure of money; a cost: *an improvement that was well worth the expense; a trip with all expenses paid.* **3. expenses.** *Abbr.* **exp. a.** Charges incurred by an employee in the performance of work: *was reimbursed for her travel expenses.* **b.** *Informal.* Money allotted for payment of such charges. **4.** Something requiring the expenditure of money: *Redecorating the house will be a considerable expense.* **5.** *Archaic.* The act of expending. **—expense** *tr.v.* **-pensed, -pens·ing, -pens·es. 1.** To charge with expenses. **2.** To write off as an expense. ***—idiom.*** **at (one's) expense.** To (one's) detriment or chagrin: *telling jokes at my expense.* [Middle English, from Anglo-Norman, from Latin *(pecunia) expēnsa,* (money) paid out, from feminine past participle of *expendere,* to pay out. See EXPEND.]

expense account *n.* An account of expenses for repayment to an employee.

ex·pen·sive (ĭk-spĕn′sĭv) *adj.* **1.** Requiring a large expenditure; costly. **2.** Marked by high prices: *expensive stores.* **—ex·pen′sive·ly** *adv.* **—ex·pen′sive·ness** *n.*

ex·pe·ri·ence (ĭk-spîr′ē-əns) *n.* **1.** The apprehension of an object, a thought, or an emotion through the senses or mind: *a child's first experience of snow.* **2.a.** Active participation in events or activities, leading to the accumulation of knowledge or skill: *a lesson taught by experience; a carpenter with experience in wall and roof repair.* **b.** The knowledge or skill so derived. **3.a.** An event or a series of events participated in or lived through. **b.** The totality of such events in the past of an individual or a group. **—experience** *tr.v.* **-enced, -enc·ing, -enc·es.** To participate in personally; undergo: *experience a great adventure; experienced loneliness.* [Middle English, from Old French, from Latin *experientia,* from *experiēns, experient-,* present participle of *experīrī,* to try. See **per-**[3] in Appendix.] **—ex·pe′ri·enc·er** *n.*

SYNONYMS: *experience, suffer, sustain, taste, undergo.* The central meaning shared by these verbs is "to encounter or partake of personally": *experience happiness; suffer a loss; sustained an injury; tasted freedom; has undergone a religious conversion.*

ex·pe·ri·enced (ĭk-spîr′ē-ənst) *adj.* **1.** Having had experience in an activity or in life in general: *a highly experienced traveler.* **2.** Skilled or knowledgeable as the result of active participation or practice: *consulted an experienced investment counselor.*

ex·pe·ri·en·tial (ĭk-spîr′ē-ĕn′shəl) *adj.* Relating to or derived from experience. **—ex·pe′ri·en′tial·ly** *adv.*

ex·per·i·ment (ĭk-spĕr′ə-mənt) *n. Abbr.* **exp., expt.** **1.a.** A test under controlled conditions that is made to demonstrate a known truth, examine the validity of a hypothesis, or determine the efficacy of something previously untried. **b.** The process of conducting such a test; experimentation. **2.** An innovative act or procedure: *"Democracy is only an experiment in government"* (William Ralph Inge). **3.** The result of experimentation: *"We are not* [nature's] *only experiment"* (R. Buckminster Fuller). **—experiment** (-mĕnt′) *intr.v.* **-ment·ed, -ment·ing, -ments. 1.** To conduct an experiment. **2.** To try something new, especially in order to gain experience: *experiment with new methods of teaching.* [Middle English, from Old French, from Latin *experīmentum,* from *experīrī,* to try. See **per-**[3] in Appendix.] **—ex·per′i·ment′er** *n.*

ex·per·i·men·tal (ĭk-spĕr′ə-mĕn′tl) *adj. Abbr.* **exp., expt., X, x** **1.a.** Relating to or based on experiment: *experimental procedures; experimental results.* **b.** Given to experimenting. **2.** Of the nature of an experiment; constituting or undergoing a test: *an experimental drug.* **3.** Founded on experience; empirical. **—ex·per′i·men′tal·ly** *adv.*

ex·per·i·men·tal·ism (ĭk-spĕr′ə-mĕn′tl-ĭz′əm) *n.* Use of empirical or experimental methods in determining the validity of ideas. **—ex·per′i·men′tal·ist** *n.*

ex·per·i·men·ta·tion (ĭk-spĕr′ə-mĕn-tā′shən) *n.* The act, process, or practice of experimenting.

experiment station *n.* An establishment in which scientific experiments are conducted in a specific field, such as agriculture, and practical uses are developed.

ex·pert (ĕk′spûrt′) *n.* **1.** A person with a high degree of skill in or knowledge of a certain subject. **2.a.** The highest grade that can be achieved in marksmanship. **b.** A person who has achieved this grade. **—expert** (ĕk′spûrt, ĭk-spûrt′) *adj.* Having or demonstrating great skill, dexterity, or knowledge as the result of experience or training. See Synonyms at **proficient.** [Middle English, from Old French, experienced, from Latin *expertus,* past participle of *experīrī,* to try. See **per-**[3] in Appendix.] **—ex′pert′ly** *adv.* **—ex′pert′ness** *n.*

ex·per·tise (ĕk′spûr-tēz′) *n.* **1.** Expert advice or opinion. **2.** Skill or knowledge in a particular area. See Synonyms at **art**[1]. [French, from *expert,* experienced. See EXPERT.]

expert system *n. Computer Science.* A program that uses available information, heuristics, and inference to suggest solutions to problems in a particular discipline.

ex·pi·a·ble (ĕk′spē-ə-bəl) *adj.* Possible to expiate: *expiable offenses.*

ex·pi·ate (ĕk′spē-āt′) *v.* **-at·ed, -at·ing, -ates.** —*tr.* To make amends or reparation for; atone: *expiate one's sins by acts of penance.* —*intr.* To make amends; atone. [Latin *expiāre, expiāt-* : *ex-,* intensive pref.; see EX– + *piāre,* to atone (from *pius,* devout).] **—ex′pi·a′tor** *n.*

ex·pi·a·tion (ĕk′spē-ā′shən) *n.* **1.** The act of expiating; atonement. **2.** A means of expiating or atoning. **—ex′pi·a·to′ry** (-ə-tôr′ē, -tōr′ē) *adj.*

ex·pi·ra·tion (ĕk′spə-rā′shən) *n. Abbr.* **exp.** **1.** The act of coming to a close; termination. **2.** The act of breathing out; exhalation. **3.** *Archaic.* Death.

ex·pi·ra·to·ry (ĭk-spī′rə-tôr′ē, -tōr′ē) *adj.* Of, relating to, or involving the expiration of air from the lungs.

ex·pire (ĭk-spīr′) *v.* **-pired, -pir·ing, -pires.** —*intr.* **1.** To come to an end; terminate: *My membership in the club has expired.* **2.** To breathe one's last breath; die: *The patient expired early this morning.* **3.** To exhale; breathe out. —*tr.* **1.** To breathe (something) out. **2.** *Archaic.* To give (something) off. [Middle English *expiren,* from Old French *expirer,* from Latin *exspīrāre* : *ex-,* ex- + *spīrāre,* to breathe.]

ex·pi·ry (ĭk-spīr′ē) *n., pl.* **-ries.** **1.** An expiration, especially of a contract or an agreement. **2.** Death.

ex·plain (ĭk-splān′) *v.* **-plained, -plain·ing, -plains.** —*tr.* **1.** To make plain or comprehensible. **2.** To define; expound: *We explained our plan to the committee.* **3.a.** To offer reasons for or a cause of; justify: *explain an error.* **b.** To offer reasons for the actions, beliefs, or remarks of (oneself). —*intr.* To make something plain or comprehensible: *Let me explain.* **—*phrasal verb.*** **explain away.** **1.** To dismiss or get rid of by or as if by explaining. **2.** To minimize by explanation. [Middle English *explanen,* from Latin *explānāre* : *ex-,* intensive pref.; see EX– + *plānus,* clear; see **pelə-**[2] in Appendix.] **—ex·plain′a·ble** *adj.*

SYNONYMS: *explain, elucidate, expound, explicate, interpret, construe.* These verbs mean to make understandable the nature or meaning of something. *Explain* is the most widely applicable: *explained the difficult words and obscure symbols; tried to explain himself.* To *elucidate* is to throw light on something complex: *"Man's whole life and environment have been laid open and elucidated"* (Thomas Carlyle). *Expound* and *explicate* imply detailed and usually learned and lengthy exploration or analysis: *"We must never forget that it is a constitution we are expounding"* (John Marshall). *"Ordinary language philosophers tried to explicate the standards of usage underlying the linguistic behavior of those who do not abuse this freedom"* (Jerrold J. Katz). To *interpret* is to reveal the underlying meaning of something by the application of special knowledge or insight: *"If a poet interprets a poem of his own he limits its suggestibility"* (William Butler Yeats). *Construe* involves putting a particular construction or interpretation on something: *"I take the official oath today . . . with no purpose to construe the Constitution or laws by any hypercritical rules"* (Abraham Lincoln). *Why do you construe my silence as a sign of disapproval?*

ex·pla·na·tion (ĕk′splə-nā′shən) *n.* **1.** The act or process of explaining: *launched into a detailed explanation.* **2.** Something that explains: *That was supposedly the explanation for their misdeeds.* **3.** A mutual clarification of misunderstandings; a reconciliation.

ex·plan·a·tive (ĭk-splăn′ə-tĭv) *adj.* Explanatory. **—ex·plan′a·tive·ly** *adv.*

ex·plan·a·to·ry (ĭk-splăn′ə-tôr′ē, -tōr′ē) *adj.* Serving or intended to explain: *an explanatory paragraph.* **—ex·plan′a·to′ri·ly** *adv.*

ex·plant (ĕk-splănt′) *tr.v.* **-plant·ed, -plant·ing, -plants.** To remove (living tissue) from the natural site of growth and place in a medium for culture. **—explant** (ĕks′plănt′) *n.* Explanted tissue. **—ex′plan·ta′tion** *n.*

ex·ple·tive (ĕk′splĭ-tĭv) *n.* **1.** An exclamation or oath, especially one that is profane, vulgar, or obscene. **2.a.** A word or phrase that does not contribute any meaning but is added only to fill out a sentence or a metrical line. **b.** A word that stands in place of and anticipates a following word or phrase. In the sentence *There are many books on the table,* the word *there* functions as an expletive. **—expletive** *adj.* Added or inserted in order to fill out something, such as a sentence or a metrical line. [From Late Latin *explētīvus,* serving to fill out, from Latin *explētus,* past participle of *explēre,* to fill out : *ex-,* ex- + *plēre,* to fill; see **pelə-**[1] in Appendix.]

ex·ple·to·ry (ĕk′splĭ-tôr′ē, -tōr′ē) *adj.* Expletive.

ex·pli·ca·ble (ĕk′splĭ-kə-bəl) *adj.* Possible to explain: *explicable phenomena; explicable behavior.* **—ex′pli·ca·bly** *adv.*

ex·pli·cate (ĕk′splĭ-kāt′) *tr.v.* **-cat·ed, -cat·ing, -cates.** To make clear the meaning of; explain. See Synonyms at **explain.** [Latin *explicāre, explicāt-,* to unfold, explain : *ex-,* ex- + *plicāre,* to fold; see **plek-** in Appendix.] **—ex·pli·ca′tion** *n.* **—ex′pli·ca′tor** *n.*

ex·pli·ca·tion de texte (ĕk-splē-kä-syôɴ də tĕkst′) *n., pl.* **ex·pli·ca·tions de texte** (ĕk-splē-kä-syôɴ də tĕkst′). A method of literary criticism in which the interrelated details of a written work are examined and analyzed in an effort to understand its structure and discover meanings. [French : *explication,* explanation + *de,* of + *texte,* text.]

ex·pli·ca·tive (ĕk′splĭ-kā′tĭv, ĭk-splĭk′ə-tĭv) *adj.* Serving to explain; explanatory. **—ex′pli·ca′tive** *n.* **—ex′pli·ca′tive·ly** *adv.*

ex·plic·it (ĭk-splĭs′ĭt) *adj.* **1.a.** Fully and clearly expressed; leaving nothing implied. **b.** Fully and clearly defined or formulated: *"generalizations that are powerful, precise, and explicit"* (Frederick Turner). **2.** Forthright and unreserved in expression: *They were explicit in their criticism.* **3.a.** Readily observable: *an explicit sign of trouble.* **b.** Describing or portraying nudity or sexual activity in graphic detail. [Latin *explicitus,* past participle of *explicāre,* to unfold. See EXPLICATE.] **—ex·plic′it·ly** *adv.* **—ex·plic′it·ness** *n.*

SYNONYMS: *explicit, categorical, definite, express, specific.* The central meaning shared by these adjectives is "entirely clear and unambiguous": *explicit statements; a categorical refusal; a definite answer; my express wishes; a specific purpose.*
ANTONYM: *ambiguous.*

explicit function *n. Mathematics.* A function, such as $y = 4x + 3$, whose value may be computed from the independent variable.

ex·plode (ĭk-splōd′) *v.* **-plod·ed, -plod·ing, -plodes.** —*intr.* **1.** To release mechanical, chemical, or nuclear energy by the sudden production of gases in a confined space: *The bomb exploded.* **2.** To burst violently as a result of internal pressure. **3.** To shatter with a loud noise: *I threw the vase on the floor and it exploded into tiny pieces.* **4.** To burst forth or break out suddenly and often violently: *My neighbor exploded in rage at the trespassers.* **5.** To increase suddenly, sharply, and without control: *The population level in this area has exploded during the past 12 years.* **6.** *Sports.* To hit a golf ball out of a sand trap with a shot that scatters the sand. —*tr.* **1.** To cause to release energy or burst violently and noisily: *The children exploded three firecrackers.* **2.** To show to be false or unreliable: *explode a hypothesis.* **3.** *Sports.* To hit (a golf ball) out of a sand trap with an explosive shot. [Latin *explōdere,* to drive out by clapping : *ex-,* ex- + *plaudere,* to clap.] **—ex·plod′er** *n.*

explode
Jack Nicklaus during a practice round at the U.S. Open golf tournament in 1986

ex·plod·ed view (ĕk-splō′dĭd) *n.* An illustration or a diagram of a construction that shows its parts separately but in positions that indicate their proper relationships to the whole.

ex·ploit (ĕk′sploit′, ĭk-sploit′) *n.* An act or deed, especially a brilliant or heroic one. See Synonyms at **feat**[1]. **—exploit** (ĭk-sploit′, ĕk′sploit′) *tr.v.* **-ploit·ed, -ploit·ing, -ploits.** **1.** To employ to the greatest possible advantage: *exploit one's talents.* **2.** To make use of selfishly or unethically: *a country that exploited peasant labor.* See Synonyms at **manipulate.** **3.** To advertise; promote. [Middle English, from Old French *esploit,* from Latin *explicitum,* neuter past participle of *explicāre,* to unfold. See EXPLICATE.] **—ex·ploit′a·bil′i·ty** *n.* **—ex·ploit′a·ble** *adj.* **—ex·**

ă pat	oi boy
ā pay	ou out
âr care	o͝o took
ä father	o͞o boot
ĕ pet	ŭ cut
ē be	ûr urge
ĭ pit	th thin
ī pie	*th* this
îr pier	hw which
ŏ pot	zh vision
ō toe	ə about, item
ô paw	♦ regionalism

Stress marks: ′ (primary); ′ (secondary), as in **dictionary** (dĭk′shə-nĕr′ē)

exposure meter

expressionism
No More War!
by Käthe Kollwitz

ploit′a·tive, ex·ploit′ive *adj.* **—ex·ploit′a·tive·ly, ex·ploit′ive·ly** *adv.* **—ex·ploit′er** *n.*

ex·ploi·ta·tion (ĕk′sploi-tā′shən) *n.* **1.** The act of employing to the greatest possible advantage: *exploitation of copper deposits.* **2.** Utilization of another person or group for selfish purposes: *exploitation of unwary consumers.* **3.** An advertising or a publicity program.

ex·plo·ra·tion (ĕk′splə-rā′shən) *n.* The act or an instance of exploring: *Arctic exploration; exploration of new theories.* **—ex·plor′a·to′ry** (ĭk-splôr′ə-tôr′ē, -splōr′ə-tōr′ē) *adj.*

ex·plore (ĭk-splôr′, -splōr′) *v.* **-plored, -plor·ing, -plores.** —*tr.* **1.** To investigate systematically; examine: *explore every possibility.* **2.** To search into or travel in for the purpose of discovery: *exploring outer space.* **3.** *Medicine.* To examine for diagnostic purposes. —*intr.* To make a careful examination or search: *scientists who have been known to explore in this region of the earth.* [Latin *explōrāre* : *ex-*, ex- + perhaps *plōrāre*, to cry out, as to rouse game.]

ex·plor·er (ĭk-splôr′ər, -splōr′-) *n.* **1.** One that explores, especially one that explores a geographic area. **2.** An implement or a tool used for exploring; a probe. **3. Explorer.** A person aged 14–20 who is a participant in the exploring program of the Boy Scouts of America.

ex·plo·sion (ĭk-splō′zhən) *n.* **1.a.** A release of mechanical, chemical, or nuclear energy in a sudden and often violent manner with the generation of high temperature and usually with the release of gases. **b.** A violent bursting as a result of internal pressure. **c.** The loud, sharp sound made as a result of either of these actions. **2.** A sudden, often vehement outburst: *an explosion of rage.* **3.** A sudden, great increase: *a population explosion; the explosion of illegal drug use.* **4.** *Linguistics.* See **plosion.** [Latin *explōsiō*, *explōsiōn-*, a driving off, from *explōsus*, past participle of *explōdere*, to drive out by clapping. See EXPLODE.]

ex·plo·sive (ĭk-splō′sĭv) *adj.* **1.** Relating to or having the nature of an explosion. **2.** Tending to explode. **—explosive** *n.* **1.** A substance, especially a prepared chemical, that explodes or causes explosion. **2.** *Linguistics.* A plosive. **—ex·plo′sive·ly** *adv.* **—ex·plo′sive·ness** *n.*

ex·po (ĕk′spō) *n., pl.* **-pos.** *Informal.* An exposition.

ex·po·nent (ĭk-spō′nənt, ĕk′spō′nənt) *n.* **1.** One that expounds or interprets. **2.** One that speaks for, represents, or advocates: *Our senator is an exponent of free trade.* **3.** *Abbr.* **exp** *Mathematics.* A number or symbol, as 3 in $(x + y)^3$, placed to the right of and above another number, symbol, or expression, denoting the power to which that number, symbol, or expression is to be raised. In this sense, also called *power.* **—exponent** *adj.* Expository; explanatory. [Latin *expōnēns*, *expōnent-*, present participle of *expōnere*, to expound. See EXPOUND.]

ex·po·nen·tial (ĕk′spə-nĕn′shəl) *adj.* *Abbr.* **exp 1.** Of or relating to an exponent. **2.** *Mathematics.* **a.** Containing, involving, or expressed as an exponent. **b.** Expressed in terms of a designated power of *e*, the base of natural logarithms. **—ex′po·nen′tial·ly** *adv.*

ex·po·nen·ti·a·tion (ĕk′spə-nĕn′shē-ā′shən) *n.* *Mathematics.* The act of raising a quantity to a power.

ex·port (ĭk-spôrt′, -spōrt′, ĕk′spôrt′, -spōrt′) *v.* **-port·ed, -port·ing, -ports.** —*tr.* **1.** To send or transport (a commodity, for example) abroad, especially for trade or sale. **2.** To cause the spread of (an idea, for example) in another part of the world; transmit. —*intr.* To send or transport abroad merchandise, especially for sale or trade. **—export** (ĕk′spôrt′, -spōrt′) *n.* *Abbr.* **exp.** Exportation. [Middle English *exsport*, from Latin *exportāre* : *ex-*, ex- + *portāre*, to carry; see **per-**[2] in Appendix.] **—ex·port′a·bil′i·ty** *n.* **—ex·port′a·ble** *adj.* **—ex·port′er** *n.*

ex·por·ta·tion (ĕk′spôr-tā′shən, -spōr-) *n.* **1.** The act of exporting. **2.** Something exported; an export.

ex·pose (ĭk-spōz′) *tr.v.* **-posed, -pos·ing, -pos·es. 1.a.** To subject or allow to be subjected to an action or an influence: *exposed themselves to disease; exposed their children to classical music.* **b.** To subject (a photographic film, for example) to the action of light. **2.** To make visible: *Cleaning exposed the grain of the wood.* See Synonyms at **show. 3.a.** To make known (something discreditable). **b.** To reveal the guilt or wrongdoing of: *expose a criminal.* See Synonyms at **reveal**[1]. **4.a.** To deprive of shelter or protection. **b.** To subject to needless risk: *an officer who exposed the troops to enemy crossfire.* [Middle English *exposen*, from Old French *exposer*, alteration (influenced by *poser*, to put, place; see POSE[1]) of Latin *expōnere*, to set forth. See EXPOUND.] **—ex·pos′er** *n.*

ex·po·sé (ĕk′spō-zā′) *n.* **1.** An exposure or a revelation of something discreditable. **2.** A formal exposition of facts. [French, past participle of *exposer*, to expose, from Old French. See EXPOSE.]

ex·po·si·tion (ĕk′spə-zĭsh′ən) *n.* **1.** A setting forth of meaning or intent. **2.a.** A statement or rhetorical discourse intended to give information about or an explanation of difficult material. **b.** The art or technique of composing such discourses. **3.** *Music.* **a.** The first part of a composition in sonata form that introduces the themes. **b.** The opening section of a fugue. **4.** The part of a play that provides the background information needed to understand the characters and the action. **5.** An act or example of exposing. **6.** A public exhibition or show, as of artistic or industrial developments. [Middle English *exposicioun*, from Old French *exposition*, from Latin *expositiō*, *expositiōn-*, from *expositus*, past participle of *expōnere*, to expound. See EXPOUND.] **—ex·pos′i·tive** (ĭk-spŏz′ĭ-tĭv), **ex·pos′i·to′ry** (-tôr′ē, -tōr′ē) *adj.* **—ex·pos′i·tor** *n.*

ex post fac·to (ĕks′ pōst făk′tō) *adj.* Formulated, enacted, or operating retroactively. Used especially of a law. [Latin *ex postfactō* : *ex*, from + *postfactō*, ablative of *postfactum*, that which is done afterward.]

ex·pos·tu·late (ĭk-spŏs′chə-lāt′) *intr.v.* **-lat·ed, -lat·ing, -lates.** To reason earnestly with someone in an effort to dissuade or correct; remonstrate. See Synonyms at **object.** [Latin *expostulāre*, *expostulāt-* : *ex-*, intensive pref.; see EX– + *postulāre*, to demand; see **prek-** in Appendix.] **—ex·pos′tu·la′tion** *n.* **—ex·pos′tu·la′tor** *n.* **—ex·pos′tu·la·to′ry** (-lə-tôr′ē, -tōr′ē), **ex·pos′tu·la′tive** *adj.*

ex·po·sure (ĭk-spō′zhər) *n.* **1.** The act or an instance of exposing, as: **a.** An act of subjecting or an instance of being subjected to an action or an influence: *their first exposure to big city life.* **b.** Appearance in public or in the mass media: *an actor with much recent exposure in television.* **c.** Revelation, especially of crime or guilt: *exposure of graft in county government.* **2.** The condition of being exposed, especially to severe weather or other forces of nature: *was hospitalized for the effects of exposure.* **3.** A position in relation to climatic or weather conditions or points of the compass: *Our house has a southern exposure.* **4.a.** The act of exposing sensitized photographic film or plate. **b.** A photographic plate or a piece of film so exposed. **c.** The amount of radiant energy needed to expose a photographic film.

exposure meter *n.* A photoelectric instrument that measures the light intensity in a given area and, in photographic use, indicates the correct settings for an optimum exposure. Also called *light meter.*

ex·pound (ĭk-spound′) *v.* **-pound·ed, -pound·ing, -pounds.** —*tr.* **1.** To give a detailed statement of; set forth: *expounded the intricacies of the new tax law.* **2.** To explain in detail; elucidate: *The speaker expounded the approach of positive thinking.* See Synonyms at **explain.** —*intr.* To make a detailed statement: *The professor was expounding on a favorite topic.* [Middle English *expounden*, from Anglo-Norman *espoundre*, from Latin *expōnere* : *ex-*, ex- + *pōnere*, to place; see **apo-** in Appendix.] **—ex·pound′er** *n.*

ex·press (ĭk-sprĕs′) *tr.v.* **-pressed, -press·ing, -press·es. 1.** To set forth in words; state. **2.** To manifest or communicate, as by a gesture; show. See Synonyms at **vent**[1]. **3.** To make known the feelings or opinions of (oneself), as by statement or art. **4.** To convey or suggest a representation of; depict: *The painting expresses the rage of war victims.* **5.** To represent by a sign or a symbol; symbolize: *express a fraction as a decimal.* **6.** To squeeze or press out, as juice from an orange. **7.** To send by special messenger or rapid transport: *express a package to Los Angeles.* **8.** *Genetics.* **a.** To cause (itself) to produce an effect or a phenotype. Used of a gene: *The gene expressed itself under specific environmental conditions.* **b.** To manifest the effects of (a gene): *Half of the people who inherit the gene express it.* **c.** To manifest (a genetic trait): *All the mice in the study expressed the defect.* **—express** *adj.* *Abbr.* **ex., exp. 1.** Definitely and explicitly stated: *their express wish.* See Synonyms at **explicit. 2.** Particular; specific: *an express plan.* **3.a.** Sent out with or moving at high speed. **b.** Direct, rapid, and usually nonstop: *express delivery of packages; an express bus.* **c.** Of, relating to, or appropriate for rapid travel: *express lanes on a freeway.* **—express** *adv.* By express delivery or transport. **—express** *n.* *Abbr.* **ex., exp. 1.a.** A rapid, efficient system for the delivery of goods and mail. **b.** Goods and mail conveyed by such a system. **2.** A means of transport, such as a train, that travels rapidly and makes few or no stops before its destination. **3.** *Chiefly British.* **a.** A special messenger. **b.** A message delivered by special courier. [Middle English *expressen*, from Old French *expresser*, from Medieval Latin *expressāre*, frequentative of Latin *exprimere* : Latin *ex-*, ex- + Latin *premere*, to press; see **per-**[4] in Appendix.] **—ex·press′er** *n.* **—ex·press′i·ble** *adj.*

ex·pres·sion (ĭk-sprĕsh′ən) *n.* **1.** The act of expressing, conveying, or representing in words, art, music, or movement; a manifestation: *an expression of rural values.* **2.** Something that expresses or communicates: *Let this plaque serve as an expression of our esteem.* **3.** *Mathematics.* An operation or a quantity stated in symbolic form, such as $\sqrt{x}$, y^2, or $x + y$. **4.** The manner in which one expresses oneself, especially in speaking, depicting, or performing. **5.** A particular word or phrase: *"an old Yankee expression . . . 'Stand up and be counted'"* (Charles Kuralt). **6.** The outward manifestation of a mood or a disposition: *My tears are an expression of my grief.* **7.** A facial aspect or a look that conveys a special feeling: *an expression of scorn.* **8.** The act of pressing or squeezing out. **9.** The act or process of expressing a gene.

ex·pres·sion·ism (ĭk-sprĕsh′ə-nĭz′əm) *n.* A movement in the arts during the early part of the 20th century that emphasized subjective expression of the artist's inner experiences. **—ex·pres′sion·ist** *n.* **—ex·pres′sion·is′tic** *adj.* **—ex·pres′sion·is′ti·cal·ly** *adv.*

ex·pres·sion·less (ĭk-sprĕsh′ən-lĭs) *adj.* Lacking expression: *Their faces remained expressionless as they listened to the bad news.*

ex·pres·sive (ĭk-sprĕs′ĭv) *adj.* **1.** Of, relating to, or characterized by expression. **2.** Serving to express or indicate: *actions expressive of frustration.* **3.** Full of expression; significant: *an expressive glance.* **—ex·pres′sive·ly** *adv.* **—ex·pres′sive·ness** *n.*

SYNONYMS: *expressive, eloquent, meaningful, significant.* The central meaning shared by these adjectives is "effectively conveying a feeling, an idea, or a mood": *an expressive gesture; an eloquent speech; a meaningful look; a significant smile.*

ex·pres·siv·i·ty (ĕk′sprĕ-sĭv′ĭ-tē) *n., pl.* **-ties. 1.** The quality of being expressive. **2.** *Genetics.* The degree to which an expressed gene produces its effects in an organism.

ex·press·ly (ĭk-sprĕs′lē) *adv.* **1.** In an express or a definite manner; explicitly: *I expressly ordered the visitor to leave.* **2.** Especially; particularly: *tools designed expressly for left-handed workers.*

ex·pres·so (ĭk-sprĕs′ō, ĕk-) *n.* Variant of **espresso.**

ex·press·way (ĭk-sprĕs′wā′) *n. Abbr.* **expy** A major divided highway designed for high-speed travel. Also called *freeway, superhighway, thruway.*

ex·pro·pri·ate (ĕk-sprō′prē-āt′) *tr.v.* **-at·ed, -at·ing, -ates. 1.** To deprive of possession: *expropriated the property owners who lived in the path of the new highway.* **2.** To transfer (property) to oneself. [Medieval Latin *expropriāre, expropriāt-* : Latin *ex-*, ex- + Latin *propriāre*, to appropriate (from *proprius*, one's own; see PROPER).] **—ex·pro′pri·a′tion** *n.* **—ex·pro′pri·a′tor** *n.* **—ex·pro′pri·a·to′ry** (-ə-tôr′ē, -tōr′ē) *adj.*

expt. *abbr.* Experiment.

exptl. *abbr.* Experimental.

ex·pul·sion (ĭk-spŭl′shən) *n.* The act of expelling or the state of being expelled. [Middle English *expulsioun*, from Old French *expulsion*, from Latin *expulsiō, expulsiōn-*, from *expulsus*, past participle of *expellere*, to expel. See EXPEL.]

ex·punc·tion (ĭk-spŭngk′shən, -spŭng′shən) *n.* The act of expunging or the condition of being expunged: *expunction of the records of the crime.* [Late Latin *expunctiō, expunctiōn-*, execution, from Latin *expunctus*, past participle of *expungere*, to strike out. See EXPUNGE.]

ex·punge (ĭk-spŭnj′) *tr.v.* **-punged, -pung·ing, -pung·es. 1.** To erase or strike out: *"I have corrected some factual slips, expunged some repetitions"* (Kenneth Tynan). **2.** To eliminate completely; annihilate. See Synonyms at **erase.** [Latin *expungere* : *ex-*, ex- + *pungere*, to prick; see **peuk-** in Appendix.] **—ex·pung′er** *n.*

ex·pur·gate (ĕk′spər-gāt′) *tr.v.* **-gat·ed, -gat·ing, -gates.** To remove erroneous, vulgar, obscene, or otherwise objectionable material from (a book, for example) before publication. [Latin *expūrgāre, expūrgāt-*, to purify : *ex-*, intensive pref.; see EX– + *pūrgāre*, to cleanse; see **peuə-** in Appendix.] **—ex′pur·ga′tion** *n.* **—ex′pur·ga′tor** *n.*

ex·pur·ga·to·ry (ĭk-spûr′gə-tôr′ē, -tōr′ē) also **ex·pur·ga·to·ri·al** (-tôr′ē-əl, -tōr′-) *adj.* Of or relating to expurgation or an expurgator.

expy *abbr.* Expressway.

ex·qui·site (ĕk′skwĭ-zĭt, ĭk-skwĭz′ĭt) *adj.* **1.** Characterized by intricate and beautiful design or execution: *an exquisite chalice.* **2.** Of such beauty or delicacy as to arouse delight: *an exquisite sunset.* See Synonyms at **delicate. 3.** Excellent; flawless: *plays the piano with exquisite technique.* **4.** Acutely perceptive or discriminating: *an exquisite sense of color.* **5.** Intense; keen: *suffered exquisite pain.* **6.** *Obsolete.* Ingeniously devised or thought out. **—exquisite** *n.* One who is excessively fastidious in dress, manners, or taste. [Middle English *exquisit*, carefully chosen, from Latin *exquīsītus*, past participle of *exquīrere*, to search out : *ex-*, ex- + *quaerere*, to seek.] **—ex′qui·site·ly** *adv.* **—ex′qui·site·ness** *n.*

exr. *abbr.* Executor.

exrx. *abbr.* Executrix.

ex·san·gui·nate (ĕks-săng′gwə-nāt′) *tr.v.* **-nat·ed, -nat·ing, -nates.** To drain of blood. [From Latin *exsanguinātus*, drained of blood : *ex-*, ex- + *sanguis, sanguin-*, blood.] **—ex·san′gui·na′tion** *n.*

ex·san·guine (ĕks-săng′gwĭn) *adj.* Lacking blood; anemic. [Latin *exsanguis, exsanguin-* : *ex-*, ex- + *sanguis*, blood.]

ex·scind (ĭk-sĭnd′) *tr.v.* **-scind·ed, -scind·ing, -scinds.** To cut out; excise. [Latin *exscindere* : *ex-*, ex- + *scindere*, to cut; see **skei-** in Appendix.]

ex·sert (ĭk-sûrt′) *tr.v.* **-sert·ed, -sert·ing, -serts.** To thrust (something) out or forth; cause to protrude. **—exsert** Also **ex·sert·ed** (-sûr′tĭd) *adj.* Thrust outward or protruding, as stamens projecting beyond petals. [Latin *exserere, exsert-*. See EXERT.] **—ex·ser′tion** *n.*

ex·sic·cate (ĕk′sĭ-kāt′) *intr. & tr.v.* **-cat·ed, -cat·ing, -cates.** To dry up or cause to dry up. [Middle English *exsiccaten*, from Latin *exsiccāre, exsiccāt-* : *ex-*, ex- + *siccāre*, to dry (from *siccus*, dry).] **—ex′sic·ca′tion** *n.* **—ex′sic·ca′tive** *adj.* **—ex′sic·ca′tor** *n.*

ex·stip·u·late (ĕks-stĭp′yə-lĭt) *adj. Botany.* Having no stipules.

ext. *abbr.* **1.** Extension. **2.a.** External. **b.** Externally. **3.** Extinct. **4.** Extra. **5.** Extract.

ex·tant (ĕk′stənt, ĕk-stănt′) *adj.* **1.** Still in existence; not destroyed, lost, or extinct: *extant manuscripts.* **2.** *Archaic.* Standing out; projecting. [Latin *exstāns, exstant-*, present participle of *exstāre*, to stand out : *ex-*, ex- + *stāre*, to stand; see **stā-** in Appendix.]

ex·tem·po·ral (ĭk-stĕm′pər-əl) *adj. Archaic.* Extemporaneous. [Latin *extemporālis*, from *ex tempore.* See EXTEMPORE.]

ex·tem·po·ra·ne·ous (ĭk-stĕm′pə-rā′nē-əs) *adj.* **1.** Carried out or performed with little or no preparation; impromptu: *an extemporaneous piano recital.* **2.** Prepared in advance but delivered without notes or text: *an extemporaneous speech.* **3.** Skilled at or given to unrehearsed speech or performance: *an accomplished extemporaneous speaker.* **4.** Provided, made, or adapted as an expedient; makeshift: *an extemporaneous policy decision.* [From Late Latin *extemporāneus*, from Latin *ex tempore.* See EXTEMPORE.] **—ex·tem′po·ra·ne′i·ty** (-pər-ə-nē′ĭ-tē) *n.* **—ex·tem′po·ra′ne·ous·ly** *adv.* **—ex·tem′po·ra′ne·ous·ness** *n.*

SYNONYMS: *extemporaneous, extemporary, extempore, impromptu, offhand, unrehearsed, unpremeditated, ad-lib.* These adjectives mean spoken, performed, done, or composed with little or no preparation or forethought. *Extemporaneous, extemporary,* and *extempore* most often apply to discourse, as a public speech, that is delivered without the assistance of a written text, though it may have been planned in advance: *an extemporaneous address; an extemporary lecture; an extempore skit. Impromptu* even more strongly suggests action or expression that comes on the spur of the moment in response to an unforeseen need: *an impromptu speech; an impromptu dinner. Offhand* implies not only spontaneity but also a casual or even cavalier manner: *an offhand remark.* What is *unrehearsed* is said or done without rehearsal or practice though not necessarily without forethought: *a few unrehearsed comments. Unpremeditated* applies to action taken without prior thought or plan; often the term implies impulsiveness prompted by strong feeling: *asked an unpremeditated question.* Something that is *ad-lib* is spontaneous and improvised and therefore not part of a prepared script or score: *an ad-lib joke; an ad-lib solo.*

ex·tem·po·rar·y (ĭk-stĕm′pə-rĕr′ē) *adj.* Spoken, done, or composed with little or no preparation or forethought. See Synonyms at **extemporaneous.** [From EXTEMPORE.] **—ex·tem′po·rar′i·ly** (-râr′ə-lē) *adv.*

ex·tem·po·re (ĭk-stĕm′pə-rē) *adj.* Spoken, carried out, or composed with little or no preparation or forethought. See Synonyms at **extemporaneous. —extempore** *adv.* In an extemporaneous manner. [Latin *ex tempore* : *ex*, of; see EX– + *tempore*, ablative of *tempus*, time.]

ex·tem·po·rize (ĭk-stĕm′pə-rīz′) *v.* **-rized, -riz·ing, -riz·es.** *—tr.* To do or perform (something) without prior preparation or practice: *extemporized an acceptance speech.* *—intr.* To perform an act or utter something in an impromptu manner; improvise: *"bravely demonstrating his ability to extemporize intelligently"* (William Safire). **—ex·tem′po·ri·za′tion** (-pər-ĭ-zā′shən) *n.* **—ex·tem′po·riz′er** *n.*

ex·tend (ĭk-stĕnd′) *v.* **-tend·ed, -tend·ing, -tends.** *—tr.* **1.** To open or straighten (something) out; unbend: *extended the legs of the folding table.* **2.** To stretch or spread (something) out to greater or fullest length: *extended the radio antenna.* **3.a.** To exert (oneself) vigorously or to full capacity: *Few mountain climbers have extended themselves as those two have.* **b.** To cause to move at full gallop. Used of a horse. **4.a.** To increase in quantity or bulk by adding a cheaper substance: *used rice or pasta to extend leftover casseroles.* **b.** To adulterate. **5.a.** To enlarge the area, scope, or range of. **b.** To expand the influence of. **c.** To make more comprehensive or inclusive. See Synonyms at **increase. 6.a.** To offer: *extend one's greetings.* **b.** To make available; provide: *extend credit to qualified purchasers.* **7.a.** To cause (something) to be or last longer: *extended our visit by a day.* **b.** To prolong the time allowed for payment of: *extend a loan for three more months.* **8.** *Chiefly British.* **a.** To appraise or assess; value. **b.** To seize or make a levy on for the purpose of settling a debt. *—intr.* To be or become long, large, or comprehensive: *influence that extended to other continents; table legs that extend by unscrewing.* [Middle English *extenden*, from Old French *extendre*, from Latin *extendere* : *ex-*, ex- + *tendere*, to stretch; see **ten-** in Appendix.] **—ex·tend′i·bil′i·ty** *n.* **—ex·tend′a·ble, ex·tend′i·ble** *adj.*

ex·tend·ed (ĭk-stĕn′dĭd) *adj.* **1.** Stretched or pulled out: *an extended telescope.* **2.** Continued for a long period of time; protracted: *had an extended vacation in the Alps.* **3.** Enlarged or broad in meaning, scope, or influence: *an extended sense of the word* honest. **—ex·tend′ed·ly** *adv.*

extended family *n.* **1.** A family group that consists of parents, children, and other close relatives, often living in close proximity. **2.** A group of relatives, such as those of three generations, who live in close geographic proximity rather than under the same roof.

ex·tend·er (ĭk-stĕn′dər) *n.* A substance added to another substance to modify, dilute, or adulterate it: *meat loaf that contained oatmeal as an extender.*

ex·ten·si·ble (ĭk-stĕn′sə-bəl) *adj.* **1.** Capable of being extended or protruded: *an extensible tongue; extensible tables.* **2.** *Computer Science.* Of or relating to a programming language or a system that can be modified by changing or adding features. **—ex·ten′si·bil′i·ty** *n.*

ex·ten·sile (ĭk-stĕn′sĭl) *adj.* Extensible.

ex·ten·sion (ĭk-stĕn′shən) *n. Abbr.* **ext. 1.** The act of ex-

ă pat	oi boy
ā pay	ou out
âr care	ŏŏ took
ä father	ōō boot
ĕ pet	ŭ cut
ē be	ûr urge
ĭ pit	th thin
ī pie	*th* this
îr pier	hw which
ŏ pot	zh vision
ō toe	ə about, item
ô paw	♦ regionalism

Stress marks: ′ (primary); ′ (secondary), as in **dictionary** (dĭk′shə-nĕr′ē)

tending or the condition of being extended. **2.** The amount, degree, or range to which something extends or can extend: *The wire has an extension of 50 feet.* **3.a.** The act of straightening or extending a limb. **b.** The position assumed by an extended limb. **4.** *Medicine.* The application of traction to a fractured or dislocated limb to restore the normal position. **5.a.** An addition that increases the area, influence, operation, or contents of something: *an extension for the vacuum cleaner; built a new extension onto the hospital wing.* **b.** An additional telephone connected to a main line. **6.a.** An allowance of extra time, especially for the repayment of a debt. **b.** The period of this extra time: *three months' extension on the loan.* **7.** The property of an object by which it occupies space. **8.** A program in a university, college, or school that offers instruction, as by television or correspondence, to persons unable to attend at the usual time or in the usual place. **9.** *Logic.* The class of objects designated by a specific term or concept; denotation. **10.** *Mathematics.* A set that includes a given and similar set as a subset. —*attributive.* Often used to modify another noun: *an extension ladder; an extension cord.* [Middle English *extensioun,* from Old French *extension,* from Latin *extēnsiō, extēnsiōn-,* from *extēnsus,* past participle of *extendere,* to extend. See EXTEND.] **—ex·ten′sion·al** *adj.*

ex·ten·si·ty (ĭk-stĕn′sĭ-tē) *n., pl.* **-ties. 1.a.** The quality of having extension or being extensive. **b.** A specific degree or range of extension. **2.** The attribute of sensation that enables one to perceive space or size.

ex·ten·sive (ĭk-stĕn′sĭv) *adj.* **1.** Large in extent, range, or amount. **2.** Of or relating to the cultivation of vast areas of land with a minimum of labor or expense. **—ex·ten′sive·ly** *adv.* **—ex·ten′sive·ness** *n.*

ex·ten·som·e·ter (ĕk′stĕn-sŏm′ĭ-tər) *n.* An instrument used to measure minute deformations in a test specimen of a material. [EXTENS(ION) + -METER.]

ex·ten·sor (ĭk-stĕn′sər) *n.* A muscle that extends or straightens a limb or body part. [New Latin, from Latin *extēnsus,* past participle of *extendere,* to stretch out. See EXTEND.]

ex·tent (ĭk-stĕnt′) *n.* **1.a.** The range, magnitude, or distance over which a thing extends: *landowners unaware of the extent of their own holdings.* **b.** The degree to which a thing extends: *prosecuted to the fullest extent of the law.* **2.** An extensive space or area: *an extent of desert.* **3.** *Law.* **a.** A writ allowing a creditor to assume temporary ownership of a debtor's property. **b.** In Great Britain, a writ allowing a creditor to seize a debtor's property temporarily. **c.** The seizure in execution of such a writ. **4.** *Archaic.* An assessment or a valuation, as of land in Britain, especially for taxation. [Middle English *extente,* assessment on land, from Anglo-Norman, from feminine past participle of *extendre,* to extend, from Latin *extendere.* See EXTEND.]

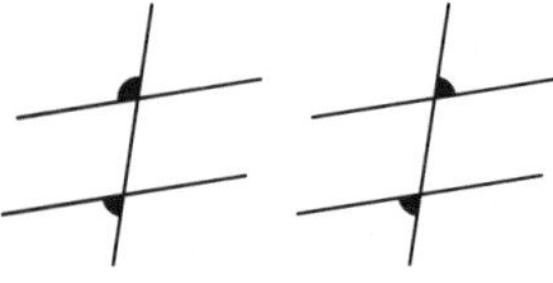

exterior angle
Left: Exterior angles on the same side
Right: Exterior opposite angles

ex·ten·u·ate (ĭk-stĕn′yo͞o-āt′) *tr.v.* **-at·ed, -at·ing, -ates. 1.** To lessen or attempt to lessen the magnitude or seriousness of, especially by providing partial excuses. See Synonyms at **palliate. 2.** *Archaic.* **a.** To make thin or emaciated. **b.** To reduce the strength of. **3.** *Obsolete.* To belittle; disparage. [Latin *extenuāre, extenuāt-* : *ex-,* ex- + *tenuāre,* to make thin (from *tenuis,* thin; see **ten-** in Appendix).] **—ex·ten′u·a′tive** *adj. & n.* **—ex·ten′u·a′tor** *n.* **—ex·ten′u·a·to′ry** (-ə-tôr′ē, -tōr′ē) *adj.*

ex·ten·u·a·tion (ĭk-stĕn′yo͞o-ā′shən) *n.* **1.** The act of extenuating or the condition of being extenuated; partial justification. **2.** A partial excuse.

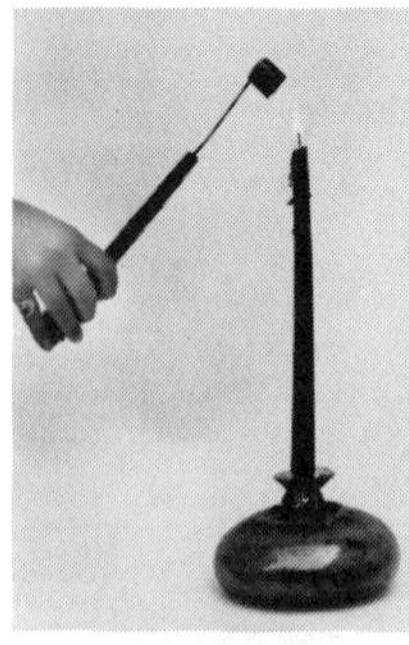

extinguisher
Candle snuffer

ex·te·ri·or (ĭk-stîr′ē-ər) *adj.* **1.** Outer; external: *the exterior door.* **2.** Originating or acting from the outside: *exterior influences on the negotiations.* **3.** Suitable for use outside: *an exterior paint.* **—exterior** *n.* **1.** A part or a surface that is outside: *the exterior of the house.* **2.** An external or outward appearance: *a friendly exterior.* **3.** A representation in visual art of the outdoors: *The film includes some striking exteriors.* [Latin, comparative of *exter,* outward. See **eghs** in Appendix.] **—ex·te′ri·or·ly** *adv.*

exterior angle *n. Mathematics.* **1.** The angle between any side of a polygon and an extended adjacent side. **2.** Any of the four angles that do not include a region of the space between two lines intersected by a transversal.

ex·te·ri·or·i·ty (ĭk-stîr′ē-ôr′ĭ-tē, -ŏr′-) *n.* Outwardness; externality.

ex·te·ri·or·ize (ĭk-stîr′ē-ə-rīz′) *tr.v.* **-ized, -iz·ing, -iz·es.** To turn outward; externalize.

ex·ter·mi·nate (ĭk-stûr′mə-nāt′) *tr.v.* **-nat·ed, -nat·ing, -nates.** To get rid of by destroying completely; extirpate. See Synonyms at **abolish.** [Latin *extermināre, extermināt-,* to drive out : *ex-,* ex- + *termināre,* to mark boundaries (from *terminus,* boundary marker).] **—ex·ter′mi·na′tion** *n.* **—ex·ter′mi·na′tive, ex·ter′mi·na·to′ry** (-nə-tôr′ē, -tōr′ē) *adj.*

ex·ter·mi·na·tor (ĭk-stûr′mə-nā′tər) *n.* One that exterminates, especially one whose occupation is the extermination of vermin.

ex·tern or **ex·terne** (ĕk′stûrn′) *n.* A person associated with but not officially residing in an institution, especially a nonresident physician on a hospital staff. [Latin *externus,* external. See EXTERNAL.] **—ex′tern·ship′** *n.*

ex·ter·nal (ĭk-stûr′nəl) *adj. Abbr.* **ext. 1.** Relating to, existing on, or connected with the outside or an outer part; exterior. **2.** Suitable for application to the outside: *external paints.* **3.** Existing independently of the mind. **4.** Acting or coming from the outside: *external pressures.* **5.** Of or relating chiefly to outward appearance; superficial: *"An internal sense of righteousness dwindles into an external concern for reputation"* (A.R. Gurney, Jr.). **6.** Of or relating to foreign affairs or foreign countries: *the country's minister of external affairs.* **—external** *n.* **1.** An exterior part or surface. **2. externals. a.** Outer circumstances. **b.** Outward appearances: *was charming as far as the externals went.* [Middle English, from Latin *externus,* outward, from *exter.* See **eghs** in Appendix.] **—ex·ter′nal·ly** *adv.*

external auditory canal *n.* See **ear canal.**

ex·ter·nal-com·bus·tion engine (ĭk-stûr′nəl-kəm-bŭs′chən) *n.* An engine, such as a steam engine, in which the fuel is burned outside the engine cylinder.

external ear *n.* The outer portion of the ear including the auricle and the passage leading to the eardrum. Also called *outer ear.*

ex·ter·nal·ism (ĭk-stûr′nə-lĭz′əm) *n.* Excessive concern with outer circumstances or appearances. **—ex·ter′nal·ist** *n.*

ex·ter·nal·i·ty (ĕk′stər-năl′ĭ-tē) *n., pl.* **-ties. 1.** The condition or quality of being external or externalized. **2.a.** Something that is external. **b.** An incidental condition that may affect a course of action: *"Our economic system treats environmental degradation as an externality—a cost that does not enter into the conventional arithmetic that determines how we use our resources"* (Barry Commoner).

ex·ter·nal·ize (ĭk-stûr′nə-līz′) *tr.v.* **-ized, -iz·ing, -iz·es. 1.a.** To make external. **b.** To manifest externally: *"Marriage is a nice way to externalize the private commitments made between you"* (Patti Davis). **2.** To attribute to outside causes. **3.** To project or attribute (inner conflicts or feelings) to external circumstances or causes. **—ex·ter′nal·i·za′tion** (-nə-lĭ-zā′shən) *n.*

external respiration *n.* The exchange of oxygen and carbon dioxide between the environment and respiratory organs such as gills or lungs.

ex·ter·o·cep·tor (ĕk′stə-rō-sĕp′tər) *n.* A sense organ, such as the ear, that receives and responds to stimuli originating from outside the body. [Latin *exter,* outside; see EXTERIOR + (RE)CEPTOR.] **—ex′ter·o·cep′tive** *adj.*

ex·ter·ri·to·ri·al (ĕks′tĕr-ĭ-tôr′ē-əl, -tōr′-) *adj.* Extraterritorial. **—ex′ter·ri·to′ri·al′i·ty** (-ăl′ĭ-tē) *n.* **—ex′ter·ri·to′ri·al·ly** *adv.*

ex·tinct (ĭk-stĭngkt′) *adj. Abbr.* **ext. 1.** No longer existing or living: *an extinct species.* **2.** No longer burning or active: *an extinct volcano.* **3.** No longer in use: *an extinct custom.* See Synonyms at **dead. 4.** *Law.* Lacking a claimant; void: *an extinct title.* [Middle English, from Latin *exstīnctus,* past participle of *exstinguere,* to extinguish. See EXTINGUISH.]

ex·tinc·tion (ĭk-stĭngk′shən) *n.* **1.a.** The act of extinguishing. **b.** The condition of being extinguished. **2.** The fact of being extinct or the process of becoming extinct: *"The most effective agent in the extinction of species is the pressure of other species"* (Alfred R. Wallace). **3.** *Psychology.* A reduction or a loss in the strength or rate of a conditioned response when the unconditioned stimulus or reinforcement is withheld. **4.** *Physiology.* A gradual decrease in the excitability of a nerve to a previously adequate stimulus, usually resulting in total loss of excitability.

ex·tinc·tive (ĭk-stĭngk′tĭv) *adj.* Tending to extinguish or make extinct.

ex·tin·guish (ĭk-stĭng′gwĭsh) *tr.v.* **-guished, -guish·ing, -guish·es. 1.** To put out (a fire, for example); quench. **2.** To put an end to (hopes, for example); destroy. See Synonyms at **abolish. 3.** To obscure; eclipse. **4.** *Law.* **a.** To settle or discharge (a debt). **b.** To nullify: *extinguished their title to the property.* **5.** *Psychology.* To bring about the extinction of (a conditioned response). [Latin *exstinguere* : *ex-,* intensive pref.; see EX- + *stinguere,* to quench; see **steig-** in Appendix.] **—ex·tin′guish·a·ble** *adj.* **—ex·tin′guish·ment** *n.*

ex·tin·guish·er (ĭk-stĭng′gwĭ-shər) *n.* One that extinguishes, especially: **a.** Any of various portable mechanical devices for spraying and extinguishing a fire with chemicals. **b.** A small metal cone or cup on a long handle, used for snuffing out candles; a snuffer.

ex·tir·pate (ĕk′stər-pāt′) *tr.v.* **-pat·ed, -pat·ing, -pates. 1.** To pull up by the roots. **2.** To destroy totally; exterminate. See Synonyms at **abolish. 3.** To remove by surgery. [Latin *exstirpāre, exstirpāt-* : *ex-,* ex- + *stirps,* root.] **—ex′tir·pa′tion** *n.* **—ex′tir·pa′tive** *adj.* **—ex′tir·pa′tor** *n.*

ex·tol also **ex·toll** (ĭk-stōl′) *tr.v.* **-tolled, -tol·ling, -tols** also **-tolled, -toll·ing, -tolls.** To praise highly; exalt. See Synonyms at **praise.** [Middle English *extollen,* from Latin *extollere,* to lift up, praise : *ex-,* up from; see EX- + *tollere,* to lift; see **tele-** in Appendix.] **—ex·tol′ler** *n.* **—ex·tol′ment** *n.*

ex·tort (ĭk-stôrt′) *tr.v.* **-tort·ed, -tort·ing, -torts.** To obtain from another by coercion or intimidation. [Latin *extorquēre, extort-,* to wrench out, extort : *ex-,* ex- + *torquēre,* to twist; see **terk**ʷ- in Appendix.] **—ex·tort′er** *n.* **—ex·tor′tive** *adj.*

ex·tor·tion (ĭk-stôr′shən) *n.* **1.** The act or an instance of extorting. **2.** Illegal use of one's official position or powers to obtain property, funds, or patronage. **3.** An excessive or exorbitant charge. **4.** Something extorted. **—ex·tor′tion·ar′y** (-shə-nĕr′ē) *adj.* **—ex·tor′tion·ist, ex·tor′tion·er** *n.*

ex·tor·tion·ate (ĭk-stôr′shə-nĭt) *adj.* **1.** Characterized by extortion. **2.** Exorbitant; immoderate: *extortionate interest rates.* **—ex·tor′tion·ate·ly** *adv.*

ex·tra (ĕk′strə) *adj. Abbr.* **ext., ex., X** **1.** More than or beyond what is usual, normal, expected, or necessary. See Synonyms at **superfluous.** **2.** Better than ordinary; superior: *extra fineness.* **3.** Subject to an additional charge: *a pizza with extra cheese.* —**extra** *n.* **1.** Something more than is usual or necessary. **2.** Something, such as an accessory on a motor vehicle, for which an additional charge is made. **3.** A special edition of a newspaper. **4.a.** An additional or alternate worker. **b.** A performer hired to play a minor part, as in a crowd scene. **5.** Something of exceptional quality. —**extra** *adv.* To an exceptional extent or degree; unusually: *extra dry.* [Probably short for EXTRAORDINARY.]

extra– or **extro–** *pref.* Outside; beyond: *extraterritorial.* [Late Latin, from Latin *extrā.* See **eghs** in Appendix.]

ex·tra-base hit (ĕk′strə-bās′) *n. Baseball.* A double, a triple, or a home run.

ex·tra·cel·lu·lar (ĕk′strə-sĕl′yə-lər) *adj.* Located or occurring outside a cell or cells: *extracellular fluid.* —**ex′tra·cel′lu·lar·ly** *adv.*

ex·tra·chro·mo·so·mal (ĕk′strə-krō′mə-sō′məl) *adj. Genetics.* Occurring or operating outside the chromosomes.

ex·tra·code (ĕk′strə-kōd′) *n. Computer Science.* A sequence of machine code instructions used to simulate hardware functions.

ex·tra·con·sti·tu·tion·al (ĕk′strə-kŏn′stĭ-to͞o′shə-nəl, -tyo͞o′-) *adj.* Beyond what is provided for in a constitution.

ex·tra·cor·po·re·al (ĕk′strə-kôr-pôr′ē-əl, -pōr′-) *adj.* Situated or occurring outside the body. —**ex′tra·cor·po′re·al·ly** *adv.*

ex·tra·cra·ni·al (ĕk′strə-krā′nē-əl) *adj.* Located or occurring outside the cranium.

ex·tract (ĭk-străkt′) *tr.v.* **-tract·ed, -tract·ing, -tracts.** **1.** To draw or pull out, using great force or effort: *extract a wisdom tooth.* **2.** To obtain despite resistance: *extract a promise.* **3.** To obtain from a substance by chemical or mechanical action, as by pressure, distillation, or evaporation. **4.** To remove for separate consideration or publication; excerpt. **5.a.** To derive or obtain (information, for example) from a source. **b.** To deduce (a principle or doctrine); construe (a meaning). **c.** To derive (pleasure or comfort) from an experience. **6.** *Mathematics.* To determine or calculate (the root of a number). —**extract** (ĕk′străkt′) *n. Abbr.* **ext.** **1.** A passage from a literary work; an excerpt. **2.** A concentrated preparation of the essential constituents of a food, a flavoring, or another substance; a concentrate: *maple extract.* [Middle English *extracten,* from Latin *extrahere, extract-* : *ex-,* ex- + *trahere,* to draw.] —**ex·tract′a·ble, ex·tract′i·ble** *adj.* —**ex·trac′tor** *n.*

ex·trac·tion (ĭk-străk′shən) *n.* **1.** The act of extracting or the condition of being extracted. **2.** Something obtained by extracting; an extract. **3.** Origin; lineage: *of Spanish extraction.*

ex·trac·tive (ĭk-străk′tĭv) *adj.* **1.** Used in or obtained by extraction. **2.** Possible to extract. —**extractive** *n.* **1.** Something that may be extracted. **2.** The insoluble portion of an extract. —**ex·trac′tive·ly** *adv.*

ex·tra·cur·ric·u·lar (ĕk′strə-kə-rĭk′yə-lər) *adj.* **1.** Being outside the regular curriculum of a school or college: *Sports and drama are the school's most popular extracurricular activities.* **2.** Being outside the usual duties of a job or profession: *The attorney's work for the legal aid society was extracurricular.* **3.** *Informal.* Extramarital.

ex·tra·dit·a·ble (ĕk′strə-dī′tə-bəl) *adj.* **1.** Subject to extradition: *extraditable fugitives.* **2.** Making liable to extradition: *an extraditable crime.*

ex·tra·dite (ĕk′strə-dīt′) *Law. v.* **-dit·ed, -dit·ing, -dites.** —*tr.* **1.** To give up or deliver (a fugitive, for example) to the legal jurisdiction of another government or authority. **2.** To obtain the extradition of. See Synonyms at **banish.** —*intr.* To perform the act of extradition or engage in the process of extradition: *"Rio or Uruguay or wherever it is that they do not extradite for murder"* (Scott Turow). [Back-formation from EXTRADITION.]

ex·tra·di·tion (ĕk′strə-dĭsh′ən) *n. Law.* Legal surrender of a fugitive to the jurisdiction of another state, country, or government for trial. [French : Latin *ex-,* ex- + Latin *trāditiō, trāditiōn-,* a handing over; see TRADITION.]

ex·tra·dos (ĕk′strə-dŏs′, -dō′, -dōs′) *n., pl.* **-dos** (-dōz′) or **-dos·es.** The upper or exterior curve of an arch. [French : Latin *extrā,* outside; see EXTRA– + French *dos,* back (from Latin *dorsum*).]

ex·tra·ga·lac·tic (ĕk′strə-gə-lăk′tĭk) *adj.* Located or originating beyond the Milky Way.

ex·tra·he·pat·ic (ĕk′strə-hĭ-păt′ĭk) *adj.* Originating or occurring outside the liver.

ex·tra-high voltage (ĕk′strə-hī′) *n. Abbr.* **EHV** A voltage higher than 345 kilovolts.

ex·tra·ju·di·cial (ĕk′strə-jo͞o-dĭsh′əl) *adj. Law.* **1.** Outside of the authority of a court. **2.** Outside of the usual judicial proceedings. —**ex′tra·ju·di′cial·ly** *adv.*

ex·tra·le·gal (ĕk′strə-lē′gəl) *adj. Law.* Not permitted or governed by law. —**ex′tra·le′gal·ly** *adv.*

ex·tra·mar·i·tal (ĕk′strə-măr′ĭ-tl) *adj.* Being in violation of marriage vows; adulterous: *an extramarital affair.*

ex·tra·mun·dane (ĕk′strə-mŭn-dān′, -mŭn′dān′) *adj.* Occurring or existing outside of the physical world or universe.

ex·tra·mu·ral (ĕk′strə-myo͝or′əl) *adj.* Occurring or situated outside of the walls or boundaries, as of a community: *the university's extramural courses.*

ex·tra·mu·si·cal (ĕk′strə-myo͞o′zĭ-kəl) *adj.* Not relating to music: *the extramusical importance of the opera.*

ex·tra·ne·ous (ĭk-strā′nē-əs) *adj.* **1.** Not constituting a vital element or part. **2.** Inessential or unrelated to the topic or matter at hand; irrelevant. See Synonyms at **irrelevant.** **3.** Coming from the outside: *extraneous interference.* See Synonyms at **extrinsic.** [From Latin *extrāneus,* from *extrā,* outside. See EXTRA–.] —**ex·tra′ne·ous·ly** *adv.* —**ex·tra′ne·ous·ness** *n.*

ex·tra·nu·cle·ar (ĕk′strə-no͞o′klē-ər, -nyo͞o′-) *adj.* **1.** Located or occurring outside the nucleus of a cell. **2.** Existing or acting outside the nucleus of an atom.

ex·tra·oc·u·lar muscle (ĕk′strə-ŏk′yə-lər) *n.* Any of the six small muscles that control movement of the eyeball within the socket.

ex·tra·or·di·naire (ĕk′strə-ôr′dn-âr′, -dē-nâr′) *adj.* Extraordinary: *a jazz singer extraordinaire.* [French, from Old French, from Latin *extrāordinārius.* See EXTRAORDINARY.]

ex·traor·di·nar·y (ĭk-strôr′dn-ĕr′ē, ĕk′strə-ôr′-) *adj.* **1.** Beyond what is ordinary or usual: *extraordinary authority.* **2.** Highly exceptional; remarkable: *an extraordinary achievement.* **3.** Employed or used for a special service, function, or occasion: *a minister extraordinary; an extraordinary professor.* [Middle English *extraordinarie,* from Latin *extraordinārius* : *extrā,* outside; see EXTRA– + *ōrdō, ōrdin-,* order; see ORDER.] —**ex·traor′di·nar′i·ly** (-dn-âr′ə-lē) *adv.*

ex·trap·o·late (ĭk-străp′ə-lāt′) *v.* **-lat·ed, -lat·ing, -lates.** —*tr.* **1.** To infer or estimate by extending or projecting known information. **2.** *Mathematics.* To estimate (a value of a variable outside a known range) from values within a known range by assuming that the estimated value follows logically from the known values. —*intr.* To engage in the process of extrapolating. [EXTRA– + (INTER)POLATE.] —**ex·trap′o·la′tion** *n.* —**ex·trap′o·la′tive** *adj.* —**ex·trap′o·la′·tor** *n.*

ex·tra·py·ram·i·dal (ĕk′strə-pĭ-răm′ĭ-dl) *adj.* Relating to or involving neural pathways situated outside or independent of the pyramidal tracts.

ex·tra·sen·so·ry (ĕk′strə-sĕn′sə-rē) *adj.* Being outside the normal range or bounds of the senses.

extrasensory perception *n.* ESP.

ex·tra·sys·to·le (ĕk′strə-sĭs′tə-lē) *n. Medicine.* A premature contraction of the heart, resulting in momentary cardiac arrhythmia.

ex·tra·ter·res·tri·al (ĕk′strə-tə-rĕs′trē-əl) *adj.* Originating, located, or occurring outside Earth or its atmosphere: *intelligent extraterrestrial life.* —**ex′tra·ter·res′tri·al** *n.*

ex·tra·ter·ri·to·ri·al (ĕk′strə-tĕr′ĭ-tôr′ē-əl, -tōr′-) *adj.* **1.** Located outside territorial boundaries: *fishing in extraterritorial waters.* **2.** Of or relating to persons exempt from the legal jurisdiction of the country in which they reside. —**ex′tra·ter′ri·to′ri·al·ly** *adv.*

ex·tra·ter·ri·to·ri·al·i·ty (ĕk′strə-tĕr′ĭ-tôr′ē-ăl′ĭ-tē, -tōr′-) *n.* Exemption from local legal jurisdiction, such as that granted to foreign diplomats.

ex·tra·u·ter·ine (ĕk′strə-yo͞o′tər-ĭn, -tə-rīn′) *adj.* Located or occurring outside the uterus: *an extrauterine pregnancy.*

ex·trav·a·gance (ĭk-străv′ə-gəns) *n.* **1.** The quality of being extravagant. **2.** Immoderate expense or display. **3.** Something extravagant. See Synonyms at **luxury.**

ex·trav·a·gan·cy (ĭk-străv′ə-gən-sē) *n., pl.* **-cies.** **1.** Extravagance. **2.** Something extravagant.

ex·trav·a·gant (ĭk-străv′ə-gənt) *adj.* **1.** Given to lavish or imprudent expenditure: *extravagant members of the imperial court.* **2.** Exceeding reasonable bounds: *extravagant demands.* See Synonyms at **excessive.** **3.** Extremely abundant; profuse: *extravagant vegetation.* **4.** Unreasonably high; exorbitant: *extravagant fees.* **5.** *Archaic.* Straying beyond limits or bounds; wandering. [Middle English, unusual, rambling, from Old French, from Medieval Latin *extrāvagāns, extrāvagant-,* present participle of *extrāvagārī,* to wander : Latin *extrā,* outside; see EXTRA– + Latin *vagārī,* to wander.] —**ex·trav′a·gant·ly** *adv.* —**ex·trav′a·gant·ness** *n.*

ex·trav·a·gan·za (ĭk-străv′ə-găn′zə) *n.* **1.** An elaborate, spectacular entertainment or display: *"Washington is an extravaganza of great buildings, greenery, and monuments"* (Larry Griffin). **2.** *Music.* A light orchestral composition marked by freedom and diversity of form, often with burlesque elements. [Italian *estravaganza,* extravagance, from *estravagante,* extravagant, from Medieval Latin *extrāvagāns, extrāvagant-,* present participle of *extrāvagārī,* to wander. See EXTRAVAGANT.]

ex·trav·a·gate (ĭk-străv′ə-gāt′) *intr.v.* **-gat·ed, -gat·ing, -gates.** *Archaic.* To exceed reasonable limits or bounds. [Medieval Latin *extrāvagārī, extrāvagāt-,* to wander. See EXTRAVAGANT.]

ex·trav·a·sate (ĭk-străv′ə-sāt′) *v.* **-sat·ed, -sat·ing, -sates.** —*tr.* **1.** *Pathology.* To force the flow of (blood or lymph) from a vessel out into surrounding tissue. **2.** *Geology.* To cause (molten lava) to pour forth from a volcanic vent. —*intr.* **1.** *Pathology.* To exude from a vessel into surrounding tissue. **2.** *Geology.* To erupt. [EXTRA– + VAS(O)– + –ATE[1].] —**ex·trav′a·sa′tion** *n.*

ex·tra·vas·cu·lar (ĕk′strə-văs′kyə-lər) *adj.* **1.** Located or

ă pat	oi boy
ā pay	ou out
âr care	o͝o took
ä father	o͞o boot
ĕ pet	ŭ cut
ē be	ûr urge
ĭ pit	th thin
ī pie	*th* this
îr pier	hw which
ŏ pot	zh vision
ō toe	ə about, item
ô paw	♦ regionalism

Stress marks: ′ (primary); ′ (secondary), as in **dictionary** (dĭk′shə-nĕr′ē)

occurring outside a blood or lymph vessel. **2.** Lacking vessels; nonvascular.

extravehicular activity
Astronaut James van Hoften on the end of the Discovery robot arm launching repaired communications satellite

ex·tra·ve·hic·u·lar activity (ĕk′strə-vē-hĭk′yə-lər) *n.* *Abbr.* **EVA** Activity or maneuvers performed by an astronaut outside a spacecraft in space.

ex·tra·ver·sion (ĕk′strə-vûr′zhən) *n.* Variant of **extroversion.**

ex·tra·vert (ĕk′strə-vûrt′) *n.* Variant of **extrovert.**

ex·tra·vert·ed (ĕk′strə-vûr′tĭd) *adj.* Variant of **extroverted.**

ex·treme (ĭk-strēm′) *adj.* **1.** Most remote in any direction; outermost or farthest: *the extreme edge of the field.* **2.** Being in or attaining the greatest or highest degree; very intense: *extreme pleasure; extreme pain.* **3.** Extending far beyond the norm: *an extreme conservative.* See Synonyms at **excessive. 4.** Of the greatest severity; drastic: *took extreme measures to conserve fuel.* **5.** *Archaic.* Final; last. **—extreme** *n.* **1.** The greatest or utmost degree or point. **2.** Either of the two things situated at opposite ends of a range: *the extremes of boiling and freezing.* **3.** An extreme condition. **4.** An immoderate, drastic expedient: *resorted to extremes in the emergency.* **5.** *Mathematics.* **a.** The first or last term of a ratio or a series. **b.** A maximum or minimum value of a function. **6.** *Logic.* The major or minor term of a syllogism. [Middle English, from Old French, from Latin *extrēmus.* See **eghs** in Appendix.] **—ex·treme′ly** *adv.* **—ex·treme′ness** *n.*

extremely high frequency *n.* *Abbr.* **EHF** A radio-frequency band with a range of 30,000 to 300,000 megahertz.

extremely low frequency *n.* *Abbr.* **ELF** A radio frequency below 300 hertz.

extreme unction *n.* *Roman Catholic Church.* The rite formerly in practice in which a priest anointed and prayed for a sick or an injured person, especially one in danger of death. In 1972 the name and rite were changed to Anointing of the Sick.

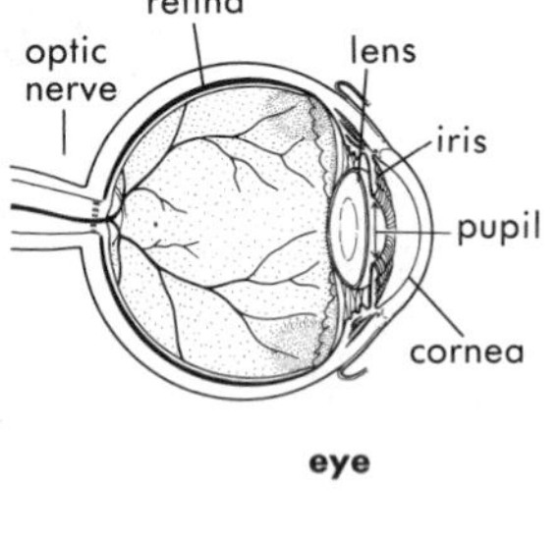

eye

ex·trem·ist (ĭk-strē′mĭst) *n.* One who advocates or resorts to measures beyond the norm, especially in politics. **—ex·trem′ism** *n.* **—ex·trem′ist** *adj.*

ex·trem·i·ty (ĭk-strĕm′ĭ-tē) *n., pl.* **-ties. 1.** The outermost or farthest point or portion. **2.** The greatest or utmost degree: *the extremity of despair.* **3. a.** Grave danger, necessity, or distress. **b.** A moment at which death or ruin is imminent. **4.** An extreme or severe measure. **5. a.** A bodily limb or appendage. **b.** A hand or foot.

ex·tri·cate (ĕk′strĭ-kāt′) *tr.v.* **-cat·ed, -cat·ing, -cates. 1.** To release from an entanglement or difficulty; disengage. **2.** *Archaic.* To distinguish from something related. [Latin *extrīcāre, extrīcāt-* : *ex-*, ex- + *trīcae,* hindrances, perplexities.] **—ex′tri·ca·ble** (-kə-bəl) *adj.* **—ex′tri·ca′tion** *n.*

SYNONYMS: *extricate, disengage, disentangle, untangle.* The central meaning shared by these verbs is "to free from something that entangles": *extricated himself from an embarrassing situation; trying to disengage her attention from the subject that obsesses her; disentangled the oar from the water lilies; the efforts of a trapped animal to untangle itself from a net.*

E 1

F P 2

T O Z 3

L P E D 4

E D F C Z P 5

D E F P O T E C 6

L E F O D P C T 7

eye chart

ex·trin·sic (ĭk-strĭn′sĭk, -zĭk) *adj.* **1.** Not forming an essential or inherent part of a thing; extraneous. **2.** Originating from the outside; external. [Latin *extrīnsecus,* from outside : *exter,* outside; see EXTERIOR + *-im,* adv. suff. + *secus,* alongside; see **sekʷ-¹** in Appendix.] **—ex·trin′si·cal·ly** *adv.*

SYNONYMS: *extrinsic, extraneous, foreign, alien.* These adjectives mean not part of the essential nature of a thing. *Extrinsic* applies to what is either outside of a thing or derived from something external to it: *"How is it possible to write about Frank Sinatra in a manner that suggests his music is in some way extrinsic to him?"* (Barbara Grizzuti Harrison). What is *extraneous* comes from without and is inessential or irrelevant: *an issue extraneous to the debate.* Something *foreign* is markedly different from and incompatible with the thing in question: *Jealousy is foreign to his nature.* What is *alien* is irreconcilably different: *an economic theory alien to the spirit of capitalism.*

extrinsic factor *n.* See **vitamin B_{12}.**

extro– *pref.* Variant of **extra–.**

ex·trorse (ĕk′strôrs′) *adj.* *Botany.* Facing outward; turned away from the axis: *extrorse anthers.* [Late Latin *extrōrsus,* turned outward, blend of Latin *extrā,* outside; see EXTRA–, and Latin *versus,* past participle of *vertere,* to turn; see **wer-²** in Appendix.]

ex·tro·ver·sion also **ex·tra·ver·sion** (ĕk′strə-vûr′zhən) *n.* **1.** Interest in one's environment or in others as opposed to or to the exclusion of oneself. **2.** A turning inside out, as of an organ or a part. **—ex′tro·ver′sive** *adj.* **—ex′tro·ver′sive·ly** *adv.*

ex·tro·vert also **ex·tra·vert** (ĕk′strə-vûrt′) *n.* An individual interested in others or in the environment as opposed to or to the exclusion of self. [Alteration (influenced by INTROVERT) of *extravert* : EXTRA– + Latin *vertere, vers-,* to turn; see **wer-²** in Appendix.]

ex·tro·vert·ed also **ex·tra·vert·ed** (ĕk′strə-vûr′tĭd) *adj.* Marked by interest in others or in the environment as opposed to or to the exclusion of self; gregarious or outgoing: *"the hearty and extroverted types who dominated public life in Boston"* (Thomas P. O'Neill, Jr.).

ă pat	oi boy
ā pay	ou out
âr care	o͝o took
ä father	o͞o boot
ĕ pet	ŭ cut
ē be	ûr urge
ĭ pit	th thin
ī pie	*th* this
îr pier	hw which
ŏ pot	zh vision
ō toe	ə about, item
ô paw	♦ regionalism

Stress marks: **′** (primary); ′ (secondary), as in **dictionary** (dĭk′shə-nĕr′ē)

ex·trude (ĭk-stro͞od′) *v.* **-trud·ed, -trud·ing, -trudes.** *—tr.* **1.** To push or thrust out. **2.** To shape (a plastic, for instance) by forcing it through a die. *—intr.* To protrude or project. [Latin *extrūdere* : *ex-*, ex- + *trūdere,* to thrust; see **treud-** in Appendix.]

ex·tru·sion (ĭk-stro͞o′zhən) *n.* **1.** The act or process of pushing or thrusting out. **2.** The act or process of shaping by forcing through a die. **3.** An object or material produced by extruding. [Medieval Latin *extrūsiō, extrūsiōn-,* from Latin *extrūsus,* past participle of *extrūdere,* to thrust out. See EXTRUDE.]

ex·tru·sive (ĭk-stro͞o′sĭv, -zĭv) *adj.* **1.** Tending to push or thrust out. **2.** Tending to protrude or project. **3.** Derived from magma poured out or ejected at the earth's surface. Used of igneous rocks.

ex·u·ber·ance (ĭg-zo͞o′bər-əns) *n.* **1.** The quality or condition of being exuberant. **2.** An exuberant act or expression.

ex·u·ber·ant (ĭg-zo͞o′bər-ənt) *adj.* **1.** Full of unrestrained enthusiasm or joy. **2.** Lavish; extravagant. **3.** Extreme in degree, size, or extent. **4.** Growing, producing, or produced abundantly; plentiful: *"Threads of her exuberant hair showed up at the bottom of the sink"* (Anne Tyler). See Synonyms at **profuse.** [Middle English, overabundant, from Old French, from Latin *exūberāns, exūberant-,* present participle of *exūberāre,* to exuberate. See EXUBERATE.] **—ex·u′ber·ant·ly** *adv.*

ex·u·ber·ate (ĭg-zo͞o′bə-rāt′) *intr.v.* **-at·ed, -at·ing, -ates. 1.** *Usage Problem.* To be exuberant. **2.** *Archaic.* To abound; overflow. [Middle English *exuberaten,* to make fruitful, from Latin *exūberāre, exūberāt-* : *ex-*, intensive pref.; see EX– + *ūberāre,* to be fruitful (from *ūber,* fertile; see **euə-dh-r̥** in Appendix).]

USAGE NOTE: *Exuberate* is not well established in its use to mean "to be exuberant." In an earlier survey it was unacceptable to a majority of the Usage Panel.

ex·u·date (ĕks′yo͞o-dāt′) *n.* A substance that has oozed forth. [Latin *exsūdātum,* neuter past participle of *exsūdāre,* to exude. See EXUDE.]

ex·u·da·tion (ĕks′yo͞o-dā′shən) *n.* **1.** The act or an instance of oozing forth. **2.** An exudate. **—ex′u·da′tive** *adj.*

ex·ude (ĭg-zo͞od′, ĭk-so͞od′) *v.* **-ud·ed, -ud·ing, -udes.** *—intr.* To ooze forth. *—tr.* **1.** To discharge or emit (a liquid or gas, for example) gradually. **2.** To exhibit in abundance: *a face that exuded self-satisfaction.* [Latin *exsūdāre* : *ex-*, ex- + *sūdāre,* to sweat; see **sweid-** in Appendix.]

ex·ult (ĭg-zŭlt′) *intr.v.* **-ult·ed, -ult·ing, -ults. 1.** To rejoice greatly; be jubilant or triumphant. **2.** *Obsolete.* To leap upward, especially for joy. [Latin *exsultāre* : *ex-*, ex- + *saltāre,* to dance, frequentative of *salīre,* to leap; see **sel-** in Appendix.] **—ex·ul′tance, ex·ul′tan·cy** *n.* **—ex·ult′ing·ly** *adv.*

ex·ul·tant (ĭg-zŭl′tənt) *adj.* Marked by great joy or jubilation; triumphant. **—ex·ul′tant·ly** *adv.*

ex·ul·ta·tion (ĕk′səl-tā′shən, ĕg′zəl-) *n.* The act or condition of rejoicing greatly.

ex·urb (ĕk′sûrb′) *n.* A region lying beyond the suburbs of a city, especially one inhabited principally by wealthy people. [EX– + (SUB)URB.] **—ex·ur′ban** *adj.*

ex·ur·ban·ite (ĕk-sûr′bə-nīt′, ĕg-zûr′-) *n.* A resident of an exurb.

ex·ur·bi·a (ĕk-sûr′bē-ə, ĕg-zûr′-) *n.* A typically exurban area.

ex·u·vi·ae (ĭg-zo͞o′vē-ē′) *pl.n.* The cast-off skins or coverings of various organisms, such as the shells of crabs or the external coverings of the larvae and nymphs of insects. [Latin, from *exuere,* to take off. See **eu-¹** in Appendix.] **—ex·u′vi·al** (-vē-əl) *adj.*

ex·u·vi·ate (ĭg-zo͞o′vē-āt′) *v.* **-at·ed, -at·ing, -ates.** *—tr.* To shed or cast off (a covering). *—intr.* To shed or cast off exuviae; molt. [EXUVI(AE) + –ATE¹.] **—ex·u′vi·a′tion** *n.*

–ey *suff.* Variant of **–y¹.**

ey·as (ī′əs) *n.* A nestling hawk or falcon, especially one to be trained for falconry. [Middle English *eias,* from *an eias,* alteration of **a nias,* an eyas, from Old French *niais,* from Latin *nīdus,* nest.]

Eyck (īk), **Jan van.** 1390?–1441. Flemish painter who with his brother **Hubert** (died 1426) founded the Flemish school of painting. Jan's works, characterized by brilliant coloring and minute realistic detail, include *Arnolfini and His Wife* (1434). No existing works can be positively attributed to Hubert.

♦**eye** (ī) *n.* **1.** An organ of vision or of light sensitivity. **2. a.** The vertebrate organ of vision; either of a pair of hollow structures located in bony sockets of the skull, functioning together or independently, each having a lens capable of focusing incident light on an internal photosensitive retina from which nerve impulses are sent to the brain. **b.** The external, visible portion of this organ together with its associated structures, especially the eyelids, eyelashes, and eyebrows. **c.** The pigmented iris of this organ. **3.** The faculty of seeing; vision. **4.** The ability to make intellectual or aesthetic judgments: *has a good eye for understated fashion.* **5. a.** A way of regarding something; a point of view: *To my eye, the decorations are excellent.* **b.** Attention: *The lavish window display immediately got my eye.* **6.** Something suggestive of the vertebrate organ of vision, especially: **a.** An opening in a needle. **b.** The aperture of a camera. **c.** A loop, as of metal, rope, or thread. **d.** A circular marking on a peacock's feather. **e.** *Chiefly*

Southern U.S. The round flat cover over the hole on a wood-burning stove. **7.** A photosensitive device, such as a photoelectric cell. **8.** *Botany.* **a.** A bud on a twig or tuber: *the eye of a potato.* **b.** The often differently colored center of the corolla of some flowers. **9. a.** *Meteorology.* The circular area of relative calm at the center of a cyclone. **b.** The center or focal point of attention or action: *right in the eye of the controversy.* **10.** *Informal.* A detective, especially a private detective. **11.** A choice center cut of meat, as of beef: *eye of the round.* —**eye** *tr.v.* **eyed, eye·ing** or **ey·ing** (ī′ĭng), **eyes. 1.** To look at: *eyed the passing crowd with indifference.* **2.** To watch closely: *eyed the shark's movements.* **3.** To supply with an eye. —***idioms.*** **all eyes.** Fully attentive. **an eye for an eye.** Punishment in which an offender suffers what the victim has suffered. **clap** (or **lay** or **set**) **(one's) eyes on.** To look at. **eye to eye.** In agreement: *We're eye to eye on all the vital issues.* **have eyes for.** To be interested in. **have (one's) eye on. 1.** To look at, especially attentively or continuously. **2.** To have as one's objective. **in a pig's eye.** *Slang.* Under no condition; never: *In a pig's eye will I ever do that.* **in the eye of the wind.** *Nautical.* In a direction opposite that of the wind; close to the wind. **in the public eye. 1.** Frequently seen in public or in the media. **2.** Widely publicized; well-known. **my eye.** *Slang.* In no way; not at all. Used interjectionally. **with an eye to.** With a view to: *redecorated the room with an eye to its future use as a nursery.* **with (one's) eyes closed.** Unaware of the risks involved. **with (one's) eyes open.** Aware of the risks involved. [Middle English, from Old English *ēge, ēage.* See **okʷ-** in Appendix.]

eye·ball (ī′bôl′) *n.* **1.** The globe-shaped portion of the eye surrounded by the socket and covered externally by the eyelids. **2.** The eye itself. —**eyeball** *tr.v.* **-balled, -ball·ing, -balls.** *Informal.* **1.** To look over carefully; scrutinize. **2.** To measure or estimate roughly by sight: *eyeballed the area of the wall that needed paint.*

eye·ball-to-eye·ball (ī′bôl′tə-ī′bôl′) *adv. & adj. Informal.* Face to face.

eye bank *n.* A place at which corneas obtained from human bodies immediately after death are stored and preserved for subsequent transplantation to patients with corneal defects.

eye bath *n.* See **eyecup** (sense 1).

eye·bolt (ī′bōlt′) *n.* A bolt having a looped head designed to receive a hook or rope.

eye·bright (ī′brīt′) *n.* Any of several plants of the genus *Euphrasia,* having small, opposite, toothed leaves and white and purplish flowers grouped in spikes.

eye·brow (ī′brou′) *n.* **1.** The bony ridge extending over the eye. **2.** The arch of short hairs covering this ridge.

eyebrow pencil *n.* A cosmetic pencil used for extending or darkening the eyebrows.

eye-catch·ing (ī′kăch′ĭng) *adj.* Visually attractive: *an eye-catching dress.* —**eye′-catch′er** *n.*

eye chart *n.* A chart of letters and figures of various sizes, used to test visual acuity.

eye contact *n.* Direct visual contact with another's eyes: *"He managed to say hello to 12 people in five seconds without making eye contact with a single one"* (Village Voice).

eye·cup (ī′kŭp′) *n.* **1.** A small cup with a rim contoured to fit the socket of the eye, used for applying a liquid medicine or wash to the eye. Also called *eye bath, eyeglass.* **2.** *Embryology.* See **optic cup.**

eyed (īd) *adj.* Having eyes of a specified number or kind. Often used in combination: *one-eyed; blue-eyed.*

eye dialect *n.* The use of misspellings, such as *wimmin* for *women,* to represent dialectal or nonstandard speech.

eyed·ness (īd′nĭs) *n.* A preference for use of one eye rather than the other.

eye·drop·per (ī′drŏp′ər) *n.* A dropper for administering liquid medicines, especially into the eye.

eye·ful (ī′fo͝ol′) *n.* **1.** A complete view. **2.** One that is pleasing to the sight, especially an attractive person. **3.** Sufficient observation to discover more than one had expected or enough to be satisfied: *After an eyeful of his art collection, she decided to leave.* **4.** An amount of material blown or directed into the eye: *got an eyeful of water from the squirt gun.*

eye·glass (ī′glăs′) *n.* **1. a. eyeglasses.** Glasses for the eyes. **b.** A single lens in a pair of glasses; a monocle. **2.** See **eyepiece. 3.** See **eyecup** (sense 1).

eye·hole (ī′hōl′) *n.* **1.** The socket of an eye. **2.** See **peephole.**

eye·hook (ī′ho͝ok′) *n.* A hook attached to a ring at the end of a rope or chain.

eye·lash (ī′lăsh′) *n.* **1.** Any of the short hairs fringing the edge of the eyelid. **2.** A row of the hairs fringing the eyelid.

eye·let (ī′lĭt) *n.* **1. a.** A small hole or perforation, usually rimmed with metal, cord, fabric, or leather, used for fastening with a cord or hook. **b.** A metal ring designed to reinforce such a hole; a grommet. **2.** A small hole edged with embroidered stitches as part of a design. **3.** A peephole. **4.** A small eye. [Alteration (influenced by EYE) of Middle English *oilet,* from Old French *oillet,* diminutive of *oil,* eye, from Latin *oculus.* See **okʷ-** in Appendix.]

eyelet

eye·lid also **eye-lid** (ī′lĭd′) *n.* Either of two folds of skin and muscle that can be closed over the exposed portion of the eyeball.

eye·lift (ī′lĭft′) *n.* Cosmetic plastic surgery of the tissue surrounding the eye to reduce or eliminate folds, wrinkles, and sags.

eye·lin·er (ī′lī′nər) *n.* Makeup used to outline the eyes.

eye opener *n. Informal.* **1.** A startling or shocking revelation. **2.** A drink of liquor, taken to stimulate, especially upon awakening.

eye·piece (ī′pēs′) *n.* The lens or lens group closest to the eye in an optical instrument; an ocular. Also called *eyeglass.*

eye-pop·ping (ī′pŏp′ĭng) *adj. Informal.* Eliciting wonder or astonishment: *an eye-popping display of fireworks.* —**eye′-pop′per** *n.*

eye rhyme *n.* A rhyme consisting of words, such as *lint* and *pint,* with similar spellings but different sounds. Also called *sight rhyme.*

eye·shade (ī′shād′) *n.* A visor fastened about the head and used for protection against glare.

eyeshade
Worn by Sinclair Lewis, 1938

eye shadow *n.* A cosmetic available in various colors or tints and applied especially to the eyelids to enhance the eyes.

eye·shot (ī′shŏt′) *n.* The range of vision; sight.

eye·sight (ī′sīt′) *n.* **1.** The faculty of sight; vision. **2.** Range of vision; view.

eyes-on·ly (īz′ōn′lē) *adj.* Of or relating to privileged information: *"Never before . . . had he been ordered to write a secret eyes-only memo"* (Jeff Kamen).

eye·sore (ī′sôr′, ī′sōr′) *n.* Something, such as a distressed building, that is unpleasant or offensive to view.

eye·spot (ī′spŏt′) *n.* **1.** A small, light-sensitive patch of pigment in certain algae and unicellular organisms. **2.** A simple visual organ of certain invertebrates consisting of a sensory ending covered by light-sensitive, pigmented cells. **3.** A rounded eyelike marking, as on the tail of a peacock. **4.** *Botany.* Either of two fungal diseases that affect grasses and are characterized by oval lesions.

eye·stalk (ī′stôk′) *n.* A movable stalklike structure in certain crustaceans, such as crabs and shrimp, that bears an eye at the tip.

eye·strain (ī′strān′) *n.* Pain and fatigue of the eyes, often accompanied by headache, resulting from prolonged use of the eyes, uncorrected defects of vision, or an imbalance of the eye muscles.

eye·tooth (ī′to͞oth′) *n.* A canine tooth of the upper jaw. [Perhaps so called from its location immediately below the eye.]

eye·wash (ī′wŏsh′, ī′wôsh′) *n.* **1.** A solution, medicated or nonmedicated, applied as a cleanser for the eyes. **2.** *Informal.* Actions or remarks intended to conceal the facts of a situation.

eye·wear (ī′wâr′) *n.* **1.** Eyeglasses, goggles, or other objects worn over the eyes. **2.** Fashionable eyeglasses.

eye·wink (ī′wĭngk′) *n.* **1.** A wink of the eye. **2.** An instant. **3.** *Obsolete.* A glance.

eye·wit·ness (ī′wĭt′nĭs) *n.* A person who has seen someone or something and can bear witness to the fact.

eyespot

ey·ra (âr′ə) *n.* The reddish-brown color phase of the jaguarundi. [American Spanish *eirá,* a kind of fox, from Guarani *eirara.*]

eyre (âr) *n.* A circuit court held by itinerant royal justices in medieval England. [Middle English, from Anglo-Norman *eire,* from Latin *iter,* journey. See **ei-** in Appendix.]

Eyre (âr), **Lake.** A shallow salt lake of south-central Australia. It is the largest lake in the country and the lowest point on the continent.

Eyre Peninsula. A peninsula of southern Australia between Spencer Gulf and the Great Australian Bight.

ey·rie (âr′ē, îr′ē) *n.* Variant of **aerie.**

ey·rir (ā′rîr′) *n., pl.* **au·rar** (ou′rär′, œ′rär′). See table at **currency.** [Icelandic, from Old Norse, money, probably from Latin *aurum,* gold.]

eyr·y (âr′ē, îr′ē) *n.* Variant of **aerie.**

Ezek. *abbr. Bible.* Ezekiel.

Ez·e·ki·as (ĕz′ĭ-kī′əs). See **Hezekiah.**

E·ze·ki·el (ĭ-zē′kē-əl) *n. Bible.* **1.** A Hebrew prophet of the sixth century B.C. who called for the Jews exiled in Babylon to return to godliness and faith. **2.** *Abbr.* **Ezek., Ezk** See table at **Bible.**

Ez·ra (ĕz′rə) *n. Bible.* **1.** A Hebrew high priest of the fifth century B.C. who led many Jews back to Jerusalem after their Babylonian exile. **2.** *Abbr.* **Ezr** See table at **Bible.**

eyestalk

Phoenician
The Phoenicians used a single sign for the initial sound in *wāw*, "hook" or "peg," and the related vowel *u*.

Early Greek
This sign was altered into two different shapes by the Greeks. One form became the ancestor of Roman V and Y (see V), while the other stood for the sound of *w*. Although this sound and the corresponding letter *digamma* (F) were lost in classical Greek, they survived in the West Greek dialects from which the Latin alphabet is derived.

F

Roman
When the Romans needed a sign for the sound of *f*, they made use of the combination FH, which was soon shortened to the F that is still in use.

f[1] or **F** (ĕf) *n., pl.* **f's** or **F's. 1.** The sixth letter of the modern English alphabet. **2.** Any of the speech sounds represented by the letter *f*. **3.** The sixth in a series. **4. F.** A failing grade in schoolwork. **5.** Something shaped like the letter F. **6.** Or **F.** *Music.* **a.** The fourth tone in the scale of C major or the sixth tone in the relative minor scale. **b.** A key or scale in which F is the tonic. **c.** A written or printed note representing this tone. **d.** A string, key, or pipe tuned to the pitch of this tone.

f[2] *abbr.* **1.** Focal length. **2.** Or **F.** *Music.* Forte. **3.** *Mathematics.* Function.

F[1] The symbol for the element **flourine.**

F[2] *abbr.* **1.** Fahrenheit. **2.** Farad. **3.** Or **F.** Fellow (of a university or another institution). **4.** Filial generation.

f. *abbr.* **1.** Farthing. **2.** Or **F.** Female. **3.** Or **F.** *Grammar.* Feminine. **4.** Or **F.** *Metallurgy.* Fine. **5.** Or **F.** Folio. **6.** Following. **7.** *Sports.* Foul. **8.** Franc.

F. *abbr.* **1.** French. **2.** Friday.

f/ *abbr.* Relative aperture of a lens.

fa (fä) *n. Music.* The fourth tone of the diatonic scale in solfeggio. [Middle English, from Medieval Latin. See GAMUT.]

FA *abbr.* **1.** Or **F.A.** Fine art. **2.** *Sports.* Football Association.

f.a. *abbr.* Fire alarm.

FAA *abbr.* Federal Aviation Administration.

f.a.a. or **F.A.A.** *abbr.* Free of all average.

fab[1] (făb) *n. Informal.* Fabrication: *a shed of metal fab.*

fab[2] (făb) *adj. Slang.* Fabulous; wonderful.

Fa·ber·gé (făb′ər-zhā′), **Peter Carl.** 1846–1920. Russian goldsmith and jeweler who created ornate gifts, notably a series of jeweled and enameled Easter eggs for European royalty.

Fa·bi·an (fā′bē-ən) *adj.* **1.a.** Of or relating to the caution and avoidance of direct confrontation typical of the Roman general Quintus Fabius Maximus. **b.** Cautious or dilatory, as in taking action. **2.** Of, relating to, or being a member of the Fabian Society, which was committed to gradual rather than revolutionary means for spreading socialist principles. [Latin *Fabiānus,* after Quintus FABIUS MAXIMUS VERRUCOSUS.] **—Fa′bi·an** *n.* **—Fa′bi·an·ism** *n.* **—Fa′bi·an·ist** *n.*

Fa·bi·us Max·i·mus Ver·ru·co·sus (fā′bē-əs măk′sə-məs vĕr-yo͞o-kō′səs, -o͞o-), **Quintus.** Known as "the Cunctator." Died 203 B.C. Roman general who ultimately defeated (209) the superior forces of Hannibal through delay tactics.

fa·ble (fā′bəl) *n.* **1.** A usually short narrative making an edifying or cautionary point and often employing as characters animals that speak and act like human beings. **2.** A story about legendary persons and exploits. **3.** A falsehood; a lie. **—fable** *v.* **-bled, -bling, -bles.** *—tr.* To recount as if true. *—intr. Archaic.* To compose fables. [Middle English, from Old French, from Latin *fābula,* from *fārī,* to speak. See **bhā-**[2] in Appendix.] **—fa′bler** *n.*

fa·bled (fā′bəld) *adj.* **1.** Made known or famous by fables; legendary. **2.** Existing only in fables; fictitious.

fab·li·au (făb′lē-ō′) *n., pl.* **-li·aux** (-lē-ō′, -ōz′). A medieval verse tale characterized by comic, ribald treatment of themes drawn from life. [French, from Old North French, from Old French *fablel,* diminutive of *fable,* fable. See FABLE.]

fab·ric (făb′rĭk) *n.* **1.a.** A cloth produced especially by knitting, weaving, or felting fibers. **b.** The texture or quality of such cloth. **2.** A complex underlying structure: *destroyed the very fabric of the ancient abbey during wartime bombing; needs to protect the fabric of civilized society.* **3.a.** A method or style of construction. **b.** A structural material, such as masonry or timber. **c.** A physical structure; a building. [Middle English *fabryke,* something constructed, from Old French *fabrique,* from Latin *fabrica,* craft, workshop, from *faber, fabr-,* workman, artificer.]

fab·ric·a·ble (făb′rĭ-kə-bəl) *adj.* Capable of being shaped or formed: *a fabricable alloy; fabricable materials.* **—fab′ric·a·bil′i·ty** *n.*

fab·ri·cant (făb′rĭ-kənt) *n.* A manufacturer.

fab·ri·cate (făb′rĭ-kāt′) *tr.v.* **-cat·ed, -cat·ing, -cates. 1.** To make; create. **2.** To construct by combining or assembling diverse, typically standardized parts: *fabricate small boats.* **3.** To concoct in order to deceive: *fabricated an excuse.* [Middle English *fabricaten,* from Latin *fabricārī, fabricāt-,* to make, from *fabrica,* craft. See FABRIC.] **—fab′ri·ca′tion** *n.* **—fab′ri·ca′tor** *n.*

fab·u·late (făb′yə-lāt′) *intr.v.* **-lat·ed, -lat·ing, -lates.** To engage in the composition of fables or stories, especially those in which the element of fantasy comes into play: *"a land which . . . had given itself up to dreaming, to fabulating, to tale-telling"* (Lawrence Durrell). [Latin *fābulārī, fābulāt-,* to talk, from *fābula,* tale, talk. See FABLE.] **—fab′u·la′tion** *n.* **—fab′u·la′tor** *n.*

fab·u·list (făb′yə-lĭst) *n.* **1.** A composer of fables. **2.** An inventor or teller of falsehoods; a liar. [French *fabuliste,* from Latin *fābula,* fable. See FABLE.]

fab·u·lous (făb′yə-ləs) *adj.* **1.** Barely credible; astonishing: *the fabulous endurance of a marathon runner.* **2.** Extremely pleasing or successful: *a fabulous vacation.* **3.a.** Of the nature of a fable or myth; legendary. **b.** Told of or celebrated in fables or legends. [Middle English, mythical, from Old French *fabuleux,* from Latin *fābulōsus,* from *fābula,* fable. See FABLE.] **—fab′u·lous·ly** *adv.* **—fab′u·lous·ness** *n.*

fac. *abbr.* **1.** Facsimile. **2.** Faculty.

fa·çade also **fa·cade** (fə-säd′) *n.* **1.** *Architecture.* The face of a building, especially the principal face. **2.** An artificial or deceptive front: *ideological slogans that were a façade for geopolitical power struggles.* [French, from Italian *facciata,* from *faccia,* face, from Vulgar Latin **facia,* from Latin *faciēs.* See **dhē-** in Appendix.]

fa·çad·ism also **fa·cad·ism** (fə-sä′-dĭz′əm) *n. Architecture.* The technique of preserving the fronts of notable old buildings while demolishing the backs and interiors, often constructing modern interiors behind the old façades.

face (fās) *n.* **1.a.** The surface of the front of the head from the top of the forehead to the base of the chin and from ear to ear. **b.** A person: *We saw many new faces on the first day of classes.* **2.** A person's countenance. **3.** A contorted facial expression; a grimace: *made a face at the prospect of eating lemons.* **4.** Outward appearance: *the modern face of the city.* **5.a.** Value or standing in the eyes of others; prestige: *lose face.* **b.** Self-assurance; confidence: *The team managed to maintain a firm face even in times of great adversity.* **6.** Effrontery; impudence: *had the face to question my judgment.* **7.** The most significant or prominent surface of an object, especially: **a.** The surface presented to view; the front. **b.** A façade. **c.** Outer surface: *the face of the earth.* **d.** A marked side: *the face of a clock; the face of a playing card.* **e.** The right side, as of fabric. **8.** *Geometry.* A planar surface of a geometric solid. **9.** Any of the surfaces of a rock or crystal. **10.** The end, as of a mine or tunnel, at which work is advancing. **11.** The appearance and geologic surface features of an area of land; topography. **12.** *Printing.* A typeface or range of typefaces. **—face** *v.* **faced, fac·ing, fac·es.** *—tr.* **1.** To occupy a position with the face toward: *stood and faced the audience.* **2.** To front on: *a window that faces the south.* **3.a.** To confront with complete awareness: *had to face the facts.* **b.** To overcome by confronting boldly or bravely: *"What this generation must do is face its problems"* (John F. Kennedy). **c.** To confront with impudence. **4.a.** To be certain to encounter; have in store: *An unskilled youth faces a difficult life.* **b.** To bring or to be brought face to face with: *"The prospect of military conflict . . . faced us with nightmarish choices"* (Henry A. Kissinger). **5.** To cause (troops) to change direction by giving a command. **6.** *Games.* To turn (a playing card) so that the face is up. **7.** To furnish with a surface or cover of a different material: *bronze that is faced with gold foil.* **8.** To line or trim the edge of, especially with contrasting material: *face a hem with lace.* **9.** To treat the surface of so as to smooth. *—intr.* **1.** To be turned or placed with the front toward a specified direction. **2.** To turn the face in a specified direction. **—*phrasal verbs.* face down.** To attain mastery over or overcome by confronting in a resolute, determined manner: *face down an opponent in a debate; faced the enemy down.* **face off.** *Sports.* To start play in ice hockey, lacrosse, and other games by releasing the puck or ball between two opposing players. **face up.** To confront, an unpleasant situation, for example, with resolution and assurance: *had to face up or get out; finally faced up to the prob-*

lem. —*idioms.* **face the music.** To accept the unpleasant consequences, especially of one's own actions. **face to face. 1.** In each other's presence; in direct communication: *The two world leaders at last spoke face to face.* **2.** Directly confronting: *We were face to face with death during the avalanche.* **in (the) face of.** Despite the opposition of; notwithstanding: *"This statement flies in the face of accepted wisdom"* (S. Fred Singer). **on the face of it.** From appearances alone; apparently: *On the face of it, the problem seems minor.* **show (one's) face.** To make an appearance: *Don't show your face on my property again.* **to (one's) face.** In the view or hearing of: *criticized the supervisor to her face.* [Middle English, from Old French, from Vulgar Latin **facia,* from Latin *faciēs.* See **dhē-** in Appendix.] —**face′a·ble** *adj.* —**face′less** *adj.* —**face′less·ness** *n.*

SYNONYMS: *face, countenance, kisser, mug, pan, physiognomy, puss, visage.* The central meaning shared by these nouns is "the front surface of the head": *turned her face away; a happy countenance; punched him in the kisser; caught a glimpse of his ugly mug; tripped and fell on her pan; caught him staring at my physiognomy; a menacing look on his puss; a noble-looking visage.* See also Synonyms at **defy.**

face angle *n. Mathematics.* The angle formed between two edges of a polyhedral angle.

face card *n. Games.* A king, queen, or jack of a deck of playing cards. Also called *picture card.*

face·cloth also **face cloth** (fās′klôth′, -klŏth′) *n.* See **washcloth.**

face·down (fās′doun′) *n.* A determined, resolute, often hostile confrontation with an opponent or enemy: *tried to avert a facedown between the two nations; a political facedown during the primaries.* —**facedown** (fās′doun′) *adv.* In a position so that the face is down: *a victim floating facedown in the water.*

face-hard·en (fās′här′dn) *tr.v.* **-hard·ened, -hard·en·ing, -hard·ens.** To harden the surface of (a metal).

face-lift (fās′lĭft′) also **face-lift·ing** (-lĭf′tĭng) *n.* **1.** Plastic surgery to remove facial wrinkles, sagging skin, fat deposits, or other visible signs of aging for cosmetic purposes. Also called *rhytidectomy.* **2.** A restyling or modernization, as of a building.

face·mask (fās′măsk′) *n.* A protective or disguising cover for the face, often enveloping the entire head: *wore a facemask while diving; a skier's facemask; armed robbers who wore facemasks.*

face-off (fās′ôf′, -ŏf′) *n.* **1.** *Sports.* A method of starting play in ice hockey, lacrosse, and other games in which an official drops the puck or ball between two opposing players who contend for its control. **2.** A confrontation: *"Marshall's face-off with Jefferson in* Marbury v. Madison *in 1803"* (Newsweek).

face·plate (fās′plāt′) *n.* **1.** A disk attached to the mandrel of a lathe to hold the work to be turned. **2.** The glass front of a cathode-ray tube upon which the image is displayed. **3.** A protective plate covering the human face, as of a welder or diver.

fac·er (fā′sər) *n.* **1.** One that faces, especially a device used in smoothing or dressing a surface. **2.** An unexpected, stunning blow or defeat.

face-sav·er (fās′sā′vər) *n.* Something that prevents loss of dignity or self-esteem: *The compromise was a face-saver for all concerned.* —**face′-sav′ing** *n.*

fac·et (făs′ĭt) *n.* **1.** One of the flat polished surfaces cut on a gemstone or occurring naturally on a crystal. **2.** *Anatomy.* A small, smooth, flat surface, as on a bone or tooth. **3.** *Biology.* One of the lenslike visual units of a compound eye, as of an insect. **4.** One of numerous aspects, as of a subject; a phase. See Synonyms at **phase.** [French *facette,* from Old French, diminutive of *face,* face. See FACE.] —**fac′et·ed, fac′et·ted** *adj.*

fa·cete (fə-sēt′) *adj. Archaic.* Facetious. [Latin *facētus.*]

fa·ce·ti·ae (fə-sē′shē-ē′) *pl.n.* Witty or humorous writings and sayings. [Latin, pl. of *facētia,* jest. See FACETIOUS.]

fa·ce·tious (fə-sē′shəs) *adj.* Playfully jocular; humorous: *facetious remarks.* [French *facétieux,* from *facétie,* jest, from Latin *facētia,* from *facētus,* witty.] —**fa·ce′tious·ly** *adv.*

face·up (fās′ŭp′) *adv.* In a position so that the face is up: *a patient lying faceup on the stretcher.*

face value *n.* **1.** The value printed or written on the face, as of a bill or bond. **2.** Apparent significance or value: *took their compliments at face value.*

fa·cial (fā′shəl) *adj.* Of or concerning the face: *facial cosmetics; facial hair.* —**facial** *n.* A treatment for the face, usually consisting of a massage and the application of cosmetic creams. —**fa′cial·ly** *adv.*

facial index *n.* The ratio of facial length to facial width multiplied by 100.

facial nerve *n.* Either of the seventh pair of cranial nerves that control facial muscles and relay sensation from the taste buds of the front part of the tongue.

-facient *suff.* **1.** Causing; bringing about: *somnifacient.* **2.** Something that causes or brings about: *abortifacient.* [From Latin *faciēns, facient-,* present participle of *facere,* to do. See **dhē-** in Appendix.]

fa·ci·es (fā′shē-ēz′, -shēz) *n., pl.* **facies. 1.** *Biology.* The general aspect or outward appearance, as of a given growth of flora. **2.** *Medicine.* The appearance or expression of the face, especially when typical of a certain disorder or disease. **3.** *Geology.* A rock or stratified body distinguished from others by its appearance or composition. [Latin *faciēs.* See **dhē-** in Appendix.]

fac·ile (făs′əl) *adj.* **1.** Done or achieved with little effort or difficulty; easy. See Synonyms at **easy. 2.** Working, acting, or speaking with effortless ease and fluency. See Synonyms at **nimble. 3.** Arrived at without due care, effort, or examination; superficial: *proposed a facile solution to a complex problem.* **4.** Readily manifested, together with an aura of insincerity and lack of depth: *a facile slogan devised by politicians.* **5.** *Archaic.* Pleasingly mild, as in disposition or manner. [Middle English, from Old French, from Latin *facilis.* See **dhē-** in Appendix.] —**fac′ile·ly** *adv.* —**fac′ile·ness** *n.*

fa·cil·i·tate (fə-sĭl′ĭ-tāt′) *tr.v.* **-tat·ed, -tat·ing, -tates.** To make easy or easier: *political agreements that facilitated troop withdrawals.* [From French *faciliter,* from Old French, from Italian *facilitare,* from *facile,* facile, from Latin *facilis.* See FACILE.] —**fa·cil′i·ta′tive** (-tā′tĭv) *adj.* —**fa·cil′i·ta′tor** *n.*

fa·cil·i·ta·tion (fə-sĭl′ĭ-tā′shən) *n.* **1.a.** The act of making easy or easier. **b.** The state of being made easy or easier. **2.** *Physiology.* The process of lowering the threshold for propagation of the action potential of a neuron, especially by repeated use of a neural pathway or the summation of two or more subthreshold impulses.

fa·cil·i·ty (fə-sĭl′ĭ-tē) *n., pl.* **-ties. 1.** Ease in moving, acting, or doing; aptitude: *"an extreme facility in acquiring new dialects"* (W.H. Hudson). **2.** Readiness to be persuaded; pliability. **3.** Often **facilities.** Something that facilitates an action or process. See Synonyms at **amenity. 4.** Something created to serve a particular function: *hospitals and other health care facilities.*

fac·ing (fā′sĭng) *n.* **1.a.** A piece of material sewn to the edge of a garment, such as a dress or coat, as lining or decoration. **b.** Material used for such a lining or decoration. **2.** An outer layer or coating applied to a surface for protection or decoration.

FACP or **F.A.C.P.** *abbr.* Fellow of the American College of Physicians.

FACS or **F.A.C.S.** *abbr.* Fellow of the American College of Surgeons.

fac·sim·i·le (făk-sĭm′ə-lē) *n. Abbr.* **fac. 1.** An exact copy or reproduction, as of a document. **2.a.** A method of transmitting images or printed matter by electronic means. **b.** An image so transmitted. In this sense, also called *fax.* —**facsimile** *adj. Abbr.* **fac. 1.** Of or used to produce exact reproductions, as of documents. **2.** Exactly reproduced; duplicate. [Latin *fac simile,* make similar : *fac,* imperative of *facere,* to make; see **dhē-** in Appendix + *simile,* neuter of *similis,* similar; see SIMILAR.]

fact (făkt) *n.* **1.** Information presented as objectively real. **2.** A real occurrence; an event: *had to prove the facts of the accident.* **3.a.** Something having real, demonstrable existence: *Genetic engineering is now a fact.* **b.** The quality of being real or actual: *a blur of fact and fancy.* **4.** A thing that has been done, especially a crime: *an accessory before the fact.* **5.** *Law.* The aspect of a case at law comprising events determined by evidence: *The jury made a finding of fact.* —*idiom.* **in (point of) fact.** In reality or in truth; actually. [Latin *factum,* deed, from neuter past participle of *facere,* to do. See **dhē-** in Appendix.]

USAGE NOTE: *Fact* has a long history of usage in the sense "allegation of fact," as in *"This tract was distributed to thousands of American teachers, but the facts and the reasoning are wrong"* (Albert Shanker). This practice has led inevitably to the introduction of the phrases *true facts* and *real facts,* as in *The true facts of the case may never be known.* These usages may occasion qualms among critics who hold that facts cannot be other than true, but they often serve a useful purpose.

fact-find·ing (făkt′fīn′dĭng) *n.* Discovery or determination of facts or accurate information. —**fact-finding** *adj.* Of, relating to, or used in the discovery or determination of facts: *a fact-finding committee; a fact-finding tour.* —**fact′-find′er** *n.*

fac·tic·i·ty (făk-tĭs′ĭ-tē) *n.* The quality or condition of being a fact: *historical facticity.*

fac·tion¹ (făk′shən) *n.* **1.** A group of persons forming a cohesive, usually contentious minority within a larger group. **2.** Conflict within an organization or nation: *"Our own beloved country . . . is now afflicted with faction and civil war"* (Abraham Lincoln). [French, from Latin *factiō, factiōn-,* from *factus,* past participle of *facere,* to do. See **dhē-** in Appendix.] —**fac′tion·al** *adj.* —**fac′tion·al·ism** *n.* —**fac′tion·al·ly** *adv.*

fac·tion² (făk′shən) *n.* **1.** A form of literature or filmmaking that treats real people or events as if they were fictional or uses real people or events as essential elements in an otherwise fictional rendition. **2.** A literary work or film that is a mix of fact and fiction. [Blend of FACT and FICTION.]

-faction *suff.* Production; making: *petrifaction.* [Middle English *-faccioun,* from Old French *-faction,* from Latin *-factiō, -factiōn-,* from *factus,* past participle of *facere,* to make. See **dhē-** in Appendix.]

fac·tion·al·ize (făk′shə-nə-līz′) *tr.v.* **-ized, -iz·ing, -iz·es.** To split (a group, for example) into disputatious factions: *"Once a faculty is factionalized, of course, the process of appointments becomes partly a competition for allies"* (Calvin Trillin).

fac·tious (făk′shəs) *adj.* **1.** Of, relating to, produced by, or characterized by internal dissension. **2.** Given to or promoting

facemask
Top: Ski mask
Bottom: Field hockey goalie's mask

ă pat	oi boy
ā pay	ou out
âr care	ŏŏ took
ä father	ōō boot
ĕ pet	ŭ cut
ē be	ûr urge
ĭ pit	th thin
ī pie	*th* this
îr pier	hw which
ŏ pot	zh vision
ō toe	ə about, item
ô paw	♦ regionalism

Stress marks: ′ (primary); ′ (secondary), as in **dictionary** (dĭk′shə-nĕr′ē)

internal dissension. See Synonyms at **insubordinate.** **—fac′ti·tious·ly** *adv.* **—fac′tious·ness** *n.*

fac·ti·tious (făk-tĭsh′əs) *adj.* **1.** Produced artificially rather than by a natural process. **2.** Lacking authenticity or genuineness; sham: *speculators responsible for the factitious value of some stocks.* [Latin *factīcius,* from *factus,* past participle of *facere,* to make. See **dhē-** in Appendix.] **—fac·ti′tious·ly** *adv.*

fac·ti·tive (făk′tĭ-tĭv) *adj.* Of or constituting a transitive verb, such as *elect,* that in some constructions takes an objective complement to modify its direct object. [New Latin *factitīvus,* from Latin *factitāre,* to do, practice, frequentative of *facere,* to do. See **dhē-** in Appendix.] **—fac′ti·tive·ly** *adv.*

fact of life *n., pl.* **facts of life. 1.** Something unavoidable that must be faced or dealt with. **2. facts of life.** The basic physiological functions involved in sex and reproduction. Often used with *the.*

fac·toid (făk′toid) *n.* Unverified or inaccurate information that is presented in the press as factual, often as part of a publicity effort, and that is then accepted as true because of constant repetition: *"What one misses finally is what might have emerged beyond both facts and factoids—a profound definition of the Marilyn Monroe phenomenon"* (Christopher Lehmann-Haupt). **—fac·toid′al** *adj.*

fac·tor (făk′tər) *n.* **1.** One that actively contributes to an accomplishment, a result, or a process: *"Surprise is the greatest factor in war"* (Tom Clancy). See Synonyms at **element. 2.a.** One who acts for someone else; an agent. **b.** A person or firm that accepts accounts receivable as security for short-term loans. **3.** *Mathematics.* One of two or more quantities that divides a given quantity without a remainder: *2 and 3 are factors of 6; a and* b *are factors of* ab. **4.** A quantity by which a stated quantity is multiplied or divided, so as to indicate an increase or decrease in a measurement: *The rate increased by a factor of ten.* **5.** A gene. No longer in technical usage. **6.** *Physiology.* A substance that functions in a specific biochemical reaction or bodily process, such as blood coagulation. **—factor** *tr.v.* **-tored, -tor·ing, -tors.** To determine or indicate explicitly the factors of. ***—phrasal verb.*** **factor in.** To figure in: *We factored sick days and vacations in when we prepared the work schedule.* [Middle English *factour,* perpetrator, agent, from Old French *facteur,* from Latin *factor,* maker, from *facere,* to make. See **dhē-** in Appendix.] **—fac′tor·a·ble** *adj.* **—fac′tor·ship′** *n.*

factor VIII *n.* See **antihemophilic factor.**

factor IX *n.* A protein substance in blood plasma that participates in and is essential for the blood-clotting process. A deficiency of this factor is the cause of Christmas disease.

fac·tor·age (făk′tər-ĭj) *n.* **1.** The business of a factor. **2.** The commission or fee paid to a factor.

fac·to·ri·al (făk-tôr′ē-əl, -tōr′-) *n.* The product of all the positive integers from 1 to a given number: *4 factorial, usually written 4!, is equal to 24 (1 × 2 × 3 × 4 = 24).* **—factorial** *adj.* Of or relating to a factor or factorial.

fac·tor·ize (făk′tə-rīz′) *tr.v.* **-ized, -iz·ing, -iz·es.** *Mathematics.* To factor. **—fac′tor·i·za′tion** (-tər-ĭ-zā′shən) *n.*

fac·to·ry (făk′tə-rē) *n., pl.* **-ries. 1.a.** A building or group of buildings in which goods are manufactured; a plant. **b.** A vessel in which newly caught seafood is prepared for shipment and sale: *a floating fish factory.* **2.** A business establishment for commercial agents or factors in a foreign country. **3.** The source of prolific production: *a group of singers who really were a hit-tune factory; an old house that served as an illegal drug factory.* [Late Latin *factōria,* oil press, mill, and Medieval Latin *factōria,* establishment for factors, both from Latin *factor,* factor. See FACTOR.]

fac·to·tum (făk-tō′təm) *n.* An employee or assistant who serves in a wide range of capacities. [Medieval Latin *factōtum* : Latin *fac,* imperative of *facere,* to do; see **dhē-** in Appendix + Latin *tōtum,* everything, from neuter of *tōtus,* all; see **teutā-** in Appendix.]

fac·tu·al (făk′cho͞o-əl) *adj.* **1.** Of the nature of fact; real. **2.** Of or containing facts. **—fac′tu·al′i·ty** (-ăl′ĭ-tē) *n.* **—fac′tu·al·ly** *adv.* **—fac′tu·al·ness** *n.*

fac·tu·al·ism (făk′cho͞o-ə-lĭz′əm) *n.* Devotion or adherence to fact. **—fac′tu·al·ist** *n.*

fac·u·la (făk′yə-lə) *n., pl.* **-lae** (-lē′). Any of various large, bright spots or veined patches on the sun's photosphere, usually near sunspots. [Latin, small torch, diminutive of *fax, fac-,* torch.]

fac·ul·ta·tive (făk′əl-tā′tĭv) *adj.* **1.** Of or relating to a mental faculty. **2.a.** Capable of occurring or not occurring; contingent. **b.** Not required or compulsory; optional. **3.** Granting permission or authority. **4.** *Biology.* Capable of functioning under varying environmental conditions. Used of certain organisms, such as bacteria that can live with or without oxygen. **—fac′ul·ta′tive·ly** *adv.*

facultative apomict *n.* A plant capable of reproducing either sexually or asexually.

fac·ul·ty (făk′əl-tē) *n., pl.* **-ties.** *Abbr.* **fac. 1.** An inherent power or ability. **2.** Any of the powers or capacities possessed by the human mind. See Synonyms at **ability. 3.** The ability to perform or act. **4.a.** Any of the divisions or comprehensive branches of learning at a college or university: *the faculty of law.* **b.** The teachers and instructors within such a division. **c.** A body of teachers. **5.** All of the members of a learned profession: *the medical faculty.* **6.** Authorization granted by authority; conferred power. **7.** *Archaic.* An occupation; a trade. [Middle English *faculte,* from Old French, from Latin *facultās,* power, ability, from *facilis,* easy. See **dhē-** in Appendix.]

fad (făd) *n.* A fashion that is taken up with great enthusiasm for a brief period of time; a craze. [Possibly from *fidfad,* fussy person, fussy, from FIDDLE-FADDLE.] **—fad′dism** *n.* **—fad′dist** *n.*

WORD HISTORY: Although we do not know for certain the origin of *fad,* first recorded in 1834 with the sense "whim, crotchet," we can suggest one possibility. In 1754, 80 years before this occurrence of *fad,* we find an instance of the word *fidfad,* meaning "a fussy person": "The youngest . . . is, in everything she does, an absolute fidfad." *Fidfad* is found in the latter part of the 19th century with the sense "small detail, frill," and the adjective *fidfad,* meaning "frivolous, fussy, petty," is recorded in 1830. *Fad* could thus be a shortened form of *fidfad,* itself shortened from *fiddle-faddle.*

FAD *abbr.* Flavin adenine dinucleotide.

fad·dish (făd′ĭsh) *adj.* **1.** Having the nature of a fad. **2.** Given to fads. **—fad′dish·ly** *adv.* **—fad′dish·ness** *n.*

fade (fād) *v.* **fad·ed, fad·ing, fades.** —*intr.* **1.** To lose brightness, loudness, or brilliance gradually; dim: *The lights and music faded as we set sail from the harbor.* **2.** To lose freshness; wither: *summer flowers that had faded.* **3.** To lose strength or vitality; wane: *youthful energy that had faded over the years.* **4.** To disappear gradually; vanish: *a hope that faded.* See Synonyms at **disappear.** —*tr.* **1.** To cause to lose brightness, freshness, or strength: *Time has faded her beauty.* **2.** *Football.* To move back from the scrimmage line. Used of a quarterback. **3.** *Games.* To meet the bet of (an opposing player) in dice. **—fade** *n.* **1.** A gradual diminution in the brightness or visibility of an image in cinema or television. **2.** A periodic reduction in the received strength of a radio transmission. ***—phrasal verbs.*** **fade in. 1.** To appear gradually. **2.** To cause to appear or be heard gradually. Used of a cinematic or television image or of a sound. **fade out. 1.** To disappear gradually. **2.** To cause to disappear gradually. Used of a cinematic or television image or of a sound. [Middle English *faden,* from Old French *fader,* from *fade,* faded, probably from Vulgar Latin **fatidus,* alteration of Latin *fatuus,* insipid.]

fade·a·way (fād′ə-wā′) *n.* **1.** The act or an instance of gradually diminishing in brightness, loudness, or strength until actual disappearance occurs. **2.** *Baseball.* **a.** A screwball. **b.** An act of sliding by a base runner during which the runner veers sideways to avoid being tagged.

fade-in or **fade·in** (fād′ĭn′) *n.* A gradual increase in the visibility of an image or the audibility of a sound, as in cinema, television, or radio.

fade·less (fād′lĭs) *adj.* Not fading or not subject to fading: *fadeless fabric.* **—fade′less·ly** *adv.*

fade-out or **fade·out** (fād′out′) *n.* **1.** A gradual disappearance of an image or a sound, as in cinema, television, or radio. **2.** A gradual and temporary loss in reception of a radio or television signal, often generated by interference in transmission.

fad·ing (fā′dĭng) *n.* **1.** A waning; a decline: *"The final factor in the fading of the Renaissance was the Counter Reformation"* (Will Durant). **2.** Fluctuation in the strength of radio signals because of variations in the transmission medium.

fa·do (fä′*th*o͞o, făth′ō) *n., pl.* **-dos.** *Music.* A sad Portuguese folksong. [Portuguese, from Latin *fātum,* fate. See FATE.]

fa·e·na (fä-ā′nä) *n.* The series of final passes performed by a matador preparatory to killing a bull in a bullfight. [Spanish, manual labor, from Catalan *feyna,* from Latin *facienda,* things to be done, neuter pl. gerundive of *facere,* to do. See FACT.]

Fa·en·za (fä-ĕn′zə). A city of north-central Italy southwest of Ravenna. It is noted for its richly colored pottery, produced here since the 12th century. Population, 39,700.

fa·er·ie also **fa·er·y** (fā′ə-rē, fâr′ē) *n., pl.* **-ies. 1.** A tiny, mischievous, imaginary form; a fairy. **2.** The land or realm of the fairies. [Middle English *faierie, fairie.* See FAIRY.] **—fa′er·ie, fa′er·y** *adj.*

Faer·oe Islands or **Far·oe Islands** (fâr′ō). A group of volcanic islands in the northern Atlantic Ocean between Iceland and the Shetland Islands. Originally settled by Celtic peoples, the islands passed to Denmark in 1380.

Faer·o·ese or **Far·o·ese** (fâr′ō-ēz′, -ēs′) *n., pl.* **Faeroese** or **Faroese. 1.** A member of the Scandinavian people inhabiting the Faeroe Islands. **2.** The North Germanic language spoken by the inhabitants of the Faeroe Islands. **—Fae′ro·ese′** *adj.*

FAF *abbr.* Financial Aid Form.

Faf·nir (fäv′nər, -nĭr′) *n.* *Mythology.* The Norse dragon that guarded the treasure of the Nibelungs and was slain by Sigurd.

fag¹ (făg) *n.* **1.a.** A student at a British public school who is required to perform menial tasks for a student in a higher class. **b.** A drudge. **2.** *Chiefly British.* Fatiguing or tedious work; drudgery. **—fag** *v.* **fagged, fag·ging, fags.** —*intr.* **1.** To work to exhaustion; toil. **2.** To function as the servant of another student in a British public school. —*tr.* To exhaust; weary: *Four hours on the tennis court fagged me out.* [From *fag,* to droop (obsolete), perhaps from Middle English *fagge.* See FAG END.]

fag² (făg) *n.* *Slang.* A cigarette. [Short for FAG END.]

fag³ (făg) *n.* *Offensive Slang.* Used as a disparaging term for a gay or homosexual man. [Short for FAGGOT².]

fag end *n.* **1.** The frayed end of a length of cloth or rope. **2.a.** An inferior or worn-out remnant. **b.** The last part: *"the fag end of this crisis-ridden century"* (Wallace Irwin, Jr.). [Middle English *fagge, fag,* broken thread in cloth, something that hangs loose.]

fag·got¹ (făg′ət) *n. & v.* Variant of **fagot.**

fag·got² (făg′ət) *n. Offensive Slang.* Used as a disparaging term for a gay or homosexual man. [Perhaps from *faggot,* variant of FAGOT, bundle, lump, old woman.]

fag·got·ing (făg′ə-tĭng) *n.* Variant of **fagoting.**

fag·ot also **fag·got** (făg′ət) *—n.* **1.** A bundle of twigs, sticks, or branches bound together. **2.** A bundle of pieces of iron or steel to be welded or hammered into bars. *—tr.v.* **-ot·ed, -ot·ing, -ots** also **-got·ed, -got·ing, -gots. 1.** To collect or bind into a fagot; bundle. **2.** To decorate with fagoting. [Middle English, from Old French, from Old Provençal, possibly from Vulgar Latin **facus,* from Greek *phakelos,* bundle.]

fag·ot·ing also **fag·got·ing** (făg′ə-tĭng) *n.* **1.** A method of decorating cloth by pulling out horizontal threads and tying the remaining vertical threads into hourglass-shaped bunches. **2.** A method of joining hemmed edges by crisscrossing thread over an open seam.

Fahd (fäd). Full name Fahd ibn Abdel Aziz al-Saud. Born 1922. King of Saudi Arabia (since 1982).

Fahr·en·heit (făr′ən-hīt′) *adj. Abbr.* **F, Fahr.** Of or relating to a temperature scale that registers the freezing point of water as 32°F and the boiling point as 212°F at one atmosphere of pressure. See table at **measurement.** [After Gabriel Daniel FAHRENHEIT.]

Fahr·en·heit (făr′ən-hīt′, fär′-), **Gabriel Daniel.** 1686–1736. German-born physicist who invented the mercury thermometer (1714) and devised the Fahrenheit temperature scale.

FAIA or **F.A.I.A.** *abbr.* Fellow of the American Institute of Architects.

Fa·ial also **Fa·yal** (fə-yäl′, fä-). An island of the central Azores in the northern Atlantic Ocean.

fa·ience also **fa·ïence** (fī-äns′, -äɴs′, fā-) *n.* **1.** Earthenware decorated with colorful, opaque glazes. **2.** A moderate to strong greenish blue. [French *faïence,* after *Faïence,* Faenza, Italy.]

fail (fāl) *v.* **failed, fail·ing, fails.** *—intr.* **1.** To prove deficient or lacking; perform ineffectively or inadequately. **2.** To be unsuccessful: *a valiant attempt that failed.* **3.** To receive an academic grade below the acceptable minimum. **4.a.** To prove insufficient in quantity or duration; give out: *The water supply failed during the drought.* **b.** To fall short, as in what is expected of one: *failed in her obligations to the family.* **5.** To decline, as in strength or effectiveness: *The patient's heart failed.* **6.** To cease functioning properly: *The engine failed.* **7.** To become bankrupt or insolvent: *Our family business failed in 1929.* *—tr.* **1.** To disappoint or prove undependable to: *Our sentries failed us.* **2.** To abandon; forsake: *His strength failed him.* **3.** To omit to perform (an expected duty, for example): *"We must . . . hold . . . those horrors up to the light of justice. Otherwise we would fail our inescapable obligation to the victims of Nazism: to remember"* (Anthony Lewis). **4.** To leave (something) undone; neglect: *failed to wash the dishes.* **5.a.** To receive an academic grade below the acceptable minimum in (a course, for example): *failed algebra twice.* **b.** To give such a grade of failure to (a student): *failed me in algebra.* **—fail** *n.* **1.** Failure to deliver securities to a purchaser within a specified time. **2.** Failure to receive the proceeds of a transaction, as in the sale of stock or securities, by a specified date. **—*idiom.* without fail.** With no chance of failure: *Be here at noon without fail.* [Middle English *failen,* from Old French *faillir,* from Vulgar Latin **fallīre,* variant of Latin *fallere,* to deceive.]

failed (fāld) *adj.* Having undergone failure: *new economic policies intended to replace the failed ones of a past administration.*

fail·ing (fā′lĭng) *n.* **1.** The act of a person or thing that fails; a failure. **2.** A minor fault. See Synonyms at **fault.** **—failing** *adj.* Undergoing failure: *failing health; failing kidneys; a failing business.* **—failing** *prep.* In the absence of; without: *Failing a rainstorm, the game will be played this afternoon.*

faille (fīl) *n.* A slightly ribbed, woven fabric of silk, cotton, or rayon. [French, from Old North French, cloth head-covering worn by women in Flanders, possibly from Middle Dutch *falie,* scarf.]

fail-safe (fāl′sāf′) *adj.* **1.** Capable of compensating automatically and safely for a failure, as of a mechanism or power source. **2.** Acting to discontinue a military attack on the occurrence of any of a variety of predetermined conditions. **3.** Guaranteed not to fail: *"There is no fail-safe mechanism guaranteed either to contain or to restore presidential authority"* (Arthur M. Schlesinger, Jr.). **—fail-safe** *n.* A fail-safe mechanism. **—fail-safe** *intr.v.* **-safed, -saf·ing, -safes.** To compensate automatically for failure.

fail-soft (fāl′sôft′, -sŏft′) *adj.* Capable of operating at a reduced level of efficiency after the failure of a component or power source. Used of electronic equipment.

fail·ure (fāl′yər) *n.* **1.** The condition or fact of not achieving the desired end or ends: *the failure of an experiment.* **2.** One that fails: *a failure at one's career.* **3.** The condition or fact of being insufficient or falling short: *a crop failure.* **4.** A cessation of proper functioning or performance: *a power failure.* **5.** Nonperformance of what is requested or expected; omission: *failure to report a change of address.* **6.** The act or fact of failing to pass a course, a test, or an assignment. **7.** A decline in strength or effectiveness. **8.** The act or fact of becoming bankrupt or insolvent. [Alteration of *failer,* default, from Anglo-Norman, from Old French *faillir,* to fail. See FAIL.]

fain (fān) *adv.* **1.** Happily; gladly: *"I would fain improve every opportunity to wonder and worship, as a sunflower welcomes the light"* (Henry David Thoreau). **2.** *Archaic.* Preferably; rather. **—fain** *adj. Archaic.* **1.** Ready; willing. **2.** Pleased; happy. **3.** Obliged or required. [Middle English, from Old English *fægen,* joyful, glad.]

fai·né·ant (fā′nā-äɴ′) *adj.* Given to doing nothing; idle. See Synonyms at **lazy.** **—fainéant** *n.* An irresponsible idler; a sluggard. [French, alteration (influenced by *fait néant,* does nothing) of Old French *faignant,* idler, from present participle of *faindre, feindre,* to feign. See FEIGN.]

faint (fānt) *adj.* **faint·er, faint·est. 1.** Lacking strength or vigor; feeble. **2.** Lacking conviction, boldness, or courage; timid. **3.a.** Lacking brightness: *a faint light in the gloom.* **b.** Lacking clarity or distinctness: *a faint recollection.* **4.** Likely to fall into a faint; dizzy and weak: *felt faint for a moment.* **—faint** *n.* An abrupt, usually brief loss of consciousness, generally associated with failure of normal blood circulation. See Synonyms at **blackout.** **—faint** *intr.v.* **faint·ed, faint·ing, faints. 1.** To fall into a usually brief state of unconsciousness. **2.** *Archaic.* To weaken in purpose or spirit. [Middle English, deceitful, cowardly, from Old French, past participle of *feindre,* to feign. See FEIGN.] **—faint′er** *n.* **—faint′ly** *adv.* **—faint′ness** *n.*

faint-heart·ed (fānt′här′tĭd) *adj.* Deficient in conviction or courage; timid. **—faint′-heart′ed·ly** *adv.* **—faint′-heart′ed·ness** *n.*

♦fair¹ (fâr) *adj.* **fair·er, fair·est. 1.** Of pleasing appearance, especially because of a pure or fresh quality; comely. **2.a.** Light in color, especially blond: *fair hair.* **b.** Of light complexion: *fair skin.* **3.** Free of clouds or storms; clear and sunny: *fair skies.* **4.** Free of blemishes or stains; clean and pure: *one's fair name.* **5.** Promising; likely: *We're in a fair way to succeed.* **6.a.** Having or exhibiting a disposition that is free of favoritism or bias; impartial: *a fair mediator.* **b.** Just to all parties; equitable: *a compromise that is fair to both factions.* **7.** Being in accordance with relative merit or significance: *She wanted to receive her fair share of the proceeds.* **8.** Consistent with rules, logic, or ethics: *a fair tactic.* **9.** Moderately good; mildly satisfying: *gave only a fair performance of the sonata.* **10.** Superficially true or appealing; specious: *Don't trust his fair promises.* **11.** Lawful to hunt or attack: *fair game.* **12.** *Archaic.* Free of all obstacles. **—fair** *adv.* **1.** In a proper or legal manner: *playing fair.* **2.** Directly; straight: *a blow caught fair in the stomach.* **—fair** *tr.v.* **faired, fair·ing, fairs.** To join (pieces) so as to be smooth, even, or regular: *faired the aircraft's wing into the fuselage.* **—fair** *n.* **1.** *Archaic.* A beautiful or beloved woman. **2.** *Obsolete.* Loveliness; beauty. **—*phrasal verb.* fair off** (or **up**). *Chiefly Southern U.S.* To become clear. Used of weather. **—*idioms.* fair and square.** Just and honest. **for fair.** To the greatest or fullest extent possible: *Our team was beaten for fair in that tournament.* **no fair.** Something contrary to the rules: *That was no fair.* [Middle English, from Old English *fæger,* lovely, pleasant.] **—fair′ness** *n.*

SYNONYMS: *fair, just, equitable, impartial, unprejudiced, unbiased, objective, dispassionate.* These adjectives mean free from favoritism, self-interest, or bias in judgment. *Fair* is the most general: *a fair referee; a fair deal; a fair fight; on a fair footing. Just* stresses conformity with what is legally or ethically right or proper: *a kind and just man; "a just and lasting peace"* (Abraham Lincoln). *Equitable* also implies justice, but justice dictated by reason, conscience, and a natural sense of what is fair to all concerned: *an equitable distribution of gifts among the children. Impartial* emphasizes lack of favoritism: *"the cold neutrality of an impartial judge"* (Edmund Burke). *Unprejudiced* means without favorable or unfavorable preconceived opinions or judgments: *an unprejudiced evaluation of the arguments for and against the proposal. Unbiased* implies absence of the preference or inclination inhibiting impartiality: *gave an unbiased account of her family problems. Objective* implies detachment that permits observation and judgment without undue reference to one's personal feelings or thoughts: *Try to be objective as you listen to the testimony. Dispassionate* means free from or unaffected by strong personal emotions: *A journalist should be a dispassionate reporter of fact.* See also Synonyms at **average, beautiful.**

♦*REGIONAL NOTE:* American folk speech puts Standard English to shame in its wealth of words for describing weather conditions. When the weather goes from fair to cloudy, New Englanders say that it's "breedin' up a storm" (Maine informant in the *Linguistic Atlas of New England*). If the weather is clear, however, a New Englander might call it *open.* Southern *fair off* and *fair up,* meaning "to become clear," were originally Northeastern terms and were brought to the South as settlement expanded southward and westward. They are now "regionalized to the South," according to Craig M. Carver, author of *American Regional Dialects.* These phrases may be the origin of modern and less regional coinings, such as *mild up,* used on a television weather forecast: "The Southwest is beginning to mild up just a tad."

WORD HISTORY: The history of the word *fair* illustrates how words can weaken in meaning over time. In Old English the ancestor of *fair, fæger,* had senses such as "lovely, beautiful, pleas-

Fahd ibn Abdel Aziz al-Saud
Photographed in 1987

ă pat	oi boy
ā pay	ou out
âr care	ŏŏ took
ä father	ōō boot
ĕ pet	ŭ cut
ē be	ûr urge
ĭ pit	th thin
ī pie	*th* this
îr pier	hw which
ŏ pot	zh vision
ō toe	ə about, item
ô paw	♦ regionalism

Stress marks: ′ (primary); ′ (secondary), as in **dictionary** (dĭk′shə-nĕr′ē)

ant, agreeable," a far cry from our modern sense "mildly good or satisfying." The Old English senses passed into Middle English, where the word *fair* started to take a slight turn in the direction already alluded to. *Fair* could mean "highly to be approved of, splendid, good," but it could also be used ironically, as in Chaucer's observation after a horse threw the Cook on the pilgrimage to Canterbury: "that was a fair feat of horsemanship by the Cook." This ironic use was probably not responsible for the semantic weakening of *fair,* but it shows how a positive word can have its meaning reversed. The weakening of *fair* was most likely caused by "the determined optimism which led to the use of *fair* . . . rather than direct expression of discontent," in the words of George H. McKnight. One might add as another cause the desire to avoid hurting other people's feelings.

fairlead

fair² (fâr) *n.* **1.** A gathering held at a specified time and place for the buying and selling of goods; a market. **2.** An exhibition, as of farm products or manufactured goods, usually accompanied by various competitions and entertainments: *a state fair.* **3.** An exhibition intended to inform people about a product or business opportunity: *a computer fair; a job fair.* **4.** An event, usually for the benefit of a charity or public institution, including entertainment and the sale of goods; a bazaar: *a church fair.* [Middle English *faire,* from Old French *feire,* from Late Latin *fēria,* sing. of Latin *fēriae,* holidays. See **dhēs-** in Appendix.]

fair ball *n. Baseball.* A batted ball that first strikes the ground or leaves the playing field beyond first or third base within the foul lines or that is within the foul lines as it bounces past first or third base or that comes to rest or is touched by a fielder in front of first or third base within the foul lines.

Fair·banks (fâr′băngks′). A city of central Alaska north-northeast of Anchorage. It was founded in 1902 as a gold-mining camp. Population, 22,645.

Fairbanks, Charles Warren. 1852–1918. Vice President of the United States (1905–1909) under Theodore Roosevelt.

Fairbanks, Douglas. 1883–1939. American actor known for his swashbuckling roles in silent films such as *Robin Hood* (1922).

Fair·born (fâr′bôrn′). A city of southwest Ohio northeast of Dayton. It was formed in 1950 by the consolidation of two former villages. Population, 29,702.

fair catch *n. Football.* A catch of a punt on the fly by a defensive player who has signaled that he or she will not run with the ball and who therefore may not be tackled.

Fair·fax (fâr′făks′). An independent city of northeast Virginia, a residential suburb of Washington, D.C. Population, 19,390.

Fair·field (fâr′fēld′). **1.** A city of western California north-northeast of Oakland. It was founded in 1859. Population, 58,099. **2.** A town of southwest Connecticut on Long Island Sound southwest of Bridgeport. Settled in 1639, it is mainly residential. Population, 54,849. **3.** A city of southwest Ohio north of Cincinnati. It is an industrial center. Population, 30,777.

fairwater
Nuclear-powered *Polaris* submarine

fair·ground (fâr′ground′) *n.* Open land where fairs or exhibitions are held.

fair-haired (fâr′hârd′) *adj.* **1.** Having blond hair: *a fair-haired toddler.* **2.** Favorite: *"master linguist, Yale dropout and fair-haired boy of the OSS"* (Edward Klein).

fair·ing¹ (fâr′ĭng) *n.* An auxiliary structure or the external surface of a vehicle, such as an aircraft, that serves to reduce drag.

fair·ing² (fâr′ĭng) *n. Chiefly British.* A gift, especially one bought or given at a fair.

fair·ish (fâr′ĭsh) *adj.* Of moderately large size or good quality. **—fair′ish·ly** *adv.*

Fair Lawn (fâr). A borough of northeast New Jersey across the Passaic River from Paterson. Population, 32,229.

fair·lead (fâr′lēd′) also **fair·lead·er** (-lē′dər) *n. Nautical.* A device such as a ring or block of wood with a hole in it through which rigging is passed to hold it in place or prevent it from snagging or chafing.

fair·ly (fâr′lē) *adv.* **1. a.** In a fair or just manner; equitably. **b.** Legitimately; suitably. **2.** Clearly; distinctly. **3.** Actually; fully: *The walls fairly shook with their bellowing.* **4. a.** Moderately; rather: *a fairly good dinner.* **b.** To a reasonable degree: *I was fairly sure that I would go to the party.* **5.** *Obsolete.* **a.** Gently. **b.** Courteously.

fair-mar·ket value (fâr′mär′kĭt) *n.* The price, as of a commodity or service, at which both buyers and sellers agree to do business.

fair-mind·ed (fâr′mīn′dĭd) *adj.* Just and impartial; not prejudiced. **—fair′-mind′ed·ly** *adv.* **—fair′-mind′ed·ness** *n.*

Fair·mont (fâr′mŏnt′). A city of northern West Virginia near the Pennsylvania border northeast of Clarksburg. It was settled in 1793 around Prickett's Fort (built 1774). Population, 23,863.

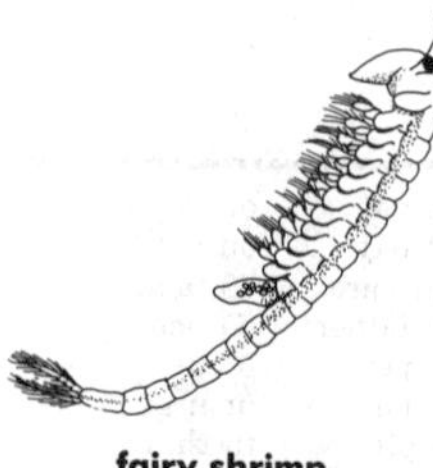

fairy shrimp

fairness doctrine *n.* A basic tenet of the licensed broadcasting industry in the United States that ensures reasonable opportunity for the airing of opposing viewpoints on controversial issues.

Fair Oaks. A locality just east of Richmond, Virginia, where Union troops defeated the Confederates at the Battle of Seven Pines (May 31–June 1, 1862).

fair play *n.* Conformity to established rules.

fair shake *n. Informal.* A fair chance, as at achieving success.

fair-spo·ken (fâr′spō′kən) *adj.* Civil, courteous, and gentle in speech.

fair trade *n.* Trade that conforms to a fair-trade agreement.

fair-trade (fâr′trād′) *tr.v.* **-trad·ed, -trad·ing, -trades.** To sell at a price consistent with a fair-trade agreement.

fair-trade agreement *n.* A commercial agreement under which distributors sell products of a given class at no less than a minimum price set by the manufacturer.

Fair·view Park (fâr′vyo͞o′). A city of northeast Ohio, a residential suburb of Cleveland. Population, 19,311.

fair·wa·ter (fâr′wô′tər, -wŏt′ər) *n. Nautical.* **1.** A device used to fair the lines of an underwater fitting. **2.** The bridge and conning tower on a submarine.

fair·way (fâr′wā′) *n.* **1.** A stretch of ground free of obstacles to movement. **2.** *Sports.* The part of a golf course covered with short grass and extending from the tee to the putting green. **3.** *Nautical.* **a.** A navigable deep-water channel in a river or harbor or along a coastline. **b.** The usual course taken by vessels through a harbor or coastal waters.

fair-weath·er (fâr′wĕth′ər) *adj.* **1.** Suitable or used only during fair weather: *fair-weather hiking gear.* **2.** Present and dependable only in good times: *fair-weather friends.*

Fair·weath·er (fâr′wĕth′ər), **Mount.** A peak, 4,666.5 m (15,300 ft) high, on the border between southeast Alaska and western British Columbia, Canada.

fair·y (fâr′ē) *n., pl.* **-ies.** **1.** A tiny imaginary being in human form, depicted as clever, mischievous, and possessing magical powers. **2.** *Offensive Slang.* Used as a disparaging term for a gay or homosexual man. [Middle English *fairie,* fairyland, enchanted being, from Old French *faerie,* from *fae,* fairy, from Vulgar Latin *Fāta,* goddess of fate, from Latin *fātum,* fate. See FATE.]

fairy godmother *n.* A generous benefactor.

fair·y·land (fâr′ē-lănd′) *n.* **1.** The imaginary land of fairies. **2.** A charming, enchanting place.

fairy lily *n.* See **zephyr lily.**

fairy primrose *n.* A Chinese ornamental *(Primula malcoides)* grown for its large, rose to pink flowers.

fairy ring *n.* A circle of mushrooms in a grassy area, marking the periphery of perennial underground mycelial growth. [From the belief that it is a dancing place for fairies.]

fairy shrimp *n.* Any of various transparent freshwater crustaceans of the order Anostraca that lack a carapace and characteristically swim upside-down.

fairy tale *n.* **1.** A fanciful tale of legendary deeds and creatures, usually intended for children. **2.** A fictitious, highly fanciful story or explanation.

fair·y-tale (fâr′ē-tāl′) *adj.* **1.** Of or relating to a fairy tale. **2.** Likened to a fairy tale: *a fairy-tale romance.*

Fai·sal also **Fei·sal** or **Fei·sul** (fī′səl). Full name Faisal ibn Abdel Aziz al-Saud. 1906?–1975. King of Saudi Arabia (1964–1975) who used oil revenue to increase industrialization and improve educational and medical facilities.

Fai·sa·la·bad (fī′sä-lə-bäd′). Formerly **Ly·all·pur** (lī′əl-po͝or′). A city of northeast Pakistan west of Lahore. Founded in 1892, it is a cloth and grain market. Population, 1,092,000.

fait ac·com·pli (fā′tä-kôN-plē′, fĕt′ä-) *n., pl.* **faits ac·com·plis** (fā′tä-kôN-plē′, -plēz′, fĕt′ä-). An accomplished, presumably irreversible deed or fact. [French : *fait,* fact + *accompli,* accomplished.]

faith (fāth) *n.* **1.** Confident belief in the truth, value, or trustworthiness of a person, an idea, or a thing. **2.** Belief that does not rest on logical proof or material evidence. See Synonyms at **belief, trust.** **3.** Loyalty to a person or thing; allegiance: *keeping faith with one's supporters.* **4.** Often **Faith.** *Theology.* The theological virtue defined as secure belief in God and a trusting acceptance of God's will. **5.** The body of dogma of a religion: *the Moslem faith.* **6.** A set of principles or beliefs. **—*idiom.* in faith.** Indeed; truly. [Middle English, from Anglo-Norman *fed,* from Latin *fidēs.* See **bheidh-** in Appendix.]

faith·ful (fāth′fəl) *adj.* **1.** Adhering firmly and devotedly, as to a person, a cause, or an idea; loyal. **2.** Having or full of faith. **3.** Worthy of trust or belief; reliable. **4.** Consistent with truth or actuality: *a faithful reproduction of the portrait.* **—faithful** *n., pl.* **faithful** or **-fuls.** **1.** The practicing members of a religious faith, especially of Christianity or Islam: *a pilgrimage to Mecca made by the faithful.* **2.** A steadfast adherent of a faith or cause: *a meeting of the party faithful.* **—faith′ful·ly** *adv.* **—faith′ful·ness** *n.*

SYNONYMS: *faithful, loyal, true, constant, fast, steadfast, staunch.* These adjectives mean adhering firmly and devotedly to someone or something, such as a person, cause, or duty, that elicits or demands one's fidelity. *Faithful* and *loyal* both suggest undeviating attachment; the words are often interchangeable, though *loyal* is the term more often applied to political allegiance: *a faithful employee; gave faithful service; a loyal companion; a loyal citizen. True* implies steadiness, sincerity, and reliability: *"I would be true, for there are those who trust me"* (Howard Arnold Walter). *Constant* stresses uniformity and invariability: *"But I am constant as the northern star"* (Shakespeare). *Fast* suggests loyalty that is not easily deflected: *fast friends. Steadfast* strongly implies fixed, unswerving loyalty: *a steadfast ally. Staunch* even more strongly suggests unshakable attachment or allegiance: *"He lived and died a staunch loyalist"* (Harriet Beecher Stowe).

faith healer *n.* One who treats disease with prayer. **—faith healing** *n.*

faith•less (fāth′lĭs) *adj.* **1.** Not true to duty or obligation; disloyal. **2.** Having no religious faith. **3.** Unworthy of faith or trust; unreliable. **—faith′less•ly** *adv.* **—faith′less•ness** *n.*

SYNONYMS: *faithless, unfaithful, false, disloyal, traitorous, treacherous, perfidious, recreant.* These adjectives mean not true to duty or obligation. *Faithless* and *unfaithful* are approximately interchangeable and imply failure to adhere to promises, obligations, or allegiances: *has never been faithless to her ideals; an unfaithful spouse. False* emphasizes a tendency to be faithless or deceitful: *a false friend. "To thine own self be true,/And it must follow, as the night the day,/Thou canst not then be false to any man"* (Shakespeare). One who is *disloyal* is false to persons or things that are due allegiance: *Disloyal staff members exposed the senator's indiscretions to the press. Traitorous* most commonly refers to disloyalty to a government or nation: *a lying, traitorous insurrectionist. Treacherous* suggests a propensity for betraying trust or faith: *"She gave the treacherous impulse time to subside"* (Henry James). *Perfidious* applies to what is abominably treacherous; it suggests vileness of behavior and often deceitfulness: *the victim of a perfidious murder. Recreant* implies a reprehensible, often cowardly disloyalty: *"while* [Holland's] *sister provinces had proved recreant to* [William of Orange]*"* (John Lothrop Motley).

fai•tour (fā′tər) *n. Archaic.* An impostor. [Middle English, from Anglo-Norman, from Latin *factor,* maker. See FACTOR.]

fa•ji•ta (fə-hē′tə, fä-hē′tä) *n., pl.* **-tas.** An appetizer consisting of marinated skirt steak or other meat, such as chicken, fish, or duck, that is grilled over an open fire and then placed in a tortilla. [American Spanish, diminutive of *faja,* band, strip, from Latin *fascia,* band, bandage.]

fake¹ (fāk) *adj.* Having a false or misleading appearance; fraudulent. **—fake** *n.* **1.** One that is not authentic or genuine; a sham. **2.** *Sports.* A brief feint or aborted change of direction intended to mislead one's opponent or the opposing team. **—fake** *v.* **faked, fak•ing, fakes.** *—tr.* **1.** To contrive and present as genuine; counterfeit. **2.** To simulate; feign. See Synonyms at **pretend. 3.** *Music.* To improvise (a passage). **4.** *Sports.* To deceive (an opponent) with a fake. *—intr.* **1.** To engage in feigning, simulation, or other deceptive activity. **2.** *Sports.* To perform a fake. [Origin unknown.]

fake² (fāk) *n.* One loop or winding of a coiled rope or cable. **—fake** *tr.v.* **faked, fak•ing, fakes.** To coil (a rope or cable). [Middle English *faken,* to coil a rope.]

fak•er (fā′kər) *n.* One who fakes or produces fakes. See Synonyms at **impostor. —fak′er•y** (-kə-rē) *n.*

fa•kir (fə-kîr′, fä-, fā-) *n.* **1.** A Moslem religious mendicant. **2.** A Hindu ascetic or religious mendicant, especially one who performs feats of magic or endurance. [Arabic *faqīr,* from *faqura,* to be poor.]

fa•la•fel or **fe•la•fel** (fə-lä′fəl) *n.* **1.** Ground spiced chickpeas and fava beans shaped into balls and fried. **2.** A sandwich filled with such a mixture. [Arabic *falāfil,* pl. of *filfil,* pepper, probably from Sanskrit *pippalī,* from *pippalam,* peppercorn.]

Fa•lan•gist (fə-lăn′gĭst, fā′lăn′-) *n.* A member of a fascist organization constituting the official ruling party of Spain after 1939. [Spanish *Falangista,* from *Falange (Española),* (Spanish) Phalanx, from Latin *phalanx, phalang-.* See PHALANX.]

Fa•la•sha (fə-lä′shə, fä-) *n., pl.* **Falasha** or **-shas.** *Offensive.* Used as a disparaging term for an Ethiopian Jew. [Amharic *fälasha,* from *fälasi,* stranger.]

fal•cate (făl′kāt′) also **fal•cat•ed** (-kā′tĭd) *adj.* Curved and tapering to a point; sickle-shaped. [Latin *falcātus,* from *falx, falc-,* sickle.]

fal•ces (făl′sēz′, fôl′-) *n.* Plural of **falx.**

fal•chion (fôl′chən) *n.* **1.** A short, broad sword with a convex cutting edge and a sharp point, used in medieval times. **2.** *Archaic.* A sword. [Middle English *fauchoun,* from Old French *fauchon,* from Vulgar Latin **falciō, falciōn-,* from Latin *falx, falc-,* sickle.]

fal•ci•form (făl′sə-fôrm′) *adj.* Curved or sickle-shaped; falcate. [Latin *falx, falc-,* sickle + -FORM.]

fal•con (făl′kən, fôl′-, fô′kən) *n.* **1. a.** Any of various birds of prey of the family Falconidae and especially of the genus *Falco,* having a short, curved beak and long, pointed, powerful wings adapted for swift flight. **b.** Any of several species of these birds or related birds such as hawks, trained to hunt small game. **c.** A female bird of this type used in falconry. **2.** A small cannon in use from the 15th to the 17th century. [Middle English, from Old French *faucon, falcun,* from Late Latin *falcō, falcōn-.* See **pel-¹** in Appendix.]

fal•con•er (făl′kə-nər, fôl′-, fô′kə-) *n.* **1.** One that breeds and trains falcons. **2.** One that hunts with falcons.

fal•con•et (făl′kə-nĕt′, fôl′-, fô′kə-) *n.* **1.** A small or young falcon. **2.** Any of several small falcons, especially of the genus *Microhierax* native to tropical Asia.

fal•con-gen•tle (făl′kən-jĕn′tl, fôl′-, fô′kən-) *n.* A female falcon, especially a peregrine falcon. [Middle English *faucon gentil,* from Old French *faucon gentil,* noble falcon.]

fal•con•ry (făl′kən-rē, fôl′-, fô′kən-) *n. Sports.* **1.** Hunting of game with falcons. **2.** The art of training falcons for hunting. [Alteration of French *fauconnerie,* from Old French, from *faucon,* falcon. See FALCON.]

fal•de•ral (făl′də-răl′) *n.* Variant of **folderol.**

fald•stool (fôld′sto͞ol′) *n.* **1.** A folding or small desk stool at which worshipers kneel to pray, especially one on which the British sovereign kneels at the time of coronation. **2.** A folding chair or stool, especially one used by a bishop when not occupying the throne or when presiding away from the cathedral. **3.** A desk at which the litany is recited. [Partial translation of Medieval Latin *faldistolium,* folding stool, of Germanic origin. See **pel-²** in Appendix.]

Fa•lis•can (fə-lĭs′kən) *n.* **1.** A member of an ancient Italic people of southern Etruria. **2.** The language of this people, closely related to Latin and known from place and personal names and from inscriptions. **—Faliscan** *adj.* Of or relating to the Faliscans or their language or culture. [From Latin *Faliscus,* from *Falerii,* a city of ancient Etruria.]

Fal•kirk (fôl′kûrk′). A burgh of central Scotland west of Edinburgh. At the Battle of Falkirk (1298), the troops of Edward I defeated the Scots. Population, 37,800.

Falk•land Islands (fôk′lənd, fôlk′-). A group of islands in the southern Atlantic Ocean east of the Strait of Magellan. Controlled by Great Britain since the 1830's, the islands are also claimed by Argentina and were occupied briefly by Argentinian troops in 1982.

Falk•ner (fôk′nər), **William.** See William **Faulkner.**

fall (fôl) *v.* **fell** (fĕl), **fall•en** (fô′lən), **fall•ing, falls.** *—intr.* **1.** To drop or come down freely under the influence of gravity. **2.** To drop oneself to a lower or less erect position: *I fell back in my chair. The pilgrims fell to their knees.* **3. a.** To lose an upright or erect position suddenly. **b.** To drop wounded or dead, especially in battle. **4.** To go or come as if by falling: *All grief fell from our hearts. Night fell quickly.* **5.** To come to rest; settle: *The light fell on my book.* **6.** To hang down: *The child's hair fell in ringlets.* **7.** To be cast down: *Her eyes fell.* **8.** To assume an expression of consternation or disappointment: *His face fell when he heard the report.* **9.** To undergo conquest or capture, especially as the result of an armed attack: *The city fell after a long siege.* **10. a.** To experience defeat or ruin: *After 300 years the dynasty fell.* **b.** To lose office: *The disgraced prime minister fell from power.* **11.** To slope downward: *The rolling hills fall gently toward the coast.* **12. a.** To lessen in amount or degree: *The air pressure is falling.* **b.** To decline in financial value: *Last year, stock prices fell sharply.* **c.** To lose weight. *The patient's weight fell away rapidly.* **13.** To diminish in pitch or volume: *My friend's voice fell to a whisper.* **14. a.** To give in to temptation; sin. **b.** To lose one's chastity. **15.** To pass into a particular state, condition, or situation: *fell silent; fall in love.* **16.** To occur at a specified time: *New Year's Day falls on a Tuesday this year.* **17.** To occur at a specified place: *The stress falls on the last syllable.* **18.** To come, as by chance. **19. a.** To be given by assignment or distribution: *The greatest task fell to me.* **b.** To be given by right or inheritance. **20.** To be included within the range or scope of something: *The specimens fall into three categories.* **21.** To come into contact; strike: *My gaze fell on a small book in the corner.* **22.** To come out; issue: *Insincere compliments fell from their lips.* **23.** To begin vigorously: *fell to work immediately.* **24.** To be born. Used chiefly of lambs. *—tr.* To cut down (a tree); fell. **—fall** *n.* **1.** The act or an instance of falling. **2.** A sudden drop from a relatively erect to a less erect position. **3.** Something that has fallen: *a fall of hail.* **4. a.** An amount that has fallen: *a fall of two inches of rain.* **b.** The distance that something falls: *The victim suffered a fall of three stories to the ground.* **5.** Autumn. **6. falls** *(used with a sing. or pl. verb).* A waterfall. **7.** A downward movement or slope. **8.** Any of several pendent articles of dress, especially: **a.** A veil hung from a woman's hat and down her back. **b.** An ornamental cascade of lace or trimming attached to a dress, usually at the collar. **c.** A woman's hairpiece with long, free-hanging hair. **9. a.** An overthrow; a collapse: *the fall of a government.* **b.** Armed capture of a place under siege: *the fall of Dien Bien Phu.* **10.** A reduction in value, amount, or degree. **11.** A marked, often sudden, decline in status, rank, or importance: *"turned them in, set them up for prosecution; positioned them, as it were, for the fall"* (Joan Didion). **12. a.** A moral lapse. **b.** A loss of chastity. **13.** Often **Fall.** *Theology.* The loss of innocence and grace resulting from Adam's eating the forbidden fruit in the Garden of Eden. **14.** *Sports.* **a.** The act of throwing or forcing a wrestling opponent down on his or her back. Also called *pin.* **b.** Any of various wrestling maneuvers so used. **15.** *Nautical.* **a.** A break or rise in the level of a deck. **b. falls.** The apparatus used to hoist and transfer cargo or lifeboats. **16.** The end of a cable, rope, or chain that is pulled by the power source in hoisting. **17. a.** The birth of an animal, especially a lamb. **b.** All the animals born at one birth; a litter. **18.** A family of woodcock in flight. See Synonyms at **flock¹. 19.** *Botany.* The outer series of perianth in the irises and related plants. **—*phrasal verbs.* fall apart.** To break down; collapse: *The rickety chair fell apart. He fell apart after years as a POW.* **fall away. 1.** To withdraw one's friendship and support. **2.** To become gradually diminished in size. **3.** To drift off an established course. **fall back. 1.** To give ground; retreat. **2.** To recede: *The waves fell back.* **fall behind. 1.** To fail to keep up a pace; lag behind. **2.** To be financially in arrears. **fall down.** To fail to meet expectations; lag in performance: *fell down on the job.* **fall for. 1.** To feel love for. **2.** To be deceived or swindled by: *fell for the con artist's scheme and lost $200,000.* **fall in. 1.** To take one's place

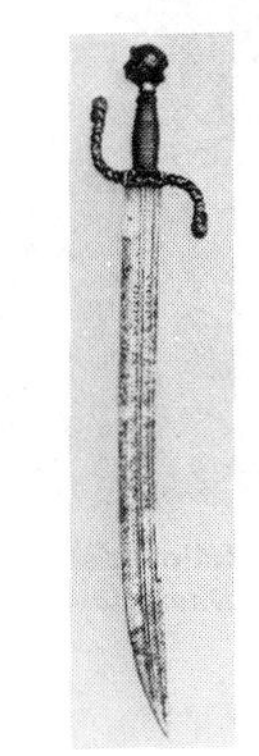

falchion
16th-century Islamic

ă pat	oi boy
ā pay	ou out
âr care	o͝o took
ä father	o͞o boot
ĕ pet	ŭ cut
ē be	ûr urge
ĭ pit	th thin
ī pie	*th* this
îr pier	hw which
ŏ pot	zh vision
ō toe	ə about, item
ô paw	♦ regionalism

Stress marks: ′ (primary); ′ (secondary), as in **dictionary** (dĭk′shə-nĕr′ē)

fallow deer
Dama dama

in a military formation. **2.** To sink inward; cave in: *The roof of the old barn fell in.* **fall off. 1.** To become less; decrease: *Stock prices have fallen off. The number of staff meetings fell off after a few months.* **2.** *Nautical.* To change course to leeward. **fall on** (or **upon**). **1.** To attack suddenly and viciously: *Snipers and irregulars fell on the hapless patrol.* **2.** To meet with; encounter: *a stockbroker who fell on hard times.* **fall out. 1.a.** To leave a barracks, for example, in order to take one's place in a military formation. **b.** To leave a military formation. **2.** To quarrel: *The siblings fell out over their inheritance.* **3.** To happen; occur. **fall through.** To fail; miscarry: *Our plans fell through at the last minute.* **fall to.** To begin an activity energetically: *"The press fell to with a will"* (Russell Baker). —***idioms.*** **fall back on** (or **upon**). **1.** To rely on: *fall back on old friends in time of need.* **2.** To resort to: *I had to fall back on my savings when I was unemployed.* **fall between (the) two stools.** To fail because of an inability to reconcile or choose between two courses of action. **fall flat. 1.** To fail miserably when attempting to achieve a result. **2.** To have no effect: *The jokes fell flat.* **fall foul** (or **afoul**). **1.** *Nautical.* To collide. Used of vessels. **2.** To clash: *fell foul of the law.* **fall from grace.** To experience a major reduction in status or prestige. **fall into line.** To adhere to established rules or predetermined courses of action. **fall in with. 1.** To agree with or be in harmony with: *Their views fall in with ours.* **2.** To associate or begin to associate with: *fell in with the wrong crowd.* **fall on deaf ears.** To go unheeded; be ignored completely: *"Moscow's own familiar charges . . . will also fall on deaf ears"* (Foreign Affairs). **fall over backward** (or **backwards**). To overexert oneself to do or accomplish something: *We fell over backward to complete the project on time.* **fall over (oneself).** To display inordinate, typically effusive, enthusiasm: *fell over themselves to impress the general's wife.* **fall prey to.** To be put into such a vulnerable position as to be at risk of harm, destruction, or invasion: *a person who fell prey to swindlers; did not want the country to fall prey to terrorists.* **fall short. 1.** To fail to attain a specified amount, level, or degree: *an athlete whose skill fell far short of expectations.* **2.** To prove inadequate: *Our supplies of sugar and rice fell short.* **fall through the cracks.** To pass unnoticed, neglected, or unchecked: *"Much of the wisdom . . . seems to have fallen through the cracks"* (Boston Globe). [Middle English *fallen,* from Old English *feallan.*]

fal·la·cious (fə-lā′shəs) *adj.* **1.** Containing or based on a fallacy: *a fallacious assumption.* **2.** Tending to mislead; deceptive: *fallacious testimony.* —**fal·la′cious·ly** *adv.*

fal·la·cy (făl′ə-sē) *n., pl.* **-cies. 1.** A false notion. **2.** A statement or an argument based on a false or an invalid inference. **3.** Incorrectness of reasoning or belief; erroneousness. **4.** The quality of being deceptive. [Alteration of Middle English *fallace,* from Old French, from Latin *fallācia,* deceit, from *fallāx, fallāc-,* deceitful, from *fallere,* to deceive.]

fal·lal (fă-lăl′, făl′ăl′) *n.* A showy article of dress. [Origin unknown.] —**fal·lal′er·y** *n.*

fall·back (fôl′băk′) *n.* **1.a.** Something to which one can resort or retreat. **b.** A retreat. **2.** *Computer Science.* A mechanism for carrying forth programmed instructions despite malfunction or failure of the primary device. **3.** Something that falls back: *the fallback of a huge explosion.* —**fallback** *adj.* Of, relating to, or constituting a resort or place of retreat: *a fallback proposal; a fallback position behind our own lines.*

fall·board (fôl′bôrd′, -bōrd′) *n. Music.* The hinged cover protecting the keyboard of a piano.

fall·en (fô′lən) *v.* Past participle of **fall.**

fall·fish (fôl′fĭsh′) *n., pl.* **fallfish** or **-fish·es.** A small, silvery freshwater fish *(Semotilus corporalis)* of streams and rivers in eastern North America.

fall guy *n. Slang.* **1.** A scapegoat. **2.** A gullible victim; a dupe.

fal·li·ble (făl′ə-bəl) *adj.* **1.** Capable of making an error: *Human beings are only fallible.* **2.** Tending or likely to be erroneous: *fallible hypotheses.* [Middle English, from Medieval Latin *fallibilis,* from Latin *fallere,* to deceive.] —**fal′li·bil′i·ty, fal′li·ble·ness** *n.* —**fal′li·bly** *adv.*

fall·ing action (fô′lĭng) *n.* The events of a dramatic or narrative plot following the climax.

fall·ing-out (fô′lĭng-out′) *n., pl.* **fall·ings-out** or **fall·ing-outs.** A disagreement; a quarrel: *a falling-out among family members.*

falling rhythm *n.* A rhythmic pattern in which the stress regularly occurs on the first syllable of each foot, as in *Jack and Jill went up the hill.*

falling star *n.* See **meteor.**

fall line *n.* **1.** A line connecting the waterfalls of nearly parallel rivers that marks a drop in land level. **2.** The natural line of descent, as for skiing, between two points on a slope.

fall·off (fôl′ôf′, -ŏf′) *n.* A reduction or decrease: *a falloff in car sales.*

fal·lo·pi·an tube also **Fal·lo·pi·an tube** (fə-lō′pē-ən) *n.* Either of a pair of slender ducts through which ova pass from the ovaries to the uterus in the female reproductive system of human beings and higher mammals. [After Gabriele *Fallopio* (1523–1562), Italian anatomist.]

Fal·lot's tetralogy (fă-lōz′) *n.* Tetralogy of Fallot.

fall·out (fôl′out′) *n.* **1.a.** The slow descent of minute particles of debris in the atmosphere following an explosion, especially the descent of radioactive debris after a nuclear explosion. **b.** The particles that descend in this fashion. **2.** An incidental result or side effect: *"Other social trends also have psychiatric fallout, and the people who suffer can't afford treatment"* (Martha Farnsworth Riche).

fal·low (făl′ō) *adj.* **1.** Plowed but left unseeded during a growing season: *fallow farmland.* **2.** Characterized by inactivity: *a fallow gold market.* —**fallow** *n.* **1.** Land left unseeded during a growing season. **2.** The act of plowing land and leaving it unseeded. **3.** The condition or period of being unseeded. —**fallow** *tr.v.* **-lowed, -low·ing, -lows. 1.** To plow (land) without seeding it afterward. **2.** To plow and till (land), especially to eradicate or reduce weeds. [Middle English *falow,* from Old English *fealh,* fallow land.] —**fal′low·ness** *n.*

fallow deer *n.* A small Eurasian deer *(Dama dama)* having a yellowish-red coat spotted with white in summer and broad, flattened antlers in the male. [Obsolete *fallow,* reddish-yellow, from Middle English *falow, falwe,* from Old English *fealu.* See **pel-**[1] in Appendix.]

Fall River. A city of southeast Massachusetts on the Rhode Island border west-northwest of New Bedford. Formerly a textile center, it now has diversified industries. Population, 92,574.

Fal·mouth (făl′məth). A town of southeast Massachusetts on southwest Cape Cod. Once a whaling and shipbuilding center, it is now a popular summer resort. Population, 23,640.

false (fôls) *adj.* **fals·er, fals·est. 1.** Contrary to fact or truth: *false tales of bravery.* **2.** Deliberately untrue: *delivered false testimony under oath.* **3.** Arising from mistaken ideas: *false hopes of writing a successful novel.* **4.** Intentionally deceptive: *a suitcase with a false bottom; false promises.* **5.** Not keeping faith; treacherous: *a false friend.* See Synonyms at **faithless. 6.** Not genuine or real: *false teeth; false documents.* **7.** Erected temporarily, as for support during construction. **8.** Resembling but not accurately or properly designated as such: *a false thaw in January; the false dawn peculiar to the tropics.* **9.** *Music.* Of incorrect pitch. **10.** Unwise; imprudent: *Don't make a false move or I'll shoot.* —**false** *adv.* In a treacherous or faithless manner: *play a person false.* [Middle English *fals,* from Old French, from Latin *falsus,* from past participle of *fallere,* to deceive.] —**false′ly** *adv.* —**false′ness** *n.*

false alarm *n.* **1.** An emergency alarm, such as a fire alarm, that is set off unnecessarily. **2.** A signal or warning that is groundless.

false arrest *n. Law.* Unlawful or unjustifiable arrest.

false fruit *n.* **1.** See **accessory fruit. 2.** See **pome.**

false-heart·ed (fôls′här′tĭd) *adj.* Of a deceitful nature; treacherous. —**false′-heart′ed·ness** *n.*

false·hood (fôls′ho͝od′) *n.* **1.** An untrue statement; a lie. **2.** The practice of lying. **3.** Lack of conformity to truth or fact; inaccuracy.

false imprisonment *n. Law.* Detention or imprisonment of a person contrary to the provisions of law.

false indigo *n.* **1.** A shrub *(Amorpha fruticosa)* of eastern North America, having compound leaves with numerous leaflets and long clusters of purplish flowers. **2.** A plant *(Baptisia australis)* of the southeast United States, having compound leaves with three leaflets and deep blue or purplish flowers.

false ipecac *n.* A shrubby plant *(Psychotria emetica)* native to Central and South America, having small white flowers and strong-smelling roots that are the source of an inferior ipecac.

false miterwort *n.* See **foamflower.**

false pretense *n. Law.* False representation of fact or circumstance, calculated to mislead.

false rib *n.* Any of the lower ribs that do not unite directly with the sternum. The five lower pairs of ribs in human beings are false ribs.

false Sol·o·mon's seal (sŏl′ə-mənz) *n.* Any of several plants of the genus *Smilacina,* native to North America and Asia and having a plumelike cluster of small greenish-white flowers with a persistent perianth. Also called *Solomon's feather, Solomon's plume.*

false spikenard *n.* A perennial herb *(Smilacina racemosa)* native to eastern North America, having fleshy rhizomes, white flowers, and usually red fruits. Also called *Solomon's zigzag.*

fal·set·to (fôl-sĕt′ō) *n., pl.* **-tos.** *Music.* **1.** A male singing voice marked by artificially produced tones in an upper register beyond the normal range especially of a tenor. **2.** One that sings in this way. —*attributive.* Often used to modify another noun: *a falsetto voice; falsetto singers.* [Italian, diminutive of *falso,* false, from Latin *falsus.* See FALSE.] —**fal·set′to** *adv.*

fals·ie (fôl′sē) *n. Informal.* Padding or a pad worn inside a brassiere to make the breasts appear larger. Often used in the plural.

fal·si·fy (fôl′sə-fī′) *v.* **-fied, -fy·ing, -fies.** —*tr.* **1.** To state untruthfully; misrepresent. **2.a.** To make false by altering or adding to: *falsify testimony.* **b.** To counterfeit; forge: *falsify a visa.* **3.** To declare or prove to be false. —*intr.* To make untrue statements; lie. [Middle English *falsifien,* from Old French *falsifier,* from Late Latin *falsificāre* : Latin *falsus,* false; see FALSE + Latin *-ficāre,* -fy.] —**fal′si·fi·ca′tion** (-fĭ-kā′shən) *n.* —**fal′si·fi′er** *n.*

fal·si·ty (fôl′sĭ-tē) *n., pl.* **-ties. 1.** The quality or condition of being false. **2.** Something false; a lie.

Fal·staff·i·an (fôl-stăf′ē-ən) *adj.* Characterized by joviality and conviviality. [After Sir John *Falstaff,* a character in *Henry*

IV, Parts I and II, and *The Merry Wives of Windsor* by William Shakespeare.]

Fal·ster (fäl′stər, fôl′-). An island of southeast Denmark in the Baltic Sea off the southern tip of Sjaelland.

falt·boat (fält′bōt′, fôlt′-) *n. Nautical.* See **foldboat.** [Partial translation of German *Faltboot,* folding boat : *falten,* to fold (from Middle High German *valten,* from Old High German *faldan;* see **pel-**[2] in Appendix) + *Boot,* boat.]

fal·ter (fôl′tər) *intr.v.* **-tered, -ter·ing, -ters. 1.** To be unsteady in purpose or action, as from loss of courage or confidence; waver. See Synonyms at **hesitate. 2.** To speak hesitatingly; stammer. **3.a.** To move ineptly or haltingly; stumble. **b.** To operate or perform unsteadily or with a loss of effectiveness: *The automobile engine faltered.* **—falter** *n.* **1.** Unsteadiness in speech or action. **2.** A faltering sound. [Middle English *falteren,* to stagger, possibly from Old Norse *faltrask,* to be puzzled, hesitate.] **—fal′ter·er** *n.* **—fal′ter·ing·ly** *adv.*

falx (fălks, fôlks) *n., pl.* **fal·ces** (făl′sēz′, fôl′-). A sickle-shaped anatomical structure. [Latin, sickle.]

FAM *abbr.* Free and Accepted Masons.

fam. *abbr.* **1.** Familiar. **2.** Family.

fame (fām) *n.* **1.a.** Great renown: *a concert violinist of international fame.* **b.** Public estimation; reputation: *a politician of ill fame.* **2.** *Archaic.* Rumor. **—fame** *tr.v.* **famed, fam·ing, fames. 1.** To make renowned or famous. **2.** *Archaic.* To report to be. [Middle English, from Old French, from Latin *fāma.* See **bhā-**[2] in Appendix.]

famed (fāmd) *adj.* Having great fame. See Synonyms at **noted.**

fa·mil·ial (fə-mĭl′yəl) *adj.* **1.** Of or relating to a family. **2.** Occurring or tending to occur among members of a family, usuallly by heredity: *familial traits; familial disease.*

fa·mil·iar (fə-mĭl′yər) *adj. Abbr.* **fam. 1.** Often encountered or seen; common. **2.** Having fair knowledge; acquainted: *was familiar with those roads.* **3.** Of established friendship; intimate: *on familiar terms.* **4.** Natural and unstudied; informal: *lectured in a familiar style.* **5.** Taking undue liberties; presumptuous: *Students should not try to be familiar in their behavior toward an instructor.* **6.** Familial. **7.** Domesticated; tame. Used of animals. **—familiar** *n. Abbr.* **fam. 1.** A close friend or associate. **2.** An attendant spirit, often taking animal form. **3.** One who performs domestic service in the household of a high official. **4.** A person who frequents a place. [Middle English, from Old French *familier,* from Latin *familiāris,* domestic, from *familia,* family. See FAMILY.] **—fa·mil′iar·ly** *adv.*

SYNONYMS: *familiar, close, intimate, confidential, chummy.* These adjectives describe relationships marked by intimacy. *Familiar* implies an easy, often informal association based on frequent contact or shared interests: *a familiar song; a familiar guest. Close* implies strong emotional attachment: *close friendship; close to my brothers and sisters. Intimate* suggests bonds of affection or understanding resulting from the sharing of interests, problems, and experiences: *intimate friends; on an intimate footing. Confidential* suggests closeness founded on trust: *the prime minister's confidential secretary. Chummy* implies the comfortable, casual sociability shared by close friends: *The bartender was chummy with the regular customers.*

fa·mil·iar·i·ty (fə-mĭl′yăr′ĭ-tē, -mĭl′ē-ăr′-) *n., pl.* **-ties. 1.** Considerable acquaintance with. **2.** Established friendship; intimacy. **3.a.** An excessively familiar or informal act; an impropriety. **b.** A sexual advance. **4.** The quality or condition of being familiar.

fa·mil·iar·ize (fə-mĭl′yə-rīz′) *tr.v.* **-ized, -iz·ing, -iz·es. 1.** To make known, recognized, or familiar. **2.** To make acquainted with. **—fa·mil′iar·i·za′tion** (-yər-ĭ-zā′shən) *n.* **—fa·mil′iar·iz′er** *n.*

fam·i·ly (făm′ə-lē, făm′lē) *n., pl.* **-lies.** *Abbr.* **fam. 1.a.** A fundamental social group in society typically consisting of a man and woman and their offspring. **b.** Two or more people who share goals and values, have long-term commitments to one another, and reside usually in the same dwelling place. **2.** All the members of a household under one roof. **3.** A group of persons sharing common ancestry. See Usage Note at **collective noun. 4.** Lineage, especially distinguished lineage. **5.** A locally independent organized crime unit, as of the Cosa Nostra. **6.a.** A group of like things; a class. **b.** A group of individuals derived from a common stock: *the family of human beings.* **7.** *Biology.* A taxonomic category of related organisms ranking below an order and above a genus. A family usually consists of several genera. See table at **taxonomy. 8.** *Linguistics.* A group of languages descended from the same parent language, such as the Indo-European language family. **9.** *Mathematics.* A set of functions or surfaces that can be generated by varying the parameters of a general equation. **10.** *Chemistry.* A group of elements with similar chemical properties. **11.** *Chemistry.* A vertical column in the periodic table of elements. **—family** *adj.* **1.** Of or having to do with a family: *family problems.* **2.** Being suitable for a family: *family movies.* [Middle English *familie,* from Latin *familia,* household, servants of a household, from *famulus,* servant.]

family Bible *n.* A Bible with special pages to record births, deaths, and marriages.

family circle *n.* A section of theater seats that are less expensive than some others.

family doctor *n.* **1.** A physician who practices the specialty of family medicine. Also called *family physician, family practitioner.* **2.** See **general practitioner.**

family hour *n.* A period of time during the evening, typically between 6 and 8 P.M., during which television and radio programs suitable for family viewing and listening are broadcast. Also called *family time.*

family man *n.* **1.** A man having a wife and children. **2.** A man devoted to his family.

family medicine *n.* The branch of medicine that deals with provision of comprehensive health care to people regardless of age or sex while placing particular emphasis on the family unit. Also called *family practice.*

family name *n.* See **surname** (sense 1).

family physician *n.* See **family doctor** (sense 1).

family plan·ning (plăn′ĭng) *n.* A program to regulate the number and spacing of children in a family through the practice of contraception or other methods of birth control.

family practice *n.* See **family medicine.**

family practitioner *n.* See **family doctor** (sense 1).

family room *n.* A recreation room especially for the use of family members.

family style *adv. & adj.* Having serving dishes of food placed on the table at a sit-down meal so that each participant in the meal can select his or her own portions: *students eating family style in the dorm; a family style restaurant.*

family therapy *n.* A form of psychotherapy in which the interrelationships of family members are examined in group sessions in order to identify and alleviate the problems of one or more members of the family.

family time *n.* See **family hour.**

family tree *n.* **1.** A genealogical diagram of a family's ancestry. **2.** The ancestors and descendants of a family considered as a group.

family way *n. Informal.* The state of being pregnant: *My neighbor is in a family way.*

fam·ine (făm′ĭn) *n.* **1.** A drastic, wide-reaching food shortage. **2.** A drastic shortage; a dearth. **3.** Severe hunger; starvation. **4.** *Archaic.* Extreme appetite. [Middle English, from Old French, from *faim,* hunger, from Latin *famēs.*]

fam·ish (făm′ĭsh) *v.* **-ished, -ish·ing, -ish·es.** *—tr.* **1.** To cause to endure severe hunger. **2.** To cause to starve to death. *—intr.* **1.** To endure severe deprivation, especially of food. **2.** To undergo starvation and die. [Middle English *famishen,* alteration of Middle English *famen,* from Old French *afamer,* from Vulgar Latin **affamāre* : Latin *ad-,* ad- + Latin *famēs,* hunger.] **—fam′ish·ment** *n.*

fa·mous (fā′məs) *adj.* **1.** Well or widely known. See Synonyms at **noted. 2.** *Informal.* First-rate; excellent: *had a famous old time at the party.* [Middle English, from Anglo-Norman, from Latin *fāmōsus,* from *fāma,* fame. See **bhā-**[2] in Appendix.] **—fa′mous·ly** *adv.* **—fa′mous·ness** *n.*

fam·u·lus (făm′yə-ləs) *n., pl.* **-li** (-lī′). A private secretary or other close attendant. [German, from Latin.]

fan[1] (făn) *n.* **1.** A device for creating a current of air or a breeze, especially: **a.** A machine using an electric motor to rotate thin, rigid vanes in order to move air, as for cooling. **b.** A collapsible, usually wedge-shaped device made of a light material such as silk, paper, or plastic. **2.** A machine for winnowing. **3.** Something resembling an open fan in shape: *a peacock's fan.* **—fan** *v.* **fanned, fan·ning, fans.** *—tr.* **1.** To move or cause a current of (air) with or as if with a fan. **2.** To direct a current of air or a breeze upon, especially in order to cool: *fan one's face.* **3.** To stir (something) up by or as if by fanning: *fanned the flames in the fireplace; an otherwise quiet employee who fanned resentment among her colleagues.* **4.** To open (something) out into the shape of a fan: *The bird fanned its colorful tail.* **5.a.** To fire (an automatic gun) in a continuous sweep by keeping one's finger on the trigger. **b.** To fire (a nonautomatic gun) rapidly by chopping the hammer with the palm. **6.** To winnow. **7.** *Baseball.* To strike out (a batter). *—intr.* **1.** To spread out like a fan: *The troops fanned out in a northerly direction.* **2.** *Baseball.* To strike out. [Middle English, winnowing fan, from Old English *fann,* from Latin *vannus.* See **wet-**[1] in Appendix.]

fan[2] (făn) *n. Informal.* An ardent devotee; an enthusiast. [Short for FANATIC.]

fan·ac or **FAN·AC** (făn′ăk′) *n. Slang.* The activities of fans, especially fans of science fiction or skateboarding, usually involving the organization of conventions or writing of articles. [Perhaps FAN[2] + AC(TIVITY).]

fa·nat·ic (fə-năt′ĭk) *n.* A person marked or motivated by an extreme, unreasoning enthusiasm, as for a cause. **—fanatic** *adj.* Fanatical. [Latin *fānāticus,* inspired by orgiastic rites, pertaining to a temple, from *fānum,* temple. See **dhēs-** in Appendix.]

SYNONYMS: *fanatic, zealot, enthusiast.* These nouns denote persons who are ardently and usually excessively devoted to a particular cause, subject, or activity. *Fanatic* implies the pursuit of a given interest to inordinate and even irrational lengths, often to the exclusion of all other interests: *"A fanatic is one who can't change his mind and won't change the subject"* (Winston S. Churchill). A *zealot* is immoderately devoted to a cause or goal and seeks to advance it with passionate fervor: *"those furious zealots*

fan[1]
Top: Hand-held fan
Bottom: Comanche peyote fan with beaded handle and macaw and pheasant feathers

ă pat	oi boy
ā pay	ou out
âr care	ŏŏ took
ä father	ōō boot
ĕ pet	ŭ cut
ē be	ûr urge
ĭ pit	th thin
ī pie	*th* this
îr pier	hw which
ŏ pot	zh vision
ō toe	ə about, item
ô paw	♦ regionalism

Stress marks: ′ (primary); ′ (secondary), as in **dictionary** (dĭk′shə-nĕr′ē)

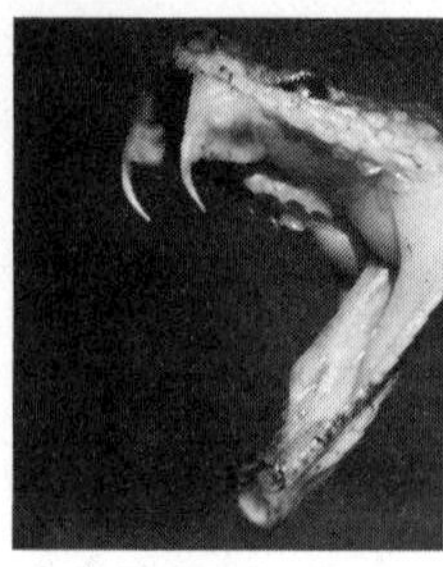
fang

who blow the bellows of faction until the whole furnace of politics is red-hot" (Washington Irving). *Enthusiast* can denote a religious zealot holding visionary opinions: *"It is unfortunate, considering that enthusiasm moves the world, that so few enthusiasts can be trusted to speak the truth"* (A.J. Balfour). More commonly, however, it merely implies strong interest in something, such as a hobby, and lacks the unfavorable connotations of the other terms: *a hockey enthusiast.*

---

fa·nat·i·cal (fə-năt′ĭ-kəl) *adj.* Possessed with or motivated by excessive, irrational zeal. **—fa·nat′i·cal·ly** *adv.* **—fa·nat′i·cal·ness** *n.*

fa·nat·i·cism (fə-năt′ĭ-sĭz′əm) *n.* Excessive, irrational zeal.

fa·nat·i·cize (fə-năt′ĭ-sīz′) *v.* **-cized, -ciz·ing, -ciz·es.** *—tr.* To make fanatical. *—intr.* To behave as a fanatic.

fan belt *n.* A taut rubber belt that transfers torque from the crankshaft to the shaft of the cooling fan on an engine.

fan·ci·er (făn′sē-ər) *n.* **1.** One who has a special enthusiasm for or interest in something: *a fancier of antiques.* **2.** One who breeds a plant or an animal for those features held to be desirable.

fan·ci·ful (făn′sĭ-fəl) *adj.* **1.** Created in the fancy; unreal: *a fanciful story.* **2.** Tending to indulge in fancy: *a fanciful mind.* **3.** Showing invention or whimsy in design; imaginative. See Synonyms at **fantastic.** **—fan′ci·ful·ly** *adv.* **—fan′ci·ful·ness** *n.*

fan·cy (făn′sē) *n., pl.* **-cies. 1.** The mental faculty through which whims, visions, and fantasies are summoned up; imagination, especially of a whimsical or fantastic nature. See Synonyms at **imagination. 2.** An image or a fantastic invention created by the mind. **3.** A capricious notion; a whim. **4.** A capricious liking or inclination. **5.** Critical sensibility; taste. **6.** Amorous or romantic attachment; love. **7. a.** The enthusiasts or fans of a sport or pursuit considered as a group. **b.** The sport or pursuit, such as boxing, engaging the interest of such a group. **—fancy** *adj.* **-ci·er, -ci·est. 1.** Highly decorated: *a fancy hat.* **2.** Arising in the fancy; capricious. **3.** Executed with skill; complex or intricate: *the fancy footwork of a figure skater.* **4.** *Abbr.* **fcy.** Of superior grade; fine: *fancy preserves.* **5.** Excessive or exorbitant: *paid a fancy price for the car.* **6.** Bred for unusual qualities or special points. **—fancy** *tr.v.* **-cied, -cy·ing, -cies. 1.** To visualize; imagine: *"She tried to fancy what the flame of a candle looks like after the candle is blown out"* (Lewis Carroll). **2.** To take a fancy to; like. See Synonyms at **like[1]**. **3.** To suppose; guess. [From Middle English *fantsy,* imagination, fantasy, from *fantasie.* See FANTASY.] **—fan′ci·ly** *adv.* **—fan′ci·ness** *n.*

fantail

fancy dress *n.* A masquerade costume.

fan·cy-free (făn′sē-frē′) *adj.* **1.** Having no commitments or restrictions; carefree. **2.** Not in love or married; unattached.

fan·cy·work (făn′sē-wûrk′) *n.* Decorative needlework, such as embroidery.

fan·dan·go (făn-dăng′gō) *n., pl.* **-gos. 1. a.** An animated Spanish or Spanish-American dance in triple time. **b.** A piece of music for this dance. **2.** *Informal.* Nonsense; tomfoolery. [Spanish, possibly alteration of **fadango,* from *fado,* from Portuguese, sad song. See FADO.]

fan·dom (făn′dəm) *n.* All the fans of a sport, an activity, or a famous person.

fan·fare (făn′fâr′) *n.* **1.** *Music.* A loud flourish of brass instruments, especially trumpets. **2.** *Informal.* A spectacular public display. [French, possibly of imitative origin.]

fan·far·o·nade (făn′făr-ə-näd′, -näd′) *n.* **1.** Bragging or blustering manner or behavior. **2.** A fanfare. [French *fanfaronnade,* from Spanish *fanfarronada,* bluster, from *fanfarrón,* a braggart, perhaps from Arabic *farfār.*]

fang (făng) *n.* **1.** A long, pointed tooth, especially: **a.** Any of the hollow or grooved teeth of a venomous snake with which it injects its poison. **b.** Any of the canine teeth of a carnivorous animal with which it seizes and tears its prey. **2.** A fanglike structure, especially a chelicera of a venomous spider. **3.** The root of a tooth. [Middle English, booty, spoils, something seized, from Old English. See **pag-** in Appendix.] **—fanged** *adj.*

Fang (făng, fäng, fäN) *n., pl.* **Fang** or **Fangs. 1.** A member of a people inhabiting Gabon, Equatorial Guinea, and Cameroon. **2.** The Bantu language of the Fang.

fan-in (făn′ĭn′) *n.* *Computer Science.* The number of inputs available to a given logic circuit.

fan·ion (făn′yən) *n.* A small flag for marking a position, used especially by surveyors or soldiers. [French, alteration of **fanillon,* diminutive of *fanon,* maniple, from Old French, from Frankish **fanō.*]

fan·jet also **fan-jet** (făn′jĕt′) *n.* **1.** A jet engine that provides extra thrust by means of a ducted fan in its forward end that draws in extra air. **2.** An airplane with such an engine.

fan letter *n.* A piece of fan mail.

fan·light (făn′līt′) *n.* **1.** *Architecture.* A half-circle window, often with sash bars arranged like the ribs of a fan. **2.** *Chiefly British.* A transom.

fan mail *n.* Mail sent to a public figure by admirers.

fan·ny (făn′ē) *n., pl.* **-nies.** *Slang.* The buttocks. [Perhaps from *Fanny,* a nickname for *Frances.*]

fan-out (făn′out′) *n.* *Computer Science.* The number of circuits that can be fed input signals from an output device.

fan palm *n.* A palm tree having palmately divided, fanlike leaves.

fan·tab·u·lous (făn-tăb′yə-ləs) *adj.* *Slang.* Marvelously excellent: *"a really fantabulous find, just magnificent"* (Mel Fisher). [Blend of FANTASTIC and FABULOUS.]

fan·tail (făn′tāl′) *n.* **1.** Any of a breed of domestic pigeons having a rounded, fan-shaped tail. **2.** Any of several birds of the genus *Rhipidura* of eastern Asia and Australia, having a long, fan-shaped tail. **3.** Any of a breed of goldfish having a wide, fanlike double tail fin. **4.** A fanlike tail or end. **5.** *Nautical.* The stern overhang of a ship. **—fan′tailed′** *adj.*

fan-tan (făn′tăn′) *n.* *Games.* **1.** A Chinese betting game in which the players lay wagers on the number of counters that will remain when a hidden pile of them has been divided by four. **2.** A card game in which sevens and their equivalent are played in sequence and the first player out of cards is the winner. [Chinese *fān tān* : *fān,* turn, chance + *tān,* to spread out.]

fan·ta·sia (făn-tā′zhə, -zhē-ə, făn′tə-zē′ə) *n.* *Music.* **1.** A free composition structured according to the composer's fancy. Also called *fantasy.* **2.** A medley of familiar themes, with variations and interludes. [Italian, from Latin *phantasia,* fantasy. See FANTASY.]

fan·ta·sist (făn′tə-sĭst) *n.* One that creates a fantasy.

fan·ta·size (făn′tə-sīz′) *v.* **-sized, -siz·ing, -siz·es.** *—tr.* To portray in the mind; imagine. *—intr.* To indulge in fantasies.

fan·tast (făn′tăst′) *n.* A visionary; a dreamer. [German, from Medieval Latin *phantasta,* from Greek *phantastēs,* boaster, from *phantasia,* imagination. See FANTASY.]

fan·tas·tic (făn-tăs′tĭk) also **fan·tas·ti·cal** (-tĭ-kəl) *adj.* **1.** Quaint or strange in form, conception, or appearance. **2. a.** Unrestrainedly fanciful; extravagant: *fantastic hopes.* **b.** Bizarre, as in form or appearance; strange: *fantastic attire; fantastic behavior.* **c.** Based on or existing only in fantasy; unreal. **3.** Wonderful or superb; remarkable: *a fantastic trip to Europe.* [Middle English *fantastik,* imagined, from Old French *fantastique,* from Late Latin *phantasticus,* imaginary, from Greek *phantastikos,* able to create mental images, from *phantazesthai,* to appear. See FANTASY.] **—fan·tas′ti·cal′i·ty** (-tĭ-kăl′ĭ-tē) *n.* **—fan·tas′ti·cal·ly** *adv.* **—fan·tas′ti·cal·ness** *n.*

SYNONYMS: *fantastic, bizarre, grotesque, fanciful, exotic.* These adjectives apply to what is very strange or strikingly unusual. *Fantastic* in this comparison describes what seems to have slight relation to the real world because of its strangeness or extravagance: *fantastic imaginary beasts such as the unicorn. Bizarre* stresses oddness of character or appearance that is heightened by striking contrasts and incongruities and that shocks or fascinates: *a bizarre art nouveau façade. Grotesque* refers principally to appearance or aspect in which deformity and distortion approach the point of caricature or even absurdity: *rainspouts terminating in gargoyles and other grotesque creatures. Fanciful* applies to a character, nature, or design strongly influenced by imagination, caprice, or whimsy: *a fanciful pattern with intertwined vines and flowers.* Something *exotic* is unusual and intriguing in appearance or effect: *exotic birds.*

---

fan·tas·ti·cate (făn-tăs′tĭ-kāt′) *tr.v.* **-cat·ed, -cat·ing, -cates.** To make fantastic: "[his] *splendidly baroque style adorns and fantasticates his thought"* (New York Times). **—fan·tas′ti·ca′tion** *n.*

fan·tas·ti·co (făn-tăs′tĭ-kō) *n., pl.* **-coes.** *Informal.* An extremely bizarre person. [Italian, imaginary, from Late Latin *phantasticus.* See FANTASTIC.]

fan·ta·sy (făn′tə-sē, -zē) *n., pl.* **-sies. 1.** The creative imagination; unrestrained fancy. See Synonyms at **imagination. 2.** Something, such as an invention, that is a creation of the fancy. **3.** A capricious or fantastic idea; a conceit. **4. a.** Fiction characterized by highly fanciful or supernatural elements. **b.** An example of such fiction. **5.** An imagined event or sequence of mental images, such as a daydream, usually fulfilling a wish or psychological need. **6.** *Music.* See **fantasia** (sense 1). **7.** A coin issued especially by a questionable authority and not intended for use as currency. **8.** *Obsolete.* A hallucination. **—fantasy** *tr.v.* **-sied, -sy·ing, -sies.** To imagine; visualize. [Middle English *fantasie, fantsy,* from Old French *fantasie,* from Latin *phantasia,* from Greek, appearance, imagination, from *phantazesthai,* to appear, from *phantos,* visible, from *phainesthai,* to appear. See **bhā-[1]** in Appendix.]

fan·ta·sy·land (făn′tə-sē-lănd′, -zē-) *n.* A place conjured up by the imagination, often populated by bizarre inhabitants: *the fantasyland of an operetta; television's latest excursion into fantasyland.*

Fan·te or **Fan·ti** (făn′tē, făn′-) *n., pl.* **Fante** or **Fanti** also **-tes** or **-tis. 1.** A member of a people inhabiting Ghana. **2.** The variety of Akan spoken by this people.

fan·toc·ci·ni (făn′tə-chē′nē) *pl.n.* **1.** Puppets animated by moving wires or mechanical means. **2.** A play or show employing such puppets. [Italian, pl. of *fantoccino,* diminutive of *fantoccio,* puppet, augmentative of *fante,* child, short for *infante,* from Latin *infāns, infant-,* infant. See INFANT.]

fan·tod (făn′tŏd′) *n.* **1. fantods. a.** A state of nervous irritability. **b.** Nervous movements caused by tension. **2.** An outburst of emotion; a fit. [Origin unknown.]

fan·tom (făn′təm) *n. & adj.* Variant of **phantom.**

fan vaulting *n.* *Architecture.* An intricate style of traceried vaulting, common in late English Gothic, in which ribs arch out like a fan.

fan·wort (făn′wûrt′, -wôrt′) *n.* Any of several aquatic plants of the genus *Cabomba,* having opposite, finely divided, fanlike submersed leaves and alternate, entire, peltate floating leaves. Also called *cabomba.*

fan·zine (făn′zēn) *n.* An amateur-produced fan magazine distributed by mail to a subculture readership and devoted to the coverage of interests such as science fiction, rock music, or skateboarding. [FAN[2] + (MAGA)ZINE.]

FAQ *abbr.* Fair average quality.

far (fär) *adv.* **far·ther, far·thest** or **fur·ther, fur·thest. 1.** To, from, or at considerable distance: *a cat that had strayed far from home.* **2.** To or at a specific distance, degree, or position: *Just how far are you taking this argument?* **3.** To a considerable degree; much: *felt far better yesterday; eyes that seemed far too close together.* **4.** Not at all; anything but: *seems far from content; a test of strength that was far from a failure.* **5.** To an advanced point or stage: *a brilliant student who will go far.* **—far** *adj.* **farther, farthest** or **further, furthest. 1.a.** Being at considerable distance; remote: *a far country.* **b.** Going back a considerable extent in time: *the far past.* See Synonyms at **distant. 2.** More distant than another: *the far corner.* **3.** Extensive or lengthy: *a far trek.* **4.** Far-seeing and comprehensive in thought or outlook: *a commander of far vision.* **5.** Marked by political views of the most advanced or extreme nature: *the far right; the far left.* **6.** Being on the right side of an animal or a vehicle. **7.** Being the animal or vehicle on the right. **—*idioms.* as far as.** To or at a specific point, degree, or extent: *They will arrive at nine, as far as we know.* **by far.** To the most extreme or evident degree: *She is by far the best executive in the company.* **far and away.** By a great margin: *"That made him, far and away, the best known of the Democrats who started the presidential race this year"* (Tom Wicker). **far cry.** A long way: *The climate in Alaska is a far cry from that of Florida.* **how far.** To what degree, distance, or extent: *didn't know how far to believe them; tried to decide how far she could ski in such cold.* **so far. 1.** Up to the present moment: *So far there's been no word from them.* **2.** To a limited extent: *You can go only so far on five dollars.* **thus far.** Up to this point; so far: *Our success has been limited thus far.* [Middle English, from Old English *feor.* See **per**[1] in Appendix.]

Far. *abbr.* Faraday.

far·ad (făr′əd, -ăd′) *n. Abbr.* **F** The unit of capacitance in the meter-kilogram-second system equal to the capacitance of a capacitor having an equal and opposite charge of 1 coulomb on each plate and a potential difference of 1 volt between the plates. See table at **measurement.** [After Michael FARADAY.]

far·a·da·ic (făr′ə-dā′ĭk) *adj.* Variant of **faradic.**

far·a·day (făr′ə-dā′) *n. Abbr.* **Far.** The quantity of electricity that is capable of depositing or liberating 1 gram equivalent weight of a substance in electrolysis, approximately 9.6494×10^4 coulombs. [After Michael FARADAY.]

Far·a·day (făr′ə-dā′, -dē), **Michael.** 1791–1867. British physicist and chemist who discovered electromagnetic induction (1831) and proposed the field theory later developed by Maxwell and Einstein.

Faraday effect *n.* The rotation of the plane of polarization of either a plane-polarized light beam passed through a transparent isotropic medium or a plane-polarized microwave passing through a magnetic field along the lines of that field. Also called *Faraday rotation.* [After Michael FARADAY.]

fa·rad·ic (fə-răd′ĭk) also **far·a·da·ic** (făr′ə-dā′ĭk) *adj.* Of, relating to, or using an intermittent asymmetrical alternating electric current produced by an induction coil. [After Michael FARADAY.]

far·a·dism (făr′ə-dĭz′əm) *n.* Faradization.

far·a·di·za·tion (făr′ə-dĭ-zā′shən) *n.* The application of faradic current to stimulate muscles and nerves.

far·a·dize (făr′ə-dīz′) *tr.v.* **-dized, -diz·ing, -diz·es.** To treat or stimulate (a muscle or nerve) with faradic current.

far·an·dole (făr′ən-dōl′) *n.* **1.** A spirited circle dance of Provençal derivation. **2.** The music for this circle dance. [French, from Provençal *farandoulo.*]

far and wide *adv.* Everywhere: *looked far and wide for the lost puppy.*

far·a·way (fär′ə-wā′) *adj.* **1.** Very distant; remote. See Synonyms at **distant. 2.** Abstracted; dreamy: *a faraway look.*

farce (färs) *n.* **1.a.** A light dramatic work in which highly improbable plot situations, exaggerated characters, and often slapstick elements are used for humorous effect. **b.** The broad or spirited humor characteristic of such works. **2.** A ludicrous, empty show; a mockery: *The election was a farce, for it was fixed.* **3.** A seasoned stuffing, as for roasted turkey. **—farce** *tr.v.* **farced, farc·ing, farc·es. 1.** To pad or fill out (a speech, for example) with jokes or witticisms. **2.** To stuff, as for roasting. [Middle English *farse,* stuffing, from Old French *farce,* stuffing, interpolation, interlude, from Vulgar Latin **farsa,* from Latin *farsa,* feminine past participle of *farcīre,* to stuff.]

far·ceur (fär-sœr′) *n.* **1.** One who acts in or writes a farce. **2.** A comic; a wag. [French, from Old French, from *farcer,* to joke, from *farce,* farce. See FARCE.]

far·ci or **far·cie** (fär-sē′) *adj.* Stuffed, especially with finely ground meat: *mushrooms farci.* [French, past participle of *farcir,* to stuff, from Old French, from Latin *farcīre.*]

far·ci·cal (fär′sĭ-kəl) *adj.* **1.** Of or relating to farce. **2.a.** Resembling a farce; ludicrous. **b.** Ridiculously clumsy; absurd. **—far′ci·cal′i·ty** (-kăl′ĭ-tē) *n.* **—far′ci·cal·ly** *adv.*

far·cie (fär-sē′) *adj.* Variant of **farci.**

far·cy (fär′sē) *n. Veterinary Medicine.* A chronic form of glanders that affects chiefly the skin and superficial lymph vessels. [Middle English *farsi, farsin,* from Old French *farcin,* from Latin *farcīmen,* sausage, from *farcīre,* to stuff.]

farcy bud *n. Veterinary Medicine.* A craterlike ulcer characteristic of farcy.

far·del (fär′dl) *n.* **1.** A pack; a bundle. **2.** A burden. [Middle English, from Old French, diminutive of *farde,* package, from Arabic *fardah.*]

fare (fâr) *intr.v.* **fared, far·ing, fares. 1.** To get along: *How are you faring with your project?* **2.** To travel; go. **3.** To dine; eat. **—fare** *n.* **1.** A transportation charge, as for a bus. **2.** A passenger transported for a fee. **3.** Food and drink; diet: *simple home-cooked fare.* [Middle English *faren,* from Old English *faran.* See **per-**[2] in Appendix.] **—far′er** *n.*

Far East (fär). The countries and regions of eastern and southeast Asia, especially China, Japan, North Korea, South Korea, and Mongolia. **—Far′ East′ern** *adj.*

Far Eastern U.S.S.R. A historical region of the U.S.S.R., bordering on the Pacific Ocean.

fare·beat (fâr′bēt′) *intr.v.* **-beat, -beat·en** (-bēt′n) or **-beat, -beat·ing, -beats.** *Slang.* To avoid paying the fare for public transportation, especially subway transportation. **—fare′beat·er** *n.*

Fare·ham (fâr′əm). An urban district of southern England on Portsmouth harbor north-northwest of Portsmouth. It is a shipbuilding center. Population, 88,100.

fare-thee-well (fâr′*th*ē-wĕl′) *n.* **1.** A condition of utmost perfection: *played the part of the martyr to a fare-thee-well.* **2.** The most extreme degree: *beat his opponent in the match to a veritable fare-thee-well.*

fare·well (fâr-wĕl′) *interj.* Used to express good-bye. **—farewell** *n.* **1.** An acknowledgment at parting; a good-bye. **2.** The act of departing. *—attributive.* Often used to modify another noun: *a farewell party.* [Middle English *fare wel* : imperative of *faren,* to fare; see FARE + *wel,* well; see WELL[2].]

Fare·well (fâr-wĕl′, fâr′wĕl′), **Cape.** The southernmost point of Greenland.

far·fel or **far·fal** (fär′fəl) *n.* Noodles shaped like small grains or pellets. [Yiddish *farfl,* from Middle High German *varveln.*]

far-fetched (fär′fĕcht′) *adj.* Not readily believable because of improbable elements therein: *a far-fetched analogy; a far-fetched excuse.*

far-flung (fär′flŭng′) *adj.* **1.** Remote; distant. **2.** Widely distributed; wide-ranging.

Far·go (fär′gō). A city of eastern North Dakota on the Red River east of Bismarck. Founded with the coming of the railroad in 1871, it is the largest city in the state. Population, 61,383.

far-gone (fär′gôn′, -gŏn′) *adj.* Very close to or nearing the end: *a drug addict too far-gone for rehabilitation.*

Far·i·bault (făr′ə-bō′). A city of southeast Minnesota south of Minneapolis. It was built on the site of a trading post established in 1826. Population, 16,241.

Fa·ri·da·bad (fə-rē′də-băd′). A city of north-central India south-southeast of New Delhi. It is a grain and cotton market. Population, 330,864.

fa·ri·na (fə-rē′nə) *n.* Fine meal prepared from cereal grain and various other plant products and often used as a cooked cereal or in puddings. [Middle English, from Latin *farīna,* from *far,* a kind of grain. See **bhares-** in Appendix.]

far·i·na·ceous (făr′ə-nā′shəs) *adj.* **1.** Made from, rich in, or consisting of starch. **2.** Having a mealy or powdery texture. [Latin *farīnāceus,* mealy, from *farīna,* farina. See FARINA.]

far·i·nose (făr′ə-nōs′) *adj.* **1.** Similar to or yielding farina. **2.** *Biology.* Covered with mealy dust or powder. [Late Latin *farīnōsus,* mealy, from Latin *farīna,* farina. See FARINA.]

farkleberry
Vaccinium arboreum

far·kle·ber·ry (fär′kəl-bĕr′ē) *n.* A shrub or small tree *(Vaccinium arboreum)* of the southeast United States, having leathery leaves and hard black berries. Also called *sparkleberry.* [*farkle* (of unknown origin) + BERRY.]

farm (färm) *n.* **1.** A tract of land cultivated for the purpose of agricultural production. **2.a.** A tract of land devoted to the raising and breeding of domestic animals. **b.** An area of water devoted to the raising, breeding, or production of a specific aquatic animal: *a trout farm; an oyster farm.* **3.** An area of land devoted to the storage of a commodity or the emplacement of a group of devices: *a tank farm; an antenna farm.* **4.** *Baseball.* A minor-league club affiliated with a major-league club for the training of recruits and the maintenance of temporarily unneeded players. **5.** *Obsolete.* **a.** The system of leasing out the rights of collecting and retaining taxes in a certain district. **b.** A district so leased. *—attributive.* Often used to modify another noun: *farm machinery; farm buildings; farm policy.* **—farm** *v.* **farmed, farm·ing, farms.** *—tr.* **1.** To cultivate or produce a crop on. **2.** To pay a fixed sum in order to have the right to collect and retain profits from (a business, for example). **3.** To turn over (a business, for example) to another in return for the payment of a fixed sum.

ă pat	oi boy
ā pay	ou out
âr care	o͝o took
ä father	o͞o boot
ĕ pet	ŭ cut
ē be	ûr urge
ĭ pit	th thin
ī pie	*th* this
îr pier	hw which
ŏ pot	zh vision
ō toe	ə about, item
ô paw	♦ regionalism

Stress marks: ′ (primary); ′ (secondary), as in **dictionary** (dĭk′shə-nĕr′ē)

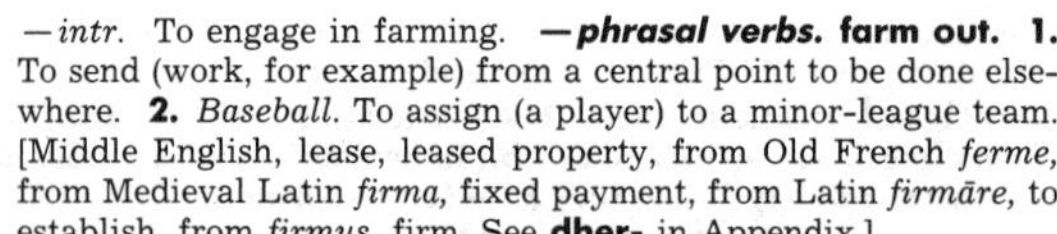

—*intr.* To engage in farming. —***phrasal verbs.*** **farm out. 1.** To send (work, for example) from a central point to be done elsewhere. **2.** *Baseball.* To assign (a player) to a minor-league team. [Middle English, lease, leased property, from Old French *ferme,* from Medieval Latin *firma,* fixed payment, from Latin *firmāre,* to establish, from *firmus,* firm. See **dher-** in Appendix.]

Fannie Farmer

farm·er (fär′mər) *n.* **1.** One who works on or operates a farm. **2.** One who has paid for the right to collect and retain certain revenues or profits.

Far·mer (fär′mər), **Fannie Merritt.** 1857–1915. American cookery expert who edited the *Boston Cooking School Cook Book* (1896), which has undergone many revisions as the *Fannie Farmer Cookbook.*

Farmer, James Leonard. Born 1920. American civil rights leader who founded the Congress of Racial Equality (1942) and served as its national director (1961–1966).

farmer cheese *n.* An unripened cheese similar to cottage cheese but drier and firmer in texture.

Far·mers Branch (fär′mərz). A town of northeast Texas, a residential and industrial suburb of Dallas. Population, 24,863

farm·er's lung (fär′mərz) *n.* An occupational disease affecting the lungs and characterized by chronic shortness of breath caused by an allergic reaction to fungal spores present in moldy hay dust that has been inhaled.

farm·ers' market (fär′mərz) *n.* A public market at which farmers and often other vendors sell produce directly to consumers. Also called *greenmarket.*

farm hand *n.* A hired farm laborer.

farm·house (färm′hous′) *n.* A dwelling on a farm.

Far·ming·ton (fär′mĭng-tən). **1.** A town of central Connecticut southwest of Hartford. Settled in 1640, it is chiefly residential. Population, 16,407. **2.** A city of northwest New Mexico south-southwest of Durango, Colorado. It is the trade center of an irrigated farming area. Population, 31,222.

Farmington Hills. A city of southeast Michigan, an industrial suburb of Detroit. Population, 58,056.

farm·land (färm′lănd′, -lənd) *n.* An expanse of land suitable or used for farming.

farm·stead (färm′stĕd′) *n.* A farm, including its land and buildings.

farm·wom·an (färm′wo͝om′ən) *n.* A woman who works on or operates a farm.

farm·yard (färm′yärd′) *n.* An area surrounded by or adjacent to farm buildings.

Eileen Farrell
In character for Cherubini's *Medea*

far·o (fâr′ō) *n.* *Games.* A card game in which the players lay wagers on the top card of the dealer's pack. [Alteration of PHARAOH.]

Far·oe Islands (fâr′ō). See **Faeroe Islands.**

Far·o·ese (fâr′ō-ēz′, -ēs′) *n.* Variant of **Faeroese.**

far-off (fär′ôf′, -ŏf′) *adj.* Remote in space or time. See Synonyms at **distant.**

♦ **fa·ro·li·to** (făr′ə-lē′tō, fär′-) *n., pl.* **-tos.** *Southwestern U.S.* See **luminaria** (sense 1). [Spanish, paper lantern, diminutive of *farol,* lantern, from *faro,* lighthouse, lantern, from Latin *pharus,* from *Pharus,* Pharos.]

fa·rouche (fä-ro͞osh′) *adj.* **1.** Fierce; wild: *an artist who was farouche even in everyday life.* **2.** Exhibiting withdrawn temperament and shyness coupled with an air of cranky, often sullen fey charm: *"small, farouche poems illustrated with doodles, a cross between Ogden Nash and Blake"* (Rosemary Dinnage). [French, from Old French *faroche,* alteration of *forasche,* from Late Latin *forāsticus,* belonging outside, from Latin *forās,* out of doors. See FOREIGN.]

Fa·rouk I also **Fa·ruk I** (fə-ro͞ok′). 1920–1965. King of Egypt (1936–1952) who lost support of his army after Egypt's military loss to Israel (1948) and was ousted (1952) by a coup d'état.

far-out (fär′out′) *adj.* *Slang.* Extremely unconventional: *"all kinds of far-out and unique inventions"* (Peter Nissenson).

far point *n.* The farthest point at which an object can be seen distinctly by the eye.

farthingale

Far·quhar (fär′kwər), **George.** 1678–1707. Irish playwright whose comedic works include *The Recruiting Officer* (1706).

far·rag·i·nous (fə-răj′ə-nəs) *adj.* Composed of a variety of substances. [From Latin *farrāgō, farrāgin-,* medley, hodgepodge. See FARRAGO.]

far·ra·go (fə-rä′gō, -rā′-) *n., pl.* **-goes.** An assortment or a medley; a conglomeration: *"their special farrago of resentments"* (William Safire). [Latin *farrāgō,* mixed fodder, hodgepodge, from *far, farr-,* a kind of grain. See **bhares-** in Appendix.]

fasces

Far·ra·gut (făr′ə-gət), **David Glasgow.** 1801–1870. American admiral who commanded Union ships on daring Civil War missions, including the capture of New Orleans (1862) and the taking of Mobile Bay (1864).

far-reach·ing (fär′rē′chĭng) *adj.* Having a wide range, influence, or effect: *the far-reaching implications of a major new epidemic.*

far-red (fär′rĕd′) *adj.* **1.** Of, relating to, or being electromagnetic radiation in the infrared spectrum farthest from visible red light, having wavelengths between 50,000 nanometers and 1 millimeter. **2.** Of, relating to, or being electromagnetic radiation in the infrared spectrum closest to visible red light, having a wavelength of about 0.8 micron.

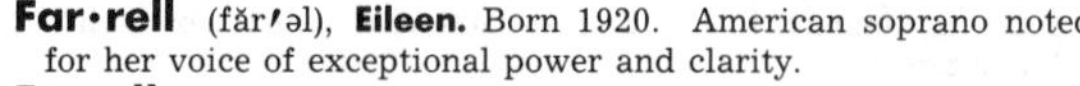

Far·rell (făr′əl), **Eileen.** Born 1920. American soprano noted for her voice of exceptional power and clarity.

Farrell, James Thomas. 1904–1979. American writer best known for his *Studs Lonigan* trilogy of novels (1932–1935).

far·ri·er (făr′ē-ər) *n.* One that shoes horses. [Obsolete French *ferrier,* from Latin *ferrārius,* of iron, blacksmith, from *ferrum,* iron.] —**far′ri·er·y** *n.*

far·row¹ (făr′ō) *n.* A litter of pigs. —**farrow** *v.* **-rowed, -row·ing, -rows.** —*tr.* To give birth to (a litter of pigs). —*intr.* To produce a litter of pigs. [Ultimately from Old English *fearh.* See **porko-** in Appendix.]

far·row² (făr′ō) *adj.* Not pregnant. Used of a cow. [Middle English *ferow.*]

Fars (färz, färs) or **Far·si·stan** (fär′sĭ-stăn′, -stän′). A historical region of southern Iran along the Persian Gulf. It was more or less identical with the ancient province of Pars, which formed the nucleus of the Persian Empire. The Arabs changed the name after they conquered the region in the seventh century.

far·see·ing (fär′sē′ĭng) *adj.* **1.** Prudent; foresighted. **2.** Able to see far; keen-sighted.

Far·si (fär′sē) *n.* **1.** The modern Iranian language, dating from about the ninth century A.D., that is the national language of Iran and is written in an Arabic alphabet; Persian. **2. a.** A speaker of Farsi. **b.** A member of the predominant ethnic group of Iran. [Persian *fārsī,* from Arabic *Fārs,* Persia.]

far·sight·ed or **far-sight·ed** (fär′sī′tĭd) *adj.* **1.** Able to see distant objects better than objects at close range; hyperopic. **2.** Capable of seeing to a great distance. **3.** Planning prudently for the future; foresighted: *large goals that required farsighted policies.* —**far′sight′ed·ly** *adv.*

far·sight·ed·ness (fär′sī′tĭd-nĭs) *n.* See **hyperopia.**

Far·si·stan (fär′sĭ-stăn′, -stän′). See **Fars.**

fart (färt) *Vulgar Slang. intr.v.* **fart·ed, fart·ing, farts. 1.** To expel intestinal gas through the anus; break wind. **2.** To fool around; fritter time away. —**fart** *n.* **1.** A usually audible discharge of intestinal gas. **2.** A person regarded as annoying or foolish. [Middle English *farten,* from Old English **feortan.* See **perd-** in Appendix.]

far·ther (fär′thər) *Usage Problem. adv.* A comparative of **far. 1.** To or at a more distant or remote point. **2.** To or at a more advanced point or stage. **3.** To a greater extent or degree. —**farther** *adj.* A comparative of **far.** More distant; remoter: *the farther shore.* [Middle English, variant (influenced by *far;* far; see FAR) of *further.* See FURTHER.]

USAGE NOTE: *Farther* and *further* have been used interchangeably by many writers since the Middle English period. According to a rule of relatively recent origin, however, *farther* should be reserved for physical distance and *further* for advancement along a nonphysical dimension. Thus 74 percent of the Usage Panel prefers *farther* in the sentence *If you are planning to drive any farther than Ukiah, you'd better carry chains;* whereas 64 percent prefers *further* in the sentence *We won't be able to answer these questions until we are further along in our research.* In many cases, however, the distinction is not easy to draw. If we may speak metaphorically of *a statement that is far from the truth,* for example, the analogous use of *farther* should be allowed in a sentence such as *Nothing could be farther from the truth,* though *Nothing could be further from the truth* is also justifiable.

far·ther·most (fär′thər-mōst′) *adj.* Most distant; farthest.

far·thest (fär′thĭst) *adj.* A superlative of **far.** Most remote or distant. —**farthest** *adv.* A superlative of **far. 1.** To or at the most distant or remote point. **2.** To or at the most advanced point or stage. **3.** By the greatest extent or degree. [Middle English *ferthest,* superlative of *farther.* See FARTHER.]

far·thing (fär′thĭng) *n.* *Abbr.* **f. 1.** A coin formerly used in Great Britain worth one fourth of a penny. **2.** Something of very little value. [Middle English *ferthing,* from Old English *fēorthung.* See **kʷetwer-** in Appendix.]

far·thin·gale (fär′thĭn-gāl′, -thĭng-) *n.* A support, such as a hoop, worn beneath a skirt to extend it horizontally from the waist, used by European women in the 16th and 17th centuries. [Alteration of obsolete *verdynggale,* from Old French *verdugale,* from Old Spanish *verdugado,* from *verdugo,* stick, shoot of a tree, from *verde,* green, from Latin *viridis,* from *virēre,* to be green.]

Fa·ruk I (fə-ro͞ok′). See **Farouk I.**

Far West. A U.S. region originally comprising all territories west of the Mississippi River. It is now generally restricted to the area west of the Great Plains. —**Far′ West′ern** *adj.*

f.a.s. also **F.A.S.** *abbr.* Free alongside ship.

fasc. *abbr.* Fascicle.

fas·ces (făs′ēz′) *pl.n.* A bundle of rods bound together around an ax with the blade projecting, carried before ancient Roman magistrates as an emblem of authority. [Latin, pl. of *fascis,* bundle.]

fas·ci·a (făsh′ē-ə) *n., pl.* **fas·ci·ae** (făsh′-ē-ē′, fā′shē-ē). **1.** *Anatomy.* A sheet or band of fibrous connective tissue enveloping, separating, or binding together muscles, organs, and other soft structures of the body. **2.** A broad and distinct band of color. **3.** (*also* fā′shē-ə). *Architecture.* A flat horizontal band or member between moldings, especially in a classical entablature. **4.** (fā′-

shə). *Chiefly British.* The dashboard of a motor vehicle. [Latin, band.] **—fas′ci·al** *adj.*

fas·ci·ate (făsh′ē-āt′) also **fas·ci·at·ed** (-ā′tĭd) *adj.* **1.** *Botany.* Abnormally flattened or coalesced, as certain stems. **2.** *Zoology.* Marked by broad bands of color, as certain insects. [Latin *fasciātus,* from *fascia,* band.]

fas·ci·a·tion (făs′ē-ā′shən, făsh′ē-) *n.* **1.** The act of binding up or fastening, as with bandages. **2.** The manner in which something is bound up or fastened. **3.** *Botany.* An abnormal flattening or coalescence of stems, as in broccoli.

fas·ci·cle (făs′ĭ-kəl) *n. Abbr.* **fasc. 1.** A small bundle. **2.** One of the parts of a book published in separate sections. Also called *fascicule.* **3.** *Botany.* A bundle or cluster of stems, flowers, or leaves. **4.** See **fasciculus.** [Latin *fasciculus,* diminutive of *fascis,* bundle.] **—fas′ci·cled** *adj.*

fas·cic·u·lar (fə-sĭk′yə-lər) *adj.* Of, relating to, or composed of fascicles. **—fas·cic′u·lar·ly** *adv.*

fascicular cambium *n. Botany.* Cambium that develops within the vascular bundle.

fas·cic·u·late (fə-sĭk′yə-lĭt) also **fas·cic·u·lat·ed** (-lā′tĭd) *adj.* Arranged in or formed of fascicles; fascicular. **—fas·cic′u·late·ly** *adv.* **—fas·cic′u·la′tion** *n.*

fas·ci·cule (făs′ĭ-kyo͞ol′) *n.* See **fascicle** (sense 2).

fas·cic·u·lus (fə-sĭk′yə-ləs) *n., pl.* **-li** (-lī′). A bundle of anatomical fibers, as of muscle or nerve. Also called *fascicle.* [Latin, fascicle. See FASCICLE.]

fas·ci·nate (făs′ə-nāt′) *v.* **-nat·ed, -nat·ing, -nates.** *—tr.* **1.** To hold an intense interest or attraction for. See Synonyms at **charm. 2.** To hold motionless; spellbind. **3.** *Obsolete.* To bewitch. *—intr.* To be irresistibly charming or attractive. [Latin *fascināre, fascināt-,* to cast a spell on, from *fascinum,* an evil spell, a phallic-shaped amulet.]

fas·ci·nat·ing (făs′ə-nā′tĭng) *adj.* Possessing the power to charm or allure; captivating. **—fas′ci·nat′ing·ly** *adv.*

fas·ci·na·tion (făs′ə-nā′shən) *n.* **1.** The capability of eliciting intense interest or of being very attractive. **2.** The state of being intensely interested or attracted: *listened in fascination.* **3.** An intensely interesting, attractive quality or trait.

fas·ci·na·tor (făs′ə-nā′tər) *n.* **1.** One that fascinates. **2.** A woman's head scarf.

fas·cine (fă-sēn′, fə-) *n.* A cylindrical bundle of sticks bound together for use in construction, as of fortresses, earthworks, sea walls, or dams. [French, from Latin *fascīna,* from *fascis,* bundle.]

fas·ci·o·li·a·sis (fə-sē′ə-lī′ə-sĭs, -sī′-) *n., pl.* **-ses** (-sēz′). Infestation with parasitic flukes of the family Fasciolidae, especially infestation of the liver and bile ducts with the liver fluke. [New Latin *Fasciola,* genus name (from Latin, diminutive of *fascia,* band) + -IASIS.]

fas·cism (făsh′ĭz′əm) *n.* **1.** Often **Fascism. a.** A system of government marked by centralization of authority under a dictator, stringent socioeconomic controls, suppression of the opposition through terror and censorship, and typically a policy of belligerent nationalism and racism. **b.** A political philosophy or movement based on or advocating such a system of government. **2.** Oppressive, dictatorial control. [Italian *fascismo,* from *fascio,* group, from Late Latin *fascium,* neuter of Latin *fascis,* bundle.] **—fas·cis′tic** (fə-shĭs′tĭk) *adj.*

fas·cist (făsh′ĭst) *n.* **1.** Often **Fascist.** An advocate or adherent of fascism. **2.** A reactionary or dictatorial person. **—fascist** *adj.* **1.** Often **Fascist.** Of, advocating, or practicing fascism. **2. Fascist.** Of or relating to the regime of the Fascisti. [Italian *fascista,* from *fascio,* group. See FASCISM.]

Fa·scis·ti (fă-shē′stē) *pl.n.* The members of an Italian political organization that controlled Italy under the fascist dictatorship of Benito Mussolini from 1922 to 1943. [Italian, pl. of *fascista,* fascist. See FASCIST.]

fash·ion (făsh′ən) *n.* **1.** The prevailing style or custom, as in dress or behavior: *out of fashion.* **2.** Something, such as a garment, that is in the current mode: *Her dress is the latest fashion.* **3.** The style characteristic of the social elite: *a man of fashion.* **4. a.** Manner or mode; way: *Set the table in this fashion.* **b.** A personal, often idiosyncratic manner: *played the violin in his own curious fashion.* **5.** Kind or variety; sort: *people of all fashions.* **6.** Shape or form; configuration. **—fashion** *tr.v.* **-ioned, -ion·ing, -ions. 1.** To give shape or form to; make: *fashioned a table from a redwood burl.* **2.** To train or influence into a particular state or character. **3.** To adapt, as to a purpose or an occasion; accommodate. **4.** *Obsolete.* To contrive. ***—idiom.* after** (or **in**) **a fashion.** In some way or other, especially to a limited extent: *She sings after a fashion.* [Middle English *facioun,* from Old French *façon,* appearance, manner, from Latin *factiō, factiōn-,* a making, from *factus,* past participle of *facere,* to make, do. See **dhē-** in Appendix.] **—fash′ion·er** *n.*

SYNONYMS: *fashion, style, mode, vogue.* These nouns refer to a prevailing or preferred manner of dress, adornment, behavior, or way of life at a given time. *Fashion,* the broadest term, usually refers to what accords with conventions adopted by polite society or set by those in the forefront of the artistic or intellectual sphere: *wears clothes in the height of fashion; a time when pop art was very much in fashion. Style* is sometimes used interchangeably with *fashion* (*a gown that is out of style*), but *style,* like *mode,* often stresses adherence to standards of elegance: *The couple travels in style. Miniskirts were the mode in the late sixties. Vogue* is applied to fashion that prevails widely (*the voluptuous figure in vogue at the time of Rubens*); the term often suggests enthusiastic but short-lived acceptance (*a game that enjoyed a vogue in its day*). See also Synonyms at **method.**

fash·ion·a·ble (făsh′ə-nə-bəl) *adj.* **1.** Conforming to the current style; stylish. **2.** Associated with or frequented by persons of fashion. **—fashionable** *n.* A stylish person. **—fash′ion·a·bil·i·ty, fash′ion·a·ble·ness** *n.* **—fash′ion·a·bly** *adv.*

SYNONYMS: *fashionable, chic, dashing, in, modish, posh, sharp, smart, stylish, swank, trendy.* The central meaning shared by these adjectives is "being or in accordance with the current fashion": *a fashionable restaurant; a chic dress; a dashing hat; the in place to go; modish jewelry; a posh address; a sharp jacket; a smart hotel; stylish clothes; a swank apartment; a trendy neighborhood.*
ANTONYM: *unfashionable.*

fash·ion·mon·ger (făsh′ən-mŭng′gər, -mŏng′-) *n.* One concerned with following, spreading, or setting the fashion.

fashion plate *n.* **1.** A person who consistently wears the latest fashions. **2.** An illustration of current styles in dress.

fast[1] (făst) *adj.* **fast·er, fast·est. 1.** Acting, moving, or capable of acting or moving quickly; swift. **2.** Accomplished in relatively little time: *a fast visit.* **3.** Indicating a time somewhat ahead of the actual time: *The clock is fast.* **4.** Adapted to or suitable for rapid movement: *a fast running track.* **5.** Designed for or compatible with a short exposure time: *fast film.* **6. a.** Disposed to dissipation; wild: *ran with a fast crowd.* **b.** Flouting conventional moral standards; sexually promiscuous. **7.** Resistant, as to destruction or fading: *fast colors.* **8.** Firmly fixed or fastened: *a fast grip.* **9.** Fixed firmly in place; secure: *shutters that are fast against the rain.* **10.** Firm in loyalty: *fast friends.* **11.** Lasting; permanent: *fast rules and regulations.* **12.** Deep; sound: *in a fast sleep.* **—fast** *adv.* **1.** In a secure manner; tightly: *hold fast.* **2.** To a sound degree; deeply: *fast asleep.* **3.** In a rapid manner; quickly. **4.** In quick succession: *New ideas followed fast.* **5.** Ahead of the correct or expected time: *a watch that runs fast.* **6.** In a dissipated, immoderate way: *living fast.* **7.** *Archaic.* Close by; near. [Middle English, from Old English *fæst,* firm, fixed. See **past-** in Appendix.]

SYNONYMS: *fast, rapid, swift, fleet, speedy, quick, hasty, expeditious.* These adjectives refer to something, such as activity or movement, marked by great speed. *Fast* and *rapid* are often used interchangeably, though *fast* is more often applied to the person or thing in motion, and *rapid,* to the activity or movement involved: *a fast car; a fast plane; a rapid mountain stream; rapid development; a fast runner; rapid strides. Swift* suggests smoothness and sureness of movement (*a swift current; swift but unclear handwriting*), and *fleet,* lightness of movement (*The cheetah is the fleetest of animals*). *Speedy* refers to velocity (*a speedy worker*) or to promptness or hurry (*hoped for a speedy resolution to the problem*). *Quick* most often applies to what takes little time or to promptness of response or action: *Let's eat a quick snack. Only her quick reaction prevented an accident. Hasty* implies hurried action (*a hasty visit*) and often a lack of care or thought (*regretted the hasty decision*). *Expeditious* suggests rapid efficiency: *sent the package by the most expeditious means.* See also Synonyms at **faithful.**

fastback

fast[2] (făst) *intr.v.* **fast·ed, fast·ing, fasts. 1.** To abstain from food. **2.** To eat very little or abstain from certain foods, especially as a religious discipline. **—fast** *n.* **1.** The act or practice of abstaining from or eating very little food. **2.** A period of such abstention or self-denial. [Middle English *fasten,* from Old English *fæstan.* See **past-** in Appendix.]

fast·back (făst′băk′) *n.* An automobile designed with a curving downward slope from roof to rear.

fast·ball (făst′bôl′) *n. Baseball.* A pitch thrown at the pitcher's maximum speed.

fast break *n. Sports.* A rush by the offense, as in basketball, toward the goal in an attempt to score before the opposing team readies a defense.

fast-breed·er reactor (făst′brē′dər) *n.* A breeder reactor that requires high-speed neutrons to produce fissionable material.

fast buck *n. Slang.* Money acquired quickly with little effort and sometimes unscrupulously.

fas·ten (făs′ən) *v.* **-tened, -ten·ing, -tens.** *—tr.* **1.** To attach firmly to something else, as by pinning or nailing. **2. a.** To make fast or secure. **b.** To close, as by fixing firmly in place. **3.** To fix or direct steadily: *fastened her gaze on the stranger.* **4.** To place; attribute: *fastened the blame on the weather.* **5.** To impose (oneself) without welcome. *—intr.* **1.** To become attached, fixed, or joined. **2.** To take firm hold; cling fast: *fasten on a notion.* **3.** To focus steadily; concentrate: *All eyes fastened on the speaker.* [Middle English *fastnen,* from Old English *fæstnian.* See **past-** in Appendix.] **—fas′ten·er** *n.*

SYNONYMS: *fasten, anchor, fix, moor, secure.* The central meaning shared by these verbs is "to cause to remain firmly or fast in position or place": *fastened our seat belts; anchored the television antenna to the roof; fixed the flagpole in concrete; mooring the rowboat at the dock; secures her chignon with hairpins.*
ANTONYM: *unfasten.*

ă pat	oi boy
ā pay	ou out
âr care	o͝o took
ä father	o͞o boot
ĕ pet	ŭ cut
ē be	ûr urge
ĭ pit	th thin
ī pie	*th* this
îr pier	hw which
ŏ pot	zh vision
ō toe	ə about, item
ô paw	♦ regionalism

Stress marks: ′ (primary); ′ (secondary), as in **dictionary** (dĭk′shə-nĕr′ē)

fas·ten·ing (făs′ə-nĭng) *n.* Something, such as a hook, used to attach one thing to another firmly.

fast food *n.* Inexpensive food, such as hamburgers and fried chicken, prepared and served quickly for consumption on the premises or elsewhere. **—fast′-food′** (făst′fo͞od′) *adj.*

fast-for·ward (făst-fôr′wərd) or **fast forward** *n.* **1.a.** A function on an electronic recording device, such as a videocassette or tape player, that permits rapid advancement of the tape. **b.** The mechanism, such as a button, used to activate this function. **2.** *Informal.* A rapidly changing situation or series of events: *"The trial was on fast forward"* (Nelson DeMille). **—fast-forward** *v.* **-ward·ed, -ward·ing, -wards.** *—intr.* To advance a tape rapidly on an electronic recording device. *—tr.* To advance (a tape) rapidly on such a device.

fas·tid·i·ous (fă-stĭd′ē-əs, fə-) *adj.* **1.** Possessing or displaying careful, meticulous attention to detail. **2.** Difficult to please; exacting. **3.** Excessively scrupulous or sensitive, especially in matters of taste or propriety. See Synonyms at **meticulous. 4.** *Microbiology.* Having complicated nutritional requirements. [Middle English, squeamish, particular, haughty, from Old French *fastidieux,* from Latin *fastīdiōsus,* from *fastīdium,* squeamishness, haughtiness, probably from *fastus,* disdain.] **—fas·tid′i·ous·ly** *adv.* **—fas·tid′i·ous·ness** *n.*

fas·tig·i·ate (fă-stĭj′ē-ĭt) also **fas·tig·i·at·ed** (-ē-ā′tĭd) *adj.* *Botany.* Having erect and almost parallel branches tapering toward the top, as in the Lombardy poplar. [Medieval Latin *fastīgiātus,* high, from Latin *fastīgium,* apex, height.] **—fas·tig′i·ate·ly** *adv.*

fas·tig·i·um (fă-stĭj′ē-əm) *n.* The period of maximum severity or intensity of a disease or fever. [Latin, apex, height.]

fast lane *n.* *Informal.* A reckless, self-indulgent, and free-spending sphere of activity, often involving dissipation: *"the culinary fast lane . . . where sea urchins and arugula salads flourish"* (Boston Globe). **—fast′-lane′** (făst′lān′) *adj.*

fast·ness (făst′nĭs) *n.* **1.** The condition or quality of being fast, especially: **a.** Firmness; security. **b.** Rapidity; swiftness. **2.** The quality or condition of color retention; colorfastness. **3.a.** A secure or fortified place; a stronghold. **b.** A remote, secret place.

fast one *n.* *Informal.* A shrewd trick or swindle; a deceitful or treacherous act.

fast-talk (făst′tôk′) *tr.v.* **-talked, -talk·ing, -talks.** *Informal.* To persuade, mislead, or obtain with a smooth line of talk: *fast-talked him out of his money; fast-talked her way into the show.* **—fast′-talk′er** *n.*

fast track *n.* *Informal.* The quickest and most direct route to achievement of a goal, as in competing for professional advancement: *"Making complaints against the public is hardly the fast track to elective office"* (New Yorker). **—fast′-track′** (făst′trăk′) *adj.* **—fast track′er** *n.*

fat (făt) *n.* **1.a.** The ester of glycerol and one, two, or three fatty acids. **b.** Any of various soft, solid, or semisolid organic compounds constituting the esters of glycerol and fatty acids and their associated organic groups. **c.** A mixture of such compounds occurring widely in organic tissue, especially in the adipose tissue of animals and in the seeds, nuts, and fruits of plants. **d.** Animal tissue containing such substances. **e.** A solidified animal or vegetable oil. **2.** Obesity; corpulence. **3.** The best or richest part: *living off the fat of the land.* **4.** Unnecessary excess: *"would drain the appropriation's fat without cutting into education's muscle"* (New York Times). **—fat** *adj.* **fat·ter, fat·test. 1.** Having much or too much fat or flesh; plump or obese. **2.** Full of fat or oil; greasy. **3.** Abounding in desirable elements. **4.** Fertile or productive; rich: *"It was a fine, green, fat landscape"* (Robert Louis Stevenson). **5.** Having an abundance or amplitude; well-stocked: *a fat larder.* **6.a.** Yielding profit or plenty; lucrative or rewarding: *a fat promotion.* **b.** Prosperous; wealthy: *grew fat on illegal profits.* **7.a.** Thick; large: *a fat book.* **b.** Puffed up; swollen: *a fat lip.* **—fat** *tr. & intr.v.* **fat·ted, fat·ting, fats.** To make or become fat; fatten. **—*idioms.* a fat lot.** *Slang.* Very little or none at all: *a fat lot of good it will do him.* **fat chance.** *Slang.* Very little or no chance. [Middle English, from Old English *fǣtt.* See **peiə-** in Appendix.] **—fat′ly** *adv.* **—fat′ness** *n.*

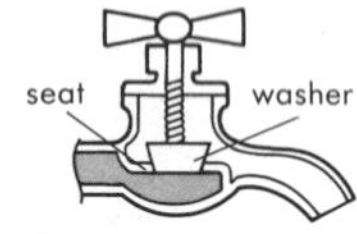

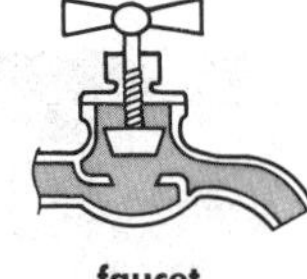

faucet

SYNONYMS: *fat, obese, corpulent, fleshy, portly, stout, pudgy, rotund, plump, chubby.* These adjectives mean having an abundance and often an excess of flesh. *Fat* implies excessive weight and is generally unfavorable in its connotations: *not merely overweight but downright fat. Obese* and *corpulent* imply gross overweight: *"a woman of robust frame . . . though stout, not obese"* (Charlotte Brontë). *Her father is too corpulent to play handball. Fleshy* implies a not necessarily excessive abundance of flesh: *firm, fleshy arms. Portly* and *stout* are sometimes used as polite terms to describe fatness. In stricter application *portly* refers to a person whose bulk is combined with a stately or imposing bearing, and *stout,* to a person with a thickset, bulky figure: *"a portly, rubicund man of middle age"* (Winston Churchill). *Even slim girls can become stout matrons. Pudgy* means short and fat: *pudgy fingers. Rotund* suggests roundness of figure, often in a squat person: *"this pink-faced rotund specimen of prosperity"* (George Eliot). *Plump* applies to a pleasing fullness of figure: *a plump, rosy little girl.* A *chubby* person is round and plump: *a chubby toddler.*

fa·tal (făt′l) *adj.* **1.** Causing or capable of causing death. **2.** Causing ruin or destruction; disastrous: *"Such doctrines, if true, would be absolutely fatal to my theory"* (Charles Darwin). **3.** Of decisive importance; fateful. **4.** Determining destiny; controlled by fate. **5.** *Obsolete.* Having been destined; fated. [Middle English, fateful, from Old French, from Latin *fātālis,* from *fātum,* prophecy, doom. See FATE.]

SYNONYMS: *fatal, deadly, mortal, lethal.* These adjectives apply to what causes or is likely to cause death. *Fatal* describes conditions, circumstances, or events that have caused or are destined inevitably to cause death or dire consequences: *a fatal accident; a fatal illness. "It is fatal to enter any war without the will to win it"* (Douglas MacArthur). *Deadly* means capable of killing: *a deadly weapon; a deadly poison. Mortal* describes a condition or action that has produced or is about to produce death: *a mortal wound. Lethal* refers to a sure agent of death that may have been created solely for the purpose of killing: *execution by lethal injection; a lethal dose of barbiturates.*

fa·tal·ism (făt′l-ĭz′əm) *n.* **1.** The doctrine that all events are predetermined by fate and are therefore unalterable. **2.** Acceptance of the belief that all events are predetermined. **—fa′tal·ist** *n.* **—fa′tal·is′tic** *adj.* **—fa′tal·is′ti·cal·ly** *adv.*

fa·tal·i·ty (fā-tăl′ĭ-tē, fə-) *n., pl.* **-ties. 1.a.** A death resulting from an accident or a disaster: *highway fatalities.* **b.** One that is killed as a result of such an occurrence: *The driver was one of the fatalities.* **2.** The ability to cause death or disaster. **3.** The quality of being determined by fate. **4.** A decree made by fate; destiny. **5.** The quality of being doomed to disaster.

fatality rate *n.* See **death rate.**

fa·tal·ly (făt′l-ē) *adv.* **1.** So as to cause death; mortally: *fatally injured.* **2.** So as to result in disaster or ruin. **3.** According to the decree of fate; inevitably.

fa·ta mor·ga·na (fä′tə môr-gä′nə) *n.* See **mirage** (sense 1). [Italian, mirage, Morgan le Fay (from the belief that the mirage was caused by her witchcraft) : *fata,* fairy (from Vulgar Latin *fāta,* goddess of fate; see FAIRY) + *Morgana,* Morgan (probably from Old Irish *Morrigain*).]

fat·back (făt′băk′) *n.* The strip of fat from the upper part of a side of pork, usually dried and salt-cured.

fat body *n.* **1.** A food reserve of fatty tissue in the larval stages of certain insects. **2.** A mass of fatty tissue located near the genital glands in some amphibians, including the frogs and toads.

fat cat *n.* *Slang.* **1.** A wealthy and highly privileged person. **2.** A wealthy contributor to a political campaign.

fat cell *n.* Any of various cells found in adipose tissue that are specialized for the storage of fat. Also called *adipocyte.*

Fat City or **fat city** *n.* *Slang.* A condition or set of circumstances characterized by great prosperity.

fate (fāt) *n.* **1.a.** The supposed force, principle, or power that predetermines events. **b.** The inevitable events predestined by this force. **2.** A final result or consequence; an outcome. **3.** Unfavorable destiny; doom. **4. Fates.** *Greek & Roman Mythology.* The three goddesses, Clotho, Lachesis, and Atropos, who control human destiny. Used with *the.* [Middle English, from Old French *fat,* from Latin *fātum,* prophecy, doom, neuter past participle of *fārī,* to speak. See **bhā-**[2] in Appendix.]

SYNONYMS: *fate, destiny, kismet, lot, portion.* The central meaning shared by these nouns is "something that is inevitably destined to happen to a person": *deserved a worse fate; complained about their miserable destiny; a meeting foreordained by kismet; has a happy lot; success that was her portion.*

fat·ed (fā′tĭd) *adj.* **1.** Governed by fate; predetermined. **2.** Condemned to death or destruction; doomed: *the fated city of Troy.*

fate·ful (fāt′fəl) *adj.* **1.** Vitally affecting subsequent events; being of great consequence; momentous: *a fateful decision to counterattack.* **2.** Controlled by or as if by fate; predetermined. **3.** Bringing death or disaster; fatal. **4.** Ominously prophetic; portentous: *a fateful sign.* **—fate′ful·ly** *adv.* **—fate′ful·ness** *n.*

fath or **fath.** *abbr.* Fathom.

fat·head (făt′hĕd′) *n.* *Slang.* A person regarded as stupid. **—fat′head′ed** *adj.* **—fat′head′ed·ly** *adv.*

fa·ther (fä′*th*ər) *n.* **1.** A man who begets or raises or nurtures a child. **2.** A male parent of an animal. **3.** A male ancestor. **4.** A man who creates, originates, or founds something: *Chaucer is considered the father of English poetry.* **5.** An early form; a prototype. **6. Father. a.** God. **b.** The first person of the Christian Trinity. **7.** An elderly or venerable man. Used as a title of respect. **8.** A member of the senate in ancient Rome. **9.** One of the leading men, as of a city: *the town fathers.* **10.** Or **Father.** A church father. **11.** *Abbr.* **Fr. a.** A priest or clergyman in the Roman Catholic or Anglican churches. **b.** Used as a title and form of address with or without the clergyman's name. **—father** *v.* **-thered, -ther·ing, -thers.** *—tr.* **1.** To procreate (offspring) as the male parent. **2.** *Usage Problem.* To act or serve as a father to (a child). **3.** To create, found, or originate. **4.** To acknowledge responsibility for. **5.a.** To attribute the paternity, creation, or origin of. **b.** To assign falsely or unjustly; foist. *—intr. Usage Problem.* To act or serve as a father. [Middle English *fader,* from Old English *fæder.* See **pəter-** in Appendix.]

ă pat	oi boy
ā pay	ou out
âr care	o͝o took
ä father	o͞o boot
ĕ pet	ŭ cut
ē be	ûr urge
ĭ pit	th thin
ī pie	*th* this
îr pier	hw which
ŏ pot	zh vision
ō toe	ə about, item
ô paw	♦ regionalism

Stress marks: **′** (primary); ′ (secondary), as in **dictionary** (dĭk′shə-nĕr′ē)

USAGE NOTE: The verb *father* has come to be used widely to mean specifically to "perform the child-rearing functions of a father," particularly in the gerund *fathering,* as in *Fathering a stepchild takes considerable tact and understanding.* This usage reflects the same social changes that have led to the analogous use of the verb *parent* and has met with the same kinds of critical resistance. In the most recent survey the example cited was rejected by 64 percent of the Usage Panel. A problem particular to this use of *father* is that it may occasion opportunities for humorous misconstruction, since it is in direct competition with the older sense of "beget." • It is notable that the analogous use of *mother* as a verb meaning specifically "to perform the child-rearing functions of a mother" is encountered only rarely. It is likely that the discrepancy in the frequency of these new uses of *mother* and *father* reflects the fact that recent writers on family life have tended to place more emphasis on a reconceptualization of the traditional paternal role in child-rearing. See Usage Note at **parent.**

Father Christmas *n. Chiefly British.* Santa Claus.

father confessor *n.* **1.** A priest who hears confessions. **2.** A person in whom one confides.

father figure *n.* An older man, often one in a position of power or influence, who elicits the emotions usually reserved for a father.

fa·ther·hood (fä′*thər*-ho͝od′) *n.* **1.** The state of being a father. **2.** The qualities of a father. **3.** Fathers considered as a group.

fa·ther-in-law (fä′*thər*-ĭn-lô′) *n., pl.* **fa·thers-in-law** (fä′*thərz*-). **1.** The father of one's husband or wife. **2.** *Archaic.* A stepfather.

fa·ther·land (fä′*thər*-lănd′) *n.* **1.** One's native land. **2.** The land of one's ancestors.

fa·ther·less (fä′*thər*-lĭs) *adj.* **1.** Having no living father. **2.** Having no known father. **—fa′ther·less·ness** *n.*

fa·ther·ly (fä′*thər*-lē) *adj.* **1.** Of, like, or appropriate to a father: *fatherly love.* **2.** Showing the affection of a father. **—fatherly** *adv.* In a manner befitting a father. **—fa′ther·li·ness** *n.*

Fa·ther's Day (fä′*thərz*) *n.* The third Sunday in June, observed in the United States in honor of fathers.

fath·om (făth′əm) *n., pl.* **fathom** or **fath·oms.** *Abbr.* **fath, fath., fm., fth.** A unit of length equal to 6 feet (1.83 meters), used principally in the measurement and specification of marine depths. **—fathom** *tr.v.* **-omed, -om·ing, -oms. 1.** To determine the depth of; sound. **2.** To penetrate to the meaning or nature of; comprehend. [Middle English *fathme,* from Old English *fæthm,* outstretched arms. See **pet-** in Appendix.]

Fa·thom·e·ter (fă-*thŏm*′ĭ-tər). A trademark used for a sonic depth finder.

fath·om·less (făth′əm-lĭs) *adj.* **1.** Too deep to be fathomed or measured. **2.** Too obscure or complicated to be understood. **—fath′om·less·ly** *adv.* **—fath′om·less·ness** *n.*

fa·tid·ic (fə-tĭd′ĭk) also **fa·tid·i·cal** (-ĭ-kəl) *adj.* Relating to or characterized by prophecy; prophetic. [Latin *fātidicus* : *fātum,* prophecy, doom; see FATE + *dīcere,* to say; see **deik-** in Appendix.]

fat·i·ga·ble (făt′ĭ-gə-bəl) *adj.* Subject to fatigue. [French, from Old French, from Late Latin *fatīgābilis,* from Latin *fatīgāre,* to fatigue.] **—fat′i·ga·bil′i·ty** *n.*

fa·tigue (fə-tēg′) *n.* **1.** Physical or mental weariness resulting from exertion. **2.** Something, such as tiring effort or activity, that causes weariness: *the fatigue of a long hike.* **3.** *Physiology.* The decreased capacity or complete inability of an organism, an organ, or a part to function normally because of excessive stimulation or prolonged exertion. **4.** The weakening or failure of a material, such as metal or wood, resulting from prolonged stress. **5.a.** Manual or menial labor, such as barracks cleaning, assigned to soldiers. **b. fatigues.** Clothing worn by military personnel for labor or for field duty. **—fatigue** *v.* **-tigued, -tigu·ing, -tigues.** —*tr.* **1.** To tire with physical or mental exertion; weary. **2.** To create fatigue in (a metal or other material). —*intr.* To be or become fatigued. See Synonyms at **tire[1].** [French, from Old French, from *fatiguer,* to fatigue, from Latin *fatīgāre.*]

Fat·i·ma also **Fat·i·mah** (făt′ə-mə). 616?–633. Daughter of the Islamic prophet Mohammed. She is considered by Moslems to be one of the Four Perfect Women.

Fá·ti·ma (făt′ə-mə). A village of west-central Portugal north-northeast of Lisbon. It became a pilgrimage site after the reported appearance of the Virgin Mary to three children in 1917.

Fat·i·mah (făt′ə-mə). See **Fatima.**

Fat·i·mid (făt′ə-mĭd′) also **Fat·i·mite** (-mīt′). A Moslem dynasty that ruled North Africa and parts of Egypt (909–1171).

fat·ling (făt′lĭng) *n.* A young animal, such as a lamb or calf, fattened for slaughter.

♦**fat pine** *n. Chiefly Southern U.S.* Easily ignited, resin-rich kindling. Also called ♦*fatwood.* See Regional Note at **lightwood.**

fat·so (făt′sō) *n., pl.* **-soes.** *Slang.* A fat person.

fat-sol·u·ble (făt′sŏl′yə-bəl) *adj.* Soluble in fats or fat solvents.

fat·ten (făt′n) *v.* **-tened, -ten·ing, -tens.** —*tr.* **1.** To make plump or fat. **2.** To fertilize (land). **3.** To increase the amount or substance of; swell: *fatten one's bank account.* —*intr.* To grow fat or fatter. **—fat′ten·er** *n.*

fat·tish (făt′ĭsh) *adj.* Somewhat fat. **—fat′tish·ness** *n.*

fat·ty (făt′ē) *adj.* **-ti·er, -ti·est. 1.** Containing or composed of fat: *fatty food; fatty deposits.* **2.** Characteristic of fat; greasy. **3.** Derived from or chemically related to fat. **—fatty** *n., pl.* **-ties.** *Informal.* A fat person. **—fat′ti·ly** *adv.* **—fat′ti·ness** *n.*

fatty acid *n.* Any of a large group of monobasic acids, especially those found in animal and vegetable fats and oils, having the general formula $C_nH_{2n+1}COOH$. Characteristically made up of saturated or unsaturated aliphatic compounds with an even number of carbon atoms, this group of acids includes palmitic, stearic, and oleic acids.

fatty alcohol *n.* Any of various alcohols derived from plant or animal oils and fats and used in plastics and pharmaceuticals.

fatty degeneration *n. Pathology.* The accumulation of fat globules within the cells of a bodily organ, such as the liver or heart, resulting in deterioration of tissue and diminished functioning of the affected organ.

fa·tu·i·ty (fə-to͞o′ĭ-tē, -tyo͞o′-, fă-) *n., pl.* **-ties. 1.** Smug stupidity; utter foolishness. **2.** Something that is utterly stupid or silly. [Latin *fatuitās,* from *fatuus,* silly, foolish.]

fat·u·ous (făch′o͞o-əs) *adj.* **1.** Vacuously, smugly, and unconsciously foolish. See Synonyms at **foolish. 2.** Delusive; unreal: *fatuous hopes.* [From Latin *fatuus.*] **—fat′u·ous·ly** *adv.* **—fat′u·ous·ness** *n.*

♦**fat·wood** (făt′wo͝od′) *n. Chiefly Southern U.S.* See **fat pine.** See Regional Note at **lightwood.**

♦**fau·bourg** (fō′bo͝or′, -bo͝org′) *n. New Orleans.* A district of metropolitan New Orleans lying outside the original city limits. See Regional Note at **beignet.** [Middle English *faubourgh,* from Old French *faubourg,* alteration (influenced by *faux,* false, from Latin *falsus;* see FALSE) of *forsborc* : *fors,* outside (from Latin *forīs;* see **dhwer-** in Appendix) + *borc,* town (from Late Latin *burgus,* fort, of Germanic origin; see **bhergh-[2]** in Appendix).]

♦ ***REGIONAL NOTE:*** The close political ties between Scotland and France during the 15th through 17th centuries were reflected in linguistic borrowing from French to Scots, as in the case of *faubourg,* a synonym for *suburb.* In England *faubourg* seems to have lost the competition with the more popular *suburb.* However, in contemporary American English the word still exists, although it is virtually confined to the city of New Orleans, where, in fact, *faubourg* remains in use because of the city's French background. Even there it is used not as a common noun like *suburb* but in combination in the names of various quarters of the city, for example, *Faubourg Sainte Marie.* These city districts, like their counterparts in Paris, such as *Faubourg Saint-Germain* and *Faubourg Saint-Antoine,* originally lay outside the city limits, hence the designation *faubourg,* originally from Old French *fors,* "outside," and *borc,* "town." As the population grew outward, these former suburbs became part of the city proper.

fau·cal (fô′kəl) *adj. Botany.* Relating to the throat of a corolla with fused petals. [From Latin *faux, fauc-,* throat.]

fau·ces (fô′sēz′) *pl.n. (used with a sing. or pl. verb).* The passage from the back of the mouth to the pharynx, bounded by the soft palate, the base of the tongue, and the palatine arches. [Middle English, from Latin *faucēs.*] **—fau′cal** (-kəl), **fau′cial** (-shəl) *adj.*

fau·cet (fô′sĭt) *n.* A device for regulating the flow of a liquid from a reservoir such as a pipe or drum. [Middle English, from Old French *fausset,* cask stopper, from *fausser,* to break in, from Late Latin *falsāre,* to falsify, from Latin *falsus,* false. See FALSE.]

Faulk·ner also **Falk·ner** (fôk′nər), **William.** 1897–1962. American writer who set many of his works, such as the novels *The Sound and the Fury* (1929) and *The Unvanquished* (1938), in the imaginary Yoknapatawpha County, a microcosm of the postbellum South. He won the 1949 Nobel Prize for literature. **—Faulk·ner′i·an** (fôk-nîr′ē-ən) *adj.*

fault (fôlt) *n.* **1.a.** A character weakness, especially a minor one. **b.** Something that impairs or detracts from physical perfection; a defect. **c.** A mistake; an error. **d.** A minor offense or misdeed. **2.** Responsibility for a mistake or an offense; culpability. **3.** *Geology.* A fracture in the continuity of a rock formation caused by a shifting or dislodging of the earth's crust, in which adjacent surfaces are differentially displaced parallel to the plane of fracture. Also called *shift.* **4.** *Electronics.* A defect in a circuit or wiring caused by imperfect connections, poor insulation, grounding, or shorting. **5.** *Sports.* A bad service, as in tennis. **6.** *Obsolete.* A lack or deficiency. **—fault** *v.* **fault·ed, fault·ing, faults.** —*tr.* **1.** To find error or defect in; criticize or blame. **2.** *Geology.* To produce a fault in; fracture. —*intr.* **1.** To commit a mistake or an error. **2.** *Geology.* To shift so as to produce a fault. **—*idioms.* at fault. 1.** Deserving of blame; guilty: *admitted to being at fault.* **2.** Confused and puzzled. **find fault.** To seek, find, and complain about faults; criticize: *found fault with his speech.* **to a fault.** To an excessive degree: *generous to a fault.* [Middle English *faulte,* from Old French, from Vulgar Latin **fallita,* feminine past participle of Latin *fallere,* to deceive, fail.]

SYNONYMS: *fault, failing, weakness, frailty, foible, vice.* These nouns denote an imperfection or deficiency of character. A *fault* is a quality or trait that detracts from moral excellence: *"If we had no faults of our own, we would not take so much pleasure in noticing those of others"* (La Rochefoucauld). A *failing* is a minor

William Faulkner
Photographed in 1950

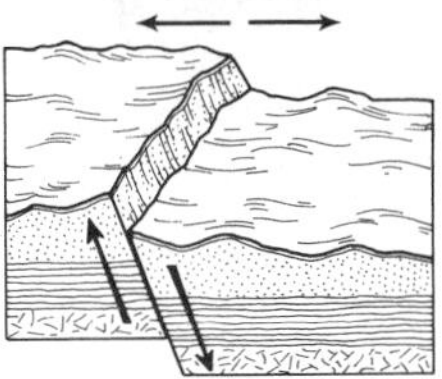

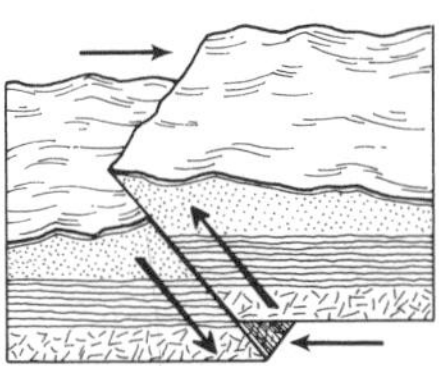

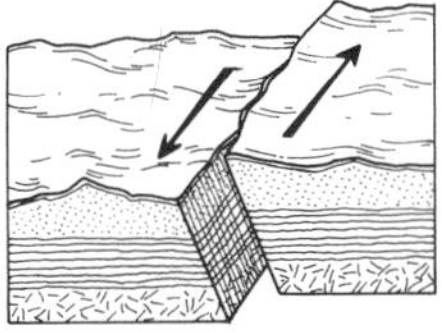

fault
Top: Photograph of the San Andreas Fault, California
Bottom: Diagrams illustrating normal (*top*), thrust (*center*), and strike-slip (*bottom*) faults

fault or shortcoming: *"An inability to stay quiet . . . is one of the most conspicuous failings of mankind"* (Walter Bagehot). *Weakness* suggests deficiency of moral strength or force of character: *"We must touch his weaknesses with a delicate hand. There are some faults so nearly allied to excellence, that we can scarce weed out the fault without eradicating the virtue"* (Oliver Goldsmith). The term is related to but stronger than *frailty,* which implies the likelihood of yielding to temptation: *"Our frailties are invincible, our virtues barren"* (Robert Louis Stevenson). Even weaker in imputing censure is *foible,* which refers to a minor defect that is easily overlooked and may even be endearing: *"Science is his forte, and omniscience his foible"* (Sydney Smith). *Vice* in this comparison refers to a moral flaw or in a weaker sense to a defect of character: *"Lord, Lord, how subject we old men are to this vice of lying!"* (Shakespeare). *"Obstinacy, Sir, is certainly a great vice"* (Edmund Burke). See also Synonyms at **blame, blemish.**

Faust

fault·find·er (fôlt′fīn′dər) *n.* One who is given to petty criticism and constant complaint.

fault·find·ing (fôlt′fīn′dĭng) *n.* Petty or nagging criticism; carping. **—faultfinding** *adj.* Disposed to find fault. See Synonyms at **critical.**

fault·less (fôlt′lĭs) *adj.* Being without fault. See Synonyms at **perfect.** **—fault′less·ly** *adv.* **—fault′less·ness** *n.*

fault plane *n. Geology.* The plane along which the break or shear of a fault occurs.

fault·y (fôl′tē) *adj.* **-i·er, -i·est. 1.** Containing a fault or defect; imperfect or defective. **2.** *Obsolete.* Deserving of blame; guilty. **—fault′i·ly** *adv.* **—fault′i·ness** *n.*

faun (fôn) *n. Roman Mythology.* Any of a group of rural deities represented as having the body of a man and the horns, ears, tail, and sometimes legs of a goat. [Middle English, from Old French, from Latin *Faunus,* Faunus.]

fau·na (fô′nə) *n., pl.* **-nas** or **-nae** (-nē′). **1.** Animals, especially the animals of a particular region or period, considered as a group. **2.** A catalogue of the animals of a specific region or period. [Late Latin *Fauna,* sister of Faunus.] **—fau′nal** *adj.* **—fau′nal·ly** *adv.*

fau·nis·tic (fô-nĭs′tĭk) *adj.* Of or relating to the geographic distribution of animals. **—fau·nis′ti·cal·ly** *adv.*

Fau·nus (fô′nəs) *n. Roman Mythology.* A god of nature and fertility. [Latin.]

Fau·ré (fō-rā′), **Gabriel Urbain.** 1845–1924. French composer chiefly noted for his songs, including the cycle *La Bonne Chanson* (1891–1892), and for his Requiem (1887).

Faust (foust) also **Faus·tus** (fou′stəs, fô′-) *n.* A magician and alchemist in German legend who sells his soul to the devil in exchange for power and knowledge. [German, after Johann *Faust* (1480?–1540?), German magician and alchemist.] **—Faust′i·an** (fou′stē-ən) *adj.*

faute de mieux (fōt də myœ′) *adv.* For lack of something better. [French : *faute,* lack + *de,* of + *mieux,* better.]

fau·teuil (fō′tĭl, fō-tœ′yə) *n.* An upholstered armchair usually having open sides. [French, from Old French *faldestoel,* of Germanic origin. See **pel-²** in Appendix.]

fau·vism (fō′vĭz′əm) *n.* An early 20th-century movement in painting begun by a group of French artists and marked by the use of bold, often distorted forms and vivid colors. [French *fauvisme,* from *fauve,* wild animal, from *fauve,* wild, reddish-yellow, from Old French *falve,* reddish-yellow, from Frankish *falw-.* See **pel-¹** in Appendix.] **—fauv′ist** *adj.*

faux (fō) *adj.* Artificial; fake: *faux pearls.* [French, from Old French *fals.* See FALSE.]

faux-na·ïf also **faux-naif** (fō-nä-ēf′) *adj.* Marked by a false show of innocent simplicity: *"Their gee-whiz, faux-naif comportment is not always convincing"* (Madison Bell). [French : *faux,* false + *naïf,* naive.]

faux pas (fō pä′) *n., pl.* **faux pas** (fō päz′). A social blunder. [French : *faux,* false + *pas,* step.]

fa·va bean (fä′və) *n.* See **broad bean.** [Italian *fava,* from Latin *faba,* broad bean. See **bha-bhā-** in Appendix.]

fa·ve·la (fə-vĕl′ə) *n.* A shantytown or slum, especially in Brazil. [Portuguese, possibly from diminutive of *favo,* honeycomb (from Latin *favus*) or from *favelas,* probably from pl. of *favela,* spurge (from *fava,* bean, from Latin *faba;* see FAVA BEAN).]

fa·ve·o·late (fə-vē′ə-lāt′) *adj.* Pitted with cavities or cells; honeycombed. [From New Latin *faveolus* : Latin *favus,* honeycomb + (ALV)EOLUS.]

fa·vo·ni·an (fə-vō′nē-ən) *adj.* **1.** Of or relating to the west wind. **2.** Mild; benign. [Latin *Favōniānus,* from *Favōnius,* the west wind.]

♦**fa·vor** (fā′vər) *n.* **1.** A gracious, friendly, or obliging act that is freely granted: *do someone a favor.* **2.a.** Friendly or favorable regard; approval or support: *won the favor of the monarch; looked with favor on the plan.* **b.** A state of being held in such regard: *a style currently in favor.* **3.** Unfair partiality; favoritism. **4.a.** A privilege or concession. **b. favors.** Sexual privileges, especially as granted by a woman. **5.a.** Something given as a token of love, affection, or remembrance. **b.** A small decorative gift given to each guest at a party. **6.** Advantage; benefit: *sailed under favor of cloudless skies.* **7.** Behalf; interest: *an error in our favor.* **8.** *Obsolete.* A communication, especially a letter. **9.** *Archaic.* **a.** Aspect or appearance. **b.** Countenance; face. **10.** *Obsolete.* A facial feature. **—favor** *v.* **-vored, -vor·ing, -vors.** *—tr.* **1.** To perform a kindness or service for; oblige. See Synonyms at **oblige. 2.** To treat or regard with friendship, approval, or support. **3.** To be partial to; indulge a liking for: *favors bright colors.* **4.** To be or tend to be in support of. **5.** To make easier or more possible; facilitate: *Darkness favored their escape.* **6.** To treat with care; be gentle with: *favored my wounded leg.* **7.** *Chiefly Southern U.S.* To resemble in appearance: *She favors her father.* *—intr. Chiefly Southern U.S.* To resemble another in appearance: *She and her father favor.* ***—idiom.* in favor of. 1.** In support of; approving: *We are in favor of her promotion to president.* **2.** To take advantage of: *The court decided in favor of the plaintiff.* **3.** Inscribed or made out to the benefit of: *a check in favor of a charity.* [Middle English, from Old French, from Latin, from *favēre,* to be favorable.] **—fa′vor·er** *n.* **—fa′vor·ing·ly** *adv.*

♦ ***REGIONAL NOTE:*** When a Southerner *favors* a relative, he or she is not giving that person special privileges; rather, the Southerner looks like that relative. *Favor* can be either transitive—*She favors her father*—or intransitive with a compound subject: *She and her father favor.* This sense of *favor* goes back to early modern English: *"This young lord Chamont/Favors my mother"* (Ben Jonson). The verb derives from the noun *favor,* which was used from the 15th to the 19th century to mean "appearance, aspect; the countenance, face": *"What makes thy favor like the bloodless head/Fall'n on the block?"* (Tennyson). This sense of the noun is now archaic, but the verb thrives in the English of the Southern United States.

fa·vor·a·ble (fā′vər-ə-bəl, fāv′rə-) *adj.* **1.** Advantageous; helpful: *favorable winds.* **2.** Encouraging; propitious: *a favorable diagnosis.* **3.** Manifesting approval; commendatory: *a favorable report.* **4.** Winning approval; pleasing: *a favorable impression.* **5.** Granting what has been desired or requested: *a favorable reply.* **6.** Indulgent or partial: *listened with a favorable ear.* **—fa′vor·a·ble·ness** *n.* **—fa′vor·a·bly** *adv.*

SYNONYMS: *favorable, propitious, auspicious, benign, conducive.* These adjectives describe what is indicative of a successful outcome. *Favorable* can refer to people, conditions, or circumstances that contribute in a positive way to the attainment of a goal: *I hope you will give favorable consideration to my suggestion. The performance received a favorable review. Propitious* implies a favorable tendency or inclination: *"Miracles are propitious accidents, the natural causes of which are too complicated to be readily understood"* (George Santayana). *Auspicious* refers to what by its favorable nature presages good fortune: *The project had an auspicious beginning. Benign* applies to people or things that exert a beneficial influence: *"I lingered round them, under that benign sky . . . and wondered how anyone could ever imagine unquiet slumbers, for the sleepers in that quiet earth"* (Emily Brontë). Something *conducive* contributes to a result, often a desirable one: *"Nothing is more conducive to happiness than the free exercise of the mind in pursuits congenial to it"* (Macaulay).

fa·vored (fā′vərd) *adj.* **1.** Treated or thought of with great kindness or partiality: *the favored child.* **2.** Endowed with special gifts, talents, or advantages. **3.** Having an appearance of a specified kind. Often used in combination: *ill-favored; well-favored.*

fa·vor·ite (fā′vər-ĭt, fāv′rĭt) *n.* **1.a.** One that enjoys special favor or regard. **b.** One that is trusted, indulged, or preferred above all others, especially by a superior: *a favorite of the monarch.* **2.** A contestant or competitor regarded as most likely to win. **—favorite** *adj.* Liked or preferred above all others; regarded with special favor. [Obsolete French *favorit,* from Old Italian *favorito,* past participle of *favorire,* to favor, from *favore,* favor, from Latin *favor.* See FAVOR.]

favorite son *n.* **1.** A man favored for nomination as a presidential candidate by his own state delegates at a national political convention. **2.** A famous man viewed with much favor by his hometown for his achievements.

fa·vor·it·ism (fā′vər-ĭ-tĭz′əm, fāv′rĭ-) *n.* **1.** A display of partiality toward a favored person or group. **2.** The state of being held in special favor.

fa·vour (fā′vər) *n. & v. Chiefly British.* Variant of **favor.**

fa·vus (fā′vəs) *n.* A chronic skin infection, usually of the scalp, caused by fungi of the genus *Trichophyton* and characterized by the development of thick, yellow crusts over the hair follicles. [Latin, honeycomb.]

Fawkes (fôks), **Guy.** 1570–1606. English conspirator executed for his role in the Gunpowder Plot, an attempt to kill James I and blow up Parliament on November 5, 1605, to avenge the persecution of Roman Catholics in England.

fawn¹ (fôn) *intr.v.* **fawned, fawn·ing, fawns. 1.** To exhibit affection or attempt to please, as a dog does by wagging its tail, whining, or cringing. **2.** To seek favor or attention by flattery and obsequious behavior. [Middle English *faunen,* from Old English *fagnian,* to rejoice, from *fagen, fægen,* glad.] **—fawn′er** *n.* **—fawn′ing·ly** *adv.*

SYNONYMS: *fawn, apple-polish, bootlick, kowtow, slaver, toady, truckle.* The central meaning shared by these verbs is "to curry favor by behaving obsequiously and submissively": *fawned on her superior; students apple-polishing the teacher; bootlicked to get a* *promotion; lawyers kowtowing to a judge; slavered over his rich uncle; toadying to members of the occupation force; nobles truckling to the king.*

fawn² (fôn) *n.* **1.** A young deer, especially one less than a year old. **2.** *Color.* A grayish yellow brown to light grayish or moderate reddish brown. [Middle English, from Old French *foun, faon, feon,* young animal, from Vulgar Latin **fētō, *fētōn-,* from Latin *fētus,* offspring. See **dhē(i)-** in Appendix.]

fawn lily *n.* Any of several North American lilies of the genus *Erythronium,* especially *E. californicum* of western North America, having nodding, usually yellow flowers and often mottled leaves.

fax (făks) *n.* See **facsimile** (sense 2). **—fax** *tr.v.* **faxed, fax·ing, fax·es.** To transmit (printed matter or an image) by electronic means. [Shortening and alteration of FACSIMILE.]

fay¹ (fā) *tr. & intr.v.* **fayed, fay·ing, fays.** To join or fit closely or tightly. [Middle English *feien,* from Old English *fēgan.* See **pag-** in Appendix.]

fay² (fā) *n.* A fairy or an elf. [Middle English *faie,* enchanted person or place, from Old French *fae.* See FAIRY.]

fay³ (fā) *n.* *Archaic.* Faith: *"Sirrah, by my fay, it waxes late"* (Shakespeare). [Middle English *fai,* from Anglo-Norman *fei, fed.* See FAITH.]

Fa·yal (fə-yälʹ, fä-). See **Faial.**

fay·a·lite (fāʹə-lītʹ) *n.* A yellowish to black mineral, Fe_2SiO_4, of the olivine group. [German *Fayalit,* from *Fayal,* Faial.]

Fay·ette·ville (fāʹĭt-vĭlʹ, -vəl). **1.** A city of northwest Arkansas in the Ozark Plateau north-northeast of Fort Smith. The University of Arkansas (established 1871) is here. Population, 36,608. **2.** A city of south-central North Carolina south-southwest of Raleigh. Founded by Scottish colonists in 1739, it was a Tory center during the American Revolution. Population, 59,507.

faze (fāz) *tr.v.* **fazed, faz·ing, faz·es.** To disrupt the composure of; disconcert. See Synonyms at **embarrass.** [Middle English *fesen,* to drive away, frighten, from Old English *fēsian.*]

fb also **f.b.** *abbr.* *Sports.* Fullback.

F.B. *abbr.* **1.** Foreign body. **2.** Freight bill.

FBI also **F.B.I.** *abbr.* Federal Bureau of Investigation.

fc *abbr.* Foot-candle.

f.c. *abbr.* *Printing.* Follow copy.

FCA *abbr.* Farm Credit Administration.

fcap. *abbr.* Foolscap.

FCC *abbr.* Federal Communications Commission.

F clef *n.* *Music.* See **bass clef.**

fcp. *abbr.* Foolscap.

FCS or **F.C.S.** *abbr.* Fellow of the Chemical Society.

fcy. *abbr.* Fancy.

FD *abbr.* **1.** Fatal dose. **2.** Fire department. **3.** Focal distance.

F.D. *abbr.* *Latin.* Fidei Defensor (Defender of the Faith).

FDA *abbr.* Food and Drug Administration.

FDIC *abbr.* Federal Deposit Insurance Corporation.

Fe The symbol for the element **iron** (sense 1). [Latin *ferrum,* iron.]

fe·al·ty (fēʹəl-tē) *n., pl.* **-ties. 1.a.** The fidelity owed by a vassal to his feudal lord. **b.** The oath of such fidelity. **2.** Faithfulness; allegiance. See Synonyms at **fidelity.** [Middle English *fealtye,* from Old French *fealte,* from Latin *fidēlitās,* faithfulness, from *fidēlis,* faithful, from *fidēs,* faith. See **bheidh-** in Appendix.]

fear (fîr) *n.* **1.a.** A feeling of agitation and anxiety caused by the presence or imminence of danger. **b.** A state or condition marked by this feeling: *living in fear.* **2.** A feeling of disquiet or apprehension: *a fear of looking foolish.* **3.** Extreme reverence or awe, as toward a supreme power. **4.** A reason for dread or apprehension: *Being alone is my greatest fear.* **—fear** *v.* **feared, fear·ing, fears.** —*tr.* **1.** To be afraid or frightened of. **2.** To be uneasy or apprehensive about: *feared the test results.* **3.** To be in awe of; revere. **4.** To consider probable; expect: *I fear you are wrong. I fear I have bad news for you.* **5.** *Archaic.* To feel fear within (oneself). —*intr.* **1.** To be afraid. **2.** To be uneasy or apprehensive. [Middle English *fer,* from Old English *fǣr,* danger, sudden calamity. See **per-³** in Appendix.] **—fearʹer** *n.*

SYNONYMS: *fear, fright, dread, terror, horror, panic, alarm, dismay, consternation, trepidation.* These nouns all denote the agitation and anxiety caused by the presence or imminence of danger. *Fear* is the most general term: *fear of change; fear of flying; fear of death. "Fear is the parent of cruelty"* (J.A. Froude). *Fright* is sudden, usually momentary fear characterized by great agitation: *In her fright she forgot to lock the door. Dread* is strong fear of something impending, especially of what one is powerless to avoid: *He looked forward with dread to the scheduled surgery. Terror* is intense, overpowering fear: *"the weapon which most readily conquers reason: terror and violence"* (Adolf Hitler). *Horror* is a combination of fear and aversion or repugnance: *Murder arouses widespread horror. Panic* is sudden frantic fear, often groundless: *The fire caused a panic among the horses. Rumors of the President's illness resulted in panic on the world stock markets. Alarm* is fright aroused by the first realization of danger: *I watched with alarm as the current carried the raft and its passengers toward the dam. Dismay* is apprehension that robs one of courage or the power to act effectively: *The appearance of a comet caused universal dismay in the ancient world. Consternation* is a state of often paralyzing dismay characterized by confusion and helplessness: *Consternation spread throughout the city as the invading army approached. Trepidation* is dread marked by trembling or hesitancy: *"They were . . . full of trepidation about things that were never likely to happen"* (John Morley).

WORD HISTORY: Old English *fǣr,* the ancestor of our word *fear,* meant "calamity, disaster," but not the emotion engendered by such an event. This is in line with the meaning of the prehistoric Common Germanic word **fēraz,* "danger," which is the source of words with similar senses in other Germanic languages, such as Old Saxon and Old High German *fār,* "ambush, danger," and Old Icelandic *fār,* "treachery, damage." Scholars, in fact, have determined the form and meaning of Germanic **fēraz* by working backward from the forms and the meanings of its descendants. The most important cause of the change of meaning in the word *fear* was probably the existence in Old English of the related verb *fǣran,* which meant "to terrify, take by surprise." *Fear* is first recorded in Middle English with the sense "emotion of fear" in a work composed around 1290.

Fear (fîr), **Cape.** A promontory on Smith Island off the coast of southeast North Carolina at the mouth of the Cape Fear River.

fear·ful (fîrʹfəl) *adj.* **1.** Causing or capable of causing fear; frightening: *a fearful howling.* **2.** Experiencing fear; frightened. See Synonyms at **afraid. 3.** Feeling or inclined to feel anxiety or apprehension; timid; nervous. **4.** Indicating anxiety, fear, or terror: *a fearful, nervous glance.* **5.** Feeling reverence, dread, or awe. **6.** Extreme, as in degree or extent; dreadful: *a fearful blunder; fearful poverty.* **—fearʹful·ly** *adv.* **—fearʹful·ness** *n.*

fear·less (fîrʹlĭs) *adj.* Without fear; brave. See Synonyms at **brave. —fearʹless·ly** *adv.* **—fearʹless·ness** *n.*

fear·some (fîrʹsəm) *adj.* **1.** Causing or capable of causing fear: *"The Devil is a fearsome enemy"* (Jimmy Breslin). **2.** Fearful; timid. **—fearʹsome·ly** *adv.* **—fearʹsome·ness** *n.*

fea·si·ble (fēʹzə-bəl) *adj.* **1.** Capable of being accomplished or brought about; possible: *a feasible plan.* See Synonyms at **possible. 2.** Used or dealt with successfully; suitable: *feasible new sources of energy.* **3.** Logical; likely: *a feasible explanation.* [Middle English *fesable,* from Old French *faisable,* from *faire, fais-,* to do, from Latin *facere.* See **dhē-** in Appendix.] **—feaʹsi·bilʹi·ty, feaʹsi·ble·ness** *n.* **—feaʹsi·bly** *adv.*

feast (fēst) *n.* **1.a.** A large, elaborately prepared meal, usually for many persons and often accompanied by entertainment; a banquet. **b.** A meal that is well prepared and abundantly enjoyed. **2.** A periodic religious festival commemorating an event or honoring a god or saint. **3.** Something giving great pleasure or satisfaction: *a book that is a veritable feast for the mind.* **—feast** *v.* **feast·ed, feast·ing, feasts.** —*tr.* To give a feast for; entertain or feed sumptuously: *feasted the guests on venison.* —*intr.* **1.** To partake of a feast; eat heartily. **2.** To experience something with gratification or delight: *feasted on the view.* ***—idiom.*** **feast (one's) eyes on.** To be delighted or gratified by the sight of: *We feasted our eyes on the paintings.* [Middle English *feste,* from Old French, from Vulgar Latin **fēsta,* from Latin, pl. of *fēstum,* from *fēstus,* festive. See **dhēs-** in Appendix.] **—feastʹer** *n.*

Feast of Dedication (fēst) *n.* *Judaism.* See **Hanukkah.**

Feast of Lights *n.* *Judaism.* See **Hanukkah.**

feat¹ (fēt) *n.* **1.** A notable act or deed, especially an act of courage; an exploit. **2.** An act of skill, endurance, imagination, or strength; an achievement. **3.** *Obsolete.* A specialized skill; a knack. [Middle English *fet,* from Anglo-Norman, from Latin *factum,* from neuter past participle of *facere,* to make, do. See **dhē-** in Appendix.]

SYNONYMS: *feat, achievement, exploit, masterstroke.* The central meaning shared by these nouns is "an extraordinary deed or action": *feats of bravery; achievements of diplomacy; military exploits; a masterstroke of entrepreneurship.*

feat² (fēt) *adj.* **feat·er, feat·est.** *Archaic.* **1.** Adroit; dexterous. **2.** Neat; trim. [Middle English *fet,* suitable, from Old French *fait,* from Latin *factus,* done, made. See FEATURE.] **—featʹly** *adv.*

feath·er (fĕ*th*ʹər) *n.* **1.** One of the light, flat growths forming the plumage of birds, consisting of numerous slender, closely arranged parallel barbs forming a vane on either side of a horny, tapering, partly hollow shaft. **2. feathers.** Plumage. **3. feathers.** Clothing; attire. **4.** A feathery tuft or fringe of hair, as on the legs or tail of some dogs. **5.** Character, kind, or nature: *Birds of a feather flock together.* **6.** Something small, trivial, or inconsequential. **7.a.** A strip, wedge, or flange used as a strengthening part. **b.** A wedge or key that fits into a groove to make a joint. **8.** The vane of an arrow. **9.** A feather-shaped flaw, as in a precious stone. **10.** The wake made by a submarine's periscope. **11.** The act of feathering the blade of an oar in rowing. **—feather** *v.* **-ered, -er·ing, -ers.** —*tr.* **1.** To cover, dress, or decorate with or as if with feathers. **2.** To fit (an arrow) with a feather. **3.a.** To thin, reduce, or fringe the edge of by cutting, shaving, or wearing away. **b.** To shorten and taper (hair) by cutting and thinning. **4.** To connect with a tongue-and-groove joint. **5.** To turn (an oar blade) almost horizontal as it is carried back after each stroke. **6.a.** To alter the pitch of (a propeller) so that the chords of the blades are parallel with the line of flight. **b.** To alter the pitch of (the rotor of a helicoptor) while in forward flight. **7.** To turn off (an aircraft engine) while in flight. —*intr.* **1.** To grow feathers or

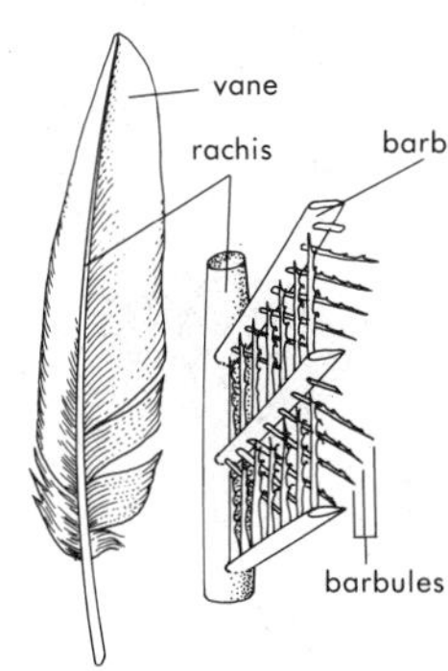

feather

ă pat	oi boy
ā pay	ou out
âr care	ŏŏ took
ä father	ōō boot
ĕ pet	ŭ cut
ē be	ûr urge
ĭ pit	th thin
ī pie	*th* this
îr pier	hw which
ŏ pot	zh vision
ō toe	ə about, item
ô paw	♦ regionalism

Stress marks: **ʹ** (primary); ʹ (secondary), as in **dictionary** (dĭkʹshə-nĕrʹē)

feather duster

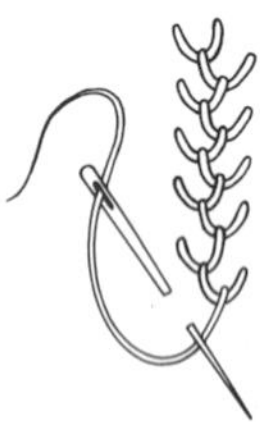

featherstitch

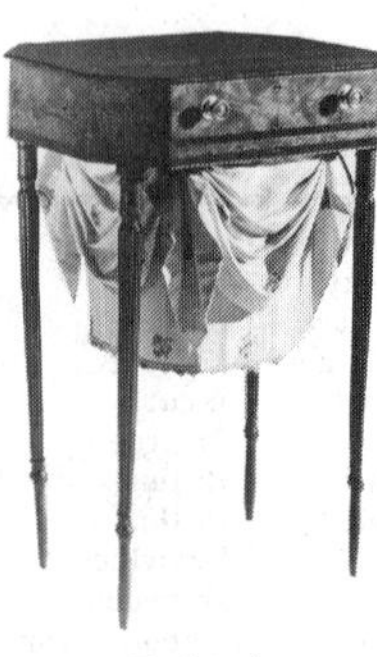

Federal
Early 19th-century sewing table attributed to Nehemiah Adams (fl. 1790-1840)

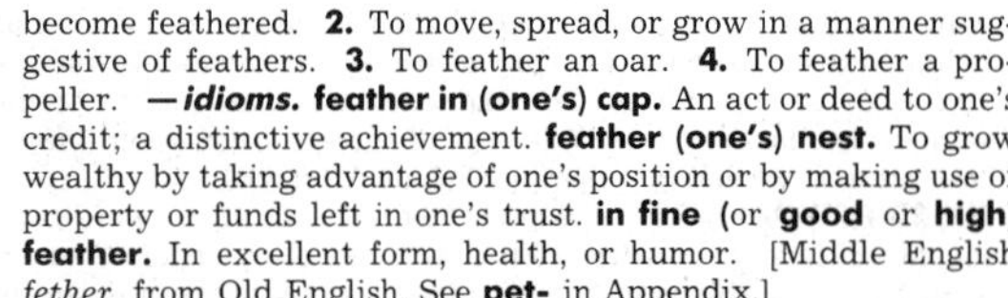

become feathered. **2.** To move, spread, or grow in a manner suggestive of feathers. **3.** To feather an oar. **4.** To feather a propeller. **—*idioms.* feather in (one's) cap.** An act or deed to one's credit; a distinctive achievement. **feather (one's) nest.** To grow wealthy by taking advantage of one's position or by making use of property or funds left in one's trust. **in fine** (or **good** or **high**) **feather.** In excellent form, health, or humor. [Middle English *fether,* from Old English. See **pet-** in Appendix.]

feath•er•bed (fĕth′ər-bĕd′) *intr.v.* **-bed•ded, -bed•ding, -beds.** To engage in or promote featherbedding. **—featherbed** *adj.* Relating to or promoting featherbedding: *featherbed rules.*

feather bed *n.* **1.** A mattress stuffed with feathers. **2.** A bed having a feather mattress.

feath•er•bed•ding (fĕth′ər-bĕd′ĭng) *n.* The practice of requiring an employer to hire more workers than are needed or to limit their production in keeping with a safety regulation or union rule.

feath•er•bone (fĕth′ər-bōn′) *n.* A lightweight corset bone originally made from the quills of domestic fowl as a substitute for whalebone.

feath•er•brain (fĕth′ər-brān′) *n.* A silly, flighty, or empty-headed person. **—feath′er•brained′** *adj.*

feather duster *n.* A brush made of a bundle of long feathers fastened to the end of a stick, used for dusting delicate objects.

feath•ered (fĕth′ərd) *adj.* **1.** Covered, provided, or adorned with feathers. **2.** Moving swiftly: *feathered feet.* **3.** Having the chords of propeller blades parallel to the line of flight.

feath•er•edge (fĕth′ər-ĕj′) *n.* **1.** A thin fragile edge, especially a tapering edge of a board. **2.** See **deckle edge.**

feather grass *n.* Any of various grasses of the genus *Stipa,* having clusters of featherlike spikelets. Also called *needle grass, spear grass.*

feath•er•head (fĕth′ər-hĕd′) *n.* A featherbrain. **—feath′er•head′ed** *adj.*

feath•er•ing (fĕth′ər-ĭng) *n.* **1.** Plumage. **2.** The feathers fitted to an arrow. **3.** A fringe of hair on an animal's coat, especially on the leg of a dog.

feather palm *n.* A palm having pinnately compound, featherlike leaves.

feather rot *n.* A disease of tree trunks caused by the fungus *Poria subacida* that causes the trunk to become spongy or stringy.

feather star *n.* Any of numerous crinoids of the genus *Antedon* and related genera, having a free-swimming, stalkless adult stage with branched, feathery arms.

feath•er•stitch (fĕth′ər-stĭch′) *n.* An embroidery stitch that produces a decorative zigzag line. **—feath′er•stitch′** *v.*

feath•er•weight (fĕth′ər-wāt′) *n.* **1.** *Sports.* **a.** A professional boxer weighing more than 118 and not more than 126 pounds (approximately 53.5–57 kilograms), heavier than a bantamweight and lighter than a lightweight. **b.** A contestant in various other sports in a similar weight class. **2.** A person or thing of little weight or size. **3.** An insignificant person: *a political featherweight.* **—featherweight** *adj.* **1.** Of or relating to featherweights. **2.** Unimportant; trivial.

feath•er•y (fĕth′ə-rē) *adj.* **1.** Covered with or consisting of feathers. **2.** Resembling or suggestive of a feather, as in form or lightness. **—feath′er•i•ness** *n.*

fea•ture (fē′chər) *n.* **1.a.** Any of the distinct parts of the face, as the eyes, nose, or mouth. **b.** Often **features.** The overall appearance of the face or its parts. **2.** A prominent or distinctive aspect, quality, or characteristic: *a feature of one's personality; a feature of the landscape.* **3.a.** The main film presentation at a theater. **b.** A special attraction at an entertainment. **4.** A prominent or special article, story, or department in a newspaper or periodical. **5.** An item advertised or offered as particularly attractive or as an inducement: *a washing machine with many features.* **6.** *Archaic.* **a.** Outward appearance; form or shape. **b.** Physical beauty. **—feature** *tr.v.* **-tured, -tur•ing, -tures. 1.** To give special attention to; display, publicize, or make prominent. **2.** To have or include as a prominent part or characteristic: *The play featured two well-known actors.* **3.** To depict or outline the features of. **4.** *Informal.* To picture mentally; imagine: *Can you feature her in that hat?* [Middle English *feture,* from Old French *faiture,* from Latin *factūra,* a working or making, from *factus,* past participle of *facere,* to make, do. See **dhē-** in Appendix.]

fea•tured (fē′chərd) *adj.* **1.** Given special prominence, attention, or publicity: *a featured item at a sale; a featured actor.* **2.** Having a specified kind of facial features. Often used in combination: *sharp-featured; plain-featured.*

fea•ture•less (fē′chər-lĭs) *adj.* Lacking distinguishing characteristics or features: *the featureless landscape of the steppe.*

Feb. also **Feb** *abbr.* February.

fe•bric•i•ty (fĭ-brĭs′ĭ-tē) *n.* The condition of having a fever. [Medieval Latin *febrīcitās,* from Latin *febrīcitāre,* to have a fever, from *febris,* fever.]

feb•ri•fa•cient (fĕb′rə-fā′shənt) *n.* A substance that produces fever. **—febrifacient** *adj.* Causing or producing fever. [Latin *febris,* fever + –FACIENT.]

fe•brif•ic (fĭ-brĭf′ĭk) *adj.* **1.** Producing fever. **2.** Having a fever; feverish. [Latin *febris,* fever + –FIC.]

feb•ri•fuge (fĕb′rə-fyo͞oj′) *n.* An agent or a medication that reduces a fever; an antipyretic. **—febrifuge** *adj.* Acting to reduce fever. [Latin *febris,* fever + –FUGE.]

feb•rile (fĕb′rəl, fē′brəl) *adj.* Of, relating to, or characterized by fever; feverish. [Late Latin *febrīlis,* from Latin *febris,* fever.]

Feb•ru•ar•y (fĕb′ro͞o-ĕr′ē, fĕb′yo͞o-) *n., pl.* **-ies.** *Abbr.* **Feb., Feb** The second month of the year in the Gregorian calendar. See table at **calendar.** [Middle English *Februarie,* from *Februārius (mēnsis),* (month) of purification, from *februa,* expiatory offerings, possibly of Sabine origin.]

fec. *abbr. Latin.* Fecit (he or she made or did it).

fe•cal (fē′kəl) *adj.* Of, relating to, or composed of feces.

fe•ces (fē′sēz) *pl.n.* Waste matter eliminated from the bowels; excrement. [Middle English, from Latin *faecēs,* pl. of *faex,* dregs.]

feck•less (fĕk′lĭs) *adj.* **1.** Lacking purpose or vitality; feeble or ineffective. **2.** Careless and irresponsible. [Scots *feck,* effect (alteration of EFFECT) + –LESS.] **—feck′less•ly** *adv.* **—feck′less•ness** *n.*

fec•u•lent (fĕk′yə-lənt) *adj.* Full of foul or impure matter; fecal. [Middle English, from Latin *faeculentus,* heavy with sediment, from *faex, faec-,* dregs.] **—fec′u•lence** *n.*

fe•cund (fē′kənd, fĕk′ənd) *adj.* **1.** Capable of producing offspring or vegetation; fruitful. **2.** Marked by intellectual productivity. See Synonyms at **fertile.** [Middle English, from Old French *fecond,* from Latin *fēcundus.* See **dhē(i)-** in Appendix.]

fe•cun•date (fē′kən-dāt′, fĕk′ən-) *tr.v.* **-dat•ed, -dat•ing, -dates. 1.** To make fecund or fruitful. **2.** To impregnate; fertilize. [Latin *fēcundāre, fēcundāt-,* from *fēcundus,* fruitful. See FECUND.] **—fe′cun•da′tion** *n.*

fe•cun•di•ty (fĭ-kŭn′dĭ-tē) *n.* **1.** The quality or power of producing abundantly; fertility. **2.** The capacity for producing offspring, especially in abundance; productiveness. **3.** Productive or creative power: *fecundity of the mind.*

fed (fĕd) *v.* Past tense and past participle of **feed.**

Fed (fĕd) *n. Informal.* **1.a.** The Federal Reserve System. **b.** The Federal Reserve Board. **2.** Often **fed.** A federal agent or official.

fed. *abbr.* **1.** Federal. **2.** Federated. **3.** Federation.

fe•da•yee (fĕ-dä′yē′, -dä′ē′, -dă′-) *n., pl.* **-yeen** (-yēn′, -ēn′). A commando or guerrilla, especially an Arab commando operating in the Middle East. [Arabic *fedā'yūn,* commandos, from *fidā'iy,* one who sacrifices himself for his country, from *fidā',* sacrifice, ransom.]

fed•er•a•cy (fĕd′ər-ə-sē) *n., pl.* **-cies.** *Archaic.* An alliance; a confederacy. [Short for CONFEDERACY.]

fed•er•al (fĕd′ər-əl, fĕd′rəl) *adj. Abbr.* **fed. 1.** Of, relating to, or being a form of government in which a union of states recognizes the sovereignty of a central authority while retaining certain residual powers of government. **2.** Of or constituting a form of government in which sovereign power is divided between a central authority and a number of constituent political units. **3.** Of or relating to the central government of a federation as distinct from the governments of its member units. **4.** Favorable to or advocating federation: *The senator's federal leanings were well known.* **5.** Relating to or formed by a treaty or compact between constituent political units. **6. Federal. a.** Of, relating to, or supporting Federalism or the Federalist Party. **b.** Of, relating to, or loyal to the Union cause during the American Civil War. **7.** Often **Federal.** Of, relating to, or being the central government of the United States. **8. Federal.** Relating to or characteristic of a style of architecture, furniture, and decoration produced in the United States especially in the late 18th and early 19th centuries and characterized by adaptations of classical forms combined with typically American motifs. **—federal** *n.* **1. Federal. a.** A supporter of the Union during the American Civil War, especially a Union soldier. **b.** A Federalist. **2.** Often **Federal.** A federal agent or official. [From Latin *foedus, foeder-,* league, treaty. See **bheidh-** in Appendix.] **—fed′er•al•ly** *adv.*

federal case *n.* **1.** *Law.* An action or a cause that falls under the jurisdiction of a federal court. **2.** *Informal.* A major issue that has evolved from a minor problem or complaint: *made a federal case out of our tardiness.*

federal district also **Federal District** *n.* An area, such as the District of Columbia, that is reserved as the site of the national capital of a federation.

fed•er•al•ism (fĕd′ər-ə-lĭz′əm, fĕd′rə-) *n.* **1.a.** A system of government in which power is divided between a central authority and constituent political units. **b.** Advocacy of such a system of government. **2. Federalism.** The doctrine of the Federalist Party.

fed•er•al•ist (fĕd′ər-ə-lĭst, fĕd′rə-) *n.* **1.** An advocate of federalism. **2. Federalist.** A member or supporter of the Federalist Party. **—federalist** *adj.* **1.** Of or relating to federalism or its advocates. **2. Federalist.** Of or relating to Federalism or Federalists.

Federalist Party *n.* A U.S. political party founded in 1787 to advocate the establishment of a strong federal government and the adoption by the states of the Constitution. The party gained prominence in the 1790's under the leadership of Alexander Hamilton.

fed•er•al•ize (fĕd′ər-ə-līz′, fĕd′rə-) *tr.v.* **-ized, -iz•ing, -iz•es. 1.** To unite in a federal union. **2.** To subject to the authority of a federal government; put under federal control. **—fed′er•al•i•za′tion** (-lĭ-zā′shən) *n.*

Federal Reserve System *n.* A U.S. banking system that consists of 12 federal reserve banks, with each one serving member banks in its own district. This system, supervised by the Federal Reserve Board, has broad regulatory powers over the money supply and the credit structure.

fed·er·ate (fĕd′ə-rāt′) *v.* **-at·ed, -at·ing, -ates.** —*tr.* To cause to join into a league, federal union, or similar association. —*intr.* To become united into a federal union. —**federate** (fĕd′ər-ĭt, fĕd′rĭt) *adj.* United in a federation. [Latin *foederāre, foederāt-,* to ratify an agreement, from *foedus, foeder-,* league, treaty. See **bheidh-** in Appendix.]

fed·er·a·tion (fĕd′ə-rā′shən) *n. Abbr.* **fed. 1.** The act of federating, especially a joining together of states into a league or federal union. **2.** A league or association formed by federating, especially a government or political body established through federal union.

fed·er·a·tive (fĕd′ə-rā′tĭv, fĕd′ər-ə-, fĕd′rə-) *adj.* Forming, belonging to, or of the nature of a federation; federal.

fe·do·ra (fĭ-dôr′ə, -dōr′ə) *n.* A soft felt hat with a fairly low crown creased lengthwise and a brim that can be turned up or down. [After *Fédora,* a play by Victorien Sardou.]

fed up *adj.* Unable or unwilling to put up with something any longer: *She was fed up with their complaints. I resigned from the company because I was fed up.*

fee (fē) *n.* **1.** A fixed sum charged, as by an institution or by law, for a privilege: *a license fee; tuition fees.* **2.** A charge for professional services: *a surgeon's fee.* **3.** A tip; a gratuity. **4.** *Law.* An inherited or heritable estate in land. **5.a.** In feudal law, an estate in land granted by a lord to his vassal on condition of homage and service. Also called *feud, fief.* **b.** The land so held. —**fee** *tr.v.* **feed, fee·ing, fees. 1.** To give a tip to. **2.** *Scots.* To hire. —***idiom.*** **in fee.** *Law.* In absolute and legal possession. [Middle English *fe,* from Anglo-Norman *fee,* fief, from Old French *fie, fief,* of Germanic origin. See **peku-** in Appendix.]

fee·ble (fē′bəl) *adj.* **-bler, -blest. 1.a.** Lacking strength; weak. **b.** Indicating weakness. **2.** Lacking vigor, force, or effectiveness; inadequate. See Synonyms at **weak.** [Middle English *feble,* from Old French, from Latin *flēbilis,* lamentable, from *flēre,* to weep.] —**fee′ble·ness** *n.* —**fee′bly** *adv.*

fee·ble-mind·ed (fē′bəl-mīn′dĭd) *adj.* **1.** *Offensive.* Deficient in intelligence. **2.** Exhibiting a marked lack of intelligent consideration and forethought: *feeble-minded excuses.* **3.** *Obsolete.* Irresolute and weak-willed. —**fee′ble-mind′ed·ly** *adv.* —**fee′ble-mind′ed·ness** *n.*

feed (fēd) *v.* **fed** (fĕd), **feed·ing, feeds.** —*tr.* **1.a.** To give food to; supply with nourishment: *feed the children.* **b.** To provide as food or nourishment: *fed fish to the cat.* **2.a.** To serve as food for: *The turkey is large enough to feed a dozen.* **b.** To produce food for: *The valley feeds an entire county.* **3.a.** To provide for consumption, utilization, or operation: *feed logs to a fire; feed data into a computer.* **b.** To supply with something essential for growth, maintenance, or operation: *Melting snow feeds the reservoirs.* **c.** To distribute (a local radio or television broadcast) to a larger audience or group of receivers by way of a network or satellite. **4.a.** To minister to; gratify: *fed their appetite for the morbid.* **b.** To support or promote; encourage: *His unexplained absences fed our suspicions.* **5.** To supply as a cue: *feed lines to an actor.* **6.** *Sports.* To pass a ball or puck to (a teammate), especially in order to score. —*intr.* **1.** To eat: *pigs feeding at a trough.* **2.** To be nourished or supported: *an ego that feeds on flattery.* **3.a.** To move steadily, as into a machine for processing. **b.** To be channeled; flow: *This road feeds into the freeway.* —**feed** *n.* **1.a.** Food for animals or birds. **b.** The amount of such food given at one time. **2.** *Informal.* A meal, especially a large one. **3.** The act of eating. **4.a.** Material or an amount of material supplied, as to a machine or furnace. **b.** The act of supplying such material. **5.a.** An apparatus that supplies material to a machine. **b.** The aperture through which such material enters a machine. **6.** Distribution of a locally broadcast radio or television program by way of a network or satellite to a larger audience or group of receivers. —***idiom.*** **off (one's) feed.** Suffering a lack of appetite; sick: *The dog is off its feed this week.* [Middle English *feden,* from Old English *fēdan.* See **pā-** in Appendix.]

feed·back (fēd′băk′) *n.* **1.a.** The return of a portion of the output of a process or system to the input, especially when used to maintain performance or to control a system or process. **b.** The portion of the output so returned. **2.** The return of information about the result of a process or activity; an evaluative response: *asked the students for feedback on the new curriculum.*

feedback inhibition *n.* A cellular control mechanism in which an enzyme that catalyzes the production of a particular substance in the cell is inhibited when that substance has accumulated to a certain level, thereby balancing the amount provided with the amount needed.

feed·bag (fēd′băg′) *n.* A bag that fits over a horse's muzzle and holds feed. Also called *nosebag.*

feed·er (fē′dər) *n.* **1.** One that supplies food: *a nation that is the feeder of millions in developing countries.* **2.** One that is fed, especially an animal that is being fattened for market. **3.** A worker or device that feeds materials into a machine for further processing. **4.** Something that contributes to the operation, maintenance, or supply of something else, especially: **a.** A tributary stream. **b.** A branch line of a transport system, as of an airline or a railroad. **5.** Any of the medium-voltage lines used to distribute electric power from a substation to consumers or to smaller substations. **6.** A transmission line between an antenna and a transmitter.

feed·hole (fēd′hōl′) *n. Computer Science.* One of a noninformational series of holes in a paper tape that engages a driving sprocket to carry the tape through a reading or punching device.

feed·lot (fēd′lŏt′) *n.* A plot of ground on which livestock are fattened for market.

feed·stock (fēd′stŏk′) *n.* Raw material required for an industrial process.

feed·stuff (fēd′stŭf′) *n.* Food for livestock; fodder.

feed·through (fēd′thrōō′) *n.* A conductor connecting two circuits on opposite sides of a printed circuit board.

feel (fēl) *v.* **felt** (fĕlt), **feel·ing, feels.** —*tr.* **1.a.** To perceive through the sense of touch: *feel the velvety smoothness of a peach.* **b.** To perceive as a physical sensation: *feel a sharp pain; feel the cold.* **2.a.** To touch. **b.** To examine by touching. See Synonyms at **touch. 3.** To test or explore with caution: *feel one's way in a new job.* **4.a.** To undergo the experience of: *felt my interest rising; felt great joy.* **b.** To be aware of; sense: *felt the anger of the crowd.* **c.** To be emotionally affected by: *She still feels the loss of her dog.* **5.a.** To be persuaded of (something) on the basis of intuition, emotion, or other indefinite grounds: *I feel that what the informant says may well be true.* **b.** To believe; think: *She felt his answer to be evasive.* —*intr.* **1.** To experience sensations of touch. **2.a.** To produce a particular sensation, especially through the sense of touch: *The sheets felt smooth.* **b.** To produce a particular impression; appear to be; seem: *It feels good to be home.* See Usage Note at **well**[2]. **3.** To be conscious of a specified kind or quality of physical, mental, or emotional state: *felt warm and content; feels strongly about the election.* **4.** To seek or explore something by the sense of touch: *felt for the light switch in the dark.* **5.** To have compassion or sympathy: *I feel for him in his troubles.* —**feel** *n.* **1.** Perception by or as if by touch; sensation: *a feel of autumn in the air.* **2.** The sense of touch: *a surface that is rough to the feel.* **3.** The nature or quality of something as perceived by or as if by the sense of touch: *"power steering that seems overassisted, eliminating road feel"* (Mark Ginsburg). **4.** Overall impression or effect; atmosphere: *"gives such disparate pictures . . . a crazily convincing documentary feel"* (Stephen King). **5.** Intuitive awareness or natural ability: *has a feel for decorating.* —***phrasal verbs.*** **feel out.** To try cautiously or indirectly to ascertain the viewpoint or nature of. **feel up.** *Vulgar Slang.* To touch or fondle (someone) sexually. —***idioms.*** **feel in (one's) bones.** To have an intuition of. **feel like.** *Informal.* To have an inclination or desire for: *felt like going for a walk.* **feel like (oneself).** To sense oneself as being in one's normal state of health or spirits: *I just don't feel like myself today.* [Middle English *felen,* from Old English *fēlan.* See **pōl-** in Appendix.]

feel·er (fē′lər) *n.* **1.** Something, such as a hint or question, designed to elicit the attitudes or intentions of others. **2.** *Zoology.* A sensory or tactile organ, such as an antenna, a tentacle, or a barbel.

feel·ing (fē′lĭng) *n.* **1.a.** The sensation involving perception by touch. **b.** A sensation experienced through touch. **c.** A physical sensation: *a feeling of warmth.* **2.** An affective state of consciousness, such as that resulting from emotions, sentiments, or desires: *experienced a feeling of excitement.* **3.** An awareness or impression: *He had the feeling that he was being followed.* **4.a.** An emotional state or disposition; an emotion: *expressed deep feeling.* **b.** A tender emotion; a fondness. **5.a.** Capacity to experience the higher emotions; sensitivity; sensibility: *a man of feeling.* **b. feelings.** Susceptibility to emotional response; sensibilities: *The child's feelings are easily hurt.* **6.** Opinion based more on emotion than on reason; sentiment. **7.** A general impression conveyed by a person, place, or thing: *The stuffy air gave one the feeling of being in a tomb.* **8.a.** Appreciative regard or understanding: *a feeling for propriety.* **b.** Intuitive awareness or aptitude; a feel: *has a feeling for language.* —**feeling** *adj.* **1.** Having the ability to react or feel emotionally; sentient; sensitive. **2.** Easily moved emotionally; sympathetic: *a feeling heart.* **3.** Expressive of sensibility or emotion: *a feeling glance.* —**feel′ing·ly** *adv.*

SYNONYMS: *feeling, emotion, passion, sentiment.* These nouns refer to complex and usually strong subjective human response, such as love or hate. Although *feeling* and *emotion* are sometimes interchangeable, *feeling* is the more general and neutral: *feelings of hope and joy; a feeling of inferiority; religious feelings. "I have said that poetry is the spontaneous overflow of powerful feelings: it takes its origin from emotion recollected in tranquillity"* (William Wordsworth). *Emotion* is often considered to be the stronger of the two terms and to imply the presence of excitement or agitation: *He has difficulty controlling his emotions. "Poetry is not a turning loose of emotion, but an escape from emotion"* (T.S. Eliot). *Passion* is intense, compelling emotion: *"They seemed like ungoverned children inflamed with the fiercest passions of men"* (Francis Parkman). *Sentiment* often applies to a thought or opinion arising from or influenced by emotion: *What are your sentiments about the government's policies?* The word can also refer to the delicate, sensitive, or higher or more refined feelings: *"The mystic reverence, the religious allegiance, which are essential to a true monarchy, are imaginative sentiments that no legislature can manufacture in any people"* (Walter Bagehot). See also Synonyms at **opinion.**

fee simple *n., pl.* **fees simple.** *Law.* **1.** An estate in land of which the inheritor has unqualified ownership and power of disposition. **2.** Private ownership of real estate in which the owner has the right to control, use, and transfer the property at will.

fee splitting *n.* The practice of sharing fees with professional

fedora
Worn by Humphrey Bogart

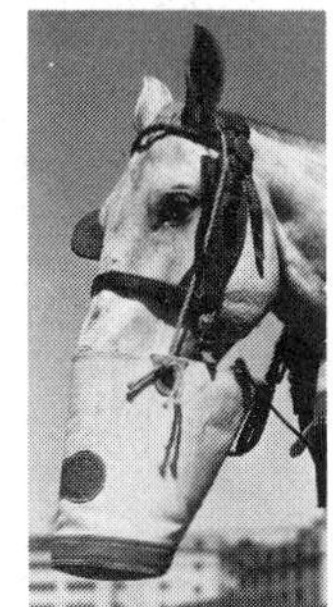

feedbag

ă **pat**	oi **boy**
ā **pay**	ou **out**
âr **care**	ŏŏ **took**
ä **father**	ōō **boot**
ĕ **pet**	ŭ **cut**
ē **be**	ûr **urge**
ĭ **pit**	th **thin**
ī **pie**	*th* **this**
îr **pier**	hw **which**
ŏ **pot**	zh **vision**
ō **toe**	ə **about, item**
ô **paw**	♦ **regionalism**

Stress marks: ′ (primary); ′ (secondary), as in **dictionary** (dĭk′shə-nĕr′ē)

colleagues, such as physicians, for patient or client referrals.

feet (fēt) *n.* Plural of **foot.**

fee tail *n., pl.* **fees tail.** *Law.* An estate in land limited in inheritance to a particular class of heirs.

Feh·ling's solution (fā′lĭngz) *n.* An aqueous solution of copper sulfate, sodium hydroxide, and potassium sodium tartrate used to test for the presence of sugars and aldehydes in a substance, such as urine. [After Hermann von *Fehling* (1812–1885), German chemist.]

Feif·fer (fī′fər), **Jules.** Born 1929. American cartoonist who won a 1986 Pulitzer Prize for his sarcastic comic strip.

feign (fān) *v.* **feigned, feign·ing, feigns.** —*tr.* **1.a.** To give a false appearance of: *feign sleep.* **b.** To represent falsely; pretend to: *feign authorship of a novel.* See Synonyms at **pretend. 2.** To imitate so as to deceive: *feign another's voice.* **3.** To fabricate: *feigned an excuse.* **4.** *Archaic.* To invent or imagine. —*intr.* To pretend; dissemble. [Middle English *feinen,* from Old French *feindre,* from Latin *fingere,* to shape, form. See **dheigh-** in Appendix.]

feigned (fānd) *adj.* **1.** Not real; pretended: *a feigned modesty.* **2.** Made-up; fictitious.

fei·jo·a·da (fā′zho͞o-ä′dä, -jwä′də) *n.* A dish of black beans cooked with meat such as sausage, served with rice and traditionally garnished with cassava meal, collard greens or kale, onions, oranges, and a hot pepper sauce. [Portuguese, from *feijão,* bean, from Latin *phaseolus.* See FRIJOL.]

Fei·ning·er (fī′nĭng-ər), **Lyonel Charles Adrian.** 1871–1956. American-born artist who was influenced by cubism and the Bauhaus movement and developed a delicate geometric style with intersecting planes of translucent colors.

felucca
On the Nile River, Luxor, Egypt

feint (fānt) *n.* **1.** A feigned attack designed to draw defensive action away from an intended target. **2.** A deceptive action calculated to divert attention from one's real purpose. See Synonyms at **artifice.** —**feint** *v.* **feint·ed, feint·ing, feints.** —*intr.* To make a feint. —*tr.* **1.** To deceive with a feint. **2.** To make a deceptive show of. [French *feinte,* from Old French, from past participle of *feindre,* to feign. See FEIGN.]

Fei·sal (fī′səl). See **Faisal.**

♦**feist** (fīst) also **fice** (fīs) *n. Chiefly Southern U.S.* A small mongrel dog. [Variant of obsolete *fist,* short for *fisting dog,* from Middle English *fisten,* to break wind. See **pezd-** in Appendix.]

♦***REGIONAL NOTE:*** *Feist,* also *fice,* is one of several regional terms for a small mixed-breed dog or mongrel. Used throughout the Midland and Southern states, *feist* connotes a snappy, nervous, belligerent little dog—hence the derived adjective *feisty,* meaning "touchy, quarrelsome, or spirited," applicable to animals and to people.

♦**feist·y** (fī′stē) *adj.* **-i·er, -i·est. 1.** Touchy; quarrelsome. **2.** Full of spirit or pluck; frisky or spunky. See Regional Note at **feist.** [From FEIST.] —**feist′i·ness** *n.*

Fei·sul (fī′səl). See **Faisal.**

fe·la·fel (fə-lä′fəl) *n.* Variant of **falafel.**

feld·spar (fĕld′spär′, fĕl′-) also **fel·spar** (fĕl′-) *n.* Any of a group of abundant rock-forming minerals occurring principally in igneous, plutonic, and some metamorphic rocks, and consisting of silicates of aluminum with potassium, sodium, calcium, and, rarely, barium. About 60 percent of the earth's outer crust is composed of feldspar. [Partial translation of obsolete German *Feldspath* : *Feld,* field (from Middle High German *veld,* from Old High German *feld;* see **pelə-[2]** in Appendix) + *Spath,* spar.]

feld·spath·ic (fĕld-spăth′ĭk, fĕl-) *adj.* Of, relating to, or containing feldspar. [From obsolete German *Feldspath,* feldspar. See FELDSPAR.]

fe·li·cif·ic (fē′lĭ-sĭf′ĭk) *adj.* Producing or intended to produce happiness. [Latin *fēlix, fēlīc-,* fortunate; see **dhē(i)-** in Appendix + –FIC.]

fe·lic·i·tate (fĭ-lĭs′ĭ-tāt′) *tr.v.* **-tat·ed, -tat·ing, -tates. 1.** To offer congratulations to: *"I felicitate you on your memory, sir"* (John Fowles). **2.** *Archaic.* To make happy. —**felicitate** *adj. Obsolete.* Made happy. [Late Latin *fēlīcitāre, fēlīcitāt-,* to make happy, from *fēlīx, fēlīc-,* fortunate. See **dhē(i)-** in Appendix.] —**fe·lic′i·ta′tor** *n.*

fe·lic·i·ta·tion (fĭ-lĭs′ĭ-tā′shən) *n.* Congratulations. Often used in the plural.

fe·lic·i·tous (fĭ-lĭs′ĭ-təs) *adj.* **1.** Admirably suited; apt: *a felicitous comparison.* See Synonyms at **fit[1]. 2.** Exhibiting an agreeably appropriate manner or style: *a felicitous writer.* **3.** Marked by happiness or good fortune: *a felicitous life.* —**fe·lic′i·tous·ly** *adv.* —**fe·lic′i·tous·ness** *n.*

fe·lic·i·ty (fĭ-lĭs′ĭ-tē) *n., pl.* **-ties. 1.a.** Great happiness; bliss. **b.** An instance of great happiness. **2.** A cause or source of happiness. **3.a.** An appropriate and pleasing manner or style: *felicity of expression.* **b.** An instance of appropriate and pleasing manner or style. **4.** *Archaic.* Good fortune. [Middle English *felicite,* from Old French *felicite,* from Latin *fēlīcitās,* from *fēlīx, fēlīc-,* fortunate. See **dhē(i)-** in Appendix.]

fe·lid (fē′lĭd) *adj.* Feline. [From New Latin *Fēlidae,* family name, from *Fēlis,* type genus, from Latin *fēlēs,* cat.] —**fe′lid** *n.*

fe·line (fē′līn′) *adj.* **1.** Of or belonging to the family Felidae, which includes the lions, tigers, jaguars, and wild and domestic cats; felid. **2.** Suggestive of a cat, as in suppleness or stealthiness. —**feline** *n.* An animal of the family Felidae. [Latin *fēlīnus* or Late Latin *fēlīneus,* both from Latin *fēlēs,* cat.] —**fe′line′ly** *adv.* —**fe′line′ness, fe·lin′i·ty** (fĭ-lĭn′ĭ-tē) *n.*

feline distemper *n.* See **distemper[1]** (sense 1b).

fell[1] (fĕl) *tr.v.* **felled, fell·ing, fells. 1.a.** To cause to fall by striking; cut or knock down: *fell a tree; fell an opponent in boxing.* **b.** To kill: *was felled by an assassin's bullet.* **2.** To sew or finish (a seam) with the raw edges flattened, turned under, and stitched down. —**fell** *n.* **1.** The timber cut down in one season. **2.** A felled seam. [Middle English *fellen,* from Old English *fellan, fyllan.*] —**fell′a·ble** *adj.*

fell[2] (fĕl) *adj.* **1.** Of an inhumanly cruel nature; fierce: *fell hordes.* **2.** Capable of destroying; lethal: *a fell blow.* **3.** Dire; sinister: *by some fell chance.* **4.** *Scots.* Sharp and biting. —***idiom.* at** (or **in**) **one fell swoop.** All at once. [Middle English *fel,* from Old French, nominative of *felon.* See FELON[1].] —**fell′ness** *n.*

fell[3] (fĕl) *n.* **1.** The hide of an animal; a pelt. **2.** A thin membrane directly beneath the hide. [Middle English *fel,* from Old English *fell.* See **pel-[3]** in Appendix.]

fell[4] (fĕl) *n. Chiefly British.* **1.** An upland stretch of open country; a moor. **2.** A barren or stony hill. [Middle English *fel,* from Old Norse *fell, fjall,* mountain, hill.]

fell[5] (fĕl) *v.* Past tense of **fall.**

fel·la (fĕl′ə) *n. Informal.* A man or boy; a fellow.

fel·lah (fĕl′ə, fə-lä′) *n., pl.* **fel·la·hin** or **fel·la·heen** (fĕl′ə-hēn′, fə-lä-hēn′). A peasant or agricultural laborer in an Arab country, such as Syria or Egypt. [Arabic *fellāḥ,* dialectal variant of *fallāḥ,* from *falaḥa,* to cultivate, till.]

fel·late (fə-lāt′) *v.* **-lat·ed, -lat·ing, -lates.** —*tr.* To perform fellatio on. —*intr.* To engage in fellatio. [Latin *fellāre, fellāt-,* to suck. See FELLATIO.] —**fel·la′tion** (-lā′shən) *n.* —**fel·la′tor** *n.*

fel·la·ti·o (fə-lā′shē-ō′, -lä′tē-ō′, fĕ-) *n.* Oral stimulation of the penis. [New Latin, from Latin *fellātus,* past participle of *fellāre,* to suck. See **dhē(i)-** in Appendix.]

fell·er[1] (fĕl′ər) *n.* **1.** A lumberjack. **2.** One that fells seams.

fel·ler[2] (fĕl′ər) *n. Informal.* A man or boy; a fellow.

Fel·li·ni (fə-lē′nē, fĕl-), **Federico.** Born 1920. Italian filmmaker whose works include *La Dolce Vita* (1960).

fel·loe (fĕl′ō) *n.* Variant of **felly.**

fel·low (fĕl′ō) *n.* **1.a.** A man or boy. **b.** *Informal.* A boyfriend. **2.** A comrade or an associate. **3.a.** A person of equal rank, position, or background; a peer. **b.** One of a pair; a mate: *found the lost shoe and its fellow.* **4.** *Abbr.* **F, F.** A member of a learned society. **5.** *Abbr.* **F, F.** A graduate student appointed to a position granting financial aid and providing for further study. **6.** *Abbr.* **F, F.** *Chiefly British.* **a.** An incorporated senior member of certain colleges and universities. **b.** A member of the governing body of certain colleges and universities. **7.** *Obsolete.* A person of a lower social class. —**fellow** *adj.* Being of the same kind, group, occupation, society, or locality; having in common certain characteristics or interests: *fellow workers.* [Middle English *felau,* from Old English *fēolaga,* from Old Norse *fēlagi,* business partner, fellow, from *fēlag,* partnership : *fē,* property, money; see **peku-** in Appendix + *lag,* a laying down; see **legh-** in Appendix.]

WORD HISTORY: A jolly good fellow might or might not be the ideal business associate, but the ancestor of our word *fellow* definitely referred to a business partner. *Fellow,* borrowed into English from Old Norse, is related to the Old Icelandic word *fēlagi,* meaning "a partner or shareholder of any kind." Old Icelandic *fēlagi* is derived from *fēlag,* "partnership," a compound made up of *fē,* "livestock, property, money," and *lag,* "a laying in order" and "fellowship." The notion of putting one's property together lies behind the senses of *fēlagi* meaning "partner" and "consort." In Old Icelandic *fēlagi* also had the general sense "fellow, mate, comrade," which fellow has as well, indicating perhaps that most partnerships turned out all right for speakers of Old Icelandic.

fellow feeling *n.* **1.** Sympathetic awareness of others; rapport. **2.** Community of interest.

fellow man also **fel·low·man** (fĕl′ō-măn′) *n.* A kindred human being.

fellow servant *n. Law.* One of a group of employees working together under such circumstances that the employer, under common law, is not considered liable for injury to one worker resulting from the negligence of another.

fel·low·ship (fĕl′ō-shĭp′) *n.* **1.a.** The condition of sharing similar interests, ideals, or experiences, as by reason of profession, religion, or nationality. **b.** The companionship of individuals in a congenial atmosphere and on equal terms. **2.** A close association of friends or equals sharing similar interests. **3.** Friendship; comradeship. **4.a.** The financial grant made to a fellow in a college or university. **b.** The status of having been awarded such a grant. **c.** A foundation established for the awarding of such a grant.

fellow traveler *n.* One who sympathizes with or supports the tenets and program of an organized group, such as the Communist Party, without being a member.

fel·ly (fĕl′ē) also **fel·loe** (fĕl′ō) *n., pl.* **-lies** also **-loes.** The rim or a section of the rim of a wheel supported by spokes. [Middle English *felie, felwe,* from Old English *felg.*]

fel·on[1] (fĕl′ən) *n.* **1.** *Law.* One who has committed a felony. **2.** *Archaic.* An evil person. —**felon** *adj. Archaic.* Evil; cruel.

ă pat	oi boy
ā pay	ou out
âr care	o͝o took
ä father	o͞o boot
ĕ pet	ŭ cut
ē be	ûr urge
ĭ pit	th thin
ī pie	*th* this
îr pier	hw which
ŏ pot	zh vision
ō toe	ə about, item
ô paw	♦ regionalism

Stress marks: ′ (primary); ′ (secondary), as in **dictionary** (dĭk′shə-nĕr′ē)

[Middle English *feloun,* from Old French *felon,* wicked, a wicked person, from Medieval Latin *fellō, fellōn-,* possibly of Germanic origin.]

fel·on² (fĕl′ən) *n.* A painful, purulent infection at the end of a finger or toe in the area surrounding the nail. Also called *whitlow.* [Middle English *feloun,* probably from Latin *fel,* gall, bile. See **ghel-²** in Appendix.]

fe·lo·ni·ous (fə-lō′nē-əs) *adj.* **1.** *Law.* Having the nature of, relating to, or concerning a felony: *felonious intent.* **2.** *Archaic.* Evil; wicked. **—fe·lo′ni·ous·ly** *adv.* **—fe·lo′ni·ous·ness** *n.*

fel·o·ny (fĕl′ə-nē) *n., pl.* **-nies.** *Law.* **1.** One of several grave crimes, such as murder, rape, or burglary, punishable by a more stringent sentence than that given for a misdemeanor. **2.** Any of several crimes in early English law punishable by forfeiture of land or goods and by possible loss of life or a bodily part.

fel·sic (fĕl′sĭk) *n.* Relating to or containing a group of light-colored silicate minerals that occur in igneous rocks. [FEL(DSPAR) + S(ILICA) + -IC.]

fel·site (fĕl′sīt′) *n.* A fine-grained, light-colored igneous rock, composed chiefly of feldspar and quartz. [FELS(PAR) + -ITE¹.] **—fel·sit′ic** (-sĭt′ĭk) *adj.*

fel·spar (fĕl′spär′) *n.* Variant of **feldspar.**

felt¹ (fĕlt) *n.* **1.a.** A fabric of matted, compressed animal fibers, such as wool or fur, sometimes mixed with vegetable or synthetic fibers. **b.** A material resembling this fabric. **2.** Something made of this fabric. **—felt** *adj.* Made of, relating to, or resembling felt. **—felt** *v.* **felt·ed, felt·ing, felts.** *—tr.* **1.** To make into felt. **2.** To cover with felt. **3.** To press or mat (something) together. *—intr.* To become like felt; mat together. [Middle English, from Old English. See **pel-⁵** in Appendix.] **—felt′y** *adj.*

felt² (fĕlt) *v.* Past tense and past participle of **feel.**

felt·ing (fĕl′tĭng) *n.* **1.** The practice or process of making felt. **2.** The materials from which felt is made. **3.** Felted fabric.

fe·luc·ca (fə-lo͞o′kə, -lŭk′ə) *n. Nautical.* A narrow, swift, lateen-rigged sailing vessel, such as that used on the Nile or in the Mediterranean Sea. [Italian *feluca,* from Arabic *fulk,* ship.]

fel·wort (fĕl′wûrt′, -wôrt′) *n.* An annual gentian *(Gentianella amarella)* having small, lilac to creamy white flowers with fringed corollas. [Middle English **feldwort,* from Old English *feldwyrt* : *feld,* field; see FIELD + *wyrt,* wort; see WORT¹.]

fem. *abbr.* Female; feminine.

fe·male (fē′māl′) *adj. Abbr.* **fem., f., F** **1.a.** Of, relating to, or denoting the sex that produces ova or bears young. **b.** Characteristic of or appropriate to this sex; feminine. See Synonyms at **feminine. c.** Consisting of members of this sex. **2.** *Botany.* **a.** Relating to or designating an organ, such as a pistil or an ovary, that functions in producing seeds after fertilization. **b.** Bearing pistils but not stamens; pistillate: *female flowers.* **3.** Having a recessed part, such as a slot or receptacle, designed to receive a complementary male part: *the female section of an electrical outlet.* **—female** *n. Abbr.* **fem., f., F** **1.** A member of the sex that produces ova or bears young. **2.** A woman or girl. **3.** *Botany.* A plant having only pistillate flowers. [Middle English, alteration (influenced by *male,* male; see MALE) of *femelle,* from Old French, from Latin *fēmella,* diminutive of *fēmina,* woman. See **dhē(i)-** in Appendix.] **—fe′male′ness** *n.*

feme (fĕm) *n.* **1.** *Law.* A wife. **2.** *Obsolete.* A woman. [Anglo-Norman, from Latin *fēmina.* See FEMALE.]

feme cov·ert (kŭv′ərt) *n. Law.* A married woman. [Anglo-Norman : *feme,* woman + Old French *covert,* covered.]

feme sole *n. Law.* A single woman, whether divorced, widowed, or never married. [Anglo-Norman *feme soule* : *feme,* woman + *soule,* single.]

fem·i·nine (fĕm′ə-nĭn) *adj.* **1.** Of or relating to women or girls; female. **2.** Characterized by or possessing qualities generally attributed to a woman. **3.** Effeminate; womanish. **4.** *Abbr.* **fem., f., F.** *Grammar.* Designating or belonging to the gender of words or grammatical forms that refer chiefly to females or to things classified as female. **—feminine** *n. Abbr.* **fem., f., F.** *Grammar.* **1.** The feminine gender. **2.** A word or form belonging to the feminine gender. [Middle English, from Old French, from Latin *fēminīnus,* from *fēmina,* woman. See **dhē(i)-** in Appendix.] **—fem′i·nine·ly** *adv.* **—fem′i·nine·ness** *n.*

SYNONYMS: *feminine, female, womanly, womanish, effeminate, ladylike.* These adjectives mean "of, relating to, characteristic of, or appropriate to women." *Feminine* as the opposite of *masculine* often refers to what is considered characteristic of women: *feminine intuition. Female,* like *male,* categorizes by gender or sex; the term is not limited in application to human beings: *the female population; a female kitten; a female plant. Womanly* describes qualities regarded as becoming to a woman: *womanly virtue; womanly sympathy. Womanish* applies to qualities associated with women and traditionally considered undesirable in men: *womanish tears. Effeminate* is largely restricted in reference to men and implies lack of manliness or strength: *an effeminate walk. Ladylike* is applicable to what befits women of good breeding: *ladylike manners.*

feminine ending *n.* **1.** An extra unstressed syllable at the end of a line of verse. **2.** *Grammar.* A final syllable or termination that marks or forms words in the feminine gender.

feminine rhyme *n.* A rhyme in which the final syllable is unstressed, as in *feather/heather.*

fem·i·nin·i·ty (fĕm′ə-nĭn′ĭ-tē) *n., pl.* **-ties. 1.** The quality or condition of being feminine. **2.** A characteristic or trait traditionally held to be female. **3.** Women considered as a group. **4.** Effeminacy.

fem·i·nism (fĕm′ə-nĭz′əm) *n.* **1.** Belief in the social, political, and economic equality of the sexes. **2.** The movement organized around this belief.

fem·i·nist (fĕm′ə-nĭst) *n.* A person whose beliefs and behavior are based on feminism. **—feminist** *adj.* Of or relating to feminism. **—fem′i·nis′tic** *adj.*

USAGE NOTE: The term *feminist* may be applied to a person of either sex, according to 86 percent of the Usage Panel.

fem·i·nize (fĕm′ə-nīz′) *tr.v.* **-nized, -niz·ing, -niz·es. 1.** To give a feminine appearance or character to. **2.** To cause (a male) to assume feminine characteristics. **—fem′i·ni·za′tion** (-nĭ-zā′shən) *n.*

femme (fĕm) *n. Informal.* A woman or girl. [French, from Old French, from Latin *fēmina.* See FEMININE.]

femme fa·tale (fĕm′ fə-tăl′, -täl′, făm′) *n., pl.* **femmes fa·tales** (fĕm′ fə-tăl′, -tălz′, -täl′, -tälz′, făm′). **1.** A woman of great seductive charm who leads men into compromising or dangerous situations. **2.** An alluring and mysterious woman. [French : *femme,* woman + *fatale,* deadly.]

fem·o·ra (fĕm′ər-ə) *n.* A plural of **femur.**

fem·o·ral (fĕm′ər-əl) *adj.* Of, relating to, or located in the thigh or femur. [From Latin *femur, femor-,* thigh.]

femoral artery *n.* The main artery of the thigh, supplying blood to the groin and lower extremity.

femto– *pref.* One quadrillionth (10^{-15}): *femtovolt.* [From Danish and Norwegian *femten,* fifteen, from Old Norse *fimmtān.* See **penkʷe** in Appendix.]

fe·mur (fē′mər) *n., pl.* **fe·murs** or **fem·o·ra** (fĕm′ər-ə). **1.** A bone of the leg situated between the pelvis and knee in human beings. It is the largest and strongest bone in the body. Also called *thighbone.* **2.** A functionally similar bone in the leg or hind limb of a vertebrate animal. **3.** The thick, most muscular segment of the insect leg, situated between the trochanter and the tibia. [Latin, thigh.]

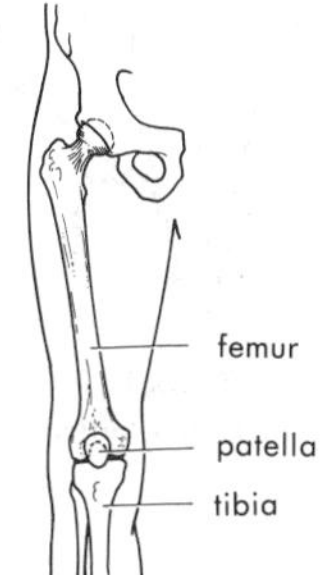

femur

fen (fĕn) *n.* Low, flat, swampy land; a bog or marsh. [Middle English, from Old English *fenn.*]

fence (fĕns) *n.* **1.** A structure serving as an enclosure, a barrier, or a boundary, usually made of posts or stakes joined together by boards, wire, or rails. **2.** The art or sport of fencing. **3.a.** One who receives and sells stolen goods. **b.** A place where stolen goods are received and sold. **4.** *Archaic.* A means of defense; a protection. **—fence** *v.* **fenced, fenc·ing, fenc·es.** *—tr.* **1.** To enclose with or as if with a fence. See Synonyms at **enclose. 2.** To separate or close off by or as if by means of a fence. **3.a.** To ward off; keep away. **b.** To defend. **4.** To sell (stolen goods) to a fence. *—intr.* **1.** To practice the art or sport of fencing. **2.** To use tactics similar to the parry and thrust of fencing. **3.** To avoid giving direct answers; hedge. **4.** To act as a conduit for stolen goods. ***—idiom.* on the fence.** *Informal.* Undecided as to which of two sides to support; uncommitted or neutral. [Middle English *fens,* short for *defens,* defense. See DEFENSE.] **—fenc′er** *n.*

fencing
Lunging and standing on guard

fence·row (fĕns′rō′) *n.* The uncultivated land on each side of a fence.

fence sitter *n. Informal.* One who takes a position of neutrality or indecision, as in a controversial matter. **—fence′-sit′ting** (fĕns′sĭt′ĭng) *n.*

fenc·ing (fĕn′sĭng) *n.* **1.** The art or sport of using a foil, an épée, or a saber in attack and defense. **2.** Skillful repartee, especially as a defense against having to give direct answers. **3.** Material, such as wire, stakes, and rails, used in the construction of fences. **4.** A barrier or an enclosure of fences.

fend (fĕnd) *v.* **fend·ed, fend·ing, fends.** *—tr.* **1.** To ward off. Often used with *off: fend off an attack.* **2.** *Archaic.* To defend. *—intr.* **1.** To make an effort to resist: *fend against the cold.* **2.** To attempt to manage without assistance: *The children had to fend for themselves while their parents worked.* [Middle English *fenden,* short for *defenden,* to defend. See DEFEND.]

fend·er (fĕn′dər) *n.* **1.a.** A guard over each wheel of a motor vehicle, for example, that is shaped and positioned so as to block the splashing of water or mud. **b.** A device at the front end of a locomotive or streetcar designed to push aside obstructions. **2.** A cushioning device, such as a bundle of rope or a piece of timber, used on the side of a vessel or dock to absorb impact or friction. **3.** A screen or metal framework placed in front of a fireplace to keep hot coals and debris from falling out.

fender

fend·er-bend·er or **fender bender** (fĕn′dər-bĕn′dər) *n. Informal.* A collision involving motor vehicles that results in minor damage.

Fé·ne·lon (fā-nə-lôɴ′), **François de Salignac de la Mothe.** 1651–1715. French prelate and writer who tutored the grandson of Louis XIV and created controversy with his epic *Télémaque* (1699), which the king considered to be a satire of his court.

fe·nes·tra (fə-nĕs′trə) *n., pl.* **-trae** (-trē′). **1.** *Anatomy.* A small opening, especially either of two windowlike apertures in the medial wall of the middle ear. **2.** The opening in a bone made by surgical fenestration. **3.** *Zoology.* A transparent spot or marking, as on the wing of a moth or butterfly. **4.** *Architecture.* A

fennel
Foeniculum vulgare

fermata

ferret[1]
Black-footed ferret
Mustela nigripes
(near extinction)

ă pat	oi boy
ā pay	ou out
âr care	o͝o took
ä father	o͞o boot
ĕ pet	ŭ cut
ē be	ûr urge
ĭ pit	th thin
ī pie	*th* this
îr pier	hw which
ŏ pot	zh vision
ō toe	ə about, item
ô paw	◆ regionalism

Stress marks: **ʹ** (primary); ʹ (secondary), as in **dictionary** (dĭkʹshə-nĕrʹē)

windowlike opening. [Latin, window.] **—fe·nesʹtral** *adj.*

fen·es·trat·ed (fĕnʹĭ-strāʹtĭd) also **fen·es·trate** (fĕnʹĭ-strātʹ, fĭ-nĕsʹtrātʹ) *adj.* **1.** *Architecture.* Having windows or windowlike openings. **2.** *Biology.* Having fenestrae. [From Latin *fenestrātus,* past participle of *fenestrāre,* to furnish with windows, from *fenestra,* window.]

fen·es·tra·tion (fĕnʹĭ-strāʹshən) *n.* **1.** *Architecture.* The design and placement of windows in a building. **2.** An opening in the surface of a structure, as in a membrane. **3.** The surgical creation of an artificial opening in the bony part of the inner ear so as to improve or restore hearing.

Fe·ni·an (fēʹnē-ən) *n.* **1.** One of a legendary group of heroic Irish warriors of the second and third centuries A.D. **2.** A member of a secret revolutionary organization in the United States and Ireland in the mid-19th century, dedicated to the overthrow of British rule in Ireland. [From alteration (influenced by *féne,* body of freemen under early Irish law) of Irish Gaelic *fianna,* bands of young warriors, from Old Irish *fíanna,* pl. of *fían.*] **—Feʹni·an** *adj.* **—Feʹni·an·ism** *n.*

fen·nec (fĕnʹĭk) *n.* A small nocturnal fox *(Vulpes zerda,* formerly *Fennecus zerda)* of desert regions of northern Africa, having fawn-colored fur and large, pointed ears. [Arabic dialectal *fenek,* fox, small furry animal.]

fen·nel (fĕnʹəl) *n.* **1.** A Eurasian plant *(Foeniculum vulgare)* having pinnate leaves, clusters of small yellow flowers grouped in umbels, and aromatic seeds used as flavoring. **2.** The edible seeds or stalks of this plant. [Middle English *fenel,* from Old English *fenol,* from Latin *fēnuculum,* variant of *faeniculum,* diminutive of *faenum, fēnum,* hay. See **dhē(i)-** in Appendix.]

fen·ny (fĕnʹē) *adj.* **1.** Having the nature of a fen; marshy. **2.** Relating to or found in fens.

Fens (fĕnz). A lowland district of eastern England west and south of the Wash. Early attempts by the Romans to drain the area were abandoned by Anglo-Saxon times.

fen·ta·nyl (fĕnʹtə-nil) *n.* A narcotic analgesic used in combination with other drugs before, during, or following surgery. [Alteration of *phentanyl,* alteration of the chemical name.]

fen·u·greek (fĕnʹyə-grēkʹ, fĕnʹə-) *n.* **1.** A cloverlike Eurasian plant *(Trigonella foenum-graecum)* having white flowers and pungent, aromatic seeds used as flavoring. **2.** The seeds of this plant. [Middle English *fenigrek,* from Old French *fenegrec,* from Latin *fēnugraecum,* from *fēnum graecum* : *fēnum,* hay; see FENNEL + *Graecus,* Greek; see GREEK.]

fen·u·ron (fĕnʹyə-rŏnʹ) *n.* A white compound, $C_9H_{12}N_2O$, used as a herbicide. [*fen-* (alteration of PHEN–) + UR(EA) + –ON[3].]

feoff·ee (fĕf-ēʹ, fē-fēʹ) *n.* *Law.* One to whom a feoffment is granted.

feoff·er also **feof·for** (fĕfʹər, fēʹfər) *n.* *Law.* One who grants a feoffment.

feoff·ment (fĕfʹmənt, fēfʹ-) *n.* *Law.* A grant of lands as a fee.

feof·for (fĕfʹər, fēʹfər) *n.* *Law.* Variant of **feoffer.**

FEP *abbr.* *Computer Science.* Front-end processor.

FEPC *abbr.* Fair Employment Practices Commission.

–fer *suff.* One that bears: *aquifer.* [Latin, bearer, bearing, from *ferre,* to carry. See **bher-**[1] in Appendix.]

FERA *abbr.* Federal Emergency Relief Administration.

fe·ral (fîrʹəl, fĕrʹ-) *adj.* **1.a.** Existing in a wild or untamed state. **b.** Having returned to an untamed state from domestication. **2.** Of or suggestive of a wild animal; savage: *a feral grin.* [From Latin *fera,* wild animal, from *ferus,* wild. See **ghwer-** in Appendix.]

fer·bam (fûrʹbămʹ) *n.* A black powder, $C_9H_{18}FeN_3S_6$, used as an agricultural fungicide. [*fer(ric dimethyl-dithiocar)bam(ate).*]

Fer·ber (fûrʹbər), **Edna.** 1887–1968. American writer who wrote several popular novels, including *So Big* (1924).

fer-de-lance (fĕrʹdl-ănsʹ, -änsʹ) *n., pl.* **fer-de-lance.** A venomous tropical American pit viper *(Bothrops atrox)* having brown and grayish markings. [French, from *fer de lance,* spearhead : *fer,* iron + *de,* of + *lance,* spear.]

Fer·di·nand I[1] (fûrʹdn-ăndʹ). Known as "Ferdinand the Great." Died 1065. King of Castile (1035–1065) and León (1037–1065) who reconquered much of Portugal from the Moors.

Ferdinand I[2]**.** 1503–1564. Holy Roman emperor (1558–1564) and king of Bohemia and Hungary (1526–1564).

Ferdinand II. 1578–1637. Holy Roman emperor (1619–1637) and king of Bohemia (1617–1619 and 1620–1627) and Hungary (1618–1625). A leader of the Counter Reformation, he waged constant war against Protestant forces.

Ferdinand III. 1608–1657. Holy Roman emperor (1637–1657) and king of Hungary (1625–1647) and Bohemia (1627–1656). He signed the Peace of Westphalia (1648), thus ending the Thirty Years' War.

Ferdinand V. Known as "Ferdinand the Catholic." 1452–1516. King of Castile and León (1474–1504) who ruled jointly with his wife, Isabella I. He was also king of Sicily (1468–1516) and Aragon (1479–1516) as Ferdinand II and of Naples (1504–1516) as Ferdinand III. His marriage to Isabella (1469) marked the beginning of the modern Spanish state.

fere (fîr) *n.* *Archaic.* **1.** A companion. **2.** A spouse. [Middle English, from Old English *gefēra.* See **per-**[2] in Appendix.]

fer·e·to·ry (fĕrʹĭ-tôrʹē, -tōrʹē) *n., pl.* **-ries. 1.** A receptacle to hold the relics of saints; a reliquary. **2.** An area of a church in which reliquaries are kept. [Middle English, from Anglo-Norman *fertre,* from Latin *feretrum,* from Greek *pheretron,* from *pherein,* to carry. See **bher-**[1] in Appendix.]

Fer·ga·na also **Fer·gha·na** (fər-gäʹnə, fyĭr-gə-näʹ). A city of eastern Uzbekistan southwest of Andizhan. It is the center of the fertile **Fergana Valley,** a densely populated agricultural and industrial region controlled by Russia after 1876. Population, 195,000.

Fer·gu·son (fûrʹgə-sən). A city of eastern Missouri, a suburb of St. Louis. Population, 24,740.

fe·ri·a (fîrʹē-ə, fĕrʹ-) *n., pl.* **-ri·as** or **-ri·ae** (-ē-ēʹ). A weekday on a church calendar on which no feast is observed. [Medieval Latin, ordinary day, weekday, from Late Latin, feast day (used with ordinals to name the days of the week), from Latin *fēriae,* religious festival, holidays. See **dhēs-** in Appendix.] **—feʹri·al** *adj.*

fe·rine (fîrʹīnʹ) *adj.* Untamed; feral. [Latin *ferīnus,* from *fera,* wild animal. See FERAL.]

fer·i·ty (fĕrʹĭ-tē) *n.* **1.** The state of being wild or untamed. **2.** The state of being savage; ferocity. [Latin *feritās,* from *ferus,* wild. See FERAL.]

fer·ma·ta (fĕr-mäʹtə) *n.* *Music.* **1.** The prolongation of a tone, chord, or rest beyond its indicated time value. **2.** The sign indicating this prolongation. [Italian, from feminine past participle of *fermare,* to stop, from Latin *firmāre,* to make firm, from *firmus,* firm. See **dher-** in Appendix.]

fer·ment (fûrʹmĕntʹ) *n.* **1.** Something, such as a yeast, a bacterium, a mold, or an enzyme, that causes fermentation. **2.** Fermentation. **3.a.** A state of agitation or of turbulent change or development. **b.** An agent that precipitates or is capable of precipitating such a state. See Synonyms at **catalyst. —ferment** (fər-mĕntʹ) *v.* **-ment·ed, -ment·ing, -ments.** *—tr.* **1.** To produce by or as if by fermentation. **2.** To cause to undergo fermentation. **3.** To make turbulent; excite or agitate. *—intr.* **1.** To undergo fermentation. **2.** To be in an excited or agitated state; seethe. [Middle English, from Old French, from Latin *fermentum.* See **bhreu-** in Appendix.] **—fer·mentʹa·bilʹi·ty** *n.* **—fer·mentʹa·ble** *adj.*

fer·men·ta·tion (fûrʹmən-tāʹshən, -mĕn-) *n.* **1.** Any of a group of chemical reactions induced by living or nonliving ferments that split complex organic compounds into relatively simple substances, especially the anaerobic conversion of sugar to carbon dioxide and alcohol by yeast. **2.** Unrest; agitation.

fer·men·ta·tive (fər-mĕnʹtə-tĭv) *adj.* **1.a.** Causing fermentation. **b.** Capable of causing or undergoing fermentation. **2.** Relating to or of the nature of fermentation.

fer·ment·er (fər-mĕnʹtər) *n.* **1.** An organism that causes fermentation. **2.** Also **fer·men·tor.** An apparatus that maintains optimal conditions for the growth of microorganisms, used in large-scale fermentation and in the commercial production of antibiotics and hormones.

fer·mi (fûrʹmē, fĕrʹ-) *n.* A unit of length equal to one femtometer (10^{-15} meter). [After Enrico FERMI.]

Fer·mi (fĕrʹmē), **Enrico.** 1901–1954. Italian-born American physicist. He won a 1938 Nobel Prize for his work on artificial radioactivity caused by neutron bombardment.

fer·mi·on (fûrʹmē-ŏnʹ, fĕrʹ-) *n.* A particle, such as an electron, a proton, or a neutron, having half-integral spin and obeying statistical rules requiring that not more than one in a set of identical particles may occupy a particular quantum state. [After Enrico FERMI.]

fer·mi·um (fûrʹmē-əm, fĕrʹ-) *n.* *Symbol* **Fm** A synthetic transuranic metallic element (atomic number 100) having 10 isotopes with mass numbers ranging from 248 to 257 and corresponding half-lives ranging from 0.6 minute to approximately 100 days. See table at **element.** [After Enrico FERMI.]

fern (fûrn) *n.* Any of numerous flowerless, seedless vascular plants having roots, stems, and fronds and reproducing by spores. [Middle English, from Old English *fearn.* See **per-**[2] in Appendix.] **—fernʹy** *adj.*

Fer·nán·dez (fər-nănʹdĕz, fĕr-nänʹdĕth, -dĕs), **Juan.** 1536?–1602? Spanish navigator who discovered the Juan Fernández Islands off the coast of Chile (1563).

Fernández de Cór·do·ba (də kôrʹdə-bə, *th*ĕ kôrʹthô-vä), **Gonzalo.** Known as "El Gran Capitán." 1453–1515. Spanish general who was instrumental in driving the Moors from Granada (1492) and brought all of Naples under Spanish rule (1503).

Fer·nan·do de No·ro·nha (fər-nănʹdō də nə-rōnʹyə, fĕr-näNʹdo͞o də nô-rôʹnyə). An island group in the Atlantic Ocean off the northeast coast of Brazil.

Fer·nan·do Po (fər-nănʹdō pōʹ). See **Bioko.**

Fern·dale (fûrnʹdālʹ). A city of southeast Michigan, a residential suburb of Detroit. Population, 26,227.

fern·er·y (fûrʹnə-rē) *n., pl.* **-ies. 1.** A place or container in which ferns are grown. **2.** A bed or collection of ferns.

◆**fer·ninst** (fər-nĭnstʹ) also **for·nent** (fər-nĕntʹ) *prep.* *Upper Southern U.S.* Opposite, near to, or against: *Their barn is ferninst the house.* [Dialectal *fornent, fornenst* : FORE + *anent, anenst* (from Middle English; see ANENT).]

◆***REGIONAL NOTE:*** *Ferninst,* meaning "opposite, next to, against," has been attributed to Irish English, brought over during the peak years of Irish immigration to the United States in the mid-19th century. However, other, earlier citations with various spellings date further back: *"I walked with them to a room nearly fornent the old state-house"* (Davy Crockett). These variant forms are traceable to the American colonial period, when the source of *ferninst* was probably Scotland or other parts of the British Isles. The term is now dying out; Craig M. Carver, in his book *American Regional Dialects,* reports that "only nine [*DARE*] informants, all well over sixty-five years of age, used this term." A derived noun *ferninster,* meaning "someone who is deliberately contrary," is also used: *"The trouble with the Republican leaders in Congress . . . is that they are just ferninsters"* (William Allen White).

fern seed *n.* The dustlike spores of ferns, once thought to have the power of making their possessor invisible.

fe·ro·cious (fə-rō′shəs) *adj.* **1.** Extremely savage; fierce. See Synonyms at **cruel. 2.** Marked by unrelenting intensity; extreme: *ferocious heat.* [From Latin *ferōx, ferōc-,* fierce. See **ghwer-** in Appendix.] **—fe·ro′cious·ly** *adv.* **—fe·ro′cious·ness** *n.*

fe·roc·i·ty (fə-rŏs′ĭ-tē) *n.* The state or quality of being ferocious; fierceness.

–ferous *suff.* Bearing; producing; containing: *carboniferous.* [–FER + –OUS.]

ferr– *pref.* Variant of **ferro–.**

Fer·ra·ra (fə-rär′ə, fĕ-rä′rä). A city of northern Italy southwest of Venice. In the early 13th century the Este family established a powerful principality here and made it a flourishing center of Renaissance learning and the arts. Population, 123,200.

fer·rate (fĕr′āt′) *n.* See **ferrite** (sense 1).

fer·re·dox·in (fĕr′ĭ-dŏk′sĭn) *n.* An iron-containing protein present in green plants and certain anaerobic bacteria that functions in electron transport reactions in biochemical processes, such as photosynthesis. [FER(RO)– + REDOX + –IN.]

fer·ret[1] (fĕr′ĭt) *n.* **1.** A weasellike, usually albino mammal *(Mustela putorius furo)* related to the polecat and often trained to hunt rats or rabbits. **2.** A black-footed ferret. **—ferret** *v.* **-ret·ed, -ret·ing, -rets.** *—tr.* **1.a.** To hunt (rabbits, for example) with ferrets. **b.** To drive out, as from a hiding place; expel. **2.** To uncover and bring to light by searching. Often used with *out: ferret out the solution to a mystery.* **3.** To hound or harry persistently; worry. *—intr.* **1.** To engage in hunting with ferrets. **2.** To search intensively. [Middle English *furet, ferret,* from Old French *furet,* from Vulgar Latin **fūrittus,* diminutive of Latin *fūr,* thief. See **bher-[1]** in Appendix.] **—fer′ret·er** *n.* **—fer′ret·y** *adj.*

fer·ret[2] (fĕr′ĭt) also **fer·ret·ing** (-ĭ-tĭng) *n.* A narrow piece of tape used to bind or edge fabric. [Probably alteration of Italian *fioretti,* floss silk, pl. of *fioretto,* diminutive of *fiore,* flower, from Latin *flōs, flōr-,* flower. See **bhel-[3]** in Appendix.]

ferri– *pref.* Iron, especially ferric iron: *ferricyanide.* [From Latin *ferrum,* iron.]

fer·ri·age (fĕr′ē-ĭj) *n.* **1.** The act or business of carrying by ferry. **2.** The toll charged for a ferry passage.

fer·ric (fĕr′ĭk) *adj.* Of, relating to, or containing iron, especially with a valence of 3 or a valence higher than in a corresponding ferrous compound.

ferric ammonium citrate *n.* An iron-containing salt, $Fe(NH_4)_3(C_6H_5O_7)_2$, used in treating some forms of anemia.

ferric chloride *n.* A salt, $FeCl_3$, used medicinally as an astringent and a hematinic and industrially as a coagulent.

ferric oxide *n.* A dark red compound, Fe_2O_3, occurring naturally as hematite ore and rust and used in pigments and metal polishes and on magnetic tapes.

fer·ri·cy·a·nide (fĕr′ĭ-sī′ə-nīd′, fĕr′ĭ-) *n.* Any of various salts containing the negative trivalent radical $Fe(CN)_6$ and used in making blue pigments.

fer·rif·er·ous (fə-rĭf′ər-əs, fĕ-) *adj.* Containing or yielding iron.

Fer·ris wheel also **fer·ris wheel** (fĕr′ĭs) *n.* An amusement ride consisting of a large upright, rotating wheel having suspended seats that remain in a horizontal position as the wheel revolves. [After George Washington Gale *Ferris* (1859–1896), American engineer.]

fer·rite (fĕr′īt′) *n.* **1.** Any of a group of nonmetallic, ceramiclike, usually ferromagnetic compounds of ferric oxide with other oxides, especially such a compound characterized by extremely high electrical resistivity and used in computer memory elements, permanent magnets, and various solid-state devices. Also called *ferrate.* **2.** Iron that has not combined with carbon, occurring commonly in steel, cast iron, and pig iron below 910°C.

ferrite core *n.* A magnetic core used in a computer core memory.

fer·ri·tin (fĕr′ĭ-tĭn) *n.* An iron-containing protein complex, found principally in the intestinal mucosa, spleen, and liver, that functions as the primary form of iron storage in the body.

ferro– or **ferr–** *pref.* **1.** Iron: *ferromagnetic.* **2.** Ferrous iron: *ferrocyanide.* [From Latin *ferrum,* iron.]

fer·ro·al·loy (fĕr′ō-ăl′oi′, -ə-loi′) *n.* Any of various alloys of iron and one or more other elements, such as manganese or silicon, used as a raw material in the production of steel.

fer·ro·con·crete (fĕr′ō-kŏn′krēt′, -kŏng′-, -kŏn-krēt′, -kŏng-) *n.* See **reinforced concrete.**

fer·ro·cy·a·nide (fĕr′ō-sī′ə-nīd′) *n.* A salt containing the negative tetravalent radical $Fe(CN)_6$, used in making blue pigments, blueprint paper, and ferricyanide.

fer·ro·e·lec·tric (fĕr′ō-ĭ-lĕk′trĭk) *adj.* Of or relating to a crystalline dielectric that can be given a permanent electric polarization by application of an electric field. **—ferroelectric** *n.* A ferroelectric substance. **—fer′ro·e·lec·tric′i·ty** (-ĭ-lĕk-trĭs′ĭ-tē, -ē′lĕk-) *n.*

fer·ro·mag·ne·sian (fĕr′ō-măg-nē′zhən, -shən) *adj.* Containing iron and magnesium.

fer·ro·mag·net (fĕr′ō-măg′nĭt) *n.* **1.a.** A ferromagnetic substance. **b.** A substance with magnetic properties resembling those of iron. **2.** A ferromagnetic magnet.

fer·ro·mag·net·ic (fĕr′ō-măg-nĕt′ĭk) *adj.* Relating to or characteristic of substances such as iron, nickel, or cobalt and various alloys that exhibit extremely high magnetic permeability, the ability to acquire high magnetization in relatively weak magnetic fields, a characteristic saturation point, and magnetic hysteresis. **—fer′ro·mag′ne·tism** (-măg′nĭ-tĭz′əm) *n.*

fer·ro·man·ga·nese (fĕr′ō-măng′gə-nēz′, -nēs′) *n.* An alloy of iron and manganese used in the production of steel.

fer·ro·sil·i·con (fĕr′ō-sĭl′ĭ-kən, -kŏn′) *n.* An alloy of iron and silicon used in the production of carbon steel.

fer·ro·type (fĕr′ə-tīp′) *n.* **1.** A positive photograph made directly on an iron plate varnished with a thin sensitized film. Also called *tintype.* **2.** The process by which such photographs are made.

fer·rous (fĕr′əs) *adj.* Of, relating to, or containing iron, especially with a valence of 2 or a valence lower than in a corresponding ferric compound.

ferrous oxide *n.* A black powder, FeO, used in the manufacture of steel, green heat-absorbing glass, and enamels.

ferrous sulfate *n.* A greenish crystalline compound, $FeSO_4{\cdot}7H_2O$, used as a pigment, fertilizer, and feed additive, in sewage and water treatment, and as a medicine in the treatment of iron deficiency. Also called *copperas.*

ferrous sulfide *n.* A black to brown sulfide of iron, FeS, used in making hydrogen sulfide.

fer·ru·gi·nous (fə-ro͞o′jə-nəs, fĕ-) *adj.* **1.** Of, containing, or similar to iron. **2.** Having the color of iron rust; reddish-brown. [From Latin *ferrūginus,* from *ferrūgō, ferrūgin-,* iron rust, from *ferrum,* iron.]

fer·rule (fĕr′əl) *n.* **1.** A metal ring or cap placed around a pole or shaft for reinforcement or to prevent splitting. **2.** A bushing used to secure a pipe joint. [Alteration (influenced by Latin *ferrum,* iron) of Middle English *verrele,* from Old French *virole,* from Latin *viriola,* little bracelet, diminutive of *viriae,* bracelets. See **wei-** in Appendix.] **—fer′rule** *v.*

fer·ry (fĕr′ē) *v.* **-ried, -ry·ing, -ries.** *—tr.* **1.** *Nautical.* **a.** To transport (people, vehicles, or goods) by boat across a body of water. **b.** To cross (a body of water) by a ferry. **2.a.** To deliver (a vehicle, especially an aircraft) under its own power to its eventual user. **b.** To transport (people or goods) especially by aircraft. *—intr.* To cross a body of water on or as if on a ferry. **—ferry** *n., pl.* **-ries. 1.** *Nautical.* **a.** A ferryboat. **b.** A place where passengers or goods are transported across a body of water, such as a river, by a ferry. **2.** A franchise or legal right to operate a ferrying service for a fee. **3.** A service and route for delivering an aircraft under its own power to its eventual user. [Middle English *ferien,* from Old English *ferian.* See **per-[2]** in Appendix.]

fer·ry·boat (fĕr′ē-bōt′) *n.* *Nautical.* A boat used to ferry passengers, vehicles, or goods.

fer·tile (fûr′tl) *adj.* **1.** *Biology.* **a.** Capable of initiating, sustaining, or supporting reproduction. **b.** Capable of growing and developing; able to mature: *a fertile egg.* **2.** *Botany.* Bearing functional reproductive structures such as seeds or fruit or material such as spores or pollen. **3.** Bearing or producing crops or vegetation abundantly; fruitful. **4.** Rich in material needed to sustain plant growth: *fertile soil.* **5.** Highly or continuously productive; prolific: *a fertile imagination; a fertile source of new ideas.* **6.** *Physics.* Capable of producing fissionable material: *fertile thorium 232.* [Middle English *fertil,* from Old French *fertile,* from Latin *fertilis,* from *ferre,* to bear. See **bher-[1]** in Appendix.] **—fer′tile·ly** *adv.* **—fer′tile·ness** *n.*

SYNONYMS: *fertile, fecund, fruitful, productive, prolific.* The central meaning shared by these adjectives is "marked by great productivity": *fertile farmland; a fecund imagination; fruitful efforts; a productive meeting; a prolific writer.*
ANTONYM: *infertile.*

Fer·tile Cres·cent (fûr′tl krĕs′ənt). A region of the Middle East arching across the northern part of the Syrian Desert and extending from the Nile Valley to the Tigris and Euphrates rivers.

fer·til·i·ty (fər-tĭl′ĭ-tē) *n.* **1.** The condition, quality, or degree of being fertile. **2.** The birthrate of a population.

fertility factor *n.* See **sex factor** (sense 1).

fer·til·i·za·tion (fûr′tl-ĭ-zā′shən) *n.* **1.** The act or process of initiating biological reproduction by insemination or pollination. **2.** The union of male and female gametes to form a zygote. **3.** The act or process of applying a fertilizer. **—fer′til·i·za′tion·al** *adj.*

fer·til·ize (fûr′tl-īz′) *v.* **-ized, -iz·ing, -iz·es.** *—tr.* **1.** To cause the fertilization of (an ovum, for example). **2.** To make (soil, for example) fertile: *Compost fertilizes the soil.* **3.** To

Ferris wheel
Detail of photograph showing Ferris wheel at 1893 World's Columbian Exposition, Chicago

ferrule
Top: Household brush
Center: Round brush
Bottom: Flat-edged brush

ferryboat

fess¹

festoon

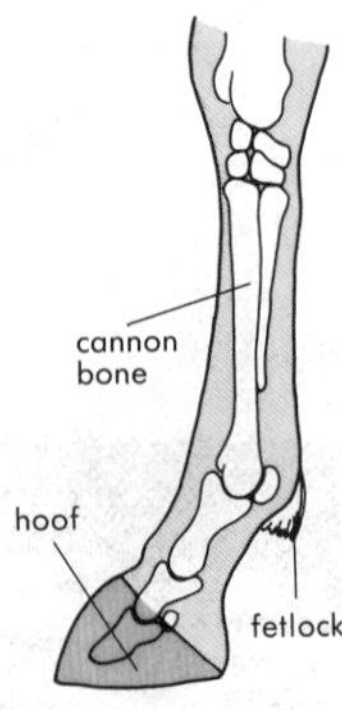

fetlock

spread fertilizer on: *used a mechanical spreader to fertilize the lawn.* —*intr.* To spread fertilizer. **—fer′til·iz′a·ble** *adj.*

fer·til·iz·er (fûr′tl-ī′zər) *n.* Any of a large number of natural and synthetic materials, including manure and nitrogen, phosphorus, and potassium compounds, spread on or worked into soil to increase its capacity to support plant growth.

fer·ule (fĕr′əl) *n.* An instrument, such as a cane, stick, or flat piece of wood, used in punishing children. **—ferule** *tr.v.* **-uled, -ul·ing, -ules.** To punish with a ferule. [Middle English *ferul,* fennel stalk, from Latin *ferula,* fennel stalk, rod.]

fe·ru·lic acid (fə-ro͞o′lĭk) *n.* A compound, $C_{10}H_{10}O_4$, related to vanillin and obtained from certain plants. [From New Latin *Ferula,* plant genus, from Latin *ferula,* giant fennel.]

fer·ven·cy (fûr′vən-sē) *n., pl.* **-cies.** The condition or quality of being fervent.

fer·vent (fûr′vənt) *adj.* **1.** Having or showing great emotion or zeal; ardent: *fervent protests; a fervent admirer.* **2.** Extremely hot; glowing. [Middle English, from Old French, from Latin *fervēns, fervent-,* present participle of *fervēre,* to boil. See **bhreu-** in Appendix.] **—fer′vent·ly** *adv.* **—fer′vent·ness** *n.*

fer·vid (fûr′vĭd) *adj.* **1.** Marked by great passion or zeal: *a fervid patriot.* **2.** Extremely hot; burning. [Latin *fervidus,* from *fervēre,* to boil. See **bhreu-** in Appendix.] **—fer′vid·ly** *adv.*

fer·vor (fûr′vər) *n.* **1.** Great warmth and intensity of emotion. See Synonyms at **passion. 2.** Intense heat. [Middle English *fervour,* from Old French, from Latin *fervor,* from *fervēre,* to boil. See FERVID.]

fer·vour (fûr′vər) *n. Chiefly British.* Variant of **fervor.**

Fès (fĕs). See **Fez.**

fes·cen·nine (fĕs′ə-nīn′, -nēn′) *adj.* Licentious; obscene. [Latin *Fescinnīnus,* of Fescennia, a town of ancient Etruria known for its licentious poetry.]

fes·cue (fĕs′kyo͞o) *n.* Any of various grasses of the genus *Festuca,* often cultivated as pasturage. [Alteration of Middle English *festu,* straw, from Old French, from Late Latin *festūcum,* from Latin *festūca.*]

fess¹ also **fesse** (fĕs) *n. Heraldry.* A wide horizontal band forming the middle section of an escutcheon. [Middle English *fesse,* from Old French, from Latin *fascia,* band.]

fess² (fĕs) *intr.v.* **fessed, fess·ing, fess·es.** *Informal.* To admit to something; confess: *"won't fess up to being even vaguely liberal"* (Jonathan Alter). [Short for CONFESS.]

fesse (fĕs) *n. Heraldry.* Variant of **fess¹.**

fess point *n. Heraldry.* The center point of an escutcheon.

fest (fĕst) *n.* A gathering or an occasion characterized by a specified activity. Often used in combination: *a music fest; a food fest.* [From German *Fest,* festival, from Middle High German *vëst,* from Latin *fēstum.* See FEAST.]

fes·tal (fĕs′təl) *adj.* Of, relating to, or of the nature of a feast or festival; festive. [Middle English, from Old French, from Late Latin *fēstālis,* from Latin *fēstum,* feast. See FEAST.] **—fes′tal·ly** *adv.*

fes·ter (fĕs′tər) *v.* **-tered, -ter·ing, -ters.** —*intr.* **1.** To generate pus; suppurate. **2.** To form an ulcer. **3.** To undergo decay; rot. **4.a.** To be or become an increasing source of irritation or poisoning; rankle: *bitterness that festered and grew.* **b.** To be subject to or exist in a condition of decline: *allowed the once beautiful park to fester.* —*tr.* To infect, inflame, or corrupt. **—fester** *n.* A small festering sore or ulcer; a pustule. [Middle English *festren,* from *festre,* fistula, from Old French, from Latin *fistula.*]

fes·ti·nate (fĕs′tə-nīt) *adj.* Hasty. **—festinate** (-nāt′) *intr.v.* **-nat·ed, -nat·ing, -nates.** To hasten. [Latin *festīnātus,* past participle of *festīnāre,* to hasten.] **—fes′ti·nate·ly** *adv.*

fes·ti·val (fĕs′tə-vəl) *n.* **1.** An occasion for feasting or celebration, especially a day or time of religious significance that recurs at regular intervals. **2.** An often regularly recurring program of cultural performances, exhibitions, or competitions: *a film festival; a high-school music festival.* **3.** Revelry; conviviality. **—festival** *adj.* Of, relating to, or suitable for a feast or festival; festive. [From Middle English, festive, from Old French, from Medieval Latin *fēstivālis,* from Latin *fēstīvus,* from *fēstus.* See **dhēs-** in Appendix.]

fes·ti·val·go·er (fĕs′tə-vəl-gō′ər) *n.* One who attends a festival.

fes·tive (fĕs′tĭv) *adj.* **1.** Of, relating to, or appropriate for a feast or festival. **2.** Merry; joyous: *The birthday party was a festive occasion.* [Latin *fēstīvus,* from *fēstus.* See **dhēs-** in Appendix.] **—fes′tive·ly** *adv.* **—fes′tive·ness** *n.*

fes·tiv·i·ty (fĕ-stĭv′ĭ-tē) *n., pl.* **-ties. 1.** A joyous feast, holiday, or celebration; a festival. **2.** The pleasure, joy, and gaiety of a festival or celebration. **3. festivities.** The proceedings or events of a festival.

fes·toon (fĕ-sto͞on′) *n.* **1.** A string or garland, as of leaves or flowers, suspended in a loop or curve between two points. **2.** A representation of such a string or garland, as in painting or sculpture. **—festoon** *tr.v.* **-tooned, -toon·ing, -toons. 1.** To decorate with or as if with festoons; hang festoons on. **2.** To form or make into festoons. [French *feston,* from Italian *festone,* from *festa,* feast, from Vulgar Latin **fēsta.* See FEAST.]

fes·toon·er·y (fĕ-sto͞o′nə-rē) *n., pl.* **-ies. 1.** An arrangement of festoons. **2.** Festoons considered as a group.

fest·schrift (fĕst′shrĭft′) *n., pl.* **-schrif·ten** (-shrĭf′tən) or **-schrifts.** A volume of learned articles or essays by colleagues and admirers, serving as a tribute or memorial especially to a scholar. [German : *Fest,* festival; see FEST + *Schrift,* writing, from Middle High German *schrift,* from Old High German *scrift,* from *scrīban,* to write, from Latin *scrībere.* See **skrībh-** in Appendix.]

FET *abbr.* **1.** Federal estate tax. **2.** Also **F.E.T.** Federal Excise Tax. **3.** Field-effect transistor.

fet– *pref.* Variant of **feto–.**

fet·a (fĕt′ə, fē′tə) *n.* A white semisoft Greek cheese made usually of goat's or ewe's milk and preserved in brine. [Modern Greek *(turi) pheta,* (cheese) slice, from Italian *fetta,* slice, from **offetta,* diminutive of **offa,* from Latin *offa,* morsel of food.]

fe·tal also **foe·tal** (fēt′l) *adj.* Of, relating to, characteristic of, or being a fetus.

fetal alcohol syndrome *n.* A complex of birth defects including cardiac, cranial, facial, or neural abnormalities and physical and mental growth retardation, occurring in an infant as a result of excess alcohol consumed by the mother in pregnancy.

fetal distress syndrome *n.* An abnormal condition of a fetus during gestation or at the time of delivery, marked by altered heart rate or rhythm and leading to compromised blood flow or changes in blood chemistry.

fetal hemoglobin *n.* The predominant form of hemoglobin in a fetus and a newborn. Normally present in small amounts in an adult, it may be abnormally elevated in certain forms of anemia.

fetal position *n.* A position of the body at rest in which the spine is curved, the head is bowed forward, and the arms and legs are drawn in toward the chest. [From its resemblance to the position of a fetus in the womb.]

fetch¹ (fĕch) *v.* **fetched, fetch·ing, fetch·es.** —*tr.* **1.** To come or go after and take or bring back: *The puppy fetched the stick that we had tossed.* **2.a.** To cause to come. **b.** To bring in as a price: *fetched a thousand dollars at auction.* **c.** To interest or attract. **3.a.** To draw in (breath); inhale. **b.** To bring forth (a sigh, for example) with obvious effort. **4.** *Informal.* To deliver (a blow) by striking; deal. **5.** *Nautical.* To arrive at; reach: *fetched port after a month at sea.* —*intr.* **1.a.** To go after something and return with it. **b.** To retrieve killed game. Used of a hunting dog. **2.** To take an indirect route. **3.** *Nautical.* **a.** To hold a course. **b.** To turn about; veer. **—fetch** *n.* **1.** The act or an instance of fetching. **2.** *Computer Science.* A program routine that brings a module of a program from storage into main memory for immediate use. **3.** A stratagem or trick. **4.a.** The distance over which a wind blows. **b.** The distance traveled by waves with no obstruction. ***—phrasal verb.*** **fetch up. 1.** To reach a stopping place or goal; end up. **2.** To make up (lost time, for example). **3.** To bring forth; produce. **4.** To bring to a halt; stop. [Middle English *fecchen,* from Old English *feccean.* See **ped-** in Appendix.] **—fetch′er** *n.*

fetch² (fĕch) *n. Chiefly British.* **1.** A ghost; an apparition. **2.** A doppelgänger. [Origin unknown.]

fetch·ing (fĕch′ĭng) *adj.* Very attractive; charming: *a fetching new hairstyle.* **—fetch′ing·ly** *adv.*

fete also **fête** (fāt, fĕt) —*n.* **1.** A festival or feast. **2.a.** An elaborate, often outdoor entertainment. **b.** An elaborate party. —*tr.v.* **fet·ed, fet·ing, fetes** also **fêt·ed, fêt·ing, fêtes. 1.** To celebrate or honor with a festival, a feast, or an elaborate entertainment. **2.** To pay honor to. [French *fête,* from Old French *feste.* See FEAST.]

fet·er·i·ta (fĕt′ə-rē′tə) *n.* A grass *(Sorghum vulgare* var. *caudatum)* native to Sudan, grown in warm regions for its grain and as forage. [Arabic dialectal.]

feti– *pref.* Variant of **feto–.**

fet·ich (fĕt′ĭsh, fē′tĭsh) *n.* Variant of **fetish.**

fet·ich·ism (fĕt′ĭ-shĭz′əm, fē′tĭ-) *n.* Variant of **fetishism.**

fe·ti·cide (fē′tĭ-sīd′) *n.* Intentional destruction of a human fetus. **—fe′ti·cid′al** (-sīd′l) *adj.*

fet·id (fĕt′ĭd, fē′tĭd) also **foe·tid** (fē′tĭd) *adj.* Having an offensive odor. [Middle English, from Latin *fētidus,* from *fētēre,* to stink.] **—fet′id·ly** *adv.* **—fet′id·ness** *n.*

fet·ish also **fet·ich** (fĕt′ĭsh, fē′tĭsh) *n.* **1.** An object that is believed to have magical or spiritual powers, especially such an object associated with animistic or shamanistic religious practices. **2.** An object of unreasonably excessive attention or reverence: *made a fetish of punctuality.* **3.** Something, such as a material object or a nonsexual part of the body, that arouses sexual desire and may become necessary for sexual gratification. **4.** An abnormally obsessive preoccupation or attachment; a fixation. [French *fétiche,* from Portuguese *feitiço,* artificial, charm, from Latin *factīcius,* artificial. See FACTITIOUS.]

fet·ish·ism also **fet·ich·ism** (fĕt′ĭ-shĭz′əm, fē′tĭ-) *n.* **1.** Worship of or belief in magical fetishes. **2.** Excessive attachment or regard. **3.** The displacement of sexual arousal or gratification to a fetish. **—fet′ish·ist** *n.* **—fet′ish·is′tic** *adj.* **—fet′ish·is′ti·cal·ly** *adv.*

fet·ish·ize (fĕt′ĭ-shīz′) *tr.v.* **-ized, -iz·ing, -iz·es.** To make a fetish of: *"The American public schools . . . have in the space of a few years gone from neglecting computers to fetishizing them"* (James Traub).

fet·lock (fĕt′lŏk′) *n.* **1.a.** A projection on the lower part of the leg of a horse or related animal, above and behind the hoof. **b.** A tuft of hair on such a projection. **2.** The joint marked by such a projection. [Middle English *fitlok.* See **ped-** in Appendix.]

feto– or **feti–** or **fet–** *pref.* Fetus; fetal: *fetology.* [From FETUS.]

fe·tol·o·gy (fē-tŏl′ə-jē) *n.* The medical study and treatment of the fetus, especially within the uterus. **—fe·tol′o·gist** *n.*

fe·to·pro·tein (fē′tə-prō′tēn, -tē-ĭn) *n.* Any of several antigens normally present in a fetus and occurring abnormally in adults as a result of certain neoplastic conditions or diseases of the liver.

fe·tor (fē′tər, -tôr′) also **foe·tor** (fē′tər) *n.* An offensive odor; a stench. See Synonyms at **stench.** [Middle English *fetoure,* from Latin *fētor,* from *fētēre,* to stink.]

fe·to·scope (fē′tə-skōp′) *n.* A flexible fiberoptic device used to view a fetus in utero. **—fe·tos′co·py** (fē-tŏs′kə-pē) *n.*

fet·ter (fĕt′ər) *n.* **1.** A chain or shackle for the ankles or feet. **2.** Something that serves to restrict; a restraint. **—fetter** *tr.v.* **-tered, -ter·ing, -ters. 1.** To put fetters on; shackle. **2.** To restrict the freedom of. See Synonyms at **hamper**[1]. [Middle English *feter,* from Old English. See **ped-** in Appendix.]

fet·ter·bush (fĕt′ər-bo͝osh′) *n.* Any of several deciduous or evergreen shrubs of the genus *Leucothoe,* having clusters of white to pink flowers and many-seeded capsules with five valves.

fet·tle (fĕt′l) *n.* **1.a.** Proper or sound condition. **b.** Mental or emotional state; spirits: *was in fine fettle.* **2.** *Metallurgy.* Loose sand or ore used to line the hearth of a reverberatory furnace in preparation for pouring molten metal. **—fettle** *tr.v.* **-tled, -tling, -tles.** *Metallurgy.* To line the hearth of (a reverberatory furnace) with loose sand or ore in preparation for pouring molten metal. [From Middle English *fetlen,* to make ready, possibly from Old English *fetel,* girdle.]

fet·tling (fĕt′lĭng) *n.* *Metallurgy.* Fettle.

fet·tuc·ci·ne (fĕt′ə-chē′nē) *n.* **1.** Pasta in narrow, flat strips. **2.** A dish made with such strips of pasta. [Italian, pl. diminutive of *fettucia,* ribbon, possibly diminutive of *fetta,* slice. See FETA.]

fettuccine Al·fre·do (ăl-frā′dō, äl-) *n.* A dish consisting of fettuccine in a rich cream sauce with Parmesan cheese. [After *Alfredo all'Augusteo,* a restaurant in Rome.]

fe·tus also **foe·tus** (fē′təs) *n., pl.* **-tus·es. 1.** The unborn young of a viviparous vertebrate having a basic structural resemblance to the adult animal. **2.** In human beings, the unborn young from the end of the eighth week after conception to the moment of birth, as distinguished from the earlier embryo. [Middle English, from Latin. See **dhē(i)-** in Appendix.]

feud[1] (fyo͞od) *n.* A bitter, often prolonged quarrel or state of enmity, especially such a state of hostilities between two families or clans. **—feud** *intr.v.* **feud·ed, feud·ing, feuds.** To carry on or perpetuate a bitter quarrel or state of enmity. [Alteration (probably influenced by FEUD[2]) of Middle English *fede,* from Old French *faide,* of Germanic origin.]

feud[2] (fyo͞od) *n.* See **fee** (sense 5a). [Medieval Latin *feudum,* of Germanic origin. See **peku-** in Appendix.]

feud. *abbr.* Feudal; feudalism.

feu·dal (fyo͞od′l) *adj.* *Abbr.* **feud. 1.** Of, relating to, or characteristic of feudalism. **2.** Of or relating to lands held in fee or to the holding of such lands. **—feu′dal·ly** *adv.*

feu·dal·ism (fyo͞od′l-ĭz′əm) *n.* *Abbr.* **feud. 1.** A political and economic system of Europe from the 9th to about the 15th century, based on the holding of all land in fief or fee and the resulting relation of lord to vassal and characterized by homage, legal and military service of tenants, and forfeiture. **2.** A political, economic, or social order resembling this medieval system. **—feu′dal·ist** *n.* **—feu′dal·is′tic** *adj.*

feu·dal·i·ty (fyo͞o-dăl′ĭ-tē) *n., pl.* **-ties. 1.** The quality or state of being feudal. **2.** A feudal holding, system, or regime.

feu·dal·ize (fyo͞od′l-īz′) *tr.v.* **-ized, -iz·ing, -iz·es.** To make feudal. **—feu′dal·i·za′tion** (-ĭ-zā′shən) *n.*

feu·da·to·ry (fyo͞o′də-tôr′ē, -tōr′ē) *n., pl.* **-ries. 1.** A person holding land by feudal fee; a vassal. **2.** A feudal fee. **—feudatory** *adj.* **1.** Of, relating to, or characteristic of the feudal relationship between vassal and lord. **2.** Owing feudal homage or allegiance. [Medieval Latin *feudatōrius,* from *feudātus,* past participle of *feudāre,* to enfeoff, from *feudum,* fee, fief. See FEUD[2].]

feud·ist[1] (fyo͞o′dĭst) *n.* A participant in a feud.

feud·ist[2] (fyo͞o′dĭst) *n.* A specialist in feudal law.

feuil·le·ton (fœ′yə-tôɴ′) *n.* **1.a.** The part of a European newspaper devoted to light fiction, reviews, and articles of general entertainment. **b.** An article appearing in such a section. **2.a.** A novel published in installments. **b.** A light, popular work of fiction. **3.** A short literary essay or sketch. [French, from *feuillet,* sheet of paper, little leaf, diminutive of *feuille,* leaf, from Old French *foille,* from Latin *folium.* See **bhel-**[3] in Appendix.] **—feuil′le·ton′ism** (-tôn′ĭz′əm, -tôɴ′nĭz′-) *n.* **—feuil′le·ton′ist** *n.* **—feuil′le·ton·is′tic** *adj.*

fe·ver (fē′vər) *n.* **1.a.** Abnormally high body temperature. **b.** Any of various diseases characterized by abnormally high body temperature. **2.a.** A condition of heightened activity or excitement: *a fever of anticipation.* **b.** A contagious, usually short-lived enthusiasm or craze: *disco fever.* **—fever** *v.* **-vered, -ver·ing, -vers.** —*tr.* To effect fever in. —*intr.* To be or become feverish. [Middle English, from Old English *fefor* and from Old French *fievre,* both from Latin *febris.*]

fever blister *n.* See **cold sore.**

fe·ver·few (fē′vər-fyo͞o′) *n.* An aromatic plant *(Chrysanthemum parthenium)* native to Eurasia, having clusters of buttonlike, white-rayed flower heads. [Middle English *feverfu,* from Old English *feferfuge* and from Anglo-Norman **fevrefue,* both from Late Latin *febrifugia* : *febris,* fever + *fuga,* flight.]

fe·ver·ish (fē′vər-ĭsh) *adj.* **1.a.** Of, relating to, or resembling a fever. **b.** Having a fever or symptoms characteristic of a fever. **c.** Causing or tending to cause fever. **2.** Marked by intense agitation, emotion, or activity: *worked at a feverish pace.* **—fe′ver·ish·ly** *adv.* **—fe′ver·ish·ness** *n.*

fever pitch *n.* A state of extreme agitation or excitement.

fever tree *n.* Any of several trees, such as certain species of eucalyptus or *Pinckneya pubens,* of the southeast United States, having leaves or bark used to allay fever.

fe·ver·weed (fē′vər-wēd′) *n.* Any of various plants considered to have medicinal properties.

fe·ver·wort (fē′vər-wûrt′, -wôrt′) *n.* See **horse gentian.**

few (fyo͞o) *adj.* **few·er, few·est. 1.** Amounting to or consisting of a small number: *one of my few bad habits.* **2.** Being more than one but indefinitely small in number: *bowled a few strings.* **—few** *n. (used with a pl. verb).* **1.** An indefinitely small number of persons or things: *A few of the books have torn jackets.* **2.** An exclusive or limited number: *the discerning few; the fortunate few.* **—few** *pron. (used with a pl. verb).* A small number of persons or things: *"For many are called, but few are chosen"* (Matthew 22:14). [Middle English *fewe,* from Old English *fēawe.* See **pau-** in Appendix.] **—few′ness** *n.*

USAGE NOTE: The traditional rule holds that *fewer* is used with expressions denoting things that can be counted (*fewer than four players*), while *less* is used with mass terms denoting things of measurable extent (*less paper; less than a gallon of paint*). However, *less* is idiomatic in certain constructions where *fewer* would occur according to the traditional rule. *Less than* is used before a plural noun that denotes a measure of time, amount, or distance: *less than three weeks; less than $400; less than 50 miles. Less* is sometimes used with plural nouns in the expressions *no less than* (as in *No less than 30 of his colleagues signed the letter*) and *or less* (as in *Give your reasons in 25 words or less*).

fey (fā) *adj.* **1.a.** Having or displaying an otherworldly, magical, or fairylike aspect or quality: *"She's got that fey look as though she's had breakfast with a leprechaun"* (Dorothy Burnham). **b.** Having visionary power; clairvoyant. **c.** Appearing touched or crazy, as if under a spell. **2.** *Scots.* **a.** Fated to die soon. **b.** Full of the sense of approaching death. [Middle English *feie,* fated to die, from Old English *fǣge.*] **—fey′ly** *adv.* **—fey′ness** *n.*

WORD HISTORY: The history of the words *fey* and *fay* illustrates a rather fey coincidence. Our word *fay,* "fairy, elf," the descendant of Middle English *faie,* "a person or place possessed of magical properties," and first recorded around 1390, goes back to Old French *fae,* "fairy," the same word that has given us *fairy. Fae* in turn comes from Vulgar Latin *Fāta,* "the goddess of fate," from Latin *fātum,* "fate." If *fay* goes back to fate, so does *fey* in a manner of speaking, for its Old English ancestor *fǣge* meant "fated to die." The sense we are more familiar with, "magical or fairylike in quality," seems to have arisen partly because of the resemblance in sound between *fay* and *fey.*

fez

Feyn·man (fīn′mən), **Richard Phillips.** 1918–1988. American physicist. He shared a 1965 Nobel Prize for research in quantum electrodynamics.

fez (fĕz) *n., pl.* **fez·zes.** A man's felt cap in the shape of a flat-topped cone, usually red with a black tassel hanging from the crown, worn chiefly in the eastern Mediterranean region. [French, from Turkish *fes,* from FEZ.]

Fez (fĕz) also **Fès** (fĕs). A city of north-central Morocco northeast of Casablanca. The oldest part of the city was founded in the 9th century. Population, 448,823.

Fez·zan (fə-zăn′). A region of southwest Libya. It was under Turkish control from the 16th century until 1912.

ff *abbr.* *Music.* Fortissimo.

ff. *abbr.* **1.** Folios. **2.** Following.

FFA *abbr.* Future Farmers of America.

F.F.A. or **f.f.a.** *abbr.* *Business.* Free from alongside.

f factor *n.* See **sex factor** (sense 1). [F(ERTILITY) FACTOR.]

fff *abbr.* *Music.* Fortississimo.

FFV *abbr.* First Family of Virginia.

FG *abbr.* **1.** *Football & Basketball.* Field goal. **2.** Fine grain.

FHA *abbr.* **1.** Federal Housing Administration. **2.** Future Homemakers of America.

FHLBB *abbr.* Federal Home Loan Bank Board.

fhp or **f.hp.** *abbr.* Friction horsepower.

fi·a·cre (fē-ä′krə) *n.* A small hackney carriage. [French, after the Hôtel de Saint *Fiacre* in Paris.]

fi·an·cé (fē′än-sā′, fē-än′sā′) *n.* A man engaged to be married. [French, from past participle of *fiancer,* to betroth, from Old French *fiancier,* from *fiance,* trust, from *fier,* to trust, from Vulgar Latin **fīdāre,* from Latin *fīdere.* See **bheidh-** in Appendix.]

fi·an·cée (fē′än-sā′, fē-än′sā′) *n.* A woman engaged to be married. [French, feminine of *fiancé,* fiancé. See FIANCÉ.]

fi·an·chet·to (fē′ən-kĕt′ō, -chĕt′ō) *Games. n., pl.* **-chet·ti** (-kĕt′ē, -chĕt′ē). The development in chess of a bishop from its

ă pat	oi boy
ā pay	ou out
âr care	o͝o took
ä father	o͞o boot
ĕ pet	ŭ cut
ē be	ûr urge
ĭ pit	th thin
ī pie	*th* this
îr pier	hw which
ŏ pot	zh vision
ō toe	ə about, item
ô paw	♦ regionalism

Stress marks: ′ (primary); ′ (secondary), as in **dictionary** (dĭk′shə-nĕr′ē)

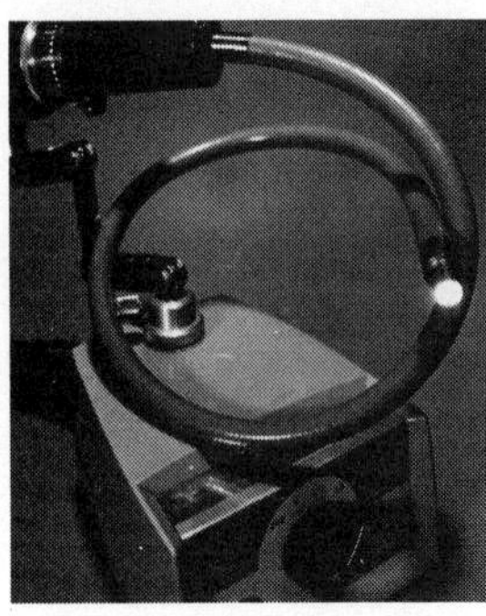
fiberscope

original position to the second square of the adjacent knight's file. **—fianchetto** *tr. & intr.v.* **-chet·toed, -chet·to·ing, -chet·tos.** To develop as or set up a fianchetto. [Italian, diminutive of *fianco,* flank, from Old Italian, from Old French *flanc.* See FLANK.]

fi·as·co (fē-ăs′kō, -ä′skō) *n., pl.* **-coes** or **-cos.** A complete failure. [French, from Italian *fare fiasco,* to make a bottle, fail, from *fiasco,* bottle (translation of French *bouteille,* bottle, error, used by the French for linguistic errors committed by Italian actors on the 18th-century French stage), from Late Latin *flascō.* See FLASK.]

fi·at (fē′ət, -ăt′, -ät′, fī′ăt′, -ət) *n.* **1.** An arbitrary order or decree. **2.** Authorization or sanction: *government fiat.* [Medieval Latin, from Latin, let it be done, third person sing. present subjunctive of *fierī,* to become, to be done. See **bheuə-** in Appendix.]

fiat money *n.* Legal tender, especially paper currency, authorized by a government but not based on or convertible into gold or silver.

fib (fĭb) *n.* An insignificant or childish lie. **—fib** *intr.v.* **fibbed, fib·bing, fibs.** To tell a fib. See Synonyms at **lie²**. [Perhaps from obsolete and dialectal *fible-fable,* nonsense, reduplication of FABLE.] **—fib′ber** *n.*

fi·ber (fī′bər) *n.* **1.** A slender, elongated, threadlike object or structure. **2.** *Botany.* One of the elongated, thick-walled cells that give strength and support to plant tissue. **3.** *Anatomy.* **a.** Any of the filaments constituting the extracellular matrix of connective tissue. **b.** Any of various elongated cells or threadlike structures, especially a muscle fiber or a nerve fiber. **4. a.** A natural or synthetic filament, as of cotton or nylon, capable of being spun into yarn. **b.** Material made of such filaments. **5. a.** Something that provides substance or texture. **b.** Essential character or structure: *"stirred the deeper fibers of my nature"* (Oscar Wilde). **c.** Basic strength or toughness; fortitude: *lacking in moral fiber.* **6.** Coarse, indigestible plant matter, consisting primarily of polysaccharides such as cellulose, that when eaten stimulates intestinal peristalsis. In this sense, also called *bulk, roughage.* [French *fibre,* from Old French, from Latin *fibra.*] **—fi′bered** *adj.*

fi·ber·board (fī′bər-bôrd′, -bōrd′) *n.* A building material composed of wood chips or plant fibers bonded together and compressed into rigid sheets.

fi·ber·fill (fī′bər-fĭl′) *n.* Lightweight synthetic fiber used as filling or insulation, as in comforters, pillows, and outerwear.

Fi·ber·glas (fī′bər-glăs′). A trademark used for a type of fiberglass and for goods made of fiberglass.

fi·ber·glass (fī′bər-glăs′) *n.* A material consisting of extremely fine glass fibers, used in making various products, such as yarns, fabrics, insulators, and structural objects or parts. Also called *spun glass.*

fi·ber·ize (fī′bə-rīz′) *tr.v.* **-ized, -iz·ing, -iz·es.** To break into fibers. **—fi′ber·i·za′tion** (-bər-ĭ-zā′shən) *n.*

fiber optics *n. (used with a sing. verb).* **1.** The science or technology of light transmission through very fine, flexible glass or plastic fibers. **2.** A bundle of optical fibers. **—fi′ber-op′tic** (fī′bər-ŏp′tĭk) *adj.*

fi·ber·scope (fī′bər-skōp′) *n.* A flexible fiber-optic instrument used to view an object or area, such as a body cavity, that would otherwise be inaccessible.

Fi·bo·nac·ci number (fē′bə-nä′chē) *n.* A number in the Fibonacci sequence.

Fibonacci sequence *n.* The sequence of numbers, 1, 1, 2, 3, 5, 8, 13, . . . , in which each successive number is equal to the sum of the two preceding numbers. [After Leonardo *Fibonacci* (died c. 1250), Italian mathematician.]

fibr– *pref.* Variant of **fibro–.**

fi·branne (fī′brăn′) *n.* A linenlike fabric made of spun-rayon yarn. [French, from *fibre,* fiber. See FIBER.]

fi·bre (fī′bər) *n. Chiefly British.* Variant of **fiber.**

fi·bril (fī′brəl, fĭb′rəl) *n.* **1.** A small, slender fiber or filament. **2.** *Anatomy.* Any threadlike fiber or filament, such as a myofibril or neurofibril, that is a constituent of a cell or larger structure. [New Latin *fibrilla,* diminutive of Latin *fibra,* fiber.] **—fi′bril·lar** (-lər), **fi′bril·lar′y** (-lĕr′ē) *adj.* **—fi′bril·lose′** (-lōs′) *adj.*

fib·ril·late (fĭb′rə-lāt′, fī′brə-) *intr. & tr.v.* **-lat·ed, -lat·ing, -lates.** To undergo or cause to undergo fibrillation. [New Latin *fibrilla,* fibril; see FIBRIL + –ATE¹.]

fib·ril·la·tion (fĭb′rə-lā′shən, fī′brə-) *n.* **1.** The forming of fibers. **2. a.** Fine, rapid twitching of individual muscle fibers with little or no movement of the muscle as a whole. **b.** Rapid, uncoordinated twitching movements that replace the normal rhythmic contraction of the heart and may cause a lack of circulation and pulse.

fi·brin (fī′brĭn) *n.* An elastic, insoluble, whitish protein produced by the action of thrombin on fibrinogen and forming an interlacing fibrous network in the coagulation of blood. **—fi′brin·ous** *adj.*

fi·brin·o·gen (fī-brĭn′ə-jən) *n.* A protein in the blood plasma that is essential for the coagulation of blood and is converted to fibrin by the action of thrombin in the presence of ionized calcium. **—fi′bri·nog′e·nous** (fī′brə-nŏj′ə-nəs) *adj.*

fi·brin·o·gen·ic (fī′brə-nō-jĕn′ĭk) *adj.* **1.** Of or relating to fibrinogen. **2.** Producing fibrin. **—fi′brin·o·gen′i·cal·ly** *adv.*

fi·bri·noid (fī′brə-noid′, fĭb′rə-) *adj.* Of or resembling fibrin. **—fibrinoid** *n.* A homogenous, acellular material similar to fibrin, found normally in the placenta and formed in connective tissue and in the walls of blood vessels in certain disease states.

fi·bri·nol·y·sin (fī′brə-nŏl′ĭ-sĭn) *n.* See **plasmin.**

fi·bri·nol·y·sis (fī′brə-nŏl′ĭ-sĭs) *n., pl.* **-ses** (-sēz′). The breakdown of fibrin, usually by the enzymatic action of plasmin. **—fi′bri·no·lyt′ic** (-nə-lĭt′ĭk) *adj.*

fibro– or **fibr–** *pref.* Fiber, especially fibrous tissue: *fibroma.* [From Latin *fibra,* fiber.]

fi·bro·blast (fī′brə-blăst′) *n.* A cell that gives rise to connective tissue. **—fi′bro·blast′ic** *adj.*

fi·bro·car·ti·lage (fī′brō-kär′tl-ĭj) *n.* Cartilage that contains numerous thick bundles of collagen fibers.

fi·bro·cys·tic (fī′brō-sĭs′tĭk) *adj. Medicine.* Characterized by increased fibrosis and cystic spaces, especially in glandular tissue: *fibrocystic disease of the breast.*

fi·broid (fī′broid′) *adj.* Composed of or resembling fibrous tissue. **—fibroid** *n.* A fibroma or myoma occurring especially in the uterine wall.

fi·bro·in (fī′brō-ĭn) *n.* An insoluble white protein that is the essential component of raw silk and spider-web filaments.

fi·bro·ma (fī-brō′mə) *n., pl.* **-mas** or **-ma·ta** (-mə-tə). A benign, usually enclosed neoplasm composed primarily of fibrous tissue. **—fi·brom′a·tous** (-brŏm′ə-təs, -brō′mə-) *adj.*

fi·bro·pla·sia (fī′brə-plā′zhə, -zhē-ə) *n.* The formation of fibrous tissue, as normally occurs in the healing of wounds. **—fi′bro·plas′tic** (-plăs′tĭk) *adj.*

fi·bro·sis (fī-brō′sĭs) *n. Pathology.* The formation of excessive fibrous tissue, as in a reparative or reactive process. **—fi·brot′ic** (-brŏt′ĭk) *adj.*

fi·bro·si·tis (fī′brə-sī′tĭs) *n. Pathology.* Inflammatory hyperplasia of white fibrous connective tissue, especially surrounding the muscles and causing pain and stiffness. [New Latin *fibrōsus,* fibrous (from Latin *fibra,* fiber) + –ITIS.]

fi·brous (fī′brəs) *adj.* **1.** Having or resembling fibers. **2.** Full of sinews; tough. **—fi′brous·ly** *adv.* **—fi′brous·ness** *n.*

fibrous root *n.* A root system made up of many threadlike members of more or less equal length, as in most grasses.

fi·bro·vas·cu·lar (fī′brō-văs′kyə-lər) *adj. Botany.* Having fibrous tissue and vascular tissue, as in the woody tissue of plants.

fibrovascular bundle *n. Botany.* See **vascular bundle.**

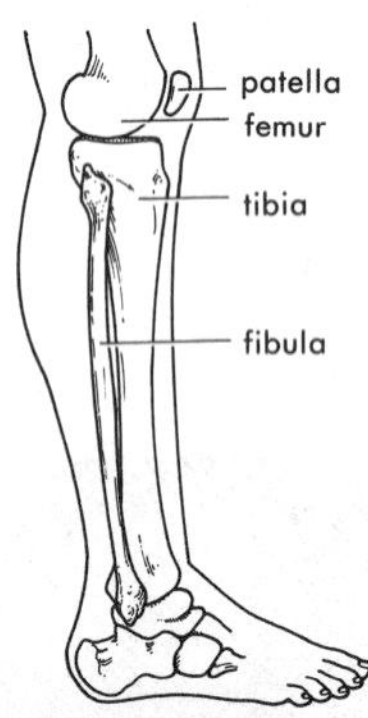

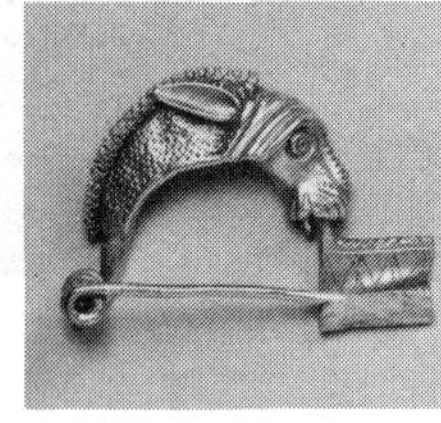
fibula
Top: Of a leg
Bottom: c. A.D. 400 Hunnish fibula with stylized horse's head

fib·u·la (fĭb′yə-lə) *n., pl.* **-lae** (-lē′) or **-las.** **1. a.** The outer and narrower of two bones of the human lower leg, extending from the knee to the ankle. **b.** The corresponding bone in the hind leg of an animal. **2.** An often ornamented clasp or brooch used in ancient Greece and Rome to fasten clothing. [Latin *fībula,* clasp, from *fīgere,* to fasten. See **dhīgʷ-** in Appendix.]

–fic *suff.* Causing; making: *soporific.* [Latin *-ficus,* from *facere,* to do. See **dhē-** in Appendix.]

FICA *abbr.* Federal Insurance Contributions Act.

–fication *suff.* Production; making: *jollification.* [Latin *-ficātiō, -ficātiōn-,* from *-ficātus,* past participle of *-ficāre,* to make, from *-ficus,* -fic.]

♦ **fice** (fīs) *n. Chiefly Southern U.S.* Variant of **feist.**

fiche (fēsh) *n.* A microfiche.

Fich·te (fĭk′tə, fĭKH′-), **Johann Gottlieb.** 1762–1814. German philosopher whose concept of the moral order of the universe and the moral nature of societies was an important influence on Hegel.

fich·u (fĭsh′o͞o, fē-sho͞o′) *n.* A woman's triangular scarf of lightweight fabric, worn over the shoulders and crossed or tied in a loose knot at the breast. [French, from past participle of *ficher,* to fix, from Vulgar Latin **figicāre,* from Latin *fīgere.* See **dhīgʷ-** in Appendix.]

fick·le (fĭk′əl) *adj.* Characterized by erratic changeableness or instability, especially with regard to affections or attachments; capricious. [Middle English *fikel,* from Old English *ficol,* deceitful.] **—fick′le·ness** *n.* **—fick′ly** *adv.*

fict. *abbr.* **1.** Fiction. **2.** Fictitious.

fic·tile (fĭk′təl, -tīl′) *adj.* **1. a.** Capable of being molded; plastic. **b.** Formed of a moldable substance, such as clay or earth. **2.** Of or relating to earthenware or pottery. [Latin *fictilis,* made of clay, from *fictus,* past participle of *fingere,* to mold. See **dheigh-** in Appendix.]

fic·tion (fĭk′shən) *n. Abbr.* **fict.** **1. a.** An imaginative creation or a pretense that does not represent actuality but has been invented. **b.** The act of inventing such a creation or pretense. **2.** A lie. **3. a.** A literary work whose content is produced by the imagination and is not necessarily based on fact. **b.** The category of literature comprising works of this kind, including novels and short stories. **4.** *Law.* Something untrue that is intentionally represented as true by the narrator. [Middle English *ficcioun,* from Old French *fiction,* from Latin *fictiō, fictiōn-,* from *fictus,* past participle of *fingere,* to form. See **dheigh-** in Appendix.] **—fic′tion·al** *adj.* **—fic′tion·al′i·ty** (-shə-năl′ĭ-tē) *n.* **—fic′tion·al·ly** *adv.*

WORD HISTORY: "The latest fiction" to most people means the latest novels or stories rather than the most recently invented pretense or latest lie. All three senses of the word *fiction* point back to its source, Latin *fictiō,* "the action of shaping, a feigning, that which is feigned." *Fictiō* in turn was derived from *fingere,* "to make by shaping, feign, make up or invent a story or excuse." Our first instance of *fiction,* recorded in a work composed around

ă pat	oi boy
ā pay	ou out
âr care	o͝o took
ä father	o͞o boot
ĕ pet	ŭ cut
ē be	ûr urge
ĭ pit	th thin
ī pie	*th* this
îr pier	hw which
ŏ pot	zh vision
ō toe	ə about, item
ô paw	♦ regionalism

Stress marks: **′** (primary); ′ (secondary), as in **dictionary** (dĭk′shə-nĕr′ē)

1412, was used in the sense "invention of the mind, that which is imaginatively invented." It is not a far step from this meaning to the sense "imaginative literature," first recorded in 1599.

fic·tion·al·ize (fĭk′shə-nə-līz′) *tr.v.* **-ized, -iz·ing, -iz·es.** To treat as or make into fiction: *"has fictionalized his people and their town, but we know they are real"* (Harper's). **—fic′tion·al·i·za′tion** (-shə-nə-lĭ-zā′shən) *n.*

fic·tion·eer (fĭk′shə-nîr′) *n.* One who writes fiction, especially a prolific creator of commercial or pulp fiction. **—fic′tion·eer′ing** *n.*

fic·tion·ist (fĭk′shə-nĭst) *n.* A writer of fiction, especially a novelist.

fic·tion·ize (fĭk′shə-nīz′) *tr.v.* **-ized, -iz·ing, -iz·es.** To fictionalize. **—fic′tion·i·za′tion** (-shə-nĭ-zā′shən) *n.*

fic·ti·tious (fĭk-tĭsh′əs) *adj. Abbr.* **fict. 1.** Of, relating to, or characterized by fiction; imaginary. **2. a.** Accepted or assumed for the sake of convention: *a fictitious belief.* **b.** Adopted or assumed in order to deceive: *a fictitious name.* **3.** Not genuinely believed or felt; sham: *greeted me with a fictitious enthusiasm.* [From Latin *fictīcius,* from *fictus,* past participle of *fingere,* to form. See FICTION.] **—fic·ti′tious·ly** *adv.* **—fic·ti′tious·ness** *n.*

fic·tive (fĭk′tĭv) *adj.* **1.** Of, relating to, or able to engage in imaginative invention. **2.** Of, relating to, or being fiction; fictional. **3.** Not genuine; sham. **—fic′tive·ly** *adv.*

fi·cus (fī′kəs) *n., pl.* **ficus** or **-cus·es.** Any of numerous tropical trees, shrubs, or climbers of the genus *Ficus,* having pearlike multiple fruits. [Latin *fīcus,* fig.]

fid (fĭd) *n.* **1.** *Nautical.* A square bar used as a support for a topmast. **2.** A large, tapering pin used to open the strands of a rope before splicing. [Origin unknown.]

fid. *abbr.* Fidelity.

–fid *suff.* Divided into parts or lobes: *pinnatifid.* [Latin *-fidus,* from *findere, fid-,* to split. See **bheid-** in Appendix.]

fid·dle (fĭd′l) *n.* **1.** *Music.* **a.** A violin. **b.** A member of the violin family. **2.** *Nautical.* A guardrail used on a table during rough weather to prevent things from slipping off. **3.** *Informal.* Nonsensical, trifling matters: *"There are things that are important/beyond all this fiddle"* (Marianne Moore). **4.** The act or an instance of cheating or swindling; fraud. **—fiddle** *v.* **-dled, -dling, -dles.** —*intr.* **1.** *Music.* To play a violin. **2. a.** To move one's fingers or hands in a nervous fashion. **b.** To occupy oneself in an aimless or desultory way: *liked to fiddle with all the knobs and dials.* **c.** To meddle or tamper: *a reporter who fiddled with the facts.* **3.** To commit a fraud, especially to steal from one's employer. —*tr.* **1.** *Music.* To play (a tune) on a violin. **2.** To cheat or swindle. **3.** To alter or falsify (accounts, for example) for dishonest gain. **—*phrasal verb.* fiddle away.** To waste or squander: *fiddled away the morning with unnecessary tasks.* [Middle English *fidle,* from Old English *fithele.*] **—fid′dler** *n.*

fid·dle-de-dee (fĭd′l-dē-dē′) *interj.* Used to express mild annoyance or impatience. [From FIDDLE.]

fid·dle-fad·dle (fĭd′l-făd′l) *n.* Nonsense. **—fiddle-faddle** *intr.v.* **-dled, -dling, -dles.** To fritter away one's time; dally. [Reduplication of FIDDLE.] **—fid′dle-fad′dler** *n.*

fid·dle-foot·ed (fĭd′l-fo͝ot′ĭd) *adj.* **1.** Excitable or nervous: *fiddle-footed ponies.* **2.** Inclined to roam or wander.

fid·dle·head (fĭd′l-hĕd′) *n.* **1.** *Nautical.* A curved, scroll-like ornamentation at the top of a ship's bow that resembles the neck of a violin. **2.** *Botany.* The coiled young frond of any of various ferns, some of which are considered a delicacy when cooked. In this sense, also called *crosier.*

fiddler crab *n.* Any of various burrowing crabs of the genus *Uca* of coastal areas, the male of which has a greatly enlarged anterior claw.

fid·dle·sticks (fĭd′l-stĭks′) *interj.* Used to express mild annoyance or impatience.

fid·dling (fĭd′lĭng) *adj.* Trivial; petty.

fi·de·ism (fē′dā-ĭz-əm, fī′dē-) *n.* Reliance on faith alone rather than scientific reasoning or philosophy in questions of religion. [Probably from French *fidéisme,* from Latin *fidēs,* faith. See FIDELITY.] **—fi′de·ist** *n.* **—fi′de·is′tic** *adj.*

fi·del·i·ty (fĭ-dĕl′ĭ-tē, fī-) *n., pl.* **-ties.** *Abbr.* **fid. 1.** Faithfulness to obligations, duties, or observances. **2.** Exact correspondence with fact or with a given quality, condition, or event; accuracy. **3.** The degree to which an electronic system accurately reproduces the sound or image of its input signal. [Middle English *fidelite,* from Old French, from Latin *fidēlitās,* from *fidēlis,* faithful, from *fidēs,* faith. See **bheidh-** in Appendix.]

SYNONYMS: *fidelity, allegiance, fealty, loyalty.* These nouns denote faithfulness, as to a person or a cause. *Fidelity* implies the unfailing fulfillment of one's duties and obligations and strict adherence to vows or promises: *fidelity to one's spouse; fidelity to one's word of honor. Allegiance* is faithfulness, as to a government or state to which one is subject, considered as a duty: *"I know no South, no North, no East, no West, to which I owe any allegiance. . . . The Union, Sir, is my country"* (Henry Clay). *Fealty,* once applied to the obligation of a tenant or vassal to a feudal lord, now suggests faithfulness that one has pledged to uphold: *swore fealty to the laws and Constitution of the United States. Loyalty* implies a steadfast and devoted attachment that is not easily turned aside: *loyalty to an oath; loyalty to one's family; party loyalty; loyalty to an ideal.*

fidg·et (fĭj′ĭt) *v.* **-et·ed, -et·ing, -ets.** —*intr.* **1.** To behave or move nervously or restlessly. **2.** To play or fuss; fiddle: *He fidgeted with his notes while lecturing.* —*tr.* To cause to behave or move nervously or restlessly. **—fidget** *n.* **1.** Often **fidgets.** A condition of restlessness as manifested by nervous movements. Often used with *the.* **2.** One that fidgets. [From obsolete and dialectal *fidge,* to move restlessly, perhaps from Middle English *fiken,* of Scandinavian origin.]

fidg·et·y (fĭj′ĭ-tē) *adj.* **1.** Tending to fidget. **2.** Creating unnecessary fuss. **—fidg′et·i·ness** *n.*

fi·do (fī′dō) *n., pl.* **-dos.** A coin containing a minting error. [*f(reaks), i(rregulars), d(efects), o(ddities).*]

fi·du·cial (fĭ-do͞o′shəl, -dyo͞o′-, fī-) *adj.* **1.** Based on or relating to faith or trust. **2.** Relating to or characteristic of a legal trust; fiduciary. **3.** Regarded or employed as a standard of reference, as in surveying. [Late Latin *fīdūciālis,* from Latin *fīdūcia,* trust, from *fīdere,* to trust. See **bheidh-** in Appendix.] **—fi·du′cial·ly** *adv.*

fi·du·ci·ar·y (fĭ-do͞o′shē-ĕr′ē, -shə-rē, -dyo͞o′-, fī-) *adj.* **1. a.** Of or relating to a holding of something in trust for another: *a fiduciary heir; a fiduciary contract.* **b.** Of, relating to, or being a trustee or trusteeship. **c.** Held in trust. **2.** Of, relating to, or consisting of fiat money. **3.** Of, relating to, or being a system of marking in the field of view of an optical instrument that is used as a reference point or measuring scale. **—fiduciary** *n., pl.* **-ies.** One, such as an agent of a principal or a company director, that stands in a special relation of trust, confidence, or responsibility in certain obligations to others. [Latin *fīdūciārius,* from *fīdūcia,* trust. See FIDUCIAL.]

fie (fī) *interj.* Used to express distaste or disapproval.

Fied·ler (fēd′lər), **Arthur.** 1894–1979. American conductor who as director of the Boston Pops Orchestra (1930–1979) blended works of classical and popular music in his concerts.

fief (fēf) *n.* **1.** See **fee** (sense 5a). **2.** A fiefdom. [French, from Old French *feu, fief,* probably from Vulgar Latin **feudum.* See FEUD[2].]

fief·dom (fēf′dəm) *n.* **1.** The estate or domain of a feudal lord. **2.** Something over which one dominant person or group exercises control: *"long the independent head of a powerful fiefdom within the Police Department"* (David Burnham).

field (fēld) *n. Abbr.* **fld. 1. a.** A broad, level, open expanse of land. **b.** A meadow: *a field of buttercups.* **c.** A cultivated expanse of land, especially one devoted to a particular crop: *a field of corn.* **d.** A portion of land or a geologic formation containing a specified natural resource. **e.** A wide, unbroken expanse, as of ice. **2. a.** A battleground. **b.** A battle. **c.** The scene or an area of military operations or maneuvers. **d.** A military area away from headquarters. **3. a.** A background area, as on a flag, painting, or coin: *a blue insignia on a field of red.* **b.** *Heraldry.* The background of a shield or one of the divisions of the background. **4.** *Sports.* **a.** An area in which an athletic event takes place. **b.** The portion of a playing field having specific dimensions on which the action of a game takes place. **c.** All the contestants or participants in an event, especially all the contestants except the favorite or the winner in a contest of more than two. **d.** The members of a team engaged in active play. **e.** The body of riders following a pack of hounds in hunting. **5. a.** An area of human activity or interest: *several fields of endeavor.* **b.** A topic, a subject, or an area of academic interest or specialization. **c.** Profession, employment, or business. **d.** An area or a setting of practical activity or application outside an office, a school, a factory, or a laboratory: *biologists working in the field; a product tested in the field.* **e.** An area or a region where business activities are conducted: *sales representatives in the field.* **6.** *Mathematics.* A set of elements having two operations, designated addition and multiplication, satisfying the conditions that multiplication is distributive over addition and that both operations are associative and commutative for all elements of the set, with the exception of the additive identity element, which is not commutative in respect to multiplication. **7.** *Physics.* A region of space characterized by a physical property, such as gravitational or electromagnetic force or fluid pressure, having a determinable value at every point in the region. **8.** The usually circular area in which the image is rendered by the lens system of an optical instrument. Also called *field of view.* **9.** *Computer Science.* **a.** A defined area of a storage medium, such as a set of bit locations or a set of adjacent columns on a punch card, used to record a type of information consistently. **b.** An element of a database record in which one piece of information is stored. **—field** *adj.* **1.** Growing, cultivated, or living in fields or open land. **2.** Made, used, or carried on in the field: *field operations.* **3.** Working, operating, or active in the field: *field representatives of a firm.* **—field** *v.* **field·ed, field·ing, fields.** —*tr.* **1.** *Sports.* **a.** To retrieve (a ball) and perform the required maneuver, especially in baseball. **b.** To place in the field to play: *field a team.* **2.** To give an unrehearsed response to: *fielded tough questions from the press.* **3. a.** To place in competition. **b.** To put into action: *field an army of campaign workers.* —*intr.* *Sports.* To play as a fielder. **—*idiom.* take the field.** To begin or resume activity, as in military operations or in a sport. [Middle English, from Old English *feld.* See **pele-**[2] in Appendix.]

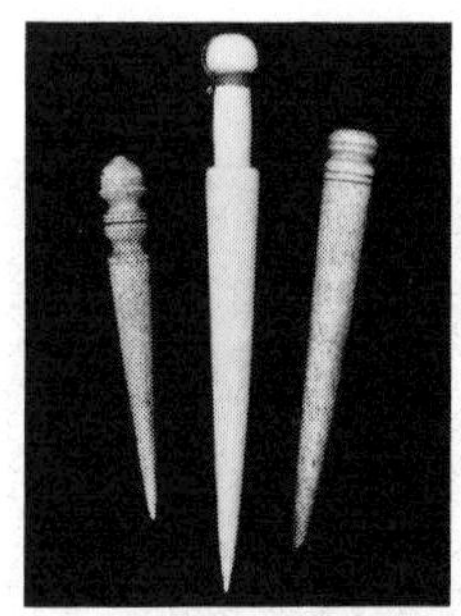
fid
Whalebone splicing implements

fiddlehead
Maidenhair fern

fiddler crab
Male fiddler crab

Arthur Fiedler

field hockey

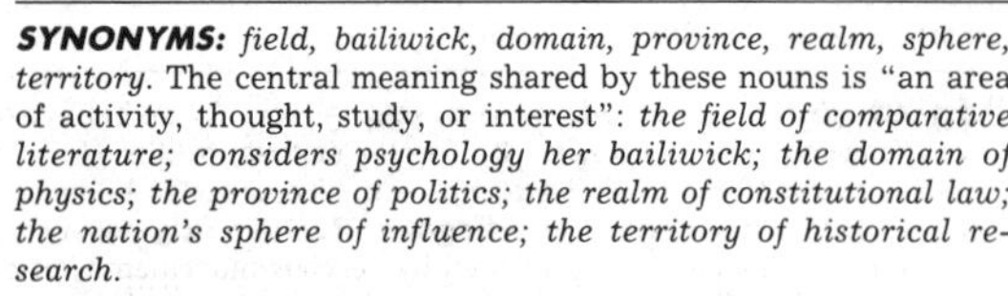

SYNONYMS: *field, bailiwick, domain, province, realm, sphere, territory.* The central meaning shared by these nouns is "an area of activity, thought, study, or interest": *the field of comparative literature; considers psychology her bailiwick; the domain of physics; the province of politics; the realm of constitutional law; the nation's sphere of influence; the territory of historical research.*

Field (fēld), **Cyrus West.** 1819–1892. American merchant and financier who planned and oversaw the laying of the transatlantic telegraph cable (completed 1866).

Field, Eugene. 1850–1895. American writer best known for his children's verse, especially the lullabies "Wynken, Blynken, and Nod" and "Little Boy Blue."

Field, Stephen Johnson. 1816–1899. American jurist who served as an associate justice of the U.S. Supreme Court (1863–1897).

field artillery *n.* Artillery other than antiaircraft artillery that is light enough to be mounted for use in the field.

field capacity *n.* The maximum amount of water that a particular soil can hold.

field coil *n.* An electric coil around a field magnet used to generate a magnetic field, as in an electric motor or generator. Also called *field winding.*

field corn *n.* Corn used primarily as feed for livestock.

field day *n.* **1.a.** *Sports.* A day set aside for sports or athletic competition. **b.** An outdoor meeting, social event, or festivity. **c.** A day for military exercises, maneuvers, or display. **2.** *Informal.* A time of great pleasure, activity, or opportunity: *The media had a field day with the sensational story.*

field-ef·fect transistor (fēld′ĭ-fĕkt′) *n. Abbr.* **FET** A transistor in which the output current is controlled by a variable electric field.

field emission *n.* The emission of electrons from the surface of a conductor, caused by a strong electric field.

field·er (fēl′dər) *n. Sports.* One who plays a position in the field, especially an outfielder in baseball.

field·er's choice (fēl′dərz) *n. Baseball.* A play made on a ground ball in which the fielder chooses to put out an advancing base runner, thus allowing the batter to reach first base safely.

field event *n. Sports.* A throwing or jumping event of a track-and-field meet.

field·fare (fēld′fâr′) *n.* An Old World thrush *(Turdus pilaris)* having gray and reddish-brown plumage. [Middle English *feldfare,* from Old English *feldeware,* error for **feldefare* : *felde,* field; see FIELD + *-*fare,* goer (from *faran,* to go; see **per-**[2] in Appendix).]

field glass *n.* A portable binocular telescope without prisms used especially outdoors for viewing distant objects. Often used in the plural.

field goal *n. Abbr.* **FG 1.** *Football.* A score worth three points made on an ordinary down by place-kicking or drop-kicking the ball over the crossbar and between the goal posts. **2.** *Basketball.* A score made by throwing the ball through the basket in regulation play, worth two points or, if attempted from beyond a specified distance, three points.

W.C. Fields

field-grade officer (fēld′grād′) *n. Abbr.* **FO, F.O.** A military officer, such as a major, lieutenant colonel, or colonel, ranking above a captain and below a brigadier general. Also called *field officer.*

field hand *n.* An outdoor worker on a farm.

field hockey *n. Sports.* A game played on turf in which two opposing teams of players, using curved sticks, try to drive a ball into the opponents' goal.

field hospital *n.* A hospital established on a temporary basis to serve troops in a combat zone.

field house *n. Sports.* **1.** A building having locker rooms and storage and training facilities, located at an athletic field. **2.** A building having one or more areas for different athletic events and usually grandstands for spectators.

Field·ing (fēl′dĭng), **Henry.** 1707–1754. British writer whose works include *Joseph Andrews* (1742) and *Tom Jones* (1749).

field-i·on microscope (fēld′ī′ən, -ī′ŏn) *n.* A microscope that produces an image of the atoms on a metal surface by means of ions formed in a high-voltage electric field.

field lens *n.* The lens positioned farthest from the eye in a compound eyepiece.

field magnet *n.* A magnet used to produce a magnetic field in an electrical device such as a generator or motor.

field marshal *n. Abbr.* **FM, F.M.** An officer in some European armies, usually ranking just below the commander in chief.

field mouse *n.* Any of various small mice or voles, especially of the genus *Microtus,* inhabiting meadows and fields and often causing damage to crops. Also called *meadow mouse.*

field officer *n.* See **field-grade officer.**

field of force *n., pl.* **fields of force.** A region of space throughout which the force produced by a single agent, such as an electric current, is operative. Also called *force field.*

field of honor *n., pl.* **fields of honor. 1.** The scene of a duel. **2.** A battlefield.

field of view *n., pl.* **fields of view.** See **field** (sense 8).

field of vision *n., pl.* **fields of vision.** See **visual field.**

Fields (fēldz), **W.C.** 1880–1946. American entertainer known for his raspy voice, bulbous nose, and sardonic disposition. His films include *My Little Chickadee* (1940).

fields·man (fēldz′mən) *n. Sports.* A fielder in cricket.

field·stone (fēld′stōn′) *n.* A stone occurring naturally in fields, often used as a building material. —*attributive.* Often used to modify another noun: *a fieldstone fireplace.*

field·strip (fēld′strĭp′) *tr.v.* **-stripped, -strip·ping, -strips. 1.** To disassemble (a weapon) for cleaning, repair, or inspection. **2.** To leave no trace of (a cigarette butt) by rolling up the paper and scattering the tobacco.

field-test (fēld′tĕst′) *tr.v.* **-test·ed, -test·ing, -tests.** To test (a technique or product, for example) under conditions of actual operation or use.

field theory *n. Physics.* An explicit mathematical description of physical phenomena that takes into account the effects of one or more fields.

field trial *n.* **1.** A test for young, untried hunting dogs to determine their competence in pointing and retrieving. Often used in the plural. **2.** A trial of a new product in actual situations of use.

field trip *n.* A group excursion for the purpose of firsthand observation, as to a museum, the woods, or a historic place.

field wind·ing (wīn′dĭng) *n.* See **field coil.**

field·work (fēld′wûrk′) *n.* **1.** A temporary military fortification erected in the field. **2.** Work done or firsthand observations made in the field as opposed to that done or observed in a controlled environment. **3.** The collecting of sociological or anthropological data in the field. **—field′work′er** *n.*

fiend (fēnd) *n.* **1.a.** An evil spirit; a demon. **b.** The Devil; Satan. **c.** A diabolically evil or wicked person. **2.** *Informal.* One who is addicted to something: *a dope fiend.* **3.** *Informal.* One who is completely absorbed in or obsessed with a given job or pastime: *a crossword-puzzle fiend.* **4.** *Informal.* One who is particularly adept at something: *a fiend with computers.* [Middle English, from Old English *fēond.* See **pē(i)-** in Appendix.]

fiend·ish (fēn′dĭsh) *adj.* **1.** Of, relating to, or suggestive of a fiend; diabolical. **2.** Extremely wicked or cruel. **3.** Extremely bad, disagreeable, or difficult: *a fiendish blizzard; a fiendish problem.* **—fiend′ish·ly** *adv.* **—fiend′ish·ness** *n.*

fierce (fîrs) *adj.* **fierc·er, fierc·est. 1.** Having a savage and violent nature; ferocious. See Synonyms at **cruel. 2.** Extremely severe or violent; terrible: *"the fierce thunders roar me their music"* (Ezra Pound). **3.** Extremely intense or ardent: *fierce loyalty.* See Synonyms at **intense. 4.** Strenuously active or resolute: *a fierce attempt to escape.* **5.** *Informal.* Very difficult or unpleasant: *a fierce exam.* **6.** Savage or threatening in appearance. [Middle English *fiers,* from Old French, from Latin *ferus.* See **ghwer-** in Appendix.] **—fierce′ly** *adv.* **—fierce′ness** *n.*

fi·er·i fa·ci·as (fī′ə-rē fā′shē-əs, fā′shəs) *n. Law.* A writ of execution authorizing a sheriff to lay a claim to and seize the goods and chattels of a debtor to fulfill a judgment against the debtor. [Middle English, from Medieval Latin : Latin *fierī,* to be done + Latin *faciās,* second person sing. present subjunctive of *facere,* to do, cause (words used in the writ).]

fier·y (fīr′ē, fī′ə-rē) *adj.* **-i·er, -i·est. 1.a.** Consisting of or containing fire. **b.** Burning or glowing. **c.** Using or effected with fire. **d.** Easily ignited; flammable. **2.** Having the color of fire; brightly red: *fiery hair; a fiery sunset.* **3.a.** Torridly hot. **b.** Feverishly hot and flushed: *fiery cheeks.* **c.** Being in an inflamed, usually painful condition: *a fiery boil.* **4.a.** Easily excited or emotionally volatile; tempestuous: *a fiery temper.* **b.** Charged with emotion; spirited: *a fiery denunciation.* [Middle English, from *fier,* fire. See FIRE.] **—fier′i·ly** *adv.* **—fier′i·ness** *n.* **—fier′y** *adv.*

Fie·so·le (fē-ā′zə-lē, fyĕ′zô-lĕ). A town of central Italy overlooking the Arno River. Population, 14,774.

Fie·so·le (fyĕ′zō-lā, -zô-lĕ), **Giovanni Angelica da.** See Fra **Angelico.**

fi·es·ta (fē-ĕs′tə) *n.* A festival or religious holiday, especially a saint's day celebrated in Spanish-speaking countries. [Spanish, from Vulgar Latin **fēsta.* See FEAST.]

fife (fīf) *n. Music.* A small, high-pitched, transverse flute used primarily to accompany drums in a military or marching band. [Probably German *Pfeife,* from Middle High German *pfīfe,* from Old High German *pfīffa,* from Vulgar Latin **pīpa,* from Latin *pīpāre,* to chirp.] **—fif′er** *n.*

Fife (fīf). A region of eastern Scotland between the Firths of Forth and Tay. It was once a Pict kingdom.

fife rail *n. Nautical.* A rail around the lower part of a ship's mast to which the belaying pins for the rigging are secured. [Possibly from its use by the ship's fifer.]

FIFO (fī′fō) *n. Accounting.* See **first-in, first-out.**

fif·teen (fĭf-tēn′) *n.* **1.** The cardinal number equal to 14 + 1. **2.** The 15th in a set or sequence. [Middle English *fiftene,* from Old English *fīftēne.* See **penkʷe** in Appendix.] **—fif·teen′** *adj. & pron.*

fif·teenth (fĭf-tēnth′) *n.* **1.** The ordinal number matching the number 15 in a series. **2.** One of 15 equal parts. **—fif·teenth′** *adv. & adj.*

fifth (fĭfth) *n.* **1.** The ordinal number matching the number five in a series. **2.** One of five equal parts. **3.** One fifth of a gallon or four fifths of a quart of liquor. **4.** *Music.* **a.** An interval encompassing five diatonic tones, such as C, D, E, F, and G. **b.** The harmonic combination of the two tones constituting the extremities of such an interval. **c.** The dominant in a given key or tonality. **5. Fifth.** The Fifth Amendment. Used with *the.* [Middle English, from Old English *fīfta.* See **penkʷe** in Appendix.] **—fifth** *adv. & adj.* **—fifth′ly** *adv.*

Fifth Amendment *n.* An amendment to the Constitution of the United States, ratified in 1791, that deals with the rights of accused criminals by providing for due process of law, forbidding double jeopardy, and stating that no person may be forced to testify as a witness against himself or herself.

fifth column *n.* A clandestine subversive organization working within a country to further an invading enemy's military and political aims. [First applied in 1936 to rebel sympathizers inside Madrid when four columns of rebel troops were attacking that city.] **—fifth columnist** *n.*

fifth estate *n.* A class or group in society other than the nobility, the clergy, the middle class, and the press.

fifth wheel *n.* **1.a.** A wheel or portion of a wheel placed horizontally over the forward axle of a carriage to provide support and stability during turns. **b.** A similar device over the rear axle or axles of a tractor or pickup truck, serving as a coupling for a semitrailer. **2.** An additional wheel carried on a four-wheeled vehicle as a spare. **3.** An extra and unnecessary person or thing.

fif·ti·eth (fĭf′tē-ĭth) *n.* **1.** The ordinal number matching the number 50 in a series. **2.** One of 50 equal parts. **—fif′ti·eth** *adv. & adj.*

fif·ty (fĭf′tē) *n.* **1.** The cardinal number equal to 5 × 10. **2. fifties. a.** *Often* **Fifties.** The decade from 50 to 59 in a century. **b.** A decade or the numbers from 50 to 59: *They began playing golf in their fifties. With the sunshine, the temperature reached the fifties.* [Middle English *fifti,* from Old English *fīftig.* See **penkʷe** in Appendix.] **—fif′ty** *adj. & pron.*

fif·ty-fif·ty (fĭf′tē-fĭf′tē) *adj.* **1.** Divided or shared in two equal portions: *a fifty-fifty split.* **2.** Being equally likely and unlikely or favorable and unfavorable: *had a fifty-fifty chance of surviving.* **—fif′ty-fif′ty** *adv.*

fig[1] (fĭg) *n.* **1.a.** Any of several trees or shrubs of the genus *Ficus,* especially *F. carica,* native to the Mediterranean region and widely cultivated for its edible multiple fruit. **b.** The sweet, hollow, pear-shaped, multiple fruit of this plant, having numerous tiny seedlike fruits. **2.a.** Any of several plants bearing similar fruit. **b.** The fruit of such a plant. **3.** A trivial or contemptible amount: *not worth a fig; didn't care a fig.* [Middle English, from Old French *figue,* from Old Provençal *figa,* from Vulgar Latin **fīca,* from Latin *fīcus.*]

fig[2] (fĭg) *n.* **1.** Dress; array: *in full fig.* **2.** Physical condition; shape: *in fine fig.* [Perhaps from *fig,* to trot out a horse in lively condition, dress up, variant of *feague,* to make a horse lively, probably from Dutch *vegen,* to brush, from Middle Dutch *vēghen.*]

fig. *abbr.* **1.** Figurative. **2.** Figure.

fight (fīt) *v.* **fought** (fôt), **fight·ing, fights.** *—intr.* **1.a.** To attempt to harm or gain power over an adversary by blows or with weapons. **b.** *Sports.* To engage in boxing or wrestling. **2.** To engage in a quarrel; argue: *They are always fighting about money.* **3.** To strive vigorously and resolutely: *fought against graft; fighting for her rights.* *—tr.* **1.a.** To contend with physically or in battle. **b.** To wage or carry on (a battle). **c.** To contend for, by or as if by combat: *"I now resolved that Calais should be fought to the death"* (Winston S. Churchill). **2.a.** *Sports.* To box or wrestle against in a ring. **b.** To participate in (a boxing match, for example). **3.** To set (a boxer, for example) in combat with another. See Synonyms at **oppose. 4.** To contend with or struggle against: *fight cancer; fight temptation.* **5.** To try to prevent the development or success of. **6.** To gain by struggle or striving: *fought my way to the top.* **—fight** *n.* **1.** A confrontation between opposing groups in which each attempts to harm or gain power over the other, as with bodily force or weapons. **2.** A quarrel or conflict. **3.a.** A physical conflict between two or more individuals. **b.** *Sports.* A boxing or wrestling match. **4.** A struggle to achieve an objective. See Synonyms at **conflict. 5.** The power or inclination to fight; pugnacity: *I just didn't have any fight left in me.* ***—phrasal verb.*** **fight off.** To defend against or drive back (a hostile force, for example). ***—idioms.*** **fight fire with fire.** To combat one evil or one set of negative circumstances by reacting in kind. **fight shy of.** To avoid meeting or confronting. [Middle English *fighten,* from Old English *feohtan, fihtan.*] **—fight′a·bil′i·ty** *n.* **—fight′a·ble** *adj.* **—fight′ing·ly** *adv.*

fight·er (fī′tər) *n.* **1.** One that fights, as: **a.** A soldier; a warrior. **b.** *Sports.* A boxer; a pugilist. **c.** A fast, maneuverable combat aircraft used to engage enemy aircraft. **2.** A pugnacious, unyielding, or determined person.

fight·er-bomb·er (fī′tər-bŏm′ər) *n.* A versatile aircraft capable of functioning as a fighter and a bomber chiefly in tactical and defensive operations.

fight·ing chair (fī′tĭng) *n.* A chair, often padded and equipped with a harness, used on a boat by a saltwater angler for support while landing a large fish.

fighting chance *n.* A chance to win but only with a struggle: *had a fighting chance to recover.*

fight-or-flight reaction (fīt′ôr-flīt′) *n.* A set of physiological changes, such as increases in heart rate, arterial blood pressure, and blood glucose, initiated by the sympathetic nervous system to mobilize body systems in response to stress.

fig leaf *n.* **1.** A stylized representation of the leaf of a fig, used especially to conceal the genitalia depicted on statues of men and boys. **2.** Something that serves as a usually insufficient concealment or camouflage: *"Many fallen executives are still allowed the fig leaf of 'resignation'"* (David Pauly).

fig marigold *n.* Any of various plants of the genus *Mesembryanthemum,* native to southern Africa and having thick, fleshy leaves and variously colored flowers. Also called *icicle plant, pebble plant.*

fig·ment (fĭg′mənt) *n.* Something invented, made up, or fabricated: *just a figment of the imagination.* [Middle English, from Latin *figmentum,* from *fingere,* to form. See **dheigh-** in Appendix.]

fig·ur·al (fĭg′yər-əl) *adj.* Of, relating to, consisting of, or forming a pictorial composition or design of human or animal figures.

fig·u·rant (fĭg′yə-ränt′, -rănt′, -räɴ′) *n.* **1.** A member of a corps de ballet who does not perform solos. **2.** A stage performer having no speaking part. [French, from present participle of *figurer,* to represent, from Old French, from Latin *figūrāre,* to form, from *figūra,* figure. See FIGURE.]

fig·u·ra·tion (fĭg′yə-rā′shən) *n.* **1.** The act of forming something into a particular shape. **2.** A shape, a form, or an outline. **3.** The act of representing with figures. **4.** A figurative representation. **5.** *Music.* Ornamentation of a passage by the use of embellishing and often repeating figures.

fig·u·ra·tive (fĭg′yər-ə-tĭv) *adj. Abbr.* **fig. 1.a.** Based on or making use of figures of speech; metaphorical: *figurative language.* **b.** Containing many figures of speech; ornate. **2.** Represented by a figure or resemblance; emblematic. **3.** Of or relating to artistic representation by means of animal or human figures. **—fig′u·ra·tive·ly** *adv.* **—fig′u·ra·tive·ness** *n.*

fig·ure (fĭg′yər) *n. Abbr.* **fig. 1.a.** A written or printed symbol representing something other than a letter, especially a number. **b. figures.** Mathematical calculations: *good at figures.* **c.** An amount represented in numbers: *sold for a large figure.* **2.a.** *Mathematics.* A geometric form consisting of any combination of points, lines, or planes: *A triangle is a plane figure.* **b.** The outline, form, or silhouette of a thing. **c.** The shape or form of a human body. **d.** An indistinct object or shape: *saw figures dashing down the street.* **3.a.** A person, especially a well-known one: *a famous historical figure.* **b.** A person's public image or presence: *became a tragic figure overnight.* **4.** Impression or appearance made: *cuts a dashing figure.* **5.** A person, an animal, or an object that symbolizes something. **6.** A pictorial or sculptural representation, especially of the human body. **7.a.** A diagram. **b.** A design or pattern, as in a textile: *silk with a paisley figure.* **8.** An illustration printed from an engraved plate or block. **9.a.** A configuration or distinct group of steps in a dance. **b.** A pattern traced by a series of movements, as in ice skating. **10.** *Music.* A brief melodic or harmonic unit often constituting the base for a larger phrase or structure. **11.** *Logic.* Any one of the forms that a syllogism can take, depending on the position of the middle term. **—figure** *v.* **-ured, -ur·ing, -ures.** *—tr.* **1.** *Mathematics.* To calculate with numbers. **2.** To make a likeness of; depict. **3.** To adorn with a design or figures. **4.** *Music.* To indicate the chordal structure of (a bass line of single notes) with a sequence of conventionalized numbers. **5.** *Informal.* **a.** To conclude, believe, or predict: *I never figured that this would happen.* **b.** To consider or regard: *figured them as con artists.* *—intr.* **1.** *Mathematics.* To calculate; compute. **2.a.** To be or seem important or prominent. **b.** To be pertinent or involved: *politicians who figured in the scandal.* **3.** *Informal.* To seem reasonable or expected: *It figures.* ***—phrasal verbs.*** **figure in.** To include, as in making an account: *figured in travel expenses.* **figure on.** *Informal.* **1.** To depend on: *We figured on your support.* **2.** To take into consideration; expect: *I figured on an hour's delay.* **3.** To plan: *We figure on leaving at noon.* **figure out.** *Informal.* **1.** To discover or decide: *Let's figure out a way to help.* **2.** To solve or decipher: *Can you figure out this puzzle?* [Middle English, from Old French, from Latin *figūra.* See **dheigh-** in Appendix.] **—fig′ur·er** *n.*

SYNONYMS: *figure, design, device, motif, pattern.* The central meaning shared by these nouns is "an element or a component in a decorative composition": *a tapestry with a floral figure; a rug with a geometric design; a brooch with a fanciful and intricate device; a scarf with a heart motif; fabric with a plaid pattern.* See also Synonyms at **calculate, form.**

fig·ured (fĭg′yərd) *adj.* **1.** Shaped or fashioned in a particular way. **2.** Decorated with a design; patterned: *"My dress is richly figured"* (Amy Lowell). **3.** Represented, as in graphic art or sculpture; depicted.

figured bass (bās) *n. Music.* See **continuo.**

figure eight *n.* A form or representation, such as a knot or an ice-skating maneuver, that has the shape of the numeral 8.

fig·ure·head (fĭg′yər-hĕd′) *n.* **1.** A person given a position of nominal leadership but having no actual authority. **2.** *Nautical.* A carved figure on the prow of a ship.

figure of speech *n., pl.* **figures of speech.** An expression such as a metaphor or simile or a device such as personification or hyperbole in which words are used in a nonliteral way to achieve an effect beyond the range of ordinary language.

figure skat·ing (skā′tĭng) *n. Sports.* Ice skating in which

fig[1]

figurehead

figure skating
Scott Hamilton, photographed in 1983

ă pat	oi boy
ā pay	ou out
âr care	o͝o took
ä father	o͞o boot
ĕ pet	ŭ cut
ē be	ûr urge
ĭ pit	th thin
ī pie	*th* this
îr pier	hw which
ŏ pot	zh vision
ō toe	ə about, item
ô paw	♦ regionalism

Stress marks: ′ (primary); ′ (secondary), as in **dictionary** (dĭk′shə-nĕr′ē)

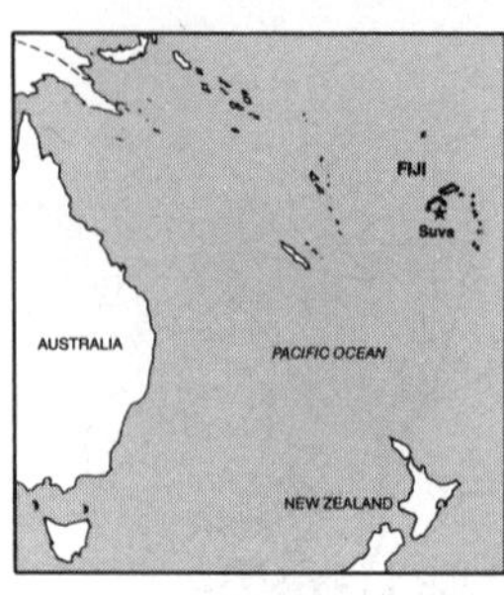

Fiji

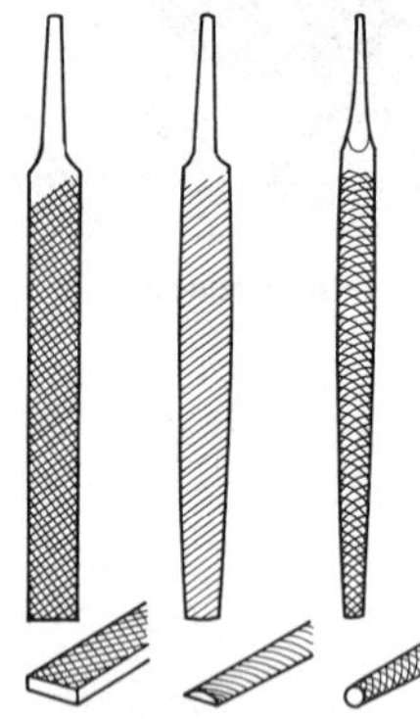

file[2]
Left to right: Flat, half-rounded, and round tipped files

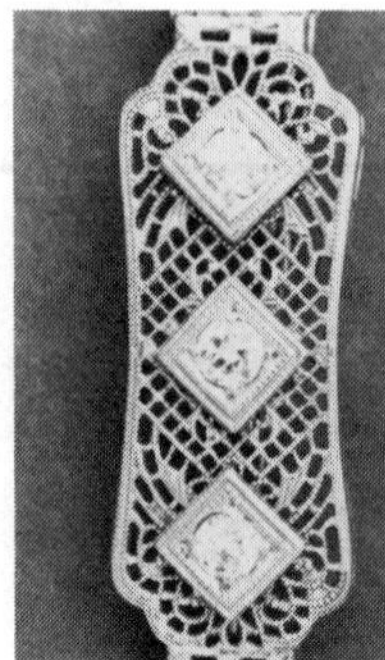

filigree
Detail of a bracelet

the skater traces prescribed, usually elaborate figures. **—figure skater** *n.*

fig·ures shift (fĭg′yərz) *n.* **1.** A shift in a typewriter to uppercase. **2.** *Computer Science.* A data control character after which characters are interpreted as having been typed in the uppercase mode.

fig·u·rine (fĭg′yə-rēn′) *n.* A small molded or sculptured figure; a statuette. [French, from Italian *figurina,* diminutive of *figura,* figure, from Latin *figūra.* See FIGURE.]

fig wasp *n.* A small wasp belonging to the family Agonidae, especially *Blastophaga psenes,* that breeds in caprifig and is active in the pollination of fig trees and shrubs.

fig·wort (fĭg′wûrt′, -wôrt′) *n.* Any of various plants of the genus *Scrophularia* having loose, branching clusters of small greenish or purple flowers. [FIG[1], piles (obsolete) + WORT[1] (from its use as a folk medicine).]

Fi·ji (fē′jē). An island country of the southwest Pacific Ocean comprising about 320 islands. The islands were annexed by Great Britain in 1874 and became independent in 1970. Suva, on the island of Viti Levu, is the capital. Population, 686,000.

Fi·ji·an (fē′jē-ən) *n.* **1.** A native or inhabitant of Fiji. **2.** The Austronesian language of Fiji. **—Fijian** *adj.* Of or relating to Fiji or its people, language, or culture.

fi·la (fī′lə) *n.* Plural of **filum.**

fil·a·ment (fĭl′ə-mənt) *n.* **1.** A fine or thinly spun thread, fiber, or wire. **2.** *Botany.* **a.** The stalk that bears the anther in a stamen. **b.** A chainlike series of cells, as in many algae. **3. a.** A fine wire heated electrically to incandescence in an electric lamp. **b.** *Electronics.* A high-resistance wire or ribbon forming the cathode in some thermionic tubes. [New Latin *filāmentum,* from Late Latin *filāre,* to spin, from Latin *fīlum,* thread. See **gʷhī-** in Appendix.] **—fil′a·men′tous** (-mĕn′təs), **fil′a·men′ta·ry** (-mĕn′tə-rē, -mĕn′trē) *adj.*

fi·lar (fī′lər) *adj.* **1.** Of or relating to a thread. **2.** Having fine threads across the field of view for measuring small distances, as in the eyepiece of a telescope. [From Latin *fīlum,* thread. See **gʷhī-** in Appendix.]

fil·a·ree (fĭl′ə-rē′) *n.* See **alfilaria.** [Alteration of ALFILARIA.]

fi·lar·i·a (fə-lâr′ē-ə) *n., pl.* **-i·ae** (-ē-ē′). Any of various slender, threadlike nematode worms of the superfamily Filarioidea that are parasitic in vertebrates and are often transmitted as larvae by mosquitos and other biting insects. The adult form lives in the blood and lymphatic tissues, causing inflammation and obstruction that can lead to elephantiasis. [New Latin *Fīlāria,* former genus name, from Latin *fīlum,* thread. See **gʷhī-** in Appendix.] **—fi·lar′i·al** (-ē-əl), **fi·lar′i·an** (-ē-ən) *adj.*

fil·a·ri·a·sis (fĭl′ə-rī′ə-sĭs) *n., pl.* **-ses** (-sēz′). Disease caused by infestation of tissue with filariae. [FILAR(IA) + -IASIS.]

fil·a·ture (fĭl′ə-cho͝or′, -chər) *n.* **1.** The act or process of spinning, drawing, or twisting into threads. **2.** The act or process of reeling raw silk from cocoons. **3.** A reel used in drawing silk from cocoons. **4.** An establishment where silk is reeled. [French, from Late Latin *fīlātus,* past participle of *fīlāre,* to spin. See FILAMENT.]

fil·bert (fĭl′bərt) *n.* **1.** See **hazel** (sense 1). **2.** See **hazelnut.** [Middle English, from Anglo-Norman *philber,* after Saint *Philibert* (died 684), whose feast day in late August coincides with the ripening of the nut.]

filch (fĭlch) *tr.v.* **filched, filch·ing, filch·es.** To take (something, especially something of little value) in a furtive manner; snitch. See Synonyms at **steal.** [Middle English *filchen.*] **—filch′er** *n.*

Filch·ner Ice Shelf (fĭlk′nər). An area of Antarctica bordering on Coats Land at the head of Weddell Sea.

file[1] (fīl) *n.* **1.** A container, such as a cabinet or folder, for keeping papers in order. **2. a.** A collection of papers or published materials kept or arranged in convenient order. **b.** *Computer Science.* A collection of related data or program records. **3. a.** A line of persons, animals, or things positioned one behind the other. **b.** A line of troops or military vehicles so positioned. **4.** *Games.* Any of the rows of squares that run vertically or between players on a playing board in chess or checkers. **5.** *Archaic.* A list or roll. **—file** *v.* **filed, fil·ing, files.** *—tr.* **1.** To put or keep (papers, for example) in useful order for storage or reference. **2.** To enter (a legal document) on public official record. **3.** To send or submit (copy) to a newspaper. **4.** To carry out the first stage of (a lawsuit, for example): *filed charges against my associate.* *—intr.* **1.** To march or walk in a line. **2.** To put items in a file. **3.** To make application; apply: *filed for a job with the state; file for a divorce.* **4.** To enter one's name in a political contest: *filed for Congress.* **—*idiom.* on file.** In or as if in a file for easy reference: *We will keep your résumé on file.* [From Middle English *filen,* to put documents on file, from Old French *filer,* to spin thread, to put documents on a thread, from Late Latin *fīlāre,* to spin, draw out in a long line, from Latin *fīlum,* thread. See **gʷhī-** in Appendix.]

file[2] (fīl) *n.* **1.** Any of several hardened steel tools with cutting ridges for forming, smoothing, or reducing especially metallic surfaces. **2.** A nail file. **3.** *Chiefly British.* A crafty or artful person. **—file** *tr.v.* **filed, fil·ing, files.** To smooth, reduce, or remove with or as if with a file. [Middle English, from Old English *fīl.* See **peig-** in Appendix.]

file[3] (fīl) *tr.v.* **filed, fil·ing, files.** *Archaic.* To make sullied or corrupt; defile. [Middle English *filien,* from Old English *fȳlan.* See **pū̆-** in Appendix.]

fi·lé (fē′lā, fĭ-lā′) *n.* Powdered sassafras leaves used to thicken and season soups, stews, and gumbos. [Louisiana French, from French, past participle of *filer,* to spin thread (from its effect when added to hot liquids), from Old French. See FILE[1].]

file clerk *n.* One who is employed to maintain the files and records of an office.

file·fish (fīl′fĭsh′) *n., pl.* **filefish** or **-fish·es.** Any of various chiefly tropical marine fishes of the family Balistidae, related to and resembling the triggerfishes, with a flat body and rough, spiny scales.

fi·let[1] (fĭ-lā′, fĭl′ā′) *n.* A net or lace with a simple pattern of squares. [French, from Old French, diminutive of *fil,* thread, from Latin *fīlum.* See FILE[1].]

fi·let[2] (fĭ-lā′, fĭl′ā′) *n.* Variant of **fillet** (sense 2). **—filet** *v.* Variant of **fillet** (sense 2).

fi·let mi·gnon (fĭ-lā′ mēn-yôɴ′, fĭl′ā′) *n., pl.* **fi·lets mi·gnons** (fĭ-lā′ mēn-yôɴ′, fĭl′ā). A small, round, very choice cut of beef from the loin. [French : *filet,* fillet + *mignon,* dainty.]

fil·i·al (fĭl′ē-əl) *adj.* **1.** Of, relating to, or befitting a son or daughter: *filial respect.* **2.** Having or assuming the relationship of child or offspring to parent. **3.** *Genetics.* Of or relating to a generation or the sequence of generations following the parental generation. [Middle English, from Old French, from Late Latin *fīliālis,* from Latin *fīlius,* son. See **dhē(i)-** in Appendix.] **—fil′i·al·ly** *adv.*

fil·i·ate (fĭl′ē-āt′) *tr.v.* **-at·ed, -at·ing, -ates.** *Law.* To determine judicially the paternity of (a child born out of wedlock, for example). [Medieval Latin *fīliāre, fīliāt-,* to acknowledge as a son, from Latin *fīlius,* son. See **dhē(i)-** in Appendix.]

fil·i·a·tion (fĭl′ē-ā′shən) *n.* **1. a.** The condition or fact of being the child of a certain parent. **b.** *Law.* Judicial determination of paternity. **2.** A line of descent; derivation. **3. a.** The act or fact of forming a new branch, as of a society or language group. **b.** The branch thus formed.

fil·i·bus·ter (fĭl′ə-bŭs′tər) *n.* **1. a.** The use of obstructionist tactics, especially prolonged speechmaking, for the purpose of delaying legislative action. **b.** An instance of the use of this delaying tactic. **2.** An adventurer who engages in a private military action in a foreign country. **—filibuster** *v.* **-tered, -ter·ing, -ters.** *—intr.* **1.** To use obstructionist tactics in a legislative body. **2.** To take part in a private military action in a foreign country. *—tr.* To use obstructionist tactics against (a legislative measure, for example). [Spanish *filibustero,* freebooter, from French *flibustier,* from Dutch *vrijbuiter,* pirate. See FREEBOOTER.] **—fil′i·bus′ter·er** *n.*

fil·i·form (fĭl′ə-fôrm′, fī′lə-) *adj.* Having the form of or resembling a thread or filament. [Latin *fīlum,* thread; see **gʷhī-** in Appendix + -FORM.]

fil·i·gree (fĭl′ĭ-grē′) *n.* **1.** Delicate and intricate ornamental work made from gold, silver, or other fine twisted wire. **2. a.** An intricate, delicate, or fanciful ornamentation. **b.** A design resembling such ornamentation: *filigrees of frosting on a cake.* **—filigree** *tr.v.* **-greed, -gree·ing, -grees.** To decorate with or as if with filigree. [Alteration of French *filigrane,* from Italian *filigrana* : Latin *fīlum,* thread; see **gʷhī-** in Appendix + Latin *grānum,* grain; see **gr̥-no-** in Appendix.]

fil·ing (fī′lĭng) *n.* **1.** The act or an instance of using a file. **2.** A particle or shaving removed by a file: *metal filings.*

fil·i·o·pi·e·tis·tic (fĭl′ē-ō-pī′ĭ-tĭs′tĭk) *adj.* Of or relating to an often immoderate reverence for forebears or tradition. [Latin *fīlius,* son; see FILIAL + PIETISTIC.]

Fil·i·pi·no (fĭl′ə-pē′nō) *n., pl.* **-nos.** **1.** A native or inhabitant of the Philippines. **2.** Used as the name for the Austronesian language that is based on Tagalog, draws its lexicon from other Philippine languages, and is the official language of the Philippines. **—Filipino** *adj.* Of or relating to the Philippines or its peoples, languages, or cultures. [Spanish, from *(Islas) Filipinas,* Philippine (Islands).]

fill (fĭl) *v.* **filled, fill·ing, fills.** *—tr.* **1. a.** To put into as much as can be held: *fill a glass with milk.* **b.** To supply to the fullest extent: *fill a concert hall.* **c.** To build up the level of (low-lying land) with material such as earth or gravel. **d.** To stop or plug up (an opening, for example). **e.** To repair a cavity of (a tooth). **f.** To add a foreign substance to (cloth or wood, for example). **2. a.** To satiate, as with food and drink. **b.** To satisfy or meet; fulfill: *fill the requirements.* See Synonyms at **satisfy.** **c.** To complete (something) by insertion or addition: *fill in the blanks.* **d.** To supply with material, such as writing, an inscription, or an illustration: *filled the blank spaces on the page with notes.* **3.** To supply as required: *fill a prescription; fill an order.* **4. a.** To place a person in: *fill a job vacancy.* **b.** To possess and discharge the duties of; hold: *fill a post.* **5. a.** To occupy the whole of; pervade: *Music filled the room.* **b.** To spread throughout: *Fear filled the city.* **c.** To engage or occupy completely; make full: *filled the child's mind with strange ideas; a story that filled our hearts with joy.* **6.** To cover the surface of (an inexpensive metal) with a layer of precious metal, such as gold. **7.** *Nautical.* **a.** To cause (a sail) to swell. **b.** To adjust (a yard) so that wind will cause a sail to swell. *—intr.* To become full. **—fill** *n.* **1.** An amount needed to make full, complete, or satisfied: *eat one's fill.* **2.** Material for filling a container, cavity, or passage. **3. a.** A built-up piece of land; an embankment. **b.** The material, such as earth or gravel, used for fill. **—*phrasal verbs.* fill in. 1.** *Informal.* To provide with information that is essential or newly acquired: *I wasn't* *there—would you fill me in?* **2.** To act as a substitute; stand in: *an understudy who filled in at the last minute.* **fill out. 1.** To complete (a form, for example) by providing required information: *carefully filled out the job application.* **2.** To become or make more fleshy: *He filled out after age 35.* **—*idioms.* fill (someone's) shoes.** To assume someone's position or duties. **fill the bill.** *Informal.* To serve a particular purpose. [Middle English *fillen,* from Old English *fyllan.* See **pele-**[1] in Appendix.]

filled gold (fĭld) *n.* A relatively inexpensive metal such as brass with a surface layer of bonded gold.

filled milk *n.* Skim milk with vegetable oils added to substitute for butterfat.

fill·er (fĭl′ər) *n.* One that fills, as: **a.** Something added in order to augment weight or size or fill space. **b.** A composition, especially a semisolid that hardens on drying, used to fill pores, cracks, or holes in wood, plaster, or other construction surfaces before finishing. **c.** Tobacco used to form the body of a cigar. **d.** A short item used to fill space in a publication. **e.** Something, such as a news item, public-service message, or music, used to fill time in a radio or television presentation. **f.** A sheaf of loose papers used to fill a notebook or binder. **g.** *Architecture.* An element, such as a plate, used to fill the space between two supporting members.

fil·lér (fĭl′âr′) *n., pl.* **fillér** or **-lérs.** See table at **currency.** [Hungarian.]

fil·let (fĭl′ĭt) *n.* **1.** A narrow strip of ribbon or similar material, often worn as a headband. **2.** Also **fi·let** (fĭ-lā′, fĭl′ā′). **a.** A strip or compact piece of boneless meat or fish, especially the beef tenderloin. **b.** A boneless strip of meat rolled and tied, as for roasting. **3.** *Architecture.* **a.** A thin, flat molding used as separation between or ornamentation for larger moldings. **b.** A ridge between the indentations of a fluted column. **4.** A narrow decorative line impressed onto the cover of a book. **5.** *Heraldry.* A narrow horizontal band placed in the lower fourth area of the chief. **6.** *Anatomy.* A loop-shaped band of fibers, such as the lemniscus. **—fillet** *tr.v.* **-let·ed, -let·ing, -lets. 1.** To bind or decorate with or as if with a fillet. **2.** Also **fi·let** (fĭ-lā′, fĭl′ā′). To slice, bone, or make into fillets. [Middle English *filet,* from Old French, diminutive of *fil,* thread, from Latin *fīlum.* See **gʷhī-** in Appendix.]

fill-in (fĭl′ĭn′) *n. Informal.* **1.** One that serves as a substitute for another. **2.** A short, informative summary.

fill·ing (fĭl′ĭng) *n.* **1.** An act or instance of filling. **2.** Something used to fill a space, cavity, or container: *a gold filling in a tooth.* **3.** An edible mixture used to fill pastries, sandwiches, or cakes: *a pie filling.* **4.** The horizontal threads that cross the warp in weaving; weft.

filling station *n.* See **service station** (sense 1).

fil·lip (fĭl′əp) *n.* **1.** A snap or light blow made by pressing a fingertip against the thumb and suddenly releasing it. **2.** A slight goad or incentive; a small stimulus. **—fillip** *tr.v.* **-liped, -lip·ing, -lips.** To strike, propel, arouse, or stimulate. [Imitative.]

Fill·more (fĭl′môr′, -mōr′), **Millard.** 1800–1874. The 13th President of the United States (1850–1853), who succeeded to office after the death of Zachary Taylor. He struggled to keep the nation unified but lost the support of his Whig Party by attempting to enforce the Fugitive Slave Act in the North.

fil·ly (fĭl′ē) *n., pl.* **-lies. 1.** A young female horse. **2.** *Informal.* A lively, high-spirited girl. [Middle English *filli,* from Old Norse *fylja.* See **pau-** in Appendix.]

film (fĭlm) *n.* **1.** A thin skin or membrane. **2.** A thin, opaque, abnormal coating on the cornea of the eye. **3.** A thin covering or coating: *a film of dust on the piano.* **4.** A thin, flexible, transparent sheet, as of plastic, used in wrapping or packaging. **5.a.** A thin sheet or strip of flexible material, such as a cellulose derivative or a thermoplastic resin, coated with a photosensitive emulsion and used to make photographic negatives or transparencies. **b.** A thin sheet or strip of developed photographic negatives or transparencies. **6.a.** A movie. **b.** Movies considered as a group. **7.** A coating of magnetic alloys on glass used in manufacturing computer storage devices. **—film** *v.* **filmed, film·ing, films.** *—tr.* **1.** To cover with or as if with a film. **2.** To make a movie of or based on: *film a rocket launch; film a scene from a ballet.* *—intr.* **1.** To become coated or obscured with or as if with a film: *The window filmed over with moisture.* **2.** To make or shoot scenes for a movie. [Middle English, from Old English *filmen.* See **pel-**[3] in Appendix.]

WORD HISTORY: One indication of the gulf between us and our Victorian predecessors is that the *Oxford English Dictionary* fascicle containing the word *film,* published in 1896, does not have the sense "a motion picture." The one hint of the future to be found among still familiar older senses of the word, such as "a thin skin or membranous coating" or "an abnormal thin coating on the cornea," is the sense of *film* used in photography, a sense referring to a coating of material, such as gelatin, that could substitute for a photographic plate or be used on a plate or on photographic paper. Thus a word that has been with us since Old English times took on this new use, first recorded in 1845, which has since developed and now refers to an art form, a sense first recorded in 1920.

film·card (fĭlm′kärd′) *n.* A microfiche.

film·dom (fĭlm′dəm) *n.* **1.** The movie industry. **2.** The people employed in the movie industry. Also called *moviedom.*

film·go·er (fĭlm′gō′ər) *n.* One who frequently goes to see movies. **—film′go′ing** *adj.*

film·ic (fĭl′mĭk) *adj.* Of, relating to, or characteristic of movies; cinematic. **—film′i·cal·ly** *adv.*

film·mak·er (fĭlm′mā′kər) *n.* One who directs or produces movies.

film·mak·ing (fĭlm′mā′kĭng) *n.* The making of movies.

film·og·ra·phy (fĭl-mŏg′rə-fē) *n., pl.* **-phies. 1.** Writings about movies. **2.** A list of movies, as of a given director or actor. **—film·og′ra·pher** *n.*

film pack *n.* A pack of photographic sheet films that can be exposed in succession and withdrawn from the exposure position for storage at the rear of the pack.

film·set·ting (fĭlm′sĕt′ĭng) *n.* Photocomposition.

film·strip (fĭlm′strĭp′) *n.* A length of film containing photographs, diagrams, or other graphic matter prepared for still projection. Also called *stripfilm.*

film·y (fĭl′mē) *adj.* **-i·er, -i·est. 1.** Of, resembling, or consisting of film; gauzy. See Synonyms at **airy. 2.** Covered by or as if by a film; hazy. **—film′i·ly** *adv.* **—film′i·ness** *n.*

fil·o·plume (fĭl′ə-plo͞om′, fī′lə-) *n.* A hairlike feather having few or no barbs, usually located between contour feathers. [Latin *fīlum,* thread; see **gʷhī-** in Appendix + PLUME.]

fi·lose (fī′lōs′) *adj.* **1.** Threadlike. **2.** Having or ending in a threadlike part or process. [Latin *fīlum,* thread; see **gʷhī-** in Appendix + –OSE[1].]

fils[1] (fēs) *n.* Used to distinguish a son from his father when they have the same given name. [French, from Latin *fīlius,* son. See **dhē(i)-** in Appendix.]

fils[2] (fĭls) *n., pl.* **fils.** See table at **currency.** [Arabic *fals, fils,* from Latin *follis,* bellows, windbag, purse, piece of money. See **bhel-**[2] in Appendix.]

fil·ter (fĭl′tər) *n.* **1.a.** A porous material through which a liquid or gas is passed in order to separate the fluid from suspended particulate matter. **b.** A device containing such a substance. **2.** Any of various electric, electronic, acoustic, or optical devices used to reject signals, vibrations, or radiations of certain frequencies while passing others. **—filter** *v.* **-tered, -ter·ing, -ters.** *—tr.* **1.** To pass (a liquid or gas) through a filter. **2.** To remove by passing through a filter: *filter out impurities.* *—intr.* **1.** To pass through or as if through a filter: *Light filtered through the blinds.* **2.** To come or go gradually and in small groups: *The audience filtered back into the hall.* [Middle English *filtre,* from Old French, from Medieval Latin *filtrum,* of Germanic origin. See **pel-**[5] in Appendix.] **—fil′ter·er** *n.* **—fil′ter·less** *adj.*

fil·ter·a·ble (fĭl′tər-ə-bəl, fĭl′trə-) also **fil·tra·ble** (-trə-bəl) *adj.* **1.** That can be filtered or separated by filtering: *filterable solutions of granular matter.* **2.** That can pass through a given pore size. **—fil′ter·a·bil′i·ty** *n.*

filterable virus *n.* A virus that is small enough to pass through a fine-pored filter, as of diatomite or porcelain. Also called *ultravirus.*

filter bed *n.* A layer of sand or gravel on the bottom of a reservoir or tank, used to filter water or sewage.

filter feeder *n.* An aquatic animal, such as a clam, barnacle, or sponge, that feeds by filtering particulate organic material from water.

filter paper *n.* Porous paper suitable for use as a filter.

filth (fĭlth) *n.* **1.a.** Foul or dirty matter. **b.** Disgusting garbage or refuse. **2.** A dirty or corrupt condition; foulness. **3.** Something, such as language or printed matter, considered obscene, prurient, or immoral. [Middle English, from Old English *fȳlth.* See **pū̆-** in Appendix.]

filth·y (fĭl′thē) *adj.* **-i·er, -i·est. 1.** Covered with or smeared with filth; disgustingly dirty. See Synonyms at **dirty. 2.** Obscene; scatological. **3.** Vile; nasty: *a filthy traitor.* **—filth′i·ly** *adv.* **—filth′i·ness** *n.*

fil·tra·ble (fĭl′trə-bəl) *adj.* Variant of **filterable.**

fil·trate (fĭl′trāt′) *tr. & intr.v.* **-trat·ed, -trat·ing, -trates.** To put or go through a filter. **—filtrate** *n.* Material, especially liquid, that has passed through a filter. [New Latin *filtrāre, filtrāt-,* to filter, from Medieval Latin *filtrum,* filter. See FILTER.]

fil·tra·tion (fĭl-trā′shən) *n.* The act or process of filtering.

fi·lum (fī′ləm) *n., pl.* **-la** (-lə). A threadlike anatomical structure; a filament. [Latin *fīlum,* thread. See **gʷhī-** in Appendix.]

fim·bri·a (fĭm′brē-ə) *n., pl.* **-bri·ae** (-brē-ē′). A fringelike part or structure, as at the opening of the fallopian tubes. [Late Latin *fimbria,* fringe, feminine sing. of Latin *fimbriae,* threads, fringe.] **—fim′bri·al** *adj.*

fim·bri·ate (fĭm′brē-ĭt, -āt′) also **fim·bri·at·ed** (-ā′tĭd) *adj.* Fringed, as the edge of a petal or the opening of a duct. [Latin *fimbriātus,* from *fimbriae,* fringe.] **—fim′bri·a′tion** *n.*

fin[1] (fĭn) *n.* **1.** A membranous appendage extending from the body of a fish or other aquatic animal, used for propelling, steering, or balancing the body in the water. **2.** Something resembling a fin in shape or function, as: **a.** A fixed or movable airfoil used to stabilize an aircraft, a missile, or a projectile in flight. **b.** A projecting vane used for cooling, as on a radiator or an engine cylinder. **c.** See **tail fin** (sense 2). **3.** See **flipper** (sense 2). **—fin**

Millard Fillmore

fin[1]
Angelfish

ă pat	oi boy
ā pay	ou out
âr care	o͝o took
ä father	o͞o boot
ĕ pet	ŭ cut
ē be	ûr urge
ĭ pit	th thin
ī pie	*th* this
îr pier	hw which
ŏ pot	zh vision
ō toe	ə about, item
ô paw	♦ regionalism

Stress marks: ′ (primary); ′ (secondary), as in **dictionary** (dĭk′shə-nĕr′ē)

v. **finned, fin·ning, fins.** —*tr.* To equip with fins. —*intr.* **1.** To emerge with the fins above water. **2.** To swim, as a fish. **3.** To lash the water with the fins. Used of a dying whale. [Middle English, from Old English *finn.*]

fin[2] (fĭn) *n. Slang.* A five-dollar bill. [Yiddish *finf,* five, from Old High German *funf, finf.* See **penk^{w}e** in Appendix.]

fin. *abbr.* **1.** Finance; financial. **2.** Finish.

Fin. *abbr.* Finland; Finnish.

fi·na·gle (fə-nā′gəl) *v.* **-gled, -gling, -gles.** *Informal.* —*tr.* **1.** To obtain or achieve by indirect, usually deceitful methods: *finagle a day off from work.* **2.** To cheat; swindle: *shady stockbrokers who finagle their clients out of fortunes.* —*intr.* To use crafty, deceitful methods. [Probably from dialectal *fainaigue,* to cheat.] —**fi·na′gler** *n.*

fi·nal (fī′nəl) *adj.* **1.** Forming or occurring at the end; last: *the final scene of a film.* **2.** Of or constituting the end result of a succession or process; ultimate: *an act with an immediate purpose and a final purpose.* **3.** Not to be changed or reconsidered; unalterable: *The judge's decision is final.* See Synonyms at **last[1].** —**final** *n.* Something that comes at or forms the end, especially: **a.** The last or one of the last of a series of contests: *the finals of a state spelling bee.* **b.** The last examination of an academic course. [Middle English, from Old French, from Latin *fīnālis,* from *fīnis,* end.] —**fi′nal·ly** *adv.*

fi·nal·e (fə-năl′ē, -nä′lē) *n.* The concluding part, especially of a musical composition. [Italian, from Latin *fīnālis,* final. See FINAL.]

fi·nal·ist (fī′nə-lĭst) *n.* A contestant in the final session of a competition.

fi·nal·i·ty (fī-năl′ĭ-tē, fə-) *n., pl.* **-ties. 1.** The condition or fact of being final. **2.** A final, conclusive, or decisive act or utterance.

fi·nal·ize (fī′nə-līz′) *tr.v.* **-ized, -iz·ing, -iz·es.** *Usage Problem.* To put into final form; complete or conclude: *"They have jointly agreed . . . to drop all litigation when the merger is finalized"* (Springfield MA Union-News). —**fi′nal·i·za′tion** (-nə-lĭ-zā′shən) *n.* —**fi′nal·iz′er** *n.*

USAGE NOTE: *Finalize* is frequently associated with the language of bureaucracy and so is objected to by many writers. The sentence *We will finalize plans for a class reunion* was unacceptable to 71 percent of the Usage Panel. Although *finalize* has no single exact synonym, a substitute can always be found from among *complete, conclude, make final,* and *put into final form.* See Usage Note at **-ize.**

Final Solution also **final solution** *n.* The Nazi program of exterminating Jews during the German Third Reich: *"The SS Jewish section kept the account books of the Final Solution"* (Emanuel Litvinoff). [Translation of German *Endlösung* : *end-,* final + *Lösung,* solution.]

fi·nance (fə-năns′, fī-, fī′năns′) *n.* **1.** *Abbr.* **fin.** The science of the management of money and other assets. **2.** The management of money, banking, investments, and credit. **3. finances.** Monetary resources; funds, especially those of a government or corporate body. **4.** The supplying of funds or capital. —**finance** *tr.v.* **-nanced, -nanc·ing, -nanc·es. 1.** To provide or raise the funds or capital for: *financed a new car.* **2.** To supply funds to: *financing a daughter through law school.* **3.** To furnish credit to. [Middle English *finaunce,* settlement, money supply, from Old French *finance,* payment, from *finer,* to pay ransom, from *fin,* end, from Latin *fīnis.*] —**fi·nance′a·ble** *adj.*

finance bill *n.* A legislative act to raise public revenues.

finance company *n.* A company that makes loans to clients.

fi·nan·cial (fə-năn′shəl, fī-) *adj. Abbr.* **fin.** Of, relating to, or involving finance, finances, or financiers. —**fi·nan′cial·ly** *adv.*

SYNONYMS: *financial, pecuniary, fiscal, monetary.* These adjectives mean of or relating to money (*a financial adviser; pecuniary motives; a fiscal year; monetary considerations*), but they often differ in application. *Financial* frequently refers to transactions involving money on a large scale: *Many computer-software corporations are experiencing financial reverses. Pecuniary* is more appropriate to the private, small-scale dealings of individuals: *He received thanks but no pecuniary compensation for his services. Fiscal* applies especially to a nation's financial practices and policies: *The Secretary of the Treasury is the chief fiscal officer of our government. Monetary* has special reference to the coinage, printing, or circulation of currency: *The basic monetary unit of the United States is the dollar.*

fin·an·cier (fĭn′ən-sîr′, fə-năn′-, fī′nən-) *n.* One who is occupied with or expert in large-scale financial affairs. [French, from Old French, from *finance,* payment. See FINANCE.]

fin·back (fĭn′băk′) *n.* A rorqual, especially *Balaenoptera physalus* of the Atlantic and Pacific coasts, that attains a length of about 21 meters (70 feet). Also called *fin whale.*

fin·ca (fĭng′kə, fĕng′kä) *n.* A rural property, especially a large farm or ranch, in Spanish America. [American Spanish, from Spanish, real estate, from Old Spanish *fincar,* to pitch tents, reside, from Vulgar Latin **fingicāre,* from Latin *fīgere,* to fasten. See **dhīg^w-** in Appendix.]

finch (fĭnch) *n.* Any of various relatively small birds of the family Fringillidae, including the goldfinches, sparrows, cardinals, grosbeaks, and canaries, having a short, stout bill adapted for cracking seeds. [Middle English, from Old English *finc.*]

find (fīnd) *v.* **found** (found), **find·ing, finds.** —*tr.* **1.** To come upon, often by accident; meet with. **2.** To come upon after a search: *found the hidden leak in the pipe.* **3.** To discover or ascertain through observation, experience, or study: *found a solution; find the product of two numbers; found that it didn't really matter.* **4. a.** To perceive to be, after experience or consideration: *found the gadget surprisingly useful; found the book entertaining.* **b.** To experience or feel: *found comfort in her smile.* **5.** To recover (something lost): *found her keys.* **6.** To recover the use of; regain: *found my voice and replied.* **7.** To succeed in reaching; arrive at: *The dart found its mark.* **8.** To obtain or acquire by effort: *found the money by economizing.* **9.** To decide on and make a declaration about: *The jury deliberated and found a verdict of guilty. All but one of the jurors found him guilty.* **10.** To furnish; supply. **11. a.** To bring (oneself) to an awareness of what one truly wishes to be and do in life. **b.** To perceive (oneself) to be in a specific place or condition: *found herself at home that night; found himself drawn to the stranger.* —*intr.* To come to a legal decision or verdict: *The jury found for the defendant.* —**find** *n.* **1.** The act of finding. **2.** Something that is found, especially an unexpectedly valuable discovery: *the Rosetta stone, that providential archaeological find.* —***phrasal verb.* find out. 1.** To ascertain (something), as through examination or inquiry: *I found out the phone number by looking it up. If you're not sure, find out.* **2.** To detect the true nature or character of; expose: *Liars risk being found out.* **3.** To detect and apprehend; catch: *Most embezzlers are found out in the end.* [Middle English *finden,* from Old English *findan.* See **pent-** in Appendix.] —**find′a·ble** *adj.*

find·er (fīn′dər) *n.* **1.** One that finds: *a finder of great hidden treasure.* **2.** A viewfinder. **3.** A low-power, wide-angle telescope fixed to the body of a more powerful telescope and pointed in the same direction for initially locating an object to be observed.

find·er's fee (fīn′dərz) *n., pl.* **finders' fees.** A fee paid to the finder of financial backing for a venture or to a party that brings the principals in a venture together.

fin-de-siè·cle (făɴ′dəsē-ĕk′lə) *adj.* Of or characteristic of the last part of the 19th century, especially with reference to its artistic climate of effete sophistication. [French : *fin,* end + *de,* of + *siècle,* century.]

find·ing (fīn′dĭng) *n.* **1.** Something that has been found. **2. a.** A conclusion reached after examination or investigation: *the finding of a grand jury; a coroner's findings.* **b.** A statement or document containing an authoritative decision or conclusion: *a presidential finding that authorized the covert operation.* **3. findings.** Small tools and materials used by an artisan: *a jeweler's findings.*

Find·lay (fĭnd′lē). A city of northwest Ohio south of Toledo. It is a manufacturing center. Population, 35,594.

fine[1] (fīn) *adj.* **fin·er, fin·est. 1.** Of superior quality, skill, or appearance: *a fine day; a fine writer.* **2.** Very small in size, weight, or thickness: *fine type; fine paper.* **3. a.** Free from impurities. **b.** *Abbr.* **f., F.** *Metallurgy.* Containing pure metal in a specified proportion or amount: *gold 21 carats fine.* **4.** Very sharp; keen: *a blade with a fine edge.* **5.** Thin; slender: *fine hairs.* **6.** Exhibiting careful and delicate artistry: *fine china.* See Synonyms at **delicate. 7.** Consisting of very small particles; not coarse: *fine dust.* **8. a.** Subtle or precise: *a fine difference.* **b.** Able to make or detect effects of great subtlety or precision; sensitive: *has a fine eye for color.* **9.** Trained to the highest degree of physical efficiency: *a fine racehorse.* **10.** Characterized by refinement or elegance. **11.** Being in a state of satisfactory health; quite well: *I'm fine. And you?* **12.** Used as an intensive: *a fine mess.* —**fine** *adv.* **1.** Finely. **2.** *Informal.* Very well: *doing fine.* —**fine** *tr. & intr.v.* **fined, fin·ing, fines.** To make or become finer, purer, or cleaner. [Middle English *fin,* from Old French, from Latin *fīnis,* end.] —**fine′ness** *n.*

fine[2] (fīn) *n.* **1.** A sum of money required to be paid as a penalty for an offense. **2.** *Law.* **a.** A forfeiture or penalty to be paid to the offended party in a civil action. **b.** An amicable settlement of a suit over land ownership. **3.** *Obsolete.* An end; a termination. —**fine** *tr.v.* **fined, fin·ing, fines.** To require the payment of a fine from; impose a fine on. —***idiom.* in fine. 1.** In conclusion; finally. **2.** In summation; in brief. [Middle English *fin,* from Old French, settlement, compensation, from Medieval Latin *fīnis,* from Latin *fīnis,* end.] —**fin′a·ble, fine′a·ble** *adj.*

fi·ne[3] (fē′nā) *n. Music.* The end. [Italian, from Latin *fīnis,* end.]

fine art (fīn) *n.* **1.** *Abbr.* **FA, F.A. a.** Art produced or intended primarily for beauty rather than utility. **b.** Often **fine arts.** Any of the art forms, such as sculpture, painting, and music, that are used to create this art. **2.** Something requiring highly developed techniques and skills: *the fine art of teaching.*

fine-drawn (fīn′drôn′) *adj.* **1.** Drawn out to a slender, threadlike state: *fine-drawn wire.* **2.** Subtly or precisely fashioned: *a fine-drawn theory.* **3.** Delicately formed: *fine-drawn features.*

fine-grained (fīn′grānd′) *adj.* Having a fine, smooth, even grain: *fine-grained wood.*

fine·ly (fīn′lē) *adv.* **1.** In a fine manner; splendidly. **2.** To a fine point; discriminatingly. **3.** In small pieces or parts; minutely: *finely chopped nuts.*

fine print (fīn) *n.* **1.** The portion of a document, especially a contract, that contains qualifications or restrictions in small type or obscure language. **2.** Something presented in a deliberately ambiguous or obscure manner. Also called *small print.*

fin·er·y (fīʹnə-rē) *n., pl.* **-ies.** Elaborate adornment, especially fine clothing and accessories.

fines herbes (fēn zĕrbʹ, fēn ĕrbʹ) *pl.n.* Finely chopped herbs, specifically parsley, chives, tarragon, and thyme, mixed together and used as a seasoning. [French : *fines,* feminine pl. of *fin,* fine + *herbes,* pl. of *herbe,* herb.]

fine-spun (fīnʹspŭnʹ) *adj.* **1.** Developed to extreme fineness or subtlety; elaborate. **2.** Developed to excessive fineness or subtlety; overwrought.

fi·nesse (fə-nĕsʹ) *n.* **1.** Refinement and delicacy of performance, execution, or artisanship. **2.** Skillful, subtle handling of a situation; tactful, diplomatic maneuvering. **3.** *Games.* The playing of a card in a suit in which one holds a nonsequential higher card, either to induce an opponent to play an intermediate card that one's partner can then top or to win the trick economically. **4.** A stratagem in which one appears to decline an advantage. **—finesse** *v.* **-nessed, -ness·ing, -ness·es.** *—tr.* **1.** To accomplish by the use of finesse. **2.** To handle with a deceptive or evasive strategy. **3.** *Games.* To play (a card) as a finesse. *—intr.* **1.** To use finesse. **2.** *Games.* To make a finesse in cards. [French, fineness, subtlety, from *fin,* fine. See FINE[1].]

fine structure (fīn) *n.* **1.** *Physics.* The splitting of spectral lines caused by the magnetic moments of orbiting electrons in the atomic nucleus. **2.** *Biology.* See **ultrastructure.**

fine-toothed comb (fīnʹto͞otht′, -to͞othdʹ) *n.* **1.** A comb with teeth set close together. **2.** A method of searching or investigating in minute detail: *examined the figures with a fine-toothed comb but found no errors.*

fine-tune (fīnʹto͞onʹ, -tyo͞onʹ) *tr.v.* **-tuned, -tun·ing, -tunes.** To make small adjustments in for optimal performance or effectiveness: *"Advertising agencies kept fine-tuning the coolly calculated machinery of merchandising and hype"* (New Yorker).

fin·fish (fĭnʹfĭsh′) *n.* An aquatic vertebrate of the superclass Pisces.

Fin·gal's Cave (fĭngʹgəlz). A cavern of western Scotland on Staffa Island in the Inner Hebrides.

fin·ger (fĭngʹgər) *n.* **1.** One of the five digits of the hand, especially one other than the thumb. **2.** The part of a glove designed to cover a finger. **3.** Something, such as an oblong peninsula, that resembles one of the digits of the hand. **4.** The length or width of a finger. **5.** A degree of participation; a share: *"seems almost sure to have a finger or two in crafting the final blueprint"* (George B. Merry). **6.** An obscene gesture of defiance or derision made by pointing or jabbing the middle finger upward. Often used with *the.* **—finger** *v.* **-gered, -ger·ing, -gers.** *—tr.* **1.** To touch with the fingers; handle. See Synonyms at **touch. 2.** *Music.* **a.** To mark (a score) with indications of which fingers are to play the notes. **b.** To play (an instrument) by using the fingers in a particular order or way. **3.** *Slang.* **a.** To inform on. **b.** To designate, especially as an intended victim. *—intr.* **1.** To handle something with the fingers. **2.** *Music.* To use the fingers in playing an instrument. ***—idioms.*** **have** (or **keep**) **(one's) fingers crossed.** To hope for a successful or advantageous outcome. **twist** (or **wrap**) **around (one's) little finger.** To dominate utterly and effortlessly. [Middle English, from Old English. See **penkʷe** in Appendix.] **—finʹger·er** *n.* **—finʹger·less** *adj.*

fin·ger·board (fĭngʹgər-bôrd′, -bōrd′) *n. Music.* A strip of wood on the neck of a stringed instrument against which the strings are pressed in playing.

finger bowl *n.* A small bowl that holds water for rinsing the fingers at the table.

fin·ger·breadth (fĭngʹgər-brĕdth′) *n.* The breadth of one finger.

fin·gered (fĭngʹgərd) *adj.* Having a finger or fingers, especially of a specific number, kind, or appearance. Often used in combination: *four-fingered; rosy-fingered.*

finger hole *n.* **1.** *Music.* Any of the holes on a wind instrument that cause a change in pitch when covered by a finger. **2.** A hole for a finger, as in a bowling ball or on the dial of a telephone.

fin·ger·ing (fĭngʹgər-ĭng) *n. Music.* **1.** The technique used in playing an instrument with the fingers. **2.** The indication on a score of which fingers are to be used in playing.

Fin·ger Lakes (fĭngʹgər). A group of 11 elongated glacial lakes in west-central New York, including Cayuga and Seneca, the largest and deepest of the lakes.

fin·ger·ling (fĭngʹgər-lĭng) *n.* A young or small fish, especially a young salmon or trout.

finger millet *n.* An annual plant *(Eleusine coracana)* in the grass family, native to the Old World tropics and an important cereal in India and Africa. Also called *ragi.*

fin·ger·nail (fĭngʹgər-nāl′) *n.* The nail on a finger.

fin·ger-paint (fĭngʹgər-pānt′) *tr. & intr.v.* **-paint·ed, -paint·ing, -paints.** To make by or engage in finger painting.

finger painting *n.* **1.** The technique of painting by applying color to moistened paper with the fingers. **2.** A picture made with this technique.

fin·ger·pick (fĭngʹgər-pĭk′) *v.* **-picked, -pick·ing, -picks.** *Music. —intr.* To play a stringed instrument, such as the guitar or banjo, by plucking individual strings with the fingers. *—tr.* To play (a stringed instrument) by plucking individual strings with the fingers. **—finʹger·pick′er** *n.*

finger pick *n.* A pointed, slightly curved plectrum worn on the fingertip, used in playing a stringed instrument such as the guitar or banjo.

finger post *n.* A guidepost in the shape of a pointing hand.

fin·ger·print (fĭngʹgər-prĭnt′) *n.* **1.** An impression on a surface of the curves formed by the ridges on a fingertip, especially such an impression made in ink and used as a means of identification. **2.** A distinctive or identifying mark or characteristic: *"the invisible fingerprint that's used on labels and packaging to sort out genuine products from counterfeits"* (Gene G. Marcial). **—fingerprint** *tr.v.* **-print·ed, -print·ing, -prints. 1.** To take the fingerprints of. **2.** To identify by means of a distinctive mark or characteristic.

fingerprint

fin·ger·spell·ing (fĭngʹgər-spĕl′ĭng) *n.* Communication by means of a manual alphabet. **—finʹger·spell′** *v.*

fin·ger·tip (fĭngʹgər-tĭp′) *n.* The extreme end or tip of a finger. ***—idiom.*** **at (one's) fingertips.** Readily available.

finger wave *n.* A wave set into dampened hair using only the fingers and a comb.

fin·i·al (fĭnʹē-əl) *n.* **1.** *Architecture.* An ornament fixed to the peak of an arch or arched structure. **2.** An ornamental terminating part, such as the screw on top of a lampshade. [Middle English, last, finial, variant of *final.* See FINAL.]

fin·i·cal (fĭnʹĭ-kəl) *adj.* Finicky. [Probably from FINE[1].] **—finʹi·cal·ly** *adv.* **—finʹi·cal·ness** *n.*

fin·ick·y (fĭnʹĭ-kē) *adj.* **-i·er, -i·est.** Insisting capriciously on getting just what one wants; fastidious: *a finicky eater.* [From *finick,* a finical person, from FINICAL.] **—finʹick·i·ness** *n.*

fin·is (fĭnʹĭs, fīʹnĭs, fē-nēʹ) *n.* The end; the conclusion: *setbacks that wrote finis to our venture.* [Middle English, from Latin *fīnis.*]

fin·ish (fĭnʹĭsh) *v.* **-ished, -ish·ing, -ish·es.** *—tr.* **1.** To arrive at or attain the end of: *finish a race.* **2.** To bring to an end; terminate: *finished cleaning the room.* **3.** To consume all of; use up: *finish a pie.* **4.** To bring to a desired or required state: *finish a painting.* **5.** To give (wood, for example) a desired or particular surface texture. **6.** To destroy; kill. **7.** To bring about the ruin of: *The stock market crash finished many speculators. —intr.* **1.** To come to an end; stop. **2.** To reach the end of a task, course, or relationship. **—finish** *n.* **1.** *Abbr.* **fin.** The final part; the conclusion: *racers neck-and-neck at the finish.* **2.** The reason for one's ruin; downfall. **3.** Something that completes, concludes, or perfects, especially: **a.** The last treatment or coating of a surface: *applied a shellac finish to the cabinet.* **b.** The surface texture produced by such a treatment or coating. **c.** A material used in surfacing or finishing. **4.** Completeness, thoroughness, refinement, or smoothness of execution; polish. [Middle English *finishen,* from Old French *finir, finiss-,* to complete, from Latin *fīnīre,* from *fīnis,* end.] **—finʹish·er** *n.*

fin·ished (fĭnʹĭsht) *adj.* **1.** Highly accomplished or skilled; polished: *a finished artist.* **2.** Exhibiting a high degree of skill or polish: *an essay that was a finished piece of work.*

fin·ish·ing school (fĭnʹĭ-shĭng) *n.* A private girls' school that stresses training in cultural subjects and social activities.

finishing touch *n.* A small change or addition that serves to complete something.

finish line *n. Sports.* A line that marks the end of a course for racing.

fi·nite (fīʹnīt′) *adj.* **1.a.** Having bounds; limited: *a finite list of choices; our finite fossil fuel reserves.* **b.** Existing, persisting, or enduring for a limited time only; impermanent. **2.** *Mathematics.* **a.** Being neither infinite nor infinitesimal. **b.** Having a positive or negative numerical value; not zero. **c.** Possible to reach or exceed by counting. Used of a number. **d.** Having a limited number of elements. Used of a set. **3.** *Grammar.* Limited by person, number, tense, and mood. Used of a verb that can serve as a predicate or the initial element of one. **—finite** *n.* A finite thing. [Middle English *finit,* from Latin *fīnītus,* past participle of *fīnīre,* to limit, from *fīnis,* end.] **—fiʹnite′ly** *adv.* **—fiʹnite′ness** *n.*

Finland

fin·i·tude (fĭnʹĭ-to͞od′, -tyo͞od′, fīʹnĭ-) *n.* The quality or condition of being finite.

fink (fĭngk) *Slang. n.* **1.** A contemptible person. **2.** An informer. **3.** A hired strikebreaker. **—fink** *intr.v.* **finked, fink·ing, finks. 1.** To inform against another person. **2.** To withhold promised support or participation; back down: *They said they would help us, but then finked out.* [Origin unknown.]

Fin·land (fĭnʹlənd). *Abbr.* **Fin.** A country of northern Europe bordering on the Gulf of Bothnia and the Gulf of Finland. Controlled from the 13th century by Sweden and from the 19th century by Russia, it became independent in 1919. Helsinki is the capital and the largest city. Population, 4,893,748.

Finland, Gulf of. An arm of the Baltic Sea bordered by Finland, Russia, and Estonia. An important shipping lane, the shallow gulf is usually frozen from December to March.

Fin·land·ize (fĭnʹlən-dīz′) *tr.v.* **-ized, -iz·ing, -iz·es.** To cause (a country or other political unit) to adopt a neutral or conciliatory posture and policy in its relations with a great power. **—Finʹland·i·zaʹtion** *n.*

Fin·lay River (fĭnʹlē). A river of northern British Columbia, Canada, flowing about 402 km (250 mi) to the Peace River.

Finn (fĭn) *n.* **1.** A native or inhabitant of Finland. **2.** One who speaks Finnish or a Finnic language. [From Swedish *Finne.*]

fin·nan had·die (fĭnʹən hădʹē) *n.* Smoked haddock. Also

ă pat	oi boy
ā pay	ou out
âr care	o͝o took
ä father	o͞o boot
ĕ pet	ŭ cut
ē be	ûr urge
ĭ pit	th thin
ī pie	*th* this
îr pier	hw which
ŏ pot	zh vision
ō toe	ə about, item
ô paw	♦ regionalism

Stress marks: **ʹ** (primary); **′** (secondary), as in **dictionary** (dĭkʹshə-nĕr′ē)

called *finnan haddock*. [From alteration of *Findon* or *Findhorn*, villages of northeast Scotland.]

Finn·bog·a·dót·tir (fĭn′bō-gə-dô′tər, -gä-dō′tĭr), **Vigdís.** Born 1930. President of Iceland (since 1980) and the first democratically elected woman head of state.

Vigdís Finnbogadóttir
Photographed in 1987

finned (fĭnd) *adj.* Having a fin, fins, or finlike parts. Often used in combination: *single-finned; multifinned.*

Fin·nic (fĭn′ĭk) *adj.* Of or relating to Finland or the Finns. **—Finnic** *n.* A branch of Finno-Ugric that includes Finnish, Estonian, and Lapp.

Finn·ish (fĭn′ĭsh) *adj. Abbr.* **Fin.** Of or relating to Finland or its people, language, or culture. **—Finnish** *n.* The Finno-Ugric language of the Finns.

Fin·no-U·gric (fĭn′ō-o͞o′grĭk, -yo͞o′-) also **Fin·no-U·gri·an** (-o͞o′grē-ən, -yo͞o′-) *—n.* A subfamily of the Uralic language family that includes Finnish, Hungarian, and other languages of eastern Europe and the northwest Soviet Union. *—adj.* **1.** Of or relating to the Finns and the Ugrians. **2.** Of or relating to Finno-Ugric.

fin·ny (fĭn′ē) *adj.* **-ni·er, -ni·est. 1.** Having a fin or fins. **2.** Resembling a fin; finlike. **3.** Of, relating to, or full of fish.

fi·noc·chi·o also **fi·no·chi·o** (fə-nō′kē-ō′) *n.* A variety of fennel *(Foeniculum vulgare* var. *dulce)* whose blanched aromatic, celerylike stalks are eaten as a vegetable. Also called *Florence fennel, sweet fennel.* [Italian, from Latin *fēniculum,* fennel, diminutive of *fēnum,* hay. See **dhē(i)-** in Appendix.]

Fin·ster·aar·horn (fĭn′stər-är′hôrn′). A peak, 4,276.7 m (14,022 ft) high, of the Bernese Alps in south-central Switzerland. It is the highest elevation in the range.

fin whale *n.* See **finback.**

fiord (fyôrd, fyōrd) *n.* Variant of **fjord.**

fip·ple (fĭp′əl) *n. Music.* **1.** A whistlelike mouthpiece for certain wind instruments, such as a recorder or flageolet, that channels the breath toward the sounding edge of a side opening. **2.** An object similar to a fipple in an organ pipe. [Origin unknown.]

fipple flute *n. Music.* A flute, such as a recorder, with a fipple.

fir (fûr) *n.* **1.a.** Any of various evergreen trees of the genus *Abies,* having single, flattened needles and erect cones with deciduous scales. **b.** Any of several similar or related trees, such as the Douglas fir. **2.** The wood of these trees. [Middle English *firre,* probably of Scandinavian origin. See **perkʷu-** in Appendix.] **—fir′ry** *adj.*

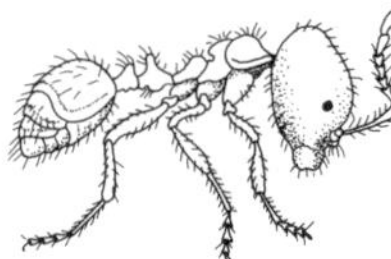

fire ant

Fir·dau·si (fîr-dou′sē) also **Fir·du·si** (fər-do͞o′-). Pen name of Abul Kasim Mansur. 940?–1020? Persian epic poet whose *Book of Kings* (1010) recounts the history of Persia from the arrival of the Persians to the Arab conquest.

fire (fīr) *n.* **1.a.** A rapid, persistent chemical change that releases heat and light and is accompanied by flame, especially the exothermic oxidation of a combustible substance. **b.** Burning fuel or other material: *a cooking fire; a forest fire.* **2.a.** Burning intensity of feeling; ardor. See Synonyms at **passion. b.** Enthusiasm. **3.** Luminosity or brilliance, as of a cut and polished gemstone. **4.** Liveliness and vivacity of imagination; brilliance. **5.** A severe test; a trial or torment. **6.** A fever or bodily inflammation. **7.a.** The discharge of firearms or artillery: *heard the fire of cannon.* **b.** The launching of a missile, rocket, or similar ballistic body. **c.** Discharged bullets or other projectiles: *subjected enemy positions to heavy mortar fire; struck by rifle fire.* **8.** Intense, repeated attack or criticism: *answered the fire from her political critics.* *—attributive.* Often used to modify another noun: *a fire chief; fire prevention.* **—fire** *v.* **fired, fir·ing, fires.** *—tr.* **1.a.** To cause to burn; ignite. **b.** To light (something) up as if by fire: *The morning sun fired the tops of the trees.* **2.a.** To add fuel to (something burning). **b.** To maintain or fuel a fire in. **3.a.** To bake in a kiln: *fire pottery.* **b.** To dry by heating. **4.** To arouse the emotions of; make enthusiastic or ardent: *warriors who were fired by patriotism.* **5.a.** To discharge (a firearm, for example). **b.** To detonate (an explosive). **6.a.** To propel (a projectile); launch (a missile). **b.** *Informal.* To throw with force and speed; hurl: *fire a ball at a batter.* **c.** To utter or direct with insistence: *fired questions at the senator.* **7.** *Games.* To score (a number) in a game or contest. **8.** *Informal.* To discharge from a position; dismiss. See Synonyms at **dismiss.** *—intr.* **1.** To become ignited; flame up. **2.a.** To become excited or ardent. **b.** To become angry or annoyed. **3.** To tend a fire. **4.a.** To shoot a weapon: *aimed and fired at the target.* **b.** To detonate an explosive. **c.** To ignite fuel, as in an engine. **5.** *Informal.* To project or hurl a missile: *The pitcher wound up and fired.* **6.** *Physiology.* To generate an electrical impulse. Used of a neuron. **7.** To become yellowed or brown before reaching maturity, as grain. ***—phrasal verbs.*** **fire away.** *Informal.* To start to talk or ask questions. **fire off. 1.** To utter or ask rapidly. **2.** To write and send (a letter, for example) in haste. ***—idioms.*** **between two fires.** Being attacked from two sources or sides simultaneously. **on fire. 1.** Ignited; ablaze. **2.** Filled with enthusiasm or excitement. **start** (or **light** or **build**) **a fire under.** *Slang.* To urge or goad to action. **under fire. 1.** Exposed or subjected to enemy attack. **2.** Exposed or subjected to critical attack or censure: *an official who was under fire for mismanagement.* [Middle English *fir,* from Old English *fȳr.* See **pūr-** in Appendix.] **—fire′a·ble** *adj.* **—fir′er** *n.*

fire pink
Silene virginica

fire alarm *n. Abbr.* **f.a. 1.** A device, such as a siren, used in announcing the outbreak of a fire. **2.** The signal, especially the noise, produced by such a device.

fire ant *n.* Any of several ants of the genus *Solenopsis,* especially *S. geminata* or *S. saevissima* of the southern United States and tropical America, that build large mounds and are capable of inflicting a painful sting.

fire·arm (fīr′ärm′) *n.* A weapon, especially a pistol or rifle, capable of firing a projectile and using an explosive charge as a propellant.

fire·ball (fīr′bôl′) *n.* **1.** A brilliantly burning sphere. **2.** A highly luminous, intensely hot spherical cloud of dust, gas, and vapor generated by a nuclear explosion. **3.** A meteor that is as bright or brighter than the brightest planets. **4.** See **ball of fire.**

fire·base (fīr′bās′) *n.* A military base or site from which heavy fire is directed against the enemy.

fire beetle *n.* Any of various tropical American click beetles of the genus *Pyrophorus,* especially *P. noctilucus,* having bright, luminous spots.

fire·bird (fīr′bûrd′) *n.* Any of various birds, such as the Baltimore oriole, having bright scarlet or orange plumage.

fire blight *n.* A destructive disease of apple and pear trees, caused by a bacterium *(Erwinia amylovora)* that blackens the leaves and kills the branches.

♦**fire·board** (fīr′bôrd′, -bōrd′) *n. Upper Southern U.S.* See **mantel** (sense 2).

fire·boat (fīr′bōt′) *n. Nautical.* A boat equipped to fight fires along waterfronts and on ships.

fire·bomb (fīr′bŏm′) *n.* A bomb used to start a fire; an incendiary bomb. *—tr.* **-bombed, -bomb·ing, -bombs.** To attack (a target) with a firebomb. *—intr.* To launch an attack against a target, using a firebomb. **—fire′bomb′er** *n.*

fire·box (fīr′bŏks′) *n.* **1.** A chamber, such as the furnace of a steam locomotive, in which fuel is burned. **2.** A box containing a fire alarm.

fire·brand (fīr′brănd′) *n.* **1.** A person who stirs up trouble or kindles a revolt. **2.** A piece of burning wood.

fire·brat (fīr′brăt′) *n.* A small, wingless insect *(Thermobia domestica)* related to the silverfish and inhabiting warm areas of buildings, as around furnaces or boilers.

fire·break (fīr′brāk′) *n.* A strip of cleared or plowed land used to stop the spread of a fire. Also called *fireguard.*

fire·brick (fīr′brĭk′) *n.* A refractory brick, usually made of fire clay, used for lining furnaces, fireboxes, chimneys, or fireplaces.

fire brigade *n.* An organized body of firefighters.

fire·bug (fīr′bŭg′) *n. Informal.* An arsonist; a pyromaniac.

fire clay also **fire·clay** (fīr′klā′) *n.* A type of clay that is able to withstand intense heat, used to make firebricks, crucibles, and other objects that are exposed to high temperatures.

fire control *n.* The control of the delivery of gunfire on military targets.

fire·crack·er (fīr′krăk′ər) *n.* A small explosive charge and a fuse in a heavy paper casing, exploded to make noise, as at celebrations.

fire·damp (fīr′dămp′) *n.* **1.** A combustible gas, chiefly methane, occurring naturally in mines from the decomposition of coal. **2.** The explosive mixture of firedamp and air.

fire department *n. Abbr.* **FD** A department, especially of a municipal government, whose purpose is preventing and putting out fires.

♦**fire·dog** (fīr′dôg′, -dŏg′) *n. Chiefly South Atlantic U.S.* See **andiron.**

fire door *n.* A door made of fire-resistant material that can be closed to prevent the spread of fire.

fire·drake (fīr′drāk′) *n.* A fiery dragon of Germanic mythology. [Middle English *firdrake,* from Old English *fȳrdraca* : *fȳr,* fire; see FIRE + *draca,* dragon; see DRAKE[2].]

fire drill *n.* An exercise in the use of firefighting equipment or the evacuation of a building in case of a fire.

fire-eat·er (fīr′ē′tər) *n.* **1.** A performer who pretends to swallow fire. **2.** A belligerent person or a militant partisan. **—fire′-eat′ing** *adj.*

fire engine *n.* Any of various large motor vehicles that carry firefighters and equipment to a fire and support extinguishing operations, as by pumping water.

fire escape *n.* A structure or device, such as an outside stairway attached to a building, erected for emergency exit in the event of fire.

fire extinguisher *n.* A portable apparatus containing chemicals that can be discharged in a jet to extinguish a small fire.

fire·fight (fīr′fīt′) *n.* An exchange of gunfire, as between infantry units.

fire·fight·er also **fire fighter** (fīr′fī′tər) *n.* A member of a fire department who fights fires. **—fire′fight′ing** *adj. & n.*

fire·flood (fīr′flŭd′) or **fire·flood·ing** (-flŭd′ĭng) *n.* A procedure for extracting additional oil from a well by injecting compressed air into the petroleum reservoir and burning some of the oil to increase the flow.

fire·fly (fīr′flī′) *n.* Any of various nocturnal beetles of the family Lampyridae, characteristically having luminescent chemicals in the posterior tip of the abdomen that produce a flashing light. Also called *lightning bug.*

fire·guard (fīr′gärd′) *n.* **1.** A metal screen placed in front of an open fireplace to catch sparks. Also called *fire screen.* **2.** See **firebreak.**

fire•house (fīr′hous′) *n.* See **fire station.**

fire hydrant *n.* An upright pipe with a nozzle or spout for drawing water from a water main. Also called *fireplug.*

fire irons *pl.n.* Implements, such as tongs, a shovel, and a poker, used to tend a fireplace.

Fire Island (fīr). A narrow barrier island off the southern shore of Long Island in southeast New York.

fire•light (fīr′līt′) *n.* The light from a fire, as in a fireplace.

fire•lock (fīr′lŏk′) *n.* See **flintlock** (sense 2).

fire•man (fīr′mən) *n.* **1.** A firefighter. **2.** A man who tends fires; a stoker. **3.** An enlisted man in the U.S. Navy engaged in the operation of engineering machinery. **4.** *Baseball.* A relief pitcher.

fire marshal *n.* **1.** The head of a department or an office that is charged with the prevention and investigation of fires. **2.** A person in charge of firefighting personnel and equipment at an industrial plant.

Fi•ren•ze (fē-rĕn′dzĕ). See **Florence** (sense 1).

fire opal *n.* An opal with brilliant flamelike yellow, orange, and red colors. Also called *girasol.*

fire pink *n.* A perennial herb *(Silene virginica)* of eastern North America, having red flowers with narrow, deeply notched petals.

fire•place (fīr′plās′) *n. Abbr.* **fpl 1.** An open recess for holding a fire at the base of a chimney; a hearth. **2.** A structure, usually of stone or brick, for holding an outdoor fire.

fire•plug (fīr′plŭg′) *n.* See **fire hydrant.**

fire•pow•er (fīr′pou′ər) *n.* **1.** The capacity, as of a weapon, weapons system, military unit, or position, for delivering fire. **2.** The ability to deliver fire against an enemy in combat.

fire•proof (fīr′pro͞of′) *adj.* Impervious or resistant to damage by fire. **—fireproof** *tr.v.* **-proofed, -proof•ing, -proofs.** To make fireproof.

fire sale *n.* A sale of merchandise damaged by fire.

fire screen *n.* See **fireguard** (sense 1).

fire ship *n.* A military vessel loaded with explosives and combustible material and set adrift among enemy ships or fortifications to destroy them.

fire•side (fīr′sīd′) *n.* **1.** The area immediately surrounding a fireplace or hearth. **2.** A home. **—fireside** *adj.* At or as if at a fireside: *a fireside chat.*

fire station *n.* A building for fire equipment and firefighters. Also called *firehouse.*

fire•stone (fīr′stōn′) *n.* **1.** A flint or pyrite used to strike a fire. **2.** A fire-resistant stone, such as certain sandstones.

fire•storm (fīr′stôrm′) *n.* **1.** A fire of great size and intensity that generates and is fed by strong inrushing winds from all sides: *the firestorm that leveled Hiroshima after the atomic blast.* **2.** An intense outburst from many sources: *a firestorm of criticism.*

fire thorn *n.* Any of various thorny shrubs of the genus *Pyracantha,* native to Asia and often cultivated for their evergreen foliage and showy reddish or orange berries.

fire tower *n.* A tower in which a lookout for fires is posted.

fire•trap (fīr′trăp′) *n.* A building that can catch fire easily or is difficult to escape from in the event of fire.

fire•wall (fīr′wôl) *n.* A fireproof wall used as a barrier to prevent the spread of fire. **—firewall** *intr.v.* **-walled, -wall•ing, -walls.** *Slang.* To apply maximum acceleration or thrust. Used of motor vehicles or aircraft.

fire•wa•ter (fīr′wô′tər, -wŏt′ər) *n. Slang.* Strong liquor, especially whiskey. [Translation of Ojibwa *ishkodewaaboo,* whiskey.]

fire•weed (fīr′wēd′) *n.* **1.** Any of various plants of the genus *Epilobium,* especially *E. angustifolium,* having long, terminal, spikelike clusters of pinkish-purple flowers. Also called *willow herb.* **2.** Any of several weedy North American plants of the genus *Erechtites,* having small white or greenish flowers grouped in discoid heads.

fire•wood (fīr′wo͝od′) *n.* Wood used as fuel.

fire•work (fīr′wûrk′) *n.* **1.a.** A device consisting of a combination of explosives and combustibles, set off to generate colored lights, smoke, and noise for amusement. **b. fireworks.** A display of such devices. **2. fireworks. a.** An exciting or spectacular display, as of musical virtuosity. **b.** A display of rage or fierce contention.

fir•ing (fīr′ĭng) *n.* **1.** The process of applying fire or heat, as in the hardening or glazing of ceramics. **2.** Fuel for fires.

firing line *n.* **1.** The line of positions from which fire is directed at a target. **2.** The forefront of an activity or pursuit; the vanguard.

firing pin *n.* The part of the bolt or breech of a firearm that strikes the primer and detonates the charge of a projectile.

firing squad *n.* **1.** A detachment assigned to shoot persons condemned to death. **2.** A detachment of soldiers chosen to fire a salute at a military funeral.

fir•kin (fûr′kĭn) *n.* **1.** A small wooden barrel or covered vessel. **2.** Any of several British units of capacity, usually equal to about ¼ of a barrel or 9 gallons (34 liters). [Middle English *ferken, ferdekin,* probably from Middle Dutch **verdelkijn,* diminutive of *veerdel,* one-fourth : *veerde,* fourth; see **kʷetwer-** in Appendix + *deel,* part; see **dail-** in Appendix.]

firm[1] (fûrm) *adj.* **firm•er, firm•est. 1.** Resistant to externally applied pressure. **2.** Marked by or indicating the tone and resiliency of healthy tissue: *firm muscles.* **3.** Securely fixed in place: *Despite being hit by the car, the post was still firm.* **4.** Indicating or possessed of determination or resolution: *a firm voice.* **5.** Constant; steadfast: *a firm ally.* **6.a.** Not subject to change; fixed and definite: *a firm bargain; a firm offer.* **b.** Unfluctuating; steady: *Stock prices are still firm.* **7.** Strong and sure: *a firm grasp.* **—firm** *tr. & intr.v.* **firmed, firm•ing, firms.** To make or become firm. **—firm** *adv.* **firmer, firmest.** Without wavering; resolutely: *stand firm.* [Middle English *ferm,* from Old French, from Latin *firmus.* See **dher-** in Appendix.] **—firm′ly** *adv.* **—firm′ness** *n.*

SYNONYMS: *firm, hard, solid.* The central meaning shared by these adjectives is "tending not to yield to external pressure, touch, or force": *a firm mattress; hard as granite; solid ice.*
ANTONYM: *soft.*

firm[2] (fûrm) *n.* **1.** A commercial partnership of two or more persons, especially when unincorporated. **2.** The name under which a company transacts business. [Italian *firma,* from *firmare,* to ratify by signature, from Medieval Latin *firmāre,* from Latin, to confirm, from *firmus,* firm. See **dher-** in Appendix.]

WORD HISTORY: In these days of agribusiness, a farm and a firm are probably closer than they have been since the time before the words *farm* and *firm* developed from the same Latin word, *firmāre,* "to strengthen, make fast, confirm, attest," which is derived from Latin *firmus,* the source of *firm,* meaning "secure." In Medieval Latin *firmāre* came to mean "to ratify by signature," from which sense eventually came our word *firm,* first recorded in 1574 with the meaning "signature." This word *firm* later added the senses "designation under which a firm transacts business" and "commercial house." Latin *firmāre* by way of Old French also gave us Middle English *ferme,* the ancestor of our word *farm.*

fir•ma•ment (fûr′mə-mənt) *n.* The vault or expanse of the heavens; the sky. [Middle English, from Old French, from Late Latin *firmāmentum,* from Latin, support, from *firmāre,* to strengthen. See FIRM[2].] **—fir′ma•ment′al** (-mĕn′tl) *adj.*

fir•mer chisel (fûr′mər) *n.* A chisel or gouge with a thin blade, used to shape and finish wood by hand. [French *fermoir,* from Old French, alteration (influenced by *fermer,* to make firm, from Latin *firmāre*; see FIRM[2]) of *formoir,* from *former,* to form, from Latin *formāre,* from *forma,* form.]

firm•ware (fûrm′wâr′) *n. Computer Science.* Programming instructions that are stored in a read-only memory unit rather than being implemented through software.

firn (fîrn) *n.* Granular, partially consolidated snow that has passed through one summer melt season but is not yet glacial ice. Also called *old snow.* [German, from German dialectal, of last year, from Old High German *firni,* old.]

first (fûrst) *n.* **1.** The ordinal number matching the number one in a series. **2.** The one coming, occurring, or ranking before or above all others. **3.** The beginning; the outset: *from the first; at first.* **4.** *Music.* The voice or instrument highest in pitch or carrying the principal part. **5.** The transmission gear or corresponding gear ratio used to produce the range of lowest drive speeds in a motor vehicle. **6.** The winning position in a contest: *finished the season in first.* **7.** *Baseball.* **a.** First base. **b.** A first baseman. **—first** *adj.* **1.** Corresponding in order to the number one. **2.** Coming before all others in order or location: *the first house on your left.* **3.** Occurring or acting before all others in time; earliest: *the first day of spring.* **4.** Ranking above all others, as in importance or quality; foremost: *was first in the class.* **5.** *Music.* Being highest in pitch or carrying the principal part: *first trumpet.* **6.** Of, relating to, or being the transmission gear or corresponding gear ratio used to produce the range of lowest drive speeds in a motor vehicle. **—first** *adv.* **1.** Before or above all others in time, order, rank, or importance: *arrived first; forgot to light the oven first.* **2.** For the first time. **3.** Rather; preferably: *would die first.* **4.** In the first place; to begin with. See Usage Note at **firstly.** [Middle English, from Old English *fyrst.* See **per**[1] in Appendix.]

first aid *n.* Emergency treatment administered to an injured or sick person before professional medical care is available. **—first′-aid′** (fûrst′ād′) *adj.*

first base *n.* **1.** *Baseball.* **a.** The first of the bases in the infield, counterclockwise from home plate. **b.** The fielding position occupied by the first baseman. **2.** *Slang.* The first stage or step toward completion or success: *"He never got to first base with any of his big wheels and deals"* (Ross Macdonald).

first baseman *n. Baseball.* The infielder stationed near first base.

first-born (fûrst′bôrn′) *adj.* First in order of birth; born first. **—first-born** *n.* The child in a family who is born first.

first class *n.* **1.** The first, highest, or best group in a system of classification: *a restaurant of the first class.* **2.** The most luxurious and most expensive class of accommodations on a train, passenger ship, airplane, or other conveyance. **3.** A class of mail including letters, post cards, and packages sealed against inspection.

first-class (fûrst′klăs′) *adj.* **1.** Constituting or belonging to the first, highest, or best group in a system of classification: *a first-class hotel; first-class mail.* **2.** Of the foremost excellence or highest quality; first-rate: *a first-class mind.* **—first′ class′** *adv.*

fire tower

fireworks
Over the Charles River, Boston, Massachusetts

firkin
Mid 19th-century American Shaker firkin

ă pat	oi boy
ā pay	ou out
âr care	o͝o took
ä father	o͞o boot
ĕ pet	ŭ cut
ē be	ûr urge
ĭ pit	th thin
ī pie	*th* this
îr pier	hw which
ŏ pot	zh vision
ō toe	ə about, item
ô paw	♦ regionalism

Stress marks: **′** (primary); ′ (secondary), as in **dictionary** (dĭk′shə-nĕr′ē)

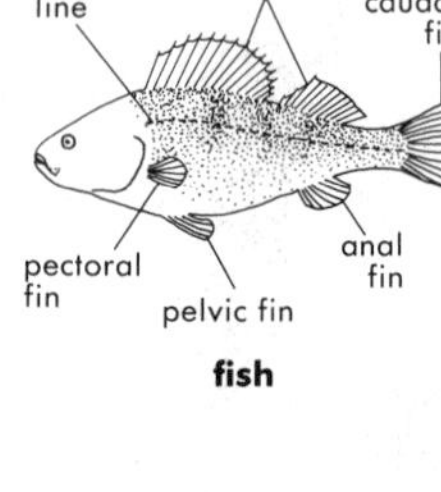

fish

first cousin *n.* See **cousin** (sense 1).

first-de·gree burn (fûrst′dĭ-grē′) *n.* A mild burn that produces redness of the skin but no blistering.

first down *n. Football.* **1.** The first in the series of four downs in which an offensive team must advance ten yards to retain possession of the ball. **2.** A gain of ten or more yards entitling the offensive team to a new series of downs.

first edition *n.* **1.a.** The first published copies of a literary work printed from the same type and distributed at the same time. **b.** A single copy from a group published first. **2.** The day's first press run of a newspaper.

first family also **First Family** *n.* **1.** A family having high social status, often because of descent from the first settlers of a place. **2.** The family of the chief executive of a city, state, or country.

first finger *n.* See **index finger.**

first floor *n.* **1.** The ground floor of a building. **2.** *Chiefly British.* The floor immediately above the ground floor.

first fruits also **first·fruits** (fûrst′fro͞ots′) *pl.n.* **1.** The first gathered fruits of a harvest, offered to God in gratitude. **2.** The first results of an undertaking.

first generation *n.* **1.** Persons who have left one country and settled in another. **2.** Persons whose parents are immigrants. **3.** *Computer Science.* The period of computer technology during the late 1940's and early 1950's, when computers were built with vacuum tubes.

first-gen·er·a·tion (fûrst′jĕn′ə-rā′shən) *adj.* **1.** Of or relating to a person who has left one country and settled in another. **2.** Of or relating to a person or persons whose parents are immigrants. **3.** *Computer Science.* Of, relating to, or being the period of computer technology distinguished by the use of vacuum tubes.

first·hand (fûrst′hănd′) *adj.* Received from the original source: *firsthand information.* **—first′hand′** *adv.*

first-in, first-out (fûrst′ĭn′ fûrst′out′) *n. Accounting.* A method of inventory accounting in which the oldest items are assumed to have been the first sold. In a period of rising prices, this method yields a higher ending inventory, a lower cost of goods sold, a higher gross profit (assuming constant price), and a higher taxable income. Also called *FIFO.*

first lady *n.* **1.** Often **First Lady.** The wife or hostess of the chief executive of a country, state, or city. **2.** The foremost woman of a profession or art: *the first lady of the American theater.*

first lieutenant *n.* **1.** A commissioned rank in the U.S. Army, Air Force, and Marines that is above second lieutenant and below captain. **2.** One who holds this rank.

first·ling (fûrst′lĭng) *n.* **1.** The first of a kind or category. **2.** A first-born offspring.

first·ly (fûrst′lē) *adv.* In the first place; to begin with.

USAGE NOTE: There is ample reputable precedent for using both *first* and *firstly* to begin an enumeration: *Our objectives are, first* (or *firstly*), *to recover from last year's slump.* Whichever is chosen, however, consistency is best served if any succeeding items are introduced by a parallel form, as in *first . . . second . . . third* or *firstly . . . secondly . . . thirdly.*

first mate *n.* An officer on a merchant ship ranking immediately below the captain.

first name *n.* The name that occurs first in a person's full name.

first night *n.* **1.** The opening performance of a theatrical production. **2.** The performance presented on such a night.

first night·er (nī′tər) *n.* A member of the audience at a first night.

first offender *n.* One convicted of a legal offense for the first time.

first papers *pl.n.* The documents first filed by one applying for U.S. citizenship.

first person *n.* **1.a.** A category of linguistic forms, such as verbs and pronouns, designating the speaker or writer of the sentence in which they appear. **b.** One of the forms of this category. **2.** A style of writing in which forms in the first person are used: *a novel written in the first person.*

first-rate (fûrst′rāt′) *adj.* Foremost in quality, rank, or importance. **—first-rate** *adv. Informal.* Very well; excellently.

first sergeant *n.* The senior noncommissioned officer of a U.S. Army or Marine Corps unit, who is equivalent in rank to a master sergeant and performs administrative duties.

first strike *n.* The initial use of strategic nuclear weapons against a nuclear-armed adversary, theorized as feasible only if the attacker can destroy the adversary's retaliatory capacity. **—first′-strike′** (fûrst′strīk′) *adj.*

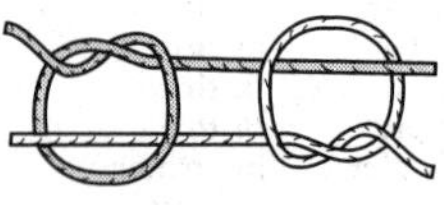
fisherman's knot

first-string (fûrst′strĭng′) *adj.* **1.** *Sports.* Of, relating to, or being a regular member, as of a football team, rather than a substitute. **2.** First-rate. **—first′-string′er** *n.*

first water *n.* **1.** The highest degree of quality or purity in diamonds or pearls. **2.** The foremost rank or quality: *a pianist of the first water.* [Probably translation of Arabic *mā',* water, water luster.]

First World also **first world** (fûrst) *n.* The industrialized non-Communist countries of the world. **—first′-world′** (fûrst′-wûrld′) *adj.*

First World War *n.* World War I.

firth (fûrth) *n. Scots.* A long, narrow inlet of the sea. [Middle English *furth,* from Old Norse *fjördhr.* See **per-**[2] in Appendix.]

fisc (fĭsk) *n.* The treasury of a kingdom or state. [French, from Latin *fiscus,* money basket, treasury.]

fis·cal (fĭs′kəl) *adj.* **1.** Of or relating to government expenditures, revenues, and debt: *a fiscal policy of incurring budget deficits to stimulate a weak economy.* **2.** Of or relating to finance or finances. See Synonyms at **financial.** [French, from Latin *fiscālis,* from *fiscus,* money basket, treasury.] **—fis′cal·ly** *adv.*

fiscal year *n. Abbr.* **FY** A 12-month period for which an organization plans the use of its funds.

Fi·scher (fĭsh′ər), **Emil Hermann.** 1852–1919. German chemist. He won a 1902 Nobel Prize for his work on the structure and synthesis of sugars and purines.

Fischer, Hans. 1881–1945. German chemist. He won a 1930 Nobel Prize for his work on the synthesis of hemin.

fish (fĭsh) *n., pl.* **fish** or **fish·es. 1.** Any of numerous cold-blooded aquatic vertebrates of the superclass Pisces, characteristically having fins, gills, and a streamlined body and including specifically: **a.** Any of the class Osteichthyes, having a bony skeleton. **b.** Any of the class Chondrichthyes, having a cartilaginous skeleton and including the sharks, rays, and skates. **2.** The flesh of such animals used as food. **3.** Any of various primitive aquatic vertebrates of the class Cyclostomata, lacking jaws and including the lampreys and hagfishes. **4.** Any of various unrelated aquatic animals, such as a jellyfish, cuttlefish, or crayfish. **5.** *Informal.* A person who is deficient in something: *a cold fish; a poor fish.* *—attributive.* Often used to modify another noun: *fish parts; fish gaffs.* **—fish** *v.* **fished, fish·ing, fish·es.** *—intr.* **1.** To catch or try to catch fish. **2.** To look for something by feeling one's way; grope: *fished in both pockets for a coin.* **3.** To seek something in a sly or indirect way: *fish for compliments.* *—tr.* **1.a.** To catch or try to catch (fish). **b.** To catch or try to catch fish in: *fish mountain streams.* **2.** To catch or pull as if fishing: *deftly fished the corn out of the boiling water.* ***—phrasal verb.*** **fish out.** To deplete (a lake, for example) of fish by fishing. ***—idioms.*** **fish in troubled waters.** To try to take advantage of a confused situation. **fish or cut bait.** *Informal.* To proceed with an activity or abandon it altogether. **like a fish out of water.** Completely unfamiliar with one's surroundings or activity. **neither fish nor fowl.** Having no specific characteristics; indefinite. **other fish to fry.** *Informal.* Other matters to attend to: *He declined to come along to the movie, saying he had other fish to fry.* [Middle English, from Old English *fisc.*]

Fish (fĭsh), **Hamilton.** 1808–1893. American politician who negotiated the settlement of the Civil War *Alabama* Claims with Great Britain (1871).

fish and chips *pl.n.* Fried fillets of fish and French-fried potatoes.

fish·bowl also **fish bowl** (fĭsh′bōl′) *n.* **1.** A transparent bowl in which live fish are kept. **2.** *Informal.* A place that is lacking in privacy.

fish cake *n.* A fried cake or patty of chopped fish, often mixed with potato, bread crumbs, or rice.

fish crow *n.* A crow *(Corvus ossifragus)* native to the coastal regions and rivers of the eastern United States.

fish·er (fĭsh′ər) *n.* **1.** One that fishes, as a person or ship engaged in fishing. **2.a.** A carnivorous mammal *(Martes pennanti)* of northern North America, having thick, dark-brown fur. Also called *pekan, wejack.* **b.** The fur of this animal.

fish·er·man (fĭsh′ər-mən) *n.* **1.** One who fishes as an occupation or for sport. **2.** A commercial fishing vessel.

fish·er·man's bend (fĭsh′ər-mənz) *n.* A knot used to secure the end of a line to a ring or spar, made by two turns with the end passed back under both.

fisherman's knot *n.* A knot used to join two lines, made by securing either end to the opposite standing part by an overhand knot.

fish·er·y (fĭsh′ə-rē) *n., pl.* **-ies. 1.** The industry or occupation devoted to the catching, processing, or selling of fish, shellfish, or other aquatic animals. **2.** A place where fish or other aquatic animals are caught. **3.** A fishing business. **4.** A hatchery for fish. **5.** The legal right to fish in specified waters or areas.

Fish·es (fĭsh′ĭz) *pl.n. (used with a sing. verb).* See **Pisces** (senses 1, 2a).

fish·eye (fĭsh′ī′) *adj.* **1.** Of, relating to, or being a wide-angle photographic lens that covers an angle of about 180°, producing a circular image with exaggerated foreshortening in the center and increasing distortion toward the periphery. **2.** *Slang.* A suspicious, unfriendly glance or look.

fish farm *n.* A commercial facility consisting of tanks or ponds in which fish are raised for food.

fish flour *n.* A flour made of dried and powdered fish.

fish fry *n.* **1.** A cookout or other meal at which fried fish is the main course. **2.** A piece of fried fish.

fish·gig (fĭsh′gĭg′) *n.* A pronged instrument for spearing fish. [Alteration (influenced by FISH) of obsolete *fisgig,* from Spanish *fisga,* ultimately from Latin *fīxus,* fixed. See FIX.]

fish hawk *n.* See **osprey** (sense 1).

fish·hook (fĭsh′ho͝ok′) *n.* A barbed hook for catching fish.

fish·ing (fĭsh′ĭng) *n.* **1.** The act, occupation, or sport of catching fish. **2.** A place for catching fish.

fishing rod *n.* A rod of wood, steel, or fiberglass used with a line for catching fish.

fish joint *n.* A joint formed by bolting a fishplate to each side of two abutting rails, timbers, or beams. [From FISH(PLATE).]

fish ladder *n.* A series of pools arranged like ascending steps at the side of a stream, enabling migrating fish to swim upstream around a dam or other obstruction.

fish•meal (fĭsh′mēl′) *n.* A nutritive mealy substance produced from fish or fish parts and used as animal feed and fertilizer.

fish•mon•ger (fĭsh′mŭng′gər, -mŏng′-) *n. Chiefly British.* One that sells fish.

fish•net (fĭsh′nĕt′) *n.* **1.** Netting used to catch fish. **2.** A mesh fabric resembling such netting.

fish•plate (fĭsh′plāt′) *n.* A metal or wooden plate bolted to the sides of two abutting rails or beams, used especially in the laying of railroad track. [Probably from French *fiche,* peg (from Old French; see MICROFICHE) + PLATE.]

fish•pond (fĭsh′pŏnd′) *n.* A pond containing or stocked with edible fish.

fish protein concentrate *n. Abbr.* **FPC** A flour or paste rich in protein that is prepared from ground fish and used as a nutritional additive to foods.

fish•skin disease (fĭsh′skĭn′) *n.* See **ichthyosis.**

fish stick *n.* An oblong piece of breaded fish fillet.

fish story *n. Informal.* An implausible, boastful story. [From the fact that fishermen traditionally exaggerate the size of their catch.]

fish•tail (fĭsh′tāl′) *adj.* Resembling or suggestive of the tail of a fish in shape or movement. **—fishtail** *intr.v.* **-tailed, -tail•ing, -tails. 1.** To have the rear end of a forward-moving vehicle swerve from side to side out of control: *I stepped hard on the gas, and the truck fishtailed on the icy road.* **2.** To swing the tail of an airplane from side to side in order to reduce speed.

fishtail palm *n.* Any of several tropical Asiatic palms of the genus *Caryota,* particularly *C. mitis,* having bipinnate leaves with toothed, oblique leaflet apices.

fish•wife (fĭsh′wīf′) *n.* **1.** A woman who sells fish. **2.** A woman regarded as coarse and shrewishly abusive.

fish•y (fĭsh′ē) *adj.* **-i•er, -i•est. 1.** Resembling or suggestive of fish, as in taste or odor. **2.** Cold or expressionless: *a fishy stare.* **3.** *Informal.* Inspiring doubt or suspicion: *Something is fishy about the accident.* **—fish′i•ly** *adv.* **—fish′i•ness** *n.*

Fisk (fĭsk), **James.** 1834–1872. American railroad financier and speculator who attempted in 1869 to corner the gold market with Jay Gould, leading to Black Friday, a day of nationwide panic.

Fiske (fĭsk), **John.** 1842–1901. American historian and philosopher known for his writings on religion and science, especially *Excursions of an Evolutionist* (1884).

fissi– *pref.* **1.** Fission: *fissiparous.* **2.** Split; cleft: *fissipalmate.* [From Latin *fissus,* past participle of *findere,* to split. See **bheid-** in Appendix.]

fis•sile (fĭs′əl, -īl′) *adj.* **1.** Possible to split. **2.** *Physics.* Fissionable, especially by neutrons of all energies. **3.** *Geology.* Easily split along close parallel planes. [Latin *fissilis,* from *fissus,* split. See FISSI–.] **—fis•sil′i•ty** (fĭ-sĭl′ĭ-tē) *n.*

fis•sion (fĭsh′ən) *n.* **1.** The act or process of splitting into parts. **2.** A nuclear reaction in which an atomic nucleus, especially a heavy nucleus such as an isotope of uranium, splits into fragments, usually two fragments of comparable mass, with the evolution of from 100 million to several hundred million electron volts of energy. **3.** *Biology.* An asexual reproductive process in which a unicellular organism divides into two or more independently maturing daughter cells. [Latin *fissiō, fissiōn-,* a cleaving, from *fissus,* split. See FISSI–.]

fis•sion•a•ble (fĭsh′ə-nə-bəl) *adj.* Capable of undergoing fission: *fissionable nuclear material.* **—fis′sion•a•bil′i•ty** *n.*

fission bomb *n.* See **atom bomb** (sense 1).

fis•si•pal•mate (fĭs′ə-păl′māt′) *adj.* Having lobed or partially webbed separated toes, as in the feet of certain birds.

fis•sip•a•rous (fĭ-sĭp′ər-əs) *adj.* **1.** Reproducing by biological fission. **2.** Tending to break up into parts or break away from a main body; factious. **—fis•sip′a•rous•ly** *adv.* **—fis•sip′a•rous•ness** *n.*

fis•si•ped (fĭs′ə-pĕd′) *adj.* Having the toes separated from one another, as in the feet of certain carnivorous mammals. **—fissiped** *n.* A carnivorous mammal, such as a bear, dog, or cat, that has such toes.

fis•sure (fĭsh′ər) *n.* **1.** A long, narrow opening; a crack or cleft. **2.** The process of splitting or separating; division. **3.** A separation into subgroups or factions; a schism. **4.** *Anatomy.* A normal groove or furrow, as in the liver or brain, that divides an organ into lobes or separates it into parts. **5.** *Medicine.* A break in the skin, usually where it joins a mucous membrane, producing a cracklike sore or ulcer. **—fissure** *intr. & tr.v.* **-sured, -sur•ing, -sures.** To form a crack or cleft or cause a crack or cleft in. [Middle English, cut, from Old French, from Latin *fissūra,* from *fissus,* split. See FISSI–.]

fist (fĭst) *n.* **1.** The hand closed tightly with the fingers bent against the palm. **2.** *Informal.* A grasp; a clutch: *had a fortune in their fists and let it go.* **3.** *Printing.* See **index** (sense 3). **—fist** *tr.v.* **fist•ed, fist•ing, fists. 1.** To clench into a fist. **2.** To grasp with the fist. [Middle English, from Old English *fȳst.* See **penkʷe** in Appendix.]

fist•fight (fĭst′fīt′) *n.* A fight with the bare fists.

fist•ful (fĭst′fo͝ol′) *n., pl.* **-fuls.** The amount a fist can hold.

fist•ic (fĭs′tĭk) *adj. Sports.* Of or relating to boxing; pugilistic.

fist•i•cuffs (fĭs′tĭ-kŭfs′) *pl.n.* **1.** A fistfight. **2.** *Sports.* Boxing. [From *fisty cuffs* : *fisty,* with the fists (from FIST) + CUFF[2].] **—fist′i•cuff′er** *n.*

fis•tu•la (fĭs′chə-lə) *n., pl.* **-las** or **-lae** (-lē′). An abnormal duct or passage resulting from injury, disease, or a congenital disorder that connects an abscess, a cavity, or a hollow organ to the body surface or to another hollow organ. [Middle English, from Latin.]

fis•tu•lous (fĭs′chə-ləs) or **fis•tu•lar** (-lər) *adj.* **1.** Of or resembling a fistula. **2.** Tubular and hollow, as the leaves of a scallion. **3.** Made of or containing tubular parts.

fit[1] (fĭt) *v.* **fit•ted** or **fit, fit•ted, fit•ting, fits.** —*tr.* **1.a.** To be the proper size and shape for: *These shoes fit me.* **b.** To cause to be the proper size and shape: *The tailor fitted the trousers by shortening them.* **c.** To measure for proper size: *She fitted me for a new jacket.* **2.** To be appropriate to; suit: *music that fits your mood.* **3.** To be in conformity or agreement with: *observations that fit the theory nicely.* **4.** To make suitable; adapt: *fitted the shelves for large books.* **5.** To make ready; prepare: *Specialized training fitted her for the job.* **6.** To equip; outfit: *fit out a ship.* **7.** To provide a place or time for: *You can't fit any more toys in the box. The doctor can fit you in today.* **8.** To insert or adjust so as to be properly in place: *fit a handle on a door.* —*intr.* **1.** To be the proper size and shape. **2.** To be suited; belong: *doesn't fit in with these people.* **3.** To be in harmony; agree: *His good mood fit in with the joyful occasion.* **—fit** *adj.* **fit•ter, fit•test. 1.** Suited, adapted, or acceptable for a given circumstance or purpose: *not a fit time for flippancy.* **2.** Appropriate; proper: *Do as you see fit.* **3.** Physically sound; healthy: *keeps fit with diet and exercise.* **—fit** *n.* **1.** The state, quality, or way of being fitted: *the proper fit of means to ends.* **2.** The manner in which clothing fits: *a jacket with a tight fit.* **3.** The degree of precision with which surfaces are adjusted or adapted to each other in a machine or collection of parts. ***—idioms.*** **fit to be tied.** Roused to great anger or indignation; outraged. **fit to kill.** *Slang.* To an extreme or elaborate degree: *dressed up fit to kill.* [Middle English *fitten,* to be suitable, marshal troops.] **—fit′ly** *adv.* **—fit′ter** *n.*

SYNONYMS: *fit, suitable, meet, proper, appropriate, apt, fitting, happy, felicitous.* These adjectives mean right or correct in view of existing circumstances. They are often interchangeable. *Fit* refers to what is adapted for or suited to a purpose, occasion, or use: *a meal fit for a gourmet; a tractor fit for heavy duty; not a fit time or place for an argument. Suitable* implies ability to meet a requirement, fill a need, or answer a purpose: *an overcoat suitable for everyday wear; a book not suitable for children. Meet* applies to what is precisely suitable and often suggests the sense of being right or just: *a meet reward. Proper* describes what is harmonious, either by nature or because it accords with reason, custom, or propriety: *the proper time to plant a crop; the proper form of address for a cleric.* What is *appropriate* to a thing or for an occasion especially befits it: *a funeral conducted with appropriate solemnity.* What is *apt* is notably to the point: *an apt reply. Fitting* suggests close agreement, as with a prevailing mood or spirit: *"We have come to dedicate a portion of that field, as a final resting place for those who here gave their lives . . . It is altogether fitting and proper that we should do this"* (Abraham Lincoln). *Happy* and *felicitous* are applicable to what seems especially suitable, as by its nature: *a happy turn of phrase; a felicitous comment.* See also Synonyms at **adapt.**

fit[2] (fĭt) *n.* **1.** *Medicine.* **a.** A seizure or a convulsion, especially one caused by epilepsy. **b.** The sudden appearance of a symptom such as coughing or sneezing. **2.** A sudden outburst of emotion: *a fit of jealousy.* **3.** A sudden period of vigorous activity. ***—idiom.*** **by** (or **in**) **fits and starts.** With irregular intervals of action and inaction; intermittently. [Middle English, hardship, probably from Old English *fitt,* struggle.]

fit[3] (fĭt) *n. Archaic.* A section of a poem or ballad. [Middle English, from Old English.]

fitch (fĭch) *n.* **1.** See **polecat** (sense 1a). **2.** The fur of this animal. [Middle English *fiche,* from Middle Dutch *vitsche, visse.*]

Fitch (fĭch), **John.** 1743–1798. American steamboat pioneer whose early designs (1787–1790) were successful but received insufficient financial backing for large-scale production.

Fitch, (William) Clyde. 1865–1909. American playwright whose works include *Beau Brummel* (1890) and *The Climbers* (1901).

Fitch•burg (fĭch′bûrg′). A city of north-central Massachusetts north of Worcester. It was settled in 1740. Population, 39,580.

fitch•ew (fĭch′o͞o) also **fitch•et** (-ĭt) *n. Archaic.* The Old World polecat or its fur. [Middle English *ficheux,* possibly from Walloon *ficheau,* diminutive of Middle Dutch *vitsche, visse.*]

fit•ful (fĭt′fəl) *adj.* Occurring in or characterized by intermittent bursts, as of activity; irregular. See Synonyms at **periodic.** **—fit′ful•ly** *adv.* **—fit′ful•ness** *n.*

fit•ness (fĭt′nĭs) *n.* The state or condition of being physically fit, especially as the result of exercise and proper nutrition. —*attributive.* Often used to modify another noun: *fitness equipment; fitness centers.*

fitness walking *n. Sports.* The aerobic sport of brisk, rhythmic, vigorous walking, intended to improve cardiovascular effi-

fish ladder
At Bonneville Dam on the Columbia River

ă pat	oi boy
ā pay	ou out
âr care	o͝o took
ä father	o͞o boot
ĕ pet	ŭ cut
ē be	ûr urge
ĭ pit	th thin
ī pie	*th* this
îr pier	hw which
ŏ pot	zh vision
ō toe	ə about, item
ô paw	♦ regionalism

Stress marks: **′** (primary); ′ (secondary), as in **dictionary** (dĭk′shə-nĕr′ē)

ciency, strengthen the heart, control weight gain, and reduce stress.

fit·ting (fĭtʹĭng) *adj.* Being in keeping with a situation; appropriate. See Synonyms at **fit**[1]. **—fitting** *n.* **1.** The act of trying on clothes whose fit is being adjusted. **2.** A small detachable part for a machine or an apparatus. **3. fittings.** *Chiefly British.* Furnishings or fixtures. **—fitʹting·ly** *adv.* **—fitʹting·ness** *n.*

Ella Fitzgerald

Fitz·ger·ald (fĭts-jĕrʹəld), **Ella.** Born 1918. American jazz singer known for her scat singing.

Fitzgerald, F(rancis) Scott (Key). 1896–1940. American writer who epitomized the Jazz Age. His best-known novels are *The Great Gatsby* (1925) and *Tender Is the Night* (1934).

Fitz·Ger·ald (fĭts-jĕrʹəld), **Edward.** 1809–1883. British poet and noted translator of *The Rubáiyát of Omar Khayyám* (1859).

FitzGerald, George Francis. 1851–1901. Irish physicist who made significant discoveries in electromagnetic radiation.

Fiu·me (fyo͞oʹmā, -mĕ). See **Rijeka.**

five (fīv) *n.* **1.** The cardinal number equal to 4 + 1. **2.** The fifth in a set or sequence. **3.** Something, such as a quintet or a basketball team, that has five parts, units, or members. **4.** A five-dollar bill. **5. fives** *(used with a sing. verb). Sports.* One of several forms of handball originating in England and played mainly at British schools and universities, in which only the receiving side can score points. [Middle English, from Old English *fīf.* See **penkʷe** in Appendix.] **—five** *adj. pron.*

five-and-dime (fīvʹən-dīmʹ) *n.* See **five-and-ten.**

five-and-ten (fīvʹən-tĕnʹ) *n.* A retail store selling a wide variety of inexpensive articles. Also called *dime store, five-and-dime, ten-cent store.* [Short for *five-and-ten-cent store.*]

Five Civilized Nations (fīv) *pl.n.* The Cherokee, Chickasaw, Choctaw, Creek, and Seminole peoples. Also called *Five Civilized Tribes.*

F. Scott Fitzgerald

five-fin·ger (fīvʹfĭngʹgər) *n.* Any of several plants having palmately compound leaves with five leaflets, such as the cinquefoil.

Five Forks. A crossroads in southeast Virginia southwest of Petersburg where the last important Civil War battle was fought on April 1, 1865. The Union victory led to the fall of Petersburg and the capture of Richmond.

Five Nations *pl.n.* The Iroquois confederacy as originally formed by the Mohawk, Oneida, Onondaga, Cayuga, and Seneca peoples.

fiv·er (fīʹvər) *n.* **1.** *Informal.* A five-dollar bill. **2.** *Chiefly British.* A five-pound note.

♦ **five-way chili** (fīvʹwāʹ) *n. Cincinnati.* A main dish consisting of layers of noodles, chili con carne, kidney beans, chopped onions, and grated cheese.

♦ **fix** (fĭks) *v.* **fixed, fix·ing, fix·es.** *—tr.* **1. a.** To place securely; make stable or firm: *fixed the tent poles in the ground.* See Synonyms at **fasten. b.** To secure to another; attach: *fixing the notice to the board with tacks.* **2. a.** To put into a stable or unalterable form: *tried to fix the conversation in her memory.* **b.** To make (a chemical substance) nonvolatile or solid. **c.** *Biology.* To convert (nitrogen) into stable, biologically assimilable compounds. **d.** To kill and preserve (a specimen) intact for microscopic study. **e.** To prevent discoloration of (a photographic image) by washing or coating with a chemical preservative. **3.** To direct steadily: *fixed her eyes on the road ahead.* **4.** To capture or hold: *The man with the long beard fixed our attention.* **5. a.** To set or place definitely; establish: *fixed her residence in a coastal village.* **b.** To determine with accuracy; ascertain: *fixed the date of the ancient artifacts.* **c.** To agree on; arrange: *fix a time to meet.* **6.** To assign; attribute: *fixing the blame.* **7. a.** To correct or set right; adjust: *fix a misspelling; fix the out-of-date accounts.* **b.** To restore to proper condition or working order; repair: *fix a broken machine.* **c.** *Computer Science.* To convert (data) from floating-point notation to fixed-point notation. **8.** To make ready; prepare: *fixed the room for the guests; fix lunch for the kids; fixed himself a milkshake.* **9.** To spay or castrate (an animal). **10.** *Informal.* To take revenge upon; get even with. **11.** To influence the outcome or actions of by improper or unlawful means: *fix a prizefight; fix a jury.* *—intr.* **1.** To direct one's efforts or attention; concentrate: *We fixed on the immediate goal.* **2.** To become stable or firm; harden: *Fresh plaster will fix in a few hours.* **3.** *Chiefly Southern U.S.* To be on the verge of; to be making preparations for. Used in progressive tenses with the infinitive: *We were fixing to leave without you.* **—fix** *n.* **1. a.** The act of adjusting, correcting, or repairing. **b.** *Informal.* Something that repairs or restores; a solution: *no easy fix for an intractable problem.* **2.** The position, as of a ship or aircraft, determined by visual observations with the aid of equipment. **3.** A clear determination or understanding: *a briefing that gave us a fix on the current situation.* **4.** An instance of arranging a special consideration, such as an exemption from a requirement, or an improper or illegal outcome, especially by means of bribery. **5.** A difficult or embarrassing situation; a predicament. See Synonyms at **predicament. 6.** *Slang.* An intravenous injection of a narcotic. ***—phrasal verbs.* fix up. 1.** To improve the appearance or condition of; refurbish. **2.** To provide; equip. *Informal.* To provide a companion on a date for: *fixed me up with an escort at the last minute.* [Middle English *fixen,* from *fix,* fixed in position, from Latin *fixus,* past participle of *fīgere,* to fasten. See **dhīgʷ-** in Appendix.] **—fixʹa·ble** *adj.* **—fixʹer** *n.*

fjord

ă pat	oi boy
ā pay	ou out
âr care	o͝o took
ä father	o͞o boot
ĕ pet	ŭ cut
ē be	ûr urge
ĭ pit	th thin
ī pie	*th* this
îr pier	hw which
ŏ pot	zh vision
ō toe	ə about, item
ô paw	♦ regionalism

Stress marks: ʹ (primary); ʹ (secondary), as in **dictionary** (dĭkʹshə-nĕrʹē)

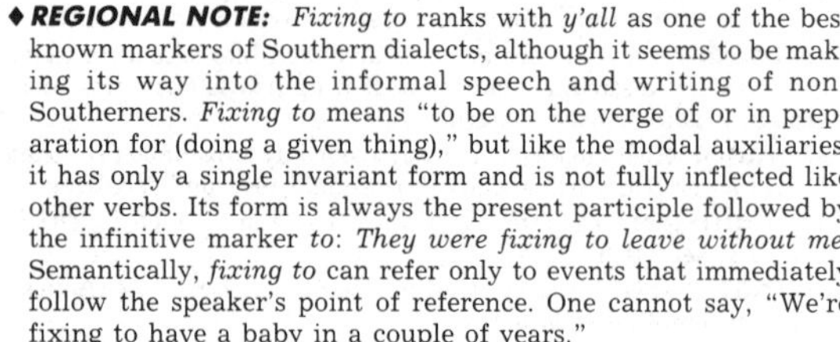

♦ ***REGIONAL NOTE:*** *Fixing to* ranks with *y'all* as one of the best known markers of Southern dialects, although it seems to be making its way into the informal speech and writing of non-Southerners. *Fixing to* means "to be on the verge of or in preparation for (doing a given thing)," but like the modal auxiliaries, it has only a single invariant form and is not fully inflected like other verbs. Its form is always the present participle followed by the infinitive marker *to*: *They were fixing to leave without me.* Semantically, *fixing to* can refer only to events that immediately follow the speaker's point of reference. One cannot say, "We're fixing to have a baby in a couple of years."

fix·ate (fĭkʹsātʹ) *v.* **-at·ed, -at·ing, -ates.** *—tr.* **1.** To make fixed, stable, or stationary. **2.** To focus one's eyes or attention on. **3.** To command the attention of exclusively or repeatedly; preoccupy obsessively: *"Movies and television seem especially fixated on the troubled Vietnam veteran"* (James Hall-Sheehy). **4.** *Psychology.* **a.** To attach (oneself) to a person or thing in an immature or neurotic fashion. **b.** To cause (the libido) to be arrested at an early stage of psychosexual development. *—intr.* **1.** To focus the eyes or attention. **2.** *Psychology.* **a.** To form a fixation; become attached to in an immature or neurotic way. **b.** To be arrested at an early stage of psychosexual development.

fix·a·tion (fĭk-sāʹshən) *n.* **1.** The act or process of fixing or fixating. **2.** An obsessive preoccupation. **3.** *Psychology.* A strong attachment to a person or thing, especially such an attachment formed in childhood or infancy and manifested in immature or neurotic behavior that persists throughout life.

fix·a·tive (fĭkʹsə-tĭv) *n.* Something that fixes, protects, or preserves, especially: **a.** A liquid preservative applied to artwork, such as watercolor paintings or charcoal drawings. **b.** A solution used to preserve and harden fresh tissue for microscopic examination. **c.** A liquid mixed with perfume to prevent rapid evaporation. **—fixʹa·tive** *adj.*

fixed (fĭkst) *adj.* **1.** Firmly in position; stationary. **2.** Determined; established; set: *at a fixed time; a fixed price.* **3.** Not subject to change or variation; constant: *pensioners on a fixed income.* **4.** *Chemistry.* **a.** Not readily evaporating; nonvolatile. **b.** Being in a stable, combined form: *fixed nitrogen.* **5.** Firmly, often dogmatically held: *fixed notions.* **6.** Supplied, especially with funds or needs. Often used in combination: *a well-fixed bachelor.* **7.** Illegally prearranged as to outcome: *a fixed election.* **—fixʹed·ly** (fĭkʹsĭd-lē) *adv.* **—fixʹed·ness** *n.*

fixed head *n.* A stationary device, such as a tape-recording head, that reads and imprints information on a single track of magnetic tape.

fixed macrophage *n.* See **histiocyte.**

fixed oil *n.* A nonvolatile oil, especially a fatty oil of vegetable origin.

fixed-point (fĭkstʹpointʹ) *adj.* Of, relating to, or being a method of writing numerical quantities with a predetermined number of digits and with the decimal located at a single, unchanging position.

fixed star *n.* A star so distant from Earth that its position in relation to other stars appears not to change. Its movements can be measured only by precise observations over long periods of time.

fix·ings (fĭkʹsĭngz) *pl.n. Informal.* Accessories; trimmings: *a Mexican dinner with all the fixings.*

fix·i·ty (fĭkʹsĭ-tē) *n., pl.* **-ties. 1.** The quality or condition of being fixed. **2.** Something fixed or immovable.

fix·ture (fĭksʹchər) *n.* **1.** Something securely fixed in place. **2.** Something attached as a permanent appendage, apparatus, or appliance: *plumbing fixtures.* **3.** *Law.* A chattel bound to realty. **4.** One that is invariably present in and long associated with a place: *a journalist who became a Washington fixture.* **5. a.** The act or process of fixing. **b.** The condition of being fixed. [Variant of obsolete *fixure,* from Late Latin *fīxūra,* from Latin *fīxus,* fixed. See FIX.]

fizz (fĭz) *intr.v.* **fizzed, fizz·ing, fizz·es.** To make a hissing or bubbling sound. **—fizz** *n.* **1.** A hissing or bubbling sound. **2.** Effervescence. **3.** An effervescent beverage. [Imitative.] **—fizzʹy** *adj.*

fiz·zle (fĭzʹəl) *intr.v.* **-zled, -zling, -zles. 1.** To make a hissing or sputtering sound. **2.** *Informal.* To fail or end weakly, especially after a hopeful beginning. **—fizzle** *n. Informal.* A failure; a fiasco. [Probably from obsolete *fist,* to break wind, from Middle English *fisten.* See **pezd-** in Appendix.]

WORD HISTORY: In Philemon Holland's 1601 translation of Pliny's *Natural History,* we are surprised by the use of the word *fizzle* in the statement that if asses eat a certain plant, "they will fall a fizling and farting." *Fizzle* was first used in English to mean, in the decorous parlance of the *Oxford English Dictionary,* "to break wind without noise." During the 19th century *fizzle* took on a related but more respectable sense, "to hiss, as does a piece of fireworks," illustrated by a quotation from the November 7, 1881, issue of the *London Daily News:* "unambitious rockets which fizzle doggedly downwards." In the same century *fizzle* also took on figurative senses, one of which seems to have been popular at Yale. The *Yale Literary Magazine* for 1849 helpfully defines the word as follows: "*Fizzle,* to rise with modest reluctance, to hesitate often, to decline finally; generally, to misunderstand the question." The figurative sense of *fizzle* that has caught on is the one with which we are most familiar today, "to fall or die out."

---

fjeld (fyĕld) *n.* A high, barren plateau in the Scandinavian countries. [Danish, from Old Norse *fjall.*]

fjord or **fiord** (fyôrd, fyōrd) *n.* A long, narrow, deep inlet of the sea between steep slopes. [Norwegian, from Old Norse *fjördhr.* See **per-²** in Appendix.]

fl or **fl.** *abbr.* Fluid.

fL *abbr.* Foot-lambert.

FL *abbr.* **1.** Florida. **2.** Focal length. **3.** Foreign languages.

fl. *abbr.* **1.** *Football.* Flankerback. **2.** Floor. **3.** Florin. **4.** Floruit. **5.** Flute.

Fla. *abbr.* Florida.

flab (flăb) *n.* Soft, fatty body tissue. [Back-formation from FLABBY.]

flab·ber·gast (flăb′ər-găst′) *tr.v.* **-gast·ed, -gast·ing, -gasts.** To cause to be overcome with astonishment; astound. See Synonyms at **surprise.** [Origin unknown.]

flab·by (flăb′ē) *adj.* **-bi·er, -bi·est. 1.** Lacking firmness; flaccid: *getting flabby around the waist.* See Synonyms at **limp. 2.** Lacking force or vitality; ineffectual: *flabby self-pity.* [Alteration of *flappy,* tending to flap, from FLAP.] **—flab′bi·ly** *adv.* **—flab′bi·ness** *n.*

fla·bel·la (flə-bĕl′ə) *n.* Plural of **flabellum.**

fla·bel·late (flə-bĕl′ĭt, flăb′ə-lāt′) also **fla·bel·li·form** (flə-bĕl′ə-fôrm′) *adj.* Fan-shaped. [Latin *flābellum,* fan; see FLABELLUM + –ATE¹.]

fla·bel·lum (flə-bĕl′əm) *n., pl.* **-bel·la** (-bĕl′ə). A fan-shaped anatomical structure. [Latin *flābellum,* fan, diminutive of *flābra,* breeze, from *flāre,* to blow. See **bhlē-** in Appendix.]

flac·cid (flăk′sĭd, flăs′ĭd) *adj.* **1.** Lacking firmness, resilience, or muscle tone. See Synonyms at **limp. 2.** Lacking vigor or energy: *flaccid management.* [Latin *flaccidus,* from *flaccus,* flabby.] **—flac·cid′i·ty** (-sĭd′ĭ-tē), **flac′cid·ness** *n.* **—flac′cid·ly** *adv.*

flack¹ (flăk) *Informal. n.* A press agent; a publicist. **—flack** *v.* **flacked, flack·ing, flacks.** *—intr.* To act as a press agent: *flacking for a movie studio.* *—tr.* To act as a press agent for; promote: *authors who tour the country flacking their books.* [Origin unknown.] **—flack′er·y** *n.*

flack² (flăk) *n.* Variant of **flak.**

flac·on (flăk′ən, -ŏn′) *n.* A small, often decorative bottle with a tight-fitting stopper or cap. [French, from Old French. See FLAGON.]

flag¹ (flăg) *n.* **1.** A piece of cloth, usually rectangular, of distinctive color and design, used as a symbol, a standard, a signal, or an emblem. **2.** National or other allegiance, as symbolized by a flag: *ships of the same flag.* **3.** A ship carrying the flag of an admiral; a flagship. **4.** A marking device, such as a gummed strip of paper, attached to an object to attract attention or ease identification; a tab. **5.** The masthead of a newspaper. **6.** *Music.* A cross stroke added to a note that is less than a quarter note in value. **7.** A distinctively shaped or marked tail, as of a dog or deer. **8.** *Computer Science.* A bit or series of bits with two stable states, used in software to indicate a single piece of information. **—flag** *tr.v.* **flagged, flag·ging, flags. 1.** To mark with a flag or flags for identification or ornamentation: *flag a parade route; flagging parts of a manuscript for later review.* **2.a.** To signal with or as if with a flag. **b.** To signal to stop: *flag down a passing car.* [Origin unknown.] **—flag′ger** *n.*

flag² (flăg) *n.* A plant, such as an iris or a cattail, that has long, sword-shaped leaves. [Middle English *flagge,* reed, of Scandinavian origin.]

flag³ (flăg) *intr.v.* **flagged, flag·ging, flags. 1.** To hang limply; droop. **2.** To decline in vigor or strength: *My appetite flags in the hot weather.* **3.** To decline in interest: *The conversation flagged.* [Possibly of Scandinavian origin; akin to Old Norse *flögra,* to flap about.]

flag⁴ (flăg) *n.* A flagstone. **—flag** *tr.v.* **flagged, flag·ging, flags.** To pave with slabs of flagstone. [Middle English *flagge,* piece of turf, from Old Norse *flaga,* slab of stone. See **plāk-¹** in Appendix.]

Flag Day (flăg) *n.* June 14, observed in the United States in commemoration of the adoption in 1777 of the official U.S. flag.

fla·gel·la (flə-jĕl′ə) *n.* Plural of **flagellum.**

flag·el·lant (flăj′ə-lənt, flə-jĕl′ənt) *n.* **1.** One who whips, especially one who scourges oneself for religious discipline or public penance. **2.** One who seeks sexual gratification in beating or being beaten by another person. [Latin *flagellāns, flagellant-,* from present participle of *flagellāre,* to whip. See FLAGELLATE.] **—flag′el·lant** *adj.* **—flag′el·lant·ism** *n.*

fla·gel·lar (flə-jĕl′ər) *adj.* Of or relating to a flagellum.

flag·el·late (flăj′ə-lāt′) *tr.v.* **-lat·ed, -lat·ing, -lates. 1.** To whip or flog; scourge. **2.** To punish or impel as if by whipping. **—flagellate** (-lĭt, -lāt′, flə-jĕl′ĭt) *adj.* **1.** *Biology.* Flagellated. **2.** Resembling or having the form of a flagellum; whiplike. **3.** Relating to or caused by a flagellate organism. **—flagellate** (-lĭt, -lāt′, flə-jĕl′ĭt) *n.* An organism, such as a euglena, that is equipped with a flagellum. [Latin *flagellāre, flagellāt-,* to whip, from *flagellum,* diminutive of *flagrum,* whip.]

flag·el·lat·ed (flăj′ə-lā′tĭd) *adj. Biology.* Having a flagellum or flagella.

flag·el·la·tion (flăj′ə-lā′shən) *n.* **1.** The act of flagellating. **2.** *Biology.* The flagellar arrangement on an organism.

fla·gel·li·form (flə-jĕl′ə-fôrm′) *adj.* Long, thin, and tapering; whip-shaped: *flagelliform appendages.* [Latin *flagellum,* little whip; see FLAGELLUM + –FORM.]

fla·gel·lin (flə-jĕl′ĭn) *n.* The chief protein component of bacterial flagella.

fla·gel·lum (flə-jĕl′əm) *n., pl.* **-gel·la** (-jĕl′ə). **1.** *Biology.* A long, threadlike appendage, especially a whiplike extension of certain cells or unicellular organisms that functions as an organ of locomotion. **2.** A whip. [Latin, diminutive of *flagrum,* whip.]

flag·eo·let (flăj′ə-lĕt′, -lā′) *n. Music.* A small flutelike instrument with a cylindrical mouthpiece, four finger holes, and two thumbholes. [French, diminutive of Old French *flajol,* flute, from Vulgar Latin **flābeolum,* possibly alteration of Latin *flābellum,* diminutive of *flābrum,* gust of wind, from *flāre,* to blow. See INFLATE.]

Flagg (flăg), **James Montgomery.** 1877–1960. American artist and writer best known for his World War I recruiting poster of Uncle Sam saying "I Want You."

flag·ging¹ (flăg′ĭng) *adj.* **1.** Declining; weakening: *flagging strength.* **2.** Languid; drooping. **—flag′ging·ly** *adv.*

flag·ging² (flăg′ĭng) *n.* A pavement laid with flagstones.

fla·gi·tious (flə-jĭsh′əs) *adj.* **1.** Characterized by extremely brutal or cruel crimes; vicious. **2.** Infamous; scandalous: *"That remorseless government persisted in its flagitious project"* (Robert Southey). [Middle English *flagicious,* wicked, from Latin *flāgitiōsus,* from *flāgitium,* shameful act, protest, from *flāgitāre,* to importune, to demand vehemently.] **—fla·gi′tious·ly** *adv.* **—fla·gi′tious·ness** *n.*

Flag·ler (flăg′lər), **Henry Morrison.** 1830–1913. American capitalist who built resorts and railroad lines in Florida to promote it as a recreational area.

flag·man (flăg′mən) *n.* One who signals with or carries a flag.

flag of convenience *n., pl.* **flags of convenience.** A foreign flag under which a merchant vessel is registered for purposes of reducing operating costs or avoiding government regulations.

flag officer *n.* An officer in the navy or coast guard holding a rank higher than captain, such as rear admiral, vice admiral, or admiral.

flag of truce *n., pl.* **flags of truce.** A white flag brought or displayed to an enemy as a request for a conference or as a signal of surrender.

flag·on (flăg′ən) *n.* **1.** A large vessel, usually of metal or pottery, with a handle and spout and often a lid, used for holding wine or other liquors. **2.** The quantity of liquid that such a vessel can hold. [Middle English, from Old French *flacon,* from Late Latin *flascō, flascōn-,* bottle. See FLASK.]

flag·pole (flăg′pōl′) *n.* A pole on which a flag is raised. Also called *flagstaff.* ***—idiom.*** **run (something) up the flagpole.** *Slang.* To test (a plan, a suggestion, a draft, or an idea) and then measure the response to it.

fla·grant (flā′grənt) *adj.* **1.** Conspicuously bad, offensive, or reprehensible: *a flagrant miscarriage of justice; flagrant cases of wrongdoing at the highest levels of government.* See Usage Note at **blatant. 2.** *Obsolete.* Flaming; blazing. [Latin *flagrāns, flagrant-,* present participle of *flagrāre,* to burn. See **bhel-¹** in Appendix.] **—fla′gran·cy, fla′grance** *n.* **—fla′grant·ly** *adv.*

SYNONYMS: *flagrant, glaring, gross, egregious, rank.* These adjectives refer to what is conspicuously bad or offensive. *Flagrant* applies to what is so offensive that it cannot escape notice: *in flagrant disregard of the law.* What is *glaring* is blatantly and painfully manifest: *a glaring error; glaring contradictions. Gross* suggests a magnitude of offense or failing that cannot be condoned or forgiven: *gross ineptitude; gross injustice.* What is *egregious* is outrageously bad: *an egregious lie. Rank* implies that the term it qualifies is as indicated to an extreme, violent, or gross degree: *rank stupidity; rank treachery.* See also Synonyms at **outrageous.**

---

fla·gran·te de·lic·to (flə-grăn′tē dĭ-lĭk′tō) *adv.* In the very act; red-handed. [Medieval Latin *flagrante dēlictō,* while the crime is blazing : *flagrante,* ablative of *flagrāns,* blazing + *dēlictō,* ablative of *dēlictum,* offense.]

flag·ship (flăg′shĭp′) *n.* **1.** A ship that carries a fleet or squadron commander and bears the commander's flag. **2.** The chief one of a related group: *the flagship of a newspaper chain; the flagship of a line of reference books.*

Flag·stad (flăg′stăd′, fläg′stä′), **Kirsten Marie.** 1895–1962. Norwegian operatic soprano known for her performances as Wagnerian heroines.

flag·staff (flăg′stăf′) *n.* See **flagpole.**

Flag·staff (flăg′stăf′). A city of north-central Arizona northeast of Prescott. It is a health resort and the site of Lowell Observatory (founded 1894). Population, 34,743.

flag·stick (flăg′stĭk′) *n. Sports.* A removable pole with a numbered flag marking the placement of each hole on the putting greens of a golf course.

flag·stone (flăg′stōn′) *n.* **1.** A flat slab of stone used as a paving material. **2.** An evenly layered sedimentary rock that can be split into paving stones.

flag¹

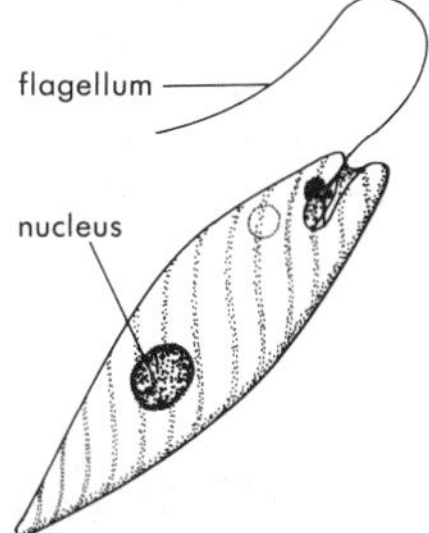

flagellum

flagon
c. 1780 pewter flagon attributed to Thomas Carpenter

flagstick
On a putting green

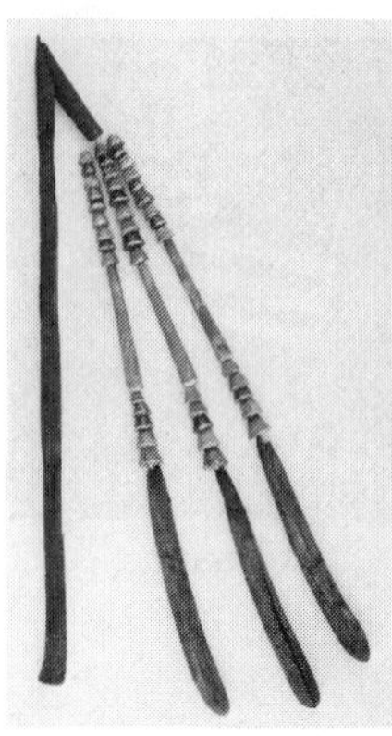
flail
Egyptian flail of the Middle Kingdom

flake[2]
Fish drying on a flake

flambé

flamenco

flag-wav·ing (flăg′wā′vĭng) *n.* Excessive or fanatical patriotism; chauvinism. **—flag′-wav′er** *n.*

Fla·her·ty (flă′ər-tē, flä′-), **Robert Joseph.** 1884–1951. American explorer and filmmaker whose works, including *Nanook of the North* (1922), were the first major documentaries.

flail (flāl) *n.* A manual threshing device consisting of a long wooden handle or staff and a shorter, free-swinging stick attached to its end. **—flail** *v.* **flailed, flail·ing, flails.** *—tr.* **1.** To beat or strike with or as if with a flail: *flailed our horses with the reins.* **2.** To wave or swing vigorously; thrash: *flailed my arms to get their attention.* **3.** To thresh using a flail. *—intr.* **1.** To move vigorously or erratically; thrash about: *arms flailing helplessly in the water.* **2.** To strike or lash out violently: *boxers flailing at each other in the ring.* **3.** To thresh grain. [Middle English, from Old English *flegil* and from Old French *flaiel,* both from Late Latin *flagellum,* threshing tool, from Latin *flagrum,* whip.]

flair (flâr) *n.* **1.** A natural talent or aptitude; a knack: *a flair for interior decorating.* **2.** Instinctive discernment; keenness: *a flair for the exotica.* **3.** Distinctive elegance or style: *served us with flair.* [Middle English, fragrance, from Old French, from *flairer,* to scent, from Late Latin *flāgrāre,* alteration of Latin *frāgrāre,* to emit an odor.]

flak also **flack** (flăk) *n.* **1.a.** Antiaircraft artillery. **b.** The bursting shells fired from such artillery. **2.** *Informal.* **a.** Excessive or abusive criticism. **b.** Dissension; opposition. [German, from *Fl(ieger)a(bwehr)k(anone),* aircraft-defense gun.]

flake[1] (flāk) *n.* **1.** A flat, thin piece or layer; a chip. **2.** A small piece; a bit. **3.** A small crystalline bit of snow. **4.** *Slang.* A somewhat eccentric person; an oddball. **5.** *Slang.* Cocaine. **—flake** *v.* **flaked, flak·ing, flakes.** *—tr.* **1.** To break flat, thin pieces or layers from; chip. **2.** To cover, mark, or overlay with or as if with flakes. *—intr.* To come off in flat, thin pieces or layers; chip off. ***—phrasal verb.*** **flake out.** *Slang.* **1.** To fall asleep or collapse from fatigue or exhaustion. **2.** To act in an odd or eccentric manner. [Middle English. See **plāk-[1]** in Appendix.] **—flak′er** *n.*

flake[2] (flāk) *n.* **1.** A frame or platform for drying fish or produce. **2.** A scaffold lowered over the side of a ship to support workers or caulkers. [Middle English *fleke,* from Old Norse *fleki,* hurdle, shield used for defense in battle. See **plāk-[1]** in Appendix.]

flake white *n.* A pigment made of flakes of white lead.

flak·ey (flā′kē) *adj.* Variant of **flaky.**

flak jacket *n.* A bulletproof jacket or vest.

flak·y also **flak·ey** (flā′kē) *adj.* **-i·er, -i·est. 1.** Made of or resembling flakes. **2.** Forming or tending to form flakes or thin, crisp fragments: *flaky pastry.* **3.** *Slang.* Somewhat eccentric; odd: *"that slightly flakey quality, in joy as well as in grief, that prepares us subtly for the mad scenes to come"* (Village Voice). **—flak′i·ly** *adv.* **—flak′i·ness** *n.*

flam[1] (flăm) *n.* *Informal.* **1.** A lie or hoax; a deception. **2.** Nonsense; drivel. [Short for FLIMFLAM.]

flam[2] (flăm) *n.* *Music.* A drumbeat consisting of two almost simultaneous strokes of which the first is a very rapid grace note. [Probably of imitative origin.]

flam·bé (fläm-bā′, flän-) *tr.v.* **-béed, -bé·ing, -bés.** To drench with a liquor, such as brandy, and ignite: *flambéed the steak at the table.* **—flambé** *adj.* Served flaming in ignited liquor: *steak flambé.* [From French, past participle of *flamber,* to flame, from Old French, from *flambe,* flame. See FLAME.]

flam·beau (flăm′bō′) *n., pl.* **-beaux** (-bōz′) or **-beaus. 1.** A lighted torch. **2.** A large ornamental candlestick. [French, from Old French, from *flambe,* flame. See FLAME.]

flam·boy·ant (flăm-boi′ənt) *adj.* **1.** Highly elaborate; ornate. See Synonyms at **ornate. 2.** Richly colored; resplendent. **3.** *Architecture.* Of, relating to, or having wavy lines and flamelike forms characteristic of 15th- and 16th-century French Gothic architecture. **4.** Marked by striking audacity or verve. **5.** Given to ostentatious display; showy. See Synonyms at **showy. —flamboyant** *n.* See **royal poinciana.** [French, from Old French, present participle of *flamboyer,* to blaze, from *flambe,* flame. See FLAME.] **—flam·boy′ance, flam·boy′an·cy** *n.* **—flam·boy′ant·ly** *adv.*

flame (flām) *n.* **1.** The zone of burning gases and fine suspended matter associated with rapid combustion; a hot, glowing mass of burning gas or vapor. **2.** The condition of active, blazing combustion: *burst into flame.* See Synonyms at **blaze[1]. 3.** Something resembling a flame in motion, brilliance, intensity, or shape. **4.** A violent or intense passion. **5.** *Informal.* A sweetheart. **—flame** *v.* **flamed, flam·ing, flames.** *—intr.* **1.** To burn brightly; blaze. **2.** To color or flash suddenly: *cheeks that flamed with embarrassment.* *—tr.* **1.** To burn, ignite, or scorch (something) with a flame. **2.** *Obsolete.* To foment; incite. [Middle English, from Anglo-Norman *flaumbe,* variant of Old French *flambe,* from *flamble,* from Latin *flammula,* diminutive of *flamma.* See **bhel-[1]** in Appendix.] **—flam′er** *n.*

flame cell *n.* A hollow cell in the excretory system of certain invertebrates, including flatworms and rotifers, containing a tuft of rapidly beating cilia that serve to propel waste products into excretory tubules.

fla·men (flā′mən) *n., pl.* **fla·mens** or **flam·i·nes** (flăm′ə-nēz′). A priest, especially of an ancient Roman deity. [Middle English *flamin,* from Latin *flāmen.*]

fla·men·co (flə-mĕng′kō) *n., pl.* **-cos. 1.a.** A dance style of the Andalusian Gypsies characterized by forceful, often improvised rhythms. **b.** A dance in this style. **2.** The guitar music that usually accompanies a dance in this style. [Spanish, Flemish, from Middle Dutch *Vlāming,* Fleming.]

WORD HISTORY: The origin of the word *flamenco* is to be sought variously in the realms of ornithology and northern Europe. Spanish contains two homographs spelled *flamenco,* one of which means "Flemish, Andalusian Gypsy," and the other, "flamingo." *Flamenco* in the former sense comes from the Middle Dutch word *Vlāming,* meaning "Fleming." *Flamenco,* "flamingo," comes ultimately from Latin *flamma,* "flame," referring to the fiery red plumage of the bird. Is the dance named for its flamingolike fieriness or its Flemishness? It would seem that some kind of association between Gypsies and people of Flemish extraction explains the use of *flamenco,* "Fleming, Andalusian Gypsy," as the name of a dance originally associated with the Andalusian Gypsies. The English word *flamenco,* borrowed from Spanish, is first recorded in 1896.

flame nettle *n.* See **coleus.**

flame·out (flām′out′) *n.* Failure of a jet aircraft engine, especially in flight, caused by the extinction of the flame in the combustion chamber.

flame·proof (flām′pro͞of′) *adj.* Resistant to catching fire. **—flameproof** *tr.v.* **-proofed, -proof·ing, -proofs.** To make resistant to catching fire. **—flame′proof′er** *n.*

flame-re·tard·ant (flām′rĭ-tär′dnt) *adj.* Resistant to catching fire. **—flame′-re·tard′ant** *n.*

flame·throw·er (flām′thrō′ər) *n.* A weapon that projects ignited incendiary fuel, such as napalm, in a steady stream.

flam·i·nes (flăm′ə-nēz′) *n.* A plural of **flamen.**

flam·ing (flā′mĭng) *adj.* **1.** On fire; ablaze. **2.** Resembling a flame in brilliance, color, or form: *flaming autumn leaves.* **3.** Intense; ardent: *flaming passions.* **4.** *Informal.* Used as an intensive: *a flaming liberal.* **—flam′ing·ly** *adv.*

fla·min·go (flə-mĭng′gō) *n., pl.* **-gos** or **-goes. 1.** Any of several large, gregarious wading birds of the family Phoenicopteridae of tropical regions, having reddish or pinkish plumage, long legs, a long flexible neck, and a bill turned downward at the tip. **2.** *Color.* A moderate reddish orange. [Portuguese *flamengo* or Spanish *flamenco,* both probably from Old Provençal *flamenc,* from *flama,* flame, from Latin *flamma.* See **bhel-[1]** in Appendix.]

flamingo flower *n.* A short-stemmed perennial *(Anthurium scherzeranum)* native to Costa Rica and Guatemala, having a reflex, shiny, scarlet spathe and a spirally contorted, vermilion spadix. Also called *pigtail.*

flaming sword *n.* A widely cultivated bromeliad *(Vriesea splendens)* native to French Guiana, having long, unbranched inflorescences with red imbricated bracts and yellow flowers.

Fla·min·i·an Way (flə-mĭn′ē-ən). An ancient Roman road that was the principal artery between Rome and Cisalpine Gaul. It was begun in 220 B.C. by Gaius Flaminius (died 217).

flam·ma·ble (flăm′ə-bəl) *adj.* Easily ignited and capable of burning rapidly; inflammable. [From Latin *flammāre,* to set fire to, from *flamma,* flame. See **bhel-[1]** in Appendix.] **—flam′ma·bil′i·ty** *n.* **—flam′ma·ble** *n.*

USAGE NOTE: Historically, *flammable* and *inflammable* mean the same thing. However, the presence of the prefix *in–* has misled many people into assuming that *inflammable* means "not flammable" or "noncombustible." In the circumstances, it is therefore advisable to use only *flammable* in contexts imparting warnings or on product labels, where a misinterpretation might have more serious consequences for the reader than an etymological mistake would deserve.

Flam·ma·rion (flə-mâr′ē-ôN′), **Camille.** 1842–1925. French astronomer who founded the French Astronomical Society (1887).

flam·y (flā′mē) *adj.* **-i·er, -i·est.** Resembling a flame.

flan (flăn, flän, fläN) *n.* **1.** A tart with a filling of custard, fruit, or cheese. **2.** A dessert of firm, smooth custard with a topping of caramel syrup. **3.** A metal disk to be stamped as a coin; a blank. [French, from Old French *flaon,* from Late Latin *fladō, fladōn-,* flat cake, of Germanic origin. See **plat-** in Appendix.]

Flan·a·gan (flăn′ə-gən), **Edward Joseph.** 1886–1948. American priest who founded Boys Town (1917), a community for underprivileged boys.

Flan·ders (flăn′dərz). A historical region of northwest Europe including parts of northern France, western Belgium, and southwest Netherlands along the North Sea. For many centuries it enjoyed virtual independence and great prosperity as a center of the cloth industry. The Hapsburg wars in the Low Countries caused the eventual division of the region.

flâ·ne·rie (flän-rē′, flä′nə-rē′) *n.* Aimless idling; dawdling. [French, from *flâner,* to idle about, stroll. See FLÂNEUR.]

flâ·neur (flä-nûr′) *n.* An aimless idler; a loafer. [French, from *flâner,* to idle about, stroll, of Germanic origin. See **pele-[2]** in Appendix.]

flange (flănj) *n.* A protruding rim, edge, rib, or collar, as on a wheel or a pipe shaft, used to strengthen an object, hold it in place, or attach it to another object. [Possibly variant of *flanch,* device at the side of an escutcheon, perhaps from French *flanche,* feminine of *flanc,* side. See FLANK.] **—flange** *v.*

flank (flăngk) *n.* **1.** The section of flesh on the body of a person or an animal between the last rib and the hip; the side. **2.** A cut of meat from the flank of an animal. **3.** A lateral part or side: *the flank of a mountain.* **4.a.** The right or left side of a military formation: *an attack on both flanks.* **b.** The right or left side of a bastion. **—flank** *tr.v.* **flanked, flank·ing, flanks.** **1.** To protect or guard the flank of. **2.** To menace or attack the flank of. **3.** To be placed or situated at the flank or side of: *Two stone lions flanked the entrance.* **4.** To put (something) on each side of: *flanked the driveway with tall shrubs.* [Middle English, from Old English *flanc,* from Old French *flanc,* of Germanic origin.]

flan·ken (flăng′kən) *n.* **1.** A cut of meat taken from the short ribs of beef. **2.** A dish prepared from this cut of beef by boiling or stewing, often served with horseradish. [Yiddish, from German, pl. of *Flanke,* flank, side, from French *flanc.* See FLANK.]

flank·er (flăng′kər) *n.* **1.** One that flanks, especially a soldier so positioned as to protect the flank of a column of troops on the march. **2.** *Business.* An extension product, such as a diet version of a soft drink, added to a line to support the sales of the main product. **3.** *Football.* A flankerback.

flank·er·back (flăng′kər-băk′) *n. Abbr.* **fl.** *Football.* An offensive halfback stationed just behind the line of scrimmage and slightly wide of the formation, used chiefly as a pass receiver.

flan·nel (flăn′əl) *n.* **1.** A soft woven cloth of wool or a blend of wool and cotton or synthetics. **2. flannels. a.** Outer clothing, especially trousers, made of this cloth. **b.** Underclothing made of this cloth. [Middle English, a kind of woolen cloth or garment, perhaps variant of *flanyn,* sackcloth, probably from Old French *flaine,* a kind of coarse wool.]

flannel bush *n.* Any of various shrubs or small trees of the genus *Fremontodendron* of California and northern Mexico, having downy, lobed leaves and showy yellow flowers.

flannel cake *n.* See **pancake.**

flan·nel·ette (flăn′ə-lĕt′) *n.* A soft cotton cloth with a nap, used chiefly for baby clothes and underclothing.

flannel leaf *n.* See **mullein.**

Flan·ner (flăn′ər), **Janet.** Pen name Genêt. 1892–1978. American journalist who was the Paris correspondent for the *New Yorker* (1925–1975).

flap (flăp) *n.* **1.** A flat, usually thin piece attached at only one side. **2.** A projecting or hanging piece usually intended to double over and protect or cover: *the flap of an envelope.* **3.a.** The act of waving or fluttering: *the flap of the flag in the wind.* **b.** The sound produced by this motion. **4.** A blow given with something flat; a slap. **5.** A variable control surface on the trailing edge of an aircraft wing, used primarily to increase lift or drag. **6.** Either of the folded ends of a book jacket that fit inside the front and back covers. **7.** *Medicine.* Tissue that has been partially detached and used in surgical grafting to fill an adjacent defect or cover the cut end of a bone after amputation. **8.** *Informal.* A commotion or disturbance: *a flap in Congress over the defense budget.* **—flap** *v.* **flapped, flap·ping, flaps.** —*tr.* **1.** To wave (the arms, for example) up and down. **2.** To cause to move or sway with a fluttering or waving motion. **3.** To hit with something broad and flat; slap. **4.** *Informal.* To fling down; toss. —*intr.* **1.** To move or sway while fixed at one edge or corner; flutter: *banners flapping in the breeze.* **2.** To wave arms or wings up and down. **3.** To fly by beating the air with the wings. **4.** *Informal.* To become upset or flustered. [Middle English *flappe,* slap.]

flap·doo·dle also **flap-doo·dle** (flăp′do͞od′l) *n. Slang.* Foolish talk; nonsense: *"Behind the tourist flap-doodle, authentic* [Key West] *cooking is produced by the descendants of Bahamian English and Cubans, who migrated to this coral reef over a century ago"* (Betty Fussell). [Origin unknown.]

flap·jack (flăp′jăk′) *n.* See **pancake.**

flap·pa·ble (flăp′ə-bəl) *adj. Informal.* Easily excited or upset.

flap·per (flăp′ər) *n.* **1.** A broad, flexible part, such as a flipper. **2.** A young woman, especially one in the 1920's who showed disdain for conventional dress and behavior. [Sense 2, British Slang, very young female prostitute, flapper, possibly from *flapper,* fledgling partridge or duck (from FLAP) or from dialectal *flap,* loose or flighty girl.]

flare (flâr) *v.* **flared, flar·ing, flares.** —*intr.* **1.** To flame up with a bright, wavering light. **2.** To burst into intense, sudden flame. **3.a.** To erupt or intensify suddenly: *Tempers flared at the meeting.* **b.** To become suddenly angry: *The candidate flared at the reporter's question.* **4.** To expand or open outward in shape: *a skirt that flares from the waist; nostrils that flared with anger.* —*tr.* **1.** To cause to flame up. **2.** To signal with a blaze of light. **—flare** *n.* **1.** A brief, wavering blaze of light. See Synonyms at **blaze¹.** **2.** A device that produces a bright light for signaling, illumination, or identification. **3.** An outbreak, as of emotion or activity. **4.** An expanding or opening outward. **5.** An unwanted reflection within an optical system or the resultant fogging of the image. **6.** A solar flare. **7.** *Football.* A quick pass to a back running toward the sideline. **8.** *Medicine.* An area of redness on the skin surrounding the primary site of infection or irritation. [Origin unknown.]

flare·back (flâr′băk′) *n.* **1.** A flame produced in the breech of a gun by ignition of residual gases. **2.** A burst of something aimed back at its origin; a backfire: *a flareback of bad publicity.*

flare-up (flâr′ŭp′) *n.* **1.** A sudden outbreak of flame or light: *a flare-up of the embers.* **2.** An outburst or eruption: *a flare-up of anger.* **3.** A recurrence or an intensification: *a flare-up of rheumatism.*

flash (flăsh) *v.* **flashed, flash·ing, flash·es.** —*intr.* **1.** To burst forth into or as if into flame. **2.** To give off light or be lighted in sudden or intermittent bursts. **3.** To appear or occur suddenly: *The image flashed onto the screen.* **4.** To move or proceed rapidly: *The cars flashed by.* **5.** *Slang.* To think of or remember something suddenly: *flashed on that time we got caught in the storm.* **6.** *Slang.* To expose oneself in an indecent manner. —*tr.* **1.a.** To cause (light) to appear suddenly or in intermittent bursts. **b.** To cause to burst into flame. **c.** To reflect (light). **d.** To cause to reflect light from (a surface). **2.** To make known or signal by flashing lights. **3.** To communicate or display at great speed: *flashed the news to the world capitals.* **4.** To exhibit briefly. **5.** To display ostentatiously; flaunt. **6.** To fill suddenly with water. **7.** To cover with a thin protective layer. **—flash** *n.* **1.** A sudden, brief, intense display of light. **2.** A sudden perception: *a flash of insight.* **3.** A split second; an instant: *I'll be on my way in a flash.* **4.** A brief news dispatch or transmission. **5.** *Slang.* Gaudy or ostentatious display: *"The antique flash and trash of an older southern California have given way to a sleeker age of cultural hip"* (Newsweek). **6.** A flashlight. **7.a.** Instantaneous illumination for photography: *photograph by flash.* **b.** A device, such as a flashbulb, flashgun, or flash lamp, used to produce such illumination. **8.** *Slang.* The pleasurable sensation that accompanies the use of a drug; a rush. **9.** *Obsolete.* The language or cant of thieves, tramps, or underworld figures. **—flash** *adj.* **1.** Happening suddenly or very quickly: *flash freezing.* **2.** *Slang.* Ostentatious; showy: *a flash car.* **3.** Of or relating to figures of quarterly economic growth released by the government and subject to later revision. **4.** Of or relating to photography using instantaneous illumination. **5.** Of or relating to thieves, swindlers, and underworld figures. ***—idiom.*** **flash in the pan.** One that promises great success but fails. [Middle English *flashen,* to splash, variant of *flasken,* of imitative origin.]

SYNONYMS: *flash, gleam, glance, glint, sparkle, glitter, glisten, shimmer, glimmer, twinkle, scintillate.* These verbs mean to send forth light. *Flash* refers to a sudden and brilliant but short-lived outburst of light: *A bolt of lightning flashed across the horizon. Gleam* implies transient or constant light that often appears against a dark background: *"The light gleams an instant, then it's night once more"* (Samuel Beckett). *Glance* refers most often to light reflected obliquely: *Moonlight glanced off the windows of the darkened building. Glint* applies to briefly gleaming or flashing light: *Rays of sun glinted among the autumn leaves. Sparkle* suggests a rapid succession of little flashes of high brilliance (*crystal that sparkled in the candlelight; frost sparkling on the pavement*), and *glitter,* a similar succession of even greater intensity (*glittering mirrors*). To *glisten* is to shine with a sparkling luster: *The snow glistened in the dawn light. Shimmer* means to shine with a soft, tremulous light: *"Everything about her shimmered and glimmered softly, as if her dress had been woven out of candle-beams"* (Edith Wharton). *Glimmer* refers to faint, fleeting light: *"On the French coast, the light/Gleams, and is gone; the cliffs of England stand,/ Glimmering and vast, out in the tranquil bay"* (Matthew Arnold). To *twinkle* is to shine with quick, intermittent flashes or gleams: *"a few stars, twinkling faintly in the deep blue of the night sky"* (Hugh Walpole). *Scintillate* is applied to what flashes as if emitting sparks in a continuous stream: *"ammonium chloride . . . depositing minute scintillating crystals on the windowpanes"* (Primo Levi). See also Synonyms at **blaze¹, moment.**

flash·back (flăsh′băk′) *n.* **1.a.** A literary or cinematic device in which an earlier event is inserted into the normal chronological order of a narrative. **b.** The episode or scene depicted by means of this device. **2.** An unexpected recurrence of the effects of a hallucinogenic drug long after its original use. **3.** *Psychology.* A recurring, intensely vivid mental image of a past traumatic experience: *"Another study shows that women who served in Vietnam still struggle with depression, anxiety, and painful flashbacks from the war"* (New York Times).

flash·board (flăsh′bôrd′, -bōrd′) *n.* A board or structure of boards extending above a dam to increase its capacity.

flash·bulb or **flash bulb** (flăsh′bŭlb′) *n.* A glass bulb filled with finely shredded aluminum or magnesium foil that is ignited by electricity to produce a short-duration high-intensity light flash for taking photographs. Also called *photoflash.*

flash burn *n.* A burn resulting from brief exposure to intense radiation.

flash butt weld·ing (wĕl′dĭng) *n.* A technique for joining segments of metal rail or pipe in which segments aligned end to end are electronically charged, producing an electric arc that melts and welds the ends of the segments, yielding an exceptionally strong and smooth joint. Also called *flash welding.*

flash card also **flash·card** (flăsh′kârd′) *n.* A card printed with words or numbers and briefly displayed in a learning drill.

flash·cube (flăsh′kyo͞ob′) *n.* A small cube that contains four flashbulbs and that rotates automatically to the next unused bulb when a picture is taken with the camera to which it is attached.

flash·er (flăsh′ər) *n.* **1.** A device that automatically switches an electric lamp off and on, as in a commercial display sign. **2.** *Slang.* One who engages in indecent exposure; an exhibitionist.

flash flood also **flash·flood** (flăsh′flŭd′) *n.* A sudden flood of great volume, usually caused by a heavy rain.

flamingo

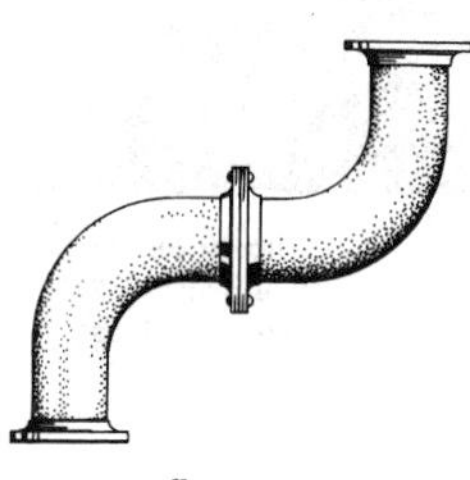
flange

ă pat	oi boy
ā pay	ou out
âr care	o͝o took
ä father	o͞o boot
ĕ pet	ŭ cut
ē be	ûr urge
ĭ pit	th thin
ī pie	*th* this
îr pier	hw which
ŏ pot	zh vision
ō toe	ə about, item
ô paw	♦ regionalism

Stress marks: ′ (primary); ′ (secondary), as in **dictionary** (dĭk′shə-nĕr′ē)

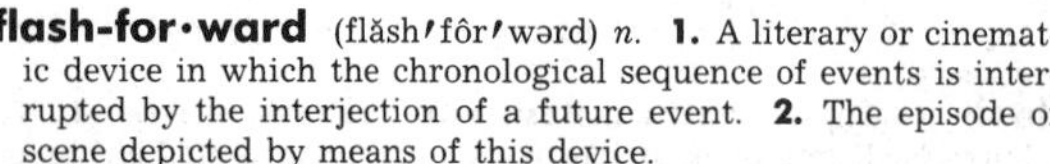

flask
1888 American silver flask by the Gorham Manufacturing Company

flatboat
1870 print by Currier and Ives

ă pat	oi boy
ā pay	ou out
âr care	o͝o took
ä father	o͞o boot
ĕ pet	ŭ cut
ē be	ûr urge
ĭ pit	th thin
ī pie	*th* this
îr pier	hw which
ŏ pot	zh vision
ō toe	ə about, item
ô paw	♦ regionalism

Stress marks: ′ (primary); ′ (secondary), as in **dictionary** (dĭk′shə-nĕr′ē)

flash-for·ward (flăsh′fôr′wərd) *n.* **1.** A literary or cinematic device in which the chronological sequence of events is interrupted by the interjection of a future event. **2.** The episode or scene depicted by means of this device.

flash·gun (flăsh′gŭn′) *n.* A dry-cell powered photographic apparatus that holds and electrically triggers a flashbulb. Also called *flash unit.*

flash·ing (flăsh′ĭng) *n.* Sheet metal used to reinforce and weatherproof the joints and angles of a roof.

flash lamp *n.* An electric lamp for producing a high-intensity light of very short duration for use in photography.

flash·light (flăsh′līt′) *n.* **1.** A small, portable lamp usually powered by batteries. **2.** A brief, brilliant flood of light from a photographic lamp. **3.** A bright light, as of a beacon or signal lamp, that flashes at regular intervals.

flash·o·ver (flăsh′ō′vər) *n.* **1.** An unintended electric arc, as between two pieces of apparatus. **2.** The temperature point at which the heat in an area or a region is high enough to ignite all flammable material simultaneously.

flash photolysis *n.* A method of investigating fast photochemical reactions in gases in which a gas is exposed to very brief, intense flashes of light and the resulting products are analyzed spectroscopically.

flash point also **flash·point** (flăsh′point′) *n.* **1.** The lowest temperature at which the vapor of a combustible liquid can be made to ignite momentarily in air. **2.** The point at which eruption into significant action, creation, or violence occurs: *"The shootdown did not increase international tensions to the flash point"* (Seymour M. Hersh).

flash·tube also **flash tube** (flăsh′to͞ob′) *n.* A gas discharge tube used in an electronic flash to produce a brief, intense flash of light.

flash unit *n.* **1.** An electronic flash system containing both a power supply and a flashtube in a single compact unit. **2.a.** See **flashgun. b.** A flashgun and reflector.

flash weld·ing (wĕl′dĭng) *n.* See **flash butt welding.**

flash·y (flăsh′ē) *adj.* **-i·er, -i·est. 1.** Cheap and showy; gaudy. See Synonyms at **gaudy**[1]. **2.** Giving a momentary or superficial impression of brilliance. **—flash′i·ly** *adv.* **—flash′i·ness** *n.*

flask (flăsk) *n.* **1.** A small container, such as a bottle, having a narrow neck and usually a cap, especially: **a.** A flat, relatively thin container for liquor. **b.** A container or case for carrying gunpowder or shot. **c.** A vial or round long-necked vessel for laboratory use. **2.** A frame for holding a sand mold in a foundry. [Middle English, cask, keg, from Old French *flasque,* from Late Latin *flascō,* of Germanic origin.]

flat[1] (flăt) *adj.* **flat·ter, flat·test. 1.** Having a horizontal surface without a slope, tilt, or curvature. **2.** Having a smooth, even, level surface: *a skirt sewed with fine flat seams.* **3.** Having a relatively broad surface in relation to thickness or depth: *a flat board.* See Synonyms at **level. 4.** Stretched out or lying at full length along the ground; prone. **5.** Free of qualification; absolute: *a flat refusal.* **6.** Fixed; unvarying: *a flat rate.* **7.** Lacking interest or excitement; dull: *a flat scenario.* **8.a.** Lacking in flavor: *a flat stew that needs salt.* **b.** Having lost effervescence or sparkle: *flat beer.* **9.a.** Deflated. Used of a tire. **b.** Electrically discharged. Used of a storage battery. **10.** Of or relating to a horizontal line that displays no ups or downs and signifies the absence of physiological activity: *A flat electroencephalogram indicates a loss of brain function.* **11.** Commercially inactive; sluggish: *flat sales for the month.* **12.** Unmodulated; monotonous: *a flat voice.* **13.** Lacking variety in tint or shading; uniform: *"The sky was bright but flat, the color of oyster shells"* (Anne Tyler). **14.** Not glossy; mat: *flat paint.* **15.** *Music.* **a.** Being below the correct pitch. **b.** Being one half step lower than the corresponding natural key: *the key of B flat.* **16.** Designating the vowel *a* as pronounced in *bad* or *cat.* **17.** *Nautical.* Taut. Used of a sail. **—flat** *adv.* **1.a.** Level with the ground; horizontally. **b.** On or up against a flat surface; at full length. **2.** So as to be flat. **3.a.** Directly; completely: *went flat against the rules; flat broke.* **b.** Exactly; precisely: *arrived in six minutes flat.* **4.** *Music.* Below the intended pitch. **5.** *Business.* Without interest charge. **—flat** *n.* **1.** A flat surface or part. **2.** Often **flats.** A stretch of level ground: *salt flats.* **3.** A shallow frame or box for seeds or seedlings. **4.** Stage scenery on a movable wooden frame. **5.** A flatcar. **6.** A deflated tire. **7.** A shoe with a flat heel. **8.** A large flat piece of mail. **9.** A horse that competes in a flat race. Also called *runner.* **10.** *Music.* **a.** A sign (♭) affixed to a note to indicate that it is to be lowered by a half step. **b.** A note that is lowered a half step. **11.** *Football.* The area of the field to either side of an offensive formation. **—flat** *v.* **flat·ted, flat·ting, flats.** —*tr.* **1.** To make flat; flatten. **2.** *Music.* To lower (a note) a semitone. —*intr. Music.* To sing or play below the proper pitch. [Middle English, from Old Norse *flatr.* See **plat-** in Appendix.] **—flat′ly** *adv.* **—flat′ness** *n.*

flat[2] (flăt) *n.* **1.** An apartment on one floor of a building. **2.** *Archaic.* A story in a house. [Alteration of Scots *flet,* inner part of a house, from Middle English, from Old English, floor, dwelling. See **plat-** in Appendix.]

flat·bed (flăt′bĕd′) *n.* **1.** An open truck bed or trailer with no sides, used to carry large objects such as heavy machinery, cars, or houses. **2.** A railroad flatcar.

flat-bed press (flăt′bĕd′) *n. Printing.* A press in which the type, locked into a chase, is supported by a flat surface or bed and the paper is applied to the type either by a flat platen or by a cylinder against which the bed moves.

flat·boat (flăt′bōt′) *n. Nautical.* A boat with a flat bottom and square ends used for transporting freight on inland waterways.

flat·bot·tom (flăt′bŏt′əm) or **flat·bot·tomed** (-bŏt′əmd) *adj.* Having a flat bottom: *a flatbottom boat.*

flat·bread (flăt′brĕd′) *n.* Any of various breads made from usually unleavened dough and baked in flat, often round loaves.

flat·car (flăt′kär′) *n.* A railroad freight car without sides or a roof.

flat-coat·ed retriever (flăt′kō′tĭd) *n.* A medium-sized sporting dog of a breed originally developed in England, having a thick, smooth coat that is black or deep reddish brown.

flat·fish (flăt′fĭsh′) *n., pl.* **flatfish** or **-fish·es.** Any of numerous chiefly marine fishes of the order Pleuronectiformes, including the flounders, soles, and halibuts, having a laterally compressed body with both eyes on the upper side.

flat·foot (flăt′fo͝ot′) *n.* **1.** *pl.* **-feet** (-fēt′). A condition in which the arch of the foot is abnormally flattened down so that the entire sole makes contact with the ground. **2.** *pl.* **-foots. a.** *Informal.* A person with flat feet. **b.** *Slang.* A police officer. **—flatfoot** *intr.v.* **-foot·ed, -foot·ing, -foots.** To walk in a flat-footed manner: *"He flatfooted along, twirling his club"* (James T. Farrell).

flat-foot·ed (flăt′fo͝ot′ĭd) *adj.* **1.** Of or afflicted with flatfoot. **2.a.** Steady on the feet. **b.** *Informal.* Without reservation; forthright: *a flat-footed refusal.* **3.** Unable to react quickly; unprepared: *The new product caught their competitors flat-footed.* **—flat′-foot′ed·ly** *adv.* **—flat′-foot′ed·ness** *n.*

Flat·head (flăt′hĕd′) *n., pl.* **Flathead** or **-heads. 1.a.** A Native American people inhabiting western Montana and northern Idaho, now located principally on Flathead Lake. **b.** A member of this people. **c.** The Salishan language of the Flathead. **2.** See **Interior Salish.**

flat·head catfish (flăt′hĕd′) *n.* A large American catfish *(Pylodictis olivaris)* having a yellowish body with brown markings and common in streams of the Mississippi Valley and southeast United States.

Flathead River. A river rising in southeast British Columbia, Canada, and flowing about 386 km (240 mi) generally southward across the Montana border to **Flathead Lake** then south and west to the Clark Fork River.

flat·i·ron (flăt′ī′ərn) *n.* An iron for pressing clothes, especially one that is heated externally, as on a hearth or stove.

flat·land (flăt′lănd′, -lənd) *n.* **1.** Land that varies little in elevation. **2. flatlands.** A geographic area composed chiefly of land that varies little in elevation. **—flat′land′er** *n.*

flat·let (flăt′lĭt) *n. Chiefly British.* An efficiency apartment.

flat·ling (flăt′lĭng) also **flat·lings** (-lĭngs) *adv. Chiefly British.* With the flat side or edge of a sword.

flat out *adv. Informal.* **1.** In a direct manner; bluntly: *told me the truth flat out.* **2.** At top speed: *running flat out.*

flat-out (flăt′out′) *adj. Informal.* Thoroughgoing; out-and-out: *a flat-out promotional campaign; a flat-out deception.*

flat pick *n. Music.* A flat, often triangular plectrum held between the finger and thumb, used in picking and strumming a guitar or similar stringed instrument. **—flat′-pick′** (flăt′pĭk′) *v.* **—flat′-pick′er** *n.* **—flat′-pick′ing** *n.*

flat race *n.* A horserace run over level ground with no obstacles such as fences or hazards.

flat silver *n.* Utensils, such as knives, forks, or spoons, made of silver or silver plate.

flat·ten (flăt′n) *v.* **-tened, -ten·ing, -tens.** —*tr.* **1.** To make flat or flatter. **2.** To knock down; lay low: *The boxer was flattened with one punch.* —*intr.* To become flat or flatter. **—flat′ten·er** *n.*

flat·ter[1] (flăt′ər) *v.* **-tered, -ter·ing, -ters.** —*tr.* **1.** To compliment excessively and often insincerely, especially in order to win favor. **2.** To please or gratify the vanity of: *"What really flatters a man is that you think him worth flattering"* (George Bernard Shaw). **3.a.** To portray favorably: *a photograph that flatters its subject.* **b.** To show off becomingly or advantageously. —*intr.* To practice flattery. [Middle English *flateren,* from Old French *flater,* of Germanic origin. See **plat-** in Appendix.] **—flat′ter·er** *n.* **—flat′ter·ing·ly** *adv.*

flat·ter[2] (flăt′ər) *n.* **1.** A flat-faced swage or hammer used by blacksmiths. **2.** A die plate for flattening metal into strips, as in the manufacture of watch springs.

flat·ter·y (flăt′ə-rē) *n., pl.* **-ies. 1.** The act or practice of flattering. **2.** Excessive or insincere praise.

flat·tish (flăt′ĭsh) *adj.* Somewhat flat.

flat·top (flăt′tŏp′) *n. Informal.* **1.** An aircraft carrier. **2.** A short haircut in which the hair is brushed straight up and cropped flat across the top.

flat·u·lence (flăch′ə-ləns) *n.* **1.** The presence of excessive gas in the digestive tract. **2.** Self-importance; pomposity.

flat·u·len·cy (flăch′ə-lən-sē) *n.* Flatulence.

flat·u·lent (flăch′ə-lənt) *adj.* **1.** Of, afflicted with, or caused by flatulence. **2.** Inducing or generating flatulence. **3.** Pompous;

bloated. [French, from Latin *flātus*, fart. See FLATUS.] **—flat′u·lent·ly** *adv.*

fla·tus (flā′təs) *n.* Gas generated in or expelled from the digestive tract, especially the stomach or intestines. [Latin *flātus*, wind, fart, from *flāre*, to blow. See **bhlē-** in Appendix.]

flat·ware (flăt′wâr′) *n.* **1.** Tableware that is fairly flat and fashioned usually of a single piece, as plates. **2.** Table utensils such as knives, forks, and spoons.

flat-wa·ter (flăt′wô′tər, -wŏt′ər) *adj.* Of or on a level or slow-moving watercourse: *flat-water canoeing; a flat-water race.*

flat·wise (flăt′wīz′) also **flat·ways** (-wāz′) *adv.* With the flat side down or in contact with a surface.

flat·work (flăt′wûrk′) *n.* Laundry, such as sheets and linens, that can be ironed by a mangle rather than by hand.

flat·worm (flăt′wûrm′) *n.* Any of various parasitic and nonparasitic worms of the phylum Platyhelminthes, such as a tapeworm or a planarian, characteristically having a soft, flat, bilaterally symmetrical body and no body cavity. Also called *platyhelminth.*

Flau·bert (flō-bâr′), **Gustave.** 1821–1880. French writer considered a forerunner of naturalism and known for his precise literary style. His works include *Madame Bovary* (1857) and "A Simple Heart" (1877). **—Flau·ber′tian** (-shən, -tē-ən) *adj.*

flaunt (flônt) *v.* **flaunt·ed, flaunt·ing, flaunts.** *—tr.* **1.** To exhibit ostentatiously or shamelessly: *flaunts his knowledge.* See Synonyms at **show.** **2.** *Usage Problem.* To show contempt for; scorn. *—intr.* **1.** To parade oneself ostentatiously; show oneself off. **2.** To wave grandly: *pennants flaunting in the wind.* [Origin unknown.] **—flaunt′er** *n.* **—flaunt′ing·ly** *adv.*

USAGE NOTE: *Flaunt* as a transitive verb means "to exhibit ostentatiously": *She flaunted her diamonds.* To *flout* is "to show contempt for": *She flouted the proprieties.* For some time now *flaunt* has been used in the sense "to show contempt for," even by educated users of English. This usage is still widely seen as erroneous and is best avoided.

flaunt·y (flôn′tē) *adj.* **-i·er, -i·est.** Inclined to flaunt; ostentatious. **—flaunt′i·ly** *adv.* **—flaunt′i·ness** *n.*

flau·ta (flou′tä) *n.* A tortilla rolled around a filling such as beef, chicken, or cheese into a flutelike shape and sometimes deep-fried. [Spanish, flute, probably from Old Provençal *flaüt.* See FLUTE.]

flau·tist (flô′tĭst, flou′-) *n. Music.* A flutist. [Italian *flautista*, from *flauto*, flute, from Old Provençal *flaüt.*]

flav– *pref.* Variant of **flavo–.**

fla·va·none (flā′və-nōn′) *n.* A colorless crystalline compound, $C_{15}H_{12}O_2$, derived from flavone. [FLAV(O)– + –AN(E) + –ONE.]

fla·ves·cent (flə-vĕs′ənt) *adj.* Turning yellow; yellowish. [Latin *flāvēscēns, flāvēscent-*, present participle of *flāvēscere*, to turn yellow, inchoative of *flāvēre*, to be yellow, from *flāvus*, yellow. See **bhel-**[1] in Appendix.]

fla·vin (flā′vĭn) also **fla·vine** (-vēn′) *n.* **1.** Any of various water-soluble yellow pigments, including riboflavin, found in plant and animal tissue as coenzymes of flavoprotein. **2.** A ketone, $C_{10}H_6N_4O_2$, that gives color to various natural yellow pigments.

flavin adenine dinucleotide *n. Abbr.* **FAD** A coenzyme, $C_{27}H_{33}N_9O_{15}P_2$, that is a derivative of riboflavin and functions in certain oxidation-reduction reactions in the body.

fla·vine (flā′vēn′) *n.* **1.** A brownish-red crystalline powder, $C_{14}H_{15}N_3Cl_2$, used as an antiseptic. **2.** Variant of **flavin.**

flavin mononucleotide *n. Abbr.* **FMN** A derivative of riboflavin, $C_{17}H_{21}N_4O_9P$, that functions as a coenzyme of various flavoproteins in certain oxidation-reduction reactions in the body.

flavo– or **flav–** *pref.* **1.** Yellow: *flavin.* **2.** Flavin: *flavoprotein.* [Latin *flāvus*, yellow. See **bhel-**[1] in Appendix.]

fla·vone (flā′vōn′) *n.* A crystalline compound, $C_{15}H_{10}O_2$, the parent substance of a number of important yellow pigments, occurring on the leaves or in the stems and seed capsules of many primroses.

fla·vo·noid (flā′və-noid′) *n.* Any of a large group of plant substances that includes the anthocyanins.

fla·vo·pro·tein (flā′vō-prō′tēn′, -tē-ĭn) *n.* Any of a group of enzymes containing flavin bound to protein and acting as dehydrogenation catalysts in biological reactions.

fla·vor (flā′vər) *n.* **1.** Distinctive taste; savor: *a flavor of smoke in bacon.* See Synonyms at **taste.** **2.** A distinctive yet intangible quality felt to be characteristic of a given thing: *"What matters in literature . . . is surely the idiosyncratic, the individual, the flavor or color of a particular human suffering"* (Harold Bloom). **3.** A flavoring: *contains no artificial flavors.* **4.** *Archaic.* Aroma; fragrance. **—flavor** *tr.v.* **-vored, -vor·ing, -vors.** To give flavor to. [Middle English *flavour*, aroma, from Old French *flaor*, from Vulgar Latin **flātor*, from Latin *flāre*, to blow. See **bhlē-** in Appendix.] **—fla′vor·er** *n.* **—fla′vor·less** *adj.* **—fla′vor·ous** (-əs), **fla′vor·some** (-səm) *adj.* **—fla′vor·y** *adj.*

fla·vor·ful (flā′vər-fəl) *adj.* Full of flavor; savory. **—fla′vor·ful·ly** *adv.*

fla·vor·ing (flā′vər-ĭng) *n.* A substance, such as an extract or a spice, that imparts flavor.

fla·vor·ist (flā′vər-ĭst) *n.* One whose profession is blending artificially isolated chemicals to create the taste and smell of a particular food.

fla·vour (flā′vər) *n. & v. Chiefly British.* Variant of **flavor.**

flaw[1] (flô) *n.* **1.** An imperfection, often concealed, that impairs soundness: *a flaw in the crystal that caused it to shatter.* See Synonyms at **blemish.** **2.** A defect or shortcoming in something intangible: *They share the character flaw of arrogance.* **3.** A defect in a legal document that can render it invalid. **—flaw** *tr. & intr.v.* **flawed, flaw·ing, flaws.** To make or become defective. [Middle English *flaue*, splinter, perhaps from Old Norse *flaga*, slab of stone. See **plāk-**[1] in Appendix.]

flaw[2] (flô) *n.* **1.a.** A brief gust or blast of wind. **b.** A passing storm; a squall. **2.** *Obsolete.* A burst of passion. [Probably of Scandinavian origin; akin to Swedish *flaga*, gust of wind.] **—flaw′y** *adj.*

flaw·less (flô′lĭs) *adj.* Being entirely without flaw or imperfection; perfect. See Synonyms at **perfect.** **—flaw′less·ly** *adv.* **—flaw′less·ness** *n.*

flax (flăks) *n.* **1.a.** Any of several plants of the genus *Linum*, especially the widely cultivated *L. usitatissimum*, having blue flowers, seeds that yield linseed oil, and slender stems from which a textile fiber is obtained. **b.** The fine, light-colored textile fiber obtained from this plant. **c.** Any of several similar plants. **2.** *Color.* A pale grayish yellow. [Middle English, from Old English *fleax.* See **plek-** in Appendix.]

flax·en (flăk′sən) *adj.* **1.** Made of or resembling flax. **2.** Having the pale grayish-yellow color of flax fiber: *flaxen braids.*

flax·seed (flăks′sēd′) *n.* The seed of flax, the source of linseed oil and emollient medicinal preparations.

flax·y (flăk′sē) *adj.* **-i·er, -i·est.** Resembling flax, as in texture.

flay (flā) *tr.v.* **flayed, flay·ing, flays.** **1.** To strip off the skin or outer covering of. **2.** To strip of money or goods; fleece. **3.** To whip or lash. **4.** To assail with stinging criticism; excoriate. [Middle English *flen*, from Old English *flēan.*] **—flay′er** *n.*

F layer *n.* **1.** The highest zone of the ionosphere, extending at night from about 190 to 400 kilometers (120 to 250 miles) and during the day from about 145 to 400 kilometers (90 to 250 miles) above the earth's surface. Also called *F region.* **2.** Either of two layers, designated F_1 and F_2, into which the F layer is divided during the day, extending respectively from about 145 to 240 kilometers (90 to 150 miles) and from about 190 to 400 kilometers (120 to 250 miles) above the earth's surface.

fld. *abbr.* Field.

fl dr *abbr.* Fluid dram.

flea (flē) *n.* **1.** Any of various small, wingless, bloodsucking insects of the order Siphonaptera that have legs adapted for jumping and are parasitic on warm-blooded animals. **2.** Any of various small crustaceans that resemble or move like fleas, such as the water flea. ***—idiom.* a flea in (one's) ear.** An annoying hint or a stinging rebuke. [Middle English *fle*, from Old English *flēah.*]

flea·bag (flē′băg′) *n. Informal.* A seedy, run-down hotel or other lodging place.

flea·bane (flē′bān′) *n.* Any of various plants of the genus *Erigeron*, having variously colored, many-rayed, daisylike flower heads.

flea beetle *n.* Any of various small beetles of the subfamily Alticinae that have hind legs adapted for jumping and feed on the foliage of certain plants.

flea·bite (flē′bīt′) *n.* **1.a.** The bite of a flea. **b.** The small red mark caused by a flea's bite. **2.** A trifling loss, inconvenience, or annoyance.

flea-bit·ten (flē′bĭt′n) *adj.* **1.** Covered with fleas or fleabites. **2.** *Informal.* Seedy; delapidated: *A flea-bitten couch.* **3.** Having a pale coat with reddish-brown flecks. Used of horses.

flea collar *n.* A collar, as for a cat or dog, containing a substance that repels or kills fleas.

flea market *n.* A market, usually held outdoors, where antiques, used household goods, and curios are sold. [Translation of French *marché aux puces.*]

flea·pit (flē′pĭt′) *n. Chiefly British.* A cheap or squalid theater.

flèche (flĕsh, flāsh) *n.* A slender spire, especially one on a church above the intersection of the nave and transepts. [French, arrow, flèche, from Old French, arrow, of Germanic origin. See **pleu-** in Appendix.]

flé·chette (flā-shĕt′, flĕ-) *n.* A steel missile or dart dropped from an aircraft. [French, diminutive of *flèche*, arrow. See FLÈCHE.]

fleck (flĕk) *n.* **1.** A tiny mark or spot: *flecks of mica in the rock.* **2.** A small bit or flake: *flecks of foam; a fleck of dandruff.* **—fleck** *tr.v.* **flecked, fleck·ing, flecks.** To spot or streak: *the path was flecked with sunlight.* [Probably from Middle English *flekked*, spotted; akin to Old Norse *flekkr*, spot.]

flec·tion (flĕk′shən) *n. Anatomy.* Variant of **flexion** (sense 1). **—flec′tion·al** *adj.*

fled (flĕd) *v.* Past tense and past participle of **flee.**

fledge (flĕj) *v.* **fledged, fledg·ing, fledg·es.** *—tr.* **1.** To take care of (a young bird) until it is ready to fly. **2.** To cover with or as if with feathers. **3.** To provide (an arrow) with feathers. *—intr.* To grow the plumage necessary for flight. [Probably from obsolete *fledge*, feathered, from Middle English *flegge*, from Old English **flycge.* See **pleu-** in Appendix.]

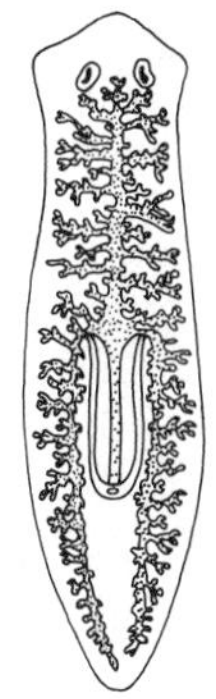
flatworm

Gustave Flaubert

flax

flèche
Amiens Cathedral, France

fledg·ling also **fledge·ling** (flĕj′lĭng) —*n.* **1.** A young bird that has recently acquired its flight feathers. **2.** A young or inexperienced person. —*adj.* New and untried or inexperienced: *a fledgling enterprise; a fledgling skier.*

flee (flē) *v.* **fled** (flĕd), **flee·ing, flees.** —*intr.* **1.** To run away, as from trouble or danger: *fled from the house into the night.* **2.** To pass swiftly away; vanish: *"of time fleeing beneath him"* (William Faulkner). —*tr.* To run away from: *flee the scene of an accident.* [Middle English *flen,* from Old English *flēon.* See **pleu-** in Appendix.] —**fle′er** *n.*

fleece (flēs) *n.* **1.a.** The coat of wool of a sheep or similar animal. **b.** The yield of wool shorn from a sheep at one time. **2.** A soft, woolly covering or mass. **3.** Fabric with a soft, deep pile. —**fleece** *tr.v.* **fleeced, fleec·ing, fleec·es. 1.** To defraud of money or property; swindle. **2.** To shear the fleece from. **3.** To cover with or as if with fleece. [Middle English *fles,* from Old English *flēos.*] —**fleec′er** *n.*

fleec·y (flē′sē) *adj.* **-i·er, -i·est.** Of, resembling, or covered with fleece: *fleecy clouds.* —**fleec′i·ly** *adv.* —**fleec′i·ness** *n.*

fleer (flîr) *intr.v.* **fleered, fleer·ing, fleers.** To smirk or laugh in contempt or derision. —**fleer** *n.* A taunting, scoffing, or derisive look or gibe. [Middle English *flerien,* of Scandinavian origin.] —**fleer′ing·ly** *adv.*

fleet¹ (flēt) *n.* **1.** A number of warships operating together under one command. **2.** A group of vessels or vehicles, such as taxicabs or fishing boats, owned or operated as a unit. [Middle English *flete,* from Old English *flēot,* from *flēotan,* to float. See **pleu-** in Appendix.]

fleur-de-lis
On a gold florin

fleet² (flēt) *adj.* **fleet·er, fleet·est. 1.** Moving swiftly; rapid or nimble. See Synonyms at **fast¹. 2.** Fleeting; evanescent. —**fleet** *v.* **fleet·ed, fleet·ing, fleets.** —*intr.* **1.** To move or pass swiftly. **2.** To fade out; vanish. **3.** *Archaic.* To flow. **4.** *Obsolete.* To drift. —*tr.* **1.** To cause (time) to pass quickly. **2.** *Nautical.* To alter the position of (tackle or rope, for example). [Probably from Old Norse *fljōtr.* V., from Middle English *fleten,* to drift, float, from Old English *flēotan.* See **pleu-** in Appendix.] —**fleet′ly** *adv.* —**fleet′ness** *n.*

Fleet Admiral (flēt) *n.* See **Admiral of the Fleet.**

fleet·ing (flē′tĭng) *adj.* Passing quickly; ephemeral: *"fleeting passions of fantasy"* (Gloria Vanderbilt). See Synonyms at **transient.** —**fleet′ing·ly** *adv.* —**fleet′ing·ness** *n.*

Fleet Street *n.* British journalism. [After *Fleet Street* in central London, long the headquarters for many British newspaper publishers.]

flei·shig (flā′shĭk) *adj.* Consisting of, prepared with, or relating to meat or meat products. [Yiddish *fleyshik,* from *fleysh,* meat, from Middle High German *vleisch,* meat, from Old High German *fleisk,* flesh.]

Flem. *abbr.* Flemish.

Flem·ing (flĕm′ĭng) *n.* **1.** A native or inhabitant of Flanders. **2.** A Belgian who speaks Flemish. [Middle English, from Middle Dutch *Vlāming.*]

Fleming, Sir **Alexander.** 1881–1955. British bacteriologist who discovered penicillin in 1928. He shared a 1945 Nobel Prize for this achievement.

Fleming, Ian Lancaster. 1908–1964. British writer noted for his spy novels featuring the fictional secret agent James Bond.

Flem·ish (flĕm′ĭsh) *adj. Abbr.* **Flem.** Of or relating to Flanders, the Flemings, or their language or culture. —**Flemish** *n. Abbr.* **Flem. 1.** The West Germanic language of the Flemings. **2.** The Flemings.

Flens·burg (flĕnz′bûrg, flĕns′bo͝ork′). A city of northern Germany on **Flensburg Fjord,** an arm of the Baltic Sea at the Danish border. Founded c. 1200, the city is a port and shipbuilding center. Population, 86,873.

flense (flĕns) *tr.v.* **flensed, flens·ing, flens·es.** To strip the blubber or skin from (a whale, for example). [Danish.] —**flens′er** *n.*

flesh (flĕsh) *n.* **1.a.** The soft tissue of the body of a vertebrate, covering the bones and consisting mainly of skeletal muscle and fat. **b.** The surface or skin of the human body. **2.** The meat of animals as distinguished from the edible tissue of fish or fowl. **3.** *Botany.* The pulpy, usually edible part of a fruit or vegetable. **4.** Excess fatty tissue; plumpness. **5.a.** The body as opposed to the mind or soul. **b.** The physical or carnal nature of humankind. **c.** Sensual appetites. **6.** Humankind in general; humanity. **7.** One's family; kin. **8.** Substance; reality: *"The maritime strategy has an all but unstoppable institutional momentum behind it . . . that has given force and flesh to the theory"* (Jack Beatty). —**flesh** *v.* **fleshed, flesh·ing, flesh·es.** —*tr.* **1.** To give substance or detail to; fill out: *fleshed out the novel with a subplot.* **2.** To clean (a hide) of adhering flesh. **3.** To encourage (a falcon, for example) to participate in the chase by feeding it flesh from a kill. **4.** To inure to battle or bloodshed. **5.** To plunge or thrust (a weapon) into flesh. —*intr.* To become plump or fleshy; gain weight. —***idiom.*** **in the flesh. 1.** Alive. **2.** In person; present. [Middle English, from Old English *flǣsc.*] —**flesh′less** *adj.*

flesh and blood *n.* **1.** Human nature or physical existence, together with its weaknesses. **2.** A person's blood relatives; kin. **3.** Substance and depth in artistic portrayal; lifelikeness: *characters lacking in flesh and blood.*

flesh fly *n.* Any of various flies of the family Sarcophagidae whose larvae are parasitic in animal tissue or feed on carrion.

flesh·ly (flĕsh′lē) *adj.* **-li·er, -li·est. 1.** Of or relating to the body; corporeal. See Synonyms at **bodily. 2.** Of, relating to, or inclined to carnality; sensual. **3.** Not spiritual; worldly: *fleshly pleasures.* **4.** Tending to plumpness; fleshy. —**flesh′li·ness** *n.*

flesh·pot (flĕsh′pŏt′) *n.* **1.** Often **fleshpots.** A district or an establishment offering sensual pleasures or entertainment. **2.** Physical or sensual gratification.

flesh wound (wo͞ond) *n.* A wound that penetrates the flesh but does not damage underlying bones or vital organs.

flesh·y (flĕsh′ē) *adj.* **-i·er, -i·est. 1.a.** Relating to, consisting of, or resembling flesh. **b.** Having abundant flesh; plump. See Synonyms at **fat. 2.** Having a juicy or pulpy texture: *ripe, fleshy peaches.* **3.** Fleshly; carnal: *"the fleshy fringes of show business"* (Newsweek). —**flesh′i·ness** *n.*

fleshy fruit *n.* A fruit, such as the grape, cucumber, or cherry, that has a soft and pulpy wall.

fletch (flĕch) *tr.v.* **fletched, fletch·ing, fletch·es.** To feather (an arrow). [Probably back-formation from FLETCHER.]

fletch·er (flĕch′ər) *n.* One who makes arrows. [Middle English *fleccher,* from Old French *flechier,* from *fleche,* arrow, of Germanic origin. See **pleu-** in Appendix.]

Fletch·er (flĕch′ər), **Alice Cunningham.** 1838–1923. Cuban-born American ethnologist noted for her studies of Native American culture.

Fletcher, John. 1579–1625. English playwright who collaborated with Francis Beaumont on romantic tragicomedies, including *Philaster* (1610) and *The Maid's Tragedy* (1611).

fleur-de-lis or **fleur-de-lys** (flûr′də-lē′, flo͝or′-) *n., pl.* **fleurs-de-lis** or **fleurs-de-lys** (flûr′də-lēz, flo͝or′-). **1.** An iris, especially a white-flowered form of *Iris germanica.* **2.** *Heraldry.* A device consisting of a stylized three-petaled iris flower, used as the armorial emblem of the kings of France. [Middle English *flour de lice,* from Old French *flor de lis* : *flor,* flower + *de,* of + *lis,* lily.]

Fleu·ry (flœ-rē′), **André Hercule de.** 1653–1743. French prelate and politician who became a cardinal in 1726 and served as prime minister (1726–1743) under Louis XV.

flew (flo͞o) *v.* Past tense of **fly¹.**

flews (flo͞oz) *pl.n.* The pendulous corners of the upper lip of certain dogs, such as the bloodhound. [Origin unknown.]

flex (flĕks) *v.* **flexed, flex·ing, flex·es.** —*tr.* **1.** To bend (something pliant or elastic). **2.a.** To bend (a joint). **b.** To bend (a joint) repeatedly. **3.a.** To contract (a muscle, for example). **b.** To move by muscular control: *"Sandy flexes his brow characteristically, one of those Latin gestures reflecting something too delicate or imprecise to say"* (Scott Turow). **4.** To exhibit or show off the strength of: *"They had spent six years since the lightning Six Day War flexing their invincibility"* (Howard Kaplan). —*intr.* To bend: *"His hands flexed nervously as he spoke"* (Mary McCarthy). —**flex** *n.* **1.** *Chiefly British.* Flexible insulated electric cord. **2.** The act or an instance of flexing; a bending. **3.** Pliancy; flexibility: *"'Resolution' has none of that modern flex we favor, with generous, built-in amounts of 'maybe'"* (Melvin Maddocks). —***idiom.*** **flex (one's) muscles.** *Informal.* To exhibit or show off one's strength. [Latin *flectere, flex-,* to bend.]

flex– *pref.* Variant of **flexi–.**

flex·a·gon (flĕk′sə-gŏn′) *n.* A folded paper construction that can be flexed along its folds to reveal and conceal its faces alternately.

flexi– or **flex–** *pref.* Flexible: *flexitime.* [From FLEXIBLE.]

flex·i·ble (flĕk′sə-bəl) *adj.* **1.a.** Capable of being bent or flexed; pliable. **b.** Capable of being bent repeatedly without injury or damage. **2.** Susceptible to influence or persuasion; tractable. **3.** Responsive to change; adaptable: *a flexible schedule.* [From Latin *flexibilis,* from *flexus,* past participle of *flectere,* to bend.] —**flex′i·bil′i·ty, flex′i·ble·ness** *n.* —**flex′i·bly** *adv.*

SYNONYMS: *flexible, elastic, resilient, springy, supple.* These adjectives refer literally to what is capable of withstanding stress without injury and figuratively to what can undergo change or modification. Something that is *flexible* can be bent, twisted, or turned (*flexible wire*); the word can also refer to adaptability to change or the need for change (*a flexible administrator; flexible plans*). What is *elastic* returns to an original shape, form, or position, as after being stretched (*an elastic band*), can adapt or be adapted to differing circumstances (*an elastic clause in a contract*), is quick to recover, as from illness or misfortune (*an elastic spirit*), or is stretched beyond strict or proper bounds (*an elastic interpretation of a law*). *Resilient,* like *elastic,* implies a springing back to an original shape, especially after compression (*thin, resilient copper*); it also suggests a buoyant capacity to revive, as from depression (*a resilient temperament*). *Springy* describes what is marked by resilience and elasticity: *springy curls; a springy stride. Supple* applies to what is easily bent or twisted (*a supple birch rod; supple suede*), bends or twists with agility (*a supple body; supple limbs*), or is marked by easy adaptability (*a supple mind*).

flexible time *n.* See **flextime.**

flex·ile (flĕk′səl, -sīl′) *adj.* Flexible.

flex·ion (flĕk′shən) *n.* **1.** Also **flec·tion.** *Anatomy.* **a.** The act of bending a joint or limb in the body by the action of flexors. **b.** The resulting condition of being bent. **2.** A part that is bent.

[Latin *flexiō, flexiōn-,* a bending, from *flexus,* past participle of *flectere,* to bend.]

flex·i·time (flĕk′sĭ-tīm′) *n.* See **flextime.**

flex·og·ra·phy (flĕk-sŏg′rə-fē) *n.* A system of printing on a rotary press employing water-based ink, used for printing on plastic, paper, or cardboard. **—flex·og′ra·pher** *n.* **—flex′o·graph′ic** (-sə-grăf′ĭk) *adj.* **—flex′o·graph′i·cal·ly** *adv.*

flex·or (flĕk′sər) *n.* A muscle that when contracted acts to bend a joint or limb in the body. [New Latin, from Latin *flexus,* past participle of *flectere,* to bend.]

flex·time (flĕks′tīm′) *n.* An arrangement by which employees may set their own work schedules, especially their starting and finishing hours. Also called *flexible time, flexitime.*

flex·u·ous (flĕk′shōō-əs) *adj.* Bending or winding alternately from side to side; sinuous. [From Latin *flexuōsus,* from *flexus,* a bending, a turning, from *flectere,* to bend.] **—flex′u·os′i·ty** (-ŏs′ĭ-tē) *n.* **—flex′u·ous·ly** *adv.*

flex·ure (flĕk′shər) *n.* **1.** A curve, turn, or fold, such as a bend in a tubular organ: *a flexure of the colon.* **2.** The act or an instance of bending or flexing; flexion. **—flex′ur·al** *adj.*

fley (flā) *tr.v.* **fleyed, fley·ing, fleys.** *Scots.* To frighten. [Middle English *fleien,* from Old English *flȳgan, flēgan.* See **pleu-** in Appendix.]

flib·ber·ti·gib·bet (flĭb′ər-tē-jĭb′ĭt) *n.* A silly, scatterbrained, or garrulous person. [Middle English *flipergebet.*]

flic (flĭk) *n. Slang.* A police officer, especially in France. [French.]

flick[1] (flĭk) *n.* **1.a.** A light, quick blow, jerk, or touch: *a flick of the wrist; gave my horse a flick with the reins.* **b.** The sound accompanying this motion. **2.** A light splash, dash, or daub. **—flick** *v.* **flicked, flick·ing, flicks.** *—tr.* **1.** To touch or hit with a light, quick blow: *flicked him with his hand.* See Synonyms at **brush**[1]. **2.** To cause to move with a light blow; snap: *flicked the light switch on.* **3.** To remove with a light, quick blow: *flicked the lint off the coat.* *—intr.* To twitch or flutter. [Imitative.]

flick[2] (flĭk) *n. Slang.* A movie. [Short for FLICKER[1].]

flick·er[1] (flĭk′ər) *v.* **-ered, -er·ing, -ers.** *—intr.* **1.** To move waveringly; flutter: *shadows flickering on the wall.* See Synonyms at **flutter. 2.** To burn unsteadily or fitfully. *—tr.* To cause to move waveringly. **—flicker** *n.* **1.** A brief movement; a tremor. **2.** An inconstant or wavering light. **3.** A brief or slight sensation: *a flicker of doubt.* **4.** *Slang.* A movie. [Middle English *flikeren,* to flutter, from Old English *fliceran.*]

flick·er[2] (flĭk′ər) *n.* Any of various large North American woodpeckers of the genus *Colaptes,* especially *C. auratus,* the common flicker, having a brown back, spotted breast, and white rump. [Perhaps from FLICK[1].]

flick·er·tail (flĭk′ər-tāl′) *n.* See **Richardson's ground squirrel.**

flied (flīd) *intr.v.* Past tense and past participle of **fly**[1] (sense 7).

fli·er also **fly·er** (flī′ər) *n.* **1.** One, such as an insect or a bird, that flies with wings. **2.** The pilot of an aircraft. **3.** A passenger in an aircraft: *business fliers who travel 100,000 miles or more per year.* **4.** A pamphlet or circular for mass distribution. **5.** A step in a straight stairway. **6.** *Informal.* A daring venture. **7.** Often **flyer.** *Australian.* An exceptionally swift kangaroo.

flies (flīz) *v.* Third person singular present tense of **fly**[1].

flight[1] (flīt) *n.* **1.a.** The motion of an object in or through a medium, especially through the earth's atmosphere or through space. **b.** An instance of such motion. **c.** The distance covered in such motion. **2.a.** The act or process of flying through the air by means of wings. **b.** The ability to fly. **3.** A swift passage or movement. **4.** A scheduled airline run or trip. **5.** A group, especially of birds or aircraft, flying together. See Synonyms at **flock**[1]. **6.** A number of aircraft in the U.S. Air Force forming a subdivision of a squadron. **7.** An exuberant or transcendent effort or display: *a flight of the imagination; flights of oratory.* **8.** A series of stairs rising from one landing to another. **—flight** *intr.v.* **flight·ed, flight·ing, flights.** To migrate or fly in flocks. [Middle English, from Old English *flyht.* See **pleu-** in Appendix.]

flight[2] (flīt) *n.* The act or an instance of running away; an escape. [Middle English, from Old English **flyht.* See **pleu-** in Appendix.]

flight attendant *n.* A person who assists passengers in an aircraft.

flight bag *n.* A lightweight, flexible piece of luggage with zippered outside pockets.

flight deck *n.* **1.** The upper deck of an aircraft carrier, used as a runway. **2.** An elevated compartment in certain aircraft, used by the pilot, copilot, and flight engineer.

flight engineer *n.* The crew member responsible for the mechanical performance of an aircraft in flight.

flight feather *n.* Any of the comparatively large, stiff feathers of a bird's wing or tail that are necessary for flight.

flight·less (flīt′lĭs) *adj.* Incapable of flying. Used of certain birds, such as the penguin.

flight line *n.* The area of an airfield, specifically the parking area and the maintenance hangars, where aircraft are onloaded, offloaded, and serviced.

flight surgeon *n.* An air force physician who specializes in aeromedicine.

flight-test (flīt′tĕst′) *tr.v.* **-test·ed, -test·ing, -tests.** To test (an aircraft, for example) during flight.

flight·wor·thy (flīt′wûr′thē) *adj.* Denoting an aircraft that is fit to fly. **—flight′wor′thi·ness** *n.*

flight·y (flī′tē) *adj.* **-i·er, -i·est. 1.a.** Given to capricious or unstable behavior. **b.** Characterized by irresponsible or silly behavior. **2.** Easily excited; skittish. **—flight′i·ly** *adv.* **—flight′i·ness** *n.*

flim·flam (flĭm′flăm′) *Informal. n.* **1.** Nonsense; humbug. **2.** A deception; a swindle. **—flimflam** *tr.v.* **-flammed, -flam·ming, -flams.** To swindle; cheat. [Probably of Scandinavian origin.] **—flim′flam′mer** *n.* **—flim′flam′mer·y** *n.*

flim·sy (flĭm′zē) *adj.* **-si·er, -si·est. 1.** Light, thin, and insubstantial: *a flimsy fabric.* **2.** Lacking solidity or strength: *a flimsy table.* **3.** Lacking plausibility; unconvincing: *a flimsy excuse.* **—flimsy** *n., pl.* **-sies. 1.** Thin paper usually used to make multiple copies. **2.** Something written on this thin paper. [Origin unknown.] **—flim′si·ly** *adv.* **—flim′si·ness** *n.*

WORD HISTORY: The origin of *flimsy,* although uncertain, is not completely obscure. The word is first recorded in English in the 17th century in a dictionary of cant, the jargon of people such as thieves and beggars. Its early senses "frail" and "trivial" as well as its form may link it with *flim-flam,* recorded first around 1538. The noun *flim-flam* could mean "a piece of nonsense or idle talk," and the adjective could mean "frivolous." *Flim-flam* itself is a reduplication in which the pattern *fl—m* occurs twice, the first time with the sound (ĭ); the second, with the sound (ă). *Flim* may be related to the Old Norse word *flim,* meaning "a lampoon, libel."

flight deck
Of the U.S.S. *Constellation*

flinch (flĭnch) *intr.v.* **flinched, flinch·ing, flinch·es. 1.** To start or wince involuntarily, as from surprise or pain. **2.** To recoil, as from something unpleasant or difficult; shrink. See Synonyms at **recoil. —flinch** *n.* An act or instance of starting, wincing, or recoiling. [Obsolete French *flenchir,* of Germanic origin.] **—flinch′er** *n.* **—flinch′ing·ly** *adv.*

flin·ders (flĭn′dərz) *pl.n.* Bits, fragments, or splinters. [Middle English *flendris,* possibly of Scandinavian origin; akin to Norwegian *flindra,* splinter.]

Flin·ders (flĭn′dərz), Sir **Matthew.** 1774–1814. British explorer who sailed to New South Wales (1795) and subsequently made a thorough study of the Australian coast.

Flinders Range. A mountain range of south-central Australia east of Lake Torrens. The highest peak is 1,189.5 m (3,900 ft).

Flinders River. An intermittent river of northeast Australia flowing about 837 km (520 mi) to the Gulf of Carpentaria.

fling (flĭng) *v.* **flung** (flŭng), **fling·ing, flings.** *—tr.* **1.** To throw with violence: *flung the dish against the wall.* See Synonyms at **throw. 2.** To put or send suddenly or unexpectedly: *troops that were flung into battle.* **3.** To throw (oneself) into an activity with abandon and energy. **4.** To cast aside; discard: *fling propriety away.* *—intr.* To move quickly, violently, or impulsively. **—fling** *n.* **1.** The act of flinging. **2.** A brief period of indulging one's impulses. See Synonyms at **binge. 3.** *Informal.* A usually brief attempt or effort: *You take a fling at it.* [Middle English *flingen,* of Scandinavian origin. See **plāk-**[2] in Appendix.]

flint (flĭnt) *n.* **1.** A very hard, fine-grained quartz that sparks when struck with steel. **2.a.** A piece of flint used to produce a spark. **b.** A small solid cylinder of a spark-producing alloy, used in lighters to ignite the fuel. **3.** A piece of flint used as a tool by primitive human beings. **4.** Something resembling flint in hardness: *a jaw of flint.* [Middle English, from Old English.]

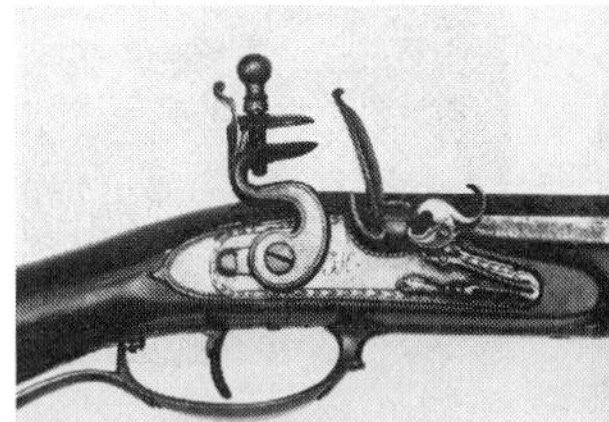

flintlock
Late 18th-century American Kentucky rifle

Flint (flĭnt). A city of southeast-central Michigan north-northwest of Detroit. Founded on the site of a fur-trading post established in 1819, it became an automobile-manufacturing center in the early 1900's. Population, 159,611.

♦ **flint corn** *n.* A variety of corn *(Zea mays* var. *indurata)* having small, hard grains. See Regional Note at **johnnycake.**

flint glass *n.* A soft, fusible, lustrous, brilliant lead-oxide optical glass with high refraction and low dispersion. Also called *lead glass.*

flint·head (flĭnt′hĕd′) *n.* See **wood ibis.**

flint·lock (flĭnt′lŏk′) *n.* **1.** A gunlock in which a flint embedded in the hammer produces a spark that ignites the charge. **2.** A firearm having this type of gunlock. In this sense, also called *firelock.*

Flint River. A river of western Georgia flowing about 531 km (330 mi) generally southward to join the Chattahoochee River and form the Apalachicola River at the Florida border.

flint·y (flĭn′tē) *adj.* **-i·er, -i·est. 1.** Containing or composed of flint. **2.** Unyielding; stern: *a flinty manner.* **—flint′i·ly** *adv.* **—flint′i·ness** *n.*

flip (flĭp) *v.* **flipped, flip·ping, flips.** *—tr.* **1.** To throw or toss with a light, brisk motion: *flipped me the ball; flipped his hair out of his eyes.* **2.** To toss in the air, imparting a spin: *flip a coin.* **3.a.** To turn over or around, especially with a light, quick motion: *flip over a card; flipped the record to play the other side.* **b.** To turn through; leaf: *flipped the pages of the report.* **4.** To strike quickly or lightly; flick. **5.** To move or act on with a quick motion: *flip a switch; flipped open her briefcase.* *—intr.* **1.** To turn over: *The canoe flipped over in the rapids.* **2.** To turn a somersault in the air. **3.** To move in twists and turns: *fish flipping about in the net.* **4.** To move quickly and lightly; snap: *The lid*

ă **pat**	oi **boy**
ā **pay**	ou **out**
âr **care**	ŏŏ **took**
ä **father**	ōō **boot**
ĕ **pet**	ŭ **cut**
ē **be**	ûr **urge**
ĭ **pit**	th **thin**
ī **pie**	*th* **this**
îr **pier**	hw **which**
ŏ **pot**	zh **vision**
ō **toe**	ə **about, item**
ô **paw**	♦ **regionalism**

Stress marks: ′ (primary); ′ (secondary), as in **dictionary** (dĭk′shə-nĕr′ē)

flipped open. **5.** To leaf; browse: *flipped through the catalogue.* **6.** *Slang.* **a.** To go crazy. Often used with *out.* **b.** To react strongly and especially enthusiastically: *She flipped over the new car.* **—flip** *n.* **1.** The act of flipping, especially: **a.** A flick or tap. **b.** A short, quick movement: *a flip of the wrist.* **c.** A somersault. **2.** *Informal.* A reversal; a flipflop. **3.** A mixed drink made with any of various alcoholic beverages and often including beaten eggs. **—flip** *adj.* **flip·per, flip·pest.** *Informal.* Marked by casual disrespect; impertinent: *a flip answer to a serious question.* **—*idiom.* flip (one's) lid.** *Slang.* **1.** To react strongly, as with anger or enthusiasm. **2.** To go crazy. [Perhaps imitative.]

flip·book (flĭp′bo͝ok′) *n.* A small book consisting of a series of images that give the illusion of continuous movement when the edges of the pages are flipped quickly.

flip chart *n.* A chart consisting of sheets hinged at the top that can be flipped over to present information sequentially.

flip-flop (flĭp′flŏp′) *n.* **1.** The movement or sound of repeated flapping. **2.** A backward somersault or handspring. **3.** *Informal.* A reversal, as of a stand or position: *a foreign policy flip-flop.* **4.** A backless, often foam rubber sandal held to the foot at the big toe by means of a thong. **5.** *Electronics.* An electronic circuit or mechanical device capable of assuming either of two stable states, especially a computer circuit used to store a single bit of information. **—flip′-flop′** *v.*

flip·pant (flĭp′ənt) *adj.* **1.** Marked by disrespectful levity or casualness; pert. **2.** *Archaic.* Talkative; voluble. [Probably from FLIP.] **—flip′pan·cy** *n.* **—flip′pant·ly** *adv.*

flip·per (flĭp′ər) *n.* **1.** A wide, flat limb, as of a seal, whale, or other aquatic mammal, adapted for swimming. **2.** A rubber covering for the foot having a flat, flexible portion that widens as it extends forward from the toes, used in swimming and diving. In this sense, also called *fin.*

flipper
Worn by a scuba diver

flip side *n.* *Informal.* **1.** The reverse side, as of a phonograph record. **2.** The opposite side: *"The flip side of retrospectively savaging the loser is beatifying . . . the winner"* (Charles Krauthammer).

flirt (flûrt) *v.* **flirt·ed, flirt·ing, flirts.** *—intr.* **1.** To make playfully romantic or sexual overtures. **2.** To deal playfully, triflingly, or superficially with: *flirt with danger.* **3.** To move abruptly or jerkily. *—tr.* **1.** To toss or flip suddenly. **2.** To move quickly. **—flirt** *n.* **1.** One given to flirting. **2.** An abrupt, jerking movement. [Origin unknown.]

SYNONYMS: *flirt, dally, play, toy, trifle.* The central meaning shared by these verbs is "to deal lightly, casually, or flippantly with someone or something": *flirted with the idea of getting a job; dallying with music; can't play with life; toyed with the problem; a person not to be trifled with.*

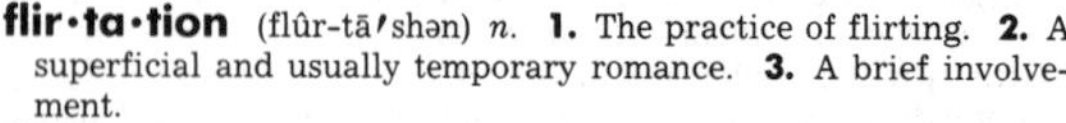

flir·ta·tion (flûr-tā′shən) *n.* **1.** The practice of flirting. **2.** A superficial and usually temporary romance. **3.** A brief involvement.

flir·ta·tious (flûr-tā′shəs) *adj.* **1.** Given to flirting. **2.** Full of playful allure: *a flirtatious glance.* **—flir·ta′tious·ly** *adv.*

flit (flĭt) *intr.v.* **flit·ted, flit·ting, flits.** **1.** To move about rapidly and nimbly. **2.** To move quickly from one condition or location to another. See Synonyms at **flutter.** **—flit** *n.* **1.** A fluttering or darting movement. **2.** *Informal.* An empty-headed, silly, often erratic person. [Middle English *flitten,* from Old Norse *flytja,* to carry about, convey. See **pleu-** in Appendix.] **—flit′ter** *n.*

flitch (flĭch) *n.* **1.** A salted and cured side of bacon. **2.** A longitudinal cut from the trunk of a tree. **3.** One of several planks secured together to form a single beam. [Middle English *flicche,* from Old English *flicce.*]

flit·ter (flĭt′ər) *intr.v.* **-tered, -ter·ing, -ters.** To flutter. See Synonyms at **flutter.** [Frequentative of FLIT.]

♦**float** (flōt) *v.* **float·ed, float·ing, floats.** *—intr.* **1.a.** To remain suspended within or on the surface of a fluid without sinking. **b.** To be suspended in or move through space as if supported by a liquid. **2.** To move from place to place, especially at random. **3.** To move easily or lightly: *"Miss Golightly . . . floated round in their arms light as a scarf"* (Truman Capote). **4.** *Economics.* To find a level in relationship to other currencies solely in response to the law of supply and demand: *allowed the dollar to float.* *—tr.* **1.** To cause to remain suspended without sinking or falling. **2.a.** To put into the water; launch: *float a ship; float a navy.* **b.** To start or establish (a business enterprise, for example). **3.** To flood (land), as for irrigation. **4.** *Economics.* To allow (the exchange value of a currency) to find freely its real level in relationship to other currencies. **5.** To release (a security) for sale. **6.** To arrange for (a loan). **7.** To make the surface of (plaster, for example) level or smooth. **8.** *Computer Science.* To convert data from fixed-point notation to floating-point notation. **—float** *n.* **1.** Something that floats, as: **a.** A raft. **b.** A buoy. **c.** A life preserver. **d.** A buoyant object, such as a cork, used to hold a net or fishing line afloat. **e.** A landing platform attached to a wharf and floating on the water. **f.** A floating ball attached to a lever to regulate the water level in a tank. **2.** *Biology.* An air-filled sac or structure that aids in the flotation of an aquatic organism. Also called *air bladder, air vesicle.* **3.** A decorated exhibit or scene mounted on a mobile platform and pulled or driven in a parade. **4.** A sum of money representing checks that are outstanding. **5.** A tool for smoothing the surface of plaster or cement. **6.** A soft drink with ice cream floating in it. See Regional Note at **milk shake.** [Middle English *floten,* from Old English *flotian.* See **pleu-** in Appendix.] **—float′a·ble** *adj.*

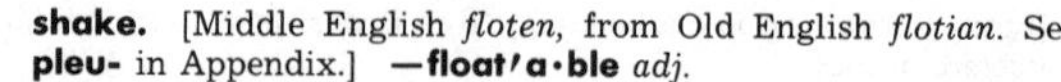

float·age (flō′tĭj) *n.* Variant of **flotage.**

float·a·tion (flō-tā′shən) *n.* Variant of **flotation.**

float·er (flō′tər) *n.* **1.** One, such as a person or an object, that floats or is capable of floating. **2.** One who wanders; a drifter. **3.** An employee who is reassigned from job to job or shift to shift within an operation. **4.** One who votes illegally in different polling places. **5.** An insurance policy that protects movable property in transit or regularly subject to use in varying places. **6.** *Slang.* A corpse that is recovered from a body of water, especially when it has been there for some time. **7. floaters.** Specks or small threads in the visual field, usually perceived to be moving, that are caused by minute aggregations of cells or proteins in the vitreous humor of the eye.

float·ing (flō′tĭng) *adj.* **1.** Buoyed on or suspended in or as if in a fluid. **2.** Not secured in place; unattached. **3.** Inclined to move or be moved about: *a floating meeting; floating crap games.* **4.** *Economics.* **a.** Available for use; in circulation. Used of capital. **b.** Short-term and usually unfunded. Used of a debt. **5.** Designed or constructed to operate smoothly and without vibration. **6.** Of or relating to an organ of the body that is movable or out of normal position: *a floating kidney.*

floating dock *n.* **1.** A structure that can be submerged to permit the entry and docking of a ship and then raised to lift the ship from the water for repairs. Also called *floating drydock.* **2.** A dock that is supported by metal pipes on which it can move up and down with the rise and fall of the water level.

floating island *n.* A dessert of soft custard with mounds of beaten egg whites or whipped cream floating on its surface.

float·ing-point (flō′tĭng-point′) *adj.* Of, relating to, or being a method of writing numeric quantities with a mantissa representing the value of the digits and a characteristic indicating the power of the number base, such as 3×10^{-5}.

floating rib *n.* A false rib whose anterior end is unattached. The lowest two pairs of human ribs are floating ribs.

float·plane (flōt′plān′) *n.* An aircraft equipped with one or more floats for landing on or taking off from a body of water.

floc (flŏk) *n.* A flocculent mass formed in a fluid through precipitation or aggregation of suspended particles. [Short for FLOCCULUS.]

floc·cose (flŏk′ōs) *adj.* *Botany.* Covered with tufts of soft hair, as the fruits of quince. [Late Latin *floccōsus,* from Latin *floccus,* tuft of wool.]

floc·cu·late (flŏk′yə-lāt′) *v.* **-lat·ed, -lat·ing, -lates.** *—tr.* **1.** To cause (soil) to form lumps or masses. **2.** To cause (clouds) to form fluffy masses. *—intr.* To form lumpy or fluffy masses. **—flocculate** *n.* Something that has formed lumpy or fluffy masses. **—floc′cu·la′tion** *n.*

floc·cule (flŏk′yo͞ol) *n.* A small, loosely held mass or aggregate of fine particles, resembling a tuft of wool and suspended in or precipitated from a solution. Also called *flock.* [New Latin *flocculus,* flocculus. See FLOCCULUS.]

floc·cu·lent (flŏk′yə-lənt) *adj.* **1.** Having a fluffy or woolly appearance. **2.** *Chemistry.* Made up of or containing woolly masses. **3.** *Zoology.* Having a soft, waxy, and woollike covering, as certain insects. **—floc′cu·lence** *n.* **—floc′cu·lent·ly** *adv.*

floc·cu·lus (flŏk′yə-ləs) *n., pl.* **-li** (-lī′). **1.** A small fluffy mass or tuft. **2.** *Anatomy.* Either of two small lobes on the lower posterior border of the cerebellum. **3.** *Astronomy.* Any of various cloudlike masses of gases appearing as bright or dark patches on the surface of the sun. [New Latin, diminutive of Latin *floccus,* tuft of wool.]

flock¹ (flŏk) *n.* **1.** A group of animals that live, travel, or feed together. **2.** A group of people under the leadership of one person, especially the members of a church. **3.** A large crowd or number: *had a flock of questions.* See Usage Note at **collective noun.** **—flock** *intr.v.* **flocked, flock·ing, flocks.** To congregate or travel in a flock or crowd. [Middle English *flok,* from Old English *floc.*]

SYNONYMS: *flock, flight, herd, drove, pack, gang, gaggle, bevy, brood.* These nouns denote a number of animals, birds, or fish considered collectively, and some have human connotations. *Flock* is applied to a congregation of animals of one kind, especially sheep or goats herded by human beings, and to any congregation of wild or domesticated birds, especially when on the ground. It is also applicable to people who form the membership of a church or to people under someone's care or supervision. *Flight* refers to a flock of birds in flight. *Herd* is used of a number of animals, especially cattle, herded by human beings; or of wild animals such as antelope, elephants, and zebras; or of whales and seals. Applied to people, it is used disparagingly of a crowd or of the masses and suggests the gregarious aspect of crowd psychology. *Drove* is used of a herd or flock of cattle, sheep, geese, or the like, that are being moved or driven from one place to another; less often it refers to a crowd of people in movement. *Pack* is applicable to any body of animals, especially wolves, or of birds, especially grouse, and to a body of hounds trained to hunt as a unit. It also refers disparagingly to a band or group of persons. *Gang* refers to a herd, especially of buffalo or elk; to a pack of wolves or wild dogs; or to various associations of persons, especially when engaged in violent or criminal pursuits. *Gaggle* denotes a flock of geese. *Bevy* is used of a company of roe deer, larks, or quail. *Brood* is applicable to offspring that are still under the care of a mother, especially the offspring of domestic and game birds or, less formally, of human beings. • The following related terms are used as indicated: *cast,* the number of hawks or falcons cast off at one time, usually a pair; *cete,* a company of badgers; *covert,* a flock of coots; *covey,* a family of grouse, partridges, or other game birds; *drift,* a drove or herd, especially of hogs; *exaltation,* a flight of larks; *fall,* a family of woodcock in flight; *gam,* a school of whales, or a social congregation of whalers, especially at sea; *kennel,* a number of hounds or dogs housed in one place or under the same ownership; *kindle,* a brood or litter, especially of kittens; *litter,* the total number of offspring produced at a single birth by a multiparous mammal; *muster,* a flock of peacocks; *nide,* a brood of pheasants; *pod,* a small herd of seals or whales; *pride,* a company of lions; *rout,* a company of people or animals in movement, especially knights or wolves; *school,* a congregation of fish, or aquatic mammals such as dolphins or porpoises; *shrewdness,* a company of apes; *skein,* a flight of wildfowl, especially geese; *skulk,* a congregation of vermin, especially foxes, or of thieves; *sloth,* a company of bears; *sord,* a flight of mallards; *sounder,* a herd of wild boar; *stable,* a number of horses housed in one place or under the same ownership; *swarm,* a colony of insects, such as ants, bees, or wasps, especially when migrating to a new nest or hive; *troop,* a number of animals, birds, or people, especially when on the move; *warren,* the inhabitants, such as rabbits, of a warren; *watch,* a flock of nightingales; and *wisp,* a flock of birds, especially of snipe. See also Synonyms at **crowd.**

---

flock² (flŏk) *n.* **1.** A tuft, as of fiber or hair. **2.** Waste wool or cotton used for stuffing furniture and mattresses. **3.** An inferior grade of wool added to cloth for extra weight. **4.** Pulverized wool or felt that is applied to paper, cloth, or metal to produce a texture or pattern. **5.** See **floccule.** —**flock** *tr.v.* **flocked, flock·ing, flocks. 1.** To stuff with waste wool or cotton. **2.** To texture or pattern with pulverized wool or felt. [Middle English *flok,* from Old French *floc,* from Latin *floccus,* tuft of wool.]

Flod·den (flŏd′n). A hill of northern England near the Scottish border. It was the site of the Battle of Flodden Field (September 9, 1513) in which the English defeated the Scots under James IV.

floe (flō) *n.* **1.** An ice floe. **2.** A segment that has separated from such an ice mass. [Probably from Norwegian *flo,* layer, from Old Norse *flō.* See **plāk-¹** in Appendix.]

flog (flŏg, flôg) *tr.v.* **flogged, flog·ging, flogs. 1.** To beat severely with a whip or rod. **2.** *Informal.* To publicize aggressively: *flogging a new book.* [Perhaps from alteration of Latin *flagellāre.* See FLAGELLATE.] —**flog′ger** *n.*

flood (flŭd) *n.* **1.** An overflowing of water onto land that is normally dry. **2.** A flood tide. **3.** An abundant flow or outpouring: *received a flood of applications.* See Synonyms at **flow. 4.** A floodlight, specifically a unit that produces a beam of intense light. **5. Flood.** The universal deluge recorded in the Old Testament as having occurred during the life of Noah. Often used with *the.* —**flood** *v.* **flood·ed, flood·ing, floods.** —*tr.* **1.** To cover or submerge with or as if with a flood; inundate: *My desk is flooded with paper.* **2.** To fill with an abundance or an excess: *flood the market with cheap foreign goods.* —*intr.* **1.** To become inundated or submerged. **2.** To pour forth; overflow. [Middle English *flod,* from Old English *flōd.* See **pleu-** in Appendix.]

flood·gate (flŭd′gāt′) *n.* **1.** A gate used to control the flow of a body of water. Also called *water gate.* **2.** Something that restrains a flood or an outpouring: *a ruling that opened the floodgates to refugees seeking asylum.*

flood·light (flŭd′līt′) *n.* **1.** Artificial light in an intensely bright and broad beam. **2.** A unit that produces a beam of intense light; a flood. —**floodlight** *tr.v.* **-light·ed** or **-lit** (-lĭt′), **-light·ing, -lights.** To illuminate with a floodlight.

flood·plain also **flood plain** (flŭd′plān′) *n.* A plain bordering a river and subject to flooding.

flood tide also **flood·tide** (flŭd′tīd′) *n.* **1.** The incoming or rising tide; the period between low water and the succeeding high water. **2.** A climax or high point: *a flood tide of fears.*

flood·wall (flŭd′wôl′) *n.* A wall built along a shore or bank to protect an area from floods.

flood·wat·er (flŭd′wô′tər, -wŏt′ər) *n.* The water of a flood. Often used in the plural.

floor (flôr, flōr) *n. Abbr.* **fl. 1.a.** The surface of a room on which one stands. **b.** The lower or supporting surface of a structure. **2.a.** A story or level of a building. **b.** The occupants of such a story: *The entire floor complained about the noise.* **3.** A level surface or area used for a specified purpose: *a dance floor; a threshing floor.* **4.** The surface of a structure on which vehicles travel. **5.a.** The part of a legislative chamber or meeting hall where members are seated and from which they speak. **b.** The right to address an assembly, as granted under parliamentary procedure. **c.** The body of assembly members: *a motion from the floor.* **6.** The part of a room or building where the principal business or work takes place, especially: **a.** The area of an exchange where securities are traded. **b.** The part of a retail store in which merchandise is displayed and sales are made. **c.** The area of a factory where the product is manufactured or assembled. **7.** The ground or lowermost surface, as of a forest or an ocean. **8.** A lower limit or base: *a pricing floor; a bidding floor.* —**floor** *tr.v.* **floored, floor·ing, floors. 1.** To provide with a floor. **2.** *Informal.* To press (the accelerator of a motor vehicle) to the floor. **3.a.** To knock down. **b.** To stun; overwhelm: *The very idea floored me.* [Middle English *flor,* from Old English *flōr.* See **pelə-²** in Appendix.] —**floor′er** *n.*

floor·age (flôr′ĭj, flōr′-) *n.* Floor space.

floor·board (flôr′bôrd′, flōr′bōrd′) *n.* **1.** A board in a floor. **2.** The floor of a motor vehicle.

floor exercise *n. Sports.* An event in competitive gymnastics that consists of various tumbling maneuvers performed on a mat.

floor·ing (flôr′ĭng, flōr′-) *n.* **1.** A floor. **2.** Material, such as lumber or tile, used in making floors.

floor lamp *n.* A tall lamp with a base that stands on the floor.

floor leader *n.* The member of a legislature chosen by fellow party members to be in charge of the party's activities on the floor.

floor manager *n.* **1.** See **floorwalker. 2.** A person who is in charge of directing something, such as activities at a political convention, from the floor.

floor plan *n.* A scale diagram of a room or building drawn as if seen from above.

floor sample *n.* Merchandise sold at a reduced price because it has been a display or demonstration model.

floor·show (flôr′shō′, flōr′-) *n.* A series of entertainments presented in a nightclub.

floor·walk·er (flôr′wô′kər, flōr′-) *n.* An employee of a department store who supervises sales personnel and assists customers. Also called *floor manager.*

floo·zy also **floo·zie** (flo͞o′zē) *n., pl.* **-zies.** *Slang.* A woman regarded as gaudy or tawdry. [Origin unknown.]

flop (flŏp) *v.* **flopped, flop·ping, flops.** —*intr.* **1.** To fall or lie down heavily and noisily. **2.** To move about loosely or limply: *The dog's ears flopped when it ran.* **3.** *Informal.* To fail utterly: *The play flopped.* **4.** *Slang.* **a.** To rest idly; lounge. **b.** To go to bed. —*tr.* To drop or lay (something) down heavily and noisily: *flopped the steak onto a platter.* —**flop** *n.* **1.** The act of flopping. **2.** The sound made when flopping. **3.** *Informal.* An utter failure. [Alteration of FLAP.] —**flop′per** *n.*

flop·house (flŏp′hous′) *n.* A cheap, run-down hotel or boarding house.

flop·py (flŏp′ē) *adj.* **-pi·er, -pi·est.** Tending to flop; loose and flexible. See Synonyms at **limp.** —**floppy** *n., pl.* **-pies.** *Computer Science.* A floppy disk. —**flop′pi·ly** *adv.* —**flop′pi·ness** *n.*

floppy disk *n. Computer Science.* A flexible plastic disk coated with magnetic material and covered by a protective jacket, used primarily in microcomputers and minicomputers to store data magnetically. Also called *diskette.*

flo·ra (flôr′ə, flōr′ə) *n., pl.* **flo·ras** or **flo·rae** (flôr′ē′, flōr′ē′). **1.** Plants considered as a group, especially the plants of a particular country, region, or time. **2.** A treatise describing the plants of a region or time. **3.** The bacteria and other microorganisms that normally inhabit a bodily organ or part: *intestinal flora.* [From FLORA.]

Flo·ra (flôr′ə, flōr′ə) *n. Roman Mythology.* The goddess of flowers. [Latin *Flōra,* from *flōs, flōr-,* flower. See **bhel-³** in Appendix.]

flo·rae (flôr′ē′, flōr′ē′) *n.* A plural of **flora.**

flo·ral (flôr′əl, flōr′-) *adj.* Of, relating to, or suggestive of a flower: *a fabric with a floral pattern.* —**flo′ral·ly** *adv.*

floral cup *n.* A tubular or cup-shaped structure of a flower, bearing on its rim the sepals, petals, and stamens.

floral envelope *n.* The perianth of a flower.

Flo·ral Park (flôr′əl, flōr′-). A village of southeast New York on western Long Island, a residential suburb of New York City. Population, 16,805.

floral tube *n.* A tube usually formed by the basal fusion of the perianth and stamens, as in the flowers of the daffodil.

flo·re·at·ed (flôr′ē-ā′tĭd, flōr′-) *adj.* Variant of **floriated.**

Flor·ence (flôr′əns, flŏr′-) **1.** Also **Fi·ren·ze** (fē-rĕn′dzĕ). A city of central Italy on the Arno River east of Pisa. Originally an Etruscan settlement, then a Roman town, Florence was a powerful city-state under the Medici family during the Italian Renaissance. Population, 453,293. **2.** A city of northwest Alabama on the Tennessee River west-northwest of Decatur. Founded in 1818, it is highly industrialized. Population, 37,029. **3.** A city of northeast South Carolina east-northeast of Columbia. It has been a transportation center since the Civil War. Population, 29,176.

Florence fennel *n.* See **finocchio.**

Flor·en·tine (flôr′ən-tēn′, -tīn′, flŏr′-) *adj.* **1.** Of or relating to Florence, Italy. **2.** Of or relating to the style of art and architecture that flourished in Florence, Italy, during the Renaissance. **3.** Often **florentine.** Having or characterizing a dull chased or rubbed finish. Used of gold. **4.** Prepared, cooked, or served with spinach. —**Florentine** *n.* A native or inhabitant of Florence, Italy. [Latin *Flōrentīnus,* from *Flōrentia,* Florence, Italy.]

Flo·res (flôr′ĭs, -ēz, flōr′-). An island of eastern Indonesia in the Lesser Sundas on the **Flores Sea,** between the eastern end of the Java Sea and the western end of the Banda Sea south of Sulawesi. The island came under Dutch influence in the 17th century, although the Portuguese held the eastern end until 1851.

Flo·res (flô′rĕs), **Juan José.** 1800–1864. Ecuadorian general and politician who was appointed Ecuador's first president in 1830 and served two terms (1830–1835 and 1839–1845).

flo·res·cence (flô-rĕs′əns, flə-) *n.* A condition, time, or pe-

floe
In Antarctica

floppy disk

ă pat	oi boy
ā pay	ou out
âr care	o͝o took
ä father	o͞o boot
ĕ pet	ŭ cut
ē be	ûr urge
ĭ pit	th thin
ī pie	*th* this
îr pier	hw which
ŏ pot	zh vision
ō toe	ə about, item
ô paw	♦ regionalism

Stress marks: ′ (primary); ′ (secondary), as in **dictionary** (dĭk′shə-nĕr′ē)

riod of flowering. See Synonyms at **bloom**[1]. [New Latin *flōrēscentia,* from Latin *flōrēscēns, flōrēscent-,* present participle of *flōrēscere,* inchoative of *flōrēre,* to flower, bloom. See FLOURISH.] **—flo·res′cent** *adj.*

flo·ret (flôr′ĭt, flōr′-) *n.* A small or reduced flower, especially one of the grasses and composite plants, such as a daisy. [Middle English *flouret,* from Old French *florete,* diminutive of *flor,* flower. See FLOWER.]

Flo·rey (flôr′ē, flōr′ē), Sir **Howard Walter.** Baron Florey of Adelaide. 1898–1968. Australian-born British pathologist. He shared a 1945 Nobel Prize for isolating and purifying penicillin.

Flo·ri·a·nó·po·lis (flôr′ē-ə-nŏp′ə-lĭs, flōr-, flô′ryə-nô′po͝o-lēs′). A city of southeast Brazil on an island just off the coast. It is a port linked to the mainland by a suspension bridge. Population, 153,652.

flo·ri·at·ed also **flo·re·at·ed** (flôr′ē-ā′tĭd, flōr′-) *adj.* Decorated with floral designs. [From Latin *flōs, flōr-,* flower. See **bhel-**[3] in Appendix.]

flo·ri·bun·da (flôr′ə-bŭn′də, flōr′-) *n.* Any of several hybrid roses bearing numerous single or double flowers. [New Latin, feminine of *floribundus,* blossoming freely, from Latin *flōs, flōr-,* flower. See FLOWER.]

flo·ri·cane (flôr′ĭ-kān′, flōr′-) *n.* The flowering and fruiting stem of a biennial plant, especially of a bramble. [Latin *flōs, flōr-,* flower; see FLOWER + CANE.]

flo·ri·cul·ture (flôr′ĭ-kŭl′chər, flōr′-) *n.* The cultivation of flowering and ornamental plants. [Latin *flōs, flōr-,* flower; see FLOWER + CULTURE.] **—flo′ri·cul′tur·al** *adj.* **—flo′ri·cul′tur·al·ly** *adv.* **—flo′ri·cul′tur·ist** *n.*

flor·id (flôr′ĭd, flŏr′-) *adj.* **1.** Flushed with rosy color; ruddy. **2.** Very ornate; flowery: *a florid prose style.* See Synonyms at **ornate. 3.** *Archaic.* Healthy. **4.** *Obsolete.* Abounding in or covered with flowers. [French *floride,* from Latin *flōridus,* from *flōs, flōr-,* flower. See **bhel-**[3] in Appendix.] **—flo·rid′i·ty** (flə-rĭd′ĭ-tē, flô-), **flor′id·ness** *n.* **—flor′id·ly** *adv.*

Flor·i·da (flôr′ĭ-də, flŏr′-). *Abbr.* **FL, Fla.** A state of the southeast United States bordering on the Atlantic Ocean and the Gulf of Mexico. It was admitted as the 27th state in 1845. The peninsula was first discovered by Juan Ponce de León in 1513 and became the center of a Spanish settlement that included the southeast part of the present-day United States. Spain finally ceded the area in 1819. Tallahassee is the capital and Jacksonville the largest city. Population, 9,746,421. **—Flo·rid′i·an** (flə-rĭd′ē-ən), **Flor′i·dan** (-ĭd-n) *adj. n.*

flotilla
On the Indian Ocean

Florida, Straits of. Also **Florida Strait.** A sea passage between Cuba and the Florida Keys, linking the Gulf of Mexico with the Atlantic Ocean.

Florida arrowroot *n.* Coontie.

Florida Keys. A chain of small coral and limestone islands and reefs extending about 241 km (150 mi) in a southwestward arc from south of Miami to Key West.

flo·rid·e·an starch (flə-rĭd′ē-ən) *n. Botany.* The storage carbohydrate of the red algae. [From New Latin *Florideae,* subclass of red algae, from Latin *flōridus,* flowery. See FLORID.]

flo·rif·er·ous (flô-rĭf′ər-əs) *adj.* Bearing flowers. [From Latin *flōrifer,* bearing flowers : *flōs, flōr-,* flower; see FLOWER + *-fer,* -fer.] **—flo·rif′er·ous·ly** *adv.* **—flo·rif′er·ous·ness** *n.*

flor·i·gen (flôr′ə-jən, flōr′-) *n.* A plant hormone that promotes flowering. [Latin *flōs, flōr-,* flower; see **bhel-**[3] in Appendix + –GEN.] **—flor′i·gen′ic** (-jĕn′ĭk) *adj.*

flor·in (flôr′ĭn, flŏr′-) *n. Abbr.* **fl. 1.** A guilder. **2.** A British coin worth two shillings. **3.a.** A gold coin first issued at Florence, Italy, in 1252. **b.** Any of several gold coins similar to the Florentine florin, formerly used in Europe. [Middle English, from Old French, from Old Italian *fiorino,* from *fiore,* flower (from the lily on the coins), from Latin *flōs, flōr-,* flower. See **bhel-**[3] in Appendix.]

Flor·in (flôr′ĭn, flŏr′-). A community of central California, a suburb of Sacramento. Population, 16,523.

Flo·ri·o (flôr′ē-ō′, flōr′-), **John.** 1553?–1625. English lexicographer noted for his Italian-English dictionary (1598).

Flor·is·sant (flôr′ĭ-sənt, flōr′-). A city of eastern Missouri, a residential suburb of St. Louis. It was settled by French farmers and fur trappers in the 1760's. Population, 55,372.

flo·rist (flôr′ĭst, flōr′-, flŏr′-) *n.* One in the business of raising or selling flowers and ornamental plants. [Latin *flōs, flōr-,* flower; see **bhel-**[3] in Appendix + –IST.] **—flo′rist·ry** *n.*

flo·rist·ics (flô-rĭs′tĭks, flō-) *n.* (*used with a sing. verb*). The study of the number, distribution, and relationships of plant species in one or more areas.

–florous *suff.* Having a specified kind or number of flowers: *tubuliflorous.* [From Late Latin *-flōrus,* from Latin *flōs, flōr-,* flower. See **bhel-**[3] in Appendix.]

flo·ru·it (flôr′yo͞o-ĭt, -o͞o-, flōr′-, flŏr′-) *n. Abbr.* **fl.** The period during which a person, school, or movement was most active or flourishing. [Latin *flōruit,* third person sing. perfect tense of *flōrēre,* to flourish. See FLOURISH.]

Flo·ry (flôr′ē, flōr′ē), **Paul John.** 1910–1985. American chemist. He won a 1974 Nobel Prize for developing methods of studying long-chain molecules.

floss (flôs, flŏs) *n.* **1.** Dental floss. **2.** Short or waste silk fibers, especially from the outer surface of the cocoon of a silkworm. **3.** Soft, loosely twisted thread, as of silk or cotton, used in embroidery. **4.** A downy or silky fibrous substance, such as corn silk or silk cotton. **—floss** *v.* **flossed, floss·ing, floss·es.** —*tr.* To clean between (teeth) with dental floss. —*intr.* To use dental floss. [Perhaps alteration of French *floche,* tuft of wool, from Old French *floc, floche,* from Latin *floccus.*] **—floss′er** *n.*

floss·y (flô′sē, flŏs′ē) *adj.* **-i·er, -i·est. 1.** Superficially stylish; slick: *wrote flossy articles about the lifestyles of the rich.* **2.** Of, relating to, or resembling floss. **—floss′i·ly** *adv.* **—floss′i·ness** *n.*

flo·tage also **float·age** (flō′tĭj) *n.* **1.** See **flotation** (sense 1). **2.** Floating objects or material; flotsam.

flo·ta·tion also **float·a·tion** (flō-tā′shən) *n.* **1.** The act, process, or condition of floating. Also called *flotage.* **2.** The act or an instance of launching or initiating, especially the floating of stocks or bonds or the financing of a business venture by floating stocks or bonds. **3.** The process of separating different materials, especially minerals, by agitating a pulverized mixture of the materials with water, oil, and chemicals. Differential wetting of the suspended particles causes unwetted particles to be carried by air bubbles to the surface for collection. **4.** The capability, especially of a vehicle tread or tire, to remain on top of a soft surface, such as sand, wet ground, or snow.

flotation device *n.* A life preserver.

flo·til·la (flō-tĭl′ə) *n.* **1.a.** A small fleet. **b.** A fleet of small craft. **2.** A U.S. Navy organizational unit of two or more squadrons of small warships. **3.** *Informal.* A group of vehicles owned or operated as a unit: *"Now* [the limousine service] *has a flotilla of about 150 cars, more than 200 uniformed chauffeurs"* (People). [Spanish, diminutive of *flota,* fleet, from Old French *flote,* from Old Norse *floti.* See **pleu-** in Appendix.]

flot·sam (flŏt′səm) *n.* **1.a.** Wreckage or cargo that remains afloat after a ship has sunk. **b.** Floating refuse or debris. **2.** Discarded odds and ends. **3.** Vagrant, usually destitute people. [Anglo-Norman *floteson,* from Old French *floter,* to float, of Germanic origin. See **pleu-** in Appendix.]

USAGE NOTE: *Flotsam,* in maritime law, applies to wreckage or cargo left floating on the sea after a shipwreck. *Jetsam* applies to cargo or equipment thrown overboard (jettisoned) from a ship in distress and either sunk or washed ashore. The common phrase *flotsam and jetsam* is now used loosely to describe any objects found floating or washed ashore.

flounce[1] (flouns) *n.* A strip of decorative, usually gathered or pleated material attached by one edge, as on a garment or curtain. **—flounce** *tr.v.* **flounced, flounc·ing, flounc·es.** To trim with a strip or strips of gathered or pleated material. [Alteration of *frounce,* from Middle English, pleat, from Old French *fronce,* of Germanic origin. See **sker-**[2] in Appendix.]

flounce[2] (flouns) *intr.v.* **flounced, flounc·ing, flounc·es. 1.a.** To move in a lively or bouncy manner: *The children flounced around the room in their costumes.* **b.** To move with exaggerated or affected motions: *flounced petulantly out of the house.* **2.** To move clumsily; flounder. **—flounce** *n.* The act or motion of flouncing. [Possibly of Scandinavian origin.]

flounc·ing (floun′sĭng) *n.* **1.** Material used to make flounces. **2.** A flounce or an arrangement of flounces, as on a curtain.

floun·der[1] (floun′dər) *intr.v.* **-dered, -der·ing, -ders. 1.** To make clumsy attempts to move or regain one's balance. **2.** To move or act clumsily and in confusion. See Synonyms at **blunder.** See Usage Note at **founder**[1]. **—flounder** *n.* The act of floundering. [Probably alteration of FOUNDER[1].]

floun·der[2] (floun′dər) *n., pl.* **flounder** or **-ders.** Any of various marine flatfishes of the families Bothidae and Pleuronectidae, which include important food fishes. [Middle English, from Anglo-Norman *floundre,* of Scandinavian origin. See **plat-** in Appendix.]

flour (flour) *n.* **1.** A fine, powdery foodstuff obtained by grinding and sifting the meal of a grain, especially wheat, used chiefly in baking. **2.** Any of various similar finely ground or powdered foodstuffs, as of cassava, fish, or bananas. **3.** A soft, fine powder. **—flour** *tr.v.* **floured, flour·ing, flours. 1.** To cover or coat with flour. **2.** To make into flour. [Middle English. See FLOWER.] **—flour′y** *adj.*

flour·ish (flûr′ĭsh, flŭr′-) *v.* **-ished, -ish·ing, -ish·es.** —*intr.* **1.** To grow well or luxuriantly; thrive: *The crops flourished in the rich bottomland.* **2.** To do or fare well; prosper: *"No village on the railroad failed to flourish"* (John Kenneth Galbraith). **3.** To be in a period of highest productivity, excellence, or influence: *an anonymous poet who flourished in the tenth century; painted when Impressionism was flourishing.* **4.** To make bold, sweeping movements: *The banner flourished in the wind.* —*tr.* To wield, wave, or exhibit dramatically. **—flourish** *n.* **1.** A dramatic or stylish movement, as of waving or brandishing: *"A few . . . musicians embellish their performance with a flourish of the fingers"* (Frederick D. Bennett). **2.** An embellishment or ornamentation: *signed her name with a distinctive flourish; a long speech with many rhetorical flourishes.* **3.** An ostentatious act or gesture: *a flourish of generosity.* **4.** *Music.* A showy or ceremonious passage, such as a fanfare. [Middle English *florishen,* from Old French *florir, floriss-,* from Vulgar Latin **flōrīre,* from Latin *flōrēre,* from *flōs, flōr-,* flower. See **bhel-**[3] in Appendix.] **—flour′ish·er** *n.*

SYNONYMS: *flourish, brandish, wave.* The central meaning shared by these verbs is "to swing back and forth boldly and dramatically": *flourished her newly signed contract; brandish a sword; waving a baton.*

flout (flout) *v.* **flout·ed, flout·ing, flouts.** —*tr.* To show contempt for; scorn: *flout a law; behavior that flouted convention.* See Usage Note at **flaunt.** —*intr.* To be scornful. —**flout** *n.* A contemptuous action or remark; an insult. [Perhaps from Middle English *flouten,* to play the flute, from Old French *flauter,* from *flaute,* flute. See FLUTE.] —**flout′er** *n.* —**flout′ing·ly** *adv.*

flow (flō) *v.* **flowed, flow·ing, flows.** —*intr.* **1.a.** To move or run smoothly with unbroken continuity, as in the manner characteristic of a fluid. **b.** To issue in a stream; pour forth: *Sap flowed from the gash in the tree.* **2.** To circulate, as the blood in the body. **3.** To move with a continual shifting of the component particles: *wheat flowing into the bin; traffic flowing through the tunnel.* **4.** To proceed steadily and easily: *The preparations flowed smoothly.* **5.** To exhibit a smooth or graceful continuity: *The cadence of the poem flowed gracefully.* **6.** To hang loosely and gracefully: *The cape flowed from his shoulders.* **7.** To rise. Used of the tide. **8.** To arise; derive: *Several conclusions flow from this hypothesis.* **9.a.** To abound or teem: *coffers flowing with treasure.* **b.** To stream copiously; flood: *Contributions flowed in from all parts of the country.* **10.** To menstruate. **11.** To undergo plastic deformation without cracking or breaking. Used of rocks, metals, or minerals. —*tr.* **1.** To release as a flow: *trees flowing thin sap.* **2.** To cause to flow: *"One of the real keys to success is developing a system where you can flow traffic to yourselves"* (Marc Klee). —**flow** *n.* **1.a.** The act of flowing. **b.** The smooth motion characteristic of fluids. **2.a.** A stream or current. **b.** A flood or an overflow. **c.** A residual mass that has stopped flowing: *a hardened lava flow.* **3.a.** A continuous output or outpouring: *a flow of ideas; produced a steady flow of articles and stories.* **b.** A continuous movement or circulation: *the flow of traffic; a flow of paperwork across his desk.* **4.** The amount that flows in a given period of time. **5.** The rising of the tide. **6.** Continuity and smoothness of appearance. **7.** A general movement or tendency: *As the lone dissenter in the group, she was going against the flow of opinion.* **8.** The sequence in which operations are performed. **9.** An apparent ease or effortlessness of performance: *"An athlete must learn to forget the details of his or her training to achieve the instinctive sense of flow that characterizes a champion"* (Frederick Turner). **10.** Menstrual discharge. [Middle English *flouen,* from Old English *flōwan.* See **pleu-** in Appendix.] —**flow′ing·ly** *adv.*

SYNONYMS: *flow, current, flood, flux, rush, stream, tide.* The central meaning shared by these nouns is "something suggestive of running water": *a flow of thought; the current of history; a flood of ideas; a flux of words; a rush of sympathy; a stream of complaints; a tide of immigration.* See also Synonyms at **stem**[1].

flow·age (flō′ĭj) *n.* **1.** The act of flowing or overflowing. **2.a.** The state of being flooded. **b.** A body of water, such as a lake or reservoir, formed by usually deliberate flooding. **3.** An outflow or overflow. **4.** The gradual plastic deformation of a solid body, as by heat.

flow chart also **flow·chart** (flō′chärt′) *n.* A schematic representation of a sequence of operations, as in a manufacturing process or computer program. Also called *flow diagram, flow sheet.*

flow-chart (flō′chärt′) *tr.v.* **-chart·ed, -chart·ing, -charts.** To design a flow chart for: *"Carson put away the papers on which he had been flow-charting a system . . . for a prospering little manufacturer"* (John Updike). —**flow′-chart′ing** *n.*

flow diagram *n.* See **flow chart.**

flow·er (flou′ər) *n.* **1.a.** The reproductive structure of some seed-bearing plants, characteristically having either specialized male or female organs or both male and female organs, such as stamens and a pistil, enclosed in an outer envelope of petals and sepals. **b.** Such a structure having showy or colorful parts; a blossom. **2.** A plant that is cultivated or appreciated for its blossoms. **3.** The condition or a time of having developed flowers: *The azaleas were in full flower.* **4.** Something, such as an ornament or a figure of speech, that resembles a flower in shape, fineness, or attractiveness. **5.** The period of highest development; the peak. See Synonyms at **bloom**[1]. **6.** The highest example or best representative: *the flower of our generation.* **7.** A natural development or outgrowth: *"His attitude was simply a flower of his general good nature"* (Henry James). **8. flowers.** *Chemistry.* A fine powder produced by condensation or sublimation of a compound. —**flower** *v.* **-ered, -er·ing, -ers.** —*intr.* **1.** To produce a flower or flowers; blossom. **2.** To develop naturally or fully; mature: *His artistic talents flowered early.* —*tr.* To decorate with flowers or with a floral pattern. [Middle English *flour,* flower, best of anything, flour, from Old French *flor,* from Latin *flōs, flōr-.* See **bhel-**[3] in Appendix.] —**flow′er·er** *n.* —**flow′er·less** *adj.*

flow·er·age (flou′ər-ĭj) *n.* **1.** Flowers considered as a group. **2.** The process or state of flowering.

flower bud *n.* A bud that will develop into a flower.

flower bug *n.* Any of a group of bugs in the family Anthocoridae, which feed on insects that infest flowers.

flower child *n.* *Informal.* A hippie, especially one advocating universal peace and love as antidotes to social or political ills. [From the custom of carrying or wearing flowers to symbolize peace and love.] —**flow′er-child′** (flou′ər-chīld′) *adj.*

flow·er·et (flou′ər-ĭt) *n.* A small flower; a floret.

flower girl *n.* A young girl who carries flowers in a procession, especially at a wedding.

flower head *n.* **1.** *Botany.* A dense, short, compact cluster of sessile flowers, as of composite plants or clover. Also called *capitulum.* **2.** A very dense grouping of flower buds, as in broccoli and cauliflower.

flow·er·ing dogwood (flou′ər-ĭng) *n.* See **dogwood.**

flowering maple *n.* Any of various tropical plants of the genus *Abutilon,* having leaves resembling those of the maple and variously colored flowers. Also called *abutilon, Indian mallow.*

flowering plant *n.* A plant that produces flowers and fruit; an angiosperm.

flowering quince *n.* Any of several shrubs of the genus *Chaenomeles,* native to Asia and having spiny branches and red or pink flowers.

flowering wintergreen *n.* See **fringed polygala.**

flower people *pl.n.* *Informal.* Hippies, especially ones advocating universal peace and love.

flow·er·pot (flou′ər-pŏt′) *n.* A pot in which plants are grown.

flower power *n.* *Informal.* A movement among hippies and especially flower people in the 1960's and 1970's, expressing countercultural or antiestablishment beliefs and ideals.

flow·er·y (flou′ə-rē) *adj.* **-i·er, -i·est.** **1.** Of, relating to, or suggestive of flowers: *a flowery perfume.* **2.** Abounding in or covered with flowers. **3.** Full of ornate or grandiloquent expressions; highly embellished: *a flowery speech.* —**flow′er·i·ness** *n.*

flow meter *n.* An instrument for monitoring, measuring, or recording the rate of flow, pressure, or discharge of a fluid, as of a gaseous fuel.

flown[1] (flōn) *v.* Past participle of **fly**[1].

flown[2] (flōn) *adj.* *Archaic.* Filled to excess. [Obsolete, past participle of FLOW.]

flow sheet *n.* See **flow chart.**

flow·stone (flō′stōn′) *n.* A layered deposit of calcium carbonate on rock where water has flowed or dripped, as on the walls of a cave.

fl oz or **fl. oz.** *abbr.* Fluid ounce.

flu (flo͞o) *n.* *Informal.* Influenza. [Short for INFLUENZA.]

flub (flŭb) *Informal. tr.v.* **flubbed, flub·bing, flubs.** To botch; bungle. —**flub** *n.* The act or an instance of botching or bungling: *"Their literature leans toward a comedy of small social flubs and withered chastity"* (James Wolcott). [Origin unknown.] —**flub′ber** *n.*

flub·dub (flŭb′dŭb′) *n.* *Informal.* Pretentious nonsense; bunkum. [Origin unknown.]

fluc·tu·ate (flŭk′cho͞o-āt′) *v.* **-at·ed, -at·ing, -ates.** —*intr.* **1.** To vary irregularly. See Synonyms at **swing.** **2.** To rise and fall in or as if in waves; undulate. —*tr.* To cause to rise and fall or vary irregularly. [Latin *fluctuāre, fluctuāt-,* from *fluctus,* a flowing, from past participle of *fluere, fluc-,* to flow. See **bhleu-** in Appendix.] —**fluc′tu·ant** (-ənt) *adj.* —**fluc′tu·a′tion** *n.*

flue[1] (flo͞o) *n.* **1.** A pipe, tube, or channel for conveying hot air, gas, steam, or smoke, as from a furnace or fireplace to a chimney. **2.** *Music.* **a.** An organ pipe sounded by means of a current of air striking a lip in the side of the pipe and causing the air within to vibrate. Also called *labial.* **b.** The lipped opening in such a pipe. [Origin unknown.]

flue[2] (flo͞o) *n.* A fishing net. [Middle English, from Middle Dutch *vlūwe.* See **pleu-** in Appendix.]

flue·gel·horn (flo͞o′gəl-hôrn′, flü′-) *n.* *Music.* Variant of **flügelhorn.**

flu·ent (flo͞o′ənt) *adj.* **1.a.** Able to express oneself readily and effortlessly: *a fluent speaker; fluent in three languages.* **b.** Flowing effortlessly; polished: *speaks fluent Russian.* **2.** Flowing or moving smoothly; graceful: *a yacht with long, fluent curves.* **3.** Flowing or capable of flowing; fluid. [Latin *fluēns, fluent-,* present participle of *fluere,* to flow. See **bhleu-** in Appendix.] —**flu′en·cy** *n.* —**flu′ent·ly** *adv.*

flue pipe *n.* *Music.* An organ pipe with a lipped opening; a flue.

flu·er·ic (flo͞o-ĕr′ĭk) *adj.* Fluidic. [Latin *fluere,* to flow; see **bhleu-** in Appendix + -IC.]

flu·er·ics (flo͞o-ĕr′ĭks) *n.* *(used with a sing. verb).* Fluidics.

flue stop *n.* *Music.* An organ stop controlling a set of flue pipes.

fluff (flŭf) *n.* **1.** Light down or fuzz, as on a young bird or on a dandelion or milkweed seed. **2.** Something having a very light, soft, or frothy consistency or appearance: *a fluff of meringue; a fluff of cloud.* **3.** Something of little substance or consequence, especially: **a.** Light or superficial entertainment: *The movie was just another bit of fluff from Hollywood.* **b.** Inflated or padded material: *The report was mostly fluff, with little new information.* **4.** *Informal.* An error, especially in the delivery of lines, as by an actor or announcer. —**fluff** *v.* **fluffed, fluff·ing, fluffs.** —*tr.* **1.** To make fluffy: *fluff a pillow; a squirrel fluffing out its tail.* **2.** *Informal.* **a.** To ruin or mar by a mistake or blunder: *They fluffed their chance to participate in the playoffs by losing their last three*

ă pat	oi boy
ā pay	ou out
âr care	o͝o took
ä father	o͞o boot
ĕ pet	ŭ cut
ē be	ûr urge
ĭ pit	th thin
ī pie	*th* this
îr pier	hw which
ŏ pot	zh vision
ō toe	ə about, item
ô paw	♦ regionalism

Stress marks: ′ (primary); ′ (secondary), as in **dictionary** (dĭk′shə-nĕr′ē)

games. **b.** To forget or botch (one's lines). —*intr.* **1.** To become fluffy. **2.** *Informal.* To make an error, especially to forget or botch one's lines. [Origin unknown.]

fluff·y (flŭf′ē) *adj.* **-i·er, -i·est. 1.a.** Of, relating to, or resembling fluff. **b.** Covered with fluff. **2.** Light and airy; soft: *fluffy curls; a fluffy soufflé.* **3.a.** Light or frivolous: *a fluffy musical comedy.* **b.** Lacking depth or precision; fuzzy: *fluffy thinking.* —**fluff′i·ly** *adv.* —**fluff′i·ness** *n.*

flü·gel·horn or **flue·gel·horn** (flo͞o′gəl-hôrn′, flü′-) *n. Music.* A bugle with valves, similar to the cornet but having a wider bore. [German : *Flügel,* flank (from its use to summon flanks during a battle) (from Middle High German *vlügel,* wing, flank; see **pleu-** in Appendix) + *Horn,* horn (from Middle High German, from Old High German; see **ker-**[1] in Appendix).] —**flü′gel·horn′ist** *n.*

flu·id (flo͞o′ĭd) *n. Abbr.* **fl, fl.** A continuous, amorphous substance whose molecules move freely past one another and that has the tendency to assume the shape of its container; a liquid or gas. —**fluid** *adj.* **1.** Of, relating to, or characteristic of a fluid. **2.** Readily reshaped; pliable. **3.** Smooth and flowing; graceful: *the fluid motion of a cat.* **4.a.** Changing or tending to change; variable: *a fluid situation fraught with uncertainty.* **b.** Characterized by or allowing social mobility: *"Everyone seems to . . . share in an intricate set of lore from the past and present whose deliciousness somehow would be ruined if Britain were a truly fluid society"* (Nicholas Lemann). **5.** Convertible into cash: *fluid assets.* [From Middle English, flowing, from Old French *fluide,* from Latin *fluidus,* from *fluere,* to flow. See **bhleu-** in Appendix.] —**flu·id′i·ty** (-ĭd′ĭ-tē), **flu′id·ness** *n.* —**flu′id·ly** *adv.*

fluid clutch *n.* See **fluid drive.**

fluid dram *n. Abbr.* **fl dr** A unit of volume or capacity in the apothecary system, equal to ⅛ of a fluid ounce (3.70 milliliters).

fluid drive *n.* An automotive transmission coupling that provides a smooth start, consisting of two separate turbines that rotate on the same axis in a surrounding liquid, such that the turbine connected to the engine drives the turbine connected to the transmission. Also called *fluid clutch.*

fluid dynamics *n. (used with a sing. verb).* The branch of applied science that is concerned with the movement of gases and liquids.

flu·id·ex·tract (flo͞o′ĭd-ĕk′străkt′) *n.* A concentrated alcohol solution of a vegetable drug of such strength that each milliliter contains the equivalent of one gram of the dry form of the drug.

flu·id·ic (flo͞o-ĭd′ĭk) *adj.* **1.** Of, relating to, or characteristic of a fluid. **2.** Relating to or controlled by fluidics.

flu·id·ics (flo͞o-ĭd′ĭks) *n. (used with a sing. verb).* The technology of using the flows and pressures of fluids in sensing, control, and information-processing systems with no moving parts.

flu·id·ize (flo͞o′ĭ-dīz′) *tr.v.* **-ized, -iz·ing, -iz·es. 1.** To make fluid. **2.** To pulverize (a solid) so finely that it takes on most of the properties of a fluid. —**flu′id·i·za′tion** (-ĭ-dĭ-zā′shən) *n.*

fluid mechanics *n. (used with a sing. verb).* The branch of mechanics concerned with the properties of gases and liquids.

fluid ounce *n. Abbr.* **fl oz, fl. oz. 1.** A unit of volume or capacity in the U.S. Customary System, used in liquid measure, equal to 29.57 milliliters (1.804 cubic inches). **2.** A unit of volume or capacity in the British Imperial System, used in liquid and dry measure, equal to 28.41 milliliters (1.734 cubic inches).

fluke[1] (flo͞ok) *n.* **1.** Any of various flatfishes, especially a flounder of the genus *Paralichthys.* **2.** See **trematode.** [Middle English, from Old English *flōc.* See **plāk-**[1] in Appendix.]

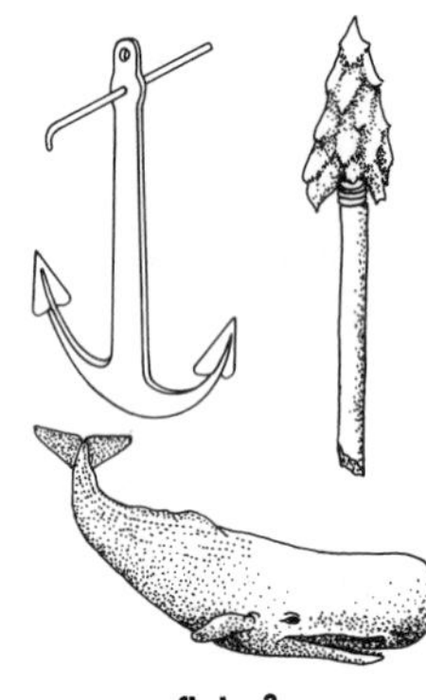

fluke[2]
Of an admiralty anchor (*top left*), an arrowhead (*top right*), and a sperm whale (*bottom*)

fluke[2] (flo͞ok) *n.* **1.** *Nautical.* The triangular blade at the end of an arm of an anchor, designed to catch in the ground. **2.** A barb or barbed head, as on an arrow or a harpoon. **3.** Either of the two horizontally flattened divisions of the tail of a whale. [Possibly from FLUKE[1].]

fluke[3] (flo͞ok) *n.* **1.** A stroke of good luck. **2.** A chance occurrence; an accident. **3.** *Games.* An accidentally good or successful stroke in billiards or pool. [Origin unknown.]

fluk·y also **fluk·ey** (flo͞o′kē) *adj.* **-i·er, -i·est. 1.** Resulting from or depending on mere chance. **2.** Constantly shifting; uncertain: *a fluky wind.* [From FLUKE[3].] —**fluk′i·ly** *adv.* —**fluk′i·ness** *n.*

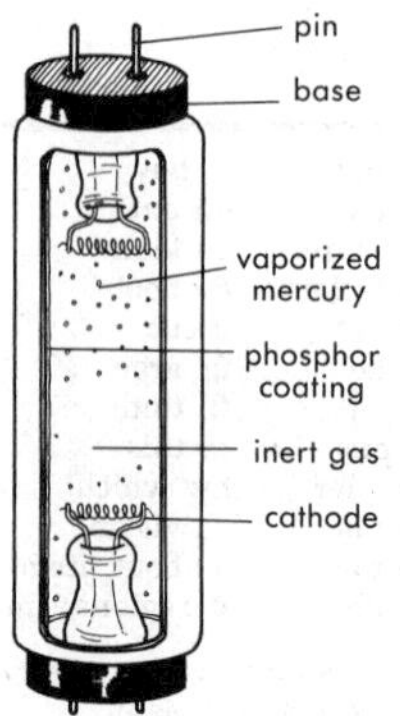

fluorescent lamp

flume (flo͞om) *n.* **1.** A narrow gorge, usually with a stream flowing through it. **2.** An open artificial channel or chute carrying a stream of water, as for furnishing power or conveying logs. [Middle English *flum,* river, from Old French, from Latin *flūmen,* from *fluere,* to flow. See **bhleu-** in Appendix.]

flum·mer·y (flŭm′ə-rē) *n., pl.* **-ies. 1.** Meaningless or deceptive language; humbug. **2.a.** Any of several soft, sweet, bland foods, such as custard. **b.** A sweet, gelatinous pudding made by straining boiled oatmeal or flour. [Welsh *llymru,* soft jelly from sour oatmeal.]

flum·mox (flŭm′əks) *tr.v.* **-moxed, -mox·ing, -mox·es.** *Informal.* To confuse; perplex. [Probably of English dialectal origin.]

flung (flŭng) *v.* Past tense and past participle of **fling.**

flunk (flŭngk) *Informal. v.* **flunked, flunk·ing, flunks.** —*intr.* To fail, especially in a course or an examination. —*tr.* **1.** To fail (an examination or course). **2.** To give a failing grade to. —**flunk** *n.* **1.** The act or an instance of flunking. **2.** A failing grade. —***phrasal verb.*** **flunk out.** To expel or be expelled from a school or course because of work that does not meet required standards. [Origin unknown.] —**flunk′er** *n.*

flun·key (flŭng′kē) *n.* Variant of **flunky.**

flunk·out (flŭngk′out′) *n. Informal.* One expelled from a school for failure to meet the required standards.

flun·ky also **flun·key** (flŭng′kē) *n., pl.* **-kies** also **-keys. 1.** A person of slavish or unquestioning obedience; a lackey. **2.** One who does menial or trivial work; a drudge. **3.** A liveried manservant. [Scots, perhaps from FLANKER, an attendant at one's flank.] —**flun′ky·ism** *n.*

WORD HISTORY: The word *flunky* has come into Standard English from Scots, in which the word meant "liveried manservant, footman," coming at least by the 19th century to be a term of contempt. The word is first recorded and defined in a work about Scots published in 1782. The definition states that a *flunky* is "literally a sidesman or attendant at your flank," which gives support to the suggestion that *flunky* is a derivative and alteration of *flanker,* "one who stands at a person's flank."

flu·or (flo͞o′ôr′, -ər) *n.* See **fluorite.** [New Latin, mineral belonging to a group used as fluxes, from Latin, a flowing, from *fluere,* to flow. See **bhleu-** in Appendix.]

fluor– *pref.* Variant of **fluoro–.**

fluo·resce (flo͞o-rĕs′, flô-, flō-) *intr.v.* **-resced, -resc·ing, -resc·es.** To undergo, produce, or show fluorescence. [Back-formation from FLUORESCENCE.] —**fluo·resc′er** *n.*

fluo·res·ce·in (flo͞o-rĕs′ē-ĭn, flô-, flō-) *n.* An orange-red compound, $C_{20}H_{12}O_5$, that exhibits intense fluorescence in alkaline solution and is used in medicine, in oceanography, and as a textile dye.

fluo·res·cence (flo͞o-rĕs′əns, flô-, flō-) *n.* **1.** The emission of electromagnetic radiation, especially of visible light, stimulated in a substance by the absorption of incident radiation and persisting only as long as the stimulating radiation is continued. **2.** The property of emitting such radiation. **3.** The radiation so emitted. [FLUOR(SPAR) + –ESCENCE.]

fluo·res·cent (flo͞o-rĕs′ənt, flô-, flō-) *adj.* **1.a.** Of or relating to fluorescence. **b.** Exhibiting or produced by fluorescence: *fluorescent plankton; fluorescent light.* **2.** Glowing as if with fluorescence; vivid: *bright fluorescent colors.* —**fluorescent** *n.* A fluorescent lamp.

fluorescent lamp *n.* A lamp that produces visible light by fluorescence, especially a glass tube whose inner wall is coated with a material that fluoresces when an electrical current causes a vapor within the tube to discharge electrons.

fluor·i·date (flo͝or′ĭ-dāt′, flôr′-, flōr′-) *tr.v.* **-dat·ed, -dat·ing, -dates.** To add a fluorine compound to (a drinking water supply, for example) for the purpose of reducing tooth decay.

fluor·i·da·tion (flo͝or′ĭ-dā′shən, flôr′-, flōr′-) *n.* The addition of a fluorine compound to a drinking water supply for the purpose of reducing tooth decay.

fluor·ide (flo͝or′īd′, flôr′-, flōr′-) *n.* A binary compound of fluorine with another element. [FLUOR(INE) + –IDE.]

fluor·i·na·tion (flo͝or′ĭ-nā′shən, flôr′-, flōr′-) *n.* A chemical reaction that introduces fluorine into a compound.

fluor·ine (flo͝or′ēn′, -ĭn, flôr′-, flōr′-) *n. Symbol* **F** A pale-yellow, highly corrosive, poisonous, gaseous halogen element, the most electronegative and most reactive of all the elements, used in a wide variety of industrially important compounds. Atomic number 9; atomic weight 18.9984; freezing point −219.62°C; melting point −223°C; boiling point −188.14°C; specific gravity of liquid 1.108 (at boiling point); valence 1. See table at **element.**

fluor·ite (flo͝or′īt′, flôr′-, flōr′-) *n.* A mineral, essentially CaF_2, that is often fluorescent in ultraviolet light and occurs in light green, blue, yellow, brown, and colorless forms. Also called *fluor, fluorspar.*

fluoro– or **fluor–** *pref.* **1.** Fluorine: *fluorosis.* **2.** Fluorescence: *fluoroscope.* [From FLUORINE and from FLUOR.]

fluor·o·car·bon (flo͝or′ō-kär′bən, flôr′-, flōr′-) *n.* An inert liquid or gaseous halocarbon compound in which fluorine replaces some or all hydrogen molecules, used as aerosol propellants, refrigerants, solvents, and lubricants and in making plastics and resins.

fluor·o·chem·i·cal (flo͝or′ō-kĕm′ĭ-kəl, flôr′-, flōr′-) *n.* A compound containing fluorine, especially a fluorocarbon.

fluor·o·chrome (flo͝or′ə-krōm′, flôr′-, flōr′-) *n.* Any of a group of fluorescent dyes used to stain biological specimens.

fluo·rog·ra·phy (flo͞o-rŏg′rə-fē, flô-, flō-) *n.* See **photofluorography.**

fluo·rom·e·ter (flo͞o-rŏm′ĭ-tər, flô-, flō-) *n.* An instrument for detecting and measuring fluorescence. —**fluo·rom′e·try** *n.*

fluor·o·scope (flo͝or′ə-skōp′, flôr′-, flōr′-) *n.* A device equipped with a fluorescent screen on which the internal structures of an optically opaque object, such as the human body, may be viewed as shadowy images formed by the differential transmission of x-rays through the object. Also called *roentgenoscope.* —**fluoroscope** *tr.v.* **-scoped, -scop·ing, -scopes.** To examine the interior of (an object) with a fluoroscope. —**fluor′o·scop′ic** (-skŏp′ĭk) *adj.* —**fluor′o·scop′i·cal·ly** *adv.*

fluo·ros·co·py (flo͞o-rŏs′kə-pē, flô-, flō-) *n., pl.* **-pies.** Examination by means of a fluoroscope. —**fluo·ros′co·pist** *n.*

fluo·ro·sis (flo͞o-rō′sĭs, flô-, flō-) *n.* An abnormal condition caused by excessive intake of fluorine, as from fluoridated drinking water, characterized chiefly by mottling of the teeth. **—fluo·rot′ic** (-rŏt′ĭk) *adj.*

fluor·o·u·ra·cil (flo͝or′ō-yo͝or′ə-sĭl, flôr′-, flōr′-) *n.* An antineoplastic agent, $C_4H_3FN_2O_2$, used especially in the treatment of cancers of the skin, breast, and digestive system.

flu·or·spar (flo͞o′ər-spär′, flo͝or′spär′) *n.* See **fluorite.**

flu·phen·a·zine (flo͞o-fĕn′ə-zēn′) *n.* A tranquilizing drug, $C_{22}H_{26}F_3N_3OS$, used especially in the form of its hydrochloride in psychotherapy. [FLU(ORO)– + PHENAZINE.]

flu·raz·e·pam (flo͞o-răz′ə-păm′) *n.* A mild hypnotic drug, $C_{21}H_{23}ClFN_3O$, used especially in the form of its hydrochloride in the treatment of insomnia. [FLU(O)R(O)– + (DI)AZEPAM.]

flur·ry (flûr′ē, flŭr′ē) *n., pl.* **-ries. 1.** A brief, light snowfall. **2.a.** A sudden gust of wind. **b.** A stirring mass, as of leaves or dust; a shower. **3.** A sudden burst or commotion; a stir: *a flurry of interest in the new product; a flurry of activity when the plane landed.* **4.** A short period of active trading, as on a stock exchange. **—flurry** *v.* **-ried, -ry·ing, -ries.** —*tr.* To agitate, stir, or confuse. —*intr.* To move or come down in a flurry. [Perhaps from *flurr,* to scatter.]

flush[1] (flŭsh) *v.* **flushed, flush·ing, flush·es.** —*intr.* **1.** To turn red, as from fever, embarrassment, or strong emotion; blush. **2.** To glow, especially with a reddish color: *The sky flushed pink at dawn.* **3.** To flow suddenly and abundantly, as from containment; flood. **4.** To be emptied or cleaned by a rapid flow of water, such as a toilet. —*tr.* **1.** To cause to redden or glow. **2.** To excite or elate: *The negotiators were flushed with the success of their final meeting.* **3.a.** To clean, rinse, or empty with a rapid flow of a liquid, especially water: *flush a toilet; flush a wound with iodine.* **b.** To remove or eliminate by or as if by flushing: *"The weakness in demand and productivity will at least . . . flush out some of the inflation premium that has been built into interest rates"* (Fortune). **—flush** *n.* **1.a.** A flooding flow or rush, as of water. **b.** The act of cleaning or rinsing by or as if by flushing. **2.** A blush or glow: *"here and there a flush of red on the lip of a little cloud"* (Willa Cather). **3.a.** A reddening of the skin, as with fever, emotion, or exertion. **b.** A brief sensation of heat over all or part of the body. **4.** A rush of strong feeling: *He felt a flush of pride as he watched his children.* **5.** A state of freshness or vigor. See Synonyms at **bloom[1]**. **—flush** *adj.* **flush·er, flush·est. 1.** Having a healthy reddish color; flushed. **2.** Having an abundant supply of money; affluent. See Synonyms at **rich. 3.** Marked by abundance; plentiful: *flush times resulting from the oil boom.* **4.** Swelling; overflowing: *rivers flush with the spring rains.* **5.a.** Having surfaces in the same plane; even. **b.** Arranged with adjacent sides, surfaces, or edges close together: *a sofa flush against the wall.* See Synonyms at **level. c.** *Printing.* Aligned evenly with a margin, as along the left or right edge of a typeset page; not indented. **6.** Direct, straightforward, or solid: *knocked out by a flush blow to the jaw.* **7.** Designed to be emptied or cleaned by flushing: *a flush toilet.* **—flush** *adv.* **1.** So as to be even, in one plane, or aligned with a margin. **2.** Squarely or solidly: *The ball hit him flush on the face.* [Probably from FLUSH[3], to dart out.] **—flush′er** *n.* **—flush′ness** *n.*

flush[2] (flŭsh) *n. Games.* A hand in which all the cards are of the same suit but not in numerical sequence, ranked above a straight and below a full house in poker. [French *flux, flus,* from Old French *flux,* from Latin *flūxus,* flux. See FLUX.]

flush[3] (flŭsh) *v.* **flushed, flush·ing, flush·es.** —*tr.* **1.** To frighten (a game bird, for example) from cover. **2.** To drive or force into the open: *The police fired tear gas to flush out the terrorists.* —*intr.* To dart out or fly from cover. **—flush** *n.* A bird or flock of birds that has been frightened from cover. [Middle English *flusshen.*]

Flush·ing (flŭsh′ĭng). **1.** A section of New York City in northern Queens on western Long Island. **2.** See **Vlissingen.**

flush·less toilet (flŭsh′lĭs) *n.* A toilet that disposes of waste without using water, especially one that utilizes bacteria to break down waste matter.

flush·om·e·ter (flŭsh-ŏm′ĭ-tər) *n.* A device for flushing toilets and urinals that utilizes pressure from the water supply system rather than the force of gravity to discharge water into the bowl, designed to use less water than conventional flush toilets.

flus·ter (flŭs′tər) *tr. & intr.v.* **-tered, -ter·ing, -ters.** To make or become nervous or upset. **—fluster** *n.* A state of agitation, confusion, or excitement. [From Middle English *flostring,* agitation, probably of Scandinavian origin. See **pleu-** in Appendix.]

flute (flo͞ot) *n. Abbr.* **fl. 1.** *Music.* **a.** A high-pitched woodwind instrument consisting of a slender tube closed at one end with keys and finger holes on the side and an opening near the closed end across which the breath is blown. Also called *transverse flute.* **b.** Any of various similar reedless woodwind instruments, such as the recorder. **c.** An organ stop whose flue pipe produces a flutelike tone. **2.a.** *Architecture.* A long, usually rounded groove incised as a decorative motif on the shaft of a column, for example. **b.** A similar groove or furrow, as in a pleated ruffle of cloth or on a piece of furniture. **3.** A tall, narrow wineglass, often used for champagne. **—flute** *v.* **flut·ed, flut·ing, flutes.** —*tr.* **1.** *Music.* To play (a tune) on a flute. **2.** To produce in a flutelike tone. **3.** To make flutes in (a column, for example). —*intr.* **1.** *Music.* To play a flute. **2.** To sing, whistle, or speak with a flutelike tone. [Middle English *floute,* from Old French *flaute* and from Middle Dutch *flute* (Middle Dutch, from Old French) from Old Provençal, perhaps a blend of *flaujol,* flageolet (from Vulgar Latin **flābeolum;* see FLAGEOLET), and *laut,* lute; see LUTE[1].] **—flut′er** *n.* **—flut′ey, flut′y** *adj.*

flut·ing (flo͞o′tĭng) *n.* **1.a.** *Architecture.* A decorative motif consisting of a series of uniform, usually vertical flutes, as those incised in the surface of a column. **b.** The act of incising or making grooves. **2.** The grooves formed by narrow pleats in cloth, as in a ruffle.

flut·ist (flo͞o′tĭst) *n. Music.* One who plays the flute.

flut·ter (flŭt′ər) *v.* **-tered, -ter·ing, -ters.** —*intr.* **1.** To wave or flap rapidly in an irregular manner: *curtains that fluttered in the breeze.* **2.a.** To fly by a quick, light flapping of the wings. **b.** To flap the wings without flying. **3.** To move or fall in a manner suggestive of tremulous flight: *"Her arms rose, fell, and fluttered with the rhythm of the song"* (Evelyn Waugh). **4.** To vibrate or beat rapidly or erratically: *My heart fluttered wildly.* **5.** To move quickly in a nervous, restless, or excited fashion; flit. —*tr.* To cause to flutter: *"fluttering her bristly black lashes as swiftly as butterflies' wings"* (Margaret Mitchell). **—flutter** *n.* **1.** The act of fluttering. **2.** A condition of nervous excitement or agitation: *Everyone was in a flutter over the news that the director was resigning.* **3.** A commotion; a stir. **4.** *Pathology.* Abnormally rapid pulsation, especially of the atria or ventricles of the heart. **5.** Rapid fluctuation in the pitch of a sound reproduction resulting from variations in the speed of the recording or reproducing equipment. **6.** *Chiefly British.* A small bet; a gamble: *"If they like a flutter, Rick will get them better odds than the bookies"* (John le Carré). [Middle English *floteren,* from Old English *floterian.* See **pleu-** in Appendix.] **—flut′ter·er** *n.* **—flut′ter·y** *adj.*

SYNONYMS: *flutter, flicker, flit, flitter, hover.* The central meaning shared by these verbs is "to move quickly, lightly, and irregularly like a bird in flight": *children fluttering around a birthday cake; flames that flickered in the night; guests flitting from table to table; sunlight flittering over the ocean; admirers hovering around a celebrity.*

flutter kick *n. Sports.* A swimming kick in which the legs are held horizontally and alternately moved up and down in rapid strokes without bending the knees.

flu·vi·al (flo͞o′vē-əl) *adj.* **1.** Of, relating to, or inhabiting a river or stream. **2.** Produced by the action of a river or stream. [Middle English, from Latin *fluviālis,* from *fluvius,* river, from *fluere,* to flow. See **bhleu-** in Appendix.]

flu·vi·a·tile (flo͞o′vē-ə-tīl′) *adj.* Fluvial. [French, from Latin *fluviātilis,* from *fluvius,* river. See FLUVIAL.]

flu·vi·o·ma·rine (flo͞o′vē-ō-mə-rēn′) *adj.* Relating to or being deposits, especially near the mouth of a river, formed by the combined action of river and sea. [Latin *fluvius,* river (from *fluere,* to flow; see **bhleu-** in Appendix) + MARINE.]

flux (flŭks) *n.* **1.a.** A flow or flowing. **b.** A continued flow; a flood. See Synonyms at **flow. 2.** The flowing in of the tide. **3.** *Medicine.* The discharge of large quantities of fluid material from the body, especially the discharge of watery feces from the intestines. **4.a.** The rate of flow of fluid, particles, or energy through a given surface. **b.** See **flux density. c.** The lines of force of a magnetic field. **5.** Constant or frequent change; fluctuation: *"The newness and flux of the computer industry has meant many opportunities for women and minorities"* (Connie Winkler). **6.** *Chemistry & Metallurgy.* A substance that aids, induces, or otherwise actively participates in fusing or flowing, as: **a.** A substance applied to a surface to be joined by welding, soldering, or brazing to facilitate the flowing of solder and prevent formation of oxides. **b.** A mineral added to the metals in a furnace to promote fusing or to prevent the formation of oxides. **c.** An additive that improves the flow of plastics during fabrication. **d.** A readily fusible glass or enamel used as a base in ceramic work. **—flux** *v.* **fluxed, flux·ing, flux·es.** —*tr.* **1.** To melt; fuse. **2.** To apply a flux to. —*intr.* **1.** To become fluid. **2.** To flow; stream. [Middle English, from Old French, from Latin *flūxus,* from past participle of *fluere,* to flow. See **bhleu-** in Appendix.]

flux density *n. Physics.* The rate of flux per unit area. Also called *flux.*

flux gate *n. Physics.* A detector used to indicate the direction of the earth's magnetic field.

flux·ion (flŭk′shən) *n.* **1.a.** A flow or flowing. **b.** Continual change. **2.** *Archaic.* **a.** See **derivative** (sense 3). **b. fluxions.** Differential calculus. [French, from Late Latin *flūxiō, flūxiōn-,* from Latin *flūxus,* flux. See FLUX.] **—flux′ion·al, flux′ion·ar′y** (flŭk′shə-nĕr′ē) *adj.* **—flux′ion·al·ly** *adv.*

fly[1] (flī) *v.* **flew** (flo͞o), **flown** (flōn), **fly·ing, flies** (flīz). —*intr.* **1.** To engage in flight, especially: **a.** To move through the air by means of wings or winglike parts. **b.** To travel by air: *We flew to Dallas.* **c.** To operate an aircraft or spacecraft. **2.a.** To rise in or be carried through the air by the wind: *a kite flying above the playground.* **b.** To float or flap in the air: *pennants flying from the masthead.* **3.** To move or be sent through the air with great speed: *bullets flying in every direction; a plate that flew from my hands when I stumbled.* **4.a.** To move with great speed; rush or dart: *The children flew down the hall. Rumors were flying during their absence.* **b.** To flee; escape. **c.** To hasten; spring: *flew to her students' defense.* **5.** To pass by swiftly: *a vacation flying by; youth that is soon flown.* **6.** To be dissipated; vanish: *Their small inheritance had quickly flown.* **7.** *past tense and past participle* **flied** (flīd). *Baseball.* To hit a fly ball. **8.** To undergo

flute

fluting

ă pat	oi boy
ā pay	ou out
âr care	o͝o took
ä father	o͞o boot
ĕ pet	ŭ cut
ē be	ûr urge
ĭ pit	th thin
ī pie	*th* this
îr pier	hw which
ŏ pot	zh vision
ō toe	ə about, item
ô paw	♦ regionalism

Stress marks: **′** (primary); ′ (secondary), as in **dictionary** (dĭk′shə-nĕr′ē)

an explosive reaction; burst: *The dropped plate flew into pieces. The motorist flew into a rage.* **9.** *Informal.* To gain acceptance or approval; go over: *"However sophisticated the reasoning, this particular notion may not fly"* (New York Times). —*tr.* **1.a.** To cause to fly or float in the air: *fly a kite; fly a flag.* **b.** *Nautical.* To operate under (a particular flag): *a tanker that flies the Liberian flag.* **2.a.** To pilot (an aircraft or a spacecraft). **b.** To carry or transport in an aircraft or a spacecraft: *fly emergency supplies to a stricken area.* **c.** To pass over or through in flight: *flew the coastal route in record time.* **d.** To perform in a spacecraft or an aircraft: *flew six missions into space.* **3.a.** To flee or run from: *fly a place in panic.* **b.** To avoid; shun: *fly temptation.* —**fly** *n., pl.* **flies. 1.** The act of flying; flight. **2.a.** A fold of cloth that covers a fastening of a garment, especially one on the front of trousers. **b.** The fastening or opening covered by such a fold. **3.** A flap that covers an entrance or forms a rooflike extension for a tent or the canopy of a vehicle. **4.** A flyleaf. **5.** *Baseball.* A fly ball. **6.a.** The span of a flag from the staff to the outer edge. **b.** The outer edge of a flag. **7.** A flywheel. **8. flies.** The area directly over the stage of a theater, containing overhead lights, drop curtains, and equipment for raising and lowering sets. **9.** *Chiefly British.* A one-horse carriage, especially one for hire. —***phrasal verb.* fly at.** To attack fiercely; assault: *The dogs flew at each other's throats.* —***idioms.* fly high.** To be elated: *They were flying high after their first child was born.* **fly off the handle.** *Informal.* To become suddenly enraged: *flew off the handle when the train was finally canceled.* **let fly. 1.** To shoot, hurl, or release: *The troops let fly a volley of gunfire.* **2.** To lash out; assault: *The mayor let fly with an angry attack on her critics.* **on the fly. 1.** On the run; in a hurry: *took lunch on the fly.* **2.** While in the air; in flight: *caught the ball on the fly.* [Middle English *flien,* from Old English *flēogan.* See **pleu-** in Appendix.] —**fly′a·ble** *adj.*

fly agaric
Amanita muscaria

fly² (flī) *n., pl.* **flies. 1.a.** Any of numerous two-winged insects of the order Diptera, especially any of the family Muscidae, which includes the housefly. **b.** Any of various other flying insects, such as the caddis fly. **2.** A fishing lure simulating a fly, made by attaching materials such as feathers, tinsel, and colored thread to a fishhook. —***idiom.* fly in the ointment.** A detrimental circumstance or detail; a drawback. [Middle English *flie,* from Old English *flēoge.* See **pleu-** in Appendix.]

fly³ (flī) *adj. Chiefly British.* Mentally alert; sharp. [Probably from FLY¹.]

fly agaric *n.* A poisonous mushroom *(Amanita muscaria)* usually having a red or orange cap with white gills and patches.

fly ash *n.* Fine particulate ash sent up by the combustion of a solid fuel, such as coal, and discharged as an airborne emission or recovered as a byproduct for various commercial uses.

fly·a·way (flī′ə-wā′) *adj.* **1.** Made or worn loose or draped, as to allow or suggest fluttering in the wind: *a flyaway coat; long, flyaway hair.* **2.a.** Prepared for immediate flight: *a plane in flyaway condition.* **b.** Designed for air travel: *flyaway bags.* **3.** Given to frivolity; flighty. —**flyaway** *n. Sports.* An aerial gymnastic move performed on the parallel bars, rings, or other apparatus, especially a flying dismount with a somersault.

flycatcher
Acadian flycatcher
Empidonax virescens

fly ball *n. Baseball.* A ball that is batted in a high arc, usually to the outfield.

fly·blow (flī′blō′) *n.* The egg or larva of a blowfly, usually deposited on meat. —**flyblow** *tr.v.* **-blew** (-blo͞o′), **-blown** (-blōn′), **-blow·ing, -blows. 1.** To deposit flyblows on. **2.** To contaminate; taint.

fly·blown (flī′blōn′) *adj.* **1.** Contaminated with flyblows. **2.a.** Tainted; corrupt: *a flyblown reputation.* **b.** Dirty or rundown; squalid: *a flyblown bar on the edge of town.*

fly·boat (flī′bōt′) *n. Nautical.* Any of various small, swift boats. [Alteration and partial translation of Dutch *vlieboot* : *Vlie,* a channel off the island of Vlieland in the northern Netherlands + *boot,* boat.]

fly book *n.* A case, usually in the form of a book, in which artificial flies for fishing are carried.

fly·boy or **fly-boy** (flī′boi′) *n. Slang.* A member of an air force, especially a pilot.

fly bridge *n. Nautical.* See **flying bridge.**

fly·by also **fly-by** (flī′bī′) *n., pl.* **-bys.** A flight passing close to a specified target or position, especially a maneuver in which a spacecraft or satellite passes sufficiently close to a body to make detailed observations without orbiting or landing.

fly-by-night (flī′bī-nīt′) *Informal. adj.* **1.** Unreliable or unscrupulous, especially with regard to business dealings: *"fly-by-night telephone companies that open up shop, sell some systems, then disappear when service is needed"* (Mary Ellen Jordan). **2.** Of an impermanent or insubstantial nature: *fly-by-night fashions in clothing.* —**fly-by-night** also **fly-by-night·er** (-nī′tər) *n.* **1.** An unscrupulous or undependable person, especially one who leaves secretly without paying creditors. **2.** Something of a shaky or impermanent nature.

flying bridge

fly-cast (flī′kăst′) *intr.v.* **-cast, -cast·ing, -casts.** To cast artificial flies with a fly rod, as in fishing. —**fly′-cast′er** *n.*

fly-cast·ing (flī′kăs′tĭng) *n.* The art or sport of casting artificial flies with a fly rod.

fly·catch·er (flī′kăch′ər, -kĕch′-) *n.* **1.** Any of various Eurasian birds of the family Muscicapidae that feed on insects, usually catching the insects in flight. **2.** Any of various similar American birds of the family Tyrannidae. In this sense, also called *tyrant flycatcher.*

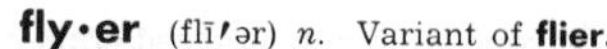

fly·er (flī′ər) *n.* Variant of **flier.**

fly-fish (flī′fĭsh′) *intr.v.* **-fished, -fish·ing, -fish·es.** To angle using artificial flies for bait and usually a fly rod for casting. —**fly′-fish′er·man, fly′-fish′er** *n.*

fly-fish·ing (flī′fĭsh′ĭng) *n.* The art or sport of angling with artificial flies for bait.

fly front *n.* A garment front that has a fly concealing the fastenings.

fly gallery *n.* A narrow elevated platform at the side of the stage in a theater, from which a stagehand works the ropes controlling equipment in the flies.

fly·ing (flī′ĭng) *adj.* **1.** Of or relating to aviation: *a flying time of three hours between cities.* **2.** Capable of or engaged in flight: *The bat is a flying mammal.* **3.** Situated, extending, or functioning in the air: *a flying deck.* **4.a.** Swiftly moving; fleet: *played the difficult passage with flying fingers.* **b.** Done or performed swiftly in or as if in the air: *crossed the goal line with a flying leap.* **5.** Brief; hurried: *made a flying visit to the neighbors' house; took a flying glance at the report.* **6.** Capable of swift deployment or response; extremely mobile. **7.** *Nautical.* Not secured by spars or stays. Used of a sail. —**flying** *n.* **1.** Flight in an aircraft or a spacecraft. **2.** The piloting or navigation of an aircraft or a spacecraft. —***idiom.* with flying colors.** With complete or outstanding success: *passed the Latin examination with flying colors.*

flying boat *n.* A large seaplane that floats on its hull rather than on pontoons.

flying bomb *n.* See **robot bomb.**

flying bridge *n. Nautical.* A small, usually open platform located above the main bridge, as on a powerboat, equipped with a secondary set of navigational controls. Also called *fly bridge.*

flying buttress *n. Architecture.* A masonry support consisting usually of a pier or buttress standing apart from the main structure and connected to it by an arch along which the thrust, as from the vaulting, is borne. Also called *arc-boutant.*

flying dragon *n.* See **flying lizard.**

Fly·ing Dutchman (flī′ĭng) *n.* **1.** A spectral ship said to appear in storms near the Cape of Good Hope. **2.** The captain of this ship, a legendary Dutch mariner condemned to sail the seas against the wind until Judgment Day.

flying field *n.* A graded field on which airplanes may land and take off.

flying fish *n.* Any of various marine fishes of the family Exocoetidae, having enlarged, winglike pectoral fins capable of sustaining them in brief, gliding flight over the water.

flying fox *n.* Any of various fruit-eating bats of the suborder Megachiroptera, chiefly inhabiting tropical Africa, Asia, and Australia and having a foxlike muzzle and small, pointed ears.

flying frog *n.* Either of two arboreal frogs *(Rhacophorus reinwardtii* or *R. nigropalmatus)* of southeast Asia, having toes connected by webbing and capable of making long, gliding leaps.

flying gecko *n.* Any of various small lizards of the genus *Ptychozoon* of southeast Asia, having extensions of skin along each side of the body that enable it to glide short distances.

flying gurnard *n.* Any of various chiefly tropical marine fishes of the family Dactylopteridae, having greatly enlarged, winglike pectoral fins that facilitate gliding through the water.

flying head *n.* A device that is designed to read and write information on a moving magnetic surface, as on a disk or drum, while being supported above the surface by a thin cushion of air.

flying jib *n. Nautical.* A light sail that extends beyond the jib and is attached to an extension of the jib boom.

flying lemur *n.* Either of two arboreal mammals, *Cynocephalus volans* of the Philippines or *C. variegatus* of southeast Asia, that are sustained in gliding leaps by a wide, fur-covered membrane extending from each side of the body. Also called *colugo.*

flying lizard *n.* Any of various small tropical Asian lizards of the genus *Draco,* having winglike membranes on each side of the body that may be spread to enable it to glide through the air. Also called *flying dragon.*

flying machine *n.* A machine designed for flight, especially an early experimental type of aircraft.

flying mare *n. Sports.* A wrestling throw in which one grabs one's opponent's wrist, turns one's back to the opponent, and flips the opponent over one's shoulder onto the ground.

flying phalanger *n.* Any of several small marsupials of the family Petauridae, especially one of the genus *Petaurus,* native to Australia, New Guinea, and Tasmania and having large folds of skin between the forelegs and hind legs that enable it to glide through the air.

flying saucer *n.* Any of various unidentified flying objects of presumed extraterrestrial origin, typically described as luminous moving disks.

flying squad *n. Chiefly British.* A small mobile unit, especially of motorized police, capable of moving quickly into action, as during an emergency.

flying squirrel *n.* Any of various nocturnal squirrels of the genera *Pteromys, Petaurista, Glaucomys,* and related genera, having membranes along each side of the body between the forelegs and hind legs that enable it to glide between trees.

flying start *n.* **1.** *Sports.* A racing start in which the contestants are already in full motion when they cross the starting line.

2. A quick or auspicious beginning. Also called *running start.*

flying wedge *n.* A compact, wedge-shaped formation, as of police or guards, moving as a body and used especially for penetrating crowds.

fly·leaf (flī′lēf′) *n.* A blank or specially printed leaf at the beginning or end of a book.

fly net *n.* A net covering used for protection from flying insects.

fly-o·ver (flī′ō′vər) *n.* **1.** A flight over a specific location, usually at low altitude, as by a formation of military aircraft. **2.** *Chiefly British.* An overpass, as on a highway.

fly·pa·per (flī′pā′pər) *n.* Paper coated with a sticky, sometimes poisonous substance, used to catch flies.

fly-past (flī′păst′) *n. Chiefly British.* A fly-over, as by military aircraft.

fly-poi·son (flī′poi′zən) *n.* A poisonous lily *(Amianthium muscitoxicum)* of the eastern United States, having narrow basal leaves and a terminal raceme of small white or greenish flowers.

Fly River (flī). A river, about 1,046 km (650 mi) long, rising in western Papua New Guinea and flowing generally southeastward to the Gulf of Papua.

fly rod *n.* A long, flexible fishing rod used in fly-fishing.

fly·sheet (flī′shēt′) *n.* A printed sheet or pamphlet; a handbill.

fly·speck (flī′spĕk′) *n.* **1.** A small dark speck or stain made by the excrement of a fly. **2.** A minute or insignificant spot. **—flyspeck** *tr.v.* **-specked, -speck·ing, -specks. 1.** To mark or foul with flyspecks. **2.** *Slang.* To examine closely or in minute detail; scrutinize: "[The company's] *performance will be flyspecked for clues as to how well it will do over the calendar year"* (Harry A. Stark).

♦**fly swat** *n. Chiefly Southern U.S.* See **fly swatter.**

♦**fly swatter** *n.* An implement used to kill flies or other insects, usually consisting of a piece of plastic or wire mesh attached to a long handle. Also called ♦*fly swat.*

fly·trap (flī′trăp′) *n.* **1.** A trap for catching flies. **2.** An insectivorous plant, such as the Venus's-flytrap.

fly-ty·ing (flī′tī′ĭng) *n.* The art or hobby of making artificial fishing flies. **—fly′-ti′er** (-tī′ər) *n.*

fly·way (flī′wā′) *n.* A seasonal route followed by birds migrating to and from their breeding areas.

fly·weight (flī′wāt′) *n.* **1.** *Sports.* **a.** A professional boxer weighing not more than 112 pounds (approximately 51 kilograms) or less than a bantamweight. **b.** A contestant in various other sports in the lightest weight class. **2.** Something that is particularly small, light, or inconsequential.

fly·wheel (flī′hwēl′, -wēl′) *n.* **1.** A heavy-rimmed rotating wheel used to minimize variations in angular velocity and revolutions per minute, as in a machine subject to fluctuation in drive and load. **2.** An analogous device, especially one used to regulate the speed of clockwork.

fly·whisk (flī′hwĭsk′, -wĭsk′) *n.* A whisk, as of hair, used for brushing away flies.

Fm The symbol for the element **fermium.**

FM *abbr.* **1.** Field manual. **2.** Also **F.M.** Field marshal. **3.** Also **fm.** Frequency modulation.

fm. *abbr.* **1.** Fathom. **2.** From.

FMB *abbr.* Federal Maritime Board.

FMCS *abbr.* Federal Mediation and Conciliation Service.

FMN *abbr.* Flavin mononucleotide.

FN *abbr.* Foreign national.

fn. *abbr.* Footnote.

FNMA *abbr.* Federal National Mortgage Association.

f-num·ber (ĕf′nŭm′bər) *n.* The ratio of the focal length of a lens or lens system to the effective diameter of its aperture. Also called *f-stop.* [F(OCAL LENGTH) + NUMBER.]

FO *abbr.* **1.** Also **F.O.** Field-grade officer. **2.** Field order. **3.** Finance officer. **4.** Also **F/O.** Flight officer. **5.** Also **F.O.** Foreign office.

foal (fōl) *n.* The young offspring of a horse or other equine animal, especially one under a year old. **—foal** *intr.v.* **foaled, foal·ing, foals.** To give birth to a foal. [Middle English *fole,* from Old English *fola.* See **pau-** in Appendix.]

foam (fōm) *n.* **1.a.** A mass of bubbles of air or gas in a matrix of liquid film, especially an accumulation of fine, frothy bubbles formed in or on the surface of a liquid, as from agitation or fermentation. **b.** A thick chemical froth, such as shaving cream or a substance used to fight fires. **2.a.** Frothy saliva produced especially as a result of physical exertion or a pathological condition. **b.** The frothy sweat of a horse or other equine animal. **3.** The sea. **4.** Any of various light, porous, semirigid or spongy materials used for thermal insulation or shock absorption, as in packaging. **—foam** *v.* **foamed, foam·ing, foams.** —*intr.* **1.** To produce or issue as foam; froth. **2.a.** To produce foam from the mouth, as from exertion or a pathological condition. **b.** To be extremely angry; rage: *was foaming over the disastrous budget cuts.* **3.** To teem; seethe: *a playground foaming with third graders.* —*tr.* **1.** To cause to produce foam. **2.** To cause to become foam. [Middle English *fom,* from Old English *fām.*]

foam·flow·er (fōm′flou′ər) *n.* A woodland plant *(Tiarella cordifolia)* of eastern North America, having a narrow cluster of small white flowers. Also called *false miterwort.*

foam rubber *n.* A light, firm, spongy rubber made by beating air into latex and then curing it. Foam rubber has a wide range of uses including upholstery and insulation.

foam·y (fō′mē) *adj.* **-i·er, -i·est. 1.** Of, relating to, or resembling foam. **2.** Consisting of or covered with foam. **—foam′i·ly** *adv.* **—foam′i·ness** *n.*

fob¹ (fŏb) *n.* **1.** A small pocket at the front waistline of a man's trousers or in the front of a vest, used especially to hold a watch. **2.a.** A short chain or ribbon attached to a pocket watch and worn hanging in front of the vest or waist. **b.** An ornament attached to such a chain or ribbon. [Probably of Germanic origin.]

fob² (fŏb) *tr.v.* **fobbed, fob·bing, fobs.** *Archaic.* To cheat or deceive (another). ***—phrasal verb.* fob off. 1.** To dispose of (goods) by fraud or deception; palm off: *fobbed off the zircon as a diamond.* **2.** To put off or appease by deceitful or evasive means: *needed help but was fobbed off with promises.* [Middle English *fobben,* probably from *fob,* trickster.]

f.o.b. also **F.O.B.** *abbr.* Free on board.

fo·cal (fō′kəl) *adj.* **1.** Of or relating to a focus. **2.** Placed at or measured from a focus. **—fo′cal·ly** *adv.*

focal distance *n. Abbr.* **FD** See **focal length.**

focal infection *n.* A bacterial infection localized in a specific part of the body, such as the tonsils, that may spread to another part of the body.

fo·cal·ize (fō′kə-līz′) *tr. & intr.v.* **-ized, -iz·ing, -iz·es. 1.** To adjust or come to a focus. **2.** To bring or be brought to a focus; sharpen. **3.** To concentrate or be concentrated; localize. **—fo′cal·i·za′tion** (-kə-lĭ-zā′shən) *n.*

focal length *n. Abbr.* **f, FL** The distance from the surface of a lens or mirror to its focal point. Also called *focal distance, focus.*

focal point *n.* See **focus** (sense 1a).

Foch (fôsh, fŏsh), **Ferdinand.** 1851–1929. French marshal and commander in chief on the western front during World War I.

fo·ci (fō′sī′, -kī′) *n.* A plural of **focus.**

fo'c's'le (fōk′səl) *n. Nautical.* Variant of **forecastle.**

fo·cus (fō′kəs) *n., pl.* **-cus·es** or **-ci** (-sī′, -kī′). **1.a.** A point at which rays of light or other radiation converge or from which they appear to diverge, as after refraction or reflection in an optical system: *the focus of a lens.* Also called *focal point.* **b.** See **focal length. 2.a.** The distinctness or clarity of an image rendered by an optical system. **b.** The state of maximum distinctness or clarity of such an image: *in focus; out of focus.* **c.** An apparatus used to adjust the focal length of an optical system in order to make an image distinct or clear: *a camera with automatic focus.* **3.** A center of interest or activity. See Synonyms at **center. 4.** Close or narrow attention; concentration: *"He was forever taken aback by* [New York's] *pervasive atmosphere of purposefulness—the tight focus of its drivers, the brisk intensity of its pedestrians"* (Anne Tyler). **5.** A condition in which something can be clearly apprehended or perceived: *couldn't get the problem into focus.* **6.** *Pathology.* The region of a localized bodily infection or disease. **7.** *Geology.* The point of origin of an earthquake. **8.** *Mathematics.* A fixed point whose relationship with a directrix determines a conic section. **—focus** *v.* **-cused, -cus·ing, -cus·es** or **-cussed, -cus·sing, -cus·ses.** —*tr.* **1.** To cause (light rays, for example) to converge on or toward a central point; concentrate. **2.a.** To render (an object or image) in clear outline or sharp detail by adjustment of one's vision or an optical device; bring into focus. **b.** To adjust (a lens, for example) to produce a clear image. **3.** To direct toward a particular point or purpose: *focused all their attention on finding a solution to the problem.* —*intr.* **1.** To converge on or toward a central point of focus; be focused. **2.** To adjust one's vision or an optical device so as to render a clear, distinct image. **3.** To concentrate attention or energy: *a campaign that focused on economic issues.* [Latin, hearth.] **—fo′cus·er** *n.*

focus group *n.* A small group selected from a wider population and sampled, as by open discussion, for its members' opinions about or emotional response to a particular subject or area, used especially in market research or political analysis.

fod·der (fŏd′ər) *n.* **1.** Feed for livestock, especially coarsely chopped hay or straw. **2.** Raw material, as for artistic creation. **3.** A consumable, often inferior item or resource that is in demand and usually abundant supply: *romantic novels intended as fodder for the pulp fiction market.* **—fodder** *tr.v.* **-dered, -der·ing, -ders.** To feed with fodder. [Middle English, from Old English *fōdor.* See **pā-** in Appendix.]

foe (fō) *n.* **1.** A personal enemy. **2.** An enemy in war. **3.** An adversary; an opponent: *a foe of tax reform.* See Synonyms at **enemy. 4.** Something that serves to oppose, injure, or impede: *endemic diseases that were the foe of economic development.* [Middle English *fo,* from Old English *gefā,* from *fāh,* hostile.]

foehn also **föhn** (fœn, fān) *n.* A warm, dry wind coming off the lee slopes of a mountain range, especially off the northern slopes of the Alps. [German *Föhn,* from Middle High German *fœnne,* from Old High German *phōno,* from Vulgar Latin **faōnius,* from Latin *favōnius,* the west wind, from *favēre,* to be favorable.]

foe·man (fō′mən) *n.* A foe in battle; an enemy.

foe·tal (fēt′l) *adj.* Variant of **fetal.**

foe·tid (fē′tĭd) *adj.* Variant of **fetid.**

foe·tor (fē′tər) *n.* Variant of **fetor.**

foe·tus (fē′təs) *n.* Variant of **fetus.**

fog¹ (fôg, fŏg) *n.* **1.** Condensed water vapor in cloudlike masses lying close to the ground and limiting visibility. **2.a.** An obscuring haze, as of atmospheric dust or smoke. **b.** A mist or film

flying buttress
Amiens Cathedral, France

flying squirrel

foal

ă pat	oi boy
ā pay	ou out
âr care	ŏŏ took
ä father	ōō boot
ĕ pet	ŭ cut
ē be	ûr urge
ĭ pit	th thin
ī pie	*th* this
îr pier	hw which
ŏ pot	zh vision
ō toe	ə about, item
ô paw	♦ regionalism

Stress marks: ′ (primary); ′ (secondary), as in **dictionary** (dĭk′shə-nĕr′ē)

clouding a surface, as of a window, lens, or mirror. **3.** A cloud of vaporized liquid, especially a chemical spray used in fighting fires. **4.a.** A state of mental vagueness or bewilderment. **b.** Something that obscures or conceals; a haze: *shrouded their actions in a fog of disinformation.* **5.** A blur on a developed photographic image. **—fog** *v.* **fogged, fog·ging, fogs.** *—tr.* **1.** To cover or envelop with or as if with fog. **2.** To cause to be obscured; cloud. **3.** To make vague, hazy, or confused: *a memory that had been fogged by time.* **4.** To obscure or dim (a photographic image). *—intr.* **1.** To be covered with or as if with fog. **2.** To be blurred, clouded, or obscured: *My glasses fogged in the warm air.* **3.** To be dimmed or obscured. Used of a photographic image. [Perhaps of Scandinavian origin.] **—fog′ger** *n.*

fog² (fôg, fŏg) *n.* **1.** A new growth of grass appearing on a field that has been mowed or grazed. **2.** Tall, decaying grass left standing after the cutting or grazing season. [Middle English *fogge,* tall grass. See **pŭ-** in Appendix.]

fog bank *n.* A dense mass of fog defined against clearer surrounding air, often as viewed from a distance at sea.

fog·bound (fôg′bound′, fŏg′-) *adj.* **1.** Immobilized by heavy fog: *a fogbound fleet.* **2.** Enveloped or obscured by fog: *fogbound cliffs.*

fog·bow (fôg′bō′, fŏg′-) *n.* A faint white or yellowish arc-shaped light, similar to a rainbow, that sometimes appears in fog opposite the sun. Also called *seadog.*

fog·dog (fôg′dôg′, -dŏg′, fŏg′-) *n.* A bright or clear spot that appears in breaking fog. [From the fact that it accompanies fog as a dog accompanies its owner.]

fo·gey (fō′gē) *n.* Variant of **fogy.**

Fog·gia (fô′jə). A city of southern Italy northeast of Naples. It is a transportation and industrial center. Population, 157,126.

fog·gy (fô′gē, fŏg′ē) *adj.* **-gi·er, -gi·est.** **1.a.** Full of or surrounded by fog. **b.** Resembling or suggestive of fog. **2.** Clouded or blurred by or as if by fog; vague: *had only a foggy memory of what had taken place; hasn't the foggiest idea how to get home.* **—fog′gi·ly** *adv.* **—fog′gi·ness** *n.*

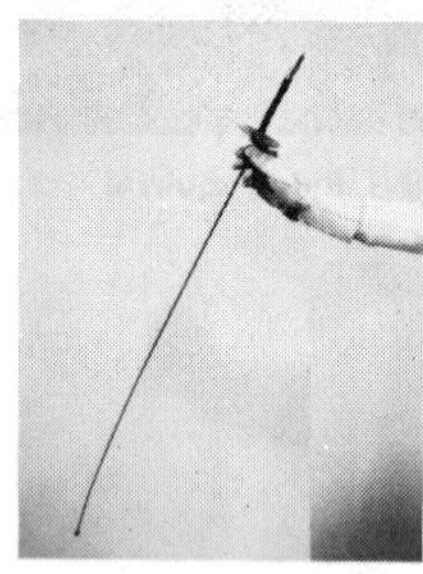

foil³

Fog·gy Bottom (fŏg′ē) *n.* The U.S. Department of State. [From the location of the Department of State in a low-lying area of Washington, D.C., near the Potomac River.]

fog·horn (fôg′hôrn′, fŏg′-) *n.* **1.** *Nautical.* A horn for sounding warning signals in fog or darkness, used especially on ships, buoys, and coastal installations. **2.** A booming, insistent voice.

fo·gy also **fo·gey** (fō′gē) *n., pl.* **-gies** also **-geys.** A person of stodgy or old-fashioned habits and attitudes. [Scots *fogey.*] **—fo′gy·ish** *adj.* **—fo′gy·ism** *n.*

föhn (fœn, fān) *n.* Variant of **foehn.**

foi·ble (foi′bəl) *n.* **1.** A minor weakness or failing of character. See Synonyms at **fault.** **2.** The weaker section of a sword blade, from the middle to the tip. [Obsolete French *foible,* weak point of a sword, weak, from Old French *feble,* weak. See FEEBLE.]

foil¹ (foil) *tr.v.* **foiled, foil·ing, foils.** **1.** To prevent from being successful; thwart. See Synonyms at **frustrate.** **2.** To obscure or confuse (a trail or scent) so as to evade pursuers. **—foil** *n. Archaic.* **1.** A repulse; a setback. **2.** The trail or scent of an animal. [Middle English *foilen,* to trample, defile, variant of *filen,* to defile. See FILE³.]

foil² (foil) *n.* **1.** A thin, flexible leaf or sheet of metal: *aluminum foil.* **2.** A thin layer of polished metal placed under a displayed gem to lend it brilliance. **3.** One that by contrast underscores or enhances the distinctive characteristics of another: *"I am resolved my husband shall not be a rival, but a foil to me"* (Charlotte Brontë). **4.** The reflective metal coating on the back of a glass mirror. **5.** *Architecture.* A curvilinear, often lobelike figure or space formed between the cusps of intersecting arcs, found especially in Gothic tracery and Moorish ornament. **6.a.** An airfoil. **b.** *Nautical.* A hydrofoil. **—foil** *tr.v.* **foiled, foil·ing, foils.** **1.** To cover or back with foil. **2.** To set off by contrast. [Middle English, from Old French *foille,* from Latin *folia,* pl. of *folium,* leaf. See **bhel-³** in Appendix.]

folding door

foil³ (foil) *n.* **1.** A fencing sword having a usually circular guard and a thin, flexible four-sided blade with a button on the tip to prevent injury. **2.** Often **foils.** The art or sport of fencing with such a sword: *a contest at foils.* [Origin unknown.]

foin (foin) *Archaic. intr.v.* **foined, foin·ing, foins.** To thrust with a pointed weapon. **—foin** *n.* A thrust with a pointed weapon. [Middle English *foinen,* from *foin,* a thrust, from Old French *foine,* pitchfork, from Latin *fuscina,* three-pronged fish spear.]

foi·son (foi′zən) *n.* **1.** *Scots.* Physical strength or power. **2.** *Archaic.* A plentiful harvest; abundance. **3. foisons.** *Obsolete.* Reserves of power; resources. [Middle English *foisoun,* from Old French *foison,* from Latin *fūsiō, fūsiōn-,* a pouring, from *fūsus,* past participle of *fundere,* to pour. See **gheu-** in Appendix.]

foist (foist) *tr.v.* **foist·ed, foist·ing, foists.** **1.** To pass off as genuine, valuable, or worthy: *"I can usually tell whether a poet . . . is foisting off on us what he'd like to think is pure invention"* (J.D. Salinger). **2.** To impose (something or someone unwanted) upon another by coercion or trickery: *They had extra work foisted on them because they couldn't say no to the boss.* **3.** To insert fraudulently or deceitfully: *foisted unfair provisions into the contract.* [Probably Dutch dialectal *vuisten,* to take in hand, from Middle Dutch, from *vuist,* fist. See **penkʷe** in Appendix.]

Fo·kine (fô-kēn′, fō-), **Michel.** 1880–1942. Russian-born American choreographer often considered the founder of modern ballet.

Fok·ker (fŏk′ər, fô′kər), **Anthony Herman Gerard.** 1890–1939. Dutch-born American aircraft designer and manufacturer who revolutionized aerial warfare by synchronizing a front-mounted machine gun (1915).

fol. *abbr.* **1.** Folio. **2.** Following.

fol·a·cin (fŏl′ə-sĭn) *n.* See **folic acid.** [FOL(IC) AC(ID) + -IN.]

fo·late (fō′lāt′) *n.* **1.** A salt or ester of folic acid. **2.** See **folic acid.** [FOL(IC ACID) + -ATE².]

fold¹ (fōld) *v.* **fold·ed, fold·ing, folds.** *—tr.* **1.** To bend over or double up so that one part lies on another part: *fold a sheet of paper.* **2.** To make compact by doubling or bending over parts: *folded the laundry; folded the chairs for stacking.* **3.** To bring from an extended to a closed position: *The hawk folded its wings.* **4.** To bring from a compact to an extended position; unfold: *a suitcase that folds out to become a display table; folded the ironing board down from the wall.* **5.** To place together and intertwine: *fold one's arms.* **6.** To envelop or clasp; enfold: *folded his children to his breast; folded the check into the letter.* **7.** To blend in (a cooking ingredient) by gently turning a mixture on top of it: *folded the beaten egg whites into the batter.* **8.a.** *Informal.* To discontinue operating; close: *They had to fold the company a year after they started it.* **b.** *Games.* To withdraw (one's hand) in defeat, as by laying cards face down on a table. **9.** *Geology.* To form bends in (a stratum of rock). *—intr.* **1.a.** To become folded. **b.** To be capable of being folded: *a bed that folds for easy storage.* **2.** *Informal.* To close, especially for lack of financial success; fail. **3.** *Games.* To withdraw from a game in defeat. **4.** *Informal.* **a.** To give in; buckle: *a team that never folded under pressure.* **b.** To weaken or collapse from exertion. **—fold** *n.* **1.** The act or an instance of folding. **2.** A part that has been folded over or against another: *the loose folds of the drapery; clothes stacked in neat folds.* **3.** A line or mark made by folding; a crease: *tore the paper carefully along the fold.* **4.** A coil or bend, as of rope. **5.** *Chiefly British.* A hill or dale in undulating country. **6.** *Geology.* A bend in a stratum of rock. **7.** *Anatomy.* A crease or ridge apparently formed by folding, as of a membrane; a plica. [Middle English *folden,* from Old English *fealdan, faldan.* See **pel-²** in Appendix.] **—fold′a·ble** *adj.*

fold² (fōld) *n.* **1.** A fenced enclosure for domestic animals, especially sheep. **2.** A flock of sheep. **3.a.** A group of people or institutions bound together by common beliefs and aims: *"He is a living testament to the wisdom of admitting lay psychoanalysts into the official fold"* (Jerome Bruner). **b.** A religious congregation: *The priest welcomed new parishioners into the fold.* **—fold** *tr.v.* **fold·ed, fold·ing, folds.** To place or keep (sheep, for example) in a fenced enclosure. [Middle English, from Old English *fald.*]

-fold *suff.* **1.** Divided into a specified number of parts: *fivefold.* **2.** Multiplied by a specified number: *fiftyfold.* [Middle English, from Old English *-feald, -fald.* See **pel-²** in Appendix.]

fold·a·way (fōld′ə-wā′) *adj.* Designed to be folded up for easy storage: *a foldaway bed.* **—fold′a·way′** *n.*

fold·boat (fōld′bōt′) *n. Nautical.* A small boat resembling a kayak, consisting of rubberized canvas stretched over a collapsible frame. Also called *faltboat.* [Translation of German *Faltboot.*]

fold·er (fōl′dər) *n.* **1.** One that folds or is folded, such as a booklet or pamphlet made of one or more folded sheets of paper. **2.** A flexible cover folded in the center and used as a holder for loose paper: *a file folder; a hanging folder.*

fol·de·rol (fŏl′də-rŏl′) also **fal·de·ral** (făl′də-răl′) *n.* **1.** Foolishness; nonsense. **2.** A trifle; a gewgaw. [From a nonsense refrain in some old songs.]

fold·ing door (fōl′dĭng) *n.* A door with hinged or pleated sections that fold together when the door is opened.

folding money *n.* Paper money.

fold·out (fōld′out′) *n.* **1.** *Printing.* A folded insert or section, as of a cover, whose full size exceeds that of the regular page. **2.** A piece or part, as of furniture, that folds out or down from a closed position. **—fold′out′** *adj.*

fold·up (fōld′ŭp′) *adj.* Designed to fold up, as for storage or carrying; collapsible: *a foldup umbrella; a foldup crib.* **—foldup** *n.* **1.** An object that folds up. **2.** *Informal.* A complete failure or breakdown; a collapse: *"The Giants are hoping that* [he] *can avoid his foldup of last season and help them remain in the race"* (Los Angeles Times).

fo·li·a (fō′lē-ə) *n.* *Geology & Mathematics.* Plural of **folium.**

fo·li·a·ceous (fō′lē-ā′shəs) *adj.* **1.** Of, relating to, or resembling the leaf of a plant. **2.** Having leaves or leaflike structures. **3.** *Geology.* Consisting of thin, leaflike layers, as of minerals. [From Latin *foliāceus,* from *folium,* leaf. See FOLIUM.]

fo·li·age (fō′lē-ĭj, fō′lĭj) *n.* **1.a.** Plant leaves, especially tree leaves, considered as a group. **b.** A cluster of leaves. **2.** An ornamental representation of leaves, stems, and flowers, especially in architecture. [Alteration (influenced by Latin *folium,* leaf) of Middle English *foilage,* from Old French *foillage,* from *foille,* leaf. See FOIL².] **—fo′li·aged** *adj.*

foliage plant *n.* A plant cultivated chiefly for its ornamental leaves.

fo·li·ar (fō′lē-ər) *adj.* Of or relating to a leaf or leaves. [New Latin *foliāris,* from Latin *folium,* leaf. See FOLIUM.]

fo·li·ate (fō′lē-ĭt, -āt′) *adj.* **1.** Of or relating to leaves. **2.**

Shaped like a leaf. **3.** *Geology.* Foliated. **—foliate** (-āt′) *v.* **-at·ed, -at·ing, -ates.** —*tr.* **1.** To hammer or cut (metal) into thin leaf or foil. **2.a.** To coat (glass, for example) with metal foil. **b.** To furnish or adorn with metal foil. **3.** To separate into thin layers or laminae. **4.** To decorate with foliage or foils: *an arch that is foliated in the Gothic style.* **5.** To number the leaves of (a manuscript, for example). —*intr.* **1.** To produce foliage. **2.** To split into thin leaflike layers or folia. [Latin *foliātus,* bearing foliage, from *folium,* leaf. See FOLIUM.]

–foliate *suff.* Having a specified kind or number of leaves: *trifoliate.* [From FOLIATE.]

fo·li·at·ed (fō′lē-ā′tĭd) *adj. Geology.* Of or relating to rock that exhibits a layered structure.

fo·li·a·tion (fō′lē-ā′shən) *n.* **1.** The state of being in leaf. **2.** Decoration with sculpted or painted foliage. **3.** *Architecture.* Decoration of an opening with cusps and foils, as in Gothic tracery. **4.a.** The act, process, or product of forming metal into thin leaf or foil. **b.** The act or process of coating glass with metal foil. **5.a.** The process of numbering consecutively the leaves of a book or manuscript. **b.** The leaves so numbered. **6.** *Geology.* The layered structure common to metamorphic rocks.

fo·lic acid (fō′lĭk, fŏl′ĭk) *n.* A yellowish-orange compound, $C_{19}H_{19}N_7O_6$, of the vitamin B complex group, occurring in green plants, fresh fruit, liver, and yeast. Also called *folacin, folate, vitamin B_c.* [Latin *folium,* leaf; see FOLIUM + –IC.]

fo·lie à deux (fô-lē′ ä dœ′, fŏl′ē) *n.* A condition in which symptoms of a mental disorder, such as delusive beliefs or ideas, occur simultaneously in two individuals who share a close relationship or association. [French : *folie,* madness + *à,* between + *deux,* two.]

fo·li·ic·o·lous (fō′lē-ĭk′ə-ləs) *adj.* Thriving on or parasitic to leaves. [Latin *folium,* leaf; see **bhel-**[3] in Appendix + –COLOUS.]

fo·li·o (fō′lē-ō′) *n., pl.* **-os.** *Abbr.* **f., F., fol. 1.a.** A large sheet of paper folded once in the middle, making two leaves or four pages of a book or manuscript. **b.** A book or manuscript of the largest common size, usually about 38 centimeters (15 inches) in height, consisting of such folded sheets. **2.a.** A leaf of a book numbered only on the front side. **b.** A number on such a leaf. **c.** A page number. **3.** *Accounting.* A page in a ledger or two facing pages that are assigned a single number. **4.** *Law.* A specific number of words used as a unit for measuring the length of the text of a document. **—folio** *tr.v.* **-oed, -o·ing, -os.** To number consecutively the pages or leaves of (a book, for example). [Middle English, from Late Latin *foliō,* ablative of *folium,* leaf of paper, from Latin, leaf. See **bhel-**[3] in Appendix.]

–foliolate *suff.* Having a specified kind or number of leaflets: *bifoliolate.* [New Latin *foliolātus,* from French *foliole,* leaflet, from Late Latin *foliolum,* diminutive of Latin *folium,* leaf. See FOLIUM.]

fo·li·ose (fō′lē-ōs′) *adj.* **1.** Bearing numerous leaves; leafy. **2.** Of, relating to, or resembling a leaf. **3.** Of or relating to a lichen whose thallus is flat and leafy. [Latin *foliōsus,* from *folium,* leaf. See FOLIUM.]

fo·li·um (fō′lē-əm) *n., pl.* **-li·a** (-lē-ə). **1.** *Geology.* A thin, leaflike layer or stratum occurring especially in metamorphic rock. **2.** *Mathematics.* A plane cubic curve having a single loop, a node, and two ends asymptotic to the same line. [Latin, leaf. See **bhel-**[3] in Appendix.]

folk (fōk) *n., pl.* **folk** or **folks. 1.a.** The common people of a society or region considered as the representatives of a traditional way of life and especially as the originators or carriers of the customs, beliefs, and arts that make up a distinctive culture: *a leader who came from the folk.* **b.** *Archaic.* A nation; a people. **2. folks.** *Informal.* People in general: *Folks around here will always lend a hand if you need it.* **3.** Often **folks.** People of a specified group or kind: *city folks; rich folk.* **4. folks.** *Informal.* **a.** The members of one's family or childhood household; one's relatives. **b.** One's parents: *My folks are always forgetting my allowance.* **—folk** *adj.* Of, occurring in, or originating among the common people: *folk culture; a folk hero.* **—*idiom.* just folks.** *Informal.* Down-to-earth, open-hearted. [Middle English, from Old English *folc.* See **pele-**[1] in Appendix.]

folk art also **folk-art** (fōk′ärt′) *n.* Art originating among the common people of a nation or region and usually reflecting their traditional culture, especially everyday or festive items produced or decorated by unschooled artists. **—folk artist** *n.*

folk dance or **folk-dance** also **folk·dance** (fōk′dăns′) *n.* **1.a.** A traditional dance originating among the common people of a nation or region. **b.** The music accompanying such a dance. **2.** A social gathering at which folk dances are performed. **—folk′-dance′** *adj.* **—folk dancer** *n.* **—folk danc′ing** (dăn′sĭng) *n.*

folk etymology also **folk-et·y·mol·o·gy** (fōk′ĕt-ə-mŏl′ə-jē) *n.* A change in the form of a word or phrase resulting from a mistaken assumption about its composition or meaning, as in *shamefaced* for earlier *shamfast,* "bound by shame," or *cutlet* from French *côtelette,* "little rib."

folk·ie also **folk·y** (fō′kē) *Music.* —*n., pl.* **-ies.** A folk singer or musician. —*adj.* **-i·er, -i·est.** Of, relating to, or in the style of folk music.

folk·ish (fō′kĭsh) *adj.* **1.** Of or characteristic of folk music, art, or literature. **2.** Simple or natural; folksy: *charmed us with his folkish wit and humor.* **—folk′ish·ly** *adv.* **—folk′ish·ness** *n.*

folk linguistics *n.* *(used with a sing. verb).* Popular belief or speculation about how language is used, especially by a group or an element of a population.

folk·lore (fōk′lôr′, -lōr′) *n.* **1.** The traditional beliefs, myths, tales, and practices of a people, transmitted orally. **2.** The comparative study of folk knowledge and culture. Also called *folkloristics.* **3.a.** A body of widely accepted but usually specious notions about a place, a group, or an institution: *Rumors of their antics became part of the folklore of Hollywood.* **b.** A popular but unfounded belief. **—folk′lor′ic** *adj.* **—folk′lor′ish** *adj.* **—folk′lor′ist** *n.* **—folk′lor·is′tic** *adj.*

folk·lor·is·tics (fōk′lô-rĭs′tĭks, -lō-) *n.* *(used with a sing. verb).* See **folklore** (sense 2).

folk Mass also **folk mass** *n.* A Mass in which folk music is used as part of the service instead of liturgical music.

folk medicine *n.* Traditional medicine as practiced by nonprofessional healers or embodied in local custom or lore, generally involving the use of natural and especially herbal remedies.

folk·moot (fōk′mo͞ot′) or **folk·mote** (-mōt′) *n.* A general assembly of the people of a town, district, or shire in medieval England. [Middle English, from Old English *folcmōt* : *folc,* folk; see FOLK + *mōt,* meeting.]

folk music *n. Music.* **1.** Music originating among the common people of a nation or region and spread about or passed down orally, often with considerable variation. **2.** Contemporary music in the style of traditional folk music. **—folk′-mu′sic** (fōk′myo͞o′zĭk) *adj.*

folk-rock or **folk rock** (fōk′rŏk′) *n. Music.* A variety of popular music combining elements of rock 'n' roll and folk music. **—folk′-rock′** *adj.*

folk·sing·er or **folk-sing·er** also **folk sing·er** (fōk′sĭng′ər) *n. Music.* A singer of folksongs. **—folk sing′ing** (sĭng′ĭng) *n.*

folk·song or **folk-song** also **folk song** (fōk′sông′, -sŏng′) *n. Music.* **1.** A song belonging to the folk music of a people or area, often existing in several versions or with regional variations. **2.** A song composed in the style of traditional folk music.

folk·sy (fōk′sē) *adj.* **-si·er, -si·est.** *Informal.* **1.** Simple and unpretentious in behavior. **2.** Characterized by informality and affability: *a friendly, folksy town.* **3.** Modest; low-key: *folksy humor; a folksy style that masked a keen business mind.* **—folk′si·ly** *adv.* **—folk′si·ness** *n.*

folk·tale or **folk-tale** also **folk tale** (fōk′tāl′) *n.* A story or legend forming part of an oral tradition.

folk·way (fōk′wā′) *n.* A practice, custom, or belief shared by the members of a group as part of their common culture. Often used in the plural.

folk·y (fō′kē) *n. & adj. Music.* Variant of **folkie.**

fol·li·cle (fŏl′ĭ-kəl) *n.* **1.** *Anatomy.* **a.** A small bodily cavity or sac: *a hair follicle.* **b.** A cavity in the ovary containing a maturing ovum surrounded by its encasing cells. **2.** *Botany.* A dry, single-chambered fruit that splits along only one seam to release its seeds, as in larkspur and milkweed. [Latin *folliculus,* little bag, diminutive of *follis,* bellows. See **bhel-**[2] in Appendix.]

follicle mite *n.* Any of various tiny mites of the genus *Demodex* that infest the hair follicles of mammals.

fol·li·cle-stim·u·lat·ing hormone (fŏl′ĭ-kəl-stĭm′yə-lā′tĭng) *n. Abbr.* **FSH** A gonadotropic hormone of the anterior pituitary gland that stimulates the growth of follicles in the ovary and induces the formation of sperm in the testis.

fol·lic·u·lar (fə-lĭk′yə-lər) *adj.* **1.** Relating to, having, or resembling a follicle or follicles. **2.** Affecting or growing out of a follicle or follicles.

fol·lic·u·late (fə-lĭk′yə-lĭt) also **fol·lic·u·lat·ed** (-lā′tĭd) *adj.* Having or consisting of a follicle or follicles.

fol·lic·u·li·tis (fə-lĭk′yə-lī′tĭs) *n.* Inflammation of a follicle, especially of a hair follicle. [Latin *folliculus,* follicle; see FOLLICLE + –ITIS.]

fol·low (fŏl′ō) *v.* **-lowed, -low·ing, -lows.** —*tr.* **1.** To come or go after; proceed behind: *Follow the usher to your seat.* **2.a.** To go after in or as if in pursuit: *"The wrong she had done followed her and haunted her dream"* (Katherine Anne Porter). **b.** To keep under surveillance: *followed the suspect for a week before making the arrest.* **3.a.** To move along the course of; take: *We followed a path to the shore.* **b.** To go in the direction of; be guided by: *followed the sun westward across the plains; followed the signs to the monkey house.* **4.** To accept the guidance, command, or leadership of: *follow a spiritual master; rebels who refused to follow their commander.* **5.** To adhere to; practice: *followed the ancient customs of their people.* **6.** To take as a model or precedent; imitate: *followed her new friends in everything they did; followed my example and resigned.* **7.a.** To act in agreement or compliance with; obey: *follow the rules; follow one's instincts.* **b.** To keep to or stick to: *followed the recipe; follow a diet.* **8.** To engage in (a trade or occupation); work at. **9.** To come after in order, time, or position: *Night follows day.* **10.** To bring something about at a later time than or as a consequence of: *She followed her lecture with a question-and-answer period. The band followed its hit record with a national tour.* **11.** To occur or be evident as a consequence of: *Your conclusion does not follow your premise.* **12.a.** To watch or observe closely: *followed the bird through binoculars.* **b.** To be attentive to; pay close heed to: *too sleepy to follow the sermon.* **c.** To keep oneself informed of the course, progress, or fortunes of: *follow the stock market; followed*

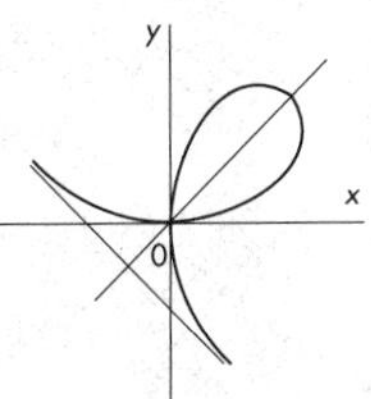

folium
Folium of Descartes

folk dance

ă pat	oi boy
ā pay	ou out
âr care	o͝o took
ä father	o͞o boot
ĕ pet	ŭ cut
ē be	ûr urge
ĭ pit	th thin
ī pie	*th* this
îr pier	hw which
ŏ pot	zh vision
ō toe	ə about, item
ô paw	♦ regionalism

Stress marks: ′ (primary); ′ (secondary), as in **dictionary** (dĭk′shə-nĕr′ē)

Henry Fonda
Holding his American Film Institute's Life Achievement Award; photographed with daughter Jane in 1978

the local teams. **13.** To grasp the meaning or logic of; understand: *Do you follow my argument?* —*intr.* **1.** To come, move, or take place after another person or thing in order or time. **2.** To occur or be evident as a consequence; result: *If you ignore your diet, trouble will follow.* **3.** To grasp the meaning or reasoning of something; understand. **—follow** *n.* **1.** The act or an instance of following. **2.** *Games.* A billiards shot in which the cue ball is struck above center so that it follows the path of the object ball after impact. **—*phrasal verbs.* follow along.** To move or proceed in unison or in accord with an example: *followed along with the song.* **follow through. 1.** *Sports.* To carry a stroke to natural completion after hitting or releasing a ball or other object. **2.** To carry an act, a project, or an intention to completion; pursue fully: *followed through on her promise to reorganize the department.* **follow up. 1.** To carry to completion; follow through on: *followed up their recommendations with concrete proposals.* **2.** To increase the effectiveness or enhance the success of by further action: *followed up her interview with a telephone call.* **—*idioms.* as follows.** As will be stated next. Used to introduce a specified enumeration, explanation, or command. **follow (one's) nose. 1.** To move straight ahead or in a direct path. **2.** *Informal.* To be guided by instinct: *had no formal training but became a success by following his nose.* **follow suit. 1.** *Games.* To play a card of the same suit as the one led. **2.** To do as another has done. [Middle English *folowen,* from Old English *folgian.*]

SYNONYMS: *follow, succeed, ensue, result, supervene.* These verbs mean to come after something or someone. *Follow,* which has the widest application, can refer to coming after in time or order, as a consequence or result, or by the operation of logic: *Night follows day. If you disregard the doctor's orders, a relapse will follow. Though he disapproves of violence, it doesn't follow that he won't defend himself.* To *succeed* is to come next after another in time or order, especially in planned order determined by considerations such as rank, inheritance, or election: *"The son of a mandarin has no prescriptive right to succeed his father"* (H.G. Wells). *The heir apparent succeeded to the throne. Ensue* applies to what follows something, usually as a consequence or by way of logical development: *If a forest fire cannot be extinguished, devastation is sure to ensue. Result* implies that what follows is caused by what has preceded: *Failure to file an income tax return can result in a fine. Supervene,* in contrast, refers to the coming after of a thing that has little relation to what has preceded and that is often unexpected: *"A bad harvest supervened. Distress reached its climax"* (Charlotte Brontë).

USAGE NOTE: *As follows* (not *as follow*) is the established form of the idiom, no matter whether the noun that precedes it is singular or plural: *The regulations are as follows.*

fondue

fol·low·er (fŏl′ō-ər) *n.* **1.** One who subscribes to the teachings or methods of another; an adherent: *a follower of Gandhi.* **2.** A servant; a subordinate. **3.** A fan; an enthusiast. **4.** One that imitates or copies another: *A successful marketing campaign will have many followers.* **5.** A machine element moved by another machine element.

fol·low·er·ship (fŏl′ō-ər-shĭp′) *n.* **1.** The act or condition of following a leader; adherence: *"It was not a crisis of leadership. It was a crisis of followership"* (Christian Science Monitor). **2.** A group of followers; a following: *"It is hard to have leadership when you have a divided followership"* (Joseph Badaracco).

fol·low·ing (fŏl′ō-ĭng) *adj. Abbr.* **fol., ff., f. 1.** Coming next in time or order: *in the following chapter.* **2.** Now to be enumerated: *The following people will report for duty.* **3.** Blowing in the same direction as the course of a ship or an aircraft. Used of wind. **—following** *n.* A group or gathering of admirers, adherents, or disciples: *a lecturer with a large following.* **—following** *prep.* Subsequent to; after: *Following dinner, brandy was served in the study.*

fol·low-on (fŏl′ō-ŏn′, -ôn′) *adj.* Following as a related or consequent aspect or development: *"Such contracts involve follow-on sales of maintenance services"* (Christian Science Monitor). **—fol′low-on′** *n.*

follow shot *n.* **1.** A shot in a movie in which the camera follows behind or along with a moving subject. **2.** *Games.* A follow in billiards.

fol·low-through or **fol·low·through** (fŏl′ō-thro͞o′) *n.* **1.** The act or an instance of following through: *a book promotion campaign with no follow-through.* **2.** *Sports.* The concluding part of a stroke, after a ball or other object has been hit or released.

fol·low-up or **fol·low·up** (fŏl′ō-ŭp′) —*n.* **1.** The act or an instance of following up, as to further an end or review new developments: *The follow-up is often as important as the initial contact in gaining new clients. The social worker's emphasis on followup reassured her clients.* **2.** One that follows so as to further an end or increase effectiveness: *The software was a successful follow-up to the original product.* **3.** An article or a report giving further information on a previously reported item of news. —*adj.* Intended to follow up, as to reinforce or evaluate previous action: *follow-up services that are provided by the sales department; a followup examination after the surgery.*

font¹
Baptismal font

fol·ly (fŏl′ē) *n., pl.* **-lies. 1.** A lack of good sense, understanding, or foresight. **2.a.** An act or instance of foolishness: *regretted the follies of his youth.* **b.** A costly undertaking having an absurd or ruinous outcome. **3. follies.** *(used with a sing. or pl. verb).* An elaborate theatrical revue consisting of music, dance, and skits.

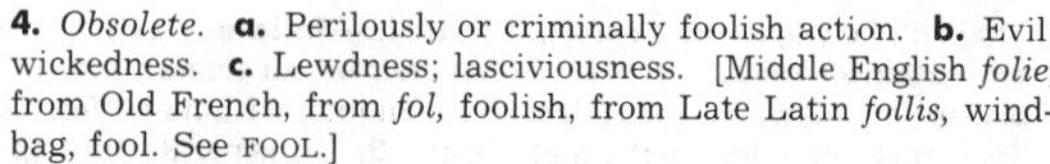

4. *Obsolete.* **a.** Perilously or criminally foolish action. **b.** Evil; wickedness. **c.** Lewdness; lasciviousness. [Middle English *folie,* from Old French, from *fol,* foolish, from Late Latin *follis,* windbag, fool. See FOOL.]

Fol·som (fōl′səm) *adj.* Of or relating to a culture that flourished in western North America east of the Rocky Mountains during the late Pleistocene period, notable chiefly for the use of grooved, leaf-shaped flint projectile points. [After *Folsom,* a town of northeast New Mexico.]

Fo·mal·haut (fō′məl-hôt′) *n.* The brightest star in the constellation Piscis Austrinus, 24 light-years from Earth. [Arabic *fum al-hūt,* mouth of the fish, Fomalhaut.]

fo·ment (fō-mĕnt′) *tr.v.* **-ment·ed, -ment·ing, -ments. 1.** To promote the growth of; incite. See Synonyms at **incite. 2.** To treat (the skin, for example) by fomentation. [Middle English *fomenten,* to apply warm liquids to the skin, from Old French *fomenter,* from Late Latin *fōmentāre,* from Latin *fōmentum,* from **fovementum,* from *fovēre,* to warm.] **—fo·ment′er** *n.*

fo·men·ta·tion (fō′mən-tā′shən, -mĕn-) *n.* **1.** The act of fomenting; incitement. **2.a.** A substance or material used as a warm, moist medicinal compress; a poultice. **b.** The therapeutic application of warmth and moisture, as to relieve pain.

fo·mite (fō′mīt′) *n.* An inanimate object or substance that is capable of transmitting infectious organisms from one individual to another. [Back-formation from New Latin *fōmitēs,* pl. of Latin *fōmes,* tinder, from **fovemēs,* from *fovēre,* to warm.]

Fon (fŏn) *n., pl.* **Fon** or **Fons. 1.** A people of Benin and neighboring parts of Nigeria. **2.** The Gbe language of the Fon.

fond¹ (fŏnd) *adj.* **fond·er, fond·est. 1.** Having a strong liking, inclination, or affection: *fond of ballet; fond of my nieces and nephews.* **2.** Affectionate; tender: *a fond embrace.* **3.** Immoderately affectionate or indulgent; doting: *fond grandparents who tended to spoil the child.* **4.** Cherished; dear: *my fondest hopes.* **5.** *Archaic.* Naively credulous or foolish. [Middle English *fonned,* foolish, probably from past participle of *fonnen,* to be foolish, probably from *fonne,* fool.] **—fond′ly** *adv.*

fond² (fŏnd) *n.* The background of a design in lace. [French, from Old French *fonds, fond,* from Latin *fundus,* bottom.]

Fon·da (fŏn′də), **Henry.** 1905–1982. American actor noted for films such as *The Grapes of Wrath* (1940) and *On Golden Pond* (1981). His daughter **Jane** (born 1937) won an Academy Award for *Klute* (1971) and *Coming Home* (1978).

fon·dant (fŏn′dənt) *n.* **1.** A sweet, creamy sugar paste used in candies and icings. **2.** A candy containing this paste. [French, from present participle of *fondre,* to melt, from Latin *fundere.* See **gheu-** in Appendix.]

Fond du Lac (fŏn′ də lăk′, dyə). A city of eastern Wisconsin at the southern end of Lake Winnebago south-southeast of Oshkosh. It is an industrial center in a resort region. Population, 35,863.

fon·dle (fŏn′dl) *v.* **-dled, -dling, -dles.** —*tr.* **1.** To handle, stroke, or caress lovingly. See Synonyms at **caress. 2.** *Obsolete.* To treat with indulgence and solicitude; pamper. —*intr.* To show fondness or affection by caressing. [Frequentative of FOND¹, to show fondness for (obsolete).] **—fon′dler** *n.*

fond·ness (fŏnd′nĭs) *n.* **1.** Warm affection or liking. See Synonyms at **love. 2.** A strong inclination or preference; a taste: *a fondness for sweets; a fondness for travel.* **3.** *Archaic.* Naive trustfulness; credulity.

fon·due also **fon·du** (fŏn-do͞o′, -dyo͞o′) *n.* **1.a.** A hot dish made of melted cheese and wine and eaten with bread. **b.** A similar dish, especially one consisting of a melted sauce in which pieces of food, such as bread, meat, or fruit, are dipped or cooked: *chocolate fondue.* **2.** A soufflé usually made with cheese and bread crumbs. [French, from feminine past participle of *fondre,* to melt. See FONDANT.] **—fon·due′** *v.*

Fon·se·ca (fôn-sā′kə, -sĕ′kä), **Gulf of.** An inlet of the Pacific Ocean in western Central America bordered by El Salvador, Honduras, and Nicaragua.

font¹ (fŏnt) *n.* **1.** A basin for holding baptismal water in a church. **2.** A receptacle for holy water; a stoup. **3.** The oil reservoir in an oil-burning lamp. **4.** An abundant source; a fount: *She was a font of wisdom and good sense.* [Middle English, from Old English, from Late Latin *fōns, font-,* from Latin, fountain.] **—font′al** (fŏn′tl) *adj.*

font² (fŏnt) *n. Printing.* A complete set of type of one size and face. [French *fonte,* casting, from Old French (from Vulgar Latin **fundita,* from Late Latin, feminine of **funditus,* past participle of Latin *fundere,* to pour forth; see FONDANT) or from Old French *fondre,* to melt (from Latin *fundere,* to pour forth).]

Fon·taine·bleau (fŏn′tĭn-blō′, fôN-tĕn-blō′). A town of northern France southeast of Paris. Its chateau (built by Francis I) was long a royal palace and is now the summer residence of the president of France. Population, 15,679.

Fon·tan·a (fŏn-tăn′ə). A city of southern California west of San Bernardino. It is an industrial center. Population, 37,107.

fon·ta·nel also **fon·ta·nelle** (fŏn′tə-nĕl′) *n.* Any of the soft membranous gaps between the incompletely formed cranial bones of a fetus or an infant. Also called *soft spot.* [Middle English *fontinel,* from Old French *fontanele,* diminutive of *fontaine,* fountain. See FOUNTAIN.]

Fon·tanne (fŏn-tăn′), **Lynn.** 1887?–1983. British-born American actress who in 1922 married Alfred Lunt, with whom she performed in many productions, including *Pygmalion* (1926).

Fon·teyn (fŏn-tān′), Dame **Margot.** 1919–1991. British ballerina who joined the Royal Ballet in 1934 and began her acclaimed partnership with Rudolf Nureyev in 1962.

fon·ti·na (fŏn-tē′nə) *n.* A ripened cheese of variable texture and flavor, originally produced in Italy. [Italian.]

Foo·chow (fo͞o′jō′, -chou′). See **Fuzhou.**

food (fo͞od) *n.* **1.** Material, usually of plant or animal origin, that contains or consists of essential body nutrients, such as carbohydrates, fats, proteins, vitamins, or minerals, and is ingested and assimilated by an organism to produce energy, stimulate growth, and maintain life. **2.** A specified kind of nourishment: *breakfast food; plant food.* **3.** Nourishment eaten in solid form: *food and drink.* **4.** Something that nourishes or sustains in a way suggestive of physical nourishment: *food for thought; food for the soul.* —*attributive.* Often used to modify another noun: *food allergies; food additives.* [Middle English *fode,* from Old English *fōda.* See **pā-** in Appendix.]

food chain *n.* A succession of organisms in an ecological community that constitutes a continuation of food energy from one organism to another as each consumes a lower member and in turn is preyed upon by a higher member.

food cycle *n.* See **food web.**

food fish *n.* A fish that may be used as food for human beings.

food·ie (fo͞o′dē) *n. Slang.* A person who has an ardent or refined interest in food; a gourmet: *"in the culinary fast lane, where surprises are expected and foodies beg to be thrilled"* (Boston Globe).

food poi·son·ing (poi′zə-nĭng) *n.* **1.** An acute, often severe gastrointestinal disorder characterized by vomiting and diarrhea and caused by eating food contaminated with bacteria, especially bacteria of the genus *Salmonella,* or the toxins they produce. **2.** Poisoning caused by ingesting substances, such as certain mushrooms, that contain natural toxins.

food processor *n.* An appliance consisting of a container housing interchangeable rotating blades and used for preparing foods, as by shredding, slicing, chopping, or blending.

food pyramid *n. Ecology.* A graphic representation of the structure of a food chain, depicted as a pyramid having a broad base formed by producers and tapering to a point formed by end consumers. Between successive levels, total biomass decreases as energy is lost from the system.

food service or **food·serv·ice** (fo͞od′sûr′vĭs) *n.* The practice or business of making, transporting, and serving or dispensing prepared foods, as in a restaurant or commissary.

food stamp *n.* A stamp or coupon, issued by the government to persons with low incomes, that can be redeemed for food at stores.

food·stuff (fo͞od′stŭf′) *n.* A substance that can be used or prepared for use as food.

food vacuole *n. Biology.* A vacuole in which phagocytized food is digested.

food web *n.* A complex of interrelated food chains in an ecological community. Also called *food cycle.*

foo·fa·raw (fo͞o′fə-rô′) *n.* **1.** Excessive or flashy ornamentation. **2.** A fuss over a trifling matter. [Probably from Spanish *fanfarrón,* boaster, and from French *frou-frou,* rustling, both of imitative origin.]

fool (fo͞ol) *n.* **1.** One who is regarded as deficient in judgment, sense, or understanding. **2.** One who acts unwisely on a given occasion: *I was a fool to have refused the job.* **3.** One who has been tricked or made to appear ridiculous; a dupe: *They made a fool of me by pretending I won the award.* **4.** *Informal.* A person with a talent or an enthusiasm for a certain activity: *a dancing fool; a fool for skiing.* **5.** A member of a royal or noble household who provided entertainment, as with jokes or antics; a jester. **6.** A dessert made of stewed or puréed fruit mixed with cream or custard and served cold. **7.** *Archaic.* A mentally deficient person; an idiot. —**fool** *v.* **fooled, fool·ing, fools.** —*tr.* **1.** To deceive or trick; dupe: *"trying to learn how to fool a trout with a little bit of floating fur and feather"* (Charles Kuralt). **2.** To confound or prove wrong; surprise, especially pleasantly: *We were sure they would fail, but they fooled us.* —*intr.* **1.** *Informal.* **a.** To speak or act facetiously or in jest; joke: *I was just fooling when I said you couldn't have any of my candy.* **b.** To behave comically; clown. **c.** To feign; pretend: *He said he had a toothache but it turned out he was only fooling.* **2.** To engage in idle or frivolous activity. **3.** To toy, tinker, or mess: *shouldn't fool with matches.* —**fool** *adj. Informal.* Foolish; stupid: *off on some fool errand or other.* —***phrasal verbs.*** **fool around.** *Informal.* **1.** To engage in idle or casual activity; putter: *was fooling around with some figures in hopes of balancing the budget.* **2.** To engage in frivolous activity; make fun. **3.** To engage in casual, often promiscuous sexual acts. **fool away.** To waste (time or money) foolishly; squander: *fooled away the week's pay on Friday night.* —***idiom.*** **play** (or **act**) **the fool. 1.** To act in an irresponsible or foolish manner. **2.** To behave in a playful or comical manner. [Middle English *fol,* from Old French, from Late Latin *follis,* windbag, fool, from Latin *follis,* bellows. See **bhel-**[2] in Appendix.]

WORD HISTORY: The pejorative nature of the term *fool* is only strengthened by a knowledge of its etymology. Its source, the Latin word *follis,* meant "a bag or sack, a large inflated ball, a pair of bellows." Users of the word in Late Latin, however, saw a resemblance between the bellows or the inflated ball and a person who was what we would call "a windbag" or "an airhead." The word, which passed into English by way of French, is first recorded in English in a work written around the beginning of the 13th century with the sense "a foolish or ignorant person."

fool·er·y (fo͞o′lə-rē) *n., pl.* **-ies. 1.** Foolish behavior or speech. **2.** An instance of foolish behavior or speech; a jest.

fool·har·dy (fo͞ol′här′dē) *adj.* **-di·er, -di·est.** Unwisely bold or venturesome; rash. See Synonyms at **reckless.** [Middle English *folhardi,* from Old French *fol hardi* : *fol,* fool; see FOOL + *hardi,* bold; see HARDY[1].] —**fool′har′di·ly** *adv.* —**fool′har′di·ness** *n.*

fool·ish (fo͞o′lĭsh) *adj.* **1.** Lacking or exhibiting a lack of good sense or judgment; silly: *foolish remarks.* **2.** Resulting from stupidity or misinformation; unwise: *a foolish decision.* **3.** Arousing laughter; absurd or ridiculous: *a foolish grin.* **4.** Immoderate or stubborn; unreasonable: *foolish pride; foolish love.* **5.** Embarrassed; abashed: *I feel foolish telling you this.* **6.** Insignificant; trivial: *spent all their money on foolish little knickknacks.* —**fool′ish·ly** *adv.* —**fool′ish·ness** *n.*

SYNONYMS: *foolish, silly, fatuous, absurd, preposterous, ridiculous, ludicrous.* These adjectives are applied to what is so devoid of wisdom or good sense as to be laughable. *Foolish,* the least emphatic and derogatory, usually implies poor judgment or lack of wisdom or soundness: *a foolish young fellow; a foolish expenditure of time and energy. Silly* suggests lack of point or purpose: *a silly argument; silly mistakes; suggestions that aren't brilliant but aren't silly either. Fatuous* applies especially to what is foolish in a vacuous, smug, and unconscious way: *seems to take pride in making fatuous remarks. Absurd, preposterous, ridiculous,* and *ludicrous* apply to what is risible because of a departure from reason, logic, or common sense: *It would be absurd for us both to drive, since we're headed for the same destination. Preposterous* describes what is contrary to reason or sense: *"It would be preposterous to take so grave a step on the advice of an enemy"* (J.A. Froude). *Ridiculous* refers to what inspires ridicule: *"Clara's conceited assumption of a universal interest in her dull children was ridiculous"* (Arnold Bennett). *Ludicrous* applies to what causes scornful laughter: *It is ludicrous to call a simple split-level house a mansion.*

fool·proof (fo͞ol′pro͞of′) *adj.* **1.** Designed so as to be impervious to human incompetence, error, or misuse: *a foolproof safety lock.* **2.** Effective; infallible: *a foolproof scheme.*

fools·cap (fo͞olz′kăp′) *n.* **1.** *Abbr.* **fcp., fcap., fp.** *Chiefly British.* A sheet of writing or printing paper measuring approximately 13 by 16 inches. **2.** A fool's cap. [From the watermark of a fool's cap with bells originally used for this paper.]

fool's cap (fo͞olz) *n.* **1.** A gaily decorated cap, usually with a number of loose peaks tipped with bells, formerly worn by court jesters and clowns. **2.** See **dunce cap.**

fool's errand *n., pl.* **fools' errands.** A fruitless mission or undertaking.

fool's gold *n.* See **pyrite.**

fool's paradise *n.* A state of delusive contentment or false hope.

fool's-pars·ley (fo͞olz′pär′slē) *n.* A poisonous European weed *(Aethusa cynapium)* having finely divided leaves, umbels of small white flowers, and an unpleasant odor.

foon (fo͞on) *n.* A spoon with broad tines at the end of its bowl, adapted for spearing and scooping food. [Blend of FORK and SPOON.]

foot (fo͝ot) *n., pl.* **feet** (fēt). **1.** The lower extremity of the vertebrate leg that is in direct contact with the ground in standing or walking. **2.** A structure used for locomotion or attachment in an invertebrate animal, such as the muscular organ extending from the ventral side of a mollusk. **3.** Something suggestive of a foot in position or function, especially: **a.** The lowest part; the bottom: *the foot of a mountain; the foot of a page.* **b.** The end opposite the head, top, or front: *the foot of a bed; the foot of a parade.* **c.** The termination of the leg of a piece of furniture, especially when shaped or modeled. **d.** The part of a sewing machine that holds down and guides the cloth. **e.** *Nautical.* The lower edge of a sail. **f.** *Botany.* The base of the sporophyte in mosses and liverworts. **4.** The inferior part or rank: *at the foot of the class.* **5.** The part of a stocking or high-topped boot that encloses the foot. **6. a.** A manner of moving; a step: *walks with a light foot.* **b.** Speed or momentum, as in a race: *"the only other Democrats who've demonstrated any foot till now"* (Michael Kramer). **7.** *(used with a pl. verb).* Foot soldiers; infantry: *A regiment of foot are descending the hill.* **8.** A unit of poetic meter consisting of stressed and unstressed syllables in any of various set combinations. For example, an iambic foot has an unstressed followed by a stressed syllable. **9.** *Abbr.* **ft., ft** A unit of length in the U.S. Customary and British Imperial systems equal to 12 inches (0.3048 meter). See table at **measurement. 10. foots.** Sediment that forms during the refining of oil and other liquids; dregs. —**foot** *v.* **foot·ed, foot·ing, foots.** —*intr.* **1.** To go on foot; walk. Often used with *it: When their car broke down, they had to foot it the rest of the way.* **2.** To dance. Often used with *it: "We foot it all the night/weaving olden dances"* (William Butler Yeats). **3.** *Nautical.* To make headway; sail. —*tr.* **1.** To go by foot over, on, or through; tread. **2.** To execute the steps of (a dance). **3.** To add up (a column of numbers) and write the sum at the bottom; total: *footed up the bill.* **4.** To pay; defray: *footed the expense of their*

food processor

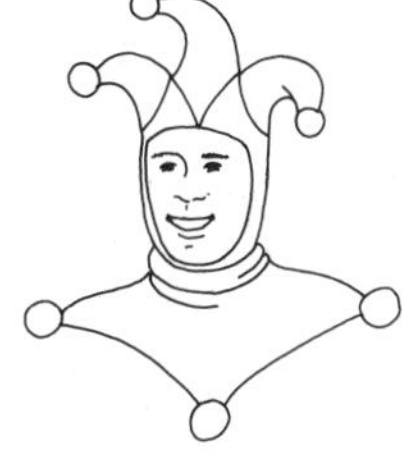

fool's cap

ă pat	oi boy
ā pay	ou out
âr care	o͝o took
ä father	o͞o boot
ĕ pet	ŭ cut
ē be	ûr urge
ĭ pit	th thin
ī pie	*th* this
îr pier	hw which
ŏ pot	zh vision
ō toe	ə about, item
ô paw	♦ regionalism

Stress marks: **′** (primary); ′ (secondary), as in **dictionary** (dĭk′shə-nĕr′ē)

football
Cincinnati Bengals
playing the New York Jets

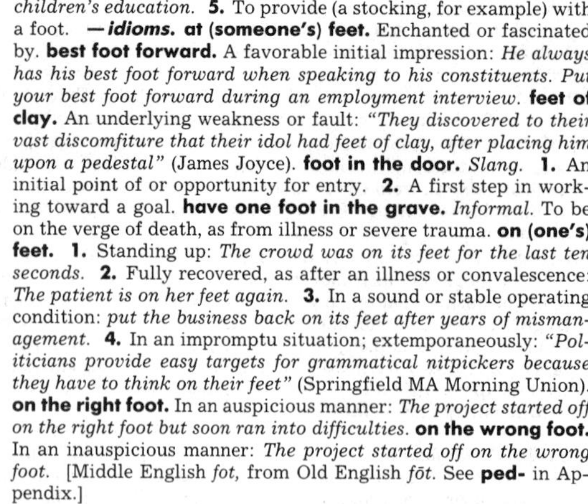

children's education. **5.** To provide (a stocking, for example) with a foot. **—*idioms.* at (someone's) feet.** Enchanted or fascinated by. **best foot forward.** A favorable initial impression: *He always has his best foot forward when speaking to his constituents. Put your best foot forward during an employment interview.* **feet of clay.** An underlying weakness or fault: *"They discovered to their vast discomfiture that their idol had feet of clay, after placing him upon a pedestal"* (James Joyce). **foot in the door.** *Slang.* **1.** An initial point of or opportunity for entry. **2.** A first step in working toward a goal. **have one foot in the grave.** *Informal.* To be on the verge of death, as from illness or severe trauma. **on (one's) feet. 1.** Standing up: *The crowd was on its feet for the last ten seconds.* **2.** Fully recovered, as after an illness or convalescence: *The patient is on her feet again.* **3.** In a sound or stable operating condition: *put the business back on its feet after years of mismanagement.* **4.** In an impromptu situation; extemporaneously: *"Politicians provide easy targets for grammatical nitpickers because they have to think on their feet"* (Springfield MA Morning Union). **on the right foot.** In an auspicious manner: *The project started off on the right foot but soon ran into difficulties.* **on the wrong foot.** In an inauspicious manner: *The project started off on the wrong foot.* [Middle English *fot,* from Old English *fōt.* See **ped-** in Appendix.]

USAGE NOTE: Used in combination with numbers to form expressions denoting units of measure, *foot* and *feet* are used typically in the following: *a four-foot plank; a plank four feet* (less frequently, *four foot*) *long; a plank four feet six inches long* (or *four foot six inches long*). When *foot* is combined with greater numbers than one to refer to simple distance, however, only the plural *feet* is used: *a ledge 20 feet* (not *foot*) *away. At that speed, a car moves 88 feet* (not *foot*) *in a second.*

foot·age (fo͝ot′ĭj) *n.* **1.** Length, extent, or amount based on measurement in feet: *estimated the square footage of new office space.* **2. a.** An amount or length of film or videotape. **b.** A shot or series of shots of a specified nature or subject: *news footage; some good footage of the royal wedding.*

foot-and-mouth disease (fo͝ot′n-mouth′) *n.* An acute, highly contagious degenerative viral disease of cattle and other cloven-hoofed animals, characterized by fever and the eruption of vesicles around the mouth and hoofs. It is usually not fatal. Also called *hoof-and-mouth disease.*

footbridge
McMinnville's Airport
Park, Oregon

foot·ball (fo͝ot′bôl′) *n.* **1.** *Sports.* **a.** A game played by two teams of 11 players each on a rectangular, 100-yard-long field with goal lines and goal posts at either end, the object being to gain possession of the ball and advance it in running or passing plays across the opponent's goal line or kick it through the air between the opponent's goal posts. **b.** The inflated oval ball used in this game. **2.** *Chiefly British.* **a.** Rugby. **b.** Soccer. **c.** The ball used in Rugby or soccer. **3.** *Informal.* A problem or issue that is discussed among groups or persons without being settled: *The issue of tax reform became a political football.* **—foot′ball′er** *n.*

foot·bath (fo͝ot′băth′, -bäth′) *n.* A small bath, such as a basin or shallow pool, for washing or disinfecting the feet.

foot·board (fo͝ot′bôrd′, -bōrd′) *n.* **1.** An upright board across the foot of a bedstead. **2.** A board or small raised platform on which to support or rest the feet, as in a carriage.

foot·boy (fo͝ot′boi′) *n.* A youth employed as a servant or page.

foot brake *n.* A brake operated by pressure of the foot on a pedal, as in an automobile.

foot·bridge (fo͝ot′brĭj′) *n.* A bridge designed for pedestrians.

foot-can·dle (fo͝ot′kăn′dl) *n.* *Abbr.* **fc, ft-c** A unit of measure of the intensity of light falling on a surface, equal to one lumen per square foot and originally defined with reference to a standardized candle burning at one foot from a given surface.

foot·cloth (fo͝ot′klôth′, -klŏth′) *n.* *Archaic.* A richly ornamented cloth draped over the back of a horse and touching the ground on both sides.

foot-drag·ging (fo͝ot′drăg′ĭng) *n.* Failure to take prompt or required action: *"The inquiry should be thorough and objective, while working fast enough to avoid any suspicion of foot-dragging"* (Economist). **—foot′-drag′ger** *n.*

foot·ed (fo͝ot′ĭd) *adj.* Having feet or a foot: *a footed sofa.* Often used in combination: *web-footed; four-footed.*

foot·er (fo͝ot′ər) *n.* **1.** One that is an indicated number of feet in height or length. Often used in combination: *a six-footer.* **2.** Printed matter positioned in the bottom margin of a page, especially a title, page number, or date that is repeated throughout a document created on a word-processing system. **3.** See **footing** (sense 4).

foot·fall (fo͝ot′fôl′) *n.* See **footstep** (sense 1).

foot fault *n.* *Sports.* A fault against the server, as in tennis, called for failure to keep both feet behind the base line.

footpath

foot·gear (fo͝ot′gîr′) *n.* Sturdy footwear, such as shoes or boots.

foot·hill (fo͝ot′hĭl′) *n.* A hill near the base of a mountain or mountain range.

foot·hold (fo͝ot′hōld′) *n.* **1.** A place providing support for the foot in climbing or standing. **2.** A firm or secure position that provides a base for further advancement.

foot·ing (fo͝ot′ĭng) *n.* **1.** Secure placement of the feet in standing or moving. **2. a.** A surface or its condition with respect to its suitability for walking or running, especially the condition of a racetrack. **b.** A secure place for the feet; a foothold. **3.** The act of moving on foot. **4.** *Architecture.* The supporting base or groundwork of a structure, as for a monument or wall. Also called *footer.* **5.** A basis or foundation: *a business begun on a good footing.* **6. a.** Position or rank in relation to others; standing: *Everyone began on an equal footing.* **b.** Terms of social interaction: *neighbors on a friendly footing.* **7.** The act of making a foot for something, such as a stocking. **8.** The sum of a column of figures.

foot-lam·bert (fo͝ot′lăm′bərt) *n.* *Abbr.* **fL** A unit of luminance equal to 1/ξ candela per square foot.

foo·tle (fo͝ot′l) *Informal. intr.v.* **-tled, -tling, -tles. 1.** To waste time; trifle. **2.** To talk nonsense. **—footle** *n.* Nonsense; foolishness. [Probably variant of *footer,* to screw around, from obsolete *fouter,* a fuck, from French *foutre,* to fuck, from Latin *futuere.* See **bhau-** in Appendix.] **—foo′tler** *n.*

foot·less (fo͝ot′lĭs) *adj.* **1.** Having no feet. **2.** Lacking a firm support or basis; unsubstantial. **3.** *Informal.* Not competent or skillful; inept. **—foot′less·ly** *adv.* **—foot′less·ness** *n.*

foot·lights (fo͝ot′līts′) *pl.n.* **1.** Lights placed in a row along the front of a stage floor. **2.** The theater as a profession.

foo·tling (fo͝ot′lĭng) *adj.* *Informal.* **1.** Lacking importance or significance; trifling: *a footling gesture.* **2.** Stupid; inept. [Present participle of FOOTLE.]

foot·lock·er (fo͝ot′lŏk′ər) *n.* A trunk for storing personal belongings, especially one kept at the foot of a bed, as in a barracks.

foot·long (fo͝ot′lông′, -lŏng′) *adj.* Being about one foot in length: *a footlong hot dog.*

foot·loose (fo͝ot′lo͞os′) *adj.* Having no attachments or ties; free to do as one pleases.

foot·man (fo͝ot′mən) *n.* **1.** A man employed as a servant to wait at table, attend the door, and run various errands, as in a palace. **2.** *Archaic.* **a.** A foot soldier; an infantryman. **b.** One who travels on foot; a pedestrian.

foot·mark (fo͝ot′märk′) *n.* See **footprint** (sense 1).

foot·note (fo͝ot′nōt′) *n.* **1.** *Abbr.* **fn.** A note placed at the bottom of a page of a book or manuscript that comments on or cites a reference for a designated part of the text. **2.** Something related to but of lesser importance than a larger work or occurrence: *a political scandal that was but a footnote to modern history.* **—footnote** *tr.v.* **-not·ed, -not·ing, -notes.** To furnish with or comment on in footnotes.

foot·pace (fo͝ot′pās′) *n.* **1.** A walking pace. **2.** A raised platform in a room, as for a lecturer; a dais.

foot·pad¹ (fo͝ot′păd′) *n.* A thief who preys on pedestrians. [FOOT + obsolete *pad,* highwayman (probably from Middle Dutch *pad,* path; see **pent-** in Appendix).]

foot·pad² (fo͝ot′păd′) *n.* A plate or similar structure on the leg of a spacecraft that distributes weight and helps prevent sinking after landing.

foot·path (fo͝ot′păth′, -päth′) *n.* A narrow path for persons on foot.

foot-pound (fo͝ot′pound′) *n.* *Abbr.* **ft-lb** A unit of work equal to the work done by a force of one pound acting through a distance of one foot in the direction of the force.

foot-pound·al (fo͝ot′poun′dl) *n.* A unit of work equal to the work done by a force of one poundal acting through a distance of one foot in the direction of the force.

foot-pound-sec·ond (fo͝ot′pound′sĕk′ənd) *adj.* *Abbr.* **fps, f.p.s.** Of, relating to, or characteristic of the British, Canadian, or U.S. system of units based on the foot, the pound, and the second as the fundamental units of length, mass, and time.

foot·print (fo͝ot′prĭnt′) *n.* **1.** An outline or indentation left by a foot on a surface. Also called *footmark, footstep.* **2.** An area within which a spacecraft is supposed to land. **3.** A designated area affected or covered by a device or phenomenon: *the footprint of a microcomputer; the footprint of a communications satellite.*

foot·race or **foot race** (fo͝ot′rās′) *n.* *Sports.* A race run by contestants on foot. **—foot′rac′ing** *n.*

foot·rest (fo͝ot′rĕst′) *n.* A support on which to rest the feet.

foot·rope (fo͝ot′rōp′) *n.* *Nautical.* **1.** A rope attached to the lower border of a sail. **2.** A rope, rigged beneath a yard, for sailors to stand on during the reefing or furling of sail.

foot rot *n.* **1.** A degenerative bacterial infection of the feet in certain hoofed animals, especially cattle or sheep, often resulting in loss of the hoof. **2.** A disease of plants in which the stem or trunk rots at its base.

foot·sie also **foot·sy** (fo͝ot′sē) *n.* *Informal.* The act of flirting in which one secretly touches the feet or legs of another with one's own, as under a table. **—*idiom.* play footsie with. 1.** To flirt with, especially in secret. **2.** To cooperate or curry favor with in a sly or devious way. [From diminutive of FOOT.]

foot·slog (fo͝ot′slŏg′) *intr.v.* **-slogged, -slog·ging, -slogs.** To trudge through or as if through mud. **—foot′slog′ger** *n.*

foot soldier *n.* A soldier who fights on foot.

foot·sore (fo͝ot′sôr′, -sōr′) *adj.* Having sore or tired feet, as from too much walking. **—foot′sore′ness** *n.*

foot·stalk (fo͝ot′stôk′) *n.* A supporting stalk, such as a peduncle or pedicel.

foot·stall (fo͝ot′stôl′) *n.* The pedestal, plinth, or base of a pillar, column, or statue.

foot·step (fo͝ot′stĕp′) *n.* **1.a.** A step with the foot. **b.** The sound of a foot stepping. Also called *footfall.* **2.** The distance covered by a step: *a footstep away.* **3.** See **footprint** (sense 1). **4.** A step on which to go up or down. —***idiom.*** **follow in (someone's) footsteps.** To carry on the behavior, work, or tradition of.

foot·stone (fo͝ot′stōn′) *n.* A marking stone placed at the foot of a grave.

foot·stool (fo͝ot′sto͞ol′) *n.* A low stool for supporting the feet.

foot·sy (fo͝ot′sē) *n. Informal.* Variant of **footsie.**

foot·wall (fo͝ot′wôl′) *n.* The mass of rock underlying a mineral deposit in a mine.

foot·way (fo͝ot′wā′) *n.* A walk or path for pedestrians.

foot·wear (fo͝ot′wâr′) *n.* Attire, such as shoes or slippers, for the feet.

foot·work (fo͝ot′wûrk′) *n.* **1.** *Sports.* The manner in which the feet are used or maneuvered, as in boxing or in figure skating. **2.** Work that involves moving around on foot; legwork. **3.** *Informal.* Skillful dealing or maneuvering; tactics: *"They've built a corporate empire on dazzling financial footwork"* (Christopher Farrell).

foo·zle (fo͞o′zəl) *tr.v.* **-zled, -zling, -zles.** To manage clumsily; bungle. —**foozle** *n.* The act of bungling, especially a poor stroke in golf. [Perhaps from German dialectal *fuseln,* to work poorly or slowly.] —**foo′zler** *n.*

fop (fŏp) *n.* A man who is preoccupied with and often vain about his clothes and manners; a dandy. [Middle English, fool; probably akin to Middle English *fob,* trickster, cheat. See FOB[2].]

fop·per·y (fŏp′ə-rē) *n., pl.* **-ies. 1.** Foolish quality or action. **2.** The dress or manner of a fop.

fop·pish (fŏp′ĭsh) *adj.* Of, relating to, or characteristic of a fop; dandified. —**fop′pish·ly** *adv.* —**fop′pish·ness** *n.*

for (fôr; fər *when unstressed*) *prep.* **1.a.** Used to indicate the object, aim, or purpose of an action or activity: *trained for the ministry; put the house up for sale; plans to run for senator.* **b.** Used to indicate a destination: *headed off for town.* **2.** Used to indicate the object of a desire, an intention, or a perception: *had a nose for news; eager for fame and fortune.* **3.a.** Used to indicate the recipient or beneficiary of an action: *prepared lunch for us.* **b.** On behalf of: *spoke for all the members.* **c.** In favor of: *Were they for or against the proposal?* **d.** In place of: *a substitute for eggs.* **4.a.** Used to indicate equivalence or equality: *paid ten dollars for a ticket; repeated the conversation word for word.* **b.** Used to indicate correlation or correspondence: *took two steps back for every step forward.* **5.a.** Used to indicate amount, extent, or duration: *a bill for five dollars; walked for miles; stood in line for several minutes.* **b.** Used to indicate a specific time: *had an appointment for two o'clock.* **6.a.** As being: *take for granted; mistook me for the librarian.* **b.** Used to indicate an actual or implied listing or choosing: *For one thing, we can't afford it.* **7.** As a result of; because of: *jumped for joy.* **8.** Used to indicate appropriateness or suitability: *It will be for the judge to decide.* **9.** Notwithstanding; despite: *For all the problems, it was a valuable experience.* **10.a.** As regards; concerning: *a stickler for neatness.* **b.** Considering the nature or usual character of: *was spry for his advanced age.* **c.** In honor of: *named for her grandmother.* —**for** *conj.* Because; since. [Middle English, from Old English. See **per[1]** in Appendix.]

FOR *abbr.* Free on rail.

for. *abbr.* **1.** Foreign. **2.** Forest; forestry.

for– *pref.* Completely; excessively, especially with destructive or detrimental effect: *forworn.* [Middle English, from Old English. See **per[1]** in Appendix.]

fo·ra (fôr′ə, fōr′ə) *n.* A plural of **forum.**

for·age (fôr′ĭj, fŏr′-) *n.* **1.** Food for domestic animals; fodder. **2.** The act of looking or searching for food or provisions. —**forage** *v.* **-aged, -ag·ing, -ag·es.** —*intr.* **1.** To wander in search of food or provisions. **2.** To make a raid, as for food: *soldiers foraging near an abandoned farm.* **3.** To conduct a search; rummage. —*tr.* **1.** To collect forage from; strip of food or supplies: *troops who were foraging the countryside.* **2.** *Informal.* To obtain by foraging: *foraged a snack from the refrigerator.* [Middle English, from Old French *fourrage,* from *forrer,* to forage, from *feurre,* fodder, of Germanic origin. See **pā-** in Appendix.] —**for′ag·er** *n.*

For·a·ker (fôr′ə-kər, fŏr′-), **Mount.** A peak, 5,307 m (17,400 ft) high, in the Alaska Range of south-central Alaska.

for·am (fôr′əm, fŏr′-) *n.* A foraminifer. [Short for FORAMINIFER.]

fo·ra·men (fə-rā′mən) *n., pl.* **-ram·i·na** (-răm′ə-nə) or **-ra·mens.** An opening or orifice, as in a bone or in the covering of the ovule of a plant. [Latin *forāmen,* an opening, from *forāre,* to bore.] —**fo·ram′i·nal** (-răm′ə-nəl), **fo·ram′i·nous** (-nəs) *adj.*

foramen magnum *n.* The large orifice in the base of the skull through which the spinal cord passes to the cranial cavity and becomes continuous with the medulla oblongata. [New Latin *forāmen magnum* : Latin *forāmen,* opening + Latin *magnus,* large.]

foramen o·val·e (ō-văl′ē, -vā′lē, -vä′-) *n.* An opening in the septum between the right and left atria of the heart, present in the fetus but usually closed soon after birth. [New Latin *forāmen ōvāle* : Latin *forāmen,* opening + Medieval Latin *ōvālis,* oval.]

fo·ram·i·na (fə-răm′ə-nə) *n.* A plural of **foramen.**

for·a·min·i·fer (fôr′ə-mĭn′ə-fər, fŏr′-) also **for·a·min·i·fer·an** (-mĭn′ə-fər-ən) *n., pl.* **fo·ram·i·nif·er·a** (fə-răm′ə-nĭf′ər-ə) or **for·a·min·i·fers.** Any of the chiefly marine protozoans of the order Foraminifera, characteristically having a calcareous shell with perforations through which numerous pseudopods protrude. [From New Latin *Forāminifera,* order name : Latin *forāmen, forāmin-,* an opening + Latin *-fer,* -fer.] —**fo·ram′i·nif′er·ous** (fə-răm′ə-nĭf′ər-əs), **fo·ram′i·nif′er·al** *adj.*

for·as·much as (fôr′əz-mŭch′ əz) *conj.* Inasmuch as; since.

for·ay (fôr′ā′, fŏr′ā′, fŏr′ā′) *n.* **1.** A sudden raid or military advance. **2.** A venture or an initial attempt, especially outside one's usual area: *an actor's foray into politics.* —**foray** *v.* **-ayed, -ay·ing, -ays.** —*intr.* **1.** To make a raid. **2.** To make inroads, as for profit or adventure. —*tr. Archaic.* To pillage in search of spoils. [Middle English *forrai,* from *forraien,* to plunder, probably back-formation from *forreour,* raider, plunderer, from Old French *forrier,* from *forrer,* to forage. See FORAGE.]

forb (fôrb) *n.* A broad-leaved herb other than a grass, especially one growing in a field, prairie, or meadow. [From Greek *phorbē,* fodder, from *pherbein,* to graze.]

for·bad (fər-băd′, fôr-) *v.* A past tense of **forbid.**

for·bade (fər-băd′, -bād′, fôr-) *v.* A past tense of **forbid.**

for·bear[1] (fôr-bâr′) *v.* **-bore** (-bôr′, -bōr′), **-borne** (-bôrn′, -bōrn′), **-bear·ing, -bears.** —*tr.* **1.** To refrain from; resist: *forbear replying.* See Synonyms at **refrain[1]. 2.** To desist from; cease. **3.** *Obsolete.* To avoid or shun. —*intr.* **1.** To hold back; refrain. **2.** To be tolerant or patient in the face of provocation. [Middle English *forberen,* from Old English *forberan,* to endure. See **bher-[1]** in Appendix.] —**for·bear′er** *n.*

for·bear[2] (fôr′bâr′, fŏr′-) *n.* Variant of **forebear.**

for·bear·ance (fôr-bâr′əns) *n.* **1.** The act of forbearing. **2.** Tolerance and restraint in the face of provocation; patience. See Synonyms at **patience. 3.** The quality of being forbearing. **4.** *Law.* The act of a creditor who refrains from enforcing a debt when it falls due.

for·bid (fər-bĭd′, fôr-) *tr.v.* **-bade** (-băd′, -bād′) or **-bad** (-băd′), **-bid·den** (-bĭd′n) or **-bid, -bid·ding, -bids. 1.** To command (someone) not to do something: *I forbid you to go.* **2.** To command against the doing or use of (something); prohibit: *forbid smoking on trains.* **3.** To have the effect of preventing; preclude: *Discretion forbids a reply.* [Middle English *forbidden, forbeden,* from Old English *forbēodan.* See **bheudh-** in Appendix.] —**for·bid′dance** *n.* —**for·bid′der** *n.*

SYNONYMS: *forbid, ban, enjoin, interdict, prohibit, proscribe.* The central meaning shared by these verbs is "to refuse to allow": *laws that forbid speeding; banned smoking; was enjoined from broadcasting the news item; interdict trafficking in drugs; rules that prohibit swimming in the reservoir; proscribed the importation of raw fruits and vegetables.*
ANTONYM: *permit.*

for·bid·den (fər-bĭd′n, fôr-) *v.* A past participle of **forbid.** —**forbidden** *adj. Physics.* Having a low probability of occurrence. Used of quantum phenomena: *a forbidden transition.*

For·bid·den City (fər-bĭd′n, fôr-). A walled enclosure of central Beijing, China, containing the palaces of former Chinese emperors.

forbidden fruit *n.* An indulgence or a pleasure that is illegal or is believed to be immoral. [From the story of the fruit of the tree of knowledge of good and evil, forbidden to Adam and Eve in Genesis 2:16–3:19.]

for·bid·ding (fər-bĭd′ĭng, fôr-) *adj.* **1.** Tending or threatening to impede progress: *forbidding rapids.* **2.** Unpleasant; disagreeable: *a forbidding scowl.* **3.** Having a menacing aspect: *forbidding thunderclouds.* —**for·bid′ding·ly** *adv.*

for·bore (fôr-bôr′, -bōr′) *v.* Past tense of **forbear[1].**

for·borne (fôr-bôrn′, -bōrn′) *v.* Past participle of **forbear[1].**

force (fôrs, fōrs) *n.* **1.** The capacity to do work or cause physical change; energy, strength, or active power: *the force of an explosion.* **2.a.** Power made operative against resistance; exertion: *use force in driving a nail.* **b.** The use of physical power or violence to compel or restrain: *a confession obtained by force.* **3.a.** Intellectual power or vigor, especially as conveyed in writing or speech. **b.** Moral strength. **c.** A capacity for affecting the mind or behavior; efficacy: *the force of logical argumentation.* **d.** One that possesses such capacity: *the forces of evil.* **4.a.** A body of persons or other resources organized or available for a certain purpose: *a large labor force.* **b.** A person or group capable of influential action: *a retired senator who is still a force in national politics.* **5.a.** Military strength. **b.** The entire military strength, as of a nation. **c.** Units of a nation's military personnel, especially those deployed into combat: *Our forces have at last engaged the enemy.* **6.** *Law.* Legal validity. **7.** *Physics.* A vector quantity that tends to produce an acceleration of a body in the direction of its application. —**force** *tr.v.* **forced, forc·ing, forc·es. 1.** To compel through pressure or necessity: *I forced myself to practice daily. He was forced to take a second job.* **2.a.** To gain by the use of force or coercion: *force a confession.* **b.** To move or effect against resistance or inertia: *forced my foot into the shoe.* **c.** To inflict or impose relentlessly: *He forced his ideas upon the group.* **3.a.** To put undue strain on: *She forced her voice despite being hoarse.* **b.** To increase or accelerate (a pace, for example) to the

footrope

Forbidden City

ă pat	oi boy
ā pay	ou out
âr care	o͝o took
ä father	o͞o boot
ĕ pet	ŭ cut
ē be	ûr urge
ĭ pit	th thin
ī pie	*th* this
îr pier	hw which
ŏ pot	zh vision
ō toe	ə about, item
ô paw	♦ regionalism

Stress marks: ′ (primary); ′ (secondary), as in **dictionary** (dĭk′shə-nĕr′ē)

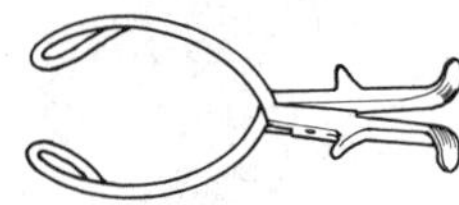

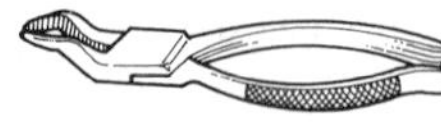

forceps
Top: Obstetrical
Bottom: Dental

maximum. **c.** To produce with effort and against one's will: *force a laugh in spite of pain.* **d.** To use (language) with obvious lack of ease and naturalness. **4. a.** To move, open, or clear by force: *forced our way through the crowd.* **b.** To break down or open by force: *force a lock.* **5.** To rape. **6.** *Botany.* To cause to grow or mature by artificially accelerating normal processes. **7.** *Baseball.* **a.** To put (a runner) out on a force play. **b.** To allow (a run) to be scored by walking a batter when the bases are loaded. **8.** *Games.* To cause an opponent to play (a particular card). —***idioms.*** **force (someone's) hand.** To force to act or speak prematurely or unwillingly. **in force.** **1.** In full strength; in large numbers: *Demonstrators were out in force.* **2.** In effect; operative: *a rule that is no longer in force.* [Middle English, from Old French, from Medieval Latin *fortia,* from neuter pl. of Latin *fortis,* strong. See **bhergh-**[2] in Appendix.] —**force′a·ble** *adj.* —**forc′er** *n.*

SYNONYMS: *force, compel, coerce, constrain, oblige, obligate.* These verbs mean to cause a person or thing to follow a prescribed or dictated course. *Force,* the most general, usually implies the exertion of strength, especially physical power, or the operation of circumstances that permit no alternative to compliance: *Tear gas forced the fugitives out of their hiding place. Lack of funds will eventually force him to look for work. Compel* is often interchangeable with *force,* but it applies especially to an act dictated by one in authority: *Say nothing unless you're compelled to. His playing compels respect, if not enthusiasm. Coerce* invariably implies the use of strength or harsh measures in securing compliance: *"The way in which the man of genius rules is by persuading an efficient minority to coerce an indifferent and self-indulgent majority"* (James Fitzjames Stephen). *Constrain* suggests that one is bound to a course of action by physical or moral means or by the operation of compelling circumstances: *"I am your anointed Queen. I will never be by violence constrained to do anything"* (Elizabeth I). *Oblige* is applicable when compliance is brought about by the operation of authority, necessity, or moral or ethical considerations: *"Work consists of whatever a body is* obliged *to do"* (Mark Twain). *Obligate* applies when force is exerted by the terms of a legal contract or promise or by the dictates of one's conscience or sense of propriety: *I am obligated to repay the loan.* See also Synonyms at **strength.**

Betty Ford
Photographed in 1982

forced (fôrst, fōrst) *adj.* **1.** Imposed by force; involuntary: *was condemned to a life of forced labor; a plane that made a forced landing.* **2.** Produced under strain; not spontaneous: *forced laughter.* See Usage Note at **forceful.**

forced march *n.* A march that is longer or faster than usual, as for a critical destination.

force-feed (fôrs′fēd′, fōrs′-) *tr.v.* **-fed** (-fĕd′), **-feed·ing, -feeds.** **1.** To compel to ingest food; feed forcibly, especially by mechanical means. **2.** To force to assimilate: *prisoners of war being force-fed the party line.*

force field *n.* See **field of force.**

force·ful (fôrs′fəl, fōrs′-) *adj.* Characterized by or full of force; effective. —**force′ful·ly** *adv.* —**force′ful·ness** *n.*

USAGE NOTE: *Forceful, forcible,* and *forced* have distinct, though related meanings. *Forceful* is used to describe someone or something that possesses or is filled with strength or force: *a forceful speaker; a forceful personality. Forceful measures* may or may not involve the use of actual physical force. *Forcible,* by contrast, is most often used of actions accomplished by the application of physical force: *There had been a forcible entry. The police had to use forcible restraint in order to arrest the suspect. Forced* is used to describe an act or a condition brought about by control or an outside influence: *a forced smile; a forced landing; forced labor.*

Gerald Ford

force ma·jeure (fôrs′ mä-zhûr′, fōrs′) *n.* **1.** Superior or overpowering force. **2.** An unexpected or uncontrollable event. [French : *force,* force + *majeure,* greater.]

force-march (fôrs′märch′, fōrs′-) *intr. & tr.v.* **-marched, -march·ing, -march·es.** To undertake or subject to a forced march. [Back-formation from *forced march.*]

force·meat (fôrs′mēt′, fōrs′-) *n.* Finely ground and highly spiced meat, fish, or poultry that is served alone or used in stuffing. [*Force* (alteration of FARCE) + MEAT.]

force of habit *n.* Behavior that has become automatic through long practice or frequent repetition.

force-out (fôrs′out′, fōrs′-) *n.* *Baseball.* The act or fact of putting out a base runner on a force play.

force play *n.* *Baseball.* A play in which a runner is put out when forced by the batter to move to the next base and a fielder holding the ball touches that base first.

for·ceps (fôr′səps, -sĕps) *n., pl.* **forceps.** **1.** An instrument resembling a pair of pincers or tongs, used for grasping, manipulating, or extracting, especially such an instrument used by a surgeon. **2.** A pincerlike pair of movable appendages at the posterior end of the abdomen in certain insects, such as earwigs. [Latin, fire tongs, pincers. See **gʷher-** in Appendix.]

force pump *n.* A pump with a solid piston and valves used to raise a liquid or expel it under pressure.

forc·i·ble (fôr′sə-bəl, fōr′-) *adj.* **1.** Effected against resistance through the use of force: *a forcible entry.* **2.** Characterized by force; powerful. See Usage Note at **forceful.** —**forc′i·ble·ness** *n.* —**forc′i·bly** *adv.*

for·ci·pate (fôr′sə-pāt′) *adj.* Shaped like or resembling forceps. [Latin *forceps, forcip-,* pincers; see **gʷher-** in Appendix + -ATE[1].]

ford (fôrd, fōrd) *n.* A shallow place in a body of water, such as a river, where one can cross by walking or riding on an animal or in a vehicle. —**ford** *tr.v.* **ford·ed, ford·ing, fords.** To cross (a body of water) at a ford. [Middle English, from Old English. See **per-**[2] in Appendix.] —**ford′a·ble** *adj.*

Ford (fôrd, fōrd), **Elizabeth Bloomer.** Known as "Betty." Born 1918. First Lady of the United States (1974–1977) as the wife of President Gerald R. Ford. She supported the Equal Rights Amendment and programs for disabled children.

Ford, Ford Madox. Originally Ford Hermann Hueffer. 1873–1939. British writer and editor whose works include *The Good Soldier* (1915) and the tetralogy *Parade's End* (1924–1928).

Ford, Gerald Rudolph. Born 1913. The 38th President of the United States (1974–1977), who was appointed Vice President on the resignation of Spiro Agnew (1973) and became President after Richard Nixon's resignation over the Watergate scandal.

Ford, Henry. 1863–1947. American automobile manufacturer who developed a gasoline-powered automobile (1893), founded the Ford Motor Company (1903), and mass-produced the Model T (1908–1927). His son **Edsel Bryant Ford** (1893–1943) ran the company from 1919 to 1943, as did his grandson **Henry Ford II** (1917–1987) from 1945 to 1980.

Ford, John[1]**.** 1586–1639. English playwright whose works include *'Tis Pity She's a Whore* (1633).

Ford, John[2]**.** 1895–1973. American filmmaker whose works include *The Informer* (1935), *The Grapes of Wrath* (1940), *How Green Was My Valley* (1941), and *The Quiet Man* (1952).

for·do also **fore·do** (fôr-do͞o′, fōr-) *tr.v.* **-did** (-dĭd′), **-done** (-dŭn′), **-do·ing, -does** (-dŭz′). *Archaic.* **1.** To bring to ruin; destroy. **2.** To exhaust utterly. [Middle English *fordon,* from Old English *fordōn* : *for-,* for- + *dōn,* to do; see **dhē-** in Appendix.]

fore (fôr, fōr) *adj.* **1.** Located at or toward the front; forward. **2.** Earlier in order of occurrence; former. —**fore** *n.* **1.** Something that is located at or toward the front. **2.** The front part. —**fore** *adv.* **1.** At, toward, or near the front; forward. **2.** At an earlier time. —**fore** also **'fore** *prep.* Before. —**fore** *interj.* *Sports.* Used by a golfer to warn those ahead that a ball is headed in their direction. —***idiom.*** **to the fore.** In, into, or toward a position of prominence: *A new virtuoso has come to the fore.* [Middle English, beforehand, before, in front of, from Old English. See **per**[1] in Appendix.]

fore– *pref.* **1.** Before; earlier: *foredoom.* **2.** In front of; front: *foredeck.* [Middle English *for-, fore-,* from Old English, from *fore,* in front. See **per**[1] in Appendix.]

fore and aft *adv.* **1.** *Nautical.* **a.** From the bow of a ship to the stern; lengthwise. **b.** In, at, or toward both ends of a ship. **2.** In or at the front and back.

fore-and-aft (fôr′ən-ăft′, fōr′-) *adj.* Parallel with the length of a structure, such as a ship or house; running lengthwise.

fore-and-aft·er (fôr′ən-ăf′tər, fōr′-) *n.* *Nautical.* A sailing ship, such as a schooner, with a fore-and-aft rig.

fore-and-aft rig *n.* *Nautical.* A rig on a sailing ship that has quadrilateral and triangular sails set to the fore-and-aft line and that can be trimmed to leeward.

fore-and-aft sail *n.* *Nautical.* A sail set parallel with the keel of a vessel, having the foremost edge or luff attached to the mast with travelers and the upper edge set on a gaff or stay.

fore·arm[1] (fôr-ärm′, fōr-) *tr.v.* **-armed, -arm·ing, -arms.** To arm or prepare in advance of a conflict.

fore·arm[2] (fôr′ärm′, fōr′-) *n.* **1.** The part of the arm between the wrist and the elbow. **2.** The corresponding part of the foreleg in certain quadrupeds, such as a horse.

fore·bear also **for·bear** (fôr′bâr′, fōr′-) *n.* A person from whom one is descended; an ancestor. See Synonyms at **ancestor.** [Middle English : *fore-,* fore- + *beer,* one who is (from *been,* to be; see BE).]

fore·bode (fôr-bōd′, fōr-) *v.* **-bod·ed, -bod·ing, -bodes.** —*tr.* **1.** To indicate the likelihood of; portend: *harsh words that foreboded estrangement.* **2.** To have a premonition of (a future misfortune). —*intr.* To prophesy or predict. —**fore·bod′er** *n.*

fore·bod·ing (fôr-bō′dĭng, fōr-) *n.* **1.** A sense of impending evil. See Synonyms at **apprehension.** **2.** An evil omen; a portent. —**foreboding** *adj.* Marked by or indicative of foreboding; ominous. —**fore·bod′ing·ly** *adv.* —**fore·bod′ing·ness** *n.*

fore·brain (fôr′brān′, fōr′-) *n.* **1.** The most anterior of the three primary regions of the embryonic brain from which the telencephalon and diencephalon develop. **2.** The segment of the adult brain that develops from the embryonic forebrain and includes the cerebrum, thalamus, and hypothalamus.

fore·cad·die (fôr′kăd′ē, fōr′-) *n.* *Sports.* A golf caddie who is positioned in the fairway and points out the location of balls on the course.

fore·cast (fôr′kăst′, fōr′-) *v.* **-cast** or **-cast·ed, -cast·ing, -casts.** —*tr.* **1.** To estimate or calculate in advance, especially to predict (weather conditions) by analysis of meteorological data. See Synonyms at **predict.** **2.** To serve as an advance indication of; foreshadow: *price increases that forecast inflation.* —*intr.* To calculate or estimate something in advance; predict the future.

—**forecast** *n.* A prediction, as of coming events or conditions. [Middle English *forecasten,* to plan beforehand : *fore-,* fore- + *casten,* to throw, calculate, prepare; see CAST.] —**fore·cast′a·ble** *adj.* —**fore′cast′er** *n.*

fore·cas·tle (fōk′səl, fôr′kăs′əl, fōr′-) also **fo'c's'le** (fōk′səl) *n. Nautical.* **1.** The section of the upper deck of a ship located at the bow forward of the foremast. **2.** A superstructure at the bow of a merchant ship where the crew is housed. [Middle English *forecastel* : *fore-,* fore- + *castel,* fortification; see CASTLE.]

fore-check (fôr′chĕk′, fōr′-) *intr.v.* **-checked, -check·ing, -checks.** *Sports.* To check an ice-hockey opponent in the opponent's own defensive zone. —**fore′-check′er** *n.*

fore·close (fôr-klōz′, fōr-) *v.* **-closed, -clos·ing, -clos·es.** —*tr.* **1.a.** To deprive (a mortgagor) of the right to redeem mortgaged property, as when payments have not been made. **b.** To bar an equity or a right to redeem (a mortgage). **2.** To exclude or rule out; bar. **3.** To settle or resolve beforehand. —*intr.* To bar an equity or a right to redeem a mortgage. [Middle English *forclosen,* to exclude from an inheritance, from Old French *forclos,* shut out, past participle of *forclore,* to exclude : *fors-,* outside (from Latin *forīs;* see **dhwer-** in Appendix) + *clore,* to close (from Latin *claudere*).] —**fore·clos′a·ble** *adj.*

fore·clo·sure (fôr-klō′zhər, fōr-) *n.* The act of foreclosing, especially a legal proceeding by which a mortgage is foreclosed.

fore·court (fôr′kôrt′, fōr′kōrt′) *n.* **1.** A courtyard in front of a building. **2.** *Sports.* The part of a court nearest the net or wall, as in tennis or handball.

fore·deck (fôr′dĕk′, fōr′-) *n. Nautical.* The forward part of the deck of a ship, usually the main deck.

fore·do (fôr-do͞o′, fōr-) *v.* Variant of **fordo.**

fore·doom (fôr-do͞om′, fōr-) *tr.v.* **-doomed, -doom·ing, -dooms.** To doom or condemn beforehand.

fore-edge painting (fôr′ĕj′, fōr′-) *n.* A technique of painting a picture on the front outer edges of the leaves of a book, so that the picture is visible only when the leaves are fanned open.

fore·face (fôr′fās′, fōr′-) *n.* The part of the head of a four-legged mammal that is in front of the eyes.

fore·fa·ther (fôr′fä′*th*ər, fōr′-) *n.* **1.** An ancestor. See Synonyms at **ancestor. 2.** A person who is from an earlier time and has originated or contributed to a common tradition shared by a particular group.

fore·feel (fôr-fēl′, fōr-) *tr.v.* **-felt** (-fĕlt′), **-feel·ing, -feels.** To feel beforehand; have a premonition of.

fore·fend (fôr-fĕnd′, fōr-) *v.* Variant of **forfend.**

fore·fin·ger (fôr′fĭng′gər, fōr′-) *n.* See **index finger.**

fore·foot (fôr′fo͝ot′, fōr′-) *n.* **1.** Either of the front feet of a quadruped. **2.** *Nautical.* The part of a ship at which the prow joins the keel.

fore·front (fôr′frŭnt′, fōr′-) *n.* **1.** The foremost part or area. **2.** The position of most importance, prominence, or responsibility; the vanguard: *in the forefront of the liberation movement.* In this sense, also called *foreground.*

fore·gath·er (fôr-găth′ər, fōr-) *v.* Variant of **forgather.**

fore·go[1] (fôr-gō′, fōr-) *tr.v.* **-went** (-wĕnt′), **-gone** (-gôn′, -gŏn′), **-go·ing, -goes** (-gōz′). To precede, as in time or place. [Middle English *foregon,* from Old English *foregān* : *fore-,* fore- + *gān,* go; see **ghē-** in Appendix.] —**fore·go′er** *n.*

fore·go[2] (fôr-gō′, fōr-) *v.* Variant of **forgo.**

fore·go·ing (fôr-gō′ĭng, fōr-, fôr′gō′ĭng, fōr′-) *adj.* Said, written, or encountered just before; previous: *Refer to the foregoing figures.*

fore·gone (fôr-gôn′, -gŏn′, fōr-)*v.* Past participle of **forego**[1]. —**foregone** (fôr′gôn′, -gŏn′, fōr′-) *adj.* Having gone before; previous. [Past participle of FOREGO[1].]

foregone conclusion *n.* **1.** An end or a result regarded as inevitable: *The victory was a foregone conclusion.* **2.** A conclusion formed in advance of argument or consideration.

fore·ground (fôr′ground′, fōr′-) *n.* **1.** The part of a scene or picture that is nearest to and in front of the viewer. **2.** See **forefront** (sense 2).

fore·gut (fôr′gŭt′, fōr′-) *n.* **1.** The anterior part of the embryonic alimentary canal of a vertebrate from which the pharynx, lungs, esophagus, stomach, liver, pancreas, and duodenum develop. **2.** The first part of the alimentary canal of an arthropod or annelid, which includes the buccal cavity, esophagus, crop, and gizzard.

fore·hand (fôr′hănd′, fōr′-) *adj.* **1.** Made or done with the hand moving palm forward: *a forehand tennis stroke.* **2.** *Obsolete.* Taking place, done, or given beforehand; prior. —**forehand** *n.* **1.** A forehand stroke, as in tennis. **2.** The part of a horse in front of the rider. —**forehand** *adv.* With a forehand stroke or motion.

fore·hand·ed (fôr′hăn′dĭd, fōr′-) *adj.* **1.** Forehand, as in tennis. **2.a.** Looking or planning ahead; circumspect. **b.** Having ample financial resources; well-off. —**fore′hand′ed·ly** *adv.* —**fore′hand′ed·ness** *n.*

fore·head (fôr′ĭd, -hĕd′, fōr′-) *n.* **1.** The part of the face between the eyebrows, the normal hairline, and the temples. **2.** The front part of something. [Middle English *forhed,* from Old English *forhēafod* : *for-,* fore- + *hēafod,* head; see HEAD.]

for·eign (fôr′ĭn, fōr′-) *adj. Abbr.* **for. 1.** Located away from one's native country: *on business in a foreign city.* **2.** Of, characteristic of, or from a place or country other than the one being considered: *a foreign custom.* **3.** Conducted or involved with other nations or governments; not domestic: *foreign trade.* **4.** Situated in an abnormal or improper place in the body and typically introduced from outside: *a foreign object in the eye.* **5.** Not natural; alien: *Jealousy is foreign to her nature.* **6.** Not germane; irrelevant. **7.** Subject to the jurisdiction of another political unit. [Middle English *forein,* from Old French *forain,* from Late Latin *forānus,* on the outside, from Latin *forās,* outside. See **dhwer-** in Appendix.] —**for′eign·ness** *n.*

SYNONYMS: *foreign, alien, exotic, strange.* The central meaning shared by these adjectives is "of, from, or characteristic of another place or part of the world": *a foreign accent; alien customs; exotic birds; moved to a strange city.* See also Synonyms at **extrinsic.**

foreign affairs *pl.n.* Affairs concerning international relations and national interests in foreign countries.

foreign aid *n.* Aid, such as economic or military assistance, offered by one nation to another.

foreign bill *n.* A draft for a sum of money to be paid in another country.

for·eign-born (fôr′ĭn-bôrn′, fŏr′-) *adj.* Foreign by birth; not native to the country in which one resides.

foreign correspondent *n.* A correspondent who sends news reports or commentary from a foreign country for broadcast or publication.

for·eign·er (fôr′ə-nər, fŏr′-) *n.* **1.** One who is from a foreign country or place. **2.** One who is from outside a particular group or community; an outsider.

foreign exchange *n. Abbr.* **FX 1.** Transaction of international monetary business, as between governments or businesses of different countries. **2.** Negotiable bills drawn in one country to be paid in another country.

for·eign·ism (fôr′ĭ-nĭz′əm, fŏr′-) *n.* A foreign idiom or custom.

foreign minister *n.* A cabinet minister in charge of a nation's foreign affairs.

foreign mission *n.* **1.** A permanent diplomatic legation established in a foreign country. **2.** A religious group especially of Christians sent to a foreign country for missionary service.

foreign office *n. Abbr.* **FO, F.O.** The governmental department in charge of foreign affairs in certain countries.

foreign policy *n.* The diplomatic policy of a nation in its interactions with other nations.

For·eign Service (fôr′ĭn, fŏr′-) *n. Abbr.* **FS 1.** The diplomatic and consular staff of the United States. **2. foreign service.** The diplomatic and consular personnel of a nation's foreign office.

fore·judge also **for·judge** (fôr-jŭj′, fōr-) *tr.v.* **-judged, -judg·ing, -judg·es.** To judge beforehand without adequate examination or evidence; prejudge. —**fore·judg′ment** *n.*

fore·know (fôr-nō′, fōr-) *tr.v.* **-knew** (-no͞o′, -nyo͞o′), **-known** (-nōn′), **-know·ing, -knows.** To have foreknowledge of, especially by supernatural means or through revelation.

fore·knowl·edge (fôr-nŏl′ĭj, fōr-, fôr′nŏl′-, fōr′-) *n.* Knowledge or awareness of something before its existence or occurrence; prescience.

fore·known (fôr-nōn′, fōr-) *v.* Past participle of **foreknow.**

fore·la·dy (fôr′lā′dē, fōr′-) *n.* See **forewoman.**

fore·land (fôr′lənd, fōr′-) *n.* A projecting land mass; a promontory.

fore·leg (fôr′lĕg′, fōr′-) *n.* Either of the front legs of a quadruped.

fore·limb (fôr′lĭm′, fōr′-) *n.* An anterior appendage, such as a leg, wing, or flipper.

fore·lock[1] (fôr′lŏk′, fōr′-) *n.* A lock of hair that grows from or falls on the forehead, especially the part of a horse's mane that falls forward between the ears.

fore·lock[2] (fôr′lŏk′, fōr′-) *n.* A cotter pin; a linchpin.

fore·man (fôr′mən, fōr′-) *n.* **1.** A man who serves as the leader of a work crew, as in a factory. **2.** A man who chairs and speaks for a jury. —**fore′man·ship′** *n.*

fore·mast (fôr′məst, -măst′, fōr′-) *n. Nautical.* The forward mast on a sailing vessel.

fore·milk (fôr′mĭlk′, fōr′-) *n.* See **colostrum.**

fore·most (fôr′mōst′, fōr′-) *adj.* **1.** First in time or place. **2.** Ahead of all others, especially in position or rank. —**foremost** *adv.* **1.** In the front or first position. **2.** So as to be most important. [Alteration of Middle English *formest,* superlative of *forme,* first, from Old English *forma.* See **per**[1] in Appendix.]

fore·moth·er (fôr′mŭth′ər, fōr′-) *n.* A woman ancestor.

fore·name (fôr′nām′, fōr′-) *n.* A name before one's surname; a first name.

fore·named (fôr′nāmd′, fōr′-) *adj.* Named previously; aforementioned.

fore·noon (fôr′no͞on′, fōr′-, fôr-no͞on′, fōr-) *n.* The period of time between sunrise and noon; morning.

fo·ren·sic (fə-rĕn′sĭk, -zĭk) *adj.* **1.** Relating to, used in, or appropriate for courts of law or for public discussion or argumentation. **2.** Of, relating to, or used in debate or argument; rhetorical. [From Latin *forēnsis,* public, of a forum, from *forum,* forum. See **dhwer-** in Appendix.] —**fo·ren′si·cal·ly** *adv.*

forehand

ă pat	oi boy
ā pay	ou out
âr care	o͝o took
ä father	o͞o boot
ĕ pet	ŭ cut
ē be	ûr urge
ĭ pit	th thin
ī pie	*th* this
îr pier	hw which
ŏ pot	zh vision
ō toe	ə about, item
ô paw	♦ regionalism

Stress marks: ′ (primary); ′ (secondary), as in **dictionary** (dĭk′shə-nĕr′ē)

forensic medicine *n.* The branch of medicine that interprets or establishes the facts in civil or criminal law cases. Also called *medical jurisprudence.*

fo·ren·sics (fə-rĕn′sĭks, -zĭks) *n. (used with a sing. verb).* The art or study of formal debate; argumentation.

fore·or·dain (fôr′ôr-dān′, fōr′-) *tr.v.* **-dained, -dain·ing, -dains.** To determine or appoint beforehand; predestine. **—fore′or·dain′ment, fore·or′di·na′tion** (-ôr′dn-ā′shən) *n.*

fore·part (fôr′pärt′, fōr′-) *n.* **1.** The first or early part of a period of time. **2.** The anterior part, as of an object or organism.

fore·paw (fôr′pô′, fōr′-) *n.* The paw of an animal's foreleg.

fore·peak (fôr′pēk′, fōr′-) *n. Nautical.* The section of the hold of a ship that is within the angle made by the bow and is used for trimming or for storage of cargo.

fore·per·son (fôr′pûr′sən, fōr′-) *n.* **1.** The chair and spokesperson for a jury: *"A jury gives no reasons for its decision; it reaches a collective result, announced by the foreperson"* (Hiller B. Zobel). **2.** The leader of a work crew, as in a factory.

fore·play (fôr′plā′, fōr′-) *n.* Sexual stimulation preceding intercourse.

fore·quar·ter (fôr′kwôr′tər, fōr′-) *n.* **1.** The front section of a side of meat. **2.** The foreleg, shoulder, and adjacent lateral parts of an animal, especially a horse.

fore·ran (fôr-răn′, fōr-) *v.* Past tense of **forerun.**

fore·reach (fôr-rēch′, fōr-) *v.* **-reached, -reach·ing, -reach·es.** *Nautical.* *—tr.* To gain on or get ahead of (a sailing vessel). *—intr.* **1.** To gain on or go ahead of a sailing vessel. **2.** To continue moving forward after taking in sail, as when coming about.

fore·run (fôr-rŭn′, fōr-) *tr.v.* **-ran** (-răn′), **-run, -run·ning, -runs. 1.** To run before. **2.** To precede as an indication of what is to follow; foreshadow. **3.** To prevent from arriving or occurring; forestall.

fore·run·ner (fôr′rŭn′ər, fōr′-) *n.* **1.a.** One that precedes, as in time; a predecessor. **b.** An ancestor; a forebear. **2.a.** One that comes before and indicates the approach of another; a harbinger. **b.** A warning sign or symptom. **3.** *Sports.* One who skis the course before the beginning of a race.

fore·said (fôr′sĕd′, fōr′-) *adj. Archaic.* Aforesaid.

fore·sail (fôr′səl, -sāl′, fōr′-) *n. Nautical.* **1.** The principal square sail hung to the foremast of a square-rigged vessel. **2.** The principal triangular sail hung to the mast of a fore-and-aft-rigged vessel. **3.** The triangular sail hung to the forestay of a cutter or sloop.

fore·see (fôr-sē′, fōr-) *tr.v.* **-saw** (-sô′), **-seen** (-sēn′), **-see·ing, -sees.** To see or know beforehand: *foresaw the increase in unemployment.* **—fore·see′a·ble** *adj.* **—fore·se′er** *n.*

fore·shad·ow (fôr-shăd′ō, fōr-) *tr.v.* **-owed, -ow·ing, -ows.** To present an indication or a suggestion of beforehand; presage. **—fore·shad′ow·er** *n.*

fore·sheet (fôr′shēt′, fōr′-) *n. Nautical.* **1.** A rope used in trimming a foresail. **2. foresheets.** The space near the bow of an open boat.

fore·shock (fôr′shŏk′, fōr′-) *n.* A minor tremor of the earth that precedes a larger earthquake originating at approximately the same location.

fore·shore (fôr′shôr′, fōr′shōr′) *n.* **1.** The part of a shore that lies between high and low watermarks. **2.** The part of a shore between the water and occupied or cultivated land.

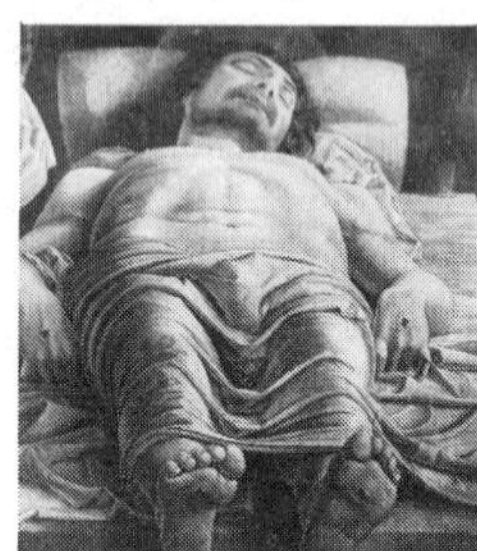

foreshorten
Detail of *The Dead Christ* by Andrea Mantegna

fore·short·en (fôr-shôr′tn, fōr-) *tr.v.* **-ened, -en·ing, -ens. 1.** To shorten the lines of (an object) in a drawing or other representation so as to produce an illusion of projection or extension in space. **2.** To reduce the length of; curtail or abridge.

fore·show (fôr-shō′, fōr-) *tr.v.* **-showed, -shown** (-shōn′), or **-showed, -show·ing, -shows.** To show in advance.

fore·side (fôr′sīd′, fōr′-) *n.* The front or upper side or part.

fore·sight (fôr′sīt′, fōr′-) *n.* **1.** Perception of the significance and nature of events before they have occurred. **2.** Care in providing for the future; prudence. See Synonyms at **prudence. 3.** The act of looking forward. **—fore′sight′ed** *adj.* **—fore′sight′ed·ly** *adv.* **—fore′sight′ed·ness** *n.* **—fore′sight′ful** *adj.*

fore·skin (fôr′skĭn′, fōr′-) *n.* The loose fold of skin that covers the glans of the penis. Also called *prepuce.*

fore·speak (fôr-spēk′, fōr-) *tr.v.* **-spoke** (-spōk′), **-spo·ken** (-spō′kən), **-speak·ing, -speaks. 1.** To predict. **2.** To arrange for in advance.

for·est (fôr′ĭst, fŏr′-) *n. Abbr.* **for. 1.** A dense growth of trees, plants, and underbrush covering a large area. **2.** Something that resembles a large, dense growth of trees, as in density, quantity, or profusion: *a forest of skyscrapers.* **3.** A defined area of land formerly set aside in England as a royal hunting ground. *—attributive.* Often used to modify another noun: *forest management; forest fires.* **—forest** *tr.v.* **-est·ed, -est·ing, -ests.** To plant trees on. [Middle English, from Old French, from Medieval Latin *forestis (silva),* outside (forest), from Latin *forīs,* outside. See **dhwer-** in Appendix.] **—for′est·al, fo·res′tial** (fə-rĕs′chəl) *adj.* **—for′es·ta′tion** *n.*

fore·stage (fôr′stāj′, fōr′-) *n.* The part of a stage in front of the closed curtain.

fore·stall (fôr-stôl′, fōr-) *tr.v.* **-stalled, -stall·ing, -stalls. 1.** To delay, hinder, or prevent by taking precautionary measures beforehand. See Synonyms at **prevent. 2.** To deal with or think of beforehand; anticipate. **3.** To prevent or hinder normal sales in (a market) by buying up merchandise, discouraging persons from bringing their goods to market, or encouraging an increase in prices in goods already on sale. [Middle English *forestallen,* to waylay and rob, from *forestal,* highway robbery, ambush, from Old English *foresteall* : *fore,* fore- + *steall,* position; see **stel-** in Appendix.] **—fore·stall′er** *n.* **—fore·stall′ment** *n.*

fore·stay (fôr′stā′, fōr′-) *n. Nautical.* A stay extending from the head of the foremast to the bowsprit of a ship.

fore·stay·sail (fôr′stā′səl, -sāl′, fōr′-) *n. Nautical.* A triangular sail set on the forestay.

for·est·er (fôr′ĭ-stər, fŏr′-) *n.* **1.** One who is trained in forestry. **2.** One that inhabits a forest. **3.** Any of various chiefly black moths of the family Agaristidae.

For·est·er (fôr′ĭ-stər, fŏr′-), **C(ecil) S(cott).** 1899–1966. British writer known for his adventure novels set during the Napoleonic Wars and featuring Horatio Hornblower.

For·est Hills (fôr′ĭst, fŏr′-). A residential section of New York City in central Queens on western Long Island. Until 1978 the U.S. Open Championship matches were held here.

for·est·land (fôr′ĭst-lănd′, fŏr′-) *n.* A section of land covered with forest or set aside for the cultivation of forests.

Forest Park. 1. A city of northwest Georgia, an industrial suburb of Atlanta. Population, 18,782. **2.** A city of southwest Ohio, a residential suburb of Cincinnati. Population, 18,675.

forest ranger *n.* An officer in charge of protecting or managing a section of a public forest.

for·est·ry (fôr′ĭ-strē, fŏr′-) *n. Abbr.* **for. 1.a.** The science and art of cultivating, maintaining, and developing forests. **b.** The management of a forestland. **2.** A forestland.

fore·swear (fôr-swâr′, fōr-) *v.* Variant of **forswear.**

fore·taste (fôr′tāst′, fōr′-) *n.* **1.** An advance token or warning. **2.** A slight taste or sample in anticipation of something to come. **—foretaste** (fôr-tāst′, fōr-, fôr′tāst′, fōr′-) *tr.v.* **-tast·ed, -tast·ing, -tastes.** To have an anticipatory taste of.

fore·tell (fôr-tĕl′, fōr-) *tr.v.* **-told** (-tōld′), **-tell·ing, -tells.** To tell of or indicate beforehand; predict. **—fore·tell′er** *n.*

SYNONYMS: *foretell, augur, divine, prophesy, vaticinate.* The central meaning shared by these verbs is "to tell about something beforehand by or as if by supernatural means": *foretelling the future; augured scandal from a distance; divined the enemy's victory; prophesying a stock-market boom; atrocities vaticinated by the antifascists.* See also Synonyms at **predict.**

fore·thought (fôr′thôt′, fōr′-) *n.* **1.** Deliberation, consideration, or planning beforehand. **2.** Preparation or thought for the future. See Synonyms at **prudence. —fore′thought′ful** *adj.* **—fore′thought′ful·ly** *adv.* **—fore′thought′ful·ness** *n.*

fore·to·ken (fôr-tō′kən, fōr-) *tr.v.* **-kened, -ken·ing, -kens.** To indicate or give warning of beforehand; presage. **—foretoken** (fôr′tō′kən, fōr′-) *n.* An advance sign; a warning.

fore·told (fôr-tōld′, fōr-) *v.* Past tense and past participle of **foretell.**

fore·top (fôr′tŏp′, fōr′-) *n.* **1.** (*also* -təp). *Nautical.* A platform at the top of a ship's foremast. **2.** A forelock, especially of a horse.

fore·top·gal·lant (fôr′tŏp-găl′ənt, fōr′-, fôr′təp-, fōr′-) *adj. Nautical.* Of, relating to, or being the mast directly above the foremast.

fore·top·mast (fôr′tŏp′məst, fōr′-, fôr′təp-măst′, fōr′-) *n. Nautical.* The mast that is above the foretop.

fore·top·sail (fôr′tŏp′səl, fōr′-, fôr′təp-, fōr′-) *n. Nautical.* The sail hung from the foretopmast.

for·ev·er (fôr-ĕv′ər, fər-) *adv.* **1.** For everlasting time; eternally: *No one can live forever.* **2.** At all times; incessantly: *was forever complaining about the job.* **—forever** *n.* A seemingly very long time: *It has taken forever to resolve these problems.*

for·ev·er·more (fôr-ĕv′ər-môr′, -mōr′, fər-) *adv.* Forever.

fore·warn (fôr-wôrn′, fōr-) *tr.v.* **-warned, -warn·ing, -warns.** To warn in advance. See Synonyms at **warn.**

fore·went (fôr-wĕnt′, fōr-) *v.* Past tense of **forego**[1]**.**

fore·wing (fôr′wĭng′, fōr′-) *n.* Either of a pair of anterior wings of a four-winged insect.

fore·wom·an (fôr′wo͝om′ən, fōr′-) *n.* **1.** A woman who serves as the leader of a work crew, as in a factory. **2.** A woman who chairs and speaks for a jury. Also called *forelady.*

fore·word (fôr′wərd, fōr′-) *n.* A preface or an introductory note, as for a book, especially by a person other than the author.

fore·worn (fôr-wôrn′, fōr-wōrn′) *adj.* Variant of **forworn.**

fore·yard (fôr′yärd′, fōr′-) *n. Nautical.* The lowest yard on a foremast.

for·feit (fôr′fĭt) *n.* **1.** Something surrendered or subject to surrender as punishment for a crime, an offense, an error, or a breach of contract. **2.** *Games.* **a.** Something placed in escrow and then redeemed after payment of a fine. **b. forfeits.** A game in which forfeits are demanded. **3.** A forfeiture. **—forfeit** *adj.* Lost or subject to loss through forfeiture. **—forfeit** *tr.v.* **-feit·ed, -feit·ing, -feits. 1.** To surrender, be deprived of, or give up the right to on account of a crime, an offense, an error, or a breach of contract. **2.** To subject to seizure as a forfeit. [Middle English *forfet,* crime, penalty, from Old French *forfait,* past participle of *forfaire,* to commit a crime, act outside the law : *fors,* beyond (from Latin *forīs,* outside; see **dhwer-** in Appendix) + *faire,* to do (from Latin *facere;* see **dhē-** in Appendix).] **—for′feit·a·ble** *adj.* **—for′feit·er** *n.*

for·fei·ture (fôr′fĭ-cho͝or′, -chər) *n.* **1.** The act of surrendering something as a forfeit. **2.** Something that is forfeited; a penalty.

for·fend also **fore·fend** (fôr-fĕnd′, fōr-) *tr.v.* **-fend·ed, -fend·ing, -fends. 1.a.** To keep or ward off; avert. **b.** *Archaic.* To forbid. **2.** To defend or protect. [Middle English *forfenden* : *for-,* for- + *fenden,* to ward off; see FEND.]

for·fi·cate (fôr′fĭ-kĭt, -kāt′) *adj.* Deeply forked or notched, as the tails of certain birds. [Latin *forfex, forfic-,* scissors + -ATE[1].]

for·gath·er also **fore·gath·er** (fôr-găth′ər, fōr-) *intr.v.* **-ered, -er·ing, -ers. 1.** To gather together; assemble. **2.** To meet another usually by accident.

for·gave (fər-gāv′, fôr-) *v.* Past tense of **forgive.**

forge[1] (fôrj, fōrj) *n.* **1.** A furnace or hearth where metals are heated or wrought; a smithy. **2.** A workshop where pig iron is transformed into wrought iron. **—forge** *v.* **forged, forg·ing, forg·es.** *—tr.* **1.a.** To form (metal, for example) by heating in a forge and beating or hammering into shape. **b.** To form (metal) by a mechanical or hydraulic press. **2.** To give form or shape to, especially by means of careful effort: *forge a treaty; forge a close relationship.* **3.** To fashion or reproduce for fraudulent purposes; counterfeit: *forge a signature.* *—intr.* **1.** To work at a forge or smithy. **2.** To make a forgery or counterfeit. [Middle English, from Old French, from Latin *fabrica,* from *faber,* worker.] **—forge′a·bil′i·ty** *n.* **—forge′a·ble** *adj.* **—forg′er** *n.*

forge[2] (fôrj, fōrj) *intr.v.* **forged, forg·ing, forg·es. 1.** To advance gradually but steadily: *forged ahead through throngs of shoppers.* **2.** To advance with an abrupt increase of speed: *forged into first place with seconds to go.* [Probably from FORGE[1].]

for·ger·y (fôr′jə-rē, fōr′-) *n., pl.* **-ies. 1.** The act of forging, especially the illegal production of something counterfeit. **2.** Something counterfeit, forged, or fraudulent.

for·get (fər-gĕt′, fôr-) *v.* **-got** (-gŏt′), **-got·ten** (-gŏt′n) or **-got, -get·ting, -gets.** *—tr.* **1.** To be unable to remember (something). **2.** To treat with thoughtless inattention; neglect: *forget one's family.* **3.** To leave behind unintentionally. **4.** To fail to mention. **5.a.** To banish from one's thoughts: *forget a disgrace.* **b.** *Informal.* To disregard on purpose. Usually used in the imperative: *Oh, forget it. I refuse to go!* *—intr.* **1.** To cease remembering: *Let's forgive and forget.* **2.** To fail or neglect to become aware at the proper or specified moment: *forgot about my appointment.* ***—idiom.*** **forget oneself.** To lose one's reserve, temper, or self-restraint. [Middle English *forgeten,* from Old English *forgietan.* See **ghend-** in Appendix.] **—for·get′ter** *n.*

for·get·ful (fər-gĕt′fəl, fôr-) *adj.* **1.** Tending or likely to forget. **2.** Marked by neglectful or heedless failure to remember: *forgetful of one's responsibilities.* **3.** Causing one to be unable to remember. **—for·get′ful·ly** *adv.* **—for·get′ful·ness** *n.*

SYNONYMS: *forgetful, unmindful, oblivious.* These adjectives refer to inability or failure to remember. *Forgetful* usually implies a faulty memory or a tendency not to remember: *As I grow older I become increasingly forgetful.* Less often the word is used as the equivalent of *unmindful,* which applies principally to failure to keep in mind what should be remembered, as through deliberate oversight, heedlessness, or inattentiveness: *She ought not to be forgetful of her duties. Each passenger rushed toward the exit, unmindful of the others. Oblivious* refers to failure rather than inability to remember, as because one is preoccupied or because one has chosen to disregard something: *Fortunately for the author, he was soon oblivious of the vitriolic criticism.* Sometimes the term implies lack of awareness: *For a person who has known them so long you are strangely oblivious to their faults.*

for·ge·tive (fôr′jĭ-tĭv, fōr′-) *adj. Archaic.* Capable of imagining or inventing. [Possibly from FORGE[1] + *-tive* (as in *inventive,* or *creative*).]

for·get-me-not (fər-gĕt′mē-nŏt′, fôr-) *n.* **1.** Any of various herbaceous plants of the genus *Myosotis,* having clusters of small blue flowers. Also called *scorpion grass.* **2.** Any of several similar or related plants. [Translation of Old French *ne m'oubliez mie.*]

for·get·ta·ble (fər-gĕt′ə-bəl, fôr-) *adj.* Fit or apt to be forgotten: *a movie with very forgettable characters.*

for·give (fər-gĭv′, fôr-) *v.* **-gave** (-gāv′), **-giv·en** (-gĭv′ən), **-giv·ing, -gives.** *—tr.* **1.** To excuse for a fault or an offense; pardon. **2.** To renounce anger or resentment against. **3.** To absolve from payment of (a debt, for example). *—intr.* To accord forgiveness. [Middle English *forgiven,* from Old English *forgiefan.* See **ghabh-** in Appendix.] **—for·giv′a·ble** *adj.* **—for·giv′a·bly** *adv.* **—for·giv′er** *n.*

SYNONYMS: *forgive, pardon, excuse, condone.* These verbs mean to refrain from imposing punishment on an offender or demanding satisfaction for an offense. The first three can be used as conventional ways of offering apology, as for minor infractions of social proprieties: *Please forgive me for being late. I hope you'll pardon the length of this letter. Excuse me, but I disagree with you.* More strictly, to *forgive* is to grant pardon without harboring resentment: *"Children begin by loving their parents; as they grow older they judge them; sometimes they forgive them"* (Oscar Wilde). *Pardon* more strongly implies release from the liability for or penalty entailed by an offense: *After the revolution all political prisoners were pardoned. "God may pardon you, but I never can"* (Elizabeth I). To *excuse* is to pass over a mistake or fault without demanding punishment or redress: *"There are some acts of injustice which no national interest can excuse"* (J.A. Froude). To *condone* is to overlook an offense, usually a serious one; the word often suggests tacit forgiveness: *Failure to protest police brutality may indicate a willingness to condone it.*

for·give·ness (fər-gĭv′nĭs, fôr-) *n.* The act of forgiving; pardon.

for·giv·ing (fər-gĭv′ĭng, fôr-) *adj.* **1.** Inclined or able to forgive. **2.** Providing a margin for error or shortcomings. **—for·giv′ing·ly** *adv.* **—for·giv′ing·ness** *n.*

for·go also **fore·go** (fôr-gō′, fōr-) *tr.v.* **-went** (-wĕnt′), **-gone** (-gôn′, -gŏn′), **-go·ing, -goes.** To abstain from; relinquish: *unwilling to forgo dessert.* [Middle English *forgon,* from Old English *forgān,* go away, forgo : *for-,* for- + *gān,* to go; see **ghē-** in Appendix.] **—for·go′er** *n.*

forget-me-not

for·got (fər-gŏt′, fôr-) *v.* Past tense and a past participle of **forget.**

for·got·ten (fər-gŏt′n, fôr-) *v.* A past participle of **forget.**

forgotten man *n.* A person or class of persons that is treated with undeserved neglect or disregard.

fo·rint (fôr′ĭnt′) *n.* See table at **currency.** [Hungarian, from Italian *fiorino,* florin. See FLORIN.]

for·judge (fôr-jŭj′, fōr-) *v.* Variant of **forejudge.**

fork (fôrk) *n.* **1.** A utensil with two or more prongs, used for eating or serving food. **2.** An implement with two or more prongs used for raising, carrying, piercing, or digging. **3.a.** A bifurcation or separation into two or more branches or parts. **b.** The point at which such a bifurcation or separation occurs: *a fork in a road.* **c.** One of the branches of such a bifurcation or separation: *the right fork.* See Synonyms at **branch. 4.** *Games.* An attack by one chess piece on two pieces at the same time. **—fork** *v.* **forked, fork·ing, forks.** *—tr.* **1.** To raise, carry, pitch, or pierce with a fork. **2.** To give the shape of a fork to (one's fingers, for example). **3.** *Games.* To launch an attack on (two chess pieces). **4.** *Informal.* To pay: *forked over $50 for front-row seats; forked up the money owed.* *—intr.* **1.** To divide into two or more branches: *The river forks here.* **2.a.** To use a fork, as in working. **b.** To turn at or travel along a fork. [Middle English *forke,* digging fork, from Old English *forca* and from Old North French *forque,* both from Latin *furca.*] **—fork′er** *n.* **—fork′ful′** *n.*

fork·ball (fôrk′bôl′) *n. Baseball.* A pitch with the ball placed between the index and middle fingers so that the ball takes a sharp dip near home plate. **—fork′ball′er** *n.*

forked (fôrkt, fôr′kĭd) *adj.* **1.** Containing or characterized by a fork: *a forked river.* **2.** Shaped like or similar to a fork: *forked lightning; a forked tail.*

fork·lift (fôrk′lĭft′) *n.* A small industrial vehicle with a power-operated pronged platform that can be raised and lowered for insertion under a load to be lifted and moved. **—forklift** *tr.v.* **-lift·ed, -lift·ing, -lifts.** To move or stack by use of a vehicle with a power-operated pronged platform.

fork·y (fôr′kē) *adj.* **-i·er, -i·est.** Forked.

For·lì (fôr-lē′). A city of northern Italy southeast of Bologna. A Roman trade center, it became a free commune in the 11th century. Population, 91,900.

forklift

for·lorn (fər-lôrn′, fôr-) *adj.* **1.a.** Appearing sad or lonely because deserted or abandoned. **b.** Forsaken or deprived: *forlorn of all hope.* **2.** Wretched or pitiful in appearance or condition: *forlorn roadside shacks.* **3.** Nearly hopeless; desperate. See Synonyms at **despondent.** [Middle English *forloren,* past participle of *forlesen,* to abandon, from Old English *forlēosan.* See **leu-** in Appendix.] **—for·lorn′ly** *adv.* **—for·lorn′ness** *n.*

forlorn hope *n.* **1.** An arduous or nearly hopeless undertaking. **2.** An advance guard of troops sent on a hazardous mission. [By folk etymology from Dutch *verloren hoop,* advance guard : *verloren,* past participle of *verliezen,* to lose; see **leu-** in Appendix + *hoop,* troop.]

form (fôrm) *n.* **1.a.** The shape and structure of an object. **b.** The body or outward appearance of a person or an animal considered separately from the face or head; figure. **2.a.** The essence of something. **b.** The mode in which a thing exists, acts, or manifests itself; kind: *a form of animal life; a form of blackmail.* **3.a.** Procedure as determined or governed by regulation or custom. **b.** A fixed order of words or procedures, as for use in a ceremony; a formula. **4.** A document with blanks for the insertion of details or information: *insurance forms.* **5.a.** Manners or conduct as governed by etiquette, decorum, or custom. **b.** Behavior according to a fixed or accepted standard: *Tardiness is considered bad form.* **c.** Performance considered with regard to acknowledged criteria: *a good jump shooter having an unusual form.* **6.a.** Proven ability to perform: *a musician at the top of her form.* **b.** Fitness, as of an athlete or animal, with regard to health or training. **c.** The past performance of a racehorse. **d.** A racing form. **7.a.** Method of arrangement or manner of coordinating elements in literary or musical composition or in organized discourse: *presented my ideas in outline form; a treatise in the form of a dialogue.* **b.** A particular type or example of such arrangement: *The essay is a literary form.* **c.** The design, structure, or pattern of a

ă pat	oi boy
ā pay	ou out
âr care	o͝o took
ä father	o͞o boot
ĕ pet	ŭ cut
ē be	ûr urge
ĭ pit	th thin
ī pie	*th* this
îr pier	hw which
ŏ pot	zh vision
ō toe	ə about, item
ô paw	♦ regionalism

Stress marks: ′ (primary); ′ (secondary), as in **dictionary** (dĭk′shə-nĕr′ē)

work of art: *symphonic form.* **8. a.** A mold for the setting of concrete. **b.** A model of the human figure or part of it used for displaying clothes. **c.** A proportioned model that may be adjusted for fitting clothes. **9.** A grade in a British secondary school or in some American private schools: *the sixth form.* **10. a.** A linguistic form. **b.** The external aspect of words with regard to their inflections, pronunciation, or spelling: *verb forms.* **11. a.** *Chiefly British.* A long seat; a bench. **b.** The resting place of a hare. **12.** *Botany.* A subdivision of a variety usually differing in one trivial characteristic, such as flower color. **—form** *v.* **formed, form·ing, forms.** —*tr.* **1. a.** To give form to; shape: *form clay into figures.* **b.** To develop in the mind; conceive: *form an opinion.* **2. a.** To shape or mold (dough, for example) into a particular form. **b.** To arrange oneself in: *Holding out his arms, the cheerleader formed a T. The acrobats formed a pyramid.* **c.** To organize or arrange: *The environmentalists formed their own party.* **d.** To fashion, train, or develop by instruction or precept: *form a child's mind.* **3.** To come to have; develop or acquire: *form a habit.* **4.** To constitute or compose a usually basic element, part, or characteristic of. **5. a.** To produce (a tense, for example) by assuming an inflection: *form the pluperfect.* **b.** To make (a word) by derivation or composition. **6.** To put in order; arrange. —*intr.* **1.** To become formed or shaped. **2.** To come into being by taking form; arise. **3.** To assume a specified form, shape, or pattern. [Middle English *forme,* from Latin *fōrma.*] **—form′a·bil′i·ty** *n.* **—form′a·ble** *adj.*

SYNONYMS: *form, figure, shape, configuration, contour, profile.* These nouns refer to the external outline of a thing. *Form* is the outline and structure of a thing as opposed to its substance: *stalactites of curious forms; a garden in the form of a lovers' knot. Figure* refers usually to form as established by bounding or enclosing lines: *The cube is a solid geometric figure. "Europe is disclosed as a prone and emaciated figure, the Alps shaping like a backbone, and the branching mountain chains like ribs, the peninsular plateau of Spain forming a head"* (Thomas Hardy). *Shape* implies three-dimensional definition that indicates both outline and bulk or mass: *"Rowing* [at night], *he faced her, a hooded and cloaked shape"* (Joseph Conrad). *Configuration* stresses the pattern formed by the arrangement of parts within an outline: *The map shows the configuration of the North American continent, with its mountains, rivers, and plains. Contour* refers especially to the outline of a three-dimensional figure: *I ran my finger along the soft, curving contour of the child's cheek. Profile* denotes the outline of something viewed against a background and especially the outline of the human face in side view: *We glimpsed the profile of the church steeple against the last glow of the sunset. The profile of the old warrior was characterized by a strong jaw and an aquiline nose.*

-form *suff.* Having the form of: *plexiform.* [New Latin *-fōrmis,* from Latin *fōrma,* form.]

for·mal (fôr′məl) *adj.* **1. a.** Relating to or involving outward form or structure. **b.** Being or relating to essential form or constitution: *a formal principle.* **2. a.** Following or being in accord with accepted forms, conventions, or regulations: *had little formal education; went to a formal party.* **b.** Executed, carried out, or done in proper or regular form: *a formal reprimand; a formal document.* **3. a.** Characterized by strict or meticulous observation of forms; methodical: *very formal in their business transactions.* **b.** Stiffly ceremonious: *a formal manner; a formal greeting; a formal bow to the monarch.* **4.** Having the outward appearance but lacking in substance: *a formal requirement that is usually ignored.* **—formal** *n.* Something, such as a gown or social affair, that is formal in nature. [Middle English, from Latin *fōrmālis,* from *fōrma,* shape.] **—for′mal·ly** *adv.* **—for′mal·ness** *n.*

for·mal·de·hyde (fôr-măl′də-hīd′) *n.* A colorless, gaseous compound, HCHO, the simplest aldehyde, used for manufacturing melamine and phenolic resins, fertilizers, dyes, and embalming fluids and in aqueous solution as a preservative and disinfectant. [FORM(IC ACID) + ALDEHYDE.]

for·ma·lin (fôr′mə-lĭn) *n.* An aqueous solution of formaldehyde that is 37 percent by weight. [Originally a trademark.]

for·mal·ism (fôr′mə-lĭz′əm) *n.* **1.** Rigorous or excessive adherence to recognized forms, as in religion or art. **2.** An instance of rigorous or excessive adherence to recognized forms. **—for′mal·ist** *adj.* & *n.* **—for′mal·is′tic** *adj.*

for·mal·i·ty (fôr-măl′ĭ-tē) *n., pl.* **-ties. 1.** The quality or condition of being formal. **2.** Rigorous or ceremonious adherence to established forms, rules, or customs. **3.** An established form, rule, or custom, especially one followed merely for the sake of procedure or decorum.

for·mal·ize (fôr′mə-līz′) *tr.v.* **-ized, -iz·ing, -iz·es. 1.** To give a definite form or shape to. **2. a.** To make formal. **b.** To give formal standing or endorsement to; make official or legitimate by the observance of proper procedure. **—for′mal·iz′a·ble** *adj.* **—for′mal·i·za′tion** (-mə-lĭ-zā′shən) *n.* **—for′mal·iz′er** *n.*

formal logic *n.* The study of the properties of propositions and deductive reasoning by abstraction and analysis of the form rather than the content of propositions under consideration.

for·mal·wear (fôr′məl-wâr′) *n.* Attire, such as evening gowns and tuxedos, for wear on formal occasions.

for·mant (fôr′mənt) *n.* Any of several frequency regions of relatively great intensity in a sound spectrum, which together determine the characteristic quality of a vowel sound. [German, from Latin *fōrmāns, fōrmant-,* present participle of *fōrmāre,* to form, from *fōrma,* form.]

for·mat (fôr′măt′) *n.* **1.** A plan for the organization and arrangement of a specified production. **2.** The material form or layout of a publication. **3.** *Computer Science.* **a.** The arrangement of data for storage or display. **b.** A method for achieving such an arrangement. **—format** *tr.v.* **-mat·ted, -mat·ting, -mats. 1.** To plan or arrange in a specified form: *They formatted the conference so that each speaker had less than 15 minutes to deliver a paper.* **2.** *Computer Science.* **a.** To divide (a disk) into marked sectors so that it may store data. **b.** To determine the arrangement of (data) for storage or display. [French, ultimately from Latin *fōrmātus,* past participle of *fōrmāre,* to form, from *fōrma,* form.]

for·mate (fôr′māt′) *n.* A compound, such as a salt or an ester of formic acid, that contains the $HCOO^-$ radical. [FORM(IC ACID) + -ATE[2].]

for·ma·tion (fôr-mā′shən) *n.* **1.** The act or process of forming something or of taking form. **2.** Something formed: *beautiful cloud formations.* **3.** The manner or style in which something is formed; structure: *the distinctive formation of the human eye.* **4.** A specified arrangement or deployment, as of troops. **5.** *Geology.* The primary unit of lithostratigraphy, consisting of a succession of strata useful for mapping or description. **—for·ma′tion·al** *adj.*

form·a·tive (fôr′mə-tĭv) *adj.* **1.** Forming or capable of forming. **2. a.** Susceptible to transformation by growth and development. **b.** *Biology.* Capable of producing new cells or tissue. **3.** Of or relating to formation, growth, or development: *the formative stages of a plot.* **4.** *Linguistics.* Relating to the formation or inflection of words. **—formative** *n.* *Grammar.* A derivational or inflectional affix. **—form′a·tive·ly** *adv.*

form class *n.* *Linguistics.* A set of words that have one or more grammatical or syntactic characteristics in common, such as the class of transitive verbs in English.

form criticism *n.* A method of textual criticism, applied especially to the Bible, for tracing the origin and history of certain passages through systematic study of the writings in terms of conventional literary forms, such as parables, proverbs, and love poems. **—form critic** *n.* **—form critical** *adj.*

form·er[1] (fôr′mər) *n.* **1.** One that forms; a maker or creator: *a former of ideas.* **2.** *Chiefly British.* A member of a school form: *a fifth former.*

for·mer[2] (fôr′mər) *adj.* **1. a.** Occurring earlier in time. **b.** Of, relating to, or taking place in the past. **2.** Coming before in place or order; foregoing. **3.** Being the first of two mentioned. **4.** Having been in the past: *a former ambassador.* [Middle English, comparative of *forme,* first, from Old English *forma.* See **per**[1] in Appendix.]

USAGE NOTE: Grammarians have often insisted that the phrases *the former* and *the latter* should be used only to refer to the first of two things and the second of two things, respectively: *"But Flynn preceded Casey, as did also Jimmy Blake, and the former was a lulu and the latter was a fake."* It is not difficult to find examples of violations of this rule in the works of reputable writers. But the fact that *former* and *latter* are plainly comparatives will make many readers uneasy when the words are used in enumerations of more than two things, much as would the analagous incorrect use of a comparative in a sentence such as *Her boys are 7, 9, and 13; only the younger was born in California.*

for·mer·ly (fôr′mər-lē) *adv.* At an earlier time; once.

form·fit·ting (fôrm′fĭt′ĭng) *adj.* Snugly fitting the contours of the body: *formfitting jeans.*

form genus *n.* *Botany.* A genus of fossil plants or imperfect fungi classified according to their asexual organs.

for·mic (fôr′mĭk) *adj.* **1.** Of or relating to ants. **2.** Of, derived from, or containing formic acid. [From Latin *formīca,* ant.]

For·mi·ca (fôr-mī′kə). A trademark used for a variety of high-pressure laminated plastic sheets of synthetic resin employed especially as a heat-resistant and chemical-resistant surface on tables and counters. This trademark sometimes occurs in print in attributive uses: *"The restaurant was dimly lit, with plain Formica tables and cushioned booths"* (Chicago Tribune).

formic acid *n.* A colorless caustic fuming liquid, HCOOH, used in dyeing and finishing textiles and paper and in the manufacture of fumigants, insecticides, and refrigerants. [From its natural occurrence in ants.]

for·mi·car·y (fôr′mĭ-kĕr′ē) *n., pl.* **-ies.** A nest of ants; an anthill. [Medieval Latin *formīcārium,* from Latin *formīca,* ant.]

for·mi·civ·o·rous (fôr′mĭ-sĭv′ər-əs) *adj.* Feeding on ants. [Latin *formīca,* ant + -VOROUS.]

for·mi·da·ble (fôr′mĭ-də-bəl) *adj.* **1.** Arousing fear, dread, or alarm: *the formidable prospect of major surgery.* **2.** Inspiring awe, admiration, or wonder: *"Though a true hero, he was also a thoroughgoing bureaucrat and politician, a formidable combination"* (Mario Puzo). **3.** Difficult to undertake, surmount, or defeat: *a formidable challenge; a formidable opponent.* [Middle English, from Old French, from Latin *formīdābilis,* from *formīdāre,* to fear, from *formīdō,* fear.] **—for′mi·da·bil′i·ty, for′mi·da·ble·ness** *n.* **—for′mi·da·bly** *adv.*

form·less (fôrm′lĭs) *adj.* **1.** Having no definite form. See Synonyms at **shapeless.** **2.** Lacking order. **3.** Having no material existence. **—form′less·ly** *adv.* **—form′less·ness** *n.*

form letter *n.* A usually impersonal letter in a standardized format that may be sent to different people or to large numbers of recipients.

For·mo·sa (fôr-mō′sə). See **Taiwan.**

Formosa Strait also **Tai·wan Strait** (tī′wän′). An arm of the Pacific Ocean between Taiwan and China.

for·mu·la (fôr′myə-lə) *n., pl.* **-las** or **-lae** (-lē′). **1.a.** An established form of words or symbols for use in a ceremony or procedure. **b.** An utterance of conventional notions or beliefs; a hackneyed expression. **2.** A method of doing or treating something that relies on an established, uncontroversial model or approach: *a new situation comedy that simply uses an old formula.* **3.** *Chemistry.* **a.** A symbolic representation of the composition or of the composition and structure of a compound. **b.** The compound so represented. **4.a.** A prescription of ingredients in fixed proportion; a recipe. **b.** A liquid food for infants, containing most of the nutrients in human milk. **5.** *Mathematics.* A statement, especially an equation, of a fact, rule, principle, or other logical relation. **6. Formula.** *Sports.* A set of specifications, including engine displacement, fuel capacity, and weight, that determine a class of racing car. [Latin *fōrmula,* diminutive of *fōrma,* form.] **—for′mu·la′ic** (-lā′ĭk) *adj.* **—for′mu·la′i·cal·ly** *adv.*

for·mu·la·rize (fôr′myə-lə-rīz′) *tr.v.* **-rized, -riz·ing, -riz·es.** To express as or reduce to a formula; formulate. **—for′mu·la·ri·za′tion** (-lər-ĭ-zā′shən) *n.* **—for′mu·la·riz′er** *n.*

for·mu·lar·y (fôr′myə-lĕr′ē) *n., pl.* **-ies. 1.** A book or other collection of stated and fixed forms, such as prayers. **2.** A statement expressed in formulas. **3.** A fixed form or pattern; a formula. **4.** A book containing a list of pharmaceutical substances along with their formulas, uses, and methods of preparation.

for·mu·late (fôr′myə-lāt′) *tr.v.* **-lat·ed, -lat·ing, -lates. 1.a.** To state as or reduce to a formula. **b.** To express in systematic terms or concepts. **c.** To devise or invent: *formulate strategy.* **2.** To prepare according to a specified formula. **—for′mu·la′tion** *n.* **—for′mu·la′tor** *n.*

formula weight *n.* See **molecular weight.**

for·mu·lize (fôr′myə-līz′) *tr.v.* **-lized, -liz·ing, -liz·es.** To formulate. **—for′mu·li·za′tion** (-lĭ-zā′shən) *n.* **—for′mu·liz′er** *n.*

form word *n. Grammar.* See **function word.**

form·work (fôrm′wûrk′) *n.* The structure of boards that make up a form for pouring concrete in construction.

for·myl (fôr′mĭl′) *n.* The negative univalent radical HCO, characteristic of aldehydes. [FORM(IC ACID) + –YL.]

For·nax (fôr′năks′) *n.* A constellation in the Southern Hemisphere near Sculptor and Eridanus. [Latin *fornāx,* furnace, oven. See **gʷher-** in Appendix.]

♦**for·nent** (fər-nĕnt′) *prep. Upper Southern U.S.* Variant of **fernimst.**

for·ni·cate (fôr′nĭ-kāt′) *intr.v.* **-cat·ed, -cat·ing, -cates.** To commit fornication. [Late Latin *fornicārī, fornicāt-,* from *fornix, fornic-,* vault, vaulted cellar, brothel. See **gʷher-** in Appendix.] **—for′ni·ca′tor** *n.*

for·ni·ca·tion (fôr′nĭ-kā′shən) *n.* Sexual intercourse between partners who are not married to each other.

WORD HISTORY: The Latin word *fornix,* from which *fornicātiō,* the ancestor of *fornication,* is derived, meant "a vault, an arch." The term also referred to a vaulted cellar or similar place where prostitutes plied their trade. This sense of *fornix* in Late Latin yielded the verb *fornicārī,* "to commit fornication," from which is derived *fornicātiō,* "whoredom, fornication." Our word is first recorded in Middle English about 1303.

for·nix (fôr′nĭks) *n., pl.* **-ni·ces** (-nĭ-sēz′). An archlike anatomical structure or fold, such as the arched band of white matter located beneath the corpus callosum of the brain. [Latin, arch, vault. See **gʷher-** in Appendix.]

for-prof·it (fər-prŏf′ĭt, fôr-) *adj.* Established or operated with the intention of making a profit: *a for-profit hospital.*

For·rest (fôr′ĭst, fŏr′-), **Edwin.** 1806–1872. American actor noted for his portrayal of Othello.

Forrest, Nathan Bedford. 1821–1877. American Confederate general who was active at the battles of Shiloh (1862) and Chickamauga (1863).

for·sake (fôr-sāk′, fər-) *tr.v.* **-sook** (-so͝ok′), **-sak·en** (-sā′kən), **-sak·ing, -sakes. 1.** To give up (something formerly held dear); renounce: *forsook liquor.* **2.** To leave altogether; abandon: *forsook Hollywood and returned to the legitimate stage.* [Middle English *forsaken,* from Old English *forsacan.* See **sāg-** in Appendix.]

for·sooth (fôr-so͞oth′, fər-) *adv.* In truth; indeed. [Middle English *forsoth,* from Old English *forsōth* : *for,* for; see FOR + *sōth,* truth; see SOOTH.]

for·spent (fôr-spĕnt′, fər-) *adj. Archaic.* Worn out, as from exertion; exhausted.

For·ster (fôr′stər), **E(dward) M(organ).** 1879–1970. British writer whose novels, such as *Howards End* (1910), explore the emotional and moral shortcomings of England's upper classes.

for·swear also **fore·swear** (fôr-swâr′, fōr-) *v.* **-swore** (fôr-swôr′, fōr-swōr′), **-sworn** (fôr-swôrn′, fōr-swōrn′), **-swear·ing, -swears.** —*tr.* **1.a.** To renounce or repudiate under oath. **b.** To renounce seriously. **2.** To disavow under oath; deny. **3.** To make (oneself) guilty of perjury. —*intr.* To swear falsely; commit perjury. [Middle English *forsweren,* from Old English *forswerian* : *for-,* wrongly; see FOR– + *swerian,* to swear; see SWEAR.]

for·syth·i·a (fôr-sĭth′ē-ə, -sī′thē-ə, fər-) *n.* Any of several shrubs of the genus *Forsythia,* native to Asia and widely cultivated for their early-blooming yellow flowers. [New Latin, genus name, after William *Forsyth* (1737–1804), Scottish horticulturist.]

fort (fôrt, fōrt) *n. Abbr.* **ft., Ft. 1.** A fortified place or position stationed with troops. **2.** A permanent army post. [Middle English, strength, stronghold, from Old French, strong, strength, from Latin *fortis.* See **bhergh-²** in Appendix.]

fort. *abbr.* Fortification.

For·ta·le·za (fôr′tl-ā′zə, -tə-lĕ′-). A city of northeast Brazil northwest of Natal on the Atlantic Ocean. Founded in 1609, it is a thriving port and industrial center. Population, 1,307,611.

for·ta·lice (fôr′tə-lĭs) *n. Archaic.* **1.** A defensive structure or position; a fortress. **2.** A small fort. [Middle English, from Medieval Latin *fortalitia.* See FORTRESS.]

For·tas (fôr′təs), **Abraham.** Known as "Abe." 1910–1982. American jurist who served as an associate justice of the U.S. Supreme Court (1965–1969).

Fort Col·lins (fôrt kŏl′ĭnz, fōrt). A city of northern Colorado north-northeast of Boulder. It is a trade, shipping, and processing center. Population, 65,092.

Fort-de-France (fôr-də-fräNs′). The capital and largest city of Martinique, on the western coast of the island on **Fort-de-France Bay,** an inlet of the Caribbean Sea. Population, 99,844.

Fort Dodge (dŏj). A city of central Iowa on the Des Moines River north-northwest of Des Moines. It was settled in the 1840's. Population, 29,423.

forte¹ (fôrt, fōrt, fôr′tā′) *n.* **1.** Something in which a person excels. **2.** The strong part of a sword blade, between the middle and the hilt. [French *fort,* from Old French, strong, from Latin *fortis.* See **bhergh-²** in Appendix.]

SYNONYMS: *forte, métier, specialty, thing.* The central meaning shared by these nouns is "something at which a person is particularly skilled": *Writing fiction is her forte. The theater is his métier. The professor made the description of the Semitic languages her specialty. Mountain climbing is really her thing.*

for·te² (fôr′tā′) *Music. adv. & adj. Abbr.* **f, F.** In a loud, forceful manner. Used chiefly as a direction. **—forte** *n.* A note, passage, or chord played forte. [Italian, strong, forte, from Latin *fortis.* See **bhergh-²** in Appendix.]

for·te-pi·an·o (fôr′tā-pē-ăn′ō, -ä′nō) *adv. & adj. Music.* In a loud, then suddenly soft, manner. Used chiefly as a direction. [Italian : *forte,* loud; see FORTE² + *piano,* soft; see PIANO².]

Fort E·rie (îr′ē). A town of southern Ontario, Canada, on the Niagara River opposite Buffalo, New York. It is on the site of a fort established in 1764. Population, 24,096.

forth (fôrth, fōrth) *adv.* **1.** Forward in time, place, or order; onward: *from this time forth.* **2.** Out into view: *A stranger came forth from the crowd; put my ideas forth.* **3.** *Obsolete.* Away from a specified place; abroad. **—forth** *prep. Archaic.* Out of; forth from. [Middle English, from Old English. See **per¹** in Appendix.]

Forth (fôrth, fōrth). A river of south-central Scotland flowing about 187 km (116 mi) eastward to the **Firth of Forth,** a wide inlet of the North Sea.

forth·com·ing (fôrth-kŭm′ĭng, fōrth-) *adj.* **1.** About to appear or take place; approaching: *the forthcoming elections.* **2.a.** Available when required or as promised: *Federal funds were not forthcoming.* **b.** Affable and outgoing: *a considerate, forthcoming person.* **c.** Candid and willing to cooperate. **—forthcoming** (fôrth′kŭm′ĭng, fōrth′-) *n.* The act or an instance of coming forth.

forth·right (fôrth′rīt′, fōrth′-) *adj.* **1.** Direct and without evasion; straightforward: *a forthright appraisal; forthright criticism.* **2.** *Archaic.* Proceeding straight ahead. **—forthright** *adv.* **1.a.** Directly ahead. **b.** Directly and frankly. **2.** *Archaic.* At once. **—forth′right′ly** *adv.* **—forth′right′ness** *n.*

forth·with (fôrth-wĭth′, -wĭth′, fōrth-) *adv.* At once; immediately.

for·ti·eth (fôr′tē-ĭth) *n.* **1.** The ordinal number matching the number 40 in a series. **2.** One of 40 equal parts. **—for′ti·eth** *adv. & adj.*

for·ti·fi·ca·tion (fôr′tə-fĭ-kā′shən) *n. Abbr.* **fort., ft. 1.a.** The science of fortifying. **b.** The act or process of fortifying. **2.** Something that serves to fortify, especially military works erected to fortify a position or place.

for·ti·fied wine (fôr′tə-fīd′) *n.* Wine, such as sherry, to which alcohol, usually in the form of brandy, has been added.

for·ti·fy (fôr′tə-fī′) *v.* **-fied, -fy·ing, -fies.** —*tr.* To make strong, as: **a.** To strengthen and secure (a position) with fortifications. **b.** To reinforce by adding material. **c.** To impart physical strength or endurance to; invigorate. **d.** To give emotional, moral or mental strength to; encourage: *Prayer fortified us during our crisis.* **e.** To strengthen or enrich (food, for example), as by adding vitamins. —*intr.* To build fortifications. [Middle English

ă pat	oi boy
ā pay	ou out
âr care	o͝o took
ä father	o͞o boot
ĕ pet	ŭ cut
ē be	ûr urge
ĭ pit	th thin
ī pie	*th* this
îr pier	hw which
ŏ pot	zh vision
ō toe	ə about, item
ô paw	♦ regionalism

Stress marks: ′ (primary); ′ (secondary), as in **dictionary** (dĭk′shə-nĕr′ē)

fortifien, from Old French *fortifier,* from Late Latin *fortificāre,* from Latin *fortis,* strong. See **bhergh-**[2] in Appendix.] **—for′ti·fi′a·ble** *adj.* **—for′ti·fi′er** *n.* **—for′ti·fy′ing·ly** *adv.*

for·tis (fôr′tĭs) *Linguistics. adj.* Articulated with relatively strong pressure or tension of the respiratory muscles, as in English *p* and *t* compared with *b* and *d.* **—fortis** *n.* A fortis consonant. [Latin, strong. See **bhergh-**[2] in Appendix.]

for·tis·si·mo (fôr-tĭs′ə-mō′) *Music. adv. & adj. Abbr.* **ff** In a very loud manner. Used chiefly as a direction. **—fortissimo** *n., pl.* **-mos.** A note, chord, or passage played fortissimo. [Italian, superlative of *forte,* strong. See FORTE[2].]

for·tis·sis·si·mo (fôr′tĭ-sĭs′ə-mō) *adv. & adj. Abbr.* **fff** *Music.* In the loudest manner. Used chiefly as a direction. [Italian, superlative of *fortissimo.* See FORTISSIMO.]

for·ti·tude (fôr′tĭ-to͞od′, -tyo͞od′) *n.* Strength of mind that allows one to endure pain or adversity with courage. [Middle English, from Latin *fortitūdō,* from *fortis,* strong. See **bhergh-**[2] in Appendix.] **—for′ti·tu′di·nous** (-to͞od′n-əs, -tyo͞od′-) *adj.*

Fort-La·my (fôr-lä-mē′). See **Ndjamena.**

Fort Lau·der·dale (lô′dər-dāl′). A city of southeast Florida on the Atlantic coast north of Miami Beach. It has long been a favorite vacation spot for college students. Population, 153,279.

Fort Lee (lē). A borough of northeast New Jersey on the Hudson River opposite Manhattan. Settled around 1700, it was an early center of the motion-picture industry. Population, 32,449.

Fort Mc·Mur·ray (mĭk-mûr′ē, -mŭr′ē). A city of northeast Alberta, Canada, at the conjunction of the Athabasca and Clearwater rivers. Population, 31,000.

Fort My·ers (mī′ərz). A city of southwest Florida on an estuary of the Caloosahatchee River north-northeast of Cape Coral. It is a shipping and tourist center. Population, 36,638.

Fort Nel·son (nĕl′sən). A river, about 418 km (260 mi) long, of northeast British Columbia, Canada.

fort·night (fôrt′nīt′) *n.* A period of 14 days; two weeks. [Middle English *fourtenight,* alteration of *fourtene night,* fourteen nights : Old English *fēowertēne,* fourteen; see FOURTEEN + Old English *niht,* night; see NIGHT.]

fort·night·ly (fôrt′nīt′lē) *adj.* Happening or appearing once in or every two weeks. **—fortnightly** *adv.* Once in a fortnight. **—fortnightly** *n., pl.* **-lies.** A publication issued once every two weeks.

Fort Pierce (pîrs). A city of east-central Florida on the Indian River lagoon north-northwest of Palm Beach. It is a distribution center in a cattle and farming region. Population, 33,802.

FOR·TRAN (fôr′trăn′) *n. Computer Science.* A high-level programming language for problems that can be expressed algebraically, used mainly in mathematics, science, and engineering. [FOR(MULA) + TRAN(SLATION).]

for·tress (fôr′trĭs) *n.* A fortified place, especially a large, permanent military stronghold that often includes a town. [Middle English *forteress,* from Old French, from Medieval Latin *fortalitia,* from Latin *fortis,* strong. See **bhergh-**[2] in Appendix.]

Fort Smith (smĭth). **1.** A region of southwest Northwest Territories, Canada, including Great Slave Lake and most of Great Bear Lake. **2.** A city of western Arkansas on the Oklahoma border west-northwest of Little Rock. Population, 71,626.

Fort Thom·as (tŏm′əs). A city of northern Kentucky, a residential suburb of Covington. Population, 16,012.

for·tu·i·tous (fôr-to͞o′ĭ-təs, -tyo͞o′-) *adj.* **1.** Happening by accident or chance. See Synonyms at **accidental. 2.** *Usage Problem.* **a.** Happening by a fortunate accident or chance. **b.** Lucky or fortunate. [Latin *fortuitus,* from *forte,* by chance, ablative of *fors,* chance.] **—for·tu′i·tous·ly** *adv.* **—for·tu′i·tous·ness** *n.*

USAGE NOTE: In its best-established sense, *fortuitous* means "happening by accident or chance," with no implication as to the desirability of the outcome: *a fortuitous meeting* may have either fortunate or unfortunate consequences. In this century, however, the word is often used with particular reference to happy accidents, as in *The company's third-quarter profits were enhanced as the result of a fortuitous drop in the cost of RAM chips.* This use may have arisen because *fortuitous* resembles both *fortunate* and *felicitous;* it is well established in the writing of reputable authors. More controversial is the use of *fortuitous* to mean simply "lucky or fortunate," as in *He came to the Giants in June as the result of a fortuitous trade that sent two minor-league players to the Reds' organization.* This use dates back at least to the 1920's, when H.W. Fowler labeled it a malapropism. It is still widely regarded as incorrect, and writers who are unwilling to risk censure are advised to avoid it.

for·tu·i·ty (fôr-to͞o′ĭ-tē, -tyo͞o′-) *n., pl.* **-ties. 1.** A chance occurrence. **2.** The quality or condition of being fortuitous.

For·tu·na (fôr-to͞o′nə, -tyo͞o′-) *n. Roman Mythology.* The goddess of fortune.

for·tu·nate (fôr′chə-nĭt) *adj.* **1.** Bringing something good and unforeseen; auspicious. **2.** Having unexpected good fortune; lucky. See Synonyms at **happy. —fortunate** *n.* One who has good fortune, especially a wealthy person. [Latin *fortūnātus,* from *fortūna,* chance. See FORTUNE.] **—for′tu·nate·ly** *adv.* **—for′tu·nate·ness** *n.*

for·tune (fôr′chən) *n.* **1.a.** The chance happening of fortunate or adverse events; luck: *He decided to go home for the holidays, and his fortune turned for the worse.* **b. fortunes.** The turns of luck in the course of one's life. **c.** Success, especially when at least partially resulting from luck: *No matter what they tried, it ended in fortune.* **2.a.** A person's condition or standing in life determined by material possessions or financial wealth: *She pursued her fortune in another country.* **b.** Extensive amounts of material possessions or money; wealth. **c.** A large sum of money: *spent a fortune on the new car.* **3.** Often **Fortune.** A hypothetical, often personified force or power that favorably or unfavorably governs the events of one's life: *We believe that Fortune is on our side.* **4.a.** Fate; destiny: *told my fortune with tarot cards.* **b.** A foretelling of one's destiny. **—fortune** *v.* **-tuned, -tun·ing, -tunes.** *—tr.* **1.** *Archaic.* To endow with wealth. **2.** *Obsolete.* To ascribe or give good or bad fortune to. *—intr. Archaic.* To occur by chance; happen. [Middle English, from Old French, from Latin *fortūna,* from *fors, fort-,* chance.]

fortune cookie *n.* A cookie made from a thin layer of dough folded and baked around a slip of paper bearing a prediction of fortune or a maxim.

fortune hunter *n.* A person who seeks wealth, especially through marriage.

for·tune·tell·er (fôr′chən-tĕl′ər) *n.* One who professes to predict future events. **—for′tune·tell′ing** *adj. & n.*

Fort Wal·ton Beach (wôl′tən). A city of northwest Florida in the Panhandle east of Pensacola. It is a year-round resort on the Gulf of Mexico. Population, 20,829.

Fort Wayne (wān). A city of northeast Indiana northeast of Indianapolis. A French trading post and fort were built on the site in the late 17th century. Population, 172,028.

Fort Worth (wûrth). A city of northeast Texas west of Dallas. Built on the site of a military post established in the 1840's, it is a major industrial center. Population, 385,164.

for·ty (fôr′tē) *n., pl.* **-ties. 1.** The cardinal number equal to 4 × 10. **2. forties. a.** *Often* **Forties.** The decade from 40 to 49 in a century. **b.** A decade or the numbers from 40 to 49: *They stopped smoking in their forties. At night the temperature fell into the forties.* [Middle English, from Old English *fēowertig.* See **k^w^etwer-** in Appendix.] **—for′ty** *adj. & pron.*

for·ty-five (fôr′tē-fīv′) *n.* **1.** A .45-caliber pistol. **2.** A phonograph record designed to be played at 45 revolutions per minute. **—for′ty-five′** *adj.*

for·ty-nin·er (fôr′tē-nī′nər) *n.* One who took part in the 1849 California gold rush.

forty winks *pl.n. (used with a sing. or pl. verb). Informal.* A short nap.

fo·rum (fôr′əm, fōr′-) *n., pl.* **fo·rums** also **fo·ra** (fôr′ə, fōr′ə). **1.a.** The public square or marketplace of an ancient Roman city that was the assembly place for judicial activity and public business. **b.** A public meeting place for open discussion. **c.** A medium of open discussion or voicing of ideas, such as a newspaper or a radio or television program. **2.** A public meeting or presentation involving a discussion usually among experts and often including audience participation. **3.** A court of law; a tribunal. [Middle English, from Latin. See **dhwer-** in Appendix.]

for·ward (fôr′wərd) *adj.* **1.a.** At, near, or belonging to the front or forepart; fore: *the forward section of the aircraft.* **b.** Located ahead or in advance: *kept her eye on the forward horizon.* **2.a.** Going, tending, or moving toward a position in front: *a forward plunge down a flight of stairs.* **b.** *Sports.* Advancing toward an opponent's goal. **c.** Moving in a prescribed direction or order for normal use: *forward rolling of the cassette tape.* **3.a.** Ardently inclined; eager. **b.** Lacking restraint or modesty; presumptuous or bold: *a forward child.* **4.a.** Being ahead of current economic, political, or technological trends; progressive: *a forward concept.* **b.** Deviating radically from convention or tradition; extreme. **5.** Exceptionally advanced; precocious. **6.** Of, relating to, or done in preparation for the future: *bidding on forward contracts for corn.* **—forward** *adv.* **1.** Toward or tending to the front; frontward: *step forward.* **2.** Into consideration: *put forward a new proposal.* **3.** In or toward the future: *looking forward to seeing you.* **4.a.** In the prescribed direction or sequence for normal use: *rolled the tape forward.* **b.** In an advanced position or a configuration registering a future time: *set the clock forward.* **c.** At or to a different time; earlier or later: *moved the appointment forward, from Friday to Thursday.* **—forward** *n. Abbr.* **fwd** *Sports.* **1.** A player in certain games, such as basketball, soccer, or hockey, who is part of the forward line of the offense. **2.** The position played by such a person. **—forward** *tr.v.* **-ward·ed, -ward·ing, -wards. 1.** To send on to a subsequent destination or address. See Synonyms at **send**[1]. **2.** To help advance; promote. See Synonyms at **advance.** [Middle English, from Old English *foreweard* : *fore-,* fore- + *-weard,* -ward.] **—for′ward·ly** *adv.* **—for′ward·ness** *n.*

for·ward·er (fôr′wər-dər) *n.* One that forwards, especially an agent that facilitates and assures the passage of received goods to their destination.

for·ward-look·ing (fôr′wərd-lo͝ok′ĭng) *adj.* Concerned with or making provision for the future: *forward-looking educators; a forward-looking corporate plan.*

forward pass *n. Football.* A pass thrown from behind the line of scrimmage to a receiver who is closer to the opponent's end line than the passer.

for·wards (fôr′wərdz, fōr′-) *adv.* To or tending to the front; forward.

fossil
Top: Fish
Bottom: Leaf

ă pat	oi boy
ā pay	ou out
âr care	o͝o took
ä father	o͞o boot
ĕ pet	ŭ cut
ē be	ûr urge
ĭ pit	th thin
ī pie	*th* this
îr pier	hw which
ŏ pot	zh vision
ō toe	ə about, item
ô paw	♦ regionalism

Stress marks: ′ (primary); ′ (secondary), as in **dictionary** (dĭk′shə-nĕr′ē)

for·went (fôr-wĕnt′, fōr-) *v.* Past tense of **forgo.**

for·worn also **fore·worn** (fôr-wôrn′, fōr-wōrn′) *adj. Archaic.* Worn-out.

for·zan·do (fôrt-sän′dō) *adv., adj., & n. Abbr.* **forz** *Music.* Variant of **sforzando.**

FOS *abbr.* Free on steamer.

foss (fŏs) *n.* Variant of **fosse.**

fos·sa (fŏs′ə) *n., pl.* **fos·sae** (fŏs′ē′). *Anatomy.* A small cavity or depression, as in a bone. [Latin, ditch, from feminine past participle of *fodere,* to dig.] **—fos′sate′** (fŏs′āt′) *adj.*

fosse also **foss** (fŏs) *n.* A ditch or moat. [Middle English, from Old French, from Latin *fossa.* See FOSSA.]

fos·sick (fŏs′ĭk) *v.* **-sicked, -sick·ing, -sicks.** *Australian.* *—intr.* **1.** To search for gold, especially by reworking washings or waste piles. **2.** To rummage or search around, especially for a possible profit. *—tr.* To search for by or as if by rummaging. [English dialectal, to find out, dig up.] **—fos′sick·er** *n.*

fos·sil (fŏs′əl) *n.* **1.** A remnant or trace of an organism of a past geologic age, such as a skeleton or leaf imprint, embedded and preserved in the earth's crust. **2.** One, such as a rigid theory, that is outdated or antiquated. **3.** *Linguistics.* **a.** A word or morpheme that is used only in certain restricted contexts, as *kempt* in *unkempt,* but is otherwise obsolete. **b.** An archaic syntactic rule or pattern used only in idioms, as *so be it.* **—fossil** *adj.* **1.** Characteristic of or having the nature of a fossil. **2.** Being or similar to a fossil. **3.** Belonging to the past; antiquated. [From Latin *fossilis,* dug up, from *fossus,* past participle of *fodere,* to dig.]

fossil fuel *n.* A hydrocarbon deposit, such as petroleum, coal, or natural gas, derived from living matter of a previous geologic time and used for fuel.

fos·sil·if·er·ous (fŏs′ə-lĭf′ər-əs) *adj.* Containing fossils.

fos·sil·ize (fŏs′ə-līz′) *v.* **-ized, -iz·ing, -iz·es.** *—tr.* **1.** To convert into a fossil. **2.** To make outmoded or inflexible with time; antiquate. *—intr.* To become a fossil. **—fos′sil·i·za′tion** (-sə-lĭ-zā′shən) *n.*

fos·so·ri·al (fŏ-sôr′ē-əl, -sōr′-) *adj. Zoology.* Adapted for or used in burrowing or digging: *the fossorial forefeet of a mole.* [From Late Latin *fossōrius,* from Latin *fossus,* past participle of *fodere,* to dig.]

fos·ter (fô′stər, fŏs′tər) *tr.v.* **-tered, -ter·ing, -ters. 1.** To bring up; nurture: *bear and foster offspring.* See Synonyms at **nurture. 2.** To promote the growth and development of; cultivate: *detect and foster artistic talent.* See Synonyms at **advance. 3.** To nurse; cherish: *foster a secret hope.* **—foster** *adj.* **1.** Providing parental care and nurture to children not related through legal or blood ties: *foster parents; foster grandparents; a foster home.* **2.** Receiving parental care and nurture from those not related to one through legal or blood ties: *foster children.* [Middle English *fostren,* from Old English **fōstrian,* to nourish, from *fōstor,* food, nourishing. See **pā-** in Appendix.]

Fos·ter (fô′stər, fŏs′tər), **Stephen Collins.** 1826–1864. American songwriter whose works, such as "Oh! Susannah" (1848), reflect the sentiment of pre-Civil War America.

Foster City. A city of western California, a suburb of San Mateo. Population, 23,287.

Fou·cault (fo͞o-kō′), **Jean Bernard Léon.** 1819–1868. French physicist who estimated the speed of light and determined that it travels more slowly in water than in air (1850).

Foucault pendulum *n.* A simple pendulum suspended from a long wire and set into motion along a meridian. The plane of motion appears to turn clockwise in the Northern Hemisphere and counterclockwise in the Southern Hemisphere, demonstrating the axial rotation of the earth. [After Jean Bernard Léon FOUCAULT.]

Fouc·quet (fo͞o-kā′). See **Fouquet.**

fou·droy·ant (fo͞o-droi′ənt, fo͞o′drwä-yäɴ′) *adj.* **1.** Dazzling or stunning in effect. **2.** *Medicine.* Occurring suddenly and severely. Used of a disease. [French, from present participle of *foudroyer,* to strike with lightning, from *foudre,* lightning, from Old French *fouldre,* from Latin *fulgur,* from *fulgēre,* to flash. See **bhel-**[1] in Appendix.]

fought (fôt) *v.* Past tense and past participle of **fight.**

foul (foul) *adj.* **foul·er, foul·est. 1.** Offensive to the senses; revolting. **2.** Having an offensive odor; smelly. **3.** Rotten or putrid: *foul meat.* **4.a.** Full of dirt or mud; dirty. See Synonyms at **dirty. b.** Full of impurities; polluted: *foul air.* **5.** Morally detestable; wicked: *foul deeds.* **6.** Of a vulgar or obscene nature: *foul language.* **7.** Very disagreeable or displeasing; horrid: *a foul movie.* **8.** Bad or unfavorable: *in fair weather or foul.* **9.** Violating accepted standards or rules; dishonorable: *used foul means to gain power.* **10.a.** *Sports.* Contrary to the rules of a game or sport: *a foul boxing punch.* **b.** *Baseball.* Outside the foul lines: *a foul fly ball.* **11.** Entangled or twisted: *a foul anchor.* **12.** Clogged or obstructed; blocked: *a foul ventilator shaft.* **13.** *Archaic.* Ugly; unattractive. **—foul** *n.* **1.a.** *Abbr.* **f.** *Sports.* An infraction or a violation of the rules of play. **b.** *Baseball.* A foul ball. **2.** An entanglement or a collision. **3.** An instance of clogging or obstructing. **—foul** *adv.* In a foul manner. **—foul** *v.* **fouled, foul·ing, fouls.** *—tr.* **1.** To make dirty or foul; pollute. See Synonyms at **contaminate. 2.** To bring into dishonor; besmirch. **3.** To clog or obstruct. **4.** To entangle or catch (a rope, for example). **5.** *Nautical.* To encrust (a ship's hull) with foreign matter, such as barnacles. **6.a.** *Sports.* To commit a foul against. **b.** *Baseball.* To hit (a ball) outside the foul lines. *—intr.* **1.** To become foul. **2.a.** *Sports.* To commit a foul. **b.** *Baseball.* To hit a ball outside the foul lines: *fouled twice and then struck out; fouled out to the catcher.* **3.** To become entangled or twisted: *The anchor line fouled on a rock.* **4.** To become clogged or obstructed. ***—phrasal verbs.* foul out.** *Sports.* To be put out of a game for exceeding the number of permissible fouls. **foul up.** To blunder or cause to blunder because of mistakes or poor judgment. [Middle English, from Old English *fūl.* See **pū̆-** in Appendix.] **—foul′ly** *adv.* **—foul′ness** *n.*

fou·lard (fo͞o-lärd′) *n.* **1.** A lightweight twill or plain-woven fabric of silk or silk and cotton, usually having a small printed design. **2.** An article of clothing, especially a necktie or scarf, made of this fabric. [French.]

foul ball *n. Baseball.* A batted ball that touches the ground outside of fair territory.

foul·brood (foul′bro͝od′) *n.* A fatal disease of honeybee larvae caused by one of several types of bacteria, including *Bacillus alvei.*

foul line *n.* **1.** *Baseball.* Either of two straight lines extending from the rear of home plate to the outer edge of the playing field and indicating the area in which a fair ball can be hit. **2.** *Basketball.* A line 15 feet in front of each backboard from which players shoot foul shots. Also called *free-throw line.* **3.** *Sports.* A boundary limiting the permissible movements of a player, as on a bowling alley or in a field event.

foul-mouthed (foul′mouthd′, -moutht′) *adj.* Using abusive or obscene language.

foul play *n.* Unfair or treacherous action, especially when involving violence.

foul shot *n. Basketball.* An unobstructed shot from the foul line awarded to a fouled player and scored as one point if successful. Also called *free throw.*

foul tip *n. Baseball.* A pitched ball that is deflected slightly off the bat toward the catcher.

foul-up (foul′ŭp′) *n.* **1.** A condition of confusion caused by mistakes or poor judgment. **2.** A mechanical failure.

found[1] (found) *tr.v.* **found·ed, found·ing, founds. 1.** To establish or set up, especially with provision for continuing existence: *The college was founded in 1872.* **2.** To establish the foundation or basis of; base: *found a theory on firm evidence.* [Middle English *founden,* from Old French *fonder,* from Latin *fundāre,* from *fundus,* bottom.]

SYNONYMS: *found, create, establish, institute, organize.* The central meaning shared by these verbs is "to bring something into existence and set it in operation": *founded a colony; created a trust fund; establishing an advertising agency; instituted an annual ball to benefit the homeless; organizing the metal-trading division of a bank.*

Stephen Foster
c. 1850 portrait attributed to Thomas Hicks (1823–1890)

found[2] (found) *tr.v.* **found·ed, found·ing, founds. 1.** To melt (metal) and pour into a mold. **2.** To make (objects) by pouring molten material into a mold. [Middle English *founden,* from Old French *fondre,* from Latin *fundere.* See **gheu-** in Appendix.]

found[3] (found) *v.* Past tense and past participle of **find.**

foun·da·tion (foun-dā′shən) *n.* **1.** The act of founding, especially the establishment of an institution with provisions for future maintenance. **2.** The basis on which a thing stands, is founded, or is supported. See Synonyms at **base**[1]. **3.a.** Funds for the perpetual support of an institution; an endowment. **b.** An institution founded and supported by an endowment. **4.** A foundation garment. **5.** A cosmetic used as a base for facial makeup. **—foun·da′tion·al** *adj.*

foundation garment *n.* A woman's supporting undergarment, such as a corset or girdle.

foun·der[1] (foun′dər) *v.* **-dered, -der·ing, -ders.** *—intr.* **1.** To sink below the water: *The ship struck a reef and foundered.* **2.** To cave in; sink: *The platform swayed and then foundered.* **3.** To fail utterly; collapse: *a marriage that soon foundered.* **4.** To stumble, especially to stumble and go lame. Used of horses. **5.** To become ill from overeating. Used of livestock. **6.** To be afflicted wtih laminitis. Used of horses. *—tr.* To cause to founder. **—founder** *n.* See **laminitis.** [Middle English *foundren,* to sink to the ground, from Old French *fondrer,* from Vulgar Latin **funderāre,* from **fundus,* **funder-,* bottom, from Latin *fundus, fund-.*]

USAGE NOTE: The verbs *founder* and *flounder* are often confused. *Founder* comes from a Latin word meaning "bottom" (as in *foundation*) and originally referred to knocking enemies down; it is now used as well to mean "to fail utterly, collapse." *Flounder* means "to move clumsily, thrash about," and hence "to proceed in confusion." If John is *foundering* in Chemistry 1, he had better drop the course; if he is *floundering,* he may yet pull through.

found·er[2] (found′ər) *n.* One who establishes something or formulates the basis for something: *the founder of a university; the founders of a new nation.*

Found·ing Father (foun′dĭng) *n.* **1.** A member of the convention that drafted the U.S. Constitution in 1787. **2. founding father.** A man who founds or establishes something.

found·ling (found′lĭng) *n.* A deserted or abandoned child of unknown parentage. [Middle English, from *found,* past participle of *finden,* to find. See FIND.]

found object *n.* A natural object or an artifact not originally

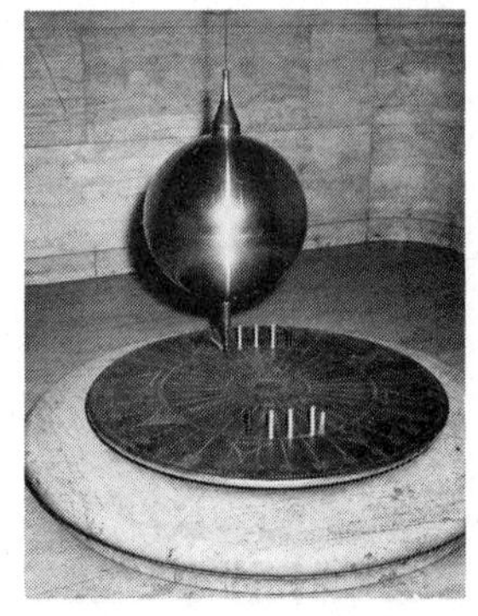
Foucault pendulum

foundry

fountain

four-poster

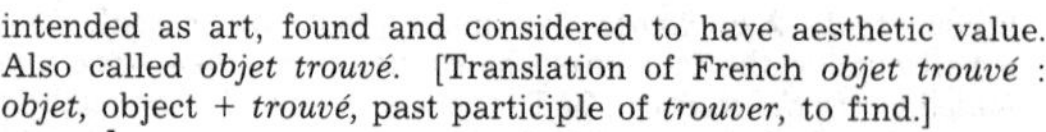

intended as art, found and considered to have aesthetic value. Also called *objet trouvé.* [Translation of French *objet trouvé* : *objet,* object + *trouvé,* past participle of *trouver,* to find.]

foun·dry (foun′drē) *n., pl.* **-dries. 1.** An establishment in which metal is melted and poured into molds. **2. a.** The skill or operation of founding. **b.** The castings made by founding.

fount[1] (fount) *n.* **1.** A fountain. **2.** One that initiates or dispenses; a source: *Damascus—the fount of modern Arab nationalism.* [Middle English, from Old English and Old French *font,* both from Latin *fōns, font-.*]

fount[2] (fount) *n. Chiefly British.* Variant of **font**[2].

foun·tain (foun′tən) *n.* **1. a.** An artificially created jet or stream of water. **b.** A structure, often decorative, from which a jet or stream of water issues. **2.** A spring, especially the source of a stream. **3.** A reservoir or chamber containing a supply of liquid that can be siphoned off as needed. **4.** A soda fountain. **5.** A point of origin or dissemination; a source: *the library, a fountain of information.* **—fountain** *intr. & tr.v.* **-tained, -tain·ing, -tains.** To flow or cause to flow like a fountain. [Middle English, from Old French *fontaine,* from Late Latin *fontāna,* from Latin, feminine of *fontānus,* of a spring, from *fōns, font-,* spring.]

foun·tain·head (foun′tən-hĕd′) *n.* **1.** A spring that is the source or head of a stream. **2.** A chief and copious source; an originator: *"the intellectual fountainhead of the black conservatives"* (Jerrold K. Footlick).

fountain pen *n.* A pen filled from an external source and containing an ink reservoir that automatically feeds the writing point.

Foun·tain Valley (foun′tən). A city of southern California southeast of Los Angeles. Population, 55,080.

Fou·quet also **Fouc·quet** (fo͞o-kā′), **Jean.** 1420?–1480? French artist who produced religious paintings, unidealized portraits, and book illuminations.

Fouquet also **Foucquet, Nicolas.** 1615–1680. French superintendent of finance (1653–1661) who was convicted of embezzlement (1664) and imprisoned for life.

four (fôr, fōr) *n.* **1.** The cardinal number equal to 3 + 1. **2.** The fourth in a set or sequence. **3.** Something having four parts, units, or members, such as a musical quartet or a four-cylinder engine. ***—idiom.* all fours.** All four limbs of an animal or person: *a baby crawling on all fours.* [Middle English, from Old English *fēower.* See **kʷetwer-** in Appendix.] **—four** *adj. & pron.*

four-bag·ger (fôr′băg′ər, fōr′-) *n. Baseball.* A home run.

four-by-four or **4 × 4** (fôr′bī-fôr′, fōr′bī-fōr′) *n.* A four-wheel drive motor vehicle.

four·chette (fo͝or-shĕt′) *n.* **1.** A narrow, forked strip of material joining the front and back sections of the fingers of gloves. **2.** *Anatomy.* A small band or fold of mucous membrane forming the posterior margin of the vulva and connecting the posterior ends of the labia majora. **3.** *Zoology.* See **furcula.** [French, from Old French *forchete,* fork, diminutive of *forche,* pitchfork, from Latin *furca.*]

four-col·or (fôr′kŭl′ər, fōr′-) *adj.* Of or being an overprinting or photographic process in which three primary colors and black are transferred by four different plates or filters to a surface, reproducing the colors of the subject matter.

Four Cor·ners (fôr kôr′nərz). A location in the southwest United States where the boundaries of four states—Colorado, New Mexico, Arizona, and Utah—meet.

four-cy·cle (fôr′sī′kəl, fōr′-) *adj.* Requiring four strokes of the piston for a cycle: *a four-cycle internal-combustion engine.*

four-di·men·sion·al (fôr′dĭ-mĕn′shə-nəl, fōr′-) *adj.* Specified by or exhibiting four dimensions, especially the three spatial dimensions and single temporal dimension of the relativity theory.

four-eyed fish (fôr′īd′, fōr′-) *n.* Either of two freshwater fishes *(Anableps anableps* or *A. microlepis)* of tropical America, having bulging eyes divided horizontally, with the upper part adapted for vision above the water and the lower part for vision below the water.

four flush *n. Games.* A five-card poker hand containing four cards in the same suit.

four-flush (fôr′flŭsh′, fōr′-) *intr.v.* **-flushed, -flush·ing, -flush·es. 1.** *Games.* To bluff in poker with a four flush. **2.** *Slang.* To make empty claims; bluff. **—four′-flush′er** *n.*

four-foot·ed (fôr′fo͝ot′ĭd, fōr′-) *adj.* Having four feet.

four·gon (fo͝or-gôɴ′) *n., pl.* **-gons** (-gôɴ′, -gôɴz′). A wagon for carrying baggage. [French.]

four·hand·ed (fôr′hăn′dĭd, fōr′-) *adj.* **1.** *Games.* Involving or requiring four players: *fourhanded bridge.* **2.** Designed for four hands, as a piano duet.

Four-H Club (fôr′āch′, fōr′-) *n.* A youth organization sponsored by the Department of Agriculture and offering instruction in agriculture and home economics. [From its four goals: to improve head, heart, hands, and health.]

Four Hundred also **four hundred** *n.* The wealthiest and most exclusive social set of a community.

Fou·rier (fo͝or′ē-ā′, fo͞o-ryā′), **(François Marie) Charles.** 1772–1837. French social theorist who believed that universal harmony could be achieved by reorganizing society into self-sustaining units called "phalanxes."

Fourier, Baron **Jean Baptiste Joseph.** 1768–1830. French mathematician and physicist who formulated a method for analyzing periodic functions and studied the conduction of heat.

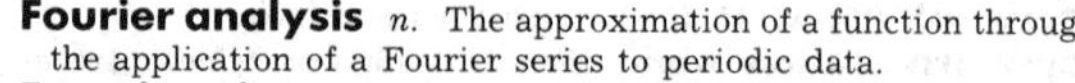

Fourier analysis *n.* The approximation of a function through the application of a Fourier series to periodic data.

Fou·ri·er·ism (fo͝or′ē-ə-rĭz′əm) *n.* A system for social reform advocated by Charles Fourier in the early 19th century, proposing that society be organized into small self-sustaining communal groups. **—Fou′ri·er·ist, Fou′ri·er·ite′** (-ə-rīt′) *n.*

Fourier series *n. Mathematics.* An infinite series whose terms are constants multiplied by sine and cosine functions and that can, if uniformly convergent, approximate a wide variety of functions. [After Baron Jean Baptiste Joseph FOURIER.]

four-in-hand (fôr′ĭn-hănd′, fōr′-) *n.* **1.** A team of four horses controlled by one driver. **2.** A vehicle drawn by four horses. **3.** A necktie tied in a slipknot with long ends left hanging one in front of the other.

four-leaf clover (fôr′lēf′, fōr′-) *n.* A clover leaf having four leaflets instead of the normal three, considered to be an omen of good luck.

four-let·ter word (fôr′lĕt′ər, fōr′-) *n.* Any of several short English words generally regarded as vulgar or obscene.

four-o'clock (fôr′ə-klŏk′, fōr′-) *n.* Any of several plants of the genus *Mirabilis,* especially *M. jalapa,* native to tropical America and widely cultivated for its funnel-shaped or tubular, variously colored flowers that open late in the afternoon.

four·pen·ny nail (fôr′pĕn′ē, -pə-nē, fōr′-) *n.* A nail 1½ inches (3.8 centimeters) long.

four-post·er (fôr′pō′stər, fōr′-) *n.* A bed having tall corner posts originally intended to support curtains or a canopy.

four·ra·gère (fo͝or′ə-zhâr′) *n.* An ornamental braided cord usually looped around the left shoulder of a uniform, sometimes awarded to an entire military unit. [French, from *fourrage,* forage, from Old French *forrage.* See FORAGE.]

four·score (fôr′skôr′, fōr′skōr′) *adj.* Four times twenty; eighty.

four·some (fôr′səm, fōr′-) *n.* **1.** A group of four persons or things, especially two couples. **2.** *Sports & Games.* **a.** A game, especially a golf match, played by four persons, two on each side. **b.** The players in such a game. [Middle English *four-som,* from Old English *fēowra sum,* one of four : *fēowra,* genitive pl. of *fēower,* four; see FOUR + *sum,* one; see –SOME[2].]

four·square (fôr′skwâr′, fōr′-) *adj.* **1.** Having four equal sides and four right angles; square. **2.** Marked by firm, unwavering conviction or expression; forthright: *a foursquare refusal to yield.* **—foursquare** *adv.* In a forthright manner; squarely.

four-star (fôr′stär′, fōr′-) *adj.* Of superlative quality: *a four-star restaurant.*

four·teen (fôr-tēn′, fōr-) *n.* **1.** The cardinal number equal to 13 + 1. **2.** The 14th in a set or sequence. **3.** Something having 14 parts, units, or members. [Middle English *fourtene,* from Old English *fēowertēne.* See **kʷetwer-** in Appendix.] **—four·teen′** *adj. & pron.*

four·teenth (fôr-tēnth′, fōr-) *n.* **1.** The ordinal number matching the number 14 in a series. **2.** One of 14 equal parts. **—four·teenth′** *adv. & adj.*

fourth (fôrth, fōrth) *n.* **1.** The ordinal number matching the number four in a series. **2.** One of four equal parts. **3.** *Music.* **a.** A tone four degrees above or below a given tone in a diatonic scale. **b.** The interval between two such tones. **c.** The harmonic combination of these tones. **d.** The subdominant in a scale. **4.** The transmission gear or gear ratio used to produce forward speeds next higher to those of third in a motor vehicle. **5. Fourth.** The Fourth of July; Independence Day. [Middle English *fourthe,* from Old English *fēorthā.* See **kʷetwer-** in Appendix.] **—fourth** *adv. & adj.*

fourth-class (fôrth′klăs′, fōrth′-) *adj.* Of or being a class of mail consisting of merchandise and some printed matter weighing over eight ounces and not sealed against inspection. **—fourth-class** *adv.* As or by fourth-class mail.

fourth dimension *n.* Time regarded as a coordinate dimension and required by relativity theory, along with three spatial dimensions, to specify completely the location of any event.

fourth estate *n.* Journalists considered as a group.

Fourth of July *n.* See **Independence Day.**

Fourth World also **fourth world** *n.* The least-developed countries of the Third World, especially those in Africa and Asia.

4WD *abbr.* Four-wheel drive.

four-wheel (fôr′hwēl′, -wēl′, fōr′-) *adj.* **1.** Having or running on four wheels. **2.** Of or relating to four-wheel drive.

four-wheel drive *n. Abbr.* **FWD, 4WD** An automotive drive system in which mechanical power is transmitted from the drive shaft to all four wheels.

four-wheel·er (fôr′hwē′lər, -wē′-, fōr′-) *n.* A small, all-terrain motor vehicle seating one person and having four wheels with large tires.

fo·ve·a (fō′vē-ə) *n., pl.* **-ve·ae** (-vē-ē′). **1.** A small cuplike depression or pit in a bone or an organ. **2.** The fovea centralis. [Latin, small pit.] **—fo′ve·al** (-əl), **fo′ve·ate′** (-āt′) *adj.* **—fo′ve·i·form′** (-ə-fôrm′) *adj.*

fovea cen·tra·lis (sĕn-trā′lĭs) *n.* A small depression near the center of the retina, constituting the area of most acute vision. [New Latin : Latin *fovea,* small pit + Latin *centrālis,* central.]

fo·ve·ae (fō′vē-ē′) *n.* Plural of **fovea.**

fo·ve·o·la (fō-vē′ə-lə) *n., pl.* **-lae** (-lē′) or **-las.** A small fovea. [New Latin, diminutive of Latin *fovea,* small pit.]

fowl (foul) *n., pl.* **fowl** or **fowls. 1.** Any of various birds of the order Galliformes, especially the common, widely domesticated chicken *(Gallus gallus).* **2.a.** A bird, such as the duck, goose, turkey, or pheasant, that is used as food or hunted as game. **b.** The flesh of such birds used as food. **3.** A bird of any kind. **—fowl** *intr.v.* **fowled, fowl·ing, fowls.** To hunt, trap, or shoot wildfowl. [Middle English *foul,* from Old English *fugol.* See **pleu-** in Appendix.] **—fowl′er** *n.*

Fow·ler (fou′lər), **Henry Watson.** 1858–1933. British lexicographer who collaborated with his brother **Francis** (1870–1918) on *The King's English* (1906). He also wrote *A Dictionary of Modern English Usage* (1926).

fowl·ing piece (fou′lĭng) *n.* A light shotgun for shooting birds and small animals.

fox (fŏks) *n., pl.* **fox·es** also **fox. 1.a.** Any of various carnivorous mammals of the genus *Vulpes* and related genera, related to the dogs and wolves and characteristically having upright ears, a pointed snout, and a long, bushy tail. **b.** The fur of one of these mammals. **2.** A crafty, sly, or clever person. **3.** *Slang.* An attractive young person. **4.** *Nautical.* Small cordage made by twisting together two or more strands of tarred yarn. **5.** *Archaic.* A sword. **—fox** *v.* **foxed, fox·ing, fox·es.** *—tr.* **1.** To trick or fool by ingenuity or cunning; outwit. **2.** To baffle or confuse. **3.** To make (beer) sour by fermenting. **4.** To repair (a shoe) by attaching a new upper. **5.** *Obsolete.* To intoxicate. *—intr.* **1.** To act slyly or craftily. **2.** To turn sour in fermenting. Used of beer. [Middle English, from Old English.]

Fox (fŏks) *n., pl.* **Fox** or **Fox·es. 1.a.** A Native American people formerly inhabiting various parts of southern Michigan, southern Wisconsin, northern Illinois, and eastern Iowa, with present-day populations in central Iowa and with the Sauk in Oklahoma. **b.** A member of this people. **2.** The Algonkian language of the Fox.

Fox, Charles James. 1749–1806. British politician who supported American independence and the French Revolution.

Fox, George. 1624–1691. English religious leader who founded the Society of Friends, or Quakers (1647–1648).

Foxe (fŏks), **John.** 1516–1587. English martyrologist who wrote *The Book of Martyrs* (1563).

foxed (fŏkst) *adj.* Discolored with yellowish-brown stains: *"Their set of George Eliot was foxed and buckled by the rain"* (John Cheever). [Perhaps from the color of foxes.]

fox·fire (fŏks′fīr′) *n.* A phosphorescent glow, especially that produced by certain fungi found on rotting wood.

fox·glove (fŏks′glŭv′) *n.* **1.** Any of several herbs of the genus *Digitalis,* especially *D. purpurea* of Europe, having a long cluster of large, tubular, pinkish-purple flowers and leaves that are the source of the drug digitalis. **2.** Any of several related plants.

fox grape *n.* A wild grape *(Vitis labrusca)* of the eastern United States that bears purplish-black berries and is the source of many cultivated grape varieties. Also called *skunk grape.*

fox·hole (fŏks′hōl′) *n.* A shallow pit dug by a soldier in combat for immediate refuge against enemy fire.

fox·hound (fŏks′hound′) *n.* Any of various medium-sized short-haired hounds developed for fox hunting, especially either of two breeds, the English foxhound and the American foxhound.

fox snake *n.* A rat snake *(Elaphe vulpina)* common to the north-central United States, having dark brown or black blotches on the back and a reddish head.

fox sparrow *n.* A large sparrow *(Passerella iliaca)* of the western United States, Canada, and Alaska, having a rufous tail and streaked underparts.

fox squirrel *n.* A large North American squirrel *(Sciurus niger)* having rusty or grayish fur.

fox·tail (fŏks′tāl′) *n.* Any of several grasses of the genus *Alopecurus,* having dense, silky or bristly flowering spikes.

foxtail lily *n.* Eremurus.

fox terrier *n.* Any of various small terriers of a breed originating in England, having a white coat with dark markings and developed in both wire-haired and smooth-coated varieties. They were formerly used to drive foxes out of hiding.

fox·trot (fŏks′trŏt′) *intr.v.* **-trot·ted, -trot·ting, -trots.** To dance the fox trot.

fox trot *n.* **1.a.** A ballroom dance in 2/4 or 4/4 time, encompassing a variety of slow and fast steps. **b.** The music for this dance. **2.** A slow broken gait of a horse, between a trot and a walk.

fox·y (fŏk′sē) *adj.* **-i·er, -i·est. 1.a.** Of or resembling a fox. **b.** Slyly clever; crafty: *a foxy scheme.* See Synonyms at **sly. 2.** Having a reddish-brown color. **3.** Discolored, as by age or decay; foxed. **4.** *Slang.* Sensually attractive; sexy. **5.** Having a distinctive sharp flavor or aroma: *foxy American grapes.* **—fox′i·ly** *adv.* **—fox′i·ness** *n.*

foy (foi) *n. Scots.* A farewell feast, drink, or gift, as at a wedding. [Dutch dialectal *fooi,* from Middle Dutch *foye,* journey, from Old French *voie,* from Latin *via,* road. See **wegh-** in Appendix.]

foy·er (foi′ər, foi′ā′, fwä′yā′) *n.* **1.** A lobby or an anteroom, as of a theater or hotel. **2.** An entrance hall; a vestibule. [French, social center, from Old French *foier,* fireplace, from Vulgar Latin **focārium,* from Late Latin, neuter of *focārius,* of the hearth (unattested sense), from Latin *focus,* fire.]

fp or **f.p.** *abbr.* Freezing point.

fp. *abbr.* Foolscap.

FPC *abbr.* **1.** Federal Power Commission. **2.** Fish protein concentrate. **3.** Friends Peace Committee.

fpl *abbr.* Fireplace.

fpm or **f.p.m.** *abbr.* Feet per minute.

FPO *abbr.* Fleet post office.

fps or **f.p.s.** *abbr.* **1.** Feet per second. **2.** Foot-pound-second. **3.** Frames per second.

Fr The symbol for the element **francium.**

fr. *abbr.* **1.** Frame. **2.** Franc. **3.** From.

Fr. *abbr.* **1.** Father (cleric). **2.** France; French. **3.** Frau. **4.** Friar. **5.** Friday.

f.r. *abbr. Latin.* Folio recto (right-hand page).

Fra (frä) *n. Roman Catholic Church.* Used as a title for an Italian monk or friar; brother. [Italian, short for *frate,* brother, from Latin *frāter.* See **bhrāter-** in Appendix.]

fra·cas (frā′kəs, frăk′əs) *n. Informal.* A noisy, disorderly fight or quarrel; a brawl. See Synonyms at **brawl.** [French, from Italian *fracasso,* from *fracassare,* to make an uproar.]

frac·tal (frăk′təl) *n.* A geometric pattern that is repeated at ever smaller scales to produce irregular shapes and surfaces that cannot be represented by classical geometry. Fractals are used especially in computer modeling of irregular patterns and structures in nature. [French, from Latin *frāctus,* past participle of *frangere,* to break. See FRACTION.]

fract·ed (frăk′tĭd) *adj. Obsolete.* Broken. [From Latin *frāctus,* past participle of *frangere,* to break. See FRACTION.]

frac·tion (frăk′shən) *n.* **1.** *Mathematics.* An expression that indicates the quotient of two quantities. **2.** A disconnected piece; a fragment. **3.** A small part; a bit: *moved a fraction of a step.* **4.** A chemical component separated by fractionation. [Middle English *fraccioun,* a breaking, from Anglo-Norman, from Late Latin *frāctiō, frāctiōn-,* from Latin *frāctus,* past participle of *frangere,* to break. See **bhreg-** in Appendix.]

WORD HISTORY: One might think that a word like *fraction* as well as its ancestors might have always referred to the mathematical fraction. Certainly the mathematical notion of a fraction was known to the Babylonians, perhaps as early as 2000 B.C. But our word *fraction* goes back only to the Latin word *frangere,* "to break." From the stem of the past participle *frāctus* is derived Late Latin *frāctiō,* "a breaking" or "a breaking in pieces," as in the breaking of the Eucharistic Host. In Medieval Latin the word *frāctiō* developed its mathematical sense, which was taken into Middle English along with the word. The earliest recorded sense of our word is "an aliquot part of a unit, a fraction or subdivision," found in a work by Chaucer written about 1400. One of the next recorded instances of the word recalls its origins, referring to the "brekying or fraccioun" of a bone.

frac·tion·al (frăk′shə-nəl) *adj.* **1.** Of, relating to, or constituting a fraction. **2.** Very small; insignificant: *a minor candidate's fractional share of the vote.* **3.** Being in fractions or pieces. **—frac′tion·al·ly** *adv.*

fractional currency *n.* Coin or paper currency in a denomination less than a standard monetary unit.

fractional distillation *n.* Distillation to separate volatile chemical substances in which the products are collected in a series of separate fractions, each with a higher boiling point than the previous fraction.

frac·tion·al·ize (frăk′shə-nə-līz′) *tr.v.* **-ized, -iz·ing, -iz·es.** To divide into separate parts or sections: *conflicting interests that tend to fractionalize a society.* **—frac′tion·al·i·za′tion** (-shə-nə-lĭ-zā′shən) *n.*

frac·tion·ate (frăk′shə-nāt′) *tr.v.* **-at·ed, -at·ing, -ates. 1.** To divide or separate into parts; break up: *"In the post-Watergate era, power has been fractionated on Capitol Hill"* (Evan Thomas). **2.** To separate (a chemical compound) into components, as by distillation or crystallization. **—frac′tion·a′tion** *n.* **—frac′tion·a′tor** *n.*

frac·tion·ize (frăk′shə-nīz′) *tr. & intr.v.* **-ized, -iz·ing, -iz·es.** To divide into parts or fractions; fractionalize. **—frac′tion·i·za′tion** (-shə-nĭ-zā′shən) *n.*

frac·tious (frăk′shəs) *adj.* **1.** Inclined to make trouble; unruly. **2.** Having a peevish nature; cranky. [From FRACTION, discord (obsolete).] **—frac′tious·ly** *adv.* **—frac′tious·ness** *n.*

frac·ture (frăk′chər) *n.* **1.a.** The act or process of breaking. **b.** The condition of having been broken or ruptured: *"a sudden and irreparable fracture of the established order"* (W. Bruce Lincoln). **2.** A break, rupture, or crack, especially in bone or cartilage. **3.** *Mineralogy.* **a.** The characteristic manner in which a mineral breaks. **b.** The characteristic appearance of the surface of a broken mineral. **4.** *Geology.* A crack or fault in a rock. **—fracture** *v.* **-tured, -tur·ing, -tures.** *—tr.* **1.** To cause to break: *fracture a bone.* **2.** To disrupt or destroy as if by breaking: *fractured the delicate balance of power.* **3.** To abuse or misuse flagrantly, as by violating rules: *ignorant writers who fracture the language.* **4.** *Slang.* To cause to laugh heartily: *"Jack Benny fractured audiences . . . for more than 50 years"* (Newsweek). *—intr.* To undergo a fracture. See Synonyms at **break.** [Middle English, from Old French, from Latin *frāctūra,* from *frāctus,* past participle of *frangere,* to break. See **bhreg-** in Appendix.]

foxglove

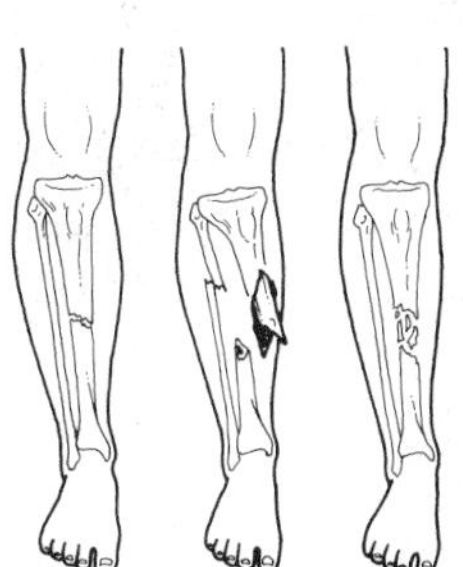

fracture
Left to right: Simple, compound, and comminuted fractures

ă pat	oi boy
ā pay	ou out
âr care	ŏŏ took
ä father	ōō boot
ĕ pet	ŭ cut
ē be	ûr urge
ĭ pit	th thin
ī pie	*th* this
îr pier	hw which
ŏ pot	zh vision
ō toe	ə about, item
ô paw	♦ regionalism

Stress marks: ′ (primary); ′ (secondary), as in **dictionary** (dĭk′shə-nĕr′ē)

Jean Fragonard

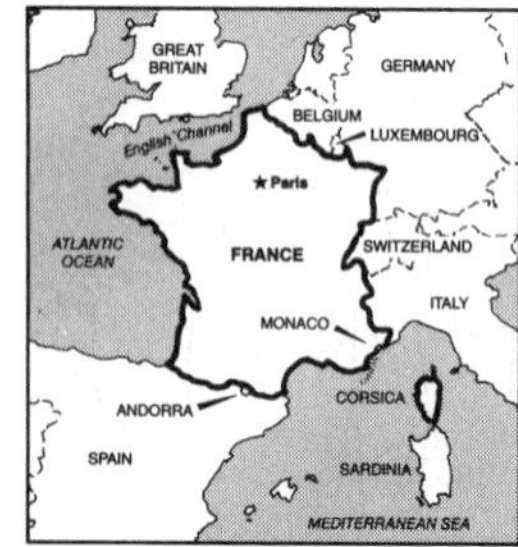

France

ă pat	oi boy
ā pay	ou out
âr care	ŏŏ took
ä father	ōō boot
ĕ pet	ŭ cut
ē be	ûr urge
ĭ pit	th thin
ī pie	*th* this
îr pier	hw which
ŏ pot	zh vision
ō toe	ə about, item
ô paw	♦ regionalism

Stress marks: ′ (primary); **′** (secondary), as in **dictionary** (dĭk′shə-nĕr′ē)

frae (frā) *prep. Scots.* From. [Middle English *fra,* from Old Norse *frā.* See FRO.]

frag (frăg) *Slang. n.* A fragmentation grenade. **—frag** *tr.v.* **fragged, frag·ging, frags.** To wound or kill (a fellow soldier) by throwing a grenade or similar explosive at the victim: *"He got fragged. Blown away"* (Bobbie Ann Mason). **—frag′ger** *n.*

frag·ile (frăj′əl, -īl′) *adj.* **1.** Easily broken, damaged, or destroyed; frail. **2.** Lacking physical or emotional strength; delicate. **3.** Lacking substance; tenuous or flimsy: *a fragile claim to fame.* [French, from Old French, from Latin *fragilis,* from *frangere, frag-,* to break. See **bhreg-** in Appendix.] **—frag′ile·ly** *adv.* **—fra·gil′i·ty** (frə-jĭl′ĭ-tē), **frag′ile·ness** *n.*

SYNONYMS: *fragile, breakable, frangible, delicate, brittle.* These adjectives mean easily broken or damaged. *Fragile* applies to objects whose lightness or delicacy of material requires that they be handled with great care: *a collection of fragile porcelain plates. Breakable* and *frangible,* which are identical in meaning, mean capable of being broken but do not necessarily imply inherent weakness: *Even earthenware pottery is breakable. The museum stored all frangible articles in a locked showcase. Delicate* refers to what is so soft, tender, or fine as to be susceptible to injury: *The peach is a delicate fruit. Brittle* refers to hardness and inelasticity of material that makes something especially likely to fracture or snap when it is subjected to pressure: *brittle bones.* See also Synonyms at **weak.**

frag·ment (frăg′mənt) *n.* **1.** A small part broken off or detached. **2.** An incomplete or isolated portion; a bit: *overheard fragments of their conversation; extant fragments of an old manuscript.* **—fragment** (-mĕnt′) *v.* **-ment·ed, -ment·ing, -ments.** *—tr.* To break or separate (something) into fragments. *—intr.* To become broken into fragments: *After the election, the coalition fragmented.* [Middle English, from Latin *fragmentum,* from *frangere, frag-,* to break. See **bhreg-** in Appendix.]

frag·men·tal (frăg-mĕn′tl) *adj.* **1.** Fragmentary. **2.** *Geology.* Consisting of broken rock, coal, or ore moved from its place of origin. **—frag·men′tal·ly** *adv.*

frag·men·tar·y (frăg′mən-tĕr′ē) *adj.* Consisting of small, disconnected parts: *a picture that emerges from fragmentary information.* **—frag′men·tar′i·ly** (-târ′ə-lē) *adv.* **—frag′men·tar′i·ness** *n.*

frag·men·ta·tion (frăg′mən-tā′shən, -mĕn-) *n.* **1.** The act or process of breaking into fragments. **2.** The scattering of the fragments of an exploding bomb or other projectile.

fragmentation bomb *n.* An aerial antipersonnel bomb that scatters shrapnel over a wide area upon explosion.

fragmentation grenade *n.* A grenade that scatters shrapnel over a wide area upon explosion.

frag·men·tize (frăg′mən-tīz′) *tr. & intr.v.* **-tized, -tiz·ing, -tiz·es.** To break or become broken into fragments. **—frag′men·tiz′er** *n.*

Fra·go·nard (frăg′ə-när′, frä-gô-), **Jean Honoré.** 1732–1806. French artist best known for his rococo paintings of exotic landscapes and love scenes.

fra·grance (frā′grəns) *n.* **1.** The state or quality of having a pleasant odor. **2.** A sweet or pleasant odor; a scent.

SYNONYMS: *fragrance, aroma, bouquet, perfume, redolence, scent.* The central meaning shared by these nouns is "a pleasant or sweet odor": *the fragrance of lilacs; the aroma of sizzling bacon; the bouquet of a fine Burgundy wine; the perfume of roses; the redolence of freshly brewed coffee; the scent of newly mown hay.*

fragrance strip *n.* A sealed or folded strip, as on an envelope or a magazine page, designed to release an aroma when broken or torn open.

fra·grant (frā′grənt) *adj.* Having a pleasant odor. [Middle English, from Latin *frāgrāns, frāgrant-,* past participle of *frāgrāre,* to emit an odor.] **—fra′grant·ly** *adv.*

fraid·y cat (frā′dē) *n. Slang.* A timid or fearful person.

frail[1] (frāl) *adj.* **frail·er, frail·est. 1.** Physically weak; delicate: *an invalid's frail body.* **2.** Not strong or substantial; slight: *evidence too frail to stand up in court.* **3.** Easily broken or destroyed; fragile. **4.** Easily led astray; morally weak. See Synonyms at **weak.** [Middle English *frele,* from Old French, from Latin *fragilis,* from *frangere, frag-,* to break. See **bhreg-** in Appendix.] **—frail′ly** *adv.* **—frail′ness** *n.*

frail[2] (frāl) *n.* **1.** A rush basket for holding fruit, especially dried fruit. **2.** The quantity of fruit, such as raisins or figs, that such a basket can hold. [Middle English *fraiel,* from Old French.]

frail·ty (frāl′tē) *n., pl.* **-ties. 1.** The condition or quality of being frail. **2.** A fault, especially weakness of resolution, arising from the imperfections of human nature. See Synonyms at **fault.**

fraise (frāz) *n.* **1.** A defensive barrier of pointed, inclined stakes or barbed wire. **2.** A ruff for the neck worn in the 16th century. [French, from Old French, mesentery (from its pleated shape), from *(feves) frasees,* shelled (beans), from the resemblance between the mesentery and the peel surrounding individual broad beans, from Latin *(faba) frēsa,* ground (bean), feminine past participle of *frendere,* to crush. See FRENUM.]

frak·tur (fräk-tŏŏr′) *n.* A style of black letter formerly used in German manuscripts and printing. [German, from Latin *fractūra,* a breaking (from the curlicues that appear to break up the word). See FRACTURE.]

fram·be·sia (frăm-bē′zhə, -zhē-ə) *n.* See **yaws.** [New Latin, from French *framboise,* raspberry (from the appearance of the excrescence), from Old French, of Germanic origin. See **bhā-**[1] in Appendix.]

frame (frām) *v.* **framed, fram·ing, frames.** *—tr.* **1.** To build by putting together the structural parts of; construct: *frame a house.* **2.** To conceive or design: *framed an alternate proposal.* **3.** To arrange or adjust for a purpose: *The question was framed to draw only one answer.* **4. a.** To put into words; formulate: *frame a reply.* **b.** To form (words) silently with the lips. **5.** To enclose in or as if in a frame: *frame a painting.* **6.** *Informal.* **a.** To make up evidence or contrive events so as to incriminate (a person) falsely. **b.** To prearrange (a contest) so as to ensure a desired fraudulent outcome; fix: *frame a prizefight.* *—intr.* **1.** *Archaic.* To go; proceed. **2.** *Obsolete.* To manage; contrive. **—frame** *n. Abbr.* **fr. 1.** Something composed of parts fitted and joined together. **2.** A structure that gives shape or support: *the frame of a house.* **3. a.** An open structure or rim for encasing, holding, or bordering: *a window frame; the frame of a mirror.* **b.** A closed, often rectangular border of drawn or printed lines. **4.** Often **frames.** A pair of eyeglasses, excluding the lenses. **5.** The structure of a human or animal body; physique: *a worker's sturdy frame.* **6.** A cold frame. **7.** A general structure or system: *the frame of government.* **8.** A general state or condition: *The news put me into a better frame of mind.* **9.** *Sports & Games.* **a.** A round or period of play in some games, such as bowling and billiards. **b.** *Baseball.* An inning. **10.** A single picture on a roll of movie film. **11.** The total area of a complete picture in television broadcasting. **12.** *Informal.* A frame-up. **13.** A single step in a sequence of programmed instruction. **14.** *Obsolete.* Shape; form. [Middle English *framen,* from Old English *framian,* to further, from *fram,* forward. See FROM.]

frame of reference *n., pl.* **frames of reference. 1.** A set of coordinate axes in terms of which position or movement may be specified or with reference to which physical laws may be mathematically stated. **2.** A set of ideas, as of philosophical or religious doctrine, in terms of which other ideas are interpreted or assigned meaning.

fram·er (frā′mər) *n.* **1.** One that frames: *a picture framer; a framer of new laws.* **2.** Often **Framer.** One of the people who wrote the U.S. Constitution.

frame·shift mutation (frām′shĭft′) *n. Genetics.* A mutation in a DNA chain caused by the insertion or deletion of one or more nucleotides, except in a number that is a multiple of three, which alters every codon beyond the point of insertion or deletion.

frame story *n.* A narrative structure containing or connecting a series of otherwise unrelated tales.

frame-up (frām′ŭp′) *n. Informal.* **1.** A scheme to incriminate an innocent person. **2.** A contest or deliberation the outcome of which is fraudulently prearranged.

frame·work (frām′wûrk′) *n.* **1.** A structure for supporting or enclosing something else, especially a skeletal support used as the basis for something being constructed. **2.** An external work platform; a scaffold. **3.** A fundamental structure, as for a written work or a system of ideas.

fram·ing (frā′mĭng) *n.* A frame, framework, or system of frames.

Fra·ming·ham (frā′mĭng-hăm′). A town of east-central Massachusetts west-southwest of Boston. Population, 65,113.

franc (frăngk) *n. Abbr.* **f., fr.** See table at **currency.** [French, from Old French, from Medieval Latin *Francōrum rēx,* king of the Franks (from the legend on the first of these coins). See FRANK.]

France (frăns). *Abbr.* **Fr.** A country of western Europe on the Atlantic Ocean and the English Channel. It was settled by the Franks after the retreat of the Romans, who had conquered Celtic Gaul in 58–51 B.C. Charlemagne made it the center of his Empire of the West after A.D. 800. In the Middle Ages France was split into numerous fiefdoms and kingdoms, most of which were incorporated into the royal domain by the time of Louis XI (reigned 1461–1483). Widespread poverty and discontent led to the French Revolution (1789), the excesses of which contributed to the rise of Napoleon Bonaparte (1799). Much of France was occupied by the Germans in World War II. Paris is the capital and the largest city. Population, 54,334,871.

France (frăns, fräɴs), **Anatole.** Pen name of Jacques Anatole François Thibault. 1844–1924. French critic and writer of sophisticated, often satirical short stories and novels, including *Penguin Island* (1908). He won the 1921 Nobel Prize for literature.

Fran·ce·sca (frăn-chĕs′kə, frän-), **Piero della.** See **Piero della Francesca.**

Francesca da Ri·mi·ni (də rĭm′ĭ-nē, dä rē′mē-nē). Died c. 1285. Italian noblewoman. Unhappily married, she fell in love with her brother-in-law. When her husband learned of the affair, he murdered his wife and brother, a tragedy recounted by Dante.

Franche-Com·té (fräɴsh-kōɴ-tā′). A historical region and former province of eastern France. The region became part of France after 1676.

fran·chise (frăn′chīz′) *n.* **1.** A privilege or right officially granted a person or a group by a government, especially: **a.** The constitutional or statutory right to vote. **b.** The establishment of a corporation's existence. **c.** The granting of certain rights and powers to a corporation. **d.** Legal immunity from servitude, certain burdens, or other restrictions. **2.a.** Authorization granted to someone to sell or distribute a company's goods or services in a certain area. **b.** A business or group of businesses established or operated under such authorization. **3.** The territory or limits within which immunity, a privilege, or a right may be exercised. **4.** *Informal.* A professional sports team. **—franchise** *tr.v.* **-chised, -chis·ing, -chis·es.** To grant a franchise to. [Middle English *fraunchise,* from Old French *franchise,* from *franche,* feminine of *franc,* free, exempt. See FRANK[1].]

fran·chis·ee (frăn′chī-zē′) *n.* One that is granted a franchise, as to market a company's goods or services in a certain local area.

fran·chis·er or **fran·chi·sor** (frăn′chī′zər) *n.* One that grants a franchise.

Fran·cis I (frăn′sĭs). 1494–1547. King of France (1515–1547) who waged four wars against Holy Roman Emperor Charles V from 1521 to 1544.

Francis II. 1768–1835. Last Holy Roman emperor (1792–1806) and emperor of Austria (1804–1835) as Francis I.

Fran·cis·can (frăn-sĭs′kən) *n. Roman Catholic Church.* A member of a religious mendicant order founded by Saint Francis of Assisi in 1209 and now divided into three independent branches. **—Franciscan** *adj.* Of or relating to Saint Francis of Assisi or to the order founded by him. [New Latin *Franciscānus,* from Medieval Latin *Franciscus,* from Saint FRANCIS OF ASSISI.]

Francis Fer·di·nand (fûr′dn-ănd′). 1863–1914. Austrian archduke whose assassination by a Serbian nationalist precipitated World War I.

Francis Jo·seph I (jō′zəf, -səf, yō′zĕf) also **Franz Jo·sef I** (frănz jō′zəf, -səf, frănts, fränts yō′zĕf). 1830–1916. Emperor of Austria (1848–1916) and king of Hungary (1867–1916) who divided (1867) his empire into a dual monarchy, Austria-Hungary.

Francis of As·si·si (ə-sē′zē, -sē, ə-sĭs′ē), Saint. 1182?–1226. Italian Roman Catholic monk who founded the Franciscan order (1209). He was canonized in 1228.

Francis of Sales (sälz, säl), Saint. 1567–1622. French ecclesiastic who maintained that spiritual perfection is possible not just for religious contemplatives but also for people involved in secular pursuits.

Fran·cis·town (frăn′sĭs-toun′). A city of eastern Botswana near the Zimbabwe border. Population, 32,000.

fran·ci·um (frăn′sē-əm) *n. Symbol* **Fr** An extremely unstable radioactive element of the alkali metals, produced artificially from actinum or thorium, having approximately 19 isotopes, the most stable of which is Fr 223 with a half-life of 21 minutes. Atomic number 87; valence 1. See table at **element.** [After FRANCE.]

Franck (frängk, fräɴk), **César Auguste.** 1822–1890. French organist and composer who exerted great influence as a teacher. His most acclaimed work is his Symphony in D minor (1889).

Fran·co (frăng′kō, fräng′-), **Francisco.** Known as "El Caudillo." 1892–1975. Spanish soldier and political leader who directed the Nationalist government and rebel armed forces that defeated the Republicans in the Spanish Civil War (1936–1939). He ruled as dictator (1939–1975) until his death.

Franco– *pref.* French: *Francophone.* [From Late Latin *Francus,* a Frank. See FRANK.]

Fran·co-A·mer·i·can (frăng′kō-ə-mĕr′ĭ-kən) *n.* An American of French or French-Canadian descent. **—Franco-American** *adj.* **1.** Of or relating to the Franco-Americans. **2.** Of or relating to France and America: *Franco-American relations.*

fran·co·lin (frăng′kə-lĭn) *n.* Any of various Eurasian or African birds of the genus *Francolinus,* related to and resembling the quails and partridges. [French, from Italian *francolino.*]

Fran·co·ni·a (frăng-kō′nē-ə, -kōn′yə, frăn-). A region and former duchy of southern Germany. **—Fran·co′ni·an** *adj. & n.*

Fran·co·phile (frăng′kə-fīl′) also **Fran·co·phil** (-fĭl′) *n.* A person who admires France, its people, or its culture. **—Fran′co·phile′** *adj.* **—Fran′co·phil′i·a** (-fĭl′ē-ə, -fēl′yə) *n.*

Fran·co·phobe (frăng′kə-fōb′) *n.* A person who dislikes or fears France, its people, or its culture. **—Fran′co·phobe′, Fran′co·pho′bic** *adj.* **—Fran′co·pho′bi·a** *n.*

Fran·co·phone or **fran·co·phone** (frăng′kə-fōn′) *—n.* A French-speaking person, especially in a region where two or more languages are spoken. *—adj.* French-speaking. **—Fran′co·phon′ic** (-fŏn′ĭk) *adj.*

fran·gi·ble (frăn′jə-bəl) *adj.* Capable of being broken; breakable. See Synonyms at **fragile.** [Middle English, from Old French, from Medieval Latin *frangibilis,* from Latin *frangere,* to break. See **bhreg-** in Appendix.] **—fran′gi·bil′i·ty, fran′gi·ble·ness** *n.*

fran·gi·pan·i (frăn′jə-păn′ē, -pä′nē) *n., pl.* **-pan·is. 1.** Any of various tropical American deciduous shrubs or trees of the genus *Plumeria,* having milky sap and showy, fragrant, funnel-shaped, variously colored flowers. Also called *temple tree.* **2.** A perfume derived from or similar in scent to the flowers of one of these shrubs or trees. **3.** Also **fran·gi·pane** (frăn′jə-pān′). A creamy pastry filling flavored with almonds. [French *frangipane,* after Muzio *Frangipani,* 16th-century Italian marquis.]

Fran·glais (fräɴ-glā′) *n.* French characterized by numerous borrowings from English. [Blend of French *français,* French (from Old French *franceis,* from *France,* France), and *anglais,* English (from Old French *englois,* from Old English *Angel,* from Latin *Anglī,* the Angles; see ANGLE).]

frank[1] (frăngk) *adj.* **frank·er, frank·est. 1.** Open and sincere in expression; straightforward. **2.** Clearly manifest; evident: *frank enjoyment.* **—frank** *tr.v.* **franked, frank·ing, franks. 1.a.** To put an official mark on (a piece of mail) so that it can be sent free of charge. **b.** To send (mail) free of charge. **2.** To place a stamp or mark on (a piece of mail) to show the payment of postage. **3.** To enable (a person) to come and go freely. **—frank** *n.* **1.a.** A mark or signature placed on a piece of mail to indicate the right to send it free of charge. **b.** The right to send mail free. **2.** A franked piece of mail. [Middle English, free, from Old French *franc,* from Late Latin *Francus,* Frank. See FRANK.] **—frank′ness** *n.*

SYNONYMS: *frank, candid, outspoken, straightforward, open.* These adjectives mean revealing or disposed to reveal one's thoughts freely and honestly. *Frank* implies forthrightness of expression, sometimes to the point of bluntness: *You can tell me what you think, and you may just as well be frank. Candid* stresses openness and sincerity and often suggests refusal to evade difficult or unpleasant issues: *"Save, save, oh save me from the candid friend!"* (George Canning). *Outspoken* usually implies bold lack of reserve: *It is possible to be outspoken without being rude. Straightforward* denotes directness of manner and expression: *"George was a straightforward soul . . . 'See here!' he said. 'Are you engaged to anybody?'"* (Booth Tarkington). *Open* suggests freedom from all trace of reserve or secretiveness: *"I will be open and sincere with you"* (Joseph Addison).

Francis I
Portrait of Francis I, King of France
by Joos van Cleve
(1490?–1540?)

frank[2] (frăngk) *n. Informal.* A frankfurter.

Frank (frăngk) *n.* A member of one of the Germanic tribes of the Rhine region in the early Christian era, especially one of the Salian Franks who conquered Gaul about A.D. 500 and established an extensive empire that reached its greatest power in the ninth century. [Middle English, from Old English *Franca* and Old French *Franc,* both from Late Latin *Francus,* of Germanic origin.]

Frank (frăngk, frängk), **Anne.** 1929–1945. German Jewish diarist who fled from Nazi Germany to Amsterdam with her family (1933) and kept a diary during her years in hiding (1942–1944). She and her family were captured (August 1944) and sent to concentration camps. Anne died of typhus in the camp at Belsen.

Frank·en·stein (frăng′kən-stīn′) *n.* **1.** An agency or a creation that slips from the control of and ultimately destroys its creator. **2.** A monster having the appearance of a man. [From *Frankenstein,* the creator of the artificial monster in *Frankenstein* by Mary Wollstonecraft Shelley.]

Francis Ferdinand

WORD HISTORY: The word *Frankenstein* has taken on a life of its own, somewhat like the monster created from parts of corpses by the Swiss student Frankenstein, whose name serves as the title of Mary Shelley's novel, published in 1818. People have persisted in calling the monster Frankenstein; in fact, the first recorded use of the name as a common noun in 1838 refers to mules as "Frankensteins." The word has gone on to refer to "a monster having the appearance of a man" and "an agency that slips from the control of and ultimately destroys its creator." Since most people have given the name of the novel's protagonist to his creation, Frankenstein's monster has, in a sense, destroyed its creator.

Frank·en·thal·er (frăng′kən-thô′lər, -thŏl′ər), **Helen.** Born 1928. American abstract expressionist painter noted for her innovative techniques and brilliant use of color.

Frank·fort (frăngk′fərt). The capital of Kentucky, in the north-central part of the state northwest of Lexington. It was chosen as capital in 1792. Population, 25,973.

frank·for·ter (frăngk′fər-tər) *n.* Variant of **frankfurter.**

Frank·furt (frănk′fərt, frängk′fo͝ort′). **1.** Also **Frankfurt an der O·der** (än dər ō′dər). A city of eastern Germany on the Oder River and the Polish border. It was chartered in 1253. Population, 84,072. **2.** Also **Frankfurt am Main** (äm mīn′). A city of west-central Germany on the Main River. Founded in the first century B.C. by the Romans, it was the virtual capital of Germany from 1816 to 1866. Population, 599,634.

frank·furt·er also **frank·fort·er** (frăngk′fər-tər) *n.* A smoked sausage of beef or beef and pork made in long, reddish links. [After FRANKFURT, West Germany.]

Frank·furt·er (frăngk′fər-tər), **Felix.** 1882–1965. Austrian-born American jurist who served as an associate justice of the U.S. Supreme Court (1939–1962).

frank·in·cense (frăng′kĭn-sĕns′) *n.* An aromatic gum resin obtained from African and Asian trees of the genus *Boswellia* and used chiefly as incense and in perfumes. [Middle English *frank encens,* from Old French *franc encens* : *franc,* free, pure; see FRANK[1] + *encens,* incense; see INCENSE[2].]

Frank·ish (frăng′kĭsh) *adj.* Of or relating to the Franks or their language. **—Frankish** *n.* The West Germanic language of the Franks.

frank·lin (frăng′klĭn) *n.* A medieval English freeholder of non-noble birth holding extensive property. [Middle English *frankelein,* from Anglo-Norman *fraunclein,* from Anglo-Norman *franc.* See FRANK[1].]

Frank·lin (frăngk′lĭn). **1.** A former district of northeast Northwest Territories, Canada. Created in 1895, it is now in the Baffin Region. **2.** A town of southeast Massachusetts near the Rhode Island border southwest of Boston. It was settled in 1660. Popu-

Francisco Franco

Benjamin Franklin
c. 1785 portrait by Joseph Siffred Duplessis (1725–1802)

lation, 18,217. **3.** A city of southeast Wisconsin, a residential suburb of Milwaukee. Population, 16,871.

Franklin, Aretha. Born 1942. American singer whose popular songs of the mid-1960's include "Respect."

Franklin, Benjamin. 1706–1790. American public official, writer, scientist, and printer. After the success of his *Poor Richard's Almanac* (1732–1757), he entered politics and played a major part in the American Revolution. Franklin negotiated French support for the colonists, signed the Treaty of Paris (1783), and helped draft the Constitution (1787–1789).

Franklin, Sir **John.** 1786–1847. British explorer who led a search for the Northwest Passage (1845–1847) on which he and his 129-man crew perished.

Franklin, John Hope. Born 1915. American historian noted for his studies of Black American history, such as *From Slavery to Freedom* (1947).

frank·lin·ite (frăng′klĭ-nīt′) *n.* A black, slightly magnetic mineral of zinc, iron, and manganese, $ZnFe_2O_4$, that is a source of zinc. [After *Franklin,* a borough of northern New Jersey.]

Franklin Square. A community of southeast New York on southeast Long Island. It is mainly residential. Population, 32,800.

Franklin stove *n.* A cast-iron heating stove shaped like a fireplace but employing metal baffles to increase its heating efficiency. [After Benjamin FRANKLIN.]

Franklin tree *n.* A deciduous tree or shrub *(Franklinia alatamaha)* originally native to Georgia but now known only in cultivation, having large, white, fragrant flowers and woody capsules. [After Benjamin FRANKLIN.]

frank·ly (frăngk′lē) *adv.* **1.** In a frank manner; candidly. **2.** In truth; honestly: *Frankly, I don't care.*

frank·pledge (frăngk′plĕj′) *n.* **1.** An Anglo-Saxon legal system in which units or tithings composed of ten households were formed, in each of which members were held responsible for one another's conduct. **2.** A member of a unit in frankpledge. [Middle English *frankplegge,* from Anglo-Norman *frauncpledge* : Old French *franc,* free, frank; see FRANK¹ + Old French *plege,* pledge; see PLEDGE.]

fran·se·ri·a (frăn-sîr′ē-ə) *n.* Any of various herbs or shrubs of the genus *Franseria,* native to western North America. [New Latin *Franseria,* genus name, after Antonio *Franseri,* 18th-century Spanish botanist.]

fran·tic (frăn′tĭk) *adj.* **1.** Highly excited with strong emotion or frustration; frenzied: *frantic with worry.* **2.** Characterized by rapid and disordered or nervous activity: *made a frantic last-minute search for the lost key.* **3.** *Archaic.* Mad; insane. [Middle English *frantik,* from Old French *frenetique,* from Latin *phrenēticus.* See FRENETIC.] **—fran′ti·cal·ly, fran′tic·ly** *adv.* **—fran′tic·ness** *n.*

Franz Jo·sef I (frănz jō′zəf, -səf, frănts, fränts yō′zĕf). See **Francis Joseph I.**

Franz Josef Land (lănd, länt). An archipelago in the Arctic Ocean north of Novaya Zemlya. The islands were claimed by the U.S.S.R. in 1926.

frap (frăp) *tr.v.* **frapped, frap·ping, fraps.** *Nautical.* **1.** To make secure by lashing: *frap a sail.* **2.** To take up the slack of; tighten. [Middle English *frapen,* to strike, from Old French *fraper.* See FRAPPÉ.]

♦**frap·pé** (fră-pā′, frăp) *n.* **1.** A frozen, fruit-flavored mixture that is similar to sherbet and served as a dessert or appetizer. **2.** A beverage, usually a liqueur, poured over shaved ice. **3.** Often **frappe.** (frăp). *New England.* See **milk shake** (sense 1). See Regional Note at **milk shake.** [French, from past participle of *frapper,* to strike, chill, from Old French *fraper,* to strike, probably of imitative origin.]

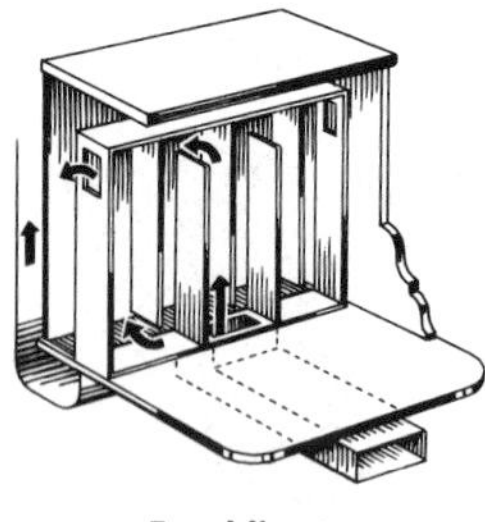
Franklin stove

Fra·ser (frā′zər), **James Earle.** 1876–1953. American sculptor whose works include the design for the buffalo nickel (1913).

Fraser River. A river of British Columbia, Canada, flowing about 1,368 km (850 mi) from the Rocky Mountains near the Alberta boundary to the Strait of Georgia at Vancouver.

frat (frăt) *n. Informal.* A college fraternity.

fra·ter·nal (frə-tûr′nəl) *adj.* **1. a.** Of or relating to brothers: *a close fraternal tie.* **b.** Showing comradeship; brotherly. **2.** Of or constituting a fraternity: *a fraternal association.* **3.** *Biology.* Of, relating to, or being a twin developed from two separately fertilized ova; dizygotic. [Middle English, from Old French *fraternel,* from Medieval Latin *frāternālis,* from Latin *frāternus,* from *frāter,* brother. See **bhrāter-** in Appendix.] **—fra·ter′nal·ism** *n.* **—fra·ter′nal·ly** *adv.*

fra·ter·ni·ty (frə-tûr′nĭ-tē) *n., pl.* **-ties. 1.** A body of people associated for a common purpose or interest, such as a guild. **2.** A group of people joined by similar backgrounds, occupations, interests, or tastes: *the fraternity of bird watchers.* **3.** A chiefly social organization of men students at a college or university, usually designated by Greek letters. **4.** The quality or condition of being brothers; brotherliness. [Middle English *fraternite,* from Old French *fraternite,* from Latin *frāternitās,* from *frāternus,* fraternal. See FRATERNAL.]

frat·er·nize (frăt′ər-nīz′) *intr.v.* **-nized, -niz·ing, -niz·es. 1.** To associate with others in a brotherly or congenial way. **2.** To associate on friendly terms with an enemy or opposing group, often in violation of discipline or orders. [French *fraterniser,* from Medieval Latin *frāternizāre,* from Latin *frāternus,* fraternal. See FRATERNAL.] **—frat′er·ni·za′tion** (-nĭ-zā′shən) *n.* **—frat′er·niz′er** *n.*

frat·ri·cide (frăt′rĭ-sīd′) *n.* **1.** The killing of one's brother or sister. **2.** One who has killed one's brother or sister. [Middle English, from Old French, from Latin *frātricīdium* and *frātricīda* : *frāter, frātr-,* brother; see **bhrāter-** in Appendix + *-cīdium* and *-cīda,* -cide.] **—frat′ri·cid′al** (-sīd′l) *adj.*

Frau (frou) *n., pl.* **Frau·en** (frou′ən). *Abbr.* **Fr.** Used as a courtesy title in a German-speaking area before the surname or professional title of a married woman. [German, from Middle High German *vrowe,* from Old High German *frouwa.* See **per¹** in Appendix.]

fraud (frôd) *n.* **1.** A deception deliberately practiced in order to secure unfair or unlawful gain. **2.** A piece of trickery; a trick. **3. a.** One that defrauds; a cheat. **b.** One who assumes a false pose; an impostor. [Middle English *fraude,* from Old French, from Latin *fraus, fraud-.*]

fraud·u·lent (frô′jə-lənt) *adj.* **1.** Engaging in fraud; deceitful. **2.** Characterized by, constituting, or gained by fraud: *fraudulent business practices.* [Middle English, from Old French, from Latin *fraudulentus,* from *fraus, fraud-,* deceit.] **—fraud′u·lence** *n.* **—fraud′u·lent·ly** *adv.*

fraught (frôt) *adj.* **1.** Filled with a specified element or elements; charged: *an incident fraught with danger; an evening fraught with high drama.* **2.** Fully provided: *"a work so full with various learning fraught"* (John Dryden). **3.** Marked by distress; upsetting: *"an account of a fraught mother-daughter relationship"* (Francesca Simon). **—fraught** *n. Scots.* Freight; cargo. [Middle English, past participle of *fraughten,* to load, from *fraght,* cargo; see FREIGHT, and from Middle Dutch *vrachten,* to load (from *vracht,* freight; see **ēik-** in Appendix).]

Fräu·lein (froi′līn′, frou′-) *n., pl.* **Fräulein. 1.** *Abbr.* **Frl.** Used as a courtesy title in a German-speaking area before the name of an unmarried woman or girl. **2. fräulein.** Used as a form of polite address for a girl or young woman in a German-speaking area. **3.** *Chiefly British.* A German governess. [German, diminutive of *Frau,* wife. See FRAU.]

Fraun·ho·fer lines (froun′hō′fər) *pl.n.* A set of several hundred dark lines appearing against the bright background of the continuous solar spectrum and produced by absorption of light by the cooler gases in the sun's outer atmosphere at frequencies corresponding to the atomic transition frequencies of these gases. [After Joseph von *Fraunhofer* (1787–1826), German physicist.]

frax·i·nel·la (frăk′sə-nĕl′ə) *n.* See **gas plant.** [New Latin, diminutive of Latin *fraxinus,* ash tree. See **bhereg-** in Appendix.]

fray¹ (frā) *n.* **1.** A scuffle; a brawl. See Synonyms at **brawl. 2.** A heated dispute or contest. **—fray** *tr.v.* **frayed, fray·ing, frays.** *Archaic.* **1.** To alarm; frighten. **2.** To drive away. [Middle English *frai,* alteration of *affrai.* See AFFRAY.]

fray² (frā) *v.* **frayed, fray·ing, frays.** —*tr.* **1.** To strain; chafe: *repeated noises that fray the nerves.* **2.** To wear away (the edges of fabric, for example) by rubbing. —*intr.* To become worn away or tattered along the edges. **—fray** *n.* A frayed or threadbare spot, as on fabric. [Middle English *fraien,* to wear, bruise, from Old French *fraier,* to rub, from Latin *fricāre.*]

Fra·zer (frā′zər), Sir **James George.** 1854–1941. British anthropologist who examined the importance of magic, religion, and science to the development of human thought in his most famous work, *The Golden Bough* (1890).

fraz·zle (frăz′əl) *Informal. v.* **-zled, -zling, -zles.** —*tr.* **1.** To wear away along the edges; fray. **2.** To exhaust physically or emotionally. —*intr.* **1.** To become worn away along the edges. **2.** To become exhausted physically or emotionally. **—frazzle** *n.* **1.** A frayed or tattered condition. **2.** A condition of exhaustion: *worked themselves to a frazzle.* [Perhaps a blend of FRAY² and dialectal *fazzle,* to unravel (from Middle English *facelyn,* to fray, from *fasel,* frayed edge, probably diminutive of *fas,* rootlets, from Old English *fæs*).]

FRB *abbr.* Federal Reserve Board.

FRCP or **F.R.C.P.** *abbr.* Fellow of the Royal College of Physicians.

FRCS or **F.R.C.S.** *abbr.* Fellow of the Royal College of Surgeons.

freak¹ (frēk) *n.* **1.** A thing or an occurrence that is markedly unusual or irregular: *A freak of nature produced the midsummer snow.* **2.** An abnormally formed organism, especially a person or animal regarded as a curiosity or monstrosity. **3.** A sudden capricious turn of mind; a whim: *"The freaks of the psyche can no more be explained than the Devil"* (Maurice Collis). See Synonyms at **caprice. 4.** *Slang.* **a.** A drug user or addict: *a speed freak.* **b.** An eccentric or nonconformist person, especially a member of a counterculture. **c.** An enthusiast: *rock music freaks.* **—freak** *intr. & tr.v.* **freaked, freak·ing, freaks.** *Slang.* **1.** To experience or cause to experience frightening hallucinations or feelings of paranoia, especially as a result of taking a drug. Often used with *out.* **2.** To behave or cause to behave irrationally and uncontrollably. Often used with *out.* **3.** To become or cause to become greatly excited or upset. Often used with *out.* [Origin unknown.]

freak² (frēk) *n.* A fleck or streak of color. **—freak** *tr.v.* **freaked, freak·ing, freaks.** To speckle or streak with color: *"the white Pink, and the Pansy freaked with jet"* (John Milton). [From FREAK¹.]

freak·ing (frē′kĭng) *adj. Slang.* Used as an intensive: *"It brought back the whole freaking Nam to me"* (Jimmy Breslin). [Alteration of *frigging,* present participle of FRIG.]

freak·ish (frē′kĭsh) *adj.* **1.** Markedly unusual or abnormal; strange: *freakish weather; a freakish combination of styles.* **2.** Relating to or being a freak: *a freakish extra toe.* **3.** Capricious or whimsical. **—freak′ish·ly** *adv.* **—freak′ish·ness** *n.*

freak-out or **freak·out** (frēk′out′) *n. Slang.* **1.** An experience of frightening feelings or hallucinations, especially as a result of taking a drug. **2.** An experience or scene of unrestrained excitement or irrational behavior. **3.** One having such an experience or participating in such a scene.

freak·y (frē′kē) *adj.* **-i·er, -i·est. 1.** Strange or unusual; freakish. **2.** *Slang.* Frightening. **—freak′i·ly** *adv.*

freck·le (frĕk′əl) *n.* A small brownish spot on the skin, often turning darker or increasing in number upon exposure to the sun. **—freckle** *tr. & intr.v.* **-led, -ling, -les.** To dot or become dotted with freckles or spots of color. [From Middle English *frakles,* freckles, alteration of *fraknes,* probably of Scandinavian origin; akin to Old Icelandic *freknōttr,* freckly.] **—freck′ly** *adj.*

Fred·er·ick (frĕd′rĭk, -ər-ĭk). A city of northern Maryland west of Baltimore. It is a processing center in a farming region. Population, 28,086.

Frederick I. Known as "Frederick Barbarossa." 1123?–1190. Holy Roman emperor (1152–1190) and king of Germany and Italy. After quelling the rebellious German nobility, he failed to subdue papal authority in Italy and conceded supremacy to Pope Alexander III (1177). He drowned while leading the Third Crusade.

Frederick II[1]. 1194–1250. Holy Roman emperor (1212–1250) and king of Sicily (1198–1250) as Frederick I. He led the Sixth Crusade (1228–1229), capturing Jerusalem.

Frederick II[2]. Known as "Frederick the Great." 1712–1786. King of Prussia (1740–1786). Successful in the War of the Austrian Succession (1740–1748) and the Seven Years' War (1756–1763), he brought Prussia great military prestige in Europe.

Frederick IX. 1899–1972. King of Denmark (1947–1972) who signed a constitutional amendment allowing the succession of a woman to the throne.

Fred·er·icks·burg (frĕd′rĭks-bûrg′, -ər-ĭks-). An independent city of northeast Virginia north of Richmond. In the Battle of Fredericksburg (December 1862) Ambrose Burnside's Union forces were defeated by Robert E. Lee's smaller Confederate army in one of the bloodiest battles of the Civil War. Population, 15,322.

Frederick the Great. See **Frederick II[2].**

Frederick Wil·liam (wĭl′yəm). Known as "the Great Elector." 1620–1688. Elector of Brandenburg (1640–1688) who reorganized and rebuilt his domain after its devastation in the Thirty Years' War.

Frederick William I. 1688–1740. King of Prussia (1713–1740) who strengthened the army and diversified the economy of his dominion.

Frederick William II. 1744–1797. King of Prussia (1786–1797) whose mismanaged reign was marked by a costly war with Revolutionary France (1792–1795).

Frederick William III. 1770–1840. King of Prussia (1797–1840) whose long, turbulent reign included participation in the Napoleonic Wars and the suppression of democratic movements.

Frederick William IV. 1795–1861. King of Prussia (1840–1861) who crushed the Revolution of 1848.

Fred·er·ic·ton (frĕd′rĭk-tən, -ər-ĭk-). The capital of New Brunswick, Canada, in the south-central part of the province northwest of St. John. Population, 43,723.

Fred·er·iks·berg (frĕd′rĭks-bûrg′, -ər-ĭks-, frĕ′*th*ə-rēks-bărKH′). A city of eastern Denmark, a suburb of Copenhagen on Sjaelland Island. Population, 88,114.

free (frē) *adj.* **fre·er, fre·est. 1.** Not imprisoned or enslaved; being at liberty. **2.** Not controlled by obligation or the will of another: *felt free to go.* **3.a.** Having political independence: *"America . . . is the freest and wealthiest nation in the world"* (Rudolph W. Giuliani). **b.** Governed by consent and possessing or granting civil liberties: *a free citizenry.* **c.** Not subject to arbitrary interference by a government: *a free press.* **4.a.** Not affected or restricted by a given condition or circumstance: *a healthy animal, free of disease; free from need.* **b.** Not subject to a given condition; exempt: *income that is free of all taxes.* **5.** Not subject to external restraint: *"Comment is free but facts are sacred"* (Charles Prestwich Scott). **6.** Not literal or exact: *a free translation.* **7.a.** Costing nothing; gratuitous: *a free meal.* **b.** Publicly supported: *free education.* **8.a.** Not occupied or used: *a free locker.* **b.** Not taken up by scheduled activities: *free time between classes.* **9.** Unobstructed; clear: *a free lane.* **10.** Unguarded in expression or manner; open; frank. **11.** Taking undue liberties; forward or overfamiliar. **12.** Liberal or lavish: *tourists who are free with their money.* **13.** Given, made, or done of one's own accord; voluntary or spontaneous: *a free act of the will; free choices.* **14.** *Chemistry & Physics.* **a.** Unconstrained; unconfined: *free expansion.* **b.** Not fixed in position; capable of relatively unrestricted motion: *a free electron.* **c.** Not chemically bound in a molecule: *free oxygen.* **d.** Involving no collisions or interactions: *a free path.* **e.** Empty: *a free space.* **f.** Unoccupied: *a free energy level.* **15.** *Nautical.* Favorable: *a free wind.* **16.** Not bound, fastened, or attached: *the free end of a chain.* **17.** *Linguistics.* Being a vowel in an open syllable unchecked by a consonant, as the *o* in *go.* **—free** *adv.* **1.** In a free manner; without restraint. **2.** Without charge. **—free** *tr.v.* **freed, free·ing, frees. 1.** To set at liberty; make free: *freed the slaves; free the imagination.* **2.** To relieve of a burden, an obligation, or a restraint: *a people who were at last freed from fear.* **3.** To remove obstructions or entanglements from; clear: *free a path through the jungle.* **—*idiom.* for free.** *Informal.* Without charge. [Middle English *fre,* from Old English *frēo.* V., from Middle English *freen,* from Old English *frēon,* to love, set free. See **prī-** in Appendix.] **—free′ly** *adv.* **—free′ness** *n.*

free agent *n. Sports.* A professional player who is free to sign a contract with any team. **—free agency** *n.*

free alongside ship *adv. & adj. Abbr.* **f.a.s., F.A.S.** Without charge to the purchaser for delivery to the point of loading aboard ship.

free-as·so·ci·ate (frē′ə-sō′shē-āt′, -sē-) *intr.v.* **-at·ed, -at·ing, -ates.** To engage in free association.

free association *n.* **1.** A spontaneous, logically unconstrained and undirected association of ideas, emotions, and feelings. **2.** A psychoanalytic technique in which a patient's articulation of free associations is encouraged in order to reveal unconscious thoughts and emotions, such as traumatic experiences that have been repressed.

free·base or **free-base** (frē′bās′) *—v.* **-based, -bas·ing, -bas·es.** *—tr.* **1.** To purify (cocaine) by dissolving it in a heated solvent and separating and drying the precipitate. **2.** To use (cocaine purified in this way) by burning it and inhaling the fumes. *—intr.* To prepare or use cocaine purified in this way. *—n.* Cocaine purified by this method. **—free′bas′er** *n.*

free·bie also **free·bee** (frē′bē) *n. Slang.* An article or service given free: *"such freebies as subway and bus maps"* (New York). [From FREE.]

free·board (frē′bôrd′, -bōrd′) *n.* **1.** *Nautical.* The distance between the water line and the uppermost full deck of a ship. **2.** The distance between the ground and the undercarriage of an automobile. [Probably ultimately partial translation of Anglo-Norman *franc bord,* land claimed outside the fence of a park or forest : *franc,* free + *bord,* border.]

freeboard deck *n. Nautical.* The uppermost deck that is officially considered completely watertight.

free·boot (frē′bo͞ot′) *intr.v.* **-boot·ed, -boot·ing, -boots.** To act as a freebooter. [Back-formation from FREEBOOTER.]

free·boot·er (frē′bo͞o′tər) *n.* A person who pillages and plunders, especially a pirate. [Dutch *vrijbuiter,* from *vrijbuit,* plunder : *vrij,* free; see **prī-** in Appendix + *buit,* booty (from Middle Dutch *būte,* of Middle Low German origin).]

free·born (frē′bôrn′) *adj.* **1.** Born as a free person, not as a slave or serf. **2.** Relating to or befitting a person born free.

free central placentation *n. Botany.* The arrangement of ovules on a central column that is not connected to the ovary wall by partitions, as in the ovaries of the carnation and primrose.

free city *n.* A city governed as an autonomous political unit under international auspices.

freed·man (frēd′mən) *n.* A man who has been freed from slavery.

free·dom (frē′dəm) *n.* **1.** The condition of being free of restraints. **2.** Liberty of the person from slavery, detention, or oppression. **3.a.** Political independence. **b.** Possession of civil rights; immunity from the arbitrary exercise of authority. **4.** Exemption from an unpleasant or onerous condition: *freedom from want.* **5.** The capacity to exercise choice; free will: *We have the freedom to do as we please all afternoon.* **6.** Ease or facility of movement: *loose sports clothing, giving the wearer freedom.* **7.** Frankness or boldness; lack of modesty or reserve: *the new freedom in movies and novels.* **8.a.** The right to unrestricted use; full access: *was given the freedom of their research facilities.* **b.** The right of enjoying all of the privileges of membership or citizenship: *the freedom of the city.* [Middle English *fredom,* from Old English *frēodōm* : *frēo,* free; see FREE + *-dōm,* -dom.]

SYNONYMS: *freedom, liberty, license.* These nouns refer to the power to act, speak, or think without externally imposed restraints. *Freedom* is the most general term: *"In giving freedom to the slave, we assure freedom to the free"* (Abraham Lincoln). *"The freedom of the press is one of the great bulwarks of liberty"* (George Mason). *Liberty* is often used interchangeably with *freedom;* often, however, it especially stresses the power of free choice: *liberty of opinion; liberty of worship; at liberty to choose whatever occupation she wishes; "liberty, perfect liberty, to think, feel, do just as one pleases"* (William Hazlitt). *License* sometimes denotes deliberate deviation from normally applicable rules or practices to achieve a desired effect, as in literature or art: *poetic license.* Frequently, though, it denotes undue freedom: *"the intolerable license with which the newspapers break . . . the rules of decorum"* (Edmund Burke).

freedom fighter *n.* One engaged in armed rebellion or resistance against an oppressive government.

freedom march *n.* An organized protest march in support of civil rights, especially one aimed at ending racial segregation. **—freedom marcher** *n.*

freedom of the seas *n.* **1.** The doctrine that ships of any nation may travel through international waters unhampered. **2.**

ă pat	oi boy
ā pay	ou out
âr care	o͝o took
ä father	o͞o boot
ĕ pet	ŭ cut
ē be	ûr urge
ĭ pit	th thin
ī pie	*th* this
îr pier	hw which
ŏ pot	zh vision
ō toe	ə about, item
ô paw	♦ regionalism

Stress marks: **′** (primary); ′ (secondary), as in **dictionary** (dĭk′shə-nĕr′ē)

freesia

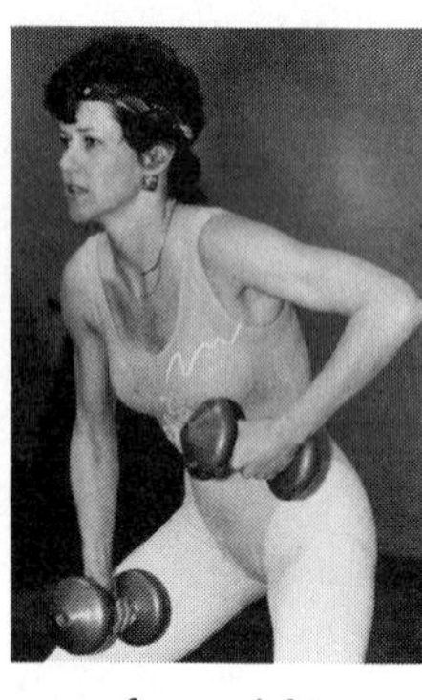
free-weight

ă pat	oi boy
ā pay	ou out
âr care	o͝o took
ä father	o͞o boot
ĕ pet	ŭ cut
ē be	ûr urge
ĭ pit	th thin
ī pie	*th* this
îr pier	hw which
ŏ pot	zh vision
ō toe	ə about, item
ô paw	♦ regionalism

Stress marks: **ʹ** (primary); ʹ (secondary), as in **dictionary** (dĭkʹshə-nĕrʹē)

The right of neutral shipping in wartime to trade at will except where blockades are established.

freedom rider *n.* One of an interracial group of civil rights activists in the early 1960's who rode buses through parts of the southern United States for the purpose of challenging racial segregation. **—freedom ride** *n.*

freed·wom·an (frēdʹwo͝omʹən) *n.* A woman who has been freed from slavery.

free energy *n.* **1.** A thermodynamic quantity that is the difference between the internal energy of a system and the product of its absolute temperature and entropy. **2.** A thermodynamic quantity that is the difference between the enthalpy and the product of the absolute temperature and entropy of a system. In this sense, also called *Gibbs free energy.*

free enterprise *n.* The freedom of private businesses to operate competitively for profit with minimal government regulation. **—freeʹ-enʹter·priseʹ** (frēʹĕnʹtər-prīzʹ) *adj.*

free fall or **free-fall** (frēʹfôlʹ) *n.* **1.** The fall of a body within the atmosphere without a drag-producing device such as a parachute. **2.** The ideal falling motion of a body that is subject only to the earth's gravitational field. **3.** Rapid, uncontrolled decline: *"The markets threatened to go into free fall and we came within an eyelash of . . . an uncontrollable panic"* (Felix Rohatyn).

free-fire zone (frēʹfīrʹ) *n.* A battle area or combat zone in which no restrictions are placed on the use of arms or explosives.

free flight *n.* Flight, as of an aircraft or a spacecraft, after termination of powered flight.

free-float·ing (frēʹflōʹtĭng) *adj.* **1.** Not committed or decided. **2.** Experienced without an obvious basis or cause: *free-floating anxiety.*

free-for-all (frēʹfər-ôlʹ) *n.* A disorderly fight, argument, or competition in which everyone present takes part. See Synonyms at **brawl.**

free·form (frēʹfôrmʹ) *adj.* **1.** Having or characterized by a usually flowing asymmetrical shape or outline: *freeform sculpture.* **2.** Characterized by an unconventional or variable form: *their own freeform teaching methods.* **—freeʹformʹ** *adv.*

free form *n. Linguistics.* A morpheme, such as *cat* or *write,* that is capable of standing alone and retaining meaning.

free·hand (frēʹhăndʹ) *adj.* Drawn by hand without the aid of tracing or drafting devices. **—freeʹhandʹ** *adv.*

free hand *n.* Freedom to do or decide as one sees fit.

free·hand·ed (frēʹhănʹdĭd) *adj.* Openhanded; generous. See Synonyms at **liberal. —freeʹhandʹed·ly** *adv.* **—freeʹhandʹed·ness** *n.*

free·heart·ed (frēʹhärʹtĭd) *adj.* **1.** Unreserved; open. **2.** Generous; liberal. **—freeʹheartʹed·ly** *adv.*

free·hold (frēʹhōldʹ) *n.* **1.** *Law.* **a.** An estate held in fee or for life. **b.** The tenure by which such an estate is held. **2.** A tenure of an office or a dignity for life. [Middle English *frehold,* translation of Anglo-Norman *fraunc tenement* : *fraunc,* free + *tenement,* possession.] **—freeʹholdʹer** *n.*

free·lance (frēʹlănsʹ) also **free lance** *n.* **1.** A person, especially a writer or an artist, who sells his or her services to employers without a long-term commitment to any one of them. **2.** An uncommitted independent, as in politics or social life. **3.** A medieval mercenary. **—freelance** *v.* **-lanced, -lanc·ing, -lanc·es.** —*intr.* To work as a freelance: *a journalist who freelances.* —*tr.* To produce and sell as a freelance: *freelanced the article to a magazine publisher.* **—freelance** *adj.* Of, relating to, or working as a freelance. **—freeʹlancʹer** *n.*

free-liv·ing (frēʹlĭvʹĭng) *adj.* **1.** Given to self-indulgence. **2.** *Biology.* **a.** Living independently of another organism; not part of a parasitic or symbiotic relationship. **b.** Moving independently; not sessile.

free·load (frēʹlōdʹ) *intr.v.* **-load·ed, -load·ing, -loads.** *Slang.* To take advantage of the charity, generosity, or hospitality of others. **—freeʹloadʹer** *n.*

free love *n.* The belief in or practice of sexual relations without marriage and without formal obligations.

free lunch *n. Slang.* Something acquired without due effort or without cost.

free·man (frēʹmən) *n.* **1.** A person not in slavery or serfdom. **2.** One who possesses the rights or privileges of a citizen.

free·mar·tin (frēʹmärʹtn) *n.* A sterile or otherwise sexually imperfect female calf born as the twin of a bull calf. [Origin unknown.]

free·ma·son (frēʹmāʹsən) *n.* **1. Freemason.** A member of the Free and Accepted Masons, an international fraternal and charitable organization with secret rites and signs. **2.** A member of a guild of skilled itinerant masons during the Middle Ages.

free·ma·son·ry (frēʹmāʹsən-rē) *n.* **1. Freemasonry.** The institutions, precepts, and rites of the Freemasons. **2.** Spontaneous fellowship and sympathy among a number of people.

free on board *adj. & adv. Abbr.* **f.o.b., F.O.B.** Without charge to the purchaser for delivery on board or into a carrier at a specified point or location.

free port *n.* A port or an area of a port in which imported goods can be held or processed free of customs duties before reexport.

Free·port (frēʹpôrtʹ, -pōrtʹ). **1.** A city of northwest Illinois west of Rockford. The second Lincoln-Douglas debate occurred here in 1858. Population, 29,266. **2.** A village of southeast New York on the southern shore of Long Island. It is mainly residential. Population, 38,272.

free radical *n.* **1.** An atom or group of atoms having at least one unpaired electron, which makes it highly reactive. **2.** An organic compound in which some of the valence electrons are unpaired, occurring as a normal byproduct of oxidation reactions in metabolism.

free rein *n.* Unlimited freedom to act or make decisions: *gave me free rein to reorganize the department.*

free ride *n. Slang.* Something acquired without the ordinary effort or cost. **—free rider** *n.*

free·sia (frēʹzhə, -zhē-ə, -zē-ə) *n.* Any of several plants of the genus *Freesia,* native to southern Africa, having one-sided clusters of fragrant, variously colored flowers. [New Latin, after Friedrich Heinrich Theodor *Freese* (1795–1876), German physician.]

free silver *n.* The free coinage of silver, especially at a fixed ratio to gold.

free skat·ing (skāʹtĭng) *n. Sports.* Freestyle ice skating. **—free skater** *n.*

free soil *n.* U.S. territory in which slavery was prohibited before the Civil War.

free-soil (frēʹsoilʹ) *adj.* **1.** Prohibiting slavery: *free-soil states.* **2.a.** Opposing the extension of slavery before the U.S. Civil War. **b. Free-Soil.** Of or being a U.S. political party founded in 1848 to oppose the extension of slavery into U.S. territories and the admission of slave states into the Union.

free speech *n.* The right to express any opinion in public without censorship or restraint by the government.

free spirit *n.* One who is not restrained, as by convention or obligation.

free-spo·ken (frēʹspōʹkən) *adj.* Candid in expression; outspoken. **—freeʹ-spoʹken·ness** *n.*

free·stand·ing (frēʹstănʹdĭng) *adj.* Standing or operating independently of anything else: *a freestanding bell tower; a freestanding maternity clinic.*

free·stone (frēʹstōnʹ) *n.* **1.** A stone, such as limestone, that is soft enough to be cut easily without shattering or splitting. **2.** A fruit, especially a peach, that has a stone not adhering to the pulp. [Middle English *freston,* translation of Old French *franche pere,* high-grade stone : *franche,* high-grade, feminine of *franc,* noble, freeborn + *pere,* stone.]

free·style (frēʹstīlʹ) *n. Sports.* **1.a.** A swimming event in which the contestants may choose any stroke. **b.** The crawl. **2.** A competition, as in figure skating, skiing, or surfing, in which any maneuver or movement is allowed and competitors are judged on their artistic expression, acrobatic skill, and athletic expertise. **3.** A style of wrestling in which all noninjurious holds or tactics are permitted. **—freeʹstyleʹ** *adv. & adj.*

free-swim·ming (frēʹswĭmʹĭng) *adj.* Able to swim freely; not sessile or attached: *the free-swimming larva of the oyster.*

free-swing·ing (frēʹswĭngʹĭng) *adj.* Bold and uninhibited: *a lawyer with a free-swinging courtroom style.*

free·think·er (frēʹthĭngʹkər) *n.* One who has rejected authority and dogma, especially in religious thinking, in favor of rational inquiry and speculation. **—freeʹthinkʹing** *adj. & n.*

free thought *n.* Thought that rejects authority and dogma, especially in religion; freethinking.

free throw *n. Basketball.* See **foul shot.**

free-throw line (frēʹthrōʹ) *n. Basketball.* See **foul line** (sense 2).

Free·town (frēʹtounʹ). The capital and largest city of Sierra Leone, in the western part of the country on the Atlantic Ocean. Population, 300,000.

free trade *n.* Trade between nations without protective customs tariffs. **—free trader** *n.*

free university *n.* An independent unaccredited organization established by students within a university for the study of nontraditional subjects.

free verse *n.* Verse composed of variable, usually unrhymed lines having no fixed metrical pattern. [Translation of French *vers libre* : *vers,* verse + *libre,* free.]

free·way (frēʹwāʹ) *n.* **1.** See **expressway. 2.** A highway without tolls.

free-weight or **free weight** (frēʹwātʹ) *n. Sports.* A weight, such as a barbell or dumbbell, that is unattached to another structural device and can be raised and lowered by use of the hands and arms.

free·wheel (frēʹhwēlʹ, -wēlʹ) *intr.v.* **-wheeled, -wheel·ing, -wheels. 1.** To continue turning or spinning after disengagement from the drive mechanism. **2.** To live or move freely and sometimes aimlessly or irresponsibly. **3.** To operate independently or free of restraints.

free wheel *n.* **1.** A power-transmission device that allows the drive shaft of a motor vehicle to continue turning when its speed is greater than that of the engine shaft. **2.** A clutch in the rear-wheel hub of a bicycle that permits the wheel to turn without pedal action, as in coasting.

free·wheel·ing (frēʹhwēʹlĭng, -wēʹ-) *adj.* **1.a.** Free of restraints or rules in organization, methods, or procedure. **b.** Heedless of consequences; carefree. **2.** Relating to or equipped with a free wheel.

free·will (frē′wĭl′) *adj.* Done of one's own accord; voluntary.

free will *n.* **1.** The ability or discretion to choose; free choice: *chose to remain behind of my own free will.* **2.** The power, attributed especially to human beings, of making free choices that are unconstrained by external circumstances or by an agency such as divine will. [Middle English *fre wil,* translation of Late Latin *liberum arbitrium* : Latin *liberum,* free + Latin *arbitrium,* will.]

free world *n.* The countries of the world that have democratic and capitalistic or moderately socialistic systems rather than communist or totalitarian systems.

freeze (frēz) *v.* **froze** (frōz), **fro·zen** (frō′zən), **freez·ing, freez·es.** —*intr.* **1.a.** To pass from the liquid to the solid state by loss of heat. **b.** To acquire a surface or coat of ice from cold: *The lake froze over in January. Bridges freeze before the adjacent roads.* **2.** To become clogged or jammed because of the formation of ice: *The pipes froze in the basement.* **3.** To be at that degree of temperature at which ice forms: *It may freeze tonight.* **4.** To be killed or harmed by cold or frost: *They almost froze to death. Mulch keeps garden plants from freezing.* **5.** To be or feel uncomfortably cold: *Aren't you freezing without a coat?* **6.** To become fixed, stuck, or attached by or as if by frost: *The lock froze up with rust.* **7.a.** To become motionless or immobile, as from surprise or attentiveness: *I heard a sound and froze in my tracks.* **b.** To become unable to act or react, as from fear: *froze in front of the audience.* **8.** To become icily silent in manner: *froze at the rebuke.* **9.** To become rigid and inflexible; solidify: *an opinion that froze into dogma.* —*tr.* **1.a.** To convert into ice. **b.** To cause ice to form upon. **c.** To cause to congeal or stiffen from extreme cold: *winter cold that froze the ground.* **2.** To preserve (foods, for example) by subjecting to freezing temperatures. **3.** To damage, kill, or make inoperative by cold or by the formation of ice. **4.** To make very cold; chill. **5.** To immobilize, as with fear or shock. **6.** To chill with an icy or formal manner: *froze me with one look.* **7.** To stop the motion or progress of: *The negotiations were frozen by the refusal of either side to compromise.* **8.a.** To fix (prices or wages, for example) at a given or current level. **b.** To prohibit further manufacture or use of. **c.** To prevent or restrict the exchange, withdrawal, liquidation, or granting of by governmental action: *freeze investment loans during a depression; froze foreign assets held by U.S. banks.* **9.** To capture or preserve a likeness of, as on film. **10.a.** To photograph (a subject) in mid-action so as to produce a still image. **b.** To stop (a moving film) at a particular image. **11.** To anesthetize by chilling. **12.** *Sports.* To keep possession of (a ball or puck) so as to deny an opponent the opportunity to score. —**freeze** *n.* **1.a.** The act of freezing. **b.** The state of being frozen. **2.** A spell of cold weather; a frost. **3.** A restriction that forbids a quantity from rising above a given or current level: *a freeze on city jobs; a proposed freeze on the production of nuclear weapons.* —***phrasal verb.*** **freeze out.** To shut out or exclude, as by cold or unfriendly treatment: *The others tried to freeze me out of the conversation.* —***idiom.*** **freeze (someone's) blood.** To affect with terror or dread; horrify: *a scream that froze my blood.* [Middle English *fresen,* from Old English *frēosan.* See **preus-** in Appendix.] —**freez′a·ble** *adj.*

freeze-dry (frēz′drī′) *tr.v.* **-dried, -dry·ing, -dries.** To preserve (food, for example) by rapid freezing and drying in a high vacuum.

freeze-etch·ing (frēz′ĕch′ĭng) *n.* A method of specimen preparation for electron microscopy in which a replica is made from a sample that has been rapidly frozen and then fractured along natural planes of weakness to reveal its internal structure. —**freeze′-etched′** (-ĕcht′) *adj.*

freeze-frame or **freeze frame** (frēz′frām′) *n.* **1.** A still picture in the course of a movie or television film, made by running a series of identical frames or by stopping a reel or videotape at one desired frame. **2.** A vivid, motionless scene or image. —**freeze′-frame′** *v.*

freez·er (frē′zər) *n.* A thermally insulated compartment, cabinet, or room in which a subfreezing temperature is maintained for the rapid freezing and storing of perishable food.

freez·ing point (frē′zĭng) *n.* *Abbr.* **fp, f.p.** **1.** The temperature at which a liquid of specified composition solidifies under a specified pressure. **2.** The temperature at which the liquid and solid phases of a substance of specified composition are in equilibrium at atmospheric pressure.

free zone *n.* An area at a port or city where goods may be received and held without the payment of duty.

F region *n.* See **F layer** (sense 1).

Frei·burg (frī′bûrg′, -bo͝ork′). Also **Freiburg im Breis·gau** (ĭm brīs′gou′). A city of southwest Germany near the Rhine River at the edge of the Black Forest. Population, 181,304.

freight (frāt) *n.* *Abbr.* **frt.** **1.** Goods carried by a vessel or vehicle, especially by a commercial carrier; cargo. **2.** A burden; a load. **3.a.** Commercial transportation of goods. **b.** The charge for transporting goods. Also called *freightage.* **4.** A railway train carrying goods only. —**freight** *tr.v.* **freight·ed, freight·ing, freights.** **1.** To convey commercially as cargo. **2.** To load with goods to be transported. **3.** To load; charge. See Synonyms at **charge.** [Middle English *fraught, freight,* from Middle Dutch or Middle Low German *vracht, vrecht;* see **ēik-** in Appendix.]

freight·age (frā′tĭj) *n.* **1.** See **freight** (sense 3). **2.** Cargo.

freight car *n.* A railroad car designed for carrying freight.

freight·er (frā′tər) *n.* **1.** A vehicle, especially a ship, used for carrying freight. **2.** A shipper of cargo.

freight train *n.* A railroad train made up of freight cars.

frem·i·tus (frĕm′ĭ-təs) *n.,* *pl.* **fremitus.** A palpable vibration, as felt by the hand placed on the chest during coughing. [Latin, a murmuring, from past participle of *fremere,* to murmur.]

Fre·mont (frē′mŏnt′). **1.** A city of western California on San Francisco Bay southeast of Oakland. It is a manufacturing and shipping center. Population, 131,945. **2.** A city of east-central Nebraska on the Platte River west-northwest of Omaha. It is a processing center in an agricultural region. Population, 23,979. **3.** A city of northern Ohio southeast of Toledo. Population, 17,834.

Fré·mont (frē′mŏnt′), **John Charles.** 1813–1890. American explorer, soldier, and politician who explored and mapped much of the American West and Northwest.

fre·mont·i·a (frē-mŏn′tē-ə, -chə, frĭ-) *n.* The flannel bush. [New Latin, after John Charles FRÉMONT.]

fre·na (frē′nə) *n.* *Anatomy.* A plural of **frenum.**

french (frĕnch) *tr.v.* **frenched, french·ing, french·es.** **1.** To cut (green beans, for example) into thin strips before cooking. **2.** To trim fat or bone from (a chop, for example). [From FRENCH.]

French curve

French (frĕnch) *adj.* *Abbr.* **Fr., F.** **1.** Of, relating to, or characteristic of France or its people or culture. **2.** Of or relating to the French language. —**French** *n.* **1.** *Abbr.* **Fr., F.** The Romance language of France, parts of Switzerland and Belgium, and other countries formerly under French influence or control. **2.** The people of France. [Middle English, from Old English *frencisc,* Frankish, from *Franca,* Frank. See FRANK.]

French, Daniel Chester. 1850–1931. American sculptor whose many public statues include the seated marble figure of Abraham Lincoln at the Lincoln Memorial in Washington, D.C.

French bulldog *n.* Any of a breed of small, muscular dogs developed in France from toy English bulldogs and native breeds.

French Cam·e·roons (kăm′ə-ro͞onz′). A region and former French protectorate of west-central Africa. It was ceded to France by Germany in 1919.

French-Ca·na·di·an also **French Ca·na·di·an** (frĕnch′-kə-nā′dē-ən) *n.* A Canadian of French descent. —**French′-Ca·na′di·an** *adj.*

French chalk *n.* Chalk made of a soft, white variety of talc, used by tailors for marking fabrics and by dry cleaners for removing grease spots.

French chop *n.* A rib chop with the meat and fat trimmed from the end of the rib.

French Con·go (kŏng′gō). See **French Equatorial Africa.**

French cuff *n.* A wide cuff for a shirt sleeve that is folded back and fastened with a cuff link.

French curve *n.* A flat drafting instrument with curved edges and several scroll-shaped cutouts, used as a guide in drawing curves when constructing graphs or making engineering drawings.

French door
Doorway with two French doors

French door *n.* A door, usually one of a pair, of light construction with glass panes extending for most of its length.

French dressing *n.* **1.** A salad dressing of oil, vinegar, and seasonings. **2.** A commercially prepared creamy salad dressing that is usually pinkish in color and often sweet.

French E·qua·to·ri·al Af·ri·ca (ē′kwə-tôr′ē-əl ăf′rĭ-kə, -tōr′-, ĕk′wə-). Formerly **French Con·go** (kŏng′gō). A former federation of west-central Africa (1910–1958) comprising the present-day countries of Chad, Gabon, Congo, and Central African Republic.

French fry *n.* A thin strip of potato fried in deep fat. Often used in the plural.

French-fry (frĕnch′frī′) *tr.v.* **-fried, -fry·ing, -fries.** To fry (potato strips, for example) in deep fat.

French Gui·a·na (gē-ăn′ə, -ä′nə, gī-). A French overseas department of northeast South America on the Atlantic Ocean. Settlement by the French began in 1604. Cayenne is the capital and the largest city. Population, 72,012.

French heel *n.* A curved, moderately high heel used on women's shoes.

French horn

French horn *n.* *Music.* A valved brass wind instrument that produces a mellow tone from a long, narrow tube that is coiled in a circle before ending in a flaring bell.

French·i·fy (frĕn′chə-fī′) *tr.v.* **-fied, -fy·ing, -fies.** To make French in character or quality. —**French′i·fi·ca′tion** (-fĭ-kā′shən) *n.*

French kiss *n.* *Slang.* A kiss in which the tongue enters the partner's mouth.

French knot *n.* A decorative embroidery stitch made by looping the thread two or more times around the needle, which is then inserted into the fabric.

French leave *n.* An informal, unannounced, or abrupt departure. [From the 18th-century French custom of leaving without saying good-bye to the host or hostess.]

French·man (frĕnch′mən) *n.* A man who is a native or inhabitant of France.

French marigold *n.* A widely cultivated plant *(Tagetes patula)* native to Mexico and Guatemala, having divided leaves, yellow rays usually with reddish markings, and large flower heads.

French pastry *n.* Any of a wide variety of rich and elaborate pastries prepared in individual portions.

French Pol·y·ne·sia (pŏl′ə-nē′zhə, -shə). A French overseas territory in the south-central Pacific Ocean comprising some 120 islands, including the Society and Marquesas islands and the

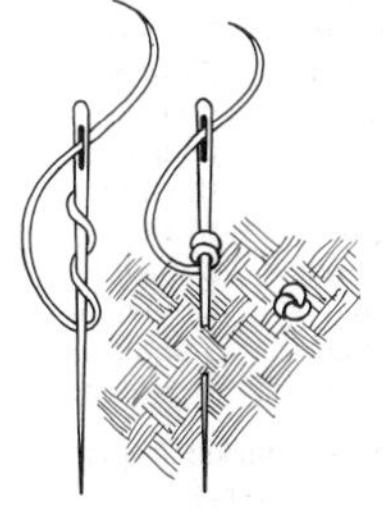

French knot

fret[3]

Tuamotu archipelago. It was organized as a territory in 1903. Papeete, on the island of Tahiti, is the capital. Population, 166,753.

French provincial *n.* A style of architecture or furniture characteristic of the provinces in 17th- and 18th-century France.

French seam *n.* A seam stitched first on the right side and then turned in and stitched on the wrong side so that the raw edges are enclosed in the seam.

French toast *n.* Sliced bread soaked in a batter of milk and egg and lightly fried.

French West Af·ri·ca (ăf′rĭ-kə). A former federation of western Africa (1895–1959) comprising the present-day countries of Benin, Guinea, Ivory Coast, Mali, Mauritania, Niger, Senegal, and Burkina Faso.

French West In·dies (ĭn′dēz). The French overseas departments of Guadeloupe and Martinique in the Lesser Antilles.

French window *n.* **1.** A pair or one of a pair of windows extending to the floor and opening in the middle. **2.** A casement window.

French·wom·an (frĕnch′wo͝om′ən) *n.* A woman who is a native or inhabitant of France.

Fre·neau (frĭ-nō′), **Philip Morin.** Known as "the poet of the American Revolution." 1752–1832. American poet noted for his satirical attacks on the British.

fre·net·ic or **phre·net·ic** (frə-nĕt′ĭk) also **fre·net·i·cal** or **phre·net·i·cal** (-ĭ-kəl) *adj.* Wildly excited or active; frantic; frenzied. [Middle English *frenetik,* from Old French *frenetique,* from Latin *phrenēticus,* from Greek *phrenitikos,* from *phrenitis,* brain disease, from *phrēn,* mind. See **gʷhren-** in Appendix.] —**fre·net′i·cal·ly** *adv.* —**fre·net′i·cism** (-ĭ-sĭz′əm) *n.*

Sigmund Freud

fren·u·lum (frĕn′yə-ləm) *n., pl.* **-la** (-lə). **1.** *Anatomy.* A small frenum. **2.** *Entomology.* A bristly structure on the hind wings of certain moths and butterflies that holds the forewings and hind wings together during flight. [New Latin, diminutive of Latin *frēnum,* bridle, from *frendere,* to grind. See **ghrendh-** in Appendix.]

fre·num (frē′nəm) *n., pl.* **-nums** or **-na** (-nə). *Anatomy.* A membranous fold of skin or mucous membrane that supports or restricts the movement of a part or organ, such as the small band of tissue that connects the underside of the tongue to the floor of the mouth. [Latin *frēnum,* bridle, from *frendere,* to grind. See **ghrendh-** in Appendix.]

fren·zied (frĕn′zēd) *adj.* Affected with or marked by frenzy; frantic: *a frenzied rush for the exits.* —**fren′zied·ly** *adv.*

fren·zy (frĕn′zē) *n., pl.* **-zies. 1.** A state of violent mental agitation or wild excitement. **2.** Temporary madness or delirium. **3.** A mania; a craze. —**frenzy** *tr.v.* **-zied, -zy·ing, -zies.** To drive into a frenzy. [Middle English *frenesie,* from Old French, from Medieval Latin *phrenēsia,* from Latin *phrenēsis,* back-formation from *phrenēticus,* delirious. See FRENETIC.]

Frey

Fre·on (frē′ŏn′). A trademark used for a variety of nonflammable gaseous or liquid fluorinated hydrocarbons employed primarily as working fluids in refrigeration and air conditioning and as aerosol propellants.

freq. *abbr.* **1.** Frequency. **2.** *Grammar.* Frequentative. **3.** Frequently.

fre·quence (frē′kwəns) *n.* Frequency. [Middle English, multitude, from Old French, from Latin *frequentia.* See FREQUENCY.]

fre·quen·cy (frē′kwən-sē) *n., pl.* **-cies.** *Abbr.* **freq. 1.** The property or condition of occurring at frequent intervals. **2.** *Mathematics & Physics.* The number of times a specified phenomenon occurs within a specified interval, as: **a.** The number of repetitions of a complete sequence of values of a periodic function per unit variation of an independent variable. **b.** The number of complete cycles of a periodic process occurring per unit time. **c.** The number of repetitions per unit time of a complete waveform, as of an electric current. **3.** *Statistics.* **a.** The number of measurements in an interval of a frequency distribution. **b.** The ratio of the number of times an event occurs in a series of trials of a chance experiment to the number of trials of the experiment performed. [Latin *frequentia,* multitude, from *frequēns, frequent-,* crowded, numerous, frequent.]

Freya
With attendants

frequency distribution *n. Statistics.* A set of intervals, usually adjacent and of equal width, into which the range of a statistical distribution is divided, each associated with a frequency indicating the number of measurements in that interval.

frequency modulation *n. Abbr.* **FM, fm** The encoding of a carrier wave by variation of its frequency in accordance with an input signal.

fre·quent (frē′kwənt) *adj.* Occurring or appearing quite often or at close intervals: *frequent errors of judgment.* —**frequent** (*also* frē-kwĕnt′) *tr.v.* **-quent·ed, -quent·ing, -quents.** To pay frequent visits to; be in or at often: *frequent a restaurant.* [Middle English, ample, profuse, from Old French, from Latin *frequēns, frequent-,* crowded, numerous, frequent.] —**fre′quen·ta′tion** *n.* —**fre·quent′er** (-kwĕn′tər) *n.* —**fre′quent·ness** *n.*

fre·quen·ta·tive (frē-kwĕn′tə-tĭv) *Grammar. adj. Abbr.* **freq.** Expressing repeated action. —**frequentative** *n. Abbr.* **freq.** A frequentative verb or verb form.

frequent flier *n.* One who travels often by air, especially on one airline.

fre·quent·ly (frē′kwənt-lē) *adv. Abbr.* **freq.** At frequent intervals; often.

fres·co (frĕs′kō) *n., pl.* **-coes** or **-cos. 1.** The art of painting on fresh, moist plaster with pigments dissolved in water. **2.** A painting executed in this way. —**fresco** *tr.v.* **-coed, -co·ing, -coes.** To paint in fresco. [Italian, fresh (plaster), of Germanic origin.] —**fres′co·er, fres′co·ist** *n.*

fresh (frĕsh) *adj.* **fresh·er, fresh·est. 1.** New to one's experience; not encountered before. **2.** Novel; different: *a fresh slant on the problem.* See Synonyms at **new. 3.** Recently made, produced, or harvested; not stale or spoiled: *fresh bread.* **4.** Not preserved, as by canning, smoking, or freezing: *fresh vegetables.* **5.** Not saline or salty: *fresh water.* **6.** Not yet used or soiled; clean: *a fresh sheet of paper.* **7.** Free from impurity or pollution; pure: *fresh air.* **8.** Additional; new: *fresh evidence.* **9.** Bright and clear; not dull or faded: *a fresh memory.* **10.** Having the glowing, unspoiled appearance of youth: *a fresh complexion.* **11.** Untried; inexperienced: *fresh recruits.* **12.** Having just arrived; straight: *fashions fresh from Paris.* **13.** Revived or reinvigorated; refreshed: *I was fresh as a daisy after the nap.* **14.** Fairly strong; brisk: *a fresh wind.* **15.** *Informal.* Bold and saucy; impudent. **16.** Having recently calved and therefore with milk. Used of a cow. —**fresh** *adv.* Recently; newly: *fresh out of milk; muffins baked fresh daily.* —**fresh** *n.* **1.** The early part: *the fresh of the day.* **2.** A freshet. [Middle English, from Old English *fersc,* pure, not salty, and from Old French *freis* (feminine *fresche*), new, recent, of Germanic origin.] —**fresh′ly** *adv.* —**fresh′ness** *n.*

fresh breeze *n. Meteorology.* A wind with a speed of from 19 to 24 miles (30 to 38 kilometers) per hour, according to the Beaufort scale.

fresh·en (frĕsh′ən) *v.* **-ened, -en·ing, -ens.** —*intr.* **1.** To become fresh, as in vigor or appearance: *freshened up after the day's work.* **2.** To become brisk; increase in strength. Used of the wind. **3.** To lose saltiness. **4.** To calve and therefore begin to produce milk. Used of a cow. —*tr.* **1.** To make fresh. **2.** To add to or strengthen (a drink). —**fresh′en·er** *n.*

fresh·et (frĕsh′ĭt) *n.* **1.** A sudden overflow of a stream resulting from a heavy rain or a thaw. **2.** A stream of fresh water that empties into a body of salt water.

fresh gale *n. Meteorology.* A wind with a speed of from 39 to 46 miles (62 to 74 kilometers) per hour, according to the Beaufort scale.

fresh·man (frĕsh′mən) *n.* **1.** A student in the first-year class of a high school, college, or university. **2.** A beginner; a novice. See Usage Note at **man.** —*attributive.* Often used to modify another noun: *in my freshman year; a freshman senator.*

fresh·wa·ter (frĕsh′wô′tər, -wŏt′ər) *adj.* **1.** Of, relating to, living in, or consisting of water that is not salty: *freshwater fish; freshwater lakes.* **2.** Situated away from the sea; inland. **3.** *Nautical.* Accustomed to sailing on inland waters only: *a freshwater sailor.*

Fres·nel (frā-nĕl′), **Augustin Jean.** 1788–1827. French physicist who supported the wave theory of light, investigated polarized light, and developed a compound lens for use in lighthouses.

Fres·nel lens (frə-nĕl′) *n.* A thin optical lens consisting of concentric rings of segmental lenses and having a short focal length, used primarily in spotlights, beacons, and the headlights of motor vehicles. [After Augustin Jean FRESNEL.]

Fres·no (frĕz′nō). A city of central California south-southeast of Sacramento in the San Joaquin Valley. Population, 217,289.

fret[1] (frĕt) *v.* **fret·ted, fret·ting, frets.** —*tr.* **1.** To cause to be uneasy; vex: *"fret thy soul with crosses and with cares"* (Edmund Spenser). **2. a.** To gnaw or wear away; erode. **b.** To produce a hole or worn spot in; corrode. See Synonyms at **chafe. 3.** To form (a passage or channel) by erosion. **4.** To disturb the surface of (water or a stream); agitate. —*intr.* **1.** To be vexed or troubled; worry. See Synonyms at **brood. 2.** To be worn or eaten away; become corroded. **3.** To move agitatedly. **4.** To gnaw with the teeth in the manner of a rodent. —**fret** *n.* **1.** The act or an instance of fretting. **2.** A hole or worn spot made by abrasion or erosion. **3.** Irritation of mind; agitation. [Middle English *freten,* from Old English *fretan,* to devour. See **ed-** in Appendix.]

fret[2] (frĕt) *Music. n.* One of several ridges set across the fingerboard of a stringed instrument, such as a guitar. —**fret** *tr.v.* **fret·ted, fret·ting, frets. 1.** To provide with frets. **2.** To press (the strings of an instrument) against the frets. [Origin unknown.]

fret[3] (frĕt) *n.* **1.** An ornamental design consisting of repeated and symmetrical figures, often in relief, contained within a band or border. **2.** A headdress, worn by women of the Middle Ages, consisting of interlaced wire. —**fret** *tr.v.* **fret·ted, fret·ting, frets.** To provide with such a design or headdress. [Middle English, interlaced work, from Old French *frete.*]

fret·ful (frĕt′fəl) *adj.* **1.** Inclined to be vexed or troubled; peevish. **2.** Marked by worry and distress; troublesome: *"Of all the fretful stages of human development, adolescence is the most infamous"* (David Gelman). —**fret′ful·ly** *adv.* —**fret′ful·ness** *n.*

fret saw *n.* A long, narrow-bladed saw with fine teeth, used in making curved cuts in thin wood or metal.

fret·work (frĕt′wûrk′) *n.* **1.** Ornamental work consisting of three-dimensional frets; geometric openwork. **2.** Such ornamental work represented two dimensionally by chiaroscuro.

Freud (froid), **Anna.** 1895–1982. Austrian-born British psychoanalyst noted for her theories about child therapy.

Freud, Sigmund. 1856–1939. Austrian physician and founder of psychoanalysis who theorized that the symptoms of hysterical patients represent forgotten and unresolved infantile psychosexual conflicts.

ă pat	oi boy
ā pay	ou out
âr care	o͝o took
ä father	o͞o boot
ĕ pet	ŭ cut
ē be	ûr urge
ĭ pit	th thin
ī pie	*th* this
îr pier	hw which
ŏ pot	zh vision
ō toe	ə about, item
ô paw	♦ regionalism

Stress marks: ′ (primary); ′ (secondary), as in **dictionary** (dĭk′shə-nĕr′ē)

Freu·di·an (froi′dē-ən) *adj.* Relating to or being in accordance with the psychoanalytic theories of Sigmund Freud. —**Freudian** *n.* A person who accepts the basic tenets of the psychoanalytic theories of Sigmund Freud, especially a psychiatrist who applies Freudian theory and method in conducting psychotherapy. —**Freu′di·an·ism** *n.*

Freudian slip *n.* A verbal mistake that is thought to reveal an unconscious belief, thought, or emotion.

Freund's adjuvant (froindz) *n.* A substance consisting of killed microorganisms, such as mycobacteria, in an oil and water emulsion that is administered to induce and enhance the formation of antibodies. [After Jules T. *Freund* (1890–1960), Hungarian-born American immunologist.]

Frey (frā) also **Freyr** (frâr) *n. Mythology.* The Norse god who dispenses peace, good weather, prosperity, and bountiful crops; the brother of Freya.

Frey·a also **Frey·ja** (frā′ə) *n. Mythology.* The Norse goddess of love and beauty; the sister of Frey.

Freyr (frâr) *n. Mythology.* Variant of **Frey.**

F.R.G. or **FRG** *abbr.* Federal Republic of Germany.

Fri. *abbr.* Friday.

fri·a·ble (frī′ə-bəl) *adj.* Readily crumbled. [Latin *friābilis,* from *friāre,* to crumble.] —**fri′a·bil′i·ty, fri′a·ble·ness** *n.*

fri·ar (frī′ər) *n. Abbr.* **Fr.** A member of a usually mendicant Roman Catholic order. [Middle English *frere,* from Old French, from Latin *frāter,* brother. See **bhrāter-** in Appendix.] —**fri′ar·ly** *adj.*

fri·ar·bird (frī′ər-bûrd′) *n.* Any of various honeyeaters of the genus *Philemon* of Australia and adjacent regions, having a partly naked, featherless head. Also called *leatherhead.*

fri·ar's lantern (frī′ərz) *n.* See **ignis fatuus** (sense 1).

fri·ar·y (frī′ə-rē) *n., pl.* **-ies.** A monastery of friars.

frib·ble (frĭb′əl) *v.* **-bled, -bling, -bles.** —*tr.* To waste (time, for example); fritter (something) away. —*intr.* To waste time; trifle. —**fribble** *n.* **1.** A frivolity; a trifle. **2.** A frivolous person. [Origin unknown.] —**frib′bler** *n.*

fric·an·deau (frĭk′ən-dō′) *n.* A cut of veal that has been larded and braised. [French, from *fricasser,* to fricassee. See FRICASSEE.]

fric·as·see (frĭk′ə-sē′, frĭk′ə-sē′) *n.* Poultry or meat cut into pieces and stewed in gravy. —*tr.* **-seed, -see·ing, -sees.** To prepare (poultry or meat) by cutting into pieces and stewing in gravy. [French *fricassée,* from Old French, from feminine past participle of *fricasser,* to fricassee : probably *frire,* to fry (from Latin *frīgere,* to roast, fry) + *casser,* to break, crack (from Latin *quassāre,* to shake, shatter; see SQUASH[2]) or Vulgar Latin **coāctiāre,* to press together (from Latin *coāctus,* past participle of *cōgere,* to drive or bring together; see COGENT).]

fric·a·tive (frĭk′ə-tĭv) *Linguistics. n.* A consonant, such as *f* or *s* in English, produced by the forcing of breath through a constricted passage. Also called *spirant.* —**fricative** *adj.* Of, relating to, or being a fricative consonant. [New Latin *fricātīvus,* from Latin *fricātus,* past participle of *fricāre,* to rub.]

Frick (frĭk), **Henry Clay.** 1849–1919. American industrialist who amassed a fortune in the steel industry.

fric·tion (frĭk′shən) *n.* **1.** The rubbing of one object or surface against another. **2.** Conflict, as between persons having dissimilar ideas or interests; clash. **3.** *Physics.* A force that resists the relative motion or tendency to such motion of two bodies in contact. [Latin *frictiō, frictiōn-,* from *frictus,* past participle of *fricāre,* to rub.] —**fric′tion·al** *adj.* —**fric′tion·al·ly** *adv.*

friction clutch *n.* A mechanical clutch that transmits torque through surface friction between the faces of the clutch.

friction drive *n.* An automotive transmission system in which motion is transmitted from one part to another by the surface friction of rolling contact.

friction match *n.* A match that ignites when struck on an abrasive surface.

friction tape *n.* A sturdy, moisture-resistant adhesive tape, usually made of cloth, used to insulate electrical conductors.

Fri·day (frī′dē, -dā′) *n. Abbr.* **Fri., Fr., F.** The sixth day of the week. [Middle English *Fridai,* from Old English *Frīgedæg.* See **prī-** in Appendix.]

fridge (frĭj) *n. Informal.* A refrigerator.

Frid·ley (frĭd′lē). A city of eastern Minnesota, a suburb of Minneapolis on the Mississippi River. Population, 30,228.

fried (frīd) *v.* Past tense and past participle of **fry**[1].

Fried (frēd, frēt), **Alfred Hermann.** 1864–1921. Austrian pacifist. He shared the 1911 Nobel Peace Prize.

Frie·dan (frĭ-dăn′), **Betty Naomi.** Born 1921. American feminist who wrote *The Feminine Mystique* (1963) and founded the National Organization for Women (1966).

Fried·land·er's bacillus (frēd′lĕn′dərz) *n.* A pathogenic bacterium *(Klebsiella pneumoniae)* that often causes pneumonia. [After Karl *Friedländer* (1847–1887), German pathologist.]

Fried·man (frēd′mən), **Milton.** Born 1912. American economist. He won a 1976 Nobel Prize for his theories of monetary control and governmental nonintervention in the economy.

friend (frĕnd) *n.* **1.** A person whom one knows, likes, and trusts. **2.** A person whom one knows; an acquaintance. **3.** A person with whom one is allied in a struggle or cause; a comrade. **4.** One who supports, sympathizes with, or patronizes a group, cause, or movement: *friends of the clean air movement.* **5. Friend.** A member of the Society of Friends; a Quaker. —**friend** *tr.v.* **friend·ed, friend·ing, friends.** *Archaic.* To befriend. [Middle English, from Old English *frēond.* See **prī-** in Appendix.] —**friend′less** *adj.* —**friend′less·ness** *n.*

friend·ly (frĕnd′lē) *adj.* **-li·er, -li·est. 1.** Of, relating to, or befitting a friend: *friendly advice.* **2.** Favorably disposed; not antagonistic: *a government friendly to our interests.* **3.** Warm; comforting. **4. a.** *Computer Science.* User-friendly. **b.** *Informal.* Easy to understand or use for a specified agent. Often used in combination: *a reader-friendly novel; a consumer-friendly policy.* —**friendly** *adv.* In the manner of a friend. —**friendly** *n., pl.* **-lies.** *Informal.* One fighting on or favorable to one's own side: *"If I read this right, you're the only friendly we have there right now"* (Tom Clancy). —**friend′li·ly** *adv.* —**friend′li·ness** *n.*

Friend·ly Islands (frĕnd′lē). See **Tonga.**

fri·er (frī′ər) *n.* Variant of **fryer.**

fries (frīz) *v.* Third person singular present tense of **fry**[1]. —**fries** *n.* Plural of **fry**[1].

Frie·sian (frē′zhən) *n.* Variant of **Frisian.**

Fries·land (frēz′lənd, -lănd′, frēs′-). A region of northern Europe on the North Sea between the Scheldt and Weser rivers. The Frisians, a Germanic people, were conquered by the Franks in the eighth century.

frieze[1] (frēz) *n. Architecture.* **1.** A plain or decorated horizontal part of an entablature between the architrave and cornice. **2.** A decorative horizontal band, as along the upper part of a wall in a room. [French *frise,* from Medieval Latin *frisium, frigium,* embroidery, from Latin *Phrygium (opus),* Phrygian (work), from PHRYGIA.]

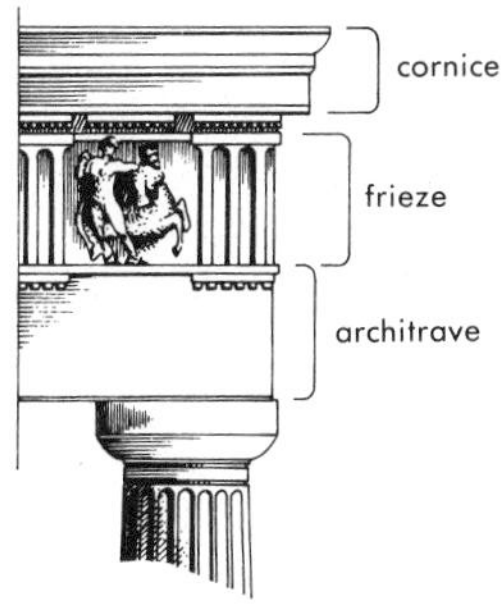

frieze[1]

frieze[2] (frēz) *n.* **1.** A coarse, shaggy woolen cloth with an uncut nap. **2.** A dense, low-pile surface, as in carpeting, resembling such cloth. Also called *frisé.* [Middle English *frise,* from Old French, from Medieval Latin *(pannī) frisiī,* woolen garments. See FRISIAN.]

frig (frĭg) *v.* **frigged, frig·ging, frigs.** *Vulgar Slang.* —*tr.* To have sexual intercourse with. —*intr.* To have sexual intercourse. [Middle English, to quiver, possibly from Old French *friquer,* to rub, from Latin *fricāre.*]

frig·ate (frĭg′ĭt) *n.* **1.** A U.S. warship of 4,000 to 9,000 displacement tons, larger than a destroyer and smaller than a cruiser, used primarily for escort duty. **2.** A high-speed, medium-sized sailing war vessel of the 17th, 18th, and 19th centuries. **3.** *Archaic.* A fast, light vessel, such as a sailboat. [French *frégate,* from Italian *fregata.*]

frigate bird *n.* Any of various tropical sea birds of the family Fregatidae that have long, powerful wings, dark plumage, and a hooked beak and characteristically snatch food from other birds in flight. Also called *man-o'-war bird.*

frigate
Top: Modern U.S. Navy frigate
Bottom: Painting of the U.S.S. *Constitution,* also called "Old Ironsides"

Frigg (frĭg) also **Frig·ga** (frĭg′ə) *n. Mythology.* The Norse goddess of the heavens and wife of Odin. [Old Norse. See **prī-** in Appendix.]

fright (frīt) *n.* **1.** Sudden, intense fear, as of something immediately threatening; alarm. See Synonyms at **fear. 2.** *Informal.* Something extremely unsightly, alarming, or strange: *Brush your hair; you look a fright.* —**fright** *tr.v.* **fright·ed, fright·ing, frights.** *Archaic.* To frighten. [Middle English, from Old English *fyrhto, fryhto.* V., from Middle English *frighten,* to frighten, be afraid, from Old English *fyrhtan.*]

fright·en (frīt′n) *v.* **-ened, -en·ing, -ens.** —*tr.* **1.** To fill with fear; alarm. **2.** To drive or force by arousing fear: *The suspect was frightened into confessing.* —*intr.* To become afraid. —**fright′en·er** *n.* —**fright′en·ing·ly** *adv.*

SYNONYMS: *frighten, scare, alarm, terrify, terrorize, startle, panic.* These verbs mean to cause a person to experience fear. *Frighten* and the less formal *scare* are the most widely applicable terms: *"Better be killed than frightened to death"* (Robert Smith Surtees). *Don't let the size of the task scare you. Alarm* implies the often sudden onset of fear or apprehension: *Her sudden and inexplicable loss of weight alarmed her doctor. Terrify* implies overwhelming, often paralyzing fear: *"The regulars, terrified by the yells of the Indians . . . gathered themselves into a body"* (George Bancroft). *Terrorize* implies fear that intimidates; the word sometimes suggests deliberate coercion: *"premeditated and systematized terrorizing of the civil populations"* (Edith Wharton). *Startle* suggests fear that shocks momentarily and may cause a sudden, involuntary movement of the body: *The clap of thunder startled us. Panic* implies sudden frantic fear that often impairs self-control and rationality: *The radio drama was so realistic that it panicked listeners who tuned in after it had begun.*

fright·ful (frīt′fəl) *adj.* **1.** Causing disgust or shock; horrifying. **2.** Causing fright; terrifying. **3.** *Informal.* **a.** Excessive; extreme: *a frightful liar.* **b.** Disagreeable; distressing: *frightful weather.* —**fright′ful·ly** *adv.* —**fright′ful·ness** *n.*

fright wig *n.* A wig with hair, especially long or frizzy hair, standing up from the surface.

frig·id (frĭj′ĭd) *adj.* **1.** Extremely cold. See Synonyms at **cold. 2.** Lacking warmth of feeling. **3.** Stiff and formal in manner: *a frigid refusal to a request.* **4.** Persistently averse to sexual intercourse. [Latin *frīgidus,* cold, from *frīgus,* the cold.] —**fri·gid′i·ty** (frĭ-jĭd′ĭ-tē), **frig′id·ness** *n.* —**frig′id·ly** *adv.*

Frigg

Frig·i·daire (frĭj′ĭ-dâr′). A trademark used for electric refrigerators and other household appliances.

Frig·id Zone (frĭj′ĭd). Either of two extreme latitude zones of the earth, the **North Frigid Zone,** between the North Pole and the Arctic Circle, or the **South Frigid Zone,** between the South Pole and the Antarctic Circle.

frig·o·rif·ic (frĭg′ə-rĭf′ĭk) also **frig·o·rif·i·cal** (-ĭ-kəl) *adj.* Causing coldness; chilling. [Latin *frīgorificus* : *frīgus, frīgor-*, the cold + *-ficus*, -fic.]

♦ **fri·jol** (frē-hōl′, frē′hōl′) also **fri·jo·le** (frē-hō′lē) *n., pl.* **fri·jo·les** (frē-hō′lēz, frē′hō′-). *Southwestern U.S.* A bean cultivated and used for food. [Spanish, variant of *fréjol*, from Old Spanish *frisol*, from Catalan *fesol*, from Latin *phaseolus*, diminutive of *phasēlus*, a type of legume, from Greek *phasēlos*.]

frill (frĭl) *n.* **1.** A ruffled, gathered, or pleated border or projection, such as a fabric edge used to trim clothing or a curled paper strip for decorating the end of the bone of a piece of meat. **2.** A ruff of hair or feathers about the neck of an animal or a bird. **3.** A wrinkling of the edge of a photographic film. **4.** *Informal.* Something that is desirable but not a necessity; a luxury. See Synonyms at **luxury.** —**frill** *v.* **frilled, frill·ing, frills.** —*tr.* **1.** To make into a ruffle or frill. **2.** To add a ruffle or frill to. —*intr.* To become wrinkled along the edge. [Origin unknown.] —**frill′i·ness** *n.* —**frill′y** *adj.*

frilled lizard (frĭld) *n.* An Australian lizard *(Chlamydosaurus kingi)* having a broad, contractile membrane extending from the neck and throat that can be extended like a ruff when the mouth is opened.

Friml (frĭm′əl), **(Charles) Rudolf.** 1879–1972. Czechoslovakian-born American pianist and composer of 33 light operas.

fringe (frĭnj) *n.* **1.** A decorative border or edging of hanging threads, cords, or strips, often attached to a separate band. **2.** Something that resembles such a border or edging. **3.** A marginal, peripheral, or secondary part: *"They like to hang out on the geographical fringes, the seedy outposts"* (James Atlas). **4.** Those members of a group or political party holding extreme views: *the lunatic fringe.* **5.** Any of the light or dark bands produced by the diffraction or interference of light. **6.** A fringe benefit. —**fringe** *tr.v.* **fringed, fring·ing, fring·es. 1.** To decorate with or as if with a fringe: *The weaver fringed the edge of the scarf.* **2.** To serve as a fringe to: *Ferns fringed the pool.* [Middle English *frenge*, from Old French, from Vulgar Latin **frimbia*, alteration of Late Latin *fimbria*. See FIMBRIA.] —**fring′y** *adj.*

fringe area *n.* A zone just outside of the range of a broadcasting station in which signals are weakened and distorted.

fringe benefit *n.* An employment benefit given in addition to one's wages or salary.

fringed gentian (frĭnjd) *n.* A biennial or annual plant *(Gentianopsis crinita)* of eastern North America, having blue, bell-shaped flowers with fringed petals.

fringed orchis *n.* Any of various orchids of the genus *Habenaria,* having variously colored flowers with a fringed lip and a spurred base.

fringed polygala *n.* A perennial plant *(Polygala paucifolia)* of eastern North America, having fringed, reddish-purple flowers. Also called *flowering wintergreen.*

fringe tree *n.* A shrub or small tree *(Chionanthus virginicus)* of the southeast United States, having drooping clusters of white flowers and dark blue fruit. Also called *old-man's-beard.*

fring·ing reef (frĭn′jĭng) *n.* A coral reef formed close to a shoreline.

frip·per·y (frĭp′ə-rē) *n., pl.* **-ies. 1.** Pretentious, showy finery. **2.** Pretentious elegance; ostentation. **3.** Something trivial or nonessential. [French *friperie*, from Old French *freperie*, old clothes, from *felpe, frepe*, from Medieval Latin *faluppa*, worthless material.]

Fris. *abbr.* Frisian.

Fris·bee (frĭz′bē). A trademark used for a plastic disk-shaped toy that players throw and catch. This trademark sometimes occurs in print meaning "a throw-and-catch game played with this toy": *"The Mall is a better place to play Frisbee with a dog"* (Los Angeles Times).

fri·sé (frē-zā′) *n.* See **frieze²**. [French, from past participle of *friser*, to curl. See FRIZZ¹.]

fri·sée (frĭ-zā′) *n.* See **endive** (sense 1). [French, from feminine past participle of *friser*, to curl. See FRIZZ¹.]

fri·sette also **fri·zette** (frĭ-zĕt′) *n.* A fringe of curled, often artificial hair, usually worn on the forehead by a woman. [French *frisette*, from *friser*, to curl. See FRIZZ¹.]

fri·seur (frē-zûr′, -zœr′) *n.* A hairdresser; a coiffeur. [French, from *friser*, to curl. See FRIZZ¹.]

Fri·sian (frĭzh′ən, frē′zhən) also **Frie·sian** (frē′zhən) *n.* *Abbr.* **Fris., Frs. 1.** A native or inhabitant of the Frisian Islands or Friesland. **2.** The West Germanic language of the Frisians. It is the language most closely related to English. [From Latin *Frīsiī*, the Frisians, of Germanic origin.] —**Fri′sian** *adj.*

Frisian Islands. A chain of islands in the North Sea off the coast of the Netherlands, Germany, and Denmark. The **West Frisian Islands** belong to the Netherlands. The **East Frisian Islands** and most of the **North Frisian Islands** are part of Germany; the other North Frisians are Danish.

frisk (frĭsk) *v.* **frisked, frisk·ing, frisks.** —*intr.* To move about briskly and playfully; frolic. —*tr.* To search (a person) for something concealed, especially a weapon, by passing the hands quickly over clothes or through pockets. —**frisk** *n.* **1.** An energetic, playful movement; a gambol. **2.** The act of frisking. [From Middle English *frisk*, lively, from Old French *frisque*, of Germanic origin.] —**frisk′er** *n.*

fringe

frisk·y (frĭs′kē) *adj.* **-i·er, -i·est.** Energetic, lively, and playful: *a frisky kitten.* —**frisk′i·ly** *adv.* —**frisk′i·ness** *n.*

fris·son (frē-sōN′) *n., pl.* **-sons** (-sōNz′, -sōN′). A moment of intense excitement; a shudder: *The story's ending arouses a frisson of terror.* [French, from Old French *friçons*, pl. of *friçon*, a trembling, from Vulgar Latin **frīctiō*, **frīctiōn-*, from Latin *frīgēre*, to be cold.]

frit (frĭt) *n.* **1.** The fused or partially fused materials used in making glass. **2.** A vitreous substance used in making porcelain, glazes, or enamels. —**frit** *tr.v.* **frit·ted, frit·ting, frits.** To make into frit. [Italian *fritta*, from feminine past participle of *friggere*, to fry, from Latin *frīgere*, to roast, fry.]

frit fly *n.* Any of several small flies of the family Chloropidae, especially *Oscinella frit*, having larvae that are destructive to cereal plants such as oats and wheat. [Origin unknown.]

frith (frĭth) *n.* *Scots.* A firth. [Alteration of FIRTH.]

frit·il·lar·y (frĭt′l-ĕr′ē) *n., pl.* **-ies. 1.** Any of various bulbous plants of the genus *Fritillaria*, having nodding, variously colored, often spotted or checkered flowers. **2.** Any of various butterflies of the family Nymphalidae, especially of the genera *Speyeria* and *Boloria*, having brownish wings marked with black or silvery spots on the underside. [New Latin *Fritillāria*, genus name, from Latin *fritillus*, dice-box.]

frit·ta·ta (frĭ-tä′tə, frēt-tä′tə) *n.* An open-faced omelet, often cooked with meat, cheese, or vegetables. [Italian, from *fritto*, past participle of *friggere*, to fry. See FRIT.]

frit·ter¹ (frĭt′ər) *tr.v.* **-tered, -ter·ing, -ters. 1.** To reduce or squander little by little: *frittered his inheritance away.* See Synonyms at **waste. 2.** To break, tear, or cut into bits; shred. [Probably from *fritter*, fragment, probably alteration of *fitters*, from *fitter*, to break into small pieces.]

frit·ter² (frĭt′ər) *n.* A small cake made of batter, often containing fruit, vegetables, or fish, sautéed or deep-fried. [Middle English *friture*, from Old French, from Late Latin *frīctūra*, from Latin *frīctus*, past participle of *frīgere*, to roast, fry.]

fritz (frĭts) *n.* *Informal.* A condition in which something does not work properly: *Our television is on the fritz.* [Origin unknown.]

Fri·u·li (frē′ə-lē′, frē-ōō′lē). A historical region and former duchy of Italy in present-day northeast Italy and northwest Yugoslavia.

Fri·u·li-Ve·ne·zia Giu·lia (frē′ə-lē′və-nĕt′sē-ə jōōl′yə, frē-ōō′lē-vĕ-nĕt′syä). A region of northeast Italy bounded by Austria in the north and Yugoslavia in the east.

friv·ol (frĭv′əl) *intr.v.* **-oled, -ol·ing, -ols** or **-olled, -ol·ling, -ols.** To behave frivolously. [Back-formation from FRIVOLOUS.] —**friv′ol·er** *n.*

fri·vol·i·ty (frĭ-vŏl′ĭ-tē) *n., pl.* **-ties. 1.** The quality or condition of being frivolous. **2.** A frivolous act or thing.

friv·o·lous (frĭv′ə-ləs) *adj.* **1.** Unworthy of serious attention; trivial: *a frivolous novel.* **2.** Inappropriately silly: *a frivolous purchase.* [Middle English, probably from Latin *frīvolus*, of little value, probably from *friāre*, to crumble.] —**friv′o·lous·ly** *adv.* —**friv′o·lous·ness** *n.*

fri·zette (frĭ-zĕt′) *n.* Variant of **frisette.**

frizz¹ (frĭz) *tr. & intr.v.* **frizzed, frizz·ing, frizz·es.** To form or be formed into small, tight curls or tufts. —**frizz** *n.* **1.** The condition of being frizzed. **2.** A small, tight curl or tuft. [Alteration (influenced by FRIZZLE²) of French *friser*, from Old French, possibly from *frire, fris-*, to fry, from Latin *frīgere*, to roast, fry.]

frizz² (frĭz) *v.* **frizzed, frizz·ing, frizz·es.** —*tr.* To fry or burn with a sizzling noise. —*intr.* To make a sizzling noise while frying or searing. [Possibly back-formation from FRIZZLE¹.]

friz·zle¹ (frĭz′əl) *v.* **-zled, -zling, -zles.** —*tr.* **1.** To fry (something) until crisp and curled: *frizzled the bacon.* **2.** To scorch or sear with heat. —*intr.* To fry or sear with a sizzling noise. [Possibly blend of FRY¹ and SIZZLE.]

friz·zle² (frĭz′əl) *tr. & intr.v.* **-zled, -zling, -zles.** To form or cause to be formed into small, tight curls; frizz. —**frizzle** *n.* A small, tight curl. [Origin unknown.]

friz·zly (frĭz′lē) *adj.* **-zli·er, -zli·est.** Tightly curled.

friz·zy (frĭz′ē) *adj.* **-zi·er, -zi·est.** Tightly curled; frizzly. —**friz′zi·ly** *adv.* —**friz′zi·ness** *n.*

Frl. *abbr.* Fräulein.

fro (frō) *adv.* Away; back: *moving to and fro.* —**fro** *prep.* *Scots.* From. [Middle English, probably from Old Norse *frā*. See **per¹** in Appendix.]

Frö·bel (frœ′bəl), **Friedrich Wilhelm August.** See Friedrich Wilhelm August **Froebel.**

Fro·bish·er (frō′bĭ-shər, frŏb′ĭ-), Sir **Martin.** 1535?–1594. English explorer who made three voyages to the Canadian Arctic (1576, 1577, and 1578) in search of the Northwest Passage.

Frobisher Bay. An arm of the Atlantic Ocean extending into southeast Baffin Island in Northwest Territories, Canada.

frock (frŏk) *n.* **1.** A woman's dress. **2.** A long, loose outer garment, as that worn by artists and craftspeople; a smock. **3.** A woolen garment formerly worn by sailors. **4.** A robe worn by monks, friars, and other clerics; a habit. —**frock** *tr.v.* **frocked, frock•ing, frocks. 1.** To clothe in a frock. **2.** To invest with clerical office. [Middle English *frok,* a monk's habit, from Old French *froc,* from Medieval Latin *froccus,* of Germanic origin.]

frock coat *n.* A man's dress coat or suit coat with knee-length skirts.

froe also **frow** (frō) *n.* A cleaving tool having a heavy blade set at right angles to the handle. [From *frower,* possibly from FROWARD.]

Froe•bel also **Frö•bel** (frœ′bəl), **Friedrich Wilhelm August.** 1782–1852. German educator who established the first kindergarten (1837).

frog (frôg, frŏg) *n.* **1.** Any of numerous tailless, aquatic, semiaquatic, or terrestrial amphibians of the order Anura and especially of the family Ranidae, characteristically having a smooth, moist skin, webbed feet, and long hind legs adapted for leaping. **2.** A wedge-shaped, horny prominence in the sole of a horse's hoof. **3.** A loop fastened to a belt to hold a tool or weapon. **4.** An ornamental looped braid or cord with a button or knot for fastening the front of a garment. **5.** A device on intersecting railroad tracks that permits wheels to cross the junction. **6.** A spiked or perforated device used to support stems in a flower arrangement. **7.** *Informal.* Hoarseness or phlegm in the throat. **8.** *Offensive Slang.* Used as a disparaging term for a French person. [Middle English *frogge,* from Old English *frogga.*]

frog•eye (frôg′ī′, frŏg′ī′) *n.* A plant disease caused by fungi and characterized by rounded spots on the leaves.

frog•fish (frôg′fĭsh′, frŏg′-) *n., pl.* **frogfish** or **-fish•es.** Any of various bottom-dwelling fishes of the family Antennariidae of tropical and temperate seas, characteristically having a prickly or warty globose body and pectoral fins adapted for grasping.

frog•hop•per (frôg′hŏp′ər, frŏg′-) *n.* See **spittlebug.**

frog kick *n. Sports.* A swimming kick used in the breaststroke in which the knees are drawn up close to the hips and the feet are thrust outward and backward so that the legs come together when fully extended.

frog•man (frôg′măn′, -mən, frŏg′-) *n.* A swimmer provided with breathing apparatus and other equipment to execute underwater maneuvers, especially military maneuvers.

frog•mouth (frôg′mouth′, frŏg′-) *n.* Any of various brown or gray nocturnal birds of the family Podargidae of southeast Asia and Australia, having a wide mouth and a hooked bill.

frog spit *n.* **1.** A foamlike aggregation of small aquatic plants, such as green algae, on the surface of a pond. Also called *frog spittle.* **2.** See **cuckoo spit.**

Frois•sart (froi′särt′, frwä-sär′), **Jean.** 1333?–1405? French historian noted for his vivid accounts of Europe during the Hundred Years' War.

frol•ic (frŏl′ĭk) *n.* **1.** Gaiety; merriment: *fun and frolic.* **2.** A gay, carefree time. **3.** A playful antic. —**frolic** *intr.v.* **-icked, -ick•ing, -ics. 1.** To behave playfully and uninhibitedly; romp. **2.** To engage in merrymaking, joking, or teasing. —**frolic** *adj. Archaic.* Merry. [From Dutch *vrolijk,* merry, from Middle Dutch *vrolijc* : *vro,* happy + *-lijc,* -like; see **līk-** in Appendix.] —**frol′ick•er** *n.*

frol•ic•some (frŏl′ĭk-səm) *adj.* Full of high-spirited fun; frisky and playful. See Synonyms at **playful.**

♦**from** (frŭm, frŏm; frəm *when unstressed*) *prep. Abbr.* **fm., fr. 1.a.** Used to indicate a specified place or time as a starting point: *walked home from the station; from six o'clock on.* See Usage Notes at **escape, whence. b.** Used to indicate a specified point as the first of two limits: *from grades four to six.* **2.** Used to indicate a source, a cause, an agent, or an instrument: *a note from the teacher; taking a book from the shelf.* **3.** Used to indicate separation, removal, or exclusion: *keep someone from making a mistake; liberation from bondage.* **4.** Used to indicate differentiation: *know right from wrong.* **5.** Because of: *faint from hunger.* —***idiom.* from away.** *Maine.* Not native to Maine. [Middle English, from Old English. See **per**[1] in Appendix.]

Fromm (frōm, frŏm), **Erich.** 1900–1980. German-born American psychoanalyst who emphasized the role of social conditioning in human behavior.

frond (frŏnd) *n.* **1.** The leaf of a fern. **2.** A large compound leaf of a palm. **3.** A leaflike thallus, as of a seaweed or lichen. [Latin *frōns, frond-,* foliage.] —**frond′ed** *adj.*

fron•des•cent (frŏn-dĕs′ənt) *adj.* Bearing, resembling, or having a profusion of leaves or fronds; leafy. [Latin *frondēscēns, frondēscent-,* present participle of *frondēscere,* to become leafy, inchoative of *frondēre,* to put forth leaves, from *frōns, frond-,* foliage.] —**fron•des′cence** *n.*

fron•dose (frŏn′dōs′) *adj.* **1.** Bearing fronds. **2.** Resembling a frond. [Latin *frondōsus,* abounding in foliage, from *frōns, frond-,* foliage.] —**fron′dose′ly** *adv.*

frons (frŏnz) *n., pl.* **fron•tes** (frŏn′tēz). The anterior, uppermost part of the head of an insect. [Latin *frōns, front-,* forehead, front.]

front (frŭnt) *n.* **1.** The forward part or surface, as of a building. **2.** The area, location, or position directly before or ahead. **3.** A position of leadership or superiority. **4.** The forehead or face, especially of a bird or other animal. **5.a.** Demeanor or bearing, especially in the presence of danger or difficulty. **b.** An outward, often feigned, appearance or manner: *They put up a good front.* **6.a.** Land bordering a lake, river, or street. **b.** A promenade along the water at a resort. **7.** A detachable part of a man's dress shirt covering the chest; a dickey. **8.a.** The most forward line of a combat force. **b.** The area of contact between opposing combat forces; a battlefront. **9.** *Meteorology.* The interface between air masses of different temperatures or densities. **10.** A field of activity: *the economic front.* **11.a.** A group or movement uniting various individuals or organizations for the achievement of a common purpose; a coalition. **b.** A nominal leader lacking in real authority; a figurehead. **c.** An apparently respectable person, group, or business used as a cover for secret or illegal activities. **12.** *Archaic.* **a.** The first part; the beginning. **b.** The face; the countenance. —**front** *adj.* **1.** Of, relating to, aimed at, or located in the front: *the front lines; the front row; front property on Lake Tahoe.* **2.** *Linguistics.* Designating vowels produced at or toward the front of the oral cavity, such as the vowels of *green* and *get.* —**front** *v.* **front•ed, front•ing, fronts.** —*tr.* **1.** To look out on; face: *a house that fronts the ocean.* **2.** To meet in opposition; confront. See Synonyms at **defy. 3.** To provide a front for. **4.** To serve as a front for. **5.** *Music.* To lead (a group of musicians): *"Goodman . . . became the first major white bandleader to front an integrated group"* (Bill Barol). **6.** *Informal.* To provide before payment: *"In . . . personal liability suits, a lawyer is fronting both time and money"* (Richard Faille). —*intr.* **1.** To have a front; face onto something else: *Her property fronts on the highway.* **2.** To provide an apparently respectable cover for secret or illegal activities: *fronting for organized crime.* —**front** *interj.* Used by a desk clerk in a hotel to summon a bellhop. —***idiom.* front and center.** In the most prominent position. [Middle English, from Old French, from Latin *frōns, front-.*]

frog
Bullfrog
Rana catesbeiana

front. *abbr.* Frontispiece.

front•age (frŭn′tĭj) *n.* **1.a.** The front part of a piece of property. **b.** The land between a building and the street. **c.** Land adjacent to something, such as a building, street, or body of water. **2.** The direction in which something faces.

frontage road *n.* See **service road.**

fron•tal[1] (frŭn′tl) *adj.* **1.** Of, relating to, directed toward, or situated at the front: *a frontal attack.* **2.** *Anatomy.* **a.** Of or relating to the forehead or frontal bone. **b.** Of or relating to the frontal plane. **3.** Of or relating to a meteorological front. —**fron′tal•ly** *adv.*

fron•tal[2] (frŭn′tl) *n.* **1.** A drapery covering the front of an altar. **2.** The façade of a building. [Middle English *frontel,* from Old French, from Medieval Latin *frontāle,* from Latin *frōns, front-,* forehead, front.]

frontal bone *n. Anatomy.* A cranial bone consisting of a vertical portion corresponding to the forehead and a horizontal portion that forms the roofs of the orbital and nasal cavities.

frontal lobe *n. Anatomy.* The largest and most anterior part of each cerebral hemisphere.

frontal lobotomy *n.* A prefrontal lobotomy.

frontal plane *n. Anatomy.* A plane parallel to the long axis of the body and perpendicular to the sagittal plane that separates the body into front and back portions.

front bench *n.* The first bench on either side of the aisle in a parliament, reserved for ministers and leaders of the principal political parties.

front burner *n. Informal.* A position of relatively great importance: *put consideration of the question on the front burner.*

front•court (frŭnt′kôrt′, -kōrt′) *n. Basketball.* **1.** The half of the court having the basket at which the offensive team shoots. **2.** The forwards and center on a team. In this sense, also called *frontline.*

Fron•te•nac (frŏn′tə-năk′, frôN-näk′), Comte de. Title of Louis de Buade. 1620?–1698. French colonial administrator who governed New France (1672–1682 and 1689–1698).

front-end (frŭnt′ĕnd′) *adj.* **1.** Of or relating to the initial phase of a project: *a front-end investment.* **2.** Of or relating to the forward parts of a vehicle: *a front-end alignment.*

front-end load *n.* The amount deducted from early payments made to a mutual fund purchase plan that covers expenses such as sales commissions.

front-end loader *n.* An earthmoving machine with a hydraulic scoop in front for lifting and loading earth or rubble.

front-end processor *n. Abbr.* **FEP** *Computer Science.* A computer used to process data before it is sent to a mainframe computer for analysis or further processing.

fron•ten•is (frŭn-tĕn′ĭs, frŏn′tĕn′ĭs) *n. Sports.* A Latin-American tennis game played on a three-walled court. [American Spanish, blend of Spanish *frontón,* jai alai court; see FRONTON, and Spanish *tenis,* tennis (from English TENNIS).]

fron•tes (frŏn′tēz) *n.* Plural of **frons.**

fron•tier (frŭn-tîr′, frŏn-, frŭn′tîr′, frŏn′-) *n.* **1.a.** An international border. **b.** The area along an international border. See Synonyms at **boundary. 2.** A region just beyond or at the edge of a settled area. **3.** An undeveloped area or field for discovery or research: *theories on the frontier of astrophysics.* —*attributive.* Often used to modify another noun: *frontier towns; frontier law.* [Middle English *frountier,* from Old French *frontier,* from *front,* forehead, front. See FRONT.]

fron•tiers•man (frŭn-tîrz′mən, frŏn-) *n.* A man who lives on the frontier.

fron•tiers•wom•an (frŭn-tîrz′wo͝om′ən, frŏn-) *n.* A woman who lives on the frontier.

ă pat	oi boy
ā pay	ou out
âr care	o͝o took
ä father	o͞o boot
ĕ pet	ŭ cut
ē be	ûr urge
ĭ pit	th thin
ī pie	*th* this
îr pier	hw which
ŏ pot	zh vision
ō toe	ə about, item
ô paw	♦ regionalism

Stress marks: ′ (primary); ′ (secondary), as in **dictionary** (dĭk′shə-nĕr′ē)

fron·tis·piece (frŭn′tĭ-spēs′) *n. Abbr.* **front. 1.** An illustration that faces or immediately precedes the title page of a book, book section, or magazine. **2.** *Architecture.* **a.** A façade, especially an ornamental façade. **b.** A small ornamental pediment, as on top of a door. **3.** *Archaic.* A title page. [Alteration (influenced by PIECE) of French *frontispice,* from Late Latin *frontispicium,* façade of a building : Latin *frontis,* genitive of *frōns,* forehead, front + Latin *specere,* to look at; see **spek-** in Appendix.]

front·let (frŭnt′lĭt) *n.* **1.** An ornament or a band worn on the forehead as a phylactery. **2.** The forehead of an animal. **3.** The forehead of a bird when of a different color or texture of plumage. **4.** An ornamental border for a frontal. [Middle English, from Old French *frontelet,* diminutive of *frontel,* ornament worn on the forehead. See FRONTAL[2].]

front·line also **front line** (frŭnt′līn′) —*n.* **1.** A front or boundary, especially one between military, political, or ideological positions. **2.** *Basketball.* See **frontcourt** (sense 2). **3.** *Football.* The linemen of a team. —*adj.* or **front-line. 1.** Located or used at a military front. **2.** Of or relating to the most advanced or important position or activity in a field or undertaking: *"leaders of the six black 'front-line states' bordering South Africa"* (Boston Globe). **3.** *Sports.* **a.** Of or relating to the frontline. **b.** Being a member of the regular team; first-string: *a team in need of a frontline catcher.*

front-load (frŭnt′-lōd′) *v.* **-load·ed, -load·ing, -loads.** —*tr.* To concentrate costs or benefits of (a financial obligation or deal) in an early period: *They front-loaded their tax deductions.* —*intr.* To concentrate costs or benefits in an early period.

front man *n.* **1.** A man who serves as a nominal leader but who lacks real authority. **2.** *Music.* A leading singer with a group.

front matter *n.* The material, such as the preface, frontispiece, and title page, preceding the text in a book.

front money *n.* Money paid in advance, as for contracted goods or services.

front office *n.* The executive or policymaking officers of an organization.

fron·to·gen·e·sis (frŭn′tō-jĕn′ĭ-sĭs) *n., pl.* **-ses** (-sēz′). Formation or intensification of a meteorological front.

fron·tol·y·sis (frŭn-tŏl′ĭ-sĭs) *n., pl.* **-ses** (-sēz′). Dissipation of a meteorological front.

fron·ton (frŏn′tŏn′, frôn-tôn′) *n. Sports.* An arena for jai alai. [Spanish *frontón,* wall, fronton, augmentative of *frente,* forehead, face, from Old Spanish *fruente,* from Latin *frōns, front-.*]

front-page (frŭnt′pāj′) *adj.* Worthy of coverage on the front page of a newspaper: *front-page news.* **—front-page** *tr.v.* **-paged, -pag·ing, -pag·es.** To place or report on the front page of a newspaper.

Front Range (frŭnt). A range of the Rocky Mountains in north-central Colorado. It rises to 4,352.4 m (14,270 ft) at Grays Peak.

front room *n.* See **living room.**

front-run·ner also **front·run·ner** (frŭnt′rŭn′ər) *n.* **1.** One that is in a leading position in a race or other competition: *the front-runner for the presidential nomination.* **2.** A competitor who performs best when in the lead. **—front′-run′ning** *adj.*

front·ward (frŭnt′wərd) *adv. & adj.* Toward, to, or at the front. **—front′wards** *adv.*

front-wheel drive (frŭnt′hwēl′, -wēl′) *n. Abbr.* **FWD** An automotive drive system in which only the front pair of wheels receives power from the engine.

frore (frôr, frōr) *adj. Archaic.* Extremely cold; frosty. [Middle English, past participle of *fresen,* to freeze, from Old English *frēosan.* See FREEZE.]

frosh (frŏsh) *n., pl.* **frosh.** *Informal.* A freshman, as in college. [Shortening and alteration of FRESHMAN.]

frost (frôst, frŏst) *n.* **1.** A deposit of minute ice crystals formed when water vapor condenses at a temperature below freezing. **2.** A temperature low enough to cause freezing. **3.** The process of freezing. **4.** A cold or icy manner. —*attributive.* Often used to modify another noun: *the frost season; frost damage to crops.* **—frost** *v.* **frost·ed, frost·ing, frosts.** —*tr.* **1.** To cover with frost. **2.** To damage or kill by frost. **3.** To cover (glass, for example) with a roughened or speckled decorative surface. **4.** To cover or decorate with icing: *frost a cake.* **5.** *Slang.* To anger or upset: *What really frosted me about the incident was the fact that you lied.* —*intr.* To become covered with or as if with frost. [Middle English, from Old English. See **preus-** in Appendix.]

Frost (frôst, frŏst), **Robert Lee.** 1874–1963. American poet whose collections include *A Boy's Will* (1913) and *In the Clearing* (1962).

Frost·belt also **Frost Belt** (frôst′bĕlt′, frŏst′-). The north-central and northeast United States.

frost·bite (frôst′bīt′, frŏst′-) *n.* Injury or destruction of skin and underlying tissue, most often that of the nose, ears, fingers, or toes, resulting from prolonged exposure to freezing or subfreezing temperatures. **—frostbite** *tr.v.* **-bit** (-bĭt′), **-bit·ten** (-bĭt′n), **-bit·ing, -bites.** To injure or damage by freezing.

frost·fish (frôst′fĭsh′, frŏst′-) *n., pl.* **frostfish** or **-fish·es.** Any of several North American fishes, especially the tamcod, that appear during the fall frost season.

frost-free (frôst′frē′, frŏst′-) *adj.* Requiring little or no defrosting: *a frost-free refrigerator.*

♦**frost heave** *n. New England.* Ruptured pavement caused by the expansion of freezing water under the road: *"We've got the worst frost heaves in 20 years"* (Wallace E. Stickney).

frost·ing (frô′stĭng, frŏs′tĭng) *n.* **1.** Icing, as on a cake. **2.** A roughened or speckled surface imparted to glass or metal.

frost line *n.* The depth to which frost penetrates the earth.

frost·work (frôst′wûrk′, frŏst′-) *n.* **1.** The intricate patterns produced by frost, as on a windowpane. **2.** Artificially made ornamental patterns similar to those produced by frost, applied to the surface of metal or glass.

frost·y (frô′stē, frŏs′tē) *adj.* **-i·er, -i·est. 1.** Producing or characterized by frost; freezing. See Synonyms at **cold. 2.** Covered with or as if with frost. **3.** Silvery white; hoary. **4.** Cold in manner: *a frosty look; a frosty farewell.* **—frost′i·ly** *adv.* **—frost′i·ness** *n.*

froth (frôth, frŏth) *n.* **1.** A mass of bubbles in or on a liquid; foam. **2.** Salivary foam released as a result of disease or exhaustion. **3.** Something unsubstantial or trivial. **4.** A fit of resentment or vexation: *was in a froth over the long delay.* **—froth** (*also* frôth, frŏth) *v.* **frothed, froth·ing, froths.** —*tr.* **1.** To cover with foam. **2.** To cause to foam. —*intr.* To exude or expel foam. [Middle English, from Old Norse *frodha.*]

froth·y (frô′thē, frŏth′ē) *adj.* **-i·er, -i·est. 1.** Made of, covered with, or resembling froth; foamy. **2.** Playfully frivolous in character or content: *a frothy French farce.* **—froth′i·ly** *adv.* **—froth′i·ness** *n.*

frot·tage (frô-täzh′) *n.* **1.** The act of rubbing against the body of another person, as in a crowd, to attain sexual gratification. **2. a.** A method of making a design by placing a piece of paper on top of an object and then rubbing over it, as with a pencil or charcoal. **b.** A design so made. [French, from *frotter,* to rub, from Old French *froter.*]

Froude (fro͞od), **James Anthony.** 1818–1894. British historian and biographer noted for his works on Thomas Carlyle.

frou·frou also **frou-frou** (fro͞o′fro͞o) *n.* **1.** Fussy or showy dress or ornamentation. **2.** A rustling sound, as of silk. [French, of imitative origin.]

frow (frō) *n.* Variant of **froe.**

fro·ward (frō′wərd, -ərd) *adj.* Stubbornly contrary and disobedient; obstinate. **—fro′ward·ly** *adv.* **—fro′ward·ness** *n.*

Fro·ward (frō′wərd, -ərd), **Cape.** The southernmost point of mainland South America, on the Strait of Magellan.

frown (froun) *v.* **frowned, frown·ing, frowns.** —*intr.* **1.** To wrinkle the brow, as in thought or displeasure. **2.** To regard something with disapproval or distaste: *frowned on the use of so much salt in the food.* —*tr.* To express (disapproval, for example) by wrinkling the brow. **—frown** *n.* A wrinkling of the brow in thought or displeasure; a scowl. [Middle English *frounen,* from Old French *froigner,* to turn up one's nose, from *frogne,* grimace, of Celtic origin.] **—frown′er** *n.* **—frown′ing·ly** *adv.*

SYNONYMS: *frown, glower, lower, scowl.* The central meaning shared by these verbs is "to contract the brows in displeasure": *frowns when he is annoyed; glowered sullenly at being interrupted; lowering at the rambunctious child; scowled at me when I came home late.*

WORD HISTORY: Caesar's division of Gaul into three parts used to be known by every child who learned Latin, but perhaps even classically trained schoolchildren did not always realize that in spite of the conquest of Gaul by the Romans, some Gaulish elements lived on, such as our word *frown.* This word is descended from Gaulish, a Celtic language that is related to Welsh and Irish. *Frown,* first recorded in Middle English in a work composed around 1395, came from Old French *froigner,* which meant "to turn up one's nose." The Old French word was derived from *frogne,* "grimace," which in turn came from the hypothetical Gaulish word **frogna,* "nose," which is related to Welsh *ffroen,* "nose," and Old Irish *srōn,* "nose."

frows·ty (frou′stē) *adj.* **-ti·er, -ti·est.** *Chiefly British.* Having a stale smell; musty. [Origin unknown.]

frow·zy also **frow·sy** (frou′zē) *adj.* **-zi·er, -zi·est** also **-si·er, -si·est. 1.** Unkempt; slovenly: *frowzy clothes; a frowzy professor.* **2.** Having an unpleasant smell; musty: *a frowzy pantry.* [Origin unknown.] **—frow′zi·ness** *n.*

froze (frōz) *v.* Past tense of **freeze.**

fro·zen (frō′zən) *v.* Past participle of **freeze. —frozen** *adj.* **1.** Made into, covered with, or surrounded by ice. **2.** Very cold: *the frozen North.* **3.** Preserved by freezing: *frozen meat.* **4.** Rendered immobile: *frozen in their tracks with fear.* **5.** Expressive of cold unfriendliness or disdain: *a frozen look on their faces.* **6. a.** Kept at a fixed level: *frozen rents.* **b.** Impossible to withdraw, sell, or liquidate: *frozen assets.*

frozen food *n.* Food that has undergone freezing and is intended to remain frozen until used.

FRS *abbr.* **1.** Federal Reserve System. **2.** Or **F.R.S.** Fellow of the Royal Society.

Frs. *abbr.* Frisian.

frt. *abbr.* Freight.

fruc·tif·er·ous (frŭk-tĭf′ər-əs, fro͝ok-) *adj.* Bearing fruit. [Latin *frūctifer* (*frūctus,* fruit; see FRUIT + *-fer,* -fer) + -OUS.]

fruc·ti·fi·ca·tion (frŭk′tə-fĭ-kā′shən, fro͝ok′-) *n.* **1.** The producing of fruit. **2.** A seed-bearing or spore-bearing structure.

fruc·ti·fy (frŭk′tə-fī′, fro͝ok′-) *v.* **-fied, -fy·ing, -fies.** —*tr.*

To make fruitful or productive. —*intr.* To bear fruit. [Middle English *fructifien,* to bear fruit, from Old French *fructifier,* from Latin *frūctificāre* : *frūctus,* fruit; see FRUIT + *-ficāre,* -fy.]

fruc·tose (frŭk′tōs′, fro͝ok′-) *n.* A very sweet sugar, $C_6H_{12}O_6$, occurring in many fruits and honey and used as a preservative for foodstuffs and as an intravenous nutrient. Also called *fruit sugar, levulose.* [Latin *frūctus,* fruit; see FRUIT + –OSE[2].]

fruc·tu·ous (frŭk′cho͞o-əs, fro͝ok′-) *adj.* Fruitful; productive. [Middle English, from Old French, from Latin *frūctuōsus,* from *frūctus,* fruit. See FRUIT.]

fru·gal (fro͞o′gəl) *adj.* **1.** Practicing or marked by economy, as in the expenditure of money or the use of material resources. See Synonyms at **sparing. 2.** Costing little; inexpensive: *a frugal lunch.* [Latin *frūgālis,* virtuous, thrifty, from *frūx, frūg-,* fruit, virtue.] **—fru·gal′i·ty** (fro͞o-găl′ĭ-tē), **fru′gal·ness** *n.*

fru·gi·vore (fro͞o′jə-vôr′, -vōr′) *n.* An animal, such as a chimpanzee or fruit bat, that feeds primarily on fruit. [From FRUGIVOROUS.]

fru·giv·o·rous (fro͞o-jĭv′ər-əs) *adj.* Feeding on fruit; fruit-eating. [Latin *frūx, frūg-,* fruit + –VOROUS.]

fruit (fro͞ot) *n., pl.* **fruit** or **fruits. 1.a.** The ripened ovary or ovaries of a seed-bearing plant, together with accessory parts, containing the seeds and occurring in a wide variety of forms. **b.** An edible, usually sweet and fleshy form of such a structure. **c.** A part or an amount of such a plant product, served as food: *fruit for dessert.* **2.** The fertile, often spore-bearing structure of a plant that does not bear seeds. **3.** A plant crop or product: *the fruits of the earth.* **4.** Result; outcome: *the fruit of their labor.* **5.** Offspring; progeny. **6.** A fruity aroma or flavor in a wine. **7.** *Offensive Slang.* Used as a disparaging term for a gay or homosexual man. —*attributive.* Often used to modify another noun: *fruit trees; fruit growers.* **—fruit** *intr. & tr.v.* **fruit·ed, fruit·ing, fruits.** To produce or cause to produce fruit. [Middle English, from Old French, from Latin *frūctus,* enjoyment, fruit, from past participle of *fruī,* to enjoy.]

fruit·age (fro͞o′tĭj) *n.* **1.a.** The process, time, or condition of bearing fruit. **b.** A yield of fruit. **2.** A result or an effect.

fruit·ar·i·an (fro͞o-târ′ē-ən) *n.* One whose diet includes fruits, seeds, and nuts but no vegetables, grains, or animal products. [Blend of FRUIT and (VEGET)ARIAN.]

fruit bat *n.* Any of various fruit-eating bats of the suborder Megachiroptera, inhabiting chiefly tropical and subtropical regions of Africa, Asia, and Australia.

fruit·cake (fro͞ot′kāk′) *n.* **1.** A heavy, spiced cake containing nuts and candied or dried fruits. **2.** *Slang.* A crazy or an eccentric person: *"a fruitcake under the delusion that he was Saint Nicholas"* (John Strahinich).

fruit cocktail *n.* A mixture of fresh or preserved fruits cut into pieces and served as an appetizer or dessert. Also called *fruit cup.*

fruit fly *n.* **1.** Any of various small flies of the family Drosophilidae, having larvae that feed on ripening or fermenting fruits and vegetables, especially the common species *Drosophila melanogaster,* often used in genetic research. Also called *pomace fly, vinegar fly.* **2.** Any of various flies of the family Tephritidae, having larvae that hatch in and damage plant tissue.

fruit·ful (fro͞ot′fəl) *adj.* **1.a.** Producing fruit. **b.** Conducive to productivity; causing to bear in abundance: *fruitful soil.* **2.** Producing something in abundance; prolific: *a fruitful author of fiction.* **3.** Producing results; profitable. See Synonyms at **fertile. —fruit′ful·ly** *adv.* **—fruit′ful·ness** *n.*

fruit·ing body (fro͞o′tĭng) *n.* A specialized spore-producing structure, especially of a fungus.

fru·i·tion (fro͞o-ĭsh′ən) *n.* **1.** Realization of something desired or worked for; accomplishment: *labor finally coming to fruition.* **2.** Enjoyment derived from use or possession. **3.** The condition of bearing fruit. [Middle English *fruicioun,* from Old French *fruicion,* from Late Latin *fruitiō, fruitiōn-,* enjoyment, from Latin *fruitus,* past participle of *fruī,* to enjoy.]

fruit·less (fro͞ot′lĭs) *adj.* **1.** Producing no fruit. **2.** Unproductive of success: *a fruitless search.* See Synonyms at **futile. —fruit′less·ly** *adv.* **—fruit′less·ness** *n.*

fruit·let (fro͞ot′lĭt) *n.* **1.** A small fruit. **2.** *Botany.* A single member of a multiple fruit.

fruit sugar *n.* See **fructose.**

fruit·wood (fro͞ot′wo͝od′) *n.* The wood of any of several fruit-bearing trees, such as the apple, cherry, or pear, used especially in cabinetmaking.

fruit·y (fro͞o′tē) *adj.* **-i·er, -i·est. 1.** Of, containing, or relating to fruit. **2.** Tasting or smelling richly of or as if of fruit: *"My nose filled with the smells of leather, polish, wax—the fat, fruity smell of rich car"* (Anthony Hyde). **3.** Excessively sentimental or sweet. **4.** *Slang.* Crazy; eccentric. **5.** *Offensive Slang.* Gay or homosexual. **—fruit′i·ness** *n.*

fru·men·ta·ceous (fro͞o′mən-tā′shəs, -mĕn-) *adj.* Resembling or consisting of grain, especially wheat. [From Late Latin *frūmentāceus,* from Latin *frūmentum,* grain.]

fru·men·ty (fro͞o′mən-tē) also **fur·mi·ty** (fûr′mĭ-tē) *n., pl.* **-ties.** Hulled wheat boiled in milk and flavored with sugar and spices. [Middle English *frumente,* from Old French *froumentee,* from *froument,* grain, from Latin *frūmentum.*]

frump (frŭmp) *n.* **1.** A girl or woman regarded as dull, plain, or unfashionable. **2.** A person regarded as colorless and primly sedate. [Possibly short for Middle English *frumple,* wrinkle, from Middle Dutch *verrompelen,* to wrinkle : *ver-,* completely; see **per**[1] in Appendix + *rompelen,* to wrinkle.] **—frump′i·ly** *adv.* **—frump′i·ness** *n.* **—frump′y** *adj.*

frump·ish (frŭm′pĭsh) *adj.* **1.** Dull or plain. **2.** Prim and sedate. **—frump′ish·ly** *adv.* **—frump′ish·ness** *n.*

Frun·ze (fro͞on′zə). The capital of Kirghiz, in the north-central part of the region on the Chu River. It was incorporated into Russia in 1862. Population, 604,000.

frus·ta (frŭs′tə) *n. Mathematics.* A plural of **frustum.**

frus·trate (frŭs′trāt′) *tr.v.* **-trat·ed, -trat·ing, -trates. 1.a.** To prevent from accomplishing a purpose or fulfilling a desire; thwart: *A persistent wind frustrated my attempt to rake the lawn.* **b.** To cause feelings of discouragement or bafflement in. **2.** To make ineffectual or invalid; nullify. [Middle English *frustraten,* from Latin *frūstrārī, frūstrāt-,* from *frūstrā,* in vain.] **—frus′trat′er** *n.* **—frus′trat′ing·ly** *adv.*

SYNONYMS: *frustrate, thwart, foil, balk.* These verbs mean to prevent the attainment or fulfillment of a goal or purpose. To *frustrate* is to cause to be completely unavailing: *A poor memory frustrated her efforts to become an actress. Thwart* suggests defeat by direct opposition: *"He was thwarted at every step by political obstacles"* (William E.H. Lecky). To *foil* is to defeat by or as if by outwitting, confounding, or disconcerting: *The conspirators will be foiled in their intrigue. Balk* implies the placing of barriers or hindrances in another's way: *"Time after time our hopes are balked"* (Herbert Spencer).

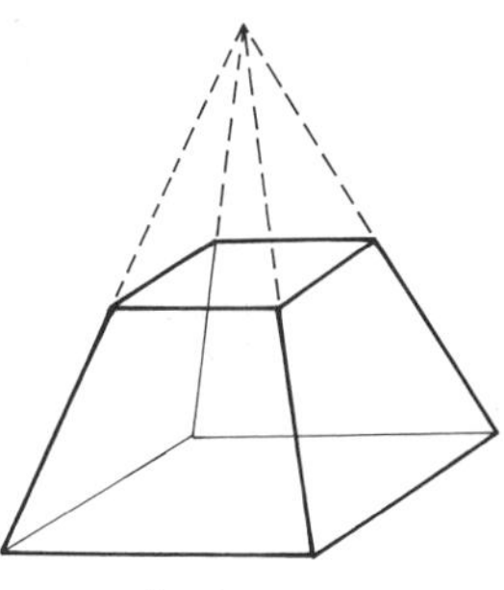
frustum

frus·tra·tion (frŭ-strā′shən) *n.* **1.a.** The act of frustrating or an instance of being frustrated. **b.** The state of being frustrated. **2.** Something that serves to frustrate.

frus·tule (frŭs′cho͞ol, -tyo͞ol) *n.* The hard, siliceous bivalve shell of a diatom. [French, from Latin *frustulum,* diminutive of *frustum,* piece broken off.]

frus·tum (frŭs′təm) *n., pl.* **-tums** or **-ta** (-tə). *Mathematics.* The part of a solid, such as a cone or pyramid, between two parallel planes cutting the solid, especially the section between the base and a plane parallel to the base. [Latin, piece broken off.]

fru·tes·cent (fro͞o-tĕs′ənt) *adj.* Relating to, resembling, or assuming the form of a shrub; shrubby. [Latin *frutex,* shrub, bush + –ESCENT.] **—fru·tes′cence** *n.*

fru·ti·cose (fro͞o′tĭ-kōs′) *adj.* Resembling a shrub, especially in having woody stems and branches. [Latin *fruticōsus,* from *frutex, frutic-,* shrub, bush.]

fry[1] (frī) *v.* **fried, fry·ing, fries** (frīz). —*tr.* **1.** To cook over direct heat in hot oil or fat. **2.** *Slang.* To destroy (electronic circuitry) with excessive heat or current: *"a power surge to the computer that fried a number of sensitive electronic components"* (Erik Sandberg-Diment). —*intr.* **1.** To be cooked in a pan over direct heat in hot oil or fat. **2.** *Slang.* To undergo execution in an electric chair. **—fry** *n., pl.* **fries** (frīz). **1.** A French fry. Often used in the plural. **2.** A dish of a fried food. **3.** A social gathering at which food is fried and eaten: *a fish fry.* [Middle English *frien,* from Old French *frire,* from Latin *frīgere.*]

fry[2] (frī) *pl.n.* **1.a.** Small fish, especially young, recently hatched fish. **b.** The young of certain other animals. **2.** Individuals, especially young or insignificant persons: *"These pampered public school boys . . . had managed to evade the long prison sentences that lesser fry were serving"* (Noel Annan). [Middle English *fri,* probably from Anglo-Norman *frie,* from *frier,* to rub, from Latin *fricāre.*]

Fry (frī), **Christopher.** Born 1907. British playwright who revitalized modern verse drama with his comic and religious works, such as *A Phoenix Too Frequent* (1946) and *Curtmantle* (1962).

fry·er also **fri·er** (frī′ər) *n.* **1.** One that fries, as a deep utensil usually equipped with a basket and used for frying foods. **2.** A small young chicken suitable for frying.

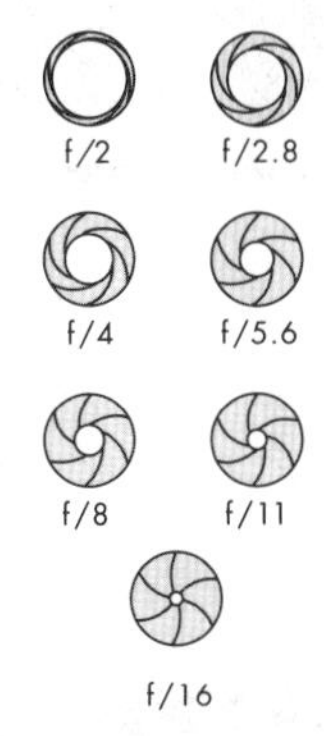

f-stop

♦fry·ing pan (frī′ĭng) *n.* A shallow, long-handled pan used for frying food. Also called *♦fry pan, ♦skillet, ♦spider.*

♦ *REGIONAL NOTE:* The terms *frying pan* and *skillet* are now virtually interchangeable, but there was a time when they were so regional as to be distinct dialect markers. *Frying pan* and the shortened version *fry pan* were once New England terms; *frying pan* is now in general use. *Skillet* seems to have been confined to the Midland section of the country, including the Upper South. Its use is still concentrated there, but it is no longer used in that area alone, probably because of the national marketing of skillet dinner mixes. The term *spider,* originally denoting a type of frying pan that had long legs to hold it up over the coals, spread from New England westward to the Upper Northern states and down the coast to the South Atlantic states. It is still well known in both these regions, although it is now considered old-fashioned.

♦fry pan *n. Chiefly New England.* See **frying pan.** See Regional Note at **frying pan.**

FS *abbr.* **1.** Foreign Service. **2.** Forest Service.

FSH *abbr.* Follicle-stimulating hormone.

FSLIC *abbr.* Federal Savings and Loan Insurance Corporation.

f-stop (ĕf′stŏp′) *n.* **1.** A camera lens aperture setting that corresponds to an f-number. **2.** See **f-number.** [F(OCAL LENGTH) + STOP.]

f-sys·tem (ĕf′sĭs′təm) *n.* A method of indicating the relative aperture of a camera lens based on the f-number.

ă pat	oi boy
ā pay	ou out
âr care	o͝o took
ä father	o͞o boot
ĕ pet	ŭ cut
ē be	ûr urge
ĭ pit	th thin
ī pie	*th* this
îr pier	hw which
ŏ pot	zh vision
ō toe	ə about, item
ô paw	♦ regionalism

Stress marks: **′** (primary); ′ (secondary), as in **dictionary** (dĭk′shə-nĕr′ē)

ft. *abbr.* **1.** Or **ft.** Foot. **2.** Also **Ft.** Fort. **3.** Fortification.

FTA *abbr.* Future Teachers of America.

FTC *abbr.* Federal Trade Commission.

ft-c *abbr.* Foot-candle.

fth. *abbr.* Fathom.

ft-lb *abbr.* Foot-pound.

fub·sy (fŭb′zē) *adj.* **-si·er, -si·est.** *Chiefly British.* Somewhat fat and squat. [From obsolete *fubs,* chubby person.]

Fu·chou (fo͞o′jō′, -chou′). See **Fuzhou.**

fuch·sia (fyo͞o′shə) *n.* **1.** Any of various tropical shrubs or trees of the genus *Fuchsia,* widely cultivated for their showy, drooping purplish, reddish, or white flowers. **2.** *Color.* A strong, vivid purplish red. [New Latin *Fuchsia,* genus name, after Leonhard *Fuchs* (1501–1566), German botanist.] **—fuch′sia** *adj.*

fuch·sin (fyo͝ok′sĭn) also **fuch·sine** (-sĭn, -sēn′) *n.* A dark green synthetic dyestuff, $C_{20}H_{19}N_3HCl$, used to make a purple-red dye employed in coloring textiles and leather and as a bacterial stain. Also called *magenta.* [FUCHS(IA) + –IN.]

fuck (fŭk) *Obscene. v.* **fucked, fuck·ing, fucks.** *—tr.* **1.** To have sexual intercourse with. **2.** To victimize. **3.** Used in the imperative as a signal of angry dismissal. *—intr.* **1.** To engage in sexual intercourse. **2.** To act wastefully or foolishly. **—fuck** *n.* **1.** An act of sexual intercourse. **2.** A partner in sexual intercourse. **3.** A despised person. **—fuck** *interj.* Used to express extreme displeasure. ***—phrasal verbs.*** **fuck off. 1.** Used in the imperative as a signal of angry dismissal. **2.** To spend time idly. **3.** To masturbate. **fuck over.** To treat unfairly; take advantage of. **fuck up. 1.** To bungle. **2.** To act carelessly, foolishly, or incorrectly. [Middle English, attested in pseudo-Latin *fuccant,* (they) fuck, deciphered from *gxddbov.*]

WORD HISTORY: The obscenity *fuck* is a very old word, first recorded in English in the 15th century. Age has not dimmed its shock value, even though it is seen in print much more often now than in the past. Its first known occurrence, in a poem entitled "Flen flyys" written sometime before 1500, is in code, illustrating the unacceptability of the word even then. The poem, composed in a mixture of Latin and English, satirizes the Carmelite friars of Cambridge, England, with the title taken from the first words of the poem, "Flen, flyys, and freris," that is, "fleas, flies, and friars." The line that contains *fuck* reads "Non sunt in coeli, quia gxddbov xxkxzt pg ifmk." The Latin words "Non sunt in coeli, quia" mean "they [the friars] are not in heaven, since." The code *"gxddbov xxkxzt pg ifmk"* is easily broken by simply writing the preceding letter in the alphabet. As we decode, we must watch for differences in the alphabet and in spelling between then and now. For *g* write *f;* for *x, v* (used for *u* and *v*); *d, c; b, a; o, n; v, t; xx, vv* (which equals *w*); *k, i; x, v; z, y; t, s; p, o; g, f; i, h; f, e; m, l;* and for *k, i.* This yields "fvccant [a fake Latin form] vvivys of heli." The whole thus reads in translation: "They are not in heaven because they fuck wives of Ely [a town near Cambridge]."

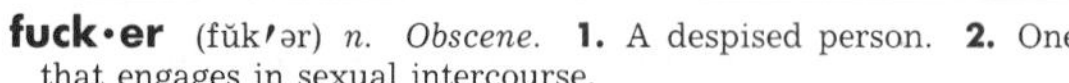

Carlos Fuentes

fuck·er (fŭk′ər) *n. Obscene.* **1.** A despised person. **2.** One that engages in sexual intercourse.

fuck·ing (fŭk′ĭng) *Obscene. adv. & adj.* Used as an intensive.

fuck·up (fŭk′ŭp′) *n. Obscene.* **1.** One who acts carelessly or foolishly; a bungler. **2.** A blunder; a bungle.

fu·coid (fyo͞o′koid′) *adj.* Of or belonging to the order Fucales, which includes brown algae such as gulfweed and rockweed. **—fucoid** *n.* **1.** A member of the order Fucales. **2.** A fossilized cast or impression of such an organism. [FUC(US) + –OID.]

fu·cose (fyo͞o′kōs′) *n.* An aldose, $C_6H_{12}O_5$, present in certain brown algae and in the polysaccharides associated with some blood groups. [FUC(US) + –OSE[2].]

fu·co·xan·thin (fyo͞o′kō-zăn′thĭn) *n.* A brown carotenoid pigment, $C_{40}H_{60}O_6$, found in brown algae. [FUC(US) + XANTH(O)– + –IN.]

fu·cus (fyo͞o′kəs) *n.* Any of various brown algae of the genus *Fucus,* which includes many of the rockweeds. [Latin *fūcus,* seaweed, orchil, from Greek *phukos.*]

fud·dle (fŭd′l) *v.* **-dled, -dling, -dles.** *—tr.* **1.** To put into a state of confusion; befuddle. See Synonyms at **confuse. 2.** To make drunk; intoxicate. *—intr.* To drink; tipple. **—fuddle** *n.* A state of confusion or intoxication. [Origin unknown.]

Mount Fuji

fud·dy-dud·dy (fŭd′ē-dŭd′ē) *n., pl.* **-dies.** An old-fashioned, fussy person. [Origin unknown.]

fudge (fŭj) *n.* **1.** A soft, rich candy made of sugar, milk, butter, and flavoring. **2.** Nonsense; humbug. **—fudge** *v.* **fudged, fudg·ing, fudg·es.** *—tr.* **1.** To fake or falsify: *fudge casualty figures.* **2.** To evade (an issue, for example); dodge. *—intr.* **1.** To act in an indecisive manner: *always fudged on the important questions.* **2. a.** To go beyond the proper limits of something: *fudged on the building code requirements.* **b.** To act dishonestly; cheat. [Possibly alteration of *fadge,* to fit.]

fueh·rer (fyo͝or′ər) *n.* Variant of **führer.**

fu·el (fyo͞o′əl) *n.* **1.** Something consumed to produce energy, especially: **a.** A material such as wood, coal, gas, or oil burned to produce heat or power. **b.** Fissionable material used in a nuclear reactor. **c.** Nutritive material metabolized by a living organism; food. **2.** Something that maintains or stimulates an activity or emotion: *"Money is the fuel of a volunteer organization"* (Natalie de Combray). *—attributive.* Often used to modify another noun: *a fuel pump; fuel tanks.* **—fuel** *v.* **-eled, -el·ing, -els** also **-elled, -el·ling, -els.** *—tr.* **1.** To provide with fuel. **2.** To support or stimulate the activity or existence of: *rhetoric that fueled the dissenters.* *—intr.* To take in fuel. [Middle English *feuel,* from Old French *fouaille, feuaile,* from Vulgar Latin **focālia,* neuter pl. of **focālis,* of the hearth or fireplace, from Latin *focus,* hearth, fireplace.] **—fu′el·er** *n.*

fuel cell *n.* An electrochemical cell in which the energy of a reaction between a fuel, such as liquid hydrogen, and an oxidant, such as liquid oxygen, is converted directly and continuously into electrical energy.

fu·el-ef·fi·cient (fyo͞o′əl-ĭ-fĭsh′ənt) *adj.* Operable using comparatively little fuel. **—fu′el-ef·fi′cien·cy** *n.*

fuel injection *n.* Any of several methods or mechanical systems by which a fuel is reduced to a fine spray and injected directly into the cylinders of an internal-combustion engine.

fuel oil *n.* A liquid or liquefiable petroleum product that is used to generate heat or power.

fuel rod *n.* A protective metal tube containing pellets of fuel for a nuclear reactor.

Fu·en·tes (fo͞o-ĕn′tās′, fwĕn′tĕs), **Carlos.** Born 1928. Mexican writer known for his metaphysical stories and novels.

fug (fŭg) *n.* A heavy, stale atmosphere, especially the musty air of an overcrowded or poorly ventilated room: *"In spite of the open windows the stench had become a reeking fug"* (Colleen McCullough). [Perhaps alteration of *fogo,* stench.]

fu·ga·cious (fyo͞o-gā′shəs) *adj.* **1.** Passing away quickly; evanescent. **2.** *Botany.* Withering or dropping off early. [From Latin *fugāx, fugāc-,* from *fugere,* to flee.] **—fu·ga′cious·ly** *adv.* **—fu·ga′cious·ness, fu·gac′i·ty** (-găs′ĭ-tē) *n.*

–fuge *suff.* One that expels or drives away: *vermifuge.* [French, from New Latin *-fugus,* driving away, fleeing, from Latin, fleeing (from *fugere,* to flee) and from Latin *fugāre,* to drive away (from *fuga,* flight).]

Fug·ger (fo͝og′ər). Family of German financiers who exerted great economic and political influence in the 15th and 16th centuries. Founded by **Johannes** (1348–1409), the family business was greatly expanded by his son **Jakob** (died 1469).

fu·gi·tive (fyo͞o′jĭ-tĭv) *adj.* **1.** Running away or fleeing, as from the law. **2. a.** Lasting only a short time; fleeting: *fugitive hours.* See Synonyms at **transient. b.** Difficult to comprehend or retain; elusive: *fugitive solutions to the problem.* **c.** Given to change or disappearance; perishable: *fugitive beauty.* **3.** Tending to wander; vagabond. **4.** Having to do with topics of temporary interest; ephemeral. **—fugitive** *n.* **1.** One who flees; a refugee. **2.** Something fleeting or ephemeral. [Middle English *fugitif,* from Old French, from Latin *fugitīvus,* from *fugitus,* past participle of *fugere,* to flee.] **—fu′gi·tive·ly** *adv.* **—fu′gi·tive·ness** *n.*

fu·gle (fyo͞o′gəl) *intr.v.* **-gled, -gling, -gles.** *Archaic.* **1.** To act as a fugleman. **2.** To make signals. [Back-formation from FUGLEMAN.]

fu·gle·man (fyo͞o′gəl-mən) *n.* **1.** A leader, especially a political leader. **2.** *Archaic.* A soldier who once served as a guide and model for his company. [Alteration of German *Flügelmann,* file leader : *Flügel,* wing (from Middle High German *vlügel;* see **pleu-** in Appendix) + *Mann,* man (from Middle High German *man,* from Old High German; see **man-**[1] in Appendix).]

fu·gu (fo͞o′go͞o) *n.* Any of various poisonous fish related to the puffers that are used as food, especially in Japan, after the poisonous skin and organs have been removed. [Japanese.]

fugue (fyo͞og) *n.* **1.** *Music.* A polyphonic composition in which themes or a theme stated successively by a number of voices in imitation are developed contrapuntally. **2.** *Psychiatry.* A pathological amnesiac condition during which one is apparently conscious of one's actions but has no recollection of them after returning to a normal state. This condition, usually resulting from severe mental stress, may persist for as long as several months. [Italian *fuga* (influenced by French *fugue,* from Italian *fuga*), from Latin, flight.] **—fu′gal** (fyo͞o′gəl) *adj.* **—fu′gal·ly** *adv.*

füh·rer also **fueh·rer** (fyo͝or′ər) *n.* A leader, especially one exercising the powers of a tyrant. [German, from Middle High German *vüerer,* from *vüeren,* to lead, from Old High German *fuoren.* See **per-**[2] in Appendix.]

Fu·jai·rah (fə-jī′rə, fo͞o-jī′rä). A sheikdom of the United Arab Emirates on the Gulf of Oman. Population, 32,191.

Fu·ji (fo͞o′jē), **Mount.** Also **Fu·ji·ya·ma** (fo͞o′jē-yä′mə, -mä) or **Fu·ji·no·ya·ma** (-nō-) or **Fu·ji·san** (-sän′). The highest peak, 3,778.6 m (12,389 ft), in Japan, in central Honshu west-southwest of Tokyo. An almost perfectly symmetrical snow-capped cone, it is a sacred mountain and dormant volcano.

Fu·jian[1] (fo͞o′jyän′, fü′-) also **Fu·kien** (kyĕn′). A province of southeast China on the East China Sea and the Formosa Strait. Agriculture and fishing are important to its economy. Fuzhou is the capital. Population, 27,130,000.

Fu·jian[2] (fo͞o′jyän′, fü′-) also **Fu·kien** (-kyĕn′) *n.* A dialect of Chinese spoken in Fujian province, eastern Guangdong province, and Taiwan.

Fu·ji·sa·wa (fo͞o′jē-sä′wə, -wä). A city of east-central Honshu, Japan, an industrial and residential suburb of Tokyo. Population, 328,387.

Fu·kien (fo͞o′kyĕn′). See **Fujian**[1]**.**

Fu·ku·o·ka (fo͞o′ko͞o-ō′kə, -kä). A city of northwest Kyushu,

Japan, on an inlet of the Sea of Japan. It is an industrial and educational center. Population, 1,160,402.

Fu·ku·ya·ma (fo͞o′kə-yä′mə, -ko͞o-yä′mä). A city of southwest Honshu, Japan, on the Inland Sea east of Kure. Population, 360,264.

–ful *suff.* **1.** Full of: *playful.* **a.** Characterized by; resembling: *masterful.* **b.** Tending, given, or able to: *useful.* **2.** A quantity that fills: *armful.* [Middle English, from Old English, from *full,* full. See FULL[1].]

USAGE NOTE: The plurals of nouns ending in *–ful* are usually formed by adding the letter *s* to the end of the suffix: *cupfuls; glassfuls; spoonfuls.*

Fu·la·ni (fo͞o′lä′nē, fo͞o-lä′-) also **Fu·la** (fo͞o′lə) *n., pl.* **Fulani** or **-nis** also **Fula** or **-las. 1.** A member of a pastoral, largely Moslem people inhabiting parts of West Africa from northern Nigeria to Mali and the Atlantic coast. **2.** The West Atlantic language of this people.

Ful·bright (fo͝ol′brīt′), **J(ames) William.** Born 1905. American politician who as U.S. senator from Arkansas (1945–1975) proposed the Fulbright Act (1946), which established an exchange program for American and foreign educators and students.

ful·crum (fo͝ol′krəm, fŭl′-) *n., pl.* **-crums** or **-cra** (-krə). **1.** The point or support on which a lever pivots. **2.** *Zoology.* An anatomical structure that acts as a hinge or a point of support. **3.** An agent through which vital powers are exercised. [Latin, bedpost, from *fulcīre,* to support.]

Ful·da (fo͝ol′də). A city of central Germany south-southeast of Kassel on the **Fulda River,** about 217 km (135 mi) long. The city grew around a Benedictine abbey founded in 744. Population, 55,441.

ful·fill also **ful·fil** (fo͝ol-fĭl′) *tr.v.* **-filled, -fill·ing, -fills** also **-fils. 1.** To bring into actuality; effect: *fulfilled their promises.* **2.** To carry out (an order, for example). **3.** To measure up to; satisfy. See Synonyms at **perform, satisfy. 4.** To bring to an end; complete. [Middle English *fulfillen,* from Old English *fullfyllan* : *full,* full; see FULL[1] + *fyllan,* to fill; see FILL.] **—ful·fill′er** *n.* **—ful·fill′ment, ful·fil′ment** *n.*

ful·gent (fo͝ol′jənt, fŭl′-) *adj.* Shining brilliantly; radiant: *"tower searchlights . . . as fulgent as half a billion candles"* (Nicholas Proffitt). [Middle English, from Latin *fulgēns, fulgent-,* present participle of *fulgēre,* to flash, shine. See **bhel-**[1] in Appendix.] **—ful′gent·ly** *adv.*

ful·gu·rant (fo͝ol′gyər-ənt, -gər-, fŭl′-) *adj.* Flashing like lightning; dazzlingly bright. [Latin *fulgurāns, fulgurant-,* present participle of *fulgurāre,* to lighten. See FULGURATE.]

ful·gu·rate (fo͝ol′gyə-rāt′, -gə-, fŭl′-) *v.* **-rat·ed, -rat·ing, -rates.** *—intr.* To emit flashes of lightning. *—tr.* **1.** To emit (light) in flashes. **2.** *Medicine.* To destroy (abnormal tissue, for example) by electric current. [Latin *fulgurāre, fulgurāt-,* from *fulgur,* lightning. See **bhel-**[1] in Appendix.] **—ful′gu·ra′tion** *n.*

ful·gu·rite (fo͝ol′gyə-rīt′, -gə-, fŭl′-) *n.* A slender, usually tubular body of glassy rock produced by lightning striking and then fusing dry sandy soil. [Latin *fulgur,* lightning; see FULGURATE + –ITE[1].]

ful·gu·rous (fo͝ol′gyər-əs, -gər-, fŭl′-) *adj.* **1.** Emitting flashes of lightning. **2.** Emitting in flashes similar to lightning. [Latin *fulgur,* lightning; see FULGURATE + –OUS.]

fu·lig·i·nous (fyo͞o-lĭj′ə-nəs) *adj.* **1.** Sooty. **2.** Colored by or as if by soot. [Late Latin *fūlīginōsus,* from Latin *fūlīgō, fūlīgin-,* soot.] **—fu·lig′i·nous·ly** *adv.*

full[1] (fo͝ol) *adj.* **full·er, full·est. 1.** Containing all that is normal or possible: *a full pail.* **2.** Complete in every particular: *a full account.* **3.** *Baseball.* **a.** Amounting to three balls and two strikes. Used of a count. **b.** Having a base runner at first, second, and third base: *The bases were full when the slugger stepped up to bat.* **4.a.** Of maximum or highest degree: *at full speed.* **b.** Being at the peak of development or maturity: *in full bloom.* **5.** Having a great deal or many: *a book full of errors.* **6.** Totally qualified, accepted, or empowered: *a full member of the club.* **7.a.** Rounded in shape; plump: *a full figure.* **b.** Having or made with a generous amount of fabric: *full draperies.* **8.a.** Having an appetite completely satisfied, especially for food or drink: *was full after the Thanksgiving dinner.* **b.** Providing an abundance, especially of food. **9.** Having depth and body; rich: *a full aroma; full tones.* **10.** Completely absorbed or preoccupied: *"He was already pretty full of himself"* (Ron Rosenbaum). **11.** Possessing both parents in common: *full brothers; full sisters.* **—full** *adv.* **1.** To a complete extent; entirely. **2.** Exactly; directly: *full in the path of the moon.* **—full** *v.* **fulled, full·ing, fulls.** *—tr.* To make (a garment) full, as by pleating or gathering. *—intr.* To become full. Used of the moon. **—full** *n.* **1.** The maximum or complete size or amount: *repaid in full.* **2.** The highest degree or state: *living life to the full.* [Middle English *ful,* from Old English *full.* See **pelə-**[1] in Appendix.] **—full′ness, ful′ness** *n.*

full[2] (fo͝ol) *tr.v.* **fulled, full·ing, fulls.** To increase the weight and bulk of (cloth) by shrinking and beating or pressing. [Middle English *fullen,* from Old French *fouler,* from Vulgar Latin **fullāre,* from Latin *fullō,* fuller. See **bhel-**[2] in Appendix.]

full·back (fo͝ol′băk′) *n. Abbr.* **fb, f.b. 1.** *Football.* **a.** An offensive backfield player whose position is behind the quarterback and halfbacks and who primarily performs offensive blocking and line plunges. **b.** The position of this player. **2.** *Sports.* **a.** A primarily defensive backfield player in field hockey, soccer, or rugby whose position is near the defensive goal or goal line. **b.** The position of this player.

full blood *n.* **1.** Relationship established through having the same set of parents. **2.** A person or an animal of unmixed race or breed.

full-blood·ed (fo͝ol′blŭd′ĭd) *adj.* **1.a.** Of unmixed ancestry; purebred. **b.** Related by way of having the same parents. **2.a.** Not pale or anemic; florid or ruddy. **b.** Vigorous and vital. **3.** Complete in all respects. **—full′-blood′ed·ness** *n.*

full-blown (fo͝ol′blōn′) *adj.* **1.** Having blossomed or opened completely: *full-blown roses.* **2.** Fully developed or matured. **3.** Having or displaying all the characteristics necessary for completeness: *a full-blown financial crisis.*

full-bod·ied (fo͝ol′bŏd′ēd) *adj.* **1.** Having richness and intensity of flavor or aroma: *a full-bodied wine.* **2.** Rich and intense: *a full-bodied performance of the aria.*

full-bore (fŭl′bôr′, -bōr′) *adj.* Thoroughgoing: *"a full-bore investigation into the damaging leak"* (Tom Morganthau).

full circle *adv.* Back to one's starting point: *We've come full circle from wealth to poverty to wealth again.*

full-court press (fo͝ol′kôrt′, -kōrt′) *n.* **1.** *Basketball.* An aggressive defensive strategy in which one or two players harass the ball handler in the backcourt while the rest of the team maintains a close man-to-man or zone defense. **2.** A strong, diversified effort: *"The Administration undertook a full-court press to secure congressional approval"* (Abraham F. Lowenthal).

full dress *n.* Attire appropriate for formal or ceremonial events.

full-dress (fo͝ol′drĕs′) *adj.* **1.** Of, appropriate for, or requiring full dress; formal: *a full-dress uniform; a full-dress ceremony.* **2.** Complete in every respect: *a full-dress debate.* **3.** Characterized by exhaustive thoroughness: *a full-dress investigation.*

full·er[1] (fo͝ol′ər) *n.* One that fulls cloth.

full·er[2] (fo͝ol′ər) *n.* **1.** A hammer used by a blacksmith for grooving or spreading iron. **2.** A groove made by such a hammer. [Possibly from FULL[1], to pleat.]

Ful·ler (fo͝ol′ər), **Melville Weston.** 1833–1910. American jurist who served as the chief justice of the U.S. Supreme Court (1888–1910).

Fuller, R(ichard) Buckminster. 1895–1983. American architect and inventor who sought to solve practical problems with simple designs that require a minimum of materials and energy.

Fuller, (Sarah) Margaret. 1810–1850. American writer and critic who edited the transcendentalist periodical *Dial* (1840–1842) and wrote *Woman in the Nineteenth Century* (1845).

full·er's earth (fo͝ol′ərz) *n.* A highly adsorbent claylike substance consisting of hydrated aluminum silicates, used predominantly in fulling woolen cloth, in talcum powders, as a filter, and as a catalyst.

fuller's teasel *n.* A prickly Eurasian plant *(Dipsacus fullonum)* having bristly flower heads used by fullers to raise the nap on cloth.

Ful·ler·ton (fo͝ol′ər-tən). A city of southern California southeast of Los Angeles. Population, 102,034.

full-fash·ioned (fo͝ol′făsh′ənd) *adj.* Knitted in a shape that conforms closely to body lines.

full-fledged (fo͝ol′flĕjd′) *adj.* **1.** Having reached full development; mature. **2.** Having full status or rank: *a full-fledged lawyer.* **3.** Having fully developed adult plumage.

full gainer *n. Sports.* A forward dive in which the diver executes a full back somersault before entering the water.

full house *n. Games.* A poker hand containing three of a kind and a pair, ranked above a flush and below four of a kind.

full-length (fo͝ol′lĕngkth′, -lĕngth′) *adj.* **1.** Showing or fitted to the entire length, especially of the human body: *a full-length mirror; a full-length robe.* **2.** Of a normal or standard length: *a full-length novel.*

full moon *n.* **1.** The moon when it is visible as a fully illuminated disk. **2.** The period of the month when such a moon occurs.

full-mouthed (fo͝ol′mouthd′, -moutht′) *adj.* **1.** Having a complete set of teeth. Used of cattle and other livestock. **2.** Uttered loudly or noisily.

full nelson *n. Sports.* A wrestling hold in which both hands are thrust under the opponent's arms from behind and then pressed against the back of the opponent's neck.

full rhyme *n.* See **perfect rhyme** (sense 1).

full-scale (fo͝ol′skāl′) *adj.* **1.** Of actual or full size; not reduced: *a full-scale model.* **2.** Employing all resources; not limited or partial: *a full-scale campaign against nuclear power plants.*

full-serv·ice (fo͝ol′sûr′vĭs) *adj.* Associated with or offering complete service: *full-service gasoline pumps; full-service banks.*

full-size (fo͝ol′sīz′) *adj.* **1.** Of the standard or normal size: *a full-size car.* **2.a.** Measuring 54 by 75 inches. Used of a bed: *a full-size bed.* **b.** Being of a size that will fit such a bed: *full-size fitted sheets.*

full stop *n.* **1.** A period indicating the end of a sentence. **2.** A complete halt, as one made by a motor vehicle.

full-time (fo͝ol′tīm′) *adj.* Employed for or involving a standard number of hours of working time: *a full-time administrative assistant.* **—full′-time′** *adv.*

ful·ly (fo͝ol′ē) *adv.* **1.** Totally or completely: *fully grown.* **2.** At least: *Fully half of the volunteers did not appear.*

ă pat	oi boy
ā pay	ou out
âr care	o͝o took
ä father	o͞o boot
ĕ pet	ŭ cut
ē be	ûr urge
ĭ pit	th thin
ī pie	*th* this
îr pier	hw which
ŏ pot	zh vision
ō toe	ə about, item
ô paw	♦ regionalism

Stress marks: ′ (primary); ′ (secondary), as in **dictionary** (dĭk′shə-nĕr′ē)

ful·mar (fo͝ol′mər, -mär′) *n.* **1.** A gull-like bird *(Fulmarus glacialis)* of Arctic regions, having smoky gray plumage. **2.** Any of several similar or related birds. [Dialectal : probably from Old Norse *fūll,* foul; see **pū-** in Appendix + *mār,* mew; akin to Old English *mǣw.*]

ful·mi·nant (fo͝ol′mə-nənt, fŭl′-) *adj.* **1.** Exploding or detonating. **2.** *Pathology.* Occurring suddenly, rapidly, and with great severity or intensity. [Latin *fulmināns, fulminant-,* present participle of *fulmināre,* to strike with lightning. See FULMINATE.]

ful·mi·nate (fo͝ol′mə-nāt′, fŭl′-) *v.* **-nat·ed, -nat·ing, -nates.** —*intr.* **1.** To issue a thunderous verbal attack or denunciation: *fulminated against political chicanery.* **2.** To explode or detonate. —*tr.* **1.** To issue (a denunciation, for example) thunderously. **2.** To cause to explode. —**fulminate** *n.* An explosive salt of fulminic acid, especially fulminate of mercury. [Middle English *fulminaten,* from Latin *fulmināre, fulmināt-,* to strike with lightning, from *fulmen, fulmin-,* lightning that strikes. See **bhel-**[1] in Appendix.] —**ful′mi·na′tion** *n.* —**ful′mi·na′tor** *n.* —**ful′mi·na·to′ry** (-nə-tôr′ē, -tōr′ē) *adj.*

fulminate of mercury *n.* A gray crystalline powder, $HgC_2N_2O_2$, that when dry explodes under percussion or heat and is used in detonators and as a high explosive.

ful·mine (fo͝ol′mĭn, fŭl′-) *tr. & intr.v.* **-mined, -min·ing, -mines.** *Archaic.* To fulminate. [From Latin *fulmināre,* to strike with lightning. See FULMINATE.]

ful·min·ic acid (fo͝ol-mĭn′ĭk, fŭl-) *n.* An unstable acid, HONC, that forms highly explosive salts. [Latin *fulmen, fulmin-,* lightning that strikes; see FULMINATE + –IC.]

ful·some (fo͝ol′səm) *adj.* **1.** Offensively flattering or insincere. See Synonyms at **unctuous. 2.** Offensive to the taste or sensibilities. **3.** *Usage Problem.* Copious or abundant. [Middle English *fulsom,* abundant, well-fed, arousing disgust : *ful,* full; see FULL[1] + *-som,* adj. suff.; see –SOME[1].] —**ful′some·ly** *adv.* —**ful′some·ness** *n.*

USAGE NOTE: The word *fulsome* is often used, particularly in the expression *fulsome praise,* to mean simply "abundant," without any implication of excess or insincerity. This usage is etymologically justified but may invite misunderstandings in contexts in which a deprecatory interpretation might also be available. The sentence *I offer you my most fulsome apologies* may unintentionally raise an eyebrow, where the use of an adjective like *full* or *abundant* would leave no room for doubt as to the sincerity of the speaker's intentions.

Ful·ton (fo͝ol′tən). A city of central Missouri east-southeast of Columbia. On March 5, 1946, Winston Churchill delivered his Iron Curtain speech here. Population, 11,046.

Fulton, Robert. 1765–1815. American engineer and inventor who developed the first useful submarine and torpedo (1800) and produced the first practical steamboat, the *Clermont* (1807).

Fu Man·chu mustache (fo͞o′ măn-cho͞o′) *n.* A mustache with ends that hang downward toward or below the chin. [After *Fu Manchu,* character in novels by Sax Rohmer, pen name of Arthur Sarsfield Ward (1886–1959), British mystery writer.]

fu·ma·rate (fyo͞o′mə-rāt′) *n.* A salt or ester of fumaric acid. [FUMAR(IC ACID) + –ATE[2].]

fu·mar·ic acid (fyo͞o-măr′ĭk) *n.* An organic acid, $C_4H_4O_4$, found in various plants and produced synthetically and used mainly in resins, paints, varnishes, and inks. [From New Latin *Fūmāria,* genus of herbaceous plants (from Late Latin *fūmāria,* fumitory, from Latin *fūmus,* smoke) + –IC.]

fu·ma·role (fyo͞o′mə-rōl′) *n.* A hole in a volcanic area from which hot smoke and gases escape. [Italian *fumarola,* from Late Latin *fūmāriolum,* smoke hole, diminutive of Latin *fūmārium,* smoke chamber, from *fūmus,* smoke.] —**fu′ma·rol′ic** (-rŏl′ĭk) *adj.*

fu·ma·to·ri·um (fyo͞o′mə-tôr′ē-əm, -tōr′-) *n., pl.* **-to·ri·ums** or **-to·ri·a** (-tôr′ē-ə, -tōr′-). An airtight fumigation chamber in which chemical vapors are used to destroy insects and fungi on plants. Also called *fumatory.* [New Latin, from Latin *fūmāre,* to smoke, from *fūmus,* smoke.]

fu·ma·to·ry (fyo͞o′mə-tôr′ē, -tōr′ē) *adj.* Of or relating to smoke or fumigation. —**fumatory** *n., pl.* **-ries.** See **fumatorium.** [From Latin *fūmāre,* to smoke, from *fūmus,* smoke.]

fum·ble (fŭm′bəl) *v.* **-bled, -bling, -bles.** —*intr.* **1.** To touch or handle nervously or idly: *fumble with a necktie.* **2.** To grope awkwardly to find or to accomplish something: *fumble for a key.* **3.** To proceed awkwardly and uncertainly; blunder: *fumble through a speech.* **4.a.** *Football.* To drop a ball that is in play. **b.** *Baseball.* To mishandle a ground ball. —*tr.* **1.** To touch or handle clumsily or idly: *"fumbled the receiver into its cradle"* (Howard Kaplan). **2.** To make a mess of; bungle. See Synonyms at **botch. 3.** To feel or make (one's way) awkwardly. **4.a.** *Football.* To drop (a ball) while in play. **b.** *Baseball.* To mishandle (a ground ball). —**fumble** *n.* **1.** The act or an instance of fumbling. **2.** *Sports.* A ball that has been fumbled. [Middle English *fomelen,* to grope.]

fume (fyo͞om) *n.* **1.** Vapor, gas, or smoke, especially if irritating, harmful, or strong. **2.** A strong or acrid odor. **3.** A state of resentment or vexation. —**fume** *v.* **fumed, fum·ing, fumes.** —*tr.* **1.** To subject to or treat with fumes. **2.** To give off in or as if in fumes. —*intr.* **1.** To emit fumes. **2.** To rise in fumes. **3.** To feel or show resentment or vexation. [Middle English, from Old French *fum,* from Latin *fūmus.*]

fu·mi·gant (fyo͞o′mĭ-gənt) *n.* A chemical compound used in its gaseous state as a pesticide or disinfectant. [Latin *fūmigāns, fūmigant-,* present participle of *fūmigāre,* to smoke. See FUMIGATE.]

fu·mi·gate (fyo͞o′mĭ-gāt′) *v.* **-gat·ed, -gat·ing, -gates.** —*tr.* To subject to smoke or fumes, usually in order to exterminate pests or disinfect. —*intr.* To employ smoke or fumes in order to exterminate or disinfect. [Latin *fūmigāre, fūmigāt-,* to smoke : *fūmus,* smoke + *agere,* to drive, make; see **ag-** in Appendix.] —**fu′mi·ga′tion** *n.* —**fu′mi·ga′tor** *n.*

fu·mi·to·ry (fyo͞o′mĭ-tôr′ē, -tōr′ē) *n., pl.* **-ries.** An herb *(Fumaria officinalis)* native to Eurasia, having finely divided leaves and small, spurred, purplish flowers. Also called *earth smoke.* [Middle English *fumetere,* from Old French *fumeterre,* from Medieval Latin *fūmus terrae* : Latin *fūmus,* smoke + Latin *terrae,* genitive of *terra,* dry land, earth; see **ters-** in Appendix.]

fun (fŭn) *n.* **1.** A source of enjoyment, amusement, or pleasure. **2.** Enjoyment; amusement: *have fun at the beach.* **3.** Playful, often noisy, activity. —**fun** *intr.v.* **funned, fun·ning, funs.** *Informal.* To behave playfully; joke. —**fun** *adj. Informal.* Enjoyable; amusing: *"You're a real fun guy"* (Margaret Truman). —***idiom.* for** (or **in**) **fun.** As a joke; playfully. [Possibly from *fon,* to make a fool of, from Middle English *fonnen,* to fool, possibly from *fonne,* fool.]

USAGE NOTE: The use of *fun* as an attributive adjective, as in *a fun time, a fun place,* most likely originated in a playful reanalysis of the use of the word in sentences such as *It is fun to ski,* where *fun* behaves syntactically like an adjective such as *amusing* or *swell.* The usage became popular in the 1950's and 1960's, though there is some evidence to suggest that it has 19th-century antecedents. Certainly the sense of this word makes it particularly susceptible to jocular treatment. But as with other such reanalyses (for example, in the expression *a whole 'nother*), the usage appears to have persisted after the original flavor had been lost. Thus there is no intimation of humorous intent in a press release that announces: *The corporation believes that a spelling bee is a fun way to emphasize the critical importance of good basic communication skills in America's workplace.* The day may come when this usage is entirely unremarkable, just as the word *talkative* has lost all taint of its originally jocular formation from the attachment of a Latinate suffix to a native Anglo-Saxon root. At present, however, the attributive use of *fun* may still raise eyebrows, and writers who want to stay on the safe side are advised to avoid it in contexts in which a light tone would not be appropriate.

Fu·na·ba·shi (fo͞o′nə-bä′shē, -nä-). A city of east-central Honshu, Japan, a suburb of Tokyo on Tokyo Bay. Population, 506,967.

fu·nam·bu·list (fyo͞o-năm′byə-lĭst) *n.* One who performs on a tightrope or a slack rope. [From Latin *fūnambulus* : *fūnis,* rope + *ambulāre,* to walk; see **ambhi** in Appendix.] —**fu·nam′bu·lism** *n.*

func·tion (fŭngk′shən) *n.* **1.** The action for which one is particularly fitted or employed. **2.a.** Assigned duty or activity. **b.** A specific occupation or role: *in my function as chief editor.* **3.** An official ceremony or a formal social occasion. **4.** Something closely related to another thing and dependent on it for its existence, value, or significance: *Growth is a function of nutrition.* **5.** *Abbr.* **f** *Mathematics.* **a.** A variable so related to another that for each value assumed by one there is a value determined for the other. **b.** A rule of correspondence between two sets such that there is a unique element in the second set assigned to each element in the first set. —*intr.* **-tioned, -tion·ing, -tions.** To have or perform a function; serve: *functioned as ambassador.* [Latin *fūnctiō, fūnctiōn-,* performance, execution, from *fūnctus,* past participle of *fungī,* to perform, execute.] —**func′tion·less** *adj.*

SYNONYMS: *function, duty, office, role.* The central meaning shared by these nouns is "the actions and activities assigned to, required of, or expected of a person": *the function of a teacher; a bank clerk's duty; assumed the office of financial adviser; the role of a parent.*

func·tion·al (fŭngk′shə-nəl) *adj.* **1.a.** Of or relating to a function. **b.** Of, relating to, or indicating a mathematical function or functions. **2.** Designed for or adapted to a particular function or use: *functional architecture.* **3.** Capable of performing; operative: *a functional set of brakes.* **4.** *Pathology.* Involving functions rather than a physiological or structural cause. —**func′tion·al′i·ty** (-shə-năl′ĭ-tē) *n.* —**func′tion·al·ly** *adv.*

functional group *n.* An atom or group of atoms, such as a carboxyl group, that replaces hydrogen in an organic compound and that defines the structure of a family of compounds and determines the properties of the family.

functional illiterate *n.* A person whose skills in reading and writing are insufficient for ordinary practical needs.

func·tion·al·ism (fŭngk′shə-nə-lĭz′əm) *n.* **1.** The doctrine that the function of an object should determine its design and materials. **2.** A doctrine stressing purpose, practicality, and utility. —**func′tion·al·ist′** *adj. & n.*

functional shift *n. Linguistics.* A shift in the syntactic function of a word, as when a noun serves as a verb.

func·tion·ar·y (fŭngk′shə-nĕr′ē) *n., pl.* **-ies.** One who holds an office or a trust or performs a particular function.

function word *n. Grammar.* A word, such as a preposition, a conjunction, or an article, that has little semantic content of its own and chiefly indicates a grammatical relationship. Also called *form word, functor.*

func·tor (fŭngk′tər) *n.* **1.** One that performs an operation or a function. **2.** *Grammar.* See **function word.** [New Latin, from Latin *fūnctiō,* performance, function. See FUNCTION.]

fund (fŭnd) *n.* **1.** A source of supply; a stock: *a fund of goodwill.* **2.a.** A sum of money or other resources set aside for a specific purpose: *a pension fund.* **b. funds.** Available money; ready cash: *short on funds.* **3. funds.** The stock of the British permanent national debt, considered as public securities. Used with *the.* **4.** An organization established to administer and manage a sum of money. **—fund** *tr.v.* **fund·ed, fund·ing, funds. 1.** To provide money for paying off the interest or principal of (a debt). **2.** To convert into a long-term or floating debt with fixed interest payments. **3.** To place in a fund for accumulation. **4.** To furnish a fund for: *funded the space program.* [Latin *fundus,* bottom, piece of land.]

fun·da·ment (fŭn′də-mənt) *n.* **1.a.** The buttocks. **b.** The anus. **2.** The natural features of a land surface unaltered by human beings. **3.** A foundation, as of a building. **4.** An underlying theoretical basis or principle: *"All neighbor states . . . must revise . . . their policy fundaments"* (C.L. Sulzberger). [Middle English *foundement,* from Old French *fondement,* from Latin *fundāmentum,* from *fundāre,* to lay the foundation, from *fundus,* bottom.]

fun·da·men·tal (fŭn′də-mĕn′tl) *adj.* **1.a.** Of or relating to the foundation or base; elementary: *the fundamental laws of the universe.* **b.** Forming or serving as an essential component of a system or structure; central: *an example that was fundamental to the argument.* **c.** Of great significance or entailing major change: *a book that underwent fundamental revision.* **2.** *Physics.* **a.** Of or relating to the component of lowest frequency of a periodic wave or quantity. **b.** Of or relating to the lowest possible frequency of a vibrating element or system. **3.** *Music.* Having the root in the bass: *a fundamental chord.* **—fundamental** *n.* **1.** Something that is an essential or necessary part of a system or object. **2.** *Physics.* The lowest frequency of a periodically varying quantity or of a vibrating system. **—fun′da·men′tal·ly** *adv.*

fun·da·men·tal·ism (fŭn′də-mĕn′tl-ĭz′əm) *n.* **1.a.** Often **Fundamentalism.** An organized, militant Evangelical movement originating in the United States in 1920 in opposition to Liberalism and secularism. **b.** Adherence to the theology of this movement. **2.** A movement or point of view characterized by rigid adherence to fundamental or basic principles. **—fun′da·men′tal·ist** *adj. & n.* **—fun′da·men′tal·ist′ic** *adj.*

fundamental particle *n.* See **elementary particle.**

fun·di (fŭn′dī′) *n. Anatomy.* Plural of **fundus.**

fund·raise or **fund-raise** also **fund raise** (fŭnd′rāz′) *intr.v.* **-raised, -rais·ing, -rais·es.** To engage in fundraising.

fund·rais·er also **fund-rais·er** (fŭnd′rā′zər) *n.* **1.** One, such as a person or an organization, that raises funds. **2.** A social function, such as a dinner, held for raising funds.

fund·rais·ing or **fund-rais·ing** (fŭnd′rā′zĭng) *n.* The organized activity or an instance of soliciting money or pledges, as for charitable organizations or political campaigns. **—fund′rais′ing** *adj.*

fun·dus (fŭn′dəs) *n., pl.* **-di** (-dī′). *Anatomy.* The portion of a hollow organ opposite or farthest from its opening. [Latin, bottom.] **—fun′dic** *adj.*

Fun·dy (fŭn′dē), **Bay of.** An inlet of the Atlantic Ocean in southeast Canada between New Brunswick and Nova Scotia.

fu·ner·al (fyōō′nər-əl) *n.* **1.a.** The ceremonies held in connection with the burial or cremation of a dead person. **b.** *Archaic.* The eulogy delivered or the sermon preached at such a ceremony. **2.** The burial procession accompanying a body to the grave. **3.** An end or a cessation of existence. **4.** *Slang.* A source of concern or care: *If he doesn't meet the deadline, it's his funeral.* **—funeral** *adj.* Of, relating to, or resembling a funeral. [Middle English *funerelles,* funeral rites, from Old French *funerailles,* from Medieval Latin *fūnerālia,* neuter pl. of *fūnerālis,* funereal, from Late Latin, from Latin *fūnus, fūner-,* death rites.]

funeral director *n.* One whose business is to arrange for the burial or cremation of the dead and assist at the funeral rites and who is usually an embalmer. Also called *mortician, undertaker.*

funeral home *n.* An establishment in which the dead are prepared for burial or cremation and in which wakes and funerals may be held.

fu·ner·ar·y (fyōō′nə-rĕr′ē) *adj.* Of or suitable for a funeral or burial. [Latin *fūnerārius,* from *fūnus, fūner-,* funeral.]

fu·ne·re·al (fyōō-nîr′ē-əl) *adj.* **1.** Of or relating to a funeral. **2.** Appropriate for or suggestive of a funeral; mournful: *funereal gloom.* [From Latin *fūnereus,* from *fūnus, fūner-,* funeral.] **—fu·ne′re·al·ly** *adv.*

fun fair *n. Chiefly British.* An amusement park.

fun·fest (fŭn′fĕst′) *n. Slang.* A party or gathering for amusement.

fun·gal (fŭng′gəl) also **fun·gous** (-gəs) *adj.* **1.** Of, relating to, resembling, or characteristic of a fungus. **2.** Caused by a fungus.

fun·gi (fŭn′jī, fŭng′gī) *n.* A plural of **fungus.**

fun·gi·ble (fŭn′jə-bəl) *adj.* **1.** *Law.* Returnable or negotiable in kind or by substitution, as a quantity of grain for an equal amount of the same kind of grain. **2.** Interchangeable. **—fungible** *n.* Something that is exchangeable or substitutable. Often used in the plural. [Medieval Latin *fungibilis,* from Latin *fungī (vice),* to perform (in place of).] **—fun′gi·bil′i·ty** *n.*

fun·gi·cide (fŭn′jĭ-sīd′, fŭng′gĭ-) *n.* A chemical substance that destroys or inhibits the growth of fungi. **—fun′gi·cid′al** (-sīd′l) *adj.* **—fun′gi·cid′al·ly** *adv.*

fun·gi·form (fŭn′jə-fôrm′, fŭng′gə-) *adj.* Shaped like a mushroom. [FUNG(US) + –FORM.]

fun·gi·stat (fŭn′jĭ-stăt′, fŭng′gĭ-) *n.* A substance that inhibits the growth of fungi.

fun·giv·or·ous (fŭn-jĭv′ər-əs, fŭng-gĭv′-) *adj.* Feeding on fungi.

fun·go (fŭng′gō) *n., pl.* **-goes.** *Baseball.* A fly ball hit for fielding practice by a player who tosses the ball up and hits it on its way down with a long, thin, light bat. [Origin unknown.]

fun·goid (fŭng′goid′) *adj.* Of, relating to, resembling, or being a fungus. **—fungoid** *n.* A fungus.

fun·gous (fŭng′gəs) *adj.* Variant of **fungal.** [Middle English, tender (as mushrooms), from Latin *fungōsus,* spongy, from *fungus,* fungus. See FUNGUS.]

fun·gus (fŭng′gəs) *n., pl.* **fun·gi** (fŭn′jī, fŭng′gī) or **fun·gus·es.** Any of numerous eukaryotic organisms of the kingdom Fungi, which lack chlorophyll and vascular tissue and range in form from a single cell to a body mass of branched filamentous hyphae that often produce specialized fruiting bodies. The kingdom includes the yeasts, molds, smuts, and mushrooms. [Latin; perhaps akin to Greek *spongos, sphongos,* sponge.]

fun house also **fun·house** (fŭn′hous′) *n.* A building or an attraction in an amusement park or a carnival that features various devices intended to surprise, frighten, bewilder, or amuse.

fu·ni·cle (fyōō′nĭ-kəl) *n.* Variant of **funiculus.**

fu·nic·u·lar (fyōō-nĭk′yə-lər, fə-) *adj.* **1.** Of, relating to, or resembling a rope or cord. **2.** Operated or moved by a cable. **3.** Of, relating to, or constituting a funiculus. **—funicular** *n.* A cable railway on a steep incline, especially such a railway with simultaneously ascending and descending cars counterbalancing one another.

funicular

fu·nic·u·lus (fyōō-nĭk′yə-ləs, fə-) also **fu·ni·cle** (fyōō′nĭ-kəl) *n., pl.* **-li** (-lī′) also **-cles. 1.** *Anatomy.* A slender cordlike strand or band, especially: **a.** A bundle of nerve fibers in a nerve trunk. **b.** One of three major divisions of white matter in the spinal cord, consisting of fasciculi. **c.** The umbilical cord. **2.** *Botany.* A stalk connecting an ovule or a seed with the placenta. [Latin *fūniculus,* slender rope, diminutive of *fūnis,* rope.]

funk¹ (fŭngk) *n.* **1.a.** A state of cowardly fright; a panic. **b.** A state of severe depression. **2.** A cowardly, fearful person. **—funk** *v.* **funked, funk·ing, funks.** *—tr.* **1.** To shrink from in fright or dread. **2.** To be afraid of. *—intr.* To shrink in fright. [Probably from obsolete Flemish *fonck,* disturbance, agitation.]

funk² (fŭngk) *n.* **1.** *Music.* **a.** An earthy quality appreciated in music such as jazz or soul. **b.** A type of popular music combining elements of jazz, blues, and soul and characterized by syncopated rhythm and a heavy, repetitive bass line. **2.** *Slang.* An unsophisticated quality or atmosphere of a region or locality: *"The setting is country funk"* (Nina Martin). [Back-formation from FUNKY².]

Funk (fŭngk, fōōngk), **Casimir.** 1884–1967. Polish-born American biochemist whose research of deficiency diseases led to his discovery of vitamins, which he named in 1912.

funk hole *n.* A dugout or similar place of shelter or refuge. [From FUNK¹.]

funk·y¹ (fŭng′kē) *adj.* **-i·er, -i·est.** Frightened; panicky.

funk·y² (fŭng′kē) *adj.* **-i·er, -i·est. 1.a.** Having a moldy or musty smell: *funky cheese; funky cellars.* **b.** Having a strong, offensive, unwashed odor. **2.** *Slang.* **a.** Of or relating to music that has an earthy quality reminiscent of the blues: *funky jazz.* **b.** Earthy and uncomplicated; natural: *"At the opposite end of Dallas's culinary spectrum is funky regional fare"* (Jacqueline Friedrich). **3.** *Slang.* **a.** Characterized by self-expression, originality, and modishness; unconventional: *funky clothes.* **b.** Outlandishly vulgar or eccentric in a humorous or tongue-in-cheek manner; campy: *"funky caricatures of sexpot glamour"* (Pauline Kael). [From *funk,* strong smell, tobacco smoke, perhaps from French dialectal *funquer,* to give off smoke, from Old French *fungier,* from Latin *fūmigāre.* See FUMIGATE.] **—funk′i·ness** *n.*

WORD HISTORY: When asked which words in the English language are the most difficult to define precisely, a lexicographer would surely mention *funky.* The meaning of *funky* seems well captured by Geneva Smitherman in *Talkin and Testifyin: The Language of Black America,* where she states that *funky* means "[related to] the blue notes or blue mood created in jazz, blues, and soul music generally, down-to-earth soulfully expressed sounds; by extension [related to] the real nitty-gritty or fundamental essence of life, soul to the max." Be that as it may, *funky* is first recorded in 1784 in a reference to musty, old, moldy cheese. *Funky* then developed the sense "smelling strong or bad," which could be used to describe body odor. But *funky* was applied to jazz, too—a usage explained in 1959 by one F. Newton in *Jazz Scene*: "Critics are on the search for something a little more like the old, original, passion-laden blues: the trade-name which has been suggested for it is 'funky' (literally: 'smelly,' i.e. symbolizing the return from the upper atmosphere to the physical, down-to-earth reality)." *Funky* comes from the earlier noun *funk,* which

ă **pat**	oi **boy**
ā **pay**	ou **out**
âr **care**	ŏŏ **took**
ä **father**	ōō **boot**
ĕ **pet**	ŭ **cut**
ē **be**	ûr **urge**
ĭ **pit**	th **thin**
ī **pie**	*th* **this**
îr **pier**	hw **which**
ŏ **pot**	zh **vision**
ō **toe**	ə **about, item**
ô **paw**	♦ **regionalism**

Stress marks: ′ (primary); ′ (secondary), as in **dictionary** (dĭk′shə-nĕr′ē)

meant "a strong smell or stink." This noun can probably be traced back to the Latin word *fūmus,* "smoke."

fun•nel (fŭn′əl) *n.* **1.a.** A conical utensil having a small hole or narrow tube at the apex and used to channel the flow of a substance, as into a small-mouthed container. **b.** Something resembling this utensil in shape. **2.** A shaft, flue, or stack for ventilation or the passage of smoke, especially the smokestack of a ship or locomotive. **—funnel** *v.* **-neled, -nel•ing, -nels** or **-nelled, -nel•ling, -nels.** *—intr.* **1.** To take the shape of a funnel. **2.** To move through or as if through a funnel: *tourists funneling slowly through customs.* *—tr.* **1.** To cause to take the shape of a funnel. **2.** To cause to move through or as if through a funnel. [Middle English *fonel,* from Provençal *fonilh,* from Late Latin *fundibulum,* from Latin *īnfundibulum,* from *īnfundere,* to pour in. See INFUSE.]

fun•nel•form (fŭn′əl-fôrm′) *adj. Botany.* Shaped like a funnel, as the corolla of a petunia or a morning glory.

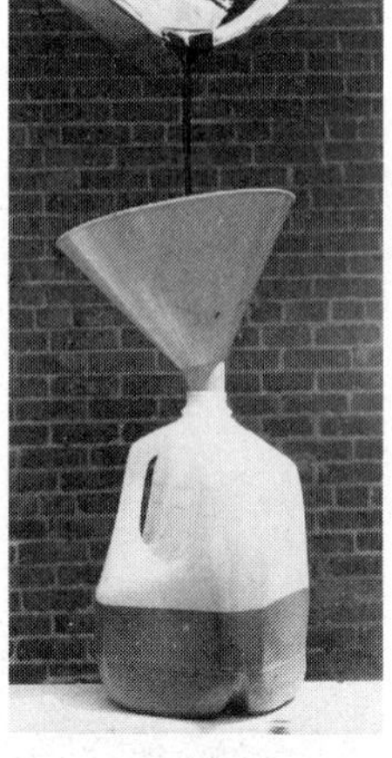

funnel

fun•ny (fŭn′ē) *adj.* **-ni•er, -ni•est. 1.a.** Causing laughter or amusement. **b.** Intended or designed to amuse. **2.** Strangely or suspiciously odd; curious. **3.** Tricky or deceitful. **—funny** *n., pl.* **-nies.** *Informal.* **1.** A joke; a witticism. **2. funnies. a.** Comic strips. **b.** The section of a newspaper containing comic strips. [From FUN.] **—fun′ni•ly** *adv.* **—fun′ni•ness** *n.*

funny bone *n. Informal.* **1.** A point on the elbow where the ulnar nerve runs close to the surface and produces a sharp tingling sensation if knocked against the bone. **2.** A sense of humor.

funny book *n.* See **comic book.**

funny farm *n. Slang.* A mental health facility or hospital.

fun•ny•man (fŭn′ē-măn′) *n.* A humorous person, especially a professional comedian.

funny money *n. Informal.* **1.** Counterfeit currency. **2.** Money from an obscure or questionable source.

funny paper *n.* A section or supplement of a newspaper containing comic strips.

fur (fûr) *n.* **1.** The thick coat of soft hair covering the skin of a mammal, such as a fox or beaver. **2.** The hair-covered, dressed pelt of such a mammal, used in the making of garments and as trimming or decoration. **3.** A garment made of or lined with the dressed pelt of a mammal. **4.** A coating similar to the pelt of a mammal. *—attributive.* Often used to modify another noun: *a fur coat; fur hats.* **—fur** *tr.v.* **furred, fur•ring, furs. 1.** To cover, line, or trim with fur. **2.** To provide fur garments for. **3.** To cover or coat as if with fur. **4.** To line (a wall or floor) with furring. [Middle English *furre,* probably from *furren,* to line with fur, from Old French *forrer,* from *forre, fuerre,* sheath, lining, of Germanic origin. See **pā-** in Appendix.]

fur. *abbr.* Furlong.

fu•ran (fyo͝or′ăn′, fyo͝o-răn′) *n.* **1.** One of a group of colorless, volatile, heterocyclic organic compounds containing a ring of four carbon atoms and one oxygen atom, obtained from wood oils and used in the synthesis of furfural and other organic compounds. **2.** The simplest such compound, C_4H_4O. In this sense, also called *furfuran.* [FUR(FURAL) + -AN[2].]

fu•ra•nose (fyo͝or′ə-nōs′) *n.* A sugar having a cyclic structure resembling that of furan.

fur•bear•er also **fur-bear•er** (fûr′bâr′ər) *n.* An animal whose skin is covered with fur, especially fur that is commercially valuable. **—fur′bear′ing** *adj.*

fur•be•low (fûr′bə-lō′) *n.* **1.** A ruffle or flounce on a garment. **2.** A piece of showy ornamentation. **—furbelow** *tr.v.* **-lowed, -low•ing, -lows.** To decorate with a ruffle or flounce. [Probably alteration of Provençal *farbello, farbella,* fringe, perhaps alteration of Italian *faldella,* pleat, diminutive of *falda,* flap, loose end, of Germanic origin. See **pel-**[2] in Appendix.]

fur•bish (fûr′bĭsh) *tr.v.* **-bished, -bish•ing, -bish•es. 1.** To brighten by cleaning or rubbing; polish. **2.** To restore to attractive or serviceable condition; renovate. [Middle English *furbishen,* from Old French *fourbir, fourbiss-,* from Frankish **furbjan.*] **—fur′bish•er** *n.*

fur•cate (fûr′kāt′) *intr.v.* **-cat•ed, -cat•ing, -cates.** To divide into branches; fork. **—furcate** *adj.* Divided into branches; forked. [Late Latin *furcātus,* forked, from Latin *furca,* fork.] **—fur′cate′ly** *adv.* **—fur•ca′tion** *n.*

fur•cu•la (fûr′kyə-lə) *n., pl.* **-lae** (-lē′). *Zoology.* A forked part or bone, such as the wishbone of a bird. Also called *fourchette.* [Latin, diminutive of *furca,* fork.] **—fur′cu•lar** *adv.*

fur•fur (fûr′fər) *n., pl.* **-fu•res** (-fyə-rēz′). An epidermal scale, as that associated with dandruff. [Latin, bran, scales.]

fur•fu•ra•ceous (fûr′fə-rā′shəs, -fyə-) *adj.* **1.** Made of or covered with scaly particles, such as dandruff. **2.** Relating to or resembling bran. [Late Latin *furfurāceus,* branlike, scaly : Latin *furfur,* bran + Latin *-āceus,* -aceous.]

fur•fu•ral (fûr′fə-răl′, -fyə-) *n.* A colorless, sweet-smelling, mobile liquid, C_4H_3OCHO, made from corncobs and used in the synthesis of furan, as a solvent for nitrocellulose, and as a fungicide and weed killer. [FURFUR + -AL[3].]

fur•fu•ran (fûr′fə-răn′, -fyə-) *n.* See **furan** (sense 2). [FURFUR(AL) + -AN[2].]

fur•fu•res (fûr′fyə-rēz′) *n.* Plural of **furfur.**

fu•ri•o•so (fyo͝or′ē-ō′sō, -zō) *adv. & adj. Music.* In a tempestuous and vigorous manner. Used chiefly as a direction. [Italian, from Latin *furiōsus,* furious. See FURIOUS.]

fu•ri•ous (fyo͝or′ē-əs) *adj.* **1.** Full of or characterized by extreme anger; raging. **2.** Suggestive of extreme anger in action or appearance; fierce. See Synonyms at **angry.** [Middle English, from Old French *furieus,* from Latin *furiōsus,* from *furia,* fury. See FURY.] **—fu′ri•ous•ly** *adv.*

furl (fûrl) *v.* **furled, furl•ing, furls.** *—tr.* To roll up and secure (a flag or sail, for example) to something else. *—intr.* To be or become rolled up. **—furl** *n.* **1.** The act or an instance of rolling up. **2.** A single roll or a rolled section. [Perhaps from French *ferler,* from Old French *ferlier,* to fasten : *ferm,* firm; see FIRM[1] + *lier,* to bind (from Latin *ligāre;* see **leig-** in Appendix).]

fur•long (fûr′lông′, -lŏng′) *n. Abbr.* **fur.** A unit for measuring distance, equal to ⅛ mile (201 meters). See table at **measurement.** [Middle English, from Old English *furlang* : *furh,* furrow + *lang,* long; see LONG[1].]

fur•lough (fûr′lō) *n.* **1.a.** A leave of absence or vacation, especially one granted to a member of the armed forces. **b.** A usually temporary layoff from work. **c.** A leave of absence from prison granted to a prisoner. **2.** The papers or documents authorizing a leave: *The soldiers had their furloughs in their breast pockets.* **—furlough** *tr.v.* **-loughed, -lough•ing, -loughs. 1.** To grant a leave to. **2.** To lay off (workers). [Alteration of *vorloffe, furlogh,* from Dutch *verlof,* from Middle Dutch. See **leubh-** in Appendix.]

fur•mi•ty (fûr′mĭ-tē) *n.* Variant of **frumenty.**

furn. *abbr.* Furnished.

fur•nace (fûr′nĭs) *n.* **1.** An enclosure in which energy in a nonthermal form is converted to heat, especially such an enclosure in which heat is generated by the combustion of a suitable fuel. **2.** An intensely hot place: *the furnace of the sun; an attic room that is a furnace in the summer.* **3.** A severe test or trial: *endured the furnace of his friends' blame after the accident.* [Middle English, from Old French *fornais,* from Latin *fornāx, fornāc-,* oven. See **g^{w}her-** in Appendix.]

fur•nish (fûr′nĭsh) *tr.v.* **-nished, -nish•ing, -nish•es. 1.** To equip with what is needed, especially to provide furniture for. **2.** To supply; give: *"The story of Orpheus has furnished Pope with an illustration"* (Thomas Bulfinch). [Middle English *furnisshen,* from Old French *fournir, fourniss-,* of Germanic origin. See **per**[1] in Appendix.] **—fur′nish•er** *n.*

SYNONYMS: *furnish, equip, outfit, appoint, accouter.* These verbs mean to provide with what is necessary for an activity or a purpose. *Furnish* refers primarily to the provision of basic necessities: *furnished the new apartment; furnish a boat with care. Equip* usually implies the provision of more specialized items for a particular need or a particular service: *equip a car with snow tires. Outfit* suggests comprehensive provision of necessary items for a larger purpose, as for an expedition: *outfitting the children for summer camp.* To *appoint* is to provide with furnishings and often accessories, usually of a tasteful kind: *a library that was appointed in leather. Accouter* refers most often to providing with articles of equipment, especially for military service: *knights who were accoutered for battle.*

fur•nish•ing (fûr′nĭ-shĭng) *n.* **1.** A piece of equipment necessary or useful for comfort or convenience. **2. furnishings.** The furniture, appliances, and other movable articles in a home or other building. **3. furnishings.** Wearing apparel and accessories.

fur•ni•ture (fûr′nĭ-chər) *n.* **1.** The movable articles in a room or an establishment that make it fit for living or working. **2.** *Archaic.* The necessary equipment for a saddle horse. [Old French *fourniture,* from *fournir,* to furnish. See FURNISH.]

Fur•ni•vall (fûr′nə-vəl), **Frederick James.** 1825–1910. British philologist who as a member of the Philological Society proposed the *Oxford English Dictionary* in 1857.

fu•ror (fyo͝or′ôr′, -ər) *n.* **1.** A general commotion; public disorder or uproar. **2.** Violent anger; frenzy. **3.** A fashion adopted enthusiastically by the public; a fad. **4.** A state of intense excitement or ecstasy. [Middle English *furour,* wrath, fury, from Old French *fureur,* from Latin *furor,* from *furere,* to rage.]

fu•rore (fyo͝or′ôr′, -ōr′) *n. Chiefly British.* Variant of **furor** (senses 1, 3). [Italian, from Latin *furor,* frenzy. See FUROR.]

fu•ro•se•mide (fyo͝o-rō′sə-mīd′) *n.* A white to yellow crystalline powder, $C_{12}H_{11}ClN_2O_5S$, used as a diuretic. [FUR(FURAL) + S(ULF)- + *-emide* (alteration of AMIDE).]

furred (fûrd) *adj.* **1.** Bearing fur. **2.** Made, covered, or trimmed with fur. **3.** Wearing fur garments. **4.** Covered or coated as if with fur. **5.** Provided with furring, as a wall, ceiling, or floor.

fur•ri•er (fûr′ē-ər) *n.* **1.** One that deals in furs. **2.** One whose occupation is the dressing, designing, cleaning, or repairing of furs. [Alteration (influenced by CLOTHIER) of Middle English *furrer,* from Anglo-Norman *furrere,* from Old French *forrer,* to line with fur. See FUR.]

fur•ri•er•y (fûr′ē-ə-rē) *n., pl.* **-ies. 1.** Fur garments and trimmings considered as a group. **2.** The business of a furrier.

fur•ring (fûr′ĭng) *n.* **1.** Trimming or lining made of fur. **2.** A furlike coating, as on the tongue. **3.a.** The preparation of a wall, ceiling, or floor with strips of wood or metal to provide a level substratum for plaster, flooring, or another surface or to create an air space. **b.** Strips of material used in this process.

fur•row (fûr′ō, fŭr′ō) *n.* **1.** A long, narrow, shallow trench made in the ground by a plow. **2.** A rut, groove, or narrow depression: *snow drifting in furrows.* **3.** A deep wrinkle in the skin, as on the forehead. **—furrow** *v.* **-rowed, -row·ing, -rows.** *—tr.* **1.** To make long, narrow, shallow trenches in; plow. **2.** To form grooves or deep wrinkles in. *—intr.* To become furrowed or wrinkled. [Middle English *forwe,* from Old English *furh.*]

fur·ry (fûr′ē, fŭr′ē) *adj.* **-ri·er, -ri·est. 1.** Consisting of or similar to fur. **2.a.** Covered with, wearing, or trimmed with fur. **b.** Covered with a furlike substance. **3.** Having a furlike quality, as in tone; fuzzy: *a furry voice.* **—fur′ri·ness** *n.*

fur seal *n.* Any of several eared seals of the genera *Callorhinus* or *Arctocephalus,* having thick, soft underfur that is valued commercially for use in making garments.

Fürth (fo͝ort, fürt). A city of south-central Germany, an industrial suburb of Nuremberg. Population, 97,623.

fur·ther (fûr′*th*ər) *adj.* A comparative of **far. 1.** More distant in degree, time, or space: *a result that was further from our expectations than last time; the further lamppost.* **2.** Additional: *a further example; a further delay.* **—further** *adv.* A comparative of **far. 1.** To a greater extent; more: *considered further the consequences of her actions.* **2.** In addition; furthermore: *He stated further that he would not cooperate with the committee.* **3.** At or to a more distant or advanced point: *went only three miles further; reading five pages further tonight.* See Usage Note at **farther. —further** *tr.v.* **-thered, -ther·ing, -thers.** To help the progress of; advance. See Synonyms at **advance.** [Middle English, from Old English *furthra,* from *furthor,* farther. Adv., from Middle English, from Old English *furthor.* See **per**[1] in Appendix.] **—fur′ther·er** *n.*

fur·ther·ance (fûr′*th*ər-əns) *n.* The act of furthering or helping forward: *"Pakistan does not aspire to any . . . role in furtherance of the strategies of other powers"* (Ismail Patel).

fur·ther·more (fûr′*th*ər-môr′, -mōr′) *adv.* In addition; moreover. See Synonyms at **also.**

fur·ther·most (fûr′*th*ər-mōst′) *adj.* Most distant or remote.

fur·thest (fûr′*th*ĭst) *adj.* A superlative of **far.** Most distant in degree, time, or space: *That's the furthest thing from my mind. They explored the furthest reaches of space.* **—furthest** *adv.* A superlative of **far. 1.** To the greatest extent or degree: *went the furthest of all the children in her education.* **2.** At or to the most distant point in space or time: *He swam the furthest.* [Middle English, from *further,* more distant. See FURTHER.]

fur·tive (fûr′tĭv) *adj.* **1.** Characterized by stealth; surreptitious. **2.** Expressive of hidden motives or purposes; shifty. See Synonyms at **secret.** [French *furtif,* from Old French, from Latin *furtīvus,* from *furtum,* theft, from *fūr,* thief. See **bher-**[1] in Appendix.] **—fur′tive·ly** *adv.* **—fur′tive·ness** *n.*

fu·run·cle (fyo͝or′ŭng′kəl) *n.* See **boil**[2]. [Latin *fūrunculus,* knob on a vine that "steals" the sap, diminutive of *fūr,* thief. See **bher-**[1] in Appendix.] **—fu·run′cu·lar** (fyo͞o-rŭng′kyə-lər), **fu·run′cu·lous** (-ləs) *adj.*

fu·run·cu·lo·sis (fyo͞o-rŭng′kyə-lō′sĭs) *n.* A skin condition characterized by the development of recurring boils. [Latin *fūrunculus,* furuncle; see FURUNCLE + -OSIS.]

fu·ry (fyo͝or′ē) *n., pl.* **-ries. 1.** Violent anger; rage. See Synonyms at **anger. 2.** Violent, uncontrolled action; turbulence. **3. Furies.** *Greek & Roman Mythology.* The three terrible, winged goddesses with serpentine hair, Alecto, Megaera, and Tisiphone, who pursue and punish doers of unavenged crimes. **4.** A woman regarded as angry or spiteful. [Middle English *furie,* from Old French, from Latin *furia,* from *furere,* to rage.]

furze (fûrz) *n.* See **gorse.** [Middle English *furse,* from Old English *fyrs.*]

fu·sain (fyo͞o-zān′, fyo͞o′zān) *n.* **1.a.** Fine charcoal in stick form, made from the wood of the spindle tree. **b.** A sketch or drawing made with this charcoal. **2.** A dull dark-gray, brittle, porous type of bituminous coal resembling charcoal. [French, spindle tree, charcoal made from its wood, from Vulgar Latin *fūsāgō, *fūsāgin-, spindle (formerly made from the wood of a spindle tree), from Latin *fūsus.*]

Fu·san (fo͞o′sän′). See **Pusan.**

fu·sar·i·um (fyo͞o-zâr′ē-əm) *n., pl.* **-i·a** (-ē-ə). Any of various pathogenic fungi of the genus *Fusarium,* chiefly inhabiting temperate climates and infecting both plants and animals. In human beings, infection may cause inflammation of the cornea and external ear. [New Latin, genus name, possibly from Latin *fūsus,* spindle (from its shape).]

fus·cous (fŭs′kəs) *adj.* Dark brownish-gray in color. [From Latin *fuscus.*]

fuse[1] also **fuze** (fyo͞oz) *—n.* **1.** A cord of readily combustible material that is lighted at one end to carry a flame along its length to detonate an explosive at the other end. **2.** Often **fuze.** A mechanical or electrical mechanism used to detonate an explosive charge or device such as a bomb or grenade: *"A mechanical . . . switch is used to initiate the fuzes"* (International Defense Review). *—tr.v.* **fused, fus·ing, fus·es** also **fuzed, fuz·ing, fuz·es.** To equip with a mechanical or electrical fuse: *"The bomb . . . was fuzed and timed to explode after the aircraft had taken off"* (Aviation Week & Space Technology). [From Italian *fuso,* spindle (originally from its shape), from Latin *fūsus.*]

fuse[2] (fyo͞oz) *v.* **fused, fus·ing, fus·es.** *—tr.* **1.** To liquefy or reduce to a plastic state by heating; melt. **2.** To mix (constituent elements) together by or as if by melting; blend. *—intr.* **1.** To become liquefied from heat. **2.** To become mixed or united by or as if by melting together: *"There was no separation between joy and sorrow: they fused into one"* (Henry Miller). See Synonyms at **melt, mix. —fuse** *n.* A safety device that protects an electric circuit from excessive current, consisting of or containing a metal element that melts when current exceeds a specific amperage, thereby opening the circuit. [Latin *fundere, fūs-,* to melt. See **gheu-** in Appendix.]

fused quartz (fyo͞ozd) *n.* See **quartz glass.**

fused silica *n.* See **quartz glass.**

fu·see also **fu·zee** (fyo͞o-zē′) *n.* **1.** A friction match with a large head capable of burning in a wind. **2.** A colored flare used as a warning signal for trucks and railroad trains. **3.** A cone-shaped pulley with a spiral groove, used in a cord- or chain-winding clock to maintain even travel in the timekeeping mechanism as the force of the mainspring lessens in unwinding. **4.** A combustible fuse for detonating explosives. [From French *fusée,* spindle, rocket, flare, fuse, from Old French, spindleful of thread, from *fus,* spindle, from Latin *fūsus.*]

fu·se·lage (fyo͞o′sə-läzh′, -zə-) *n.* The central body of an aircraft, to which the wings and tail assembly are attached and which accommodates the crew, passengers, and cargo. [French, from *fuselé,* spindle-shaped, from Old French *fusel,* spindle, from Vulgar Latin **fūsellus,* diminutive of Latin *fūsus.*]

Fu·sel·i (fyo͞o′zə-lē′), **Henry.** 1741–1825. Swiss-born British painter whose works, including *The Nightmare* (1781), display a fantastic, macabre quality.

fu·sel oil (fyo͞o′zəl) *n.* An acrid, oily, poisonous liquid mixture of amyl alcohols, occurring in incompletely distilled alcoholic liquids and used as a solvent and in the manufacture of explosives and pure amyl alcohols. [German *Fusel,* bad liquor, from Low German.]

Fu·shun (fo͞o′sho͝on′, fü′shün′). A city of northeast China east of Shenyang. It was formerly controlled by Russia and Japan. Population, 1,240,000.

fu·si·ble (fyo͞o′zə-bəl) *adj.* Capable of being fused or melted by heating. **—fu′si·bil′i·ty** *n.* **—fu′si·ble·ness** *n.*

fusible metal *n.* A metal alloy having a low melting point, used as solder and for safety plugs and fuses.

fu·si·form (fyo͞o′zə-fôrm′) *adj.* Tapering at each end; spindle-shaped. [Latin *fūsus,* spindle + -FORM.]

fu·sil (fyo͞o′zəl) *n.* A light flintlock musket. [French, steel in a flintlock, firearm, from Old French *fuisil,* steel for a tinderbox, from Vulgar Latin **focīlis (petra),* fire-(stone), from Late Latin *focus,* fire, from Latin, hearth.]

fu·sile (fyo͞o′zəl, -zīl′) *adj. Archaic.* **1.** Formed by melting or casting. **2.** Capable of being fused; fusible. [Middle English, from Latin *fūsilis,* from *fūsus,* past participle of *fundere,* to melt. See **gheu-** in Appendix.]

fu·sil·ier also **fu·sil·eer** (fyo͞o′zə-lîr′) *n.* **1.** A soldier in any of certain British army regiments formerly armed with fusils. **2.** A soldier armed with a fusil. [French, musketeer, from *fusil,* musket. See FUSIL.]

fu·sil·lade (fyo͞o′sə-läd′, -lād′, -zə-, fyo͞o′sə-läd′, -lād′, -zə-) *n.* **1.** A discharge from a number of firearms, fired simultaneously or in rapid succession. **2.** A rapid outburst or barrage: *a fusillade of insults.* **—fusillade** *tr.v.* **-lad·ed, -lad·ing, -lades.** To attack with a fusillade. [French, from *fusiller,* to shoot, from *fusil,* firearm. See FUSIL.]

Fu·sin (fo͞o′shĭn′, fü′-). See **Fuxin.**

fu·sion (fyo͞o′zhən) *n.* **1.** The act or procedure of liquefying or melting by the application of heat. **2.** The liquid or melted state induced by heat. **3.a.** The merging of different elements into a union: *fusion of metals in an alloy; the difficult fusion of conflicting factions.* **b.** A union resulting from fusing: *A fusion of religion and politics emerged.* **4.** *Physics.* A nuclear reaction in which nuclei combine to form more massive nuclei with the simultaneous release of energy. **5.** *Music.* Jazz-rock. [Latin *fūsiō, fūsiōn-,* from *fūsus,* past participle of *fundere,* to melt. See **gheu-** in Appendix.]

fusion bomb *n.* A nuclear bomb, especially a hydrogen bomb, that derives its released energy principally from fusion reactions among light nuclei.

fu·sion·ism (fyo͞o′zhə-nĭz′əm) *n.* The theory or practice of forming coalitions, especially of political groups or factions. **—fu′sion·ist** *n.*

fuss (fŭs) *n.* **1.** Needlessly nervous or useless activity; commotion: *There was a lot of fuss on moving day.* **2.a.** A state of excessive and unwarranted concern over an unimportant matter: *made a big fuss over one low test grade.* **b.** An objection; a protest: *The longer working hours caused a big fuss.* **3.** A quarrel. **4.** A display of affectionate excitement and attention: *Everyone made a fuss over the new baby.* **—fuss** *v.* **fussed, fuss·ing, fuss·es.** *—intr.* **1.** To trouble or worry over trifles. **2.** To be excessively careful or solicitous: *fussed over their children.* **3.** To get into or be in a state of nervous or useless activity: *fussed with the collar of his coat.* **4.** To object; complain. *—tr.* To disturb or vex with unimportant matters. [Origin unknown.] **—fuss′er** *n.*

fuss·budg·et also **fuss-bud·get** (fŭs′bŭj′ĭt) *n.* A person who fusses over trifles. Also called *fusspot.*

fuss·pot (fŭs′pŏt′) *n.* See **fussbudget.**

fuss·y (fŭs′ē) *adj.* **-i·er, -i·est. 1.** Easily upset; given to bouts of ill temper: *a fussy baby.* **2.** Paying great or excessive attention to personal tastes and appearance; fastidious: *He was always*

fur seal
Antarctic fur seal
Arctocephalus gazella

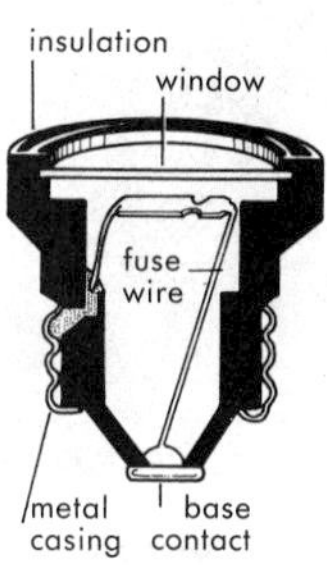

fuse[2]

ă pat	oi boy
ā pay	ou out
âr care	o͝o took
ä father	o͞o boot
ĕ pet	ŭ cut
ē be	ûr urge
ĭ pit	th thin
ī pie	*th* this
îr pier	hw which
ŏ pot	zh vision
ō toe	ə about, item
ô paw	♦ regionalism

Stress marks: ′ (primary); ′ (secondary), as in **dictionary** (dĭk′shə-nĕr′ē)

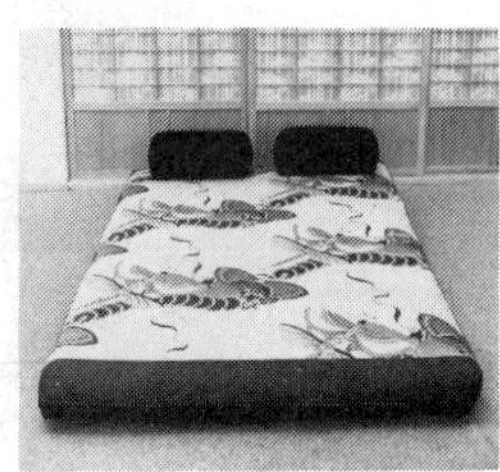

futon

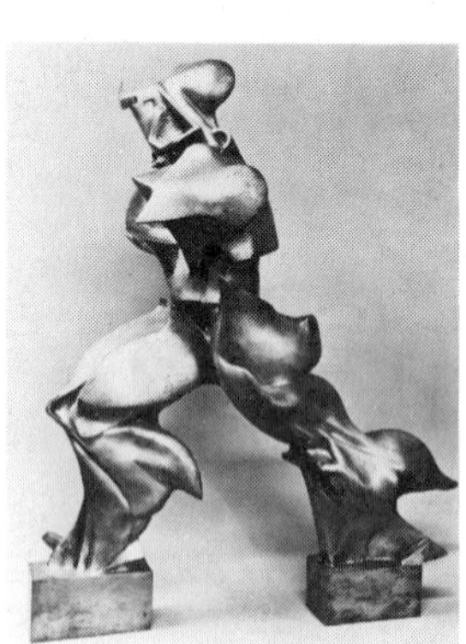

futurism
Unique Forms of Continuity in Space, 1913, by Umberto Boccioni. *Bronze (cast 1931), 43⅞" × 34⅞" × 15¾". The Museum of Modern Art, New York. Acquired through the Lillie P. Bliss Bequest.*

ă pat	oi boy
ā pay	ou out
âr care	o͝o took
ä father	o͞o boot
ĕ pet	ŭ cut
ē be	ûr urge
ĭ pit	th thin
ī pie	*th* this
îr pier	hw which
ŏ pot	zh vision
ō toe	ə about, item
ô paw	♦ regionalism

Stress marks: **′** (primary); ′ (secondary), as in **dictionary** (dĭk′shə-nĕr′ē)

fussy about clothes. **3.** Calling for or requiring great attention to sometimes trivial details. **4.** Full of superfluous details: *"It can indeed be fussy, filling with ornament what should be empty space"* (H.D.F. Kitto). **—fuss′i·ly** *adv.* **—fuss′i·ness** *n.*

Fust (fo͞ost), **Johann.** 1400?–1466. German printer who was the financial partner (1450?–1455) and successor (1455) of Gutenberg.

fus·tian (fŭs′chən) *n.* **1.a.** A coarse, sturdy cloth made of cotton and flax. **b.** Any of several thick, twilled cotton fabrics, such as corduroy, having a short nap. **2.** Pretentious speech or writing; pompous language. See Synonyms at **bombast.** **—fustian** *adj.* **1.** Made of or as if of fustian: "[He] *disliked the heavy, fustian . . . and brocaded decor of Soviet officialdom"* (Frederick Forsyth). **2.** Pompous, bombastic, and ranting: *"Yossarian was unmoved by the fustian charade of the burial ceremony"* (Joseph Heller). [Middle English, from Old French *fustaigne,* from Medieval Latin *fustāneum,* possibly from Latin *fūstis,* wooden stick, club (loan translation of Greek *xulina (lina),* wood-linen, cotton) or from *El Fostat* (El Fustat), a section of Cairo, Egypt.]

fus·tic (fŭs′tĭk) *n.* **1.** A small dioecious tropical American tree *(Chlorophora tinctoria)* having wood that yields a yellow dyestuff. **2.** The wood of this plant. **3.** A dyestuff obtained from the wood of this plant. [Middle English *fustik,* from Old French *fustoc,* from Arabic *fustuq,* from Greek *pistakē,* pistachio. See PISTACHIO.]

fus·ti·gate (fŭs′tĭ-gāt′) *tr.v.* **-gat·ed, -gat·ing, -gates. 1.** To beat with a club; cudgel. **2.** To criticize harshly: *"We followed* [Ibsen] *as he fustigates himself and us"* (Patrice Chereau). [Late Latin *fūstigāre, fūstigāt-* : from Latin *fūstis,* club + *agere,* to do; see **ag-** in Appendix.] **—fus′ti·ga′tion** *n.*

fus·ty (fŭs′tē) *adj.* **-ti·er, -ti·est. 1.** Smelling of mildew or decay; musty. **2.** Old-fashioned; antique. [Middle English, from Old French *fust,* piece of wood, wine cask, from Latin *fūstis,* stick, club.] **—fus′ti·ly** *adv.* **—fus′ti·ness** *n.*

fu·su·ma (fo͞o-so͞o′mä) *n., pl.* **fusuma.** Light, sliding partitions of thick paper mounted in grooves on the floor and the ceiling of a Japanese house and moved into various positions to form rooms. [Japanese.]

fut. *abbr.* **1.** *Grammar.* Future. **2.** *Business.* Futures.

fu·thark (fo͞o′thärk′) *n.* **1.** The common Germanic runic alphabet. **2.** Also **fu·thorc** or **fu·thork** (-thôrk′). The Old English runic alphabet. [From the first six letters of the alphabet: *f, u, th, a, r, k* (or c).]

fu·tile (fyo͞ot′l, fyo͞o′tīl′) *adj.* **1.** Having no useful result. **2.** Trifling and frivolous; idle: *the futile years after her artistic peak.* [Latin *fūtilis.* See **gheu-** in Appendix.] **—fu′tile·ly** *adv.* **—fu′tile·ness** *n.*

SYNONYMS: *futile, barren, bootless, fruitless, unavailing, useless, vain.* The central meaning shared by these adjectives is "producing no result or effect": *a futile effort; a barren search; bootless entreaties; fruitless labors; an unavailing attempt; a useless discussion; vain regrets.*
ANTONYM: *useful.*

fu·til·i·tar·i·an (fyo͞o-tĭl′ĭ-târ′ē-ən) *adj.* Holding or based on the view that human endeavor is futile. **—futilitarian** *n.* One who holds the view that human endeavor is futile. [FUTILIT(Y) + -ARIAN.] **—fu·til′i·tar′i·an·ism** *n.*

fu·til·i·ty (fyo͞o-tĭl′ĭ-tē) *n., pl.* **-ties. 1.** The quality of having no useful result; uselessness. **2.** Lack of importance or purpose; frivolousness. **3.** A futile act.

fu·ton (fo͞o′tŏn) *n., pl.* **futon** or **-tons.** An article of bedding consisting of a pad of tufted cotton batting or similar material, used on a floor or on a raised frame as a mattress or comforter. [Japanese, bedclothes, bedding.]

fut·tock (fŭt′ək) *n. Nautical.* One of the curved timbers that forms a rib in the frame of a ship. [Middle English *fottek,* perhaps alteration of *fothok* : *fot,* foot; see FOOT + *hok,* hook; see HOOK.]

futtock plate *n. Nautical.* An iron plate attached horizontally to the top of the lower mast to secure the topmast rigging and the upper ends of the futtock shrouds.

futtock shroud *n. Nautical.* One of the iron rods extending from a band on the lower mast to the futtock plate, used to brace the base of the topmast.

Fu·tu·na Islands (fə-to͞o′nə, fo͞o-) also **Hoorn Islands** (hôrn, hōrn). An island group of the southwest Pacific Ocean northeast of Fiji. Part of the French overseas territory of Wallis and Futuna, the islands were annexed by France in 1887.

fu·ture (fyo͞o′chər) *n.* **1.** The indefinite time yet to come: *will try to do better in the future.* **2.** Something that will happen in time to come: *"The future comes apace"* (Shakespeare). **3.** A prospective or expected condition, especially one considered with regard to growth, advancement, or development: *a business with no future.* **4. futures.** *Abbr.* **fut.** *Business.* Commodities or stocks bought or sold upon agreement of delivery in time to come. **5.** *Abbr.* **fut.** *Grammar.* **a.** The form of a verb used in speaking of action that has not yet occurred or of states not yet in existence. **b.** A verb form in the future tense. **—future** *adj.* That is to be or to come; of or existing in later time. [Middle English, from Old French *futur,* from Latin *futūrus,* about to be. See **bheuə-** in Appendix.]

fu·ture·less (fyo͞o′chər-lĭs) *adj.* Having no prospect or hope of success in one's future. **—fu′ture·less·ness** *n.*

future perfect *n. Grammar.* A verb tense that expresses action completed by a specified time in the future and that is formed in English by combining *will have* or *shall have* with a past participle.

future shock *n.* A condition of distress and disorientation brought on by the inability to cope with rapid societal and technological change. [After the book *Future Shock* by Alvin Toffler (born 1928).]

future tense *n. Grammar.* A verb tense expressing future time.

fu·tur·ism (fyo͞o′chə-rĭz′əm) *n.* **1.** A belief that the meaning of life and one's personal fulfillment lie in the future and not in the present or past. **2.** An artistic movement originating in Italy around 1910 whose aim was to express the energetic, dynamic, and violent quality of contemporary life, especially as embodied in the motion and force of modern machinery. **—fu′tur·ist** *n.*

fu·tur·is·tic (fyo͞o′chə-rĭs′tĭk) *adj.* **1.** Of or relating to the future. **2.a.** Of, characterized by, or expressing a vision of the future: *futuristic decor.* **b.** Being ahead of the times; innovative or revolutionary: *futuristic computer software.* **3.** Of or relating to futurism. **—fu′tur·is′ti·cal·ly** *adj.*

fu·tur·ist·ics (fyo͞o′chə-rĭs′tĭks) *n. (used with a sing. verb).* Futurology.

fu·tu·ri·ty (fyo͞o-to͝or′ĭ-tē, -tyo͝or′-, -cho͝or′-) *n., pl.* **-ties. 1.** The future. **2.** The quality or condition of being in or of the future. **3.** A future event or possibility. **4.** *Sports.* A futurity race.

futurity race *n. Sports.* **1.** A race that competitors enter well in advance. **2.** A race for horses in which the competitors are entered at or before their birth.

futurity stakes *pl.n. Sports.* **1.** The stakes awarded to the winner or winners in a futurity race. **2.** A futurity race.

fu·tur·ol·o·gy (fyo͞o′chə-rŏl′ə-jē) *n.* The study or forecasting of potential developments, as in science, technology, and society, using current conditions and trends as a point of departure. **—fu′tur·o·log′i·cal** (fyo͞o′chər-ə-lŏj′ĭ-kəl) *adj.* **—fu′tu·rol′o·gist** *n.*

futz (fŭts) *intr.v.* **futzed, futz·ing, futz·es.** *Slang.* To waste time or effort on frivolities; fool. Often used with *around*: *"would like to return to the days when Americans believed: 'By golly, you don't futz around with Uncle Sam'"* (Wall Street Journal). [Possibly blend of FUCK and PUTZ.]

Fu·xin also **Fu·sin** (fo͞o′shĭn′, fü′-). A city of northeast China west-northwest of Shenyang. Population, 551,300.

fuze (fyo͞oz) *n. & v.* Variant of **fuse¹.**

fu·zee (fyo͞o-zē′) *n.* Variant of **fusee.**

Fu·zhou (fo͞o′jō′) also **Foo·chow** or **Fu·chou** (fo͞o′jō′, -chou′). A city of southeast China on the Min River delta. An ancient walled city, Fuzhou has been the capital of Fujian province since the tenth century. Population, 754,500.

fuzz¹ (fŭz) *n.* A mass or coating of fine, light fibers, hairs, or particles; down: *the fuzz on a peach.* **—fuzz** *v.* **fuzzed, fuzz·ing, fuzz·es.** *—tr.* **1.** To cover with fine light fibers, hairs, or particles. **2.** To make blurred or indistinct: *fuzzing the difference between the two candidates; worked quickly to fuzz up the details of the scandal.* *—intr.* To become blurred or obscure. [Perhaps back-formation from FUZZY.]

fuzz² (fŭz) *n. Slang.* The police. [Origin unknown.]

fuzz·y (fŭz′ē) *adj.* **-i·er, -i·est. 1.** Covered with fuzz. **2.** Of or resembling fuzz. **3.** Not clear; indistinct: *a fuzzy recollection of past events.* **4.** Not coherent; confused: *a fuzzy plan of action.* [Perhaps from Low German *fussig,* spongy. See **pū̆-** in Appendix.] **—fuzz′i·ly** *adv.* **—fuzz′i·ness** *n.*

fuzz·y·head·ed (fŭz′ē-hĕd′ĭd) *adj.* **1.a.** Marked by unclear, confused thinking. **b.** Giddy; silly. **2.** Having a head covered with fuzz. **—fuzz′y·head′ed·ness** *n.*

f.v. *abbr. Latin.* Folio verso (on the back of the page).

FWB *abbr.* Four-wheel brake.

fwd *abbr. Sports.* Forward.

FWD *abbr.* **1.** Four-wheel drive. **2.** Front-wheel drive.

FX *abbr.* Foreign exchange.

FY *abbr.* Fiscal year.

-fy or **-ify** *suff.* Cause to become; make. *basify.* [Middle English *-fien,* from Old French *-fier,* from Latin *-ficāre, -ficārī,* from *-ficus,* -fic.]

FYI *abbr.* For your information.

fyke (fīk) *n.* A long, bag-shaped fishing net held open by hoops. [Dutch *fuik,* from Middle Dutch *fūke.*]

fyl·fot (fĭl′fŏt′) *n.* A swastika. [Originally perhaps a device for the foot of a painted window : FILL + FOOT.]

Fyn (fĭn, fün). An island of south-central Denmark west of Sjaelland. Its chief products are dairy goods and cereals.

FZS or **F.Z.S.** *abbr.* Fellow of the Zoological Society.

Gg

g[1] or **G** (jē) *n., pl.* **g's** or **G's. 1.** The seventh letter of the modern English alphabet. **2.** Any of the speech sounds represented by the letter *g.* **3.** *Music.* **a.** The fifth tone in the scale of C major or the seventh tone in the relative minor scale. **b.** A key or scale in which G is the tonic. **c.** A written or printed note representing this tone. **d.** A string, key, or pipe tuned to the pitch of this tone. **4.** A unit of acceleration equal to the acceleration caused by gravity at the earth's surface, about 9.8 meters (32 feet) per second per second.

g[2] *abbr.* **1.** Acceleration of gravity. **2.** Gram.

G[1] (jē) *n.* A movie rating that allows admission to persons of all ages. —*attributive.* Often used to modify another noun: *a G movie.* [Short for GENERAL.]

G[2] (jē) *n., pl.* **G's.** *Slang.* One thousand dollars. [G(RAND), one thousand dollars.]

G[3] The symbol for **conductance.**

G[4] *abbr.* **1.** *Physics.* Gauss. **2.** Also **G.** Good. **3.** Gravitational constant. **4.** Guanine.

g. *abbr.* **1.** *Grammar.* Gender. **2.** *Grammar.* Genitive. **3.** Also **G.** Gourde. **4.** Also **G.** Guilder. **5.** Also **G.** Guinea. **6.** Also **G.** Gulf.

Ga[1] The symbol for the element **gallium.**

Ga[2] *abbr. Bible.* Galatians.

GA *abbr.* **1.** General agent. **2.** Also **G.A.** General Assembly. **3.** Also **Ga.** Georgia.

ga. *abbr.* Gauge.

G.A. *abbr.* General average.

gab (găb) *Slang. intr.v.* **gabbed, gab·bing, gabs.** To talk idly or incessantly, as about trivial matters. **—gab** *n.* Idle talk; chatter. [Middle English *gabben,* to scoff, speak foolishly, from Old Norse *gabba,* to scoff.] **—gab′ber** *n.*

GABA *abbr.* Gamma-aminobutyric acid.

gab·ar·dine (găb′ər-dēn′, găb′ər-dēn′) *n.* **1.** A sturdy, tightly woven fabric of cotton, wool, or rayon twill. Also called *gaberdine.* **2.** See **gaberdine** (sense 1). **3.** *Chiefly British.* A laborer's long, loose smock; a gaberdine. [Alteration of GABERDINE.]

gab·ble (găb′əl) *v.* **-bled, -bling, -bles.** —*intr.* **1.** To speak rapidly or incoherently; jabber. **2.** To make rapid, low muttering or quacking sounds, as a goose or duck. —*tr.* To utter rapidly or incoherently. **—gabble** *n.* **1.** Rapid, incoherent, or meaningless speech. **2.** The low muttering sound of a goose or duck. [Probably frequentative of GAB.] **—gab′bler** *n.*

gab·bro (găb′rō) *n., pl.* **-bros.** A usually coarse-grained igneous rock composed chiefly of calcic plagioclase and pyroxene. Also called *norite.* [Italian, perhaps from Latin *glaber,* bald, beardless.] **—gab·bro′ic** (gă-brō′ĭk) *adj.*

gab·broid (găb′roid′) *adj.* Resembling gabbro.

gab·by (găb′ē) *adj.* **-bi·er, -bi·est.** *Slang.* Tending to talk excessively; garrulous. **—gab′bi·ness** *n.*

ga·belle (gə-bĕl′) *n.* A tax, especially the salt tax imposed in France before 1790. [Middle English *gabel,* from Old French, from Old Italian *gabella,* from Arabic *qabāla,* tribute, from *qabila,* to receive.]

gab·er·dine (găb′ər-dēn′, găb′ər-dēn′) *n.* **1.** A long, coarse cloak or frock worn especially by Jews during the Middle Ages. Also called *gabardine.* **2.** *Chiefly British.* A loose smock worn by laborers. **3.** See **gabardine** (sense 1). [Obsolete French *gauvardine,* from Old French *galvardine,* perhaps from Middle High German *wallevart,* pilgrimage : *wallen,* to roam; see **wel-**[2] in Appendix + *vart,* journey (from Middle High German, from Old High German, from *faran,* to go; see **per-**[2] in Appendix).]

gab·fest (găb′fĕst′) *n. Slang.* **1.** An informal gathering or session for the exchange of news, opinions, and gossip. **2.** A long, animated conversation or discussion.

ga·bi·on (gā′bē-ən) *n.* **1.** A cylindrical wicker basket filled with earth and stones, formerly used in building fortifications. **2.** A hollow metal cylinder used especially in constructing dams and foundations. [French, from Italian *gabbione,* augmentative of *gabbia,* cage, from Latin *cavea.*]

ga·ble (gā′bəl) *n.* **1. a.** The generally triangular section of wall at the end of a pitched roof, occupying the space between the two slopes of the roof. **b.** The whole end wall of a building or wing having a gable roof. **2.** A triangular, usually ornamental architectural section, as one above an arched door or window. [Middle English *gable, gavel,* from Norman French *gable* (perhaps of Celtic origin) and from Old Norse *gafl;* see **ghebh-el-** in Appendix.] **—ga′bled** *adj.*

Ga·ble (gā′bəl), **(William) Clark.** 1901–1960. American actor who received an Academy Award for his performance in *It Happened One Night* (1934).

gable roof *n.* A pitched roof having a gable at each end.

Ga·bo (gä′bō, -bə), **Naum.** 1890–1977. Russian-born American sculptor and designer known for his sculptural experiments with constructivism.

Ga·bon (gă-bōɴ′). A country of west-central Africa on the Atlantic Ocean. Settled by the French in 1841, it became part of French Equatorial Africa in 1910 and achieved independence in 1960. Libreville is the capital and the largest city. Population, 1,312,000.

Ga·bor (gä′bôr, gə-bôr′), **Dennis.** 1900–1979. Hungarian-born British physicist. He won a 1971 Nobel Prize for his work on holography.

Ga·bo·riau (gä-bô-ryō′), **Émile.** 1832?–1873. French writer who is considered a founder of the detective novel. His works include *Monsieur Lecoq* (1868) and *L'Argent des Autres* (1874).

Ga·bo·rone (gä′bə-rōn′, -rō′nē). The capital of Botswana, in the southeast part of the country near the South African border. It was founded c. 1890. Population, 72,000.

Ga·bri·el (gā′brē-əl) *n. Bible.* An archangel acting as the messenger of God.

ga·by (gā′bē) *n., pl.* **-bies.** *Chiefly British.* A person of deficient intelligence. [Origin unknown.]

gad[1] (găd) *intr.v.* **gad·ded, gad·ding, gads.** To move about restlessly and with little purpose. See Synonyms at **wander.** [Middle English *gadden,* to hurry.] **—gad′der** *n.*

gad[2] (găd) *n.* **1.** A pointed tool, such as a spike or chisel, used for breaking rock or ore. **2.** A goad, as for prodding cattle. **—gad** *tr.v.* **gad·ded, gad·ding, gads.** To break up (ore, for example) with a gad. [Middle English, from Old Norse *gaddr.*]

Gad[1] (găd). In the Old Testament, a son of Jacob and the forebear of one of the tribes of Israel.

Gad[2] (găd) *interj.* Used to express surprise or dismay. [Alteration of GOD.]

gad·a·bout (găd′ə-bout′) *n.* One who roams or roves about, as in search of amusement or social activity.

Gad·da·fi (gə-dä′fē), **Muammar al-.** See Muammar al- **Qaddafi.**

gad·fly (găd′flī′) *n., pl.* **-flies. 1.** A persistent, irritating critic; a nuisance. **2.** One that acts as a provocative stimulus; a goad. **3.** Any of various flies, especially of the family Tabanidae, that bite or annoy livestock and other animals.

gadg·et (găj′ĭt) *n.* A small specialized mechanical or electronic device; a contrivance. [Origin unknown.] **—gadg′et·y** *adv.*

gadg·e·teer (găj′ĭ-tîr′) *n.* A person who designs, builds, or delights in the use of gadgets.

gadg·et·ry (găj′ĭ-trē) *n.* **1.** Gadgets considered as a group. **2.** The design or construction of gadgets.

ga·doid (gā′doid′, găd′oid′) also **ga·did** (gā′dĭd) —*adj.* Of or belonging to the fish family Gadidae, which includes the cods and the hakes. —*n.* A fish of the family Gadidae. [New Latin *Gadus,* fish genus (from Greek *gados,* a kind of fish) + -OID.]

gad·o·lin·ite (găd′l-ə-nīt′) *n.* A dark green or greenish-black silicate mineral, $Be_2FeY_2Si_2O_{10}$, containing several of the rare earths in combination with iron. [After Johan *Gadolin* (1760–1852), Finnish chemist.]

gad·o·lin·i·um (găd′l-ĭn′ē-əm) *n. Symbol* **Gd** A silvery-white, malleable, ductile, metallic rare-earth element obtained from monazite and bastnaesite and used in improving high-temperature characteristics of iron, chromium, and related alloys.

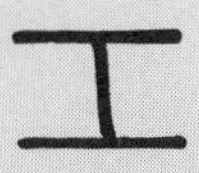

Phoenician

The third letter of the Phoenician alphabet stood for the sound of *g* in *gīmel* or *gaml,* "camel."

Early Greek

Adopting the letter with little change, the Greeks called it *gamma.*

Roman

The Romans at first used their version of this sign for both *g* (writing *Caius* or *C.* for the name *Gaius*) and *k* and only later developed the modified form G for the sound *g.* The modern "soft" value of G results from changes in the pronunciation of *g* before *e, i,* and *y* in Latin, the Romance languages, and Old English.

gable roof

Three of the gables on the House of the Seven Gables, Salem, Massachusetts

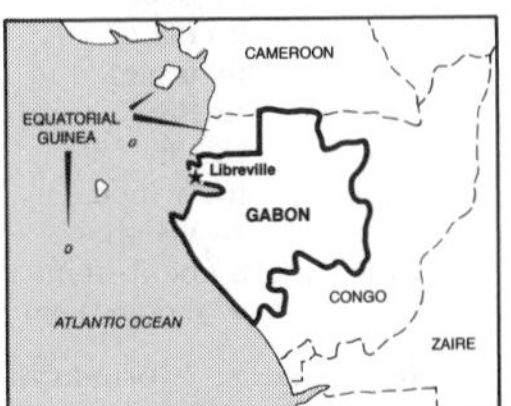

Gabon

gaff[1]

Yuri Gagarin

Thomas Gainsborough
1754 self-portrait

ă pat	oi boy
ā pay	ou out
âr care	ŏŏ took
ä father	ōō boot
ĕ pet	ŭ cut
ē be	ûr urge
ĭ pit	th thin
ī pie	*th* this
îr pier	hw which
ŏ pot	zh vision
ō toe	ə about, item
ô paw	♦ regionalism

Stress marks: ʹ (primary); ʹ (secondary), as in **dictionary** (dĭkʹshə-nĕrʹē)

Atomic number 64; atomic weight 157.25; melting point 1,312°C; boiling point approximately 3,000°C; specific gravity from 7.8 to 7.896; valence 3. See table at **element.** [After Johan *Gadolin* (1760–1852), Finnish chemist.]

ga·droon (gə-dro͞onʹ) *n.* **1.** *Architecture.* A band of convex molding carved with ornamental beading or reeding. **2.** An ornamental band, used especially in silverwork, embellished with fluting, reeding, or another continuous pattern. [French *godron,* from Old French *goderon,* perhaps from *godet,* cup without base or handle, from Middle Dutch *kodde,* log, from Old Provençal *got,* cup, from Latin *guttus,* flask, from *gutta,* drop.] **—ga·drooned**ʹ *adj.* **—ga·droonʹing** *n.*

Gads·den (gădzʹdən). A city of northeast Alabama northeast of Birmingham. It is an industrial center. Population, 47,565.

Gadsden Purchase. An area in extreme southern New Mexico and Arizona south of the Gila River. It was purchased by the United States from Mexico in 1853 to ensure territorial rights for a practicable southern railroad route to the Pacific Coast.

gad·wall (gădʹwôlʹ) *n.* A widely distributed North American duck *(Anas strepera)* having gray or brown plumage. [Origin unknown.]

gad·zooks (găd'zo͞oksʹ) *interj.* Used as a mild or ironic oath: *"Gadzooks! Is there a panic detector, akin to a smoke detector, that sniffs anxiety in the air?"* (George F. Will). [Perhaps alteration for *God's hooks,* the nails of the crucifixion of Christ.]

Gae·a (jēʹə) also **Gai·a** (gāʹə) *n. Greek Mythology.* The goddess of the earth, who bore and married Uranus and became the mother of the Titans and the Cyclopes.

Gael (gāl) *n.* **1.** A Gaelic-speaking Celt of Scotland, Ireland, or the Isle of Man. **2.** A Scottish Highlander. [Scottish Gaelic *Gaidheal* and Irish Gaelic *Gaedheal,* both from Old Irish *Goídil.* See GOIDELIC.]

Gael·ic (gāʹlĭk) *adj.* Of or relating to the Gaels or their culture or languages. **—Gaelic** *n.* **1.** Goidelic. **2.** Any of the Goidelic languages.

gaff[1] (găf) *n.* **1.** A large iron hook attached to a pole or handle and used to land large fish. **2.** *Nautical.* A spar attached to the mast and used to extend the upper edge of a fore-and-aft sail. **3.a.** A sharp metal spur fastened to the leg of a gamecock. **b.** A climbing hook used by telephone and electric line workers. **4.** *Slang.* A trick or gimmick, especially one used in a swindle or to rig a game. **5.** *Slang.* Harshness of treatment; abuse. **—gaff** *tr.v.* **gaffed, gaf·fing, gaffs. 1.** To hook or land (a fish) using a gaff. **2.** To equip (a gamecock) with a gaff. **3.** *Slang.* **a.** To take in or defraud; swindle. **b.** To rig or fix in order to cheat: *knew that the carnival games had been gaffed.* [Middle English *gaffe,* from Old French, from Old Provençal *gaf,* from *gafar,* to seize, of Germanic origin. See **kap-** in Appendix.]

gaff[2] (găf) *n. Chiefly British.* A public place of entertainment, especially a cheap or disreputable music hall or theater. [Origin unknown.]

gaff[3] (găf) *n.* Variant of **gaffe.**

gaffe also **gaff** (găf) *n.* **1.** A clumsy social error; a faux pas: *"The excursion had in his eyes been a monstrous gaffe, a breach of sensibility and good taste"* (Mary McCarthy). **2.** A blatant mistake or misjudgment. [French, from Old French, hook. See GAFF[1].]

gaf·fer (găfʹər) *n.* **1.** An electrician in charge of lighting on a movie or television set. **2.** *Chiefly British.* An old man or a rustic. **3.** *Chiefly British.* A boss or foreman. [Probably alteration (influenced by GRANDFATHER) of GODFATHER.]

gaff rig *n. Nautical.* A rig with a fore-and-aft sail that has its upper edge supported by a gaff.

gaff-top·sail (găfʹtŏpʹsəl, -sālʹ) *n. Nautical.* A light triangular or quadrilateral sail set over a gaff.

gag (găg) *n.* **1.** Something forced into or put over the mouth to prevent speaking or crying out. **2.** An obstacle to or a censoring of free speech. **3.** A device placed in the mouth to keep it open, as in dentistry. **4.a.** A practical joke. **b.** A comic effect or remark. See Synonyms at **joke. 5.** The act or an instance of gagging or choking. **—gag** *v.* **gagged, gag·ging, gags.** *—tr.* **1.** To prevent from speaking or crying out by using a gag. **2.** To stop or restrain from exercising free speech: *censorship laws aimed at gagging the press.* **3.** To cause to choke, retch, or undergo a regurgitative spasm. **4.** To keep (the mouth) open by using a gag. **5.** To block off or obstruct (a pipe or valve, for example). *—intr.* **1.a.** To experience a regurgitative spasm in the throat, as from revulsion to a food or smell or in reflexive response to an introduced object. **b.** To retch or choke. **2.** To make jokes or quips. [From Middle English *gaggen,* to suffocate, perhaps of imitative origin.]

ga·ga (gäʹgäʹ) *adj. Informal.* **1.** Silly; crazy. **2.** Completely absorbed, infatuated, or excited: *They were gaga over the rock group's new album.* **3.** Senile; doddering. [French, old fool, gaga, of imitative origin.]

Ga·ga·rin (gə-gärʹĭn), **Yuri Alekseyevich.** 1934–1968. Soviet cosmonaut. In 1961 he became the first person to travel in space.

gage[1] (gāj) *n.* **1.** Something deposited or given as security against an obligation; a pledge. **2.** Something, such as a glove, that is offered or thrown down as a pledge or challenge to fight. **3.** A challenge. **—gage** *tr.v.* **gaged, gag·ing, gag·es.** *Archaic.* **1.** To pledge as security. **2.** To offer as a stake in a bet; wager. [Middle English, from Old French, of Germanic origin.]

gage[2] (gāj) *n.* Any of several varieties of plum, such as the greengage. [After Sir William *Gage,* 18th-century British botanist.]

gage[3] (gāj) *n. & v.* Variant of **gauge.**

Gage (gāj), **Thomas.** 1721–1787. British general and colonial administrator. As governor of Massachusetts (1774–1775) his attempts to suppress colonial resistance led to the start of the American Revolution.

gag·er (gāʹjər) *n.* Variant of **gauger.**

gag·ger (găgʹər) *n.* One that gags, as a piece of metal used to keep the core in position in a foundry mold.

gag·gle (găgʹəl) *n.* **1.** A flock of geese. See Synonyms at **flock**[1]. **2.** A cluster or group: *"A gaggle of photographers huddled on the sidewalk beside a swelling crowd of onlookers"* (Gioia Diliberto). [Middle English *gagel,* from *gagelen,* to cackle, probably of imitative origin.]

gag law *n.* **1.** *Law.* A law intended to limit freedom of the press, as by instituting censorship or restricting access to information. **2.** See **gag rule.**

gag line *n.* A line, as in a comedy routine or speech, intended to provoke laughter.

gag·man (găgʹmănʹ) *n.* **1.** A man employed to write jokes or comedy routines, as for a professional entertainer or show. **2.** A comedian who uses gags, especially a standup comedian.

gag order *n. Law.* A court order forbidding public reporting or commentary, as by the news media, on a case currently before the court.

gag rule *n.* A rule, as in a legislative body, limiting discussion or debate on an issue. Also called *gag law.*

gag·ster (găgʹstər) *n.* **1.** A gagman, especially a standup comedian. **2.** One who tells or plays jokes; a joker.

Ga·han·na (gə-hănʹə). A city of central Ohio, a suburb of Columbus. Population, 18,001.

gahn·ite (gäʹnītʹ) *n.* A dark green to brown or black mineral, $ZnAl_2O_4$. Also called *zinc spinel.* [After Johan Gottlieb *Gahn* (1745–1818), Swedish mineralogist.]

Gai·a (gāʹə) *n. Greek Mythology.* Variant of **Gaea.**

gai·e·ty also **gay·e·ty** (gāʹĭ-tē) *n., pl.* **-ties. 1.** A state of joyful exuberance or merriment; vivacity. **2.** Merry or joyful activity; festivity: *making preparations for the holiday gaieties.* **3.** Bright color or showiness, as of dress; finery. [French *gaieté,* from Old French, from *gai,* cheerful. See GAY.]

Gail·lard Cut (gĭl-yärdʹ, gāʹlärdʹ). Formerly **Cu·le·bra Cut** (ko͞o-lāʹbrə). An excavation, about 13 km (8 mi) long and 14 m (45 ft) deep, through Culebra Mountain, a hill in the Canal Zone, Panama. The cut forms the southeast section of the Panama Canal.

gail·lar·di·a (gə-lärʹdē-ə) *n.* Any of several New World plants of the genus *Gaillardia* in the composite family, having red or yellow florets grouped into large solitary flower heads. Also called *blanket flower.* [New Latin *Gaillardia,* genus name, after *Gaillard* de Marentonneau, 18th-century French botanist.]

gai·ly also **gay·ly** (gāʹlē) *adv.* **1.** In a joyful, cheerful, or happy manner; merrily. **2.** With bright colors or trimmings; showily: *gaily dressed in ribbons and flounces.*

gain[1] (gān) *v.* **gained, gain·ing, gains.** *—tr.* **1.** To come into possession or use of; acquire: *gained a small fortune in real estate; gained important information about the enemy's plans.* **2.** To attain in competition or struggle; win: *gained a decisive victory; gained control of the company.* **3.** To obtain through effort or merit; achieve: *gain recognition; gain a hearing for the proposal.* **4.** To secure as profit or reward; earn: *gain a living; gain extra credits in school.* **5.a.** To manage to achieve an increase of: *a movement that gained strength; gained wisdom with age.* **b.** To increase by (a specific amount): *gained 15 pounds; the market gained 30 points.* **6.** To come to; reach: *gained the top of the mountain.* See Synonyms at **reach. 7.** To become fast by (a specified amount of time). Used of a timepiece: *My watch gains four minutes a day.* *—intr.* **1.** To increase; grow: *gained in experience and maturity; a painting that gained in value.* **2.** To become better; improve: *gaining in health.* **3.** To obtain a profit or advantage; benefit: *stood to gain politically by his opponent's blunder.* **4.a.** To close a gap; get closer: *The runners in the back were steadily gaining on the leader.* **b.** To increase a lead. **5.** To put on weight: *I began to gain when I went off my diet.* **6.** To operate or run fast. Used of a timepiece. **—gain** *n.* **1.a.** Something gained or acquired: *territorial gains.* **b.** Progress; advancement: *The country made social and political gains under the new government.* **2.** The act of acquiring; attainment. **3.** An increase in amount or degree: *a gain in operating income.* **4.** *Electronics.* An increase in signal power, voltage, or current by an amplifier, expressed as the ratio of output to input. Also called *amplification.* ***—idiom.*** **gain time. 1.** To run too fast. Used of a timepiece. **2.** To delay or prolong something until a desired event occurs. [From Middle English *gayne,* booty (from Old French *gaigne, gain,* gain, from *gaaignier,* to gain, of Germanic origin) and Middle English *gein,* advantage (from Old Norse *gegn,* ready, and from Old French *gain,* gain).]

gain[2] (gān) *n.* A notch or mortise cut into a board to receive another part. **—gain** *tr.v.* **gained, gain·ing, gains. 1.** To cut out a gain in. **2.** To join by or fit into a gain. [Origin unknown.]

gain·er (gāʹnər) *n.* **1.** One that gains: *a gainer of weight.* **2.**

Sports. A dive in which the diver leaves the board facing forward, does a back somersault, and enters the water feet first.

Gaines (gānz), **Edmund Pendleton.** 1777–1849. American general who defended Fort Erie in the War of 1812.

Gaines•ville (gānz′vĭl′, -vəl). A city of north-central Florida southwest of Jacksonville. The University of Florida (founded 1853) is important to its economy. Population, 81,371.

gain•ful (gān′fəl) *adj.* Providing a gain; profitable: *gainful employment.* **—gain′ful•ly** *adv.* **—gain′ful•ness** *n.*

gain•say (gān-sā′, gān′sā′) *tr.v.* **-said** (-săd′, -sĕd′), **-say•ing, -says** (-sāz′, -sĕz′). **1.** To declare false; deny. See Synonyms at **deny. 2.** To oppose, especially by contradiction. [Middle English *gainsayen* : *gain-*, against (from Old English *gegn-*) + *sayen,* to say (from Old English *secgan;* see SAY).]

Gains•bor•ough (gānz′bûr′ō, -bər-ə), **Thomas.** 1727–1788. British portrait and landscape painter. His masterpieces include *The Blue Boy* and *The Harvest Wagon* (both c. 1770).

'gainst also **gainst** (gĕnst, gānst) *prep.* Against.

Gai•ser•ic (gī′zə-rĭk′). See **Genseric.**

gait (gāt) *n.* **1.** A particular way or manner of moving on foot: *a person who ran with a clumsy, hobbling gait.* **2.** Any of the ways, such as a canter, trot, or walk, by which a horse can move by lifting the feet in different order or rhythm. **3.** Rate or manner of proceeding: *The project went forward at a steady gait.* **—gait** *tr.v.* **gait•ed, gait•ing, gaits.** To train (a horse) in a particular gait or gaits. [Middle English *gate,* path, gait, from Old Norse *gata,* path. See **ghē-** in Appendix.]

gait•ed (gā′tĭd) *adj.* Having a specified gait. Often used in combination: *smooth-gaited; slow-gaited.*

gai•ter (gā′tər) *n.* **1.a.** A heavy cloth or leather covering for the legs extending from the instep to the ankle or knee. **b.** A similar covering of lightweight, moisture-resistant fabric, used by skiers in conditions of deep snow. **2.** An ankle-high shoe with elastic sides. **3.** An overshoe with a cloth top. [French *guêtre,* from Old French *guietre,* of Germanic origin. See **wer-**[2] in Appendix.]

Gai•thers•burg (gā′*th*ərz-bûrg′). A city of western Maryland north-northwest of Washington, D.C. It is a residential city with light industries. Population, 26,424.

Ga•ius (gā′əs, gī′-) also **Ca•ius** (kā′-, kī′-). fl. A.D. 130–180. Roman jurist whose chief work, the *Institutes,* is a major source of information on Roman law.

Gaj•du•sek (gī′də-shĕk′), **D(aniel) Carleton.** Born 1923. American virologist. He shared a 1976 Nobel Prize for research on the origin and spread of infectious diseases.

gal (găl) *n. Informal.* A girl. [Alteration of GIRL.]

gal. *abbr.* Gallon.

Gal. *abbr. Bible.* Galatians.

ga•la (gā′lə, găl′ə, gä′lə) *n.* **1.** A festive occasion, especially a lavish social event or entertainment. **2.** *Chiefly British.* An athletic competition, especially a swimming contest. **—gala** *adj.* **1.** Marked by lavish or festive celebration: *a gala ball after the inaugural ceremony.* **2.** Characterized by sumptuous social pleasure: *the gala life of the very rich.* [Italian and French, both ultimately from Old French *gale,* rejoicing, from *galer,* to make merry. See GALLANT.]

ga•la•bi•a (jə-lä′bē-ə) *n.* Variant of **djellaba.**

galact– *pref.* Variant of **galacto–.**

ga•lac•tic (gə-lăk′tĭk) *adj.* **1.** Of or relating to a galaxy, especially the Milky Way. **2.** Of enormous size; immense.

galactic equator *n.* The great circle of the celestial sphere that lies in the plane bisecting the band of the Milky Way, inclined at an angle of approximately 62° to the celestial equator. Also called *galactic circle.*

galactic noise *n.* Radio-frequency radiation originating outside the solar system.

galacto– or **galact–** *pref.* Milk: *galactose.* [From Greek *galakto-,* from *gala, galakt-,* milk. See **melg-** in Appendix.]

ga•lac•to•poi•e•sis (gə-lăk′tə-poi-ē′sĭs) *n.* Secretion and continued production of milk by the mammary glands. **—ga•lac′to•poi•et′ic** (-ĕt′ĭk) *adj.*

ga•lac•tor•rhe•a (gə-lăk′tə-rē′ə) *n.* **1.** Excessive flow of milk from the breasts during lactation. **2.** Spontaneous milk flow not associated with childbirth or the nursing of an infant.

gal•ac•tos•am•ine (găl′ək-tō′sə-mēn′, gə-lăk-) *n.* An amino-acid derivative of galactose.

ga•lac•tose (gə-lăk′tōs′) *n.* A monosaccharide, CH_2OH-$(CHOH)_4CHO$, commonly occurring in lactose and in certain pectins, gums, and mucilages.

ga•lac•to•se•mi•a (gə-lăk′tə-sē′mē-ə) *n.* An inherited metabolic disorder characterized by the deficiency of an enzyme that is necessary for the metabolism of galactose. The disorder results in elevated levels of galactose in the blood and, if untreated, can lead to mental retardation and eye and liver abnormalities. **—ga•lac′to•se′mic** *adj.*

ga•lac•to•si•dase (gə-lăk′tō-sĭ-dās′, -dāz′, -lăk-tō′-) *n.* An enzyme that catalyzes the hydrolysis of a galactoside.

ga•lac•to•side (gə-lăk′tə-sīd′) *n.* Any of a group of glycosides that yield galactose on hydrolysis.

ga•la•go (gə-lā′gō, -lä′-) *n., pl.* **-gos.** See **bush baby.** [New Latin *Galago,* genus name, perhaps from Wolof *golo,* monkey.]

ga•lah (gə-lä′) *n.* **1.** An Australian cockatoo *(Cacatua roseicapilla)* having pale blue-gray plumage and a pink breast. **2.** *Australian.* A fool; an idiot. [Yuwaalaraay (Aboriginal language of southeast Australia) *gilaa.*]

Gal•a•had (găl′ə-hăd′) *n.* **1.** In Arthurian legend, the purest of the Knights of the Round Table who alone succeeded in the quest for the Holy Grail. **2.** One considered to be noble, pure, or chivalrous.

ga•lan•gal (gə-lăng′gəl) *n.* **1.** A plant *(Alpinia officinarum)* of eastern Asia, having pungent, aromatic roots used medicinally and as seasoning. **2.** The dried roots of this plant. [Variant of GALINGALE.]

gal•an•tine (găl′ən-tēn′) *n.* A dish of boned, stuffed meat or fish that is poached and served cold coated with aspic. [Middle English *galauntine,* a kind of sauce, from Old French *galatine, galentine,* aspic, fish sauce, diminutive of Medieval Latin *gelāta,* jelly, from feminine past participle of Latin *gelāre,* to freeze, coagulate. See GELATIN.]

ga•lan•ty show (gə-lăn′tē) *n.* A shadow play performed by casting the shadows of miniature figures on a screen or wall. [Perhaps from Italian *galanti,* pl. of *galante,* a gallant, from Old French *galant.* See GALLANT.]

Ga•lá•pa•gos Islands (gə-lä′pə-gəs, -lăp′ə-). A group of volcanic islands in the Pacific Ocean west of the mainland of Ecuador. The islands are famous for their rare species of fauna, including the giant tortoises for which they are named.

gal•a•te•a (găl′ə-tē′ə) *n.* A durable, often striped cotton fabric used in making clothing. [After the *Galatea,* a 19th-century English warship (from the fabric's use for children's sailor suits).]

Gal•a•te•a (găl′ə-tē′ə) *n. Greek Mythology.* A maiden who was originally a statue carved by Pygmalion and who was brought to life by Aphrodite in answer to the sculptor's pleas.

Ga•la•ţi (gä-läts′, -lät′sē) or **Ga•latz** (gä′läts′). A city of eastern Romania on the lower Danube River northeast of Bucharest. It is a major inland port. Population, 285,077.

Ga•la•tia (gə-lā′shə, -shē-ə). An ancient country of central Asia Minor in the region surrounding modern Ankara, Turkey. Settled by Gauls in the third century B.C., it became a Roman province in 25 B.C. **—Ga•la′tian** *adj. & n.*

Ga•la•tians (gə-lā′shənz) *pl.n.* *(used with a sing. verb). Abbr.* **Gal., Ga** *Bible.* See table at **Bible.**

Ga•latz (gä′läts′). See **Galaţi.**

gal•a•vant (găl′ə-vănt′) *v.* Variant of **gallivant.**

ga•lax (gā′lăks′) *n.* A stemless, evergreen, perennial plant *(Galax urceolata)* of the eastern United States, having a rosette of glossy, heart-shaped leaves and small, white flowers in spikelike clusters. Also called *beetleweed, coltsfoot, wandflower.* [New Latin *Galax,* genus name, from Greek *gala,* milk. See GALAXY.]

gal•ax•y (găl′ək-sē) *n., pl.* **-ies. 1.a.** Any of numerous large-scale aggregates of stars, gas, and dust that constitute the universe, containing an average of 100 billion (10^{11}) solar masses and ranging in diameter from 1,500 to 300,000 light-years. Also called *nebula.* **b.** Often **Galaxy.** The Milky Way. **2.** An assembly of brilliant, glamorous, or distinguished persons or things: *a galaxy of theatrical performers.* [Middle English *galaxie,* the Milky Way, from Late Latin *galaxias,* from Greek, milky, from *gala, galakt-,* milk. See **melg-** in Appendix.]

Gal•ba (găl′bə, gôl′-), **Servius Sulpicius.** 3 B.C.–A.D. 69. Emperor of Rome (68–69) who was assassinated after naming an unpopular successor.

gal•ba•num (găl′bə-nəm, gôl′-) *n.* A bitter, aromatic gum resin extracted from an Asiatic plant *(Ferula galbaniflua)* or any of several related plants and used in incense and medicinally as a counterirritant. [Middle English, from Latin, from Greek *khalbanē,* from Hebrew *ḥelbĕnâ.*]

Gal•braith (găl′brāth′), **John Kenneth.** Born 1908. Canadian-born American economist, writer, and diplomat who served as U.S. ambassador to India (1961–1963).

gale[1] (gāl) *n.* **1.** A very strong wind. **2.** *Meteorology.* **a.** Any of four winds with speeds of from 32 to 63 miles (51 to 102 kilometers) per hour, according to the Beaufort scale. **b.** A fresh gale. **3.** A forceful outburst: *gales of laughter.* **4.** *Archaic.* A breeze. [Origin unknown.]

gale[2] (gāl) *n.* The sweet gale. [Middle English *gail,* from Old English *gagel.*]

ga•le•a (gā′lē-ə) *n., pl.* **-le•ae** (-lē-ē′). A helmet-shaped part, such as the upper petal of certain plants or part of the maxilla of an insect. [Latin, helmet.]

ga•le•ate (gā′lē-āt′) also **ga•le•at•ed** (-ā′tĭd) *adj.* **1.** *Biology.* Having a galea. **2.** Helmet-shaped. [Latin *galeātus,* past participle of *galeāre,* to cover with a helmet, from *galea,* helmet.]

Ga•len (gā′lən). A.D. 130?–200? Greek anatomist, physician, and writer. His theories formed the basis of European medicine until the Renaissance.

ga•le•na (gə-lē′nə) *n.* A gray mineral, essentially PbS, the principal ore of lead. [Latin *galēna,* lead ore.]

ga•len•i•cal (gā-lĕn′ĭ-kəl, gə-) *n.* A medicinal preparation composed mainly of herbal or vegetable matter. **—galenical** *adj.* Of, relating to, or being a drug or agent made up chiefly of herbal or vegetable matter. [After GALEN.]

Ga•len•ism (gā′lə-nĭz′əm) *n.* The medical system based on the theories or practices of Galen. **—Ga′len•ist** *adj. & n.*

gaiter
A pair of gaiters

galaxy
Top: Andromeda galaxy
Bottom: Whirlpool galaxy

John Kenneth Galbraith

Gales·burg (gālz′bûrg′). A city of northwest-central Illinois west-northwest of Peoria. The poet Carl Sandburg was born here in 1878. Population, 35,305.

gal Friday *n. Informal.* A girl Friday.

Ga·li·bi (gə-lē′bē) *n., pl.* **Galibi** or **-bis. 1.** A member of the Carib people of French Guiana. **2.** The language of the Galibi. [Carib, strong man, Galibi. See CANNIBAL.]

Galileo

Ga·li·cia (gə-lĭsh′ə, -ē-ə). **1.** A historical region of central Europe in southeast Poland and western Ukraine. An independent principality after 1087, it was conquered by the Russians in the 12th century and later passed to Poland and Austria. The territory was returned to Poland after World War I, and the eastern portion was ceded to the U.S.S.R. after World War II. **2.** A region and ancient kingdom of northwest Spain on the Atlantic Ocean south of the Bay of Biscay. Exploited by the Romans for its mineral resources, it later became a Goth kingdom and a stronghold of the Moors.

Ga·li·cian¹ (gə-lĭsh′ən) *adj.* Of or relating to Polish Galicia or its people, language, or culture. **—Galician** *n.* A native or inhabitant of Polish Galicia.

Ga·li·cian² (gə-lĭsh′ən) *adj.* Of or relating to Spanish Galicia or its people, language, or culture. **—Galician** *n.* **1.** A native or inhabitant of Spanish Galicia. **2.** The Portuguese dialect spoken in Spanish Galicia.

Gal·i·le·an also **Gal·i·lae·an** (găl′ə-lē′ən) *—n.* **1.** A native or inhabitant of Galilee. **2.** A Christian. **3.** Jesus. *—adj.* Of or relating to Galilee or its people.

gal·i·lee (găl′ə-lē′) *n.* A small chapel or porch at the western end of a medieval English church. [Middle English *galile,* from Old North French *galilee,* from Medieval Latin *galilaea,* from Latin *Galilea,* Galilee.]

Gal·i·lee (găl′ə-lē′). A region of northern Israel. The northernmost part of Palestine and the ancient kingdom of Israel, Galilee was the center of Jesus's ministry.

Galilee, Sea of. Formerly **Lake Ti·be·ri·as** (tī-bîr′ē-əs). A freshwater lake of northeast Israel. About 214 m (700 ft) below sea level, it is fed and drained by the Jordan River.

Ga·li·le·o Ga·li·lei (găl′ə-lē′ō găl′ə-lā′, -lā′ō). 1564–1642. Italian astronomer and physicist. The first to use a telescope to study the stars (1610), he was an outspoken advocate of Copernicus's theory that the sun forms the center of the universe, which led to his persecution and imprisonment by the Inquisition (1633). **—Gal′i·le′an** *adj.*

gal·i·ma·ti·as (găl′ə-mā′shē-əs, -măt′ē-əs) *n.* Nonsense; gibberish. [French.]

gal·in·gale (găl′ĭn-gāl′) *n.* Any of various sedges of the genus *Cyperus,* especially *C. longus* of Europe, having rough-edged leaves, reddish spikelets, and aromatic roots. [Middle English, a kind of root, from Old French *galingal,* from Arabic *ḫulunjān,* from Chinese (Mandarin) *Gāo liáng jiāng,* a kind of ginger : *Gāo liáng,* an area in Guangdong province + *jiāng,* ginger.]

gal·i·ot also **gal·li·ot** (găl′ē-ət) *n. Nautical.* **1.** A light, swift galley formerly used in the Mediterranean. **2.** A light, single-masted, flat-bottomed Dutch merchant ship. [Middle English, from Old French, from *galee, galie.* See GALLEY.]

gal·i·pot (găl′ə-pŏt′, -pō′) *n.* Crude turpentine obtained from the cluster pine tree *(Pinus pinaster)* of southern Europe. [French.]

gall¹ (gôl) *n.* **1.** See **bile** (sense 1). **2.a.** Bitterness of feeling; rancor. **b.** Something bitter to endure: *the gall of defeat.* **3.** Outrageous insolence; effrontery. See Synonyms at **temerity.** [Middle English, from Old English *gealla, galla.* See **ghel-²** in Appendix.]

gall² (gôl) *n.* **1.** A skin sore caused by friction and abrasion: *a saddle gall.* **2.a.** Exasperation; vexation. **b.** The cause of such vexation. **—gall** *v.* **galled, gall·ing, galls.** *—tr.* **1.** To make (the skin) sore by abrasion; chafe. **2.** To damage or break the surface of by or as if by friction; abrade: *the bark of saplings galled by improper staking.* See Synonyms at **chafe. 3.** To irk or exasperate; vex: *It galled me to have to wait outside.* *—intr.* To become irritated, chafed, or sore. [Middle English *galle,* from Old English *gealla,* possibly from Latin *galla,* gallnut.]

gall³ (gôl) *n.* An abnormal swelling of plant tissue caused by insects, microorganisms, or external injury. [Middle English *galle,* from Old French, from Latin *galla,* gallnut.]

Gal·la (găl′ə) *n., pl.* **Galla** or **-las.** See **Oromo.** [Perhaps from Arabic *ġalīẓ,* rough.] **—Gal′la** *adj.*

gal·lant (găl′ənt) *adj.* **1.** Smartly or boldly stylish; dashing: *a gallant feathered hat; cut a gallant figure at the coronation.* **2.a.** Unflinching in battle or action; valiant: *put up a gallant resistance to the attackers.* **b.** Nobly or selflessly resolute: *made a gallant attempt to save his friend's reputation.* **3.** Stately; majestic. **4.** (gə-lănt′, -länt′). **a.** Courteously attentive especially to women; chivalrous. **b.** Flirtatious; amorous. **—gallant** (gə-lănt′, -länt′, găl′ənt) *n.* **1.** A fashionable young man. **2.a.** A man courteously attentive to women. **b.** A woman's lover; a paramour. **—gallant** (gə-lănt′, -länt′) *v.* **-lant·ed, -lant·ing, -lants.** *—tr.* To woo or pay court to (a lady). *—intr.* To play the gallant. [Middle English *galaunt,* from Old French *galant,* present participle of *galer,* to rejoice, of Germanic origin. See **wel-¹** in Appendix.] **—gal′lant·ly** *adv.*

gal·lant·ry (găl′ən-trē) *n., pl.* **-ries. 1.** Nobility of spirit or action; courage. **2.** Chivalrous attention toward women; courtliness: *"the air of faintly mocking gallantry with which he habitually treated mother"* (Louis Auchincloss). **3.** The act or an instance of gallant speech or behavior. **4.** *Archaic.* A bold or stylish appearance.

Gal·la·tin (găl′ĭ-tn). A city of northern Tennessee northeast of Nashville. It is a trade and market center. Population, 17,191.

Gal·la·tin (găl′ə-tĭn), **(Abraham Alfonse) Albert.** 1761–1849. Swiss-born American financier and politician who served as U.S. representative from New York (1795–1801), secretary of the treasury (1801–1814), and minister to France (1816–1823) and Great Britain (1826–1827).

Gal·lau·det (găl′ə-dĕt′), **Thomas Hopkins.** 1787–1851. American educator who established the first free American school for the hearing-impaired (1817).

gall·blad·der also **gall bladder** (gôl′blăd′ər) *n.* A small, pear-shaped muscular sac, located under the right lobe of the liver, in which bile secreted by the liver is stored until needed by the body for digestion.

Galle (gäl, găl). A city of southern Sri Lanka on the Indian Ocean. It was a trade center for the Chinese and Arabs by 100 B.C. and later flourished as a Portuguese and Dutch port. Population, 77,183.

gal·le·ass (găl′ē-ăs′, -əs) *n. Nautical.* A large, fast, heavily armed three-masted Mediterranean galley of the 16th and 17th centuries. [French *galeasse,* from Old French, from Old Italian *galeaza,* augmentative of *galea,* galley, from Old Provençal or Catalan. See GALLEY.]

gal·lein (găl′ē-ĭn, găl′ēn′) *n.* A brown or metallic green dye, $C_{20}H_{12}O_7$, used as a pH indicator and in dyeing textiles. [GALL(IC ACID) + (PHTHAL)EIN.]

gal·le·on (găl′ē-ən, găl′yən) *n. Nautical.* A large three-masted sailing ship with a square rig and usually two or more decks, used from the 15th to 17th century especially by Spain as a merchant ship or warship. [Spanish *galeon,* from Old Spanish, augmentative of *galea,* galley, from Old French *galie.* See GALLEY.]

gal·le·ri·a (găl′ə-rē′ə) *n.* A roofed passageway or indoor court usually containing a variety of shops or businesses. [Italian, from Old Italian. See GALLERY.]

♦**gal·ler·y** (găl′ə-rē) *n., pl.* **-ies. 1.** A roofed promenade, especially one extending along the wall of a building and supported by arches or columns on the outer side. **2.** A long enclosed passage, such as a hallway or corridor. **3.a.** A narrow balcony, usually having a railing or balustrade, along the outside of a building. **b.** A projecting or recessed passageway along an upper story on the interior or exterior of a large building, especially a church, generally marked by a colonnade or an arcade. **4.** *Lower Southern U.S.* See **veranda. 5.a.** An upper section, often with a sloping floor, projecting from the rear or side walls of a theater or an auditorium to provide additional seating. **b.** The seats in such a section, usually cheaper than those on the main floor. **c.** The cheapest seats in a theater, generally those of the uppermost gallery. **d.** The audience occupying a gallery or cheap section of a theater. **6.** A large audience or group of spectators, as at a tennis or golf match. **7.** The general public, usually considered as exemplifying a lack of discrimination or sophistication: *accused the administration of playing to the gallery on the defense issue.* **8.a.** A building, an institution, or a room for the exhibition of artistic work. **b.** An establishment that displays and sells works of art. **c.** A photographer's studio. **9.** A collection; an assortment: *The trial featured a gallery of famous and flamboyant witnesses.* **10.a.** An underground tunnel or passageway, as in a cave or one dug for military or mining purposes. **b.** A passage made by a tunneling insect or animal. **11.** *Nautical.* A platform or balcony at the stern or quarters of some early sailing ships. **12.** A decorative upright trimming or molding along the edge of a table top, tray, or shelf. [Middle English *galerie,* from Old French, from Old North French *galilee,* galilee. See GALILEE.] **—gal′ler·ied** *adj.*

♦***REGIONAL NOTE:*** In Texas, Arkansas, Louisiana, Mississippi, and southern Alabama, an open roofed porch that runs along at least one side of a house is called a *gallery: "Out on the small front gallery she had hung Bobinôt's Sunday clothes to air"* (Kate Chopin). Craig M. Carver, the author of *American Regional Dialects,* points out that the word *gallery,* from Old French *galerie,* was borrowed into British English in the 15th century and was brought over to the American colonies by English-speaking settlers. Although the word in the sense "porch" did not survive in the American English of the East Coast, it was borrowed separately, probably from Acadian French, into the English of 18th-century Louisiana and there survived as part of the Gulf Southern dialect.

gal·ley (găl′ē) *n., pl.* **-leys. 1.** *Nautical.* **a.** A large, usually single-decked medieval ship of shallow draft, propelled by sails and oars and used as a merchant ship or warship in the Mediterranean. **b.** An ancient Mediterranean seagoing vessel propelled by oars. **c.** A large rowboat formerly used by British customs officers. **2.** The kitchen of an airliner or a ship. **3.** *Printing.* **a.** A long tray, usually of metal, used for holding composed type. **b.** Galley proof. [Middle English *galei,* from Old French *galie,* from Old Provençal or Catalan *galea,* from Medieval Greek, probably variant of Greek *galeos,* shark, perhaps from *galeē,* weasel.]

galley proof *n. Printing.* A proof taken from composed type before page composition to allow for the detection and correction of errors.

galley slave *n.* **1.** A slave or convict forced to ply an oar of a galley. **2.** A person assigned to perform tedious or menial tasks; a drudge.

gall·fly (gôl′flī′) *n.* Any of various small insects, such as the gall midge or gall wasp, that deposit their eggs on plant stems or in the bark of trees, causing the formation of galls in which their larvae grow.

Gal·li·a (găl′ē-ä). See **Gaul**[2].

gal·liard (găl′yərd) *n.* **1.** A spirited dance popular in France in the 16th and 17th centuries. **2.** The triple-time music for this dance. **—galliard** *adj. Archaic.* Spirited; lively; gay. [Middle English *gaillard,* from Old French *gaillart,* probably of Celtic origin.]

Gal·lic (găl′ĭk) *adj.* Of or relating to Gaul or France; French. [Latin *Gallicus,* from *Gallus,* a Gaul.]

gal·lic acid (găl′ĭk, gô′lĭk) *n.* A colorless crystalline compound, $C_7H_6O_5$, derived from tannin and used as a tanning agent, as an ink dye, and in photography and the manufacture of paper. [French *acide gallique,* from *galle,* plant gall. See GALL[3].]

Gal·li·can (găl′ĭ-kən) *adj.* **1.** Relating to or characteristic of Gallicanism. **2.** Gallic. **—Gallican** *n.* A supporter of Gallicanism.

Gal·li·can·ism (găl′ĭ-kə-nĭz′əm) *n.* A movement originating among the French Roman Catholic clergy that favored the restriction of papal control and the achievement by each nation of individual administrative autonomy.

Gal·li·cism (găl′ĭ-sĭz′əm) *n.* **1.** A French phrase or idiom appearing in another language. **2.** A characteristic French trait.

Gal·li·cize (găl′ĭ-sīz′) *tr. & intr.v.* **-cized, -ciz·ing, -ciz·es.** To make or become French, as in form, character, or custom. **—Gal′li·ci·za′tion** (-sĭ-zā′shən) *n.*

gal·li·gas·kins (găl′ĭ-găs′kĭnz) *pl.n.* **1.** Loosely fitting hose or breeches worn in the 16th and 17th centuries. **2.** Loose trousers. **3.** *Chiefly British.* Leggings. [Perhaps alteration (influenced by GALLEY, and GASCON) of French *garguesques,* variant of *greguesques,* from Spanish *gregüescos,* from *griego,* Greek, from Latin *Graecus.* See GREEK.]

gal·li·mau·fry (găl′ə-mô′frē) *n., pl.* **-fries.** A jumble; a hodgepodge. [French *galimafrée,* from Old French *galimafree,* sauce, ragout : probably *galer,* to make merry; see GALLANT + *mafrer,* to gorge oneself (from Middle Dutch *moffelen,* to open one's mouth wide, of imitative origin).]

gal·li·na·ceous (găl′ə-nā′shəs) *adj.* **1.** Of, belonging to, or characteristic of the order Galliformes, which includes the common domestic fowl as well as the pheasants, turkeys, and grouse. **2.** Relating to or resembling the domestic fowl. [From Latin *gallīnāceus,* of poultry, from *gallīna,* hen, feminine of *gallus,* cock. See **gal-** in Appendix.] **—gal′li·na′cean** *n.*

Gal·li·nas (gä-yē′näs), **Point.** A cape of northern Colombia, the northernmost point of South America.

gall·ing (gô′lĭng) *adj.* Causing extreme irritation or chagrin; vexing: *a galling delay; a galling setback to their plans.* **—gall′ing·ly** *adv.*

gal·li·nip·per (găl′ə-nĭp′ər) *n.* A large mosquito or other insect capable of inflicting a painful bite. [Origin unknown.]

gal·li·nule (găl′ə-no͞ol′, -nyo͞ol′) *n.* Any of various wading and swimming birds of the family Rallidae, frequenting swampy regions and characteristically having dark, iridescent plumage and a red bill tipped with yellow. [Latin *gallīnula,* pullet, diminutive of *gallīna,* hen. See GALLINACEOUS.]

gal·li·ot (găl′ē-ət) *n. Nautical.* Variant of **galiot.**

gal·li·pot (găl′ə-pŏt′) *n.* A small glazed earthenware jar formerly used by druggists for medicaments. [Middle English *galy pott* : probably *galei,* galley; see GALLEY + *pott,* pot; see POT[1].]

gal·li·um (găl′ē-əm) *n. Symbol* **Ga** A rare metallic element that is liquid near room temperature, expands on solidifying, and is found as a trace element in coal, bauxite, and other minerals. It is used in semiconductor technology and as a component of various low-melting alloys. Atomic number 31; atomic weight 69.72; melting point 29.78°C; boiling point 2,403°C; specific gravity 5.907; valence 2, 3. See table at **element.** [From Latin *gallus,* cock, translation of surname of Paul Émile *Lecoq* de Boisbaudran (1838–1912), French chemist : *le,* the + *coq,* rooster.]

gallium arsenide *n.* A dark-gray crystalline compound, GaAs, used in transistors, solar cells, and semiconducting lasers.

gal·li·vant also **gal·a·vant** (găl′ə-vănt′) *intr.v.* **-vant·ed, -vant·ing, -vants. 1.** To roam about in search of pleasure or amusement. See Synonyms at **wander. 2.** To play around amorously; flirt. [Perhaps alteration of GALLANT.]

WORD HISTORY: Ladies' men and gambling are no strangers, as the history of the word *gallivant* may attest. *Gallivant,* which is first recorded in English in 1819, is thought possibly to be an alteration of the word *gallant,* "to play the gallant or dandy, flirt," under the influence of the word *levant,* "to leave quickly and secretly, especially as a gambler might do to avoid payment of debts." The word *levant* may hark back to the notion of the Levant, the countries of the Near East, as a far-off place where someone might go to hide. In French the phrase *faire voile en Levant,* which means literally "to sail into the Levant," actually means "to be stolen." When a person gallivanted, the person was at one time playing the gallant, perhaps with the intention of stealing away with a heart or two. One can still gallivant with others or simply gallivant on one's own.

gal·li·wasp (găl′ə-wŏsp′, -wôsp′) *n.* Any of several long-bodied lizards of the genus *Diploglossus,* native to marshy regions of Central America and the West Indies. [Origin unknown.]

gall midge *n.* Any of various small, mosquitolike flies of the family Cecidomyiidae, having larvae that cause the formation of galls in plants.

gall mite *n.* Any of various mites of the family Eriophyidae that produce galls on plants.

gall·nut (gôl′nŭt′) *n.* See **nutgall.**

gal·lo·glass or **gal·low·glass** (găl′ō-glăs′) *n.* An armed retainer or mercenary in the service of an Irish chieftain. [Irish Gaelic *galloglach* : *gall,* foreigner + *oglach,* soldier (from *ōg,* from Old Irish *ōac;* see **yeu-** in Appendix).]

Gal·lo·ma·ni·a (găl′ō-mā′nē-ə, -mān′yə) *n.* A strong predilection for anything French. [French *gallomanie* : *gallo-,* France (from Latin *Gallus,* a Gaul) + *-manie,* mania (from Late Latin *mania;* see MANIA).]

gal·lon (găl′ən) *n. Abbr.* **gal. 1.a.** A unit of volume in the U.S. Customary System, used in liquid measure, equal to 4 quarts (3.785 liters). **b.** A unit of volume in the British Imperial System, used in liquid and dry measure, equal to 4 quarts (4.546 liters). See table at **measurement. 2.** A container with a capacity of one gallon. [Middle English, a liquid measure, from Old North French *galon.*]

gal·lon·age (găl′ə-nĭj) *n.* An amount measured in gallons.

gal·loon (gə-lo͞on′) *n.* A narrow braid or braid used as trimming and commonly made of lace, metallic thread, or embroidery. [French *galon,* from Old French *galonner,* to decorate the hair with ribbons.] **—gal·looned′** *adj.*

gal·loot (gə-lo͞ot′) *n. Slang.* Variant of **galoot.**

gal·lop (găl′əp) *n.* **1.a.** A natural three-beat gait of a horse, faster than a canter, in which all four feet are off the ground at the same time during each stride. **b.** A fast running motion of other quadrupeds. **2.** A ride taken at a gallop. **3.** A rapid pace: *Events were proceeding at a gallop.* **—gallop** *v.* **-loped, -lop·ing, -lops.** *—tr.* **1.** To cause to gallop. **2.** To transport at or as if at a gallop: *gallop the mail to the next station.* *—intr.* **1.** To ride a horse at a gallop. **2.** To move or progress swiftly: *Summer was galloping by.* [From Middle English *galopen,* to go at a gallop, from Old French *galoper,* of Germanic origin. See **wel-**[1] in Appendix.] **—gal′lop·er** *n.*

gal·lo·pade (găl′ə-pād′, -päd′) *n.* Variant of **galop.**

gal·lop·ing (găl′ə-pĭng) *adj.* **1.** Of or resembling a gallop, especially in rhythm or rapidity. **2.** Developing at an accelerated rate and leading to death. Used of certain diseases.

Gal·lo·way (găl′ə-wā′). A region of southwest Scotland. The **Mull of Galloway,** a promontory on a peninsula on its southwest coast, is the southernmost point in Scotland.

gal·low·glass (găl′ō-glăs′) *n.* Variant of **galloglass.**

gal·lows (găl′ōz) *n., pl.* **gallows** or **-lows·es. 1.a.** A device usually consisting of two upright posts supporting a crossbeam from which a noose is suspended and used for execution by hanging; a gallows tree. **b.** A similar structure used for supporting or suspending. **2.** Execution by hanging: *a crime punishable by the gallows.* [Middle English *galwes,* pl. of *galwe,* gallows, from Old English *gealga, galga.*]

gallows bird *n. Informal.* One who is destined or deserves to be hanged.

gallows humor *n.* Humorous treatment of a grave or dire situation: *"conveying with gallows humor the utter insanity of the nuclear-arms race"* (New York).

gallows tree *n.* A device used for hanging a person until dead; a gallows.

gall·stone (gôl′stōn′) *n.* A small, hard, pathological concretion, composed chiefly of cholesterol, calcium salts, and bile pigments, formed in the gallbladder or in a bile duct.

Gal·lup (găl′əp). A city of northwest New Mexico near the Arizona border west-northwest of Albuquerque. It is a trade center in a ranching and mining area. Population, 18,167.

Gallup, George Horace. 1901–1984. American public-opinion analyst. Through his techniques of polling the public, he accurately predicted the outcome of the 1936 presidential election.

gal·lus·es (găl′ə-sĭz) *pl.n.* Suspenders for trousers. [Variant of *gallowses,* pl. of GALLOWS.]

gall wasp *n.* Any of various wasps of the family Cynipidae whose larvae produce distinctively shaped galls on oaks and other plants.

Ga·lois (găl-wä′), **Évariste.** 1811–1832. French mathematician who made valuable contributions to number theory algebra before being killed in a duel at the age of 21.

Ga·lois theory (găl-wä′) *n.* The part of mathematical group theory concerned with the conditions under which a polynomial equation of power *n* with coefficients in a given mathematical field can be solved by repeating given operations and extracting the *n*th roots. [After Évariste GALOIS.]

ga·loot also **gal·loot** (gə-lo͞ot′) *n. Slang.* A person, especially a clumsy or uncouth one. [Origin unknown.]

gal·op (găl′əp) also **gal·o·pade** or **gal·lo·pade** (găl′ə-pād′, -päd′) *n.* **1.** A lively round dance in duple time, popular in

ă pat	oi boy
ā pay	ou out
âr care	o͝o took
ä father	o͞o boot
ĕ pet	ŭ cut
ē be	ûr urge
ĭ pit	th thin
ī pie	*th* this
îr pier	hw which
ŏ pot	zh vision
ō toe	ə about, item
ô paw	♦ regionalism

Stress marks: **′** (primary); ′ (secondary), as in **dictionary** (dĭk′shə-nĕr′ē)

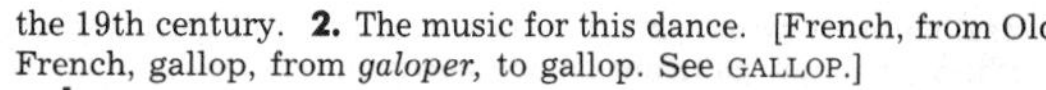

the 19th century. **2.** The music for this dance. [French, from Old French, gallop, from *galoper,* to gallop. See GALLOP.]

ga·lore (gə-lôr′, -lōr′) *adj.* In great numbers; in abundance: *"with balloons and hot dogs . . . and fireworks galore"* (Anne Armstrong). [Irish Gaelic *go leór,* enough : *go,* adv. particle + *leór,* enough (from Old Irish *lour,* alteration of *roar;* see **wērə-** in Appendix).]

ga·losh (gə-lŏsh′) *n.* **1.** A waterproof overshoe. **2.** *Obsolete.* A sturdy heavy-soled boot or shoe. [Middle English *galoche,* wooden soled shoe, from Old French.]

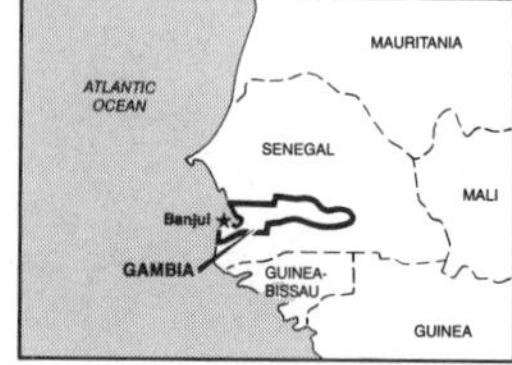

Gambia

Gals·wor·thy (gălz′wûr′*thē*), **John.** 1867–1933. British writer. Author of *The Forsyte Saga* (1906–1921) and many other *Forsyte* stories, he won the 1932 Nobel Prize for literature.

ga·lumph (gə-lŭmf′) *intr.v.* **-lumphed, -lumph·ing, -lumphs.** To move or run clumsily or heavily. [Perhaps blend of GALLOP and TRIUMPH.]

galv. *abbr.* Galvanized.

Gal·va·ni (găl-vä′nē, gäl-), **Luigi.** 1737–1798. Italian physiologist and physician who asserted that animal tissues generate electricity. Although he was proved wrong, his experiments stimulated research on electricity.

gal·van·ic (găl-văn′ĭk) *adj.* **1.** Of or relating to direct-current electricity, especially when produced chemically. **2. a.** Having the effect of an electric shock: *a galvanic revelation.* **b.** Produced as if by an electric shock: *The new leader had a galvanic effect on our morale.* [GALVAN(ISM) + –IC.] **—gal·van′i·cal·ly** *adv.*

galvanic cell *n.* See **primary cell.**

galvanic couple *n.* See **voltaic couple.**

galvanic skin response *n.* *Abbr.* **GSR** A change in the ability of the skin to conduct electricity, caused by an emotional stimulus, such as fright.

gal·va·nism (găl′və-nĭz′əm) *n.* **1.** Direct-current electricity, especially when produced chemically. Also called *voltaism.* **2.** Therapeutic application of direct-current electricity, especially the electric stimulation of nerves and muscle. [After Luigi GALVANI.]

gal·va·nize (găl′və-nīz′) *tr.v.* **-nized, -niz·ing, -niz·es. 1.** To stimulate or shock with an electric current. **2.** To arouse to awareness or action; spur: *"Issues that once galvanized the electorate fade into irrelevance"* (Arthur M. Schlesinger, Jr.). **3.** To coat (iron or steel) with rust-resistant zinc. **—gal′va·ni·za′tion** (-nĭ-zā′shən) *n.* **—gal′va·niz′er** *n.*

galvano– *pref.* Galvanism; galvanic: *galvanometer.* [From GALVANIC or GALVANISM.]

gal·va·no·mag·net·ic (găl′və-nō-măg-nĕt′ĭk, găl-văn′ō-) *adj.* Of or relating to the generation of an electric field by a magnetic field in semiconductors and metals.

gal·va·nom·e·ter (găl′və-nŏm′ĭ-tər) *n.* An instrument used to detect, measure, and determine the direction of small electric currents by means of mechanical effects produced by a coil in a magnetic field. **—gal′va·no·met′ric** (-nō-mĕt′rĭk), **gal′va·no·met′ri·cal** *adj.* **—gal′va·nom′e·try** *n.*

gal·va·no·scope (găl′və-nə-skōp′, găl-văn′ə-) *n.* An instrument used to detect the presence and determine the direction of electric currents by the deflection of a magnetic needle. **—gal′·va·no·scop′ic** (-skŏp′ĭk) *adj.* **—gal′va·nos′co·py** (găl′və-nŏs′kə-pē) *n.*

Gal·ves·ton (găl′vĭ-stən). A city of southeast Texas south-southeast of Houston on **Galveston Island** at the entrance to **Galveston Bay,** an arm of the Gulf of Mexico. The Spanish explorer Cabeza de Vaca may have been shipwrecked on the island in 1528. Population, 61,902.

gambrel roof

Gal·way (gôl′wā′). A region of west-central Ireland bordering on **Galway Bay,** an inlet of the Atlantic Ocean. The city of **Galway** (population, 37,835) was incorporated in the late 14th century and is today an important industrial and tourist center.

gal·yak (găl′yăk′) *n.* A flat, glossy fur made from the pelt of a stillborn lamb or kid. [Russian dialectal *golyak,* sheepskin coat of smooth fur, from Russian *golyĭ,* smooth, bald, naked.]

gam[1] (găm) *n.* **1.** A social visit or friendly interchange, especially between whalers or seafarers. **2.** A herd of whales or a social congregation of whalers, especially at sea. See Synonyms at **flock[1]**. **—gam** *v.* **gammed, gam·ming, gams.** —*intr.* To hold a visit, especially while at sea. —*tr.* **1.** To visit with. **2.** To spend (time) talking or visiting. [Perhaps short for GAMMON[2] or variant of GAME[1].]

gam[2] (găm) *n.* *Slang.* A person's leg. [Probably from Polari (theatrical argot), from Italian *gamba,* from Late Latin *gamba,* hoof. See GAMBOL.]

gam– *pref.* Variant of **gamo–.**

Ga·ma (găm′ə, gä′mə), **Vasco da.** 1460?–1524. Portuguese explorer and colonial administrator. The first European to sail to India (1497–1498), he opened the rich lands of the East to Portuguese trade and colonization.

ga·may (gă-mā′, găm′ā) *n.* A variety of red grape used for making red wines, especially Beaujolais. [French, after *Gamay,* a village of east-central France.]

gam·ba (gäm′bə, găm′-) *n.* *Music.* See **viola da gamba** (sense 1).

gam·ba·do[1] (găm-bā′dō) *n., pl.* **-does** or **-dos. 1.** A low leap of a horse in which all four feet are off the ground. **2.** A leaping or gamboling movement. [Alteration (influenced by GAMBADO[2]) of French *gambade,* from Italian *gambata,* from Old Italian *gambata.* See GAMBOL.]

gam·ba·do[2] (găm-bā′dō) *n., pl.* **-does** or **-dos. 1.** Either of a pair of protective leather gaiters attached to a saddle. **2.** A rider's legging. [From Italian *gamba,* leg, from Old Italian. See GAMBOL.]

Gam·bi·a (găm′bē-ə). A country of western Africa on the Atlantic Ocean. It was a British protectorate after 1894 and became independent in 1965. Banjul is the capital and the largest city. Population, 696,000. **—Gam′bi·an** *adj. & n.*

Gambia River. A river of western Africa flowing about 1,126 km (700 mi) from northern Guinea through southeast Senegal and Gambia to the Atlantic Ocean at Banjul.

gam·bier also **gam·bir** (găm′bîr) *n.* A resinous, astringent extract obtained from the leaves of a woody vine *(Uncaria gambir)* of Malaysia and Indonesia, used medicinally and in tanning and dyeing. [Malay *gambir.*]

Gam·bier Islands (găm′bîr′). An island group of the south-central Pacific Ocean, part of French Polynesia.

gam·bit (găm′bĭt) *n.* **1.** *Games.* An opening in chess in which a minor piece, or pieces, usually a pawn, is offered in exchange for a favorable position. **2.** A maneuver, stratagem, or ploy, especially one used at an initial stage. **3.** A remark intended to open a conversation. [Ultimately from Spanish *gambito,* from Italian *gambetto,* act of tripping someone up in wrestling, from *gamba,* leg, from Old Italian. See GAMBOL.]

USAGE NOTE: Critics familiar with the nature of chess gambits have sometimes maintained that the word should not be used in an extended sense except to refer to maneuvers that involve the tactical sacrifice of some advantage. But *gambit* is well established in the general sense of "maneuver" and in the related sense of "a remark intended to open a conversation," which usually carries no implication of sacrifice.

gam·ble (găm′bəl) *v.* **-bled, -bling, -bles.** —*intr.* **1. a.** To bet on an uncertain outcome, as of a contest. **b.** *Games.* To play a game of chance for stakes. **2.** To take a risk in the hope of gaining an advantage or a benefit. **3.** To engage in reckless or hazardous behavior: *You are gambling with your health by continuing to smoke.* —*tr.* **1.** *Games.* To put up as a stake in gambling; wager. **2.** To expose to hazard; risk: *gambled their lives in a dangerous rescue mission.* **—gamble** *n.* **1.** *Games.* A bet, wager, or other gambling venture. **2.** An act or undertaking of uncertain outcome; a risk: *I took a gamble that stock prices would rise.* [Perhaps from obsolete *gamel,* to play games, from Middle English *gamen, gamenen,* to play, from Old English *gamenian,* from *gamen,* fun.] **—gam′bler** *n.*

gam·boge (găm-bōj′, -bo͞ozh′) *n.* **1.** A brownish or orange resin obtained from several trees of the genus *Garcinia* of south-central Asia and yielding a golden-yellow pigment. **2.** *Color.* A strong yellow. [New Latin *cambugium, gambogium,* after CAMBODIA.] **—gam·boge′** *adj.*

gam·bol (găm′bəl) *intr.v.* **-boled, -bol·ing, -bols** or **-bolled, -bol·ling, -bols.** To leap about playfully; frolic. **—gambol** *n.* A playful skipping or frolicking about. [Alteration of French *gambade,* horse's jump, from Old French, perhaps from Old Italian *gambata,* from *gamba,* leg, from Late Latin, hoof, perhaps from Greek *kampē,* bend.]

gam·brel (găm′brəl) *n.* **1.** The hock of a horse or other animal. **2.** A frame used by butchers for hanging carcasses by the legs. [French dialectal *gamberel,* from Old North French, from *gambe,* leg, from Late Latin *gamba,* hoof. See GAMBOL.]

gambrel roof *n.* A ridged roof with two slopes on each side, the lower slope having the steeper pitch.

gam·bu·sia (găm-byo͞o′zhə) *n.* Any of various small livebearers of the genus *Gambusia* that feed on mosquito larvae and are often used in mosquito control. [New Latin *Gambusia,* genus name, from American Spanish *gambusino,* idle fisherman.]

game[1] (găm) *n.* **1.** An activity providing entertainment or amusement; a pastime: *party games; word games.* **2. a.** A competitive activity or sport in which players contend with each other according to a set of rules: *the game of basketball; the game of gin rummy.* **b.** A single instance of such an activity: *We lost the first game.* **c. games.** An organized athletic program or contest: *track-and-field games; took part in the winter games.* **d.** A period of competition or challenge: *It was too late in the game to change the schedule of the project.* **3. a.** The total number of points required to win a game: *One hundred points is game in bridge.* **b.** The score accumulated at any given time in a game: *The game is now 14 to 12.* **4.** The equipment needed for playing certain games: *packed the children's games in the car.* **5.** A particular style or manner of playing a game: *improved my tennis game with practice.* **6.** *Informal.* **a.** An active interest or pursuit, especially one involving competitive engagement or adherence to rules: *"the way the system operates, the access game, the turf game, the image game"* (Hedrick Smith). **b.** A business or occupation; a line: *the insurance game.* **c.** An illegal activity; a racket. **7.** *Informal.* **a.** Evasive, trifling, or manipulative behavior: *wanted a straight answer, not more of their tiresome games.* **b.** A calculated strategy or approach; a scheme: *I saw through their game from the very beginning.* **8.** *Mathematics.* A model of a competitive situation that identifies interested parties and stipulates rules governing all aspects of the competition, used in game theory to determine the optimal course of action for an interested party. **9.a.** Wild animals, birds, or fish hunted for food or sport. **b.** The flesh of these animals, eaten as food. **10.a.** An object of attack, ridicule, or pursuit: *The press considered the candidate's indiscretions to be game.* **b.** Mockery; sport: *The older children teased and made game of the newcomer.* **—game** *v.* **gamed, gam·ing, games.** —*tr. Archaic.* To waste or lose by gambling. —*intr.* To play for stakes; gamble. **—game** *adj.* **gam·er, gam·est. 1.** Plucky and unyielding in spirit; resolute: *She put up a game fight against her detractors.* **2.** Ready and willing: *Are you game for a swim?* **—*idiom.* the only game in town.** *Informal.* The only alternative: *"The Anglo-Irish Agreement is the only game in town available to political leaders seeking a graceful way out of the Ulster morass"* (Boston Globe). *"He's the only game in town for the press to write about"* (Leonard Garment). [Middle English, from Old English *gamen.*] **—game′ly** *adv.* **—game′ness** *n.*

game² (gām) *adj.* **gam·er, gam·est.** Crippled; lame: *a game leg.* [Origin unknown.]

game bird *n.* A bird, such as a pheasant or grouse, that is widely hunted for sport.

game·cock (gām′kŏk′) *n.* A rooster trained for cockfighting.

game fish *n.* A fish prized for the sport involved in catching it.

game fowl *n.* Any of several breeds of domestic fowl raised especially for cockfighting.

game·keep·er (gām′kē′pər) *n.* One who is employed to protect and maintain game birds and animals, especially on an estate or a game preserve.

gam·e·lan (găm′ə-lăn′) *n. Music.* An Indonesian orchestra composed mainly of tuned percussion instruments such as bamboo xylophones, wooden or metal chimes, and gongs. [Javanese : *gamêl,* to make music + *-an,* suff. indicating means.]

game law *n.* A regulation intended for the management or conservation of game animals, as one determining the season in which a species may be hunted or fished or one placing restrictions on the method of capture or the number of animals that may be taken.

game of chance *n. Games.* A game, usually played for money or stakes, in which the winner is determined by a chance event, as by drawing numbers or throwing dice.

game plan *n.* **1.** *Sports.* The strategy devised before or used during an event. **2.** A strategy for reaching an objective: *"Harvey decided the best game plan was to stay loose"* (Cyra McFadden).

game point *n. Sports & Games.* **1.** A situation in a game, especially tennis, in which one side or player needs only one point to win. **2.** The winning point.

game room *n.* A recreation room, especially a room used for table games, such as pool or table tennis.

game show *n. Games.* A television show in which contestants compete for prizes by playing games of knowledge or chance.

games·man (gāmz′mən) *n. Sports & Games.* **1.** One who plays a sport or game, especially skillfully or avidly. **2.** One who practices gamesmanship.

games·man·ship (gāmz′mən-shĭp′) *n.* **1.** The art or practice of using tactical maneuvers to further one's aims or better one's position: *"a sometimes wry, sometimes savage look at the players, political gamesmanship, turf battles and outright chaos that permeated Washington"* (David M. Alpern). **2.** *Sports & Games.* The use in a sport or game of aggressive, often dubious tactics, such as psychological intimidation or disruption of concentration, to gain an advantage over one's opponent.

game·some (gām′səm) *adj.* Frolicsome; playful. **—game′some·ly** *adv.* **—game′some·ness** *n.*

game·ster (gām′stər) *n. Games.* One who plays games, especially a gambler.

gamet– *pref.* Variant of **gameto–.**

gam·e·tan·gi·um (găm′ĭ-tăn′jē-əm) *n., pl.* **-gi·a** (-jē-ə). An organ or a cell in which gametes are produced. [GAMET(O)– + Greek *angeion,* vessel, diminutive of *angos,* vessel + –IUM.] **—gam′e·tan′gi·al** (-əl) *adj.*

gam·ete (găm′ēt′, gə-mēt′) *n.* A reproductive cell having the haploid number of chromosomes, especially a mature sperm or egg capable of fusing with a gamete of the opposite sex to produce the fertilized egg. [New Latin *gameta,* from Greek *gametē,* wife, and *gametēs,* husband, from *gamein,* to marry, from *gamos,* marriage. See **gemə-** in Appendix.] **—ga·met′ic** (-mĕt′ĭk) *adj.* **—ga·met′i·cal·ly** *adv.*

game theory *n.* A mathematical method of decision-making in which a competitive situation is analyzed to determine the optimal course of action for an interested party, often used in political, economic, and military planning. Also called *theory of games.*

gameto– or **gamet–** *pref.* Gamete: *gametogenesis.* [From New Latin *gameta,* gamete. See GAMETE.]

ga·me·to·cyte (gə-mē′tə-sīt′) *n.* A cell from which gametes develop by meiotic division, especially a spermatocyte or an oocyte.

ga·me·to·gen·e·sis (gə-mē′tə-jĕn′ĭ-sĭs) *n.* The formation or production of gametes. **—ga·me′to·gen′ic, gam′e·tog′e·nous** (găm′ĭ-tŏj′ə-nəs) *adj.*

ga·me·to·phore (gə-mē′tə-fôr′, -fōr′) *n.* A structure, as in liverworts and mosses, on which gametangia are borne. **—ga·me′to·phor′ic** (-fôr′ĭk, -fōr′-) *adj.*

ga·me·to·phyte (gə-mē′tə-fīt′) *n. Botany.* The gamete-producing phase in a plant characterized by alternation of generations. **—ga·me′to·phyt′ic** (-fĭt′ĭk) *adj.*

game warden *n.* An official in charge of managing game animals or wildlife, especially by the enforcement of game laws.

gam·ey (gā′mē) *adj.* Variant of **gamy.**

gam·ic (găm′ĭk) *adj.* Of or requiring fertilization to reproduce; sexual.

gam·in (găm′ĭn) *n.* An often homeless boy who roams about the streets; an urchin. [French.]

ga·mine (gă-mēn′, găm′ēn) *n.* **1.** An often homeless girl who roams about the streets; an urchin. **2.** A girl or woman of impish appeal. [French, feminine of *gamin,* gamin.]

gam·ing (gā′mĭng) *n. Games.* The playing of games of chance; gambling.

gam·ma (găm′ə) *n.* **1.** The third letter of the Greek alphabet. See table at **alphabet. 2.** The third item in a series or system of classification. **3.** A unit of magnetic field strength equal to one hundred thousandth (10^{-5}) of an oersted. **4.** A unit of mass equal to one millionth (10^{-6}) of a gram. **5.** *Chemistry.* The third position from a designated carbon atom in an organic molecule at which an atom or a radical may be substituted. [Middle English, from Greek, of Phoenician origin; akin to Hebrew *gīmel,* gimel.]

gam·ma-a·mi·no·bu·tyr·ic acid (găm′ə-ə-mē′nō-byo͞o-tîr′ĭk, -ăm′ə-nō-) *n. Abbr.* **GABA** An amino acid, $C_4H_9NO_2$, that occurs in the central nervous system and is associated with the transmission of nerve impulses.

gamma camera *n.* An electronic instrument used in medical diagnostics to visualize the distribution of radioactive compounds in animal tissue.

gamma decay *n.* **1.** A radioactive process in which an atomic nucleus loses energy by emitting a gamma ray without a change in its atomic or mass numbers. **2.** The decay of an unstable elementary particle by photon emission.

gamma globulin *n.* A protein fraction of blood serum containing numerous antibodies, used in the prevention and treatment of certain diseases, such as measles and hepatitis.

gamma ray *n.* Electromagnetic radiation emitted by radioactive decay and having energies in a range from ten thousand (10^4) to ten million (10^7) electron volts.

gam·ma-ray astronomy (găm′ə-rā′) *n.* Astronomy that deals with the origin and nature of periodic gamma-ray emissions from extraterrestrial sources.

gam·mer (găm′ər) *n. Chiefly British.* An elderly woman. [Probably alteration (influenced by GRANDMOTHER) of GODMOTHER.]

gam·mon¹ (găm′ən) *Games. n.* A victory in backgammon reached before the loser has succeeded in removing a single piece. **—gammon** *tr.v.* **-moned, -mon·ing, -mons.** To defeat in backgammon by scoring a gammon. [Probably from Middle English *gamen, gammen,* game, from Old English *gamen.*]

gam·mon² (găm′ən) *Chiefly British. n.* Misleading or nonsensical talk; humbug. **—gammon** *v.* **-moned, -mon·ing, -mons.** —*tr.* To mislead by deceptive talk. —*intr.* To talk misleadingly or deceptively. [Origin unknown.] **—gam′mon·er** *n.*

gam·mon³ (găm′ən) *n.* **1.** A cured or smoked ham. **2.** The lower part of a side of bacon. [Middle English *gambon,* from Old North French, from *gambe,* leg, from Late Latin *gamba,* hoof. See GAMBOL.]

gam·mon⁴ (găm′ən) *tr.v.* **-moned, -mon·ing, -mons.** *Nautical.* To fasten (a bowsprit) to the stem of a ship. [Origin unknown.]

gamo– or **gam–** *pref.* **1.** United; joined: *gamopetalous.* **2.** Sexual: *gamogenesis.* [Greek, marriage, from *gamos.* See **gemə-** in Appendix.]

gam·o·gen·e·sis (găm′ə-jĕn′ĭ-sĭs) *n.* Sexual reproduction. **—gam′o·ge·net′ic** (-jə-nĕt′ĭk) *adj.* **—gam′o·ge·net′i·cal·ly** *adv.*

gam·o·pet·al·ous (găm′ə-pĕt′l-əs) *adj. Botany.* Having or characterizing a corolla with partially or wholly fused petals.

gam·o·phyl·lous (găm′ə-fĭl′əs) *adj. Botany.* Having or designating united leaves or leaflike parts.

gam·o·sep·al·ous (găm′ə-sĕp′ə-ləs) *adj. Botany.* Having the sepals united or partly united.

–gamous *suff.* **1.a.** Having a specified number of marriages: *monogamous.* **b.** Practicing a specified kind of marriage: *exogamous.* **2.** Having a specified kind of reproduction or reproductive organs: *heterogamous.* [From Greek *-gamos,* from *gamos,* marriage. See **gemə-** in Appendix.]

Ga·mow (gă′mou, găm′ôf, -ŏf), **George.** 1904–1968. Russian-born American nuclear physicist known for his work on radioactivity and genetic information.

gamp (gămp) *n. Chiefly British.* A large, baggy umbrella. [After the umbrella of Mrs. Sarah *Gamp,* a character in the novel *Martin Chuzzlewit* by Charles Dickens.]

gam·ut (găm′ət) *n.* **1.** A complete range or extent: *a face that expressed a gamut of emotions, from rage to peaceful contentment.* **2.** *Music.* The entire series of recognized notes. [Middle English, the musical scale, from Medieval Latin *gamma ut,* low G : *gamma,* lowest note of the medieval scale (from Greek *gamma,* gamma; see GAMMA) + *ut,* first note of the lowest hexachord (after *ut,* first word in a Latin hymn to Saint John the Baptist, the initial syllables of successive lines of which were sung to the notes of an

gamelan

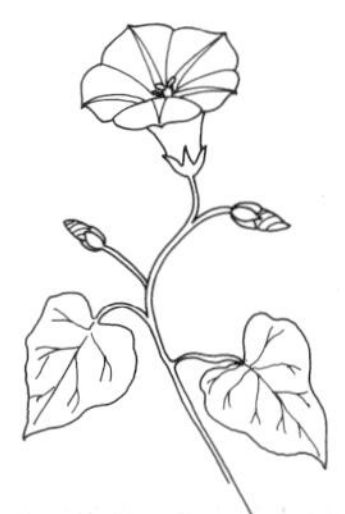

gamopetalous
Wild potato vine
Ipomoea pandurata

ă pat	oi boy
ā pay	ou out
âr care	o͝o took
ä father	o͞o boot
ĕ pet	ŭ cut
ē be	ûr urge
ĭ pit	th thin
ī pie	*th* this
îr pier	hw which
ŏ pot	zh vision
ō toe	ə about, item
ô paw	♦ regionalism

Stress marks: ′ (primary); ′ (secondary), as in **dictionary** (dĭk′shə-nĕr′ē)

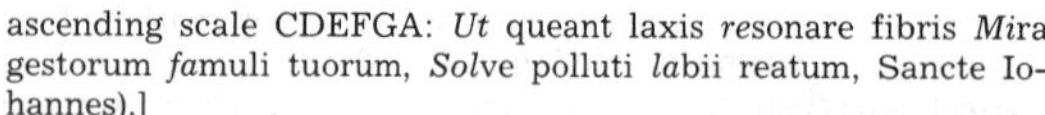

ascending scale CDEFGA: *Ut* queant laxis *re*sonare fibris *Mi*ra gestorum *fa*muli tuorum, *Sol*ve polluti *la*bii reatum, Sancte Iohannes).]

Indira Gandhi
Photographed in 1982

gam·y also **gam·ey** (gā′mē) *adj.* **-i·er, -i·est. 1.a.** Having the flavor or odor of game, especially game that is slightly spoiled. **b.** Ill-smelling; rank. **2.** Showing an unyielding spirit; plucky: *a gamy little mare that loved to run.* **3.a.** Corrupt; tainted: *"those considerable forces in America that appear to be tired of the old politics (particularly the gamy municipal variety)"* (Tom Wicker). **b.** Sordid; seamy. **—gam′i·ly** *adv.* **—gam′i·ness** *n.*

-gamy *suff.* **1.** Marriage: *exogamy.* **2.** Procreative or propagative union: *allogamy.* **3.** The possession of a specified manner of fertilization or specified reproductive organs: *apogamy.* [Greek *-gamia,* from *gamos,* marriage. See **gemə-** in Appendix.]

gan·der (găn′dər) *n.* **1.** A male goose. **2.** *Informal.* A look or glance: *"Everyone turns and takes a gander at the yokels"* (Garrison Keillor). **3.** *Informal.* A simpleton; a ninny. [Middle English, from Old English *gandra.* See **ghans-** in Appendix.]

Gan·der (găn′dər). A town of northeast Newfoundland, Canada. Its airport was strategically important during World War II and was long used as a refueling stop for transatlantic flights. Population, 10,404.

Gan·dhi (gän′dē, găn′-), **Indira Nehru.** 1917–1984. Indian political leader who served as prime minister (1966–1977 and 1980–1984). She was assassinated by Sikh extremists.

Gandhi, Mohandas Karamchand. Known as "Mahatma." 1869–1948. Indian nationalist and spiritual leader who developed the practice of nonviolent disobedience that forced Great Britain to grant independence to India (1947). He was assassinated by a Hindu fanatic.

gan·dy dancer (găn′dē) *n. Slang.* **1.** A railroad worker. **2.** An itinerant laborer. [Origin unknown.]

ga·nef or **ga·nof** also **gon·if** (gä′nəf) *n.* A thief, scoundrel, or rascal. [Yiddish; akin to Hebrew *gannāb.*]

Mahatma Gandhi

gang[1] (găng) *n.* **1.** A group of criminals or hoodlums who band together for mutual protection and profit. **2.** A group of adolescents who band together, especially a group of delinquents. **3.** *Informal.* A group of people who associate regularly on a social basis: *The whole gang from the office went to a clambake.* **4.** A group of laborers organized together on one job or under one foreperson: *a railroad gang.* **5.** A matched or coordinated set, as of tools: *a gang of chisels.* **6.a.** A pack of wolves or wild dogs. **b.** A herd, especially of buffalo or elk. See Synonyms at **flock**[1]. **—gang** *v.* **ganged, gang·ing, gangs.** *—intr.* To band together as a group or gang. *—tr.* **1.** To arrange or assemble into a group, as for simultaneous operation or production: *gang several pages onto one printing plate.* **2.** To attack as an organized group. ***—phrasal verb.* gang up. 1.** To join together in opposition or attack: *The older children were always ganging up on the little ones.* **2.** To act together as a group: *various agencies ganging up to combat the use of illicit drugs.* [Middle English, band of men, from Old English, journey, and Old Norse *gangr,* journey, group, as in *thjofagangr,* gang of thieves.]

gang[2] (găng) *n.* Variant of **gangue.**

Gan·ga (gŭng′gə). See **Ganges.**

gang·bang or **gang-bang** (găng′băng′) *n. Vulgar Slang.* **1.** Sexual intercourse, often rape, involving one person or victim and several others who have relations with that person in rapid succession. **2.** Sexual intercourse involving several people who select and change partners in an indiscriminate manner. **—gang′bang′** *v.*

gang·bus·ter (găng′bŭs′tər) *n. Slang.* A law enforcement officer who works to break up organized criminal groups. ***—idiom.* like gangbusters.** *Slang.* With great impact, vigor, or zeal: *came on like gangbusters at the start of his campaign; a career that took off like gangbusters.*

Gan·ges (găn′jēz′) also **Gan·ga** (gŭng′gə). A river of northern India and Bangladesh rising in the Himalaya Mountains and flowing about 2,510 km (1,560 mi) generally eastward to the Bay of Bengal. The river is sacred to Hindus.

Ganymede
19th-century
white marble sculpture
Hebe and Ganymede
by Thomas Crawford

gang·land (găng′lănd′, -lənd) *n.* The underworld of organized criminal gangs. **—gangland** *adj.* Of, relating to, or carried out by organized criminals: *gangland turf; a gangland slaying.*

gan·gli·a (găng′glē-ə) *n.* A plural of **ganglion.**

gan·gli·at·ed (găng′glē-ā′tĭd) also **gan·gli·ate** (-ĭt, -āt′) *adj.* Having ganglia.

gan·gling (găng′glĭng) *adj.* Awkwardly tall or long-limbed; rangy: *gangling adolescents.* [Perhaps from dialectal *gang,* to go, from Middle English *gangen,* from Old English *gangan.*]

gan·gli·on (găng′glē-ən) *n., pl.* **-gli·a** (-glē-ə) or **-gli·ons. 1.** *Anatomy.* A group of nerve cells forming a nerve center, especially one located outside the brain or spinal cord. **2.** A center of power, activity, or energy. **3.** *Pathology.* A benign cystic lesion resembling a tumor, occurring in a tendon sheath or joint capsule. [From Greek, cystlike tumor, nerve bundle.] **—gan′gli·on′ic** (-ŏn′ĭk) *adj.*

gan·gli·on·at·ed (găng′-glē-ə-nā′tĭd) *adj.* Gangliated.

gan·gli·o·side (găng′glē-ə-sīd′) *n.* Any of a group of galactose-containing cerebrosides found in the surface membranes of nerve cells. [GANGLI(ON) + –OS(E)[2] + –IDE.]

gan·gly (găng′glē) *adj.* **-gli·er, -gli·est.** Gangling. [Alteration of GANGLING.]

gang·plank (găng′plăngk′) *n. Nautical.* A board or ramp used as a removable footway between a ship and a pier. Also called *gangway.* [From GANG[1], way (obsolete and dialectal).]

gang·plow (găng′plou′) *n.* A plow equipped with several blades that make parallel furrows.

gang·punch (găng′pŭnch′) *tr.v.* **-punched, -punch·ing, -punch·es.** *Computer Science.* To duplicate (information) from a punched card onto succeeding cards.

gang rape *n.* Rape of a victim by several attackers in rapid succession. **—gang′-rape′** (găng′rāp′) *v.*

gan·grel (găng′rəl) *n. Scots.* A vagabond; a drifter. [Middle English, probably from *gangen,* to go. See GANGLING.]

gan·grene (găng′grēn′, găng-grēn′) *n.* Death and decay of body tissue, often occurring in a limb, caused by insufficient blood supply and usually following injury or disease. **—gangrene** *tr. & intr.v.* **-grened, -gren·ing, -grenes.** To affect or become affected with gangrene. [Medieval Latin *cancrēna,* from Latin *gangraena, gangrēna,* from Greek *gangraina.*] **—gan′gre·nous** (găng′grə-nəs) *adj.*

gang saw *n.* A saw fitted with several blades for making simultaneous parallel cuts.

gang·ster (găng′stər) *n.* A member of an organized group of criminals. **—gang′ster·dom** *n.* **—gang′ster·ism** *n.*

gangue also **gang** (găng) *n.* Worthless rock or other material in which valuable minerals are found. [French, from German *Gang,* lode, from Middle High German *ganc,* from Old High German *gang,* a going.]

gang·way (găng′wā′) *n.* **1.** *Nautical.* **a.** A passage along either side of a ship's upper deck. **b.** See **gangplank. c.** An opening in the bulwark of a ship through which passengers may board. **2.** A narrow passageway, as of boards laid on the ground. **3.** The main level of a mine. **4.** *Chiefly British.* **a.** The aisle that divides the front and rear seating sections of the House of Commons. **b.** An aisle between seating sections, as in a theater. **—gangway** *interj.* Used to clear a passage through a crowded area. [From GANG[1], way, passage (obsolete and dialectal).]

gan·is·ter also **gan·nis·ter** (găn′ĭ-stər) *n.* **1.** A fine-grained quartzite used to line refractory furnaces. **2.** A mixture of fire clay and ground quartz, used to line metallurgical furnaces. [Origin unknown.]

gan·ja (gän′jə) *n.* Marijuana, especially a highly resinous form of marijuana prepared from the flowering tops and leaves of selected plants and usually ingested by smoking. [Hindustani *gāṁjhā,* hemp resin, from Sanskrit *gañjyā-,* of hemp, from *gañjaḥ,* hemp, alteration of *gṛñjaḥ.*]

Gan Jiang (gän′ jyäng′) also **Kan River** (kăn). A river of southeast China flowing about 885 km (550 mi) generally north into the Yangtze River (Chang Jiang) north of Nanchang.

gan·net (găn′ĭt) *n.* Any of several large sea birds of the genus *Morus,* especially *M. bassanus* of northern Atlantic coastal regions, having white plumage with black wingtips. Also called *solan.* [Middle English *ganet,* from Old English *ganot.* See **ghans-** in Appendix.]

gan·nis·ter (găn′ĭ-stər) *n.* Variant of **ganister.**

ga·nof (gä′nəf) *n.* Variant of **ganef.**

gan·oid (găn′oid′) *adj.* Of, relating to, or characteristic of certain bony fishes, such as the sturgeon and the gar, that have armorlike scales consisting of bony plates covered with layers of dentine and enamel. **—ganoid** *n.* A ganoid fish. [From New Latin *Ganoidei,* subclass name, from Greek *ganos,* brightness, gladness, from *ganusthai,* to rejoice. See **gāu-** in Appendix.]

Gan·su (gän′sōō′) also **Kan·su** (kän′sōō′, gän′-). A province of north-central China. It was long a corridor for the Silk Road to Turkistan, India, and Persia. Lanzhou is the capital. Population, 20,410,000.

gant·let[1] (gônt′lĭt, gänt′-) *n.* A section of double railroad tracks formed by the temporary convergence of two parallel tracks in such a way that each set remains independent while traversing the same ground, affording passage at a narrow place without need of switching. **—gantlet** *tr.v.* **-let·ed, -let·ing, -lets.** To converge (railroad tracks) to form a gantlet. [Variant of GAUNTLET[2].]

gant·let[2] (gônt′lĭt, gänt′-) *n.* Variant of **gauntlet**[1].

gant·let[3] (gônt′lĭt, gänt′-) *n.* Variant of **gauntlet**[2].

gant·line (gănt′līn′, -lĭn) *n. Nautical.* A rope passed through an overhead pulley, as at the top of a mast, that is used for hoisting. [Perhaps alteration of *girtline,* gantline : *girt* (variant of GIRTH) + LINE[1].]

gan·try (găn′trē) *n., pl.* **-tries. 1.** A mount for a traveling crane consisting of a large archlike or bridgelike frame designed to move along a set of tracks. **2.** A similar spanning frame supporting a group of railway signals over several tracks. **3.** *Aerospace.* A massive vertical frame structure used in assembling or servicing a rocket, especially at a launch site. **4.** A support for a barrel lying on its side. [Middle English *ganter, gauntre,* wooden stand for barrels, from Old North French *gantier,* wooden frame, from Latin *canthērius,* from Greek *kanthēlios,* pack ass, from *kanthēlia,* panniers at the side of a pack-saddle.]

Gantt chart (gănt) *n.* A chart that depicts progress in relation to time, often used in planning and tracking a project. [After Henry Laurence *Gantt* (1861–1919), American engineer.]

Gan·y·mede (găn′ə-mēd′) *n.* **1.** *Greek Mythology.* A Trojan boy of great beauty whom Zeus carried away to be cupbearer to the gods. **2.** One of the four brightest satellites of Jupiter and the eighth in distance from the planet. Originally sighted by Galileo, it is one of the largest satellites in the solar system. [Latin *Ganymēdēs,* from Greek *Ganumēdēs.*]

GAO *abbr.* General Accounting Office.

gaol (jāl) *n. & v. Chiefly British.* Variant of **jail.**

gap (găp) *n.* **1.a.** An opening in a solid structure or surface; a cleft or breach: *wriggled through a gap in the fence; a large gap in the wall where the artillery shell had exploded.* **b.** A break in a line of defense. **2.** An opening through mountains; a pass. **3.** A space between objects or points; an aperture: *a gap between his front teeth.* **4.** An interruption of continuity: *a nine-minute gap in the recorded conversation; needed to fill in the gaps in her knowledge.* **5.a.** A conspicuous difference or imbalance; a disparity: *a gap between revenue and spending; the widening gap between rich and poor.* **b.** A problematic situation resulting from such a disparity: *the budget gap; the technology gap.* **6.** A spark gap. **7.** *Computer Science.* An absence of information on a recording medium, often used to signal the end of a segment of information. **8.** *Electronics.* The distance between the head of a recording device and the surface of the recording medium. **—gap** *v.* **gapped, gap·ping, gaps.** *—tr.* To make an opening in. *—intr.* To be or become open. [Middle English, from Old Norse, chasm.]

GAPA *abbr.* Ground-to-air pilotless aircraft.

gape (gāp, găp) *intr.v.* **gaped, gap·ing, gapes. 1.** To open the mouth wide; yawn. **2.** To stare wonderingly or stupidly, often with the mouth open. See Synonyms at **gaze. 3.** To open wide: *The curtains gaped when the wind blew.* **—gape** *n.* **1.** The act or an instance of gaping. **2.** A large opening. **3.** *Zoology.* The width of the space between the open jaws or mandibles of a vertebrate. **4. gapes** *(used with a sing. verb). Veterinary Medicine.* A disease of birds, especially young domesticated chickens and turkeys, caused by gapeworms and resulting in obstructed breathing. **5. gapes.** A fit of yawning. [Middle English *gapen,* from Old Norse *gapa.*]

gape·worm (gāp′wûrm′, găp′-) *n.* A nematode worm *(Syngamus trachea)* that infects the tracheas of certain birds and causes gapes.

gap·ing (gā′pĭng) *adj.* Deep and wide open: *a gaping wound; a gaping hole.* **—gap′ing·ly** *adv.*

gar[1] (gär) *n.* **1.** Any of several ganoid fishes of the family Lepisosteidae of fresh and brackish waters of North and Central America, having long narrow jaws, an elongated body, and a long snout. **2.** A similar or related fish, such as the needlefish. In this sense, also called *garfish, garpike.* [Short for GARFISH.]

gar[2] (gär) *tr.v.* **garred, gar·ring, gars.** *Scots.* To cause or compel. [Middle English *geren,* from Old Norse *gera,* to make.]

GAR or **G.A.R.** *abbr.* Grand Army of the Republic.

ga·rage (gə-räzh′, -räj′) *n.* **1.** A building or indoor space in which to park or keep a motor vehicle. **2.** A commercial establishment where cars are repaired, serviced, or parked. **—garage** *tr.v.* **-raged, -rag·ing, -rag·es.** To put or store in a garage. [French, from *garer,* to shelter, from Old French *garer, guerrer,* of Germanic origin. See **wer-**[4] in Appendix.]

WORD HISTORY: It is difficult for a 20th-century imagination to envision a world without garages or a language without the word *garage.* However, probably before the 19th and certainly before the 18th century the word did not exist, and possibly before the end of the 19th century the thing itself did not exist. Our word is a direct borrowing of French *garage,* which is first recorded in 1802 in the sense "place where one docks." The verb *garer,* from which *garage* was derived, originally meant "to put merchandise under shelter," then "to moor a boat," and then "to put a vehicle into a place for safekeeping," that is, a *garage,* a sense first recorded in French in 1901. English almost immediately borrowed this French word, the first instance being found in 1902.

garage sale *n.* A sale of used household items or clothing held at the home of the seller. Also called *tag sale.*

Gar·a·mond (găr′ə-mŏnd′, gä-rä-môɴ′), **Claude.** 1480?–1561. French type designer known for establishing the roman-style letter as the standard in printing.

garb (gärb) *n.* **1.** A distinctive style or form of clothing; dress: *clerical garb.* **2.** An outward appearance; a guise: *presented their radical ideas in the garb of moderation.* **—garb** *tr.v.* **garbed, garb·ing, garbs.** To cover with or as if with clothing; dress. [Obsolete French *garbe,* grace, from Italian *garbo,* from *garbare,* to please, of Germanic origin.]

gar·bage (gär′bĭj) *n.* **1.a.** Food wastes, as from a kitchen. **b.** Refuse; trash. **2.a.** Worthless or nonsensical matter; rubbish: *Their advice turned out to be nothing but garbage.* **b.** Inferior or offensive literary or artistic material. **3.** *Computer Science.* Incorrect, meaningless, or unwanted information in input, output, or memory. *—attributive.* Often used to modify another noun: *garbage collection.* [Middle English, offal from fowls.]

gar·ban·zo (gär-bän′zō) *n., pl.* **-zos.** See **chickpea.** [Spanish, alteration of Old Spanish *arvanço,* perhaps from Greek *erebinthos.*]

gar·ble (gär′bəl) *tr.v.* **-bled, -bling, -bles. 1.** To mix up or distort to such an extent as to make misleading or incomprehensible: *She garbled all the historical facts.* **2.** To scramble (a signal or message), as by erroneous encoding or faulty transmission. **3.** *Archaic.* To sort out; cull. **—garble** *n.* The act or an instance of garbling. [Middle English *garbelen,* to inspect and remove refuse from spices, from Anglo-Norman *garbeler,* to sift, and from Medieval Latin *garbellāre,* both from Arabic *ġarbala,* to select, from *ġirbāl,* sieve, from Late Latin *crībellum,* diminutive of Latin *crībrum.* See **krei-** in Appendix.] **—gar′bler** (-blər) *n.*

Gar·bo (gär′bō), **Greta.** 1905–1990. Swedish-born American actress known for her reclusiveness and her performances in such films as *Queen Christina* (1933) and *Camille* (1937).

Greta Garbo

gar·board (gär′bôrd′, -bōrd′) *n. Nautical.* The first range or strake of planks laid next to a ship's keel. [Obsolete Dutch *gaarboord* : possibly Dutch *gaar,* cooked, done (from Middle Dutch *gaer*) + *boord,* board (from Middle Dutch *boort*).]

gar·boil (gär′boil′) *n. Archaic.* Confusion; uproar. [Obsolete French *garbouil,* from Old French, from Old Italian *garbuglio,* perhaps from Latin *bullīre,* to boil.]

gar·bol·o·gy (gär-bŏl′ə-jē) *n.* The study of a society or culture by examining or analyzing its refuse. [GARB(AGE) + -LOGY.] **—gar·bol′o·gist** *n.*

Gar·cí·a Lor·ca (gär-sē′ə lôr′kä, gär-thē′ä), **Federico.** 1898–1936. Spanish writer considered Spain's leading modern poet for works such as *Lament for the Death of a Bullfighter* (1935).

Gar·cí·a Már·quez (gär-sē′ə mär′kəs, -kĕs), **Gabriel.** Born 1928. Colombian-born writer known especially for his novel *One Hundred Years of Solitude* (1967). He won the 1982 Nobel Prize for literature.

Gar·cí·a Ro·bles (gär-sē′ə rō′bləs, -blĕs), **Alfonso.** 1911–1991. Mexican diplomat. He shared the 1982 Nobel Peace Prize for his role in United Nations nuclear disarmament negotiations.

gar·çon (gär-sôɴ′) *n., pl.* **-çons** (-sôɴ′). A waiter. [French, from Old French *garçun,* servant, accusative of *gars,* boy, soldier, probably of Germanic origin.]

Gar·da (gär′də), **Lake.** A lake of northern Italy east of Milan. Its shoreline is dotted with resorts and vineyards.

gar·dant (gär′dnt) *adj. Heraldry.* Variant of **guardant.**

gar·den (gär′dn) *n.* **1.** A plot of land used for the cultivation of flowers, vegetables, herbs, or fruit. **2.** Often **gardens.** Grounds laid out with flowers, trees, and ornamental shrubs and used for recreation or display: *public gardens; a botanical garden.* **3.** A yard or lawn. **4.** A fertile, well-cultivated region. **5.a.** An open-air establishment where refreshments are served: *a beer garden.* **b.** A large public auditorium or arena. **—garden** *v.* **-dened, -den·ing, -dens.** *—tr.* **1.** To cultivate (a plot of ground) as a garden. **2.** To furnish with a garden. *—intr.* **1.** To plant or tend a garden. **2.** To work as a gardener. **—garden** *adj.* **1.** Of, suitable to, or used in a garden: *garden tools; garden vegetables.* **2.** Provided with open areas and greenery: *a garden community.* **3.** Garden-variety. ***—idiom.* lead** (or **take**) **down the garden path.** To mislead or deceive (another). [Middle English *gardin,* from Old North French, from *gart,* of Germanic origin. See **gher-**[1] in Appendix.]

Federico García Lorca

Gar·den (gär′dn), **Alexander.** 1730?–1791. Scottish-born American naturalist and physician who contributed to the classification of New World plants. The gardenia is named after him.

Gar·de·na (gär-dē′nə). A city of southern California, an industrial suburb of Los Angeles. Population, 45,165.

garden apartment *n.* A unit in a low-rise apartment complex that includes a substantial amount of open, usually landscaped ground.

garden city *n.* A residential suburb or community planned so as to provide a pleasant environment with low-density housing and open public land.

Garden City. 1. A city of southwest Kansas west-northwest of Dodge City. It is a trade and industrial center in an irrigated farming area. Population, 18,256. **2.** A city of southeast Michigan, a chiefly residential suburb of Detroit. Population, 35,640. **3.** A village of southeast New York on western Long Island. Roosevelt Field, the starting point for Charles A. Lindbergh's 1927 transatlantic flight, is in the village. Population, 22,927.

gardenia

garden cress *n.* An annual herb *(Lepidium sativum)* of the mustard family, having pungent leaves and usually grown as a salad plant.

gar·den·er (gärd′nər, gär′dn-ər) *n.* One who works in or tends a garden for pleasure or hire.

Garden Grove. A city of southern California, a residential suburb of Long Beach and Los Angeles. Population, 123,307.

garden heliotrope *n.* A widely cultivated valerian *(Valeriana officinalis)* having clusters of small, fragrant, purplish, pink, or white flowers and strong-smelling rhizomes formerly used in medicine.

gar·de·nia (gär-dēn′yə) *n.* **1.** Any of various shrubs and trees of the Old World tropics that belong to the genus *Gardenia,* especially *G. jasminoides* native to China, having glossy evergreen leaves and large, fragrant, usually white flowers. **2.** The flower of this plant. Also called *Cape jasmine.* [New Latin, genus name, after Alexander GARDEN.]

Garden of Eden *n.* See **Eden**[1] (sense 1).

gar·den-va·ri·e·ty (gär′dn-və-rī′ĭ-tē) *adj.* Common; unremarkable: *situation comedies, game shows, and other garden-variety television fare.*

garde·robe (gärd′rōb′) *n. Archaic.* **1.a.** A chamber for storing clothes; a wardrobe. **b.** The contents of a wardrobe. **2.** A

ă pat	oi boy
ā pay	ou out
âr care	o͝o took
ä father	o͞o boot
ĕ pet	ŭ cut
ē be	ûr urge
ĭ pit	th thin
ī pie	*th* this
îr pier	hw which
ŏ pot	zh vision
ō toe	ə about, item
ô paw	♦ regionalism

Stress marks: ′ (primary); ′ (secondary), as in **dictionary** (dĭk′shə-nĕr′ē)

James A. Garfield

gargoyle
On the Cathedral of Notre Dame, Paris

Giuseppe Garibaldi
Wearing the shirt he made popular

Judy Garland
In a scene from *Meet Me in St. Louis*, 1944

private chamber. [Middle English, from Old French : *garder,* to keep (of Germanic origin; see GUARD) + *robe,* robe (of Germanic origin; see ROBE).]

Gar·di·ner (gärd′nər, gär′dn-ər), **Samuel Rawson.** 1829–1902. British historian, educator, and editor known for his *History of England from the Accession of James I to the Restoration* (10 volumes, 1863–1882).

Gar·di·ners Island (gärd′nərz, gär′dn-ərz). An island of southeast New York in **Gardiners Bay** between two peninsulas of eastern Long Island. Settled in 1639, it is a reputed burial place of Captain Kidd's pirate treasure.

Gard·ner (gärd′nər). A city of north-central Massachusetts west of Fitchburg. Its furniture industry dates from c. 1805. Population, 17,900.

Gardner, Erle Stanley. 1889–1970. American lawyer and detective novelist known for creating the character of Perry Mason.

Gardner, Isabella Stewart. 1840–1924. American collector and patron of the arts. She built a magnificent villa and gallery in Boston to house her exceptional collection of art objects and opened it to the public in 1903.

Gar·eth (găr′ĭth) *n.* In Arthurian legend, a nephew of King Arthur and one of the Knights of the Round Table.

Gar·field (gär′fēld′). A city of northeast New Jersey on the Passaic River southeast of Paterson. It was settled by the Dutch in 1679. Population, 26,803.

Garfield, James Abram. 1831–1881. The 20th President of the United States (1881). He was assassinated by Charles Guiteau (1841–1882), a frustrated office-seeker.

Garfield Heights. A city of northeast Ohio, an industrial suburb of Cleveland. Population, 34,938.

gar·fish (gär′fĭsh′) *n., pl.* **garfish** or **-fish·es.** See **gar**[1] (sense 2). [Middle English : *gare,* spear (from Old English *gār*) + *fish,* fish; see FISH.]

gar·ga·ney (gär′gə-nē) *n., pl.* **-neys.** A small European duck *(Anas querquedula)* having a conspicuous white stripe over each eye and down the back of the head in the male. [Italian dialectal *gargenei,* variant of *garganello,* ultimately from Late Latin *gargala,* tracheal artery.]

gar·gan·tu·a (gär-găn′cho͞o-ə) *n.* A person of great size or stature and of voracious physical or intellectual appetites. [After the giant hero of *Gargantua and Pantagruel* by François Rabelais.]

gar·gan·tu·an (gär-găn′cho͞o-ən) *adj.* Of immense size, volume, or capacity; gigantic. See Synonyms at **enormous.**

gar·get (gär′gĭt) *n.* Mastitis of domestic animals, especially cattle. [Perhaps from Middle English, throat, from Old French *gargate.*]

gar·gle (gär′gəl) *v.* **-gled, -gling, -gles.** —*intr.* **1.** To force exhaled air through a liquid held in the back of the mouth, with the head tilted back, in order to cleanse or medicate the mouth or throat. **2.** To produce the sound of gargling when speaking or singing. —*tr.* **1.** To rinse or medicate (the mouth or throat) by gargling. **2.** To circulate or apply (a medicine or solution) by gargling. **3.** To utter with a gargling sound. —**gargle** *n.* **1.** A medicated solution for gargling. **2.** A gargling sound. [French *gargouiller,* from Old French.]

gar·goyle (gär′goil′) *n.* **1.** A roof spout in the form of a grotesque or fantastic creature projecting from a gutter to carry rainwater clear of the wall. **2.** A grotesque ornamental figure or projection. **3.** A person of bizarre or grotesque appearance. [Middle English *gargoile,* from Old French *gargole, gargouille,* throat, waterspout.]

gar·i·bal·di (găr′ə-bôl′dē) *n.* **1.** A loose, high-necked blouse styled after the red shirts worn by Garibaldi and his soldiers. **2.** A bright orange or yellow-orange damselfish *(Hypsypops rubicundus)* native to coastal marine waters of southern California. [After Giuseppe GARIBALDI.]

Gar·i·bal·di (găr′ə-bôl′dē, gä′rē-bäl′dē), **Giuseppe.** 1807–1882. Italian general and nationalist who led 1,000 volunteers in the capture of Sicily and Naples (1860). His conquest led to the formation of the kingdom of Italy (1861).

gar·ish (gâr′ĭsh, găr′-) *adj.* **1.a.** Marred by strident color or excessive ornamentation; gaudy. **b.** Loud and flashy: *garish makeup.* See Synonyms at **gaudy**[1]. **2.** Glaring; dazzling: *"Hide me from Day's garish eye"* (John Milton). [Origin unknown.] —**gar′ish·ly** *adv.* —**gar′ish·ness** *n.*

gar·land (gär′lənd) *n.* **1.a.** A wreath or festoon, especially one of plaited flowers or leaves, worn on the body or draped as a decoration. **b.** A representation of such a wreath or festoon, used as an architectural ornament or a heraldic device. **2.** A mark of honor or tribute; an accolade: *received garlands of praise from the critics.* **3.** *Nautical.* A ring or collar of rope used to hoist spars or prevent fraying. **4.** An anthology, as of ballads or poems. —**garland** *tr.v.* **-land·ed, -land·ing, -lands. 1.** To ornament or deck with a garland. **2.** To form into a garland. [Middle English, from Old French *garlande,* perhaps of Germanic origin. See **wei-** in Appendix.]

Gar·land (gär′lənd). A city of northeast Texas, an industrial suburb of Dallas. Population, 138,857.

Garland, (Hannibal) Hamlin. 1860–1940. American writer whose stories and novels include the autobiographical *A Son of the Middle Border* (1917).

Garland, Judy. 1922–1969. American actress and singer best remembered for her performance as Dorothy in *The Wizard of Oz* (1939).

garland chrysanthemum *n.* An annual Mediterranean herb *(Chrysanthemum coronarium)* of the composite family, having yellow florets grouped in small rayed flower heads and aromatic, bipinnately lobed leaves. Also called *crown daisy.*

garland flower *n.* A European evergreen shrub *(Daphne cneorum)* having fragrant rose, pink, or white flowers grouped in dense terminal heads.

gar·lic (gär′lĭk) *n.* **1.** An onionlike plant *(Allium sativum)* of southern Europe having a bulb that breaks up into separable cloves with a strong, distinctive odor and flavor. **2.** The bulb of this plant. —**garlic** *tr.v.* **-licked, -lick·ing, -licks.** To season or flavor (a food) with garlic. [Middle English, from Old English *gārlēac* : *gār,* spear + *lēac,* leek.]

garlic chive *n.* See **Chinese chive.**

gar·lick·y (gär′lĭ-kē) *adj.* Containing, tasting of, or smelling of garlic.

garlic mustard *n.* A Eurasian weed *(Alliaria petiolata)* having small white flowers and an odor of garlic.

gar·ment (gär′mənt) *n.* An article of clothing. —*attributive.* Often used to modify another noun: *garment factories; the garment district.* —**garment** *tr.v.* **-ment·ed, -ment·ing, -ments.** To clothe. [Middle English, from Old French *garnement,* from *garnir,* to equip, of Germanic origin. See **wer-**[4] in Appendix.]

garment bag *n.* A long, zippered bag used to carry and protect suits, dresses, and coats when traveling.

gar·ner (gär′nər) *tr.v.* **-nered, -ner·ing, -ners. 1.** To gather and store in or as if in a granary. **2.** To amass; acquire. See Synonyms at **reap.** —**garner** *n.* A granary. [Middle English, from *garner, gerner,* granary, from Old French *gernier, grenier,* from Latin *grānārium.* See GRANARY.]

Gar·ner (gär′nər), **John Nance.** 1868–1967. Vice President of the United States (1933–1941) during Franklin D. Roosevelt's first two terms.

gar·net[1] (gär′nĭt) *n.* **1.** Any of several common, widespread aluminum or calcium silicate minerals occurring in two internally isomorphic series, $(Mg, Mn, Fe)_3Al_2Si_3O_{12}$ and $Ca_3(Cr, Al, Fe)_2Si_3O_{12}$, generally crystallized, often embedded in igneous and metamorphic rocks, and colored red, brown, black, green, yellow, or white and used both as gemstones and as abrasives. **2.** *Color.* A dark to very dark red. [Middle English, from Old French *grenate,* from *grenat,* pomegranate-red, probably from Latin *grānātum,* pomegranate, from neuter of *grānātus,* seedy. See POMEGRANATE.]

gar·net[2] (gär′nĭt) *n. Nautical.* A tackle for hoisting light cargo. [Middle English *garnett,* probably from Middle Dutch *garnaat.*]

gar·net·if·er·ous (gär′nĭ-tĭf′ər-əs) *adj.* Containing garnets.

gar·ni·er·ite (gär′nē-ə-rīt′) *n.* A pale green or apple-green mineral, $(Ni, Mg)_3Si_2O_5(OH)_4$, used as a gemstone and as an important nickel ore. [After Jules *Garnier,* 19th-century French geologist.]

gar·nish (gär′nĭsh) *tr.v.* **-nished, -nish·ing, -nish·es. 1.a.** To enhance in appearance by adding decorative touches; embellish. **b.** To decorate (prepared food or drink) with small colorful or savory items, such as parsley or lemon slices. **2.** *Law.* To garnishee. —**garnish** *n.* **1.a.** Ornamentation; embellishment. **b.** An embellishment added to a prepared food or drink for decoration or added flavor. **2.** *Slang.* An unwarranted fee, such as one extorted from a new prisoner by a jailer. [Middle English *garnishen,* from Old French *garnir, garniss-,* of Germanic origin. See **wer-**[4] in Appendix.]

gar·nish·ee (gär′nĭ-shē′) *Law. n.* A third party who has been notified that money or property in his or her hands but belonging to a defendant has been attached. —**garnishee** *tr.v.* **-eed, -ee·ing, -ees. 1.** To attach by garnishment: *garnishee a debtor's wages.* **2.** To serve with a garnishment: *garnishee an employer.*

gar·nish·ment (gär′nĭsh-mənt) *n.* **1.** *Law.* **a.** A legal proceeding whereby money or property due a debtor but in the possession of another is applied to the payment of the debt owed to the plaintiff. **b.** A court order directing a third party who holds money or property belonging to a defendant to withhold it and appear in court to answer inquiries. **2.** Ornamentation; embellishment.

gar·ni·ture (gär′nĭ-chər) *n.* Something that garnishes; an embellishment. [French, from Old French, from *garnir,* to garnish. See GARNISH.]

Ga·ronne (gä-rôn′). A river of southwest France flowing about 563 km (350 mi) generally northwest from the Spanish Pyrenees to the Dordogne River north of Bordeaux.

gar·pike (gär′pīk′) *n.* See **gar**[1] (sense 2).

gar·ret (găr′ĭt) *n.* A room on the top floor of a house, typically under a pitched roof; an attic. [Middle English, from Old French *garite,* watchtower, from *garir,* to defend, of Germanic origin. See **wer-**[4] in Appendix.]

Gar·rick (găr′ĭk), **David.** 1717–1779. British actor and theater manager who was considered the foremost Shakespearean player of his time.

gar·ri·son (găr′ĭ-sən) *n.* **1.** A military post, especially one that is permanently established. **2.** The troops stationed at a military post. —**garrison** *tr.v.* **-soned, -son·ing, -sons. 1.** To assign (troops) to a military post. **2.** To supply (a post) with troops. **3.** To occupy as or convert into a military post. [Middle English *garison,* fortified place, from Old French, from *garir,* to defend, of Germanic origin. See **wer-⁴** in Appendix.]

Gar·ri·son (găr′ĭ-sən), **William Lloyd.** 1805–1879. American abolitionist leader who founded and published *The Liberator* (1831–1865), an antislavery journal.

garrison cap *n.* A soft cloth cap without a visor, worn as part of a military uniform. Also called *overseas cap.*

Garrison finish *n. Sports.* A finish in a contest or race in which the winner comes from behind at the last moment. [After Edward ("Snapper") *Garrison,* 19th-century American jockey.]

gar·rote or **gar·rotte** (gə-rŏt′, -rōt′) —*n.* **1.a.** A method of execution formerly practiced in Spain, in which a tightened iron collar is used to strangle or break the neck of a condemned person. **b.** The iron collar used for such an execution. **2.a.** Strangulation, especially in order to rob. **b.** A cord or wire used for strangling. —*tr.v.* **-rot·ed, -rot·ing, -rotes** or **-rot·ted, -rot·ting, -rottes. 1.** To execute by garrote. **2.** To strangle in order to rob. [Spanish cudgel, instrument of torture, possibly from Old French *garrot,* perhaps from *garoquier,* to struggle.] —**gar·rot′er** *n.*

gar·ru·li·ty (gə-rōō′lĭ-tē) *n.* Excessive talkativeness; loquaciousness.

gar·ru·lous (găr′ə-ləs, găr′yə-) *adj.* **1.** Given to excessive and often trivial or rambling talk; tiresomely talkative. See Synonyms at **talkative. 2.** Wordy and rambling: *a garrulous speech.* [From Latin *garrulus,* from *garrīre,* to chatter.] —**gar′ru·lous·ly** *adv.* —**gar′ru·lous·ness** *n.*

gar·ter (gär′tər) *n.* **1.a.** An elasticized band worn around the leg to hold up a stocking or sock. **b.** A suspender strap with a fastener attached to a girdle or belt to hold up a woman's stocking. **c.** An elasticized band worn around the arm to keep the sleeve pushed up. **2. Garter. a.** The badge of the Order of the Garter. **b.** The order itself. **c.** Membership in the order. —**garter** *tr.v.* **-tered, -ter·ing, -ters. 1.** To fasten and hold with a garter. **2.** To put a garter on. [Middle English, band to support socks, from Old North French *gartier,* from *garet,* bend of the knee, probably of Celtic origin.]

garter snake *n.* Any of various nonvenomous North and Central American snakes of the genus *Thamnophis,* having longitudinal stripes.

garth (gärth) *n.* **1.** A grassy quadrangle surrounded by cloisters. **2.** *Archaic.* A yard, garden, or paddock. [Middle English, enclosed yard, from Old Norse *gardhr.* See **gher-¹** in Appendix.]

Gar·vey (gär′vē), **Marcus (Moziah) Aurelius.** 1887–1940. Jamaican Black nationalist active in America in the 1920's.

Gar·y (gâr′ē, găr′ē). A city of northwest Indiana on Lake Michigan near the Illinois border. Founded on land purchased by the U.S. Steel Corporation in 1905, it is a highly industrialized port of entry. Population, 151,953.

gas (găs) *n., pl.* **gas·es** or **gas·ses. 1.a.** The state of matter distinguished from the solid and liquid states by relatively low density and viscosity, relatively great expansion and contraction with changes in pressure and temperature, the ability to diffuse readily, and the spontaneous tendency to become distributed uniformly throughout any container. **b.** A substance in the gaseous state. **2.** A gaseous fuel, such as natural gas. **3.** Gasoline. **4.** The speed control of a gasoline engine: *Step on the gas.* **5.** A gaseous asphyxiant, irritant, or poison. **6.** A gaseous anesthetic, such as nitrous oxide. **7.a.** Flatulence. **b.** Flatus. **8.** *Slang.* Idle or boastful talk. **9.** *Slang.* Someone or something exceptionally exciting or entertaining: *The party was a gas.* —*attributive.* Often used to modify another noun: *gas tanks; gas stoves.* —**gas** *v.* **gassed, gas·sing, gas·es** or **gas·ses.** —*tr.* **1.** To treat chemically with gas. **2.** To overcome, disable, or kill with poisonous fumes. —*intr.* **1.** To give off gas. **2.** *Slang.* To talk excessively. —***phrasal verb.*** **gas up.** To supply a vehicle with gas or gasoline: *gas up a car; gassed up before the trip.* [Dutch, an occult physical principle supposed to be present in all bodies, alteration of Greek *khaos,* chaos, empty space, coined by Jan Baptista van Helmont (1577–1644), Flemish chemist.]

gas·bag (găs′băg′) *n.* **1.** An expansible bag for holding gas. **2.** *Slang.* One given to empty or boastful talk.

gas burner *n.* A nozzle or jet on a fitting through which combustible gas is released to burn. Also called *gas jet.*

gas chamber *n.* A sealed enclosure in which condemned prisoners are executed by poison gas.

gas chromatograph *n.* An instrument used in gas chromatography to separate a sample of a volatile substance into its components.

gas chromatography *n.* Chromatography in which the substance to be separated into its components is diffused along with a carrier gas through a liquid or solid adsorbent for differential adsorption. —**gas′-chro·mat′o·graph′ic** (găs′krō-măt′ə-grăf′ĭk) *adj.*

gas·con (găs′kən) *n.* A boastful person; a braggart. [From GASCON (from the traditional stereotype of Gascons as braggarts).]

Gas·con (găs′kən) *n.* A native or inhabitant of Gascony. —**Gascon** *adj.* Of or relating to Gascony, the Gascons, or their language or culture.

gas·con·ade (găs′kə-nād′) *n.* Boastfulness; bravado. [French *gasconnade,* from *Gascon,* Gascon, from Latin *Vascō, Vascon-.*] —**gas′con·ade′** *v.* —**gas′con·ad′er** *n.*

Gas·con·ade (găs′kə-nād′). A river rising in the Ozark Plateau of south-central Missouri and flowing about 426 km (265 mi) generally northeast to the Missouri River east of Jefferson City.

gas constant *n. Symbol* **R** *Physics.* A constant, equal to 8.314 joules per Kelvin or 1.985 calories per degree Celsius, that is the constant of proportionality (R) in the equation Pressure × Volume = (R) × Temperature, relating the pressure and volume of a quantity of gas to the absolute temperature.

Gas·co·ny (găs′kə-nē). A historical region and former province of southwest France. Settled originally by Basque peoples, it was conquered by the Romans and later by the Visigoths and Franks. A new wave of Basque invaders from south of the Pyrenees established the duchy of Vasconia in the sixth century A.D. In 1052 Gascony passed to the duchy of Aquitaine and finally became part of the French royal domain in 1607.

gas·dy·nam·ics (găs′dī-năm′ĭks) *n.* (*used with a sing. verb*). The branch of dynamics that deals with the motion of gases and the thermal effects of this motion. —**gas′dy·nam′ic** *adj.* —**gas′dy·nam′i·cist** (-ĭ-sĭst) *n.*

gas·e·ous (găs′ē-əs, găsh′əs) *adj.* **1.** Of, relating to, or existing as a gas. **2.** Lacking substance or concreteness; tenuous or indefinite. **3.** Full of or containing gas. —**gas′e·ous·ness** *n.*

gas fitter *n.* One who installs or repairs gas pipes, fixtures, or appliances.

gas gangrene *n.* Gangrene occurring in a wound infected with bacteria of the genus *Clostridium,* especially *C. perfringens,* and characterized by the presence of gas in the affected tissue.

gas-guz·zler (găs′gŭz′lər) *n. Informal.* An automotive vehicle that gets relatively low gas mileage. —**gas′-guz′zling** *adj.*

gash (găsh) *tr.v.* **gashed, gash·ing, gash·es.** To make a long, deep cut in; slash deeply. —**gash** *n.* **1.** A long, deep cut. **2.** A deep flesh wound. [Alteration of Middle English *garsen,* to scarify, from Old North French *garser,* from Late Latin *charaxāre,* to scratch, engrave, from Greek *kharassein.*]

Gash·er·brum (gŭsh′ər-brōōm′, -brōōm′). A series of four peaks in the Karakoram Range of the Himalaya Mountains in northern Kashmir. **Gasherbrum I** is the highest, at 8,073.4 m (26,470 ft), although **Gasherbrum IV,** 7,930 m (26,000 ft), has been called more difficult than Everest for mountain climbers.

gas·hold·er (găs′hōl′dər) *n.* A storage container for fuel gas, especially a large, telescoping, cylindrical tank. Also called *gasometer.*

gas·house (găs′hous′) *n.* See **gasworks.**

gas·i·form (găs′ə-fôrm′) *adj.* Having the form of gas; gaseous.

gas·i·fy (găs′ə-fī′) *tr. & intr.v.* **-fied, -fy·ing, -fies.** To convert into or become gas. —**gas′i·fi′a·ble** *adj.* —**gas′i·fi·ca′tion** (-fĭ-kā′shən) *n.* —**gas′i·fi′er** *n.*

gas jet *n.* **1.** See **gas burner. 2.** The flame of burning gas from a gas burner.

Gas·kell (găs′kəl), **Elizabeth Cleghorn Stevenson.** 1810–1865. British writer noted for her *Life of Charlotte Brontë* (1857).

gas·ket (găs′kĭt) *n.* **1.** Any of a wide variety of seals or packings used between matched machine parts or around pipe joints to prevent the escape of a gas or fluid. **2.** *Nautical.* A cord or canvas strap used to secure a furled sail to a yard boom or gaff. [Perhaps alteration of French *garcette,* small cord, diminutive of *garce,* girl, from Old French, feminine of *gars,* boy, soldier. See GARÇON.]

gas·kin (găs′kĭn) *n.* **1.** The part of the hind leg of a horse or related animal between the stifle and the hock. **2. gaskins.** *Obsolete.* Galligaskins. [Probably short for GALLIGASKINS.]

gas·light (găs′līt′) *n.* **1.** Light produced by burning illuminating gas. **2.** A gas burner or lamp.

gas log *n.* A gas burner designed to look like a log for use in a fireplace.

gas main *n.* A major pipeline conveying gas to smaller pipes for distribution to consumers.

gas mask *n.* A respirator that contains a chemical air filter and is worn over the face as protection against toxic gases and aerosols.

gas·o·hol (găs′ə-hôl′) *n.* A fuel consisting of a blend of ethyl alcohol and unleaded gasoline, especially a blend of 10 percent ethanol and 90 percent gasoline. [GAS(OLINE) + (ALC)OHOL.]

gas·o·line (găs′ə-lēn′, găs′ə-lēn′) *n.* A volatile mixture of flammable liquid hydrocarbons derived chiefly from crude petroleum and used principally as a fuel for internal-combustion engines and as a solvent, an illuminant, and a thinner. [GAS + -OL(E) + -INE².]

gas·om·e·ter (gă-sŏm′ĭ-tər) *n.* **1.** An apparatus for measuring gases. **2.** See **gasholder.** [French *gazomètre* : *gaz,* gas (from Dutch *gas;* see GAS) + *-mètre,* -meter.]

gasp (găsp) *v.* **gasped, gasp·ing, gasps.** —*intr.* **1.** To draw in the breath sharply, as from shock. **2.** To breathe convulsively or laboriously. —*tr.* To utter in a breathless manner. —**gasp** *n.* A short convulsive intake or catching of the breath. [Middle English *gaspen, gaispen,* to gape, yawn, from Old Norse *geispa,* to yawn.]

Gas·par (găs′pär, -pər). See **Caspar.**

Gas·pé (găs-pā′). A city of eastern Quebec, Canada, on **Gaspé**

garlic
Allium sativum

gas mask

ă pat	oi boy
ā pay	ou out
âr care	ŏŏ took
ä father	ōō boot
ĕ pet	ŭ cut
ē be	ûr urge
ĭ pit	th thin
ī pie	*th* this
îr pier	hw which
ŏ pot	zh vision
ō toe	ə about, item
ô paw	♦ regionalism

Stress marks: ′ (primary); ′ (secondary), as in **dictionary** (dĭk′shə-nĕr′ē)

Bay, an inlet of the Gulf of St. Lawrence near the eastern tip of the Gaspé Peninsula. Population, 17,261.

Gaspé Peninsula. A peninsula of eastern Quebec, Canada, between Chaleur Bay and the mouth of the St. Lawrence River. Jacques Cartier landed here in 1534.

gasp·er (găs′pər) *n. Chiefly British.* A cigarette.

gas plant *n.* A Eurasian plant *(Dictamnus albus)* having aromatic foliage and white flowers and emitting a flammable vapor. Also called *burning bush, dittany, fraxinella.*

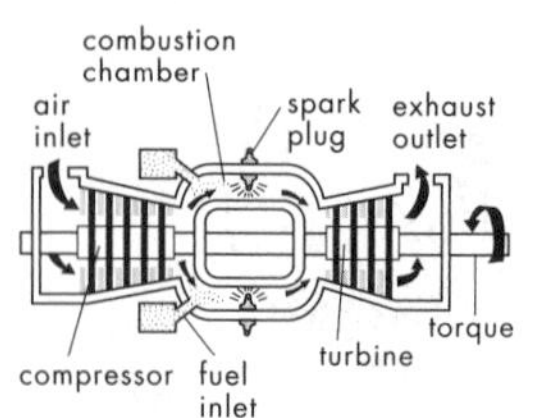

gas turbine
Simple, open-cycle gas turbine

gas·ser (găs′ər) *n.* **1.** A well or drilling that yields natural gas. **2.** *Slang.* Something highly entertaining or remarkable. **3.** *Slang.* A talkative or boastful person.

gas station *n.* See **service station** (sense 1).

gas·sy (găs′ē) *adj.* **-si·er, -si·est. 1.** Containing or full of gas. **2.** Resembling gas. **3.** *Slang.* Bombastic; boastful. **—gas′si·ness** *n.*

gast (găst) *tr.v.* **gast·ed, gast·ing, gasts.** *Obsolete.* To frighten; scare. [Middle English *gasten,* from Old English *gǣstan,* from *gāst,* ghost.]

gas·tight (găs′tīt′) *adj.* Impermeable by gas. **—gas′tight′-ness** *n.*

Gas·to·ni·a (gă-stō′nē-ə). A city of southern North Carolina near the South Carolina border west of Charlotte. It is a textile center. Population, 47,333.

gastr– *pref.* Variant of **gastro–.**

gas·trec·to·my (gă-strĕk′tə-mē) *n., pl.* **-mies.** Surgical excision of part or all of the stomach.

gas·tric (găs′trĭk) *adj.* Of, relating to, or associated with the stomach.

gastric juice *n.* The colorless, watery, acidic digestive fluid that is secreted by various glands in the mucous membrane of the stomach and consists chiefly of hydrochloric acid, pepsin, rennin, and mucin.

gastric ulcer *n.* An ulcer occurring in the mucous membrane of the stomach.

gas·trin (găs′trĭn) *n.* A hormone secreted by glands in the mucous membrane of the stomach that stimulates the production of gastric juice.

gate¹
Floodgate

gas·tri·tis (gă-strī′tĭs) *n.* Chronic or acute inflammation of the stomach, especially of the mucous membrane of the stomach.

gastro– or **gastr–** *pref.* **1.a.** Belly: *gastropod.* **b.** Stomach: *gastritis.* **2.** Gastric: *gastrin.* [Greek, from *gastēr, gastr-,* belly.]

gas·troc·ne·mi·us (găs′trŏk-nē′mē-əs, găs′trə-) *n., pl.* **-mi·i** (-mē-ī′). The largest, most prominent muscle of the calf of the leg, the action of which extends the foot and bends the knee. [New Latin, from Greek *gastroknēmia,* calf of the leg : *gastro-,* gastro- + *knēmē,* leg.]

gas·tro·en·ter·ic (găs′trō-ĕn-tĕr′ĭk) *adj.* Gastrointestinal.

gas·tro·en·ter·i·tis (găs′trō-ĕn′tə-rī′tĭs) *n.* Inflammation of the mucous membrane of the stomach and intestines.

gas·tro·en·ter·ol·o·gy (găs′trō-ĕn′tə-rŏl′ə-jē) *n.* The branch of medicine that deals with the study of disorders affecting the stomach, intestines, and associated organs. **—gas′tro·en′-ter·o·log′ic** (-ə-lŏj′ĭk), **gas′tro·en′ter·o·log′i·cal** *adj.* **—gas′tro·en′ter·ol′o·gist** *n.*

gas·tro·in·tes·ti·nal (găs′trō-ĭn-tĕs′tə-nəl) *adj. Abbr.* **GI** Of or relating to the stomach and intestines: *the gastrointestinal tract.*

gas·tro·lith (găs′trə-lĭth′) *n.* **1.** A pathological stony mass formed in the stomach; gastric calculus. **2.** A small stone found in the stomach of some reptiles, fish, and birds that aids in digestion by helping grind ingested food material.

gas·trol·o·gy (gă-strŏl′ə-jē) *n.* The medical study of the stomach and its diseases. **—gas′tro·log′i·cal, gas′tro·log′ic** *adj.* **—gas′tro·log′i·cal·ly** *adv.* **—gas·trol′o·gist** *n.*

gas·tro·nome (găs′trə-nōm′) also **gas·tron·o·mer** (gă-strŏn′ə-mər) *n.* A connoisseur of good food and drink; a gourmet. Also called *gastronomist.* [French, back-formation from *gastronomie,* gastronomy. See GASTRONOMY.]

gas·tro·nom·ic (găs′trə-nŏm′ĭk) also **gas·tro·nom·i·cal** (-ĭ-kəl) *adj.* Of or relating to gastronomy. **—gas′tro·nom′-i·cal·ly** *adv.*

gas·tron·o·mist (gă-strŏn′ə-mĭst) *n.* See **gastronome.**

gas·tron·o·my (gă-strŏn′ə-mē) *n., pl.* **-mies. 1.** The art or science of good eating. **2.** A style of cooking, as of a particular region. [French *gastronomie,* from Greek *gastronomia* : *gastro-,* gastro- + *-nomia,* -nomy.]

gatehouse

gas·tro·pod (găs′trə-pŏd′) *n.* Any of various mollusks of the class Gastropoda, such as the snail, slug, cowrie, or limpet, characteristically having a single, usually coiled shell or no shell at all, a ventral muscular foot for locomotion, and eyes and feelers located on a distinct head. **—gastropod** *adj.* Of or belonging to the class Gastropoda. [From New Latin *Gastropoda,* class name : GASTRO– + *-poda,* -pod.] **—gas·trop′o·dan** (gă-strŏp′ə-dn), **gas·trop′o·dous** (-dəs) *adj.*

gas·tro·scope (găs′trə-skōp′) *n.* An endoscope that is inserted through the mouth and used for examining the interior of the stomach. **—gas′tro·scop′ic** (-skŏp′ĭk) *adj.* **—gas·tros′-co·pist** (gă-strŏs′kə-pĭst) *n.* **—gas·tros′co·py** (-kə-pē) *n.*

gas·tros·to·my (gă-strŏs′tə-mē) *n., pl.* **-mies.** Surgical construction of a permanent opening from the external surface of the abdominal wall into the stomach, usually for inserting a feeding tube.

gas·trot·o·my (gă-strŏt′ə-mē) *n., pl.* **-mies.** A surgical incision into the stomach.

gas·tro·trich (găs′trə-trĭk) *n.* Any of various minute aquatic animals of the phylum Gastrotricha, having a wormlike, ciliated body. [From New Latin *Gastrotricha,* phylum name : GASTRO– + Greek *-trikha,* neuter pl. of *-trikhos,* -trichous.]

gas·tro·vas·cu·lar (găs′trō-văs′kyə-lər) *adj.* Having both a digestive and a circulatory function. Used especially to describe the body cavity of a coelenterate.

gas·tru·la (găs′trə-lə) *n., pl.* **-las** or **-lae** (-lē′). An embryo at the stage following the blastula, consisting of a hollow, two-layered sac of ectoderm and endoderm surrounding an archenteron that communicates with the exterior through the blastopore. [New Latin : Greek *gastēr, gastr-,* belly + Latin *-ula,* feminine diminutive suff.] **—gas′tru·lar** (-lər) *adj.*

gas·tru·late (găs′trə-lāt′) *intr.v.* **-lat·ed, -lat·ing, -lates.** To form or become a gastrula.

gas·tru·la·tion (găs′trə-lā′shən) *n.* The process of forming a gastrula.

gas turbine *n.* An internal-combustion engine consisting essentially of an air compressor, a combustion chamber, and a turbine wheel turned by the expanding products of combustion.

gas·works (găs′wûrks′) *pl.n. (used with a sing. verb).* A factory where gas for heating and lighting is produced. Also called *gashouse.*

gat¹ (găt) *n.* A narrow passage extending inland from a shore; a channel. [Probably Dutch, from Middle Dutch.]

gat² (găt) *n. Slang.* A pistol. [Short for GAT(LING GUN).]

gat³ (găt) *v. Archaic.* A past tense of **get.**

gate¹ (gāt) *n.* **1.** A structure that can be swung, drawn, or lowered to block an entrance or a passageway. **2.a.** An opening in a wall or fence for entrance or exit. **b.** The structure surrounding such an opening, such as the monumental or fortified entrance to a palace or walled city. **3.a.** A means of access: *the gate to riches.* **b.** A passageway, as in an airport terminal, through which passengers proceed for embarkation. **4.** A mountain pass. **5.** The total paid attendance or admission receipts at a public event: *a good gate at the football game.* **6.** A device for controlling the passage of water or gas through a dam or conduit. **7.** The channel through which molten metal flows into a shaped cavity of a mold. **8.** *Sports.* A passage between two upright poles through which a skier must go in a slalom race. **9.** *Electronics.* A circuit with multiple inputs and one output that is energized only when a designated set of input pulses is received. **—gate** *tr.v.* **gat·ed, gat·ing, gates. 1.** *Chiefly British.* To confine (a student) to the grounds of a college as punishment. **2.** *Electronics.* To select part of (a wave) for transmission, reception, or processing by magnitude or time interval. ***—idioms.*** **get the gate.** *Slang.* To be dismissed or rejected. **give (someone) the gate.** *Slang.* **1.** To discharge from a job. **2.** To reject or jilt. [Middle English, from Old English *geat.*]

gate² (gāt) *n.* **1.** *Chiefly British.* A particular way of acting or doing; manner. **2.** *Archaic.* A path or way. [Middle English, from Old Norse *gata.* See **ghē-** in Appendix.]

gâ·teau or **ga·teau** (gă-tō′, gä-) *n., pl.* **gâ·teaux** or **ga·teaux** (gă-tō′, gä-). A cake or pastry, especially a light one filled with custard, fruit, or nuts. [French, from Old French *gastel,* cake, from Frankish **wastil,* food.]

gate·crash·er (gāt′krăsh′ər) *n. Slang.* One who gains admittance, as to a party or concert, without being invited or without paying. **—gate′crash′** *v.*

gate·fold (gāt′fōld′) *n. Printing.* A foldout, especially one that opens to double the page size.

gate·house (gāt′hous′) *n.* **1.** A lodge at the entrance to the driveway of an estate. **2.** A fortified structure built over the gateway to a city or castle. **3.** A building that houses the controls of a dam or canal lock.

gate·keep·er (gāt′kē′pər) *n.* **1.** One that is in charge of passage through a gate. **2.** One who monitors or oversees the actions of others.

gate-leg table (gāt′lĕg′) *n.* A drop-leaf table with paired legs that swing out to support the leaves.

gate·post (gāt′pōst′) *n.* An upright post on which a gate is hung or against which it closes.

ga·ter also **′ga·ter** (gā′tər) *n. Informal.* Variants of **gator.**

Gates (gāts). A community of western New York, a suburb of Rochester. Population, 29,756.

Gates, Horatio. 1728?–1806. American Revolutionary general who became a hero after winning the Battle of Saratoga (1777) but suffered a humiliating defeat at Camden, South Carolina (1780).

Gates·head (gāts′hĕd′). A borough of northeast England on the Tyne River opposite Newcastle. Dating probably to Saxon times, it has an iron and steel industry that developed in the 19th century. Population, 214,100.

gate·way (gāt′wā′) *n.* **1.** An opening or a structure framing an opening, such as an arch, that may be closed by a gate. **2.** Something that serves as an entrance or a means of access: *a gateway to success; the gateway to the West.*

gateway drug *n.* A habit-forming substance whose use may lead to the abuse of drugs that are more addictive or more dangerous: *Marijuana is considered a gateway drug for cocaine.*

Gath (găth). An ancient city of Palestine east-northeast of Gaza. It was one of the five Philistine city-kingdoms.

gath·er (găth′ər) *v.* **-ered, -er·ing, -ers.** —*tr.* **1.** To cause to come together; convene. **2.a.** To accumulate (something) gradually; amass. **b.** To harvest or pick: *gather flowers; gather wild foods.* **3.** To gain by a process of gradual increase: *gather speed.* **4.** To collect into one place; assemble. **5.** To pick up and enfold: *gathered the kittens into her arms.* **6.** *Printing.* To arrange (signatures) in sequence for bookbinding. **7.a.** To draw into small folds or puckers, as by pulling a thread through cloth. **b.** To contract and wrinkle (the brow). **8.** To draw about or bring (one thing) closer to something else: *gathered the shawl about my shoulders.* **9.** To conclude; infer: *I gather that a decision has not been reached.* **10.** To summon up; muster: *gathered up his courage.* **11.** To attract or be a center of attraction for: *The parade gathered a large crowd.* —*intr.* **1.** To come together in a group; assemble. **2.** To accumulate: *Dark clouds are gathering.* **3.** To grow or increase by degrees. **4.** To come to a head, as a boil; fester. **5.** To forage for wild foodstuffs. —**gather** *n.* **1.a.** The act or an instance of gathering. **b.** A quantity gathered. **2.** A small fold or pucker made by gathering cloth. [Middle English *getheren, gaderen,* from Old English *gadrian.* See **ghedh-** in Appendix.] —**gath′er·er** *n.*

SYNONYMS: *gather, collect, assemble, congregate, accumulate, amass.* These verbs mean to bring or come together in a group or mass. *Gather* is the most general term and therefore the most widely applicable: *The tour guide gathered the visitors in the hotel lobby. A group of students gathered in front of the administration building to demand divestiture. I gathered sticks as kindling for the fire. Clouds gather before a thunderstorm. Collect* is often interchangeable with *gather: A proctor will collect* (or *gather*) *the examination papers at the end of the hour. Tears collected* (or *gathered*) *in her eyes.* Frequently, however, *collect* refers to the careful selection of like or related things that become part of an organized whole: *collects antiques; collected stamps. Assemble* in all of its senses implies that the persons or things involved have a definite and usually close relationship. With respect to persons the term suggests convening out of common interest or purpose: *Assembling an able staff was more difficult than raising the funds to finance the venture. The new legislature will assemble in January.* With respect to things *assemble* implies gathering and fitting together components, as of a structure or machine: *The curator is devoting time and energy to assembling an interesting exhibit of Stone Age artifacts. Congregate* refers chiefly to the coming together of a large number of persons or animals: *After the lecture the physicians congregated in the library to compare notes. Accumulate* applies to the increase of like or related things over an extended period: *They gradually accumulated enough capital to be financially secure after retirement. Old newspapers and magazines are accumulating in the basement. Amass* refers to the collection or accumulation of things, especially valuable things, to form an imposing quantity: *families who amassed great fortunes in the days before income tax.* See also Synonyms at **reap.**

gath·er·ing (găth′ər-ĭng) *n.* **1.a.** The action of one that gathers. **b.** That which is gathered or amassed; a collection or an accumulation. **2.** An assembly of persons; a meeting. **3.** The collecting of food that grows wild, such as berries, roots, and grains. **4.** A gather in cloth. **5.** A suppurated swelling; a boil or an abscess.

Gat·i·neau (găt′n-ō′, gä-tē-nō′). A town of southwest Quebec, Canada, northeast of Hull near the mouth of the **Gatineau River,** about 386 km (240 mi) long. The river rises in the Laurentian Plateau and flows generally southwest to the Ottawa River. The city is an industrial center. Population, 74,988.

Gat·ling (găt′lĭng), **Richard Jordan.** 1818–1903. American firearms inventor remembered for inventing the first rapid-firing gun (patented 1862).

Gatling gun *n.* A machine gun having a cluster of barrels that are fired in sequence as the cluster is rotated. [After Richard Jordan GATLING.]

ga·tor or **ga·ter ′ga·tor, ′ga·ter** (gā′tər) *n. Informal.* An alligator.

Gat·or·ade (gā′tə-rād′). A trademark used for a thirst-quenching beverage drunk especially by athletes.

GATT *abbr.* General Agreement on Tariffs and Trade.

Ga·tún Lake (gə-to͞on′, gä-). An artificial lake of central Panama formed by the impounding of the Chagres River. It is a major link in the Panama Canal system.

gauche (gōsh) *adj.* Lacking social polish; tactless. See Synonyms at **awkward.** [French, awkward, lefthanded, from Old French, from *gauchir,* to turn aside, walk clumsily, of Germanic origin.] —**gauche′ly** *adv.* —**gauche′ness** *n.*

gau·che·rie (gō′shə-rē′) *n.* **1.** An awkward or tactless act, manner, or expression. **2.** A lack of tact; awkwardness. [French, from *gauche,* gauche. See GAUCHE.]

gau·cho (gou′chō) *n., pl.* **-chos. 1.** A cowboy of the South American pampas. **2. gauchos.** Calf-length pants with flared legs. [American Spanish, probably from Quechua *wáhcha,* poor person, orphan, vagabond.]

gaud (gôd) *n.* A gaudy or showy ornament or trinket. [Middle English *gaud, gaudi,* sing. of *gaudies,* large, ornamental beads on a rosary, trinkets, from Medieval Latin *gaudia,* from Latin, pl. of *gaudium,* joy (referring to the Joyful Mysteries of the Virgin Mary), from *gaudēre,* to rejoice. See **gāu-** in Appendix.]

gaud·er·y (gô′də-rē) *n., pl.* **-ies.** Showy or gaudy decoration; ostentatious or pretentious show.

Gau·dí (gou′dē, gou-dē′), **Antonio.** 1852–1926. Spanish architect who worked mainly in Barcelona, developing a startling new style that paralleled developments in art nouveau and incorporated color as well as odd bits of material.

gaud·y¹ (gô′dē) *adj.* **-i·er, -i·est.** Showy in a tasteless or vulgar way. [Possibly from GAUDY² (influenced by GAUD).] —**gaud′i·ly** *adv.* —**gaud′i·ness** *n.*

SYNONYMS: *gaudy, flashy, garish, loud, meretricious, tawdry.* The central meaning shared by these adjectives is "tastelessly showy": *a gaudy costume; a flashy ring; garish colors; a loud sport shirt; a meretricious yet stylish book; tawdry ornaments.*

gaucho

gaud·y² (gô′dē) *n., pl.* **-ies.** *Chiefly British.* A feast, especially an annual university dinner. [Middle English *gaudi, gaud,* prank, trick, possibly from Old French *gaudie,* merriment (from *gaudir,* to enjoy, make merry, from Latin *gaudēre,* to rejoice) and from Latin *gaudium,* enjoyment, merry-making (from *gaudēre,* to rejoice; see **gāu-** in Appendix).]

gauf·fer (gŏf′ər, gô′fər) *v. & n.* Variant of **goffer.**

Gau·ga·me·la (gô′gə-mē′lə). An ancient village of Assyria northeast of Nineveh. Alexander the Great defeated the Persians under Darius III here in 331 B.C.

gauge also **gage** (gāj) —*n. Abbr.* **ga. 1.a.** A standard or scale of measurement. **b.** A standard dimension, quantity, or capacity. **2.** An instrument for measuring or testing. **3.** A means of estimating or evaluating; a test: *a gauge of character.* See Synonyms at **standard. 4.** *Nautical.* The position of a vessel in relation to another vessel and the wind. **5.a.** The distance between the two rails of a railroad. **b.** The distance between two wheels on an axle. **6.** The interior diameter of a shotgun barrel as determined by the number of lead balls of a size exactly fitting the barrel that are required to make one pound. Often used in combination: *a 12-gauge shotgun.* **7.** The amount of plaster of Paris combined with common plaster to speed setting of the mixture. **8.** Thickness or diameter, as of sheet metal or wire. **9.** The fineness of knitted cloth as determined by the number of loops per 1½ inches. —*tr.v.* **gauged, gaug·ing, gaug·es** also **gaged, gag·ing, gag·es. 1.** To measure precisely. **2.** To determine the capacity, volume, or contents of. **3.** To evaluate or judge: *gauge a person's ability.* **4.** To adapt to a specified measurement. **5.** To mix (plaster) in specific proportions. **6.** To chip or rub (bricks or stones) to size. [Middle English, from Old North French, gauging rod, of Germanic origin.] —**gauge′a·ble** *adj.*

gaug·er also **gag·er** (gā′jər) *n. Chiefly British.* A revenue officer who inspects bulk goods subject to duty.

Gau·guin (gō-găɴ′), **(Eugène Henri) Paul.** 1848–1903. French artist whose paintings are characterized by simplified forms and brilliant colors.

Gaul¹ (gôl) *n.* **1.** A Celt of ancient Gaul. **2.** A French person.

Gaul² (gôl). Formerly **Gal·li·a** (găl′ē-ä). An ancient region of western Europe south and west of the Rhine River, west of the Alps, and north of the Pyrenees, corresponding roughly to modern-day France and Belgium. The Romans extended the designation to include northern Italy, particularly after Julius Caesar's conquest of the area in the Gallic Wars (58–51 B.C.).

Gaul·ish (gô′lĭsh) *n.* The Celtic language of ancient Gaul.

Gaull·ism (gō′lĭz′əm, gô′-) *n.* **1.** The political movement supporting Gen. Charles de Gaulle as leader of the French government in exile during World War II. **2.a.** The political movement headed by Charles de Gaulle after World War II. **b.** The political principles and goals of Charles de Gaulle and his followers. —**Gaull′ist** *n.*

gaum (gôm) *tr.v.* **gaumed, gaum·ing, gaums.** *Upper Southern U.S.* To smudge or smear. [Perhaps alteration of obsolete *gome,* grease, variant of *coom,* soot, mixture of dirt and axle grease, variant of CULM².]

gauntlet¹

gaunt (gônt) *adj.* **gaunt·er, gaunt·est. 1.** Thin and bony; angular. See Synonyms at **lean². 2.** Emaciated and haggard; drawn. **3.** Bleak and desolate; barren. [Middle English, perhaps from Old French *gant,* possibly of Scandinavian origin.] —**gaunt′ly** *adv.* —**gaunt′ness** *n.*

gaunt·let¹ also **gant·let** (gônt′lĭt, gänt′-) *n.* **1.** A protective glove worn with medieval armor. **2.** A protective glove with a flared cuff, used in manual labor, in certain sports, and for driving. **3.** A challenge: *throw down the gauntlet.* **4.** A dress glove cuffed above the wrist. [Middle English, from Old French *gantelet,* diminutive of *gant,* glove, from Frankish **want.*]

WORD HISTORY: In the first and second editions of *The American Heritage Dictionary* Usage Notes explained why the spelling *gauntlet* is acceptable for both *gauntlet*¹ and *gauntlet*². Such has not always been the case. The story of *gauntlet*¹, as in *to throw down the gauntlet,* is unexciting: it comes from the Old French word *gantelet,* a diminutive of *gant,* "glove." From the time of its appearance in Middle English (in a work composed in 1449), the word has been spelled with an *au* as well as an *a,* still a possible spelling. But the other *gauntlet,* as in *to run the gauntlet,* is an alteration of the earlier English form *gantlope,* which came from the Swedish word *gatlopp,* a compound of *gata,* "lane," and *lopp,*

ă pat	oi boy
ā pay	ou out
âr care	o͝o took
ä father	o͞o boot
ĕ pet	ŭ cut
ē be	ûr urge
ĭ pit	th thin
ī pie	*th* this
îr pier	hw which
ŏ pot	zh vision
ō toe	ə about, item
ô paw	♦ regionalism

Stress marks: ′ (primary); ′ (secondary), as in **dictionary** (dĭk′shə-nĕr′ē)

"course." The earliest recorded form of the English word, found in 1646, is *gantelope,* showing that alteration of the Swedish word had already occurred. The English word was then influenced by the spelling of the word *gauntlet,* "glove," and in 1676 we find the first recorded instance of the spelling *gauntlet* for this word, although *gantelope* is found as late as 1836. From then on spellings with *au* and *a* are both found. The *au* seems to have won out, although one could say that the *a* is preferable because it reflects the Swedish source. In regard to a word that has been so altered in form, this seems a rather fine point.

gaur
Bos gaurus

gaunt·let² also **gant·let** (gônt′lĭt, gänt′-) *n.* **1.a.** A form of punishment in which men armed with sticks or other weapons arrange themselves in two lines facing each other and beat the person forced to run between them. **b.** The lines of men so arranged. **2.** An onslaught or attack from all sides: *"The hostages . . . ran the gauntlet of insult on their way to the airport"* (Harper's). **3.** A severe trial; an ordeal. [Alteration (influenced by GAUNTLET¹) of *gantlope,* from Swedish *gatlopp* : *gata,* lane (from Old Swedish; see **ghē-** in Appendix) + *lopp,* course, running (from Middle Low German *lōp*).]

gaur (gour) *n.* A large, dark-coated wild ox *(Bos gaurus)* of hilly areas of southeast Asia. Also called *seladang.* [Hindi, from Sanskrit *gauraḥ.* See **gʷou-** in Appendix.]

gauss (gous) *n., pl.* **gauss** or **gauss·es.** *Abbr.* **G** *Physics.* The centimeter-gram-second unit of magnetic induction, equal to one maxwell per square centimeter. [After Karl Friedrich GAUSS.]

Gauss (gous), **Karl Friedrich.** 1777–1855. German mathematician and astronomer known for his contributions to algebra, differential geometry, probability theory, and number theory.

Gauss·i·an distribution (gou′sē-ən) *n.* See **normal distribution.** [After Karl Friedrich GAUSS.]

Gau·ta·ma (gô′tə-mə, gou′-), **Siddhartha.** See **Buddha.**

Gau·tier (gō-tyā′), **Théophile.** 1811–1872. French writer who influenced French literature during its shift from romanticism to aestheticism and naturalism.

gauze (gôz) *n.* **1.a.** A thin, transparent fabric with a loose open weave, used for curtains and clothing. **b.** A thin, loosely woven surgical dressing, usually made of cotton. **c.** A thin plastic or metal woven mesh. **2.** A mist or haze. [French *gaze,* possibly from Spanish *gasa* (from Arabic *qazz,* raw silk, possibly from Persian *kazh*).] **—gauz′i·ly** *adv.* **—gauz′i·ness** *n.*

gauz·y (gô′zē) *adj.* **-i·er, -i·est.** Resembling gauze in thinness or transparency. See Synonyms at **airy.** **—gauz′i·ly** *adv.* **—gauz′i·ness** *n.*

gavel¹

ga·vage (gə-väzh′) *n.* Introduction of nutritive material into the stomach by means of a tube. [French, from *gaver,* to force down the throat, ultimately from Old French *gave,* throat, from Old Latin **gaba.*]

gave (gāv) *v.* Past tense of **give.**

gav·el¹ (găv′əl) *n.* **1.** A small mallet used by a presiding officer or an auctioneer to signal for attention or order or to mark the conclusion of a transaction. **2.** A maul used by masons in fitting stones. **—gavel** *tr.v.* **-eled, -el·ing, -els** also **-elled, -el·ling, -els.** To bring about or compel by using a gavel: *"The chairman . . . tries to gavel the demonstration to an end"* (New Yorker). [Origin unknown.]

gav·el² (găv′əl) *n.* Tribute or rent in ancient and medieval England. [Middle English, from Old English *gafol.* See **ghabh-** in Appendix.]

gazebo

gav·el·kind (găv′əl-kīnd′) *n.* An English system of land tenure from Anglo-Saxon times to 1926 that provided for the equal division of land among all qualified heirs. [Middle English *gavelkinde* : Old English *gafol,* gavel; see GAVEL² + Old English *gecynd,* kind; see KIND².]

gav·el-to-gav·el (găv′əl-tə-găv′əl) *adj. Informal.* Extending from the opening to the close, as of a political convention: *gavel-to-gavel television coverage.*

ga·vi·al (gā′vē-əl) *n.* A large reptile *(Gavialis gangeticus)* of southern Asia, related to and resembling the crocodiles and having a long, slender snout. Also called *gharial.* [French, from Hindi *ghaṛiyāl.*]

ga·votte (gə-vŏt′) *n.* **1.** A French peasant dance resembling the minuet. **2.** Music for this dance in moderately quick 4/4 time. [French, from Provençal *gavoto,* from *gavot,* native of the Alps, possibly from *gava,* crop of a bird, from Old Latin **gaba,* gullet, throat.] **—ga·votte′** *v.*

GAW *abbr.* Guaranteed annual wage.

Ga·wain (gə-wān′, gä′wān′, gou′ən, gä′wən) *n.* In Arthurian legend, a nephew of Arthur and a Knight of the Round Table.

gawk (gôk) *n.* An awkward, loutish person; an oaf. **—gawk** *intr.v.* **gawked, gawk·ing, gawks.** To stare or gape stupidly. [Perhaps alteration (influenced by *gawk hand,* left hand, from dialectal *gaulic,* left-handed, clumsy) of obsolete *gaw,* to gape, from Middle English *gawen,* from Old Norse *gā,* to heed.]

gawk·y (gô′kē) *adj.* **-i·er, -i·est.** Awkward; ungainly. **—gawk′i·ly** *adv.*

gay (gā) *adj.* **gay·er, gay·est.** **1.** Showing or characterized by cheerfulness and lighthearted excitement; merry. **2.** Bright or lively, especially in color: *a gay, sunny room.* **3.** Of, relating to, or sharing the lifestyle and concerns of the homosexual community. **4.** Homosexual. **5.** Given to social pleasures. **6.** Dissolute; licentious. **—gay** *n.* A gay person, especially an openly gay person in contemporary society. [Middle English *gai,* from Old French, possibly of Germanic origin.] **—gay′ness** *n.*

USAGE NOTE: The word *gay* is now standard in its use to refer to the American homosexual community and its members; in this use it is generally lowercased. *Gay* is distinguished from *homosexual* in emphasizing the cultural and social aspects of homosexuality. Many writers reserve *gay* for male homosexuals, but the word is also used to refer to homosexuals of both sexes; when the intended meaning is not clear in the context, the phrase *gay and lesbian* should be used. Like the other names of social groups that are derived from adjectives (e.g., *Black*), *gay* may be regarded as offensive when used as a noun to refer to particular individuals, as in *There were two gays on the panel;* here a phrase such as *gay people* should be used instead. But there is no objection to the use of the noun in the plural to refer to the general gay community, as in *Gays have united in opposition to the policy.*

Gay (gā), **John.** 1685–1732. English writer known especially for his play *The Beggar's Opera* (1728).

Ga·ya (gə-yä′, gī′ə). A city of northeast India south of Patna. The surrounding area is sacred to Buddhist and Hindu pilgrims. Population, 247,075.

ga·yal (gə-yäl′) *n.* A domesticated bovine mammal *(Bos frontalis)* of India and Burma, having thick, pointed horns, a dark coat, and a tufted tail. [Bengali *gayāl,* probably from Sanskrit *gauḥ,* ox. See **gʷou-** in Appendix.]

gay·e·ty (gā′ĭ-tē) *n.* Variant of **gaiety.**

gay feather *n.* See **blazing star** (sense 2).

Gay-Lus·sac (gā′lə-săk′, -lü-săk′), **Joseph Louis.** 1778–1850. French chemist and physicist who isolated the element boron (1809) and formulated a law that explains the behavior of a gas under constant pressure.

gay·ly (gā′lē) *adv.* Variant of **gaily.**

gaz. *abbr.* Gazette; gazetteer.

Ga·za (gä′zə, găz′ə, gā′zə). A city of southwest Asia in the **Gaza Strip,** a narrow coastal area along the Mediterranean Sea adjoining Israel and Egypt. The territory was part of the British mandate for Palestine (1917–1948), passed to Egypt in 1949, and was occupied by Israel in 1967. The city of Gaza was one of the five major Philistine city-kingdoms. Population, 118,272.

ga·zar (gə-zär′) *n.* A loosely woven silk with a crisp finish. [Probably ultimately from Arabic *qazz,* raw silk. See GAUZE.]

gaze (gāz) *intr.v.* **gazed, gaz·ing, gaz·es.** To look steadily, intently, and with fixed attention. **—gaze** *n.* A steady, fixed look. [Middle English *gasen,* probably of Scandinavian origin.] **—gaz′er** *n.*

SYNONYMS: *gaze, stare, gape, glare, peer, ogle.* These verbs mean to look long and intently. *Gaze* refers to prolonged looking that is often indicative of wonder, fascination, awe, or admiration: *gazing at the stars; gazed into her eyes.* To *stare* is to gaze fixedly; the word can indicate curiosity, boldness, insolence, or stupidity: *stared at them in disbelief; staring into the distance. Gape* suggests a prolonged open-mouthed look reflecting amazement, awe, or lack of intelligence: *tourists gaping at the sights.* To *glare* is to fix another with a hard, piercing stare: *He glared furiously at me when I contradicted him.* To *peer* is to look narrowly, searchingly, and seemingly with difficulty: *peered through her spectacles at the contract.* To *ogle* is to stare in an amorous, usually impertinent manner: *construction workers on their lunch hour ogling passing women.*

ga·ze·bo (gə-zā′bō, -zē′-) *n., pl.* **-bos** or **-boes.** **1.** A freestanding, roofed, usually open-sided structure providing a shady resting place. **2.** See **belvedere.** [Origin unknown.]

gaze·hound (gāz′hound′) *n.* A dog, such as the Afghan hound, that hunts its prey by sight rather than by scent.

ga·zelle (gə-zĕl′) *n.* Any of various small, swift antelopes of the genus *Gazella* and related genera of Africa and Asia, characteristically having a slender neck and annulate horns. [French, from Old French, from Arabic *ġazāl.*]

ga·zette (gə-zĕt′) *n. Abbr.* **gaz.** **1.** A newspaper. **2.** An official journal. **3.** *Chiefly British.* An announcement in an official journal. **—gazette** *tr.v.* **-zet·ted, -zet·ting, -zettes.** *Chiefly British.* To announce or publish in an official journal or in a newspaper. [French, from Italian *gazzetta,* probably from Italian dialectal *gazeta,* a small coin (possibly from the price).]

gaz·et·teer (găz′ĭ-tîr′) *n. Abbr.* **gaz.** **1.** A geographic dictionary or index. **2.** *Archaic.* A writer for a gazette; a journalist.

Ga·zi·an·tep (gä′zē-än-tĕp′). Formerly **Ain·tab** (īn-tăb′). A city of southern Turkey north of Aleppo, Syria. An ancient Hittite center, it was strategically important during the Crusades. Population, 374,290.

gaz·pa·cho (gə-spä′chō, gəz-pä′-) *n., pl.* **-chos.** A chilled soup made with chopped tomatoes, cucumbers, onions, peppers, and herbs. [Spanish.]

G.B. *abbr.* Great Britain.

Gbe (bĕ, gbĕ) *n.* A closely related group of languages, including Ewe and Fon, that are spoken in coastal Ghana, Togo, Benin, and Nigeria. [Gbe, language, voice.]

GC *abbr.* Gigacycle.

ă pat	oi boy
ā pay	ou out
âr care	o͝o took
ä father	o͞o boot
ĕ pet	ŭ cut
ē be	ûr urge
ĭ pit	th thin
ī pie	*th* this
îr pier	hw which
ŏ pot	zh vision
ō toe	ə about, item
ô paw	♦ regionalism

Stress marks: ′ (primary); ′ (secondary), as in **dictionary** (dĭk′shə-nĕr′ē)

GCA *abbr.* Ground-controlled approach.

G.C.B. *abbr.* Knight of the Grand Cross, Order of the Bath.

gcd or **g.c.d.** *abbr. Mathematics.* Greatest common divisor.

gcf or **g.c.f.** *abbr. Mathematics.* Greatest common factor.

G clef *n. Music.* See **treble clef.**

GCT *abbr.* Greenwich civil time.

Gd The symbol for the element **gadolinium.**

gd. *abbr.* Good.

G.D. *abbr.* Grand duchy.

Gdańsk (gə-dänsk′, -dănsk′, -dīnsk′) also **Dan·zig** (dăn′sĭg, dän′tsĭk). A city of northern Poland near the mouth of the Vistula River on the **Gulf of Gdańsk,** an inlet of the Baltic Sea. An old Slavic settlement, Gdańsk was a part of the Hanseatic League after the 13th century and was later ruled by Poland and Prussia. The Treaty of Versailles (1919) declared it a free city, although it came under Nazi control in 1935. Hitler's demand that Gdańsk be returned to Germany led to his invasion of Poland and the beginning of World War II (September 1939). Population, 467,200.

G.D.R. or **GDR** *abbr.* German Democratic Republic.

gds. *abbr.* Goods.

Gdy·ni·a (gə-dĭn′ē-ə, -dĭn′yə). A city of northern Poland on the Gulf of Gdańsk northwest of Gdańsk. It has been a major Baltic port since the 1930's. Population, 243,100.

Ge The symbol for the element **germanium.**

ge– *pref.* Variant of **geo–.**

ge·an·ti·cline (jē-ăn′tĭ-klīn′) *n.* A large upward fold of the earth's crust. **—ge·an′ti·cli′nal** *adj.*

gear (gîr) *n.* **1.a.** A toothed machine part, such as a wheel or cylinder, that meshes with another toothed part to transmit motion or to change speed or direction. **b.** A complete assembly that performs a specific function in a larger machine. **c.** A transmission configuration for a specific ratio of engine to axle torque in a motor vehicle. **2.** Equipment, such as tools or clothing, used for a particular activity; paraphernalia: *fishing gear.* See Synonyms at **equipment. 3.a.** Clothing and accessories: *the latest gear for teenagers.* **b.** Personal belongings, including clothing: *keeps her gear in a trunk.* **4.** The harness for a horse. **5.** *Nautical.* **a.** A ship's rigging. **b.** A sailor's personal effects. **—gear** *v.* **geared, gear·ing, gears.** —*tr.* **1.a.** To equip with gears. **b.** To connect by gears. **c.** To put into gear. **2.** To adjust or adapt so as to make suitable: *geared the speech to a conservative audience.* **3.** To provide with gear; equip. —*intr.* **1.** To come into or be in gear. **2.** To become adjusted so as to fit or blend. ***—phrasal verb.* gear up.** To get ready for a coming action or event: *a group of investors who had geared up for the takeover fight.* [Middle English *gere,* equipment, from Old Norse *gervi*; akin to *gera,* to do, make, make ready.]

gear·box (gîr′bŏks′) *n.* **1.** See **transmission** (sense 3). **2.** A protective casing for a system of gears.

gear·ing (gîr′ĭng) *n.* **1.** A system of gears and associated elements by which motion is transferred within a machine. **2.** The act or technique of providing with gears.

gear ratio *n.* The ratio of the speed of rotation of the powered gear of a gear train to that of the final or driven gear.

gear·shift (gîr′shĭft′) *n.* A mechanism for changing from one gear to another in a transmission.

gear train *n.* A system of interconnected gears.

gear·wheel also **gear wheel** (gîr′hwēl′, -wēl′) *n.* A wheel with a toothed rim.

Geat (gēt, yăt) *n.* A member of an ancient Germanic people of southern Sweden conquered by the Swedes in the 6th century. [Old English *Gēat.*]

Ge·bel Mu·sa (jĕb′əl mo͞o′sə, -sä). See **Jebel Musa.**

Ge·ber (jē′bər, gā′-) also **Ja·bir** (jä′bər, jä′bîr). fl. eighth century? Arab scholar and alchemist who wrote a number of influential books of alchemical theory.

geck·o (gĕk′ō) *n., pl.* **-os** or **-oes.** Any of various usually small tropical and subtropical lizards of the family Gekkonidae, having toes padded with setae containing numerous suction cups that enable them to climb on vertical surfaces. [Malay (Javanese) *ge'kok.*]

GED *abbr.* **1.** General equivalency diploma. **2.** General educational development.

Ged·des (gĕd′ēz), **Norman Bel.** 1893–1958. American architect and theatrical and industrial designer who popularized the concept of streamlining.

gee[1] (jē) *n.* The letter *g.*

gee[2] (jē) *interj.* Used to command a horse or an ox to turn to the right. **—gee** *intr.v.* **geed, gee·ing, gees.** To turn to the right.

gee[3] also **jee** (jē) *interj.* Used as a mild expletive or exclamation, as of surprise, enthusiasm, or sympathy. [Alteration of JE-SUS.]

gee[4] (jē) *n. Slang.* A thousand dollars. [From GEE[1], from the first letter of GRAND.]

♦**Gee·chee** (gē′chē) *n.* **1.** *Southeastern U.S.* Gullah. **2.** The local dialect of English spoken in Charleston, South Carolina. [After the OGEECHEE River.]

geek (gēk) *n. Slang.* **1.** An odd or ridiculous person. **2.** A carnival performer whose show consists of bizarre acts, such as biting the head off a live chicken. [Perhaps alteration of dialectal *geck,* fool, from Low German *gek,* from Middle Low German.] **—geek′y** *adj.*

Gee·long (jə-lông′). A city of southeast Australia southwest of Melbourne. It is a manufacturing center with a thriving tourist industry. Metropolitan area population, 137,173.

geese (gēs) *n.* Plural of **goose.**

gee whiz *interj.* Used to express mild surprise, amazement, or enthusiasm.

gee-whiz (jē′hwĭz′, -wĭz′) *adj. Informal.* Marked by or inducing a sense of wide-eyed wonder or excitement, as in response to an amazing achievement: *"The book seems a little too gee-whiz even for describing what everyone does admit is a revolution"* (Savvy).

gee·zer (gē′zər) *n.* An eccentric old man. See Usage Note at **adage.** [Probably alteration of dialectal *guiser,* masquerader, from Middle English *gysar,* from *gysen,* to dress, from *gyse, guise,* fashion. See GUISE.]

WORD HISTORY: A relationship with a word we know well is disguised in the word *geezer.* A clue to this relationship is found in British dialect. The *English Dialect Dictionary* defines *geezer* as "a queer character, a strangely-acting person," and refers the reader to *guiser,* "a mummer, masquerader." The citations for *guiser* refer to practices such as the following: "People, usually children . . . go about on Christmas Eve, singing, wearing masks, or otherwise disguised," the last word of this passage being the one to which *geezer* is related.

gecko

ge·fil·te fish (gə-fĭl′tə) *n.* Finely chopped fish, usually whitefish, pike, or carp, mixed with crumbs, eggs, and seasonings, cooked in a broth in the form of balls or oval-shaped cakes and usually served chilled. [Yiddish : *gefilt,* past participle of *filn,* to fill, stuff + *fish,* fish.]

ge·gen·schein (gā′gən-shīn′) *n.* A faint, glowing spot in the sky, exactly opposite the position of the sun. Also called *counterglow.* [German : *gegen,* against (from Middle High German, from Old High German *gegin*) + *Schein,* light (from Middle High German *schīn,* from Old High German *schīn,* from *scīnan,* to shine).]

Ge·hen·na (gĭ-hĕn′ə) *n.* **1.** A place or state of torment or suffering. **2.** The abode of condemned souls; hell. [Late Latin, from Greek *Geenna,* from Hebrew *Gê' Hinnōm,* possibly short for *Gē ben Hinnōm,* valley of the son of Hinnom, a valley south of Jerusalem.]

Geh·rig (gĕr′ĭg), **Henry Louis.** Known as "Lou." 1903–1941. American baseball player. In 14 seasons with the New York Yankees (1925–1939), Gehrig was the American League's most valuable player 4 times. He earned a career batting average of .340.

Lou Gehrig
Photographed in the late 1930's

Gei·ger counter (gī′gər) *n.* An instrument that detects and measures the intensity of radiation, such as particles from radioactive material, consisting of a Geiger tube and associated electronic equipment. [After Hans Wilhelm *Geiger* (1882–1945), German physicist.]

gei·ger tree (gī′gər) *n.* A small evergreen tree *(Cordia sebestena)* native to the Florida Keys, the West Indies, and northern South America, having large orange and scarlet flowers in terminal clusters. [After John *Geiger* (fl. c. 1832), American friend of John James Audubon.]

Geiger tube *n.* A metal or glass tube filled with gas that is ionized by passing charged particles, producing within the tube an electric charge indicative of a particular particle. [After Hans Wilhelm *Geiger* (1882–1945), German physicist.]

Gei·sel (gī′zəl), **Theodor Seuss.** Pen name Dr. Seuss. 1904–1991. American writer and illustrator of children's books, including *The Cat in the Hat* (1957).

gei·sha (gā′shə, gē′-) *n., pl.* **geisha** or **-shas.** One of a class of professional women in Japan trained from girlhood in conversation, dancing, and singing in order to lend an atmosphere of chic and gaiety to professional or social gatherings of men. [Japanese : *gei,* art + *sha,* person.]

gel (jĕl) *n.* **1.** A colloid in which the disperse phase has combined with the dispersion medium to produce a semisolid material, such as a jelly. **2.** A gelatin used in theatrical lighting. **3.** A jellylike substance used in styling hair. **—gel** *intr.v.* **gelled, gel·ling, gels.** To become a gel. [Short for GELATIN.] **—gel′a·ble** *adj.*

ge·län·de·sprung (gə-lĕn′də-shpro͝ong′) *n. Sports.* A jump in skiing made from a crouching position with the use of both poles. [German : *Gelände,* open field (from Middle High German *gelende,* from Old High German *gilanti,* from *lant,* land; see **lendh-** in Appendix) + *Sprung,* jump (from Middle High German *spruc,* from Old High German, from *springan,* to jump).]

gel·ate (jĕl′āt′) *intr.v.* **-at·ed, -at·ing, -ates.** To gel.

gel·a·tin also **gel·a·tine** (jĕl′ə-tn) *n.* **1.a.** A colorless or slightly yellow, transparent, brittle protein formed by boiling the specially prepared skin, bones, and connective tissue of animals and used in foods, drugs, and photographic film. **b.** Any of various similar substances. **2.** A jelly made with gelatin, used as a dessert or salad base. **3.** A thin, transparent membrane used over a theatrical light to color it. [French *gélatine,* from Italian *gelatina,* diminutive of *gelata,* jelly, from feminine past participle of *gelare,* to freeze, from Latin *gelāre.* See **gel-** in Appendix.]

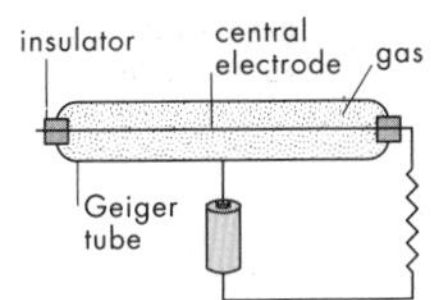

Geiger tube
Schematic diagram

ge·lat·i·nize (jə-lăt′n-īz′, jĕl′ə-tn-īz′) *v.* **-nized, -niz·ing, -niz·es.** —*tr.* **1.** To convert to gelatin or jelly. **2.** To coat with gelatin. —*intr.* To become gelatinous. **—ge·lat′i·ni·za′tion** (-lăt′n-ĭ-zā′shən) *n.*

ge·lat·i·nous (jə-lăt′n-əs) *adj.* **1.** Resembling gelatin; viscous. **2.** Of, relating to, or containing gelatin. **—ge·lat′i·nous·ly** *adv.* **—ge·lat′i·nous·ness** *n.*

ge·la·tion (jĕ-lā′shən) *n.* **1.** Solidification by cooling or freezing. **2.** The process of forming a gel. [Latin *gelātiō, gelātiōn-,* from *gelātus,* past participle of *gelāre,* to freeze. See **gel-** in Appendix.]

ge·la·to (jə-lä′tō, jĕ-) *n., pl.* **-ti** (-tē). An Italian ice cream or ice. [Italian, from past participle of *gelare,* to freeze. See GELATIN.]

geld[1] (gĕld) *tr.v.* **geld·ed** or **gelt** (gĕlt), **geld·ing, gelds. 1.** To castrate (a horse, for example). **2.** To deprive of strength or vigor; weaken. [Middle English *gelden,* from Old Norse *gelda.*]

geld[2] (gĕld) *n.* A tax paid to the crown by English landholders under Anglo-Saxon and Norman kings. [Middle English *geld* and Medieval Latin *geldum,* both from Old English *geld, gield,* payment.]

Gel·der·land (gĕl′dər-lănd′, KHĕl′dər-länt′). A region and former duchy of east-central Netherlands. The duchy was formed in 1339 and passed to the Hapsburgs in 1543. It became part of the Netherlands in 1579.

geld·ing (gĕl′dĭng) *n.* A castrated animal, especially a male horse. [Middle English, from Old Norse *geldingr,* from *gelda,* to geld.]

gel·id (jĕl′ĭd) *adj.* Very cold; icy: *gelid ocean waters.* See Synonyms at **cold.** [Latin *gelidus,* from *gelū,* frost. See **gel-** in Appendix.] **—ge·lid′i·ty** (jə-lĭd′ĭ-tē), **gel′id·ness** *n.* **—gel′id·ly** *adv.*

gel·ig·nite (jĕl′ĭg-nīt′) *n.* An explosive mixture composed of nitroglycerine, guncotton, wood pulp, and potassium nitrate. [GEL(ATIN) + Latin *ignis,* fire + –ITE[1].]

Gell-Mann (gĕl′män′), **Murray.** Born 1929. American physicist. He won a 1969 Nobel Prize for his study of subatomic particles.

Gel·sen·kir·chen (gĕl′zən-kîr′kən, -KHən). A city of west-central Germany in the Ruhr Valley northeast of Essen. It is a major industrial and coal-mining center. Population, 287,956.

gelt[1] (gĕlt) *n. Slang.* Money. [Yiddish, from Middle High German *geld,* from Old High German *gelt,* recompense.]

gelt[2] (gĕlt) *v.* A past tense and a past participle of **geld**[1].

gem (jĕm) *n.* **1.** A pearl or mineral that has been cut and polished for use as an ornament. **2. a.** Something that is valued for its beauty or perfection: *a little gem of a book.* **b.** A beloved or highly prized person. **3.** A type of muffin. **—gem** *tr.v.* **gemmed, gem·ming, gems.** To adorn with or as if with precious or semiprecious stones. [Middle English *gemme,* from Old French, from Latin *gemma.* See **gembh-** in Appendix.]

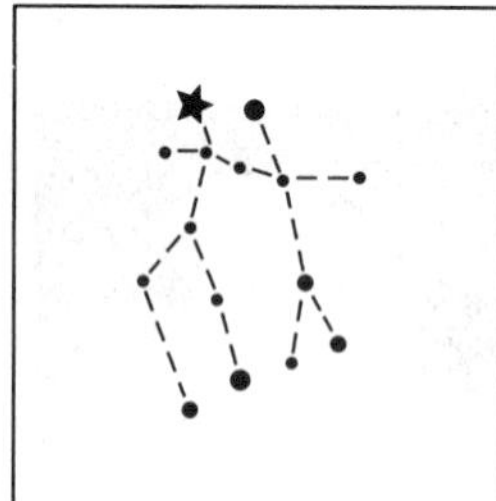
Gemini

GEM *abbr.* Ground-effect machine.

Ge·ma·ra (gə-mär′ə, -môr′ə) *n.* The second part of the Talmud, consisting primarily of commentary on the Mishnah. [Aramaic *gĕmārā,* completion, from *gĕmar,* to complete.] **—Ge·ma′ric** *adj.* **—Ge·ma′rist** *n.*

♦**gem clip** *n. Chiefly Southern U.S.* See **paper clip.** [Origin unknown.]

gem·i·nate (jĕm′ə-nāt′) *v.* **-nat·ed, -nat·ing, -nates.** *—tr.* **1.** To double. **2.** To arrange in pairs. *—intr.* To occur in pairs. **—geminate** (-nĭt, -nāt′) *adj.* Forming a pair; doubled. **—geminate** (-nĭt, -nāt′) *n. Linguistics.* A double or long consonant. [Latin *gemināre, gemināt-,* from *geminus,* twin.] **—gem′i·na′tion** *n.*

Gem·i·ni (jĕm′ə-nī′, -nē′) *pl.n. (used with a sing. verb).* **1.** A constellation in the Northern Hemisphere containing the stars Castor and Pollux. Also called *Twins.* **2. a.** The third sign of the zodiac in astrology. Also called *Twins.* **b.** One who is born under this sign. [Middle English, from Latin *Geminī,* pl. of *geminus,* twin.]

Gem·i·ni·an (jĕm′ə-nī′ən, -nē′-) *n.* One who is born under the sign of Gemini.

gem·ma (jĕm′ə) *n., pl.* **gem·mae** (jĕm′ē′). An asexual budlike propagule as in liverworts, capable of developing into a new individual; a bud. [Latin, bud. See **gembh-** in Appendix.]

gemsbok
Oryx gazella

gem·mate (jĕm′āt′) *adj.* Having or reproducing by gemmae. **—gemmate** *intr.v.* **-mat·ed, -mat·ing, -mates.** To produce gemmae or reproduce by means of gemmae. [From Latin *gemmātus,* past participle of *gemmāre,* to bud, from *gemma,* bud. See **gembh-** in Appendix.] **—gem·ma′tion** (jĕ-mā′shən) *n.*

gem·mip·a·rous (jĕ-mĭp′ər-əs) *adj. Botany.* Reproducing by buds or gemmae. [Latin *gemma,* bud; see GEMMA + –PAROUS.] **—gem·mip′a·rous·ly** *adv.*

gem·mol·o·gy (jĕ-mŏl′ə-jē) *n.* Variant of **gemology.**

gem·mu·la·tion (jĕm′yə-lā′shən) *n.* Production of or reproduction by gemmules.

gem·mule (jĕm′yo͞ol) *n.* **1.** A small gemma or similar structure, especially a reproductive structure in some sponges that remains dormant through the winter and later develops into a new individual. **2.** A hypothetical particle of heredity postulated to be the mediating factor in the production of new cells in the theory of pangenesis. [French, from Latin *gemmula,* diminutive of *gemma,* bud. See **gembh-** in Appendix.] **—gem′mu·lif′er·ous** (jĕm′yo͞o-lĭf′ər-əs) *adj.*

gem·my (jĕm′ē) *adj.* **1.** Full of or set with gems. **2.** Glittering like a gem.

gem·ol·o·gy or **gem·mol·o·gy** (jĕ-mŏl′ə-jē) *n.* The study of gems. **—gem′o·log′i·cal** (jĕm′ə-lŏj′ĭ-kəl) *adj.* **—gem·ol′o·gist** *n.*

ge·mot also **ge·mote** (gə-mōt′) *n.* A public meeting or local judicial assembly in Anglo-Saxon England. [Old English *gemōt* : *ge-,* collective pref.; see **kom** in Appendix + *mōt,* assembly.]

gems·bok (gĕmz′bŏk′) *n.* A large antelope *(Oryx gazella)* of arid regions of southern Africa, having long, sharp, straight horns, a tufted tail, and distinctive black and white markings on the head. [Afrikaans, from Dutch, from German *Gemsbock* : *Gemse,* chamois (from Middle High German *gemeze,* from Old High German **gamiza,* from Late Latin *camox*) + *Bock,* buck (from Middle High German *boc,* from Old High German).]

gem·stone (jĕm′stōn′) *n.* A precious or semiprecious stone that may be used as a jewel when cut and polished.

ge·müt·lich (gə-mo͞ot′lĭk, -müt′lĭKH) *adj.* Warm and congenial; pleasant or friendly. [German, from Middle High German *gemüetlich,* from *gemüete,* spirit, feelings, from Old High German *gimuoti,* from *muot,* mind, spirit, joy. See **mē-**[1] in Appendix.]

ge·müt·lich·keit (gə-müt′lĭKH-kīt′, -mo͞ot′-) *n.* Warm friendliness; amicability. [German, from *gemütlich,* congenial. See GEMÜTLICH.]

gen. *abbr.* **1.** Gender. **2.** General; generally. **3.** Generator. **4.** Generic. **5.** *Grammar.* Genitive. **6.** Genus.

Gen. *abbr.* **1.** General. **2.** *Bible.* Genesis.

–gen or **–gene** *suff.* **1.** Producer: *androgen.* **2.** One that is produced: *phosgene.* [French *-gène,* from Greek *-genēs,* born. See **genə-** in Appendix.]

gen·darme (zhän′därm′) *n.* **1.** A member of the French national police organization constituting a branch of the armed forces with responsibility for general law enforcement. **2.** *Slang.* A police officer. [French, from Old French *gent d'armes,* sing. of *gens d'armes,* mounted soldiers, men-at-arms : *gens,* people, men (from Latin *gentes,* pl. of *gēns,* clan; see **genə-** in Appendix) + *de,* of (from Latin *dē;* see DE–) + *armes,* pl. of *arme,* weapon; see ARM[2].]

gen·dar·me·rie (zhän-där′mə-rē) *n.* **1.** A body of French gendarmes. **2.** *Slang.* A group of police officers. [French, from Old French, calvary, from *gent d'armes, gendarme,* mounted soldier. See GENDARME.]

gen·der (jĕn′dər) *n. Abbr.* **g., gen. 1.** *Grammar.* **a.** A grammatical category used in the analysis of nouns, pronouns, adjectives, and, in some languages, verbs that may be arbitrary or based on characteristics such as sex or animacy and that determines agreement with or selection of modifiers, referents, or grammatical forms. **b.** One category of such a set. **c.** The classification of a word or grammatical form in such a category. **d.** The distinguishing form or forms used. **2.** Sexual identity, especially in relation to society or culture. *—attributive.* Often used to modify another noun: *"Women entered graduate schools . . . and encountered gender discrimination when they applied for the few academic positions"* (New York Times). **—gender** *tr.v.* **-dered, -der·ing, -ders.** To engender. [Middle English *gendre,* from Old French, kind, gender, from Latin *genus, gener-.* See **genə-** in Appendix.] **—gen′der·less** *adj.*

USAGE NOTE: Traditionally, *gender* has been used primarily to refer to the grammatical categories of "masculine," "feminine," and "neuter"; but in recent years the word has become well established in its use to refer to sex-based categories, as in phrases such as *gender gap* and *the politics of gender.* This usage is supported by the practice of many anthropologists, who reserve *sex* for reference to biological categories, while using *gender* to refer to social or cultural categories. According to this rule, one would say *The effectiveness of the medication appears to depend on the sex* (not *gender*) *of the patient,* but *In peasant societies, gender* (not *sex*) *roles are likely to be more clearly defined.* This distinction is useful in principle, but it is by no means widely observed, and considerable variation in usage occurs at all levels.

gender bender or **gen·der-ben·der** (jĕn′dər-bĕn′dər) *n. Slang.* **1.** One who dresses or acts in an androgynous manner. **2.** Something, such as a theatrical performance or a book, whose portrayal of gender roles is nontraditional or androgynous.

gender gap or **gen·der-gap** (jĕn′dər-găp′) *n.* A disproportionate difference, as in attitudes and voting preferences, between the sexes. *—attributive.* Often used to modify another noun: *"His gender-gap troubles multiplied after an impromptu speech about 'women's place'"* (Newsweek).

gen·der-neu·tral (jĕn′dər-no͞o′trəl, -nyo͞o′-) *adj.* Free of explicit or implicit reference to gender or sex, as is the term *police officer* (instead of *policewoman* or *policeman*) or the term *crewed* (instead of *manned*).

gene (jēn) *n.* A hereditary unit that occupies a specific location on a chromosome and determines a particular characteristic in an organism. Genes exist in a number of different forms and can undergo mutation. [From Greek *genos,* race, offspring. See **genə-** in Appendix.]

–gene *suff.* Variant of **–gen.**

ge·ne·al·o·gy (jē′nē-ŏl′ə-jē, -ăl′-, jĕn′ē-) *n., pl.* **-gies. 1.** A record or table of the descent of a person, family, or group from an ancestor or ancestors; a family tree. **2.** Direct descent from an ancestor; lineage or pedigree. **3.** The study or investigation of ancestry and family histories. [Middle English *genealogie,* from

Old French, from Late Latin *geneālogia*, from Greek : *genea*, family; see **genə-** in Appendix + *-logia*, -logy.] **—ge′ne·a·log′i·cal** (-ə-lŏj′ĭ-kəl) *adj.* **—ge′ne·a·log′i·cal·ly** *adv.* **—ge′ne·al′o·gist** *n.*

gene amplification *n.* A cellular process characterized by the production of multiple copies of a particular gene or genes to amplify the phenotype that the gene confers on the cell. Drug resistance in cancer cells is linked to amplification of the gene that prevents absorption of the chemotherapeutic agent by the cell.

gene flow *n.* Transfer of genes from one population to another of the same species, as by migration or the dispersal of seeds and pollen.

gene frequency *n.* The frequency of occurrence of an allele in relation to that of other alleles of the same gene in a population.

gene pool *n.* The collective genetic information contained within a population of sexually reproducing organisms.

gen·er·a (jĕn′ər-ə) *n.* Plural of **genus.**

gen·er·a·ble (jĕn′ər-ə-bəl) *adj.* Capable of being generated: *generable ideas.* [Latin *generābilis*, from *generāre*, to produce. See GENERATE.]

gen·er·al (jĕn′ər-əl) *adj. Abbr.* **gen., genl. 1.** Concerned with, applicable to, or affecting the whole or every member of a class or category: *"subduing all her impressions as a woman, to something more general"* (Virginia Woolf). **2.** Affecting or characteristic of the majority of those involved; prevalent: *general discontent.* **3.** Being usually the case; true or applicable in most instances but not all: *the general correctness of her decisions.* **4.a.** Not limited in scope, area, or application: *as a general rule.* **b.** Not limited to or dealing with one class of things; diversified: *general studies.* **5.** Involving only the main features rather than precise details: *a general grasp of the subject.* **6.** Highest or superior in rank: *the general manager.* **—general** *n.* **1.** *Abbr.* **Gen. a.** A commissioned rank in the U.S. Army, Air Force, or Marine Corps that is above lieutenant general. **b.** One who holds this rank or a similar rank in another military organization. **2.** A general officer. **3.** A statement, principle, or fact that embraces or is applicable to the whole. **4.** *Archaic.* The public. **—*idiom.* in general.** Generally. [Middle English, from Latin *generālis*, from *genus, gener-*, kind. See **genə-** in Appendix.] **—gen′er·al·ness** *n.*

SYNONYMS: *general, common, generic, universal.* The central meaning shared by these adjectives is "belonging to, relating to, or affecting the whole": *the general welfare; a common enemy; generic differences between birds and reptiles; universal military conscription.*
ANTONYM: *particular.*

Gen·er·al American (jĕn′ər-əl) *n.* The speech of native English speakers of the upper Midwestern United States, considered by some to be representative of that of the majority of the country, excluding the Southeast, New York City, and eastern New England.

general anesthetic *n.* An anesthetic that causes loss of sensation in the entire body and induces unconsciousness.

general assembly *n.* **1.** A legislative body, especially a U.S. state legislature. **2. General Assembly.** *Abbr.* **GA, G.A.** The principal deliberative body of the United Nations, in which each member nation is represented and has one vote. **3.** The supreme governing body of some religious denominations.

General Court *n.* **1.** A legislative body having judicial powers in colonial New England. **2.** The state legislature of Massachusetts and New Hampshire.

general court-martial *n.* A court-martial consisting of at least five officers for trying major offenses.

gen·er·al·cy (jĕn′ər-əl-sē) *n., pl.* **-cies.** The rank, appointment, authority, or tenure of a general.

general delivery *n.* **1.** A department of a post office that holds mail for addressees until it is called for. **2.** Mail directed to this department.

general election *n.* An election involving all or most constituencies of a state or nation in the choice of candidates.

gen·er·al·is·si·mo (jĕn′ər-ə-lĭs′ə-mō′) *n., pl.* **-mos.** The commander in chief of all the armed forces in certain countries. [Italian, superlative of *generale*, a general, from Latin *generālis*, general. See GENERAL.]

gen·er·al·ist (jĕn′ər-ə-lĭst) *n.* One who has broad general knowledge and skills in several areas.

gen·er·al·i·ty (jĕn′ə-răl′ĭ-tē) *n., pl.* **-ties. 1.** The state or quality of being general. **2.** An observation or a principle having general application. **3.** An imprecise or vague statement or idea. **4.** The greater portion or number; the majority.

gen·er·al·i·za·tion (jĕn′ər-ə-lĭ-zā′shən) *n.* **1.** The act or an instance of generalizing. **2.** A principle, a statement, or an idea having general application.

gen·er·al·ize (jĕn′ər-ə-līz′) *v.* **-ized, -iz·ing, -iz·es.** *—tr.* **1.a.** To reduce to a general form, class, or law. **b.** To render indefinite or unspecific. **2.a.** To infer from many particulars. **b.** To draw inferences or a general conclusion from. **3.a.** To make generally or universally applicable. **b.** To popularize. *—intr.* **1.a.** To form a concept inductively. **b.** To form general notions or conclusions. **2.** To deal in generalities; speak or write vaguely. **3.** *Medicine.* To spread through the body. Used of a usually localized disease.

gen·er·al·ized (jĕn′ər-ə-līzd′) *adj.* **1.** *Biology.* Not specifically adapted to a particular environment or function; not specialized. **2.** Generally prevalent: *observed a state of generalized discontent.*

gen·er·al·ly (jĕn′ər-ə-lē) *adv. Abbr.* **gen. 1.** Popularly; widely: *generally known.* **2.a.** As a rule; usually: *The child generally has little to say.* **b.** For the most part: *a generally boring speech.* **3.** Without reference to particular instances or details; not specifically: *generally speaking.*

general officer *n.* An officer in the U.S. Army, Air Force, or Marine Corps ranking above colonel.

General of the Air Force *n.* **1.** The highest commissioned rank in the U.S. Air Force. **2.** One who holds this rank.

General of the Army *n.* **1.** The highest commissioned rank in the U.S. Army. **2.** One who holds this rank.

general paresis *n.* A brain disease occurring as a late consequence of syphilis, characterized by dementia, progressive muscular weakness, and paralysis.

general practitioner *n. Abbr.* **G.P., GP** A physician whose practice is not oriented to a specific medical specialty but instead covers a variety of medical problems in patients of all ages. Also called *family doctor.*

gen·er·al-pur·pose (jĕn′ər-əl-pûr′pəs) *adj.* Designed for or suitable to more than one use; broadly useful: *a general-purpose loan.*

general relativity *n.* The geometric theory of gravitation developed by Albert Einstein, incorporating and extending the theory of special relativity to accelerated frames of reference and introducing the principle that gravitational and inertial forces are equivalent.

general semantics *n. (used with a sing. verb).* A discipline developed by Alfred Korzybski that proposes to improve human behavioral responses through a more critical use of words and symbols.

gen·er·al·ship (jĕn′ər-əl-shĭp′) *n.* **1.** The rank, office, or tenure of a general. **2.** Leadership or skill in the conduct of a war. **3.** Skillful management or leadership.

general staff *n.* A group of military officers charged with assisting the commander of a division or higher unit in planning, coordinating, and supervising operations.

general store *n.* A retail store, usually located in a rural community, that sells a wide variety of merchandise but is not divided into departments.

general strike *n.* A strike by all or most of the workers in an industry or throughout a country or an area.

gen·er·ate (jĕn′ə-rāt′) *tr.v.* **-at·ed, -at·ing, -ates. 1.a.** To bring into being; give rise to: *generate a discussion.* **b.** To produce as a result of a chemical or physical process: *generate heat.* **2.** To engender (offspring); procreate. **3.** *Mathematics.* To form (a geometric figure) by describing a curve or surface. **4.** *Computer Science.* To produce (a program) by instructing a computer to follow given parameters with a skeleton program. [Latin *generāre, generāt-*, to produce, from *genus, gener-*, birth. See **genə-** in Appendix.]

gen·er·a·tion (jĕn′ə-rā′shən) *n.* **1.** All of the offspring that are at the same stage of descent from a common ancestor: *Mother and daughters represent two generations.* **2.** *Biology.* A form or stage in the life cycle of an organism: *asexual generation of a fern.* **3.** The average interval of time between the birth of parents and the birth of their offspring. **4.a.** A group of individuals born and living about the same time. **b.** A group of generally contemporaneous individuals regarded as having common cultural or social characteristics and attitudes: *"They're the television generation"* (Roger Enrico). **5.a.** A period of sequential technological development and innovation. **b.** A class of objects derived from a preceding class: *a new generation of computers.* **6.** The act or process of generating; origination, production, or procreation. **—gen·er·a′tion·al** *adj.*

generation gap *n.* A broad difference in values and attitudes between one generation and another, especially between young people and their parents.

gen·er·a·tive (jĕn′ər-ə-tĭv, -ə-rā′-) *adj.* **1.** Having the ability to originate, produce, or procreate. **2.** Of or relating to the production of offspring. **—gen′er·a·tive·ly** *adv.* **—gen′er·a·tive·ness** *n.*

generative cell *n. Botany.* A cell of the male gametophyte or pollen grain in seed plants that divides to give rise directly or indirectly to sperm.

generative grammar *n.* A linguistic theory that attempts to describe a native speaker's tacit grammatical knowledge by a system of rules that in an explicit and well-defined way specify all of the well-formed, or grammatical, sentences of a language while excluding all ungrammatical, or impossible, sentences.

gen·er·a·tor (jĕn′ə-rā′tər) *n. Abbr.* **gen. 1.a.** One that generates, especially a machine that converts mechanical energy into electrical energy. **b.** An apparatus that generates vapor or gas. **2.** A circuit that generates a specified waveform. **3.** *Mathematics.* See **generatrix. 4.** *Computer Science.* A program that produces specific programs from the definition of an operation.

gen·er·a·trix (jĕn′ə-rā′trĭks) *n., pl.* **-er·a·tri·ces** (-ə-rā′trĭ-sēz′, -ər-ə-trī′sēz). *Mathematics.* A geometric element

generator
At a hydroelectric power plant

ă pat	oi boy
ā pay	ou out
âr care	ŏŏ took
ä father	ōō boot
ĕ pet	ŭ cut
ē be	ûr urge
ĭ pit	th thin
ī pie	*th* this
îr pier	hw which
ŏ pot	zh vision
ō toe	ə about, item
ô paw	♦ regionalism

Stress marks: **′** (primary); ′ (secondary), as in **dictionary** (dĭk′shə-nĕr′ē)

that generates a geometric figure, especially a straight line that generates a surface by moving in a specified fashion. Also called *generator.*

ge·ner·ic (jə-nĕr′ĭk) *adj. Abbr.* **gen. 1.** Relating to or descriptive of an entire group or class; general. See Synonyms at **general. 2.** *Biology.* Of or relating to a genus. **3.** Not having a trademark or brand name. **—generic** *n.* **1.** A product, such as a drug or detergent, that is sold without a brand name or trademark. **2.** A wine that is a blend of several grape varieties and does not carry the name of any specific grape. [From Latin *genus, gener-,* kind. See **genə-** in Appendix.] **—ge·ner′i·cal·ly** *adv.*

gen·er·os·i·ty (jĕn′ə-rŏs′ĭ-tē) *n., pl.* **-ties. 1.** Liberality in giving or willingness to give: *"Uncommon generosity causes neglect rather than ingratitude"* (Héloise). **2.** Nobility of thought or behavior; magnanimity. **3.** Amplitude; abundance. **4.** A generous act. [Middle English *generosite,* from Old French, from Latin *generōsitās,* from *generōsus.* See GENEROUS.]

gen·er·ous (jĕn′ər-əs) *adj.* **1.** Liberal in giving or sharing. See Synonyms at **liberal. 2.** Characterized by nobility and forbearance in thought or behavior; magnanimous. **3.** Marked by abundance; ample: *a generous slice of cake.* **4.** Having a rich bouquet and flavor: *a generous wine.* **5.** *Obsolete.* Of noble lineage. [French *genereux,* of noble birth, magnanimous, from Latin *generōsus,* from *genus, gener-,* birth. See **genə-** in Appendix.] **—gen′er·ous·ly** *adv.* **—gen′er·ous·ness** *n.*

Gen·e·see (jĕn′ĭ-sē′, jĕn′ĭ-sē′). A river rising in northern Pennsylvania and flowing about 241 km (150 mi) generally northward across western New York to Lake Ontario.

gen·e·sis (jĕn′ĭ-sĭs) *n., pl.* **-ses** (-sēz′). **1.** The coming into being of something; the origin. See Synonyms at **beginning. 2. Genesis.** *Abbr.* **Gen., Gn.** *Bible.* See table at **Bible.** [Latin, from Greek. See **genə-** in Appendix.]

-genesis *suff.* Origin; production: *abiogenesis.* [Latin, from Greek, birth, origin. See **genə-** in Appendix.]

gene-splic·ing (jēn′splī′sĭng) *n.* The process in which fragments of DNA from one or more different organisms are combined to form recombinant DNA and are made to function within the cells of a host organism.

gen·et¹ (jĕn′ĭt, jə-nĕt′) *n.* Any of several Old World carnivorous mammals of the genus *Genetta,* having grayish or yellowish fur with dark spots and a long, ringed tail. [Middle English, from Old French *genete.*]

gen·et² (jĕn′ĭt) *n.* Variant of **jennet.**

Ge·net (zhə-nā′), **Jean.** 1910–1986. French writer who is best known for his absurdist plays, including *The Balcony* (1956).

Ge·nêt (zhə-nā′). See Janet **Flanner.**

Genêt or **Genet, Edmond Charles Edouard.** Known as "Citizen Genêt." 1763–1834. French diplomat who attempted (1793) to draw the United States into France's war against Great Britain and Spain.

Genghis Khan
Portrait from a 16th-century Persian manuscript

ge·net·ic (jə-nĕt′ĭk) also **ge·net·i·cal** (-ĭ-kəl) *adj.* **1.a.** Of or relating to genetics or genes. **b.** Affecting or affected by genes: *a genetic disorder.* **2.** Of, relating to, or influenced by the origin or development of something. **3.** *Linguistics.* Of or relating to the relationship between or among languages that are descendants of a protolanguage. [From Greek *genetikos,* genitive, from *genesis,* origin. See GENESIS.] **—ge·net′i·cal·ly** *adv.*

genetic code *n.* The sequence of nucleotides in the DNA molecule of a chromosome that specifies the amino acid sequence in the synthesis of proteins. It is the basis of heredity. **—genetic coding** *n.*

genetic coun·sel·ing (koun′sə-lĭng, koun′slĭng) *n.* The counseling of prospective parents on the probabilities and dangers of inherited diseases occurring in their offspring and on the diagnosis and treatment of such diseases. **—genetic counselor** *n.*

genetic drift *n.* Random fluctuations in the frequency of the appearance of a gene in a small, isolated population, presumably owing to chance rather than natural selection.

genetic engineering *n.* Scientific alteration of the structure of genetic material in a living organism. It involves the production and use of recombinant DNA and has been employed to create bacteria that synthesize insulin and other human proteins. **—genetic engineer** *n.*

ge·net·i·cist (jə-nĕt′ĭ-sĭst) *n.* One who specializes in genetics.

genetic load *n.* The difference in fitness between the theoretically most fit genotype within a population and the average genotype.

genetic map *n.* A graphic representation of the arrangement of genes or mutable sites on a chromosome.

genetic marker *n.* A known DNA sequence associated with a particular gene or trait that is used to indicate the presence of that gene or trait. Genetic markers associated with certain diseases can often be detected in the blood serum, where their presence is used to determine whether an individual is at high risk for developing a disease.

ge·net·ics (jə-nĕt′ĭks) *n.* **1.** *(used with a sing. verb).* The branch of biology that deals with heredity, especially the mechanisms of hereditary transmission and the variation of inherited characteristics among similar or related organisms. **2.** *(used with a pl. verb).* The genetic constitution of an individual, a group, or a class.

Ge·ne·va (jə-nē′və). A city of southwest Switzerland located on Lake Geneva and bisected by the Rhone River. Originally an ancient Celtic settlement, it was a focal point of the Reformation after the arrival of John Calvin in 1536. Geneva was the headquarters of the League of Nations (1920–1946) and is still the home of many international organizations. Population, 159,500.

Geneva, Lake. Also **Lake Le·man** (lē′mən, lə-măN′). A lake on the Swiss-French border between the Alps and the Jura Mountains. It is traversed east to west by the Rhone River.

Geneva bands *pl.n.* Two strips of white cloth that hang from the front of the collar of some clerical and academic robes. [After GENEVA, Switzerland.]

Geneva Convention *n.* One of a series of agreements first formulated at an international convention held in Geneva, Switzerland, in 1864, establishing rules for the treatment of prisoners of war, the sick, and the wounded.

Geneva cross *n.* A red Greek or St. George's cross on a white ground, used as a symbol by the Red Cross and as a sign of neutrality. [After GENEVA, Switzerland.]

Geneva gown *n.* A loose black academic or clerical gown with wide sleeves. [After GENEVA, Switzerland.]

Ge·ne·van (jə-nē′vən) also **Gen·e·vese** (jĕn′ə-vēz′, -vēs′) *—adj.* **1.** Of or relating to Geneva, Switzerland, or its inhabitants. **2.** Of or relating to the teachings of John Calvin in Geneva; Calvinistic. *—n.* **1.** A native or inhabitant of Geneva, Switzerland. **2.** A Calvinist.

Gen·ghis Khan (jĕng′gĭs kän′, gĕng′-) also **Jen·ghis Khan** or **Jen·ghiz Khan** (jĕn′gĭz kän′, -gĭs, jĕng′-). Originally Temujin. 1162?–1227. Mongol conqueror who united the Mongol tribes and in 1206 took the name Genghis Khan ("supreme conqueror").

gen·ial¹ (jēn′yəl) *adj.* **1.** Having a pleasant or friendly disposition or manner; cordial and kindly. See Synonyms at **gracious. 2.** Conducive to life, growth, or comfort; mild: *"the genial sunshine . . . saturating his miserable body with its warmth"* (Jack London). **3.** *Obsolete.* Relating to or marked by genius. **4.** *Obsolete.* Of or relating to marriage; nuptial. [Latin *geniālis,* festive, from *genius,* spirit of festivity. See **genə-** in Appendix.] **—ge′ni·al′i·ty** (jē′nē-ăl′ĭ-tē), **gen′ial·ness** *n.* **—gen′ial·ly** *adv.*

ge·ni·al² (jĭ-nī′əl) *n.* Of or relating to the chin. [From Greek *geneion,* chin, from *genus,* jaw. See **genu-²** in Appendix.]

gen·ic (jē′nĭk, jĕn′ĭk) *adj.* Of, relating to, produced by, or being genes or a gene. **—gen′i·cal·ly** *adv.*

-genic *suff.* **1.** Producing; generating: *dysgenic.* **2.** Produced or generated by: *cryptogenic.* **3.** Suitable for production or reproduction by a specified medium: *photogenic.* [-GEN + -IC.]

ge·nic·u·late (jə-nĭk′yə-lĭt) also **ge·nic·u·lat·ed** (-lā′tĭd) *adj.* **1.** Bent abruptly, as a knee. **2.** Having kneelike joints; able to bend at an abrupt angle. [Latin *geniculātus,* with bended knee, from *geniculum,* diminutive of *genū,* knee. See **genu-¹** in Appendix.] **—ge·nic′u·late·ly** *adv.* **—ge·nic′u·la′tion** *n.*

ge·nie (jē′nē) *n.* **1.** A supernatural creature who does one's bidding when summoned. **2.** A jinni. [French *génie,* spirit, from Latin *genius,* guardian spirit. See GENIUS.]

ge·ni·i (jē′nē-ī′) *n. Roman Mythology.* Plural of **genius** (sense 4).

gen·ip (jĕn′əp) *n.* **1.** A tropical American tree *(Melicoccus bijugatus)* having small, fragrant, greenish-white flowers and small fruits with a green, leathery rind and a juicy, yellowish, translucent pulp. **2.** The sweet, edible fruit of this plant. Also called *honeyberry, Spanish lime.* **3.** See **genipap** (sense 2). [Possibly alteration of GENIPAP.]

gen·i·pap (jĕn′ə-păp′) *n.* **1.** A tropical American evergreen tree *(Genipa americana)* having yellowish-white flowers and edible fruits used in preserves or drinks. The fruits yield dark blue dye that is used extensively as a body paint by Indians of tropical America. **2.** The reddish-brown fruit of this plant. Also called *genip, marmalade box.* [Portuguese *genipapo,* from Tupi *jenipapo,* from *yandi-ipab,* genipap fruit.]

genit. *abbr. Grammar.* Genitive.

gen·i·tal (jĕn′ĭ-tl) *adj.* **1.** Of or relating to biological reproduction. **2.** Of or relating to the genitalia. **3.** *Psychology.* Of or relating to the stage of psychosexual development in psychoanalytic theory beginning in puberty and during which the genitals become the focus of sexual gratification. **—genital** *n.* A reproductive organ, especially one of the external sex organs. Often used in the plural. [Middle English, from Latin *genitālis,* from *genitus,* past participle of *gignere,* to beget. See **genə-** in Appendix.] **—gen′i·tal·ly** *adv.*

genital herpes *n.* A highly contagious, sexually transmitted viral infection of the genital and anal regions caused by herpes simplex and characterized by small clusters of painful lesions.

gen·i·ta·li·a (jĕn′ĭ-tā′lē-ə, -tāl′yə) *pl.n.* The reproductive organs, especially the external sex organs; the genitals. [Latin *genitālia,* from neuter pl. of *genitālis,* genital. See GENITAL.]

genital wart *n.* A pointed papilloma typically found on the skin or mucous membranes of the anus and external genitalia. It is caused by a virus that is transmitted through sexual contact. Also called *condyloma acuminatum, venereal wart.*

gen·i·ti·val (jĕn′ĭ-tī′vəl) *adj. Grammar.* Of, relating to, or in the genitive case. **—gen′i·ti′val·ly** *adv.*

gen·i·tive (jĕn′ĭ-tĭv) *Grammar. adj. Abbr.* **gen., genit., g., G. 1.** Of, relating to, or designating a case that expresses possession, measurement, or source. **2.** Of or relating to an affix or a construction, such as a prepositional phrase, characteristic of the genitive case. **—genitive** *n.* **1.** The genitive case. **2.** A form or construction in this case. [Middle English *genetif,* from Latin *genetīvus,* from *genitus,* past participle of *gignere,* to beget. See **gena-** in Appendix.]

gen·i·tor (jĕn′ĭ-tər) *n.* **1.** One who produces or creates. **2.** *Anthropology.* A natural father or mother. [Middle English *genitour,* from Old French *genitor,* from Latin, from *genitus,* past participle of *gignere,* to beget. See **gena-** in Appendix.]

gen·i·to·u·ri·nar·y (jĕn′ĭ-tō-yo͝or′ə-nĕr′ē) *adj.* *Abbr.* **GU** Of or relating to the genital and urinary organs or their functions. [GENIT(AL) + URINARY.]

gen·ius (jēn′yəs) *n., pl.* **-ius·es. 1.a.** Extraordinary intellectual and creative power. **b.** A person of extraordinary intellect and talent: *"One is not born a genius, one becomes a genius"* (Simone de Beauvoir). **c.** A person who has an exceptionally high intelligence quotient, typically above 140. **2.a.** A strong natural talent, aptitude, or inclination: *has a genius for choosing the right words.* **b.** One who has such a talent or inclination: *a genius at diplomacy.* **3.** The prevailing spirit or distinctive character, as of a place, a person, or an era: *the genius of Elizabethan England.* **4.** *pl.* **ge·ni·i** (jē′nē-ī′) *Roman Mythology.* A tutelary deity or guardian spirit of a person or place. **5.** A person who has great influence over another. **6.** A jinni in Moslem mythology. [Middle English, guardian spirit, from Latin. See **gena-** in Appendix.]

ge·ni·us lo·ci (jē′nē-əs lō′sī′, -kē, -kī) *n.* **1.** The distinctive atmosphere or pervading spirit of a place. **2.** The guardian deity of a place. [Latin *genius locī* : *genius,* spirit + *locī,* genitive sing. of *locus,* place.]

genl. *abbr.* General.

gen·o·a (jĕn′ō-ə) *n.* *Nautical.* A large jib used on a racing yacht. Also called *genoa jib.* [After GENOA.]

Gen·o·a (jĕn′ō-ə). A city of northwest Italy on the **Gulf of Genoa,** an arm of the Ligurian Sea. An ancient settlement, Genoa flourished under the Romans and enjoyed great prosperity during the Crusades. Population, 760,300. **—Gen′o·ese′** (-ēz′, -ēs′), **Gen′o·vese′** (-vēz′, -vēs′) *adj. & n.*

genoa jib *n.* *Nautical.* See **genoa.**

gen·o·cide (jĕn′ə-sīd′) *n.* The systematic and planned extermination of an entire national, racial, political, or ethnic group. [Greek *genos,* race; see **gena-** in Appendix + -CIDE.] **—gen′o·cid′al** (-sīd′l) *adj.* **—gen′o·cid′al·ly** *adv.*

ge·noise (zhə-nwŏz′) *n.* A delicate, buttery sponge cake. [French, from feminine of *genois,* Genoese, after GENOA.]

ge·nome (jē′nōm′) also **ge·nom** (-nŏm) *n.* A complete haploid set of chromosomes with its associated genes. [GEN(E) + -OME.] **—ge·nom′ic** (-nŏm′ĭk) *adj.*

gen·o·type (jĕn′ə-tīp′, jē′nə-) *n.* **1.** The genetic constitution of an organism or a group of organisms. **2.** A group or class of organisms having the same genetic constitution. [Greek *genos,* race; see **gena-** in Appendix + Latin *typus,* type; see TYPE.] **—gen′o·typ′ic** (-tĭp′ĭk), **gen′o·typ′i·cal** *adj.* **—gen′o·typ′i·cal·ly** *adv.* **—gen′o·ty·pic′i·ty** (-tī-pĭs′ĭ-tē) *n.*

-genous *suff.* **1.** Producing; generating: *hematogenous.* **2.** Produced by or in a specified manner: *hypogenous.* [-GEN + -OUS.]

gen·re (zhän′rə) *n.* **1.** A type or class: *"Emaciated famine victims . . . on television focused a new genre of attention on the continent"* (Helen Kitchen). **2.a.** A category of artistic composition, as in music or literature, marked by a distinctive style, form, or content: *"his six String Quartets . . . the most important works in the genre since Beethoven's"* (Time). **b.** A realistic style of painting that depicts scenes from everyday life. [French, from Old French, kind, from Latin *genus, gener-.* See **gena-** in Appendix.]

gen·ro (gĕn′rō′) *n., pl.* **-ros.** Any of a group of elder male politicians of Japan who were formerly advisers to the emperor. [Japanese *genrō* : Chinese *yuán,* first + Chinese *lǎo,* elder.]

gens (jĕnz) *n., pl.* **gen·tes** (jĕn′tēz′). **1.** A patrilineal clan of ancient Rome composed of several families of the same name claiming a common ancestor and belonging to a common religious cult. **2.** *Anthropology.* An exogamous patrilineal clan. [Latin *gēns.* See **gena-** in Appendix.]

Gen·ser·ic (jĕn′sə-rĭk′, gĕn′-) also **Gai·ser·ic** (gī′zə-). Died A.D. 477. King of the Vandals (428–477) who invaded Africa (429), captured Carthage (439), and sacked Rome (455).

gent¹ (jĕnt) *adj.* *Archaic.* Graceful; elegant. [Middle English, noble, excellent, from Old French, well-born, from Latin *genitus,* past participle of *gignere,* to beget. See **gena-** in Appendix.]

gent² (jĕnt) *n.* *Informal.* A gentleman. [Short for GENTLEMAN.]

Gent (gĕnt, KHĕnt). See **Ghent.**

gen·ta·mi·cin (jĕn′tə-mī′sĭn) *n.* A broad-spectrum antibiotic derived from an actinomycete of the genus *Micromonospora,* used in its sulfate form to treat various infections. [Alteration of *gentamycin* : GENT(I)A(N VIOLET) + -MYCIN.]

gen·teel (jĕn-tēl′) *adj.* **1.** Refined in manner; well-bred and polite. **2.** Free from vulgarity or rudeness. **3.** Elegantly stylish: *genteel manners and appearance.* **4.a.** Striving to convey a manner or an appearance of refinement and respectability. See Synonyms at **polite. b.** Marked by affected and somewhat prudish refinement. [French *gentil,* from Old French. See GENTLE.] **—gen·teel′ly** *adv.* **—gen·teel′ness** *n.*

gen·teel·ism (jĕn-tēl′ĭz′əm) *n.* A word or an expression thought by its user to be more refined than another, as in *expectorate* for *spit.*

gen·tes (jĕn′tēz′) *n.* Plural of **gens.**

gen·tian (jĕn′shən) *n.* **1.** Any of numerous plants of the genus *Gentiana,* characteristically having showy, variously colored flowers. **2.** The dried rhizome and roots of a yellow-flowered European gentian, *G. lutea,* sometimes used as a tonic. [Middle English *gencian,* from Old French *genciane,* from Latin *gentiāna,* perhaps after *Gentius,* second-century B.C. king of Illyria.]

gentian violet *n.* A dye used in microscopy as a biological stain and in medicine as a bactericide, a fungicide, and an anthelmintic.

gen·tile (jĕn′tīl′) *n.* **1.** Often **Gentile.** One who is not of the Jewish faith or is of a non-Jewish nation. **2.** Often **Gentile.** A Christian. **3.** A pagan or heathen. **4.** Often **Gentile.** *Mormon Church.* A non-Mormon. **—gentile** *adj.* **1.** Of or relating to a Gentile. **2.** Of or relating to a gens, tribe, or people. **3.** *Grammar.* Expressing national or local origins. [Middle English *gentil,* from Late Latin *gentīlis,* pagan, from Latin, of the same clan. See GENTLE.]

gen·ti·lesse (jĕn′tə-lĕs′) *n.* *Archaic.* Refinement and courtesy resulting from good breeding. [Middle English, from Old French, from *gentil,* noble. See GENTLE.]

gen·til·i·ty (jĕn-tĭl′ĭ-tē) *n.* **1.** The quality of being well-mannered; refinement. **2.** The condition of being born to the gentry. **3.** Persons of high social standing considered as a group. **4.** An attempt to convey or maintain the appearance of refinement and elegance. [Middle English *gentilete,* nobility of birth, from Old French, from Latin *gentīlitās,* from *gentīlis,* of the same clan. See GENTLE.]

gen·tle (jĕn′tl) *adj.* **-tler, -tlest. 1.** Considerate or kindly in disposition; amiable and tender. **2.** Not harsh or severe; mild and soft: *a gentle scolding; a gentle tapping at the window.* **3.** Easily managed or handled; docile: *a gentle horse.* **4.** Not steep or sudden; gradual: *a gentle incline.* **5.a.** Of good family; wellborn. **b.** Suited to one of good breeding; refined and polite. **6.** *Archaic.* Noble; chivalrous: *a gentle knight.* **—gentle** *n.* *Archaic.* One of good birth or relatively high station. **—gentle** *tr.v.* **-tled, -tling, -tles. 1.** To make less severe or intense: *The peaceful sunset gentled her dreadful mood.* **2.** To soothe, as by stroking; pacify. **3.** To tame or break (a domestic animal, for instance): *gentle a horse.* **4.** To raise to the status of a noble. [Middle English *gentil,* courteous, noble, from Old French, from Latin *gentīlis,* of the same clan, from *gēns, gent-,* clan. See **gena-** in Appendix.] **—gen′tle·ness** *n.* **—gen′tly** *adv.*

gentle breeze *n.* *Meteorology.* A wind with a speed from 8 to 12 miles (13 to 19 kilometers) per hour, according to the Beaufort scale.

gen·tle·folk (jĕn′tl-fōk′) also **gen·tle·folks** (-fōks′) *pl.n.* Persons of good family and relatively high station.

gen·tle·man (jĕn′tl-mən) *n.* **1.** A man of gentle or noble birth or superior social position: *"He's too much a gentleman to be a scholar"* (Aphra Behn). **2.** A well-mannered and considerate man with high standards of proper behavior. See Usage Note at **lady. 3.** A man of independent means who does not need to have a wage-paying job. **4.** A man: *Do you know this gentleman?* **5. gentlemen.** Used as a form of address for a group of men. **6.** A manservant; a valet. **—gen′tle·man·ly** *adj.*

gen·tle·man-at-arms (jĕn′tl-mən-ət-ärmz′) *n., pl.* **gen·tle·men-at-arms** (-mĭn-ət-ärmz′). One of a military corps of 40 gentlemen who attend the British sovereign as a ceremonial guard on state occasions.

gentleman farmer *n., pl.* **gentlemen farmers.** A man of independent means who farms chiefly for pleasure rather than income.

gen·tle·man's agreement or **gen·tle·men's agreement** (jĕn′tl-mənz) *n., pl.* **gentleman's agreements** or **gentlemen's agreements.** An unwritten agreement guaranteed only by the pledged word or secret understanding of the participants.

gentleman's gentleman *n.* A manservant; a valet.

gen·tle·men's agreement (jĕn′tl-mənz) *n.* Variant of **gentleman's agreement.**

gen·tle·peo·ple (jĕn′tl-pē′pəl) *n.* Used as a form of address for a group of people.

gen·tle·per·son (jĕn′tl-pûr′sən) *n.* A person of good breeding; a lady or a gentleman.

gen·tle·wom·an (jĕn′tl-wo͝om′ən) *n.* **1.** A woman of gentle or noble birth or superior social position. **2.** A well-mannered and considerate woman with high standards of proper behavior. **3.** A woman acting as a personal attendant to a lady of rank.

gen·tri·fi·ca·tion (jĕn′trə-fĭ-kā′shən) *n.* The restoration and upgrading of deteriorated urban property by the middle classes, often resulting in displacement of lower-income people.

gen·tri·fy (jĕn′trə-fī′) *tr.v.* **-fied, -fy·ing, -fies.** To subject to gentrification: *gentrify a row of Victorian houses.* [GENTR(Y) + -FY.] **—gen′tri·fi′er** *n.*

gen·try (jĕn′trē) *n., pl.* **-tries. 1.** People of gentle birth, good breeding, or high social position. **2.a.** An upper or ruling class. **b.** The class of English landowners ranking just below the nobility. **3.** People of a particular class or group: *another commuter from the suburban gentry.* [Middle English *gentri,* nobility of birth, from Old French *genterie,* variant of *genterise, gentilise,* from *gentil,* noble. See GENTLE.]

ă pat	oi boy
ā pay	ou out
âr care	o͝o took
ä father	o͞o boot
ĕ pet	ŭ cut
ē be	ûr urge
ĭ pit	th thin
ī pie	*th* this
îr pier	hw which
ŏ pot	zh vision
ō toe	ə about, item
ô paw	♦ regionalism

Stress marks: ′ (primary); ′ (secondary), as in **dictionary** (dĭk′shə-nĕr′ē)

geode

geodesic dome

Saint George
Early 15th-century Italian tempera painting by an unknown artist of the Byzantine School

George III

gen·u·flect (jĕn′yə-flĕkt′) *intr.v.* **-flect·ed, -flect·ing, -flects. 1.** To bend the knee or touch one knee to the floor or ground, as in worship. **2.** To be servilely respectful or deferential; grovel. [Late Latin *genūflectere* : Latin *genū*, knee; see **genu-**[1] in Appendix + Latin *flectere*, to bend.] **—gen′u·flec′tion** (-flĕk′shən) *n.*

gen·u·ine (jĕn′yo͞o-ĭn) *adj.* **1.** Actually possessing the alleged or apparent attribute or character: *genuine leather.* **2.** Not spurious or counterfeit; authentic. See Synonyms at **authentic. 3.a.** Honestly felt or experienced: *genuine devotion.* **b.** Actual; real: *a genuine dilemma.* **4.** Free from hypocrisy or dishonesty; sincere. **5.** Being of pure or original stock: *a genuine Hawaiian.* [Latin *genuīnus*, natural, possibly from alteration of *ingenuus*, native, freeborn. See INGENUOUS.] **—gen′u·ine·ly** *adv.* **—gen′u·ine·ness** *n.*

ge·nus (jē′nəs) *n., pl.* **gen·er·a** (jĕn′ər-ə). *Abbr.* **gen. 1.** *Biology.* A taxonomic category ranking below a family and above a species and generally consisting of a group of species exhibiting similar characteristics. In taxonomic nomenclature the genus name is used, either alone or followed by a Latin adjective or epithet, to form the name of a species. See table at **taxonomy. 2.** *Logic.* A class of objects divided into subordinate species having certain common attributes. **3.** A class, group, or kind with common attributes. [Latin, kind. See **genə-** in Appendix.]

-geny *suff.* Production; generation; origin: *ontogeny.* [Greek *-geneia*, from *-genēs*, born. See **genə-** in Appendix.]

geo– or **ge–** *pref.* **1.** Earth: *geocentric.* **2.** Geography: *geopolitical.* [Greek *geō-*, from *gē*, earth.]

ge·o·bot·a·ny (jē′ō-bŏt′n-ē) *n.* See **phytogeography. —ge′o·bo·tan′ic** (-bə-tăn′ĭk), **ge′o·bo·tan′i·cal** *adj.* **—ge′o·bot′a·nist** (-bŏt′n-ĭst) *n.*

ge·o·cen·tric (jē′ō-sĕn′trĭk) *adj.* **1.** Relating to, measured from, or with respect to the center of the earth. **2.** Having the earth as a center. **—ge′o·cen′tri·cal·ly** *adv.*

ge·o·chem·is·try (jē′ō-kĕm′ĭ-strē) *n.* The chemistry of the composition and alterations of the solid matter of the earth or a celestial body. **—ge′o·chem′i·cal** (-ĭ-kəl) *adj.* **—ge′o·chem′i·cal·ly** *adv.* **—ge′o·chem′ist** *n.*

ge·o·chro·nol·o·gy (jē′ō-krə-nŏl′ə-jē) *n.* The chronology of the earth's history as determined by geologic events. **—ge′o·chron′o·log′ic** (-krŏn′ə-lŏj′ĭk), **ge′o·chron′o·log′i·cal** *adj.* **—ge′o·chron′o·log′i·cal·ly** *adv.* **—ge′o·chro·nol′o·gist** *n.*

ge·o·chro·nom·e·try (jē′ō-krə-nŏm′ĭ-trē) *n.* Measurement of geologic time, as through isotopic radioactive decay. **—ge′o·chron′o·met′ric** (-krŏn′ə-mĕt′rĭk) *adj.*

ge·o·code (jē′ə-kōd′) *n.* The demographic characterization of a neighborhood or locality, especially as used in marketing.

ge·o·co·ro·na (jē′ō-kə-rō′nə) *n.* The outermost region of the earth's atmosphere, consisting chiefly of ionized hydrogen.

ge·ode (jē′ōd′) *n.* A hollow, usually spheroidal rock with crystals lining the inside wall. [French *géode*, from Latin *geōdēs*, a precious stone, from Greek, earthlike : *gē*, earth + *-ōdēs*, *-oeidēs*, -oid.]

ge·o·des·ic (jē′ə-dĕs′ĭk, -dē′sĭk) *adj.* **1.** *Mathematics.* Of or relating to the geometry of geodesics. **2.** Of or relating to geodesy. **—geodesic** *n. Mathematics.* The shortest line between two points on any mathematically defined surface. [From GEODESY.]

geodesic dome *n.* A domed or vaulted structure of lightweight straight elements that form interlocking polygons.

ge·od·e·sy (jē-ŏd′ĭ-sē) *n.* The geologic science of the size and shape of the earth. [New Latin *geōdaesia*, from Greek *geōdaisia* : *geō-*, geo- + *daiesthai*, to divide; see **dā-** in Appendix.] **—ge·od′e·sist** *n.*

ge·o·det·ic (jē′ə-dĕt′ĭk) also **ge·o·det·i·cal** (-ĭ-kəl) *adj.* Geodesic. **—ge′o·det′i·cal·ly** *adv.*

geodetic survey *n.* A survey of a large area of land in which corrections are made to account for the curvature of the earth.

geo·duck also **gwe·duc** (go͞o′ē-dŭk′) *n.* A very large, edible clam *(Panope generosa)* of the Pacific coast of northwest North America. [From Puget Salish *g*^{w}*ídəq*.]

ge·o·ec·o·nom·ics also **ge·o-ec·o·nom·ics** (jē′ō-ĕk′ə-nŏm′ĭks, -ē′kə-) *n. (used with a sing. verb).* **1.** The study of the relationship between politics and economics, especially on an international scale. **2.** A governmental policy employing geoeconomics. **3.** A combination of international economic and political factors relating to or influencing a nation or region. **—ge′o·ec′o·nom′ic** *adj.* **—ge′o·ec′o·nom′i·cal·ly** *adv.* **—ge′o·e·con′o·mist** (-ĭ-kŏn′ə-mĭst) *n.*

Geof·frey of Mon·mouth (jĕf′rē; mŏn′məth). 1100?–1154. English prelate and chronicler whose *Historia Regum Britanniae* (c. 1139) is a source of Arthurian legend.

geog. *abbr.* **1.a.** Geographer. **b.** Geography. **2.** Geographic.

ge·o·graph·ic (jē′ə-grăf′ĭk) also **ge·o·graph·i·cal** (-ĭ-kəl) *adj. Abbr.* **geog. 1.** Of or relating to geography. **2.** Concerning the topography of a region. **—ge′o·graph′i·cal·ly** *adv.*

geographic mile *n.* A nautical mile.

ge·og·ra·phy (jē-ŏg′rə-fē) *n., pl.* **-phies.** *Abbr.* **geog. 1.** The study of the earth and its features and of the distribution of life on the earth, including human life and the effects of human activity. **2.** The physical characteristics, especially the surface features, of an area. **3.** A book on geography. **4.** An ordered arrangement of constituent elements: *charting a geography of the mind.* [Latin *geōgraphia*, from Greek : *geō-*, geo- + *-graphia*, -graphy.] **—ge·og′ra·pher** *n.*

ge·oid (jē′oid′) *n.* The hypothetical surface of the earth that coincides everywhere with mean sea level. [German, from Greek *geoeidēs*, earthlike : *gē*, earth + *-oeidēs*, -oid.] **—ge·oid′al** (-oid′l) *adj.*

geol. *abbr.* **1.** Geologic; geological. **2.a.** Geologist. **b.** Geology.

geologic time *n.* The period of time covering the physical formation and development of the earth, especially the period prior to human history.

ge·ol·o·gize (jē-ŏl′ə-jīz′) *intr.v.* **-gized, -giz·ing, -giz·es.** To study geology or make geologic investigations.

ge·ol·o·gy (jē-ŏl′ə-jē) *n., pl.* **-gies.** *Abbr.* **geol. 1.** The scientific study of the origin, history, and structure of the earth. **2.** The structure of a specific region of the earth's crust. **3.** A book on geology. **4.** The scientific study of the origin, history, and structure of the solid matter of a celestial body. [Medieval Latin *geōlogia*, study of earthly things : Greek *geō-*, geo- + Greek *-logia*, -logy.] **—ge′o·log′ic** (jē′ə-lŏj′ĭk), **ge′o·log′i·cal** *adj.* **—ge′o·log′i·cal·ly** *adv.* **—ge·ol′o·gist** *n.*

geom. *abbr.* **1.** Geometric. **2.** Geometry.

geomagnetic equator *n.* The imaginary great circle on the earth's surface formed by the intersection of a plane passing through the earth's center perpendicular to the axis connecting the north and south magnetic poles.

geomagnetic storm *n.* See **magnetic storm.**

ge·o·mag·ne·tism (jē′ō-măg′nĭ-tĭz′əm) *n.* **1.** The magnetism of the earth. **2.** The study of the earth's magnetism. **—ge′o·mag·net′ic** (-nĕt′ĭk) *adj.* **—ge′o·mag·net′i·cal·ly** *adv.*

ge·o·man·cy (jē′ə-măn′sē) *n.* Divination by means of lines and figures or by geographic features. [Middle English *geomancie*, from Medieval Latin *geōmantia*, from Late Greek *geōmanteia*, divination by signs from the earth : Greek *geō-*, geo- + Greek *manteia*, divination; see -MANCY.] **—ge′o·man′cer** *n.* **—ge′o·man′tic** (-tĭk) *adj.*

ge·o·met·ric (jē′ə-mĕt′rĭk) also **ge·o·met·ri·cal** (-rĭ-kəl) *adj. Abbr.* **geom. 1.** *Mathematics.* **a.** Of or relating to geometry and its methods and principles. **b.** Increasing or decreasing in a geometric progression. **2.** Using simple geometric forms such as circles and squares in design and decoration. **—ge′o·met′ri·cal·ly** *adv.*

geometric isomer *n.* Any of a set of isomers that differ because of a structural asymmetry about a double bond in the molecule.

ge·o·met·ri·cize (jē′ə-mĕt′rĭ-sīz′) *tr.v.* **-cized, -ciz·ing, -ciz·es.** To design or form in geometric patterns or figures.

geometric mean *n. Mathematics.* The *n*th root, usually the positive *n*th root, of a product of *n* factors.

geometric pace *n.* See **pace**[1] (sense 3a).

geometric progression *n. Mathematics.* A sequence, such as the numbers 1, 3, 9, 27, 81, in which each term is multiplied by the same factor in order to obtain the following term.

ge·o·met·rics (jē′ə-mĕt′rĭks) *n. (used with a pl. verb).* **1.** *Mathematics.* Geometric qualities or properties. **2.** A pattern or design characterized by the use of geometric figures: *Bright geometrics enhance the appearance of the cloth.*

geometric series *n. Mathematics.* An infinite series of the form $a + ax + ax^2 + ax^3 + \ldots$

ge·om·e·trid (jē-ŏm′ĭ-trĭd) *n.* Any of various moths of the family Geometridae, having caterpillars commonly known as measuring worms that move by looping the body in alternate contractions and expansions. **—geometrid** *adj.* Of or belonging to the Geometridae. [From New Latin *Geōmetridae*, family name, from Latin *geōmetrēs*, geometrician, land-measurer, from Greek, from *geōmetrein*, to measure land. See GEOMETRY.]

ge·om·e·trize (jē-ŏm′ĭ-trīz′) *v.* **-trized, -triz·ing, -triz·es.** *Mathematics.* —*intr.* **1.** To study geometry. **2.** To apply the methods of geometry. —*tr.* **1.** To present in geometric form. **2.** To bring into conformance with the laws and principles of geometry.

ge·om·e·try (jē-ŏm′ĭ-trē) *n., pl.* **-tries.** *Abbr.* **geom. 1.** *Mathematics.* **a.** The mathematics of the properties, measurement, and relationships of points, lines, angles, surfaces, and solids. **b.** A system of geometry: *Euclidean geometry.* **c.** A geometry restricted to a class of problems or objects: *solid geometry.* **d.** A book on geometry. **2.a.** Configuration; arrangement. **b.** A surface shape. **3.** A physical arrangement suggesting geometric forms or lines. [Middle English *geometrie*, from Old French, from Latin *geōmetria*, from Greek, from *geōmetrein*, to measure land : *gē*, earth + *metron*, measure; see **mē-**[2] in Appendix.] **—ge·om′e·tri′cian** (jē-ŏm′ĭ-trĭsh′ən, jē′ə-mĭ-), **ge·om′e·ter** *n.*

ge·o·mor·phic (jē′ə-môr′fĭk) *adj.* Of or resembling the earth, its shape, or surface configuration.

ge·o·mor·phol·o·gy (jē′ō-môr-fŏl′ə-jē) *n.* The study of the evolution and configuration of land forms. **—ge′o·mor′pho·log′ic** (-môr′fə-lŏj′ĭk), **ge′o·mor′pho·log′i·cal** (-ĭ-kəl) *adj.* **—ge′o·mor′pho·log′i·cal·ly** *adv.* **—ge′o·mor·phol′o·gist** *n.*

ge·oph·a·gy (jē-ŏf′ə-jē) *n.* The eating of earthy substances, such as clay or chalk, practiced among various peoples as a custom or for dietary or subsistence reasons. **—ge·oph′a·gism** *n.* **—ge·oph′a·gist** *n.*

ge·o·phone (jē′ə-fōn′) *n.* An electronic receiver designed to pick up seismic vibrations.

ge·o·phys·ics (jē′ō-fĭz′ĭks) *n. (used with a sing. verb).* The physics of the earth and its environment, including the physics of fields such as meteorology, oceanography, and seismology. —**ge′o·phys′i·cal** *adj.* —**ge′o·phys′i·cal·ly** *adv.* —**ge′o·phys′i·cist** (-ĭ-sĭst) *n.*

ge·o·phyte (jē′ə-fīt′) *n.* A perennial plant, such as a crocus or tulip, propagated by buds on underground bulbs, tubers, or corms.

ge·o·pol·i·tics (jē′ō-pŏl′ĭ-tĭks) *n. (used with a sing. verb).* **1.** The study of the relationship among politics and geography, demography, and economics, especially with respect to the foreign policy of a nation. **2.a.** A governmental policy employing geopolitics. **b.** A Nazi doctrine holding that the geographic, economic, and political needs of Germany justified its invasion and seizure of other lands. **3.** A combination of geographic and political factors relating to or influencing a nation or region. —**ge′o·po·lit′i·cal** (-pə-lĭt′ĭ-kəl) *adj.* —**ge′o·po·lit′i·cal·ly** *adv.* —**ge′o·pol′i·ti′cian** (-tĭsh′ən) *n.*

ge·o·pon·ic (jē′ə-pŏn′ĭk) *adj.* Of or relating to agriculture or farming. [Greek *geōponikos,* from *geōponein,* to till : *gē,* earth + *ponein,* to toil; see **(s)pen-** in Appendix.]

ge·o·pon·ics (jē′ə-pŏn′ĭks) *n. (used with a sing. verb).* The study or science of agriculture.

ge·o·pres·sured (jē′ō-prĕsh′ərd) also **ge·o·pres·sur·ized** (jē′ō-prĕsh′ə-rīzd′) *adj.* Being under high pressure within the earth.

Geor·die[1] (jôr′dē) *n. Chiefly British.* **1.** A native or inhabitant of Newcastle upon Tyne, England, or its environs. **2.** The dialect of English spoken by Geordies. [Scots, diminutive of *George.*]

Geor·die[2] (jôr′dē) *n. Scots.* A formerly used British gold coin worth one pound and five pence; a guinea. [Scots, diminutive of *George,* after Saint GEORGE, whose image was once stamped on it.]

George (jôrj) *n.* **1.** A jeweled figure of Saint George killing the dragon, used as an insignia of the Knights of the Garter. **2.** An English coin during the reign of Henry VIII, imprinted with a figure of Saint George.

George, Saint. Died c. A.D. 303. Christian martyr and patron of England who, according to legend, slew a fearsome dragon.

George I[1]**.** 1660–1727. Elector of Hanover (1698–1727) and king of Great Britain and Ireland (1714–1727) who left the affairs of his country in the hands of Sir Robert Walpole.

George I[2]**.** 1845–1913. King of Greece (1863–1913) who was elected by the Greek Assembly and introduced a democratic constitution (1864).

George II[1]**.** 1683–1760. King of Great Britain and Ireland and elector of Hanover (1727–1760). His 1743 victory at the Battle of Dettingen (a village of present-day south-central Germany) was the last time that a British monarch led his troops in the field.

George II[2]**.** 1890–1947. King of Greece (1922–1923 and 1935–1947). He was deposed by a military junta in 1923 but returned to the throne in 1935 after a plebiscite.

George III. 1738–1820. King of Great Britain and Ireland (1760–1820) and of Hanover (1815–1820). His government's policies fed American discontent, leading to revolution in 1776.

George IV. 1762–1830. King of Great Britain and Ireland and of Hanover (1820–1830) who caused controversy when he attempted to divorce his estranged wife.

George V. 1865–1936. King of Great Britain and Northern Ireland and emperor of India (1910–1936) who gave up his German titles during World War I.

George V Coast also **George V Land.** A section of the coastal area of Antarctica between Wilkes Land and Victoria Land. It is claimed by Australia.

George VI. 1895–1952. King of Great Britain and Northern Ireland (1936–1952) and emperor of India (1936–1947). He acceded to the throne on the abdication of Edward VIII.

George, Henry. 1839–1897. American journalist and reformer known for his theories on taxation, contained in *Progress and Poverty* (1879).

George, Lake. 1. A lake of northeast Florida formed by a widening of the St. Johns River. **2.** A glacial lake of northeast New York in the foothills of the Adirondack Mountains south of Lake Champlain.

George River. A river of northeast Quebec, Canada, rising on the Quebec-Labrador border and flowing about 563 km (350 mi) northward to Ungava Bay.

Geor·ges Bank (jôr′jĭz). A submerged sandbank in the Atlantic Ocean east of Cape Cod, Massachusetts. It is a highly productive fishing ground.

George·town (jôrj′toun′). **1.** Also **George Town.** The capital of the Cayman Islands, on Grand Cayman in the West Indies west of Jamaica. It is an international banking center. Population, 7,617. **2.** The capital and largest city of Guyana, in the northern part of the country on the Atlantic Ocean. Founded by the British in 1781, it was called Stabroek while it was controlled by the Dutch and was renamed Georgetown in 1812. Population, 78,500. **3.** A section of western Washington, D.C. Settled c. 1665, it was incorporated as a town in 1789 but lost its charter in 1871 and was annexed by Washington, D.C., in 1878.

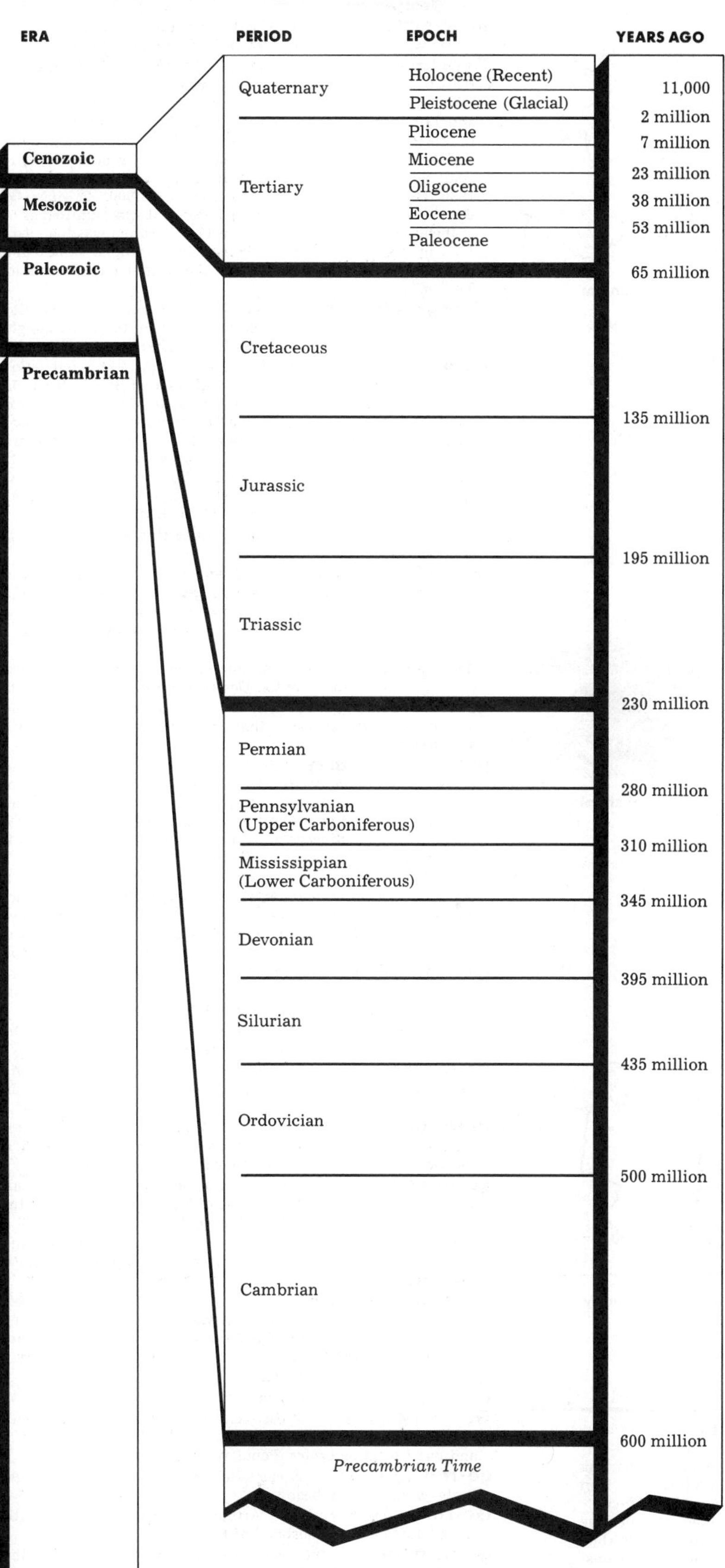

GEOLOGIC TIME SCALE
ERA
PERIOD
EPOCH
YEARS AGO
Cenozoic
Mesozoic
Paleozoic
Precambrian
Quaternary
Holocene (Recent)
Pleistocene (Glacial)
11,000
2 million
Tertiary
Pliocene
Miocene
Oligocene
Eocene
Paleocene
7 million
23 million
38 million
53 million
65 million
Cretaceous
135 million
Jurassic
195 million
Triassic
230 million
Permian
280 million
Pennsylvanian
(Upper Carboniferous)
310 million
Mississippian
(Lower Carboniferous)
345 million
Devonian
395 million
Silurian
435 million
Ordovician
500 million
Cambrian
600 million
Precambrian Time

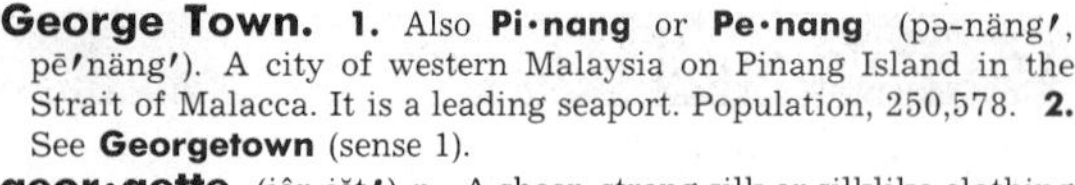

George Town. **1.** Also **Pi·nang** or **Pe·nang** (pə-năng′, pē′năng′). A city of western Malaysia on Pinang Island in the Strait of Malacca. It is a leading seaport. Population, 250,578. **2.** See **Georgetown** (sense 1).

geor·gette (jôr-jĕt′) *n.* A sheer, strong silk or silklike clothing fabric with a dull, creped surface. [Originally a trademark.]

Geor·gia (jôr′jə). **1.** A region of Asia Minor in the Caucasus on the Black Sea south of Russia. It developed as a kingdom c. 4th century B.C. and reached the height of its prosperity in the 12th and 13th centuries. Acquired by Russia between 1801 and 1829, the region was briefly independent (1918–1921). Invaded by the Red Army in 1921, it was proclaimed a soviet republic and officially joined the U.S.S.R. in 1922. It became a separate republic in 1936. The capital is Tbilisi. Population, 5,201,000. **2.** *Abbr.* **GA, Ga.** A state of the southeast United States. It was admitted as one of the original Thirteen Colonies in 1788. Georgia was founded in 1732 by a group led by the British philanthropist James Oglethorpe. Atlanta is the capital and the largest city. Population, 5,463,087.

geranium

Georgia, Strait of. A channel between Vancouver Island, Canada, and mainland British Columbia and northern Washington State. It links Puget Sound with Queen Charlotte Sound.

Geor·gian (jôr′jən) *adj.* **1.** Of, relating to, or characteristic of the reigns of the four Georges who ruled Great Britain from 1714 to 1830. **2.** Of or relating to the U.S. state of Georgia or its inhabitants. **3.** Of or relating to the Georgian republic or its people, language, or culture. **—Georgian** *n.* **1.** A native or inhabitant of the U.S. state of Georgia. **2.a.** A native or inhabitant of the Georgian republic. **b.** The non-Indo-European language of the Georgians. **3.** A person of, or whose style is imitative of, the period of the first four Georges of Great Britain.

Georgian Bay. An extension of Lake Huron in southeast Ontario, Canada.

geor·gic (jôr′jĭk) also **geor·gi·cal** (-jĭ-kəl) *adj.* Of or relating to agriculture or rural life. **—georgic** *n.* A poem concerning farming or rural life. [Latin *geōrgicus,* from Greek *geōrgikos,* from *geōrgos,* farmer : *geō-,* geo- + *ergon,* work; see **werg-** in Appendix.]

Geor·gi·na (jôr-jē′nə). An intermittent river, about 1,126 km (700 mi) long, of the Simpson Desert in north-central Australia.

ge·o·sci·ence (jē′ō-sī′əns) *n.* Any one of the sciences, such as geology or geochemistry, that deals with the earth. **—ge′o·sci′en·tist** *n.*

German shepherd

ge·o·sta·tion·ar·y (jē′ō-stā′shə-nĕr′ē) *adj.* **1.** Of, relating to, or being a satellite that travels above Earth's equator from west to east at an altitude of approximately 35,900 kilometers (22,300 miles) and at a speed matching that of Earth's rotation, thus remaining stationary in relation to Earth. **2.** Of, relating to, or being the orbit of such a satellite.

ge·o·strat·e·gy (jē′ō-străt′ə-jē) *n., pl.* **-gies. 1.** The branch of geopolitics that deals with strategy. **2.** The geopolitical and strategic factors that together characterize a certain geographic area. **3.** Governmental strategy based on geopolitics. **—ge′o·stra·te′gic** (-strə-tē′jĭk) *adj.* **—ge′o·strat′e·gist** *n.*

ge·o·stroph·ic (jē′ə-strŏf′ĭk) *adj.* Of or relating to force caused by the earth's rotation. [GEO– + Greek *strophē,* a turning; see STROPHE + –IC.] **—ge′o·stroph′i·cal·ly** *adv.*

ge·o·syn·chro·nous (jē′ō-sĭng′krə-nəs, -sĭn′-) *adj.* Geostationary. **—ge′o·syn′chro·nous·ly** *adv.*

ge·o·syn·cline (jē′ō-sĭn′klīn′) *n.* An extensive, usually linear depression in the earth's crust. **—ge′o·syn·cli′nal** (-sĭn-klī′nəl) *adj.*

Germany

ge·o·tax·is (jē′ō-tăk′sĭs) *n. Biology.* Movement of a motile organism using the earth's gravity for orientation. **—ge′o·tac′tic** (-tĭk) *adj.* **—ge′o·tac′ti·cal·ly** *adv.*

ge·o·tec·ton·ic (jē′ō-tĕk-tŏn′ĭk) *adj.* Of or relating to the shape, structure, and arrangement of the rock masses resulting from structural deformation of the earth's crust.

ge·o·ther·mal (jē′ō-thûr′məl) also **ge·o·ther·mic** (-mĭk) *adj.* Of or relating to the internal heat of the earth. **—ge′o·ther′mal·ly** *adv.*

ge·ot·ro·pism (jē-ŏt′rə-pĭz′əm) *n. Biology.* The growth of a living organism in response to gravity, as the downward growth of plant roots. **—ge′o·tro′pic** (jē′ə-trō′pĭk, -trŏp′ĭk) *adj.* **—ge′o·tro′pi·cal·ly** *adv.*

ger. *abbr. Grammar.* Gerund.

Ger. *abbr.* German; Germany.

Ge·ra (gĕr′ə). A city of east-central Germany south-southwest of Leipzig. Chartered in the early 13th century, it is an industrial and transportation center. Population, 129,891.

ge·rah (gîr′ə) *n.* An ancient Hebrew coin and unit of weight. [Hebrew *gērâ,* grain, bean.]

Ge·raint (jə-rānt′) *n.* In Arthurian legend, a Knight of the Round Table and the husband of Enid.

ge·ra·ni·al (jə-rā′nē-əl) *n.* A structural isomer of citral that is obtained from the oxidation of geraniol. [GERANI(OL) + –AL[3].]

ge·ra·ni·ol (jə-rā′nē-ôl′, -ōl′, -ŏl′) *n.* A fragrant, pale yellow liquid alcohol, $C_9H_{17}COH$, derived chiefly from the oils of geranium and citronella and used in cosmetics and flavorings. [GERANI(UM) + –OL[1].]

ge·ra·ni·um (jə-rā′nē-əm) *n.* **1.** Any of various plants of the genus *Geranium,* having palmately divided leaves and pink or purplish flowers. Also called *cranesbill.* **2.** Any of various plants of the genus *Pelargonium,* native chiefly to southern Africa and widely cultivated for their rounded, often variegated leaves and showy clusters of red, pink, or white flowers. Also called *storksbill.* **3.** *Color.* A strong to vivid red. [New Latin *Geranium,* genus name, from Latin *geranium,* crane's-bill, from Greek *geranion,* diminutive of *geranos,* crane. See **gerə-**[2] in Appendix.]

ger·bil (jûr′bəl) *n.* **1.** Any of various small, mouselike rodents of the genus *Gerbillus* and related genera of arid regions of Africa and Asia Minor, having long hind legs and a long tail. **2.** The Mongolian gerbil *(Meriones unguiculatus),* having large dark eyes and a long furry tail and often kept as a pet. [French *gerbille,* from New Latin *Gerbillus,* genus name, diminutive of *gerbō,* jerboa. See JERBOA.]

ge·rent (jîr′ənt) *n.* One that rules or manages. [From Latin *gerēns, gerent-,* present participle of *gerere,* to manage.]

ger·e·nuk (gĕr′ə-no͝ok′) *n.* An African gazelle *(Litocranius walleri)* having long legs, a long slender neck, and backward curving horns in the male. [Somali *garanūg,* Waller's gazelle.]

ger·fal·con (jûr′făl′kən, -fôl′-, -fô′-) *n.* Variant of **gyrfalcon.**

ger·i·at·ric (jĕr′ē-ăt′rĭk) *adj.* **1.** Of or relating to geriatrics. **2.** Of or relating to the aged or to characteristics of the aging process. **—geriatric** *n.* An aged person. [Back-formation from GERIATRICS.]

ger·i·a·tri·cian (jĕr′ē-ə-trĭsh′ən) also **ger·i·at·rist** (-ăt′rĭst) *n.* A physician who specializes in geriatrics.

ger·i·at·rics (jĕr′ē-ăt′rĭks) *n. (used with a sing. verb).* The branch of medicine that deals with the diagnosis and treatment of diseases and problems specific to the aged. [Greek *gēras,* old age; see **gerə-**[1] in Appendix + –IATRICS.]

Gé·ri·cault (zhā-rē-kō′), **(Jean Louis André) Théodore.** 1791–1824. French painter whose boldly colored, unorthodox works introduced romanticism to French painting.

germ (jûrm) *n.* **1.** *Biology.* A small mass of protoplasm or cells from which a new organism or one of its parts may develop. **2.** The earliest form of an organism; a seed, bud, or spore. **3.** A microorganism, especially a pathogen. **4.** Something that may serve as the basis of further growth or development: *the germ of a project.* [Middle English, from Old French *germe,* from Latin *germen,* bud. See **genə-** in Appendix.]

ger·man[1] (jûr′mən) *n.* **1.** An intricate dance for many couples. **2.** A party for dancing at which this dance is featured. [Short for *German cotillion.*]

ger·man[2] (jûr′mən) *adj.* Having the same parents or the same grandparents on either the mother's or the father's side. Often used in combination: *a cousin-german; a brother-german.* [Middle English *germain,* from Old French, from Latin *germānus,* from *germen,* offshoot. See **genə-** in Appendix.]

Ger·man (jûr′mən) *adj. Abbr.* **Ger. 1.** Of, relating to, or characteristic of Germany or its people. **2.** Of or relating to the German language. **—German** *n. Abbr.* **Ger. 1.a.** A native or inhabitant of Germany. **b.** A person of German ancestry. **2.** The West Germanic language of Germany, Austria, and part of Switzerland. In this sense, also called *High German.* [Middle English, from Latin *Germānus.*]

German cockroach *n.* A small, light brown cockroach *(Blatella germanica)* that is a common household pest. Also called *Croton bug.*

ger·man·der (jər-măn′dər) *n.* Any of various usually aromatic plants of the genus *Teucrium,* with purplish or reddish flowers. [Middle English *germandre,* from Old French *germandree,* alteration of Medieval Latin *germandrea,* from Late Greek *khamandrua,* from Greek *khamaidrus* : *khamai,* on the ground; see **dhghem-** in Appendix + *drus,* oak; see **deru-** in Appendix.]

ger·mane (jər-mān′) *adj.* Being both pertinent and fitting. See Synonyms at **relevant.** [Middle English *germain,* having the same parents, closely connected. See GERMAN[2].] **—ger·mane′ly** *adv.* **—ger·mane′ness** *n.*

German East Af·ri·ca (ăf′rĭ-kə). A former German protectorate of eastern Africa comprising much of what is now Tanzania, Rwanda, and Burundi. The protectorate was declared in 1885 and lasted until the Allies captured the territory in World War I.

Ger·ma·ni·a (jər-mā′nē-ə, -mān′yə). **1.** An ancient region of central Europe north of the Danube and east of the Rhine. **2.** A part of the Roman Empire west of the Rhine River corresponding to northeast France and sections of Belgium and the Netherlands.

Ger·man·ic (jər-măn′ĭk) *adj.* **1.a.** Of, relating to, or characteristic of Germany or its people, language, or culture. **b.** Of or relating to the Teutons. **c.** Of or relating to speakers of a Germanic language. **2.** Of, relating to, or constituting the Germanic languages. **—Germanic** *n.* A branch of the Indo-European language family that comprises North Germanic, West Germanic, and the extinct East Germanic.

Ger·man·i·cus Cae·sar (jər-măn′ĭ-kəs sē′zər). 15 B.C.–A.D. 19. Roman general. Highly popular after his military triumphs in the Rhineland (A.D. 11–16), he was recalled to Rome by Emperor Tiberius and died there, possibly from poison.

Ger·man·ism (jûr′mə-nĭz′əm) *n.* **1.** An attitude, a custom, or a feature that seems characteristically German. **2.** A German idiom or phrasing that appears in another language. **3.** Esteem for Germany and emulation of German ways.

ă pat	oi boy
ā pay	ou out
âr care	o͝o took
ä father	o͞o boot
ĕ pet	ŭ cut
ē be	ûr urge
ĭ pit	th thin
ī pie	*th* this
îr pier	hw which
ŏ pot	zh vision
ō toe	ə about, item
ô paw	♦ regionalism

Stress marks: ′ (primary); ′ (secondary), as in **dictionary** (dĭk′shə-nĕr′ē)

Ger·man·ist (jûr′mə-nĭst) *n.* A specialist in the study of German or Germanic culture, literature, or language.

ger·ma·ni·um (jər-mā′nē-əm) *n. Symbol* **Ge** A brittle, crystalline, gray-white metalloid element, widely used as a semiconductor, as an alloying agent and catalyst, and in certain optical glasses. Atomic number 32; atomic weight 72.59; melting point 937.4°C; boiling point 2,830°C; specific gravity 5.323 (at 25°C); valence 2, 4. See table at **element.** [After GERMANIA.]

Ger·man·ize (jûr′mə-nīz′) *v.* **-ized, -iz·ing, -iz·es.** —*tr.* **1.** To give a German quality to. **2.** *Archaic.* To translate into German. —*intr.* To have or adopt German customs or attitudes. **—Ger′man·i·za′tion** (-mə-nĭ-zā′shən) *n.* **—Ger′man·iz′er** *n.*

German measles *n. (used with a sing. or pl. verb).* See **rubella.**

Ger·man·o·phile (jər-măn′ə-fīl′) *n.* One who admires Germany, its people, and its culture. **—Ger·man′o·phile′** *adj.*

Ger·man·o·phobe (jər-măn′ə-fōb′) *n.* One who dislikes or fears Germany, its people, and its culture. **—Ger·man′o·phobe′** *adj.* **—Ger·man′o·pho′bi·a** *n.*

German shepherd *n.* Any of a breed of large dog developed in Germany, having a dense grayish to brownish or black coat and often trained to assist the police and guide the blind. Also called *police dog.*

German shorthaired pointer *n.* Any of a breed of medium to large sporting and hunting dog, developed in Germany and having a short, smooth coat with white and reddish to tan markings.

German silver *n.* See **nickel silver.**

German Southwest Af·ri·ca (ăf′rĭ-kə). A former German colony of southwest Africa. It was annexed by Germany in 1885 and awarded to South Africa as the mandate of South-West Africa (now Namibia) by the League of Nations in 1919.

Ger·man·town (jûr′mən-toun′). **1.** A residential section of Philadelphia, Pennsylvania. Settled in 1683, it was the site of a Revolutionary War battle (October 4, 1777) in which George Washington's troops unsuccessfully attacked the British encampment. **2.** A town of extreme southwest Tennessee, a suburb of Memphis. Population, 21,482.

German wirehaired pointer *n.* Any of a breed of medium to large sporting and hunting dog, developed in Germany and having a wiry coat with white and reddish to tan markings.

Ger·ma·ny (jûr′mə-nē). *Abbr.* **Ger.** A country of north-central Europe bordered on the north by the Baltic and North seas. Occupied since c. 500 B.C. by Germanic tribes, it was part of the kingdom of the Franks by the time of Charlemagne and later became a loose federation of principalities and the nucleus of the Holy Roman Empire after the coronation of Otto I in 962. Religious strife and dynastic feuds weakened the imperial state, which was broken up by Napoleon in 1806. After 1815 Germany became a confederation, then an empire centered around Prussia (1871–1918). The Weimar Republic, proclaimed after Germany's defeat in World War I, collapsed under the rise of Adolf Hitler and the Nazis. Hitler's megalomaniac dream of a Third Reich led to World War II and to yet another defeat by Allied forces. From 1949 to 1990 the territory was divided between **West Germany** and **East Germany.** Berlin is the capital and largest city and Bonn the seat of government. Population, 77,750,743.

germ cell *n.* An ovum or a sperm cell or one of its developmental precursors.

germ·free (jûrm′frē′) *adj.* Free of microorganisms.

ger·mi·cide (jûr′mĭ-sīd′) *n.* An agent that kills germs, especially pathogenic microorganisms; a disinfectant. **—ger′mi·ci′dal** (-sīd′l) *adj.*

ger·mi·nal (jûr′mə-nəl) *adj.* **1.** Of, relating to, or having the nature of a germ cell. **2.** Of, relating to, or occurring in the earliest stage of development: *was active in the germinal stages of the space program.* [French, from Latin *germen, germin-,* seed. See **genə-** in Appendix.] **—ger′mi·nal·ly** *adv.*

germinal disk *n. Embryology.* A flattened, disklike region of cells from which the embryo begins to develop in the fertilized ovum of many vertebrate species. Also called *blastodisk, embryonic disk.*

germinal vesicle *n.* The enlarged nucleus of an oocyte before meiotic division is completed.

ger·mi·nate (jûr′mə-nāt′) *v.* **-nat·ed, -nat·ing, -nates.** —*tr.* To cause to sprout or grow. —*intr.* **1.** To begin to sprout or grow. **2.** To come into existence: *An idea began to germinate in his mind.* [Latin *germināre, germināt-,* to sprout, from *germen, germin-,* seed. See **genə-** in Appendix.] **—ger′mi·na′tion** *n.* **—ger′mi·na′tive** *adj.* **—ger′mi·na′tor** *n.*

germ layer *n.* Any of three cellular layers, the ectoderm, endoderm, or mesoderm, into which most animal embryos differentiate and from which the organs and tissues of the body develop through further differentiation.

germ plasm *n.* **1.** The cytoplasm of a germ cell, especially that part containing the chromosomes. **2.** Germ cells as distinguished from other body cells. **3.** Hereditary material; genes. In this sense, also called *plasm.*

germ theory *n.* The doctrine holding that infectious diseases are caused by the activity of microorganisms within the body.

germ warfare *n.* The use of injurious microorganisms, such as bacteria or viruses, as weapons in warfare.

germ·y (jûr′mē) *adj.* **-i·er, -i·est.** Full of germs. **—germ′i·ness** *n.*

ger·o·don·tics (jĕr′ə-dŏn′tĭks) *n.* The branch of dentistry that deals with the diagnosis, prevention, and treatment of diseases and problems specific to the aged. [Greek *gēras,* old age; see GERIATRICS + ODONT(O)– + –ICS.] **—ger′o·don′tic** *adj.*

Ge·ron·i·mo (jə-rŏn′ə-mō′). 1829–1909. Apache leader who resisted the U.S. government policy to consolidate his people on reservations by leading a series of raids against Mexican and American settlements in the Southwest (1876–1886).

Geronimo
1907 photogravure by Edward Sheriff Curtis (1868–1952)

geront– *pref.* Variant of **geronto–.**

ge·ron·tic (jə-rŏn′tĭk) *adj.* Of or relating to the last phase of life.

geronto– or **geront–** *pref.* Old age; aged one: *gerontology.* [French *géronto-,* from Greek *geronta-,* from *gerōn, geront-,* old man. See **gerə-¹** in Appendix.]

ger·on·toc·ra·cy (jĕr′ən-tŏk′rə-sē) *n., pl.* **-cies. 1.** Government based on rule by elders. **2.** A governing group of elders. **—ge·ron′to·crat′** (jə-rŏn′tə-krăt′) *n.* **—ge·ron′to·crat′ic** *adj.*

ger·on·tol·o·gy (jĕr′ən-tŏl′ə-jē) *n.* The scientific study of the biological, psychological, and sociological phenomena associated with old age and aging. **—ge·ron′to·log′i·cal** (jə-rŏn′tə-lŏj′ĭ-kəl), **ge·ron′to·log′ic** (-lŏj′ĭk) *adj.* **—ger′on·tol′o·gist** *n.*

Ger·ry (gĕr′ē), **Elbridge.** 1744–1814. American politician. A signer of the Declaration of Independence (1776), he served as governor of Massachusetts (1810–1811) and as Vice President of the United States (1813–1814) under James Madison.

ger·ry·man·der (jĕr′ē-măn′dər, gĕr′-) *tr.v.* **-dered, -der·ing, -ders.** To divide (a geographic area) into voting districts so as to give unfair advantage to one party in elections. **—gerrymander** *n.* **1.** The act, process, or an instance of gerrymandering. **2.** A district or configuration of districts differing widely in size or population because of gerrymandering. [After Elbridge GERRY + (SALA)MANDER (from the shape of an election district created while Gerry was governor of Massachusetts).]

WORD HISTORY: "An official statement of the returns of voters for senators give[s] twenty nine friends of peace, and eleven gerrymanders." So reported the May 12, 1813, edition of the *Massachusetts Spy.* A gerrymander sounds like a strange political beast, which in fact it is, considered from a historical perspective. This beast was named by combining the word *salamander,* "a small lizardlike amphibian," with the last name of Elbridge Gerry, a former governor of Massachusetts—a state noted for its varied, often colorful political fauna. Gerry (whose name, incidentally, was pronounced with a hard *g,* though *gerrymander* is now commonly pronounced with a soft *g*) was immortalized in this way because an election district created by members of his party in 1812 looked like a salamander. According to one version of how *gerrymander* was coined, the shape of the district attracted the eye of the painter Gilbert Stuart, who noticed it on a map hanging in a newspaper editor's office. Stuart decorated the map with a head, wings, and claws and then said to the editor, "That will do for a salamander!" "Gerrymander!" came the reply. A new political beast was created then and there. The word is first recorded in April 1812 with respect to the creature or its caricature, but it soon came to mean not only "the action of shaping a district to gain political advantage" but also "any representative elected from such a district by that method." Within the same year *gerrymander* was also recorded as a verb.

gerrymander
Gerrymandering of northeast Massachusetts in the early 19th century

Gersh·win (gûrsh′wĭn), **George.** 1898–1937. American composer who brought jazz idiom to classical music forms in his orchestral works, such as *Rhapsody in Blue* (1924), and composed the scores for many musical comedies. His collaborations with his brother, lyricist **Ira Gershwin** (1896–1983), include the opera *Porgy and Bess* (1935).

ger·und (jĕr′ənd) *n. Abbr.* **ger.** *Grammar.* **1.** In Latin, a noun derived from a verb and having all case forms except the nominative. **2.** In other languages, a verbal noun analogous to the Latin gerund, such as the English form ending in *-ing* when used as a noun, as in *singing* in *We admired the choir's singing.* [Late Latin *gerundium,* from Latin *gerundum,* variant of *gerendum,* gerundive of *gerere,* to carry on.] **—ge·run′di·al** (jə-rŭn′dē-əl) *adj.*

ge·run·dive (jə-rŭn′dĭv) *n.* A verbal adjective in Latin that in the nominative case expresses the notion of fitness or obligation and in other cases functions as a future passive participle. [Middle English *gerundif,* from Late Latin *gerundīvus,* from *gerundium,* gerund. See GERUND.]

Ge·ry·on (jîr′ē-ən, gĕr′-) *n. Greek Mythology.* A monster with three bodies that was slain by Hercules.

Ge·sell (gĭ-zĕl′), **Arnold Lucius.** 1880–1961. American psychologist noted for his research on child development.

Ges·ner (gĕs′nər), **Konrad von.** 1516–1565. Swiss encyclopedist and naturalist whose *Historia Animalium* (1551–1558) is considered the basis of modern zoology.

ges·ne·ri·ad (gĕs-nîr′ē-ăd′, jĕs-) *n.* Any of numerous, mostly tropical herbs or shrubs of the family Gesneriaceae, including African violets, the Cape primrose, and gloxinia. [From New Latin *Gesneria,* type genus, after Konrad von GESNER.]

George and Ira Gershwin
Photographed in the 1930's

ges·so (jĕs′ō) *n., pl.* **-soes. 1.** A preparation of plaster of

Paris and glue used as a base for low relief or as a surface for painting. **2.** A surface of gesso. [Italian, from Latin *gypsum,* gypsum. See GYPSUM.] **—ges′soed** *adj.*

gest or **geste** (jĕst) *n.* **1.** A notable adventure or exploit. **2. a.** A verse romance or tale. **b.** A prose romance. [Middle English *geste.* See JEST.]

ge•stalt or **Ge•stalt** (gə-shtält′, -shtôlt′, -stält′, -stôlt′) *n., pl.* **-stalts** or **-stalt•en** (-shtält′n, -shtôlt′n, -stält′n, -stôlt′n). A physical, biological, psychological, or symbolic configuration or pattern of elements so unified as a whole that its properties cannot be derived from a simple summation of its parts. [German, shape, from Middle High German, from past participle of *stellen,* to place, from Old High German. See **stel-** in Appendix.]

Ge•stalt•ist (gə-shtäl′tĭst, -shtôl′-, -stäl′-, -stôl′-) *n.* An adherent or a practitioner of the principles of Gestalt psychology.

Gestalt psychology *n.* The school or theory in psychology holding that psychological, physiological, and behavioral phenomena are irreducible experiential configurations not derivable from a simple summation of perceptual elements such as sensation and response.

Ge•sta•po (gə-stä′pō, -shtä′-) *n.* **1.** The German internal security police as organized under the Nazi regime, known for its terrorist methods directed against those suspected of treason or questionable loyalty. **2. gestapo** *pl.* **-pos.** A police organization that employs terroristic methods to control a populace. **—Gestapo** *adj.* **1.** Of, relating to, or characteristic of the German security police organized under the Nazi regime. **2. gestapo.** Of, relating to, or characteristic of terroristic police methods or operations: *gestapo tactics.* [German *Ge(heime) Sta(ats)po(lizei),* secret state police : *geheim,* secret + *Staat,* state + *Polizei,* police.]

ges•tate (jĕs′tāt′) *v.* **-tat•ed, -tat•ing, -tates.** *—tr.* **1.** To carry within the uterus from conception to delivery. **2.** To conceive and develop in the mind. *—intr.* **1.** To gestate offspring. **2.** To develop gradually. [Back-formation from GESTATION.]

ges•ta•tion (jĕ-stā′shən) *n.* **1.** The period of development in the uterus from conception until birth; pregnancy. **2.** The conception and development of a plan or an idea in the mind. [Late Latin *gestātiō, gestātiōn-,* from Latin, a carrying, from *gestātus,* past participle of *gestāre,* freqentative of *gerere,* to carry.] **—ges′ta•to′ry** (jĕs′tə-tôr′ē, -tōr′ē), **ges•ta′tion•al** *adj.*

geste (jĕst) *n.* Variant of **gest.**

geta
A pair of geta

ges•tic (jĕs′tĭk) *adj.* Relating to bodily movements or gestures, especially in dancing. [From obsolete *gest,* bearing, from French *geste,* from Old French, from Latin *gestus.* See GESTURE.]

ges•tic•u•late (jĕ-stĭk′yə-lāt′) *v.* **-lat•ed, -lat•ing, -lates.** *—intr.* To make gestures especially while speaking, as for emphasis. *—tr.* To say or express by gestures. [Latin *gesticulārī, gesticulāt-,* from *gesticulus,* gesticulation, diminutive of *gestus,* gesture, bearing. See GESTURE.] **—ges•tic′u•la′tive** *adj.* **—ges•tic′u•la′tor** *n.* **—ges•tic′u•la•to′ry** (-lə-tôr′ē, -tōr′ē) *adj.*

ges•tic•u•la•tion (jĕ-stĭk′yə-lā′shən) *n.* **1.** The act of gesticulating. **2.** A deliberate, vigorous motion or gesture. See Synonyms at **gesture.**

ges•ture (jĕs′chər) *n.* **1.** A motion of the limbs or body made to express or help express thought or to emphasize speech. **2.** The act of moving the limbs or body as an expression of thought or emphasis. **3.** An act or a remark made as a formality or as a sign of intention or attitude: *sent flowers as a gesture of sympathy.* **—gesture** *v.* **-tured, -tur•ing, -tures.** *—intr.* To make gestures. *—tr.* To show, express, or direct by gestures. [Middle English, from Medieval Latin *gestūra,* bearing, from Latin *gestus,* from past participle of *gerere,* to behave.] **—ges′tur•al** *adj.* **—ges′tur•al•ly** *adv.* **—ges′tur•er** *n.*

SYNONYMS: *gesture, gesticulation, sign, signal.* The central meaning shared by these nouns is "an expressive, meaningful bodily motion": *an emphatic gesture of disapproval; frantic gesticulations in an attempt to get help; made a sign for silence; giving the signal to advance.*

ge•sund•heit (gə-zo͝ont′hīt′) *interj.* Used to wish good health to a person who has just sneezed. [German, health, from Middle High German *gesuntheit,* from *gesunt,* healthy, from Old High German *gisunt.*]

♦ **get** (gĕt) *v.* **got** (gŏt), **got•ten** (gŏt′n), or **got, get•ting, gets.** *—tr.* **1. a.** To come into possession or use of; receive: *got a poodle for her birthday.* **b.** To meet with or incur: *got nothing but trouble for her efforts.* **2. a.** To go after and obtain: *got a book at the library; got breakfast in town.* **b.** To go after and bring: *Get me a pillow.* **c.** To purchase; buy: *get groceries.* **3. a.** To acquire as a result of action or effort: *He got his information out of an encyclopedia. You can't get water out of a stone.* **b.** To earn: *got high marks in math and science.* **c.** To accomplish or attain as a result of military action. **4.** To obtain by concession or request: *couldn't get the time off; got permission to leave.* **5. a.** To arrive at; reach: *When did you get home?* **b.** To reach and board; catch: *She got her plane two minutes before takeoff.* **6.** To succeed in communicating with, as by telephone: *couldn't get me at the office until nine.* **7.** To become affected with (an illness, for example) by infection or exposure; catch: *get the flu; got the mumps.* **8. a.** To be subjected to; undergo: *got a severe concussion.* **b.** To receive as retribution or punishment: *got six years in prison for embezzling funds.* **c.** To sustain a stated injury to: *got my arm broken.* **9. a.** To gain or have understanding of: *Do you get this question?* **b.** To learn (a poem, for example) by heart; memorize. **c.** To find or reach by calculating: *get a total; can't get the answer.* **d.** To perceive by hearing: *I didn't get your name when we were introduced.* **10.** To procreate; beget. **11. a.** To cause to become or be in a specified state or condition: *got the children tired and cross; got the shirt clean.* **b.** To make ready; prepare: *get lunch for a crowd.* **c.** To cause to come or go: *somehow got the car through traffic.* **d.** To cause to move or leave: *Get me out of here!* **12.** To cause to undertake or perform; prevail on: *got the guide to give us the complete tour.* **13. a.** To take, especially by force; seize: *The detective got the suspect as he came out of the restaurant.* **b.** *Informal.* To overcome or destroy: *The ice storm got the rose bushes.* **c.** To evoke an emotional response or reaction in: *Romantic music really gets me.* **d.** To annoy or irritate: *What got me was his utter lack of self-discipline.* **e.** To present a difficult problem to; puzzle. **f.** To take revenge on, especially to kill in revenge for a wrong. **g.** *Informal.* To hit or strike: *She got him on the chin. The bullet got him in the shoulder.* **14.** *Baseball.* To put out. **15.** To begin or start. Used with the present participle: *I have to get working on this or I'll miss my deadline.* **16. a.** To have current possession of. Used in the present perfect form with the meaning of the present: *We've got plenty of cash.* **b.** To have as an obligation. Used in the present perfect form with the meaning of the present: *I have got to leave early. You've got to do the dishes.* *—intr.* **1. a.** To become or grow to be: *eventually got well.* **b.** To be successful in coming or going: *When will we get to New York?* **2.** To be able or permitted: *never got to see Europe; finally got to work at home.* **3. a.** To be successful in becoming: *get free of a drug problem.* **b.** Used with the past participle of transitive verbs as a passive voice auxiliary: *got stuck in the elevator.* **c.** To become drawn in, entangled, or involved: *got into debt; get into a hassle.* **4.** *Informal.* To depart immediately: *yelled at the dog to get.* **5.** To work for gain or profit; make money: *puts all his energy into getting and spending.* **—get** *n.* **1. a.** The act of begetting. **b.** Progeny; offspring. **2.** *Sports.* A return in tennis on a shot that seems impossible to reach. ***—phrasal verbs.*** **get about.** To be out of bed and beginning to walk again, as after an illness. **get across. 1.** To make understandable or clear: *I have tried to get my point across.* **2.** To be convincing or understandable: *How can I get across to the students?* **get after.** To urge or scold: *You should get after them to mow the lawn.* **get along. 1.** To be or continue to be on harmonious terms: *gets along with the in-laws.* **2.** To manage or fare with reasonable success: *can't get along on those wages.* **3. a.** To make progress. **b.** To advance, especially in years. **4.** To go away; leave. **get around. 1.** To circumvent or evade: *managed to get around the real issues.* **2.** *Informal.* To convince or win over by flattering or cajoling. **3.** To travel from place to place: *It is hard to get around without a car.* **4.** To become known; circulate: *Word got around.* **get at. 1.** To touch or reach successfully: *The cat hid where we couldn't get at it.* **2.** To try to make understandable; hint at or suggest: *I don't know what you're getting at.* **3.** To discover or understand: *If we could only get at the cause of the problem!* **4.** *Informal.* To bribe or influence by improper or illegal means: *He got at the judge, and the charges were dismissed.* **get away. 1.** To break free; escape. **2.** To leave or go away: *wanted to come along, but couldn't get away.* **get back.** To return to a person, place, or condition: *getting back to the subject.* **get by. 1.** To pass or outstrip. **2.** To succeed at a level of minimal acceptability or with the minimal amount of effort: *just got by in high school.* **3.** To succeed in managing; survive: *We'll get by if we economize.* **4.** To be unnoticed or ignored by: *His mistake got by the editor but was caught by the proofreader.* **get down. 1.** To descend. **2.** To give one's attention. Often used with *to: Let's get down to work.* **3.** To exhaust, discourage, or depress: *The heat was getting me down.* **4.** To swallow: *got the pill down on the first try.* **5.** To describe in writing. **6.** *Informal.* To lose one's inhibitions; enjoy oneself wholeheartedly. **get in. 1. a.** To enter. **b.** To arrive: *We got in late last night.* **2.** To become or cause to become involved: *She got in with the wrong crowd. Repeated loans from the finance company got me in deeper and deeper.* **3.** To become accepted, as in a club. **4.** To succeed in making or doing: *got in six deliveries before noon.* **get into. 1.** To become involved in: *got into trouble by stealing cars.* **2.** *Informal.* To be interested in: *got into gourmet cooking.* **get off. 1.** To start, as on a trip; leave. **2. a.** To fire (a round of ammunition, for example): *got off two shots before the deer disappeared.* **b.** To write and send, as a letter. **3.** To escape, as from punishment or danger: *got off scot-free.* **4.** To obtain a release or lesser penalty for: *The attorney got her client off with a slap on the wrist.* **5.** *Slang.* To act or speak with effrontery. Used in the imperative to express contempt or disdainful disbelief. **6.** *Slang.* To have an orgasm. **7.** *Slang.* **a.** To feel great pleasure or gratification. **b.** To experience euphoria, for example, as a result of taking a drug. **8.** To get permission to leave one's workplace: *got off early and went fishing.* **get on. 1.** To be or continue on harmonious terms: *She gets on well with the neighbors.* **2.** To manage or fare with reasonable success. **3. a.** To make progress; continue: *get on with a performance.* **b.** To advance in years. **4.** To acquire understanding or knowledge: *got on to the con game.* **get out. 1. a.** To leave or escape. **b.** To cause to leave or escape. **2.** To become known: *Somehow the secret got out.* **3.** To publish, as a newspaper. **get over. 1.** To prevail against; overcome. **2.** To recover from: *finally got over the divorce.* **3.** To get across. **get through. 1.** To arrive at the end of; finish or complete. **2. a.** To succeed in making contact; reach. **b.** To make oneself under-

ă pat	oi boy
ā pay	ou out
âr care	o͝o took
ä father	o͞o boot
ĕ pet	ŭ cut
ē be	ûr urge
ĭ pit	th thin
ī pie	*th* this
îr pier	hw which
ŏ pot	zh vision
ō toe	ə about, item
ô paw	♦ regionalism

Stress marks: **′** (primary); ′ (secondary), as in **dictionary** (dĭk′shə-nĕr′ē)

stood. **get to. 1.a.** To begin. Used with the present participle: *got to reminiscing.* **b.** To start to deal with: *didn't get to the housework until Sunday.* **2.** To influence or affect, especially adversely: *The noise really gets to me.* **get together. 1.** To bring together; gather. **2.** To come together. **3.** To arrive at an agreement. **get up. 1.a.** To arise from bed or rise to one's feet. **b.** To climb. **2.** To act as the creator or organizer of: *got up a petition against rezoning.* **3.** To dress or adorn: *She got herself up in a bizarre outfit.* **4.** To find within oneself: *trying to get up the nerve to quit.* **—*idioms.* get around to.** To find the time or occasion for. **get away with.** To escape the consequences of (a blameworthy act, for example): *got away with cheating but was later caught.* **get back at.** To take revenge on. **get cracking.** To begin to work; get started. **get even.** To obtain revenge. **get even with.** To repay with an equivalent act, as for revenge. **get going.** To make a beginning; get started. **get it.** *Informal.* To be punished or scolded. **get it on.** *Slang.* **1.** To become filled with energy or excitement. **2.** To engage in sexual intercourse. **get nowhere.** To make no progress. **get on the stick.** To begin to work. **get (someone's) goat.** To make angry or vexed. **get somewhere.** *Informal.* To make progress. **get there.** *Informal.* To make progress or achieve success. **get wind of.** To learn of: *got wind of the scheme.* [Middle English *geten,* from Old Norse *geta.* See **ghend-** in Appendix.] **—get′a·ble, get′ta·ble** *adj.*

USAGE NOTE: The use of *get* in the passive, as in *We got sunburned at the beach,* is generally avoided in formal writing. In less formal contexts, however, the construction does provide a useful distinction in attributing a more active role to its subject than would the corresponding passive with *be.* Thus if Jones has committed a flagrant breach of law in order to test a particular statute, the situation might best be described by the sentence *Jones got arrested by the police;* whereas if Jones did nothing to provoke the police action, the sentence *Jones was arrested by the police* would be preferred.

ge·ta (gĕt′ə, gĕ′tä) *n., pl.* **geta** or **ge·tas.** A wooden-soled shoe worn by the Japanese. [Japanese.]

Ge·ta·fe (hĕ-tä′fĕ). A town of central Spain south of Madrid. It is an industrial and agricultural center. Population, 128,522.

get·a·way (gĕt′ə-wā′) *n.* **1.** The act or an instance of escaping: *made a quick getaway.* **2.** The start, as of a race. **3.** A place appropriate for a vacation.

geth·sem·a·ne (gĕth-sĕm′ə-nē) *n.* An instance or a place of great suffering.

Geth·sem·a·ne (gĕth-sĕm′ə-nē). In the New Testament, a garden east of Jerusalem near the foot of the Mount of Olives. It was the scene of Jesus's agony and betrayal.

get·ter (gĕt′ər) *n.* A material added in small amounts during a chemical or metallurgical process to absorb impurities.

get-to·geth·er (gĕt′tə-gĕth′ər) *n. Informal.* **1.** A meeting. **2.** A casual social gathering.

get-tough (gĕt′tŭf′) *adj. Informal.* Marked by resoluteness, aggressiveness, or austerity: *the government's new get-tough policy on organized crime.*

Get·tys·burg (gĕt′ēz-bûrg′). A town of southern Pennsylvania east-southeast of Chambersburg. It was the site of a major Union victory in the Civil War (July 1–3, 1863), which checked Robert E. Lee's invasion of the North. The battle and Abraham Lincoln's famous Gettysburg Address (delivered at the dedication of a cemetery here on November 19, 1863) are commemorated by a national park. Population, 7,194.

get·up (gĕt′ŭp′) *n.* **1.** *Informal.* An outfit or a costume. **2.** *Printing.* Arrangement and production style, as of a magazine or book.

get-up-and-go (gĕt′ŭp′ən-gō′) *n. Informal.* Initiation of action motivated by energy and ambition.

get-well (gĕt′wĕl′) *adj.* Expressing wishes for one's recovery: *a get-well card.*

GeV *abbr. Physics.* Giga-electron volts.

gew·gaw (gyo͞o′gô′, go͞o′-) *n.* A decorative trinket; a bauble. [Middle English *giuegaue.*]

Ge·würz·tra·mi·ner (gə-vo͝orts′trə-mē′nər, -wûrts′-) *n.* **1.** A dry white table wine with a spicy bouquet, produced in the Alsace region of France. **2.** A similar wine produced elsewhere. [German : *Gewürz,* spice (from *würze,* from Middle High German *wirze,* from Old High German *wurz,* plant; see **wrād-** in Appendix) + *Traminer,* grape variety (from *Tramin,* wine-growing district of the southern Tyrol).]

gey·ser (gī′zər) *n.* **1.** A natural hot spring that intermittently ejects a column of water and steam into the air. **2.** (gē′zər). *Chiefly British.* A gas-operated hot-water heater. [After Icelandic *Geysir,* name of a hot spring of southwest Iceland, from *geysa,* to gush, from Old Norse. See **gheu-** in Appendix.]

gey·ser·ite (gī′zə-rīt′) *n.* A white or grayish opaline siliceous deposit formed around natural hot springs.

Ge·zer (gē′zər). An ancient city of Canaan on the coastal Plain of Sharon northwest of Jerusalem. Excavations here have revealed many levels of prehistoric cultures.

Ge·zi·ra (jə-zîr′ə), **El.** A region of east-central Sudan between the Blue Nile and the White Nile.

GFE *abbr.* Government-furnished equipment.

GFWC *abbr.* General Federation of Women's Clubs.

GGPA *abbr.* Graduate grade-point average.

GH *abbr.* Growth hormone.

Gha·gha·ra (gä′gə-rä′) or **Gha·ghra** (gä′grə, -grä) also **Gog·ra** (gŏg′rə, -rä). A river rising in southwest Tibet and flowing about 965 km (600 mi) south through the Himalaya Mountains into northern India, where it joins the Ganges River.

Gha·na (gä′nə, găn′ə). **1.** A medieval African kingdom in what is now eastern Senegal, southwest Mali, and southern Mauritania. It was founded probably in the 6th century A.D. and prospered because of its location astride the trans-Saharan caravan routes. The kingdom declined after the 11th century. **2.** A country of western Africa on the Gulf of Guinea. Ghana was a British colony after the 1870's and became independent in 1957. Accra is the capital and the largest city. Population, 12,205,574. **—Gha′na·ian, Gha′ni·an** *adj. & n.*

gha·ri·al (gŭr′ē-əl) *n.* See **gavial.**

ghast·ly (găst′lē) *adj.* **-li·er, -li·est. 1.** Inspiring shock, revulsion, or horror by or as if by suggesting death; terrifying: *a ghastly murder.* **2.** Suggestive of or resembling ghosts. **3.** Extremely unpleasant or bad: *"in the most abominable passage of his ghastly little book"* (Conor Cruise O'Brien). **4.** Very serious or great: *a ghastly error.* [Alteration (influenced by GHOST) of Middle English *gastli,* from *gasten,* to terrify. See AGHAST.] **—ghast′li·ness** *n.* **—ghast′ly** *adv.*

SYNONYMS: *ghastly, grim, gruesome, grisly, macabre, lurid.* These adjectives describe what is shockingly repellent in aspect or appearance. *Ghastly* applies to what inspires shock or horror because it suggests death: *ghastly wounds; a ghastly pallor; a ghastly shriek. Grim* refers to what repels because of its stern or fierce aspect or its harsh, relentless nature: *the grim task of burying the victims of the earthquake. Gruesome* and *grisly* describe what horrifies or revolts because of its appalling crudity or utter inhumanity: *a gruesome murder; gruesome evidence of human sacrifice; grisly jokes about cadavers and worms; "the grisly gang who work* [Hitler's] *wicked will"* (Winston S. Churchill). *Macabre* suggests the gruesome, often grotesque horror of death and decay: *macabre stories about tortures conceived by a madman. Lurid* sometimes refers to what is of a ghastly or unnatural hue suggestive of death: *As her illness worsened her skin took on a pallid, greenish, lurid appearance.* More often the term describes what shocks because of its terrible and ghastly nature: *lurid crimes.* At other times it merely refers to glaring and usually unsavory sensationalism: *a lurid, melodramatic, but accurate account of the accident.*

ghat also **ghaut** (gôt, gät) *n.* A broad flight of steps leading down to the bank of a river in India, used especially by bathers. [Hindi *ghāt,* from Sanskrit *ghaṭṭaḥ,* from *ghaṭṭate,* he shakes, rubs.]

Ghats (gôts). Two mountain ranges of southern India. The **Eastern Ghats** extend about 1,448 km (900 mi) along the coast of the Bay of Bengal. The **Western Ghats** extend about 1,609 km (1,000 mi) along the coast of the Arabian Sea.

ghaut (gôt, gät) *n.* Variant of **ghat.**

gha·zi (gä′zē) *n., pl.* **-zies.** *Islam.* **1.** A man who has fought successfully against infidels. **2.** Often used as a title for such a warrior. [Arabic *ġāzī,* participle of *ġazā,* to raid.]

ghee (gē) *n.* A clarified, semifluid butter used especially in Indian cooking. [Hindi *ghī,* from Sanskrit *ghṛtam,* possibly from *gharati,* he sprinkles.]

Ghent (gĕnt) also **Gent** (gĕnt, KHĕnt). A city of western Belgium west-northwest of Brussels. Founded in the seventh century, it remained virtually independent until its capture by the Hapsburgs in 1584. Population, 236,540.

gher·kin (gûr′kĭn) *n.* **1.a.** A West Indian vine *(Cucumis anguria)* having prickly, mature fruits that are sold as curiosities. The immature fruits are widely used for pickling. **b.** The fruit of this plant. Also called *gooseberry gourd.* **2.** A small cucumber, especially one used for pickling. [Dutch *gurken,* pl. of *gurk,* cucumber, short for *agurk,* possibly from Polish *ogorek,* perhaps from Late Greek *angourion.*]

ghet·to (gĕt′ō) *n., pl.* **-tos** or **-toes. 1.** A section of a city occupied by a minority group who live there especially because of social, economic, or legal pressure. **2.** A section or quarter in a European city to which Jews were formerly restricted. **3.** Something that resembles the restriction or isolation of a city ghetto: *"trapped in ethnic or pink-collar managerial job ghettoes"* (Diane Weathers). [Italian.]

ghetto blaster *n. Slang.* A portable stereo.

ghet·to·ize (gĕt′ō-īz′) *tr.v.* **-ized, -iz·ing, -iz·es. 1.** To set apart in or as if in a ghetto; isolate. **2.** To make into or similar to a ghetto: *"He left a city ghettoized and strangled by highways and the auto"* (New York). **—ghet′to·i·za′tion** (-ĭ-zā′shən) *n.*

Ghib·el·line (gĭb′ə-lēn′, -līn′, -lĭn) *n.* A member of the aristocratic political faction who fought during the Middle Ages for German imperial control of Italy, in opposition to the Guelphs and the papacy. [Italian *Ghibellino,* from Middle High German **wībeling,* name of a Hohenstaufen estate.]

Ghi·ber·ti (gē-bĕr′tē), **Lorenzo.** 1378?–1455. Florentine sculptor whose series of bronze panels *Gates of Paradise* (1425–1452) for the doors of the baptistery of Florence Cathedral are among the greatest works of early Renaissance art.

♦**ghil·lie** (gĭl′ē) *n.* Variant of **gillie.**

geyser
Old Faithful,
Yellowstone National Park

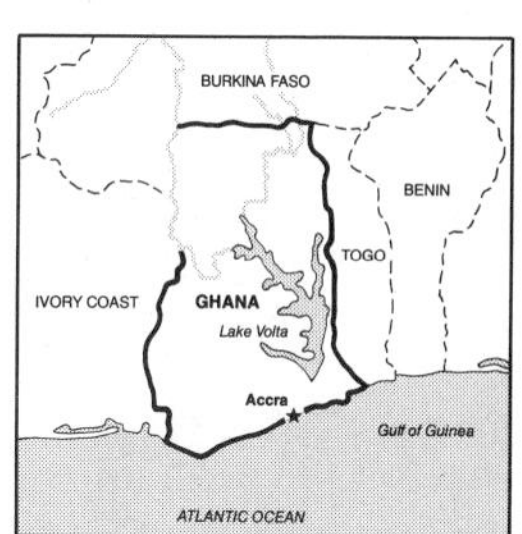

Ghana

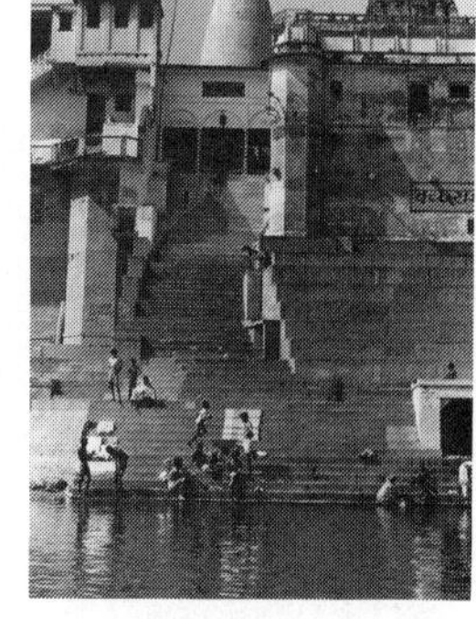
ghat
On the banks of the
Ganges River

giant sequoia
Sequoiadendron giganteum

Ghir·lan·da·io also **Ghir·lan·da·jo** (gîr-län-dä′yō), **Domenico.** Originally Domenico Bigordi. 1449–1494. Florentine painter known especially for his narrative frescoes.

ghost (gōst) *n.* **1.** The spirit of a dead person, especially one believed to appear in bodily likeness to living persons or to haunt former habitats. **2.** The center of spiritual life; the soul. **3.** A demon or spirit. **4.** A returning or haunting memory or image. **5.a.** A slight or faint trace: *just a ghost of a smile.* **b.** The tiniest bit: *not a ghost of a chance.* **6.** A faint, false image, as: **a.** A secondary image on a television or radar screen caused by reflected waves. **b.** A displaced image in a photograph caused by the optical system of the camera. **c.** A false spectral line caused by imperfections in the diffraction grating. **d.** A displaced image in a mirror caused by reflection from the front of the glass. **7.** *Informal.* A ghostwriter. **8.a.** A nonexistent publication listed in bibliographies. **b.** A fictitious employee or business. **9.** *Physiology.* A red blood cell having no hemoglobin. **—ghost** *v.* **ghost·ed, ghost·ing, ghosts.** *—intr.* **1.** *Informal.* To engage in ghostwriting. **2.** To move noiselessly like a ghost: *"Two young deer ghosted out of the woods"* (Nancy M. Debevoise). *—tr.* **1.** To haunt. **2.** *Informal.* To ghostwrite: *was hired to ghost the memoirs of a famous executive.* [Middle English *gost,* from Old English *gāst,* breath, spirit.] **—ghost′y** *adj.*

ghost crab *n.* Any of several light-colored burrowing crabs of the genus *Ocypoda* frequenting the tide line along sandy shores from the northeast United States to Brazil. Also called *white crab.*

ghost dance *n.* Either of two group dances associated with a messianic religious movement among Native American peoples of the Southwest and Great Plains in the late 19th century. Ghost dance prophets foretold the imminent disappearance of whites, the restoration of traditional lands and ways of life, and the resurrection of dead ancestors.

ghost·ing (gō′stĭng) *n.* The appearance of one or more false images on a television screen.

ghost·ly (gōst′lē) *adj.* **-li·er, -li·est. 1.** Of, relating to, or resembling a ghost, a wraith, or an apparition; spectral. **2.** Of or relating to the soul or spirit; spiritual. **—ghost′li·ness** *n.* **—ghost′ly** *adv.*

ghost net *n.* A plastic drift net that has been abandoned by a fishing boat and that entangles and kills fish, porpoises, seabirds, and other marine life.

ghost story *n.* A story having supernatural or frightening elements, especially a story featuring ghosts or spirits of the dead.

ghost town *n.* A once thriving town, especially a boomtown of the American West, that has been completely abandoned.

ghost·weed (gōst′wēd′) *n.* See **snow-on-the-mountain.**

ghost word *n.* A word that has come into a language through the perpetuation of a misreading of a manuscript, a typographical error, or a misunderstanding.

ghost·write (gōst′rīt′) *v.* **-wrote** (-rōt′), **-writ·ten** (-rĭt′n), **-writ·ing, -writes.** *—intr.* To work as a ghostwriter. *—tr.* To write (a speech, for example) as a ghostwriter. See Usage Note at **author.**

ghost·writ·er (gōst′rī′tər) *n.* One who writes for and gives credit of authorship to another.

ghost·writ·ten (gōst′rĭt′n) *v.* Past participle of **ghostwrite.**

ghost·wrote (gōst′rōt′) *v.* Past tense of **ghostwrite.**

ghoul (go͞ol) *n.* **1.** One who delights in the revolting, morbid, or loathsome. **2.** A grave robber. **3.** An evil spirit or demon in Moslem folklore believed to plunder graves and feed on corpses. [Arabic *ġūl,* from *ġāla,* to seize suddenly.] **—ghoul′ish** *adj.* **—ghoul′ish·ly** *adv.* **—ghoul′ish·ness** *n.*

GHQ *abbr.* General headquarters.

GHz *abbr.* Gigahertz.

gi *abbr.* Gill (liquid measure).

gibbon
Lar gibbon
Hylobates lar

GI[1] (jē′ī′) *n., pl.* **GIs** or **GI's.** An enlisted person in or a veteran of any of the U.S. armed forces, especially a person enlisted in the army. **—GI** *adj.* **1.** Relating to or characteristic of an enlisted person. **2.** Conforming to or in accordance with U.S. military regulations or procedures. **3.** Issued by an official U.S. military supply department. **—GI** *adv.* In strict accordance with military regulations or practices. **—GI** *tr.v.* **GI'd, GI'ing, GI's.** *Slang.* To clean (barracks, for example) thoroughly for or as if for an inspection. [From abbreviation of *galvanized iron* (applied to trash cans, etc.), later reinterpreted as *government issue.*]

GI[2] *abbr.* **1.** Galvanized iron. **2.** Gastrointestinal. **3.** General issue. **4.** Also **G.I.** Government Issue.

Gia·co·met·ti (jä-kə-mĕt′ē, -kô-mĕt′tē), **Alberto.** 1901–1966. Swiss sculptor, painter, and exponent of surrealism who is best known for his elongated sculptures of human figures.

gi·ant (jī′ənt) *n.* **1.a.** A person or thing of great size. **b.** A person of extraordinary power, significance, or importance: *a giant in the field of physics; an intellectual giant.* **2.a.** *Greek Mythology.* One of a race of humanlike beings of enormous strength and stature who were destroyed in battle with the Olympians. **b.** A being in folklore or myth similar to one of these beings. **—giant** *adj.* Marked by exceptionally great size, magnitude, or power: *a giant wave; a giant impact.* [Middle English, from Old French *geant, jaiant,* from Vulgar Latin **gagās, gagant-,* from Latin *gigās,* from Greek *gigas.*]

giant chinquapin *n.* See **chinquapin** (sense 2).

gi·ant·ess (jī′ən-tĭs) *n.* A female giant.

gi·ant·ism (jī′ən-tĭz′əm) *n.* **1.** The quality or condition of being a giant. **2.** See **gigantism** (sense 2).

giant panda *n.* See **panda** (sense 1).

giant redwood *n.* See **giant sequoia.**

Gi·ant's Causeway (jī′ənts). A basaltic formation on the northern coast of Northern Ireland. It consists of thousands of columns of volcanic origin forming three natural platforms. According to legend, it was once a bridge for giants crossing between Ireland and Scotland.

giant schnauzer *n.* Any of a breed of dog developed in Germany, similar in appearance to but larger than the standard schnauzer and used chiefly in police work.

giant sequoia *n.* A very tall, coniferous evergreen tree *(Sequoiadendron giganteum)* native to the high western slopes of the Sierra Nevada in southern California and having a massive trunk and light-colored, reddish wood. Also called *big tree, giant redwood.*

giant slalom *n. Sports.* A downhill skiing race in which participants must pass between pairs of gates set along a course that is larger and often steeper than a slalom course.

giant star *n.* Any of a class of highly luminous, exceptionally massive stars.

giaour (jour) *n. Islam.* A nonbeliever; an infidel. [Alteration of obsolete *gower, gour,* from Turkish *gâvur,* from Persian *gabr,* infidel, Zoroastrian, from Arabic *kāfir,* infidel, from *kafara,* not to believe.]

gi·ar·di·a (jē-är′dē-ə, jär′-) *n.* Any of various flagellated, usually nonpathogenic protozoa of the genus *Giardia* that may be parasitic in the intestines of vertebrates including human beings and most domestic animals. [New Latin, after Alfred Mathieu *Giard* (1846–1908), French zoologist.]

gi·ar·di·a·sis (jē′är-dī′ə-sĭs) *n.* Intestinal infection with the protozoan *Giardia lamblia.* It is usually asymptomatic in human beings but may produce abdominal cramps, diarrhea, and nausea.

gib[1] (gĭb) *n.* A plain or notched, often wedge-shaped piece of wood or metal designed to hold parts of a machine or structure in place or provide a bearing surface, usually adjusted by a screw or key. **—gib** *tr.v.* **gibbed, gib·bing, gibs.** To fasten with a gib. [Origin unknown.]

gib[2] (gĭb) *n.* A male cat, especially a castrated one. [Middle English, probably short for the personal name *Gilbert.*]

Gib. *abbr.* Gibraltar.

gib·ber (jĭb′ər) *intr.v.* **-bered, -ber·ing, -bers.** To prattle and chatter unintelligibly. **—gibber** *n.* Unintelligible or foolish talk. [Probably back-formation from GIBBERISH.]

gib·ber·el·lic acid (jĭb′ə-rĕl′ĭk) *n.* A hormone, $C_{19}H_{22}O_6$, obtained from the fungus *Gibberella fujikuroi* and used to promote the growth of plants, especially seedlings. [From GIBBERELLIN.]

gib·ber·el·lin (jĭb′ə-rĕl′ĭn) *n.* Any of several plant hormones, such as gibberellic acid, used to promote stem elongation. [From New Latin *Gibberella (fujikoroi),* the fungus from which gibberellin was first isolated, from Latin *gibberella,* feminine diminutive of *gibber,* hump.]

gib·ber·ish (jĭb′ər-ĭsh) *n.* **1.** Unintelligible or nonsensical talk or writing. **2.a.** Highly technical or esoteric language. **b.** Unnecessarily pretentious or vague language. [Probably *gibber-,* of imitative origin + –ISH.]

gib·bet (jĭb′ĭt) *n.* **1.** A device used for hanging a person until dead; a gallows. **2.** An upright post with a crosspiece, forming a T-shaped structure from which executed criminals were formerly hung for public viewing. **—gibbet** *tr.v.* **-bet·ed, -bet·ing, -bets** or **-bet·ted, -bet·ting, -bets. 1.** To execute by hanging on a gibbet. **2.a.** To hang on a gibbet for public viewing. **b.** To expose to infamy or public ridicule. [Middle English *gibet,* from Old French, diminutive of *gibe,* staff, probably from Frankish **gibb,* forked stick.]

gib·bon (gĭb′ən) *n.* Any of several small, arboreal apes of the genus *Hylobates* of southeast Asia and the East Indies, having a slender body, long arms, and no tail. [French.]

Gib·bon (gĭb′ən), **Edward.** 1737–1794. British historian who wrote the classic text *The History of the Decline and Fall of the Roman Empire* (1776–1788).

gib·bos·i·ty (gĭ-bŏs′ĭ-tē) *n., pl.* **-ties. 1.** The condition of being gibbous. **2.** A rounded hump or protuberance.

gib·bous (gĭb′əs) *adj.* **1.a.** Characterized by convexity; protuberant. **b.** More than half but less than fully illuminated. Used of the moon or a planet: *"the gibbous moon, its light reflecting whitely"* (John Barth). **2.** Having a hump; humpbacked. [Middle English, bulging, from Late Latin *gibbōsus,* hunch-backed, from Latin *gibbus,* hump.] **—gib′bous·ly** *adv.* **—gib′bous·ness** *n.*

Gibbs (gĭbz), **Josiah Willard.** 1839–1903. American mathematician and physicist who formulated the theoretical foundation of physical chemistry and developed vector analysis.

Gibbs free energy *n.* See **free energy** (sense 2). [After Josiah Willard GIBBS.]

gibe also **jibe** (jīb) *—v.* **gibed, gib·ing, gibes** also **jibed, jib·ing, jibes.** *—intr.* To make taunting, heckling, or jeering remarks. See Synonyms at **ridicule.** *—tr.* To deride with taunting remarks. *—n.* A derisive remark. [Possibly from obsolete French *giber,* to handle roughly, play, from Old French.] **—gib′er** *n.* **—gib′ing·ly** *adv.*

Gib·e·on (gĭbʹē-ən). An ancient village of Palestine near Jerusalem. In the Old Testament, its inhabitants were condemned to serve as manual laborers for the Israelites. **—Gibʹe·o·niteʹ** *n.*

gib·lets (jĭbʹlĭts) *pl.n.* The edible heart, liver, or gizzard of a fowl. [From Middle English *gibelet,* from Old French, game stew, perhaps alteration of **giberet,* from *gibier,* game.]

Gi·bral·tar[1] (jə-brôlʹtər). *Abbr.* **Gib.** A British colony at the northwest end of the **Rock of Gibraltar,** a peninsula on the south-central coast of Spain in the **Strait of Gibraltar,** connecting the Mediterranean Sea and the Atlantic Ocean between Spain and northern Africa. Gibraltar was captured by Arabs in 711 and passed to the Spanish in 1462. Great Britain took control in 1704 during the War of the Spanish Succession, although Spain has made repeated claims to regain the territory. The population of the colony is 29,648.

Gi·bral·tar[2] (jĭ-brôlʹtər) *n.* An invincible fortress or stronghold.

Gibraltar fever *n.* See **brucellosis** (sense 1).

Gib·ran (jə-bränʹ), **(Gibran) Kahlil.** 1883–1931. Syrian-born American mystic poet and painter best known for *The Prophet* (1923).

Gib·son (gĭbʹsən) *n.* A dry martini garnished with a small pickled onion. [From the name *Gibson.*]

Gibson, Althea. Born 1927. American tennis player. The first Black American to play at Wimbledon (1951), she won the U.S. women's singles title and the singles and doubles titles at Wimbledon in 1957 and 1958.

Gibson Desert. A desert of west-central Australia bounded by the Great Sandy Desert on the north and Great Victoria Desert on the south. The area includes a number of salt lakes.

Gibson girl *n.* The American young woman of the 1890's as idealized in sketches by the American illustrator Charles Dana Gibson (1867–1944). **—Gibson girl** *adj.* Of or relating to a clothing style marked by a high neck, puffed sleeves, and a tightly fitted waistline.

gid (gĭd) *n.* A disease of herbivores, especially sheep, caused by the presence of the larvae of the tapeworm *Multiceps multiceps* in the brain and resulting in a staggering gait. Also called *sturdy.* [Back-formation from GIDDY.]

gid·dap (gĭ-dăpʹ, -dŭpʹ) also **gid·dy·ap** (gĭdʹē-ăpʹ, -ŭpʹ) or **gid·dy·up** (-ŭpʹ) *interj.* Used to command a horse to go ahead or go at a faster pace. [Alteration of *get up.*]

gid·dy (gĭdʹē) *adj.* **-di·er, -di·est. 1.a.** Having a reeling, lightheaded sensation; dizzy. **b.** Causing or capable of causing dizziness: *a giddy climb to the topmast.* **2.** Frivolous and lighthearted; flighty. **—giddy** *intr. & tr.v.* **-died, -dy·ing, -dies.** To become or make giddy. [Middle English *gidi,* crazy, from Old English *gidig.* See **gheu(ə)-** in Appendix.] **—gidʹdi·ly** *adv.* **—gidʹdi·ness** *n.*

SYNONYMS: *giddy, dizzy, vertiginous.* The central meaning shared by these adjectives is "producing a sensation of whirling and a tendency to fall": *a giddy precipice; a dizzy pinnacle; a vertiginous height.*

WORD HISTORY: The word *giddy* refers to fairly lightweight experiences or situations, but at one time it had to do with profundities. *Giddy* can be traced back to the same Germanic root **gud-* that has given us the word *God.* The Germanic word **gudigaz* formed on this root meant "possessed by a god." Such possession can be a rather unbalancing experience, and so it is not surprising that the Old English representative of **gudigaz, gidig,* meant "mad, possessed by an evil spirit," or that the Middle English development of *gidig, gidi,* meant the same thing, as well as "foolish; mad (used of an animal); dizzy; uncertain, unstable." Our sense "lighthearted, frivolous," represents the ultimate secularization of *giddy.*

gid·dy·ap (gĭdʹē-ăpʹ, -ŭpʹ) or **gid·dy·up** (-ŭpʹ) *interj.* Variants of **giddap.**

Gide (zhēd), **André.** 1869–1951. French writer noted for his diaries and novels, such as *The Immoralist* (1902) and *Lafcadio's Adventures* (1914). He won the 1947 Nobel Prize for literature.

Gid·e·on[1] (gĭdʹē-ən). In the Old Testament, a Hebrew judge who opposed the Baal cult and defeated the Midianites.

Gid·e·on[2] (gĭdʹē-ən) *n.* A member of an interdenominational and international society known for placing Bibles in hotel rooms. [From *Gideons International,* formerly the *Gideon Society,* after GIDEON[1].]

gie (gē) *v. Scots.* Variant of **give.**

Giel·gud (gĭlʹgo͝odʹ, gēlʹ-), Sir **(Arthur) John.** Born 1904. British actor and director particularly noted for his performances in and productions of Shakespearean plays.

gift (gĭft) *n.* **1.** Something that is bestowed voluntarily and without compensation. **2.** The act, right, or power of giving. **3.** A talent, an endowment, an aptitude, or a bent. **—gift** *tr.v.* **gift·ed, gift·ing, gifts. 1.** *Usage Problem.* To present with a gift. **2.** To endow with. [Middle English, from Old Norse. See **ghabh-** in Appendix.]

USAGE NOTE: *Gift* has a long history of use as a verb meaning "to present as a gift; endow." The practice appears to provide a useful distinction, inasmuch as the verb *give* can sometimes be ambiguous between "to transfer physical possession" and "to transfer ownership"; and in fact a verb analogous to *gift* is found in a number of other languages (for example, Italian *regalare,* "to give as a gift," from *regalo,* "gift, present"). Unfortunately the verbal use of *gift* in Modern English is irredeemably tainted (as is its derivative *giftable*) by its association with the language of advertising and publicity (as in *Gift her with this copper warming plate*). In an earlier survey the usage was rejected by a large majority of the Usage Panel. Where clarity is required, substitutes such as *give as a gift, bestow,* or *donate* are recommended. • The phrase *free gift* should, of course, be considered redundant. But the increasing currency of its use is indicative mainly of the degree to which the word *gift* itself has been expropriated by advertisers to refer to merchandise offerings to which an obligation is attached—if not a direct price, then taking a test drive, sitting through a sales pitch, or enrolling in a book club. It is perhaps to this use of *gift,* rather than to the redundancy *free gift,* that critics ought most strenuously to object.

gift·a·ble (gĭfʹtə-bəl) *Usage Problem. adj.* Appropriate for a gift. **—giftable** *n.* Something suitable for giving as a gift.

gift certificate *n.* A certificate usually presented as a gift that entitles the recipient to select merchandise of an indicated cash value at a commercial establishment.

gift·ed (gĭfʹtĭd) *adj.* **1.** Endowed with great natural ability, intelligence, or talent: *a gifted child; a gifted pianist.* **2.** Revealing special talent: *a gifted rendition of the aria.* **—giftʹed·ly** *adv.* **—giftʹed·ness** *n.*

gift of gab *n.* The ability to talk readily, glibly, and convincingly.

gift of tongues *n.* An ecstatic utterance that is partly or wholly unintelligible to hearers, especially such an utterance considered as a charismatic gift in certain Christian congregations. Also called *glossolalia, speaking in tongues.* [From the Apostles' speaking in tongues in Acts 2:4.]

gift·ware (gĭftʹwârʹ) *n.* Wares or merchandise appropriate for gifts.

gift-wrap (gĭftʹrăpʹ) *tr.v.* **-wrapped, -wrap·ping, -wraps.** To wrap (something intended as a gift) in a decorative manner. **—gift-wrap** *n.* Gift-wrapping.

gift-wrap·ping (gĭftʹrăpʹĭng) *n.* Decorative wrapping paper.

Gi·fu (gēʹfo͞oʹ). A city of central Honshu, Japan, north-northwest of Nagoya. A manufacturing center, the city was rebuilt after an earthquake and fire in 1891. Population, 411,740.

gig[1] (gĭg) *n.* **1.** A light, two-wheeled carriage drawn by one horse. **2.** *Nautical.* **a.** A long, light ship's boat, usually reserved for use by the ship's captain. **b.** A fast, light rowboat. **3.a.** An object that whirls. **b.** *Games.* A three-digit selection in a numbers game. **—gig** *intr.v.* **gigged, gig·ging, gigs.** To ride in a gig. [Perhaps from obsolete *gig,* spinning top, from Middle English *gyg-,* possibly of Scandinavian origin.]

gig[2] (gĭg) *n.* **1.** An arrangement of barbless hooks that is dragged through a school of fish to hook them in their bodies. **2.** A pronged spear for fishing or catching frogs. **—gig** *v.* **gigged, gig·ging, gigs.** *—tr.* To fish for or catch with a gig. *—intr.* To catch a fish or frog with a gig. [Short for FISHGIG.]

gig[3] (gĭg) *Slang. n.* A demerit given in the military. **—gig** *tr.v.* **gigged, gig·ging, gigs.** To give a military demerit to. [Origin unknown.]

gig[4] (gĭg) *Slang. n.* A job, especially a booking for musicians. **—gig** *intr.v.* **gigged, gig·ging, gigs.** To work as a musician: *"gigging weekends as a piano player in the ski joints"* (Joel Oppenheimer). [Origin unknown.]

giga– *pref.* One billion (10^9): *gigahertz.* [From Greek *gigas,* giant.]

gig·a·bit (jĭgʹə-bĭtʹ, gĭgʹ-) *n. Computer Science.* A unit of information equal to one billion (10^9) bits.

gig·a·byte (jĭgʹə-bītʹ, gĭgʹ-) *n. Computer Science.* A unit of information equal to one billion (10^9) bytes.

gig·a·cy·cle (jĭgʹə-sīʹkəl, gĭgʹ-) *n. Abbr.* **GC** See **gigahertz.**

gig·a·hertz (jĭgʹə-hûrtzʹ, gĭgʹ-) *n. Abbr.* **GHz** A unit of frequency equal to one billion (10^9) hertz. Also called *gigacycle, kilomegacycle.*

gi·gan·tesque (jīʹgăn-tĕskʹ) *adj.* Of enormous size or magnitude; huge. [French, from Italian *gigantesco,* from *gigante,* giant, from Latin *gigās, gigant-.* See GIANT.]

gi·gan·tic (jī-gănʹtĭk) *adj.* **1.** Relating to or suggestive of a giant. **2.a.** Exceedingly large of its kind: *a gigantic toadstool.* **b.** Very large or extensive: *a gigantic corporation.* See Synonyms at **enormous.** [From Latin *gigās, gigant-,* giant; see GIANT, or from Greek *gigantikos* (from *gigas, gigant-,* giant).] **—gi·ganʹti·cal·ly** *adv.*

gi·gan·tism (jī-gănʹtĭzʹəm) *n.* **1.** The quality or state of being gigantic; abnormally large size. **2.** Excessive growth of the body or any of its parts, especially as a result of oversecretion of the growth hormone by the pituitary gland. In this sense, also called *giantism.*

gig·a·ton (jĭgʹə-tŭnʹ, gĭgʹ-) *n.* A unit of explosive force equal to that of one billion (10^9) tons of TNT.

gig·a·watt (jĭgʹə-wŏtʹ, gĭgʹ-) *n. Abbr.* **GW** One billion (10^9) watts.

gig·gle (gĭgʹəl) *v.* **-gled, -gling, -gles.** *—intr.* To laugh with repeated short, spasmodic sounds. *—tr.* To utter while giggling. **—giggle** *n.* A short, spasmodic laugh. [Of imitative origin.] **—gigʹgler** *n.* **—gigʹgling·ly** *adv.* **—gigʹgly** *adj.*

Gibson girl
Created by
Charles Dana Gibson

ă pat	oi boy
ā pay	ou out
âr care	o͝o took
ä father	o͞o boot
ĕ pet	ŭ cut
ē be	ûr urge
ĭ pit	th thin
ī pie	*th* this
îr pier	hw which
ŏ pot	zh vision
ō toe	ə about, item
ô paw	♦ regionalism

Stress marks: **ʹ** (primary); ʹ (secondary), as in **dictionary** (dĭkʹshə-nĕrʹē)

GIGO (gī′gō, gē′-) *n. Computer Science.* An informal rule holding that the integrity of output is dependent on the integrity of input. [*g(arbage) i(n) g(arbage) o(ut).*]

gig·o·lo (jĭg′ə-lō′, zhĭg′-) *n., pl.* **-los. 1.** A man who has a continuing sexual relationship with and receives financial support from a woman. **2.** A man who is hired as an escort or a dancing partner for a woman. [French, perhaps from *gigolette,* dancing girl, prostitute, from *giguer,* to dance, from *gigue,* fiddle, from Old French. See GIGOT.]

gig·ot (jĭg′ət, zhē-gō′) *n.* **1.** A leg of mutton, lamb, or veal for cooking. **2.** A leg-of-mutton sleeve. [French, from Old French, diminutive of *gigue,* fiddle, from Middle High German *gīge,* from Old High German *gīga.*]

gigue (zhēg) *n.* See **jig** (sense 1). [French, probably from JIG.]

Gi·jón (hē-hōn′). A city of northwest Spain on the Bay of Biscay west of Santander. Of pre-Roman origin, it is a major port and industrial center. Population, 262,395.

Gi·ku·yu (gĭ-kōō′yōō) *n.* Variant of **Kikuyu.**

Gila monster
Heloderma suspectum

Gi·la monster (hē′lə) *n.* A venomous lizard *(Heloderma suspectum)* of arid regions of the southwest United States and western Mexico, having black and orange or yellow scales. [After the GILA RIVER.]

Gila River. A river rising in the mountains of western New Mexico and flowing about 1,014 km (630 mi) generally westward across southern Arizona to the Colorado River at Yuma.

gil·bert (gĭl′bərt) *n.* The centimeter-gram-second electromagnetic unit of magnetomotive force, equal to $10/4\pi$ ampere-turn. [After William GILBERT.]

Gil·bert (gĭl′bərt), **Cass.** 1859–1934. American architect whose design of the 60-story Woolworth Building in New York City (1913) greatly influenced the development of the skyscraper.

Gilbert, Sir **Humphrey.** 1539?–1583. English navigator who urged exploration for the Northwest Passage, established in Newfoundland (1583) the first English colony in North America, and was lost at sea during a homeward voyage.

Gilbert, William. 1544–1603. English court physician noted for his studies of electricity and magnetism.

Gilbert, Sir **William Schwenck.** 1836–1911. British playwright and lyricist known for a series of comic operas, including *H.M.S. Pinafore* (1878), written with composer Sir Arthur Sullivan.

Gilbert Islands. A group of islands of western Kiribati in the central Pacific Ocean. First visited by the British in 1765, the islands were made a protectorate in 1892 and later became part of the **Gilbert and Ellice Islands Colony** (1915–1976). Full independence as the main islands of Kiribati was achieved in 1979.

gild[1] (gĭld) *tr.v.* **gild·ed** or **gilt** (gĭlt), **gild·ing, gilds. 1.** To cover with or as if with a thin layer of gold. **2.** To give an often deceptively attractive or improved appearance to. **3.** *Archaic.* To smear with blood. —***idiom.* gild the lily. 1.** To adorn unnecessarily something already beautiful. **2.** To make superfluous additions to what is already complete. [Middle English *gilden,* from Old English *gyldan.* See **ghel-[2]** in Appendix.] —**gild′er** *n.*

gild[2] (gĭld) *n.* Variant of **guild.**

gild·ing (gĭl′dĭng) *n.* **1.** The art or process of applying gilt to a surface. **2.** Gold leaf or a paint containing or simulating gold; gilt. **3.** Something used to give a superficially attractive appearance.

Gil·e·ad (gĭl′ē-əd). A mountainous region of ancient Palestine east of the Jordan River in what is now northwest Jordan.

Gil·ga·mesh (gĭl′gə-mĕsh′) *n. Mythology.* The semidivine king of Erech, a city of southern Babylonia, and hero of an epic collection of mythic tales, one of which tells of a flood that covered the earth.

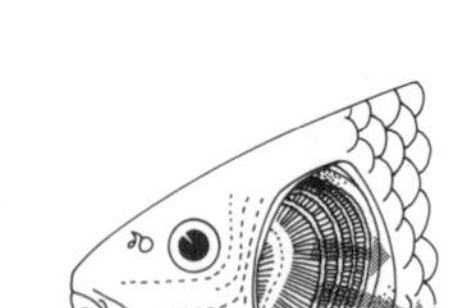

gill[1]

gill[1] (gĭl) *n.* **1.** *Zoology.* The respiratory organ of most aquatic animals that breathe water to obtain oxygen, consisting of a filamentous structure of vascular membranes across which dissolved gases are exchanged. **2. a.** Often **gills.** The wattle of a bird. **b. gills.** *Informal.* The area around the chin and neck. **3.** *Botany.* One of the thin, platelike structures on the underside of the cap of a mushroom or similar fungus. —**gill** *v.* **gilled, gill·ing, gills.** —*tr.* **1.** To catch (fish) in a gill net. **2.** To gut or clean (fish). —*intr.* To become entangled in a gill net. Used of fish. —***idiom.* to the gills.** *Informal.* As full as possible; completely. [Middle English *gile,* of Scandinavian origin.] —**gilled** *adj.*

gill[2] (jĭl) *n. Abbr.* **gi 1.** A unit of volume or capacity in the U.S. Customary System, used in liquid measure, equal to ¼ of a pint or four ounces (118 milliliters). **2.** A unit of volume or capacity, used in dry and liquid measure, equal to ¼ of a British Imperial pint (142 milliliters). See table at **measurement.** [Middle English *gille,* from Old French, wine measure, from Late Latin *gillō,* vessel for cooling liquids.]

gill[3] (gĭl) *n. Chiefly British.* **1.** A ravine. **2.** A narrow stream. [Middle English *gille,* from Old Norse *gil.*]

gill[4] also **jill** or **Gill** (jĭl) *n.* A girl, often one's sweetheart. [Middle English *gille,* from *Gille,* a woman's name.]

gill arch (gĭl) *n.* **1.** One of several bony or cartilaginous arches located on either side of the pharynx and supporting the gills in fish and amphibians. **2.** *Embryology.* One of several corresponding arches in the embryo of a higher vertebrate that develop into structures of the ear and neck. Also called *branchial arch.*

gill cleft (gĭl) *n.* See **gill slit** (sense 1).

Gilles de la Tour·ette syndrome (zhēl də lä tōō-rĕt′) *n.* See **Tourette's syndrome.**

Gil·lette (jə-lĕt′), **King Camp.** 1855–1932. American inventor and manufacturer who developed the safety razor (c. 1895).

gill fungus (gĭl) *n.* A fleshy fungus having a cap with gills on the underside.

◆**gil·lie** also **ghil·lie** (gĭl′ē) *n., pl.* **-lies. 1.** *Scots.* A professional fishing and hunting guide. See Regional Note at **mozo. 2.** A low-cut sports shoe with fringed laces. [Scottish Gaelic *gille,* boy, servant, from Old Irish *gilla,* from *gildae.*]

gill·net (gĭl′nĕt′) *tr.v.* **-net·ted, -net·ting, -nets.** To catch (fish) by means of a gill net.

gill net (gĭl) *n.* A fishing net set vertically in the water so that fish swimming into it are entangled by the gills in its mesh.

gill-net·ter (gĭl′nĕt′ər) *n.* **1.** One who uses a gill net to catch fish. **2.** *Nautical.* A boat used in fishing with gill nets.

gill slit (gĭl) *n.* **1.** One of several narrow external openings connecting with the pharynx, characteristic of sharks and related fishes, through which water passes to the exterior, thereby bathing the gills. Also called *branchial cleft, gill cleft.* **2.** *Embryology.* One of several rudimentary invaginations in the surface of the embryo, present during development of all air-breathing vertebrates and corresponding to the functional gill slits of aquatic species. Also called *branchial groove.*

gil·ly·flow·er (gĭl′ē-flou′ər) *n.* **1.** The carnation or a similar plant of the genus *Dianthus.* **2.** Any of several plants, such as the wallflower, that have fragrant flowers. [Alteration (influenced by FLOWER) of Middle English *gilofre,* from Old French *gilofre, girofle,* clove, from Late Latin *gariofilum,* from Greek *karuophullon* : *karuon,* nut; see **kar-** in Appendix + *phullon,* leaf; see **bhel-[3]** in Appendix.]

Gil·man (gĭl′mən), **Charlotte Anna Perkins.** 1860–1935. American feminist, writer, and editor best known for *Women and Economics* (1898).

Gil·mer (gĭl′mər), **Elizabeth Meriwether.** Pen name Dorothy Dix. 1870–1951. American journalist noted for her syndicated advice column for the lovelorn (1896–1949).

Gil·roy (gĭl′roi′). A city of western California southeast of San Jose. Located in the fertile Santa Clara Valley, the city is a trade center with varied industries. Population, 21,641.

Gil·son·ite (gĭl′sə-nīt′). A trademark used for a natural black bitumen employed in the manufacture of acid, alkali, and waterproof coatings.

gilt[1] (gĭlt) *v.* A past tense and a past participle of **gild[1]**. —**gilt** *adj.* **1.** Covered with gold or gilt. **2.** Resembling gold, as in color or luster. —**gilt** *n.* **1.** *Abbr.* **gt.** A thin layer of gold or something simulating gold that is applied in gilding. **2.** Superficial brilliance or gloss. **3.** *Slang.* Money.

gilt[2] (gĭlt) *n.* A young sow that has not farrowed. [Middle English, young sow, from Old Norse *gyltr.*]

gilt-edged (gĭlt′ĕjd′) also **gilt-edge** (-ĕj′) *adj.* **1.** Having gilded edges, as the pages of a book. **2.** Of the highest quality or value: *gilt-edged securities; gilt-edged credentials.* **3.** Very wealthy: *"Barricades prevented the curious from coming any closer to the gathering of gilt-edged mourners"* (Edward Rothstein).

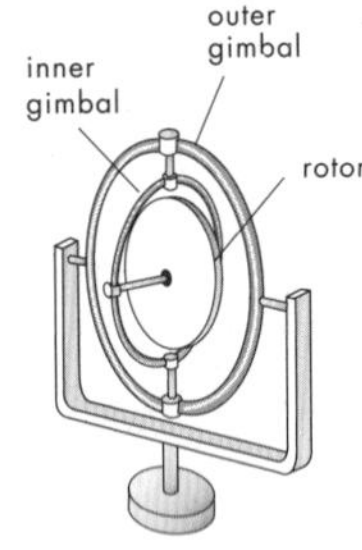

gimbal
Two-degree-of-freedom gyroscope

gim·bal (gĭm′bəl, jĭm′-) *n.* A device consisting of two rings mounted on axes at right angles to each other so that an object, such as a ship's compass, will remain suspended in a horizontal plane between them regardless of any motion of its support. Often used in the plural. Also called *gimbal ring.* —**gimbal** *tr.v.* **-baled, -bal·ing, -bals** or **-balled, -bal·ling, -bals.** To supply with or support on gimbals. [Alteration of obsolete *gemel,* double ring. See GIMMAL.]

gim·crack (jĭm′krăk′) *n.* A cheap and showy object of little or no use; a gewgaw. —**gimcrack** *adj.* Cheap and tasteless; gaudy: *"The shelves groan with an array of gimcrack gifts from fans: a stuffed piranha fish . . . a papier-mâché replica of an Apollo moonwalker"* (Harry F. Waters). [Possibly alteration of Middle English *gibecrake,* small ornament.] —**gim′crack′er·y** *n.*

gim·el (gĭm′əl) *n.* The third letter of the Hebrew alphabet. See table at **alphabet.** [Hebrew *gīmel.*]

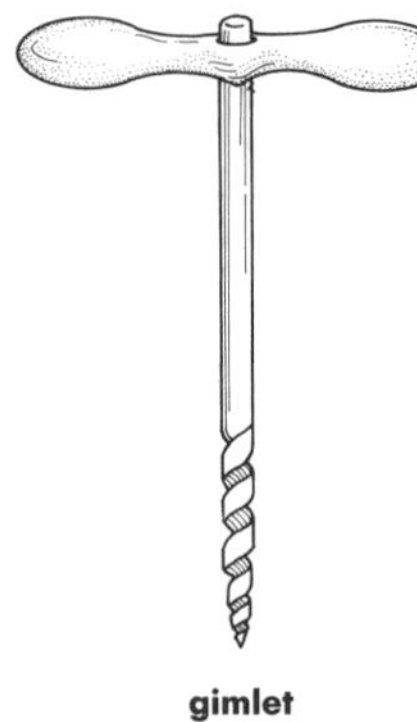
gimlet

gim·let (gĭm′lĭt) *n.* **1.** A small hand tool having a spiraled shank, a screw tip, and a cross handle and used for boring holes. **2.** A cocktail made with vodka or gin, sweetened lime juice, and sometimes effervescent water and garnished with a slice of lime. —**gimlet** *tr.v.* **-let·ed, -let·ing, -lets.** To penetrate with or as if with a gimlet. —**gimlet** *adj.* Having a penetrating or piercing quality: *gimlet eyes.* [Middle English, from Anglo-Norman *guimbelet,* perhaps from Middle Dutch *wimmelkijn,* diminutive of *wimmel,* auger.]

gim·let-eyed (gĭm′lĭt-īd′) *adj.* Having keen vision.

gim·mal (gĭm′əl, jĭm′-) *n.* **1.** A ring made of two or more interlocked rings. **2.** Any of various linkages allowing one part to rotate within another rotating part, used especially in clockworks. [Alteration of *gemel,* from Middle English, sing. of *gemeles,* twins, from Old French, from Latin *gemellus,* diminutive of *geminus,* twin.]

gim·me (gĭm′ē) *adj. Slang.* Demanding material things or especially money; acquisitive: *today's gimme society; tired of gimme letters.* —**gimme** *n. Sports.* A putt that is considered made in an informal game of golf. [Alteration of *give me.*]

gimme cap *n. Slang.* A cloth cap with a bill, adorned with the name of an organization or a product logo: *"one-size-fits-all gimme caps"* (Charles Leerhsen).

gim·mick (gĭm′ĭk) *n.* **1. a.** A device employed to cheat, de-

ă pat	oi boy
ā pay	ou out
âr care	ŏŏ took
ä father	ōō boot
ĕ pet	ŭ cut
ē be	ûr urge
ĭ pit	th thin
ī pie	*th* this
îr pier	hw which
ŏ pot	zh vision
ō toe	ə about, item
ô paw	◆ regionalism

Stress marks: ′ (primary); ′ (secondary), as in **dictionary** (dĭk′shə-nĕr′ē)

ceive, or trick, especially a mechanism for the secret and dishonest control of gambling apparatus. **b.** An innovative or unusual mechanical contrivance; a gadget. **2.a.** An innovative stratagem or scheme employed especially to promote a project: *an advertising gimmick.* **b.** A significant feature that is obscured, misrepresented, or not readily evident; a catch. **3.** A small object whose name does not come readily to mind. **—gimmick** *tr.v.* **-micked, -mick·ing, -micks. 1.** To add gimmicks to; clutter with gadgets or attention-getting details. Often used with *up.* **2.** To change or affect by means of a gimmick. [Origin unknown.] **—gim′mick·y** *adj.*

gim·mick·ry (gĭm′ĭk-rē) *n., pl.* **-ries. 1.** An array or abundance of gimmicks. **2.** The use of gimmicks.

gimp¹ (gĭmp) *n.* A narrow flat braid or rounded cord of fabric used for trimming. Also called *guimpe, guipure.* [Perhaps from French *guimpe.* See GUIMPE.]

gimp² (gĭmp) *Slang. n.* **1.** A limp or a limping gait. **2.** A person who limps. **—gimp** *intr.v.* **gimped, gimp·ing, gimps.** To walk with a limp. [Origin unknown.] **—gimp′y** *adj.*

gimp³ (gĭmp) *n.* Spirit; pep. [Origin unknown.]

gin¹ (jĭn) *n.* A strong, colorless alcoholic beverage made by distilling or redistilling rye or other grain spirits and adding juniper berries or aromatics such as anise, caraway seeds, or angelica root as flavoring. [Alteration of *geneva,* from Dutch *jenever,* from Middle Dutch *geniver,* juniper, from Old French *geneivre,* from Vulgar Latin **iiniperus,* from Latin *iūniperus.*] **—gin′ny** *adj.*

gin² (jĭn) *n.* **1.** Any of several machines or devices, especially: **a.** A machine for hoisting or moving heavy objects. **b.** A pile driver. **c.** A snare or trap for game. **d.** A pump operated by a windmill. **2.** A cotton gin. **—gin** *tr.v.* **ginned, gin·ning, gins. 1.** To remove the seeds from (cotton) with a cotton gin. **2.** To trap in a gin. [Middle English, from Old French, short for *engin,* skill. See ENGINE.]

gin³ (jĭn) *n. Games.* Gin rummy.

gin and tonic *n.* A drink made of gin and quinine water and usually garnished with a slice of lemon or lime.

gin·ger (jĭn′jər) *n.* **1.** A plant *Zingiber officinale* of tropical southeast Asia having yellowish-green flowers and a pungent, aromatic rhizome. **2.** The rhizome of this plant, often dried and powdered and used as a spice. Also called *gingerroot.* **3.a.** Any of several related plants having variously colored, often fragrant flowers. **b.** Wild ginger. **4.** *Color.* A strong brown. **5.** *Informal.* Spirit and liveliness; vigor. **—ginger** *tr.v.* **-gered, -ger·ing, -gers. 1.** To spice with ginger. **2.** *Informal.* To make lively: *A steel drum band gingered up the party.* [Middle English *gingivere,* from Old English *gingifer* and from Old French *gingivre,* both from Medieval Latin *gingiber,* from Latin *zingiberi,* from Greek *zingiberis,* of Middle Indic origin (akin to Pali *singiveram*), from Dravidian : akin to Tamil *iñci,* ginger (of southeast Asian origin) + Tamil *vēr,* root.] **—gin′ger·y** *adj.*

ginger ale *n.* An effervescent, sweetened soft drink flavored with ginger.

ginger beer *n.* A nonalcoholic drink similar to ginger ale but flavored with fermented ginger.

gin·ger·bread (jĭn′jər-brĕd′) *n.* **1.a.** A dark molasses cake flavored with ginger. **b.** A soft molasses and ginger cookie cut in various shapes, sometimes elaborately decorated. **2.a.** Elaborate ornamentation. **b.** Superfluous or tasteless embellishment, especially in architecture. [Middle English *gingebred,* a stiff pudding, preserved ginger, alteration (influenced by *bred, bread,* bread; see BREAD) of Old French *gingembrat,* from Medieval Latin **gingibrātum,* from *gingiber,* ginger. See GINGER.] **—gin′ger·bread′** *adj.* **—gin′ger·bread′y** *adj.*

gingerbread palm *n.* See **doom palm.**

ginger group *n. Chiefly British.* A highly active or galvanizing group within a larger organization or body.

gin·ger·ly (jĭn′jər-lē) *adv.* With great care or delicacy; cautiously. **—gingerly** *adj.* Cautious; careful. [Possibly alteration of obsolete French *gensor,* delicate, from Old French, comparative of *gent,* gentle. See GENT¹.] **—gin′ger·li·ness** *n.*

gin·ger·root (jĭn′jər-ro͞ot′, -ro͝ot′) *n.* See **ginger** (sense 2).

gin·ger·snap (jĭn′jər-snăp′) *n.* A flat, brittle cookie spiced with ginger and sweetened with molasses.

ging·ham (gĭng′əm) *n.* A yarn-dyed cotton fabric woven in stripes, checks, plaids, or solid colors. [Dutch *ginggang,* from Malay, from *genggang,* at intervals.]

gin·gi·va (jĭn′jə-və, jĭn-jī′-) *n., pl.* **-vae** (-vē′). See **gum².** [Latin *gingīva.*]

gin·gi·val (jĭn′jə-vəl, jĭn-jī′-) *adj.* **1.** Of or relating to the gums. **2.** *Linguistics.* Alveolar.

gin·gi·vec·to·my (jĭn′jə-vĕk′tə-mē) *n., pl.* **-mies.** Surgical removal of gum tissue.

gin·gi·vi·tis (jĭn′jə-vī′tĭs) *n.* Inflammation of the gums, characterized by redness and swelling.

ging·ko (gĭng′kō) *n.* Variant of **ginkgo.**

gink (gĭnk) *n. Slang.* A man, especially one regarded as foolish or contemptible. [Origin unknown.]

gink·go also **ging·ko** (gĭng′kō) *n., pl.* **-goes** also **-koes.** A deciduous, dioecious tree *(Ginkgo biloba)* native to China and having fan-shaped leaves and fleshy yellowish seeds with a disagreeable odor. The male plants are often grown as ornamental street trees. Also called *maidenhair tree.* [Japanese *ginkyō.*]

gin mill *n. Slang.* A bar or saloon.

gin rummy *n. Games.* A variety of rummy for two or more persons in which a player may win by matching all his or her cards or may end the game by melding with unmatched cards that add up to ten points or fewer.

Gins·berg (gĭnz′bərg), **Allen.** Born 1926. American poet of the beat generation. His works include *Howl* (1956).

gin·seng (jĭn′sĕng′) *n.* **1.** Any of several plants of the genus *Panax,* especially *P. pseudoginseng* of eastern Asia or *P. quinquefolius* of North America, having small greenish flowers grouped in umbels, palmately compound leaves, and forked roots believed to have medicinal properties. **2.** The roots of these plants. [Chinese (Mandarin) *rén shēn* : *rén,* man + *shēn,* ginseng (perhaps from the forked shape of the root).]

Gin·za (gĭn′zə). A major shopping and entertainment district of Tokyo, Japan.

gin·zo (gĭn′zō) *n., pl.* **-zoes.** *Offensive Slang.* Used as a disparaging term for a person of Italian ancestry. [Origin unknown.]

Gior·gio·ne (jôr-jō′nē, -nĕ). Originally Giorgio Barbarelli. Also known as Giorgio da Castelfranco. 1478?–1510. Italian painter of the Venetian school. Among the works ascribed to him are *The Tempest* (c. 1505) and *Sleeping Venus* (c. 1510).

Giot·to (jô′tō, jŏt′ō). 1267?–1337. Florentine painter, architect, and sculptor. Considered the greatest painter of pre-Renaissance Italy, he turned from the formulaic Byzantine style to a more natural representation of human expression and movement.

gip (jĭp) *v. & n. Slang.* Variant of **gyp.**

Gip·sy (jĭp′sē) *n.* Variant of **Gypsy.**

gi·raffe (jə-răf′) *n., pl.* **-raffes** or **giraffe.** An African ruminant mammal *(Giraffa camelopardalis)* having a very long neck and legs, a tan coat with orange-brown to black blotches, and short horns. It is the tallest land animal, often reaching a height of 5 meters (16½ feet), and feeds principally by browsing in the tree canopy of wooded grasslands. [French *girafe,* from Italian *giraffa,* from Arabic dialectal *zirāfah,* probably of African origin.] **—gi·raff′ish** *adj.*

gir·an·dole (jĭr′ən-dōl′) *n.* **1.** A composition or structure in radiating form or arrangement, such as a rotating display of fireworks. **2.** An ornamental branched candleholder, sometimes backed by a mirror. [French, from Italian *girandola,* from *girare,* to turn, from Late Latin *gȳrāre.* See GYRATE.]

Gi·rard (jə-rärd′), **Stephen.** 1750–1831. French-born American financier and philanthropist who bought out the Bank of the United States (1812) and helped finance the War of 1812.

gir·a·sol (jĭr′ə-sôl′, -sōl′, -sŏl′) *n.* **1.** Also **gir·o·sol.** See **fire opal. 2.** Also **gir·a·sole.** See **Jerusalem artichoke.** [Italian *girasole,* sunflower, opal : *girare,* to turn (from Late Latin *gȳrāre;* see GYRATE) + *sole,* sun (from Latin *sōl;* see **sāwel-** in Appendix).]

Gi·rau·doux (zhē-rō-do͞o′), **(Hippolyte) Jean.** 1882–1944. French writer primarily known for his dramas, such as *Electra* (1937), that are based on Greek mythology or biblical stories.

gird¹ (gûrd) *v.* **gird·ed** or **girt** (gûrt), **gird·ing, girds.** *—tr.* **1.a.** To encircle with a belt or band. **b.** To fasten or secure (clothing, for example) with a belt or band. **c.** To surround. See Synonyms at **surround. 2.** To equip or endow. **3.** To prepare (oneself) for action. *—intr.* To prepare for action: *"Men still spoke of peace but girded more sternly for war"* (W. Bruce Lincoln). ***—idiom.* gird (up) (one's) loins.** To summon up one's inner resources in preparation for action. [Middle English *girden,* from Old English *gyrdan.* See **gher-¹** in Appendix.]

gird² (gûrd) *intr. & tr.v.* **gird·ed, gird·ing, girds.** To jeer or jeer at. **—gird** *n.* A sarcastic remark. [Middle English *girden,* to strike.]

gird·er (gûr′dər) *n.* A horizontal beam, as of steel or wood, used as a main support for a building or bridge.

gir·dle (gûr′dl) *n.* **1.a.** A belt or sash worn around the waist. **b.** Something that encircles like a belt. **c.** A woman's elasticized, flexible undergarment worn over the waist and hips. **2.** A band made around the trunk of a tree by the removal of a strip of bark. **3.** The edge of a cut gem held by the setting. **4.** *Anatomy.* The pelvic or pectoral girdle. **—girdle** *tr.v.* **-dled, -dling, -dles. 1.** To encircle with or as if with a belt. See Synonyms at **surround. 2.** To circle around: *a ring of hills that girdled the city.* **3.** To remove a band of bark and cambium from the circumference of (a tree), usually in order to kill it. [Middle English *girdel,* from Old English *gyrdel.* See **gher-¹** in Appendix.]

gird·ler (gûrd′lər) *n.* **1.** One that makes girdles. **2.** Any of several insects that chew circular bands around twigs or stems in preparing a nesting site.

girl (gûrl) *n.* **1.** A female child. **2.** An immature or inexperienced woman, especially a young woman. **3.** A daughter: *our youngest girl.* **4.** *Informal.* A grown woman: *a night out with the girls.* **5.** A female who comes from or belongs to a particular place: *a city girl.* **6.** *Offensive.* A female servant, such as a maid. **7.** A female sweetheart: *cadets escorting their girls to the ball.* [Middle English *girle,* child, girl.] **—girl′hood′** *n.*

girl Friday *n. Informal.* An efficient and faithful woman aide or employee. [GIRL + (MAN) FRIDAY.]

girl·friend also **girl friend** (gûrl′frĕnd′) *n.* **1.** A favored female companion or sweetheart. **2.** A female friend.

Girl Guide (gûrl) *n.* A member of the Girl Guides, a British organization of young women and girls founded in 1910.

girl·ie also **girl·y** (gûr′lē) *adj. Informal.* Featuring minimally

ginkgo
Ginkgo biloba

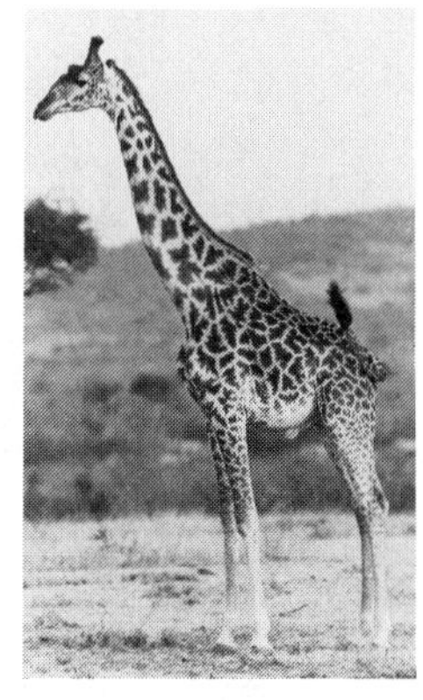

Giotto

giraffe
Masai giraffe
Giraffa tippelskirchi

girandole
c. 1810 American

clothed or naked women typically in pornographic contexts: *girlie magazines.*

girl·ish (gûr′lĭsh) *adj.* Characteristic of or befitting a girl: *girlish charm.* —**girl′ish·ly** *adv.* —**girl′ish·ness** *n.*

Girl Scout *n.* A member of the Girl Scouts, an organization of young women and girls, founded in the United States in 1912 on the plan of the Girl Guides, for character development and citizenship training.

girl wonder *n.* An extremely talented and accomplished young woman.

girl·y (gûr′lē) *adj.* Variant of **girlie.**

girn (gûrn) *intr.v.* **girned, girn·ing, girns.** *Scots.* **1.** To complain in a whining voice. **2.** To contort one's face; grimace. [Middle English *girnen,* variant of *grinnen, grennan.* See GRIN.] —**girn** *n.*

Gi·ronde[1] (jə-rŏnd′, zhē-rōNd′). An estuary of southwest France formed by the Garonne and Dordogne rivers and opening into the Bay of Biscay.

Gi·ronde[2] (jə-rŏnd′, zhĭ-) *n.* A moderate republican political party of Revolutionary France (1791–93). [After *Gironde,* a department of southwest France.] —**Gi·rond′ist** *n.*

gir·o·sol (jĭr′ə-sôl′, -sōl′, -sŏl′) *n.* Variant of **girasol** (sense 1).

girt[1] (gûrt) *v.* **girt·ed, girt·ing, girts.** —*tr.* **1.** To gird. **2.** To secure with a girth. **3.** To measure the girth of. —*intr.* To measure in girth. [Variant of GIRD[1].]

girt[2] (gûrt) *v.* A past tense and a past participle of **gird[1].**

girth (gûrth) *n.* **1.** The distance around something; the circumference. **2.** Size; bulk: *a person of large girth.* **3.** A strap encircling an animal's body in order to secure a load or saddle on its back; a cinch. —**girth** *tr.v.* **girthed, girth·ing, girths.** **1.** To measure the circumference of. **2.** To encircle. **3.** To secure with a girth. [Middle English *gerth,* girth strap, from Old Norse *gjördh,* girdle. See **gher-[1]** in Appendix.]

gi·sarme (gĭ-zärm′) *n.* A halberd with a long shaft and two-sided blade, carried by medieval foot soldiers. [Middle English, from Old French *guisarme,* possibly from Old High German *getīsarn* : *getan,* to weed + *īsarn,* iron; see **eis-** in Appendix.]

Gis·card d'Es·taing (zhĭ-skär′ dĕs-tăng′, -tăN′), **Valéry.** Born 1926. French political leader who as president of France (1974–1981) struggled against rising inflation and unemployment.

Gish (gĭsh), **Lillian Diana.** Born 1896. American actress best known for her roles in silent films, such as *The Birth of a Nation* (1915). Her sister **Dorothy** (1898–1968) was also a film actress.

gis·mo (gĭz′mō) *n.* Variant of **gizmo.**

Gis·sing (gĭs′ĭng), **George Robert.** 1857–1903. British writer best known for his novels about poverty and hardship.

gist (jĭst) *n.* **1.** The central idea; the essence. See Synonyms at **substance.** **2.** *Law.* The grounds for action in a suit. [From Anglo-Norman *(cest action) gist,* (this action) lies, third person sing. of *gesir,* to lie, from Latin *iacēre.* See **yē-** in Appendix.]

gite (zhēt) *n.* A simple, usually inexpensive rural vacation retreat especially in France. [French *gîte,* lodging, lair, from Old French *giste,* from feminine past participle of *gesir,* to lie. See GIST.]

git·tern (gĭt′ərn) *n. Music.* A medieval guitar. [Middle English *giterne,* from Old French *guiterne,* from Latin *cithara.* See CITHARA.]

give (gĭv) *v.* **gave** (gāv), **giv·en** (gĭv′ən), **giv·ing, gives.** —*tr.* **1.** To make a present of: *We gave her flowers for her birthday.* **2.** To place in the hands of; pass: *Give me the scissors.* **3. a.** To deliver in exchange or recompense; pay: *will give five dollars for the book.* **b.** To let go for a price; sell. **4. a.** To administer: *give him some cough medicine.* **b.** To convey by a physical action: *gave me a punch in the nose.* **c.** To inflict as punishment: *gave the child a spanking; was given life imprisonment for the crime.* **d.** *Law.* To accord by verdict: *A decision was given for the plaintiff.* **5. a.** To bestow, especially officially; confer: *The Bill of Rights gives us freedom of speech.* **b.** To accord or tender to another: *Give him your confidence.* **c.** To put temporarily at the disposal of: *gave them the cottage for a week.* **d.** To entrust to another, usually for a specified reason: *gave me the keys for safekeeping.* **e.** To convey or offer for conveyance: *Give him my best wishes.* **f.** *Law.* To execute and deliver. Used especially in the phrase *give bond.* **6. a.** To endure the loss of; sacrifice: *gave her son to the war; gave her life for her country.* **b.** To devote or apply completely: *gives herself to her work.* **c.** To furnish or contribute: *gave their time to help others.* **d.** To offer in good faith; pledge: *Give me your word.* **7. a.** To allot as a portion or share. **b.** To bestow as a name. **c.** To attribute (blame, for example) to someone; assign. **d.** To award as due: *gave us first prize.* **8.** To emit or utter: *gave a groan; gave a muted response.* **9.** To submit for consideration, acceptance, or use: *give an opinion; give an excuse.* **10. a.** To proffer to another: *gave the toddler my hand.* **b.** To consent to engage (oneself) in sexual intercourse with a man. **11. a.** To perform for an audience: *give a recital.* **b.** To present to view: *gave the sign to begin.* **12. a.** To offer as entertainment: *give a dinner party.* **b.** To propose as a toast. **13. a.** To be a source of; afford: *His remark gave offense. Music gives her pleasure.* **b.** To cause to catch or be subject to (a disease or bodily condition): *The draft gave me a cold.* **c.** To guide or direct, as by persuasion or behavior. Used with an infinitive phrase: *You gave me to imagine you approved of my report.* **14. a.** To yield or produce: *Cows give milk.* **b.** To bring forth or bear: *trees that give fruit.* **c.** To produce as a result of calculation: *5 × 12 gives 60.* **15. a.** To manifest or show: *gives promise of brilliance; gave evidence of tampering.* **b.** To carry out (a physical movement): *give a wink; give a start.* **16.** To permit one to have or take: *gave us an hour to finish.* **17.** To take an interest to the extent of: *"My dear, I don't give a damn"* (Margaret Mitchell). —*intr.* **1.** To make gifts or donations: *gives generously to charity.* **2. a.** To yield to physical force. **b.** To collapse from force or pressure: *The roof gave under the weight of the snow.* **c.** To yield to change: *Both sides will have to give on some issues.* **3.** To afford access to or a view of; open: *The doors give onto a terrace.* **4.** *Slang.* To be in progress; happen: *What gives?* —**give** *n.* **1.** Capacity or inclination to yield under pressure. **2.** The quality or condition of resilience; springiness: *"Fruits that have some give . . . will have more juice than hard ones"* (Elizabeth Schneider). —***phrasal verbs.*** **give away. 1.** To make a gift of. **2.** To present (a bride) to the bridegroom at a wedding ceremony. **3. a.** To reveal or make known, often accidentally. **b.** To betray. **give back.** To return: *gave me back my book.* **give in. 1.** To hand in; submit: *She gave in her report.* **2.** To cease opposition; yield. **give of.** To devote or contribute: *She really gave of her time to help. They give of themselves to improve the quality of education.* **give off.** To send forth; emit: *chemical changes that give off energy.* **give out. 1.** To allow to be known; declare publicly: *gave out the bad news.* **2.** To send forth; emit: *gave out a steady buzzing.* **3.** To distribute: *gave out the surplus food.* **4.** To stop functioning; fail. **5.** To become used up or exhausted; run out: *Their determination finally gave out.* **give over. 1.** To hand over; entrust. **2. a.** To devote to a particular purpose or use: *gave the day over to merrymaking.* **b.** To surrender (oneself) completely; abandon: *finally gave myself over to grief.* **3.** To cause an activity to stop: *ordered the combatants to give over.* **give up. 1. a.** To surrender: *The suspects gave themselves up.* **b.** To devote (oneself) completely: *gave herself up to her work.* **2. a.** To cease to do or perform: *gave up their search.* **b.** To desist from; stop: *gave up smoking.* **3.** To part with; relinquish: *gave up the apartment; gave up all hope.* **4. a.** To lose hope for: *We had given the dog up as lost.* **b.** To lose hope of seeing: *We'd given you up an hour ago.* **5.** To admit defeat. **6.** To abandon what one is doing or planning to do. Often used with *on: gave up on writing the novel.* —***idioms.*** **give a good account of (oneself).** To behave or perform creditably. **give birth to. 1.** To bear as offspring. **2.** To be the origin of: *a hobby that gave birth to a successful business.* **give ground.** To yield to a more powerful force; retreat. **give it to.** *Informal.* To punish or reprimand severely: *My parents really gave it to me for coming in late.* **give or take.** Plus or minus a small specified amount: *The chalet is close to the road, give or take a few hundred yards.* **give rise to.** To be the cause or origin of; bring about. **give (someone) the eye.** To look at admiringly or invitingly. **give the lie to. 1.** To show to be inaccurate or untrue. **2.** To accuse of lying. **give up the ghost.** To cease living or functioning; die. **give way. 1. a.** To retreat or withdraw. **b.** To yield the right of way: *gave way to an oncoming car.* **c.** To relinquish ascendancy or position: *as day gives way slowly to night.* **2. a.** To collapse from or as if from physical pressure: *The ladder gave way.* **b.** To yield to urging or demand; give in. **3.** To abandon oneself: *give way to hysteria.* [Middle English *given,* from Old English *giefan* and Old Norse *gefa.* See **ghabh-** in Appendix.]

give-and-take also **give and take** (gĭv′ən-tāk′) *n.* **1.** The practice of compromise. **2.** Lively exchange of ideas or conversation: *"the raucous give and take of American democracy"* (Charles Kuralt).

give·a·way (gĭv′ə-wā′) *n. Informal.* **1.** The act or an instance of giving something away, especially the appropriation of natural resources or public lands for private gain. **2.** Something given away at no charge, especially a premium. **3.** Something that accidentally exposes or betrays. **4.** A radio or television program on which prizes are given away to contestants. **5.** Legislation, such as a tax law, that benefits only one segment of the population.

give·back (gĭv′băk′) *n.* **1.** A cutback in employee wages or benefits conceded by a labor union in acknowledgment of unfavorable economic conditions or in exchange for other benefits. **2.** Something that is rebated or returned.

giv·en (gĭv′ən) *v.* Past participle of **give.** —**given** *adj.* **1. a.** Specified; fixed: *We will meet at a given time and location.* **b.** Granted as a supposition; acknowledged or assumed: *Given the condition of the engine, it is a wonder that it even starts.* **2.** Having a tendency; inclined: *My neighbor is given to lavish spending.* **3.** Bestowed as a gift; presented. **4.** *Law.* Issued on a specified date. Used of legal documents. —**given** *n.* Something assumed or taken for granted. Often used in the plural.

given name *n.* A name given to a person at birth or at baptism.

giv·er (gĭv′ər) *n.* **1.** One that gives: *a giver of gifts.* **2.** A donor or contributor. Often used in combination: *almsgivers.*

give-up (giv′ŭp′) *n.* **1.** A commission shared among two or more stockbrokers on a trade from one firm to another. **2.** Something relinquished or conceded; a giveback.

Gi·za (gē′zə). A city of northern Egypt, an industrial suburb of Cairo on the Nile River. The Great Pyramids and the Sphinx are nearby. Population, 1,608,400.

giz·mo also **gis·mo** (gĭz′mō) *n., pl.* **-mos.** A mechanical device or part whose name is forgotten or unknown; a gadget. [Origin unknown.]

giz·zard (gĭz′ərd) *n.* **1.** A modified muscular pouch immediately behind the stomach in the alimentary canal of birds, having a thick lining and often containing ingested grit, which aids in the mechanical breakdown of seeds before digestion. **2.** A similar digestive organ found in certain invertebrates, such as the earthworm. [Alteration of Middle English *giser,* from Old French, from Vulgar Latin **gicērium,* from Latin *gigēria,* cooked entrails of poultry, probably from Persian *jigar,* liver. See **yĕkʷr** in Appendix.]

Gjel·le·rup (gĕl′ə-ro͝op′), **Karl.** 1857–1919. Danish writer whose novels include *An Idealist* (1878) and *The Pilgrim Kamanoto* (1906). He shared the 1917 Nobel Prize for literature.

Gk. *abbr.* Greek.

gl. *abbr.* Gloss (explanatory note).

gla·bel·la (glə-bĕl′ə) *n., pl.* **-bel·lae** (-bĕl′ē). The smooth area between the eyebrows just above the nose. [New Latin, from Latin *glabellus,* hairless, diminutive of *glaber.*] **—gla·bel′lar** *adj.*

gla·brate (glā′brāt′, -brĭt) or **gla·bres·cent** (glā-brĕs′ənt) *adj. Botany.* Almost glabrous or becoming glabrous with age or maturity: *glabrate stems.* [GLABR(OUS) + –ATE [1].]

gla·brous (glā′brəs) *adj.* Having no hairs, projections, or pubescence; smooth: *a glabrous scalp; glabrous leaves.* [From Latin *glaber, glabr-,* bald.] **—gla′brous·ness** *n.*

gla·cé (glă-sā′) *adj.* **1.** Having a smooth, glazed or glossy surface, such as certain silks or leathers. **2.** Coated with a sugar glaze. **—glacé** *tr.v.* **-céed, -cé·ing, -cés. 1.** To glaze. **2.** To candy. [French, from past participle of *glacer,* to glaze, freeze, from Old French, to freeze, from Latin *glaciāre.* See GLACIATE.]

Glace Bay (glās). A town of northeast Nova Scotia, Canada, on the Atlantic coast of Cape Breton Island. It is a mining center and fishing port. The first transatlantic wireless message was transmitted from nearby Table Head in 1902. Population, 21,466.

gla·cial (glā′shəl) *adj.* **1.a.** Of, relating to, or derived from a glacier. **b.** Suggesting the extreme slowness of a glacier: *Work proceeded at a glacial pace.* **2.a.** *Often* **Glacial.** Characterized or dominated by the existence of glaciers. Used of a geologic epoch. **b.** Pleistocene. See table at **geologic time. 3.** Extremely cold; icy: *glacial waters.* See Synonyms at **cold. 4.** Having the appearance of ice. **5.a.** Lacking warmth and friendliness: *a glacial stare.* **b.** Coldly detached: *a glacial composure.* [French, from Old French, icy, from Latin *glaciālis,* from *glaciēs,* ice. See **gel-** in Appendix.] **—gla′cial·ly** *adv.*

glacial acetic acid *n.* Acetic acid that is at least 99.8 percent pure.

gla·ci·ate (glā′shē-āt′, -sē-) *tr.v.* **-at·ed, -at·ing, -ates. 1.a.** To cover with ice or a glacier. **b.** To subject to or affect by glacial action. **2.** To freeze. [Latin *glaciāre, glaciāt-,* to freeze, from *glaciēs,* ice. See **gel-** in Appendix.] **—gla′ci·a′tion** *n.*

gla·cier (glā′shər) *n.* A huge mass of ice slowly flowing over a land mass, formed from compacted snow in an area where snow accumulation exceeds melting and sublimation. [French, from Old French, cold place, from *glace,* ice, from Vulgar Latin **glacia,* from Latin *glaciēs.* See **gel-** in Appendix.] **—gla′ciered** *adj.*

Gla·cier Bay (glā′shər). A narrow inlet of the Pacific Ocean in southeast Alaska northwest of Juneau. It is surrounded by towering mountain peaks with spectacular glaciers.

glacier meal *n.* See **rock flour.**

gla·ci·ol·o·gy (glā′shē-ŏl′ə-jē, -sē-) *n.* The scientific study of glaciers and their effects on the landscape. [GLACI(ER) + –LOGY.] **—gla′ci·o·log′ic** (-ə-lŏj′ĭk), **gla′ci·o·log′i·cal** *adj.* **—gla′ci·ol′o·gist** *n.*

gla·cis (glā-sē′, glăs′ē, glā′sĭs) *n., pl.* **glacis. 1.a.** A gentle slope; an incline. **b.** A slope extending down from a fortification. **2.** A neutral area separating conflicting forces. [French, from Old French, from *glacer,* to slide, from *glace,* ice, from Latin *glaciēs.* See **gel-** in Appendix.]

Glack·ens (glăk′ənz), **William James.** 1870–1938. American painter noted for his realistic depictions of street life, such as *Chez Mouquin* (1905), and his later impressionistic works.

glad[1] (glăd) *adj.* **glad·der, glad·dest. 1.a.** Experiencing or exhibiting joy and pleasure. **b.** Appreciative: *was glad of the fire's warmth.* **2.** Providing joy and pleasure: *a glad occasion.* **3.** Very willing; pleased: *glad to help.* **4.** Bright and cheerful: *a glad May morning.* **5.** *Archaic.* Having a naturally cheerful disposition. **—glad** *tr. & intr.v.* **glad·ded, glad·ding, glads.** *Archaic.* To gladden. [Middle English, from Old English *glæd.* See **ghel-**[2] in Appendix.] **—glad′ly** *adv.* **—glad′ness** *n.*

SYNONYMS: *glad, happy, cheerful, lighthearted, joyful, joyous.* These adjectives mean being in or showing good spirits. *Glad* often refers to the feeling that results from the gratification of a wish or from satisfaction with immediate circumstances: *is glad of her success; was glad he had seen her. "Some folks rail against other folks, because other folks have what some folks would be glad of"* (Henry Fielding). *Happy* applies to a pleasurable feeling of contentment, as from a sense of fulfillment: *"Ask yourself whether you are happy, and you cease to be so"* (John Stuart Mill). *Cheerful* suggests the good spirits characteristic of a person who is pleased with something or who has a naturally outgoing nature: *She was as cheerful as anyone confined to a hospital bed could be. Lighthearted* stresses the absence of care: *"He whistles as he goes, lighthearted wretch,/Cold and yet cheerful"* (William Cowper). *Joyful* and *joyous* suggest lively, often exultant happiness: *a joyful heart; a joyful state of affairs; joyous laughter; joyous news.*

glad[2] (glăd) *n. Botany.* A gladiolus.

glad·den (glăd′n) *v.* **-dened, -den·ing, -dens.** *—tr.* To make glad. See Synonyms at **please.** *—intr. Archaic.* To be glad.

glade (glād) *n.* **1.** An open space in a forest. **2.** An everglade. [Middle English, perhaps from *glad,* bright and shining. See GLAD [1].]

glad hand *n. Informal.* A warm and hearty, but often insincere welcome or greeting.

glad-hand (glăd′hănd′) *v.* **-hand·ed, -hand·ing, -hands.** *Informal. —tr.* To extend a glad hand to: *presidential hopefuls glad-handing the factory workers. —intr.* To extend a glad hand: *was whistle-stopping and glad-handing for the last five months.* **—glad′-hand′er** *n.*

glad·i·ate (glăd′ē-āt′, -ĭt, glā′dē-) *adj.* Sword-shaped, as a leaf of an iris. [New Latin *gladiātus,* from Latin *gladius,* sword. See GLADIATOR.]

glad·i·a·tor (glăd′ē-ā′tər) *n.* **1.** A person, usually a professional combatant, a captive, or a slave, trained to entertain the public by engaging in mortal combat with another person or a wild animal in the ancient Roman arena. **2.** A person engaged in a controversy or debate, especially in public; a disputant. **3.** *Sports.* A professional boxer. [Middle English, from Latin *gladiātor,* from *gladius,* sword, of Celtic origin.] **—glad′i·a·to′ri·al** (-ə-tôr′ē-əl, -tōr′-) *adj.*

glad·i·o·lus (glăd′ē-ō′ləs) *n., pl.* **-li** (-lī, -lē) or **-lus·es. 1.** Also **glad·i·o·la** (-lə). *Botany.* Any of numerous plants of the genus *Gladiolus,* native chiefly to tropical and southern Africa and having sword-shaped leaves and showy, variously colored, irregular flowers arranged in one-sided spikes. Also called *sword lily.* **2.** *Anatomy.* The large middle section of the sternum. [Middle English *gladiol,* from Latin *gladiolus,* wild iris, diminutive of *gladius,* sword. See GLADIATOR.]

glad rags *pl.n. Slang.* Stylish clothes.

glad·some (glăd′səm) *adj.* Causing or showing gladness or joy: *a gladsome occasion; a gladsome smile.* **—glad′some·ly** *adv.* **—glad′some·ness** *n.*

Glad·stone[1] (glăd′stōn′, -stən). A city of western Missouri, an industrial suburb surrounded by Kansas City. Population, 24,990.

Glad·stone[2] (glăd′stōn′, -stən) *n.* **1.** A light four-wheeled convertible carriage with two interior seats and places outside for a driver and footman. **2.** A Gladstone bag. [After William Ewart GLADSTONE.]

Gladstone, William Ewart. 1809–1898. British political leader who served as Liberal prime minister four times (1868–1874, 1880–1885, 1886, and 1892–1894).

Gladstone bag *n.* A piece of light hand luggage consisting of two hinged compartments. [After William Ewart GLADSTONE.]

Glag·o·lit·ic (glăg′ə-lĭt′ĭk) also **Glag·o·lith·ic** (-lĭth′ĭk) *adj.* Belonging to or written in an uncial cursive alphabet attributed to Saint Cyril, formerly used in the writing of various Slavic languages but now limited to the Catholic liturgical books used by some communities along the Dalmation coast. [From Serbo-Croatian *glagoljica,* from *glagol,* word; akin to Old Church Slavonic *glagolŭ,* speech, word. See **gal-** in Appendix.]

glair also **glaire** (glâr) *n.* **1.** A sizing or glaze made of egg white. **2.** A viscous substance resembling egg white. [Middle English *glaire,* from Old French, from Vulgar Latin **clāria,* from Latin *clārus,* clear. See **kelə-**[2] in Appendix.]

glaive (glāv) *n. Archaic.* A sword, especially a broadsword. [Middle English, from Old French, from Latin *gladius.*]

Glå·ma (glô′mə) also **Glom·ma** (-mə, -mä). A river of eastern Norway flowing about 587 km (365 mi) generally southward to the Skagerrak.

glam·or (glăm′ər) *n.* Variant of **glamour.**

glam·or·ize also **glam·our·ize** (glăm′ə-rīz′) *tr.v.* **-ized, -iz·ing, -iz·es. 1.** To make glamorous: *tried to glamorize the bathroom with expensive fixtures.* **2.** To treat or portray in a romantic manner; idealize or glorify: *a show that glamorizes police work.* **—glam′or·i·za′tion** (-ər-ĭ-zā′shən) *n.* **—glam′or·iz′er** *n.*

glam·or·ous also **glam·our·ous** (glăm′ər-əs) *adj.* Full of or characterized by glamour. **—glam′or·ous·ly** *adv.* **—glam′or·ous·ness** *n.*

glam·our also **glam·or** (glăm′ər) *n.* **1.** An air of compelling charm, romance, and excitement, especially when delusively alluring. **2.** *Archaic.* A magic spell; enchantment. *—attributive.* Often used to modify another noun: *a glamour job; a glamour stock.* [Scots, magic spell, alteration of GRAMMAR (from the association of learning with magic).]

USAGE NOTE: Many words, such as *honor, vapor,* and *labor,* are usually spelled with an *–or* ending in American English but with an *–our* ending in British English. The preferred spelling of *glamour,* however, is *–our,* making it an exception to the usual American practice. The adjective is more often spelled *glamorous* in both American and British usage.

glam·our·ize (glăm′ə-rīz′) *v.* Variant of **glamorize.**

glacier

gladiator
Detail of an engraving after Jean Léon Gérôme's painting *Thumbs Down!*

ă pat	oi boy
ā pay	ou out
âr care	o͝o took
ä father	o͞o boot
ĕ pet	ŭ cut
ē be	ûr urge
ĭ pit	th thin
ī pie	*th* this
îr pier	hw which
ŏ pot	zh vision
ō toe	ə about, item
ô paw	♦ regionalism

Stress marks: **′** (primary); ′ (secondary), as in **dictionary** (dĭk′shə-nĕr′ē)

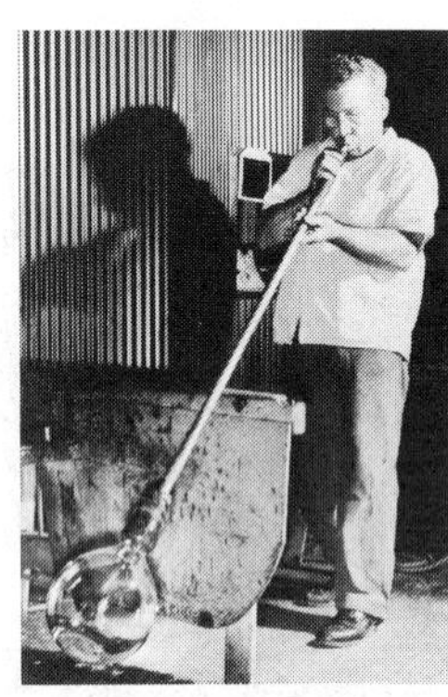

glass blowing

glam·our·ous (glăm′ər-əs) *adj.* Variant of **glamorous.**

glance¹ (glăns) *v.* **glanced, glanc·ing, glanc·es.** —*intr.* **1.a.** To direct the gaze briefly: *glance at the menu; glanced in the rear-view mirror.* **b.** To move rapidly from one thing to another. Used of the eyes. **2.** To shine briefly; glint. See Synonyms at **flash. 3.** To strike a surface at such an angle as to be deflected: *A pebble glanced off the windshield.* See Synonyms at **brush¹. 4.** To make a passing reference; touch briefly: *a history course that only glanced at the Korean conflict.* —*tr.* **1.** To strike (a surface) at an angle; graze: *The arrow glanced the target but didn't stick.* **2.** To cause to strike a surface at an angle: *glanced a stone off the wall.* —**glance** *n.* **1.** A brief or cursory look: *gave the paper a glance before breakfast.* **2.** A quick flash of light; a gleam. **3.** An oblique movement following impact; a deflection: *The car struck the barrier and went off at a glance.* —***idiom.* at first glance.** On initial consideration: *At first glance the plan seemed unworkable.* [Middle English *glauncen,* alteration (influenced by *glenten,* to shine; see **ghel-²** in Appendix) of *glacen,* from Old French *glacer,* to slide. See GLACIS.]

glance² (glăns) *n.* Any of various minerals that have a brilliant luster: *silver glance.* [German *Glanz,* from Middle High German *glanz,* from Old High German, bright. See **ghel-²** in Appendix.]

glanc·ing (glăn′sĭng) *adj.* **1.** Oblique in direction; slanting or deflected: *struck him a glancing blow.* **2.** Not straightforward: *made glancing allusions to the scandal.* —**glanc′ing·ly** *adv.*

gland¹ (glănd) *n.* **1.a.** A cell, a group of cells, or an organ that produces a secretion for use elsewhere in the body or in a body cavity or for elimination from the body. **b.** Any of various organs, such as lymph nodes, that resemble true glands but perform a nonsecretory function. **2.** *Botany.* An organ or a structure that secretes a substance. [French *glande,* from Old French *glandre,* alteration of Latin *glandula,* diminutive of *glāns, gland-,* acorn.]

gland² (glănd) *n.* A device, such as the outer sleeve of a stuffing box, designed to prevent a fluid from leaking past a moving machine part. [Origin unknown.]

glan·dered (glăn′dərd) *adj.* Affected with glanders.

glan·ders (glăn′dərz) *n. (used with a sing. or pl. verb).* A contagious, usually fatal disease of horses and other equine species, caused by the bacterium *Pseudomonas mallei* and symptomized by swollen lymph nodes, nasal discharge, and ulcers of the respiratory tract and skin. The disease is communicable to other mammals, including human beings. [Middle English *glaundres,* from Old French *glandres,* glandular swelling, pl. of *glandre,* gland. See GLAND¹.] —**glan′der·ous** *adj.*

glan·des (glăn′dēz) *n.* Plural of **glans.**

glan·du·lar (glăn′jə-lər) *adj.* **1.a.** Of, relating to, affecting, or resembling a gland or its secretion. **b.** Functioning as a gland. **2.** Having glands. **3.** Resulting from the abnormal function of glands or a gland. **4.a.** Innate; visceral: *has a glandular aversion to materialistic values.* **b.** Carnal; sensual. [French *glandulaire,* from *glandule,* small gland, from Latin *glandula.* See GLAND¹.] —**glan′du·lar·ly** *adv.*

glandular fever *n.* See **infectious mononucleosis.**

glans (glănz) *n., pl.* **glan·des** (glăn′dēz). **1.** The glans penis. **2.** The glans clitoridis. [Latin *glāns, gland-,* acorn, glans (from its shape).]

glans cli·tor·i·dis (klĭ-tôr′ĭ-dĭs, klī-) *n.* The small mass of erectile tissue at the tip of the clitoris. [New Latin *glāns clītoridis* : Latin *glāns,* glans + Greek *kleitoridos,* genitive of *kleitoris,* clitoris.]

glans penis *n.* The bulbous head or tip of the penis. [New Latin *glāns pēnis* : Latin *glāns,* glans + Latin *pēnis,* genitive of *pēnis,* penis.]

glare¹ (glâr) *v.* **glared, glar·ing, glares.** —*intr.* **1.** To stare fixedly and angrily. See Synonyms at **gaze. 2.** To shine intensely and blindingly: *A hot sun glared down on the desert.* **3.** To be conspicuous; stand out obtrusively: *The headline glared from the page.* —*tr.* To express by staring angrily: *He glared his disapproval.* —**glare** *n.* **1.** A fierce or angry stare. **2.a.** An intense, blinding light. See Synonyms at **blaze¹. b.** Garish or showy brilliance; gaudiness. [Middle English *glaren,* to glitter; akin to Middle Low German *glaren,* to glisten. See **ghel-²** in Appendix.]

glare² (glâr) *n.* A sheet or surface of glassy and very slippery ice. [Probably from GLARE¹.]

glar·ing (glâr′ĭng) *adj.* **1.** Shining intensely and blindingly: *the glaring noonday sun.* **2.** Tastelessly showy or bright; garish. **3.** Conspicuous; obvious: *a glaring error.* See Synonyms at **flagrant. 4.** Staring with anger, fierceness, or hostility: *glaring eyes.* —**glar′ing·ly** *adv.* —**glar′ing·ness** *n.*

glar·y (glâr′ē) *adj.* **-i·er, -i·est.** Dazzlingly bright; glaring.

Gla·ser (glā′zər), **Donald Arthur.** Born 1926. American physicist. He won a 1960 Nobel Prize for his invention of the bubble chamber, an apparatus used to study subatomic particles.

Glas·gow (glăs′kō, -gō, glăz′-). A city of southwest Scotland on the Clyde River. Founded in the late sixth century, Glasgow is the largest city in Scotland. Population, 767,456.

Glasgow, Ellen Anderson Gholson. 1873?–1945. American writer known for her realistic, historical novels of Virginia.

glas·nost (gläs′nəst, -nôst) *n.* An official policy of the Soviet government emphasizing candor with regard to discussion of social problems and shortcomings. [Russian *glasnost',* public information, publicity, from *glas,* voice; akin to Old Church Slavonic *glasŭ.* See **gal-** in Appendix.]

glass (glăs) *n.* **1.** Any of a large class of materials with highly variable mechanical and optical properties that solidify from the molten state without crystallization, are typically made by silicates fusing with boric oxide, aluminum oxide, or phosphorus pentoxide, are generally hard, brittle, and transparent or translucent, and are considered to be supercooled liquids rather than true solids. **2.** Something usually made of glass, especially: **a.** A drinking vessel. **b.** A mirror. **c.** A barometer. **d.** A window or windowpane. **3.a. glasses.** A pair of lenses mounted in a light frame, used to correct faulty vision or protect the eyes. **b.** *Often* **glasses.** A binocular or field glass. **c.** A device, such as a monocle or spyglass, containing a lens or lenses and used as an aid to vision. **4.** The quantity contained by a drinking vessel; a glassful. **5.** Objects made of glass; glassware. —**glass** *v.* **glassed, glass·ing, glass·es.** —*tr.* **1.a.** To enclose or encase with glass. **b.** To put into a glass container. **c.** To provide with glass or glass parts. **2.** To make glassy; glaze. **3.a.** To see reflected, as in a mirror. **b.** To reflect. **4.** To scan (a tract of land or forest, for example) with an optical instrument. —*intr.* **1.** To become glassy. **2.** To use an optical instrument, as in looking for game. [Middle English *glas,* from Old English *glæs.* See **ghel-²** in Appendix.]

glass blow·ing (blō′ĭng) *n.* The art or process of shaping an object from molten glass by blowing air into it through a tube. —**glass blower** *n.*

glassed-in (glăst′ĭn′) *adj.* Enclosed by glass or panels of glass: *a glassed-in porch; a glassed-in bookcase.*

glass eel *n.* An eel in its transparent, postlarval stage. Also called *elver.*

glass eye *n.* **1.** An artificial eye fashioned of glass. **2.** An eye whose iris is whitish, pale, or colorless.

glass·fish (glăs′fĭsh′) *n., pl.* **glassfish** or **-fish·es.** Any of various small, semitransparent Old World fishes of the genera *Ambassis* or *Chanda,* used to stock aquariums.

glass·ful (glăs′fo͝ol′) *n.* The quantity that a glass can hold.

glass harmonica *n. Music.* An instrument consisting of a set of graduated glass bowls on a rotating spindle that produce tones when a finger is pressed to their moistened rims.

glass·house (glăs′hous′) *n.* **1.** See **glasswork** (sense 3). **2.** *Chiefly British.* A greenhouse. **3.** A place, position, or situation involving intense public scrutiny.

glass·ine (glă-sēn′) *n.* A nearly transparent, resilient glazed paper resistant to the passage of air and grease.

glass jaw *n.* **1.** *Sports.* Vulnerability of a boxer to a knockout punch. **2.** Vulnerability, especially of a public figure, to destructive criticism.

glass·mak·er (glăs′mā′kər) *n.* One that makes glass. —**glass′mak′ing** *n.*

glass snake *n.* Any of several slender, limbless, snakelike lizards of the genus *Ophisaurus,* having a tail that breaks or snaps off readily and later regenerates. [From the brittleness of its tail.]

glass·ware (glăs′wâr′) *n.* Objects, especially containers, made of glass. Also called *glasswork.*

glass wool *n.* Fine-spun fibers of glass used especially for insulation and in air filters.

glass·work (glăs′wûrk′) *n.* **1.a.** The manufacture of glassware or glass. **b.** The cutting and fitting of glass panes; glaziery. **2.** See **glassware. 3. glassworks** *(used with a sing. verb).* An establishment where glass is manufactured. In this sense, also called *glasshouse.*

glass·wort (glăs′wûrt′, -wôrt′) *n.* Any of various plants of the genus *Salicornia,* growing in salt marshes and having fleshy stems and rudimentary, scalelike leaves. Also called *samphire.* [From its former use in making glass.]

glass·y (glăs′ē) *adj.* **-i·er, -i·est. 1.** Characteristic of or resembling glass. **2.** Lifeless; expressionless: *"the face changing to a demon's face with a fixed glassy grin"* (Katherine Anne Porter). —**glass′i·ly** *adv.* —**glass′i·ness** *n.*

Glas·ton·bur·y (glăs′tən-bĕr′ē). **1.** A municipal borough of southwest England south-southwest of Bristol. Glastonbury is the traditional site of King Arthur's Isle of Avalon. Population, 6,773. **2.** A city of central Connecticut southeast of Hartford. Settled in 1650, it is a manufacturing center. Population, 24,327.

Glas·we·gian (glăs-wē′jən, glăz-) *adj.* Of or relating to Glasgow, Scotland. —**Glaswegian** *n.* A native or resident of Glasgow, Scotland. [GLAS(GOW) + *Galwegian,* person from Galloway (Medieval Latin *Galwidia,* Galloway, a region of southern Scotland + -IAN).]

Glau·ber's salt (glou′bərz) *n.* A colorless hydrated sodium sulfate, $Na_2SO_4 \cdot 10H_2O$, used in paper and glass manufacturing and as a cathartic and diuretic. [After Johann Rudolf *Glauber* (1604–1668), German chemist.]

glau·co·ma (glou-kō′mə, glô-) *n.* Any of a group of eye diseases characterized by abnormally high intraocular fluid pressure, damaged optic disk, hardening of the eyeball, and partial to complete loss of vision. [Latin *glaucōma,* cataract, from Greek *glaukōma,* from *glaukos,* gray.] —**glau·co′ma·tous** (-kō′mə-təs) *adj.*

glau·co·nite (glô′kə-nīt′) *n.* A greenish clay mineral, a hydrous silicate of potassium, iron, aluminum, or magnesium, $(K,Na)(Al,Fe,Mg)_2(Al,Si)_4O_{10}(OH)_2$, found in greensand and used as a fertilizer and water softener. [Greek *glaukon,* neuter of *glaukos,* gray + -ITE¹.] —**glau′co·nit′ic** (-nĭt′ĭk) *adj.*

glau·cous (glô′kəs) *adj.* **1.** Of a pale grayish or bluish green.

2. *Botany.* Covered with a grayish, bluish, or whitish waxy coating or bloom that is easily rubbed off: *glaucous leaves.* [Latin *glaucus,* from Greek *glaukos.*] **—glau′cous·ness** *n.*

glaze (glāz) *n.* **1.** A thin, smooth, shiny coating. **2.** A thin, glassy coating of ice. **3.a.** A coating of colored, opaque, or transparent material applied to ceramics before firing. **b.** A coating, as of syrup, applied to food. **c.** A transparent coating applied to the surface of a painting to modify the color tones. **4.** A glassy film, as one over the eyes. **—glaze** *v.* **glazed, glaz·ing, glaz·es.** *—tr.* **1.** To fit, furnish, or secure with glass: *glaze a window.* **2.** To apply a glaze to: *glaze a doughnut; glaze pottery.* **3.** To coat or cover thinly with ice. **4.** To give a smooth, lustrous surface to. *—intr.* **1.** To be or become glazed or glassy: *His eyes glazed over from boredom.* **2.** To form a glaze. [From Middle English *glasen,* from *glas,* glass, from Old English *glæs.* See **ghel-²** in Appendix.] **—glaz′er** *n.*

gla·zier (glā′zhər) *n.* One that cuts and fits glass, as for doors and windows. [Middle English *glasier,* from *glas,* glass. See GLAZE.] **—gla′zier·y** (-zhə-rē) *n.*

glaz·ing (glā′zĭng) *n.* **1.a.** Glasswork. **b.** Glass set or made to be set in frames. **2.a.** A glaze. **b.** The act or process of applying a glaze.

Gla·zu·nov (glăz′ə-nôf′, -nôv′, glə-zo͞o-nôf′), **Aleksandr Konstantinovich.** 1865–1936. Russian composer who studied under Rimski-Korsakov, with whom he completed Borodin's opera *Prince Igor* (1890).

gld. *abbr.* Guilder.

gleam (glēm) *n.* **1.** A brief beam or flash of light: *saw gleams of daylight through the cracks.* **2.** A steady but subdued shining; a glow: *the gleam of burnished gold.* **3.** A brief or dim indication; a trace: *a gleam of intelligence.* **—gleam** *v.* **gleamed, gleam·ing, gleams.** *—intr.* **1.** To emit a gleam; flash or glow: *"It shone with gold and gleamed with ivory"* (Edith Hamilton). See Synonyms at **flash. 2.** To be manifested or indicated briefly or faintly. *—tr.* To cause to emit a flash of light. [Middle English *glem,* from Old English *glǣm.* See **ghel-²** in Appendix.] **—gleam′er** *n.*

glean (glēn) *v.* **gleaned, glean·ing, gleans.** *—intr.* To gather grain left behind by reapers. *—tr.* **1.** To gather (grain) left behind by reapers. **2.** To collect bit by bit: *"records from which historians glean their knowledge"* (Kemp Malone). See Synonyms at **reap.** [Middle English *glenen,* from Old French *glener,* from Late Latin *glennāre,* probably of Celtic origin.] **—glean′er** *n.*

glean·ings (glē′nĭngz) *pl.n.* Things that have been collected bit by bit: *the gleanings of patient scholars.*

gle·ba (glē′bə) *n., pl.* **-bae** (-bē′). The fleshy, spore-bearing inner mass of a puffball. [Latin *glēba,* clod.]

glebe (glēb) *n.* **1.** A plot of land belonging or yielding profit to an English parish church or an ecclesiastical office. **2.** *Archaic.* The soil or earth; land. [Latin *glēba,* clod.]

glede (glēd) *n.* Any of several birds of prey, especially a European kite *(Milvus milvus).* [Middle English, from Old English *glida.* See **ghel-²** in Appendix.]

glee (glē) *n.* **1.** Jubilant delight; joy. See Synonyms at **mirth. 2.** *Music.* An unaccompanied part song scored for three or more male voices that was popular in the 18th century. [Middle English *gle,* entertainment, from Old English *glēo.* See **ghel-²** in Appendix.]

glee club *n.* *Music.* A group of singers who perform usually short pieces of choral music.

gleed (glēd) *n.* *Archaic.* A glowing coal; an ember. [Middle English *glede,* from Old English *glēd.* See **ghel-²** in Appendix.]

glee·ful (glē′fəl) *adj.* Full of jubilant delight; joyful. **—glee′ful·ly** *adv.* **—glee′ful·ness** *n.*

glee·man (glē′mən) *n.* *Music.* A medieval itinerant singer; a minstrel. [Middle English *gleman,* from Old English *glēoman* : *glēo,* minstrelsy; see GLEE + *man,* man; see MAN.]

glee·some (glē′səm) *adj.* *Archaic.* Gleeful.

gleet (glēt) *n.* **1.** Inflammation of the urethra resulting from chronic gonorrhea and characterized by a mucopurulent discharge. **2.** The discharge that is characteristic of this inflammation. [Middle English *glet,* slime, from Old French *glette,* from Latin *glittus,* sticky.] **—gleet′y** *adj.*

gleg (glĕg) *adj.* *Scots.* Alert and quick to respond. [Middle English, clear-sighted, from Old Norse *glöggr.* See **ghel-²** in Appendix.]

glen (glĕn) *n.* A valley. [Middle English, from Scottish Gaelic *gleann,* from Old Irish *glenn.*]

Glen Bur·nie (glĕn bûr′nē). A community of north-central Maryland south of Baltimore. Population, 30,000.

Glen Cove. A city of southeast New York on northwest Long Island north of Mineola. Chiefly residential, it also has light industries. Population, 24,618.

Glen·dale (glĕn′dāl′). **1.** A city of south-central Arizona, an industrial suburb of Phoenix in an irrigated agricultural area. Population, 97,172. **2.** A city of southern California, an industrial suburb of Los Angeles. Population, 139,060.

Glendale Heights. A village of northeast Illinois, a suburb of Chicago. Population, 23,163.

Glen·do·ra (glĕn-dôr′ə, -dōr′ə). A city of southern California at the foot of the San Gabriel Mountains east-northeast of Los Angeles. It is mainly residential. Population, 38,500.

Glen·dow·er (glĕn′dou′ər, glĕn-dou′-), **Owen.** 1359?–1416? Welsh rebel who led a revolt against Henry IV (1400), controlled most of Wales, and summoned his own parliament (1405) before being effectively crushed by English forces (1409).

Glen El·lyn (ĕl′ĭn). A village of northeast Illinois, a residential suburb of Chicago. Population, 23,717.

Glen·gar·ry (glĕn-găr′ē) *n., pl.* **-ries.** A woolen cap that is creased lengthwise and often has short ribbons at the back. [After *Glengarry,* a valley of central Scotland.]

Glenn (glĕn), **John Herschel, Jr.** Born 1921. American astronaut and politician. On February 20, 1962, aboard *Friendship 7,* he became the first American to orbit the earth. He was elected U.S. senator from Ohio in 1974, 1980, and 1986.

Glen·side (glĕn′sīd′). A community of southeast Pennsylvania, a manufacturing suburb of Philadelphia. Population, 17,400.

Glen·view (glĕn′vyo͞o′). A village of northeast Illinois, a chiefly residential suburb of Chicago. Population, 32,060.

gley (glā) *n.* A sticky, bluish-gray subsurface layer of clay found in some waterlogged soils. [Russian dialectal *gleĭ,* clay.]

gli·a (glē′ə, glī′ə) *n.* See **neuroglia. —gli′al** *adj.*

gli·a·din (glī′ə-dĭn) *n.* Any of several simple proteins derived from rye or wheat gluten. [Italian *gliadina,* from Medieval Greek *glia,* glue. See ZOOGLEA.]

glib (glĭb) *adj.* **glib·ber, glib·best. 1.a.** Performed with a natural, offhand ease: *glib conversation.* **b.** Showing little thought, preparation, or concern: *a glib response to a complex question.* **2.** Marked by ease and fluency of speech or writing that often suggests or stems from insincerity, superficiality, or deceitfulness. [Possibly of Low German origin. See **ghel-²** in Appendix.] **—glib′ly** *adv.* **—glib′ness** *n.*

SYNONYMS: *glib, slick, smooth-tongued.* The central meaning shared by these adjectives is "being, marked by, or engaging in ready but often insincere or superficial discourse": *a glib denial; a slick commercial; a smooth-tongued hypocrite.* See also Synonyms at **talkative.**

glide (glīd) *v.* **glid·ed, glid·ing, glides.** *—intr.* **1.** To move in a smooth, effortless manner: *a submarine gliding through the water.* See Synonyms at **slide. 2.** To move silently and furtively. **3.** To occur or pass imperceptibly. **4.** To fly without propulsion. Used of an aircraft. **5.** *Music.* To blend one tone into the next; slur. **6.** *Linguistics.* To articulate a glide in speech. *—tr.* To cause to move or pass smoothly, silently, or imperceptibly. **—glide** *n.* **1.** The act of gliding. **2.** *Music.* A slur. **3.** *Linguistics.* **a.** The transitional sound produced by passing from the articulatory position of one speech sound to that of another. **b.** See **semivowel.** [Middle English *gliden,* from Old English *glīdan.* See **ghel-²** in Appendix.]

glide path *n.* The path of descent of an aircraft, delineated by a radio beam that directs the pilot in landing the craft.

glid·er (glī′dər) *n.* **1.** A light, engineless aircraft designed to glide after being towed aloft or launched from a catapult. **2.** A swinging couch suspended from a vertical frame. **3.** A device that aids gliding.

glim (glĭm) *n.* **1.** A source of light, as a candle. **2.** The illumination given off by such a source. [Perhaps short for GLIMMER.]

glim·mer (glĭm′ər) *n.* **1.** A dim or intermittent flicker or flash of light. **2.** A faint manifestation or indication; a trace: *a glimmer of understanding.* **—glimmer** *intr.v.* **-mered, -mer·ing, -mers. 1.** To emit a dim or intermittent light. See Synonyms at **flash. 2.** To appear faintly or indistinctly: *Hope still glimmered in our minds.* [Middle English *glimeren.* See **ghel-²** in Appendix.]

glimpse (glĭmps) *n.* **1.** A brief, incomplete view or look. **2.** *Archaic.* A brief flash of light. **—glimpse** *v.* **glimpsed, glimps·ing, glimps·es.** *—tr.* To obtain a brief, incomplete view of. *—intr.* To look briefly; glance: *glimpsed at the headlines.* [Middle English *glimsen.* See **ghel-²** in Appendix.] **—glimps′er** *n.*

Glin·ka (glĭng′kə, glyĕn′kə), **Mikhail Ivanovich.** 1804–1857. Russian composer whose works include *Russlan and Ludmilla* (1842).

glint (glĭnt) *n.* **1.** A momentary flash of light; a sparkle. **2.** A faint or fleeting indication; a trace. **—glint** *v.* **glint·ed, glint·ing, glints.** *—intr.* To gleam or flash briefly. See Synonyms at **flash.** *—tr.* To cause to gleam or flash. [Middle English *glent,* of Scandinavian origin. See **ghel-²** in Appendix.]

glint·y (glĭn′tē) *adj.* **-i·er, -i·est. 1.** Sparkling; glittery. **2.** Cheap and flashy.

gli·o·ma (glē-ō′mə, glī-) *n., pl.* **-mas** or **-ma·ta** (-mä′tə). A tumor originating in the neuroglia of the brain or spinal cord.

glis·sade (glĭ-säd′, -sād′) *n.* **1.** A gliding step in ballet. **2.** A controlled slide, in either a standing or sitting position, used in descending a steep icy or snowy incline. **—glissade** *intr.v.* **-sad·ed, -sad·ing, -sades.** To perform a glissade. [French, from *glisser,* to slide, from Old French, possibly alteration (influenced by *glacer,* to slide; see GLACIS) of *glier,* to glide, of Germanic origin. See **ghel-²** in Appendix.] **—glis·sad′er** *n.*

glis·san·do (glĭ-sän′dō) *n., pl.* **-di** (-dē) or **-dos.** *Music.* A rapid slide through a series of consecutive tones in a scalelike passage. [French *glissade;* see GLISSADE + *-ando,* as in ACCELERANDO or DIMINUENDO.]

glis·ten (glĭs′ən) *intr.v.* **-tened, -ten·ing, -tens.** To shine by reflection with a sparkling luster. See Synonyms at **flash. —glisten** *n.* A sparkling, lustrous shine. [Middle English *glisnen,* from Old English *glisnian.* See **ghel-²** in Appendix.]

glean
Detail from *Summer, The Gleaners* by Jean François Millet

John Glenn

ă pat	oi boy
ā pay	ou out
âr care	o͝o took
ä father	o͞o boot
ĕ pet	ŭ cut
ē be	ûr urge
ĭ pit	th thin
ī pie	*th* this
îr pier	hw which
ŏ pot	zh vision
ō toe	ə about, item
ô paw	♦ regionalism

Stress marks: ′ (primary); ′ (secondary), as in **dictionary** (dĭk′shə-nĕr′ē)

globe

glis·ter (glĭs′tər) *intr.v.* **-tered, -ter·ing, -ters.** To glisten. **—glister** *n.* Glitter; brilliance. [Middle English *glisteren,* probably from Middle Dutch *glinsteren* or Middle Low German *glisteren;* see **ghel-²** in Appendix.]

glitch (glĭch) *n.* **1.** A minor malfunction, mishap, or technical problem; a snag: *a computer glitch; a navigational glitch; a glitch in the negotiations.* **2.** A false or spurious electronic signal caused by a brief, unwanted surge of electric power. **3.** *Astronomy.* A sudden change in the period of rotation of a neutron star. [Probably from Yiddish *glitsh,* a slip, lapse, from *glitshn,* to slip, from Middle High German *glitschen,* alteration of *glīten,* to glide, from Old High German *glītan.* See **ghel-²** in Appendix.] **—glitch′y** *adj.*

WORD HISTORY: Although in retrospect *glitch* seems to be a word that people would always have found useful, it is first recorded in English in 1962 in the writing of John Glenn: "Another term we adopted to describe some of our problems was 'glitch.'" Glenn then gives the technical sense of the word the astronauts had adopted: "Literally, a glitch is a spike or change in voltage in an electrical current." In this very passage we see how the word moved from its narrow, technical electronic sense to a more general sense, even if the astronauts were not necessarily the first to extend the meaning of *glitch.* Since then the word has passed beyond technical use and now covers a wide variety of malfunctions and mishaps.

glit·ter (glĭt′ər) *n.* **1.** A sparkling or glistening light. **2.** Brilliant or showy, often superficial attractiveness. **3.** Small pieces of light-reflecting decorative material. **—glitter** *intr.v.* **-tered, -ter·ing, -ters. 1.a.** To sparkle brilliantly; glisten. See Synonyms at **flash. b.** To sparkle coldly or malevolently: *eyes that glittered at the prospect of revenge.* **2.** To be brilliantly, often deceptively, attractive. [Middle English *gliteren,* from Old Norse *glitra.* See **ghel-²** in Appendix.] **—glit′ter·ing·ly** *adv.* **—glit′ter·y** *adj.*

glit·te·ra·ti (glĭt′ə-rä′tē) *pl.n. Informal.* Highly fashionable celebrities; the smart set: *"private parties on Park Avenue and Central Park West, where the literati mingled with glitterati"* (Skylines). [GLITTER + (LITER)ATI.]

glitz (glĭts) *Informal. n.* Ostentatious showiness; flashiness: *"a garish barrage of show-biz glitz"* (Peter G. Davis). **—glitz** *tr.v.* **glitz·ed, glitz·ing, glitz·es.** To invest with an ostentatiously showy quality: *"have started to glitz up their shows with filmed backdrops"* (Bill Barol). [Back-formation from *glitzy,* flashy, showy, probably from German *glitzern,* to glitter, from Middle High German *glitzen,* to shine, from Old High German *glīzan.* See **ghel-²** in Appendix.] **—glitz′i·ness** *n.* **—glitz′y** *adj.*

Gli·wi·ce (glĭ-vēt′sə, glē-vē′tsĕ). A city of south-central Poland west-northwest of Katowice. Chartered in 1276, it was ceded by Austria to Prussia in 1742 and assigned to Poland by the Potsdam Conference in 1945. Population, 212,500.

gloam (glōm) *n. Archaic.* Twilight; gloaming. [Back-formation from GLOAMING.]

gloam·ing (glō′mĭng) *n.* Twilight; dusk. [Middle English *gloming,* from Old English *glōmung,* from *glōm,* dusk. See **ghel-²** in Appendix.]

gloat (glōt) *intr.v.* **gloat·ed, gloat·ing, gloats.** To feel or express great, often malicious, pleasure or self-satisfaction: *Don't gloat over your rival's misfortune.* **—gloat** *n.* **1.** The act of gloating. **2.** A feeling of great, often malicious, pleasure or self-satisfaction. [Perhaps of Scandinavian origin. See **ghel-²** in Appendix.] **—gloat′er** *n.*

glob (glŏb) *n.* **1.** A small drop; a globule. **2.** A soft, thick lump or mass: *a glob of mashed potatoes; globs of red mud.* [Middle English *globbe,* large mass, from Latin *globus,* globular mass.]

glob·al (glō′bəl) *adj.* **1.** Having the shape of a globe; spherical. **2.** Of, relating to, or involving the entire earth; worldwide: *global war; global monetary policies.* **3.** Comprehensive; total: *"a . . . global, generalized sense of loss"* (Maggie Scarf). **4.** *Computer Science.* Of or relating to an entire program, document, or file. **—glob′al·ly** *adv.*

glob·al·ism (glō′bə-lĭz′əm) *n.* A national geopolitical policy in which the entire world is regarded as the appropriate sphere for a state's influence. **—glob′al·ist** *n.*

glob·al·ize (glō′bə-līz′) *tr.v.* **-ized, -iz·ing, -iz·es.** To make global or worldwide in scope or application. **—glob′al·i·za′tion** *n.* **—glob′al·iz′er** *n.*

global village *n.* The entire world and its inhabitants: *"The global village has come to understand that no society that seeks respect can support or tolerate . . . savagery"* (Hugh Sidey).

globe (glōb) *n.* **1.** A body with the shape of a sphere, especially a representation of the earth in the form of a hollow ball. **2.a.** The earth. **b.** A planet. **3.** A spherical or bowllike container, especially a glass cover for a light bulb. **4.** A sphere emblematic of sovereignty; an orb. **—globe** *intr. & tr.v.* **globed, glob·ing, globes.** To assume the shape of or form into a sphere. [Middle English, from Old French, from Latin *globus.*]

globe amaranth *n.* A widely cultivated ornamental plant *(Gomphrena globosa)* native to the Old World tropics, having colorful scalelike perianths and numerous flowers grouped in heads.

globe artichoke *n.* See **artichoke** (sense 1).

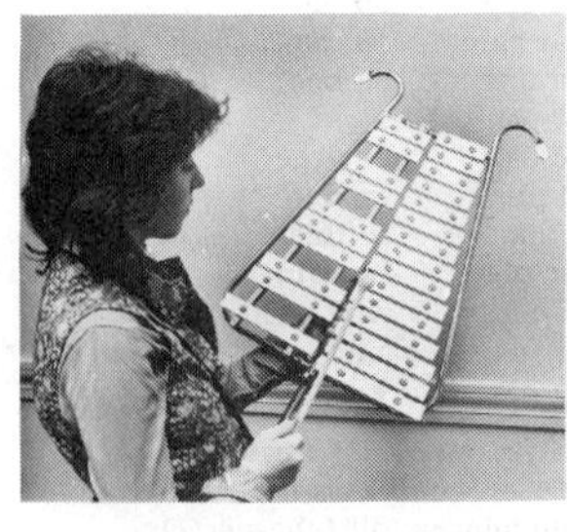
glockenspiel

globe·fish (glōb′fĭsh′) *n., pl.* **globefish** or **-fish·es.** Any of various fishes, especially the ocean sunfish or puffer, having or capable of assuming a globular shape.

globe·flow·er (glōb′flou′ər) *n.* Any of several plants of the genus *Trollius* having palmately lobed leaves, solitary, usually yellow flowers, and many follicles.

globe mallow *n.* Any of several herbs or shrubs of the genus *Sphaeralcea,* native to the arid regions of North and South America and having colorful cuplike corollas and numerous stamens fused into tubes.

globe thistle *n.* Any of several Eurasian plants of the genus *Echinops* having bipinnately dissected leaves with prickly margins and dense, bluish, globose flower heads.

globe·trot (glōb′trŏt′) *intr.v.* **-trot·ted, -trot·ting, -trots.** To travel often and widely, especially for sightseeing. [Back-formation from *globetrotter.*] **—globe′trot′er** *n.* **—globe′trot′ting** *n.*

glo·bin (glō′bĭn) *n.* The protein that is a constituent of hemoglobin. [Back-formation from HEMOGLOBIN.]

glo·boid (glō′boid′) *adj.* Having a globelike shape; spheroid. **—globoid** *n.* A globe-shaped object.

glo·bose (glō′bōs′) also **glo·bous** (-bəs) *adj.* Spherical; globular. **—glo′bose′ly** *adv.* **—glo′bose′ness, glo·bos′i·ty** (-bŏs′ĭ-tē) *n.*

glob·u·lar (glŏb′yə-lər) *adj.* **1.** Having the shape of a globe or globule; spherical. **2.** Consisting of globules. **3.** Worldwide; global. **—glob′u·lar·ly** *adv.* **—glob′u·lar·ness** *n.*

globular cluster *n. Astronomy.* A system of stars, generally smaller in size than a galaxy, that is more or less globular in conformation.

glob·ule (glŏb′yo͞ol) *n.* A small spherical mass, especially a small drop of liquid. [French, from Latin *globulus,* diminutive of *globus,* sphere.]

glob·u·lif·er·ous (glŏb′yə-lĭf′ər-əs) *adj.* Composed of or producing globules.

glob·u·lin (glŏb′yə-lĭn) *n.* Any of a class of proteins found extensively in blood plasma, milk, muscle, and plant seeds that are insoluble in pure water, soluble in dilute salt solution, and coagulable by heat. [GLOBUL(E) + –IN.]

glo·chid·i·um (glō-kĭd′ē-əm) *n., pl.* **-i·a** (-ē-ə). **1.** *Zoology.* The parasitic larva of certain freshwater mussels of the family Unionidae, having hooks for attaching to the gills or other external parts of a host fish. **2.** Also **glo·chid** (glō′kĭd). *Botany.* One of the minute barbed hairs or bristles on certain plants, such as the prickly pear. [New Latin *glōchidium,* from Greek *glōkhis, glōkhid-,* barb of an arrow.] **—glo·chid′i·ate** (-ĭt, -āt′) *adj.*

glock·en·spiel (glŏk′ən-spēl′, -shpēl′) *n. Music.* A percussion instrument with a series of metal bars tuned to the chromatic scale and played with two light hammers. [German : *Glocken,* pl. of *Glocke,* bell (from Middle High German, from Old High German *glocka,* of imitative origin) + *Spiel,* play; see SPIEL.]

glogg (glŏg) also **glögg** (glœg) *n.* A hot punch made of red wine, brandy, and sherry flavored with almonds, raisins, and orange peel. [Swedish *glögg,* alteration of *glödgat (vin),* mulled (wine), from past participle of *glödga,* to mull, from *glöd,* ember. See **ghel-²** in Appendix.]

glom (glŏm) *Slang. v.* **glommed, glom·ming, gloms.** *—tr.* **1.** To steal. **2.** To seize; grab. **3.** To look or stare at. *—intr.* To seize upon or latch onto something: *"The country has glommed onto the spectacle of a wizard showman turning the tables on his inquisitors"* (Mary McGrory). **—glom** *n.* A glimpse. [Probably from Scots *glam,* to snatch at, from Scottish Gaelic.]

glom·er·a (glŏm′ər-ə) *n.* Plural of **glomus.**

glom·er·ate (glŏm′ər-ĭt) *adj.* Formed into a compact, rounded mass; tightly clustered; conglomerate. [Latin *glomerātus,* past participle of *glomerāre,* to wind into a ball, from *glomus, glomer-,* ball.]

glom·er·ule (glŏm′ə-ro͞ol′, glŏm′yə-) *n.* **1.** *Botany.* A compact, cymose cluster of flowers. **2.** *Anatomy.* A glomerulus. [New Latin *glomerulus.* See GLOMERULUS.] **—glo·mer′u·late** (glō-mĕr′yə-lĭt) *adj.*

glo·mer·u·lus (glō-mĕr′yə-ləs) *n., pl.* **-li** (-lī′). *Anatomy.* **1.** A small cluster or mass of blood vessels or nerve fibers. **2.** A tuft of capillaries situated within a Bowman's capsule at the end of a renal tubule in the vertebrate kidney that filters waste products from the blood and thus initiates urine formation. [New Latin, diminutive of Latin *glomus, glomer-,* ball.]

Glom·ma (glô′mə, -mä). See **Glåma.**

glo·mus (glō′məs) *n., pl.* **glom·er·a** (glŏm′ər-ə). A small body surrounded by many nerve fibers, consisting of an anastomosis between fine arterioles and veins. [Latin.]

gloom (glo͞om) *n.* **1.a.** Partial or total darkness; dimness: *switched on a table lamp to banish the gloom of a winter afternoon.* **b.** A partially or totally dark place, area, or location. **2.a.** An atmosphere of melancholy or depression: *Gloom pervaded the office.* **b.** A state of melancholy or depression; despondency. **—gloom** *v.* **gloomed, gloom·ing, glooms.** *—intr.* **1.** To be or become dark, shaded, or obscure. **2.** To feel, appear, or act despondent, sad, or mournful. *—tr.* **1.** To make dark, shaded, or obscure. **2.** *Archaic.* To make despondent; sadden. [Probably from Middle English *gloumen,* to become dark, look glum.]

gloom·y (glo͞o′mē) *adj.* **-i·er, -i·est. 1.** Partially or totally dark, especially dismal and dreary: *a damp, gloomy day.* **2.** Showing or filled with gloom: *gloomy faces.* **3.a.** Causing or producing gloom; depressing: *gloomy news.* **b.** Marked by hopelessness; very pessimistic: *gloomy predictions.* See Synonyms at **glum.** —**gloom′i·ly** *adv.* —**gloom′i·ness** *n.*

glop (glŏp) *n. Slang.* **1.** A soft, soggy mixture, as of food: *cafeterias serving nondescript glop.* **2.** Something, such as a piece of writing, that is judged to be worthless. [Probably imitative of the sound of food being mixed.] —**glop** *v.* —**glop′py** *adj.*

Glo·ri·a (glôr′ē-ə, glōr′-) *n.* **1.a.** A Latin doxology beginning with the words *Gloria Patri.* **b.** A Latin doxology forming part of the Ordinary of the Mass and beginning with the words *Gloria in excelsis Deo.* **c.** A musical setting for either of these doxologies. **2. gloria.** A halo or nimbus. [Middle English, from Late Latin *Glōria,* from Latin *glōria,* glory.]

glo·ri·fy (glôr′ə-fī′, glōr′-) *tr.v.* **-fied, -fy·ing, -fies. 1.** To give glory, honor, or high praise to; exalt. **2.** To cause to be or seem more glorious or excellent than is actually the case: *Your descriptions have glorified an average house into a mansion.* **3.** To give glory to, especially through worship. [Middle English *glorifien,* from Old French *glorefier,* from Latin *glōrificāre* : *glōria,* glory + *-ficāre,* -fy.] —**glo′ri·fi·ca′tion** (-fĭ-kā′shən) *n.* —**glo′ri·fi′er** *n.*

glo·ri·ole (glôr′ē-ōl′, glōr′-) *n.* See **glory** (sense 8). [French, from Latin *glōriola,* diminutive of *glōria,* glory.]

glo·ri·ous (glôr′ē-əs, glōr′-) *adj.* **1.** Having or deserving glory; famous. **2.** Conferring or advancing glory: *a glorious achievement.* **3.** Marked by great beauty and splendor; magnificent: *a glorious sunset.* **4.** Delightful; wonderful: *had a glorious visit with old friends.* —**glo′ri·ous·ly** *adv.* —**glo′ri·ous·ness** *n.*

glo·ry (glôr′ē, glōr′ē) *n., pl.* **-ries. 1.** Great honor, praise, or distinction accorded by common consent; renown. **2.** Something conferring honor or renown. **3.** A highly praiseworthy asset: *Your hair is your crowning glory.* **4.** Adoration, praise, and thanksgiving offered in worship. **5.** Majestic beauty and splendor; resplendence: *The sun set in a blaze of glory.* **6.** The splendor and bliss of heaven; perfect happiness. **7.** A height of achievement, enjoyment, or prosperity: *Paris in its greatest glory.* **8.** A halo, nimbus, or aureole. In this sense, also called *gloriole.* —**glory** *intr.v.* **-ried, -ry·ing, -ries.** To rejoice triumphantly; exult: *a sports team that gloried in its hard-won victory.* [Middle English *glorie,* from Old French, from Latin *glōria.*]

glo·ry-of-the-snow (glôr′ē-əv-*th*ə-snō′, glōr′-) *n.* A small bulbous plant *(Chionodoxa luciliae)* native to southwest Asia, Crete, and Cyprus, cultivated for its early-blooming blue flowers.

gloss[1] (glôs, glŏs) *n.* **1.** A surface shininess or luster. **2.** A superficially or deceptively attractive appearance. —**gloss** *v.* **glossed, gloss·ing, gloss·es.** —*tr.* **1.** To give a bright sheen or luster to. **2.** To make attractive or acceptable by deception or superficial treatment: *a résumé that glossed over the applicant's lack of experience.* See Synonyms at **palliate.** —*intr.* To become shiny or lustrous. [Perhaps of Scandinavian origin; akin to Icelandic *glossi,* a spark. See **ghel-[2]** in Appendix.]

gloss[2] (glôs, glŏs) *n. Abbr.* **gl. 1.a.** A brief explanatory note or translation of a difficult or technical expression usually inserted in the margin or between lines of a text or manuscript. **b.** A collection of such notes; a glossary. **2.** An extensive commentary, often accompanying a text or publication. **3.** A purposefully misleading interpretation or explanation. —**gloss** *tr.v.* **glossed, gloss·ing, gloss·es. 1.** To provide (an expression or a text) with a gloss or glosses. **2.** To give a false interpretation to. [Middle English *glose,* from Old French, from Medieval Latin *glōsa,* from Late Latin *glōssa,* foreign word requiring explanation, from Greek, tongue, language.] —**gloss′er** *n.*

gloss. *abbr.* Glossary.

glos·sa (glô′sə, glŏs′ə) *n., pl.* **glos·sae** (glô′sē, glŏs′ē) or **glos·sas. 1.** *Anatomy.* The tongue. **2.** *Zoology.* A tonguelike structure in the labium of an insect. [Greek *glōssa,* tongue.]

glos·sal (glô′səl, glŏs′əl) *adj.* Of or relating to the tongue.

glos·sa·ry (glô′sə-rē, glŏs′ə-) *n., pl.* **-ries.** *Abbr.* **gloss.** A list of difficult or specialized words with their definitions, often placed at the back of a book. [Middle English *glosarie,* from Latin *glōssārium,* from *glōssa,* foreign word. See GLOSS[2].] —**glos·sar′i·al** (glô-sâr′ē-əl, glŏ-) *adj.* —**glos′sa·rist** *n.*

glos·si·tis (glô-sī′tĭs, glŏ-) *n.* Inflammation of the tongue. —**glos·sit′ic** (-sĭt′ĭk) *adj.*

glos·sog·ra·phy (glô-sŏg′rə-fē, glŏ-) *n.* The compilation of glosses or glossaries. —**glos·sog′ra·pher** *n.*

glos·so·la·li·a (glô′sə-lā′lē-ə, glŏs′ə-) *n.* **1.** Fabricated and nonmeaningful speech, especially such speech associated with a trance state or certain schizophrenic syndromes. **2.** See **gift of tongues.** [New Latin : Greek *glōssa,* tongue + Greek *lalein,* to babble.]

glos·so·pha·ryn·ge·al nerve (glô′sō-fə-rĭn′jē-əl, -jəl, -făr′ən-jē′əl, glŏs′ō-) *n.* Either of the ninth pair of cranial nerves that contain both sensory and motor fibers and supply the tongue, soft palate, pharynx, and parotid gland.

gloss·y (glô′sē, glŏs′ē) *adj.* **-i·er, -i·est. 1.** Having a smooth, shiny, lustrous surface: *glossy satin.* See Synonyms at **sleek. 2.** Superficially and often speciously attractive; showy: *glossy trendsetters.* —**glossy** *n., pl.* **-ies. 1.** A photographic print on smooth, shiny paper. **2.** *Chiefly British.* A popular magazine printed on smooth-coated stock. —**gloss′i·ly** *adv.* —**gloss′i·ness** *n.*

glot·tal (glŏt′l) *adj. Linguistics.* Relating to or articulated in the glottis.

glottal stop *n. Linguistics.* A speech sound produced by a momentary complete closure of the glottis, followed by an explosive release.

glot·tis (glŏt′ĭs) *n., pl.* **-tis·es** or **-ti·des** (-tĭ-dēz′). **1.** The opening between the vocal cords at the upper part of the larynx. **2.** The vocal apparatus of the larynx. [Greek *glōttis,* from *glōtta, glōssa,* tongue.]

Glouces·ter (glŏs′tər, glô′stər). **1.** A borough of southwest-central England on the Severn River west-northwest of London. On the site of the Roman city Glevum, it was the Saxon capital of Mercia. Population, 91,600. **2.** A city of northeast Massachusetts on Cape Ann and the Atlantic Ocean northeast of Boston. Its sheltered harbor has been used by fishing fleets for three centuries. Population, 27,768.

glove (glŭv) *n.* **1.a.** A fitted covering for the hand with a separate sheath for each finger and the thumb. **b.** A gauntlet. **2.a.** *Baseball.* An oversized padded leather covering for the hand, used in catching balls, especially one with more finger sheaths than the catcher's or first baseman's mitt. **b.** *Sports.* A boxing glove. —**glove** *v.* **gloved, glov·ing, gloves.** —*tr.* **1.** To furnish with gloves. **2.** To cover with or as if with a glove. —*intr.* To don gloves, as before performing an operation on a patient. [Middle English, from Old English *glōf.*]

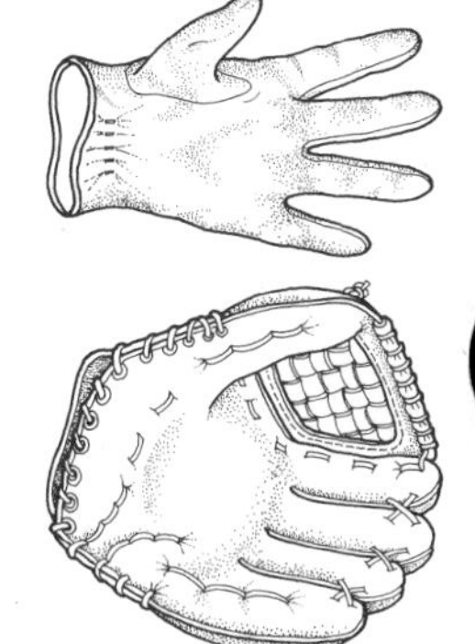

glove
Top: Winter glove
Bottom: Baseball outfielder's glove

glove compartment *n.* A small storage container in the dashboard of an automobile. Also called *glove box.*

Glov·ers·ville (glŭv′ərz-vĭl′). A city of east-central New York northwest of Schenectady. Its glove-making industry dates to the late 18th century. Population, 17,836.

glow (glō) *intr.v.* **glowed, glow·ing, glows. 1.** To shine brightly and steadily, especially without a flame: *Embers glowed in the furnace.* **2.a.** To have a bright, warm, usually reddish color: *The children's cheeks glowed from the cold.* **b.** To flush; blush. **3.** To be exuberant or radiant: *parents glowing with pride.* —**glow** *n.* **1.** A light produced by a body heated to luminosity; incandescence. See Synonyms at **blaze[1]. 2.** Brilliance or warmth of color, especially redness: *"the evening glow of the city streets when the sun has gone behind the tallest houses"* (Seán O'Faoláin). **3.** A sensation of physical warmth. **4.** A warm feeling, as of pleasure or well-being. [Middle English *glouen,* from Old English *glōwan.* See **ghel-[2]** in Appendix.]

glow·er (glou′ər) *intr.v.* **-ered, -er·ing, -ers.** To look or stare angrily or sullenly. See Synonyms at **frown.** —**glower** *n.* An angry or sullen look or stare. [Middle English *gloren,* probably of Scandinavian origin. See **ghel-[2]** in Appendix.] —**glow′er·ing·ly** *adv.*

glow plug *n.* A small electric heating element in an internal-combustion engine that facilitates starting by preheating the air in a cylinder and is used especially in diesel engines.

glow·worm (glō′wûrm′) *n.* Any of various luminous female beetles or beetle larvae of the families Phengodidae and Lampyridae, especially the larva or wingless grublike female of a firefly.

glox·in·i·a (glŏk-sĭn′ē-ə) *n.* Any of several tropical South American plants of the genus *Sinningia,* especially *S. speciosa,* cultivated as a houseplant for its showy, variously colored flowers. [New Latin, after Benjamin Peter *Gloxin,* 18th-century German botanist.]

gloze (glōz) *v.* **glozed, gloz·ing, gloz·es.** —*tr.* To minimize or underplay; gloss: *glozed over the embarrassing part.* See Synonyms at **palliate.** —*intr. Archaic.* To use flattery or cajolery. [Middle English *glosen,* to interpret, explain away, from Old French *gloser,* from *glose,* gloss. See GLOSS[2].]

glowworm

gluc– *pref.* Variant of **gluco–.**

glu·ca·gon (glo͞o′kə-gŏn′) *n.* A hormone produced by the pancreas that stimulates an increase in blood sugar levels, thus opposing the action of insulin. [Probably GLUC(O)– + Greek *agōn,* present participle of *agein,* to lead, drive; see **ag-** in Appendix.]

Gluck (glo͝ok), **Christoph Willibald.** 1714–1787. German operatic composer noted for his emphasis on dramatic impact and musical simplicity. His works include *Orfeo ed Euridice* (1762).

gluco– or **gluc–** *pref.* Glucose: *glucagon.* [From GLUCOSE.]

glu·co·cor·ti·coid (glo͞o′kō-kôr′tĭ-koid′) *n.* Any of a group of steroid hormones, such as cortisone, that are produced by the adrenal cortex, are involved in carbohydrate, protein, and fat metabolism, and have anti-inflammatory properties.

glu·co·ne·o·gen·e·sis (glo͞o′kə-nē′ə-jĕn′ĭ-sĭs) *n.* The formation of glucose, especially by the liver, from noncarbohydrate sources, such as amino acids and the glycerol portion of fats. —**glu′co·ne′o·ge·net′ic** (-ō-jə-nĕt′ĭk) *adj.*

glu·cose (glo͞o′kōs′) *n.* **1.** A monosaccharide sugar, $C_6H_{12}O_6$, occurring widely in most plant and animal tissue. It is the principal circulating sugar in the blood and the major energy source of the body. **2.** A colorless to yellowish syrupy mixture of dextrose, maltose, and dextrins containing about 20 percent water, used in confectionery, alcoholic fermentation, tanning, and treating tobacco. In this sense, also called *starch syrup.* [French, from Greek *gleukos,* sweet wine.]

glu·co·side (glo͞o′kə-sīd′) *n.* A glycoside, the sugar component of which is glucose. —**glu′co·sid′ic** (-sĭd′ĭk) *adj.* —**glu′co·sid′i·cal·ly** *adv.*

glue (glo͞o) *n.* **1.a.** A strong liquid adhesive obtained by boiling

ă pat	oi boy
ā pay	ou out
âr care	o͝o took
ä father	o͞o boot
ĕ pet	ŭ cut
ē be	ûr urge
ĭ pit	th thin
ī pie	*th* this
îr pier	hw which
ŏ pot	zh vision
ō toe	ə about, item
ô paw	♦ regionalism

Stress marks: ′ (primary); ′ (secondary), as in **dictionary** (dĭk′shə-nĕr′ē)

collagenous animal parts such as bones, hides, and hooves into hard gelatin and then adding water. **b.** Any of various similar adhesives, such as paste, mucilage, or epoxy. **2.** An adhesive force or factor: *Idealism was the glue that held our group together.* **—glue** *tr.v.* **glued, glu•ing, glues. 1.** To stick or fasten with or as if with glue. **2.** To fasten on something attentively: *Our eyes were glued to the stage.* [Middle English *glu,* from Old French, from Late Latin *glūs, glūt-,* from Latin *glūten.*] **—glu′ey** *adj.* **—glu′i•ness** *n.*

glum (glŭm) *adj.* **glum•mer, glum•mest. 1.** Moody and melancholy; dejected. **2.** Gloomy; dismal. **—glum** *n.* **1.** The quality or state of being moody, melancholy, and gloomy or an instance of it: *"He was a charming mixture of glum and glee"* (Lillian Hellman). **2. glums.** *Chiefly British.* The blues. Often used with *the: "Most other publications have got the glums"* (Tina Brown). [Probably akin to Middle English *gloumen,* to become dark. See GLOOM.] **—glum′ly** *adv.* **—glum′ness** *n.*

SYNONYMS: *glum, gloomy, morose, dour, saturnine.* These adjectives mean having a broodingly cheerless aspect or disposition. *Glum* implies silent dejection: *Why so glum? The votes haven't been counted yet. Gloomy* suggests somber melancholy: *She takes a gloomy view of the future. Morose* implies sourness of temper and a tendency to be uncommunicative: *He stared down at his dinner plate in a morose and unsociable manner. Dour* especially suggests grimness or humorlessness and sometimes an obstinate nature: *"To a Western eye,* [they] *seem poorly dressed, ill-groomed, dour and preoccupied"* (Peter Lewis). *Saturnine* suggests gloominess or melancholy of temperament and often a tendency to be bitter or sardonic: *the saturnine faces of the judges.*

glu•ma•ceous (glo͞o-mā′shəs) *adj.* Having or resembling glumes.

glume (glo͞om) *n.* One of the two chaffy basal bracts of a grass spikelet. [Latin *glūma,* husk. See **gleubh-** in Appendix.]

glu•on (glo͞o′ŏn) *n.* A hypothetical massless, neutral elementary particle believed to mediate the strong interaction that binds quarks together. [GLU(E) + –ON[1].]

glut (glŭt) *v.* **glut•ted, glut•ting, gluts.** *—tr.* **1.** To fill beyond capacity, especially with food; satiate. See Synonyms at **satiate. 2.** To flood (a market) with an excess of goods so that supply exceeds demand. *—intr.* To eat or indulge in something excessively. **—glut** *n.* An oversupply. [Middle English *glotten,* probably from Old French *glotoiier,* to eat greedily, from Latin *gluttīre.*]

glu•tam•ic acid (glo͞o-tăm′ĭk) *n.* A nonessential amino acid, $C_5H_9NO_4$, occurring widely in plant and animal tissue and having a salt, sodium glutamate, that is used as a flavor-intensifying seasoning. [GLUT(EN) + AM(IDE) + –IC.]

glu•ta•mine (glo͞o′tə-mēn′) *n.* A nonessential amino acid, $C_5H_{10}N_2O_3$, occurring widely in plant and animal tissue and produced commercially for use in medicine and biochemical research. [GLUT(EN) + AMINE.]

glu•tar•al•de•hyde (glo͞o′tə-răl′də-hīd′) *n.* A water-soluble oily liquid, $OHC(CH_2)_3CHO$, containing two aldehyde groups, used in tanning leather and as a fixative for biological tissues. [Blend of *glutaric acid* (from GLUTEN) and ALDEHYDE.]

glu•te•i (glo͞o′tē-ī′, glo͞o-tē′ī′) *n.* Plural of **gluteus.**

glutei max•i•mi (măk′sə-mī′) *n.* Plural of **gluteus maximus.**

glu•ten (glo͞ot′n) *n.* A mixture of plant proteins occurring in cereal grains, chiefly corn and wheat, used as an adhesive and as a flour substitute. [French, from Latin *glūten,* glue.] **—glu′ten•ous** *adj.*

glu•teth•i•mide (glo͞o-tĕth′ə-mīd′) *n.* A nonbarbiturate sedative and hypnotic drug, $C_{13}H_{15}NO_2$. [GLUTE(N) + THI(O)– + (A)MIDE.]

glyph
Top: Road construction ahead
Bottom: Pedestrian crossing ahead

glu•te•us (glo͞o′tē-əs, glo͞o-tē′-) *n., pl.* **glu•te•i** (glo͞o′tē-ī′, glo͞o-tē′ī′). Any of the three large muscles of each buttock, especially the gluteus maximus, that extend, abduct, and rotate the thigh. [New Latin, from Greek *gloutos,* buttock.] **—glu′te•al** *adj.*

gluteus max•i•mus (măk′sə-məs) *n., pl.* **glutei max•i•mi** (măk′sə-mī′). The largest and outermost gluteus. [New Latin : *gluteus,* gluteus + *maximus,* largest.]

glu•ti•nous (glo͞ot′n-əs) *adj.* Of the nature of or resembling glue; sticky. [Middle English, from Latin *glūtinōsus,* from *glūten, glūtin-,* glue.] **—glu′ti•nous•ly** *adv.* **—glu′ti•nous•ness, glu′ti•nos′i•ty** (-ŏs′ĭ-tē) *n.*

glut•ton (glŭt′n) *n.* **1.** A person who eats or consumes immoderate amounts of food and drink. **2.** A person with an inordinate capacity to receive or withstand something: *a glutton for punishment.* **3.** See **wolverine** (sense 1). [Middle English *glotoun,* from Old French *gloton,* from Latin *gluttō, gluttōn-.*]

glut•ton•ous (glŭt′n-əs) *adj.* **1.** Given to or marked by gluttony. **2.** Indulging in something, such as an activity, to excess; voracious. See Synonyms at **voracious. —glut′ton•ous•ly** *adv.*

glut•ton•y (glŭt′n-ē) *n., pl.* **-ies.** Excess in eating or drinking.

glyc– *pref.* Variant of **glyco–.**

glyc•er•al•de•hyde (glĭs′ə-răl′də-hīd′) *n.* A sweet, colorless, crystalline solid, $C_3H_6O_3$, that is an intermediate compound in carbohydrate metabolism. [GLYCER(IN) + ALDEHYDE.]

gly•cer•ic acid (glĭ-sĕr′ĭk) *n.* A colorless, syrupy acid, $C_3H_6O_4$, obtained from oxidation of glycerol. [From GLYCERIN.]

glyc•er•ide (glĭs′ə-rīd′) *n.* A natural or synthetic ester of glycerol and fatty acids. [GLYCER(IN) + –IDE.]

glyc•er•in also **glyc•er•ine** (glĭs′ər-ĭn) *n.* Glycerol or a preparation of glycerol. [French *glycérine,* from Greek *glukeros,* sweet.]

glyc•er•ol (glĭs′ə-rôl′, -rōl′, -rŏl′) *n.* A syrupy, sweet, colorless or yellowish liquid, $C_3H_8O_3$, obtained from fats and oils as a byproduct of saponification and used as a solvent, an antifreeze, a plasticizer, and a sweetener and in the manufacture of dynamite, cosmetics, liquid soaps, inks, and lubricants. [GLYCER(IN) + –OL[1].]

glyc•er•yl (glĭs′ər-əl) *n.* A trivalent radical, CH_2CHCH_2, obtained from glycerol by the removal of hydroxyl groups. [GLYCER(IN) + –YL.]

gly•cin (glī′sĭn) also **gly•cine** (-sēn′, -sĭn) *n.* A poisonous crystalline compound, $C_8H_9NO_3$, used as a photographic developer. [Probably from GLYCINE.]

gly•cine (glī′sēn′, -sĭn) *n.* **1.** A sweet-tasting crystalline nonessential amino acid, $C_2H_5NO_2$, that is the principal amino acid occurring in sugar cane. It is derived from the alkaline hydrolysis of gelatin and used in biochemical research and medicine. **2.** Variant of **glycin.** [GLYC(O)– + –INE[2].]

glyco– or **glyc–** *pref.* **1.** Sugar: *glycoprotein.* **2.** Glycogen: *glycogenesis.* [From Greek *glukus,* sweet.]

gly•co•gen (glī′kə-jən) *n.* A polysaccharide, $(C_6H_{10}O_5)_n$, that is the main form of carbohydrate storage in animals and occurs primarily in the liver and muscle tissue. It is readily converted to glucose as needed by the body to satisfy its energy needs. Also called *animal starch.* **—gly′co•gen′ic** (-jĕn′ĭk) *adj.*

gly•co•gen•e•sis (glī′kə-jĕn′ĭ-sĭs) *n.* The formation or synthesis of glycogen. [GLYCO– + –GENESIS.] **—gly′co•ge•net′ic** (-jə-nĕt′ĭk) *adj.*

gly•co•gen•ol•y•sis (glī′kə-jə-nŏl′ĭ-sĭs) *n., pl.* **-ses** (-sēz′). The biomedical breakdown of glycogen to glucose. **—gly′co•gen′o•lyt′ic** (-jĕn′ə-lĭt′ĭk) *adj.*

gly•col (glī′kôl′, -kōl′, -kŏl′) *n.* **1.** Ethylene glycol. **2.** Any of various alcohols containing two hydroxyl groups.

gly•col•ic acid (glī-kŏl′ĭk) *n.* A colorless crystalline compound, $C_2H_4O_3$, found in sugar beets, cane sugar, and unripe grapes that is used in leather dyeing and tanning and in pharmaceuticals, pesticides, adhesives, and plasticizers.

gly•co•lip•id (glī′kə-lĭp′ĭd) *n.* A lipid that contains carbohydrate groups.

gly•col•y•sis (glī-kŏl′ə-sĭs) *n.* The ATP-generating metabolic process that occurs in nearly all living cells by which carbohydrates and sugars, typically glucose, are converted in a series of steps to pyruvic acid. **—gly′co•lyt′ic** *adj.*

gly•co•pro•tein (glī′kō-prō′tēn′, -tē-ĭn) *n.* Any of a group of conjugated proteins that contain a carbohydrate as the nonprotein component.

gly•cos•a•mi•no•gly•can (glī′kōs-ə-mē′nō-glī′kăn) *n.* Any of a group of polysaccharides with high molecular weight that contain amino sugars and often form complexes with proteins. Also called *mucopolysaccharide.* [GLYC(O)– + (HEX)OS(E) + AMIN(E) + *glycan,* polysaccharide (GLYC(O)– + –AN[2]).]

gly•co•side (glī′kə-sīd′) *n.* Any of a group of organic compounds, occurring abundantly in plants, that yield a sugar and one or more nonsugar substances on hydrolysis. [*Glycose* (variant of GLUCOSE) + –IDE.] **—gly′co•sid′ic** (-sĭd′ĭk) *adj.*

gly•co•su•ri•a (glī′kə-so͝or′ē-ə, -sho͝or′-) *n.* Excess sugar in the urine, often associated with diabetes mellitus. [*Glycose* (variant of GLUCOSE) + –URIA.] **—gly′co•su′ric** *adj.*

Glyn (glĭn), **Elinor (Sutherland).** 1864–1943. British writer noted for her sensational romance novels, including *It* (1927).

glyph (glĭf) *n.* **1.** *Architecture.* A vertical groove, especially in a Doric column or frieze. **2.** A symbolic figure that is usually engraved or incised. **3.** A symbol, such as a stylized human figure on a public sign, that imparts information nonverbally. [Greek *gluphē,* carving, from *gluphein,* to carve. See **gleubh-** in Appendix.] **—glyph′ic** *adj.*

glyp•tic (glĭp′tĭk) *adj.* Of or relating to engraving or carving, especially on precious stones. [Greek *gluptikos,* from *gluptos,* carved, from *gluphein,* to carve. See **gleubh-** in Appendix.]

glyp•tics (glĭp′tĭks) *n.* (*used with a sing. verb*). The art of engraving or carving, especially on precious stones; glyptography.

glyp•to•graph (glĭp′tə-grăf′) *n.* An engraved inscription on a precious stone. [Greek *gluptos,* carved; see GLYPTIC + –GRAPH.]

glyp•tog•ra•phy (glĭp-tŏg′rə-fē) *n.* The art or process of carving or engraving on precious stones. **—glyp•tog′ra•pher** *n.* **—glyp′to•graph′ic** (-tə-grăf′ĭk), **glyp′to•graph′i•cal** *adj.*

GM or **G.M.** *abbr.* **1.** General manager. **2.** *Games.* Grand master.

gm. *abbr.* Gram.

G-man (jē′măn′) *n.* An agent of the Federal Bureau of Investigation. [G(OVERNMENT) + MAN.]

GMAT *abbr.* **1.** Graduate Management Admissions Test. **2.** Or **G.m.a.t.** Greenwich mean astronomical time.

gmel•i•na (gmĕl′ĭ-nə, gmā′lĭ-) *n.* A deciduous tree *(Gmelina arborea)* native to southeast Asia, having large opposite leaves, brownish-yellow flowers grouped in cymose panicles, and yellow drupes. [New Latin, genus name, after Johann Georg *Gmelin* (1709–1755), German botanist.]

GMP (jē′ĕm-pē′) *n.* A nucleotide composed of guanine, ribose, and one phosphate group that is formed during protein synthesis. Also called *guanylic acid.* [G(UANOSINE) M(ONO)P(HOSPHATE).]

GMT or **G.m.t.** *abbr.* Greenwich mean time.

GMW *abbr.* Gram molecular weight.

Gn *abbr. Bible.* Genesis.

gnar also **gnarr** (när) *intr.v.* **gnarred, gnar·ring, gnars.** To snarl; growl. [Imitative.]

gnarl[1] (närl) *intr.v.* **gnarled, gnarl·ing, gnarls.** To snarl; growl. [Frequentative of GNAR.]

gnarl[2] (närl) *n.* A protruding knot on a tree. **—gnarl** *tr.v.* **gnarled, gnarl·ing, gnarls.** To make knotted; twist. [Back-formation from GNARLED.]

gnarled (närld) *adj.* **1.** Having gnarls; knotty or misshapen: *gnarled branches.* **2.** Morose or peevish; crabbed. **3.** Rugged and roughened, as from old age or work: *the gnarled hands of a carpenter.* [Probably variant of *knarled,* from *knarl,* tangle, knot, alteration of Middle English *knarre,* knot in wood. See KNAR.]

gnarr (när) *v.* Variant of **gnar.**

gnash (năsh) *tr.v.* **gnashed, gnash·ing, gnash·es. 1.** To grind or strike (the teeth, for example) together. **2.** To bite (something) by grinding the teeth. [Alteration of Middle English *gnasten, gnaisten,* possibly of Scandinavian origin; akin to Old Norse *gnastan,* a gnashing.] **—gnash** *n.*

gnat (năt) *n.* Any of various small, biting, two-winged flies, such as a punkie or black fly. [Middle English, from Old English *gnæt.*]

gnat·catch·er (năt′kăch′ər, -kĕch′-) *n.* Any of several tiny North American birds of the genus *Polioptila,* having bluish-gray and white plumage, a long tail, and a small, slender bill.

gna·thal (nā′thəl, năth′əl) *adj.* Gnathic. [Greek *gnathos,* jaw; see **genu-**[2] in Appendix + –AL[1].]

gnath·ic (năth′ĭk) *adj.* Of or relating to the jaw. [Greek *gnathos,* jaw; see **genu-**[2] in Appendix + –IC.]

gna·thite (nā′thīt′, năth′īt′) *n.* A jawlike appendage of an arthropod. [Greek *gnathos,* jaw; see GNATHIC + –ITE[1].]

-gnathous *suff.* Having a specified kind of jaw: *metagnathous.* [New Latin *-gnathus,* from Greek *-gnathos,* from *gnathos,* jaw. See **genu-**[2] in Appendix.]

gnaw (nô) *v.* **gnawed, gnaw·ing, gnaws.** *—tr.* **1.a.** To bite, chew on, or erode with the teeth. **b.** To produce by gnawing: *gnaw a hole.* See Synonyms at **bite. c.** To erode or diminish gradually as if by gnawing: *waves gnawing the rocky shore.* **2.** To afflict or worry persistently: *fear that constantly gnawed me.* *—intr.* **1.** To bite or chew persistently: *The dog gnawed at the bone.* **2.** To cause erosion or gradual diminishment. **3.** To cause persistent worry or pain: *Hunger gnawed at the prisoners.* [Middle English *gnauen,* from Old English *gnagan.*] **—gnaw′er** *n.*

gnd. *abbr.* Ground (electricity).

gneiss (nīs) *n.* A banded or foliated metamorphic rock, usually of the same composition as granite. [German *Gneis,* probably alteration of Middle High German *gneist,* spark (from its appearance), from Old High German *gneisto.*] **—gneiss′ic** (nī′sĭk), **gneiss′oid′** (nī′soid′), **gneiss′ose′** (nī′sōs′) *adj.*

gnoc·chi (nyô′kē) *pl.n.* Dumplings made of flour, semolina, or potatoes, boiled or baked and served with grated cheese or a sauce. [Italian, pl. of *gnocco,* probably alteration of *nocchio,* knot in wood.]

gnome[1] (nōm) *n.* One of a fabled race of dwarflike creatures who live underground and guard treasure hoards. [French, from New Latin *gnomus.*] **—gnom′ish** *adj.*

gnome[2] (nōm) *n.* A pithy saying that expresses a general truth or fundamental principle; an aphorism. [Greek *gnōmē,* from *gignōskein,* to know. See **gnō-** in Appendix.]

gno·mic (nō′mĭk) *adj.* Marked by aphorisms; aphoristic: *gnomic verse; a gnomic style.*

gno·mon (nō′mŏn′, -mən) *n.* **1.** An object, such as the style of a sundial, that projects a shadow used as an indicator. **2.** The geometric figure that remains after a parallelogram has been removed from a similar but larger parallelogram with which it shares a corner. [Latin *gnōmōn,* from Greek, from *gignōskein,* to know. See **gnō-** in Appendix.] **—gno·mon′ic, gno·mon′i·cal** *adj.*

gno·sis (nō′sĭs) *n.* Intuitive apprehension of spiritual truths, an esoteric form of knowledge sought by the Gnostics. [Greek *gnōsis,* knowledge, from *gignōskein,* to know. See **gnō-** in Appendix.]

Gnos·tic (nŏs′tĭk) *adj.* **1. gnostic.** Of, relating to, or possessing intellectual or spiritual knowledge. **2.** Of or relating to Gnosticism. **—Gnostic** *n.* A believer in Gnosticism. [Late Latin *Gnōsticus,* a Gnostic, from Late Greek *Gnōstikos,* from Greek *gnōstikos,* concerning knowledge, from *gnōsis,* knowledge. See GNOSIS.]

Gnos·ti·cism (nŏs′tĭ-sĭz′əm) *n.* The doctrines of certain pre-Christian pagan, Jewish, and early Christian sects that valued the revealed knowledge of God and of the origin and end of the human race as a means to attain redemption for the spiritual element in human beings and that distinguished the Demiurge from the unknowable Divine Being.

GNP *abbr.* Gross national product.

GnRH *abbr.* Gonadotropin-releasing hormone.

gnu (no͞o, nyo͞o) *n.* Either of two large African antelopes *(Connochaetes gnou* or *C. taurinus)* having a drooping mane and beard, a long tufted tail, and curved horns in both sexes. Also called *wildebeest.* [Probably from Dutch *gnoe,* from Nguni (Xhosa) *i-ngu,* white-tailed gnu, from San *!nu,* black wildebeest.]

go[1] (gō) *v.* **went** (wĕnt), **gone** (gôn, gŏn), **go·ing, goes** (gōz). *—intr.* **1.** To move or travel; proceed: *We will go by bus. Solicitors went from door to door seeking donations. How fast can the boat go?* **2.** To move away from a place; depart: *Go before I cry.* **3.a.** To pursue a certain course: *messages that go through diplomatic channels to the ambassador.* **b.** To resort to another, as for aid: *went directly to the voters of her district.* See Synonyms at **resort. 4.a.** To extend between two points or in a certain direction; run: *curtains that go from the ceiling to the floor.* **b.** To give entry; lead: *a stairway that goes to the basement.* **5.** To function properly: *The car won't go.* **6.a.** To have currency. **b.** To pass from one person to another; circulate: *Wild rumors were going around the office.* **7.** To pass as the result of a sale: *The gold watch went to the highest bidder.* **8.** *Informal.* Used as an intensifier when joined by *and* to a coordinate verb: *She went and complained to Personnel.* **9.** Used in the progressive tense with an infinitive to indicate future intent or expectation: *I am going to learn how to dance.* **10.a.** To be in a certain condition. **b.** To come to be in a certain condition: *go mad; hair that had gone gray.* **c.** To continue to be in a certain condition or continue an activity: *go barefoot all summer.* **d.** To carry out an action to a certain point or extent: *Your parents went to great expense to put you through college.* **11.a.** To be customarily located; belong: *The fork goes to the left of the plate. Where do the plates go?* **b.** To be capable of entering or fitting: *Will the suitcase go into the trunk of your car?* **12.a.** To pass into someone's possession: *All the jewelry went to her heirs.* **b.** To be allotted: *How much of your salary goes for rent?* **13.** To be a contributing factor: *It all goes to show us that the project can be completed on time.* **14.a.** To have a particular form: *as the saying goes.* **b.** To be such, by and large: *well behaved, as big dogs go.* **15.a.** To pass by; elapse: *The day went pleasantly enough until I received your call.* **b.** To be used up. **c.** To be discarded or abolished: *All luxuries will have to go.* **16.a.** To become weak; fail: *His hearing has started to go.* **b.** To come apart; break up. **17.** To cease living; die. **18.a.** To get along; fare: *How are things going?* **b.** To have a successful outcome: *creativity that made the advertising campaign really go.* **19.** To be suitable or appropriate as an accessory or accompaniment: *a color that goes beautifully with your complexion.* **20.a.** To have authority: *Whatever I say goes.* **b.** To be valid, acceptable, or adequate. **21.** *Informal.* To excrete waste from the bladder or bowels. **22.** *Informal.* To begin an act: *Here goes!* **23.** *Obsolete.* To walk. *—tr.* **1.** To proceed or move according to: *I was free to go my own way.* **2.** To traverse: *Only two of the runners went the entire distance.* **3.** *Informal.* **a.** To bet: *go $20 on the black horse.* **b.** To bid: *I'll go $500 on the vase.* **4.** *Informal.* **a.** To take on the responsibility or obligation for: *go bail for a client.* **b.** To participate to (a given extent): *Will you go halves with me if we win the lottery?* **5.** To amount to; weigh: *a shark that went 400 pounds.* **6.** *Informal.* To enjoy: *I could go a cold beer right now.* **7.** *Usage Problem.* To say. Used chiefly in verbal narration: *First I go, "Thank you," then he goes, "What for?"* **—go** *n., pl.* **goes. 1.** The act or an instance of going. **2.** An attempt; an effort: *had a go at acting.* **3.** The time or period of an activity. **4.** *Informal.* Energy; vitality: *had lots of go.* **5.** *Informal.* **a.** The go-ahead. **b.** *Often* **Go.** The starting point: *"And from Go there was something deliciously illicit about the whole affair"* (Erica Abeel). **c.** *Informal.* A situation in which planned operations can be effectuated. *The space mission is a go.* **—go** *adj. Informal.* Functioning correctly and ready for action: *All systems are go.* **—*phrasal verbs.* go about.** To set about to do; undertake: *Go about your chores in a responsible way.* **go along.** To cooperate: *They get along by going along.* **go around. 1.** To satisfy a demand or requirement: *just enough food to go around.* **2.** To go here and there; move from place to place. **3.** To have currency: *rumors going around.* **go at. 1.** To attack, especially with energy. **2.** To approach; undertake: *He went at the job with a lot of energy.* **go by. 1.** To elapse; pass: *as time goes by.* **2.** To pay a short visit: *My parents were away when we went by last week.* **go down. 1.a.** To drop below the horizon; set: *The sun went down.* **b.** To fall to the ground: *The helicopter went down in a ball of fire.* **c.** To sink: *The torpedoed battleship went down.* **d.** To experience defeat or ruin. **2.** To admit of easy swallowing: *a cough syrup that goes down readily.* **3.** *Chiefly British.* To leave a university. **4.** *Slang.* To occur; happen: *"a collection of memorable pieces about the general craziness that was going down in those days"* (James Atlas). **5.a.** To be accepted or tolerated: *How will your ideas go down as far as corporate marketing is concerned?* **b.** To come to be remembered in posterity: *a debate that will go down as a turning point in the campaign.* **go for. 1.** *Informal.* To have a special liking for: *I really go for progressive jazz.* **2.** To attack: *an opponent who is known to go for the jugular in arguments.* **3.** To pass for or serve as: *a couch that also goes for a bed.* **go in. 1.** To take part in a cooperative venture: *went in with the others to buy a present.* **2.** To make an approach, as before an attack: *Troops went in at dawn.* **go off. 1.** To undergo detonation; explode. **2.** To make a noise; sound: *The siren went off at noon.* **3.** To leave: *Don't go off mad.* **4.** *Informal.* To adhere to the expected course of events or the expected plan: *The project went off smoothly.* **go on. 1.** To take place; happen: *didn't know what was going on.* **2.a.** To continue: *Life*

gnu
Brindled gnu
Connochaetes taurinus

ă **pat**	oi **boy**
ā **pay**	ou **out**
âr **care**	o͝o **took**
ä **father**	o͞o **boot**
ĕ **pet**	ŭ **cut**
ē **be**	ûr **urge**
ĭ **pit**	th **thin**
ī **pie**	*th* **this**
îr **pier**	hw **which**
ŏ **pot**	zh **vision**
ō **toe**	ə **about, item**
ô **paw**	♦ **regionalism**

Stress marks: ′ (primary); ′ (secondary), as in **dictionary** (dĭk′shə-nĕr′ē)

goalkeeper
Field hockey goalkeeper

goatee

goat's rue
Tephrosia virginiana

must go on. **b.** To keep on doing (something): *Don't go on talking.* **c.** To proceed: *She went on to become a senator.* **3.** *Informal.* To talk volubly: *My, you do go on.* **go out. 1.** To become extinguished. **2. a.** To go outdoors; leave one's residence: *He went out at seven.* **b.** To take part in social life outside the home: *goes out a lot.* **3.** To become unfashionable: *High boots went out last year.* **4.** To undergo structural collapse: *The bridge went out.* **go over. 1.** To gain acceptance or approval: *a new style that didn't go over.* **2.** To examine: *go over the test scores.* **go through. 1.** To examine carefully: *went through the students' papers.* **2.** To experience: *We went through hell while working on this project.* **3.** To perform: *I went through the sonata in 30 minutes.* **go under. 1.** To suffer defeat or destruction; fail. **2.** To lose consciousness. **go up.** *Chiefly British.* To go to a university. **go with.** To date regularly. **—*idioms.* go all the way.** To engage in sex. **go back on.** To fail to honor or keep: *go back on a promise.* **go begging.** To be in little or no demand: *"Prestige or no prestige, directors' jobs at some companies have actually gone begging"* (Bill Powell). **go belly up.** *Informal.* To undergo total financial failure: *"A record number of . . . banks went belly up"* (New Republic). **go bust.** *Informal.* To undergo financial collapse: *"Railroads were in the news mainly when they were going bust"* (Christian Science Monitor). **go by the board.** To be discarded or ignored: *old dress codes that have now gone by the board.* **go down on.** *Vulgar Slang.* To perform oral sex on. **go down the line.** To provide strong support. **go fly a kite.** *Informal.* To cease being an annoyance. Often used in the imperative. **go for broke.** *Informal.* To commit or expend all of one's available resources toward achievement of a goal: *"Why not go for broke and take on somebody who is quite young and see what he does?"* (Roger L. Stevens). **go for it.** *Informal.* To expend all one's strength and resources toward achievement of an end or purpose. **go in for. 1.** To have interest in: *goes in for classical music.* **2.** To take part in: *goes in for water skiing.* **go it alone.** To undertake a project, trip, or responsibility without the presence or help of others. **go off the deep end.** To behave hysterically or very recklessly. **go one better.** To surpass or outdo by one degree: *He's gone me one better.* **go out for.** To seek to become a participant in: *go out for varsity soccer.* **go out of (one's) way.** To inconvenience oneself in doing something beyond what is required. **go out the window.** *Informal.* To become insignificant or inoperative: *"As soon as a third body is introduced to the Newtonian system, all lawful ordering of processes goes out the window"* (Fusion). **go places.** *Informal.* To be on the way to success: *a young executive who is clearly going places.* **go steady.** To date someone exclusively. **go the distance.** To carry a course of action through to completion. **go the vole.** To risk all of one's resources in the prospect of achieving great gains. **go to pieces. 1.** To lose one's self-control. **2.** To suffer the loss of one's health. **go to the mat.** *Informal.* To fight or dispute until one side or another is victorious: *The governor will go to the mat with the legislature over the controversial spending bill.* **go to town.** *Informal.* **1.** To work or perform efficiently and rapidly. **2.** To be highly successful. **go up in flames** (or **smoke).** To be utterly destroyed. **go without saying.** To be self-evident: *It goes without saying that success is the product of hard work.* **on the go.** Constantly busy or active. **to go.** To be taken out, as restaurant food or drink: *coffee and doughnuts to go.* [Middle English *gon,* from Old English *gān.* See **ghē-** in Appendix.]

USAGE NOTE: *Go* has long been used to describe the production of nonlinguistic noises, as in *The train went "toot." The cow goes "moo."* In recent years, however, younger speakers have extended this use of *go* to the report of speech, as in *Then he goes, "You think you're* real *smart, don't you."* For speakers young enough to get away with it, this usage serves a useful purpose in informal spoken narrative as an explicit indicator of a direct quotation, particularly when the speaker wishes to mimic the accent or intonation of the original spoken source. Largely restricted to the "narrative present" used in vivid description, it is highly inappropriate in formal speech or writing.

go² (gō) *n. Games.* A Japanese game for two, played with counters on a board that is ruled with 19 vertical and 19 horizontal lines. [Japanese.]

go·a (gō′ə) *n.* A gazelle *(Procapra picticaudata)* native to Tibet and having backward-curving horns in the male. [Tibetan *dgoba.*]

Go·a (gō′ə). A former Portuguese colony (1510–1961) of southwest India on the Malabar Coast.

goad (gōd) *n.* **1.** A long stick with a pointed end used for prodding animals. **2.** An agent or means of prodding or urging; a stimulus. **—goad** *tr.v.* **goad·ed, goad·ing, goads.** To prod or urge with or as if with a long pointed stick. [Middle English *gode,* from Old English *gād.*]

Goa, Da·man, and Di·u (də-män′; dē′o͞o). A union territory of southwest India on the Malabar Coast of the Arabian Sea. Formerly three noncontiguous Portuguese colonies, the territory was formally annexed by India in 1962.

go-a·head (gō′ə-hĕd′) *Informal. n.* **1.** Permission to proceed: *waiting for the go-ahead from the control tower.* **2.** Energetic assertiveness. **—go-ahead** *adj.* Characterized by energy and assertiveness: *a go-ahead marketing strategy.*

goal (gōl) *n.* **1.** The purpose toward which an endeavor is directed; an objective. See Synonyms at **intention. 2.** *Sports.* **a.** The finish line of a race. **b.** A specified structure or zone into or over which players endeavor to advance a ball or puck. **c.** The score awarded for such an act. [Middle English *gol,* boundary, possibly from Old English **gāl,* barrier.]

goal·ie (gō′lē) *n. Sports.* See **goalkeeper.**

goal·keep·er (gōl′kē′pər) *n. Sports.* A player assigned to protect the goal in various sports. Also called *goalie, goaltender, netkeeper.*

goal kick *n. Sports.* A free kick that is awarded to a defensive soccer player when the ball has been driven out of bounds over the end line by an opponent.

goal line *n. Sports.* **1.** A line located at either end and typically running the width of a playing area, on which a goal post or goal is positioned. **2.** *Football.* A line at either end of the playing field over which the ball must be carried or passed to score a touchdown.

goal post *n. Sports.* One of a pair of posts often joined with a crossbar and set at each end of a playing field to form a goal.

goal·tend·er (gōl′tĕn′dər) *n. Sports.* See **goalkeeper.**

goal·tend·ing (gōl′tĕn′dĭng) *n.* **1.** *Sports.* The act of protecting a goal, as in hockey and other such sports. **2.** *Basketball.* An illegal play in which a player deflects a ball that is on the downward path to the basket or that is already on the rim of the basket, carrying the penalty of an automatic score when committed by the defense or nullifying the field goal when committed by the offense.

go-a·round (gō′ə-round′) *n.* **1.** An argument; a go-round. **2.** An evasive excuse; a runaround.

goat (gōt) *n.* **1.** Any of various hollow-horned, bearded ruminant mammals of the genus *Capra,* originally of mountainous regions of the Old World, especially any of the domesticated forms of *C. hircus,* raised for wool, milk, and meat. **2.** A lecherous man. **3.** A scapegoat. [Middle English *got,* from Old English *gāt.*]

Goat (gōt) *n.* See **Capricorn.**

goat antelope *n.* Any of various wild ruminant mammals, such as the mountain goat or the chamois, having characteristics of both goats and antelopes.

goat·ee (gō-tē′) *n.* A small chin beard trimmed into a point. [Alteration of *goaty* (from GOAT, from its resemblance to a goat's beard).]

WORD HISTORY: When assessing American contributions to the English language and to fashion, let us not forget the *goatee.* Early comments on this style of beard appear first in American writings, making this word an Americanism. Although the style raises few eyebrows now, the early comments were not favorable: "One chap's . . . rigged out like a show monkey, with a little tag of hair hangin down under his chin jest like our old billy goat, that's a leetle too smart for this latitude, I think." This 1842 description, found in William Tappan Thompson's *Major Jones's Courtship,* also reveals the etymology of the word. The first actual recorded occurrence of the word, found in Daniel Lee and Joseph H. Frost's *Ten Years in Oregon,* published in 1844, also sounds disapproving: "A few individuals . . . leave what is called, by some of their politer neighbors, a 'goaty' under the chin."

goat·fish (gōt′fĭsh′) *n., pl.* **goatfish** or **-fish·es.** Any of various brightly colored fishes of the family Mullidae of warm seas, having two sensory barbels on the chin. Also called *red mullet, surmullet.*

Goat Island. An island of western New York in the Niagara River dividing Niagara Falls into the American and Canadian falls.

goats·beard also **goat's-beard** (gōts′bîrd′) *n.* **1.** A European weed *(Tragopogon pratensis)* widely naturalized in eastern North America, having grasslike leaves and yellow, dandelionlike flower heads. **2.** A tall dioecious plant *(Aruncus dioicus)* native to the eastern United States, having bipinnately compound leaves and a large panicle of small white flowers.

goat·skin (gōt′skĭn′) *n.* **1.** The skin of a goat. **2.** Leather made from a goatskin. **3.** A container, as for wine, made from a goatskin.

goat's rue (gōts′) *n.* **1.** A North American plant *(Tephrosia virginiana)* having large yellow flowers marked with purple and grouped in a terminal raceme or panicle. **2.** A Eurasian plant *(Galega officinalis)* cultivated for its showy, variously colored flowers or as food for livestock.

goat·suck·er (gōt′sŭk′ər) *n.* Any of various chiefly nocturnal, insectivorous birds of the family Caprimulgidae, which includes the nighthawk and the whippoorwill. [Translation of Greek *aigothēlas* : *aigos,* goat + *-thēlas,* sucker (from *thēlē,* teat, from the belief that the bird sucked milk from goats).]

gob¹ (gŏb) *n.* **1.** A small mass or lump. **2.** Often **gobs.** *Informal.* A large quantity: *a gob of money; gobs of time.* [Middle English *gobbe,* probably from Old French *gobe,* mouthful, from *gober,* to gulp, of Celtic origin.]

gob² (gŏb) *n. Slang.* The mouth. [Perhaps from Scottish and Irish Gaelic.]

gob³ (gŏb) *n. Slang.* A sailor. [Origin unknown.]

Go·bat (gō-bä′), **Charles Albert.** 1834–1914. Swiss politician. He shared the 1902 Nobel Peace Prize.

gob·bet (gŏb′ĭt) *n.* **1.** A piece or chunk, especially of raw meat. **2.** A bit or morsel: *a diary containing gobbets of useful information.* **3.** A small amount of liquid; a drop. [Middle English *gobet,* from Old French, diminutive of *gobe,* mouthful. See GOB¹.]

gob·ble¹ (gŏb′əl) *v.* **-bled, -bling, -bles.** —*tr.* **1.** To devour in large, greedy gulps. **2.** To take greedily; grab: *gobbled up the few remaining tickets.* —*intr.* To eat greedily or rapidly. [Frequentative of Middle English *gobben,* to drink greedily, probably from *gobbe,* lump, mouthful. See GOB¹.]

gob·ble² (gŏb′əl) *n.* The guttural, chortling sound of a male turkey. —**gobble** *intr.v.* **-bled, -bling, -bles.** To make this sound. [Imitative.]

gob·ble·dy·gook also **gob·ble·de·gook** (gŏb′əl-dē-go͝ok′) *n.* Unclear, wordy jargon. [Imitative of the gobbling of a turkey.]

gob·bler (gŏb′lər) *n.* A male turkey.

Go·be·lin (gō′bə-lĭn, gŏb′ə-) *n.* A tapestry of a kind woven at the Gobelin works in Paris, France, noted for rich pictorial design.

go-be·tween (gō′bĭ-twēn′) *n.* One who acts as an intermediary or messenger between two sides.

Go·bi (gō′bē). A desert of southeast Mongolia and northern China. It consists mainly of a series of shallow alkaline basins.

gob·let (gŏb′lĭt) *n.* **1.** A drinking vessel, such as a glass, that has a stem and base. **2.** *Archaic.* A drinking bowl without handles. [Middle English *gobelet,* from Old French, diminutive of *gobel,* cup, probably of Celtic origin.]

goblet cell *n.* Any of the specialized epithelial cells found in the mucous membrane of the stomach, intestines, and respiratory passages that secrete mucus. [From its shape.]

gob·lin (gŏb′lĭn) *n.* A grotesque, elfin creature of folklore, thought to work mischief or evil. [Middle English *gobelin,* from Norman French **gobelin,* name of a ghost that supposedly haunted the town of Évreux in the 12th century.]

go·by (gō′bē) *n., pl.* **goby** or **-bies.** Any of numerous usually small spiny-finned fishes of the family Gobiidae, having the pelvic fins united to form a suction disk. [Latin *gōbius,* gudgeon, from Greek *kōbios.*]

go-by (gō′bī′) *n. Informal.* An intentional slight; a snub.

go-cart (gō′kärt′) *n.* **1.** A small wagon for children to ride in, drive, or pull. **2.** A small frame on casters designed to help support a child learning to walk. **3.** A handcart. **4.** A stroller.

♦**go cup** *n. New Orleans.* An alcoholic beverage provided in a plastic cup for a patron who wishes to take the drink out.

god (gŏd) *n.* **1. God. a.** A being conceived as the perfect, omnipotent, omniscient originator and ruler of the universe, the principal object of faith and worship in monotheistic religions. **b.** The force, effect, or a manifestation or aspect of this being. **c.** *Christian Science.* "Infinite Mind; Spirit; Soul; Principle; Life; Truth; Love" (Mary Baker Eddy). **2.** A being of supernatural powers or attributes, believed in and worshiped by a people, especially a male deity thought to control some part of nature or reality. **3.** An image of a supernatural being; an idol. **4.** One that is worshiped, idealized, or followed: *money was their god.* **5.** A very handsome man. **6.** A powerful ruler or despot. [Middle English, from Old English. See **gheu(ə)-** in Appendix.]

God·al·might·y (gŏd′ôl-mī′tē) *interj.* Used to express extreme surprise or dismay.

Go·dard (gō-där′), **Jean Luc.** Born 1930. French filmmaker known for his innovative cinematic and narrative technique in films such as *Breathless* (1959) and *Every Man for Himself* (1980).

Go·da·va·ri (gō-dä′və-rē). A river of central India flowing about 1,448 km (900 mi) from the Western Ghats southeast across the Deccan Plateau to the Bay of Bengal.

God-aw·ful (gŏd′ô′fəl) *adj. Slang.* Extremely trying; atrocious.

god·child (gŏd′chīld′) *n.* A person for whom another serves as sponsor at baptism.

god·damn also **God·damn** (gŏd′dăm′) —*interj.* Used to express extreme displeasure, anger, or surprise. —*n.* Damn. —*tr. & intr.v.* **-damned, -damn·ing, -damns.** To damn. —*adj.* Variant of **goddamned.**

god·damned (gŏd′dămd′) or **god·damn** (-dăm′) *adj.* Damned. —**god′damned′, god′dam′** *adv.*

God·dard (gŏd′ərd), **Robert Hutchings.** 1882–1945. American physicist who developed and launched the first successful liquid-fueled rocket (1926).

god·daugh·ter (gŏd′dô′tər) *n.* A female godchild.

god·dess (gŏd′ĭs) *n.* **1.** A female being of supernatural powers or attributes, believed in and worshiped by a people. **2.** An image of a female supernatural being; an idol. **3.** Something, such as fame or wealth, that is worshiped or idealized. **4.** A woman of great beauty or grace.

go-dev·il (gō′dĕv′əl) *n.* **1.** A logging sled. **2.** A railway handcar. **3.** A jointed tool for cleaning an oil pipeline and disengaging obstructions. **4.** An iron dart dropped into an oil well to explode a charge of dynamite.

god·fa·ther (gŏd′fä′*th*ər) *n.* **1.** A man who sponsors a person at baptism. **2.** One that has a relationship to another person or to something that is the equivalent of being a baptismal sponsor: *the godfather of a new generation of nuclear physicists.* **3.** *Slang.* The leader of an organized crime family. —**godfather** *tr.v.* **-thered, -ther·ing, -thers.** To serve as or as if a godfather to.

god·for·sak·en also **God·for·sak·en** (gŏd′fər-sā′kən) *adj.* **1.** Located in a dismal or remote area. **2.** Desolate; forlorn.

God·frey of Bouil·lon (gŏd′frē; bo͞o-yôɴ′). 1061?–1100. French leader of the First Crusade (1096–1099).

god·head (gŏd′hĕd′) *n.* **1.** Divinity; godhood. **2. Godhead. a.** The Christian God, especially the Trinity. **b.** The essential and divine nature of God, regarded abstractly. [Middle English *godhode, godhede,* from Old English *godhād* : *god,* god; see GOD + *-hād,* -hood.]

god·hood (gŏd′ho͝od′) *n.* The quality or state of being a god; divinity.

god·less (gŏd′lĭs) *adj.* **1.** Recognizing or worshiping no god. **2.** Wicked, impious, or immoral. —**god′less·ly** *adv.* —**god′less·ness** *n.*

god·like (gŏd′līk′) *adj.* Resembling or of the nature of a god or God; divine. —**god′like′ness** *n.*

god·ling (gŏd′lĭng) *n.* A minor god.

god·ly (gŏd′lē) *adj.* **-li·er, -li·est. 1.** Having great reverence for God; pious. **2.** Divine. —**god′li·ness** *n.*

god·moth·er (gŏd′mŭ*th*′ər) *n.* **1.** A woman who sponsors a person at baptism. **2.** One that has a relationship to another person or to something that is the equivalent of being a baptismal sponsor: *the godmother to a new generation of physicians.* —**godmother** *tr.v.* **-ered, -er·ing, -ers.** To serve as or as if a godmother to.

god·ox·ious (gŏd-ŏk′shəs) *adj. Informal.* Extremely distasteful and repellent: *"sixteen godoxious syrups in a thimble of soda"* (Padgett Powell). [Probably GOD(-AWFUL) + (OBN)OXIOUS.]

god·par·ent (gŏd′pâr′ənt, -păr′-) *n.* A godfather or a godmother.

God's acre (gŏdz) *n.* A churchyard or burial ground. [Translation of German *Gottesacker* : *Gottes,* genitive of *Gott,* god + *Acker,* field.]

god·send (gŏd′sĕnd′) *n.* Something wanted or needed that comes or happens unexpectedly. [Alteration of Middle English *goddes sand,* God's message : *goddes,* genitive of *God,* God; see GOD + *sand,* message (from Old English; see **sent-** in Appendix).]

god·son (gŏd′sŭn′) *n.* A male godchild.

God·speed (gŏd′spēd′) *n.* Success or good fortune. [Middle English *God spede (you),* may God prosper (you) : *God,* god; see GOD + *spede,* third person sing. present subjunctive of *speden,* to prosper (from Old English *spēdan,* from *spēd,* success; see SPEED).]

Godt·håb (gôt′hôp′). The capital of Greenland, on the southwest coast of the island on **Godthåb Fjord.** The town was founded in 1721. Population, 10,559.

Go·du·nov (go͞od′n-ôf′, gŏd′-, gə-do͞o-nôf′), **Boris Fyodorovich.** 1551?–1605. Czar of Russia (1598–1605) who became regent for Fyodor I (1557–1598) on the death of Ivan IV (1584) and was chosen czar on Fyodor's death.

God·win (gŏd′wĭn), **William.** 1756–1836. British writer and political theorist who believed in the perfectibility of human nature and maintained that people could live harmoniously without laws and institutions.

Godwin Aus·ten (ô′stən), **Mount.** See **K2.**

god·wit (gŏd′wĭt′) *n.* Any of various large shore birds of the genus *Limosa,* having a long, slender, slightly upturned bill. [Origin unknown.]

Goeb·bels (gœ′bəls), **(Paul) Joseph.** 1897–1945. German Nazi propaganda minister (1933–1945) who exploited the German radio, press, cinema, and theater to launch propaganda against the Jews and other groups.

Goe·ring (gĕr′ĭng, gûr′-, gœ′rĭng), **Hermann Wilhelm.** See Hermann Wilhelm **Göring.**

goes (gōz) *v.* Third person singular present tense of **go¹.**

Goe·thals (gō′thəlz), **George Washington.** 1858–1928. American army officer and engineer who directed the construction of the Panama Canal (1907–1914).

Goe·the (gœ′tə), **Johann Wolfgang von.** 1749–1832. German writer and scientist. A master of poetry, drama, and the novel, he spent 50 years on his two-part dramatic poem *Faust* (published 1808 and 1832). —**Goe′the·an** (-tē-ən) *adj.*

goe·thite (gō′thīt′, gœ′tīt′) *n.* A red, yellow, or brown mineral, essentially $HFeO_2$, one of the common constituents of rust. [After Johann Wolfgang von GOETHE.]

go-fast (gō′făst′) *n. Nautical.* A sleek, high-performance motorboat, often used in smuggling operations.

go·fer also **go-fer** (gō′fər) *n. Slang.* An employee who runs errands in addition to performing regular duties. [Alteration of *go for,* from that person's having to go for or after things.]

gof·fer also **gauf·fer** (gŏf′ər, gô′fər) —*tr.v.* **-fered, -fer·ing, -fers.** To press ridges or narrow pleats into (a frill, for example). —*n.* **1.** An iron used for pressing ridges or narrow pleats. **2.** Ridges or pleats produced in this manner. [French *gaufrer,* to emboss, from Old French, from *gaufre,* honeycomb, waffle; akin to Middle Low German *wāfel.* See **webh-** in Appendix.]

go-get·ter (gō′gĕt′ər, -gĕt′-) *n. Informal.* An enterprising person.

gog·gle (gŏg′əl) *v.* **-gled, -gling, -gles.** —*intr.* **1.** To stare with wide and bulging eyes. **2.** To roll or bulge. Used of the eyes. —*tr.* To roll or bulge (the eyes). —**goggle** *n.* **1.** A stare or leer. **2. goggles.** A pair of tight-fitting eyeglasses, often tinted or having side shields, worn to protect the eyes from hazards such as

goblet
Early 19th-century German silver goblet by Carl Moritz Stumpf

Jean Luc Godard
Photographed in 1988 at the Cannes Film Festival

goggles

ă pat	oi boy
ā pay	ou out
âr care	o͝o took
ä father	o͞o boot
ĕ pet	ŭ cut
ē be	ûr urge
ĭ pit	th thin
ī pie	*th* this
îr pier	hw which
ŏ pot	zh vision
ō toe	ə about, item
ô paw	♦ regionalism

Stress marks: ′ (primary); ′ (secondary), as in **dictionary** (dĭk′shə-nĕr′ē)

golden club
Orontium aquaticum

dust, glare, or flying debris. [Middle English *gogelen,* to squint.] **—gog′gly** *adj.*

gog·gle-eyed (gŏg′əl-īd′) *adj.* Having prominent or rolling eyes.

Gogh (gō, gôKH, KHôKH), **Vincent van.** See Vincent **van Gogh.**

go-go[1] also **go·go** (gō′gō′) *adj. Informal.* Of or relating to discotheques or to the energetic music and dancing performed at discotheques. [From À GOGO.]

go-go[2] also **go·go** (gō′gō′) *adj. Informal.* **1.** Marked by assertive action: *a go-go sales executive.* **2.a.** Of, relating to, or engaging in a type of speculative, short-term stock-market operation: *a go-go fund.* **b.** Characterized by the fast growth and development that invites speculative investment: *go-go industries such as microprocessing and laser technology.* [Intensive reduplication (influenced by GO-GO[1]) of GO[1].]

Go·gol (gô′gəl, gō′gôl), **Nikolai Vasilievich.** 1809–1852. Russian writer considered the founder of realism in Russian literature. His works include the novel *Dead Souls* (1842).

Gog·ra (gŏg′rə, -rä). See **Ghaghara.**

Goi·â·ni·a (goi-ăn′ē-ə, -ä′nē-ə). A city of south-central Brazil southwest of Brasília. It is a shipping and processing center in an agricultural and cattle-raising region. Population, 702,858.

Goi·del·ic (goi-dĕl′ĭk) *n.* A branch of the Celtic languages that includes Irish Gaelic, Scottish Gaelic, and Manx. **—Goidelic** *adj.* **1.** Of or relating to the Gaels. **2.** Of, relating to, or characteristic of Goidelic. [From Old Irish *Goídil,* Gael, possibly from Old Welsh *-guoidel, Gwyddel.*]

go·ing (gō′ĭng) *n.* **1.** Departure: *comings and goings.* **2.** The condition underfoot as it affects one's headway in walking or riding: *Once we left the trail the going was rough.* **3.** *Informal.* Progress toward a goal; headway: *It was easy going during my senior year.* **—going** *adj.* **1.** Working; running: *a machine in going order.* **2.** In full operation; flourishing: *a going business.* **3.** Current; prevailing: *The going rates are high.* **4.** To be found; available: *the best products going.* ***—idiom.*** **going on.** Approaching: *The child is six, going on seven years of age.*

go·ing-o·ver (gō′ĭng-ō′vər) *n., pl.* **go·ings-o·ver** (gō′ĭngz-). *Informal.* **1.** An examination; an inspection. **2.a.** A severe beating. **b.** A severe reprimand.

go·ings-on (gō′ĭngz-ŏn′, -ôn′) *pl.n. Informal.* Actions or behavior, especially when regarded with disapproval: *"cool observers of nutty goings-on"* (Variety).

goi·ter (goi′tər) *n.* A noncancerous enlargement of the thyroid gland, visible as a swelling at the front of the neck, that is often associated with iodine deficiency. Also called *struma.* [French *goitre,* from Provençal *goitron,* from Vulgar Latin **guttūriō, guttūriōn-,* throat, from Latin *guttur.*] **—goi′trous** (-trəs) *adj.*

Go·lan Heights (gō′län′). An upland region between northeast Israel and southwest Syria northeast of the Sea of Galilee. Fortified by Syria after 1948, the area was captured by Israel in the 1967 Arab-Israeli War and formally annexed in 1981.

golden eagle
Aquila chrysaetos

Gol·con·da[1] (gŏl-kŏn′də). A ruined city of south-central India west of Hyderabad. Capital of an ancient kingdom (c. 1364–1512), it was later one of the five Moslem kingdoms of the Deccan until its capture by Aurangzeb's forces in 1687.

Gol·con·da[2] (gŏl-kŏn′də) *n.* A source of great riches, such as a mine. [After GOLCONDA[1].]

gold (gōld) *n.* **1.a.** *Symbol* **Au** A soft, yellow, corrosion-resistant element, the most malleable and ductile metal, occurring in veins and alluvial deposits and recovered by mining or by panning or sluicing. A good thermal and electrical conductor, gold is generally alloyed to increase its strength, and it is used as an international monetary standard, in jewelry, for decoration, and as a plated coating on a wide variety of electrical and mechanical components. Atomic number 79; atomic weight 196.967; melting point 1,063.0°C; boiling point 2,966.0°C; specific gravity 19.32; valence 1, 3. See table at **element. b.** Coinage made of this element. **c.** A gold standard. **2.** Money; riches. **3.** *Color.* A light olive-brown to dark yellow, or a moderate, strong to vivid yellow. **4.** Something regarded as having great value or goodness: *a heart of gold.* **5.a.** A medal, as in the Olympics, made of gold: *won 9 golds in 13 events.* **b.** A gold record. **—gold** *adj.* Having the color of gold. [Middle English, from Old English. See **ghel-**[2] in Appendix.]

gold·beat·ing (gōld′bē′tĭng) *n.* The act, process, or art of beating sheets of gold into gold leaf. **—gold′beat′er** *n.*

gold beetle *n.* See **gold bug** (sense 1).

Gold·berg (gōld′bərg), **Arthur Joseph.** 1908–1990. American jurist and diplomat who served as an associate justice of the U.S. Supreme Court (1962–1965) and a U.S. representative to the United Nations (1965–1968).

Goldberg, Reuben Lucius. Known as "Rube." 1883–1970. American cartoonist noted for his intricate diagrams of complicated, impractical contraptions designed to effect comparatively simple results.

gold·brick (gōld′brĭk′) *Slang. n.* A person, especially a soldier, who avoids assigned duties or work; a shirker. **—goldbrick** *v.* **-bricked, -brick·ing, -bricks.** *—intr.* To shirk one's assigned duties or responsibilities. *—tr.* To cheat; swindle. **—gold′brick′er** *n.*

gold brick *n.* **1.** A bar of gilded cheap metal that appears to be genuine gold. **2.** A fraudulent, worthless substitute.

gold bug *n.* **1.** Any of several North American beetles, especially *Metriona bicolor,* having a golden metallic luster. Also called *gold beetle.* **2.** A supporter of the gold standard. **3.** A speculator in or a purchaser of gold.

gold coast *n. Informal.* **1.** A rich neighborhood. **2.** The executive suite or suites in a company's headquarters. [After GOLD COAST.]

Gold Coast (gōld). **1.** A section of coastal western Africa along the Gulf of Guinea on the southern shore of Ghana. It was named for the large quantities of gold formerly found in the area and brought to the coast for sale. **2.** A former British colony in the southern part of the Gold Coast, now part of Ghana.

gold digger *n. Informal.* A woman who seeks money and expensive gifts from men.

gold dust *n.* Gold in powdered form.

gold·en (gōl′dən) *adj.* **1.** Of, relating to, made of, or containing gold. **2.a.** *Color.* Having the color of gold or a yellow color suggestive of gold. **b.** Lustrous; radiant: *the golden sun.* **c.** Suggestive of gold, as in richness or splendor: *a golden voice.* **3.** Of the greatest value or importance; precious. **4.** Marked by peace, prosperity, and often creativeness: *a golden era.* **5.** Very favorable or advantageous; excellent: *a golden opportunity.* **6.** Having a promising future; seemingly assured of success: *a golden generation.* **7.** Of or relating to a 50th anniversary. **—gold′en·ly** *adv.* **—gold′en·ness** *n.*

golden age *n.* **1.** A period of great peace, prosperity, and happiness. **2.** *Greek & Roman Mythology.* The first age of the world, an untroubled and prosperous era during which people lived in ideal happiness.

golden ager *n.* A senior citizen.

golden Al·ex·an·ders (ăl′ĭg-zăn′dərz) *n. (used with a sing. or pl. verb).* An herb *(Zizia aurea)* of eastern North America, having compound umbels of small yellow flowers and ternately compound leaves. [Middle English *alisaundre,* probably from Medieval Latin *(petroselīnum) Alexandrīnum,* horse-parsley, after ALEXANDER III[1].]

golden aster *n.* Any of various North American plants of the genus *Chrysopsis* having yellow, rayed flower heads.

golden bantam *n.* A variety of corn having large, bright-yellow kernels on a relatively small ear.

golden calf *n.* **1.** A golden image of a sacrificial calf fashioned by Aaron and worshiped by the Israelites. **2.a.** Money as an objec of worship; mammon. **b.** The subject of intense veneration: *"Arms control . . . has evolved* [into] *the golden calf of liberalism"* (Patrick J. Buchanan).

golden chinquapin *n.* See **chinquapin** (sense 2).

golden club *n.* An aquatic plant *(Orontium aquaticum)* of the eastern United States, having a clublike, golden-yellow spadix, small blue-green berries, and floating leaves.

golden eagle *n.* A large eagle *(Aquila chrysaetos)* of mountainous areas of the Northern Hemisphere, having dark plumage with brownish-yellow feathers on the back of the head and neck.

gol·den·eye (gōl′dən-ī′) *n.* **1.** Either of two diving ducks *(Bucephala clangula* or *B. islandica)* of northern regions, having a short black bill, a rounded head, and yellow eyes. **2.** Any of various lacewings of the family Chrysopidae having yellow or copper-colored eyes. [From their golden-yellow eyes.]

Gold·en Fleece (gōl′dən) *n. Greek Mythology.* The fleece of the golden ram, stolen by Jason and the Argonauts from the king of Colchis.

Golden Gate. A strait in western California connecting the Pacific Ocean and San Francisco Bay. Discovered in 1579 by Sir Francis Drake, it was known as the Golden Gate long before the name gained new popularity during the gold rush of 1849.

golden glow *n.* A tall plant *(Rudbeckia laciniata)* cultivated for its large, yellow, many-rayed double flower heads.

golden handcuffs *pl.n. (used with a sing. verb). Slang.* A lucrative incentive to an executive intended to discourage resignation or ensure long-term cooperation after departure.

golden handshake *n. Slang.* A lucrative severance agreement offered to an employee typically as an inducement to retire.

Golden Horde *n.* The Mongol army that swept over eastern Europe in the 13th century and established a suzerain in Russia. [From the golden tent of their commander.]

Golden Horn. An inlet of the Bosporus in northwest Turkey forming the harbor of Istanbul.

golden mean *n.* The course between extremes.

golden needles *pl.n. (used with a sing. or pl. verb).* See **enokidake.**

golden oak mushroom *n.* See **shiitake.**

golden oldie *n.* A recording, movie, or other form of entertainment that was very popular in the past.

golden parachute *n. Slang.* An employment agreement that guarantees a key executive lucrative severance benefits if control of the company changes hands followed by management shifts.

golden pheasant *n.* A pheasant *(Chrysolophus pictus)* of China and Tibet that has a long tail and varicolored plumage.

gold·en·rod (gōl′dən-rŏd′) *n.* Any of numerous chiefly North American plants of the genus *Solidago,* having clusters of small yellow flower heads that bloom in late summer or fall.

golden rule *n.* The biblical teaching that one should behave toward others as one would have others behave toward oneself.

gold·en·seal (gōl′dən-sēl′) *n.* A woodland plant *(Hydrastis* *canadensis)* of eastern North America, having small greenish-white flowers and a yellow root formerly used medicinally. Also called *orangeroot.*

golden section *n.* A ratio, observed especially in the fine arts, between the two dimensions of a plane figure or the two divisions of a line such that the smaller is to the larger as the larger is to the sum of the two, a ratio of roughly three to five.

golden umbrella *n. Slang.* A golden parachute.

Golden Valley. A city of southeast Minnesota, a suburb of Minneapolis. Population, 22,775.

gold·field (gōld′fēld′) *n.* An area containing abundant deposits of gold or gold ore.

gold-filled (gōld′fĭld′) *adj.* Made of a hard base metal with an outer layer of gold.

gold·finch (gōld′fĭnch′) *n.* **1.** Any of several small American finches of the genus *Carduelis,* especially *C. tristis,* of which the male has yellow plumage with a black forehead, wings, and tail. **2.** A small Eurasian finch *(Carduelis carduelis)* having brownish plumage with black wings boldly marked with yellow and a red patch across the face.

gold·fish (gōld′fĭsh′) *n., pl.* **goldfish** or **-fish·es.** A freshwater fish *(Carassius auratus)* native to eastern Asia, characteristically having brassy or reddish coloring and bred in many ornamental forms as an aquarium fish.

gold foil *n.* Gold rolled or beaten into sheets somewhat thicker than gold leaf.

gold·i·locks (gōl′dē-lŏks′) *pl.n. (used with a sing. or pl. verb).* A European plant *(Aster linosyris)* having narrow, sessile leaves and dense corymbs of small, bright yellow, discoid flower heads. [Middle English *goldi,* golden (from *gold,* gold; see GOLD) + *locks,* pl. of LOCK[2].]

Gold·ing (gōl′dĭng), **William Gerald.** Born 1911. British writer noted for his novels, such as *The Lord of the Flies* (1954). He won the 1983 Nobel Prize for literature.

gold leaf *n.* Gold beaten into extremely thin sheets used especially for gilding.

Gold·man (gōld′mən), **Emma.** 1869–1940. Russian-born American anarchist. Jailed repeatedly for her advocacy of birth control and opposition to military conscription, she was deported to the Soviet Union in 1919.

gold mine *n. Informal.* A rich or plentiful source of something desired.

gold-of-pleas·ure (gōld′əv-plĕzh′ər) *n.* A Eurasian plant *(Camelina sativa)* having yellow flowers and seeds rich in oil.

Gol·do·ni (gŏl-dō′nē), **Carlo.** 1707–1793. Italian dramatist who wrote more than 250 plays, including 150 comedies.

gold rush *n.* **1.** A rush of migrants to an area where gold has been discovered. **2.** Headlong pursuit of wealth and success: *a gold rush on Wall Street.*

Golds·bor·o (gōldz′bûr′ō). A city of east-central North Carolina southeast of Raleigh. It is a manufacturing center and marketplace for a tobacco-growing region. Population, 31,871.

gold·smith (gōld′smĭth′) *n.* **1.** An artisan who fashions objects of gold. **2.** A trader or dealer in gold articles.

Gold·smith (gōld′smĭth′), **Oliver.** 1730?–1774. British writer whose literary reputation rests on his novel *The Vicar of Wakefield* (1766), the pastoral poem *The Deserted Village* (1770), and the dramatic comedy *She Stoops to Conquer* (1773).

goldsmith beetle *n.* Either of two scarabaeid beetles *(Cotalpa lanigera* or *Cetonia aurata)* having metallic greenish-yellow coloring.

gold standard *n.* A monetary standard under which the basic unit of currency is equal in value to and exchangeable for a specified amount of gold.

gold·stone (gōld′stōn′) *n.* An aventurine with gold-colored inclusions.

gold·thread (gōld′thrĕd′) *n.* Any of several plants of the genus *Coptis,* having white flowers, slender yellow roots, ternately divided evergreen leaves, and clusters of follicles.

Gold·wa·ter (gōld′wô′tər, -wŏt′ər), **Barry Morris.** Born 1909. American politician. A conservative Republican, he served as U.S. senator from Arizona (1953–1965 and 1969–1987) and ran unsuccesfully for President in 1964.

Gold·wyn (gōld′wĭn), **Samuel.** 1882–1974. Polish-born American film producer who founded his own film company (1917) and merged with Louis B. Mayer to form Metro-Goldwyn-Mayer (1925).

go·lem (gō′ləm) *n.* In Jewish folklore, an artificially created human being supernaturally endowed with life. [Hebrew *gōlem,* lump, clod, fool, from *gālam,* to wrap up.]

Go·le·ta (gō-lē′tə). A city of southern California on the Pacific Ocean west of Santa Barbara. It is a trade center for an agricultural region. Population, 28,100.

golf (gŏlf, gôlf) *n. Sports.* A game played on a large outdoor course with a series of 9 or 18 holes spaced far apart, the object being to propel a small, hard ball with the use of various clubs into each hole with as few strokes as possible. **—golf** *intr.v.* **golfed, golf·ing, golfs.** To play this game. [Middle English.] **—golf′er** *n.*

golf club *n. Sports.* **1.** One of a set of clubs having a slender shaft and a head of wood or iron, used in golf. **2.** An organization of golfers.

golf course *n. Sports.* A large tract of land laid out for golf. Also called *golflinks.*

golf·links (gŏlf′lĭngks′, gôlf′-) *pl.n. Sports.* See **golf course.**

Gol·gi (gôl′jē), **Camillo.** 1844?–1926. Italian histologist. He shared a 1906 Nobel Prize for research on the structure of the nervous system.

Golgi apparatus *n.* A network of stacked membranous vesicles present in most living cells that functions in the formation of secretions within the cell. Also called *Golgi body, Golgi complex.* [After Camillo GOLGI.]

gol·go·tha (gŏl′gə-thə) *n.* A place or occasion of great suffering. [After *Golgotha* (Calvary).]

Gol·go·tha (gŏl′gə-thə, gŏl-gŏth′ə). See **Calvary**[1].

gol·iard (gōl′yərd, -yärd′) *n.* A wandering student in medieval Europe disposed to conviviality, license, and the making of ribald and satirical Latin songs. [Middle English, from Old French, glutton, goliard, from *gole,* throat, from Latin *gula.*] **—gol·iar′dic** (gōl-yär′dĭk) *adj.*

Go·li·ath[1] (gə-lī′əth). In the Old Testament, a giant Philistine warrior who was slain by David with a stone and sling.

Go·li·ath[2] (gə-lī′əth) *n.* A person or thing of colossal power or achievement.

gol·li·wog or **gol·li·wogg** (gŏl′ē-wŏg′) *n.* A doll fashioned in grotesque caricature of a Black male. [After *Golliwog,* a character in books by Florence Upton (died 1922), American illustrator.]

gol·ly (gŏl′ē) *interj.* Used to express mild surprise or wonder. [Alteration of GOD.]

gom·been (gŏm-bēn′) *n. Irish.* Usury. [Irish Gaelic *gaimbín,* diminutive of *gamba,* leg, lump (perhaps influenced by *glamba,* heap).]

Go·mel (gō′məl, gô′-, gô′myĭl). A city of Belorussia southeast of Minsk. First mentioned in 1142, it was controlled alternately by Russia and Poland, passing finally to Russia in 1772. Population, 465,000.

Go·mor·rah[1] (gə-môr′ə, -mŏr′ə). An ancient city of Palestine near Sodom, possibly covered by the waters of the Dead Sea. According to the Old Testament, the city was destroyed by fire because of its wickedness.

Go·mor·rah[2] (gə-môr′ə, -mŏr′ə) *n.* A wicked or depraved place: *"confirmed my fantasy of Hollywood as both Oz and Gomorrah"* (Julie Salamon).

Gom·pers (gŏm′pərz), **Samuel.** 1850–1924. British-born American labor leader who was president of the American Federation of Labor (1886–1924, except 1895).

gom·pho·sis (gŏm-fō′sĭs) *n., pl.* **-ses** (-sēz). *Anatomy.* A type of immovable articulation, as of a tooth inserted into its bony socket. [Greek *gomphōsis,* from *gomphoun,* to fasten with bolts, from *gomphos,* bolt. See **gembh-** in Appendix.]

gon– *pref.* Variant of **gono–.**

–gon *suff.* A figure having a specified kind or number of angles: *isogon.* [Greek *-gōnon,* from neuter of *gōnos,* angled, from *gōnia,* angle. See **genu-**[1] in Appendix.]

go·nad (gō′năd′) *n.* An organ in animals that produces gametes, especially a testis or an ovary. [New Latin *gonas, gonad-,* from Greek *gonos,* procreation, genitals. See **gene-** in Appendix.] **—go·nad′al** (gō-năd′l), **go·nad′ic** *adj.*

go·nad·o·trop·ic (gō-năd′ə-trŏp′ĭk, -trō′pĭk) also **go·nad·o·troph·ic** (-trŏf′ĭk, -trō′fĭk) *adj.* Acting on or stimulating the gonads: *a gonadotropic hormone.*

go·nad·o·tro·pin (gō-năd′ə-trō′pĭn, -trŏp′ĭn) also **go·nad·o·tro·phin** (-trō′fĭn, -trō′pĭn) *n.* A hormone that stimulates the growth and activity of the gonads, especially any of several pituitary hormones that stimulate the function of the ovaries and testes.

go·nad·o·tro·pin-re·leas·ing hormone (gō-năd′ə-trō′pĭn-rĭ-lēs′ĭng, -trŏp′ĭn-) *n. Abbr.* **GnRH** A hormone produced by the hypothalamus that signals the anterior pituitary gland to begin secreting luteinizing hormone and follicle-stimulating hormone. Also called *luteinizing hormone-releasing hormone.*

Go·na·ïves (gō′nə-ēv′, gô-nä-). A city of western Haiti on an arm of the Caribbean Sea north-northwest of Port-au-Prince. Haitian independence was proclaimed here in 1804. Population, 34,209.

Gon·court (gôN-ko͝or′), **Edmond Louis Antoine Huot de.** 1822–1896. French writer who collaborated with his brother **Jules Alfred Huot de Goncourt** (1830–1870) on numerous works, most notably novels such as *Madame Gervaisais* (1869).

Gond (gŏnd) *n.* A member of a Dravidian people inhabiting central India.

Gon·dar (gŏn′dər, -där′) also **Gon·der** (-dər). A town of northwest Ethiopia on Lake Tana. An early capital of Ethiopia, it flourished c. 1630 to c. 1860. Population, 85,941.

Gon·di (gŏn′dē) *n.* The Dravidian language of the Gonds.

gon·do·la (gŏn′dl-ə, gŏn-dō′lə) *n.* **1.** *Nautical.* **a.** A lightweight narrow barge with ends that curve up into a point and often a small cabin in the middle, propelled with a single oar from the stern and used on the canals of Venice. **b.** A flat-bottomed river boat. **2.** A gondola car. **3.** A basket, an enclosure, or an instrument sling suspended from and carried aloft by a balloon. **4.** An enclosed structure suspended from a cable, used for con-

golf
Preparing to putt

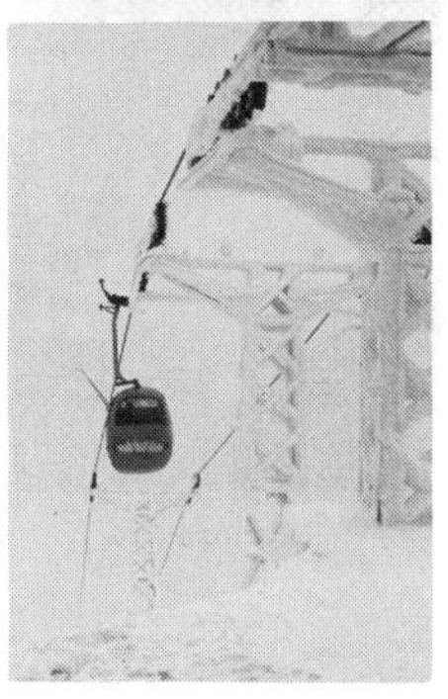

gondola
Top: Venetian gondola
Bottom: Ski lift gondola

ă pat	oi boy
ā pay	ou out
âr care	o͝o took
ä father	o͞o boot
ĕ pet	ŭ cut
ē be	ûr urge
ĭ pit	th thin
ī pie	*th* this
îr pier	hw which
ŏ pot	zh vision
ō toe	ə about, item
ô paw	♦ regionalism

Stress marks: ′ (primary); ′ (secondary), as in **dictionary** (dĭk′shə-nĕr′ē)

veying passengers, as to and from a ski slope. [Italian, from Old Italian *gondula*.]

gondola car *n.* An open railroad freight car with low sides.

gon·do·lier (gŏn′dl-îr′) *n. Nautical.* The person who propels a gondola. [French, from Italian *gondoliere*, from *gondola*, gondola. See GONDOLA.]

Gond·wa·na·land (gŏnd-wä′nə-lănd′) *n.* The protocontinent of the Southern Hemisphere, a hypothetical landmass that according to the theory of plate tectonics broke up into India, Australia, Antarctica, Africa, and South America. [After *Gondwana*, a region of central India, from GOND.]

gone (gôn, gŏn) *v.* Past participle of **go**[1]. **—gone** *adj.* **1.** Past; bygone. **2.** Advanced beyond hope or recall. **3.** Dying or dead. **4.** Ruined; lost: *a gone cause.* **5.** Carried away; absorbed. **6.** Used up; exhausted. **7.** *Slang.* Infatuated: *gone on the girl.* **8.** *Slang.* Pregnant: *is five months gone.*

gon·er (gô′nər, gŏn′ər) *n. Slang.* One that is ruined or doomed. [From GONE.]

gonfalon

gon·fa·lon (gŏn′fə-lŏn′, -lən) *n.* A banner suspended from a crosspiece, especially as a standard in an ecclesiastical procession or as the ensign of a medieval Italian republic. [Italian *gonfalone*, of Germanic origin. See **gʷhen-** in Appendix.]

gon·fa·lon·ier (gŏn′fə-lə-nîr′) *n.* The bearer of a gonfalon. [French, from Italian *gonfaloniere*, from *gonfalone*, gonfalon. See GONFALON.]

gong (gông, gŏng) *n.* **1.** A rimmed metal disk that produces a loud, sonorous tone when struck with a padded mallet. **2.** A usually saucer-shaped bell that is struck with a mechanically operated hammer. **—gong** *intr.v.* **gonged, gong·ing, gongs.** To make the sound of a gong. [Malay *gōng*.]

Gon·gor·ism (gŏng′gə-rĭz′əm) *n.* A florid, ornate literary style, often employing elaborate puns and conceits. [After Luis de *Góngora* y Argote (1561–1627), Spanish poet.] **—Gon′gor·is′tic** (-rĭs′tĭk) *adj.*

go·nid·i·um (gō-nĭd′ē-əm) *n., pl.* **-i·a** (-ē-ə). **1.** An asexually produced reproductive cell, such as a zeospore, found in certain algae. **2.** An algal cell filled with chlorophyll, formed in the thallus of a lichen. [New Latin, from Greek *gonos*, seed, offspring. See GONO–.] **—go·nid′i·al** *adj.*

gon·if (gä′nəf) *n.* Variant of **ganef.**

go·ni·om·e·ter (gō′nē-ŏm′ĭ-tər) *n.* **1.** An optical instrument for measuring crystal angles, as between crystal faces. **2.** A radio receiver and directional antenna used as a system to determine the angular direction of incoming radio signals. [Greek *gōnia*, angle; see **genu-**[1] in Appendix + –METER.] **—go′ni·o·met′ric** (-nē-ə-mĕt′rĭk), **go′ni·o·met′ri·cal** *adj.* **—go′ni·om′e·try** *n.*

go·ni·on (gō′nē-ŏn′) *n.* The outer point on either side of the lower jaw at which the jawbone angles upward. [French, from Greek *gōnia*, angle. See **genu-**[1] in Appendix.]

Gonne (gŏn, gŭn), **Maud.** 1865–1953. Irish patriot and actress. A leader of the Irish independence movement, she was a founder (1906) of Sinn Fein.

goose

gono– or **gon–** *pref.* Sexual; reproductive: *gonophore.* [Greek, from *gonos*, seed, procreation. See **gene-** in Appendix.]

gon·o·coc·cus (gŏn′ə-kŏk′əs) *n., pl.* **-coc·ci** (-kŏk′sī′, -kŏk′ī′). The bacterium *Neisseria gonorrhoeae*, which is the causative agent of gonorrhea. **—gon′o·coc′cal** (-kŏk′əl), **gon′o·coc′cic** (-kŏk′ĭk, -kŏk′sĭk) *adj.*

go-no-go (gō-nō′gō) *adj.* Of, relating to, or involving a mandatory decision to continue or abort a course of action: *a go-no-go launch of the space shuttle.*

gon·o·phore (gŏn′ə-fôr′, -fōr′) *n.* A structure bearing or consisting of a reproductive organ or part, such as a reproductive polyp or bud in a hydroid colony. **—gon′o·pho′ric** (-fôr′ĭk, -fōr′-), **go·noph′o·rous** (gə-nŏf′ər-əs) *adj.*

gon·o·pore (gŏn′ə-pôr′, -pōr′) *n.* A reproductive aperture or pore, especially of certain insects and worms.

gon·or·rhe·a (gŏn′ə-rē′ə) *n.* A sexually transmitted disease caused by gonococcal bacteria that affects the mucous membrane chiefly of the genital and urinary tracts and is characterized by an acute purulent discharge and painful or difficult urination, though women often have no symptoms. [Late Latin, spermatorrhea, from Greek *gonorrhoia* : *gono-*, gono- + *-rhoia*, -rrhea.] **—gon′or·rhe′al, gon′or·rhe′ic** *adj.*

–gony *suff.* Generation; reproduction; manner of origin: *heterogony.* [Latin *-gonia*, from Greek *-goneia*, from *gonos*, offspring. See **gene-** in Appendix.]

gon·zo (gŏn′zō) *adj. Slang.* **1.** Using exaggerated, often highly subjective or self-indulgent style and tending toward bizarre or unconventional subjects, chiefly in journalism: *"a hyperkinetic, gonzo version of Graham Greene"* (New Yorker). **2.** Bizarre; unconventional. [Perhaps Italian, simpleton (perhaps short for *Borgonzone*, Burgundian) or Spanish *ganso*, dullard, goose (of Germanic origin; see **ghans-** in Appendix).]

goo (go͞o) *n. Informal.* **1.** A sticky, wet, viscous substance. **2.** Sentimental drivel. [Perhaps short for BURGOO.]

♦ **goo·ber** (go͞o′bər) *n. Chiefly Southern U.S.* See **peanut** (sense 2). [Of Bantu origin; akin to Kongo or Kimbundu *n-guba*.]

♦ ***REGIONAL NOTE:*** Most Southerners recognize the terms *goober* and *goober pea* as other names for the peanut. *Goober* is related to Kongo or Kimbundu *n-guba*, "peanut." The word is especially interesting as one of a small stock of African language borrowings brought over by slaves. Most of these words have to do with the food items imported from Africa for the slaves to eat. In this category are *gumbo*, "okra," which is of Bantu origin, and *yam*, which is of West African origin. The noun *cooter* is related to the Mandingo word *kuta* and the Tshiluba word *nkudu*, both meaning "turtle." *Cooter* is still used in South Carolina, Georgia, and the Gulf States to denote the edible freshwater turtle of the genus *Chrysemys* and, by extension, other turtles and tortoises.

♦ **goober pea** *n. Chiefly Southern U.S.* See **peanut** (sense 2). See Regional Note at **goober.**

good (go͝od). *Abbr.* **gd., G, G.** *adj.* **bet·ter** (bĕt′ər), **best** (bĕst). **1.** Being positive or desirable in nature; not bad or poor: *a good experience; good news from the hospital.* **2. a.** Having the qualities that are desirable or distinguishing in a particular thing: *a good exterior paint; a good joke.* **b.** Serving the desired purpose or end; suitable: *Is this a good dress for the party?* **3. a.** Not spoiled or ruined: *The milk is still good.* **b.** In excellent condition; sound: *a good tooth.* **4. a.** Superior to the average; satisfactory: *a good student.* **b.** Used formerly to refer to the U.S. Government grade of meat higher than standard and lower than choice. **5. a.** Of high quality: *good books.* **b.** Discriminating: *good taste.* **6.** Worthy of respect; honorable: *ruined the family's good name.* **7.** Attractive; handsome: *good looks.* **8.** Beneficial to health; salutary: *a good night's rest.* **9.** Competent; skilled: *a good machinist.* **10.** Complete; thorough: *a good workout.* **11. a.** Reliable; sure: *a good investment.* **b.** Valid or true: *a good reason.* **c.** Genuine; real: *a good dollar bill.* **12. a.** In effect; operative: *a warranty good for two years; a driver's license that is still good.* **b.** Able to continue in a specified activity: *I'm good for another round of golf.* **13. a.** Able to pay or contribute: *Is she good for the money that you lent her?* **b.** Able to elicit a specified reaction: *He is always good for a laugh.* **14. a.** Ample; substantial: *a good income.* **b.** Bountiful: *a good table.* **15.** Full: *It is a good mile from here.* **16. a.** Pleasant; enjoyable: *had a good time at the party.* **b.** Propitious; favorable: *good weather; a good omen.* **17. a.** Of moral excellence; upright: *a good person.* **b.** Benevolent; kind: *a good soul; a good heart.* **c.** Loyal; staunch: *a good Republican.* **18. a.** Well-behaved; obedient: *a good child.* **b.** Socially correct; proper: *good manners.* **19.** *Sports.* Having landed within bounds or within a particular area of a court: *The first serve was wide, but the second was good.* **20.** Used to form exclamatory phrases expressing surprise or dismay: *Good heavens! Good grief!* **—good** *n.* **1. a.** Something that is good. **b.** A good, valuable, or useful part or aspect. **2.** Welfare; benefit: *for the common good.* **3.** Goodness; virtue: *There is much good to be found in people.* **4. goods. a.** Commodities; wares: *frozen goods.* **b.** Portable personal property. **c.** *(used with a sing. or pl. verb).* Fabric; material. **5. goods.** *Slang.* Incriminating information or evidence: *tried to get the goods on the crook.* **—good** *adv. Informal.* Well. **—*idioms.* as good as.** Practically; nearly: *as good as new.* **for good.** Permanently; forever: *I'm moving to Europe for good.* **good and.** *Informal.* Very; thoroughly: *I'll do it when I'm good and ready.* **no good.** *Informal.* **1.** Worthless. **2.** Futile; useless: *It's no good arguing with them.* **to the good. 1.** For the best; advantageous. **2.** In an advantageous financial position: *ended up to the good.* [Middle English, from Old English *gōd*. See **ghedh-** in Appendix.]

USAGE NOTE: *Good* is properly used as an adjective with linking verbs such as *be, seem,* or *appear: The future looks good. The soup tastes good.* It should not be used as an adverb with other verbs: *The car runs well* (not *good*). Thus, *The dress fits well and looks good.* See Usage Note at **well**[2]**.**

Good Book (go͝od) *n.* The Bible.

good-bye or **good·bye** also **good-by** (go͝od-bī′) *—interj.* Used to express farewell. *—n., pl.* **-byes** also **-bys.** An expression of farewell. [Alteration (influenced by *good day*) of *God be with you*.]

WORD HISTORY: More than one reader has no doubt wondered exactly how *good-bye* is derived from the phrase "God be with you." To understand this, it is helpful to see earlier forms of the expression, such as *God be wy you, b'w'y, godbwye, god buy' ye,* and *good-b'wy.* It is no mistake to think that the first word of the expression is now *good* and not *God,* for *good* replaced *God* by analogy with such expressions as *good day,* perhaps after people no longer had a clear idea of the original sense of the expression. A letter of 1573 written by Gabriel Harvey contains the first recorded use of *good-bye*: "To requite your gallonde [gallon] of *godbwyes,* I regive you a pottle of howdyes," recalling another contraction that is still used.

good faith *n.* Compliance with standards of decency and honesty: *bargained in good faith.*

good-fel·low·ship (go͝od′fĕl′ō-shĭp′) *n.* Pleasant sociability; comradeship.

good-for-noth·ing (go͝od′fər-nŭth′ĭng) *n.* A person of little worth or usefulness. **—good-for-nothing** *adj.* Having little worth; useless.

Good Friday *n.* The Friday before Easter, observed by Christians in commemoration of the crucifixion of Jesus.

ă pat	oi boy
ā pay	ou out
âr care	o͝o took
ä father	o͞o boot
ĕ pet	ŭ cut
ē be	ûr urge
ĭ pit	th thin
ī pie	*th* this
îr pier	hw which
ŏ pot	zh vision
ō toe	ə about, item
ô paw	♦ regionalism

Stress marks: ′ (primary); ′ (secondary), as in **dictionary** (dĭk′shə-nĕr′ē)

good·heart·ed (go͝od′här′tĭd) *adj.* Kind and generous. **—good′heart′ed·ly** *adv.* **—good′heart′ed·ness** *n.*

Good Hope (go͝od′ hōp′), **Cape of.** A promontory on the southwest coast of South Africa south of Cape Town. It was first circumnavigated in 1488 by Bartolomeu Dias.

good-hu·mored (go͝od′hyo͞o′mərd) *adj.* Cheerful; amiable. **—good′-hu′mored·ly** *adv.* **—good′-hu′mored·ness** *n.*

good·ie (go͝od′ē) *n.* Variant of **goody** [1].

good·ish (go͝od′ĭsh) *adj.* **1.** Somewhat good. **2.** Somewhat large or big; goodly.

good-look·ing (go͝od′lo͝ok′ĭng) *adj.* Of a pleasing or attractive appearance; handsome.

good·ly (go͝od′lē) *adj.* **-li·er, -li·est. 1.** Of pleasing appearance; comely. **2.** Somewhat large; considerable: *a goodly sum.* **—good′li·ness** *n.*

good·man (go͝od′mən) *n. Archaic.* **1.a.** The male head of a household. **b.** A husband. **2. Goodman.** Used formerly as a courtesy title before the surname of a man not of noble birth.

Goodman, Benjamin David. Called "Benny." Known as "the King of Swing." 1909–1986. American clarinetist whose band, formed in 1934, introduced swing, a style of jazz that was greatly popular in the 1930's and 1940's.

good nature *n.* A cheerful, obliging disposition.

good-na·tured (go͝od′nā′chərd) *adj.* Having an easygoing, cheerful disposition. See Synonyms at **amiable. —good′-na′tured·ly** *adv.* **—good′-na′tured·ness** *n.*

good·ness (go͝od′nĭs) *n.* **1.** The state or quality of being good. **2.** The beneficial or nutritious part. **—goodness** *interj.* Used to express mild surprise.

good offices *pl.n.* Beneficial acts performed for another, especially acts performed by a mediator in a dispute.

good old boy also **good ol′ boy** or **good ole boy** (ōl) *n. Slang.* A man who follows the stereotypical behavior of his peers, especially one who embodies the revelry, camaraderie, or bigotry regarded as typical of some white men of the rural southern United States.

Good Samaritan *n.* A compassionate person who unselfishly helps others. [After the passerby in the New Testament parable who was the only person to aid a man who had been beaten and robbed (Luke 10:30–37).]

good-sized (go͝od′sīzd′) *adj.* Of a fairly large size.

good-tem·pered (go͝od′tĕm′pərd) *adj.* Having an even temper; not easily irritated. **—good′-tem′pered·ly** *adv.* **—good′-tem′pered·ness** *n.*

good·wife (go͝od′wīf′) *n. Archaic.* **1.** The female head of a household. **2. Goodwife.** Used formerly as a courtesy title before the surname of a married woman not of noble birth.

good·will also **good will** (go͝od′wĭl′) *n.* **1.** An attitude of kindness or friendliness; benevolence. **2.** Cheerful acquiescence or willingness. **3.** A good relationship, as of a business enterprise with its customers or a nation with other nations.

Good·win Sands (go͝od′wĭn). A stretch of dangerous shoals in the Strait of Dover off the southeast coast of England.

good·y [1] (go͝od′ē) *Informal. interj.* Used to express delight. **—goody** also **good·ie** *n., pl.* **-ies.** Something attractive or delectable, especially something sweet to eat.

good·y [2] (go͝od′ē) *n., pl.* **good·ies.** *Archaic.* A goodwife. [Short for GOODWIFE.]

Good·year (go͝od′yîr′), **Charles.** 1800–1860. American inventor who developed vulcanized rubber (1839).

good·y-good·y (go͝od′ē-go͝od′ē) *adj.* Affectedly sweet, good, or virtuous. **—goody-goody** *n., pl.* **-ies.** One who is affectedly sweet, good, or virtuous.

goody two-shoes (to͞o′sho͞oz′) *n., pl.* **goody two-shoes.** *Informal.* A goody-goody. [After the title character in *The History of Little Goody Two-Shoes*, a nursery tale perhaps by Oliver Goldsmith.]

goo·ey (go͞o′ē) *adj.* **-i·er, -i·est.** Sticky and viscous.

goof (go͞of) *Slang. n.* **1.** An incompetent, foolish, or stupid person. **2.** A careless mistake; a slip. **—goof** *v.* **goofed, goof·ing, goofs.** *—intr.* **1.** To make a silly mistake; blunder. **2.** To waste or kill time. *—tr.* To spoil, as through clumsiness; bungle: *goof up a job.* [Possibly alteration of dialectal *goff*, fool, from obsolete French *goffe*, stupid.]

goof·ball or **goof ball** (go͞of′bôl′) *Slang.—n.* **1.** A foolish, incompetent, or stupid person. **2.** A barbiturate or tranquilizer in the form of a pill, especially when taken for nonmedical purposes. *—adj.* Silly or outlandish: *"Underneath his goofball braggadocio lies a kind of purity"* (David Ansen).

goof-off (go͞of′ôf′, -ŏf′) *n. Slang.* One who shirks work or responsibility.

goof·proof (go͞of′pro͞of′) *adj. Slang.* Protected against mistakes: *a goofproof recipe.*

goof·y (go͞o′fē) *adj.* **-i·er, -i·est.** *Slang.* Silly; ridiculous: *a goofy hat.* **—goof′i·ly** *adv.* **—goof′i·ness** *n.*

goo·gol (go͞o′gôl′) *n.* The number 10 raised to the power 100 (10^{100}), written out as the numeral 1 followed by 100 zeros. [Coined at the age of nine by Milton Sirotta, nephew of Edward Kasner (1878–1955), American mathematician.]

goo·gol·plex (go͞o′gôl-plĕks′) *n.* The number 10 raised to the power googol, written out as the numeral 1 followed by 10^{100} zeros. [GOOGOL + *-plex*, as in DUPLEX.]

goo-goo (go͞o′go͞o′) *adj. Slang.* Amorous, often humorously so: *made goo-goo eyes at her.* [Perhaps alteration of GOGGLE.]

gook [1] (go͝ok, go͞ok) *n.* Variant of **guck.**

gook [2] (go͞ok) *n. Offensive Slang.* **1.** Used as a disparaging term for an Asian person. **2.** Used as a disparaging term for a North Vietnamese soldier or guerrilla in the Vietnam War. [Origin unknown.]

goom·bah (go͞om′bä, go͞om′-) *n. Slang.* A companion or an associate, especially an older friend who acts as a patron, a protector, or an adviser. [Origin unknown.]

goon (go͞on) *n. Slang.* **1.** A thug hired to intimidate or harm opponents. **2.** A stupid or oafish person. [Probably ultimately short for GOONEY, simpleton.]

goo·ney also **goo·ny** (go͞o′nē) *n., pl.* **-neys** also **-nies.** An albatross, especially the black-footed albatross. Also called *gooney bird.* [Origin unknown.]

goop (go͞op) *n. Slang.* A sticky, wet, viscous substance. [Perhaps alteration of GOO.] **—goop′y** *adj.*

goos·an·der (go͞o-săn′dər) *n. Chiefly British.* A fish-eating duck *(Mergus merganser)*, the male of which has a glossy greenish-black head and a white body. [Origin unknown.]

goose (go͞os) *n., pl.* **geese** (gēs). **1.a.** Any of various wild or domesticated water birds of the family Anatidae, and especially of the genera *Anser* and *Branta*, characteristically having a shorter neck than that of a swan and a shorter, more pointed bill than that of a duck. **b.** The female of such a bird. **c.** The flesh of such a bird used as food. **2.** *Informal.* A silly person. **3.** *pl.* **goos·es.** A tailor's pressing iron with a long curved handle. **4.** *Slang.* A poke, prod, or pinch between or on the buttocks. **—goose** *tr.v.* **goosed, goos·ing, goos·es.** *Slang.* **1.** To poke, prod, or pinch (a person) between or on the buttocks. **2.** To move to action, spur: *"The pilot goosed his craft, powering away"* (Nicholas Proffitt). [Middle English *goos*, from Old English *gōs*. See **ghans-** in Appendix.]

goose barnacle *n.* Any of various barnacles of the genus *Lapas*, having a fleshy stalk that attaches to rocks or floating objects such as ship hulls. Also called *gooseneck barnacle.*

goose·ber·ry (go͞os′bĕr′ē, -bə-rē, go͞oz′-) *n.* **1.a.** A spiny European shrub *(Ribes uva-crispa)*, having lobed leaves, greenish flowers, and edible greenish to yellow or red berries. **b.** The fruit of this plant. **2.** Any of several plants bearing similar fruit.

gooseberry gourd *n.* See **gherkin** (sense 1b).

goose bumps *pl.n.* Momentary roughness of the skin caused by erection of the papillae in response to cold or fear. Also called *goose flesh, goose pimples.*

Goose Creek (go͞os). A city of southeast South Carolina, a suburb of Charleston. Population, 17,811.

goose egg *n. Slang.* Zero, especially when written as a numeral to indicate that no points have been scored.

goose·fish (go͞os′fĭsh′) *n., pl.* **goosefish** or **-fish·es.** Any of several anglerfishes of the genus *Lophius*, such as *L. americanus* of North American Atlantic waters. Also called *monkfish.*

goose flesh *n.* See **goose bumps.**

goose·foot (go͞os′fo͝ot′) *n., pl.* **-foots.** Any of various weeds of the genus *Chenopodium*, having small greenish flowers. [From the shape of its leaves.]

goose grass *n.* **1.** See **silverweed. 2.** See **yard grass.**

goose·neck (go͞os′nĕk′) *n.* A slender, curved object or part, such as the flexible shaft of a type of desk lamp. **—goose′-necked′** *adj.*

gooseneck barnacle *n.* See **goose barnacle.**

goose pimples *pl.n.* See **goose bumps.**

goose step *n.* A military parade step executed by swinging the legs sharply from the hips and keeping the knees locked.

goose-step (go͞os′stĕp′) *intr.v.* **-stepped, -step·ping, -steps.** To march in such a way that the legs swing sharply from the hips and the knees are locked.

goos·y also **goos·ey** (go͞o′sē) *adj.* **-i·er, -i·est. 1.** Relating to or resembling a goose. **2.** Foolish or scatterbrained.

GOP or **G.O.P.** *abbr.* Grand Old Party.

go·pher (gō′fər) *n.* **1.** Any of various short-tailed, burrowing rodents of the family Geomyidae of North America, having furlined external cheek pouches. Also called *pocket gopher.* **2.** Any of various ground squirrels of the genus *Citellus* of North American prairies. **3.** Any of several burrowing tortoises of the genus *Gopherus*, especially *G. polyphemus* of the southeast United States. [Probably short for earlier *megopher*, gopher tortoise, of unknown origin.]

gopher ball *n. Baseball.* A pitched ball that is hit for a home run. [Origin unknown.]

gopher snake *n.* See **bull snake.**

Go·rakh·pur (gôr′ək-po͝or′, gōr′-). A city of northern India east of Lucknow. It was founded c. 1400. Population, 290,814.

Gor·ba·chev (gôr′bə-chôf′, -chŏf′, gər-bə-chôf′), **Mikhail Sergeyevich.** Born 1931. Soviet politician who served as general secretary of the Communist Party (1985–1991) and became president of the U.S.S.R. in 1989. He won the 1990 Nobel Peace Prize.

Gor·di·an knot (gôr′dē-ən) *n.* **1.** An exceedingly complicated problem or deadlock. **2.** An intricate knot tied by King

gooseberry
Ribes uva-crispa

goose step

Mikhail Gorbachev
Photographed in 1987

gorge
Royal Gorge, near Canon City, Colorado

Gordius of Phrygia and cut by Alexander the Great with his sword after hearing an oracle promise that whoever could undo it would be the next ruler of Asia.

Gor·don (gôr′dn), **Charles George.** Known as "Chinese Gordon." 1833–1885. British army officer who took part in the capture of Peking (Beijing) in 1860 and commanded the Chinese force that quashed the Taiping Rebellion (1863–1864).

Gordon setter *n.* A medium-sized hunting dog of a breed originating in Scotland, and having a silky black-and-tan coat. [After Alexander, Fourth Duke of *Gordon* (1745?–1827), Scottish hunter.]

gore¹ (gôr) *tr.v.* **gored, gor·ing, gores.** To pierce or stab with a horn or tusk. [Middle English *goren,* probably from *gore,* spear, from Old English *gār.*]

gore² (gôr) *n.* **1.** A triangular or tapering piece of cloth forming a part of something, as in a skirt or sail. **2.** A small triangular piece of land. **—gore** *tr.v.* **gored, gor·ing, gores. 1.** To provide with a gore. **2.** To cut into a gore. [Middle English, from Old English *gāra,* triangular piece of land.]

gore³ (gôr) *n.* Blood, especially coagulated blood from a wound. [Middle English, filth, from Old English *gor.*]

Gore-Tex (gôr′tĕks). A trademark used for a water-repellant, breathable laminated fabric used primarily in outerwear and shoes.

Gor·gas (gôr′gəs), **William Crawford.** 1854–1920. American army surgeon who suppressed yellow fever in Havana (1898) and the Panama Canal Zone (1904–1913).

gorge (gôrj) *n.* **1.** A deep, narrow passage with steep rocky sides; a ravine. **2.** A narrow entrance into the outwork of a fortification. **3.** The throat; the gullet. **4.** The crop of a hawk. **5.** An instance of gluttonous eating. **6.** The contents of the stomach; something swallowed. **7.** A mass obstructing a narrow passage: *a shipping lane blocked by an ice gorge.* **—gorge** *v.* **gorged, gorg·ing, gorg·es.** *—tr.* **1.** To stuff with food; glut: *gorged themselves with candy.* See Synonyms at **satiate. 2.** To devour greedily. *—intr.* To eat gluttonously. [Middle English, throat, from Old French, from Late Latin *gurga,* perhaps from Latin *gurges,* whirlpool, abyss.] **—gorg′er** *n.*

Gorgon

gor·geous (gôr′jəs) *adj.* **1.a.** Dazzlingly beautiful or magnificent: *wore a gorgeous Victorian gown.* **b.** Characterized by magnificence or virtuosic brilliance: *the pianist's gorgeous technique.* **2.** *Informal.* Wonderful; delightful. [Middle English *gorgeouse,* probably from Old French *gorgias,* jewelry-loving, elegant, from *gorge,* throat. See GORGE.] **—gor′geous·ly** *adv.* **—gor′geous·ness** *n.*

gor·ger·in (gôr′jər-ĭn) *n. Architecture.* The necking of a column. [French, from Old French, from *gorge,* throat. See GORGE.]

gor·get (gôr′jĭt) *n.* **1.** A piece of armor protecting the throat. **2.** An ornamental collar. **3.** The scarflike part of a wimple covering the neck and shoulders. **4.** A band or patch of distinctive color on the throat of an animal, especially an area of brightly colored feathers on the throat of a bird. [Middle English, from Old French *gorgete,* diminutive of *gorge,* throat. See GORGE.]

Gor·gon (gôr′gən) *n.* **1.** *Greek Mythology.* Any of the three sisters Stheno, Euryale, and the mortal Medusa who had snakes for hair and eyes that if looked into turned the beholder into stone. **2. gorgon.** A woman regarded as ugly or terrifying. [Middle English, from Latin *Gorgō, Gorgon-,* from Greek, from *gorgos,* terrible.] **—Gor·go′ni·an** (-gō′nē-ən) *adj.*

gor·go·ni·an (gôr-gō′nē-ən) *n.* Any of various corals of the order Gorgonacea, having a flexible, often branching skeleton of horny material. **—gorgonian** *adj.* Of or belonging to the order Gorgonacea. [From Latin *gorgonia,* coral, from *Gorgō, Gorgon-,* Gorgon. See GORGON.]

gor·gon·ize (gôr′gə-nīz′) *tr.v.* **-ized, -iz·ing, -iz·es.** To have a paralyzing or stupefying effect on.

Gor·gon·zo·la (gôr′gən-zō′lə) *n.* A pungent, blue-veined, pressed Italian cheese made of cow's milk. [After *Gorgonzola,* a town of northern Italy.]

gorilla
Endangered mountain gorilla
Gorilla beringei

go·ril·la (gə-rĭl′ə) *n.* **1.** The largest of the anthropoid apes *(Gorilla gorilla)* native to the forests of equatorial Africa, having a stocky body and coarse, dark brown or black hair. **2.** *Slang.* **a.** A brutish man. **b.** A thug. [New Latin, from Greek *Gorillai,* a tribe of hairy women, perhaps of African origin.]

WORD HISTORY: Two traditions of exploration come together in the history of the word *gorilla,* which also illustrates how knowledge of the classics has influenced scientific terminology. Dr. Thomas S. Savage, an American missionary to western Africa, first described the gorilla in 1847, giving it the New Latin name *Troglodytes gorilla.* In doing so he was using his knowledge of Greek literature, in which there exists a fourth-century B.C. translation of a report written by Hanno, another visitor to western Africa. This Carthaginian navigator, who voyaged before 480 B.C., went as far as Sierra Leone in his explorations. In the Greek translation of his report he tells of seeing *Gorillai,* the name of which he allegedly learned from local informants and which he thought were members of a tribe of hairy women. In fact they were probably the same creatures that Thomas Savage described about 24 centuries later.

goshawk
Northern goshawk
Accipiter gentilis

Gö·ring also **Goe·ring** (gĕr′ĭng, gûr′-, gœ′rĭng), **Hermann Wilhelm.** 1893–1946. German Nazi politician and military leader who was responsible for the buildup of German air forces, directed the German wartime economy, and was named Hitler's successor (1939). Severely criticized for Germany's military decline, he lost favor with Hitler and was stripped of his command (1943).

Gor·ki (gôr′kē), **Maksim.** See Maksim **Gorky.**

Gor·ky or **Gor·ki** (gôr′kē). Formerly **Nizh·ny Nov·go·rod** (nĭzh′nē nŏv′gə-rŏd′, nyē′zhnē nôv′gə-rət). A city of western Russia on the Volga River west of Kazan. Founded as a frontier post in 1221, it was formerly famous for its trade fairs. Population, 1,399,000.

Gorky, Arshile. 1904–1948. Armenian-born American painter considered a transitional figure between surrealism and abstract expressionism.

Gorky also **Gor·ki** (gôr′kē), **Maksim** also **Maxim.** Pen name of Aleksei Maksimovich Peshkov. 1868–1936. Russian writer who supported the Bolshevik Revolution of 1917 and helped develop socialist realism as the officially accepted literary aesthetic.

Gör·litz (gûr′lĭts′, gœr′-). A city of east-central Germany east of Dresden on the Polish border. It was founded c. 1200 and grew as a cloth-weaving center. Population, 80,216.

Gor·lov·ka (gôr-lôf′kə, gôr′ləf-kə). A city of southeast Ukraine in the Donets Basin north of Donetsk. It is a major coal-mining and industrial center. Population, 342,000.

♦ **gorm** (gôrm) *n. Upper Southern U.S.* Variant of **gaum.**

gor·mand·ize (gôr′mən-dīz′) *v.* **-ized, -iz·ing, -iz·es.** *—intr.* To eat gluttonously; gorge. *—tr.* To devour (food) gluttonously. [From GOURMANDISE, gluttony (obsolete).] **—gor′mand·iz′er** *n.*

gorm·less (gôrm′lĭs) *adj. Chiefly British.* Lacking intelligence and vitality; dull. [From dialectal *gawm,* sense, from Middle English *gome,* notice, from Old Norse *gaumr.*]

go-round (gō′round′) *n.* An argument; a go-around.

gorp (gôrp) *n.* A mixture of high-energy foods, such as dried fruit, nuts, and seeds, eaten especially as a snack. [Origin unknown.]

gorse (gôrs) *n.* Any of several spiny shrubs of the genus *Ulex,* especially *U. europaeus,* native to Europe and having fragrant yellow flowers and black pods. Also called *furze, whin.* [Middle English *gorst, gors,* from Old English.]

go·ry (gôr′ē, gōr′ē) *adj.* **-ri·er, -ri·est. 1.** Covered or stained with gore; bloody. **2.** Full of or characterized by bloodshed and violence. See Synonyms at **bloody. —gor′i·ly** *adv.* **—gor′i·ness** *n.*

gosh (gŏsh) *interj.* Used to express mild surprise or delight. [Alteration of GOD.]

gos·hawk (gŏs′hôk′) *n.* **1.** A large, powerful hawk *(Accipiter gentilis)* having broad, rounded wings, a long tail, and gray or brownish plumage. **2.** Any of several similar or related hawks. [Middle English *goshauk,* from Old English *gōshafoc* : *gōs,* goose; see GOOSE + *hafoc,* hawk; see HAWK¹.]

Go·shen (gō′shən). **1.** A region of ancient Egypt on the eastern delta of the Nile River. According to the Old Testament, it was inhabited by the Israelites from the time of Jacob until the Exodus. **2.** A city of northern Indiana east-southeast of South Bend. It is a manufacturing center. Population, 19,665.

Go·siute (gō′sho͞ot) *n., pl.* **Gosiute** or **-siutes. 1.a.** A Native American people inhabiting an area southwest of Great Salt Lake. **b.** A member of this people. **2.** The Uto-Aztecan language of this people, a dialect of Shoshone.

gos·ling (gŏz′lĭng) *n.* **1.** A young goose. **2.** A naive or inexperienced young person. [Middle English, variant (influenced by *gos,* goose; see GOOSE) of *gesling,* from Old Norse *gæslingr,* diminutive of *gās.* See **ghans-** in Appendix.]

go-slow (gō′slō′) *adj. Informal.* Deliberate and careful, as in behavior or viewpoint: *"a go-slow effort to maintain a sense of continuity and order"* (Christian Science Monitor).

gos·pel (gŏs′pəl) *n.* **1.** Often **Gospel.** The proclamation of the redemption preached by Jesus and the Apostles, which is the central content of Christian revelation. **2.a. Gospel.** *Bible.* One of the first four books of the New Testament, describing the life, death, and resurrection of Jesus and recording his teaching. **b.** A similar narrative. **3.** Often **Gospel.** A lection from any of the first four books of the New Testament included as part of a religious service. **4.** A teaching or doctrine of a religious teacher. **5.** *Music.* Gospel music. **6.** Something, such as an idea or a principle, accepted as unquestionably true: *The teacher said it, and that made it gospel.* *—attributive.* Often used to modify another noun: *a gospel meeting; a gospel singer.* [Middle English, from Old English *gōdspel* (ultimately translation of Greek *euangelion;* see EVANGEL) : *gōd,* good; see GOOD + *spel,* news.]

gos·pel·er also **gos·pel·ler** (gŏs′pə-lər) *n.* **1.** One who teaches or professes faith in a gospel. **2.** One who reads or sings the Gospel as part of a church service.

gospel music *n. Music.* A kind of distinctively American religious music that is associated with evangelism and is based on the simple melodies of folk music blended with melodic and rhythmic elements of spirituals and jazz.

gospel side also **Gospel side** *n.* The left side of an altar or a chancel as the congregation faces it. [So called from the practice in some churches of reading the Gospel and the Epistle from different sides.]

gos·port (gŏs′pôrt′, -pōrt′) *n.* A flexible speaking tube used for one-way communication between individual compartments or cockpits of an airplane. [After GOSPORT.]

Gos·port (gŏs′pôrt′, -pōrt′). A municipal borough of southern England west of Portsmouth. Formerly a victualing station for the Royal Navy, it was an embarkation point for the invasion of France in 1944. Population, 77,400.

gos·sa·mer (gŏs′ə-mər) *n.* **1.** A soft, sheer, gauzy fabric. **2.** Something delicate, light, or flimsy. **3.** A fine film of cobwebs often seen floating in the air or caught on bushes or grass. **—gossamer** *adj.* Sheer, light, delicate, or tenuous. See Synonyms at **airy.** [Middle English *gossomer* : *gos,* goose; see GOOSE + *somer,* summer (probably from the abundance of gossamer during early autumn when geese are in season); see SUMMER[1].] **—gos′sa·mer·y** *adj.*

gos·sip (gŏs′əp) *n.* **1.** Rumor or talk of a personal, sensational, or intimate nature. **2.** A person who habitually spreads intimate or private rumors or facts. **3.** Trivial, chatty talk or writing. **4.** A close friend or companion. **5.** *Chiefly British.* A godparent. **—gossip** *intr.v.* **-siped, -sip·ing, -sips.** To engage in or spread gossip. [Middle English *godsib, gossip,* godparent, from Old English *godsibb* : *god,* god; see GOD + *sibb,* kinsman; see **s(w)e-** in Appendix.] **—gos′sip·er** *n.* **—gos′sip·ry** *n.* **—gos′sip·y** *adj.*

SYNONYMS: *gossip, blab, tattle.* The central meaning shared by these verbs is "to engage in or communicate idle, indiscreet talk": *gossiping about the neighbors' domestic problems; can't be trusted with a secret—he always blabs; is disliked by her classmates for tattling on mischief makers.*

gos·sip·mon·ger (gŏs′əp-mŭng′gər, -mŏng′-) *n.* One who relates gossip.

gos·sy·pol (gŏs′ə-pôl′, -pōl′, -pŏl′) *n.* A toxic pigment, $C_{30}H_{30}O_8$, obtained from cottonseed oil and detoxified by heating, that has been experimentally shown to inhibit sperm production. [New Latin *Gossypium,* genus name (from Latin *gossypion,* cotton plant) + -OL[1].]

got (gŏt) *v.* Past tense and a past participle of **get.**

Gö·ta Canal (yœ′tə). A system of rivers, lakes, and canals of southern Sweden extending from the Kattegat at the mouth of the **Göta River,** about 93 km (58 mi) long, to the Baltic Sea.

Gö·te·borg (yœ′tə-bôr′ē). A city of southwest Sweden on the Kattegat at the starting point of the Göta Canal system. Founded in 1604, it is a major port. Population, 424,085.

Goth (gŏth) *n.* A member of a Germanic people who invaded the Roman Empire in the early centuries of the Christian era. [From Middle English *Gothes,* Goths, from Late Latin *Gothī* (of Germanic origin) and from Old English *Gotan.*]

Goth. *abbr.* Gothic.

Go·tha (gō′thə, -tä). A city of central Germany west of Erfurt. First mentioned in the tenth century, it is an industrial and cultural center. The *Almanach de Gotha,* a record of Europe's aristocratic and royal houses, was first published here in 1763. Population, 57,662.

Goth·am (gŏth′əm). New York City. The nickname was popularized by Washington Irving and others in *Salmagundi,* a series of satirical sketches (1807–1808). **—Goth′am·ite′** (-ə-mīt′) *n.*

Goth·ic (gŏth′ĭk) *adj. Abbr.* **Goth. 1.a.** Of or relating to the Goths or their language. **b.** Germanic; Teutonic. **2.** Of or relating to the Middle Ages; medieval. **3.a.** Of or relating to an architectural style prevalent in western Europe from the 12th through the 15th century and characterized by pointed arches, rib vaulting, and flying buttresses. **b.** Of or relating to an architectural style derived from medieval Gothic. **4.** Of or relating to painting, sculpture, or other art forms prevalent in northern Europe from the 12th through the 15th century. **5.** Often **gothic.** Of or relating to a style of fiction that emphasizes the grotesque, mysterious, and desolate. **6. gothic.** Barbarous; crude. **—Gothic** *n.* **1.** The extinct East Germanic language of the Goths. **2.** Gothic art or architecture. **3.** Often **gothic.** *Printing.* **a.** See **black letter. b.** See **sans serif. 4.** A novel in a style emphasizing the grotesque, mysterious, and desolate. **—Goth′i·cal·ly** *adv.*

WORD HISTORY: The combination *Gothic romance* represents a union of two of the major influences in the development of European culture, the Roman Empire and the Germanic tribes that invaded it. The Roman origins of *romance* must be sought in the etymology of that word, but we can see clearly that *Gothic* is related to the name *Goth* used for one of the Germanic tribes that invaded the Roman Empire. The word *Gothic,* which is first recorded in 1611 in a reference to the language of the Goths, was extended in sense in several ways, meaning "Germanic," "medieval, not classical," "barbarous," and also an architectural style that was not Greek or Roman. *Gothic,* originally in the sense "medieval, not classical," was applied by Horace Walpole to his novel *The Castle of Otranto, a Gothic Story,* published in 1765. From this novel, filled with scenes of terror and gloom in a medieval setting, have descended the Gothic romances of today.

Gothic arch *n.* A pointed arch, especially one with a jointed apex.

Goth·i·cism (gŏth′ĭ-sĭz′əm) *n.* **1.** The use or imitation of Gothic style, as in architecture. **2.** A barbarous or crude manner or style.

Goth·i·cize also **goth·i·cize** (gŏth′ĭ-sīz′) *tr.v.* **-cized, -ciz·ing, -ciz·es.** To make Gothic.

Got·land (gŏt′lənd, gôt′lŭnd). A region of southeast Sweden comprising several islands in the Baltic Sea, including **Gotland Island.** Inhabited since the Stone Age, Gotland is the traditional homeland of the Goths.

got·ten (gŏt′n) *v.* A past participle of **get.**

göt·ter·däm·mer·ung or **Göt·ter·däm·mer·ung** (gŏt′ər-dăm′ə-rŭng′, gœt′ər-dĕm′ə-ro͝ong′) *n.* A turbulent ending of a regime or an institution: *"The nation had been flirting with forms of götterdämmerung, with extremes of vocabulary and behavior and an appetite for violent resolution"* (Lance Morrow). [After *Götterdämmerung,* an opera by Richard Wagner : German *Götter-,* genitive pl. of *Gott,* god (from Middle High German *got,* from Old High German; see **gheu(ə)-** in Appendix) + German *Dämmerung,* twilight (from Middle High German *dëmerunge,* from Old High German *demerunga,* from *demar,* twilight).]

Göt·tin·gen (gœt′ĭng-ən). A city of central Germany northeast of Kassel. Chartered in 1210, the city is noted for its university, founded in the 1730's. Population, 132,454.

Gott·schalk (gŏch′ôk′, gŏt′shôk′), **Louis Moreau.** 1829–1869. American composer and pianist whose compositions often incorporate Black and Creole rhythms.

gouache (gwäsh, go͞o-äsh′) *n.* **1.a.** A method of painting with opaque water colors mixed with a preparation of gum. **b.** An opaque pigment used when painting in this way. **2.** A painting executed in this manner. [French, from Italian *guazzo,* from Latin *aquātiō,* watering, from *aquātus,* past participle of *aquārī,* to fetch water, from *aqua,* water. See **akʷ-ā-** in Appendix.]

Gou·da[1] (gou′də, go͞o′-, KHOU′dä). A city of western Netherlands northeast of Rotterdam. Chartered in 1272, it is noted for its cheese market. Population, 60,026.

Gou·da[2] (go͞o′də, gou′-) *n.* A mild, close-textured, pale yellow cheese made from whole or partially skimmed milk. [After GOUDA[1].]

Gou·dy (gou′dē), **Frederic William.** 1865–1947. American printer and designer of more than 90 typefaces.

gouge (gouj) *n.* **1.** A chisel with a rounded, troughlike blade. **2.a.** A scooping or digging action, as with such a chisel. **b.** A groove or hole scooped with or as if with such a chisel. **3.** *Informal.* A large amount, as of money, exacted or extorted. **—gouge** *tr.v.* **gouged, goug·ing, goug·es. 1.** To cut or scoop out with or as if with a gouge: *"He began to gouge a small pattern in the sand with his cane"* (Vladimir Nabokov). **2.a.** To force out the eye of (a person) with one's thumb. **b.** To thrust one's thumb into the eye of. **3.** *Informal.* To extort from. **4.** *Slang.* To swindle. [Middle English, from Old French, from Late Latin *gubia,* variant of *gulbia,* of Celtic origin.] **—goug′er** *n.*

gou·lash (go͞o′läsh′, -lăsh′) *n.* A stew of beef or veal and vegetables, seasoned mainly with paprika. [Hungarian *gulyás (hús),* herdsman's (meat), goulash, from *gulya,* herdsman.]

Gould (go͞old), **Jay.** 1836–1892. American financier and speculator who with James Fisk and Daniel Drew wrested control of the Erie Railroad from Cornelius Vanderbilt (1867–1868). With Fisk, he caused the financial panic of September 24, 1869, with an attempt to corner the gold market.

Gou·nod (go͞o′nō, go͞o-nō′), **Charles François.** 1818–1893. French composer particularly noted for his ecclesiastical music and the operas *Faust* (1859) and *Romeo and Juliet* (1867).

gou·ra·mi (go͞o-rä′mē, go͝or′ə-) *n., pl.* **-mis.** Any of various freshwater fishes of the family Anabantidae of southeast Asia, capable of breathing air and popular in home aquariums. [Malay *gurami,* carp, of Javanese origin.]

gourd (gôrd, gōrd, go͝ord) *n.* **1.** Any of several trailing or climbing plants related to the pumpkin, squash, and cucumber and bearing fruits with a hard rind. **2.a.** The fruit of such a plant, often of irregular and unusual shape. **b.** The dried and hollowed-out shell of one of these fruits, often used as a drinking utensil. [Middle English *gourde,* from Anglo-Norman, ultimately from Latin *cucurbita.*]

gourde (go͝ord) *n. Abbr.* **g., G.** See table at **currency.** [Haitian, from feminine of French *gourd,* dull, from Late Latin *gurdus,* blunt, from Latin, dullard.]

gour·mand (go͝or-mänd′, go͝or′mənd) *n.* **1.** A lover of good food. **2.** A gluttonous eater. See Usage Note at **gourmet.** [Middle English *gourmant,* glutton, from Old French *gormant.*]

gour·man·dise (go͝or′mən-dēz′) *n.* A taste and relish for good food: *"You could see the gourmandise shining on his rosy lips"* (Glenway Wescott). [Middle English *gromandise,* gluttony, from Old French *gormandise,* from *gormant,* glutton.]

gour·met (go͝or-mā′, go͝or′mā′) *n.* A connoisseur of fine food and drink. *—attributive.* Often used to modify another noun: *gourmet cooking; gourmet restaurants.* [French, from Old French, alteration (influenced by *gourmand,* glutton; see GOURMAND) of *groumet,* servant, valet in charge of wines, from Middle English *grom,* boy, valet.]

USAGE NOTE: A *gourmet* is a person with discriminating taste in food and wine, as is a *gourmand. Gourmand* can also mean one who enjoys food in great quantities. An *epicure* is much the same as a *gourmet,* but the word may sometimes carry overtones of excessive refinement.

Gothic
Cathedral of Notre Dame, Rheims, France

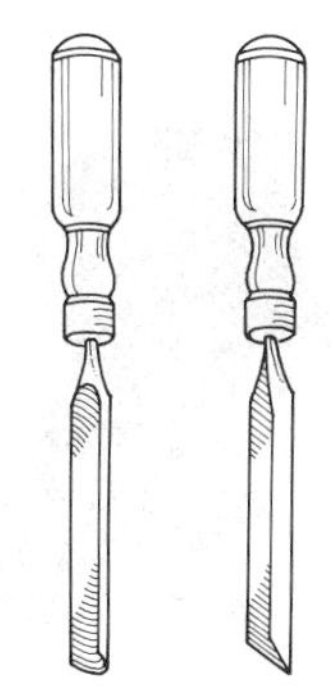

gouge
Left: Hollow gouge
Right: Parting gouge

gourd

ă pat	oi boy
ā pay	ou out
âr care	o͝o took
ä father	o͞o boot
ĕ pet	ŭ cut
ē be	ûr urge
ĭ pit	th thin
ī pie	*th* this
îr pier	hw which
ŏ pot	zh vision
ō toe	ə about, item
ô paw	♦ regionalism

Stress marks: **′** (primary); ′ (secondary), as in **dictionary** (dĭk′shə-nĕr′ē)

Gour•mont (go͝or-môN′), **Rémy de.** 1858–1915. French writer known for his symbolic novels, such as *A Virgin Heart* (1907).

gout (gout) *n.* **1.** *Pathology.* A disturbance of uric-acid metabolism occurring predominantly in males, characterized by painful inflammation of the joints, especially of the feet and hands, and arthritic attacks resulting from elevated levels of uric acid in the blood and the deposition of urate crystals around the joints. The condition can become chronic and result in deformity. **2.** A large blob or clot: *"and makes it bleed great gouts of blood"* (Oscar Wilde). [Middle English *goute,* from Old French, drop, gout, from Medieval Latin *gutta,* from Latin, drop (from the belief that gout was caused by drops of morbid humors).] **—gout′i•ness** *n.* **—gout′y** *adj.*

gout•weed (gout′wēd′) *n.* A European plant *(Aegopodium podagraria)* widely naturalized in eastern North America, having small white flowers grouped in compound umbels. A variegated form is commonly grown as an edging or a ground cover. Also called *bishop's weed.*

gov. *abbr.* **1.** Government. **2.** Or **Gov.** Governor.

gov•ern (gŭv′ərn) *v.* **-erned, -ern•ing, -erns.** *—tr.* **1.** To make and administer the public policy and affairs of; exercise sovereign authority in. **2.** To control the speed or magnitude of; regulate: *a valve governing fuel intake.* **3.** To control the actions or behavior of: *Govern yourselves like civilized human beings.* **4.** To keep under control; restrain: *a child who could not be governed.* **5.** To exercise a deciding or determining influence on: *Chance usually governs the outcome of the game.* **6.** *Grammar.* To require (a specific morphological form) of accompanying words. *—intr.* **1.** To exercise political authority. **2.** To have or exercise a determining influence. [Middle English *governen,* from Old French *governer,* from Latin *gubernāre,* from Greek *kubernan.*] **—gov′ern•a•ble** *adj.*

Go•ver•na•dor Va•la•da•res (guv′ər-nə-dôr′ văl′ə-där′ĭs, gô′vĭr-nä-dôr′ vä′lä-där′ĭs). A city of eastern Brazil northeast of Belo Horizonte. It is a processing center in a lumbering and agricultural region. Population, 173,624.

Francisco Goya
1799 self-portrait from a series of satirical paintings and prints entitled *Los Caprichos*

gov•er•nance (gŭv′ər-nəns) *n.* **1.** The act, process, or power of governing; government: *"Regaining a sense of the state is thus an absolute priority, not only for an effective policy against . . . terrorism, but also for governance itself"* (Moorhead Kennedy). **2.** The state of being governed.

gov•er•ness (gŭv′ər-nĭs) *n.* A woman employed to educate and train the children of a private household. [Middle English *governesse,* short for *governouresse,* from Old French *governeresse,* feminine of *governeor,* governor, from Latin *gubernātor.* See GUBERNATORIAL.]

gov•er•nes•sy (gŭv′ər-nĭs′ē, -nĭ-sē) *adj.* Fastidious, especially about matters of learning; prim.

gov•ern•ment (gŭv′ərn-mənt) *n. Abbr.* **gov., govt. 1.** The act or process of governing, especially the control and administration of public policy in a political unit. **2.** The office, function, or authority of one who governs or of a governing body. **3.** Exercise of authority in a political unit; rule. **4.** The agency or apparatus through which an individual or a body that governs exercises authority and performs its functions. **5.** A governing body or organization, as: **a.** The ruling political party or coalition of political parties in a parliamentary system. **b.** The cabinet in a parliamentary system. **c.** The persons who make up a governing body. **6.** A system or policy by which a political unit is governed. **7.** Management or administration of an organization, a business, or an institution. **8.** Political science. **—gov′ern•ment′al** (-mĕn′tl) *adj.* **—gov′ern•ment′al•ly** *adv.*

USAGE NOTE: In American usage *government* always takes a singular verb. In British usage *government,* in the sense of a governing group of officials, is usually construed as a plural collective and therefore takes a plural verb: *The government are determined to follow this course.* See Usage Note at **collective noun.**

Gov•ern•ment Issue (gŭv′ərn-mənt) *n. Abbr.* **GI, G.I.** Something, such as military equipment, that is issued by a government.

gov•er•nor (gŭv′ər-nər) *n. Abbr.* **gov., Gov. 1.** A person who governs, especially: **a.** The chief executive of a state in the United States. **b.** An official appointed to govern a colony or territory. **c.** A member of a governing body. **2.** The manager or administrative head of an organization, a business, or an institution. **3.** A military commandant. **4.** *Chiefly British.* Used as a form of polite address for a man. **5.** A feedback device on a machine or an engine that is used to provide automatic control, as of speed, pressure, or temperature.

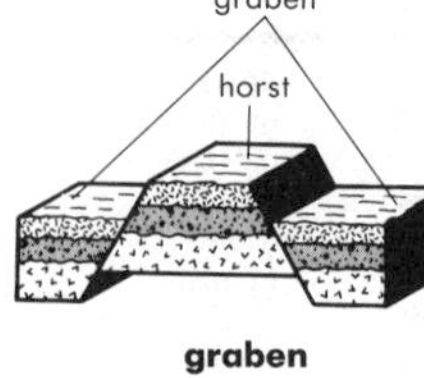

graben

WORD HISTORY: The American Revolution did away with much that was British, but it neglected to discard an important British political term. The word *governor* certainly seems to denote a very American office, and England has no corresponding official with that title for its counties. Nonetheless, *governor* has had a long history in English with reference to political rulers. In Middle English *governour,* the ancestor of *governor,* meant both "a sovereign ruler" and "a subordinate or substitute ruler." In the later sense it was a natural term to use for heads of the British colonies in North America as well as elsewhere. During our colonial period royal governors were often unpopular, yet the word was not dropped after the Revolutionary War and in fact was chosen to designate the executive head of a state when the United States of America was created.

gov•er•nor-gen•er•al (gŭv′ər-nər-jĕn′ər-əl) *n., pl.* **gov•er•nors-gen•er•al** (gŭv′ər-nərz-) or **gov•er•nor-gen•er•als** (-jĕn′ər-əlz). A governor of a large territory who has other subordinate governors under his or her jurisdiction. **—gov′er•nor-gen′er•al•ship′** *n.*

gov•er•nor•ship (gŭv′ər-nər-shĭp′) *n.* The office, term, or jurisdiction of a governor.

Gov•er•nors Island (gŭv′ər-nərz). An island of southeast New York in Upper New York Bay south of Manhattan.

govt. *abbr.* Government.

gow•an (gou′ən) *n. Scots.* A yellow or white wildflower, especially the Old World daisy. [Probably alteration of Middle English *gollan,* a plant with yellow flowers; akin to Old Norse *gullinn,* golden, from *gull,* gold. See **ghel-**[2] in Appendix.]

Gow•er (gou′ər, gôr′, gōr′), **John.** 1325?–1408. English poet who wrote allegorical, didactic works, such as *Vox Clamantis* (1382?–1384), in Latin, French, and English.

gown (goun) *n.* **1.** A long, loose, flowing garment, such as a robe or nightgown. **2.** A long, usually formal dress for a woman. **3.** A robe or smock worn in operating rooms and other parts of hospitals as a guard against contamination. **4.** A distinctive outer robe worn on ceremonial occasions, as by scholars or clerics. **5.** The faculty and student body of a university: *perfect accord between town and gown.* **—gown** *intr. & tr.v.* **gowned, gown•ing, gowns.** To dress oneself in or invest (another) with a gown. [Middle English *goune,* from Old French, from Late Latin *gunna,* leather garment.]

gowns•man (gounz′mən) *n.* One who wears a distinctive gown as a mark of profession or office.

goy (goi) *n., pl.* **goy•im** (goi′ĭm) or **goys.** *Offensive.* Used as a disparaging term for one who is not a Jew. [Yiddish, from Hebrew *gôy,* nation, one who is not Jewish, non-Jew, Jew ignorant of the Jewish religion.] **—goy′ish** *adj.*

Go•ya y Lu•ci•en•tes (goi′ə ē lo͞o-syĕn′tēs, gô′yä ē lo͞o-thyĕn′tĕs), **Francisco José de.** 1746–1828. Spanish painter and etcher whose art reflected the political and social turmoil of his times. His highly influential works include portraits of Spanish nobility and *The Third of May 1808* (1814).

G.P. or **GP** *abbr.* General practitioner.

GPA *abbr.* Grade point average.

g.p.d. *abbr.* Gallons per day.

g.p.m. *abbr.* Gallons per minute.

GPO *abbr.* **1.** General post office. **2.** Government Printing Office.

g.p.s. *abbr.* Gallons per second.

GQ *abbr.* General quarters.

gr. *abbr.* **1.** Grade. **2.** Grain. **3.** Gram. **4.** Gravity. **5.** Great. **6.** Gross. **7.** Group.

Gr. *abbr.* Greece; Greek.

Graaf•i•an follicle (grä′fē-ən, grăf′ē-) *n.* Any of the fluid-filled vesicles in the mammalian ovary containing a maturing ovum. [After Regnier de *Graaf* (1641–1673), Dutch physician and anatomist.]

grab[1] (grăb) *v.* **grabbed, grab•bing, grabs.** *—tr.* **1.** To take or grasp suddenly: *grabbed the letter from me.* **2.** To capture or restrain; arrest. **3.** To obtain or appropriate unscrupulously or forcibly: *grab public funds; grab power.* **4.** To take hurriedly: *grabbed my coat and hat and left.* **5.** *Slang.* To capture the attention of: *a plot that grabs the reader.* *—intr.* To make a grasping or snatching motion: *We grabbed for the life raft.* **—grab** *n.* **1.** Sudden seizure of something or someone; a snatch: *"The imminence of death is reflected in every last power-stroke and grab of the great money bosses"* (Dylan Thomas). **2.** One that is grabbed. **3.** A mechanical device for gripping an object. ***—idiom.*** **up for grabs.** *Slang.* Available for anyone to take or win: *"The reputation of the . . . king is still up for grabs"* (William Zinsser). [Obsolete Dutch or Low German *grabben,* from Middle Dutch or Middle Low German. See **ghrebh-**[1] in Appendix.] **—grab′ber** *n.*

grab[2] (grăb) *n. Nautical.* An Oriental coastal vessel with two or three masts. [Arabic *ġurāb,* raven, swift galley.]

grab bag *n.* **1.** A container filled with articles, such as party gifts, to be drawn unseen. **2.** *Slang.* A miscellaneous collection: *The meeting evolved into a grab bag of petty complaints.*

grab•ble (grăb′əl) *intr.v.* **-bled, -bling, -bles. 1.** To feel around with the hands; grope. **2.** To fall down; sprawl. [Probably from Dutch *grabbelen,* from Middle Dutch, frequentative of *grabben,* to grab. See GRAB[1].] **—grab′bler** *n.*

grab•by (grăb′ē) *adj.* **-bi•er, -bi•est.** *Informal.* Inclined to grab; greedy. **—grab′bi•ness** *n.*

gra•ben (grä′bən) *n.* A usually elongated depression between geologic faults. [German *Graben,* from Middle High German *grabe,* trench, from Old High German *grabo,* from *graban,* to dig. See **ghrebh-**[2] in Appendix.]

Grac•chi (grăk′ī). See **Gracchus.**

Grac•chus (grăk′əs), **Tiberius Sempronius.** 163–133 B.C. Roman social reformer. Known with his brother **Gaius Sempronius Gracchus** (153–121 B.C.) as "the Gracchi," he sought to aid poor farmers through greater subdivision of land but was killed in a riot. Gaius assumed his brother's work and met a similar fate.

grace (grās) *n.* **1.** Seemingly effortless beauty or charm of movement, form, or proportion. See Synonyms at **elegance. 2.** A characteristic or quality pleasing for its charm or refinement. **3.** A sense of fitness or propriety. **4.a.** A disposition to be generous or helpful; good will. **b.** Mercy; clemency. **5.** A favor rendered by one who need not do so; indulgence. **6.** A temporary immunity or exemption; a reprieve. **7. Graces.** *Greek & Roman Mythology.* Three sister goddesses, known in Greek mythology as Aglaia, Euphrosyne, and Thalia, who dispense charm and beauty. **8.** *Theology.* **a.** Divine love and protection bestowed freely on people. **b.** The state of being protected or sanctified by the favor of God. **c.** An excellence or a power granted by God. **9.** A short prayer of blessing or thanksgiving said before or after a meal. **10. Grace.** Used with *His, Her,* or *Your* as a title and form of address for a duke, a duchess, or an archbishop. **11.** *Music.* An embellishment such as an appoggiatura or a trill. **—grace** *tr.v.* **graced, grac·ing, grac·es. 1.** To honor or favor: *You grace our table with your presence.* **2.** To give beauty, elegance, or charm to. **3.** *Music.* To embellish with grace notes. ***—idioms.* in the good graces of.** In favor with. **in the bad graces of.** Out of favor with. **with bad grace.** In a grudging manner. **with good grace.** In a willing manner. [Middle English, from Old French, from Latin *grātia,* from *grātus,* pleasing. See **g^{w}erə-[2]** in Appendix.]

grace cup *n.* **1.** A cup used at the end of a meal, usually after grace, for the final toast. **2.** The final toast of a meal.

grace·ful (grās′fəl) *adj.* Showing grace of movement, form, or proportion: *"England's slow, graceful economic collapse"* (J.C. Winters). **—grace′ful·ly** *adv.* **—grace′ful·ness** *n.*

grace·less (grās′lĭs) *adj.* **1.** Lacking grace; clumsy. **2.** Having or exhibiting no sense of propriety or decency. **3.** Inferior or clumsy in treatment or performance: *a graceless production of the play.* **—grace′less·ly** *adv.* **—grace′less·ness** *n.*

grace note *n. Music.* A note, especially an appoggiatura, added as an embellishment.

grace period *n.* **1.** A period in which a debt may be paid without accruing further interest or penalty. **2.** A period in which an insurance policy is effective even though the premium is past due.

grac·ile (grăs′əl, -īl′) *adj.* **1.** Gracefully slender. **2.** Graceful. [Latin *gracilis.*] **—gra·cil′i·ty** (grə-sĭl′ĭ-tē) *n.*

gra·ci·o·so (grä′sē-ō′sō, -zō) *n., pl.* **-sos.** A clown or buffoon in Spanish comedies. [Spanish, amiable, clown, from Latin *grātiōsus.* See GRACIOUS.]

gra·cious (grā′shəs) *adj.* **1.** Characterized by kindness and warm courtesy. **2.** Characterized by tact and propriety: *responded to the insult with gracious humor.* **3.** Of a merciful or compassionate nature. **4.** Condescendingly courteous; indulgent. **5.** Characterized by charm or beauty; graceful. **6.** Characterized by elegance and good taste: *gracious living.* **7.** *Archaic.* Enjoying favor or grace; acceptable or pleasing. **—gracious** *interj.* Used to express surprise or mild emotion. [Middle English, from Old French *gracieus,* from Latin *grātiōsus,* from *grātia,* good will. See GRACE.] **—gra′cious·ly** *adv.* **—gra′cious·ness** *n.*

SYNONYMS: *gracious, cordial, genial, sociable.* The central meaning shared by these adjectives is "marked by kindness, sympathy, and unaffected politeness": *gracious even to unexpected visitors; a cordial welcome; a genial guest; enjoyed a sociable chat.* ***ANTONYM:*** *ungracious.*

grack·le (grăk′əl) *n.* **1.** Any of several American blackbirds of the family Icteridae, especially of the genus *Quiscalus,* having iridescent blackish plumage. Also called *crow blackbird.* **2.** Any of several Asian mynas of the genus *Gracula.* [New Latin *Grăcula,* genus name, from Latin *grāculus,* jackdaw. See **gerə-[2]** in Appendix.]

grad (grăd) *n. Informal.* A graduate of a school or college.

grad. *abbr.* **1.** Gradient. **2.** Graduated.

gra·date (grā′dāt′) *v.* **-dat·ed, -dat·ing, -dates.** *—intr.* To pass imperceptibly from one degree, shade, or tone to another. *—tr.* **1.** To cause to pass imperceptibly from one degree, shade, or tone to another. **2.** To arrange in or according to grades. [Back-formation from GRADATION.]

gra·da·tion (grā-dā′shən) *n.* **1.a.** A series of gradual, successive stages; a systematic progression. **b.** A degree or stage in such a progression. **2.** A passing by barely perceptible degrees from one tone or shade to another. See Synonyms at **nuance. 3.** The act of gradating or arranging in grades. **4.** *Linguistics.* See **ablaut.** [Latin *gradātiō, gradātiōn-,* from *gradus,* step. See GRADE.] **—gra·da′tion·al** *adj.* **—gra·da′tion·al·ly** *adv.*

grade (grād) *n. Abbr.* **gr. 1.** A stage or degree in a process. **2.** A position in a scale of size, quality, or intensity. **3.** An accepted level or standard. **4.** A set of persons or things all falling in the same specified limits; a class. **5.a.** A class at an elementary school or the pupils in it. **b. grades.** Elementary school. **6.** A mark indicating a student's level of accomplishment. **7.** A military, naval, or civil service rank. **8.** The degree of inclination of a slope, road, or other surface. **9.** A slope or gradual inclination, especially of a road or railroad track. **10.** The level at which the ground surface meets the foundation of a building. **11.** A domestic animal produced by crossbreeding one of purebred stock with one of ordinary stock. **12.** *Linguistics.* A degree of ablaut. **—grade** *v.* **grad·ed, grad·ing, grades.** *—tr.* **1.** To arrange in steps or degrees. **2.** To arrange in a series or according to a scale. **3.a.** To determine the quality of (academic work, for example); evaluate. **b.** To give a grade to (a student, for example). **4.** To level or smooth to a desired or horizontal gradient. **5.** To gradate. **6.** To improve the quality of (livestock) by crossbreeding with purebred stock. *—intr.* **1.** To hold a certain rank or position. **2.** To change or progress gradually. [French, from Latin *gradus.* See **ghredh-** in Appendix.]

grade crossing *n.* An intersection of railroad tracks, roads, walkways, or a combination of these at the same level.

grade point *n.* A point assigned to a course credit, as in a university, that corresponds to the letter grade made in a course. Also called *grade index.*

grade point average *n. Abbr.* **GPA** The average grade earned by a student, figured by dividing the grade points earned by the number of credits attempted. Also called *grade point index.*

grad·er (grā′dər) *n.* **1.** One that grades, especially: **a.** One who grades students' work. **b.** A piece of heavy equipment used to level or smooth road or other surfaces to the desired gradient. **2.** A student in a specified class in an elementary or high school. Often used in combination: *tenth graders.*

grade school *n.* See **elementary school. —grade′-school′er** (grād′sko͞o′lər) *n.*

gra·di·ent (grā′dē-ənt) *n. Abbr.* **grad. 1.** A rate of inclination; a slope. **2.** An ascending or descending part; an incline. **3.** *Physics.* The rate at which a physical quantity, such as temperature or pressure, changes relative to change in a given variable, especially distance. **4.** *Mathematics.* A vector having coordinate components that are the partial derivatives of a function with respect to its variables. **5.** *Biology.* A series of progressively increasing or decreasing differences in the growth rate, metabolism, or physiological activity of a cell, an organ, or an organism. [Perhaps GRADE + *-ient,* as in QUOTIENT.]

gra·din (grād′n) also **gra·dine** (grā′dēn′, grə-dēn′) *n.* One of a series of steps or tiered seats, as in an amphitheater. [French, from Italian *gradino,* diminutive of *grado,* step, from Latin *gradus.* See GRADE.]

grad·u·al (grăj′o͞o-əl) *adj.* Advancing or progressing by regular or continuous degrees: *gradual erosion; a gradual slope.* **—gradual** *n. Roman Catholic Church.* **1.** A book containing the choral portions of the Mass. **2.** A biblical text sung between the Epistle and the Gospel of the Mass. [Middle English, having steps, from Medieval Latin *graduālis,* from Latin *gradus,* step. See GRADE. N., Middle English, from Medieval Latin *graduāle,* the part of the service sung by the choir from the altar steps, gradual, from neuter sing. of *graduālis,* having steps.] **—grad′u·al·ly** *adv.* **—grad′u·al·ness** *n.*

grad·u·al·ism (grăj′o͞o-ə-lĭz′əm) *n.* The belief in or the policy of advancing toward a goal by gradual, often slow stages. **—grad′u·al·ist** *n.* **—grad′u·al·is′tic** *adj.*

grad·u·ate (grăj′o͞o-āt′) *v.* **-at·ed, -at·ing, -ates.** *—intr.* **1.** To be granted an academic degree or diploma: *Two thirds of the entering freshmen stayed to graduate.* **2.a.** To change gradually or by degrees. **b.** To advance to a new level of skill, achievement, or activity: *After a summer of diving instruction, they had all graduated to back flips.* *—tr.* **1.a.** To grant an academic degree or diploma to: *The teachers hope to graduate her this spring.* **b.** *Usage Problem.* To receive an academic degree from. **2.** To arrange or divide into categories, steps, or grades. **3.** To divide into marked intervals, especially for use in measurement. **—graduate** (-ĭt) *n.* **1.** One who has received an academic degree or diploma. **2.** A graduated container, such as a cylinder or beaker. **—graduate** (-ĭt) *adj.* **1.** Possessing an academic degree or diploma. **2.** Of or relating to studies beyond a bachelor's degree: *graduate courses.* [Middle English *graduaten,* to confer a degree, from Medieval Latin *graduārī, graduāt-,* to take a degree, from Latin *gradus,* step. See GRADE.] **—grad′u·a′tor** *n.*

USAGE NOTE: The verb *graduate* has denoted the action of conferring an academic degree or diploma since at least 1421, as in *She was graduated from Yale in 1980.* This earlier pattern of use is still defensible, if slightly old-fashioned, and is acceptable to 78 percent of the Usage Panel. In general usage, however, it has largely yielded to the much more recent active pattern (first attested in 1807): *She graduated from Yale in 1980.* This pattern, which no longer bears any taint of incorrectness, is acceptable to 89 percent of the Panel. It has the advantage of ascribing the accomplishment to the student, rather than to the institution, as is usually appropriate in discussions of individual cases. When the institution's responsibility is emphasized, however, the older pattern may still be recommended. A sentence such as *The university graduated more computer science majors in 1987 than in the entire previous decade* stresses the university's accomplishment, say, of its computer science program. On the other hand, the sentence *More computer science majors graduated in 1987 than in the entire previous decade* implies that the class of 1987 was in some way a remarkable group. • The transitive use of *graduate,* as in *She graduated Yale in 1980,* was unacceptable to 77 percent of the Usage Panel.

grad·u·a·tion (grăj′o͞o-ā′shən) *n.* **1.a.** Conferral or receipt of an academic degree or diploma marking completion of studies. **b.** A ceremony at which degrees or diplomas are conferred; a commencement. **2.a.** A division or an interval on a graduated scale.

Graces
Aglaia, Euphrosyne, and Thalia in a detail from *Spring* by Botticelli

ă pat	oi boy
ā pay	ou out
âr care	o͝o took
ä father	o͞o boot
ĕ pet	ŭ cut
ē be	ûr urge
ĭ pit	th thin
ī pie	*th* this
îr pier	hw which
ŏ pot	zh vision
ō toe	ə about, item
ô paw	♦ regionalism

Stress marks: ′ (primary); ′ (secondary), as in **dictionary** (dĭk′shə-nĕr′ē)

b. A mark indicating the boundary of such an interval. **3.** An arrangement in or a division into stages or degrees.

Graeco– *pref.* Variant of **Greco–.**

graf·fi·ti (grə-fē′tē) *n.* Plural of **graffito.**

graf·fi·tist (grə-fē′tĭst) *n.* One who produces graffiti.

graf·fi·to (grə-fē′tō) *n., pl.* **-ti** (-tē). *Usage Problem.* A drawing or an inscription made on a wall or other surface, usually so as to be seen by the public. Often used in the plural. [Italian, diminutive of *graffio,* a scratching, scribble, probably from *graffiare,* to scratch, scribble, probably from Vulgar Latin **graphiāre,* to write with a stylus, from Latin *graphium,* stylus, from Greek *grapheion, graphion,* from *graphein,* to write. See **gerbh-** in Appendix.]

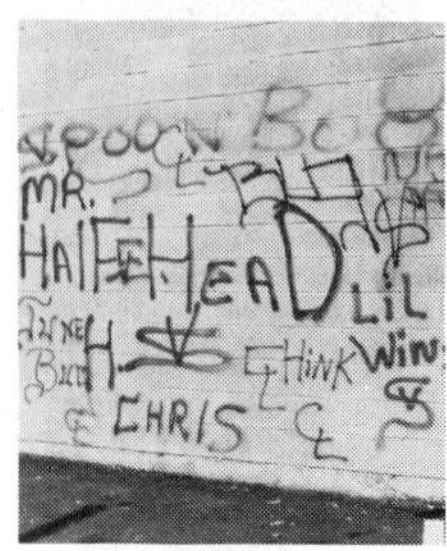
graffito
Graffiti on a wall

USAGE NOTE: The form *graffiti,* based on the Italian plural, is far more common than the singular form *graffito. Graffiti* is often used as a singular noun. When the reference is to a particular inscription (as in *There was a bold graffiti on the wall*), the form *graffito* would be etymologically correct but might strike some readers as pedantic outside an archaeological context. There is no substitute for the singular use of *graffiti* when the word is used as a mass noun to refer to inscriptions in general or to the related social phenomenon. The sentence *Graffiti is a major problem for the Transit Authority Police* cannot be reworded *Graffito is . . .* (since *graffito* can refer only to a particular inscription) or *Graffiti are . . . ,* which suggests that the police problem involves only the physical marks and not the larger issue of vandalism. In such contexts, the use of *graffiti* as a singular is justified by both utility and widespread precedent.

graft¹ (grăft) *v.* **graft·ed, graft·ing, grafts.** —*tr.* **1.a.** To unite (a shoot or bud) with a growing plant by insertion or by placing in close contact. **b.** To join (a plant or plants) by such union. **2.** To transplant or implant (living tissue, for example) surgically into a bodily part to replace a damaged part or compensate for a defect. **3.** To join or unite closely: *graft new customs onto old.* —*intr.* **1.** To make a graft. **2.** To be or become joined. —**graft** *n.* **1.a.** A detached shoot or bud united or to be united with a growing plant. **b.** The union or point of union of a detached shoot or bud with a growing plant by insertion or attachment. **c.** A plant produced by such union. **2.a.** Material, especially living tissue or an organ, surgically attached to or inserted into a bodily part to replace a damaged part or compensate for a defect. **b.** The procedure of implanting or transplanting such material. **c.** The configuration or condition resulting from such a procedure. [Middle English *graften,* alteration of *graffen,* probably from Old French *grafier,* from *graffe,* stylus, graft (from its shape), from Latin *graphium,* stylus. See GRAFFITO. N., Middle English *grafte,* alteration of *graffe,* from Old French *graffe.*]

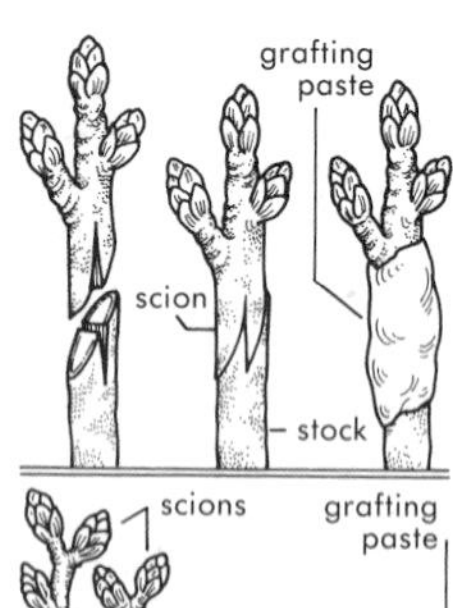

graft¹
Top: Whip grafting
Bottom: Cleft grafting

graft² (grăft) *n.* **1.** Unscrupulous use of one's position to derive profit or advantages; extortion. **2.** Money or an advantage gained or yielded by unscrupulous means. —**graft** *tr. & intr.v.* **graft·ed, graft·ing, grafts.** To gain by or practice unscrupulous use of one's position. [Origin unknown.]

graft·age (grăf′tĭj) *n.* The process of making a graft in horticulture.

graft·er¹ (grăf′tər) *n.* One that grafts: *a grafter of roses.*

graft·er² (grăf′tər) *n.* One who gains profit or advantage by unscrupulous use of position: *"the cheats and grafters in Wall Street and Washington"* (Alex Brummer).

graft-ver·sus-host disease or **graft versus host disease** (grăft′vûr′səs-hōst′, -səz-) *n.* A pathological condition in which cells from the transplanted tissue of a donor initiate an immunologic attack on the cells and tissue of the recipient.

gra·ham (grā′əm) *n.* Whole-wheat flour. [After Sylvester *Graham* (1794–1851), American cleric and social reformer.]

Gra·ham (grā′əm), **John.** First Viscount Dundee. 1649?–1689. Scottish Jacobite leader and long-time persecutor of the Covenanters, whom he defeated in a bloody battle in which he was mortally wounded (1689).

Graham, Martha. 1894–1991. American dancer and choreographer. A central figure in modern dance, she founded the Dance Repertory Theatre in New York City in 1930.

Graham, William Franklin. Known as "Billy." Born 1918. American religious leader who has conducted evangelical tours throughout the world.

graham cracker *n.* A slightly sweet, usually rectangular cracker made with whole-wheat flour.

Gra·hame (grā′əm), **Kenneth.** 1859–1932. British writer known for his essays and children's books, notably *The Wind in the Willows* (1908).

Graham Island. An island off western British Columbia, Canada, in the Pacific Ocean. It is the largest and northernmost of the Queen Charlotte Islands.

Graham Land. A region of Antarctica near the tip of the Antarctic Peninsula. Part of the British Antarctic Territory, it is also claimed by Argentina and Chile.

Gra·ian Alps (grā′ən grī′ən). A section of the western Alps on the border between southeast France and northwest Italy.

grain elevator
In Kansas

grail (grāl) *n.* **1. Grail.** A cup or plate that, according to medieval legend, was used by Jesus at the Last Supper and that later became the object of many chivalrous quests. Also called *Holy Grail.* **2.** Often **Grail.** The object of a prolonged endeavor. [Middle English *greal,* from Old French *graal,* from Medieval Latin *gradālis,* flat dish.]

grain (grān) *n. Abbr.* **gr. 1.a.** A small, dry, one-seeded fruit of a cereal grass, having the fruit and the seed walls united. Also called *caryopsis.* **b.** The fruits of cereal grasses especially after having been harvested, considered as a group. **2.** Cereal grasses considered as a group: *a field of grain.* **3.a.** A relatively small discrete particulate or crystalline mass: *a grain of sand.* **b.** A small amount or the smallest amount possible: *hasn't a grain of sense.* **4.** *Aerospace.* A mass of solid propellant. **5.** A unit of weight in the U.S. Customary System, an avoirdupois unit equal to 0.002285 ounce (0.065 gram). See table at **measurement. 6.** The arrangement, direction, or pattern of the fibrous tissue in wood. **7.a.** The side of a hide or piece of leather from which the hair or fur has been removed. **b.** The pattern or markings on this side of leather. **8.** The pattern produced, as in stone, by the arrangement of particulate constituents. **9.** The relative size of the particles composing a substance or pattern: *a coarse grain.* **10.** A painted, stamped, or printed design that imitates the pattern found in wood, leather, or stone. **11.** The direction or texture of fibers in a woven fabric. **12.** A state of fine crystallization. **13.a.** Basic temperament or nature; disposition. **b.** An essential quality or characteristic. **14.** *Archaic.* Color; tint. —**grain** *v.* **grained, grain·ing, grains.** —*tr.* **1.** To cause to form into grains; granulate. **2.** To paint, stamp, or print with a design imitating the grain of wood, leather, or stone. **3.** To give a granular or rough texture to. **4.** To remove the hair or fur from (hides) in preparation for tanning. —*intr.* To form grains. —***idiom.* with a grain of salt.** With reservations; skeptically: *Take that advice with a grain of salt.* [Middle English, from Old French *graine,* from Latin *grānum.* See **grə-no-** in Appendix.] —**grain′er** *n.*

grain alcohol *n.* See **alcohol** (sense 1).

Grain Coast (grān). A historical region of western Africa along the coast of the Atlantic Ocean, roughly identical with present-day Liberia. It was named for its once-thriving trade in grains of paradise.

grain elevator *n.* A building equipped with mechanical lifting devices and used for storing grain.

grains of paradise (grānz) *pl.n.* **1.** The pungent, aromatic seeds of a tropical African plant *(Aframomum melegueta)* used medicinally and for flavoring beverages. **2.** The seeds of cardamom.

grain·y (grā′nē) *adj.* **-i·er, -i·est. 1.** Made of or resembling grain; granular. **2.** Resembling the grain of wood. **3.** Having sharp divisions between light and dark patches; not smooth. Used of photographs and film. —**grain′i·ness** *n.*

gram¹ (grăm) *n. Abbr.* **g, gm., gr.** A metric unit of mass equal to one thousandth (10^{-3}) of a kilogram. See table at **measurement.** [French *gramme,* from Late Latin *gramma,* a small weight, from Greek, something written, small weight. See **gerbh-** in Appendix.]

gram² (grăm) *n.* **1.** Any of several plants, such as the chickpea, bearing seeds widely used as food in tropical Asia. **2.** The seeds of such a plant. [Obsolete Portuguese, from Latin *grānum,* seed. See **grə-no-** in Appendix.]

–gram *suff.* Something written or drawn; a record: *cardiogram.* [Greek *-gramma,* from *gramma,* letter. See **gerbh-** in Appendix.]

gra·ma also **gram·ma** (grä′mə, grăm′ə) *n.* Any of various grasses of the genus *Bouteloua* of western North America and South America, forming dense tufts or mats and often used as pasturage. [American Spanish, from Spanish, Bermuda grass, quitch grass, from Latin *grāmen, grāmin-,* grass.]

gram·a·rye (grăm′ə-rē) *n.* Occult learning; magic. [Middle English *gramarie,* probably from Old French *gramaire,* grammar, book of magic. See GRAMMAR.]

gram atom *n.* One mole of atoms of an element.

gram-a·tom·ic mass (grăm′ə-tŏm′ĭk) *n.* The mass of one mole of atoms of an element. Also called *gram-atomic weight.*

gram calorie *n.* See **calorie** (sense 1).

gram equivalent *n.* The amount of a substance whose weight in grams is numerically equal to its equivalent weight.

gra·mer·cy (grə-mûr′sē, grăm′ər-) *interj. Archaic.* Used to express surprise or gratitude. [Middle English *gramerci,* from Old French *grand merci* : *grand,* great; see GRAND + *merci,* thanks; see MERCY.]

gram·i·ci·din (grăm′ĭ-sīd′n) *n.* An antibiotic produced by the soil bacterium *Bacillus brevis* and used to treat infections caused by certain gram-positive bacteria. [GRAM(-POSITIVE) + –CID(E) + –IN.]

gra·min·e·ous (grə-mĭn′ē-əs) *adj.* **1.** Of, relating to, or characteristic of grasses. **2.** Of or belonging to the grass family. [From Latin *grāmineus,* grassy, from *grāmen, grāmin-,* grass.] —**gra·min′e·ous·ness** *n.*

gram·i·niv·o·rous (grăm′ə-nĭv′ər-əs) *adj.* Feeding on grasses. [Latin *grāmen, grāmin-,* grass + –VOROUS.]

gram·ma (grä′mə, grăm′ə) *n.* Variant of **grama.**

gram·mar (grăm′ər) *n. Abbr.* **gram. 1.a.** The study of how words and their component parts combine to form sentences. **b.** The study of structural relationships in language or in a language, sometimes including pronunciation, meaning, and linguistic history. **2.a.** The system of inflections, syntax, and word formation of a language. **b.** The system of rules implicit in a language, viewed as a mechanism for generating all sentences possible in that language. **3.a.** A normative or prescriptive set of rules setting forth the current standard of usage for pedagogical or reference purposes. **b.** Writing or speech judged with regard to such a set of rules. **4.** A book containing the morphologic, syntactic, and semantic rules for a specific language. **5.a.** The basic principles of an area of knowledge: *the grammar of music.* **b.** A book dealing with such principles. [Middle English *gramere,* from Old French *gramaire,* alteration of Latin *grammatica,* from Greek *grammatikē,* from feminine of *grammatikos,* of letters, from *gramma, grammat-,* letter. See **gerbh-** in Appendix.]

gram·mar·ian (grə-mâr′ē-ən) *n.* A specialist in grammar.

grammar school *n.* **1.** See **elementary school. 2.** *Chiefly British.* A secondary or preparatory school. **3.** A school stressing the study of classical languages.

gram·mat·i·cal (grə-măt′ĭ-kəl) *adj.* **1.** Of or relating to grammar. **2.** Conforming to the rules of grammar: *a grammatical sentence.* [Late Latin *grammaticālis,* from Latin *grammaticus,* from Greek *grammatikos,* of letters. See GRAMMAR.] **—gram·mat′i·cal′i·ty** (-kăl′ĭ-tē) *n.* **—gram·mat′i·cal·ly** *adv.*

grammatical gender *n.* Gender assigned to a word arbitrarily or on the basis of its grammatical form.

Gram·mat·i·cus (grə-măt′ĭ-kəs). See **Aelfric.**

gram·ma·tol·o·gy (grăm′ə-tŏl′ə-jē) *n.* The study and science of systems of graphic script. [Greek *gramma, grammat-,* letter; see GRAMMAR + –LOGY.] **—gram′ma·to·log′ic** (-tə-lŏj′ĭk), **gram′ma·to·log′i·cal** *adj.* **—gram′ma·tol′o·gist** *n.*

gramme (grăm) *n. Chiefly British.* Variant of **gram**[1].

gram-mo·lec·u·lar weight (grăm′mə-lĕk′yə-lər) *n. Abbr.* **GMW** See **mole**[5] (sense 2).

gram molecule *n.* See **mole**[5] (sense 1).

Gram·my (grăm′ē). A service mark used for any of the statuettes awarded by the National Academy of Recording Arts and Sciences for excellence in the recording industry.

gram-neg·a·tive or **Gram-neg·a·tive** (grăm′nĕg′ə-tĭv) *adj.* Of, relating to, or being a bacterium that does not retain the violet stain used in Gram's method.

gram·o·phone (grăm′ə-fōn′) *n.* A record player; a phonograph. [Originally a trademark.]

gramp (grămp) or **gramps** (grămps) *n. Informal.* A grandfather. [Alteration of GRANDP(A).]

Gram·pi·an Mountains (grăm′pē-ən). A mountain range of central Scotland extending northeast to southwest and forming a natural barrier between the Highlands and the Lowlands. Ben Nevis, 1,343.8 m (4,406 ft), is the highest point.

gram-pos·i·tive or **Gram-pos·i·tive** (grăm′pŏz′ĭ-tĭv) *adj.* Of, relating to, or being a bacterium that retains the violet stain used in Gram's method.

gram·pus (grăm′pəs) *n.* **1.** A cetacean *(Grampus griseus)* related to and resembling the dolphins but lacking a beaklike snout. **2.** Any of various similar cetaceans, such as the killer whale. [Alteration (perhaps influenced by GRAND) of Middle English *graspeis,* from Old French *craspois, graspeis,* from Medieval Latin *crassus piscis, craspiscis* : Latin *crassus,* fat + Latin *piscis,* fish.]

Gram's method (grămz) *n.* A staining technique used to classify bacteria in which a bacterial specimen is first stained with crystal violet, then treated with an iodine solution, decolorized with alcohol, and counterstained with safranine. Gram-positive bacteria retain the violet stain; gram-negative bacteria do not. [After Hans Christian Joachim *Gram* (1853–1938), Danish physician.]

gra·na (grā′nə) *n. Botany.* Plural of **granum.**

Gra·na·da (grə-nä′də, grä-nä′thä). A city of southern Spain southeast of Córdoba. Founded by the Moors in the eighth century, it became the center of an independent kingdom in 1238. The city was captured by Castilian troops in 1492, ending Moorish control in Spain. Population, 256,191.

gran·a·dil·la (grăn′ə-dĭl′ə, -dē′yə) *n.* **1.** Any of various tropical American passionflowers, especially *Passiflora quadrangularis,* bearing edible fruit. **2.** The egg-shaped, fleshy fruit of such a plant. [Spanish, diminutive of *granada,* pomegranate, from Latin *grānātum,* from neuter of *grānātus,* seedy, from *grānum,* seed. See **gr̥ə-no-** in Appendix.]

Gra·na·dos (grə-nä′dōs, grä-nä′thôs), **Enrique.** 1867–1916. Spanish pianist and composer noted for his nationalistic music, such as *Goyescas* (1912–1914).

gran·a·ry (grăn′ə-rē, grā′nə-) *n., pl.* **-ries. 1.** A building for storing threshed grain. **2.** A region yielding much grain. [Latin *grānārium,* from *grānum,* grain. See **gr̥ə-no-** in Appendix.]

Gran·by (grăn′bē). A city of southern Quebec, Canada, east of Montreal. It is a manufacturing center. Population, 38,069.

Gran Cha·co (grän′ chä′kō). A lowland plain of central South America divided among Paraguay, Bolivia, and Argentina.

grand (grănd) *adj.* **grand·er, grand·est. 1.** Large and impressive in size, scope, or extent; magnificent. **2.a.** Rich and sumptuous: *A grand meal was laid before them.* **b.** Of a solemn, stately, or splendid nature. **3.a.** Dignified or noble in appearance or effect: *a grand old face that bespeaks suffering but not defeat.* **b.** Noble or admirable in conception or intent: *a grand purpose.* **c.** Lofty or sublime in character: *a speech delivered in the grand style of the great orators.* **4.** Wonderful or very pleasing: *had a grand time.* **5.** Having higher rank than others of the same category: *a grand admiral.* **6.** Having more importance than others; principal: *the grand ballroom of a hotel.* **7.** Of a haughty or pretentious nature. **8.** Including or covering all units or aspects: *the grand total.* **—grand** *n.* **1.** *Music.* A grand piano. **2.** *Slang.* A thousand dollars. [Middle English, from Old French, from Latin *grandis.*] **—grand′ly** *adv.* **—grand′ness** *n.*

SYNONYMS: *grand, magnificent, imposing, stately, majestic, august, grandiose.* These adjectives mean strikingly large in size, scope, or extent. Both *grand* and *magnificent* apply to what is physically or aesthetically impressive. *Grand* implies dignity, sweep, or eminence: *buildings on a grand scale; a grand coronation ceremony; a performance in the grand manner. Magnificent* suggests splendor, sumptuousness, and grandeur: *a magnificent cathedral; magnificent jewels; a magnificent poem. Imposing* describes what impresses by virtue of its size, bearing, or power: *an imposing residence; mountain peaks of imposing height. Stately* refers principally to what is dignified and handsome, as in size or proportions: *stately homes; stately columns; a stately oak. Majestic* suggests lofty dignity or nobility: *the majestic Alps; a majestic wave of the hand. August* describes what inspires solemn reverence or awe, as because of exalted rank or character: *was ushered into the archbishop's august presence. Grandiose* refers to what is marked by imposing largeness (*simple but grandiose architecture*); it often suggests pretentiousness, affectation, or pompousness (*grandiose ideas; a grandiose writing style*).

gran·dad·dy (grăn′dăd′ē) *n.* Variant of **granddaddy.**

gran·dam (grăn′dăm′, -dəm) also **gran·dame** (-dām′, -dăm, -dəm) *n.* **1.** See **grandmother** (sense 1). **2.** An old woman. [Middle English *grandame,* from Old French *dame-grant* : *dame,* lady; see DAME + *grant,* great; see GRAND.]

grand·aunt (grănd′ănt′, -änt′) *n.* See **great-aunt.**

grand·ba·by (grănd′bā′bē, grăn′-) *n. Informal.* A grandchild.

Grand Ba·ha·ma (grănd bə-hä′mə, -hā′-). An island of the Bahamas in the Atlantic Ocean east of West Palm Beach, Florida.

Grand Banks. An extensive area of shoals in the western Atlantic Ocean off southeast Newfoundland, Canada. The mingling of the cold Labrador Current and the warmer Gulf Stream make the area a major source of food fish.

Grand Canal. 1. An inland waterway, about 1,609 km (1,000 mi) long, of eastern China extending from Tianjin in the north to Hangzhou in the south. Begun in the 6th to 5th century B.C., it was completed in the 13th century A.D. **2.** The principal waterway of Venice, Italy. Crossed by the Rialto and other bridges, the canal is lined with impressive buildings.

Grand Ca·na·ry (kə-nâr′ē). One of the Canary Islands in the Atlantic Ocean east-southeast of Tenerife Island.

Grand Canyon. A gorge of the Colorado River in northwest Arizona. It is up to 1.6 km (1 mi) deep, from 6.4 to 29 km (4 to 18 mi) wide, and more than 321.8 km (200 mi) long.

Grand Cay·man (kā-măn′, kā′mən). See **Cayman Islands.**

grand·child (grănd′chīld′, grăn′-) *n.* A child of one's son or daughter.

Grand Cou·lee (kōō′lē). A gorge, about 48 km (30 mi) long, of north-central Washington, carved by the Columbia River. It is fed by water from the Grand Coulee Dam.

grand·dad (grăn′dăd′) *n. Informal.* A grandfather.

grand·dad·dy also **gran·dad·dy** (grăn′dăd′ē) *n. Informal.* **1.** A grandfather. **2.** One that is the first, oldest, or most respected of its kind: *the granddaddy of modern computers.*

grand·daugh·ter (grăn′dô′tər) *n.* A daughter of one's son or daughter.

grand duchess *n.* **1.** The wife or widow of a grand duke. **2.** A woman who is the sovereign of a grand duchy. **3.** The daughter or granddaughter of a czar in the male line. **4.** Used as the title for such a noblewoman.

grand duchy *n. Abbr.* **G.D.** A territory ruled by a grand duke or a grand duchess.

grand duke *n.* **1.** A nobleman who is the sovereign of a grand duchy. **2.** A son or grandson of a czar in the male line. **3.** Used as the title for such a nobleman.

Gran·de (grăn′də, grăɴ′dĭ), **Rio.** A river, about 1,046 km (650 mi) long, flowing from southeast Brazil generally northwest to the Paranaíba River, with which it forms the Paraná River.

grande dame (grănd′ dăm′, grănd′ däm′) *n., pl.* **grandes dames** also **grand dames** (grănd′ dăm′, grănd′ däm′). **1.** A highly respected elderly or middle-aged woman. **2.** A respected woman having extensive experience in her field: *the grande dame of women's professional tennis.* [French : *grande,* great + *dame,* lady.]

gran·dee (grăn-dē′) *n.* **1.a.** A nobleman of the highest rank in Spain or Portugal. **b.** Used as the title for such a nobleman. **2.** A person of eminence or high rank. [Spanish *grande,* from Latin *grandis,* great.]

grande luxe *n.* Great luxury. *—attributive.* Often used to modify another noun: *a grande luxe hotel; a grande luxe lifestyle.* [French : *grande,* great + *luxe,* luxury.]

Grande Prairie (grănd). A city of western Alberta, Canada, northwest of Edmonton. It is a trade center in a farming region. Population, 24,263.

Grande-Terre (grăn′târ′, grăɴd-). An island of eastern Guadeloupe in the Leeward Islands of the West Indies.

gran·deur (grăn′jər, -jŏŏr′) *n.* **1.** The quality or condition of

granary

Grand Canal
Venice, Italy

Grand Canyon

ă pat	oi boy
ā pay	ou out
âr care	ŏŏ took
ä father	ōō boot
ĕ pet	ŭ cut
ē be	ûr urge
ĭ pit	th thin
ī pie	*th* this
îr pier	hw which
ŏ pot	zh vision
ō toe	ə about, item
ô paw	♦ regionalism

Stress marks: ′ (primary); ′ (secondary), as in **dictionary** (dĭk′shə-nĕr′ē)

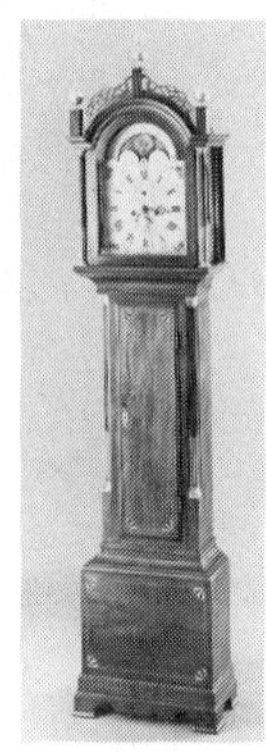
grandfather clock
c. 1800 American by Simon Willard (1753–1848)

being grand; magnificence: *"The world is charged with the grandeur of God"* (Gerard Manley Hopkins). **2.** Nobility or greatness of character. [Middle English, from Old French, from *grand,* great, from Latin *grandis.*]

Grand Falls. See **Churchill Falls.**

grand·fa·ther (grănd′fä′*th*ər, grăn′-) *n.* **1.** The father of one's mother or father. **2.** A forefather; an ancestor. **3.** *Computer Science.* A stored file of data from which two successive files have been derived, used for comparison with or as a backup copy for the newer files. **—grandfather** *tr.v.* **-thered, -ther·ing, -thers.** To exempt (one already involved in an activity or a business) from new regulations concerning that activity or business: *The city passed an ordinance restricting the size of advertising signs, but grandfathered all those signs erected before 1982.* [V., from GRANDFATHER CLAUSE.]

grandfather clause *n.* **1.** A provision in a statute that exempts those already involved in a regulated activity or business from the new regulations established by the statute. **2.** A clause in the constitutions of several southern states before the year 1915, intended to disfranchise Black people by exempting from stringent voting requirements all lineal descendants of persons who were registered voters before 1867.

grandfather clock *n.* A pendulum clock enclosed in a tall, narrow cabinet. [From the song *My Grandfather's Clock* by Henry C. Work.]

grand·fa·ther·ly (grănd′fä′*th*ər-lē, grăn′-) *adj.* **1.** Characteristic of or befitting a grandfather. **2.** Having the qualities of a grandfather.

Grand Forks. A city of eastern North Dakota on the Red River north of Fargo. Established as a fur-trading post in 1801, it is the seat of the University of North Dakota (founded 1883). Population, 43,765.

Grand Gui·gnol (grän gē-nyôl′) *n.* Drama that emphasizes the horrifying or the macabre. [After Le *Grand Guignol,* a theater in Paris.]

gran·dil·o·quence (grăn-dĭl′ə-kwəns) *n.* Pompous or bombastic speech or expression. [From *grandiloquent,* from Latin *grandiloquus* : *grandis,* great + *loquī,* to speak; see **tolkʷ-** in Appendix.] **—gran·dil′o·quent** *adj.* **—gran·dil′o·quent·ly** *adv.*

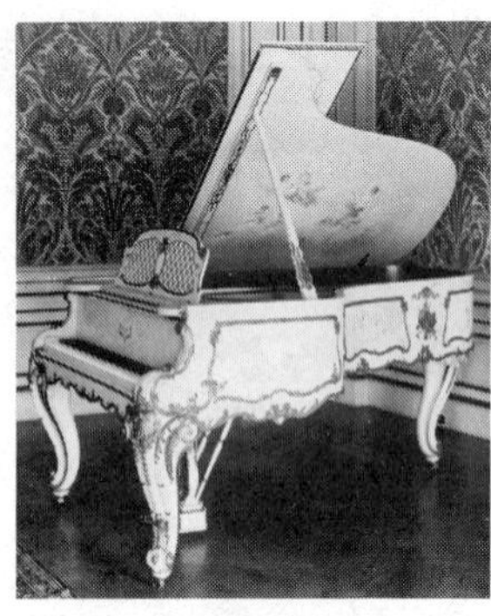
grand piano
Rococo style

gran·di·ose (grăn′dē-ōs′, grăn′dē-ōs′) *adj.* **1.** Characterized by greatness of scope or intent; grand. See Synonyms at **grand. 2.** Characterized by feigned or affected grandeur; pompous. [French, from Italian *grandioso,* from *grande,* great, from Latin *grandis.*] **—gran′di·ose′ly** *adv.* **—gran′di·os′i·ty** (-ŏs′ĭ-tē), **gran′di·ose′ness** *n.*

gran·di·o·so (grän′dē-ō′sō, -zō, grăn′) *adv. & adj. Music.* In a grand and noble style. Used chiefly as a direction. [Italian. See GRANDIOSE.]

Grand Island. A city of southeast-central Nebraska west of Lincoln. It was settled on the Platte River in 1857 and moved to its present location in 1866. Population, 33,180.

Grand Junc·tion (jŭngk′shən). A city of western Colorado at the junction of the Gunnison and Colorado rivers near the Utah border. It is a trade and manufacturing center in an irrigated farming region. Population, 27,956.

grand jury *n. Law.* A jury of 12 to 23 persons convened in private session to evaluate accusations against persons charged with crime and to determine whether the evidence warrants a bill of indictment.

grand·kid (grănd′kĭd′, grăn′-) *n. Informal.* A grandchild.

Grand Lama *n.* Either of two traditionally reincarnating high lamas of Tibetan Buddhism, the Dalai Lama or the Panchen Lama.

grand larceny *n. Law.* The theft of property of a value exceeding the amount constituting petit larceny.

grand·ma (grănd′mä′, grăn′-, grăm′mä′, grăm′ə) *n. Informal.* A grandmother.

grand mal (grän mäl′, grän, grănd′ măl′) *n.* A severe form of epilepsy characterized by seizures involving spasms and loss of consciousness. [French : *grand,* great + *mal,* illness.]

Grand·ma Mo·ses (grănd′mä mō′zĭz, -zĭs). See Anna Mary Robertson **Moses.**

Grand Ma·nan Island (mə-năn′). An island of southern New Brunswick, Canada, in the Bay of Fundy. **Grand Manan Channel** separates the island from the coast of Maine.

grand march *n.* A ceremonial march at a ball in which all couples take part.

grand master or **grand·mas·ter** (grănd′măs′tər) *n.* **1.** *Abbr.* **GM, G.M.** *Games.* A chess player regarded as having the highest level of ability. **2.** A person of the highest competence or achievement in a field: *a grand master of foreign diplomacy.*

grand·moth·er (grănd′mŭ*th*′ər, grăn′-) *n.* **1.** The mother of one's father or mother. Also called *grandam.* **2.** A female ancestor.

grand·moth·er·ly (grănd′mŭ*th*′ər-lē, grăn′-) *adj.* **1.** Characteristic of or befitting a grandmother. **2.** Having the qualities of a grandmother.

grand·neph·ew (grănd′nĕf′yo͞o, grăn′-) *n.* A son of one's nephew or niece.

grand·niece (grănd′nēs′, grăn′-) *n.* A daughter of one's nephew or niece.

grand opera *n. Music.* A serious or melodramatic drama having the entire text set to music.

grand·pa (grănd′pä′, grăn′-, grăm′pä′, grăm′pə) *n. Informal.* A grandfather.

grand·par·ent (grănd′pâr′ənt, -păr′-, grăn′-) *n.* A parent of one's mother or father; a grandmother or grandfather. **—grand′pa·ren′tal** (-pə-rĕn′tl) *adj.* **—grand′par′ent·hood′** *n.*

grand piano *n. Music.* A piano having the strings strung in a horizontal harp-shaped frame supported usually on three legs.

Grand Prairie. A city of northeast Texas halfway between Dallas and Fort Worth. Located in a highly urbanized area, the city has an aerospace industry. Population, 71,462.

Grand Pré (grăn′ prā′, grän′). A village of western Nova Scotia, Canada, on an arm of the Bay of Fundy. Settled by Acadians, it is the setting for Longfellow's poem *Evangeline* (1847).

Grand Prix (grän′ prē′) *n., pl.* **Grand Prix** (prēz′, prē′). *Sports.* Any of several competitive international road races for sports cars of specific engine size over an exacting, usually risky course. [French, short for *Grand Prix de Paris,* originally an international horserace established in 1863 at Longchamp in Paris.]

Grand Rapids (grănd). A city of west-central Michigan on the Grand River west-northwest of Lansing. Built on the site of an Ottawa village, it has been a furniture-manufacturing center since the mid-1800's. Population, 181,843.

Grand River. 1. A river rising in southeast Iowa and flowing about 483 km (300 mi) southeast across northwest Missouri to the Missouri River. **2.** A river, about 418 km (260 mi) long, of southern Michigan flowing north and northwest to Lake Michigan.

grand·sire (grănd′sīr′, grăn′-) also **grand·sir** (-sər) *n. Archaic.* **1.** A grandfather. **2.** A male ancestor; a forefather. **3.** An old man.

grand slam *n.* **1.** *Games.* The winning of all the tricks during the play of one hand in bridge and other whist-derived card games. **2.** *Sports.* The winning of all the major or specified events, especially on a professional circuit. **3.** *Baseball.* A home run hit when three runners are on base.

grand·son (grănd′sŭn′, grăn′-) *n.* A son of one's son or daughter.

grand·stand (grănd′stănd′, grăn′-) *n.* **1.** A roofed stand for spectators at a stadium or racetrack. **2.** The spectators or audience at an event. **—grandstand** *intr.v.* **-stand·ed, -stand·ing, -stands.** To perform ostentatiously so as to impress an audience. **—grand′stand′er** *n.*

Grand Te·ton (tē′tŏn′, tēt′n). A mountain, 4,198.6 m (13,766 ft) high, of the Teton Range in northwest Wyoming.

grand tour *n.* **1.** A comprehensive tour or survey. **2.** An extended tour of continental Europe formerly considered a finishing course in the education of young men of the English upper class.

Grand Turk (tûrk). The chief island of the Turks and Caicos Islands in the Atlantic Ocean southeast of the Bahamas. The town of **Grand Turk** (population, 3,146) is the capital of the island group.

grand·un·cle (grănd′ŭng′kəl) *n.* See **great-uncle.**

Grand·view (grănd′vyo͞o′). A city of western Missouri surrounded on three sides by southern Kansas City. It is a manufacturing center. Population, 24,502.

grange (grānj) *n.* **1. Grange. a.** An association of farmers founded in the United States in 1867. **b.** One of the branch lodges of this association. **2.** *Chiefly British.* A farm, especially the residence and outbuildings of a gentleman farmer. **3.** *Archaic.* A granary. [Middle English, granary, from Old French *grange,* from Vulgar Latin **grānica,* from Latin *grānum,* seed. See **gr̥ə-no-** in Appendix.]

grani– *pref.* Grain; seed: *granivorous.* [Latin *grāni-,* from *grānum,* seed. See GRAM[2].]

gran·ite (grăn′ĭt) *n.* **1.** A common, coarse-grained, light-colored, hard igneous rock consisting chiefly of quartz, orthoclase or microcline, and mica, used in monuments and for building. **2.** Unyielding endurance; steadfastness: *a will of granite.* [Italian *granito,* from past participle of *granire,* to make grainy, from *grano,* grain, from Latin *grānum.* See **gr̥ə-no-** in Appendix.] **—gra·nit′ic** (grā-nĭt′ĭk, grə-), **gran′it·oid′** (grăn′ĭ-toid′) *adj.*

Gran·ite City (grăn′ĭt). A city of southwest Illinois, an industrial suburb of East St. Louis. Population, 36,815.

gran·ite·ware (grăn′ĭt-wâr′) *n.* **1.** Iron utensils with a mottled enamel resembling granite. **2.** Earthenware with a speckled glaze resembling granite.

gra·niv·o·rous (grə-nĭv′ər-əs) *adj.* Feeding on grain and seeds.

♦ **gran·ny** or **gran·nie** (grăn′ē) *n., pl.* **-nies. 1.** *Informal.* A grandmother. **2.** *Informal.* A fussy person. **3.** *Chiefly Southern U.S.* See **midwife** (sense 1). [Short for GRANDMOTHER or GRANDAM.]

granny flat *n.* See **accessory apartment.**

granny knot *n.* A knot resembling a square knot but with the second tie crossed incorrectly. [So called in contempt.]

grano– *pref.* Granite: *granolith.* [German, from *Granit,* granite, from Italian *granito.* See GRANITE.]

gra·no·la (grə-nō′lə) *n.* Rolled oats mixed with various ingredients, such as dried fruit, brown sugar, and nuts, and used especially as a breakfast cereal. [Originally a trademark.]

gran·o·lith (grăn′ə-lĭth′) *n.* A paving stone of crushed granite and cement. **—gran′o·lith′ic** *adj.*

gran·o·phyre (grăn′ə-fīr′) *n.* A fine-grained granite porphyry having a groundmass with irregular intergrowths of quartz and feldspar. [German *Granophyr* : *grano-*, grano- + *Porphyr*, porphyry (from Medieval Latin *porphyrium;* see PORPHYRY).] **—gran′o·phyr′ic** (-fīr′ĭk) *adj.*

grant (grănt) *tr.v.* **grant·ed, grant·ing, grants. 1.** To consent to the fulfillment of: *grant a request.* **2.** To accord as a favor, prerogative, or privilege: *granted the franchise to all citizens.* **3.a.** To bestow; confer: *grant aid.* **b.** To transfer (property) by a deed. **4.** To concede; acknowledge: *I grant the genius of your plan, but you still will not find backers.* **—grant** *n.* **1.** The act of granting. **2.a.** Something granted. **b.** A giving of funds for a specific purpose: *federal grants for medical research.* **3.** *Law.* **a.** A transfer of property by deed. **b.** The property so transferred. **c.** The deed by which the property is so transferred. **4.** One of several tracts of land in New Hampshire, Maine, and Vermont originally granted to an individual or a group. [Middle English *granten,* from Old French *granter,* variant of *creanter,* from Vulgar Latin **crēdentāre,* to assure, from Latin *crēdēns, crēdent-,* present participle of *crēdere,* to believe. See **kerd-** in Appendix.] **—grant′a·ble** *adj.* **—grant′er** *n.*

SYNONYMS: *grant, vouchsafe, concede, accord, award.* These verbs mean to give as a favor, prerogative, or privilege. *Grant* usually implies that the giver is in a higher position, as one of authority, than the receiver and that he or she acts out of justice, mercy, or generosity: *granted the petitioner's request; granting permission. Vouchsafe* emphasizes more strongly the giver's superior position and connotes condescension: *won't vouchsafe an answer to your question. Concede* usually implies giving reluctantly in response to a strong claim: *had to concede the mayor's incorruptible honesty. Accord* and *award* suggest that what is granted is proper, merited, or appropriate: *must accord the senator the respect she is due; hopes to be awarded a stipend for further research.*

Grant (grănt), **Cary.** 1904–1986. British-born American actor who was the epitome of the elegant leading man in films such as *The Philadelphia Story* (1940) and *North by Northwest* (1959).

Grant, Ulysses Simpson. Originally Hiram Ulysses Grant. 1822–1885. The 18th President of the United States (1869–1877) and a Civil War general. After his victorious Vicksburg campaign (1862–1863), he was made commander in chief of the Union Army (1864) and accepted the surrender of Gen. Robert E. Lee at Appomattox (1865). Grant's two-term presidency was marred by widespread graft and corruption.

grant·ee (grăn-tē′) *n. Law.* One to whom a grant is made.

grant-in-aid (grănt′ĭn-ād′) *n., pl.* **grants-in-aid** (grănts′-). **1.** A giving of federal funds to a state or local government to subsidize a public project. **2.** A giving of funds to an institution or a person in order to subsidize a project or program.

gran·tor (grăn′tər, -tôr′) *n. Law.* One that makes a grant.

Grant's gazelle (grănts) *n.* A large gazelle *(Gazella granti)* of East Africa that has long, curved horns. [After James Augustus *Grant* (1827–1892), Scottish explorer.]

grants·man·ship (grănts′mən-shĭp′) *n.* The art of obtaining grants-in-aid. [GRANT + (GAME)SMANSHIP.]

gran·u·lar (grăn′yə-lər) *adj.* **1.** Composed or appearing to be composed of granules or grains. **2.** Having a grainy texture. **3.** *Biology.* Containing granules: *granular cells.* **—gran′u·lar′i·ty** (-lăr′ĭ-tē) *n.* **—gran′u·lar·ly** *adv.*

gran·u·late (grăn′yə-lāt′) *v.* **-lat·ed, -lat·ing, -lates.** —*tr.* **1.** To form into grains or granules. **2.** To make rough and grainy. —*intr.* To become granular or grainy. **—gran′u·la′tive** *adj.* **—gran′u·la′tor** *n.*

gran·u·la·tion (grăn′yə-lā′shən) *n.* **1.a.** The act or process of granulating. **b.** The condition or appearance of being granulated. **2.** *Physiology.* **a.** Small, fleshy, beadlike protuberances, consisting of outgrowths of new capillaries, on the surface of a wound that is healing. Also called *granulation tissue.* **b.** The formation of these protuberances. **3.** *Astronomy.* The small, transient, brilliant granular markings on the photosphere of the sun.

gran·ule (grăn′yo͞ol) *n.* **1.** A small grain or pellet; a particle. **2.** *Geology.* A rock or mineral fragment larger than a sand grain and smaller than a pebble, between 2 and 4 millimeters in diameter. **3.** *Astronomy.* One of the small, transient, brilliant markings in the photosphere of the sun. **4.** *Biology.* A cellular or cytoplasmic particle, especially one that stains readily. [Late Latin *grānulum,* diminutive of Latin *grānum,* grain. See **grə-no-** in Appendix.]

gran·u·lite (grăn′yə-līt′) *n.* A fine-grained metamorphic rock often banded in appearance and composed chiefly of feldspar, quartz, and garnet. **—gran′u·lit′ic** (-lĭt′ĭk) *adj.*

gran·u·lo·cyte (grăn′yə-lō-sīt′) *n.* Any of a group of white blood cells having granules in the cytoplasm. **—gran′u·lo·cyt′ic** (-sĭt′ĭk) *adj.*

gran·u·lo·ma (grăn′yə-lō′mə) *n., pl.* **-mas** or **-ma·ta** (-mə-tə). A mass of inflamed granulation tissue, usually associated with ulcerated infections. **—gran′u·lo′ma·tous** (-mə-təs) *adj.*

gran·u·lose (grăn′yə-lōs′) *adj.* Having a surface covered with granules.

gra·num (grā′nəm) *n. Botany.* A stacked membranous structure within a chloroplast that contains the chlorophyll and is the site of the light reactions of photosynthesis. [Latin *grānum,* seed. See GRAIN.]

Gran·ville-Bar·ker (grăn′vĭl-bär′kər), **Harley Granville.** 1877–1946. British actor, playwright, manager, and critic noted for his productions of Shakespeare.

grape (grāp) *n.* **1.** Any of numerous woody vines of the genus *Vitis,* bearing clusters of edible berries and widely cultivated in many species and varieties. **2.** The fleshy, smooth-skinned, purple, red, or green berry of a grape, eaten raw or dried as a raisin and widely used in winemaking. **3.** *Color.* A dark violet to dark grayish purple. **4.** Grapeshot. [Middle English, from Old French, bunch of grapes, hook, of Germanic origin.]

grape fern *n.* Any of various ferns of the genus *Botrychium,* having a fertile frond bearing small, grapelike clusters of spore cases. Also called *moonwort.*

grape·fruit (grāp′fro͞ot′) *n.* **1.** A tropical or semitropical evergreen *(Citrus paradisi)* cultivated for its edible fruit. **2.** The large, round fruit of this tree, having a yellow rind and juicy, somewhat acid pulp. [Probably so called because the fruit grows in clusters.]

grape hyacinth *n.* Any of various plants of the genus *Muscari,* native to Eurasia and having narrow leaves and dense terminal racemes of rounded, usually blue flowers.

grape·shot (grāp′shŏt′) *n.* A cluster of small iron balls formerly used as a cannon charge. [From its resemblance to a cluster of grapes.]

grape sugar *n.* Dextrose obtained from grapes.

grape·vine (grāp′vīn′) *n.* **1.** A vine on which grapes grow. **2.a.** The informal transmission of information, gossip, or rumor from person to person. **b.** A usually unrevealed source of confidential information.

grap·ey or **grap·y** (grā′pē) *adj.* **-i·er, -i·est.** Of or resembling grapes: *a wine with a grapey taste.* **—grap′i·ness** *n.*

graph¹ (grăf) *n.* **1.** A diagram that exhibits a relationship, often functional, between two sets of numbers as a set of points having coordinates determined by the relationship. Also called *plot.* **2.** A pictorial device, such as a pie chart or bar graph, used to illustrate quantitative relationships. Also called *chart.* **—graph** *tr.v.* **graphed, graph·ing, graphs. 1.** To represent by a graph. **2.** To plot (a function) on a graph. [Short for *graphic formula.*]

graph² (grăf) *n.* **1.** The spelling of a word. **2.** Any of the possible forms of a grapheme. **3.** A written character that represents a vowel, consonant, syllable, word, or other expression and cannot be further analyzed. [Greek *graphē,* writing. See GRAPHIC.]

-graph *suff.* **1.** Something written or drawn: *monograph.* **2.** An instrument for writing, drawing, or recording: *seismograph.* [French *-graphe,* from Late Latin *-graphus,* from Greek *-graphos,* from *graphein,* to write. See **gerbh-** in Appendix.]

graph·eme (grăf′ēm′) *n.* **1.** A letter of an alphabet. **2.** All of the letters and letter combinations that represent a phoneme, as *f, ph,* and *gh* for the phoneme /f/. [GRAPH² + -EME.] **—gra·phe′mic** (gră-fē′mĭk) *adj.* **—gra·phe′mi·cal·ly** *adv.*

-grapher *suff.* One who writes about a specified subject or in a specified manner: *stenographer.* [From Late Latin *-graphus,* from Greek *-graphos,* from *graphein,* to write. See **gerbh-** in Appendix.]

graph·ic (grăf′ĭk) also **graph·i·cal** (-ĭ-kəl) *adj.* **1.a.** Of or relating to written representation. **b.** Of or relating to pictorial representation. **2.** Of, relating to, or represented by or as if by a graph. **3.a.** Described in vivid detail. **b.** Clearly outlined or set forth. **4.** Of or relating to the graphic arts. **5.** Of or relating to graphics. **6.** *Geology.* Having crystals resembling printed characters. **—graphic** *n.* **1.** A work of graphic art. **2.** A pictorial device used for illustration, as in a lecture. **3.** A graphic display generated by a computer or an imaging device. [Latin *graphicus,* from Greek *graphikos,* from *graphē,* writing, from *graphein,* to write. See **gerbh-** in Appendix.] **—graph′i·cal·ly** *adv.* **—graph′ic·ness** *n.*

SYNONYMS: *graphic, lifelike, realistic, vivid.* The central meaning shared by these adjectives is "strikingly sharp and accurate": *a graphic account of the battle; a lifelike portrait; a realistic description; a vivid recollection of the accident.*

graphic arts *pl.n.* **1.** The fine or applied visual arts and associated techniques involving the application of lines and strokes to a two-dimensional surface. **2.** The fine or applied visual arts and associated techniques in which images are produced from blocks, plates, or type, as in engraving and lithography.

graph·ics (grăf′ĭks) *n.* **1.a.** *(used with a sing. verb).* The making of drawings in accordance with the rules of mathematics, as in engineering or architecture. **b.** *(used with a pl. verb).* Calculations, as of structural stress, from such drawings. **2.** *Computer Science.* **a.** *(used with a sing. or pl. verb).* The pictorial representation and manipulation of data, as used in computer-aided design and computer-aided manufacture, in typesetting and the graphic arts, and in educational and recreational programs. **b.** *(used with a sing. verb).* The process by which a computer displays data pictorially.

Ulysses S. Grant

grape

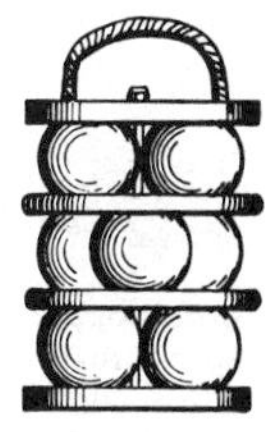

grapeshot

ă pat	oi boy
ā pay	ou out
âr care	o͝o took
ä father	o͞o boot
ĕ pet	ŭ cut
ē be	ûr urge
ĭ pit	th thin
ī pie	*th* this
îr pier	hw which
ŏ pot	zh vision
ō toe	ə about, item
ô paw	♦ regionalism

Stress marks: ′ (primary); ′ (secondary), as in **dictionary** (dĭk′shə-nĕr′ē).

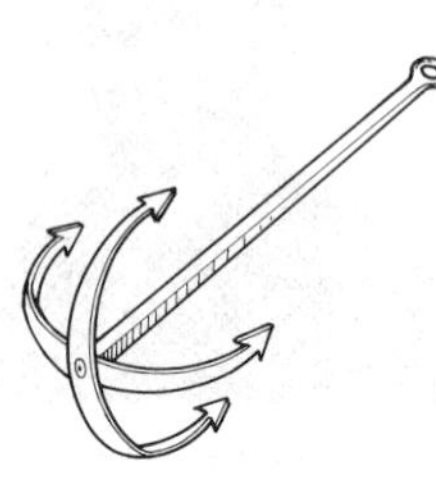
grapnel

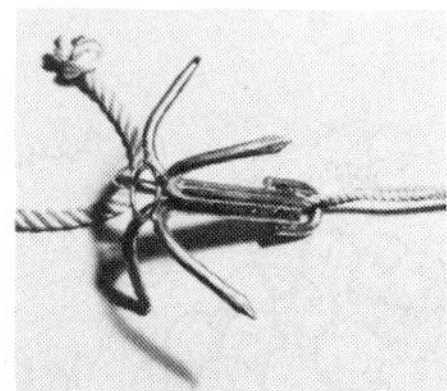
grapple

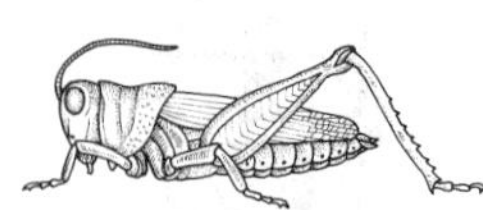
grasshopper
Spur-throated grasshopper
Schistocerca americana

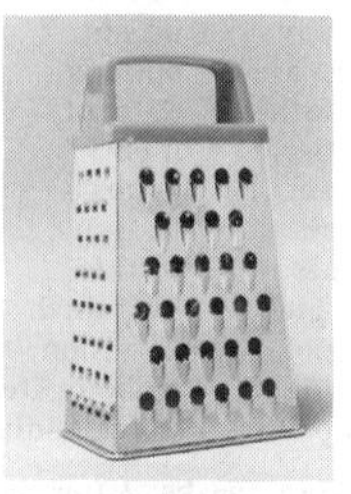
grater
Food grater

graph·ite (grăf′īt′) *n.* A soft, steel-gray to black, hexagonally crystallized allotrope of carbon with a metallic luster and a greasy feel, used in lead pencils, lubricants, paints, and coatings, that is fabricated into a variety of forms such as molds, bricks, electrodes, crucibles, and rocket nozzles. Also called *black lead, plumbago.* [Greek *graphein,* to write; see **gerbh-** in Appendix + –ITE[1].] **—gra·phit′ic** (gră-fĭt′ĭk) *adj.*

graph·i·tize (grăf′ĭ-tīz′) *tr.v.* **-tized, -tiz·ing, -tiz·es. 1.** To convert into graphite. **2.** To coat or impregnate with graphite. **—graph′i·ti·za′tion** (-tĭ-zā′shən) *n.*

gra·phol·o·gy (gră-fŏl′ə-jē) *n.* The study of handwriting, especially when employed as a means of analyzing character. [Greek *graphē,* writing; see GRAPHIC + –LOGY.] **—graph′o·log′i·cal** (grăf′ə-lŏj′ĭ-kəl) *adj.* **—gra·phol′o·gist** *n.*

graph paper *n.* Paper ruled usually into small squares of equal size for use in drawing charts, graphs, or diagrams.

–graphy *suff.* **1.** A writing or representation produced in a specified manner or by a specified process: *photography.* **2.a.** A writing about a specified subject: *oceanography.* **b.** A representation of a specified object: *phonography.* [Latin *-graphia,* from Greek, from *graphein,* to write. See **gerbh-** in Appendix.]

grap·nel (grăp′nəl) *n.* **1.** *Nautical.* A small anchor with three or more flukes, especially one used for anchoring a small vessel. Also called *grapple, grappling.* **2.** See **grapple** (sense 1a). [Middle English *grapenel,* probably ultimately from Old French *grapin,* hook, diminutive of *grape.* See GRAPE.]

grap·pa (grä′pə) *n.* An Italian brandy distilled from the pomace of grapes used in winemaking. [Italian, from Italian dialectal, grape stalk, brandy, of Germanic origin.]

grap·ple (grăp′əl) *n.* **1.a.** An iron shaft with claws at one end, usually thrown by a rope and used for grasping and holding, especially one for drawing and holding an enemy ship alongside. Also called *grapnel, grappling, grappling hook, grappling iron.* **b.** *Nautical.* See **grapnel** (sense 1). **2.** The act of grappling. **3.** *Sports.* **a.** A contest in which the participants attempt to clutch or grip each other. **b.** A grasp or grip in such a contest. **—grapple** *v.* **-pled, -pling, -ples.** *—tr.* **1.** To seize and hold, as with a grapple. **2.** To seize firmly, as with the hands. *—intr.* **1.** To hold onto something with or as if with a grapple. **2.** To use a grapple or similar device, as for dragging. **3.** To struggle, in or as if in wrestling: *grappled with their consciences.* [Middle English *grapel,* from Old French *grapil,* diminutive of *grape,* hook. See GRAPE.] **—grap′pler** *n.*

grap·pling (grăp′lĭng) *n.* **1.** See **grapple** (sense 1a). **2.** *Nautical.* See **grapnel** (sense 1).

grappling hook *n.* See **grapple** (sense 1a).

grappling iron *n.* See **grapple** (sense 1a).

grap·to·lite (grăp′tə-līt′) *n.* Any of numerous extinct colonial marine animals chiefly of the orders Dendroidea and Graptoloidea of the late Cambrian to the early Mississippian periods, whose fossil remains are often used to date the rocks of the Silurian and Ordovician ages. [Greek *graptos,* written (from *graphein,* to write; see GRAPHIC) + –LITE (from the resemblance of the fossils' impressions on shale to markings on a slate).]

grap·y (grā′pē) *adj.* **-i·er, -i·est.** Variant of **grapey.**

GRAS *abbr.* Generally recognized as safe. Used by the U.S. Food and Drug Administration as a label designating food ingredients or additives not known to be harmful to human beings when used as intended.

Gras·mere (grăs′mîr′). A lake of northwest England in the Lake District. Dove Cottage, in the former village of **Grasmere,** was the home of William Wordsworth from 1799 to 1808.

grasp (grăsp) *v.* **grasped, grasp·ing, grasps.** *—tr.* **1.** To take hold of or seize firmly with or as if with the hand. **2.** To clasp firmly with or as if with the hand. **3.** To take hold of intellectually; comprehend. See Synonyms at **apprehend.** *—intr.* **1.** To make a motion of seizing, snatching, or clutching. **2.** To show eager and prompt willingness or acceptance: *grasps at any opportunity.* **—grasp** *n.* **1.** The act of grasping. **2.a.** A firm hold or grip. **b.** An embrace. **3.** The ability or power to seize or attain; reach: *Victory in the election was within her grasp.* **4.** Understanding; comprehension: *"only a vague intuitive grasp of the meaning of greatness in literature"* (Gilbert Highet). [Middle English *graspen.* See **ghrebh-**[1] in Appendix.]

grasp·ing (grăs′pĭng) *adj.* Exceedingly eager for material gain; avaricious. **—grasp′ing·ly** *adv.* **—grasp′ing·ness** *n.*

grass (grăs) *n.* **1.a.** The grass family. **b.** The members of the grass family considered as a group. **2.** Any of various plants having slender leaves characteristic of the grass family. **3.** An expanse of ground, such as a lawn, covered with grass or similar plants. **4.** Grazing land; pasture. **5.** *Slang.* Marijuana. **6.** *Electronics.* Small variations in amplitude of an oscilloscope display caused by electrical noise. **—grass** *v.* **grassed, grass·ing, grass·es.** *—tr.* **1.a.** To cover with grass. **b.** To grow grass on. **2.** To feed (livestock) with grass. *—intr.* **1.** To become covered with grass. **2.** To graze. [Middle English *gras,* from Old English *græs.* See **ghrē-** in Appendix.]

Grass (gräs), **Günter Wilhelm.** Born 1927. German writer whose novels, notably *The Tin Drum* (1959) and *Dog Years* (1963), concern the political and social climate of Germany during and after World War II.

Grasse (grăs, gräs). A town of southeast France west of Nice. Probably founded in Roman times, it was an independent republic in the 12th century. The city has long been noted for its perfume industry. Population, 24,553.

Grasse, Comte **François Joseph Paul de.** Marquis de Grasse-Tilly. 1722?–1788. French naval officer who during the American Revolution commanded the French fleet in Chesapeake Bay.

grass family *n.* A large and widespread family of plants, the Gramineae (or Poaceae), characterized by usually hollow stems, sheath-forming leaves in two longitudinal rows, and minute flowers arranged in spikelets. The grasses include important food plants such as wheat, rice, corn, barley, oats, and sorghum and also plants for turf and fodder.

grass green *n.* *Color.* A moderate yellow-green to strong or dark yellowish-green. **—grass′-green′** (grăs′grēn′) *adj.*

♦ **grass·hop·per** (grăs′hŏp′ər) *n.* **1.** Any of numerous orthopteran insects of the families Locustidae (or Acrididae) and Tettigoniidae, often destructive to plants and characteristically having long, powerful hind legs adapted for jumping. Also called ♦*hoppergrass.* **2.** A light, usually unarmed airplane used for liaison and scouting. **3.** A cocktail consisting of crème de menthe, crème de cacao, and cream.

grass·land (grăs′lănd′) *n.* An area, such as a prairie or meadow, of grass or grasslike vegetation.

Gras·so (grăs′ō, grä′sō), **Ella Tambussi.** 1919–1981. American public official who served as governor of Connecticut (1975–1981).

grass·roots (grăs′ro͞ots′, -ro͝ots′) *pl.n. (used with a sing. or pl. verb).* **1.** People or society at a local level rather than at the center of major political activity. Often used with *the.* **2.** The groundwork or source of something. *—attributive.* Often used to modify another noun: *a grassroots movement; a grassroots constituency.*

grass snake *n.* Any of several greenish, nonvenomous snakes, especially *Opheodrys vernalis* of eastern North America or *Natrix natrix* of Europe.

grass tree *n.* Any of several woody-stemmed Australian plants of the genus *Xanthorrhoea,* having stiff grasslike leaves, palmlike stems, and a spike of small white flowers.

grass widow *n.* **1.** A woman who is divorced or separated from her husband. **2.** A woman whose husband is temporarily absent. **3.** An abandoned mistress. **4.** The mother of an illegitimate child. [Perhaps in allusion to a bed of grass or hay.]

WORD HISTORY: The term *grass widow* cries out for explanation as to what *grass* means and how *grass widow* came to have its varied though related senses. *Grass* probably refers to a bed of grass or hay as opposed to a real bed. This association would help explain the earliest recorded sense of the word (1528), "an unmarried woman who has lived with one or more men," as well as the related senses "an abandoned mistress" and "the mother of an illegitimate child." Later on, after the sense of *grass* had been obscured, people may have interpreted *grass* as equivalent to the figurative use of *pasture,* as in *out to pasture.* Hence *grass widow* could have developed the senses "a divorced or separated wife" or "a wife whose husband is temporarily absent."

grass widower *n.* **1.** A man who is divorced or separated from his wife. **2.** A man whose wife is temporarily absent.

grass·y (grăs′ē) *adj.* **-i·er, -i·est. 1.** Covered with or abounding in grass. **2.** Resembling or suggestive of grass, as in color or odor.

grate[1] (grāt) *v.* **grat·ed, grat·ing, grates.** *—tr.* **1.** To reduce to fragments, shreds, or powder by rubbing against an abrasive surface. **2.** To cause to make a harsh grinding or rasping sound through friction: *grated her teeth in anger.* **3.** To irritate or annoy persistently. **4.** *Archaic.* To rub or wear away. *—intr.* **1.** To make a harsh rasping sound by or as if by scraping or grinding. **2.** To cause irritation or annoyance: *a noise that grates on one's nerves.* **—grate** *n.* A harsh rasping sound made by scraping or rubbing: *the grate of a key in a lock.* [Middle English *graten,* from Old French *grater,* to scrape, of Germanic origin.]

grate[2] (grāt) *n.* **1.** A framework of parallel or latticed bars for blocking an opening. **2.** A framework of metal bars used to hold fuel or food in a stove, furnace, or fireplace. **3.** A fireplace. **4.** A perforated iron plate or screen for sieving and grading crushed ore. **—grate** *tr.v.* **grat·ed, grat·ing, grates.** To equip with a grate. [Middle English, from Medieval Latin *grāta,* alteration of Latin *crātis,* wickerwork.]

grate·ful (grāt′fəl) *adj.* **1.** Appreciative of benefits received; thankful. **2.** Expressing gratitude. **3.** Affording pleasure or comfort; agreeable. [From obsolete *grate,* pleasing, from Latin *grātus.* See **gʷerə-**[2] in Appendix.] **—grate′ful·ly** *adv.* **—grate′ful·ness** *n.*

grat·er (grā′tər) *n.* One that grates, as an implement with sharp-edged slits and perforations on which to grate foods.

Gra·tian (grā′shən, -shē-ən). A.D. 359–383. Emperor of Rome (367–383) who ruled jointly (from 379) with Theodosius I. He was murdered by followers of the usurper Maximus (died 383).

grat·i·fi·ca·tion (grăt′ə-fĭ-kā′shən) *n.* **1.a.** The act of gratifying. **b.** The condition of being gratified. **2.** An instance or a cause of being gratified. **3.** *Archaic.* **a.** A reward. **b.** A gratuity.

grat·i·fy (grăt′ə-fī′) *tr.v.* **-fied, -fy·ing, -fies. 1.** To please or satisfy: *His achievement gratified his father.* See Synonyms at

please. **2.** To give what is desired to; indulge: *gratified her curiosity.* **3.** *Archaic.* To reward. [Middle English *gratifien,* to favor, from Latin *grātificārī* : *grātus,* pleasing; see **gʷerə-[2]** in Appendix + *-ficārī,* -fy.] **—grat′i·fi′er** *n.* **—grat′i·fy′ing** *adj.* **—grat′i·fy′ing·ly** *adv.*

gra·tin (grät′n, grăt′n, grä-tăɴ′) *n.* A crust consisting of browned crumbs and butter, often with grated cheese. [French, from obsolete *grater,* to scratch, scrape, from Old French. See GRATE[1].]

grat·ing (grā′tĭng) *n.* **1.** A grill or network of bars set in a window or door or used as a partition; a grate. **2.** A diffraction grating.

grat·is (grăt′ĭs, grä′tĭs, grā′-) *adv. & adj.* Without charge. [Middle English, from Latin *grātīs,* alteration of *grātiīs,* out of kindness, free, ablative pl. of *grātia,* kindness. See **gʷerə-[2]** in Appendix.]

grat·i·tude (grăt′ĭ-to͞od′, -tyo͞od′) *n.* The state of being grateful; thankfulness. [Middle English, from Old French, probably from Late Latin *grātitūdō, grātitūdin-,* from Latin *grātus,* pleasing. See **gʷerə-[2]** in Appendix.]

Grat·tan (grăt′n), **Henry.** 1746–1820. Irish politician who opposed the union of Ireland with England (1800).

gra·tu·i·tous (grə-to͞o′ĭ-təs, -tyo͞o′-) *adj.* **1.** Given or granted without return or recompense; unearned. **2.** Given or received without cost or obligation; free. **3.** Unnecessary or unwarranted; unjustified: *gratuitous criticism.* [From Latin *grātuītus.* See **gʷerə-[2]** in Appendix.] **—gra·tu′i·tous·ly** *adv.* **—gra·tu′i·tous·ness** *n.*

gra·tu·i·ty (grə-to͞o′ĭ-tē, -tyo͞o′-) *n., pl.* **-ties.** A favor or gift, usually in the form of money, given in return for service. See Synonyms at **bonus.** [French *gratuité,* from Old French *gratuite,* from Medieval Latin *grātuītās,* probably from Latin *grātuītus,* voluntary. See GRATUITOUS.]

grat·u·late (grăch′ə-lāt′) *Archaic. tr.v.* **-lat·ed, -lat·ing, -lates.** To congratulate. [Latin *grātulārī, grātulāt-,* ultimately from *grātārī,* to rejoice with. See GRATEFUL.] **—grat′u·la′tion** *n.* **—grat′u·la·to′ry** (-lə-tôr′ē, -tōr′ē) *adj.*

grau·pel (grou′pəl) *n.* See **snow pellet.** [German *Graupel,* diminutive of *Graupe,* hulled grain, probably of Slavic origin; akin to Russian *krupa,* groats.]

gra·va·men (grə-vā′mən) *n., pl.* **-va·mens** or **-vam·i·na** (-văm′ə-nə). *Law.* The part of a charge or an accusation that weighs most substantially against the accused. [Medieval Latin *gravāmen,* injury, accusation, from Late Latin, encumbrance, obligation, from Latin *gravāre,* to burden, from *gravis,* heavy. See GRAVE[2].]

grave[1] (grāv) *n.* **1.a.** An excavation for the interment of a corpse. **b.** A place of burial. **2.** Death or extinction: *faced the grave with calm resignation.* [Middle English, from Old English *græf.* See **ghrebh-[2]** in Appendix.]

grave[2] (grāv) *adj.* **grav·er, grav·est. 1.** Requiring serious thought; momentous: *a grave decision in a time of crisis.* **2.** Fraught with danger or harm: *a grave wound.* **3.** Dignified and somber in conduct or character: *a grave procession.* See Synonyms at **serious. 4.** Somber or dark in hue. **5.** (*also* gräv). *Linguistics.* **a.** Written with or modified by the mark (`), as the è in *Sèvres.* **b.** Of or referring to a phonetic feature that distinguishes sounds produced at the periphery of the vocal tract, as in labial and velar consonants and back vowels. **—grave** (*also* gräv) *n. Linguistics.* A mark (`) indicating a pronounced *e* for the sake of meter in the usually nonsyllabic ending *-ed* in English poetry. [French, from Old French, from Latin *gravis.* See **gʷerə-[1]** in Appendix.] **—grave′ly** *adv.* **—grave′ness** *n.*

grave[3] (grāv) *tr.v.* **graved, grav·en** (grā′vən), or **graved, grav·ing, graves. 1.** To sculpt or carve; engrave. **2.** To stamp or impress deeply; fix permanently. [Middle English *graven,* from Old English *grafan.* See **ghrebh-[2]** in Appendix.]

grave[4] (grāv) *tr.v.* **graved, grav·ing, graves.** To clean and coat (the bottom of a wooden ship) with pitch. [Middle English *graven.*]

gra·ve[5] (grä′vā) *adv. & adj. Music.* In a slow and solemn manner. Used chiefly as a direction. [Italian, from Latin *gravis,* heavy. See GRAVE[2].]

grave·dig·ger (grāv′dĭg′ər) *n.* One that digs graves.

grav·el (grăv′əl) *n.* **1.** An unconsolidated mixture of rock fragments or pebbles. **2.** *Pathology.* The sandlike granular material of urinary calculi. **—gravel** *tr.v.* **-eled, -el·ing, -els** or **-elled, -el·ling, -els. 1.** To apply a surface of rock fragments or pebbles to. **2.** To confuse; perplex. **3.** *Informal.* To irritate. [Middle English, from Old French *gravele,* diminutive of *grave,* pebbly shore, of Celtic origin.]

grav·el-blind (grăv′əl-blīnd′) *adj.* Having minimal vision. [On the model of SAND-BLIND.]

grav·el·ly (grăv′ə-lē) *adj.* **1.** Of, full of, or covered with rock fragments or pebbles: *a gravelly beach.* **2.** Having a harsh rasping sound: *a gravelly voice.*

grav·en (grā′vən) *v.* A past participle of **grave[3].**

graven image *n.* An idol or a fetish carved in wood or stone.

grav·er (grā′vər) *n.* **1.** One who carves or engraves. **2.** An engraver's cutting tool.

grave robber *n.* One who plunders valuables from tombs or graves or who steals corpses after burial, as for illicit dissection.

Graves (gräv′). A region of southwest France in the Garonne River valley. The area is known for its fine table wines.

Graves, (grāvz), **Robert Ranke.** 1895–1985. British writer and critic whose works include love poems and the critical work *The White Goddess* (1948).

Graves' disease (grāvz) *n.* A condition usually caused by excessive production of thyroid hormone and characterized by an enlarged thyroid gland, protrusion of the eyeballs, a rapid heartbeat, and nervous excitability. Also called *exophthalmic goiter.* [After Robert J. *Graves* (1797–1853), Irish physician.]

Graves·end (grāvz′ĕnd′). A municipal borough of southeast England on the Thames River east of London. It is an industrial and shipping center. Pocahontas is buried here. Population, 96,300.

grave·side (grāv′sīd′) *n.* The area beside a grave. *—attributive.* Often used to modify another noun: *a graveside ceremony; a graveside oration.*

grave·site (grāv′sīt′) *n.* A place used for graves or a grave.

grave·stone (grāv′stōn′) *n.* A stone placed over a grave as a marker; a tombstone.

grave·yard (grāv′yärd′) *n.* A burial ground; a cemetery.

graveyard shift *n.* **1.** A work shift that runs during the early morning hours, as from midnight to 8 A.M. **2.** The workers on an early-morning shift.

grav·id (grăv′ĭd) *adj.* Carrying developing young or eggs: *a gravid uterus; a gravid female.* [Latin *gravidus,* from *gravis,* heavy. See **gʷerə-[1]** in Appendix.] **—gra·vid′i·ty** (grə-vĭd′ĭ-tē), **grav′id·ness** *n.* **—grav′id·ly** *adv.*

gra·vim·e·ter (gră-vĭm′ĭ-tər, grăv′ə-mē′-) *n.* **1.** An instrument used to measure specific gravity. **2.** An instrument used to measure variations in a gravitational field. [French *gravimètre* : Latin *gravis,* heavy; see GRAVITY + *-mètre,* -meter.] **—gra·vim′e·try** (gră-vĭm′ĭ-trē, grə-) *n.*

grav·i·met·ric (grăv′ə-mĕt′rĭk) also **grav·i·met·ri·cal** (-rĭ-kəl) *adj.* **1.** Of or relating to measurement by weight. **2.** Of or relating to measurement of variations in a gravitational field. [From *gravimetry,* measurement of specific gravity, from GRAVIMETER.] **—grav′i·met′ri·cal·ly** *adv.*

grav·ing dock (grā′vĭng) *n.* A dry dock where the hulls of ships are repaired and maintained.

grav·i·sphere (grăv′ĭ-sfîr′) *n.* The spherical region of space dominated by the gravitational field of a celestial body. [GRAVI(TY) + SPHERE.]

grav·i·tate (grăv′ĭ-tāt′) *intr.v.* **-tat·ed, -tat·ing, -tates. 1.** To move in response to the force of gravity. **2.** To move downward. **3.** To be attracted by or as if by an irresistible force: *"My excuse must be that all Celts gravitate towards each other"* (Oscar Wilde). [New Latin *gravitāre, gravitāt-,* from Latin *gravitās,* heaviness. See GRAVITY.] **—grav′i·tat′er** *n.*

grav·i·ta·tion (grăv′ĭ-tā′shən) *n.* **1.** *Physics.* **a.** The natural phenomenon of attraction between massive bodies. **b.** The act or process of moving under the influence of this attraction. **2.** A movement toward a source of attraction: *the gravitation of the middle classes to the suburbs.* **—grav′i·ta′tion·al** *adj.* **—grav′i·ta′tion·al·ly** *adv.* **—grav′i·ta′tive** *adj.*

gravitational collapse *n. Astronomy.* **1.** The implosion of a star or other celestial body under the influence of its own gravity, resulting in a body that is many times smaller and denser than the original body. **2.** The process by which stars, star clusters, and galaxies form from interstellar gas under the influence of gravity.

gravitational constant *n. Abbr.* **G** *Physics.* The constant in Newton's law of gravitation that yields the rate of acceleration of a less massive body toward a more massive body when multiplied by the product of the masses of the two bodies and divided by the square of the distance between them.

gravitational interaction *n. Physics.* A hypothetical weak, fundamental interaction between elementary particles.

gravitational wave *n. Physics.* A hypothetical wave that is held to propagate the force of gravity and to travel at the speed of light. Also called *gravity wave.*

grav·i·ton (grăv′ĭ-tŏn′) *n. Physics.* A hypothetical particle postulated to be the quantum of gravitational interaction and presumed to have an indefinitely long lifetime, zero electric charge, and zero rest mass. See table at **subatomic particle.** [GRAVIT(ATION) + –ON[1].]

grav·i·ty (grăv′ĭ-tē) *n.* **1.** *Abbr.* **gr.** *Physics.* **a.** The natural force of attraction exerted by a celestial body, such as Earth, upon objects at or near its surface, tending to draw them toward the center of the body. **b.** The natural force of attraction between any two massive bodies, which is directly proportional to the product of their masses and inversely proportional to the square of the distance between them. **c.** Gravitation. **2.** Grave consequence; seriousness or importance: *They are still quite unaware of the gravity of their problems.* **3.** Solemnity or dignity of manner. [French *gravité,* heaviness, from Old French, from Latin *gravitās,* from *gravis,* heavy. See **gʷerə-[1]** in Appendix.]

gravity wave *n. Physics.* See **gravitational wave.**

grav·lax (gräv′läks) *n.* Raw, thinly sliced salmon marinated in spices, especially dill, and served usually as an appetizer. [Swedish : *grava,* to bury (from the original process of curing it in the ground); see **ghrebh-[2]** in Appendix + *lax,* salmon; see **laks-** in Appendix.]

ă pat	oi boy
ā pay	ou out
âr care	o͝o took
ä father	o͞o boot
ĕ pet	ŭ cut
ē be	ûr urge
ĭ pit	th thin
ī pie	*th* this
îr pier	hw which
ŏ pot	zh vision
ō toe	ə about, item
ô paw	♦ regionalism

Stress marks: ′ (primary); ′ (secondary), as in **dictionary** (dĭk′shə-nĕr′ē)

gray wolf
Canis lupus

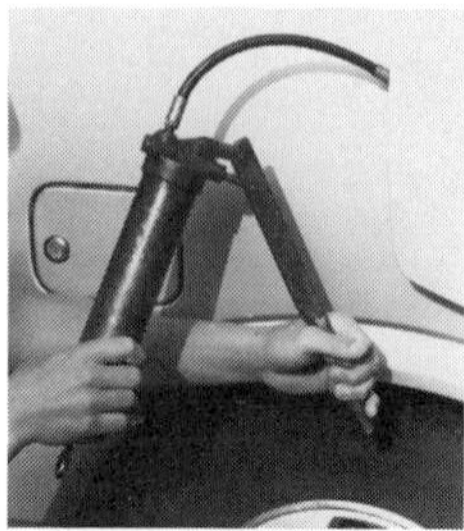
grease gun

great auk
Detail from a painting by John James Audubon

ă pat	oi boy
ā pay	ou out
âr care	o͝o took
ä father	o͞o boot
ĕ pet	ŭ cut
ē be	ûr urge
ĭ pit	th thin
ī pie	*th* this
îr pier	hw which
ŏ pot	zh vision
ō toe	ə about, item
ô paw	♦ regionalism

Stress marks: **ʹ** (primary); ʹ (secondary), as in **dictionary** (dĭkʹshə-nĕrʹē)

gra·vure (grə-vyo͝orʹ) *n.* **1.a.** A method of printing with etched plates or cylinders; intaglio printing. **b.** Photogravure. **2.a.** A plate used in the process of gravure. **b.** A reproduction produced by gravure. [French, from *graver,* to engrave, from Old French, of Germanic origin. See **ghrebh-**[2] in Appendix.]

gra·vy (grāʹvē) *n., pl.* **-vies. 1.a.** The juices that drip from cooking meat. **b.** A sauce made by thickening and seasoning these juices. **2.** *Slang.* **a.** Money, profit, or benefit easily or illicitly gained. **b.** Payment or benefit in excess of what is expected or required. [Middle English *grave,* from Old French, possibly a misreading of *grane,* stew, sauce, from Latin *grānātus,* having many seeds. See POMEGRANATE.]

gravy boat *n.* An elongated dish or pitcher for serving gravy.

gravy train *n. Slang.* An occupation or other source of income that requires little effort while yielding considerable profit.

gray also **grey** (grā) —*adj.* **gray·er, gray·est** also **grey·er, grey·est. 1.** *Color.* Of or relating to an achromatic color of any lightness between the extremes of black and white. **2.a.** Dull or dark: *a gray, rainy afternoon.* **b.** Lacking in cheer; gloomy: *a gray mood.* **3.a.** Having gray hair; hoary. **b.** Old or venerable. **4.** Intermediate in character or position, as with regard to a subjective matter: *the gray area between their differing opinions on the film's morality.* —*n.* **1.** *Color.* An achromatic color of any lightness between the extremes of black and white. **2.** An object or animal of the color gray. **3.** Often **Gray. a.** A member of the Confederate Army in the Civil War. **b.** The Confederate Army. —*tr. & intr.v.* **grayed, gray·ing, grays** also **greyed, grey·ing, greys.** To make or become gray. [Middle English *grei,* from Old English *grǣg.*] —**grayʹly** *adj.* —**grayʹness** *n.*

Gray (grā), **Asa.** 1810–1888. American botanist who greatly enlarged and improved the description of North American flora and was the chief American advocate of Charles Darwin's theories.

Gray, Horace. 1828–1902. American jurist who served as an associate justice of the U.S. Supreme Court (1882–1902).

Gray, Robert. 1755–1806. American explorer who twice circumnavigated the globe (1787–1790 and 1790–1793) and discovered Grays Harbor and the Columbia River (1792).

Gray, Thomas. 1716–1771. British poet considered a forerunner of English romanticism. His most famous work is *Elegy Written in a Country Courtyard* (1751).

gray·beard (grāʹbîrdʹ) *n.* An old man.

gray eminence *n.* See **éminence grise.**

gray·fish (grāʹfĭshʹ) *n., pl.* **grayfish** or **-fish·es.** See **dogfish** (sense 1).

gray·ish (grāʹĭsh) *adj.* Somewhat gray.

gray jay *n.* A bird *(Perisoreus canadensis)* of North American conifer forests, having gray plumage and a black-capped head. Also called *camp robber, Canada jay, moosebird, whiskey jack.*

gray·lag also **grey·lag** (grāʹlăgʹ) *n.* A wild gray goose *(Anser anser)* of Europe. [Possibly GRAY + LAG[1], lingering behind (obsolete), from its being the last of the geese to leave England on its annual migration.]

gray·ling (grāʹlĭng) *n., pl.* **grayling** or **-lings.** Any of several freshwater food and game fishes of the genus *Thymallus* of the Northern Hemisphere, having a large dorsal fin.

gray·mail (grāʹmālʹ) *n.* A defensive tactic in an espionage trial whereby the accused threatens to reveal secret information unless the charges are dropped. [GRAY + (BLACK)MAIL.]

gray market *n.* The business of buying or selling goods, such as imports, at prices below those set by an official regulatory agency. [GRAY + (BLACK) MARKET.]

gray matter *n.* **1.** Brownish-gray nerve tissue, especially of the brain and spinal cord, composed of nerve cell bodies and their dendrites and some supportive tissue. **2.** *Informal.* Brains; intellect.

gray mullet *n.* See **mullet** (sense 1).

grays·by (grāzʹbē) *n.* A tropical grouper *(Epinephelus cruentatus),* abundant among the coral reefs of the Florida Keys and the West Indies. [Origin unknown.]

Grays Harbor (grāz). An inlet of the Pacific Ocean in western Washington. It is the shipping point for a lumbering area.

Grays Peak. A mountain, 4,352.4 m (14,270 ft) high, in the Front Range of the Rocky Mountains in central Colorado.

gray squirrel *n.* A common squirrel *(Sciurus carolinensis)* of eastern North America, having grayish or blackish fur.

gray·wacke (grāʹwăkʹ, -wăkʹə) *n.* Any of various dark gray sandstones that contain shale. [Partial translation of German *Grauwacke* : *grau,* gray + *Wacke,* rock (from Middle High German, from Old High German *waggo,* boulder; see **wegh-** in Appendix).]

gray whale *n.* A whalebone whale *(Eschrichtius robustus)* of northern Pacific waters, having grayish-black coloring with white blotches. Also called *devilfish.*

gray wolf *n.* A large, tawny gray wolf *(Canis lupus)* that formerly occupied diverse habitats throughout northern North America and Eurasia but now lives in fewer, more limited areas because of human encroachment. Also called *timber wolf.*

Graz (gräts). A city of southeast Austria on the Mur River south-southwest of Vienna. It was probably founded in the 12th century. Population, 243,166.

graze[1] (grāz) *v.* **grazed, graz·ing, graz·es.** —*intr.* **1.** To feed on growing grasses and herbage. **2.** *Informal.* **a.** To eat a variety of appetizers as a full meal. **b.** To eat snacks throughout the day in place of full meals. —*tr.* **1.** To feed on (herbage) in a field or on pastureland. **2.** To feed on the herbage of (a piece of land). **3.** To afford herbage for the feeding of: *This field will graze 30 head of cattle.* **4.** To put (livestock) out to feed. **5.** To tend (feeding livestock) in a pasture. [Middle English *grasen,* from Old English *grasian,* from *græs,* grass. See **ghrē-** in Appendix.] —**grazeʹa·ble, grazʹa·ble** *adj.* —**grazʹer** *n.*

graze[2] (grāz) *v.* **grazed, graz·ing, graz·es.** —*tr.* **1.** To touch lightly in passing; brush. See Synonyms at **brush**[1]. **2.** To scrape or scratch slightly; abrade. —*intr.* To scrape or touch something lightly in passing. —**graze** *n.* **1.** The act of brushing or scraping along a surface. **2.** A minor scratch or abrasion. [Perhaps from GRAZE[1].]

gra·zier (grāʹzhər) *n.* A person who grazes cattle. [Middle English *grasier,* from *grasen,* to graze. See GRAZE[1].]

gra·zi·o·so (grätʹsē-ōʹsō, -zō) *adv. & adj. Music.* In a graceful, smooth manner. Used chiefly as a direction. [Italian, from Latin *grātiōsus,* gracious, agreeable. See GRACIOUS.]

Gr. Brit. *abbr.* Great Britain.

♦**grease** (grēs) *n.* **1.** Soft or melted animal fat, especially after rendering. **2.** A thick oil or viscous substance, especially when used as a lubricant. **3.a.** The oily substance present in raw wool; suint. **b.** Raw wool that has not been cleansed of this oily substance. **4.** *Slang.* Something, such as money or influence, that facilitates the attainment of an object or a desire: *accepted some grease to fix the outcome of the race.* —**grease** (grēs, grēz) *tr.v.* **greased, greas·ing, greas·es. 1.** To coat, smear, or soil with grease: *greased the pie pan.* **2.** To lubricate with grease. **3.** To facilitate the progress of. **4.** *Slang.* To kill. See Regional Note at **greasy.** —*idiom.* **grease (someone's) palm** (or **hand).** *Slang.* To bribe. [Middle English *grese,* from Anglo-Norman *grece,* from Vulgar Latin **crassia,* from Latin *crassus,* fat, thick.] —**greaseʹless** *adj.* —**greaseʹproofʹ** *adj.*

grease gun *n.* **1.** A hand-powered pump used to force grease under pressure into bearings. **2.** A submachine gun.

grease monkey *n. Slang.* A mechanic, especially one who works on motor vehicles or aircraft.

grease·paint also **grease paint** (grēsʹpāntʹ) *n.* Theatrical makeup, especially a preparation of grease mixed with colorings.

grease pencil *n.* A pencil of hard grease mixed with colorings, used especially for marking on glossy or glazed surfaces.

greas·er (grēʹsər, -zər) *n.* **1.** One who greases, such as a worker who greases working parts in a machine. **2.** *Slang.* A tough young man, especially one from a white working-class background who is much involved with motorcycles or cars. **3.** *Offensive Slang.* Used as a disparaging term for a Latin American, especially a Mexican.

grease·wood (grēsʹwo͝odʹ) *n.* A spiny shrub *(Sarcobatus vermiculatus)* of western North America, having small alternate leaves, white stems, and small greenish flowers.

♦**greas·y** (grēʹsē, -zē) *adj.* **-i·er, -i·est. 1.** Coated or soiled with grease. **2.** Containing grease, especially too much grease: *a greasy hamburger.* **3.** Suggestive of grease, as in slipperiness: *a greasy character.* —**greasʹi·ly** *adv.* —**greasʹi·ness** *n.*

♦***REGIONAL NOTE:*** In the Southern states the adjective *greasy* and the verb *grease* are pronounced with a (z) rather than with an (s) sound. This pronunciation is so stable and so characteristic of Southern dialects that dialect scholars use it to trace the migration of Southern speakers into other dialect areas, such as southern Indiana.

greasy spoon *n. Slang.* A small, inexpensive, often unsanitary restaurant.

great (grāt) *adj.* **great·er, great·est.** *Abbr.* **gr., gt. 1.** Very large in size. **2.** Larger in size than others of the same kind. **3.** Large in quantity or number: *A great throng awaited us.* See Synonyms at **large. 4.** Extensive in time or distance: *a great delay.* **5.** Remarkable or outstanding in magnitude, degree, or extent: *a great crisis.* **6.** Of outstanding significance or importance: *a great work of art.* **7.** Chief or principal: *the great house on the estate.* **8.** Superior in quality or character; noble: *"For he was great, ere fortune made him so"* (John Dryden). **9.** Powerful; influential: *one of the great nations of the West.* **10.** Eminent; distinguished: *a great leader.* **11.** Grand; aristocratic. **12.** *Informal.* Enthusiastic: *a great lover of music.* **13.** *Informal.* Very skillful: *great at algebra.* **14.** *Informal.* Very good; first-rate: *We had a great time at the dance.* **15.** Being one generation removed from the relative specified. Often used in combination: *a great-granddaughter.* **16.** *Archaic.* Pregnant. —**great** *n.* **1.** *pl.* **greats** or **great** One that is great: *a composer considered among the greats.* **2.** *Music.* **a.** A division of most pipe organs, usually containing the most powerful ranks of pipes. **b.** A similar division of other organs. —**great** *adv. Informal.* Very well: *got along great with the teacher.* [Middle English *grete,* from Old English *grēat,* thick, coarse.] —**greatʹly** *adv.* —**greatʹness** *n.*

Great A·ba·co (grātʹ ăbʹə-kōʹ). The largest island of the Abaco and Cays group in the northern Bahamas.

Great Al·föld (ôlʹfəld). See **Alföld.**

great ape *n.* Any of various anthropoid apes of the family Pongidae, which includes the chimpanzees, gorillas, and orangutans.

great auk *n.* A large, flightless sea bird *(Pinguinus impennis)* formerly common on northern Atlantic coasts but extinct since the middle of the 19th century.

great-aunt or **great aunt** (grāt′ănt′, -änt′) *n.* A sister of one's grandparent. Also called *grandaunt.*

Great Aus·tra·lian Bight (ô-strāl′yən). A wide bay of the Indian Ocean on the southern coast of Australia. Much of the coastline consists of high cliffs extending inland to form the Nullarbor Plain.

Great Barrier Reef. The largest coral reef in the world, about 2,011 km (1,250 mi) long, off the northeast coast of Australia. Its banks are known for their exotic fish and crustaceans.

Great Basin. A desert region of the western United States comprising most of Nevada and parts of Utah, California, Idaho, Wyoming, and Oregon.

Great Bear *n.* See **Ursa Major.**

Great Bear Lake. A lake of northwest mainland Northwest Territories, Canada. The **Great Bear River,** about 113 km (70 mi) long, flows westward from the lake to the Mackenzie River.

Great Bend (bĕnd). A city of central Kansas on the Arkansas River northwest of Wichita. It is located on the old Santa Fe Trail. Population, 16,608.

great blue heron *n.* A large American heron *(Ardea herodias)* having blue-gray plumage and a predominantly white head with a dark crest.

Great Brit·ain (brĭt′n). *Abbr.* **G.B., Gr. Brit., Gt. Brit. 1.** An island off the western coast of Europe comprising England, Scotland, and Wales. It is separated from the mainland by the English Channel and from Ireland by the Irish Sea. **2.** See **United Kingdom.**

great circle *n.* **1.** A circle described by the intersection of the surface of a sphere with a plane passing through the center of the sphere. **2.** A segment of such a circle representing the shortest distance between two terrestrial points.

great·coat (grāt′kōt′) *n.* A heavy overcoat.

Great Com·o·ro (kŏm′ə-rō′). The largest of the Comoro Islands, in the northern Mozambique Channel of the Indian Ocean.

Great Dane *n.* Any of various large, powerful dogs of a breed developed in Germany, having a muscular body, a short smooth coat, and a narrow head.

great divide *n.* **1.** A large or major watershed of a landmass. **2.** A major point of division, especially death.

Great Di·vide (dĭ-vīd′). See **Continental Divide.**

Great Di·vid·ing Range (dĭ-vī′dĭng) also **Eastern High·lands** (hī′ləndz). A chain of mountains curving along the eastern coast of Australia.

great·en (grāt′n) *tr. & intr.v.* **-ened, -en·ing, -ens.** *Archaic.* To make or become great or greater.

great·er also **Great·er** (grā′tər) *adj.* Of, relating to, or being a city considered together with its populous suburbs: *the greater metropolitan area of Dallas; Greater Los Angeles.*

Greater An·til·les (ăn-tĭl′ēz). An island group of the West Indies including Cuba, Jamaica, Hispaniola, and Puerto Rico.

greater omentum *n.* A fold of the peritoneum, passing from the stomach to the transverse colon. Also called *caul.*

Greater Sun·da Islands (sŭn′də, sōōn′-). See **Sunda Islands.**

great·est common divisor (grā′tĭst) *n. Abbr.* **gcd, g.c.d.** *Mathematics.* The largest number that divides evenly into each of a given set of numbers. Also called *greatest common factor, highest common factor.*

Great Falls. A city of central Montana on the Missouri River north-northeast of Helena. At the center of extensive hydroelectric power installations, Great Falls is popularly known as "Electric City." Population, 56,725.

great·heart·ed (grāt′här′tĭd) *adj.* **1.** Noble or courageous in spirit: *a greathearted general.* **2.** Generous; magnanimous: *a greathearted landowner.* **—great′heart′ed·ly** *adv.* **—great′heart′ed·ness** *n.*

great horned owl *n.* A large North American owl *(Bubo virginianus)* having prominent ear tufts and brownish plumage with a white throat.

Great In·di·an Desert (ĭn′dē-ən). See **Thar Desert.**

Great Kar·roo (kə-rōō′). See **Karroo.**

Great Lakes. A group of five freshwater lakes of central North America between the United States and Canada, including Lakes Superior, Huron, Erie, Ontario, and Michigan. French traders first sighted the lakes in the early 17th century.

great laurel *n.* See **rosebay** (sense 1).

Great Mi·am·i River (mī-ăm′ē, -ăm′ə). See **Miami River.**

Great Na·ma·qua·land (nə-mä′kwə-lănd′). See **Namaqualand.**

Great Ouse River (ōōz). See **Ouse River** (sense 1).

Great Pee Dee (pē′ dē′). See **Pee Dee.**

Great Plains. A vast grassland region of central North America extending from the Canadian provinces of Alberta, Saskatchewan, and Manitoba southward to Texas.

Great Power *n.* One of the nations having great political, social, and economic influence in international affairs.

Great Pyrenees *n.* Any of a breed of large, heavy-boned dogs having a thick white coat and originally developed to guard sheep.

Great Rift Valley. A geologic depression of southwest Asia and eastern Africa extending from the Jordan River valley to Mozambique. The region is marked by a series of faults caused by volcanic action.

Great Russian *n.* A member of the Russian-speaking people inhabiting the Russian Soviet Federated Socialist Republic and constituting the largest ethnic group in the U.S.S.R.

Great Saint Ber·nard Pass (sānt′ bər-närd′). An Alpine pass, 2,473.6 m (8,110 ft) high, on the Italian-Swiss border.

Great Salt Lake (sôlt). A shallow body of salt water of northwest Utah between the Wasatch Range on the east and the **Great Salt Lake Desert** on the west. The lake is a remnant of prehistoric Lake Bonneville, which covered an extensive area of the Great Basin. Great Salt Lake Desert is barren and uncultivated.

Great Sand·y Desert (săn′dē). A vast arid area of northwest Australia north of the Gibson Desert.

Great Sark (särk). See **Sark.**

great seal *n.* The principal seal of a government or state, with which official documents are stamped.

great seal
Great Seal of the United States

great skua *n.* A predatory gull-like sea bird *(Catharacta skua)* of northern regions, having brownish plumage.

Great Slave Lake (slāv). A lake of southern Northwest Territories, Canada. The British fur trader Samuel Hearne (1745–1792) first sighted the lake in 1771.

Great Smok·y Mountains (smō′kē). A range of the Appalachian Mountains on the North Carolina–Tennessee border rising to 2,026.1 m (6,643 ft) at Clingmans Dome.

Great South Bay. An arm of the Atlantic Ocean between the southern shore of Long Island and offshore barrier islands.

Great Spirit *n.* The principal deity in the religion of many Native American peoples.

great-un·cle or **great uncle** (grāt′ŭng′kəl) *n.* A brother of one's grandparent. Also called *granduncle.*

Great Vic·to·ri·a Desert (vĭk-tôr′ē-ə, -tōr′-). An arid region of south-central Australia sloping to the Nullarbor Plain on the south.

Great Vowel Shift *n.* A series of phonetic changes occurring in Early Modern English in which the Middle English low and mid long vowels were raised, (ä) and (ō) becoming (ā) and (ōō), for example, while the high long vowels (ē) and (ōō) became the diphthongs (ī) and (ou).

Great Wall of Chi·na (chī′nə). A line of fortifications extending about 2,414 km (1,500 mi) across northern China. Built in the third century B.C. by some 300,000 laborers, the wall is today a major tourist attraction.

Great Wall of China
Section at Gubeikou, northeast of Beijing

Great War *n.* World War I.

great white shark *n.* A large shark *(Carcharodon carcharias)* of temperate and tropical waters that grows to about 7 meters (23 feet). It is the only shark known to feed regularly on marine mammals.

greave (grēv) *n.* Leg armor worn below the knee. Often used in the plural. [Sing. of Middle English *greves,* from Old French, shins.]

greaves (grēvz) *pl.n. (used with a sing. or pl. verb).* The unmelted residue left after animal fat has been rendered. [From Low German *greven.*]

grebe (grēb) *n.* Any of various swimming and diving birds of the family Podicipedidae, having a pointed bill and lobed, fleshy membranes along each toe. [French *grèbe.*]

Gre·cian (grē′shən) *adj.* Greek. **—Grecian** *n.* A native or inhabitant of Greece. [From Latin *Graecia,* Greece, from *Graecus,* Greek. See GREEK.]

Gre·cism (grē′sĭz′əm) *n.* **1.** The style or spirit of Greek culture, art, or thought. **2.** Something done in imitation of Greek style or spirit. **3.** An idiom of the Greek language.

Gre·cize (grē′sīz′) *tr.v.* **-cized, -ciz·ing, -ciz·es.** To make Greek or Hellenic in form or style. [French *gréciser,* from Late Latin *graecizāre,* from Greek *graikizein,* to speak Greek, from *Graikos,* Greek.]

Gre·co (grĕk′ō), **El.** Born Doménikos Theotokópoulos. 1541–1614. Greek-born Spanish painter of religious works, such as *Christ Stripped of His Garments* (1579), characterized by elongated human figures, contrasting colors, and deep shadows.

El Greco
c. 1609 self-portrait

Greco– or **Graeco–** *pref.* Greece; Greek: *Greco-Roman.* [From Latin *Graecus,* Greek. See GREEK.]

Grec·o-Ro·man (grĕk′ō-rō′mən, grē′kō-) *adj.* Of or relating to both Greece and Rome: *Greco-Roman mythology.*

gree (grē) *n. Scots.* Superiority; mastery. [Middle English *gre,* from Old French, step, from Latin *gradus.* See GRADE.]

Greece (grēs) Formerly **Hel·las** (hĕl′əs). *Abbr.* **Gr. 1.** A country of southeast Europe on the southern Balkan Peninsula and including numerous islands in the Mediterranean, Aegean, and Ionian seas. One of the most important centers of early civilization, Greece grew and flourished as an amalgam of independent city-states, although intercity strife led to conquest by Philip II of Macedon in 338 B.C. Greece was ruled by the Ottoman Turks from the 15th century A.D. until its independence in 1829. Athens is the capital and the largest city. Population, 9,740,417. **2.** A community of western New York, a suburb of Rochester. Population, 63,700.

Greece

greed (grēd) *n.* An excessive desire to acquire or possess more than what one needs or deserves, especially with respect to material wealth: *"Many . . . attach to competition the stigma of self-*

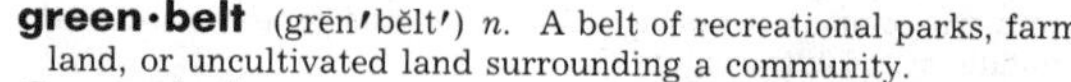

ish greed" (Henry Fawcett). [Back-formation from GREEDY.]

greed·y (grē′dē) *adj.* **-i·er, -i·est. 1.** Excessively desirous of acquiring or possessing, especially wishing to possess more than what one needs or deserves. **2.** Wanting to eat or drink more than one can reasonably consume; gluttonous. **3.** Extremely eager or desirous: *greedy for the opportunity to prove their ability.* [Middle English *gredi,* from Old English *grǣdig.* See **gher-²** in Appendix.] **—greed′i·ly** *adv.* **—greed′i·ness** *n.*

Greek (grēk) *n. Abbr.* **Gr., Gk. 1.a.** The Indo-European language of the Greeks. Greek, the sole member of the Hellenic branch, consists of several groups of ancient and modern regional, social, and literary dialects and is divided into several historical periods. **b.** Greek language and literature from the middle of the eighth century B.C. to the end of the third century A.D., especially the Attic Greek of the fifth and fourth centuries B.C.. **2.a.** A native or inhabitant of Greece. **b.** A person of Greek ancestry. **3.** *Informal.* A member of a fraternity or sorority that has its name composed of Greek letters. **4.** *Informal.* Something that is unintelligible: *Quantum mechanics is Greek to me.* **—Greek** *adj.* Of or relating to Greece or its people, language, or culture. [Middle English *Grek,* from Old English *Grēcas,* the Greeks, from Latin *Graecus,* Greek, from Greek *Graikos,* tribal name.]

Greek cross

Greek Catholic *n.* **1.** A member of the Eastern Orthodox Church. **2.** A member of a Uniat church.

Greek Church *n.* The Eastern Orthodox Church.

Greek cross *n.* A cross formed by two bars of equal length crossing in the middle at right angles to each other.

Greek fire *n.* An incendiary preparation first used by the Byzantine Greeks to set fire to enemy ships.

Greek Orthodox Church *n.* The state church of Greece, an autonomous part of the Eastern Orthodox Church.

Greek revival *n.* An architectural style imitating elements of ancient Greek temple design, popular in the United States and Europe in the first half of the 19th century.

Gree·ley (grē′lē). A city of north-central Colorado north-northeast of Denver. It was founded in 1870 as a cooperative farm and temperance center. Population, 53,006.

Greeley, Horace. 1811–1872. American journalist and politician who founded and edited the *New York Tribune* (1841–1872). In 1872 he ran unsuccessfully for President.

green (grēn) *n.* **1.** *Color.* The hue of that portion of the visible spectrum lying between yellow and blue, evoked in the human observer by radiant energy with wavelengths of approximately 490 to 570 nanometers; any of a group of colors that may vary in lightness and saturation and whose hue is that of the emerald or somewhat less yellow than that of growing grass; one of the additive or light primaries; one of the psychological primary hues. **2.** Something green in color. **3. greens.** Green growth or foliage, especially: **a.** The branches and leaves of plants used for decoration. **b.** Leafy plants or plant parts eaten as vegetables. **4.** A grassy lawn or plot, especially: **a.** A grassy area located usually at the center of a city or town and set aside for common use; a common. **b.** *Sports.* A putting green. **5. greens.** A green uniform: *"a young . . . sergeant in dress greens"* (Nelson DeMille). **6.** *Slang.* Money. **7. Green.** A supporter of a social and political movement that espouses global environmental protection, bioregionalism, social responsibility, and nonviolence. **—green** *adj.* **green·er, green·est. 1.** *Color.* Of the color green. **2.** Abounding in or covered with green growth or foliage: *the green woods.* **3.** Made with green or leafy vegetables: *a green salad.* **4.** Characterized by mild or temperate weather: *a green climate.* **5.** Youthful; vigorous: *at the green age of 18.* **6.** Not mature or ripe; young: *green tomatoes.* **7.** Brand-new; fresh. **8.** Not yet fully processed, especially: **a.** Not aged: *green wood.* **b.** Not cured or tanned: *green pelts.* **9.** Lacking training or experience. See Synonyms at **young. 10.a.** Lacking sophistication or worldly experience; naive. **b.** Easily duped or deceived; gullible. **11.** Having a sickly or unhealthy pallor indicative of nausea or jealousy, for example. **—green** *tr. & intr.v.* **greened, green·ing, greens.** To make or become green. **—*idiom.* green around** (or **about**) **the gills.** Pale or sickly in appearance. [Middle English *grene,* from Old English *grēne.* See **ghrē-** in Appendix. N., sense 7, translation of German *Grünen,* Greens, from *grün,* green.] **—green′ly** *adv.* **—green′ness** *n.*

greenhouse

Green, Paul Eliot. 1894–1981. American playwright noted for his dramas portraying Southern life, such as *In Abraham's Bosom* (1926), for which he won a Pulitzer Prize.

Green, William. 1873–1952. American labor leader who as president of the American Federation of Labor (1924–1952) led the struggle with the Congress of Industrial Organizations after the two unions split (1936).

green alga *n.* Any of the numerous algae of the division Chlorophyta, such as spirogyra and sea lettuce, that have chlorophyll unmasked by other pigments.

Gree·na·way (grē′nə-wā′), **Catherine.** Known as "Kate." 1846–1901. British artist and writer noted for her illustrations of her own children's books, such as *Under the Window* (1879).

green·back (grēn′băk′) *n.* A note of U.S. currency.

Green Bay. A city of eastern Wisconsin on **Green Bay,** an arm of Lake Michigan. Founded as a trading post in 1634, the city is a port of entry with varied industries. Population, 87,899.

green bean *n.* See **string bean** (sense 1).

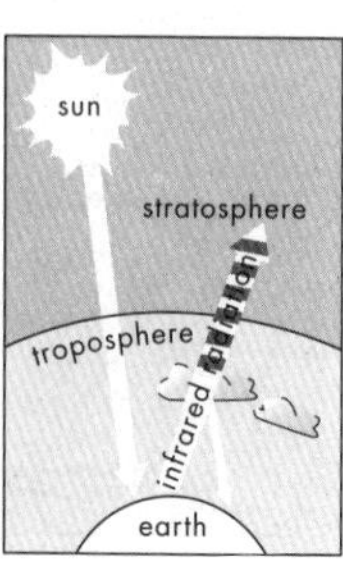

greenhouse effect

green·belt (grēn′bĕlt′) *n.* A belt of recreational parks, farmland, or uncultivated land surrounding a community.

Green·belt (grēn′bĕlt′). A city of central Maryland, a residential suburb of Washington, D.C. It was planned and built by the federal government as an experimental model community. Population, 17,332.

Green Beret *n.* A member of the U.S. Army Special Forces. [From the green beret that is part of the uniform.]

green·bri·er (grēn′brī′ər) *n.* See **catbrier.**

green card *n.* An official document issued by the U.S. government to aliens, allowing them to work legally in the United States. [Formerly a green-colored card.]

green corn *n.* Young, tender ears of sweet corn.

Green·dale (grēn′dāl′). A village of southeast Wisconsin, a suburb of Milwaukee. It was founded in the 1930's as a planned community built by the federal government. Population, 16,928.

green dragon *n.* A tuberous plant *(Arisaema dracontium)* of eastern North America, having divided leaves and minute flowers at the base of a long, slender spadix projecting from a narrow green spathe. Also called *dragonroot.*

Greene (grēn), **(Henry) Graham.** 1904–1991. British writer particularly known for his novels, such as *The Power and the Glory* (1940), which reflect his ardent Catholic beliefs.

Greene, Nathanael. 1742–1786. American Revolutionary general whose strategies in the South significantly weakened British strength in the region.

Greene, Robert. 1558?–1592. English writer noted for his plays, such as *Friar Bacon and Friar Bungay* (c. 1589).

green·er·y (grē′nə-rē) *n., pl.* **-ies. 1.a.** Green foliage; verdure. **b.** Such foliage used for decoration. **2.** A place where plants are grown.

green-eyed (grēn′īd′) *adj.* Jealous.

Green·field (grēn′fēld′). **1.** A town of northwest Massachusetts north of Northampton. The first cutlery factory in America was established here in the early 1800's. Population, 18,436. **2.** A city of southeast Wisconsin, a residential suburb of Milwaukee. Population, 31,467.

Greenfield Park. A town of southern Quebec, Canada, a residential suburb of Montreal on the opposite bank of the St. Lawrence River. Population, 18,527.

green·finch (grēn′fĭnch′) *n.* A common Eurasian finch *(Carduelis chloris)* having green and yellow plumage.

green·fly (grēn′flī′) *n.* A green aphid commonly occurring as a destructive pest of various cultivated plants.

green·gage (grēn′gāj′) *n.* A variety of plum *(Prunus domestica)* having yellowish-green skin and sweet flesh. [GREEN + *gage,* after Sir William *Gage,* 18th-century English botanist.]

green·gro·cer (grēn′grō′sər) *n. Chiefly British.* A retail seller of fresh fruits and vegetables. **—green′gro′cer·y** *n.*

green·head (grēn′hĕd′) *n.* A male mallard duck.

green·heart (grēn′härt′) *n.* **1.a.** A tropical American tree *(Ocotea rodioei)* having dark, greenish, durable wood. **b.** Any of various similar trees. **2.** The wood of any of these trees.

green·horn (grēn′hôrn′) *n.* **1.** An inexperienced or immature person, especially one who is easily deceived. **2.** A newcomer, especially one who is unfamiliar with the ways of a place or group. [Middle English *greene horn,* horn of a newly slaughtered animal : *grene,* green; see GREEN + *horn,* horn; see HORN.]

green·house (grēn′hous′) *n.* **1.** A structure, primarily of glass, in which temperature and humidity can be controlled for the cultivation or protection of plants. **2.** *Slang.* A clear plastic bubble or shell covering part of an aircraft.

greenhouse effect *n.* **1.** The phenomenon whereby the earth's atmosphere traps solar radiation, caused by the presence in the atmosphere of gases such as carbon dioxide, water vapor, and methane that allow incoming sunlight to pass through but absorb heat radiated back from the earth's surface. **2.** A similar retention of solar radiation, as by another planet or in a solar panel.

green·ie (grē′nē) *n. Slang.* An amphetamine pill that is green in color.

green·ing¹ (grē′nĭng) *n.* **1.** Restoration of vitality or freshness; rejuvenation. **2.** An adoption or alignment with the ideals or practices of the Green movement: *the greening of the mayor's platform; the greening of the cities.*

green·ing² (grē′nĭng) *n.* Any of several varieties of green-skinned apples.

green·ish (grē′nĭsh) *adj.* Somewhat green.

Green·land (grēn′lənd, -lănd′). An island of Denmark in the northern Atlantic Ocean off northeast Canada. Most of the island lies within the Arctic Circle. Discovered by Eric the Red in the tenth century, it is the largest island in the world. **—Green·land′ic** (-lăn′dĭk) *adj.*

Greenland Sea. A section of the southern Arctic Ocean off the eastern coast of Greenland.

Greenland spar *n.* See **cryolite.**

green·let (grēn′lĭt) *n.* Any of various small greenish birds of the genus *Hylophilus* of Central and South America, related to the vireos.

green light *n.* **1.** The green-colored light that signals traffic to proceed. **2.** *Informal.* Permission to proceed.

green·ling (grēnʹlĭng) *n.* Any of various marine food fishes of the family Hexagrammidae, which frequent rocky coastal areas of the northern Pacific.

green·mail (grēnʹmālʹ) *n.* An antitakeover maneuver in which the target firm purchases the raider's stock at a price above that available to other stockholders. [GREEN, money + (BLACK)MAIL.] **—greenʹmailʹer** *n.*

green manure *n.* A growing crop, such as clover or grass, that is plowed under the soil to improve fertility.

green·mar·ket (grēnʹmärʹkĭt) *n.* See **farmers' market.**

green monkey *n.* A long-tailed African monkey *(Cercopithecus aethiops* subsp. *sabaeus)* having yellowish-gray fur with a greenish tinge.

Green Mountains. A range of the Appalachian Mountains extending from southern Quebec, Canada, through Vermont to western Massachusetts. The range rises to 1,339.9 m (4,393 ft).

green·ock·ite (grēʹnə-kītʹ) *n.* A yellow to brown or red mineral, CdS, the only ore of cadmium. [After Charles Murray Cathcart, Second Earl *Greenock* (1783–1859), British soldier.]

Gree·nough (grēʹnōʹ), **Horatio.** 1805–1852. American sculptor whose principal work is the neoclassical statue of George Washington at the Smithsonian Institution in Washington, D.C.

green pepper *n.* The unripened green fruit of pepper plants of the genus *Capsicum.*

green plover *n.* See **lapwing.**

green revolution *n.* A significant increase in agricultural productivity resulting from the introduction of high-yield varieties of grains, the use of pesticides, and improved management techniques.

Green River. 1. A river rising in central Kentucky and flowing about 595 km (370 mi) generally northwest to the Ohio River near Evansville, Indiana. **2.** A river, about 1,175 km (730 mi) long, rising in western Wyoming and flowing through northwest Colorado and eastern Utah to the Colorado River.

green·room (grēnʹro͞omʹ, -ro͝omʹ) *n.* A waiting room or lounge in a theater or concert hall for the use of performers when they are off-stage. [So called because such rooms were originally painted green.]

green·sand (grēnʹsăndʹ) *n.* A sand or sediment having a dark greenish color caused by the presence of glauconite.

Greens·bor·o (grēnzʹbûrʹə, -bûrʹō). A city of north-central North Carolina east of Winston-Salem. Settled in 1749, it is a textile center. Population, 155,642.

Greens·burg (grēnzʹbûrgʹ). A city of southwest Pennsylvania east-southeast of Pittsburgh. It was settled in the late 1700's and incorporated as a city in 1928. Population, 17,558.

green·shank (grēnʹshăngkʹ) *n.* A European wading bird *(Tringa nebularia)* having greenish legs and a long bill.

green·sick·ness (grēnʹsĭkʹnĭs) *n.* See **chlorosis** (sense 2). **—greenʹsickʹ** *adj.*

green·side (grēnʹsīdʹ) *adj. Sports.* Situated beside a putting green: *a greenside bunker.*

greens·keep·er (grēnzʹkēʹpər) *n. Sports.* One who is responsible for the maintenance of a golf course.

green snake *n.* Any of several slender, yellow-green nonvenomous North American snakes of the genus *Opheodrys,* such as the grass snake.

green soap *n.* A translucent, yellowish-green soft or liquid soap made chiefly from vegetable oils and used in the treatment of skin disorders.

green·stick fracture (grēnʹstĭkʹ) *n.* A partial bone fracture, usually occurring in children, in which the bone is bent but only broken on one side.

green·stone (grēnʹstōnʹ) *n.* Any of various altered basic igneous rocks colored green by chlorite, hornblende, or epidote.

green·sward (grēnʹswôrdʹ) *n.* Ground that is green with grass; turf.

green tea *n.* Tea made from leaves that are not fermented before being dried.

green thumb *n.* An ability to make plants grow well.

green turtle *n.* A large marine turtle *(Chelonia mydas)* having greenish flesh that is prized as food, especially in turtle soup.

Green·ville (grēnʹvĭlʹ). **1.** A city of western Mississippi on the Mississippi River north of Vicksburg. It is a trade, processing, and industrial center in a fertile agricultural region. Population, 40,613. **2.** A city of eastern North Carolina southeast of Rocky Mount. Founded in 1786, the city grew as a tobacco market. Population, 35,740. **3.** A city of northwest South Carolina northwest of Columbia. Located in the Piedmont near the Blue Ridge, it was laid out in 1797 and is today a resort and manufacturing center. Population, 58,242. **4.** A city of northeast Texas northeast of Dallas. It is a manufacturing center. Population, 22,161.

green·way (grēnʹwāʹ) *n.* A corridor of undeveloped land, as along a river or between urban centers, that is reserved for recreational use or environmental preservation.

Green·wich. 1. (grĕnʹĭch, grĭnʹĭj). A borough of Greater London in southeast England on the Thames River. It is the site of the original Royal Observatory, through which passes the prime meridian, or longitude 0°. **2.** (grĕnʹĭch, grĭnʹ-, grēnʹwĭchʹ). A town of southwest Connecticut on Long Island Sound. Settled in 1640, it is mainly residential. Population, 59,578.

Green·wich time (grĕnʹĭch, grĭnʹĭj) *n.* See **universal time.**

Green·wich Village (grĕnʹĭch, -ĭj, grĭnʹ-). A mainly residential section of lower Manhattan in New York City. Settled during colonial times, the area began to attract notice as an artists' and writers' community after 1910.

green-winged teal (grēnʹwĭngdʹ) *n.* A small freshwater duck *(Anas crecca),* the male of which has gray plumage, a brown head, and an iridescent green speculum.

green·wood (grēnʹwo͝odʹ) *n.* A wood or forest with green foliage.

Green·wood (grēnʹwo͝odʹ). **1.** A city of central Indiana, a residential suburb of Indianapolis. Population, 19,327. **2.** A city of west-central Mississippi east of Greenville. It is a trade center for a cotton-growing region. Population, 20,115. **3.** A city of western South Carolina west-northwest of Columbia. The city was settled in 1824. Population, 21,613.

greet (grēt) *tr.v.* **greet·ed, greet·ing, greets. 1.** To salute or welcome in a friendly and respectful way with speech or writing, as upon meeting or in opening a letter. **2.** To receive with a specified reaction: *greet a joke with laughter.* **3.** To be perceived by: *A din greeted our ears.* [Middle English *greten,* from Old English *grētan.*] **—greetʹer** *n.*

greet·ing (grēʹtĭng) *n.* A word or gesture of welcome or salutation.

greeting card *n.* A folded card bearing a message of greeting, congratulation, or other sentiment, usually sent or given on a special occasion or holiday.

greg·a·rine (grĕgʹə-rīnʹ) *n.* Any of various sporozoan protozoans of the order Gregarinida that are parasitic within the digestive tracts of various invertebrates including arthropods and annelids. **—gregarine** *adj.* Of or belonging to the order Gregarinida. [From New Latin *Gregarīna,* type genus, from Latin *gregārius,* belonging to a flock. See GREGARIOUS.] **—gregʹa·rinʹi·an** (-rĭnʹē-ən) *adj.*

gre·gar·i·ous (grĭ-gârʹē-əs) *adj.* **1.** Seeking and enjoying the company of others; sociable. See Synonyms at **social. 2.** Tending to move in or form a group with others of the same kind: *gregarious bird species.* **3.** *Botany.* Growing in groups that are close together but not densely clustered or matted. [Latin *gregārius,* belonging to a flock, from *grex, greg-,* flock. See **ger-** in Appendix.] **—gre·garʹi·ous·ly** *adv.* **—gre·garʹi·ous·ness** *n.*

Gre·go·ri·an calendar (grĭ-gôrʹē-ən, -gōrʹ-) *n.* The solar calendar in use throughout most of the world, sponsored by Pope Gregory XIII in 1582 as a corrected version of the Julian calendar. See table at **calendar.**

Gregorian chant *n. Roman Catholic Church.* A liturgical chant that is monodic, rhythmically unstructured, and sung without accompaniment. [After Saint GREGORY I.]

Greg·o·ry I (grĕgʹə-rē), Saint. Known as "Gregory the Great." 540?–604. Pope (590–604) who increased papal authority, enforced rules of life for the clergy, and sponsored many important missionary expeditions.

Gregory VII. Original name Hildebrand. 1020?–1085. Pope (1073–1085) who sought to establish the supremacy of the pope within the Church and the authority of the Church over the state.

Gregory XIII. Originally Ugo Buoncompagni. 1502–1585. Pope (1572–1585) who sponsored the adoption of the Gregorian calendar (1582).

Gregory, Lady **Isabella Augusta Persse.** 1852–1932. Irish playwright. She was a founder (1899) and director (1904–1932) of the Abbey Theater.

Gregory of Nys·sa (nĭsʹə), Saint. A.D. 335?–394? Eastern theologian and church father who led the conservative faction during the Trinitarian controversy of the fourth century.

Gregory of Tours (to͝or, to͞or), Saint. 538–594. Frankish prelate and historian who produced a valuable history of the sixth-century Franks.

greige (grā, grāzh) *adj.* Not bleached or dyed; unfinished. Used of textiles. [French *grège,* from Italian *(seta) greggia,* raw (silk), from *greggio,* gray, of Germanic origin.]

grei·sen (grīʹzən) *n.* A granitic rock composed chiefly of quartz and mica. [German, from *greissen,* to split.]

grem·lin (grĕmʹlĭn) *n.* **1.** An imaginary gnomelike creature to whom mechanical problems, especially in aircraft, are attributed. **2.** A maker of mischief. [Perhaps blend of Irish *gruaimín,* bad-tempered little fellow (from Middle Irish *gruaim,* gloom, surliness) and GOBLIN.]

WORD HISTORY: Elves, goblins, and trolls seem to be the timeless creations of the distant past, but gremlins were born in the 20th century. In fact, *gremlin* is first recorded only in the 1920's, as a Royal Air Force term for a low-ranking officer or enlisted man saddled with oppressive assignments. Said to have been invented by members of the Royal Naval Air Service in World War I, *gremlin* is used in works written in the 1940's for "an imaginary gnomelike creature who causes difficulties in aircraft." The word seems likely to have been influenced by *goblin,* but accounts of its origin are various and none are certain. One source calls in Fremlin beer bottles to explain the word; another, the Irish Gaelic word *gruaimín,* "ill-humored little fellow." Whatever the word's origin, it is certain that gremlins have taken on a life of their own.

Gre·na·da (grə-nāʹdə). A country in the Windward Islands of the West Indies comprising the island of **Grenada** and the south-

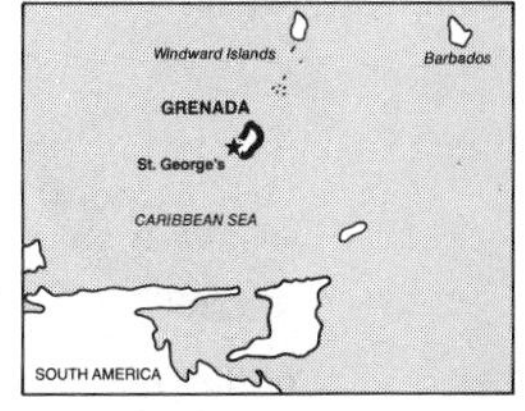

Grenada

ă pat	oi boy
ā pay	ou out
âr care	o͝o took
ä father	o͞o boot
ĕ pet	ŭ cut
ē be	ûr urge
ĭ pit	th thin
ī pie	*th* this
îr pier	hw which
ŏ pot	zh vision
ō toe	ə about, item
ô paw	♦ regionalism

Stress marks: **ʹ** (primary); ʹ (secondary), as in **dictionary** (dĭkʹshə-nĕrʹē)

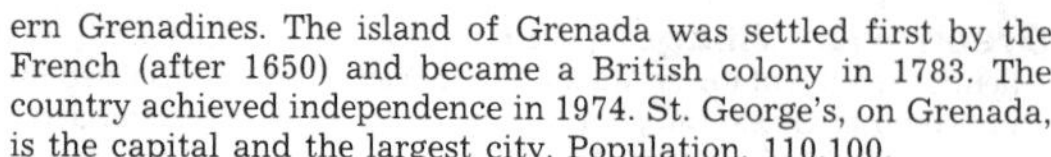

ern Grenadines. The island of Grenada was settled first by the French (after 1650) and became a British colony in 1783. The country achieved independence in 1974. St. George's, on Grenada, is the capital and the largest city. Population, 110,100.

gre·nade (grə-nād′) *n.* **1.** A missile containing priming and bursting charges, designed to be thrown by hand or deployed by a specially equipped launcher. **2.** A glass container filled with a chemical that is dispersed when the container is thrown and smashed. [French, from Old French *(pome) grenate,* pomegranate (from its shape). See POMEGRANATE.]

gren·a·dier (grĕn′ə-dîr′) *n.* **1.a.** A member of the British Grenadier Guards, the first regiment of the royal household infantry. **b.** A soldier who is a member of a special corps or regiment. **c.** A soldier equipped with grenades. **2.** Any of various deep-sea fishes of the family Macrouridae, having a long tapering tail and lacking a tail fin. In this sense, also called *rat-tail.* [French, from *grenade,* grenade. See GRENADE.]

gren·a·dine (grĕn′ə-dēn′, grĕn′ə-dēn′) *n.* **1.** A thick, sweet syrup made from pomegranates and used as a flavoring, especially in beverages. **2.** A thin, loosely woven fabric of silk, cotton, or synthetic fiber. [French, from *grenade,* pomegranate, from Old French *grenate.* See POMEGRANATE.]

Gren·a·dines (grĕn′ə-dēnz′). An archipelago in the Windward Islands of the eastern Caribbean Sea. The southern islands are part of Grenada; the other islands are part of St. Vincent and the Grenadines.

Gren·del (grĕn′dl) *n.* The male monster, descended from Cain, slain by Beowulf in the Old English epic *Beowulf.*

Gren·fell (grĕn′fĕl′, -fəl), Sir **Wilfred Thomason.** 1865–1940. British missionary and physician who ministered to fishing crews in the North Sea and later established medical and social facilities in Labrador and Newfoundland.

Gre·no·ble (grə-nō′bəl, -nôbl′). A city of southeast France on the Isère River south-southwest of Chambéry. An ancient Roman city, Grenoble is a noted tourist and skiing center and was the site of the 1968 Winter Olympics. Population, 156,637.

Gren·ville (grĕn′vĭl′, -vəl), **George.** 1712–1770. British political leader who as prime minister (1763–1765) instigated the Stamp Act (1765), which provoked rebellious activities in the American colonies.

Gren·ville (grĕn′vĭl′), Sir **Richard.** 1542?–1591. English naval officer who commanded the fleet carrying the first colonists to Virginia (1585) and organized the English defense against the Spanish Armada (1588).

Gresh·am (grĕsh′əm). A city of northwest Oregon, a mainly residential suburb of Portland. Population, 33,005.

Gresham, Sir **Thomas.** 1519–1579. English financier. A founder of the Royal Exchange, he is traditionally credited with Gresham's law.

Gresh·am's law (grĕsh′əmz) *n.* The theory holding that if two kinds of money in circulation have the same denominational value but different intrinsic values, the money with higher intrinsic value will be hoarded and eventually driven out of circulation by the money with lesser intrinsic value. [After Sir Thomas GRESHAM.]

gres·so·ri·al (grĕ-sôr′ē-əl, -sōr′-) *adj.* Adapted for walking or having limbs adapted for walking. Used of flightless birds. [From New Latin *gressōrius,* from Latin *gressus,* step, from past participle of *gradī,* to walk. See **ghredh-** in Appendix.]

Gret·na (grĕt′nə). A city of southeast Louisiana on the Mississippi River opposite New Orleans. It is a manufacturing center. Population, 20,615.

Gretna Green. A village of southern Scotland on the English border. It was famous as a place for runaway marriages from 1754 until 1856, when the Scottish law was changed to require a 21-day residence period for one of the parties before issuance of a license.

Greuze (grœz), **Jean Baptiste.** 1725–1805. French painter of moralistic genre works, such as *The Paralytic Tended by His Children* (1763).

grew (gro͞o) *v.* Past tense of **grow.**

grex (grĕks) *n. Botany.* A classification for cultivars derived from the same hybrid. [Latin, herd, flock. See GREGARIOUS.]

grey (grā) *adj., n., & v.* Variant of **gray.**

Grey (grā), **Charles.** Second Earl Grey. 1764–1845. British politician who as prime minister (1830–1834) implemented parliamentary and social reforms, notably the abolition of slavery throughout the British Empire.

Grey, Lady **Jane.** 1537–1554. Queen of England for nine days (1553). Proclaimed queen on the death of Edward VI (July 10, 1553), she was imprisoned after her short reign, replaced by the popular Mary Tudor, and subsequently beheaded for treason.

Grey, Zane. 1875–1939. American writer of Western adventure novels, including *Riders of the Purple Sage* (1912).

grey·hen (grā′hĕn′) *n.* The female of the black grouse.

grey·hound (grā′hound′) *n.* Any of a breed of tall, slender dogs, having a smooth coat, a narrow head, and long legs and capable of running swiftly. [Middle English *grehound,* from Old English *grīghund* : *grīg,* gray + *hund,* hound; see HOUND.]

greyhound

grey·lag (grā′lăg′) *n.* Variant of **graylag.**

grib·ble (grĭb′əl) *n.* Any of several small, wood-boring marine isopod crustaceans of the genus *Limnoria,* especially *L. lignorum,* which often damage underwater wooden structures. [Possibly diminutive of GRUB.]

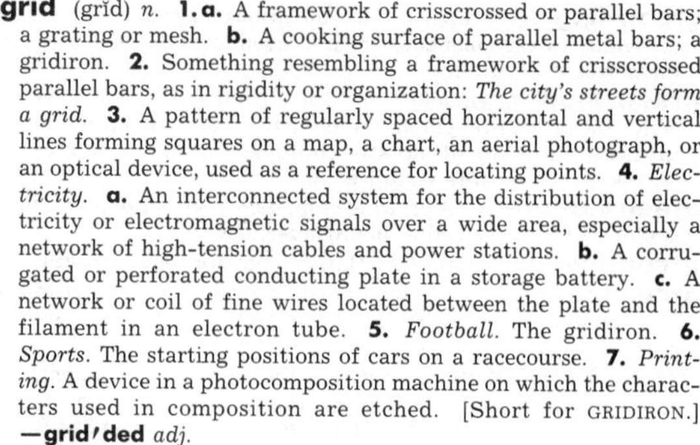

grid (grĭd) *n.* **1.a.** A framework of crisscrossed or parallel bars; a grating or mesh. **b.** A cooking surface of parallel metal bars; a gridiron. **2.** Something resembling a framework of crisscrossed parallel bars, as in rigidity or organization: *The city's streets form a grid.* **3.** A pattern of regularly spaced horizontal and vertical lines forming squares on a map, a chart, an aerial photograph, or an optical device, used as a reference for locating points. **4.** *Electricity.* **a.** An interconnected system for the distribution of electricity or electromagnetic signals over a wide area, especially a network of high-tension cables and power stations. **b.** A corrugated or perforated conducting plate in a storage battery. **c.** A network or coil of fine wires located between the plate and the filament in an electron tube. **5.** *Football.* The gridiron. **6.** *Sports.* The starting positions of cars on a racecourse. **7.** *Printing.* A device in a photocomposition machine on which the characters used in composition are etched. [Short for GRIDIRON.] **—grid′ded** *adj.*

grid·der (grĭd′ər) *n. Football.* A player.

grid·dle (grĭd′l) *n.* A flat metal surface, such as a pan, that is used for cooking by dry heat. **—griddle** *tr.v.* **-dled, -dling, -dles.** To cook on a flat metal surface. [Middle English *gridel,* gridiron, from Old North French *gredil,* from Latin *crāticula,* diminutive of *crātis,* wickerwork hurdle, lattice.]

grid·dle·cake (grĭd′l-kāk′) *n.* See **pancake.**

grid·i·ron (grĭd′ī′ərn) *n.* **1.** *Football.* **a.** The field of play. **b.** The game itself. **2.** A metal structure high above the stage of a theater, from which ropes or cables are strung to scenery and lights. **3.a.** A flat framework of parallel metal bars used for broiling meat or fish. **b.** An object resembling such a framework. [Middle English *gridirne,* alteration (influenced by *iren, irne,* iron; see IRON) of *gridere,* alteration of *gridel.* See GRIDDLE.]

grid·lock (grĭd′lŏk′) *n.* **1.** A traffic jam in which no vehicular movement is possible, especially one caused by the blockage of key intersections within a grid of streets. **2.** A complete lack of movement or progress resulting in a backup or stagnation: *"the political gridlock that prevented . . . the President and Congress from moving expeditiously to cut the budget"* (Robert D. Hormats). **—grid′lock′** *v.* **—grid′locked′** *adj.*

grief (grēf) *n.* **1.** Deep mental anguish, as that arising from bereavement. See Synonyms at **regret.** **2.** A source of deep mental anguish. **3.** Annoyance or frustration: *Trying to follow their directions was nothing but grief.* **4.** Trouble or difficulty: *the griefs of trying to meet a deadline.* **5.** *Archaic.* A grievance. [Middle English, from Old French, from *grever,* to harm, aggrieve. See GRIEVE.]

Grieg (grĕg, grĭg), **Edvard Hagerup.** 1843–1907. Norwegian composer whose works, such as the incidental music for *Peer Gynt* (1876), incorporate Norwegian folk music idioms.

Grier (grîr), **Robert Cooper.** 1794–1870. American jurist who served as an associate justice of the U.S. Supreme Court (1846–1870).

griev·ance (grē′vəns) *n.* **1.a.** An actual or supposed circumstance regarded as just cause for protest. **b.** A complaint or protestation based on such a circumstance. See Synonyms at **injustice.** **2.** Indignation or resentment stemming from a feeling of having been wronged. **3.** *Obsolete.* **a.** The act of inflicting hardship or harm. **b.** The cause of hardship or harm. [Middle English *grevaunce,* from Old French *grevance,* from *grever,* to harm. See GRIEVE.]

grieve (grēv) *v.* **grieved, griev·ing, grieves.** *—tr.* **1.** To cause to be sorrowful; distress. **2.** *Archaic.* To hurt or harm. *—intr.* To experience or express grief. [Middle English *greven,* from Old French *grever,* to harm, from Latin *gravāre,* to burden, from *gravis,* heavy. See **g^wera-¹** in Appendix.] **—griev′er** *n.* **—griev′ing·ly** *adv.*

SYNONYMS: *grieve, lament, mourn, sorrow.* The central meaning shared by these verbs is "to feel, show, or express grief, sadness, or regret": *grieved over her father's sudden death; lamenting over the decline in academic standards; mourning for lost hopes; sorrowed over the innocent victims of the dictatorship.*
ANTONYM: *rejoice.*

Grieve (grēv), **Christopher Murray.** See Hugh **MacDiarmid.**

griev·ous (grē′vəs) *adj.* **1.** Causing grief, pain, or anguish: *a grievous loss.* **2.** Serious or dire; grave: *a grievous crime.* [Anglo-Norman *grevous,* from *grever,* to harm, aggrieve, from Latin *gravāre,* to burden. See GRIEVE.] **—griev′ous·ly** *adv.* **—griev′ous·ness** *n.*

grif·fin also **grif·fon** or **gryph·on** (grĭf′ən) *n.* A fabulous beast with the head and wings of an eagle and the body of a lion. [Middle English *griffoun,* from Old French *griffon,* from *grif,* from Latin *grȳphus,* variant of *grȳps, grȳph-,* from Greek *grups.*]

griffin
Sixth- to seventh-century Persian bowl

Grif·fin (grĭf′ĭn). A city of west-central Georgia south-southeast of Atlanta. It is a textile and food-processing center in a farming region. Population, 20,728.

Grif·fith (grĭf′ĭth). A town of extreme northwest Indiana south of Hammond. It is mainly residential. Population, 17,026.

Griffith, Arthur. 1872–1922. Irish nationalist leader who was a founder of the Sinn Fein movement for Irish independence (1905).

Griffith, D(avid Lewelyn) W(ark). 1875–1948. American filmmaker who developed several cinematic techniques, such as fade-

D.W. Griffith

ins, fade-outs, close-ups, moving-camera shots, and flashbacks. *The Birth of a Nation* (1915) is among his many films.

grif·fon (grĭf′ən) *n.* **1.** Any of a breed of dog originating in Belgium and having a short, bearded muzzle. Also called *Brussels griffon.* **2.** Any of various wirehaired hunting dogs of a breed originating in the Netherlands in the late 19th century. **3.** Variant of **griffin.** [French, from Old French. See GRIFFIN.]

grift (grĭft) *Slang. n.* **1.** Money made dishonestly, as in a swindle. **2.** A swindle or confidence game. **—grift** *v.* **grift·ed, grift·ing, grifts.** *—intr.* To engage in swindling or cheating. *—tr.* To obtain by swindling or cheating. [Perhaps alteration of GRAFT[2].] **—grift′er** *n.*

grig (grĭg) *n.* A lively, bright person. [Middle English, dwarf.]

gri·gri also **gris-gris** (grē′grē) *n., pl.* **gri·gris** also **gris-gris** (grē′grē). An African charm, fetish, or amulet. [French, of West African origin; akin to Bulanda *grigri,* amulet.]

grill (grĭl) *tr.v.* **grilled, grill·ing, grills. 1.** To broil on a gridiron. **2.** To torture or afflict as if by broiling. **3.** *Informal.* To question relentlessly; cross-examine. **4.** To mark or emboss with a gridiron. **—grill** *n.* **1.** A cooking surface of parallel metal bars; a gridiron. **2.** Food cooked by broiling or grilling. **3.** An informal restaurant or a room in a restaurant where grilled foods are served; a grillroom. **4.** A series of marks grilled or embossed on a surface. **5.** Variant of **grille.** [French *griller,* from *gril,* gridiron, from Old French *greille,* from Latin *crātīcula,* diminutive of *crātis,* wickerwork, lattice.] **—grill′er** *n.*

gril·lage (grĭl′ĭj) *n.* A network or frame of timber or steel serving as a foundation, usually on ground that is wet or soft. [French, from Old French, trellis, from *greille,* gridiron. See GRILL.]

grille also **grill** (grĭl) *n.* **1.** A grating of metal, wood, or another material used as a screen, divider, barrier, or decorative element, as in a window or on the front end of an automotive vehicle. **2.** An opening covered with a grating. [French, from Old French *greille.* See GRILL.]

grill·er·y (grĭl′ə-rē) *n., pl.* **-ies.** A grill; a grillroom.

grill·room (grĭl′ro͞om′, -ro͝om′) *n.* A place where grilled foods are served to customers; a grill.

grill·work (grĭl′wûrk′) *n.* Material formed into grilles or a grille.

grilse (grĭls) *n., pl.* **grilse.** A young Atlantic salmon on its first return from the sea to fresh or brackish waters. [From Middle English *grills,* young salmon (pl.).]

grim (grĭm) *adj.* **grim·mer, grim·mest. 1.** Unrelenting; rigid. **2.** Uninviting or unnerving in aspect; forbidding: *"undoubtedly the grimmest part of him was his iron claw"* (J.M. Barrie). **3.** Ghastly; sinister: *"He made a grim jest at the horrifying nature of his wound"* (Reginald Pound). See Synonyms at **ghastly. 4.** Dismal; gloomy: *a grim, rainy day.* **5.** Ferocious; savage: *the grim advance of the pillaging army.* [Middle English, from Old English, fierce, severe.] **—grim′ly** *adv.* **—grim′ness** *n.*

grim·ace (grĭm′ĭs, grĭ-mās′) *n.* A sharp contortion of the face expressive of pain, contempt, or disgust. **—grimace** *intr.v.* **-aced, -ac·ing, -ac·es.** To make a sharp contortion of the face. [French, from Old French *grimache,* alteration of *grimuche,* probably from Frankish **grīma,* mask.] **—grim′ac·er** *n.*

gri·mal·kin (grĭ-môl′kĭn, -măl′-) *n.* **1.** A cat, especially an old female cat. **2.** An old woman considered to be ill-tempered. [Variant of *graymalkin* : GRAY + obsolete *Malkin,* diminutive of the personal name *Matilda.*]

grime (grīm) *n.* Black dirt or soot, especially such dirt clinging to or ingrained in a surface. **—grime** *tr.v.* **grimed, grim·ing, grimes.** To cover with black dirt or soot; begrime. [Middle English *grim*; akin to Middle Dutch *grīme.* See **ghrēi-** in Appendix.]

Grim·ké (grĭm′kē), **Sarah Moore.** 1792–1873. American feminist and abolitionist. She and her sister **Angelina Emily Grimké** (1805–1879) were among the first American women to speak publicly against slavery and the repression of women.

Grimm (grĭm), **Jakob Ludwig Karl.** 1785–1863. German philologist and folklorist who formulated Grimm's Law (1819), the basis for much of modern comparative linguistics. With his brother **Wilhelm Karl** (1786–1859) he collected Germanic folk tales and published them as *Grimm's Fairy Tales* (1812–1815).

Grimm's Law (grĭmz) *n.* A formula describing the regular changes undergone by Indo-European stop consonants represented in Germanic, essentially stating that Indo-European *p, t,* and *k* became Germanic *f, th,* and *h;* Indo-European *b, d,* and *g* became Germanic *p, t,* and *k;* and Indo-European *bh, dh,* and *gh* became Germanic *b, d,* and *g.* [After Jakob Ludwig Karl GRIMM.]

Grims·by (grĭmz′bē). A borough of eastern England near the mouth of the Humber River southeast of Hull. It is a major fishing port and has varied industries. Population, 91,800.

grim·y (grī′mē) *adj.* **-i·er, -i·est.** Covered with grime. See Synonyms at **dirty. —grim′i·ly** *adv.* **—grim′i·ness** *n.*

grin (grĭn) *v.* **grinned, grin·ning, grins.** *—intr.* To draw back the lips and bare the teeth, as in mirth or good humor. *—tr.* To express with a grin: *I grinned my approval.* **—grin** *n.* **1.** The act of grinning. **2.** The facial expression produced by grinning. See Synonyms at **smile.** [Middle English *grennen,* to grimace, from Old English *grennian.*] **—grin′ner** *n.* **—grin′ning·ly** *adv.*

grind (grīnd) *v.* **ground** (ground), **grind·ing, grinds.** *—tr.* **1.a.** To crush, pulverize, or reduce to powder by friction, especially by rubbing between two hard surfaces: *grind wheat into flour.* **b.** To shape, sharpen, or refine with friction: *grind a lens.* **2.** To rub (two surfaces) together harshly; gnash: *grind the teeth.* **3.** To bear down on harshly; crush. **4.** To oppress or weaken gradually: *"Laws grind the poor, and rich men rule the law"* (Oliver Goldsmith). **5.a.** To operate by turning a crank: *ground a hurdy-gurdy.* **b.** To produce or process by turning a crank: *grinding a pound of beef.* **6.** To produce mechanically or without inspiration: *The factory grinds out a uniform product.* **7.** To instill or teach by persistent repetition: *ground the truth into their heads.* *—intr.* **1.** To perform the operation of grinding something. **2.** To become crushed, pulverized, or powdered by friction. **3.** To move with noisy friction; grate: *a train grinding along rusty rails.* **4.** *Informal.* To devote oneself to study or work: *grinding for a test; grinding away at housework.* **5.** *Slang.* To rotate the pelvis erotically, as in the manner of a stripteaser. **—grind** *n.* **1.** The act of grinding. **2.** A crunching or grinding noise. **3.** A specific grade or degree of pulverization, as of coffee beans: *drip grind.* **4.** *Informal.* A laborious task, routine, or study: *the daily grind.* **5.** *Informal.* A student who works or studies excessively. **6.** *Slang.* An erotic rotation of the pelvis. [Middle English *grinden,* from Old English *grindan.* See **ghrendh-** in Appendix.] **—grind′ing·ly** *adv.*

♦**grind·er** (grīn′dər) *n.* **1.** One that grinds, especially: **a.** One who sharpens cutting edges. **b.** A mechanical device that grinds: *a meat grinder.* **2.** A molar. **3. grinders.** *Informal.* The teeth. **4.** *New England.* See **submarine** (sense 2). See Regional Note at **submarine.**

grind·stone (grīnd′stōn′) *n.* **1.** A revolving stone disk used for grinding, polishing, or sharpening tools. **2.** A millstone. ***—idiom.* put (one's) nose to the grindstone.** *Informal.* To work in earnest.

grin·go (grĭng′gō) *n., pl.* **-gos.** *Offensive Slang.* Used as a disparaging term for a foreigner in Latin America, especially an American or English person. [Spanish, foreign, foreign language, gibberish, probably alteration of *griego,* Greek, from Latin *Graecus.* See GREEK.]

WORD HISTORY: The word *gringo* is an offensive term in Latin America for a foreigner, particularly an American or English person. But the word existed in Spanish before this particular sense came into being. In fact, *gringo* may be an alteration of the word *griego,* the Spanish development of Latin *Graecus,* "Greek." *Griego* first meant "Greek, Grecian," as an adjective and "Greek, Greek language," as a noun. The saying "It's Greek to me" exists in Spanish, as it does in English, and helps us understand why *griego* came to mean "unintelligible language" and perhaps, by further extension of this idea, "stranger, that is, one who speaks a foreign language." The altered form *gringo* lost touch with Greek but has the senses "unintelligible language," "foreigner, especially an English person," and in Latin America, "North American or Britisher." Its first recorded English use (1849) is in John Woodhouse Audubon's *Western Journal:* "We were hooted and shouted at as we passed through, and called 'Gringoes.'"

gri·ot (grē-ō′, grē′ō, grē′ŏt) *n.* A storyteller in western Africa who perpetuates the oral tradition and history of a village or family. [French, alteration of *guiriot,* perhaps ultimately from Portuguese *criado,* domestic servant, from Latin *creātus,* one brought up or trained, from past participle of *creāre,* to produce, bring up. See CREATE.]

grip[1] (grĭp) *n.* **1.a.** A tight hold; a firm grasp: *a drowning swimmer now safely in the grip of a lifeguard.* **b.** The pressure or strength of such a grasp: *a wrestler with an unmatched grip.* **c.** A manner of grasping and holding: *The crate afforded no comfortable grip.* **2.a.** Intellectual hold; understanding: *a good grip on French history.* **b.** Ability to function properly or well; competence: *getting a grip on the new technique.* **3.a.** A mechanical device that grasps and holds. **b.** A part, such as a handle, that is designed to be grasped and held. **4.** A suitcase or valise. **5.a.** A stagehand who helps in shifting scenery. **b.** A member of a film production crew who adjusts sets and props and sometimes assists the camera operator. **—grip** *v.* **gripped, grip·ping, grips.** *—tr.* **1.** To secure and maintain a tight hold on; seize firmly. **2.** To hold the interest or attention of: *a scene that gripped the entire audience.* *—intr.* To maintain a secure grasp. [Middle English, from Old English *gripe,* grasp and *gripa,* handful.] **—grip′per** *n.* **—grip′ping·ly** *adv.*

grip[2] (grĭp) *n.* Variant of **grippe.**

gripe (grīp) *v.* **griped, grip·ing, gripes.** *—intr.* **1.** *Informal.* To complain naggingly or petulantly; grumble. **2.** To have sharp pains in the bowels. *—tr.* **1.** *Informal.* To irritate; annoy: *Her petty complaints really gripe me.* **2.** To cause sharp pain in the bowels of. **3.** To grasp; seize. **4.** To oppress or afflict. **—gripe** *n.* **1.** *Informal.* A complaint. **2. gripes.** Sharp, spasmodic pains in the bowels. **3.** A firm hold; a grasp. **4.** A grip; a handle. [Middle English *gripen,* to seize, from Old English *grīpan.*] **—grip′er** *n.*

grippe also **grip** (grĭp) *n.* See **influenza** (sense 1). [French, from Old French, claw, quarrel, from *gripper,* to seize, grasp, from Frankish **grīpan.*] **—grip′py** *adj.*

grip·sack (grĭp′săk′) *n.* A small suitcase.

Gris (grēs), **Juan.** Originally José Victoriano Gonzáles. 1887–1927. Spanish painter who adopted and further developed cubism. His works include *Homage to Picasso* (1912).

gri·saille (grĭ-zī′, -zāl′) *n.* **1.** A style of monochromatic paint-

grille
Top: Gateway
Bottom: Automobile grille

grindstone

ă pat	oi boy
ā pay	ou out
âr care	o͝o took
ä father	o͞o boot
ĕ pet	ŭ cut
ē be	ûr urge
ĭ pit	th thin
ī pie	*th* this
îr pier	hw which
ŏ pot	zh vision
ō toe	ə about, item
ô paw	♦ regionalism

Stress marks: **′** (primary); ′ (secondary), as in **dictionary** (dĭk′shə-nĕr′ē)

ing in shades of gray, used especially for the representation of relief sculpture. **2.** A painting or design in this style. **3.a.** Vitrifiable glass paint. **b.** A lacy pattern painted on light glass with vitrifiable paint and fired. [French, from *gris,* gray, from Old French, from Frankish **grīs.*]

gris·e·o·ful·vin (grĭz′ē-ə-fo͝ol′vĭn) *n.* An antibiotic, $C_{17}H_{17}ClO_6$, administered orally for the treatment of ringworm and other fungal infections of the skin, hair, and nails. [From New Latin *griseofulvum,* species of penicillium : Medieval Latin *grīseus,* griseous; see GRISEOUS + Latin *fulvum,* neuter of *fulvus,* tawny; see **ghel-**[2] in Appendix.]

gris·e·ous (grĭz′ē-əs, grĭs′-) *adj.* Mottled with gray, especially bluish gray; grizzled. [Medieval Latin *grīseus,* of Germanic origin.]

gri·sette (grĭ-zĕt′) *n.* A French working-class girl or young woman. [French, a cheap gray dress fabric, grisette, from *gris,* gray. See GRISAILLE.]

gris-gris (grē′grē) *n.* Variant of **grigri.**

gris·ly (grĭz′lē) *adj.* **-li·er, -li·est.** Inspiring repugnance; gruesome. See Synonyms at **ghastly.** [Middle English *grisli,* from Old English *grislīc.* See **ghrēi-** in Appendix.] **—gris′li·ness** *n.*

gri·son (grī′sən, grĭz′ən) *n.* Either of two small carnivorous mammals *(Galictis vittata* or *G. cuja)* of Central and South America, having grizzled fur, a slender body, and short legs. [French, from Old French, gray fur, from *gris,* gray. See GRISAILLE.]

grist (grĭst) *n.* **1.** Grain or a quantity of grain for grinding. **2.** Ground grain. ***—idiom.*** **grist for (one's)** (or **the**) **mill.** Something that can be used to advantage. [Middle English, Old English *grīst.* See **ghrendh-** in Appendix.]

gris·tle (grĭs′əl) *n.* Cartilage, especially when present in meat. [Middle English, from Old English.]

gris·tly (grĭs′lē) *adj.* **-tli·er, -tli·est. 1.** Composed of or containing gristle. **2.** Resembling gristle. **—gris′tli·ness** *n.*

grist·mill (grĭst′mĭl′) *n.* A mill for grinding grain.

grit (grĭt) *n.* **1.** Minute rough granules, as of sand or stone. **2.** The texture or fineness of sand or stone used in grinding. **3.** A coarse hard sandstone used for making grindstones and millstones. **4.** *Informal.* Indomitable spirit; pluck. **—grit** *v.* **grit·ted, grit·ting, grits.** *—tr.* **1.** To clamp (the teeth) together. **2.** To cover or treat with grit. *—intr.* To make a grinding noise. [Middle English *gret,* sand, from Old English *grēot.*]

grith (grĭth) *n.* Protection or sanctuary provided by Old English law to persons in certain circumstances, as when in a church or traveling on the king's highway. [Middle English, from Old English, from Old Norse *gridh,* domicile, asylum.]

grits (grĭts) *pl.n. (used with a sing. or pl. verb).* **1.** A ground, usually white meal of dried and hulled corn kernels that is boiled and served as a breakfast food or side dish. **2.** Coarsely ground grain, especially corn. [Alteration of Middle English *grutta,* coarse meal, from Old English *grytta,* pl. of *grytt.*]

grit·ty (grĭt′ē) *adj.* **-ti·er, -ti·est. 1.** Containing, covered with, or resembling grit. **2.** Showing resolution and fortitude; plucky: *a gritty decision.* **—grit′ti·ly** *adv.* **—grit′ti·ness** *n.*

grizzly bear
Ursus arctos
subsp. *horribilis*

griv·et (grĭv′ĭt) *n.* A long-tailed African monkey *(Cercopithecus aethiops)* having a greenish-gray coat and tufts of white hair on the face. [French.]

griz·zle (grĭz′əl) *tr. & intr.v.* **-zled, -zling, -zles.** To make or become gray. **—grizzle** *n.* **1.a.** The color of a grizzled animal. **b.** A grizzled animal. **2.** *Archaic.* Gray hair. **—grizzle** *adj.* **1.** Gray. **2.** Grizzled. [From Middle English *grisel,* gray, from Old French, diminutive of *gris,* gray. See GRISAILLE.]

griz·zled (grĭz′əld) *adj.* **1.** Streaked with or partly gray. **2.** Having brownish fur or hair tipped with gray.

griz·zly (grĭz′lē) *adj.* **-zli·er, -zli·est.** Grayish or flecked with gray. **—grizzly** *n., pl.* **-zlies.** A grizzly bear.

grizzly bear *n.* The brown bear of northwest North America, now considered a subspecies *(Ursus arctos* subsp. *horribilis).* Also called *silvertip.*

gro. *abbr.* Gross.

groin

groan (grōn) *v.* **groaned, groan·ing, groans.** *—intr.* **1.** To voice a deep, inarticulate sound, as of pain, grief, or displeasure. **2.** To make a sound expressive of stress or strain: *floorboards groaning.* *—tr.* To utter or express with groans or a groan. **—groan** *n.* The sound made in groaning. [Middle English *gronen,* from Old English *grānian.*] **—groan′er** *n.* **—groan′ing·ly** *adv.*

groat (grōt) *n.* An English silver coin worth four pence, used from the 14th to the 17th century. [Middle English *grot,* from Middle Dutch *groot,* a thick, large coin, translation of Medieval Latin *(dēnārius) grossus.*]

groats (grōts) *pl.n. (used with a sing. or pl. verb).* Hulled, usually crushed grain, especially oats. [Middle English *grotes,* from Old English *grotan.*]

gro·cer (grō′sər) *n.* One that sells foodstuffs and various household supplies. [Middle English, wholesaler, from Anglo-Norman *grosser,* from Medieval Latin *grossārius, grocerius,* from Late Latin *grossus,* thick.]

gro·cer·y (grō′sə-rē) *n., pl.* **-ies. 1.** A store selling foodstuffs and various household supplies. **2. groceries.** Commodities sold by a grocer.

Grod·no (grôd′nō, -nə, grŏd′-). A city of western Belorussia on the Neman River near the Polish border. Capital of an independent principality until 1398, Grodno was ruled at various times by Lithuania, Poland, and Russia. Population, 247,000.

grog (grŏg) *n.* An alcoholic liquor, especially rum diluted with water. [After Old *Grog,* nickname of Edward Vernon (1684–1757), British admiral who ordered that diluted rum be served to his sailors, from GROGRAM (from his habit of wearing a grogram cloak).]

grog·gy (grŏg′ē) *adj.* **-gi·er, -gi·est.** Unsteady and dazed; shaky. [From GROG.] **—grog′gi·ly** *adv.* **—grog′gi·ness** *n.*

grog·ram (grŏg′rəm, grō′grəm) *n.* A coarse, often stiffened fabric made of silk, mohair, wool, or a blend of them. [Alteration of French *gros grain,* coarse texture. See GROSGRAIN.]

groin (groin) *n.* **1.** *Anatomy.* The crease or hollow at the junction of the inner part of each thigh with the trunk, together with the adjacent region and often including the external genitals. **2.** *Architecture.* The curved edge at the junction of two intersecting vaults. **3.** A small jetty extending from a shore to protect a beach against erosion or to trap shifting sands. **—groin** *tr.v.* **groined, groin·ing, groins.** To provide or build with groins. [Alteration (influenced by LOIN) of Middle English *grinde,* perhaps from Old English *grynde,* abyss, hollow.]

grok (grŏk) *tr.v.* **grok·ked, grok·king, groks.** *Slang.* To understand profoundly through intuition or empathy. [Coined by Robert A. Heinlein in his *Stranger in a Strange Land.*]

grom·met (grŏm′ĭt) also **grum·met** (grŭm′-) *n.* **1.a.** A reinforced eyelet, as in cloth or leather, through which a fastener may be passed. **b.** A small metal or plastic ring used to reinforce such an eyelet. **2.** *Nautical.* A loop of rope or metal used for securing the edge of a sail to its stay. [Probably from obsolete French *gromette, gormette,* chain joining the ends of a bit, from Old French, from *gourmer,* to bridle.]

grom·well (grŏm′wəl, -wĕl′) *n.* See **puccoon** (sense 1). [Alteration of Middle English *gromil,* from Old French : *gro-*; perhaps akin to *graine,* grain + *mil,* millet (from Latin *milium;* see MILLET).]

Gro·my·ko (grə-mē′kō, grō-), **Andrei Andreyevich.** 1909–1989. Soviet political leader who served as ambassador to the United States (1943–1946) and the United Nations (1946–1948).

Gro·ning·en (grō′nĭng-ən, KHrō′-). A city of northeast Netherlands north-northeast of Apeldoorn. An important trade center, it was captured by the Dutch in 1594. Population, 167,866.

groom (gro͞om, gro͝om) *n.* **1.** A man or boy employed to take care of horses. **2.** A bridegroom. **3.** One of several officers in an English royal household. **4.** *Archaic.* **a.** A man. **b.** A male servant. *—tr.* **groomed, groom·ing, grooms. 1.** To care for the appearance of; to make neat and trim: *groomed himself carefully in front of the mirror.* **2.** To clean and brush (an animal). **3.** To prepare, as for a specific position or purpose: *groom an employee for advancement.* **4.** *Sports.* To prepare (a trail) for skiers, as by packing down new snow or leveling moguls. *—intr.* To care for one's appearance. [Middle English *grom.* N., sense 2, short for BRIDEGROOM.] **—groom′er** *n.*

grooms·man (gro͞omz′mən, gro͝omz′-) *n.* A man who attends the bridegroom at a wedding.

groove (gro͞ov) *n.* **1.** A long, narrow furrow or channel. **2.** *Slang.* A settled routine: *got into the groove of a nine-to-five job.* **3.** *Slang.* A situation or an activity that one enjoys or to which one is especially well suited: *found his groove playing bass in a trio.* **4.** *Slang.* A very pleasurable experience. **—groove** *v.* **grooved, groov·ing, grooves.** *—tr.* To cut a groove or grooves. *—intr.* *Slang.* **1.a.** To take great pleasure or satisfaction; enjoy oneself: *just sitting around, grooving on the music.* **b.** To be affected with pleasurable excitement. **2.** To react or interact harmoniously. [Middle English *groof,* mining shaft, probably from Middle Dutch *groeve,* ditch. See **ghrebh-**[2] in Appendix.]

groov·y (gro͞o′vē) *adj.* **-i·er, -i·est.** *Slang.* Very pleasing; wonderful. **—groov′i·ness** *n.*

grope (grōp) *v.* **groped, grop·ing, gropes.** *—intr.* **1.** To reach about uncertainly; feel one's way: *groped for the telephone.* **2.** To search blindly or uncertainly: *grope for an answer.* *—tr.* **1.** To make (one's way) by reaching about uncertainly. **2.** *Slang.* To handle or fondle for sexual pleasure. **—grope** *n.* The act or an instance of groping. [Middle English *gropen,* from Old English *grāpian.*] **—grop′er** *n.* **—grop′ing·ly** *adv.*

Gro·pi·us (grō′pē-əs), **Walter Adolph.** 1883–1969. German-born American architect. Founder of the Bauhaus school of design, he exerted tremendous influence on modern architecture.

gros·beak (grōs′bēk′) *n.* Any of various finches of the family Fringillidae of Europe and America, having a thick, conical bill. [Partial translation of French *grosbec* : *gros,* thick, large (from Old French; see GROSS) + *bec,* beak.]

gro·schen (grō′shən) *n., pl.* **groschen.** See table at **currency.** [German, from Middle High German *grosse,* from Medieval Latin *(dēnārius) grossus,* thick (denarius), from Late Latin *grossus,* thick.]

gros·grain (grō′grān′) *n.* **1.** A closely woven silk or rayon fabric with narrow horizontal ribs. **2.** A ribbon made of this fabric. [French *gros grain,* coarse texture : *gros,* coarse, thick (from Old French; see GROSS) + *grain,* texture, grain (from Old French *graine,* grain, seed; see GRAIN).]

gross (grōs) *adj.* **gross·er, gross·est. 1.a.** Exclusive of deductions; total: *gross profits.* See Synonyms at **whole. b.** Unmitigated in any way; utter: *gross incompetence.* **2.** Glaringly obvious; flagrant: *gross injustice.* See Synonyms at **flagrant.**

3. a. Brutishly coarse, as in behavior; crude. **b.** Offensive; disgusting. See Synonyms at **coarse. c.** Lacking sensitivity or discernment; unrefined. **d.** Carnal; sensual. **4. a.** Overweight; corpulent. **b.** Dense; profuse. **5.** Broad; general: *the gross outlines of a plan.* **—gross** *n.* **1.** *pl.* **gross·es.** The entire body or amount, as of income, before necessary deductions have been made. **2.** *pl.* **gross.** *Abbr.* **gr., gro.** A group of 144 items; 12 dozen. **—gross** *tr.v.* **grossed, gross·ing, gross·es.** To earn as a total income or profit before deductions. ***—phrasal verb.*** **gross out.** *Slang.* To fill with disgust; nauseate: *"The trick in making a family film . . . is finding ways to interest grown-ups without boring, confusing, or grossing out the younger set"* (Christian Science Monitor). [Middle English, large, from Old French *gros,* from Late Latin *grossus,* thick. N., sense 2, Middle English *grosse,* from Old French *grosse (douzain),* large (dozen), feminine of *gros.*] **—gross′er** *n.* **—gross′ly** *adv.* **—gross′ness** *n.*

gross anatomy *n.* The study of the organs, parts, and structures of a body that are visible to the naked eye. Also called *macroscopic anatomy.*

Gross·glock·ner (grōs′glŏk′nər). A peak, 3,799.4 m (12,457 ft) high, of southern Austria in the Hohe Tauern range of the Alps.

gross index *n. Computer Science.* The general index that is consulted first in locating a specific record.

gross national product *n. Abbr.* **GNP** The total market value of all the goods and services produced by a nation during a specified period.

gross-out (grōs′out′) *n. Slang.* Something that elicits disgust.

gros·su·la·rite (grŏs′yə-lə-rīt′) also **gros·su·lar** (-lər) *n.* A pale green, pink, brown, or black garnet, $Ca_3Al_2(SiO_4)_3$, occurring alone or as a constituent of the common garnet. [German *Grossularit,* from New Latin *Grossulāria,* former genus of gooseberry (from the color of some garnets), from French *groseille,* gooseberry, from Old French *grosele,* of Germanic origin; akin to Middle Dutch *kroes,* curled.]

Gros Ventre (grō′ vänt′) *n., pl.* **Gros Ventre** or **Gros Ventres** (vänt′). **1.** See **Atsina. 2.** See **Hidatsa.** [French : *gros,* big + *ventre,* belly.]

grosz (grôsh) *n., pl.* **gro·szy** (grô′shē). See table at **currency.** [Polish, from Czech *groš,* from Medieval Latin *(dēnārius) grossus,* thick (denarius). See GROSCHEN.]

Grosz (grōs), **George.** 1893–1959. German-born American artist. Associated with the Berlin Dada movement, he is best known for his biting antimilitaristic caricatures of the 1920's.

grot (grŏt) *n.* A grotto. [French *grotte,* from Italian *grotta.* See GROTTO.]

Grote (grōt), **George.** 1794–1871. British historian noted for his *History of Greece* (1846–1856).

gro·tesque (grō-tĕsk′) *adj.* **1.** Characterized by ludicrous or incongruous distortion, as of appearance or manner. **2.** Outlandish or bizarre, as in character or appearance. See Synonyms at **fantastic. 3.** Of, relating to, or being the grotesque style in art or a work executed in this style. **—grotesque** *n.* **1.** One that is grotesque. **2. a.** A style of painting, sculpture, and ornamentation in which natural forms and monstrous figures are intertwined in bizarre or fanciful combinations. **b.** A work of art executed in this style. [From French, a fanciful style of decorative art, from Italian *grottesca,* from feminine of *grottesco,* of a grotto, from *grotta,* grotto. See GROTTO.] **—gro·tesque′ly** *adv.* **—gro·tesque′ness** *n.*

gro·tes·que·ry also **gro·tes·que·rie** (grō-tĕs′kə-rē) *n., pl.* **-ries. 1.** The state of being grotesque; grotesqueness. **2.** Something grotesque.

Gro·ti·us (grō′shē-əs, -shəs), **Hugo.** Originally Huig de Groot. 1583–1645. Dutch jurist, politician, and theologian whose major work, *Of the Law of War and Peace* (1625), is considered the first comprehensive treatise on international law.

Grot·on (grŏt′n). A town of southeast Connecticut on the Thames River opposite New London. Settled c. 1650, it is a port and the site of a U.S. submarine base. Population, 41,062.

grot·to (grŏt′ō) *n., pl.* **-toes** or **-tos. 1.** A small cave or cavern. **2.** An artificial structure or excavation made to resemble a cave or cavern. [Alteration of Italian *grotta,* from Vulgar Latin **grupta,* from Latin *crypta,* vault. See CRYPT.]

grot·ty (grŏt′ē) *adj.* **-ti·er, -ti·est.** *Chiefly British.* Wretched; miserable. [Alteration of GROTESQUE.] **—grot′ti·ness** *n.*

grouch (grouch) *n.* **1.** A habitually complaining or irritable person. **2.** A grumbling or sulky mood: *in a grouch about the long line for tickets.* **3.** A complaint; a grudge: *had only one grouch against the landlord.* **—grouch** *intr.v.* **grouched, grouch·ing, grouch·es.** To grumble or sulk. [From Middle English *grucchen,* to grumble, complain. See GRUDGE.]

grouch·y (grou′chē) *adj.* **-i·er, -i·est.** Tending to complain or grumble; peevish or grumpy. **—grouch′i·ly** *adv.* **—grouch′i·ness** *n.*

ground[1] (ground) *n.* **1. a.** The solid surface of the earth. **b.** The floor of a body of water, especially the sea. **2.** Soil; earth: *level the ground for a lawn.* **3.** Often **grounds.** An area of land designated for a particular purpose: *a burial ground; parade grounds.* **4.** Often **grounds.** The land surrounding or forming part of a house or another building: *a guesthouse on the grounds of the mansion.* **5.** An area or a position that is contested in or as if in battle: *The soldiers held their ground against the enemy. Character witnesses helped the defendant stand her ground in the trial.* **6.** Something that serves as a foundation or means of attachment for something else: *a ground of white paint under the mural.* **7.** A surrounding area; a background. **8.** Often **grounds.** The foundation for an argument, a belief, or an action; a basis. **9.** Often **grounds.** The underlying condition prompting an action; a cause: *grounds for suspicion; a ground for divorce.* See Synonyms at **base**[1]. **10.** An area of reference or discussion; a subject: *The professor covered new ground in every lecture.* **11. grounds.** The sediment at or from the bottom of a liquid: *coffee grounds.* **12.** *Abbr.* **gnd.** *Electricity.* **a.** A large conducting body, such as the earth or an electric circuit connected to the earth, used as an arbitrary zero of potential. **b.** A conducting object, such as a wire, that is connected to such a position of zero potential. **—ground** *v.* **ground·ed, ground·ing, grounds.** *—tr.* **1.** To place on or cause to touch the ground. **2.** To provide a basis for (a theory, for example); justify. **3.** To supply with basic information; instruct in fundamentals. **4. a.** To prevent (an aircraft or a pilot) from flying. **b.** *Informal.* To restrict (someone) especially to a certain place as a punishment. **5.** *Electricity.* To connect (an electric circuit) to a ground. **6.** *Nautical.* To run (a vessel) aground. **7. a.** *Baseball.* To hit (a ball) onto the ground. **b.** *Football.* To throw a ball to the ground in order to stop play and avoid being tackled behind the line of scrimmage. *—intr.* **1.** To touch or reach the ground. **2.** *Baseball.* To hit a ground ball: *grounded to the second baseman.* **3.** *Nautical.* To run aground. ***—phrasal verb.*** **ground out.** *Baseball.* To be put out by hitting a ground ball that is fielded and thrown to first base. ***—idioms.*** **drive** (or **run**) **into the ground.** To belabor (an issue or a subject). **from the ground up.** From the most basic level to the highest level; completely: *designed the house from the ground up; learned the family business from the ground up.* **off the ground.** Under way, as if in flight: *Because of legal difficulties, the construction project never got off the ground.* **on (one's) own ground.** In a situation where one has knowledge or competence: *a sculptor back on her own ground after experiments with painting.* [Middle English, from Old English *grund.*]

ground[2] (ground) *v.* Past tense and past participle of **grind.**

ground ball also **ground·ball** (ground′bôl′) *n. Baseball.* A batted ball that rolls or bounces along the ground.

ground bass (bās) *n. Music.* A short musical passage that is continually repeated in the bass under the changing harmonies and melodies of the upper range.

ground beetle *n.* See **carabid.**

ground·break·er (ground′brā′kər) *n.* One that is original or innovative.

ground·break·ing (ground′brā′kĭng) *n.* The act or ceremony of breaking ground to begin a construction project. **—groundbreaking** *adj.* **1.** Of, relating to, or being a ceremony of breaking ground. **2.** Characterized by originality and innovation: *a groundbreaking technology.*

ground cedar *n.* See **ground pine.**

ground cherry *n.* Any of various chiefly New World plants of the genus *Physalis,* having small, globose, fleshy fruit enclosed in a papery, bladderlike, persistent calyx. Also called *husk tomato.*

ground cloth *n.* **1.** A waterproof cover used to protect an area of ground, such as a baseball field. **2.** A waterproof sheet placed under camp bedding as a protection against moisture. Also called *ground sheet.*

ground-con·trolled approach (ground′kən-trōld′) *n. Abbr.* **GCA** A control mode in which an aircraft is talked down for landing through the use of surveillance and precision approach radar.

ground cover also **ground·cov·er** (ground′kŭv′ər) *n.* **1.** Small plants other than saplings, such as mosses, ferns, grasses, and undershrubs, growing on a forest floor; undergrowth. **2. a.** A low-growing, dense growth of plants, such as a pachysandra or crown vetch, planted to prevent soil erosion in areas where turf is difficult or impossible to grow, as in deep shade or on a steep slope. **b.** A plant used for such a growth.

ground crew *n.* A team of mechanics and technicians that maintain and service aircraft on the ground.

ground-ef·fect machine (ground′ĭ-fĕkt′) *n. Abbr.* **GEM** See **air-cushion vehicle.** [From *ground effect,* a peculiarity of certain aircraft when landing, in which a cushion of air directed off the wings prevents touchdown.]

ground·er (groun′dər) *n. Baseball.* A ground ball.

ground fish *n.* A fish, such as a flounder or cod, that lives at the bottom of a body of water. Also called *groundling.*

ground floor *n.* **1.** The floor of a building at or nearest ground level. **2.** *Informal.* The beginning of a venture, especially regarded as a position of advantage: *investors vying to get in on the ground floor of a development project.*

ground glass *n.* **1.** Glass that has been ground or etched to create a roughened, nontransparent surface. **2.** Glass that has been ground into fine particles, as for use as an abrasive.

ground hemlock *n.* A low-growing yew *(Taxus canadensis)* of northeast North America.

♦ **ground·hog** also **ground hog** (ground′hôg′, -hŏg′) *n.* See **woodchuck.** See Regional Note at **woodchuck.**

Ground·hog Day (ground′hôg′, -hŏg′) *n.* February 2, on which according to popular legend is predicted an early spring if the groundhog does not see its shadow upon emerging from its

grotesque

ă pat	oi boy
ā pay	ou out
âr care	ŏŏ took
ä father	ōō boot
ĕ pet	ŭ cut
ē be	ûr urge
ĭ pit	th thin
ī pie	*th* this
îr pier	hw which
ŏ pot	zh vision
ō toe	ə about, item
ô paw	♦ regionalism

Stress marks: ′ (primary); ′ (secondary), as in **dictionary** (dĭk′shə-nĕr′ē)

burrow or six more weeks of winter if the groundhog does see its shadow. The day is observed each year with a celebration in Punxsutawney, Pennsylvania.

ground ivy *n.* A creeping or trailing European aromatic plant *(Glechoma hederacea),* widely naturalized in North America and having rounded, scalloped leaves and small purplish flowers.

ground·keep·er (ground′kē′pər) *n.* Variant of **groundskeeper.**

ground·less (ground′lĭs) *adj.* Having no ground or foundation; unsubstantiated: *groundless optimism.* See Synonyms at **baseless.** —**ground′less·ly** *adv.* —**ground′less·ness** *n.*

ground level *n. Physics.* See **ground state.**

ground·ling (ground′lĭng) *n.* **1.a.** A plant or an animal that lives on or close to the ground. **b.** See **ground fish. 2.** A person with uncultivated tastes. **3.** A spectator in the cheap standing-room section of an Elizabethan theater.

ground loop *n.* A sharp horizontal turn made by an aircraft on the ground when taxiing, landing, or taking off.

ground·mass (ground′măs′) *n.* The fine-grained crystalline base of porphyritic rock in which larger crystals are embedded.

ground meristem *n. Botany.* The primary meristem that differentiates into the pith and cortex.

ground·nut (ground′nŭt′) *n.* **1.a.** A climbing vine *(Apios americana)* of eastern North America, having compound leaves, clusters of fragrant brownish flowers, and small edible tubers. **b.** Any of several plants having underground tubers or nutlike parts. **c.** The tuber or nutlike part of such a plant. **2.** *Chiefly British.* A peanut.

ground·out (ground′out′) *n. Baseball.* A play in which a batter is put out at first base after hitting a ground ball to an infielder.

ground pine *n.* A club moss, especially *Lycopodium obscurum* or *L. complanatum* or a similar species. Also called *ground cedar.*

ground plan *n.* **1.** A plan of a floor of a building drawn as if seen from overhead. **2.** A preliminary plan or strategy: *the ground plan for an invasion.*

ground plum *n.* **1.** A perennial plant *(Astragalus crassicarpus)* of the central and western United States, having compound leaves, purple or white flowers, and green, plumlike, edible fruit. **2.** The fruit of this plant.

ground rent *n. Chiefly British.* Rent paid for land to be used chiefly for building.

ground robin *n.* See **towhee** (sense 1).

ground rule *n.* **1.** *Sports.* A rule governing the playing of a game on a particular field, course, or court. **2.** A basic rule of procedure or behavior. Often used in the plural.

ground·sel[1] (ground′səl, groun′-) *n.* Any of various plants of the genus *Senecio,* having rayed, usually yellow flower heads. [Middle English *groundeswille,* from Old English *grundeswylige,* alteration (influenced by *grund,* ground) of *gundeswilge* : *gund,* pus + *swelgan,* to swallow (from its use in reducing abscesses); see **swel-** in Appendix.]

ground·sel[2] (ground′səl, groun′-) *n.* Variant of **groundsill.**

ground sheet *n.* See **ground cloth.**

ground·side (ground′sīd′) *n.* The part of an airport used for operations unrelated to the departure and arrival of aircraft. —*attributive.* Often used to modify another noun: *groundside facilities; groundside personnel.*

ground·sill (ground′sĭl′) also **ground·sel** (ground′səl, groun′-) *n.* The horizontal timber nearest the ground in the frame of a building.

grounds·keep·er (groundz′kē′pər) also **ground·keep·er** (ground′-) *n.* One who maintains grounds, as of an estate, a park, or an athletic field. —**grounds′keep′ing** *n.*

ground speed also **ground·speed** (ground′spēd′) *n. Abbr.* **GS** The speed of an airborne aircraft relative to the ground it traverses in a given period of time.

ground squirrel *n.* Any of several burrowing or terrestrial squirrels of the genus *Citellus* or *Spermophilus,* including many species that hibernate during the winter.

ground state *n.* The state of least possible energy in a physical system, as of elementary particles. Also called *ground level.*

grove
California orange grove

ground·stroke (ground′strōk′) *n. Sports.* A swing of a tennis racquet at a ball that has bounced from the ground.

ground substance *n.* **1.** The intercellular material in which the cells and fibers of connective tissue are embedded. Also called *matrix.* **2.** See **hyaloplasm.**

ground·swell (ground′swĕl′) *n.* **1.** A sudden gathering of force, as of public opinion: *a groundswell of antiwar sentiment.* **2.** A broad, deep undulation of the ocean, often caused by a distant storm or an earthquake.

ground water also **ground·wa·ter** (ground′wô′tər, -wŏt′ər) *n.* Water beneath the earth's surface, often between saturated soil and rock, that supplies wells and springs.

ground wave *n.* A radio wave that travels along the surface of the earth.

ground·work (ground′wûrk′) *n.* A foundation; a basis. See Synonyms at **base**[1].

ground zero *n.* **1.** The target of a projectile, such as a missile or bomb. **2.** The site directly below, directly above, or at the point of detonation of a nuclear weapon.

group (gro͞op) *n. Abbr.* **gr. 1.** An assemblage of persons or objects gathered or located together; an aggregation: *a group of dinner guests; a group of buildings near the road.* **2.** Two or more figures that make up a unit or design, as in sculpture. **3.** A number of individuals or things considered together because of similarities: *a small group of supporters across the country.* **4.** *Linguistics.* A category of related languages that is less inclusive than a family. **5.a.** A military unit consisting of two or more battalions and a headquarters. **b.** A unit of two or more squadrons in the U.S. Air Force, smaller than a wing. **6.** A class or collection of related objects or entities, as: **a.** Two or more atoms behaving or regarded as behaving as a single chemical unit. **b.** A column in the periodic table of the elements. **c.** A stratigraphic unit, especially a unit consisting of two or more formations deposited during a single geologic era. **7.** *Mathematics.* A set with an associative binary operation under which the set is closed, which contains an identity element and an inverse for every element in the set. —**group** *adj.* Of, relating to, constituting, or being a member of a group: *a group discussion; a group effort.* —**group** *v.* **grouped, group·ing, groups.** —*tr.* To place or arrange in a group: *grouped the children according to height.* —*intr.* To belong to or form a group: *The soldiers began to group on the hillside.* [French *groupe,* from Italian *gruppo,* probably of Germanic origin.]

USAGE NOTE: *Group* as a collective noun can be followed by a singular or plural verb. It takes a singular verb when the persons or things that make up the group are considered collectively: *The dance group is ready for rehearsal. Group* takes a plural verb when the persons or things that constitute it are considered individually: *The group were divided in their sympathies.* See Usage Note at **collective noun.**

grou·per (gro͞o′pər) *n., pl.* **grouper** or **-pers.** Any of various often large food and game fishes of the genera *Epinephelus, Mycteroperca,* and related genera, which inhabit warm seas. [Portuguese *garupa.*]

group·ie (gro͞o′pē) *n. Slang.* **1.** A fan, especially a young woman, who follows a rock group around on tours. **2.** An enthusiastic supporter or follower: *a fashion groupie.*

group·ing (gro͞o′pĭng) *n.* **1.** The act or process of uniting into groups. **2.** A collection of people or things united into a group.

group insurance *n.* Insurance purchased by a group of persons, such as the employees of a company, often at a reduced individual rate.

group practice *n.* **1.** The practice of health care by an association of medical, dental, or veterinary professionals who share premises and other resources. **2.** An association of health care professionals who share premises and other resources.

group theory *n.* The branch of mathematics concerned with the discovery of groups and the description of their properties.

group therapy *n.* A form of psychotherapy that involves sessions guided by a therapist and attended by several clients who confront their personal problems together. The interaction among clients is considered to be an integral part of the therapeutic process. —**group therapist** *n.*

group·think (gro͞op′thĭngk′) *n.* **1.** The act or practice of reasoning or decision-making by a group, as by a board of directors or a research team. **2.** Conformity to the values or ethical standards of a group.

grouse[1] (grous) *n., pl.* **grouse** or **grous·es.** Any of various plump, chickenlike game birds of the family Tetraonidae, chiefly of the Northern Hemisphere and having mottled brown or grayish plumage. [Origin unknown.]

grouse[2] (grous) *Informal. intr.v.* **groused, grous·ing, grous·es.** To complain; grumble. —**grouse** *n.* A cause for complaint; a grievance. [Perhaps from French dialectal *groucer,* from Old French *grouchier.* See GRUDGE.] —**grous′er** *n.*

grout (grout) *n.* **1.a.** A thin mortar used to fill cracks and crevices in masonry. **b.** A thin plaster for finishing walls and ceilings. **2.** Often **grouts.** *Chiefly British.* Sediment; lees. —**grout** *tr.v.* **grout·ed, grout·ing, grouts.** To fill or finish with a thin mortar or plaster. [Middle English, grain used for making malt, mud, from Old English *grūt,* coarse meal.] —**grout′er** *n.*

grove (grōv) *n.* **1.** A small wood or stand of trees that lacks dense undergrowth. **2.** A group of trees planted and cultivated for the production of fruit or nuts: *an orange grove.* [Middle English, from Old English *grāf.*]

Grove (grōv), Sir **George.** 1820–1900. British musicologist whose *Dictionary of Music and Musicians* (first published 1878–1889) has become a standard reference work.

Grove City. A city of central Ohio south-southwest of Columbus. It is in a diversified farming area. Population, 16,816.

grov·el (grŏv′əl, grŭv′-) *intr.v.* **-eled, -el·ing, -els** also **-elled, -el·ling, -els. 1.** To behave in a servile or demeaning manner; cringe. **2.** To lie or creep in a prostrate position, as in subservience or humility. **3.** To give oneself over to base pleasures: *"Have we not groveled here long enough, eating and drinking like mere brutes?"* (Walt Whitman). [Back-formation from obsolete *groveling,* prone, face downward, from Middle English : *(on) grufe,* face downwards (from Old Norse *ā grūfu,* from *grūfa,* to grovel) + *-ling,* adv. suff; see –LING[2].] —**grov′el·er** *n.* —**grov′el·ing·ly** *adv.*

Groves (grōvz). A city of southeast Texas east of Port Arthur near the Louisiana border. Population, 17,090.

Groves, Leslie Richard. 1896–1970. American army officer and military director of the atomic bomb project (1942–1947).

grow (grō) *v.* **grew** (gro͞o), **grown** (grōn), **grow·ing, grows.** —*intr.* **1.** To increase in size by a natural process. **2.a.** To expand; gain: *The business grew under new management.* **b.** To increase in amount or degree; intensify: *The suspense grew.* **3.** To develop and reach maturity. **4.** To be capable of growth; thrive: *Some plants grow in deep shade.* **5.** To become attached by or as if by the process of growth: *tree trunks that had grown together.* **6.** To come into existence from a source; spring up: *love that grew from friendship.* **7.** To come to be by a gradual process or by degrees; become: *grow angry; grow closer.* —*tr.* **1.** To cause to grow; raise: *grow tulips.* **2.** To allow (something) to develop or increase by a natural process: *grow a beard.* —***phrasal verbs.*** **grow into. 1.** To develop so as to become: *A boy grows into a man.* **2.** To develop or change so as to fit: *She grew into her job. He grew into the relationship slowly.* **grow on** (or **upon**). **1.** To become gradually more evident to: *A feeling of distrust grew on me.* **2.** To become gradually more pleasurable or acceptable to: *a taste that grows on a person.* **grow up.** To become an adult. —***idiom.*** **grow out of.** To develop or come into existence from: *an article that grew out of a few scribbled notes; trust that grew out of long acquaintance.* [Middle English *growen,* from Old English *grōwan.* See **ghrē-** in Appendix.] —**grow′er** *n.* —**grow′ing·ly** *adv.*

grow·ing pains (grō′ĭng) *pl.n.* **1.** Pains in the limbs and joints of children or adolescents, often attributed to rapid growth but arising from various unrelated causes. **2.** Emotional difficulties that occur during adolescence. **3.** Problems that arise in the initiation or enlargement of an enterprise.

growl (groul) *n.* **1.** The low, guttural, menacing sound made by an animal: *the growl of a dog.* **2.** A gruff, surly utterance: *The desk officer answered my greeting with a growl.* —**growl** *v.* **growled, growl·ing, growls.** —*intr.* **1.** To emit a low, guttural sound or utterance. **2.** To speak in an angry or surly manner. —*tr.* To utter by growling: *growled the orders.* [Middle English *groule, grollen,* to rumble, growl, probably from Old French *grouler,* of Germanic origin.] —**growl′y** *adj.*

grow lamp *n.* See **grow light.**

growl·er (grou′lər) *n.* **1.** One, such as a dog, that growls. **2.** A small iceberg. **3.** *Informal.* A container, such as a pail or pitcher, that is used for carrying beer. **4.** *Electricity.* An electromagnetic device with two poles, used for magnetizing, demagnetizing, and finding short-circuited coils.

grow light *n.* A fluorescent lamp that emits a spectrum of light similar to that of the sun, used to grow plants indoors. Also called *grow lamp.*

grown (grōn) *v.* Past participle of **grow.** —**grown** *adj.* **1.** Having full growth; mature: *a grown woman.* **2.** Produced or cultivated in a certain way or place: *locally grown produce.*

grown·up also **grown-up** (grōn′ŭp′) *n.* An adult.

grown-up (grōn′ŭp′) *adj.* Of or intended for adults; mature: *a grown-up attitude toward work; grown-up movies.*

growth (grōth) *n.* **1.a.** The process of growing. **b.** Full development; maturity. **2.** Development from a lower or simpler to a higher or more complex form; evolution. **3.** An increase, as in size, number, value, or strength; extension or expansion: *population growth.* **4.** Something that grows or has grown: *a new growth of grass.* **5.** *Pathology.* An abnormal mass of tissue, such as a tumor, growing in or on a living organism. **6.** A result of growth; a product: *concerns that are a growth of the new responsibilities.*

growth company *n.* A company whose rate of growth significantly exceeds that of the average in its field or the overall rate of economic growth.

growth factor *n.* A substance that affects the growth of an organism.

growth fund *n.* A mutual fund that offers long-term capital appreciation.

growth hormone *n. Abbr.* **GH** See **somatotropin.**

growth ring *n. Botany.* A growth layer in secondary xylem seen in a cross section.

Groz·ny or **Groz·nyy** (grôz′nē). A city of southwest Russia southwest of Astrakhan. It is the center of extensive oil fields discovered in 1893. Population, 393,000.

grub (grŭb) *v.* **grubbed, grub·bing, grubs.** —*tr.* **1.** To dig up by or as if by the roots: *grubbed carrots with a stick.* **2.** To clear of roots and stumps by digging: *grubbed a small plot.* **3.** *Slang.* To obtain by importunity: *grub a cigarette.* —*intr.* **1.** To dig in the earth: *grub for potatoes.* **2.a.** To search laboriously by or as if by digging; rummage. **b.** To toil arduously; drudge: *grub for a living.* —**grub** *n.* **1.** The thick, wormlike larva of certain beetles and other insects. **2.** A drudge. **3.** *Slang.* Food. [Middle English *grubben,* from Old English **grybban.* See **ghrebh-**[2] in Appendix.] —**grub′ber** *n.*

grub·by (grŭb′ē) *adj.* **-bi·er, -bi·est. 1.** Dirty; grimy: *grubby old work clothes.* **2.** Infested with grubs. **3.** Contemptible; despicable: *has a grubby way of treating others.* —**grub′bi·ly** *adv.* —**grub′bi·ness** *n.*

grub·stake (grŭb′stāk′) *n.* Supplies or funds advanced to a mining prospector or a person starting a business in return for a promised share of the profits. —**grubstake** *tr.v.* **-staked, -stak·ing, -stakes.** To supply with funds in return for a promised share of profits. —**grub′stak′er** *n.*

Grub Street (grŭb) *n.* The world of impoverished writers and literary hacks. [After *Grub Street,* London, former name of Milton Street, where such writers lived.]

grudge (grŭj) *tr.v.* **grudged, grudg·ing, grudg·es. 1.** To be reluctant to give or admit: *even grudged the tuition money.* **2.** To resent for having; begrudge: *grudged him his good ways with the children.* —**grudge** *n.* A deep-seated feeling of resentment or rancor: *bears a grudge about the accident.* [Middle English *gruggen, grucchen,* to grumble, complain, from Old French *grouchier,* probably of Germanic origin.] —**grudg′er** *n.* —**grudg′ing·ly** *adv.*

Gru·dziadz (gro͞o′jôɴts′). A city of north-central Poland on the Vistula River northeast of Bydgoszcz. Founded by the Teutonic Knights, it passed to Poland in 1466 and was ruled by Prussia from 1772 to 1919. Population, 93,900.

gru·el (gro͞o′əl) *n.* **1.** A thin, watery porridge. **2.** *Chiefly British.* Severe punishment. [Middle English, from Old French, of Germanic origin.]

gru·el·ing also **gru·el·ling** (gro͞o′ə-lĭng, gro͞o′lĭng) *adj.* Physically or mentally demanding to the point of exhaustion: *a grueling campaign.* —**gru′el·ing·ly** *adv.*

grue·some (gro͞o′səm) *adj.* Causing horror and repugnance; frightful and shocking: *a gruesome murder.* See Synonyms at **ghastly.** [Obsolete *grue,* to shudder (from Middle English *gruen,* from Middle Dutch *grūwen,* or Middle Low German *gruwen*) + -SOME[1].] —**grue′some·ly** *adv.* —**grue′some·ness** *n.*

gruff (grŭf) *adj.* **gruff·er, gruff·est. 1.** Brusque or stern in manner or appearance: *a gruff reply.* **2.** Hoarse; harsh: *a gruff voice.* [Dutch *grof,* from Middle Dutch or Middle Low German.] —**gruff′ly** *adv.* —**gruff′ness** *n.*

SYNONYMS: *gruff, brusque, blunt, bluff, curt, crusty.* These adjectives mean abrupt and sometimes discourteous in manner or speech. *Gruff* implies roughness or surliness of manner and often harsh speech but does not necessarily suggest rudeness: *Her answer was gruff, but her eyes twinkled. Brusque* emphasizes rude abruptness: *Try to cultivate a less brusque manner. Blunt* stresses utter frankness and usually a disconcerting directness: *I have to be blunt: you're not welcome here. Bluff* refers to unpolished, unceremonious manner but usually implies hearty good nature: *He has a bluff but rather pleasant manner. Curt* denotes usually rude briefness and abruptness of speech: *I received a curt letter telling me I was in arrears on my mortgage payments. Crusty* suggests a rough and forbidding manner that sometimes conceals benevolence of spirit: *He's a crusty old gentleman who feeds stray dogs and cats.*

grum·ble (grŭm′bəl) *v.* **-bled, -bling, -bles.** —*intr.* **1.** To complain in a surly manner; mutter discontentedly: *"The governed will always find something to grumble about"* (Crane Brinton). **2.** To rumble or growl. —*tr.* To express in a grumbling, discontented manner: *grumbled a rude response.* —**grumble** *n.* **1.** A muttered complaint. **2.** A rumble; a growl. [Probably Dutch *grommelen,* to mutter, from Middle Dutch, frequentative of *grommen.*] —**grum′bler** *n.* —**grum′bling·ly** *adv.* —**grum′bly** *adj.*

grum·met (grŭm′ĭt) *n.* Variant of **grommet.**

grump (grŭmp) *n.* **1.** A cranky, complaining person. **2.** Often **grumps.** A fit of ill temper. Often used with *the.* —**grump** *intr.v.* **grumped, grump·ing, grumps. 1.** To mutter complaints. **2.** To behave in a grumpy manner. [Origin unknown.]

grump·y (grŭm′pē) *adj.* **-i·er, -i·est.** Surly and peevish; cranky. —**grump′i·ly** *adv.* —**grump′i·ness** *n.*

Grü·ne·wald (gro͞o′nə-wôld′, grü′nə-vält′), **Matthias.** Died 1528. German painter noted for his paintings of religious scenes, particularly the Crucifixion.

grunge (grŭnj) *n. Slang.* **1.** Filth; dirt. **2.** One that is dirty, inferior, obnoxious, or boring. [Back-formation from GRUNGY.]

grun·gy (grŭn′jē) *adj.* **-gi·er, -gi·est.** *Slang.* In a dirty, rundown, or inferior condition: *grungy old jeans.* [Origin unknown.]

grun·ion (grŭn′yən) *n.* A small fish *(Leuresthes tenuis)* of coastal waters of California and Mexico that spawns at night along beaches during the high tides of spring and summer. [Perhaps from Spanish *gruñón,* grumbler, from *gruñir,* to grumble, grunt, from Latin *grunnīre, grundīre,* to grunt.]

♦**grunt** (grŭnt) *v.* **grunt·ed, grunt·ing, grunts.** —*intr.* **1.** To utter a deep, guttural sound, as a hog does. **2.** To utter a sound similar to a grunt, as in disgust. —*tr.* To utter or express with a deep, guttural sound: *He merely grunted his approval.* —**grunt** *n.* **1.** A deep, guttural sound. **2.** Any of various chiefly tropical marine fishes of the family Haemulidae that, upon removal from the water, produce grunting sounds by rubbing together tooth plates in the throat. **3.** *Slang.* An infantryman in the U.S. military, especially in the Vietnam War: *"They were called grunts . . . They were the infantrymen, the foot soldiers of the war"* (Bernard Edelman). **4.** *Slang.* One who performs routine or mundane tasks. **5.** *New England & Upstate New York.* A dessert made by dropping pieces of biscuit dough onto blueberries as they boil and then covering and steaming the mixture. [Middle English *grunten,* from Old English *grunnettan;* probably akin to *grunnian.*] —**grunt′er** *n.* —**grunt′ing·ly** *adv.*

Grus (grŭs, gro͞os) *n.* A constellation in the Southern Hemi-

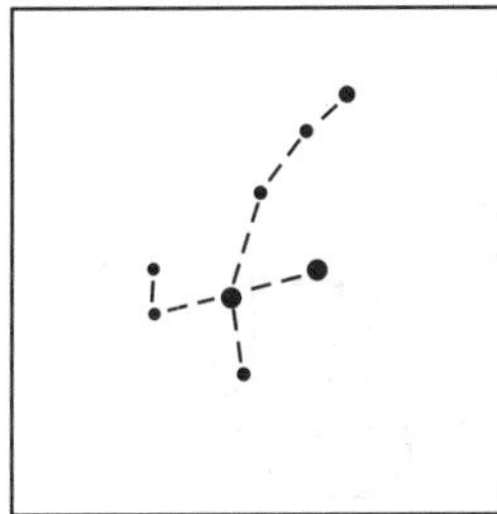

Grus

ă pat	oi boy
ā pay	ou out
âr care	o͝o took
ä father	o͞o boot
ĕ pet	ŭ cut
ē be	ûr urge
ĭ pit	th thin
ī pie	*th* this
îr pier	hw which
ŏ pot	zh vision
ō toe	ə about, item
ô paw	♦ regionalism

Stress marks: **′** (primary); ′ (secondary), as in **dictionary** (dĭk′shə-nĕr′ē)

sphere near Indus and Phoenix. [Latin *grūs,* crane. See **gerə-**[2] in Appendix.]

Gru·yère (gro͞o-yâr′, grē-) *n.* A pale yellow cheese, with or without holes, that has a firm texture and a golden-brown rind and is often used in cooking. [French, after *Gruyère,* a district of west-central Switzerland.]

gr. wt. *abbr.* Gross weight.

gryph·on (grĭf′ən) *n.* Variant of **griffin.**

GS *abbr.* **1.** General staff. **2.** Ground speed.

GSA *abbr.* **1.** General Services Administration. **2.** Girl Scouts of America.

GSC *abbr.* General staff corps.

GSO *abbr.* General staff officer.

GSR *abbr.* Galvanic skin response.

GST also **G.s.t.** *abbr.* Greenwich sidereal time.

G-string (jē′strĭng′) *n.* **1.** A narrow loincloth supported by a waistband; a breechcloth. **2.** A similar garment, usually decorated, that is worn especially by stripteasers. [Origin unknown.]

G-suit (jē′so͞ot′) *n.* A flight garment worn by astronauts and jet pilots that presses on the lower body to maintain the blood supply to the brain during rapid vertical acceleration. [G[2] + SUIT.]

gt. *abbr.* **1.** Gilt. **2.** Great. **3.** *Pharmacology.* Gutta.

Gt. Brit. *abbr.* Great Britain.

G.T.C. *abbr.* Good 'til canceled.

gtd. *abbr.* Guaranteed.

GTP (jē′tē-pē′) *n.* A nucleotide composed of guanine, ribose, and three phosphate groups and necessary for the synthesis of RNA. [G(UANOSINE) T(RI)P(HOSPHATE).]

GTS *abbr.* *Nautical.* Gas turbine ship.

gtt. *abbr.* *Pharmacology.* Guttae.

GU *abbr.* **1.** Genitourinary. **2.** Guam.

gua·ca·mo·le (gwä′kə-mō′lē) *n.* A thick paste of mashed avocado, often seasoned with tomato, peppers, or other condiments and usually served as a dip or in salads. [American Spanish, from Nahuatl *ahuacamolli* : *ahuacatl,* avocado + *molli,* sauce, paste.]

gua·cha·ro (gwä′chə-rō′) *n., pl.* **-ros.** A fruit-eating nocturnal bird *(Steatornis caripensis)* of South America, whose young have a layer of fat that yields an oil used in cooking and for lighting. Also called *oilbird.* [American Spanish *guácharo,* from *guacho,* vagabond, from Quechua *wáhcha,* poor person, orphan.]

Gua·da·la·ja·ra (gwŏd′l-ə-här′ə, gwä′*thä*-lä-hä′rä). A city of west-central Mexico west-northwest of Mexico City. At an altitude of more than 1,525 m (5,000 ft), it is noted for its glassware and pottery. Population, 1,626,152.

Gua·dal·ca·nal (gwŏd′l-kə-năl′). A volcanic island of the western Pacific Ocean, the largest of the Solomon Islands.

Gua·dal·qui·vir (gwŏd′l-kwĭv′ər, gwä′*thäl*-kē-vîr′). A river of southern Spain flowing about 644 km (400 mi) west and southwest to the Gulf of Cádiz.

Gua·da·lupe Hi·dal·go (gwäd′l-o͞op′ hĭ-däl′gō, gwä′*thä*-lo͞o′pĕ ē-*thäl*′gô). Officially **Gus·ta·vo A. Ma·de·ro** (go͞o-stä′vō ä′ mə-gâr′ō, go͞o-stä′vô ä′ mä-*thĕ*′rô). A city of south-central Mexico, a suburb of Mexico City. On February 2, 1848, a treaty ending the Mexican War was signed here. Population, 88,537.

Gua·da·lupe Mountains (gwŏd′l-o͞op′, gwŏd′l-o͞o′pē). A mountain range of southern New Mexico and western Texas rising to **Guadalupe Peak,** 2,668.4 m (8,749 ft) high, in Texas.

Guadalupe River. A river, about 402 km (250 mi) long, of southeast Texas flowing southeast to the San Antonio River near its mouth on San Antonio Bay.

Gua·de·loupe (gwŏd′l-o͞op′, gwŏd′l-o͞op′). An overseas department of France comprising the islands of Grande-Terre and Basse-Terre and smaller islands in the Leeward Islands of the West Indies. The islands were first colonized by the French in 1635. Basse-Terre is the capital. Population, 328,400.

Gua·dia·na (gwä-dyä′nə, *-thyä*′nä). A river rising in south-central Spain and flowing about 821 km (510 mi) west and south partly along the Spanish-Portuguese border to the Gulf of Cádiz.

guai·ac (gwī′ăk′) *n.* Variant of **guaiacum** (sense 2).

guai·a·col (gwī′ə-kôl′, -kōl′) *n.* A yellowish, oily, aromatic substance, $C_7H_8O_2$, derived from guaiacum or wood creosote and used chiefly as an expectorant, a local anesthetic, and an antiseptic. [GUAIAC(UM) + –OL[2].]

guai·a·cum (gwī′ə-kəm) *n.* **1.** A tree of the genus *Guaiacum;* a lignum vitae. **2.** Also **guai·ac** (gwī′ăk′). **a.** The wood of a guaiacum. **b.** A greenish-brown resin obtained from this tree, used medicinally and in varnishes. [New Latin, from Spanish *guayacán,* from Taino.]

Guam (gwäm). *Abbr.* **GU.** An unincorporated territory of the United States, the largest and most southerly of the Mariana Islands in the western Pacific Ocean. The island was ceded by Spain to the United States in 1898. Agana is the capital. Population, 105,979. **—Gua·ma′ni·an** (gwä-mā′nē-ən) *adj. & n.*

guan (gwän) *n.* Any of several large game birds of the family Cracidae, native to the jungles of tropical America and related to and resembling the curassows. [American Spanish, of South American Indian origin.]

Gua·na·ba·ra Bay (gwä′nə-bär′ə). An inlet of the Atlantic Ocean on the southeast coast of Brazil.

gua·na·co (gwə-nä′kō) *n., pl.* **-cos** or **guanaco.** A reddish-brown South American ruminant mammal *(Lama guanicoe)* related to and resembling the domesticated llama. [Spanish, from Quechua *huanaco.*]

gua·neth·i·dine (gwä-nĕth′ĭ-dēn′) *n.* A drug, $C_{10}H_{22}N_4$, used in the form of its sulfate salt in the treatment of hypertension. [Blend of GUANIDINE and ETH(YL).]

Guang·dong (gwäng′dông′) also **Kwang·tung** (kwäng′-to͝ong′, gwäng′do͝ong′). A province of southeast China on the South China Sea. It has been part of China since c. 200 B.C. Guangzhou is the capital. Population, 62,530,000.

Guang·xi Zhuang·zu (gwäng′shē′ jwäng′dzo͞o′) also **Kwang·si Chuang** (kwäng′sē′ chwäng′). An autonomous region of southern China on the Vietnamese border. Nanning is the capital. Population, 38,730,000.

Guang·zhou (gwäng′jō′) also **Kwang·chow** (kwäng′chō′). Formerly **Can·ton** (kăn′tŏn′, kăn′tŏn′). A city of southern China on a delta near the South China Sea. The capital of Guangdong province, it became a treaty port open to foreign trade after the Opium War (1839–1842). Population, 2,570,000.

gua·ni·dine (gwä′nĭ-dēn′) *n.* A strongly alkaline crystalline compound, $NHC(NH_2)_2$, formed by the oxidation of guanine and found in the urine as a normal product of protein metabolism. It is commonly used in the organic synthesis of plastics, resins, and explosives. [GUAN(INE) + –ID(E) + –INE[2].]

gua·nine (gwä′nēn′) *n.* *Abbr.* **G** A purine base, $C_5H_5ON_5$, that is an essential constituent of both RNA and DNA. [From GUANO, in which it is found.]

gua·no (gwä′nō) *n., pl.* **-nos.** **1.** A substance composed chiefly of the dung of sea birds or bats, accumulated along certain coastal areas or in caves and used as fertilizer. **2.** Any of various similar substances, such as a fertilizer prepared from ground fish parts. [Spanish, from Quechua *huanu,* dung.]

gua·no·sine (gwä′nə-sēn′, -sĭn) *n.* A nucleoside, $C_{10}H_{13}N_5O_5$, consisting of guanine and ribose. [GUAN(INE) + (RIB)OS(E) + –INE[2].]

guanosine mon·o·phos·phate (mŏn′ō-fŏs′făt′) *n.* GMP.

guanosine triphosphate *n.* GTP.

Guan·tá·na·mo (gwän-tä′nə-mo′). A city of southeast Cuba north of **Guantánamo Bay,** an inlet of the Caribbean Sea. A U.S. naval station was established on the bay in 1903. The city was founded by French settlers from Haiti in the 19th century. Population, 166,558.

gua·nyl·ic acid (gwä-nĭl′ĭk) *n.* See **GMP.** [GUAN(INE) + –YL + –IC.]

Gua·po·ré (gwä′pə-rā′, -po͞o-rĕ′, -pô-). A river of South America rising in western Brazil and flowing about 1,609 km (1,000 mi) northwest to the Mamoré River.

guar (gwär) *n.* An annual plant *(Cyamopsis tetragonolobus)* probably native to India, adapted to semiarid regions and grown as a forage crop and for its seeds, from which guar gum is obtained. Also called *cluster bean.* [Hindi *guār.*]

guar. *abbr.* Guaranteed.

gua·ra·ni (gwä′rə-nē′) *n., pl.* **guarani** or **-nis.** See table at **currency.** [Spanish *guaraní,* Guarani. See GUARANI.]

Gua·ra·ni (gwä′rə-nē′) *n., pl.* **Guarani** or **-nis.** **1.** A member of a South American Indian people of Paraguay, northern Argentina, and southern Brazil. **2.** The Tupi-Guaranian language of this people. [Spanish *guaraní,* of South American Indian origin.]

guar·an·tee (găr′ən-tē′) *n.* **1.** Something that assures a particular outcome or condition: *Lack of interest is a guarantee of failure.* **2. a.** A promise or an assurance, especially one given in writing, that attests to the quality or durability of a product or service. **b.** A pledge that something will be performed in a specified manner. **3. a.** A guaranty by which one person assumes responsibility for paying another's debts or fulfilling another's responsibilities. **b.** A guaranty for the execution, completion, or existence of something. **4.** A guarantor. **—guarantee** *tr.v.* **-teed, -tee·ing, -tees.** **1.** To assume responsibility for the debt, default, or miscarriage of. **2.** To assume responsibility for the quality or performance of: *guarantee a product.* **3.** To undertake to do, accomplish, or ensure (something) for another: *guaranteed to free the captives; guarantees freedom of speech.* **4.** To make certain: *The rain guarantees a good crop this year.* **5.** To furnish security for. **6.** To express or declare with conviction: *I guarantee that you'll like this book.* [Alteration of Middle English *garant,* warranty, from Old French. See GUARANTY.]

guar·an·tor (găr′ən-tôr′, găr′ən-tər) *n.* One, such as a person or corporation, that makes or gives a promise, assurance, or pledge typically relating to quality, durability, or performance.

guar·an·ty (găr′ən-tē) *n., pl.* **-ties.** **1.** An agreement by which one person assumes the responsibility of assuring payment or fulfillment of another's debts or obligations. **2. a.** Something given as security for the execution, completion, or existence of something else. **b.** The act of providing such security. **3. a.** A guarantee, as for a product or service: *a new refrigerator still under guaranty.* **b.** A guarantee to perform something in a specified way. **4.** A guarantee serving to assure a particular outcome or condition. **5.** A guarantor. **—guaranty** *tr.v.* **-tied, -ty·ing, -ties.** To guarantee. [Anglo-Norman *guarantie,* from Old French, from *garant, guarant,* warrant, of Germanic origin. See **wer-**[4] in Appendix.]

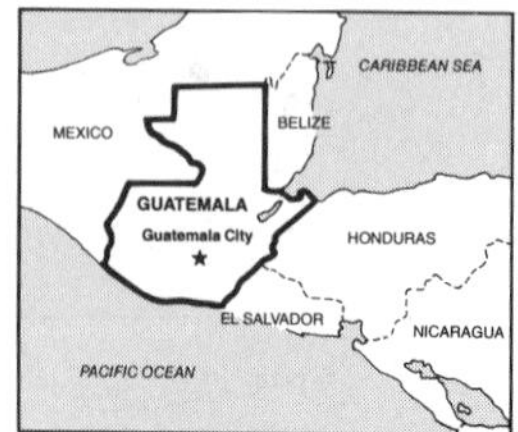

Guatemala

ă pat	oi boy
ā pay	ou out
âr care	o͝o took
ä father	o͞o boot
ĕ pet	ŭ cut
ē be	ûr urge
ĭ pit	th thin
ī pie	*th* this
îr pier	hw which
ŏ pot	zh vision
ō toe	ə about, item
ô paw	♦ regionalism

Stress marks: ′ (primary); ′ (secondary), as in **dictionary** (dĭk′shə-nĕr′ē)

guard (gärd) *v.* **guard·ed, guard·ing, guards.** —*tr.* **1.** To protect from harm by or as if by watching over: *guard a bank; guarding the President.* See Synonyms at **defend. 2.** To watch over so as to prevent escape or violence: *guarded the prisoner.* **3.** *Sports.* To keep (an opposing player) from scoring or playing effectively. **4.** To maintain control over, as to prevent indiscretion: *Guard what you say.* **5.** To supervise entry or exit through; keep watch at: *guarded the door.* **6.** To furnish (a device or object) with a protective piece. **7.** *Archaic.* To escort. —*intr.* **1.** To take precautions: *guard against infection.* **2.** To serve as a guard. —**guard** *n.* **1.** One who protects, keeps watch, or acts as a sentinel. **2.** One who supervises prisoners. **3.** A group of people serving as an escort or performing drill exhibitions on ceremonial occasions: *an honor guard.* **4.** *Chiefly British.* A railway employee in charge of a train. **5.** *Football.* One of the two offensive linemen on either side of the center. **6.** *Basketball.* Either of the two players normally positioned in the backcourt who are responsible for bringing the ball to and initiating offensive plays from the frontcourt. **7.** *Sports.* A defensive position or stance, as in boxing or fencing. **8. a.** The act or duty of guarding. **b.** Protection; watch: *a prisoner under close guard.* **9.** Something that gives protection; a safeguard: *a guard against tooth decay.* **10.** A device or an attachment that prevents injury, damage, or loss, especially: **a.** An attachment or a covering put on a machine to protect the operator or a part of the machine. **b.** A device on a foil, sword, or knife that protects the hand. **c.** A padded covering worn to protect a body part from injury: *a shin guard.* **d.** A small chain or band attached to a watch or bracelet to prevent loss. **e.** A ring worn to prevent a more valuable ring from sliding off the finger. **11.** *Electronics.* A signal that prevents accidental activation of a device or ambiguous interpretation of data. —***idioms.*** **off (one's) guard.** Not alert; unprepared. **on (one's) guard.** Alert and watchful; cautious. **stand guard. 1.** To keep watch. **2.** To act as a sentinel. [Middle English *garden,* from Old French *garder, guarder,* of Germanic origin. See **wer-**[3] in Appendix.]

guar·dant also **gar·dant** (gär′dnt) *adj. Heraldry.* Positioned so that the head is turned toward the viewer. Used of an animal depicted so that its body is viewed from the side. [Obsolete French, from Old French *guardant, gardant,* present participle of *garder,* to guard. See GUARD.]

guard cell *n. Botany.* One of the paired epidermal cells that control the opening and closing of a stoma in plant tissue.

guard·ed (gär′dĭd) *adj.* **1.** Protected; defended. **2.** Watched over; supervised. **3.** Cautious; restrained: *We view these changes with guarded optimism.* —**guard′ed·ly** *adv.* —**guard′ed·ness** *n.*

guard hair *n.* Any of the long coarse hairs forming a layer that covers and protects the soft underfur of certain mammals.

guard·house (gärd′hous′) *n.* **1.** A building that accommodates a military guard. **2.** A jail for the detention of military personnel guilty of minor offenses or awaiting court-martial.

guard·i·an (gär′dē-ən) *n.* **1.** One that guards, watches over, or protects. **2.** *Law.* One who is legally responsible for the care and management of the person or property of an incompetent or a minor. **3.** A superior in a Franciscan monastery. [Middle English *gardein,* from Anglo-Norman, from Old French *gardien,* from alteration of *gardenc,* from *garder,* to guard. See GUARD.] —**guard′i·an·ship′** *n.*

Guard·mem·ber (gärd′mĕm′bər) *n.* A National Guardmember.

guard·rail (gärd′rāl′) *n.* A protective railing, as on a staircase or along a highway.

guard·room (gärd′ro͞om′, -ro͝om′) *n.* **1.** A room used by guards on duty. **2.** A room in which military prisoners are confined.

guards·man (gärdz′mən) *n.* **1.** A person who acts as a guard. **2.** A National Guardmember. **3.** *Chiefly British.* A soldier in a regiment of household guards.

guar gum *n.* A water-soluble paste made from the seeds of the guar plant and used as a thickener and stabilizer in foods and pharmaceuticals.

Guar·ne·ri (gwär-nĕr′ē, -nyĕr′ē). Family of Italian violin makers, including **Andrea** (1626?–1698), who founded the family business, and his grandson **Guiseppe** (1687?–1745).

Guar·ne·ri·us (gwär-nâr′ē-əs, -nîr′-) *n.* A violin made by a member of the Guarneri family.

Gua·rul·hos (gwä-ro͞o′lyo͞os). A city of southeast Brazil, an industrial suburb of São Paulo. Population, 426,693.

Gua·te·ma·la (gwä′tə-mä′lə). **1.** *Abbr.* **Guat.** A country of northern Central America. Inhabited by a Mayan civilization for more than a thousand years before the Spanish conquest in 1524, Guatemala achieved independence in 1839. Guatemala is the capital and the largest city. Population, 6,054,227. **2.** Also **Guatemala City.** The capital and largest city of Guatemala, in the south-central part of the country. Founded on its present site in 1776, it was rebuilt after major earthquakes in 1917 and 1918. Population, 754,243. —**Gua′te·ma′lan** *adj. & n.*

gua·va (gwä′və) *n.* **1.** Any of various tropical American shrubs and trees of the genus *Psidium,* especially *P. guajava,* having white flowers and edible fruit. **2.** The fruit of this plant. [Spanish *guayaba,* of Caribbean Indian origin.]

Gua·via·re (gwäv-yär′ē, -yä′rĕ). A river of central and eastern Colombia flowing about 1,046 km (650 mi) east from the Andes to the Orinoco River on the Colombia-Venezuela boundary.

Gua·ya·quil (gwī′ə-kēl′). The largest city of Ecuador, in the western part of the country near the **Gulf of Guayaquil,** an inlet of the Pacific Ocean. The city was frequently subject to pirate attacks in the 17th century. Population, 1,204,532.

Guay·na·bo (gwī-nä′bō). A city of northeast Puerto Rico, a manufacturing suburb of San Juan. Population, 65,075.

gua·yu·le (gwī-o͞o′lē) *n.* A shrub *(Parthenium argentatum)* of the southwest United States and Mexico whose sap was considered a potential source of natural rubber during World War II. [American Spanish, from Nahuatl *cuauhuli* : *cuahu(itl),* tree + *uli,* latex gum.]

gu·ber·na·to·ri·al (go͞o′bər-nə-tôr′ē-əl, -tōr′-, gyo͞o′-) *adj.* Of or relating to a governor. [From Latin *gubernātor,* governor, from *gubernāre,* to govern. See GOVERN.]

guck (gŭk, go͝ok) also **gook** (go͝ok, go͞ok) *n. Slang.* A thick, messy substance, such as sludge. [Possibly G(OO) + (M)UCK.]

gudg·eon[1] (gŭj′ən) *n.* **1. a.** A small Eurasian freshwater fish *(Gobio gobio)* related to the carp and used for bait. **b.** Any of various similar or related fishes. **2.** *Slang.* One who is easily duped. [Middle English *gojoun,* from Old French *goujon,* from Latin *gōbiō, gōbiōn-,* variant of *gōbius.* See GOBY.]

gudg·eon[2] (gŭj′ən) *n.* **1.** A metal pivot or journal at the end of a shaft or an axle, around which a wheel or other device turns. **2.** The socket of a hinge into which a pin fits. **3.** A metal pin that joins two pieces of stone. **4.** *Nautical.* The socket for the pintle of a rudder. [Middle English *gudyon,* from Old French *gojon,* peg, diminutive of *goi,* gouge. See GOUGE.]

gudgeon pin *n.* See **wrist pin.**

Gud·run (go͝od′ro͞on′) also **Guth·run** (go͝oth′-) *n. Mythology.* The daughter of the king of the Nibelungs and wife of Sigurd, later of Atli, in the *Volsunga Saga.*

guel·der rose (gĕl′dər) *n.* A Eurasian shrub *(Viburnum opulus)* having clusters of white flowers and small red fruit. [After *Guelderland* (Gelderland).]

Guelph[1] (gwĕlf). A city of southern Ontario, Canada, west of Toronto. It is an industrial center in a farming area. Population, 71,207.

Guelph[2] also **Guelf** (gwĕlf) *n.* A member of a strong faction in medieval Italy that supported the power of the pope and the city-states in a struggle against the German emperors and the Ghibellines. [Italian *Guelfo,* from Middle High German *Welf,* name of the founder of a German princely family.]

Guen·e·vere (gwĕn′ə-vîr) *n.* Variant of **Guinevere.**

gue·non (gə-nōn′) *n.* Any of various chiefly arboreal African monkeys, primarily of the genus *Cercopithecus,* having long hind legs and a long tail. [French.]

guer·don (gûr′dn) *n.* A reward; recompense. —**guerdon** *tr.v.* **-doned, -don·ing, -dons.** To reward. [Middle English, from Old French, from Medieval Latin *widerdōnum,* alteration (influenced by Latin *dōnum,* gift; see DONATION) of Old High German *widarlōn* : *widar,* back, against; see **wi-** in Appendix + *lōn,* reward; see **lau-** in Appendix.]

gue·ri·don (gĕr′ĭ-dŏn′, gā-rē-dôN′) *n.* A small round table. [French *guéridon,* from the proper name *Guéridon.*]

gue·ril·la (gə-rĭl′ə) *n.* Variant of **guerrilla.**

Guer·ni·ca (gwâr′nĭ-kə, gĕr-nē′kä). A town of north-central Spain northeast of Bilbao. Its April 1937 bombing by German planes during the Spanish Civil War inspired one of Picasso's most famous paintings. Population, 12,100.

Guern·sey[1] (gûrn′zē). An island of southern Great Britain, one of the Channel Islands in the English Channel off the coast of northwest France.

Guern·sey[2] (gûrn′zē) *n., pl.* **-seys.** Any of a breed of brown and white dairy cattle originally developed on the island of Guernsey and noted for producing a rich, golden milk.

guer·ril·la or **gue·ril·la** (gə-rĭl′ə) —*n.* A member of an irregular, usually indigenous military or paramilitary unit operating in small bands in occupied territory to harass and undermine the enemy, as by surprise raids. —*attributive.* Often used to modify another noun: *guerrilla warfare; guerrilla tactics.* [Spanish, raiding party, guerrilla force, diminutive of *guerra,* war, of Germanic origin. See **wers-** in Appendix.]

guerrilla theater *n.* See **street theater.**

guess (gĕs) *v.* **guessed, guess·ing, guess·es.** —*tr.* **1. a.** To predict (a result or an event) without sufficient information. **b.** To assume, presume, or assert (a fact) without sufficient information. **2.** To form a correct estimate or conjecture of: *guessed the answer.* **3.** To suppose; think: *I guess he was wrong.* —*intr.* **1.** To make an estimate or conjecture: *We could only guess at her motives.* **2.** To estimate or conjecture correctly. See Synonyms at **conjecture.** —**guess** *n.* **1.** An act or instance of guessing. **2.** A conjecture arrived at by guessing. [Middle English *gessen,* probably of Scandinavian origin. See **ghend-** in Appendix.]

guess·ti·mate (gĕs′tə-mĭt) *n. Informal.* An estimate based on conjecture. [Blend of GUESS and ESTIMATE.] —**guess′ti·mate′** (-māt′) *v.*

guess·work (gĕs′wûrk′) *n.* **1.** The process of making guesses. **2.** An estimate or judgment made by guessing.

guest (gĕst) *n.* **1.** One who is a recipient of hospitality at the home or table of another. **2.** One to whom entertainment or hospitality has been extended by another in the role of host or hostess, as at a party. **3.** One who pays for meals or accommodations at a restaurant, hotel, or other establishment; a patron. **4.** A dis-

guava
Psidium guajava

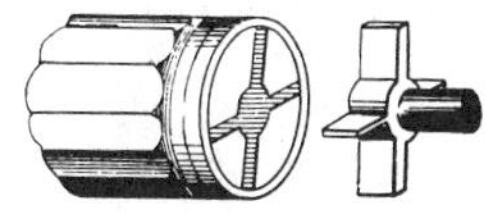
gudgeon[2]

gueridon

Guernsey[2]
Guernsey cow

guide dog

guilloche

guimpe

Guinea

tinguished visitor to whom the hospitality of an institution, a city, or a government is extended. **5.** A visiting performer, speaker, or contestant, as on a radio or television program. **6.** *Zoology.* A commensal organism, especially an insect that lives in the nest or burrow of another species. **—guest** *v.* **guest·ed, guest·ing, guests.** *—tr.* To entertain as a guest. *—intr.* To appear as a guest: *guested on a television series.* **—guest** *adj.* **1.** Provided for guests: *guest rooms.* **2.** Participating as a guest: *a guest conductor.* [Middle English *gest,* from Old Norse *gestr.* See **ghos-ti-** in Appendix.]

Guest (gĕst), **Edgar Albert.** 1881–1959. British-born American journalist known for his widely syndicated, homey rhymes, collected in books such as *A Heap o' Livin'* (1916).

guest·house (gĕst′hous′) *n.* A small house or cottage adjacent to a main house, used for lodging guests.

guest worker *n.* A foreigner who is permitted to work in a country on a temporary basis, as for farm labor. [Translation of German *Gastarbeiter.*]

Gue·va·ra (gə-vär′ə, gĕ-vä′rä), **Ernesto.** Known as "Che." 1928–1967. Argentine-born Cuban revolutionary leader who was Fidel Castro's chief lieutenant in the Cuban revolution (1956–1959). Active in other Latin American revolutions, he was captured and executed by the Bolivian army.

guff (gŭf) *n. Slang.* **1.** Nonsense; baloney. **2.** Insolent talk; back talk. [Perhaps imitative.]

guf·faw (gə-fô′) *n.* A hearty, boisterous burst of laughter. **—guffaw** *intr.v.* **-fawed, -faw·ing, -faws.** To laugh heartily and boisterously. [Probably imitative.]

Gug·gen·heim (go͝og′ən-hīm′). Family of American industrialists and philanthropists, including **Meyer** (1828–1905), who amassed the family fortune in the copper industry. His sons **Daniel** (1856–1930) and **Simon** (1867–1941) and his granddaughter **Marguerite** (1898–1979), known as "Peggy," were patrons of the arts.

Gui·an·a (gē-ăn′ə, -ä′nə, gī-). A region of northeast South America including southeast Venezuela, part of northern Brazil, and French Guiana, Suriname, and Guyana.

Guiana High·lands (hī′ləndz). A mountainous tableland region of northern South America extending from southeast Venezuela into Guyana and northern Brazil.

guid·ance (gīd′ns) *n.* **1.** The act or process of guiding. **2.** Counseling, such as that provided for students seeking advice about vocational and educational matters. **3.** Any of various processes for guiding the path of a vehicle, especially a missile, by means of built-in equipment.

guide (gīd) *n.* **1.a.** One who shows the way by leading, directing, or advising. **b.** One who serves as a model for others, as in a course of conduct. **2.** A person employed to conduct others, as through a museum, and give information about points of interest encountered. **3.a.** Something, such as a pamphlet, that offers basic information or instruction: *a shopper's guide.* **b.** A guidebook. **4.a.** Something that serves to direct or indicate. **b.** A device, such as a ruler, tab, or bar, that serves as an indicator or acts to regulate a motion or operation. **5.** A soldier stationed at the right or left of a column of marchers to control alignment, show direction, or mark the point of pivot. **—guide** *v.* **guid·ed, guid·ing, guides.** *—tr.* **1.** To serve as a guide for; conduct. **2.** To direct the course of; steer: *guide a ship through a channel.* **3.** To exert control or influence over. **4.** To supervise the training or education of. *—intr.* To serve as a guide. [Middle English, from Old French, from Old Provençal *guida,* from *guidar,* to guide, of Germanic origin. See **weid-** in Appendix.] **—guid′a·ble** *adj.* **—guid′er** *n.*

SYNONYMS: *guide, lead, pilot, shepherd, steer, usher.* The central meaning shared by these verbs is "to conduct on or direct to the way": *guided me to my seat; led the troops into battle; a teacher piloting his pupils through the museum; shepherding tourists to the chartered bus; steered the applicant to the proper department; ushering a visitor out.*

guide·book (gīd′bo͝ok′) *n.* A handbook of directions and other information, especially for travelers or tourists.

guid·ed missile (gī′dĭd) *n.* A self-propelled missile that can be guided while it is in flight.

guide dog *n.* A dog that has been specially trained to guide a visually impaired or sightless person.

guided wave *n.* An electromagnetic or acoustic wave transmitted by a process that limits its physical dispersion along the length of its transmission.

guide fossil *n.* See **index fossil.**

guide·line (gīd′līn′) *n.* A statement or other indication of policy or procedure by which to determine a course of action: *guidelines for the completion of tax returns.*

guide·post (gīd′pōst′) *n.* **1.** A post with a sign giving directions for travelers, usually placed at a crossroad. **2.** Something that serves as a guide or an example; a guideline.

guide rope *n.* A rope fastened to another rope that is lifting a load, used to guide the rope and steady the load.

guide·word (gīd′wûrd′) *n.* A word or term that appears at the top of each page or column in a reference book, such as a dictionary, to indicate the first or last entry on the page.

Gui·do d'A·rez·zo (gwē′dō dä-rĕt′sō) or **Guido A·re·ti·no** (är′ĕ-tē′nō). 990?–1050. Benedictine monk and music theorist who devised the four-line staff, thereby allowing precise musical notation.

gui·don (gī′dŏn′, gīd′n) *n.* **1.** A small flag or pennant carried as a standard by a military unit. **2.** A soldier bearing such a flag or pennant. [French, from Old French, from Old Italian *guidone,* from *guidare,* to guide, from Old Provençal *guidar.* See GUIDE.]

Gui·enne or **Guy·enne** (gē-ĕn′). A historical region and former province of southwest France. Part of England after the marriage of Eleanor of Aquitaine to Henry II in 1152, it was reconquered by France in 1453.

guild also **gild** (gĭld) *n.* **1.a.** An association of persons of the same trade or pursuits, formed to protect mutual interests and maintain standards. **b.** A similar association, as of merchants or artisans, in medieval times. **2.** *Ecology.* One of four groups of plants, the lianas, epiphytes, saprophytes, and parasites, having a characteristic mode of existence that involves some dependence on other plant life. [Middle English *gild,* from Old Norse *gildi,* payment, guild.]

guil·der (gĭl′dər) *n. Abbr.* **g., G., gld.** See table at **currency.** [Middle English *gilder,* alteration of Middle Dutch *gulden,* golden. See **ghel-**[2] in Appendix.]

guild·hall (gĭld′hôl′) *n.* **1.** The meeting hall of a guild. **2.** A town hall.

guilds·man (gĭldz′mən) *n.* **1.** A member of a guild. **2.** An advocate of guild socialism.

guild socialism *n.* An English socialist doctrine of the early 20th century according to which industry would be owned by the state but managed by guilds of workers.

guile (gīl) *n.* **1.** Treacherous cunning; skillful deceit. **2.** *Obsolete.* A trick or stratagem. **—guile** *tr.v.* **guiled, guil·ing, guiles.** *Archaic.* To beguile; deceive. [Middle English, from Old French, of Germanic origin; akin to Old English *wigle,* sorcery.]

guile·ful (gīl′fəl) *adj.* Full of guile; deceitfully or treacherously cunning. See Synonyms at **sly.** **—guile′ful·ly** *adv.* **—guile′ful·ness** *n.*

guile·less (gīl′lĭs) *adj.* Free of guile; artless. See Synonyms at **naive.** **—guile′less·ly** *adv.* **—guile′less·ness** *n.*

Guil·ford (gĭl′fərd). A town of southern Connecticut east of New Haven. It was settled in 1639. Population, 17,375.

Gui·lin (gwē′lĭn′) also **Kwei·lin** (kwā′-). A city of southeast China northwest of Guangzhou. The original city dates back to the sixth century A.D. Population, 325,000.

Guil·lain Bar·ré Syndrome (gē-yăn′ bə-rā′) *n.* A temporary inflammation of the nerves, causing pain, weakness, and paralysis in the extremities and often progressing to the chest and face. It typically occurs after recovery from a viral infection or, in rare cases, following immunization for influenza. [After Georges *Guillain* (1876–1961) and Jean Alexandre *Barré* (1880–1967), French neurologists.]

guil·le·mot (gĭl′ə-mŏt′) *n.* Any of several auks of the genus *Cepphus,* having black plumage with white markings. [French, diminutive of the personal name *Guillaume.*]

guil·loche (gĭ-lōsh′, gē-yōsh′) *n. Architecture.* An ornamental border formed of two or more curved bands that interlace to repeat a circular design. [French *guilloch.*]

guil·lo·tine (gĭl′ə-tēn′, gē′ə-) *n.* **1.** A device consisting of a heavy blade held aloft between upright guides and dropped to behead the victim below. **2.** An instrument, such as a paper cutter, similar in action to a guillotine. **—guillotine** *tr.v.* **-tined, -tin·ing, -tines.** **1.** To behead with a guillotine. **2.** To cut with or as if with a guillotine. [French, after Joseph Ignace *Guillotin* (1738–1814), French physician.]

WORD HISTORY: "At half past 12 the guillotine severed her head from her body." So reads the statement containing the first recorded use of *guillotine* in English, found in the *Annual Register* of 1793. The word occurs in a context clearly illustrating the function of the *guillotine,* "a machine with a heavy blade that falls freely between upright guides to behead a condemned person." Ironically, the guillotine, which became the most notable symbol of the excesses of the French Revolution, was named for a humanitarian physician, Joseph Ignace Guillotin. Guillotin, a member of the French Constituent Assembly, recommended in a speech to that body on October 10, 1789, that executions be performed by a beheading device rather than by hanging, the method used for commoners, or by the sword, reserved for the nobility. He argued that beheading by machine was quicker and less painful than the work of the rope and the sword. In 1791 the Assembly did indeed adopt beheading by machine as the state's preferred method of execution. A beheading device designed by Dr. Antoine Louis, secretary of the College of Surgeons, was first used on April 25, 1792, to execute a highwayman named Pelletier or Peletier. The device was called a *louisette* or *louison* after its inventor's name, but because of Guillotin's famous speech, his name became irrevocably associated with the machine. After Guillotin's death in 1814, his children tried unsuccessfully to get the device's name changed. When their efforts failed, they were allowed to change their name instead.

guilt (gĭlt) *n.* **1.** The fact of being responsible for the commission of an offense. See Synonyms at **blame.** **2.** *Law.* Culpability for a crime or lesser breach of regulations that carries a legal penalty. **3.a.** Remorseful awareness of having done something wrong. **b.**

self-reproach for supposed inadequacy or wrongdoing. **4.** Guilty conduct; sin. [Middle English *gilt,* from Old English *gylt,* crime.]

guilt·less (gĭlt′lĭs) *adj.* Free of guilt; innocent. **—guilt′less·ly** *adv.* **—guilt′less·ness** *n.*

guilt·y (gĭl′tē) *adj.* **-i·er, -i·est. 1.** Responsible for or chargeable with a reprehensible act; deserving of blame; culpable: *guilty of cheating; the guilty party.* **2.** *Law.* Adjudged to have committed a crime. **3.** Suffering from or prompted by a sense of guilt: *a guilty conscience.* **4.** Hinting at or entailing guilt: *a guilty smirk; a guilty secret.* See Synonyms at **blameworthy. —guilt′i·ly** *adv.* **—guilt′i·ness** *n.*

guimpe (gămp, gĭmp) *n.* **1.** A blouse worn under a jumper. **2.** A yoke insert for a low-necked dress. **3.** A starched cloth covering the neck and shoulders as part of a nun's habit. **4.** See **gimp[1].** [French, from Old French *guimple,* from Old High German *wimpal.* See **weip-** in Appendix.]

Guin. *abbr.* Guinea.

guin·ea (gĭn′ē) *n.* **1.** *Abbr.* **g., G. a.** A gold coin issued in England from 1663 to 1813 and worth one pound and one shilling. **b.** The sum of one pound and one shilling. **2.** *Offensive Slang.* Used as a disparaging term for an Italian or a person of Italian descent. [After the GUINEA coast of Africa, the source of the gold from which it was first made.]

Guin·ea (gĭn′ē). *Abbr.* **Guin.** A country of western Africa on the Atlantic Ocean. It was a French colony from 1898 until 1958, when it gained its independence. Conakry is the capital and the largest city. Population, 4,830,000. **—Guin′e·an** *adj.* & *n.*

Guinea, Gulf of. A broad inlet of the Atlantic Ocean formed by the great bend in the west-central coast of Africa. It includes the Bights of Benin and Biafra.

Guin·ea-Bis·sau (gĭn′ē-bĭ-sou′). A country of western Africa on the Atlantic Ocean. A Portuguese colony after 1879, it achieved independence in 1974. Bissau is the capital and the largest city. Population, 777,214.

guinea fowl *n.* Any of several pheasantlike birds of the family Numididae native to Africa, especially a widely domesticated species *(Numida meleagris)* having blackish plumage marked with many small white spots. Also called *guinea hen.* [After the GUINEA coast of Africa.]

guinea pig *n.* **1.** Any of various small, short-eared domesticated rodents of the genus *Cavia,* having variously colored hair and no visible tail. They are widely kept as pets and often used as experimental animals. **2.** *Informal.* A person who is used as a subject for experimentation or research. [Perhaps alteration (influenced by GUINEA used as a name for any faraway unknown country) of GUIANA.]

guinea worm *n.* A long, threadlike nematode worm *(Dracunculus medinensis)* of tropical Asia and Africa that is a subcutaneous parasite of human beings and other mammals and causes ulcerative lesions on the legs and feet. [After the GUINEA coast of Africa.]

Guin·e·vere (gwĭn′ə-vîr′) also **Guen·e·vere** (gwĕn′-) *n.* The wife of King Arthur and lover of Lancelot according to Arthurian legend.

Guin·ness (gĭn′ĭs), Sir **Alec.** Born 1914. British actor known for his extraordinary range of roles. His films include *Kind Hearts and Coronets* (1949) and *The Bridge on the River Kwai* (1957).

gui·pure (gĭ-pŏŏr′, -pyŏŏr′) *n.* **1.** A coarse, large-patterned lace without a net ground. **2.** See **gimp[1].** [French, from Old French, from *guiper,* to cover with silk, of Germanic origin. See **weip-** in Appendix.]

Guis·card (gē-skär′), **Robert.** See **Robert Guiscard.**

guise (gīz) *n.* **1.** Outward appearance or aspect; semblance. **2.** False appearance; pretense: *spoke to me under the guise of friendship.* **3.** Mode of dress; garb: *huddled on the street in the guise of beggars.* **4.** *Obsolete.* Custom; habit. [Middle English, manner, fashion, from Old French, of Germanic origin. See **weid-** in Appendix.]

Guise (gēz), Second Duke. Title of François de Lorraine. 1519–1563. French general who suppressed the Huguenots.

Guise, Third Duke. Title of Henri de Lorraine. 1550–1588. French military leader who helped plan the massacre of Huguenots on Saint Bartholomew's Day, 1572. His designs on the throne led to his assassination by order of Henry III.

gui·tar (gĭ-tär′) *n. Music.* An instrument having a large, flat-backed sound box similar in shape to a violin, a long fretted neck, and usually six strings, played by strumming or plucking. [French *guitare,* from Spanish *guitarra,* from alteration of Greek *kithara,* cithara.] **—gui·tar′ist** *n.*

gui·tar·fish (gĭ-tär′fĭsh′) *n., pl.* **guitarfish** or **-fish·es.** Any of several marine fishes of the family Rhinobatidae, having a guitar-shaped body and related to the skates and rays.

Gui·yang (gwē′yäng′) also **Kwei·yang** (kwā′-). A city of southwest China east-northeast of Kunming. The capital of Guizhou province, it is a major transportation and industrial center. Population, 871,000.

Gui·zhou (gwē′jō′) also **Kwei·chow** (kwā′chō′). A province of southeast China. It passed under Chinese suzerainty in the 10th century and became a province in the 17th century. Guiyang is the capital. Population, 29,680,000.

Gui·zot (gē-zō′), **François Pierre Guillaume.** 1787–1874. French historian and politician who advocated a constitutional monarchy, served as premier (1847–1848), and published several historical works.

Gu·ja·rat (gŏŏ′jə-rät′, gŏŏj′ə-). A region of western India bordering on the Arabian Sea. An independent kingdom after 1401, it was annexed by the Mogul Empire in 1572.

Gu·ja·ra·ti (gŏŏ′jə-rä′tē, gŏŏj′ə-) *n., pl.* **Gujarati** or **-tis. 1.** The Indic language of Gujarat. **2.** A native or inhabitant of Gujarat.

Guj·ran·wa·la (gŏŏj′rən-wä′lə, gŏŏj′-). A city of northeast Pakistan north of Lahore. It was an early center of Sikh influence. Population, 597,000.

gul (gōōl) *n.* A stylized octagonal motif in oriental rugs. [Persian, rose. See JULEP.]

gu·lag also **Gu·lag** (gōō′läg) *n.* **1.** A network of forced labor camps in the Soviet Union. **2.** A forced labor camp or prison, especially for political dissidents. **3.** A place or situation of great suffering and hardship, likened to the atmosphere in a prison system or a forced labor camp. [Russian *Gulag,* from *G(lavnoe) u(pravlenie) (ispravitel'no-trudovykh) lag(ereĭ),* Chief Administration of (Correctional Labor) Camps.]

gu·lar (gōō′lər, gyōō′-) *adj.* Of, relating to, or located on the throat. [Latin *gula,* throat + –AR.]

Gul·bar·ga (gŭl′bər-gä′). A city of south-central India west of Hyderabad. It is a manufacturing center in an agricultural area. Population, 221,325.

gulch (gŭlch) *n.* A small ravine, especially one cut by a torrent. [Perhaps from dialectal *gulch,* to gush, (of land) to sink in, from Middle English *gulchen,* to drink greedily, to spew.]

gul·den (gŏŏl′dən, gōōl′-) *n., pl.* **-dens** or **gulden.** A guilder. [Middle English, from Dutch *gulden (florijn),* golden (florin), from Middle Dutch. See **ghel-[2]** in Appendix.]

gules (gyōōlz) *n. Heraldry.* The color red, indicated on a blazon by vertical lines. [Middle English *goules,* from Old French, red fur neckpiece, pl. of *gole,* throat, from Latin *gula.*]

gulf (gŭlf) *n.* **1.** *Abbr.* **g., G.** A large area of a sea or ocean partially enclosed by land, especially a long landlocked portion of sea opening through a strait. **2.** A deep, wide chasm; an abyss. **3.** A wide gap, as in understanding: *"the gulf between the Victorian sensibility and our own"* (Babette Deutsch). **4.** Something, such as a whirlpool, that draws down or engulfs. **—gulf** *tr.v.* **gulfed, gulf·ing, gulfs.** To engulf. [Middle English *goulf,* from Old French *golfe,* from Old Italian *golfo,* from Late Latin *colpus, colfus,* from Greek *kolpos,* bosom, gulf.]

Gulf In·tra·coas·tal Waterway (gŭlf ĭn′trə-kō′stəl). An inland waterway of bays, canals, and rivers from northwest Florida to Brownsville, Texas. It is approximately 1,770 km (1,100 mi) long.

Gulf of. For names of actual gulfs, see the specific element of the name; for example, **Mexico, Gulf of; Lions, Gulf of.**

Gulf·port (gŭlf′pôrt′, -pōrt′). A city of southeast Mississippi on an arm of the Gulf of Mexico west of Biloxi. Settled in 1891, it developed as a port after 1902. Population, 39,676.

Gulf States. 1. The countries bordering the Persian Gulf in southwest Asia, including Iran, Iraq, Kuwait, Saudi Arabia, Bahrain, Qatar, United Arab Emirates, and Oman. **2.** The states of the southern United States with coastlines on the Gulf of Mexico. They are Florida, Alabama, Mississippi, Louisiana, and Texas.

Gulf Stream. A warm ocean current of the northern Atlantic Ocean off eastern North America. It flows from the Gulf of Mexico through the Straits of Florida and then north and northeast to merge with the North Atlantic Drift.

gulf·weed also **gulf weed** (gŭlf′wēd′) *n.* Any of several brownish seaweeds of the genus *Sargassum* of tropical Atlantic waters, having rounded air bladders and often forming dense, floating masses. Also called *sargasso, sargassum.* [After the *Gulf* of Mexico.]

gull[1] (gŭl) *n.* Any of various chiefly coastal aquatic birds of the family Laridae, having long wings, webbed feet, a thick, slightly hooked beak, and usually gray and white plumage. [Middle English *gulle,* possibly of Brythonic origin.]

gull[2] (gŭl) *n.* A person who is easily tricked or cheated; a dupe. **—gull** *tr.v.* **gulled, gull·ing, gulls.** To deceive or cheat. [Probably from *gull,* to swallow (obsolete), from Middle English *golen,* to pretend to swallow, from *gole,* throat, perhaps from Old French *goule.* See GULLET.]

Gul·lah (gŭl′ə) *n.* **1.** One of a group of people of African ancestry inhabiting the Sea Islands and coastal areas of South Carolina, Georgia, and northern Florida. **2.** The creolized language of the Gullahs, based on English but including vocabulary elements and grammatical features from several African languages and spoken in isolated communities from Georgetown in eastern South Carolina to northern Florida. [Perhaps alteration of ANGOLA, or from *Gola,* a people of Sierra Leone and Liberia.]

gul·let (gŭl′ĭt) *n.* **1.** The esophagus. **2.** The throat. **3.** *Zoology.* An invagination into the cytoplasm of certain ciliates, used for food intake. [Middle English *golet,* from Old French *goulet,* from *goule,* throat, from Latin *gula.*]

gul·li·ble (gŭl′ə-bəl) *adj.* Easily deceived or duped. [From GULL[2].] **—gul′li·bil′i·ty** *n.* **—gul′li·bly** *adv.*

Gul·li·ver (gŭl′ə-vər) *n.* An Englishman who travels to the imaginary lands of Lilliput, Brobdingnag, and Laputa, and the country of the Houyhnhnms in Jonathan Swift's satire *Gulliver's Travels* (1726).

Guinea-Bissau

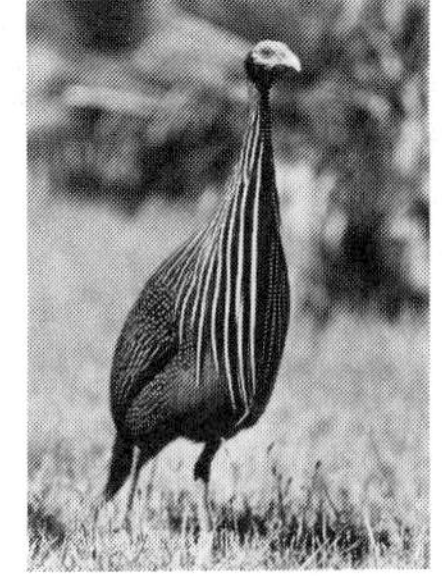

guinea fowl
Vulturine guinea fowl
Acryllium vulturinum

guitar

gull[1]
Herring gull
Larus argentatus

ă pat	oi boy
ā pay	ou out
âr care	ŏŏ took
ä father	ōō boot
ĕ pet	ŭ cut
ē be	ûr urge
ĭ pit	th thin
ī pie	*th* this
îr pier	hw which
ŏ pot	zh vision
ō toe	ə about, item
ô paw	♦ regionalism

Stress marks: **′** (primary); ′ (secondary), as in **dictionary** (dĭk′shə-nĕr′ē)

gullwing

gull·wing (gŭl′wĭng′) *adj.* Hinged at the top so as to swing upward. Used of a type of automobile door.

gul·ly[1] (gŭl′ē) *n., pl.* **-lies.** A deep ditch or channel cut in the earth by running water after a prolonged downpour. **—gully** *v.* **-lied, -ly·ing, -lies.** —*tr.* To wear a deep ditch or channel in. —*intr.* To form a deep ditch or channel. [Perhaps alteration of Middle English *golet,* throat, channel. See GULLET.]

gul·ly[2] (gŭl′ē) *n., pl.* **-lies.** *Chiefly British.* A large knife. [Short for dialectal *gully knife* : *gully* (probably alteration of Middle English *golet,* throat; see GULLET) + KNIFE.]

gulp (gŭlp) *v.* **gulped, gulp·ing, gulps.** —*tr.* **1.** To swallow greedily or rapidly in large amounts: *gulp down coffee.* **2.** To choke back by or as if by swallowing. —*intr.* **1.** To choke or gasp, as in swallowing large amounts of liquid. **2.** To swallow air audibly, as in nervousness. **—gulp** *n.* **1.** The act of gulping. **2.** A large amount swallowed at one time. **3.** *Computer Science.* A small group of bytes that may be either data or instruction. [From Middle English *gulpen* or from Flemish or Dutch *gulpen.*] **—gulp′er** *n.* **—gulp′ing·ly** *adv.*

gum[1] (gŭm) *n.* **1.a.** Any of various viscous substances that are exuded by certain plants and trees and dry into water-soluble, noncrystalline, brittle solids. **b.** A similar plant exudate, such as a resin. **c.** Any of various adhesives made from such exudates or other sticky substance. **2.** A substance resembling the viscous substance exuded by certain plants, as in stickiness. **3.a.** Any of various trees of the genera *Eucalyptus, Liquidambar,* or *Nyssa* that are sources of gum. **b.** The wood of such a tree; gumwood. **4.** Chewing gum. **—gum** *v.* **gummed, gum·ming, gums.** —*tr.* To cover, smear, seal, fill, or fix in place with or as if with gum. —*intr.* **1.** To exude or form gum. **2.** To become sticky or clogged. ***—phrasal verb.*** **gum up.** To ruin or bungle: *gum up the works.* [Middle English *gomme,* from Old French, from Late Latin *gumma,* variant of Latin *gummi, cummi,* from Greek *kommi,* perhaps from Egyptian *ḳmj-t.*]

gum[2] (gŭm) *n.* The firm connective tissue covered by mucous membrane that envelops the alveolar arches of the jaw and surrounds the bases of the teeth. Also called *gingiva.* **—gum** *tr.v.* **gummed, gum·ming, gums.** To chew (food) with toothless gums. [Middle English *gome,* from Old English *gōma,* palate, jaw.]

gum ac·croi·des (ə-kroi′dēz, ăk-roi′-) *n.* See **acaroid resin.** [Alteration of New Latin *acaroides.* See ACAROID RESIN.]

gum ammoniac *n.* See **ammoniac[2].**

gum arabic *n.* A gum exuded by various African trees of the genus *Acacia,* especially *A. senegal,* used in the preparation of pills and emulsions and the manufacture of mucilage and candies and in general as a thickener and colloidal stabilizer. Also called *acacia.*

gum·ball (gŭm′bôl′) *n.* A small ball of chewing gum with a colored sugar coating.

♦ **gum band** *n. Pennsylvania.* See **rubber band.** [Translation of German *Gummiring.*]

♦ ***REGIONAL NOTE:*** The English spoken in Pennsylvania features words borrowed directly from German. *Gum band,* the local equivalent for *rubber band,* is derived from German *Gummiring,* "rubber band." *Smearcase,* a Pennsylvania term for cottage cheese, is from *Schmierkäse,* "soft cheese that can be 'smeared,' or spread."

gully[1]

gum benjamin *n.* See **benzoin** (sense 1).

gum benzoin *n.* See **benzoin** (sense 1).

♦ **gum·bo** (gŭm′bō) *n., pl.* **-bos. 1.a.** See **okra** (sense 1). **b.** *Chiefly Southern U.S.* See **okra** (sense 2). See Regional Note at **goober. 2.** A soup or stew thickened with okra pods. Also called *okra.* **3.** A fine silty soil, common in the southern and western United States, that forms an unusually sticky mud when wet. **4. Gumbo.** A patois spoken by some Black people and Creoles in Louisiana and the French West Indies. [Louisiana French *gombo,* of Bantu origin; akin to Tshiluba *ki-ngumbo,* okra.]

gum·boil (gŭm′boil′) *n.* A small boil or abscess on the gum, often resulting from tooth decay.

gum·bo-lim·bo (gŭm′bō-lĭm′bō) *n., pl.* **-bos.** An aromatic, resinous tree *(Bursera simaruba)* of Florida, Central America, and the West Indies, having compound leaves and small white flowers. [Perhaps GUMBO + *limbo* (possibly of Bantu origin; akin to Kongo *-dimbo,* birdlime).]

gum·drop (gŭm′drŏp′) *n.* A small candy made of sweetened, colored, and flavored gum arabic or gelatin and coated with coarse granulated sugar.

gum·ma (gŭm′ə) *n., pl.* **gum·mas** or **gum·ma·ta** (gŭm′ə-tə). A small, rubbery granuloma that has a necrotic center and is enclosed by an inflamed, fibrous capsule. It is characteristic of an advanced stage of syphilis. [New Latin, from Late Latin, gum. See GUM[1].] **—gum′ma·tous** *adj.*

gum·mite (gŭm′īt) *n.* An orange-red to grayish yellow mixture of several uranium oxides, silicates, and salts occurring naturally in the oxidation and hydration of uraninite. [German *Gummit,* from *Gummi,* gum, from Middle High German, from Medieval Latin, from Latin. See GUM[1].]

gum·mose (gŭm′ōs′) *adj.* Variant of **gummous.**

gum·mo·sis (gŭ-mō′sĭs) *n.* The pathological formation of patches of gum on certain plants, such as sugar cane and some fruit trees, resulting from attack by insects, microorganisms, or adverse weather conditions. [Latin *gummi,* gum; see GUM[1] + -OSIS.]

gum·mous (gŭm′əs) also **gum·mose** (-ōs′) *adj.* Made of or resembling gum.

gum·my (gŭm′ē) *adj.* **-mi·er, -mi·est. 1.** Consisting of or containing gum. **2.** Covered or clogged with or as if with gum. **3.** Having the texture or properties of gum; sticky and viscid. **—gum′mi·ness** *n.*

gum plant *n.* Any of several North American plants of the genus *Grindelia,* especially *G. squarrosa,* having sticky leaves and bracts and yellow, rayed flower heads.

gump·tion (gŭmp′shən) *n. Informal.* **1.** Boldness of enterprise; initiative or aggressiveness. **2.** Guts; spunk. **3.** Common sense. [Scots.]

gum resin *n.* A mixture of gum and resin that exudes from some plants or trees.

gum·shoe (gŭm′shōō′) *n.* **1.** A sneaker or rubber overshoe. **2.** *Slang.* An investigator, especially a detective. **—gumshoe** *intr.v.* **-shoed, -shoe·ing, -shoes.** *Slang.* **1.** To work as a detective. **2.** To move about stealthily; sneak.

gum·wood (gŭm′wo͝od′) *n.* The wood of a gum tree.

♦ **gun** (gŭn) *n.* **1.** A weapon consisting of a metal tube from which a projectile is fired at high velocity into a relatively flat trajectory. **2.** A cannon with a long barrel and a relatively low angle of fire. **3.** A portable firearm, such as a rifle or revolver. **4.** A device resembling a firearm or cannon, as in its ability to project something, such as grease, under pressure or at great speed. **5.** A discharge of a firearm or cannon as a signal or salute. **6.** One, such as a hunter, who carries or uses a gun. **7.a.** A person skilled in the use of a gun. **b.** A professional killer: *a hired gun.* **8.** The throttle of an engine, as of an automobile. **—gun** *v.* **gunned, gun·ning, guns.** —*tr.* **1.** To shoot (a person): *a bank robber who was gunned down by the police.* **2.** To open the throttle of (an engine) so as to accelerate: *gunned the engine and sped off.* **3.** *Maine.* To hunt (game). —*intr.* To hunt with a gun. ***—phrasal verb.*** **gun for. 1.** To pursue relentlessly so as to overcome or destroy. **2.** To go after in earnest; set out to obtain: *gunning for a promotion.* ***—idioms.*** **go great guns.** To proceed or perform with great speed, skill, or success. **under the gun.** Under great pressure or under threat. [Middle English *gonne,* cannon, short for *Gunilda,* woman's name applied to a siege engine, from Old Norse *Gunnhildr,* woman's name : *gunnr,* war; see **g^{w}hen-** in Appendix + *hildr,* war.]

gun·boat (gŭn′bōt′) *n.* A small armed vessel.

gunboat diplomacy *n.* Diplomacy involving intimidation by threat or use of military force: *"in the days when gunboat diplomacy was a more accepted tool of world powers"* (Christian Science Monitor).

gun carriage *n.* A frame or structure upon which a gun is mounted for firing or maneuvering.

gun control *n.* Regulation of the sale and use of rifles and handguns.

gun·cot·ton (gŭn′kŏt′n) *n.* See **nitrocellulose.**

gun dog *n.* A dog trained or bred to assist hunters, as in flushing or retrieving game.

gun·fight (gŭn′fīt′) *n.* A duel or battle with firearms. **—gun′fight′er** *n.*

gun·fire (gŭn′fīr′) *n.* The firing of guns.

gun·flint (gŭn′flĭnt′) *n.* The piece of flint used to strike the igniting spark in a flintlock.

gung ho (gŭng′ hō′) *adj. Slang.* Extremely enthusiastic and dedicated. [Earlier *Gung Ho,* motto of certain U.S. marine forces in Asia during World War II, from Chinese (Mandarin) *gōnghé,* to work together (short for *gōngyèhézuòshè,* Chinese Industrial Co-operative Society) : *gōng,* work + *hé,* together.]

gun·ite (gŭn′īt) *n.* A concrete mixture that is sprayed from a special gun over steel reinforcements in light construction. [Originally a trademark.]

gunk (gŭngk) *n. Informal.* A thick, greasy substance. [After *Gunk,* a trademark for a degreasing solvent.]

gun·lock (gŭn′lŏk′) *n.* A device for igniting the charge of a firearm.

gun·man (gŭn′mən) *n.* **1.** A man armed with a gun, especially an armed criminal or a professional killer. Also called *gunslinger.* **2.** A man skilled in the use of a gun.

gun·met·al (gŭn′mĕt′l) *n.* **1.** An alloy of copper with 10 percent tin. **2.** Metal used for guns. **3.** *Color.* A dark gray. **—gun′met′al** *adj.*

gun moll *n. Slang.* The girlfriend of a gangster. [Obsolete British slang *gun,* thief (short for *ganef;* see GANEF) + MOLL.]

Gun·nar (go͝on′är′, -ər) *n. Mythology.* The husband of Brynhild, the brother-in-law of Sigurd, and the brother of Gudrun in the *Volsunga Saga.*

Gunn effect (gŭn) *n. Electronics.* The production of microwave oscillations when a constant voltage in excess of a critical level is applied to opposite faces of a semiconductor. [After John Battiscombe *Gunn* (born 1928), Egyptian-born British physicist.]

gun·nel[1] (gŭn′əl) *n.* Any of various small, elongated fishes of the family Pholidae, common in the tidal pools and coastal waters of northern seas. [Origin unknown.]

gun·nel[2] (gŭn′əl) *n. Nautical.* Variant of **gunwale.**

gun·ner (gŭn′ər) *n.* **1.** A member of the armed forces who operates a gun. **2.** A warrant officer in the U.S. Marine Corps having charge of ordnance. **3.** *Chiefly British.* An artillery soldier, especially a private. **4.** One who hunts with a gun.

gun•ner•a (gŭn′ər-ə, gə-nîr′ə) *n.* Any of several plants of the tropical genus *Gennera,* having gigantic leaves and small, red to purple drupes. [New Latin *Gunnera,* genus name, after Johann Ernst *Gunnerus* (1718–1773), Norwegian botanist.]

gun•ner•y (gŭn′ə-rē) *n.* **1.** The science dealing with the techniques and procedures of operating guns. **2.** The use of guns.

gunnery sergeant *n. Abbr.* **GySgt 1.** A noncommissioned rank in the U.S. Marine Corps that is above staff sergeant and below master sergeant and first sergeant. **2.** One who holds this rank.

♦**gun•ning** (gŭn′ĭng) *n. Maine.* The sport of hunting: *"Usually any kind of a tight camp will be kept available through our gunning . . . season"* (John Gould).

♦**gun•ny** (gŭn′ē) *n.* A coarse, heavy fabric made of jute or hemp, used especially for bags or sacks. See Regional Note at **gunnysack.** [Hindi *gonī,* from Sanskrit *goṇī,* sack.]

♦**gun•ny•sack** (gŭn′ē-săk′) *n. Chiefly Western U.S.* A bag or sack made of gunny. Also called ♦*crocus sack,* ♦*croker sack,* ♦*tow bag,* ♦*tow sack.*

♦***REGIONAL NOTE:*** A large sack made from loosely woven, coarse material such as burlap goes by a variety of names in regional American English. In the greater West the usual term is *gunnysack,* which ultimately comes from the Sanskrit word *goṇī,* meaning "jute or hemp fiber." In the Upper South such a sack is called a *tow sack,* and in Eastern North Carolina, a *tow bag.* (The word *tow* is another synonym for fabric made from jute or hemp and probably derives from an Old English word for "spinning.") In the Lower South the same type of bag is called a *crocus sack* or a *croker sack,* both terms deriving from the word *crocus.* According to Craig M. Carver, who draws on the research of Walter S. Avis, "*Crocus* is a coarse, loosely woven material once worn by slaves and laborers and common in colonial New England. It probably took its name from the sacks in which crocus or saffron was shipped." Though the term *crocus sack* had virtually disappeared from New England by the end of the 19th century, it survives in the South.

gun•play (gŭn′plā′) *n.* A shooting of guns with intent to inflict harm.

gun•point (gŭn′point′) *n.* The point of a gun. ***—idiom.* at gunpoint.** Under the threat of being shot.

gun•pow•der (gŭn′pou′dər) *n.* Any of various explosive powders used to propel projectiles from guns, especially a black mixture of potassium nitrate, charcoal, and sulfur.

gunpowder tea *n.* A Chinese green tea, each leaf of which is rolled into a pellet.

gun•room (gŭn′ro͞om′, -ro͝om′) *n.* The quarters of midshipmen and junior officers on a British warship.

gun•run•ner (gŭn′rŭn′ər) *n.* One that smuggles firearms and ammunition. **—gun′run′ning** *n.*

gun•sel (gŭn′səl) *n. Slang.* A hoodlum or other criminal, especially one who carries a gun. [Perhaps alteration (influenced by GUN) of Yiddish *gendzl,* gosling, diminutive of *gandz,* goose, from Middle High German *gans,* from Old High German. See **ghans-** in Appendix.]

gun•ship (gŭn′shĭp′) *n.* An armed aircraft, such as a helicopter, that is used to support troops and provide fire cover.

gun•shot (gŭn′shŏt′) *n.* **1.** The shooting of a gun. **2.** The range of a gun: *within gunshot.* **3.** Shot fired from a gun. *—attributive.* Often used to modify another noun: *a gunshot wound; gunshot victims.*

gun-shy (gŭn′shī′) *adj.* **1.** Afraid of loud noise, such as that of gunfire. **2.** Extremely distrustful or wary.

gun•sling•er (gŭn′slĭng′ər) *n.* See **gunman** (sense 1). **—gun′sling′ing** *n.*

gun•smith (gŭn′smĭth′) *n.* One that makes or repairs firearms.

gun•stock (gŭn′stŏk′) *n.* The handle of a gun.

Gun•ter (gŭn′tər), **Edmund.** 1581–1626. English astronomer and mathematician who invented a surveying chain and introduced the trigonometric terms *cosine* and *cotangent.*

Gun•ter's chain (gŭn′tərz) *n.* See **chain** (sense 8a). [After Edmund GUNTER.]

Gun•ther (go͝on′tər) *n. Mythology.* A king of Burgundy and the husband of Brunhild in the *Nibelungenlied.*

Gun•ther (gŭn′thər), **John.** 1901–1970. American writer who combined journalistic observations and personal experience in a series of books, including *Inside Europe* (1936).

Gun•tur (go͝on-to͝or′). A city of southeast India east-southeast of Hyderabad. Founded by the French in the 18th century, it was officially ceded to the British in 1823. Population, 367,699.

gun•wale also **gun•nel** (gŭn′əl) *n. Nautical.* The upper edge of the side of a vessel. [So called because guns were mounted on it.]

Guo•yu (gwô′yo͞o′) also **Kuo•yu** (kwô′-) *n.* See **Mandarin** (sense 4). [Chinese (Mandarin) : *guó,* nation, country + *yŭ,* language.]

gup•py (gŭp′ē) *n., pl.* **-pies.** A small, brightly colored livebearing freshwater fish *(Poecilia reticulata* or *Lebistes reticulatus),* native to northern South America and adjacent islands of the West Indies and popular in home aquariums. [After R.J. Lechmere *Guppy* (1836–1916), clergyman of Trinidad who first supplied specimens to the British Museum.]

gur•gi•ta•tion (gûr′jĭ-tā′shən) *n.* A whirling or surging motion, as of water. [Late Latin *gurgitāre,* to engulf (from Latin *gurges, gurgit-,* whirlpool) + -ATION.]

gur•gle (gûr′gəl) *v.* **-gled, -gling, -gles.** *—intr.* **1.** To flow in a broken, irregular current with a bubbling sound: *water gurgling from a bottle.* **2.** To make a sound similar to this: *The baby gurgled with pleasure.* *—tr.* To express or pronounce with a broken, irregular, bubbling sound. [From Middle English *gurguling,* a gurgling sound in the abdomen, from Medieval Latin **gurgulāre,* to gurgle, from Latin *gurguliō,* gullet.] **—gur′gle** *n.* **—gur′gling•ly** *adv.*

Gur•kha (go͝or′kə) *n.* **1.** A member of a Rajput ethnic group predominant in Nepal. **2.** A member of this people serving in the British or Indian armies. [Nepalese : Sanskrit *gāus,* cow + Sanskrit *rakṣati,* he guards, protects.]

gur•nard (gûr′nərd) *n., pl.* **-nards** or **gurnard. 1.** Any of various widely distributed marine fishes of the family Triglidae, having large fanlike pectoral fins and a large armored head. **2.** The flying gurnard. [Middle English, from Old French *gornart,* from *gronir,* to grunt (from its grunting when caught), from Latin *grunnīre.*]

gur•ney (gûr′nē) *n., pl.* **-neys.** A metal stretcher with wheeled legs, used for transporting patients. [Possibly from the name *Gurney.*]

gu•ru (go͞or′o͞o, go͞o-ro͞o′) *n., pl.* **-rus. 1.** *Hinduism.* A personal spiritual teacher. **2. a.** A teacher and guide in spiritual and philosophical matters. **b.** A trusted counselor and adviser; a mentor. **3. a.** A recognized leader in a field: *the guru of high finance.* **b.** An acknowledged and influential advocate, as of a movement or idea: *"In a culture that worships slimness, he was the Guru of Lean"* (Erica Abeel). [Hindi *gurū,* from Sanskrit *guruḥ,* from *guru-,* heavy, venerable. See **g**ʷ**erə-**[1] in Appendix.]

gush (gŭsh) *v.* **gushed, gush•ing, gush•es.** *—intr.* **1.** To flow forth suddenly in great volume: *water gushing from a hydrant.* **2.** To emit a sudden and abundant flow, as of tears. **3.** To make an excessive display of sentiment or enthusiasm: *gushed over the baby.* *—tr.* To emit abundantly; pour forth. **—gush** *n.* **1.** A sudden, copious outflow: *a gush of tears.* **2.** Excessively demonstrative language or behavior. [Middle English *gushen,* perhaps of Scandanavian origin. See **gheu-** in Appendix.]

gush•er (gŭsh′ər) *n.* One that gushes, especially an abundantly flowing gas or oil well.

gush•y (gŭsh′ē) *adj.* **-i•er, -i•est.** Marked by excessive displays of sentiment or enthusiasm. **—gush′i•ly** *adv.* **—gush′i•ness** *n.*

gus•set (gŭs′ĭt) *n.* **1.** A triangular insert, as in the seam of a garment, for added strength or expansion. **2.** A triangular metal bracket used to strengthen a joist. **3.** A piece of mail or plate armor protecting the joints in a suit of armor. [Middle English, from Old French *gousset,* perhaps diminutive of *gousse,* pod, husk.]

gus•sy (gŭs′ē) *tr.v.* **-sied, -sy•ing, -sies.** *Slang.* To dress or decorate elaborately; adorn or embellish: *gussied herself up in sequins and feathers.* [Perhaps from Australian slang *gussie,* an effeminate man, diminutive of the personal name *Augustus.*]

gust[1] (gŭst) *n.* **1.** A strong, abrupt rush of wind. **2.** A sudden burst, as of rain or smoke. **3.** An outburst of emotion. **—gust** *intr.v.* **gust•ed, gust•ing, gusts.** To blow in gusts. [Probably from Old Norse *gustr.* See **gheu-** in Appendix.]

gust[2] (gŭst) *n.* **1.** *Archaic.* Relish; gusto. **2.** *Obsolete.* **a.** The sense of taste. **b.** Personal taste or inclination; liking. [Middle English *guste,* taste, from Latin *gustus.* See GUSTO.]

gus•ta•tion (gŭ-stā′shən) *n.* The act or faculty of tasting. [Latin *gustātiō, gustātiōn-,* an appetizer, from *gustātus,* past participle of *gustāre,* to taste, from *gustus,* taste. See GUSTO.]

gus•ta•to•ry (gŭs′tə-tôr′ē, -tōr′ē) also **gus•ta•tive** (-tə-tĭv) *adj.* Of or relating to the sense of taste. **—gus′ta•to′ri•ly** *adv.*

Gus•ta•vo A. Ma•de•ro (go͞o-stä′vō ä′ mə-dâr′ō, go͞o-stä′vô ä′ mä-*thĕ*′rô). See **Guadalupe Hidalgo.**

Gus•ta•vus I (gŭs-tā′vəs, -tä′-). 1496–1560. King of Sweden (1523–1560) who established Lutheranism as the state religion.

Gustavus II. Known as "Gustavus Adolphus." 1594–1632. King of Sweden (1611–1632) who was drawn into the Thirty Years' War by his desire to assure Swedish control of the Baltic States and was killed at the Battle of Lützen.

Gustavus III. 1746–1792. King of Sweden (1771–1792) who increased royal power, introduced reforms, and waged an unpopular war against Russia (1788–1790).

Gustavus IV. 1778–1837. King of Sweden (1792–1809) whose tactless diplomacy and loss of Swedish possessions to France and Russia led to his dethronement.

Gustavus V. 1858–1950. King of Sweden (1907–1950) who kept Sweden neutral through both World Wars.

Gustavus VI. 1882–1973. King of Sweden (1950–1973). The last Swedish monarch with real political power, he was also an authority on Chinese art and archaeology.

gus•to (gŭs′tō) *n., pl.* **-toes. 1.** Vigorous enjoyment; zest. See Synonyms at **zest. 2.** Individual taste. **3.** *Archaic.* Artistic style. [Italian, from Latin *gustus,* taste. See **geus-** in Appendix.]

gust•y (gŭs′tē) *adj.* **-i•er, -i•est. 1.** Blowing in or marked by

ă pat	oi boy
ā pay	ou out
âr care	o͝o took
ä father	o͞o boot
ĕ pet	ŭ cut
ē be	ûr urge
ĭ pit	th thin
ī pie	*th* this
îr pier	hw which
ŏ pot	zh vision
ō toe	ə about, item
ô paw	♦ regionalism

Stress marks: ′ (primary); ′ (secondary), as in **dictionary** (dĭk′shə-nĕr′ē)

gusts: *a gusty storm.* **2.** Characterized by sudden outbursts. **—gust′i·ly** *adv.* **—gust′i·ness** *n.*

gut (gŭt) *n.* **1.a.** The alimentary canal or a portion thereof, especially the intestine or stomach. **b.** The embryonic digestive tube, consisting of the foregut, the midgut, and the hindgut. **2. guts.** The bowels; entrails; viscera. **3.** *Slang.* **a.** Innermost emotional or visceral response: *She felt in her gut that he was guilty.* **b. guts.** The essential components or inner working parts: *"The best part of a good car . . . is its guts"* (Leigh Allison Wilson). **4. guts.** *Slang.* **a.** Courage; fortitude. **b.** Nerve; audacity. **5.** *Slang.* A gut course. **6.** A thin, tough cord made from the intestines of animals, usually sheep, used as strings for musical instruments or as surgical sutures. **7.** A narrow passage or channel. **8.** Fibrous material taken from the silk gland of a silkworm before it spins a cocoon, used for fishing tackle. **—gut** *tr.v.* **gut·ted, gut·ting, guts. 1.** To remove the intestines or entrails of; eviscerate. **2.** To extract essential or major parts of: *gut a manuscript.* **3.** To destroy the interior of: *Fire gutted the house.* **4.** To reduce or destroy the effectiveness of: *A stipulation added at the last minute gutted the ordinance.* **—gut** *adj. Slang.* Arousing or involving basic emotions; visceral: *"Conservationism is a gut issue in the West"* (Saturday Review). **—*idiom.* gut it out.** *Slang.* To show pluck and perseverance in the face of opposition or adversity. [From Middle English *guttes,* entrails, from Old English *guttas.* See **gheu-** in Appendix.] **—gut′ty** *adj.*

Johann Gutenberg

gut·buck·et (gŭt′bŭk′ĭt) *n. Music.* **1.** An early type of jazz characterized by a strong beat and rollicking delivery, similar to barrelhouse. **2.** A homemade bass instrument. [From *gutbucket bass,* a type of homemade bass instrument made from a bucket.]

gut course *n. Slang.* An undemanding academic course of study. [Possibly from GUT, to extract, excerpt.]

Gu·ten·berg (go͞ot′n-bûrg′), **Johann** or **Johannes.** 1400?–1468? German printer who is traditionally considered the inventor of movable type. His *Mazarin Bible* (c. 1455) is believed to be the first book printed with such type.

Guth·rie (gŭth′rē), **Woodrow Wilson.** Known as "Woody." 1912–1967. American folk singer and composer of numerous songs, including "This Land Is Your Land" (1940).

Guth·run (go͝oth′ro͞on′) *n.* Variant of **Gudrun.**

gut·less (gŭt′lĭs) *adj. Slang.* **1.** Lacking courage or drive. **2.** Lacking substance; weak or insignificant. **—gut′less·ness** *n.*

guts·y (gŭt′sē) *adj.* **-i·er, -i·est.** *Slang.* **1.** Marked by courage or daring; plucky. **2.** Robust and uninhibited; lusty: *"the gutsy . . . intensity of her musical involvement"* (Judith Crist). **—guts′i·ly** *adv.* **—guts′i·ness** *n.*

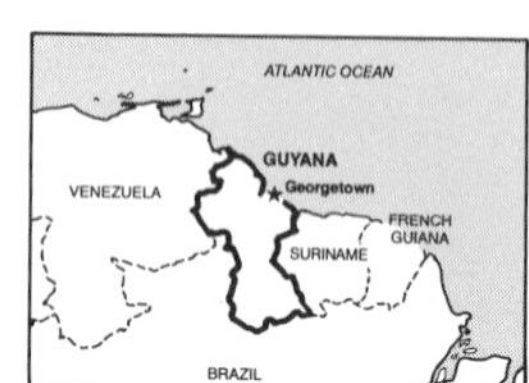

Guyana

gut·ta (gŭt′ə) *n., pl.* **gut·tae** (gŭt′ē′). **1.** *Architecture.* One of a series of small, droplike ornaments on a Doric entablature. **2.** *Abbr.* **gt.** *Pharmacology.* A drop, as of liquid medicine. [Middle English, from Latin, drop.]

gut·ta-per·cha (gŭt′ə-pûr′chə) *n.* A rubbery substance derived from the latex of any of several tropical trees of the genera *Palaquium* and *Payena,* used as an electrical insulator, as a waterproofing compound, and in golf balls. [Malay *gĕtah pĕrca* : *gĕtah,* sap + *pĕrca,* strip of cloth.]

gut·tate (gŭt′āt′) also **gut·tat·ed** (-ā′tĭd) *adj.* **1.** Having or resembling drops. **2.** Spotted as if by drops. [Latin *guttātus,* speckled, from *gutta,* drop.]

gut·ta·tion (gŭ-tā′shən) *n.* The exudation of water from leaves as a result of root pressure.

♦**gut·ter** (gŭt′ər) *n.* **1.** A channel at the edge of a street or road for carrying off surface water. **2.** A trough fixed under or along the eaves for draining rainwater from a roof. Also called ♦*eaves spout,* ♦*eaves trough,* ♦*rainspout,* ♦*spouting.* **3.** A furrow or groove formed by running water. **4.** A trough or channel for carrying something off, such as that on either side of a bowling alley. **5.** *Printing.* The white space formed by the inner margins of two facing pages, as of a book. **6.** A degraded and squalid class or state of human existence. **—gutter** *v.* **-tered, -ter·ing, -ters.** —*tr.* **1.** To form gutters or furrows in. **2.** To provide with gutters. —*intr.* **1.** To flow in channels or rivulets. **2.** To melt away through the side of the hollow formed by a burning wick. Used of a candle. **3.** To burn low and unsteadily; flicker. **—gutter** *adj.* Befitting the lowest class of human life; vulgar, sordid, or unprincipled: *gutter language; the gutter press.* [Middle English *goter, guter,* from Old French *gotier,* from *gote,* drop, from Latin *gutta.*]

Nell Gwyn
c. 1675 portrait from the studio of Sir Peter Lely

♦***REGIONAL NOTE:*** Certain household words have proved important as markers for major U.S. dialect boundaries. The channels along the edge of a roof for carrying away rainwater (normally referred to in the plural) are variously known as *eaves spouts* or *eaves troughs* in New England and the Great Lakes states, *spouting* or *rainspouts* in New Jersey, eastern Pennsylvania, and the Delmarva Peninsula, and *gutters* from Virginia southward. The transition points mark unusually clear boundaries for the three major dialect areas—Northern, Midland, and Southern—traditionally acknowledged by scholars of American dialects. Atypically, Southern *gutters* seems to have become the standard U.S. term.

gut·ter·snipe (gŭt′ər-snīp′) *n.* **1.** A street urchin. **2.** A person of the lowest class.

gut·tur·al (gŭt′ər-əl) *adj.* **1.** Of or relating to the throat. **2.** Having a harsh, grating quality, as certain sounds produced in the back of the mouth. **3.** *Linguistics.* Velar. [French, from New Latin *gutturālis,* from Latin *guttur,* throat.] **—gut′tur·al·ism, gut′tur·al′i·ty** (-ə-răl′ĭ-tē) , **gut′tur·al·ness** *n.* **—gut′tur·al·ly** *adv.*

gut·tur·al·ize (gŭt′ər-ə-līz′) *tr.v.* **-ized, -iz·ing, -iz·es. 1.** To pronounce in a guttural manner. **2.** *Linguistics.* To velarize. **—gut′tur·al·i·za′tion** (-ə-lĭ-zā′shən) *n.*

guy[1] (gī) *n.* A rope, cord, or cable used to steady, guide, or secure something. **—guy** *tr.v.* **guyed, guy·ing, guys.** To steady, guide, or secure with a rope, cord, or cable. [Partly from Middle English *gie,* guide, guy (from Old French *guie,* from *guier,* to guide; see **weid-** in Appendix) and partly from Low German; akin to Dutch *gei,* brail.]

guy[2] (gī) *n.* **1.** *Informal.* A man; a fellow. **2. guys.** *Informal.* Persons of either sex. **3.** *Chiefly British.* A person of odd or grotesque appearance or dress. **4.** Often **Guy.** An effigy of Guy Fawkes paraded through the streets of English towns and burned on Guy Fawkes Day. **—guy** *tr.v.* **guyed, guy·ing, guys.** To hold up to ridicule; mock. [After *Guy Fawkes.*]

Guy·a·na (gī-ăn′ə, -ä′nə). Formerly **Brit·ish Gui·a·na** (brĭt′ĭsh gē-ăn′ə, -ä′nə, gī-). *Abbr.* **Guy.** A country of northeast South America on the Atlantic Ocean. Settled originally by the Dutch in the 17th century, it was a British colony from 1814 until 1966, when it gained its independence. Georgetown is the capital and the largest city. Population, 918,000. **—Guy′a·nese′** (-nēz′, -nēs′) *adj. & n.*

Guy·enne (gē-ĕn′). See **Guienne.**

Guy Fawkes Day (gī′ fôks′) *n.* November 5, observed in Great Britain to commemorate the foiling of the attempt led by Guy Fawkes in 1605 to blow up the king and members of Parliament in retaliation for increasing repression of Roman Catholics in England.

guy·ot (gē′ō) *n.* A flat-topped submarine mountain. [After Arnold Henri *Guyot* (1807–1884), Swiss-born American geologist and geographer.]

guz·zle (gŭz′əl) *v.* **-zled, -zling, -zles.** —*tr.* **1.** To drink greedily or habitually: *guzzle beer.* **2.** To consume to excess: *a car that guzzles gas.* —*intr.* To drink, especially alcoholic beverages, greedily or habitually. [Origin unknown.] **—guz′zler** *n.*

GVW *abbr.* Gross vehicular weight.

GW *abbr.* Gigawatt.

Gwa·li·or (gwä′lē-ôr′). A city of north-central India south of Agra. Population, 539,015.

gwe·duc (go͞o′ē-dŭk′) *n.* Variant of **geoduck.**

Gwin·net (gwə-nĕt′), **Button.** 1735?–1777. American Revolutionary patriot primarily known for the value of his few existing autographs.

Gwyn or **Gwynne** (gwĭn), **Eleanor.** Known as "Nell." 1650?–1687. English actress who was the lover of Charles II.

gybe (jīb) *v. & n. Nautical.* Variant of **jibe**[1].

gym (jĭm) *n. Sports.* **1.** A gymnasium. **2.** A school course in physical education. **3.** A metal frame supporting equipment used in outdoor play.

gym. *abbr. Sports.* Gymnastics.

gym·kha·na (jĭm-kä′nə) *n. Sports.* **1.** Any of various meets at which contests are held to test the skill of the competitors, as in equestrianship, gymnastics, or sports car racing. **2.** The place where such an event is held. [Probably alteration (influenced by GYMNASTICS) of Hindi *gend-khānā,* racket court : *gend,* ball + *khāna,* house (from Persian).]

gym·na·si·um (jĭm-nā′zē-əm) *n., pl.* **-si·ums** or **-si·a** (-zē-ə). **1.** *Sports.* A room or building equipped for indoor sports. **2.** (gĭm-nä′zē͞oom′). An academic high school in some central European countries, especially Germany, that prepares students for the university. [Latin, school, from Greek *gumnasion,* from *gumnazein,* to exercise naked, from *gumnos,* naked. See **nog^w-** in Appendix.]

gym·nast (jĭm′năst′, -nəst) *n. Sports.* A person who is skilled in gymnastics, especially one who engages in competition. [French *gymnaste,* from Greek *gumnastēs,* trainer of professional athletes, from *gumnazein,* to exercise. See GYMNASIUM.]

gym·nas·tic (jĭm-năs′tĭk) *adj. Sports.* Of or relating to gymnastics. **—gym·nas′ti·cal·ly** *adv.*

gym·nas·tics (jĭm-năs′tĭks) *n.* **1.** *Abbr.* **gym.** *Sports.* **a.** *(used with a pl. verb).* Physical exercises designed to develop and display strength, balance, and agility, especially those performed on or with specialized apparatus. **b.** *(used with a sing. verb).* The art or practice of such exercises. **2.** *(used with a pl. verb).* **a.** Complex intellectual or artistic exercises: *mental gymnastics.* **b.** *Informal.* Feats of physical agility: *had to go through gymnastics to cross the slippery walk.*

gym·nos·o·phist (jĭm-nŏs′ə-fĭst) *n.* One of an ancient sect of Hindu ascetics who wore little or no clothing and were devoted to contemplation. [Middle English *gumnosophist,* from sing. of Latin *gymnosophistae,* from Greek *gumnosophistai* : *gumnos,* naked; see **nog^w-** in Appendix + *sophistēs,* expert; see SOPHIST.]

gym·no·sperm (jĭm′nə-spûrm′) *n.* A plant, such as a cycad or conifer, whose seeds are not enclosed within an ovary. [From New Latin *Gymnospermae,* class name, from Greek *gumnospermos* : *gumnos,* naked; see **nog^w-** in Appendix + *sperma,* seed; see SPERM[1].] **—gym′no·sper′mous** *adj.* **—gym′no·sper′my** *n.*

gyn. *abbr.* **1.** Gynecological. **2.** Gynecologist. **3.** Gynecology.

gyn– *pref.* Variant of **gyno–.**

gy·nan·dro·morph (jī-năn′drə-môrf′, gī-, jĭ-) *n.* An organism having both male and female characteristics, especially an insect exhibiting a mixture of male and female tissues or sex organs. **—gy·nan′dro·mor′phic, gy·nan′dro·mor′phous** *adj.* **—gy·nan′dro·mor′phism, gy·nan′dro·mor′phy** *n.*

gy·nan·drous (jī-năn′drəs, gī-, jĭ-) *adj.* Having the stamens and pistil united to form a column, as in orchids.

gyn·ar·chy (jĭn′är′kē, jī′när′-, gī′-) *n., pl.* **-chies.** Government by women. **—gyn·ar′chic** *adj.*

–gyne *suff.* Female reproductive organ: *trichogyne.* [From Greek *gunē,* woman. See **gʷen-** in Appendix.]

gyneco– or **gynec–** *pref.* Woman: *gynecology.* [Greek *gunaiko-,* from *gunē, gunaik-,* woman. See GYNO–.]

gyn·e·coc·ra·cy (jĭn′ĭ-kŏk′rə-sē, gī′-nĭ-, jī′-) or **gy·noc·ra·cy** (jĭ-nŏk′rə-sē, gī-, jī-) *n., pl.* **-cies. 1.** Government by women. **2.** A society ruled by women. [Greek *gunaikokratia* : *gunē, gunaik-,* woman; see **gʷen-** in Appendix + *-kratia,* -cracy.] **—gyn′e·co·crat′ic** (-kə-krăt′ĭk) *adj.*

gyn·e·coid (jĭn′ĭ-koid′, gī′nĭ-, jī′-) *adj.* Characteristic of a woman.

gynecol. *abbr.* **1.** Gynecological. **2.** Gynecologist. **3.** Gynecology.

gy·ne·col·o·gy (gī′nĭ-kŏl′ə-jē, jĭn′ĭ-, jī′nĭ-) *n. Abbr.* **gyn., gynecol.** The branch of medicine dealing with the administration of health care to women, especially the diagnosis and treatment of disorders affecting the female reproductive organs. **—gy′ne·co·log′i·cal** (-kə-lŏj′ĭ-kəl), **gy′ne·co·log′ic** *adj.* **—gy′ne·col′o·gist** *n.*

gyn·e·co·mas·ti·a (jĭn′ĭ-kō-măs′tē-ə, gī′nĭ-, jī′-) *n.* Abnormal enlargement of the breasts in a male.

gyn·e·cop·a·thy (jĭn′ĭ-kŏp′ə-thē, gī′nĭ-, jī′-) *n., pl.* **-thies.** Any of various diseases specific to women.

gyno– or **gyn–** *pref.* **1.** Woman: *gynarchy.* **2.** Female reproductive organ; pistil: *gynophore.* [From Greek *gunē,* woman. See **gʷen-** in Appendix.]

gy·noc·ra·cy (jĭ-nŏk′rə-sē, gī-, jī-) *n.* Variant of **gynecocracy.**

gyn·o·di·oe·cious (jĭn′ō-dī-ē′shəs, gī′nō-, jī′-) *adj.* Having bisexual flowers on some plants and only female flowers on other plants of the same species. **—gy′no·di·oe′cism** (jī′nō-dī-ē′sĭz′əm, gī′-) *n.*

gy·noe·ci·um (jĭ-nē′sē-əm, gī-, jī-) *n., pl.* **-ci·a** (-sē-ə). The female reproductive organs of a flower; the pistil or pistils considered as a group. [New Latin, alteration (influenced by Greek *oikos,* house; see ECOLOGY) of Latin *gynaecēum,* women's apartments, from Greek *gunaikeion,* from neuter of *gunaikeios,* of women, from *gunē, gunaik-,* woman. See **gʷen-** in Appendix.]

gyn·o·gen·e·sis (jĭn′ə-jĕn′ĭ-sĭs, gī′nə-, jī′-) *n.* Parthenogenesis in which the egg is activated by sperm, but without fusion of the egg and sperm nuclei.

gyn·o·phore (jĭn′ə-fôr′, -fōr′, gī′nə-, jī′-) *n.* The stalk of a pistil. **—gyn′o·phor′ic** (-fôr′ĭk, -fōr′-) *adj.*

–gynous *suff.* **1.** Of, relating to, or having a specified number or kind of females: *heterogynous.* **2. a.** Of, relating to, or situated in a specified place with respect to female plant organs: *epigynous.* **b.** Having a specified number or kind of female plant organs: *protogynous.* [From New Latin *-gynus,* from Greek *gunē,* woman. See **gʷen-** in Appendix.]

–gyny *suff.* **1.** The state or condition of having a specified number of women or females: *monogyny.* **2. a.** The condition of being situated in a specified place with respect to female plant organs: *epigyny.* **b.** The condition of having a specified number or kind of female plant organs: *protogyny.* [From Greek *gunē,* woman. See **gʷen-** in Appendix.]

Győr (dyûr, dyœr). A city of northwest Hungary near the Czechoslovakian border. On the site of a Roman military outpost evacuated in the fourth century A.D., it was later a Magyar stronghold and a royal free town (after 1743). Population, 128,252.

gyo·za (gyō′zə, gyô′zä′) *n.* A Japanese dish consisting of pockets of dough that are stuffed, as with minced pork or shrimp, and fried. [Japanese.]

gyp also **gip** (jĭp) *Slang.* —*tr.v.* **gypped, gyp·ping, gyps** also **gipped, gip·ping, gips.** To deprive (another) of something by fraud; cheat or swindle. —*n.* **1.** A fraud or swindle. **2.** One who defrauds; a swindler. [Probably short for GYPSY.] **—gyp′per** *n.*

gyp joint *n. Slang.* A business establishment that makes a practice of overcharging or cheating its customers.

gyp·sif·er·ous (jĭp-sĭf′ər-əs) *adj.* Containing gypsum. [GYPS(UM) + –FEROUS.]

gyp·soph·i·la (jĭp-sŏf′ə-lə) *n.* Any of various plants of the genus *Gypsophila,* having small white or pink flowers and including baby's breath. [New Latin *Gypsophila,* genus name : Greek *gupsos,* chalk; see GYPSUM + Greek *philos,* loving; see –PHILE.]

gyp·so·phile (jĭp′sə-fīl′) *n.* A plant living in gypsiferous soil. [GYPS(UM) + –PHILE.]

gyp·sum (jĭp′səm) *n.* A widespread colorless, white, or yellowish mineral, $CaSO_4 \cdot 2H_2O$, used in the manufacture of plaster of Paris, various plaster products, and fertilizers. [Middle English *gipsum,* from Latin *gypsum,* from Greek *gupsos,* probably of Semitic origin.]

gypsum board *n.* See **plasterboard.**

Gyp·sy also **Gip·sy** (jĭp′sē) *n., pl.* **-sies. 1.** A member of a nomadic people that arrived in Europe in migrations from northern India around the 14th century, now also living in North America and Australia. Many Gypsy groups have preserved elements of their traditional culture, including an itinerant existence, tribal organization, and the Romany language. **2.** See **Romany** (sense 2). **3. gypsy.** One inclined to a nomadic, unconventional way of life. **4.** A person who moves from place to place as required for employment, especially: **a.** A part-time or temporary member of a college faculty. **b.** A member of the chorus line in a theater production. [Alteration of Middle English *gypcian,* short for *Egipcien,* Egyptian (so called because they were thought to have come from Egypt).]

gypsy moth
Lymantria dispar

gypsy cab *n.* A taxicab that is licensed only to respond to calls but often cruises the streets for passengers.

gypsy moth *n.* **1.** A European moth *(Lymantria dispar)* having hairy caterpillars that feed on foliage and are destructive to trees and shrubs. It was introduced into the United States in the late 1800's. **2.** *Informal.* A moderate Republican representing a northeast or midwestern urban area in the U.S. House of Representatives.

gy·ral (jī′rəl) *adj.* **1.** Moving in a circle or spiral; gyratory. **2.** Of or relating to a gyrus. **—gy′ral·ly** *adv.*

gy·rate (jī′rāt′) *intr.v.* **-rat·ed, -rat·ing, -rates. 1.** To revolve around a fixed point or axis. **2.** To revolve in or as if in a circle or spiral. See Synonyms at **turn. —gyrate** *adj. Biology.* In rings; coiled or convoluted. [Late Latin *gȳrāre, gȳrāt-,* from Latin *gȳrus,* circle. See GYRE.] **—gy′ra′tor** *n.*

gy·ra·tion (jī-rā′shən) *n.* **1.** The act of gyrating. **2. a.** Circular or spiral motion. **b.** Circular or spiral movement resembling that of a gyrating object: *"increased volatility and unprecedented gyrations in interest rates"* (Jack Egan).

gy·ra·to·ry (jī′rə-tôr′ē, -tōr′ē) *adj.* Having a circular or spiral motion.

gyre (jīr) *n.* **1.** A circular or spiral form; a vortex: *"rain swirling the night into tunnels and gyres"* (Anthony Hyde). **2.** A circular or spiral motion, especially a circular ocean current. **—gyre** *intr.v.* **gyred, gyr·ing, gyres.** To whirl. [Latin *gȳrus,* from Greek *guros.*]

gy·rene (jī-rēn′) *n. Slang.* A member of the U.S. Marine Corps. [Perhaps alteration of GI[1] + (MA)RINE.]

gyr·fal·con also **ger·fal·con** (jûr′făl′kən, -fôl′-, -fô′-) *n.* A large falcon *(Falco rusticolus)* of Arctic regions, having color phases that range from black to gray to white. [Middle English *girfaucoun,* from Old French *girfaut, gerfaucon* : Old High German *gīr,* vulture + Old French *faucon,* falcon; see FALCON.]

gy·ri (jī′rī′) *n.* Plural of **gyrus.**

gy·ro[1] (jī′rō) *n., pl.* **-ros. 1.** A gyroscope. **2.** A gyrocompass.

gy·ro[2] (jī′rō, jē′-) *n., pl.* **-ros.** A sandwich made usually of sliced roasted lamb, onion, and tomato stuffed in pita bread. [From Modern Greek *guros,* a turning, from Greek, circle (from the turning of the meat on a spit).]

gyro– *pref.* **1.** Spinning: *gyromagnetic.* **2.** Circle; spiral: *gyroplane.* **3.** Gyroscopic: *gyrostabilizer.* [Greek *guro-,* circular, from *guros,* circle.]

gy·ro·com·pass (jī′rō-kŭm′pəs, -kŏm′-) *n.* A compass with a motorized gyroscope whose angular momentum interacts with the force produced by the earth's rotation to maintain a north-south orientation of the gyroscopic spin axis, thereby providing a stable directional reference.

gyroscope

gy·ro·mag·net·ic (jī′rō-măg-nĕt′ĭk) *adj.* Of, relating to, or resulting from the magnetic properties of a spinning, electrically charged particle.

gyromagnetic ratio *n.* The ratio of the magnetic moment to the intrinsic angular momentum of a spinning particle.

gy·ro pilot (jī′rō) *n.* An automatic pilot incorporating a gyroscope that initiates corrections to control surfaces on aircraft and thus maintains a preset course and altitude.

gy·ro·plane (jī′rə-plān′) *n.* An aircraft, such as a helicopter or autogyro, equipped with wings that rotate about an approximately vertical axis.

gy·ro·scope (jī′rə-skōp′) *n.* A device consisting of a spinning mass, typically a disk or wheel, mounted on a base so that its axis can turn freely in one or more directions and thereby maintain its orientation regardless of any movement of the base. **—gy′ro·scop′ic** (-skŏp′ĭk) *adj.* **—gy′ro·scop′i·cal·ly** *adv.*

gy·ro·sta·bi·liz·er (jī′rō-stā′bə-lī′zər) *n.* An instrument having a heavy gyroscope whose axis spins in a vertical plane to reduce the side-to-side rolling of a ship or aircraft.

gy·ro·stat (jī′rə-stăt′) *n.* A gyroscope consisting of a rotating wheel in a rigid case. **—gy′ro·stat′ic** *adj.* **—gy′ro·stat′i·cal·ly** *adv.*

gy·rus (jī′rəs) *n., pl.* **-ri** (-rī′). Any of the prominent, rounded, elevated convolutions on the surfaces of the cerebral hemispheres. [Latin *gȳrus,* circle. See GYRE.]

GySgt *abbr.* Gunnery sergeant.

gyve (jīv) *Archaic. n.* A shackle or fetter, especially for the leg. **—gyve** *tr.v.* **gyved, gyv·ing, gyves.** To shackle or fetter. [From Middle English *gives,* gyves.]

ă pat	oi boy
ā pay	ou out
âr care	ŏŏ took
ä father	ōō boot
ĕ pet	ŭ cut
ē be	ûr urge
ĭ pit	th thin
ī pie	*th* this
îr pier	hw which
ŏ pot	zh vision
ō toe	ə about, item
ô paw	♦ regionalism

Stress marks: ′ (primary); ′ (secondary), as in **dictionary** (dĭk′shə-nĕr′ē)

Phoenician
The letter *hēth* originally represented a consonant *ḥ* in Semitic languages, including Phoenician.

Early Greek
In adopting the Phoenician alphabet the Greeks used this letter for their *h* sound, or "rough breathing." In the East Ionic dialect the *h* was lost and the sign came to be used instead for the long vowel *ē* (*ēta*).

H

Roman
But the West Greek alphabets retained the *h,* and from them came the symbol that the Romans simplified to H. The letter's English name comes from French *hache,* from Latin *ach,* a graphic variant of *ah,* which is an altered form of the Roman name *ha.*

h¹ or **H** (āch) *n., pl.* **h's** or **H's. 1.** The eighth letter of the modern English alphabet. **2.** Any of the speech sounds represented by the letter *h.* **3.** The eighth in a series. **4.** Something shaped like the letter H.

h² The symbol for **Planck's constant.**

h³ *abbr.* **1.** Also **h.** Hit. **2.** Hour.

H¹ 1. The symbol for the element **hydrogen. 2.** The symbol for **enthalpy.**

H² *abbr.* **1.** *Physics.* Hamiltonian. **2.** Henry. **3.** Humidity.

h. also **H.** *abbr.* **1.** Harbor. **2.** Hard; hardness. **3.** Height. **4.** High. **5.** *Music.* Horn. **6.** Hundred. **7.** Husband.

ha¹ also **hah** (hä) *interj.* Used to express surprise, wonder, triumph, puzzlement, or pique.

ha² *abbr.* **1.** Hectare. **2.** *Latin.* Hoc anno (this year). **3.** Hour angle.

Haa·kon VII (hô′kən, -ko͝on′). 1872–1957. King of Norway (1905–1957) who headed the exiled Norwegian government in London during the Nazi occupation of his country (1940–1945).

Haar·lem (här′ləm). A city of western Netherlands near the North Sea west of Amsterdam. Chartered in 1245, it is a distribution point for bulbs, especially tulips. Population, 152,511.

Haar·lem·mer·meer (här′lə-mər-mâr′). A city of western Netherlands west-northwest of Amsterdam in an agricultural area. Population, 83,428.

Ha·bak·kuk (hăb′ə-kŭk′, -ko͝ok′, hə-băk′ək) *n. Bible.* **1.** A Hebrew prophet of the late seventh century B.C. **2.** *Abbr.* **Hab.** See table at **Bible.** [Hebrew *Ḥăbaqqûq.*]

ha·ba·ne·ra (hä′bə-nâr′ə, ä′bə-) *n.* **1.** A slow Cuban dance. **2.** The music for this dance, in duple time. [Spanish *(danza) habanera,* (dance) of Havana, from *La Habana,* Havana, Cuba.]

hab. corp. *abbr. Law.* Habeas corpus.

hab·da·lah also **Hab·da·lah** (häv′dä-lä′, häv-dô′lə) *n. Judaism.* A religious ceremony observed at the close of the Sabbath or a holy day. [Hebrew *habdālâ,* separation.]

ha·be·as corpus (hā′bē-əs) *n. Abbr.* **hab. corp.** *Law.* One of a variety of writs that may be issued to bring a party before a court or judge, having as its function the release of the party from unlawful restraint. [Middle English, from Medieval Latin *habeās corpus* : Latin *habeās,* second person sing. present subjunctive of *habēre,* to have + Latin *corpus,* body (from the first words of the writ).]

Ha·ber (hä′bər), **Fritz.** 1868–1934. German chemist. He won a 1918 Nobel Prize for the synthetic production of ammonia.

Haber-Bosch process (hä′bər-bôsh′) *n.* See **Haber process.** [After Fritz HABER and Karl BOSCH.]

hab·er·dash·er (hăb′ər-dăsh′ər) *n.* **1.** A dealer in men's furnishings. **2.** *Chiefly British.* A dealer in sewing notions and small wares. [Middle English, probably from Anglo-Norman *hapertas,* petty wares.]

hab·er·dash·er·y (hăb′ər-dăsh′ə-rē) *n., pl.* **-ies. 1.** A haberdasher's shop. **2.** The goods and wares sold by a haberdasher.

hab·er·geon (hăb′ər-jən) also **hau·ber·geon** (hô′-) *n.* **1.** A short, sleeveless coat of mail. **2.** A hauberk. [Middle English, from Old French *hauberjon,* from *hauberc,* hauberk. See HAUBERK.]

Haber process *n.* The principal commercial method of producing ammonia, by direct combination of nitrogen and hydrogen under high pressure in the presence of a catalyst, often iron. Also called *Haber-Bosch process.* [After Fritz HABER.]

hab·ile (hăb′ĭl) *adj.* Generally able or adroit; handy. [Middle English *habil,* from Old French *habile,* from Latin *habilis,* from *habēre,* to handle. See **ghabh-** in Appendix.]

ha·bil·i·ment (hə-bĭl′ə-mənt) *n.* **1.** Often **habiliments. a.** The special dress or garb associated with an occasion or office: *"shrouded from head to foot in the habiliments of the grave"* (Edgar Allan Poe). **b.** Clothes. **2. habiliments.** Characteristic furnishings or equipment; trappings: *surrounded by the habiliments of the television news industry.* [Middle English *habilement,* from Old French *habillement,* from *habiller,* to clothe, alteration (influenced by *habit,* clothing; see HABIT) of *abiller,* to prepare, strip a tree of its branches : *a-,* toward (from Latin *ad-;* see AD–) + *bille,* log; see BILLET².]

ha·bil·i·tate (hə-bĭl′ĭ-tāt′) *v.* **-tat·ed, -tat·ing, -tates.** —*tr.* **1.** To clothe. **2.** To fit out or equip (a mine) for operation. **3.** *Obsolete.* To impart an ability or capacity to. —*intr.* To qualify oneself for a post or office. [Late Latin *habilitāre, habilitāt-,* to enable, from Latin *habilitās, habilitāt-,* ability, from *habilis,* able. See HABILE.] —**ha·bil′i·ta′tion** *n.*

hab·it (hăb′ĭt) *n.* **1.a.** A recurrent, often unconscious pattern of behavior that is acquired through frequent repetition. **b.** An established disposition of the mind or character. **2.** Customary manner or practice: *a person of ascetic habits.* **3.** An addiction, especially to a narcotic drug. **4.** Physical constitution. **5.** Characteristic appearance, form, or manner of growth, especially of a plant or crystal. **6.a.** A distinctive dress or costume, especially of a religious order. **b.** A riding habit. —**habit** *tr.v.* **-it·ed, -it·ing, -its.** To clothe; dress. [Middle English, clothing, from Old French, clothing, behavior, custom, from Latin *habitus,* from past participle of *habēre,* to have. See **ghabh-** in Appendix.]

SYNONYMS: *habit, practice, custom, usage, use, wont, habitude.* These nouns denote patterns of behavior established by continual repetition. *Habit* applies to a way of acting so ingrained in an individual that it is done without conscious thought: *trying to break the smoking habit; has a habit of closing his eyes when he tells a story. "Habit rules the unreflecting herd"* (William Wordsworth). *Practice* denotes a customary, often chosen pattern of individual or group behavior: *It is our practice to eat an early dinner. "You will find it a very good practice always to verify your references, sir"* (Martin Joseph Routh). *Custom* is either individual or group behavior as established by long practice and especially by accepted conventions: *"No written law has ever been more binding than unwritten custom supported by popular opinion"* (Carrie Chapman Catt). *Usage* refers to customary practice that has become an accepted standard for a group and thus regulates individual behavior: *"laws . . . . corrected, altered, and amended by acts of parliament and common usage"* (William Blackstone). *Use* and *wont* are terms for the customary and distinctive practice of an individual or a group: *"situations where the use and wont of their fathers no longer meet their necessities"* (J.A. Froude). *Habitude* refers to an individual's habitual disposition to behave in a certain way rather than to a specific act: *"His real habitude gave life and grace/To appertainings and to ornament"* (Shakespeare).

hab·it·a·ble (hăb′ĭ-tə-bəl) *adj.* Suitable to live in or on; inhabitable: *habitable land.* [Middle English, from Old French, from Latin *habitābilis,* from *habitāre,* to dwell, frequentative of *habēre,* to have. See **ghabh-** in Appendix.] —**hab′it·a·bil′i·ty, hab′it·a·ble·ness** *n.* —**hab′it·a·bly** *adv.*

hab·i·tant (hăb′ĭ-tənt) *n.* **1.** An inhabitant. **2.** Also **ha·bi·tan** (ă′bē-tän′). An inhabitant of French descent living in Canada, especially Quebec, or in Louisiana. [Middle English, from Old French, from present participle of *habiter,* to dwell, from Latin *habitāre.* See HABITABLE.]

hab·i·tat (hăb′ĭ-tăt′) *n.* **1.** The area or type of environment in which an organism or ecological community normally lives or occurs: *a marine habitat.* **2.** The place in which a person or thing is most likely to be found. [Latin, it dwells, third person sing. present of *habitāre,* to dwell. See HABITABLE.]

hab·i·ta·tion (hăb′ĭ-tā′shən) *n.* **1.** The act of inhabiting or the state of being inhabited. **2.a.** A natural environment or locality. **b.** A place of abode; a residence. [Middle English *habitacioun,* from Latin *habitātiō, habitātiōn-,* from *habitātus,* past participle of *habitāre,* to dwell. See HABITABLE.]

hab·it-form·ing (hăb′ĭt-fôr′mĭng) *adj.* **1.** Capable of leading to physiological or psychological dependence: *a habit-forming drug.* **2.** Tending to become habitual: *The taste of success may become habit-forming.*

ha·bit·u·al (hə-bĭch′o͞o-əl) *adj.* **1.a.** Of the nature of a habit: *habitual lying.* **b.** Being such by force of habit: *a habitual liar.* See Synonyms at **chronic. 2.** Established by long use; usual: *my* *habitual place.* See Synonyms at **usual.** **—ha·bit′u·al·ly** *adv.* **—ha·bit′u·al·ness** *n.*

ha·bit·u·ate (hə-bĭch′o͞o-āt′) *v.* **-at·ed, -at·ing, -ates.** *—tr.* To accustom by frequent repetition or prolonged exposure. *—intr.* **1.** To cause physiological or psychological habituation, as to a drug. **2.** *Psychology.* To experience habituation. [From Middle English, accustomed, from Late Latin *habituātus,* past participle of *habituārī,* to be in a condition, from Latin *habitus,* condition, habit. See HABIT.]

ha·bit·u·a·tion (hə-bĭch′o͞o-ā′shən) *n.* **1.** The process of habituating or the state of being habituated. **2.a.** Physiological tolerance to a drug resulting from repeated use. **b.** Psychological dependence on a drug. **3.** *Psychology.* The decline of a conditioned response following repeated exposure to the conditioned stimulus.

hab·i·tude (hăb′ĭ-to͞od′, -tyo͞od′) *n.* A habitual tendency or way of behaving. See Synonyms at **habit.** [Middle English, from Latin *habitūdō,* condition, from *habitus.* See HABIT.]

ha·bit·u·é (hə-bĭch′o͞o-ā′, hə-bĭch′o͞o-ā′) *n.* A person who frequents a particular place, especially a place offering a specific pleasurable activity. See Synonyms at **votary.** [French, from past participle of *habituer,* to accustom, frequent, from Old French, from Late Latin *habituārī,* to be in a condition. See HABITUATE.]

hab·i·tus (hăb′ĭ-təs) *n., pl.* **habitus.** The physical and constitutional characteristics of an individual, especially as related to the tendency to develop a certain disease. [Latin, condition. See HABIT.]

ha·boob (hə-bo͞ob′) *n.* A penetrating sandstorm or dust storm with violent winds, occurring chiefly in Arabia, North Africa, and India. [Arabic *habūb,* strong wind, from *habba,* to blow.]

Habs·burg (hăps′bûrg′, häps′bo͝ork′). See **Hapsburg.**

ha·ček (hä′chĕk′) *n.* A diacritical mark (ˇ) that resembles an inverted circumflex and is used over certain letters, such as *č,* to indicate quality of pronunciation. [Czech *háček,* diminutive of *hák,* hook, from Middle High German *hāken,* from Old High German *hāko.* See **keg-** in Appendix.]

Ha·chi·o·ji (hä′chē-ō′jē). A city of east-central Honshu, Japan, west of Tokyo. It has been noted for its weaving industry since the early 18th century. Population, 426,650.

ha·chure (hă-sho͝or′, hăsh′o͝or) *n.* One of the short lines used on maps to shade or to indicate slopes and their degree and direction. **—hachure** (hă-sho͝or′) *tr.v.* **-chured, -chur·ing, -chures.** To make hatching on (a map). [French, from Old French, from *hacher,* to cross-hatch. See HATCH[3].]

ha·ci·en·da (hä′sē-ĕn′də) *n.* **1.** A large estate or plantation in Spanish-speaking countries. **2.** The house of the owner of such an estate. [Spanish, from Latin *facienda,* things to be done, neuter pl. gerundive of *facere,* to do. See **dhē-** in Appendix.]

Ha·ci·en·da Heights (hä′sē-ĕn′də). A community of southern California, a suburb of Los Angeles. Population, 49,422.

hack[1] (hăk) *v.* **hacked, hack·ing, hacks.** *—tr.* **1.** To cut or chop with repeated and irregular blows: *hacked down the saplings.* **2.** To break up the surface of (soil). **3.** *Slang.* To cut or mutilate as if by hacking: *hacked millions off the budget.* **4.** *Slang.* To cope with successfully; manage: *couldn't hack a second job.* *—intr.* **1.** To chop or cut something by hacking. **2.** *Computer Science.* To work or perform as a hacker. **3.** To cough roughly or harshly. **—hack** *n.* **1.** A rough, irregular cut made by hacking. **2.** A tool, such as a hoe, used for hacking. **3.** A blow made by hacking. **4.** A rough, dry cough. [Middle English *hakken,* from Old English *-haccian;* see **keg-** in Appendix. V., intr., sense 2, back-formation from HACKER[1].] **—hack′a·ble** *adj.*

hack[2] (hăk) *n.* **1.** A horse used for riding or driving; a hackney. **2.** A worn-out horse for hire; a jade. **3.a.** One who undertakes unpleasant or distasteful tasks for money or reward; a hireling. **b.** A writer hired to produce routine or commercial writing. **4.** A carriage or hackney for hire. **5.** *Informal.* **a.** A taxicab. **b.** See **hackie.** **—hack** *v.* **hacked, hack·ing, hacks.** *—tr.* **1.** To let out (a horse) for hire. **2.** To make banal or hackneyed with indiscriminate use. *—intr.* **1.** To drive a taxicab for a living. **2.** To work for hire as a writer. **3.** To ride on horseback at an ordinary pace. **—hack** *adj.* **1.** By, characteristic of, or designating routine or commercial writing: *hack prose.* **2.** Hackneyed; banal. [Short for HACKNEY.]

hack·a·more (hăk′ə-môr′, -mōr′) *n.* A rope or rawhide halter with a wide band that can be lowered over a horse's eyes, used in breaking horses to a bridle. [Alteration of Spanish *jáquima,* halter, from Old Spanish *xaquima,* from Arabic *šakīma,* bit of a bridle.]

hack·ber·ry (hăk′bĕr′ē) *n.* **1.** Any of various trees or shrubs of the genus *Celtis,* having inconspicuous flowers and small, usually ovoid drupes. **2.** The fruit of such a plant. **3.** The soft, yellowish wood of these trees or shrubs. Also called *sugarberry.* [Alteration of obsolete *hagberry* : *hag-* (of Scandinavian origin) + BERRY.]

hack·but (hăk′bŭt′) *n.* See **harquebus.** [French *haquebute,* from Old French *hacquebute,* alteration (influenced by *buter,* to aim at) of Middle Dutch *hakebus.* See HARQUEBUS.] **—hack′but·eer′** (-bə-tîr′), **hack′but′ter** *n.*

Hack·en·sack (hăk′ən-săk′). A city of northeast New Jersey east-southeast of Paterson on the **Hackensack River,** about 64 km (40 mi) long. The city is an industrial and residential suburb of New York City. Population, 36,039.

hack·er[1] (hăk′ər) *n.* **1.** *Computer Science.* **a.** One who is proficient at using or programming a computer; a computer buff. **b.** One who illegally gains access to or enters another's electronic system to obtain secret information or steal money. **2.** *Sports.* One who enthusiastically pursues a game or sport: *a weekend tennis hacker.* [Perhaps from *hacker,* amateurish or inept golfer or tennis player (possibly from HACK[1]), or perhaps from *hack,* practical joke, clever scheme (from dialectal *hack,* to embarrass, confuse, play a trick on).]

hack·er[2] (hăk′ər) *n.* See **hackie.**

hack·ie (hăk′ē) *n.* A taxicab driver. Also called *hack, hacker.*

hack·le[1] (hăk′əl) *n.* **1.** Any of the long, slender, often glossy feathers on the neck of a bird, especially a male domestic fowl. **2.** **hackles.** The erectile hairs along the back of the neck of an animal, especially of a dog. **3.a.** A tuft of cock feathers trimming an artificial fishing fly. **b.** A hackle fly. **—hackle** *tr.v.* **-led, -ling, -les.** To trim (an artificial fishing fly) with a hackle. ***—idiom.*** **get (one's) hackles up.** To be extremely insulted or irritated. [Middle English *hakell,* cloak, skin, plumage, possibly from Old English *hacele,* cloak, mantle.]

hack·le[2] (hăk′əl) *v.* **-led, -ling, -les.** *—tr.* To chop roughly; mangle by hacking. *—intr.* To hack. [Frequentative of HACK[1].]

hack·le·back (hăk′əl-băk′) *n.* See **shovelnose.**

hackle fly *n.* An artificial, usually wingless fishing fly trimmed with hackles.

hack·ly (hăk′lē) *adj.* Nicked or notched. [From HACKLE[2].]

hack·ma·tack (hăk′mə-tăk′) *n.* See **balsam poplar.** [Perhaps from Western Abenaki.]

hack·ney (hăk′nē) *n., pl.* **-neys. 1.** Often **Hackney.** A horse of a breed developed in England, having a gait characterized by pronounced flexion of the knee. **2.** A trotting horse suited for routine riding or driving; a hack. **3.** A coach or carriage for hire. **—hackney** *tr.v.* **-neyed, -ney·ing, -neys. 1.** To cause to become banal and trite through overuse. **2.** To hire out; let. **—hackney** *adj.* **1.** Banal; trite. **2.** Having been hired. [Middle English *hakenei,* probably after *Hakenei,* Hackney, a borough of London, England, where such horses were raised.]

hack·neyed (hăk′nēd) *adj.* Overfamiliar through overuse; trite. See Synonyms at **trite.**

hack·saw (hăk′sô′) *n.* A saw consisting of a tough, fine-toothed blade stretched taut in a frame, used especially for cutting metal. [Alteration of Middle English *hagge-saue,* a kind of saw : *haggen,* to cut, chop; see HAGGLE + *sawe,* saw; see SAW[1].] **—hack′saw′** *v.*

hack·work (hăk′wûrk′) *n.* **1.** Commissioned work, such as writing or acting, done usually by formula and in conformance with commercial standards. **2.** Tedious, monotonous, or uninteresting work of any kind.

had (hăd) *v.* Past tense and past participle of **have.**

ha·dal (hād′l) *adj.* Of or relating to the deepest regions of the ocean, below about 6,000 meters (20,000 feet). [French, from *Hadès,* Hades, from Greek *Haidēs.* See **weid-** in Appendix.]

had·dock (hăd′ək) *n., pl.* **haddock** or **-docks.** A food fish *(Melanogrammus aeglefinus)* of northern Atlantic waters, related to and resembling the cod. [Middle English *haddok.*]

hade (hād) *n. Geology.* The angle of inclination from the vertical of a vein, fault, or lode. [Origin unknown.]

Ha·des (hā′dēz) *n.* **1.** *Greek Mythology.* **a.** The god of the netherworld and dispenser of earthly riches. **b.** This netherworld kingdom, the abode of the shades of the dead. **2.** Also **hades.** Hell. [Greek *Haidēs.* See **weid-** in Appendix.]

hadj (hăj) *n. Islam.* Variant of **haj.**

hadj·i (hăj′ē) *n. Islam.* Variant of **haji.**

had·n't (hăd′nt). Had not.

Ha·dri·an (hā′drē-ən). A.D. 76–138. Emperor of Rome (117–138) who sought to end distinctions between Rome and the Roman provinces. During his visit to Britain (122), he ordered the construction of Hadrian's Wall.

Ha·dri·an's Wall (hā′drē-ənz). An ancient Roman wall, 118.3 km (73.5 mi) long, across northern England. Built by the emperor Hadrian c. A.D. 122–126 and extended by Severus a century later, the wall marked the northern boundary of Roman Britain.

had·ron (hăd′rŏn′) *n.* Any of a class of subatomic particles that are composed of quarks and take part in the strong interaction. See table at **subatomic particle.** [Greek *hadros,* thick; see **sā-** in Appendix + –ON[1].] **—had·ron′ic** *adj.*

had·ro·saur (hăd′rə-sôr′) *n.* Any of various amphibious dinosaurs of the genus *Anatosaurus* and related genera that had webbed feet and a ducklike bill. [New Latin *Hadrosaurus,* genus name : Greek *hadros,* thick; see HADRON + *sauros,* lizard.]

hadst (hădst) *v. Archaic.* A second person singular past tense of **have.**

hae (hā, hă) *tr.v.* **haed, haen** (hān, hăn), **hae·ing, haes.** *Scots.* To have.

Haeck·el (hĕk′əl), **Ernst Heinrich.** 1834–1919. German philosopher and naturalist who mapped a genealogical tree relating all animal life.

Haeck·el's law (hĕk′əlz) *n.* See **biogenetic law.** [After Ernst Heinrich HAECKEL.]

haem– also **haema–** or **haemo–** *pref.* Variants of **hemo–.**

haemat– or **haemato–** *pref.* Variants of **hemato–.**

–haemia *suff.* Variant of **–emia.**

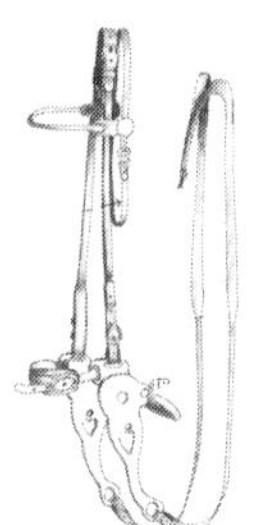
hackamore
Hackamore bit-bridle

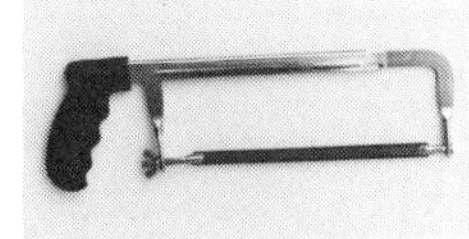
hacksaw

Hadrian

hadrosaur
Corythosaurus

ă pat	oi boy
ā pay	ou out
âr care	o͝o took
ä father	o͞o boot
ĕ pet	ŭ cut
ē be	ûr urge
ĭ pit	th thin
ī pie	*th* this
îr pier	hw which
ŏ pot	zh vision
ō toe	ə about, item
ô paw	♦ regionalism

Stress marks: ′ (primary); ′ (secondary), as in **dictionary** (dĭk′shə-nĕr′ē)

haen (hān, hăn) *v. Scots.* Past participle of **hae.**

haet (hāt) *n. Scots.* A minute amount; a jot. [Scots, short for *hae it,* take it.]

ha·fiz (hä′fĭz) *n. Islam.* **1.** One who has memorized the Koran. **2.** Used as a title of respect for such a person. [Persian, from Arabic *ḥāfiẓ,* from *ḥafiẓa,* to memorize, guard.]

Ha·fiz (hä-fĭz′, -fēz′). fl. 14th century. Persian poet whose sensuous rhyming couplets, many of which concern love, wine, and nature, are interpreted allegorically by Sufic Moslems.

haf·ni·um (hăf′nē-əm) *n. Symbol* **Hf** A brilliant, silvery, metallic element separated from ores of zirconium and used in nuclear reactor control rods, as a getter for oxygen and nitrogen, and in the manufacture of tungsten filaments. Atomic number 72; atomic weight 178.49; melting point 2,220°C; boiling point 5,400°C; specific gravity 13.3; valence 4. See table at **element.** [After *Hafnia,* Medieval Latin name for Copenhagen, Denmark.]

haft (hăft) *n.* A handle or hilt, especially the handle of a tool or weapon. **—haft** *tr.v.* **haft·ed, haft·ing, hafts.** To fit into or equip with a hilt or handle. [Middle English, from Old English *hæft.* See **kap-** in Appendix.]

haf·ta·rah or **haf·to·rah** (häf′tä-rä′, häf-tôr′ə, -tōr′ə) *n.* Variants of **haphtarah.**

Ha·fun (hă-fōōn′), **Cape.** A promontory of northeast Somalia on the Indian Ocean. It is the easternmost point of Africa.

hag¹ (hăg) *n.* **1.** An old woman considered ugly or frightful. **2.a.** A witch; a sorceress. **b.** *Obsolete.* A female demon. **3.** A hagfish. [Middle English *hagge,* perhaps short for Old English *hægtesse,* witch.] **—hag′gish** *adj.* **—hag′gish·ly** *adv.* **—hag′gish·ness** *n.*

hag² (hăg) *n. Chiefly British.* **1.** A boggy area; a quagmire. **2.** A spot in boggy land that is softer or more solid than the surrounding area. **3.** A cutting in a peat bog. [Middle English, gap, chasm, of Scandinavian origin; akin to Old Norse *högg.* See **kau-** in Appendix.]

Hag. *abbr. Bible.* Haggai.

Ha·gar (hā′gər, -gär). In the Old Testament, the Egyptian servant of Abraham's wife, Sarah. With Abraham she had a son, Ishmael.

Ha·gen (hä′gən). A city of west-central Germany northeast of Cologne. Chartered in 1746 and famous for its textiles in the late 18th century, it became an industrial and manufacturing center after 1870. Population, 207,636.

Ha·gers·town (hā′gərz-toun′). A city of northern Maryland northwest of Frederick. It is a manufacturing center in an agricultural region. Population, 34,132.

hag·fish (hăg′fĭsh′) *n., pl.* **hagfish** or **-fish·es.** Any of various primitive, eel-shaped marine fishes of the family Myxinidae, having a jawless sucking mouth equipped with rasping teeth with which they bore into and feed on other fishes. [HAG¹ + FISH.]

Hag·ga·dah also **Hag·ga·da** (hä′gä-dä′, hə-gä′də, -gô′də) *n., pl.* **-doth** (-dôt′, -dōt′, -dōs, -dəz). *Judaism.* **1.** Traditional Jewish literature, especially the nonlegal part of the Talmud. **2.** The book containing the story of the Exodus and the ritual of the Seder, read at the Passover Seder. [Hebrew *haggādâ,* narration, telling, from *higgîd,* to narrate, tell.]

hag·gad·ic also **Hag·gad·ic** (hə-găd′ĭk, -gä′dĭk, -gôdĭk) *adj. Judaism.* Of or relating to the Haggadah.

hag·ga·dist (hə-gä′dĭst, -gô′-) *n. Judaism.* **1.** A haggadic writer. **2.** A student of haggadic literature. **—hag′ga·dis′tic** (hăg′ə-dĭs′tĭk) *adj.*

Hag·ga·i (hăg′ē-ī′, hăg′ī′) *n. Bible.* **1.** A Hebrew prophet of the sixth century B.C. **2.** *Abbr.* **Hag.** See table at **Bible.** [Hebrew *Haggay.*]

hag·gard (hăg′ərd) *adj.* **1.a.** Appearing worn and exhausted; gaunt. **b.** Wild or distraught in appearance. **2.** Wild and intractable. Used of a hawk in falconry. **—haggard** *n.* An adult hawk captured for training. [French *hagard,* wild, from Old French, wild hawk, raptor, perhaps of Germanic origin.] **—hag′gard·ly** *adv.* **—hag′gard·ness** *n.*

SYNONYMS: *haggard, wasted, worn, careworn.* These adjectives mean showing the physical effects of anxiety, disease, hunger, or fatigue. *Haggard* implies thinness, tiredness, and often the expression of one seemingly distraught or harried: *Don't lose so much weight that you look haggard. Her eyes were haggard and cavernous. Wasted* stresses frailness or enfeeblement such as results from prolonged illness or extreme hardship: *"a tall, bent old man, wasted almost to a skeleton"* (W.H. Hudson). *Worn* means showing the wearing effects of overwork, care, or suffering: *"I was shocked to see the worn look of his handsome young face"* (Charles Dickens). *Careworn* applies to one whose physical appearance reveals the effects of worry or burdensome responsibility: *Her countenance looked careworn as she bent over her pile of mending.*

Hag·gard (hăg′ərd), Sir **(Henry) Rider.** 1856–1925. British writer whose romantic adventure novels include *King Solomon's Mines* (1885) and *She* (1887).

hag·gis (hăg′ĭs) *n.* A Scottish dish consisting of a mixture of the minced heart, lungs, and liver of a sheep or calf mixed with suet, onions, oatmeal, and seasonings and boiled in the stomach of the slaughtered animal. [Middle English *hagese*; perhaps akin to *haggen,* to chop. See HAGGLE.]

hag·gle (hăg′əl) *v.* **-gled, -gling, -gles.** *—intr.* **1.** To bargain, as over the price of something; dicker: *"He preferred to be overcharged than to haggle"* (W. Somerset Maugham). **2.** To argue in an attempt to come to terms. *—tr.* **1.** To cut (something) in a crude, unskillful manner; hack. **2.** *Archaic.* To harass or worry by wrangling. **—haggle** *n.* An instance of bargaining or arguing. [Frequentative of dialectal *hag,* to chop, hack, from Middle English *haggen,* from Old Norse *höggva.* See **kau-** in Appendix.] **—hag′gler** *n.*

hagi– *pref.* Variant of **hagio–.**

hag·i·ar·chy (hăg′ē-är′kē, hā′jē-) *n., pl.* **-chies.** Government by holy men, such as priests or saints. Also called *hagiocracy.*

hagio– or **hagi–** *pref.* **1.** Saint: *hagiography.* **2.** Holy: *hagioscope.* [Greek *hagios,* holy.]

hag·i·oc·ra·cy (hăg′ē-ŏk′rə-sē, hā′jē-) *n., pl.* **-cies.** See **hagiarchy.**

Hag·i·og·ra·pha (hăg′ē-ŏg′rə-fə, hā′jē-) *pl.n. (used with a sing. or pl. verb). Bible.* The Writings. [Late Latin, from Late Greek, from neuter pl. of *hagiographos,* written by inspiration, scriptural : Greek *hagio-,* hagio- + Greek *-graphos,* written (from *graphein,* to write; see –GRAPH).]

hag·i·og·ra·phy (hăg′ē-ŏg′rə-fē, hā′jē-) *n., pl.* **-phies. 1.** Biography of saints. **2.** A worshipful or idealizing biography. **—hag′i·og′raph·er** *n.* **—hag′i·o·graph′ic** (-ə-grăf′ĭk), **hag′i·o·graph′i·cal** *adj.*

hag·i·ol·a·try (hăg′ē-ŏl′ə-trē, hā′jē-) *n.* Worship of the saints.

hag·i·ol·o·gy (hăg′ē-ŏl′ə-jē, hā′jē-) *n., pl.* **-gies. 1.** Literature dealing with the lives of saints. **2.** A collection of sacred writings. **3.** An authoritative list of saints. **—hag′i·o·log′ic** (-ə-lŏj′ĭk), **hag′i·o·log′i·cal** *adj.* **—hag′i·ol′o·gist** *n.*

hag·i·o·scope (hăg′ē-ə-skōp′, hā′jē-) *n.* A small opening in an interior wall of a church, enabling those in the transept to view the main altar. **—hag′i·o·scop′ic** (-skŏp′ĭk) *adj.*

hag·rid·den (hăg′rĭd′n) *adj.* **1.** Harassed by or as if by a witch. **2.** Tormented or harassed, as by unreasoning fears: *"a man hagridden by the future—haunted by visions of an imminent heaven or hell upon earth"* (C.S. Lewis).

Hague (hāg), **The.** Also **'s Gra·ven·ha·ge** (skrä′vən-hä′gə, SKHRä′vən-hä′KHə). The de facto capital of the Netherlands, in the western part of the country near the North Sea. The Hague grew around a palace built c. 1250 by William of Holland (1228–1256) and is today the seat of the country's legislature and supreme court. Population, 445,213.

hah (hä) *interj.* Variant of **ha¹.**

ha-ha¹ (hä′hä′) also **haw-haw** (hô′hô′) *—n.* **1.** A sound made in imitation of laughter. **2. ha-ha.** *Slang.* An instance of amusement. Often used in the plural: *drove around the baseball field at midnight just for ha-has; a party that was a real ha-ha.* *—interj.* Used to express amusement or scorn.

ha-ha² (hä′hä′) also **haw-haw** (hô′hô′) *n.* A moat, walled ditch, or hedge sunk in the ground to serve as a fence without impairing the view or scenic appeal. [French (perhaps as an exclamation of surprise).]

Hahn (hän), **Otto.** 1879–1968. German chemist. He won a 1944 Nobel Prize for his work on atomic fission.

Hah·ne·mann (hä′nə-mən, -män′), **(Christian Friedrich) Samuel.** 1755–1843. German physician and founder of homeopathy. He postulated that medicine produces symptoms in healthy people that are similar to those that it relieves in sick people.

hah·ni·um (hä′nē-əm) *n.* Element 105. [After Otto HAHN.]

haick (hīk, hāk) *n.* Variant of **haik.**

Hai·da (hī′də) *n., pl.* **Haida** or **-das. 1.** A Native American people inhabiting the Queen Charlotte Islands of British Columbia, Canada, and Prince of Wales Island in Alaska. **2.** A member of this people. **3.** Any or all of the language varieties spoken by the Haida. **—Hai′dan** *adj.*

Hai·fa (hī′fə). A city of northwest Israel on the **Bay of Haifa,** an inlet of the Mediterranean Sea. Located at the foot of Mount Carmel, the city probably dates from the third century A.D. and is now a major port and industrial center. Population, 224,700.

Haig (hāg), **Douglas.** First Earl Haig. 1861–1928. British field marshal who was commander in chief of the British forces on the western front (1915–1918).

Haight-Ash·bu·ry (hāt′ăsh′bĕr-ē, -bə-rē). A section of central San Francisco. In the 1960's it was a famous gathering place for hippies and followers of the drug culture.

haik also **haick** (hīk, hāk) *n.* A large piece of cotton, silk, or wool cloth worn as an outer garment in Morocco. [Arabic *ḥā'ik,* from *ḥāka,* to weave.]

Hai·kou (hī′kou′, -kō′). A city of southern China on Hainan Island in the South China Sea. It is a seaport and an industrial center. Population, 266,302.

hai·ku (hī′kōō) *n., pl.* **haiku** also **-kus. 1.** A Japanese lyric verse form having three unrhymed lines of five, seven, and five syllables, traditionally invoking an aspect of nature or the seasons. **2.** A poem written in this form. [Japanese : *hai,* amusement (from Chinese *pá,* farce) + *ku,* sentence (from Chinese *jù*).]

hail¹ (hāl) *n.* **1.** Precipitation in the form of pellets of ice and hard snow. **2.** Something that falls with the force and quantity of a shower of ice and hard snow: *a hail of pebbles; a hail of criticism.* **—hail** *v.* **hailed, hail·ing, hails.** *—intr.* **1.** To precipitate in pellets of ice and hard snow. **2.** To fall like hailstones: *Con-*

demnations hailed down on them. —*tr.* To pour (something) down or forth: *They hailed insults at me.* [Middle English, from Old English *hægel, hagol.*]

hail² (hāl) *v.* **hailed, hail·ing, hails.** —*tr.* **1.a.** To salute or greet. **b.** To greet or acclaim enthusiastically: *The crowds hailed the boxing champion.* **2.** To call out to in order to catch the attention of: *hail a cabdriver.* —*intr. Nautical.* To signal or call to a passing ship as a greeting or as an identification. —**hail** *n.* **1.** The act of greeting or acclaiming. **2.** A shout made to catch someone's attention or to greet. **3.** Hailing distance: *told me to stay within hail.* —**hail** *interj.* Used to express a greeting or tribute. —***phrasal verb.* hail from.** To come or originate from: *She hails from Oklahoma.* [Middle English *heilen,* from *(wæs) hæil,* (be) healthy. See WASSAIL.]

hail·er (hā′lər) *n.* **1.** One that greets, acclaims, or catches someone's attention. **2.** A bullhorn.

Hai·le Se·las·sie (hī′lē sə-lăs′ē, -lä′sē). Title of Ras Taffari Makonnen. 1892–1975. Emperor of Ethiopia (1930–1974). After the Italian invasion of his country (1936), he fled to England, returned to Ethiopia with Allied troops (1941), and was restored to the throne. He was deposed in a military coup (1974).

hail-fel·low (hāl′fĕl′ō) also **hail-fel·low-well-met** (-wĕl′-mĕt′) *adj.* Heartily friendly and congenial. [From the obsolete greeting *hail, fellow!*] —**hail′-fel′low** *n.*

Hail Mar·y (hāl′ mâr′ē) *n., pl.* **Hail Mar·ys.** *Roman Catholic Church.* A prayer based on the greetings of Gabriel and Saint Elizabeth to the Virgin Mary.

hail·stone (hāl′stōn′) *n.* A hard pellet of snow and ice.

hail·storm (hāl′stôrm′) *n.* A storm with hail.

haim·ish also **heim·ish** (hā′mĭsh) *adj. Slang.* Warm and comfortable; homey; folksy: *"It is very gentle and sweet up here. It's . . . sort of haimish"* (Janet Malcolm). [Yiddish *heymish,* from Middle High German *heimisch,* from Old High German *heimisc,* from *heim,* home. See **tkei-** in Appendix.]

Hai·nan (hī′nän′). An island of southern China in the South China Sea, separated from Leizhou Peninsula by a narrow strait.

Hai·naut (hā-nō′, ĕ-nō′). A historical region of southwest Belgium and northern France. It originated in the ninth century and was later joined, through royal marriages, with Flanders and Holland. Parts of Hainaut were annexed by France in the 1600's.

♦ **haint** (hānt) *n. Chiefly Southern U.S.* Variant of **haunt** (sense 2).

Hai·phong (hī′fŏng′). A city of northeast Vietnam on the Red River delta near the Gulf of Tonkin. Established in 1874, it was shelled by the French in 1946 and heavily bombed by U.S. forces during the Vietnam War. Population, 330,755.

hair (hâr) *n.* **1.a.** Any of the cylindrical, keratinized, often pigmented filaments characteristically growing from the epidermis of a mammal. **b.** A growth of such filaments, as that forming the coat of an animal or covering the scalp of a human being. **2.** A filamentous projection or bristle similar to a hair, such as a seta of an arthropod or an epidermal process of a plant. **3.** Fabric made from the hair of certain animals: *a coat of alpaca hair.* **4.a.** A minute distance or narrow margin: *won by a hair.* **b.** A precise or exact degree: *calibrated to a hair.* [Middle English *her,* from Old English *hǣr.*]

hair·ball (hâr′bôl′) *n.* A small mass of hair located in the stomach or intestine of an animal, such as a cat, resulting from an accumulation of small amounts of hair that are swallowed each time the animal licks its coat.

hair·breadth (hâr′brĕdth′) *adj.* Extremely close: *a hairbreadth escape.* —**hairbreadth** *n.* Variant of **hairsbreadth.**

hair·brush (hâr′brŭsh′) *n.* A brush for the hair.

hair cell *n.* A cell in the organ of Corti having fine hairlike processes.

hair·cloth (hâr′klôth′, -klŏth′) *n.* A wiry fabric woven especially from horsehair or camel's hair, used for upholstering and for stiffening garments.

hair·cut (hâr′kŭt′) *n.* **1.** The act or an instance of cutting the hair. **2.** A style in which hair is cut. —**hair′cut′ter** *n.* —**hair′cut′ting** *adj. & n.*

hair·do (hâr′do͞o′) *n., pl.* **-dos.** A style in which hair is arranged.

hair·dress·er (hâr′drĕs′ər) *n.* One who cuts or arranges hair.

hair·dress·ing (hâr′drĕs′ĭng) *n.* **1.** The occupation of a hairdresser. **2.** The act of dressing or arranging the hair. **3.** A cosmetic or medicinal preparation for dressing the hair.

haired (hârd) *adj.* Having a specified kind of hair. Often used in combination: *a long-haired cat; a short-haired dog.*

hair follicle *n.* A tubular infolding of the epidermis containing the root of a hair.

hair·less (hâr′lĭs) *adj.* Having little or no hair. —**hair′less·ness** *n.*

hair·line (hâr′līn′) *n.* **1.** The outline of the growth of hair on the head, especially across the front. **2.** A very slender line. **3.** *Printing.* **a.** A very fine line on a typeface. **b.** A style of type using such lines. **4.a.** A textile design having thin, threadlike stripes. **b.** A fabric, usually a worsted, with such stripes.

hair·piece (hâr′pēs′) *n.* A covering or bunch of human or artificial hair used to conceal baldness or give shape to a coiffure.

hair·pin (hâr′pĭn′) *n.* **1.** A thin, cylindrical strip of metal or other material bent in the shape of a long U, used by women to secure a hairdo or headdress. **2.** Something shaped like a hairpin, especially a sharp turn in a road.

hair-rais·er (hâr′rā′zər) *n. Informal.* One that causes wild excitement, terror, or thrills.

hair-rais·ing (hâr′rā′zĭng) *adj.* Causing excitement, terror, or thrills.

hairs·breadth or **hair's-breadth** (hârz′brĕdth′) also **hair·breadth** (hâr′-) *n.* A small space, distance, or margin: *won by a hairsbreadth.*

hair seal *n.* Any of various seals of the family Phocidae, having a stiff, hairlike coat in the adult and ears visible only as small indentations.

hair shirt *n.* A coarse haircloth garment worn next to the skin by religious ascetics as penance.

hair space *n. Printing.* The narrowest of the metal spaces used for separating words or letters.

hair·split·ting (hâr′splĭt′ĭng) *n.* The making of unreasonably fine distinctions. —**hair′split′ter** *n.* —**hair′split′ting** *adj.*

hair spray also **hair·spray** (hâr′sprā′) *n.* A commercial product sprayed on the hair to keep it in place.

hair·spring (hâr′sprĭng′) *n.* A fine coiled spring that regulates the movement of the balance wheel in a watch or clock.

hair·streak (hâr′strēk′) *n.* Any of numerous butterflies of the subfamily Theclinae, having transverse streaks on the undersurface of the wings and fine, hairlike projections on the hind wings.

hair stroke *n.* A very fine line in writing or printing.

hair·style (hâr′stīl′) *n.* The design of a coiffure. —**hair′styl′ing** *n.* —**hair′styl′ist** *n.*

hair trigger *n.* A gun trigger adjusted to respond to a very slight pressure.

hair-trig·ger (hâr′trĭg′ər) *adj.* Responding to the slightest provocation or stimulation: *a hair-trigger temper.*

hair·weav·ing (hâr′wē′vĭng) *n.* The process of interweaving a hairpiece of human hair with the wearer's own hair. —**hair′weave′** *v.* —**hair′weav′er** *n.*

hair·worm (hâr′wûrm′) *n.* **1.** Any of various slender, parasitic nematode worms of the genus *Trichostrongylus,* which infest the stomach and small intestine of cattle, sheep, and related animals. **2.** See **horsehair worm.**

hair·y (hâr′ē) *adj.* **-i·er, -i·est.** **1.** Covered with hair or hairlike projections: *a hairy caterpillar.* **2.** Consisting of or resembling hair: *a hairy overcoat.* **3.** *Slang.* Fraught with difficulties; hazardous: *a hairy escape; hairy problems.* —**hair′i·ness** *n.*

Hai·ti (hā′tē). **1.** A country of the West Indies comprising the western part of the island of Hispaniola and two offshore islands. A French colony after 1697, the country became independent in 1804 following a slave revolt led by Toussaint L'Ouverture. Port-au-Prince is the capital and largest city. Population, 5,053,791. **2.** See **Hispaniola.**

Hai·tian (hā′shən, -tē-ən) *adj.* Of or relating to Haiti or its people or culture. —**Haitian** *n.* **1.** A native or inhabitant of Haiti. **2.** Haitian Creole.

Haitian Creole *n.* A language spoken by the majority of Haitians, based on French and various African languages.

haj or **hajj** also **hadj** (hăj) *n., pl.* **haj·es** or **hajj·es** also **hadj·es.** *Islam.* A pilgrimage to Mecca during Dhu'l Hijja, made as an objective of the religious life of a Moslem. [Arabic *ḥajj,* from *ḥajja,* to go on a pilgrimage.]

haj·i or **haj·ji** also **hadj·i** (hăj′ē) *n., pl.* **haj·is** or **haj·jis** also **hadj·is.** *Islam.* **1.** One who has made a pilgrimage to Mecca. **2.** Often used as a form of address for one who has made such a pilgrimage. [Arabic *ḥājjī,* from *ḥajj,* pilgrimage. See HAJ.]

ha·ka (hä′kä) *n.* A Maori war dance accompanied by chanting. [Maori.]

hake (hāk) *n., pl.* **hake** or **hakes.** Any of various marine food fishes of the genera *Merluccius* and *Urophycis,* related to and resembling the cod. [Middle English, possibly from Old English *haca,* hook (from the shape of its lower jaw). See **keg-** in Appendix.]

ha·keem (hä′kēm) *n.* Variant of **hakim¹.**

Ha·ken·kreuz (hä′kən-kroits′) *n.* A swastika. [German : *Haken,* hook (from Middle High German *hāken;* see HAČEK) + *Kreuz,* cross (from Middle High German *kriuze;* see KREUZER).]

ha·kim¹ also **ha·keem** (hä′kēm) *n., pl.* **-kims** also **-keems.** A Moslem physician. [Arabic *ḥakīm,* wise, wise man, from *ḥakama,* to be judicious, exercise authority.]

ha·kim² (hä′kĭm) *n., pl.* **-kims.** A Moslem ruler, provincial governor, or judge. [Arabic *ḥākim,* from *ḥakama,* to exercise authority.]

Hak·luyt (hăk′lo͞ot′), **Richard.** 1552?–1616. English geographer who collected accounts of English exploratory voyages and published them in *Principal Navigations, Voyages, and Discoveries of the English Nation* (1589).

Ha·ko·da·te (hä′kô-dä′tĕ). A city of southwest Hokkaido, Japan, on Tsugaru Strait. Its excellent harbor was first opened to foreign traders in 1854. Population, 319,190.

♦ **ha·ku** (hä′ko͞o) *n. Hawaii.* A crown made of fresh flowers. [Hawaiian, from *haku,* to put in order, make a wreath.]

hal– *pref.* Variant of **halo–.**

Ha·la·kah also **Ha·la·cha** (hä′lä-KHä′, hä-lä′KHə, -lô′-) *n. Judaism.* The legal part of Talmudic literature, an interpretation of the laws of the Scriptures. [Mishnaic Hebrew *hălākâ,* rule,

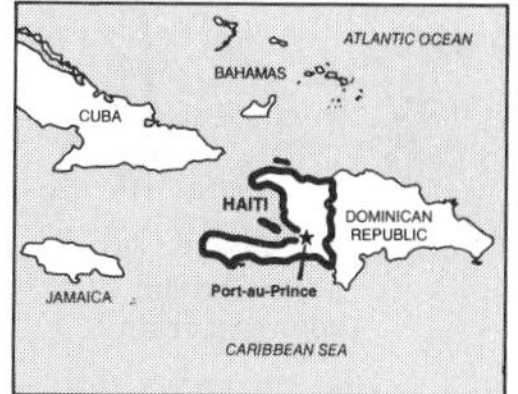

Haiti

haku

ă pat	oi boy
ā pay	ou out
âr care	o͝o took
ä father	o͞o boot
ĕ pet	ŭ cut
ē be	ûr urge
ĭ pit	th thin
ī pie	*th* this
îr pier	hw which
ŏ pot	zh vision
ō toe	ə about, item
ô paw	♦ regionalism

Stress marks: ′ (primary); ′ (secondary), as in **dictionary** (dĭk′shə-nĕr′ē)

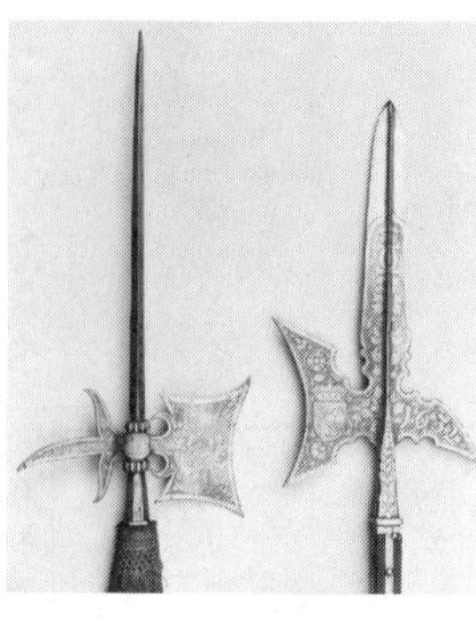

halberd
Left: German
Right: Austrian

tradition, from *hālak,* to go.] —**Ha·lak′ic** (hə-lăk′ĭk, -lä′KHĭk) *adj.*

ha·lal (hə-läl′) *Islam. n.* Meat that has been slaughtered in the manner prescribed by the shari'a. —**halal** *adj.* **1.** Of or being meat slaughtered in the prescribed way: *a halal butcher; a halal label.* **2.** In accordance with or permitted under the shari'a. [Arabic *ḥalāl,* that which is lawful.]

ha·la·la (hə-lä′lə) *n., pl.* **halala** or **-las.** A coin of Saudi Arabia worth 1/100 of a riyal. [Arabic *halalah.*]

ha·la·tion (hā-lā′shən) *n.* **1.** A blurring or spreading of light around bright areas on a photographic image. **2.** An area of glow around a bright object on a television screen. [HAL(O) + –ATION.]

ha·la·vah (hä′lə-vä′) *n.* Variant of **halvah.**

hal·berd (hăl′bərd, hôl′-) also **hal·bert** (-bərt) *n.* A weapon of the 15th and 16th centuries having an axlike blade and a steel spike mounted on the end of a long shaft. [French *hallebarde,* from Old French *alabarde,* from Old Italian *alabarda,* from Middle High German *helmbarde, halmbarte* : *helm,* handle + *barte,* ax (from Old High German *barta;* see **bhardh-ā-** in Appendix).] —**hal′ber·dier′** (-bər-dîr′) *n.*

hal·cy·on (hăl′sē-ən) *n.* **1.** A kingfisher, especially one of the genus *Halcyon.* **2.** A fabled bird, identified with the kingfisher, that was supposed to have had the power to calm the wind and the waves while it nested on the sea during the winter solstice. —**halcyon** *adj.* **1.** Calm and peaceful; tranquil. See Synonyms at **calm. 2.** Prosperous; golden: *halcyon years.* [Middle English *alcioun,* from Latin *alcyōn, halcyōn,* from Greek *halkuōn,* a mythical bird, kingfisher, alteration (influenced by *hals,* salt, sea, and *kuōn,* conceiving) of *alkuōn.*]

Hal·dane (hôl′dā′, -dən). Family of Scottish intellectuals, including **Richard Burdon Haldane** (1856–1928), a philosopher and politician; his sister **Elizabeth Sanderson Haldane** (1862–1937), a writer and Scotland's first woman justice of the peace (1920); their brother **John Scott Haldane** (1860–1936), a physiologist; and his son **John Burdon Sanderson Haldane** (1892–1964), a geneticist.

hale¹ (hāl) *adj.* **hal·er, hal·est.** Free from infirmity or illness; sound. See Synonyms at **healthy.** [Middle English, from Old English *hāl.* See **kailo-** in Appendix.] —**hale′ness** *n.*

hale² (hāl) *tr.v.* **haled, hal·ing, hales. 1.** To compel to go: *"In short order the human rights campaign was haled before a high court of indignation"* (Arthur M. Schlesinger, Jr.). **2.** *Archaic.* To pull, drag, or hoist. [Middle English *halen,* to pull, drag, from Old French *haler,* of Germanic origin. See **kelə-²** in Appendix.]

Hale (hāl), **Edward Everett.** 1822–1909. American Unitarian cleric and writer whose more than 150 literary works include the story "The Man Without a Country" (1863). His sister **Lucretia Peabody Hale** (1820–1900) wrote two noted children's books, *The Peterkin Papers* (1880) and *The Last of the Peterkins* (1886).

Hale, George Ellery. 1868–1938. American astrophysicist who invented the spectroheliograph (1891).

Hale, Nathan. 1755–1776. American Revolutionary soldier hanged by the British as a spy. According to tradition, his last words were "I only regret that I have but one life to lose for my country."

Hale, Sarah Josepha Buell. 1788–1879. American writer and editor of *Godey's Lady's Book* (1837–1877). Her own works include the poem "Mary Had a Little Lamb" (1830).

Ha·le·a·ka·la Crater (hä′lē-ä′kə-lä′). An enormous volcanic crater, 829.6 m (2,720 ft) deep, of eastern Maui, Hawaii. The mountain itself is 3,057 m (10,023 ft) high.

ha·ler (hä′lər, -lĕr′) *n., pl.* **-lers** or **-le·ru** (-lə-ro͞o′). See table at **currency.** [Czech *haléř,* from Middle High German *haller,* an early German silver coin, after Schwäbisch *Hall,* a town of southwest Germany.]

Hale·thorpe (hāl′thôrp). A community of northern Maryland, a suburb of Baltimore. Population, 20,163.

Ha·lé·vy (ä-lā-vē′), **(Jacques François) Fromental (Élie).** 1799–1862. French composer of operatic works, including *La Juive* and *L'Eclair* (both 1835).

Ha·ley (hā′lē), **Alex.** 1921–1992. American writer best known for *Roots* (1976), a fictionalized chronicle tracing his family history back to its African origins.

Haley, William John Clifton, Jr. Known as "Bill." 1925–1981. American singer who with his band, the Comets, recorded "Rock Around the Clock," "Shake, Rattle, and Roll" (both 1954), and other early and influential rock 'n' roll songs.

half (hăf, häf) *n., pl.* **halves** (hăvz, hävz). **1.** *Abbr.* **hf. a.** One of two equal parts that together constitute a whole. **b.** One part approximately equal to the remaining part. **2.** *Informal.* A 50-cent piece. **3.** *Sports.* **a.** One of the two playing periods into which certain games are divided. **b.** A halfback. **4.** *Chiefly British.* A school term; a semester. **5.** Half an hour: *a half past one.* —**half** *adj.* **1.** *Abbr.* **hf. a.** Being one of two equal parts. **b.** Being approximately a half. **2.** Partial or incomplete: *gave me a half smile.* —**half** *adv.* **1.** To the extent of exactly or nearly 50 percent: *The tank is half empty.* **2.** Not completely or sufficiently; partly: *only half right.* —***idioms.*** **by half. 1.** By a considerable extent. **2.** By an excessive amount: *too clever by half.* **by halves.** In a reluctant manner; unenthusiastically. **in half.** Into halves. **not half.** Not at all: *"Fancy housing? Not half likely, ma'am"* (Russell Baker). **not the half of.** Only a fraction or a small part of. [Middle English, from Old English *healf.* See **skel-¹** in Appendix.]

USAGE NOTE: The phrases *a half, half of,* and *half a* or *half an* are all correct, though they may differ slightly in meaning. For example, *a half day* is used when *day* has the special sense "a working day," and the phrase then means "4 hours." *Half of a day* and *half a day* are not restricted in this way and can mean either 4 or 12 hours.

half-and-half (hăf′ənd-hăf′, häf′ənd-häf′) *adj.* Being half one thing and half another: *a half-and-half mixture of linseed oil and turpentine.* —**half-and-half** *adv.* In equal portions. —**half-and-half** *n.* **1.** A mixture of two things in equal portions, especially a mixture of equal parts of milk and cream. **2.** *Chiefly British.* A blend of malt liquors, especially porter and ale.

half-assed (hăf′ăst′, häf′äst′) *adj. Vulgar Slang.* **1.** Not well planned or executed. **2.** Incompetent. —**half′-assed′** *adv.*

half·back (hăf′băk′, häf′-) *n. Abbr.* **hb, hb. 1.** *Football.* **a.** One of the two players positioned near the flanks behind the line of scrimmage. **b.** The position held by this player. **2.** *Sports.* **a.** One of several players in various sports stationed behind the forward line. **b.** The position held by this player.

half-baked (hăf′bākt′, häf′-) *adj.* **1.** Only partly baked. **2.** *Informal.* Insufficiently thought out; ill-conceived: *a half-baked scheme.* **3.** *Informal.* Exhibiting a lack of good judgment or common sense: *a half-baked visionary.*

half binding *n. Printing.* A bookbinding in which the back and often the corners of the volume are bound in a material differing from the rest of the cover.

half blood also **half-blood** (hăf′blŭd′, häf′-) *n.* **1. a.** The relationship existing between persons having only one parent in common. **b.** A person existing in such a relationship. **2.** *Offensive.* A half-breed. **3.** A half-blooded domestic animal.

half-blood·ed (hăf′blŭd′ĭd, häf′-) *adj.* **1.** Having only one parent in common. **2.** Having one parent of pedigreed stock and the other of unknown or mixed ancestry. Used of animals.

half boot *n.* A low boot extending just above the ankle.

half-bound (hăf′bound′, häf′-) *adj. Printing.* Having a half binding.

half-bred (hăf′brĕd′, häf′-) *adj.* Having only one parent that is purebred; half-blooded. Used of animals.

half-breed (hăf′brēd′, häf′-) *n. Offensive.* A person having parents of different ethnic types. —**half-breed** *adj.* Half-blooded; hybrid. Used of animals.

half brother *n.* A brother related through one parent only.

half-caste (hăf′kăst′, häf′käst′) *Offensive. n.* A person of mixed racial descent. —**half-caste** *adj.* Of mixed racial descent.

half-cell (hăf′sĕl′, häf′-) *n.* Either of the two connected parts of an electrochemical cell, consisting of one electrode in a conductive fluid.

half cock *n.* The position of the hammer of a firearm when it is raised halfway and locked by a catch so that the trigger cannot be pulled.

half·cocked (hăf′kŏkt′, häf′-) *adj.* **1.** *Informal.* Inadequately or poorly prepared: *a halfcocked plan to buy out the company.* **2.** Being at the position of half cock. Used of a firearm. —**halfcocked** *adv. Informal.* In an inadequate or poorly prepared manner: *went off halfcocked and bought all the wrong items.*

half-crown (hăf′kroun′, häf′-) *n.* A coin formerly used in Great Britain, worth two shillings and sixpence.

half-dol·lar (hăf′dŏl′ər, häf′-) *n.* A U.S. silver coin worth 50 cents.

half gainer *n. Sports.* A dive in which the diver springs from the board facing forward, rotates backward in the air in a half backward somersault, and enters the water headfirst, facing the board.

half·heart·ed (hăf′här′tĭd, häf′-) *adj.* Exhibiting or feeling little interest, enthusiasm, or heart; uninspired: *a halfhearted attempt at writing a novel.* —**half′heart′ed·ly** *adv.* —**half′heart′ed·ness** *n.*

half hitch *n.* A knot or hitch made by looping a rope or strap around an object and then back around itself, bringing the end of the rope through the loop.

half-hour (hăf′our′, häf′-) *n.* **1.** A period of 30 minutes. **2.** The middle point of an hour: *The clock chimes on the half-hour.* —**half′-hour′ly** *adv. & adj.*

half-in·te·gral (hăf′ĭn′tĭ-grəl, häf′-) *adj. Mathematics.* Having an integer as a numerator and 2 as a denominator. Used of a fraction.

half-length (hăf′lĕngkth′, -lĕngth′, häf′-) *n.* A portrait that shows only the upper half and hands of a person. —**half-length** *adj.* **1.** Of or relating to a half-length portrait. **2.** Of half the full length.

half-life (hăf′līf′, häf′-) *n.* **1.** *Physics.* The time required for half the nuclei in a sample of a specific isotopic species to undergo radioactive decay. **2.** *Biology.* **a.** The time required for half the quantity of a drug or other substance deposited in a living organism to be metabolized or eliminated by normal biological processes. Also called *biological half-life.* **b.** The time required for the radioactivity of material taken in by a living organism to be reduced to half its initial value by a combination of biological elimination processes and radioactive decay.

half-light (hăf′līt′, häf′-) *n.* The soft, subdued light seen at dusk or dawn or in dimly lit interiors.

half-line or **half line** (hăf′līn′, häf′-) *n. Mathematics.* See **ray**[1] (sense 4).

half-mast (hăf′măst′, häf′mäst′) *n.* The position about halfway up a mast or pole at which a flag is flown as a symbol of mourning for the dead or as a signal of distress. Also called *half-staff.* **—half-mast** *tr.v.* **-mast·ed, -mast·ing, -masts.** To place (a flag) halfway up a mast or pole.

half-moon (hăf′mo͞on′, häf′-) *n.* **1.** The moon when only half its disk is illuminated. **2.** Something, such as the lunula of a fingernail, that is shaped like a crescent.

half nelson *n. Sports.* A wrestling hold in which one arm is passed under the opponent's arm from behind to the back of the neck.

half note *n. Music.* A note having one half the value of a whole note.

half·pen·ny (hā′pə-nē, hāp′nē) *n., pl.* **half·pence** (hā′pəns) or **half·pen·nies. 1.a.** A British coin worth one half of a new penny. **b.** A British coin worth one half of an old penny, no longer in circulation. **2.** The sum of one half of a penny.

half-pint (hăf′pīnt′, häf′-) *n. Slang.* A small person or animal.

half relief *n.* Sculptural relief composed of modeled forms that project approximately halfway from the background. Also called *demirelief, mezzo-relievo.*

half rhyme *n.* See **off rhyme.**

half sister *n.* A sister related through one parent only.

half-slip (hăf′slĭp′, häf′-) *n.* A woman's slip that hangs from the waist.

half sole *n.* A shoe sole that extends from the shank to the toe.

half-sole (hăf′sōl′, häf′-) *tr.v.* **-soled, -sol·ing, -soles.** To fit or repair with a half sole.

half-staff (hăf′stăf′, häf′stäf′) *n.* See **half-mast.**

half step *n.* **1.** *Music.* See **semitone. 2.** A marching step of 15 inches (38 centimeters) at quick time and 18 inches (46 centimeters) at double time.

half-tim·bered (hăf′tĭm′bərd, häf′-) also **half-tim·ber** (-bər) *adj.* Having a wooden framework with plaster, brick, stone, or other masonry filling the spaces.

half·time (hăf′tīm′, häf′-) *n. Abbr.* **HT** *Sports.* The intermission between halves in certain games, such as basketball or football.

half title *n. Printing.* The title of a book printed at the top of the first page of the text or on a full page preceding the main title page.

half·tone (hăf′tōn′, häf′-) *n. Abbr.* **HT 1.** A tone or value halfway between a highlight and a dark shadow. **2.a.** A picture in which the gradations of light are obtained by the relative darkness and density of tiny dots produced by photographing the subject through a fine screen. **b.** A picture made by such a process.

half tone *n. Music.* See **semitone.**

half-track (hăf′trăk′, häf′-) *n.* A lightly armored military motor vehicle, with caterpillar treads in place of wheels.

half-truth (hăf′tro͞oth′, häf′-) *n.* A statement, especially one intended to deceive, that omits some of the facts necessary for a full description or account.

half volley *n. Sports.* A stroke in certain games, such as tennis, in which the ball is hit immediately after it bounces off the ground.

half·way (hăf′wā′, häf′-) *adj.* **1.** Midway between two points or conditions: *a halfway sign on the trail.* **2.** Reaching or including only half or a portion; partial: *halfway measures.* **—half′way′** *adv.*

halfway house *n.* **1.** A rehabilitation center where people who have left an institution, such as a hospital or prison, are helped to readjust to the outside world. **2.** A stopping place, such as an inn, that marks the midpoint of a journey.

half-wit (hăf′wĭt′, häf′-) *n. Offensive.* A person regarded as foolish or stupid. **—half′-wit′ted** *adj.* **—half′-wit′ted·ly** *adv.* **—half′-wit′ted·ness** *n.*

hal·i·but (hăl′ə-bət, hŏl′-) *n., pl.* **halibut** or **-buts.** Any of several large, edible flatfishes of the genus *Hippoglossus* and related genera, of northern Atlantic or Pacific waters. [Middle English : *hali, holi,* holy (from its being eaten on holy days); see HOLY + *butte,* flatfish (from Middle Dutch; see **bhau-** in Appendix).]

Hal·i·car·nas·sus (hăl′ĭ-kär-năs′əs). An ancient Greek city of southwest Asia Minor on the Aegean Sea in present-day Turkey. In the fourth century B.C. Queen Artemisia built a magnificent tomb here for her husband, King Mausolus. His mausoleum was considered one of the Seven Wonders of the World.

hal·ide (hăl′īd′, hā′līd′) *n.* A chemical compound of a halogen with a more electropositive element or group.

hal·i·dom (hăl′ĭ-dəm) *n. Obsolete.* **1.** Something considered holy. **2.** A sanctuary. [Middle English, from Old English *hālig-dōm* : *hālig,* holy; see HOLY + *-dōm,* -dom.]

Hal·i·fax (hăl′ə-făks′). **1.** The capital and largest city of Nova Scotia, Canada, in the south-central part of the province on the Atlantic Ocean. Founded in 1749, it served as an important naval base in the American Revolution, the War of 1812, and both World Wars. Population, 114,594. **2.** An industrial borough of northeast England northeast of Manchester. Population, 192,500.

Halifax, First Earl of. Title of Edward Frederick Lindley Wood. 1881–1959. British public official who was viceroy of India (1926–1931) and foreign secretary (1938–1940).

hal·ite (hăl′īt′, hā′līt′) *n.* **1.** A colorless or white mineral, NaCl, occurring as cubic crystals and found in dried lakebeds in acrid climates, mined or gathered for use as table salt. **2.** Rock salt.

hal·i·to·sis (hăl′ĭ-tō′sĭs) *n.* The condition of having stale or foul-smelling breath. [Latin *hālitus,* breath (akin to *hālāre,* to breathe) + –OSIS.]

hall (hôl) *n.* **1.** A corridor or passageway in a building. **2.** A large entrance room or vestibule in a building; a lobby. **3.a.** A building for public gatherings or entertainments. **b.** The large room in which such events are held. **4.** A building used for the meetings, entertainments, or living quarters of a fraternity, sorority, church, or other social or religious organization. **5.a.** A building belonging to a school, college, or university that provides classroom, dormitory, or dining facilities. **b.** A large room in such a building. **c.** The group of students using such a building: *The entire hall stayed up late studying.* **d.** *Chiefly British.* A meal served in such a building. **6.** The main house on a landed estate. **7.a.** The castle or house of a medieval monarch or noble. **b.** The principal room in such a castle or house, used for dining, entertaining, and sleeping. [Middle English *halle,* large residence, from Old English *heall.* See **kel-**[1] in Appendix.]

WORD HISTORY: The *halls of academe* and *city hall* remind us that what we commonly mean by the word *hall,* "a passageway, an entrance room," represents a shrunken version of what *hall* once commonly designated. Going back to the Indo-European root *kel-*[1], "to cover," the Old English word *heall,* ancestor of our *hall,* referred to "a large place covered by a roof, whether a royal residence, an official building, or a large private residence, or a large room in a residence where the public life of the household is carried on." These senses and related ones are still in use, as is attested by *town hall* and *halls of academe.* Our common use of the term *hall* for a vestibule or a corridor harks back to medieval times when the hall was the main public room of a residence and people lived much less privately than now. As private rooms in houses took on the importance they have today, the hall lost its function. *Hall* also had come to mean any large room, and the vestibule was at one time one of the main sitting rooms in a house, but this sort of room has largely disappeared also, and *hall* has become the designation for the small vestibule of today as well as for an entrance passage or any passageway.

Hall (hôl), **Asaph.** 1829–1907. American astronomer who discovered the two satellites of Mars, Deimos and Phobos (1877).

Hall, Charles Francis. 1821–1871. American explorer who led three expeditions to the Arctic (1860–1862, 1864–1869, and 1871).

Hall, Charles Martin. 1863–1914. American chemist who developed an electrolytic method of economically producing aluminum from bauxite (1886).

Hall, Granville Stanley. 1844–1924. American psychologist who founded child psychology and profoundly influenced educational psychology.

hal·lah (KHä′lə, hä′-) *n.* Variant of **challah.**

Hal·lam (hăl′əm), **Henry.** 1777–1859. British historian whose accurate but uncolorful works include *Europe During the Middle Ages* (1818). The death of his son **Arthur Henry Hallam** (1811–1833) inspired Tennyson's poem *In Memoriam.*

Hal·lan·dale (hăl′ən-dāl′). A city of southeast Florida on the Atlantic Ocean south of Fort Lauderdale. It is a processing center for fruits and vegetables. Population, 36,517.

Hal·le (hä′lə). A city of central Germany on the Saale River west-northwest of Leipzig. First mentioned in the 9th century, it was an important member of the Hanseatic League in the Middle Ages. Population, 236,139.

Hal·leck (hăl′ĭk, -ək), **Fitz-Greene.** 1790–1867. American poet whose Byronic works include *Fanny* (1819) and "Marcos Bozzaris" (1825).

Halleck, Henry Wager. 1815–1872. American Union general who served as general in chief (1862–1864) but was replaced by Gen. Ulysses S. Grant.

Hall effect *n.* Generation of an electric potential perpendicular to both an electric current flowing along a conducting material and an external magnetic field applied at right angles to the current upon application of the magnetic field. [After Edwin Herbert *Hall* (1855–1938), American physicist.]

hal·lel (hä-lāl′, hä′lāl) *n. Judaism.* A chant of praise consisting of Psalms 113 through 118, used during Passover and on certain other holidays. [Hebrew *hallēl,* song of praise, from *hillēl,* to praise.]

hal·le·lu·jah (hăl′ə-lo͞o′yə) *interj.* Used to express praise or joy. **—hallelujah** *n.* **1.** An exclamation of "hallelujah." **2.** *Music.* A composition expressing praise and based on the word "hallelujah." [Hebrew *hallĕlûyāh,* praise the Lord : *hallĕlu,* pl. imperative of *hillēl,* to praise + *Yāh,* God (short for *Yahweh*).]

Hal·ley (hăl′ē), **Edmund** or **Edmond.** 1656–1742. English astronomer who applied Newton's laws of motion to predict correctly the period of a comet (1705).

Edmund Halley

ă pat	oi boy
ā pay	ou out
âr care	o͝o took
ä father	o͞o boot
ĕ pet	ŭ cut
ē be	ûr urge
ĭ pit	th thin
ī pie	*th* this
îr pier	hw which
ŏ pot	zh vision
ō toe	ə about, item
ô paw	♦ regionalism

Stress marks: ′ (primary); ′ (secondary), as in **dictionary** (dĭk′shə-nĕr′ē)

Halley's comet
In 1986

halo
Detail of a chasuble

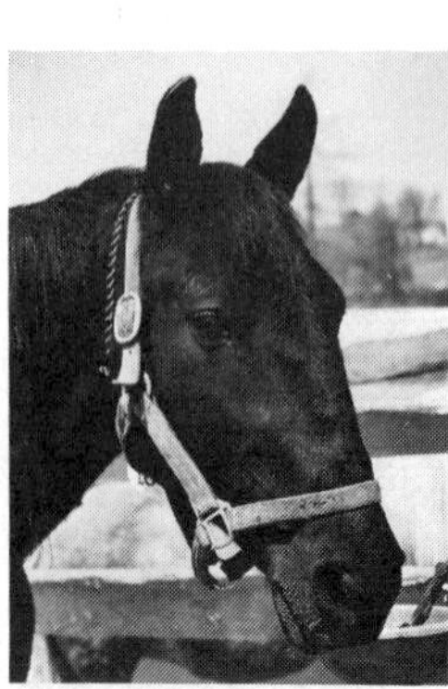
halter¹

Hal·ley's comet (hăl′ē, hā′lēz) *n.* A comet with a period of approximately 76 years, the first one for which a return was successfully predicted. It last appeared in 1986. [After Edmund HALLEY.]

hal·liard (hăl′yərd) *n. Nautical.* Variant of **halyard.**

hall·mark (hôl′märk′) *n.* **1.** A mark indicating quality or excellence. **2.** A mark used in England to stamp gold and silver articles that meet established standards of purity. **3.** A conspicuous feature or characteristic: *"The sense of guilt is the hallmark of civilized humanity"* (Theodor Reik). **—hallmark** *tr.v.* **-marked, -mark·ing, -marks.** To stamp (gold and silver articles) with a mark indicating purity. [After Goldsmith's *Hall* in London, England, where gold and silver articles were appraised and stamped.]

hal·loa (hə-lō′) *interj., n. & v.* Variant of **halloo.**

hall of fame *n., pl.* **halls of fame. 1.** A group of persons judged outstanding, as in a sport or profession. **2.** A building housing memorial items honoring illustrious persons.

hal·loo (hə-lo͞o′) also **hal·loa** (-lō′) *—interj.* **1.** Used to catch someone's attention. **2.** Used to urge on hounds in a hunt. *—n., pl.* **-loos** also **-loas.** A shout or call of "halloo." *—v.* **-looed, -loo·ing, -loos** also **-loaed, -loa·ing, -loas.** *—intr.* To shout "halloo." *—tr.* **1.** To urge on or pursue by calling "halloo" or shouting. **2.** To call out to. **3.** To shout or yell (something). [Alteration of obsolete *holla,* stop! See HELLO.]

hal·low (hăl′ō) *tr.v.* **-lowed, -low·ing, -lows. 1.** To make or set apart as holy. **2.** To respect or honor greatly. [Middle English *halwen,* from Old English *hālgian.* See **kailo-** in Appendix.]

hal·lowed (hăl′ōd) *adj.* **1.** Sanctified; consecrated: *a hallowed cemetery.* **2.** Highly venerated; sacrosanct: *our hallowed war heroes.*

Hal·low·een also **Hal·low·e'en** (hăl′ə-wēn′, hŏl′-) *n.* October 31, celebrated in the United States, Canada, and the British Isles by children going door to door while wearing costumes and begging treats and playing pranks. [Short for *All Hallow Even* : ALLHALLOW(MAS) + EVEN².]

Hal·low·mas also **Hal·low·mass** (hăl′ō-məs, -măs′) *n. Archaic.* All Saints' Day. [Short for ALLHALLOWMAS.]

Hall·statt (hôl′stăt′, häl′shtät′) *adj.* Of or relating to a dominant Iron Age culture of central and western Europe, probably Celtic, that flourished from the ninth to the fifth century B.C. [After the type-site at *Hallstatt,* a village of northern Austria.]

hal·lu·ces (hăl′yə-sēz′, hăl′ə-) *n.* Plural of **hallux.**

hal·lu·ci·nate (hə-lo͞o′sə-nāt′) *v.* **-nat·ed, -nat·ing, -nates.** *—intr.* To undergo hallucination. *—tr.* To cause to have hallucinations. [Latin *hallūcinārī, hallūcināt-,* to dream, be deceived, variant of *ālūcinārī.*] **—hal·lu′ci·na′tor** *n.*

hal·lu·ci·na·tion (hə-lo͞o′sə-nā′shən) *n.* **1.a.** False or distorted perception of objects or events with a compelling sense of their reality, usually resulting from a mental disorder or as a response to a drug. **b.** The objects or events so perceived. **2.** A false or mistaken idea; a delusion. **—hal·lu′ci·na′tion·al, hal·lu′ci·na′tive** *adj.*

hal·lu·ci·na·to·ry (hə-lo͞o′sə-nə-tôr′ē, -tōr′ē) *adj.* **1.** Of or characterized by hallucination. **2.** Inducing hallucination.

hal·lu·cin·o·gen (hə-lo͞o′sə-nə-jən) *n.* A substance that induces hallucination. [HALLUCIN(ATION) + -GEN.] **—hal·lu′cin·o·gen′ic** (-jĕn′ĭk) *adj.*

hal·lu·ci·no·sis (hə-lo͞o′sə-nō′sĭs) *n.* An abnormal condition or mental state characterized by hallucination. [HALLUCIN(ATION) + -OSIS.]

hal·lux (hăl′əks) *n., pl.* **hal·lu·ces** (hăl′yə-sēz′, hăl′ə-). **1.** The innermost or first digit on the hind foot of certain mammals. In human beings, it is commonly called the big toe. **2.** A homologous digit of a bird, a reptile, or an amphibian. In birds, it is often directed backward. [Latin *hallux, hallus.*]

hall·way (hôl′wā′) *n.* **1.** A corridor in a building. **2.** An entrance hall.

halm (hôm) *n.* Variant of **haulm.**

Hal·ma·he·ra (hăl′mə-hĕr′ə, häl′mä-hĕ′rä). An island of eastern Indonesia between New Guinea and Sulawesi. Irregular in shape, it is the largest of the Moluccas.

ha·lo (hā′lō) *n., pl.* **-los** or **-loes. 1.a.** A circular band of colored light around a light source, as around the sun or moon, caused by the refraction and reflection of light by ice particles suspended in the intervening atmosphere. **b.** Something resembling this band. **2.** A luminous ring or disk of light surrounding the heads or bodies of sacred figures, such as saints, in religious paintings; a nimbus. **3.** The aura of majesty or glory surrounding a person, a thing, or an event that is regarded with reverence, awe, or sentiment. **—halo** *tr.v.* **-loed, -lo·ing, -loes.** To encircle with or as if with a halo. [Medieval Latin *halō,* from accusative of Latin *halōs,* from Greek, threshing floor, disk of or around the sun or moon.]

halo– or **hal–** *pref.* **1.** Salt: *halophyte.* **2.** Halogen: *halocarbon.* [French, from Greek, from *hals, hal-,* salt, sea. See **sal-** in Appendix.]

hal·o·bi·ont (hăl′ō-bī′ŏnt) *n.* An organism that lives or grows in a salty environment.

hal·o·car·bon (hăl′ə-kär′bən) *n.* A compound, such as a fluorocarbon, that consists of carbon and one or more halogens.

hal·o·cline (hăl′ə-klīn′) *n.* A vertical gradient in ocean salinity.

hal·o·gen (hăl′ə-jən) *n.* Any of a group of five chemically related nonmetallic elements including fluorine, chlorine, bromine, iodine, and astatine. [Swedish : *halo-,* halo- + *-gen,* -gen.] **—ha·log′e·nous** (hă-lŏj′ə-nəs) *adj.*

hal·o·ge·nate (hăl′ə-jə-nāt′) *tr.v.* **-nat·ed, -nat·ing, -nates.** To treat or combine with a halogen. **—hal′o·ge·na′tion** *n.*

ha·lon (hā′lŏn) *n.* Any of several halocarbons used as fire-extinguishing agents.

hal·o·per·i·dol (hăl′ō-pĕr′ĭ-dôl′, -dŏl′, -dōl′) *n.* A tranquilizer, $C_{21}H_{23}ClFNO_2$, used especially in the treatment of psychotic disorders, including schizophrenia. [HALO– + (PI)PERID(INE) + -OL¹.]

hal·o·phile (hăl′ə-fīl′) *n.* An organism that requires a salty environment. **—hal′o·phil′ic** (-fĭl′ĭk), **ha·loph′i·lous** (hă-lŏf′ə-ləs) *adj.*

hal·o·phyte (hăl′ə-fīt′) *n.* A plant that grows in saline soil. **—hal′o·phyt′ic** (-fĭt′ĭk) *adj.*

hal·o·thane (hăl′ə-thān′) *n.* A colorless, nonflammable liquid, $C_2HBrClF_3$, used as an inhalational anesthetic. [HALO– + (E)THANE.]

Hals (hälz, häls), **Frans.** 1580?–1666. Dutch painter of genre scenes and portraits, such as *The Laughing Cavalier* (1624).

Hal·sey (hôl′zē), **William Frederick.** Known as "Bull." 1882–1959. American naval officer who during World War II led American naval forces to several important victories, including the Battle of Leyte Gulf (1944).

Häl·sing·borg or **Hel·sing·borg** (hĕl′sĭng-bôrg′, hĕl′sĭng-bôr′ē). A city of southwest Sweden on the Oresund opposite Sjaelland. It belonged to Denmark until the mid-1600's. Population, 104,689.

halt¹ (hôlt) *n.* A suspension of movement or progress, especially a temporary one. **—halt** *v.* **halt·ed, halt·ing, halts.** *—tr.* To cause to stop; arrest. *—intr.* To stop; pause. See Synonyms at **stop.** [German, from Middle High German, from imperative of *halten,* to stop, hold back, from Old High German *haltan.*]

halt² (hôlt) *intr.v.* **halt·ed, halt·ing, halts. 1.** To proceed or act with uncertainty or indecision; waver. **2.** To be defective or proceed poorly, as in the development of an argument in logic or in the rhythmic structure of verse. **3.** To limp or hobble. **—halt** *adj. Archaic.* Lame; crippled. [Middle English *halten,* to limp, from Old English *healtian.*]

hal·ter¹ (hôl′tər) *n.* **1.** A device made of rope or leather straps that fits around the head or neck of an animal and is used to lead or secure the animal. **2.a.** A rope with a noose used for execution by hanging. **b.** Death or execution by hanging. **3.** A bodice for women that ties behind the neck and across the back, leaving the arms, shoulders, and back bare. **—halter** *tr.v.* **-tered, -ter·ing, -ters. 1.** To put a halter on. **2.** To control with or as if with a halter. **3.** To hang (someone). [Middle English, from Old English *hælftre.*]

hal·ter² (hôl′tər, hăl′-) *n., pl.* **-ter·es** (-tîr′ēz). Either of the small, clublike balancing organs that are the rudimentary hind wings of flies and other dipterous insects. Also called *balancer.* [Latin *haltēr,* lead weights used in leaping exercises, from sing. of Greek *haltēres,* from *hallesthai,* to jump. See **sel-** in Appendix.]

hal·ter-top (hôl′tər-tŏp′) *n.* A woman's halter. **—halter-top** *adj.* Designed so as to include such a halter: *halter-top dresses.*

halt·ing (hôl′tĭng) *adj.* **1.** Hesitant or wavering: *a halting voice.* **2.** Imperfect; defective: *halting verse.* **3.** Limping; lame. **—halt′ing·ly** *adv.*

Hal·tom City (hôl′təm). A city of northeast Texas, a suburb of Fort Worth. Population, 29,014.

Hal·ton Hills (hôl′tən). A town of southeast Ontario, Canada, a suburb of Toronto. Population, 35,190.

hal·vah or **hal·va** (häl-vä′, häl′vä) also **ha·la·vah** (hä′lə-vä′) *n.* A confection consisting of crushed sesame seeds in a binder of honey. [From Turkish *helva,* from Arabic *ḥalwā.*]

halve (hăv, häv) *tr.v.* **halved, halv·ing, halves. 1.** To divide (something) into two equal portions or parts. **2.** To lessen or reduce by half: *halved the recipe to serve two.* **3.** *Informal.* To share (something) equally: *The twins halve everything.* **4.** *Sports.* To play (a golf game or hole) using the same number of strokes as one's opponent. [Middle English *halven,* from *half,* half. See HALF.]

halves (hăvz, hävz) *n.* Plural of **half.**

hal·yard also **hal·liard** (hăl′yərd) *n. Nautical.* A rope used to raise or lower a sail, flag, or yard. [Alteration (influenced by YARD¹) of Middle English *halier,* from *halen,* to pull. See HALE².]

ham (hăm) *n.* **1.** The thigh of the hind leg of certain animals, especially a hog. **2.** A cut of meat from the thigh of a hog. **3.** The back of the knee. **4.** The back of the thigh. **5. hams.** The buttocks. **6.** An actor who overacts or a performer who exaggerates. **7.** A licensed amateur radio operator. **—ham** *v.* **hammed, ham·ming, hams.** *—intr.* To overact. *—tr.* To exaggerate or overdo (a dramatic role, for example). [Middle English *hamme,* from Old English *hamm.* N., senses 6 and 7, possibly from *ham-fatter,* a poor or amateurish actor.]

Ham (hăm). In the Old Testament, a son of Noah and the brother of Japheth and Shem.

Ha·ma or **Ha·mah** (hä′mä). A city of western Syria south-southwest of Aleppo. Settled probably in the Bronze Age, it was a Hittite center in the second millennium B.C. and is frequently mentioned in the Bible as Hamath. Population, 177,208.

Ham·a·dan (hăm′ə-dăn′, -dän′). A city of western Iran west-southwest of Tehran. An ancient city, it was captured by Alexander the Great in 330 B.C. and later ruled by Seleucid kings, Romans, and Arabs (after A.D. 645). Population, 234,000.

ham·a·dry·ad (hăm′ə-drī′əd) *n., pl.* **-ads** or **-a·des** (-ə-dēz′). **1.** *Greek & Roman Mythology.* A wood nymph who lives only as long as the tree of which she is the spirit lives. **2.** See **king cobra.** [Middle English *amadriad,* from Latin *Hamadryas, Hamadryad-,* from Greek *Hamadruas* : *hama,* together with; see **sem-**[1] in Appendix + *Druas,* dryad (from *drus,* oak; see **deru-** in Appendix).]

ham·a·dry·as (hăm′ə-drī′əs) *n.* A baboon *(Papio hamadryas)* of northern Africa and Arabia, the adult male of which has a heavy mane. Also called *sacred baboon.* [Latin, hamadryad. See HAMADRYAD.]

Ha·mah (hä′mä). See **Hama.**

ha·mal also **ham·mal** (hə-mäl′) *n.* A porter or bearer in certain Moslem countries. [Arabic *ḥammāl,* from *ḥamala,* to carry.]

Ha·ma·ma·tsu (hä′mə-mät′so͞o). A city of southern Honshu, Japan, east-southeast of Nagoya. It is an industrial center. Population, 514,118.

Ha·man (hā′mən). In the Old Testament, a Persian minister who was hanged for plotting the destruction of the Jews.

ha·mar·ti·a (hä′mär-tē′ə) *n.* Tragic flaw. [Greek, from *hamartanein,* to miss the mark, err.]

ha·mate (hā′māt′) *Anatomy. adj.* Hooked at the tip. **—hamate** *n.* A small, hook-shaped carpal bone of the wrist. Also called *unciform.* [Latin *hāmātus,* from *hāmus,* hook.]

Ham·burg (hăm′bûrg′, häm′bo͝org′, -bo͝ork′). A city of northern Germany on the Elbe River northeast of Bremen. Founded by Charlemagne as a defensive citadel in the early ninth century, the city quickly grew in commercial importance and in 1241 formed an alliance with Lübeck that became the basis for the Hanseatic League. Population, 1,592,447.

ham·burg·er (hăm′bûr′gər) also **ham·burg** (-bûrg′) *n.* **1.a.** Ground meat, usually beef. **b.** A patty of such meat. **2.** A sandwich made with a patty of ground meat usually in a roll or bun. *—attributive.* Often used to modify another noun: *hamburger patties; hamburger restaurants.* [Short for *Hamburger steak,* after HAMBURG.]

WORD HISTORY: After having eaten countless hamburgers, one may perhaps be interested in knowing more about the origins of the name. By the middle of the 19th century people in Hamburg, Germany, the busiest port in West Germany today, enjoyed pounded beefsteak in some form. Perhaps brought to America by the large numbers of Germans who migrated around that time, this sort of dish with the name *Hamburg steak* may have appeared on a menu as early as 1836. The first recorded use of *Hamburg steak* is found in 1884 in the *Boston Journal,* with *hamburger steak* being first recorded in a Walla Walla, Washington, newspaper in 1889. A 1902 cookbook contains a recipe for Hamburg steak that is closer to our conception, a recipe using ground beef mixed with onion and pepper. The hamburger was on its way, as was the Americanism *hamburger.*

Ham·den (hăm′dən). A town of southern Connecticut, a suburb of New Haven. Population, 51,071.

hame (hām) *n.* One of the two curved wooden or metal pieces of a harness that fits around the neck of a draft animal and to which the traces are attached. [Middle English, from Middle Dutch. See **tkei-** in Appendix.]

Ha·meln (hä′məln) also **Ham·e·lin** (hăm′ə-lĭn, hăm′lĭn). A city of northern Germany on the Weser River southwest of Hanover. An ancient Saxon settlement, it is a manufacturing and tourist center famous as the setting for the legend of the Pied Piper of Hamelin. Population, 55,992.

ham-fist·ed (hăm′fĭs′tĭd) *adj.* Ham-handed.

ham-hand·ed (hăm′ hăn′dĭd) *adj.* **1.** Clumsy; maladroit; heavy-handed. **2.** Having unusually large hands.

Ha·mil·car Bar·ca (hə-mĭl′kär′ bär′kə, hăm′əl-). 270?–228? B.C. Carthaginian general and father of Hannibal. He led Carthaginian forces during the final years of the First Punic War (264–241). After making peace with the Romans, he returned to Carthage and quelled a rebellion of mercenary troops.

Ham·il·ton (hăm′əl-tən). **1.** The capital of Bermuda, on Bermuda Island. Founded in 1790, it is an important tourist resort. Population, 1,676. **2.** A city of southeast Ontario, Canada, at the western end of Lake Ontario southwest of Toronto. It is an industrial center and a thriving port. Population, 306,434. **3.** A burgh of south-central Scotland southeast of Glasgow in a coal and iron region. Population, 51,900. **4.** A city of southwest Ohio north of Cincinnati. It was settled on the site of Fort Hamilton, built in 1791. Population, 63,189.

Hamilton, Alexander. 1755?–1804. American politician. The first U.S. secretary of the treasury (1789–1795), he established the national bank and public credit system. Hamilton was mortally wounded in a duel with his political rival Aaron Burr. **—Ham′il·to′ni·an** (-tō′nē-ən) *adj. n.*

Hamilton, Alice. 1869–1970. American toxicologist and physician known for her research on occupational poisons and her book *Industrial Poisons in the United States* (1925).

Hamilton, Edith. 1867–1963. German-born American classicist noted for her engaging studies of ancient life, particularly *The Greek Way* (1930).

Hamilton, Lady **Emma Lyon.** 1765?–1815. British socialite. She became Horatio Nelson's lover in 1798 and had a daughter with him in 1801.

Hamilton, Mount. A peak, 1,285 m (4,213 ft) high, of western California east of San Jose. It is the site of Lick Observatory, built in 1876 to 1888 and directed by the University of California.

Ham·il·to·ni·an (hăm′əl-tō′nē-ən) *n. Abbr.* **H** *Physics.* A mathematical function that can be used systematically and with great generality to generate the equations of motion of a dynamic system, equal for many such systems to the sum of the kinetic and potential energies of the system expressed in terms of the system's coordinates and momenta treated as independent variables. [After Sir William Rowan *Hamilton* (1805–1865), Irish mathematician.]

Hamilton Inlet. A deep inlet of the northern Atlantic Ocean in southeast Labrador connecting with Lake Melville.

Ham·ite (hăm′īt′) *n.* A member of a group of peoples of northern and northeast Africa, including the Berbers, Tuaregs, and the ancient Egyptians and their descendants. [After HAM.]

Ha·mit·ic (hă-mĭt′ĭk) *adj.* Of or relating to the Hamites or their languages or cultures. **—Hamitic** *n.* A presumed language family formerly thought to include Egyptian and the Berber, Cushitic, and Chadic languages.

Ham·i·to-Se·mit·ic (hăm′ĭ-tō-sə-mĭt′ĭk) *n.* Afro-Asiatic. No longer in technical use. [HAMIT(IC) + SEMITIC.]

ham·let (hăm′lĭt) *n.* A small village. [Middle English *hamelet,* from Old French, diminutive of *hamel,* diminutive of *ham,* village, of Germanic origin. See **tkei-** in Appendix.]

Ham·lin (hăm′lən), **Hannibal.** 1809–1891. Vice President of the United States (1861–1865) under Abraham Lincoln.

Hamm (hăm, häm). A city of west-central Germany in the Ruhr district south-southeast of Münster. Founded c. 1226, it was an active member of the Hanseatic League after 1417. Population, 166,641.

ham·mal (hə-mäl′) *n.* Variant of **hamal.**

Ham·mar·skjöld (hä′mər-shōld′, -shəld, hăm′ər-, hä′mär-shœld′), **Dag Hjalmar Agné Carl.** 1905–1961. Swedish political leader and secretary-general of the United Nations (1953–1961) who greatly increased the influence of the organization through his peacekeeping efforts in Suez, Lebanon, and the Congo. He won the 1961 Nobel Peace Prize posthumously.

ham·mer (hăm′ər) *n.* **1.** A hand tool used to exert an impulsive force by striking, consisting of a handle with a perpendicularly attached head made of a relatively heavy, rigid material. **2.** A tool or device similar in function or action to this striking tool, as: **a.** The part of a gunlock that hits the primer or firing pin or explodes the percussion cap and causes the gun to fire. **b.** *Music.* One of the padded wooden pieces of a piano that strikes the strings. **c.** A part of an apparatus that strikes a gong or bell, as in a clock. **3.** *Anatomy.* See **malleus. 4.** *Sports.* A metal ball weighing 16 pounds (7.2 kilograms) and having a long wire or wooden handle by which it is thrown for distance in track-and-field competition. **5.** A small mallet used by auctioneers. **—hammer** *v.* **-mered, -mer·ing, -mers.** *—tr.* **1.** To hit, especially repeatedly, with or as if with a hammer; pound. See Synonyms at **beat. 2.** To beat into a shape with or as if with a hammer: *hammered out the dents in the fender; hammered out a contract acceptable to both sides.* **3.** To put together, fasten, or seal, particularly with nails, by hammering. **4.** To force upon by constant repetition: *hammered the information into the students' heads.* *—intr.* **1.** To deal repeated blows with or as if with a hammer; pummel: *"Wind hammered at us violently in gusts"* (Thor Heyerdahl). **2.** To undergo beating in the manner of a hammer: *My pulse hammered.* **3.** *Informal.* To keep at something continuously: *hammered away at the problem.* **—idiom. go** (or **come**) **under the hammer.** To be put up for auction. [Middle English *hamer,* from Old English *hamor.* See **ak-** in Appendix.]

hammer and sickle *n.* An emblem of the Communist movement signifying the alliance of workers and peasants.

hammer and tongs *adv.* With tremendous energy or effort; vigorously: *worked hammer and tongs to meet the deadline.*

ham·mered (hăm′ərd) *adj.* Shaped or worked with a metalworker's hammer and often showing the marks of these tools: *a bowl of hammered brass.*

Ham·mer·fest (hăm′ər-fĕst′, hä′mər-). A town of northern Norway on an island in the Arctic Ocean. It is the northernmost town of Europe, with uninterrupted daylight from May 17 to July 29. Population, 7,208.

ham·mer·head (hăm′ər-hĕd′) *n.* **1.** The head of a hammer. **2.** Any of several large predatory sharks of the genus *Sphyrna,* having the sides of the head elongated into large, fleshy extensions with the eyes at the ends. **3.** A wading bird *(Scopus umbretta)* of Africa and southwest Asia, having brown plumage, a large bladelike bill, and a long, backward-pointing crest. Also called *hammerkop, umbrette.* **4.** An African fruit bat *(Hypsignathus monstrosus),* the male of which has a distinctive, enlarged head.

ham·mer·kop (hăm′ər-kŏp′) *n.* See **hammerhead** (sense 3). [Partial translation of Afrikaans *hamerkop* : *hamer,* hammer +

hamadryas
Papio hamadryas

hame
Pair of connected hames

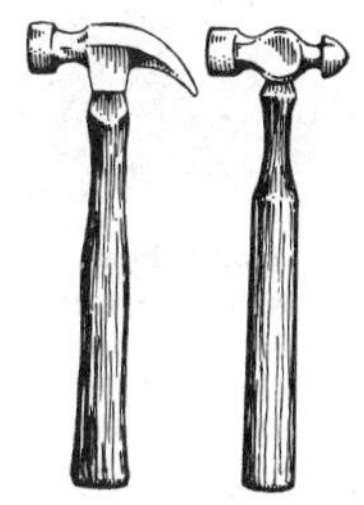

hammer
Left: Claw hammer
Right: Ball-peen hammer

ă pat	oi boy
ā pay	ou out
âr care	o͝o took
ä father	o͞o boot
ĕ pet	ŭ cut
ē be	ûr urge
ĭ pit	th thin
ī pie	*th* this
îr pier	hw which
ŏ pot	zh vision
ō toe	ə about, item
ô paw	♦ regionalism

Stress marks: ′ (primary); ′ (secondary), as in **dictionary** (dĭk′shə-nĕr′ē)

hammock[1]

Hammurabi
c. 1765 B.C. Babylonian sculpture

Hampshire
Hampshire lamb

kop, head (from Middle Dutch, probably from Late Latin *cuppa,* drinking vessel, cup).]

ham·mer·lock (hăm′ər-lŏk′) *n.* **1.** *Sports.* A wrestling hold in which the opponent's arm is pulled behind the back and twisted upward. **2.** Overwhelming dominance that is difficult if not impossible to overcome: *"has preserved its hammerlock on the business largely because of its reputation for quality"* (Fortune).

Ham·mer·stein (hăm′ər-stīn′, -stēn′), **Oscar.** 1846?–1919. German-born American operatic manager who founded opera houses in Harlem (1888) and Manhattan (1906). His grandson **Oscar Hammerstein II** (1895–1960), a lyricist, collaborated on many musicals and is best known for his efforts with Richard Rodgers, such as *Oklahoma!* (1943) and *The Sound of Music* (1959).

ham·mer·toe (hăm′ər-tō′) *n.* A toe, usually the second, that is permanently flexed downward, resulting in a clawlike shape.

Ham·mett (hăm′ĭt), **Dashiell.** 1894–1961. American writer of highly acclaimed detective fiction, including *The Maltese Falcon* (1930) and *The Thin Man* (1932).

ham·mock[1] (hăm′ək) *n.* A hanging, easily swung cot or lounge of canvas or heavy netting suspended between two trees or other supports. [Spanish *hamaca,* from Taino.]

ham·mock[2] (hăm′ək) *n.* Variant of **hummock** (sense 2).

Ham·mond[1] (hăm′ənd). Family of American engineers and inventors, including **John Hays Hammond** (1855–1936), a mining engineer who helped develop mining interests in California and South Africa, and his son **John Hays Hammond, Jr.** (1888–1965), who invented telephonic and telegraphic devices.

Ham·mond[2] (hăm′ənd). A city of northwest Indiana on the Illinois border west of Gary. It is highly industrialized. Population, 93,714.

Ham·mu·ra·bi (hăm′ə-rä′bē, hä′mo͝o-). Died 1750 B.C. Babylonian king (1792–1750) who codified the laws of Mesopotamia and Sumeria.

ham·my (hăm′ē) *adj.* **-mi·er, -mi·est.** Marked or characterized by overacting; affectedly humorous or dramatic. **—ham′mi·ly** *adv.* **—ham′mi·ness** *n.*

ham·per[1] (hăm′pər) *tr.v.* **-pered, -per·ing, -pers.** To prevent the free movement, action, or progress of. **—hamper** *n. Nautical.* Necessary but encumbering equipment on a ship. [Middle English *hamperen.*]

SYNONYMS: *hamper, fetter, handcuff, hobble, hog-tie, manacle, shackle, trammel.* The central meaning shared by these verbs is "to restrict the activity or free movement of": *a swimmer hampered by clothing; prisoners fettered by chains; handcuffed by rigid regulations; hobbled by responsibilities; an aspiring leadership that refused to be hog-tied; imagination manacled by fear; shackled by custom; trammeled by debts.* See also Synonyms at **hinder[1].**

ham·per[2] (hăm′pər) *n.* A large basket, usually with a cover. [Middle English, alteration of Anglo-Norman *hanaper,* from Old French *hanepier,* a case for holding goblets, from *hanap,* goblet, of Germanic origin.]

Hamp·shire (hămp′shîr, -shər) *n.* **1.** A large sheep of a breed originating in England. **2.** A pig of a breed developed in the United States, having a black body with a white, beltlike band. [After *Hampshire,* a county of southern England.]

Hamp·ton (hămp′tən). **1.** A historic section of London, England. It includes Hampton Court Palace, built by Cardinal Wolsey in 1515 and appropriated by Henry VIII in 1526. George II was the last to use it as a royal residence, and much of the palace is now open to the public. **2.** An independent city of southeast Virginia opposite Norfolk on **Hampton Roads,** the outlet of three rivers into Chesapeake Bay. Settled by colonists from Jamestown in 1610, the city was sacked by the British in the War of 1812. Population, 122,617.

Hampton, Lionel. Born 1913. American musician who was the first to use the vibraphone as a jazz instrument.

Hampton, Wade. 1818–1902. American Confederate general in the Civil War who later served as governor (1876–1879) and U.S. senator (1879–1891) for South Carolina.

ham·ster (hăm′stər) *n.* A small Eurasian rodent of the subfamily Cricetinae, especially *Mesocricetus auratus,* having large cheek pouches and a short tail and often kept as a pet or used in laboratory research. [German, from Middle High German *hamastra,* perhaps from Old High German *hamustro,* of Slavic origin.]

ham·string (hăm′strĭng′) *n.* **1.** Any of the tendons at the rear hollow of the human knee. **2.** Or **hamstrings.** The hamstring muscle. **3.** The large tendon in the back of the hock of a quadruped. **—hamstring** *tr.v.* **-strung** (-strŭng′), **-string·ing, -strings. 1.** To cut the hamstring of (an animal or a person) and thereby cripple. **2.** To destroy or hinder the efficiency of; frustrate.

hamstring muscle *n.* Any of the three muscles constituting the back of the upper leg that serve to flex the knee joint, adduct the leg, and extend the thigh.

ham·strung (hăm′strŭng′) *v.* Past tense and past participle of **hamstring.**

Ham·sun (häm′sən, -so͞on′), **Knut.** Pen name of Knut Pedersen. 1859–1952. Norwegian writer whose novels include *Hunger* (1890). He won the 1920 Nobel Prize for literature.

Ham·tramck (hăm-trăm′ĭk). A city of southeast Michigan surrounded by Detroit. The city is known primarily for automobile manufacturing. Population, 21,300.

ham·u·lus (hăm′yə-ləs) *n., pl.* **-li** (-lī′). A small hooklike projection or process, as at the end of a bone. [Latin, diminutive of *hāmus,* hook.]

ham·za also **ham·zah** (hăm′zə, häm′zä) *n.* A sign in Arabic orthography used to represent the sound of a glottal stop, transliterated in English as an apostrophe. [Arabic, from *hamaza,* to urge on, goad.]

Han[1] (hän) *n., pl.* **Han** or **Hans.** A member of the principal ethnic group of China, constituting about 93 percent of the population, especially as distinguished from Manchus, Mongols, Huis, and other nationalities. Also called *Chinese, Han Chinese.*

Han[2] (hän). A Chinese dynasty (206 B.C.–A.D. 220) noted for unifying and expanding its national territory and for promoting literature and the arts.

Han Chinese *n.* See **Han[1].**

Han·cock (hăn′kŏk′), **John.** 1737–1793. American politician and Revolutionary leader. He was president of the Continental Congress (1775–1777) and the first to sign the Declaration of Independence.

Hancock, Winfield Scott. 1824–1886. American Civil War general who defeated Robert E. Lee and George Pickett in the Gettysburg Campaign (1863).

hand (hănd) *n.* **1.a.** The terminal part of the human arm located below the forearm, used for grasping and holding and consisting of the wrist, palm, four fingers, and an opposable thumb. **b.** A homologous or similar part in other animals, as the terminal part of the forelimb in certain vertebrates. **2.** A unit of length equal to 4 inches (10.2 centimeters), used especially to specify the height of a horse. **3.** Something suggesting the shape or function of the human hand, especially: **a.** Any of the rotating pointers used as indexes on the face of a mechanical clock. **b.** A pointer, as on a gauge or dial. **4.** *Printing.* See **index** (sense 3). **5.** Lateral direction indicated according to the way in which one is facing: *at my right hand.* **6.** A style or individual sample of writing. **7.** A round of applause to signify approval. **8.** Physical assistance; help: *gave me a hand with the bags.* **9.** *Games.* **a.** The cards held in a card game by a given player at any time. **b.** The number of cards dealt each player; the deal. **c.** A player or participant in a card game: *We need a fourth hand for bridge.* **d.** A portion or section of a game during which all the cards dealt out are played: *a hand of poker.* **10.a.** One who performs manual labor: *a factory hand.* **b.** One who is part of a group or crew: *the ship's hands.* **11.** A participant in an activity, often one who specializes in a particular activity or pursuit: *called for more hands to decorate the Christmas tree; an old hand at labor negotiations.* **12.a.** The degree of immediacy of a source of information; degree of reliability: *probably heard the scandalous tale at third hand.* **b.** The strength or force of one's position: *negotiated from a strong hand.* **13.** Often **hands. a.** Possession, ownership, or keeping: *The books should be in your hands by noon.* **b.** Power; jurisdiction; care: *The defendant's fate is in the hands of the jury. Dinner is in the hands of the chef.* **14.a.** Involvement or participation: *"In all this was evident the hand of the counterrevolutionaries"* (John Reed). **b.** An influence or effect: *The general manager had a hand in all the major decisions.* **c.** Evidence of craft or artistic skill: *can see the hand of a genius even in the lighter poems.* **15.** An aptitude or ability: *I tried my hand at decorating.* **16.** The aesthetic feel or tactile quality of something, such as a fabric, textile, or carpeting, that indicates its fineness, texture, and durability. **17.** A manner or way of performing something: *a light hand with makeup.* **18.a.** Permission or a promise, especially a pledge to wed. **b.** A commitment or an agreement, especially when sealed by a handshake; one's word: *You have my hand on that.* **—hand** *tr.v.* **hand·ed, hand·ing, hands. 1.** To give or pass with or as if with the hands; transmit: *Hand me your keys.* **2.** To aid, direct, or conduct with the hands: *The usher handed the patron to a reserved seat.* **3.** *Nautical.* To roll up and secure (a sail); furl. ***—phrasal verbs.*** **hand down. 1.** To bequeath as an inheritance to one's heirs. **2.** To make and pronounce an official decision, especially a court verdict. **hand on.** To turn over to another. **hand out. 1.** To distribute freely; disseminate. **2.** To administer or deal out. **hand over.** To release or relinquish to another. ***—idioms.*** **at hand. 1.** Close by; near. **2.** Soon in time; imminent: *Retribution is at hand.* **at the hand** (or **hands) of.** Performed by someone or through the agency of someone. **by hand.** Performed manually. **hand it to.** *Informal.* To give credit to: *You've got to hand it to her; she knows what she's doing.* **in hand. 1.** Under control: *The project is well in hand.* **2.** Accessible at the present time. **3.** In preparation. **off (one's) hands.** No longer under one's jurisdiction, within one's responsibility, or in one's care: *We finally got that project off our hands.* **on hand.** Available. **on** (or **upon) (one's) hands.** In one's possession, often as an imposed responsibility or burden: *Now they have the grandchildren on their hands.* **on the one hand.** As one point of view; from one standpoint. **on the other hand.** As another point of view; from another standpoint. **out of hand. 1.** Out of control: *Employee absenteeism has gotten out of hand.* **2.** At once; immediately. **3.** Over and done with; finished. **4.** Uncalled for or improper; indiscreet. **to hand. 1.** Nearby. **2.** In one's possession. [Middle English, from Old English.] **—hand′er** *n.* **—hand′less** *adj.*

Hand (hănd), **(Billings) Learned.** 1872–1961. American jurist. As a federal judge (1924–1951) his influence was so great that he was sometimes called the "tenth man" of the U.S. Supreme Court.

Han·dan also **Han·tan** (hän′dän′). A city of east-central China south-southwest of Beijing. It is a flourishing industrial center. Population, 727,500.

hand and foot *adv.* With concerted, never-ending effort: *had to wait on them hand and foot.*

hand and glove *adv.* Variant of **hand in glove.**

hand·bag (hănd′băg′) *n.* **1.** A woman's purse. **2.** A piece of small hand luggage.

hand·ball (hănd′bôl′) *n. Sports.* **1.** A game similar in scoring to volleyball that is played by two or more players who hit a ball against a wall with their hands usually while wearing a special glove. **2.** The small rubber ball used in this game.

hand·bar·row (hănd′băr′ō) *n.* A flat framework or litter with carrying poles at each end.

hand·bill (hănd′bĭl′) *n.* A printed sheet or pamphlet distributed by hand.

hand·blown also **hand-blown** (hănd′blōn′) *adj.* Formed or shaped with a hand-held blowpipe: *handblown goblets.*

hand·book (hănd′bo͝ok′) *n. Abbr.* **hdbk. 1.** A concise manual or reference book providing specific information or instruction about a subject or place. **2.** *Games.* **a.** A book in which off-track bets are recorded. **b.** A place where off-track bets are taken.

hand brake *n.* See **emergency brake.**

hand·breadth (hănd′brĕdth′) also **hand's-breadth** or **hand's breadth** (hăndz′-) *n.* A linear measurement approximating the width of the palm of the hand, from 2½ to 4 inches (6.25 to 10 centimeters).

hand·car (hănd′kär′) *n.* A small open railroad car propelled by a hand pump or a small motor.

hand·cart (hănd′kärt′) *n.* A small, usually two-wheeled cart pulled or pushed by hand.

hand·clap (hănd′klăp′) *n.* A beating together of the palms of the hands to indicate applause, attract attention, or provide a rhythmic accompaniment to music.

hand·clasp (hănd′klăsp′) *n.* The act of clasping the hand of another, especially in friendship.

hand·craft (hănd′krăft′) *n.* Variant of **handicraft.** **—handcraft** (hănd-krăft′) *tr.v.* **-craft·ed, -craft·ing, -crafts.** To fashion or make by hand. **—hand·craft′er** *n.* **—hand′crafts′man·ship′, hand′craft′man·ship′** *n.*

hand·cuff (hănd′kŭf′) *n.* A restraining device consisting of a pair of strong, connected hoops that can be tightened and locked about the wrists and used on one or both arms of a prisoner in custody; a manacle. Often used in the plural. **—handcuff** *tr.v.* **-cuffed, -cuff·ing, -cuffs. 1.** To restrain with or as if with handcuffs. **2.** To render ineffective or impotent. See Synonyms at **hamper**[1].

hand·ed (hăn′dĭd) *adj.* **1.** Of or relating to dexterity, preference, or size with respect to a hand or hands. Often used in combination: *one-handed; left-handed; large-handed.* **2.** Relating to a specified number of people. Often used in combination: *a four-handed card game.*

hand·ed·ness (hăn′dĭd-nĭs) *n.* **1.** A preference for using one hand as opposed to the other. **2.** *Chemistry & Physics.* The property that distinguishes an asymmetric from its mirror image but not from a rotated object.

Han·del (hăn′dl), **George Frederick.** 1685–1759. German-born composer whose works include the English oratorio *Messiah* (1742) and the orchestral *Water Music* (1717). **—Han·del′i·an** (hăn-dē′lē-ən, -dĕl′yən, -dĕl′-ē-ən, -dĕl′yən) *adj.*

hand·fast (hănd′făst′) *n. Archaic.* A handclasp used to signify a pledge, such as a contract or marriage. [From Middle English *hondfast,* past participle of *hondfesten,* to betroth, from Old Norse *handfesta,* to strike a bargain, pledge : *hönd,* hand + *festa,* to fasten, fix, affirm; see **past-** in Appendix.]

hand·ful (hănd′fo͝ol′) *n., pl.* **-fuls. 1.** The amount that a hand can hold. **2.** A small, undefined number or quantity: *only a handful of people on the street.* **3.** *Informal.* One that is too difficult to control or handle easily: *The toddler is a real handful.*

hand glass *n.* **1.** A small magnifying glass held in the hand. **2.** A mirror with a handle.

hand·grip (hănd′grĭp′) *n.* **1.** A grip of or by the hand. **2.** Something, such as a handle, that is suited to a grip by the hand. **3. handgrips.** Hand-to-hand combat.

hand·gun (hănd′gŭn′) *n.* A firearm that can be used with one hand.

hand-held also **hand·held** (hănd′hĕld′) *adj.* Compact enough to be used or operated while being held in the hand or hands: *a hand-held calculator; a hand-held video camera.*

hand·hold (hănd′hōld′) *n.* **1.** A grip of or by the hand. **2.** Something that one can hold onto for support.

hand·hold·ing (hănd′hōl′dĭng) *n.* Strong personal support and reassurance, especially that given to alleviate tension and anxiety.

hand·i·cap (hăn′dē-kăp′) *n.* **1.** *Sports & Games.* **a.** A race or contest in which advantages or compensations are given different contestants to equalize the chances of winning. **b.** Such an advantage or penalty. See Synonyms at **advantage. 2.** A physical or mental disability. See Synonyms at **disadvantage. 3.** A hindrance. **—handicap** *tr.v.* **-capped, -cap·ping, -caps. 1.** *Sports & Games.* To assign handicaps or a handicap to (a contestant). **2.** To cause to be at a disadvantage; impede. [From obsolete *hand in cap,* a game in which forfeits were held in a cap.]

hand·i·capped (hăn′dē-kăpt′) *adj.* Physically or mentally disabled: *a pool equipped for handicapped swimmers.*

USAGE NOTE: Although *handicapped* is widely used in both law and everyday speech to refer to people having physical or mental disabilities, those described by the word tend to prefer the expressions *disabled* or *people with disabilities.* To say that people are *handicapped* may imply that they cannot function on a par with others, while to say that they have a *disability* allows more readily for the possibility that they can so function, in spite of having to do some things in different ways. It is also felt that some stigma may attach to the word *handicapped* on account of its origin in the phrase *hand in cap,* actually derived from a game of chance but sometimes mistakenly believed to involve the image of a beggar. The word *handicapped* is best reserved to describe a disabled person who is unable to function owing to some property of the environment. Thus people with a physical disability requiring a wheelchair may or may not be *handicapped,* depending on whether wheelchair ramps are made available to them.

hand·i·cap·per (hăn′dē-kăp′ər) *n.* **1.** *Sports & Games.* One who assigns handicaps. **2.** *Games.* One who predicts the winners in a horserace, especially one who publishes such predictions as a guide for bettors.

hand·i·craft (hăn′dē-krăft′) also **hand·craft** (hănd′krăft′) *n.* **1.** Skill and facility with the hands. **2.** A craft or an occupation requiring skilled use of the hands. **3.** Work produced by skilled hands. [Middle English *handecraft,* from Old English *handcræft* : *hand,* hand + *cræft,* craft.]

Han·dies Peak (hăn′dēz). A mountain, 4,284.6 m (14,048 ft) high, in the San Juan Mountains of southwest Colorado.

hand·i·ly (hăn′dĭ-lē, -dl-ē) *adv.* **1.** In an easy manner. **2.** In a convenient manner.

hand in glove or **hand and glove** *adv.* On intimate terms or in close association.

hand in hand *adv.* In cooperation; jointly.

hand·i·work (hăn′dē-wûrk′) *n.* **1.** Work performed by hand. **2.** The product of a person's efforts and actions. [Middle English *handiwerk,* from Old English *handgeweorc* : *hand,* hand + *geweorc,* work (*ge-,* collective pref.; see **kom** in Appendix + *weorc,* work; see WORK).]

hand·ker·chief (hăng′kər-chĭf, -chēf′) *n., pl.* **-chiefs** also **-chieves** (-chĭvz, -chēvz′). *Abbr.* **hdkf. 1.** A small square of cloth used especially for wiping the nose or mouth. **2.** A large piece of cloth worn as a decorative article; a scarf.

han·dle (hăn′dl) *v.* **-dled, -dling, -dles.** *—tr.* **1.** To touch, lift, or hold with the hands. **2.** To operate with the hands; manipulate. **3.** To deal with or have responsibility for; conduct: *handles matters of corporate law.* **4.** To cope with or dispose of: *handles problems efficiently.* **5. a.** To direct, execute, or dispose of: *handle an investment.* **b.** To manage, administer to, or represent: *handle a boxer.* **6.** To deal or trade in the purchase or sale of: *a branch office that handles grain exports.* *—intr.* To act or function in a given way while in operation: *a car that handles well in the snow; a boat that handles poorly in rough water.* **—handle** *n.* **1.** A part that is designed to be held or operated with the hand. **2.** An opportunity or a means for achieving a purpose. **3.** *Slang.* A person's name. **4.** *Games.* The total amount of money bet on an event or over a set period of time. ***—idiom.* get** (or **have) a handle on.** *Informal.* To achieve an understanding of: *I was finally able to get a handle on the true nature of the problem.* [Middle English *handelen,* from Old English *handlian.*] **—han′dle·less** *adj.*

SYNONYMS: *handle, manipulate, wield, ply.* These verbs mean to use or operate with or as if with the hands. *Handle* applies widely and suggests competence: *He handles an ax like a born woodsman. She handled the employee's problem with sensitivity and direction. Manipulate* connotes skillful or artful management, as of a tool or an instrument: *The radio operator manipulated the dials and changed the frequency.* When *manipulate* refers to people or personal affairs, it often implies deviousness or the use of improper influence or fraud in gaining an end: *I put forth his suggestion as my own without realizing I had been manipulated. Wield* implies freedom, skill, and ease in handling physical or figurative tools and implements: *wield a hatchet; wields a persuasive pen.* It also connotes effectiveness in the exercise of intangibles such as authority or influence: *wielded enormous power. Ply* suggests industry and persistence, as in the use of tools (*plying a knife and fork with gusto*); the term also applies to the regular and diligent engagement in a task or pursuit (*plies the baker's trade*). See also Synonyms at **touch, treat.**

han·dle·bar (hăn′dl-bär′) *n.* A curved metal steering bar, as on a bicycle. Often used in the plural.

handlebar mustache *n.* A long, curved mustache resembling a handlebar.

han·dler (hănd′lər) *n.* **1.** One that handles or directs something or someone: *the candidate's campaign handlers; the defector's handlers.* **2.** *Sports.* **a.** One who trains or exhibits an animal, such as a dog. **b.** One who acts as the trainer or second of a boxer.

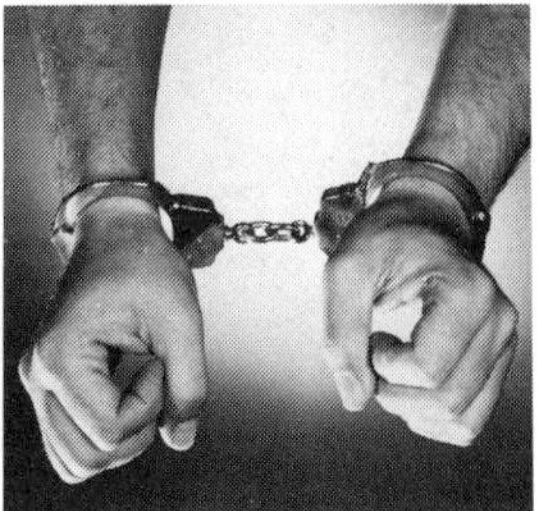

handcuff
Pair of handcuffs

George Frederick Handel

handlebar mustache

ă pat	oi boy
ā pay	ou out
âr care	o͝o took
ä father	o͞o boot
ĕ pet	ŭ cut
ē be	ûr urge
ĭ pit	th thin
ī pie	*th* this
îr pier	hw which
ŏ pot	zh vision
ō toe	ə about, item
ô paw	♦ regionalism

Stress marks: ′ (primary); ′ (secondary), as in **dictionary** (dĭk′shə-nĕr′ē)

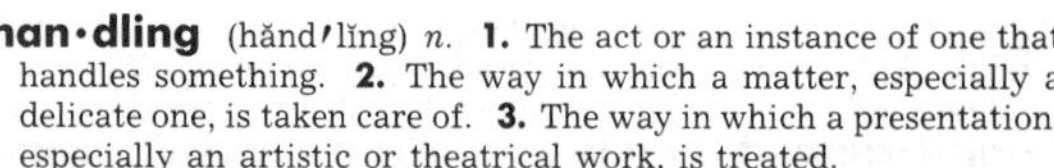

hand organ

han•dling (hănd′lĭng) *n.* **1.** The act or an instance of one that handles something. **2.** The way in which a matter, especially a delicate one, is taken care of. **3.** The way in which a presentation, especially an artistic or theatrical work, is treated.

hand•made (hănd′mād′) *adj.* Made or prepared by hand rather than by machine.

hand•maid (hănd′mād′) also **hand•maid•en** (-mād′n) *n.* **1.** A woman attendant or servant. **2.** Often **handmaiden.** Something that serves a useful but subordinate purpose: *piety as the handmaiden of religious faith.*

hand-me-down (hănd′mē-doun′) *adj.* **1.** Handed down to one person after being used and discarded by another. **2.** Of inferior quality; shabby. **—hand-me-down** *n.* Something, such as an article of clothing, passed on from one person to another.

hand•off (hănd′ôf′, -ŏf′) *n.* **1.** *Football.* A play in which one player hands the ball to another. **2.** The act or an instance of passing something or the control of it from one person or agency to another: *a handoff of the aircraft from one control tower to another.*

hand organ *n. Music.* A barrel organ operated by turning a crank by hand.

hand•out (hănd′out′) *n.* **1.** Food, clothing, or money given to the needy. **2.** A folder or leaflet circulated free of charge. **3.** A prepared news or publicity release.

hand over fist *adv.* At a tremendous rate: *made money hand over fist.* [From the way sailors haul in or climb up a rope.]

hand•pick (hănd′pĭk′) *tr.v.* **-picked, -pick•ing, -picks. 1.** To gather or pick by hand. **2.** To select personally. **—hand′-picked′** *adj.*

hand press *n.* A printing press operated by hand.

hand•print (hănd′prĭnt′) *n.* An outline or indentation left by a hand.

hand puppet *n.* A puppet operated by hand.

hand•rail (hănd′rāl′) *n.* A narrow railing to be grasped with the hand for support.

hand•saw (hănd′sô′) *n.* A small saw operated by one hand.

hand's-breadth or **hand's breadth** (hăndz′brĕdth′) *n.* Variant of **handbreadth.**

hands down (hăndz) *adv.* **1.** With no trouble; easily. **2.** Unquestionably. **—hands′-down′** (hăndz′doun′) *adj.*

hand•sel (hănd′səl) also **han•sel** (hăn′-) *Chiefly British.* —*n.* **1.** A gift to express good wishes at the beginning of a new year or enterprise. **2.** The first money or barter taken in, as by a new business or on the opening day of business, especially when considered a token of good luck. **3.a.** A first payment. **b.** A specimen or foretaste of what is to come. —*tr.v.* **-seled, -sel•ing, -sels** or **-selled, -sel•ling, -sels. 1.** To give a handsel to. **2.** To launch with a ceremonial gesture or gift. **3.** To do or use for the first time. [Middle English *hanselle,* from Old English *handselen,* a handing over (*hand,* hand + *selen,* gift) and from Old Norse *handsal,* legal transfer (*hand,* hand + *sal,* a giving).]

hand•set (hănd′sĕt′) *n.* The handle-shaped part of a telephone, containing the receiver and transmitter and often a dial or push buttons.

hand•shake (hănd′shāk′) *n.* The grasping of hands by two people, as in greeting or leave-taking.

hands-off (hăndz′ôf′, -ŏf′) *adj.* Characterized by nonintervention: *a hands-off foreign policy.*

hand•some (hăn′səm) *adj.* **-som•er, -som•est. 1.** Pleasing and dignified in form or appearance. See Synonyms at **beautiful. 2.** Generous or copious: *a handsome reward.* See Synonyms at **liberal. 3.** Marked by or requiring skill or dexterity: *did some handsome maneuvers on the skating rink.* **4.** Appropriate or fitting: *a handsome location for the new school.* **5.** Large: *a handsome price; won by a handsome margin.* [Middle English *handsom,* handy : *hand,* hand (from Old English) + *-som,* n. suff.; see —SOME[1].] **—hand′some•ly** *adv.* **—hand′some•ness** *n.*

hand press
Used by Benjamin Franklin in England, 1725–1726

hands-on (hăndz′ŏn′, -ôn′) *adj.* Involving active participation; applied, as opposed to theoretical: *"We're involved in hands-on operations, pushing levers, pushing buttons"* (Arthur R. Taylor).

hand•spike (hănd′spīk′) *n.* A bar used as a lever. [Alteration of Dutch *handspaak* : *hand,* hand (from Middle Dutch *hant*) + *spaak,* spoke (from Middle Dutch *spāke,* stick).]

hand•spring (hănd′sprĭng′) *n. Sports.* A gymnastic feat in which the body is flipped completely forward or backward from an upright position, landing first on the hands and then on the feet.

hand•stand (hănd′stănd′) *n. Sports.* The act of balancing on the hands with one's feet in the air.

hand-to-hand (hănd′tə-hănd′) *adj.* Being at close quarters: *hand-to-hand combat.* **—hand to hand** *adv.*

hand-to-mouth (hănd′tə-mouth′) *adj.* Having or providing only the bare essentials: *a hand-to-mouth way of life.*

hand wav•ing (wā′vĭng) *n.* Usually insubstantial words or actions intended to convince or impress: *resorted to hand waving in place of rational arguments.* **—hand′-wav′ing** (hănd′wā′vĭng) *adj.*

hand•work (hănd′wûrk′) *n.* Work done by hand rather than by machine.

hand•wo•ven (hănd′wō′vən) *adj.* **1.** Woven on a hand-operated loom: *handwoven rugs.* **2.** Woven by hand: *handwoven baskets.*

hand•wring•ing or **hand wringing** (hănd′rĭng′ĭng) *n.* **1.** Clasping and squeezing of the hands, often in distress. **2.** An excessive expression of distress: *handwringing by the popular press over the state of the economy.* **—hand′wring′er, hand wringer** *n.*

hand•writ•ing (hănd′rī′tĭng) *n.* **1.** Writing done with the hand. **2.** The writing characteristic of a particular person.

hand•y (hăn′dē) *adj.* **-i•er, -i•est. 1.** Skillful in using one's hands; manually adroit. See Synonyms at **dexterous. 2.** Readily accessible: *found a handy spot for the can opener.* **3.** Useful; convenient: *a handy gadget.* **4.** Easy to use or handle: *a handy reference book.* [From HAND.] **—hand′i•ness** *n.*

Han•dy (hăn′dē), **William Christopher.** Known as "W.C. Handy." 1873–1958. American musician and composer. He was the first person to publish a blues composition, "The Memphis Blues" (1911).

hand•y•man also **handy man** (hăn′dē-măn′) *n.* A man who does odd jobs or various small tasks.

Han•ford (hăn′fərd). A city of central California south-southeast of Fresno. It is a trade and processing center for the San Joaquin Valley. Population, 20,958.

hang (hăng) *v.* **hung** (hŭng), **hang•ing, hangs.** —*tr.* **1.** To fasten from above with no support from below; suspend. **2.** To suspend or fasten so as to allow free movement at or about the point of suspension: *hang a door.* **3.** *past tense and past participle* **hanged** (hăngd). **a.** To execute by suspending by the neck: *They hanged the prisoner at dawn.* **b.** Used to express exasperation or disgust: *I'll be hanged! Hang it all!* **4.** To fix or attach at an appropriate angle: *hang a scythe to its handle.* **5.** To alter the hem of (a garment) so as to fall evenly at a specified height. **6.** To furnish, decorate, or appoint by suspending objects around or about: *hang a room with curtains.* **7.** To hold or incline downward; let droop: *hang one's head in sorrow.* **8.a.** To attach to a wall: *hang wallpaper.* **b.** To display, as in a gallery or an office: *hung four new paintings in the foyer.* **9.** *Informal.* To give (a nickname or label) to someone. **10.** To deadlock (a jury) by failing to render a unanimous verdict. **11.** *Baseball.* To throw (a pitch) in such a manner as to fail to break. —*intr.* **1.** To be attached from above with no support from below. **2.** To die as a result of hanging. **3.** To remain suspended or poised over a place or an object; hover: *rain clouds hanging low over the corn fields.* **4.** To attach oneself as a dependent or an impediment; cling. **5.** To incline downward; droop. **6.** To depend: *Everything hangs on the committee's decision.* **7.** To pay strict attention: *a student who hangs on the professor's every word.* **8.** To remain unresolved or uncertain: *His future hung in the balance.* **9.** To fit the body in loose lines: *a dress that hangs well.* **10.** To be on display, as in a gallery. **11.** *Baseball.* To fail to break or move in the intended way, as a curve ball. **12.** To be imminent; loom: *the threat hanging over us.* **13.** To be or become burdensome: *Time hung heavy on my hands.* **—hang** *n.* **1.** The way in which something hangs. **2.** A downward inclination or slope. **3.** Particular meaning or significance. **4.** *Informal.* The proper method for doing, using, or handling something: *finally got the hang of it.* **5.** A suspension of motion; a slackening. ***—phrasal verbs.*** **hang around. 1.** To spend time idly; loiter. **2.** To keep company; consort. **hang back.** To be averse; hold back. **hang in.** *Informal.* To persevere: *decided to hang in despite his illness.* **hang off.** To hold back; be averse. **hang on. 1.** To cling tightly to something. **2.** To continue persistently; persevere. **3.** To keep a telephone connection open. **4.** To wait for a short period of time. **hang out.** *Slang.* **1.** To spend one's free time in a certain place: *"a group of boys who hung out together around what they called 'Barry's Corner'"* (Linda Ellerbee). **2.** To pass time idly; loiter: *spent the evening just hanging out.* **3.** To keep company; date: *hanging out with a former boyfriend.* **hang together. 1.** To stand united; stick together: *"We must all hang together, or assuredly we shall all hang separately"* (Benjamin Franklin). **2.** To constitute a coherent totality: *diverse plot lines that did not hang together.* **hang up. 1.** To suspend on a hook or hanger. **2.a.** To replace (a telephone receiver) on its base or cradle. **b.** To end a telephone conversation. **3.a.** To delay or impede; hinder: *Budget problems hung up the project for months.* **b.** To become halted or snagged: *The fishing line hung up on a rock.* **c.** *Informal.* To have or cause to have emotional difficulties or inhibitions. ***—idioms.*** **give** (or **care**) **a hang.** To be concerned or anxious: *I don't give a hang what you do.* **hang a left.** *Informal.* To make a left turn, as in an automobile. **hang a right.** *Informal.* To make a right turn, as in an automobile. **hang fire. 1.** To delay: *"They are people who hung fire even through the bloody days of the Hungarian Revolution"* (Mark Muro). **2.** To be slow in firing, as a gun. **hang in there.** *Informal.* To persevere despite difficulties; persist: *She hung in there despite pressure to resign.* **hang it up.** *Informal.* To give up; quit. **hang loose.** *Slang.* To stay calm or relaxed. **hang on to.** To hold firmly; keep fast: *Hang on to your money.* **hang tough.** *Informal.* To remain firmly resolved: *"We are going to hang tough on this"* (Donald T. Regan). **let it all hang out.** *Slang.* **1.** To be completely relaxed. **2.** To be completely candid. [Middle English *hongen,* from Old English *hangian,* to be suspended, and from Old English *hōn,* to hang; see **konk-** in Appendix.]

USAGE NOTE: *Hanged,* as a past tense and a past participle of *hang,* is used in the sense of "to put to death by hanging." In the following example *hung* would be unacceptable to a majority of the Usage Panel: *Frontier courts hanged many a prisoner after a* *summary trial.* In all other senses of the word, *hung* is the preferred form as past tense and past participle.

han·gar (hăng′ər, hăng′gər) *n.* A shelter especially for housing or repairing aircraft. [French, from Old French *hangard,* of Germanic origin. See **tkei-** in Appendix.]

Hang·chow or **Hang·chou** (hăng′chou′, hăng′jō′). See **Hangzhou.**

hang·dog (hăng′dôg′, -dŏg′) *adj.* **1.** Shamefaced or guilty. **2.** Downcast; intimidated. **—hangdog** *n.* A sneaky or despicable person.

hanged (hăngd) *v.* Past tense and past participle of **hang** (sense 3). See Usage Note at **hang.**

hang·er (hăng′ər) *n.* **1.** One who hangs something: *a house painter who also works as a paperhanger.* **2.** A contrivance to which something hangs or by which something is hung, as: **a.** A device around which a garment is draped for hanging from a hook or rod. **b.** A loop or strap by which something is hung. **3.** A bracket on the spring shackle of a motor vehicle, designed to hold it to the chassis. **4.** A decorative strip of cloth hung on a garment or wall. **5.** A short sword that may be hung from a belt.

hang·er-on (hăng′ər-ŏn′, -ôn′) *n., pl.* **hang·ers-on** (hăng′ərz-). A sycophant; a parasite.

hang-glide (hăng′glīd′) *intr.v.* **-glid·ed, -glid·ing, -glides.** To fly by means of a hang glider.

hang glider *n.* **1.** A device resembling a kite from which a harnessed rider hangs while gliding from a height. **2.** The rider of such a device.

hang·ing (hăng′ĭng) *n.* **1.** Execution on a gallows. **2.** Something, such as a tapestry, that is hung. **3.** A descending slope or an inclination. **—hanging** *adj.* **1.** Situated on a sharp declivity. **2.** Projecting downward; overhanging. **3.** Suited for holding something that hangs. **4. a.** Deserving death by hanging: *a hanging crime.* **b.** Disposed to inflict severe sentences, such as death by hanging: *a hanging judge.*

hanging indention *n.* Indention of every line in a paragraph except the first.

hang·man (hăng′mən) *n.* **1.** A man employed to execute condemned prisoners by hanging. **2.** (*also* -măn). *Games.* A game in which one player chooses a word whose letters are guessed at by another player. For each wrong guess, a new part of the stick figure of a hanging man is drawn.

hang·nail (hăng′nāl′) *n.* A small piece of dead skin at the side or the base of a fingernail that is partly detached from the rest of the skin. [Alteration of AGNAIL.]

hang·out (hăng′out′) *n. Slang.* A frequently visited place.

hang·o·ver (hăng′ō′vər) *n.* **1.** Unpleasant physical effects following the heavy use of alcohol. **2.** A letdown, as after a period of excitement. **3.** A vestige; a holdover: *hangovers from prewar legislation.*

hang·tag (hăng′tăg′) *n.* A tag attached to a piece of merchandise giving information about its composition, care, and use.

hang-up (hăng′ŭp′) *n. Informal.* **1.** A psychological or emotional difficulty or inhibition. **2.** An obstacle to smooth progress or development.

Hang·zhou (hăng′jō′) also **Hang·chow** or **Hang·chou** (hăng′chou′, hăng′jō′). A city of eastern China at the head of **Hangzhou Bay,** an inlet of the East China Sea. Founded in 606, the city was the capital of a powerful kingdom from 907 to 960. It is the capital of Zhejiang province. Population, 1,250,000.

hank (hăngk) *n.* **1.** A coil or loop. **2.** *Nautical.* A ring on a stay attached to the head of a jib or staysail. **3.** A looped bundle, as of yarn. [Middle English, from Old Norse *hönk.*]

han·ker (hăng′kər) *intr.v.* **-kered, -ker·ing, -kers.** To have a strong, often restless desire. See Synonyms at **yearn.** [Perhaps from Dutch dialectal *hankeren.* See **konk-** in Appendix.] **—hank′er·er** *n.*

han·kie also **han·ky** (hăng′kē) *n., pl.* **-kies.** *Informal.* A handkerchief.

han·ky-pan·ky (hăng′kē-păng′kē) *n. Slang.* **1.** Devious or mischievous activity. **2.** Illicit sexual activity. [Alteration of *hokey-pokey,* alteration of HOCUS-POCUS.]

Han·na (hăn′ə), **Marcus Alonzo.** Known as "Mark." 1837–1904. American financier and politician who managed the 1896 and 1900 presidential campaigns of William McKinley and served as a U.S. senator from Ohio (1897–1904).

Han·ni·bal¹ (hăn′ə-bəl). 247–183? B.C. Carthaginian general who crossed the Alps in 218 with about 35,000 men and routed Roman armies at Lake Trasimeno (217) and Cannae (216). He was later defeated at the Battle of Zama (202).

Han·ni·bal² (hăn′ə-bəl). A city of northeast Missouri on the Mississippi River northwest of St. Louis. It is famous as the boyhood home of Mark Twain. Population, 18,811.

Han·no (hăn′ō). Known as "the Great." fl. third century B.C. Carthaginian political leader who opposed the policy of conquest during the Second Punic War (218–201). After Hannibal's defeat (202) Hanno negotiated a treaty with the Romans.

Han·no·ver (hăn′ō′vər, hä-nō′-). See **Hanover².**

Ha·noi (hă-noi′, hə-). The capital of Vietnam, in the northern part of the country on the Red River. Founded before the seventh century, it became the capital of French Indochina after 1887 and the capital of North Vietnam after 1954. Population, 819,913.

Han·o·ver¹ (hăn′ō′vər). British ruling family (1714–1901). When Victoria ascended the throne in 1837, the crowns of Hanover and Great Britain were separated.

Han·o·ver² or **Han·no·ver** (hăn′ō′vər, hä-nō′-). **1.** A former kingdom and province of northwest Germany. It was an electorate of the Holy Roman Empire from 1692 to 1805. The kingdom lasted from 1815 to 1866, when Hanover became a province of Prussia (later Germany). **2.** A city of northwest Germany southeast of Bremen. Chartered in 1241, it became part of the Hanseatic League in 1386. Population, 514,010.

Han·o·ve·ri·an (hăn′ō-vîr′ē-ən) *adj.* **1.** Of, relating to, or characteristic of the royal family of Hanover. **2.** Of, belonging to, or characteristic of the kingdom or province of Hanover.

Hanover Park. A village of northeast Illinois, a suburb of Chicago. Population, 28,850.

Han River (hän). A river, about 1,126 km (700 mi) long, of east-central China flowing generally southeast to the Yangtze River (Chang Jiang).

Han·sard (hăn′sərd) *n.* The official report of the proceedings and debates of a legislature in the Commonwealth of Nations, especially of the British or Canadian parliament. [After Luke *Hansard* (1752–1828), British printer.]

Hans·ber·ry (hănz′bĕr-ē), **Lorraine.** 1930–1965. American playwright known for her play *A Raisin in the Sun* (1959).

hanse (hăns) *n.* A medieval merchant guild or trade association. [Middle English, from Old French, from Middle Low German, from Old High German *hansa,* military troop.] **—han′se·at′ic** (hăn′sē-ăt′ĭk) *adj.*

Han·se·at·ic League (hăn′sē-ăt′ĭk). A former economic and defensive confederation of free towns in northern Germany and neighboring areas. Traditionally dated to a protective alliance formed by Lübeck and Hamburg in 1241, it reached the height of its power in the 14th century and held its last assembly in 1669.

han·sel (hăn′səl) *n. & v.* Variant of **handsel.**

Han·sen's disease (hăn′sənz) *n.* Leprosy. No longer in scientific use. [After Gerhard H.A. *Hansen* (1841–1912), Norwegian physician.]

han·som (hăn′səm) *n.* A two-wheeled covered carriage with the driver's seat above and behind. Also called *hansom cab.* [After Joseph Aloysius *Hansom* (1803–1882), British architect.]

Han·tan (hän′dän′). See **Handan.**

Ha·nuk·kah or **Ha·nu·kah** also **Cha·nu·kah** (KHä′nə-kə, hä′-) *n. Judaism.* An eight-day festival beginning on the 25th day of Kislev, commemorating the victory in 165 B.C. of the Maccabees over Antiochus Epiphanes (c. 215–164 B.C.) and the rededication of the Temple at Jerusalem. Also called *Feast of Dedication, Feast of Lights.* [Hebrew *ḥănukkâ,* dedication, from *ḥānak,* to dedicate.]

han·u·man (hŭn′o͝o-män′) *n., pl.* **-mans.** A small monkey *(Presbytis entellus)* of southern Asia, having bristly hairs on the crown and the sides of the face. [Hindi *hanumān,* from Sanskrit *Hanuman,* name of a monkey-god in Hindu mythology, from *hanu,* jaw. See **genu-²** in Appendix.]

hao (hou) *n.* See table at **currency.**

♦ **hao·le** (hou′lē, -lā) *n. Hawaii.* A person, especially a white person, who is not a native Hawaiian. See Regional Note at **ukulele.** [Hawaiian.]

hap (hăp) *n.* **1.** Fortune; chance. **2.** A happening; an occurrence. **—hap** *intr.v.* **happed, hap·ping, haps.** To happen. [Middle English, from Old Norse *happ.* See **kob-** in Appendix.]

ha·pax le·go·me·non (hā′păks′ lĭ-gŏm′ə-nŏn′) *n., pl.* **ha·pax le·go·me·na** (-nə). A word or form that occurs only once in the recorded corpus of a given language. [Greek : *hapax,* once + *legomenon,* neuter sing. passive participle of *legein,* to count, say.]

hap·haz·ard (hăp-hăz′ərd) *adj.* Dependent upon or characterized by mere chance. See Synonyms at **chance.** **—haphazard** *n.* Mere chance; fortuity. **—haphazard** *adv.* By chance. **—hap·haz′ard·ly** *adv.* **—hap·haz′ard·ness** *n.*

haph·ta·rah also **haf·ta·rah** or **haf·to·rah** (häf′tä-rä′, häf-tôr′ə, -tōr′ə) *n., pl.* **-ta·roth** or **-to·roth** or **-to·rot** or **-to·ros** (-tä-rōt′, -rōs′, -tôr′ōt′, -ōs′, -tōr′-). *Judaism.* A selection from the Prophets, read in synagogue services on the Sabbath following each lesson from the Torah. [Mishnaic Hebrew *hapṭārâ,* conclusion, from *hipṭîr,* to conclude, dismiss, from Hebrew *'pāṭar,* to separate, discharge.]

hap·less (hăp′lĭs) *adj.* Luckless; unfortunate. See Synonyms at **unfortunate.** **—hap′less·ly** *adv.* **—hap′less·ness** *n.*

hap·lite (hăp′līt′) *n.* Variant of **aplite.**

hap·loid (hăp′loid′) *Genetics. adj.* **1.** Having the same number of sets of chromosomes as a germ cell or half as many as a somatic cell. **2.** Having a single set of chromosomes. **—haploid** *n.* An organism having haploid cells. [From Greek *haplous,* single; see **sem-¹** in Appendix + –OID.]

hap·loi·dy (hăp′loi′dē) *n. Genetics.* The state or condition of being haploid.

hap·lol·o·gy (hăp-lŏl′ə-jē) *n.* The loss of one of two identical or similar adjacent syllables in a word, as in Latin *nūtrīx,* "nurse," from earlier **nūtrītrīx.* [Greek *haplos, haplous,* single, simple; see HAPLOID + –LOGY.]

hang glider

hansom

ă pat	oi boy
ā pay	ou out
âr care	o͝o took
ä father	o͞o boot
ĕ pet	ŭ cut
ē be	ûr urge
ĭ pit	th thin
ī pie	*th* this
îr pier	hw which
ŏ pot	zh vision
ō toe	ə about, item
ô paw	♦ regionalism

Stress marks: ′ (primary); ′ (secondary), as in **dictionary** (dĭk′shə-nĕr′ē)

hap·lont (hăp′lŏnt) *n. Genetics.* An organism that is haploid throughout its life cycle except as a zygote, when it is diploid, as in many algae and fungi. [Greek *haplous,* single, simple; see HAPLOID + -ONT.]

hap·lo·sis (hăp-lō′sĭs) *n. Genetics.* Reduction of the diploid number of chromosomes by one half during meiosis, resulting in the haploid number. [Greek *haplos, haplous,* single; see HAPLOID + -OSIS.]

hap·ly (hăp′lē) *adv.* By chance or accident.

hap·pen (hăp′ən) *intr.v.* **-pened, -pen·ing, -pens. 1.a.** To come to pass. **b.** To come into being. **2.** To take place or occur by chance. **3.** To come upon something by chance. **4.** To come or go casually; make an appearance. [Middle English *happenen,* from *hap,* chance. See HAP.]

SYNONYMS: *happen, befall, betide, chance, occur.* The central meaning shared by these verbs is "to come about": *What would happen if you said no? Who can predict the misery that may befall humankind? Woe betide the poor soldier. It chanced that we succeeded. The accident occurred recently.*

hap·pen·chance (hăp′ən-chăns′) *n.* A happenstance.

hap·pen·ing (hăp′ə-nĭng) *n.* **1.** Something that takes place; an occurrence. See Synonyms at **occurrence. 2.** An improvised, often spontaneous spectacle or performance, especially one involving audience participation.

hap·pen·stance (hăp′ən-stăns′) *n.* A chance circumstance: *"Marriage loomed only as an outgrowth of happenstance; you met a person"* (Bruce Weber). [HAPPEN + (CIRCUM)STANCE.]

hap·pi coat (hăp′ē) *n.* A Japanese jacket made of cotton or similar material and having an open front, often fastened with ties. [Japanese *happi* : Chinese *bàn,* half + Chinese *bèi,* to wear.]

hap·py (hăp′ē) *adj.* **-pi·er, -pi·est. 1.** Characterized by good luck; fortunate. **2.** Enjoying, showing, or marked by pleasure, satisfaction, or joy. **3.** Being especially well-adapted; felicitous: *a happy turn of phrase.* **4.** Cheerful; willing: *happy to help.* **5.a.** Characterized by a spontaneous or obsessive inclination to use something. Often used in combination: *trigger-happy.* **b.** Enthusiastic about or involved with to a disproportionate degree. Often used in combination: *money-happy.* [Middle English, from *hap,* luck. See HAP.] **—hap′pi·ly** *adv.* **—hap′pi·ness** *n.*

SYNONYMS: *happy, fortunate, lucky, providential.* The central meaning shared by these adjectives is "attended by luck or good fortune": *a happy outcome; a fortunate omen; a lucky guess; a providential recovery.* See also Synonyms at **fit[1], glad[1].**
ANTONYM: *unhappy.*

hap·py-go-luck·y (hăp′ē-gō-lŭk′ē) *adj.* Taking things easily; carefree.

happy hour *n.* A period of time, usually in late afternoon and early evening, during which a bar or lounge features drinks at reduced prices.

Haps·burg also **Habs·burg** (hăps′bûrg′, häps′bo͝ork′). A royal German family that supplied rulers to a number of European states from the late Middle Ages until the 20th century. The Hapsburgs reached the height of their power under Charles V of Spain. When Charles abdicated (1558), the empire was divided between the Spanish and Austrian lines. The Spanish branch ceased to rule after 1700 and the Austrian branch after 1918.

hap·ten (hăp′tĕn′) also **hap·tene** (-tēn′) *n.* A substance that reacts with a specific antibody but cannot induce the formation of antibodies unless bound to a carrier protein or other molecule. [German : Greek *haptein,* to fasten + German *-en,* n. suff. (from Greek *-ēnē,* -ene).] **—hap·ten′ic** *adj.*

hap·tic (hăp′tĭk) *adj.* Of or relating to the sense of touch; tactile. [Greek *haptikos,* from *haptesthai,* to grasp, touch.]

hap·to·glo·bin (hăp′tə-glō′bĭn) *n.* A plasma protein that is a normal constituent of blood serum and functions in the binding of free hemoglobin in the bloodstream. [Greek *haptein,* to bind, fasten + (HEMO)GLOBIN.]

ha·ra-ki·ri (hăr′ĭ-kîr′ē, hä′rē-) also **ha·ri-ka·ri** (hăr′ē-kär′ē, hăr′ē-kăr′ē) *n., pl.* **-ris.** Ritual suicide by disembowelment formerly practiced by Japanese samurai. [Japanese : *hara,* abdomen, bowels + *kiri,* to cut.]

Ha·ran or **Har·ran** (hä-rän′). An ancient city of Mesopotamia in present-day southeast Turkey. It was an important trading post and a religious center devoted to the Assyrian moon god.

ha·rangue (hə-răng′) *n.* **1.** A long, pompous speech, especially one delivered before a gathering. **2.** A speech or piece of writing characterized by strong feeling or expression; a tirade. **—harangue** *v.* **-rangued, -rangu·ing, -rangues.** *—tr.* To deliver a harangue to. *—intr.* To deliver a harangue. [Middle English *arang,* a speech to an assembly, from Old French *harangue,* from Old Italian *aringa,* from *aringare,* to speak in public, probably from *aringo, arringa,* public square, meeting place, of Germanic origin. See **koro-** in Appendix.] **—ha·rangu′er** *n.*

Ha·rap·pa (hə-răp′ə). A locality in the Indus River valley of the Punjab in Pakistan. Archaeological finds dating back to the third millennium B.C. indicate a possible link between Indian and Sumerian cultures.

Ha·ra·re (hə-rär′ā). Formerly **Salis·bur·y** (sôlz′bĕr′ē, -brē). The capital and largest city of Zimbabwe, in the northeast part of the country. Founded by the British in 1890, it is a manufacturing and tobacco-processing center. Population, 656,011.

ha·rass (hăr′əs, hə-răs′) *tr.v.* **-rassed, -rass·ing, -rass·es. 1.** To irritate or torment persistently. **2.** To wear out; exhaust. **3.** To impede and exhaust (an enemy) by repeated attacks or raids. [French *harasser,* possibly from Old French *harer,* to set a dog on, from *hare,* interjection used to set a dog on, of Germanic origin.] **—ha·rass′er** *n.* **—ha·rass′ment** *n.*

SYNONYMS: *harass, harry, hound, badger, pester, plague, bait.* These verbs are compared as they mean to trouble persistently or incessantly. *Harass* and *harry* imply systematic persecution by besieging with repeated annoyances, threats, demands, or misfortunes: *The landlord harassed tenants who were behind in their rent. "Of all the griefs that harass the distress'd"* (Samuel Johnson). *A gang of delinquents harried the storekeeper. Hound* suggests unrelenting pursuit to gain a desired end: *Reporters hounded the celebrity for an interview.* To *badger* is to nag or tease persistently: *The child badgered his parents to buy him a new bicycle.* To *pester* is to inflict a succession of petty annoyances: *"How she would have pursued and pestered me with questions and surmises"* (Charlotte Brontë). *Plague* refers to the infliction of tribulations, such as worry or vexation, likened to an epidemic disease: *"As I have no estate, I am plagued with no tenants or stewards"* (Henry Fielding). To *bait* is to torment by or as if by taunting, insulting, or ridiculing: *Hecklers baited the speaker mercilessly.*
USAGE NOTE: Educated usage appears to be evenly divided on the pronunciation of *harass.* In a recent survey 50 percent of the Usage Panel preferred a pronunciation with stress on the first syllable, while 50 percent preferred stress on the second syllable. Curiously, the Panelists' comments appear to indicate that each side regards itself as an embattled minority.

Har·bin (här′bĭn′). A city of northeast China north of Jilin. It grew after Russia was granted a trade concession in 1896 and the completion of the railroad to Port Arthur in 1898. The city is the capital of Heilongjiang province. Population, 2,630,000.

har·bin·ger (här′bĭn-jər) *n.* One that indicates or foreshadows what is to come; a forerunner. **—harbinger** *tr.v.* **-gered, -ger·ing, -gers.** To signal the approach of; presage. [Middle English *herbengar,* person sent ahead to arrange lodgings, from Old French *herbergeor,* from *herbergier,* to provide lodging for, from *herberge,* lodging, of Germanic origin. See **koro-** in Appendix.]

har·bor (här′bər) *n. Abbr.* **h., H. 1.** A sheltered part of a body of water deep enough to provide anchorage for ships. **2.** A place of shelter; a refuge. **—harbor** *tr.v.* **-bored, -bor·ing, -bors. 1.** To give shelter to: *harbor refugees; harbor a fugitive.* **2.** To provide a place, home, or habitat for: *a basement that harbors a maze of pipes; streams that harbor trout and bass.* **3.** To entertain or nourish (a specified thought or feeling): *harbor a grudge.* [Middle English *herberwe,* probably from Old English *herebeorg,* lodging. See **koro-** in Appendix.] **—har′bor·er** *n.*

har·bor·age (här′bər-ĭj) *n.* **1.** Shelter and anchorage for ships. **2.** Shelter; refuge.

har·bor·mas·ter (här′bər-măs′tər) *n.* An officer who oversees and enforces the regulations of a harbor.

harbor seal *n.* A hair seal *(Phoca vitulina)* of coastal waters of the Northern Hemisphere, having a spotted coat. Also called *sea calf.*

har·bour (här′bər) *n. & v. Chiefly British.* Variant of **harbor.**

hard (härd) *adj.* **hard·er, hard·est.** *Abbr.* **h., H. 1.** Resistant to pressure; not readily penetrated. **2.a.** Physically toughened; rugged. **b.** Mentally toughened; strong-minded. **3.a.** Requiring great effort or endurance: *a hard assignment.* **b.** Performed with or marked by great diligence or energy: *a project that required years of hard work.* **c.** Difficult to resolve, accomplish, or finish: *That was a hard question.* **d.** Difficult to understand or impart: *Physics was the hardest of my courses. Thermodynamics is a hard course to teach.* **4.a.** Intense in force or degree: *a hard blow.* **b.** Inclement: *a long, hard winter.* **5.a.** Stern or strict in nature or comportment: *a hard taskmaster.* **b.** Resistant to persuasion or appeal; obdurate. **c.** Making few concessions: *drives a hard bargain.* **6.a.** Difficult to endure: *a hard life.* **b.** Oppressive or unjust in nature or effect: *restrictions that were hard on welfare applicants.* **c.** Lacking compassion or sympathy; callous. **7.a.** Harsh or severe in effect or intention: *said some hard things that I won't forget.* **b.** Bitter; resentful: *No hard feelings, I hope.* **8.a.** Causing damage or premature wear: *Snow and ice are hard on a car's finish.* **b.** Bad; adverse: *hard luck.* **9.** Proceeding or performing with force, vigor, or persistence; assiduous: *a hard worker.* **10.a.** Real and unassailable: *hard evidence.* **b.** Definite; firm: *a hard commitment.* **c.** Close; penetrating: *We need to take a hard look at the situation.* **d.** Free from illusion or bias; practical: *brought some hard common sense to the discussion.* **e.** Using or based on data that are readily quantified or verified: *the hard sciences.* **11.a.** Marked by sharp outline or definition; stark. **b.** Lacking in delicacy, shading, or nuance. **12.a.** Metallic, as opposed to paper. Used of currency. **b.** Backed by bullion rather than by credit. Used of currency. **c.** High and stable. Used of prices. **13.a.** Durable; lasting: *hard merchandise.* **b.** Written or printed rather than stored in electronic media: *sent the information by hard mail.* **14.** Erect; tumid. Used of a penis. **15.a.** Having high alcoholic content; intoxicating: *hard liquor.* **b.** Rendered alcoholic by fermentation; fermented: *hard cider.* **16.** Containing dissolved salts that interfere with the lathering action of soap. Used of water. **17.** *Linguistics.* Velar, as in c in *cake* or g in *log,* as opposed to palatal or soft. **18.** *Physics.* Of relatively high energy; penetrating: *hard x-rays.* **19.** High in gluten content: *hard wheat.* **20.** *Chemistry.* Resistant to biodegradation: *a hard detergent.* **21.** Physically addictive. Used of certain illegal drugs, such as heroin. **22.** Resistant to blast, heat, or radiation. Used especially of nuclear weapons. **—hard** *adv.* **1.** With strenuous effort; intently: *worked hard all day; stared hard at the accused criminal.* **2.** With great force, vigor, or energy: *pressed hard on the lever.* **3.** In such a way as to cause great damage or hardship: *industrial cities hit hard by unemployment.* **4.** With great distress, grief, or bitterness: *took the divorce hard.* **5.** Firmly; securely: *held hard to the railing.* **6.** Toward or into a solid condition: *concrete that sets hard within a day.* **7.** Near in space or time; close: *The factory stands hard by the railroad tracks.* **8.** *Nautical.* Completely; fully: *hard alee.* **—*idioms.* hard and fast.** Defined, fixed, and invariable: *hard and fast rules.* **hard of hearing. 1.** Having a partial loss of hearing. **2.** One who has a partial loss of hearing. **hard put.** Undergoing great difficulty: *Under the circumstances, he was hard put to explain himself.* **hard up.** *Informal.* In need; poor. [Middle English, from Old English *heard.* See **kar-** in Appendix.]

SYNONYMS: *hard, difficult, arduous.* These adjectives are compared as they mean requiring great physical or mental effort to do, achieve, or master. *Hard* is the most general term: *Why is it so hard for you to keep a secret? "You write with ease to show your breeding,/But easy writing's curst hard reading"* (Richard Brinsley Sheridan). *Difficult* and *hard* are interchangeable in many instances: *a difficult* (or *hard*) *subject; a book that is difficult* (or *hard*) *to find. Difficult,* however, is often preferable where the need for skill or ingenuity is implied: *"All poetry is difficult to read,/—The sense of it is, anyhow"* (Robert Browning). *Arduous* refers to what involves burdensome labor or sustained physical or spiritual effort: *"knowledge at which* [Isaac] *Newton arrived through arduous and circuitous paths"* (Macaulay). *Negotiating a reduction in nuclear arms is a long and arduous undertaking.* See also Synonyms at **firm[1]**.

hard•back (härd′băk′) *Printing. adj.* Bound in cloth, cardboard, or leather rather than paper. Used of books. **—hardback** *n.* A book bound in cloth, cardboard, or leather.

hard•ball (härd′bôl′) *n.* **1.** *Sports.* Baseball. **2.** *Informal.* The use of any means, however ruthless, to attain an objective.

hard-bit•ten (härd′bĭt′n) *adj.* Toughened by experience.

hard•board (härd′bôrd′, -bōrd′) *n.* A construction board made by compressing fibers of wood chips usually with a binder at a high temperature.

hard-boil (härd′boil′) *tr.v.* **-boiled, -boil•ing, -boils.** To boil (an egg) in the shell to a solid consistency. [Back-formation from HARD-BOILED.]

hard-boiled (härd′boild′) *adj.* **1.** Cooked by boiling in the shell to a solid consistency. Used of eggs. **2.** Callous; unfeeling. **3.** Unsentimental and practical; tough.

hard•bound (härd′bound′) *adj. & n. Printing.* Hardback.

hard coal *n.* See **anthracite.**

hard copy *n.* A printed copy of the output of a computer or word processor.

hard core *n.* **1.** The most dedicated, unfailingly loyal faction of a group or an organization: *the hard core of the separatist movement.* **2.** An intractable core or nucleus of a society, especially one that is stubbornly resistant to improvement or change.

hard-core also **hard•core** (härd′kôr′, -kōr′) *adj.* **1.** Intensely loyal; die-hard: *a hard-core secessionist; a hard-core golfer.* **2.** Stubbornly resistant to improvement or change: *hard-core poverty.* **3.** Extremely graphic or explicit: *hard-core pornography.*

hard•cov•er (härd′kŭv′ər) *adj. & n. Printing.* Hardback.

hard disk *n. Computer Science.* A rigid magnetic disk fixed permanently within a drive unit and used for storing computer data. Hard disks generally offer more storage and quicker access to data than floppy disks do.

Har•de•ca•nute or **Har•di•ca•nute** (här′dĭ-kə-no͞ot′, -nyo͞ot′). 1019?–1042. King of England (1040–1042) and of Denmark (1035–1042). The legitimate son of King Canute, he claimed the English throne after the death of Harold I, Canute's illegitimate son.

hard•edge (härd′ĕj′) *n.* A form of abstract painting characterized by clearly defined geometric shapes and often bright colors.

hard-edged (härd′ĕjd′) *adj.* Inclined to hold a position; severe: *"In those magazine pieces the children were splendidly self-willed, hard-edged, perverse, indomitable"* (Alice Munro).

hard•en (här′dn) *v.* **-ened, -en•ing, -ens.** *—tr.* **1.** To make hard or harder. **2.** To enable to withstand physical or mental hardship. **3.** To make unfeeling, unsympathetic, or callous: *"To love love and not its meaning hardens the heart in monstrous ways"* (Archibald MacLeish). **4.** To make sharp, as in outline. **5.** To protect (nuclear weapons) by surrounding with earth or concrete. *—intr.* **1.** To become hard or harder. **2.** To rise and become stable. Used of prices. **3.** To become inured.

SYNONYMS: *harden, acclimate, acclimatize, season, toughen.* The central meaning shared by these verbs is "to make resistant to hardship, especially through continued exposure": *was hardened to life on the frontier; is becoming acclimated to the tropical heat; was acclimatized by long hours to overwork; became seasoned to life in prison; toughened by experience and criticism.*
ANTONYM: *soften.*

hard•en•er (här′dn-ər) *n.* One that hardens, especially a substance added to varnish or paint to give it a harder surface or finish.

hard•en•ing (här′dn-ĭng) *n.* **1.** The act or process of becoming hard or harder. **2.** Something that hardens, as a substance added to iron to yield steel. **3.** Gradual exposure of plants to cold weather.

hardening of the arteries *n.* Arteriosclerosis.

hard-fist•ed (härd′fĭs′tĭd) *adj.* Tightfisted; stingy.

hard•hack (härd′hăk′) *n.* A woody plant *(Spiraea tomentosa)* of eastern North America, having leaves with rusty down on the undersides and spikelike clusters of small, rose-purple flowers. Also called *steeplebush.*

hard-hand•ed (härd′hăn′dĭd) *adj.* **1.** Having hands calloused or hardened by work. **2.** Oppressive; tyrannical. **—hard′-hand′ed•ness** *n.*

hard•hat or **hard-hat** (härd′hăt′) *—n.* **1.a.** A lightweight protective helmet, usually of metal or reinforced plastic, worn by workers in industrial settings. **b.** *Informal.* A construction worker. **2.** *Slang.* **a.** An ultraconservative. **b.** An extremely patriotic person with a conventional, usually unquestioning sense of morality. *—adj.* **1.** Relating to heavy industry, construction, or demolition. **2.** *Informal.* Of, relating to, or characterized by extreme conservatism. **3.** *Slang.* Extremely patriotic.

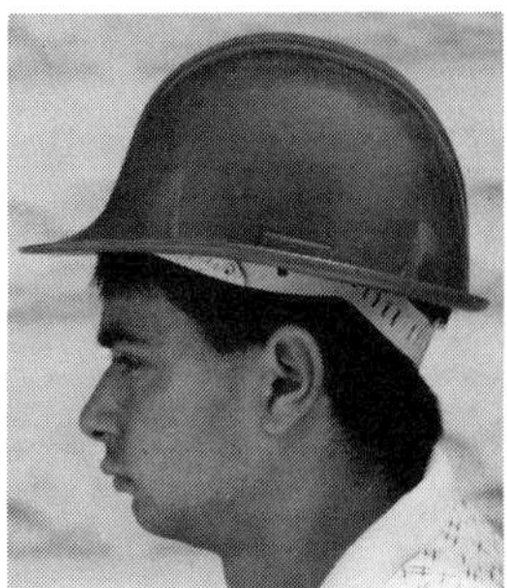

hardhat

hard•head (härd′hĕd′) *n.* **1.** A shrewd, tough person. **2.** A stubborn, unmovable person. **3.** *pl.* **hardhead** or **-heads.** Any of several fishes having a bony head, especially the Atlantic croaker.

hard•head•ed (härd′hĕd′ĭd) *adj.* **1.** Stubborn; willful. **2.** Realistic; pragmatic. **—hard′head′ed•ly** *adv.* **—hard′head′ed•ness** *n.*

hard•heart•ed (härd′här′tĭd) *adj.* Lacking in feeling or compassion; pitiless and cold. **—hard′heart′ed•ly** *adv.* **—hard′heart′ed•ness** *n.*

hard-hit•ting (härd′hĭt′ĭng) *adj.* Effective; forceful.

Har•di•ca•nute (här′dĭ-kə-no͞ot′, -nyo͞ot′). See **Hardecanute.**

har•di•hood (här′dē-ho͝od′) *n.* **1.** Boldness and daring. **2.** Impudence or insolence.

Har•ding (här′dĭng), **Chester.** 1792–1866. American portrait painter whose subjects included Daniel Webster, Daniel Boone, and John C. Calhoun.

Harding, Florence Mabel King. 1860–1924. First Lady of the United States (1921–1923) as the wife of President Warren G. Harding. She worked tirelessly for her husband's election to the presidency.

Florence Harding

Harding, Warren Gamaliel. 1865–1923. The 29th President of the United States (1921–1923), who made several misguided appointments that led to a corrupt administration. He died in office.

Warren G. Harding

hard labor *n.* Compulsory physical labor coincident with a prison term imposed as punishment for a crime.

hard landing *n.* The landing by impact of a spacecraft unequipped with or not using devices such as retrorockets to slow it down.

hard line *n.* A firm, uncompromising policy, position, or stance.

hard-line also **hard•line** (härd′līn′) *adj.* Firm and uncompromising, as in policy, position, or stance: *a hard-line foreign policy.* **—hard′-lin′er** *n.*

hard•ly (härd′lē) *adv.* **1.** Barely; just. **2.** To almost no degree; almost not: *I could hardly hear the speaker.* **3.** Probably or almost surely not: *"Easily was a man made an infidel, but hardly might he be converted to another faith"* (T.E. Lawrence). **4.** With severity; harshly. **5.** With great difficulty; painfully. [Middle English *hardli,* from Old English *heardlīce,* harshly, bravely, from *heard,* hard. See HARD.]

USAGE NOTE: The use of *hardly* with a negative is avoided in Standard English. Some critics have been puzzled that adverbs such as *hardly, rarely,* and *scarcely* should be treated as negatives in the traditional strictures against double negation, which tars sentences like *I couldn't hardly see him* with the same brush as *I didn't get none.* After all, they argue, the sentence *Mary hardly laughed* entails that Mary did laugh, not that she didn't, and therefore does not express a negative proposition. But *hardly* and *scarcely* occur with other negative expressions in a number of ways. For one thing, they combine with items such as *any* and *at all,* which are characteristically associated with negative contexts: we say *I hardly saw him at all* or *I never saw him at all* but not *I occasionally saw him at all;* we say *I hardly had any time* or *I didn't have any time* but not *I had any time,* and so on. Like other negative adverbs, *hardly* triggers inversion of the subject and auxiliary when it begins a sentence. Thus we say *Hardly had I arrived when she left,* on the pattern of *Never have I read such a book* or *At no time has he condemned the movement.* Such inversion is not

ă pat	oi boy
ā pay	ou out
âr care	o͝o took
ä father	o͞o boot
ĕ pet	ŭ cut
ē be	ûr urge
ĭ pit	th thin
ī pie	*th* this
îr pier	hw which
ŏ pot	zh vision
ō toe	ə about, item
ô paw	♦ regionalism

Stress marks: ′ (primary); ′ (secondary), as in **dictionary** (dĭk′shə-nĕr′ē)

used with other adverbs: we would not say *Occasionally has he addressed this question* or *To a slight degree have they changed their position.* The fact is that adverbs such as *hardly* are semantically negative in that they qualify a state or an event relative to the limiting case of nonoccurrence. Thus the meaning of *hardly* is, roughly, "almost not at all"; the meaning of *rarely* is "practically never"; and so forth. These adverbs are felt to have a negative component in their meaning, and it should not be surprising that grammarians have reacted to combinations of *hardly* with negatives in the same way that they have reacted to combinations of pairs of negatives such as *not* and *none.* See Usage Notes at **double negative, rarely, scarcely.**

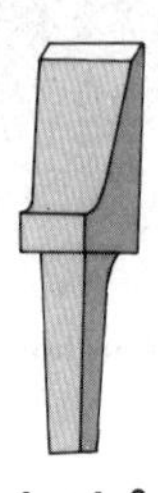

hardy²

hard maple *n.* See **sugar maple.**

hard·ness (härd′nĭs) *n. Abbr.* **h., H. 1.** The quality or condition of being hard. **2.** *Mineralogy.* The relative resistance of a mineral to scratching, as measured by the Mohs scale. **3.** The relative resistance of a metal or other material to denting, scratching, or bending.

hard news *n.* News, as in a newspaper or television report, that deals with formal or serious topics and events. **—hard′-news′** (härd′no͞oz′, -nyo͞oz′), **hard′news′** *adj.*

hard-nosed (härd′nōzd′) *adj.* Hardheaded.

hard-on (härd′ŏn′, -ôn′) *n. Vulgar Slang.* An erection of the penis.

hard palate *n.* The relatively hard, bony anterior portion of the palate.

hard·pan (härd′păn′) *n.* **1.** A layer of hard subsoil or clay. Also called *caliche.* **2.** Hard, unbroken ground. **3.** A foundation; bedrock.

hard-pressed (härd′prĕst′) *adj.* Experiencing great difficulty or distress: *financially hard-pressed.*

hard rock *n. Music.* A style of rock 'n' roll characterized by a harsh, amplified sound and frequently employing distortion, feedback, and other electronic modulations.

hard rubber *n.* Ebonite.

hard sauce *n.* A creamy sauce of butter and sugar with rum, brandy, or vanilla flavoring, served chilled with puddings, gingerbread, or fruitcakes.

hare
European hare
Lepus europaeus

hard·scrab·ble (härd′skrăb′əl) *adj.* Earning a bare subsistence, as on the land; marginal: *the sharecropper's hardscrabble life.* **—hardscrabble** *n.* Barren or marginal farmland.

hard sell *n. Informal.* **1.** Aggressive, high-pressure selling or promotion. **2.** A person or an organization that resists pressure from salespeople; a difficult sales prospect.

hard-set (härd′sĕt′) *adj.* Fixed; rigid.

hard-shell (härd′shĕl′) *n.* A hard-shell clam or crab. **—hard-shell** also **hard-shelled** (-shĕld′) *adj.* **1.** Having a thick, heavy, or hardened shell. **2.** Uncompromising; confirmed.

hard-shell clam *n.* See **quahog.**

hard-shell crab *n.* A marine crab with a fully hardened shell, especially an edible crab in this stage.

hard-shelled (härd′shĕld′) *adj.* Variant of **hard-shell.**

hard·ship (härd′shĭp′) *n.* **1.** Extreme privation; suffering. **2.** A cause of privation or suffering. See Synonyms at **difficulty.**

hard-spun (härd′spŭn′) *adj.* Twisted tightly in spinning, often to the point of curling and looping. Used of yarn.

hard·stand (härd′stănd′) *n.* A hard-surfaced area for parking aircraft or ground vehicles.

hard·tack (härd′tăk′) *n.* A hard biscuit or bread made with flour and water. Also called *sea biscuit, sea bread, ship biscuit.*

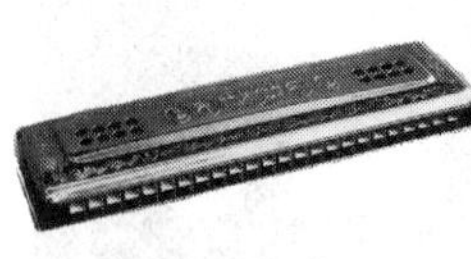

harmonica

hard·top (härd′tŏp′) *n.* An automobile designed to look like a convertible but having a rigidly fixed, hard top.

hard·ware (härd′wâr′) *n. Abbr.* **hdwe. 1.** Metal goods and utensils such as locks, tools, and cutlery. **2. a.** *Computer Science.* A computer and the associated physical equipment directly involved in the performance of data-processing or communications functions. **b.** Machines and other physical equipment directly involved in performing an industrial, technological, or military function. **3.** *Informal.* Weapons, especially military weapons. —*attributive.* Often used to modify another noun: *hardware manufacturers; hardware add-ons.*

hard-wired (härd′wīrd′) *adj.* **1.** *Computer Science.* Of, relating to, or implemented through logic circuitry permanently connected within a computer or calculator and therefore not subject to change by programming. **2.** Directly connected by electrical wires or cables. **—hard′wire′** *v.*

hard·wood (härd′wo͝od′) *n.* **1.** The wood of a dicotyledonous tree. **2.** A dicotyledonous tree.

har·dy¹ (här′dē) *adj.* **-di·er, -di·est. 1.** Being in robust and sturdy good health. See Synonyms at **healthy. 2.** Courageous; intrepid. **3.** Brazenly daring; audacious. **4.** Capable of surviving unfavorable conditions, such as cold weather or lack of moisture. Used especially of cultivated plants. [Middle English, from Old French *hardi,* past participle of *hardir,* make hard, embolden, of Germanic origin. See **kar-** in Appendix.] **—har′di·ly** *adv.* **—har′di·ness** *n.*

har·dy² (här′dē) *n., pl.* **-dies.** A square-shanked chisel that fits into a square hole in an anvil. [Probably from HARD.]

Har·dy (här′dē), **Oliver.** 1892–1957. American comedian famous for the slapstick abuse he inflicted upon his partner in the comedy team of Laurel and Hardy.

Hardy, Thomas. 1840–1928. British writer noted for his Wessex novels, including *Far from the Madding Crowd* (1874), *The Mayor of Casterbridge* (1886), and *Tess of the d'Urbervilles* (1891).

Har·dy-Wein·berg law (här′dē-wīn′bûrg) *n.* A fundamental principal in population genetics stating that the genotype frequencies and gene frequencies of a large, randomly mating population remain constant provided immigration, mutation, and selection do not take place. [After Godfrey Harold *Hardy* (1877–1947), British mathematician, and Wilhelm *Weinberg* (1862–1937), German physician.]

hare (hâr) *n.* Any of various mammals of the family Leporidae, especially of the genus *Lepus,* similar to rabbits but having longer ears and legs and giving birth to active, furred young. **—hare** *intr.v.* **hared, har·ing, hares.** To move hurriedly, as if hunting a swift quarry: *went haring off after a lower-priced car.* [Middle English, from Old English *hara.* See **kas-** in Appendix.]

hare and hounds *n. Games.* A game in which one group leaves a trail of paper scraps for a pursuing group to follow.

hare·bell (hâr′bĕl′) *n.* A perennial plant *(Campanula rotundifolia)* having slender stems, dense clusters of basal leaves, and bell-shaped blue or white flowers. Also called *bluebell.*

hare·brained (hâr′brānd′) *adj.* Foolish; flighty: *a harebrained scheme.*

USAGE NOTE: The first part of the compound *harebrained* is often misspelled *hair* in the belief that the meaning of the word is "with a hair-sized brain" rather than "with no more sense than a hare." Though *hairbrained* has a long history, this spelling is not established usage.

Ha·re Krish·na (hä′rē krĭsh′nə) *n., pl.* **Hare Krish·nas. 1.** A chant to the Hindu god Krishna. **2.** *Informal.* **a.** A member of the International Society for Krishna Consciousness (ISKCON), founded in the United States in 1966. **b.** The society itself. [From the chant *Hare Krishna* : Sanskrit *hare,* vocative of *Hariḥ,* a name of Vishnu (from *hari-,* yellow-green, tawny yellow; see **ghel-²** in Appendix) + Sanskrit *Kṛṣṇā,* Krishna.]

hare·lip (hâr′lĭp′) *n.* A congenital deformity marked by a vertical cleft or pair of clefts in the upper lip. **—hare′lipped′** *adj.*

har·em (hâr′əm, hăr′-) *n.* **1.** A house or a section of a house reserved for women members of a Moslem household. **2.** The wives, concubines, female relatives, and servants occupying such a place. **3.** A group of women sexual partners for one man. [Turkish, from Persian *ḥaram,* from Arabic *ḥarīm,* sacred, forbidden place, from *ḥarama,* to be prohibited.]

Har·greaves (här′grēvz′), **James.** Died 1778. British inventor of the spinning jenny (c. 1764). He patented his device in 1770.

har·i·cot¹ (hăr′ĭ-kō′) *n.* The edible pod or seed of any of several beans, especially the kidney bean. [French, possibly alteration (influenced by French *haricot,* stew; see HARICOT²) of Nahuatl *ayacotli.*]

har·i·cot² (hăr′ĭ-kō′) *n.* A highly seasoned mutton or lamb stew with vegetables. [French, from Old French *hericot, hericoq,* possibly from *harigoter,* to cut into pieces, probably of Germanic origin.]

ha·ri-ka·ri (här′ē-kär′ē, hăr′ē-kăr′ē) *n.* Variant of **hara-kiri.**

Ha·ri Rud (här′ē ro͞od′). A river, about 1,126 km (700 mi) long, of northwest Afghanistan, northeast Iran, and Turkmenistan.

hark (härk) *intr.v.* **harked, hark·ing, harks.** To listen attentively. **—*idiom.* hark back.** To return to a previous point, as in a narrative. [Middle English *harken, herken,* from Old English **heorcian.*]

har·ken (här′kən) *v.* Variant of **hearken.**

Har·lan (här′lən), **John Marshall.** 1833–1911. American jurist. As an associate justice of the U.S. Supreme Court (1877–1911) he was known for his outspoken dissenting opinions. His grandson **John Marshall Harlan** (1899–1971) also served as an associate justice of the Court (1955–1971).

Har·lem (här′ləm). A section of New York City in northern Manhattan bordering on the Harlem and East rivers. Peter Stuyvesant established the Dutch settlement of Nieuw Haarlem here in 1658. A rapid influx of Black people beginning c. 1910 made it one of the largest Black communities in the United States. After World War II many Hispanics settled in East (or Spanish) Harlem. **—Har′lem·ite′** *n.*

Harlem River. A channel in New York City separating the northern end of Manhattan Island from the Bronx. With Spuyten Duyvil Creek it connects the Hudson and East rivers.

har·le·quin (här′lĭ-kwĭn, -kĭn) *n.* **1. Harlequin.** A conventional buffoon of the commedia dell'arte, traditionally presented in a mask and parti-colored tights. **2.** A clown; a buffoon. **—harlequin** *adj. Abbr.* **hlqn** Having a pattern of brightly colored diamond shapes. [Obsolete French, from Old French *Herlequin, Hellequin,* a demon, perhaps from Middle English **Herleking,* from Old English *Herla cyning,* King Herla, a mythical figure identified with Woden.]

har·le·quin·ade (här′lĭ-kwə-nād′) *n.* **1.** A comedy or pantomime in which Harlequin is the main attraction. **2.** Farcical clowning or buffoonery. [Obsolete French, from *harlequin,* harlequin. See HARLEQUIN.]

harlequin bug *n.* A flat-bodied, brightly colored stinkbug

ă pat	oi boy
ā pay	ou out
âr care	o͝o took
ä father	o͞o boot
ĕ pet	ŭ cut
ē be	ûr urge
ĭ pit	th thin
ī pie	*th* this
îr pier	hw which
ŏ pot	zh vision
ō toe	ə about, item
ô paw	♦ regionalism

Stress marks: ′ (primary); ′ (secondary), as in **dictionary** (dĭk′shə-nĕr′ē)

(Murgantia histrionica) that is destructive to cabbage and other cruciferous plants. Also called *calicoback.*

Har·lin·gen (här′lĭn-jən). A city of extreme southern Texas northwest of Brownsville. It is a processing and shipping center for the lower Rio Grande valley. Population, 43,543.

har·lot (här′lət) *n.* A prostitute. [Middle English, vagabond, rogue, lecher, harlot, from Old French *arlot, herlot,* vagabond.] **—har′lot·ry** (-lə-trē) *n.*

WORD HISTORY: *Harlot* is first recorded in English in a work written around the beginning of the 13th century, meaning "a man of no fixed occupation, vagabond, beggar," also the first main sense of the word *herlot,* which we borrowed from Old French. The recorded history of a word is sometimes all we need to scotch conjectures as to its ultimate origins. William Lambarde, in a 1570–1576 work, suggested that the word *harlot* came from the name of Arletta, or "Harlothe," William the Conqueror's mother. As we have seen, Lambarde was unnecessarily besmirching her, for the history of *harlot* makes clear that "prostitute" was not its first sense. In fact, the word came to mean "male lecher" before it meant "prostitute," but by the time Lambarde wrote, "prostitute" must have been thought to have been the main sense of the word, hence his etymology.

Har·low (här′lō). An urban district of southeast England northeast of London. It was designated as a new town in 1946 to alleviate overpopulation in London. Population, 79,400.

Harlow, Jean. 1911–1937. American actress known for her beauty and sardonic wit. Her films include *Red Dust* (1932).

harm (härm) *n.* **1.** Physical or psychological injury or damage. **2.** Wrong; evil. **—harm** *tr.v.* **harmed, harm·ing, harms.** To do harm to. See Synonyms at **injure.** [Middle English, from Old English *hearm.*]

har·mat·tan (här′mə-tăn′, här-măt′n) *n.* A dry, dusty wind that blows along the northwest coast of Africa. [Akan (Twi) *haramata,* possibly from Arabic *ḥarām,* evil thing.]

harm·ful (härm′fəl) *adj.* Causing or capable of causing harm; injurious. **—harm′ful·ly** *adv.* **—harm′ful·ness** *n.*

harm·less (härm′lĭs) *adj.* **1.** Incapable of causing harm. **2.** Free from loss or legal liability: *Under the agreement, I would be held harmless if the other parties defaulted.* **—harm′less·ly** *adv.* **—harm′less·ness** *n.*

har·mo·lod·ic (här′mə-lŏd′ĭk) *adj. Music.* Relating to a style of modern improvisational music in which different, contrasting instruments are played in different keys or tempos. [Possibly from HAR(MONY) + MO(VEMENT) + (ME)LODIC.]

har·mon·ic (här-mŏn′ĭk) *adj.* **1.** *Music.* **a.** Of or relating to harmony. **b.** Pleasing to the ear: *harmonic orchestral effects.* **c.** Characterized by harmony: *a harmonic liturgical chant.* **2.** Of or relating to harmonics. **3.** Integrated in nature. **—harmonic** *n.* *Music.* **1.a.** A tone in the harmonic series of overtones produced by a fundamental tone. **b.** A tone produced on a stringed instrument by lightly touching an open or stopped vibrating string at a given fraction of its length so that both segments vibrate. Also called *overtone, partial, partial tone.* **2.** A wave whose frequency is a whole-number multiple of that of another. **3. harmonics** *(used with a sing. verb).* The theory or study of the physical properties and characteristics of musical sound. [Latin *harmonicus,* from Greek *harmonikos,* from *harmonia,* harmony. See HARMONY.] **—har·mon′i·cal·ly** *adv.*

har·mon·i·ca (här-mŏn′ĭ-kə) *n. Music.* **1.** A small, rectangular instrument consisting of a row of free reeds set back in air holes, played by exhaling or inhaling. Also called *mouth organ.* **2.** A glass harmonica. **3.** An instrument consisting of tuned strips of metal or glass fixed to a frame and struck with a hammer. [Alteration of obsolete *armonica,* glass harmonica, from Italian, feminine of *armonico,* harmonious, from Latin *harmonicus,* harmonic. See HARMONIC.]

harmonic analysis *n. Mathematics.* The representation of functions by means of linear operations such as summation or integration on characteristic sets of functions, especially such representation by Fourier series.

harmonic mean *n. Mathematics.* The reciprocal of the arithmetic mean of the reciprocals of a specified set of numbers.

harmonic motion *n.* A periodic vibration, as of a violin string, in which the motions are symmetrical about a region of equilibrium. Such a vibration may have only one frequency and amplitude or may be a combination of two or more components. Also called *simple harmonic motion.*

harmonic progression *n. Mathematics.* A sequence of quantities whose reciprocals form an arithmetic progression, such as 1, $\frac{1}{3}$, $\frac{1}{5}$, $\frac{1}{7}$, ...

harmonic series *n.* **1.** *Mathematics.* A series whose terms are in harmonic progression, as $1 + \frac{1}{3} + \frac{1}{5} + \frac{1}{7} + \ldots$. **2.** *Music.* A series of tones consisting of a fundamental tone and the overtones produced by it, and whose frequencies are consecutive integral multiples of the frequency of the fundamental.

har·mo·ni·ous (här-mō′nē-əs) *adj.* **1.** Exhibiting accord in feeling or action. **2.** Having component elements pleasingly or appropriately combined: *a harmonious blend of architectural styles.* **3.** Characterized by harmony of sound; melodious. **—har·mo′ni·ous·ly** *adv.* **—har·mo′ni·ous·ness** *n.*

har·mo·nist (här′mə-nĭst) *n. Music.* One skilled in harmony. **—har′mo·nis′tic** *adj.* **—har′mo·nis′ti·cal·ly** *adv.*

har·mo·ni·um (här-mō′nē-əm) *n. Music.* An organlike keyboard instrument that produces tones with free metal reeds actuated by air forced from a bellows. [French, from *harmonie,* harmony, from Old French *armonie, harmonie.* See HARMONY.]

har·mo·nize (här′mə-nīz′) *v.* **-nized, -niz·ing, -niz·es.** *—tr.* **1.** To bring or come into agreement or harmony. See Synonyms at **agree. 2.** *Music.* To provide harmony for (a melody). *—intr.* **1.** To be in agreement; be harmonious. **2.** *Music.* To sing or play in harmony. **—har′mo·ni·za′tion** (-nĭ-zā′shən) *n.* **—har′mo·niz′er** *n.*

har·mo·ny (här′mə-nē) *n., pl.* **-nies. 1.** Agreement in feeling or opinion; accord: *live in harmony.* **2.** A pleasing combination of elements in a whole: *color harmony; the order and harmony of the universe.* See Synonyms at **proportion. 3.** *Music.* **a.** The study of the structure, progression, and relation of chords. **b.** Simultaneous combination of notes in a chord. **c.** The structure of a work or passage as considered from the point of view of its chordal characteristics and relationships. **d.** A combination of sounds considered pleasing to the ear. **4.** A collation of parallel passages, especially from the Gospels, with a commentary demonstrating their consonance and explaining their discrepancies. [Middle English *armonie,* from Old French, from Latin *harmonia,* from Greek, articulation, agreement, harmony, from *harmos,* joint. See **ar-** in Appendix.]

harm's way (härmz) *n.* A risky position; danger: *a place for the children that is out of harm's way.*

Harms·worth (härmz′wûrth′), **Alfred Charles William.** Viscount Northcliffe. 1865–1922. British newspaper publisher who founded the *Daily Mail* (1896) and the *Daily Mirror* (1903).

har·ness (här′nĭs) *n.* **1.** The gear or tackle, other than a yoke, with which a draft animal pulls a vehicle or an implement. **2.** Something resembling such gear or tackle, as the arrangement of straps used to hold a parachute to the body. **3.** A device that raises and lowers the warp threads on a loom. **4.** *Archaic.* Armor for a man or horse. **—harness** *tr.v.* **-nessed, -ness·ing, -ness·es. 1.a.** To put a harness on (a draft animal). **b.** To fasten by the use of a harness. **2.** To bring under control and direct the force of: *If you can harness your energy, you will accomplish a great deal.* **—*idiom.* in harness.** On duty or at work. [Middle English *harnes,* from Old French *harneis,* of Germanic origin. See **nes-**[1] in Appendix.] **—har′ness·er** *n.*

har·nessed antelope (här′nĭst) *n.* See **bushbuck.**

harness race *n. Sports.* A horserace between pacers or trotters harnessed to sulkies. **—harness racing** *n.*

Har·old I (hăr′əld). Known as "Harold Harefoot." Died 1040. King of England (1035–1040). The illegitimate son of Canute, Harold claimed the English throne after his father's death.

Harold II. 1022?–1066. King of England (1066) and the last of the Anglo-Saxon monarchs. He succeeded Edward the Confessor and was killed fighting the invasion of William the Conqueror.

Harold III. 1015–1066. King of Norway (1045–1066) who invaded England in 1066 and was killed in battle.

Ha·roun al-Ra·schid (hä-ro͞on′ äl-rä-shēd′). See **Harun al-Rashid.**

harp (härp) *n.* **1.** *Music.* An instrument consisting of an upright, open triangular frame with usually 46 strings of graded lengths played by plucking with the fingers. **2.** Something, such as a pair of vertical supports for a lampshade, that resembles this musical instrument. **—harp** *intr.v.* **harped, harp·ing, harps.** To play a harp. **—*phrasal verb.* harp on.** To talk or write about to an excessive and tedious degree; dwell on. [Middle English, from Old English *hearpe* and from Old French *harpe,* of Germanic origin.] **—harp′er** *n.* **—harp′ist** *n.*

Har·per (här′pər). Family of American printers and publishers, including **James** (1795–1869), **John** (1797–1875), **Joseph Wesley** (1801–1870), and **Fletcher** (1806–1877).

Har·pers Ferry (här′pərz). A locality of extreme northeast West Virginia. It was the scene of John Brown's rebellion (1859), in which he briefly seized the U.S. arsenal.

Harper Woods. A city of southeast Michigan, a suburb of Detroit. Population, 16,361.

har·poon (här-po͞on′) *n.* A spearlike weapon with a barbed head used in hunting whales and large fish. **—harpoon** *tr.v.* **-pooned, -poon·ing, -poons.** To strike, kill, or capture with or as if with a spearlike weapon. [Probably from Dutch *harpoen,* from Middle Dutch, from Old French *harpon,* possibly from *harpe,* clamp, claw, from Latin *harpa,* sickle, from Greek *harpē.*] **—har·poon′er** *n.*

harpoon gun *n.* A small cannonlike apparatus used to fire harpoons.

harp seal *n.* An earless seal *(Pagophilus groenlandicus)* of the North Atlantic and Arctic oceans whose pups are hunted for their fine, white fur. [From the shape of the markings on its shoulders and sides.]

harp·si·chord (härp′sĭ-kôrd′, -kōrd′) *n. Music.* A keyboard instrument whose strings are plucked by means of quills or plectrums. [Alteration of obsolete French *harpechorde,* from Italian *arpicordo* : *arpa,* harp (from Late Latin *harpa,* of Germanic origin) + *corda,* string (from Latin *chorda,* from Greek *khordē;* see **ghere-** in Appendix).] **—harp′si·chord′ist** *n.*

Har·py (här′pē) *n., pl.* **-pies. 1.** *Greek Mythology.* One of several loathsome, voracious monsters with the head and trunk of

harness

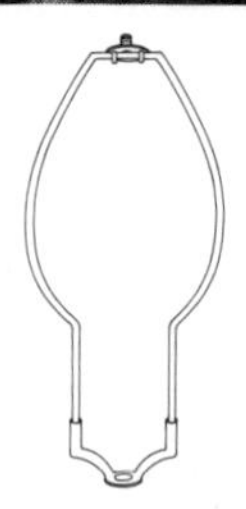

harp
Top: Musical instrument
Bottom: For a lampshade

harpoon
Eskimo hunting with a harpoon

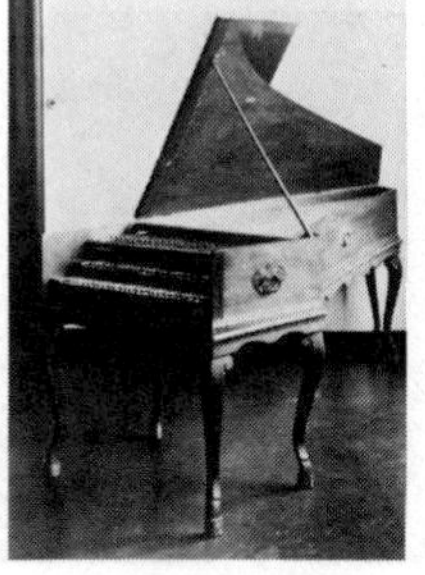

harpsichord

harquebus
c. 1550 Austrian

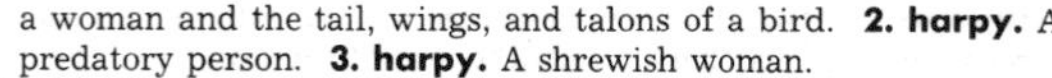

a woman and the tail, wings, and talons of a bird. **2. harpy.** A predatory person. **3. harpy.** A shrewish woman.

har·que·bus (här′kə-bəs, -kwə-) also **ar·que·bus** (är′-) *n.* A heavy, portable matchlock gun invented during the 15th century. Also called *hackbut.* [Obsolete French *harquebuse,* from Old French, alteration of Middle Dutch *hakebus* : *hake,* hook; see **keg-** in Appendix + *busse,* gun (from Late Latin *buxis,* box; see BOX[1]).]

Har·ran (hä-rän′). See **Haran.**

har·ri·dan (hăr′ĭ-dn) *n.* A woman regarded as scolding and vicious. [Possibly from French *haridelle,* gaunt woman, old horse, nag.]

har·ri·er[1] (hăr′ē-ər) *n.* **1.** One that harries. **2.** Any of various slender, narrow-winged hawks of the genus *Circus,* such as the marsh hawk, that prey on small animals. [Sense 2, alteration (influenced by HARRY) of obsolete *harrower,* from HARROW[2].]

har·ri·er[2] (hăr′ē-ər) *n.* **1.** Any of a breed of small hounds originally used in hunting hares and rabbits. **2.** *Sports.* A cross-country runner. [Middle English *hairer, eirer,* possibly alteration (influenced by *hair, hare,* hare; see HARE) of Old French *errier,* wanderer, from *errer,* to wander. See ERR.]

Har·ri·man (hăr′ə-mən), **Edward Henry.** 1848–1909. American railway magnate. He joined J.P. Morgan and James J. Hill to form the Northern Securities Company, a railroad trust that was ordered dissolved by the U.S. Supreme Court (1904).

Harriman, (William) Averell. 1891–1986. American financier and diplomat who held a number of public offices, including ambassador to the U.S.S.R. (1943–1946).

Har·ris (hăr′ĭs), **Benjamin.** fl. 1673–1713. English publisher and journalist in Massachusetts. His *Publick Occurrences* was the first newspaper printed in America (1690).

Harris, Frank. 1856–1931. Irish-born American writer known for his autobiography *My Life and Loves* (1923–1927).

Harris, Joel Chandler. 1848–1908. American writer and journalist who wrote *Uncle Remus: His Songs and His Sayings* (1880) and its many sequels.

Harris, Roy Ellsworth. 1898–1979. American composer known especially for his folk-inspired symphonies.

Harris, Townsend. 1804–1878. American diplomat who as the first U.S. consul general to Japan (1855–1860) was instrumental in opening that country to Western trade.

Benjamin Harrison[2]

Har·ris·burg (hăr′ĭs-bûrg′). The capital of Pennsylvania, in the southeast-central part of the state west-northwest of Philadelphia. Settled in the early 1700's as Harris' Ferry, it was renamed in 1785 and became the capital in 1812. Population, 53,264.

Har·ri·son (hăr′ĭ-sən). A village of southeast New York, a residential suburb of New York City. Population, 23,046.

Harrison, Benjamin[1]. 1726–1791. American Revolutionary leader who served as a member of the Continental Congress (1774–1778) and was also governor of Virginia (1782–1784).

Harrison, Benjamin[2]. 1833–1901. The 23rd President of the United States (1889–1893). The first Pan-American Conference took place (1889) during his administration.

Harrison, George. Born 1943. British singer and songwriter who was formerly lead guitarist with the Beatles. His compositions include "My Sweet Lord."

George Harrison

Harrison, Sir **Reginald Carey.** Known as "Rex." 1908–1990. British actor best remembered for his portrayal of Professor Henry Higgins in the Broadway musical and film versions of *My Fair Lady.*

Harrison, William Henry. 1773–1841. The ninth President of the United States (1841). He died of pneumonia after one month in office.

Har·ri·son·burg (hăr′ĭ-sən-bûrg′). An independent city of north-central Virginia northwest of Charlottesville. It is a processing center in an agricultural region. Population, 19,671.

har·row[1] (hăr′ō) *n.* A farm implement consisting of a heavy frame with sharp teeth or upright disks, used to break up and even off plowed ground. **—harrow** *tr.v.* **-rowed, -row·ing, -rows. 1.** To break up and level (soil or land) with a harrow. **2.** To inflict great distress or torment on. [Middle English *harwe.*] **—har′row·er** *n.*

har·row[2] (hăr′ō) *tr.v.* **-rowed, -row·ing, -rows.** *Archaic.* To plunder; sack. [Middle English *herwen,* variant of *harien.* See HARRY.]

Har·row (hăr′ō). A mainly residential district of northeast Greater London. It is the site of the public school Harrow, founded in 1571.

har·row·ing (hăr′ō-ĭng) *adj.* Extremely distressing; agonizing: *a harrowing experience.*

har·rumph (hə-rŭmf′) *intr.v.* **-rumphed, -rumph·ing, -rumphs. 1.** To make a show of clearing one's throat. **2.** To offer usually brief critical comments: *harrumphed for a while over the proposal.* [Imitative.] **—har·rumph′** *n.*

William Henry Harrison

har·ry (hăr′ē) *tr.v.* **-ried, -ry·ing, -ries. 1.** To disturb or distress by or as if by repeated attacks; harass. See Synonyms at **harass. 2.** To raid, as in war; sack or pillage. [Middle English *harien,* from Old English *hergian.* See **koro-** in Appendix.]

harsh (härsh) *adj.* **harsh·er, harsh·est. 1.** Unpleasantly coarse and rough to the touch. See Synonyms at **rough. 2.** Disagreeable to the senses, especially to the sense of hearing. **3.** Extremely severe or exacting; stern. [Middle English *harsk,* of Scandinavian origin.] **—harsh′ly** *adv.* **—harsh′ness** *n.*

harsh·en (här′shən) *tr. & intr.v.* **-ened, -en·ing, -ens.** To make or become harsh.

hars·let (här′slĭt) *n.* Variant of **haslet.**

hart (härt) *n., pl.* **harts** or **hart.** A male deer, especially a male red deer over five years old. [Middle English, from Old English *heorot.* See **ker-[1]** in Appendix.]

Hart (härt), **Lorenz Milton.** 1895–1943. American lyricist whose song credits include "The Lady Is a Tramp," "My Funny Valentine," and "Blue Moon."

Hart, Moss. 1904–1961. American playwright, librettist, and director. He wrote a number of Broadway comedies with George S. Kaufman, including *The Man Who Came to Dinner* (1939).

Harte (härt), **(Francis) Bret.** 1836–1902. American writer noted for his stories about California mining towns. *The Luck of Roaring Camp and Other Sketches* (1870) is his best-known collection.

har·te·beest (här′tə-bēst′, härt′bēst′) *n., pl.* **-beests** or **hartebeest.** Any of various large African antelopes of the genus *Alcelaphus,* characterized by a reddish-brown coat and ringed, outward-curving horns. [Obsolete Afrikaans, from Middle Dutch, variant of *hertebeest* : *hert,* deer; see **ker-[1]** in Appendix + *beest,* beast (from Old French *beste;* see BEAST).]

Hart·ford (härt′fərd). The capital of Connecticut, in the north-central part of the state on the Connecticut River. Settled 1635–1636 by Massachusetts colonists on the site of a Dutch trading post, it became the nucleus of the Connecticut Colony in 1639. From 1701 to 1875 it was joint capital with New Haven. Population, 136,392.

Har·tle·pool (härt′lē-po͞ol′, här′tl-). A borough of northeast England on the North Sea south-southeast of Newcastle. It is a seaport with iron and steel industries. Population, 94,600.

hart's-tongue (härts′tŭng′) *n.* A European evergreen fern *(Phyllitis scolopendrium)* with narrow, undivided fronds. [So called from the shape of its fronds.]

har·um-scar·um (hâr′əm-skâr′əm, hăr′əm-skăr′əm) *adj.* Lacking a sense of responsibility; reckless. **—harum-scarum** *adv.* With abandon; recklessly. [From *hare,* to frighten + SCARE.]

Ha·run al-Ra·shid or **Ha·roun al-Ra·schid** (hä-ro͞on′ äl-rä-shēd′) also **Harun ar-Ra·shid** (är′-). 763?–809. Caliph of Baghdad (786–809) noted for his participation in the Moslem holy war against the Byzantines and for the splendor of his court.

ha·rus·pex (hə-rŭs′pĕks′, hăr′ə-spĕks′) also **a·rus·pex** (ə-rŭs′pĕks′) *n., pl.* **ha·rus·pi·ces** (hə-rŭs′pĭ-sēz′) also **a·rus·pi·ces** (ə-rŭs′pĭ-sēz′). A priest in ancient Rome who practiced divination by the inspection of the entrails of animals. [Latin. See **ghere-** in Appendix.]

Har·vard (här′vərd), **John.** 1607–1638. American cleric and philanthropist who left his library and half his estate to the college in Cambridge, Massachusetts, that now bears his name.

Harvard, Mount. A peak, 4,398.1 m (14,420 ft) high, in the Sawatch Range of the Rocky Mountains in central Colorado.

har·vest (här′vĭst) *n.* **1.** The act or process of gathering a crop. **2.a.** The crop that ripens or is gathered in a season. **b.** The amount or measure of the crop gathered in a season. **c.** The time or season of such gathering. **3.** The result or consequence of an activity. *—attributive.* Often used to modify another noun: *a harvest festival; harvest gleanings.* **—harvest** *v.* **-vest·ed, -vest·ing, -vests.** *—tr.* **1.** To gather (a crop). **2.** To gather a crop from. **3.** To receive (the benefits or consequences of an action). See Synonyms at **reap.** *—intr.* To gather a crop. [Middle English, from Old English *hærfest.* See **kerp-** in Appendix.] **—har′vest·a·ble** *adj.* **—har′vest·a·bil′i·ty** *n.*

harvest bug *n.* See **chigger** (sense 1).

har·vest·er (här′vĭ-stər) *n.* **1.** One who gathers a crop. **2.** A machine for harvesting crops; a reaper.

harvest fly *n.* Any of several cicadas of the genus *Tibicen* that produce a shrill sound heard late in summer.

harvest home *n.* **1.** The completion of a harvest. **2.a.** The time of completing a harvest. **b.** A festival held at this time. **c.** A song sung at this time.

har·vest·man (här′vĭst-mən) *n.* **1.** A man who harvests. **2.** See **daddy longlegs** (sense 1).

harvest mite *n.* See **chigger** (sense 1).

harvest moon *n.* The full moon that occurs nearest the autumnal equinox.

Har·vey (här′vē). A city of northeast Illinois, an industrial suburb of Chicago. Population, 35,810.

Harvey, William. 1578–1657. English physician, anatomist, and physiologist who discovered the circulation of blood in the human body (1628).

Harz Mountains (härts). A mountain range of central Germany extending about 97 km (60 mi) between the Weser and the Elbe. The range rises to 1,142.8 m (3,747 ft).

has (hăz) *v.* Third person singular present tense of **have.**

has-been (hăz′bĭn′) *n., pl.* **has-beens.** *Informal.* One that is no longer famous, popular, successful, or useful.

Has·dru·bal (hăz′dro͞o′bəl, hăz-dro͞o′-). Died 207 B.C. Carthaginian general who attempted to establish military dominance on the Iberian Peninsula during the Second Punic War but was defeated by Roman forces (207).

ha·sen·pfef·fer (hä′zən-fĕf′ər, -sən-) *n.* A highly seasoned stew of marinated rabbit meat. [German : *Hase,* rabbit (from Middle High German, from Old High German *haso;* see **kas-** in Appendix) + *Pfeffer,* pepper (from Old High German *pfeffar,* from Latin *piper;* see PEPPER).]

hash¹ (hăsh) *n.* **1.** A dish of chopped meat, potatoes, and sometimes vegetables, usually browned. **2.a.** A jumble; a hodgepodge. **b.** *Informal.* A mess: *made a hash of the project.* **3.** A reworking or restatement of already familiar material. **—hash** *tr.v.* **hashed, hash·ing, hash·es. 1.** To chop into pieces; mince. **2.** *Informal.* To make a mess of; mangle. **3.** *Informal.* To discuss carefully; review: *hash over future plans.* **—*idiom.* settle (someone's) hash.** *Slang.* To silence or subdue. [Variant of Middle English *hache,* from Old French, past participle of *hacher, hachier,* to chop up, from *hache,* ax, of Germanic origin. See HATCHET.]

hash² (hăsh) *n. Slang.* Hashish.

hash browns (brounz) *pl.n.* Chopped cooked potatoes, fried until brown. Also called *hash brown potatoes.*

hash·eesh (hăsh′ēsh′, hă-shēsh′, hä-) *n.* Variant of **hashish.**

hash house *n. Slang.* A cheap restaurant.

hash·ish (hăsh′ēsh′, -ĭsh, hă-shēsh′, hä-) also **hash·eesh** (hăsh′ēsh′, hă-shēsh′, hä-) *n.* A purified resin prepared from the flowering tops of the female cannabis plant and smoked or chewed as a narcotic or an intoxicant. [Arabic *ḥašīš,* hemp, dried grass.]

hash mark *n.* **1.** A service stripe on the sleeve of an enlisted person's uniform. **2.** *Football.* A mark in either of two series placed on the field perpendicular to the yard lines and used for spotting the ball. [Alteration of HATCH³.]

hash slinger *n. Slang.* One who provides food in a cheap restaurant.

Ha·sid or **Has·sid** also **Chas·sid** (KHä′sĭd, KHô′-, hä′-) *n., pl.* **Ha·si·dim** or **Has·si·dim** also **Chas·si·dim** (KHä-sē′dĭm, KHô′-, hä′-). A member of a movement of popular mysticism founded in Eastern Europe in the 18th century. [From Hebrew *ḥāsîd,* pious.] **—Ha·si′dic** *adj.* **—Ha·si′dism** *n.*

has·let (hăs′lĭt, hăz′-) also **hars·let** (här′slĭt) *n.* The heart, liver, and other edible viscera of an animal, especially hog viscera. [Middle English *hastelet,* from Old French, diminutive of *haste,* roast meat, spit, perhaps from Latin *hasta,* spear, or of Germanic origin.]

has·n't (hăz′ənt). Has not.

hasp (hăsp) *n.* A metal fastener with a hinged, slotted part that fits over a staple and is secured by a pin, bolt, or padlock. **—hasp** *tr.v.* **hasped, hasp·ing, hasps.** To close or lock with such a fastener. [Middle English, from Old English *hæsp, hæpse.*]

Has·sam (hăs′əm), **(Frederick) Childe.** 1859–1935. American painter who used brilliant colors and bold brushwork to depict city street scenes and natural landscapes in works such as *Rainy Day in Boston* (1885).

Has·sel (hä′səl), **Odd.** 1897–1981. Norwegian chemist. He shared a 1969 Nobel Prize for the study of organic molecules.

Has·sid (KHä′sĭd, KHô′-, hä′-) *n.* Variant of **Hasid.**

has·sle (hăs′əl) *Informal. n.* **1.** An argument or a fight. **2.** Trouble; bother. **—hassle** *v.* **-sled, -sling, -sles.** —*intr.* To argue or fight: *customers hassling with merchants over high prices.* —*tr.* To bother or harass: *street gangs hassling passersby.* [Origin unknown.]

WORD HISTORY: It is difficult to believe that there were no hassles before 1945, but that is the year in which the noun *hassle* is first recorded in English. The origins of this word might be considered a hassle for the etymologist. An English dialect word, *hassle,* meaning "to hack at, cut with a blunt knife and with a sawing motion," is recorded at the end of the 19th century. A Southern dialect word, *hassle,* "to pant, breathe heavily," is also a possible source. A more popular notion has been that *hassle* is a blend, but here again we have a hassle. Three separate possibilities have been proposed, a combination of *harass* and *hustle, haggle* and *tussle,* and *haggle* and *wrestle.* Given all these possibilities, it is clear why words such as *hassle* end up with the etymology "origin unknown."

has·sock (hăs′ək) *n.* **1.** A thick cushion used as a footstool or for kneeling. **2.** A dense clump of grass. [Middle English *hassok,* clump of grass, from Old English *hassuc.*]

hast (hăst) *v. Archaic.* Second person singular present tense of **have.**

has·tate (hăs′tāt′) *adj. Botany.* Having the shape of an arrowhead but with the basal lobes pointing outward at right angles: *hastate leaves.* [From Latin *hasta,* spear.] **—has′tate′ly** *adv.*

haste (hāst) *n.* **1.** Rapidity of action or motion. **2.** Overeagerness to act. **3.** Rash or headlong action; precipitateness. **—haste** *intr. & tr.v.* **hast·ed, hast·ing, hastes.** To hasten or cause to hasten. **—*idiom.* make haste.** To move or act swiftly; hurry. [Middle English, from Old French, of Germanic origin.]

SYNONYMS: *haste, celerity, dispatch, expedition, hurry, speed.* The central meaning shared by these nouns is "rapidity or promptness of movement or activity": *left the room in haste; a legal system not known for celerity; advanced with all possible dispatch; cleaned up the room with remarkable expedition; worked systematically but without hurry; driving with excessive speed.*

ANTONYM: *deliberation.*

has·ten (hā′sən) *v.* **-tened, -ten·ing, -tens.** —*intr.* To move or act swiftly. —*tr.* **1.** To cause to hurry. **2.** To speed up; accelerate: *fanned the wet paint to hasten drying.* See Synonyms at **speed.**

Has·tings (hā′stĭngz). **1.** A borough of southeast England on the English Channel at the entrance to the Strait of Dover. Hastings is near the site of William the Conqueror's victory over the Saxons (October 14, 1066). Population, 75,900. **2.** A city of southern Nebraska south of Grand Island. Population, 23,045.

Hastings, Thomas. 1860–1929. American architect who with John Merven Carrère formed an important architectural firm whose designs include that of the New York Public Library (1897–1911) and numerous mansions.

Hastings, Warren. 1732–1818. British colonial administrator who as governor-general of India (1773–1785) carried out land and legal reforms and instituted British control of the Indian government.

hast·y (hā′stē) *adj.* **-i·er, -i·est. 1.** Characterized by speed; rapid. See Synonyms at **fast¹. 2.** Done or made too quickly to be accurate or wise; rash: *a hasty decision.* See Synonyms at **impetuous. 3.** Easily angered; irritable. **—hast′i·ly** *adv.* **—hast′i·ness** *n.*

hasty pudding *n.* **1.** Cornmeal mush served with maple syrup, brown sugar, or other sweetening. **2.** *Chiefly British.* A mush made with flour or oatmeal.

hat (hăt) *n.* **1.** A covering for the head, especially one with a shaped crown and brim. **2.a.** A head covering of distinctive color and shape worn as a symbol of office. **b.** The office symbolized by the wearing of such a head covering. **3.** A role or an office symbolized by or as if by the wearing of different head coverings: *wears two hats—one as parent and one as corporate executive.* **—hat** *tr.v.* **hat·ted, hat·ting, hats.** To supply or cover with a hat. **—*idioms.* at the drop of a hat.** At the slightest pretext or provocation. **hat in hand.** In a humble manner; humbly. **pass the hat.** To take up a collection of money. **take (one's) hat off to.** To respect, admire, or congratulate. **talk through (one's) hat. 1.** To talk nonsense. **2.** To bluff. **throw** (or **toss**) **(one's) hat into the ring.** To enter a political race as a candidate for office. **under (one's) hat.** As a secret or in confidence: *Keep this information under your hat.* [Middle English, from Old English *hæt, hætt.*]

hat·band (hăt′bănd′) *n.* A band of ribbon or cloth worn on a hat just above the brim.

hat·box (hăt′bŏks′) *n.* A box or case for a hat.

hatch¹ (hăch) *n.* **1.a.** An opening, as in the deck of a ship, in the roof or floor of a building, or in an aircraft. **b.** The cover for such an opening. **c.** A hatchway. **d.** *Nautical.* A ship's compartment. **2.** The hinged rear door of a hatchback. **3.** A floodgate. **—*idiom.* down the hatch.** *Slang.* Drink up. Often used as a toast. [Middle English, small door, from Old English *hæc, hæcc.*]

hatch² (hăch) *v.* **hatched, hatch·ing, hatch·es.** —*intr.* To emerge from or break out of an egg. —*tr.* **1.** To produce (young) from an egg. **2.** To cause (an egg or eggs) to produce young. **3.** To devise or originate, especially in secret: *hatch an assassination plot.* **—hatch** *n.* **1.** The act or an instance of hatching. **2.** The young hatched at one time; a brood. [Middle English *hacchen,* from Old English **hæccan.*] **—hatch′er** *n.*

hatch³ (hăch) *tr.v.* **hatched, hatch·ing, hatch·es.** To shade by drawing or etching fine parallel or crossed lines on. **—hatch** *n.* A fine line used in hatching. [Middle English *hachen,* to engrave, carve, from Old French *hacher, hachier,* to cross-hatch, cut up. See HASH¹.]

hatch·back (hăch′băk′) *n.* An automobile having a sloping back with a hatch that opens upward.

hat·check (hăt′chĕk′) *n.* A room for checking hats and other outer garments. —*attributive.* Often used to modify another noun: *a hatcheck concession; a hatcheck attendant.*

hatch·el (hăch′əl) *n.* A comb for separating flax fibers. **—hatchel** *tr.v.* **-eled, -el·ing, -els** also **-elled, -el·ling, -els.** To separate (flax fibers) with a hatchel. [Middle English *hechel,* possibly from Old English **hecel;* akin to Middle Dutch *hekel.* See HECKLE.]

hatch·er·y (hăch′ə-rē) *n., pl.* **-ies.** A place where eggs, especially those of fish or poultry, are hatched.

hatch·et (hăch′ĭt) *n.* **1.** A small, short-handled ax for use in one hand. **2.** A tomahawk. [Middle English *hachet,* from Old French *hachete,* diminutive of *hache,* ax, of Germanic origin; akin to Old High German *happa,* sickle.]

hatchet face *n.* A long, gaunt face with sharp features. **—hatch′et-faced′** (hăch′ĭt-fāst′) *adj.*

hatchet job *n. Slang.* A crude or ruthless effort usually ending in destruction: *did a hatchet job on the mayor's reputation.*

hatchet man *n. Slang.* **1.** A man hired to commit murder. **2.** A man hired or assigned to carry out a disagreeable task or an unscrupulous order.

hatch·ing (hăch′ĭng) *n.* **1.** Fine lines used in graphic arts to show shading. **2.** The process of decorating with such lines.

hatch·ling (hăch′lĭng) *n.* A newly hatched bird, amphibian, fish, or reptile.

hatch·ment (hăch′mənt) *n. Heraldry.* A panel bearing the

hartebeest
Hunter's hartebeest
Damaliscus hunteri

hatch²

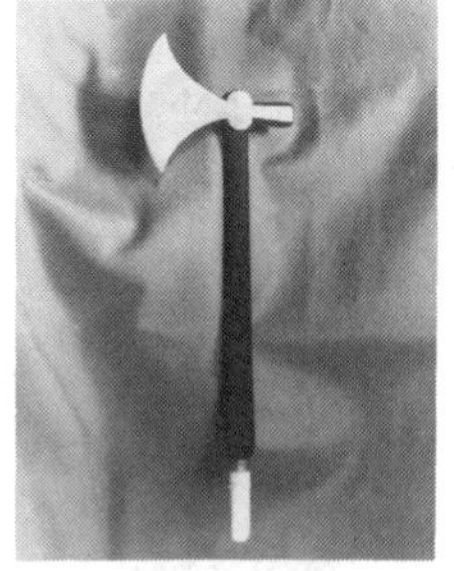

hatchet

ă pat	oi boy
ā pay	ou out
âr care	ŏŏ took
ä father	ōō boot
ĕ pet	ŭ cut
ē be	ûr urge
ĭ pit	th thin
ī pie	*th* this
îr pier	hw which
ŏ pot	zh vision
ō toe	ə about, item
ô paw	♦ regionalism

Stress marks: ′ (primary); ′ (secondary), as in **dictionary** (dĭk′shə-nĕr′ē)

coat of arms of a deceased person. [Alteration of *hachement, achiment,* from ACHIEVEMENT, escutcheon.]

hatch·way (hăch′wā′) *n.* **1.** A passage or an opening leading to a hold, compartment, or cellar. **2.** A ladder or stairway within a hatchway.

hate (hāt) *v.* **hat·ed, hat·ing, hates.** —*tr.* **1. a.** To feel hostility or animosity toward. **b.** To detest. **2.** To feel dislike or distaste for: *hates washing dishes.* —*intr.* To feel hatred. —**hate** *n.* **1.** Intense animosity or dislike; hatred. **2.** An object of detestation or hatred: *My pet hate is tardiness.* [Middle English *haten,* from Old English *hatian.* N., Middle English, from Old English *hete.*] —**hat′er** *n.*

Hatshepsut
Portrayed as the god Osiris

hate·ful (hāt′fəl) *adj.* **1.** Eliciting or deserving hatred. **2.** Feeling or showing hatred; malevolent. —**hate′ful·ly** *adv.* —**hate′ful·ness** *n.*

SYNONYMS: *hateful, detestable, odious, obnoxious, offensive, repellent.* These adjectives, which are often interchangeable, describe what elicits or deserves strong dislike, distaste, or revulsion: *Hateful* refers to what evokes hatred or deep animosity: *"No vice is universally as hateful as ingratitude"* (Joseph Priestley). *Detestable* applies to what arouses abhorrence or scorn: *detestable crimes; a detestable occupation.* Something *odious* is the object of disgust, aversion, or intense displeasure: *"a kind of slimy stuff . . . of a most nauseous, odious smell"* (Daniel Defoe); *"consequences odious to those you govern"* (Edmund Burke). *Obnoxious* is applied to something that is very objectionable: *"I know no method to secure the repeal of bad or obnoxious laws so effective as their stringent execution"* (Ulysses S. Grant). *Offensive* applies to what offends or excites displeasure: *offensive behavior; an offensive suggestion.* Something *repellent* arouses repugnance or disgust: *I find his obsequiousness repellent.*

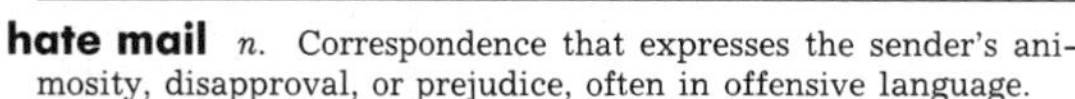

hate mail *n.* Correspondence that expresses the sender's animosity, disapproval, or prejudice, often in offensive language.

hath (hăth) *v. Archaic.* Third person singular present tense of **have.**

Hath·a·way (hăth′ə-wā′), **Anne.** 1556?–1623. The wife of William Shakespeare. She married the playwright in 1582.

hat·pin (hăt′pĭn′) *n.* A long straight pin usually with an ornamental head, used to secure a hat to the wearer's hair.

ha·tred (hā′trĭd) *n.* Intense animosity or hostility. [Middle English : *hate,* hate; see HATE + Old English *rǣden,* condition; see **ar-** in Appendix.]

Hat·shep·sut (hăt-shĕp′so͞ot′) also **Hat·shep·set** (-sĕt′). Died c. 1482 B.C. Queen of Egypt (1503–1482) who on the death of her husband, Thutmose II (c. 1504), became regent for her son Thutmose III and bestowed the title of pharaoh on herself.

hat·ter (hăt′ər) *n.* One whose occupation is the manufacture, selling, or repair of hats.

Hat·ter·as Island (hăt′ər-əs). A long barrier island off the eastern coast of North Carolina between Pamlico Sound and the Atlantic Ocean, with **Cape Hatteras** projecting from the southeast part. The cape experiences frequent storms that drive ships landward and has been called "the Graveyard of the Atlantic."

Hat·ties·burg (hăt′ēz-bûrg′). A city of southeast Mississippi southeast of Jackson. Once a lumbering center, it now has varied industries. Population, 40,829.

hat trick *n. Sports.* **1.** Three consecutive wins, hits, or goals made by one player in one game, as in ice hockey. **2.** Three wickets taken in cricket by a bowler in three consecutive balls. [From the hat with which the feat was traditionally rewarded in cricket.]

hau·ber·geon (hô′bər-jən) *n.* Variant of **habergeon.**

hau·berk (hô′bərk) *n.* A long tunic made of chain mail. [Middle English, from Old French *hauberc,* of Germanic origin. See **kʷel-**[1] in Appendix.]

hauberk

haugh (hôᴋʜ) *n. Scots.* A low-lying meadow in a river valley. [Middle English *hawch,* from Old English *healh,* secret place, small hollow. See **kel-**[1] in Appendix.]

haugh·ty (hô′tē) *adj.* **-ti·er, -ti·est.** Scornfully and condescendingly proud. See Synonyms at **proud.** [From Middle English *haut,* from Old French *haut, halt,* alteration (influenced by Frankish *hōh,* high) of Latin *altus,* high. See **al-**[2] in Appendix.] —**haugh′ti·ly** *adv.* —**haugh′ti·ness** *n.*

haul (hôl) *v.* **hauled, haul·ing, hauls.** —*tr.* **1.** To pull or drag forcibly; tug. See Synonyms at **pull.** **2.** To transport, as with a truck or cart. **3.** *Informal.* To compel to go, especially for trial: *"hauled the huge companies into court"* (Peter Matthiessen). **4.** *Nautical.* To change the course of (a ship), especially in order to sail closer into the wind. —*intr.* **1.** To pull; tug. **2.** To provide transportation; cart. **3. a.** To shift direction: *The wind hauled to the east.* **b.** To change one's mind. **4.** *Nautical.* To change the course of a ship. —**haul** *n.* **1.** The act of pulling or dragging. **2.** The act of transporting or carting. **3.** A distance, especially the distance over which something is pulled or transported. **4.** Something that is pulled or transported; a load. **5.** Everything collected or acquired by a single effort; the take: *a big haul of fish.* —***phrasal verbs.*** **haul off.** *Informal.* **1.** To draw back slightly, as in preparation for initiating an action: *"hauled off and smacked the hapless aide across the face"* (Bill Barol). **2.** To shift operations to a new place; to move away. **haul up.** To come to a halt. [Middle English *haulen,* from Old French *haler,* of Germanic origin. See **kele-**[2] in Appendix.] —**haul′er** *n.*

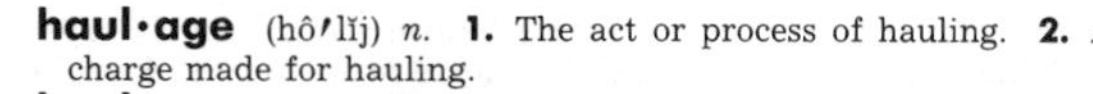

haul·age (hô′lĭj) *n.* **1.** The act or process of hauling. **2.** A charge made for hauling.

haulm (hôm) *n. Chiefly British.* The stems of peas, beans, potatoes, or grasses. [Middle English *halm,* straw, from Old English *healm.*]

haunch (hônch, hŏnch) *n.* **1.** The hip, buttock, and upper thigh in human beings and animals. **2.** The loin and leg of a four-footed animal, especially as used for food: *a haunch of venison.* **3.** *Architecture.* Either of the sides of an arch, curving down from the apex to an impost. [Middle English *haunche,* from Old French *hanche,* from Frankish **hanka.*]

♦**haunt** (hônt, hŏnt) *v.* **haunt·ed, haunt·ing, haunts.** —*tr.* **1.** To inhabit, visit, or appear to in the form of a ghost or other supernatural being. **2.** To visit often; frequent: *haunted the movie theaters.* **3.** To come to mind continually; obsess: *a riddle that haunted me all morning.* **4.** To be continually present in; pervade: *the melancholy that haunts the composer's music.* —*intr.* To recur or visit often, especially as a ghost. —**haunt** *n.* **1.** A place much frequented. **2.** (hănt). *Chiefly Southern U.S.* A ghost or other supernatural being. [Middle English *haunten,* to frequent, from Old French *hanter.* See **tkei-** in Appendix.] —**haunt′er** *n.*

haunt·ing (hôn′tĭng, hŏn′-) *adj.* Continually recurring to the mind; unforgettable: *a haunting melody.* —**haunt′ing·ly** *adv.*

Haupt·mann (houpt′män′, houp′-), **Gerhart.** 1862–1946. German writer known primarily for his naturalistic plays. He won the 1912 Nobel Prize for literature.

Hau·sa (hou′sə, -zə) *n., pl.* **Hausa** or **Hau·sas. 1.** A member of a predominantly Moslem people inhabiting northern Nigeria and southern Niger. **2.** A Chadic language spoken by the Hausa, widely used as a trade language in West Africa.

haus·frau (hous′frou′) *n.* A housewife. [German : *Haus,* house (from Middle High German *hūs,* from Old High German) + *Frau,* wife; see FRAU.]

Hauss·mann (hous′mən, ōs-män′), Baron **Georges Eugène.** 1809–1891. French public official who planned and oversaw numerous municipal improvements to Paris.

haus·tel·lum (hô-stĕl′əm) *n., pl.* **haus·tel·la** (hô-stĕl′ə). A portion of the proboscis that is adapted as a sucking organ in many insects. [New Latin, diminutive of Latin *haustrum,* scoop on a water wheel, from *haurīre,* to draw up.] —**haus·tel′late** (hô-stĕl′ĭt, hô′stə-lāt′) *adj.*

haus·to·ri·um (hô-stôr′ē-əm, -stōr′-) *n., pl.* **haus·to·ri·a** (hô-stôr′ē-ə, -stōr′-). *Botany.* A specialized absorbing structure of a parasitic plant, such as the rootlike outgrowth of the dodder, that obtains food from a host plant. [New Latin *haustōrium,* from Latin *haustus,* a drawing in, absorption, from past participle of *haurīre,* to draw up.] —**haus·to′ri·al** *adj.*

haut·boy also **haut·bois** (hō′boi′, ō′boi′) *n., pl.* **-boys** also **-bois** (-boiz′). An oboe. [French *hautbois,* from Old French : *haut,* high; see HAUGHTY + *bois,* wood (of Germanic origin).]

haute (ōt) *adj.* Fashionably elegant: *"In Washington, haute gastronomy is at least as important as the national economy"* (Ann L. Trebbe). [French, feminine of *haut,* high. See HAUTBOY.]

haute couture *n.* **1.** The leading establishments or designers for the creation of exclusive fashions for women. **2. a.** The creation of exclusive fashions for women. **b.** The fashions created. [French : *haute,* high, elegant + *couture,* sewing.]

haute cuisine *n.* **1.** Elaborate or skillfully prepared food, especially that of France. **2.** The characteristic manner or style of preparing such food. [French : *haute,* high, elegant + *cuisine,* cooking.]

haute é·cole (ā-kôl′) *n.* The art, techniques, or practice of expert equestrianship. [French : *haute,* high, advanced + *école,* school.]

hau·teur (hō-tûr′, ō-tœr′) *n.* Haughtiness in bearing and attitude; arrogance. [French, from Old French, from *haut,* high. See HAUGHTY.]

Ha·van·a (hə-văn′ə). The capital and largest city of Cuba, in the northwest part of the island country on the Gulf of Mexico. Founded in 1519, it became the capital of Spanish Cuba in 1552. Population, 1,961,674. —**Ha·van′an** *adj. & n.*

Hav·ant and Wa·ter·loo (hăv′ənt; wô′tər-lo͞o′, wŏt′ər-). An urban district of southern England near the English Channel east of Southhampton. It is a manufacturing center. Population, 114,800.

Ha·va·su·pai (hä′və-so͞o′pī) *n.* **1. a.** A Native American people inhabiting an area southeast of the Grand Canyon. **b.** A member of this people. **2.** The Yuman language of the Havasupai, closely related to Hualapai.

have (hăv) *v.* **had** (hăd), **hav·ing, has** (hăz). —*tr.* **1. a.** To be in possession of: *already had a car.* **b.** To possess as a characteristic, quality, or function: *has a beard; had a great deal of energy.* **c.** To possess or contain as a constituent part: *a car that has an automatic transmission.* **2.** To occupy a particular relation to: *had a great many disciples.* **3.** To possess knowledge of or facility in: *has very little Spanish.* **4.** To hold in the mind; entertain: *had doubts about their loyalty.* **5.** To use or exhibit in action: *have compassion.* **6. a.** To come into possession of; acquire: *Not one copy of the book was to be had in the entire town.* **b.** To receive; get: *I had a letter from my cousin.* **c.** To accept; take: *I'll have the green peas instead of the spinach.* **7. a.** To suffer from: *have defective vision.* **b.** To be subject to the experience of: *had a difficult time last winter.* **8.a.** To cause to, as by persuasion or compulsion: *had my assistant run the errand.* **b.** To cause to be: *had everyone fascinated.* **9.** To permit; allow: *I won't have that kind of behavior in my house.* **10.** To carry on, perform, or execute: *have an argument.* **11.a.** To place at a disadvantage: *Your opponent in the debate had you on every issue.* **b.** *Informal.* To get the better of, especially by trickery or deception: *They realized too late that they'd been had by a swindler.* **c.** *Informal.* To influence by dishonest means; bribe: *an incorruptible official who could not be had.* **12.a.** To procreate (offspring): *wanted to have a child.* **b.** To give birth to; bear: *She's going to have a baby.* **13.** To partake of: *have lunch.* **14.** To be obliged to; must: *We simply have to get there on time.* **15.** To engage in sexual intercourse with. —*aux.* Used with a past participle to form the present perfect, past perfect, and future perfect tenses indicating completed action: *The troublemaker has gone for good. I regretted that I had lost my temper. They will have finished by the time we arrive.* —**have** *n.* One enjoying especially material wealth: *"Almost overnight, there was a new and widespread hostility on the part of the haves toward the have-nots"* (Thomas P. O'Neill, Jr.). —***phrasal verbs.*** **have at.** To attack. **have on. 1.** To wear: *had on red shoes.* **2.** To be scheduled: *We have a dinner party on for tomorrow evening.* —***idioms.*** **have done with.** To stop; cease: *Have done with your foolish quibbling!* **have had it.** *Informal.* **1.** To have endured all that one can: *I've had it with their delays.* **2.** To be in a state beyond remedy, repair, or salvage: *That coat has had it.* **3.** To have done everything that is possible or that will be permitted. **have it in for (someone).** To intend to harm, especially because of a grudge. **have it out.** To settle decisively, especially by means of an argument or a discussion. **have (something) coming.** To deserve what one receives: *You had that reprimand coming for a very long time.* **have to do with.** To be concerned or associated with. [Middle English *haven,* from Old English *habban.* See **kap-** in Appendix.]

Ha•vel (hä′fəl). A river, about 346 km (215 mi) long, of eastern Germany flowing through Berlin to the Elbe River.

Ha•vel (hä′vəl), **Václav.** Born 1936. Czechoslovakian writer and politician. A widely known playwright, Havel became a civil rights leader after the Soviet invasion of Czechoslovakia (1968). He was elected president in December 1989.

have•lock (hăv′lŏk′, -lək) *n.* A cloth covering for a cap, having a flap to cover and protect the back of the neck. [After Sir Henry *Havelock* (1795–1857), British soldier.]

havelock

Have•lock (hăv′lŏk′). A city of southeast North Carolina east of Fayetteville. Population, 17,718.

haven (hā′vən) *n.* **1.** A harbor or an anchorage; a port. **2.** A place of refuge or rest; a sanctuary. —**haven** *tr.v.* **-vened, -ven•ing, -vens.** To put into or provide with a haven. [Middle English, from Old English *hæfen.* See **kap-** in Appendix.]

have-not (hăv′nŏt′) *n.* One enjoying little or no material wealth: *"The gap between the haves and the have-nots still shows up clearly at the polls"* (Brad Edmondson).

have•n't (hăv′ənt). Have not.

Hav•er•hill (hā′vrəl, hā′vər-əl). A city of northeast Massachusetts northeast of Lowell. It grew as a shoe-producing center but now has varied light industries. Population, 46,865.

hav•er•sack (hăv′ər-săk′) *n.* A bag carried over one shoulder to transport supplies, as on a hike. [French *havresac,* from obsolete German *Habersack* : *Haber,* oats (from Middle High German *habere,* from Old High German *habaro*) + German *Sack,* bag (from Middle High German *sac,* from Old High German, from Latin *saccus;* see SACK[1]).]

Ha•ver•sian canal (hə-vûr′zhən) *n.* Any of the tiny, interconnecting, longitudinal channels in bone tissue through which blood vessels, nerve fibers, and lymphatics pass. [After Clopton *Havers* (1650?–1702), English physician and anatomist.]

Haversian system *n.* A structural unit of bone consisting of a Haversian canal and corresponding lamellae of compact bone.

hav•oc (hăv′ək) *n.* **1.** Widespread destruction; devastation. **2.** Disorder or chaos: *a wild party that created havoc in the house.* —**havoc** *tr.v.* **-ocked, -ock•ing, -ocs.** To destroy or pillage. [Middle English *havok,* from Anglo-Norman *(crier) havok,* (to cry) havoc, variant of Old French *havot,* plundering, of Germanic origin.]

haw[1] (hô) *n.* An utterance used by a speaker who is fumbling for words. —**haw** *intr.v.* **hawed, haw•ing, haws.** To fumble in speaking. [Imitative.]

haw[2] (hô) *n.* **1.** The fruit of a hawthorn. **2.** A hawthorn or similar tree or shrub. [Middle English, from Old English *haga.*]

haw[3] (hô) *n.* **1.** A nictitating membrane, especially of a domesticated animal. **2.** An inflamed condition of this membrane. [Origin unknown.]

haw[4] (hô) *interj.* Used to command an animal to turn left. —**haw** *intr.v.* **hawed, haw•ing, haws.** To turn left.

Ha•wai•i (hə-wä′ē, -wī′ē, -wä′yə). *Abbr.* **HI** A state of the United States in the central Pacific Ocean comprising the Hawaiian Islands. The islands became a U.S. territory in 1900, which was admitted as the 50th state in 1959. Honolulu, on Ohau, is the capital and the largest city. Population, 964,691.

Ha•wai•ian (hə-wä′yən) *n.* **1.a.** A member or descendent of the indigenous Polynesian people of the Hawaiian Islands. **b.** A native or inhabitant of the Hawaiian Islands, the state of Hawaii, or Hawaii Island. **2.** The Polynesian language of Hawaii. —**Ha•wai′ian** *adj.*

Hawaiian guitar *n.* *Music.* An electric guitar consisting of a long fretted neck and six to eight steel strings that are plucked while being pressed with a movable steel bar. Also called *steel guitar.*

Hawaiian Islands. Formerly **Sand•wich Islands** (sănd′wĭch, săn′-). *Abbr.* **H.I.** A group of volcanic and coral islands in the central Pacific Ocean coextensive with the state of Hawaii. There are eight major islands and more than a hundred minor ones. The islands were settled by Polynesians in the sixth century A.D. and visited by Capt. James Cook in 1778. Petitions for annexation by the United States were approved in 1898.

Hawaii Island. The largest and southernmost of the Hawaiian Islands. It is the top of an enormous submarine mountain and has several volcanic peaks.

Hawaii Standard Time *n.* Standard time in the tenth time zone west of Greenwich, England, reckoned at 150° west and used, for example, in Hawaii and the western Aleutian Islands. Also called *Hawaii Time.*

Ha•wash River (hä′wäsh′). See **Awash River.**

haw•finch (hô′fĭnch′) *n.* **1.** A Eurasian bird *(Coccothraustes coccothraustes)* having a thick bill, a short, white-tipped tail, and brown, white, and black plumage. **2.** Any of various birds similar or related to this bird. [HAW[2] + FINCH.]

haw-haw[1] (hô′hô′) *n. & interj.* Variant of **ha-ha**[1].

haw-haw[2] (hô′hô′) *n.* Variant of **ha-ha**[2].

hawk[1] (hôk) *n.* **1.** Any of various birds of prey of the order Falconiformes and especially of the genera *Accipiter* and *Buteo,* characteristically having a short, hooked bill and strong claws adapted for seizing. **2.** Any of various similar birds of prey. **3.** A person who preys on others; a shark. **4.a.** One who demonstrates an actively aggressive or combative attitude, as in an argument. **b.** A person who favors military force or action in order to carry out foreign policy. —**hawk** *intr.v.* **hawked, hawk•ing, hawks. 1.** To hunt with trained hawks. **2.** To swoop and strike in the manner of a hawk: *"It was fun to watch the scattered snail kites . . . lifting and falling in the wind as they hawked across the shining grass and water"* (Peter Matthiessen). [Middle English *hauk,* from Old English *hafoc.* See **kap-** in Appendix.] —**hawk′ish** *adj.* —**hawk′ish•ly** *adv.* —**hawk′ish•ness** *n.*

hawk[2] (hôk) *v.* **hawked, hawk•ing, hawks.** —*intr.* To peddle goods aggressively, especially by calling out. —*tr.* To peddle (goods) aggressively, especially by calling out. [Middle English *hauken,* back-formation from *hauker.* See HAWKER.]

hawk[3] (hôk) *v.* **hawked, hawk•ing, hawks.** —*intr.* To clear or attempt to clear the throat by or as if by coughing up phlegm. —*tr.* To clear the throat of (phlegm). —**hawk** *n.* An audible effort to clear the throat by expelling phlegm. [Imitative.]

hawk•er (hô′kər) *n.* One who sells goods aggressively, especially by calling out. [Middle English *hauker,* probably from Middle Low German *höker,* from *höken,* to peddle, bend, bear on the back.]

hawk-eyed (hôk′īd′) *adj.* Having very keen eyesight.

Haw•kins (hô′kĭnz), Sir **Anthony Hope.** Pen name Anthony Hope. 1863–1933. British writer particularly known for his romantic novels, such as *The Prisoner of Zenda* (1894).

Haw•kins or **Haw•kyns** (hô′kĭnz), Sir **John.** 1532–1595. English naval hero who commanded the rear squadron in the defeat of the Spanish Armada (1588).

hawk moth *n.* Any of various thick-bodied moths of the family Sphingidae, having long narrow forewings and characteristically feeding by hovering over flowers and sucking nectar through an extended proboscis. Also called *sphinx moth.*

hawk's beard (hôks) *n.* Any of various plants of the genus *Crepis,* resembling the dandelion and having rayed, usually yellow flower heads.

hawks•bill (hôks′bĭl′) *n.* A tropical sea turtle *(Eretmochelys imbricata)* valued as a source of tortoiseshell. Also called *tortoiseshell.*

hawk•weed (hôk′wēd′) *n.* Any of numerous often hairy plants of the genus *Hieracium,* having yellow or orange dandelionlike flower heads.

Haw•kyns (hô′kĭnz), Sir **John.** See Sir John **Hawkins.**

Haw•orth (hou′ərth, härth). A village of northern England west-northwest of Bradford. The Brontë sisters lived with their father and brother in the parsonage here.

Haworth, Sir **Walter Norman.** 1883–1950. British biochemist. He shared a 1937 Nobel Prize for his research on carbohydrates and vitamin C.

ha•wor•thi•a (hô-wûr′thē-ə, *-thē-*) *n.* Any of numerous succulent South African herbs of the genus *Haworthia,* having densely imbricate, often warty leaves that are clustered in rosettes. Also called *star cactus, wart plant.* [After Adrian Hardy *Haworth* (1767–1833), British botanist.]

Haw River (hô). A river, about 209 km (130 mi) long, rising in north-central North Carolina and flowing generally southeast to join the Deep River and form the Cape Fear River.

hawse (hôz) *n.* *Nautical.* **1.** The part of a ship where the hawseholes are located. **2.** A hawsehole. **3.** The space between the bows and anchors of an anchored ship. **4.** The arrangement of a ship's anchor cables when both starboard and port anchors are secured. [Middle English *hals,* forward curve of a strake, probably from Old Norse *hāls,* neck, ship's bow. See **k**ʷ**el-**[1] in Appendix.]

ă pat	oi boy
ā pay	ou out
âr care	ŏŏ took
ä father	ōō boot
ĕ pet	ŭ cut
ē be	ûr urge
ĭ pit	th thin
ī pie	*th* this
îr pier	hw which
ŏ pot	zh vision
ō toe	ə about, item
ô paw	♦ regionalism

Stress marks: ′ (primary); ′ (secondary), as in **dictionary** (dĭk′shə-nĕr′ē)

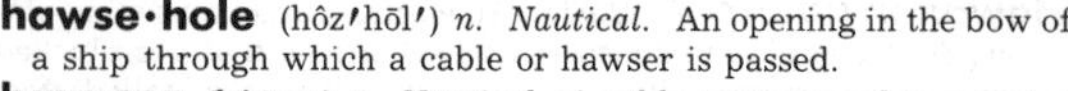

Nathaniel Hawthorne

hawse·hole (hôz′hōl′) *n. Nautical.* An opening in the bow of a ship through which a cable or hawser is passed.

haw·ser (hô′zər) *n. Nautical.* A cable or rope used in mooring or towing a ship. [Middle English, from Anglo-Norman *haucer,* from Old French *haucier,* to hoist, from Vulgar Latin **altiāre,* alteration of Late Latin *altāre,* from Latin *altus,* high. See **al-**[2] in Appendix.]

haw·thorn (hô′thôrn′) *n.* Any of various usually thorny trees or shrubs of the genus *Crataegus* having clusters of white or pinkish flowers and reddish fruits containing a few one-seeded nutlets. [Middle English, from Old English *hagathorn* : *haga,* haw + *thorn,* thorn.]

Haw·thorne (hô′thôrn′). **1.** A city of southern California, an industrial and residential suburb of Los Angeles. Population, 56,447. **2.** A borough of northeast New Jersey north-northeast of Paterson. It is primarily residential. Population, 18,200.

Hawthorne, Nathaniel. 1804–1864. American writer whose works, such as *The Scarlet Letter* (1850) and *The House of the Seven Gables* (1851), are marked by elegant prose and moralistic and spiritual themes.

hay (hā) *n.* **1.** Grass or other plants, such as clover or alfalfa, cut and dried for fodder. **2.** *Slang.* A trifling amount of money: *gets $100 an hour, which isn't hay.* —**hay** *v.* **hayed, hay·ing, hays.** —*intr.* To mow and cure grass and herbage for hay. —*tr.* **1.** To make (grass) into hay. **2.** To feed with hay. [Middle English, from Old English *hīeg.* See **kau-** in Appendix.] —**hay′er** *n.*

Hay (hā), **John Milton.** 1838–1905. American public official and writer who served as ambassador to Great Britain (1897–1898) and U.S. secretary of state (1898–1905).

Ha·ya·ka·wa (hī′ə-kou′ə), **S(amuel) I(chiye).** 1906–1992. Canadian-born American philologist, educator, and legislator. Noted for his writings on general semantics, such as *Language in Action* (1941), he was also president of San Francisco State College (1968–1973) and a U.S. senator from California (1977–1983).

hay·cock (hā′kŏk′) *n. Chiefly British.* A conical mound of hay.

Haydn (hīd′n), **Franz Joseph.** 1732–1809. Austrian composer who exerted great influence on the development of the classical symphony. A contemporary of Mozart, he wrote numerous symphonies and string quartets as well as operas and concertos.

Hay·ek (hī′ək, -ĕk), **Friedrich August von.** Born 1899. Austrian-born British economist. He shared a 1974 Nobel Prize for work on the theory of optimum allocation of resources.

Rutherford B. Hayes
Photographed by Mathew Brady

Hayes (hāz), **Helen.** Born 1900. American actress whose 50-year career included acclaimed performances on stage, as in *Dear Brutus* (1918) and *Victoria Regina* (1935–1939), and in motion pictures, such as *The Sin of Madelon Claudet* (1931).

Hayes, Rutherford Birchard. 1822–1893. The 19th President of the United States (1877–1881). Winning the controversial election of 1876 by one electoral vote, he pacified the South by removing federal troops (1877).

Hayes River. A river, about 483 km (300 mi) long, of eastern Manitoba, Canada, flowing northeast to Hudson Bay.

hay fever *n.* An allergic condition affecting the mucous membranes of the upper respiratory tract and the eyes, most often characterized by nasal discharge, sneezing, and itchy, watery eyes and usually caused by an abnormal sensitivity to airborne pollen. Also called *pollinosis.*

haystack

hay·fork (hā′fôrk′) *n.* **1.** A hand tool for pitching hay. **2.** A machine-operated fork for moving hay.

hay·loft (hā′lôft′, -lŏft′) *n.* A loft for storing hay. Also called *haymow.*

hay·mak·er (hā′mā′kər) *n. Slang.* A powerful blow with the fist.

hay·mow (hā′mou′) *n.* **1.** See **hayloft. 2.** The hay stored in a hayloft. **3.** *Archaic.* A haystack.

Hayne (hān), **Robert Young.** 1791–1839. American politician. A U.S. senator from South Carolina (1823–1832), he engaged Daniel Webster in a famous debate on the conflict between federal power and states' rights (1830).

hay·rack (hā′răk′) *n.* **1.** A rack from which livestock feed. **2.a.** A rack fitted to a wagon for carrying hay. **b.** A wagon fitted with such a rack.

hay·rick (hā′rĭk′) *n.* See **haystack.**

hay·ride (hā′rīd′) *n.* A ride taken for amusement, usually by a group of people in the evening in a wagon or other vehicle piled with hay or straw.

Hay River. A river of northwest Canada rising in northeast British Columbia and flowing about 853 km (530 mi) generally northeast across northwest Alberta to Great Slave Lake.

Hays (hāz). A city of central Kansas west of Salina. Founded near the site of Fort Hays, established in 1865, the city has a large agricultural experiment station. Population, 16,301.

Hays, Arthur Garfield. 1881–1954. American lawyer. As counsel for the American Civil Liberties Union (1912–1954) he was involved in several famous legal battles, including the Scopes trial (1925) and the Sacco-Vanzetti case (1927).

Hays, William Harrison. Known as "Will." 1879–1954. American politician and motion-picture executive who as president of the Motion Picture Producers and Distributors of America (1922–1945) established the Production Code (1930), which prescribed the moral content of American films from 1930 to 1966.

hay·seed (hā′sēd′) *n.* **1.** Grass seed shaken out of hay. **2.** Pieces of chaff or straw that fall from hay. **3.** *Slang.* A bumpkin; a yokel.

hay·stack (hā′stăk′) *n.* A large stack of hay for winter storage in the open. Also called *hayrick.*

Hay·ward (hā′wərd). A city of western California southeast of Oakland. Food processing is among its important industries. Population, 94,342.

hay·wire (hā′wīr′) *n.* Wire used in baling hay. —**haywire** *adj. Informal.* **1.** Mentally confused or erratic; crazy: *went haywire over the interminable delays.* **2.** Not functioning properly; broken. [From the use of baling wire for makeshift repairs.]

WORD HISTORY: It may seem odd that the word *haywire* should have come to describe something or someone that is not functioning properly. *Haywire* originally was in fact simply a compound of the words *hay* and *wire,* denoting wire used to bale things such as hay or straw. The term is first recorded as a noun in a debate that occurred in the Canadian House of Commons (1917); hence it is a Canadianism, or since it soon thereafter appeared in a United States publication, a North Americanism. We find an earlier (1905) attributive use, however, in the phrase *hay wire outfit,* a term used contemptuously for poorly equipped loggers. What lies behind this term is the practice of making repairs with haywire. *Haywire* is found in other contexts with the general sense "makeshift, inefficient," from which comes the extended senses "not functioning properly" and "crazy."

Hay·wood (hā′wo͝od′), **William Dudley.** Known as "Big Bill." 1869–1928. American labor leader. A socialist who helped found the Industrial Workers of the World (1905), he was ejected from the Socialist Party for his militant views (1912) and was convicted of sedition during World War I.

haz·ard (hăz′ərd) *n.* **1.** A chance; an accident. **2.** A chance of being injured or harmed; danger: *Space travel is full of hazards.* **3.** A possible source of danger: *a fire hazard.* **4.** *Games.* A dice game similar to craps. **5.** *Sports.* An obstacle, such as a sand trap, found on a golf course. —**hazard** *tr.v.* **-ard·ed, -ard·ing, -ards. 1.** To expose to danger or harm. See Synonyms at **endanger. 2.** To venture (something); dare: *hazard a guess.* [Middle English *hasard,* dice game, from Old French, possibly from Old Spanish *azar,* possibly from Arabic *az-zahr,* gaming die.]

hazard light *n.* A light on a vehicle that blinks to indicate that the vehicle poses danger to others.

haz·ard·ous (hăz′ər-dəs) *adj.* **1.** Marked by danger; perilous. **2.** Depending on chance; risky. —**haz′ard·ous·ly** *adv.* —**haz′ard·ous·ness** *n.*

hazardous waste *n.* A substance, such as nuclear waste or an industrial byproduct, that is potentially damaging to the environment and harmful to the health and well-being of human beings and other living organisms.

haze[1] (hāz) *n.* **1.a.** Atmospheric moisture, dust, smoke, and vapor that diminishes visibility. **b.** A partially opaque covering: *Let the polish dry to a haze before buffing it.* **2.** A vague or confused state of mind. —**haze** *intr.v.* **hazed, haz·ing, haz·es.** To become misty or hazy; blur. [Probably back-formation from HAZY.]

haze[2] (hāz) *tr.v.* **hazed, haz·ing, haz·es. 1.** To persecute or harass with meaningless, difficult, or humiliating tasks. **2.** To initiate, as into a college fraternity, by exacting humiliating performances from or playing rough practical jokes upon. [Perhaps from obsolete *haze,* to frighten, from obsolete French *haser,* to annoy, from Old French.] —**haz′er** *n.*

ha·zel (hā′zəl) *n.* **1.** Any of various shrubs or small trees of the genus *Corylus,* especially the European species *C. avellana* or the American species *C. americana,* bearing edible nuts enclosed in a leafy husk. Also called *filbert.* **2.** A hazelnut. **3.** *Color.* A light brown or yellowish brown. [Middle English *hasel,* from Old English *hæsel.*] —**ha′zel** *adj.*

ha·zel·nut (hā′zəl-nŭt′) *n.* The edible nut of a hazel, having a hard, smooth brown shell. Also called *filbert.*

Ha·zel Park (hā′zəl). A city of southeast Michigan, a residential suburb of Detroit. Population, 20,914.

Haz·let (hāz′lĭt). A community of east-central New Jersey east-southeast of New Brunswick. Population, 28,013.

Ha·zle·ton (hā′zəl-tən). A city of east-central Pennsylvania south of Wilkes-Barre. Population, 27,318.

Haz·litt (hăz′lĭt, hāz′-), **William.** 1778–1830. British essayist noted for his trenchant literary criticism. His works include *The Characters of Shakespeare's Plays* (1817).

HAZMAT *abbr.* Hazardous material.

haz·y (hā′zē) *adj.* **-i·er, -i·est. 1.** Marked by the presence of haze; misty: *hazy sunshine.* **2.** Not clearly defined; unclear or vague: *I'm a bit hazy on the new budget.* [Origin unknown.] —**haz′i·ly** *adv.* —**haz′i·ness** *n.*

haz·zan (KHä′zən) *n.* Variant of **chazan.**

hb or **hb.** *abbr. Sports.* Halfback.

Hb *abbr.* Hemoglobin.

H-bomb (āch′bŏm′) *n.* A hydrogen bomb.

h.c. *abbr.* Honoris causa (by reason of honor).

H.C. *abbr.* **1.** Holy Communion. **2.** House of Commons.

H.C.F. also **h.c.f.** or **hcf** *abbr. Mathematics.* Highest common factor.

HCG *abbr.* Human chorionic gonadotropin.

HD *abbr.* Heavy-duty.

hd. *abbr.* Head.

hdbk. *abbr.* Handbook.

hdkf. *abbr.* Handkerchief.

HDL *abbr.* High-density lipoprotein.

hdqrs. *abbr.* Headquarters.

HDTV *abbr.* High-definition television.

hdwe. *abbr.* Hardware.

he[1] (hē) *pron.* **1.a.** Used to refer to the man or boy previously mentioned or implied. **b.** Used to refer to a male animal. **2.** *Usage Problem.* Used to refer to a person whose gender is unspecified or unknown: *"He who desires but acts not, breeds pestilence"* (William Blake). **—he** *n.* A male person or animal: *Is the cat a he?* [Middle English, from Old English *hē.* See **ko-** in Appendix.]

USAGE NOTE: Traditionally, English speakers have used the pronouns *he, him,* and *his* generically in contexts in which the grammatical form of the antecedent requires a singular pronoun, as in *Every member of Congress is answerable to* his *constituents; A novelist should write about what* he *knows best; No one seems to take any pride in* his *work anymore,* and so on. Beginning early in the 20th century, however, the traditional usage has come under increasing criticism for reflecting and perpetuating gender discrimination. • Defenders of the traditional usage have argued that the masculine pronouns *he, his,* and *him* can be used generically to refer to men and women. This analysis of the generic use of *he* is linguistically doubtful. If *he* were truly a gender-neutral form, we would expect that it could be used to refer to the members of any group containing both men and women. But in fact the English masculine form is an odd choice when it refers to a female member of such a group. There is something plainly disconcerting about sentences such as *Each of the stars of* It Happened One Night [i.e., Clark Gable and Claudette Colbert] *won an Academy Award for his performance.* In this case, the use of *his* forces the reader to envision a single male who stands as the representative member of the group, a picture that is at odds with the image that comes to mind when we picture the stars of *It Happened One Night.* Thus *he* is not really a gender-neutral pronoun; rather, it refers to a male who is to be taken as the representative member of the group referred to by its antecedent. The traditional usage, then, is not simply a grammatical convention; it also suggests a particular pattern of thought. • Many writers sidestep the problem by avoiding the relevant constructions. In place of *Every student handed in* his *assignment,* they write *All the students handed in their assignments;* in place of *A taxpayer must appear for* his *hearing in person,* they write *Taxpayers must appear for their hearings in person,* and so on. Even when using the relevant constructions, however, many writers never use masculine pronouns as generics. In a series of sample sentences such as *A patient who doesn't accurately report* _____ *sexual history to the doctor runs the risk of misdiagnosis,* an average of 46 percent of the Usage Panel chose a coordinate form (*her/his, his or her,* and so on), 3 percent chose the plural pronoun (although the actual frequency of the plural in writing is far higher than this number would suggest), 2 percent chose the feminine pronoun, another 2 percent chose an indefinite or a definite article, and 7 percent gave no response or felt that no pronoun was needed to complete the sentence. • As a substitute for coordinate forms such as *his/her* or *her and his,* third person plural forms, such as *their,* have a good deal to recommend them: they are admirably brief and entirely colloquial and may be the only sensible choice in informal style; for example, in the radio commercial that says *"Make someone happy—give them a goosedown Christmas,"* where *him* would be misleading and *her or him* would be fussy. At least one major British publisher has recently adopted this usage for its learners' dictionaries, where one may read such sentences as *If someone says they are "winging it," they mean that they are improvising their way.* But in formal style, this option is perhaps less risky for a publisher of reference books than for an individual writer, who may be misconstrued as being careless or ignorant rather than attuned to the various grammatical and political nuances of the use of the masculine pronoun as generic pronoun. What is more, this solution ignores a persistent intuition that expressions such as *everyone* and *each student* should in fact be treated as grammatically singular. Writers who are concerned about avoiding both grammatical and social problems are best advised to use coordinate forms such as *his or her.* • Some writers see no need to use a personal pronoun implying gender unless absolutely necessary; in the sample sentence *A child who develops this sort of rash on* _____ *hands should probably be kept at home for a couple of days,* 6 percent of the Usage Panel completed the sentence with *the.* In addition, some writers have proposed other solutions to the use of *he* as a generic pronoun, such as the introduction of wholly new gender-neutral pronouns like *s/he* or *hiser,* or the switching between feminine and masculine forms in alternating sentences, paragraphs, or chapters. • In contrast to these innovations, many writers use the masculine pronoun as generic in all cases. For the same series of sample sentences, the average percentage of Usage Panel members who consistently completed the sentences with *his* was 37. This course is grammatically unexceptionable, but the writer who follows it must be prepared to incur the displeasure of readers who regard this pattern as a mark of insensitivity or gender discrimination. When a majority of writers are taking care to avoid the masculine as generic, the writer who uses it in this way may invite the inference that there is some pointed reason for referring to the representative instance as male. The entire question is unlikely to be resolved in the near future. See Usage Notes at **any, anyone, each, every, neither, one.**

he[2] (hā) *n.* The fifth letter of the Hebrew alphabet. See table at **alphabet.** [Hebrew *hē.*]

He The symbol for the element **helium.**

HE *abbr.* High explosive.

H.E. *abbr.* **1.** His Eminence. **2.** Her, or His, Excellency.

head (hĕd) *n. Abbr.* **hd. 1.a.** The uppermost or forwardmost part of the body of a vertebrate, containing the brain and the eyes, ears, nose, mouth, and jaws. **b.** The analogous part of an invertebrate organism. **c.** The length or height of such a part: *The horse lost by a head. She is two heads taller than he is.* **2.** The seat of the faculty of reason; intelligence, intellect, or mind: *I did the figuring in my head.* **3.** Mental ability or aptitude: *She has a good head for mathematics.* **4.** Freedom of choice or action: *Give the child his head and see how well he solves the problems.* **5.** *Slang.* **a.** A habitual drug user. **b.** An enthusiast **6.** A portrait or representation of a person's head. **7.** Often **heads** *(used with a sing. verb).* The side of a coin having the principal design and the date. **8.** *Informal.* A headache: *had a bad head early this morning.* **9.a.** An individual; a person: *charged five dollars a head.* **b. head.** A single animal: *20 head of cattle.* **10.a.** A person who leads, rules, or is in charge; a leader, chief, or director: *the head of the corporation.* **b.** A headmaster or headmistress. **11.** The foremost or leading position: *marched at the head of the parade.* **12.** A headwaiter. **13.a.** The difference in depth of a liquid at two given points. **b.** The measure of pressure at the lower point expressed in terms of this difference. **c.** The pressure exerted by a liquid or gas: *a head of steam.* **d.** The liquid or gas exerting the pressure. **14.** The froth or foam that rises to the top in pouring an effervescent liquid, such as beer. **15.** The tip of an abscess, a boil, or a pimple, in which pus forms. **16.** A turning point; a crisis: *bring matters to a head.* See Synonyms at **crisis. 17.a.** A projection, weight, or fixture at the end of an elongated object: *the head of a pin; a head of land overlooking the harbor.* **b.** *Anatomy.* The proximal end of a long bone: *the head of the femur.* **c.** The working end of a tool or an implement: *the head of a hammer.* **d.** The part of an explosive device that carries the explosive; a warhead. **18.a.** An attachment to or part of a machine that holds or contains the operative device. **b.** The magnetic head of a tape recorder. **19.** A rounded, compact mass, as of leaves or buds: *a head of cabbage.* **20.** *Botany.* A flower head. **21.** The uppermost part; the top: *Place the appropriate name at the head of each column.* **22.** The end considered the most important: *sat at the head of the table.* **23.** Either end of an object, such as a drum, whose two ends are interchangeable. **24.** *Nautical.* **a.** The forward part of a vessel. **b.** The top part or upper edge of a sail. **25.** A toilet, especially on a ship. **26.** A passage or gallery in a coal mine. **27.** *Printing.* **a.** The top of a book or of a page. **b.** A headline or heading. **c.** A distinct topic or category: *under the head of recent Spanish history.* **28.** Headway; progress. **29.** *Linguistics.* The word in a construction that has the same grammatical function as the construction as a whole and that determines relationships of concord to other parts of the construction or sentence in which the construction occurs. **30.** *Vulgar Slang.* Oral sex. **—head** *adj.* **1.** Of, relating to, or intended for the head. Often used in combination: *headshaking; headwrap.* **2.** Foremost in rank or importance: *the head librarian.* **3.** Placed at the top or the front: *the head name on the list.* **4.** *Slang.* Of, relating to, or for drugs or drug users. **—head** *v.* **head·ed, head·ing, heads.** *—tr.* **1.** To be in charge of; lead: *The minister headed the committee.* **2.** To be in the first or foremost position of: *Collins heads the list of job candidates.* **3.** To aim, point, or turn in a certain direction: *headed the team of horses up the hill.* **4.** To remove the head or top of. **5.** *Sports.* To hit (a soccer ball) in the air with one's head. **6.** To provide with a head: *head each column with a number; headed the flagpole with a golden ball.* *—intr.* **1.** To proceed or go in a certain direction: *head for town.* **2.** To form a head, as lettuce or cabbage. **3.** To originate, as a stream or river; rise. ***—phrasal verb.*** **head off.** To block the progress or completion of; intercept: *Try to head him off before he gets home.* ***—idioms.*** **head and shoulders above.** Far superior to: *head and shoulders above her colleagues in analytical capability.* **head over heels. 1.** Rolling, as in a somersault: *tripped and fell head over heels.* **2.** Completely; hopelessly: *head over heels in love.* **keep (one's) head.** To remain calm; remain in control of oneself. **lose (one's) head.** To lose one's poise or self-control. **off** (or **out of**) **(one's) head.** Insane; crazy. **put heads together.** To consult and plan together: *Let's put our heads together and solve this problem.* [Middle English, from Old English *hēafod.* See **kaput-** in Appendix.]

head·ache (hĕd′āk′) *n.* **1.** A pain in the head. **2.** *Informal.* Something, such as a problem, that causes annoyance or trouble. **—head′ach′y** (-ā′kē) *adj.*

head·band (hĕd′bănd′) *n.* **1.** A band worn around the head. **2.** *Printing.* An ornamental strip at the top of a page or beginning of a chapter or paragraph. **3.** *Printing.* A cloth band attached to the top of the spine of a book.

head·board (hĕd′bôrd′, -bōrd′) *n.* A board or panel that forms the head, as of a bed.

head·cheese (hĕd′chēz′) *n.* A jellied loaf or sausage made

ă pat	oi boy
ā pay	ou out
âr care	ŏŏ took
ä father	ōō boot
ĕ pet	ŭ cut
ē be	ûr urge
ĭ pit	th thin
ī pie	*th* this
îr pier	hw which
ŏ pot	zh vision
ō toe	ə about, item
ô paw	♦ regionalism

Stress marks: **′** (primary); ′ (secondary), as in **dictionary** (dĭk′shə-nĕr′ē)

from chopped and boiled parts of the feet, head, and sometimes the tongue and heart of an animal, usually a hog.

head cold *n.* A common cold mainly affecting the mucous membranes of the nasal passages, characterized by congestion, headache, and sneezing.

head·count·er (hĕd′koun′tər) *n. Informal.* A pollster.

head·dress (hĕd′drĕs′) *n.* **1.** A covering or an ornament for the head. **2.** A hairdo; a coiffure.

head·ed (hĕd′ĭd) *adj.* **1.** Growing or grown into a head. **2.** Having a head or heading. **3.** Having a specified kind or number of heads. Often used in combination: *a two-headed eagle; three-headed Cerberus.* **4.** Having a mentality of a certain type. Often used in combination: *a cool-headed fighter pilot.*

head·er (hĕd′ər) *n.* **1.** One that fits a head on an object. **2.** One that removes a head from an object, especially a machine that reaps the heads of grain and passes them into a wagon or receptacle. **3.** A pipe that serves as a central connection for two or more smaller pipes. **4.** A floor or roof beam placed between two long beams that supports the ends of the tailpieces. **5.** A brick laid across rather than parallel with a wall. **6.** *Informal.* A headlong dive or fall. **7.** *Sports.* A pass or shot made in soccer by heading the ball. **8.** *Computer Science.* Printed matter or information, such as a title, date, or page number, positioned in the top margin of a page and usually repeated throughout a document, especially a document composed on a word-processing system. **9.** A raised tank or hopper that maintains a constant pressure or supply to a system, especially the small tank that supplies water to a central heating system.

headdress
Top: Chinese
Bottom: Native American

head·fast (hĕd′făst′) *n. Nautical.* A mooring rope or chain that secures the bow of a ship to a wharf.

head·first (hĕd′fûrst′) also **head·fore·most** (-fôr′mōst′, -məst, -fōr′-) *adv.* **1.** With the head leading; headlong: *went headfirst down the stairs.* **2.** Impetuously; brashly. **—head′-first′** *adj.*

head·ful (hĕd′fo͝ol′) *n. Informal.* **1.** A relatively great amount of knowledge: *a headful of baseball trivia; a headful of good stories.* **2.** Something that covers the surface of one's head: *a headful of auburn curls; a headful of shampoo.*

head gate *n.* **1.** A control gate upstream of a lock or canal. **2.** A floodgate that controls the flow of water in a ditch, sluice, race, or channel.

head·gear (hĕd′gîr′) *n.* **1.** A covering, such as a hat or helmet, for the head. **2.** The part of a harness that fits about a horse's head. **3.** The rigging for hauling or lifting located at the head of a mine shaft. **4.** *Nautical.* The rigging on the forward sails of a craft.

head·hunt (hĕd′hŭnt′) *intr.v.* **-hunt·ed, -hunt·ing, -hunts.** To engage in headhunting. **—head′hunt′er** *n.*

head·hunt·ing (hĕd′hŭn′tĭng) *n.* **1.** The custom of cutting off and preserving the heads of enemies as trophies. **2.** *Slang.* The process of attempting to remove influence and power from enemies, especially political enemies. **3.** *Slang.* **a.** The business of recruiting personnel, especially executive personnel, as for a corporation. **b.** The act or an instance of such recruiting.

headphone
Attached to portable audiocassette player

head·ing (hĕd′ĭng) *n.* **1.** The title, subtitle, or topic that stands at the top or beginning, as of a paragraph, letter, or chapter. **2.** The course or direction in which a ship or an aircraft is moving. **3.a.** A gallery or drift in a mine. **b.** The end of a gallery or drift.

head·lamp (hĕd′lămp′) *n.* See **headlight** (sense 1).

head·land (hĕd′lənd, -lănd′) *n.* **1.** A point of land, usually high and with a sheer drop, extending out into a body of water; a promontory. **2.** The unplowed land at the end of a plowed furrow.

head·less (hĕd′lĭs) *adj.* **1.a.** Formed without a head. **b.** Decapitated. **2.** Lacking a leader or director. **3.** Lacking intelligence and prudence; stupid or foolish. **—head′less·ness** *n.*

head·light (hĕd′līt′) *n.* **1.** A light with a reflector and lens mounted on the front of a locomotive, an automobile, or another vehicle. Also called *headlamp.* **2.** A lamp mounted on a miner's or spelunker's hard hat.

head·line (hĕd′līn′) *n.* **1.** The title or caption of a newspaper article, usually set in large type. **2.** Often **headlines.** An important or sensational piece of news. **3.** A line at the head of a page or passage giving information such as the title, author, and page number. **—headline** *tr.v.* **-lined, -lin·ing, -lines. 1.** To supply (a page or passage) with a headline. **2.a.** To present or promote as a headliner: *The Palace Theater headlines a magician.* **b.** To serve as the headliner of: *He headlines the bill.*

head·lin·er (hĕd′lī′nər) *n.* A performer who receives prominent billing; a star.

head·lock (hĕd′lŏk′) *n. Sports.* A wrestling hold in which the head of one wrestler is encircled and locked by the arm and body of the other.

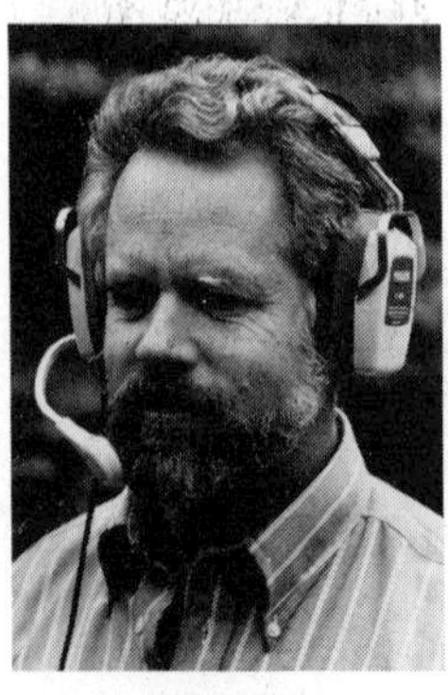

headset

head·long (hĕd′lông′, -lŏng′) *adv.* **1.** With the head leading; headfirst: *The runner slid headlong into third base.* **2.** In an impetuous manner; rashly. **3.** At breakneck speed or with uncontrolled force. **—headlong** (hĕd′lông′, -lŏng′) *adj.* **1.** Done with the head leading; headfirst: *a headlong dive.* **2.** Impetuous; rash. See Synonyms at **impetuous. 3.** Uncontrollably forceful or fast. **4.** *Archaic.* Steep; sheer. [From Middle English *(bi) hedlong,* from *hed, head,* head. See HEAD.]

head·man (hĕd′mən, -măn′) *n.* **1.** The leader or the chief man of a small, primitive village or community. **2.** A headsman.

head·mas·ter also **head master** (hĕd′măs′tər) *n.* A man who is the principal of a school, usually a private school.

head·mis·tress also **head mistress** (hĕd′mĭs′trĭs) *n.* A woman who is the principal of a school, usually a private school.

head money *n.* **1.** A reward paid for the capture and delivery of a fugitive; a bounty. **2.** A poll tax.

head·most (hĕd′mōst′, -məst) *adj.* Leading; foremost.

head-on (hĕd′ŏn′, -ôn′) *adv.* **1.** With the head or front first: *The cars crashed head-on.* **2.** In open conflict; in direct opposition: *"I have wondered since whether it would have been wiser to meet the issue head-on"* (Henry A. Kissinger). **—head-on** *adj.* **1.** Facing forward; frontal. **2.** With the front end foremost: *a head-on collision.*

head·phone (hĕd′fōn′) *n.* A receiver, as for a telephone, radio, or stereo, held to the ear by a headband.

head·piece (hĕd′pēs′) *n.* **1.** A protective covering for the head. **2.** A set of headphones; a headset. **3.** See **headstall. 4.** An ornamental design, especially at the top of a page. **5.** The seat of intelligence; brains.

head pin *n. Sports.* See **kingpin** (sense 1).

head·quar·ter (hĕd′kwôr′tər) *v.* **-tered, -ter·ing, -ters.** *Usage Problem.* —*tr.* To provide with headquarters: *"Despite the derivation of its name, the former Texas Oil Company is headquartered in White Plains, New York"* (New Republic). —*intr.* To establish headquarters.

USAGE NOTE: The verb *headquarter* occurs in both transitive and intransitive senses: *The magazine has headquartered him in a building that houses many foreign journalists. The European correspondent will headquarter in Paris.* In an earlier survey a majority of the Usage Panel found both these examples to be unacceptable in formal writing. Although ample citational evidence exists for these usages, writers who wish to avoid criticism should consider the use of alternative expressions, for example: *The magazine has just assigned him to* (or *has stationed him in*) *a building that houses many foreign journalists. The European correspondent will make her headquarters in Paris* (or *will make Paris her headquarters*).

head·quar·ters (hĕd′kwôr′tərz) *pl.n. (used with a sing. or pl. verb). Abbr.* **hdqrs., h.q., HQ, H.Q. 1.** The offices of a commander, as of a military unit, from which orders are issued. **2.** A center of operations or administration: *The company has its headquarters in the suburbs.* See Synonyms at **center.**

USAGE NOTE: The noun *headquarters* is used with either a singular or a plural verb. The plural is more common: *The headquarters are in Boston.* But the singular is sometimes preferred when reference is to authority rather than to physical location: *Battalion headquarters has approved the retreat.*

head·race (hĕd′rās′) *n.* A watercourse that feeds water into a mill, water wheel, or turbine.

head register *n.* One of the higher ranges of the voice in singing or speaking, including the falsetto.

head·rest (hĕd′rĕst′) *n.* **1.** A support for the head, as at the back of a chair. **2.** A cushion attached to the top of the back of an automotive vehicle's seat, especially to prevent whiplash. In this sense, also called *head restraint.*

head rhyme *n.* Consonantal alliteration at the beginning of words. Also called *beginning rhyme.*

head·room (hĕd′ro͞om′, -ro͝om′) *n.* **1.** Space above one's head, as in a motor vehicle, above a doorway, or in a tunnel; clearance. **2.** *Electronics.* Dynamic headroom.

head·sail (hĕd′səl, -sāl′) *n. Nautical.* A sail, such as a jib, set forward of a foremast.

head·scarf (hĕd′skärf′) *n., pl.* **-scarfs** or **-scarves** (-skärvz). A scarf, usually folded into a triangle, worn over the head and tied under the chin.

head sea *n. Nautical.* Waves or current running directly against the course of a ship.

head·set (hĕd′sĕt′) *n.* **1.** A pair of headphones. **2.** A pair of headphones with a voice transmitter attached.

head·shake (hĕd′shāk′) *n.* A turning of one's head to the right and left, signifying denial, disapproval, disbelief, doubt, or bemusement. **—head′shak′ing** *adj. & n.*

head·ship (hĕd′shĭp′) *n.* **1.** The position or office of a head or leader; primacy or command. **2.** *Chiefly British.* The position of a headmaster or headmistress.

head shop *n. Slang.* A specialty shop that sells paraphernalia for use with illegal drugs.

head·shot (hĕd′shŏt′) *n.* **1.** A photograph of the head. **2.** A bullet or shot aimed at and hitting the head.

head shrinker *n.* **1.** A headhunter who dries and shrinks the heads of victims. **2.** *Slang.* A psychiatrist, especially a psychoanalyst.

heads·man (hĕdz′mən) *n.* A public executioner who beheads condemned prisoners.

head·space (hĕd′spās′) *n.* The volume left at the top of a filled jar, tin, or other container before sealing.

head·spring (hĕd′sprĭng′) *n.* A fountainhead; a source.

head·stall (hĕd′stôl′) *n.* The section of a bridle that fits over a horse's head. Also called *headpiece.*

head·stand (hĕd′stănd′) *n.* A position, as in gymnastics or yoga, in which one supports oneself vertically on one's head with the hands braced for support on the floor or on a mat.

head start *n.* **1.** *Sports.* A start before other contestants in a race. **2.** An early start that confers an advantage.

head·stock (hĕd′stŏk′) *n.* A nonmoving part of a machine or power tool that supports a revolving part, such as the spindle of a lathe.

head·stone (hĕd′stōn′) *n.* **1.** A memorial stone set at the head of a grave. **2.** Also **head stone.** *Architecture.* See **keystone** (sense 1).

head·strong (hĕd′strông′, -strŏng′) *adj.* **1.** Determined to have one's own way; stubbornly and often recklessly willful. See Synonyms at **obstinate, unruly. 2.** Resulting from willfulness and obstinacy.

heads up (hĕdz) *interj.* Used as a warning to watch out for a potential source of danger, as at a construction site.

heads-up (hĕdz′ŭp′) *adj.* Showing an alert, competent style: *play heads-up basketball.*

heads-up display *n.* An electronically generated display of flight, navigational, attack, or other data superimposed upon a pilot's forward field of view.

head-to-head (hĕd′tə-hĕd′) *adv. & adj.* **1.** In direct confrontation or conflict at close quarters: *The two brothers went at it head-to-head. It was a head-to-head contest all the way.* **2.** Arranged in lines running in opposite directions: *The bunks were set up head-to-head.* **3.** Running close together in the same direction; neck and neck: *The horses ran mostly head-to-head.*

head-trip (hĕd′trĭp′) *n. Slang.* **1.** A mentally stimulating experience. **2.** An act or a pattern of behavior undertaken primarily for self-gratification.

head·wait·er (hĕd′wā′tər) *n.* A waiter who is in charge of the waiters and waitresses in a restaurant and is often responsible for taking reservations and seating guests.

head wall *n.* A steep slope or precipice rising at the head of a valley or glacial cirque.

head·wa·ter (hĕd′wô′tər, -wŏt′ər) *n.* The water from which a river rises; a source. Often used in the plural.

head·way (hĕd′wā′) *n.* **1.** Forward movement, especially of a ship. **2.** Progress toward a goal. **3.** The clear vertical space beneath a ceiling or archway; clearance. **4.** The distance in time or space that separates two vehicles traveling the same route.

head·wear (hĕd′wâr′) *n.* A hat or other covering for the head.

head·wind or **head wind** (hĕd′wĭnd′) *n.* A wind blowing directly against the course of an aircraft or a ship.

head·word (hĕd′wûrd′) *n.* **1.** A word, phrase, or name, usually set in boldface or other distinctive type, that serves as the heading for an entry in a dictionary, an encyclopedia, or a similar reference work. Also called *entry word.* **2.** *Linguistics.* A word that may be modified by an adjunct.

head·work (hĕd′wûrk′) *n.* Mental activity or work; thought.

head·y (hĕd′ē) *adj.* **-i·er, -i·est. 1.a.** Intoxicating or stupefying: *heady liqueur.* **b.** Tending to upset the mind or the balance of senses: *standing on a heady outcrop of rock.* **c.** Serving to exhilarate: *the heady news of triumph.* **2.a.** Impetuous and rash: *a heady outburst of anger.* **b.** Domineering; overbearing: *too heady to reason with.* **3.** Swift and violent; headlong: *a heady current.* **4.** Showing intelligence and good judgment; prudent: *heady tactics.* **5.** Suffering from a headache: *a heady, throbbing feeling.* **—head′i·ly** *adv.* **—head′i·ness** *n.*

heal (hēl) *v.* **healed, heal·ing, heals.** —*tr.* **1.** To restore to health or soundness; cure. See Synonyms at **cure. 2.** To set right; repair: *healed the rift between us.* **3.** To restore (a person) to spiritual wholeness. —*intr.* To become whole and sound; return to health. [Middle English *healen,* from Old English *hǣlan.* See **kailo-** in Appendix.] **—heal′a·ble** *adj.*

heal-all (hēl′ôl′) *n. Botany.* The self-heal.

heal·er (hē′lər) *n.* One that heals or attempts to heal, especially a faith healer.

heal·ing herb (hē′lĭng) *n.* See **comfrey.**

health (hĕlth) *n.* **1.** The overall condition of an organism at a given time. **2.** Soundness, especially of body or mind; freedom from disease or abnormality. **3.** A condition of optimal well-being: *concerned about the ecological health of the area.* **4.** A wish for someone's good health, often expressed as a toast. [Middle English *helthe,* from Old English *hǣlth.* See **kailo-** in Appendix.]

health care also **health·care** (hĕlth′kâr′) *n.* The prevention, treatment, and management of illness and the preservation of mental and physical well-being through the services offered by the medical and allied health professions. **—health care** also **health-care** *adj.* Of or relating to health care: *the health care industry.*

health food *n.* A food believed to be highly beneficial to health, especially a food grown organically and free of chemical additives.

health·ful (hĕlth′fəl) *adj.* **1.** Conducive to good health; salutary. **2.** Healthy. See Usage Note at **healthy. —health′ful·ly** *adv.* **—health′ful·ness** *n.*

health insurance *n.* Insurance against expenses incurred through illness of the insured.

health maintenance organization *n.* An HMO.

health spa *n.* A business establishment with equipment and facilities for exercising and improving physical fitness.

health walking *n. Sports.* See **race walking.**

health·y (hĕl′thē) *adj.* **-i·er, -i·est. 1.** Possessing good health. **2.** Conducive to good health; healthful: *healthy air.* **3.** Indicative of sound, rational thinking or frame of mind: *a healthy attitude.* **4.** Sizable; considerable: *a healthy portion of potatoes; a healthy raise in salary.* **—health′i·ly** *adv.* **—health′i·ness** *n.*

SYNONYMS: *healthy, sound, wholesome, hale, robust, well, hardy, vigorous.* These adjectives are compared as they mean being in or indicative of good physical or mental health. *Healthy* stresses the absence of disease and often implies energy and strength: *a rosy, healthy infant. If you exercise regularly and eat properly, you'll stay fit and healthy. Sound* emphasizes freedom from injury, imperfection, or impairment: *"You should pray for a sound mind in a sound body"* (Juvenal). *Wholesome* suggests appealing healthiness and well-being: *"a broad grin on his ugly wholesome face"* (Archibald Marshall). *"Exercise develops wholesome appetites"* (Louisa May Alcott). *Hale* stresses freedom from infirmity, especially in elderly persons, while *robust* emphasizes healthy strength and ruggedness: *"He is pretty well advanced in years, but hale, robust, and florid"* (Tobias Smollett). *Well* indicates absence of or recovery from sickness: *Her mother is not a well woman. Hardy* implies robust and sturdy good health: *hardy mountaineers of Alpine regions. Vigorous* suggests healthy, active energy and strength: *"a vigorous old man, who spent half of his day on horseback"* (W.H. Hudson).

USAGE NOTE: The distinction in meaning between *healthy* ("possessing good health") and *healthful* ("conducive to good health") was ascribed to the two terms only as late as the 1880's. This distinction, though tenaciously supported by some critics, is belied by citational evidence—evidence clearly indicating that *healthy* and *healthful* have shared the meaning "conducive to good health" since at least the mid-16th century, or for more than 400 years. Use of *healthy* in this sense is to be found in the works of a broad group of distinguished speakers and writers of English, with this example being typical: *"Gardening . . . and working in wood, are fit and healthy recreations for a man of study or business"* (John Locke). Therefore, both *healthy* and *healthful* are correct in these contexts: *a healthy climate, a healthful climate; a healthful diet, a healthy diet.*

heap (hēp) *n.* **1.** A group of things placed or thrown, one on top of the other: *a heap of dirty rags lying in the corner.* **2.** Often **heaps.** *Informal.* A great deal; a lot: *We have heaps of homework tonight.* **3.** *Slang.* An old or run-down car. **—heap** *tr.v.* **heaped, heap·ing, heaps. 1.** To put or throw in a pile. **2.** To fill completely or to overflowing: *heap a plate with vegetables.* **3.** To bestow in abundance or lavishly: *heaped praise on the rescuers.* [Middle English, from Old English *hēap.*]

SYNONYMS: *heap, bank, mound, pile, stack.* The central meaning shared by these nouns is "a group or collection of things lying one on top of the other": *a heap of old newspapers; a bank of thunder clouds; a mound of boulders; a pile of boxes; a stack of firewood.*

hear (hîr) *v.* **heard** (hûrd), **hear·ing, hears.** —*tr.* **1.** To perceive (sound) by the ear: *Can you hear the signal?* **2.** To learn by hearing; be told by others: *I heard she got married.* **3.a.** To listen to attentively: *Hear what I have to tell you.* **b.** To listen to in an official, professional, or formal capacity: *heard the last witness in the afternoon.* **c.** To listen to and consider favorably: *Lord, hear my prayer!* **d.** To attend or participate in: *hear Mass.* —*intr.* **1.** To be capable of perceiving sound. **2.** To receive news or information; learn: *I heard about your accident.* **3.** To consider, permit, or consent to something. Used only in the negative: *I won't hear of your going!* **—*phrasal verb.* hear from. 1.** To get a letter, telephone call, or transmitted communication from. **2.** To be reprimanded by: *If you don't do your homework, you're going to hear from me.* **—*idiom.* hear, hear.** Used to express approval. [Middle English *hearen,* Old English *hīeran.* See **keu-** in Appendix.] **—hear′er** *n.*

hear·ing (hîr′ĭng) *n.* **1.** The sense by which sound is perceived; the capacity to hear. **2.** Range of audibility; earshot. **3.** An opportunity to be heard. **4.** *Law.* **a.** A preliminary examination of an accused person. **b.** The trial of an equity case. **5.** A session, as of an investigatory committee or a grand jury, at which testimony is taken from witnesses.

hearing aid *n.* A small electronic apparatus that amplifies sound and is worn in or behind the ear to compensate for impaired hearing.

hearing dog *n.* A dog trained to assist a deaf or hearing-impaired person by signaling the occurrence of certain sounds, such as a ringing telephone or doorbell.

hear·ing-im·paired (hîr′ĭng-ĭm-pârd′) *adj.* **1.** Having a diminished or defective sense of hearing, but not deaf; hard of hearing. **2.** Completely incapable of hearing; deaf. **—hearing-impaired** *n. (used with a pl. verb).* Persons who are deficient in

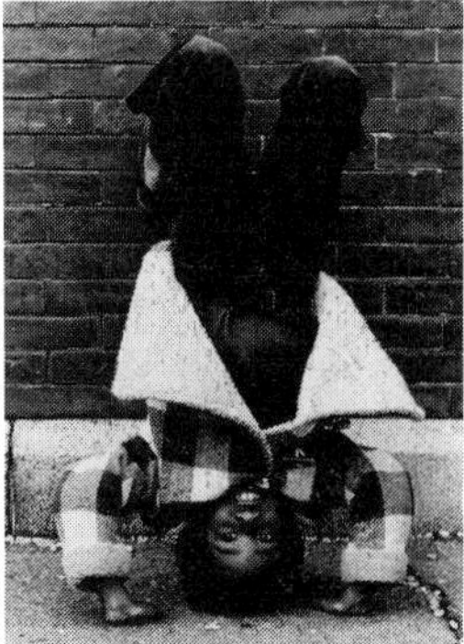

headstand

headstone

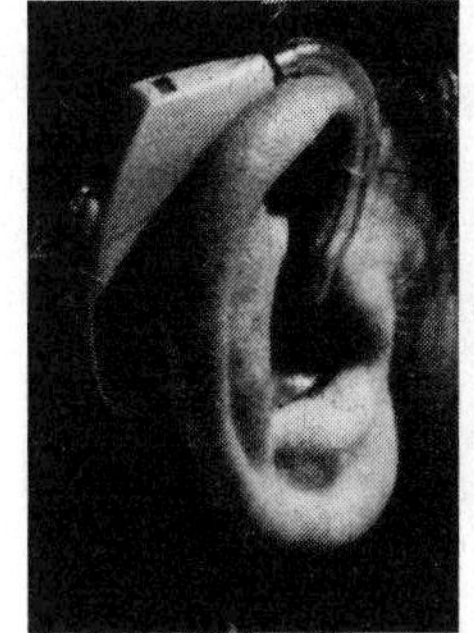

hearing aid

ă pat	oi boy
ā pay	ou out
âr care	o͝o took
ä father	o͞o boot
ĕ pet	ŭ cut
ē be	ûr urge
ĭ pit	th thin
ī pie	*th* this
îr pier	hw which
ŏ pot	zh vision
ō toe	ə about, item
ô paw	♦ regionalism

Stress marks: **′** (primary); ′ (secondary), as in **dictionary** (dĭk′shə-nĕr′ē)

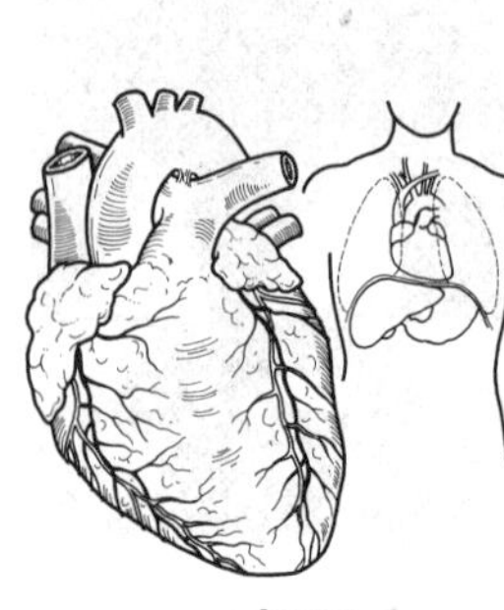

heart

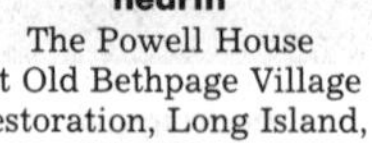

hearth
The Powell House at Old Bethpage Village restoration, Long Island, New York

hearing or are deaf: *The speech was interpreted in sign language for the hearing-impaired.*

hear·ken also **har·ken** (här′kən) *v.* **-kened, -ken·ing, -kens.** —*intr.* To listen attentively; give heed. —*tr. Archaic.* To listen to; hear. [Middle English *herknen,* from Old English *hercnian.* See **keu-** in Appendix.]

Hearn (hûrn), **Lafcadio.** 1850–1904. Greek-born American writer noted for his exotic stories and novels, such as *Chita* (1887).

hear·say (hîr′sā′) *n.* **1.** Information heard from another. **2.** *Law.* Evidence based on the reports of others rather than the personal knowledge of a witness and therefore generally not admissible as testimony.

hearse (hûrs) *n.* **1.** A vehicle for conveying a coffin to a church or cemetery. **2.** *Roman Catholic Church.* A triangular candelabrum used at Tenebrae during Holy Week. **3.** A framelike structure over a coffin or tomb on which to hang epitaphs. [Middle English *herse,* a harrow-shaped structure for holding candles over a coffin, from Old French *herce,* from Medieval Latin *hercia,* from Latin *hirpex, hirpic-,* harrow, probably from Oscan *hirpus,* wolf (alluding to its teeth).]

Hearst (hûrst), **William Randolph.** 1863–1951. American newspaper and magazine publisher. Beginning with the *San Francisco Examiner* in 1887, he built the world's largest publishing empire, comprising 28 major newspapers.

heart (härt) *n.* **1.** *Anatomy.* **a.** The chambered, muscular organ in vertebrates that pumps blood received from the veins into the arteries, thereby maintaining the flow of blood through the entire circulatory system. **b.** A similarly functioning structure in invertebrates. **2.** The area that is the approximate location of the heart in the body; the breast. **3. a.** The vital center and source of one's being, emotions, and sensibilities. **b.** The repository of one's deepest and sincerest feelings and beliefs: *an appeal from the heart; a subject dear to her heart.* **c.** The seat of the intellect or imagination: *the worst atrocities the human heart could devise.* **4. a.** Emotional constitution, basic disposition, or character: *a man after my own heart.* **b.** One's prevailing mood or current inclination: *We were light of heart. My heart is not in it.* **5. a.** Capacity for sympathy or generosity; compassion: *a leader who seems to have no heart.* **b.** Love; affection: *The child won my heart.* **6. a.** Courage; resolution; fortitude: *The soldiers lost heart and retreated.* **b.** The firmness of will or the callousness required to carry out an unpleasant task or responsibility: *hadn't the heart to send them away without food.* **7.** A person esteemed or admired as lovable, loyal, or courageous: *a dear heart.* **8. a.** The central or innermost physical part of a place or region: *the heart of the financial district.* See Synonyms at **center. b.** The core of a plant, fruit, or vegetable: *hearts of palm.* **9.** The most important or essential part: *get to the heart of the matter.* **10.** A conventionalized two-lobed representation of the heart, usually colored red or pink. **11.** *Games.* **a.** A red, heart-shaped figure on certain playing cards. **b.** A playing card with this figure. **c. hearts** *(used with a sing. or pl. verb).* The suit of cards represented by this figure. **d.** A card game in which the object is either to avoid hearts when taking tricks or to take all the hearts. —*attributive.* Often used to modify another noun: *heart surgery; heart patients.* —**heart** *tr.v.* **heart·ed, heart·ing, hearts.** *Archaic.* To encourage; hearten. —***idioms.*** **at heart.** In one's deepest feelings; fundamentally. **by heart.** Learned by rote; memorized word for word. **do (one's) heart good.** To lift one's spirits; make one happy. **from the bottom** (or **depths**) **of (one's) heart.** With the deepest appreciation; most sincerely. **have (one's) heart in (one's) mouth.** To be extremely frightened or anxious. **have (one's) heart in the right place.** To be well-intentioned. **heart and soul.** Completely; entirely. **in (one's) heart of hearts.** In the seat of one's truest feelings. **lose (one's) heart to.** To fall in love with. **near** (or **close to**) **(one's) heart.** Loved by or important to one. **steal (someone's) heart.** To win one's affection or love. **take to heart.** To take seriously and be affected or troubled by: *Don't take my criticism to heart.* **to (one's) heart's content.** To one's entire satisfaction, without limitation. **wear (one's) heart on (one's) sleeve.** To show one's feelings clearly and openly by one's behavior. **with all (one's) heart. 1.** With great willingness or pleasure. **2.** With the deepest feeling or devotion. **with half a heart.** In a half-hearted manner. [Middle English *hert,* from Old English *heorte.* See **kerd-** in Appendix.]

heart·ache (härt′āk′) *n.* Emotional anguish; sorrow. See Synonyms at **regret.**

heart attack *n.* Acute myocardial infarction typically resulting from an occlusion or obstruction of a coronary artery and characterized by sudden, severe pain in the chest that often radiates to the shoulder, arm, or jaw.

heart·beat (härt′bēt′) *n.* **1.** A single complete pulsation of the heart. **2.** A vital force or driving impulse: *Broadway is the heartbeat of the New York City theater world.*

heart block *n.* A condition in which faulty transmission of the impulses that control the heartbeat results in a lack of coordination in the contraction of the atria and ventricles of the heart.

heart·break (härt′brāk′) *n.* Overwhelming sorrow, grief, or disappointment. See Synonyms at **regret.** —**heart′break′er** *n.*

heart·break·ing (härt′brā′kĭng) *adj.* Causing overwhelming grief or distress. —**heart′break′ing·ly** *adv.*

heart·bro·ken (härt′brō′kən) *adj.* Suffering from or exhibiting overwhelming sorrow, grief, or disappointment. —**heart′bro′ken·ly** *adv.* —**heart′bro′ken·ness** *n.*

heart·burn (härt′bûrn′) *n.* A burning sensation, usually centered in the middle of the chest near the sternum, caused by the reflux of acidic stomach fluids that enter the lower end of the esophagus. Also called *cardialgia, pyrosis.*

heart disease *n.* A structural or functional abnormality of the heart, or of the blood vessels supplying the heart, that impairs its normal functioning.

heart·en (här′tn) *tr.v.* **-ened, -en·ing, -ens.** To give strength, courage, or hope to; encourage. See Synonyms at **encourage.**

heart failure *n.* **1.** Cessation of normal heart function. **2.** The inability of the heart to pump blood at an adequate rate, resulting in congestion in the lungs, shortness of breath, edema in the lower extremities, and enlargement of the liver.

heart·felt (härt′fĕlt′) *adj.* Deeply or sincerely felt; earnest. See Synonyms at **sincere.**

hearth (härth) *n.* **1.** The floor of a fireplace, usually extending into a room and paved with brick, flagstone, or cement. **2.** Family life; the home. **3.** *Metallurgy.* **a.** The lowest part of a blast furnace or cupola, from which the molten metal flows. **b.** The bottom of a reverberatory furnace, where ore is exposed to the flame. **4.** The fireplace or brazier of a blacksmith's forge. [Middle English *herth,* from Old English *heorth.* See **ker-**[3] in Appendix.]

hearth money *n. Roman Catholic Church.* See **Peter's pence** (sense 2).

hearth·rug (härth′rŭg′) *n.* A rug laid on a floor in front of a fireplace.

hearth·side (härth′sīd′) *n.* A place next to a hearth.

hearth·stone (härth′stōn′) *n.* **1.** Stone used in the construction of a hearth. **2.** Family life; the home. **3.** A soft stone or composition of pipe clay and pulverized stone used for scouring and whitening hearths or doorsteps.

heart·i·ly (här′tl-ē) *adv.* **1.** In a cordial manner; with warmth and sincerity: *She greeted us heartily.* **2.** Thoroughly; completely: *wished heartily that they would leave.* **3.** With zest or enthusiasm. **4.** With great appetite or enjoyment: *eat heartily.*

heart·land (härt′lănd′) *n.* A central region, especially one that is politically, economically, or militarily vital to a nation.

heart·leaf (härt′lēf′) *n.* See **wild ginger.**

heart·less (härt′lĭs) *adj.* **1.** Devoid of compassion or feeling; pitiless. **2.** *Archaic.* Devoid of courage or enthusiasm; spiritless. —**heart′less·ly** *adv.* —**heart′less·ness** *n.*

heart-lung machine (härt′lŭng′) *n.* An apparatus through which blood is temporarily diverted, especially during heart surgery, to oxygenate it and pump it throughout the body, thus maintaining circulation until the heart and lungs are able to return to normal functioning.

heart massage *n.* See **cardiac massage.**

heart rate *n. Abbr.* **HR** The number of heartbeats per unit of time, usually expressed as beats per minute.

heart-rend·ing or **heart·rend·ing** (härt′rĕn′dĭng) *adj.* Causing anguish or deep distress; arousing deep sympathy.

heart-search·ing (härt′sûr′chĭng) *n.* An examination of one's conscience, innermost feelings, and motives. —**heart′-search′ing** *adj.*

hearts·ease also **heart's-ease** (härts′ēz′) *n.* **1.** Peace of mind. **2.** A hybrid plant derived from crossing certain species of the genus *Viola* and having small variously colored flowers.

heart·sick (härt′sĭk′) *adj.* Profoundly disappointed; despondent. —**heart′sick′ness** *n.*

heart-strick·en (härt′strĭk′ən) also **heart-struck** (-strŭk′) *adj.* Overwhelmed with grief, dismay, or remorse.

heart·string (härt′strĭng′) *n.* **1. heartstrings.** The deepest feelings or affections: *a tug at the heartstrings.* **2.** One of the nerves or tendons formerly believed to brace and sustain the heart.

heart-struck (härt′strŭk′) *adj.* Variant of **heart-stricken.**

heart·throb (härt′thrŏb′) *n.* **1.** A pulsation of the heart; a heartbeat. **2. a.** Sentimental or tender emotion. **b.** Infatuation. **3. a.** A sweetheart. **b.** The object of one's infatuation.

heart-to-heart (härt′tə-härt′) *adj.* Candid; frank. —**heart-to-heart** *n.* An intimate conversation in private.

heart·warm·ing or **heart-warm·ing** (härt′wôr′mĭng) *adj.* Causing gladness and pleasure.

heart·wood (härt′wo͝od′) *n.* The older, inactive central wood of a tree or woody plant, usually darker and harder than the younger sapwood. Also called *duramen.*

heart·worm (härt′wûrm′) *n.* **1.** A filarial worm *(Dirofilaria immitis)* transmitted by mosquitoes and parasitic in the heart and associated blood vessels of dogs and other canids. **2.** The condition resulting from infestation with the heartworm.

heart·y (här′tē) *adj.* **-i·er, -i·est. 1.** Expressed warmly, exuberantly, and unrestrainedly: *a hearty welcome.* See Synonyms at **sincere. 2.** Complete or thorough; unequivocal: *hearty support.* **3.** Vigorous; robust: *a hearty glow of health.* **4.** Enjoying or requiring much food: *a person with a hearty appetite.* **a.** Providing abundant nourishment: *a hearty chowder.* **b.** Satisfying; substantial: *a hearty meal.* —**hearty** *n., pl.* **-ies. 1.** A good fellow; a comrade. **2.** A sailor. —**heart′i·ness** *n.*

heat (hēt) *n.* **1.** *Physics.* A form of energy associated with the motion of atoms or molecules and capable of being transmitted through solid and fluid media by conduction, through fluid media by convection, and through empty space by radiation. **2.** The sensation or perception of such energy as warmth or hotness. **3.** An abnormally high bodily temperature, as from a fever. **4. a.** The condition of being hot. **b.** A degree of warmth or hotness: *The burner was on low heat.* **5. a.** The warming of a room or building by a furnace or another source of energy: *The house was cheap to rent, but the heat was expensive.* **b.** A furnace or other source of warmth in a room or building: *The heat was on when we returned from work.* **6.** A hot season; a spell of hot weather. **7. a.** Intensity, as of passion, emotion, color, appearance, or effect. **b.** The most intense or active stage: *the heat of battle.* **c.** A burning sensation in the mouth produced by spicy flavoring in food. **8.** Estrus. **9.** One of a series of efforts or attempts. **10. a.** *Sports & Games.* One round of several in a competition, such as a race. **b.** A preliminary contest held to determine finalists. **11.** *Informal.* Pressure; stress. **12.** *Slang.* **a.** An intensification of police activity in pursuing criminals. **b.** The police. Used with *the.* **13.** *Slang.* Adverse comments or hostile criticism: *Heat from the press forced the senator to resign.* **14.** *Slang.* A firearm, especially a pistol. —*attributive.* Often used to modify another noun: *heat barriers; heat resistance.* **—heat** *v.* **heat·ed, heat·ing, heats.** —*tr.* **1.** To make warm or hot. **2.** To excite the feelings of; inflame. —*intr.* **1.** To become warm or hot. **2.** To become excited emotionally or intellectually. ***—phrasal verb.*** **heat up.** *Informal.* To become acute or intense: *"If inflation heats up, interest rates could increase"* (Christian Science Monitor). [Middle English *hete,* from Old English *hǣtu.* See **kai-** in Appendix.]

heat capacity *n.* The amount of heat required to raise the temperature of one mole or one gram of a substance by one degree Celsius without change of phase.

heat·ed (hē′tĭd) *adj.* Angry; vehement; impassioned: *a heated argument.* **—heat′ed·ly** *adv.*

heat·er (hē′tər) *n.* **1.** An apparatus that heats or provides heat. **2.** One who heats something or tends a heating apparatus. **3.** *Slang.* A pistol. **4.** *Baseball.* A fastball.

heat exchanger *n.* A device, such as an automobile radiator, used to transfer heat from a fluid on one side of a barrier to a fluid on the other side without bringing the fluids into direct contact.

heat exhaustion *n.* A condition caused by exposure to heat, resulting in the depletion of body fluids and causing weakness, dizziness, nausea, and often collapse. The condition can be alleviated by rest and the administration of fluids and electrolytes to compensate for those lost through excessive sweating. Also called *heat prostration.*

heath (hēth) *n.* **1.** Any of various usually low-growing shrubs of the genus *Erica* and related genera, native to Europe and South Africa and having small evergreen leaves and small, colorful, urn-shaped flowers. Also called *heather.* **2.** An extensive tract of uncultivated open land covered with herbage and low shrubs; a moor. [Middle English, uncultivated land, from Old English *hǣth.* See **kaito-** in Appendix.]

Heath (hēth), **Edward Richard George.** Born 1916. British politician who as prime minister (1970–1974) secured his country's entry into the Common Market (1972).

hea·then (hē′thən) *n., pl.* **-thens** or **heathen. 1. a.** One who adheres to the religion of a people or nation that does not acknowledge the God of Judaism, Christianity, or Islam. **b.** Such persons considered as a group; the unconverted. **2. a.** One who is regarded as irreligious, uncivilized, or unenlightened. **b.** Such persons considered as a group. [Middle English *hethen,* from Old English *hǣthen.* See **kaito-** in Appendix.] **—hea′then** *adj.* **—hea′then·dom, hea′then·ism, hea′then·ry** *n.*

hea·then·ish (hē′thə-nĭsh) *adj.* **1.** Of or having to do with heathens. **2.** Uncouth; barbarous. **—hea′then·ish·ly** *adv.* **—hea′then·ish·ness** *n.*

heath·er (hĕth′ər) *n.* **1.** A low-growing Eurasian shrub *(Calluna vulgaris)* growing in dense masses and having small evergreen leaves and clusters of small, bell-shaped pinkish-purple flowers. Also called *ling.* **2.** See **heath** (sense 1). **3.** *Color.* A grayish purple to purplish red. [Alteration (influenced by HEATH) of Middle English *hather,* probably from Old English **hǣddre.*]

heath·er·y (hĕth′ə-rē) *adj.* **1.** Of, relating to, or resembling heather. **2.** Flecked with various colors.

heath hen *n.* A subspecies of the prairie chicken *(Tympanuchus cupido* subsp. *cupido)* that became extinct in eastern North America during the first part of the 20th century.

heat island *n.* An area, such as a city or an industrial site, having consistently higher temperatures than surrounding areas because of a greater retention of heat, as by buildings, concrete, and asphalt.

heat lightning *n.* Intermittent flashes of light near the horizon, usually seen on a hot summer evening, unaccompanied by thunder and thought to be cloud reflections of distant lightning.

heat of combustion *n.* The amount of heat released per unit mass or unit volume of a substance when the substance is completely burned.

heat of fusion *n.* The amount of heat required to convert a unit mass of a solid at its melting point into a liquid without an increase in temperature.

heat of transformation *n.* See **latent heat.**

heat of vaporization *n.* The amount of heat required to convert a unit mass of a liquid at its boiling point into vapor without an increase in temperature.

heat·proof (hēt′pro͞of′) *adj.* Unaffected by heat. Used especially of plastic, glass, or ceramic utensils that may be used directly over a flame or in an oven.

heat prostration *n.* See **heat exhaustion.**

heat pump *n.* A device that warms or cools a building by transferring heat from a relatively low-temperature reservoir to one at a higher temperature.

heat rash *n.* An inflammatory skin condition caused by obstruction of the ducts of the sweat glands, resulting from exposure to high heat and humidity and characterized by the eruption of small, red papules accompanied by an itching or prickling sensation. Also called *miliaria, prickly heat.*

heat-seal (hēt′sēl′) *tr.v.* **-sealed, -seal·ing, -seals.** To enclose an object in a thin, clear thermoplastic sheet that is bonded by heat and pressure to form a closure against air or tampering.

heat shield *n.* A barrier that prevents the heating of a space or an object by absorbing, reflecting, or dissipating external heat, especially a protective structure on a spacecraft or missile that dissipates heat on atmospheric reentry by melting and vaporizing.

heat sink *n.* **1.** An environment capable of absorbing heat from an object with which it is in thermal contact. **2.** A protective device that absorbs and dissipates the excess heat generated by a system.

heat stroke *n.* A severe condition caused by impairment of the body's temperature-regulating abilities, resulting from prolonged exposure to excessive heat and characterized by cessation of sweating, severe headache, high fever, hot dry skin, and in serious cases, collapse and coma.

heat-treat (hēt′trēt′) *tr.v.* **-treat·ed, -treat·ing, -treats.** To treat (metal, for example) by alternate heating and cooling in order to produce desired characteristics, such as increased hardness; temper. **—heat treater** *n.* **—heat treatment** *n.*

heat wave *n.* A period of unusually hot weather.

heave (hēv) *v.* **heaved, heav·ing, heaves.** —*tr.* **1.** To raise or lift, especially with great effort or force: *heaved the box of books onto the table.* See Synonyms at **lift. 2. a.** To throw (a heavy object) with great effort; hurl: *heave the shot; heaved a brick through the window.* **b.** To throw or toss: *heaved his backpack into the corner.* **3.** To utter with effort or pain: *heaved a groan of despair.* **4.** To vomit (something). **5.** *past tense and past participle* **hove** (hōv). *Nautical.* **a.** To raise or haul up by means of a rope, line, or cable: *hove the anchor up and set sail.* **b.** To move a ship in a certain direction or into a certain position by hauling: *hove the ship astern.* **6.** To make rise or swell: *the wind heaving huge waves; an exhausted dog heaving its chest.* **7.** *Geology.* To displace or move (a vein, lode, or stratum, for example). —*intr.* **1.** To rise up or swell, as if pushed up; bulge: *The sidewalk froze and heaved.* **2.** To rise and fall in turn, as waves. **3.** To gag or vomit. **4.** *past tense and past participle* **hove.** *Nautical.* **a.** To move in a certain direction or to a specified position: *The frigate hove alongside.* **b.** To pull at or haul a rope or cable: *The brig is heaving around on the anchor.* **c.** To push at a capstan bar or lever. **—heave** *n.* **1.** The effort of heaving. **2.** An act of hurling; a throw, especially when considered in terms of distance: *a heave of 63 feet.* **3.** *Geology.* A horizontal dislocation, as of a rock stratum, at a fault. **4.** An upward movement. **5.** The act or an instance of gagging or vomiting. **6. heaves** *(used with a sing. or pl. verb).* A pulmonary disease of horses that is characterized by respiratory irregularities, such as coughing, and is noticeable especially after exercise or in cold weather. ***—phrasal verb.*** **heave to.** *Nautical.* **a.** To turn a sailing ship so that its bow heads into the wind and the ship lies motionless except for drifting, in order to meet a storm: *The brig hove to.* **b.** To turn an engine-powered vessel in a similar situation so that its bow heads into the seas while proceeding at low speed. ***—idiom.*** **heave into sight** (or **view**). To rise or seem to rise over the horizon into view, as a ship. [Middle English *heven,* from Old English *hebban.* See **kap-** in Appendix.] **—heav′er** *n.*

heave ho *interj. Nautical.* Used as a command to sailors to pull hard on a rope or cable.

heave-ho (hēv′hō′) *n. Slang.* Dismissal from one's job or from one's position: *got the heave-ho in a very unceremonious manner; gave the employee the old heave-ho.*

heav·en (hĕv′ən) *n.* **1.** Often **heavens.** The sky or universe as seen from Earth; the firmament. **2. a.** Often **Heaven.** The abode of God, the angels, and the souls of those who are granted salvation. **b.** An eternal state of communion with God; everlasting bliss. **3. a. Heaven.** God: *Heaven help you!* **b. heavens.** Used in various phrases to express surprise: *Good heavens!* **4.** Often **heavens.** The celestial powers; the gods: *The heavens favored the young prince.* **5.** A condition or place of great happiness, delight, or pleasure: *The lake was heaven.* ***—idiom.*** **move heaven and earth.** To do everything possible to bring about something desired. [Middle English *heven,* from Old English *heofon.* See **ak-** in Appendix.]

heav·en·ly (hĕv′ən-lē) *adj.* **1.** Sublime; delightful; enchanting. **2.** Of or relating to the firmament; celestial. **3.** Of or relating to the abode of God; divine. **—heav′en·li·ness** *n.*

heav·en-sent (hĕv′ən-sĕnt′) *adj.* Occurring at an opportune time; providential.

heav·en·ward (hĕv′ən-wərd) *adv. & adj.* Toward, to, or in heaven. **—heav′en·wards** (-wərdz) *adv.*

heav·i·er-than-air (hĕv′ē-ər-thən-âr′) *adj.* Being an aircraft that is heavier than the air it displaces.

ă pat	oi boy
ā pay	ou out
âr care	o͝o took
ä father	o͞o boot
ĕ pet	ŭ cut
ē be	ûr urge
ĭ pit	th thin
ī pie	*th* this
îr pier	hw which
ŏ pot	zh vision
ō toe	ə about, item
ô paw	♦ regionalism

Stress marks: **′** (primary); ′ (secondary), as in **dictionary** (dĭk′shə-nĕr′ē)

heav·i·ly (hĕv-ə-lē) *adv.* **1.** In a burdened manner: *heavily laden.* **2.** Very slowly and with difficulty; laboriously: *walking heavily through the snow.* **3.** Greatly or severely: *heavily in debt.*

Heav·i·side (hĕv′ē-sīd′), **Oliver.** 1850–1925. British physicist who predicted the existence of the ionized atmospheric layer now known as the ionosphere.

Heaviside layer *n.* See **E layer.** [After Oliver HEAVISIDE.]

heav·y (hĕv′ē) *adj.* **-i·er, -i·est.** *Abbr.* **hvy. 1.** Having relatively great weight: *a heavy load.* **2.** Having relatively high density; having a high specific gravity. **3. a.** Large, as in number or quantity: *a heavy turnout; heavy casualties.* **b.** Large in yield or output: *heavy rainfall.* **4.** Of great intensity: *heavy activity; heavy fighting.* **5. a.** Having great power or force: *a heavy punch.* **b.** Violent; rough: *heavy seas.* **6. a.** Equipped with massive armaments and weapons: *a heavy cruiser; heavy infantry.* **b.** Large enough to fire powerful shells: *heavy guns.* **7. a.** Indulging to a great degree: *a heavy drinker.* **b.** Involved or participating on a large scale: *a heavy investor.* **8.** Of great import or seriousness; grave: *heavy matters of state.* **9. a.** Having considerable thickness: *a heavy coat.* **b.** Broad or coarse: *drew the face with heavy lines.* **10. a.** Dense; thick: *a heavy fog.* **b.** Slow to dissipate; strong: *"There was a heavy fragrance of flowers and lemon trees"* (Mario Puzo). **c.** Too dense or rich to digest easily: *a heavy dessert.* **d.** Insufficiently leavened: *heavy bread.* **e.** Full of clay and readily saturated: *heavy soil.* **11. a.** Weighed down; burdened: *trees heavy with plums.* **b.** Emotionally weighed down; despondent: *a heavy heart.* **c.** Marked by or exhibiting weariness: *heavy lids.* **d.** Sad or painful: *heavy news.* **12. a.** Hard to do or accomplish; arduous: *heavy going; heavy reading.* **b.** Not easily borne; oppressive: *heavy taxes.* **13.** Lacking vitality; deficient in vivacity or grace: *a heavy gait; heavy humor.* **14.** Sharply inclined; steep: *a heavy grade.* **15.** Having a large capacity or designed for rough work: *a heavy truck.* **16.** Of, relating to, or involving the large-scale production of basic products, such as steel: *heavy industry.* **17.** Of or relating to a serious dramatic role. **18.** *Physics.* Of or relating to an isotope with an atomic mass greater than the average mass of that element. **19.** Loud; sonorous: *a heavy sound; heavy breathing.* **20.** *Linguistics.* Of, relating to, or being a syllable ending in a long vowel or in a vowel plus two consonants. **21.** *Slang.* **a.** Of great significance or profundity. **b.** Very popular or important: *a rock star who is really heavy.* **—heavy** *adv.* **-ier, -iest.** Heavily: *The snow is falling heavier tonight than last night.* **—heavy** *n., pl.* **-ies. 1. a.** A serious or tragic role in a play. **b.** An actor playing such a role. **2.** *Slang.* A villain in a story or play. **3.** *Slang.* A mobster. **4.** *Slang.* One that is very important or influential: *a media heavy.* [Middle English *hevi,* from Old English *hefig.* See **kap-** in Appendix.] **—heav′i·ness** *n.*

SYNONYMS: *heavy, weighty, hefty, massive, ponderous, cumbersome.* These adjectives mean having a relatively great weight. *Heavy* refers to what has great weight (*a heavy boulder; a heavy load*); figuratively it applies to what is burdensome or oppressive to the spirit (*heavy responsibilities; heavy losses*). *Weighty* literally denotes having considerable weight (*a weighty package*); figuratively it describes what is onerous, serious, or important (*the weighty cares of a head of state; a weighty problem; a weighty decision*). *Hefty* refers principally to physical heaviness or brawniness: *a hefty dictionary; a tall, hefty wrestler. Massive* describes what is bulky, heavy, solid, and strong: *a massive head; massive marble columns; a massive gold chain. Ponderous* refers to what has great mass and weight and usually implies unwieldiness: *ponderous prehistoric beasts.* Figuratively it describes what is complicated, involved, or lacking in grace: *a book with a ponderous plot; a ponderous compliment.* Something *cumbersome* is difficult to move, handle, or deal with because it is heavy, bulky, or clumsy: *cumbersome luggage; a cumbersome writing style.*

heav·y-dut·y (hĕv′ē-do͞o′tē, -dyo͞o′-) *adj. Abbr.* **HD** Made to withstand hard use or wear.

heav·y-foot·ed (hĕv′ē-fo͝ot′ĭd) *adj.* Having a ponderous, lumbering gait.

heav·y-hand·ed (hĕv′ē-hăn′dĭd) *adj.* **1.** Clumsy; awkward. **2.** Tactless; indiscreet. **3.** Oppressive; harsh. **—heav′y-hand′ed·ness** *n.*

heav·y-heart·ed (hĕv′ē-här′tĭd) *adj.* Melancholy; depressed; sad. **—heav′y-heart′ed·ly** *adv.* **—heav′y-heart′ed·ness** *n.*

heavy hydrogen *n.* An isotope of hydrogen with mass number greater than 1; deuterium or tritium.

heav·y-lad·en (hĕv′ē-lăd′n) *adj.* **1.** Loaded with great weight. **2.** Burdened with grievous cares.

heavy lifting *n. Slang.* Serious or difficult activities or work: *"Attention is shifting to the fall Presidential race, and with only seven months left in office, Reagan won't be doing any heavy lifting"* (Business Week).

heavy metal *n.* **1.** A metal with a specific gravity greater than about 5.0, especially one that is poisonous, such as lead or mercury. **2.** *Music.* Very loud, greatly amplified, brash rock music often with shouted, violent lyrics.

heavy particle *n.* See **baryon.**

heav·y·set (hĕv′ē-sĕt′) *adj.* Having a stout or compact build.

heavy spar *n.* See **barite.**

heavy water *n.* Any of several isotopic forms of water, especially deuterium oxide, that consists chiefly of molecules containing heavy hydrogen and is used as a moderator in certain nuclear reactors.

heav·y·weight (hĕv′ē-wāt′) *n.* **1.** One of above average weight. **2.** *Sports.* **a.** A professional boxer weighing more than 175 pounds (approximately 79.5 kilograms), heavier than a light heavyweight. **b.** A contestant in other sports in the heaviest weight class. **3.** *Informal.* A person of great importance or influence. **—heav′y·weight′** *adj.*

Heb. *abbr.* **1.** Hebrew. **2.** *Bible.* Hebrews.

Heb·bel (hĕb′əl), **(Christian) Friedrich.** 1813–1863. German dramatist whose works include *Judith* (1840) and *Maria Magdalena* (1844).

heb·do·mad (hĕb′də-măd′) *n.* **1.** A group of seven. **2.** A period of seven days; a week. [Latin *hebdomas, hebdomad-,* the number seven, from Greek, from *hebdomos,* seventh, from *hepta,* seven. See **septm̥** in Appendix.]

heb·dom·a·dal (hĕb-dŏm′ə-dəl) *adj.* Weekly. **—heb·dom′a·dal·ly** *adv.*

He·be (hē′bē) *n. Greek Mythology.* The goddess of youth and spring, cupbearer to the Olympian gods.

He·bei (hœ′bā′) also **Ho·pei** or **Ho·peh** (hō′pā′, hŭ′bā′). A province of northeast China bordering on the Gulf of Bo Hai. Shijiazhuang is the capital. Population, 55,480,000.

he·be·phre·ni·a (hē′bə-frē′nē-ə, -frĕn′ē-) *n.* A type of schizophrenia, usually starting at puberty, characterized by foolish mannerisms, senseless laughter, delusions, hallucinations, and regressive behavior. [Greek *hēbē,* youth + -PHRENIA.] **—he′be·phren′ic** (-frĕn′ĭk, -frē′nĭk) *adj.*

heb·e·tate (hĕb′ĭ-tāt′) *tr.v.* **-tat·ed, -tat·ing, -tates.** To make obtuse or dull. [Latin *hebetāre, hebetāt-,* from *hebes, hebet-,* blunt.] **—heb′e·ta′tion** *n.* **—heb′e·ta′tive** *adj.*

heb·e·tude (hĕb′ĭ-to͞od′, -tyo͞od′) *n.* Dullness of mind; mental lethargy. [Late Latin *hebetūdō,* from Latin *hebes, hebet-,* dull.] **—heb′e·tu′di·nous** (-to͞od′n-əs, -tyo͞od′-) *adj.*

Hebr. *abbr.* Hebrew.

He·bra·ic (hĭ-brā′ĭk) also **He·bra·i·cal** (-ĭ-kəl) *adj.* Of, relating to, or characteristic of the Hebrews or their language or culture. [Middle English *Ebraik,* from Late Latin *Hebrāicus,* from Greek *Hebraikos,* from *Hebraios.* See HEBREW.] **—He·bra′i·cal·ly** *adv.*

He·bra·ism (hē′brā-ĭz′əm) *n.* **1.** A manner or custom characteristic of the Hebrews. **2.** A linguistic feature typical of Hebrew occurring especially in another language. **3.** The culture, spirit, or character of the Hebrew people. **4.** Judaism.

He·bra·ist (hē′brā′ĭst) *n.* A scholar who specializes in the study of Hebrew. **—He′bra·is′tic, He′bra·is′ti·cal** *adj.* **—He′bra·is′ti·cal·ly** *adv.*

He·bra·ize (hē′brā-īz′) *v.* **-ized, -iz·ing, -iz·es.** *—tr.* To make Hebraic in form or idiom. *—intr.* To use or adopt Hebraisms. **—He′bra·i·za′tion** (-ĭ-zā′shən) *n.*

He·brew (hē′bro͞o) *n. Abbr.* **Heb., Hebr. 1.** A member or descendant of a northern Semitic people, claiming descent from Abraham, Isaac, and Jacob; an Israelite; a Jew. **2. a.** The Semitic language of the ancient Hebrews. **b.** Any of the various later forms of this language, especially the language of the Israelis. **3. Hebrews** *(used with a sing. verb). Bible.* See table at **Bible.** [Middle English *Ebreu,* from Old French, from Latin *Hebraeus,* Hebraic, from Greek *Hebraios,* from Aramaic *ʿibray,* from Hebrew *ʿibrî.*] **—He′brew** *adj.*

Hebrew Scriptures *pl.n. Bible.* The Pentateuch, the Prophets, and the Hagiographa, forming the covenant between God and the Jewish people that is the foundation and Bible of Judaism while constituting for Christians the Old Testament.

Heb·ri·des (hĕb′rĭ-dēz′) also **West·ern Islands** (wĕs′tərn). An island group of western and northwest Scotland in the Atlantic Ocean, divided into the **Inner Hebrides,** closer to the Scottish mainland, and the **Outer Hebrides,** to the northwest. The original Celtic inhabitants were conquered by Scandinavians, who ruled the islands until 1266. Native Scottish chieftains controlled the Hebrides until the 16th century, when the islands passed to the kingdom of Scotland. **—Heb′ri·de′an** *adj. & n.*

He·bron (hē′brən). A city of the West Bank south-southwest of Jerusalem. Believed to be one of the oldest cities in the world, it was Abraham's home and King David's capital for a short time. Hebron was occupied by Israel in 1967. Population, 43,000.

Hec·a·te or **Hek·a·te** (hĕk′ə-tē, hĕk′ĭt) *n. Greek Mythology.* An ancient fertility goddess who later became associated with Persephone as queen of Hades and protector of witches.

hec·a·tomb (hĕk′ə-tōm′) *n.* **1.** A large-scale sacrifice or slaughter. **2.** A sacrifice to the ancient Greek and Roman gods consisting originally of 100 oxen or cattle. [Latin *hecatombē,* from Greek *hekatombē* : *hekaton,* hundred; see **dekm̥** in Appendix + *-bē,* oxen; see **gʷou-** in Appendix.]

Hecht (hĕkt), **Ben.** 1894–1964. American writer of short stories, novels, such as *Erik Dorn* (1921), dramas, including *The Front Page* (1928), written with Charles MacArthur.

heck (hĕk) *interj.* Used as a mild oath. **—heck** *n. Slang.* Used as an intensive: *had a heck of a lot of money; was crowded as heck.* [Alteration of HELL.]

heck·el·phone (hĕk′əl-fōn′) *n. Music.* A woodwind instrument of the oboe family, with a pitch between that of an English horn and a bassoon. [German *Heckelphon,* after Wilhelm *Heckel* (1879–1952), German musical instrument maker.]

heck·le (hĕk′əl) *tr.v.* **-led, -ling, -les. 1.** To try to embarrass and annoy (another) by questions, gibes, or objections; badger. **2.** To comb (flax or hemp) with a hatchel. [Middle English *hekelen,* to comb with a hatchel, from *hekel,* hatchel, from Middle Dutch. See **keg-** in Appendix.] **—heck′ler** *n.*

heck·uv·a (hĕk′ə-və) *adj. Slang.* Used as an intensive: *You've done a heckuva good job.* [Alteration of *heck of a.*]

hect– *pref.* Variant of **hecto–.**

hec·tare (hĕk′târ′) *n. Abbr.* **ha** A metric unit of area equal to 100 ares (2.471 acres). See table at **measurement.**

hec·tic (hĕk′tĭk) *adj.* **1.** Characterized by intense activity, confusion, or haste: *"There was nothing feverish or hectic about his vigor"* (Erik Erikson). **2.** *Medicine.* Of, relating to, or being a fever that fluctuates during the day, as in tuberculosis or septicemia. **3.** Consumptive; feverish. **4.** Flushed. [Middle English *etik,* recurring, consumptive, from Old French *etique,* from Late Latin *hecticus,* from Greek *hektikos,* from *hexis,* habit, from *ekhein,* to be in a certain condition. See **segh-** in Appendix.]

WORD HISTORY: In the Usage Panel survey done for the first edition of the *American Heritage Dictionary* (1969), 92 percent of the Panel approved of the use of *hectic* in its most familiar sense, "characterized by feverish activity, confusion, or haste." The question was put to the Panel because in earlier usage that sense was sometimes deprecated as a loose extension of the term's meaning in medicine. Unless one has some medical knowledge one probably does not know the older medical uses of the term, for example, "relating to an undulating fever, such as those accompanying tuberculosis," and unless one has some acquaintance with Middle English one would not recognize the first recorded instance of the word, *etik,* in a text written before 1398. The Middle English term comes from the Old French development of the Late Latin word *hecticus,* whose form helped reshape our word in the 16th century. Late Latin *hecticus* in turn comes from Greek *hektikos,* "formed by habit or forming habit" and "consumptive," developing the last sense because of the chronic nature of tuberculous fevers. Thus a word that once simply meant "habitual" eventually had an English descendant used to refer to circumstances that would be undesirable if they were habitual.

hecto– or **hect–** *pref.* One hundred (10^2): *hectare.* [French, alteration of Greek *hekaton,* hundred. See **dekm̥** in Appendix.]

hec·to·cot·y·lus (hĕk′tō-kŏt′l-əs) *n., pl.* **-cot·y·li** (-kŏt′l-ī′). A modified arm of the male of certain cephalopods, such as the octopus, functioning as a reproductive organ in the transference of sperm to the mantle cavity of the female. [New Latin : HECTO– + Greek *kotulē,* small cup.]

hec·to·gram (hĕk′tə-grăm′) *n. Abbr.* **hg** A metric unit of mass equal to 100 grams.

hec·to·graph (hĕk′tə-grăf′) *n.* A machine employing a glycerin-coated layer of gelatin in order to make copies of typed or written material. **—hectograph** *tr.v.* **-graphed, -graph·ing, -graphs.** To copy by means of a hectograph. **—hec′to·graph′ic** *adj.* **—hec′to·graph′i·cal·ly** *adv.*

hec·to·li·ter (hĕk′tə-lē′tər) *n. Abbr.* **hl 1.** A metric unit of liquid capacity or volume equal to 100 liters. **2.** A metric unit of dry capacity or volume equal to 100 liters.

hec·to·me·ter (hĕk′tə-mē′tər, hĕk-tŏm′ĭ-tər) *n. Abbr.* **hm** A metric unit of length equal to 100 meters. See table at **measurement.**

hec·tor (hĕk′tər) *n.* A bully. **—hector** *v.* **-tored, -tor·ing, -tors.** —*tr.* To intimidate or dominate in a blustering way. —*intr.* To behave like a bully; swagger. [Latin *Hectōr,* Hector, from Greek *Hektōr.*]

Hec·tor (hĕk′tər) *n. Greek Mythology.* A Trojan prince, the eldest son of Priam and Hecuba, killed by Achilles in Homer's *Iliad.*

Hec·u·ba (hĕk′yə-bə) *n.* The wife of Priam and mother of Hector, Paris, and Cassandra in Homer's *Iliad.*

he'd (hēd). **1.** He had. **2.** He would.

hed·dle (hĕd′l) *n.* One of a set of parallel cords or wires in a loom used to separate and guide the warp threads and make a path for the shuttle. [Probably alteration of Middle English *helde,* from Old English *hefeld.* See **kap-** in Appendix.]

hedge (hĕj) *n.* **1.** A row of closely planted shrubs or low-growing trees forming a fence or boundary. **2.** A line of people or objects forming a barrier: *a hedge of spectators along the sidewalk.* **3.a.** A means of protection or defense, especially against financial loss: *a hedge against inflation.* **b.** A securities transaction that reduces the risk on an existing investment position. **4.** An intentionally noncommittal or ambiguous statement. **—hedge** *v.* **hedged, hedg·ing, hedg·es.** —*tr.* **1.** To enclose or bound with or as if with hedges. **2.** To hem in, hinder, or restrict with or as if with a hedge. **3.** To minimize or protect against the loss of by counterbalancing one transaction, such as a bet, against another. —*intr.* **1.** To plant or cultivate hedges. **2.** To take compensatory measures so as to counterbalance possible loss. **3.** To avoid making a clear, direct response or statement. [Middle English, from Old English *hecg.*] **—hedg′er** *n.* **—hedg′y** *adj.*

hedge fund *n.* An investment company that uses high-risk techniques, such as borrowing money and selling short, in an effort to make extraordinary capital gains.

hedge·hog (hĕj′hôg′, -hŏg′) *n.* **1.** Any of several small insectivorous mammals of the family Erinaceidae of Europe, Africa, and Asia, having the back covered with dense, erectile spines and characteristically rolling into a ball for protection. **2.** Any of several spiny animals, such as the porcupine, that are similar to the hedgehog.

hedgehog
European hedgehog
Erinaceus europaeus

hedge·hop (hĕj′hŏp′) *intr.v.* **-hopped, -hop·ping, -hops.** To fly an airplane close to the ground, rising above objects as they appear, as in spraying crops. **—hedge′hop′per** *n.*

hedge hyssop *n.* Any of various plants of the genus *Gratiola,* growing in damp places and having yellow or whitish flowers.

hedge·row (hĕj′rō′) *n.* A row of bushes, shrubs, or trees forming a hedge.

Hed·jaz (hē-jăz′). See **Hejaz.**

he·don·ic (hĭ-dŏn′ĭk) *adj.* **1.** Of, relating to, or marked by pleasure. **2.** Of or relating to hedonism or hedonists. [Greek *hēdonikos,* from *hēdonē,* pleasure. See **swād-** in Appendix.] **—he·don′i·cal·ly** *adv.*

he·don·ics (hĭ-dŏn′ĭks) *n. (used with a sing. verb).* **1.** The branch of psychology that studies pleasant and unpleasant sensations and states of mind. **2.** *Philosophy.* The branch of ethics that deals with the relation of pleasure to duty.

he·don·ism (hēd′n-ĭz′əm) *n.* **1.** Pursuit of or devotion to pleasure, especially to the pleasures of the senses. **2.** *Philosophy.* The ethical doctrine holding that only what is pleasant or has pleasant consequences is intrinsically good. **3.** *Psychology.* The doctrine holding that behavior is motivated by the desire for pleasure and the avoidance of pain. [Greek *hēdonē,* pleasure; see **swād-** in Appendix + –ISM.] **—he′don·ist** *n.* **—he′don·is′tic** *adj.* **—he′don·is′ti·cal·ly** *adv.*

–hedral *suff.* Having a specified kind or number of surfaces: *dihedral.* [From –HEDRON.]

–hedron *suff.* A crystal or geometric figure having a specified kind or number of surfaces: *heptahedron.* [New Latin, from Greek *-edron,* neuter of *-edros,* -sided, from *hedra,* face. See **sed-** in Appendix.]

hee·bie-jee·bies (hē′bē-jē′bēz) *pl.n. Slang.* A feeling of uneasiness or nervousness; the jitters. [Coined by William De Beck (1890–1942), American cartoonist, in his comic strip *Barney Google.*]

heed (hēd) *v.* **heed·ed, heed·ing, heeds.** —*tr.* To pay attention to; listen to and consider: *"He did not heed my gibes, and chattered on"* (Sean O'Faolain). —*intr.* To pay attention. **—heed** *n.* Close attention; notice. [Middle English *heden,* from Old English *hēdan.*]

heed·ful (hēd′fəl) *adj.* Paying close attention; mindful. See Synonyms at **careful. —heed′ful·ly** *adv.* **—heed′ful·ness** *n.*

heed·less (hēd′lĭs) *adj.* Marked by or paying little heed; unmindful or thoughtless. See Synonyms at **careless, impetuous. —heed′less·ly** *adv.* **—heed′less·ness** *n.*

hee·haw (hē′hô′) *n.* **1.** The braying sound made by a donkey. **2.** *Informal.* A noisy laugh; a guffaw. —*intr.* **-hawed, -haw·ing, -haws. 1.** To bray. **2.** *Informal.* To guffaw. [Imitative.]

heel¹ (hēl) *n.* **1.a.** The rounded posterior portion of the human foot under and behind the ankle. **b.** The corresponding part of the hind foot of other vertebrates. **c.** A similar anatomical part, such as the fleshy rounded base of the human palm or the hind toe of a bird. **2.a.** The part, as of a sock, shoe, or stocking, that covers the rounded posterior portion of the human foot. **b.** The built-up portion of a shoe or boot, supporting the heel. **3.** One of the crusty ends of a loaf of bread. **4.** *Nautical.* **a.** The lower end of a mast. **b.** The after end of a ship's keel. **5.a.** A lower, rearward surface, as of the head of a golf club where it joins the shaft. **b.** *Music.* The end of a violin bow where the handle is located. **6.** *Botany.* The basal end of a plant cutting or tuber used in propagation. **7.** Oppression; tyranny: *under the heel of Stalinism; the heel of an autocrat.* **8.** *Informal.* A dishonorable man; a cad. **—heel** *v.* **heeled, heel·ing, heels.** —*tr.* **1.a.** To furnish with a heel or heels. **b.** To repair or replace the heels, as for shoes. **2.** *Slang.* To furnish, especially with money. **3.** To arm (a gamecock) with gaffs. **4.** To press or strike with the heel: *heel a horse.* —*intr.* To follow at one's heels: *The dog won't heel.* ***—idioms.*** **down at the heels. 1.** Having one's shoe heels worn down. **2.** Shabby; run-down; poor. **lay by the heels.** To put in fetters or shackles; imprison. **on** (or **upon**) **the heels of. 1.** Directly behind. **2.** Immediately following. **out at the heel** (or **heels**). **1.** Having holes in one's socks or shoes. **2.** Run-down; shabby; seedy. **take to** (**one's**) **heels.** To run away; flee. **to heel. 1.** Close behind. **2.** Under discipline or control. [Middle English, from Old English *hēla.*]

heel² (hēl) *intr. & tr.v.* **heeled, heel·ing, heels.** To tilt or cause to tilt to one side. **—heel** *n.* A tilt, as of a boat, to one side. [Alteration of Middle English *helden,* from Old English *hieldan.*]

heel-and-toe (hēl′ən-tō′) *adj.* Characterized by a stride in which the heel of one foot touches ground before the toe of the other foot is lifted, as in walking races.

heel-and-toe·ing (hēl′ən-tō′ĭng) *n. Sports.* See **race walking.**

heel·ball (hēl′bôl′) *n.* A wax colored with lampblack that is used to stain and polish the edges of the soles and heels of shoes or take rubbings of brass or inscriptions.

heel bone *n.* See **calcaneus.**

ă pat	oi boy
ā pay	ou out
âr care	ŏŏ took
ä father	ōō boot
ĕ pet	ŭ cut
ē be	ûr urge
ĭ pit	th thin
ī pie	*th* this
îr pier	hw which
ŏ pot	zh vision
ō toe	ə about, item
ô paw	♦ regionalism

Stress marks: ′ (primary); ′ (secondary), as in **dictionary** (dĭk′shə-nĕr′ē)

heel·er (hē′lər) *n.* **1.** One who heels shoes. **2.** *Informal.* A ward heeler.

heel·piece (hēl′pēs′) *n.* A piece made for or serving as the heel of a shoe or stocking.

heel·post (hēl′pōst′) *n.* The post to which a door or gate is hinged.

heel·tap (hēl′tăp′) *n.* **1.** A layer of leather or wood added to raise the heel of a shoe; a lift. **2.** A small amount of liquor remaining in a container or drinking vessel.

heel·work (hēl′wûrk′) *n.* In flamenco dancing, a stylized tapping of the heels in time with the music.

Heer·len (hâr′lən). A city of southeast Netherlands east-northeast of Maastricht near the German border. It is a manufacturing center in a coal-mining area. Population, 93,283.

He·fei (hœ′fā′) also **Ho·fei** (hŭ′-). A city of east-central China west of Nanjing. A rapidly growing industrial center, it is the capital of Anhui province. Population, 594,200.

heft (hĕft) *n.* Weight; heaviness; bulk. **—heft** *v.* **heft·ed, heft·ing, hefts.** *—tr.* **1.** To lift (something) in order to judge or estimate its weight. **2.** To hoist (something); heave. *—intr.* To have a given weight. [Middle English, from *heven,* to lift. See HEAVE.]

heft·y (hĕf′tē) *adj.* **-i·er, -i·est. 1.** Of considerable weight; heavy. **2.** Rugged and powerful. See Synonyms at **heavy. 3.** *Informal.* Of considerable size or amount: *a hefty serving of mashed potatoes; received a hefty bonus.* **—heft′i·ly** *adv.* **—heft′i·ness** *n.*

Jascha Heifetz
Photographed in 1924

He·gel (hā′gəl), **Georg Wilhelm Friedrich.** 1770–1831. German philosopher who proposed that truth is reached by a continuing dialectic.

He·ge·li·an·ism (hā-gā′lē-ə-nĭz′əm, hĭ-jē′-) *n.* The monist, idealist philosophy of Hegel in which the dialectic of thesis, antithesis, and synthesis is used as an analytic tool in order to approach a higher unity or a new thesis. **—He·ge′li·an** *adj. & n.*

he·gem·o·ny (hĭ-jĕm′ə-nē, hĕj′ə-mō′nē) *n., pl.* **-nies.** The predominant influence of one state over others. [Greek *hēgemonia,* from *hēgemōn,* leader, from *hēgeisthai,* to lead. See **sāg-** in Appendix.] **—heg′e·mon′ic** (hĕj′ə-mŏn′ĭk) *adj.* **—he·gem′o·nism** *n.* **—he·gem′o·nist** *adj. n.*

USAGE NOTE: *Hegemony* may be stressed on either the second or first syllable, though 72 percent of the Usage Panel prefers the first pronunciation.

he·gi·ra also **he·ji·ra** (hĭ-jī′rə, hĕj′ər-ə) *n.* **1.** A flight to escape danger. **2.** Also **Hegira.** The flight of Mohammed from Mecca to Medina in 622, marking the beginning of the Moslem era. [Medieval Latin, from Arabic *hijrah,* emigration, flight, from *hajara,* to depart.]

Hei·deg·ger (hī′dĕg′ər, -dĭ-gər), **Martin.** 1889–1976. German philosopher who maintained that authentic human existence belongs only to those who react with angst to the inherent emptiness of life.

Hei·del·berg (hīd′l-bûrg′, -bĕrk′). A city of southwest Germany on the Neckar River north-northwest of Stuttgart. First mentioned in the 12th century, it was the capital of the Palatinate until the early 18th century. Population, 133,693.

Heidelberg man *n.* An early member of an extinct human species, considered closely related to *Homo erectus,* known primarily from a fossil jawbone found near Heidelberg, West Germany, in 1907.

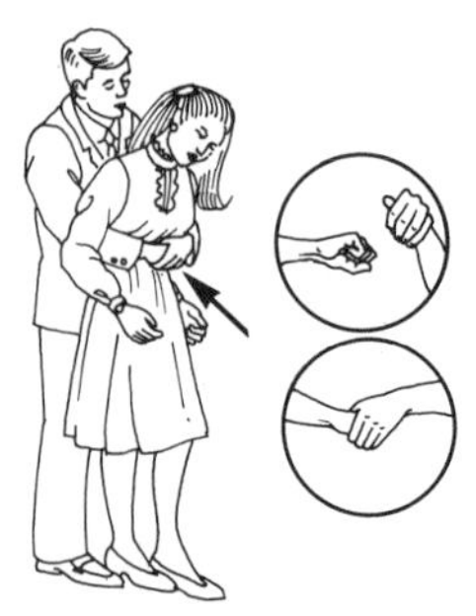

Heimlich maneuver
Stand behind victim and wrap arms around waist (*left*); grasp hands (*right*) with thumb of fist against victim's abdomen above navel but below ribs; press fist into victim's abdomen with a quick upper thrust

Hei·den·stam (hād′n-stăm′, -stäm′), **(Carl Gustaf) Verner von.** 1859–1940. Swedish writer whose subjective works of poetry and fiction led the literary reaction to Swedish naturalism. He won the 1916 Nobel Prize for literature.

heif·er (hĕf′ər) *n.* A young cow, especially one that has not yet given birth to a calf. [Middle English, from Old English *hēahfore* : *hēah-,* of unknown meaning + *fearr,* calf.]

Hei·fetz (hī′fĭts), **Jascha.** 1901–1987. Russian-born American violinist. Considered among the world's best violinists at the age of 13, he matured into a great artist, tempering his virtuoso technique with thoughtful interpretation.

heigh-ho (hī′hō′, hā′-) *interj.* Used to express fatigue, mild surprise, boredom, disappointment, or sometimes exultation.

height (hīt) *n. Abbr.* **h., H., hgt., ht 1.a.** The distance from the base of something to the top. **b.** Elevation above a given level, as of the sun or a star above the horizon; altitude. See Synonyms at **elevation. 2.a.** The condition or attribute of being relatively or sufficiently high or tall. **b.** Stature, especially of the human body. **3.** The highest or uppermost point; the summit or apex. **4.a.** The highest or most advanced degree; the zenith: *at the height of her career.* **b.** The point of highest intensity; the climax: *the height of a storm.* **5.** An eminence, such as a hill or mountain. **6.a.** A high point or position. **b.** *Obsolete.* High rank, estate, or degree. **7.a.** *Archaic.* Loftiness of mind. **b.** *Obsolete.* Arrogance; hauteur: *"He returned me a very resolute answer, and full of height"* (Oliver Cromwell). [Middle English, from Old English *hēhthu, hēahthu.*]

height·en (hīt′n) *v.* **-ened, -en·ing, -ens.** *—tr.* **1.** To raise or increase the quantity or degree of; intensify. **2.** To make high or higher; raise. *—intr.* **1.** To rise or increase in quantity or degree; intensify. **2.** To become high or higher; rise. **—height′en·er** *n.*

height-to-pa·per (hīt′tə-pā′pər) *n. Printing.* The height of type from foot to face, standardized at 0.9186 inch (2.333 centimeters).

Heil·bronn (hīl′brŏn′, -brôn′). A city of southwest Germany on the Neckar River north of Stuttgart. On the site of a 9th-century Carolingian palace, it became a free imperial city in the 14th century. Population, 110,666.

Hei·long·jiang (hā′lông′jyäng′) also **Hei·lung·kiang** (hā′lo͝ong′kyäng′). A province of extreme northeast China bordering on Russia. It was under Japanese control from 1932 to 1945. Harbin is the capital. Population, 33,110,000.

Hei·long Jiang (hā′lông′ jyäng′). See **Amur River.**

Hei·lung·kiang (hā′lo͝ong′kyäng′). See **Heilongjiang.**

hei·mish (hā′mĭsh) *adj. Slang.* Variant of **haimish.**

Heim·lich maneuver (hīm′lĭk′, -lĭKH′) *n.* An emergency technique used to eject an object, such as food, from the trachea of a choking person. The technique employs a firm upward thrust just below the rib cage to force air from the lungs. [After Henry J. *Heimlich* (born 1920), American surgeon.]

Hei·ne (hī′nə), **Heinrich.** 1797–1856. German writer who lived in Paris after 1831. His romantic poems and social essays are marked by his love for the German land and people and derision for many modern German institutions.

hei·nie (hī′nē) *n. Slang.* The buttocks. [Alteration of HINDER[2].]

Hein·lein (hīn′līn, -lĭn), **Robert Anson.** 1907–1988. American writer of science fiction whose works include *Stranger in a Strange Land* (1961) and *The Moon Is a Harsh Mistress* (1967).

hei·nous (hā′nəs) *adj.* Grossly wicked or reprehensible; abominable: *a heinous crime.* [Middle English, from Old French *haineus,* from *haine,* hatred, from *hair,* to hate, from Frankish **hatjan.*] **—hei′nous·ly** *adv.* **—hei′nous·ness** *n.*

heir (âr) *n.* **1.** *Law.* A person who inherits or is entitled by law or by the terms of a will to inherit the estate of another. **2.** A person who succeeds or is in line to succeed to a hereditary rank, title, or office. **3.** One who receives or is expected to receive a heritage, as of ideas, from a predecessor. [Middle English, from Anglo-Norman, from Latin *hērēs.* See **ghē-** in Appendix.]

heir apparent *n., pl.* **heirs apparent.** *Law.* An heir whose right to inheritance is indefeasible by law provided he or she survives an ancestor.

heir·dom (âr′dəm) *n.* **1.** Succession by right of blood; heirship. **2.** An inheritance.

heir·ess (âr′ĭs) *n.* A woman who is an heir, especially to great wealth. See Usage Note at **-ess.**

heir·loom (âr′lo͞om′) *n.* **1.** A valued possession passed down in a family through succeeding generations. **2.** *Law.* An article of personal property included in an inherited estate. [Middle English *heirlome* : *heir,* heir; see HEIR + *lome,* implement; see LOOM[2].]

heir presumptive *n., pl.* **heirs presumptive.** *Law.* An heir whose claim can be defeated by the birth of a closer relative before the death of the ancestor.

heir·ship (âr′shĭp′) *n.* **1.** The condition of being an heir. **2.** Right to inheritance; heirdom.

Hei·sen·berg (hī′zən-bûrg′, -bĕrk′), **Werner Karl.** 1901–1976. German physicist and a founder of quantum mechanics. He won a 1932 Nobel Prize for his uncertainty principle.

heist (hīst) *Slang. tr.v.* **heist·ed, heist·ing, heists. 1.** To steal: *heisted the collection of jewels from the museum.* **2.** To hold up; rob. **—heist** *n.* A robbery; a burglary. [Alteration of HOIST.]

He·jaz also **Hed·jaz** (hē-jăz′). A region of northwest Saudi Arabia on the Gulf of Aqaba and the Red Sea. It includes the holy cities of Mecca and Medina.

he·ji·ra (hĭ-jī′rə, hĕj′ər-ə) *n.* Variant of **hegira.**

Hek·a·te (hĕk′ə-tē, hĕk′ĭt) *n. Greek Mythology.* Variant of **Hecate.**

Hek·la (hĕk′lə). An active volcano, 1,492.1 m (4,892 ft) high, of southwest Iceland. In medieval Icelandic folklore, Hekla was believed to be one of the gateways to purgatory.

Hel (hĕl) *n. Mythology.* **1.** The Norse goddess of death and the underworld; the daughter of Loki. **2.** The Norse underworld of the dead not killed in battle. [Old Norse. See **kel-**[1] in Appendix.]

He·La cell (hĕl′ə) *n.* Any of the cells of the first continuously cultured human carcinoma strain, originally obtained from cancerous cervical tissue and maintained for use in studying cellular processes. [After *He(nrietta) La(cks),* who donated such cells in 1951.]

held (hĕld) *v.* Past tense and past participle of **hold**[1].

Held (hĕld), **Anna.** 1865?–1918. French-born American entertainer noted for her appearances in musical comedies produced by Florenz Ziegfeld.

Held, John, Jr. 1889–1958. American illustrator and writer known for his interpretations of Jazz Age subject matter.

hel·den·te·nor also **Hel·den·te·nor** (hĕl′dən-tə-nôr′, -nōr′) *n. Music.* **1.** A tenor voice with a striking dramatic or brilliant quality that is well suited for heroic roles, such as those in Wagnerian opera. **2.** A person with such a voice. [German : *Held,* hero (from Middle High German *helt,* from Old High German *helid*) + *Tenor,* tenor (from Italian *tenore;* see TENOR).]

Hel·e·na (hĕl′ə-nə). The capital of Montana, in the west-central part of the state north-northeast of Butte. It was founded in 1864 after the discovery of gold at Last Chance Gulch. Helena became the state capital in 1889. Population, 23,938.

ă pat	oi boy
ā pay	ou out
âr care	o͝o took
ä father	o͞o boot
ĕ pet	ŭ cut
ē be	ûr urge
ĭ pit	th thin
ī pie	*th* this
îr pier	hw which
ŏ pot	zh vision
ō toe	ə about, item
ô paw	♦ regionalism

Stress marks: ′ (primary); ′ (secondary), as in **dictionary** (dĭk′shə-nĕr′ē)

Hel·en of Troy (hĕl′ən; troi) *n. Greek Mythology.* The daughter of Zeus and Leda and wife of Menelaus. Her abduction by Paris caused the Trojan War.

Hel·go·land (hĕl′gō-lănd′, -länt′). An island of northwest Germany, one of the North Frisian Islands in **Helgoland Bay,** an inlet of the North Sea. The island belonged to Denmark and Great Britain before being ceded to Germany in 1890.

heli–[1] *pref.* Helicopter: *heliport.* [From HELICOPTER.]

heli–[2] *pref.* Variant of **helio–.**

he·li·a·cal (hĭ-lī′ə-kəl) *adj.* Of or relating to the sun, especially rising and setting with the sun. [From Late Latin *hēliacus,* from Greek *hēliakos,* from *hēlios,* sun. See **sāwel-** in Appendix.] **—he·li′a·cal·ly** *adv.*

hel·i·borne (hĕl′ə-bôrn′, -bōrn′) *adj.* Carried or transported by helicopter: *heliborne troops.*

helic– *pref.* Variant of **helico–.**

hel·i·cal (hĕl′ĭ-kəl, hē′lĭ-) *adj.* **1.** Of or having the shape of a helix; spiral. **2.** Having a shape approximating that of a helix. **—hel′i·cal·ly** *adv.*

hel·i·ces (hĕl′ĭ-sēz′, hē′lĭ-) *n.* A plural of **helix.**

helico– or **helic–** *pref.* Helix; spiral: *helicoid.* [Greek *heliko-,* from *helix, helik-,* spiral. See HELIX.]

hel·i·coid (hĕl′ĭ-koid′, hē′lĭ-) *adj.* Arranged in or having the approximate shape of a flattened coil or spiral. **—helicoid** *n. Mathematics.* A surface in the form of a coil or screw. [Greek *helikoeidēs* : *helix, helik-,* spiral; see HELIX + *-oeidēs,* -oid.]

helicoid cyme *n.* An inflorescence coiled in a bud like a snail shell and expanded superficially, as on a raceme with the flowers on one side.

hel·i·con (hĕl′ĭ-kŏn′, -kən) *n. Music.* A large spiral brass tuba that fits around the player's shoulder. [Probably from Greek *helix, helik-,* spiral.]

Hel·i·con (hĕl′ĭ-kŏn′, -kən). A mountain, 1,749.2 (5,735 ft) high, of central Greece. It was the legendary abode of the Muses and was sacred to Apollo.

hel·i·cop·ter (hĕl′ĭ-kŏp′tər) *n.* An aircraft that derives its lift from blades that rotate about an approximately vertical central axis. **—helicopter** *intr. & tr.v.* **-tered, -ter·ing, -ters.** To go or transport by helicopter. [French *hélicoptère* : Greek *helix, helik-,* spiral; see HELIX + Greek *pteron,* wing; see –PTER.]

WORD HISTORY: The origin of the word *helicopter* is apparent only upon due recognition of its Greek ancestors. *Helicopter* was borrowed from the French word *hélicoptère,* a word constructed from Greek *heliko–* and *pteron,* "wing." *Heliko–* is a form of *helix,* "spiral," that combines with other words and word forms to create new words. The consonant cluster *pt* in *pteron* begins many Greek words but relatively few English words, so English speakers who are unfamiliar with Greek do not think of the word's elements as *helico–pter.* At least some English speakers have analyzed the word into the elements *heli–copter,* as is shown by the clipped form *copter.*

hel·i·cul·ture (hĕl′ĭ-kŭl′chər, hēlĭ-) *n.* The science and occupation of growing snails for food. [Blend of New Latin *Helix,* genus of spiral-shelled mollusks (from Greek *helix, helic-,* spiral; see HELIX) and CULTURE.] **—hel′i·cul′tur·al** *adj.* **—hel′i·cul′tur·al·ist** *n.*

helio– or **heli–** *pref.* Sun: *heliocentric.* [Greek *hēlio-,* from *hēlios,* sun. See **sāwel-** in Appendix.]

he·li·o·cen·tric (hē′lē-ō-sĕn′trĭk) also **he·li·o·cen·tri·cal** (-trĭ-kəl) *adj.* **1.** Referred or with respect to the sun. **2.** Having the sun as a center. **—he′li·o·cen·tric′i·ty** (-sĕn-trĭs′ĭ-tē) *n.*

He·li·o·gab·a·lus (hē′lē-ə-găb′ə-ləs, -lē-ō-) also **El·a·gab·a·lus** (ĕl′ə-). A.D. 204–222. Emperor of Rome (218–222). A priest of Baal, he became emperor after the murder of his cousin Caracalla (217). His debauchery and the imposition of his religion on the Romans led to an insurrection in which he was killed.

he·li·om·e·ter (hē′lē-ŏm′ĭ-tər) *n.* A telescope equipped to measure small angular distances between celestial bodies. **—he′li·o·met′ric** (-ə-mĕt′rĭk), **he′li·o·met′ri·cal** *adj.* **—he′li·o·met′ri·cal·ly** *adv.* **—he′li·om′e·try** *n.*

He·li·op·o·lis (hē′lē-ŏp′ə-lĭs). **1.** An ancient city of northern Egypt in the Nile River delta north of modern Cairo. It was the center of worship of the sun god Ra until the rise of Thebes (c. 2100 B.C.). **2.** See **Baalbek.**

He·li·os (hē′lē-ŏs′) *n. Greek Mythology.* The sun god, son of Hyperion, depicted as driving his chariot across the sky from east to west daily.

he·li·o·sphere (hē′lē-ə-sfîr′) *n.* The region in space through which the sun's gases and magnetic field extend.

he·li·o·stat (hē′lē-ə-stăt′) *n.* An instrument in which a mirror is automatically moved so that it reflects sunlight in a constant direction. It is used with a pyrheliometer to make continuous measurements of solar radiation.

he·li·o·tax·is (hē′lē-ō-tăk′sĭs) *n. Biology.* The movement of an organism in response to the light of the sun. **—he′li·o·tac′tic** (-tăk′tĭk) *adj.*

he·li·o·ther·a·py (hē′lē-ō-thĕr′ə-pē) *n., pl.* **-pies.** Medical therapy involving exposure to sunlight.

he·lio·trope (hēl′yə-trōp′, hē′lē-ə-) *n.* **1.a.** Any of several plants of the genus *Heliotropium,* especially *H. arborescens,* native to Peru and having small, highly fragrant purplish flowers. Also called *turnsole.* **b.** The garden heliotrope. **c.** Any of various plants that turn toward the sun. **2.** See **bloodstone. 3.** *Color.* A moderate, light, or brilliant violet to moderate or deep reddish purple. [Middle English *elitrope* (from Old English *eliotropus*) and French *héliotrope,* both from Latin *hēliotropium,* from Greek *hēliotropion* : *hēlio-,* helio- + *tropos,* turn; see TROPE.] **—he′lio·trope′** *adj.*

he·lio·tro·pin (hēl′yə-trō′pĭn, hē′lē-ŏt′rə-pĭn) *n.* Piperonal.

he·li·ot·ro·pism (hē′lē-ŏt′rə-pĭz′əm) *n. Biology.* Growth or orientation of a sessile organism, especially a plant, toward or away from the light of the sun. **—he′li·o·trop′ic** (-ə-trŏp′ĭk) *adj.* **—he′li·o·trop′i·cal·ly** *adv.*

he·li·o·type (hē′lē-ə-tīp′) *n. Printing.* **1.** A photomechanically produced plate for pictures or type made by exposing a gelatin film under a negative, hardening it with chrome alum, and printing directly from it. **2.** Also **he·li·o·typ·y** (-tī′pē). The process of producing a heliotype. **—he′li·o·type′** *v.* **—he′li·o·typ′ic** (-tĭp′ĭk) *adj.*

he·li·o·zo·an (hē′lē-ə-zō′ən) *n.* Any of various aquatic protozoans of the order Heliozoa, having numerous spindlelike pseudopods that radiate from a central cell mass. [From New Latin *Heliozoa,* class name : HELIO– (from their shape) + *-zoa,* pl. of *-zoon,* -zoon.] **—he′li·o·zo′ic** (-zō′ĭk) *adj.*

hel·i·pad (hĕl′ə-păd′) *n.* See **heliport.**

hel·i·port (hĕl′ə-pôrt′, -pōrt′) *n.* A place for helicopters to land and take off. Also called *helipad, helistop.* [HELI(COPTER) + (AIR)PORT.]

hel·i·stop (hĕl′ĭ-stŏp′) *n.* See **heliport.**

he·li·um (hē′lē-əm) *n. Symbol* **He** A colorless, odorless inert gaseous element occurring in natural gas and with radioactive ores. It is used as a component of artificial atmospheres and laser media, as a refrigerant, as a lifting gas for balloons, and as a superfluid in cryogenic research. Atomic number 2; atomic weight 4.0026; boiling point −268.9°C; density at 0°C 0.1785 gram per liter. See table at **element.** [From Greek *hēlios,* sun (so called because its existence was deduced from the solar spectrum). See **sāwel-** in Appendix.]

helium I *n.* Liquid helium existing as a normal fluid between the superfluid transition point of approximately 2.2°K at 1 atmosphere pressure and its boiling point of 4.2°K.

helium II *n.* Liquid helium existing as a superfluid below the transition point of approximately 2.2°K at 1 atmosphere and having extremely low viscosity and high thermal conductivity.

he·lix (hē′lĭks) *n., pl.* **-lix·es** or **hel·i·ces** (hĕl′ĭ-sēz′, hē′lĭ-). **1.** *Mathematics.* A three-dimensional curve that lies on a cylinder or cone, so that its angle to a plane perpendicular to the axis is constant. **2.** A spiral form or structure. **3.** *Anatomy.* The folded rim of skin and cartilage around most of the outer ear. **4.** *Architecture.* A volute on a Corinthian or Ionic capital. [Latin, from Greek. See **wel-**[2] in Appendix.]

hell (hĕl) *n.* **1.a.** Often **Hell.** The abode of condemned souls and devils in some religions; the place of eternal punishment for the wicked after death, presided over by Satan. **b.** A state of separation from God. **2.** The abode of the dead, identified with the Hebrew Sheol and the Greek Hades; the underworld. **3. Hell.** *Christian Science.* Mortal belief; sin or error. **4.a.** A situation or place of evil, misery, discord, or destruction: *"War is hell"* (William Tecumseh Sherman). **b.** Torment; anguish: *went through hell on the job.* **5.a.** The powers of darkness and evil. **b.** *Informal.* One that causes trouble, agony, or annoyance: *The boss is hell when a job is poorly done.* **6.** A sharp scolding: *gave the student hell for cheating.* **7.** *Informal.* Excitement, mischievousness, or high spirits: *We did it for the sheer hell of it.* **8.a.** A tailor's receptacle for discarded material. **b.** *Printing.* A hellbox. **9.** *Informal.* Used as an intensive: *How the hell can I go? You did one hell of a job. He ran like hell to catch the bus.* **10.** *Archaic.* A gambling house. **—hell** *intr.v.* **helled, hell·ing, hells.** *Informal.* To behave riotously; carouse: *out all night helling around.* **—hell** *interj.* Used to express anger, disgust, or impatience. ***—idioms.*** **for the hell of it.** For no particular reason; on a whim: *walked home by the old school for the hell of it.* **hell on.** *Informal.* **1.** Damaging or destructive to: *Driving in a hilly town is hell on the brakes.* **2.** Unpleasant to or painful for. **hell or** (or **and**) **high water.** Troubles or difficulties of whatever magnitude: *We're staying, come hell or high water.* **hell to pay.** Great trouble: *If we're wrong, there'll be hell to pay.* [Middle English *helle,* from Old English. See **kel-**[1] in Appendix.]

he'll (hēl). **1.** He will. **2.** He shall.

hel·la·cious (hĕ-lā′shəs) *adj.* **1.** Distasteful and repellant: *hellacious smog.* **2.** *Slang.* Extraordinary, remarkable: *a hellacious catch of fish.* [HELL + *-acious* (as in AUDACIOUS).]

Hel·las (hĕl′əs). See **Greece.**

hell·bend·er (hĕl′bĕn′dər) *n.* A large aquatic salamander *(Cryptobranchus alleganiensis)* of the eastern and central United States.

hell-bent or **hell·bent** (hĕl′bĕnt′) *adj.* Impetuously or recklessly determined to do or achieve something: *was hell-bent on winning.*

hell·box (hĕl′bŏks′) *n. Printing.* A receptacle for broken or discarded type.

hell·cat (hĕl′kăt′) *n. Informal.* **1.a.** A woman regarded as

helicopter
Single-rotor helicopter transporting a snowmobile

Helios

helix
Cylindrical model

hellebore
White hellebore
Veratrum viride

bad-tempered and evil. **b.** A woman who practices sorcery; a witch. **2.** A person who torments others.

hell·div·er (hĕl′dī′vər) *n.* A common American grebe *(Podilymbus podiceps).*

Hel·le (hĕl′ē) *n.* *Greek Mythology.* The daughter of a Greek king who, while fleeing with her brother from their stepmother, drowned in the Hellespont, thereafter named for her.

hel·le·bore (hĕl′ə-bôr′, -bōr′) *n.* **1.** Any of various plants of the genus *Helleborus,* native to Eurasia, most species of which are poisonous. **2.** Any of various plants of the genus *Veratrum,* especially *V. viride* of North America, having large leaves and greenish flowers and yielding a toxic alkaloid used medicinally. [Middle English *ellebre,* from Old French, from Latin *elleborus,* from Greek *helleboros* : perhaps *hellos,* fawn + *-boros,* eaten (from *bibrōskein,* to eat).]

Hel·lene (hĕl′ēn′) also **Hel·le·ni·an** (hĕ-lē′nē-ən) *n.* A Greek. [Greek *Hellēn.*]

Hel·len·ic (hĕ-lĕn′ĭk) *adj.* Of or relating to the ancient Hellenes, their language, or their history; Greek. **—Hellenic** *n.* The branch of the Indo-European language family that consists only of Greek.

Hel·le·nism (hĕl′ə-nĭz′əm) *n.* **1.** An idiom or custom peculiar to the Greeks. **2.** The civilization and culture of ancient Greece. **3.** Admiration for and adoption of Greek ideas, style, or culture.

Hel·le·nist (hĕl′ə-nĭst) *n.* **1.** One in Hellenistic times who adopted the Greek language and culture, especially a Jew of the Diaspora. **2.** A devotee or student of Greek civilization, language, or literature.

Hel·le·nis·tic (hĕl′ə-nĭs′tĭk) also **Hel·le·nis·ti·cal** (-tĭ-kəl) *adj.* **1.** Of or relating to the Hellenists. **2.** Of or relating to post-classical Greek history and culture from the death of Alexander the Great to the accession of Augustus. Relating to or in the style of the Greek art or architecture of this period.

Hel·le·nize (hĕl′ə-nīz′) *v.* **-nized, -niz·ing, -niz·es.** *—intr.* To adopt Greek ways and speech; become Greek. *—tr.* To make Greek in character, culture, or civilization. **—Hel′le·ni·za′tion** (-nĭ-zā′shən) *n.* **—Hel′le·niz′er** *n.*

hell·er (hĕl′ər) *n.* A person who behaves recklessly or wildly. [From HELL.]

Hel·les·pont (hĕl′ĭ-spŏnt′). See **Dardanelles.**

hell-for-leath·er (hĕl′fər-lĕth′ər) *adv. & adj. Informal.* At breakneck speed: *"The journey back he made along the coast road, traveling hell-for-leather"* (Idival Jones).

Hell Gate. A narrow channel of the East River in New York City between Manhattan and Long Island. It was named by the Dutch navigator Adriaen Block (fl. 1610–1624), who passed through it into Long Island Sound in 1614.

hell·gram·mite (hĕl′grə-mīt′) *n.* The large, brownish aquatic larva of the dobsonfly, often used as fishing bait. Also called *dobson, snake doctor.* [Origin unknown.]

hell·hole (hĕl′hōl′) *n.* **1.** A place of extreme wretchedness or squalor. **2.** *Obsolete.* The pit of hell.

hell·hound (hĕl′hound′) *n.* **1.** A devilish person; a fiend. **2.** *Greek Mythology.* Cerberus, the watchdog of Hades.

hel·lion (hĕl′yən) *n. Informal.* A mischievous, troublesome person, especially a child. [Probably alteration (influenced by HELL) of dialectal *hallion,* worthless person.]

hell·ish (hĕl′ĭsh) *adj.* **1.** Of, resembling, or worthy of hell; fiendish. **2.** Highly unpleasant: *hellish weather.* **—hell′ish·ly** *adv.* **—hell′ish·ness** *n.*

Hell·man (hĕl′mən), **Lillian.** 1905–1984. American playwright whose works include *Toys in the Attic* (1960).

hel·lo (hĕ-lō′, hə-) also **hul·lo** (hə-) *—interj.* Used to greet someone, answer the telephone, or express surprise. *—n., pl.* **-los.** A calling or greeting of "hello." *—intr.v.* **-loed, -lo·ing, -loes.** To call "hello." [Alteration of *hallo,* alteration of obsolete *holla,* stop!, perhaps from Old French *hola* : *ho,* ho! + *la,* there (from Latin *illāc,* that way).]

Hells Canyon (hĕlz). A gorge of the Snake River on the Idaho-Oregon border. It is about 201 km (125 mi) long and has a maximum depth of approximately 2,410 m (7,900 ft).

hell·uv·a (hĕl′ə-və) *adj. Slang.* Used as an intensive: *He's a helluva great guy.* [Alteration of *hell of a.*]

helm[1] (hĕlm) *n.* **1.** *Nautical.* The steering gear of a ship, especially the tiller or wheel. **2.** A position of leadership or control: *at the helm of the government.* **—helm** *tr.v.* **helmed, helm·ing, helms.** To take the helm of; steer or direct. [Middle English, from Old English *helma.*]

helm[2] (hĕlm) *Archaic. n.* A helmet. **—helm** *tr.v.* **helmed, helm·ing, helms.** To cover or furnish with a helmet. [Middle English, from Old English. See **kel-**[1] in Appendix.]

Hel·mand (hĕl′mənd). A river, about 1,287 km (800 mi) long, rising in the Hindu Kush and flowing southwest across Afghanistan to a marshy lake on the Iranian border.

helmet
Top: Cycling helmet
Bottom: c. 550–500 B.C.
Chalcidian

hel·met (hĕl′mĭt) *n.* **1.a.** A head covering of hard material, such as leather, metal, or plastic, worn by football players, firefighters, construction workers, motorcyclists, and others to protect the head. **b.** The headgear with a glass mask worn by deep-sea divers. **c.** A pith helmet; a topi. **d.** A head covering, such as a balaclava, that is shaped like a helmet. **2.** A piece of armor, usually made of metal, designed to protect the head. **3.** *Botany.* The hood-shaped sepal or corolla of some flowers. **—helmet** *tr. & intr.v.* **-met·ed, -met·ing, -mets.** To provide with or put on a helmet. [Middle English, from Old French, diminutive of *helme,* of Germanic origin. See **kel-**[1] in Appendix.] **—hel′met·ed** *adj.*

Helm·holtz (hĕlm′hōlts′), **Hermann Ludwig Ferdinand von.** 1821–1894. German physicist and physiologist who formulated the mathematical law of the conservation of energy (1847).

hel·minth (hĕl′mĭnth′) *n.* A worm, especially a parasitic roundworm or tapeworm. [French *helminthe,* from Greek *helmins, helminth-.* See **wel-**[2] in Appendix.]

hel·min·thi·a·sis (hĕl′mĭn-thī′ə-sĭs) *n., pl.* **-ses** (-sēz′). A disease caused by infestation with parasitic worms.

hel·min·thic (hĕl-mĭn′thĭk) *adj.* **1.** Of or relating to worms, especially parasitic worms. **2.** Tending to expel worms; anthelmintic. **—helminthic** *n.* An agent that expels or destroys parasitic worms; an anthelmintic.

hel·min·thol·o·gy (hĕl′mĭn-thŏl′ə-jē) *n.* The scientific study of worms, especially parasitic worms. **—hel′min·thol′o·gist** *n.*

helms·man (hĕlmz′mən) *n. Nautical.* A person who steers a ship. **—helms′man·ship′** *n.*

hel·o (hĕl′ō) *n., pl.* **hel·os.** *Informal.* A helicopter.

Hé·lo·ise (ĕl′ə-wēz′, ā-lô-ēz′). 1098?–1164. French religious figure who secretly married Peter Abelard (c. 1118).

hel·ot (hĕl′ət) *n.* **1. Helot.** One of a class of serfs in ancient Sparta, neither a slave nor a free citizen. **2.** A person in servitude; a serf. [From Greek *Heilōtes,* pl. of *Heilōs, Heilōt-.*] **—hel′ot·ry** (-ə-trē) *n.*

hel·ot·ism (hĕl′ə-tĭz′əm) *n.* **1.** A system under which a nominally free social class or a religious, national, or racial minority is permanently oppressed and degraded. **2.** A type of symbiosis, as among certain ants, in which one species is dominant and makes the members of another species perform the tasks required for their mutual survival.

hel·ot·ry (hĕl′ə-trē) *n.* **1.** The condition of serfdom. **2.** Helots considered as a group.

help (hĕlp) *v.* **helped, help·ing, helps.** *—tr.* **1.** To give assistance to; aid: *I helped her find the book. He helped me into my coat.* **2.** To contribute to the furtherance of; promote. **3.** To give relief to: *help the needy.* **4.** To ease; relieve: *medication to help your cold.* **5.** To change for the better; improve: *A fresh coat of paint will help a scarred old table.* **6.** To refrain from; avoid or resist. Used with *can* or *cannot: couldn't help laughing.* **7.** To wait on, as in a store or restaurant. *—intr.* To be of service; give assistance. **—help** *n.* **1.a.** The act or an instance of helping. **b.** Aid or assistance. **2.** Relief; remedy. **3.** One that helps: *You've been a great help. A food processor is a help to the serious cook.* **4.** A person employed to help, especially a farm worker or domestic servant. Such employees considered as a group. Often used with *the.* **—*idiom.* help (oneself) to. 1.** To serve or provide oneself with: *Help yourself to the cookies.* **2.** *Informal.* To take (something) without asking permission: *The thief helped himself to our family silver.* [Middle English *helpen,* from Old English *helpan.*]

SYNONYMS: *help, aid, assist, succor.* These verbs mean to contribute to the fulfillment of a need, the furtherance of an effort, or the achievement of a purpose or end. *Help* and *aid,* the most general, are frequently interchangeable: *a medication that helps* (or *aids*) *the digestion; a fine sense of rhythm that helped* (or *aided*) *the student in learning music. Help,* however, sometimes conveys a stronger suggestion of effectual action: *Nothing will help. I'll help you move the piano. He helped her out of the car. Assist* usually implies making a secondary contribution or acting as a subordinate: *A team of kitchen apprentices assisted the chef in preparing the banquet. Succor* refers to going to the relief of one in want, difficulty, or distress: *"Mr. Harding thought . . . of the worn-out, aged men he had succored"* (Anthony Trollope). See also Synonyms at **improve.**

USAGE NOTE: A common use of *help* is exemplified by the sentence *Don't change it any more than you can help* (that is, "any more than you have to"). Some grammarians condemn this usage on the ground that *help* in this sense means "avoid" and logically requires a negative. But the expression is a well established idiom. See Usage Note at **cannot.**

help·er (hĕl′pər) *n.* One that helps; an assistant. See Synonyms at **assistant.**

helper T cell also **helper cell** *n. Immunology.* A T cell that activates B cells to release antibodies and killer T cells to destroy cells having a specific antigenic makeup.

help·ful (hĕlp′fəl) *adj.* Providing assistance; useful. **—help′ful·ly** *adv.* **—help′ful·ness** *n.*

help·ing (hĕl′pĭng) *n.* A single portion of food.

help·less (hĕlp′lĭs) *adj.* **1.** Unable to manage by oneself; incompetent. **2.** Lacking power or strength; impotent. **3.** Impossible to remedy; hopeless. **4.** Impossible to control; involuntary: *helpless laughter.* **—help′less·ly** *adv.* **—help′less·ness** *n.*

help·mate (hĕlp′māt′) *n.* A helper and companion, especially a spouse.

WORD HISTORY: The existence of the two words *helpmeet* and *helpmate* meaning exactly the same thing is a comedy of errors. God's promise to Adam, in Genesis 2:18 as rendered in the King James version of the Bible (1611), was to give him "an help [helper] meet [fit or suitable] for him." In 1673 the poet John Dryden used the phrase "help-meet for man," with a hyphen between *help* and *meet*. This was one step on the way toward the establishment of the phrase "help meet" as an independent word. Another was the use of "help meet" without "for man" to mean a suitable helper, usually a spouse, as Eve had been to Adam. Despite such usages, however, for the most part *helpmeet* was not thought of as a word in its own right until the 19th century. Nonetheless the phrase "help meet" probably played a role in the creation of the synonymous compound *helpmate,* from (*help* and *mate*), first recorded in 1715.

---

help•meet (hĕlp′mēt′) *n.* A helpmate. [HELP + MEET[2].]

Hel•sing•borg (hĕl′sĭng-bôrg′, hĕl′sĭng-bôr′ē). See **Hälsingborg.**

Hel•sing•or (hĕl′sĭng-ûr′, -œr′) also **El•si•nore** (ĕl′sə-nôr′, -nōr′). A city of eastern Denmark north of Copenhagen on northern Sjaelland Island and the Oresund. Known since the 13th century, it is famous as the setting for Shakespeare's *Hamlet.* Population, 56,161.

Hel•sin•ki (hĕl′sĭng′kē, hĕl-sĭng′-). The capital and largest city of Finland, in the southern part of the country on the Gulf of Finland. Founded in 1550 by Gustavus I of Sweden, it passed to Russia along with Finland in 1809 and became capital of Finland in 1812. Population, 484,263.

hel•ter-skel•ter (hĕl′tər-skĕl′tər) *adv.* **1.** In disorderly haste; confused; pell-mell. **2.** Haphazardly. **—helter-skelter** *adj.* **1.** Carelessly hurried and confused. **2.** Haphazard. **—helter-skelter** *n.* Turmoil; confusion. [Origin unknown.]

helve (hĕlv) *n.* A handle of a tool, such as an ax, a chisel, or a hammer. [Middle English, from Old English *hielfe.*]

Hel•ve•tia (hĕl-vē′shə, -shē-ə). An ancient region of central Europe occupying a plateau between the Alps and the Jura Mountains. It was named by the Romans for its predominantly Celtic inhabitants. Helvetia corresponded roughly to the western part of modern Switzerland.

Hel•ve•tian (hĕl-vē′shən) *adj.* **1.** Of or relating to Helvetia or the Helvetii. **2.** Swiss. **—Helvetian** *n.* **1.** One of the Helvetii. **2.** A Swiss. [From Latin *Helvētius,* from *Helvētiī,* Helvetii.]

Hel•ve•ti•i (hĕl-vē′shē-ī′) *pl.n.* A Celtic people inhabiting western Switzerland during the time of Julius Caesar. [Latin *Helvētiī.*]

Hel•vé•tius (hĕl-vē′shəs, -vā′-, ĕl-vā-syüs′), **Claude Adrien.** 1715–1771. French philosopher and Encyclopedist who proposed his sensationalist philosophy in *De l'Esprit* (1758), a book that was condemned by the Paris parliament to be burned publicly.

hem[1] (hĕm) *n.* **1.** An edge or a border on a piece of cloth, especially a finished edge, as for a garment or curtain, made by folding the selvage edge under and stitching it down. **2.** The height or level of the bottom edge of a skirt, dress, or coat; a hemline. **—hem** *tr.v.* **hemmed, hem•ming, hems. 1.** To fold back and stitch down the edge of. **2.** To surround and shut in; enclose: *a valley hemmed in by mountains.* See Synonyms at **enclose.** [Middle English, from Old English *hem, hemm.*] **—hem′mer** *n.*

hem[2] (hĕm) *n.* A short cough or clearing of the throat made especially to gain attention, warn another, hide embarrassment, or fill a pause in speech. **—hem** *intr.v.* **hemmed, hem•ming, hems. 1.** To utter a hem. **2.** To hesitate in speech. ***—idiom.*** **hem and haw.** To be hesitant and indecisive; equivocate: *"a leader who cannot make up his or her mind, never knows what to do, hems and haws"* (Margaret Thatcher). [From Middle English *heminge,* coughing, of imitative origin.]

hem– or **hema–** *pref.* Variants of **hemo–.**

he•ma•cy•tom•e•ter (hē′mə-sī-tŏm′ĭ-tər) *n.* An instrument for counting the number of blood cells in a measured volume of blood.

he•mag•glu•ti•nate (hē′mə-glo͞ot′n-āt′) *tr.v.* **-nat•ed, -nat•ing, -nates.** To cause agglutination of red blood cells. **—he′mag•glu′tin•a′tion** *n.*

he•mag•glu•ti•nin (hē′mə-glo͞ot′n-ĭn) *n.* A substance, such as an antibody, that causes agglutination of red blood cells.

he•mal (hē′məl) *adj.* **1.** Of or relating to the blood or blood vessels. **2.** Relating to or located on the side of the body that contains the heart and principal blood vessels.

he-man (hē′măn′) *n. Informal.* A strong, virile man.

he•man•gi•o•ma (hĭ-măn′jē-ō′mə) *n., pl.* **-mas** also **-ma•ta** (-mə-tə). A benign skin lesion consisting of dense, usually elevated masses of dilated blood vessels.

he•ma•pher•e•sis (hē′mə-fĕr′ə-sĭs, hĕm′ə-) *n. Medicine.* See **apheresis** (sense 2).

hemat– *pref.* Variant of **hemato–.**

he•ma•te•in (hē′mə-tē′ĭn, hē′mə-tēn′) *n.* A reddish-brown crystalline compound, $C_{16}H_{12}O_6$, used as an indicator and a biological stain.

he•mat•ic (hĭ-măt′ĭk) *adj.* Of, relating to, resembling, containing, or acting on blood. **—hematic** *n. Medicine.* A hematinic. [Greek *haimatikos,* from *haima,* blood.]

he•ma•tin (hē′mə-tĭn) *n.* A blue to blackish-brown compound, $C_{34}H_{32}N_4O_4{\cdot}FeOH$, formed in the decomposition of hemoglobin.

he•ma•tin•ic (hē′mə-tĭn′ĭk) *adj.* **1.** Acting to increase the amount of hemoglobin in the blood. **2.** Of, relating to, or derived from hematin. **—hematinic** *n.* A drug that increases the amount of hemoglobin in the blood.

he•ma•tite (hē′mə-tīt′) *n.* A black or blackish-red to brick-red mineral, essentially Fe_2O_3, the chief ore of iron. [Middle English *emathite, ematites,* from Latin *haematītēs,* from Greek *(lithos) haimatitēs,* bloodlike (stone), from *haima, haimat-,* blood.] **—he′ma•tit′ic** (-tĭt′ĭk) *adj.*

hemato– or **hemat–** also **haemat–** or **haemato–** *pref.* Blood: *hematology.* [Greek *haimato-,* from *haima, haimat-,* blood.]

he•ma•to•blast (hē′mə-tə-blăst′, hĭ-măt′ə-) *n.* An immature blood cell. **—he′ma•to•blas′tic** *adj.*

he•mat•o•crit (hĭ-măt′ə-krĭt′) *n.* **1.** The percentage by volume of packed red blood cells in a sample of blood after centrifugation. **2.** A centrifuge used to determine the volume of blood cells and plasma in a sample of blood. [HEMATO– + Greek *kritēs,* judge (from *krinein,* to judge; see **krei-** in Appendix).]

he•ma•to•gen•e•sis (hē′mə-tə-jĕn′ĭ-sĭs, hĭ-măt′ə-) *n.* Hematopoiesis. **—he′ma•to•gen′ic** (-jĕn′ĭk), **he′ma•to•ge•net′ic** (-jə-nĕt′ĭk) *adj.*

he•ma•tog•e•nous (hē′mə-tŏj′ə-nəs) *adj.* **1.** Producing blood. **2.** Originating in or spread by the blood.

he•ma•tol•o•gy (hē′mə-tŏl′ə-jē) *n.* The science encompassing the medical study of the blood and blood-producing organs. **—he′ma•to•log′ic** (-tə-lŏj′ĭk), **he′ma•to•log′i•cal** *adj.* **—he′ma•to•log′i•cal•ly** *adv.* **—he′ma•tol′o•gist** *n.*

he•ma•tol•y•sis (hē′mə-tŏl′ĭ-sĭs) *n.* Hemolysis.

he•ma•to•ma (hē′mə-tō′mə) *n., pl.* **-mas** or **-ma•ta** (-mə-tə). A localized swelling filled with blood resulting from a break in a blood vessel.

he•ma•to•poi•e•sis (hē′mə-tō-poi-ē′sĭs, hĭ-măt′ə-) also **he•mo•poi•e•sis** (hē′mə-poi-ē′-sĭs) *n.* The formation of blood or blood cells in the body. **—he′ma•to•poi•et′ic** (-ĕt′ĭk) *adj.*

he•ma•tox•y•lin (hē′mə-tŏk′sə-lĭn) *n.* A yellow or red crystalline compound, $C_{16}H_{14}O_6{\cdot}3H_2O$, the coloring material of logwood, used in dyes, inks, and stains. [New Latin *Haematoxylon,* a genus of plants (Greek *haimato-,* hemato- + XYL–) + –IN.]

he•ma•to•zo•on (hē′mə-tō-zō′ŏn′, hĭ-măt′ə-) *n., pl.* **-zo•a** (-zō′ə). A parasitic protozoan or similar organism that lives in the blood. **—he′ma•to•zo′al, he′ma•to•zo′ic** *adj.*

he•ma•tu•ri•a (hē′mə-to͝or′ē-ə, -tyo͝or′-) *n.* The presence of blood in the urine. **—he′ma•tu′ric** *adj.*

heme (hēm) *n.* The deep red, nonprotein, ferrous component of hemoglobin, $C_{34}H_{32}FeN_4O_4$. [Short for HEMATIN.]

he•mel•y•tron (hĕ-mĕl′ĭ-trŏn′) *n., pl.* **-tra** (-trə). One of the forewings of a hemipterous insect, having a thick membranous apex. [HEM(I)– + ELYTRON.]

hem•er•a•lo•pi•a (hĕm′ər-ə-lō′pē-ə) *n.* A visual defect characterized by the inability to see as clearly in bright light as in dim light. [New Latin, from Greek *hēmeralōps,* suffering from hemeralopia : *hēmera,* day + *alaos,* blind + *ōps,* eye; see NYCTALOPIA.] **—hem′er•a•lop′ic** (-lŏp′ĭk) *adj.*

hem•er•o•cal•lis (hĕm′ər-ə-kăl′ĭs) *n.* See **day lily.** [New Latin, from Greek *hēmerokalles,* a kind of lily : *hēmera,* day + *kallos,* beauty.]

Hem•et (hĕm′ĭt). A city of southern California east of Santa Ana. Ancient rock paintings and carvings have been found here. Population, 22,454.

hemi– *pref.* **1.** Half: *hemihedral.* **2.** Partial; partially: *hemiparasite.* [Greek *hēmi-.* See **sēmi-** in Appendix.]

–hemia *suff.* Variant of **–emia.**

hem•i•al•gi•a (hĕm′ē-ăl′jē-ə, -jə) *n.* Pain affecting one half of the body.

he•mic (hē′mĭk) *adj.* Of or relating to the blood.

hem•i•cel•lu•lose (hĕm′ĭ-sĕl′yə-lōs′, -lōz′) *n.* Any of several polysaccharides that are more complex than a sugar and less complex than cellulose, found in plant cell walls and produced commercially from corn grain hulls.

hem•i•chor•date (hĕm′ĭ-kôr′dāt′, -dĭt) *n.* Any of various wormlike marine animals of the phylum Hemichordata, having a primitive notochord and gill slits. **—hemichordate** *adj.* Of or belonging to the phylum Hemichordata.

hem•i•cy•cle (hĕm′ĭ-sī′kəl) *n.* **1.** A semicircle. **2.** A semicircular structure or arrangement. [French *hémicycle,* from Latin *hēmicyclium,* from Greek *hēmikuklion* : *hēmi-,* hemi- + *kuklion,* neuter of *kuklios,* circular (from *kuklos,* circle; see CYCLE).]

hem•i•dem•i•sem•i•qua•ver (hĕm′ē-dĕm′ē-sĕm′ē-kwā′vər) *n. Chiefly British.* A sixty-fourth note.

hem•i•he•dral (hĕm′ĭ-hē′drəl) *adj.* Exhibiting only half the faces required for complete symmetry. Used of a crystal.

hem•i•hy•drate (hĕm′ĭ-hī′drāt′) *n.* A hydrate in which the molecular ratio of water molecules to anhydrous compound is 1:2. **—hem′i•hy′drat′ed** *adj.*

hem•i•me•tab•o•lous (hĕm′ē-mə-tăb′ə-ləs) also **hem•i•met•a•bol•ic** (-mĕt′əbŏl′ĭk) *adj.* Undergoing a metamorphosis that lacks a pupal stage. Used of certain insects. [HEMI– + METABOL(IC) + –OUS.] **—hem′i•me•tab′o•lism** (-ə-lĭz′əm) *n.*

hem•i•mor•phic (hĕm′ĭ-môr′fĭk) *adj.* Asymmetrical at the axial ends. Used of a crystal.

hem•i•mor•phite (hĕm′ĭ-môr′fīt′) *n.* A usually white or colorless mineral, essentially $Zn_4Si_2O_7(OH)_2{\cdot}H_2O$, an important ore of zinc. Also called *calamine.* [HEMIMORPH(IC) + –ITE[1].]

ă pat	oi boy
ā pay	ou out
âr care	o͝o took
ä father	o͞o boot
ĕ pet	ŭ cut
ē be	ûr urge
ĭ pit	th thin
ī pie	*th* this
îr pier	hw which
ŏ pot	zh vision
ō toe	ə about, item
ô paw	♦ regionalism

Stress marks: ′ (primary); ′ (secondary), as in **dictionary** (dĭk′shə-nĕr′ē)

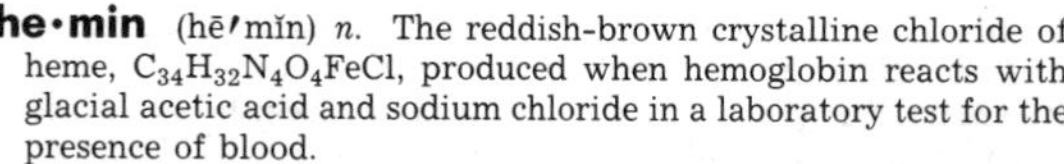

Ernest Hemingway

he•min (hē′mĭn) *n.* The reddish-brown crystalline chloride of heme, $C_{34}H_{32}N_4O_4FeCl$, produced when hemoglobin reacts with glacial acetic acid and sodium chloride in a laboratory test for the presence of blood.

Hem•ing or **Hem•minge** (hĕm′ĭng), **John.** 1556?–1630. English actor and an editor of the First Folio of Shakespeare's plays (1623).

Hem•ing•way (hĕm′ĭng-wā′), **Ernest Miller.** 1899–1961. American writer whose works include *The Sun Also Rises* (1926), *For Whom the Bell Tolls* (1940), and *The Old Man and the Sea* (1952). He won the 1954 Nobel Prize for literature.

hem•i•par•a•site (hĕm′ĭ-păr′ə-sīt′) *n.* **1.** A plant, such as mistletoe, that obtains some nourishment from its host but also photosynthesizes. Also called *semiparasite.* **2.** An organism that can live either independently or as a parasite. **—hem′i•par′a•sit′ic** (-sĭt′ĭk) *adj.*

hem•i•ple•gia (hĕm′ĭ-plē′jə, -jē-ə) *n.* Paralysis affecting only one side of the body. [Late Greek *hēmiplēgia* : Greek *hēmi-,* hemi- + Greek *-plēgia,* -plegia.] **—hem′i•ple′gic** (-plē′jĭk) *adj. & n.*

he•mip•ter•an (hĭ-mĭp′tər-ən) *adj.* Hemipterous. **—hemipteran** also **he•mip•ter•on** (-tə-rŏn′) *n.* A hemipterous insect; a true bug.

he•mip•ter•ous (hĭ-mĭp′tər-əs) *adj.* Of or belonging to the insect order Hemiptera, which includes the true bugs of the suborder Heteroptera and their allies of the suborder Homoptera, characterized by piercing or sucking mouthparts and two pairs of wings.

hem•i•sphere (hĕm′ĭ-sfîr′) *n.* **1.a.** A half of a sphere bounded by a great circle. **b.** A half of a symmetrical, approximately spherical object as divided by a plane of symmetry. **2.** Either half of the celestial sphere as divided by the ecliptic, the celestial equator, or the horizon. **3.** Either the northern or southern half of the earth as divided by the equator or the eastern or western half as divided by a meridian. **4.** *Anatomy.* Either of the lateral halves of the cerebrum; a cerebral hemisphere. **—hem′i•spher′ic** (-sfîr′ĭk, -sfĕr′-), **hem′i•spher′i•cal** *adj.* **—hem′i•spher′i•cal•ly** *adv.*

hem•i•stich (hĕm′ĭ-stĭk′) *n.* **1.** A half line of verse, especially when separated rhythmically from the rest of the line by a caesura. **2.** An incomplete or imperfect line of verse. [Latin *hemistichium,* from Greek *hēmistikhion* : *hēmi-,* hemi- + *stikhos,* line; see **steigh-** in Appendix.]

hem•line (hĕm′līn′) *n.* **1.** The bottom edge of a skirt, dress, or coat. **2.** The height of the edge of such a garment, measured from the floor.

hemlock
Eastern hemlock
Tsuga canadensis

hem•lock (hĕm′lŏk′) *n.* **1.a.** Any of various coniferous evergreen trees of the genus *Tsuga* of North America and eastern Asia, having small cones and short, flat leaves with two white bands underneath. **b.** The wood of such trees, used as a source of lumber, wood pulp, and tannic acid. **2.a.** Any of several poisonous plants of the genera *Conium* and *Cicuta,* such as the poison hemlock. **b.** A poison obtained from the poison hemlock. [Middle English *hemlok,* poisonous hemlock, from Old English *hymlice, hemlic.*]

Hem•minge (hĕm′ĭng). See John **Heming.**

hemo– or **hema–** or **hem–** also **haemo–** or **haema–** or **haem–** *pref.* Blood: *hemacyte.* [Greek *haimo-,* from *haima.*]

he•mo•chro•ma•to•sis (hē′mə-krō′mə-tō′sĭs) *n.* A hereditary disorder affecting iron metabolism in which excessive amounts of iron accumulate in the body tissues. The disorder is characterized by diabetes mellitus, liver dysfunction, and a bronze pigmentation of the skin.

he•mo•coel (hē′mə-sēl′) *n.* A cavity or series of spaces between the organs of most arthropods and mollusks through which the blood circulates.

he•mo•cy•a•nin (hē′mō-sī′ə-nĭn) *n.* A bluish, copper-containing respiratory pigment similar to hemoglobin, present in the blood of certain mollusks and arthropods.

he•mo•cyte (hē′mə-sīt′) *n.* A cellular component of the blood, especially of an invertebrate.

he•mo•di•al•y•sis (hē′mō-dī-ăl′ĭ-sĭs) *n., pl.* **-ses** (-sēz′). A procedure for removing metabolic waste products or toxic substances from the bloodstream by dialysis.

he•mo•dy•nam•ics (hē′mə-dī-năm′ĭks) *n. (used with a sing. verb).* The study of the forces involved in the circulation of blood. **—he′•mo•dy•nam′•ic** *adj.* **—he′•mo•dy•nam′•i•cal•ly** *adv.*

he•mo•flag•el•late (hē′mō-flăj′ə-lāt′, -lĭt, -flə-jĕl′ĭt) *n.* A flagellate protozoan, such as a trypanosome, that is parasitic in the blood.

he•mo•glo•bin (hē′mə-glō′bĭn) *n. Abbr.* **hg, hgb., Hb** The iron-containing respiratory pigment in red blood cells of vertebrates, consisting of about 6 percent heme and 94 percent globin. [Ultimately short for *hematinoglobulin* : HEMATIN + GLOBULIN.]

he•mo•glo•bi•nu•ri•a (hē′mə-glō′bə-no͝or′ē-ə, -nyo͝or′-) *n.* The presence of hemoglobin in the urine. **—he′mo•glo′bi•nu′ric** *adj.*

he•mo•lymph (hē′mə-lĭmf′) *n.* The circulatory fluid of certain invertebrates, analogous to blood in arthropods and to lymph in other invertebrates. **—he′mo•lym•phat′ic** (-lĭm-făt′ĭk) *adj.*

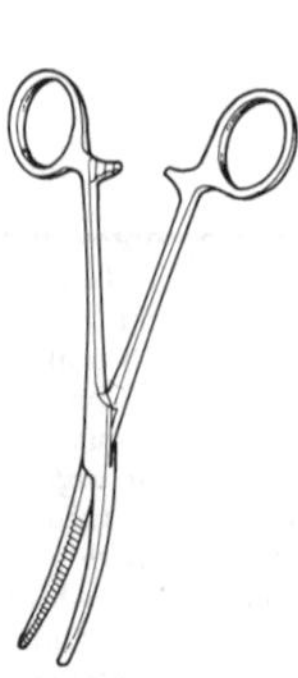

hemostat

he•mo•ly•sin (hē′mə-lī′sĭn, hĭ-mŏl′ĭ-) *n.* An agent or a substance, such as an antibody or a bacterial toxin, that causes the destruction of red blood cells, thereby liberating hemoglobin.

he•mol•y•sis (hĭ-mŏl′ĭ-sĭs, hē′mə-lī′sĭs) *n.* The destruction or dissolution of red blood cells, with subsequent release of hemoglobin. **—he′mo•lyt′ic** (hē′mə-lĭt′ĭk) *adj.*

hemolytic anemia *n.* Anemia resulting from the lysis of red blood cells, as in response to certain toxic or infectious agents and in certain inherited blood disorders.

he•mo•lyze (hē′mə-līz′) *intr. & tr.v.* **-lyzed, -lyz•ing, -lyz•es.** To undergo or cause to undergo hemolysis.

he•mo•phil•i•a (hē′mə-fĭl′ē-ə, -fēl′yə) *n.* Any of several hereditary blood-coagulation disorders in which the blood fails to clot normally because of a deficiency or an abnormality of one of the clotting factors. Hemophilia, a recessive trait associated with the X-chromosome, is manifested almost exclusively in males.

he•mo•phil•i•ac (hē′mə-fĭl′ē-ăk′, -fē′lē-) *n.* A person who is affected with hemophilia.

he•mo•phil•ic (hē′mə-fĭl′ĭk) *adj.* **1.** Of, relating to, or affected by hemophilia. **2.** Growing well in blood or in a culture containing blood. Used of certain bacteria.

he•mo•pho•bi•a (hē′mə-fō′bē-ə) *n.* An abnormal fear of blood. **—he′mo•pho′bic** *adj.*

he•mo•poi•e•sis (hē′mə-poi-ē′sĭs) *n.* Variant of **hematopoiesis.** **—he′mo•poi•et′ic** (-ĕt′ĭk) *adj.*

he•mop•ty•sis (hĭ-mŏp′tĭ-sĭs) *n.* The coughing or spitting up of blood from the respiratory tract. [HEMO– + Greek *ptusis,* a spitting (from *ptuein,* to spit).]

hem•or•rhage (hĕm′ər-ĭj) *n.* **1.** Excessive discharge of blood from the blood vessels; profuse bleeding. **2.** A copious loss of something valuable: *A hemorrhage of corporate earnings.* **—hemorrhage** *v.* **-rhaged, -rhag•ing, -rhag•es.** *—intr.* **1.** To bleed copiously. **2.** To undergo a rapid and sudden loss: *a gubernatorial candidate whose popularity hemorrhaged after a disastrous debate.* *—tr.* To lose (something valuable) rapidly and in quantity: *The company was hemorrhaging capital when it was bought by another firm.* [From obsolete *hemoragie, emorogie,* from Middle English *emorogie,* from Old French *emoragie,* from Latin *haemorrhagia,* from Greek *haimorrhagia* : *haimo-,* hemo- + *-rrhagia,* -rrhagia.] **—hem′or•rhag′ic** (hĕm′ə-răj′ĭk) *adj.*

hemorrhagic measles *n. (used with a sing. verb).* See **black measles.**

hem•or•rhoid (hĕm′ə-roid′) *n.* **1.** An itching or painful mass of dilated veins in swollen anal tissue. **2. hemorroids.** The pathological condition in which such painful masses occur. In this sense, also called *piles.* [From Middle English *emoroides,* hemorrhoids, from Old French *emoroides,* from Latin *haemorrhoidae,* from Greek *haimorrhoïdes,* pl. of *haimorrhoïs,* from *haimorrhoos,* flowing with blood : *haimo-,* hemo- + *rhein,* to flow; see **sreu-** in Appendix.]

hem•or•rhoid•al (hĕm′ə-roid′l) *adj.* **1.** Of or relating to hemorrhoids. **2.** *Anatomy.* Supplying the region of the rectum and anus. Used of certain arteries.

hem•or•rhoid•ec•to•my (hĕm′ə-roi-dĕk′tə-mē) *n., pl.* **-mies.** Surgical removal of hemorrhoids.

he•mo•sid•er•in (hē′mō-sĭd′ər-ĭn) *n.* A protein that stores iron in the body, derived chiefly from the hemoglobin released during hemolysis.

he•mo•sta•sis (hē′mə-stā′sĭs, hē-mŏs′tə-) also **he•mo•sta•sia** (hē′mə-stā′zhə, -zhē-ə, -zē-ə) *n.* **1.** The stoppage of bleeding or hemorrhage. **2.** The stoppage of blood flow through a blood vessel or body part.

he•mo•stat (hē′mə-stăt′) *n.* **1.** An agent, such as a chemical, that stops bleeding. **2.** A clamplike instrument used to compress a blood vessel in order to reduce or arrest the flow of blood during surgery.

he•mo•stat•ic (hē′mə-stăt′ĭk) *adj.* Acting to arrest bleeding or hemorrhage. **—hemostatic** *n.* A hemostatic device or agent. [HEMO– + Greek *statikos,* causing to stop; see STATIC.]

hemp (hĕmp) *n.* **1.** Cannabis. **2.** The tough, coarse fiber of the cannabis plant, used to make cordage. **3.a.** Any of various plants similar to cannabis, especially one yielding a similar fiber. **b.** The fiber of such a plant. [Middle English, from Old English *hænep.*]

hemp agrimony *n.* A Eurasian and North African plant *(Eupatorium cannabinum)* having palmately divided leaves and clusters of small reddish-purple flower heads.

hemp•en (hĕm′pən) *adj.* Of, relating to, or resembling hemp.

hemp nettle *n.* Any of various Eurasian plants of the genus *Galeopsis,* having bristly stems and white or reddish flowers with two lips.

Hemp•stead (hĕmp′stĕd′, -stĭd). A village of southeast New York on western Long Island southeast of Mineola. It is the seat of Hofstra University (founded 1935). Population, 40,404.

hem•stitch (hĕm′stĭch′) *n.* **1.** A decorative stitch usually bordering a hem, as on a handkerchief, made by drawing out several parallel threads and catching together the cross threads in uniform groups. **2.** Needlework in which this stitch is used. **—hemstitch** *tr.v.* **-stitched, -stitch•ing, -stitch•es.** To ornament or embroider with hemstitches. **—hem′stitch′er** *n.*

hen (hĕn) *n.* **1.** A female bird, especially the adult female of the domestic fowl. **2.** The female of certain aquatic animals, such as an octopus or a lobster. **3.** *Slang.* A woman, especially a fussy old woman. [Middle English, from Old English. See **kan-** in Appendix.] **—hen′nish** *adj.* **—hen′nish•ly** *adv.* **—hen′nish•ness** *n.*

He·nan (hœ′nän′) also **Ho·nan** (hō′-). A province of east-central China. It is one of the oldest inhabited regions in China and the site of many Stone Age remains. Zhengzhou is the capital. Population, 77,130,000.

hen-and-chick·ens (hĕn′ən-chĭk′ənz) *n., pl.* **hens-and-chick·ens** (hĕnz′-). Any of several plants having many runners or offshoots, especially the houseleek.

hen·bane (hĕn′bān′) *n.* A poisonous Eurasian plant *(Hyoscyamus niger)* having an unpleasant odor, sticky leaves, and funnel-shaped greenish-yellow flowers. It is a source of the drug hyoscamine.

hen·bit (hĕn′bĭt′) *n.* A Eurasian plant *(Lamium amplexicaule)* having toothed, opposite leaves and small white or purplish-red flowers with two lips. [HEN + BIT[1].]

hence (hĕns) *adv.* **1.a.** For this reason; therefore: *handmade and hence expensive.* **b.** From this source: *They grew up in the Sudan; hence their interest in Nubian art.* **2.** From this time; from now: *A year hence it will be forgotten.* **3.a.** From this place; away from here: *Get you hence!* **b.** From this life. [Middle English *hennes,* from here : *henne* (from Old English *heonan;* see **ko-** in Appendix) + *-es,* adverbial suff.; see –S[3].]

hence·forth (hĕns′fôrth′) *adv.* From this time forth; from now on.

hence·for·ward (hĕns-fôr′wərd) *adv.* Henceforth.

hench·man (hĕnch′mən) *n.* **1.** A loyal and trusted follower or subordinate. **2.** A person who supports a political figure chiefly out of selfish interests. **3.** A member of a criminal gang. **4.** *Obsolete.* A page to a prince or other person of high rank. [Middle English *hengsman, henshman,* servant to a person of rank : *hengest,* horse (from Old English) + *man,* man; see MAN.]

hen·coop (hĕn′ko͞op′) *n.* A coop or cage for poultry. Also called *hennery.*

hen·dec·a·syl·lab·ic (hĕn-dĕk′ə-sĭ-lăb′ĭk) *adj.* Containing 11 syllables. **—hendecasyllabic** *n.* A verse of 11 syllables. [From Latin *hendecasyllabus,* a line of eleven syllables, from Greek *hendekasullabos* : *hendeka,* eleven (*hen,* neuter of *heis,* one; see **sem-**[1] in Appendix + *deka,* ten; see DECADE) + *sullabē,* syllable; see SYLLABLE.] **—hen·dec′a·syl′la·ble** (-sĭl′ə-bəl) *n.*

Hen·der·son (hĕn′dər-sən). **1.** A city of northwest Kentucky on the Ohio River south of Evansville, Indiana. Settled in the late 1700's, it was the home of John J. Audubon from 1810 to 1819. Population, 24,834. **2.** A city of southeast Nevada southeast of Las Vegas. Founded in 1942, it is in a desert area surrounded by mountains. Population, 24,363.

Henderson, Arthur. 1863–1935. British politician who was president of the World Disarmament Conference (1932–1935). He won the 1934 Nobel Peace Prize.

Hen·der·son·ville (hĕn′dər-sən-vĭl′). A city of northern Tennessee northeast of Nashville. Population, 26,561.

hen·di·a·dys (hĕn-dī′ə-dĭs) *n.* A figure of speech in which two words connected by a conjunction are used to express a single notion that would normally be expressed by an adjective and a substantive, such as *grace and favor* instead of *gracious favor.* [Late Latin, from Greek *hen dia duoin,* one by means of two : *hen,* neuter of *heis,* one; see **sem-**[1] in Appendix + *dia,* through + *duoin,* genitive of *duō,* two; see **dwo-** in Appendix.]

Hen·dricks (hĕn′drĭks), **Thomas Andrews.** 1819–1885. Vice President of the United States (1885) under Grover Cleveland.

Hen·drix (hĕn′drĭks), **Jimi.** Originally James Marshall Hendrix. 1942–1970. American musician whose innovative electric guitar playing greatly influenced the development of rock music.

hen·e·quen also **hen·e·quin** (hĕn′ĭ-kwĭn) *n.* **1.** A tropical American plant *(Agave fourcroydes)* having large, thick, sword-shaped leaves that yield a coarse reddish fiber used in making rope and twine. **2.** The fiber obtained from this plant. [Spanish *henequén,* perhaps of Arawakan origin.]

Heng·e·lo (hĕng′ə-lō′). A city of eastern Netherlands near the German border northwest of Enschede. It is an industrial center. Population, 76,855.

Heng·yang (hŭng′yäng′, hœng′-). A city of southeast China south-southwest of Wuhan. It is an important transportation hub and industrial center. Population, 350,000.

hen harrier *n.* See **northern harrier.**

Hen·ie (hĕn′ē), **Sonja.** 1912–1969. Norwegian-born figure skater who won Olympic gold medals in 1928, 1932, and 1936 and ten consecutive world championships (1927–1936).

Hen·ley (hĕn′lē) or **Hen·ley-on-Thames** (-ŏn-tĕmz′, -ôn-). A municipal borough of south-central England west of London. It is the site of a famed annual rowing regatta that was established in 1839. Population, 10,976.

hen·na (hĕn′ə) *n.* **1.a.** A tree or shrub *(Lawsonia inermis)* of the Middle East, having fragrant white or reddish flowers. **b.** A reddish-orange dyestuff prepared from the dried and ground leaves of this plant, used as a cosmetic dye and for coloring leather and fabrics. **2.** *Color.* A moderate or strong reddish brown to strong brown. **—henna** *tr.v.* **-naed, -na·ing, -nas.** To dye (hair, for example) with henna. [Arabic *ḥinnā'.*] **—hen′na** *adj.*

hen·ner·y (hĕn′ə-rē) *n., pl.* **-ies. 1.** A poultry farm. **2.** See **hencoop.**

hen·o·the·ism (hĕn′ə-thē-ĭz′əm) *n.* Belief in one god without denying the existence of others. [Greek *heno-* (from *hen,* neuter of *heis,* one; see **sem-**[1] in Appendix) + THE(O)– + –ISM.] **—hen′o·the′ist** *n.* **—hen′o·the·is′tic** *adj.*

hen·peck (hĕn′pĕk′) *tr.v.* **-pecked, -peck·ing, -pecks.** *Informal.* To dominate or harass (one's husband) with persistent nagging.

Hen·ri (hĕn′rē), **Robert.** 1865–1929. American painter whose realistic works aligned him with a group of painters, known as the Eight, or the Ashcan School, who decried the artificiality and sentimentality of American painting at the turn of the century.

hen·ry (hĕn′rē) *n., pl.* **-ries** or **-rys.** *Abbr.* **H** The unit of inductance in which an induced electromotive force of one volt is produced when the current is varied at the rate of one ampere per second. See table at **measurement.** [After Joseph HENRY.]

Hen·ry I (hĕn′rē). Known as "Henry Beauclerc." 1068–1135. King of England (1100–1135). The youngest son of William the Conqueror, he restored the laws of Edward the Confessor and conquered Normandy (1106).

Henry II[1]**.** 1133–1189. King of England (1154–1189). The son of Princess Matilda, he founded the Plantagenet royal line and appointed Thomas à Becket as archbishop of Canterbury. His quarrels with Becket concerning the authority of the Crown over the Church led to the murder of the archbishop (1170).

Henry II[2]**.** 1519–1559. King of France (1547–1559). The son of Francis I, he regained Calais from the English (1558).

Henry III[1]**.** 1207–1272. King of England (1216–1272) who succeeded his father, King John. His reign was marred by baronial opposition led by Simon de Montfort.

Henry III[2]**.** 1551–1589. King of France (1574–1589) who helped his mother, Catherine de Médicis, plot the Saint Bartholomew's Day Massacre (1572).

Henry IV[1]**.** 1050–1106. Holy Roman emperor and king of Germany (1056–1106) who continually struggled for power with Pope Gregory VII. Twice excommunicated, Henry appointed an antipope (1084), had himself again crowned emperor, invaded Italy, and was ultimately dethroned by his rebellious sons.

Henry IV[2]**.** Known as "Henry Bolingbroke." 1366?–1413. King of England (1399–1413). Son of John of Gaunt and grandson of Edward III, he was banished from England by Richard II, who confiscated his estate. Henry returned, raised an army, and compelled Richard to abdicate. Parliament confirmed Henry's claim to the throne, thus establishing the Lancastrian line.

Henry IV[3]**.** Known as "Henry of Navarre." 1553–1610. King of France (1589–1610) who founded the Bourbon royal line, successfully waged war against Spain (1595–1598), and gave political rights to French Protestants in the Edict of Nantes (1598).

Henry V[1]**.** 1081–1125. Holy Roman emperor and king of Germany (1106–1125) who fought against Flanders, Bohemia, Hungary, and Poland.

Henry V[2]**.** 1387–1422. King of England (1413–1422) who succeeded his father, Henry IV, and suppressed the Lollards. He also reopened the Hundred Years' War, defeating the French at Agincourt (1415) and capturing all of Normandy by 1419.

Henry VI. 1421–1471. King of England (1422–1461 and 1470–1471) who as an infant succeeded his father, Henry V. He was taken prisoner in the Yorkist victory at Northampton (1460), and Edward IV was proclaimed king (1461). Rescued from captivity, Henry regained the throne (1470) but was recaptured at the Battle of Barnet and murdered in the Tower of London.

Henry VII. Known as "Henry Tudor." 1457–1509. King of England (1485–1509) and founder of the Tudor line. Head of the house of Lancaster, he led the opposition to Richard III, defeated Richard at Bosworth Field (August 22, 1485), and was proclaimed king. In 1486 Henry married Elizabeth, daughter of Edward IV, thereby uniting the houses of York and Lancaster.

Henry VIII. 1491–1547. King of England (1509–1547) who succeeded his father, Henry VII. His divorce from Catherine of Aragon, his first wife, compelled him to break from the Catholic Church by the Act of Supremacy (1534).

Henry, Cape. A promontory of southeast Virginia at the entrance to Chesapeake Bay east of Norfolk.

Henry, Joseph. 1791–1878. American physicist who performed extensive studies of electromagnetic phenomena.

Henry, O. See William Sydney **Porter.**

Henry, Patrick. 1736–1799. American Revolutionary leader and orator. A member of the House of Burgesses (1765) and the Continental Congress (1774–1776), he spurred the creation of the Virginia militia with his words "Give me liberty, or give me death" (1775). He also served as governor of Virginia (1776–1790).

Henry the Navigator. 1394–1460. Prince of Portugal who established an observatory and school of navigation and directed voyages that spurred the growth of Portugal's colonial empire.

hens-and-chick·ens (hĕnz′ən-chĭk′ənz) *n.* Plural of **hen-and-chickens.**

Hen·son (hĕn′sən), **Jim.** 1936–1990. American puppeteer and creator of the Muppets, a troupe of puppets including Kermit the Frog, Ernie and Bert, and Big Bird.

hent (hĕnt) *tr.v.* **hent·ed, hent·ing, hents.** *Obsolete.* To take hold of; seize. [Middle English *henten,* from Old English *hentan.*]

hep (hĕp) *adj. Slang.* Variant of **hip**[2]**.**

hep·a·rin (hĕp′ər-ĭn) *n.* A complex organic acid found especially in lung and liver tissue and having the ability to prevent the clotting of blood, used in the treatment of thrombosis. [Late Latin *hēpar,* liver (from Greek; see **yĕkʷr̥** in Appendix) + –IN.]

hepat– *pref.* Variant of **hepato–.**

Jimi Hendrix

Henry VIII

ă pat	oi boy
ā pay	ou out
âr care	o͝o took
ä father	o͞o boot
ĕ pet	ŭ cut
ē be	ûr urge
ĭ pit	th thin
ī pie	*th* this
îr pier	hw which
ŏ pot	zh vision
ō toe	ə about, item
ô paw	♦ regionalism

Stress marks: ′ (primary); ′ (secondary), as in **dictionary** (dĭk′shə-nĕr′ē)

he·pat·ic (hĭ-păt′ĭk) *adj.* **1.** Of, relating to, or resembling the liver. **2.** Acting on or occurring in the liver. **—hepatic** *n.* A drug that acts on the liver. [Middle English *epatic,* from Old French *hepatique,* from Latin *hēpaticus,* from Greek *hēpatikos,* from *hēpar, hēpat-,* liver. See **yēkʷr̥** in Appendix.]

he·pat·i·ca (hĭ-păt′ĭ-kə) *n.* Any of several woodland plants of the genus *Hepatica,* especially *H. americana* of eastern North America, having three-lobed leaves and white or lavender flowers. Also called *liverleaf.* [Middle English *epatica,* liverwort, from Medieval Latin *hēpatica,* from feminine of Latin *hēpaticus,* of the liver. See HEPATIC.]

hepatic duct *n.* The main excretory duct of the liver, which joins the cystic duct to form the common bile duct.

hep·a·ti·tis (hĕp′ə-tī′tĭs) *n., pl.* **-tit·i·des** (-tĭt′ĭ-dēz′). Inflammation of the liver, caused by infectious or toxic agents and characterized by jaundice, fever, liver enlargement, and abdominal pain.

hepatitis A *n.* A form of hepatitis caused by an RNA virus that does not persist in the blood serum and is transmitted by ingestion of infected food and water. The disease has a shorter incubation and generally milder symptoms than hepatitis B. Also called *infectious hepatitis.*

hepatitis B *n.* A form of hepatitis caused by a DNA virus that persists in the blood serum and is transmitted by infected blood, as through the use of a contaminated syringe. The disease has a long incubation and symptoms that may become severe or chronic, causing serious damage to the liver. Also called *serum hepatitis.*

hepato– or **hepat–** *pref. pref.* Liver: *hepatitis.* [Greek *hēpato-,* from *hēpar, hēpat-,* liver. See **yēkʷr̥** in Appendix.]

he·pa·to·cyte (hĕp′ə-tə-sīt′, hĭ-păt′ə-) *n.* A parenchymal cell of the liver.

hep·a·to·ma (hĕp′ə-tō′mə) *n., pl.* **-mas** or **-ma·ta** (-mə-tə). A usually cancerous tumor occurring in the liver.

hep·a·to·meg·a·ly (hĕp′ə-tə-mĕg′ə-lē, hĭpăt′ə-) *n.* Abnormal enlargement of the liver.

hep·a·to·tox·ic·i·ty (hĕp′ə-tō-tŏk-sĭs′ĭ-tē, hĭ-păt′ō-) *n.* **1.** The quality or condition of being toxic or destructive to the liver. **2.** The capacity of a substance to have damaging effects on the liver. **—hep′a·to·tox′ic** (-tŏk′sĭk) *adj.*

hep·a·to·tox·in (hĕp′ə-tō-tŏk′sĭn, hĭ-păt′ō-) *n.* A substance capable of causing damage to the liver.

Hep·burn (hĕp′bûrn′), **Katharine Houghton.** Born 1909. American actress whose unique comedic and dramatic presence marks many fine motion pictures, including *The Philadelphia Story* (1940), *Adam's Rib* (1949), and *The African Queen* (1951).

hep·cat (hĕp′kăt′) *n. Slang.* A performer or devotee of swing and jazz, especially during the 1940's.

He·phaes·tus (hĭ-fĕs′təs) *n. Greek Mythology.* The god of fire and metalworking.

Hep·ple·white (hĕp′əl-hwīt′, -wīt′) *adj.* Of, relating to, or being an English style of furniture of the late 18th century, characterized by its light, graceful lines, the use of concave curves, and the shield or heart backs of its chairs. [After George HEPPLEWHITE.]

Hepplewhite, George. Died 1786. British cabinetmaker whose elegant designs, now greatly admired, were considered unfashionable in his day.

hepta– or **hept–** *pref.* Seven: *heptarchy.* [Greek, from *hepta,* seven. See **septm̥** in Appendix.]

hep·tad (hĕp′tăd′) *n.* A group or series of seven. [Greek *heptas, heptad-,* the number seven, from *hepta,* seven. See **septm̥** in Appendix.]

hep·ta·gon (hĕp′tə-gŏn′) *n.* A polygon having seven sides. [From Greek *heptagōnon,* neuter of *heptagōnos,* having seven angles : *hepta-,* hepta- + *-gōnos,* angled; see –GON.] **—hep·tag′o·nal** (-tăg′ə-nəl) *adj.*

hep·ta·he·dron (hĕp′tə-hē′drən) *n., pl.* **-drons** or **-dra** (-drə). A polyhedron with seven faces. **—hep′ta·he′dral** (-drəl) *adj.*

hep·tam·e·ter (hĕp-tăm′ĭ-tər) *n.* **1.** A metrical unit consisting of seven feet. **2.** A line of verse consisting of seven metrical feet.

hep·tane (hĕp′tān′) *n.* A volatile, colorless, highly flammable liquid hydrocarbon, C_7H_{16}, obtained in the fractional distillation of petroleum and used as a standard in determining octane ratings, as an anesthetic, and as a solvent.

hep·tar·chy (hĕp′tär′kē) *n., pl.* **-chies. 1.a.** Government by seven persons. **b.** A state governed by seven persons. **2.** Often **Heptarchy.** The informal confederation of the Anglo-Saxon kingdoms from the fifth to the ninth century, consisting of Kent, Sussex, Wessex, Essex, Northumbria, East Anglia, and Mercia.

hep·ta·stich (hĕp′tə-stĭk′) *n.* A stanza or strophe consisting of seven lines.

Hep·ta·teuch (hĕp′tə-to͞ok′, -tyo͞ok′) *n. Bible.* The first seven books of the Old Testament. [Greek *heptateukhos,* volume containing seven books : *hepta-,* hepta- + *teukhos,* case for papyrus rolls, book; see **dheugh-** in Appendix.]

hep·tath·lon (hĕp-tăth′lən, -lŏn′) *n. Sports.* An athletic contest in which each contestant participates in seven different track and field events. [HEPT(A)– + (DEC)ATHLON.]

Hep·worth (hĕp′wûrth′), Dame **Barbara.** 1903–1975. British sculptor best known for her *Single Form (Memorial to Dag Hammarskjöld)* at the United Nations Plaza in New York City.

her (hər, ər; hûr *when stressed*) *adj.* The possessive form of **she.** Used as a modifier before a noun: *her boots; her accomplishments.* **—her** *pron.* The objective case of **she. 1.a.** Used as the direct object of a verb: *They saw her at the conference.* **b.** Used as the indirect object of a verb: *They gave her a round of applause.* **2.** Used as the object of a preposition: *This letter is addressed to her.* **3.** *Informal.* Used as a predicate nominative: *It's her.* **—her** *n.* A female: *The dog is a her.* See Usage Note at **be, I**[1]. [Middle English, from Old English *hire.* See **ko-** in Appendix.]

her. *abbr.* Heraldry.

He·ra (hîr′ə) also **He·re** (hîr′ē) *n. Greek Mythology.* The sister and wife of Zeus.

Her·a·cle·a (hĕr′ə-klē′ə). An ancient Greek city of southern Italy near the Gulf of Taranto. In 280 B.C. it was the site of one of Pyrrhus's victories over the Romans.

Her·a·cles or **Her·a·kles** (hĕr′ə-klēz′) *n. Greek & Roman Mythology.* Variants of **Hercules** (sense 1).

Her·a·cli·tus (hĕr′ə-klī′təs). fl. 500 B.C. Greek philosopher who maintained that strife and change are natural conditions of the universe. **—Her′a·cli′te·an** (-tē-ən) *adj.*

Her·a·cli·us (hĕr′ə-klī′əs, hĭ-răk′lē-). 575?–641. Emperor of the Byzantine Empire (610–641) who captured Syria, Palestine, and Egypt from Persia (613–628) but lost them all to Moslem invaders (635–641).

her·ald (hĕr′əld) *n.* **1.** A person who carries or proclaims important news; a messenger. **2.** One that gives a sign or indication of something to come; a harbinger: *The crocus is a herald of spring.* **3.** An official whose specialty is heraldry. **4.a.** An official formerly charged with making royal proclamations and bearing messages of state between sovereigns. **b.** An official who formerly made proclamations and conveyed challenges at a tournament. **—herald** *tr.v.* **-ald·ed, -ald·ing, -alds.** To proclaim; announce: *cheers that heralded the team's arrival.* [Middle English, from Anglo-Norman, of Germanic origin. See **koro-** in Appendix.]

he·ral·dic (hə-răl′dĭk) *adj.* Of or relating to heralds or heraldry. **—he·ral′di·cal·ly** *adv.*

her·ald·ry (hĕr′əl-drē) *n., pl.* **-ries. 1.** *Abbr.* **her. a.** The profession, study, or art of devising, granting, and blazoning arms, tracing genealogies, and determining and ruling on questions of rank or protocol, as exercised by an officer of arms. **b.** A branch of knowledge dealing with the history and description in proper terms of armorial bearings and their accessories. **2.** Armorial ensigns or similar insignia. **3.** Pomp and ceremony, especially attended with armorial trappings; pageantry. **—her′ald·ist** *n.*

He·rat (hĕ-rät′). A city of northwest Afghanistan on the Hari Rud east of Kabul. Located at a strategic position on an ancient trade route, it became part of Afghanistan in 1881. Population, 140,323.

herb (ûrb, hûrb) *n.* **1.** A plant whose stem does not produce woody, persistent tissue and generally dies back at the end of each growing season. **2.** Any of various often aromatic plants used especially in medicine or as seasoning. **3.** *Slang.* Marijuana. [Middle English *herbe,* from Old French *erbe,* from Latin *herba.*] **—herb′y** *adj.*

her·ba·ceous (hûr-bā′shəs, ûr-) *adj.* **1.** Relating to or characteristic of an herb as distinguished from a woody plant. **2.** Green and leaflike in appearance or texture. [From Latin *herbāceus,* from *herba,* herb.]

herb·age (ûr′bĭj, hûr′-) *n.* **1.** Herbaceous plant growth, especially grass or similar vegetation used for pasturage. **2.** The fleshy, often edible parts of plants. [Middle English, from Old French *erbage,* from *erbe,* from Latin *herba.*]

herb·al (ûr′bəl, hûr′-) *adj.* Of, relating to, or containing herbs. **—herbal** *n.* A book about plants and herbs, especially those that are useful to human beings.

herb·al·ist (ûr′bə-lĭst, hûr′-) *n.* **1.** One who grows, collects, or specializes in the use of herbs, especially medicinal herbs. **2.** See **herb doctor.**

her·bar·i·um (hûr-bâr′ē-əm, ûr-) *n., pl.* **-i·ums** or **-i·a** (-ē-ə). **1.** A collection of dried plants mounted, labeled, and systematically arranged for use in scientific study. **2.** A place or an institution where such a collection is kept. [Late Latin *herbārium,* from Latin *herbārius,* one skilled in herbs, from Latin *herba,* herb, vegetation.]

Her·bart (hĕr′bärt′), **Johann Friedrich.** 1776–1841. German philosopher and founder of modern scientific pedagogy.

herb bennet *n.* A hairy Eurasian plant *(Geum urbanum)* having small yellow flowers and an astringent root formerly used medicinally. [Middle English *herbe benet,* from Anglo-Norman, from Medieval Latin *herba benedicta* : Latin *herba,* herb + Latin *benedicta,* feminine past participle of *benedīcere,* to bless; see BENEDICTION.]

herb doctor *n.* One who practices healing with herbs. Also called *herbalist.*

herbed (ûrbd, hûrbd) *adj.* Flavored with herbs: *herbed vinaigrette.*

Her·bert (hûr′bərt), **George.** 1593–1633. English metaphysical poet whose works, including "The Collar" (1633), are religious in theme and marked by rich symbolism and inventive meter.

Herbert, Victor. 1859–1924. American musician, composer, and conductor particularly known for his comic operas, including *Babes in Toyland* (1903).

her•bi•cide (hûr′bĭ-sīd′, ûr′-) *n.* A chemical substance used to destroy or inhibit the growth of plants, especially weeds. **—her′bi•cid′al** (-sīd′l) *adj.*

her•bi•vore (hûr′bə-vôr′, -vōr′, ûr′-) *n.* An animal that feeds chiefly on plants. [From New Latin *Herbivora,* former mammalian group, from neuter pl. of *herbivorus,* plant-eating. See HERBIVOROUS.]

her•biv•o•rous (hûr-bĭv′ər-əs, ûr-) *adj.* Feeding on plants; plant-eating. [From New Latin *herbivorus* : Latin *herba,* vegetation + Latin *-vorus,* -vorous.] **—her•biv′o•rous•ly** *adv.*

herb Par•is (păr′ĭs) *n.* A European plant *(Paris quadrifolia)* having a whorl of four leaves and a solitary yellow or greenish flower. [Probably Medieval Latin *herba paris,* herb of a pair (perhaps a reference to the two pairs of leaves on the whorl) : Latin *herba,* herb + Latin *paris,* genitive of *pār,* equal; see PAR.]

herb Rob•ert (rŏb′ərt) *n.* A low-growing Eurasian plant *(Geranium robertianum)* having divided leaves and small reddish-purple flowers. [Middle English *herbe Robert,* from Old French *erbe Robert,* from Medieval Latin *herba Robertī* : Latin *herba,* herb + *Robertī,* genitive of *Robertus,* Robert.]

Her•cu•la•ne•um (hûr′kyə-lā′nē-əm). An ancient city of south-central Italy on the Bay of Naples. A popular resort during Roman times, it was completely destroyed by the eruption of Mount Vesuvius (A.D. 79).

Her•cu•le•an (hûr′kyə-lē′ən, hûr-kyo͞o′lē-) *adj.* **1.** Often **herculean.** Of unusual size, power, or difficulty. **2.** *Greek & Roman Mythology.* **a.** Of or relating to Hercules. **b.** Resembling Hercules.

Her•cu•les (hûr′kyə-lēz′) *n.* **1.** Also **Her•a•cles** or **Her•a•kles** (hĕr′ə-klēz′). *Greek & Roman Mythology.* The son of Zeus and Alcmene, a hero of extraordinary strength who won immortality by performing 12 labors demanded by Hera. **2.** A constellation in the Northern Hemisphere near Lyra and Corona Borealis. [Latin, from Greek *Hēraklēs* : *Hēra,* Hera + *kleos,* fame; see **kleu-** in Appendix.]

Her•cu•les′ club (hûr′kyə-lēz) *n.* **1.** A tree or shrub *(Aralia spinosa)* of the southeast United States, having prickly, bipinnately compound leaves and large clusters of small white flowers. Also called *angelica tree, devil's walking stick, prickly ash.* **2.** A spiny shrub or tree *(Zanthoxylum clava-herculis)* of the central and southeast United States, having terminal panicles of small greenish-yellow flowers and pinnately compound leaves. Also called *pepperwood, Southern prickly ash.* [After the spiny club of Hercules.]

herd (hûrd) *n.* **1.a.** A group of cattle or other domestic animals of a single kind kept together for a specific purpose. **b.** A number of wild animals of one species that remain together as a group: *a herd of elephants.* See Synonyms at **flock**[1]. **2.a.** A large number of people; a crowd: *a herd of stranded passengers.* **b.** The multitude of common people regarded as a mass: *"It is the luxurious and dissipated who set the fashions which the herd so diligently follow"* (Henry David Thoreau). **—herd** *v.* **herd•ed, herd•ing, herds.** *—intr.* To come together in a herd: *The sheep herded for warmth.* *—tr.* **1.** To gather, keep, or drive (animals) in a herd. **2.** To tend (sheep or cattle). **3.** To gather and place into a group or mass: *herded the children into the auditorium.* [Middle English, from Old English *heord.*]

herd•er (hûr′dər) *n.* **1.** One who tends or drives a herd. **2.** A herdsman.

Her•der (hĕr′dər), **Johann Gottfried von.** 1744–1803. German philosopher and writer whose advocacy of intuition over rationality formed the basis of German romanticism.

her•dic (hûr′dĭk) *n.* A small horse-drawn cab with two wheels, side seats, and an entrance at the back, used in the 19th century. [After Peter *Herdic* (1824–1888), American inventor.]

herds•man (hûrdz′mən) *n.* An owner or a breeder of livestock.

here (hîr) *adv.* **1.** At or in this place: *Stop here for a rest.* **2.** At this time; now: *We'll adjourn the meeting here and discuss remaining issues after lunch.* **3.** At or on this point, detail, or item: *Here I must disagree.* **4.** In the present life or condition. **5.** To this place; hither: *Come here, please.* **—here** *adj.* **1.** Used for emphasis after a demonstrative pronoun: *Which word? This one here.* **2.** Used for emphasis after a noun modified by a demonstrative pronoun: *this word here.* **3.** *Non-Standard.* Used for emphasis between a demonstrative pronoun and a noun: *this here word.* **—here** *interj.* Used to respond to a roll call, attract attention, command an animal, or rebuke, admonish, or concur. **—here** *n.* **1.** This place: *"It would be difficult from here, with the certainty of armed gunmen inside, to bring him out alive"* (Howard Kaplan). **2.** The present time or state: *We are living in the here and now and can only speculate about the hereafter.* **—idiom. neither here nor there.** Unimportant and irrelevant. [Middle English, from Old English *hēr.* See **ko-** in Appendix.]

He•re (hîr′ē) *n.* *Greek Mythology.* Variant of **Hera.**

here•a•bout (hîr′ə-bout′) also **here•a•bouts** (-bouts′) *adv.* In this general vicinity; around here.

here•af•ter (hîr-ăf′tər) *adv.* **1.** Immediately following this in time, order, or place; after this. **2.** In a future time or state: *hope to win salvation hereafter.* **—hereafter** *n.* The afterlife: *belief in a hereafter.*

here•by (hîr-bī′) *adv.* By virtue of this act, decree, bulletin, or document; by this means.

her•e•dit•a•ment (hĕr′ĭ-dĭt′ə-mənt) *n. Law.* Property that can be inherited. [Middle English, from Medieval Latin *hērēditāmentum,* from Late Latin *hērēditāre,* to inherit, from Latin *hērēs, hērēd-,* heir. See **ghē-** in Appendix.]

he•red•i•tar•i•an (hə-rĕd′ĭ-târ′ē-ən) *n.* One who supports hereditarianism. **—hereditarian** *adj.* Relating to or based on hereditarianism.

he•red•i•tar•i•an•ism (hə-rĕd′ĭ-târ′ē-ə-nĭz′əm) *n.* The doctrine or school that regards heredity as the primary factor in determining intelligence and behavior independent of environmental influences.

he•red•i•tar•y (hə-rĕd′ĭ-tĕr′ē) *adj.* **1.** *Law.* **a.** Descending from an ancestor to a legal heir; passing down by inheritance. **b.** Having title or possession through inheritance. **2.** Transmitted or capable of being transmitted genetically from parent to offspring: *a hereditary disease.* **3.a.** Appearing in or characteristic of successive generations. **b.** Derived from or fostered by one's ancestors: *a hereditary prejudice.* **4.** Ancestral; traditional: *their hereditary home.* See Synonyms at **innate.** **5.** Of or relating to heredity or inheritance. [Middle English, from Latin *hērēditārius,* from *hērēditās,* inheritance. See HEREDITY.] **—he•red′i•tar′i•ly** (-târ′ə-lē) *adv.* **—he•red′i•tar′i•ness** *n.*

he•red•i•tist (hə-rĕd′ĭ-tĭst) *n.* A hereditarian.

he•red•i•ty (hə-rĕd′ĭ-tē) *n., pl.* **-ties.** **1.** The genetic transmission of characteristics from parent to offspring. **2.** The sum of characteristics and associated potentialities transmitted genetically to an individual organism. [French *hérédité,* from Old French *heredite,* inheritance, from Latin *hērēditās,* from *hērēs, hērēd-,* heir. See **ghē-** in Appendix.]

Here•ford[1] (hûr′fərd). A city of northwest Texas in the Panhandle southwest of Amarillo. Population, 15,853.

Here•ford[2] (hûr′fərd, hĕr′ə-fərd) *n.* Any of a breed of beef cattle developed in England and having a reddish coat with white markings. [After *Hereford,* a former county of western England.]

here•in (hîr-ĭn′) *adv.* In or into this.

here•in•af•ter (hîr′ĭn-ăf′tər) *adv.* In a following part of this document, statement, or book.

here•in•be•fore (hîr′ĭn-bĭ-fôr′, -fōr′) *adv.* In a preceding part of this document, statement, or book.

here•in•to (hîr-ĭn′to͞o) *adv.* Into this matter, circumstance, situation, or place.

here•of (hîr-ŭv′, -ŏv′) *adv.* Of this.

here•on (hîr-ŏn′, -ôn′) *adv.* On this; hereupon.

He•re•ro (hə-râr′ō, hĕr′ə-rō′) *n., pl.* **Herero** or **-ros.** **1.** A member of a pastoral people inhabiting Namibia and Botswana. **2.** The Bantu language of this people.

he•re•si•arch (hə-rē′zē-ärk′, hĕr′ĭ-sē-) *n.* One who originates or is the chief proponent of a heresy or heretical movement. [Late Latin *haeresiarcha,* from Late Greek *hairesiarkhēs* : Greek *hairesis,* sect; see HERESY + Greek *-arkhēs,* -arch.]

her•e•sy (hĕr′ĭ-sē) *n., pl.* **-sies.** **1.a.** An opinion or a doctrine at variance with established religious beliefs, especially dissension from or denial of Roman Catholic dogma by a professed believer or baptized church member. **b.** Adherence to such dissenting opinion or doctrine. **2.a.** A controversial or unorthodox opinion or doctrine, as in politics, philosophy, or science. **b.** Adherence to such controversial or unorthodox opinion. [Middle English *heresie,* from Old French, from Late Latin *haeresis,* from Late Greek *hairesis,* from Greek, a choosing, faction, from *hairēisthai,* to choose, middle voice of *hairein,* to take.]

her•e•tic (hĕr′ĭ-tĭk) *n.* A person who holds controversial opinions, especially one who publicly dissents from the officially accepted dogma of the Roman Catholic Church. **—heretic** *adj.* Heretical. [Middle English *heretik,* from Old French *heretique,* from Late Latin *haereticus,* from Greek *hairetikos,* able to choose, factious, from *hairetos,* chosen, from *hairēisthai,* to choose. See HERESY.]

he•ret•i•cal (hə-rĕt′ĭ-kəl) *adj.* **1.** Of or relating to heresy or heretics. **2.** Characterized by, revealing, or approaching departure from established beliefs or standards. **—he•ret′i•cal•ly** *adv.* **—he•ret′i•cal•ness** *n.*

here•to (hîr-to͞o′) *adv.* To this document or matter.

here•to•fore (hîr′tə-fôr′, -fōr′) *adv.* Up to the present time; before this; previously. [Middle English : *here,* here; see HERE + *tofore,* previously (from Old English *tōforan* : *tō,* to; see TO + *foran,* before, from *fore;* see FORE).]

here•un•to (hîr-ŭn′to͞o) *adv.* Hereto.

here•up•on (hîr′ə-pŏn′, -pôn′) *adv.* **1.** Immediately after this. **2.** At or on this.

here•with (hîr-wĭth′, -wĭth′) *adv.* **1.** Along with this. **2.** By this means; hereby.

her•i•ot (hĕr′ē-ət) *n.* A tribute or service rendered to a feudal lord on the death of a tenant. [Middle English, from Old English *heregeatu* : *here,* army; see **koro-** in Appendix + *geatwe,* equipment, arms.]

her•i•ta•ble (hĕr′ĭ-tə-bəl) *adj.* **1.** Capable of being passed from one generation to the next; hereditary. **2.** Capable of inheriting or taking by inheritance. [Middle English, from Old French, from *heriter,* to inherit. See HERITAGE.] **—her′i•ta•bil′i•ty** *n.* **—her′i•ta•bly** *adv.*

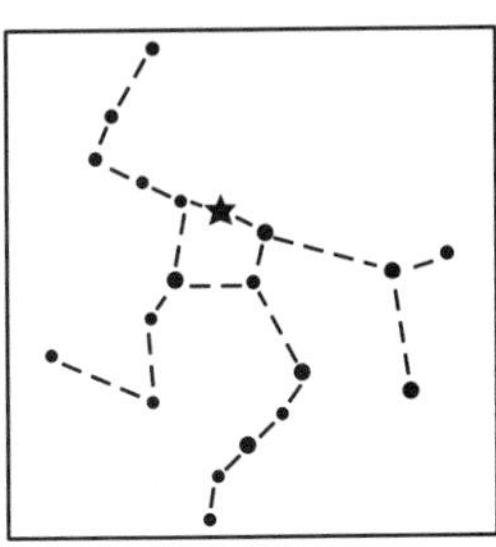

Hercules
Top: With skin of Nemean lion
Bottom: Constellation

ă pat	oi boy
ā pay	ou out
âr care	o͝o took
ä father	o͞o boot
ĕ pet	ŭ cut
ē be	ûr urge
ĭ pit	th thin
ī pie	*th* this
îr pier	hw which
ŏ pot	zh vision
ō toe	ə about, item
ô paw	♦ regionalism

Stress marks: ′ (primary); ′ (secondary), as in **dictionary** (dĭk′shə-nĕr′ē)

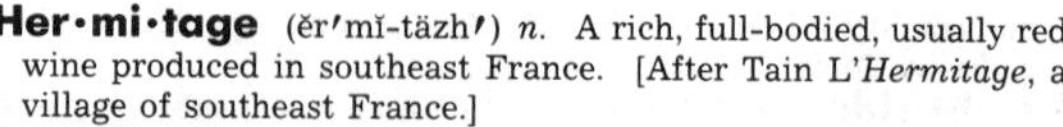

her·i·tage (hĕr′ĭ-tĭj) *n.* **1.** Property that is or can be inherited; an inheritance. **2.** Something that is passed down from preceding generations; a tradition. **3.** The status acquired by a person through birth; a birthright: *a heritage of affluence and social position.* [Middle English, from Old French, from *eritier,* heir, from Medieval Latin *hērēditārius,* from Latin, inherited. See HEREDITARY.]

SYNONYMS: *heritage, inheritance, legacy, tradition.* The central meaning shared by these nouns is "something immaterial, such as a custom, that is passed from one generation to another": *a heritage of moral uprightness; an inheritance of knowledge from the past; a legacy of philosophical thought; the tradition of noblesse oblige.*

Woody Herman

her·i·tor (hĕr′ĭ-tər) *n.* An inheritor. [Alteration of Middle English *heriter,* from Anglo-Norman, from Medieval Latin *hērēditārius.* See HEREDITARY.]

He·riz (hîr′ēz, -ēs) *n.* A strong, finely woven Persian rug that has patterns of flowers, garlands, and trees. [Alteration of *Heris,* a town of Iran.]

herk·y-jerk·y (hûr′kē-jûr′kē) *adj.* Spasmodic, irregular, and unpredictable, as in movement or manner. [Reduplication of JERKY[1].]

herl (hûrl) *n.* **1.** The barb of a feather used in trimming an artificial fly for angling. **2.** A fishing fly made with this type of barb. [Middle English *herle,* a strand or twist of hair.]

her·ma (hûr′mə) also **herm** (hûrm) *n.* A bust, usually one of Hermes mounted on a square stone post. [Latin *hermēs, herma,* from Greek *hermēs,* from *Hermēs,* Hermes.]

Her·man (hûr′mən), **Woodrow Charles.** Known as "Woody." 1913–1987. American jazz musician and bandleader who for 50 years directed a series of bands called the "Thundering Herds."

her·maph·ro·dism (hər-măf′rə-dĭz′əm) *n.* Variant of **hermaphroditism.**

her·maph·ro·dite (hər-măf′rə-dīt′) *n.* **1.** One having the reproductive organs and many of the secondary sex characteristics of both sexes. **2.** *Biology.* An organism, such as an earthworm or a monoclinous plant, having both male and female reproductive organs. **3.** Something that is a combination of disparate or contradictory elements. [Middle English *hermofrodite,* from Medieval Latin *hermofrodītus,* from Latin *hermaphrodītus,* from Greek *hermaphroditos,* Hermaphroditus, hermaphrodite. See HERMAPHRODITUS.] —**her·maph′ro·dit′ic** (-dĭt′ĭk) *adj.* —**her·maph′ro·dit′i·cal·ly** *adv.*

hermaphrodite brig *n. Nautical.* A two-masted vessel with a square-rigged foremast and a schooner-rigged mainmast.

hermaphrodite rig *n. Nautical.* See **jackass rig.**

her·maph·ro·dit·ism (hər-măf′rə-dī-tĭz′əm) also **her·maph·ro·dism** (-rə-dĭz′əm) *n.* The condition of being a hermaphrodite.

Her·maph·ro·di·tus (hər-măf′rə-dī′təs) *n. Greek Mythology.* The son of Hermes and Aphrodite, who became united in one body with the nymph Salmacis. [Greek *Hermaphroditos* : *Hermēs,* Hermes + *Aphroditē,* Aphrodite.]

her·me·neu·tic (hûr′mə-no͞o′tĭk, -nyo͞o′-) also **her·me·neu·ti·cal** (-tĭ-kəl) *adj.* Interpretive; explanatory. [Greek *hermēneutikos,* from *hermēneutēs,* interpreter, from *hermēneuein,* to interpret, from *hermēneus,* interpreter.] —**her′me·neu′ti·cal·ly** *adv.*

her·me·neu·tics (hûr′mə-no͞o′tĭks, -nyo͞o′-) *n. (used with a sing. or pl. verb).* The science and methodology of interpretation, especially of scriptural text. —**her′me·neu′tist** *n.*

Her·mes (hûr′mēz) *n. Greek Mythology.* The god of commerce, invention, cunning, and theft, who also served as messenger, scribe, and herald for the other gods.

Hermes Tris·me·gis·tus (trĭs′mə-jĭs′təs, trĭz′-) *n. Mythology.* The Egyptian god Thoth, the legendary author of works on alchemy, astrology, and magic. [Medieval Latin *Hermēs Trismegistus,* from Greek *Hermēs trismegistos* : *Hermēs,* Hermes + *trismegistos (tris,* thrice; see TRISOCTAHEDRON + *megistos,* greatest; see ALMAGEST).]

her·met·ic (hər-mĕt′ĭk) also **her·met·i·cal** (-ĭ-kəl) *adj.* **1.** Completely sealed, especially against the escape or entry of air. **2.** Impervious to outside interference or influence: *the hermetic confines of an isolated life.* **3.** Often **Hermetic.** *Mythology.* **a.** Of or relating to Hermes Trismegistus or the works ascribed to him. **b.** Having to do with the occult sciences, especially alchemy; magical. [New Latin *hermēticus,* alchemical, from Medieval Latin *Hermēs Trismegistus.* See HERMES TRISMEGISTUS.] —**her·met′i·cal·ly** *adv.*

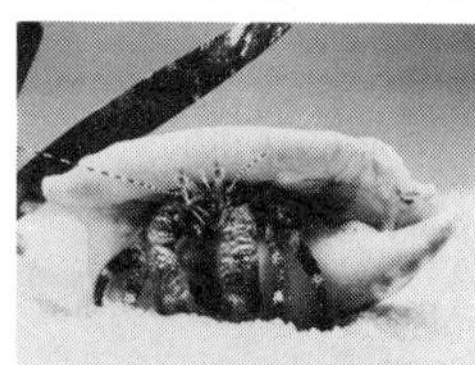

hermit crab

her·mit (hûr′mĭt) *n.* **1.** A person who has withdrawn from society and lives a solitary existence; a recluse. **2.** A spiced cookie made with molasses, raisins, and nuts. [Middle English *heremite,* from Old French, from Medieval Latin *heremīta,* from Late Latin *erēmīta,* from Greek *erēmitēs,* from *erēmia,* desert, from *erēmos,* solitary.] —**her·mit′ic, her·mit′i·cal** *adj.* —**her·mit′i·cal·ly** *adv.*

her·mit·age (hûr′mĭ-tĭj) *n.* **1. a.** The habitation of a hermit or group of hermits. **b.** A monastery or an abbey. **2.** A place where one can live in seclusion; a retreat. **3.** The condition or way of life of a hermit. [Middle English, from Old French *hermitage,* from *heremite,* hermit. See HERMIT.]

Her·mi·tage (ĕr′mĭ-täzh′) *n.* A rich, full-bodied, usually red wine produced in southeast France. [After Tain L'*Hermitage,* a village of southeast France.]

hermit crab *n.* Any of various crabs belonging to a group within the order Decapoda that protect their soft, unarmored abdomens by occupying and carrying about the empty shells of snails or other univalve mollusks.

hermit thrush *n.* A North American bird *(Catharus guttatus)* having brownish plumage, a spotted breast, a reddish tail, and a distinctive melodious song.

Her·mon (hûr′mən), **Mount.** The highest peak, 2,815.8 m (9,232 ft), of the Anti-Lebanon Range on the Syria-Lebanon border. It was sacred to the worshipers of Baal and is considered the traditional site of Jesus's transfiguration.

Her·mo·sa Beach (hər-mō′sə). A city of southern California on the Pacific Ocean south-southwest of Los Angeles. It is a resort and residential suburb. Population, 18,070.

Her·mo·sil·lo (ĕr′-mô-sē′ô). A city of northwest Mexico near the Gulf of California west of Chihuahua. Established c. 1700, it is a trade center. Population, 297,175.

hern (hûrn) *n.* A heron. [Variant of HERON.]

Her·ne (hĕr′nə). A city of west-central Germany in the Ruhr district east-northeast of Essen. It is an industrial center in a mining area. Population, 173,226.

her·ni·a (hûr′nē-ə) *n., pl.* **-ni·as** or **-ni·ae** (-nē-ē′). The protrusion of an organ or other bodily structure through the wall that normally contains it; a rupture. [Middle English, from Latin. See **ghere-** in Appendix.] —**her′ni·al** *adj.*

her·ni·ate (hûr′nē-āt′) *intr.v.* **-at·ed, -at·ing, -ates.** To form a hernia. —**her′ni·a′tion** *n.*

♦**he·ro** (hîr′ō) *n., pl.* **-roes. 1.** In mythology and legend, a man, often of divine ancestry, who is endowed with great courage and strength, celebrated for his bold exploits, and favored by the gods. **2.** A person noted for feats of courage or nobility of purpose, especially one who has risked or sacrificed his or her life: *soldiers and nurses who were heroes in an unpopular war.* **3.** A person noted for special achievement in a particular field: *the heroes of medicine.* See Synonyms at **celebrity. 4.** The principal male character in a novel, poem, or dramatic presentation. See Usage Note at **heroine. 5.** See **submarine** (sense 2). See Regional Note at **submarine.** [Probably alteration of Latin *hērōs,* from Greek. See **ser-**[1] in Appendix.]

He·ro[1] (hîr′ō) *n. Greek Mythology.* A priestess of Aphrodite beloved by Leander.

He·ro[2] (hē′rō, hîr′ō) or **He·ron** (hē′rŏn′). First century A.D. Alexandrian scientist who devised a formula for determining the area of a triangle.

Her·od (hĕr′əd). Known as "the Great." 73?–4 B.C. King of Judea (40–4) who, according to the New Testament, attempted to kill the infant Jesus by ordering the death of all children under the age of two in Bethlehem.

Herod An·ti·pas (ăn′tĭ-păs′, -pəs). Died c. A.D. 40. Ruler of Judea and tetrarch in Galilee (4 B.C. – A.D. 40). His marriage to his niece Herodias was denounced by John the Baptist, who was beheaded at the urging of Salome. It was to Herod Antipas that Pontius Pilate sent Jesus for judgment.

He·ro·di·as (hĭ-rō′dē-əs). Died c. A.D. 39. The niece and second wife of Herod Antipas and the mother of Salome.

He·rod·o·tus (hĭ-rŏd′ə-təs). Known as "the Father of History." Fifth century B.C. Greek historian whose writings, chiefly concerning the Persian Wars, are the earliest known examples of narrative history.

he·ro·ic (hĭ-rō′ĭk) also **he·ro·i·cal** (-ĭ-kəl) *adj.* **1.** Of, relating to, or resembling the heroes of literature, legend, or myth. **2.** Having, displaying, or characteristic of the qualities appropriate to a hero; courageous: *heroic deeds.* **3. a.** Impressive in size or scope; grand: *heroic undertakings.* **b.** Of a size or scale that is larger than life: *heroic sculpture.* —**heroic** *n.* **1.** A line of heroic verse. **2. heroics.** Melodramatic behavior or language: *"We trust the House . . . will come up with answers without all the political heroics"* (Atlanta Constitution). —**he·ro′i·cal·ly** *adv.* —**he·ro′i·cal·ness** *n.*

heroic couplet *n.* A verse unit consisting of two rhymed lines in iambic pentameter.

heroic drama *n.* Restoration tragedy or tragicomedy composed in heroic couplets and generally characterized by exotic settings, bombastic rhetoric, and exaggerated characterization.

heroic meter *n.* See **heroic verse.**

heroic quatrain *n.* See **elegiac stanza.**

heroic stanza *n.* A four-line stanza consisting of two heroic couplets.

heroic verse *n.* One of several verse forms traditionally used in epic and dramatic poetry, especially: **a.** The dactylic hexameter in Greek and Latin. **b.** The iambic pentameter in English. **c.** The alexandrine in French. Also called *heroic meter.*

her·o·in (hĕr′ō-ĭn) *n.* A white, odorless, bitter crystalline compound, $C_{17}H_{17}NO(C_2H_3O_2)_2$, that is derived from morphine and is a highly addictive narcotic. Also called *diacetylmorphine.* [German, originally a trademark.]

her·o·ine (hĕr′ō-ĭn) *n.* **1.** A woman noted for courage and daring action. **2.** A woman noted for special achievement in a particular field. **3.** The principal female character in a novel, poem, or dramatic presentation. [Latin *hērōīnē, hērōīna,* from Greek *hērōinē,* feminine of *hērōs,* hero. See HERO.]

USAGE NOTE: The word *hero* should no longer be regarded as restricted to men in the sense "a person noted for courageous action," though *heroine* is always restricted to women. The distinction between *heroine* and *hero* is still useful, however, in referring to the principal character of a fictional work, inasmuch as the virtues and qualities that become a traditional literary heroine like Elizabeth Bennet or Isabel Archer are generally quite different from those that become a traditional literary hero like Tom Jones or Huckleberry Finn.

her·o·in·ism (hĕr′ō-ĭ-nĭz′əm) *n.* Addiction to heroin.

her·o·ism (hĕr′ō-ĭz′əm) *n.* **1.** Heroic conduct or behavior. **2.** Heroic characteristics or qualities; courage.

her·on (hĕr′ən) *n.* Any of various wading birds of the family Ardeidae, having a long neck, long legs, a long pointed bill, and usually white, gray, or bluish-gray plumage. [Middle English, from Old French, of Germanic origin.]

He·ron (hē′rŏn′). See **Hero**[2].

her·on·ry (hĕr′ən-rē) *n., pl.* **-ries.** A place where herons nest and breed.

hero worship *n.* Intense or excessive admiration for a hero or a person regarded as a hero.

he·ro-wor·ship (hîr′ō-wûr′shĭp) *tr.v.* **-shiped, -ship·ing, -ships** or **-shipped, -ship·ping, -ships. 1.** To revere as an ideal. **2.** To adulate. **—he′ro-wor′ship·er** *n.*

her·pes (hûr′pēz) *n.* Any of several viral diseases causing the eruption of small blisterlike vesicles on the skin or mucous membranes, especially herpes simplex or herpes zoster. [Middle English, from Latin *herpēs,* from Greek, from *herpein,* to creep.] **—her·pet′ic** (hər-pĕt′ĭk) *adj.*

herpes la·bi·a·lis (lā′bē-ā′lĭs) *n.* See **cold sore.** [New Latin *herpēs labiālis* : Latin *herpēs,* herpes + Medieval Latin *labiālis,* of the lip.]

herpes sim·plex (sĭm′plĕks′) *n.* **1.** A recurrent viral disease caused by the herpes simplex virus, type one, and marked by the eruption of fluid-containing vesicles on the mouth, lips, or face. **2.** A recurrent viral disease caused by the herpes simplex virus, type two, and marked by the eruption of fluid-containing vesicles on the genitals. [New Latin *herpēs simplex* : Latin *herpēs,* herpes + Latin *simplex,* simple.]

her·pes·vi·rus (hûr′pēz-vī′rəs) *n., pl.* **-rus·es.** Any of a group of DNA-containing animal viruses that form characteristic inclusion bodies within the nuclei of host cells and cause diseases such as chickenpox, infectious mononucleosis, herpes simplex, and shingles.

herpes zos·ter (zŏs′tər, zō′stər) *n.* See **shingles.** [New Latin *herpēs zōstēr* : Latin *herpēs,* herpes + Greek *zōstēr,* girdle.]

her·pe·tol·o·gy (hûr′pĭ-tŏl′ə-jē) *n.* The branch of zoology that deals with reptiles and amphibians. [Greek *herpeton,* reptile (from *herpein,* to creep) + -LOGY.] **—her′pe·to·log′ic** (-tə-lŏj′ĭk), **her′pe·to·log′i·cal** *adj.* **—her′pe·to·log′i·cal·ly** *adv.* **—her′pe·tol′o·gist** *n.*

Herr (hĕr) *n., pl.* **Her·ren** (hĕr′ən). *Abbr.* **Hr.** Used as a courtesy title in a German-speaking area, prefixed to the surname or professional title of a man. [German, from Middle High German *hērre,* from Old High German *hērro,* lord, master, alteration of *hēriro,* older, more venerable, comparative of *hēr,* proud, holy, splendid, noble.]

Her·ren·volk (hĕr′ən-fōk′, -fôlk′) *n.* A master race. [German : *Herren,* genitive pl. of *Herr,* master; see HERR + *Volk,* people, nation; see VOLKSLIED.]

Her·rick (hĕr′ĭk), **Robert.** 1591–1674. English lyric poet whose sensuous, simple works, such as "Delight in Disorder" (1648), are marked by his affinity for Latin verse and the influence of Ben Jonson. He is considered the greatest Cavalier poet.

her·ring (hĕr′ĭng) *n., pl.* **herring** or **-rings.** Any of various fishes of the family Clupeidae, especially a commercially important food fish *(Clupea harengus)* of Atlantic and Pacific waters. [Middle English *hering,* from Old English *hǣring.*]

her·ring·bone (hĕr′ĭng-bōn′) *n.* **1.a.** A pattern consisting of rows of short, slanted parallel lines with the direction of the slant alternating row by row and used in masonry, parquetry, embroidery, and weaving. **b.** A twilled fabric woven in this pattern. **2.** *Sports.* A method of climbing a ski slope with the tips of the skis pointed outward. **—herringbone** *v.* **-boned, -bon·ing, -bones.** —*tr.* To arrange or decorate with a herringbone pattern. —*intr.* **1.** To produce a herringbone pattern. **2.** To ascend a ski slope with the ski tips pointed outward.

herring gull *n.* A common seagull *(Larus argentatus)* of the Northern Hemisphere having gray and white plumage with black wing tips.

hers (hûrz) *pron. (used with a sing. or pl. verb).* Used to indicate the one or ones belonging to her: *If you can't find your hat, take hers.* [Middle English *hires, hirs* : *hire,* her; see HER + *-es,* possessive suff.; see –'S[1].]

Her·schel (hûr′shəl). Family of British astronomers, including Sir **William Herschel** (1738–1822), who discovered Uranus (1781), was astronomer to George III, and cataloged more than 800 double stars and 2,500 nebulae. His sister **Caroline Herschel** (1750–1848) assisted in his work and published a star catalog. His son Sir **John Frederick William Herschel** (1792–1871) augmented William's work with the discovery of 525 nebulae and conducted notable research on light, photography, and astrophysics.

her·self (hûr-sĕlf′) *pron.* **1.** That one identical with her: **a.** Used reflexively as the direct or indirect object of a verb or as the object of a preposition: *She bought herself a new car. She sculpted a likeness of herself.* **b.** Used for emphasis: *She herself was certain of the facts.* **c.** Used in an absolute construction: *In office herself, she helped him get a job.* **2.** Her normal or healthy condition or state: *She's feeling herself again.* [Middle English *hire self,* from Old English *hire selfre,* dative of *hēo self* : *hēo,* she; see SHE + *self,* self; see SELF.]

her·sto·ry (hûr′stə-rē) *n., pl.* **-sto·ries. 1.** The experiences and accomplishments of women, especially as seen in a historical context: *"the rest is the stuff of an unlikely . . . herstory"* (Washington Post). **2.** The composite of experiences making up a woman's life: *"the truncated herstory of three black female students"* (Los Angeles Times).

hertz (hûrts) *n., pl.* **hertz.** *Abbr.* **Hz** A unit of frequency equal to one cycle per second. See table at **measurement.** [After Heinrich Rudolf HERTZ.]

Hertz (hûrts, hĕrts), **Gustav Ludwig.** 1887–1975. German physicist. He shared a 1925 Nobel Prize for discovering the laws that describe the impact of electrons upon atoms.

Hertz, Heinrich Rudolf. 1857–1894. German physicist who was the first to produce radio waves artificially.

Hertz·i·an wave (hûrt′sē-ən, hĕrt′-) *n.* An electromagnetic wave, usually of radio frequency, produced by the oscillation of electricity in a conductor. [After Heinrich Rudolf HERTZ.]

Hertz·sprung-Rus·sell diagram (hĕrts′sprŭng-rŭs′əl, -sprŏŏng-) *n.* A graph of the absolute magnitude of stars plotted against their surface temperature or color, used in the study of stellar evolution. [After Ejnar *Hertzsprung* (1873–1967), Danish astronomer, and Henry Norris RUSSELL.]

Herz·berg (hûrts′bûrg′), **Gerhard.** Born 1904. German-born Canadian physicist. He won a 1971 Nobel Prize for chemistry for his contributions to the understanding of the electronic structure and geometry of molecules.

Her·ze·go·vi·na (hĕrt′sə-gō-vē′nə, hûrt′-). A region of west-central Yugoslavia. Largely independent after the 10th century, it was conquered by Bosnia in the 14th century and has been closely allied with that region ever since. Herzegovina became part of the Kingdom of the Serbs, Croats, and Slovenes (later Yugoslavia) in 1918. **—Her′ze·go·vi′ni·an** *adj. n.*

Her·zl (hĕrt′səl), **Theodor.** 1860–1904. Hungarian-born Austrian who founded the Zionist World Congress in 1897.

he's (hēz). **1.** He is: *He's going to school today.* **2.** He has: *He's already been to the museum.*

Hesh·van also **Hesh·wan** (KHĕsh′vən, -vän) *n.* The second month of the year in the Jewish calendar. See table at **calendar.** [Hebrew *ḥešwān,* short for *marḥešwān,* October/November, from Akkadian *araḫsamnu.*]

He·si·od (hē′sē-əd, hĕs′ē-). fl. eighth century B.C. Greek poet. The major epics ascribed to him are *Works and Days,* a valuable account of ancient rural life, and *Theogony,* a description of the gods and the beginning of the world.

hes·i·tan·cy (hĕz′ĭ-tən-sē) *n., pl.* **-cies. 1.** The state or quality of being hesitant. **2.** An instance of hesitating.

hes·i·tant (hĕz′ĭ-tənt) *adj.* Inclined or tending to hesitate. **—hes′i·tant·ly** *adv.*

hes·i·tate (hĕz′ĭ-tāt′) *intr.v.* **-tat·ed, -tat·ing, -tates. 1.a.** To be slow to act, speak, or decide. **b.** To pause in uncertainty; waver. **2.** To be reluctant. **3.** To speak haltingly; falter. [Latin *haesitāre, haesitāt-,* to hesitate, frequentative of *haerēre,* to hold fast.] **—hes′i·tat′er** *n.* **—hes′i·tat′ing·ly** *adv.*

SYNONYMS: *hesitate, vacillate, waver, falter.* These verbs mean to be uncertain, irresolute, or indecisive. To *hesitate* is to hold back or pause because of doubt or uncertainty, as about what to do or say: *"A President either is constantly on top of events or, if he hesitates, events will soon be on top of him"* (Harry S. Truman). *Vacillate* implies going back and forth between alternative, usually conflicting courses without making a final decision: *She vacillated so long about attending the concert that when she decided to go, the tickets were sold out. Waver* suggests a delay in taking action once a choice has been made, as if the decision were being reconsidered: *After much wavering he finally gave his permission.* To *falter* is to be unsteady in resolution or action, as from fear or loss of courage: *The performer faltered in the middle of the show. The marine never faltered in his duty.*

hes·i·ta·tion (hĕz′ĭ-tā′shən) *n.* **1.** The act or an instance of hesitating. **2.** The state of being hesitant. **3.** A pause or faltering in speech.

Hes·pe·ri·an (hĕ-spîr′ē-ən) *adj.* Of or relating to the west. [From Latin *Hesperius,* from Greek *hesperios,* from *hesperos,* evening. See **wes-pero-** in Appendix.]

Hes·per·i·des (hĕ-spĕr′ĭ-dēz′) *pl.n. Greek Mythology.* **1.** The nymphs who together with a dragon watch over a garden in which golden apples grow. **2.** *(used with a sing. verb).* A garden, situated at the western end of the earth, in which golden apples grow. [Latin, from Greek, pl. of *hesperis,* feminine of *hesperios,* of the evening, western.] **—Hes′per·id′i·an, Hes′per·id′e·an** (hĕs′pə-rĭd′ē-ən) *adj.*

heron
Great egret
Casmerodius albus

ă pat	oi boy
ā pay	ou out
âr care	ŏŏ took
ä father	ōō boot
ĕ pet	ŭ cut
ē be	ûr urge
ĭ pit	th thin
ī pie	*th* this
îr pier	hw which
ŏ pot	zh vision
ō toe	ə about, item
ô paw	♦ regionalism

Stress marks: **′** (primary); ′ (secondary), as in **dictionary** (dĭk′shə-nĕr′ē)

hes·per·id·i·a (hĕs′pə-rĭd′ē-ə) *n.* Plural of **hesperidium.**

hes·per·i·din (hĕ-spĕr′ĭ-dĭn) *n.* A white or colorless crystalline compound, $C_{28}H_{34}O_{15}$, occurring in citrus fruit. [HESPERID(IUM) + –IN.]

hes·per·id·i·um (hĕs′pə-rĭd′ē-əm) *n., pl.* **-i·a** (-ē-ə). A berry having a thickened, leathery rind and juicy pulp divided into segments, as an orange or other citrus fruit. [New Latin, from HESPERIDES, land where golden apples grow.]

Hes·per·us (hĕs′pər-əs) *n.* The planet Venus in its appearance as the evening star. [Middle English, from Latin, from Greek *hesperos.* See HESPERIAN.]

Hess (hĕs), **Victor Franz.** 1883–1964. Austrian-born American physicist. He shared a 1936 Nobel Prize for his discovery of cosmic radiation.

heterocercal
Shark with heterocercal tail

Hess, (Walter Richard) Rudolf. 1894–1987. German Nazi leader. When Hitler became chancellor (1933), he named Hess as deputy führer and later (1939) as second in succession to the Nazi leadership. In May 1941 Hess was captured in Scotland, where he had flown apparently in a bid to start peace talks with Britain.

Hess, Walter Rudolf. 1881–1973. Swiss physiologist. He shared a 1949 Nobel Prize for his research on the brain's control of the body.

Hesse (hĕs). A region and former grand duchy of west-central Germany. In medieval times the territory was expanded west to the Rhine River and south to the Main River, but after 1567 it was divided into four separate regions ruled by various branches of the Hesse family.

Hes·se (hĕs′ə), **Hermann.** 1877–1962. German-born Swiss writer whose works, including *Siddhartha* (1922) and *Steppenwolf* (1927), concern the duality of human existence and the alienation of the artist. He won the 1946 Nobel Prize for literature.

Hes·sian (hĕsh′ən) *adj.* Of or relating to Hesse or its inhabitants. **—Hessian** *n.* **1.** A native or inhabitant of Hesse. **2.** A German mercenary in the British army in America during the Revolutionary War. **3.** A mercenary soldier.

Hessian boot *n.* A man's high, tasseled boot introduced into England by Hessians in the 19th century.

Hessian fly *n.* A small fly *(Mayetiola destructor)* having larvae that infest and destroy wheat and other grain plants.

hes·so·nite (hĕs′ə-nīt′) *n.* Variant of **essonite.**

hest (hĕst) *n. Archaic.* Command; behest. [Middle English, alteration of *hes,* from Old English *hǣs.* See **kei-**[2] in Appendix.]

Hes·ti·a (hĕs′tē-ə) *n. Greek Mythology.* The goddess of the hearth, daughter of Cronus and Rhea.

he·tae·ra (hĭ-tîr′ə) also **he·tai·ra** (-tīr′ə) *n., pl.* **-tae·rae** (-tîr′ē) or **-tae·ras** also **-tai·rai** (-tīr′ī′) or **-tai·ras.** An ancient Greek courtesan or concubine, especially one of a special class of cultivated female companions. [Greek *hetaira,* from *hetairos,* companion. See **s(w)e-** in Appendix.] **—he·tae′ric** *adj.*

heter– *pref.* Variant of **hetero–.**

het·er·o (hĕt′ə-rō′) *n., pl.* **-os.** *Informal.* A heterosexual person. **—het′er·o** *adj.*

hetero– or **heter–** *pref.* **1.** Other; different: *heterochromatic.* **2.** Containing different kinds of atoms: *heterocyclic.* [Greek, from *heteros,* other. See **sem-**[1] in Appendix.]

het·er·o·at·om (hĕt′ə-rō-ăt′əm) *n.* An atom other than carbon in the structure of a heterocyclic compound.

het·er·o·car·py (hĕt′ə-rō-kär′pē) *n.* Production of more than one kind of fruit. **—het′er·o·car′pous** (-kär′pəs) *adj.*

het·er·o·cer·cal (hĕt′ə-rō-sûr′kəl) *adj.* Relating to, having, or being a tail fin in which the upper lobe is larger than the lower and the vertebral column extends into the upper lobe, as in sharks. [HETERO– + Greek *kerkos,* tail + –AL[1].]

het·er·o·chro·mat·ic (hĕt′ə-rō-krō-măt′ĭk) *adj.* **1.** Of or characterized by different colors; varicolored. **2.** Consisting of different wavelengths or frequencies. **3.** Of or relating to heterochromatin. **—het′er·o·chro′ma·tism** (-krō′mə-tĭz′əm) *n.*

het·er·o·chro·ma·tin (hĕt′ə-rō-krō′mə-tĭn) *n.* Tightly coiled chromosomal material that stains deeply during interphase and is believed to be genetically inactive.

het·er·o·chro·mo·some (hĕt′ə-rō-krō′mə-sōm′) *n.* **1.** A chromosome composed primarily of heterochromatin. **2.** A sex chromosome.

het·er·o·cy·clic (hĕt′ə-rō-sī′klĭk, -sĭk′lĭk) *adj.* Containing more than one kind of atom joined in a ring. **—het′er·o·cy′cle** (-sī′kəl) *n.* **—het′er·o·cy′clic** *n.*

het·er·o·cyst (hĕt′ər-ə-sĭst′) *n.* A large, thick-walled, transparent cell that occurs at intervals along the filaments of certain cyanobacteria.

het·er·o·dox (hĕt′ər-ə-dŏks′) *adj.* **1.** Not in agreement with accepted beliefs, especially in church doctrine or dogma. **2.** Holding unorthodox opinions. [Greek *heterodoxos* : *hetero-,* hetero- + *doxa,* opinion (from *dokein,* to think; see **dek-** in Appendix).]

het·er·o·dox·y (hĕt′ər-ə-dŏk′sē) *n., pl.* **-ies. 1.** The condition or quality of being heterodox. **2.** A heterodox opinion or doctrine.

het·er·o·dyne (hĕt′ər-ə-dīn′) *adj.* Having alternating currents of two different frequencies that are combined to produce two new frequencies, the sum and difference of the original frequencies, either of which may be used in radio or television receivers by proper tuning or filtering. **—heterodyne** *tr.v.* **-dyned, -dyn·ing, -dynes.** To combine (a radio-frequency wave) with a locally generated wave of different frequency in order to produce a new frequency equal to the sum or difference of the two. [HETERO– + *-dyne,* power, frequency (from Greek *dunamis,* power; see DYNE).]

het·er·oe·cious (hĕt′ə-rē′shəs) *adj.* Spending different stages of a life cycle on different, usually unrelated hosts. Used of parasites such as rust fungi and tapeworms. [HETERO– + Greek *oikia,* house; see **weik-**[1] in Appendix + –OUS.] **—het′er·oe′cism** (-sĭz′əm) *n.*

het·er·o·gam·ete (hĕt′ə-rō-găm′ēt′, -gə-mēt′) *n.* Either of two conjugating gametes that differ in structure or behavior, such as the small, motile male spermatozoon and the larger, nonmotile female ovum. Also called *anisogamete.*

het·er·o·ga·met·ic (hĕt′ə-rō-gə-mĕt′ĭk) *adj.* **1.** Producing dissimilar gametes, such as those of human males, who produce two types of spermatozoa, one bearing the X-chromosome and the other bearing the Y-chromosome. **2.** Of or relating to heterogametes.

het·er·og·a·mous (hĕt′ə-rŏg′ə-məs) *adj.* **1.** *Biology.* **a.** Characterized by the fusion of unlike gametes in the reproductive process. **b.** Characterized by reproduction involving the alternation of sexual and parthenogenetic generations. **2.** *Botany.* Bearing male and female flowers.

het·er·og·a·my (hĕt′ə-rŏg′ə-mē) *n.* **1.** Alternation of sexual and parthenogenic generations, as in some aphids. **2.** The state or condition in which conjugating gametes are dissimilar in structure and size as well as in function. **—het′er·o·gam′ic** (-rō-găm′ĭk) *adj.*

het·er·o·ge·ne·i·ty (hĕt′ə-rō′jə-nē′ĭ-tē) *n.* The quality or state of being heterogeneous.

het·er·o·ge·ne·ous (hĕt′ər-ə-jē′nē-əs, -jēn′yəs) *adj.* **1.** Also **het·er·og·e·nous** (hĕt′ə-rŏj′ə-nəs). Consisting of dissimilar elements or parts; not homogeneous. See Synonyms at **miscellaneous. 2.** Completely different; incongruous. [From Medieval Latin *heterogeneus,* from Greek *heterogenēs* : *hetero-,* hetero- + *genos,* kind, race; see **gene-** in Appendix.] **—het′er·o·ge′ne·ous·ly** *adv.* **—het′er·o·ge′ne·ous·ness** *n.*

het·er·og·e·nous[1] (hĕt′ə-rŏj′ə-nəs) also **het·er·o·gen·ic** (-rō-jĕn′ĭk) *adj.* Not arising within the body; derived from another individual or species: *a heterogenous bone transplant.* **—het′er·og′e·ny** *n.*

het·er·og·e·nous[2] (hĕt′ə-rŏj′ə-nəs) *adj.* Variant of **heterogeneous** (sense 1).

het·er·og·o·nous (hĕt′ə-rŏg′ə-nəs) *adj.* Characterized by the alternation of sexual and parthenogenic generations. [HETERO– + –GON(Y) + –OUS.] **—het′er·og′o·ny** *n.*

het·er·o·graft (hĕt′ə-rō-grăft′) *n.* A type of tissue graft in which the donor and recipient are of different species. Also called *xenograft.*

het·er·og·y·nous (hĕt′ə-rŏj′ə-nəs) *adj.* Having two types of females, one able to reproduce sexually, the other infertile, as in ants.

het·er·o·kar·y·on (hĕt′ər-ə-kăr′ē-ŏn′, -ən) *n.* A cell having two or more genetically different nuclei. [HETERO– + KARY(O)–.] **—het′er·o·kar′y·ot′ic** (-ŏt′ĭk) *adj.*

het·er·o·lec·i·thal (hĕt′ə-rō-lĕs′ə-thəl) *adj. Embryology.* Having the yolk unevenly distributed throughout the egg. [HETERO– + Greek *lekithos,* egg yolk + –AL[1].]

het·er·ol·o·gous (hĕt′ə-rŏl′ə-gəs) *adj.* **1.** Derived from a different species: *a heterologous graft.* **2.** Of or relating to cytologic or histological elements not normally occurring in a designated part of the body. **3.** Immunologically related but not identical. Used of certain cells and antiserums. [HETERO– + Greek *logos,* word, relation; see –LOGY + –OUS.] **—het′er·ol′o·gous·ly** *adv.*

het·er·ol·o·gy (hĕt′ə-rŏl′ə-jē) *n.* Lack of correspondence between bodily parts, as in structure, arrangement, or development, arising from differences in origin.

het·er·ol·y·sis (hĕt′ə-rŏl′ĭ-sĭs, -ə-rō-lī′sĭs) *n., pl.* **-ses** (-sēz′). **1.** *Biology.* Dissolution of cells or protein components in one species by the action of lysins or enzymes from another. **2.** *Chemistry.* An organic reaction in which the breaking of bonds leads to the formation of ion pairs. **—het′er·o·lyt′ic** (-ə-rō-lĭt′ĭk) *adj.*

het·er·om·er·ous (hĕt′ə-rŏm′ər-əs) *adj.* Having unequal or differing parts within the same structure or similar structures.

het·er·o·mor·phic (hĕt′ə-rō-môr′fĭk) *adj.* **1.** Having different forms at different periods of the life cycle, as in stages of insect metamorphosis. **2.** Differing from the standard form in size or structure: *heteromorphic chromosome pairs.* **—het′er·o·mor′phism** *n.*

het·er·on·o·mous (hĕt′ə-rŏn′ə-məs) *adj.* **1.** Subject to external or foreign laws or domination; not autonomous. **2.** *Biology.* Differing in development or manner of specialization, as the dissimilar segments of certain arthropods. [HETERO– + Greek *nomos,* law; see –NOMY + –OUS.] **—het′er·on′o·mous·ly** *adv.*

het·er·o·nym (hĕt′ər-ə-nĭm′) *n.* One of two or more words that have identical spellings but different meanings and pronunciations, such as *row* (a series of objects arranged in a line), pronounced (rō), and *row* (a fight), pronounced (rou). [Back-formation from HETERONYMOUS.]

het·er·on·y·mous (hĕt′ə-rŏn′ə-məs) *adj.* **1.** Being, relating to, or of the nature of a heteronym. **2.** Being different names or terms but having correspondence or interrelationship, as *mother* and *daughter.* [From Late Greek *heterōnumos,* from Greek, with a different denominator : Greek *hetero-,* hetero- + Greek *onoma,* name; see **nō-men-** in Appendix.]

Het•er•o•ou•si•an (hĕt′ə-rō-o͞o′sē-ən, -ou′sē-ən) also **Het•er•ou•si•an** (hĕt′ə-ro͞o′-, -rou′-) *n.* A Christian who believes that the substance and nature of God the Father and God the Son are different; an Arian. [From Greek *heteroousios,* differing in substance : *hetero-,* hetero- + *ousia,* substance, nature; see HOMOIOUSIAN.] **—Het′er•o•ou′si•an, Het′er•ou′si•an** *adj.*

het•er•oph•o•ny (hĕt′ə-rŏf′ə-nē) *n. Music.* The simultaneous playing or singing of a single melody by two or more different instruments or singers. **—het′er•o•phon′ic** (-ər-ə-fŏn′ĭk) *adj.*

het•er•o•phyl•lous (hĕt′ə-rō-fĭl′əs) *adj.* Having dissimilar leaves on one plant. **—het′er•o•phyl′ly** *n.*

het•er•o•phyte (hĕt′ər-ə-fīt′) *n.* A plant, such as a parasite or saprophyte, that obtains its nourishment from other living or dead organisms. **—het′er•o•phyt′ic** (-fĭt′ĭk) *adj.*

het•er•o•plas•ty (hĕt′ər-ə-plăs′tē) *n., pl.* **-ties.** The surgical grafting of tissue obtained from one individual or species to another. **—het′er•o•plas′tic** *adj.*

het•er•o•ploid (hĕt′ər-ə-ploid′) *adj.* Having a chromosome number that is not a whole-number multiple of the haploid chromosome number for that species. **—het′er•o•ploid′** *n.* **—het′er•o•ploi′dy** *n.*

het•er•op•ter•ous (hĕt′ə-rŏp′tər-əs) *adj.* Of or belonging to the hemopterous insect suborder Heteroptera, which includes the true bugs, characterized by forewings and hind wings that differ from one another.

het•er•o•sex•ism (hĕt′ə-rō-sĕk′sĭz′əm) *n.* Discrimination or prejudice against gay or homosexual people by heterosexual people.

het•er•o•sex•u•al (hĕt′ə-rō-sĕk′sho͞o-əl) *adj.* **1.** Sexually oriented to persons of the opposite sex. **2.** Of or relating to different sexes. **—heterosexual** *n.* A heterosexual person. **—het′er•o•sex′u•al•ly** *adv.*

het•er•o•sex•u•al•i•ty (hĕt′ə-rō-sĕk′sho͞o-ăl′ĭ-tē) *n.* **1.** Sexual orientation to persons of the opposite sex. **2.** Sexual activity with another of the opposite sex.

het•er•o•sis (hĕt′ə-rō′sĭs) *n.* See **hybrid vigor.** [Late Greek *heterōsis,* alteration, alteration of Greek *heteroiōsis,* from *heteroioun,* to alter, from *heteroios,* different in kind, from *heteros,* other. See HETERO-.] **—het′er•ot′ic** (-rŏt′ĭk) *adj.*

het•er•o•spo•rous (hĕt′ər-ə-spôr′əs, -spōr′-, hĕt′ə-rŏs′pər-əs) *adj.* Producing two types of spores differing in size and sex. **—het′er•o•spo′ry** *n.*

het•er•o•styled (hĕt′ər-ə-stīld′) *adj. Botany.* Having flowers with styles of differing length, as the primrose. **—het′er•o•sty′lous** *adj.* **—het′er•o•sty′ly** *n.*

het•er•o•tax•is (hĕt′ə-rō-tăk′sĭs) also **het•er•o•tax•y** (hĕt′ər-ə-tăk′sē) or **het•er•o•tax•i•a** (hĕt′ə-rō-tăk′sē-ə) *n., pl.* **-tax•es** also **-tax•ies** or **-tax•i•as.** Abnormal structural arrangement, as of body parts. **—het′er•o•tac′tic** (-tăk′tĭk), **het′er•o•tac′tous** (-tăk′təs) *adj.*

het•er•o•thal•lic (hĕt′ə-rō-thăl′ĭk) *adj.* Producing male and female gametangia in different structures or plants, as in some algae and fungi. **—het′er•o•thal′lism** *n.*

het•er•o•to•pi•a (hĕt′ər-ə-tō′pē-ə) also **het•er•ot•o•py** (hĕt′ə-rŏt′ə-pē) *n.* Displacement of an organ or other body part to an abnormal location. **—het′er•o•top′ic** (-tŏp′ĭk) *adj.*

het•er•o•troph (hĕt′ər-ə-trŏf′, -trōf′) *n.* An organism that cannot synthesize its own food and is dependent on complex organic substances for nutrition. [HETERO- + Greek *trophos,* feeder; see -TROPHY.] **—het′er•o•tro′phic** *adj.* **—het′er•o•tro′phi•cal•ly** *adv.* **—het′er•ot′ro•phy** (-ə-rŏt′rə-fē) *n.*

het•er•o•typ•ic (hĕt′ə-rō-tĭp′ĭk) also **het•er•o•typ•i•cal** (-ĭ-kəl) *adj.* **1.** *Biology.* Of, relating to, or being the reduction division of meiosis. **2.** Of a different type or form.

het•er•o•zy•go•sis (hĕt′ə-rō-zī-gō′sĭs) *n.* **1.** The formation of a zygote by the union of genetically different gametes. **2.** The condition of being a heterozygote.

het•er•o•zy•gote (hĕt′ə-rō-zī′gōt′) *n.* An organism that has different alleles at a particular gene locus on homologous chromosomes.

het•er•o•zy•gous (hĕt′ər-ə-zī′gəs) *adj.* **1.** Having different alleles at one or more corresponding chromosomal loci. **2.** Of or relating to a heterozygote.

heth (KHĕt, KHĕs) *n.* The eighth letter of the Hebrew alphabet. See table at **alphabet.** [Hebrew *ḥēt.*]

het•man (hĕt′mən) *n., pl.* **-mans.** See **ataman.** [Ukrainian *het′man,* from Polish *hetman,* from German dialectal *hötmann, hetmann,* captain; akin to German *Hauptmann,* from Middle High German *houbetman* : Old High German *houbit,* head; see **kaput-** in Appendix + Old High German *man,* man; see FUGLEMAN.]

heu•land•ite (hyo͞o′lən-dīt′) *n.* A white, red, or yellow zeolite mineral, $CaO{\cdot}Al_2O_3{\cdot}6SiO_2{\cdot}5H_2O$. [After Henry *Heuland,* 19th-century British mineralogist.]

heu•ris•tic (hyo͞o-rĭs′tĭk) *adj.* **1.** Of or relating to a usually speculative formulation serving as a guide in the investigation or solution of a problem: *"The historian discovers the past by the judicious use of such a heuristic device as the 'ideal type'"* (Karl J. Weintraub). **2.** Of, relating to, or constituting an educational method in which learning takes place through discoveries that result from investigations made by the student. **3.** *Computer Science.* Relating to or using a problem-solving technique in which the most appropriate solution of several found by alternative methods is selected at successive stages of a program for use in the next step of the program. **—heuristic** *n.* **1.** A heuristic method or process. **2. heuristics** *(used with a sing. verb).* The study and application of heuristic methods and processes. [From Greek *heuriskein,* to find.] **—heu•ris′ti•cal•ly** *adv.*

hew (hyo͞o) *v.* **hewed, hewn** (hyo͞on) or **hewed, hew•ing, hews.** *—tr.* **1.** To make or shape with or as if with an ax: *hew a path through the underbrush.* **2.** To cut down with an ax; fell: *hew an oak.* **3.** To strike or cut; cleave. *—intr.* **1.** To cut something by repeated blows, as of an ax. **2.** To adhere or conform strictly; hold: *hew to the line.* [Middle English *hewen,* from Old English *hēawan.* See **kau-** in Appendix.] **—hew′er** *n.*

HEW *abbr.* Department of Health, Education, and Welfare.

hewn (hyo͞on) *v.* A past participle of **hew.**

hex¹ (hĕks) *n.* **1.** An evil spell; a curse. **2.** One that brings bad luck. **—hex** *tr.v.* **hexed, hex•ing, hex•es. 1.** To put a hex on. **2.** To bring or wish bad luck to: *"Chilly evening weather and a chain of minor snafus seemed to hex the $5,000-a-seat gala on Governors Island"* (Newsweek). [Pennsylvania Dutch, from German *hexen,* to hex, from *Hexe,* witch, from Middle High German *hecse,* from Old High German *hagzissa.*] **—hex′er** *n.*

WORD HISTORY: The word *hex* is a good example of the sort of borrowing into English from other languages that occurred in the English-speaking former colonies of Great Britain. German and Swiss immigrants who settled in Pennsylvania in the late 17th and 18th centuries spoke a dialect of German known as Pennsylvania Dutch. In this dialect *hexe* was the equivalent of the German verb *hexen,* "to practice sorcery." Our verb *hex,* first recorded in the sense "to practice witchcraft" in an 1830 work called *Annals of Philadelphia,* is borrowed from Pennsylvania Dutch, as is our noun.

hex² (hĕks) *adj.* Hexagonal. Used of hardware.

hex. *abbr.* Hexagon; hexagonal.

hexa– or **hex–** *pref.* **1.** Six: *hexagram.* **2.** Containing six atoms, molecules, or groups: *hexose.* [Greek, from *hex,* six. See **s(w)eks** in Appendix.]

hex•a•chlo•ro•eth•ane (hĕk′sə-klôr′ō-ĕth′ān′, -klōr′-) also **hex•a•chlor•eth•ane** (-klôr-ĕth′ān′, -klōr-) *n.* A colorless crystalline compound, Cl_3CCCl_3, used as a camphor substitute and in pyrotechnics, explosives, and veterinary medicine.

hex•a•chlo•ro•phene (hĕk′sə-klôr′ə-fēn′, -klōr′-) *n.* An almost odorless white powder, $(C_6HCl_3OH)_2CH_2$, used as a disinfectant and as an antibacterial agent in soaps. [HEXA- + CHLORO- + PHEN(OL).]

hex•a•chord (hĕk′sə-kôrd′) *n. Music.* A sequence of six tones with a semitone in the middle, the others being whole tones, that was used in medieval music. [Medieval Latin *hexachordum,* from Latin *hexachordos,* having six strings or stops : Greek *hexa-,* hexa- + Greek *-khordos,* string, note (from *khordē;* see CORD).]

hex•ad (hĕk′săd′) *n.* A group or series of six. [Late Latin *hexas, hexad-,* the number six, from Greek, from *hex,* six. See **s(w)eks** in Appendix.] **—hex•ad′ic** (hĕk-săd′ĭk) *adj.*

hex•a•dec•i•mal (hĕk′sə-dĕs′ə-məl) *adj.* **1.** Of, relating to, or based on the number 16: *the hexadecimal number system.* **2.** Of or relating to sixteenths. **—hexadecimal** *n.* A sixteenth.

hex•a•gon (hĕk′sə-gŏn′) *n. Abbr.* **hex.** A polygon having six sides. [Latin *hexagōnum,* from Greek *hexagōnon,* neuter of *hexagōnos,* having six angles : *hexa-,* hexa- + *-gōnos,* angled; see -GON.]

hex•ag•o•nal (hĕk-săg′ə-nəl) *adj. Abbr.* **hex. 1.** Having six sides. **2.** Containing a hexagon or shaped like one. **3.** *Mineralogy.* Having three equal axes intersecting at angles of 60° in one plane and one axis of variable length that is perpendicular to the others. **—hex•ag′o•nal•ly** *adv.*

hex•a•gram (hĕk′sə-grăm′) *n.* **1.** A six-pointed star formed by extending each of the sides of a regular hexagon into equilateral triangles. **2.** A figure of six lines or sides.

hex•a•he•dron (hĕk′sə-hē′drən) *n., pl.* **-drons** or **-dra** (-drə). A polyhedron, such as a cube, that has six faces. [Greek *hexaedron,* from neuter of *hexaedros,* having six sides : *hexa-,* hexa- + *-edron,* -hedron.] **—hex′a•he′dral** (-drəl) *adj.*

hex•am•er•ous (hĕk-săm′ər-əs) *adj.* **1.** Having six similar parts or divisions. **2.** *Botany.* Having flower parts, such as petals, sepals, and stamens, in sets of six. **—hex•am′er•ism** *n.*

hex•am•e•ter (hĕk-săm′ĭ-tər) *n.* **1.** A line of verse consisting of six metrical feet. **2.** In classical prosody, a line in which the first four feet are either dactylic or spondaic, the fifth dactylic, and the sixth spondaic. [Latin, from Greek *hexametros,* having six metrical feet : *hexa-,* hexa- + *metron,* meter; see METER¹.] **—hex′a•met′ric** (hĕk-sə-mĕt′rĭk), **hex′a•met′ri•cal** (-rĭ-kəl) *adj.*

hex•a•meth•yl•ene•tet•ra•mine (hĕk′sə-mĕth′ə-lēn-tĕt′rə-mēn′) *n.* See **methenamine.**

hex•ane (hĕk′sān′) *n.* A colorless, flammable liquid, C_6H_{14}, derived from the fractional distillation of petroleum and used as a solvent and in low-temperature thermometers.

ă pat	oi boy
ā pay	ou out
âr care	o͝o took
ä father	o͞o boot
ĕ pet	ŭ cut
ē be	ûr urge
ĭ pit	th thin
ī pie	*th* this
îr pier	hw which
ŏ pot	zh vision
ō toe	ə about, item
ô paw	♦ regionalism

Stress marks: ′ (primary); ′ (secondary), as in **dictionary** (dĭk′shə-nĕr′ē)

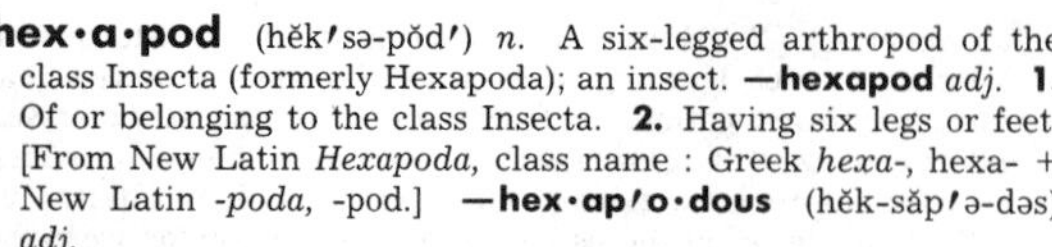

hex·a·pod (hĕk′sə-pŏd′) *n.* A six-legged arthropod of the class Insecta (formerly Hexapoda); an insect. **—hexapod** *adj.* **1.** Of or belonging to the class Insecta. **2.** Having six legs or feet. [From New Latin *Hexapoda,* class name : Greek *hexa-,* hexa- + New Latin *-poda,* -pod.] **—hex·ap′o·dous** (hĕk-săp′ə-dəs) *adj.*

hex sign
On the side of a barn

Hex·a·teuch (hĕk′sə-to͞ok′, -tyo͞ok′) *n. Bible.* The first six books of the Old Testament. [HEXA– + (PENTA)TEUCH.]

hex·o·san (hĕk′sə-săn′) *n.* Any of several polysaccharides that have the general formula $(C_6H_{10}O_5)_n$ and form a hexose on hydrolysis.

hex·ose (hĕk′sōs′) *n.* Any of various simple sugars, such as glucose and fructose, that have six carbon atoms per molecule.

hex sign *n.* Any of various painted round signs incorporating designs, such as stylized stars, rosettes, or wheels, thought to be magical. These signs were painted on barns, especially by the Pennsylvania Dutch, to ward off misfortune or evil spells.

hex·yl (hĕk′səl) *n.* The hydrocarbon radical, C_6H_{13}, having a valence of 1.

hex·yl·re·sor·ci·nol (hĕk′səl-rĭ-zôr′sə-nôl′, -nōl′, -nŏl′) *n.* A yellowish-white crystalline phenol, $C_6H_{13}C_6H_3(OH)_2$, used as an antiseptic and anthelmintic.

hey (hā) *interj.* Used to attract attention or to express surprise, appreciation, wonder, or pleasure.

hey·day (hā′dā′) *n.* The period of greatest popularity, success, or power; prime. [Perhaps alteration of *heyda,* exclamation of pleasure, probably alteration of Middle English *hey,* hey.]

Hey·er·dahl (hā′ər-däl′, hī′-), **Thor.** Born 1914. Norwegian ethnologist and explorer who led the Kon Tiki expedition (1947) on a raft across the Pacific Ocean from Peru to Tuamotu to demonstrate that Polynesians may be of South American origin.

Hey·rov·sky (hā-rôf′skē), **Jaroslav.** 1890–1967. Czechoslovakian chemist. He won a 1959 Nobel Prize for the development of polarography.

Hey·se (hī′zə), **Paul Johann Ludwig von.** 1830–1914. German writer noted for his novels, such as *Children of the World* (1873). He won the 1910 Nobel Prize for literature.

Hey·ward (hā′wərd), **(Edwin) DuBose.** 1885–1940. American writer whose novel *Porgy* (1925) and its dramatization (1927) became the basis of George Gershwin's folk opera *Porgy and Bess.*

Thor Heyerdahl

Hez·e·ki·ah (hĕz′ĭ-kī′ə) also **Ez·e·ki·as** (ĕz′ĭ-kī′əs). fl. 715?–686? B.C. King of Judah who, according to the Old Testament, sought to abolish idolatry and restore worship of Jehovah.

Hf The symbol for the element **hafnium.**

HF or **hf** *abbr.* High frequency.

hf. *abbr.* Half.

hfs *abbr.* Hyperfine structure.

hg *abbr.* **1.** Hectogram. **2.** Hemoglobin.

Hg The symbol for the element **mercury** (sense 1). [New Latin *hydrargyrum,* mercury, from Latin *hydrargyrus,* from Greek *hudrarguros* : *hydr-, hudro-,* hydro- + *arguros,* silver; see LITHARGE.]

HG or **H.G.** *abbr.* High German.

hgb. *abbr.* Hemoglobin.

HGH *abbr.* Human growth hormone.

hgt. *abbr.* Height.

hgwy. *abbr.* Highway.

H.H. *abbr.* **1.** Her Highness; His Highness. **2.** His Holiness.

hhd *abbr.* Hogshead.

HH.D. *abbr. Latin.* Humanitatum Doctor (Doctor of Humanities).

HHFA *abbr.* Housing and Home Finance Agency.

HHS *abbr.* Department of Health and Human Services.

hi (hī) *interj. Informal.* Used to express greeting.

HI *abbr.* **1.** Hawaii. **2.** High intensity. **3.** Humidity index.

H.I. *abbr.* Hawaiian Islands.

Hi·a·le·ah (hī′ə-lē′ə). A city of southeast Florida northwest of Miami. An industrial center, it is noted especially for its racetrack. Population, 145,254.

hiatal hernia *n.* A hernia in which part of the stomach protrudes through the esophageal opening of the diaphragm. Also called *hiatus hernia.*

hibiscus
Rose of Sharon
Hibiscus syriacus

hi·a·tus (hī-ā′təs) *n., pl.* **-tus·es** or **hiatus. 1.** A gap or an interruption in space, time, or continuity; a break: *"We are likely to be disconcerted by . . . hiatuses of thought"* (Edmund Wilson). **2.** *Linguistics.* A slight pause that occurs when two immediately adjacent vowels in consecutive syllables are pronounced, as in *reality* and *naive.* **3.** *Anatomy.* A separation, an aperture, a fissure, or a short passage in an organ or a body part. [Latin *hiātus,* from past participle of *hiāre,* to gape.] **—hi·a′tal** (-āt′l) *adj.*

hiatus hernia *n.* See **hiatal hernia.**

Hi·a·wa·tha (hī′ə-wŏth′ə, -wô′thə, hē′ə-). fl. 1570. Onondagan leader who is credited with the organization of the Iroquois confederacy. His name was given to the hero of Longfellow's poem *The Song of Hiawatha* (1855).

hi·ba·chi (hĭ-bä′chē) *n., pl.* **-chis.** A portable charcoal-burning brazier with a grill, used chiefly for cooking. [Japanese : *hi,* fire + *bachi,* bowl.]

Hib·bing (hĭb′ĭng). A city of northeast Minnesota in the Mesabi Range northwest of Duluth. Its mining industry was at its peak in 1917, when the town was moved 3.2 km (2 mi) south to make room for a huge open-pit iron mine. Population, 21,193.

hi·ber·nac·u·lum (hī′bər-năk′yə-ləm) *n., pl.* **-la** (-lə). *Biology.* **1.** A protective case, covering, or structure, such as a plant bud, in which an organism remains dormant for the winter. **2.** The shelter of a hibernating animal. [Latin *hībernāculum,* winter residence, from *hībernāre,* to winter, from *hībernus,* relating to winter. See **ghei-** in Appendix.]

hi·ber·nal (hī-bûr′nəl) *adj.* Of or relating to winter. [Latin *hībernālis,* from *hībernus,* wintry. See HIBERNACULUM.]

hi·ber·nate (hī′bər-nāt′) *intr.v.* **-nat·ed, -nat·ing, -nates. 1.** To pass the winter in a dormant or torpid state. **2.** To be in an inactive or dormant state or period. [Latin *hībernāre, hībernāt-,* to winter, from *hībernus,* relating to winter. See **ghei-** in Appendix.] **—hi′ber·na′tion** *n.* **—hi′ber·na′tor** *n.*

Hi·ber·ni·a (hī-bûr′nē-ə). The Latin and poetic name for the island of Ireland. **—Hi·ber′ni·an** *adj. & n.*

Hi·ber·no-Eng·lish (hī-bûr′nō-ĭng′glĭsh) *n.* See **Irish English.**

hi·bis·cus (hī-bĭs′kəs) *n.* Any of various chiefly tropical shrubs or trees of the genus *Hibiscus,* having large, showy, variously colored flowers with numerous stamens united into a tube surrounding the style. [Late Latin, variant of Latin *hibiscum,* marsh mallow, perhaps of Celtic origin.]

hic·cup also **hic·cough** (hĭk′əp) *—n.* **1.a.** A spasm of the diaphragm resulting in a rapid, involuntary inhalation that is stopped by the sudden closure of the glottis and accompanied by a sharp, distinctive sound. **b. hiccups, hiccoughs.** An attack of these spasms. Often used with *the.* **2.** The sound made by such a spasm or a sound resembling it: *"the urgent hiccup of a police siren"* (John Updike). *—intr.v.* **-cupped, -cup·ping, -cups** also **-coughed, -cough·ing, -coughs. 1.** To make a hiccup or a sound like a hiccup. **2.** To have an attack of hiccups. [Imitative.]

hick (hĭk) *Informal. n.* A person regarded as gullible or provincial: *"New Yorkers had a horrid way of making people feel like hicks"* (Louis Auchincloss). **—hick** *adj.* Provincial; unsophisticated: *a hick town.* [After *Hick,* a nickname for *Richard,* from Middle English *Hikke.*]

hick·ey (hĭk′ē) *n., pl.* **-eys.** *Informal.* **1.** A device or contrivance; a gadget. **2.a.** A reddish mark on the skin caused by kissing, biting, or sucking, as in lovemaking. **b.** A pimple. **3.** A pipe-bending apparatus. **4.** A threaded electrical fitting to connect a fixture to an outlet box. [Origin unknown.]

Hick·ok (hĭk′ŏk′), **James Butler.** Known as "Wild Bill." 1837–1876. American frontier scout and marshal whose law enforcement exploits against outlaws are the subject of folk legends.

hick·o·ry (hĭk′ə-rē) *n., pl.* **-ries. 1.** Any of several chiefly North American deciduous trees of the genus *Carya,* having smooth or shaggy bark, compound leaves, and hard smooth stones or nuts, each containing an edible seed and surrounded by a husk that splits into four valves. **2.a.** The hard, tough, heavy wood of such a tree. **b.** A walking stick or switch made from such wood. [Short for Virginia Algonquian *pocohiquara,* drink made of pressed hickory nuts.]

Hick·o·ry (hĭk′ə-rē, hĭk′rē). A city of west-central North Carolina northwest of Charlotte. Located at the foot of the Blue Ridge, it is a manufacturing center. Population, 20,757.

Hicks (hĭks), **Edward.** 1780–1849. American painter of primitive works, notably *The Peaceable Kingdom,* of which nearly 100 versions exist.

Hicks·ville (hĭks′vĭl). A community of southeast New York on western Long Island northeast of Mineola. Founded in 1648, it is mainly residential. Population, 43,245.

hid (hĭd) *v.* Past tense and a past participle of **hide[1].**

hi·dal·go (hĭ-dăl′gō, ē-thäl′gô) *n., pl.* **-gos.** A member of the minor nobility in Spain. [Spanish, alteration of *hijo dalgo,* from Old Spanish *fijo dalgo* : *fijo,* son (from Latin *fīlius;* see **dhē(i)-** in Appendix) + *de,* of (from Latin *dē;* see DE–) + *algo,* something, possession (from Latin *aliquō,* ablative of *aliquid* : *alius,* some; see **al-[1]** in Appendix + *quid,* something; see **kʷo-** in Appendix).]

Hi·dat·sa (hē-dät′sä) *n., pl.* **Hidatsa** or **-sas. 1.a.** A Native American people inhabiting an area along the Missouri River in western North Dakota. **b.** A member of this people. **2.** The Siouan language of this people. Also called *Gros Ventre.*

hid·den (hĭd′n) *v.* A past participle of **hide[1].**

hid·den·ite (hĭd′n-īt′) *n. Mineralogy.* A transparent emerald-green variety of spodumene, used as a gemstone. [After William E. *Hidden* (1832–1918), American mineralogist.]

hide[1] (hīd) *v.* **hid** (hĭd), **hid·den** (hĭd′n) or **hid, hid·ing, hides.** *—tr.* **1.** To put or keep out of sight; secrete. **2.** To prevent the disclosure or recognition of; conceal: *tried to hide the facts.* **3.** To cut off from sight; cover up: *Clouds hid the stars.* **4.** To avert (one's gaze), especially in shame or grief. *—intr.* **1.** To keep oneself out of sight. **2.** To seek refuge. ***—phrasal verb.*** **hide out.** To be in hiding, as from a pursuer: *The gangsters hid out in a remote cabin until it was safe to return to the city.* [Middle English *hiden,* from Old English *hȳdan.* See **(s)keu-** in Appendix.]

SYNONYMS: *hide, conceal, secrete, cache, screen, bury, cloak.* These verbs mean to keep from the sight or knowledge of others. *Hide* and *conceal* are the most general and are often used interchangeably: *I used a throw rug to hide* (or *conceal*) *the stain on the carpet. Don't hide* (or *conceal*) *your money in the cookie jar—it's the first place a thief would look. Fog hid* (or *concealed*) *the mountain. She smiled to hide* (or *conceal*) *her hurt feelings. "The other America, the America of poverty, is hidden today"* (Michael Harrington). *"The true use of speech is not so much to express our wants as to conceal them"* (Oliver Goldsmith). *Secrete* and *cache* involve concealment in a place unknown to others; *cache* often implies storage for later use: *The lioness secreted her cubs in the tall grass. The mountain climbers cached their provisions for the descent in a cave they could easily locate but that was inaccessible to animals.* To *screen* is to shield or block from the view of others by interposing something such as a screen: *Tall shrubs screen the actor's home from the curious. Bury* implies covering over so as to conceal: *buried the treasure; buried his hands in his pockets; buried the point of the article in a mass of details.* To *cloak* is to conceal something, such as a thought, a plan, or an intention, by masking or disguising it: *"On previously cloaked issues, the Soviets have suddenly become forthcoming"* (John McLaughlin). See also Synonyms at **block.**

---

hide² (hīd) *n.* The skin of an animal, especially the thick, tough skin or pelt of a large animal. —**hide** *tr.v.* **hid·ed, hid·ing, hides.** To beat severely; flog. —***idiom.*** **hide nor hair.** A trace; a vestige: *haven't seen hide nor hair of them since the argument.* [Middle English, from Old English *hӯd.* See **(s)keu-** in Appendix.]

hide³ (hīd) *n.* An old English measure of land, usually the amount held adequate for one free family and its dependents. [Middle English, from Old English *hīd.* See **kei-¹** in Appendix.]

hide-and-go-seek (hīd′n-gō-sēk′) *n. Games.* See **hide-and-seek.**

hide-and-seek (hīd′n-sēk′) *n. Games.* A children's game in which one player tries to find and catch others who are hiding. Also called *hide-and-go-seek.*

hide·a·way (hīd′ə-wā′) *n.* **1.** A place of concealment; a hideout. **2.** A secluded or isolated place.

hide·bound (hīd′bound′) *adj.* **1.** Stubbornly prejudiced, narrow-minded, or inflexible. **2.** Having abnormally dry, stiff skin that adheres closely to the underlying flesh. Used of domestic animals such as cattle. **3.** Having the bark so contracted and unyielding as to hinder growth. Used of trees.

hid·e·ous (hĭd′ē-əs) *adj.* **1.** Repulsive, especially to the sight; revoltingly ugly. See Synonyms at **ugly. 2.** Offensive to moral sensibilities; despicable. [Middle English, variant of *hidous,* from Anglo-Norman, from Old French *hide, hisde,* fear, possibly of Germanic origin.] —**hid′e·os′i·ty** (-ŏs′ĭ-tē) *n.* —**hid′e·ous·ly** *adv.* —**hid′e·ous·ness** *n.*

hide·out (hīd′out′) *n.* A place of shelter or concealment.

hid·ey-hole (hī′dē-hōl′) *n. Informal.* A secluded or isolated place; a hideaway.

hi·dro·sis (hĭ-drō′sĭs) *n., pl.* **-ses** (-sēz). **1.** The formation and excretion of sweat. **2.** Sweat, especially in excessive or abnormal amounts. [Greek *hidrōsis,* sweating, from *hidrōs,* sweat. See **sweid-** in Appendix.] —**hi·drot′ic** (-drŏt′ĭk) *adj.*

hie (hī) *intr. & tr.v.* **hied, hie·ing** or **hy·ing** (hī′ĭng), **hies.** To go quickly; hasten. [Middle English *hien,* from Old English *hīgian,* to strive, exert oneself.]

hi·e·mal (hī′ə-məl) *adj.* Of or relating to winter. [Latin *hiemālis,* from *hiems,* winter. See **ghei-** in Appendix.]

hier– *pref.* Variant of **hiero–.**

hi·er·arch (hī′ə-rärk′, hī′rärk′) *n.* **1.** One who occupies a position of authority in a religious hierarchy. **2.** One who occupies a high position in a hierarchy: *governmental hierarchs.* [From Middle English *jerarchis,* hierarchs, from Medieval Latin *hierarcha,* dignitary, prelate, from Greek *hierarkhēs,* high priest : *hieros,* holy; see **eis-** in Appendix + *-arkhēs,* -arch.]

hi·er·ar·chi·cal (hī′ə-rär′kĭ-kəl, hī-rär′-) or **hi·er·ar·chic** (-kĭk) or **hi·er·ar·chal** (-rär′kəl) *adj.* Of or relating to a hierarchy. —**hi′er·ar′chi·cal·ly** *adv.*

hi·er·ar·chize (hī′ə-rär-kīz′, hī′rär-) *tr.v.* **-chized, -chiz·ing, -chiz·es.** To arrange in a hierarchy. —**hi′er·ar·chi·za′tion** (-kĭ-zā′shən) *n.*

hi·er·ar·chy (hī′ə-rär′kē, hī′rär′-) *n., pl.* **-chies. 1.** A body of persons having authority. **2.a.** Categorization of a group of people according to ability or status. **b.** The group so categorized. **3.** A series in which each element is graded or ranked: *put honesty first in her hierarchy of values.* **4.a.** A body of clergy organized into successive ranks or grades with each level subordinate to the one above. **b.** Religious rule by a group of ranked clergy. **5.** One of the divisions of angels. [Middle English *ierarchie,* from Old French, from Medieval Latin *hierarchia,* from Greek *hierarkhia,* rule of a high priest, from *hierarkhēs,* high priest. See HIERARCH.]

hi·er·at·ic (hī′ə-răt′ĭk, hī-răt′-) *adj.* **1.** Of or associated with sacred persons or offices; sacerdotal. **2.** Constituting or relating to a simplified cursive style of Egyptian hieroglyphics, used in both sacred and secular writings. **3.** Extremely formal or stylized, as in a work of art. [Latin *hierāticus,* from Greek *hieratikos,* from *hierateia,* priesthood, from *hierasthai,* to be a priest, from *hiereus,* priest, from *hieros,* holy. See **eis-** in Appendix.] —**hi′er·at′i·cal·ly** *adv.*

hiero– or **hier–** *pref.* Sacred; holy: *hierology.* [Greek, from *hieros,* holy. See **eis-** in Appendix.]

hi·er·oc·ra·cy (hī′ə-rŏk′rə-sē, hī-rŏk′-) *n., pl.* **-cies.** Government by the clergy; ecclesiastical rule. —**hi′er·o·crat′ic** (hī′ər-ə-krăt′ĭk, hī′rə-krăt′-), **hi′er·o·crat′i·cal** *adj.*

hi·er·o·dule (hī′ər-ə-do͞ol′, -dyo͞ol′) *n.* An ancient Greek temple slave in the service of a specific deity. [Late Latin *hierodūlus,* from Greek *hierodoulos* : *hieron,* temple, from neuter of *hieros,* hiero- + *doulos,* slave.] —**hi′er·o·du′lic** (-do͞o′lĭk, -dyo͞o′-) *adj.*

hi·er·o·glyph (hī′ər-ə-glĭf′, hī′rə-) *n.* **1.** A picture or symbol used in hieroglyphic writing. **2.** Something that suggests a hieroglyph.

hi·er·o·glyph·ic (hī′ər-ə-glĭf′ĭk, hī′rə-) also **hi·er·o·glyph·i·cal** (-ĭ-kəl) —*adj.* **1.a.** Of, relating to, or being a system of writing, such as that of ancient Egypt, in which pictorial symbols are used to represent meaning or sounds or a combination of meaning and sound. **b.** Written with such symbols. **2.** Difficult to read or decipher. —*n.* **1.a.** A hieroglyph. **b.** Often **hieroglyphics** *(used with a sing. or pl. verb).* Hieroglyphic writing, especially that of the ancient Egyptians. **2.** Something, such as illegible or undecipherable writing, that is felt to resemble a hieroglyph. [French *hiéroglyphique,* from Late Latin *hieroglyphicus,* from Greek *hierogluphikos* : *hieros,* holy; see **eis-** in Appendix + *gluphē,* carving (from *gluphein,* to carve; see **gleubh-** in Appendix).] —**hi′er·o·glyph′i·cal·ly** *adv.*

Hi·er·o·glyph·ic Lu·vi·an (hī′ər-ə-glĭf′ĭk lo͞o′vē-ən, lo͞o′ē- hī′rə-) or **Hieroglyphic Luwian** *n.* A dialect of the Luwian branch of the extinct Anatolian branch of Indo-European, found in documents and inscriptions in an indigenous hieroglyphic script from the late second and early first millenniums B.C. in Anatolia and northern Syria.

hi·er·ol·o·gy (hī′ə-rŏl′ə-jē, hī-rŏl′-) *n., pl.* **-gies.** The sacred literature of a people.

hi·er·o·phant (hī′ər-ə-fănt′, hī′rə-, hī-ĕr′ə-fənt) *n.* **1.** An ancient Greek priest who interpreted sacred mysteries, especially the priest of the Eleusinian mysteries. **2.** An interpreter of sacred mysteries or arcane knowledge. **3.** One who explains or makes a commentary. [Late Latin *hierophanta,* from Greek *hierophantēs* : *hieros,* holy; see **eis-** in Appendix + *-phantēs,* one who shows (from *phainein, phan-,* to show; see **bhā-¹** in Appendix).] —**hi′er·o·phan′tic** *adj.*

hi·fa·lu·tin (hī′fə-lo͞ot′n) *adj. Informal.* Variant of **highfalutin.**

hi-fi (hī′fī′) *n., pl.* **-fis.** *Informal.* **1.** High fidelity. **2.** An electronic system for reproducing high-fidelity sound from radio or recordings. [HI(GH) + FI(DELITY).] —**hi′-fi′** *adj.*

Hi·ga·shi·o·sa·ka (hē-gä′shē-ō-sä′kä). A city of southern Honshu, Japan, a residential and industrial suburb of Osaka. Population, 522,798.

Hig·gin·son (hĭg′ən-sən), **Thomas Wentworth Storrow.** 1823–1911. American writer and soldier who led the first Black regiment in the Union Army (1862–1864).

hig·gle (hĭg′əl) *intr.v.* **-gled, -gling, -gles.** To haggle. [Probably alteration of HAGGLE.] —**hig′gler** *n.*

hig·gle·dy-pig·gle·dy (hĭg′əl-dē-pĭg′əl-dē) *adv.* In utter disorder or confusion: *"There is something delightfully and liberatingly ludicrous about parading higgledy-piggledy in a line of walkers of all shapes and sizes"* (Christa Worthington). —**higgledy-piggledy** *adj.* Topsy-turvy; jumbled. [Origin unknown.]

high (hī) *adj.* **high·er, high·est.** *Abbr.* **h., H. 1.a.** Having a relatively great elevation; extending far upward: *a high mountain; a high tower.* **b.** Extending a specified distance upward: *a cabinet ten feet high.* **2.a.** Being at or near the peak or culminating stage: *the high tourist season; high summer.* **b.** Advanced in development or complexity: *high forms of animal life; higher mathematics.* **c.** Far removed in time; remote: *high antiquity.* **3.a.** Slightly spoiled or tainted; gamy. Used of meat. **b.** Having a bad smell; malodorous. **4.a.** Having a pitch corresponding to a relatively large number of sound-wave cycles per second: *the high tones of a flute.* **b.** Raised in pitch; not soft or hushed: *a high voice.* **5.** Situated relatively far from the equator: *a high latitude.* **6.a.** Of great importance: *set a high priority on funding the housing program.* **b.** Eminent in rank or status: *a high official.* **c.** Serious; grave: *high crimes and misdemeanors.* **d.** Constituting a climax; crucial: *The chase scene is the high point of the film.* **e.** Characterized by lofty or stirring events or themes: *high adventure; high drama.* **7.** Lofty or exalted in quality or character: *a person of high morals.* **8.a.** Greater than usual or expected, as in quantity, magnitude, cost, or degree: *"A high price has to be paid for the happy marriage with the four healthy children"* (Doris Lessing). **b.** Favorable: *He has a high opinion of himself.* **9.** Of great force or violence: *high winds.* **10.a.** Indicating excitement or euphoria: *high spirits.* **b.** *Slang.* Intoxicated by or as if by alcohol or a drug, such as cocaine or marijuana. **11.** Luxurious; extravagant: *high living.* **12.** *Linguistics.* Of or relating to vowels produced with part of the tongue close to the palate, as in the vowel of *tree.* **13.** Of, relating to, or being the gear configuration or setting, as in an automotive transmission, that produces the greatest vehicular speed with respect to engine speed. —**high** *adv.* **higher, highest. 1.** At, in, or to a lofty position, level, or degree: *saw a plane high in the sky; prices that had gone too high.* **2.** In an extravagant or luxurious way: *made a fortune and lived high.* —**high** *n.* **1.** A lofty place or region. **2.** A lofty level or degree: *Summer temperatures reached an all-time high.* **3.** The high gear

Wild Bill Hickok

hieroglyphic
Detail from false door to the tomb of Hesire

ă pat	oi boy
ā pay	ou out
âr care	o͝o took
ä father	o͞o boot
ĕ pet	ŭ cut
ē be	ûr urge
ĭ pit	th thin
ī pie	*th* this
îr pier	hw which
ŏ pot	zh vision
ō toe	ə about, item
ô paw	♦ regionalism

Stress marks: **′** (primary); ′ (secondary), as in **dictionary** (dĭk′shə-nĕr′ē)

configuration of a transmission. **4.** A center of high atmospheric pressure; an anticyclone. **5.** *Slang.* An intoxicated or euphoric condition induced by or as if by a drug. ***—idioms.*** **high and dry. 1.** In a position of helplessness; stranded: *went off and left me high and dry.* **2.** *Nautical.* Out of water. Used of a ship, for example. **high and low.** Here and there; everywhere: *searched high and low for the keys.* **on high. 1.** High in the sky. **2.** In heaven. **3.** In a position of authority. [Middle English, from Old English *hēah.*] **—high′ly** *adv.*

SYNONYMS: *high, tall, lofty, towering, elevated.* These adjectives mean extending to a greater than usual height. *High,* the most general term, refers to what rises a considerable distance from a base or is situated at a level well above another level considered as a base: *a high building; a high ceiling; a high shelf; high standards. Tall* describes what has relatively great stature; it often refers to living things and to what has great height in relation to breadth or in comparison with like things: *a tall man; tall trees; a tall hat. Lofty* describes what is of imposing or inspiring height: *lofty mountains; lofty sentiments. Towering* suggests awe-inspiring height: *a towering oak; towering icebergs; towering ambition. Elevated* stresses height in relation to immediate surroundings; it refers principally to being raised or situated above a normal or average level: *an elevated plain; elevated praise; elevated thought.*

highboy
c. 1735 American
Queen Anne style

high altar *n.* The main altar in a church.

high-and-might·y (hī′ən-mī′tē) *adj.* Marked by arrogance; haughty and overbearing. **—high and mighty** *adv. & n.*

high·ball (hī′bôl′) *n.* **1.** A cocktail served in a tall glass and consisting of liquor, such as whiskey, mixed with water or a carbonated beverage. **2.a.** A railroad signal indicating full speed ahead. **b.** A high-speed train. **—highball** *intr.v.* **-balled, -ball·ing, -balls.** *Slang.* To move ahead at full speed.

high beam *n.* The beam of a vehicle's headlight that provides long-range illumination.

high·bind·er (hī′bīn′dər) *n.* **1.** A corrupt politician. **2.** A member of a Chinese-American secret society of paid assassins and blackmailers. [After the *Highbinders,* a group of ruffians in New York City c. 1806.]

high blood pressure *n.* Hypertension.

high·born (hī′bôrn′) *adj.* Of noble birth.

high·boy (hī′boi′) *n.* A tall chest of drawers divided into two sections and supported on four legs.

high·bred (hī′brĕd′) *adj.* Of superior breed or stock: *highbred cattle.*

highchair

high·brow (hī′brou′) also **high·browed** (-broud′) *adj.* Of, relating to, or being highly cultured or intellectual: *They only attend highbrow events such as the ballet or the opera.* **—highbrow** *n.* One who possesses or affects a high degree of culture or learning. **—high′brow′ism** *n.*

high·bush cranberry (hī′bo͝osh′) *n.* See **cranberry bush.**

high·chair (hī′châr′) *n.* A very young child's feeding chair that has long legs, a footrest, and a usually detachable tray.

High-Church (hī′chûrch′) *adj.* Of or relating to a group in the Anglican Church that stresses the historical continuity of Catholic Christianity and maintains traditional definitions of authority, the episcopacy, and the nature of the sacraments.

high-class (hī′klăs′) *adj.* Of superior quality; first-class.

high comedy *n.* Comedy of a sophisticated and witty nature, often satirizing genteel society.

high command *n.* **1.** The supreme headquarters of a military force. **2.** The most powerful leaders of an organization.

high commissioner *n.* **1.** A chief commissioner or one of high rank. **2.** A chief representative of the government of one country who is assigned to an ambassadorial post in another country.

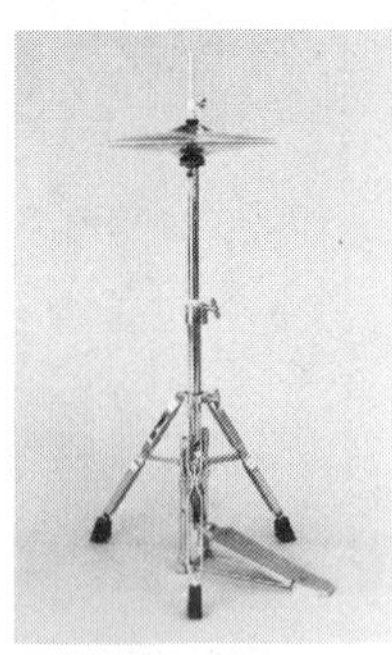

high-hat cymbals

high-count (hī′kount′) *adj.* Having a large number of warp and filling threads per square inch. Used of a woven fabric.

high-coun·try (hī′kŭn′trē) *adj.* Of, relating to, or being country that is above the piedmont and below the timberline: *"Alaska, where the quick wits, strong muscles, and nimble feet . . . can still be used in high-country logging"* (Kathryn Hobbie).

high court *n. Law.* See **Supreme Court** (sense 2).

high-def·i·ni·tion television (hī′dĕf′ə-nĭsh′ən) *n. Abbr.* **HDTV** A television system that has twice the standard number of scanning lines per frame and therefore produces pictures with greater detail.

high-den·si·ty (hī′dĕn′sĭ-tē) *adj.* Having a high concentration: *high-density urban areas.*

high-density lipoprotein *n. Abbr.* **HDL** A complex of lipids and proteins that functions as a transporter of cholesterol in the blood. High levels are associated with a decreased risk of atherosclerosis and coronary heart disease.

high jump
Fosbury flop technique

high-end (hī′ĕnd′) *adj. Informal.* **1.** Appealing to sophisticated and discerning customers: *a high-end department store; high-end video equipment.* **2.** Sophisticated and discerning: *books targeted to the high-end consumer.*

high-en·er·gy (hī′ĕn′ər-jē) *adj.* **1.** Of or relating to elementary particles with energy exceeding hundreds of thousands of electron volts. **2.** Yielding a large amount of energy upon undergoing chemical reaction. **3.** Vigorous; dynamic.

high·er criticism (hī′ər) *n.* Critical study of biblical texts to ascertain their literary origins and history and the meaning and intention of the authors. **—higher critic** *n.*

higher education *n.* Education beyond the secondary level, especially education at the college or university level.

higher law *n.* A moral or religious principle that takes precedence over the constitutions or statutes of society.

higher learning *n.* Education or academic accomplishment at the college or university level.

high·er-up (hī′ər-ŭp′) *n. Informal.* One who has a rank, position, or status superior to others.

high·est common factor (hī′ĭst) *n. Abbr.* **H.C.F., h.c.f., hcf** *Mathematics.* See **greatest common divisor.**

high explosive *n. Abbr.* **HE** An explosive, such as TNT, that combusts nearly instantaneously, thereby producing a violent, shattering effect.

♦**high·fa·lu·tin** or **hi·fa·lu·tin** (hī′fə-lo͞ot′n) also **high·fa·lu·ting** (-lo͞ot′n, -lo͞o′tĭng) *adj. Informal.* Pompous or pretentious: *"highfalutin reasons for denying direct federal assistance to the unemployed"* (Arthur M. Schlesinger, Jr.). [Origin unknown.]

♦***REGIONAL NOTE:*** H.L. Mencken, in his famous book *The American Language,* mentions *highfalutin* as an example of the many native U.S. words coined during the 19th-century period of vigorous growth. Although *highfalutin* is characteristic of American folk speech, it is not a true regionalism because it has always occurred in all regions of the country, with its use and popularity spurred by its appearance in print. The origin of *highfalutin,* like that of many folk expressions, is obscure. It has been suggested that the second element, *-falutin,* comes from the verb *flute*—hence *high-fluting,* a comical indictment of one who thinks too highly of oneself.

high fashion *n.* **1.** See **high style. 2.** Haute couture.

high fidelity *n.* The electronic reproduction of sound, especially from broadcast or recorded sources, with minimal distortion. **—high′-fi·del′i·ty** (hī′fĭ-dĕl′ĭ-tē, -fī-) *adj.*

high finance *n.* Financial transactions or institutions that are extensive in size or scope.

high-five (hī′fīv′) *n. Slang.* A gesture of greeting, elation, or victory in which one person slaps an upraised palm against that of another person.

high·fli·er also **high·fly·er** (hī′flī′ər) *n.* **1.** One who is extravagant or extreme in manner or opinions. **2.** A stock that sells well above its original value.

high-flown (hī′flōn′) *adj.* **1.** Exceedingly lofty or exalted: *high-flown ideas about the history of Christianity.* **2.** Highly pretentious or inflated: *high-flown rhetoric.*

high·fly·ing (hī′flī′ĭng) *adj.* **1.** Rising to a great height. **2.** Unusually extravagant, affected, or ambitious.

high frequency *n. Abbr.* **HF, hf** A radio frequency in the range between 3 and 30 megahertz.

high gear *n.* **1.** The high gear configuration of a transmission. **2.** *Informal.* A state of maximum activity, energy, or force: *Her mind was in high gear while studying for the examination.*

High German (hī) *n. Abbr.* **HG, H.G. 1.** German as indigenously spoken and written in central and southern Germany. **2.** See **German** (sense 2). [Translation of German *Hochdeutsch* : *hoch,* high (from the area's mountainous terrain) + *Deutsch,* German.]

high-grade (hī′grād′) *adj.* Of superior grade or quality.

high ground *n.* A position of superiority over others, especially competitors or opponents: *used negotiations as a way to gain the psychological and intellectual high ground.*

high·hand·ed (hī′hăn′dĭd) *adj.* Arrogant; overbearing. **—high′hand′ed·ly** *adv.* **—high′hand′ed·ness** *n.*

high hat *n.* **1.** See **top hat. 2.** *Music.* A set of high-hat cymbals.

high-hat (hī′hăt′) *Informal. tr.v.* **-hat·ted, -hat·ting, -hats.** To treat in a condescending or supercilious manner. **—high-hat** *adj.* Snobbish; haughty.

high-hat cymbals *pl.n. Music.* A pair of cymbals positioned to be worked by a foot pedal.

High Holy Day *n. Judaism.* Rosh Hashanah or Yom Kippur or any of the days in between. Also called *High Holiday.*

high horse *n. Informal.* A mood or an attitude of stubborn arrogance or contempt: *Get down off your high horse and apologize.*

high-in·come (hī′ĭn′kŭm) *adj.* Of or relating to individuals or groups, such as families, that are supported by or earn income considered high in comparison with that of the larger population.

high·jack (hī′jăk′) *Informal. v. & n.* Variant of **hijack.**

high jinks or **hi·jinks** (hī′jĭnks′) *pl.n.* Playful, often noisy and rowdy activity, usually involving mischievous pranks.

high jump *n. Sports.* **1.** A jump for height made over a horizontal bar in a track-and-field contest. **2.** A contest in which high jumps are made. **—high jumper** *n.*

high·land (hī′lənd) *n.* **1.** Elevated land. **2. highlands.** A mountainous or hilly section of a country. **—highland** *adj.* Of, relating to, or characteristic of a highland.

High·land (hī′lənd). A town of northwest Indiana, a suburb in the Chicago-Gary metropolitan area. Population, 25,935.

high·land·er (hī′lən-dər) *n.* One who lives in a highland.

Highland fling *n.* A lively folk dance originating in the Highlands of Scotland.

Highland Park. **1.** A city of northeast Illinois, a residential suburb of Chicago on Lake Michigan. Population, 30,611. **2.** A city of southeast Michigan surrounded by Detroit. It grew mainly after Henry Ford established an automobile factory here in 1909. Population, 27,909.

High·lands (hī′lәndz). A mountainous region of central and northern Scotland extending northwest and including the Grampian Mountains. **—High′land** *adj.* **—High′land·er** *n.*

high-lev·el (hī′lĕv′әl) *adj.* **1.** Made up of or carried out by persons having high rank or status: *a high-level corporate briefing.* **2.** Being at an elevated level in rank or importance: *a high-level official.* **3.** *Computer Science.* Of, relating to, or being a language, such as BASIC or Pascal, in which each instruction or statement corresponds to several instructions in machine language. A high-level language is translated into machine language by a computer.

high·life or **high life** (hī′līf′) *n. Informal.* An extravagant or luxurious style of living. **—high′-lif′er** *n.*

high·light (hī′līt′) *n.* **1.** An area or a spot in a drawing, painting, or photograph that is strongly illuminated. **2.** An especially significant or interesting detail or event. **—highlight** *tr.v.* **-light·ed, -light·ing, -lights. 1.** To give a highlight to (the subject of a painting, for example). **2.a.** To make prominent; emphasize. **b.** To be a highlight of. **3.** To mark important passages of text with a usually fluorescent marker as a means of memory retention or for later reference.

high·light·er (hī′lī′tәr) *n.* **1.** A usually fluorescent marker used to mark important passages of text. **2.** A cosmetic for emphasizing areas of the face, such as the eyes or cheekbones.

high-low (hī′lō′) *n. Games.* **1.** A poker game in which both high and low hands are eligible to win. **2.** A signal chiefly in bridge for one's partner to lead a suit.

high-low-jack (hī′lō′jăk′) *n. Games.* A card game in which points are scored for the high trump, low trump, jack of trumps, and either the ten of trumps or game.

High Mass *n. Roman Catholic Church.* A mass in which the celebrant is assisted by a deacon and a subdeacon and accompanied by acolytes, a thurifer, and a choir.

high-mind·ed (hī′mīn′dĭd) *adj.* Characterized by elevated ideals or conduct; noble. **—high′-mind′ed·ly** *adv.* **—high′-mind′ed·ness** *n.*

high muckamuck *n. Slang.* An important, often overbearing person. [From Chinook Jargon *hayo makamak,* plenty to eat.]

WORD HISTORY: Perhaps one would not immediately associate the word *high muckamuck* with Chinook Jargon, but it seems that English has borrowed the term. This pidgin language, which combines words from English, French, Nootka, Chinook, and the Salishan languages, was formerly used by Native Americans and fur traders in the Pacific Northwest. In this language *hayo makamak* meant "plenty to eat" and is recorded in that sense in English contexts, the first one dated 1853, in which the phrase is spelled *Hiou Muckamuck.* In 1856 we find the first recorded instance of the word meaning "pompous person, person of importance," in the *Democratic State Journal* published in Sacramento: "The professors—the high 'Muck-a-Mucks'—tried fusion, and produced confusion." In this passage the Chinook Jargon term has been Anglicized in accord with its new meaning.

high-necked (hī′nĕkt′) *adj.* Having a high neckline: *a high-necked sweater.*

high·ness (hī′nĭs) *n.* **1.** The quality or condition of being high. **2. Highness.** Used with *His, Her,* or *Your* as a title and form of address for a prince or princess: *Her Royal Highness the Princess Margaret.*

high noon *n.* **1.** Exactly noon. **2.** The highest or most advanced stage or period: *the high noon of her creativity.*

high-oc·tane (hī′ŏk′tān) *adj.* **1.** Having a high octane number and thus good antiknock properties and high efficiency: *high-octane gas.* **2.** *Slang.* High-powered; dynamic: *a high-octane sales manager; a high-octane marketing plan.*

high-pitched (hī′pĭcht′) *adj.* **1.** High in pitch, as a voice or musical tone. **2.** Steeply sloped, as a roof. **3.** Marked by or indicating intense emotion: *a high-pitched debate.*

high place *n.* In early Semitic religions, a place of worship built usually on top of a hill.

High Point. A city of north-central North Carolina southwest of Greensboro. Settled before 1750, it is a furniture-manufacturing center. Population, 63,808.

high-pow·ered (hī′pou′әrd) also **high-pow·er** (-pou′әr) *adj.* Having great power or energy; dynamic: *She's on a high-power career track.*

high-pres·sure (hī′prĕsh′әr) *adj.* **1.** Of or relating to pressures higher than normal, especially higher than atmospheric pressure. **2.** *Informal.* **a.** Using aggressive, persistent persuasive tactics: *a high-pressure salesperson.* **b.** Full of great stress or tension: *a high-pressure job.* **—high-pressure** *tr.v.* **-sured, -sur·ing, -sures.** *Informal.* To attempt to sell (something) or persuade (someone) by using aggressive, persistent tactics.

high priest *n.* **1.** *Judaism.* A chief male priest, especially of the ancient Levitical priesthood. **2.** *Mormon Church.* A male priest of the Melchizedek order. **3.** The head or chief proponent, as of a movement or doctrine. **—high priesthood** *n.*

high priestess *n.* The female head or chief proponent, as of a movement or doctrine: *the high priestess of modern art.*

high profile *n.* An intentionally conspicuous, well-publicized presence or stance: *"needs to maintain a high profile in his profession"* (Tracy Keenan Wynn). **—high′-pro′file** (hī′prō′fīl) *adj.*

high relief *n.* Sculptural relief in which the modeled forms project from the background by at least half their depth. Also called *alto-relievo.*

high-res·o·lu·tion (hī′rĕz′ә-lo͞o′shәn) *adj.* **1.** Relating to an image that has fine detail. **2.** *Computer Science.* Relating to an output device, such as a printer, whose images contain a large number of pixels and are therefore sharp and detailed.

high-rise (hī′rīz′) *adj.* **1.a.** Indicating or being a multistoried building equipped with elevators: *a high-rise apartment building.* **b.** Of, relating to, or marked by multistoried buildings: *a high-rise fire; a high-rise district.* **2.** Of, relating to, or being a bicycle with small wheels, a banana-shaped seat, and high handlebars. **—high-rise** or **high rise** *n.* **1.** A multistoried building equipped with elevators. **2.** A high-rise bicycle.

high-risk (hī′rĭsk′) *adj.* **1.** Of, relating to, or characterized by risk: *a high-risk business.* **2.** Being particularly subject to potential danger or hazard: *a high-risk surgical procedure.*

high·road or **high road** (hī′rōd′) *n.* **1.a.** The easiest or surest path or course: *the highroad to happiness.* **b.** The most positive, diplomatic, or optimistic course. **2.** *Chiefly British.* A main road; a highway.

high roller *n. Slang.* **1.** One who spends freely and extravagantly, as for luxuries or entertainment. **2.** One who gambles rashly or for high stakes. **3.** An organization, such as a large corporation, that spends or invests liberally or rashly. **—high′-roll′ing** (hī′rō′lĭng) *adj.*

high school *n. Abbr.* **HS, H.S.** A secondary school that usually includes grades 9 through 12 or 10 through 12. **—high′-school′** (hī′sko͞ol′) *adj.* **—high school′er** *n.*

high seas *pl.n.* The open waters of an ocean or a sea beyond the limits of the territorial jurisdiction of a country: *piracy on the high seas.*

high sign *n. Informal.* An often prearranged secret sign or signal intended especially to warn or inform: *gave me the high sign that it was time to leave.*

high-sound·ing (hī′soun′dĭng) *adj.* Pretentiously impressive; pompous: *high-sounding oratory.*

high-speed (hī′spēd′) *adj.* **1.** Operated or designed for operation at high speed: *a high-speed food processor.* **2.** Taking place at high speed: *a high-speed chase.* **3.** Having a speed of 50–500 frames per second, as movie film, to record events that occur too rapidly for usual photography.

high-spir·it·ed (hī′spĭr′ĭ-tĭd) *adj.* **1.** Having a proud or unbroken spirit: *a high-spirited horse.* **2.** Vivacious; lively: *a high-spirited tune.* **—high′-spir′it·ed·ly** *adv.* **—high′-spir′it·ed·ness** *n.*

high-stick·ing (hī′stĭk′ĭng) *n. Sports.* The act of carrying the blade of an ice hockey stick at a height ruled illegal.

high street *n. Chiefly British.* A main street.

high-strung (hī′strŭng′) *adj.* Tending to be very nervous and easily excited.

high style *n.* The latest in trend-setting fashion or design, usually intended for or adopted by an exclusive clientele. Also called *high fashion.* **—high′-style′** (hī′stī′) *adj.*

hight (hīt) *adj. Archaic.* Named or called. [Middle English, past participle of *highten, hihten,* to call, be called, from *hehte, hight,* past tense of *hoten,* from Old English *hātan.* See **kei-**[2] in Appendix.]

high·tail (hī′tāl′) *intr.v.* **-tailed, -tail·ing, -tails.** *Slang.* To go as fast as possible, especially in retreating: *hightailed out of town.* [From those animals that raise their tails when fleeing.]

high tea *n. Chiefly British.* A fairly substantial meal that includes tea and is served in the late afternoon or early evening.

high tech (tĕk) *Informal. n.* **1.** High technology. **2.** A style of interior decoration marked by the use of industrial materials, equipment, or design. **—high tech** also **hi-tech** (hī′tĕk′) *adj.* Of, relating to, or resembling high technology.

high technology *n.* Technology that involves highly advanced or specialized systems or devices. **—high′-tech·nol′o·gy** (hī′tĕk-nŏl′ә-jē) *adj.*

high-ten·sion (hī′tĕn′shәn) *adj. Abbr.* **HT** Having a high voltage.

high-test (hī′tĕst′) *adj.* **1.** Of or relating to highly volatile high-octane gasoline. **2.** Meeting exacting requirements.

high-tick·et (hī′tĭk′ĭt) *adj. Informal.* Very expensive: *"developing a boundless appetite for high-ticket travel"* (Eileen Keerdoja).

high tide *n.* **1.** *Abbr.* **HT a.** The tide at its fullest, when the water reaches its highest level. **b.** The time at which this tide occurs. **2.** A point of culmination; a climax. *—attributive.* Often used to modify another noun: *a high tide mark; a high tide departure.*

high-toned (hī′tōnd′) *adj.* **1.** Intellectually, morally, or so-

high relief

ă pat	oi boy
ā pay	ou out
âr care	o͝o took
ä father	o͞o boot
ĕ pet	ŭ cut
ē be	ûr urge
ĭ pit	th thin
ī pie	*th* this
îr pier	hw which
ŏ pot	zh vision
ō toe	ә about, item
ô paw	♦ regionalism

Stress marks: **′** (primary); ′ (secondary), as in **dictionary** (dĭk′shә-nĕr′ē) cially superior. **2.** *Informal.* Pretentiously elegant or fashionable: *a high-toned restaurant.*

high-tops (hī′tŏps′) *pl.n.* Sneakers or athletic shoes that lace up to the ankle. Also called *high-top shoes, high-top sneakers.*

high treason *n.* Treason against one's country or sovereign.

high water *n. Abbr.* **HW 1.** High tide. **2.** The state of a body of water that has reached its highest level.

high-wa·ter mark (hī′wô′tər, -wŏt′ər) *n.* **1.** *Abbr.* **HWM** A mark indicating the highest level reached by a body of water. **2.** The highest point, as of achievement; the apex.

high·way (hī′wā′) *n. Abbr.* **hwy, hgwy.** A main public road, especially one connecting towns and cities.

high·way·man (hī′wā′mən) *n.* A man who holds up and robs travelers on a road.

highway patrol *n.* A state law enforcement organization whose police officers patrol the public highways.

highway robbery *n.* **1.** Robbery usually of travelers on or near a public road. **2.** *Informal.* The exaction of an exorbitantly high price or fee. **—highway robber** *n.*

high wire *n.* A tightrope for aerialists that is stretched very high above the ground. ***—idiom.* high-wire act.** *Slang.* A risky job or operation. **—high′-wire′** (hī′wīr′) *adj.*

H.I.H. *abbr.* **1.** Her Imperial Highness. **2.** His Imperial Highness.

hi·jack also **high·jack** (hī′jăk′) *Informal.—tr.v.* **-jacked, -jack·ing, -jacks. 1.a.** To stop and rob (a vehicle in transit). **b.** To steal (goods) from a vehicle in transit. **c.** To seize control of (a moving vehicle) by use of force, especially in order to reach an alternate destination. **2.a.** To steal from as if by hijacking. **b.** To subject to extortion. *—n.* The act or an instance of hijacking. [Probably back-formation from *highjacker,* perhaps from *jacker,* holdup man, from JACK, to jacklight.] **—hi′jack′er** *n.*

hi·ji·ki (hē-jē′kē) *n., pl.* **-kis.** An edible seaweed with a strong flavor. [Japanese.]

hi·jinks (hī′jĭngks′) *pl.n.* Variant of **high jinks.**

hike (hīk) *v.* **hiked, hik·ing, hikes.** *—intr.* **1.** To go on an extended walk for pleasure or exercise. **2.** To rise, especially to rise upward out of place: *My coat had hiked up in the back.* *—tr.* **1.** To increase or raise in amount, especially abruptly: *shopkeepers who hiked their prices for the tourist trade.* **2.** To pull or raise with a sudden motion; hitch: *hiked myself onto the stone wall; hiked up her knee socks.* **3.** *Football.* To snap (the ball). **—hike** *n.* **1.** A long walk or march. **2.** An often abrupt increase or rise: *a price hike.* **3.** *Football.* See **snap** (sense 13). ***—phrasal verb.* hike out.** *Nautical.* To sit facing the sail and lean far backward and over the side of a small boat in order to keep the craft flat in the water. ***—idiom.* take a hike.** *Slang.* To leave because one's presence is unwanted. Often used in the imperative. [Origin unknown.] **—hik′er** *n.*

hi·la (hī′lə) *n.* Plural of **hilum.**

hi·lar·i·ous (hĭ-lâr′ē-əs, -lăr′-, hī-) *adj.* Characterized by or causing hilarity. [Latin *hilarus, hilaris,* cheerful; see HILARITY + -IOUS.] **—hi·lar′i·ous·ly** *adv.* **—hi·lar′i·ous·ness** *n.*

hi·lar·i·ty (hĭ-lăr′ĭ-tē, -lâr′-, hī-) *n.* Great merriment. See Synonyms at **mirth.** [Middle English *hilarite,* good spirits, from Old French, from Latin *hilaritās,* from *hilaris,* cheerful, from Greek *hilaros.*]

Hil·de·brand (hĭl′də-brănd′). See **Gregory VII.**

Hil·des·heim (hĭl′dəs-hīm′, -dĕs-). A city of central Germany south-southeast of Hanover. A member of the Hanseatic League, it passed to Prussia in 1866. Population, 101,017.

hill (hĭl) *n.* **1.** A well-defined natural elevation smaller than a mountain. **2.** A small heap, pile, or mound. **3.a.** A mound of earth piled around and over a plant. **b.** A plant thus covered. **4.** An incline, especially of a road; a slope. **5. Hill. a.** Capitol Hill. Often used with *the.* **b.** The U.S. Congress. Often used with *the.* **—hill** *tr.v.* **hilled, hill·ing, hills. 1.** To form into a hill, pile, or heap. **2.** To cover (a plant) with a mound of soil. ***—idiom.* over the hill.** *Informal.* Past one's prime. [Middle English *hil,* from Old English *hyll.* See **kel-²** in Appendix.] **—hill′er** *n.*

Hill, Ambrose Powell. 1825–1865. American Confederate officer active in the Seven Days' Battle, the Second Battle of Bull Run, and the Battle of Antietam (all 1862). His charge began the Battle of Gettysburg (1863).

Hill, James Jerome. Known as "J.J. Hill." 1838–1916. American railroad magnate who promoted the Great Northern Railway and with J.P. Morgan wrested control of the Northern Pacific Railroad from E.H. Harriman in a stock market struggle that provoked the Panic of 1901.

Hil·la·ry (hĭl′ə-rē), Sir **Edmund Percival.** Born 1919. New Zealand mountaineer who in 1959 with a Sherpa guide, Tenzing Norgay, first attained the summit of Mount Everest.

hill·bil·ly (hĭl′bĭl′ē) *n., pl.* **-lies.** *Informal.* A person from the backwoods or a remote mountain area. [HILL + *Billy,* a nickname for William.]

hillbilly music *n. Music.* A type of country music originating in the Appalachian Mountains and based on the traditional folk music of the British Isles.

hill·crest (hĭl′krĕst′) *n.* The summit line of a hill.

Hill·crest Center (hĭl′krĕst′). A community of south-central California, a suburb of Bakersfield. Population, 30,000.

Hillcrest Heights. A community of west-central Maryland, a suburb of Washington, D.C. Population, 17,021.

Hil·lel (hĭl′ĕl, -āl, hē-lĕl′). fl. first century B.C.–first century A.D. Palestinian rabbi who greatly influenced the interpretation of Judaic law.

Hil·liard (hĭl′yərd), **Nicholas.** 1547–1619. English painter who founded a school of miniature painting under the patronage of Elizabeth I and James I.

hill myna *n.* A starling *(Gracula religiosa)* native to Europe and North America, having the capacity to mimic human speech and often kept as a pet.

hill·ock (hĭl′ək) *n.* **1.** A small hill. **2.** *Biology.* A small protuberance or elevation, as from an organ, a tissue, or a structure. [Middle English *hillok,* from *hil,* hill. See HILL.] **—hill′ock·y** *adj.*

Hills·bor·o (hĭlz′bûr′ō, -bŭr′ō). A city of northwest Oregon west of Portland. It was settled in the 1840's. Population, 27,664.

hill·side (hĭl′sīd′) *n.* The side or slope of a hill, situated between the foot and the summit. *—attributive.* Often used to modify another noun: *hillside villas; a hillside village.*

Hill·side (hĭl′sīd′). A community of northeast New Jersey north of Elizabeth. It has varied light industries. Population, 21,440.

hill·top (hĭl′tŏp′) *n.* The crest or top of a hill. *—attributive.* Often used to modify another noun: *hilltop homes; a hilltop view.*

hill·y (hĭl′ē) *adj.* **-i·er, -i·est. 1.** Having many hills. **2.** Similar to a hill; steep. **—hill′i·ness** *n.*

Hi·lo (hē′lō). A city of Hawaii on the eastern coast of Hawaii Island on **Hilo Bay,** an inlet of the Pacific Ocean. Settled in the 1820's by American missionaries, the city is a trade and shipping center. Population, 35,269.

hilt (hĭlt) *n.* The handle of a weapon or tool. ***—idiom.* to the hilt.** To the limit; completely: *played the role to the hilt.* [Middle English, from Old English.]

Hil·ton (hĭl′tən), **James.** 1900–1954. British novelist whose best-known works are *Lost Horizon* (1933), set in the fictional land of Shangri-La, and *Goodbye, Mr. Chips* (1934).

Hilton Head Island. An island off the southern coast of South Carolina in the Sea Islands of the Atlantic Ocean.

hi·lum (hī′ləm) *n., pl.* **-la** (-lə). **1.** *Botany.* **a.** The scar on a seed, such as a bean, indicating the point of attachment to the funiculus. **b.** The nucleus of a starch grain. **2.** *Anatomy.* The area through which ducts, nerves, or blood vessels enter and leave an organ or a gland. [Latin, trifle.] **—hi′lar** (-lər) *adj.*

Hil·ver·sum (hĭl′vər-səm). A city of central Netherlands southeast of Amsterdam. It is a manufacturing and broadcasting center. Population, 88,417.

him (hĭm) *pron.* The objective case of **he. 1.** Used as the direct object of a verb: *They saw him at the meeting.* **2.** Used as the indirect object of a verb: *They offered him a ride.* **3.** Used as the object of a preposition: *This telephone call is for him.* **4.** *Informal.* Used as a predicate nominative: *It's him.* See Usage Note at **I¹. —him** *n.* A male: *The dog is a him.* [Middle English, from Old English. See **ko-** in Appendix.]

H.I.M. *abbr.* **1.** Her Imperial Majesty. **2.** His Imperial Majesty.

Him·a·la·ya Mountains (hĭm′ə-lā′ə, hĭ-mäl′yə). A mountain system of south-central Asia extending about 2,414 km (1,500 mi) through Kashmir, northern India, southern Tibet, Nepal, Sikkim, and Bhutan. **—Him′a·la′yan** *adj. & n.*

Hi·ma·lia (hĭ-mäl′yə) *n.* The satellite of Jupiter that is 11th in distance from the planet. [Greek, name of a nymph who bore three sons of Zeus, probably from *himalia,* abundance of wheatmeal, from feminine of *himalios,* abundant.]

hi·mat·i·on (hĭ-măt′ē-ŏn′) *n., pl.* **-i·a** (-ē-ə). A rectangular, woolen or linen cloak worn by men and women in ancient Greece. [Greek, diminutive of *hima, himat-,* garment, variant of *heima,* from *hennunai,* to clothe. See **wes-²** in Appendix.]

Hi·me·ji (hē′mĕ-jē′, hē-mĕ′jē). A city of southwest Honshu, Japan, west-northwest of Kobe. An industrial center, it has a large Buddhist shrine. Population, 452,916.

Himm·ler (hĭm′lər), **Heinrich.** 1900–1945. German Nazi leader. Second in power to Hitler, he directed the Nazi elite forces, the SS (1929–1945); commanded the Third Reich's police and secret police, the Gestapo (1936–1945); and coordinated the operation of the concentration and extermination camps (1941–1945).

him·self (hĭm-sĕlf′) *pron.* **1.** That one identical with him: **a.** Used reflexively as the direct or indirect object of a verb or the object of a preposition: *He congratulated himself.* **b.** Used for emphasis: *He himself found the courage.* **c.** Used in an absolute construction: *In the black himself, he could offer financial assistance to his cousin.* **2.** His normal or healthy condition or state: *He's feeling himself again.* See Usage Note at **myself.** [Middle English, from Old English *himselfum* : *him,* him; see HIM + *selfum,* dative of *self,* self; see SELF.]

Him·yar·ite (hĭm′yə-rīt′) *adj.* Of or relating to the Himyarites, their language, or their culture. **—Himyarite** *n.* **1.** A member of an ancient tribe of southwest Arabia. **2.** The Semitic language of the ancient Himyarites. [After *Himyar,* a legendary king of Yemen.] **—Him′yar·it′ic** (-rĭt′ĭk) *adj.*

hin (hĭn) *n.* A unit of liquid measure used by the ancient Hebrews, equal to about five liters. [Middle English, from Late Latin, from Greek, from Hebrew *hīn,* of Egyptian origin.]

Hi·na·ya·na (hē′nə-yä′nə) *n. Buddhism.* A small, conservative branch of Buddhism following the Pali scriptures and the nontheistic ideal of self-purification to nirvana. Also called *Theravada.* [Sanskrit *hīnayānam,* lesser vehicle : *hīna-,* inferior; see **ghē-** in Appendix + *yānam,* vehicle, way; see **ei-** in Appendix.] **—Hi'na·ya'nist** *n.* **—Hi'na·ya·nis'tic** (-yä-nĭs'tĭk) *adj.*

hind¹ (hīnd) also **hind·er** (hīn'dər) *adj.* Located at or forming the back or rear; posterior: *an animal's hind legs; the hinder part of a steer.* [Middle English *hinde,* short for *bihinde,* behind, from Old English *bihindan.* See **ko-** in Appendix.]

hind² (hīnd) *n.* **1.** A female red deer. **2.** Any of several fishes of the genus *Epinephelus* of Atlantic waters, related to and resembling the groupers. [Middle English, from Old English.]

hind³ (hīnd) *n.* **1.** *Chiefly British.* A farm laborer, especially a skilled worker. **2.** *Archaic.* A country bumpkin; a rustic. [Alteration of Middle English *hine,* household servants, possibly from Old English *hīne,* genitive of *hīgan, hīwan,* members of a household. See **kei-¹** in Appendix.]

Hind. *abbr.* **1.** Hindi. **2.** Hindustani.

hind·brain (hīnd'brān') *n.* See **rhombencephalon.**

Hin·de·mith (hĭn'də-mĭth, -mĭt), **Paul.** 1895–1963. German violist and composer of chamber music, instrumental works, and operas, such as *Mathis der Maler* (1938).

Hin·den·burg (hĭn'dən-bûrg', -bo͝ork'), **Paul von.** 1847–1934. German general and politician who as president of the Weimar Republic (1925–1934) appointed Hitler as chancellor (1933).

hin·der¹ (hĭn'dər) *v.* **-dered, -der·ing, -ders.** *—tr.* **1.** To be or get in the way of. **2.** To obstruct or delay the progress of. *—intr.* To interfere with action or progress. [Middle English *hindren,* from Old English *hindrian.* See **ko-** in Appendix.] **—hin'der·er** *n.*

SYNONYMS: *hinder, hamper, impede, obstruct, block, dam, bar.* These verbs mean to slow or prevent progress or movement. To *hinder* is to hold back, as by delaying: *The travelers were hindered by storms throughout their journey.* Often the word implies stopping or prevention: *What is to hinder you from trying?* To *hamper* is to hinder by or as if by fastening or entangling: *A suit and an overcoat hampered the efforts of the accident victim to swim to safety. She was hampered by ill health in building up her business.* To *impede* is to slow by making action or movement difficult: *"Sentiment and eloquence serve only to impede the pursuit of truth"* (Macaulay). *Obstruct* implies the presence of obstacles that interfere with progress: *A building under construction obstructs our view of the mountains. One of the mugger's accomplices tried to obstruct the police officer from upholding the law. Block* refers to complete obstruction that prevents progress, passage, or action: *A huge snowdrift is blocking the entrance to the driveway. "Do not block the way of inquiry"* (Charles S. Peirce). *Dam* suggests obstruction of the flow, progress, or release of something, such as water or emotion: *dammed the brook to form a swimming pool; dammed up his emotions.* To *bar* is to prevent entry or exit or prohibit a course of action: *mounted troops barring access to the presidential palace; laws that bar price fixing.*

hind·er² (hīn'dər) *adj.* Variant of **hind¹.**

hind·er·most (hīn'dər-mōst') *adj.* Variant of **hindmost.**

hind·gut (hīnd'gŭt') *n.* The caudal portion of the embryonic alimentary canal in vertebrates.

Hin·di (hĭn'dē) *n. Abbr.* **Hind 1.** A group of vernacular Indic dialects spoken in northern India. **2.** The literary and official language of northern India that is based on these dialects. It is written in Devanagari and uses Sanskrit as a resource language. [Hindi *Hindī,* from *Hind,* India, from Persian, from Old Persian *Hindu,* the Indus River, from Sanskrit *sindhuḥ,* river.] **—Hin'di** *adj.*

hind limb *n.* A posterior appendage, such as a leg, wing, or flipper.

hind·most (hīnd'mōst') also **hind·er·most** (hīn'dər-) *adj.* Farthest to the rear; last.

Hin·doo (hĭn'do͞o) *n. & adj. Archaic.* Variant of **Hindu.**

Hin·doo·ism (hĭn'do͞o-ĭz'əm) *n. Archaic.* Variant of **Hinduism.**

hind·quar·ter (hīnd'kwôr'tər) *n.* **1.** The posterior portion of a side of beef, lamb, veal, or mutton, including a hind leg and one or two ribs. **2. hindquarters.** The posterior part of a quadruped, adjacent to the hind legs.

hin·drance (hĭn'drəns) *n.* **1.a.** The act of hindering. **b.** The condition of being hindered. **2.** One that hinders; an impediment. See Synonyms at **obstacle.** [Middle English *hindraunce,* harm, from *hindren,* to hinder. See HINDER¹.]

hind·sight (hīnd'sīt') *n.* **1.** Perception of the significance and nature of events after they have occurred. **2.** The rear sight of a firearm.

Hin·du (hĭn'do͞o) *adj.* **1.** Of or relating to Hinduism. **2.** Of or relating to the Hindus and their culture. **—Hindu** *n.* **1.** An adherent of Hinduism. **2.** A native of India, especially northern India. [Persian *Hindū,* from *Hind,* India. See HINDI.]

Hindu calendar *n.* The lunisolar calendar governing Hindu religious life and almost all Indian festivals and dating in its classic form from the fourth century A.D. The solar year is divided into 12 lunar months in accordance with the successive entrances of the sun into the signs of the zodiac, the months varying in length from 29 to 32 days.

Hin·du·ism (hĭn'do͞o-ĭz'əm) *n.* A diverse body of religion, philosophy, and cultural practice native to and predominant in India, characterized by a belief in reincarnation and a supreme being of many forms and natures, by the view that opposing theories are aspects of one eternal truth, and by a desire for liberation from earthly evils.

Hindu Kush (ko͝osh, kŭsh). A mountain range of southwest Asia extending more than 805 km (500 mi) westward from northern Pakistan to northeast Afghanistan. The highest elevation is Tirich Mir, 7,695.2 m (25,230 ft), in Pakistan.

Hin·du·stan (hĭn'do͞o-stăn', -stän'). A historical region of India considered at various times to include only the upper Ganges River plateau or all of northern India from the Himalaya Mountains to the Deccan Plateau and from the Punjab to Assam. The term has also been applied to the entire Indian subcontinent.

Hin·du·sta·ni (hĭn'do͞o-stä'nē, -stăn'ē) *n. Abbr.* **Hind** A group of Indic dialects that includes Urdu and Hindi. **—Hindustani** *adj.* Of or relating to Hindustan, its people, or the Hindustani language.

Hines (hīnz), **Earl.** Known as "Fatha." 1905–1983. American musician. A prominent jazz pianist for 50 years, he first gained wide recognition for his recordings with Louis Armstrong in the 1920's.

hinge (hĭnj) *n.* **1.a.** A jointed or flexible device that allows the turning or pivoting of a part, such as a door or lid, on a stationary frame. **b.** A similar structure or part, such as one that enables the valves of a bivalve mollusk to open and close. **2.** A small folded paper rectangle gummed on one side, used especially to fasten stamps in an album. **3.** A point or circumstance on which subsequent events depend. **—hinge** *v.* **hinged, hing·ing, hing·es.** *—tr.* **1.** To attach by or equip with or as if with hinges or a hinge. **2.** To consider or make (something) dependent on something else; predicate: *"convenient and misleading fictions for hinging an argument"* (Stephen Jay Gould). *—intr.* To be contingent on a single factor; depend: *This plan hinges on her approval.* [Middle English. See **konk-** in Appendix.]

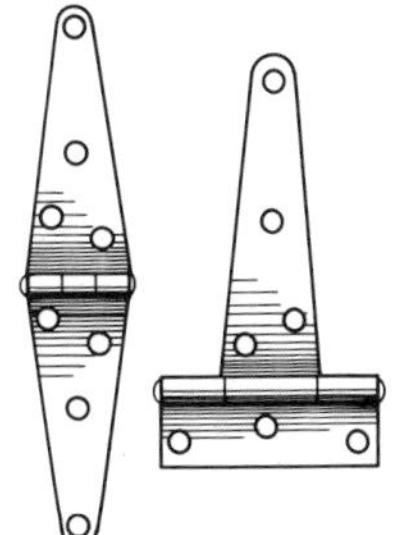

hinge
Left: Strap hinge
Right: T hinge

hinge joint *n.* A joint, such as the elbow, in which a convex part of one bone fits into a concave part of another, allowing motion in only one plane.

Hing·ham (hĭng'əm). A town of eastern Massachusetts on Massachusetts Bay southeast of Boston. It is a residential suburb and summer resort. Population, 20,339.

hin·ny (hĭn'ē) *n., pl.* **-nies.** The hybrid offspring of a male horse and a female donkey. [Alteration of Latin *hinnus,* from Greek *ginnos, innos.*]

Hin·shel·wood (hĭn'shəl-wo͝od', -chəl-), Sir **Cyril Norman.** 1897–1967. British chemist. He shared a 1956 Nobel Prize for research on the kinetics of chemical reactions.

hint (hĭnt) *n.* **1.** A slight indication or intimation: *wanted to avoid any hint of scandal.* **2.a.** A brief or indirect suggestion; a tip: *stock-trading hints.* **b.** A statement conveying information in an indirect fashion; a clue: *Give me a hint about the big news.* **3.** A barely perceptible amount: *just a hint of color.* **4.** *Archaic.* An occasion; an opportunity. **—hint** *v.* **hint·ed, hint·ing, hints.** *—tr.* To indicate or make known in an indirect manner. *—intr.* To give a hint: *wouldn't hint at the true purpose of the meeting.* See Synonyms at **suggest.** [Probably from Middle English *hinten, henten,* to catch, grasp, from Old English *hentan.*]

hin·ter·land (hĭn'tər-lănd') *n.* **1.** The land directly adjacent to and inland from a coast. **2.a.** A region remote from urban areas; backcountry. **b.** A region situated beyond metropolitan centers of culture. [German : *hinter-,* behind (from Middle High German *hinter,* from Old High German; see **ko-** in Appendix) + *Land,* land (from Middle High German *lant,* from Old High German; see **lendh-** in Appendix).]

hip¹ (hĭp) *n.* **1.a.** The laterally projecting prominence of the pelvis or pelvic region from the waist to the thigh. **b.** A homologous posterior part in quadrupeds. **c.** The hip joint. **2.** *Architecture.* The external angle formed by the meeting of two adjacent sloping sides of a roof. [Middle English, from Old English *hype.*]

hip² (hĭp) also **hep** (hĕp) *adj.* **hip·per, hip·pest** also **hep·per, hep·pest.** *Slang.* **1.** Keenly aware of, knowledgeable about, or interested in the latest trends or developments. **2.** Cognizant; wise: *I am hip to what's going on.* **3.** Very fashionable or stylish. [Perhaps from Wolof *hipi, hepi,* to open one's eyes, be aware.] **—hip** *n. & v.* **—hip'ly** *adv.* **—hip'ness** *n.*

hip³ (hĭp) *n.* A rose hip. [Middle English *hipe,* from Old English *hēope.*]

hip⁴ (hĭp) *interj.* Usually used to begin a cheer: *Hip, hip, hooray!*

hip·bone (hĭp'bōn') *n.* Either of two large flat bones each forming one of the lateral halves of the pelvis and consisting of the fused ilium, ischium, and pubis. Also called *innominate bone.*

hip boot *n.* A very high boot extending to the hips, worn especially by fishers.

hip-hop (hĭp'hŏp') *Slang. n.* The popular street culture of big-city and especially inner-city youth, characterized by graffiti art, break dancing, and rap music. **—hip-hop** *adj.* Of, relating to, or characteristic of this culture. [Probably HIP² + HOP¹.]

hip-hug·gers (hĭp'hŭg'ərz) *pl.n.* Tight-fitting pants whose waistline rests at hip level.

hip joint *n.* The ball-and-socket joint formed by the head of the femur and the cup-shaped cavity of the hipbone.

ă pat	oi boy
ā pay	ou out
âr care	o͝o took
ä father	o͞o boot
ĕ pet	ŭ cut
ē be	ûr urge
ĭ pit	th thin
ī pie	*th* this
îr pier	hw which
ŏ pot	zh vision
ō toe	ə about, item
ô paw	♦ regionalism

Stress marks: ' (primary); ' (secondary), as in **dictionary** (dĭk'shə-nĕr'ē)

Hip·par·chus¹ (hĭ-pär′kəs). Died 514 B.C. Athenian tyrant (527–514) who ruled with his brother Hippias.

Hip·par·chus² (hĭ-pär′kəs). fl. second century B.C. Greek astronomer who mapped the position of 850 stars in the earliest known star chart.

hipped¹ (hĭpt) *adj.* Having hips, especially of a given kind. Often used in combination: *slim-hipped; large-hipped.*

hipped² (hĭpt) *adj.* Interested or preoccupied to a great degree: *He is hipped on photography.* [Probably from *hip,* to make aware, from HIP².]

hipped³ (hĭpt) *adj. Chiefly British.* Melancholy; depressed. [Shortening and alteration of HYPOCHONDRIAC.]

Hip·pi·as (hĭp′ē-əs). Died 490 B.C. Athenian tyrant (527–510) who governed with his brother Hipparchus. After his brother's assassination, he ruled brutally until he was exiled by the Spartans (510).

hip·pie also **hip·py** (hĭp′ē) *n., pl.* **-pies.** *Slang.* A person who opposes and rejects many of the conventional standards and customs of society, especially one who advocates extreme liberalism in sociopolitical attitudes and lifestyles. [From HIP².] **—hip′pie·dom** *n.* **—hip′pie·hood′** *n.*

hip·po (hĭp′ō) *n., pl.* **-pos.** A hippopotamus.

Hip·po (hĭp′ō) also **Hippo Re·gi·us** (rē′jē-əs). An ancient city of northwest Africa in present-day northeast Algeria south of Annaba. Saint Augustine was its bishop from A.D. 396 to 430.

hip·po·cam·pus (hĭp′ə-kăm′pəs) *n., pl.* **-pi** (-pī′). *Anatomy.* A ridge in the floor of each lateral ventricle of the brain that consists mainly of gray matter and has a central role in memory processes. [Late Latin, a sea horse with a horse's forelegs and a dolphin's tail (from its shape in cross section), from Greek *hippokampos* : *hippos,* horse; see **ekwo-** in Appendix + *kampos,* sea monster.] **—hip′po·cam′pal** (-pəl) *adj.*

hip·po·cras (hĭp′ə-krăs′) *n.* A cordial made from wine and flavored with spices, formerly used as a medicine. [Middle English *ipocras,* from Old French *ypocras, hypocras,* from alteration of *Hippocras,* Hippocrates.]

Hip·poc·ra·tes (hĭ-pŏk′rə-tēz′). Called "the Father of Medicine." 460?–377? B.C. Greek physician who laid the foundations of scientific medicine by freeing medical study from the constraints of philosophical speculation and superstition. He is traditionally but inaccurately considered the author of the Hippocratic oath. **—Hip′po·crat′ic** (hĭp′ə-krăt′ĭk) *adj.*

Hippocratic oath *n.* An oath of ethical professional behavior sworn by new physicians, attributed to Hippocrates.

Hip·po·crene (hĭp′ə-krēn′, hĭp′ə-krē′nē) *n. Greek Mythology.* A fountain on Mount Helicon, Greece, sacred to the Muses and regarded as a source of poetic inspiration. [Latin *Hippocrēnē,* from Greek *Hippokrēnē* : *hippos,* horse (from the myth that Pegasus' hoof created it); see **ekwo-** in Appendix + *krēnē,* fountain.]

Hirohito
Photographed in 1984

hip·po·drome (hĭp′ə-drōm′) *n.* **1.** *Sports.* An arena for equestrian shows. **2.** An open-air stadium with an oval course for horse and chariot races in ancient Greece and Rome. [French, from Old French *ypodrome,* from Latin *hippodromos,* from Greek : *hippos,* horse; see **ekwo-** in Appendix + *dromos,* racecourse.]

hip·po·griff also **hip·po·gryph** (hĭp′ə-grĭf′) *n. Mythology.* A monster having the wings, claws, and head of a griffin and the body and hindquarters of a horse. [French *hippogriffe,* from Italian *ippogrifo* : *ippo-,* horse (from Greek *hippos;* see **ekwo-** in Appendix) + *grifo,* griffin (from Latin *grȳphus;* see GRIFFIN).]

Hip·pol·y·ta (hĭ-pŏl′ĭ-tə) *n. Greek Mythology.* A queen of the Amazons killed by Hercules.

Hip·pol·y·tus (hĭ-pŏl′ĭ-təs) *n. Greek Mythology.* A son of Hippolyta and Theseus who was killed by Poseidon.

Hip·pom·e·nes (hĭ-pŏm′ə-nēz) *n. Greek Mythology.* The suitor who tricked and thereby outran Atalanta.

hip·po·pot·a·mus (hĭp′ə-pŏt′ə-məs) *n., pl.* **-mus·es** or **-mi** (-mī′). **1.** A large, chiefly aquatic African herbivorous mammal *(Hippopotamus amphibius)* having thick, dark, almost hairless skin, short legs with four toes, and a broad, wide-mouthed muzzle. Also called *river horse.* **2.** The pygmy hippopotamus. [Latin, from Greek *hippopotamos* : *hippos,* horse; see **ekwo-** in Appendix + *potamos,* river; see **pet-** in Appendix.]

Hippo Re·gi·us (rē′jē-əs). See **Hippo.**

hip·py (hĭp′ē) *n. Slang.* Variant of **hippie.**

hip roof *n.* A roof having sloping edges and sides.

hip·ster (hĭp′stər) *n. Slang.* One who is exceptionally aware of or interested in the latest trends and tastes, especially a devotee of modern jazz.

hip·ster·ism (hĭp′stə-rĭz′əm) *n. Slang.* **1.** The quality or condition of being hip. **2.** The lifestyle characteristic of hipsters.

hi·ra·ga·na (hîr′ə-gä′nə) *n.* A cursive kana used for polite, informal, or casual writing. [Japanese : *hira,* ordinary, plain + *kana,* kana; see KANA.]

Hi·ra·ka·ta (hē′rä-kä′tä, hē-rä′kä-tä′). A city of southern Honshu, Japan, a suburb north-northeast of Osaka in an agricultural and lumbering area. Population, 382,257.

hir·cine (hûr′sīn′, -sĭn) *adj.* Of or characteristic of a goat, especially in strong odor. [Middle English *hircyne,* from Latin *hircīnus,* from *hircus,* goat.]

hire (hīr) *v.* **hired, hir·ing, hires.** *—tr.* **1.a.** To engage the services of (a person) for a fee; employ: *hired a new clerk.* **b.** To engage the temporary use of for a fee; rent: *hire a car for the day.* **2.** To grant the services of or the temporary use of for a fee: *hired himself out as a cook; hired out the cottage for the summer.* *—intr.* To obtain work: *She hired on as a deck hand. He hired out as a photographer.* **—hire** *n.* **1.a.** The act of hiring. **b.** The condition or fact of being hired. **2.a.** Payment for services; wages. **b.** Payment for the use of something. **3.** *Informal.* One who is hired: *two new hires in the sales department.* [Middle English *hiren,* from Old English *hӯrian.*] **—hir′a·ble, hire′a·ble** *adj.* **—hir′er** *n.*

hired gun (hīrd) *n. Slang.* **1.** One, especially a professional killer, who is hired to kill another person. **2.** One hired to fight for or protect another. **3.** One who is proficient at obtaining power for others. **4.** One with special knowledge or expertise, as in business, law, or government, who is hired to resolve particularly difficult or complex problems.

hired hand *n.* **1.** A paid employee, especially on a farm or ranch. **2.** *Informal.* A paid employee.

hire·ling (hīr′lĭng) *n.* One who works solely for compensation, especially a person willing to perform for a fee tasks considered menial or offensive.

hire purchase *n. Chiefly British.* Purchase of a commodity on an installment plan.

hi-res (hī′rĕz′) *adj. Computer Science.* High-resolution.

hir·ing hall (hīr′ĭng) *n.* A union-operated placement center where jobs from various employers are allotted to registered applicants according to a set order based usually on rotation or seniority.

Hi·ro·hi·to (hîr′ō-hē′tō). 1901–1989. Emperor of Japan (1926–1989) who advocated the Japanese government's unconditional surrender that ended World War II (1945). In 1946 he renounced his divine status.

Hi·ro·shi·ge (hîr′ō-shē′gā, hē′rô-shē′gĕ), **Ando.** 1797–1858. Japanese artist who captured the serenity of his country's landscape with his superbly composed color woodblock prints.

Hi·ro·shi·ma (hîr′ə-shē′mə, hĭ-rō′shə-mə). A city of southwest Honshu, Japan, on the Inland Sea west of Osaka. Founded in the 16th century, it was destroyed in World War II by the first atomic bomb used in warfare (August 6, 1945). The rebuilt city is an important commercial center. Population, 1,044,129.

hir·sute (hûr′so͞ot′, hîr′-, hər-so͞ot′) *adj.* **1.** Covered with hair; hairy. **2.** *Botany.* Covered with stiff or coarse hairs. [Latin *hirsūtus,* hairy, bristly.] **—hir′sute′ness** *n.*

hir·sut·ism (hûr′so͞o-tĭz′əm, hîr′-, hər-so͞o′-) *n.* Heavy growth of hair, often in abnormal distribution.

hir·u·din (hîr-o͞od′n, hîr′ə-dən, -yə-) *n.* A substance extracted from the salivary glands of leeches and used as an anticoagulant. [Originally a trademark, from Latin *hirūdō,* leech.]

his (hĭz) *adj.* The possessive form of **he.** Used as a modifier before a noun: *his boots; his accomplishments.* **—his** *pron. (used with a sing. or pl. verb).* Used to indicate the one or ones belonging to him: *If you can't find your hat, take his.* [Middle English, from Old English. See **ko-** in Appendix.]

His·pan·ic (hĭ-spăn′ĭk) *adj.* **1.** Of or relating to Spain or Spanish-speaking Latin America. **2.** Of or relating to a Spanish-speaking people or culture. **—Hispanic** *n.* **1.** A Spanish-speaking person. **2.** A U.S. citizen or resident of Latin-American or Spanish descent. [Latin *Hispānicus,* from *Hispānia,* Spain.]

USAGE NOTE: There are a number of words denoting persons who trace their origins to a Spanish-speaking country or culture. *Hispanic* is the broadest of these terms, encompassing all Spanish-speaking peoples in both hemispheres and emphasizing the common denominator of language between communities that sometimes have little else in common. It is widely used in both official and unofficial contexts and is entirely acceptable, although like the term *Spanish American,* it has occasionally been criticized as unduly emphasizing the role of European influences in shaping ethnic identity to the neglect of indigenous cultures. *Latino* is also in wide use, but it is somewhat less formal in most contexts and is generally restricted to persons of Latin-American descent. See Usage Note at **Chicano.**

Hispanic American *n.* **1.** A U.S. citizen or resident of Hispanic descent. **2.** A Spanish American. **—His·pan′ic-A·mer′i·can** (hĭ-spăn′ĭk-ə-mĕr′ĭ-kən) *adj.*

His·pan·i·cize (hĭ-spăn′ĭ-sīz′) *tr.v.* **-cized, -ciz·ing, -ciz·es.** **1.** To make Spanish in form, style, or character. **2.** To bring under Hispanic influence or control. **—His·pan′i·ci·za′tion** (-sĭ-zā′shən) *n.*

His·pan·io·la (hĭs′pən-yō′lə). Formerly **Hai·ti** (hā′tē). An island of the West Indies east of Cuba, divided between Haiti and the Dominican Republic. It was discovered by Columbus in 1492 and was originally called Española. The western part (now Haiti) was ceded to France by Spain in 1697.

His·pa·nism (hĭs′pə-nĭz′əm) or **His·pan·i·cism** (hĭ-spăn′ĭ-sĭz′əm) *n.* A Spanish word, phrase, or linguistic feature occurring in another language.

His·pa·nist (hĭs′pə-nĭst) *n.* A specialist in Spanish language or literature or in the languages and literatures of Spain, Portugal, and Latin America.

His·pa·no (hĭ-spăn′ō, -spä′nō) *n., pl.* **-nos.** **1.** A native or resident of Spanish descent living in the southwest United States.

2. A Hispanic. [Short for *Hispano-American,* from Spanish *hispano,* Spanish, from Latin *Hispānus,* from *Hispānī,* the Spaniards.]

Hispano— *pref.* Spanish; Hispanic: *Hispanophile.* [From Latin *Hispānus.* See HISPANO.]

Hispano American *n.* A Hispanic American. **—His·pa′no-A·mer′i·can** (hĭ-spăn′ō-ə-mĕr′ĭ-kən) *adj.*

His·pan·o·phile (hĭ-spăn′ə-fīl′) *n.* An admirer of Spain or of Spanish-speaking countries or peoples. **—His·pan′o·phil′i·a** (-fĭl′ē-ə).

His·pan·o·phobe (hĭ-spăn′ə-fōb′) *n.* One who has an aversion to Spain or to Spanish-speaking countries or peoples. **—His·pan′o·pho′bi·a** *n.*

his·pid (hĭs′pĭd) *adj.* Covered with stiff or rough hairs; bristly: *hispid stems.* [Latin *hispidus.*] **—his·pid′i·ty** (hĭ-spĭd′ĭ-tē) *n.*

hiss (hĭs) *n.* **1.** A sharp, sibilant sound similar to a sustained *s.* **2.** An expression of disapproval, contempt, or dissatisfaction conveyed by use of this sharp, sibilant sound. **—hiss** *v.* **hissed, hiss·ing, hiss·es.** *—intr.* To make a sharp, sibilant sound: *The audience booed and hissed. The teakettle hissed on the stove.* *—tr.* **1.** To utter with a sharp, sibilant sound. **2.** To express (a negative view or reaction) by uttering a sharp, sibilant sound: *The audience hissed its displeasure.* [Middle English *hissen,* to hiss, of imitative origin.] **—hiss′er** *n.* **—hiss′ing·ly** *adv.*

Hiss (hĭs), **Alger.** Born 1904. American public official. Accused of espionage at the height of the Communist scare, he was convicted of perjury (1950) in a controversial case.

♦ **his·sy fit** (hĭs′ē) *n. Chiefly Southern U.S.* See **tantrum.**

hist. *abbr.* **1.** Historian. **2.** Historical. **3.** History.

hist— *pref.* Variant of **histo—.**

his·tam·i·nase (hĭ-stăm′ə-nās′, -nāz′, hĭs′tə-mə-) *n.* An enzyme that inactivates histamine and is found in the digestive system.

his·ta·mine (hĭs′tə-mēn′, -mĭn) *n.* A physiologically active amine, $C_5H_9N_3$, found in plant and animal tissue. It is released from cells of the immune system in human beings as part of an allergic reaction. [HIST(IDINE) + AMINE.] **—his′ta·min′ic** (-mĭn′ĭk) *adj.*

his·ti·dine (hĭs′tĭ-dēn′, -dĭn) *n.* An essential amino acid, $C_6H_9N_3O_2$, important for the growth and repair of tissues. [HIST(O)— + —ID(E) + —INE [2].]

his·ti·o·cyte (hĭs′tē-ə-sīt′) *n.* A relatively inactive, immobile macrophage found in normal connective tissue. Also called *fixed macrophage.* [Greek *histion,* web, diminutive of *histos;* see **stā-** in Appendix + —CYTE.] **—his′ti·o·cyt′ic** (-sĭt′ĭk) *adj.*

his·ti·o·cy·to·sis (hĭs′tē-ō′sī-tō′sĭs) *n., pl.* **-ses** (-sēz). Any of several abnormal conditions characterized by the appearance of histiocytes in the blood or tissues.

histo— or **hist—** *pref.* Body tissue: *histogenesis.* [From Greek, from *histos,* web. See **stā-** in Appendix.]

his·to·chem·is·try (hĭs′tō-kĕm′ĭ-strē) *n.* The branch of science that deals with the chemical composition of the cells and tissues of the body. **—his′to·chem′i·cal** (-ĭ-kəl) *adj.* **—his′to·chem′i·cal·ly** *adv.*

his·to·com·pat·i·bil·i·ty (hĭs′tō-kəm-păt′ə-bĭl′ĭ-tē) *n., pl.* **-ties.** A state or condition in which the absence of immunological interference permits the grafting of tissue or the transfusion of blood without rejection. **—his′to·com·pat′i·ble** *adj.*

histocompatibility antigen *n.* Any of various antigens on the surface of cell membranes that serve to identify a cell as self or nonself. These antigens determine whether a tissue graft or transfusion will be accepted by a recipient.

his·to·di·al·y·sis (hĭs′tō-dī-ăl′ĭ-sĭs) *n.* See **histolysis.**

his·to·gen·e·sis (hĭs′tō-jĕn′ĭ-sĭs) *n.* The formation and development of bodily tissues. **—his′to·ge·net′ic** (-jə-nĕt′ĭk), **his′to·gen′ic** (-jĕn′ĭk) *adj.* **—his′to·ge·net′i·cal·ly, his′to·gen′i·cal·ly** *adv.*

his·to·gram (hĭs′tə-grăm′) *n.* A bar graph of a frequency distribution in which the widths of the bars are proportional to the classes into which the variable has been divided and the heights of the bars are proportional to the class frequencies.

his·tol·o·gy (hĭ-stŏl′ə-jē) *n., pl.* **-gies. 1.** The anatomical study of the microscopic structure of animal and plant tissues. **2.** The microscopic structure of tissue. **—his′to·log′i·cal** (hĭs′tə-lŏj′ĭ-kəl), **his′to·log′ic** *adj.* **—his′to·log′i·cal·ly** *adv.* **—his·tol′o·gist** *n.*

his·tol·y·sis (hĭ-stŏl′ĭ-sĭs) *n.* The breakdown and disintegration of organic tissue. Also called *histodialysis.* **—his′to·lyt′ic** (hĭs′tə-lĭt′ĭk) *adj.* **—his′to·lyt′i·cal·ly** *adv.*

his·to·mo·ni·a·sis (hĭs′tə-mə-nī′ə-sĭs) *n.* See **blackhead** (sense 2). [New Latin *Histomonas,* genus of zooflagellates (HISTO— + Greek *monas,* monad; see MONAD) + —IASIS.]

his·tone (hĭs′tōn′) *n.* Any of several small, basic proteins most commonly found in association with the DNA in chromatin.

his·to·pa·thol·o·gy (hĭs′tō-pə-thŏl′ə-jē, -pă-) *n.* The study of the microscopic anatomical changes in diseased tissue. **—his′to·path′o·log′ic** (-păth′ə-lŏj′ĭk), **his′to·path′o·log′i·cal** *adj.* **—his′to·path′o·log′i·cal·ly** *adv.* **—his′to·pa·thol′o·gist** *n.*

his·to·phys·i·ol·o·gy (hĭs′tō-fĭz′ē-ŏl′ə-jē) *n.* The branch of physiology that deals with the structure and function of tissues. **—his′to·phys′i·o·log′ic** (-ē-ə-lŏj′ĭk), **his′to·phys′i·o·log′i·cal** (-ĭ-kəl) *adj.*

his·to·plas·mo·sis (hĭs′tō-plăz-mō′sĭs) *n., pl.* **-ses** (-sēz). A disease caused by the inhalation of spores of the fungus *Histoplasma capsulatum,* most often asymptomatic but occasionally producing acute pneumonia or an influenzalike illness and spreading to other organs and systems in the body.

his·to·ri·an (hĭ-stôr′ē-ən, -stōr′-, -stŏr′-) *n. Abbr.* **hist. 1.** A writer, student, or scholar of history. **2.** One who writes or compiles a chronological record of events; a chronicler: *"The historian, registering the facts beyond doubt, and in their context, cannot but also judge"* (Robert Conquest).

his·tor·ic (hĭ-stôr′ĭk, -stŏr′-) *adj.* **1.** Having importance in or influence on history. **2.** Historical.

USAGE NOTE: *Historic* and *historical* are differentiated in usage, though their senses overlap. *Historic* refers to what is important in history: *the historic first voyage to outer space.* It is also used of what is famous or interesting because of its association with persons or events in history: *a historic house. Historical* refers to whatever existed in the past, whether regarded as important or not: *a historical character. Historical* refers also to anything concerned with history or the study of the past: *a historical novel; historical discoveries.* The differentiation between the words is not complete. They are often used interchangeably: *historic times* or *historical times.*

his·tor·i·cal (hĭ-stôr′ĭ-kəl, -stŏr′-) *adj. Abbr.* **hist. 1.a.** Of or relating to the character of history. **b.** Based on or concerned with events in history. **c.** Used in the past: *historical costumes; historical weapons.* **2.** Important or famous in history. See Usage Note at **historic. 3.** Diachronic. **—his·tor′i·cal·ly** *adv.* **—his·tor′i·cal·ness** *n.*

historical linguistics *n. (used with a sing. verb).* The study of change in language or in a particular language or language family over time, sometimes including the reconstruction of unattested forms of earlier stages of a language. Also called *philology.*

historical materialism *n.* A major tenet in the Marxist theory of history that regards material economic forces as the base on which sociopolitical institutions and ideas are built.

historical novel *n.* A novel that re-creates a period or an event in history, using fictional or actual characters or often both.

historical present *n.* The present tense used in the narration of events set in the past.

historical school *n.* A school of theorists, as in law or economics, stressing the influence of historical conditions.

his·tor·i·cism (hĭ-stôr′ĭ-sĭz′əm, -stŏr′-) *n.* **1.** A theory that events are determined or influenced by conditions and inherent processes beyond the control of human beings. **2.** A theory that stresses the significant influence of history as a criterion of value. **—his·tor′i·cist** *adj. & n.*

his·to·ric·i·ty (hĭs′tə-rĭs′ĭ-tē) *n.* Historical authenticity.

his·tor·i·cize (hĭ-stôr′ĭ-sīz′, -stŏr′-) *v.* **-cized, -ciz·ing, -ciz·es.** *—tr.* To make or make appear historical. *—intr.* To use historical details or materials. **—his·tor′i·ci·za′tion** (-sĭ-zā′shən) *n.*

his·to·ried (hĭs′tə-rēd) *adj.* Having an interesting history; storied: *an ancient and historied land.*

his·to·ri·og·ra·pher (hĭ-stôr′ē-ŏg′rə-fər, -stōr′-) *n.* **1.** A specialist in historiography. **2.** A historian, especially one designated by a group or public institution.

his·to·ri·og·ra·phy (hĭ-stôr′ē-ŏg′rə-fē, -stōr′-) *n.* **1.** The principles, theories, or methodology of scholarly historical research and presentation. **2.** The writing of history based on a critical analysis, evaluation, and selection of authentic source materials and composition of these materials into a narrative subject to scholarly methods of criticism. **3.** A body of historical literature. [French *historiographie,* from Old French, from Greek *historiographia* : *historia,* history; see HISTORY + *-graphia,* -graphy.] **—his·to′ri·o·graph′ic** (-ē-ə-grăf′ĭk), **his·to′ri·o·graph′i·cal** (-ĭ-kəl) *adj.* **—his·to′ri·o·graph′i·cal·ly** *adv.*

his·to·ry (hĭs′tə-rē) *n., pl.* **-ries.** *Abbr.* **hist. 1.** A narrative of events; a story. **2.a.** A chronological record of events, as of the life or development of a people or an institution, often including an explanation of or commentary on those events: *"The queens in history compare favorably with the kings"* (Elizabeth Cady Stanton). **b.** A formal written account of related natural phenomena: *a history of volcanoes.* **c.** A record of a patient's medical background. **3.** The branch of knowledge that records and analyzes past events: *"History has a long-range perspective"* (Elizabeth Gurley Flynn). **4.a.** The events forming the subject matter of a historical account. **b.** Something that belongs to the past: *Their troubles are history now.* **c.** An interesting past: *a house with a history.* **5.** A drama based on historical events: *the histories of Shakespeare.* [Middle English *histoire,* from Old French, from Latin *historia,* from Greek, from *historein,* to inquire, from *histōr,* learned man. See **weid-** in Appendix.]

his·tri·on·ic (hĭs′trē-ŏn′ĭk) also **his·tri·on·i·cal** (-ĭ-kəl) *adj.* **1.** Of or relating to actors or acting. **2.** Excessively dramatic or emotional; affected. See Synonyms at **dramatic.** [Late Latin *histriōnicus,* from Latin *histriō, histriōn-,* actor, probably of Etruscan origin.] **—his′tri·on′i·cal·ly** *adv.*

his·tri·on·ics (hĭs′trē-ŏn′ĭks) *n.* **1.** *(used with a pl. verb).*

ă pat	oi boy
ā pay	ou out
âr care	ŏŏ took
ä father	ōō boot
ĕ pet	ŭ cut
ē be	ûr urge
ĭ pit	th thin
ī pie	*th* this
îr pier	hw which
ŏ pot	zh vision
ō toe	ə about, item
ô paw	♦ regionalism

Stress marks: ′ (primary); ′ (secondary), as in **dictionary** (dĭk′shə-nĕr′ē)

Theatrical arts or performances. **2.** *(used with a sing. or pl. verb).* Exaggerated emotional behavior calculated for effect.

hit (hĭt) *v.* **hit, hit·ting, hits.** —*tr.* **1.a.** To come into contact with forcefully; strike: *The car hit the guardrail.* **b.** To reach with or as if with a blow: *The bullet hit the police officer in the shoulder.* **2.a.** To cause to come into contact: *She hit her hand against the wall.* **b.** To deal a blow to. **c.** To strike with a missile: *fired and hit the target.* **3.** To press or push (a key or button, for example): *hit the return key by mistake.* **4.** *Sports.* **a.** To reach with a propelled object: *hit the running back with a pass.* **b.** To score in this way: *She hit the winning goal.* **c.** To perform (a shot or maneuver) successfully: *couldn't hit the jump shot.* **d.** To propel with a stroke or blow: *hit the ball onto the green.* **5.** *Baseball.* **a.** To execute (a base hit) successfully: *hit a single.* **b.** To bat against (a pitcher or kind of pitch) successfully: *can't hit a slider.* **6.** To affect, especially adversely: *The company was hit hard by the recession.* **7.** *Informal.* To come upon or discover, especially by chance: *finally hit the right exit.* **8.a.** *Informal.* To attain or reach: *Monthly sales hit a new high. She hit 40 on her last birthday.* **b.** To accord with; suit: *The idea hit my fancy.* **c.** To produce or represent accurately: *trying to hit the right note.* **9.** *Games.* To deal cards to. **10.** *Slang.* To give a drink of liquor or a dose of a narcotic to. —*intr.* **1.** To strike or deal a blow. **2.a.** To come into contact with something; collide. **b.** To attack: *The raiders hit at dawn.* **c.** To happen or occur: *The storm hit without warning.* **3.** To achieve or find something desired or sought: *finally hit on the answer; hit upon a solution to the problem.* **4.** *Baseball.* To bat. **5.** To ignite a mixture of air and fuel in the cylinders. Used of an internal-combustion engine. —**hit** *n. Abbr.* **h, h. 1.a.** A collision or an impact. **b.** A successfully executed shot, blow, thrust, or throw. **2.** A successful or popular venture: *a Broadway hit.* **3.** An apt or effective remark. **4.** *Baseball.* A base hit. **5.** *Slang.* **a.** A dose of a narcotic drug. **b.** A puff of a cigarette or a marijuana cigarette or pipe. **6.** *Slang.* A murder planned and carried out usually by a member of an underworld syndicate. —***phrasal verbs.*** **hit on.** *Slang.* To pay unsolicited and usually unwanted sexual attention to: *can't go into a bar lately without being hit on.* **hit up.** *Slang.* To approach and ask (someone) for something, especially for money: *tried to hit me up for a loan.* —***idioms.*** **hit it big.** *Slang.* To be successful: *investors who hit it big on the stock market.* **hit it off.** *Informal.* To get along well together. **hit (someone) over the head.** *Informal.* To be so repetitive or obvious as to become redundant or insulting: *We were simply hit over the head by the poet's misogynistic imagery.* **hit the books.** *Informal.* To study, especially with concentrated effort. **hit the bottle.** *Slang.* To engage in drinking alcoholic beverages. **hit the fan.** *Slang.* To have serious, usually adverse consequences. **hit the ground running.** *Informal.* To begin a venture with great energy, involvement, and competence. **hit the hay** (or **sack).** *Slang.* To go to bed: *hit the hay well before midnight.* **hit the high points** (or **spots).** To direct attention to the most important points or places. **hit the jackpot.** To become highly and unexpectedly successful, especially to win a great deal of money. **hit the nail on the head.** To be absolutely right. **hit the road.** *Slang.* To set out, as on a trip; leave. **hit the roof** (or **ceiling).** *Slang.* To express anger, especially vehemently. **hit the spot.** To give total or desired satisfaction, as food or drink. [Middle English *hitten,* from Old English *hyttan,* from Old Norse *hitta.*] —**hit′less** *adj.* —**hit′ta·ble** *adj.*

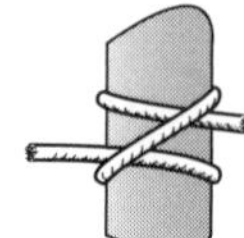

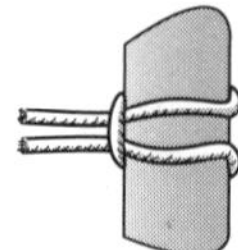

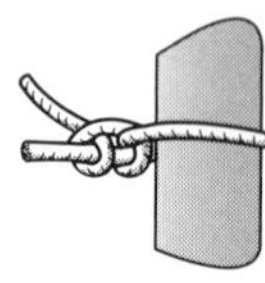

hitch
Top: Clove hitch
Center: Cow hitch
Bottom: Two half hitches

hit-and-miss (hĭt′n-mĭs′) *adj.* Sometimes succeeding and sometimes not.

hit-and-run (hĭt′n-rŭn′) *adj.* **1.** Being or involving the driver of a motor vehicle who leaves the scene of an accident, especially one in which a pedestrian or another vehicle has been struck. **2.** *Baseball.* Relating to or being a play in which a base runner starts to run on the pitch and the batter attempts to hit the ball to protect the runner. **3.** Involving or designed for swift specific action or effect: *"a day of hit-and-run disturbances by bands of dissident students"* (Alfonso Narvaez).

Alfred Hitchcock
Photographed in 1960

hitch (hĭch) *v.* **hitched, hitch·ing, hitch·es.** —*tr.* **1.** To fasten or catch temporarily with or as if with a loop, hook, or noose. **2.** To connect or attach, as to a vehicle: *hitched the horses to the sleigh.* **3.** To move or raise by pulling or jerking: *hitch up one's suspenders.* **4.** *Informal.* To hitchhike: *hitched a ride to the rally.* —*intr.* **1.** To move haltingly; hobble. **2.** To become entangled, snarled, or fastened. **3.** *Slang.* To get married: *We got hitched last weekend.* **4.** *Informal.* To hitchhike. —**hitch** *n.* **1.** Any of various knots used as a temporary fastening. **2.** A device used to connect one thing to another. **3.** A short jerking motion; a tug. **4.** A hobble or limp. **5.** An impediment or a delay: *a hitch in our plans.* **6.** A term of service, especially of military service. **7.** *Informal.* A free ride obtained along a road. [Probably from Middle English *hytchen, icchen,* to move, jerk.] —**hitch′er** *n.*

Hitch·cock (hĭch′kŏk′), Sir **Alfred Joseph.** 1899–1980. British director known for his suspense films, especially *The 39 Steps* (1935), *Strangers on a Train* (1951), and *Psycho* (1960).

hitch·hike (hĭch′hīk′) *v.* **-hiked, -hik·ing, -hikes.** —*intr.* To travel by soliciting free rides along a road. —*tr.* To solicit or get (a free ride) along a road. —**hitch′hike′** *n.* —**hitch′hik′er** *n.*

Hitch·ings (hĭch′ĭngz), **George Herbert.** Born 1905. American biochemist. He shared a 1988 Nobel Prize for developing drugs to treat leukemia and gout.

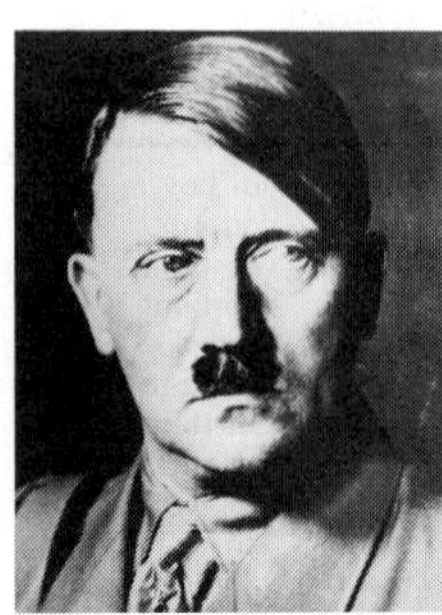

Adolf Hitler

hitch·ing post (hĭch′ĭng) *n.* A post to which an animal, especially a horse, is hitched.

hi-tech (hī′tĕk′) *adj.* Variant of **high-tech.**

hith·er (hĭth′ər) *adv.* To or toward this place: *Come hither.* —**hither** *adj.* Located on the near side. —***idiom.*** **hither and thither** (or **yon).** In or to many places; here and there: *looked hither and thither for the ring; ran hither and yon.* [Middle English, from Old English *hider.* See **ko-** in Appendix.]

hith·er·most (hĭth′ər-mōst′) *adj.* Nearest to this place or side.

hith·er·to (hĭth′ər-to͞o′, hĭth′ər-to͞o′) *adv.* Until this time: *The weather, which had hitherto been sunny and mild, suddenly turned cold.*

hith·er·ward (hĭth′ər-wərd) also **hith·er·wards** (-wərdz) *adv.* Hither.

Hit·ler (hĭt′lər), **Adolf.** Known as "Der Führer." 1889–1945. Austrian-born founder of the German Nazi Party and chancellor of the Third Reich (1933–1945). His fascist philosophy, embodied in *Mein Kampf* (1925–1927), attracted widespread support, and after 1934 he ruled as an absolute dictator. Hitler's aggressive nationalist policies resulted in the invasion of Poland (1939) and the outbreak of World War II. His regime was infamous for the extermination of millions of people, especially European Jews. He committed suicide when the collapse of the Third Reich was imminent (1945). —**Hit·ler′i·an** (hĭt-lîr′ē-ən) *adj.*

Hit·ler·ism (hĭt′lə-rĭz′əm) *n.* The fascistic and nationalistic theories and practices of Adolf Hitler and the Nazis. —**Hit′ler·ite′** (-lə-rīt′) *adj. & n.*

hit list *n. Slang.* **1.** A list of potential murder victims. **2.** A list designating a target, as for attack, coercion, or elimination: *"had a hit list of executives he wanted fired"* (New York).

hit man *n. Slang.* **1.** A man hired by a crime syndicate as a professional killer. **2.** A hatchet man.

hit-or-miss (hĭt′ər-mĭs′) *adj.* Marked by a lack of care, accuracy, or organization; random. —**hit or miss** *adv.*

hit parade *n.* **1.** *Music.* A ranked group or listing of the currently most popular songs. **2.** A collection or listing of the most popular or excellent items or people of a certain kind.

hit squad *n. Slang.* **1.** A squad or team of hired executioners, as one organized for carrying out a political assassination. **2.** A group of political terrorists.

Hitt. *abbr.* Hittite.

hit·ter (hĭt′ər) *n.* **1.** One who hits or strikes something. **2.** *Baseball.* A batter.

Hit·tite (hĭt′īt′) *n. Abbr.* **Hitt 1.** A member of an ancient people living in Anatolia and northern Syria about 2000–1200 B.C. **2.** The Indo-European language of the Hittites. —**Hittite** *adj. Abbr.* **Hitt** Of or relating to the Hittites, their language, or their culture. [From Hebrew *ḥittî,* from Akkadian *ḫatti,* from Hittite *Hatti.*]

HIV (āch′ī-vē′) *n.* A retrovirus that causes AIDS. HIV was formerly known as HTLV-III. —*attributive.* Often used to modify another noun: *an HIV infection.* [H(UMAN) I(MMUNODEFICIENCY) V(IRUS).]

Hi·va O·a (hē′və ō′ə). A volcanic island of the southern Pacific Ocean in the southeast Marquesas Islands of French Polynesia. The painter Gauguin is buried here.

hive (hīv) *n.* **1.a.** A structure for housing bees, especially honeybees. **b.** A colony of bees living in such a structure. **2.** A place swarming with activity. —**hive** *v.* **hived, hiv·ing, hives.** —*tr.* **1.** To collect into a hive. **2.** To store (honey) in a hive. **3.** To store up; accumulate. —*intr.* **1.** To enter and occupy a beehive. **2.** To live with many others in close association. —***phrasal verb.*** **hive off.** To set apart from a group: *hived off the department into another division.* [Middle English, from Old English *hȳf.*]

hives (hīvz) *pl.n. (used with a sing. or pl. verb).* A skin condition characterized by intensely itching welts and caused by an allergic reaction to internal or external agents, an infection, or a nervous condition. Also called *nettle rash, urticaria.* [Origin unknown.]

hl *abbr.* Hectoliter.

H.L. *abbr.* House of Lords.

hld. *abbr. Nautical.* Hold.

hlqn *abbr.* Harlequin.

hm *abbr.* Hectometer.

H.M. *abbr.* **1.** Her Majesty. **2.** His Majesty.

HMAS or **H.M.A.S.** *abbr.* Her, or His, Majesty's Australian Ship.

HMBS or **H.M.B.S.** *abbr.* Her, or His, Majesty's British Ship.

HMCS or **H.M.C.S.** *abbr.* Her, or His, Majesty's Canadian Ship.

HMF or **H.M.F.** *abbr.* Her, or His, Majesty's Forces.

HMO (āch′ĕm-ō′) *n.* A corporation financed by insurance premiums whose member physicians and professional staff provide curative and preventive medicine within certain financial, geographic, and professional limits to enrolled volunteer members and their families. [*H(ealth) M(aintenance) O(rganization).*]

Hmong (hmông) *n., pl.* **Hmong** or **Hmongs. 1.** A member of a people inhabiting the mountainous regions of southern China and adjacent areas of Vietnam, Laos, and Thailand. **2.** The Miao-Yao language of the Hmong. Also called *Miao.*

HMS or **H.M.S.** *abbr.* Her, or His, Majesty's Ship.

HN *abbr.* Head nurse.

hny *abbr.* Honey.

ho (hō) *interj.* Used to express surprise or joy, to attract attention to something sighted, or to urge onward: *Land ho! Westward ho!.*

Ho¹ The symbol for the element **holmium.**

Ho² *abbr. Bible.* Hosea.

ho. *abbr.* House.

♦**hoa·gie** also **hoa·gy** (hō′gē) *n., pl.* **-gies.** *Chiefly Pennsylvania & New Jersey.* See **submarine** (sense 2). See Regional Note at **submarine.** [Alteration of *hoggy.*]

hoar (hôr, hōr) *adj.* Hoary. **—hoar** *n.* Hoarfrost. [Middle English *hor,* from Old English *hār.*]

hoard (hôrd, hōrd) *n.* A hidden fund or supply stored for future use; a cache. **—hoard** *v.* **hoard·ed, hoard·ing, hoards.** *—intr.* To gather or accumulate a hoard. *—tr.* **1.** To accumulate a hoard of. **2.** To keep hidden or private. [Middle English *hord,* from Old English. See **(s)keu-** in Appendix.] **—hoard′er** *n.*

hoard·ing (hôr′dĭng, hōr′-) *n.* **1.** A temporary wooden fence around a building or structure under construction or repair. **2.** *Chiefly British.* A billboard. [Obsolete *hoard, hourd,* from French dialectal *hourd,* fence, scaffold, hurdle, from Old French, of Germanic origin.]

hoar·frost (hôr′frôst′, -frŏst′, hōr′-) *n.* Frozen dew that forms a white coating on a surface. Also called *white frost.*

hoarse (hôrs, hōrs) *adj.* **hoars·er, hoars·est. 1.** Rough or grating in sound: *a hoarse cry.* **2.** Having or characterized by a husky, grating voice: *yelled ourselves hoarse.* [Middle English *hos, hors,* from Old English *hās.*] **—hoarse′ly** *adv.* **—hoarse′ness** *n.*

hoars·en (hôr′sən, hōr′-) *tr. & intr.v.* **-ened, -en·ing, -ens.** To make or become hoarse.

hoar·y (hôr′ē, hōr′ē) *adj.* **-i·er, -i·est. 1.** Gray or white with or as if with age. **2.** Covered with grayish hair or pubescence: *hoary leaves.* **3.** So old as to inspire veneration; ancient. **—hoar′i·ly** *adv.* **—hoar′i·ness** *n.*

hoary alyssum *n.* An annual European herb *(Berteroa incana)* of the mustard family, having silvery foliage, oblong fruits, and white, deeply notched flowers. It is naturalized in eastern North America. Also called *alyssum.*

hoat·zin (wät-sēn′) *n.* A crested brownish bird *(Opisthocomus hoazin)* of tropical South America whose young have claws on the first and second digits of the wings. [American Spanish *hoazín,* from Nahuatl *uatzin,* pheasant or small game bird.]

hoax (hōks) *n.* **1.** An act intended to deceive or trick. **2.** Something that has been established or accepted by fraudulent means. **—hoax** *tr.v.* **hoaxed, hoax·ing, hoax·es.** To deceive or cheat by using a hoax. [Perhaps alteration of HOCUS.] **—hoax′er** *n.*

hob¹ (hŏb) *n.* **1.** A shelf or projection at the back or side of a fireplace, used for keeping food or utensils warm. **2.** A tool used for cutting the teeth of machine parts, as of a gearwheel. [Origin unknown.]

hob² (hŏb) *n.* **1.** *Chiefly British.* A hobgoblin, a sprite, or an elf. **2.** Mischievous behavior. [From Middle English *Hob,* a nickname for Robert.]

Ho·ban (hō′bən), **James.** 1762?–1831. Irish-born American architect who designed and supervised the construction (1793–1801) and renovation (1815–1829) of the White House.

Ho·bart. 1. (hō′bärt′). A city of southeast Tasmania, Australia, on an inlet of the Tasman Sea. It was founded in 1804 as a penal colony. Population, 47,920. **2.** (hō′bərt). A city of northwest Indiana southeast of Gary. Mainly residential, it also has varied light industries. Population, 22,987.

Ho·bart (hō′bärt′, -bərt), **Garret Augustus.** 1844–1899. Vice President of the United States (1897–1899) under William McKinley.

Hob·be·ma (hŏb′ə-mə, hô′bə-mä), **Meindert.** 1638–1709. Dutch landscape painter known for a number of works, including *The Hermitage, St. Petersburg* (1663).

Hobbes (hŏbz), **Thomas.** 1588–1679. English political philosopher who wrote *Leviathan* (1651). **—Hobbes′i·an** *adj.*

Hobb·ism (hŏb′ĭz′əm) *n.* A political theory promulgated by Thomas Hobbes, advocating absolute monarchy as the only means of adequately controlling the inevitable problems created by the inherently selfish, aggrandizing nature of human beings. **—Hobb′ist** *adj. & n.*

hob·bit (hŏb′ĭt) *n.* An imaginary creature resembling a diminutive human being, having some rabbitlike characteristics, and being naturally peace-loving, domestic, and sociable. [From pseudo-Old English *holbȳtla,* hole-builder (coined by J.R.R. Tolkien) : Old English *hol,* hole; see HOLE + Old English *bȳtla,* builder, hammerer (from *bȳtl, bīetel,* mallet; see BEETLE³).]

hob·ble (hŏb′əl) *v.* **-bled, -bling, -bles.** *—intr.* To walk or move along haltingly or with difficulty; limp. *—tr.* **1.** To put a device around the legs of (a horse, for example) so as to hamper but not prevent movement. **2.** To cause to limp. **3.** To hamper the action or progress of; impede. See Synonyms at **hamper¹. —hobble** *n.* **1.** A hobbling walk or gait. **2.** A device, such as a rope or strap, used to hobble an animal. **3.** *Archaic.* An awkward situation. [Middle English *hobblen,* of Low German origin; akin to Middle Dutch *hobbelen,* to roll.] **—hob′bler** *n.*

hob·ble·bush (hŏb′əl-bo͝osh′) *n.* A deciduous shrub *(Viburnum alnifolium)* of eastern North America, having flat clusters of white flowers with the marginal flowers larger than the others.

hob·ble·de·hoy (hŏb′əl-dē-hoi′) *n., pl.* **-hoys.** A gawky adolescent boy. [Origin unknown.]

hobble skirt *n.* A long skirt, popular between 1910 and 1914, that was so narrow below the knees that it restricted normal stride.

Hobbs (hŏbz). A city of southeast New Mexico near the Texas border southeast of Roswell. Oil and natural gas were discovered in the area in 1927. Population, 29,153.

hob·by¹ (hŏb′ē) *n., pl.* **-bies.** An activity or interest pursued outside one's regular occupation and engaged in primarily for pleasure. [Middle English *hobi, hobyn,* small horse, hobby horse, perhaps from *Hobin, Hobby,* nickname for *Robert.*] **—hob′by·ist** *n.*

hob·by² (hŏb′ē) *n., pl.* **-bies.** Any of several small falcons of the genus *Falco,* formerly used for catching small birds or game. [Middle English *hobi,* from Old French *hobe, hobel.*]

hob·by·horse (hŏb′ē-hôrs′) *n.* **1.a.** A child's riding toy that consists of a long stick with an imitation horse's head on one end. **b.** See **rocking horse. 2.a.** A figure of a horse worn attached to the waist of a mummer, as in a morris dance. **b.** A person wearing such a figure. **3.a.** A favorite hobby. **b.** A topic with which one is obsessed; a fixation.

hob·gob·lin (hŏb′gŏb′lĭn) *n.* **1.** An ugly, mischievous elf or goblin. **2.** An object or a source of fear, dread, or harassment; a bugbear: *"A foolish consistency is the hobgoblin of little minds"* (Ralph Waldo Emerson).

hob·nail (hŏb′nāl′) *n.* A short nail with a thick head used to protect the soles of shoes or boots. [HOB¹, peg, projection (obsolete) + NAIL.] **—hob′nailed′** *adj.*

hob·nob (hŏb′nŏb′) *intr.v.* **-nobbed, -nob·bing, -nobs.** To associate familiarly: *hobnobs with the executives.* [From the phrase *(drink) hob or nob,* (toast) one another alternately, from obsolete and dialectal *hab nab,* have or have not : probably Middle English *habbe,* have; see HAVE + Middle English *nabbe* (contraction of *ne habbe,* have not : Old English *ne,* not; see NOT + *habbe,* have).]

WORD HISTORY: The fact that hobnobbing with our social betters may at times be a hit-or-miss proposition has an etymological justification. The verb *hobnob* originally meant "to drink together" and occurred as a varying phrase, *hob or nob, hob-a-nob,* or *hob and nob,* the first of which is recorded in 1763. This phrasal form reflects the origins of the verb in similar phrases that were used when two people were toasting each other. The probable reason that the phrases were so used is that *hob* is a variant of *hab,* as *nob* is of *nab,* and that these in turn are probably forms of *have* and its negative. In Middle English, for example, one finds the forms *habbe,* "to have," and *nabbe,* "not to have." *Hab or nab,* or simply *hab nab,* thus meant "get or lose, hit or miss," and the variant *hob-nob* also meant "hit or miss." Used in the drinking phrase, *hob or nob* would have probably meant "give or take," and from a drinking situation *hob nob* spread to other forms of chumminess.

hive

ho·bo (hō′bō) *n., pl.* **-boes** or **-bos. 1.** A homeless person, especially an impoverished vagrant. **2.** A migrant worker. **—hobo** *intr.v.* **-boed, -bo·ing, -boes.** To live or wander like a vagrant. [Origin unknown.] **—ho′bo·ism** *n.*

Ho·bo·ken (hō′bō′kən). A city of northeast New Jersey on the Hudson River opposite Manhattan. Now a railroad hub and busy seaport, it was a resort and amusement center for New Yorkers before the mid-19th century. Population, 42,460.

Hob·son's choice (hŏb′sənz) *n.* An apparently free choice that offers no real alternative. [After Thomas *Hobson* (1544?–1630), English keeper of a livery stable, from his requirement that customers take either the horse nearest the stable door or none.]

Hoc·cleve (hŏk′lēv′) or **Oc·cleve** (ŏk′-), **Thomas.** 1369?–1450? English poet known for his detailed descriptions of life in medieval London.

Ho Chi Minh (hō′ chē′ mĭn′). 1890–1969. Vietnamese leader and first president of North Vietnam (1954–1969). His army was victorious in the French Indochina War (1946–1954), and he later led North Vietnam's struggle to defeat the U.S.-supported government in South Vietnam.

Ho Chi Minh City. Formerly **Sai·gon** (sī-gŏn′). The largest city of Vietnam, in the southern part of the country near the South China Sea. An ancient Khmer settlement, it became the capital of South Vietnam in 1954. Population, 2,441,185.

hock¹ (hŏk) *n.* **1.a.** The tarsal joint of the hind leg of a digitigrade quadruped, such as a horse, corresponding to the human ankle but bending in the opposite direction. **b.** A joint in the leg of a domestic fowl similar to the hock of a quadruped. **2.** A small cut of meat, especially ham, from the front or hind leg directly above the foot. **—hock** *tr.v.* **hocked, hock·ing, hocks.** To disable by cutting the tendons of the hock; hamstring. [Middle English, from Old English *hōh,* heel.]

hock² (hŏk) *n.* *Chiefly British.* Rhine wine. [Short for obsolete *Hockamore,* alteration of German *Hochheimer,* from *Hochheim,* a town of west-central Germany.]

hock³ (hŏk) *Slang. tr.v.* **hocked, hock·ing, hocks.** To pawn: *hock a diamond ring.* **—hock** *n.* **1.** The state of being pawned: *put the diamonds in hock.* **2.** The state of being in debt: *thought we'd never get out of hock.* [Probably from Dutch *hok,* prison.]

ă pat	oi boy
ā pay	ou out
âr care	o͝o took
ä father	o͞o boot
ĕ pet	ŭ cut
ē be	ûr urge
ĭ pit	th thin
ī pie	*th* this
îr pier	hw which
ŏ pot	zh vision
ō toe	ə about, item
ô paw	♦ regionalism

Stress marks: **′** (primary); ′ (secondary), as in **dictionary** (dĭk′shə-nĕr′ē)

hockey stick

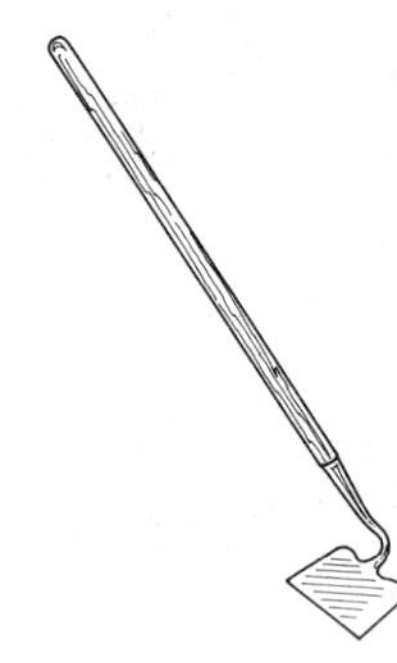
hoe
Garden hoe

hogan

hock·ey (hŏk′ē) *n. Sports.* **1.** Ice hockey. **2.** Field hockey. [Origin unknown.]

hockey stick *n. Sports.* A long-handled stick with one curved end that is used in hockey.

hock·shop (hŏk′shŏp′) *n. Slang.* A pawnshop.

ho·cus (hō′kəs) *tr.v.* **-cused, -cus·ing, -cus·es** or **-cussed, -cus·sing, -cus·ses. 1.** To fool or deceive; hoax. **2.** To infuse (food or drink) with a drug. [Short for HOCUS-POCUS.]

ho·cus-po·cus (hō′kəs-pō′kəs) *n.* **1.** Nonsense words or phrases used as a formula by quack conjurers. **2.** A trick performed by a magician or juggler; sleight-of-hand. **3.** Foolishness or empty pretense used especially to disguise deception or chicanery. **—hocus-pocus** *tr.v.* **-cused, -cus·ing, -cus·es** or **-cussed, -cus·sing, -cus·ses.** To play tricks on; deceive. [Possibly from an alteration of Latin *hoc est corpus (meum),* this is (my) body (from its use in the Eucharist at the time of transubstantiation).]

hod (hŏd) *n.* **1.** A trough carried over the shoulder for transporting loads, as of bricks or mortar. **2.** A coal scuttle. [Perhaps alteration of dialectical *hot,* from Middle English, pannier, from Old French *hotte,* of Germanic origin.]

Ho·dei·da (hō-dā′də). A city of western Yemen on the Red Sea. It is a major port and industrial center. Population, 126,400.

hodge·podge (hŏj′pŏj′) *n.* A mixture of dissimilar ingredients; a jumble. [Alteration of Middle English *hochepot,* from Old French, stew. See HOTCHPOT.]

Hodg·kin (hŏj′kĭn), Sir **Alan Lloyd.** Born 1914. British physiologist. He shared a 1963 Nobel Prize for research on nerve cells.

Hodgkin, Dorothy Mary Crowfoot. Born 1910. Egyptian-born British chemist. She won a 1964 Nobel Prize for determining the structure of compounds needed in combating pernicious anemia.

Hodg·kin's disease (hŏj′kĭnz) *n.* A malignant, progressive, sometimes fatal disease of unknown etiology, marked by enlargement of the lymph nodes, spleen, and liver. [After Thomas *Hodgkin* (1798–1866), British physician.]

hoe (hō) *n.* A tool with a flat blade attached approximately at a right angle to a long handle, used for weeding, cultivating, and gardening. **—hoe** *v.* **hoed, hoe·ing, hoes.** *—tr.* To weed, cultivate, or dig up with a hoe. *—intr.* To work with a hoe. [Middle English *howe,* from Old French *houe,* of Germanic origin. See **kau-** in Appendix.] **—ho′er** *n.*

♦**hoe·cake** (hō′kāk′) *n. Chiefly Southern U.S.* See **johnnycake.** See Regional Note at **johnnycake.** [Possibly because it was sometimes baked on the blade of a hoe.]

hoe·down (hō′doun′) *n.* **1.** A square dance. **2.** The music for a square dance. **3.** A party at which square dancing takes place.

Hoek van Hol·land (ho͝ok′ vän hô′länt). See **Hook of Holland.**

Ho·fei (hŭ′fā′). See **Hefei.**

Hof·fa (hŏf′ə), **James Riddle.** Known as "Jimmy." 1913–1975? American labor leader who became president of the Teamsters Union (1957). He was jailed for jury tampering and fraud (1967–1971) and was later abducted and presumably murdered (1975).

Hoff·man (hôf′mən), **Malvina.** 1887–1966. American sculptor who executed 110 figures of ethnic types for the Field Museum in Chicago (1930–1933).

Hoff·mann (hŏf′mən, hôf′män′), **August Heinrich.** Known as "Hoffmann von Fallersleben." 1798–1874. German writer, philologist, and literary historian noted for his patriotic verse, including "Deutschland, Deutschland über Alles" (1841).

Hoffmann, Roald. Born 1937. Polish-born American chemist. He shared a 1981 Nobel Prize for applying quantum-mechanics theories to the analysis of chemical reactions.

Hof·mann (hŏf′mən, hôf′män′), **August Wilhelm von.** 1818–1892. German chemist. Among his achievements are the discovery of formaldehyde and a method for determining molecular weights of liquids by calculating their vapor densities.

Hofmann, Hans. 1880–1966. German-born American artist who opened two art schools in New York City and Provincetown, Massachusetts (1932–1958), that were important in the development of abstract expressionism.

Hofmann, Josef Casimir. 1876–1957. Polish-born American pianist and composer who helped found the Curtis Institute in Philadelphia (1924).

Hof·manns·thal (hôf′mäns-täl′, hōf′-), **Hugo von.** 1874–1929. Austrian writer who established his reputation with lyric poems and a number of plays, including *Yesterday* (1891).

Hof·stadt·er (hŏf′stăt′ər), **Richard.** 1916–1970. American historian who won a Pulitzer Prize for *The Age of Reform* (1955).

Hofstadter, Robert. Born 1915. American physicist. He shared a 1961 Nobel Prize for determining the structure of protons and neutrons.

hog (hôg, hŏg) *n.* **1.a.** Any of various mammals of the family Suidae, which includes the domesticated pig as well as wild species, such as the boar and the wart hog. **b.** A domesticated pig, especially one weighing over 54 kilograms (120 pounds). **2.a.** A self-indulgent, gluttonous, or filthy person. **b.** One that uses too much of something. **3.** Also **hogg. a.** *Chiefly British.* A young sheep before it has been shorn. **b.** The wool from this type of sheep. **4.** *Slang.* A big, heavy motorcycle. **—hog** *v.* **hogged, hog·ging, hogs.** *—tr.* **1.** *Informal.* To take more than one's share of: *Don't hog the couch.* **2.** To cause (the back) to arch like that of a hog. **3.** To cut (a horse's mane) short and bristly. **4.** To shred (waste wood, for example) by machine. *—intr. Nautical.* To arch upward in the middle. Used of a ship's keel. ***—idiom.* high on** (or **off) the hog.** *Slang.* In a lavish or extravagant manner: *lives high on the hog since getting his share of the inheritance.* [Middle English, from Old English *hogg,* possibly of Celtic origin. See **sū-** in Appendix.]

ho·gan (hō′gän′, -gən) *n.* A usually earth-covered Navajo dwelling traditionally built with the entrance facing east. [Navajo *hooghan.*]

Ho·gan (hō′gən), **William Benjamin.** Known as "Ben." Born 1912. American golfer. He won the U.S. Open championship (1948, 1950, 1951, and 1953), the P.G.A. championship (1948), and the British Open (1953).

Ho·garth (hō′gärth′), **William.** 1697–1764. British artist whose satirical paintings attacked the contradiction of luxury and squalor in society. **—Ho·garth′i·an** *adj.*

hog·back (hôg′băk′, hŏg′-) *n.* A sharp ridge with steeply sloping sides, produced by erosion of the broken edges of highly tilted strata.

hog cholera *n.* A highly infectious, often fatal viral disease of swine, characterized by fever, loss of appetite, diarrhea, and exhaustion. Also called *African swine fever.*

hog·fish (hôg′fĭsh′, hŏg′-) *n., pl.* **hogfish** or **-fish·es. 1.** A colorful fish *(Lachnolaimus maximus)* of warm Atlantic waters, having a long snout in the adult male. **2.** See **pigfish.**

hogg (hôg, hŏg) *n. Chiefly British.* Variant of **hog** (sense 3).

Hogg (hôg, hŏg), **James.** 1770–1835. British writer known for his rustic verse, including *The Mountain Bard* (1807).

hog·gish (hô′gĭsh, hŏg′ĭsh) *adj.* **1.** Coarsely self-indulgent or gluttonous. **2.** Filthy. **—hog′gish·ly** *adv.* **—hog′gish·ness** *n.*

hog heaven *n. Slang.* A state of utter bliss or contentment: *She's in hog heaven over her new sports car.*

Hog·ma·nay (hŏg′mə-nā′, hŏg′mə-nā′) *n. Scots.* **1.** The eve of New Year's Day, on which children traditionally go from house to house asking for presents. **2.** A present requested or given on this day. [Origin unknown.]

hog·nose snake (hôg′nōz′, hŏg′-) *n.* Any of several thick-bodied, nonvenomous North American snakes of the genus *Heterodon* having an upturned snout. Also called *puff adder.*

hog peanut *n.* A twining North American vine *(Amphicarpaea bracteata)* having clusters of pinkish or white flowers and bearing three-seeded pods as well as basal or underground fleshy one-seeded pods.

hogs·head (hôgz′hĕd′, hŏgz′-). *Abbr.* **hhd** *n.* **1.** Any of various units of volume or capacity ranging from 63 to 140 gallons (238 to 530 liters), especially a unit of capacity used in liquid measure in the United States, equal to 63 gallons (238 liters). **2.** A large barrel or cask with this capacity.

hog-tie also **hog·tie** (hôg′tī′, hŏg′-) *tr.v.* **-tied, -tie·ing** or **-ty·ing, -ties. 1.** To tie together the feet or legs of. **2.** *Informal.* To impede or disrupt in movement or action. See Synonyms at **hamper**[1].

hog·wash (hôg′wôsh′, -wŏsh, hŏg′-) *n.* **1.** Worthless, false, or ridiculous speech or writing; nonsense. **2.** Garbage fed to hogs.

hog·weed (hôg′wēd′, hŏg′-) *n.* Any of certain coarse, weedy plants of the genera *Ambrosia, Erigeron,* or *Heracleum.*

hog-wild (hôg′wīld′, hŏg′-) *adj. Informal.* **1.** So wildly excited as to be irrational or devoid of good judgment: *hog-wild spending.* **2.** Wildly enthusiastic: *is hog-wild over racing cars.* **—hog′-wild′** *adv.*

Ho·hen·lo·he (hō′ən-lō′ə). German princely family in existence since the 12th century.

Ho·hen·stau·fen (hō′ən-shtou′fən). Family of German rulers of the Holy Roman Empire (1138–1208 and 1215–1254). Hohenstaufens also reigned in Sicily (1194–1268).

Ho·hen·zol·lern (hō′ən-zŏl′ərn, -tsôl′-). German royal family who ruled Brandenburg from 1415 and later extended their control to Prussia (1525). Under Frederick I (ruled 1701–1713) the family's possessions were unified as the kingdom of Prussia. From 1871 to 1918 Hohenzollern monarchs ruled the German Empire.

Ho·he Tau·ern (hō′ə tou′ərn). A range of the eastern Alps in southern Austria near the Italian border. Grossglockner, 3,799.4 m (12,457 ft), is the highest peak.

Hoh·hot (hō′hōt′) also **Hu·he·hot** (ho͞o′hā-). A city of northern China west-northwest of Beijing. An industrial city, it is also the capital of Nei Monggol (Inner Mongolia) autonomous region. Population, 542,800.

Ho·ho·kam (hə-hō′kəm) *n.* A Native American culture flourishing from about the 3rd century B.C. to the mid-15th century A.D. in south-central Arizona, noted for the construction of an extensive system of irrigation canals. [From Papago *huhugam,* those who are gone.]

ho hum (hō′ hŭm′) *interj.* Used to express boredom, weariness, or contempt.

ho-hum (hō′hŭm′) *adj. Informal.* Boring and dull; routine: *"a ho-hum speaker who couldn't capture the attention of the conventioneers"* (Chicago Tribune).

hoicks (hoiks) *interj.* Variant of **yoicks.**

hoi pol·loi (hoi′ pə-loi′) *n.* The common people; the masses. [Greek, the many : *hoi,* nominative pl. of *ho,* the; see **so-** in Appendix + *polloi,* nominative pl. of *polus,* many; see **pele-[1]** in Appendix.]

WORD HISTORY: We hoi polloi may want to be careful in our use of the term *hoi polloi* because a few pitfalls lie in wait for those without a knowledge of its background. *Hoi polloi* is a borrowing of the Greek phrase *hoi polloi,* which is made up of the form *hoi,* meaning "the" and used before a plural, and *polloi,* the plural of *polus,* "many." In Greek *hoi polloi* had a special sense, "the greater number, the people, the commonalty, the masses." This is what the phrase has tended to express in English since its first recorded instance, in an 1837 work by James Fenimore Cooper. One pitfall in the use of *hoi polloi* lies in the fact that *hoi* already expresses the sense "the," so that technically one should not add another *the* to the phrase, as in *the hoi polloi.* But this technicality has not stopped many users of the phrase, including Cooper, from doing so. The other pitfall in the use of the phrase is the misuse of it to mean "the elite," possibly brought about because *hoi* in the phrase *the hoi polloi* is reminiscent of *high* as in *high and mighty* and also because *hoi polloi* may recall *hoity-toity.*

hoi·sin sauce (hoi′sĭn, hoi-sĭn′) *n.* A thick, sweet, pungent sauce used in Chinese cooking. [Chinese (Cantonese) *hoisin,* seafood : *hoi,* ocean + *sin,* delicacy, seafood.]

hoist (hoist) *v.* **hoist·ed, hoist·ing, hoists.** —*tr.* To raise or haul up with or as if with the help of a mechanical apparatus. See Synonyms at **lift.** —*intr.* To become raised or lifted. **—hoist** *n.* **1.** An apparatus for lifting heavy or cumbersome objects. **2.** The act of hoisting; a lift. **3.** *Nautical.* **a.** The height or vertical dimension of a flag or of any square sail other than a course. **b.** A group of flags raised together as a signal. [Alteration of dialectal *hoise,* perhaps variant of Middle English *hisse,* heave!, possibly from Middle Dutch *hissen,* to haul.] **—hoist′er** *n.*

hoi·ty-toi·ty (hoi′tē-toi′tē) *adj.* **1.** Pretentiously self-important; pompous. **2.** Given to frivolity or silliness. [From reduplication of dialectal *hoit,* to romp; perhaps akin to HOYDEN.]

Ho·kan (hō′kən) *n.* A proposed grouping of a number of Native American language families of western North America.

hoke (hōk) *tr.v.* **hoked, hok·ing, hokes.** *Slang.* To give an impressive but artificial, false, or deceptive quality to: *hoked up some phony allegations.* [From HOKUM.]

hok·ey (hō′kē) *adj.* **-i·er, -i·est.** *Slang.* **1.** Mawkishly sentimental; corny. **2.** Noticeably contrived; artificial. **—hok′i·ly** *adv.* **—hok′i·ness, hok′ey·ness** *n.*

Hok·kai·do (hŏ-kī′dō, hô′kī-dō′). An island of Japan north of Honshu. It is the second largest of the Japanese islands but the least populated. Hokkaido became part of Japan in the medieval period (c. 1600) and was called Yezo or Ezo until 1868.

hok·ku (hō′ko͞o) *n., pl.* **hokku.** A haiku. [Japanese : *hok,* opening, first + *ku,* stanza.]

ho·kum (hō′kəm) *n.* **1.** Something apparently impressive or legitimate but actually untrue or insincere; nonsense. **2.** A stock technique for eliciting a desired response from an audience. [Perhaps HO(CUS-POCUS) + (BUN)KUM.]

Ho·ku·sai (hō′ko͞o-sī′, hō′ko͞o-sī′). 1760–1849. Japanese artist remembered for his historical scenes and landscapes, including *Thirty-Six Views of Mount Fuji* (1826–1833).

hol– *pref.* Variant of **holo–.**

ho·lan·dric (hō-lăn′drĭk, hŏ-) *adj.* Relating to a trait encoded by a gene or genes located on the Y-chromosome and therefore occurring only in males. [HOL(O)– + ANDR(O)– + –IC.]

Hol·arc·tic (hō-lärk′tĭk, -lär′tĭk, hŏ-) *adj.* Of, relating to, or being the zoogeographic region that includes the northern areas of the earth and is divided into Nearctic and Palearctic regions.

Hol·bein (hōl′bīn, hôl′-), **Hans[1].** Known as "the Elder." 1465?–1524. German painter. His religious works include altar pieces for the Augsburg Cathedral (1493) and for the churches of Saint Afra (c. 1495) and Saint Sebastian (1516), also in Augsburg.

Hol·bein, Hans[2]. Known as "the Younger." 1497?–1543. German-born artist in Switzerland and England noted for his portraits and religious paintings.

hold[1] (hōld) *v.* **held** (hĕld), **hold·ing, holds.** —*tr.* **1.a.** To have and keep in one's grasp: *held the reins tightly.* **b.** To aim or direct; point: *held a hose on the fire.* **c.** To keep from falling or moving; support: *a nail too small to hold the mirror; hold the horse steady; papers that were held together with tape and glue.* **d.** To sustain the pressure of: *The bridge can't hold that much weight.* **2.a.** To keep from departing or getting away: *Hold the bus! Hold the dog until I find the leash.* **b.** To keep in custody: *held the suspect for questioning.* **c.** To retain the attention or interest of: *the storyteller who held the crowd spellbound. Televised sports can't hold my interest.* **d.** To avoid letting out or expelling: *The swimmer couldn't hold her breath any longer.* **3.a.** To be filled by; contain. **b.** To be capable of holding. See Synonyms at **contain. c.** To have as a chief characteristic or quality: *The film holds a number of surprises.* **d.** To have in store: *Let's see what the future holds.* **4.a.** To have and maintain in one's possession: *holds a great deal of property.* **b.** To have as a responsible position or a privilege: *held the governorship for six years.* **c.** To have in recognition of achievement or superiority: *holds the record for the one-mile race; holds the respect of her peers.* **5.a.** To maintain control over: *The dam held the flood waters. Thieves held the stolen painting for ransom.* **b.** To maintain occupation of by force or coercion: *Students held the administrative building for a week.* **c.** To withstand the efforts or advance of (an opposing team, for example). **d.** To maintain in a given condition, situation, or action: *held himself as a gentleman at all times.* **6.a.** To impose control or restraint on; curb: *She held her temper.* **b.** To stop the movement or progress of: *Hold the presses!* **c.** To reserve or keep back from use: *Please hold two tickets for us. Please hold the relish on that hamburger.* **d.** To defer the immediate handling of: *asked the receptionist to hold all calls during the meeting.* **7.a.** To be the legal possessor of. **b.** To bind by a contract. **c.** To adjudge or decree: *The court held that the defendant was at fault.* **d.** To make accountable; obligate: *You certainly did hold me to my promise.* **8.a.** To keep in the mind or convey as a judgment, conviction, or point of view: *hold a grudge; hold it a point of honor not to reveal one's sources; holds that this economic program is the only answer to high prices.* **b.** To assert or affirm, especially formally: *This doctrine holds that people are inherently good.* **c.** To regard in a certain way: *I hold you in high esteem.* **9.a.** To cause to take place; carry on: *held the race in Florida; hold a yard sale.* **b.** To assemble for and conduct the activity of; convene: *held a meeting of the board.* **10.a.** To carry or support (the body or a bodily part) in a certain position: *Can the baby hold herself up yet? Hold up your leg.* **b.** To cover (the ears or the nose, for example) especially for protection: *held my nose against the stench.* —*intr.* **1.a.** To maintain a grasp or grip on something. **b.** To stay securely fastened: *The chain held.* **2.a.** To maintain a desired or accustomed position or condition: *hopes the weather will hold.* **b.** To withstand stress, pressure, or opposition: *The defense held. We held firm on the negotiations.* **3.** To continue in the same direction: *The ship held to a southwesterly course.* **4.** To be valid, applicable, or true: *The theory holds. This is an observation that still holds true.* **5.** To have legal right or title. Often used with *of* or *from.* **6.** To halt an intended action. Often used in the imperative. **7.** To stop the countdown during a missile or spacecraft launch. **8.** *Slang.* To have in one's possession illicit or illegally obtained material or goods, especially narcotics: *The suspect was holding.* **—hold** *n.* **1.a.** The act or a means of grasping. **b.** A manner of grasping an opponent, as in wrestling or aikido: *a neck hold; an arm hold.* **2.** Something that may be grasped or gripped, as for support. **3.a.** A bond or force that attaches or restrains, or by which something is affected or dominated: *a writer with a strong hold on the reading public.* **b.** Complete control: *has a firm hold on the complex issues.* **c.** Full understanding: *has a good hold on physics.* **4.** *Music.* **a.** The sustaining of a note longer than its indicated time value. **b.** The symbol designating this pause; a fermata. **5.a.** A direction or an indication that something is to be reserved or deferred. **b.** A temporary halt, as in a countdown. **6.a.** A prison cell. **b.** The state of being in confinement; custody. **7.** *Archaic.* A fortified place; a stronghold. **—*phrasal verbs.* hold back. 1.** To retain in one's possession or control: *held back valuable information; held back my tears.* **2.** To impede the progress of. **3.** To restrain oneself. **hold down. 1.** To limit: *Please hold the noise down.* **2.** To have (a job): *holds down two jobs.* **hold forth.** To talk at great length. **hold off. 1.** To keep at a distance; resist: *held the creditors off.* **2.** To stop or delay doing something: *Let's hold off until we have more data.* **hold on. 1.** To maintain one's grip; cling. **2.** To continue to do something; persist. **3.** To wait for something wanted or requested, especially to keep a telephone connection open. **hold out. 1.** To present or proffer as something attainable. **2.** To continue to be in supply or service; last: *Our food is holding out nicely.* **3.** To continue to resist: *The defending garrison held out for a month.* **4.** To refuse to reach or satisfy an agreement. **hold over. 1.a.** To postpone or delay. **b.** To keep in a position or state from an earlier period of time. **2.** To continue a term of office past the usual length of time. **3.** To prolong the engagement of: *The film was held over for weeks.* **hold to.** To remain loyal or faithful to: *She held to her resolutions.* **hold up. 1.** To obstruct or delay. **2.** To rob while armed, often at gunpoint. **3.** To offer or present as an example: *held up the essay up as a model for the students.* **4.** To continue to function without losing force or effectiveness; cope: *managed to hold up under the daily stress.* **hold with.** To agree with; support: *I don't hold with your theories.* **—*idioms.* get hold of. 1.** To come into possession of; find: *Where can I get hold of a copy?* **2.** To communicate with, as by telephone: *tried to get hold of you but the line was busy.* **3.** To gain control of. Often used reflexively: *You must get hold of yourself!* **hold a candle to.** To compare favorably with: *This film doesn't hold a candle to his previous ones.* **hold (one's) own.** To do reasonably well despite difficulty or criticism. **hold out on (someone).** To withhold something from: *Don't hold out on me; start telling the truth.* **hold (someone's) feet to the fire.** To pressure (someone) to consent to or undertake something. **hold sway.** To have a controlling influence; dominate. **hold the bag.** *Informal.* **1.** To be left with empty hands. **2.** To be forced to assume total responsibility when it ought to have been shared. **hold the fort.** *Informal.* **1.** To assume responsibility, especially in another's absence. **2.** To maintain a secure position. **hold the line.** To maintain the existing position or state of affairs: *had to hold the line on salary increases in the fourth quarter.* **hold the phone.** *Slang.* To stop doing what one is engaged in doing. Often used in the imperative: *Hold the phone! There's no sense in continuing this argument.* **hold water.** To stand up to critical examination: *Your theory does not hold water. The witnesses' conflicting stories held no water.* **no holds barred.** Without limits or restraints. **on hold. 1.** Into a state of temporary interruption without total disconnection during a telephone call: *had to put me*

ă pat	oi boy
ā pay	ou out
âr care	o͝o took
ä father	o͞o boot
ĕ pet	ŭ cut
ē be	ûr urge
ĭ pit	th thin
ī pie	*th* this
îr pier	hw which
ŏ pot	zh vision
ō toe	ə about, item
ô paw	♦ regionalism

Stress marks: ′ (primary); ′ (secondary), as in **dictionary** (dĭk′shə-nĕr′ē)

on hold for five minutes. **2.** *Informal.* Into a state of delay or indeterminate suspension: *had to put the romance on hold.* [Middle English *holden,* from Old English *healdan.*]

hold² (hōld) *n. Abbr.* **hld.** The lower interior part of a ship or an airplane in which cargo is stored. [Alteration (influenced by HOLD¹) of Middle English *hole,* husk, hull of a ship, from Old English *hulu.* See **kel-¹** in Appendix.]

hold·all (hōld′ôl′) *n.* **1.** A container for holding items. **2.** A case or bag for carrying miscellaneous items, as when traveling.

hold·back (hōld′băk′) *n.* **1.a.** The act of holding back. **b.** Something held back. **2.** A device that retains or restrains. **3.** A strap or an iron between the shaft and the harness on a drawn wagon, allowing the horse to stop or back up.

hold button *n.* A button on a telephone that permits the user to answer another incoming call while temporarily interrupting the previous one.

hold-down (hōld′doun′) *n.* **1.a.** The act of holding down. **b.** A limit or restraint: *"Voters want a hold-down on the Federal budget"* (Newsweek). **2.** Something, such as a clamp, used to hold an object in place.

hold·en (hōl′dən) *v. Archaic.* A past participle of **hold¹.**

hold·er (hōl′dər) *n.* **1.** One that holds, as: **a.** One that possesses something; an owner: *The holder of extensive farm land; the holder of oil fields.* **b.** One, especially a tenant, that occupies or controls something. **c.** *Law.* One that legally possesses and is entitled to the payment of a check, bill, or promissory note. **2.** A device for holding: *a towel holder.*

hold·fast (hōld′făst′) *n.* **1.** Any of various devices used to fasten something securely. **2.** *Biology.* An organ or a structure of attachment, especially the basal, rootlike formation by which certain seaweeds or other algae are attached to a substrate.

hold·ing (hōl′dĭng) *n.* **1.a.** Land rented or leased from another. **b.** Often **holdings.** Legally owned property, such as land, capital, or stocks. **2.** *Law.* A court ruling, especially a ruling on a point of law raised in an official proceeding. **3.** *Sports.* Illegal use of the arms, hands, body, or playing stick to obstruct the movements of an opponent. **—holding** *adj.* **1.** Tending to impede or delay progress: *a holding action.* **2.** Designed for usually short-term storage or retention: *a holding tank; a holding cell.*

holding company *n.* A company controlling partial or complete interest in another company or other companies.

holding pattern *n.* **1.** A usually circular pattern flown by aircraft awaiting clearance to land at an airport. **2.** *Informal.* A state of waiting or delay; a static situation: *Environmental groups succeeded in putting the nuclear industry into a holding pattern.*

hold·out (hōld′out′) *n.* One that withholds agreement or consent upon which progress is contingent.

hold·o·ver (hōld′ō′vər) *n.* One that is held over, especially an officeholder who is retained after an expired term of office.

hold·up (hōld′ŭp′) *n.* **1.** An interruption or a delay: *What's the holdup? We're in a hurry.* **2.** An armed robbery.

hole (hōl) *n.* **1.** A cavity in a solid. **2.a.** An opening or a perforation: *a hole in the clouds.* **b.** *Sports.* An opening in a defensive formation, especially the area of a baseball infield between the third base player and the shortstop. **c.** A fault or flaw: *There are holes in your argument.* **3.** A deep place in a body of water. **4.** An animal's hollowed-out habitation, such as a burrow. **5.** An ugly, squalid, or depressing dwelling. **6.** A deep or isolated place of confinement; a dungeon. **7.** An awkward situation; a predicament. **8.** *Sports.* **a.** The small pit lined with a cup into which a golf ball must be hit. **b.** One of the divisions of a golf course, from tee to cup. **9.** *Physics.* A vacant position in a crystal left by the absence of an electron, especially a position in a semiconductor that acts as a carrier of positive electric charge. In this sense, also called *electron hole.* **—hole** *v.* **holed, hol·ing, holes.** *—tr.* **1.** To put a hole in. **2.** To put or propel into a hole. *—intr.* To make a hole in something. ***—phrasal verbs.*** **hole out.** *Sports.* To hit a golf ball into the hole. **hole up.** To hibernate in or as if in a hole. *Informal.* To take refuge in or as if in a hideout. ***—idioms.*** **hole in one.** *Sports.* The driving of a golf ball from the tee into the hole in only one stroke. **in the hole. 1.** Having a score below zero. **2.** In debt. **3.** At a disadvantage. [Middle English, from Old English *hol.* See **kel-¹** in Appendix.]

SYNONYMS: *hole, hollow, cavity, pocket.* These nouns refer to an unfilled or empty space. *Hole* is applicable to an opening in or a perforation through a solid body: *dug a hole in the earth and planted the seed; a hole in the bow of the ship made by a torpedo. Hollow* denotes an unfilled area in a solid body or a dent or depression on a surface: *a hollow in the ground where ivy grows; marble steps with hollows worn by footsteps.* A *cavity* is a hollow or hollow area within a solid body or object: *a cavity in a molar; the cranial cavity. Pocket* is applied to a cavity in the earth, as one containing a mineral deposit, or to an isolated cavity or area that contains foreign or contrasting matter: *pockets of manganese in the rock; a plane that plunged into a pocket of turbulence; pockets of unemployment in an otherwise affluent society.*

hole-and-cor·ner (hōl′ən-kôr′nər) *adj.* Being in a secret place; conducted secretly.

hole card *n.* **1.** *Games.* A card in stud poker that is dealt facedown in the first round of a deal and that the holder is not obliged to reveal before the showdown. **2.** *Informal.* Something held in reserve until it can be used advantageously.

hole-in-the-wall (hōl′ĭn-thə-wôl′) *n., pl.* **holes-in-the-wall** (hōlz′-). A small, very modest, often out-of-the-way place.

hol·ey (hō′lē) *adj.* **-i·er, -i·est.** Having holes or full of holes.

Hol·guín (ôl-gēn′). A city of eastern Cuba north-northwest of Santiago de Cuba. It is a commercial and transportation center. Population, 186,236.

hol·i·day (hŏl′ĭ-dā′) *n.* **1.** A day on which custom or the law dictates a halting of general business activity to commemorate or celebrate a particular event. **2.** A religious feast day; a holy day. **3.** A day free from work that one may spend at leisure; a day off. **4.** *Chiefly British.* A vacation. *—attributive.* Often used to modify another noun: *holiday cheer; holiday travelers.* **—holiday** *intr.v.* **-dayed, -day·ing, -days.** *Chiefly British.* To pass a holiday or vacation. [Middle English *holidai,* holy day, from Old English *hālig dæg* : *hālig,* holy; see HOLY + *dæg,* day; see DAY.] **—hol′i·day′er** *n.*

Hol·i·day (hŏl′ĭ-dā′), **Eleanora.** Known as "Billie." 1915–1959. American singer. The emotional intensity of her performances made Holiday the leading female jazz vocalist of her time.

hol·i·day·mak·er (hŏl′ĭ-dā-mā′kər) *n. Chiefly British.* One who goes on vacation.

ho·li·er-than-thou (hō′lē-ər-*thən-thou*′) *adj.* Exhibiting an attitude of superior virtue; self-righteously pious.

ho·li·ness (hō′lē-nĭs) *n.* **1.** The state or quality of being holy; sanctity. **2. Holiness.** *Roman Catholic Church.* Used with *His* or *Your* as a title and form of address for a pope.

Hol·in·shed (hŏl′ən-shĕd′, -ĭnz-hĕd′) **Hol·lings·head** (-ĭngz-hĕd′), **Raphael.** Died c. 1580. English historian. His volume *Chronicles of England, Scotland, and Ireland* (1577) was used extensively by Shakespeare as well as other Elizabethan dramatists as a source of historical information.

ho·lism (hō′lĭz′əm) *n.* **1.** The theory that living matter or reality is made up of organic or unified wholes that are greater than the simple sum of their parts. **2.** A holistic investigation or system of treatment. **—ho′list** *n.*

ho·lis·tic (hō-lĭs′tĭk) *adj.* **1.** Of or relating to holism. **2.a.** Emphasizing the importance of the whole and the interdependence of its parts. **b.** Concerned with wholes rather than analysis or separation into parts: *holistic medicine; holistic ecology.* **—ho·lis′ti·cal·ly** *adv.*

Hol·la·day (hŏl′ə-dā′). A community of north-central Utah, a suburb of Salt Lake City. Population, 22,189.

hol·land (hŏl′ənd) *n.* A cotton or linen fabric, usually sized or glazed, that is used especially for window shades, bookbinding, and upholstery. [Middle English *holand,* after *Holand* (Holland), a former province of the Netherlands, from Middle Dutch.]

Hol·land (hŏl′ənd). **1.** A city of southwest Michigan southwest of Grand Rapids. Founded in 1847 by Dutch settlers, it is a manufacturing center and summer resort. Population, 26,281. **2.** See **Netherlands.**

Holland, John Philip. 1840–1914. Irish-born American inventor and nautical pioneer. His submarine was the first purchased by the U.S. government (1900).

hol·lan·daise sauce (hŏl′ən-dāz′) *n.* A rich, creamy sauce of butter, egg yolks, and lemon or vinegar. [From French *(sauce) Hollandaise,* Holland-style, from *Hollande,* Holland.]

hol·ler¹ (hŏl′ər) *v.* **-lered, -ler·ing, -lers.** *—intr.* **1.** To yell or shout. **2.** *Informal.* To complain. *—tr.* To shout out (words or phrases). See Synonyms at **shout. —holler** *n.* **1.** A yell or shout; a call. **2.** *Informal.* A complaint or gripe. [From obsolete *hollo,* hail!, stop!. See HELLO.]

♦ **hol·ler²** (hŏl′ər) *adj. & v. Upper Southern U.S.* Variant of **hollow. —holler** *n.* **1.** *Upper Southern U.S.* Variant of **hollow** (senses 1, 2, 3). **2.** *Appalachian Mountains.* Variant of **hollow** (sense 4).

♦ ***REGIONAL NOTE:*** One feature of Upper Southern English and specifically of Appalachian English is its pronunciation of the final unstressed syllable in words such as *hollow, window,* and *potato* as (-er). *Holler, winder,* and *tater* (immortalized as the name of the baby in *Snuffy Smith*) are merely variant pronunciations reflected in spelling. A noun *holler* has the specific meaning in the Appalachians of "a small valley between mountains": *They live up in the holler underneath Big Bald Mountain.*

Hol·ler·ith (hŏl′ə-rĭth′), **Herman.** 1860–1929. American inventor who created a system of recording and retrieving information on punched cards (1880).

Hollerith card *n. Computer Science.* See **punch card.** [After Herman HOLLERITH.]

Hollerith code *n. Computer Science.* A code used for recording alphanumeric information on punch cards. [After Herman HOLLERITH.]

Hol·ley (hŏl′ē), **Marietta.** 1836–1926. American writer whose satires popularized many feminist concerns.

Hol·li·day (hŏl′ĭ-dā′), **Judith Tuvim.** Known as "Judy." 1922–1965. American comedian best remembered for her performance in the play (1946–1950) and film (1950) *Born Yesterday.*

Hol·lings·head (hŏl′ĭngz-hĕd′), **Raphael.** See Raphael **Holinshed.**

♦**hol•low** (hŏl′ō) *adj.* **-er, -est. 1.** Having a cavity, gap, or space within: *a hollow wall.* **2.** Deeply indented or concave; sunken: *"His bearded face already has a set, hollow look"* (Conor Cruise O'Brien). **3.** Without substance or character: *a hollow person.* See Synonyms at **vain. 4.** Devoid of truth or validity; specious: *"Theirs is at best a hollow form of flattery"* (Annalyn Swan). **5.** Having a reverberating, sepulchral sound: *hollow footsteps.* **—hollow** *n.* **1.** A cavity, gap, or space: *a hollow behind a wall.* **2.** An indented or concave surface or area. See Synonyms at **hole. 3.** A void; an emptiness: *a hollow in one's life.* **4.** Also **hol•ler** (hŏl′ər). *Appalachian Mountains.* A small valley between mountains. **—hollow** *v.* **-lowed, -low•ing, -lows.** —*tr.* **1.** To make hollow: *hollow out a pumpkin.* **2.** To scoop or form by making concave: *hollow out a nest in the sand.* —*intr.* To become hollow or empty. [Middle English *holwe, holowe,* from *holgh,* hole, burrow (influenced by *hole,* hollow), from Old English *holh.* See **kel-**[1] in Appendix.] **—hol′low•ly** *adv.* **—hol′low•ness** *n.*

hol•low•ware (hŏl′ō-wâr′) *n.* Pieces of tableware, such as bowls, pitchers, or serving dishes, that have depth or volume.

hol•ly (hŏl′ē) *n., pl.* **-lies. 1.a.** Any of numerous trees or shrubs of the genus *Ilex,* usually having bright red berries and glossy, evergreen leaves with spiny margins. **b.** Branches of these plants, traditionally used for Christmas decoration. **2.** Any of various similar or related plants. [Middle English *holin, holi,* from Old English *holen.*]

hol•ly•hock (hŏl′ē-hŏk′) *n.* A tall plant *(Alcea rosea)* native to the Middle East and widely cultivated for its showy clusters of very large, variously colored flowers. Also called *althea.* [Middle English *holihocke,* marsh mallow : *holi,* holy; see HOLY + *hoc,* mallow (from Old English).]

holly oak *n.* See **holm oak.**

Hol•ly•wood[1] (hŏl′ē-wo͝od′). **1.** A district of Los Angeles, California. Consolidated with Los Angeles in 1910, it has long been a film and entertainment center. **2.** A city of southeast Florida on the Atlantic Ocean north of Miami Beach. It is a resort and retirement community. Population, 121,323.

Hol•ly•wood[2] (hŏl′ē-wo͝od′) *n.* **1.** The U.S. film industry. **2.** A flashy, vulgar atmosphere or tone, held to be associated with the U.S. film industry. **—Hollywood** *adj.* **1.** Of or relating to the U.S. film industry: *a Hollywood movie; a Hollywood producer.* **2.** Flashy and vulgar: *their clothes were pure Hollywood.* [After HOLLYWOOD[1], California.]

hol•ly•wood bed (hŏl′ē-wo͝od′) *n.* A mattress on a box spring supported by a metal frame or attached low legs, often with an upholstered headboard.

holm (hōm, hōlm) *n. Chiefly British.* An island in a river. [Middle English, from Old Norse *hōlmr.* See **kel-**[2] in Appendix.]

Holmes (hōmz, hōlmz), **Oliver Wendell.** 1809–1894. American physician and writer. A professor of anatomy and physiology at Harvard (1847–1882), he wrote humorous conversational pieces, including *The Autocrat of the Breakfast Table* (1858).

Holmes, Oliver Wendell, Jr. 1841–1935. American jurist who served as an associate justice of the U.S. Supreme Court (1902–1932).

hol•mic (hōl′mĭk) *adj.* Relating to holmium in its trivalent state.

hol•mi•um (hōl′mē-əm) *n. Symbol* **Ho** A relatively soft, malleable, stable rare-earth element occurring in gadolinite, monazite, and other rare-earth minerals. Atomic number 67; atomic weight 164.930; melting point 1,461°C; boiling point 2,600°C; specific gravity 8.803; valence 3. See table at **element.** [After *Holmia* (Stockholm), Sweden.]

holm oak *n.* A Mediterranean evergreen tree *(Quercus ilex)* having entire or toothed leaves with a dark green upper surface and a yellowish or white lower surface. Also called *holly oak.* [Middle English *holm,* alteration of *holin,* holly. See HOLLY.]

holo– or **hol–** *pref.* Whole; entire; entirely: *holoblastic.* [Greek, from *holos,* whole. See **sol-** in Appendix.]

hol•o•blas•tic (hŏl′ə-blăs′tĭk, hō′lə-) *adj. Embryology.* Exhibiting cleavage in which the entire egg separates into individual blastomeres. **—hol′o•blas′ti•cal•ly** *adv.*

hol•o•caust (hŏl′ə-kôst′, hō′lə-) *n.* **1.** Great or total destruction, especially by fire. **2.a.** Widespread destruction. **b.** A great disaster. **3.a. Holocaust.** The genocide of European Jews and others by the Nazis during World War II: *"Israel emerged from the Holocaust and is defined in relation to that catastrophe"* (Emanuel Litvinoff). **b.** A massive slaughter: *"an important document in the so-far sketchy annals of the Cambodian holocaust"* (Rod Nordland). **4.** A sacrificial offering that is consumed entirely by flames. [Middle English, burnt offering, from Old French *holocauste,* from Latin *holocaustum,* from Greek *holokauston,* from neuter of *holokaustos,* burnt whole : *holo-,* holo- + *kaustos,* burnt (from *kaiein,* to burn).] **—hol′o•caus′tal, hol′o•caus′tic** *adj.*

USAGE NOTE: When referring to the massive destruction of human beings by other human beings, *holocaust* has a secure place in the language. Fully 99 percent of the Usage Panel accepts the use of *holocaust* in the phrase *nuclear holocaust.* Sixty percent accepts the sentence *As many as two million people may have died in the holocaust that followed the Khmer Rouge takeover in Cambodia.* But because of its associations with genocide, extended applications of *holocaust* may not always be received with equanimity. When the word is used to refer to death brought about by natural causes, the percentage of the Panel's acceptance drops sharply. Only 31 percent of the Panel accepts the sentence *In East Africa five years of drought have brought about a holocaust in which millions have died.* Just 11 percent approved the use of *holocaust* to summarize the effects of the AIDS epidemic. This suggests that other figurative usages such as *the huge losses in the Savings and Loan holocaust* may be viewed as overblown or in poor taste.

WORD HISTORY: Totality of destruction has been central to the meaning of *holocaust* since it first appeared in Middle English in the 14th century and referred to the biblical sacrifice in which a male animal was wholly burnt on the altar in worship of God. *Holocaust* comes from Greek *holokauston* ("that which is completely burnt"), which was a translation of Hebrew *ôlâ* (literally "that which goes up," that is, in smoke). In this sense of "burnt sacrifice," *holocaust* is still used in some versions of the Bible. In the 17th century the meaning of *holocaust* broadened to "something totally consumed by fire," and the word eventually was applied to fires of extreme destructiveness. In the 20th century *holocaust* has taken on a variety of figurative meanings, summarizing the effects of war, rioting, storms, epidemic diseases, and even economic failures. Most of these usages arose after World War II, but it is unclear whether they permitted or resulted from the use of *holocaust* in reference to the mass murder of European Jews and others by the Nazis. This application of the word occurred as early as 1942, but the phrase *the Holocaust* did not become established until the late 1950's. Here it parallels and may have been influenced by another Hebrew word, *sho'ah* ("catastrophe"). In the Bible *sho'ah* has a range of meanings including "personal ruin or devastation" and "a wasteland or desert." *Sho'ah* was first used to refer to the Nazi slaughter of Jews in 1939, but its phrase *ha-sho'ah* ("the catastrophe") only became established after World War II. *Holocaust* has also been used to translate *hurban* ("destruction"), another Hebrew word used to summarize the genocide of Jews by the Nazis. This sense of *holocaust* has since broadened to include the mass slaughter of other peoples, but when capitalized it refers specifically to the destruction of Jews and other Europeans by the Nazis and may also encompass the Nazi persecution of Jews that preceded the outbreak of the war.

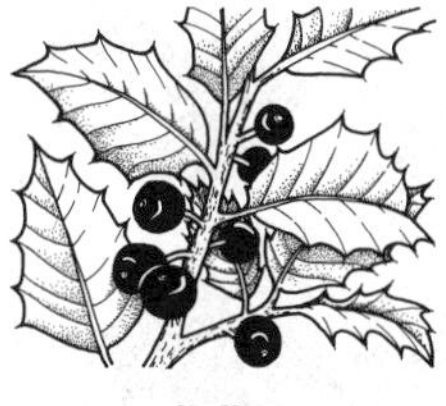
holly

Hol•o•cene (hŏl′ə-sēn′, hō′lə-) *adj.* Of, belonging to, or designating the geologic time, rock series, or sedimentary deposits of the more recent of the two epochs of the Quaternary Period, extending from the end of the Pleistocene Epoch to the present. See table at **geologic time. —Holocene** *n.* The Holocene Epoch or its system of deposits.

hol•o•crine (hŏl′ə-krĭn, -krīn′, -krēn′, hō′lə-) *adj.* Of or relating to a gland whose output consists of disintegrated secretory cells along with the secretory product itself. [HOLO– + Greek *krinein,* to separate; see ENDOCRINE.]

hol•o•en•zyme (hŏl′ō-ĕn′zīm′, hō′lō-) *n.* An active, complex enzyme consisting of an apoenzyme and a coenzyme.

ho•log•a•mous (hə-lŏg′ə-məs) *adj.* Of or relating to an organism whose germ cells morphologically resemble its somatic cells.

hol•o•gram (hŏl′ə-grăm′, hō′lə-) *n.* **1.** The pattern produced on a photosensitive medium that has been exposed by holography and then photographically developed. **2.** The photosensitive medium so exposed and so developed. Also called *holograph.*

hol•o•graph (hŏl′ə-grăf′, hō′lə-) *n.* **1.** A document written wholly in the handwriting of the person whose signature it bears. **2.** See **hologram. —holograph** *adj.* Variant of **holographic** (sense 2). [From Late Latin *holographus,* entirely written by the signer, from Greek *holographos* : *holo-,* holo- + *-graphos,* -graph.]

hol•o•graph•ic (hŏl′ə-grăf′ĭk, hō′lə-) also **hol•o•graph•i•cal** (-ĭ-kəl) *adj.* **1.** Of or relating to holography or holograms. **2.** Also **hol•o•graph** (hŏl′ə-grăf, hō′lə-). Of or being a document written wholly in the handwriting of the person whose signature it bears: *a holographic will.* **—ho′lo•graph′i•cal•ly** *adv.*

ho•log•raph•y (hō-lŏg′rə-fē) *n.* A method of producing a three-dimensional image of an object by recording on a photographic plate or film the pattern of interference formed by a split laser beam and then illuminating the pattern either with a laser or with ordinary light.

Oliver Wendell Holmes

hol•o•gyn•ic (hŏl′ə-jĭn′ĭk, -gī′nĭk, hō′lə-) *adj.* Passing to successive generations only in females: *a hologynic trait.*

hol•o•he•dral (hŏl′ə-hē′drəl, hō′lə-) *adj.* Having as many planes as required for symmetry in a given crystal system.

hol•o•me•tab•o•lism (hŏl′ō-mə-tăb′ə-lĭz′əm, hō′lō-) *n.* See **complete metamorphosis. —hol′o•me•tab′o•lous** *adj.*

Ho•lon (hō-lōn′, KHô-lôn′). A city of west-central Israel near Tel Aviv–Jaffa. It was established in 1941. Population, 137,800.

hol•o•phras•tic (hŏl′ə-frăs′tĭk, hō′lə-) *adj.* Polysynthetic. [HOLO– + Greek *phrastikos,* expressive (from *-phrastos,* speakable, thought of, from *phrazein,* to show; see **gʷhren-** in Appendix).]

hol•o•plank•ton (hŏl′ə-plăngk′tən, hō′lə-) *n.* Plankton that remains free-swimming through all stages of its life cycle.

hol•o•thu•ri•an (hŏl′ə-tho͝or′ē-ən, -thyo͝or′-, hō′lə-) *n.* Any of various echinoderms of the class Holothuroidea, which includes the sea cucumbers. [From Latin *holothūria,* water polyp, from Greek *holothourion.*] **—hol′o•thu′ri•an** *adj.*

hol•o•type (hŏl′ə-tīp′, hō′lə-) *n.* The specimen used as the basis of the original published description of a taxonomic group

ă pat	oi boy
ā pay	ou out
âr care	o͝o took
ä father	o͞o boot
ĕ pet	ŭ cut
ē be	ûr urge
ĭ pit	th thin
ī pie	*th* this
îr pier	hw which
ŏ pot	zh vision
ō toe	ə about, item
ô paw	♦ regionalism

Stress marks: ′ (primary); ′ (secondary), as in **dictionary** (dĭk′shə-nĕr′ē)

and later designated as the type specimen. **—hol′o·typ′ic** (-tĭp′ĭk) *adj.*

hol·o·zo·ic (hŏl′ə-zō′ĭk, hō′lə-) *adj.* Obtaining nourishment by the ingestion of organic material, as animals do.

holp (hōlp) *v. Archaic.* A past tense of **help.**

hol·pen (hōl′pən) *v. Archaic.* A past participle of **help.**

Hol·stein[1] (hōl′stīn′, -stēn′). A region and former duchy of northern Germany at the base of the Jutland Peninsula. It became a duchy under the suzerainty of the Holy Roman Empire in 1474 and was often controlled by Denmark in the years that followed.

Holstein[2]

Hol·stein[2] (hōl′stīn′, -stēn′) *n.* Any of a breed of large black and white dairy cattle originally developed in Friesland. [After HOLSTEIN[1].]

Hol·stein-Frie·sian (hōl′stīn-frēzhən, -stēn-) *n.* A Holstein.

hol·ster (hōl′stər) *n.* **1.** A leather case shaped to hold a pistol. **2.** A belt with loops or slots for carrying small tools or other equipment. **—holster** *tr.v.* **hol·stered, hol·ster·ing, hol·sters.** To put (a gun, for example) in a holster. [Probably Dutch, alteration of *holfter, hulfter,* from Middle High German *hulffter,* case, sheath, quiver, covering, from *hulft,* from Old High German. See **kel-**[1] in Appendix.] **—hol′stered** *adj.*

holt (hōlt) *n. Archaic.* A wood or grove; a copse. [Middle English, from Old English.]

Holt (hōlt), **Winifred.** 1870–1945. American sculptor and philanthropist who founded the first Lighthouse for the Blind in New York City (1913).

ho·ly (hō′lē) *adj.* **-li·er, -li·est. 1.** Belonging to, derived from, or associated with a divine power; sacred. **2.** Regarded with or worthy of worship or veneration; revered: *a holy book.* **3.** Living according to a strict or highly moral religious or spiritual system; saintly: *a holy person.* **4.** Specified or set apart for a religious purpose: *a holy place.* **5.** Solemnly undertaken; sacrosanct: *a holy pledge.* **6.** Regarded or deserving special respect or reverence: *The pursuit of peace is our holiest quest.* **7.** *Informal.* Used as an intensive: *raised holy hell over the mischief their children did.* [Middle English *holi,* from Old English *hālig.* See **kailo-** in Appendix.] **—ho′li·ly** *adv.* **—ho′li·ness** *n.*

Ho·ly Ark (hō′lē) *n. Judaism.* The cabinet in a synagogue in which the scrolls of the Torah are kept.

Holy Communion *n. Abbr.* **H.C.** The sacrament of the Eucharist received by a congregation.

Holy Cross (krôs′, krŏs′), **Mount of the.** A peak, 4,271.5 m (14,005 ft) high, in the Sawatch Range of the Rocky Mountains in west-central Colorado.

holster

holy day also **ho·ly·day** (hō′lē-dā′) *n.* A day specified for religious observance.

holy day of obligation also **holyday of obligation** *n., pl.* **holy days of obligation** also **holydays of obligation.** *Roman Catholic Church.* A feast on which the faithful are obliged to hear Mass and abstain from servile work.

Holy Father *n. Roman Catholic Church.* Used as a title and form of address for the pope.

Holy Ghost *n.* The Holy Spirit. [Middle English *holi gost,* holy spirit, from Old English *hālig gāst* (translation of Latin *spīritus sanctus*) : *hālig,* holy; see HOLY + *gāst,* spirit.]

Holy Grail *n.* See **grail** (sense 1).

Holy In·no·cents' Day (ĭn′ə-sənts) *n. Ecclesiastical.* December 28, observed in commemoration of the slaughter of male infants in Bethlehem during Herod the Great's attempt to kill the infant Jesus.

Holy Island or **Lin·dis·farne** (lĭn′dĭs-färn′). An island off the coast of northeast England near the Scottish border. At low tide the island is connected with the mainland by a stretch of sand.

Holy Land. The biblical region of Palestine.

Holy Office *n. Roman Catholic Church.* A Roman congregation of the Curia that is responsible for protection of the faith and morals.

holy of holies *n.* **1.** *Judaism.* The sanctuary inside the tabernacle in the Temple of Jerusalem, in which the Ark of the Covenant was kept. **2.** *Eastern Orthodox Church.* The bema or sanctuary in a church. **3.** A place of awe. [Translation of Late Latin *sanctum sanctōrum* (ultimately translation of Hebrew *qōdeš haqqodāšîm*) : *sanctum,* holy + *sanctōrum,* neuter genitive pl. of *sanctus,* holy.]

Holy Ark

holy oil *n. Ecclesiastical.* **1.** See **chrism** (sense 1). **2.** Olive oil blessed by a bishop, used to anoint the sick and in sacramentals.

Hol·yoke (hōl′yōk′). A city of southwest Massachusetts on the Connecticut River north of Springfield. Settled in 1745, it is a manufacturing center. Population, 44,678.

holy order also **Holy Order** *n. Ecclesiastical.* **1.** The sacrament or rite of ordination. Often used in the plural. **2.** The rank of an ordained Christian minister or priest. Often used in the plural. **3.** A principal order of the clergy, especially the rank of bishop, priest, and deacon, in the Roman Catholic, Eastern Orthodox, and Anglican churches. In this sense, also called *major order.*

Holy Roller *n. Offensive.* Used as a disparaging term for a member of any of various religious denominations in which spiritual fervor is expressed by shouts and violent body movements.

Holy Ro·man Empire (rō′mən). *Abbr.* **H.R.E.** A loosely federated European political entity that began with the papal coronation of the German king Otto I as the first emperor in 962 and lasted until Francis II's renunciation of the title at the instigation of Napoleon in 1806. The empire was troubled from the beginning by papal-secular squabbles over authority and after the 13th century by the rising ambitions of nationalistic states in Europe. By 1273 the empire consisted primarily of the Hapsburg domains in Austria and Spain.

Holy Saturday *n.* The Saturday before Easter.

Holy Scripture *n.* See **scripture** (sense 2).

Holy See *n. Roman Catholic Church.* **1.** The see of the bishop of Rome. **2.** The authority, jurisdiction, and governmental functions associated with the papacy.

Holy Spirit *n.* The third person of the Christian Trinity.

ho·ly·stone (hō′lē-stōn′) *n.* A piece of soft sandstone used for scouring the wooden decks of a ship. **—holystone** *tr.v.* **-stoned, -ston·ing, -stones.** To scrub or scour with a piece of soft sandstone. [Origin unknown.]

Holy Synod *n.* The governing body of any of the Eastern Orthodox churches.

Holy Thursday *n.* **1.** See **Maundy Thursday. 2.** See **Ascension Day.**

holy war also **Holy War** *n.* A war declared or fought for a religious or high moral purpose, as to extend or defend a religion.

holy water *n.* Water blessed by a priest and used for religious purposes.

Holy Week *n.* The week before Easter.

holy writ *n.* **1.** Often **Holy Writ.** The Bible. **2.** *Informal.* A document held to be the most authoritative of its kind.

hom– *pref.* Variant of **homo–.**

hom·age (hŏm′ĭj, ŏm′-) *n.* **1.** Ceremonial acknowledgment by a vassal of allegiance to his lord under feudal law. **2.** Special honor or respect shown publicly. See Synonyms at **honor.** [Middle English, from Old French, probably from *omne, homme,* man, from Latin *homō, homin-.* See **dhghem-** in Appendix.]

hom·bre[1] (ŏm′brā′, -brē) *n. Slang.* A man; a fellow. [Spanish, from Old Spanish *omne,* from Latin *homō, homin-.* See **dhghem-** in Appendix.]

hom·bre[2] (hŏm′bər, ŏm′-) *n. Games.* Variant of **ombre.**

Hom·burg also **hom·burg** (hŏm′bûrg′) *n.* A man's felt hat having a soft, dented crown and a shallow, slightly rolled brim. [After (BAD) HOMBURG.]

home (hōm) *n.* **1.** A place where one lives; a residence. **2.** The physical structure within which one lives, such as a house or an apartment. **3.** A dwelling place together with the family or social unit that occupies it; a household. **4. a.** An environment offering security and happiness. **b.** A valued place regarded as a refuge or place of origin. **5.** The place, such as a country or town, where one was born or has lived for a long period. **6.** The native habitat, as of a plant or animal. **7.** The place where something is discovered, founded, developed, or promoted; a source. **8.** A headquarters; a home base. **9. a.** *Baseball.* Home plate. **b.** *Games.* Home base. **10.** An institution where people are cared for: *a home for the elderly.* **11.** *Computer Science.* The starting position of the cursor on a computer screen, usually in the upper left corner of the screen. **—home** *adj.* **1. a.** Of or relating to a home, especially to one's household or house: *home cooking; home furnishings.* **b.** Taking place in the home: *home care for the elderly.* **2.** Of, relating to, or being a place of origin or headquarters: *the home office.* **3.** *Sports.* Relating to a team's sponsoring institution or to the place where it is franchised: *a home game; the home field advantage.* **4.** Of, relating to, or being the keys used as base positions for the fingers in touch-typing. **—home** *adv.* **1.** At, to, or toward the direction of home: *going home for lunch.* **2.** On or into the point at which something is directed: *The arrow struck home.* **3.** To the center or heart of something; deeply: *Your comments really hit home.* **—home** *v.* **homed, hom·ing, homes.** *—intr.* **1.** To go or return to one's residence or base of operations. **2.** To be guided to a target automatically, as by means of radio waves. **3.** To move or lead toward a goal: *The investigators were homing in on the truth.* *—tr.* To guide (a missile or an aircraft) to a target automatically. ***—idioms.* at home. 1.** Available to receive visitors: *at home on Thursdays.* **2.** Comfortable and relaxed; at ease: *at home in diplomatic circles.* **3.** Feeling an easy competence and familiarity: *at home in French.* **home free.** Free of tension or stress, usually after expending considerable effort: *met the schedule and was home free.* [Middle English, from Old English *hām.* See **tkei-** in Appendix.]

home base *n.* **1. a.** *Games.* An objective toward which players of certain games, such as backgammon, progress. **b.** *Baseball.* Home plate. **2.** A base of operations; a headquarters.

home·bod·y (hōm′bŏd′ē) *n., pl.* **-ies.** One whose interests center on the home.

home·bound[1] (hōm′bound′) *adj.* Heading homeward. [HOME + BOUND[4].]

home·bound[2] (hōm′bound′) *adj.* Restricted or confined to home: *homebound invalids.* [HOME + BOUND[3].]

home·boy (hōm′boi′) *n. Slang.* **1.** A male friend or acquaintance from one's hometown or neighborhood. **2.** A fellow gang member.

home·bred (hōm′brĕd′) *adj.* Raised, bred, or reared at home; domestic.

home-brew (hōm′brōō′) *n.* An alcoholic beverage, especially beer, that is made at home. **—home′-brewed′** *adj.*

home·build·er (hōm′bĭl′dər) *n.* **1.** One, such as a person or firm, whose business is the construction of dwellings. **2.** One who builds one's own home. **—home′build′ing** *n.*

home·buy·er (hōm′bī′ər) *n.* One who purchases or expects to purchase a home.

home·com·ing (hōm′kŭm′ĭng) *n.* **1.** A coming to or returning home. **2.** An annual event at schools, colleges, and universities for visiting graduates.

home computer *n. Computer Science.* A microcomputer intended for use in the home.

home economics *n. (used with a sing. or pl. verb).* The science and art of home management. Also called *household arts.* **—home economist** *n.*

home front *n.* The civilian population or the civilian activities of a country at war.

home fry *n.* A potato that has been peeled, boiled, sliced, and then fried in butter, oil, or shortening. Often used in the plural.

home ground *n.* **1.** One's familiar surroundings or habitat. **2.** An area of special strength or competence: *a company that never expected to be challenged on its home ground of software development.*

home·grown (hōm′grōn′) *adj.* **1.** Raised or grown at home. **2.** Originating in or characteristic of a locality: *"Rock is homegrown music in the United States, evolved from blues and country and Tin Pan Alley"* (Jon Pareles).

home guard *n.* A volunteer force formed to defend a homeland while the regular army is fighting elsewhere.

home-help·er (hōm′hĕl′pər) *n.* One who aids a patient requiring long-term care in the private residence rather than in a hospital or nursing home.

home invasion *n.* Burglary of a dwelling while the residents are at home.

home·land (hōm′lănd′) *n.* **1.** One's native land. **2.** A state, region, or territory that is closely identified with a particular people or ethnic group. **3.** Any of the ten regions designated by South Africa as semiautonomous territorial states for the Black population.

home·less (hōm′lĭs) *adj.* Having no home or haven. **—homeless** *n. (used with a pl. verb).* People without homes considered as a group. Often used with *the.*

home·ly (hōm′lē) *adj.* **-li·er, -li·est. 1.** Not attractive or good-looking: *a homely child.* **2.** Lacking elegance or refinement: *homely furniture.* **3.** Of a simple or unpretentious nature; plain: *homely truths.* **4.** Characteristic of the home or of home life: *homely skills.* **—home′li·ness** *n.*

home·made (hōm′mād′) *adj.* **1.** Made or prepared in the home: *homemade pie.* **2.** Made by oneself. **3.** Crudely or simply made.

home·mak·er (hōm′mā′kər) *n.* One who manages a household. **—home′mak′ing** *n.*

homeo– or **homoio–** *pref.* Like; similar: *homeostasis.* [Greek *homoio-*, from *homoios,* from *homos,* same. See **sem-**[1] in Appendix.]

ho·me·o·mor·phism (hō′mē-ə-môr′fĭz′əm) *n.* **1.** *Chemistry.* A close similarity in the crystal forms of unlike compounds. **2.** *Mathematics.* A one-to-one correspondence between the points of two geometric figures that is continuous in both directions. **—ho′me·o·mor′phous** *adj.*

ho·me·op·a·thy (hō′mē-ŏp′ə-thē) *n., pl.* **-thies.** A system for treating disease based on the administration of minute doses of a drug that in massive amounts produces symptoms in healthy individuals similar to those of the disease itself. **—ho′me·o·path′** (-ə-păth′), **ho′me·op′a·thist** *n.* **—ho′me·o·path′ic** *adj.* **—ho′me·o·path′i·cal·ly** *adv.*

ho·me·o·sta·sis (hō′mē-ō-stā′sĭs) *n.* The ability or tendency of an organism or a cell to maintain internal equilibrium by adjusting its physiological processes. **—ho′me·o·stat′ic** (-stăt′ĭk) *adj.*

ho·me·o·therm (hō′mē-ə-thûrm′) also **ho·moi·o·therm** (hō-moi′ə-) *n.* An organism, such as a mammal or bird, having a body temperature that is constant and largely independent of the temperature of its surroundings; an endotherm.

ho·me·o·ther·mal (hō′mē-ə-thûr′məl) also **ho·moi·o·ther·mal** (hō-moi′ə-) *adj.* Homeothermic.

ho·me·o·ther·mic (hō′mē-ə-thûr′mĭk) also **ho·moi·o·ther·mic** (hō-moi′ə-) *adj.* Maintaining a relatively constant body temperature that is independent of the temperature of the surrounding environment.

ho·me·o·ther·mous (hō′mē-ə-thûr′məs) also **ho·moi·o·ther·mous** (hō-moi′ə-) *adj.* Homeothermic.

home·own·er (hōm′ō′nər) *n.* One who owns a home. **—home′own′er·ship′** *n.*

home plate *n. Baseball.* A base, usually consisting of a hard rubber slab, at one of the corners of a diamond at which a batter stands when hitting and which a base runner must finally touch in order to score.

home port also **home·port** (hōm′pôrt′, -pōrt′) *—n.* **1.** The port in which a vessel is registered or permanently based. **2.** The port from which a merchant vessel primarily operates, regardless of its registry. *—tr.v.* **-port·ed, -port·ing, -ports.** To base (a ship) permanently in a given port.

hom·er[1] (hō′mər) *n.* **1.** *Baseball.* A home run. **2.** A homing pigeon. **—homer** *intr.v.* **ho·mer·ed, ho·mer·ing, ho·mers.** *Baseball.* To hit a home run: *homered in the fifth inning.*

ho·mer[2] (hō′mər) *n.* A unit of capacity used by the ancient Hebrews, equal to 10 ephahs (about 10 bushels) or 10 baths (about 100 gallons). Also called *kor.* [Hebrew *ḥōmer.*]

Ho·mer (hō′mər). fl. 850 B.C. Greek epic poet. Two of the greatest works in Western literature, the *Iliad* and the *Odyssey,* are attributed to him.

Homer, Winslow. 1836–1910. American painter known for his realistic seascapes, such as *Eight Bells* (1886).

home range *n.* The geographic area to which an organism normally confines its activity.

Ho·mer·ic (hō-mĕr′ĭk) *adj.* **1.** Of, relating to, or characteristic of Homer, his works, or the legends and age of which he wrote. **2.** Heroic in proportion, degree, or character; epic. **—Ho·mer′i·cal·ly** *adv.*

Homeric simile *n.* See **epic simile.**

home·room (hōm′ro͞om′, -ro͝om′) *n.* A school classroom to which a group of pupils of the same grade are required to report each day.

home rule *n. Abbr.* **H.R.** The principle or practice of self-government in the internal affairs of a dependent country or other political unit.

home run *n. Abbr.* **h.r.** *Baseball.* A hit that allows the batter to make a complete circuit of the diamond and score a run.

home·sick (hōm′sĭk′) *adj.* Acutely longing for one's family or home. **—home′sick′ness** *n.*

home·spun (hōm′spŭn′) *adj.* **1.** Spun or woven in the home: *homespun linen.* **2.** Made of a homespun fabric: *a homespun tablecloth.* **3.** Simple and homely; unpretentious: *"Most small towns would have gladly forfeited some of their homespun values if it meant luring a firm there"* (William Mueller). **—homespun** *n.* **1.** A plain, coarse, usually woolen cloth made of homespun yarn. **2.** A similar sturdy fabric made on a power loom.

home stand *n. Sports.* A succession of games played especially by a baseball team at the team's home field or court.

home·stead (hōm′stĕd′) *n.* **1.** A house, especially a farmhouse, with adjoining buildings and land. **2.** *Law.* Property designated by a householder as the householder's home and protected by law from forced sale to meet debts. **3.** Land claimed by a settler or squatter, especially under the Homestead Act. **4.** The place where one's home is. **—homestead** *v.* **-stead·ed, -stead·ing, -steads.** *—intr.* To settle and farm land, especially under the Homestead Act. *—tr.* To claim and settle (land) as a homestead. **—home′stead′er** *n.*

Home·stead (hōm′stĕd′). A city of southeast Florida southwest of Miami. Population, 20,668.

Homestead Act *n.* An act passed by Congress in 1862 promising ownership of a 160-acre tract of public land to a citizen or head of a family who had resided on and cultivated the land for five years after the initial claim.

homestead law *n.* Any of several laws passed in most states exempting a householder's homestead from attachment or forced sale to meet general debts.

home·stretch (hōm′strĕch′) *n.* **1.** *Sports.* The portion of a racetrack from the last turn to the finish line. **2.** *Informal.* The final stages of an undertaking.

home study *n.* A course of study in which instruction is offered at home, usually by mail.

home-style (hōm′stīl′) *adj.* Prepared or served as if in the home: *home-style apple pie.* **—home′-style′** *adv.*

home·town (hōm′toun′) *n.* The town or city of one's birth, rearing, or main residence.

home truth *n.* A key or basic truth, especially one that is discomforting to acknowledge.

home video *n.* Videotapes for viewing in the home.

home·ward (hōm′wərd) *adv. & adj.* Toward or at home. **—home′wards** (-wərdz) *adv.*

Home·wood (hōm′wo͝od′). **1.** A city of central Alabama, a suburb of Birmingham. Population, 21,412. **2.** A village of northeast Illinois, a suburb of Chicago. Population, 19,724.

home·work (hōm′wûrk′) *n.* **1.** Work, such as schoolwork or piecework, that is done at home. **2.** Preparatory or preliminary work: *did their homework before coming to the meeting.*

hom·ey also **hom·y** (hō′mē) *adj.* **-i·er, -i·est.** *Informal.* Having a feeling of home; comfortable; cozy. **—hom′ey·ness** *n.*

hom·i·cid·al (hŏm′ĭ-sīd′l, hō′mĭ-) *adj.* **1.** Of or relating to homicide. **2.** Capable of or conducive to homicide: *a homicidal rage.* **—hom′i·cid′al·ly** *adv.*

hom·i·cide (hŏm′ĭ-sīd′, hō′mĭ-) *n.* **1.** The killing of one person by another. **2.** A person who kills another person. [Middle English, from Old French, from Latin *homicīdium* and *homicīda* : *homō,* man; see **dhghem-** in Appendix + *-cīdium* and *-cīda,* -cide.]

hom·i·let·ic (hŏm′ə-lĕt′ĭk) also **hom·i·let·i·cal** (-ĭ-kəl) *adj.* **1.** Relating to or of the nature of a homily. **2.** Relating to homiletics. [Late Latin *homīlēticus,* from Greek *homilētikos,* of conversation, from *homilētos,* conversation, from *homilein,* to converse with, from *homilos,* crowd. See HOMILY.] **—hom′i·let′i·cal·ly** *adv.*

hom·i·let·ics (hŏm′ə-lĕt′ĭks) *n. (used with a sing. verb).* The art of preaching.

Homburg
Worn by Edward VII

Winslow Homer
Photographed in 1867

ă pat	oi boy
ā pay	ou out
âr care	o͝o took
ä father	o͞o boot
ĕ pet	ŭ cut
ē be	ûr urge
ĭ pit	th thin
ī pie	*th* this
îr pier	hw which
ŏ pot	zh vision
ō toe	ə about, item
ô paw	♦ regionalism

Stress marks: ′ (primary); ′ (secondary), as in **dictionary** (dĭk′shə-nĕr′ē)

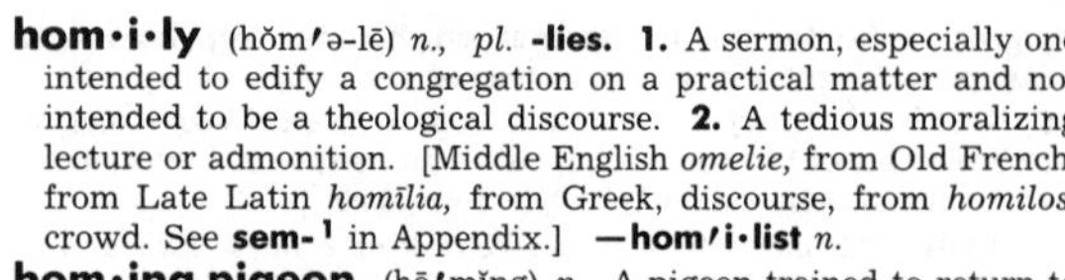

hom·i·ly (hŏm′ə-lē) *n., pl.* **-lies. 1.** A sermon, especially one intended to edify a congregation on a practical matter and not intended to be a theological discourse. **2.** A tedious moralizing lecture or admonition. [Middle English *omelie,* from Old French, from Late Latin *homīlia,* from Greek, discourse, from *homilos,* crowd. See **sem-**[1] in Appendix.] **—hom′i·list** *n.*

hom·ing pigeon (hō′mĭng) *n.* A pigeon trained to return to its home roost.

hom·i·nid (hŏm′ə-nĭd) *n.* A primate of the family Hominidae, of which *Homo sapiens* is the only extant species. **—hominid** *adj.* Of the Hominidae. [From New Latin *Hominidae,* family name, from Latin *homō, homin-,* man. See **dhghem-** in Appendix.]

hom·i·ni·za·tion (hŏm′ə-nĭ-zā′shən) *n.* The evolutionary process leading to the development of human characteristics that distinguish hominids from other primates. [Latin *homō, homin-,* man; see HOMO[1] + -IZATION.]

homocercal
Swordfish with homocercal tail

hom·i·noid (hŏm′ə-noid′) *adj.* **1.** Of or belonging to the superfamily Hominoidea, which includes apes and human beings. **2.** Resembling a human being. **—hominoid** *n.* A member of the Hominoidea. [From New Latin *Hominoidea,* superfamily name : *Homō, Homin-,* type genus (from Latin *homō,* man; see HOMO[1]) + *-oidea,* resembling (from Greek *-oeidēs,* -oid).]

hom·i·ny (hŏm′ə-nē) *n.* Hulled and dried kernels of corn, prepared as food by boiling. [Short for Virginia Algonquian *uskatahomen.*]

♦ **hominy grits** *pl.n.* Grits, especially eaten as a breakfast food. See Regional Note at **pone.**

hom·mos (ho͝om′əs, hŭm′-) *n.* Variant of **hummus.**

ho·mo[1] (hō′mō) *n.* A member of the genus *Homo,* which includes the extinct and extant species of human beings. [Latin *homō,* man. See **dhghem-** in Appendix.]

ho·mo[2] (hō′mō) *n., pl.* **-mos.** *Offensive.* Used as a disparaging term for a gay or homosexual person.

homo– or **hom–** *pref.* Same; like: *homophone.* [Greek, from *homos,* same. See **sem-**[1] in Appendix.]

ho·mo·cen·tric (hō′mə-sĕn′trĭk, hŏm′ə-) *adj.* Having the same center.

ho·mo·cer·cal (hō′mə-sûr′kəl, hŏm′ə-) *adj.* Relating to, designating, or characterized by a tail fin having two symmetrical lobes extending from the end of the vertebral column, as in most bony fishes. [HOMO– + Greek *kerkos,* tail + -AL[1].]

ho·mo·chro·mat·ic (hō′mə-krō-măt′ĭk, hŏm′ə-) *adj.* Of or characterized by one color; monochromatic. **—ho′mo·chro′ma·tism** (-krō′mə-tĭz′əm) *n.*

ho·moe·cious (hō-mē′shəs, hŏ-) *adj.* Of or being a parasite that spends all stages of its life cycle on the same host. [HOMO– + Greek *oikia,* house; see HETEROECIOUS + -OUS.]

Ho·mo e·rec·tus (hō′mō ĭ-rĕk′təs) *n.* An extinct species of human beings, regarded as an ancestor of *Homo sapiens.* [Latin *homō,* man + *ērēctus,* upright.]

ho·mo·e·rot·ic (hō′mō-ĭ-rŏt′ĭk) *adj.* **1.** Of or concerning homosexual love and desire; amatory. **2.** Tending to arouse such sexual desire.

ho·mo·e·rot·i·cism (hō′mō-ĭ-rŏt′ĭ-sĭz′əm) also **ho·mo·er·o·tism** (-ĕr′ə-tĭz′əm) *n.* A homoerotic quality or theme.

ho·mo·ga·met·ic (hō′mō-gə-mĕt′ik) *adj.* Producing gametes that contain only one type of sex chromosome.

ho·mog·a·mous (hō-mŏg′ə-məs) *adj. Botany.* **1.** Having one kind of flower on the same plant. **2.** Having stamens and pistils that mature simultaneously.

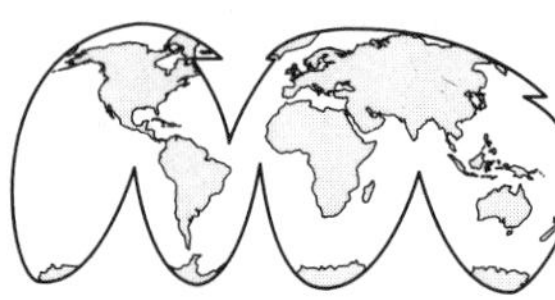

homolosine projection

ho·mo·ge·ne·i·ty (hō′mə-jə-nē′ĭ-tē, -nā′-, hŏm′ə-) *n., pl.* **-ties.** The state or quality of being homogeneous.

ho·mo·ge·ne·ous (hō′mə-jē′nē-əs, -jēn′yəs) *adj.* **1.** Of the same or similar nature or kind: *"a tight-knit, homogeneous society"* (James Fallows). **2.** Uniform in structure or composition throughout. **3.** *Mathematics.* Consisting of terms of the same degree or elements of the same dimension. [From Medieval Latin *homogeneus,* from Greek *homogenēs* : *homo-,* homo- + *genos,* kind; see HETEROGENEOUS.] **—ho′mo·ge′ne·ous·ly** *adv.* **—ho′mo·ge′ne·ous·ness** *n.*

ho·mog·e·nize (hə-mŏj′ə-nīz′, hō-) *tr.v.* **-nized, -niz·ing, -niz·es. 1.** To make homogeneous. **2. a.** To reduce to particles and disperse throughout a fluid. **b.** To make uniform in consistency, especially to render (milk) uniform in consistency by emulsifying the fat content. [From HOMOGENEOUS.] **—ho·mog′e·ni·za′tion** (-nĭ-zā′shən) *n.* **—ho·mog′e·niz′er** *n.*

ho·mog·e·nous[1] (hə-mŏj′ə-nəs, hō-) *adj. Biology.* Of or exhibiting homogeny.

ho·mog·e·nous[2] (hə-mŏj′ə-nəs, hō-) *adj.* Homogeneous. [Alteration of HOMOGENEOUS.]

ho·mog·e·ny (hə-mŏj′ə-nē, hō-) *n., pl.* **-nies.** Similarity of structure between organs or parts, possibly of dissimilar function, that are related by common descent. [Greek *homogenia,* community of origin, from *homogenēs,* of the same race, family, kind. See HOMOGENEOUS.]

ho·mo·graft (hō′mə-grăft′, hŏm′ə-) *n.* See **allograft.**

hom·o·graph (hŏm′ə-grăf′, hō′mə-) *n.* One of two or more words that have the same spelling but differ in origin, meaning, and sometimes pronunciation. **—hom′o·graph′ic** *adj.*

Ho·mo hab·i·lis (hō′mō hăb′ə-ləs) *n.* An extinct species of human beings considered to be an ancestor of modern human beings and the earliest hominid to make tools. This species existed between 1.5 and 2.0 million years ago. [Latin *homō,* man + Latin *habilis,* skillful.]

homoio– *pref.* Variant of **homeo–.**

ho·moi·o·therm (hō-moi′ə-thûrm′) *n.* Variant of **homeotherm.**

ho·moi·o·ther·mal (hō-moi′ə-thûr′məl) *adj.* Variant of **homeothermal.**

ho·moi·o·ther·mic (hō-moi′ə-thûr′mĭk) *adj.* Variant of **homeothermic.**

ho·moi·o·ther·mous (hō-moi′ə-thûr′məs) *adj.* Variant of **homeothermous.**

Ho·moi·ou·si·an (hō′moi-o͞o′sē-ən, -zē-) *n.* A member of the Semi-Arian party in the fourth century A.D. that held that Jesus the Son and God the Father were of similar but not of the same substance. [From Greek *homoiousios,* of similar substance : *homoio-,* homeo- + *ousia,* substance (from neuter present participle of *einai,* to be; see **es-** in Appendix).]

ho·mo·lec·i·thal (hō′mə-lĕs′ə-thəl) *adj.* Having a yolk that is evenly distributed throughout: *a homolecithal egg.* [HOMO– + Greek *lekithos,* egg yolk + -AL[1].]

hom·o·log (hŏm′ə-lôg′, -lŏg′, hō′mə-) *n.* Variant of **homologue.**

ho·mol·o·gate (hə-mŏl′ə-gāt′, hō-) *tr.v.* **-gat·ed, -gat·ing, -gates.** *Scots.* To approve, especially to confirm officially. [Medieval Latin *homologāre, homologāt-,* from Greek *homologein,* to agree, from *homologos,* agreeing. See HOMOLOGOUS.]

ho·mo·log·i·cal (hō′mə-lŏj′ĭ-kəl, hŏm′ə-) also **ho·mo·log·ic** (-lŏj′ĭk) *adj.* Homologous. **—ho′mo·log′i·cal·ly** *adv.*

ho·mol·o·gize (hə-mŏl′ə-jīz′, hō-) *tr.v.* **-gized, -giz·ing, -giz·es. 1.** To make homologous. **2.** To show to be homologous. **—ho·mol′o·giz′er** *n.*

ho·mol·o·gous (hə-mŏl′ə-gəs, hō-) *adj.* **1.** Corresponding or similar in position, value, structure, or function. **2.** *Biology.* Similar in structure and evolutionary origin, though not necessarily in function, as the flippers of a seal and the hands of a human being. **3.** *Immunology.* Relating to the correspondence between an antigen and the antibody produced in response to it. **4.** *Genetics.* Having the same morphology and linear sequence of gene loci as another chromosome. **5.** *Chemistry.* Belonging to or being a series of organic compounds each successive member of which differs from the preceding member by a constant increment, especially by an added CH_2 group. [From Greek *homologos,* agreeing : *homo-,* homo- + *logos,* word, proportion; see **leg-** in Appendix.]

hom·o·lo·graph·ic (hŏm′ə-lə-grăf′ĭk) *adj.* Maintaining the ratio of parts. [Greek *homalos,* even; see **sem-**[1] in Appendix + GRAPHIC.]

homolographic projection *n.* A map projection reproducing the ratios of areas as they exist on the earth's surface.

hom·o·logue also **hom·o·log** (hŏm′ə-lôg′, -lŏg′, hō′mə-) *n.* Something homologous; a homologous organ or part. [French, from Greek *homologon,* neuter of *homologos,* agreeing. See HOMOLOGOUS.]

ho·mol·o·gy (hə-mŏl′ə-jē, hō-) *n., pl.* **-gies. 1.** The quality or condition of being homologous. **2.** A homologous relationship or correspondence. **3.** *Chemistry.* **a.** The relation of the elements of a periodic family or group. **b.** The relation of the organic compounds forming a homologous series. **4.** *Mathematics.* A topologic classification of configurations into distinct types that imposes an algebraic structure or hierarchy on families of geometric figures. [Greek *homologia,* agreement, from *homologos,* agreeing. See HOMOLOGOUS.]

ho·mol·o·sine projection (hō-mŏl′ə-sīn′, -sĭn, hə-) *n.* A map of the earth's surface laid out on the basis of sinusoidal curves, with the interruptions over ocean areas distorted so that the continents appear with minimal distortion. [HOMOLO(GRAPHIC) + SINE + PROJECTION.]

ho·mo·mor·phism (hō′mə-môr′fĭz′əm, hŏm′ə-) *n.* **1.** *Biology.* Similarity of external form or appearance but not of structure or origin. **2.** *Zoology.* A resemblance in form between the immature and adult stages of an animal. **3.** *Mathematics.* A transformation of one set into another that preserves in the second set the operations between the members of the first set. **—ho′mo·mor′phic, ho′mo·mor′phous** *adj.*

hom·o·nym (hŏm′ə-nĭm′, hō′mə-) *n.* **1.** One of two or more words that have the same sound and often the same spelling but differ in meaning. **2. a.** A word that is used to designate several different things. **b.** A namesake. **3.** *Biology.* A taxonomic name that is identical to one previously applied to a different species or genus and that therefore is unacceptable in its new use. [Latin *homōnymum,* from Greek *homōnumon,* from neuter of *homōnumos,* homonymous. See HOMONYMOUS.] **—hom′o·nym′ic** *adj.*

ho·mon·y·mous (hō-mŏn′ə-məs, hə-) *adj.* **1.** Having the same name. **2.** Of the nature of a homonym; homonymic. [From Latin *homōnymus,* from Greek *homōnumos* : *homo-,* homo- + *onuma,* name; see **nō-men-** in Appendix.] **—ho·mon′y·mous·ly** *adv.*

ho·mon·y·my (hō-mŏn′ə-mē, hə-) *n., pl.* **-mies.** The quality or condition of being homonymous.

Ho·mo·ou·si·an (hō′mō-o͞o′sē-ən, -zē-) *n.* A Christian supporting the Council of Nicaea's Trinitarian definition of Jesus the Son of God as consubstantial with God the Father. [Late Latin *homoūsiānus,* from *homoūsius,* of same substance, from Greek *ho-*

moousios : *homo-*, homo- + *ousia*, substance; see HOMOIOUSIAN.]

ho·mo·phile (hō′mə-fīl′) *adj.* **1.** Gay or homosexual. **2.** Being actively concerned with the rights and welfare of gay or homosexual people. **—ho′mo·phile′** *n.*

ho·mo·pho·bi·a (hō′mə-fō′bē-ə) *n.* **1.** Aversion to gay or homosexual people or their lifestyle or culture. **2.** Behavior or an act based on this aversion. [HOMO(SEXUAL) + -PHOBIA.] **—ho′mo·phobe′** *n.* **—ho′mo·pho′bic** (-fō′bĭk) *adj.*

hom·o·phone (hŏm′ə-fōn′, hō′mə-) *n.* One of two or more words, such as *night* and *knight*, that are pronounced the same but differ in meaning, origin, and sometimes spelling. **—ho·moph′o·nous** (hō-mŏf′ə-nəs) *adj.*

hom·o·phon·ic (hŏm′ə-fŏn′ĭk, hō′mə-) *adj.* **1.** Having the same sound. **2.** *Music.* Having or characterized by a single melodic line with accompaniment. [From Greek *homophōnos* : *homo-*, homo- + *phōnē*, sound; see PHONE[2].]

ho·moph·o·ny (hō-mŏf′ə-nē) *n.*, *pl.* **-nies. 1.** The quality or condition of being homophonic. **2.** *Music.* Homophonic music.

ho·mo·phy·ly (hō′mə-fī′lē, hŏm′ə-, hō-mŏf′ə-lē) *n.*, *pl.* **-lies.** *Zoology.* Resemblance arising from common ancestry. [HOMO- + PHYL(UM) + -Y[2].] **—ho′mo·phyl′ic** (-fĭl′ĭk) *adj.*

ho·mo·plas·tic (hō′mə-plăs′tĭk, hŏm′ə-) *adj.* **1.** Of, relating to, or exhibiting homoplasy. **2.** Of, relating to, or derived from a different individual of the same species: *a homoplastic graft.* **—ho′mo·plas′ti·cal·ly** *adv.*

ho·mo·pla·sy (hō′mə-plā′sē, -plăs′ē, hŏm′ə-) *n.* Correspondence between parts or organs arising from evolutionary convergence.

ho·mop·ter·an (hō-mŏp′tər-ən) *n.* A homopterous insect. **—homopteran** *adj.* Of or belonging to the order Homoptera; homopterous. [From New Latin *Homoptera*, order name : Greek *homo-*, homo- + Greek *pteron*, wing; see -PTER.]

ho·mop·ter·ous (hō-mŏp′tər-əs) *adj.* Of or belonging to the order Homoptera, which includes the cicadas, aphids, and scale insects, characterized by sucking mouthparts. [From New Latin *Homoptera*, order name. See HOMOPTERAN.]

Ho·mo sa·pi·ens (hō′mō sā′pē-ənz, -ĕnz′) *n.* The modern species of human beings, the only extant species of the primate family Hominidae. [New Latin *Homō sapiēns* : *Homō*, genus name + Latin *sapiēns*, present participle of *sapere*, to be wise.]

ho·mo·sex·u·al (hō′mə-sĕk′shōō-əl, -mō-) *adj.* Of, relating to, or having a sexual orientation to persons of the same sex. **—homosexual** *n.* A homosexual person; a gay man or a lesbian.

ho·mo·sex·u·al·i·ty (hō′mə-sĕk′shōō-ăl′ĭ-tē, -mō-) *n.* **1.** Sexual orientation to persons of the same sex. **2.** Sexual activity with another of the same sex.

ho·mo·spo·rous (hō′mə-spôr′əs, -spōr′-, hŏm′ə-, hō-mŏs′pər-əs) *adj.* *Botany.* Producing spores of one kind only. **—ho′mo·spo′ry** *n.*

ho·mo·styled (hō′mō-stīld′) *adj.* *Botany.* Having the same relation of length between stamens and styles of different species. **—ho′mo·sty′lous** *adj.* **—ho′mo·sty′ly** *n.*

ho·mo·tax·is (hō′mō-tăk′sĭs, hŏm′ō-) *n.* Similarity of stratigraphic arrangement and fossils in noncontemporaneous or widely separated geologic deposits. **—ho′mo·tax′ic** (-tăk′sĭk), **ho′mo·tax′i·al** (-tăk′sē-əl) *adj.*

ho·mo·thal·lic (hō′mō-thăl′ĭk, hŏm′ō-) *adj.* *Botany.* Having male and female reproductive structures on the same thallus, as in some fungi and algae.

ho·mo·zy·go·sis (hō′mō-zī-gō′sĭs, -mə-, hŏm′ə-) *n.* The union of genetically identical gametes, resulting in the formation of a homozygote. **—ho′mo·zy·got′ic** (-gŏt′ĭk) *adj.*

ho·mo·zy·gote (hō′mō-zī′gōt′, -mə-, hŏm′ə-) *n.* *Genetics.* An organism that has the same alleles at a particular gene locus on homologous chromosomes.

ho·mo·zy·gous (hō′mō-zī′gəs, -mə-, hŏm′ə-) *adj.* *Genetics.* Having the same alleles at a particular gene locus on homologous chromosomes. **—ho′mo·zy·gos′i·ty** (-gŏs′ĭ-tē) *n.* **—ho′mo·zy′gous·ly** *adv.*

Homs (hômz, hôms). A city of west-central Syria north of Damascus. Birthplace of the Roman emperor Heliogabalus, it was taken by the Arabs in 636. Population, 346,871.

ho·mun·cu·lus (hō-mŭng′kyə-ləs, hə-) *n.*, *pl.* **-li** (-lī′). **1.** A diminutive human being. **2.** A miniature, fully formed individual believed by adherents of the early biological theory of preformation to be present in the sperm cell. [Latin, diminutive of *homō*, man. See **dhghem-** in Appendix.]

hom·y (hō′mē) *adj.* Variant of **homey.**

Hon. *abbr.* **1.** Honorable. **2. hon.** Honorary.

ho·nan also **Ho·nan** (hō′năn′) *n.* A pongee fabric of even color made originally from silk produced by the silkworms of Henan (formerly Honan), China.

Honan. See **Henan.**

hon·cho (hŏn′chō) *Slang.* *n.*, *pl.* **-chos.** One who is in charge; a manager or leader: *"some of the big-name honchos . . . featured in the glossy . . . magazines"* (New Yorker). **—honcho** *tr.v.* **-choed, -cho·ing, -chos.** To direct and manage (personnel and projects): *"He . . . is honchoing preparations for the forthcoming . . . economic summit"* (Newsweek). [Japanese, squad leader : *han*, squad + *chō*, chief.]

Hon·du·ras (hŏn-dŏŏr′əs, -dyŏŏr′-). *Abbr.* **Hond.** A country of northern Central America. Originally inhabited by a Mayan civilization, Honduras was colonized by the Spanish in the early 1500's and proclaimed its independence in 1821. Tegucigalpa is the capital and the largest city. Population, 4,092,000. **—Hon·du′ran** *adj.* *n.*

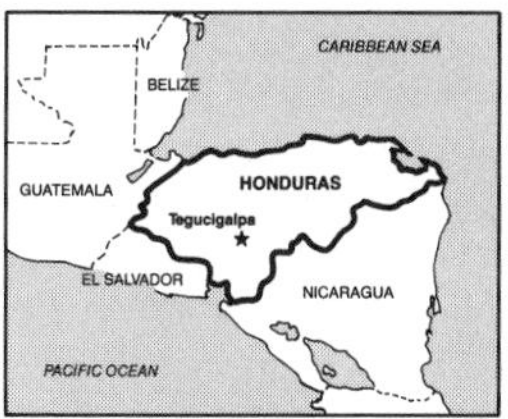

Honduras

Honduras, Gulf of. An inlet of the western Caribbean Sea bordering on Belize, Honduras, and Guatemala.

hone[1] (hōn) *n.* **1.** A fine-grained whetstone for giving a keen edge to a cutting tool. **2.** A tool with a rotating abrasive tip for enlarging holes to precise dimensions. **—hone** *tr.v.* **honed, hon·ing, hones. 1.** To sharpen on a fine-grained whetstone. **2.** To perfect or make more intense or effective: *a speaker who honed her delivery by long practice.* [Middle English, from Old English *hān*, stone. See **kō-** in Appendix.]

hone[2] (hōn) *intr.v.* **honed, hon·ing, hones.** *Informal.* **1.** To whine or moan. **2.** To hanker; yearn. [Obsolete French *hoigner*, from Old French, perhaps from *hon*, cry of discontent.]

Hon·eg·ger (hŏn′ĭ-gər, hō′nĕg′ər, ô-nĕ-gĕr′), **Arthur.** 1892–1955. French-born Swiss composer. A proponent of the modern movement in French music, he is remembered for a number of compositions, including *Pacific 231* (1923).

hon·est (ŏn′ĭst) *adj.* **1.** Marked by or displaying integrity; upright: *an honest lawyer.* **2.** Not deceptive or fraudulent; genuine: *honest weight.* **3.** Equitable; fair: *honest wages for an honest day's work.* **4. a.** Characterized by truth; not false: *honest reporting.* **b.** Sincere; frank: *an honest critique.* **5. a.** Of good repute; respectable. **b.** Without affectation; plain: *honest folk.* **6.** Virtuous; chaste. [Middle English, from Old French *honeste*, from Latin *honestus*, honorable, from *honōs*, honor.]

honest broker *n.* A neutral agent, as in mediation: *"enhanced Canada's position as honest broker in the Commonwealth"* (Kenneth McNaught).

hon·est·ly (ŏn′ĭst-lē) *adv.* **1.** In an honest manner. **2.** Used as an intensive: *I honestly don't care.* **—honestly** *interj.* Used to express mild disapproval or dismay: *Honestly! Look at the mess you've made.*

hon·es·ty (ŏn′ĭ-stē) *n.*, *pl.* **-ties. 1.** The quality or condition of being honest; integrity. **2.** Truthfulness; sincerity: *in all honesty.* **3.** *Archaic.* Chastity. **4.** *Botany.* A European plant *(Lunaria annua)* cultivated for its fragrant purplish flowers and round, flat, papery, silver-white seedpods. In this sense, also called *money plant, satin flower, silver dollar.*

SYNONYMS: *honesty, honor, integrity, probity, rectitude.* These nouns denote the quality of being upright in principle and action. *Honesty* implies truthfulness, fairness in dealing with others, and refusal to engage in fraud, deceit, or dissembling: *Honesty is the best policy. Honor* implies principled uprightness of character and a worthy adherence to a strict moral or ethical code: *"Never give in except to convictions of honor and good sense"* (Winston S. Churchill). *Integrity* is moral soundness, especially as it is revealed in dealings that test steadfastness of purpose, responsibility, or trust: *"Integrity without knowledge is weak and useless, and knowledge without integrity is dangerous and dreadful"* (Samuel Johnson). *Probity* is proven integrity: *A judge must be a person of unquestioned probity. Rectitude* is moral righteousness both in principle and in practice: *"The name of Brutus would be a guaranty to the people of rectitude of intention"* (J.A. Froude).

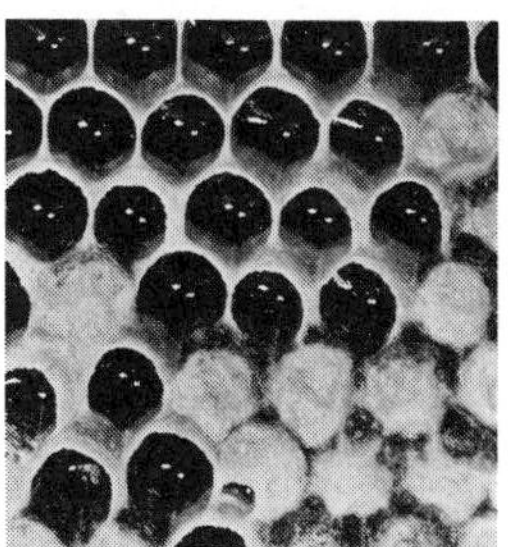
honeycomb
Close-up of hexagon-shaped cells

hone·wort (hōn′wûrt′, -wôrt′) *n.* An eastern North American perennial plant *(Cryptotaenia canadensis)* having umbels of small whitish flowers and compound leaves with larger, double serrate leaflets. [*hone-*, of unknown meaning + WORT[1].]

hon·ey (hŭn′ē) *n.*, *pl.* **-eys. 1.** *Abbr.* **hny a.** A sweet yellowish or brownish viscid fluid produced by various bees from the nectar of flowers and used as food. **b.** A similar substance made by certain other insects. **2.** A sweet substance, such as nectar. **3.** Sweetness; pleasantness. **4.** Sugary or ingratiating words; flattery. **5.** *Informal.* Sweetheart; dear. Used as a term of endearment. **6.** *Informal.* Something remarkably fine: *a honey of a car.* **—honey** *tr.v.* **-eyed** or **-ied** (hŭn′ēd), **-ey·ing, -eys. 1.** To sweeten with or as if with honey. **2.** To cajole with sweet talk. [Middle English *honi*, from Old English *hunig.*]

honey badger *n.* See **ratel.**

honey bear *n.* See **kinkajou.**

hon·ey·bee (hŭn′ē-bē′) *n.* Any of several social bees of the genus *Apis* that produce honey, especially *A. mellifera*, widely domesticated as a source of honey and beeswax.

hon·ey·ber·ry (hŭn′ē-bĕr′ē) *n.* See **genip** (sense 2).

hon·ey·comb (hŭn′ē-kōm′) *n.* **1.** A structure of hexagonal, thin-walled cells constructed from beeswax by honeybees to hold honey and larvae. **2.** Something resembling this structure in configuration or pattern. **—honeycomb** *tr.v.* **-combed, -comb·ing, -combs. 1.** To fill with holes or compartments; riddle: *cliffs that were honeycombed with caves and grottoes.* **2.** To form in or cover with a pattern like that of a honeycomb.

hon·ey·creep·er (hŭn′ē-krē′pər) *n.* **1.** Any of various small, often brightly colored tropical American birds of the family Coerebidae, having a curved bill adapted for sucking nectar from flowers. **2.** Any of several birds of the family Drepanididae of Hawaii, similar to the mainland honeycreepers.

hon·ey·dew (hŭn′ē-dōō′, -dyōō′) *n.* **1.** A sweet, sticky substance excreted by various insects, especially aphids, on the leaves of plants. **2.** A sweet exudate similar to honeydew on the leaves of plants. **3.** A honeydew melon.

ă pat	oi **boy**
ā pay	ou **out**
âr care	ŏŏ **took**
ä father	ōō **boot**
ĕ pet	ŭ **cut**
ē be	ûr **urge**
ĭ pit	th **thin**
ī pie	*th* **this**
îr pier	hw **which**
ŏ pot	zh **vision**
ō toe	ə **about, item**
ô paw	♦ **regionalism**

Stress marks: **′** (primary); ′ (secondary), as in **dictionary** (dĭk′shə-nĕr′ē)

honeydew melon *n.* A kind of melon *(Cucumis melo)* having a smooth, whitish rind and green flesh. Also called *winter melon.*

hon•ey•eat•er (hŭn′ē-ē′tər) *n.* Any of various birds of the family Meliphagidae of Australia and adjacent regions, having a long extensible tongue adapted for sucking nectar from flowers.

hon•eyed (hŭn′ēd) *v.* A past tense and a past participle of **honey.** —**honeyed** also **hon•ied** *adj.* **1.** Containing, full of, or sweetened with honey. **2.** Ingratiating; sugary: *honeyed words.* **3.** Sweet; dulcet: *a honeyed voice.*

honey guide *n.* Any of various tropical Old World birds of the family Indicatoridae, some species of which lead people or animals to the nests of wild honeybees. The birds eat the wax and larvae that remain after the nest has been destroyed for its honey.

honey locust *n.* Any of several trees of the genus *Gleditsia,* especially *G. triacanthos,* having deciduous, pinnately compound leaves, small flowers in racemes, and large, often twisted, indehiscent pods.

honey mesquite *n.* See **mesquite** (sense 1a). [From the high sugar content of its pods.]

hon•ey•moon (hŭn′ē-mo͞on′) *n.* **1.** A holiday or trip taken by a newly married couple. **2.** An early harmonious period in a relationship: *The honeymoon between the new President and the press was soon over.* —**honeymoon** *intr.v.* **-mooned, -moon•ing, -moons.** To spend a honeymoon. [Perhaps from a comparison of the moon, which wanes as soon as it is full, to the affections of a newly married couple, which are most tender right after marriage.] —**hon′ey•moon′er** *n.*

hon•ey•suck•le (hŭn′ē-sŭk′əl) *n.* **1.** Any of various shrubs or vines of the genus *Lonicera,* having opposite leaves, fragrant, usually paired tubular flowers, and small berries. **2.** Any of various similar or related plants. [Middle English *honysoukel,* alteration of *honisouke,* from Old English *hunīsūce* : *hunig,* honey + *sūcan,* to suck; see SUCK.]

Hong Ha (hông′ hä′). See **Red River** (sense 1).

Hong Kong (hŏng′kŏng′, -kŏng′, hông′kông′, -kông′). A British crown colony on the southeast coast of China southeast of Guangzhou, including **Hong Kong Island** and adjacent areas. Hong Kong Island was occupied by the British during the Opium War (1839–1842) and ceded to them by the Treaty of Nanking (1842). Other portions of the colony were acquired in 1860 and in 1898 by a 99-year lease. The colony will revert to Chinese sovereignty in 1997. Victoria is the capital. Population, 5,021,066.

Hong•shui He also **Hung•shui He** (ho͝ong′shwā′ hə′). A river, about 1,448 km (900 mi) long, rising in southwest China and flowing generally southeast to join the Xiang Jiang.

Ho•ni•a•ra (hō′nē-är′ə). The capital of the Solomon Islands, on the northwest coast of Guadalcanal. Population, 16,125.

hon•ied (hŭn′ēd) *v.* A past tense and a past participle of **honey.** —**honied** *adj.* Variant of **honeyed.**

honk (hôngk, hŏngk) *n.* **1.** The raucous, resonant sound characteristic of a wild goose. **2. a.** A sound similar to a goose's honk: *blew a loud honk on the bass saxophone.* **b.** The blaring sound of the horn on a motor vehicle. —**honk** *v.* **honked, honk•ing, honks.** —*intr.* To emit a honk. —*tr.* To cause (a horn) to produce a honk. [Imitative.] —**honk′er** *n.*

hon•ky or **hon•kie** also **hon•key** (hông′kē, hŏng′-) *n., pl.* **-kies** also **-keys.** *Offensive Slang.* Used as a disparaging term for a white person. [Possibly blend of Wolof *honq,* red, pink, of light complexion, and HUNKY.]

hon•ky-tonk (hông′kē-tôngk′, hŏng′kē-tŏngk′) *n. Slang.* A cheap, noisy bar or dance hall. —**honky-tonk** *adj.* **1.** *Slang.* Of or relating to such a bar or dance hall; tawdry: *a honky-tonk district; honky-tonk entertainers.* **2.** *Music.* Of, relating to, or being a type of ragtime characteristically played on a tinny-sounding piano. —**honky-tonk** *intr.v.* **-tonked, -tonk•ing, -tonks.** *Slang.* To visit cheap, noisy bars or dance halls. [Perhaps from HONK.]

hood¹
Academic hoods

Hon•o•lu•lu (hŏn′ə-lo͞o′lo͞o). The capital and largest city of Hawaii, on the southeast coast of Oahu. Settlement of the area began in 1816, and the city soon gained prominence as a whaling and sandalwood port. Population, 365,048.

hon•or (ŏn′ər) *n.* **1.** High respect, as that shown for special merit; esteem: *the honor shown to a Nobel laureate.* **2. a.** Good name; reputation. **b.** A source or cause of credit: *was an honor to the profession.* **3. a.** Glory or recognition; distinction. **b.** A mark, token, or gesture of respect or distinction: *the place of honor at the table.* **c.** A military decoration. **d.** A title conferred for achievement. **4.** Nobility of mind; probity. **5.** High rank. **6.** The dignity accorded to position: *awed by the honor of his office.* **7.** Great privilege: *I have the honor to present the governor.* **8. Honor.** Used with *His, Her,* or *Your* as a title and form of address for certain officials, such as judges and mayors: *Her Honor the Mayor.* **9. a.** A code of integrity, dignity, and pride, chiefly among men, that was maintained in some societies, as in feudal Europe, by force of arms. **b.** Principled uprightness of character; personal integrity. **c.** A woman's chastity or reputation for chastity. **10. honors.** Social courtesies offered to guests: *did the honors at tea.* **11. honors. a.** Special recognition for unusual academic achievement: *graduated with honors.* **b.** A program of individual advanced study for exceptional students: *planned to take honors in history.* **12.** *Sports.* The right of being first at the tee in golf. **13.** *Games.* **a.** Any of the four or five highest cards, especially the ace, king, queen, jack, and ten of the trump suit, in card games such as bridge or whist. **b.** The points allotted to these cards. Often used in the plural. —**honor** *tr.v.* **-ored, -or•ing, -ors. 1. a.** To hold in respect; esteem. **b.** To show respect for. **c.** To bow to (another dancer) in square dancing: *Honor your partner.* **2.** To confer distinction on: *He has honored us with his presence.* **3.** To accept or pay as valid: *honor a check; a store that honors all credit cards.* —***idiom.* honor bound.** Under an obligation enforced by the personal integrity of the one obliged: *I was honor bound to admit that she had done the work.* [Middle English, from Old French, from Latin.] —**hon′or•er** *n.*

SYNONYMS: *honor, homage, reverence, veneration, deference.* These nouns denote admiration, respect, or esteem accorded to another as a right or as due. *Honor,* the most general term, is applicable both to the feeling and to the expression of such sentiments: *He tried to be worthy of the honor in which he was held. Homage* is an expression of high regard and respect, often in the form of a ceremonial tribute that conveys allegiance: *"There is no country in which so absolute a homage is paid to wealth"* (Ralph Waldo Emerson). *Reverence* is a feeling of deep respect and devotion: *"Kill reverence and you've killed the hero in man"* (Ayn Rand). *Veneration* is both the feeling and the reverential expression of respect, love, and awe: *Her veneration for traditional learning never wavered. Deference* is courteous, respectful regard for another that often takes the form of yielding to his or her decisions or wishes: *Have confidence in your own judgment; don't give undue deference to the opinions and feelings of others.* See also Synonyms at **honesty.**

hon•or•a•ble (ŏn′ər-ə-bəl) *adj.* **1.** Deserving or winning honor and respect: *led an honorable life.* **2.** Bringing distinction or recognition: *honorable service to one's nation.* **3.** Possessing and characterized by honor: *an honorable person.* **4.** Consistent with honor or good name: *followed the only honorable course of action.* **5.** Distinguished; illustrious: *this honorable gathering of scholars.* **6.** Attended by marks of recognition and honor: *received an honorable burial.* **7. Honorable.** *Abbr.* **Hon. a.** Used as a title of respect for certain high government officials: *The Honorable Jane Doe, Associate Justice of the Supreme Judicial Court of Massachusetts.* **b.** Used as a courtesy title for the children of barons and viscounts and the younger sons of earls. **c.** Used in the House of Commons as a title of respect when speaking of another member. —**hon′or•a•ble•ness** *n.* —**hon′or•a•bly** *adv.*

honorable discharge *n.* Discharge from the armed forces with a commendable record.

honorable mention *n.* A citation to one who has performed well in a competition but has not been awarded a prize.

hon•o•rar•i•um (ŏn′ə-râr′ē-əm) *n., pl.* **-i•ums** or **-i•a** (-ē-ə). A payment given to a professional person for services for which fees are not legally or traditionally required. [Latin *honōrārium,* from neuter of *honōrārius,* honorary, from *honor, honōr-,* honor.]

hon•or•ar•y (ŏn′ə-rĕr′ē) *adj. Abbr.* **hon. 1.** Held or given as a mark of honor, especially conferred as an honor without the usual adjuncts: *an honorary degree.* **2. a.** Holding an office or title given as an honor, without payment: *an honorary colonel.* **b.** Voluntary: *the honorary secretary of the association.* **3.** Relying on honor and not legally enforceable, as a duty or an obligation.

hon•or•ee (ŏn′ə-rē′) *n.* The recipient of an honor.

hon•or•if•ic (ŏn′ə-rĭf′ĭk) *adj.* Conferring or showing respect or honor. —**honorific** *n.* A title, phrase, or grammatical form conveying respect, used especially when addressing a social superior. [Latin *honōrificus* : *honor, honōr-,* honor + *-ficus,* -fic.] —**hon′or•if′i•cal•ly** *adv.*

Ho•no•ri•us (hō-nôr′ē-əs, -nōr′-), **Flavius.** A.D. 384–423. Roman emperor of the West (395–423). During his reign the decline of the empire became irreversible.

honor society *n.* An organization to which students are admitted in recognition of academic achievement.

honor system *n.* A set of procedures under which persons, especially students or prisoners, are trusted to act without direct supervision in situations that might allow for dishonest behavior.

hon•our (ŏn′ər) *n. & v. Chiefly British.* Variant of **honor.**

Hon•shu (hŏn′sho͞o). The largest island of Japan, in the central part of the country between the Sea of Japan and the Pacific Ocean.

hooch¹ also **hootch** (ho͞och) *n. Slang.* **1.** Alcoholic liquor, especially inferior or bootleg liquor: *"bootleggers smashed on their own hooch"* (Christopher Hitchens). **2.** Marijuana. [Short for *hoochinoo,* from *Hoochinoo,* a Tlingit village where illegal liquor was distilled, from Tlingit *xutsnuuwú.*]

hooch² also **hootch** (ho͞och) *n. Slang.* A dwelling, especially a thatched hut. [Alteration (perhaps influenced by HUT) of Japanese *uchi,* inside, interior.]

hood¹ (ho͝od) *n.* **1.** A loose pliable covering for the head and neck, either attached to a robe or jacket or separate. **2.** An ornamental draping of cloth hung from the shoulders of an academic or ecclesiastical robe. **3.** A sack placed over a falcon's head to keep the bird quiet. **4. a.** A metal cover or cowl for a hearth or stove. **b.** A carriage top. **c.** The hinged metal lid over the engine of a motor vehicle. **5.** *Zoology.* An expanded part, crest, or marking on or near the head of an animal. —**hood** *tr.v.* **hood•ed, hood•ing, hoods.** To supply or cover with a hood. [Middle English *hod,* from Old English *hōd.*]

hood² (ho͝od) *n. Slang.* **1.** A hoodlum; a thug. **2.** A young tough. [Short for HOODLUM.]

Hood (ho͝od), **John Bell.** 1831–1879. American Confederate soldier who commanded the Atlanta Campaign (1864) and was defeated at Nashville later that year.

Hood, Mount. A volcanic peak, 3,426.7 m (11,235 ft) high, in the Cascade Range of northwest Oregon. It is the highest elevation in the state.

Hood, Thomas. 1799–1845. British poet and editor who wrote comic and topical verse, including "The Dream of Eugene Aram" (1829) and "The Song of the Shirt" (1843).

–hood *suff.* **1.a.** Condition; state; quality: *manhood.* **b.** An instance of a specified state or quality: *falsehood.* **2.** A group sharing a specified state or quality: *sisterhood.* [Middle English *-hed, -hode,* from Old English **-hǣde, -hād.*]

'hood (ho͝od) *n. Slang.* A neighborhood.

hood·ed (ho͝od′ĭd) *adj.* **1.** Covered with or having a hood. **2.** Shaped like a hood, cowl, or similar covering. **3.** *Zoology.* **a.** Having coloration or a crest suggesting a hood. **b.** Having elastic skin at the neck that, when distended, resembles a hood, as that of the cobra.

hooded seal *n.* A seal *(Cystophora cristata)* of northern seas, having a grayish, spotted coat and an inflatable hoodlike or bladderlike pouch in the region of the nose. Also called *bladdernose.*

hood·lum (ho͝od′ləm, ho͞od′-) *n.* **1.** A gangster; a thug. **2.** A tough, often aggressive or violent young man. [Origin unknown.] **—hood′lum·ism** *n.*

hood·mold (ho͝od′mōld′) *n.* See **dripstone** (sense 1).

hoo·doo (ho͞o′do͞o) *n., pl.* **-doos. 1.** See **voodoo** (sense 3). **2.a.** Bad luck. **b.** One that brings bad luck. **3.** *Geology.* A column of eccentrically shaped rock, produced by differential weathering. **—hoodoo** *tr.v.* **-dooed, -doo·ing, -doos.** To bring bad luck to. [Of West African origin, possibly from VOODOO.] **—hoo′doo·ism** *n.*

hood·wink (ho͝od′wĭngk′) *tr.v.* **-winked, -wink·ing, -winks. 1.** To take in by deceptive means; deceive. See Synonyms at **deceive. 2.** *Archaic.* To blindfold. **3.** *Obsolete.* To conceal. **—hood′wink′er** *n.*

hoo·ey (ho͞o′ē) *n. Slang.* Nonsense: *"the romantic hooey that always sold women's cosmetics"* (Jerry Adler). [Origin unknown.]

hoof (ho͝of, ho͞of) *n., pl.* **hoofs** or **hooves** (ho͝ovz, ho͞ovz). **1.a.** The horny sheath covering the toes or lower part of the foot of a mammal of the orders Perissodactyla and Artiodactyla, such as a horse, an ox, or a deer. **b.** The foot of such an animal, especially a horse. **2.** *Slang.* The human foot. **—hoof** *v.* **hoofed, hoof·ing, hoofs.** *—tr.* **1.** To trample with the hoofs. **2.** *Slang.* To walk: *We hoofed it the whole ten blocks.* *—intr. Slang.* **1.** To dance, especially as a professional entertainer. **2.** To go on foot; walk. **—*idiom.* on the hoof.** Not yet butchered; alive. Used especially of cattle: *beef on the hoof.* [Middle English *hof,* from Old English *hōf.*]

hoof-and-mouth disease (ho͝of′ən-mouth′, ho͞of′-) *n.* See **foot-and-mouth disease.**

hoof·bound (ho͝of′bound′, ho͞of′-) *adj.* Afflicted with drying and contraction of the hoof, resulting in lameness. Used of a horse.

hoofed (ho͝oft, ho͞oft) *adj.* Having hoofs; ungulate.

hoof·er (ho͝of′ər, ho͞o′fər) *n. Slang.* A professional dancer, especially a tap dancer.

Hoogh·ly (ho͞o′glē). A channel, about 257 km (160 mi) long, of the Ganges River in eastern India. The westernmost channel on the Ganges Delta, it connects Calcutta with the Bay of Bengal.

hoo-hah (ho͞o′hä′) *n. Slang.* **1.** A fuss; a disturbance: *"the subject of this last hoo-hah"* (William Safire). **2.** A chortle or laugh: *got a good hoo-hah out of that story.* [Perhaps from Yiddish *hu-ha,* to-do, uproar, exclamation.]

hook (ho͝ok) *n.* **1.a.** A curved or sharply bent device, usually of metal, used to catch, drag, suspend, or fasten something else. **b.** A fishhook. **2.** Something shaped like a hook, especially: **a.** A curved or barbed plant or animal part. **b.** A short angled or curved line on a letter. **c.** A sickle. **3.a.** A sharp bend or curve, as in a river. **b.** A point or spit of land with a sharply curved end. **4.** A means of catching or ensnaring; a trap. **5.** *Slang.* **a.** A means of attracting interest or attention; an enticement: *a sales hook.* **b.** *Music.* A catchy motif or refrain: *"sugary hard rock melodies* [and] *ear candy hooks"* (Boston Globe). **6.** *Sports.* **a.** A short swinging blow in boxing delivered with a crooked arm. **b.** A golf stroke that sends the ball to the left of a right-handed player or to the right of a left-handed player. **c.** In surfing, the lip of a breaking wave. **7.** *Baseball.* A curve ball. **8.** *Basketball.* A hook shot. **—hook** *v.* **hooked, hook·ing, hooks.** *—tr.* **1.a.** To catch, suspend, or connect with a hook. **b.** *Informal.* To snare. **c.** *Slang.* To steal; snatch. See Synonyms at **steal. 2.** To fasten by or as if by a hook. **3.** To pierce or gore with or as if with a hook. **4.** *Slang.* **a.** To take strong hold of; captivate: *a novel that hooked me on the very first page.* **b.** To cause to become addicted. **5.** To make (a rug) by looping yarn through canvas with a type of crochet hook. **6.** *Sports.* **a.** To hit with a hook in boxing. **b.** To hit (a golf ball) in a hook. **7.** *Baseball.* To pitch (a ball) with a curve. **8.** *Basketball.* To shoot (a ball) in a hook shot. *—intr.* **1.** To bend like a hook. **2.** To fasten by means of a hook or a hook and eye. **3.** *Slang.* To work as a prostitute. **—*phrasal verbs.* hook up. 1.** To assemble or wire (a mechanism). **2.** To connect a mechanism and a source of power. **3.** *Slang.* To form a tie or connection: *hooked up with the wrong crowd.* **—*idioms.* by hook or by crook.** By whatever means possible, fair or unfair. **get the hook.** *Slang.* To be unceremoniously dismissed or terminated. **hook, line, and sinker.** *Informal.* Without reservation; completely: *swallowed the excuse hook, line, and sinker.* **off the hook.** *Informal.* Freed, as from blame or a vexatious obligation: *let me off the hook with a mild reprimand.* **on (one's) own hook.** By one's own efforts. [Middle English *hok,* from Old English *hōc.* See **keg-** in Appendix.]

hook·ah (ho͝ok′ə) *n.* An Eastern smoking pipe designed with a long tube passing through an urn of water that cools the smoke as it is drawn through. Also called *hubble-bubble, narghile.* [Urdu, from Arabic *ḥuqqah,* the hookah's water urn.]

hook and eye *n.* **1.** A clothes fastener consisting of a small blunt metal hook that is inserted in a corresponding loop or eyelet. **2.** A latch consisting of a hook that is inserted in a screw eye.

hook-and-lad·der truck (ho͝ok′ən-lăd′ər) *n.* A fire engine equipped with extension ladders and hooked poles.

Hooke (ho͝ok), **Robert.** 1635–1703. English physicist, inventor, and mathematician who formulated the theory of planetary movement.

hooked (ho͝okt) *adj.* **1.** Bent or angled like a hook. **2.** Having a hook. **3.** Made by hooking yarn. *a hooked rug.* **4.** *Slang.* **a.** Captivated by or devoted to a custom or thing: *She's really hooked on gardening.* **b.** Addicted to a narcotic. **—hook′ed·ness** (ho͝ok′ĭd-nĭs) *n.*

hook·er¹ (ho͝ok′ər) *n. Nautical.* **1.** A single-masted fishing smack used off the coast of Ireland. **2.** An old worn-out or clumsy ship. [Dutch *hoeker,* from Middle Dutch *hoeckboot* : *hoec,* fishhook; see **keg-** in Appendix + *boot,* boat.]

hook·er² (ho͝ok′ər) *n.* **1.** One that hooks. **2.** *Slang.* A prostitute.

WORD HISTORY: In his *Personal Memoirs* Ulysses S. Grant described Maj. Gen. Joseph Hooker as "a dangerous man . . . not subordinate to his superiors." Hooker had his faults, of course. He may indeed have been insubordinate; undoubtedly he was an erratic leader. But there is one thing of which he is often accused that "Fighting Joe" Hooker certainly did not do: he did not give his name to prostitutes. According to a popular story, the men under Hooker's command during the Civil War were a particularly wild bunch. When his troops were on leave, we are told, they spent much of their time in brothels. For this reason, as the story goes, prostitutes came to be known as *hookers.* It is not difficult to understand how such a theory might have originated. The major general's name differs from the word *hooker* only in the capital letter that begins it. And it is true that Hooker's men were at times ill-disciplined (although it seems that liquor, not women, was the main source of their difficulties with the provost marshal). However attractive this theory may be, it cannot be true. The word *hooker,* with the sense "prostitute," is in fact older than the Civil War. It appeared in the second edition (although not in the first) of John Russell Bartlett's *Dictionary of Americanisms,* published in 1859. Bartlett defined *hooker* as "a strumpet, a sailor's trull." He also said that the word was derived from Corlear's Hook, a district in New York City, but this was only a guess. There is no evidence that the term originated in New York. Norman Ellsworth Eliason has traced this use of *hooker* back to 1845 in North Carolina. He reported the usage in *Tarheel Talk; an Historical Study of the English Language in North Carolina to 1860,* published in 1956. The fact that we have no earlier written evidence does not mean that *hooker* was never used to mean "prostitute" before 1845. The history of *hooker* is, quite simply, murky; we do not know when or where it was first used, but we can be very certain that it did not begin with Joseph Hooker. Also, we have no firm evidence that it came from Corlear's Hook. Scholarly evidence or lack thereof notwithstanding, the late Bruce Catton, the Civil War historian, did not go so far as to exonerate completely the Union general. Although "the tcrm 'hooker' did not originate during the Civil War," wrote Catton, "it certainly became popular then. During these war years, Washington developed a large [red-light district] somewhere south of Constitution Avenue. This became known as Hooker's Division in tribute to the proclivities of General Joseph Hooker and the name has stuck ever since." If the term *hooker* was derived neither from Joseph Hooker nor from Corlear's Hook, what is its derivation? It is most likely that this *hooker* is, etymologically, simply "one who hooks." The term portrays a prostitute as a person who hooks, or snares, clients.

Hook·er (ho͝ok′ər), **Joseph.** Known as "Fighting Joe." 1814–1879. American Union army officer who was defeated by Robert E. Lee at Chancellorsville (1863).

Hooker, Richard. 1554?–1600. English writer and theologian. His *Laws of Ecclesiastical Polity* (1594) was central to the formation of Anglican theology.

Hooker, Thomas. 1586?–1647. English-born American colonizer and cleric who founded Hartford, Connecticut (1636).

hook·nose (ho͝ok′nōz′) *n.* An aquiline nose. **—hook′-nosed′** *adj.*

Hook of Hol·land (ho͝ok; hŏl′ənd) also **Hoek van Hol·land** (ho͞ok′ vän hô′länt). A cape and harbor of southwest Netherlands on the North Sea west of Rotterdam, for which it serves as a port.

hook shot *n. Basketball.* A shot made by arcing the far hand upward while being positioned or moving sideways to the basket.

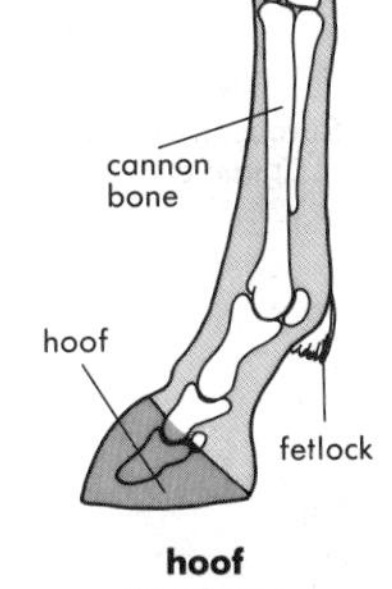

hoof
Of a horse

hookah
Portrait of a Prince, c. 1800

ă pat	oi boy
ā pay	ou out
âr care	o͝o took
ä father	o͞o boot
ĕ pet	ŭ cut
ē be	ûr urge
ĭ pit	th thin
ī pie	*th* this
îr pier	hw which
ŏ pot	zh vision
ō toe	ə about, item
ô paw	♦ regionalism

Stress marks: ′ (primary); ′ (secondary), as in **dictionary** (dĭk′shə-nĕr′ē)

hook·up (hŏŏk′ŭp′) *n.* **1.** A system of electric circuits and electrically powered equipment designed to operate together: *a nationwide telecommunications hookup.* **2.a.** A configuration of mechanical parts or devices providing a link between a supply source and a user: *a gas hookup for a mobile home.* **b.** A plan or schematic drawing of such a system or such a configuration. **3.** *Informal.* A linkage or connection, often between unlikely associates or factors.

hook·worm (hŏŏk′wûrm′) *n.* Any of numerous small parasitic nematode worms of the family Ancylostomatidae, having hooked mouthparts with which they fasten themselves to the intestinal walls of various hosts, including human beings, causing ancylostomiasis. Also called *uncinaria.*

hookworm disease *n.* See **ancylostomiasis.**

hook·y (hŏŏk′ē) *n. Informal.* Absence without leave; truancy: *play hooky from school.* [Perhaps from *hook it,* to make off.]

hoo·li·gan (hōō′lĭ-gən) *n. Informal.* A young ruffian; a hoodlum. [Origin unknown.] **—hoo′li·gan·ism** *n.*

hoop

hoop (hōōp, hŏŏp) *n.* **1.** A circular band of metal or wood put around a cask or barrel to bind the staves together. **2.** A large wooden, plastic, or metal ring, especially one used as a plaything or for trained animals to jump through. **3.** One of the lightweight circular supports for a hoop skirt. **4.** A circular, ringlike earring. **5.** One of a pair of circular wooden or metal frames used to hold material taut for embroidery or similar needlework. **6.** *Basketball.* **a.** The basket. **b.** The game of basketball. **7.** *Sports.* A croquet wicket. **—hoop** *tr.v.* **hooped, hoop·ing, hoops. 1.** To hold together or support with or as if with a hoop. **2.** To encircle. ***—idiom.*** **jump** (or **go**) **through the hoop.** To undergo a rigorous trial or examination. [Middle English *hop.*]

hoop·er (hōō′pər, hŏŏp′ər) *n.* A maker or repairer of barrels and tubs; a cooper.

hoop·la (hōōp′lä′, hŏŏp′-) *n. Slang.* **1.a.** Boisterous, jovial commotion or excitement. **b.** Extravagant publicity: *The new sedan was introduced to the public with much hoopla.* **2.** Talk intended to mislead or confuse. [Perhaps from French *houp-là,* upsy-daisy! : *houp* (of imitative origin) + *là,* there; see VOILÀ.]

hoopoe
European hoopoe
Upupa epops

hoo·poe (hōō′pōō, -pō) *n.* Any of several Old World birds of the family Upupidae, especially *Upupa epops,* having distinctively patterned plumage, a fanlike crest, and a slender, downward-curving bill. [Alteration (influenced by Latin *ūpupa*) of obsolete *hoop,* from French *huppe,* from Old French, from Vulgar Latin **ūppa,* alteration of Latin *upupa, ūpupa,* of imitative origin.]

hoop skirt
1861 American ball gown

hoop skirt *n.* A long full skirt belled out with a series of connected circular supports.

hoop snake *n.* Any of several snakes, such as the mud snake, said to grasp the tail in the mouth and move with a rolling, hooplike motion.

hoo·ray (hōō-rā′, hə-) *interj., n., & v.* Variant of **hurrah.**

Hoorn Islands (hôrn, hōrn), See **Futuna Islands.**

hoose·gow (hōōs′gou′) *n. Slang.* A jail. [Spanish *juzgado,* tribunal, courtroom, from past participle of *juzgar,* to judge, from Latin *iūdicāre,* from *iūdex, iūdic-,* judge. See JUDGE.]

Hoo·sier (hōō′zhər) *n.* Used as a nickname for a native or resident of Indiana. [Origin unknown.]

WORD HISTORY: As the fame of Indiana basketball grows ever greater, perhaps a larger number of people have become curious about the origins of the word *Hoosier,* the nickname for a native or resident of Indiana. As more than one of the curious has discovered, the origins are rather opaque. The most likely possibility is that *Hoosier* is an alteration of *hoozer,* an English dialect word recorded in Cumberland, a former county of northwest England, in the late 19th century and used to refer to anything unusually large. The transition between *hoozer* and *Hoosier* is not clear. The first recorded instance of *Hoosier* meaning "Indiana resident" is dated 1826; however, it seems possible that some senses of the word recorded later in the *Dictionary of Americanisms,* including "a big, burly, uncouth specimen or individual; a frontiersman, countryman, rustic," reflect the kind of use this word had before it settled down in Indiana.

hoot¹ (hōōt) *v.* **hoot·ed, hoot·ing, hoots.** *—intr.* **1.** To utter the characteristic cry of an owl. **2.** To make a loud raucous cry, especially of derision or contempt. *—tr.* **1.** To shout down or drive off with jeering cries: *hooted the speaker off the platform.* **2.** To express or convey by hooting: *hooted their disgust.* **—hoot** *n.* **1.a.** The characteristic cry of an owl. **b.** A sound suggesting the cry of an owl, especially the sound of a horn. **2.** A cry of scorn or derision. **3.** *Informal.* One that is hilariously funny: *"Emmett, that skirt is a hoot!"* (Bobbie Ann Mason). ***—idiom.*** **give** (or **care**) **a hoot.** To be completely indifferent to: *I don't give a hoot what you think.* [Middle English *houten,* perhaps of imitative origin.] **—hoot′er** *n.*

hoot² (hōōt, ōōt) also **hoots** (hōōts, ōōts) *interj. Scots.* Used to express annoyance or objection.

hootch¹ (hōōch) *n.* Variant of **hooch¹.**

hootch² (hōōch) *n.* Variant of **hooch².**

hootch·y-kootch·y (hōō′chē-kōō′chē) *n., pl.* **-kootch·ies.** A deliberately sensual form of belly dance, typically performed as part of a carnival. [Origin unknown.]

hoot·en·an·ny (hōōt′n-ăn′ē) *n., pl.* **-nies. 1.** *Music.* An informal performance by folk singers, typically with participation by the audience. **2.** *Informal.* An unidentified or unidentifiable gadget. [Origin unknown.]

hoot owl *n.* Any of various owls having a hooting cry.

hoots (hōōts, ōōts) *interj.* Variant of **hoot².**

Hoo·ver (hōō′vər). A city of north-central Alabama, a suburb of Birmingham. Population, 19,792.

Herbert Hoover

Hoover, Herbert Clark. 1874–1964. The 31st President of the United States (1929–1933). After the stock market crash of 1929 he was unwilling to finance employment through federal intervention and lost the presidency to Franklin D. Roosevelt in 1932.

Hoover, J(ohn) Edgar. 1895–1972. American director of the FBI (1924–1972). He is remembered for fighting gangsterism during the Prohibition era (1919–1933) and for a vigorous anti-Communist campaign after World War II.

Hoover, Lou Henry. 1874–1944. First Lady of the United States (1929–1933) as the wife of Herbert Hoover. She urged women to pursue careers and gave a series of radio talks.

Hoo·ver·ville (hōō′vər-vĭl′) *n.* A crudely built camp put up usually on the edge of a town to house the dispossessed and destitute during the depression of the 1930's. [After Herbert Clark HOOVER.]

hooves (hōōvz, hŏŏvz) *n.* A plural of **hoof.**

hop¹ (hŏp) *v.* **hopped, hop·ping, hops.** *—intr.* **1.a.** To move with light bounding skips or leaps. **b.** *Informal.* To move quickly or busily: *The shipping department is hopping this week.* **2.** To jump on one foot. **3.** To make a quick trip, especially in an airplane. *—tr.* **1.** To move over by hopping: *hop a ditch two feet wide.* **2.** *Informal.* To jump aboard: *hop a freight train.* **—hop** *n.* **1.a.** A light springy jump or leap, especially on one foot. **b.** A rebound: *The ball took a bad hop.* **2.** *Informal.* A dance; a ball. **3.a.** A short distance. **b.** A short trip, especially by air. **4.** A free ride; a lift. ***—idioms.*** **hop, skip, and (a) jump.** A short distance. **hop to it.** To begin an activity or a task quickly and energetically. [Middle English *hoppen,* from Old English *hoppian.*]

hop² (hŏp) *n.* **1.** A twining vine *(Humulus lupulus)* having lobed leaves and green female flowers arranged in conelike spikes. **2. hops.** The dried, ripe flowers of this plant, containing a bitter, aromatic oil. They are used in the brewing industry to prevent bacterial action and add the characteristic bitter taste to beer. **3.** *Slang.* Opium. **—hop** *tr.v.* **hopped, hop·ping, hops.** To flavor with hops. ***—phrasal verb.*** **hop up.** *Slang.* **1.** To increase the power or energy of: *hop up a car.* **2.** To stimulate with or as if with a narcotic. [Middle English *hoppe,* from Middle Dutch.]

HOP *abbr.* High oxygen pressure.

hop clover *n.* A Eurasian clover *(Trifolium agrarium)* or one of its relatives, having small yellow flower heads that resemble hops when withered.

hope (hōp) *v.* **hoped, hop·ing, hopes.** *—intr.* **1.** To wish for something with expectation of its fulfillment. **2.** *Archaic.* To have confidence; trust. *—tr.* **1.** To look forward to with confidence or expectation: *We hope that our children will carry on our family traditions.* **2.** To expect and desire. See Synonyms at **expect. —hope** *n.* **1.** A wish or desire accompanied by confident expectation of its fulfillment. **2.** Something that is hoped for or desired: *Success is our hope.* **3.** One that is a source of or reason for hope: *the team's only hope for victory.* **4.** Often **Hope.** The theological virtue defined as the desire and search for a future good, difficult but not impossible to attain with God's help. **5.** *Archaic.* Trust; confidence. ***—idiom.*** **hope against hope.** To hope with little reason or justification. [Middle English *hopen,* from Old English *hopian.*] **—hop′er** *n.*

Hope, Anthony. See Sir Anthony Hope **Hawkins.**

Hope, Bob. Born 1903. British-born American entertainer. He costarred with Bing Crosby in the popular "Road" films, beginning with the *Road to Singapore* (1940).

hope chest *n.* A chest used by a young woman for clothing and household goods, such as linens and silver, in anticipation of marriage.

hope·ful (hōp′fəl) *adj.* **1.** Having or manifesting hope. **2.** Inspiring hope; promising. **—hopeful** *n.* A person who aspires to success or who shows promise of succeeding, especially as a political candidate: *a group of presidential hopefuls.* **—hope′ful·ness** *n.*

hope·ful·ly (hōp′fə-lē) *adv.* **1.** In a hopeful manner. **2.** *Usage Problem.* It is to be hoped: *"Marriage is a coming together for better or for worse, hopefully enduring"* (William O. Douglas).

USAGE NOTE: Writers who use *hopefully* as a sentence adverb, as in *Hopefully the measures will be adopted,* should be aware that the usage is unacceptable to many critics, including a large majority of the Usage Panel. But it is not easy to explain why critics dislike this use of *hopefully.* It is justified by analogy to the unexceptionable uses of many other adverbs, as in *Mercifully, the play was brief* or *Frankly, I have no use for your friend.* And though this use of *hopefully* may have been a vogue word when it first gained currency 30 years ago, it has long since lost any taint of jargon or pretentiousness for the general reader. The well-attested acceptance of the usage reflects an implicit popular recognition of its usefulness; there is no precise substitute. Someone who says *Hopefully, the treaty will be ratified* makes a hopeful prediction about the fate of the treaty, whereas someone who says *I hope* (or *We hope* or *It is hoped*) *the treaty will be ratified* expresses a bald statement about what is desired. Only the latter could be continued with a clause such as *but it isn't likely.* • It might have been expected, then, that the initial flurry of objections to *hopefully* would have subsided once the usage became well established. Instead, increased currency of the usage appears only to have made the critics more adamant. In the 1969 Usage Panel survey the usage was acceptable to 44 percent of the Panel; in the most recent survey it was acceptable to only 27 percent. (By contrast, 60 percent accepted the analogous use of *mercifully* in the sentence *Mercifully, the game ended before the opponents could add another touchdown to the lopsided score.*) Yet the Panel has not shown any signs of becoming generally more conservative: in the very same survey panelists were disposed to accept once-vilified usages such as the employment of *contact* and *host* as verbs. • It seems that this use of *hopefully* has been made a litmus test, which distinguishes writers who take an active interest in questions of grammar or usage from the great mass of people who keep their own linguistic counsel. No one can be blamed who uses *hopefully* in blithe ignorance of the critics' disdain for it, since the rule could not be derived from any general concern for clarity or precision. But writers who are aware of the critical controversy face a more delicate decision. Some will simply flout the rule, seeing no reason that they should be deprived of a useful construction. Others may choose to avoid the usage, whether they are motivated by discretion or civility. • Like other sentence adverbs such as *bluntly* and *happily, hopefully* may occasionally be ambiguous. In the sentence *Hopefully, the company has launched a new venture,* the word *hopefully* might be construed as describing the point of view of either the speaker or the subject. Such ambiguities can be resolved either by repositioning the adverb (as in *The company has launched the new venture hopefully*) or by choosing a paraphrase (*One may hope that the company has launched the new venture*).

Ho·pei or **Ho·peh** (hō′pā′, hŭ′bā′). See **Hebei.**

hope·less (hōp′lĭs) *adj.* **1.** Having no hope; despairing. See Synonyms at **despondent. 2.** Offering no hope; bleak. **3.** Incurable. **4.** Having no possibility of solution; impossible. **—hope′less·ly** *adv.*

hope·less·ness (hōp′lĭs-nĭs) *n.* The condition or quality of being hopeless. See Synonyms at **despair.**

Hope·well[1] (hōp′wĕl′, -wəl) *n.* An early Native American culture centered in the Ohio River valley from about the second century B.C. to the fourth century A.D., noted for the construction of extensive earthworks and large conical burial mounds and for its highly developed arts and crafts. [After the owner of a farm in Ross County, Ohio.]

Hope·well[2] (hōp′wĕl′). An independent city of southeast Virginia south-southeast of Richmond. It was founded in 1913 as a munitions center. Population, 23,397.

hop·head (hŏp′hĕd′) *n. Slang.* A drug addict. [HOP[2] + HEAD.]

hop hornbeam *n.* Any of several deciduous trees of the genus *Ostrya,* especially *O. virginiana* of eastern North America, having unisexual flowers grouped in catkins and fruit clusters resembling hops.

Ho·pi (hō′pē) *n., pl.* **Hopi** or **-pis. 1.a.** A Pueblo people occupying a number of mesa-top pueblos on reservation land in northeast Arizona. The Hopi are noted for their sophisticated dry-farming techniques, a rich ceremonial life, and fine craftsmanship in basketry, pottery, silverwork, and weaving. **b.** A member of this people. **2.** The Uto-Aztecan language of the Hopi. [Hopi *hópi,* peaceable, a Hopi.]

Hop·kins (hŏp′kĭnz), Sir **Frederick Gowland.** 1861–1947. British biochemist. He shared a 1929 Nobel Prize for his discovery of growth-promoting vitamins.

Hopkins, Gerard Manley. 1844–1889. British poet known for a number of works published posthumously, including "The Wreck of the Deutschland" and "The Windhover."

Hopkins, Johns. 1795–1873. American financier and philanthropist who left $7 million to found the hospital and university in Baltimore that bear his name.

Hopkins, Mark. 1802–1887. American educator and theologian who was president of Williams College from 1836 to 1872.

Hop·kin·son (hŏp′kĭn-sən), **Francis.** 1737–1791. American writer and Revolutionary leader. A member of the Continental Congress and a signer of the Declaration of Independence (1776), he is also known for his political satires against the British.

Hop·kins·ville (hŏp′kĭnz-vĭl′). A city of southwest Kentucky west-southwest of Bowling Green. It is a tobacco and livestock market. Population, 27,318.

hop·lite (hŏp′līt′) *n.* A heavily armed foot soldier of ancient Greece. [Greek *hoplītēs,* from *hoplon,* armor.] **—hop·lit′ic** (-lĭt′ĭk) *adj.*

hop·per (hŏp′ər) *n.* **1.** One that hops. **2.a.** A funnel-shaped container in which materials, such as grain or fuel, are stored in readiness for dispensation. **b.** *Informal.* A place in which something is held in readiness before use or consideration: *"Several hundred protectionist bills are now piling up in the congressional hoppers"* (Christian Science Moniter). **c.** A freight car with a door in the floor through which materials are unloaded.

Hop·per (hŏp′ər), **Edward.** 1882–1967. American painter famous for his stark, realist style. Among his best-known works are *Early Sunday Morning* (1930) and *Nighthawks* (1942).

♦**hop·per·grass** (hŏp′ər-grăs′) *n. Chiefly Southern U.S.* See grasshopper (sense 1). See Regional Note at **everwhere.**

hop·sack·ing (hŏp′săk′ĭng) also **hop·sack** (-săk′) *n.* A loosely woven, coarse fabric of cotton or wool used in clothing. [From its being used for bags by hop growers.]

hop·scotch (hŏp′skŏch′) *n. Games.* A children's game in which players toss a small object into the numbered spaces of a pattern of rectangles outlined on the ground and then hop or jump through the spaces to retrieve the object. **—hopscotch** *intr.v.* **-scotched, -scotch·ing, -scotch·es.** To move in or as if in a series of irregular jumps: *"hopscotching across dozens of new cable channels"* (Harry F. Waters). [HOP[1] + SCOTCH[1], a score, line.]

hor. *abbr.* Horizontal.

ho·ra also **ho·rah** (hôr′ə, hōr′ə) *n.* A traditional round dance of Romania and Israel. [Modern Hebrew *hōrâ,* from Rumanian *horă,* from Turkish *hora,* perhaps from Modern Greek *khoro,* accusative of *khoros,* round dance, from Greek. See **gher-[1]** in Appendix.]

Hor·ace (hôr′əs, hŏr′-). 65–8 B.C. Roman lyric poet. His *Odes* and *Satires* have exerted a major influence on English poetry. **—Ho·ra′tian** (hə-rā′shən) *adj.*

ho·rah (hôr′ə, hōr′ə) *n.* Variant of **hora.**

ho·ra·ry (hôr′ə-rē, hōr′-) *adj.* **1.** Of an hour or hours. **2.** Occurring once an hour; hourly. [Medieval Latin *hōrārius,* from Latin *hōra,* hour. See HOUR.]

Horatian ode *n.* An ode in which a fixed stanzaic pattern is followed.

horde (hôrd, hōrd) *n.* **1.** A large group or crowd; a swarm: *a horde of mosquitoes.* See Synonyms at **crowd[1]**. **2.a.** A nomadic Mongol tribe. **b.** A nomadic tribe or group. [Ultimately (via Polish *horda*) from northwestern Turkic *ordï,* residence, court, from Old Turkic.]

hore·hound (hôr′hound′, hōr′-) *n.* **1.a.** An aromatic Eurasian plant *(Marrubium vulgare)* having square stems, opposite leaves with white pubescence, and numerous white flowers in axillary cymes. The leaves yield a bitter extract used in flavoring and as a cough remedy. **b.** A candy or preparation flavored with this extract. **2.** Any of similar or related plants, such as the black horehound. [Middle English, alteration (influenced by *hound,* hound; see HOUND) of *horhune,* from Old English *hārehūne* : *hār,* hoary + *hūne,* a kind of plant.]

ho·ri·zon (hə-rī′zən) *n.* **1.** The apparent intersection of the earth and sky as seen by an observer. Also called *apparent horizon.* **2.** *Astronomy.* **a.** The sensible horizon. **b.** The celestial horizon. **c.** The limit of the theoretically possible universe. **3.** The range of one's knowledge, experience, or interest. **4.** *Geology.* **a.** A specific position in a stratigraphic column, such as the location of one or more fossils, that serves to identify the stratum with a particular period. **b.** A specific layer of soil or subsoil in a vertical cross section of land. [Middle English *orizon,* from Old French, from Latin, from Greek *horizōn (kuklos),* limiting (circle), horizon, from present participle of *horizein,* to limit, from *horos,* boundary.]

hor·i·zon·tal (hôr′ĭ-zŏn′tl, hŏr′-) *adj. Abbr.* **hor. 1.** Of, relating to, or near the horizon. **2.a.** Parallel to or in the plane of the horizon. **b.** At right angles to a vertical line. **3.** Occupying or restricted to the same level in a hierarchy: *a horizontal study of verbal ability; a horizontal transfer for an employee.* **—horizontal** *n.* Something, such as a line, a plane, or an object, that is horizontal. [French, from Latin *horizōn, horizont-,* horizon. See HORIZON.] **—hor′i·zon′tal·ly** *adv.*

horizontal union *n.* See **craft union.**

hor·mo·go·ni·um (hôr′mə-gō′nē-əm) *n.* A portion of a filament of a cyanobacterium that detaches and grows by cell division into a new filament. [Greek *hormos,* chain, necklace; see **ser-[2]** in Appendix + New Latin *gonium,* germ cell during mitotic phase (GON(O)– + Latin *-ium,* n. suff.; see –IUM).]

hor·mone (hôr′mōn′) *n.* **1.** A substance, usually a peptide or steroid, produced by one tissue and conveyed by the bloodstream to another to effect physiological activity, such as growth or metabolism. **2.** Any of various similar substances found in plants and insects that regulate development. [From Greek *hormōn,* present participle of *horman,* to urge on, from *hormē,* impulse. See **er-[1]** in Appendix.] **—hor·mon′al** (-mō′nəl), **hor·mon′ic** (-mŏn′ĭk) *adj.* **—hor·mon′al·ly** *adv.*

Hor·muz (hôr′mŭz′, hôr-mo͞oz′), **Strait of.** Also **Strait of Or·muz** (ôr′mŭz′, ôr-mo͞oz′). A strategic waterway linking the Persian Gulf with the Gulf of Oman.

horn (hôrn) *n.* **1.** One of the hard, usually permanent structures projecting from the head of certain mammals, such as cattle, sheep, goats, or antelopes, consisting of a bony core covered with a sheath of keratinous material. **2.** A hard protuberance, such as an antler or a projection on the head of a giraffe or rhinoceros, that is similar to or suggestive of a horn. **3.a.** The hard, smooth keratinous material forming the outer covering of the horns of cattle or related animals. **b.** A natural or synthetic substance resembling this material. **4.** A container, such as a powder horn, made from a horn. **5.** Something having the shape of a horn, especially: **a.** A horn of plenty; a cornucopia. **b.** Either of the ends of a new moon. **c.** The point of an anvil. **d.** The pommel of a saddle. **e.** An ear trumpet. **f.** A device for projecting sound waves, as in a loudspeaker. **g.** A hollow, metallic electromagnetic transmission antenna with a circular or rectangular cross section. **6.** *Abbr.* **h., H.** *Music.* **a.** A wind instrument made of an animal horn. **b.** A brass wind instrument, such as a trombone or tuba. **c.**

Lou Hoover

Bob Hope

hoplite

hopper
At a lumberyard

ă pat	oi boy
ā pay	ou out
âr care	o͝o took
ä father	o͞o boot
ĕ pet	ŭ cut
ē be	ûr urge
ĭ pit	th thin
ī pie	*th* this
îr pier	hw which
ŏ pot	zh vision
ō toe	ə about, item
ô paw	♦ regionalism

Stress marks: **′** (primary); ′ (secondary), as in **dictionary** (dĭk′shə-nĕr′ē)

hornbill
Yellow-billed hornbill
Tockus flavirostris

Lena Horne

Vladimir Horowitz

horse
Top: Equus caballus
Bottom: Vaulting a gymnastic horse

A French horn. **d.** A wind instrument, such as a trumpet or saxophone, used in a jazz band. **7.a.** A usually electrical signaling device that produces a loud, resonant sound: *an automobile horn.* **b.** Any of various noisemakers operated by blowing or by squeezing a hollow rubber ball. **8.** *Slang.* A telephone. **—horn** *intr.v.* **horned, horn·ing, horns.** To join without being invited; intrude. Used with *in.* **—*idioms.* blow** (or **toot) (one's) own horn.** *Informal.* To brag or boast about oneself. **draw** (or **haul** or **pull) in (one's) horns.** *Informal.* **1.** To restrain oneself; draw back. **2.** To retreat from a previously taken position, view, or stance. **3.** To economize. **on the horns of a dilemma.** Faced with two equally undesirable alternatives. [Middle English, from Old English. See **ker-**[1] in Appendix.] **—horn** *adj.* **—horn′ist** *n.*

Horn (hôrn), **Cape.** A headland of extreme southern Chile in the Tierra del Fuego archipelago. The southernmost point of South America, it was first rounded in 1616 by the Dutch navigator Willem Schouten (died 1625).

horn·beam (hôrn′bēm′) *n.* **1.** Any of various trees of the genus *Carpinus,* having smooth, grayish bark and hard, whitish wood. **2.** The wood of one of these trees.

horn·bill (hôrn′bĭl′) *n.* Any of various tropical Old World birds of the family Bucerotidae, having a very large bill often surmounted by an enlarged protuberance at the base.

horn·blende (hôrn′blĕnd′) *n.* An amphibolic mineral, $CaNa(Mg,Fe)_4(Al,Fe,Ti)_3Si_6O_{22}(OH,F)_2$, commonly green or bluish green to black in color, formed in the late stages of cooling in igneous rock. [German : *Horn,* horn (from Middle High German *horn,* from Old High German; see **ker-**[1] in Appendix) + *Blende,* blende; see BLENDE.]

horn·book (hôrn′bo͝ok′) *n.* **1.** An early primer consisting of a single page protected by a transparent sheet of horn, formerly used in teaching children to read. **2.** A text that instructs in the basic skills or rudiments of a subject.

Horne (hôrn), **Lena.** Born 1917. American singer and actress. Noted for her versatile voice and classic beauty, she has performed in Broadway musicals, films, and television productions.

Horne, Marilyn. Born 1934. American operatic soprano who became a principal performer at the Metropolitan Opera in New York City after her debut there as Adalgisa in *Norma* (1970).

horned (hôrnd) *adj.* Having a horn, horns, or a hornlike growth.

horned cucumber *n.* **1.** A tropical and southern African plant *(Cucumis metuliferus)* having heart-shaped to three-lobed leaves and oblong, spiny, orange to red fruits. **2.** The fruit of this plant.

horned lizard *n.* See **horned toad.**

horned owl *n.* Any of various owls with characteristic ear tufts that resemble horns.

horned pout *n.* See **hornpout.**

horned toad *n.* Any of several lizards of the genus *Phrynosoma* of western North America and Central America, having hornlike projections on the head, a spiny flattened body, and a short tail. Also called *horned lizard.*

horned viper *n.* A venomous African snake *(Cerastes cornutus)* having a hornlike projection above each eye. Also called *sand viper.*

hor·net (hôr′nĭt) *n.* Any of various large stinging wasps of the family Vespidae, chiefly of the genera *Vespa* and *Vespula,* that characteristically build large papery nests. [Middle English *hornet,* alteration (probably influenced by *horn,* horn; see HORN) of *hernet,* from Old English *hyrnet.* See **ker-**[1] in Appendix.]

hor·nets' nest (hôr′nĭts) *n.* A violent or highly contentious situation: *"such diplomatic hornets' nests as* [the] *expulsion of Asians from Uganda"* (Christian Science Monitor).

Hor·ney (hôr′nī), **Karen Danielsen.** 1885–1952. German-born American psychoanalyst who emphasized the role of environmental and cultural factors in the development of neurosis.

horn·fels (hôrn′fĕlz′) *n., pl.* **hornfels.** A fine-grained metamorphic rock composed of quartz, feldspar, mica, and other minerals, formed by the action of intrusive rock upon sedimentary rock, especially shale. [German : *Horn,* horn; see HORNBLENDE + *Fels,* rock, cliff (from Middle High German *vels,* from Old High German *felis*).]

horn fly *n.* A small black European fly *(Haematobia irritans),* introduced into North America, that sucks blood from cattle, usually biting an animal at the base of the horn.

♦**horn·ing** (hôr′nĭng) *n. Upstate New York & Western New England.* See **shivaree.** See Regional Note at **shivaree.** [Probably because horns are blown at the shivaree.]

hor·ni·to (hôr-nē′tō) *n., pl.* **-tos.** A low mound of volcanic origin, sometimes emitting smoke or vapor. [Spanish, diminutive of *horno,* oven, from Latin *furnus.* See **g^wher-** in Appendix.]

horn of plenty *n., pl.* **horns of plenty.** See **cornucopia** (sense 1). [Translation of Late Latin *cornūcōpia.*]

horn·pipe (hôrn′pīp′) *n.* **1.** *Music.* An instrument with a single reed, finger holes, and a bell and mouthpiece made of horn. **2.a.** A spirited British folk dance originally accompanied by this instrument. **b.** The music accompanying such a dance.

horn·pout (hôrn′pout′) *n.* A freshwater catfish *(Ictalurus nebulosus)* native to eastern North America, having a large head with barbels. Also called *horned pout.*

♦**horn·swog·gle** (hôrn′swŏg′əl) *tr.v.* **-gled, -gling, -gles.** *Chiefly Northern, Midland & Western U.S.* To bamboozle; deceive. [Origin unknown.]

horn·tail (hôrn′tāl′) *n.* Any of various sawflies of the family Siricidae, the female of which has a long, stout ovipositor.

horn·worm (hôrn′wûrm′) *n.* The larva of the hawk moth, having a hornlike posterior segment.

horn·wort (hôrn′wûrt′, -wôrt′) *n.* Any of several submerged plants of the genus *Ceratophyllum,* forming branched masses in quiet water and having finely dissected, whorled leaves and minute unisexual flowers.

horn·y (hôr′nē) *adj.* **-i·er, -i·est. 1.** Having horns or hornlike projections. **2.** Made of horn or a similar substance. **3.** Tough and calloused: *horny skin.* **4.** *Vulgar Slang.* **a.** Desirous of sexual activity. **b.** Sexually aroused. [Sense 4 from HORN, an erection.] **—horn′i·ness** *n.*

horol. *abbr.* Horology.

hor·o·loge (hôr′ə-lōj′, hŏr′-) *n.* A device, such as a clock or sundial, used in telling time. [Middle English *orloge,* from Old French, from Latin *hōrologium,* from Greek *hōrologion* : *hōra,* hour, season; see **yēr-** in Appendix + *legein,* to speak; see **leg-** in Appendix.]

ho·rol·o·ger (hô-rŏl′ə-jər) *n.* Variant of **horologist.**

hor·o·log·ic (hôr′ə-lŏj′ĭk, hŏr′-) also **hor·o·log·i·cal** (-ĭ-kəl) *adj.* Of or relating to horology or a horologe.

ho·rol·o·gist (hô-rŏl′ə-jĭst) also **ho·rol·o·ger** (-jər) *n.* One who practices or is skilled in horology.

Hor·o·lo·gi·um (hôr′ə-lō′jē-əm, hŏr′-) *n.* A constellation in the Southern Hemisphere near Hydrus, Eridanus, and Reticulum. [Latin *hōrologium,* horologe. See HOROLOGE.]

ho·rol·o·gy (hô-rŏl′ə-jē) *n. Abbr.* **horol. 1.** The science of measuring time. **2.** The art of making timepieces. [Greek *hōra,* hour, season; see **yēr-** in Appendix + –LOGY.]

hor·o·scope (hôr′ə-skōp′, hŏr′-) *n.* **1.a.** The aspect of the planets and stars at a given moment, such as the moment of a person's birth, used by astrologers. **b.** A diagram of the signs of the zodiac based on such an aspect. **2.** An astrological forecast, as of a person's future, based on a diagram of the aspect of the planets and stars at a given moment. [French, from Old French, from Latin *hōroscopus,* from Greek *hōroskopos* : *hōra,* hour, season; see **yēr-** in Appendix + *skopos,* observer; see **spek-** in Appendix.]

Ho·ro·witz (hôr′ə-wĭts, hŏr′-), **Vladimir.** 1904–1989. Russian-born American pianist noted for his interpretations of Chopin and Liszt.

hor·ren·dous (hô-rĕn′dəs, hə-) *adj.* Hideous; dreadful: *"Horrendous explosions shook the whole city"* (Howard Kaplan). [From Latin *horrendus,* from gerundive of *horrēre,* to tremble.] **—hor·ren′dous·ly** *adv.*

hor·rent (hôr′ənt, hŏr′-) *adj. Archaic.* Covered with bristles; bristling. [Latin *horrēns, horrent-,* present participle of *horrēre,* to tremble, bristle.]

hor·ri·ble (hôr′ə-bəl, hŏr′-) *adj.* **1.** Arousing or tending to arouse horror; dreadful: *"War is beyond all words horrible"* (Winston S. Churchill). **2.** Very unpleasant; disagreeable. [Middle English, from Old French, from Latin *horribilis,* from *horrēre,* to tremble.] **—hor′ri·ble·ness** *n.* **—hor′ri·bly** *adv.*

hor·rid (hôr′ĭd, hŏr′-) *adj.* **1.** Causing horror; dreadful. **2.** Extremely disagreeable; offensive. **3.** *Archaic.* Bristling; rough. [Alteration (influenced by Latin *horridus,* bristling, from *horrēre,* to bristle) of Middle English *horred,* past participle of *horren,* to bristle, from Latin *horrēre,* to tremble, bristle.] **—hor′rid·ly** *adv.* **—hor′rid·ness** *n.*

hor·rif·ic (hô-rĭf′ĭk, hŏ-) *adj.* Causing horror; terrifying. [Latin *horrificus* : *horrēre,* to tremble + *-ficus,* -fic.] **—hor·rif′i·cal·ly** *adv.*

hor·ri·fy (hôr′ə-fī′, hŏr′-) *tr.v.* **-fied, -fy·ing, -fies. 1.** To cause to feel horror. See Synonyms at **dismay. 2.** To cause unpleasant surprise to; shock. [Latin *horrificāre,* from *horrificus,* horrific. See HORRIFIC.] **—hor′ri·fi·ca′tion** (-fĭ-kā′shən) *n.* **—hor′ri·fy′ing·ly** *adv.*

hor·rip·i·la·tion (hô-rĭp′ə-lā′shən, hŏ-) *n.* The bristling of the body hair, as from fear or cold; goose bumps. [Late Latin *horripilātiō, horripilātiōn-,* from Latin *horripilātus,* past participle of *horripilāre,* to bristle with hairs : *horrēre,* to tremble + *pilāre,* to grow hair (from *pilus,* hair).] **—hor·rip′i·late′** *v.*

hor·ror (hôr′ər, hŏr′-) *n.* **1.** An intense, painful feeling of repugnance and fear. See Synonyms at **fear. 2.** Intense dislike; abhorrence. **3.** A cause of horror. **4.** *Informal.* Something unpleasant, ugly, or disagreeable: *That hat is a horror.* **5. horrors.** *Informal.* Intense nervous depression or anxiety. Often used with *the.* —*attributive.* Often used to modify another noun: *a horror movie; a horror story.* [Middle English *horrour,* from Old French *horreur,* from Latin *horror,* from *horrēre,* to tremble.]

hors de com·bat (ôr′ də kôN-bä′) *adv. & adj.* Out of action; disabled. [French : *hors,* out + *de,* of + *combat,* combat.]

hors d'oeuvre (ôr dûrv′) *n., pl.* **hors d'oeuvres** (ôr dûrvz′) or **hors d'oeuvre.** An appetizer served before a meal. [French : *hors,* outside + *de,* of + *oeuvre,* (the main) work.]

horse (hôrs) *n.* **1.a.** A large hoofed mammal *(Equus caballus)* having a short-haired coat, a long mane, and a long tail, domesticated since ancient times and used for riding and for drawing or carrying loads. **b.** An adult male horse; a stallion. **c.** Any of various equine mammals, such as the wild Asian species *E. prze-*

walskii or certain extinct forms related ancestrally to the modern horse. **2.** A frame or device, usually with four legs, used for supporting or holding. **3.** *Sports.* A piece of gymnastic equipment with an upholstered body used especially for vaulting. **4.** *Slang.* Heroin. **5.** Often **horses.** Horsepower. **6.** Mounted soldiers; cavalry: *a squadron of horse.* **7.** *Geology.* **a.** A block of rock interrupting a vein and containing no minerals. **b.** A large block of displaced rock that is caught along a fault. **—horse** *v.* **horsed, hors·ing, hors·es.** *—tr.* **1.** To provide with a horse. **2.** To haul or hoist energetically. *—intr.* To be in heat. Used of a mare. **—horse** *adj.* **1.** Of or relating to a horse: *a horse blanket.* **2.** Mounted on horses: *horse guards.* **3.** Drawn or operated by a horse. **4.** Larger or cruder than others that are similar: *horse pills.* ***—phrasal verb.*** **horse around.** *Informal.* To indulge in horseplay or frivolous activity: *Stop horsing around and get to work.* ***—idioms.*** **a horse of another** (or **a different**) **color.** Another matter entirely; something else. **beat** (or **flog**) **a dead horse. 1.** To continue to pursue a cause that has no hope of success. **2.** To dwell tiresomely on a matter that has already been decided. **be** (or **get**) **on (one's) high horse.** To be or become disdainful, superior, or conceited. **hold (one's) horses.** To restrain oneself. **the horse's mouth.** A source of information regarded as original or unimpeachable. [Middle English, from Old English *hors.*]

horse·back (hôrs′băk′) *n.* **1.** The back of a horse. **2.** A natural ridge; a hogback. **—horseback** *adv. & adj.* On the back of a horse: *rode horseback to town; horseback riding.*

horse balm *n.* Any of several strongly aromatic, eastern North American plants of the genus *Collinsonia,* having opposite leaves, square stems, and axillary clusters of lemon-scented yellow flowers. [From its former use for treating ailments of horses.]

horse bean *n.* See **broad bean.**

horse chestnut *n.* **1.** Any of several trees of the genus *Aesculus,* especially the European species *A. hippocastanum,* having opposite, palmately compound leaves, erect clusters of white flowers tinged with red or yellow, and spiny or smooth capsules containing large brown seeds. **2.** The seed of any of these plants.

horse·feath·ers (hôrs′fĕth′ərz) *Slang. n. (used with a sing. verb).* Nonsense; foolishness. **—horsefeathers** *interj.* Used to express disagreement or exasperation. [Alteration of HORSESHIT.]

horse·flesh (hôrs′flĕsh′) *n.* **1.** The flesh of a horse. **2.** Horses considered as a group, especially for driving, riding, or racing.

horse·fly also **horse fly** (hôrs′flī′) *n.* Any of numerous large flies of the family Tabanidae, the females of which suck the blood of various mammals.

horse gentian *n.* Any of various plants of the genus *Triosteum,* having opposite leaves, small purplish-brown flowers, and leathery orange-yellow fruit. Also called *feverwort.*

horse·hair (hôrs′hâr′) *n.* **1.** The hair of a horse, especially from the mane or tail. **2.** Cloth made of the hair of horses. *—attributive.* Often used to modify another noun: *a horsehair sofa; horsehair upholstery.*

horsehair worm *n.* Any of various slender aquatic worms of the phylum Nematomorpha, the larvae of which are parasitic within insects. Also called *hairworm.*

horse·hide (hôrs′hīd′) *n.* **1.** The hide of a horse. **2.** Leather made from the hide of a horse.

horse latitudes *pl.n.* Either of two belts of latitudes located over the oceans at about 30° to 35° north and south, having high barometric pressure, calms, and light, changeable winds. [Possibly from Spanish *golfo de las yeguas,* mares' sea.]

horse·laugh (hôrs′lăf′, -läf′) *n. Informal.* A loud, coarse laugh; a guffaw.

horse·leech (hôrs′lēch′) *n.* Any of several large leeches of the genus *Haemopis.*

horse·less carriage (hôrs′lĭs) *n.* An automobile: *in the days when a horseless carriage was the talk of the town.*

horse mackerel *n.* **1.** See **saurel** (sense 1). **2.** Any of several tunas or related fishes.

horse·man (hôrs′mən) *n.* **1.a.** A man who rides a horse. **b.** A man skilled in equitation. **2.** A man who breeds and raises horses.

horse·man·ship (hôrs′mən-shĭp′) *n.* The skill of riding horses; equitation.

horse marine *n.* **1.a.** A marine assigned to the cavalry. **b.** A cavalryman assigned to a ship. **2.** *Informal.* One who is out of one's element; a misfit.

horse·mint (hôrs′mĭnt′) *n.* **1.** A perennial, aromatic eastern North American plant *(Monarda punctata)* having opposite leaves and yellowish flowers with purple spots. Also called *wild bergamot.* **2.** A Eurasian wild mint *(Mentha longifolia),* naturalized in the eastern United States and having long, opposite leaves and dense, spikelike elongated clusters of flowers.

horse nettle *n.* A prickly-stemmed plant *(Solanum carolinense)* of eastern and central North America, having purplish or white star-shaped flowers and yellowish berries.

horse opera *n.* A film or other theatrical work about the American West.

horse·play (hôrs′plā′) *n.* Rowdy or rough play.

horse·play·er (hôrs′plā′ər) *n. Games.* One who regularly bets on horseraces.

horse·pow·er (hôrs′pou′ər) *n. Abbr.* **hp 1.** A unit of power in the U.S. Customary System, equal to 745.7 watts or 33,000 foot-pounds per minute. **2.** The power exerted by a horse in pulling.

horse·race or **horse race** (hôrs′rās′) *n.* **1.** A contest in which horses ridden by jockeys are raced against each other. **2.** A closely fought contest. **—horse′rac′ing** *n.*

horse·rad·ish (hôrs′răd′ĭsh) *n.* **1.** A coarse Eurasian plant *(Armoracia rusticana)* in the mustard family, having a thick, whitish, pungent root, large basal leaves, and white flowers in a terminal panicle. **2.a.** The roots of this plant. **b.** A sharp condiment made of the grated roots of this plant.

horse sense *n. Informal.* Common sense; gumption.

horse·shit (hôrs′shĭt′, hôrsh′-) *n.* **1.** *Vulgar.* Excrement of a horse. **2.** *Vulgar Slang.* Meaningless or insincere talk or action; nonsense.

horse·shoe (hôrs′sho͞o′, hôrsh′-) *n.* **1.** A flat U-shaped metal plate fitted and nailed to the bottom of a horse's hoof for protection. **2.** A U-shaped object similar to a horseshoe. **3. horseshoes** *(used with a sing. verb). Games.* A game in which players toss horseshoes or horseshoe-shaped metal pieces at a stake so as to encircle it or come closer to it than the other players. **—horseshoe** *tr.v.* **-shoed, -shoe·ing, -shoes.** To fit with horseshoes.

horseshoe crab *n.* Any of various marine arthropods of the class Merostomata, especially *Limulus polyphemus* or *Xiphosura polyphemus* of eastern North America, having a large, rounded body and a stiff, pointed tail. Also called *king crab, limulus.*

Horse·shoe Falls (hôrs′sho͞o′, hôrsh′-). See **Canadian Falls.**

horse·tail (hôrs′tāl′) *n.* Any of various nonflowering plants of the genus *Equisetum,* having a jointed, hollow stem and narrow, sometimes much reduced leaves. Also called *equisetum.*

horse-trad·ing (hôrs′trā′dĭng) *n.* Negotiation characterized by hard bargaining and shrewd exchange: *political horse-trading.* **—horse trade** *n.* **—horse′-trade′** *v.* **—horse trader** *n.*

horse·weed (hôrs′wēd′) *n.* A weedy North American plant *(Erigeron canadensis)* having narrow leaves and numerous small white or greenish flower heads grouped in panicles.

horse·whip (hôrs′hwĭp′, -wĭp′) *n.* A whip used to control a horse. **—horsewhip** *tr.v.* **-whipped, -whip·ping, -whips.** To beat with or as if with a horsewhip.

horse·wom·an (hôrs′wo͝om′ən) *n.* **1.a.** A woman who rides a horse. **b.** A woman skilled in equitation. **2.** A woman who breeds and raises horses.

hors·ey (hôr′sē) *adj.* Variant of **horsy.**

horst (hôrst) *n.* A mass of the earth's crust that lies between two faults and is higher than the surrounding land. [German, from Middle High German *hurst,* thicket, from Old High German.]

hors·y also **hors·ey** (hôr′sē) *adj.* **-i·er, -i·est. 1.** Of, relating to, or resembling horses or a horse. **2.** Devoted to horses and equitation: *the horsy set.* **3.** Large and clumsy: *a horsy bureau; horsy illustrations.* **—hors′i·ly** *adv.* **—hors′i·ness** *n.*

hort. *abbr.* **1.** Horticultural. **2.** Horticulture.

hor·ta·tive (hôr′tə-tĭv) *adj.* Hortatory. [Late Latin *hortātīvus,* from Latin *hortātus,* past participle of *hortārī,* to exhort. See **gher-**[2] in Appendix.] **—hor′ta·tive·ly** *adv.*

hor·ta·to·ry (hôr′tə-tôr′ē, -tōr′ē) *adj.* Marked by exhortation or strong urging: *a hortatory speech.* [Late Latin *hortātōrius,* from Latin *hortātus,* exhorted. See HORTATIVE.]

hor·ti·cul·ture (hôr′tĭ-kŭl′chər) *n. Abbr.* **hort. 1.** The science or art of cultivating fruits, vegetables, flowers, or ornamental plants. **2.** The cultivation of a garden. [Latin *hortus,* garden; see **gher-**[1] in Appendix + (AGRI)CULTURE.] **—hor′ti·cul′tur·al** *adj.* **—hor′ti·cul′tur·al·ly** *adv.* **—hor′ti·cul′tur·ist** *n.*

Hor·ton River (hôr′tn). A river, about 443 km (275 mi) long, of northern Northwest Territories, Canada, flowing northwest into Franklin Bay, an inlet of the Beaufort Sea.

Ho·rus (hôr′əs, hōr′-) *n. Mythology.* The ancient Egyptian god of the sun, son of Osiris and Isis, represented as having the head of a hawk.

Hos. *abbr. Bible.* Hosea.

ho·san·na also **ho·san·nah** (hō-zăn′ə) *—interj.* Used to express praise or adoration to God. *—n.* **1.** A cry of "hosanna." **2.** A shout of fervent and worshipful praise. [Middle English *osanna,* from Old English, from Late Latin *ōsanna,* from Greek *hōsanna,* from Hebrew *hôša'nā',* from *hôša' nā',* save (us), I pray.]

hose (hōz) *n.* **1.** *pl.* **hose.** Stockings; socks. Used only in the plural. **2.** *pl.* **hose. a.** Close-fitting breeches or leggings reaching up to the hips and fastened to a doublet, formerly worn by men. Used only in the plural. **b.** Breeches reaching down to the knees. Used only in the plural. **3.** *pl.* **hos·es.** A flexible tube for conveying liquids or gases under pressure. **—hose** *tr.v.* **hosed, hos·ing, hos·es. 1.** To water, drench, or wash with a hose: *hosed down the deck; hosed off the dog.* **2.** *Slang.* To attack and kill (someone), typically by use of a firearm: *hosed the enemy trooper.* [Middle English, a stocking, from Old English *hosa,* leg covering. See **(s)keu-** in Appendix.]

Ho·se·a (hō-zē′ə, -zā′ə) *n. Bible.* **1.** A Hebrew prophet of the eighth century B.C. **2.** *Abbr.* **Hos., Ho** See table at **Bible.**

♦ **ho·sey** (hō′zē) *intr.v.* **-seyed, -sey·ing, -seys.** *New England.* To choose sides for a children's game. [Perhaps from French *(je) choisis,* (I) choose, first person sing. present of *choisir,* to choose, from Old French. See CHOICE.]

♦ REGIONAL NOTE: Children in New England, especially in the Boston area, use the expression *I hosey* when they are choosing

horse chestnut
Aesculus hippocastanum

horseshoe crab
Limulus polyphemus

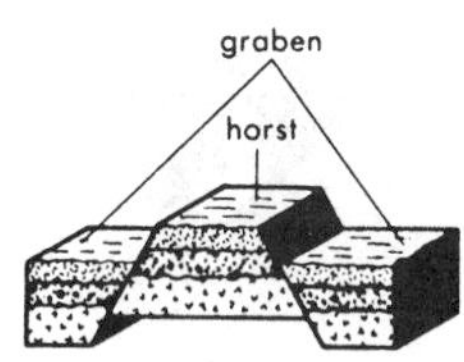

horst

Horus
Late XXVI Dynasty

ă **pat**	oi **boy**
ā **pay**	ou **out**
âr **care**	o͝o **took**
ä **father**	o͞o **boot**
ĕ **pet**	ŭ **cut**
ē **be**	ûr **urge**
ĭ **pit**	th **thin**
ī **pie**	*th* **this**
îr **pier**	hw **which**
ŏ **pot**	zh **vision**
ō **toe**	ə **about, item**
ô **paw**	♦ **regionalism**

Stress marks: ′ (primary); **′** (secondary), as in **dictionary** (dĭk′shə-nĕr′ē)

sides for a game. The *Boston Globe* asked readers about it in late 1987 and received responses from Boston; Belmont, Massachusetts; New Hampshire; and Maine. Its users agree that it is a children's expression but are unsure of its origin—some think that it derives from a pronunciation of *choose* with a heavy Irish brogue. Another possible origin of the expression is French-Canadian *choisir,* "to choose."

ho·sier·y (hō′zhə-rē) *n.* **1.** Socks and stockings; hose. **2.** *Chiefly British.* Stockings, socks, and underclothing. [*hosier,* maker of stockings (from Middle English, from *hose,* a stocking; see HOSE) + -Y[2].]

hosp. *abbr.* Hospital.

hos·pice (hŏs′pĭs) *n.* **1.** A shelter or lodging for travelers, pilgrims, foundlings, or the destitute, especially one maintained by a monastic order. **2.** A program that provides palliative care and attends to the emotional, spiritual, social, and financial needs of terminally ill patients at an inpatient facility or at the patient's home. [French, from Old French, from Latin *hospitium,* hospitality, from *hospes, hospit-,* host. See **ghos-ti-** in Appendix.]

hot cross bun

hos·pi·ta·ble (hŏs′pĭ-tə-bəl, hŏ-spĭt′ə-bəl) *adj.* **1.** Disposed to treat guests with warmth and generosity. **2.** Indicative of cordiality toward guests: *a hospitable act.* **3.** Having an open mind; receptive: *hospitable to new ideas.* **4.** Favorable to growth and development; agreeable: *a hospitable environment.* [Obsolete French, from Medieval Latin **hospitābilis,* from Latin *hospitāre,* to put up as a guest, from *hospes, hospit-,* guest, host. See **ghos-ti-** in Appendix.] **—hos′pi·ta·bly** *adv.*

hos·pi·tal (hŏs′pĭ-tl, -pĭt′l) *n. Abbr.* **hosp. 1.** An institution that provides medical, surgical, or psychiatric care and treatment for the sick or the injured. **2.** *Chiefly British.* A charitable institution, such as an orphanage or a home for the elderly. **3.** A repair shop for specified items: *a doll hospital.* **4.** *Archaic.* A hospice for travelers or pilgrims. —*attributive.* Often used to modify another noun: *hospital food; hospital patients.* [Middle English, hospice, from Old French *ospital,* from Medieval Latin *hospitāle,* from Latin *hospitālis,* of a guest, from *hospes, hospit-,* guest. See **ghos-ti-** in Appendix.]

hospital corner *n.* A tight-fitting triangular fold made by tucking a sheet and blanket securely under a mattress on the end and on each side at the corners.

Hos·pi·tal·er also **Hos·pi·tal·ler** (hŏs′pĭt′l-ər) *n.* **1.** A member of a military religious order founded among European crusaders in 12th-century Jerusalem to care for sick and needy pilgrims. **2.** A member of any of several religious orders dedicated to the care of sick or needy persons. [Middle English *Hospiteler,* from Old French *hospitalier,* from Medieval Latin *hospitālārius,* giver of hospitality, from *hospitāle,* hospice. See HOSPITAL.]

Hos·pi·ta·let (hŏs′pĭt-l-ĕt′, ôs′pē-tä-lĕt′). A city of northeast Spain, an industrial suburb of Barcelona. Population, 288,290.

hos·pi·tal·i·ty (hŏs′pĭ-tăl′ĭ-tē) *n., pl.* **-ties. 1.** Cordial and generous reception of or disposition toward guests. **2.** An instance of cordial and generous treatment of guests. [Middle English *hospitalite,* from Old French, from Latin *hospitālitās,* from *hospitālis,* of a guest. See HOSPITAL.]

hos·pi·tal·i·za·tion (hŏs′pĭ-tl-ĭ-zā′shən) *n.* **1.a.** The act of placing a person in a hospital as a patient. **b.** The condition of being hospitalized. **2.** Insurance that fully or partially covers a patient's hospital expenses.

hos·pi·tal·ize (hŏs′pĭt-l-īz′) *tr.v.* **-ized, -iz·ing, -iz·es.** To place in a hospital for treatment, care, or observation.

Hos·pi·tal·ler (hŏs′pĭt′l-ər) *n.* Variant of **Hospitaler.**

hot dog

host[1] (hōst) *n.* **1.** One who receives or entertains guests in a social or an official capacity. **2.** A person who manages an inn or a hotel. **3.** One that furnishes facilities and resources for a function or an event: *the city chosen as host for the Olympic games.* **4.** The emcee or interviewer on a radio or television program. **5.** *Biology.* The animal or plant on which or in which another organism lives. **6.** *Medicine.* The recipient of a transplanted tissue or organ. **—host** *tr.v.* **host·ed, host·ing, hosts.** *Usage Problem.* To serve as host to or at: *"the garden party he had hosted last spring"* (Saturday Review). [Middle English, host, guest, from Old French, from Late Latin *hospes, hospit-.* See **ghos-ti-** in Appendix.] **—host′ly** *adj.*

USAGE NOTE: *Host* was used as a verb in Shakespeare's time, but this usage was long obsolete when the verb was reintroduced (or perhaps reinvented) in recent years to mean "perform the role of a host." The usage occurs particularly in contexts relating to institutional gatherings or television and radio shows, where the person performing the role of host has not personally invited the guests to his or her own establishment (thus it would be odd to say *This evening we are hosting a dinner party at our house for my husband's cousins from New York*). Perhaps because the verb involves a suspect extension of the traditional conception of hospitality, it initially met with critical resistance. In a 1968 survey only 18 percent of the Usage Panel accepted the usage in the sentence *The Cleveland chapter will host this year's convention.* Over time, however, the usage has become increasingly well established and appears to serve a useful purpose in describing the activities of one who performs the ceremonial or practical role of a host (in arranging a conference or entertainment, welcoming guests, and so forth). In our most recent survey 53 percent of the Panelists

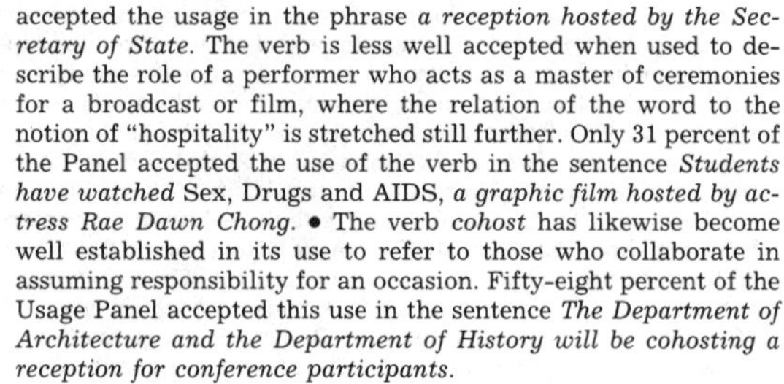

accepted the usage in the phrase *a reception hosted by the Secretary of State.* The verb is less well accepted when used to describe the role of a performer who acts as a master of ceremonies for a broadcast or film, where the relation of the word to the notion of "hospitality" is stretched still further. Only 31 percent of the Panel accepted the use of the verb in the sentence *Students have watched* Sex, Drugs and AIDS, *a graphic film hosted by actress Rae Dawn Chong.* • The verb *cohost* has likewise become well established in its use to refer to those who collaborate in assuming responsibility for an occasion. Fifty-eight percent of the Usage Panel accepted this use in the sentence *The Department of Architecture and the Department of History will be cohosting a reception for conference participants.*

host[2] (hōst) *n.* **1.** An army. **2.** A great number; a multitude. See Synonyms at **multitude.** [Middle English, from Old French, from Late Latin *hostis,* from Latin, enemy. See **ghos-ti-** in Appendix.]

host[3] also **Host** (hōst) *n. Ecclesiastical.* The consecrated bread or wafer of the Eucharist. [Middle English, from Latin *hostia,* sacrifice.]

hos·ta (hō′stə, hŏs′tə) *n.* See **plantain lily.** [New Latin *Hosta,* genus name, after Nicolaus Thomas *Host* (1761–1834), Austrian botanist.]

hos·tage (hŏs′tĭj) *n.* **1.** A person held by one party in a conflict as security that specified terms will be met by the opposing party. **2.** One that serves as security against an implied threat: *superpowers held hostage to each other by their nuclear arsenals.* **3.** One that is manipulated by the demands of another: *"National policies cannot be made hostage to another country"* (Alan D. Romberg). [Middle English, from Old French, probably from *host,* guest, host. See HOST[1].]

hos·tel (hŏs′təl) *n.* **1.** A supervised, inexpensive lodging place for travelers, especially young travelers. **2.** An inn; a hotel. **—hostel** *intr.v.* **-teled, -tel·ing, -tels.** To stay at hostels while traveling. [Middle English, lodging, from Old French, from Medieval Latin *hospitāle,* hospice, inn. See HOSPITAL.]

hos·tel·er (hŏs′tə-lər) *n.* **1.** A traveler who stays at hostels. **2.** *Archaic.* An innkeeper.

hos·tel·ry (hŏs′təl-rē) *n., pl.* **-ries.** An inn; a hotel. [Middle English *hostelrie,* from Old French *hostelerie,* from *hostel,* lodging, inn. See HOSTEL.]

host·ess (hō′stĭs) *n.* **1.** A woman who receives or entertains guests in a social or official capacity. **2.** A woman who manages an inn or a hotel. **3.** A woman who is the emcee or interviewer on a radio or television program. **4.** A woman who is employed to greet and assist patrons, as in a restaurant. **5.** A woman who is employed to dance with customers in a dance hall or nightclub. See Usage Note at **-ess.**

hos·tile (hŏs′təl, -tīl′) *adj.* **1.** Of, relating to, or characteristic of an enemy: *hostile forces; hostile acts.* **2.** Feeling or showing enmity or ill will; antagonistic: *a hostile remark.* **3.** Unfavorable to health or well-being; inhospitable or adverse: *a hostile climate.* **—hostile** *n.* **1.** An antagonistic person or thing. **2.** An enemy in warfare. [Latin *hostīlis,* from *hostis,* enemy. See **ghos-ti-** in Appendix.] **—hos′tile·ly** *adv.*

hos·til·i·ty (hŏ-stĭl′ĭ-tē) *n., pl.* **-ties. 1.** The state of being hostile; antagonism or enmity. See Synonyms at **enmity. 2.a.** A hostile act. **b. hostilities.** Acts of war; overt warfare.

hos·tler (hŏs′lər, ŏs′-) also **os·tler** (ŏs′-) *n.* **1.** One who is employed to tend horses, especially at an inn. **2.** One who services a large vehicle or engine, such as a locomotive. [Middle English, from Anglo-Norman *hostiler,* from Old French *hostel,* lodging. See HOSTEL.]

hot (hŏt) *adj.* **hot·ter, hot·test. 1.a.** Having or giving off heat capable of burning. **b.** Being at a high temperature. **2.** Being at or exhibiting a temperature that is higher than normal or desirable: *a hot forehead.* **3.** Causing a burning sensation, as in the mouth; spicy: *hot peppers; a hot curry.* **4.a.** Charged or energized with electricity: *a hot wire.* **b.** Radioactive, especially to a dangerous degree. **5.a.** Marked by intensity of emotion; ardent or fiery: *a hot temper.* **b.** Having or displaying great enthusiasm; eager: *hot for travel.* **6.a.** *Informal.* Arousing intense interest, excitement, or controversy: *a hot new book; a hot topic.* **b.** *Informal.* Marked by excited activity or energy: *a hot week on the stock market.* **c.** Violent; raging: *a hot battle.* **7.** *Slang.* Sexually excited or exciting. **8.** *Slang.* **a.** Recently stolen: *a hot car.* **b.** Wanted by the police: *a hot suspect.* **9.** Close to a successful solution or conclusion: *hot on the trail.* **10.** *Informal.* **a.** Most recent; new or fresh: *a hot news item; the hot fashions for fall.* **b.** Currently very popular or successful: *one of the hottest young talents around.* **c.** Requiring immediate action or attention: *a hot opportunity.* **11.** *Slang.* Very good or impressive. Often used in the negative: *I'm not so hot at math.* **12.** *Slang.* Funny or absurd: *told a hot one about the neighbors' dog.* **13.** *Slang.* **a.** Performing with great skill and daring: *a hot drummer.* **b.** Fast and responsive: *a hot sports car.* **c.** Unusually lucky: *hot at craps.* **14.** *Music.* Of, relating to, or being an emotionally charged style of performance marked by strong rhythms and improvisation: *hot jazz.* **15.** *Color.* Bold and bright. **— hots** *n. Slang.* Strong sexual attraction or desire. Used with *the.* **—hot** *adv.* **1.** In a hot manner; hotly. **2.** While hot: *foods that are best eaten hot.* **—hot** *tr.v.* **hot·ted, hot·ting, hots.** *Informal.* To cause to increase in intensity or excitement. Often used with *up*: *"His book is an exercise in* *the fashionable art of instant history, in which every episode is hotted up with an anecdote"* (Harper's). **—*idioms.* hot and bothered.** *Informal.* In a state of agitated excitement; flustered: *all hot and bothered before the opening performance.* **hot to trot.** *Slang.* **1.** Sexually avid; lascivious. **2.** Ready and willing; eager. **hot under the collar.** *Informal.* Angry. **make it hot for.** *Slang.* To make things uncomfortable or dangerous for: *Don't make it hot for yourself by needlessly finding fault.* [Middle English, from Old English *hāt.* See **kai-** in Appendix.] **—hot′ness** *n.*

hot air *n. Slang.* Empty, exaggerated talk.

hot·bed (hŏt′bĕd′) *n.* **1.** An environment conducive to vigorous growth or development, especially of something undesirable: *a hotbed of intrigue.* **2.** A glass-covered bed of soil heated with fermenting manure or by electricity, used for the germination of seeds or for protecting tender plants.

hot-blood·ed (hŏt′blŭd′ĭd) *adj.* Easily excited or aroused: *a hot-blooded youth.* **—hot′-blood′ed·ness** *n.*

hot·box (hŏt′bŏks′) *n.* An axle or journal box, as on a railway car, that has become overheated by excessive friction.

hot button *n. Slang.* **1.** A psychological propensity for immediate or predictable response or reaction, as to a political issue or marketing tactic: *an issue that presses voters' hot buttons.* **2.** Something that is of great interest or is known to elicit immediate or predictable response or reaction: *a new product that is a hot button among consumers.* **—hot′-but′ton** (hŏt′bŭt′n) *adj.*

hot·cake also **hot cake** (hŏt′kāk′) *n.* See **pancake.** **—*idiom.* go** (or **sell) like hotcakes.** *Informal.* To be disposed of quickly; be in great demand: *Programs for the championship game went like hotcakes.*

hotch (hŏch) *intr.v.* **hotched, hotch·ing, hotch·es.** *Scots.* To fidget. [Middle English, perhaps from Old French *hocher,* to shake, possibly of Germanic origin.]

hotch·pot (hŏch′pŏt′) *n. Law.* The gathering together of properties to ensure an equal division of the total for distribution, as among the heirs of an intestate parent. [Middle English *hochepot,* from Old French, mixture, stew : *hocher,* to shake together; see HOTCH + *pot,* pot.]

hotch·potch (hŏch′pŏch′) *n.* A hodgepodge. [Middle English *hochepoche,* alteration of *hochepot.* See HOTCHPOT.]

hot cross bun *n.* A sweet bun marked on top with a cross of frosting, traditionally eaten during Lent.

hot dog or **hot·dog** (hŏt′dôg′, -dŏg′) *—n.* **1.** A frankfurter, especially one served hot in a long soft roll. Also called *red-hot.* **2.** *Slang.* One who performs showy, often dangerous stunts, as in skiing or surfing. *—interj. Informal.* Used to express delight or enthusiasm.

hot-dog (hŏt′dôg′, -dŏg′) *intr.v.* **-dogged, -dog·ging, -dogs.** *Slang.* To perform daring stunts or acrobatic feats, especially while skiing or surfing. **—hot′-dog′ger** *n.* **—hot′-dog′ging** *adj. & n.*

ho·tel (hō-tĕl′) *n.* An establishment that provides lodging and usually meals and other services for travelers and other paying guests. *—attributive.* Often used to modify another noun: *hotel guests; hotel furnishings.* [French *hôtel,* from Old French *hostel,* hostel. See HOSTEL.]

ho·te·lier (ō′təl-yā′, hō′-) *n.* A manager or an owner of a hotel. Also called *hotelkeeper.* [French *hôtelier,* from Old French *hostilier,* from *hostel,* inn. See HOSTEL.]

ho·tel·keep·er (hō-tĕl′kē′pər) *n.* See **hotelier.**

hot flash *n.* **1.** A sudden, brief sensation of heat, often over the entire body, caused by a transient dilation of the blood vessels of the skin and experienced by some women during menopause. **2.** *Slang.* A brief, important piece of news or other information.

hot·foot (hŏt′fo͝ot′) *intr.v.* **-foot·ed, -foot·ing, -foots.** *Informal.* To go in haste. Often used with *it*: *hotfoot it out of town.* **—hotfoot** *adv.* In haste. **—hotfoot** *n., pl.* **-foots.** The practical joke of lighting a match that has been secretly inserted between the sole and upper of a victim's shoe.

hot·head (hŏt′hĕd′) *n.* A quick-tempered or impetuous person.

hot·head·ed (hŏt′hĕd′ĭd) *adj.* **1.** Easily angered; quick-tempered: *a hotheaded commander.* **2.** Impetuous; rash: *a hotheaded decision.* **—hot′head′ed·ly** *adv.* **—hot′head′ed·ness** *n.*

hot·house (hŏt′hous′) *n.* A heated greenhouse for plants that require an even, relatively warm temperature. **—hothouse** *adj.* **1.** Grown in a hothouse: *a hothouse orchid.* **2.** Delicate and sensitive, as if from growing up in a protective environment: *hothouse children; hothouse views on social progress.*

hot line or **hot·line** (hŏt′līn′) *n.* **1.** A direct and immediate telephone linkup, especially between heads of government, as for use in a crisis. **2.** A telephone line that gives quick and direct access to a source of information or help: *"This 24-hour hot line has . . . volunteers on duty to talk to callers about personal problems"* (New York).

hot·ly (hŏt′lē) *adv.* In an intense or fiery way: *a hotly contested will; answered hotly that he was innocent.*

hot metal *n. Printing.* Type cast from molten metal.

hot money *n.* Money that is moved by its owner quickly from one form or investment to another, as to take advantage of changing international exchange rates or gain high short-term returns on investments.

hot pants *pl.n.* **1.** *Vulgar Slang.* Strong sexual desire. **2.** Very brief tight shorts worn by women as an outer garment.

hot pepper *n.* **1.** The pungent fruit of any of several varieties of *Capsicum frutescens.* **2.** See **pepper** (sense 4).

hot plate *n.* **1.** An electrically heated plate for cooking or warming food. **2.** A tabletop cooking device with one or two burners.

hot pot *n. Chiefly British.* A stew of lamb or beef and potatoes cooked in a tightly covered pot.

hot potato *n. Informal.* A problem that is so controversial or sensitive that those handling it risk unpleasant consequences: *gun control—a political hot potato.*

hot rod also **hot-rod** (hŏt′rŏd′) *n. Slang.* An automobile that has been rebuilt or modified to increase its speed and acceleration. **—hot′-rod′** *v.* **—hot rodder, hot′-rod′der** *n.*

hot seat *n.* **1.** *Slang.* The electric chair. **2.** *Informal.* A position in which one is subjected to extreme stress or discomfort, as by excessive criticism.

hot·shot (hŏt′shŏt′) *n.* **1.** *Slang.* A person of impressive skill and daring, especially one who is highly successful and self-assured. **2.** A nonstop freight train. **—hot′shot′** *adj.*

hot spot also **hot·spot** (hŏt′spŏt′) *n.* **1.** An area in which there is dangerous unrest or hostile action: *"opportunities . . . for United Nations forces to play a constructive role in some of the world's hot spots"* (Paul Lewis). **2.** *Informal.* A lively and popular place, such as a nightclub. **3.** An area of intense heat, radiation, or activity.

hot spring *n.* A natural spring that issues water warmer than body temperature and therefore feels hot.

Hot Springs (hŏt). A city of west-central Arkansas west-southwest of Little Rock. It is a health resort noted for its 47 thermal springs. Population, 35,781.

Hot·ten·tot (hŏt′n-tŏt′) *n., pl.* **Hottentot** or **-tots.** *Offensive.* **1.** A Khoikhoin. **2.** Any of the Khoikhoin group of languages. [Afrikaans.]

hot·tish (hŏt′ĭsh) *adj.* Somewhat hot.

hot toddy *n.* A drink consisting of whiskey, brandy, or other liquor mixed with hot water, sugar, and spices.

hot tub *n.* A very large tub made of ceramic, acrylic, wood, or another substance and filled with hot water in which one or more bathers may soak.

hot war *n.* Armed, open conflict between nations or factions. [HOT + (COLD) WAR.]

hot water *n.* Trouble; difficulty: *is in political hot water; got into hot water over the car deal.*

hot-wa·ter bottle (hŏt′wô′tər, -wŏt′ər) *n.* A stoppered container, usually made of plastic or rubber, that is filled with hot water and applied to a part of the body for warmth. Also called *hot-water bag.*

hot-wire (hŏt′wīr′) *tr.v.* **-wired, -wir·ing, -wires.** *Informal.* To start the engine of (an automobile, for example) without a key, as by short-circuiting the ignition system.

hou·dah (hou′də) *n.* Variant of **howdah.**

Hou·dan (ho͞o′dăn′) *n.* A domesticated fowl characterized by black-and-white plumage and a V-shaped comb. [French, after *Houdan,* a village of north-central France.]

Hou·di·ni (ho͞o-dē′nē), **Harry.** 1874–1926. American magician known for his escapes from chains, handcuffs, straitjackets, and padlocked containers.

Hou·don (ho͞o′dŏn′, o͞o-dôN′), **Jean Antoine.** 1741–1828. French sculptor who executed statues of Washington and Voltaire and busts of Jefferson, Rousseau, and Lafayette.

Hough·ton (hōt′n), **Henry Oscar.** 1823–1895. American publisher who founded (1852) the printing office that became the Houghton Mifflin Company.

Hou·ma (hō′mə, ho͞o′-). A city of southeast Louisiana on the Intracoastal Waterway southwest of New Orleans. It is a processing center for seafood and sugar. Population, 32,602.

hound (hound) *n.* **1.a.** A domestic dog of any of various breeds commonly used for hunting, characteristically having drooping ears, a short coat, and a deep, resonant voice. **b.** A dog. **2.** A contemptible person; a scoundrel. **3.a.** One who eagerly pursues something: *a news hound.* **b.** A devotee or an enthusiast: *a coffee hound.* **—hound** *tr.v.* **hound·ed, hound·ing, hounds. 1.** To pursue relentlessly and tenaciously. See Synonyms at **harass. 2.** To urge insistently; nag: *hounded me until I agreed to cut my hair.* [Middle English, from Old English *hund.* See **kwon-** in Appendix.] **—hound′er** *n.*

hound's-tongue (houndz′tŭng′) *n.* Any of several Eurasian plants of the genus *Cynoglossum,* having hairy leaves, small reddish-purple flowers, and prickly, clinging fruit. [Middle English *houndes-tongue,* from Old English *hundes-tunge* (translation of Latin *cynoglōssus,* from Greek *kunoglōssos*) : *hundes,* genitive of *hund,* hound; see HOUND + *tunge,* tongue; see TONGUE.]

hounds·tooth check or **hound's-tooth check** (houndz′to͞oth′) *n.* A textile design of small broken checks.

hour (our) *n. Abbr.* **hr, h 1.** One of the 24 equal parts of a day. **2.a.** One of the points on a timepiece marking off 12 or 24 successive intervals of 60 minutes, from midnight to noon and noon to midnight or from midnight to midnight. **b.** The time of day indicated by a 12-hour clock. **c. hours.** The time of day determined on a 24-hour basis: *1730 hours is 5:30* P.M. **3.** A unit of

Harry Houdini
With shackled wrists and ankles

hound's-tongue
Burgundy hound's-tongue
Cynoglossum officinale

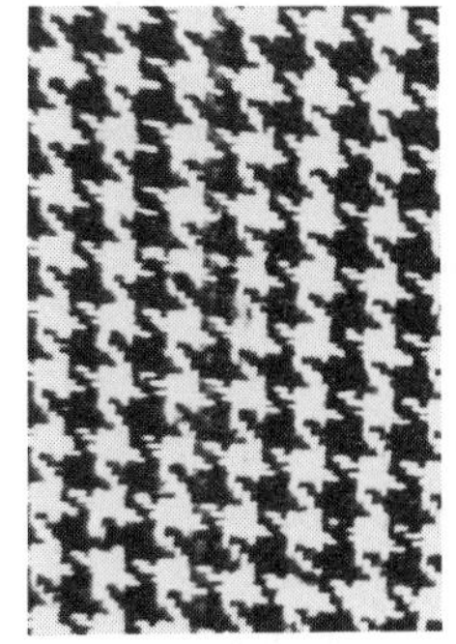

houndstooth check
Detail of fabric

ă pat	oi boy
ā pay	ou out
âr care	o͝o took
ä father	o͞o boot
ĕ pet	ŭ cut
ē be	ûr urge
ĭ pit	th thin
ī pie	*th* this
îr pier	hw which
ŏ pot	zh vision
ō toe	ə about, item
ô paw	♦ regionalism

Stress marks: ′ (primary); ′ (secondary), as in **dictionary** (dĭk′shə-nĕr′ē)

measure of longitude or right ascension, equal to 15° or 1/24 of a great circle. **4. a.** A customary or fixed time: *the dinner hour.* **b. hours.** A set period of time for a specified activity: *banking hours.* **5. a.** A particular time: *their hour of need.* **b.** A significant time: *Her hour had come.* **c.** The present time: *the man of the hour.* **6. a.** The work that can be accomplished in an hour. **b.** The distance that can be traveled in an hour. **7. a.** A single session of a school day or class. **b.** A credit hour. **8. hours.** *Ecclesiastical.* The canonical hours. [Middle English, from Old French *houre,* from Latin *hōra,* from Greek, season, time. See **yēr-** in Appendix.]

hourglass

hour angle *n. Abbr.* **ha** The angular distance, measured westward along the celestial equator, between the celestial meridian of the observer and the hour circle passing through a celestial body.

hour circle *n.* A great circle passing through the poles of the celestial sphere and intersecting the celestial equator at right angles.

hour•glass (our′glăs′) *n.* An instrument for measuring time, consisting of two glass chambers connected by a narrow neck and containing a quantity of sand, mercury, or another flowing substance that trickles from the upper chamber to the lower in a fixed amount of time, often one hour. **—hourglass** *adj.* Shaped like an hourglass: *an hourglass design; an hourglass figure.*

hou•ri (ho͝or′ē, ho͞o′rē) *n., pl.* **-ris. 1.** A voluptuous, alluring woman. **2.** One of the beautiful virgins of the Koranic paradise. [French, from Persian *ḥūrī,* from Arabic *ḥūr,* pl. of *ḥaurā',* dark-eyed woman.]

hour•long or **hour-long** (our′lông′, -lŏng′) *adj.* Lasting an hour: *an hourlong television episode.*

hour•ly (our′lē) *adj.* **1.** Occurring every hour: *hourly chimes.* **2.** Frequent; continual: *hourly changes in the plans.* **3.** By the hour as a unit: *hourly pay.* **—hourly** *adv.* **1.** At or during every hour: *The news is broadcast hourly.* **2.** Frequently; continually: *complaints that came hourly.* **—hourly** *n., pl.* **-lies.** *Informal.* An employee paid by the hour.

Hou•sa•ton•ic (ho͞o′sə-tŏn′ĭk). A river rising in the Berkshire Hills of western Massachusetts and flowing about 209 km (130 mi) generally south through Connecticut to Long Island Sound.

house (hous) *n., pl.* **hous•es** (hou′zĭz, -sĭz). *Abbr.* **ho. 1. a.** A structure serving as a dwelling for one or more persons, especially for a family. **b.** A household or family. **2.** Something, such as a burrow or shell, that serves as a shelter or habitation for a wild animal. **3.** A dwelling for a group of people, such as students or members of a religious community, who live together as a unit: *a sorority house.* **4.** A building that functions as the primary shelter or location of something: *a carriage house; the lion house at the zoo.* **5. a.** A facility, such as a theater or restaurant, that provides entertainment or food for the public: *a movie house; the specialty of the house.* **b.** The audience or patrons of such an establishment: *a full house.* **6. a.** A commercial firm: *a brokerage house.* **b.** A publishing company: *a house that specializes in cookbooks.* **c.** A gambling casino. **d.** *Slang.* A house of prostitution. **7.** A residential college within a university. **8. a.** Often **House.** A legislative or deliberative assembly. **b.** The hall or chamber in which such an assembly meets. **c.** A quorum of such an assembly. **9.** Often **House.** A family line including ancestors and descendants, especially a royal or noble family: *the House of Orange.* **10. a.** One of the 12 parts into which the heavens are divided in astrology. **b.** The sign of the zodiac indicating the seat or station of a planet in the heavens. In this sense, also called *mansion.* —*attributive.* Often used to modify another noun: *the house wine; house paint.* **—house** (houz) *v.* **housed, hous•ing, hous•es.** —*tr.* **1.** To provide living quarters for; lodge: *The cottage housed ten students.* **2.** To shelter, keep, or store in or as if in a house: *a library housing rare books.* **3.** To contain; harbor. **4.** To fit into a socket or mortise. **5.** *Nautical.* To secure or stow safely. —*intr.* **1.** To reside; dwell. **2.** To take shelter. **—*idioms.* like a house on fire** (or **afire**). *Informal.* In an extremely speedy manner: *ran away like a house on fire; tickets that sold like a house afire.* **on the house.** At the expense of the establishment; free: *food and drinks on the house.* **put** (or **set**) **(one's) house in order.** To organize one's affairs in a sensible, logical way. [Middle English, from Old English *hūs.*]

housefly
Musca domestica

house arrest *n. Law.* Confinement to one's quarters, rather than prison, by administrative or judicial order: *a prisoner under house arrest.*

♦ **house•boat** (hous′bōt′) *n.* **1.** *Nautical.* A barge designed and equipped for use as a dwelling or cruiser. **2.** See **banana split.** See Regional Note at **milk shake.**

house•bound (hous′bound′) *adj.* Confined to one's home, as by illness.

house•boy (hous′boi′) *n.* A male servant in a house.

house brand *n.* **1.** A proprietary brand of merchandise sold by one retailer and often bearing the name of the retailer. **2.** An item of merchandise sold under a house brand, usually at a lower price than an equivalent name-brand item.

house•break (hous′brāk′) *tr.v.* **-broke** (-brōk′), **-bro•ken** (-brō′kən), **-break•ing, -breaks. 1.** To train to have excretory habits that are acceptable for indoor living: *housebreak a puppy.* **2.** To subdue; tame. **—housebreak** *n.* Burglary of a dwelling: *a neighborhood in which housebreaks are a common occurrence.*

house•break•ing (hous′brā′kĭng) *n. Law.* The act of unlawfully breaking into and entering another's house. **—house′-break′er** *n.*

house•broke (hous′brōk′) *v.* Past tense of **housebreak.**

house•bro•ken (hous′brō′kən) *v.* Past participle of **housebreak. —housebroken** *adj.* **1.** Trained to have excretory habits that are appropriate for indoor living: *a fully housebroken dog.* **2.** Trained to be docile or compliant.

house call *n.* A professional visit made to a home, especially by a physician.

house•carl (hous′kärl′) *n.* A member of the bodyguard or household troops of a Danish or Anglo-Saxon king or noble.

house•clean•ing (hous′klē′nĭng) *n.* **1.** The cleaning and tidying of a house and its contents. **2.** *Informal.* Removal of unwanted personnel, methods, or policies in an effort at reform or improvement.

house•coat (hous′kōt′) *n.* A woman's garment, usually long and loose, used for informal wear at home.

house detective *n.* A detective employed by a retail store, a hotel, or another establishment to prevent theft or misconduct by patrons.

house•dress (hous′drĕs′) *n.* A simple, washable dress worn for housework.

house finch *n.* See **linnet** (sense 2).

house•fly (hous′flī′) *n.* A common, widely distributed fly *(Musca domestica)* that frequents human dwellings, breeds in moist or decaying organic matter, and transmits a wide variety of diseases.

house•ful (hous′fo͝ol) *n.* The amount or number that a house can hold or accommodate: *a houseful of Victorian furniture; a houseful of guests.*

house•guest (hous′gĕst′) *n.* A person who stays in a home as a guest.

house•hold (hous′hōld′) *n.* **1. a.** A domestic unit consisting of the members of a family who live together along with nonrelatives such as servants. **b.** The living spaces and possessions belonging to such a unit. **2.** A person or group of people occupying a single dwelling: *the rise of nonfamily households.* **—household** *adj.* **1.** Of, relating to, or used in a household: *household appliances.* **2.** Commonly known; familiar: *has become a household name.* [Middle English : *house,* house; see HOUSE + *hold,* possession, holding (from Old English, from *healdan,* to hold; see HOLD [1]).]

household arts *pl.n. (used with a sing. or pl. verb).* See **home economics.**

house•hold•er (hous′hōl′dər) *n.* **1.** One who occupies or owns a house. **2.** The head of a household.

household troops *pl.n.* The regiments of cavalry and infantry that escort and guard a sovereign and a royal family.

household word *n.* A widely known saying, name, person, or thing: *"It was an American journalist . . . who made* [T.E.] *Lawrence a household word"* (H.D.S. Greenway).

house•hus•band (hous′hŭz′bənd) *n.* A married man who manages the household as his main occupation and whose wife usually earns the family income.

house•keep•er (hous′kē′pər) *n.* **1.** One who is employed to perform or direct the domestic tasks in a household. **2.** A housewife. **3.** An employee of an establishment, such as a hospital, an inn, or a hotel, who manages other employees engaged in domestic tasks.

house•keep•ing (hous′kē′pĭng) *n.* **1.** Performance or management of household tasks. **2.** Management and maintenance of the property and equipment of an institution or organization. **3.** Routine tasks and procedures carried out in the functioning of an operation or a system. **—house′keep′** *v.*

hou•sel (hou′zəl) *Archaic. n.* The Eucharist. **—housel** *tr.v.* **-seled, -sel•ing, -sels.** To administer the Eucharist to. [Middle English, from Old English *hūsel.*]

house•leek (hous′lēk′) *n.* Any of various plants of the genus *Sempervivum* native to the Old World, especially *S. tectorum,* having a persistent, basal rosette of fleshy leaves and a branching cluster of pinkish or purplish flowers. Also called *live-forever, old-man-and-woman.*

house•lights (hous′līts′) *pl.n.* The lights that illuminate the audience section of a concert hall, a theater, or an auditorium.

house•maid (hous′mād′) *n.* A woman or girl employed to do housework.

house•maid's knee (hous′mādz′) *n.* A swelling of the bursa in front of the patella just beneath the skin, caused by trauma, such as excessive kneeling.

house•man (hous′măn′, -mən) *n.* A man employed for cleaning, maintenance, and other general work in a house or hotel.

house martin *n.* An Old World bird *(Delichon urbica)* having blue-black plumage, white rump and underparts, and a forked tail. Also called *martlet.*

house•mas•ter (hous′măs′tər) *n.* A male teacher in charge of a residence hall at a school.

house•mate (hous′māt′) *n.* One who shares a house with another.

house•moth•er (hous′mŭ*th*′ər) *n.* A woman employed as supervisor or housekeeper of a residence hall for young people.

house mouse *n.* A common gray or brownish-gray mouse *(Mus musculus)* that lives in or near buildings and often carries disease. It is frequently used in laboratory experiments.

House of Burgesses *n.* The lower house of the legislature in colonial Virginia.

House of Commons *n. Abbr.* **H.C.** The lower house of Parliament in the United Kingdom and Canada. Also called *Commons.*

house of correction *n., pl.* **houses of correction.** An institution for the confinement of persons convicted of minor criminal offenses.

House of Delegates *n.* The lower house of the state legislature in Maryland, Virginia, and West Virginia.

House of Lords *n. Abbr.* **H.L.** The upper house of Parliament in the United Kingdom, made up of members of the nobility and high-ranking clergy. Also called *Lords.*

house of prostitution *n., pl.* **houses of prostitution.** An establishment in which the services of prostitutes are available on the premises.

House of Representatives *n. Abbr.* **H.R.** The lower house of the U.S. Congress and of most state legislatures.

house organ *n.* A periodical published by a business organization for its employees or clients.

house·paint·er or **house painter** (hous′pān′tər) *n.* One whose occupation is painting houses.

house party *n.* A party at which guests stay overnight or for several days in a residence, such as the home of the one giving the party.

house physician *n.* **1.** A physician, especially an intern or a resident who cares for hospitalized patients under the supervision of the surgical and medical staff of a hospital. **2.** A physician employed by a hotel or another establishment.

house·plant (hous′plănt′) *n.* Any of a wide variety of plants grown indoors, often for decorative purposes.

house-proud (hous′proud′) *adj.* Proud of one's house or its furnishings or upkeep.

house-rais·ing (hous′rā′zĭng) *n.* The construction of a house or its framework by a group of friends or neighbors.

house·room (hous′ro͝om′, -ro͞om′) *n.* Space or accommodation in or as if in a house.

house·sit (hous′sĭt′) *intr.v.* **-sat** (-săt′), **-sit·ting, -sits.** To act as a house sitter. **—house′sit′ting** *n.*

house sitter *n.* A person who lives in and cares for a house while the regular occupant is away.

house snake *n.* See **milk snake.**

house sparrow *n.* A small bird *(Passer domesticus)* native to the Old World but widely naturalized elsewhere, having brown and gray plumage with a characteristic black throat in the adult male. Also called *English sparrow.*

house·top (hous′tŏp′) *n.* The roof of a house. ***—idiom.*** **shout.** (or **proclaim) from the housetops.** To make known publicly.

house·train also **house-train** (hous′trān′) *tr.v.* **-trained, -train·ing, -trains.** *Chiefly British.* To housebreak (an animal, for example). **—house′trained′** *adj.*

house·wares (hous′wârz′) *pl.n.* Cooking utensils, dishes, and other small articles used in a household, especially in the kitchen.

house·warm·ing (hous′wôr′mĭng) *n.* A celebration of the occupancy of a new home. *—attributive.* Often used to modify another noun: *a housewarming present; a housewarming party.*

house·wife (hous′wīf′) *n., pl.* **-wives** (-wīvz′). **1.** A woman who manages her own household as her main occupation. **2.** (hŭz′ĭf). A small container for needles, thread, and other sewing equipment. [Middle English *houswif* : *house,* house; see HOUSE + *wife,* wife; see WIFE.]

house·wife·ly (hous′wīf′lē) *adj.* Of, relating to, or suited to a housewife; domestic. **—house′wife′li·ness** *n.*

house·wif·er·y (hous′wī′fə-rē, -wīf′rē) *n.* The function or duties of a housewife; housekeeping.

house·work (hous′wûrk′) *n.* The tasks, such as cleaning and cooking, performed in housekeeping. **—house′work′er** *n.*

hous·ing¹ (hou′zĭng) *n.* **1.a.** Buildings or other shelters in which people live: *a shortage of housing in the city.* **b.** A place to live; a dwelling: *She came to college early to look for housing.* **2.** Provision of lodging or shelter: *the housing of refugees; a contract that includes housing.* **3.** Something that covers, protects, or supports, especially: **a.** A frame, bracket, or box for holding or protecting a mechanical part: *a wheel housing.* **b.** An enclosing frame in which a shaft revolves. **4.** A hole, groove, or slot in a piece of wood into which another piece is inserted. **5.** A niche for a statue. **6.** *Nautical.* **a.** The part of a mast that is below deck. **b.** The part of a bowsprit that is inside the hull.

hous·ing² (hou′zĭng) *n.* **1.** An ornamental or protective covering for a saddle. **2.** Often **housings.** Trappings for a horse. [From Middle English *house,* from Old French *houce,* from Medieval Latin *hucia, hulcia, hultia,* protective covering, of Germanic origin. See **kel-¹** in Appendix.]

housing development *n.* A group of similarly designed houses or apartment buildings, usually under a single management.

housing project *n.* A publicly funded and administered housing development, usually for low-income families.

housing start *n.* **1.** The beginning of construction of a dwelling. **2. housing starts.** The number of new dwellings begun nationwide during a particular period, used as an economic indicator: *"Housing starts . . . are well above their recession lows"* (Paul A. Samuelson).

Hous·man (hous′mən), **Alfred Edward.** 1859–1936. British poet and scholar whose works appeared in *A Shropshire Lad* (1896) and *Last Poems* (1922).

Hous·ton (hyo͞o′stən). A city of southeast Texas northwest of Galveston. Founded in 1836 and named for Sam Houston, it is a major industrial, commercial, and financial hub, the center of the U.S. aerospace industry, and a deep-water port connected with Galveston Bay and the Gulf of Mexico by the **Houston Ship Channel.** Houston is also the largest city in Texas. Population, 1,595,138. **—Hous·to′ni·an** (hyo͞o-stō′nē-ən) *n.*

Houston, Samuel. 1793–1863. American general and politician who fought in the Texan struggle for independence from Mexico and became president of the Republic of Texas (1836–1838 and 1841–1844).

Sam Houston
c. 1845 daguerreotype

hove (hōv) *v. Nautical. —tr.* Past tense and past participle of **heave** (sense 4). *—intr.* Past tense and past participle of **heave** (sense 5).

hov·el (hŭv′əl, hŏv′-) *n.* **1.** A small, miserable dwelling. **2.** An open, low shed. [Middle English, hut.]

hov·er (hŭv′ər, hŏv′-) *intr.v.* **-ered, -er·ing, -ers. 1.** To remain floating, suspended, or fluttering in the air: *gulls hovering over the waves.* **2.** To remain or linger in or near a place: *hovering around the speaker's podium.* See Synonyms at **flutter. 3.** To remain in an uncertain state; waver: *hovered between anger and remorse.* **—hover** *n.* The act or state of hovering: *a helicopter in hover.* [Middle English *hoveren,* frequentative of *hoven.*] **—hov′er·er** *n.* **—hov′er·ing·ly** *adv.*

hov·er·craft (hŭv′ər-krăft′, hŏv′-) *n.* See **air-cushion vehicle.**

how (hou) *adv.* **1.** In what manner or way; by what means: *How does this machine work?* **2.** In what state or condition: *How is she today?* **3.** To what extent, amount, or degree: *How bad was it?* **4.** For what reason or purpose; why: *How is it that he left early?* **5.** With what meaning: *How should I take that remark?* **6.** By what name: *How is she called?* **7.** By what measure; in what units: *How do you sell this corn?* **8.** What. Usually used in requesting that something be said again: *How's that again?* **9.** Used as an intensive: *How we laughed!* **—how** *conj.* **1.** The manner or way in which: *forgot how it was done.* **2.** That. **3.** In whatever way or manner; however: *Cook it how you please.* **—how** *n.* A manner or method of doing something: *"The how of research is generated by the why of the world"* (Frederick Turner). ***—idioms.*** **and how.** *Informal.* Most certainly; you bet: *She's a good dancer, and how!* **how about.** What is your thought, feeling, or desire regarding: *How about a cup of tea? How about that storm last night?* **how about that.** *Informal.* Used rhetorically to express surprise or wonder at or approval for something. **how come.** *Informal.* How is it that; why: *How come you're so late?* **how so.** How is it so: *You say the answer is wrong. How so?* [Middle English *howe,* from Old English *hū.* See **kʷo-** in Appendix.]

How·ard (hou′ərd), **Catherine.** 1520?–1542. Queen of England as the fifth wife of Henry VIII (1540–1542). She was accused of adultery and subsequently executed.

Howard, Henry. First Earl of Surrey. 1517?–1547. English poet and soldier remembered for his sonnets and his translations of two books of Virgil's *Aeneid.* In 1547 he was falsely charged with treason and executed.

Howard, Roy Wilson. 1883–1964. American journalist and publisher. He was chairman of the board (1921–1936 and 1953–1964) and president (1936–1953) of the United Press Association.

Howard, Sidney Coe. 1891–1939. American playwright best known for his play *They Knew What They Wanted* (1924).

how·be·it (hou-bē′ĭt) *adv.* Be that as it may; nevertheless. **—howbeit** *conj. Obsolete.* Although.

howdah

how·dah also **hou·dah** (hou′də) *n.* A seat, usually fitted with a canopy and railing, placed on the back of an elephant or a camel. [Urdu *haudah,* from Arabic *hawdaj,* from *hadaja,* to shuffle along, totter.]

how·dy (hou′dē) *interj.* Used to express a greeting. [From *how do ye,* how do you do.]

Howe (hou), **Elias.** 1819–1867. American inventor and manufacturer who designed early sewing machines (1845 and 1846) and subsequently won patent-infringement suits against a number of manufacturers, including Isaac M. Singer.

Howe, Julia Ward. 1819–1910. American writer and feminist who was active in the women's suffrage movement. She wrote "Battle Hymn of the Republic" (published 1862).

Howe, Richard. Earl Howe. 1726–1799. British admiral who conducted naval operations in America (1776–1778) and defeated the French at Ushant (1794).

Howe, Sir **William.** Fifth Viscount Howe. 1729–1814. British general in America. Although he defeated George Washington in a number of battles, he could not force a surrender and returned to England in 1778.

How·ells (hou′əlz), **William Dean.** 1837–1920. American writer and editor in chief (1871–1881) of the *Atlantic Monthly.* He also wrote novels, such as *The Rise of Silas Lapham* (1885).

how·ev·er (hou-ev′ər) *adv.* **1.** In whatever manner or way: *However he did it, it was very clever.* **2.** To whatever degree or extent: *"have begun, however reluctantly, to acknowledge the legitimacy of some of the concerns"* (Christopher Lasch). **3.** In

ă pat	oi **boy**
ā pay	ou **out**
âr care	o͝o **took**
ä father	o͞o **boot**
ĕ pet	ŭ **cut**
ē be	ûr **urge**
ĭ pit	th **thin**
ī pie	*th* **this**
îr pier	hw **which**
ŏ pot	zh **vision**
ō toe	ə **about, item**
ô paw	♦ regionalism

Stress marks: ′ (primary); ′ (secondary), as in **dictionary** (dĭk′shə-nĕr′ē)

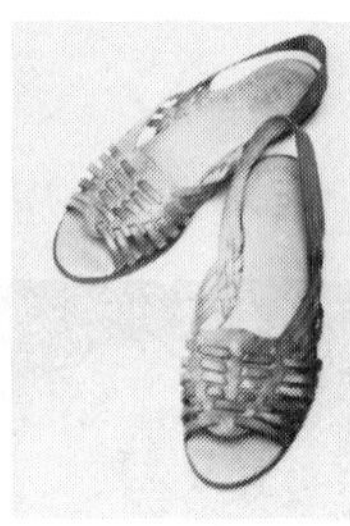
huarache

hubcap

Henry Hudson

ă pat | oi boy
ā pay | ou out
âr care | o͝o took
ä father | o͞o boot
ĕ pet | ŭ cut
ē be | ûr urge
ĭ pit | th thin
ī pie | *th* this
îr pier | hw which
ŏ pot | zh vision
ō toe | ə about, item
ô paw | ♦ regionalism

Stress marks: ʹ (primary); ʹ (secondary), as in **dictionary** (dĭkʹshə-nĕrʹē)

what way. Used as an intensive of *how: However did you get here so soon?* **4.** In spite of that; nevertheless; yet: *The book is expensive; however, it's worth it.* **5.** On the other hand; by contrast: *The first part was easy; the second, however, took hours.* **—however** *conj.* **1.** In whatever manner or way: *Dress however you like.* **2.** *Archaic.* Notwithstanding that; although.

USAGE NOTE: Although some grammarians have insisted that *however* should not be used to begin a sentence, this rule has been ignored by a number of reputable writers. See Usage Notes at **but, whatever.**

how·it·zer (houʹĭt-sər) *n.* A relatively short cannon that delivers shells at a medium muzzle velocity, usually by a high trajectory. [Dutch *houwitser,* from German *Haubitze,* alteration of obsolete *haufnitz,* catapult, from Old Czech *haufnice* : *hauf,* group, heap (of Germanic origin) + *-nice,* feminine n. suff.]

howl (houl) *v.* **howled, howl·ing, howls.** *—intr.* **1.** To utter or emit a long, mournful, plaintive sound. **2.** To cry or wail loudly, as in pain, sorrow, or anger. **3.** *Slang.* To laugh heartily. **4.** *Slang.* To go on a spree. *—tr.* To express or utter with a howl. See Synonyms at **shout. —howl** *n.* **1.** A long, wailing cry. **2.** *Slang.* Something uproariously funny or absurd. ***—phrasal verb.* howl down.** To drown out or silence by loud derisive calls: *The candidate was howled down at the town meeting.* [Middle English *houlen.*]

howl·er (houʹlər) *n.* **1.** One that howls: *a dog that turned out to be a persistent howler.* **2.** A howler monkey. **3.** *Slang.* A laughably stupid blunder.

howler monkey *n.* Any of several monkeys of the genus *Alouatta* of tropical America, having a long, prehensile tail and an extremely loud, howling call.

howl·ing (houʹlĭng) *adj.* **1.** Marked by the sound of howling: *a howling wind.* **2.** Desolate; dreary: *a howling wilderness.* **3.** *Slang.* Very great; tremendous: *a howling success.*

How·rah (houʹrə, -rä). A city of eastern India on the Hooghly River opposite Calcutta. It is a major industrial center. Population, 744,429.

how·so·ev·er (houʹsō-evʹər) *adv.* **1.** To whatever degree or extent. **2.** By whatever means.

how-to (houʹto͞oʹ) *Informal. adj.* Offering practical advice and detailed instruction in an activity. **—how-to** *n., pl.* **how-tos.** Something, such as a book or learning situation, that provides practical advice and detailed instruction in an activity: *She read a how-to on plumbing. The weekend was a real how-to for would-be campers.*

Hox·ie (hŏkʹsē), **Vinnie Ream.** 1847–1914. American sculptor known especially for her marble statue of Abraham Lincoln (unveiled 1871) in the rotunda of the Capitol in Washington, D.C.

hoy¹ (hoi) *n. Nautical.* **1.** A small sloop-rigged coasting ship. **2.** A heavy barge used for freight. [Middle English *hoie,* from Middle Dutch *hoey, hoede.*]

hoy² (hoi) *interj.* Used to attract attention.

hoy·a (hoiʹə) *n.* Any of several evergreen climbing vines or shrubs of the genus *Hoya,* with a home range from India and southern China to Australia and having opposite, simple leaves and axillary, umbellate flower clusters. Also called *porcelain flower, wax vine.* [New Latin *Hoya,* genus name, after Thomas *Hoy* (1750?–1822), British gardener.]

hoy·den (hoidʹn) *n.* A high-spirited, boisterous, or saucy girl. **—hoyden** *adj.* High-spirited; boisterous. [From earlier *hoyden,* a rude youth, probably from Dutch *heiden,* heathen, boor, from Middle Dutch. See **kaito-** in Appendix.] **—hoyʹden·ish** *adj.*

Hoyle (hoil) *n. Games.* A reference book of rules for card games and other indoor games. ***—idiom.* according to Hoyle.** In accord with the prescribed rules or regulations. [After Edmond *Hoyle* (1672?–1769), British writer on games.]

hp *abbr.* Horsepower.

HP *abbr.* High pressure.

HPF *abbr.* Highest possible frequency.

HQ or **h.q.** or **H.Q.** *abbr.* Headquarters.

hr *abbr.* Hour.

HR *abbr.* Heart rate.

Hr. *abbr.* Herr.

h.r. *abbr. Baseball.* Home run.

H.R. *abbr.* **1.** Home rule. **2.** House of Representatives.

Hra·dec Krá·lo·vé (räʹdĕts kräʹlə-və, -lô-vĕ, hräʹ-). A city of northern Czechoslovakia east of Prague. Founded in the tenth century, it was a leading town of Bohemia. Population, 98,476.

H.R.E. *abbr.* Holy Roman Empire.

H. Rept. *abbr.* House Report.

H. Res. *abbr.* House Resolution.

H.R.H. *abbr.* **1.** Her Royal Highness. **2.** His Royal Highness.

Hrolf (rŏlf, hrŏlf). See **Rollo.**

hrs *abbr.* Hours.

HS or **H.S.** *abbr.* High school.

HSGT *abbr.* High-speed ground transit.

H.S.H. *abbr.* **1.** Her Serene Highness. **2.** His Serene Highness.

Hsia (shyä). See **Xia.**

Hsian (shyän). See **Xi'an.**

Hsiang Kiang (shyängʹ kyängʹ). See **Xiang Jiang.**

Hsin·king (shĭnʹgĭngʹ). See **Changchun.**

HST *abbr.* **1.** Or **H.S.T.** Hawaiian Standard Time **2.** Hypersonic transport.

ht *abbr.* Height.

HT *abbr.* **1.** *Sports.* Halftime. **2.** Halftone. **3.** High-tension. **4.** High tide.

HTLV-I (āchʹtē-ĕlʹvē-wŭnʹ) *n.* A retrovirus that causes diseases similar to multiple sclerosis. [H(UMAN) T(-CELL) L(YMPHOTROPIC) V(IRUS) I.]

HTLV-III (āchʹtē-ĕlʹvē-thrēʹ) *n.* HIV. [H(UMAN) T(-CELL) L(YMPHOTROPIC) V(IRUS) III.]

Hts. *abbr.* Heights.

HUAC *abbr.* House Un-American Activities Committee.

Hua Guo·feng (hwäʹ gwôʹfŭngʹ) also **Hua Kuo·feng** (kwôʹfŭngʹ, gwôʹ-). Born 1920. Chinese prime minister (1976–1980). With Deng Xiaoping he initiated a program of modernization and increasing cooperation with the West.

Huai·nan (hwīʹnänʹ). A city of east-central China west-northwest of Nanjing. It grew after 1949 as the center of a coal-mining region. Population, 603,200.

Hua Kuo·feng (hwäʹ kwôʹfŭngʹ, gwôʹ-). See **Hua Guofeng.**

Hua·la·pai or **Wa·la·pai** (wäʹlə-pīʹ) *n.* **1.a.** A Native American people inhabiting northwest Arizona south of the Grand Canyon. **b.** A member of this people. **2.** The Yuman language of the Hualapai.

Hual·la·ga (wä-yäʹgä). A river rising in the Andes of west-central Peru and flowing about 1,126 km (700 mi) generally northward to the Marañón River.

Huang He (hwängʹ həʹ) also **Hwang Ho** (hōʹ) or **Yel·low River** (yĕlʹō). A river of northern China rising in the Kunlun Mountains and flowing about 4,827 km (3,000 mi) generally eastward to the Gulf of Bo Hai. It is named for the vast quantities of yellow silt it carries to its delta.

hua·ra·che (wə-räʹchē, hə-) *n.* A flat-heeled sandal with an upper of woven leather strips. [American Spanish, probably from Japanese *warachi,* straw sandal.]

Huás·car (wäsʹkärʹ). Died 1532. Incan chieftain who fought with his brother Atahualpa over the division of the empire. Atahualpa had Huascar assassinated after the Spanish conquest because he feared Huascar would return to power.

Huas·ca·rán (wäsʹkə-ränʹ, -kä-). An extinct volcano, 6,770.4 m (22,198 ft) high, in the Andes of west-central Peru.

hub (hŭb) *n.* **1.** The center part of a wheel, fan, or propeller. **2.** A center of activity or interest; a focal point. See Synonyms at **center.** [Probably alteration of HOB¹.]

hub·ba-hub·ba (hŭbʹə-hŭbʹə) *interj. Slang.* Used to express approval, pleasure, or excitement.

Hub·bard (hŭbʹərd), **Mount.** A peak, 4,559.8 m (14,950 ft) high, in the Coast Mountains of southeast Alaska.

♦ **hub·bard squash** (hŭbʹərd) *n. Northern & Western U.S.* See **winter squash.** [From the surname *Hubbard.*]

Hub·ble (hŭbʹəl), **Edwin Powell.** 1889–1953. American astronomer who discovered (1929) that the velocities of nebulae increase with distance.

hub·ble-bub·ble (hŭbʹəl-bŭbʹəl) *n.* **1.** An uproar; a hubbub. **2.** See **hookah.** [Reduplication and alteration of BUBBLE.]

Hub·ble's constant (hŭbʹəlz) *n.* A ratio expressing the rate of apparent expansion of the universe, equal to the velocity of which a typical galaxy is receding from Earth divided by its distance from Earth. [After Edwin Powell HUBBLE.]

hub·bub (hŭbʹŭbʹ) *n.* **1.** Loud noise; din. See Synonyms at **noise. 2.** Confusion; tumult. [Probably of Irish Gaelic origin; akin to Scottish Gaelic *ubub,* an interjection of aversion or contempt.]

WORD HISTORY: It has often been remarked that the Celtic inhabitants of Great Britain contributed very little to the stock of English words. Perhaps this should not be too surprising, given the difficult relations over the centuries between the people of Germanic stock and the people of Celtic stock in England and Ireland. It seems likely that a certain English contempt resides in the adoption of the word *hubbub* from a Celtic source, which is probably related to *ub ub ubub,* a Scots Gaelic interjection expressing contempt, or to *abu,* an ancient Irish war cry. In any case, *hubbub* was first recorded (1555) in the phrase *Irish hubbub* and meant "the confused shouting of a crowd." In addition to the senses it has developed, *hubbub* was again used, possibly in a non-flattering way, by the New England colonists as a term for a rambunctious game played by Native Americans.

hub·by (hŭbʹē) *n., pl.* **-bies.** *Informal.* A husband. [Alteration of HUSBAND.]

hub·cap (hŭbʹkăpʹ) *n.* A round covering over the hub of the wheel of a motor vehicle.

Hu·bei (ho͞oʹbāʹ, hüʹ-) also **Hu·pei** or **Hu·peh** (-pāʹ). A province of east-central China. It is a major agricultural region watered by the Chang Jiang (Yangtze River). Wuhan is the capital. Population, 49,310,000.

Hu·bel (hyo͞oʹbəl), **David.** Born 1926. American neurobiologist. He shared a 1981 Nobel Prize for studies on the organization and functioning of the brain.

Hu·ber Heights (hyo͞o′bər). A community of southwest Ohio, a suburb of Dayton. Population, 35,480.

Hu·bli-Dhar·war (ho͝ob′lē-där-wär′). A city of southwest India northwest of Bangalore. It was formed from two municipalities in 1961. Population, 527,108.

hu·bris (hyo͞o′brĭs) *n.* Overbearing pride or presumption; arrogance: *"There is no safety in unlimited technological hubris"* (McGeorge Bundy). [Greek, excessive pride, wanton violence. See **ud-** in Appendix.] **—hu·bris′tic** (-brĭs′tĭk) *adj.* **—hu·bris′ti·cal·ly** *adv.*

huck (hŭk) *n.* Huckaback.

huck·a·back (hŭk′ə-băk′) *n.* A coarse absorbent cotton or linen fabric used especially for toweling. [Origin unknown.]

huck·le·ber·ry (hŭk′əl-bĕr′ē) *n.* **1.** Any of various New World shrubs of the genus *Gaylussacia,* related to the blueberries and bearing edible fruit. **2.** The glossy, blackish, many-seeded berry of these plants. [Probably alteration of *hurtleberry,* whortleberry.]

huck·ster (hŭk′stər) *n.* **1.** One who sells wares or provisions in the street; a peddler or hawker. **2.** One who uses aggressive, showy, and sometimes devious methods to promote or sell a product. **3.** *Informal.* One who writes advertising copy, especially for radio or television. **—huckster** *v.* **-stered, -ster·ing, -sters.** *—tr.* **1.** To sell; peddle. **2.** To promote or attempt to sell (a commercial product, for example) in an overaggressive or showy manner. **3.** To haggle over; deal in. *—intr.* To engage in haggling. [Middle English, probably of Low German origin; akin to Middle Dutch *hokester.*] **—huck′ster·ism** *n.*

HUD *abbr.* Department of Housing and Urban Development.

Hud·ders·field (hŭd′ərz-fēld′). A borough of north-central England northeast of Manchester. First settled in Roman times, it is an industrial center specializing in textiles. Population, 125,800.

hud·dle (hŭd′l) *n.* **1.** A densely packed group or crowd, as of people or animals. **2.** *Football.* A brief gathering of a team's players behind the line of scrimmage to receive instructions for the next play. **3.** A small private conference or meeting. **—huddle** *v.* **-dled, -dling, -dles.** *—intr.* **1.** To crowd together, as from cold or fear. **2.** To draw or curl one's limbs close to one's body; crouch. **3.** *Football.* To gather in a huddle. **4.** *Informal.* To gather together for conference or consultation: *During the crisis the President's national security advisers huddled.* *—tr.* **1.** To cause to crowd together. **2.** To draw oneself together in a crouch. **3.** *Chiefly British.* To arrange, do, or make hastily or carelessly. [From *huddle,* to crowd together, possibly from Low German *hudeln.* See **(s)keu-** in Appendix.] **—hud′dler** *n.*

Hu·di·bras·tic (hyo͞o′də-brăs′tĭk) *adj.* Of or relating to a style of satirical or mock-heroic verse composed in rhymed iambic pentameter couplets. [After *Hudibras,* a satiric epic by Samuel Butler.]

Hud·son (hŭd′sən). A town of east-central Massachusetts northeast of Worcester. Population, 16,408.

Hudson, Henry. Died 1611. English navigator and explorer who discovered (1609) the Hudson River on an expedition for the East India Company.

Hudson, William Henry. 1841–1922. British naturalist and writer whose works include *Green Mansions* (1904).

Hudson Bay. An inland sea of east-central Canada connected to the Atlantic Ocean by **Hudson Strait,** lying between southern Baffin Island and northern Quebec. James Bay is the southern extension of Hudson Bay, which was explored and named by Henry Hudson in 1610.

Hudson River. A river rising in the Adirondack Mountains of northeast New York and flowing about 507 km (315 mi) generally southward to Upper New York Bay at New York City. Giovanni da Verrazano first sighted the river in 1524, but it was not explored until Henry Hudson's 1609 voyage.

Hudson seal *n.* Muskrat fur that is dyed, plucked, and sheared to resemble seal. [After HUDSON (BAY).]

hue (hyo͞o) *n.* **1.** The property of colors by which they can be perceived as ranging from red through yellow, green, and blue, as determined by the dominant wavelength of the light. **2.** A particular gradation of color; a shade or tint. **3.** Color: *all the hues of the rainbow.* **4.** Appearance; aspect: *a man of somber hue.* [Middle English, color, form, from Old English *hīw, hēo.*]

Hue (hyo͞o-ā′, hwā). A city of central Vietnam near the South China Sea northwest of Da Nang. An ancient Annamese city probably dating from the third century A.D., it was nearly destroyed during heavy fighting in the Vietnam War. Population, 165,865.

hue and cry *n.* **1.** A public clamor, as of protest or demand: *raised a great hue and cry about political corruption.* **2.a.** The pursuit of a felon announced with loud shouts to alert others who were then legally obliged to give chase. **b.** The loud outcry formerly used in such a pursuit. [Middle English *hew and cri,* from Anglo-Norman *hu e cri* : *hu,* outcry, clamor (from Old French *huer,* to shout, of imitative origin) + *cri,* cry (from Old French *crier,* to cry; see CRY).]

hued (hyo͞od) *adj.* Having a given hue, aspect, or character. Often used in combination: *rosy-hued; dark-hued.*

Huel·va (wĕl′və, -vä). A city of southwest Spain near the Gulf of Cádiz and the Portuguese border. Founded by Carthaginians, it was colonized by the Romans. Population, 137,453.

hue·vos ran·che·ros (wā′vōs răn-chĕr′ōs, hwā′-, rän-) *pl.n.* A Mexican dish consisting of fried or poached eggs covered with a spicy sauce of red or green tomatoes and usually served on a tortilla. [American Spanish : Spanish *huevos,* pl. of *huevo,* egg + American Spanish *rancheros,* pl. of *ranchero,* ranch-style.]

huff (hŭf) *n.* A fit of anger or annoyance; a pique: *stormed off in a huff.* **—huff** *v.* **huffed, huff·ing, huffs.** *—intr.* **1.** To puff; blow. **2.** To make noisy, empty threats; bluster. **3.** To react indignantly; take offense. *—tr.* **1.** To cause to puff up; inflate. **2.** To treat with insolence; bully. **3.** To anger; annoy. [Imitative of the sound of puffing.]

huff·ish (hŭf′ĭsh) *adj.* **1.** Peevish; sulky. **2.** Arrogant; insolent. **—huff′ish·ly** *adv.* **—huff′ish·ness** *n.*

huff·y (hŭf′ē) *adj.* **-i·er, -i·est.** **1.** Easily offended; touchy. **2.** Irritated or annoyed; indignant. **3.** Arrogant; haughty. **—huff′i·ly** *adv.* **—huff′i·ness** *n.*

hug (hŭg) *v.* **hugged, hug·ging, hugs.** *—tr.* **1.** To clasp or hold closely, especially in the arms, as in affection; embrace. **2.** To hold steadfastly to; cherish: *He still hugs his outmoded beliefs.* **3.** To stay close to: *a sailboat hugging the shore.* *—intr.* To embrace or cling together closely. **—hug** *n.* **1.** A close, affectionate embrace. **2.** A crushing embrace, as in wrestling. [Probably of Scandinavian origin; akin to Old Norse *hugga,* to comfort.] **—hug′ga·ble** *adj.* **—hug′ger** *n.*

Langston Hughes
Photographed in 1932 by Edward Weston

huge (hyo͞oj) *adj.* **hug·er, hug·est.** **1.** Of exceedingly great size, extent, or quantity; tremendous. See Synonyms at **enormous.** **2.** Of exceedingly great scope or nature: *the huge influence of the Hellenic world.* [Middle English, from Old French *ahuge.*] **—huge′ly** *adv.* **—huge′ness** *n.*

huge·ous (hyo͞o′jəs) *adj.* Huge. **—huge′ous·ly** *adv.* **—huge′ous·ness** *n.*

hug·ger-mug·ger or **hug·ger-mug·ger** (hŭg′ər-mŭg′ər) *—n.* **1.** Disorderly confusion; muddle. **2.** Secrecy; concealment. *—adj.* **1.** Disorderly; jumbled. **2.** Secret; clandestine. *—v.* **-gered, -ger·ing, -gers.** *—tr.* To keep secret; conceal. *—intr.* To act in a secretive manner. [Origin unknown.] **—hug′ger·mug′ger** *adv.* **—hug′ger·mug′ger·y** *n.*

Hugh Ca·pet (hyo͞o′ kā′pĭt, kăp′ĭt, kă-pā′). See **Capet.**

Hughes (hyo͞oz), **Charles Evans.** 1862–1948. American jurist and politician who was appointed an associate justice of the U.S. Supreme Court (1910) but resigned to make an unsuccessful bid for the presidency (1916). He later served as the chief justice of the Supreme Court (1930–1941).

Hughes, Howard Robard. 1905–1976. American film producer, aviator, and multimillionaire. He founded Hughes Aircraft Corporation, broke the airplane speed record (1935), and flew around the world in record time (1938).

Hughes, (James) Langston. 1902–1967. American writer. Through his poetry, prose, and drama he made important contributions to the Harlem Renaissance.

Hughes, Ted. Full name Edward James Hughes. Born 1930. British poet who was appointed poet laureate in 1984. His work is noted for its violence, passion, and natural imagery.

huipil
Made by the Cakchiquel people of south-central Guatemala

Hu·go (hyo͞o′gō, ü-gō′), **Victor Marie.** 1802–1885. French writer who went into exile after Napoleon III seized power (1851), returning to France in 1870. His novels include *The Hunchback of Notre Dame* (1831) and *Les Misérables* (1862).

Hu·gue·not (hyo͞o′gə-nŏt′) *n.* A French Protestant of the 16th and 17th centuries. [French, from Old French *huguenot,* member of a Swiss political movement, alteration (influenced by Bezanson *Hugues* (1491?–1532?), Swiss political leader) of dialectal *eyguenot,* from German dialectal *Eidgenosse,* confederate, from Middle High German *eitgenōz* : *eit,* oath (from Old High German *eid*) + *genōz,* companion (from Old High German *ginōz*).] **—Hu′gue·not′ic** *adj.* **—Hu′gue·not′ism** *n.*

huh (hŭ) *interj.* Used to express interrogation, surprise, contempt, or indifference.

Hu·he·hot (ho͞o′hā-hōt′). See **Hohhot.**

Hui (hwē) also **Hwei** (hwā) *n., pl.* **Hui** or **Huis** also **Hwei** or **Hweis.** A member of a Moslem people of northwest China, descended chiefly from the Han and an important minority of the Chinese population; a Chinese Moslem.

hui·pil (wē-pēl′) *n.* A loose, brocaded blouse worn by Maya women in Mexico and Central America. [American Spanish, from Nahuatl *huipilli.*]

Hui·zing·a (hī′zĭng-ə, hoi′zĭng-ä), **Johan.** 1872–1945. Dutch historian known for his writing on the late Middle Ages.

hu·la (ho͞o′lə) also **hu·la-hu·la** (ho͞o′lə-ho͞o′lə) *n.* A Polynesian dance characterized by undulating hips, miming movements of the arms and hands, and usually accompanied by rhythmic drumbeats and chants. [Hawaiian.]

hula

Hu·la-Hoop (ho͞o′lə-ho͞op′). A trademark used for a light plastic hoop that is whirled around the body for play or exercise by the movement of the hips. This trademark, which often occurs in print without a hyphen and in lowercase, also occurs in figurative extensions: *"His eyes swell to the size of hula hoops"* (Los Angeles Times). *"Clearly some of the current campaigning against South Africa is a fad, a moral Hula Hoop"* (George F. Will).

hu·la-hu·la (ho͞o′lə-ho͞o′lə) *n.* Variant of **hula.**

hulk (hŭlk) *n.* **1.** *Nautical.* **a.** A heavy, unwieldy ship. **b.** The hull of an old, unseaworthy, or wrecked ship. **c.** Often **hulks.** An old or unseaworthy ship used as a prison or warehouse. **2.** One, such as a person or an object, that is bulky, clumsy, or unwieldy. **—hulk** *intr.v.* **hulked, hulk·ing, hulks.** **1.** To appear as a massive or towering form; loom: *The big truck hulked out of the fog.*

2. To move clumsily. [Middle English, from Old English *hulc,* from Medieval Latin *hulcus,* probably from Greek *holkas,* merchant ship, ship that is towed, from *helkein,* to pull.]

hulk·ing (hŭl′kĭng) also **hulk·y** (hŭl′kē) *adj.* Unwieldy or bulky; massive.

hull (hŭl) *n.* **1.a.** The dry outer covering of a fruit, seed, or nut; a husk. **b.** The enlarged calyx of a fruit, such as a strawberry, that is usually green and easily detached. **2.a.** *Nautical.* The frame or body of a ship, exclusive of masts, engines, or superstructure. **b.** The main body of various other large vehicles, such as a tank, an airship, or a flying boat. **3.** The outer casing of a rocket, guided missile, or spaceship. **—hull** *tr.v.* **hulled, hull·ing, hulls.** To remove the hulls of (fruit or seeds). [Middle English *hulle,* husk, from Old English *hulu.* See **kel-**[1] in Appendix.]

Hull (hŭl). **1.** A city of southwest Quebec, Canada, opposite Ottawa, Ontario. It has a hydroelectric station and pulp, paper, and lumber mills. Population, 56,225. **2.** Also **King·ston-up·on-Hull** (kĭng′stən-ə-pŏn-hŭl′, -pôn-). A borough of northeast-central England on the northern shore of the Humber estuary at the influx of the **Hull River.** Chartered in 1299, the city has been a major seaport since the late 1700's. Population, 272,500.

Hull, Cordell. 1871–1955. American public official who as secretary of state (1933–1944) laid the groundwork for the founding of the United Nations.

Hull, Isaac. 1773–1843. American naval officer who commanded the *Constitution* during the War of 1812.

hul·la·ba·loo also **hul·la·bal·loo** (hŭl′ə-bə-lo͞o′) *n., pl.* **-loos.** Great noise or excitement; uproar. See Synonyms at **noise.** [Alteration of obsolete *hollo-ballo,* probably from *holla,* hello. See HELLO.]

hul·lo (hə-lō′) *interj., n., & v.* Variant of **hello.**

hum (hŭm) *v.* **hummed, hum·ming, hums.** —*intr.* **1.a.** To emit a continuous low droning sound like that of the speech sound (m) when prolonged. **b.** To emit the continuous droning sound of a bee on the wing; buzz. **c.** To give forth a low, continuous drone blended of many sounds: *The avenue hummed with traffic.* **2.** To be in a state of busy activity. **3.** To produce a tune without opening the lips or forming words. —*tr.* To sing (a tune) without opening the lips. **—hum** *n.* **1.** The sound produced by humming. **2.** The act of humming. **—hum** *interj.* Used to indicate hesitation, surprise, or displeasure. [Middle English *hummen,* of imitative origin.] **—hum′ma·ble** *adj.* **—hum′mer** *n.*

hu·man (hyo͞o′mən) *adj.* **1.** Of, relating to, or characteristic of human beings: *the course of human events; the human race.* **2.** Having or showing those positive aspects of nature and character that distinguish human beings from the lower animals: *an act of human kindness.* **3.** Subject to or indicative of the weaknesses, imperfections, and fragility associated with human beings: *a mistake that shows he's only human; human frailty.* **4.** Having the form of a human being. **5.** Made up of human beings: *formed a human bridge across the ice.* **—human** *n.* A human being; a person. [Middle English *humain,* from Old French, from Latin *hūmānus.* See **dhghem-** in Appendix.] **—hu′man·hood′** *n.* **—hu′man·ness** *n.*

human being *n.* **1.** A member of the genus *Homo* and especially of the species *H. sapiens.* **2.** A person: *a fine human being.*

human chorionic gonadotropin *n. Abbr.* **HCG** A hormone produced by the placenta that maintains the corpus luteum during pregnancy.

hu·mane (hyo͞o-mān′) *adj.* **1.** Characterized by kindness, mercy, or compassion: *a humane judge.* **2.** Marked by an emphasis on humanistic values and concerns: *a humane education.* [Middle English *humain,* human. See HUMAN.] **—hu·mane′ly** *adv.* **—hu·mane′ness** *n.*

SYNONYMS: *humane, compassionate, humanitarian, merciful.* The central meaning shared by these adjectives is "marked or motivated by concern with the alleviation of suffering": *a humane physician; compassionate toward disadvantaged people; released the prisoner for humanitarian reasons; is merciful to the repentant.*
ANTONYM: *inhumane.*

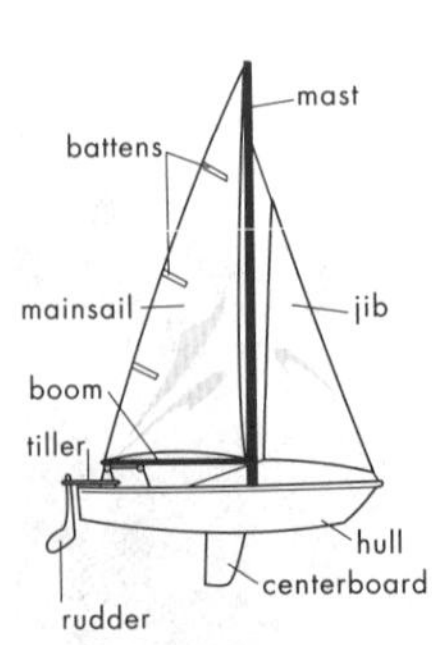

hull
Bermuda-rigged sloop

human ecology *n.* See **ecology** (senses 2, 3).

human engineering *n.* See **ergonomics** (sense 1).

human factors engineering *n.* See **ergonomics** (sense 1).

human im·mu·no·de·fi·cien·cy virus (ĭm′yə-nō-dĭ-fĭsh′-ən-sē) *n.* HIV.

hu·man-in·ter·est (hyo͞o′mən-ĭn′trĭst, -tər-ĭst, -trĕst′) *adj.* Treating people and their problems, concerns, or achievements in such a way as to arouse the interest or sympathy of the reader or viewer: *a human-interest story.*

hu·man·ism (hyo͞o′mə-nĭz′əm) *n.* **1.** A system of thought that centers on human beings and their values, capacities, and worth. **2.** Concern with the interests, needs, and welfare of human beings: *"the newest flower on the vine of corporate humanism"* (Savvy). **3.** The study of the humanities; learning in the liberal arts. **4. Humanism.** A cultural and intellectual movement of the Renaissance that emphasized secular concerns as a result of the rediscovery and study of the literature, art, and civilization of ancient Greece and Rome.

hu·man·ist (hyo͞o′mə-nĭst) *n.* **1.** A believer in the principles of humanism. **2.** One who is concerned with the interests and welfare of human beings. **3.a.** A classical scholar. **b.** A student of the liberal arts. **4. Humanist.** A Renaissance scholar devoted to Humanism. **—hu′man·is′tic** *adj.*

hu·man·i·tar·i·an (hyo͞o-măn′ĭ-târ′ē-ən) *n.* One who is devoted to the promotion of human welfare and the advancement of social reforms; a philanthropist. **—humanitarian** *adj.* Of, relating to, or characteristic of a humanitarian or humanitarianism. See Synonyms at **humane.**

hu·man·i·tar·i·an·ism (hyo͞o-măn′ĭ-târ′ē-ə-nĭz′əm) *n.* **1.** Concern for human welfare, especially as manifested through philanthropy. **2.** The belief that the sole moral obligation of humankind is the improvement of human welfare. **3.** *Theology.* The doctrine holding that Jesus was human only and not divine.

hu·man·i·ty (hyo͞o-măn′ĭ-tē) *n., pl.* **-ties. 1.** Human beings considered as a group; the human race. **2.** The condition or quality of being human; humanness. **3.** The quality of being humane; benevolence. **4.** A humane characteristic, attribute, or act. **5. humanities. a.** The languages and literatures of ancient Greece and Rome; the classics. **b.** Those branches of knowledge, such as philosophy, literature, and art, that are concerned with human thought and culture; the liberal arts. [Middle English *humanite,* from Old French, from Latin *hūmānitās,* from *hūmānus,* human. See HUMAN.]

hu·man·ize (hyo͞o′mə-nīz′) *tr.v.* **-ized, -iz·ing, -iz·es. 1.** To portray or endow with human characteristics or attributes; make human: *humanized the puppets with great skill.* **2.** To imbue with humaneness or human kindness; civilize: *acts of courtesy that humanize life in a big city.* **—hu′man·i·za′tion** (-mə-nĭ-zā′shən) *n.* **—hu′man·iz′er** *n.*

hu·man·kind (hyo͞o′mən-kīnd′) *n.* The human race: *"humankind's God-given creativity"* (New York Times).

hu·man·ly (hyo͞o′mən-lē) *adv.* **1.** In a human way. **2.** Within the scope of human means, capabilities, or powers: *not humanly possible.* **3.** According to human experience or knowledge: *Humanly speaking, the recession was not severe.*

human nature *n.* The sum of qualities and traits shared by all human beings.

hu·man·oid (hyo͞o′mə-noid′) *adj.* Having human characteristics or form. **—humanoid** *n.* **1.** A being having human form: *"humanoids from some far-flung planet"* (Robert Brustein). **2.** See **android.**

human resources *pl.n.* **1.** *(used with a pl. verb).* The persons employed in a business or an organization; personnel. **2.** *(used with a sing. verb).* The field of personnel recruitment and management.

human rights *pl.n.* The basic rights and freedoms to which all human beings are entitled, often held to include the right to life and liberty, freedom of thought and expression, and equality before the law.

human T-cell lymphotropic virus I *n.* HTLV-I.

human T-cell lymphotropic virus III *n.* HTLV-III.

Hum·ber (hŭm′bər). An estuary of the Trent and Ouse rivers in northeast-central England.

hum·ble (hŭm′bəl) *adj.* **-bler, -blest. 1.** Marked by meekness or modesty in behavior, attitude, or spirit; not arrogant or prideful. **2.** Showing deferential or submissive respect: *a humble apology.* **3.** Low in rank, quality, or station; unpretentious or lowly: *a humble cottage.* **—humble** *tr.v.* **-bled, -bling, -bles. 1.** To curtail or destroy the pride of; humiliate. **2.** To cause to be meek or modest in spirit. **3.** To give a lower condition or station to; abase. See Synonyms at **degrade.** [Middle English, from Old French, from Latin *humilis,* low, lowly, from *humus,* ground. See **dhghem-** in Appendix.] **—hum′ble·ness** *n.* **—hum′bler** *n.* **—hum′bly** *adv.*

hum·ble·bee (hŭm′bəl-bē′) *n.* See **bumblebee.** [Middle English *humbulbe* : possibly Middle Dutch *hummel* + Middle English *be, bee,* bee; see BEE[1].]

humble pie *n.* A pie formerly made from the edible organs of a deer or hog. —***idiom.* eat humble pie.** To be forced to apologize abjectly or admit one's faults in humiliating circumstances. [Alteration (influenced by HUMBLE) of obsolete *umble pie* : Middle English *umbles,* edible animal organs (variant of *numbles,* from Norman French *nombles,* from Old French, loin of veal, probably from alteration of Latin *lumbulus,* diminutive of *lumbus,* loin) + PIE[1].]

Hum·boldt (hŭm′bōlt′, ho͝om′bôlt′), Baron **(Friedrich Heinrich) Alexander von.** 1769–1859. German naturalist and writer. His expedition to South America, Cuba, and Mexico (1799–1804) advanced the science of ecology.

Humboldt, Baron **(Karl) Wilhelm von.** 1767–1835. German philologist and diplomat known for exploring the relationship between language and culture.

Hum·boldt Bay (hŭm′bōlt′). A sheltered inlet of the Pacific Ocean in northwest California.

Humboldt Current *n.* A cold ocean current of the South Pacific, flowing north along the western coast of South America. Also called *Peru Current.* [After Baron Friedrich Heinrich Alexander von HUMBOLDT.]

Humboldt Peak. A mountain, 4,289.5 m (14,064 ft) high, in the Sangre de Cristo Mountains of south-central Colorado.

Humboldt River. A river rising in the mountains of northeast Nevada and meandering about 467 km (290 mi) generally west and southwest to the **Humboldt Sink,** a lake in western Nevada.

hum·bug (hŭm′bŭg′) *n.* **1.** Something intended to deceive; a hoax or fraud. **2.** A person who claims to be other than what he or she is; an impostor. See Synonyms at **impostor. 3.** Nonsense; rubbish. **4.** Pretense; deception. **—humbug** *interj.* Used to express disbelief or disgust. **—humbug** *v.* **-bugged, -bug·ging, -bugs.** —*tr.* To deceive or trick. —*intr.* To practice deception or trickery. [Origin unknown.] **—hum′bug′ger** *n.* **—hum′bug′-ger·y** *n.*

hum·ding·er (hŭm′dĭng′ər) *n. Slang.* One that is extraordinary or remarkable: *a humdinger of a blizzard.* [Origin unknown.]

hum·drum (hŭm′drŭm′) *adj.* Lacking variety or excitement; dull. See Synonyms at **boring, dull. —humdrum** *n.* Monotonous talk or routine. [Probably from HUM.]

Hume (hyo͞om), **David.** 1711–1776. British philosopher and historian who argued that human knowledge arises only from sense experience.

hu·mec·tant (hyo͞o-mĕk′tənt) *n.* A substance that promotes retention of moisture. **—humectant** *adj.* Promoting retention of moisture. [From Latin *hūmectāns, hūmectant-,* present participle of *hūmectāre,* to moisten, from *hūmectus,* moist, from *hūmēre,* to be moist.]

hu·mer·al (hyo͞o′mər-əl) *adj.* **1.** Of, relating to, or located in the region of the humerus or the shoulder. **2.** Relating to or being a body part analogous to the humerus.

humeral veil *n. Roman Catholic Church.* A vestment resembling a shawl worn over the shoulders by a subdeacon during High Mass and by a priest when holding the monstrance.

hu·mer·us (hyo͞o′mər-əs) *n., pl.* **-mer·i** (-mə-rī′). The long bone of the arm or forelimb, extending from the shoulder to the elbow. [Latin, upper arm.]

hu·mic (hyo͞o′mĭk) *adj.* Of, relating to, or derived from humus.

hu·mid (hyo͞o′mĭd) *adj.* Containing or characterized by a high amount of water or water vapor: *humid air; a humid evening.* See Synonyms at **wet.** [Latin *hūmidus,* from *hūmēre,* to be moist.] **—hu′mid·ly** *adv.*

hu·mid·i·fi·er (hyo͞o-mĭd′ə-fī′ər) *n.* A device for increasing the humidity in a room, greenhouse, or other enclosure.

hu·mid·i·fy (hyo͞o-mĭd′ə-fī′) *tr.v.* **-fied, -fy·ing, -fies.** To make humid. **—hu·mid′i·fi·ca′tion** (-fĭ-kā′shən) *n.*

hu·mid·i·stat (hyo͞o-mĭd′ĭ-stăt′) *n.* An instrument designed to indicate or control the relative humidity of the air. Also called *hygrostat.*

hu·mid·i·ty (hyo͞o-mĭd′ĭ-tē) *n. Abbr.* **H 1.** Dampness, especially of the air. **2.** Relative humidity. [Middle English *humidite,* from Old French, from Medieval Latin *hūmiditās,* from Latin *hūmidus,* humid. See HUMID.]

hu·mi·dor (hyo͞o′mĭ-dôr′) *n.* A container designed for storing cigars or other tobacco products at a constant level of humidity. [HUMID + –OR[1].]

hu·mil·i·ate (hyo͞o-mĭl′ē-āt′) *tr.v.* **-at·ed, -at·ing, -ates.** To lower the pride, dignity, or self-respect of. See Synonyms at **degrade.** [Late Latin *humiliāre, humiliāt-,* to humble, from *humilis,* humble. See HUMBLE.]

hu·mil·i·a·tion (hyo͞o-mĭl′ē-ā′shən) *n.* **1.** The act of humiliating; degradation. **2.** The state of being humiliated or disgraced; shame. **3.** A humiliating condition or circumstance.

hu·mil·i·ty (hyo͞o-mĭl′ĭ-tē) *n.* The quality or condition of being humble. [Middle English *humilite,* from Old French, from Late Latin *humilitās,* from *humilis,* humble. See HUMBLE.]

hum·ming·bird (hŭm′ĭng-bûrd′) *n.* Any of numerous New World birds of the family Trochilidae, usually very small in size and having brilliant, iridescent plumage, a long slender bill, and wings capable of beating very rapidly, thereby enabling the bird to hover.

hum·mock (hŭm′ək) *n.* **1.** A low mound or ridge of earth; a knoll. **2.** Also **ham·mock** (hăm′ək). A tract of forested land that rises above an adjacent marsh in the southern United States. **3.** A ridge or hill of ice in an ice field. [Origin unknown.] **—hum′mock·y** *adj.*

hum·mus also **hum·us** or **hom·mos** (ho͝om′əs, hŭm′-) *n.* A smooth, thick mixture of mashed chickpeas, tahini, oil, lemon juice, and garlic, used especially as a dip for pita. [Arabic *hummus,* chickpea.]

hu·mon·gous (hyo͞o-mŏng′gəs, -mŭng′-) or **hu·mun·gous** (-mŭng′-) *adj. Slang.* Extremely large; enormous: *"humongous baked potatoes piled high with sour cream"* (Boston Globe). [Perhaps blend of HUGE and MONSTROUS or TREMENDOUS.]

hu·mor (hyo͞o′mər) *n.* **1.** The quality that makes something laughable or amusing; funniness: *could not see the humor of the situation.* **2.** That which is intended to induce laughter or amusement: *a writer skilled at crafting humor.* **3.** The ability to perceive, enjoy, or express what is amusing, comical, incongruous, or absurd. See Synonyms at **wit[1]. 4.** One of the four fluids of the body, blood, phlegm, choler, and black bile, whose relative proportions were thought in ancient physiology to determine a person's disposition and general health. **5.** *Physiology.* **a.** A body fluid, such as blood, lymph, or bile. **b.** Aqueous humor. **c.** Vitreous humor. **6.** A person's characteristic disposition or temperament: *a boy of sullen humor.* **7.** An often temporary state of mind; a mood: *I'm in no humor to argue.* **8. a.** A sudden, unanticipated whim. See Synonyms at **mood[1]. b.** Capricious or peculiar behavior. **—humor** *tr.v.* **-mored, -mor·ing, -mors. 1.** To comply with the wishes or ideas of; indulge. **2.** To adapt or accommodate oneself to. See Synonyms at **pamper.** —*idiom.* **out of humor.** In a bad mood; irritable. [Middle English, fluid, from Old French *umor,* from Latin *ūmor.*]

hu·mor·al (hyo͞o′mər-əl) *adj.* **1.** *Physiology.* Relating to bodily fluids, especially serum. **2.** Relating to or arising from any of the bodily humors.

humoral immunity *n.* The component of the immune response involving the transformation of B-lymphocytes into plasma cells that produce and secrete antibodies to a specific antigen.

hu·mor·esque (hyo͞o′mə-rĕsk′) *n. Music.* A whimsical or light-spirited composition. [German *Humoreske,* from *Humor,* humor, from English HUMOR.]

hu·mor·ist (hyo͞o′mər-ĭst) *n.* **1.** A person with a good sense of humor. **2.** A performer or writer of humorous material.

hu·mor·less (hyo͞o′mər-lĭs) *adj.* **1.** Lacking a sense of humor. **2.** Said or done without humor: *"She winked at me, but it was humorless; a wink of warning"* (Truman Capote). **—hu′mor·less·ly** *adv.* **—hu′mor·less·ness** *n.*

hu·mor·ous (hyo͞o′mər-əs) *adj.* **1.** Full of or characterized by humor; funny: *a humorous story.* **2.** Employing or showing humor; witty: *a humorous writer.* **3.** *Archaic.* Given to moods or whims; capricious. **4.** *Obsolete.* Damp; moist. **—hu′mor·ous·ly** *adv.* **—hu′mor·ous·ness** *n.*

hu·mour (hyo͞o′mər) *n. & v. Chiefly British.* Variant of **humor.**

hump (hŭmp) *n.* **1.** A rounded mass or protuberance, such as the fleshy structure on the back of a camel or of some cattle. **2.** A deformity of the back in human beings caused by an abnormal convex curvature of the upper spine. **3. a.** A low mound of earth; a hummock. **b.** A mountain range. **4.** *Chiefly British.* A fit of depression; an emotional slump. **—hump** *v.* **humped, hump·ing, humps.** —*tr.* **1.** To bend or round into a hump; arch. **2.** *Slang.* **a.** To exert (oneself). **b.** To carry, especially on the back. **3.** *Vulgar Slang.* To engage in sexual intercourse with. —*intr.* **1.** *Slang.* To exert oneself. **2.** *Slang.* To hurry. **3.** *Vulgar Slang.* To engage in sexual intercourse. —*idiom.* **over the hump.** Past the worst or most difficult part or stage: *At last I'm over the hump on my term paper.* [Probably of Low German origin.] **—humped** (hŭmpt) *adj.*

hump·back (hŭmp′băk′) *n.* **1.** See **hunchback** (sense 1). **2.** A humped upper back. **3.** A humpback whale. **—hump′-backed′** *adj.*

humpback salmon *n.* See **pink salmon.**

humpback whale *n.* A baleen whale *(Megaptera novaengliae)* having a rounded back and long, knobby flippers. Humpback whales communicate using complex, distinctive songs that identify individuals and play an important role in mating.

Hum·per·dinck (ho͝om′pər-dĭngk′, hŭm′-), **Engelbert.** 1854–1921. German composer who wrote the fairy tale opera *Hansel and Gretel* (1893).

humph (hŭmf, həmf) *interj.* Used to express doubt, displeasure, or contempt.

Hum·phrey (hŭm′frē, hŭmp′-), Duke of Gloucester and Earl of Pembroke. 1391–1447. English prince and book collector who was arrested for high treason (1447) and died in prison.

Humphrey, Hubert Horatio. 1911–1978. Vice President of the United States (1965–1969) under Lyndon Johnson. He ran unsuccessfully for the presidency in 1968.

Hum·phreys Peak (hŭm′frēz′, hŭmp′-). A mountain, 3,853.1 m (12,633 ft) high, in the San Francisco Peaks of north-central Arizona. It is the highest point in the state.

hump·y (hŭm′pē) *adj.* **-i·er, -i·est. 1.** Covered with or containing humps. **2.** Resembling a hump.

hu·mun·gous (hyo͞o-mŭng′gəs) *adj. Slang.* Variant of **humongous.**

hu·mus[1] (hyo͞o′məs) *n.* A brown or black organic substance consisting of partially or wholly decayed vegetable or animal matter that provides nutrients for plants and increases the ability of soil to retain water. [Latin, soil. See **dhghem-** in Appendix.]

hum·us[2] (ho͝om′əs, hŭm′-) *n.* Variant of **hummus.**

Hun (hŭn) *n.* **1.** A member of a nomadic pastoralist people who invaded Europe in the fourth and fifth centuries A.D. and were defeated in 455. **2.** Often **hun.** A barbarous or destructive person. **3.** *Offensive Slang.* Used as a disparaging term for a German, especially a German soldier in World War I. [From Late Latin *Hunnī,* the Huns, from Turki *Hunyü.*]

Hu·nan (ho͞o′nän′). A province of southeast-central China. Under Chinese rule since the third century B.C., the province is noted for its timber and mineral resources. Changsha is the capital. Population, 56,220,000.

hunch (hŭnch) *n.* **1.** An intuitive feeling or a premonition: *had a hunch that he would lose.* **2.** A hump. **3.** A lump or chunk. **—hunch** *v.* **hunched, hunch·ing, hunch·es.** —*tr.* **1.** To bend or draw up into a hump: *I hunched my shoulders against the wind.* **2.** To push or shove. —*intr.* **1.** To assume a crouched or cramped posture: *The cat hunched in a corner.* **2.** To thrust oneself forward. [Origin unknown.]

hunch·back (hŭnch′băk′) *n.* **1.** An individual whose back is hunched due to abnormal convex curvature of the upper spine. Also called *crookback, humpback.* **2.** An abnormally curved or hunched back. **3.** Kyphosis. **—hunch′backed′** *adj.*

hun·dred (hŭn′drĭd) *n., pl.* **hundred** or **-dreds.** *Abbr.* **h., H. 1.** The cardinal number equal to 10 × 10 or 10^2. **2.** The number

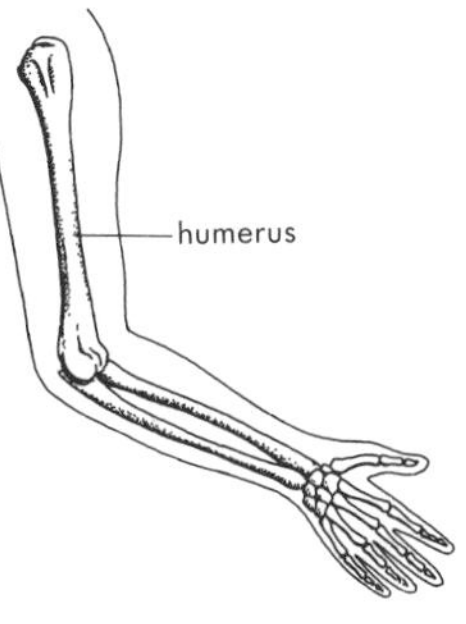

humerus

hummingbird

ă pat	oi boy
ā pay	ou out
âr care	o͝o took
ä father	o͞o boot
ĕ pet	ŭ cut
ē be	ûr urge
ĭ pit	th thin
ī pie	*th* this
îr pier	hw which
ŏ pot	zh vision
ō toe	ə about, item
ô paw	♦ regionalism

Stress marks: ′ (primary); ′ (secondary), as in **dictionary** (dĭk′shə-nĕr′ē)

Hungary

hurdle
Edwin Moses of the United States (#1114) and Allan Ince of Barbados (#77) at the Seoul Summer Olympics, 1988

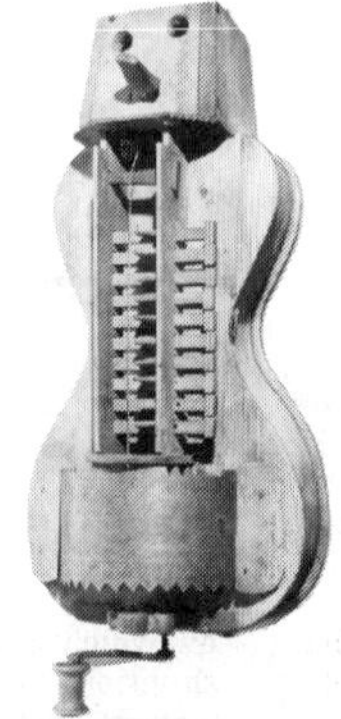
hurdy-gurdy
Early 19th-century American from northern Maine or eastern Canada

in the third position left of the decimal point in an Arabic numeral. **3.** A note of currency worth 100 dollars. **4. hundreds.** The numbers between 100 and 999: *an attendance figure estimated in the hundreds.* **5.** An administrative division of some counties in England and the United States. [Middle English, from Old English. See **dekm̥** in Appendix.] **—hun′dred** *adj.*

hun·dredth (hŭn′drĭdth) *n.* **1.** The ordinal number matching the number 100 in a series. **2.** One of 100 equal parts. **—hun′dredth** *adj.*

hun·dred·weight (hŭn′drĭd-wāt′) *n., pl.* **hundredweight** or **-weights.** *Abbr.* **cwt., cwt** **1.** A unit of weight in the U.S. Customary System equal to 100 pounds (45.36 kilograms). Also called *cental, short hundredweight.* **2.** A unit of weight in the British Imperial System equal to 112 pounds (50.80 kilograms). Also called *quintal.*

hung (hŭng) *v.* Past tense and a past participle of **hang.** See Usage Note at **hang.**

Hung. *abbr.* Hungarian; Hungary.

Hun·gar·i·an (hŭng-gâr′ē-ən) *adj. Abbr.* **Hung.** Of or relating to Hungary or its people, language, or culture. **—Hungarian** *n.* **1.** A native or inhabitant of Hungary. **2.** The Finno-Ugric language of the Magyars that is the official language of Hungary. In this sense, also called *Magyar.*

Hun·ga·ry (hŭng′gə-rē). *Abbr.* **Hung.** A country of central Europe. Hungary became an independent kingdom under Saint Stephen (ruled 997?–1038). It passed to the Turks after 1526 and was later divided between the Ottoman Empire and Austria, subsequently becoming part of the dual monarchy of Austria-Hungary from 1867 until 1918, when it achieved independence again. A Communist regime was established in 1949 and with the aid of the U.S.S.R. suppressed a counterrevolutionary uprising in 1956. A new constitution, guaranteeing free multiparty elections, was adopted in 1989. Budapest is the capital and the largest city. Population, 10,657,000.

hun·ger (hŭng′gər) *n.* **1.a.** A strong desire or need for food. **b.** The discomfort, weakness, or pain caused by a prolonged lack of food. **2.** A strong desire or craving: *a hunger for affection.* **—hunger** *v.* **-gered, -ger·ing, -gers.** *—intr.* **1.** To have a need or desire for food. **2.** To have a strong desire or craving. See Synonyms at **yearn.** *—tr.* To cause to experience hunger; make hungry. [Middle English, from Old English *hungor.*]

hunger strike *n.* A voluntary fast undertaken as a means of protest, as by a prisoner. **—hunger striker** *n.*

hung jury *n. Law.* A jury that is unable to agree on a verdict.

Hung·nam (ho͝ong′näm′). A city of east-central North Korea on the Sea of Japan north-northeast of Seoul, South Korea. It is an industrial center. Population, 260,000.

hung-over also **hung over** or **hung·o·ver** (hŭng′ō′vər) *adj.* Suffering from a hangover.

hun·gry (hŭng′grē) *adj.* **-gri·er, -gri·est.** **1.** Experiencing a desire or need for food. **2.** Extremely desirous; avid: *hungry for recognition.* **3.** Characterized by or expressing hunger or craving: *hungry eyes.* **4.** Lacking richness or fertility: *hungry soil.* [Middle English *hungri,* from Old English *hungrig,* from *hungor,* hunger.] **—hun′gri·ly** *adv.* **—hun′gri·ness** *n.*

Hung·shui He (ho͝ong′shwā′ hœ). See **Hongshui He.**

hung up *adj. Informal.* **1.** Delayed; hindered: *motorists hung up in traffic.* **2.** Also **hung-up** (hŭng′ŭp′). Anxious; nervous: *He got hung up on the details. She was all hung-up before the interview.* **3.** Over involved or preoccupied: *a teenager hung up on the latest fashions.*

hunk (hŭngk) *n.* **1.** *Informal.* A large piece; a chunk: *a hunk of fresh bread.* **2.** *Slang.* A sexually attractive man with a well-developed physique. [Perhaps from Flemish *hunke,* a piece of food.]

hun·ker (hŭng′kər) *intr.v.* **-kered, -ker·ing, -kers.** **1.** To squat close to the ground; crouch: *hunkered down to avoid the icy wind.* **2.** To hold stubbornly to a position: *"As the White House hunkered down, G.O.P. congressional unity started crumbling"* (Time). **—hunkers** *n.* The haunches. [Perhaps of Scandinavian origin; akin to Old Norse *hokra,* to crouch.]

Hunk·pa·pa (hŭngk′pä′pä) *n., pl.* **Hunkpapa** or **-pas.** **1.** A Native American people constituting a subdivision of the Teton Sioux, formerly inhabiting an area from the western Dakotas to southeast Montana, with a present-day population along the border between North and South Dakota. The Hunkpapa figured prominently in the resistance to white encroachment on the northern Great Plains. **2.** A member of this people.

hun·ky (hŭng′kē) *n., pl.* **-kies.** *Offensive Slang.* Used as a disparaging term for a person, especially a laborer, from east-central Europe. [Probably alteration of BOHUNK.]

hun·ky-do·ry (hŭng′kē-dôr′ē, -dōr′ē) *adj. Slang.* Perfectly satisfactory; fine. [Probably alteration of *hunky,* safe, all right, from obsolete *hunk,* goal, home in a game, from Dutch *honk,* from Frisian *hunk.*]

Hun·nish (hŭn′ĭsh) *adj.* **1.** Of, relating to, or characteristic of the Huns. **2.** Often **hunnish.** Barbarous; destructive. **—Hun′nish·ness** *n.*

hunt (hŭnt) *v.* **hunt·ed, hunt·ing, hunts.** *—tr.* **1.** To pursue (game) for food or sport. **2.** To search through (an area) for prey: *hunted the ridges.* **3.** To make use of (hounds, for example) in pursuing game. **4.** To pursue intensively so as to capture or kill: *hunted down the escaped convict.* **5.** To seek out; search for. See Synonyms at **seek.** **6.** To drive out forcibly, especially by harassing; chase away: *hunted the newcomers out of town.* *—intr.* **1.** To pursue game. **2.** To make a search; seek. **3.** *Aerospace.* **a.** To yaw back and forth about a flight path, as if seeking a new direction or another angle of attack. Used of an aircraft, a rocket, or a space vehicle. **b.** To rotate up and down or back and forth without being deflected by the pilot. Used of a control surface or a rocket motor in gimbals. **4.** *Engineering.* **a.** To oscillate about a selected value. Used of a machine, an instrument, or a system. **b.** To swing back and forth; oscillate. Used of an indicator on a display or an instrument panel. **—hunt** *n.* **1.** The act or sport of hunting: *an enthusiast for the hunt.* **2.a.** A hunting expedition or outing, usually with horses and hounds. **b.** Those taking part in such an expedition or outing. **3.** A diligent search or pursuit: *on a hunt for cheap gas.* [Middle English *hunten,* from Old English *huntian.*]

Hunt (hŭnt), **(James Henry) Leigh.** 1784–1859. British writer and editor of the *Examiner* (1806–1821). He is known for his essays defending romanticism.

Hunt, Richard Morris. 1827–1895. American architect who supervised an addition to the Louvre in Paris and designed an extension of the U.S. Capitol (1855).

Hunt, Ward. 1810–1886. American jurist who served as an associate justice of the U.S. Supreme Court (1873–1882).

Hunt, (William) Holman. 1827–1910. British painter who with Rossetti and Millais founded the Pre-Raphaelite Brotherhood.

hunt-and-peck (hŭnt′ən-pĕk′) *n.* A slow method of typing in which an untrained typist seeks out each key before striking it.

hunt·er (hŭn′tər) *n.* **1.** One who hunts game. **2.** A dog bred or trained for use in hunting. **3.** A horse, typically a strong fast jumper, that has been bred or trained for use in hunting. **4.** One who searches for or seeks something: *a treasure hunter.*

hunt·er-gath·er·er (hŭn′tər-găth′ər-ər) *n.* **1.** A member of a primitive people subsisting in the wild on food obtained by hunting and foraging.

hunt·er's moon (hŭn′tərz) *n.* The first full moon following the harvest moon.

hunt·ing (hŭn′tĭng) *n.* **1.** The activity or sport of pursuing game. **2.** The act of conducting a search for something: *house hunting.* **3.** *Electronics.* The periodic variation in speed of a synchronous motor with respect to the current.

Hun·ting·ton (hŭn′tĭng-tən). **1.** A city of northeast Indiana southwest of Fort Wayne. It is a trade and industrial center. Population, 16,202. **2.** A city of western West Virginia on the Ohio River west of Charleston. Founded in 1871 as a railroad terminus, it has glass and chemical industries. Population, 63,684.

Huntington, Collis Potter. 1821–1900. American transportation executive who built the western section of the first U.S. transcontinental railroad (completed 1869).

Huntington, Samuel. 1731–1796. American Revolutionary leader. He was president of the Continental Congress (1779–1781 and 1783), a signer of the Declaration of Independence, and governor of Connecticut (1786–1796).

Huntington Beach. A city of southern California on the Pacific Ocean southeast of Long Beach. Population, 170,505.

Huntington Park. A city of southern California, a residential and industrial suburb of Los Angeles. Population, 46,223.

Hun·ting·ton's chorea (hŭn′tĭng-tənz) *n.* A rare inherited disease of the central nervous system characterized by progressive dementia, abnormal posture, and involuntary movements. The typical age of onset is between 30 and 50 years. Also called *Huntington's disease.* [After George *Huntington* (1851?–1916), American physician.]

Huntington Station. A community of southeast New York on the northern shore of western Long Island. It is chiefly residential with varied light industries. Population, 30,300.

hunt·ress (hŭn′trĭs) *n.* A woman who hunts.

hunts·man (hŭnts′mən) *n.* **1.** A man who hunts. **2.** A man who manages the hounds in the hunting field.

Hunts·ville (hŭnts′vĭl′). **1.** A city of northern Alabama east-northeast of Decatur. Settled in 1805, it is a major center for space research. Population, 142,513. **2.** A city of east-central Texas north of Houston. Sam Houston's gravesite and restored home are here. Population, 23,936.

Hu·nya·di or **Hu·nya·dy** (ho͞on′yä-dē, -yô-), **János.** 1387?–1456. Hungarian general and nationalist leader who fought to protect Hungary from Turkish conquest (1437–1456).

Hu·pei or **Hu·peh** (ho͞o′pā′, hü′-). See **Hubei.**

hur·dle (hûr′dl) *n.* **1.** *Sports.* **a.** A light, portable barrier over which competitors must leap in certain races. **b. hurdles.** A race in which a series of such barriers must be jumped without the competitors' breaking their stride. **2.** An obstacle or difficulty to be overcome: *the last hurdle before graduation.* **3.** *Chiefly British.* A portable framework made of intertwined branches or wattle and used for temporary fencing. **4.** *Chiefly British.* A frame or sledge on which condemned persons were dragged to execution. **—hurdle** *v.* **-dled, -dling, -dles.** *—tr.* **1.** To leap over (a barrier) in or as if in a race. **2.** To overcome or deal with successfully; surmount: *hurdle a problem.* *—intr.* To leap over a barrier or other obstacle. [Middle English *hurdel,* portable panel for temporary fences, from Old English *hyrdel.*] **—hur′dler** *n.*

hur·dy-gur·dy (hûr′dē-gûr′dē, hûr′dē-gûr′dē) *n., pl.* **-dies.** *Music.* **1.** A medieval stringed instrument played by turning a rosined wheel with a crank and depressing keys connected to tangents on the strings. **2.** Any instrument, such as a barrel organ, played by turning a crank. [Probably imitative.]

hurl (hûrl) *v.* **hurled, hurl·ing, hurls.** —*tr.* **1.** To throw with great force; fling. See Synonyms at **throw. 2.** To send with great vigor; thrust: *hurled the army against the enemy.* **3.** To throw down; overthrow. **4.** To utter vehemently: *hurled insults at the speaker.* —*intr.* **1.** To move with great speed, force, or violence; hurtle. **2.** To throw something with force. **3.** *Baseball.* To pitch the ball. [Middle English *hurlen.*] —**hurl** *n.* —**hurl′er** *n.*

hurl·ing (hûr′lĭng) *n. Sports.* An Irish game resembling lacrosse played with a broad-bladed, netless stick.

hur·ly-bur·ly (hûr′lē-bûr′lē) *n., pl.* **-lies.** Noisy confusion; tumult. [Alteration and reduplication of *hurling,* gerund of HURL.]

Hur·ok (hyo͝or′ŏk′), **Solomon.** Known as "Sol." 1888–1974. Russian-born American impresario who sponsored a number of concert series in New York City.

Hu·ron (hyo͝or′ən, -ŏn′) *n., pl.* **Huron** or **-rons. 1.a.** A Native American confederacy formerly inhabiting southeast Ontario around Lake Simcoe, with small present-day populations in Quebec and northeast Oklahoma, where they are known as Wyandot. The Huron traded extensively throughout eastern Canada until the confederacy was destroyed by war with the Iroquois in the mid-17th century. **b.** A member of this confederacy. **2.** The Iroquoian language of the Huron. [French, boor, Huron, from Old French *hure,* bristling hair.]

Huron, Lake. The second largest of the Great Lakes, between southeast Ontario, Canada, and eastern Michigan. Part of the Great Lakes–St. Lawrence Seaway system, it is navigable for oceangoing vessels. Samuel de Champlain first sighted the lake in 1615.

hur·rah (ho͝o-rä′, -rô′, hə-) also **hoo·ray** or **hur·ray** (-rā′) —*interj.* Used as an exclamation of pleasure, approval, elation, or victory. —*n.* **1.** A shout of "hurrah." **2.** Excitement; fanfare. —*v.* **-rahed, -rah·ing, -rahs** also **-rayed, -ray·ing, -rays.** —*tr.* To applaud, cheer, or approve (someone or something) by shouting "hurrah." —*intr.* To shout "hurrah." [Alteration of HUZZAH.]

hur·ri·cane (hûr′ĭ-kān′, hŭr′-) *n.* **1.** A severe tropical cyclone originating in the equatorial regions of the Atlantic Ocean or Caribbean Sea, traveling north, northwest, or northeast from its point of origin, and usually involving heavy rains. **2.** A wind with a speed greater than 74 miles (119 kilometers) per hour, according to the Beaufort scale. **3.** Something resembling a hurricane in force or speed. [Spanish *huracán,* from Carib *huracan, furacan.*]

hurricane deck *n. Nautical.* The upper deck on a passenger steamship.

hurricane lamp *n.* A lamp with a candle, an oiled wick, or an electric bulb protected by a glass chimney.

hur·ried (hûr′ēd, hŭr′-) *adj.* **1.a.** Moving or acting rapidly. **b.** Required to move or act more rapidly; rushed. **2.** Done in great haste: *a hurried tour.* —**hur′ried·ly** *adv.* —**hur′ried·ness** *n.*

hur·ry (hûr′ē, hŭr′-) *v.* **-ried, -ry·ing, -ries.** —*intr.* To move or act with speed or haste. —*tr.* **1.** To cause to move or act with speed or haste: *hurried the children to school.* **2.** To cause to move or act with undue haste; rush: *was hurried into marriage.* **3.** To speed the progress or completion of; expedite. See Synonyms at **speed.** —**hurry** *n., pl.* **-ries. 1.** The act or an instance of hurrying; hastened progress. **2.** Activity or motion that is often unduly hurried; haste. See Synonyms at **haste. 3.** The need or wish to hurry; a condition of urgency: *in no hurry to leave.* [Possibly Middle English *horien,* perhaps variant of *harien,* to harass. See HARRY.] —**hur′ri·er** *n.*

hur·ry-scur·ry also **hur·ry-skur·ry** (hûr′ē-skûr′ē, hŭr′ē-skŭr′ē) —*intr.v.* **-ried, -ry·ing, -ries.** To move or act with undue hurry and confusion. —*n., pl.* **-ries.** Confused haste; agitation. [Reduplication of HURRY.]

Hurst (hûrst). A city of northeast Texas, an industrial and residential suburb of Fort Worth. Population, 31,420.

Hurst, Fannie. 1889–1968. American writer whose sentimental novels include *Lummox* (1923) and *Back Street* (1931).

Hur·ston (hûr′stən), **Zora Neale.** 1901?–1960. American writer whose several books and novels give detailed and sensitive accounts of Black life in the South.

hurt (hûrt) *v.* **hurt, hurt·ing, hurts.** —*tr.* **1.** To cause physical damage or pain to; injure. **2.** To cause mental or emotional suffering to; distress. **3.** To damage or impair: *The bad publicity has hurt the candidate's chances for victory.* See Synonyms at **injure.** —*intr.* **1.** To have or produce a feeling of physical pain or discomfort: *My leg hurts.* **2.a.** To cause distress or damage: *Parental neglect hurts.* **b.** To have an adverse effect: *"It never hurt to have a friend at court"* (Tom Clancy). **3.** *Informal.* To experience distress, especially of a financial kind; be in need: *"Even in a business that's hurting there's always a guy who can make a buck"* (New York). —**hurt** *n.* **1.** Something that hurts; a pain, an injury, or a wound. **2.** Mental suffering; anguish: *getting over the hurt of reading the letter.* **3.** A wrong; harm: *What hurt have you done to them?* [Middle English *hurten,* possibly from Old French *hurter,* to bang into, perhaps of Germanic origin.] —**hurt′er** *n.*

hurt·ful (hûrt′fəl) *adj.* Causing injury or suffering; damaging. —**hurt′ful·ly** *adv.* —**hurt′ful·ness** *n.*

hur·tle (hûr′tl) *v.* **-tled, -tling, -tles.** —*intr.* To move with or as if with great speed and a rushing noise: *an express train that hurtled past.* —*tr.* To fling with great force; hurl. [Middle English *hurtlen,* to collide, frequentative of *hurten,* to knock against, damage. See HURT.]

hurt·less (hûrt′lĭs) *adj.* **1.** Causing no hurt; harmless. **2.** Having no hurt; unhurt.

Hus (hŭs, ho͞os), **Jan.** See John **Huss.**

Hu·sain or **Hu·sayn** (ho͞o-sān′). See **Hussein.**

hus·band (hŭz′bənd) *n. Abbr.* **h., H. 1.** A man joined to a woman in marriage; a male spouse. **2.** *Chiefly British.* A manager or steward, as of a household. **3.** *Archaic.* A prudent, thrifty manager. —**husband** *tr.v.* **-band·ed, -band·ing, -bands. 1.** To use sparingly or economically; conserve: *husband one's energy.* **2.** *Archaic.* To find a husband for. [Middle English *huseband,* from Old English *hūsbōnda,* from Old Norse *hūsbōndi* : *hūs,* house + *bōndi, būandi,* householder, present participle of *būa,* to dwell; see **bheue-** in Appendix.]

WORD HISTORY: We gain an insight into the history of the word *husband* by considering the Old English word *hūsbōnde,* meaning "the mistress of a house." If *hūsbōnde* had survived into Modern English, *husband,* its modern form, would have been very ambiguous. The fact that *hūsbōnde* could mean "mistress of a house" helps us see the elements that make up the Old English ancestor of our word *husband. Hūs* corresponds to *house.* The element *-bōnde* is the feminine form of *-bōnda,* the second element of Old English *hūsbōnda.* The entire Old English word is a borrowing of the Old Icelandic word *hūsbōndi,* meaning "the master of a house." The second element in *hūsbōndi, bōndi,* means "a man who has land and stock" and comes from the verb *būa,* meaning "to live, dwell, have a household." The master of the house was of course usually the spouse of a wife as well, and it would seem that our main current sense of *husband* arises from this overlap.

hus·band·man (hŭz′bənd-mən) *n.* One whose occupation is husbandry; a farmer.

hus·band·ry (hŭz′bən-drē) *n.* **1.a.** The act or practice of cultivating crops and breeding and raising livestock; agriculture. **b.** The application of scientific principles to agriculture, especially to animal breeding. **2.** Careful management or conservation of resources; economy. [Middle English *husbondri,* from *huseband,* husband. See HUSBAND.]

hush (hŭsh) *v.* **hushed, hush·ing, hush·es.** —*tr.* **1.** To make silent or quiet. **2.** To calm; soothe. **3.** To keep from public knowledge; suppress mention of. Often used with *up: tried to hush up the damaging details.* —*intr.* To be or become silent or still. —**hush** *n.* A silence or stillness, especially after noise. —**hush** *adj. Archaic.* Silent; quiet. [Probably back-formation from Middle English *husht,* silent, of imitative origin.]

hush-hush (hŭsh′hŭsh′) *adj. Informal.* Secret; confidential.

Hu Shi also **Hu Shih** (ho͞o′ shœ′). 1891–1962. Chinese philosopher and diplomat. As a philosophy professor he promoted vernacular literature to replace writing in the classical style. He was also ambassador to the United States (1938–1942).

hush money *n. Informal.* A bribe paid to keep something secret.

hush·pup·py or **hush puppy** (hŭsh′pŭp′ē) *n.* A small, round or slightly oblong cake of cornmeal fried in deep fat. [Origin unknown.]

husk (hŭsk) *n.* **1.** The outer membranous or green envelope of some fruits or seeds, as that of a walnut or an ear of corn. **2.** A shell or outer covering, especially when considered worthless. **3.** A framework serving as a support. —**husk** *tr.v.* **husked, husk·ing, husks.** To remove the husk from. [Middle English; probably akin to *hose,* stocking, sheath. See HOSE.] —**husk′er** *n.*

hus·kie (hŭs′kē) *n.* Variant of **husky³.**

husk·ing bee (hŭs′kĭng) *n.* See **cornhusking** (sense 2).

husk tomato *n.* See **ground cherry.**

husk·y¹ (hŭs′kē) *adj.* **-i·er, -i·est. 1.** Hoarse or rough in quality: *a voice husky with emotion.* **2.a.** Resembling a husk. **b.** Containing husks. [From HUSK.] —**husk′i·ly** *adv.*

husk·y² (hŭs′kē) *adj.* **-i·er, -i·est. 1.** Strongly built; burly. **2.** Heavily built: *clothing sizes for husky boys.* —**husky** *n., pl.* **-ies.** A husky person. [Perhaps from HUSK.]

hus·ky³ also **hus·kie** (hŭs′kē) *n., pl.* **-kies. 1.** Often **Husky** or **Huskie.** A dog of a breed developed in Siberia for pulling sleds and having a dense, variously colored coat. Also called *Siberian husky.* **2.** A similar dog of Arctic origin. [Probably from shortening and alteration of ESKIMO.]

Huss or **Hus** (hŭs, ho͞os), **John** or **Jan.** 1372?–1415. Czechoslovakian religious reformer who was excommunicated (1409) for attacking the corruption of the clergy. His *De Ecclesia* questioned the authority and infallibility of the Catholic Church.

hus·sar (hə-zär′, -sär′) *n.* **1.** A horseman of the Hungarian light cavalry organized during the 15th century. **2.** A member of any of similar, ornately uniformed European units of light cavalry. [Hungarian *huszár,* from Serbian *husar,* highwayman, from Old Italian *corsaro.* See CORSAIR.]

Hus·sein or **Hu·sain** or **Hu·sayn** (ho͞o-sān′). Born 1935. King of Jordan (since 1952). Since he lost control of western Jordan in the Arab-Israeli War (1967), Hussein has attempted to remain neutral in Arab-Israeli conflicts.

hurricane lamp

Hussein
Photographed in 1987

ă pat	oi boy
ā pay	ou out
âr care	o͝o took
ä father	o͞o boot
ĕ pet	ŭ cut
ē be	ûr urge
ĭ pit	th thin
ī pie	*th* this
îr pier	hw which
ŏ pot	zh vision
ō toe	ə about, item
ô paw	♦ regionalism

Stress marks: **′** (primary); ′ (secondary), as in **dictionary** (dĭk′shə-nĕr′ē)

Hus·sein, Saddam. Born 1937. Iraqi military and political leader. The president of Iraq since 1979, he waged war against Iran over a territorial dispute (1980–1988) and invaded and occupied Kuwait (1990–1991).

Hus·serl (ho͝os′ərl, -ĕrl), **Edmund.** 1859–1938. Austrian-born German philosopher. A leader in the development of phenomenology, he had a major influence on the existentialists.

Huss·ite (hŭs′īt′, ho͝os′-) *n.* A follower of the religious reformer John Huss. **—Hussite** *adj.* Of or relating to John Huss or his religious theories. **—Huss′it′ism** *n.*

hus·sy (hŭz′ē, hŭs′ē) *n., pl.* **-sies. 1.** A woman considered brazen or immoral. **2.** A saucy or impudent girl. [Alteration of Middle English *houswif,* housewife. See HOUSEWIFE.]

hust·ings (hŭs′tĭngz) *pl.n. (used with a sing. or pl. verb).* **1.a.** A place where political campaign speeches are made: *a candidate out on the hustings in the farm belt.* **b.** The activities involved in political campaigning: *a veteran of the hustings.* **2.** *Chiefly British.* A court formerly held in some English cities and still held infrequently in London. **3.** *Chiefly British.* **a.** A platform on which candidates for Parliament formerly stood to address the electors. **b.** The proceedings of a parliamentary election. [From Middle English *husting,* court of common pleas, from Old English *hūsting,* court, from Old Norse *hūsthing* : *hūs,* house + *thing,* assembly.]

hus·tle (hŭs′əl) *v.* **-tled, -tling, -tles.** *—tr.* **1.** To jostle or shove roughly. **2.** To convey in a hurried or rough manner: *hustled the prisoner into a van.* **3.** To cause or urge to proceed quickly: *hustled the board into a quick decision.* **4.** To gain by energetic effort: *hustled a hot lunch.* **5.** *Slang.* **a.** To sell or get by questionable or aggressive means: *hustled stolen watches; hustling spare change.* **b.** To pressure into buying or doing something: *a barfly hustling the other customers for drinks.* *—intr.* **1.** To jostle and push. **2.** To work or move energetically and rapidly: *We hustled to get dinner ready on time.* **3.** To act aggressively, especially in business dealings. **4.** *Slang.* To obtain something by deceitful or illicit means. **5.** *Slang.* To solicit customers. Used of a pimp or prostitute. **—hustle** *n.* **1.** The act or an instance of jostling or shoving. **2.** Energetic activity; drive. **3.** *Slang.* An illicit or unethical way of doing business or obtaining money; a fraud or deceit: *"the most dangerous and wide-open drug hustle of them all"* (Newsweek). [Dutch *husselen,* to shake, from Middle Dutch *hustelen,* frequentative of *hutsen.*] **—hus′tler** *n.*

Hus·ton (hyo͞o′stən), **John.** 1906–1987. American filmmaker whose works include *The Maltese Falcon* (1941) and *The African Queen* (1951).

hut (hŭt) *n.* **1.** A crude or makeshift dwelling or shelter; a shack. **2.** A temporary structure for sheltering troops. **—hut** *tr. & intr.v.* **hut·ted, hut·ting, huts.** To shelter or take shelter in a hut. [French *hutte,* of Germanic origin. See **(s)keu-** in Appendix.]

hutch (hŭch) *n.* **1.** A pen or coop for small animals, especially rabbits. **2.** A cupboard with drawers for storage and usually open shelves on top, often used for dishes. **3.** A chest or bin for storage. **4.** A hut. [Middle English *huche,* chest, from Old French, from Medieval Latin *hūtica,* possibly of Germanic origin.]

Hutch·ins (hŭch′ĭnz), **Robert Maynard.** 1899–1977. American educator who was president (1929–1945) and chancellor (1945–1951) of the University of Chicago.

Hutch·in·son (hŭch′ĭn-sən). A city of south-central Kansas on the Arkansas River northwest of Wichita. It is a commercial and industrial center. Population, 40,284.

Hutchinson, Anne. 1591–1643. English-born American colonist and religious leader who was banished from Boston (1637) for her religious beliefs.

Hutchinson, Thomas. 1711–1780. American colonial official who was unpopular as governor of Massachusetts (1771–1774) because he supported British policies.

Hutch·in·son-Gil·ford syndrome (hŭch′ĭn-ən-gĭl′fərd) *n.* See **progeria.** [After Sir Jonathan *Hutchinson* (1828–1913) and Hastings *Gilford* (1861–1941), British physicians.]

hut·ment (hŭt′mənt) *n.* An encampment of huts.

Hut·ter·ite (hŭt′ə-rīt′, ho͝ot′-) *n.* A member of an Anabaptist sect originating in Moravia and now living communally in parts of Canada and the northwest United States. [After Jakob *Hutter* (died 1536), Moravian Anabaptist leader.]

hutz·pah (ᴋʜo͝ot′spə, ho͝ot′-) *n.* Variant of **chutzpah.**

Aldous Huxley

Hux·ley (hŭks′lē), **Aldous Leonard.** 1894–1963. British writer. His best-known work, *Brave New World* (1932), paints a grim picture of a scientifically organized utopia.

Huxley, Andrew Fielding. Born 1917. British physiologist. He shared a 1963 Nobel Prize for research on nerve cells.

Huxley, Sir **Julian Sorell.** 1887–1975. British biologist who was the first director general of UNESCO (1946–1948).

Huxley, Thomas Henry. 1825–1895. British biologist who championed Darwin's theory of evolution. His works include *Zoological Evidences as to Man's Place in Nature* (1863).

Hu Yao·bang (ho͞o′ you′băng′, hü′) also **Hu Yao-pang** (-păng′). 1915–1989. Chinese politician who served as general secretary of the Communist Party from 1980 to 1989.

Huy·gens (hī′gənz, hoi′gĕns), **Christiaan.** 1629–1695. Dutch physicist and astronomer who discovered Saturn's rings (1655), pioneered the use of the pendulum in clocks (1657), and formulated Huygens' principle.

Huy·gens' principle (hī′gənz) *n.* The principle that any point on a wave front of light may be regarded as the source of secondary waves and that the surface that is tangent to the secondary waves can be used to determine the future position of the wave front. [After Christiaan HUYGENS.]

Huys·mans (wēs-mäɴs′), **Joris Karl.** 1848–1907. French writer whose realistic novels include *En Rade* (1887).

Huy·ton-with-Ro·by (hīt′n-wĭth-rō′bē, -wĭth-). An urban district of northwest England, a residential suburb of Liverpool. Population, 174,100.

huz·zah also **huz·za** (hə-zä′) *—interj.* Used to express joy, encouragement, or triumph. *—n.* **1.** A shout of "huzzah." **2.** A cheer. [Perhaps variant of Middle English *hisse,* heave! See HOIST.]

H.V. *abbr.* **1.** High velocity. **2.** High voltage.

hvy. *abbr.* Heavy.

HW *abbr.* **1.** High water. **2.** Hot water.

Hwang Ho (hwäng′ hō′). See **Huang He.**

Hwei (hwā) *n.* Variant of **Hui.**

HWM *abbr.* High-water mark.

hwy *abbr.* Highway.

hy·a·cinth (hī′ə-sĭnth) *n.* **1.a.** A bulbous Mediterranean plant *(Hyacinthus orientalis)* having narrow leaves and a terminal raceme of variously colored, usually fragrant flowers, with a funnel-shaped perianth. Also called *jacinth.* **b.** Any of several similar or related plants, such as the grape hyacinth. **2.** *Greek Mythology.* A plant, perhaps the larkspur, gladiolus, or iris, that sprang from the blood of the slain Hyacinthus. **3.** *Color.* A deep purplish blue to vivid violet. **4.a.** A reddish or cinnamon-colored variety of transparent zircon, used as a gemstone. **b.** A blue precious stone, perhaps the sapphire, known in antiquity. [Latin *hyacinthus,* from Greek *huakinthos,* wild hyacinth.] **—hy′a·cin′thine** (-sĭn′thĭn, -thīn′) *adj.*

hyacinth bean *n.* A twining vine *(Dolichos lablab)* of the Old World tropics, having purple or white flowers and edible pods and seeds. Also called *lablab.*

Hy·a·cin·thus (hī′ə-sĭn′thəs) *n. Greek Mythology.* A beautiful youth, loved but accidentally killed by Apollo, from whose blood Apollo caused the hyacinth to grow.

Hy·a·des (hī′ə-dēz′) *pl.n.* **1.** *Greek Mythology.* The five daughters of Atlas and sisters of the Pleiades, placed by Zeus among the stars. **2.** A cluster of stars in the constellation Taurus, the five brightest of which form a V, supposed by ancient astronomers to indicate rain when they rose with the sun. [Latin, from Greek *Huades.*]

hy·ae·na (hī-ē′nə) *n.* Variant of **hyena.**

hy·a·lin (hī′ə-lĭn) also **hy·a·line** (-lĭn, -līn′) *n.* **1.** *Physiology.* The uniform matrix of hyaline cartilage. **2.** *Pathology.* A translucent product of some degenerative skin conditions. [Greek *hualos,* glass + -IN.]

hy·a·line (hī′ə-lĭn, -līn′) *adj.* Resembling glass, as in translucence or transparency; glassy. **—hyaline** *n.* **1.** Something that is translucent or transparent. **2.** Variant of **hyalin.** [Late Latin *hyalinus,* from Greek *hualinos,* of glass, from *hualos,* glass.]

hyaline cartilage *n.* Semitransparent, opalescent cartilage with a blue tint, consisting of cells that synthesize a surrounding matrix of hyaluronic acid, collagen, and protein. It forms most of the fetal skeleton and is found in the trachea, larynx, and joint surfaces of the adult.

hyaline membrane disease *n.* See **respiratory distress syndrome.**

hy·a·lite (hī′ə-līt′) *n.* A clear, colorless opal. [Greek *hualos,* glass + -ITE[1].]

hy·a·loid (hī′ə-loid′) *adj.* Glassy or transparent in appearance; hyaline. [Greek *hualoeidēs* : *hualos,* glass + *-oeidēs,* -oid.]

hy·a·lo·plasm (hī′ə-lō-plăz′əm) *n.* The clear, fluid portion of cytoplasm as distinguished from the granular and netlike components. Also called *ground substance.* [Greek *hualos,* glass + -PLASM.]

hy·al·u·ron·ic acid (hī′ə-lo͞o-rŏn′ĭk) *n.* A gellike aminoglycan that is found in the tissue space, the synovial fluid of joints, and the vitreous humor of the eyes and acts as a binding, lubricating, and protective agent. [Greek *hualos,* glass + -URONIC.]

hy·a·lu·ron·i·dase (hī′ə-lo͞o-rŏn′ĭ-dās′, -dāz′) *n.* An enzyme that inactivates hyaluronic acid in the body, thereby increasing tissue permeability to fluids. Also called *spreading factor.*

Hy·an·nis (hī-ăn′ĭs). A town of southeast Massachusetts on Nantucket Sound in south-central Cape Cod. It is a popular summer resort. Population, 8,000.

Hy·att (hī′ət), **Anna Vaugh.** 1876–1973. American sculptor known for her animal figures and works such as *Diana and the Chase* (1922) and *Don Quixote* (1942).

hy·brid (hī′brĭd) *n.* **1.** *Genetics.* The offspring of genetically dissimilar parents or stock, especially the offspring produced by breeding plants or animals of different varieties, species, or races. **2.a.** Something of mixed origin or composition. **b.** Something, such as a computer or power plant, having two kinds of components that produce the same or similar results. **3.** A word whose elements are derived from different languages. *—attributive.* Often used to modify another noun: *a hybrid tulip; a hybrid cell.* [Latin *hybrida.*] **—hy′brid·ism** *n.* **—hy′brid·ist** *n.* **—hy·brid′i·ty** (hī-brĭd′ĭ-tē) *n.*

ă pat	oi boy
ā pay	ou out
âr care	o͝o took
ä father	o͞o boot
ĕ pet	ŭ cut
ē be	ûr urge
ĭ pit	th thin
ī pie	*th* this
îr pier	hw which
ŏ pot	zh vision
ō toe	ə about, item
ô paw	♦ regionalism

Stress marks: **′** (primary); ′ (secondary), as in **dictionary** (dĭk′shə-nĕr′ē)

hy·brid·ize (hī′brĭ-dīz′) *intr. & tr.v.* **-ized, -iz·ing, -iz·es.** To produce or cause to produce hybrids; crossbreed. —**hy′brid·i·za′tion** (-brĭ-dĭ-zāshən) *n.* —**hy′brid·iz′er** *n.*

hy·brid·o·ma (hī′brĭ-dō′mə) *n.* A cell produced in the laboratory from the fusion of an antibody-producing lymphocyte and a myeloma tumor cell. It proliferates into clones that produce a continuous supply of a specific antibody.

hybrid vigor *n.* Increased vigor or other superior qualities arising from the crossbreeding of genetically different plants or animals. Also called *heterosis.*

hyd. *abbr.* **1.** Hydraulics. **2.** Hydrostatics.

hy·da·thode (hī′də-thōd′) *n.* A water-excreting microscopic epidermal structure in many plants. [Greek *hudōr, hudat-,* water; see **wed-**[1] in Appendix + *hodos,* way, road.]

hy·da·tid (hī′də-tĭd) *n.* **1.** A cyst formed as a result of infestation by larvae of the tapeworm *Echinococcus granulosus.* **2.** The encysted larva of *E. granulosus.* [Greek *hudatis, hudatid-,* watery vesicle, from *hudōr, hudat-,* water. See **wed-**[1] in Appendix.]

Hyde (hīd), **Douglas.** 1860–1949. Irish nationalist and writer who founded the Gaelic League (1893) and was president of Ireland (1938–1945).

Hyde, Edward. First Earl of Clarendon. 1609–1674. English politician who was chief adviser to Charles I during the English Civil War and served as Lord Chancellor from 1660 to 1667.

Hyde Park[1]**.** A large public park in west-central London, England famous for its soapbox orators.

Hyde Park[2]**.** A village of southeast New York on the eastern bank of the Hudson River north of Poughkeepsie. It is the birth and burial place of Franklin D. Roosevelt. Population, 2,805.

Hy·der·a·bad (hī′dər-ə-băd′, -bäd′, hī′drə-). **1.** A city of south-central India east-southeast of Bombay. Center of a former Mogul kingdom and Indian state, the city was founded in 1589 and is today a commercial center and transportation hub. Population, 2,187,262. **2.** A city of southern Pakistan on the Indus River northeast of Karachi. Founded in 1768, it was occupied by the British in 1839. Population, 745,000.

hydr– *pref.* Variant of **hydro–.**

hy·dra (hī′drə) *n.* Any of several small freshwater polyps of the genus *Hydra* and related genera, having a naked cylindrical body and an oral opening surrounded by tentacles. [New Latin *Hydra,* genus name, from Latin *Hydra,* Hydra. See HYDRA.]

Hy·dra (hī′drə) *n.* **1.** *Greek Mythology.* The many-headed monster that was slain by Hercules. **2.** A constellation in the equatorial region of the southern sky near Cancer, Libra, and Centaurus. Also called *Snake.* **3.** A persistent or multifaceted problem that cannot be eradicated by a single effort. [Middle English *Idra,* from Latin *Hydra,* from Greek *Hudra,* Hydra, a water serpent. See **wed-**[1] in Appendix.]

hy·dral·a·zine (hī-drăl′ə-zēn′) *n.* An antihypertensive drug, $C_8H_8N_4$. [HYDR(O)– + (PHTH)AL(IC ACID) + AZINE.]

hy·dra·mine (hī′drə-mēn′) *n.* A dihydric alcohol in which one hydroxyl has been replaced with an amino group.

hy·dran·gea (hī-drān′jə, -drăn′-) *n.* Any of various shrubs of the genus *Hydrangea,* having opposite leaves and large, flat-topped or rounded clusters of white, pink, or blue flowers. [New Latin *Hydrangēa,* genus name : Greek *hudro-, hudr-,* hydro- + Greek *angeion,* vessel; see ANGIO–.]

hy·drant (hī′drənt) *n.* A fire hydrant.

hy·dranth (hī′drănth′) *n.* A feeding zooid in a hydroid colony having an oral opening surrounded by tentacles. [HYDR(A) + Greek *anthos,* flower.]

hy·drarch (hī′drärk) *adj.* Originating in a wet habitat, such as a pond. Used of an ecological succession.

hy·drase (hī′drās′, -drāz′) *n.* An enzyme that catalyzes the addition or removal of water from a substrate.

hy·dras·tine (hī-drăs′tēn′, -tĭn) *n.* A poisonous white alkaloid, $C_{21}H_{21}NO_6$, obtained from the root of the goldenseal and formerly used locally to treat inflammation of mucous membranes. [New Latin *Hydrastis,* plant genus + –INE[2].]

hy·drate (hī′drāt′) *n.* A solid compound containing water molecules combined in a definite ratio as an integral part of the crystal. —**hydrate** *v.* **-drat·ed, -drat·ing, -drates.** —*tr.* **1.** To restore or maintain fluid balance. **2.** To supply water to (a person, for example) in order to restore or maintain fluid balance. —*intr.* To become a hydrate. —**hy·dra′tion** *n.* —**hy′dra′tor** *n.*

hy·drat·ed (hī′drā′tĭd) *adj.* Chemically combined with water, especially existing in the form of a hydrate.

hy·drau·lic (hī-drô′lĭk) *adj.* **1.** Of, involving, moved by, or operated by a fluid, especially water, under pressure. **2.** Able to set and harden under water, as Portland cement. **3.** Of or relating to hydraulics. [Latin *hydraulicus,* from Greek *hudraulikos,* from *hudraulis,* water organ : *hudro-, hudr-,* hydro- + *aulos,* pipe, flute.] —**hy·drau′li·cal·ly** *adv.*

hydraulic press *n.* A machine in which a large force is exerted on the larger of two pistons in a pair of hydraulically coupled cylinders by means of a relatively small force applied to the smaller piston.

hydraulic ram *n.* **1.** A water pump in which the downward flow of naturally running water is intermittently halted by a valve so that the flow is forced upward through an open pipe into a reservoir. **2.** The large output piston of a hydraulic press.

hy·drau·lics (hī-drô′lĭks) *n. (used with a sing. verb). Abbr.* **hyd.** The physical science and technology of the static and dynamic behavior of fluids.

hy·dra·zide (hī′drə-zīd′) *n.* An acyl derivative of hydrazine.

hy·dra·zine (hī′drə-zēn′, -zĭn) *n.* A colorless, fuming, corrosive hygroscopic liquid, H_2NNH_2, used in jet and rocket fuels.

hy·dric (hī′drĭk) *adj.* Relating to, characterized by, or requiring considerable moisture.

hy·dride (hī′drīd′) *n.* A compound of hydrogen with another, more electropositive element or group.

hy·dril·la (hī-drĭl′ə) *n.* A submersed Old World Plant *(Hydrilla verticillata)* having whorled, lance-shaped leaves and unisexual, solitary, axillary flowers. [New Latin, genus name, diminutive of Latin *hydra,* hydra. See HYDRA.]

hy·dri·od·ic acid (hī′drē-ŏd′ĭk) *n.* A clear, colorless or pale yellow aqueous solution of hydrogen iodide, HI, that is a strong acid and reducing agent.

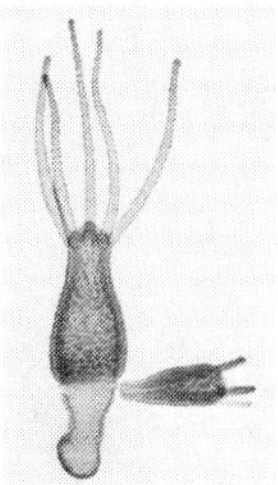
hydra

hy·dro (hī′drō) *adj.* Hydroelectric. —**hydro** *n., pl.* **-dros. 1.** Hydroelectric power. **2.** A hydroelectric power plant.

hydro– or **hydr–** *pref.* **1.a.** Water: *hydroelectric.* **b.** Liquid: *hydrodynamics.* **2.** Hydrogen: *hydrochloride.* [Greek *hudro-, hudr-,* from *hudōr.* See **wed-**[1] in Appendix.]

hy·dro·bi·ol·o·gy (hī′drō-bī-ŏl′ə-jē) *n.* The biological study of bodies of water. —**hy′dro·bi′o·log′i·cal** (-bī′ə-lŏj′ĭ-kəl) *adj.* —**hy′dro·bi·ol′o·gist** *n.*

hy·dro·bro·mic acid (hī′drə-brō′mĭk) *n.* A clear, colorless or faintly yellow, highly acidic and corrosive aqueous solution of hydrogen bromide, HBr, used in the manufacture of bromides.

hy·dro·car·bon (hī′drə-kär′bən) *n.* Any of numerous organic compounds, such as benzene and methane, that contain only carbon and hydrogen. —**hy′dro·car′bo·na′ceous** (-bə-nā′shəs), **hy′dro·car·bon′ic** (-bŏn′ĭk), **hy′dro·car′bon·ous** (-bə-nəs) *adj.*

hy·dro·cele (hī′drə-sēl′) *n.* A pathological accumulation of serous fluid in a bodily cavity, especially in the scrotal pouch. [Latin *hydrocēlē,* from Greek *hudrokēlē* : *hudro-,* hydro- + *kēlē,* tumor; see –CELE[1].]

hy·dro·ceph·a·lus (hī′drō-sĕf′ə-ləs) also **hy·dro·ceph·a·ly** (-lē) *n.* A usually congenital condition in which an abnormal accumulation of fluid in the cerebral ventricles causes enlargement of the skull and compression of the brain, destroying much of the neural tissue. [New Latin, from Greek *hudrokephalon* : *hudro-,* hydro- + *kephalē,* head; see **ghebh-el-** in Appendix.] —**hy′dro·ce·phal′ic** (-sə-făl′ĭk), **hy′dro·ceph′a·loid′** (-loid′), **hy′dro·ceph′a·lous** (-ləs) *adj.*

hy·dro·chlo·ric acid (hī′drə-klôr′ĭk, -klōr′-) *n.* A clear, colorless, fuming, poisonous, highly acidic aqueous solution of hydrogen chloride, HCl, used as a chemical intermediate and in petroleum production, ore reduction, food processing, pickling, and metal cleaning. It is found in the stomach in dilute form.

hy·dro·chlo·ride (hī′drə-klôr′īd′, -klōr′-) *n.* A compound resulting or regarded as resulting from the reaction of hydrochloric acid with an organic base.

hydrant
Fire hydrant

hy·dro·chlo·ro·thi·a·zide (hī′drə-klôr′ə-thī′ə-zīd′, -klōr′-) *n.* A diuretic drug, $C_7H_8ClN_3O_4S_2$, used in the treatment of hypertension. [HYDRO– + CHLORO– + THIAZ(OLE) + –IDE.]

hy·dro·col·loid (hī′drə-kŏl′oid′) *n.* A substance that forms a gel with water. —**hy′dro·col·loid′al** (-kə-loid′l) *adj.*

hy·dro·cor·al (hī′drə-kôr′əl, -kŏr′-) *n.* Any of various colonial marine hydrozoans of the order Hydrocorallinae, having a limestone skeleton and thus resembling the true corals.

hy·dro·cor·ti·sone (hī′drə-kôr′tĭ-sōn′, -zōn′) *n.* **1.** A steroid hormone, $C_{21}H_{30}O_5$, produced by the adrenal cortex, that regulates carbohydrate metabolism and maintains blood pressure. Also called *cortisol.* **2.** A preparation of this hormone obtained from natural sources or produced synthetically and used to treat inflammatory conditions and adrenal failure.

hy·dro·crack (hī′drə-krăk′) *tr.v.* **-cracked, -crack·ing, -cracks.** To break down (a hydrocarbon) by the process of hydrocracking. —**hy′dro·crack′er** *n.*

hy·dro·crack·ing (hī′drə-krăk′ĭng) *n.* A process by which the hydrocarbon molecules of petroleum are broken into simpler molecules, as of gasoline or kerosene, by the addition of hydrogen under high pressure and in the presence of a catalyst.

hy·dro·cy·an·ic acid (hī′drō-sī-ăn′ĭk) *n.* An aqueous solution of hydrogen cyanide. Also called *prussic acid.*

hy·dro·dy·nam·ic (hī′drō-dī-năm′ĭk) also **hy·dro·dy·nam·i·cal** (-ĭ-kəl) *adj.* **1.** Of or relating to hydrodynamics. **2.** Of, relating to, or operated by the force of liquid in motion. —**hy′dro·dy·nam′i·cal·ly** *adv.*

hy·dro·dy·nam·ics (hī′drō-dī-năm′ĭks) *n.* **1.** *(used with a sing. verb).* The branch of science that deals with the dynamics of fluids, especially incompressible fluids, in motion. **2.** *(used with a pl. verb).* The dynamics of fluids in motion. —**hy′dro·dy·nam′i·cist** (-ĭ-sĭst) *n.*

hy·dro·e·lec·tric (hī′drō-ĭ-lĕk′trĭk) *adj.* **1.** Generating electricity by conversion of the energy of running water. **2.** Of, relating to, or using electricity so generated. —**hy′dro·e·lec′tri·cal·ly** *adv.* —**hy′dro·e·lec·tric′i·ty** (-ĭ-lĕk-trĭs′ĭ-tē) *n.*

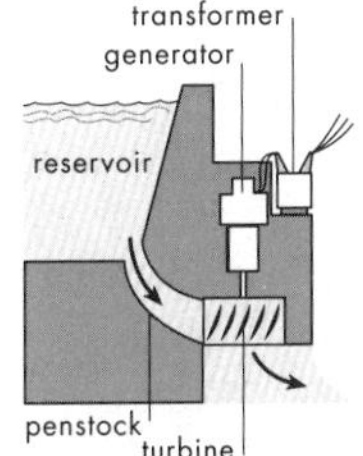

hydroelectric
Low head hydroelectric power plant

hy·dro·fluor·ic acid (hī′drō-flo͝or′ĭk, -flôr′-, -flōr′-) *n.* A colorless, fuming, corrosive, dangerously poisonous aqueous solution of hydrogen fluoride, HF, used to etch or polish glass, pickle certain metals, and clean masonry.

hy·dro·foil (hī′drə-foil′) *n. Nautical.* **1.** A winglike structure attached to the hull of a boat that raises all or part of the hull out of the water when the boat is moving forward, thus reducing drag. **2.** A boat equipped with hydrofoils. In this sense, also called *hydroplane.*

hy·dro·form·ing (hī′drə-fôr′mĭng) *n.* A process in which naphthas are converted to high-octane aromatics in the presence of hydrogen and a catalyst under pressure and heat. **—hy′dro·form′er** *n.*

hy·dro·gen (hī′drə-jən) *n. Symbol* **H** A colorless, highly flammable gaseous element, the lightest of all gases and the most abundant element in the universe, used in the production of synthetic ammonia and methanol, in petroleum refining, in the hydrogenation of organic materials, as a reducing atmosphere, in oxyhydrogen torches, and in rocket fuels. Atomic number 1; atomic weight 1.00797; melting point −259.14°C; boiling point −252.8°C; density at 0°C 0.08987 gram per liter; valence 1. See table at **element.** [French *hydrogène* : Greek *hudro-*, hydro- + *-gène*, -gen.] **—hy·drog′e·nous** (-drŏj′ə-nəs) *adj.*

hy·drog·e·nase (hī-drŏj′ə-nās′, -nāz′) *n.* An enzyme in certain microorganisms that catalyzes the formation of hydrogen.

hy·dro·gen·ate (hī′drə-jə-nāt′, hī-drŏj′ə-) *tr.v.* **-at·ed, -at·ing, -ates.** To combine with or subject to the action of hydrogen, especially to combine (an unsaturated oil) with hydrogen to produce a solid fat.

hydrogen bomb *n.* An explosive weapon of enormous destructive power caused by the fusion of the nuclei of various hydrogen isotopes in the formation of helium nuclei.

hydrogen bond *n.* A chemical bond in which a hydrogen atom of one molecule is attracted to an electronegative atom, especially a nitrogen, oxygen, or flourine atom, usually of another molecule.

hydrogen bromide *n.* An irritating colorless gas, HBr, used in the manufacture of barbiturates and synthetic hormones.

hydrogen chloride *n.* A colorless, fuming, corrosive suffocating gas, HCl, used in the manufacture of plastics.

hydrogen cyanide *n.* A colorless, volatile, extremely poisonous flammable liquid, HCN, miscible in water and used in the manufacture of dyes, fumigants, and plastics.

hydrogen fluoride *n.* A colorless, fuming corrosive liquid or a highly soluble corrosive gas, HF, used in the manufacture of hydrofluoric acid, as a reagent, catalyst, and fluorinating agent, and in the refining of uranium and the preparation of many fluorine compounds.

hydrogen iodide *n.* A corrosive, colorless suffocating gas, HI, used to manufacture hydriodic acid.

hydrogen ion *n.* The positively charged ion of hydrogen, H^+, formed by removal of the electron from atomic hydrogen and found in all aqueous solutions of acids.

hy·dro·gen·ol·y·sis (hī′drō-jə-nŏl′ĭ-sĭs) *n.* The breaking of a chemical bond in an organic molecule with the simultaneous addition of a hydrogen atom to each of the resulting molecular fragments.

hydrogen peroxide *n.* A colorless, heavy, strongly oxidizing liquid, H_2O_2, capable of reacting explosively with combustibles and used principally in aqueous solution as a mild antiseptic, a bleaching agent, an oxidizing agent, and a laboratory reagent.

hydrogen sulfide *n.* A colorless, flammable poisonous gas, H_2S, having a characteristic rotten-egg odor and used as an antiseptic, a bleach, and a reagent.

hy·dro·ge·ol·o·gy (hī′drō-jē-ŏl′ə-jē) *n.* The branch of geology that deals with the occurrence, distribution, and effect of ground water. **—hy′dro·ge′o·log′i·cal** (-jē′ə-lŏj′ĭ-kəl), **hy′dro·ge′o·log′ic** *adj.* **—hy′dro·ge·ol′o·gist** *n.*

hy·drog·ra·phy (hī-drŏg′rə-fē) *n., pl.* **-phies. 1.** The scientific description and analysis of the physical conditions, boundaries, flow, and related characteristics of the earth's surface waters. **2.** The mapping of bodies of water. **—hy·drog′ra·pher** *n.* **—hy′dro·graph′ic** (hī′drə-grăf′ĭk) *adj.* **—hy′dro·graph′i·cal·ly** *adv.*

hy·droid (hī′droid′) *n.* **1.** Any of numerous characteristically colonial hydrozoan coelenterates having a polyp rather than a medusoid form as the dominant stage of the life cycle. **2.** The asexual polyp in the life cycle of a hydrozoan. **—hydroid** *adj.* Of, relating to, or characteristic of a hydroid. [HYDRA + −OID.]

hy·dro·ki·net·ic (hī′drō-kĭ-nĕt′ĭk, -kī-) also **hy·dro·ki·net·i·cal** (-ĭ-kəl) *adj.* **1.** Of or relating to hydrokinetics. **2.** Of or relating to the kinetic energy and motion of fluids.

hy·dro·ki·net·ics (hī′drō-kĭ-nĕt′ĭks, -kī-) *n. (used with a sing. verb).* The branch of physics that deals with fluids in motion.

hydrologic cycle *n.* See **water cycle.**

hy·drol·o·gy (hī-drŏl′ə-jē) *n.* The scientific study of the properties, distribution, and effects of water on the earth's surface, in the soil and underlying rocks, and in the atmosphere. **—hy′dro·log′ic** (-drə-lŏj′ĭk), **hy′dro·log′i·cal** *adj.* **—hy′dro·log′i·cal·ly** *adv.* **—hydrol′o·gist** *n.*

hy·drol·y·sate (hī-drŏl′ĭ-sāt′, hī′drə-lī′-) also **hy·drol·y·zate** (-zāt′) *n.* A product of hydrolysis. [HYDROLYS(IS) + −ATE[2].]

hy·drol·y·sis (hī-drŏl′ĭ-sĭs) *n.* Decomposition of a chemical compound by reaction with water, such as the dissociation of a dissolved salt or the catalytic conversion of starch to glucose. **—hy′dro·lyte′** (-līt′) *n.* **—hy′dro·lyt′ic** (-drə-lĭt′ĭk) *adj.*

hy·dro·lyze (hī′drə-līz′) *tr. & intr.v.* **-lyzed, -lyz·ing, -lyz·es.** To subject to or undergo hydrolysis. **—hy′dro·lyz′a·ble** *adj.* **—hy′dro·ly·za′tion** (-lĭ-zā′shən) *n.*

hy·dro·mag·net·ics (hī′drō-măg-nĕt′ĭks) *n. (used with a sing. verb).* See **magnetohydrodynamics. —hy′dro·mag·net′ic** *adj.*

hy·dro·man·cy (hī′drə-măn′sē) *n.* Divination by the observation of water. [Middle English *ydromancy*, from Old French *ydromancie*, from Latin *hydromantīa*, from Greek *hudromanteia* : *hudro-*, hydro- + *manteia*, divination; see −MANCY.]

hy·dro·me·chan·ics (hī′drō-mĭ-kăn′ĭks) *n. (used with a sing. verb).* The study of the mechanics of fluids or the laws of equilibrium and motion concerning fluids. **—hy′dro·me·chan′i·cal** *adj.*

hy·dro·me·du·sa (hī′drō-mĭ-dōō′sə, -dyōō′-) *n., pl.* **-sas** or **-sae** (-sē). A hydrozoan in the medusoid stage of its life cycle. [HYDRO− + MEDUSA.]

hy·dro·mel (hī′drə-mĕl′) *n.* A mixture of water and honey that becomes mead when fermented. [Middle English *ydromel*, from Old French, from Latin *hydromeli*, from Greek *hudromeli* : *hudro-*, hydro- + *meli*, honey; see **melit-** in Appendix.]

hy·dro·met·al·lur·gy (hī′drō-mĕt′l-ûr′jē) *n.* The treatment of metal or the separation of metal from ores and ore concentrates by liquid processes, such as leaching, extraction, and precipitation. **—hy′dro·met′al·lur′gi·cal** *adj.*

hy·dro·me·te·or (hī′drō-mē′tē-ər, -ôr′) *n.* A precipitation product, such as rain, snow, fog, or clouds, formed from the condensation of water vapor in the atmosphere.

hy·dro·me·te·or·ol·o·gy (hī′drō-mē′tē-ə-rŏl′ə-jē) *n.* The branch of meteorology that deals with the occurrence, motion, and changes of state of atmospheric water. **—hy′dro·me′te·or′o·log′i·cal** (-ôr′ə-lŏj′ĭ-kəl, -ŏr′-) *adj.* **—hy′dro·me′te·or·ol′o·gist** *n.*

hy·drom·e·ter (hī-drŏm′ĭ-tər) *n.* An instrument used to determine specific gravity, especially a sealed, graduated tube, weighted at one end, that sinks in a fluid to a depth used as a measure of the fluid's specific gravity. **—hy′dro·met′ric** (hī′drə-mĕt′rĭk), **hy′dro·met′ri·cal** *adj.* **—hy′dro·met′ri·cal·ly** *adv.* **—hy·drom′e·try** *n.*

hy·dro·ni·um (hī-drō′nē-əm) *n.* A hydrated hydrogen ion, H_3O^+. Also called *hydronium ion.* [HYDR(O)− + (AMM)ONIUM.]

hy·drop·a·thy (hī-drŏp′ə-thē) *n., pl.* **-thies.** Internal and external use of water as a therapeutic treatment for all forms of disease. **—hy′dro·path′ic** (hī′drə-păth′ĭk), **hy′dro·path′i·cal** *adj.* **—hy·drop′a·thist, hy′dro·path′** *n.*

hy·dro·phane (hī′drə-fān′) *n.* An opal that is almost opaque when dry but transparent when wet. **—hy·droph′a·nous** (hī-drŏf′ə-nəs) *adj.*

hy·dro·phil·ic (hī′drə-fĭl′ĭk) *adj.* Having an affinity for water; readily absorbing or dissolving in water. **—hy′dro·phile′** (-fīl′) *n.* **—hy′dro·phi·lic′i·ty** (-fə-lĭs′ĭ-tē) *n.*

hy·droph·i·lous (hī-drŏf′ə-ləs) *adj. Botany.* **1.** Growing or thriving in water. **2.** Pollinated by water, as the flowers of ribbon grass and hornwort. **—hy·droph′i·ly** *n.*

hy·dro·pho·bi·a (hī′drə-fō′bē-ə) *n.* **1.** An abnormal fear of water. **2.** Rabies.

hy·dro·pho·bic (hī′drə-fō′bĭk, -fŏb′ĭk) *adj.* **1.** Repelling, tending not to combine with, or incapable of dissolving in water. **2.** Of or exhibiting hydrophobia. **—hy′dro·pho·bic′i·ty** (-bĭs′ĭ-tē) *n.*

hy·dro·phone (hī′drə-fōn′) *n.* An electrical instrument for detecting or monitoring sound under water.

hy·dro·phyte (hī′drə-fīt′) *n.* A plant adapted to grow in water. **—hy′dro·phyt′ic** (-fĭt′ĭk) *adj.*

hy·dro·plane (hī′drə-plān′) *n.* **1.** See **seaplane. 2.** *Nautical.* A motorboat designed so that the prow and much of the hull lift out of the water and skim the surface at high speeds. **3.** *Nautical.* See **hydrofoil** (sense 2). **4.** A horizontal rudder on a submarine. **—hydroplane** *intr.v.* **-planed, -plan·ing, -planes. 1.** To drive or ride in a hydroplane. **2. a.** To skim along on the surface of the water. **b.** To be or go out of control by skimming along the surface of a wet road. Used of a motor vehicle.

hy·dro·pon·ics (hī′drə-pŏn′ĭks) *n. (used with a sing. verb).* Cultivation of plants in nutrient solution rather than in soil. [HYDRO− + (GEO)PONICS.] **—hy′dro·pon′ic** *adj.* **—hy′dro·pon′i·cal·ly** *adv.* **—hy′dro·pon′i·cist** (-ĭ-sĭst), **hy′dro·pon′ist** (hī′drə-pŏn′ĭst, hī-drŏp′ə-hĭst) *n.*

hy·dro·pow·er (hī′drə-pou′ər) *n.* Hydroelectric power.

hy·dro·qui·none (hī′drō-kwĭ-nōn′, -kwĭn′ōn′) also **hy·dro·quin·ol** (-kwĭn′ôl′, -ōl′) *n.* A white crystalline compound, $C_6H_4(OH)_2$, used as a photographic developer, an antioxidant, a stabilizer, and a reagent.

hy·dro·scope (hī′drə-skōp′) *n.* An optical device used for viewing objects far below the surface of water. **—hy′dro·scop′ic** (-skŏp′ĭk) *adj.*

hy·dro·sol (hī′drə-sôl′, -sōl′, -sŏl′) *n.* A colloid with water as the dispersing medium. **—hy′dro·sol′ic** (-sŏl′ĭk) *adj.*

hy·dro·space (hī′drə-spās′) *n.* The regions beneath the ocean's surface, especially when considered as an area to be studied.

hy·dro·sphere (hī′drə-sfîr′) *n.* **1.** The waters of the earth's surface as distinguished from those of the lithosphere and the atmosphere. **2.** The water vapor in the earth's atmosphere. **—hy′dro·spher′ic** (-sfîr′ĭk, -sfĕr′-) *adj.*

hy·dro·stat·ic (hī′drə-stăt′ĭk) also **hy·dro·stat·i·cal** (-ĭ-kəl) *adj.* Of or relating to hydrostatics. **—hy′dro·stat′i·cal·ly** *adv.*

hy·dro·stat·ics (hī′drə-stăt′ĭks) *n.* *(used with a sing. verb). Abbr.* **hyd.** The branch of physics that deals with fluids at rest and under pressure.

hy·dro·sul·fate (hī′drə-sŭl′fāt′) *n.* A salt formed by the union of sulfuric acid with an alkaloid or other organic base.

hy·dro·sul·fide (hī′drə-sŭl′fīd′) *n.* A chemical compound derived from hydrogen sulfide by replacement of one of the hydrogen atoms with a basic radical or base.

hy·dro·sul·fite (hī′drə-sŭl′fīt′) *n.* **1.** A salt of hyposulfurous acid. **2.** See **sodium hydrosulfite.**

hy·dro·sul·fu·rous acid (hī′drō-sŭl-fyo͝or′əs, -sŭl′fər-əs) *n.* See **hyposulfurous acid.**

hy·dro·tax·is (hī′drə-tăk′sĭs) *n.* Movement of an organism in response to moisture. **—hy′dro·tac′tic** (-tăk′tĭk) *adj.*

hy·dro·ther·a·peu·tics (hī′drə-thĕr′ə-pyo͞o′tĭks) *n.* *(used with a sing. verb).* Hydrotherapy. **—hy′dro·ther′a·peu′tic** *adj.*

hy·dro·ther·a·py (hī′drə-thĕr′ə-pē) *n., pl.* **-pies.** External use of water in the medical treatment of certain diseases.

hy·dro·ther·mal (hī′drə-thûr′məl) *adj.* **1.** Of or relating to hot water. **2.** *Geology.* **a.** Of or relating to hot magmatic emanations rich in water. **b.** Of or relating to the rocks, ore deposits, and springs produced by such emanations. **—hy′dro·ther′mal·ly** *adv.*

hy·dro·tho·rax (hī′drə-thôr′ăks′, -thōr′-) *n.* Accumulation of serous fluid in one or both pleural cavities.

hy·drot·ro·pism (hī-drŏt′rə-pĭz′əm) *n.* Growth or movement in a sessile organism toward or away from water, as of the roots of a plant. **—hy′dro·tro′pic** (hī′drə-trō′pĭk, -trŏp′ĭk) *adj.* **—hy′dro·tro′pi·cal·ly** *adv.*

hy·drous (hī′drəs) *adj.* Containing water, especially water of crystallization or hydration.

hy·drox·ide (hī-drŏk′sīd′) *n.* A chemical compound containing the hydroxyl group.

hydroxide ion *n.* The ion OH^-, characteristic of basic hydroxides. Also called *hydroxyl ion.*

hy·drox·y (hī-drŏk′sē) *adj.* Containing the hydroxyl group. [From HYDROXYL.]

hy·drox·y·a·pa·tite (hī-drok′sē-ăp′ĭ-tīt′) *n.* The principal bone salt, $Ca_5(PO_4)_3OH$, which provides the compressional strength of vertebrate bone.

hy·drox·yl (hī-drŏk′sĭl) *n.* The univalent radical or group OH, a characteristic component of bases, certain acids, phenols, alcohols, carboxylic and sulfonic acids, and amphoteric compounds. [HYDR(O)– + OX(YGEN) + –YL.] **—hy′drox·yl′ic** (hī′drŏk-sĭl′ĭk) *adj.*

hy·drox·yl·a·mine (hī-drŏk′sə-lə-mēn′, hī′drŏk-sĭl′ə-mēn′, -sə-lăm′ĭn) *n.* A colorless crystalline compound, NH_2OH, explosive when heated, that is used as a reducing agent and in organic synthesis.

hy·drox·yl·ate (hī-drŏk′sə-lāt′) *tr.v.* **-at·ed, -at·ing, -ates.** To introduce hydroxyl into (a compound). **—hy·drox′y·la′tion** *n.*

hydroxyl ion *n.* See **hydroxide ion.**

hy·dro·zo·an (hī′drə-zō′ən) *n.* Any of numerous coelenterates of the class Hydrozoa, including the freshwater hydras, hydroids, hydrocorals, and siphonophores. **—hydrozoan** *adj.* Of, relating to, or belonging to the class Hydrozoa. [From New Latin *Hydrozoa,* class : HYDRO– + *-zoa* (pl. of –ZOON).]

Hy·drus (hī′drəs) *n.* A constellation in the Southern Hemisphere near Tucana and Mensa. [Latin, from Greek *hudros,* water snake. See **wed-**[1] in Appendix.]

hy·e·na also **hy·ae·na** (hī-ē′nə) *n.* Any of several carnivorous mammals of the family Hyaenidae of Africa and Asia, which feed as scavengers and have powerful jaws, relatively short hind limbs, and coarse hair. [Middle English *hiena,* from Old French *hiene,* from Latin *hyaena,* from Greek *huaina,* feminine of *hus,* swine. See **sū-** in Appendix.]

hy·e·tal (hī′ĭ-tl) *adj.* Of or relating to rain or rainy regions. [From Greek *huetos,* rain. See **seue-**[2] in Appendix.]

Hy·ge·ia (hī-jē′ə) *n.* *Greek Mythology.* The goddess of health.

hy·giene (hī′jēn′) *n.* **1.** The science that deals with the promotion and preservation of health. Also called *hygienics.* **2.** Conditions and practices that serve to promote or preserve health: *hygiene in the workplace; personal hygiene.* [French *hygiène* and New Latin *hygieina,* both from Greek *hugieinē (tekhnē),* (art) of health, from *hugiēs,* healthy. See **gʷei-** in Appendix.] **—hy·gien′ist** (hī-jē′nĭst, hī′jē′-, hī-jĕn′ĭst) *n.*

hy·gi·en·ic (hī′jē-ĕn′ĭk, hī-jĕn′-, -jē′nĭk) *adj.* **1.** Of or relating to hygiene. **2.** Tending to promote or preserve health. **3.** Sanitary. **—hy′gi·en′i·cal·ly** *adv.*

hy·gi·en·ics (hī′jē-ĕn′ĭks, hī-jĕn′-, -jē′nĭks) *n.* *(used with a sing. verb).* See **hygiene** (sense 1).

hygro– *pref.* Moisture; humidity: *hygroscope.* [From Greek *hugros,* wet, moist.]

hy·gro·graph (hī′grə-grăf′) *n.* An automatic hygrometer that records variations in atmospheric humidity.

hy·grom·e·ter (hī-grŏm′ĭ-tər) *n.* Any of several instruments that measure atmospheric humidity. **—hy′gro·met′ric** (hī′grə-mĕt′rĭk) *adj.* **—hy·grom′e·try** *n.*

hy·gro·scope (hī′grə-skōp′) *n.* An instrument that indicates changes in atmospheric humidity.

hy·gro·scop·ic (hī′grə-skŏp′ĭk) *adj.* Readily absorbing moisture, as from the atmosphere. **—hy′gro·scop′i·cal·ly** *adv.* **—hy′gro·sco·pic′i·ty** (-skŏ-pĭs′ĭ-tē) *n.*

hy·gro·stat (hī′grə-stăt′) *n.* See **humidistat.**

hy·ing (hī′ĭng) *v.* A present participle of **hie.**

hy·lo·zo·ism (hī′lə-zō′ĭz′əm) *n.* The philosophical doctrine holding that all matter has life, which is a property or derivative of matter. [Greek *hulē,* matter + Greek *zoē,* life; see AZO– + –ISM.] **—hy′lo·zo′ic** *adj.* **—hy′lo·zo′ist** *n.* **—hy′lo·zo·is′tic** (-zō-ĭs′tĭk) *adj.*

hy·men (hī′mən) *n.* A membranous fold of tissue that partly or completely occludes the external vaginal orifice. [Late Latin *hymēn,* from Greek *humēn,* thin skin, membrane. See **syū-** in Appendix.] **—hy′men·al** *adj.*

Hy·men (hī′mən) *n.* *Greek Mythology.* The god of marriage.

hy·me·ne·al (hī′mə-nē′əl) *adj.* Of or relating to a wedding or marriage. **—hymeneal** *n.* **1.** A wedding song or poem. **2. hymeneals.** *Archaic.* A wedding; nuptials. [From Latin *hymenaeus,* wedding song, wedding, from Greek *humēnaios,* from *Humēn,* Hymen, from *humēn,* membrane. See HYMEN.] **—hy′me·ne′al·ly** *adv.*

hy·me·ni·um (hī-mē′nē-əm) *n., pl.* **-ni·a** (-nē-ə) or **-ni·ums.** The spore-bearing layer of the fruiting body of certain fungi, containing asci or basidia. [New Latin, from Greek *humenion,* diminutive of *humēn,* membrane. See HYMEN.] **—hy·me′ni·al** (-əl) *adj.*

hy·me·nop·ter·an (hī′mə-nŏp′tər-ən) *adj.* Of or belonging to the Hymenoptera. **—hymenopteran** also **hy·me·nop·ter·on** (-tə-rŏn′) *n.* An insect of the order Hymenoptera, including the bees, wasps, and ants, often living in complex social groups and characteristically having two pairs of membranous wings. [From New Latin *Hymenoptera,* order name, from Greek *humenopteros,* membrane-winged : *humēn,* membrane; see HYMEN + *pteron,* wing; see –PTER.] **—hy′me·nop′ter·ous** (-tər-əs) *adj.*

Hy·met·tus (hī-mĕt′əs). A mountain ridge, rising to about 1,028 m (3,370 ft), in east-central Greece near Athens. Marble has been quarried here since antiquity.

Hy·mie (hī′mē) *n.* *Offensive Slang.* Used as a disparaging term for a Jew. [Probably from *Hymie,* nickname for *Hyman.*]

hymn (hĭm) *n.* **1.** A song of praise or thanksgiving to God or a deity. **2.** A song of praise or joy; a paean. **—hymn** *v.* **hymned, hymn·ing, hymns.** —*tr.* To praise, glorify, or worship in or as if in a hymn. —*intr.* To sing hymns. [Middle English *imne,* from Old French *ymne,* from Latin *hymnus,* song of praise, from Greek *humnos.*]

hym·nal (hĭm′nəl) *n.* A book or collection of church hymns. Also called *hymnary, hymnbook.* [Middle English *himnale,* from Medieval Latin *hymnāle,* from Latin *hymnus,* hymn. See HYMN.]

hymnal stanza *n.* See **common measure** (sense 3).

hym·na·ry (hĭm′nə-rē) *n.* See **hymnal.**

hymn·book (hĭm′bo͝ok′) *n.* See **hymnal.**

hym·no·dy (hĭm′nə-dē) *n., pl.* **-dies. 1.** The singing of hymns. **2.** The composing or writing of hymns. **3.** The hymns of a particular period or church. [Medieval Latin *hymnōdia,* from Greek *humnōidia* : *humnos,* hymn + *ōidē,* song; see **wed-**[2] in Appendix.] **—hym′no·dist** (-dĭst) *n.*

hym·nol·o·gy (hĭm-nŏl′ə-jē) *n.* **1.** Hymnody. **2.** The study of hymns. [Greek *humnologia,* singing of hymns : *humnos,* hymn + *-logia,* -logy.] **—hym′no·log′ic** (hĭm′nə-lŏj′ĭk), **hym′no·log′i·cal** (-ĭ-kəl) *adj.* **—hym·nol′o·gist** *n.*

hy·oid (hī′oid′) *adj.* Of or relating to the hyoid bone. **—hyoid** *n.* The hyoid bone. [New Latin *hyoidēs,* the hyoid bone, from Greek *huoeidēs,* shaped like the letter upsilon : *hu,* name of the letter upsilon + *-oeidēs,* -oid.]

hyoid bone *n.* A U-shaped bone at the base of the tongue that supports the muscles of the tongue.

hy·o·scine (hī′ə-sēn′) *n.* See **scopolamine.** [German *Hyoscin,* from New Latin *Hyoscyamus,* henbane genus, from Greek *huoskuamos,* henbane : *huos,* genitive of *hus,* swine; see **sū-** in Appendix + *kuamos,* bean.]

hy·o·scy·a·mine (hī′ə-sī′ə-mēn′) *n.* A poisonous white crystalline alkaloid, $C_{17}H_{23}NO_3$, isometric with atropine and having similar uses but more potent effects. [New Latin *Hyoscyamus,* henbane genus; see HYOSCINE + –INE[2].]

hyp. *abbr.* **1.** *Mathematics.* Hypotenuse. **2.** Hypothesis. **3.** Hypothetical.

hyp– *pref.* Variant of **hypo–.**

hyp·a·bys·sal (hĭp′ə-bĭs′əl, hī′pə-) *adj.* *Geology.* Solidifying chiefly as a minor intrusion, especially as a dike or sill, before reaching the earth's surface. Used of rocks. **—hyp′a·bys′sal·ly** *adv.*

hy·pae·thral also **hy·pe·thral** (hī-pē′thrəl) *adj.* Wholly or partly open to the sky: *an ancient hypaethral temple.* [From Lat-

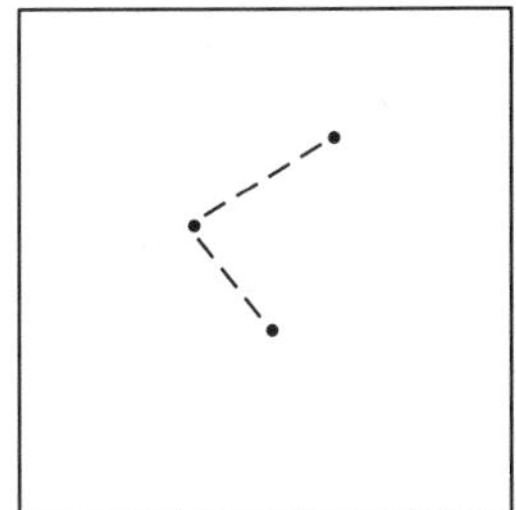

Hydrus

hyena
Spotted hyena
Crocuta crocuta

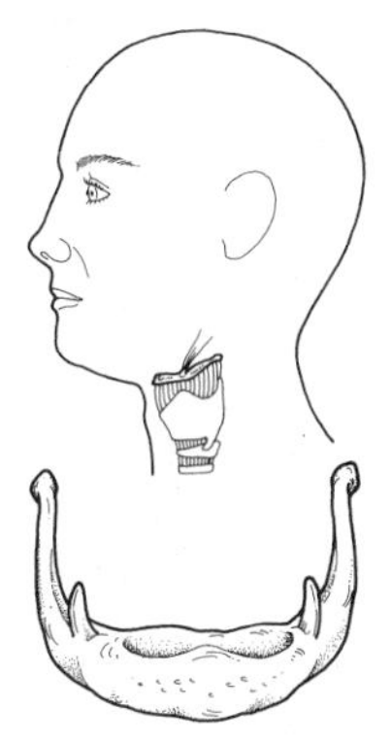

hyoid bone

ă pat	oi boy
ā pay	ou out
âr care	o͝o took
ä father	o͞o boot
ĕ pet	ŭ cut
ē be	ûr urge
ĭ pit	th thin
ī pie	*th* this
îr pier	hw which
ŏ pot	zh vision
ō toe	ə about, item
ô paw	♦ regionalism

Stress marks: ′ (primary); ′ (secondary), as in **dictionary** (dĭk′shə-nĕr′ē)

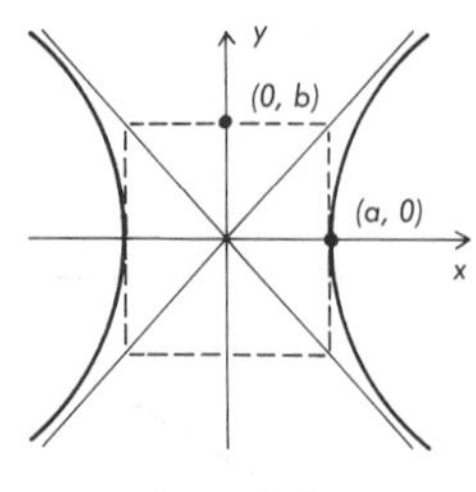

hyperbola
$y = \frac{1}{x}$

in *hypaethrus,* from Greek *hupaithros* : *hupo,* under; see HYPO– + *aithēr,* sky, air.]

hy·pan·thi·um (hī-păn′thē-əm) *n., pl.* **-thi·a** (-thē-ə). The ringlike, cup-shaped, or tubular structure of a flower on which the sepals, petals, and stamens are borne, as in the flowers of the rose or cherry. [New Latin : HYP(O)– + Greek *anthos,* flower.] **—hy·pan′thi·al** *adj.*

hype¹ (hīp) *Slang. n.* **1.** Excessive publicity and the ensuing commotion: *the hype surrounding the murder trial.* **2.** Exaggerated or extravagant claims made especially in advertising or promotional material: *"It is pure hype, a gigantic PR job"* (Saturday Review). **3.** An advertising or promotional ploy: *"Some restaurant owners in town are cooking up a $75,000 hype to promote New York as 'Restaurant City, U.S.A.'"* (New York). **4.** Something deliberately misleading; a deception: "[He] *says that there isn't any energy crisis at all, that it's all a hype, to maintain outrageous profits for the oil companies"* (Joel Oppenheimer). **—hype** *tr.v.* **hyped, hyp·ing, hypes.** To publicize or promote, especially by extravagant, inflated, or misleading claims: *hyped the new book by sending its author on a promotional tour.* [Partly from *hype,* a swindle (perhaps from HYPER–) and partly from HYPE(RBOLE).]

hype² (hīp) *Slang. n.* **1.** A hypodermic injection, syringe, or needle. **2.** A drug addict. **—hype** *tr.v.* **hyped, hyp·ing, hypes.** To stimulate with or as if with a hypodermic injection: *"hyped the country up to a purposeless pitch"* (Newsweek). [Shortening and alteration of HYPODERMIC.]

hyped-up (hīpt′ŭp′) *adj. Slang.* Stimulated with or as if with a hypodermic injection: *"hyped-up rhetoric to dramatize the strike"* (New York Times).

hy·per (hī′pər) *adj. Slang.* **1.** Having a very excitable or nervous temperament; high-strung. **2.** Emotionally stimulated or overexcited. [Short for HYPERACTIVE.]

hyper– *pref.* **1.** Over; above; beyond: *hypercharge.* **2.** Excessive; excessively: *hypercritical.* [Greek *huper-,* from *huper,* over, beyond. See **uper** in Appendix.]

hy·per·ac·id (hī′pər-ăs′ĭd) *adj.* Containing excessive acid; excessively acidic: *a hyperacid stomach.* **—hy′per·a·cid′i·ty** (-ə-sĭd′ĭ-tē) *n.*

hy·per·ac·tive (hī′pər-ăk′tĭv) *adj.* **1.** Highly or excessively active: *a hyperactive new drug; a hyperactive thyroid gland.* **2. a.** Having behavior characterized by constant overactivity. **b.** Afflicted with attention deficit disorder. **—hy′per·ac′tive·ly** *adv.* **—hy′per·ac·tiv′i·ty** (-ăk-tĭv′ĭ-tē) *n.*

hy·per·aes·the·sia (hī′pər-ĭs-thē′zhə) *n.* Variant of **hyperesthesia.**

hy·per·bar·ic (hī′pər-băr′ĭk) *adj.* Of, relating to, producing, operating, or occurring at pressures higher than normal atmospheric pressure: *a hyperbaric chamber; hyperbaric therapy.* **—hy′per·bar′i·cal·ly** *adv.*

hy·per·ba·ton (hī-pûr′bə-tŏn′) *n.* A figure of speech, such as anastrophe or hysteron proteron, using deviation from normal or logical word order to produce an effect. [Greek *huperbaton,* from neuter of *huperbatos,* transposed, from *huperbainein,* to step over : *huper-,* over, across; see HYPER– + *bainein,* to step; see **gʷā-** in Appendix.]

hy·per·bo·la (hī-pûr′bə-lə) *n., pl.* **-las** or **-lae** (-lē). *Mathematics.* A plane curve having two branches, formed by the intersection of a plane with both halves of a right circular cone at an angle parallel to the axis of the cone. It is the locus of points for which the difference of the distances from two given points is a constant. [New Latin, from Greek *huperbolē,* a throwing beyond, excess (from the relationship between the line joining the vertices of a conic and the line through its focus and parallel to its directrix). See HYPERBOLE.]

hy·per·bo·le (hī-pûr′bə-lē) *n.* A figure of speech in which exaggeration is used for emphasis or effect, as in *I could sleep for a year* or *This book weighs a ton.* [Latin *hyperbolē,* from Greek *huperbolē,* excess, from *huperballein,* to exceed : *huper,* beyond; see HYPER– + *ballein,* to throw; see **gʷelə-** in Appendix.]

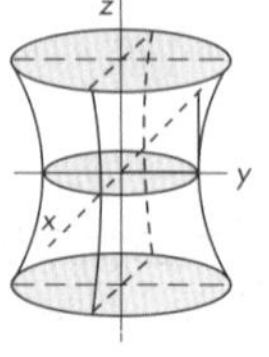

hy·per·bol·ic (hī′pər-bŏl′ĭk) also **hy·per·bol·i·cal** (-ĭ-kəl) *adj.* **1.** Of, relating to, or employing hyperbole. **2.** *Mathematics.* **a.** Of, relating to, or having the form of a hyperbola. **b.** Of or relating to a geometric system in which two or more lines can be drawn through any point in a plane and not intersect a given line in the plane. **c.** Of or relating to a hyperbolic function: *hyperbolic cosine.* **—hy′per·bol′i·cal·ly** *adv.*

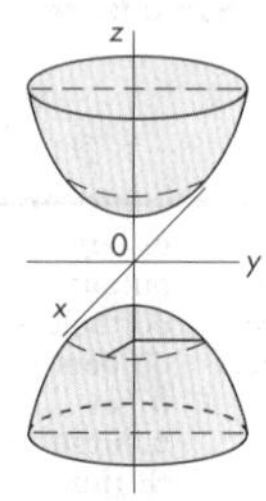

hyperboloid
Top: Hyperboloid of one sheet
Bottom: Hyperboloid of two sheets

hyperbolic function *n. Mathematics.* Any of a set of six functions related, for a real variable *z,* to the hyperbola as the trigonometric functions are to the circle: **a.** The hyperbolic sine of *z,* $\sinh z = \frac{1}{2}(e^z - e^{-z})$. **b.** The hyperbolic cosine of *z,* $\cosh z = \frac{1}{2}(e^z + e^{-z})$. **c.** The hyperbolic tangent of *z,* $\tanh z = \sinh z/\cosh z$. **d.** The hyperbolic cotangent of *z,* $\coth z = \cosh z/\sinh z$. **e.** The hyperbolic secant of *z,* $\operatorname{sech} z = 1/\cosh z$. **f.** The hyperbolic cosecant of *z,* $\operatorname{csch} z = 1/\sinh z$.

hyperbolic paraboloid *n. Mathematics.* A surface of which all sections parallel to one coordinate plane are hyperbolas and all sections parallel to another coordinate plane are parabolas.

hy·per·bo·lism (hī-pûr′bə-lĭz′əm) *n.* **1.** The use of hyperbole. **2.** An instance of hyperbole.

hy·per·bo·lize (hī-pûr′bə-līz′) *v.* **-lized, -liz·ing, -liz·es.** —*intr.* To use hyperbole; exaggerate. —*tr.* To express with hyperbole.

hy·per·bo·loid (hī-pûr′bə-loid′) *n. Mathematics.* Either of two quadric surfaces generated by rotating a hyperbola about either of its main axes and having a finite center with certain plane sections that are hyperbolas and others that are ellipses or circles. **—hy·per′bo·loid′al** (-loid′l) *adv.*

Hy·per·bo·re·an (hī′pər-bôr′ē-ən, -bōr′-, -bə-rē′ən) *n. Greek Mythology.* One of a people known to the ancient Greeks from the earliest times, living in a perpetually warm and sunny land north of the source of the north wind. **—Hyperborean** *adj.* **1.** Of or relating to the Hyperboreans. **2. hyperborean. a.** Of or relating to the far north; Arctic. **b.** Very cold; frigid. [From Latin *Hyperboreus,* from *Hyperboreī,* the Hyperboreans, from Greek *Huperboreoi* : *huper-,* hyper- + *boreios,* northern; or *Boreas,* the north wind, the north.]

hy·per·cal·ce·mia (hī′pər-kăl-sē′mē-ə) *n.* An excessive amount of calcium in the blood.

hy·per·cap·ni·a (hī′pər-kăp′nē-ə) *n.* An increased amount of carbon dioxide in the blood as a result of hypoventilation. [HYPER– + Greek *kapnos,* smoke + –IA².]

hy·per·cat·a·lec·tic (hī′pər-kăt′l-ĕk′tĭk) *adj.* Having an extra syllable or syllables at the end of a metrically complete line of verse or in a metrical foot. [Latin *hypercatalēcticus,* from Greek *huperkatalēktikos* : *huper-,* hyper- + *katalēktikos,* incomplete; see CATALECTIC.] **—hy′per·cat′a·lex′is** (-ĕk′sĭs) *n.*

hy·per·charge (hī′pər-chärj′) *n. Symbol* **Y** A quantum number equal to twice the average electric charge of a particle multiplet or, equivalently, to the sum of the strangeness and the baryon number.

hy·per·cho·les·ter·ol·e·mi·a (hī′pər-kə-lĕs′tər-ə-lē′mē-ə) *n.* **1.** An excess of cholesterol in the blood. **2.** A familial disorder characterized by a high level of cholesterol in the blood.

hy·per·cor·rect (hī′pər-kə-rĕkt′) *adj.* Of, relating to, or marked by hypercorrection. **—hy′per·cor·rect′ly** *adv.* **—hy′per·cor·rect′ness** *n.*

hy·per·cor·rec·tion (hī′pər-kə-rĕk′shən) *n. Linguistics.* **1.** A construction or pronunciation produced by mistaken analogy with standard usage out of a desire to be correct, as in the substitution of *I* for *me* in *on behalf of my wife and I.* **2.** The production of such a construction or pronunciation.

hy·per·crit·ic (hī′pər-krĭt′ĭk) *n.* A person who is excessively critical.

hy·per·crit·i·cal (hī′pər-krĭt′ĭ-kəl) *adj.* Excessively critical; captious. See Synonyms at **critical. —hy′per·crit′i·cal·ly** *adv.* **—hy′per·crit′i·cism** (-ĭ-sĭz′əm) *n.*

hy·per·e·mi·a (hī′pə-rē′mē-ə) *n.* An increase in the quantity of blood flow to a body part; engorgement. **—hy′per·e′mic** (-mĭk) *adj.*

hy·per·es·the·sia also **hy·per·aes·the·sia** (hī′pər-ĭs-thē′zhə) *n.* An abnormal or pathological increase in sensitivity to sensory stimuli, as of the skin to touch or the ear to sound. **—hy′per·es·thet′ic** (-thĕt′ĭk) *adj.*

hy·per·eu·tec·tic (hī′pər-yo͞o-tĕk′tĭk) *adj.* Having the minor component present in a larger amount than in the eutectic composition of the same components.

hy·per·ex·ten·sion (hī′pər-ĭk-stĕn′shən) *n.* Extension of a bodily joint beyond its normal range of motion. **—hy′per·ex·tend′** (-ĭk-stĕnd′) *v.*

hy·per·fine structure (hī′pər-fīn′) *n. Abbr.* **hfs** The splitting of a spectral line into two or more components as a result of the spin or magnetic moment of the atomic nucleus.

hy·per·gly·ce·mi·a (hī′pər-glī-sē′mē-ə) *n.* The presence of an abnormally high concentration of glucose in the blood. **—hy′per·gly·ce′mic** (-mĭk) *adj.*

hy·per·gol·ic (hī′pər-gŏl′ĭk) *adj.* **1.** Of or relating to a rocket propellant consisting of fuel and an oxidizer that ignite spontaneously on contact. **2.** Using such a fuel. [From German *Hypergol,* a hypergolic fluid propellant : from *hyper-,* extreme (from Greek *huper-;* see HYPER–) + Greek *ergon,* work; see ERG.] **—hy′per·gol′** (hī′pər-gôl′, -gōl′, -gŏl′) *n.* **—hy′per·gol′i·cal·ly** *adv.*

hy·per·in·fla·tion (hī′pər-ĭn-flā′shən) *n.* Extremely high monetary inflation. **—hy′per·in·fla′tion·ar′y** *adj.*

hy·per·in·su·lin·ism (hī′pər-ĭn′sə-lə-nĭz′əm) *n.* An abnormally high level of insulin in the blood, resulting in hypoglycemia.

Hy·pe·ri·on (hī-pîr′ē-ən) *n.* **1.** *Greek Mythology.* A Titan, the son of Gaea and Uranus and the father of Helios. **2.** The satellite of Saturn that is 15th in distance from the planet. [Greek *Huperiōn.*]

hy·per·ir·ri·ta·bil·i·ty (hī′pər-ĭr′ĭ-tə-bĭl′ĭ-tē) *n.* Excessive response to a stimulus. **—hy′per·ir′ri·ta·ble** *adj.*

hy·per·ker·a·to·sis (hī′pər-kĕr′ə-tō′sĭs) *n.* Hypertrophy of the cornea or the horny layer of the skin. **—hy′per·ker′a·tot′ic** (-tŏt′ĭk) *adj.*

hy·per·ki·ne·sia (hī′pər-kĭ-nē′zhə) also **hy·per·ki·ne·sis** (-sĭs) *n.* Pathologically increased muscular movement. [HYPER– + Greek *kinēsis,* movement (from *kinein,* to move; see **kei-**² in Appendix) + –IA¹.] **—hy′per·ki·net′ic** (-nĕt′ĭk) *adj.*

hy·per·li·pe·mi·a (hī′pər-lĭ-pē′mē-ə, -lī-) *n.* An excess of fat or lipids in the blood. Also called *hyperlipidemia.*

hy·per·li·pi·de·mi·a (hī′pər-lĭp′ĭ-dē′mē-ə, -lī′pĭ-) *n.* See **hyperlipemia.**

hy·per·mar·ket (hī′pər-mär′kĭt) *n.* A very large commercial establishment that is a combination of a department store and a supermarket.

hy·per·me·di·a (hī′pər-mē′dē-ə) *n.* A computer-based information retrieval system that enables a user to gain or provide access to texts, audio and video recordings, photographs, and computer graphics related to a particular subject.

hy·per·met·ric (hī′pər-mĕt′rĭk) *adj.* **1.** Having one or more syllables in addition to those found in a standard metrical unit or line of verse. **2.** Being one of these additional syllables. **—hy·per′me·ter** (hī-pûr′mĭ-tər) *n.* **—hy′per·met′ri·cal** *adj.*

hy·per·me·tro·pi·a (hī′pər-mĭ-trō′pē-ə) *n.* See **hyperopia.** [Greek *hupermetros,* beyond measure (*huper-,* hyper- + *metron,* measure; see METER²) + –OPIA.] **—hy′per·me·tro′pic** (-trō′pĭk, -trŏp′ĭk), **hy′per·me·tro′pi·cal** *adj.* **—hy′per·met′ro·py** (-mĕt′rə-pē) *n.*

hy·perm·ne·sia (hī′pərm-nē′zhə) *n.* Exceptionally exact or vivid memory, especially as associated with certain mental illnesses. [HYPER– + (A)MNESIA.] **—hy′perm·ne′sic** (-zĭk, -sĭk) *adj.*

hy·per·on (hī′pə-rŏn′) *n.* A semistable or unstable baryon with mass greater than the neutron. See table at **subatomic particle.**

hy·per·o·pi·a (hī′pə-rō′pē-ə) *n.* An abnormal condition of the eye in which vision is better for distant objects than for near objects. It results from the eyeball being too short from front to back, causing images to be focused behind the retina. Also called *farsightedness, hypermetropia.* **—hy′per·ope′** (hī′pə-rōp′) *n.* **—hy′per·o′pic** (-ō′pĭk, -ŏp′ĭk) *adj.*

hy·per·os·to·sis (hī′pər-ŏ-stō′sĭs) *n., pl.* **-ses** (-sēz). Excessive or abnormal thickening or growth of bone tissue. [HYPER– + OST(EO)– + –OSIS.] **—hy′per·os·tot′ic** (-ŏ-stŏt′ĭk) *adj.*

hy·per·pi·tu·i·ta·rism (hī′pər-pĭ-to͞o′ĭ-tə-rĭz′əm, -tyo͞o′-) *n.* **1.** Pathologically excessive production of anterior pituitary hormones, especially growth hormones. **2.** The condition resulting from an excess of pituitary hormones, characterized by gigantism in children and acromegaly in adults. **—hy′per·pi·tu′i·tar′y** (-tĕr′ē) *adj.*

hy·per·pla·sia (hī′pər-plā′zhə) *n.* An abnormal increase in the number of cells in an organ or a tissue with consequent enlargement. **—hy′per·plas′tic** (-plăs′tĭk) *adj.*

hy·per·ploid (hī′pər-ploid′) *adj.* Having a chromosome number greater than but not an exact multiple of the normal euploid number. **—hy′per·ploid′** *n.* **—hy′per·ploi′dy** *n.*

hy·perp·ne·a (hī′pərp-nē′ə, hī′pər-nē′ə) *n.* Abnormally deep or rapid breathing. [HYPER– + Greek *pnoia, pnoē,* breath, breathing (from *pnein,* to breathe; see **pneu-** in Appendix).] **—hy′perp·ne′ic** (-ĭk) *adj.*

hy·per·po·lar·ize (hī′pər-pō′lə-rīz′) *tr.v.* **-ized, -iz·ing, -iz·es.** *Physiology.* To cause an increase in polarity, as across a biological membrane.

hy·per·py·rex·i·a (hī′pər-pī-rĕk′sē-ə) *n.* Abnormally high fever. **—hy′per·py·rex′i·al, hy′per·py·ret′ic** (-rĕt′ĭk) *adj.*

hy·per·re·al·ism (hī′pər-rē′ə-lĭz′əm) *n.* An artistic style characterized by highly realistic graphic representation. **—hy′per·re′al·ist** *adj. & n.* **—hy′per·re′al·ist′ic** *adj.*

hy·per·sen·si·tive (hī′pər-sĕn′sĭ-tĭv) *adj.* Highly or excessively sensitive. **—hy′per·sen′si·tive·ness, hy′per·sen′si·tiv′i·ty** (-tĭv′ĭ-tē) *n.*

hy·per·sex·u·al (hī′pər-sĕk′sho͞o-əl) *adj.* Excessively interested or involved in sexual activity. **—hy′per·sex′u·al′i·ty** (-sĕk′sho͞o-ăl′ĭ-tē) *n.*

hy·per·son·ic (hī′pər-sŏn′ĭk) *adj.* Of, relating to, or capable of speed equal to or exceeding five times the speed of sound. **—hy′per·son′i·cal·ly** *adv.*

hy·per·space (hī′pər-spās′) *n.* Space that has four or more dimensions.

hy·per·sthene (hī′pərs-thēn′) *n.* A green, brown, or black splintery, cleavable pyroxene mineral, essentially $(Fe,Mg)_2Si_2O_6$. [French *hypersthène* : *hyper-,* extreme (from Greek *huper-;* see HYPER–) + Greek *sthenos,* strength.] **—hy′per·sthen′ic** (-thĕn′ĭk) *adj.*

hy·per·ten·sion (hī′pər-tĕn′shən) *n.* **1.** Arterial disease in which chronic high blood pressure is the primary symptom. **2.** Abnormally high blood pressure. **—hy′per·ten′sive** *adj. & n.*

hy·per·text (hī′pər-tĕkst′) *n. Computer Science.* A computer-based text retrieval system that enables the user to provide access to or gain information related to a particular text.

hy·per·ther·mi·a (hī′pər-thûr′mē-ə) *n.* Unusually high body temperature. **—hy′per·ther′mal** *adj.*

hy·per·thy·roid (hī′pər-thī′roid′) *adj.* Of, relating to, or affected with hyperthyroidism.

hy·per·thy·roid·ism (hī′pər-thī′roi-dĭz′əm) *n.* **1.** Pathologically excessive production of thyroid hormones. **2.** The condition resulting from excessive activity of the thyroid gland, characterized by increased basal metabolism.

hy·per·to·ni·a (hī′pər-tō′nē-ə) *n. Pathology.* The state of being hypertonic.

hy·per·ton·ic (hī′pər-tŏn′ĭk) *adj.* **1.** *Pathology.* Having extreme muscular or arterial tension. **2.** *Chemistry.* Having the higher osmotic pressure of two solutions. **—hy′per·to·nic′i·ty** (-tə-nĭs′ĭ-tē, -tō-) *n.*

hy·per·tro·phy (hī-pûr′trə-fē) *n., pl.* **-phies.** A nontumorous enlargement of an organ or a tissue as a result of an increase in the size rather than the number of constituent cells: *muscle hypertrophy.* **—hypertrophy** *intr. & tr.v.* **-phied, -phy·ing, -phies.** To grow or cause to grow abnormally large. **—hy′per·tro′phic** (-trō′fĭk, -trŏf′ĭk) *adj.*

hy·per·ven·ti·late (hī′pər-vĕn′tl-āt′) *v.* **-lat·ed, -lat·ing, -lates.** —*intr.* **1.** To breathe abnormally fast or deeply so as to effect hyperventilation. **2.** To breathe in this manner as from excitement or anxiety. —*tr.* To subject to hyperventilation.

hy·per·ven·ti·la·tion (hī′pər-vĕn′tl-ā′shən) *n.* Abnormally fast or deep respiration, which results in the loss of carbon dioxide from the blood, thereby causing a fall in blood pressure, tingling of the extremities, and sometimes fainting.

hy·per·vi·ta·min·o·sis (hī′pər-vī′tə-mə-nō′sĭs) *n., pl.* **-ses** (-sēz). Any of various abnormal conditions in which the physiological effect of a vitamin is produced to a pathological degree by excessive intake of the vitamin.

hy·pes·the·sia (hī′pĭs-thē′zhə) *n.* Variant of **hypoesthesia.**

hy·pe·thral (hī-pē′thrəl) *adj.* Variant of **hypaethral.**

hy·pha (hī′fə) *n., pl.* **-phae** (-fē). Any of the threadlike filaments forming the mycelium of a fungus. [New Latin, from Greek *huphē,* web. See **webh-** in Appendix.] **—hy′phal** *adj.*

hy·phen (hī′fən) *n.* A punctuation mark (-) used between the parts of a compound word or name or between the syllables of a word, especially when divided at the end of a line of text. **—hyphen** *tr.v.* **-phened, -phen·ing, -phens.** To hyphenate. [Late Latin, from Greek *huphen,* a sign indicating a compound or two words which are to be read as one, from *huph' hen,* in one : *hupo,* under; see HYPO– + *hen,* neuter of *heis,* one; see **sem-**¹ in Appendix.]

hy·phen·ate (hī′fə-nāt′) *tr.v.* **-at·ed, -at·ing, -ates.** To divide or connect (syllables, word elements, or names) with a hyphen. **—hy′phen·a′tion** *n.*

hypn– *pref.* Variant of **hypno–.**

hyp·na·gog·ic also **hyp·no·gog·ic** (hĭp′nə-gŏj′ĭk, -gō′jĭk) *adj.* **1.** Inducing sleep; soporific. **2.** Of or relating to the state of drowsiness preceding sleep. [French *hypnagogique* : Greek *hupnos,* sleep; see HYPNO– + Greek *agōgos,* leading (from *agein,* to lead; see **ag-** in Appendix).]

hypno– or **hypn–** *pref.* **1.** Sleep: *hypnophobia.* **2.** Hypnosis: *hypnoanalysis.* [From Greek *hupnos,* sleep. See **swep-** in Appendix.]

hyp·no·a·nal·y·sis (hĭp′nō-ə-năl′ĭ-sĭs) *n., pl.* **-ses** (-sēz′). The use of hypnosis in conjunction with psychoanalytic techniques.

hyp·no·gen·e·sis (hĭp′nō-jĕn′ĭ-sĭs) *n.* The process of inducing or entering sleep or a hypnotic state. **—hyp′no·ge·net′ic** (-jə-nĕt′ĭk) *adj.* **—hyp′no·ge·net′i·cal·ly** *adv.*

hyp·no·gog·ic (hĭp′nə-gŏj′ĭk, -gō′jĭk) *adj.* Variant of **hypnagogic.**

hyp·noid (hĭp′noid′) also **hyp·noi·dal** (hĭp-noid′l) *adj.* Of or resembling hypnosis or sleep.

hyp·no·pe·di·a (hĭp′nə-pē′dē-ə) *n.* See **sleep-learning.** [HYPNO– + Greek *paideia,* education; see ENCYCLOPEDIA.]

hyp·no·pho·bi·a (hĭp′nə-fō′bē-ə) *n.* An abnormal fear of falling asleep. **—hyp′no·pho′bic** *adj.*

hyp·no·pom·pic (hĭp′nə-pŏm′pĭk) *adj.* Of or relating to the partially conscious state that precedes complete awakening from sleep. [From HYPNO– + Greek *pompē,* a sending away; see POMP.]

Hyp·nos (hĭp′nŏs′) *n. Greek Mythology.* The god of sleep.

hyp·no·sis (hĭp-nō′sĭs) *n., pl.* **-ses** (-sēz). **1.** A sleeplike state usually induced by another person in which the subject may experience forgotten or suppressed memories, hallucinations, and heightened suggestibility. **2.** Hypnotism. **3.** A sleeplike condition.

hyp·no·ther·a·py (hĭp′nō-thĕr′ə-pē) *n., pl.* **-pies.** Therapy based on or using hypnosis, especially for treatment of chronic pain.

hyp·not·ic (hĭp-nŏt′ĭk) *adj.* **1.a.** Of or relating to hypnosis. **b.** Of or relating to hypnotism. **2.** Inducing or tending to induce sleep; soporific: *read the bedtime story in a hypnotic voice.* **—hypnotic** *n.* **1.a.** A person who is hypnotized. **b.** A person who can be hypnotized. **2.** An agent that causes sleep; a soporific. [French *hypnotique,* from Late Latin *hypnōticus,* inducing sleep, from Greek *hupnōtikos,* from *hupnoun,* to put to sleep, from *hupnos,* sleep. See **swep-** in Appendix.] **—hyp·not′i·cal·ly** *adv.*

hyp·no·tism (hĭp′nə-tĭz′əm) *n.* **1.** The theory or practice of inducing hypnosis. **2.** The act of inducing hypnosis. **—hyp′no·tist** *n.*

hyp·no·tize (hĭp′nə-tīz′) *tr.v.* **-tized, -tiz·ing, -tiz·es. 1.** To put into a state of hypnosis. **2.** To fascinate by or as if by hypnosis. **—hyp′no·tiz′a·bil′i·ty** *n.* **—hyp′no·tiz′a·ble** *adj.* **—hyp′no·ti·za′tion** (-tĭ-zā′shən) *n.* **—hyp′no·tiz′er** *n.*

hy·po¹ (hī′pō) *n.* See **sodium thiosulfate.** [Short for HYPOSULFITE.]

hy·po² (hī′pō) *Informal. n., pl.* **-pos. 1.** A hypodermic syringe. **2.** A hypodermic injection. **—hypo** *tr.v.* **-poed, -po·ing,**

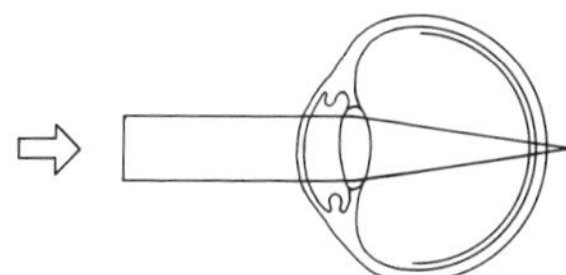

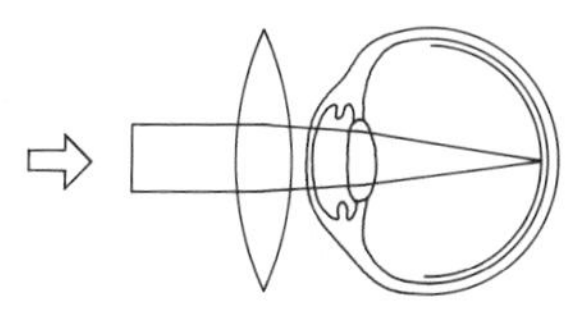

hyperopia
Top: Before correction
Bottom: After correction

ă pat	oi boy
ā pay	ou out
âr care	o͝o took
ä father	o͞o boot
ĕ pet	ŭ cut
ē be	ûr urge
ĭ pit	th thin
ī pie	*th* this
îr pier	hw which
ŏ pot	zh vision
ō toe	ə about, item
ô paw	♦ regionalism

Stress marks: ′ (primary); ′ (secondary), as in **dictionary** (dĭk′shə-nĕr′ē)

-pos. To stimulate by or as if by hypodermic injection: *"pandering to community fears in order to hypo ratings"* (Variety).

hypo– or **hyp–** *pref.* **1.** Below; beneath; under: *hypodermic.* **2.** Less than normal; deficient: *hypoesthesia.* **3.** In the lowest state of oxidation: *hypoxanthine.* [Greek *hupo-,* from *hupo,* under, beneath. See **upo** in Appendix.]

hy·po·a·cid·i·ty (hī′pō-ə-sĭd′ĭ-tē) *n., pl.* **-ties. 1.** *Chemistry.* Slight acidity. **2.** *Medicine.* A condition of less than normal acidity, especially in the stomach.

hy·po·al·ler·gen·ic (hī′pō-ăl′ər-jĕn′ĭk) *adj.* Having a decreased tendency to provoke an allergic reaction: *hypoallergenic cosmetics.*

hy·po·bar·ic (hī′pə-băr′ĭk) *adj.* Below normal pressure. **—hy′po·bar′ism** *n.*

hy·po·blast (hī′pə-blăst′) *n.* See **endoderm. —hy′po·blas′tic** *adj.*

hy·po·caust (hī′pə-kôst′) *n.* A space under the floor of an ancient Roman building where heat from a furnace was accumulated to heat a room or a bath. [Latin *hypocaustum,* from Greek *hupokauston,* from *hupokaiein,* to light a fire beneath : *hupo-,* hypo- + *kaiein,* to burn.]

hy·po·cen·ter (hī′pə-sĕn′tər) *n.* The surface position directly beneath the center of a nuclear explosion. **—hy′po·cen′tral** (-sĕn′trəl) *adj.*

hy·po·chlo·rite (hī′pə-klôr′īt′, -klōr′-) *n.* A salt or ester of hypochlorous acid.

hy·po·chlo·rous acid (hī′pə-klôr′əs, -klōr′-) *n.* A weak, unstable acid, HOCl, occurring only in solution and used as a bleach, an oxidizer, a deodorant, and a disinfectant.

hy·po·chon·dri·a (hī′pə-kŏn′drē-ə) *n.* **1.** The persistent neurotic conviction that one is or is likely to become ill, often involving experiences of real pain when illness is neither present nor likely. Also called *hypochondriasis.* **2.** Plural of **hypochondrium.** [Late Latin, abdomen, from Greek *hupokhondria,* pl. of *hupokhondrion,* abdomen (held to be the seat of melancholy), neuter of *hupokhondrios,* under the cartilage of the breastbone : *hupo-,* hypo- + *khondros,* cartilage; see **ghrendh-** in Appendix.]

hy·po·chon·dri·ac (hī′pə-kŏn′drē-ăk′) *n.* A person afflicted with hypochondria. **—hypochondriac** *adj.* **1.** Relating to or affected with hypochondria. **2.** *Anatomy.* Relating to or located in the hypochondrium. **—hy′po·chon·dri′a·cal** (-kŏn-drī′ə-kəl) *adj.* **—hy′po·chon·dri′a·cal·ly** *adv.*

hy·po·chon·dri·a·sis (hī′pə-kən-drī′ə-sĭs) *n., pl.* **-ses** (-sēz′). See **hypochondria** (sense 1). [HYPOCHONDR(IA) + –IASIS.]

hy·po·chon·dri·um (hī′pə-kŏn′drē-əm) *n., pl.* **-dri·a** (-drē-ə). The upper lateral region of the abdomen, marked by the lower ribs. [New Latin, from Greek *hupokhondrion,* abdomen. See HYPOCHONDRIA.]

hy·poc·o·rism (hī-pŏk′ə-rĭz′əm, hī′pə-kôr′ĭz′əm, -kōr′-) *n.* **1.** A name of endearment; a pet name. **2.** The use of such names. [Late Latin *hypocorisma,* from Greek *hupokorisma,* from *hupokorizesthai,* to call by endearing names : *hypo,* beneath, secretly; see HYPO– + *korizesthai,* to caress (from *koros,* boy, and *korē,* girl; see **ker-²** in Appendix.)] **—hy′po·co·ris′tic** (hī′pə-kə-rĭs′tĭk), **hy′po·co·ris′ti·cal** (-tĭ-kəl) *adj.*

hy·po·cot·yl (hī′pə-kŏt′l) *n.* The part of the axis of a plant embryo or seedling plant that is below the cotyledons. [HYPO– + COTYL(EDON).]

hy·poc·ri·sy (hĭ-pŏk′rĭ-sē) *n., pl.* **-sies. 1.** The practice of professing beliefs, feelings, or virtues that one does not hold or possess; falseness. **2.** An act or instance of such falseness. [Middle English *ipocrisie,* from Old French, from Late Latin *hypocrisis,* play-acting, pretense, from Greek *hupokrisis,* from *hupokrinesthai,* to play a part, pretend : *hupo-,* hypo- + *krinesthai,* to explain (from *krinein,* to decide, judge; see **krei-** in Appendix).]

hyp·o·crite (hĭp′ə-krĭt′) *n.* A person given to hypocrisy. [Middle English *ipocrite,* from Old French, from Late Latin *hypocrita,* from Greek *hupocritēs,* actor, from *hupokrinesthai,* to play a part, pretend. See HYPOCRISY.]

hy·po·crit·i·cal (hĭp′ə-krĭt′ĭ-kəl) *adj.* **1.** Characterized by hypocrisy: *hypocritical praise.* **2.** Being a hypocrite: *a hypocritical rogue.* **—hyp′o·crit′i·cal·ly** *adv.*

hy·po·cy·cloid (hī′pō-sī′kloid′) *n. Mathematics.* The plane locus of a point fixed on a circle that rolls on the inside circumference of a fixed circle.

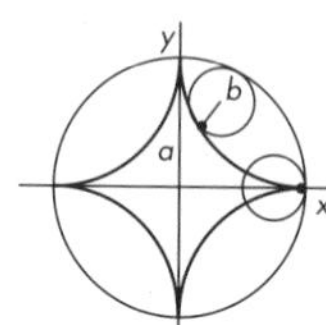

hypocycloid
a = radius of fixed circle
b = radius of rotating circle

hy·po·derm (hī′pə-dûrm′) *n.* Variant of **hypodermis.**

hy·po·der·mal (hī′pə-dûr′məl) *adj.* **1.** Of or relating to the hypodermis. **2.** Lying below the epidermis.

hy·po·der·mic (hī′pə-dûr′mĭk) *adj.* **1.** Of or relating to the layer just beneath the epidermis. **2.** Relating to the hypodermis. **3.** Injected beneath the skin. **—hypodermic** *n.* **1.** A hypodermic injection. **2.** A hypodermic needle. **3.** A hypodermic syringe. **—hy′po·der′mi·cal·ly** *adv.*

hypodermic injection *n.* A subcutaneous, intracutaneous, intramuscular, or intravenous injection by means of a hypodermic syringe and needle.

hypodermic needle *n.* **1.** A hollow needle used with a hypodermic syringe. **2.** A hypodermic syringe including the needle.

hypodermic syringe *n.* A piston syringe that is fitted with a hypodermic needle for giving injections.

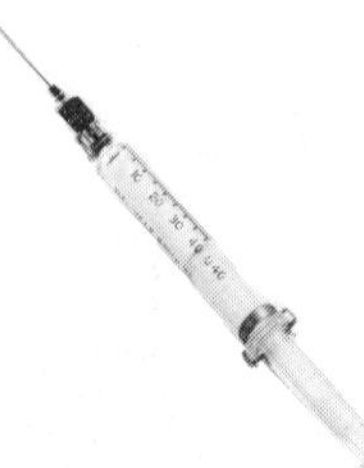
hypodermic syringe

hy·po·der·mis (hī′pə-dûr′mĭs) also **hy·po·derm** (hī′pə-dûrm′) *n.* **1.** An epidermal layer of cells that secretes an overlying chitinous cuticle, as in arthropods. **2.** *Botany.* A layer of cells lying immediately below the epidermis. **3.** *Anatomy.* A subcutaneous layer of loose connective tissue containing a varying number of fat cells.

hy·po·es·the·sia (hī′pō-ĭs-thē′zhə) also **hy·pes·the·sia** (hī′pĭs-) *n.* Partial loss of sensation; diminished sensibility.

hy·po·eu·tec·tic (hī′pō-yo͞o-tĕk′tĭk) *adj. Chemistry.* Having the minor component present in a smaller amount than in the eutectic composition of the same components.

hy·po·gas·tri·um (hī′pə-găs′trē-əm) *n., pl.* **-tri·a** (-trē-ə). The lowest of the three median regions of the abdomen. [New Latin, from Greek *hypogastrion* : *hupo,* hypo- + *gastrion,* diminutive of *gastēr,* belly.] **—hy′po·gas′tric** *adj.*

hy·po·ge·a (hī′pə-jē′ə) *n.* Plural of **hypogeum.**

hy·po·ge·al (hī′pə-jē′əl) also **hy·po·ge·an** (-ən) or **hy·po·ge·ous** (-əs) *adj.* **1.** Located under the earth's surface; underground. **2.** *Botany.* Of or relating to seed germination in which the cotyledons remain below the surface of the ground. [From Latin *hypogēus,* from Greek *hupogeios* : *hupo,* hypo- + *gē,* earth.] **—hy′po·ge′al·ly** *adv.*

hy·po·gene (hī′pə-jēn′) *adj.* Formed or situated below the earth's surface. Used of rocks.

hy·pog·e·nous (hī-pŏj′ə-nəs) *adj. Botany.* Growing on a lower surface of a structure, as fungi on leaves.

hy·po·ge·ous (hī′pə-jē′əs) *adj.* Variant of **hypogeal.**

hy·po·ge·um (hī′pə-jē′əm) *n., pl.* **-ge·a** (-jē′ə). **1.** A subterranean chamber of an ancient building. **2.** An ancient subterranean burial chamber, such as a catacomb. [Latin *hypogēum,* from Greek *hupogeion,* from neuter of *hupogeios,* underground. See HYPOGEAL.]

hy·po·glos·sal (hī′pə-glŏs′əl) *adj.* **1.** Of or relating to the area under the tongue. **2.** Of or relating to the hypoglossal nerve. [HYPO– + Greek *glōssa,* tongue.]

hypoglossal nerve *n.* Either of the 12th pair of cranial nerves that innervate the muscles of the tongue.

hy·po·gly·ce·mi·a (hī′pō-glī-sē′mē-ə) *n.* An abnormally low level of glucose in the blood.

hy·po·gly·ce·mic (hī′pō-glī-cē′mĭk) *adj.* **1.** Of or relating to hypoglycemia. **2.** Lowering the concentration of glucose in the blood: *a hypoglycemic drug.*

hy·pog·y·nous (hī-pŏj′ə-nəs) *adj. Botany.* Having the floral parts, such as sepals, petals, and stamens, borne on the receptacle beneath the ovary. **—hy·pog′y·ny** (-nē) *n.*

hy·po·lim·ni·on (hī′pə-lĭm′nē-ŏn′, -ən) *n.* The layer of water in a thermally stratified lake that lies below the thermocline, is noncirculating, and remains perpetually cold. [HYPO– + Greek *limnion,* diminutive of *limnē,* lake, pool.] **—hy′po·lim·net′ic** (-lĭm-nĕt′ĭk), **hy′po·lim′ni·al** *adj.*

hy·po·ma·ni·a (hī′pə-mā′nē-ə, -măn′yə) *n.* A mild state of mania, especially as a phase of a manic-depressive cycle. **—hy′po·man′ic** (-măn′ĭk) *adj.*

hy·po·nas·ty (hī′pə-năs′tē) *n., pl.* **-ties.** An upward bending of leaves or other plant parts, resulting from growth of the lower side. **—hy′po·nas′tic** *adj.*

hy·po·phos·phite (hī′pō-fŏs′fīt′) *n.* A salt of hypophosphorous acid.

hy·po·phos·pho·rous acid (hī′pō-fŏs′fər-əs, -fŏs-fôr′əs, -fōr′-) *n.* A clear, colorless or slightly yellow liquid, H_3PO_2, used as a reducing agent.

hy·poph·y·sis (hī-pŏf′ĭ-sĭs) *n., pl.* **-ses** (-sēz′). See **pituitary gland.** [New Latin, from Greek *hupophusis,* attachment underneath, from *hupophuein,* to grow up beneath : *hupo-,* hypo- + *phuein,* to make grow; see **bheue-** in Appendix.] **—hy·poph′y·se′al** (hī-pŏf′ĭ-sē′əl), **hy′po·phys′i·al** (hī′pə-fĭz′ē-əl) *adj.*

hy·po·pi·tu·i·ta·rism (hī′pō-pĭ-to͞o′ĭ-tə-rĭz′əm, -tyo͞o′-) *n.* **1.** Deficient or diminished production of pituitary hormones. **2.** The condition resulting from a deficiency in pituitary hormone, especially growth hormone, characterized by dwarfism in children and sometimes by decreased activity of the thyroid, adrenal, or gonadal glands. **—hy′po·pi·tu′i·tar′y** (-tĕr′ē) *adj.*

hy·po·pla·sia (hī′pō-plā′zhə, -zhē-ə) *n.* Incomplete or arrested development of an organ or a part. **—hy′po·plas′tic** (-plăs′tĭk) *adj.*

hy·po·ploid (hī′pō-ploid′) *adj. Genetics.* Having a chromosome number lower by only a few chromosomes than the normal diploid number. **—hy′po·ploi′dy** *n.*

hy·pop·ne·a (hī-pŏp′nē-ə, hī′pō-nē′ə) *n.* Abnormally slow, shallow breathing. [HYPO– + Greek *pnoia, pnoē,* breath, breathing (from *pnein,* to breathe; see **pneu-** in Appendix.)] **—hy′-pop·ne′ic** *adj.*

hy·po·sen·si·tiv·i·ty (hī′pō-sĕn′sĭ-tĭv′ĭ-tē) *n., pl.* **-ties.** Less than the normal ability to respond to stimuli. **—hy′po·sen′si·tive** *adj.*

hy·po·sen·si·tize (hī′pō-sĕn′sĭ-tīz′) *tr.v.* **-tized, -tiz·ing, -tiz·es.** To make less sensitive, as to an allergen; desensitize. **—hy′po·sen′si·ti·za′tion** (-tĭ-zā′shən) *n.*

hy·pos·ta·sis (hī-pŏs′tə-sĭs) *n., pl.* **-ses** (-sēz′). **1.** *Philosophy.* The substance, essence, or underlying reality. **2.** *Theology.* **a.** Any of the persons of the Trinity. **b.** The essential person of Jesus in which his human and divine natures are united. **3.**

Something that has been hypostatized. **4.a.** A settling of solid particles in a fluid. **b.** Something that settles to the bottom of a fluid; sediment. **5.** *Medicine.* The settling of blood in the lower part of an organ or the body as a result of decreased blood flow. **6.** *Genetics.* A condition in which the action of one gene conceals or suppresses the action of another gene that is not its allele but that affects the same part or biochemical process in an organism. [Late Latin, from Greek *hupostasis* : *hupo-*, hypo- + *stasis*, a standing; see **stā-** in Appendix.] **—hy′po·stat′ic** (hī′pə-stăt′ĭk), **hy′po·stat′i·cal** *adj.* **—hy′po·stat′i·cal·ly** *adv.*

hy·pos·ta·tize (hī-pŏs′tə-tīz′) *tr.v.* **-tized, -tiz·ing, -tiz·es.** To ascribe material existence to. [From Greek *hupostatos*, placed under, substantial, from *huphistasthai*, to stand under, exist : *hupo*, beneath; see HYPO– + *histasthai*, middle voice of *histanai*, to set, place; see EPISTASIS.] **—hy·pos′ta·ti·za′tion** (-tĭ-zā′shən) *n.*

hy·po·sthe·ni·a (hī′pəs-thē′nē-ə) *n.* An abnormal lack of strength; weakness. [HYPO– + Greek *sthenos*, strength + –IA[1].] **—hy′po·sthen′ic** (-pəs-thĕn′ĭk) *adj.*

hy·po·style (hī′pə-stīl′) *adj.* Having a roof or ceiling supported by rows of columns. **—hypostyle** *n.* A building with a roof or ceiling supported by rows of columns. [From Greek *hupostulos*, resting upon pillars : *hupo-*, hypo- + *stulos*, pillar; see **stā-** in Appendix.]

hy·po·sul·fite (hī′pō-sŭl′fīt′) *n.* See **sodium thiosulfate.**

hy·po·sul·fu·rous acid (hī′pō-sŭl-fyo͝or′əs, -sŭl′fər-əs) *n.* An unstable acid, $H_2S_2O_4$, known only in aqueous solution and used as a bleaching and reducing agent. Also called *hydrosulfurous acid.*

hy·po·tax·is (hī′pə-tăk′sĭs) *n.* *Grammar.* The dependent or subordinate relationship of clauses with connectives. [Greek *hupotaxis*, subjection, from *hupotassein*, to arrange under : *hupo-*, hypo- + *tassein, tag-*, to arrange.] **—hy′po·tac′tic** (-tăk′tĭk) *adj.*

hy·po·ten·sion (hī′pə-tĕn′shən) *n.* Abnormally low blood pressure.

hy·pot·e·nuse (hī-pŏt′n-o͞os′, -yo͞os′) also **hy·poth·e·nuse** (-pŏth′ə-no͞os′, -nyo͞os′) *n.* *Abbr.* **hyp.** *Mathematics.* The side of a right triangle opposite the right angle. [Latin *hypotēnūsa*, from Greek *hupoteinousa*, feminine sing. present participle of *hupoteinein*, to stretch or extend under : *hupo-*, hypo- + *teinein*, to stretch; see **ten-** in Appendix.]

hypoth. *abbr.* Hypothesis.

hy·po·thal·a·mus (hī′pō-thăl′ə-məs) *n.* The part of the brain that lies below the thalamus, forming the major portion of the ventral region of the diencephalon and functioning to regulate bodily temperature, certain metabolic processes, and other autonomic activities. **—hy′po·tha·lam′ic** (-thə-lăm′ĭk) *adj.*

hy·poth·e·cate (hī-pŏth′ĭ-kāt′) *tr.v.* **-cat·ed, -cat·ing, -cates.** To pledge (property) as security for a debt without transfer of title or possession. [Medieval Latin *hypothēcāre*, *hypothēcāt-*, from Latin *hypothēca*, pledge, deposit, from Greek *hupothēkē*, from *hupotithenai*, to give as a pledge, suppose. See HYPOTHESIS.] **—hy·poth′e·ca′tion** *n.* **—hy·poth′e·ca′tor** *n.*

hy·poth·e·nuse (hī-pŏth′ə-no͞os′, -nyo͞os′) *n.* Variant of **hypotenuse.**

hy·po·ther·mal (hī′pō-thûr′məl) *adj.* *Geology.* Of, relating to, or being mineral deposits formed at great depths and high temperatures.

hy·po·ther·mi·a (hī′pə-thûr′mē-ə) *n.* Abnormally low body temperature. [HYPO– + Greek *thermē*, heat; see **g[w]her-** in Appendix + –IA[1].] **—hy′po·ther′mic** (-mĭk) *adj.*

hy·poth·e·sis (hī-pŏth′ĭ-sĭs) *n.*, *pl.* **-ses** (-sēz′). *Abbr.* **hyp., hypoth. 1.** A tentative explanation that accounts for a set of facts and can be tested by further investigation; a theory. **2.** Something taken to be true for the purpose of argument or investigation; an assumption. **3.** The antecedent of a conditional statement. [Latin, subject for a speech, from Greek *hupothesis*, proposal, supposition, from *hupotithenai*, to suppose : *hupo-*, hypo- + *tithenai*, to place; see **dhē-** in Appendix.]

hy·poth·e·size (hī-pŏth′ĭ-sīz′) *v.* **-sized, -siz·ing, -siz·es.** —*tr.* To assert as a hypothesis. —*intr.* To form a hypothesis.

hy·po·thet·i·cal (hī′pə-thĕt′ĭ-kəl) also **hy·po·thet·ic** (-thĕt′ĭk) *adj.* *Abbr.* **hyp. 1.** Of, relating to, or based on a hypothesis: *a hypothetical situation.* See Synonyms at **theoretical. 2.a.** Suppositional; uncertain. See Synonyms at **supposed. b.** Conditional; contingent. [From Greek *hupothetikos*, from *hupothetos*, placed under, supposed, from *hupotithenai*, to suppose. See HYPOTHESIS.] **—hy′po·thet′i·cal** *n.* **—hy′po·thet′i·cal·ly** *adv.*

hypothetical imperative *n.* In the ethical system of Immanuel Kant, a moral command that is conditional on personal motive or desire.

hy·po·thy·roid (hī′pō-thī′roid′) *adj.* Affected by or manifesting hypothyroidism.

hy·po·thy·roid·ism (hī′pō-thī′roi-dĭz′əm) *n.* **1.** Insufficient production of thyroid hormones. **2.** A pathological condition resulting from severe thyroid insufficiency, which may lead to cretinism or myxedema.

hy·po·ton·ic (hī′pō-tŏn′ĭk) *adj.* **1.** *Pathology.* Having less than normal tone or tension, as of muscles or arteries. **2.** *Chemistry.* Having the lower osmotic pressure of two fluids. **—hy′po·to·nic′i·ty** (-tə-nĭs′ĭ-tē) *n.*

hy·pot·ro·phy (hī-pŏt′rə-fē) *n.*, *pl.* **-phies.** Progressive degeneration of an organ or tissue caused by loss of cells. **—hy′po·tro′phic** (hī′pə-trō′fĭk) *adj.*

hy·po·ven·ti·la·tion (hī′pə-vĕn′tl-ā′shən) *n.* Abnormally slow and shallow respiration, resulting in an increased level of carbon dioxide in the blood.

hy·po·xan·thine (hī′pō-zăn′thēn′) *n.* A white powder, $C_5H_4N_4O$, that is an intermediate in the metabolism of animal purines.

hy·pox·e·mi·a (hī′pŏk-sē′mē-ə) *n.* Insufficient oxygenation of the blood.

hy·pox·i·a (hī-pŏk′sē-ə, hĭ-) *n.* Deficiency in the amount of oxygen reaching body tissues. **—hy·pox′ic** *adj.*

hypso– or **hyps–** *pref.* Height: *hypsometer.* [From Greek *hupsos*, height, top. See **upo** in Appendix.]

hyp·sog·ra·phy (hĭp-sŏg′rə-fē) *n.*, *pl.* **-phies. 1.a.** The scientific study of the earth's topologic configuration above sea level, especially the measurement and mapping of land elevations. **b.** A representation or description of the earth's topologic features above sea level, as on a map. **2.** Hypsometry. **—hyp′so·graph′ic** (hĭp′sə-grăf′ĭk), **hyp′so·graph′i·cal** *adj.*

hyp·som·e·ter (hĭp-sŏm′ĭ-tər) *n.* An instrument using the atmospheric pressure as measured by the change in the boiling point of water to determine land elevations.

hyp·som·e·try (hĭp-sŏm′ĭ-trē) *n.* The measurement of elevation relative to sea level. **—hyp′so·met′ric** (hĭp′sə-mĕt′rĭk), **hyp′so·met′ri·cal** *adj.* **—hyp′so·met′ri·cal·ly** *adv.* **—hyp·som′e·trist** *n.*

hy·rax (hī′răks′) *n.*, *pl.* **-rax·es** or **-ra·ces** (-rə-sēz′). Any of several herbivorous mammals of the family Procaviidae within the order Hyraoidea of Africa and adjacent Asia, resembling woodchucks or similar rodents but more closely related to the hoofed mammals. Also called *coney, dassie.* [Greek *hurax*, shrew mouse.]

hy·son (hī′sən) *n.* A type of Chinese green tea with twisted leaves. [Chinese (Mandarin) *xī chūn* : *xī*, warm, sunny + *chūn*, springlike.]

hys·sop (hĭs′əp) *n.* **1.** A woody Eurasian plant *(Hyssopus officinalis)* having spikes of small blue flowers and aromatic leaves used in perfumery and as a condiment. **2.** Any of several similar or related plants. **3.** An unidentified plant mentioned in the Bible as the source of twigs used for sprinkling in certain Hebraic purificatory rites. [Middle English *ysope*, from Old English *ȳsōpe*, from Latin *hȳsōpum, hyssōpus*, from Greek *hussōpos*, probably of Semitic origin; akin to Hebrew *'ēzôb*.]

hyster– *pref.* Variant of **hystero–.**

hys·ter·ec·to·my (hĭs′tə-rĕk′tə-mē) *n.*, *pl.* **-mies.** Surgical removal of part or all of the uterus.

hys·ter·e·sis (hĭs′tə-rē′sĭs) *n.*, *pl.* **-ses** (-sēz). The lagging of an effect behind its cause, as when the change in magnetism of a body lags behind changes in the magnetic field. [Greek *husterēsis*, a shortcoming, from *husterein*, to come late, from *husteros*, late. See **ud-** in Appendix.] **—hys′ter·et′ic** (-rĕt′ĭk) *adj.*

hys·ter·i·a (hĭ-stĕr′ē-ə, -stîr′-) *n.* **1.** A neurosis characterized by the presentation of a physical ailment without an organic cause, sleepwalking, amnesia, episodes of hallucinations, and other mental and behavioral aberrations. **2.** Excessive or uncontrollable emotion, such as panic. [New Latin : HYSTER(IC) + –IA[1].]

hys·ter·ic (hĭ-stĕr′ĭk) *n.* **1.** A person suffering from hysteria. **2. hysterics** *(used with a sing. or pl. verb).* **a.** A fit of uncontrollable laughing or crying. **b.** An attack of hysteria. **—hysteric** *adj.* Hysterical. [From Latin *hystericus*, hysterical, from Greek *husterikos*, from *hustera*, womb (from the former idea that disturbances in the womb caused hysteria).]

hys·ter·i·cal (hĭ-stĕr′ĭ-kəl) *adj.* **1.** Of, characterized by, or arising from hysteria. **2.** Having or prone to having hysterics. **3.** *Informal.* Extremely funny: *told a hysterical story.* **—hys·ter′i·cal·ly** *adv.*

hystero– or **hyster–** *pref.* **1.** Uterus: *hysterectomy.* **2.** Hysteria: *hysteroid.* [From Greek *hustera*, womb.]

hys·ter·o·gen·ic (hĭs′tə-rō-jĕn′ĭk) *adj.* Inducing hysteria.

hys·ter·oid (hĭs′tə-roid′) *adj.* Resembling hysteria.

hys·ter·on prot·er·on (hĭs′tə-rŏn′ prŏt′ə-rŏn′) *n.* **1.** A figure of speech in which the natural or rational order of its terms is reversed, as in *bred and born* instead of *born and bred.* **2.** The logical fallacy of assuming as true and using as a premise a proposition that is yet to be proved. [Late Latin, from Greek *husteron proteron*, latter first : *husteron*, neuter sing. of *husteros*, latter, later; see **ud-** in Appendix + *proteron*, neuter sing. of *proteros*, former; see **per**[1] in Appendix.]

hys·ter·ot·o·my (hĭs′tə-rŏt′ə-mē) *n.*, *pl.* **-mies.** Surgical incision of the uterus, as in a cesarean section.

Hz *abbr.* Hertz.

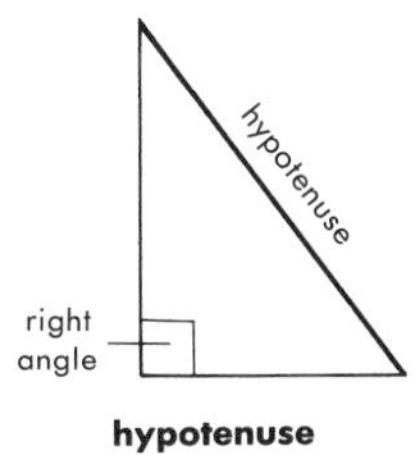

hypotenuse

hyrax

ă pat	oi boy
ā pay	ou out
âr care	o͝o took
ä father	o͞o boot
ĕ pet	ŭ cut
ē be	ûr urge
ĭ pit	th thin
ī pie	*th* this
îr pier	hw which
ŏ pot	zh vision
ō toe	ə about, item
ô paw	♦ regionalism

Stress marks: ′ (primary); ′ (secondary), as in **dictionary** (dĭk′shə-nĕr′ē)

Ii

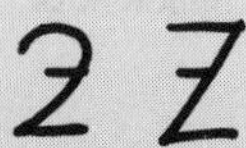

Phoenician
The seventh letter of the Phoenician alphabet stood for the consonantal sound at the beginning of *yōdh,* "arm."

Early Greek
In adapting the Phoenician alphabet to their own language the Greeks applied this letter, which they called *iōta,* to the related vowel *i.*

Roman
The Romans used it for both sounds, *i* and *y,* and it was not until the 16th century that the medieval cursive variant J was used systematically to distinguish the consonant from the vowel (see J).

ibex
Capra ibex

i[1] or **I** (ī) *n., pl.* **i's** or **I's. 1.** The ninth letter of the modern English alphabet. **2.** Any of the speech sounds represented by the letter *i.* **3.** The ninth in a series. **4.** Something shaped like the letter I.

i[2] *abbr. Mathematics.* Imaginary unit.

I[1] (ī) *pron.* Used to refer to oneself as speaker or writer. **—I** *n., pl.* **I's.** The self; the ego. [Middle English, from Old English *ic.* See **eg** in Appendix.]

USAGE NOTE: The question of when to use nominative forms of the personal pronouns (for example, *I, she, they*) and when to use objective forms (for example, *me, her, them*) has always created controversy among grammarians and uncertainty among speakers and writers. There is no problem when the pronoun stands alone in combination with a single verb or preposition: every native speaker says *I* (not *me*) *read the book; They told him* (not *he*); *The company bought a computer for us* (not *we*); and so forth. But the decision is more problematic in other environments. • When pronouns are joined with other nouns or pronouns by *and* or *or,* there is a widespread tendency to use the objective form even when the phrase is the subject of the sentence: *Robert and her are not speaking to each other.* This usage is natural in colloquial speech, but the nominative forms should be used in formal speech and writing: *John and she* (not *her*) *will be giving the talk.* • When pronouns joined by a conjunction occur as the object of a preposition such as *between, according to,* or *like,* many people use the nominative form where the traditional grammatical rule would require the objective; they say *between you and I* rather than *between you and me,* and so forth. Many critics have seen this construction as originating in a hypercorrection, whereby speakers who have been taught to say *It is I* instead of *It is me* come further to assume that correctness also requires *between you and I* in place of *between you and me.* This explanation of the tendency cannot be the whole story, inasmuch as the phrase *between you and I* occurs in Shakespeare, centuries before the prescriptive rules requiring *It is I* and the like were formulated. But the *between you and I* construction is nonetheless widely regarded as a marker of grammatical ignorance and is best avoided. • In other contexts the traditional insistence that the nominative form be used is more difficult to defend. The objective form sounds most natural when the pronoun is not grammatically related to an accompanying verb or preposition. Thus, in response to the question *"Who cut down the cherry tree?"* we more colloquially say *"Me,"* even though some grammarians have argued that *I* must be correct here by analogy to the form *"I did"*; and few speakers would accept that the sentence *What, me worry?* is improved if it is changed to *What, I worry?* The prescriptive insistence that the nominative be used in such a construction is grammatically questionable and is apt to lead to almost comical pedantries. • There is also a widespread tendency to use the objective form when a pronoun is used as a subject together with a noun in apposition, as in *Us engineers were left without any technical support.* In formal speech or writing the nominative *we* would be preferable here. But when the pronoun itself appears in apposition to a subject noun phrase, the use of nominative may sound pedantic in a sentence such as *The remaining members of the admissions committee, namely we, will have to meet on another day.* A writer who is uncomfortable about using the objective *us* here would be best advised to rewrite the sentence to avoid the difficulty. See Usage Notes at **be, but, we.**

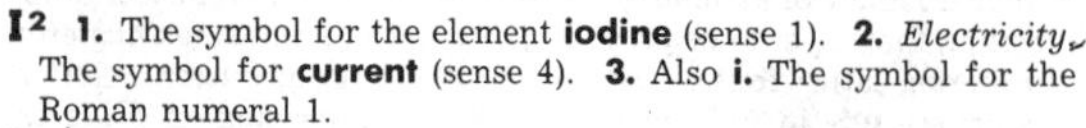

I[2] **1.** The symbol for the element **iodine** (sense 1). **2.** *Electricity.* The symbol for **current** (sense 4). **3.** Also **i.** The symbol for the Roman numeral 1.

I[3] *abbr.* **1.** Institute. **2.** Intelligence. **3.** Interstate. **4.** Isospin.

i. *abbr.* **1.** Incisor. **2.** Interest. **3.** *Grammar.* Intransitive. **4.** Or **I.** Island; isle.

—i—. Used as a connective to join word elements: *setiform.* [Middle English, from Old French, from Latin, stem vowel of nouns and adjectives used in combination.]

IA or **Ia.** *abbr.* Iowa.

i.a. *abbr.* In absentia.

—ia[1] *suff.* **1.** Disease; pathological or abnormal condition: *anoxia.* **2.** Territory; country: *Australia.* [New Latin, from Latin and Greek, n. suff.]

—ia[2] *suff.* Things derived from, relating to, or belonging to: *personalia.* [Latin, neuter pl. of *-ius,* and Greek, neuter pl. of *-ios,* n. and adj. suffixes.]

IAA *abbr.* Indoleacetic acid.

IAAF *abbr.* International Amateur Athletic Federation.

IABA *abbr.* International Amateur Boxing Association.

IADB *abbr.* Inter-American Defense Board.

—ial *suff.* Of, relating to, or characterized by: *baronial.* [Middle English, from Old French, from Latin *-iālis.*]

IALC *abbr.* Instrument approach and landing chart.

IAMAW *abbr.* International Association of Machinists and Aerospace Workers.

i·amb (ī′ămb′, ī′ăm′) also **i·am·bus** (ī-ăm′bəs) *n., pl.* **i·ambs** also **-bus·es** or **-bi** (-bī′). A metrical foot consisting of an unstressed syllable followed by a stressed syllable or a short syllable followed by a long syllable, as in *delay.* [French *iambe,* from Latin *iambus,* from Greek *iambos.*]

i·am·bic (ī-ăm′bĭk) *adj.* Consisting of iambs or characterized by their predominance: *iambic pentameter.* **—iambic** *n.* **1.** An iamb. **2.** Often **iambics.** A verse, stanza, or poem written in iambs.

i·am·bus (ī-ăm′bəs) *n.* Variant of **iamb.**

—ian *suff.* **1.** Of, relating to, or resembling: *Bostonian.* **2.** One relating to, belonging to, or resembling: *academician.* [Middle English *-ien, -ian,* from Old French *-ien,* from Latin *-iānus,* adj. and n. suff.]

—iana *suff.* Variant of **—ana.**

IAP *abbr.* International airport.

I·ap·e·tus (ī-ăp′ĭ-təs, ē-ăp′-) *n.* **1.** *Greek Mythology.* A Titan who was the father of Prometheus and Atlas and an ancestor of the human race. **2.** The satellite of Saturn that is 16th in distance from the planet. [Latin *Īapetus,* from Greek *Iapetos.*]

IARU *abbr.* International Amateur Radio Union.

IAS *abbr.* Indicated air speed.

Ia·şi (yäsh, yä′shē). A city of northeast Romania north-northeast of Bucharest. It was the capital of the country until 1861 and temporarily during World War I. Population, 305,598.

—iasis *suff.* A pathological condition characterized or produced by: *teniasis.* [New Latin, from Greek, n. suff.]

IATA *abbr.* International Air Transport Association.

—iatric *suff.* Of or relating to a specified kind of medical practice, treatment, or healing: *geriatric.* [From Greek *iatrikos,* medical, from *iatros,* physician, from *iasthai,* to heal.]

—iatrics *suff.* Medical treatment: *pediatrics.* [From —IATRIC.]

i·at·ro·gen·ic (ī-ăt′rə-jĕn′ĭk) *adj.* Induced in a patient by a physician's activity, manner, or therapy. Used especially of an infection or other complication of treatment. [Greek *iatros,* physician; see —IATRIC + —GENIC.] **—i·at′ro·gen′i·cal·ly** *adv.*

—iatry *suff.* Medical treatment: *psychiatry.* [Greek *-iatreia,* art of healing, from *iatros,* physician. See —IATRIC.]

IAU *abbr.* **1.** International Association of Universities. **2.** International Astronomical Union.

IB *abbr.* **1.** In bond. **2.** Incendiary bomb.

ib. *abbr.* Ibidem.

I·ba·dan (ē-băd′n, ē-bä′dän). A city of southwest Nigeria north-northwest of Lagos. Founded in the 1830's as a military camp, it developed into a powerful Yoruba city-state and is now a major commercial and industrial center. Population, 1,009,400.

I·ba·gué (ē-bä-gĕ′). A city of west-central Colombia west of Bogotá. It grew rapidly in the 1890's as the result of a coffee boom. Population, 265,598.

I-beam (ī′bēm′) *n.* A steel joist or girder with short flanges and a cross section formed like the letter I.

I·be·ri·a (ī-bîr′ē-ə). **1.** An ancient country of Transcaucasia roughly equivalent to the eastern part of present-day Georgia. Iberia was allied to Rome and later ruled by a Persian dynasty.

It became a Byzantine province in the sixth century A.D. **2.** See **Iberian Peninsula.**

I·be·ri·an (ī-bîr′ē-ən) *adj.* **1.** Of or relating to ancient Iberia in Transcaucasia or its peoples, languages, or cultures. **2.a.** Of or relating to the Iberian Peninsula or its modern peoples, languages, or cultures. **b.** Of or relating to the ancient peoples that inhabited the Iberian Peninsula or their languages or cultures. **—Iberian** *n.* **1.** A native or inhabitant of ancient Iberia in Transcaucasia. **2.a.** A native or inhabitant of the Iberian Peninsula. **b.** A member of one of the ancient peoples that inhabited the Iberian Peninsula. **3.** Any of the languages of these peoples.

Iberian Peninsula also **I·be·ri·a** (ī-bîr′ē-ə). A peninsula of southwest Europe occupied by Spain and Portugal. It is separated from the rest of Europe by the Pyrenees and from Africa by the Strait of Gibraltar.

I·ber·ville (ē-bĕr-vēl′), **Pierre Le Moyne.** Sieur d'Iberville. 1661–1706. Canadian-born French explorer who established settlements in what is now southern Louisiana.

i·bex (ī′bĕks′) *n., pl.* **ibex** or **i·bex·es.** Any of several wild goats of the genus *Capra,* especially *C. ibex,* native to mountainous regions of Eurasia and northern Africa and having long, ridged, backward-curving horns. [Latin.]

I·bib·i·o (ĭ-bĭb′ē-ō) *n., pl.* **Ibibio** or **-os. 1.** A member of a people of southeast Nigeria, noted for their woodcarving. **2.** The South Central Niger Congo language of the Ibibio, closely related to Efik.

i·bi·dem (ĭb′ĭ-dĕm′, ĭ-bī′dəm) *adv. Abbr.* **ib., ibid.** In the same place. Used in footnotes and bibliographies to refer to the book, chapter, article, or page cited just before. [Latin *ibīdem.* See **i-** in Appendix.]

–ibility *suff.* Variant of **–ability.**

i·bis (ī′bĭs) *n., pl.* **ibis** or **i·bis·es. 1.** Any of various storklike wading birds of the family Threskiornithidae of temperate and tropical regions, having a long, slender, downward-curving bill. **2.** The wood ibis. [Middle English *ibin,* from Latin *ībis,* from Greek, from Egyptian *hbj.*]

I·bi·za also **I·vi·za** (ē-bē′sə, ē-vē′thä). A Spanish island of the Balearic Islands in the western Mediterranean Sea southwest of Majorca. The island attracts tourists and artists and has Roman, Phoenician, and Carthaginian ruins.

I·bi·zan hound (ĭ-bē′zən, -zän) *n.* A swift, slender, medium-sized hunting dog, bred primarily in the Balearic Islands and having a short, solid, or spotted red and white or tawny coat. [After IBIZA.]

–ible *suff.* Variant of **–able.**

ibn-Khal·dun (ĭb′ən-kăl-do͞on′, -KHäl-). 1332–1406. Arab historian. His *Muqaddimah* (c. 1375) is an important work on the theory of history.

ibn-Sa·ud (ĭb′ən-sä-o͞od′), **Abdul Aziz.** 1880?–1953. Arab leader who was the first king of Saudi Arabia (1932–1953).

I·bo (ē′bō) also **Ig·bo** (ĭg′bō) *n., pl.* **Ibo** or **I·bos** also **Igbo** or **-bos. 1.** A member of a people inhabiting southeast Nigeria. **2.** The South Central Niger Congo language of the Ibo.

IBRD *abbr.* International Bank for Reconstruction and Development.

Ib·sen (ĭb′sən, ĭp′-), **Henrik.** 1828–1906. Norwegian playwright who influenced the development of modern drama with his realistic masterpieces. His major works include *Peer Gynt* (1867), *A Doll's House* (1879), and *Ghosts* (1881). **—Ib·sen′i·an** (-sē′nē-ən, -sĕn′ē-) *adj.*

i·bu·pro·fen (ī′byo͞o-prō′fən) *n.* A nonsteroidal anti-inflammatory medication, $C_{13}H_{18}O_2$, used especially in the treatment of arthritis and commonly taken for its analgesic and antipyretic properties. [Alteration of chemical name *i(so)bu(tyl)phen(yl) pro(pionic acid).*]

IBY *abbr.* International Biological Year.

IC *abbr.* Integrated circuit.

–ic *suff.* **1.** Of, relating to, or characterized by: *seismic.* **2.** Having a valence higher than that of a specified element in compounds or ions named with adjectives ending in *–ous: sulfuric acid.* **3.** One relating to or characterized by: *academic.* [Middle English, from Old French *-ique,* from Latin *-icus,* from Greek *-ikos.*]

I·ca (ē′kə, ē′kä). A city of southwest Peru south-southeast of Lima. Settled by the Spanish in 1563, it is now a commercial center. The surrounding area was inhabited by Inca peoples in pre-Columbian times. Population, 114,786.

ICAO *abbr.* International Civil Aeronautics Organization.

I·car·i·a (ĭ-kâr′ē-ə, ī-kâr′-). See **Ikaria.**

Ic·a·rus (ĭk′ər-əs) *n.* **1.** *Greek Mythology.* The son of Daedalus who, in escaping from Crete on artificial wings made for him by his father, flew so close to the sun that the wax with which his wings were fastened melted, and he fell into the Aegean Sea. **2.** An asteroid with an eccentric orbit approaching within 30 million kilometers (19 million miles) of the sun. [Latin, from Greek *Ikaros.*]

ICBM *abbr.* Intercontinental ballistic missile.

ICC *abbr.* **1.** Indian Claims Commission. **2.** International Chamber of Commerce. **3.** Interstate Commerce Commission.

ice (īs) *n.* **1.** Water frozen solid. **2.** A surface, layer, or mass of frozen water. **3.** Something resembling frozen water. **4.** A dessert consisting of sweetened and flavored crushed ice. **5.** Cake frosting; icing. **6.** *Slang.* Diamonds. **7.** *Sports.* The playing field in ice hockey; the rink. **8.** Extreme unfriendliness or reserve. **9.** *Slang.* A payment over the listed price of a ticket for a public event. *—attributive.* Often used to modify another noun: *ice cubes; ice fragments.* **—ice** *v.* **iced, ic·ing, ic·es.** *—tr.* **1.** To coat or slick with solidly frozen water. **2.** To cause to become ice; freeze. **3.** To chill by setting in or as if in ice. **4.** To cover or decorate (a cake, for example) with a sugar coating. **5.** *Slang.* To ensure of victory, as in a game; clinch. **6.** *Sports.* To shoot (the puck) far out of defensive territory in ice hockey. **7.** *Slang.* To kill; murder. *—intr.* To turn into or become coated with ice; freeze: *The pond iced over in November.* **—*idiom.* on ice.** *Slang.* **1.** In reserve or readiness. **2.** Held incommunicado. [Middle English *ise,* from Old English *īs.*] **—ice′less** *adj.*

ICE *abbr.* **1.** Internal-combustion engine. **2.** International Cultural Exchange.

Ice. *abbr.* Iceland; Icelandic.

ice age *n.* **1.** A cold period marked by episodes of extensive glaciation alternating with episodes of relative warmth. **2. Ice Age.** The most recent glacial period, which occurred during the Pleistocene epoch.

ice ax *n.* An ax used by mountaineers for cutting steps in ice.

ice bag *n.* See **ice pack** (sense 2).

ice barrier *n. Geology.* A section of the Antarctic ice shelf that extends beyond the coastline, resting partly on the ocean floor.

ice·berg (īs′bûrg′) *n.* **1.** A massive floating body of ice broken away from a glacier. Only about 10 percent of its mass is above the surface of the water. **2.** *Informal.* A cold, aloof person. [Partial translation of Dutch *ijsberg,* from Middle Dutch *ijsbergh* : *ijs,* ice + *bergh,* mountain (from Middle Dutch; see **bhergh-**[2] in Appendix).]

iceberg lettuce *n.* A crisp, round, compact head of lettuce with light green, tightly folded leaves. [From its pale color.]

ice·blink (īs′blĭngk′) *n.* **1.** A yellowish glare in the sky over an ice field. Also called *blink.* **2.** A coastal ice cliff.

ice blue (īs′blo͞o′) *n.* A very pale blue. **—ice′-blue′** *adj.*

ice·boat (īs′bōt′) *n. Nautical.* **1.** A boatlike vehicle set on sharp runners, used for sailing on ice. **2.** See **icebreaker** (sense 1). **—ice′boat′er** *n.* **—ice′boat′ing** *n.*

ice·bound (īs′bound′) *adj.* Locked in or covered over by ice.

ice·box (īs′bŏks′) *n.* **1.** An insulated chest or box into which ice is placed, used for cooling and preserving food. **2.** A refrigerator.

ice·break·er (īs′brā′kər) *n.* **1.** *Nautical.* A sturdy ship built for breaking a passage through icebound waters. Also called *iceboat.* **2.** A protective pier or dock apron used as a buffer against floating ice. **3.a.** Something done or said to relax an unduly formal atmosphere or situation. **b.** A beginning; a start. **—ice′break′ing** *n.*

ice bucket *n.* **1.** A small insulated container with a lid for holding ice. **2.** A similar container without a lid used to cool bottles placed inside it.

ice·cap or **ice cap** (īs′kăp′) *n.* An extensive dome-shaped or platelike perennial cover of ice and snow that spreads out from a center and covers a large area, especially of land.

ice-cold (īs′kōld′) *adj.* Extremely cold.

ice cream *n.* A smooth, sweet, cold food prepared from a frozen mixture of milk products, containing a minimum of 10 percent milk fat and flavorings and eaten as a snack or dessert.

WORD HISTORY: Since Americans eat about 15 quarts of ice cream per capita each year, it is appropriate that the first recorded instance of the word (1744) occurs in the writings of an American, who mentions "fine ice cream . . . with . . . strawberries and milk." The history of ice cream itself can be traced much further back, to the Roman Empire, China, and India. Ice cream was introduced to England in the 17th century and to America in the 18th. It seems to have been called *iced cream* at first (1673), in line with such expressions as *iced tea* and *iced coffee,* which we still use, but the form *ice cream* has taken over.

ice-cream chair (īs′krēm′) *n.* An armless wire chair with a round seat, originally used at tables in ice-cream parlors.

ice-cream cone *n.* **1.** A conical wafer used to hold a scoop of ice cream. **2.** A cone with ice cream in it.

ice-cream parlor *n.* An establishment where ice cream is served.

♦**ice-cream social** *n. Northern U.S.* A picnic featuring ice cream, often held for the purpose of raising money for charity. Also called *ice-cream sociable.*

ice-cream soda *n.* A refreshment consisting of scoops of ice cream in a mixture of soda water and syrup.

iced (īst) *adj.* **1.** Covered over with ice. **2.** Chilled with ice. **3.** Decorated or coated with icing.

ice·fall (īs′fôl′) *n.* **1.** The part of a glacier resembling a frozen waterfall that flows down a steep slope. **2.** An avalanche of ice.

ice field *n.* A large, level expanse of floating ice that is more than eight kilometers (five miles) in its greatest dimension.

ice floe *n.* A flat expanse of floating ice that is smaller than an ice field.

ice fog *n.* A fog of ice particles. Also called *pogonip.*

ibis
White ibis
Eudocimus albus

Henrik Ibsen

iceboat

ice-cream chair

ă pat	oi boy
ā pay	ou out
âr care	o͝o took
ä father	o͞o boot
ĕ pet	ŭ cut
ē be	ûr urge
ĭ pit	th thin
ī pie	*th* this
îr pier	hw which
ŏ pot	zh vision
ō toe	ə about, item
ô paw	♦ regionalism

Stress marks: ′ (primary); ′ (secondary), as in **dictionary** (dĭk′shə-nĕr′ē)

ice hockey

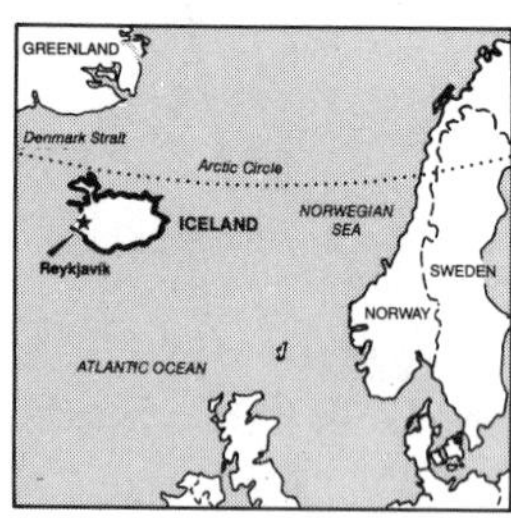

Iceland

ichthyosaur

icicle

ice foot *n.* A belt or ledge of ice that forms along the shoreline in Arctic regions.

ice-free (īs′frē′) *adj.* **1.** Free of ice and open to travel or navigation: *an ice-free channel in the river.* **2.** Marked by a lack of obstructive ice: *a three-month ice-free period during the summer.*

ice hockey *n. Sports.* A game played on ice in which two opposing teams of skaters, using curved sticks, try to drive a puck into the opponent's goal.

ice·house (īs′hous′) *n.* A place where ice is made, stored, or sold.

Icel. *abbr.* Iceland; Icelandic.

Ice·land (īs′lənd). *Abbr.* **Ice., Icel.** An island country in the North Atlantic near the Arctic Circle. Norse settlers arrived c. 850–875, and Christianity was introduced c. 1000. The feudal state was united with Norway in 1262 and with Denmark in 1380. In 1918 it became a sovereign state in personal union with Denmark, which lasted until the Icelanders voted for full independence in 1944. Reykjavík is the capital and the largest city. Population, 240,443. **—Ice′land·er** *n.*

Ice·land·ic (īs-lăn′dĭk) *adj. Abbr.* **Ice., Icel.** Of or relating to Iceland or its people, language, or culture. **—Icelandic** *n. Abbr.* **Ice., Icel.** The North Germanic language of Iceland.

Iceland moss *n.* A brittle, grayish-brown, Arctic lichen *(Cetraria islandica)* sometimes used as a food or in medicine.

Iceland spar *n.* A doubly refracting transparent calcite used in optical instruments.

ice·mak·er (īs′mā′kər) *n.* A machine, often built into a refrigerator, that freezes water into ice cubes. Also called *ice machine.*

ice·man (īs′mən) *n.* **1.** A man who cuts, sells, or delivers ice. **2.** *Slang.* A hired killer.

ice milk *n.* A smooth, sweet, cold food prepared from a frozen mixture of milk products, usually containing 3 to 6 percent butterfat, 11 to 14 percent nonfat milk solids, and 12 to 15 percent sugar.

ice-mi·nus (īs′mī′nəs) *adj.* Of or relating to a strain of genetically altered bacteria that are applied to crop plants to inhibit the formation of frost.

ice needle *n.* A thin ice crystal floating high in the atmosphere in certain conditions of clear, cold weather.

I·ce·ni (ī-sē′nī′) *pl.n.* An ancient Celtic tribe of eastern Britain who under Queen Boudicca fought unsuccessfully against the Romans about A.D. 60. [Latin *Icēnī.*] **—I·ce′nic** (-nĭk) *adj.*

ice-out (īs′out′) *n.* The thawing of ice on the surface of a body of water, such as a lake.

ice pack *n.* **1.** A floating mass of compacted ice fragments. **2.** A folded sac filled with crushed ice and applied to sore or swollen parts of the body to reduce pain and inflammation. In this sense, also called *ice bag.*

ice pick *n.* A pointed awl for chipping or breaking ice.

ice plant *n.* A succulent annual *(Mesembryanthemum crystallinum)* native to southern Africa, having white or pink flowers, fleshy leaves, and stems covered with glistening papillae.

ice point *n.* The temperature, equal to 1.0°C (33.8°F), at which pure water and ice are in equilibrium in a mixture at 1 atmosphere of pressure.

ice·scape (īs′skāp′) *n.* A wide view or vista of a region of ice and snow: *"the vast and empty icescape now called Antarctica"* (Sharon Begley).

ice show *n.* An entertainment consisting of figure skating, ice dancing, and acrobatic stunts performed by ice skaters.

ice skate *n. Sports.* A shoe or light boot with a metal runner or blade fitted to the sole, used for skating on ice.

ice-skate (īs′skāt′) *intr.v.* **-skat·ed, -skat·ing, -skates.** *Sports.* To engage in skating on ice. **—ice skater** *n.*

ice storm *n.* A storm in which snow or rain freezes on contact, forming a coat of ice on the surfaces it touches.

ice water *n.* **1.** Very cold or chilled water, especially for drinking, often with ice in it. **2.** Melted ice.

ice wine also **ice-wine** (īs′wīn′) *n.* A sweet wine made from grapes that have been left to freeze on the vines. They are picked and pressed while still frozen so that the grape sugar and acid remain intensely concentrated.

ICFTU *abbr.* International Confederation of Free Trade Unions.

ich (ĭk) *n.* A contagious disease of tropical marine and freshwater fishes, caused by a protozoan *(Ichthyophthirius multifiliis)* and characterized by small white pustules on the skin and eyes. [Short for New Latin *Ichthyophthirius,* genus name : ICHTHYO– + Greek *phtheir,* louse.]

I·chi·ka·wa (ē-chē′kä-wä′). A city of east-central Honshu, Japan, an industrial suburb of Tokyo. Population, 397,806.

I Ching (ē jĭng) *n.* A Chinese book of ancient origin consisting of 64 interrelated hexagrams along with commentaries. The hexagrams embody Taoist philosophy by describing all nature and human endeavor in terms of the interaction of yin and yang, and the book may be consulted as an oracle. [Chinese (Mandarin) *Yì Jīng* : *Yì,* divination + *Jīng,* classic, book.]

I·chi·no·mi·ya (ē′chē-nō′mē-ä′, -yä′). A city of central Honshu, Japan, a textile-manufacturing suburb of Nagoya. Population, 257,392.

ich·neu·mon (ĭk-no͞o′mən, -nyo͞o′-) *n.* **1.** A large mongoose *(Herpestes ichneumon)* of Africa and southern Europe, having a gray coat and black tail tufts. Also called *Egyptian mongoose.* **2.** The ichneumon fly. [Latin *ichneumōn,* weasel, ichneumon fly, from Greek *ikhneumōn,* from *ikhneuein,* to track, from *ikhnos,* track.]

ichneumon fly *n.* Any of various wasplike insects of the family Ichneumonidae, having larvae that are parasitic on the larvae of other insects. Also called *ichneumon wasp.*

ich·nite (ĭk′nīt′) **ich·no·lite** (-nō-līt′) *n.* A fossilized footprint. [Greek *ikhnos,* track + –ITE [1].]

ich·nog·ra·phy (ĭk-nŏg′rə-fē) *n., pl.* **-phies. 1.** The art or process of drawing ground plans. **2.** A ground plan of a building. [Latin *ichnographia* : Greek *ikhnos,* track + Latin *-graphia,* -graphy.]

ich·no·lite (ĭk′nō-līt′) *n.* Variant of **ichnite.**

i·chor (ī′kôr′, ī′kər) *n.* **1.** *Greek Mythology.* The rarefied fluid said to run in the veins of the gods. **2.** *Pathology.* A watery, acrid discharge from a wound or ulcer. [Middle English *icor,* from Late Latin *īchōr,* from Greek *ikhōr.*] **—i′chor·ous** (ī′kər-əs) *adj.*

ichth. *abbr.* Ichthyology.

ichthy– *pref.* Variant of **ichthyo–.**

ich·thy·ic (ĭk′thē-ĭk) *adj.* Of, relating to, or characteristic of fishes.

ichthyo– or **ichthy–** *pref.* Fish: *ichthyophagous.* [Latin, from Greek *ikhthuo-,* from *ikhthus,* fish.]

ich·thy·o·fau·na (ĭk′thē-ə-fô′nə) *n.* The fish of a particular region.

ich·thy·oid (ĭk′thē-oid′) *n.* A fish or fishlike vertebrate. **—ichthyoid** also **ich·thy·oi·dal** (ĭk′thē-oid′l) *adj.* Characteristic of or resembling a fish.

ich·thy·ol·o·gy (ĭk′thē-ŏl′ə-jē) *n. Abbr.* **ichth., ichthyol.** The branch of zoology that deals with the study of fishes. **—ich′thy·o·log′ic** (-ə-lŏj′ĭk), **ich′thy·o·log′i·cal** *adj.* **—ich′thy·ol′o·gist** *n.*

ich·thy·oph·a·gous (ĭk′thē-ŏf′ə-gəs) *adj.* Feeding on fish; fish-eating.

ich·thy·or·nis (ĭk′thē-ôr′nĭs) *n.* Any of various extinct, toothed birds of the genus *Ichthyornis* that existed during the Cretaceous Period. [ICHTHY(O)– + Greek *ornis,* bird; see **or-** in Appendix.]

ich·thy·o·saur (ĭk′thē-ə-sôr′) also **ich·thy·o·sau·rus** (ĭk′thē-ə-sôr′əs) *n., pl.* **-saurs** also **-sau·ri** (-sôr′ī′). Any of various extinct fishlike marine reptiles of the order Ichthyosauria of the Triassic Period to the Cretaceous Period, having a porpoise-like head and an elongated, toothed snout. [From New Latin *ichthyosaurus* : Greek *ikhthuo-,* ichthyo- + Greek *sauros,* lizard.]

ich·thy·o·sis (ĭk′thē-ō′sĭs) *n.* A congenital, often hereditary skin disease characterized by dry, thickened, scaly skin. Also called *fishskin disease.*

–ician *suff.* One who practices; a specialist: *technician.* [Middle English, from Old French *-icien* : *-ique,* n. suff.; see –IC + *-ien,* adj. and n. suff.; see –IAN.]

i·ci·cle (ī′sĭ-kəl) *n.* **1.** A tapering spike of ice formed by the freezing of dripping or falling water. **2.** *Informal.* An aloof or emotionally unresponsive person. [Middle English *isikel* : *is,* ice; see ICE + *ikel,* icicle (from Old English *gicel;* see **yeg-** in Appendix).]

icicle plant *n.* See **fig marigold.** [From its glistening papillae.]

ic·ing (ī′sĭng) *n.* **1.** A sweet glaze made of sugar, butter, water, and egg whites or milk, often flavored and cooked and used to cover or decorate baked goods, such as cakes or cookies. **2.** *Sports.* The act of intentionally shooting the puck far out of defensive territory in ice hockey.

ICJ *abbr. Law.* International Court of Justice.

ick·y (ĭk′ē) *adj.* **-i·er, -i·est.** *Informal.* **1.** Disagreeably sticky: *icky candy.* **2.** Offensive; distasteful: *icky sentimentality.* [Origin unknown.] **—ick′i·ness** *n.*

i·con also **i·kon** (ī′kŏn′) *n.* **1.a.** An image; a representation. **b.** A simile or symbol: *"Voyager will take its place . . . alongside such icons of airborne adventure as The Spirit of St. Louis and* [the] *Bell X-1"* (William D. Marbach). **2.** A representation or picture of a sacred or sanctified Christian personage, traditional to the Eastern Church. **3.** One who is the object of great attention and devotion; an idol: *"He is . . . a pop icon designed and manufactured for the video generation"* (Harry F. Waters). **4.** *Computer Science.* A picture on a screen that represents a specific command. [Ultimately from Greek *eikōn.*]

icon– *pref.* Variant of **icono–.**

i·con·ic (ī-kŏn′ĭk) *adj.* **1.** Of, relating to, or having the character of an icon. **2.** Having a conventional formulaic style. Used of certain memorial statues and busts.

icono– or **icon–** *pref.* Image; icon: *iconolatry.* [Greek *eikono-,* from *eikōn,* image.]

i·con·o·clasm (ī-kŏn′ə-klăz′əm) *n.* The beliefs, practices, or doctrine of an iconoclast. [From ICONOCLAST.]

i·con·o·clast (ī-kŏn′ə-klăst′) *n.* **1.** One who attacks and seeks to overthrow traditional or popular ideas or institutions. **2.** One who destroys sacred religious images. [French *iconoclaste,* from Medieval Greek *eikonoklastēs,* smasher of religious images : Greek *eikono-,* icono- + *-klastēs,* breaker (from Greek *klan, klas-,* to break).] **—i·con′o·clas′tic** *adj.* **—i·con′o·clas′ti·cal·ly** *adv.*

WORD HISTORY: An iconoclast can be unpleasant company, but at least the modern iconoclast only attacks such things as ideas and institutions. The original iconoclasts destroyed countless works of art. *Eikonoklastēs,* the ancestor of our word, was first formed in Medieval Greek from the elements *eikōn,* "image, likeness," and *-klastēs,* "breaker," from *klan,* "to break." The images referred to by the word are religious images, which were the subject of controversy among Christians of the Byzantine Empire in the 8th and 9th centuries, when iconoclasm was at its height. Those who opposed images did not, of course, simply destroy them, although many were demolished; they also attempted to have the images barred from display and veneration. During the Protestant Reformation images in churches were again felt to be idolatrous and were once more banned and destroyed. It is around this time that *iconoclast,* the descendant of the Greek word, is first recorded in English (1641), with reference to the Greek iconoclasts. In the 19th century *iconoclast* took on the secular sense that it has today, as in "Kant was the great iconoclast" (James Martineau).

i·co·nog·ra·phy (ī′kə-nŏg′rə-fē) *n., pl.* **-phies. 1.a.** Pictorial illustration of a subject. **b.** The collected representations illustrating a subject. **2.** A set of specified or traditional symbolic forms associated with the subject or theme of a stylized work of art. **3.** A treatise or book dealing with iconography. [Late Latin *īconographia,* description, verbal sketch, from Greek *eikonographia* : *eikono-,* icono- + *-graphia,* -graphy.] **—i′co·nog′ra·pher** *n.* **—i·con′o·graph′ic** (ī-kŏn′ə-grăf′ĭk), **i·con′o·graph′i·cal** *adj.*

i·co·nol·a·try (ī′kə-nŏl′ə-trē) *n.* Worship of icons or images. **—i′co·nol′a·ter** *n.* **—i′con·o·lat′ric** (ī′kŏn-ə-lăt′rĭk) *adj.*

i·co·nol·o·gy (ī′kə-nŏl′ə-jē) *n.* The branch of art history that deals with the description, analysis, and interpretation of icons or iconic representations. **—i·con′o·log′i·cal** (ī-kŏn′ə-lŏj′ĭ-kəl) *adj.* **—i′co·nol′o·gist** *n.*

i·con·o·scope (ī-kŏn′ə-skōp′) *n.* An early form of a television-camera tube, equipped for rapid scanning of an information-storing, photoactive mosaic. [Originally a trademark.]

i·co·nos·ta·sis (ī′kə-nŏs′tə-sĭs) *n., pl.* **-ses** (-sēz′). The screen decorated with icons that divides the sanctuary from the nave of an Eastern Orthodox church. [From Late Greek *eikonostasion,* shrine : *eikono-,* icono- + Greek *stasis,* a standing; see **stā-** in Appendix.]

i·co·sa·he·dron (ī-kō′sə-hē′drən, ī-kŏs′ə-) *n., pl.* **-drons** or **-dra** (-drə). A polyhedron having 20 faces. [Greek *eikosaedron* : *eikosi,* twenty; see **wīkm̥tī** in Appendix + *-edron,* -hedron.] **—i·co′sa·he′dral** (-drəl) *adj.*

ICRC *abbr.* International Committee of the Red Cross.

-ics *suff.* **1.** Science; art; study; knowledge; skill: *graphics.* **2.** Actions, activities, or practices of: *athletics.* **3.** Qualities or operations of: *mechanics.* [-IC + -S[1] (translation of Greek *-ika,* from neuter pl. of *-ikos,* adj. suff.).]

ic·ter·ic (ĭk-tĕr′ĭk) *adj.* **1.** Relating to or affected with jaundice. **2.** Used to treat jaundice. **—icteric** *n.* A remedy for jaundice. [Latin *ictericus,* from Greek *ikterikos,* from *ikteros,* jaundice.]

ic·ter·us (ĭk′tər-əs) *n.* See **jaundice.** [New Latin, from Greek *ikteros.*]

Ic·ti·nus (ĭk-tī′nəs). fl. fifth century B.C. Greek architect and the chief designer of the Parthenon at Athens.

ic·tus (ĭk′təs) *n., pl.* **ictus** or **-tus·es.** *Medicine.* **1.** A sudden attack, blow, stroke, or seizure. **2.** The accent that falls on a stressed syllable in a line of scanned verse. [Latin, stroke, from past participle of *īcere,* to strike.]

ICU *abbr.* Intensive care unit.

ic·y (ī′sē) *adj.* **ic·i·er, ic·i·est. 1.** Containing or covered with ice: *an icy road.* **2.** Bitterly cold; freezing: *an icy day.* See Synonyms at **cold. 3.a.** Resembling ice: *icy fingers.* **b.** Chilling in manner: *an icy smile.* **—ic′i·ly** *adv.* **—ic′i·ness** *n.*

id (ĭd) *n.* In Freudian theory, the division of the psyche that is totally unconscious and serves as the source of instinctual impulses and demands for immediate satisfaction of primitive needs. [New Latin (translation of German *Es,* a special use of *es,* it, as a psychoanalytic term), from Latin, it. See **i-** in Appendix.]

ID[1] (ī′dē′) *n., pl.* **ID's** or **IDs.** *Informal.* An ID card.

ID[2] *abbr.* **1. Id.** Idaho. **2.** Also **I.D.** Identification. **3.** Intelligence Department.

id. *abbr.* Idem.

i.d. *abbr.* Inner diameter; inside diameter; internal diameter.

-id *suff.* Body; particle: *chromatid.* [Latin *-is, -id-,* feminine patronymic suff., from Greek.]

I'd (īd). **1.** I had. **2.** I would. **3.** I should.

I·da (ī′də), **Mount.** A peak, 2,457.7 m (8,058 ft) high, of central Crete. It is the highest elevation on the island and in ancient times was closely associated with the worship of Zeus.

I·da·ho (ī′də-hō′). *Abbr.* **ID, Id.** A state of the northwest United States. It was admitted as the 43rd state in 1890. First explored by the Lewis and Clark expedition in 1805, the region was held jointly by Great Britain and the United States from 1818 to 1846. Idaho became a separate territory in 1863. Boise is the capital and the largest city. Population, 944,038. **—I′da·ho′an** *adj. & n.*

Idaho Falls. A city of southeast Idaho north-northeast of Pocatello. The site was originally a miner's fording point over the Snake River. Population, 39,590.

ID card *n.* A card, often bearing a photograph, that gives identifying data, such as name, age, or organizational membership, about a person.

IDDD *abbr.* International direct distance dialing.

-ide *suff.* **1.** Group of related chemical compounds: *monosaccharide.* **2.** Binary compound: *sodium chloride, hydrogen cyanide.* **3.** Chemical element with properties similar to another: *lanthanide.* [From (OX)IDE.]

i·de·a (ī-dē′ə) *n.* **1.** Something, such as a thought or conception, that potentially or actually exists in the mind as a product of mental activity. **2.** An opinion, a conviction, or a principle: *has some strange political ideas.* **3.** A plan, scheme, or method. **4.** The gist of a specific situation; significance: *The idea is to finish the project on time and under budget.* **5.** A notion; a fancy. **6.** *Music.* A theme or motif. **7.** *Philosophy.* **a.** In the philosophy of Plato, an archetype of which a corresponding being in phenomenal reality is an imperfect replica. **b.** In the philosophy of Kant, a concept of reason that is transcendent but nonempirical. **c.** In the philosophy of Hegel, absolute truth; the complete and ultimate product of reason. **8.** *Obsolete.* A mental image of something remembered. [Middle English, from Latin, from Greek. See **weid-** in Appendix.] **—i·de′a·less** *adj.*

SYNONYMS: *idea, thought, notion, concept, conception.* These nouns refer to what is formed or represented in the mind as the product of mental activity. *Idea* has the widest range: *Fruit is not her idea of a dessert. Don't get any ideas about revenge. "Human history is in essence a history of ideas"* (H.G. Wells). *Thought* is applied to what is distinctively intellectual and thus especially to what is produced by contemplation and reasoning as distinguished from mere perceiving, feeling, or willing: *Quiet—she's trying to collect her thoughts. I have no thought of going to Europe. "Language is the dress of thought"* (Samuel Johnson). *Notion* often refers to a vague, general, or even fanciful idea: *"She certainly has some notion of drawing"* (Rudyard Kipling). *Concept* and *conception* are applied to mental formulations on a broad scale: *He seems to have absolutely no concept of time. "Every succeeding scientific discovery makes greater nonsense of old-time conceptions of sovereignty"* (Anthony Eden).

i·de·al (ī-dē′əl, ī-dēl′) *n.* **1.** A conception of something in its absolute perfection. **2.** One that is regarded as a standard or model of perfection or excellence. **3.** An ultimate object of endeavor; a goal. **4.** An honorable or worthy principle or aim. **—ideal** *adj.* **1.a.** Of, relating to, or embodying an ideal. **b.** Conforming to an ultimate form or standard of perfection or excellence. **2.** Considered the best of its kind. **3.** Completely or highly satisfactory: *The location of the new house is ideal.* **4.a.** Existing only in the mind; imaginary. **b.** Lacking practicality or the possibility of realization. **5.** Of, relating to, or consisting of ideas or mental images. **6.** *Philosophy.* **a.** Existing as an archetype or pattern, especially as a Platonic idea or perception. **b.** Of or relating to idealism. [From Middle English, pertaining to the divine archetypes of things, from Late Latin *ideālis,* from Latin *idea,* idea. See IDEA.]

SYNONYMS: *ideal, model, example, exemplar, standard, pattern.* These nouns refer to someone or something worthy of imitation or duplication. An *ideal* is a sometimes unattainable standard of perfection: *"Religion is the vision of . . . something which is the ultimate ideal, and the hopeless quest"* (Alfred North Whitehead). A *model* is something to be imitated and often something deserving of imitation: *"Our fellow countryman is a model of a man"* (Charles Dickens). An *example* is a model that is likely to be imitated; the term often refers to something that serves rather as a deterrent or warning than as something to be emulated: *"Our Government is the potent, the omnipresent teacher. For good or for ill, it teaches the whole people by its example"* (Louis D. Brandeis). An *exemplar* is a person or thing that serves as an ideal example by reason of being either very worthy or truly representative of a type, admirable or otherwise: *"He is indeed the perfect exemplar of all nobleness"* (Jane Porter). A *standard* is an established criterion or recognized level of excellence regarded as being proper, fitting, or right: *"It wouldn't be quite fair to test him by our standards"* (William Dean Howells). A *pattern* serves as a model, plan, or guide in the creation of something: *"I will be the pattern of all patience"* (Shakespeare).

ideal gas *n.* A gas that, when kept at a constant temperature, would obey the gas laws exactly. No known gas is an ideal gas.

i·de·al·ism (ī-dē′ə-lĭz′əm) *n.* **1.** The act or practice of envisioning things in an ideal form. **2.** Pursuit of one's ideals. **3.** Idealized treatment of a subject in literature or art. **4.** *Philosophy.* The theory that the object of external perception, in itself or as perceived, consists of ideas.

i·de·al·ist (ī-dē′ə-lĭst) *n.* **1.** One whose conduct is influenced by ideals that often conflict with practical considerations. **2.** One who is unrealistic and impractical; a visionary. **3.** An artist or a writer whose work is imbued with idealism. **4.** An adherent of any system of philosophical idealism.

i·de·al·is·tic (ī-dē′ə-lĭs′tĭk) *adj.* Of, relating to, or having the nature of an idealist or idealism. **—i′de·al·is′ti·cal·ly** *adv.*

icon

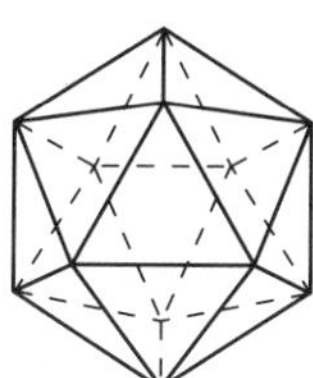

icosahedron

ă pat	oi boy
ā pay	ou out
âr care	o͝o took
ä father	o͞o boot
ĕ pet	ŭ cut
ē be	ûr urge
ĭ pit	th thin
ī pie	*th* this
îr pier	hw which
ŏ pot	zh vision
ō toe	ə about, item
ô paw	♦ regionalism

Stress marks: **′** (primary); ′ (secondary), as in **dictionary** (dĭk′shə-nĕr′ē)

i·de·al·i·ty (ī′dē-ăl′ĭ-tē) *n., pl.* **-ties. 1.** The state or quality of being ideal. **2.** Existence in idea only.

i·de·al·ize (ī-dē′ə-līz′) *v.* **-ized, -iz·ing, -iz·es.** —*tr.* **1.** To regard as ideal. **2.** To make or envision as ideal. —*intr.* **1.** To render something as an ideal. **2.** To conceive ideals or an ideal. **—i·de′al·i·za′tion** (-ə-lĭ-zā′shən) *n.* **—i·de′al·iz′er** *n.*

i·de·al·ly (ī-dē′ə-lē) *adv.* **1.** In conformity with an ideal; perfectly. **2.** In theory or imagination; theoretically.

i·de·ate (ī′dē-āt′) *v.* **-at·ed, -at·ing, -ates.** —*tr.* To form an idea of; imagine or conceive: *"Such characters represent a grotesquely blown-up aspect of an ideal man . . . if not realizable, capable of being ideated"* (Anthony Burgess). —*intr.* To conceive mental images; think. **—i′de·a′tion** *n.* **—i′de·a′tion·al** *adj.*

i·dée fixe (ē-dā fēks′) *n., pl.* **i·dées fixes** (ē-dā fēks′). A fixed idea; an obsession. [French : *idée,* idea + *fixe,* fixed.]

i·dem (ī′dĕm′) *pron. Abbr.* **id.** Something that has been mentioned previously; the same. [Latin *idem,* from *id,* it. See **i-** in Appendix.]

i·den·tic (ī-dĕn′tĭk) *adj.* **1.** Being or constituting a diplomatic action or diplomatic language in which two or more governments agree to use the same forms in their relations with other governments. **2.** Identical. [Medieval Latin *identicus,* identical. See IDENTICAL.]

i·den·ti·cal (ī-dĕn′tĭ-kəl) *adj.* **1.** Being the same: *another orator who used the senator's identical words.* See Synonyms at **same. 2.** Exactly equal and alike. **3.** Having such a close similarity or resemblance as to be essentially equal or interchangeable. **4.** *Biology.* Of or relating to a twin or twins developed from the same fertilized ovum and having the same genetic makeup and similar appearance; monozygotic. [From Medieval Latin *identicus,* from Late Latin *identitās,* identity. See IDENTITY.] **—i·den′ti·cal·ly** *adv.* **—i·den′ti·cal·ness** *n.*

USAGE NOTE: Some authorities on usage specify *with* as the preferred preposition after *identical.* But either *with* or *to* is now acceptable.

identical rhyme *n.* **1.** Repetition of the same word in the rhyme position. **2.** See **rime riche.**

i·den·ti·fi·ca·tion (ī-dĕn′tə-fĭ-kā′shən) *n.* **1.a.** The act of identifying. **b.** The state of being identified. **2.** *Abbr.* **ID, I.D.** Proof or evidence of identity. **3.** *Psychology.* **a.** A person's association with the qualities, characteristics, or views of another person or group. **b.** An unconscious process by which a person transfers the response appropriate to a particular person or group to a different person or group.

identification card *n.* An ID card.

i·den·ti·fi·er (ī-dĕn′tə-fī′ər) *n. Computer Science.* A symbol that serves to identify, indicate, or name a body of data.

i·den·ti·fy (ī-dĕn′tə-fī′) *v.* **-fied, -fy·ing, -fies.** —*tr.* **1.** To establish the identity of. **2.** To ascertain the origin, nature, or definitive characteristics of. **3.** *Biology.* To determine the taxonomic classification of (an organism). **4.** To consider as identical or united; equate. **5.** To associate or affiliate (oneself) closely with a person or group. —*intr.* To establish an identification with another or others. [Medieval Latin *identificāre,* to make to resemble : Late Latin *identitās,* identity; see IDENTITY + Latin *-ficāre,* -fy.] **—i·den′ti·fi′a·ble** *adj.* **—i·den′ti·fi′a·bly** *adv.* **—i·den′ti·fi′er** *n.*

USAGE NOTE: In the sense "to associate or affiliate (oneself) closely with a person or group," *identify* has developed two distinct subsenses. In one, the verb suggests a psychological empathy with the feelings or experiences of another person, as in *Most young readers readily identify* (or *identify themselves*) *with Holden Caulfield.* This usage derives originally from psychoanalytic writing, where it has a specific technical sense, but like other terms from that field, it was widely regarded as jargon when introduced into the wider discourse. In particular, critics seized on the fact that in this sense the verb was often used intransitively, with no reflexive pronoun. As Wilson Follett wrote in 1966, "The critic . . . could help restore the true notion in these words if he would give up *identifying* at large and resume *identifying himself with* Ivan Karamazov, Don Quixote, Mary Poppins, or whomever." In recent years, however, this use of *identify with* without the reflexive has become a standard locution. Eighty-two percent of the Usage Panel accepts the sentence *I find it hard to identify with any of his characters;* whereas only 63 percent now accepts this same usage when the reflexive pronoun is used, as in *I find it hard to identify myself with any of his characters.* • Omission of the reflexive with this use of *identify* serves among other things to distinguish it from use of the verb to mean "to associate (oneself) with the goals, interests, or principles of a group." This use of the verb can be traced back to the 18th century, but it is now somewhat less acceptable to the Panel than the first sense under discussion: 58 percent of the Panel accepts the sentence *She identified herself with the campaign against drug abuse,* and only 40 percent accepts *She identified with the campaign against drug abuse,* where no reflexive pronoun is used.

i·den·ti·ty (ī-dĕn′tĭ-tē) *n., pl.* **-ties. 1.** The collective aspect of the set of characteristics by which a thing is definitively recognizable or known: *"If the broadcast group is the financial guts of the company, the news division is its public identity"* (Bill Powell). **2.** The set of behavioral or personal characteristics by which an individual is recognizable as a member of a group. **3.** The quality or condition of being the same as something else. **4.** The distinct personality of an individual regarded as a persisting entity; individuality. **5.** *Mathematics.* **a.** An equation that is satisfied by any number that replaces the letter for which the equation is defined. **b.** Identity element. [French *identité,* from Old French *identite,* from Late Latin *identitās,* from Latin *idem,* the same (influenced by Late Latin *essentitās,* being, and *identidem,* repeatedly), from *id,* it. See **i-** in Appendix.]

identity crisis *n.* **1.** A psychosocial state or condition of disorientation and role confusion occurring especially in adolescents as a result of conflicting pressures and expectations and often producing acute anxiety. **2.** An analogous state of confusion occurring in a social structure, such as a corporation.

identity element *n. Mathematics.* The element of a set of numbers that when combined with another number in an operation leaves that number unchanged. For example, 0 is the identity element under addition for the real numbers, since if a is any real number, $a + 0 = 0 + a = a$. Similarly, 1 is the identity element under multiplication for the real numbers, since $a \times 1 = 1 \times a = a$. Also called *unity.*

identity matrix *n. Mathematics.* A square matrix with numeral 1's along the diagonal from upper left to lower right and 0's in all other positions.

identity sign *n. Mathematics.* The symbol (≡), used to designate identity rather than equality.

ideo– *pref.* Idea: *ideography.* [French *idéo-,* from Greek *idea,* form, idea. See **weid-** in Appendix.]

id·e·o·gram (ĭd′ē-ə-grăm′, ī′dē-) *n.* **1.** A character or symbol representing an idea or a thing without expressing the pronunciation of a particular word or words for it, as in the traffic sign commonly used for "no parking" or "parking prohibited." Also called *ideograph.* **2.** See **logogram. 3.** A graphic symbol, such as &, $, or @. **—id′e·o·gram·mat′ic** (grə-măt′ĭk) *adj.* **—id′e·o·gram·mat′i·cal·ly** *adv.*

id·e·o·graph (ĭd′ē-ə-grăf′) *n.* See **ideogram** (sense 1). **—id′e·o·graph′ic** *adj.* **—id′e·o·graph′i·cal·ly** *adv.*

id·e·og·ra·phy (ĭd′ē-ŏg′rə-fē, ī′dē-) *n.* **1.** The representation of ideas by graphic symbols. **2.** The use of ideograms to express ideas.

i·de·o·log·i·cal (ī′dē-ə-lŏj′ĭ-kəl, ĭd′ē-) also **i·de·o·log·ic** (-lŏj′ĭk) *adj.* **1.** Of or relating to ideology. **2.** Of or concerned with ideas.

i·de·o·logue (ī′dē-ə-lôg′, -lŏg′, ĭd′ē-) *n.* An advocate of a particular ideology, especially an official exponent of that ideology. [French *idéologue,* back-formation from *idéologie,* ideology. See IDEOLOGY.]

i·de·ol·o·gy (ī′dē-ŏl′ə-jē, ĭd′ē-) *n., pl.* **-gies. 1.** The body of ideas reflecting the social needs and aspirations of an individual, a group, a class, or a culture. **2.** A set of doctrines or beliefs forming the basis of a political or economic system. [French *idéologie* : *idéo-,* ideo- + *-logie,* -logy.] **—i′de·ol′o·gist** *n.*

i·de·o·mo·tor (ī′dē-ə-mō′tər, ĭd′ē-) *adj. Psychology.* Of or relating to an unconscious or involuntary bodily movement made in response to a thought or an idea rather than to a sensory stimulus.

ides (īdz) *pl.n. (used with a sing. or pl. verb).* The 15th day of March, May, July, or October or the 13th day of the other months in the ancient Roman calendar. [Middle English, from Old French, from Latin *Īdūs.*]

idio– *pref.* **1.** One's own; private; personal: *idiolect.* **2.** Distinct; separate: *idioblast.* [Greek, from *idios,* personal, private. See **s(w)e-** in Appendix.]

id·i·o·blast (ĭd′ē-ə-blăst′) *n.* A plant cell that differs noticeably in form from neighboring cells. **—id′i·o·blas′tic** *adj.*

id·i·o·cy (ĭd′ē-ə-sē) *n., pl.* **-cies. 1.** Extreme folly or stupidity. **2.** A foolish or stupid utterance or deed. **3.** *Psychology.* The state or condition of being an idiot; profound mental retardation. [From IDIOT.]

id·i·o·lect (ĭd′ē-ə-lĕkt′) *n.* The speech of an individual, considered as a linguistic pattern unique among speakers of his or her language or dialect. [IDIO– + (DIA)LECT.] **—id′i·o·lec′tal, id′i·o·lec′tic** *adj.*

id·i·om (ĭd′ē-əm) *n.* **1.** A speech form or an expression of a given language that is peculiar to itself grammatically or cannot be understood from the individual meanings of its elements, as in *keep tabs on.* **2.** The specific grammatical, syntactic, and structural character of a given language. **3.** Regional speech or dialect. **4.a.** A specialized vocabulary used by a group of people; jargon: *legal idiom.* **b.** A style or manner of expression peculiar to a given people: *"Also important is the uneasiness I've always felt at cutting myself off from my idiom, the American habits of speech and jest and reaction, all of them entirely different from the local variety"* (S.J. Perelman). **5.** A style of artistic expression characteristic of a particular individual, school, period, or medium: *the idiom of the French impressionists; the punk rock idiom.* [Late Latin *idiōma, idiōmat-,* from Greek, from *idiousthai,* to make one's own, from *idios,* own, personal, private. See **s(w)e-** in Appendix.]

id·i·o·mat·ic (ĭd′ē-ə-măt′ĭk) *adj.* **1.** Peculiar to or characteristic of a given language. **2.** Resembling or having the nature of an idiom. **3.** Using many idioms. **4.** Peculiar to or characteristic of the style or manner of a particular group or people. **—id′i·o·mat′i·cal·ly** *adv.*

id·i·o·path·ic (ĭd′ē-ə-păth′ĭk, ĭd′ē-ō-) *adj. Medicine.* Of, relating to, or designating a disease having no known cause. **—id′i·o·path′i·cal·ly** *adv.*

id·i·op·a·thy (ĭd′ē-ŏp′ə-thē) *n. Medicine.* **1.** A disease of unknown origin or cause. **2.** A primary disease arising spontaneously with no apparent external cause. [New Latin *idiopathīa*, primary disease, from Greek *idiopatheia* : *idio-*, idio- + *-patheia*, -pathy.]

id·i·o·syn·cra·sy (ĭd′ē-ō-sĭng′krə-sē) *n., pl.* **-sies. 1.** A structural or behavioral characteristic peculiar to an individual or a group. See Synonyms at **eccentricity. 2.** A physiological or temperamental peculiarity. **3.** An unusual individual reaction to food or a drug. [Greek *idiosunkrasia* : *idio-*, idio- + *sunkrasis*, mixture, temperament (*sun-*, syn- + *krasis*, a mixing; see **kerə-** in Appendix).] **—id′i·o·syn·crat′ic** (-sĭn-krăt′ĭk) *adj.* **—id′i·o·syn·crat′i·cal·ly** *adv.*

id·i·ot (ĭd′ē-ət) *n.* **1.** A foolish or stupid person. **2.** A person of profound mental retardation having a mental age below three years and generally being unable to learn connected speech or guard against common dangers. The term belongs to a classification system no longer in use and is now considered offensive. [Middle English, ignorant person, from Old French *idiote*, from Latin *idiōta*, from Greek *idiōtēs*, private person, layman, from *idios*, own, private. See **s(w)e-** in Appendix.]

idiot box *n. Slang.* A television.

id·i·ot·ic (ĭd′ē-ŏt′ĭk) *adj.* **1.** Showing foolishness or stupidity. **2.** Exhibiting idiocy. **—id′i·ot′i·cal·ly** *adv.*

idiot light *n. Slang.* A light on the instrument panel of a motor vehicle that gives forewarning, as of an overheated engine.

id·i·ot-proof (ĭd′ē-ət-pro͞of′) *adj. Slang.* Made or designed to be used or operated with very little risk of breakage or failure: *"These point-and-shoot cameras are almost idiot-proof"* (Donald H. Dunn).

idiot savant *n., pl.* **idiot savants.** A mentally retarded person who exhibits genius in a highly specialized area, such as mathematics or music. [French : *idiot*, idiot + *savant*, learned.]

i·dle (īd′l) *adj.* **i·dler, i·dlest. 1.a.** Not employed or busy: *idle carpenters.* See Synonyms at **inactive. b.** Avoiding work or employment; lazy: *shiftless, idle youth.* See Synonyms at **lazy. c.** Not in use or operation: *idle hands.* **2.** Lacking substance, value, or basis. See Synonyms at **baseless, vain. —idle** *v.* **i·dled, i·dling, i·dles.** —*intr.* **1.** To pass time without working or while avoiding work. **2.** To move lazily and without purpose. **3.** To run at a slow speed or out of gear. Used of a motor vehicle. —*tr.* **1.** To pass (time) without working or while avoiding work; waste: *idle the afternoon away.* **2.** To make or cause to be unemployed or inactive. **3.** To cause (a motor, for example) to idle. [Middle English *idel*, from Old English *īdel*.] **—i′dle·ness** *n.* **—i′dler** (īd′lər) *n.* **—i′dly** *adv.*

idle character *n. Computer Science.* An alphanumeric or digital character that is transmitted over a communications line but does not appear in the output of the receiving terminal.

idle pulley also **idler pulley** *n.* A pulley on a shaft that rests on or presses against a drive belt to guide it or take up slack. Also called *idle wheel.*

idle wheel *n.* **1.** A gear, wheel, or roller interposed between two similar parts to convey motion from one to the other without change in speed or direction of motion. **2.** See **idle pulley.**

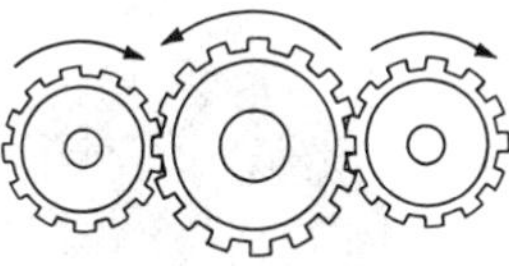

idle wheel

i·do·crase (ī′də-krās′, -krāz′, ĭd′ə-) *n.* See **vesuvianite.** [French : Greek *eidos*, form; see **weid-** in Appendix + *krasis*, mixture; see IDIOSYNCRASY.]

i·dol (īd′l) *n.* **1.a.** An image used as an object of worship. **b.** A false god. **2.** One that is adored, often blindly or excessively. **3.** Something visible but without substance. [Middle English, from Old French *idole*, from Late Latin *īdōlum*, from Greek *eidōlon*, phantom, idol, from *eidos*, form. See **weid-** in Appendix.]

i·dol·a·ter or **i·dol·a·tor** (ī-dŏl′ə-tər) *n.* **1.** One who worships idols. **2.** One who blindly or excessively admires or adores another. [Middle English *idolatre*, from Old French, from Latin *īdōlolatrēs*, from Greek *eidōlolatrēs* : *eidōlon*, idol; see IDOL + *-latrēs*, worshiper.]

i·dol·a·trous (ī-dŏl′ə-trəs) *adj.* **1.** Of or having to do with idolatry. **2.** Given to blind or excessive devotion to something: *"The religiosity of the* [group] *is self-righteous and idolatrous. It perceives no virtue in its opponents and magnifies its own"* (Christopher Lasch). **3.** Constituting idolatry. **—i·dol′a·trous·ly** *adv.* **—i·dol′a·trous·ness** *n.*

i·dol·a·try (ī-dŏl′ə-trē) *n., pl.* **-tries. 1.** Worship of idols. **2.** Blind or excessive devotion to something. [Middle English *idolatrie*, from Old French, from Latin *īdōlolatrīa*, from Greek *eidōlolatria* : *eidōlon*, idol; see IDOL + *latreia*, service.]

i·dol·ize (īd′l-īz′) *tr.v.* **-ized, -iz·ing, -iz·es. 1.** To regard with blind admiration or devotion. See Synonyms at **revere**[1]. **2.** To worship as an idol. **—i′dol·i·za′tion** (-ĭ-zā′shən) *n.* **—i′dol·iz′er** *n.*

IDP *abbr.* **1.** *Computer Science.* Integrated data processing. **2.** International driving permit.

i·dyll also **i·dyl** (īd′l) *n.* **1.a.** A short poem or prose piece depicting a rural or pastoral scene, usually in idealized terms. **b.** A narrative poem treating an epic or romantic theme. **2.** A scene or an event of a simple and tranquil nature. **3.a.** A carefree episode or experience: *a summer idyll on the coast of France.* **b.** A romantic interlude. [Latin *īdyllium*, from Greek *eidullion*, diminutive of *eidos*, form, figure. See **weid-** in Appendix.] **—i·dyl′li·cal·ly** *adv.*

i·dyl·lic (ī-dĭl′ĭk) *adj.* **1.** Of or having the nature of an idyll. **2.** Simple and carefree: *an idyllic vacation in a seashore cottage.*

i·dyl·list (īd′l-ĭst) *n.* A writer of idylls.

IE or **I.E.** *abbr.* **1.** Industrial engineer. **2.** Industrial engineering.

i.e. *abbr. Latin.* Id est (that is).

–ie *suff.* Variant of **–y**[3].

IEEE or **I.E.E.E.** *abbr.* Institute of Electrical and Electronics Engineers.

Ie·per (yā′pər) also **Y·pres** (ē′prə). A city of western Belgium near the French border south of Ostend. A famous cloth-weaving center in medieval times, it was the site of three major World War I battles (1914, 1915, and 1917). Population, 21,200.

if (ĭf) *conj.* **1.a.** In the event that: *If I were to go, I would be late.* **b.** Granting that: *If that is true, what should we do?* **c.** On the condition that: *She will play the piano only if she is paid.* **2.** Although possibly; even though: *It is a handsome if useless trinket.* **3.** Whether: *Ask if he plans to come to the meeting.* **4.** Used to introduce an exclamatory clause, indicating a wish: *If they had only come earlier!* **—if** *n.* A possibility, condition, or stipulation: *There will be no ifs, ands, or buts in this matter.* [Middle English, from Old English *gif*. See **i-** in Appendix.]

USAGE NOTE: In informal writing both *if* and *whether* are standard in their use to introduce a clause indicating uncertainty after a verb such as *ask, doubt, know, learn,* or *see: We shall soon learn whether* (or *if*) *it is true.* In such contexts, however, the use of *if* can sometimes create ambiguities. Depending on the intended meaning, the sentence *Let her know if she is invited* might be better paraphrased as *Let her know whether she is invited* or *If she is invited, let her know.* • In conditional sentences the clause introduced by *if* may contain either a past subjunctive verb (*if I were going*) or an indicative verb (*if I am going; if I was going*), depending on the intended meaning. According to the traditional rule, the subjunctive should be used to describe an occurrence that is presupposed to be contrary to fact, as in *if I were ten years younger* or *if Napoleon had won at Waterloo.* The main verb of such a sentence must then contain the modal verb *would* or (less frequently) *should: If America were still a British colony, we would have an anthem that human voices could sing. If I were the President, I should* (or *would*) *declare November 1 a national holiday.* When the situation described by the *if* clause is not presupposed to be false, however, that clause must contain an indicative verb, and the choice of verb in the main clause will depend on the intended meaning: *If Hamlet was really written by Marlowe, as many have argued, then we have underestimated Marlowe's genius. If Kevin was out all day, then it makes sense that he couldn't answer the phone.* Note also that the presence of the modal verb *would* in the main clause should not be taken as a sign that the verb in the *if* clause must be in the subjunctive, if the content of that clause is not presupposed to be false: *If I was* (not *were*) *to accept their offer—which I'm still considering—I would have to start the new job on May 2. He would always call her from the office if he was* (not *were*) *going to be late for dinner.* • Again according to the traditional rule, the subjunctive is not correctly used following verbs such as *ask* or *wonder* in *if* clauses that express indirect questions, even if the content of the question is presumed to be contrary to fact: *We wondered if dinner was* (not *were*) *included in the room price. Some of the people we met even asked us if California was* (not *were*) *an island.* • With all deference to the traditional rules governing the use of the subjunctive, it should be noted that a survey of the prose of reputable writers over the past 200 years would reveal a persistent tendency to use the indicative *was* where the traditional rule would require the subjunctive *were.* A sentence beginning *If I was the only boy in the world,* while not strictly correct, is wholly unremarkable. But the corresponding practice of using the subjunctive in place of the indicative may be labeled a hypercorrection. • In spoken English there is a growing tendency to use *would have* in place of the subjunctive in contrary-to-fact clauses, as in *if I would have been the President,* but this usage is still widely considered incorrect. See Usage Notes at **doubt, should, wish.**

IF or **i.f.** *abbr.* Intermediate frequency.

I·fe (ē′fā). A city of southwest Nigeria east of Ibadan. Center of a powerful Yoruba kingdom until the late 17th century, it is an agricultural market with varied industries. Population, 209,100.

IFF *abbr.* Identification, friend or foe.

if·fy (ĭf′ē) *adj.* **-fi·er, -fi·est.** *Informal.* Doubtful; uncertain: *an iffy proposition.* [From IF.] **—if′fi·ness** *n.*

If·ni (ēf′nē). A former Spanish possession on the Atlantic coast of southwest Morocco. It was ceded to Spain in 1860 and returned to Morocco in 1969.

IFO *abbr.* Identified flying object.

I formation *n. Football.* An alignment of the offensive team in which all the backs line up in single file behind the center.

IFR *abbr.* Instrument flight rules.

–ify *suff.* Variant of **–fy.**

Ig *abbr.* Immunoglobulin.

IG or **I.G.** *abbr.* Inspector general.

ă pat	oi boy
ā pay	ou out
âr care	o͝o took
ä father	o͞o boot
ĕ pet	ŭ cut
ē be	ûr urge
ĭ pit	th thin
ī pie	*th* this
îr pier	hw which
ŏ pot	zh vision
ō toe	ə about, item
ô paw	♦ regionalism

Stress marks: **′** (primary); ′ (secondary), as in **dictionary** (dĭk′shə-nĕr′ē)

Ignatius of Loyola

♦ **igg** (ĭg) *tr.v.* **igged, igg·ing, iggs.** *Northern U.S.* To ignore.

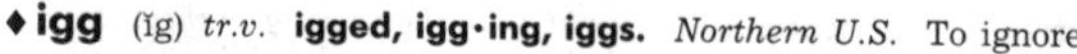

♦ ***REGIONAL NOTE:*** *Igg,* a shortened form of *ignore,* seems to have come into American speech from jive, the special jargon of Black jazz musicians in the 1930's. Its use has spread from the musicians' exclusive jargon into the Black communities of Northern U.S. cities. The reduction of a word to its initial syllable is a common source of slang or informal words, especially among groups of speakers who for reasons of exclusivity like to remain avant garde in their speech. Often such words come into general use, as in *mike* for *microphone.*

Ig·bo (ĭg′bō) *n.* Variant of **Ibo.**

ig·loo (ĭg′lo͞o) *n., pl.* **-loos. 1.** An Eskimo dwelling, especially a dome-shaped winter dwelling built of blocks of packed snow. **2.** A dome-shaped structure or building. [Canadian Eskimo *iglu,* house.]

ign. *abbr.* Ignition.

Ig·na·tius (ĭg-nā′shəs), Saint. Died c. A.D. 110. Bishop of Antioch noted especially for his epistles. He was martyred during the reign of the Roman emperor Trajan.

Ignatius of Loy·o·la (loi-ō′lə), Saint. 1491–1556. Spanish ecclesiastic who founded the Jesuits and was a leader of the Counter Reformation.

ig·ne·ous (ĭg′nē-əs) *adj.* **1.** Of, relating to, or characteristic of fire. **2.** *Geology.* **a.** Formed by solidification from a molten state. Used of rocks. **b.** Of or relating to rock so formed; pyrogenic. [From Latin *igneus,* from *ignis,* fire.]

ig·nes fat·u·i (ĭg′nēz făch′o͞o-ī′) *n.* Plural of **ignis fatuus.**

ig·nim·brite (ĭg′nĭm-brīt′) *n.* A volcanic rock formed by the welding together of tuff material from an explosive volcanic eruption. [Latin *ignis,* fire + *imber, imbr-,* rain + –ITE¹.]

ig·nis fat·u·us (ĭg′nĭs făch′o͞o-əs) *n., pl.* **ig·nes fat·u·i** (ĭg′nēz făch′o͞o-ī′). **1.** A phosphorescent light that hovers or flits over swampy ground at night, possibly caused by spontaneous combustion of gases emitted by rotting organic matter. Also called *friar's lantern, will-o'-the-wisp, wisp.* **2.** Something that misleads or deludes; an illusion. [Medieval Latin : Latin *ignis,* fire + Latin *fatuus,* foolish.]

ig·nite (ĭg-nīt′) *v.* **-nit·ed, -nit·ing, -nites.** —*tr.* **1.a.** To cause to burn. **b.** To set fire to. **2.** To subject to great heat, especially to make luminous by heat. **3.** To arouse the passions of; excite: *The insults ignited my anger.* —*intr.* **1.** To begin to burn. **2.** To begin to glow. [Late Latin *ignīre, ignīt-,* from Latin *ignis,* fire.] —**ig·nit′a·ble, ig·nit′i·ble** *adj.* —**ig·nit′er, ig·ni′tor** *n.*

iguana
Common iguana
Iguana iguana

ig·ni·tion (ĭg-nĭsh′ən) *n.* **1.** The raising of a substance to its ignition point, as by electric current, friction, or mechanical shock. **2.** *Abbr.* **ign. a.** An electrical system, typically powered by a battery or magneto, that provides the spark to ignite the fuel mixture in an internal-combustion engine. **b.** A switch that activates this system.

ignition point *n.* The minimum temperature at which a substance will continue to burn without additional application of external heat. Also called *kindling point.*

ig·ni·tron (ĭg-nī′trŏn′, ĭg′nĭ-) *n.* A single-anode, mercury-vapor rectifier in which current passes as an arc between the anode and a mercury-pool cathode, used in power rectification. [IG-NI(TE) + –TRON.]

ig·no·ble (ĭg-nō′bəl) *adj.* **1.** Not noble in quality, character, or purpose; base or mean. See Synonyms at **mean².** **2.** Not of the nobility; common. [Middle English, of low birth, from Old French, from Latin *ignōbilis* : *i-, in-,* not; see IN–¹ + *nōbilis, gnōbilis,* noble; see NOBLE.] —**ig′no·bil′i·ty** (-bĭl′ĭ-tē), **ig·no′ble·ness** *n.* —**ig·no′bly** *adv.*

ig·no·min·i·ous (ĭg′nə-mĭn′ē-əs) *adj.* **1.** Marked by shame or disgrace: *"It was an ignominious end. . . . as a desperate mutiny by a handful of soldiers blossomed into full-scale revolt"* (Angus Deming). **2.** Deserving disgrace or shame; despicable. **3.** Degrading; debasing: *"The young people huddled with their sodden gritty towels and ignominious goosebumps inside the gray-shingled bathhouse"* (John Updike). —**ig′no·min′i·ous·ly** *adv.* —**ig′no·min′i·ous·ness** *n.*

ig·no·min·y (ĭg′nə-mĭn′ē, -mə-nē) *n., pl.* **-ies. 1.** Great personal dishonor or humiliation. See Synonyms at **disgrace. 2.** Shameful or disgraceful action, conduct, or character. [French *ignominie,* from Old French, from Latin *ignōminia* : *i-, in-,* not; see IN–¹ + *nōmen, nōmin-,* name, reputation; see **nō-men-** in Appendix.]

iguanodon
Ouranosaurus

ig·no·ra·mus (ĭg′nə-rā′məs) *n., pl.* **-mus·es.** An ignorant person. [New Latin *ignōrāmus,* a grand jury's endorsement upon a bill of indictment when evidence is deemed insufficient to send the case to a trial jury, from Latin, we do not know, first person pl. present tense of *ignōrāre,* to be ignorant. See IGNORE.]

ig·no·rance (ĭg′nər-əns) *n.* The condition of being uneducated, unaware, or uninformed.

ig·no·rant (ĭg′nər-ənt) *adj.* **1.** Lacking education or knowledge. **2.** Showing or arising from a lack of education or knowledge: *an ignorant mistake.* **3.** Unaware or uninformed. [Middle English *ignoraunt,* from Old French *ignorant,* from Latin *ignōrāns, ignōrant-,* present participle of *ignōrāre,* to be ignorant, not to know. See **gnō-** in Appendix.] —**ig′no·rant·ly** *adv.*

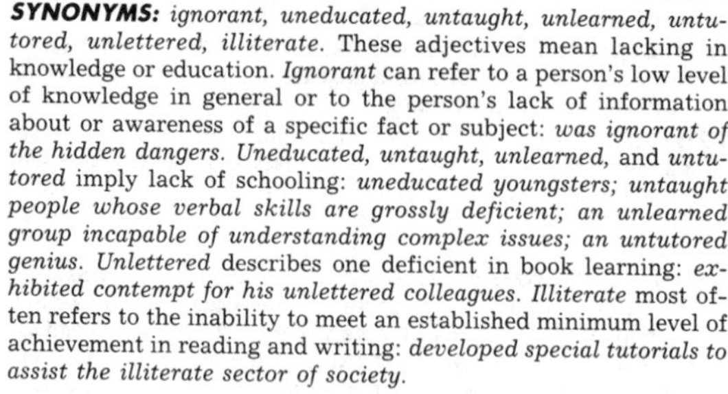

SYNONYMS: *ignorant, uneducated, untaught, unlearned, untutored, unlettered, illiterate.* These adjectives mean lacking in knowledge or education. *Ignorant* can refer to a person's low level of knowledge in general or to the person's lack of information about or awareness of a specific fact or subject: *was ignorant of the hidden dangers. Uneducated, untaught, unlearned,* and *untutored* imply lack of schooling: *uneducated youngsters; untaught people whose verbal skills are grossly deficient; an unlearned group incapable of understanding complex issues; an untutored genius. Unlettered* describes one deficient in book learning: *exhibited contempt for his unlettered colleagues. Illiterate* most often refers to the inability to meet an established minimum level of achievement in reading and writing: *developed special tutorials to assist the illiterate sector of society.*

♦ **ig·nore** (ĭg-nôr′, -nōr′) *tr.v.* **-nored, -nor·ing, -nores.** To refuse to pay attention to; disregard. See Regional Note at **igg.** [French *ignorer,* from Old French, from Latin *ignōrāre.* See **gnō-** in Appendix.] —**ig·nor′a·ble** *adj.* —**ig·nor′er** *n.*

I·go·rot (ĭg′ə-rōt′, ē′gə-) *n., pl.* **Igorot** or **-rots. 1.** A member of any of several peoples of the mountains of northern Luzon in the Philippines. **2.** Any of the Austronesian languages of the Igorot.

I·gua·çú also **I·guas·sú** (ē′gwə-so͞o′). A river, about 1,199 km (745 mi) long, of southern Brazil flowing west to the Paraná River at the Argentina-Paraguay-Brazil border. Just above the border it forms **Iguaçú Falls,** consisting of a series of cataracts averaging 61 m (200 ft) high and separated by rocky crags and islands.

i·gua·na (ĭ-gwä′nə) *n.* Any of various large tropical American lizards of the family Iguanidae, often having spiny projections along the back. [Spanish, from Arawak *iwana.*]

i·guan·o·don (ĭ-gwä′nə-dŏn′) *n.* Any of various large dinosaurs of the genus *Iguanodon,* of the Jurassic Period and Cretaceous Period. [New Latin *Iguanodon,* genus name : IGUANA + –ODON.]

I·guas·sú (ē′gwə-so͞o′). See **Iguaçú.**

IGY *abbr.* International Geophysical Year.

ihp or **i.hp.** *abbr.* Indicated horsepower.

ih·ram (ē-räm′) *n. Islam.* **1.** The sacred dress of Moslem pilgrims, consisting of two lengths of white cotton, one wrapped around the loins, the other thrown over the left shoulder. **2.** The sacred state of Moslem pilgrims in wearing this dress, during which time they practice great self-denial. [Arabic *'iḥrām,* prohibition, ihram, from *'aḥrama,* to consecrate.]

IHS *abbr.* Jesus (Greek ΙΗΣΟΥΣ with S for sigma).

Ijs·sel or **IJs·sel** (ī′səl). A river, about 113 km (70 mi) long, of eastern Netherlands flowing from the Lower Rhine River northward to the Ijsselmeer.

Ijs·sel·meer or **IJs·sel·meer** (ī′səl-mâr′, -mär′). A shallow, dike-enclosed lake of northwest Netherlands. It was formed from the Zuider Zee by the construction of two dams (completed in 1932).

I·ka·ri·a (ē′kä-rē′ä) also **I·car·i·a** (ĭ-kâr′ē-ə, ī-kâr′-). An island of southeast Greece in the Aegean Sea west of Samos. According to Greek legend, Icarus plummeted into the sea near the island.

i·ke·ba·na (ē′kĕ-bä′nä, ĭk′ə-) *n.* The Japanese art of formal flower arrangement with special regard shown to balance, harmony, and form. [Japanese : *ikeru,* to arrange + *hana,* flower.]

Ikh·na·ton (ĭk-nät′n). See **Akhenaton.**

i·kon (ī′kŏn′) *n.* Variant of **icon.**

IL *abbr.* Illinois.

il–¹ *pref.* Variant of **in–¹.**

il–² *pref.* Variant of **in–².**

IL–1 *abbr.* Interleukin–1.

IL–2 *abbr.* Interleukin–2.

ILA *abbr.* International Longshoremen's Association.

i·lang-i·lang (ē′läng-ē′läng) *n.* Variant of **ylang-ylang.**

–ile¹ *suff.* Of, relating to, or capable of: *audile.* [Middle English, from Old French, from Latin *-ilis, -īlis.*]

–ile² *suff.* A division of a specified size in the range of a statistic: *percentile.* [Probably from –ILE¹.]

il·e·a (ĭl′ē-ə) *n.* Plural of **ileum.**

il·e·ac¹ (ĭl′ē-ăk′) *adj.* Of, relating to, or having the nature of ileus.

il·e·ac² (ĭl′ē-ăk′) *adj.* Of, relating to, or involving the ileum.

Île-de-France (ēl′də-fräns′). A historical region and former province of north-central France in the Paris basin. In 987 with the choice of Hugh Capet, Count of Paris, as the French king, the Île-de-France became the nucleus of the crown lands.

il·e·i·tis (ĭl′ē-ī′tĭs) *n.* Inflammation of the ileum. [ILE(UM) + –ITIS.]

il·e·os·to·my (ĭl′ē-ŏs′tə-mē) *n., pl.* **-mies. 1.** Surgical construction of an artificial excretory opening through the abdominal wall into the ileum. **2.** The opening created by such a surgical procedure. [ILE(UM) + –STOMY.]

I·le·sha (ĭ-lĕsh′ə). A city of southwest Nigeria east-northeast of Ibadan. Formerly a caravan trade center, it is now an agricultural market. Population, 266,700.

il·e·um (ĭl′ē-əm) *n., pl.* **-e·a** (-ē-ə). The terminal portion of the small intestine extending from the jejunum to the cecum. [Late Latin *īleum,* groin, flank, variant of Latin *īlia.*] **—il′e·al** *adj.*

il·e·us (ĭl′ē-əs) *n.* Intestinal obstruction causing colic, vomiting, and constipation. [Latin *īleus,* from Greek *eileos,* from *eilein,* to squeeze, hold in check. See **wel-**^{2} in Appendix.]

i·lex (ī′lĕks′) *n.* Any of various trees or shrubs of the genus *Ilex*; holly. [Middle English, holm oak, from Latin *īlex.*]

ILGWU or **I.L.G.W.U.** *abbr.* International Ladies' Garment Workers' Union.

I·li (ē′lē′). A river, about 1,287 km (800 mi) in total length, of northwest China and southeast Kazakhstan flowing west and northwest into Lake Balkhash.

il·i·a (ĭl′ē-ə) *n.* Plural of **ilium.**

il·i·ac (ĭl′ē-ăk′) *adj.* Of, relating to, or situated near the ilium.

Il·i·am·na Lake (ĭl′ē-ăm′nə). A lake of southwest Alaska at the base of the Alaska Peninsula. Nearby is **Iliamna Peak,** a volcano rising to 3,054.9 m (10,016 ft).

Il·i·on (ĭl′ē-ən, -ŏn′). See **Troy** (sense 1).

il·i·um (ĭl′ē-əm) *n., pl.* **-i·a** (-ē-ə). The uppermost and widest of the three bones constituting either of the lateral halves of the pelvis. [Late Latin *īlium,* groin, flank, variant of Latin *īlia.*] **—il′i·ac′** (-ăk′) *adj.*

Il·i·um (ĭl′ē-əm). See **Troy** (sense 1).

ilk^{1} (ĭlk) *n.* Type or kind: *can't trust people of that ilk.* See Synonyms at **type. —ilk** *pron. Scots.* The same. Used following a name to indicate that the one named resides in an area bearing the same name: *Duncan of that ilk.* [Middle English, same, from Old English *ilca.* See **i-** in Appendix.]

WORD HISTORY: When one uses *ilk,* as in the phrase *men of his ilk,* one is using a word with an ancient pedigree even though the sense of *ilk,* "kind or sort," is actually quite recent, having been recorded no earlier than the end of the 18th century. This sense grew out of an older use of *ilk* in the phrase *of that ilk,* meaning "of the same place, territorial designation, or name." This phrase was used chiefly in names of landed families, *Guthrie of that ilk* meaning "Guthrie of Guthrie." "Same" is the fundamental meaning of the word. The ancestors of *ilk,* Old English *ilca* and Middle English *ilke,* were common words, usually appearing with such words as *the* or *that,* but the word hardly survived the Middle Ages in those uses.

ilk^{2} (ĭlk) *adj.* Variant of **ilka.**

il·ka (ĭl′kə) also **ilk** (ĭlk) *adj. Scots.* Each; every. [Middle English *ilk a,* each one : *ilk* (variant of *ech,* each; see EACH) + *a,* one, a; see A^{2}.]

ill (ĭl) *adj.* **worse** (wûrs), **worst** (wûrst). **1.** Not healthy; sick: *I began to feel ill last week.* **2.** Not normal; unsound: *an ill condition of body and mind.* **3.** Resulting in suffering; distressing: *ill effects.* **4.a.** Having evil intentions; hostile or unfriendly: *You certainly did me an ill turn.* **b.** Ascribing an objectionable quality: *holds an ill view of that political group.* **c.** Harmful; cruel. **5.** Not favorable; unpropitious: *ill predictions.* **6.** Not measuring up to recognized standards of excellence, as of behavior or conduct. **—ill** *adv.* **worse, worst. 1.** In a sickly or unsound manner; not well. **2.** Scarcely or with difficulty. **—ill** *n.* **1.** Evil; sin. **2.** Disaster, distress, or harm. **3.** Something that causes suffering; trouble: *the social ills of urban life.* **4.** Something that reflects in an unfavorable way on one: *Please don't speak ill of me when I'm gone.* [Middle English, from Old Norse *illr,* bad.]

ill. *abbr.* **1.** Illustrated. **2.** Illustration. **3.** Illustrator.

Ill. *abbr.* Illinois.

I'll (īl). **1.** I will. **2.** I shall.

ill-ad·vised (ĭl′əd-vīzd′) *adj.* Performed, carried out, or done without the benefit of wise counsel or careful prior deliberation. **—ill′-ad·vis′ed·ly** (-vī′zĭd-lē) *adv.*

Il·lam·pu (ē-yäm′po͞o). A peak, 6,366.3 m (20,873 ft) high, in the Andes of western Bolivia northwest of La Paz.

ill at ease *adj.* Nervously uncomfortable.

il·la·tion (ĭ-lā′shən) *n.* **1.** The act of inferring or drawing conclusions. **2.** A conclusion drawn; a deduction. In this sense, also called *illative.* [Late Latin *illātiō, illātiōn-,* from Latin *illātus,* past participle of *īnferre,* to carry in, infer : *in-,* in + *lātus,* brought; see **tele-** in Appendix.]

il·la·tive (ĭl′ə-tĭv, ĭ-lā′-) *adj.* **1.** Of, relating to, or of the nature of an illation. **2.** Expressing or preceding an inference. Used of a word. **3.** *Linguistics.* Of, relating to, or being a grammatical case indicating motion toward or into in some languages, as in Finnish *Helsinkiin,* "to Helsinki." **—illative** *n.* **1.** A word or phrase, such as *hence* or *for that reason,* that expresses an inference. **2.** See **illation** (sense 2). **—il′la·tive·ly** *adv.*

ill-be·ing (ĭl′bē′ĭng) *n.* Lack of prosperity, happiness, or health.

ill-bod·ing (ĭl′bō′dĭng) *adj.* Portending evil; inauspicious.

ill-bred (ĭl′brĕd′) *adj.* **1.** Badly brought up; impolite and crude. **2.** Not thoroughbred; underbred. Used of animals.

ill-con·ceived (ĭl′kən-sēvd′) *adj.* Poorly conceived or planned: *an ill-conceived scheme to take over the company.*

ill-con·sid·ered (ĭl′kən-sĭd′ərd) *adj.* Unwise; foolish: *ill-considered actions sure to result in disaster.*

ill-de·fined (ĭl′dĭ-fīnd′) *adj.* Not defined clearly or distinctly: *an ill-defined concept; an ill-defined view across the foggy moor.*

ill-dis·guised (ĭl′dĭs-gīzd′) *adj.* Poorly hidden or concealed: *ill-disguised animosity.*

ill-dressed (ĭl′drĕst′) *adj.* Clothed in a shabby or inappropriate manner.

il·le·gal (ĭ-lē′gəl) *adj.* **1.** Prohibited by law. **2.** Prohibited by official rules: *an illegal pass in football.* **3.** *Computer Science.* Unacceptable to or not performable by a computer: *an illegal operation.* **—illegal** *n.* An illegal immigrant. **—il·le′gal·ly** *adv.*

il·le·gal·i·ty (ĭl′ē-găl′ĭ-tē) *n., pl.* **-ties. 1.** The quality or state of being illegal. **2.** An illegal act.

il·leg·i·ble (ĭ-lĕj′ə-bəl) *adj.* Not legible or decipherable. **—il·leg′i·bil′i·ty, il·leg′i·ble·ness** *n.* **—il·leg′i·bly** *adv.*

il·le·git·i·ma·cy (ĭl′ĭ-jĭt′ə-mə-sē) *n.* **1.** The quality or condition of being illegitimate. **2.** Bastardy.

il·le·git·i·mate (ĭl′ĭ-jĭt′ə-mĭt) *adj.* **1.** Against the law; illegal. **2.** Born out of wedlock. **3.** *Grammar.* Not in correct usage. **4.** Incorrectly deduced; illogical. **5.** *Biology.* Unacceptable as a scientific name because of contradiction to the international rules of nomenclature. **—il′le·git′i·mate·ly** *adv.*

ill-fat·ed (ĭl′fā′tĭd) *adj.* **1.** Destined for misfortune; doomed. **2.** Marked by or causing misfortune; unlucky. See Synonyms at **unfortunate.**

ill-fa·vored (ĭl′fā′vərd) *adj.* **1.** Having an ugly or unattractive face. See Synonyms at **ugly. 2.** Objectionable; offensive.

ill feeling *n.* A feeling of animosity or rancor.

ill-fit·ting (ĭl′fĭt′ĭng) *adj.* **1.** Not fitting well or correctly: *ill-fitting trousers.* **2.** Unsuitable or inappropriate: *ill-fitting levity.*

ill-found·ed (ĭl′foun′dĭd) *adj.* Having no factual basis.

ill-got·ten (ĭl′gŏt′n) *adj.* Obtained in an evil manner or by dishonest means: *ill-gotten gains.*

ill health *n.* Poor health; sickness.

ill-housed (ĭl′houzd′) *adj.* Having inadequate, improper, or bad housing.

ill humor *n.* An irritable state of mind; surliness.

ill-hu·mored (ĭl′hyo͞o′mərd) *adj.* Irritable; surly. **—ill′-hu′mored·ly** *adv.*

il·lib·er·al (ĭ-lĭb′ər-əl) *adj.* **1.** Narrow-minded; bigoted. **2.** *Archaic.* Ungenerous, mean, or stingy. **3.** *Archaic.* **a.** Lacking liberal culture. **b.** Ill-bred; vulgar. [Latin *illīberālis* : *in-,* not; see IN–^{1} + *līberālis,* liberal; see LIBERAL.] **—il·lib′er·al·ism** *n.* **—il·lib′er·al′i·ty** (-ə-răl′ĭ-tē), **il·lib′er·al·ness** *n.* **—il·lib′er·al·ly** *adv.*

il·lic·it (ĭ-lĭs′ĭt) *adj.* Not sanctioned by custom or law; unlawful. [Latin *illicitus* : *in-,* not; see IN–^{1} + *licitus,* lawful; see LICIT.] **—il·lic′it·ly** *adv.* **—il·lic′it·ness** *n.*

Il·li·ma·ni (ē′yē-mä′nē). A mountain, 6,461.1 m (21,184 ft) high, in the Andes of western Bolivia east of La Paz. It was first scaled in 1898.

il·lim·it·a·ble (ĭ-lĭm′ĭ-tə-bəl) *adj.* Impossible to limit or circumscribe; limitless. See Synonyms at **infinite. —il·lim′it·a·bil′i·ty, il·lim′it·a·ble·ness** *n.* **—il·lim′it·a·bly** *adv.*

Il·li·noi·an (ĭl′ə-noi′ən) *adj.* Of or relating to the third glacial stage of the Pleistocene in North America. [After ILLINOIS^{2}.]

Il·li·nois^{1} (ĭl′ə-noi′, -noiz′) *n., pl.* **Illinois. 1.a.** A confederacy of Native American peoples formerly inhabiting southern Wisconsin, northern Illinois, and parts of eastern Iowa and Missouri, with present-day descendants mostly in Oklahoma. **b.** A member of this confederacy. **2.** The Algonquian language of the Illinois. [French, of Algonquian origin.]

Il·li·nois^{2} (ĭl′ə-noi′, -noiz′). *Abbr.* **IL, Ill.** A state of the north-central United States. It was admitted as the 21st state in 1818. The area was explored by the French in the late 1600's, ceded by France to the British in 1763, and ceded by them to the newly formed United States in 1783. Springfield is the capital and Chicago the largest city. Population, 11,427,414. **—Il′li·nois′an** (-noi′ən, -zən) *adj. & n.*

Illinois River. A river rising in northeast Illinois and flowing about 439 km (273 mi) generally southwest to the Mississippi River in west-central Illinois.

Illinois Waterway. A system of rivers and canals of northern and western Illinois, linking Chicago and Lake Michigan with the Mississippi River.

il·liq·uid (ĭ-lĭk′wĭd) *adj.* **1.** Not readily converted into cash. **2.** Lacking cash or liquid assets. **—il′li·quid′i·ty** *n.*

il·lit·er·a·cy (ĭ-lĭt′ər-ə-sē) *n., pl.* **-cies. 1.** The condition of being unable to read and write. **2.** An error, as in writing or speech, made by or thought to be characteristic of one who is illiterate. See Usage Note at **literate.**

il·lit·er·ate (ĭ-lĭt′ər-ĭt) *adj.* **1.a.** Unable to read and write. See Synonyms at **ignorant. b.** Having little or no formal education. **2.a.** Marked by inferiority to an expected standard of familiarity with language and literature. **b.** Violating prescribed standards of speech or writing. **3.** Ignorant of the fundamentals of a given art or branch of knowledge: *musically illiterate.* See Usage Note at **literate.** [Middle English, from Latin *illīterātus* : *in-,* not; see IN–^{1} + *līterātus,* literate; see LITERATE.] **—il·lit′er·ate** *n.* **—il·lit′er·ate·ly** *adv.* **—il·lit′er·ate·ness** *n.*

ill-man·nered (ĭl′măn′ərd) *adj.* Lacking or indicating a lack of good manners; rude. **—ill′-man′nered·ly** *adv.*

ill nature *n.* A disagreeable, irritable, or malevolent disposition.

ikebana

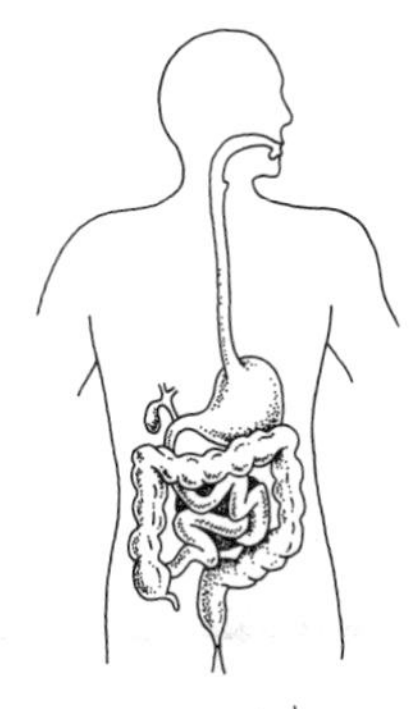

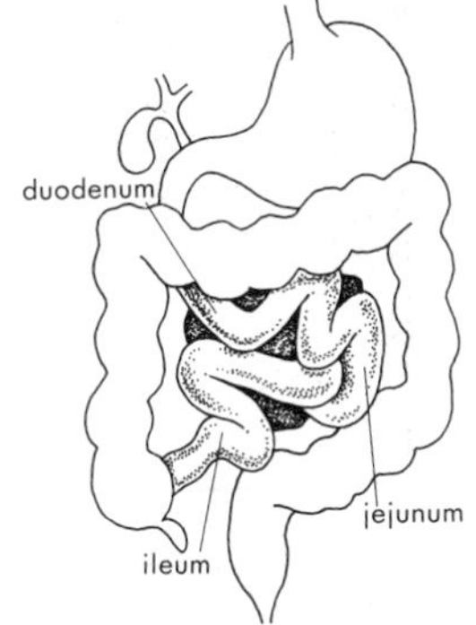

ileum

ă pat	oi boy
ā pay	ou out
âr care	o͝o took
ä father	o͞o boot
ĕ pet	ŭ cut
ē be	ûr urge
ĭ pit	th thin
ī pie	*th* this
îr pier	hw which
ŏ pot	zh vision
ō toe	ə about, item
ô paw	♦ regionalism

Stress marks: ′ (primary); ′ (secondary), as in **dictionary** (dĭk′shə-nĕr′ē)

ill-na·tured (ĭl′nā′chərd) *adj.* **1.** Having a disagreeable, irritable, or malevolent disposition. **2.** Spiteful; nasty: *an ill-natured retort.* —**ill′-na′tured·ly** *adv.*

ill·ness (ĭl′nĭs) *n.* **1.a.** Disease of body or mind; poor health; sickness. **b.** A disease. **2.** *Obsolete.* Evil; wickedness.

ill-nour·ished (ĭl′nûr′ĭsht, -nŭr′-) *adj.* Inadequately or poorly nourished; malnourished.

ill-off (ĭl′ôf′, -ŏf′) *n.* *(used with a pl. verb).* Poor or needy people: *"If the ill-off and well-to-do lived cheek by jowl, the well-to-do might do better by their brothers"* (William H. Gass).

il·log·ic (ĭ-lŏj′ĭk) *n.* A lack of logic.

il·log·i·cal (ĭ-lŏj′ĭ-kəl) *adj.* **1.** Contradicting or disregarding the principles of logic. **2.** Without logic; senseless. —**il·log′i·cal′i·ty** (-kăl′ĭ-tē), **il·log′i·cal·ness** *n.* —**il·log′i·cal·ly** *adv.*

ill-o·mened (ĭl′ō′mənd) *adj.* Marked by bad omens; inauspicious.

ill-shap·en (ĭl′shā′pən) *adj.* Unattractive, deformed, or distorted in shape; misshapen.

ill-sort·ed (ĭl′sôr′tĭd) *adj.* Badly matched.

ill-starred (ĭl′stärd′) *adj.* Ill-fated; unlucky. See Synonyms at **unfortunate.**

ill-tem·pered (ĭl′tĕm′pərd) *adj.* Having a bad temper; irritable. —**ill′-tem′pered·ly** *adv.*

ill-timed (ĭl′tīmd′) *adj.* Done or occurring at an inappropriate time; untimely.

ill-treat (ĭl′trēt′) *tr.v.* **-treat·ed, -treat·ing, -treats.** To treat unkindly or harshly; maltreat. See Synonyms at **abuse.** —**ill′-treat′ment** *n.*

il·lume (ĭ-lo͞om′) *tr.v.* **-lumed, -lum·ing, -lumes.** To illuminate. [Short for ILLUMINE.]

il·lu·mi·nance (ĭ-lo͞o′mə-nəns) *n.* *Physics.* See **illumination** (sense 7).

il·lu·mi·nant (ĭ-lo͞o′mə-nənt) *n.* Something that gives off light. [Latin *illūmināns, illūminant-,* present participle of *illūmināre,* to illuminate. See ILLUMINATE.]

il·lu·mi·nate (ĭ-lo͞o′mə-nāt′) *v.* **-nat·ed, -nat·ing, -nates.** —*tr.* **1.** To provide or brighten with light. **2.** To decorate or hang with lights. **3.** To make understandable; clarify: *"Cleverly made attacks can often serve to illuminate important differences between candidates, as well as entertain the voters"* (New Republic). **4.** To enlighten intellectually or spiritually; enable to understand. **5.** To endow with fame or splendor; celebrate. **6.** To adorn (a page of a book, for example) with ornamental designs, miniatures, or lettering in brilliant colors or precious metals. **7.** To expose to or reveal by radiation. —*intr.* **1.** To become lighted; glow. **2.** To provide intellectual or spiritual enlightenment and understanding: *"Once you decide to titillate instead of illuminate, you're on a slippery slope"* (Bill Moyers). **3.** To be exposed to or revealed by radiation. —**illuminate** (-nĭt) *n.* One who has or professes to have an unusual degree of enlightenment. [Middle English *illuminaten,* from Latin *illūmināre, illūmināt-* : *in-,* in; see IN–[2] + *lūmināre,* to light up (from *lūmen, lūmin-,* light; see **leuk-** in Appendix).] —**il·lu′mi·nat′ing·ly** *adv.*

illumination
From *The Hours of Jeanne d'Evreaux* illuminated by Jean Pucelle (1300?–1355)

il·lu·mi·na·ti (ĭ-lo͞o′mə-nä′tē) *pl.n.* **1.** People claiming to be unusually enlightened with regard to a subject. **2. Illuminati.** Any of various groups claiming special religious enlightenment. [Latin, pl. of *illūminātus,* past participle of *illūmināre,* to illuminate. See ILLUMINATE.]

il·lu·mi·na·tion (ĭ-lo͞o′mə-nā′shən) *n.* **1.a.** The act of illuminating. **b.** The state of being illuminated. **2.** A source of light. **3.** Decorative lighting. **4.** Spiritual or intellectual enlightenment. **5.** Clarification; elucidation. **6.a.** The art or act of decorating a text, a page, or an initial letter with ornamental designs, miniatures, or lettering. **b.** An example of this art. **7.** *Physics.* The luminous flux per unit area at any point on a surface exposed to incident light. In this sense, also called *illuminance.*

il·lu·mi·na·tive (ĭ-lo͞o′mə-nā′tĭv) *adj.* Of, causing, or capable of causing illumination.

il·lu·mi·na·tor (ĭ-lo͞o′mə-nā′tər) *n.* **1.** One that illuminates, especially a device for producing, concentrating, or reflecting light. **2.** One who illuminates manuscripts or other objects.

il·lu·mine (ĭ-lo͞o′mĭn) *tr.v.* **-mined, -min·ing, -mines.** To give light to; illuminate. [Middle English *illuminen,* from Old French *illuminer,* from Latin *illūmināre,* to illuminate. See ILLUMINATE.] —**il·lu′min·a·ble** *adj.*

il·lu·mi·nism (ĭ-lo͞o′mə-nĭz′əm) *n.* **1.** Belief in or proclamation of a special personal enlightenment. **2. Illuminism.** The ideas and principles of various groups of Illuminati. [French *illuminisme,* from *illuminé,* an illuminist, from past participle of *illuminer,* to illuminate, from Old French. See ILLUMINE.] —**il·lu′mi·nist** *n.*

illus. *abbr.* **1.** Illustrated. **2.** Illustration. **3.** Illustrator.

ill-us·age (ĭl′yo͞o′sĭj, -zĭj) *n.* Bad treatment; ill-use.

ill-use (ĭl′yo͞oz′) *tr.v.* **-used, -us·ing, -us·es.** To maltreat. —**ill-use** (ĭl′yo͞os′) *n.* Unjust or poor treatment; ill-usage.

il·lu·sion (ĭ-lo͞o′zhən) *n.* **1.a.** An erroneous perception of reality. **b.** An erroneous concept or belief. **2.** The condition of being deceived by a false perception or belief. **3.** Something, such as a fantastic plan or desire, that causes an erroneous belief or perception. **4.** Illusionism in art. **5.** A fine transparent cloth, used for dresses or trimmings. [Middle English, from Old French, from Late Latin *illūsiō, illūsiōn-,* from Latin, a mocking, irony, from *illūsus,* past participle of *illūdere,* to mock : *in-,* against; see IN–[2] + *lūdere,* to play; see **leid-** in Appendix.] —**il·lu′sion·al, il·lu′sion·ar′y** (-zhə-nĕr′ē) *adj.* —**il·lu′sion·less** *adj.*

il·lu·sion·ism (ĭ-lo͞o′zhə-nĭz′əm) *n.* **1.** *Philosophy.* The doctrine that the material world is an immaterial product of the senses. **2.** The use of illusionary techniques and devices in art or decoration. —**il·lu′sion·is′tic** *adj.* —**il·lu′sion·is′ti·cal·ly** *adv.*

il·lu·sion·ist (ĭ-lo͞o′zhə-nĭst) *n.* **1.** *Philosophy.* An adherent of the doctrine of illusionism. **2.** An artist whose work is marked by illusionism. **3.** A magician or ventriloquist.

il·lu·sive (ĭ-lo͞o′sĭv) *adj.* Illusory. —**il·lu′sive·ly** *adv.* —**il·lu′sive·ness** *n.*

il·lu·so·ry (ĭ-lo͞o′sə-rē, -zə-rē) *adj.* Produced by, based on, or having the nature of an illusion; deceptive: *"Secret activities offer presidents the alluring but often illusory promise that they can achieve foreign policy goals without the bothersome debate and open decision that are staples of democracy"* (Tom Wicker).

il·lus·trate (ĭl′ə-strāt′, ĭ-lŭs′trāt′) *v.* **-trat·ed, -trat·ing, -trates.** —*tr.* **1.a.** To clarify, as by use of examples or comparisons. **b.** To clarify by serving as an example or comparison. **2.** To provide (a publication) with explanatory or decorative features. **3.** *Obsolete.* To illuminate. —*intr.* To present a clarification, an example, or an explanation. [Latin *illūstrāre, illūstrāt-* : *in-,* in; see IN–[2] + *lūstrāre,* to make bright; see **leuk-** in Appendix.] —**il′lus·trat′a·ble** *adj.* —**il′lus·tra′tor** *n.*

il·lus·tra·tion (ĭl′ə-strā′shən) *n.* *Abbr.* **ill., illus. 1.a.** The act of clarifying or explaining. **b.** The state of being clarified or explained. **2.** Material used to clarify or explain. See Synonyms at **example. 3.** Visual matter used to clarify or decorate a text. **4.** *Obsolete.* Illumination. —**il′lus·tra′tion·al** *adj.*

il·lus·tra·tive (ĭ-lŭs′trə-tĭv, ĭl′ə-strā′tĭv) *adj.* Acting or serving as an illustration. —**il·lus′tra·tive·ly** *adv.*

il·lus·tri·ous (ĭ-lŭs′trē-əs) *adj.* **1.** Well known and very distinguished; eminent. See Synonyms at **noted. 2.** *Obsolete.* Shining brightly. [From Latin *illūstris,* from *illūstrāre,* to give glory to, shine upon. See ILLUSTRATE.] —**il·lus′tri·ous·ly** *adv.* —**il·lus′tri·ous·ness** *n.*

il·lu·vi·ate (ĭ-lo͞o′vē-āt′) *intr.v.* **-at·ed, -at·ing, -ates.** To undergo illuviation. [Back-formation from ILLUVIATION.]

il·lu·vi·a·tion (ĭ-lo͞o′vē-ā′shən) *n.* The deposition in an underlying soil layer of colloids, soluble salts, and mineral particles leached out of an overlying soil layer. [*illuvial,* resulting from illuviation (IN–[2] + *-luvial,* relating to the action of flowing water, as in ALLUVIAL) + –ATION.]

ill will *n.* Unfriendly feeling; enmity.

ill-wish·er (ĭl′wĭsh′ər) *n.* One who wishes no good fortune for another or others.

il·ly (ĭl′lē) *adv.* Badly; ill: *"Beauty is jealous, and illy bears the presence of a rival"* (Thomas Jefferson).

Il·lyr·i·a (ĭ-lîr′ē-ə) also **Il·lyr·i·cum** (-ĭ-kəm). An ancient region of the Balkan Peninsula on the Adriatic coast. Occupied in prehistoric times by an Indo-European-speaking people, the area became the Roman province of Illyricum after the final conquest of the Illyrians in 35–33 B.C. The name was revived by Napoleon for the provinces of Illyria (1809–1815) and retained for the kingdom of Illyria, a division of Austria from 1816 to 1849.

Il·lyr·i·an (ĭ-lîr′ē-ən) *adj.* Of or relating to ancient Illyria or its peoples, languages, or cultures. —**Illyrian** *n.* **1.** A member of one of the ancient peoples that inhabited Illyria. **2.** Any of the Indo-European languages of these peoples.

Il·lyr·i·cum (ĭ-lîr′ĭ-kəm). See **Illyria.**

il·men·ite (ĭl′mə-nīt′) *n.* A lustrous black to brownish titanium ore, essentially $FeTiO_3$. [After the *Ilmen* Mountains, a range of the southern Ural Mountains.]

ILO *abbr.* International Labor Organization.

I·lo·ca·no also **I·lo·ka·no** (ē′lō-kä′nō) —*n., pl.* **Ilocano** or **-nos** also **Ilokano** or **-nos. 1.** A member of an agricultural people of northern Luzon in the Philippines. **2.** The Austronesian language of the Ilocano. —*adj.* Of or relating to the Ilocano or their language or culture. [Spanish *Ilócano,* from *Iloko,* Austronesian people of the Philippines.]

I·lo·i·lo (ē′lō-ē′lō). A city of southeast Panay, Philippines, on **Iloilo Strait,** an inlet of the Sulu Sea. Iloilo is a major port noted for its delicate, handwoven fabrics. Population, 244,827.

I·lo·ka·no (ē′lō-kä′nō) *n.* Variant of **Ilocano.**

I·lo·rin (ē′lə-rēn′, ĭ-lôr′ən). A city of southwest Nigeria north-northeast of Lagos. Capital of a Yoruba kingdom c. 1800–1825, it is now an industrial center. Population, 355,400.

ILS *abbr.* Instrument landing system.

im–[1] *pref.* Variant of **in–[1].**

im–[2] *pref.* Variant of **in–[2].**

I'm (īm). I am.

im·age (ĭm′ĭj) *n.* **1.** A reproduction of the form of a person or an object, especially a sculptured likeness. **2.** *Physics.* An optically formed duplicate, counterpart, or other representative reproduction of an object, especially an optical reproduction of an object formed by a lens or mirror. **3.** One that closely or exactly resembles another; a double: *He is the image of his uncle.* **4.a.** The opinion or concept of something that is held by the public. **b.** The character projected to the public, as by a person or an institution, especially as interpreted by the mass media. **5.** A personification of something specified: *That child is the image of good health.* **6.** A mental picture of something not real or present. **7.a.** A vivid description or representation. **b.** A figure of speech, especially a metaphor or simile. **c.** A concrete representation, as in art, literature, or music, that is expressive or evocative of something else: *night as an image of death.* **8.** *Mathematics.* A set of values of a function corresponding to a particular subset of a domain. **9.** *Computer Science.* An exact copy of data in a file transferred to another medium. **10.** *Obsolete.* An apparition. **—image** *tr.v.* **-aged, -ag•ing, -ag•es. 1.** To make or produce a likeness of. **2.** To mirror or reflect. **3.** To symbolize or typify. **4.** To picture (something) mentally; imagine. **5.** To describe, especially so vividly as to evoke a mental picture of. **6.** *Computer Science.* To translate (photographs or other pictures) by computer into numbers that can be transmitted to a remote location and then reconverted into pictures by another computer. **7.** To visualize (something), as by magnetic resonance imaging. [Middle English, from Old French, from Latin *imāgō*.] **—im′age•less** *adj.*

image intensifier *n.* A type of image tube that is capable of increasing the brightness of an image up to 10,000 times.

im•age-mak•er (ĭm′ĭj-mā′kər) *n. Informal.* One who uses skillful techniques in publicity and advertising, especially by way of the mass media, to create a favorable public view, as of a person or an institution. **—im′age-mak′ing** *n.*

image orthicon *n.* See **orthicon.**

im•age•ry (ĭm′ĭj-rē) *n., pl.* **-ries. 1.** A set of mental pictures or images. **2.a.** The use of vivid or figurative language to represent objects, actions, or ideas. **b.** The use of expressive or evocative images in art, literature, or music. **c.** A group or body of related images, as in a painting or poem. **3.a.** Representative images, particularly statues or icons. **b.** The art of making such images.

image tube *n.* An electronic device that uses a photoelectric surface to release electrons and ultimately produce an image.

i•mag•i•na•ble (ĭ-măj′ə-nə-bəl) *adj.* Conceivable in or by the imagination: *imaginable exploits.* **—i•mag′i•na•bil′i•ty** *n.* **—i•mag′i•na•bly** *adv.*

i•ma•gi•nal (ĭ-mā′gə-nəl, ĭ-mä′-) *adj.* Of, relating to, or having the form of an insect imago.

i•mag•i•nar•y (ĭ-măj′ə-nĕr′ē) *adj.* **1.** Having existence only in the imagination; unreal. **2.** *Mathematics.* **a.** Of, relating to, or being the coefficient of the imaginary unit in a complex number. **b.** Of, relating to, involving, or being an imaginary number. **c.** Involving only a complex number of which the real part is zero. **—imaginary** *n., pl.* **-ies.** *Mathematics.* An imaginary number. **—i•mag′i•nar′i•ly** *adv.* **—i•mag′i•nar′i•ness** *n.*

imaginary number *n. Mathematics.* A complex number in which the real part is zero and the coefficient of the imaginary unit is not zero.

imaginary unit *n. Abbr.* **i** *Mathematics.* The positive square root of −1.

i•mag•i•na•tion (ĭ-măj′ə-nā′shən) *n.* **1.a.** The formation of a mental image of something that is neither perceived as real nor present to the senses. **b.** The mental image so formed. **c.** The ability or tendency to form such images. **2.** The ability to confront and deal with reality by using the creative power of the mind; resourcefulness: *handled the problems with great imagination.* **3.** A traditional or widely held belief or opinion. **4.** *Archaic.* **a.** An unrealistic idea or notion; a fancy. **b.** A plan or scheme. **—i•mag′i•na′tion•al** *adj.*

SYNONYMS: *imagination, fancy, fantasy.* These nouns refer to the power of the mind to form images, especially of what is not present to the senses. *Imagination* is the most broadly applicable: *The actor rehearsed the lines in his imagination. The glorious music haunts my imagination. "In the world of words, the imagination is one of the forces of nature"* (Wallace Stevens). *Fancy* especially suggests mental invention that is whimsical, capricious, or playful and that is characteristically well removed from reality: *"which . . . claims to be founded not on fancy . . . but on Fact"* (Arthur P. Stanley). *Is world peace only the fancy of idealists? Fantasy* is applied principally to the product of imagination given free rein and especially to elaborate or extravagant fancy: *The sitting room was a kind of Victorian fantasy, full of cabbage roses, fringe, and tassels. "The poet is in command of his fantasy, while it is exactly the mark of the neurotic that he is possessed by his fantasy"* (Lionel Trilling).

i•mag•i•na•tive (ĭ-măj′ə-nə-tĭv, -nā′tĭv) *adj.* **1.** Having a lively imagination, especially a creative imagination. **2.** Created by, indicative of, or characterized by imagination or creativity. **3.** Tending to indulge in the fanciful or in make-believe. **4.** Having no truth; false. **—i•mag′i•na•tive•ly** *adv.* **—i•mag′i•na•tive•ness** *n.*

i•mag•ine (ĭ-măj′ĭn) *v.* **-ined, -in•ing, -ines.** *—tr.* **1.** To form a mental picture or image of. **2.** To think; conjecture: *I imagine you're right.* **3.** To have a notion of or about without adequate foundation; fancy: *She imagines herself to be a true artist.* *—intr.* **1.** To employ the imagination. **2.** To make a guess; conjecture. [Middle English *imaginen,* from Old French *imaginer,* from Latin *imāginārī,* from *imāgō, imāgin-,* image.] **—i•mag′in•er** *n.*

i•ma•gi•nes (ĭ-mā′gə-nēz′) *n.* A plural of **imago.**

im•ag•ing (ĭm′ĭ-jĭng) *n.* **1.** *Medicine.* Visualization of internal bodily organs, tissues, or cavities using specialized instruments and techniques, such as ultrasonography, for diagnostic purposes. **2.** *Psychology.* The use of mental images to influence bodily processes, especially to control pain.

im•a•gism also **Im•a•gism** (ĭm′ə-jĭz′əm) *n.* A literary movement launched by British and American poets early in the 20th century in reaction against Victorian sentimentalism that advocated the use of free verse, common speech patterns, and clear concrete images. **—im′a•gist** *n.* **—im′a•gis′tic** *adj.* **—im′a•gis′ti•cal•ly** *adv.*

i•ma•go (ĭ-mā′gō, ĭ-mä′-) *n., pl.* **-goes** or **-gi•nes** (-gə-nēz′). **1.** An insect in its sexually mature adult stage after metamorphosis. **2.** *Psychology.* An often idealized image of a person, usually a parent, formed in childhood and persisting unconsciously into adulthood. [Latin *imāgō, imāgin-,* image.]

i•mam also **I•mam** (ĭ-mäm′) *n. Islam.* **1.a.** In law and theology, the caliph who is successor to Mohammed as the lawful supreme leader of the Islamic community. **b.** The male prayer leader in a mosque. **c.** The Moslem worshiper who leads the recitation of prayer when two or more worshipers are present. **2.a.** A male leader regarded by Shiites as a descendant of Mohammed divinely appointed to guide human beings. **b.** An earthly representative of the 12 such leaders recognized by the majority form of Shiism. **3.** A ruler claiming descent from Mohammed and exercising authority in an Islamic state. **4.a.** Any one of the founders of the four schools of law and theology. **b.** An authoritative scholar who founds a school of law or theology. **5.** Used as a title for such a man. [Arabic *'imām,* leader, imam, from *'amma,* to lead.]

i•mam•ate (ĭ-mä′māt′) *n. Islam.* The office of an imam.

i•ma•ret (ĭ-mä′rĕt) *n.* An inn or hostel for pilgrims in Turkey. [Turkish, from Arabic *'imārah,* from *'amara,* to build.]

im•bal•ance (ĭm-băl′əns) *n.* A lack of balance, as in distribution or functioning. **—im•bal′anced** *adj.*

im•be•cile (ĭm′bə-sĭl, -səl) *n.* **1.** A stupid or silly person; a dolt. **2.** A person whose mental acumen is well below par. **3.** A person of moderate to severe mental retardation having a mental age of from three to seven years and generally being capable of some degree of communication and performance of simple tasks under supervision. The term belongs to a classification system no longer in use and is now considered offensive. **—imbecile** also **im•be•cil•ic** (ĭm′bə-sĭl′ĭk) *adj.* **1.** Stupid; silly. **2.** Well below par in mental acumen. [From obsolete French *imbécille,* weak, feeble, from Old French, from Latin *imbēcillus* : *in-,* not; see IN−[1] + possibly *bacillum,* staff, diminutive of *baculum,* rod; see **bak-** in Appendix.] **—im′be•cile•ly** *adv.*

im•be•cil•i•ty (ĭm′bə-sĭl′ĭ-tē) *n., pl.* **-ties. 1.a.** Great stupidity or foolishness. **b.** Something, such as conduct or an act, that is stupid or foolish. **2.** *Psychology.* The state or condition of being an imbecile; moderate or severe mental retardation.

im•bed (ĭm-bĕd′) *v.* Variant of **embed.**

im•bibe (ĭm-bīb′) *v.* **-bibed, -bib•ing, -bibes.** *—tr.* **1.** To drink. **2.** To absorb or take in as if by drinking: *"The whole body . . . imbibes delight through every pore"* (Henry David Thoreau). **3.** To receive and absorb into the mind: *"Gladstone had . . . imbibed a strong prejudice against Americans"* (Philip Magnus). **4.** *Obsolete.* To permeate; saturate. *—intr.* To drink alcoholic beverages. [Middle English *embiben,* to soak up, saturate, from Latin *imbibere,* to drink in, imbibe : *in-,* in; see IN−[2] + *bibere,* to drink; see **pō(i)-** in Appendix.] **—im•bib′er** *n.*

im•bi•bi•tion (ĭm′bə-bĭsh′ən) *n.* **1.** The act of imbibing. **2.** *Chemistry.* Absorption of fluid by a solid or colloid that results in swelling.

im•bri•cate (ĭm′brĭ-kāt′) *adj.* Having the edges overlapping in a regular arrangement, as roof tiles or the scales of a fish. **—imbricate** *v.* **-cat•ed, -cat•ing, -cates.** *—tr.* To overlap in a regular pattern. *—intr.* To be arranged with regular overlapping edges. [Late Latin *imbricātus,* past participle of *imbricāre,* to cover with roof tiles, from *imbrex, imbric-,* roof tile, from *imber, imbr-,* rain.] **—im′bri•ca′tion** *n.*

imbricate
Roof tiles

im•bro•glio (ĭm-brōl′yō) *n., pl.* **-glios. 1.a.** A difficult or intricate situation; an entanglement. **b.** A confused or complicated disagreement. **2.** A confused heap; a tangle. [Italian, from Old Italian, from *imbrogliare,* to tangle, confuse : *in-,* in (from Latin; see IN−[2]) + *brogliare,* to mix, stir (probably from Old French *brooiller, brouiller;* see BROIL[2]).]

im•brue (ĭm-bro͞o′) also **em•brue** (ĕm-) *tr.v.* **-brued, -bru•ing, -brues. 1.** To saturate. **2.** To stain. [Middle English *embrewen,* from Old French *embreuver,* from Vulgar Latin **imbiberāre* : *in-,* in; see IN−[2] + Late Latin *biber,* beverage (from Latin *bibere,* to drink; see BEVERAGE).]

im•brute (ĭm-bro͞ot′) *tr. & intr.v.* **-brut•ed, -brut•ing, -brutes.** To make or become brutal.

im•bue (ĭm-byo͞o′) *tr.v.* **-bued, -bu•ing, -bues. 1.** To inspire, permeate, or invade: *work imbued with the revolutionary spirit.* See Synonyms at **charge. 2.** To stain or dye deeply. [Middle English *enbuen, imbeuen,* from Latin *imbuere,* to moisten, stain.]

IMD *abbr.* Intermodulation distortion.

IMF *abbr.* International Monetary Fund.

im•id•az•ole (ĭm′ĭ-dăz′ōl′) *n.* An organic crystalline base, $C_3H_4N_2$, that is an inhibitor of histamine. [IMID(E) + AZOLE.]

im•ide (ĭm′īd′) *n.* A compound derived from ammonia and containing the bivalent NH group combined with a bivalent acid

ă pat	oi boy
ā pay	ou out
âr care	o͝o took
ä father	o͞o boot
ĕ pet	ŭ cut
ē be	ûr urge
ĭ pit	th thin
ī pie	*th* this
îr pier	hw which
ŏ pot	zh vision
ō toe	ə about, item
ô paw	♦ regionalism

Stress marks: **′** (primary); ′ (secondary), as in **dictionary** (dĭk′shə-nĕr′ē)

group or two monovalent acid groups. [Alteration of AMIDE.]

im·i·do (ĭm′ĭ-dō′) *adj.* Of or relating to imides or an imide. [From *imido-*, from IMIDE.]

im·ine (ĭm′ēn′, -ĭn, ĭ-mēn′) *n.* A compound derived from ammonia and containing the bivalent NH group combined with a bivalent nonacid group. [Alteration of AMINE.]

im·i·no (ĭm′ə-nō′) *adj.* Of or relating to imines or an imine. [From *imino-*, from IMINE.]

i·mip·ra·mine (ĭ-mĭp′rə-mēn′) *n.* A tricyclic compound, $C_{19}H_{24}N_2$, used to treat depression and enuresis. [IMI(DE) + PR(OPYL) + AMINE.]

imit. *abbr.* Imitation; imitative.

im·i·ta·ble (ĭm′ĭ-tə-bəl) *adj.* **1.** That can be imitated: *the imitable sounds of a bird.* **2.** Worthy of imitation: *imitable behavior.*

im·i·tate (ĭm′ĭ-tāt′) *tr.v.* **-tat·ed, -tat·ing, -tates. 1.** To use or follow as a model. **2. a.** To copy the actions, appearance, mannerisms, or speech of; mimic: *amused friends by imitating the teachers.* **b.** To copy or use the style of: *brushwork that imitates Rembrandt.* **3.** To copy exactly; reproduce. **4.** To appear like; resemble. [Latin *imitārī, imitāt-*.] **—im′i·ta′tor** *n.*

SYNONYMS: *imitate, copy, mimic, ape, parody, simulate.* These verbs mean to follow something or someone taken as a model. To *imitate* is to act like or follow a pattern or style set by another: *The adults drank their tea in a ceremonious manner, and the children imitated them. The decorator had the wood paneling painted to imitate marble. "Art imitates Nature"* (Richard Franck). To *copy* is to duplicate an original as precisely as possible: *tried to copy her cultivated accent; a building that evokes the neoclassic style of architecture without copying it.* To *mimic* is to make a close imitation, as of another's actions, speech, or mannerisms, often with an intent to ridicule: *"fresh carved cedar, mimicking a glade/Of palm and plaintain"* (John Keats). *In private the candidate mimicked his opponent's stammer.* To *ape* is to follow another's lead slavishly but often with an absurd result: *"Those* [superior] *states of mind do not come from aping an alien culture"* (John Russell). To *parody* is either to imitate with comic effect or to attempt a serious imitation and fail: *"All these peculiarities* [of Samuel Johnson's literary style] *have been imitated by his admirers and parodied by his assailants"* (Macaulay). To *simulate* is to feign or falsely assume the appearance or character of something: *"I . . . lay there simulating death"* (W.H. Hudson).

im·i·ta·tion (ĭm′ĭ-tā′shən) *n. Abbr.* **imit. 1.** The act or an instance of imitating. **2.** Something derived or copied from an original. **3.** *Music.* Repetition of a phrase or sequence often with variations in key, rhythm, and voice. **—imitation** *adj.* Made to resemble another, usually superior material: *imitation fur.* **—im′i·ta′tion·al** *adj.*

im·i·ta·tive (ĭm′ĭ-tā′tĭv) *adj. Abbr.* **imit. 1.** Of or involving imitation. **2.** Not original; derivative. **3.** Tending to imitate. **4.** Onomatopoeic. **—im′i·ta′tive·ly** *adv.* **—im′i·ta′tive·ness** *n.*

im·mac·u·la·cy (ĭ-măk′yə-lə-sē) *n.* The quality or condition of being immaculate.

im·mac·u·late (ĭ-măk′yə-lĭt) *adj.* **1.** Impeccably clean; spotless. See Synonyms at **clean. 2.** Free from stain or blemish; pure. **3.** Free from fault or error: *an immaculate record.* **4.** Having no markings. [Middle English *immaculat*, from Latin *immaculātus* : *in-*, not; see IN–[1] + *maculātus*, past participle of *maculāre*, to blemish (from *macula*, spot).] **—im·mac′u·late·ly** *adv.* **—im·mac′u·late·ness** *n.*

Im·mac·u·late Conception (ĭ-măk′yə-lĭt) *n.* **1.** *Roman Catholic Church.* The doctrine that the Virgin Mary was conceived free from all stain of original sin. **2.** December 8, on which the feast of the Immaculate Conception is celebrated.

im·ma·nent (ĭm′ə-nənt) *adj.* **1.** Existing or remaining within; inherent: *believed in a God immanent in human beings.* **2.** Restricted entirely to the mind; subjective. [Late Latin *immanēns, immanent-*, present participle of *immanēre*, to remain in : Latin *in-*, in; see IN–[2] + Latin *manēre*, to remain; see **men-**[3] in Appendix.] **—im′ma·nence, im′ma·nen·cy** *n.* **—im′ma·nent·ly** *adv.*

im·ma·nent·ism (ĭm′ə-nən-tĭz′əm) *n.* Any of various religious theories postulating that a deity, mind, or spirit is immanent in the world and in the individual. **—im′ma·nent·ist** *adj. & n.*

im·ma·te·ri·al (ĭm′ə-tîr′ē-əl) *adj.* **1.** Of no importance or relevance; inconsequential or irrelevant. **2.** Having no material body or form. **—im′ma·te′ri·al·ly** *adv.* **—im′ma·te′ri·al·ness** *n.*

SYNONYMS: *immaterial, incorporeal, insubstantial, metaphysical, spiritual.* The central meaning shared by these adjectives is "lacking material body, form, or substance": *immaterial apparitions; an incorporeal spirit; insubstantial victories; metaphysical forces; spiritual beings.* See also Synonyms at **irrelevant.**
ANTONYM: *material.*

WORD HISTORY: The word *immaterial*, meaning "of no importance or relevance," has made its way in the world in spite of the opposition of no less a figure than Samuel Johnson. Johnson stated that "this sense has crept into the conversation and writings of barbarians; but ought to be utterly rejected." More than two centuries later it is difficult for us to recover Johnson's strength of feeling, and this tale might in fact serve as a warning to those who believe that the usages they abominate will not survive and become standard. Although Johnson was a man of immense learning, he did not have the lexicographical resources available today. If Johnson had had access to the *Oxford Latin Dictionary* and the *Middle English Dictionary*, among other works, he would have seen that from *māter*, meaning "a mother," "a plant as the source of things such as cuttings or fruit," and "a source," was derived the word *māteria*, meaning "wood as a building material," "any substance of which a physical object is made," "the subject matter of a speech or book," and "the condition whereby an action is effected." The adjective *māteriālis* derived from *māteria* only meant "of or concerned with subject matter" in Classical Latin, but its descendant in Late and Medieval Latin and its descendants in Old French (*materiel*) and Middle English (*material*) developed other meanings, such as "consisting of matter." One Middle English sense, "important, relevant," that probably harks back to senses of Classical Latin *māteria* such as "subject matter" continued in existence after Middle English times. So it was natural for the English word *immaterial*, first recorded in the 15th century, to come to mean "not important," in spite of Johnson's wrath.

im·ma·te·ri·al·ism (ĭm′ə-tîr′ē-ə-lĭz′əm) *n.* A metaphysical doctrine asserting the nonexistence of corporeal reality. **—im′ma·te′ri·al·ist** *adj. & n.*

im·ma·te·ri·al·i·ty (ĭm′ə-tîr′ē-ăl′ĭ-tē) *n., pl.* **-ties. 1.** The state or quality of being immaterial. **2.** Something immaterial.

im·ma·te·ri·al·ize (ĭm′ə-tîr′ē-ə-līz′) *tr.v.* **-ized, -iz·ing, -iz·es.** To render immaterial.

im·ma·ture (ĭm′ə-tyo͝or′, -to͝or′, -cho͝or′) *adj.* **1.** Not fully grown or developed. See Synonyms at **young. 2.** Marked by or suggesting a lack of normal maturity: *silly, immature behavior.* [Latin *immātūrus* : *in-*, not; see IN–[1] + *mātūrus*, mature; see **mā-**[1] in Appendix.] **—im′ma·ture′ly** *adv.* **—im′ma·tur′i·ty, im′ma·ture′ness** *n.*

im·meas·ur·a·ble (ĭ-mĕzh′ər-ə-bəl) *adj.* **1.** Impossible to measure. See Synonyms at **incalculable. 2.** Vast; limitless. **—im·meas′ur·a·bil′i·ty, im·meas′ur·a·ble·ness** *n.* **—im·meas′ur·a·bly** *adv.*

im·me·di·a·cy (ĭ-mē′dē-ə-sē) *n., pl.* **-cies. 1.** The condition or quality of being immediate. **2.** Lack of an intervening or mediating agency; directness: *the immediacy of live television coverage.* **3.** Something immediate, as in importance.

im·me·di·ate (ĭ-mē′dē-ĭt) *adj.* **1.** Occurring at once; instant: *gave me an immediate response.* **2. a.** Of or near the present time: *in the immediate future.* **b.** Of or relating to the present time and place; current: *"It is probable that, apart from the most immediate, pragmatic, technical revisions, the writer's effort to detach himself from his work is quixotic"* (Joyce Carol Oates). **3.** Close at hand; near: *in the immediate vicinity.* See Synonyms at **close. 4.** Next in line or relation: *is an immediate successor to the president of the company.* **5.** Directly apprehended or perceived: *had immediate awareness of the scope of the crisis.* **6.** Acting or occurring without the interposition of another agency or object; direct. [Middle English *immediat*, from Old French, from Late Latin *immediātus* : Latin *in-*, not; see IN–[1] + *mediātus*, past participle of *mediāre*, to be in the middle; see MEDIATE.] **—im·me′di·ate·ness** *n.*

immediate constituent *n. Grammar.* A meaningful constituent, such as a word, that enters directly into the formation of a linguistic construction, such as a phrase.

im·me·di·ate·ly (ĭ-mē′dē-ĭt-lē) *adv.* **1.** Without delay. **2.** Without an intermediary; directly: *met with the parties immediately involved in the suit.* **—immediately** *conj.* As soon as; directly: *They phoned immediately they reached home.*

im·med·i·ca·ble (ĭ-mĕd′ĭ-kə-bəl) *adj.* Incurable.

Im·mel·mann turn (ĭm′əl-mən, -män′) *n.* A maneuver in which an airplane first completes half a loop and then half a roll in order to gain altitude and change flight direction simultaneously. [After Max *Immelmann* (1890–1916), German aviator.]

im·me·mo·ri·al (ĭm′ə-môr′ē-əl, -mōr′-) *adj.* Reaching beyond the limits of memory, tradition, or recorded history. [Medieval Latin *immemoriālis* : Latin *in-*, not; see IN–[1] + Latin *memoriālis*, memorial; see MEMORIAL.] **—im′me·mo′ri·al·ly** *adv.*

im·mense (ĭ-mĕns′) *adj.* **1.** Extremely large; huge. **2.** Of boundless or immeasurable size or extent. See Synonyms at **enormous. 3.** *Informal.* Surpassingly good; excellent. [Middle English, from Old French, from Latin *immēnsus* : *in-*, not; see IN–[1] + *mēnsus*, past participle of *mētīrī*, to measure; see **mē-**[2] in Appendix.] **—im·mense′ly** *adv.* **—im·mense′ness** *n.*

im·men·si·ty (ĭ-mĕn′sĭ-tē) *n., pl.* **-ties. 1.** The quality or state of being immense. **2.** Something immense: *"the empty immensity of earth, sky, and water"* (Joseph Conrad).

im·men·sur·a·ble (ĭ-mĕn′shər-ə-bəl) *adj.* Immeasurable.

im·merge (ĭ-mûrj′) *intr.v.* **-merged, -merg·ing, -merg·es.** To submerge or disappear in or as if in a liquid. [Latin *immergere.* See IMMERSE.] **—im·mer′gence** *n.*

im·merse (ĭ-mûrs′) *tr.v.* **-mersed, -mers·ing, -mers·es. 1.** To cover completely in a liquid; submerge. See Synonyms at **dip. 2.** To baptize by submerging in water. **3.** To engage wholly or deeply; absorb: *scholars who immerse themselves in their subjects.* [From Middle English *immersed*, embedded deeply, from Latin *immersus*, past participle of *immergere*, to immerse : *in-*, in; see IN–[2] + *mergere*, to dip.]

im·mers·i·ble (ĭ-mûr′sə-bəl) *adj.* Capable of being completely immersed in water without suffering damage: *an immersible hot plate.*

im·mer·sion (ĭ-mûr′zhən, -shən) *n.* **1.a.** The act or an instance of immersing. **b.** The condition of being immersed. **2.** Baptism performed by totally submerging a person in water. **3.** *Astronomy.* The obscuring of a celestial body by another or by the shadow of another.

im·mesh (ĭm-mĕsh′) *v.* Variant of **enmesh.**

im·mi·grant (ĭm′ĭ-grənt) *n.* **1.** A person who leaves one country to settle permanently in another. **2.** A plant or an animal that establishes itself in an area where it previously did not exist.

im·mi·grate (ĭm′ĭ-grāt′) *v.* **-grat·ed, -grat·ing, -grates.** —*intr.* To enter and settle in a country or region to which one is not native. See Usage Note at **migrate.** —*tr.* To send or introduce as immigrants: *Britain immigrated many colonists to the New World.* [Latin *immigrāre, immigrāt-*, to go into : *in-*, in; see IN–[2] + *migrāre,* to depart.] —**im′mi·gra′tion** *n.*

im·mi·nence (ĭm′ə-nəns) *n.* **1.** The quality or condition of being about to occur. **2.** Something about to occur.

im·mi·nen·cy (ĭm′ə-nən-sē) *n., pl.* **-cies.** Imminence.

im·mi·nent (ĭm′ə-nənt) *adj.* About to occur; impending: *in imminent danger.* [Middle English *iminent,* from Old French *imminent,* from Latin *imminēns, imminent-*, present participle of *imminēre,* to overhang : *in-*, in; see IN–[2] + *-minēre,* to jut, threaten; see **men-**[2] in Appendix.] —**im′mi·nent·ly** *adv.* —**im′mi·nent·ness** *n.*

im·mis·ci·ble (ĭ-mĭs′ə-bəl) *adj.* That cannot undergo mixing or blending: *immiscible elements.* —**im·mis′ci·bil′i·ty** *n.* —**im·mis′ci·bly** *adv.*

im·mit·i·ga·ble (ĭ-mĭt′ĭ-gə-bəl) *adj.* That cannot be mitigated: *immitigable circumstances.* —**im·mit′i·ga·bil′i·ty, im·mit′i·ga·ble·ness** *n.* —**im·mit′i·ga·bly** *adv.*

im·mit·tance (ĭ-mĭt′ns) *n.* Electrical impedance or admittance. [IM(PEDANCE) + (AD)MITTANCE.]

im·mix (ĭ-mĭks′) *tr.v.* **-mixed, -mix·ing, -mix·es.** To commingle; blend. [Back-formation from Middle English *immixte,* past participle of *immixten,* to intermingle with, from Latin *immīxtus,* past participle of *immīscēre,* to blend : *in-*, in; see IN–[2] + *mīscēre,* to mix; see **meik-** in Appendix.] —**im·mix′ture** (-mĭks′chər) *n.*

im·mo·bile (ĭ-mō′bəl, -bēl′, -bīl′) *adj.* **1.** Immovable; fixed. **2.** Not moving; motionless. —**im′mo·bil′i·ty** (-bĭl′ĭ-tē) *n.*

im·mo·bi·lize (ĭ-mō′bə-līz′) *tr.v.* **-lized, -liz·ing, -liz·es.** **1.** To render immobile. **2.** To fix the position of (a joint or fractured limb), as with a splint or cast. **3.** To impede movement or use of: *Severe weather immobilized the rescue team.* **4.** *Economics.* **a.** To withdraw (specie) from circulation and reserve as security for other money. **b.** To convert (floating capital) into fixed capital. —**im·mo′bi·li·za′tion** (-lĭ-zā′shən) *n.* —**im·mo′bi·liz′er** *n.*

im·mod·er·a·cy (ĭ-mŏd′ər-ə-sē) *n., pl.* **-cies.** **1.** The quality or condition of being extreme or immoderate. **2.** Something extreme or immoderate.

im·mod·er·ate (ĭ-mŏd′ər-ĭt) *adj.* Exceeding normal or appropriate bounds; extreme: *immoderate spending; immoderate laughter.* See Synonyms at **excessive.** [Middle English, from Latin *immoderātus* : *in-*, not; see IN–[1] + *moderātus,* past participle of *moderārī,* to moderate; see **med-** in Appendix.] —**im·mod′er·ate·ly** *adv.* —**im·mod′er·ate·ness, im·mod′er·a′tion** *n.*

im·mod·est (ĭ-mŏd′ĭst) *adj.* **1.** Lacking modesty. **2.a.** Offending against sexual mores in conduct or appearance; indecent: *a bathing suit considered immodest by the local people.* **b.** Not properly restrained in expression or self-assertion; boastful: *immodest claims in advertising and promotion.* **3.** Arrogant. [Latin *immodestus* : *in-*, not; see IN–[1] + *modestus,* moderate, modest; see **med-** in Appendix.] —**im·mod′est·ly** *adv.* —**im·mod′es·ty** *n.*

im·mo·late (ĭm′ə-lāt′) *tr.v.* **-lat·ed, -lat·ing, -lates.** **1.** To kill as a sacrifice. **2.** To kill (oneself) by fire. **3.** To destroy. [Latin *immolāre, immolāt-*, to sacrifice, sprinkle with sacrificial meal : *in-*, on; see IN–[2] + *mola,* meal, millstone; see **melə-** in Appendix.] —**im′mo·la′tion** *n.* —**im′mo·la′tor** *n.*

im·mor·al (ĭ-môr′əl, -mŏr′-) *adj.* Contrary to established moral principles. —**im·mor′al·ly** *adv.*

im·mor·al·ist (ĭ-môr′ə-lĭst, -mŏr′-) *n.* An advocate of immorality.

im·mor·al·i·ty (ĭm′ô-răl′ĭ-tē, ĭm′ə-) *n., pl.* **-ties.** **1.** The quality or condition of being immoral. **2.** An immoral act or practice.

im·mor·tal (ĭ-môr′tl) *adj.* **1.** Not subject to death: *immortal deities; the immortal soul.* **2.** Never to be forgotten; everlasting: *immortal words.* **3.** Of or relating to immortality. **4.** *Biology.* Capable of indefinite growth or division. Used of cells in culture. —**immortal** *n.* **1.** One not subject to death. **2.** One whose fame is enduring. [Middle English, from Old French *immortel,* from Latin *immortālis.* See **mer-** in Appendix.] —**im·mor′tal·ly** *adv.*

im·mor·tal·i·ty (ĭm′ôr-tăl′ĭ-tē) *n.* **1.** The quality or condition of being immortal. **2.** Endless life or existence. **3.** Enduring fame.

im·mor·tal·ize (ĭ-môr′tl-īz′) *tr.v.* **-ized, -iz·ing, -iz·es.** To make immortal.

im·mor·telle (ĭm′ôr-tĕl′) *n.* A plant with flowers that retain their color when dried. [French, from feminine of *immortel,* immortal, from Old French. See IMMORTAL.]

im·mo·tile (ĭ-mōt′l, ĭ-mō′tīl′) *adj.* Not moving or lacking the ability to move. —**im′mo·til′i·ty** (-tĭl′ĭ-tē) *n.*

im·mov·a·ble (ĭ-mo͞o′və-bəl) *adj.* **1.a.** Impossible to move. **b.** Incapable of movement. **2.** Impossible to alter: *immovable plans.* **3.** Unyielding in principle, purpose, or adherence; steadfast. **4.** Incapable of being moved emotionally. **5.** *Law.* Not liable to be removed; permanent: *immovable property.* —**immovable** *n.* **1.** One that cannot move or be moved. **2.** Often **immovables.** *Law.* Property that cannot be moved; real property. —**im·mov′a·bil′i·ty, im·mov′a·ble·ness** *n.* —**im·mov′a·bly** *adv.*

immun. *abbr.* **1.** Immunity. **2.** Immunization.

im·mune (ĭ-myo͞on′) *adj.* **1.** Not subject to an obligation imposed on others; exempt: *immune from taxation; immune from criminal prosecution.* **2.** Not affected by a given influence; unresponsive: *immune to persuasion.* **3.** *Immunology.* Of, relating to, or having immunity to infection by a specific pathogen. —**immune** *n.* A person who is immune. [Middle English, from Latin *immūnis.* See **mei-**[1] in Appendix.]

immune reaction *n.* The reaction resulting from the recognition and binding of an antigen by its specific antibody or by a previously sensitized lymphocyte. Also called *immunoreaction.*

immune response *n.* An integrated bodily response to an antigen, especially one mediated by lymphocytes and involving recognition of antigens by specific antibodies or previously sensitized lymphocytes.

immune system *n.* The integrated body system of organs, tissues, cells, and cell products such as antibodies that differentiates self from nonself and neutralizes potentially pathogenic organisms or substances.

im·mu·ni·ty (ĭ-myo͞o′nĭ-tē) *n., pl.* **-ties.** *Abbr.* **immun.** **1.** The quality or condition of being immune. **2.** *Immunology.* Inherited, acquired, or induced resistance to infection by a specific pathogen. **3.** *Law.* **a.** Exemption from normal legal duties, penalties, or liabilities, granted to a special group of people: *legislative immunity.* **b.** Exemption from legal prosecution, often granted a witness in exchange for self-incriminating testimony.

im·mu·nize (ĭm′yə-nīz′) *tr.v.* **-nized, -niz·ing, -niz·es.** **1.** To render immune. **2.** To produce immunity in, as by inoculation. **3.** *Law.* To grant immunity from prosecution: *immunize a witness.* —**im′mu·ni·za′tion** (-nĭ-zā′shən) *n.*

immuno– *pref.* Immune; immunity: *immunoelectrophoresis.* [From IMMUNE.]

im·mu·no·as·say (ĭm′yə-nō-ăs′ā, ĭ-myo͞o′-) *n.* A laboratory or clinical technique that makes use of the specific binding between an antigen and its homologous antibody in order to identify and quantify a substance in a sample.

im·mu·no·chem·is·try (ĭm′yə-nō-kĕm′ĭ-strē, ĭ-myo͞o′-) *n.* The chemistry of immunologic phenomena, as of antigen-antibody reactions.

im·mu·no·com·pe·tent (ĭm′yə-nō-kŏm′pĭ-tənt, ĭ-myo͞o′-) *adj.* Having the normal bodily capacity to develop an immune response following exposure to an antigen. —**im′mu·no·com′pe·tence** *n.*

im·mu·no·com·pro·mised (ĭm′yə-nō-kŏm′prə-mīzd, ĭ-myo͞o′-) *adj.* Incapable of developing a normal immune response, usually as a result of disease, malnutrition, or immunosuppressive therapy.

im·mu·no·de·fi·cien·cy (ĭm′yə-nō-dĭ-fĭsh′ən-sē, ĭ-myo͞o′-) *n., pl.* **-cies.** An innate, acquired, or induced inability to develop a normal immune response. —**im′mu·no·de·fi′cient** *adj.*

im·mu·no·de·pres·sion (ĭm′yə-nō-dĭ-prĕsh′ən, ĭ-myo͞o′-) *n.* See **immunosuppression.** —**im′mu·no·de·pres′sant** (-prĕs′ənt) *n.* —**im′mu·no·de·pres′sive** *adj.*

im·mu·no·e·lec·tro·pho·re·sis (ĭm′yə-nō-ĭ-lĕk′trə-fə-rē′sĭs, ĭ-myo͞o′-) *n.* The separation and identification of proteins based on differences in electrical charge and reactivity with antibodies.

im·mu·no·fluo·res·cence (ĭm′yə-nō-flo͝o-rĕs′əns, -flô-, -flō-) *n.* Any of various techniques that use antibodies chemically linked to a fluorescent dye to identify or quantify antigens in a tissue sample. —**im′mu·no·fluo·res′cent** *adj.*

im·mu·no·ge·net·ics (ĭm′yə-nō-jə-nĕt′ĭks) *n.* *(used with a sing. verb).* **1.** The study of the interrelation between immunity to disease and genetic makeup. **2.** The branch of immunology that deals with the molecular and genetic bases of the immune response. —**im′mu·no·ge·net′i·cist** (-ĭ-sĭst) *n.*

im·mu·no·gen·ic (ĭm′yə-nō-jĕn′ĭk, ĭmyo͞o′-) *adj.* Producing an immune response; antigenic.

im·mu·no·glob·u·lin (ĭm′yə-nō-glŏb′yə-lĭn, ĭ-myo͞o′-) *n.* *Abbr.* **Ig** Any of a group of large glycoproteins secreted by plasma cells in vertebrates that function as antibodies in the immune response by binding the specific antigens. Immunoglobulins are found along the respiratory and intestinal tracts, on mucosal surfaces, and in milk, saliva, tears, and blood serum.

im·mu·nol·o·gy (ĭm′yə-nŏl′ə-jē) *n.* The branch of biomedicine that is concerned with the structure and function of the immune system, innate and acquired immunity, the bodily distinction of self from nonself, and laboratory techniques involving the interaction of antigens with specific antibodies. —**im′mu·no·**

ă pat	oi boy
ā pay	ou out
âr care	o͝o took
ä father	o͞o boot
ĕ pet	ŭ cut
ē be	ûr urge
ĭ pit	th thin
ī pie	*th* this
îr pier	hw which
ŏ pot	zh vision
ō toe	ə about, item
ô paw	♦ regionalism

Stress marks: ′ (primary); ′ (secondary), as in **dictionary** (dĭk′shə-nĕr′ē)

impala
Male impala
Aepyceros melampus

log′ic (-nə-lŏj′ĭk), **im′mu·no·log′i·cal** *adj.* **—im′mu·no·log′i·cal·ly** *adv.* **—im′mu·nol′o·gist** *n.*

im·mu·no·re·ac·tion (ĭm′yə-nō-rē-ăk′shən, ĭ-myo͞o′-) *n.* See **immune reaction. —im′mu·no·re·ac′tive** *adj.* **—im′mu·no·re·ac·tiv′i·ty** *n.*

im·mu·no·sup·pres·sion (ĭm′yə-nō-sə-prĕsh′ən, ĭ-myo͞o′-) *n.* Suppression of the immune response, as by drugs or radiation, in order to prevent the rejection of grafts or transplants or control autoimmune diseases. Also called *immunodepression.* **—im′mu·no·sup·pres′sant** (-prĕs′ənt) *n.* **—im′mu·no·sup·pres′sive** *adj.*

im·mu·no·ther·a·py (ĭm′yə-nō-thĕr′ə-pē, ĭ-myo͞o′-) *n., pl.* **-pies.** Treatment of disease by inducing, enhancing, or suppressing an immune response. **—im′mu·no·ther′a·peu′tic** (-pyo͞o′tĭk) *adj.* **—im′mu·no·ther′a·pist** *n.*

im·mure (ĭ-myo͝or′) *tr.v.* **-mured, -mur·ing, -mures. 1.** To confine within or as if within walls; imprison. **2.** To build into a wall: *immure a shrine.* **3.** To entomb in a wall. [Medieval Latin *immūrāre* : Latin *in-*, in; see IN–[2] + Latin *mūrus,* wall.] **—im·mure′ment** *n.*

im·mu·ta·ble (ĭ-myo͞o′tə-bəl) *adj.* Not subject or susceptible to change. **—im·mu′ta·bil′i·ty, im·mu′ta·ble·ness** *n.* **—im·mu′ta·bly** *adv.*

imp (ĭmp) *n.* **1.** A mischievous child. **2.** A small demon. **3.** *Obsolete.* A graft. **—imp** *tr.v.* **imped, imp·ing, imps. 1.** To graft (new feathers) onto the wing of a trained falcon or hawk to repair damage or increase flying capacity. **2.** To furnish with wings. [Middle English *impe,* scion, sprig, offspring, from Old English *impa,* young shoot, from *impian,* to graft, ultimately from Medieval Latin *impotus,* graft, from Greek *emphutos,* grafted, from Greek *emphuein,* to implant : *en-,* in; see EN–[2] + *phuein,* to make grow; see **bheuə-** in Appendix.]

imp. *abbr.* **1.** Imperative. **2.** Imperfect. **3.** Imperial. **4.a.** Import. **b.** Imported; importer. **5.** Important. **6.** Imprimatur.

im·pact (ĭm′păkt′) *n.* **1.** The striking of one body against another; collision. **2.** The force or impetus transmitted by a collision. **3.** The effect or impression of one thing on another: *still gauging the impact of automation on the lives of factory workers.* **4.** The power of making a strong, immediate impression: *a speech that lacked impact.* **—impact** (ĭm-păkt′) *v.* **-pact·ed, -pact·ing, -pacts.** *—tr.* **1.** To pack firmly together. **2.** To strike forcefully: *meteorites impacting the lunar surface.* **3.** *Usage Problem.* To have an effect or impact on. *—intr. Usage Problem.* To have an effect or impact. [From Latin *impāctus,* past participle of *impingere,* to push against. See IMPINGE.] **—im·pac′tion** *n.*

SYNONYMS: *impact, repercussion.* The central meaning shared by these nouns is "a strong effect exerted by one person or thing on another": *the far-reaching impact of an oil embargo; a strike that had dire repercussions.* See also Synonyms at **collision.**

USAGE NOTE: Each generation of critics seems to select one particular usage to stand as the emblem of what they view as linguistic crassness. Thirty years ago it was the use of *contact* as a verb, but opposition to that form has more or less disappeared, and attention now focuses on the verbal use of *impact* meaning "have an effect, affect." Eighty-four percent of the Usage Panel disapproves of the construction *to impact on,* as in the phrase *social pathologies, common to the inner city, that impact heavily on such a community;* and fully 95 percent disapproves of the use of *impact* as a transitive verb in the sentence *Companies have used disposable techniques that have a potential for impacting our health.* But even these figures do not reflect the degree of distaste with which critics view the usage: in their comments some Panelists labeled the usage as "bureaucratic," "pretentious," "vile," and "a vulgarism." • It may be that the particular pretentiousness associated with the verbal use of *impact* is caused by its derivation from an already questionable metaphoric use of the noun *impact,* as in phrases such as *the political impact of the decision* or *the impact of the program on the community,* in which no more is usually meant than might have been expressed by *effects* or *consequences.* But though *impact* may have begun life a generation ago as an inflated substitute for "affect significantly," it has by now become so common in corporate and institutional contexts that younger speakers appear to regard it as wholly standard and straightforward usage. Within a few years, accordingly, the usage is likely to be no more objectionable than *contact* is now, since it will no longer betray any particular pretentiousness on the part of those who use it. See Usage Note at **contact.**

WORD HISTORY: The often criticized use of *impact,* as in the passage "social pathologies, common to the inner city, that impact heavily on such a community," illustrates how one part of speech can have an impact on another part of speech spelled the same way. The usage also reflects the role played by science in the formation of new senses of words. The noun *impact* comes from the past participle *impāctus* of the Latin verb *impingere,* which means "to bring into violent contact," "to drive persons or other creatures onto or against," and "to fix, fasten onto." Our noun, first recorded in 1781, derived its sense from the "contact" sense of *impingere.* First recorded in a scientific context having to do with the collision of bodies, it was much used in scientific contexts and later, in the 19th century, took on a figurative sense, "the effect of one thing upon another." The verb *impact,* on the other hand, also coming from Latin *impāctus,* is found much earlier than the noun, that is, it is first recorded in 1601, deriving its sense from the "driving" and "fixing" senses of *impingere* and meaning "to press

impatiens
Spotted jewelweed
Impatiens capensis

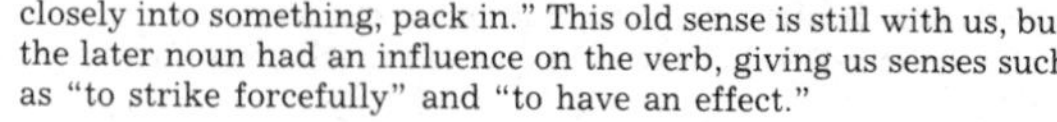

closely into something, pack in." This old sense is still with us, but the later noun had an influence on the verb, giving us senses such as "to strike forcefully" and "to have an effect."

im·pact·ed (ĭm-păk′tĭd) *adj.* **1.** Wedged together at the broken ends. Used of a fractured bone. **2.** Placed in the alveolus in a manner prohibiting eruption into a normal position. Used of a tooth. **3.** Wedged or packed in, so as to fill or block an organ or a passage: *impacted feces.*

impact zone *n. Sports.* The spot on a wave where the water is just about to collapse and explode, the spot of greatest danger to and opportunity for a surfer.

im·pair (ĭm-pâr′) *tr.v.* **-paired, -pair·ing, -pairs.** To cause to diminish, as in strength, value, or quality: *an injury that impaired my hearing; a severe storm impairing communications.* See Synonyms at **injure.** [Middle English *empairen,* from Old French *empeirer,* from Vulgar Latin **impēiōrāre* : Latin *in-,* causative pref.; see IN–[2] + Late Latin *pēiōrāre,* to worsen (from Latin *pēior, pēiōr-,* worse; see **ped-** in Appendix).] **—im·pair′ment** *n.*

im·pa·la (ĭm-pä′lə) *n.* A reddish African antelope *(Aepyceros melampus)* noted for its leaping ability and having ridged, curved horns in the male. [Nguni (Zulu) *im-pala.*]

im·pale (ĭm-pāl′) also **em·pale** (ĕm-) *tr.v.* **-paled, -pal·ing, -pales. 1.a.** To pierce with a sharp stake or point. **b.** To torture or kill by impaling. **2.** To render helpless as if by impaling. [Medieval Latin *impālāre* : Latin *in-,* in; see IN–[2] + Latin *pālus,* stake; see **pag-** in Appendix.] **—im·pal′er** *n.*

im·pal·pa·ble (ĭm-păl′pə-bəl) *adj.* **1.** Not perceptible to the touch; intangible. **2.** Difficult to perceive or grasp by the mind. **—im·pal′pa·bil′i·ty** *n.* **—im·pal′pa·bly** *adv.*

im·pan·el (ĭm-păn′əl) also **em·pan·el** (ĕm-) *tr.v.* **-eled, -el·ing, -els** or **-elled, -el·ling, -els.** *Law.* To enroll (a jury) upon a panel or list. [Middle English *empanellen,* from Anglo-Norman *empaneller* : *en-,* in (from Latin *in-;* see IN–[2]) + *panel,* piece of paper listing jurors, jury; see PANEL.] **—im·pan′el·ment** *n.*

im·par·i·ty (ĭm-păr′ĭ-tē) *n., pl.* **-ties.** Inequality; disparity. [Late Latin *imparitās,* from Latin *impār,* not equal : *in-,* not; see IN–[1] + *pār,* equal; see **pere-[2]** in Appendix.]

im·part (ĭm-pärt′) *tr.v.* **-part·ed, -part·ing, -parts. 1.** To grant a share of; bestow: *impart a subtle flavor; impart some advice.* **2.** To make known; disclose: *persuaded to impart the secret.* [Middle English *imparten,* from Old French *impartir,* from Latin *impertīre, impartīre* : *in-,* in; see IN–[2] + *partīre,* to share (from *pars, part-,* part; see **pere-[2]** in Appendix).]

im·par·tial (ĭm-pär′shəl) *adj.* Not partial or biased; unprejudiced. See Synonyms at **fair[1]. —im′par·ti·al′i·ty** (-shē-ăl′ĭ-tē), **im·par′tial·ness** *n.* **—im·par′tial·ly** *adv.*

im·part·i·ble (ĭm-pär′tə-bəl) *adj.* Not partible; indivisible: *an impartible inheritance.* **—im·part′i·bil′i·ty** *n.* **—im·part′i·bly** *adv.*

im·pass·a·ble (ĭm-păs′ə-bəl) *adj.* Impossible to pass, cross, or overcome: *impassable roads; impassable problems.* **—im·pass′a·bil′i·ty, im·pass′a·ble·ness** *n.* **—im·pass′a·bly** *adv.*

im·passe (ĭm′păs′) *n.* **1.** A road or passage having no exit; a cul-de-sac. **2.** A situation that is so difficult that no progress can be made; a deadlock or a stalemate: *reached an impasse in the negotiations.* [French : *in-,* not (from Latin *in-;* see IN–[1]) + *passe,* a passing (from Old French, from *passer,* to pass; see PASS).]

im·pas·si·ble (ĭm-păs′ə-bəl) *adj.* **1.** Not subject to suffering or pain. **2.** Unfeeling; impassive. [Middle English, from Old French, from Late Latin *impassibilis* : *in-,* not; see IN–[1] + *passibilis,* passible; see PASSIBLE.] **—im·pas′si·bil′i·ty, im·pas′si·ble·ness** *n.* **—im·pas′si·bly** *adv.*

im·pas·sion (ĭm-păsh′ən) *tr.v.* **-sioned, -sion·ing, -sions.** To arouse the passions of. [Italian *impassionare* : *in-,* in (from Latin; see IN–[2]) + *passione,* passion (from Latin *passiō, passiōn-,* emotion; see PASSION).]

im·pas·sioned (ĭm-păsh′ənd) *adj.* Filled with passion; fervent: *an impassioned plea for justice.*

im·pas·sive (ĭm-păs′ĭv) *adj.* **1.** Devoid of or not subject to emotion. **2.** Revealing no emotion; expressionless. **3.** Incapable of physical sensation. **4.** Motionless; still. [IN–[1] + PASSIVE, suffering (obsolete).] **—im·pas′sive·ly** *adv.* **—im·pas′sive·ness, im′pas·siv′i·ty** *n.*

im·paste (ĭm-păst′) *tr.v.* **-past·ed, -past·ing, -pastes. 1.** To enclose with or as if with a paste or crust. **2.** To paint by applying thick layers of pigment.

im·pas·to (ĭm-păs′tō, -pä′stō) *n., pl.* **-tos. 1.** The application of thick layers of pigment to a canvas or other surface in painting. **2.** The paint so applied. [Italian, from *impastare,* to make into a paste : *in-,* in (from Latin; see IN–[2]) + *pasta,* paste (from Late Latin; see PASTE[1]).]

im·pa·tience (ĭm-pā′shəns) *n.* The quality or condition of being impatient.

im·pa·tiens (ĭm-pā′shənz, -shəns) *n.* Any of various plants of the genus *Impatiens,* which includes the jewelweed. [Latin *impatiēns,* impatient (so called because the ripe pods burst open when touched). See IMPATIENT.]

im·pa·tient (ĭm-pā′shənt) *adj.* **1.** Unable to wait patiently or tolerate delay; restless. **2.** Unable to endure irritation or opposition; intolerant: *impatient of criticism.* **3.** Expressing or produced by impatience: *an impatient scowl.* **4.** Restively eager or desirous; anxious: *impatient to begin.* [Middle English *impacient,* from Old French *impatient,* from Latin *impatiēns, impatient-* : *in-,* not; see IN–[1] + *patiēns,* present participle of *patī,* to suffer, endure; see PATIENT.] **—im·pa′tient·ly** *adv.*

im·peach (ĭm-pēch′) *tr.v.* **-peached, -peach·ing, -peach·es. 1.a.** To make an accusation against. **b.** To charge (a public official) with improper conduct in office before a proper tribunal. **2.** To challenge the validity of; try to discredit: *impeach a witness's credibility.* [Middle English *empechen,* to impede, accuse, from Anglo-Norman *empecher,* from Late Latin *impedicāre,* to entangle : Latin *in-,* in; see IN–[2] + Latin *pedica,* fetter; see **ped-** in Appendix.] **—im·peach′er** *n.* **—im·peach′ment** *n.*

WORD HISTORY: Nothing hobbles a President so much as impeachment, and there is an etymological as well as procedural reason for this. The word *impeach* can be traced back through Anglo-Norman *empecher* to Late Latin *impedicāre,* "to catch, entangle," from Latin *pedica,* "fetter for the ankle, snare." Thus we find that Middle English *empechen,* the ancestor of our word, means such things as "to cause to get stuck fast," "hinder or impede," "interfere with," and "criticize unfavorably." A legal sense of *empechen* is first recorded in 1384. This sense, which had previously developed in Old French, was "to accuse, bring charges against." A further development of the sense had specific reference to Parliament and its formal accusation of treason or other high crimes, a process that the United States borrowed from the British. Although we have used it rarely at the federal level, impeachment stands as the ultimate snare for those who would take advantage of the public trust.

im·peach·a·ble (ĭm-pē′chə-bəl) *adj.* **1.** Capable of being impeached: *venal, impeachable public servants.* **2.** Being such as to make one liable to impeachment: *an impeachable offense.* **—im·peach′a·bil′i·ty** *n.*

im·pearl (ĭm-pûrl′) *tr.v.* **-pearled, -pearl·ing, -pearls. 1.** To form (something) into pearls. **2.** To adorn with or as if with pearls.

im·pec·ca·ble (ĭm-pĕk′ə-bəl) *adj.* **1.** Having no flaws; perfect. See Synonyms at **perfect. 2.** Incapable of sin or wrongdoing. [Latin *impeccābilis* : *in-,* not; see IN–[1] + *peccāre,* to sin; see **ped-** in Appendix.] **—im·pec′ca·bil′i·ty** *n.* **—im·pec′ca·bly** *adv.*

im·pe·cu·ni·ous (ĭm′pĭ-kyo͞o′nē-əs) *adj.* Lacking money; penniless. See Synonyms at **poor.** [IM–[1] + *pecunious,* rich (from Middle English, from Old French *pecunios,* from Latin *pecūniōsus,* from *pecūnia,* money, wealth; see **peku-** in Appendix).] **—im′pe·cu′ni·ous·ly** *adv.* **—im′pe·cu′ni·ous·ness, im′pe·cu′ni·os′i·ty** (-ŏs′ĭ-tē) *n.*

im·pe·dance (ĭm-pēd′ns) *n. Symbol* **Z** A measure of the total opposition to current flow in an alternating current circuit, made up of two components, ohmic resistance and reactance, and usually represented in complex notation as $Z = R + iX$, where R is the ohmic resistance and X is the reactance.

impedance match·ing (măch′ĭng) *n.* The use of electric circuits, transmission lines, and other devices to make the impedance of a load equal to the internal impedance of the source of power, thereby making possible the most efficient transfer of power.

im·pede (ĭm-pēd′) *tr.v.* **-ped·ed, -ped·ing, -pedes.** To retard or obstruct the progress of. See Synonyms at **hinder[1].** [Latin *impedīre.* See **ped-** in Appendix.] **—im·ped′er** *n.*

im·ped·i·ment (ĭm-pĕd′ə-mənt) *n.* **1.** Something that impedes; a hindrance or an obstruction. See Synonyms at **obstacle. 2.** An organic defect preventing clear articulation: *a speech impediment.* **3.** *Law.* Something that obstructs the making of a legal contract. [Middle English, from Old French, from Latin *impedīmentum,* from *impedīre,* to impede. See IMPEDE.] **—im·ped′i·men′tal** (-mĕn′tl), **im·ped′i·men′ta·ry** (-mĕn′tə-rē) *adj.*

im·ped·i·men·ta (ĭm-pĕd′ə-mĕn′tə) *pl.n.* Objects, such as provisions or baggage, that impede or encumber. [Latin *impedīmenta,* pl. of *impedīmentum,* impediment. See IMPEDIMENT.]

im·pel (ĭm-pĕl′) *tr.v.* **-pelled, -pel·ling, -pels. 1.** To urge to action through moral pressure; drive: *We were impelled by circumstances to take a stand.* **2.** To drive forward; propel. [Middle English *impellen,* from Latin *impellere* : *in-,* against; see IN–[2] + *pellere,* to drive; see **pel-[5]** in Appendix.]

im·pel·ler (ĭm-pĕl′ər) *n.* **1.** One that impels, as a rotating device used to force a fluid in a desired direction under pressure. **2.** A rotor or rotor blade.

im·pend (ĭm-pĕnd′) *intr.v.* **-pend·ed, -pend·ing, -pends. 1.** To be about to take place: *Her retirement is impending.* **2.** To threaten to happen; menace: *discouraged by the trouble that impended.* **3.** *Archaic.* To jut out; hang suspended. [Latin *impendēre* : *in-,* over; see IN–[2] + *pendēre,* to hang; see **(s)pen-** in Appendix.]

im·pen·e·tra·bil·i·ty (ĭm-pĕn′ĭ-trə-bĭl′ĭ-tē) *n.* **1.** The quality or condition of being impenetrable. **2.** The inability of two bodies to occupy the same space at the same time.

im·pen·e·tra·ble (ĭm-pĕn′ĭ-trə-bəl) *adj.* **1.** Impossible to penetrate or enter: *an impenetrable fortress.* **2.** Impossible to understand; incomprehensible: *impenetrable jargon.* **3.** Impervious to sentiment or argument: *an impenetrable heart.* **—im·pen′e·tra·ble·ness** *n.* **—im·pen′e·tra·bly** *adv.*

im·pen·i·tent (ĭm-pĕn′ĭ-tənt) *adj.* Not penitent; unrepentant. **—im·pen′i·tence** *n.* **—im·pen′i·tent** *n.* **—im·pen′i·tent·ly** *adv.*

im·per·a·tive (ĭm-pĕr′ə-tĭv) *adj. Abbr.* **imp. 1.** Expressing a command or plea; peremptory: *requests that grew more and more imperative.* **2.** Having the power or authority to command or control. **3.** *Grammar.* Of, relating to, or constituting the mood that expresses a command or request. **4.** Impossible to deter or evade; pressing: *imperative needs.* See Synonyms at **urgent. —imperative** *n. Abbr.* **imp. 1.a.** A command; an order. **b.** An obligation; a duty: *social imperatives.* **2.** A rule, a principle, or an instinct that compels a certain behavior: *a people driven to aggression by territorial imperatives.* **3.** *Grammar.* **a.** The imperative mood. **b.** A verb form of the imperative mood. [Middle English *imperatif,* relating to the imperative mood, from Old French, from Late Latin *imperātīvus,* from Latin *imperātus,* past participle of *imperāre,* to command. See EMPEROR.] **—im·per′a·tive·ly** *adv.* **—im·per′a·tive·ness** *n.*

im·pe·ra·tor (ĭm′pə-rä′tôr′, -tər) *n.* **1.a.** An army commander in the Roman Republic. **b.** Used as a form of address and salutation by soldiers to a victorious Roman general. **2.** The supreme power of the Roman emperor. **3.** The head of state and supreme commander in the Roman Empire, in whose name all victories were won. [Latin *imperātōr.* See EMPEROR.] **—im·per′a·to′ri·al** (ĭm-pĕr′ə-tôr′ē-əl, -tōr′-) *adj.*

im·per·cep·ti·ble (ĭm′pər-sĕp′tə-bəl) *adj.* **1.** Impossible or difficult to perceive by the mind or senses: *an imperceptible drop in temperature.* **2.** So subtle, slight, or gradual as to be barely perceptible: *an imperceptible nod.* **—im′per·cep′ti·bil′i·ty, im′per·cep′ti·ble·ness** *n.* **—im′per·cep′ti·bly** *adv.*

im·per·cep·tive (ĭm′pər-sĕp′tĭv) *adj.* Lacking perception. **—im′per·cep′tive·ness, im′per·cep·tiv′i·ty** *n.*

im·per·fect (ĭm-pûr′fĭkt) *adj. Abbr.* **imp., imperf. 1.** Not perfect. **2.** *Grammar.* Of or being the tense of a verb that shows, usually in the past, an action or a condition as incomplete, continuous, or coincident with another action. **3.** *Botany.* Having either stamens or a pistil only. Used of a flower. **4.** *Law.* Not legally enforceable: *an imperfect contract.* **—imperfect** *n. imp., imperf.* **1.** A piece of merchandise having a minor flaw that does not impair its use, usually sold at a discount. **2.** *Grammar.* **a.** The imperfect tense. **b.** A verb in the imperfect tense. [Middle English *imparfit,* from Old French *imparfait,* from Latin *imperfectus* : *in-,* not; see IN–[1] + *perfectus,* perfect; see PERFECT.] **—im·per′fect·ly** *adv.* **—im·per′fect·ness** *n.*

imperfect fungus *n.* Any of various fungi of the order Fungi Imperfecti, which reproduce only by asexual means.

im·per·fec·tion (ĭm′pər-fĕk′shən) *n.* **1.** The quality or condition of being imperfect. **2.** Something imperfect; a defect or flaw. See Synonyms at **blemish.**

im·per·fec·tive (ĭm′pər-fĕk′tĭv) *adj. Grammar.* Of, relating to, or being action without regard to its beginning or completion.

im·per·fo·rate (ĭm-pûr′fər-ĭt) *adj.* **1.** Having no opening; not perforated. **2.** Not separated by rows of perforations: *imperforate sheets of stamps.* **3.** *Medicine.* Lacking a normal opening: *an imperforate anus.* **—imperforate** *n.* An imperforate stamp.

im·pe·ri·a (ĭm-pîr′ē-ə) *n.* Plural of **imperium.**

im·pe·ri·al (ĭm-pîr′ē-əl) *adj. Abbr.* **imp. 1.** Of, relating to, or suggestive of an empire or a sovereign, especially an emperor or empress: *imperial rule; the imperial palace.* **2.** Ruling over extensive territories or over colonies or dependencies: *imperial nations.* **3.a.** Having supreme authority; sovereign. **b.** Regal; majestic. **4.** Outstanding in size or quality. **5.** Of or belonging to the British Imperial System of weights and measures. **—imperial** *n.* **1.** An emperor or empress. **2.** The top of a carriage. **3.** Something outstanding in size or quality. **4.** A variable size of paper, usually 23 by 33 inches. **5.** A pointed beard grown from the lower lip and chin. [Middle English, from Old French, from Latin *imperiālis,* from *imperium,* command. See EMPIRE. N., sense 5, after the beard of NAPOLEON III.] **—im·pe′ri·al·ly** *adv.*

imperial

Im·pe·ri·al Beach (ĭm-pîr′ē-əl). A city of southern California on the Pacific Ocean at the Mexican border. It is a residential and resort community. Population, 22,689.

im·pe·ri·al·ism (ĭm-pîr′ē-ə-lĭz′əm) *n.* **1.** The policy of extending a nation's authority by territorial acquisition or by the establishment of economic and political hegemony over other nations. **2.** The system, policies, or practices of such a government. **—im·pe′ri·al·ist** *adj. & n.* **—im·pe′ri·al·is′tic** *adj.* **—im·pe′ri·al·is′ti·cal·ly** *adv.*

imperial moth *n.* A large New World moth *(Eacles imperialis)* having yellow wings with purplish or brownish markings.

Imperial Valley. A fertile, irrigated region of southeast California and northeast Baja California, Mexico. Mostly below sea level, it includes the Salton Sea.

im·per·il (ĭm-pĕr′əl) *tr.v.* **-iled, -il·ing, -ils** or **-illed, -il·ling, -ils.** To put into peril; endanger. See Synonyms at **endanger. —im·per′il·ment** *n.*

im·pe·ri·ous (ĭm-pîr′ē-əs) *adj.* **1.** Arrogantly domineering or overbearing. See Synonyms at **dictatorial. 2.** Urgent; pressing. **3.** *Obsolete.* Regal; imperial. [From Latin *imperiōsus,* from *imperium,* imperium. See EMPIRE.] **—im·pe′ri·ous·ly** *adv.* **—im·pe′ri·ous·ness** *n.*

im·per·ish·a·ble (ĭm-pĕr′ĭ-shə-bəl) *adj.* Not perishable: *imperishable food; imperishable hopes.* **—im·per′ish·a·bil′i·ty, im·per′ish·a·ble·ness** *n.* **—im·per′ish·a·bly** *adv.*

ă pat	oi boy
ā pay	ou out
âr care	o͝o took
ä father	o͞o boot
ĕ pet	ŭ cut
ē be	ûr urge
ĭ pit	th thin
ī pie	*th* this
îr pier	hw which
ŏ pot	zh vision
ō toe	ə about, item
ô paw	♦ regionalism

Stress marks: **′** (primary); ′ (secondary), as in **dictionary** (dĭk′shə-nĕr′ē)

im·pe·ri·um (ĭm-pîr′ē-əm) *n., pl.* **-pe·ri·a** (-pîr′ē-ə). **1.** Absolute rule; supreme power. **2.** A sphere of power or dominion; an empire. **3.** *Law.* The right or power of a state to enforce the law. [Latin. See EMPIRE.]

im·per·ma·nent (ĭm-pûr′mə-nənt) *adj.* Not lasting or durable. **—im·per′ma·nence, im·per′ma·nen·cy** *n.*

im·per·me·a·ble (ĭm-pûr′mē-ə-bəl) *adj.* Impossible to permeate: *an impermeable fortress.* **—im·per′me·a·bil′i·ty, im·per′me·a·ble·ness** *n.* **—im·per′me·a·bly** *adv.*

im·per·mis·si·ble (ĭm′pər-mĭs′ə-bəl) *adj.* Not permitted; not permissible: *impermissible behavior.* **—im′per·mis′si·bil′i·ty** *n.* **—im′per·mis′si·bly** *adv.*

im·per·son·al (ĭm-pûr′sə-nəl) *adj.* **1.** Lacking personality; not being a person: *an impersonal force.* **2. a.** Showing no emotion or personality: *an aloof, impersonal manner.* **b.** Having no personal reference or connection: *an impersonal remark.* **c.** Not responsive to or expressive of human personalities: *a large, impersonal corporation.* **3.** *Grammar.* **a.** Of, relating to, or being the action of a verb that expresses the action of an unspecified subject, as in *methinks,* "it seems to me"; Latin *pluit,* "it rains"; or, with an expletive subject, English *it snowed.* **b.** Indefinite. Used of pronouns. **—im·per′son·al′i·ty** (-sə-năl′ĭ-tē) *n.* **—im·per′son·al·ly** *adv.*

im·per·son·al·ize (ĭm-pûr′sə-nə-līz′) *tr.v.* **-ized, -iz·ing, -iz·es.** To make impersonal.

im·per·son·ate (ĭm-pûr′sə-nāt′) *tr.v.* **-at·ed, -at·ing, -ates. 1.** To assume the character or appearance of, especially fraudulently: *impersonate a police officer.* **2.** To imitate the appearance, voice, or manner of; mimic: *an entertainer who impersonates celebrities.* **3.** *Archaic.* To embody; personify. **—im·per′son·a′tion** *n.* **—im·per′son·a′tor** *n.*

im·per·ti·nence (ĭm-pûr′tn-əns) *n.* **1.** The quality or condition of being impertinent, especially: **a.** Insolence. **b.** Irrelevance. **2.** An impertinent act or statement.

im·per·ti·nen·cy (ĭm-pûr′tn-ən-sē) *n., pl.* **-cies.** Impertinence.

im·per·ti·nent (ĭm-pûr′tn-ənt) *adj.* **1.** Exceeding the limits of propriety or good manners; improperly forward or bold: *impertinent of a child to lecture a grownup.* **2.** Not pertinent; irrelevant. See Synonyms at **irrelevant.** [Middle English, irrelevant, from Old French, from Late Latin *impertinēns, impertinent-* : Latin *in-,* not; see IN–[1] + *pertinēns,* pertinent; see PERTINENT.] **—im·per′ti·nent·ly** *adv.*

im·per·turb·a·ble (ĭm′pər-tûr′bə-bəl) *adj.* Unshakably calm and collected. See Synonyms at **cool. —im′per·turb′a·bil′i·ty, im′per·turb′a·ble·ness** *n.* **—im′per·turb′a·bly** *adv.*

im·per·vi·ous (ĭm-pûr′vē-əs) *adj.* **1.** Incapable of being penetrated: *a material impervious to water.* **2.** Incapable of being affected: *impervious to fear.* [From Latin *impervius* : *in-,* not; see IN–[1] + *pervius,* pervious; see PERVIOUS.] **—im·per′vi·ous·ly** *adv.* **—im·per′vi·ous·ness** *n.*

im·pe·ti·go (ĭm′pĭ-tī′gō) *n., pl.* **-gos.** A contagious bacterial skin infection, usually of children, that is characterized by the eruption of superficial pustules and the formation of thick yellow crusts, commonly on the face. [Middle English, from Latin *impetīgō,* from *impetere,* to attack. See IMPETUS.]

im·pet·u·os·i·ty (ĭm-pĕch′o͞o-ŏs′ĭ-tē) *n., pl.* **-ties. 1.** The quality or condition of being impetuous. **2.** An impetuous act.

im·pet·u·ous (ĭm-pĕch′o͞o-əs) *adj.* **1.** Characterized by sudden and forceful energy or emotion; impulsive and passionate. **2.** Having or marked by violent force: *impetuous, heaving waves.* [Middle English, violent, from Old French *impetueux,* from Late Latin *impetuōsus,* from Latin *impetus,* impetus. See IMPETUS.] **—im·pet′u·ous·ly** *adv.* **—im·pet′u·ous·ness** *n.*

SYNONYMS: *impetuous, heedless, hasty, headlong, precipitate, sudden.* These adjectives describe people and their actions when they are marked by abruptness or lack of deliberation. *Impetuous* suggests forceful impulsiveness or impatience: "[a race driver who was] *flamboyant, impetuous, disdainful of death*" (Jim Murray). *Heedless* implies carelessness or lack of a sense of responsibility or proper regard for consequences: *"Hobbling down stairs with heedless haste, I set my foot full in a pail of water"* (Richard Steele). *Hasty* and *headlong* both stress hurried, often reckless action: *"Hasty marriage seldom proveth well"* (Shakespeare). *The soldiers made a headlong rush for cover. Precipitate* suggests impulsiveness and lack of due reflection: *"Some of the fickle populace began to doubt whether they had not been rather precipitate in deposing his brother"* (Washington Irving). *Sudden* applies to what becomes apparent abruptly or unexpectedly: *The patient is given to sudden and inexplicable paroxysms of anger.*

im·pe·tus (ĭm′pĭ-təs) *n., pl.* **-tus·es. 1.** An impelling force; an impulse. **2.** The force or energy associated with a moving body. **3. a.** Something that incites; a stimulus. **b.** Increased activity in response to a stimulus: *The approaching deadline gave impetus to the investigation.* [Latin, from *impetere,* to attack : *in-,* against; see IN–[2] + *petere,* to go towards, seek; see **pet-** in Appendix.]

im·pi·e·ty (ĭm-pī′ĭ-tē) *n., pl.* **-ties. 1.** The quality or state of being impious. **2.** An impious act. **3.** Undutifulness.

im·pinge (ĭm-pĭnj′) *v.* —*intr.* **-pinged, -ping·ing, -ping·es. 1.** To collide or strike: *Sound waves impinge on the eardrum.* **2.** To encroach; trespass: *Do not impinge on my privacy.* —*tr.* To encroach upon: *"One of a democratic government's continuing challenges is finding a way to protect . . . secrets without impinging the liberties that democracy exists to protect"* (Christian Science Monitor). [Latin *impingere* : *in-,* against; see IN–[2] + *pangere,* to fasten; see **pag-** in Appendix.] **—im·pinge′ment** *n.* **—im·ping′er** *n.*

im·pi·ous (ĭm′pē-əs, ĭm-pī′-) *adj.* **1.** Lacking reverence; not pious. **2.** Lacking due respect or dutifulness: *impious toward one's parents.* [From Latin *impius* : *in-,* not; see IN–[1] + *pius,* dutiful.] **—im′pi·ous·ly** *adv.* **—im′pi·ous·ness** *n.*

imp·ish (ĭm′pĭsh) *adj.* Of or befitting an imp; mischievous. See Synonyms at **playful. —imp′ish·ly** *adv.* **—imp′ish·ness** *n.*

im·pi·toy·a·ble (ăɴ-pē-toi-ä′blə) *n.* A large wine-tasting glass configured so as to enhance taste and amplify aroma. [French, pitiless, from Old French : *in-,* not (from Latin *in-;* see IN–[1]) + *piteable,* capable of pity (from *piteer,* to pity, from *pite,* pity; see PITY).]

im·plac·a·ble (ĭm-plăk′ə-bəl, -plā′kə-) *adj.* Impossible to placate or appease: *implacable foes; implacable suspicion.* [Middle English, from Old French, from Latin *implācābilis* : *in-,* not; see IN–[1] + *plācābilis,* placable; see PLACABLE.] **—im·plac′a·bil′i·ty, im·plac′a·ble·ness** *n.* **—im·plac′a·bly** *adv.*

im·plant (ĭm-plănt′) *v.* **-plant·ed, -plant·ing, -plants.** —*tr.* **1.** To set in firmly, as into the ground: *implant fence posts.* **2.** To establish securely, as in the mind or consciousness; instill. *habits that had been implanted early in childhood.* **3.** *Medicine.* **a.** To insert or embed (an object or a device) surgically: *implant a pacemaker; implant a drug capsule.* **b.** To graft or insert (a tissue) within the body. —*intr. Embryology.* To become attached to and embedded in the uterine lining. Used of a fertilized egg. **—implant** (ĭm′plănt′) *n.* Something implanted, especially a surgically implanted tissue or device: *a dental implant; a subcutaneous implant.* [Middle English *implanten,* from Medieval Latin *implantāre* : Latin *in-,* in; see IN–[2] + Latin *plantāre,* to plant (from *planta,* a shoot; see PLANT).] **—im·plant′a·ble** *adj.*

im·plan·ta·tion (ĭm′plăn-tā′shən) *n.* **1. a.** The act or an instance of implanting. **b.** The condition of being implanted. **2.** *Embryology.* The process by which a fertilized egg implants in the uterine lining.

im·plau·si·ble (ĭm-plô′zə-bəl) *adj.* Difficult to believe; not plausible. **—im·plau′si·bil′i·ty, im·plau′si·ble·ness** *n.* **—im·plau′si·bly** *adv.*

im·plead (ĭm-plēd′) *tr.v.* **-plead·ed, -plead·ing, -pleads.** *Law.* To sue in court in response to an earlier pleading. [Middle English *empleden,* from Anglo-Norman *empleder,* variant of Old French *emplaider* : *en-,* intensive pref. (from Latin *in-;* see IN–[2]) + *plaidier,* to plead; see PLEAD.]

im·ple·ment (ĭm′plə-mənt) *n.* **1.** A tool or an instrument used in doing work: *a gardening implement.* See Synonyms at **tool. 2.** An article used to outfit or equip. **3.** A means of achieving an end; an instrument or agent. **—implement** (-mĕnt′) *tr.v.* **-ment·ed, -ment·ing, -ments. 1.** To put into practical effect; carry out: *implement the new procedures.* See Synonyms at **enforce. 2.** To supply with implements. [Middle English, supplementary payment, from Old French *emplement,* act of filling, from Late Latin *implēmentum,* from Latin *implēre,* to fill up : *in-,* intensive pref.; see IN–[2] + *plēre,* to fill; see **pele-**[1] in Appendix.] **—im′ple·men·ta′tion** (-mən-tā′shən, -mĕn-) *n.* **—im′ple·ment′er** *n.*

USAGE NOTE: The verb *implement,* meaning "to put into practice, carry out," has in fact been in use since the 19th century. Critics have sometimes objected to the verb as jargon, but its obvious usefulness appears to have outweighed their reservations. Eighty-nine percent of the Usage Panel accepts the usage in the sentence *The mayor's office announced the creation of a special task force responsible for implementing the new policy.*

im·pli·cate (ĭm′plĭ-kāt′) *tr.v.* **-cat·ed, -cat·ing, -cates. 1.** To involve or connect intimately or incriminatingly: *evidence that implicates others in the plot.* **2.** To have as a consequence or an inference; imply. **3.** *Archaic.* To interweave or entangle; entwine. [Middle English, to convey a truth bound up in a fable, from Latin *implicāre, implicāt-,* to entangle, unite : *in-,* in; see IN–[2] + *plicāre,* to fold; see **plek-** in Appendix.]

im·pli·ca·tion (ĭm′plĭ-kā′shən) *n.* **1.** The act of implicating or the condition of being implicated. **2.** The act of implying or the condition of being implied. **3.** Something that is implied, especially: **a.** An indirect indication; a suggestion. **b.** An implied meaning; implicit significance. **c.** An inference. **—im′pli·ca′tive** *adj.* **—im′pli·ca′tive·ly** *adv.*

im·plic·it (ĭm-plĭs′ĭt) *adj.* **1.** Implied or understood though not directly expressed: *an implicit agreement not to raise the touchy subject.* **2.** Contained in the nature of something though not readily apparent: *"Frustration is implicit in any attempt to express the deepest self"* (Patricia Hampl). **3.** Having no doubts or reservations; unquestioning: *implicit trust.* [Latin *implicitus,* variant of *implicātus,* past participle of *implicāre,* to entangle. See IMPLICATE.] **—im·plic′it·ly** *adv.* **—im·plic′it·ness** *n.*

implicit differentiation *n. Mathematics.* The process of isolating the derivative of a dependent variable of an implicit function by differentiating each term of the function separately, expressing the desired derivative as a symbol, and solving the resulting expression for the symbol.

implicit function *n. Mathematics.* An equation in which the variable being solved for is not directly expressed but must be arrived at by manipulation of the expression. For example, in the equation $2x + 3y = 0$, x is an implicit function of y.

im·plode (ĭm-plōd′) *v.* **-plod·ed, -plod·ing, -plodes.** —*intr.* To collapse inward violently. —*tr.* **1.** To cause to collapse inward violently. **2.** To demolish (a building) by causing to collapse inward. [IN–² + (EX)PLODE.]

im·plore (ĭm-plôr′, -plōr′) *v.* —*tr.* **-plored, -plor·ing, -plores. 1.** To appeal to in supplication; beseech: *implored the tribunal to have mercy.* **2.** To beg for urgently; entreat. —*intr.* To make an earnest appeal. See Synonyms at **beg.** [Latin *implōrāre* : *in-*, toward; see IN–² + *plōrāre*, to weep.] **—im′plo·ra′tion** *n.* **—im·plor′er** *n.* **—im·plor′ing·ly** *adv.*

im·plo·sion (ĭm-plō′zhən) *n.* **1.** A violent collapse inward, as of a highly evacuated glass vessel. **2.** Violent compression. **3.** The inward collapse of a building that is being demolished in a controlled fashion by the weakening and breaking of structural members by explosives. **4.** *Linguistics.* The pronunciation of a stop consonant with the breath drawn in. [IN–² + (EX)PLOSION.]

im·plo·sive (ĭm-plō′sĭv) *n. Linguistics.* A stop consonant pronounced with the breath drawn in. **—im·plo′sive** *adj.*

im·ply (ĭm-plī′) *tr.v.* **-plied, -ply·ing, -plies. 1.** To involve by logical necessity; entail: *Life implies growth and death.* **2.** To express or indicate indirectly: *His tone implied disapproval.* See Synonyms at **suggest.** See Usage Note at **infer. 3.** *Obsolete.* To entangle. [Middle English *implien*, from Old French *emplier*, to enfold, from Latin *implicāre*. See IMPLICATE.]

im·po·lite (ĭm′pə-līt′) *adj.* Not polite; discourteous. [Latin *impolītus*, unpolished, inelegant : *in-*, not; see IN–¹ + *polītus*, polished, past participle of *polīre*, to polish; see POLISH.] **—im′po·lite′ly** *adv.* **—im′po·lite′ness** *n.*

im·pol·i·tic (ĭm-pŏl′ĭ-tĭk) *adj.* Not wise or expedient: *an impolitic approach to a sensitive issue.* **—im·pol′i·tic·ly** *adv.*

im·pon·der·a·ble (ĭm-pŏn′dər-ə-bəl) *adj.* That cannot undergo precise evaluation: *imponderable problems.* **—im·pon′der·a·ble** *n.* **—im·pon′der·a·bil′i·ty, im·pon′der·a·ble·ness** *n.* **—im·pon′der·a·bly** *adv.*

im·port (ĭm-pôrt′, -pōrt′, ĭm′pôrt′, -pōrt′) *v.* **-port·ed, -port·ing, -ports.** —*tr.* **1.** To bring or carry in from an outside source, especially to bring in (goods or materials) from a foreign country for trade or sale. **2.** *Computer Science.* To transfer (a file, for example) from one database to another. **3.** To carry or hold the meaning of; signify: *a high inflation rate importing hard times for the consumer.* See Synonyms at **mean¹. 4.** To imply. **5.** *Archaic.* To have importance for. —*intr.* To be significant. See Synonyms at **count¹.** **—import** (ĭm′pôrt′, -pōrt′) *n.* **1.** *Abbr.* **imp.** Something imported. **2.** The act or occupation of importing goods or materials. **3.** Meaning; signification. See Synonyms at **meaning. 4.** Importance; significance: *a legal decision of far-reaching import.* See Synonyms at **importance.** [Middle English *importen*, to convey a meaning, from Medieval Latin *importāre* and from Old French *importer*, to cause, both from Latin *importāre*, to carry in, cause : *in-*, in; see IN–² + *portāre*, to carry; see **per-²** in Appendix.] **—im·port′a·bil′i·ty** *n.* **—im·port′a·ble** *adj.* **—im·port′er** *n.*

im·por·tance (ĭm-pôr′tns) *n.* **1.** The quality or condition of being important; significance. **2.** Personal status; standing. **3.** *Obsolete.* An important matter. **4.** *Obsolete.* Meaning; import. **5.** *Obsolete.* Importunity.

SYNONYMS: *importance, consequence, moment, significance, import, weight.* These nouns refer to the state or quality of being significant, influential, or worthy of note or esteem. *Importance* is the most general term: *The importance of a proper diet in maintaining health should not be disregarded. In this profession, training and experience are of equal importance. Cartoonists are considered by some to be artists of secondary importance. Consequence* is especially applicable to persons or things of notable rank or position (*scholars of consequence*) and to what is important because of its possible outcome, result, or effect (*Changes in the tax law are of consequence to all investors*). *Moment* implies importance or consequence that is readily apparent: *Heads of state are confronted with making decisions of great moment. Significance* and *import* refer to the quality of something, often not obvious, that gives it special meaning or value: *Your vote can be of real significance in the outcome of the election. The works of John Locke are of great social import. Weight* is frequently used when a personal evaluation or judgment of importance is suggested: *"The popular faction at Rome . . . was led by men of weight"* (J.A. Froude).

im·por·tant (ĭm-pôr′tnt) *adj. Abbr.* **imp. 1.** Strongly affecting the course of events or the nature of things; significant: *an important message that must get through; close friends who are important to me.* **2.** Having or suggesting a consciousness of high position or authority; authoritative: *recited the decree with an important air.* **3.** *Obsolete.* Importunate. [Middle English, from Old French, from Medieval Latin *importāns*, *important-*, present participle of *importāre*, to mean, from Latin, to import. See IMPORT.] **—im·por′tant·ly** *adv.*

USAGE NOTE: Some critics have objected to the use of the phrase *more importantly* in place of *more important* as a means of introducing an assertion, as in *More importantly, there is no party ready to step into the vacuum left by the Communists.* But both forms are widely used by reputable writers, and there is no obvious reason for preferring one or the other. In an earlier survey the introductory use of *more importantly* was acceptable to half of the members of the Usage Panel.

im·por·ta·tion (ĭm′pôr-tā′shən, -pōr-) *n.* **1.a.** The act or business of importing. **b.** The condition or process of being imported. **2.** Something imported; an import.

im·por·tu·nate (ĭm-pôr′chə-nĭt) *adj.* Troublesomely urgent or persistent in requesting or entreating: *an importunate job seeker.* **—im·por′tu·nate·ly** *adv.* **—im·por′tu·nate·ness** *n.*

im·por·tune (ĭm′pôr-to͞on′, -tyo͞on′, ĭm-pôr′chən) *v.* **-tuned, -tun·ing, -tunes.** —*tr.* **1.** To beset with insistent or repeated requests; entreat pressingly. **2.** *Archaic.* To ask for urgently or repeatedly. **3.** To annoy; vex. —*intr.* To plead or urge irksomely, often persistently. See Synonyms at **beg.** **—importune** *adj.* Importunate. [French *importuner*, from Old French *importun*, inopportune, from Latin *importūnus* : *in-*, not; see IN–¹ + *portus*, port, refuge; see **per-²** in Appendix.] **—im′por·tune′ly** *adv.* **—im′por·tun′er** *n.*

im·por·tu·ni·ty (ĭm′pôr-to͞o′nĭ-tē, -tyo͞o′-) *n., pl.* **-ties. 1.** An importunate request; an insistent or pressing demand. **2.** The quality of being importunate.

im·pose (ĭm-pōz′) *v.* **-posed, -pos·ing, -pos·es.** —*tr.* **1.** To establish or apply as compulsory; levy: *impose a tax.* **2.** To apply or make prevail by or as if by authority: *impose a peace settlement.* See Synonyms at **dictate. 3.** To obtrude or force (oneself, for example) on another or others. **4.** *Printing.* To arrange (type or plates) on an imposing stone. **5.** To offer or circulate fraudulently; pass off: *imposed a fraud on consumers.* —*intr.* To take unfair advantage: *You are always imposing on their generosity.* [Middle English *imposen*, from Old French *imposer*, alteration (influenced by *poser*, to put, place; see POSE¹) of Latin *impōnere*, to place upon : *in-*, on; see IN–² + *pōnere*, to place; see **apo-** in Appendix.] **—im·pos′er** *n.*

im·pos·ing (ĭm-pō′zĭng) *adj.* Impressive, as by virtue of size, bearing, or power: *the monarch's imposing presence.* See Synonyms at **grand.** **—im·pos′ing·ly** *adv.*

imposing stone *n. Printing.* A stone or metal slab on which material to be printed is arranged. Also called *imposing table.*

im·po·si·tion (ĭm′pə-zĭsh′ən) *n.* **1.** The act of imposing or the condition of being imposed. **2.** Something imposed, such as a tax, an undue burden, or a fraud. **3.** A burdensome or unfair demand, as upon someone's time: *listened to the telephone solicitor but resented the imposition.* **4.** *Printing.* The arrangement of printed matter to form a sequence of pages.

im·pos·si·bil·i·ty (ĭm-pŏs′ə-bĭl′ĭ-tē) *n., pl.* **-ties. 1.** The condition or quality of being impossible. **2.** Something impossible.

im·pos·si·ble (ĭm-pŏs′ə-bəl) *adj.* **1.** Incapable of having existence or of occurring. **2.** Not capable of being accomplished: *an impossible goal.* **3.** Unacceptable; intolerable: *impossible behavior.* **4.** Extremely difficult to deal with or tolerate: *an impossible child; an impossible situation.* [Middle English, from Old French, from Latin *impossibilis* : *in-*, not; see IN–¹ + *possibilis*, possible; see POSSIBLE.] **—im·pos′si·bly** *adv.*

im·post¹ (ĭm′pōst′) *n.* **1.** Something, such as a tax or duty, that is imposed. **2.** *Sports.* The weight a horse must carry in a handicap race. [Obsolete French, from Old French, from Medieval Latin *impostum*, from Latin, neuter of *impostus*, variant of *impositus*, past participle of *impōnere*, to place upon. See IMPOSE.]

im·post² (ĭm′pōst′) *n. Architecture.* The uppermost part of a column or pillar supporting an arch. [French *imposte*, from Italian *imposta*, from Latin, feminine past participle of *impōnere*, to place upon. See IMPOSE.]

im·pos·tor (ĭm-pŏs′tər) *n.* One who engages in deception under an assumed name or identity. [French *imposteur*, from Late Latin *impostor*, variant of *impositor*, one who assigns a name, from *impositus*, past participle of *impōnere*, to place upon. See IMPOSE.]

SYNONYMS: *impostor, quack, faker, humbug, mountebank, charlatan.* These nouns denote people who pretend to be other than what they are or to have abilities or qualifications that they do not really have. An *impostor* assumes the character or identity of another for the purpose of deceiving: *He succeeded in his profession, but he always secretly considered himself an impostor. Quack* refers especially to one who practices medicine without being properly qualified: *"He who has once been under the hands of a quack, is for ever after prone to dabble in drugs"* (Washington Irving). A *faker* simulates or feigns the appearance of being what he or she is not: *The brokerage executive was unmasked as a faker.* A *humbug* is a self-important or self-deluded faker: *"What a humbug that woman is!"* (Thackeray). A *mountebank* is a flamboyant, unscrupulous dealer or promoter: *"I remember . . . there was an impudent mountebank who sold pills which (as he told the country people) were very good against an earthquake"* (Joseph Addison). A *charlatan* makes false claims to skill or knowledge and hides his or her deficiency by an elaborate, fraudulent, often voluble display: *It was difficult to discern that despite all the abstruse vocabulary the professor was really a charlatan.*

im·pos·ture (ĭm-pŏs′chər) *n.* The act or instance of engaging

implosion
Four stages of demolition by implosion; Abraham Lincoln Hotel, Springfield, Illinois, December 17, 1978

ă **pat**	oi **boy**
ā **pay**	ou **out**
âr **care**	o͝o **took**
ä **father**	o͞o **boot**
ĕ **pet**	ŭ **cut**
ē **be**	ûr **urge**
ĭ **pit**	th **thin**
ī **pie**	*th* **this**
îr **pier**	hw **which**
ŏ **pot**	zh **vision**
ō **toe**	ə **about, item**
ô **paw**	♦ **regionalism**

Stress marks: **′** (primary); ′ (secondary), as in **dictionary** (dĭk′shə-nĕr′ē)

in deception under an assumed name or identity. [French, from Old French, from Late Latin *impostūra,* from Latin *impostus,* variant of *impositus,* past participle of *impōnere,* to place upon. See IMPOSE.]

im·po·tence (ĭm′pə-təns) also **im·po·ten·cy** (-tən-sē) *n.* The quality or condition of being impotent.

im·po·tent (ĭm′pə-tənt) *adj.* **1.** Lacking physical strength or vigor; weak. **2.** Lacking in power, as to act effectively; helpless: *"Technology without morality is barbarous; morality without technology is impotent"* (Freeman J. Dyson). **3.a.** Incapable of sexual intercourse, often because of an inability to achieve or sustain an erection. **b.** Sterile. Used of males. See Synonyms at **sterile.** **4.** *Obsolete.* Lacking self-restraint. [Middle English, from Old French, from Latin *impotēns, impotent-* : *in-,* not; see IN–[1] + *potēns,* potent; see POTENT.] **—im′po·tent·ly** *adv.*

im·pound (ĭm-pound′) *tr.v.* **im·pound·ed, im·pound·ing, im·pounds.** **1.** To confine in or as if in a pound: *capture and impound stray dogs.* **2.** To seize and retain in legal custody: *impounding disputed electoral ballots.* **3.** To set aside in a fund rather than spend as prescribed: *a governor who impounded monies designated for the use of cities and towns.* **4.** To accumulate and store in a reservoir: *By damming the stream, the engineers impounded its waters for irrigation.* **—im·pound′age, im·pound′ment** *n.* **—im·pound′er** *n.*

im·pov·er·ish (ĭm-pŏv′ər-ĭsh) *tr.v.* **-ished, -ish·ing, -ish·es.** **1.** To reduce to poverty; make poor. **2.** To deprive of natural richness or strength: *impoverish the soil by overuse.* See Synonyms at **deplete.** [Middle English *empoverishen,* from Old French *empovrir, empovriss-* : *en-,* causative pref.; see IN–[2] + *povre,* poor (from Latin *pauper;* see PAUPER).] **—im·pov′er·ish·ment** *n.*

im·pov·er·ished (ĭm-pŏv′ər-ĭsht) *adj.* **1.** Reduced to poverty; poverty-stricken. See Synonyms at **poor.** **2.** Deprived of natural richness or strength; depleted: *an impoverished speech; a region impoverished by drought.*

im·prac·ti·ca·ble (ĭm-prăk′tĭ-kə-bəl) *adj.* **1.** Impossible to do or carry out: *Refloating the sunken ship intact proved impracticable because of its fragility.* **2.** Unfit for passage: *roads impracticable in winter.* **3.** *Archaic.* Unmanageable; intractable. **—im·prac′ti·ca·bil′i·ty, im·prac′ti·ca·ble·ness** *n.* **—im·prac′ti·ca·bly** *adv.*

USAGE NOTE: *Impracticable* applies to a course of action that is impossible to carry out or put into practice; *impractical,* though it can be used in this way, also can be weaker in sense, suggesting that the course of action would yield an insufficient return or would have little practical value. A plan for a new baseball stadium might be rejected as *impracticable* if the site was too marshy to permit safe construction; but if the objection was merely that the site was too remote for patrons to attend games easily, the plan would better be described as *impractical.* See Usage Note at **practicable.**

impressionism
Mother and Children,
1874, by Pierre Auguste
Renoir

im·prac·ti·cal (ĭm-prăk′tĭ-kəl) *adj.* **1.** Unwise to implement or maintain in practice: *Refloating the sunken ship proved impractical because of the great expense.* **2.** Incapable of dealing efficiently with practical matters, especially finances. **3.** Not a part of experience, fact, or practice; theoretical. **4.** Impracticable. See Usage Note at **impracticable.** **—im·prac′ti·cal′i·ty** (-kăl′ĭ-tē), **im·prac′ti·cal·ness** *n.*

im·pre·cate (ĭm′prĭ-kāt′) *tr.v.* **-cat·ed, -cat·ing, -cates.** To invoke evil upon; curse. [Latin *imprecārī, imprecāt-* : *in-,* towards; see IN–[2] + *precārī,* to pray, ask; see **prek-** in Appendix.] **—im′pre·ca′tor** *n.* **—im′pre·ca·to′ry** (-kə-tôr′ē, -tōr′ē) *adj.*

im·pre·ca·tion (ĭm′prĭ-kā′shən) *n.* **1.** The act of imprecating. **2.** A curse.

im·pre·cise (ĭm′prĭ-sīs′) *adj.* Not precise. **—im′pre·cise′ly** *adv.* **—im′pre·ci′sion** (-sĭzh′ən) *n.*

im·preg·na·ble[1] (ĭm-prĕg′nə-bəl) *adj.* **1.** Impossible to capture or enter by force: *an impregnable fortress.* **2.** Difficult or impossible to attack, challenge, or refute with success: *an impregnable argument.* [Middle English, from Old French *imprenable* : *in-,* not (from Latin *in-;* see IN–[1]) + *pregnable,* pregnable; see PREGNABLE.]

im·preg·na·ble[2] (ĭm-prĕg′nə-bəl) *adj.* Capable of being impregnated. [IMPREGN(ATE) + –ABLE.]

im·preg·nate (ĭm-prĕg′nāt′) *tr.v.* **-nat·ed, -nat·ing, -nates.** **1.** To make pregnant; inseminate. **2.** To fertilize (an ovum, for example). **3.** To fill throughout; saturate: *a cotton wad that was impregnated with ether.* **4.** To permeate or imbue: *impregnate a speech with optimism.* See Synonyms at **charge.** **—impregnate** (*also* -nĭt) *adj.* Saturated or filled. [Probably from Late Latin *impraegnātus,* pregnant : Latin *in-,* in; see IN–[2] + Latin *praegnātus,* variant of *praegnās,* pregnant. See PREGNANT[1].] **—im′preg·na′tion** *n.* **—im·preg′na′tor** *n.*

im·pre·sa (ĭm-prā′zə) *n.* An emblem or a device with a motto. [Italian, undertaking, impresa. See IMPRESARIO.]

im·pre·sa·ri·o (ĭm′prĭ-sär′ē-ō′, -sâr′-) *n., pl.* **-os.** **1.** One who sponsors or produces entertainment, especially the director of an opera company. **2.** A manager; a producer. [Italian, from *impresa,* undertaking, from feminine past participle of *imprendere,* to undertake, from Vulgar Latin **imprendere.* See EMPRISE.]

im·press[1] (ĭm-prĕs′) *tr.v.* **-pressed, -press·ing, -press·es.** **1.** To affect strongly, often favorably: *wrote down whatever impressed me during the journey; was impressed by the child's sincerity.* See Synonyms at **affect[1].** **2.** To produce or attempt to produce a vivid impression or image of: *a scene that impressed itself on his memory; tries to impress the value of money on the students.* **3.** To mark or stamp with or as if with pressure: *impressed a design on the hot wax.* **4.** To apply with pressure; press. **—impress** (ĭm′prĕs′) *n.* **1.** The act of impressing. **2.** A mark or pattern produced by or as if by impressing. See Synonyms at **impression.** **3.** A stamp or seal meant to be impressed. [Middle English *impressen,* to imprint, from Old French *empresser,* from Latin *impressus,* past participle of *imprimere* : *in-,* in; see IN–[2] + *premere,* to press; see **per-[4]** in Appendix.]

im·press[2] (ĭm-prĕs′) *tr.v.* **-pressed, -press·ing, -press·es.** **1.** To compel (a person) to serve in a military force. **2.** To seize (property) by force or authority; confiscate. **—impress** (ĭm′prĕs) *n.* Impressment. [IN–[2] + PRESS[2] (influenced by IMPREST, advance on a soldier's pay (obsolete)).]

im·press·i·ble (ĭm-prĕs′ə-bəl) *adj.* Susceptible to impressions; malleable: *impressible young minds.* **—im·press′i·bil′i·ty** *n.* **—im·press′i·bly** *adv.*

im·pres·sion (ĭm-prĕsh′ən) *n.* **1.** An effect, a feeling, or an image retained as a consequence of experience. **2.** A vague notion, remembrance, or belief: *I have the impression that we have met once before.* **3.** A mark produced on a surface by pressure. **4.** The act or process of impressing. **5.** *Printing.* **a.** All the copies of a publication printed at one time from the same set of type. **b.** A single copy of such a printing. **6.** A humorous imitation of the voice and mannerisms of a famous person done by an entertainer. **7.** An initial or single coat of color or paint. **8.** *Dentistry.* An imprint of the teeth and surrounding tissues, formed with a plastic material that hardens into a mold for use in making dentures, inlays, or plastic models.

SYNONYMS: *impression, impress, imprint, print, stamp.* The central meaning shared by these nouns is "a visible mark made on a surface by pressure": *an impression of a notary's seal on wax; the impress of bare feet in the sand; a medal marked with the imprint of a bald eagle; a tar driveway with the print of automobile tires; a gold ingot with the refiner's stamp.*

im·pres·sion·a·ble (ĭm-prĕsh′ə-nə-bəl) *adj.* **1.** Readily or easily influenced; suggestible: *impressionable young people.* **2.** Capable of receiving an impression; plastic: *impressionable plaster.* **—im·pres′sion·a·bil′i·ty, im·pres′sion·a·ble·ness** *n.*

im·pres·sion·ism (ĭm-prĕsh′ə-nĭz′əm) *n.* **1.** Often **Impressionism.** A theory or style of painting originating and developed in France during the 1870's, characterized by concentration on the immediate visual impression produced by a scene and by the use of unmixed primary colors and small strokes to simulate actual reflected light. **2.** A literary style characterized by the use of details and mental associations to evoke subjective and sensory impressions rather than the re-creation of objective reality. **3.** *Music.* A style of the late 19th and early 20th centuries, using lush and somewhat vague harmony and rhythm to evoke suggestions of mood, place, and natural phenomena. **4.** The practice of expressing or developing one's subjective response to a work of art or to actual experience.

im·pres·sion·ist (ĭm-prĕsh′ə-nĭst) *n.* **1.** An artist, a composer, or a writer who practices or upholds the theories of impressionism. **2.** An entertainer who does impressions. **—impressionist** *adj.* Of, relating to, or practicing impressionism, especially in painting; impressionistic.

im·pres·sion·is·tic (ĭm-prĕsh′ə-nĭs′tĭk) *adj.* **1.** Of, relating to, or practicing impressionism. **2.** Of, relating to, or predicated on impression as opposed to reason or fact: *impressionistic memories of early childhood.* **3.** Impressionable. **—im·pres′sion·is′ti·cal·ly** *adv.*

im·pres·sive (ĭm-prĕs′ĭv) *adj.* Making a strong or vivid impression; striking or remarkable: *an impressive ceremony.* **—im·pres′sive·ly** *adv.* **—im·pres′sive·ness** *n.*

im·press·ment (ĭm-prĕs′mənt) *n.* The act or policy of seizing people or property for public service or use.

im·pres·sure (ĭm-prĕsh′ər) *n.* *Archaic.* A mark produced by pressure; an impression.

im·prest (ĭm-prĕst′) *n.* An advance or a loan of funds, especially for services rendered to a government. [From obsolete Italian *impresto,* loan, from past participle of *imprestare,* to lend : *in-,* toward (from Latin; see IN–[2]) + *prestare,* to lend (from Latin *praestāre,* to give, from *praestō,* at hand).]

im·pri·ma·tur (ĭm′prə-mä′to͝or, -mā′tər) *n.* **1.** *Abbr.* **imp.** Official approval or license to print or publish, especially under conditions of censorship. **2.a.** Official approval; sanction. **b.** A mark of official approval: *a directive bearing the imprimatur of high officials.* [New Latin *imprimātur,* let it be printed, third person sing. present subjunctive passive of Latin *imprimere,* to imprint. See IMPRESS[1].]

im·pri·mis (ĭm-prī′mĭs) *adv.* In the first place. [Middle English *in primis,* from Latin *in prīmīs* : *in,* among; see IN–[2] + *prīmīs,* ablative pl. of *prīmus,* first; see **per[1]** in Appendix.]

im·print (ĭm-prĭnt′) *tr.v.* **-print·ed, -print·ing, -prints.** **1.** To produce (a mark or pattern) on a surface by pressure. **2.** To produce a mark on (a surface) by pressure. **3.** To impart a strong or vivid impression of: *"We imprint our own ideas onto acts"* (Ellen Goodman). **4.** To fix firmly, as in the mind: *He tried to im-*

print the number on his memory. **—imprint** (ĭm′prĭnt′) *n.* **1.** A mark or pattern produced by imprinting. See Synonyms at **impression. 2.** A distinguishing influence or effect: *Spanish architecture that shows the imprint of Islamic rule.* **3.** A publisher's name, often with the date, address, and edition, printed at the bottom of a title page of a publication. [Middle English *emprenten,* from Old French *empreinter,* from *empreinte,* impression, from feminine past participle of *empreindre,* to print, from Latin *imprimere,* to impress. See IMPRESS[1].]

im·print·ing (ĭm′prĭn′tĭng) *n.* A learning process occurring early in the life of a social animal in which a specific behavior pattern is established through association with a parent or other role model.

im·pris·on (ĭm-prĭz′ən) *tr.v.* **-oned, -on·ing, -ons.** To put in or as if in prison; confine. [Middle English *emprisonen,* from Old French *emprisoner* : *en-,* in (from Latin *in-;* see IN–[2]) + *prison,* prison; see PRISON.] **—im·pris′on·a·ble** *adj.* **—im·pris′on·ment** *n.*

im·prob·a·bil·i·ty (ĭm-prŏb′ə-bĭl′ĭ-tē) *n., pl.* **-ties. 1.** The quality or condition of being improbable. **2.** Something improbable.

im·prob·a·ble (ĭm-prŏb′ə-bəl) *adj.* Unlikely to take place or be true. **—im·prob′a·ble·ness** *n.* **—im·prob′a·bly** *adv.*

im·pro·bi·ty (ĭm-prō′bĭ-tē) *n.* Lack of probity; dishonesty. [Middle English *improbite,* shameless persistence, from Old French, dishonesty, from Latin *improbitās,* from *improbus,* dishonest : *in-,* not; see IN–[1] + *probus,* honest, good; see **per**[1] in Appendix.]

im·promp·tu (ĭm-prŏmp′to͞o, -tyo͞o) *adj.* **1.** Prompted by the occasion rather than being planned in advance: *an impromptu party.* **2.** Spoken, performed, done, or composed with little or no preparation; extemporaneous: *a few impromptu remarks.* See Synonyms at **extemporaneous. —impromptu** *adv.* With little or no preparation; extemporaneously. **—impromptu** *n.* **1.** Something, such as a speech, that is made or done extemporaneously. **2.** *Music.* A short lyrical composition especially for the piano. [French, from Latin *in prōmptū,* at hand : *in,* in; see IN–[2] + *prōmptū,* ablative of *prōmptus,* readiness, from past participle of *prōmere,* to bring forth; see PROMPT.]

im·prop·er (ĭm-prŏp′ər) *adj.* **1.** Not suited to circumstances or needs; unsuitable: *improper shoes for a walk on the beach; improper medical treatment.* **2.** Not in keeping with conventional mores; indecorous: *improper behavior.* **3.** Not consistent with established truth, fact, or rule; incorrect. **4.** Irregular or abnormal. **—im·prop′er·ly** *adv.* **—im·prop′er·ness** *n.*

SYNONYMS: *improper, unbecoming, unseemly, indelicate, indecent, indecorous.* These adjectives mean not in keeping with accepted standards of what is right or proper. *Improper* often refers to unethical conduct, a breach of etiquette, or morally offensive behavior: *pleasant but slightly improper to dine alone with a married person. Unbecoming* suggests what is beneath the standard implied by one's character or position: *language unbecoming to a gentleman.* What is *unseemly* or *indelicate* is in gross violation of good taste; *indelicate* especially suggests immodesty, coarseness, or tactlessness: *unseemly to use profanity; an indelicate suggestion. Indecent* refers to what is morally offensive or harmful: *an earthy but not indecent story. Indecorous* implies violation of the mores or manners of polite society: *indecorous behavior; an indecorous proposition.*

improper fraction *n. Mathematics.* A fraction in which the numerator is larger than or equal to the denominator.

improper integral *n. Mathematics.* An integral having at least one nonfinite limit or an integrand that becomes infinite between the limits of integration.

im·pro·pri·e·ty (ĭm′prə-prī′ĭ-tē) *n., pl.* **-ties. 1.** The quality or condition of being improper. **2.** An improper act. **3.** An improper or unacceptable usage in speech or writing.

im·prove (ĭm-pro͞ov′) *v.* **-proved, -prov·ing, -proves.** *—tr.* **1.** To raise to a more desirable or more excellent quality or condition; make better. **2.** To increase the productivity or value of (land or property). **3.** To put to good use; use profitably. *—intr.* **1.** To become better. **2.** To make beneficial additions or changes: *improve on the translation.* [Middle English *improwen,* to enclose land for cultivation, from Anglo-Norman *emprouwer,* to turn to profit : Old French *en-,* causative pref. (from Latin *in;* see IN–[2]) + *prou,* profit (from Late Latin *prōde,* advantageous; see PROUD).]

SYNONYMS: *improve, better, help, ameliorate.* These verbs mean to advance to a more desirable, valuable, or excellent state. *Improve* and *better,* the most general terms, are often interchangeable: *improve* (or *better*) *the mind through study; had a haircut to improve* (or *better*) *his appearance; practicing to improve* (or *better*) *her golf game. It is sometimes difficult for disadvantaged people to improve* (or *better*) *their situation in life. Help* in this sense usually implies limited relief or change for the better: *Gargling helps a sore throat.* To *ameliorate* is to improve or better circumstances that demand change: *Volunteers could do little to ameliorate conditions in the refugee camp.*

im·prove·ment (ĭm-pro͞ov′mənt) *n.* **1.a.** The act or process of improving. **b.** The state of being improved. **2.** A change or an addition that improves.

im·prov·i·dent (ĭm-prŏv′ĭ-dənt) *adj.* **1.** Not providing for the future; thriftless. **2.** Rash; incautious. **—im·prov′i·dence** *n.* **—im·prov′i·dent·ly** *adv.*

im·prov·i·sa·tion (ĭm-prŏv′ĭ-zā′shən, ĭm′prə-vĭ-) *n.* **1.** The act of improvising. **2.** Something improvised, especially a dramatic skit.

im·prov·i·sa·tor (ĭm-prŏv′ĭ-zā′tər) *n.* One who improvises.

im·prov·i·sa·to·ry (ĭm-prŏv′ĭ-zə-tôr′ē, -tōr′ē, ĭm′prə-vĭ′-) also **im·prov·i·sa·to·ri·al** (ĭm-prŏv′ĭ-zə-tôr′ē-əl, -tōr′-) *adj.* **1.** Made up without preparation; improvised. **2.** Of or relating to improvisation: *improvisatory skill.*

im·pro·vise (ĭm′prə-vīz′) *v.* **-vised, -vis·ing, -vis·es.** *—tr.* **1.** To invent, compose, or recite without preparation. **2.** To make or provide from available materials: *improvised a dinner for the unexpected guests; improvise a makeshift tourniquet. —intr.* To invent, compose, recite, or execute something offhand. [French *improviser,* from Italian *improvvisare,* from *improvviso,* unforeseen, from Latin *imprōvīsus* : *in-,* not; see IN–[1] + *prōvīsus,* past participle of *prōvidēre,* to foresee; see PROVIDE.] **—im′pro·vis′er** *n.*

im·pru·dence (ĭm-pro͞od′ns) *n.* **1.** The quality or condition of being unwise or indiscreet. **2.** An unwise or indiscreet act.

im·pru·dent (ĭm-pro͞od′nt) *adj.* Unwise or indiscreet; not prudent.

im·pu·dence (ĭm′pyə-dəns) also **im·pu·den·cy** (-dən-sē) *n.* **1.** The quality of being offensively bold. **2.** Offensively bold behavior.

im·pu·dent (ĭm′pyə-dənt) *adj.* **1.** Characterized by offensive boldness; insolent or impertinent. See Synonyms at **shameless. 2.** *Obsolete.* Immodest. [Middle English, from Latin *impudēns, impudent-* : *in-,* not; see IN–[1] + *pudēns,* present participle of *pudēre,* to be ashamed.] **—im′pu·dent·ly** *adv.*

im·pu·dic·i·ty (ĭm′pyo͞o-dĭs′ĭ-tē) *n.* Immodesty; shamelessness. [Late Latin *impudīcitās,* from Latin *impudīcus,* immodest : *in-,* not; see IN–[1] + *pudīcus,* modest (from *pudēre,* to be ashamed).]

im·pugn (ĭm-pyo͞on′) *tr.v.* **-pugned, -pugn·ing, -pugns.** To attack as false or questionable; challenge in argument: *impugn a political opponent's record.* [Middle English *impugnen,* from Old French *impugner,* from Latin *impugnāre* : *in-,* against; see IN–[2] + *pugnāre,* to fight; see **peuk-** in Appendix.] **—im·pugn′a·ble** *adj.* **—im·pugn′er** *n.*

im·pu·is·sance (ĭm-pyo͞o′ĭ-səns, ĭm-pwĭs′əns) *n.* Lack of power or effectiveness; weakness. [Middle English *impuissaunce,* from Old French *impuissance* : *in-,* not; see IN–[1] + *puissance,* power; see PUISSANCE.] **—im·pu′is·sant** *adj.*

im·pulse (ĭm′pŭls′) *n.* **1.a.** An impelling force; an impetus. **b.** The motion produced by such a force. **2.** A sudden wish or urge that prompts an unpremeditated act or feeling; abrupt inclination: *had an impulse to run away; an impulse of regret that made me hesitate; bought a hat on impulse.* **3.** A motivating force or tendency: *"Respect for the liberty of others is not a natural impulse in most men"* (Bertrand Russell). **4.** *Electronics.* A surge of electrical power in one direction. **5.** *Physics.* The product obtained by multiplying the average value of a force by the time during which it acts. The impulse equals the change in momentum produced by the force in this time interval. **6.** *Physiology.* The electrochemical transmission of a signal along a nerve fiber that produces an excitatory or inhibitory response at a target tissue, such as a muscle or another nerve. **—impulse** *adj.* Characterized by impulsiveness or acting on impulse: *an impulse shopper; impulse buying.* [Latin *impulsus,* from past participle of *impellere,* to impel. See IMPEL.]

im·pul·sion (ĭm-pŭl′shən) *n.* **1.** The act of impelling or the condition of being impelled: *"I do not move . . . unless it be under the impulsion of a third party"* (Samuel Beckett). **2.** An impelling force; a thrust. **3.** Motion produced by an impelling force; momentum. **4.** A wish or an urge from within; an impulse.

im·pul·sive (ĭm-pŭl′sĭv) *adj.* **1.** Inclined to act on impulse rather than thought. **2.** Motivated by or resulting from impulse: *such impulsive acts as hugging strangers; impulsive generosity.* See Synonyms at **spontaneous. 3.** Having force or power to impel or incite; forceful. **4.** *Physics.* Acting within brief time intervals. Used especially of a force. **—im·pul′sive·ly** *adv.* **—im·pul′sive·ness, im′pul·siv′i·ty** *n.*

im·pu·ni·ty (ĭm-pyo͞o′nĭ-tē) *n., pl.* **-ties.** Exemption from punishment, penalty, or harm. [Latin *impūnitās,* from *impūne,* without punishment : *in-,* not; see IN–[1] + *poena,* penalty (from Greek *poinē;* see **kʷei-**[1] in Appendix).]

im·pure (ĭm-pyo͝or′) *adj.* **-pur·er, -pur·est. 1.** Not pure or clean; contaminated. **2.** Not purified by religious rite; unclean. **3.** Immoral or obscene. **4.** Mixed with another, usually inferior substance; adulterated. **5.** *Color.* Being a composite of more than one color or mixed with black or white. **6.** Deriving from more than one source, style, or convention; eclectic: *an impure art form.* **7.** Not consistent in grammar, vocabulary, idiom, or usage: *an impure style.* **—im·pure′ly** *adv.* **—im·pure′ness** *n.*

im·pu·ri·ty (ĭm-pyo͝or′ĭ-tē) *n., pl.* **-ties. 1.** The quality or condition of being impure, especially: **a.** Contamination or pollution. **b.** Lack of consistency or homogeneity; adulteration. **c.** A state of immorality; sin. **2.** Something that renders something else impure; an inferior component or additive.

im·put·a·ble (ĭm-pyo͞o′tə-bəl) *adj.* Possible to impute or ascribe; attributable: *imputable oversights.* **—im·put′a·bly** *adv.*

ă **pat**	oi **boy**
ā **pay**	ou **out**
âr **care**	o͝o **took**
ä **father**	o͞o **boot**
ĕ **pet**	ŭ **cut**
ē **be**	ûr **urge**
ĭ **pit**	th **thin**
ī **pie**	*th* **this**
îr **pier**	hw **which**
ŏ **pot**	zh **vision**
ō **toe**	ə **about, item**
ô **paw**	♦ **regionalism**

Stress marks: ′ (primary); ′ (secondary), as in **dictionary** (dĭk′shə-nĕr′ē)

im·pu·ta·tion (ĭm′pyo͞o-tā′shən) *n.* **1.** The act of imputing or ascribing; attribution. **2.** Something imputed, ascribed, or attributed. **—im·pu′ta·tive** (ĭm-pyo͞o′tə-tĭv) *adj.* **—im·pu′ta·tive·ly** *adv.*

im·pute (ĭm-pyo͞ot′) *tr.v.* **-put·ed, -put·ing, -putes. 1.** To charge with the fault or responsibility for: *imputed the rocket failure to a faulty gasket; kindly imputed my clumsiness to inexperience.* **2.** To attribute; credit: *the gracefulness so often imputed to cats.* See Synonyms at **attribute.** [Middle English *imputen,* from Old French *emputer,* from Latin *imputāre* : *in-,* in; see IN–[2] + *putāre,* to settle an account; see **peu-** in Appendix.]

in[1] (ĭn) *prep.* **1.a.** Within the limits, bounds, or area of: *was hit in the face; born in the spring; a chair in the garden.* **b.** From the outside to a point within; into: *threw the letter in the wastebasket.* **2.** To or at a situation or condition of: *was split in two; in debt; a woman in love.* **3.a.** Having the activity, occupation, or function of: *a life in politics; the officer in command.* **b.** During the act or process of: *tripped in racing for the bus.* **4.a.** With the arrangement or order of: *fabric that fell in luxuriant folds; arranged to purchase the car in equal payments.* **b.** After the style or form of: *a poem in iambic pentameter.* **5.** With the characteristic, attribute, or property of: *a tall man in an overcoat.* **6.a.** By means of: *paid in cash.* **b.** Made with or through the medium of: *a statue in bronze; a note written in German.* **7.** With the aim or purpose of: *followed in pursuit.* **8.** With reference to: *six inches in depth; has faith in your judgment.* **9.** Used to indicate the second and larger term of a ratio or proportion: *saved only one in ten.* **—in** *adv.* **1.** To or toward the inside: *opened the door and stepped in.* **2.** To or toward a destination or goal: *The mob closed in.* **3.** *Baseball.* To home base; so as to score: *runs batted in; singled the runner in.* **4.** Within a place, as of business or residence: *The manager is in before anyone else.* **5.** So as to include or incorporate: *Fold in the egg whites.* **6.** So as to occupy a position of success or favor: *campaigned hard and was voted in.* **7.** In a particular relationship: *got in bad with their supervisor.* **—in** *adj.* **1.** Located inside; inner. **2.** Incoming; inward: *took the in bus.* **3.** Holding office; having power: *the in party.* **4.** *Informal.* **a.** Currently fashionable: *the in thing to wear this season.* **b.** Concerned with or attuned to the latest fashions: *the in crowd.* See Synonyms at **fashionable. —in** *n.* **1.** One that has position, influence, or power: *the ins against the outs.* **2.** *Informal.* Influence; power: *had an in with the authorities.* **—*idioms.* in for.** Guaranteed to get or have: *You're in for a big surprise.* **in that.** For the reason that. [Middle English, from Old English. See **en** in Appendix.]

in[2] or **in.** *abbr.* Inch.

In The symbol for the element **indium.**

IN *abbr.* Indiana.

in–[1] or **il–** or **im–** or **ir–** *pref.* Not: *inarticulate.* Before *l, in-* is usually assimilated to *il-,* before *r* to *ir-,* and before *b, m,* and *p* to *im-.* See Usage Note at **un–**[1]. [Middle English, from Old French, from Latin. See **ne** in Appendix.]

in–[2] or **il–** or **im–** or **ir–** *pref.* **1.** In; into; within: *illuviation.* Before *l, in-* is usually assimilated to *il-,* before *r* to *ir-,* and before *b, m,* and *p* to *im-.* **2.** Variant of **en–**[1]. [Middle English, from Old English (from *in,* in; see IN[1]) and from Old French (from Latin, from *in,* in, within; see **en** in Appendix).]

–in *suff.* **1.** Neutral chemical compound, especially: **a.** Neutral carbohydrate: *inulin.* **b.** Protein or protein derivative: *albumin.* **c.** Lipid or lipid derivative: *lecithin.* **d.** Enzyme: *pancreatin.* **e.** Glycoside: *chitin.* **2.** A pharmaceutical: *rifampin.* **3.** An antibiotic: *penicillin.* **4.** Antigen: *tuberculin.* **5.** Variant of **–ine**[2] (sense 1). [Variant of –INE[2].]

in·a·bil·i·ty (ĭn′ə-bĭl′ĭ-tē) *n.* Lack of ability or means.

in ab·sen·tia (ĭn ăb-sĕn′shə, -shē-ə) *adv.* *Abbr.* **i.a.** While or although not present; in absence: *was tried and convicted in absentia.* [Latin *in absentiā* : *in,* in + *absentiā,* ablative of *absentia,* absence.]

in·ac·ces·si·ble (ĭn′ăk-sĕs′ə-bəl) *adj.* Not accessible; unapproachable: *inaccessible executives.* **—in′ac·ces′si·bil′i·ty** *n.* **—in′ac·ces′si·bly** *adv.*

in·ac·cu·ra·cy (ĭn-ăk′yər-ə-sē) *n., pl.* **-cies. 1.** The quality or condition of being inaccurate. **2.** An instance of being inaccurate; an error.

in·ac·cu·rate (ĭn-ăk′yər-ĭt) *adj.* Mistaken or incorrect; not accurate. **—in·ac′cu·rate·ly** *adv.* **—in·ac′cu·rate·ness** *n.*

in·ac·tion (ĭn-ăk′shən) *n.* Lack or absence of action.

in·ac·ti·vate (ĭn-ăk′tə-vāt′) *tr.v.* **-vat·ed, -vat·ing, -vates.** To render inactive. **—in·ac′ti·va′tion** *n.*

in·ac·tive (ĭn-ăk′tĭv) *adj.* **1.** Not active or tending to be active. **2.a.** Not functioning or operating; out of use: *inactive machinery.* **b.** Not being in continuous use or operation: *an inactive brokerage account.* **3.** Retired from duty or service. **4.** *Chemistry.* Not readily participating in chemical reactions. **5.** *Biology.* Having no significant effect on or interaction with living organisms. **6.** *Medicine.* Quiescent. Used especially of a disease. **7.** *Physics.* Showing no optical activity in polarized light. **—in·ac′tive·ly** *adv.* **—in′ac·tiv′i·ty, in·ac′tive·ness** *n.*

SYNONYMS: *inactive, idle, inert, passive, dormant, torpid, supine.* These adjectives mean not involved in or disposed to activity. *Inactive* simply indicates absence of activity: *retired but not inactive; an inactive and unhappy life; an inactive factory. Idle* refers to persons who are doing nothing or are not busy, as through unemployment or choice (*employees idle because of the strike; can't bear being idle*); it also refers to what is not in use or operation (*idle machinery; idle hands*). *Inert* describes things powerless to move themselves or to produce a desired effect (*an inert mass of soil*); applied to persons, it implies lethargy or sluggishness, especially of mind or spirit: *"The Honorable Mrs. Jamieson . . . was fat and inert, and very much at the mercy of her old servants"* (Elizabeth C. Gaskell). *Passive* implies being acted on by external force or provocation without reacting positively: *"in an hour like this, when the mind has a passive sensibility, but no active strength"* (Nathaniel Hawthorne). *"Much benevolence of the passive order may be traced to a disinclination to inflict pain upon oneself"* (George Meredith). *Dormant* refers principally to a state of suspended activity but often implies the possibility of renewal: *Her feelings of affection are dormant but easily awakened. Torpid* suggests sluggishness or apathy: *"It is a man's own fault, it is from want of use, if his mind grows torpid in old age"* (Samuel Johnson). *Supine* implies abject lack of will, as that resulting from indifference: *"No other colony showed such supine, selfish helplessness in allowing her own border citizens to be mercilessly harried"* (Theodore Roosevelt).

in·ad·e·qua·cy (ĭn-ăd′ĭ-kwə-sē) *n., pl.* **-cies. 1.** The quality or condition of being inadequate. **2.** An instance of being inadequate; a failing or lack.

in·ad·e·quate (ĭn-ăd′ĭ-kwĭt) *adj.* Not adequate to fulfill a need or meet a requirement; insufficient. **—in·ad′e·quate·ly** *adv.*

in·ad·mis·si·ble (ĭn′əd-mĭs′ə-bəl) *adj.* Not admissible: *inadmissible evidence.* **—in′ad·mis′si·bil′i·ty** *n.* **—in′ad·mis′si·bly** *adv.*

in·ad·ver·tence (ĭn′əd-vûr′tns) *n.* **1.** The quality of being inadvertent. **2.** An instance of being inadvertent; an oversight or a slip. [Middle English, from Old French, from Medieval Latin *inadvertentia* : Latin *in-,* not; see IN–[1] + Latin *advertēns, advertent-,* present participle of *advertere,* to turn toward; see ADVERSE.]

in·ad·ver·ten·cy (ĭn′əd-vûr′tn-sē) *n., pl.* **-cies.** Inadvertence.

in·ad·ver·tent (ĭn′əd-vûr′tnt) *adj.* **1.** Not duly attentive. **2.** Marked by unintentional lack of care. See Synonyms at **careless. —in′ad·ver′tent·ly** *adv.*

in·ad·vis·a·ble (ĭn′əd-vī′zə-bəl) *adj.* Not recommended; unwise: *Running on the ice is inadvisable.* **—in′ad·vis′a·bil′i·ty** *n.*

in ae·ter·num (ē-tûr′nəm) *adv.* To eternity; forever. [Latin : *in,* in + *aeternum,* forever, from neuter of *aeternus,* eternal.]

in·al·ien·a·ble (ĭn-āl′yə-nə-bəl, -ā′lē-ə-) *adj.* That cannot be transferred to another or others: *inalienable rights.* **—in·al′ien·a·bil′i·ty** *n.* **—in·al′ien·a·bly** *adv.*

in·al·ter·a·ble (ĭn-ôl′tər-ə-bəl) *adj.* Impossible to alter; unchangeable: *the inalterable routine of a physician.* **—in·al′ter·a·bil′i·ty** *n.* **—in·al′ter·a·bly** *adv.*

in·am·o·ra·ta (ĭn-ăm′ə-rä′tə) *n., pl.* **-tas.** A woman with whom one is in love or has an intimate relationship. [Italian, feminine of *inamorato,* inamorato. See INAMORATO.]

in·am·o·ra·to (ĭn-ăm′ə-rä′tō) *n., pl.* **-tos.** A man with whom one is in love or has an intimate relationship. [Italian, from past participle of *inammorare,* to enamor : *in-,* into (from Latin; see IN–[2]) + *amore,* love (from Latin *amor,* from *amāre,* to love).]

in-and-in (ĭn′ənd-ĭn′) *adv.* Repeatedly within the same or closely related stocks: *to breed pigs in-and-in.* **—in′-and-in′** *adj.*

in-and-out (ĭn′ənd-out′) *adj.* Involving the purchase and sale of a single security within a short period of time.

in·ane (ĭn-ān′) *adj.* **-an·er, -an·est.** Lacking sense or substance; empty: *an inane comment.* [Latin *inānis,* empty, lacking sense.] **—in·ane′ly** *adv.*

in·an·i·mate (ĭn-ăn′ə-mĭt) *adj.* **1.** Not having the qualities associated with active, living organisms; not animate. See Synonyms at **dead. 2.** Not animated or energetic; dull. **3.** *Grammar.* Belonging to the class of nouns that stand for nonliving things: *The word* car *is inanimate; the word* dog *is animate.* **—in·an′i·mate·ly** *adv.* **—in·an′i·mate·ness** *n.*

in·a·ni·tion (ĭn′ə-nĭsh′ən) *n.* **1.** Exhaustion, as from lack of nourishment or vitality. **2.** The condition or quality of being empty. [Middle English *inanisioun,* emptiness, from Old French *inanicion,* exhaustion from hunger, from Late Latin *inānītiō, inānītiōn-,* emptiness, from *inānītus,* past participle of *inānīre,* to make empty, from *inānis,* empty.]

in·an·i·ty (ĭ-năn′ĭ-tē) *n., pl.* **-ties. 1.** The condition or quality of being inane. **2.** Something empty of meaning or sense.

in·ap·peas·a·ble (ĭn′ə-pē′zə-bəl) *adj.* Difficult or impossible to appease: *inappeasable resentment.*

in·ap·pe·tence (ĭn-ăp′ĭ-təns) also **in·ap·pe·ten·cy** (-tən-sē) *n.* Lack of appetite. **—in·ap′pe·tent** *adj.*

in·ap·pli·ca·ble (ĭn-ăp′lĭ-kə-bəl, ĭn′ə-plĭk′ə-) *adj.* Not applicable: *rules inapplicable to day students.* **—in·ap′pli·ca·bil′i·ty** *n.* **—in·ap′pli·ca·bly** *adv.*

in·ap·po·site (ĭn-ăp′ə-zĭt) *adj.* Not pertinent; unsuitable. **—in·ap′po·site·ly** *adv.* **—in·ap′po·site·ness** *n.*

in·ap·pre·cia·ble (ĭn′ə-prē′shə-bəl) *adj.* Too small to be

ă pat	oi boy
ā pay	ou out
âr care	o͝o took
ä father	o͞o boot
ĕ pet	ŭ cut
ē be	ûr urge
ĭ pit	th thin
ī pie	*th* this
îr pier	hw which
ŏ pot	zh vision
ō toe	ə about, item
ô paw	♦ regionalism

Stress marks: **′** (primary); ′ (secondary), as in **dictionary** (dĭk′shə-nĕr′ē)

noticed or make a significant difference; negligible: *inappreciable fluctuations in temperature.* **—in′ap·pre′cia·bly** *adv.*

in·ap·pre·cia·tive (ĭn′ə-prē′shə-tĭv, -shē-ā′tĭv, shē-ə-) *adj.* Feeling or showing no appreciation; unappreciative. **—in′ap·pre′cia·tive·ly** *adv.* **—in′ap·pre′cia·tive·ness** *n.*

in·ap·proach·a·ble (ĭn′ə-prō′chə-bəl) *adj.* Not approachable: *an inapproachable bastion; a cold, inapproachable person.* **—in′ap·proach′a·bil′i·ty** *n.* **—in′ap·proach′a·bly** *adv.*

in·ap·pro·pri·ate (ĭn′ə-prō′prē-ĭt) *adj.* Unsuitable or improper; not appropriate. **—in′ap·pro′pri·ate·ly** *adv.* **—in′ap·pro′pri·ate·ness** *n.*

in·apt (ĭn-ăpt′) *adj.* **1.** Inappropriate: *always making inapt remarks.* **2.** Inept: *inapt handling of the project.* **—in·apt′ly** *adv.* **—in·apt′ness** *n.*

in·ap·ti·tude (ĭn-ăp′tĭ-to͞od′, -tyo͞od′) *n.* **1.** Lack of talent or ability. **2.** The quality or state of being inappropriate.

I·na·ri (ĭn′ə-rē, ē′när′ē), **Lake.** A lake of northern Finland with an outlet to the Arctic Ocean.

in·ar·tic·u·late (ĭn′är-tĭk′yə-lĭt) *adj.* **1.** Uttered without the use of normal words or syllables; incomprehensible as speech or language: *"a cry . . . that . . . sank down into an inarticulate whine"* (Jack London). **2.** Unable to speak; speechless: *inarticulate with astonishment.* See Synonyms at **dumb. 3.** Unable to speak with clarity or eloquence: *an inarticulate debater.* **4.** Going unexpressed: *inarticulate sorrow.* **5.** *Biology.* Not having joints or segments. **—in′ar·tic′u·late·ly** *adv.* **—in′ar·tic′u·late·ness, in′ar·tic′u·la·cy** (-lə-sē) *n.*

in·ar·tis·tic (ĭn′är-tĭs′tĭk) *adj.* **1.** Not conforming to the principles or criteria of art. **2.** Lacking taste or interest in art. **—in′ar·tis′tic·al·ly** *adv.*

in·as·much as (ĭn′əz-mŭch′) *conj.* **1.** Because of the fact that; since. **2.** To the extent that; insofar as.

in·at·ten·tion (ĭn′ə-tĕn′shən) *n.* Lack of attention, notice, or regard.

in·at·ten·tive (ĭn′ə-tĕn′tĭv) *adj.* Exhibiting a lack of attention; not attentive. **—in′at·ten′tive·ly** *adv.* **—in′at·ten′tive·ness** *n.*

in·au·di·ble (ĭn-ô′də-bəl) *adj.* Impossible to hear: *an inaudible conversation.* **—in·au′di·bil′i·ty** *n.* **—in·au′di·bly** *adv.*

in·au·gu·ral (ĭn-ô′gyər-əl) *adj.* **1.** Of, relating to, or characteristic of an inauguration. **2.** Initial; first: *the inaugural issue of a magazine.* **—inaugural** *n.* **1.** An inauguration. **2.** A speech given by a person being formally inducted into office.

in·au·gu·rate (ĭn-ô′gyə-rāt′) *tr.v.* **-rat·ed, -rat·ing, -rates. 1.** To induct into office by a formal ceremony. **2.** To cause to begin, especially officially or formally: *inaugurate a new immigration policy.* See Synonyms at **begin. 3.** To open or begin use of formally with a ceremony; dedicate: *inaugurate a community center.* [Latin *inaugurāre, inaugurāt-* : *in-*, intensive pref.; see IN–[2] + *augurāre*, to augur (from *augur*, soothsayer; see **aug-** in Appendix).] **—in·au′gu·ra′tor** *n.*

in·au·gu·ra·tion (ĭn-ô′gyə-rā′shən) *n.* **1.** Formal induction into office. **2.** A formal beginning or introduction.

in·aus·pi·cious (ĭn′ô-spĭsh′əs) *adj.* Not favorable; not auspicious. **—in′aus·pi′cious·ly** *adv.* **—in′aus·pi′cious·ness** *n.*

in·au·then·tic (ĭn′ô-thĕn′tĭk) *adj.* Not genuine or authentic. **—in′au·then·tic′i·ty** (-tĭs′ĭ-tē) *n.*

inbd. *abbr.* Inboard.

in between *prep. & adv.* Between: *Mortar in between the bricks; two crackers with a filling in between.*

in-be·tween (ĭn′bĭ-twēn′) *adj.* Intermediate: *Adolescence is an awkward, in-between age.* **—in-between** *n.* An intermediate: *conservatives, radicals, and in-betweens.*

in·board (ĭn′bôrd′, -bōrd′) *adj. Abbr.* **inbd. 1.** *Nautical.* Within the hull or toward the center of a vessel. **2.** Relatively close to the fuselage of an aircraft: *the inboard engines.* **—inboard** *n. Nautical.* A motor attached to the inside of the hull of a boat. **—in′board′** *adv.*

in·born (ĭn′bôrn′) *adj.* **1.** Possessed by an organism at birth. See Synonyms at **innate. 2.** Inherited or hereditary.

in·bound[1] (ĭn′bound′) *adj.* Bound inward; incoming: *inbound commuter traffic.*

in·bound[2] (ĭn′bound′) *v.* **-bound·ed, -bound·ing, -bounds.** *Basketball. —tr.* To put (the ball) into play by passing it from out of bounds to a teammate on the court. *—intr.* To execute an inbounds pass.

in·bounds (ĭn′boundz′) *adj.* **1.** *Basketball.* Involving putting the ball into play by passing it from out of bounds to a teammate on the court. **2.** *Sports.* Within the designated boundaries.

in·breathe (ĭn′brēth′) *tr.v.* **-breathed, -breath·ing, -breathes.** To breathe (something) in; inhale.

in·bred (ĭn′brĕd′) *adj.* **1.** Produced by inbreeding. **2.** Fixed in the character or disposition as if inherited; deep-seated: *an inbred distrust of radicalism.* See Synonyms at **innate.**

in·breed (ĭn′brēd′) *tr.v.* **-bred** (-brĕd′), **-breed·ing, -breeds. 1.** To breed by the continued mating of closely related individuals, especially to preserve desirable traits in a stock. **2.** To breed or develop within; engender. **—in·breed′er** *n.*

in·breed·ing (ĭn′brē′dĭng) *n.* **1.** The breeding of related individuals within an isolated or a closed group of organisms or people. **2.** The continued breeding of closely related individuals so as to preserve desirable traits in a stock.

in·built (ĭn′bĭlt′) *adj.* Built-in; inherent.

inc. *abbr.* **1.** Income. **2.** Incomplete. **3.** Also **Inc.** Incorporated. **4.** Increase.

In·ca (ĭng′kə) *n., pl.* **Inca** or **-cas. 1.a.** A member of the group of Quechuan peoples of highland Peru who established an empire from northern Ecuador to central Chile before the Spanish conquest. **b.** A ruler or high-ranking member of the Inca empire. **2.** A member of any of the peoples ruled by the Incas. [Spanish, from Quechua *inka*, ruler, man of royal lineage.]

In·ca·ic (ĭn-kā′ĭk) *adj.* Incan.

in·cal·cu·la·ble (ĭn-kăl′kyə-lə-bəl) *adj.* **1.a.** Impossible to calculate: *a mass of incalculable figures.* **b.** Too great to be calculated or reckoned: *incalculable wealth.* **2.** Impossible to foresee; unpredictable: *"The motions of her mind were as incalculable as the flit of a bird"* (Edith Wharton). **—in·cal′cu·la·bil′i·ty, in·cal′cu·la·ble·ness** *n.* **—in·cal′cu·la·bly** *adv.*

SYNONYMS: *incalculable, countless, immeasurable, incomputable, inestimable, infinite, innumerable, measureless.* The central meaning shared by these adjectives is "being greater than can be calculated or reckoned": *incalculable riches; countless hours; an immeasurable distance; an incomputable amount; jewels of inestimable value; an infinite number of reasons; innumerable difficulties; measureless power.*
ANTONYM: *calculable.*

inauguration
Swearing in
George Bush as President,
January 20, 1989

in·ca·les·cent (ĭn′kə-lĕs′ənt) *adj.* Growing hotter or more ardent. [Latin *incalēscēns, incalēscent-*, present participle of *incalēscere*, to grow warm : *in-*, intensive pref.; see IN–[2] + *calēscere*, to grow warm, inchoative of *calēre*, to be warm; see **kelə-[1]** in Appendix.] **—in′ca·les′cence** *n.*

in cam·er·a (kăm′ər-ə) *adv.* **1.** In secret; privately. **2.** *Law.* In private with a judge rather than in open court. [New Latin *in camerā* : Latin *in*, in + Medieval Latin *camerā*, ablative of *camera*, chamber.]

In·can (ĭng′kən) *adj.* Of or relating to the Inca, their civilization, or their language. **—Incan** *n.* **1.** An Inca. **2.** Quechua.

in·can·desce (ĭn′kən-dĕs′) *tr. & intr.v.* **-desced, -desc·ing, -desc·es.** To make or become incandescent. [Latin *incandēscere*, to glow : *in-*, intensive pref.; see IN–[2] + *candēscere*, to glow, inchoative of *candēre*, to shine; see **kand-** in Appendix.]

in·can·des·cence (ĭn′kən-dĕs′əns) *n.* **1.** The emission of visible light by a hot object. **2.** The light emitted by an incandescent object. See Synonyms at **blaze[1]. 3.** A high degree of emotion, intensity, or brilliance.

in·can·des·cent (ĭn′kən-dĕs′ənt) *adj.* **1.** Emitting visible light as a result of being heated. **2.** Shining brilliantly, very bright. See Synonyms at **bright. 3.** Characterized by ardent emotion, intensity, or brilliance: *an incandescent performance.* **—in′can·des′cent·ly** *adv.*

incandescent lamp *n.* An electric lamp in which a filament is heated to incandescence by an electric current.

in·can·ta·tion (ĭn′kăn-tā′shən) *n.* **1.** Ritual recitation of verbal charms or spells to produce a magic effect. **2.a.** A formula used in ritual recitation; a verbal charm or spell. **b.** A conventionalized utterance repeated without thought or aptness; a formula: *the pious incantations of the administration.* [Middle English *incantacioun*, from Old French *incantation*, from Late Latin *incantātiō, incantātiōn-*, spell, from Latin *incantātus*, past participle of *incantāre*, to enchant. See ENCHANT.] **—in′can·ta′tion·al** *adj.* **—in·can′ta·to′ry** (-tə-tôr′ē, -tōr′ē) *adj.*

Incan
Ruins of
Machu Picchu, Peru

in·ca·pa·ble (ĭn-kā′pə-bəl) *adj.* **1.a.** Lacking the necessary ability, capacity, or power: *incapable of carrying a tune; incapable of love.* **b.** Unable to perform adequately; incompetent: *an incapable administrator.* **2.** Not admitting or permitting; not susceptible: *a unique feat, incapable of duplication.* **3.** *Law.* Lacking legal qualifications or requirements; ineligible. **—in·ca′pa·bil′i·ty, in·ca′pa·ble·ness** *n.* **—in·ca′pa·bly** *adv.*

in·ca·pac·i·tant (ĭn′kə-păs′ĭ-tənt) *n.* A device or substance, such as tear gas, used to incapacitate individuals temporarily, as in riot control.

in·ca·pac·i·tate (ĭn′kə-păs′ĭ-tāt′) *tr.v.* **-tat·ed, -tat·ing, -tates. 1.** To deprive of strength or ability; disable. **2.** To make legally ineligible; disqualify. **—in′ca·pac′i·ta′tion** *n.*

in·ca·pac·i·ty (ĭn′kə-păs′ĭ-tē) *n., pl.* **-ties. 1.** Inadequate strength or ability; lack of capacity. **2.** A defect or handicap; a disability. **3.** *Law.* Something that renders one legally ineligible; a disqualification.

in·cap·su·late (ĭn-kăp′sə-lāt′) *v.* Variant of **encapsulate.**

in·car·cer·ate (ĭn-kär′sə-rāt′) *tr.v.* **-at·ed, -at·ing, -ates. 1.** To put into jail. **2.** To shut in; confine. [Medieval Latin *incarcerāre, incarcerāt-* : Latin *in-*, in; see IN–[2] + Latin *carcer*, prison.] **—in·car′cer·a′tion** *n.* **—in·car′cer·a′tor** *n.*

in·car·na·dine (ĭn-kär′nə-dīn′, -dēn′, -dĭn) *adj.* **1.** Flesh-colored. **2.** Blood-red. **—incarnadine** *tr.v.* **-dined, -din·ing, -dines.** To make incarnadine, especially to redden. [French *incarnadin*, from Italian *incarnadino*, variant of *incarnatino*, diminutive of *incarnato* : *in*, in (from Latin; see IN–[2]) + *carne*, flesh (from Latin *carō, carn-*; see INCARNATE, influenced by Italian *incarnato*, incarnate).]

in·car·nate (ĭn-kär′nĭt) *adj.* **1.a.** Invested with bodily nature and form: *an incarnate spirit.* **b.** Embodied in human form; personified: *a villain who is evil incarnate.* **2.** Incarnadine.

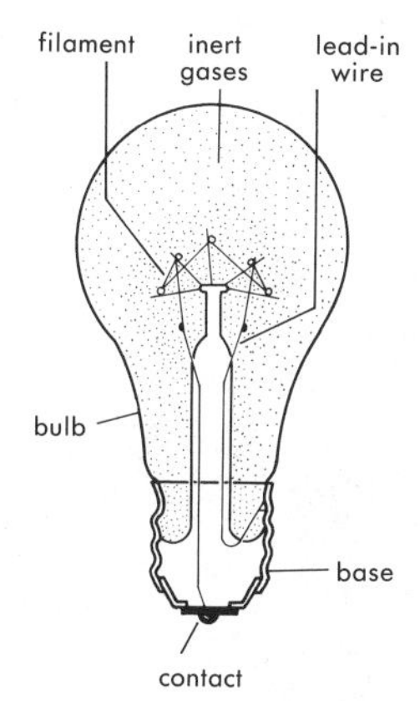

incandescent lamp

—incarnate (-nāt′) *tr.v.* **-nat·ed, -nat·ing, -nates. 1.a.** To give bodily, especially human, form to. **b.** To personify. **2.** To realize in action or fact; actualize: *a community that incarnates its founders' ideals.* [Middle English, from Late Latin *incarnātus,* past participle of *incarnāre,* to make flesh : Latin *in-,* causative pref.; see IN–[2] + Latin *carō, carn-,* flesh; see **sker-**[1] in Appendix.] **—in·car′na′tor** *n.*

in·car·na·tion (ĭn′kär-nā′shən) *n.* **1.a.** The act of incarnating. **b.** The condition of being incarnated. **2. Incarnation.** *Theology.* The Christian doctrine that the Son of God was conceived in the womb of Mary and that Jesus is true God and true man. **3.** A bodily manifestation of a supernatural being. **4.** One who is believed to personify a given abstract quality or idea. **5.** A period of time passed in a given bodily form or condition: *hopes for a better life in another incarnation.*

in·case (ĭn-kās′) *v.* Variant of **encase.**

in·cau·tious (ĭn-kô′shəs) *adj.* Not cautious; rash. **—in·cau′tious·ly** *adv.* **—in·cau′tious·ness** *n.*

in·cen·di·ar·y (ĭn-sĕn′dē-ĕr′ē) *adj.* **1.a.** Causing or capable of causing fire. **b.** Of or containing chemicals that produce intensely hot fire when exploded: *an incendiary bomb.* **c.** Of or involving arson. **2.** Tending to inflame; inflammatory. **—incendiary** *n., pl.* **-ies. 1.** An arsonist. **2.** An incendiary device. **3.** One who creates or stirs up factionism or sedition; an agitator. [Middle English, from Latin *incendiārius,* from *incendium,* fire, from *incendere,* to set on fire. See INCENSE[1].] **—in·cen′di·a·rism** (-ə-rĭz′əm) *n.*

in·cense[1] (ĭn-sĕns′) *tr.v.* **-censed, -cens·ing, -cens·es.** To cause to be extremely angry; infuriate. [Middle English *encensen,* from Old French *incenser,* from Late Latin *incēnsāre,* to sacrifice, burn, from Latin *incēnsus,* past participle of *incendere,* to set on fire. See **kand-** in Appendix.]

in·cense[2] (ĭn′sĕns′) *n.* **1.a.** An aromatic substance, such as wood or a gum, that is burned to produce a pleasant odor. **b.** The smoke or odor produced by the burning of such a substance. **2.** A pleasant smell. **3.** Flattering or fawning attention; homage. **—incense** *tr.v.* **-censed, -cens·ing, -cens·es. 1.** To perfume with incense. **2.** To burn incense to, as a ritual offering. [Middle English *encens,* from Old French, from Latin *incēnsum,* from neuter past participle of *incendere,* to set on fire. See **kand-** in Appendix.]

incense cedar *n.* Any of several coniferous evergreen trees of the genera *Calocedrus* and *Libocedrus,* having flattened branches with scalelike leaves.

in·cen·tive (ĭn-sĕn′tĭv) *n.* Something, such as the fear of punishment or the expectation of reward, that induces action or motivates effort. **—incentive** *adj.* Serving to induce or motivate: *an incentive bonus for high productivity.* [Middle English, from Late Latin *incentīvum,* from neuter of *incentīvus,* inciting, from Latin, setting the tune, from *incentus,* past participle of *incinere,* to sound : *in-,* intensive pref.; see IN–[2] + *canere,* to sing; see **kan-** in Appendix.]

in·cen·tiv·ize (ĭn-sĕn′tə-vīz′) *tr.v.* **-ized, -iz·ing, -iz·es.** *Usage Problem.* To offer incentives or an incentive to; motivate: *"This bill will help incentivize everybody to solve that part of the problem"* (Richard A. Gephardt). See Usage Note at **-ize.**

in·cept (ĭn-sĕpt′) *tr.v.* **-cept·ed, -cept·ing, -cepts.** To take in; ingest. [Latin *incipere, incept-,* to begin, take up. See INCEPTION.] **—in·cep′tor** *n.*

in·cep·tion (ĭn-sĕp′shən) *n.* The beginning of something, such as an undertaking; a commencement. See Synonyms at **origin.** [Middle English *incepcion,* from Latin *inceptiō, inceptiōn-,* from *inceptus,* past participle of *incipere,* to begin, take up : *in-,* in; see IN–[2] + *capere,* to take; see **kap-** in Appendix.]

in·cep·tive (ĭn-sĕp′tĭv) *adj.* **1.** Incipient; beginning. **2.** *Grammar.* Inchoative. **—inceptive** *n. Grammar.* An inchoative verb.

in·cer·ti·tude (ĭn-sûr′tĭ-to͞od′, -tyo͞od′) *n.* **1.** Uncertainty. **2.** Absence of confidence; doubt. **3.** Insecurity or instability.

in·ces·sant (ĭn-sĕs′ənt) *adj.* Continuing without interruption. See Synonyms at **continual.** [Middle English *incessaunte,* from Late Latin *incessāns, incessant-* : Latin *in-,* not; see IN–[1] + Latin *cessāns,* present participle of *cessāre,* to stop; see CEASE.] **—in·ces′san·cy** *n.* **—in·ces′sant·ly** *adv.*

in·cest (ĭn′sĕst′) *n.* **1.** Sexual relations between persons who are so closely related that their marriage is illegal or forbidden by custom. **2.** The statutory crime of sexual relations with such a near relative. [Middle English, from Latin *incestum,* neuter of *incestus,* impure, unchaste : *in-,* not; see IN–[1] + *castus,* pure, chaste; see **kes-** in Appendix.]

in·ces·tu·ous (ĭn-sĕs′cho͞o-əs) *adj.* **1.** Of, involving, or suggestive of incest. **2.** Having committed incest. **3.** Improperly intimate or interconnected: *"Press-politics relations are notoriously incestuous"* (Boston Globe). **—in·ces′tu·ous·ly** *adv.* **—in·ces′tu·ous·ness** *n.*

inch[1] (ĭnch) *n. Abbr.* **in, in. 1.** A unit of length in the U.S. Customary and British Imperial systems, equal to 1/12 of a foot (2.54 centimeters). See table at **measurement. 2.** A fall, as of rain or snow, sufficient to cover a surface to the depth of one inch. **3.** A unit of atmospheric pressure that is equal to the pressure exerted by a one-inch column of mercury at the earth's surface at a temperature of 0°C. **4.** A very small degree or amount: *won't budge an inch.* **—inch** *intr. & tr.v.* **inched, inch·ing, inch·es.** To move or cause to move slowly or by small degrees: *inching along through stalled traffic; inched the chair forward.* **—*idioms.* every inch.** In every respect; entirely: *"Ay, every inch a king!"* (Shakespeare). **inch by inch.** Very gradually or slowly. **within an inch of.** Almost to the point of: *came within an inch of death.* [Middle English, from Old English *ynce,* from Latin *uncia,* one twelfth of a unit. See **oi-no-** in Appendix.]

inch[2] (ĭnch) *n. Scots.* A small island. [Middle English, from Scottish Gaelic *innis,* from Old Irish *inis.*]

inch·er (ĭn′chər) *n.* Something measuring a specified number of inches, as in length or height. Often used in combination: *an 18-incher.*

inch·meal (ĭnch′mēl′) *adv.* Little by little; gradually. [INCH[1] + (PIECE)MEAL.]

in·cho·ate (ĭn-kō′ĭt) *adj.* **1.** In an initial or early stage; incipient. **2.** Imperfectly formed or developed: *a vague, inchoate idea.* [Latin *inchoātus,* past participle of *inchoāre,* to begin, alteration of *incohāre* : *in-,* in; see IN–[2] + *cohum,* strap from yoke to harness.] **—in·cho′ate·ly** *adv.* **—in·cho′ate·ness** *n.*

in·cho·a·tive (ĭn-kō′ə-tĭv) *adj.* **1.** Beginning; initial. **2.** *Grammar.* Of or being a verb or verbal form that designates the beginning of an action, a state, or an event. **—in·cho′a·tive** *n.* **—in·cho′a·tive·ly** *adv.*

In·chon (ĭn′chŏn′). A city of northwest South Korea on an inlet of the Yellow Sea southwest of Seoul. It was opened to foreign trade in 1883. Population, 1,387,000.

inch·worm (ĭnch′wûrm′) *n.* See **measuring worm.**

in·ci·dence (ĭn′sĭ-dəns) *n.* **1.** The act or an instance of happening; occurrence: *did not expect criticism and was surprised by its incidence.* **2.** Extent or frequency of occurrence: *a high incidence of malaria in the tropics.* **3.** *Physics.* **a.** The arrival of radiation or a projectile at a surface. **b.** Angle of incidence.

in·ci·dent (ĭn′sĭ-dənt) *n.* **1.** A definite and separate occurrence; an event. See Synonyms at **occurrence. 2.** A usually minor event or condition that is subordinate to another. **3.** Something contingent on or related to something else. **4.** An occurrence or event that interrupts normal procedure or precipitates a crisis: *an international incident.* **—incident** *adj.* **1.** Tending to arise or occur as a result or an accompaniment: *"There is a professional melancholy . . . incident to the occupation of a tailor"* (Charles Lamb). **2.** Related to or dependent on another thing. **3.** *Physics.* Falling upon or striking a surface: *incident radiation.* [Middle English, from Old French, apt to happen, an incident, from Latin *incidēns, incident-,* present participle of *incidere,* to happen : *in-,* on; see IN–[2] + *cadere,* to fall; see **kad-** in Appendix.]

in·ci·den·tal (ĭn′sĭ-dĕn′tl) *adj.* **1.** Occurring or likely to occur as an unpredictable or minor accompaniment: *the snags incidental to a changeover in upper management.* See Synonyms at **accidental. 2.** Of a minor, casual, or subordinate nature: *incidental expenses.* **—incidental** *n.* A minor accompanying item or expense: *a pocket in the suitcase for incidentals.*

in·ci·den·tal·ly (ĭn′sĭ-dĕn′tl-ē) *adv.* **1.** As a minor or subordinate matter: *by profession a lawyer and incidentally a musician.* **2.** (*also* -dĕnt′lē). Apart from the main subject; parenthetically.

incidental music *n. Music.* Music composed to accompany the action or dialogue of a drama or to fill intervals between scenes or acts.

in·cin·er·ate (ĭn-sĭn′ə-rāt′) *v.* **-at·ed, -at·ing, -ates.** *—tr.* To cause to burn to ashes. *—intr.* To burn completely. [Medieval Latin *incinerāre, incinerāt-* : Latin *in-,* causative pref.; see IN–[2] + Latin *cinis, ciner-,* ashes.] **—in·cin′er·a′tion** *n.*

in·cin·er·a·tor (ĭn-sĭn′ə-rā′tər) *n.* One that incinerates, especially an apparatus, such as a furnace, for burning waste.

in·cip·i·ent (ĭn-sĭp′ē-ənt) *adj.* Beginning to exist or appear: *detecting incipient tumors; an incipient personnel problem.* [Latin *incipiēns, incipient-,* present participle of *incipere,* to begin. See INCEPTION.] **—in·cip′i·en·cy, in·cip′i·ence** *n.* **—in·cip′i·ent·ly** *adv.*

in·ci·pit (ĭn′sĭ-pĭt′, ĭng′kĭ-) *n.* The beginning or opening words of the text of a medieval manuscript or early printed book. [Latin, third person sing. present tense of *incipere,* to begin. See INCEPTION.]

in·cise (ĭn-sīz′) *tr.v.* **-cised, -cis·ing, -cis·es. 1.** To cut into, as with a sharp instrument: *incised the tablet with chisels; a plateau that had been deeply incised by streams.* **2.a.** To engrave (designs or writing, for example) into a surface; carve. **b.** To engrave designs, writing, or other marks into. [French *inciser,* from Old French *enciser,* from Vulgar Latin **incīsāre,* frequentative of Latin *incīdere, incīs-* : *in-,* in; see IN–[2] + *caedere,* to cut; see **kae-id-** in Appendix.]

in·cised (ĭn-sīzd′) *adj.* **1.** Cut into a surface; engraved. **2.** Made with or as if with a sharp instrument. **3.** Deeply and sharply cut: *the incised margin of a leaf.*

in·ci·sion (ĭn-sĭzh′ən) *n.* **1.** The act of incising. **2.** *Medicine.* **a.** A cut into a body tissue or organ, especially one made during surgery. **b.** The scar resulting from such a cut. **3.** A notch, as in the edge of a leaf. **4.** The condition or quality of being incisive; incisiveness.

in·ci·sive (ĭn-sī′sĭv) *adj.* Penetrating, clear, and sharp, as in operation or expression: *an incisive mind; incisive comments.* **—in·ci′sive·ly** *adv.* **—in·ci′sive·ness** *n.*

SYNONYMS: *incisive, trenchant, biting, cutting, crisp, clear-cut.* These adjectives are synonymous when they refer to keenness and forcefulness of thought, expression, or intellect. *Incisive* and *trenchant* suggest penetration to the heart of a subject and clear, sharp, and vigorous expression: *an incisive and piquant style of writing; trenchant wit. Biting* and *cutting* apply to penetration and discernment that often have a sarcastic or sardonic quality capable of wounding or stinging: *"Biting remarks revealed her attitude of contempt"* (D.H. Lawrence). *"He can say the driest, most cutting things in the quietest of tones"* (Charlotte Brontë). *Crisp* suggests clarity, conciseness, and briskness: *a crisp retort; crisp banter. Clear-cut* specifies distinctness and sharpness of definition: *The wording of the lease is so clear-cut that no one could possibly misinterpret its meaning.*

in·ci·sor (ĭn-sīʹzər) *n. Abbr.* **i.** A tooth adapted for cutting or gnawing, located at the front of the mouth along the apex of the dental arch.

in·ci·ta·tion (ĭnʹsī-tāʹshən) *n.* **1.** The act or an instance of inciting; stimulation. **2.** Something that incites.

in·cite (ĭn-sītʹ) *tr.v.* **-cit·ed, -cit·ing, -cites.** To provoke and urge on: *troublemakers who incite riots; inciting workers to strike.* [Middle English *encyten,* from Old French *enciter,* from Latin *incitāre,* to urge forward : *in-,* intensive pref.; see IN–[2] + *citāre,* to stimulate, frequentative of *ciēre,* to put in motion; see **kei-[2]** in Appendix.] **—in·citeʹment** *n.* **—in·citʹer** *n.*

SYNONYMS: *incite, instigate, foment, abet.* These verbs mean to stir or give support to action. *Incite* is applied primarily to arousing the will and spirit to act: *Their leader tried to incite the dissidents to overthrow the government.* To *instigate* is to conceive and encourage the implementation of a plan of action, usually an evil or illegal one: *instigating a prison riot. "Commonly, though not always, we* exhort *to good actions, we* instigate *to ill"* (Samuel Johnson). *Foment* usually refers to the systematic fostering of feelings, as of discord or rebellion, that produce violent action: *foment discontent; foment civil insurrection.* To *abet* is to approve, encourage, and support actions, especially those in violation of what is right or proper: *The treasurer, aided and abetted by an assistant, misappropriated company funds.* See also Synonyms at **provoke.**

in·ci·vil·i·ty (ĭnʹsĭ-vĭlʹĭ-tē) *n., pl.* **-ties. 1.** The quality or condition of being uncivil. **2.** An uncivil or discourteous act.

incl. *abbr.* **1.** Including. **2.** Inclusive.

in·clasp (ĭn-klăspʹ) *v.* Variant of **enclasp.**

in·clem·ent (ĭn-klĕmʹənt) *adj.* **1.** Stormy: *inclement weather.* **2.** Showing no clemency; unmerciful. **—in·clemʹen·cy** *n.* **—in·clemʹent·ly** *adv.*

in·clin·a·ble (ĭn-klīʹnə-bəl) *adj.* **1.** Having a specified tendency or disposition; inclined: *inclinable to laziness.* **2.** Favorably disposed; amenable: *inclinable to our urgings.*

in·cli·na·tion (ĭnʹklə-nāʹshən) *n.* **1.** The act of inclining or the state of being inclined; a bend or tilt: *The inclination of the child's head suggested sleep.* **2. a.** A deviation or the degree of deviation from the horizontal or vertical; a slant: *the steep inclination of a roof.* **b.** An inclined surface; a slope. **3.** A tendency toward a certain condition or character: *the alkaline inclination of the local waters.* **4.** A characteristic disposition to do, prefer, or favor one thing rather than another; a propensity: *"I shall indulge the inclination so natural in old men, to be talking of themselves"* (Benjamin Franklin). See Synonyms at **tendency.**

in·cline (ĭn-klīnʹ) *v.* **-clined, -clin·ing, -clines.** *—intr.* **1.** To deviate from the horizontal or vertical; slant. **2.** To be disposed to a certain preference, opinion, or course of action. **3.** To lower or bend the head or body, as in a nod or bow. *—tr.* **1.** To cause to lean, slant, or slope. **2.** To influence to have a certain tendency; dispose: *Recent events incline us to distrust all politicians.* **3.** To bend or lower in a nod or bow: *inclined her head in acquiescence.* **—incline** (ĭnʹklīnʹ) *n.* An inclined surface; a slope or gradient. [Middle English *enclinen,* from Old French *encliner,* from Latin *inclīnāre* : *in-,* into, toward; see IN–[2] + *-clīnāre,* to lean; see **klei-** in Appendix.] **—in·clinʹer** *n.*

SYNONYMS: *incline, bias, dispose, predispose.* The central meaning shared by these verbs is "to influence or be influenced toward a particular attitude or course of action": *wasn't inclined to believe the excuse; is unjustly biased in her favor; an accomplishment that disposes us to admire him; isn't predisposed to the study of history.* See also Synonyms at **slant.**
ANTONYM: *disincline.*

in·clined (ĭn-klīndʹ) *adj.* **1.** Sloping, slanting, or leaning. **2.** Having a preference, disposition, or tendency.

inclined plane *n.* A plane set at an angle to the horizontal, especially a simple machine used to raise or lower a load by rolling or sliding.

in·cli·nom·e·ter (ĭnʹklə-nŏmʹĭ-tər) *n.* **1.** An instrument used to determine the angle of the earth's magnetic field in respect to the horizontal plane. **2.** An instrument for showing the inclination of an aircraft or a ship relative to the horizontal. **3.** See **clinometer.**

in·close (ĭn-klōzʹ) *v.* Variant of **enclose.**

in·clude (ĭn-klo͞odʹ) *tr.v.* **-clud·ed, -clud·ing, -cludes. 1.** To take in as a part, an element, or a member. **2.** To contain as a secondary or subordinate element. **3.** To consider with or place into a group, class, or total: *thanked the host for including us.* [Middle English *includen,* from Latin *inclūdere,* to enclose : *in-,* in; see IN–[2] + *claudere,* to close.] **—in·cludʹa·ble, in·cludʹi·ble** *adj.*

SYNONYMS: *include, comprise, comprehend, embrace, involve.* These verbs mean to take in or contain as part of something larger. *Include* and *comprise* both take as their objects things or persons that are constituent parts. *Comprise* usually implies that all of the components are stated: *The book comprises* (that is, consists of or is composed of) *15 chapters. Include,* like the remaining terms, more often implies an incomplete listing: *included a reference to the accompanist in the review of the concert; will include an amount for postage in my payment. "Through the process of amendment, interpretation and court decision I have finally been included in 'We, the people'"* (Barbara C. Jordan). *Comprehend* and *embrace* usually refer to the taking in of subordinate elements as part of something broader: *The study of art comprehends both aesthetic and intellectual considerations. No single theory can embrace and explain every facet of human behavior. Involve* usually suggests inclusion as a logical consequence or necessary condition: *"Every argument involves some assumptions"* (Brooke F. Westcott).

USAGE NOTE: Some writers have insisted that *include* be used only when it is followed by a partial list of the contents of the referent of the subject. On this account, one may write *New England includes Connecticut and Rhode Island,* but one must use *comprise* or *consist of* when a full enumeration is provided: *New England comprises* (not *includes*) *Connecticut, Rhode Island, Massachusetts, Vermont, New Hampshire, and Maine.* This restriction is too strong. *Include* does not rule out the possibility of a complete listing. Thus the sentence *The bibliography should include all the journal articles you have used* does not entail that the bibliography must contain something other than journal articles, though it does leave that possibility open. When one wants to make clear that the listing is exhaustive, however, the use of *comprise* or *consist of* will avoid ambiguity. Thus the sentence *The task force includes all of the Navy units on active duty in the region* allows for the possibility that Marine and Army units are also taking part, where the same sentence with *comprise* would entail that the task force contained only Navy forces. See Usage Note at **comprise.**

in·clud·ed (ĭn-klo͞oʹdĭd) *adj.* **1.** *Botany.* Not protruding beyond a surrounding part, as stamens that do not project from a corolla. **2.** *Mathematics.* Formed by and between two intersecting straight lines: *an included angle.*

in·clu·sion (ĭn-klo͞oʹzhən) *n.* **1.** The act of including or the state of being included. **2.** Something included. **3.** *Geology.* A solid, liquid, or gaseous foreign body enclosed in a mineral or rock. **4.** *Biology.* A nonliving mass, such as a droplet of fat, in the cytoplasm of a cell. **5.** *Computer Science.* A logical operation that assumes the second statement of a pair is true if the first one is true. [Latin *inclūsiō, inclūsiōn-,* from *inclūsus,* past participle of *inclūdere,* to enclose. See INCLUDE.] **—in·cluʹsion·arʹy** (-zhə-nĕrʹē) *adj.*

inclusion body *n.* An abnormal structure in a cell nucleus or cytoplasm having characteristic staining properties and associated especially with certain viral infections, such as rabies and smallpox.

in·clu·sive (ĭn-klo͞oʹsĭv) *adj. Abbr.* **incl. 1.** Taking a great deal or everything within its scope; comprehensive: *an inclusive survey of world affairs.* **2.** Including the specified extremes or limits as well as the area between them: *the numbers one to ten, inclusive.* **—in·cluʹsive·ly** *adv.* **—in·cluʹsive·ness** *n.*

inclusive of *prep.* Taking into consideration or account; including.

in·co·er·ci·ble (ĭnʹkō-ûrʹsə-bəl) *adj.* Difficult or impossible to coerce or control forcibly: *incoercible rebel leaders.*

incog. *abbr.* Incognita; incognito.

in·cog·i·tant (ĭn-kŏjʹĭ-tənt) *adj.* Thoughtless; inconsiderate. [Latin *incōgitāns, incōgitant-* : *in-,* not; see IN–[1] + *cōgitāns,* present participle of *cōgitāre,* to think; see COGITATE.]

in·cog·ni·ta (ĭnʹkŏg-nēʹtə, ĭn-kŏgʹnĭ-tə) *adv. & adj. Abbr.* **incog.** With one's identity disguised or concealed. Used of a woman. **—incognita** *n.* A woman or girl whose identity is disguised or concealed. [Italian, feminine of *incognito,* incognito. See INCOGNITO.]

in·cog·ni·to (ĭnʹkŏg-nēʹtō, ĭn-kŏgʹnĭ-tōʹ) *adv. & adj. Abbr.* **incog.** With one's identity disguised or concealed. **—incognito** *n., pl.* **-tos. 1.** One whose identity is disguised or concealed. **2.** The condition of having a disguised or concealed identity. [Italian, from Latin *incognitus,* unknown : *in-,* not; see IN–[1] + *cognitus,* past participle of *cognōscere,* to learn, recognize; see COGNITION.]

in·cog·ni·zant (ĭn-kŏgʹnĭ-zənt) *adj.* Lacking knowledge or awareness; unaware: *incognizant of the new political situation.*

in·co·her·ence (ĭnʹkō-hîrʹəns) *n.* **1.** The condition or quality of being incoherent. **2.** Something incoherent.

in·co·her·en·cy (ĭnʹkō-hîrʹən-sē) *n., pl.* **-cies.** Incoherence.

ă pat	oi boy
ā pay	ou out
âr care	o͝o took
ä father	o͞o boot
ĕ pet	ŭ cut
ē be	ûr urge
ĭ pit	th thin
ī pie	*th* this
îr pier	hw which
ŏ pot	zh vision
ō toe	ə about, item
ô paw	♦ regionalism

Stress marks: ʹ (primary); ʹ (secondary), as in **dictionary** (dĭkʹshə-nĕrʹē)

in·co·her·ent (ĭn′kō-hîr′ənt) *adj.* **1.** Lacking cohesion, connection, or harmony; not coherent: *incoherent fragments of a story.* **2.** Unable to think or express one's thoughts in a clear or orderly manner: *incoherent with grief.* **—in′co·her′ent·ly** *adv.* **—in′co·her′ent·ness** *n.*

in·com·bus·ti·ble (ĭn′kəm-bŭs′tə-bəl) *adj.* Incapable of burning. **—incombustible** *n.* An incombustible object or material. **—in′com·bus′ti·bil′i·ty** *n.* **—in′com·bus′ti·bly** *adv.*

in·come (ĭn′kŭm′) *n.* **1.** *Abbr.* **inc.** The amount of money or its equivalent received during a period of time in exchange for labor or services, from the sale of goods or property, or as profit from financial investments. **2.** The act of coming in; entrance. [Middle English, arrival, entrance, from *incomen,* to come in, from Old English *incuman* : *in,* in; see IN[1] + *cuman,* to come; see COME.]

income tax *n.* A tax levied on net personal or business income.

income tax return *n.* See **return** (sense 16).

in·com·ing (ĭn′kŭm′ĭng) *adj.* **1.** Coming in or about to come in; entering: *incoming trains; incoming mail; incoming mortar fire.* **2.** About to assume an office or a position: *the incoming governor.* **—incoming** *n.* **1.** The act of coming in; arrival. **2.** Often **incomings.** Income; revenue.

in·com·men·su·ra·ble (ĭn′kə-mĕn′sər-ə-bəl, -shər-) *adj.* **1.a.** Impossible to measure or compare. **b.** Lacking a common quality on which to make a comparison. **2.** *Mathematics.* Having no common measure or number of which all the given lengths or measures are integral multiples. **—incommensurable** *n.* One that is incommensurable. **—in′com·men′su·ra·bil′i·ty** *n.* **—in′com·men′su·ra·bly** *adv.*

in·com·men·su·rate (ĭn′kə-mĕn′sər-ĭt, -shər-) *adj.* **1.a.** Not commensurate; disproportionate: *a reward incommensurate with their efforts.* **b.** Inadequate. **2.** Incommensurable. **—in′com·men′su·rate·ly** *adv.* **—in′com·men′su·rate·ness** *n.*

in·com·mode (ĭn′kə-mōd′) *tr.v.* **-mod·ed, -mod·ing, -modes.** To cause to be inconvenienced; disturb. [French *incommoder,* from Old French, from Latin *incommodāre,* from *incommodus,* inconvenient : *in-,* not; see IN–[1] + *commodus,* convenient; see COMMODIOUS.]

in·com·mo·di·ous (ĭn′kə-mō′dē-əs) *adj.* Inconvenient or uncomfortable, as by not affording sufficient space. **—in′com·mo′di·ous·ly** *adv.* **—in′com·mo′di·ous·ness** *n.*

in·com·mod·i·ty (ĭn′kə-mŏd′ĭ-tē) *n., pl.* **-ties. 1.** Inconvenience. **2.** Something inconvenient.

in·com·mu·ni·ca·ble (ĭn′kə-myo͞o′nĭ-kə-bəl) *adj.* **1.** Impossible to be transmitted; not communicable: *an incommunicable disease.* **2.** Incommunicative: *an executive who was virtually incommunicable.* **—in′com·mu′ni·ca·bil′i·ty** *n.* **—in′com·mu′ni·ca·bly** *adv.*

in·com·mu·ni·ca·do (ĭn′kə-myo͞o′nĭ-kä′dō) *adv. & adj.* Without the means or right of communicating with others: *a prisoner held incommunicado; incommunicado political detainees.* [Spanish *incomunicado,* past participle of *incomunicar,* to deny communication : *in-,* not (from Latin; see IN–[1]) + *comunicar,* to communicate (from Latin *commūnicāre;* see COMMUNICATE).]

in·com·mu·ni·ca·tive (ĭn′kə-myo͞o′nĭ-kə-tĭv, -kā′tĭv) *adj.* Not disposed to be forthcoming or communicative; uncommunicative: *an incommunicative press secretary.* **—in′com·mu′ni·ca·tive·ly** *adv.* **—in′com·mu′ni·ca·tive·ness** *n.*

in·com·mut·a·ble (ĭn′kə-myo͞o′tə-bəl) *adj.* **1.** Not able to be exchanged one for another: *a rare, incommutable skill.* **2.** That cannot be changed; unalterable: *an incommutable death sentence.* **—in′com·mut′a·bil′i·ty, in′com·mut′a·ble·ness** *n.* **—in′com·mut′a·bly** *adv.*

in·com·pa·ra·ble (ĭn-kŏm′pər-ə-bəl) *adj.* **1.** Being such that comparison is impossible; incommensurable. **2.** So outstanding as to be beyond comparison; unsurpassed. **—in·com′pa·ra·bil′i·ty, in·com′pa·ra·ble·ness** *n.* **—in·com′pa·ra·bly** *adv.*

in·com·pat·i·bil·i·ty (ĭn′kəm-păt′ə-bĭl′ĭ-tē) *n., pl.* **-ties. 1.** The state or quality of being incompatible. **2. incompatibilities.** Mutually exclusive or antagonistic qualities or things.

in·com·pat·i·ble (ĭn′kəm-păt′ə-bəl) *adj.* **1.** Incapable of associating or blending or of being associated or blended because of disharmony, incongruity, or antagonism: *incompatible views on religion.* **2.** Impossible to be held simultaneously by one person: *the incompatible offices of prosecutor and judge.* **3.** *Logic.* That cannot be simultaneously true; mutually exclusive. See Synonyms at **inconsistent. 4.** *Medicine.* **a.** Producing an undesirable effect when used in combination with a particular substance: *a medication that is incompatible with alcohol.* **b.** Not immunologically compatible: *incompatible blood types.* **—incompatible** *n.* One that is incompatible. **—in′com·pat′i·ble·ness** *n.* **—in′com·pat′i·bly** *adv.*

in·com·pe·tent (ĭn-kŏm′pĭ-tənt) *adj.* **1.** Not qualified in legal terms: *a defendant who was incompetent to stand trial.* **2.** Inadequate for or unsuited to a particular purpose or application. **3.** Devoid of those qualities requisite for effective conduct or action. **—incompetent** *n.* An incompetent person. **—in·com′pe·tence, in·com′pe·ten·cy** *n.* **—in·com′pe·tent·ly** *adv.*

in·com·plete (ĭn′kəm-plēt′) *adj. Abbr.* **inc. 1.** Not complete. **2.** *Football.* Not caught or not caught in bounds: *an incomplete forward pass.* **—in′com·plete′ly** *adv.* **—in′com·plete′ness, in′com·ple′tion** *n.*

incomplete dominance *n. Genetics.* A heterozygous condition in which both alleles at a gene locus are partially expressed, often producing an intermediate phenotype.

incomplete flower *n.* A flower lacking sepals, petals, stamens, or pistils.

incomplete fracture *n.* A fracture that does not extend through the full transverse width of a bone.

incomplete metamorphosis *n.* A life cycle of certain insects, such as crickets and grasshoppers, characterized by the absence of a pupal stage between the immature and adult stages.

in·com·pli·ant (ĭn′kəm-plī′ənt) *adj.* Not willing to comply; unyielding. **—in′com·pli′ance, in′com·pli′an·cy** *n.* **—in′com·pli′ant·ly** *adv.*

in·com·pre·hen·si·ble (ĭn′kŏm-prĭ-hĕn′sə-bəl, ĭn-kŏm′-) *adj.* **1.a.** Difficult or impossible to understand or comprehend; unintelligible: *incomprehensible jargon.* **b.** Impossible to know or fathom: *incomprehensible mysteries.* **2.** *Archaic.* Having no limits; boundless. **—in′com·pre·hen′si·bil′i·ty, in′com·pre·hen′si·ble·ness** *n.* **—in′com·pre·hen′si·bly** *adv.*

in·com·pre·hen·sion (ĭn′kŏm-prĭ-hĕn′shən, ĭn-kŏm′-) *n.* Lack of comprehension or understanding.

in·com·pre·hen·sive (ĭn′kŏm-prĭ-hĕn′sĭv, ĭn-kŏm′-) *adj.* Limited in scope; not all-inclusive. **—in′com·pre·hen′sive·ly** *adv.* **—in′com·pre·hen′sive·ness** *n.*

in·com·press·i·ble (ĭn′kəm-prĕs′ə-bəl) *adj.* Impossible to compress; resisting compression: *mounds of incompressible garbage.* **—in′com·press′i·bil′i·ty** *n.*

in·com·put·a·ble (ĭn′kəm-pyo͞o′tə-bəl) *adj.* Impossible to compute or be computed; incalculable. See Synonyms at **incalculable. —in′com·put′a·bil′i·ty** *n.*

in·con·ceiv·a·ble (ĭn′kən-sē′və-bəl) *adj.* **1.** Impossible to comprehend or grasp fully: *inconceivable folly; an inconceivable disaster.* **2.** So unlikely or surprising as to have been thought impossible; unbelievable: *an inconceivable victory against all odds.* **—in′con·ceiv′a·bil′i·ty, in′con·ceiv′a·ble·ness** *n.* **—in′con·ceiv′a·bly** *adv.*

in·con·cin·ni·ty (ĭn′kən-sĭn′ĭ-tē) *n.* Lack of congruity or harmony; unsuitability.

in·con·clu·sive (ĭn′kən-klo͞o′sĭv) *adj.* Not conclusive: *inconclusive evidence.* **—in′con·clu′sive·ly** *adv.* **—in′con·clu′sive·ness** *n.*

in·con·den·sa·ble also **in·con·den·si·ble** (ĭn′kən-dĕn′sə-bəl) *adj.* Difficult or impossible to condense: *an incondensable judicial opinion.* **—in′con·den′sa·bil′i·ty** *n.*

in·con·dite (ĭn-kŏn′dĭt, -dīt′) *adj.* Badly constructed; crude. [Latin *inconditus* : *in-,* not; see IN–[1] + *conditus,* past participle of *condere,* to put together; see **dhē-** in Appendix.] **—in·con′dite·ly** *adv.*

in·con·form·i·ty (ĭn′kən-fôr′mĭ-tē) *n.* Lack of conformity; disagreement.

in·con·gru·ent (ĭn-kŏng′gro͞o-ənt, ĭn′kŏn-gro͞o′ənt) *adj.* **1.** Not congruent. **2.** Incongruous. **—in·con′gru·ence** *n.* **—in·con′gru·ent·ly** *adv.*

in·con·gru·i·ty (ĭn′kŏn-gro͞o′ĭ-tē) *n., pl.* **-ties. 1.** Lack of congruence. **2.** The state or quality of being incongruous. **3.** Something incongruous.

in·con·gru·ous (ĭn-kŏng′gro͞o-əs) *adj.* **1.** Lacking in harmony; incompatible: *a joke that was incongruous with polite conversation.* **2.** Not in agreement, as with principles; inconsistent: *a plan incongruous with reason.* **3.** Not in keeping with what is correct, proper, or logical; inappropriate: *incongruous behavior.* See Synonyms at **inconsistent.** [From Latin *incongruus* : *in-,* not; see IN–[1] + *congruus,* congruous; see CONGRUOUS.] **—in·con′gru·ous·ly** *adv.* **—in·con′gru·ous·ness** *n.*

in·con·se·quent (ĭn-kŏn′sĭ-kwənt) *adj.* **1.** Having no importance or significance. **2.** Inconsistent or illogical: *displayed stunningly inconsequent reasoning.* **3.** Proceeding without a natural or logical sequence; haphazard: *a speech full of inconsequent statements.* [Late Latin *incōnsequēns, incōnsequent-* : Latin *in-,* not; see IN–[1] + Latin *cōnsequēns, cōnsequent-,* consequent; see CONSEQUENT.] **—in·con′se·quence** *n.* **—in·con′se·quent·ly** *adv.*

in·con·se·quen·tial (ĭn-kŏn′sĭ-kwĕn′shəl, ĭn′kŏn-) *adj.* **1.** Lacking importance. **2.** Not following from premises or evidence; illogical. **—inconsequential** *n.* A triviality. **—in·con′se·quen′ti·al′i·ty** (-kwĕn′shē-ăl′ĭ-tē), **in·con′se·quen′tial·ness** (-shəl-nĭs) *n.* **—in·con′se·quen′tial·ly** *adv.*

in·con·sid·er·a·ble (ĭn′kən-sĭd′ər-ə-bəl) *adj.* Too small or unimportant to merit attention or consideration; trivial. **—in′con·sid′er·a·ble·ness** *n.* **—in′con·sid′er·a·bly** *adv.*

in·con·sid·er·ate (ĭn′kən-sĭd′ər-ĭt) *adj.* **1.** Thoughtless of others; displaying a lack of consideration. **2.** Not well considered or carefully thought out; ill-advised. **—in′con·sid′er·ate·ly** *adv.* **—in′con·sid′er·ate·ness, in′con·sid′er·a′tion** (-ā′shən) *n.*

in·con·sis·tence (ĭn′kən-sĭs′təns) *n.* Inconsistency.

in·con·sis·ten·cy (ĭn′kən-sĭs′tən-sē) *n., pl.* **-cies. 1.** The state or quality of being inconsistent. **2.** Something inconsistent: *many inconsistencies in your proposal.*

in·con·sis·tent (ĭn′kən-sĭs′tənt) *adj.* **1.** Displaying or marked by a lack of consistency, especially: **a.** Not regular or predictable; erratic: *inconsistent behavior.* **b.** Lacking in correct logical relation; contradictory: *inconsistent statements.* **c.** Not in agreement or harmony; incompatible: *an intersection inconsistent* *with the road map.* **2.** *Mathematics.* Not solvable for the unknowns by the same set of values. Used of two or more equations or inequalities. **—in′con·sis′tent·ly** *adv.*

SYNONYMS: *inconsistent, incongruous, incompatible, discordant, uncongenial, discrepant.* These adjectives mean being in marked disagreement. *Inconsistent* implies lack of uniformity, as in overall purpose, design, or content: *Occasional hostility is inconsistent with true friendship. Incongruous* suggests a lack of harmony and especially a lack of suitability or appropriateness, as between one person or thing and another: *Negotiating with terrorists is incongruous with national policy. Incompatible* implies conflict or an inability to coexist, as between persons of differing temperaments or things marked by fundamental differences or contradictions: *"Here are two, not only different, but incompatible things, called by the same name, liberty"* (Abraham Lincoln). *Discordant* implies a clash, as of temperaments, opinions, or principles: "[Imagination] *reveals itself in the balance or reconciliation of opposite or discordant qualities"* (Samuel Taylor Coleridge). *Uncongenial* suggests a lack of sympathy, as in character or nature: *"Realpolitik thinking is uncongenial to American political discourse"* (Christopher Layne). *Discrepant* stresses divergence where similarity or consistency is expected: *The two witnesses gave widely discrepant testimony.*

in·con·sol·a·ble (ĭn′kən-sō′lə-bəl) *adj.* Impossible or difficult to console; despondent: *was inconsolable after his pet died.* **—in′con·sol′a·bil′i·ty, in′con·sol′a·ble·ness** *n.* **—in′con·sol′a·bly** *adv.*

in·con·so·nant (ĭn-kŏn′sə-nənt) *adj.* Lacking harmony, agreement, or compatibility; discordant. **—in·con′so·nance** *n.* **—in·con′so·nant·ly** *adv.*

in·con·spic·u·ous (ĭn′kən-spĭk′yo͞o-əs) *adj.* Not readily noticeable. **—in′con·spic′u·ous·ly** *adv.* **—in′con·spic′u·ous·ness** *n.*

in·con·stan·cy (ĭn-kŏn′stən-sē) *n., pl.* **-cies. 1.** The state or quality of being eccentrically variable or fickle. **2.** An instance of being eccentrically variable or fickle.

in·con·stant (ĭn-kŏn′stənt) *adj.* **1.** Changing or varying, especially often and without discernible pattern or reason. **2.** Fickle; faithless. **—in·con′stant·ly** *adv.*

in·con·sum·a·ble (ĭn′kən-so͞o′mə-bəl) *adj.* That cannot be consumed: *seemingly inconsumable natural resources.* **—in′con·sum′a·bly** *adv.*

in·con·test·a·ble (ĭn′kən-tĕs′tə-bəl) *adj.* Impossible to contest; unquestionable: *incontestable proof of the defendant's guilt.* **—in′con·test′a·bil′i·ty, in′con·test′a·ble·ness** *n.* **—in′con·test′a·bly** *adv.*

in·con·ti·nence (ĭn-kŏn′tə-nəns) *n.* The quality or state of being incontinent.

in·con·ti·nent (ĭn-kŏn′tə-nənt) *adj.* **1.** Not restrained; uncontrolled: *incontinent rage.* **2.** Lacking normal voluntary control of excretory functions. **3.** Lacking sexual restraint; unchaste. [Middle English, from Old French, from Latin *incontinēns, incontinent-,* unrestrained : *in-,* not; see IN–[1] + *continēns,* continent; see CONTINENT[2].] **—in·con′ti·nent·ly** *adv.*

in·con·trol·la·ble (ĭn′kən-trō′lə-bəl) *adj.* Being such that control is impossible: *incontrollable rage; incontrollable children.*

in·con·tro·vert·i·ble (ĭn-kŏn′trə-vûr′tə-bəl, ĭn′kŏn-) *adj.* Impossible to dispute; unquestionable: *incontrovertible proof of the defendant's innocence.* **—in·con′tro·vert′i·bil′i·ty, in·con′tro·vert′i·ble·ness** *n.* **—in·con′tro·vert′i·bly** *adv.*

in·con·ven·ience (ĭn′kən-vēn′yəns) *n.* **1.** The state or quality of being inconvenient. **2.** Something inconvenient. **—inconvenience** *tr.v.* **-ienced, -ienc·ing, -ienc·es.** To cause inconvenience to; trouble: *The snow inconvenienced the holiday travelers.*

in·con·ven·ient (ĭn′kən-vēn′yənt) *adj.* Not convenient, especially: **a.** Not accessible; hard to reach. **b.** Not suited to one's comfort, purpose, or needs: *inconvenient to have no telephone in the kitchen.* **c.** Inopportune: *An early departure date is inconvenient for us.* **—in′con·ven′ient·ly** *adv.*

in·con·vert·i·ble (ĭn′kən-vûr′tə-bəl) *adj.* Not redeemable for money in coin: *inconvertible paper currency.* **—in′con·vert′i·bil′i·ty, in′con·vert′i·ble·ness** *n.* **—in′con·vert′i·bly** *adv.*

in·con·vinc·i·ble (ĭn′kən-vĭn′sə-bəl) *adj.* Impossible to convince: *was inconvincible as to the validity of our idea.*

in·co·or·di·nate (ĭn′kō-ôr′dn-ĭt, -āt′) *adj.* Lacking coordination; uncoordinated. **—in′co·or′di·nate·ly** *adv.*

in·co·or·di·na·tion (ĭn′kō-ôr′dn-ā′shən) *n.* Lack of coordination, especially a lack of normal voluntary and harmonious control of muscular movement.

in·cor·po·rate (ĭn-kôr′pə-rāt′) *v.* **-rat·ed, -rat·ing, -rates.** *—tr.* **1.** To unite (one thing) with something else already in existence: *incorporated the letter into her diary.* **2.** To admit as a member to a corporation or similar organization. **3.** To cause to merge or combine together into a united whole. **4.** To cause to form into a legal corporation: *incorporate a business.* **5.** To give substance or material form to; embody. *—intr.* **1.** To become united or combined into an organized body. **2.** To become or form a legal corporation: *San Antonio incorporated as a city in 1837.* **—incorporate** (-pər-ĭt) *adj.* **1.** Combined into one united body; merged. **2.** Formed into a legal corporation. [Middle English *incorporaten,* from Late Latin *incorporāre, incorporāt-,* to form into a body : Latin *in-,* in; see IN–[2] + Latin *corpus, corpor-,* body; see CORPUS.] **—in·cor′po·ra·ble** (-pər-ə-bəl) *adj.* **—in·cor′po·ra′tion** *n.* **—in·cor′po·ra′tive** *adj.* **—in·cor′po·ra′tor** *n.*

in·cor·po·rat·ed (ĭn-kôr′pə-rā′tĭd) *adj.* **1.** United into one body; combined. **2.** *Abbr.* **inc., Inc.** Formed into or organized and maintained as a legal corporation.

in·cor·po·rat·ing (ĭn-kôr′pə-rā′tĭng) *adj. Linguistics.* Polysynthetic.

in·cor·po·re·al (ĭn′kôr-pôr′ē-əl, -pōr′-) *adj.* **1.** Lacking material form or substance. See Synonyms at **immaterial. 2.** *Law.* Intangible, as a right or patent. [Middle English *incorporealle,* from Latin *incorporeus* : *in-,* not; see IN–[1] + *corporeus,* consisting of a body; see CORPOREAL.] **—in′cor·po′re·al′i·ty** (ăl′ĭ-tē) *n.* **—in′cor·po′re·al·ly** *adv.*

in·cor·po·re·i·ty (ĭn-kôr′pə-rē′ĭ-tē) *n.* The state or quality of being incorporeal; immateriality. [Medieval Latin *incorporeitās,* from Latin *incorporeus,* incorporeal. See INCORPOREAL.]

in·cor·rect (ĭn′kə-rĕkt′) *adj.* **1.** Not correct; erroneous or wrong: *an incorrect answer.* **2.** Defective; faulty: *incorrect programming of the computer.* **3.** Improper; inappropriate: *incorrect behavior.* **—in′cor·rect′ly** *adv.* **—in′cor·rect′ness** *n.*

in·cor·ri·gi·ble (ĭn-kôr′ĭ-jə-bəl, -kŏr′-) *adj.* **1.** Incapable of being corrected or reformed: *an incorrigible criminal.* **2.** Firmly rooted; ineradicable: *incorrigible faults.* **3.** Difficult or impossible to control or manage: *an incorrigible, spoiled child.* **—incorrigible** *n.* One that cannot be corrected or reformed. [Middle English, from Latin *incorrigibilis* : *in-,* not; see IN–[1] + *corrigere,* to correct; see CORRECT.] **—in·cor′ri·gi·bil′i·ty, in·cor′ri·gi·ble·ness** *n.* **—in·cor′ri·gi·bly** *adv.*

in·cor·rupt (ĭn′kə-rŭpt′) *adj.* **1.** Free of corruption or immorality. **2.** Not decayed; unspoiled. **3.** Free of errors or faults. **—in′cor·rupt′ly** *adv.* **—in′cor·rupt′ness** *n.*

in·cor·rupt·i·ble (ĭn′kə-rŭp′tə-bəl) *adj.* **1.** Incapable of being morally corrupted. **2.** Not subject to corruption or decay. **—in′cor·rupt′i·bil′i·ty** *n.* **—in′cor·rupt′i·bly** *adv.*

incr. *abbr.* **1.** Increase. **2.** Incremental.

in·crease (ĭn-krēs′) *v.* **-creased, -creas·ing, -creas·es.** *—intr.* **1.** To become greater or larger. **2.** To multiply; reproduce. *—tr.* To make greater or larger. **—increase** (ĭn′krēs′) *n. Abbr.* **inc., incr. 1.** The act of increasing: *a steady increase in temperature.* **2.** The amount or rate by which something is increased: *a tax increase of 15 percent.* **3.** *Obsolete.* Reproduction and spread; propagation. **—*idiom.* on the increase.** Increasing, especially in frequency of occurrence: *Crime is on the increase.* [Middle English *encresen,* from Old French *encreistre, encreiss-,* from Latin *increscere* : *in-,* intensive pref.; see IN–[2] + *crēscere,* to grow; see **ker-**[2] in Appendix.] **—in·creas′a·ble** *adj.* **—in·creas′er** *n.* **—in·creas′ing·ly** *adv.*

SYNONYMS: *increase, expand, enlarge, extend, augment, multiply.* These verbs mean to make or become greater or larger. *Increase* applies most widely; it sometimes suggests steady growth: *"Absence diminishes mediocre passions and increases great ones"* (La Rochefoucauld). *The mayor's political influence rapidly increased.* To *expand* is to increase in size, area, volume, bulk, or range: *He does exercises to expand his chest. "Work expands so as to fill the time available for its completion"* (C. Northcote Parkinson). *Enlarge* refers to expansion in size, extent, capacity, or scope: *The landowner enlarged her property by repeated purchases. Our group of friends is enlarging by leaps and bounds.* To *extend* is to lengthen in space or time or to broaden in range, as of application: *The transit authority extended the subway line to the next town. The baseball season may be extended. "His* [Jefferson's] *eye, like his mind, sought an extended view"* (Dumas Malone). *Augment* usually applies to what is already developed or well under way: *augmented her collection of books; depression that augments with each visit to the hospital.* To *multiply* is to increase in number, especially by propagation or procreation: *"As for my cats, they multiplied"* (Daniel Defoe). *"May thy days be multiplied!"* (Sir Walter Scott).

in·cre·ate (ĭn′krē-āt′, ĭn-krē′ĭt) *adj.* Existing without having been created. [Middle English *increat,* from Late Latin *increātus* : Latin *in-,* not; see IN–[1] + Latin *creātus,* past participle of *creāre,* to create; see CREATE.] **—in′cre·ate′ly** *adv.*

in·cred·i·ble (ĭn-krĕd′ə-bəl) *adj.* **1.** So implausible as to elicit disbelief: *gave an incredible explanation of the cause of the accident.* **2.** Astonishing: *dressed with incredible speed.* [Middle English, from Latin *incrēdibilis* : *in-,* not; see IN–[1] + *crēdibilis,* believable; see CREDIBLE.] **—in·cred′i·bil′i·ty, in·cred′i·ble·ness** *n.* **—in·cred′i·bly** *adv.*

in·cre·du·li·ty (ĭn′krĭ-do͞o′lĭ-tē, -dyo͞o′-) *n.* The state or quality of being incredulous; disbelief.

in·cred·u·lous (ĭn-krĕj′ə-ləs) *adj.* **1.** Skeptical; disbelieving: *incredulous of stories about flying saucers.* **2.** Expressive of disbelief: *an incredulous stare.* [From Latin *incrēdulus* : *in-,* not; see IN–[1] + *crēdulus,* believing; see CREDULOUS.] **—in·cred′u·lous·ly** *adv.* **—in·cred′u·lous·ness** *n.*

in·cre·ment (ĭn′krə-mənt, ĭng′-) *n.* **1.** The process of increasing in number, size, quantity, or extent. **2.** Something added or gained: *a force swelled by increments from allied armies.* **3.** A slight, often barely perceptible augmentation. **4.** One of a series

ă pat	oi boy
ā pay	ou out
âr care	o͝o took
ä father	o͞o boot
ĕ pet	ŭ cut
ē be	ûr urge
ĭ pit	th thin
ī pie	*th* this
îr pier	hw which
ŏ pot	zh vision
ō toe	ə about, item
ô paw	♦ regionalism

Stress marks: **′** (primary); ′ (secondary), as in **dictionary** (dĭk′shə-nĕr′ē)

incubator

incuse
1793 copper penny

of regular additions or contributions: *accumulating a fund by increments.* **5.** *Mathematics.* A small positive or negative change in the value of a variable. [Middle English, from Latin *incrēmentum,* from *incrēscere,* to increase. See INCREASE.] **—in′cre·men′tal** (-mĕn′tl) *adj.* **—in′cre·men′tal·ly** *adv.*

in·cre·men·tal·ism (ĭn′krə-mĕn′tl-ĭz′əm) *n.* Social or political gradualism. **—in′cre·men′tal·ist** *n.*

in·cres·cent (ĭn-krĕs′ənt) *adj.* Showing a progressively larger lighted surface; waxing: *the increscent moon.* [Latin *incrēscēns, incrēscent-,* present participle of *incrēscere,* to increase. See INCREASE.]

in·cre·tion (ĭn-krē′shən) *n.* **1.** The process of internal secretion characteristic of endocrine glands. **2.** The product of this process; a hormone. [IN–[2] + (SE)CRETION[1].]

in·crim·i·nate (ĭn-krĭm′ə-nāt′) *tr.v.* **-nat·ed, -nat·ing, -nates.** **1.** To accuse of a crime or other wrongful act. **2.** To cause to appear guilty of a crime or fault; implicate: *testimony that incriminated the defendant.* [Late Latin *incrīmināre, incrīmināt-* : Latin *in-,* causative pref.; see IN–[2] + Latin *crīmen, crīmin-,* crime; see CRIME.] **—in·crim′i·na′tion** *n.* **—in·crim′i·na·to′ry** (-nə-tôr′ē, -tōr′ē) *adj.*

in·crust (ĭn-krŭst′) *v.* Variant of **encrust.**

in·crust·a·tion (ĭn′krŭ-stā′shən) also **en·crust·a·tion** (ĕn′-) *n.* **1.a.** The act of encrusting. **b.** The state of being encrusted. **2.** A material encrusted on a surface. **3.** *Biology.* A coating of hardened exudate or other material on a body or body part; a scale or scab.

in·cu·bate (ĭn′kyə-bāt′, ĭng′-) *v.* **-bat·ed, -bat·ing, -bates.** *—tr.* **1.** To sit on (eggs) to provide heat, so as to promote embryonic development and the hatching of young; brood. **2.a.** To maintain (eggs, organisms, or living tissue) at optimal environmental conditions for growth and development. **b.** To maintain (a chemical or biochemical system) under specific conditions in order to promote a particular reaction. **3.** To form or consider slowly and protectively, as if hatching: *incubated the idea for a while, then announced it.* *—intr.* **1.** To brood eggs. **2.** To develop and hatch. **3.** To undergo incubation. [Latin *incubāre, incubāt-,* to lie down on : *in-,* on; see IN–[2] + *cubāre,* to lie down.] **—in′cu·ba′tive** *adj.*

in·cu·ba·tion (ĭn′kyə-bā′shən, ĭng′-) *n.* **1.a.** The act of incubating. **b.** The state of being incubated. **2.** *Medicine.* The development of an infection from the time the pathogen enters the body until signs or symptoms first appear. **3.** *Medicine.* The maintenance of an infant, especially a premature infant, in an environment of controlled temperature, humidity, and oxygen concentration in order to provide optimal conditions for growth and development. **—in′cu·ba′tion·al** *adj.*

in·cu·ba·tor (ĭn′kyə-bā′tər, ĭng′-) *n.* **1.** An apparatus in which environmental conditions, such as temperature and humidity, can be controlled, often used for growing bacterial cultures, hatching eggs artificially, or providing suitable conditions for a chemical or biological reaction. **2.** *Medicine.* An apparatus for maintaining an infant, especially a premature infant, in an environment of controlled temperature, humidity, and oxygen concentration. **3.** A place or situation that permits or encourages the formation and development, as of new ideas: *the college campus as an incubator of radical new sociological concepts.*

in·cu·bus (ĭn′kyə-bəs, ĭng′-) *n., pl.* **-bus·es** or **-bi** (-bī′). **1.** An evil spirit believed to descend upon and have sexual intercourse with women as they sleep. **2.** A nightmare. **3.** An oppressive or nightmarish burden. [Middle English, from Late Latin, from Latin *incubō,* from *incubāre,* to lie down on. See INCUBATE.]

in·cu·des (ĭng-kyo͞o′dēz) *n.* Plural of **incus.**

in·cul·cate (ĭn-kŭl′kāt′, ĭn′kŭl-) *tr.v.* **-cat·ed, -cat·ing, -cates.** **1.** To impress (something) upon the mind of another by frequent instruction or repetition; instill: *inculcating sound principles.* **2.** To teach (others) by frequent instruction or repetition; indoctrinate: *inculcate the young with a sense of duty.* [Latin *inculcāre, inculcāt-,* to force upon : *in-,* on; see IN–[2] + *calcāre,* to trample (from *calx, calc-,* heel).] **—in′cul·ca′tion** *n.* **—in·cul′ca′tor** *n.*

in·cul·pa·ble (ĭn-kŭl′pə-bəl) *adj.* Free of guilt; blameless.

in·cul·pate (ĭn-kŭl′pāt′, ĭn′kŭl-) *tr.v.* **-pat·ed, -pat·ing, -pates.** To incriminate. [Latin *inculpāre, inculpāt-* : *in-,* on; see IN–[2] + *culpāre,* to blame (from *culpa,* fault).] **—in′cul·pa′tion** *n.* **—in·cul′pa·to′ry** (-pə-tôr′ē, -tōr′ē) *adj.*

in·cult (ĭn-kŭlt′) *adj.* Not cultured; coarse. [Latin *incultus* : *in-,* not; see IN–[1] + *cultus,* past participle of *colere,* to till, cultivate; see **kʷel-**[1] in Appendix.]

in·cum·ben·cy (ĭn-kŭm′bən-sē) *n., pl.* **-cies.** **1.** The quality or condition of being incumbent. **2.** Something incumbent; an obligation. **3.a.** The holding of an office or ecclesiastical benefice. **b.** The term of an office or a benefice.

in·cum·bent (ĭn-kŭm′bənt) *adj.* **1.** Imposed as an obligation or a duty; obligatory: *felt it was incumbent on us all to help.* **2.** Lying, leaning, or resting on something else: *incumbent rock strata.* **3.** Currently holding a specified office: *the incumbent mayor.* **—incumbent** *n.* A person who holds an office or ecclesiastical benefice: *defeated the incumbent in a close election.* [Middle English, holder of an office, from Medieval Latin *incumbēns, incumbent-,* from Latin, present participle of *incumbere,* to lean upon, apply oneself to : *in-,* on; see IN–[2] + *-cumbere,* to recline.] **—in·cum′bent·ly** *adv.*

in·cu·na·ble (ĭn-kyo͞o′nə-bəl) *n.* An incunabulum. [French, from New Latin *incūnābulum.* See INCUNABULUM.]

in·cu·nab·u·lum (ĭn′kyə-năb′yə-ləm, ĭng′-) *n., pl.* **-la** (-lə). **1.** A book printed before 1501; an incunable. **2.** An artifact of an early period. [New Latin *incūnābulum,* from sing. of Latin *incūnābula,* swaddling clothes, cradle : *in-,* in; see IN–[2] + *cūnābula,* cradle, infancy (from *cūnae,* cradle; see **kei-**[1] in Appendix).] **—in′cu·nab′u·lar** (-lər) *adj.*

in·cur (ĭn-kûr′) *tr.v.* **-curred, -cur·ring, -curs.** **1.** To acquire or come into (something usually undesirable); sustain: *incurred substantial losses during the stock market crash.* **2.** To become liable or subject to as a result of one's actions; bring upon oneself: *incur the anger of a friend.* [Middle English *incurren,* from Old French *encorir,* from Latin *incurrere,* to run upon : *in-,* on; see IN–[2] + *currere,* to run; see **kers-** in Appendix.]

in·cur·a·ble (ĭn-kyo͝or′ə-bəl) *adj.* **1.** Being such that a cure is impossible; not curable: *an incurable disease.* **2.** Incapable of being altered, as in disposition or habits: *an incurable optimist; an incurable smoker.* **—in·cur′a·bil′i·ty, in·cur′a·ble·ness** *n.* **—in·cur′a·ble** *n.* **—in·cur′a·bly** *adv.*

in·cu·ri·ous (ĭn-kyo͝or′ē-əs) *adj.* Lacking intellectual inquisitiveness or natural curiosity; uninterested. See Synonyms at **indifferent.** **—in·cu′ri·os′i·ty** (-ŏs′ĭ-tē), **in·cu′ri·ous·ness** *n.* **—in·cu′ri·ous·ly** *adv.*

in·cur·rent (ĭn-kûr′ənt, -kŭr′-) *adj.* Affording passage to an inflowing current. [Latin *incurrēns, incurrent-,* present participle of *incurrere,* to run upon. See INCUR.]

in·cur·sion (ĭn-kûr′zhən, -shən) *n.* **1.** An aggressive entrance into foreign territory; a raid or an invasion. **2.** The act of entering another's territory or domain. **3.** The act of entering or running into: *homes damaged by the incursion of floodwater.* [Middle English, from Old French, from Latin *incursiō, incursiōn-,* from *incursus,* past participle of *incurrere,* to run upon. See INCUR.]

in·cur·vate (ĭn-kûr′vāt′, ĭn′kûr-) *tr.v.* **-vat·ed, -vat·ing, -vates.** To cause to bend into an inward curve. **—incurvate** *adj.* Curved inward. **—in′cur·va′tion** *n.* **—in·cur′va·ture′** (-və-cho͝or′, -chər) *n.*

in·curve (ĭn-kûrv′, ĭn′kûrv′) *tr. & intr.v.* **-curved, -curv·ing, -curves.** To cause to bend or to bend into an inward curve. **—incurve** (ĭn′kûrv′) *n.* An inward curve. [Middle English *incurven,* to twist, distort, from Latin *incurvāre,* to curve in, be crooked : *in-,* in; see IN–[2] + *curvus,* curve; see CURVE.]

in·cus (ĭng′kəs) *n., pl.* **in·cu·des** (ĭng-kyo͞o′dēz). **1.** *Anatomy.* An anvil-shaped bone between the malleus and the stapes in the mammalian middle ear. Also called *anvil.* **2.** A thunderhead. [Latin *incūs, incūd-,* anvil, from *incūsus,* past participle of *incūdere,* to forge with a hammer : *in-,* intensive pref.; see IN–[2] + *cūdere,* to beat, forge; see **kau-** in Appendix.]

in·cuse (ĭn-kyo͞oz′, -kyo͞os′) *adj.* Formed by hammering, stamping, or pressing: *an incuse design on a coin.* [Latin *incūdere, incūs-,* to forge with a hammer. See INCUS.]

ind. *abbr.* **1.** Independence; independent. **2.** Index. **3.** Indigo. **4.** Industrial; industry.

Ind. *abbr.* **1.** Indian. **2.** Indiana. **3.** Indies.

in·da·ba (ĭn-dä′bə) *n.* A conference of indigenous peoples of southern Africa. [Nguni (Zulu) *in-daba,* topic, conference.]

in·da·mine (ĭn′də-mēn′) *n.* Any of a group of organic bases forming unstable bluish or greenish salts and used in making dyes. [IND(IGO) + AMINE.]

in·debt·ed (ĭn-dĕt′ĭd) *adj.* Morally, socially, or legally obligated to another; beholden. [Middle English *endetted,* from Old French *endette,* past participle of *endetter,* to oblige : *en-,* causative pref.; see EN–[1] + *dette,* debt; see DEBT.]

in·debt·ed·ness (ĭn-dĕt′ĭd-nĭs) *n.* **1.** The state of being indebted. **2.** Something owed to another.

in·de·cen·cy (ĭn-dē′sən-sē) *n., pl.* **-cies.** **1.** The state or quality of being unseemly or immodest. **2.** Something indecent.

in·de·cent (ĭn-dē′sənt) *adj.* **1.** Offensive to good taste; unseemly. **2.** Offensive to public moral values; immodest. See Synonyms at **improper.** **—in·de′cent·ly** *adv.*

in·de·ci·pher·a·ble (ĭn′dĭ-sī′fər-ə-bəl) *adj.* Impossible to decipher: *indecipherable handwriting; an indecipherable message.* **—in′de·ci′pher·a·bil′i·ty, in′de·ci′pher·a·ble·ness** *n.* **—in′de·ci′pher·a·bly** *adv.*

in·de·ci·sion (ĭn′dĭ-sĭzh′ən) *n.* Reluctance or an inability to make up one's mind; irresolution.

in·de·ci·sive (ĭn′dĭ-sī′sĭv) *adj.* **1.** Prone to or characterized by indecision; irresolute: *an indecisive manager.* **2.** Inconclusive: *an indecisive contest; an indecisive battle.* **3.** Not clearly defined; indefinite: *indecisive boundaries running through mountainous terrain.* **—in′de·ci′sive·ly** *adv.* **—in′de·ci′sive·ness** *n.*

in·de·clin·a·ble (ĭn′dĭ-klī′nə-bəl) *adj.* **1.** Without grammatical inflection. **2.** Of, relating to, or being a word that lacks grammatical inflection though belonging to a form class whose members are usually inflected.

in·de·com·pos·a·ble (ĭn-dē′kəm-pō′zə-bəl) *adj.* That cannot be separated into components: *indecomposable matter.*

in·dec·o·rous (ĭn-dĕk′ər-əs) *adj.* Lacking propriety or good taste. See Synonyms at **improper.** **—in·dec′o·rous·ly** *adv.* **—in·dec′o·rous·ness** *n.*

in·de·cor·um (ĭn′dĭ-kôr′əm, -kōr′-) *n.* **1.** Lack of propriety or good taste; impropriety. **2.** An instance of indecorous behavior or action.

in·deed (ĭn-dēd′) *adv.* **1.** Without a doubt; certainly: *very cold indeed; was indeed grateful.* **2.** In fact; in reality: *said the car would break down, and indeed it did.* **—indeed** *interj.* Used to express surprise, skepticism, or irony. [Middle English *in dede,* in fact : *in,* in; see IN[1] + *dede,* deed, fact; see DEED.]

indef. *abbr.* Indefinite.

in·de·fat·i·ga·ble (ĭn′dĭ-făt′ĭ-gə-bəl) *adj.* Incapable or seemingly incapable of being fatigued; tireless. See Synonyms at **tireless.** [Obsolete French *indéfatigable,* from Latin *indēfatīgābilis* : *in-,* not; see IN–[1] + *dēfatīgāre,* to tire out (*dē-,* intensive pref.; see DE– + *fatīgāre,* to weary).] **—in′de·fat′i·ga·bil′i·ty, in′de·fat′i·ga·ble·ness** *n.* **—in′de·fat′i·ga·bly** *adv.*

in·de·fea·si·ble (ĭn′dĭ-fē′zə-bəl) *adj.* That cannot be annulled or made void: *an indefeasible claim; indefeasible rights.* **—in′de·fea′si·bil′i·ty** *n.* **—in′de·fea′si·bly** *adv.*

in·de·fec·ti·ble (ĭn′dĭ-fĕk′tə-bəl) *adj.* **1.** Having the ability to resist decay or failure; lasting. **2.** Having no flaw or defect; perfect. **—in′de·fec′ti·bil′i·ty** *n.* **—in′de·fec′ti·bly** *adv.*

in·de·fen·si·ble (ĭn′dĭ-fĕn′sə-bəl) *adj.* **1.** Inexcusable; unpardonable: *indefensible behavior.* **2.** Invalid; untenable: *an indefensible assumption.* **3.** Vulnerable to physical attack: *indefensible borders.* **—in′de·fen′si·bil′i·ty, in′de·fen′si·ble·ness** *n.* **—in′de·fen′si·bly** *adv.*

in·de·fin·a·ble (ĭn′dĭ-fī′nə-bəl) *adj.* Impossible to define, describe, or analyze. See Synonyms at **unspeakable.** **—indefinable** *n.* One that is indefinable. **—in′de·fin′a·bil′i·ty, in′de·fin′a·ble·ness** *n.* **—in′de·fin′a·bly** *adv.*

in·def·i·nite (ĭn-dĕf′ə-nĭt) *adj. Abbr.* **indef.** Not definite, especially: **a.** Unclear; vague. **b.** Lacking precise limits: *an indefinite leave of absence.* **c.** Uncertain; undecided: *indefinite about their plans.* **—in·def′i·nite·ly** *adv.* **—in·def′i·nite·ness** *n.*

indefinite article *n. Grammar.* An article, such as English *a* or *an,* that does not fix the identity of the noun modified.

indefinite integral *n. Mathematics.* A function whose derivative is a given function.

indefinite number *n. Abbr.* **n** *Mathematics.* A variable number.

indefinite pronoun *n. Grammar.* A pronoun, such as English *any* or *some,* that does not specify the identity of its object.

in·de·his·cent (ĭn′dĭ-hĭs′ənt) *adj. Botany.* Not splitting open at maturity: *indehiscent fruit.* **—in′de·his′cence** *n.*

in·del·i·ble (ĭn-dĕl′ə-bəl) *adj.* **1.** Impossible to remove, erase, or wash away; permanent: *indelible ink.* **2.** Making a mark not easily erased or washed away: *an indelible pen for labeling clothing.* [Latin *indēlēbilis* : *in-,* not; see IN–[1] + *dēlēbilis,* capable of being effaced (from *dēlēre,* to wipe out).] **—in·del′i·bil′i·ty, in·del′i·ble·ness** *n.* **—in·del′i·bly** *adv.*

in·del·i·ca·cy (ĭn-dĕl′ĭ-kə-sē) *n., pl.* **-cies. 1.** The quality or condition of being indelicate. **2.** Something indelicate.

in·del·i·cate (ĭn-dĕl′ĭ-kĭt) *adj.* **1.** Offensive to established standards of propriety; improper. See Synonyms at **improper. 2.** Marked by a lack of good taste; coarse. See Synonyms at **coarse. 3.** Lacking in consideration for the feelings of others; tactless. **4.** See Synonyms at **improper.** **—in·del′i·cate·ly** *adv.* **—in·del′i·cate·ness** *n.*

in·dem·ni·fi·ca·tion (ĭn-dĕm′nə-fĭ-kā′shən) *n.* **1.a.** The act of indemnifying. **b.** The condition of being indemnified. **2.** Something that indemnifies; a compensation for loss.

in·dem·ni·fy (ĭn-dĕm′nə-fī′) *tr.v.* **-fied, -fy·ing, -fies. 1.** To protect against damage, loss, or injury; insure. **2.** To make compensation to for damage, loss, or injury suffered. [Latin *indemnis,* uninjured (*in-,* not; see IN–[1] + *damnum,* harm, damage entailing liability) + –FY.] **—in·dem′ni·fi′er** *n.*

in·dem·ni·ty (ĭn-dĕm′nĭ-tē) *n., pl.* **-ties. 1.** Security against damage, loss, or injury. **2.** A legal exemption from liability for damages. **3.** Compensation for damage, loss, or injury suffered. See Synonyms at **reparation.** [Middle English *indempnite,* from Anglo-Norman, from Late Latin *indemnitās,* from Latin *indemnis,* uninjured. See INDEMNIFY.]

in·de·mon·stra·ble (ĭn′dĭ-mŏn′strə-bəl) *adj.* Impossible to prove or demonstrate: *a seemingly valid but indemonstrable hypothesis.* **—in′de·mon′stra·ble·ness, in′de·mon′stra·bil′i·ty** *n.* **—in′de·mon′stra·bly** *adv.*

in·dene (ĭn′dēn′) *n.* A colorless organic liquid, C_9H_8, obtained from coal tar and used in preparing synthetic resins. [IND(OLE) + –ENE.]

in·dent[1] (ĭn-dĕnt′) *v.* **-dent·ed, -dent·ing, -dents.** —*tr.* **1.** *Printing.* To set (the first line of a paragraph, for example) in from the margin. **2.a.** To cut or tear (a document with two or more copies) along an irregular line so that the parts can later be matched for establishing authenticity. **b.** To draw up (a document) in duplicate or triplicate. **3.a.** To notch or serrate the edge of; make jagged. **b.** To make notches, grooves, or holes in (wood, for example) for the purpose of mortising. **c.** To fit or join together by or as if by mortising. **4.** *Chiefly British.* To order (goods) by purchase order or official requisition. —*intr.* **1.** To make or form an indentation. **2.** *Chiefly British.* To draw up or order an indent. **—indent** (ĭn-dĕnt′, ĭn′dĕnt′) *n.* **1.** The act of indenting or the condition of being indented. **2.** *Printing.* A blank space before the beginning of an indented line: *a two-pica indent.* **3.** An indenture. **4.** A U.S. certificate issued at the close of the American Revolution for interest due on the public debt. **5.** *Chiefly British.* An official requisition or purchase order for goods. [Middle English *endenten,* to notch, from Anglo-Norman and Old French *endenter,* both from Medieval Latin *indentāre* : Latin *in-,* in; see IN–[2] + Latin *dēns, dent-,* tooth; see **dent-** in Appendix.]

in·dent[2] (ĭn-dĕnt′) *tr.v.* **-dent·ed, -dent·ing, -dents. 1.** To make a dent in: *a bay that indents the southern coast.* **2.** To impress (a design, for example); stamp. **—indent** (ĭn-dĕnt′, ĭn′-dĕnt′) *n.* An indentation.

in·den·ta·tion (ĭn′dĕn-tā′shən) *n.* **1.a.** The act of indenting. **b.** The condition of being indented. **2.** *Printing.* The blank space between a margin and the beginning of an indented line. **3.** A notch or jagged cut in an edge. **4.** A recess, as in a border or coastline.

in·den·tion (ĭn-dĕn′shən) *n.* **1.a.** The act of indenting. **b.** The condition of being indented. **2.** *Printing.* The blank space between a margin and the beginning of an indented line. **3.** *Archaic.* An indentation or a dent.

in·den·ture (ĭn-dĕn′chər) *n.* **1.** Often **indentures.** A contract binding one party into the service of another for a specified term. **2.a.** A document in duplicate having indented edges. **b.** A deed or legal contract executed between two or more parties. **c.** An official or authenticated inventory, list, or voucher. **3.** Indentation. **—indenture** *tr.v.* **-tured, -tur·ing, -tures. 1.** To bind into the service of another by indenture. **2.** *Archaic.* To form a small depression in (a surface). [Middle English *endenture,* a written agreement, from Anglo-Norman, from *endenter,* to indent (from the matching notches on multiple copies of the documents). See INDENT[1].]

in·de·pend·ence (ĭn′dĭ-pĕn′dəns) *n.* **1.** *Abbr.* **ind.** The state or quality of being independent. **2.** *Archaic.* Sufficient income for comfortable self-support; a competence.

In·de·pend·ence (ĭn′dĭ-pĕn′dəns). A city of western Missouri, a suburb of Kansas City. A starting point for the Santa Fe and Oregon trails during the 19th century, it was the home of President Harry S. Truman. Population, 111,806.

Independence Day *n.* July 4, celebrated in the United States to commemorate the adoption in 1776 of the Declaration of Independence. Also called *Fourth of July.*

in·de·pend·en·cy (ĭn′dĭ-pĕn′dən-sē) *n., pl.* **-cies. 1.** Independence. **2.** An independent territory or state. **3. Independency.** The Independent movement in 17th-century England.

in·de·pend·ent (ĭn′dĭ-pĕn′dənt) *adj. Abbr.* **ind. 1.** Not governed by a foreign power; self-governing. **2.** Free from the influence, guidance, or control of another or others; self-reliant: *an independent mind.* **3.** Not determined or influenced by someone or something else; not contingent: *a decision independent of the outcome of the study.* **4.** Often **Independent.** Affiliated with or loyal to no one political party or organization. **5.** Not dependent on or affiliated with a larger or controlling group or system: *an independent food store.* **6.a.** Not relying on others for support, care, or funds; self-supporting. **b.** Providing or being sufficient income to enable one to live without working: *a person of independent means.* **7.** *Mathematics.* **a.** Not dependent on other variables. **b.** Of or relating to a system of equations no one of which can be derived from another equation in the system. **8. Independent.** Of or relating to the 17th-century English Independents. **—independent** *n.* **1.** Often **Independent.** One that is independent, especially a voter, an officeholder, or a political candidate who is not committed to a political party. **2. Independent.** A member of a movement in England in the 17th century advocating the political and religious independence of individual congregations. **3. Independent.** *Chiefly British.* A Congregationalist.

independent clause *n. Grammar.* See **main clause.**

independent variable *n.* **1.** *Mathematics.* A variable whose value determines the value of other variables. **2.** *Statistics.* A manipulated variable in an experiment or a study whose presence or degree determines the change in the dependent variable.

in-depth (ĭn′dĕpth′) *adj.* Detailed; thorough: *an in-depth study.*

In·der·al (ĭn′də-rôl′, -rŏl′). A trademark used for a beta-adrenergic blocking agent for the treatment of certain cardiovascular conditions.

in·de·scrib·a·ble (ĭn′dĭ-skrī′bə-bəl) *adj.* **1.** Impossible to describe: *indescribable views.* **2.** Exceeding description: *experienced indescribable delight.* See Synonyms at **unspeakable.** **—in′de·scrib′a·bil′i·ty, in′de·scrib′a·ble·ness** *n.* **—in′de·scrib′a·bly** *adv.*

in·de·struc·ti·ble (ĭn′dĭ-strŭk′tə-bəl) *adj.* Impossible to destroy: *indestructible furniture; indestructible faith.* [Late Latin *indēstrūctibilis* : Latin *in-,* not; see IN–[1] + *dēstrūctibilis,* destructible (from Latin *dēstrūctus,* past participle of *dēstruere,* to destroy; see DESTROY).] **—in′de·struc′ti·bil′i·ty, in′de·struc′ti·ble·ness** *n.* **—in′de·struc′ti·bly** *adv.*

in·de·ter·min·a·ble (ĭn′dĭ-tûr′mə-nə-bəl) *adj.* **1.** Impossible to fix or measure: *indeterminable traces of poison; indeterminable assets.* **2.** Impossible to settle or decide with finality: *indeterminable questions.* **—in′de·ter′min·a·bly** *adv.*

in·de·ter·mi·na·cy (ĭn′dĭ-tûr′mə-nə-sē) *n.* The state or quality of being indeterminate.

in·de·ter·mi·nate (ĭn′dĭ-tûr′mə-nĭt) *adj.* **1.a.** Not precisely determined, determinable, or established: *a person of indeterminate age.* **b.** Not precisely fixed, as to extent, size, nature, or

ă pat	oi boy
ā pay	ou out
âr care	ŏŏ took
ä father	ōō boot
ĕ pet	ŭ cut
ē be	ûr urge
ĭ pit	th thin
ī pie	*th* this
îr pier	hw which
ŏ pot	zh vision
ō toe	ə about, item
ô paw	♦ regionalism

Stress marks: **′** (primary); ′ (secondary), as in **dictionary** (dĭk′shə-nĕr′ē)

India

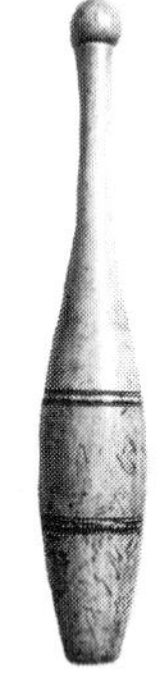
Indian club

Indian tobacco
Lobelia inflata

number: *an indeterminate number of plant species in the jungle.* **c.** Lacking clarity or precision, as in meaning; vague: *an indeterminate turn of phrase.* **d.** Not fixed or known in advance: *an indeterminate future.* **e.** Not leading up to a definite result or ending: *an indeterminate campaign.* **2.** *Botany.* Not terminating in a flower and continuing to grow at the apex: *an indeterminate inflorescence.* [Middle English, from Latin *indēterminātus* : *in-*, not; see IN–[1] + *dēterminātus,* determined; see DETERMINATE.] **—in′de·ter′mi·nate·ly** *adv.* **—in′de·ter′mi·nate·ness, in′de·ter′mi·na′tion** (-nā′shən) *n.*

indeterminate vowel *n.* *Linguistics.* See **schwa** (sense 1).

in·de·ter·min·ism (ĭn′dĭ-tûr′mə-nĭz′əm) *n.* **1.** Unpredictability. **2.** *Philosophy.* The doctrine that the will is free and that human action is not necessarily or not at all predetermined by physiological and psychological antecedents. **—in′de·ter′min·ist** *n.* **—in′de·ter′min·is′tic** *adj.*

in·dex (ĭn′dĕks′) *n., pl.* **-dex·es** or **-di·ces** (-dĭ-sēz′). **1.** *Abbr.* **ind.** Something that serves to guide, point out, or otherwise facilitate reference, especially: **a.** An alphabetized list of names, places, and subjects treated in a printed work, giving the page or pages on which each item is mentioned. **b.** A thumb index. **c.** A table, file, or catalog. **2.** Something that reveals or indicates; a sign: *"Her face . . . was a fair index to her disposition"* (Samuel Butler). **3.** *Printing.* A character (☞) used in printing to call attention to a particular paragraph or section. Also called *fist, hand.* **4.** An indicator or a pointer, as on a scientific instrument. **5. a.** *Mathematics.* A number or symbol, often written as a subscript or superscript to a mathematical expression, that indicates an operation to be performed on, an ordering relation involving, or a use of the associated expression. **b.** A number derived from a formula, used to characterize a set of data. **6. Index.** *Roman Catholic Church.* A list formerly published by Church authority, restricting or forbidding the reading of certain books. **—index** *tr.v.* **-dexed, -dex·ing, -dex·es. 1.** To furnish with an index: *index a book.* **2.** To enter in an index. **3.** To indicate or signal. **4.** To adjust through indexation. [Middle English, forefinger, from Latin. See **deik-** in Appendix.] **—in′dex′er** *n.*

in·dex·a·tion (ĭn′dĕk-sā′shən) *n.* The automatic adjustment of an economic variable, such as wages, taxes, or pension benefits, to a cost-of-living index, so that the variable rises or falls in accordance with the rate of inflation.

index case *n.* The earliest documented case of a disease included in an epidemiologic study.

index finger *n.* The finger next to the thumb. Also called *first finger, forefinger.*

index fossil *n.* The fossil remains of an organism that lived in a particular geologic age, used to identify or date the rock or rock layer in which it is found. Also called *guide fossil.*

index number *n.* A number indicating change in magnitude, as of price, wage, employment, or production shifts, relative to the magnitude at a specified point usually taken as 100.

index of refraction *n.* The ratio of the speed of light in a vacuum to the speed of light in a medium under consideration. Also called *refractive index.*

In·di·a (ĭn′dē-ə). **1.** A peninsula and subcontinent of southern Asia south of the Himalaya Mountains, occupied by India, Nepal, Bhutan, Sikkim, Pakistan, and Bangladesh. **2.** A country of southern Asia. India was the site of one of the oldest civilizations in the world, centered in the Indus River valley c. 2500 to 1500 B.C. Parts of India were overrun by the Aryans and later occupied or controlled by various powers, including the Moguls, European states, and local nawabs and rajahs. The British finally assumed authority over "the Jewel in the Crown" in 1857, although Queen Victoria did not assume the title of empress until 1876. In the 20th century increasing unrest led to Britain's withdrawal and independence for the country (1947). New Delhi is the capital and Calcutta the largest city. Population, 685,184,692.

India ink *n.* **1.** A black pigment made from lampblack mixed with a binding agent and molded into cakes or sticks. **2.** A liquid ink made from this pigment. In this sense, also called *Chinese ink.*

In·di·a·man (ĭn′dē-ə-mən) *n.* *Nautical.* A large merchant ship formerly used on trade routes to India.

In·di·an (ĭn′dē-ən) *adj.* *Abbr.* **Ind. 1.** Of or relating to India or the East Indies or to their peoples, languages, or cultures. **2.** Of or relating to any of the Native American peoples. **—Indian** *n.* *Abbr.* **Ind. 1.** A native or inhabitant of India or of the East Indies. **2.** See **Native American.** See Usage Note at **Native American. 3.** Any of the languages of the Native Americans. **4.** See **Indus**[2]**.**

In·di·an·a (ĭn′dē-ăn′ə). **1.** *Abbr.* **IN, Ind.** A state of the north-central United States. It was admitted as the 19th state in 1816. The area was controlled by France until 1763 and then by Great Britain until 1783. The Indiana Territory was formed in 1800. Indianapolis is the capital and the largest city. Population, 5,490,260. **2.** A borough of west-central Pennsylvania east-northeast of Pittsburgh. It is an industrial center. Population, 16,051. **—In′di·an′an, In′di·an′i·an** *adj. & n.*

Indiana, Robert. Born 1928. American pop artist known for his "Love" theme in paintings and sculpture.

Indian almond *n.* An Asiatic tree *(Terminalia catappa)* widely cultivated and naturalized in the tropics and having fruit with edible seeds. Also called *myrobalan, tropical almond.*

In·di·an·ap·o·lis (ĭn′dē-ə-năp′ə-lĭs). The capital and largest city of Indiana, in the central part of the state. It was settled in 1820 as the site of a new state capital, which was moved here in 1825. Population, 700,807.

Indian bean *n.* See **catalpa.**

Indian bread *n.* Any of various plants, such as the breadroot, having edible parts used by certain Native American peoples for food.

Indian club *n.* *Sports.* A bottle-shaped wooden club swung in the hand for gymnastic exercise.

Indian corn *n.* See **corn**[1] (sense 1).

Indian currant *n.* See **coralberry** (sense 1).

Indian file *n.* See **single file. —Indian file** *adv.*

Indian giver *n.* *Offensive.* One who gives something to another and then takes or demands the gift back.

Indian hemp *n.* Cannabis.

Indian licorice *n.* See **rosary pea.**

Indian mallow *n.* See **flowering maple.**

Indian meal *n.* See **cornmeal.**

Indian mustard *n.* An annual plant *(Brassica juncea)* in the mustard family, having yellow flowers, petiolate leaves, and oil-rich seeds. Also called *brown mustard.*

Indian Ocean. A body of water extending from southern Asia to Antarctica and from eastern Africa to southeast Australia.

Indian paintbrush *n.* Any of various partly parasitic plants of the genus *Castilleja,* having spikes of flowers surrounded by showy, brightly colored bracts. Also called *painted cup.*

Indian pipe *n.* A waxy white or sometimes pinkish saprophytic woodland plant *(Monotropa uniflora)* having scalelike leaves and a solitary, nodding flower.

Indian pony *n.* A small, hardy horse of western North America, often used for crossbreeding.

♦ **Indian pudding** *n.* *New England.* A pudding consisting of milk, cornmeal, egg, and molasses baked for several hours in a heavy casserole. [So called because it is made with Indian meal.]

Indian red *n.* An iron oxide used as a paint and cosmetic pigment.

Indian River. A lagoon extending about 265 km (165 mi) along the coast of east-central Florida.

Indian summer *n.* **1.** A period of mild weather occurring in late autumn. **2.** A pleasant, tranquil, or flourishing period occurring near the end of something: *the Indian summer of the administration.*

Indian Territory. A region and former territory of the south-central United States, mainly in present-day Oklahoma. It was set aside by the government as a homeland for forcibly displaced Native Americans in 1834. The western section was opened to general settlement in 1889 and became part of the Oklahoma Territory in 1890. The two territories were merged in 1907 to form the state of Oklahoma.

Indian tobacco *n.* A poisonous North American plant *(Lobelia inflata)* having light blue to white flowers and rounded seedpods enclosed by an inflated, persistent calyx.

♦ **Indian turnip** *n.* *Midland U.S.* See **jack-in-the-pulpit.**

Indian wrestling *n.* *Sports.* **1.** See **arm wrestling. 2.** A form of wrestling in which two opponents, lying supine in reversed position, lock their near arms, raise and lock their near legs, and attempt to force the other's leg down. **3.** A form of wrestling in which two opponents stand facing each other with usually right hands interlocked and the outsides of their near feet set together and attempt to unbalance each other.

India paper *n.* **1.** A thin, uncoated, delicate paper made of vegetable fiber, used especially for taking impressions of engravings. **2.** See **Bible paper.**

India rubber *n.* See **rubber**[1] (sense 1).

In·dic (ĭn′dĭk) *adj.* **1.** Of or relating to India or its peoples or cultures. **2.** Of, relating to, or constituting the Indo-European languages of the Indian subcontinent and Sri Lanka. **—Indic** *n.* A branch of the Indo-European language family that comprises the languages of the Indian subcontinent and Sri Lanka. Also called *Sanskritic.*

indic. *abbr.* **1.** *Grammar.* Indicative. **2.** Indicator.

in·di·can (ĭn′dĭ-kăn′) *n.* **1.** A potassium salt, $C_8H_6NO_4SK$, found in sweat and urine and formed by the conversion of tryptophan to indole by intestinal bacteria. **2.** A glucoside, $C_{14}H_{17}NO_6$, occurring in the indigo plant and used as a source for indigo dye. [Latin *indicum,* indigo; see INDIGO + –AN[2].]

in·di·cant (ĭn′dĭ-kənt) *n.* Something, such as a typographical device, that serves to indicate.

in·di·cate (ĭn′dĭ-kāt′) *tr.v.* **-cat·ed, -cat·ing, -cates. 1.** To show the way to or the direction of; point out: *an arrow indicating north; indicated the right road by nodding toward it.* **2.** To serve as a sign, symptom, or token of; signify: *"The cracking and booming of the ice indicate a change of temperature"* (Henry David Thoreau). **3.** To suggest or demonstrate the necessity, expedience, or advisability of: *The symptoms indicate immediate surgery.* **4.** To state or express briefly: *indicated his wishes in a letter; indicating her approval with a nod.* [Latin *indicāre, indicāt-,* to show, from *index,* forefinger, indicator. See **deik-** in Appendix.] **—in′di·ca·to′ry** (-kə-tôr′ē, -tōr′ē) *adj.*

SYNONYMS: *indicate, argue, attest, bespeak, betoken, testify, witness.* The central meaning shared by these verbs is "to give grounds for supposing or inferring the existence or presence of something": *a fever indicating illness; a shabby house that argues poverty; paintings that attest the artist's genius; disorder that bespeaks negligence; melting snows that betoken spring floods; a comment testifying ignorance; a stunned silence that witnessed his astonishment.*

in·di·ca·tion (ĭn′dĭ-kā′shən) *n. Abbr.* **indn. 1.** The act of indicating. **2.** Something that serves to indicate; a sign: *smiles, frowns, and other indications of emotion.* **3.** Something indicated as necessary or expedient: *Bed rest is usually the indication for flu cases.* **4.** The degree indicated by a measuring instrument.

in·dic·a·tive (ĭn-dĭk′ə-tĭv) *adj.* **1.** Serving to indicate: *symptoms indicative of anemia; an insignia indicative of high rank.* **2.** *Abbr.* **indic.** *Grammar.* Of, relating to, or being the mood of the verb used in ordinary objective statements. **—indicative** *n. Abbr.* **indic.** *Grammar.* **1.** The indicative mood. **2.** A verb in the indicative mood. **—in·dic′a·tive·ly** *adv.*

in·di·ca·tor (ĭn′dĭ-kā′tər) *n. Abbr.* **indic. 1.** One that indicates, especially: **a.** A pointer or an index. **b.** An instrument used to monitor the operation or condition of an engine, a furnace, an electrical network, a reservoir, or another physical system; a meter or gauge. **c.** The needle, dial, or other registering device on such an instrument. **2.** *Chemistry.* Any of various substances, such as litmus or phenolphthalein, that indicate the presence, absence, or concentration of another substance or the degree of reaction between two or more substances by means of a characteristic change, especially in color. **3.** Any of various statistical values that together provide an indication of the condition or direction of the economy.

in·di·ces (ĭn′dĭ-sēz′) *n.* A plural of **index.**

in·di·cia (ĭn-dĭsh′ə, -dĭsh′ē-ə) *pl.n.* **1.** Identifying marks; indications. **2.** Markings on bulk mailings used as a substitute for stamps or cancellations. [Latin, pl. of *indicium,* sign, from *index, indic-,* indicator. See INDEX.]

in·di·ci·um (ĭn-dĭsh′ē-əm) *n.* Singular of **indicia.**

in·dict (ĭn-dīt′) *tr.v.* **-dict·ed, -dict·ing, -dicts. 1.** To accuse of wrongdoing; charge: *a book that indicts modern values.* **2.** *Law.* To make a formal accusation or indictment against (a party) by the findings of a jury, especially a grand jury. [Alteration of Middle English *enditen,* to accuse, write a document. See INDITE.] **—in′dict·ee′** (ĭn′dī-tē′) *n.* **—in·dict′er, in·dict′or** *n.*

in·dict·a·ble (ĭn-dī′tə-bəl) *adj.* **1.** Capable of being indicted: *Evidence suggested that the official was indictable for the crime.* **2.** Making one liable to indictment: *an indictable offense.*

in·dic·tion (ĭn-dĭk′shən) *n.* A 15-year cycle used as a chronological unit in ancient Rome and incorporated in some medieval systems. [Middle English *indiccioun,* from Late Latin *indictiō, indictiōn-,* proclamation, period of 15 years, from Latin *indictus,* past participle of *indīcere,* to proclaim. See INDITE.]

in·dict·ment (ĭn-dīt′mənt) *n.* **1. a.** The act of indicting. **b.** The condition of being indicted. **2.** *Law.* A written statement charging a party with the commission of a crime or other offense, drawn up by a prosecuting attorney and found and presented by a grand jury.

In·dies (ĭn′dēz). *Abbr.* **Ind. 1.** See **East Indies. 2.** See **West Indies.**

in·dif·fer·ence (ĭn-dĭf′ər-əns, -dĭf′rəns) *n.* The state or quality of being indifferent.

in·dif·fer·en·cy (ĭn-dĭf′ər-ən-sē, -dĭf′rən-) *n. Archaic.* Indifference.

in·dif·fer·ent (ĭn-dĭf′ər-ənt, -dĭf′rənt) *adj.* **1.** Characterized by a lack of partiality; unbiased: *a properly indifferent jury.* **2.** Not mattering one way or the other. **3.** Having no marked feeling for or against. **4.** Having no particular interest in or concern for; apathetic: *indifferent to the sufferings of others.* **5.** Being neither too much nor too little; moderate. **6.** Being neither good nor bad; mediocre: *an indifferent performance.* **7.** Being neither right nor wrong. **8.** Not active or involved; neutral: *an indifferent chemical in a reaction.* **9.** *Biology.* Undifferentiated, as cells or tissue. [Middle English, from Old French, from Latin *indifferēns, indifferent-* : *in-,* not; see IN–[1] + *differēns,* different; see DIFFERENT.] **—in·dif′fer·ent·ly** *adv.*

SYNONYMS: *indifferent, unconcerned, incurious, detached, uninterested.* These adjectives mean marked by an absence of interest. *Indifferent* applies most broadly; it can suggest lack of partiality, bias, or preference or a lack of feeling one way or another: *"The universe is not hostile, nor yet is it friendly. It is simply indifferent"* (John H. Holmes). *Unconcerned* implies not only a lack of interest but also a lack of solicitude, feeling, concern, or care: *blithely unconcerned about his friend's plight. Incurious* stresses absence of intellectual inquisitiveness or natural curiosity: *strangely incurious about the causes of the political upheaval surrounding her. Detached* suggests absence of involvement together with an impersonal point of view: "[His] *maturity appears in the detached clear-sightedness with which he could observe his own character"* (David Cecil). *Uninterested* merely denotes lack of interest: *an uninterested spectator; an uninterested glance.* See also Synonyms at **average.**

in·dif·fer·ent·ism (ĭn-dĭf′ər-ən-tĭz′əm, -dĭf′rən-) *n.* The belief that all religions are of equal validity. **—in·dif′fer·ent·ist** *n.*

in·di·gen (ĭn′dĭ-jən, -jĕn′) also **in·di·gene** (-jən, -jēn′) *n.* One that is native or indigenous to an area. [French *indigène,* native, a native, from Latin *indigena.* See **gene-** in Appendix.]

in·di·gence (ĭn′dĭ-jəns) *n.* Poverty; neediness.

in·di·gene (ĭn′dĭ-jən, -jēn′) *n.* Variant of **indigen.**

in·dig·e·nous (ĭn-dĭj′ə-nəs) *adj.* **1.** Originating and growing or living in an area or environment. See Synonyms at **native. 2.** Intrinsic; innate. [From Latin *indigena,* a native. See INDIGEN.] **—in·dig′e·nous·ly** *adv.* **—in·dig′e·nous·ness** *n.*

in·di·gent (ĭn′dĭ-jənt) *adj.* **1.** Experiencing want or need; impoverished. See Synonyms at **poor. 2.** *Archaic.* Lacking or deficient. **—indigent** *n.* A needy or destitute person. [Middle English, from Old French, from Latin *indigēns, indigent-,* present participle of *indigēre,* to need : *indu-,* in; see **en** in Appendix + *egēre,* to lack.] **—in′di·gent·ly** *adv.*

in·di·gest·ed (ĭn′dī-jĕs′tĭd, -dĭ-) *adj.* **1.** Not digested; undigested: *indigested food.* **2.** *Archaic.* **a.** Not carefully thought over or considered. **b.** Formless or shapeless.

in·di·gest·i·ble (ĭn′dī-jĕs′tə-bəl, -dĭ-) *adj.* Difficult or impossible to digest: *an indigestible meal.* **—in′di·gest′i·bil′i·ty** *n.* **—in′di·gest′i·bly** *adv.*

in·di·ges·tion (ĭn′dī-jĕs′chən, -dĭ-) *n.* **1.** Inability to digest or difficulty in digesting something, especially food. **2.** Discomfort or illness resulting from this inability or difficulty.

In·di·gir·ka (ĭn′dĭ-gîr′kə). A river, about 1,789 km (1,112 mi) long, of northeast Russia flowing generally northward to the East Siberian Sea.

in·dign (ĭn-dīn′) *adj.* **1.** *Archaic.* Unworthy. **2.** *Obsolete.* Shameful; disgraceful. [Middle English *indigne,* from Old French, from Latin *indignus* : *in-,* not; see IN–[1] + *dignus,* worthy; see **dek-** in Appendix.]

in·dig·nant (ĭn-dĭg′nənt) *adj.* Characterized by or filled with indignation. See Synonyms at **angry.** [Latin *indignāns, indignant-,* present participle of *indignārī,* to be indignant, from *indignus,* unworthy. See INDIGN.] **—in·dig′nant·ly** *adv.*

in·dig·na·tion (ĭn′dĭg-nā′shən) *n.* Anger aroused by something unjust, mean, or unworthy. See Synonyms at **anger.** [Middle English *indignacioun,* from Old French *indignation,* from Latin *indignātiō, indignātiōn-,* from *indignātus,* past participle of *indignārī,* to regard as unworthy, from *indignus,* unworthy. See INDIGN.]

in·dig·ni·ty (ĭn-dĭg′nĭ-tē) *n., pl.* **-ties. 1.** Humiliating, degrading, or abusive treatment. **2.** A source of offense, as to a person's pride or sense of dignity; an affront. **3.** *Obsolete.* Lack of dignity or honor. [French *indignité,* from Old French, from Latin *indignitās,* from *indignus,* unworthy. See INDIGN.]

in·di·go (ĭn′dĭ-gō′) *n., pl.* **-gos** or **-goes. 1. a.** Any of various shrubs or herbs of the genus *Indigofera* in the pea family, having odd-pinnate leaves and usually red or purple flowers in axillary racemes. **b.** A blue dye obtained from these plants or produced synthetically. **2.** Any of several related plants, especially those of the genera *Amorpha* or *Baptisia.* **3.** *Abbr.* **ind.** *Color.* The hue of that portion of the visible spectrum lying between blue and violet, evoked in the human observer by radiant energy with wavelengths of approximately 420 to 450 nanometers; a dark blue to grayish purple blue. [Spanish *índigo* and Dutch *indigo* (from Portuguese *endego*), both from Latin *indicum,* from Greek *Indikon (pharmakon),* Indian (dye), from neuter of *Indikos,* of India, from *India,* India, from *Indos,* the Indus River, from Old Persian *Hindu.* See HINDI.] **—in′di·go′** *adj.*

indigo bunting *n.* A small common finch *(Passerina cyanea)* of North and Central America, the male of which has deep blue plumage.

indigo snake *n.* A nonvenomous bluish-black snake *(Drymarchon corais)* of the southern United States and northern Mexico.

indigo squill *n.* See **eastern camass.**

in·dig·o·tin (ĭn-dĭg′ə-tĭn, ĭn′dĭ-gō′-) *n.* A dark blue crystalline compound, $C_{16}H_{10}N_2O_2$, the principal coloring matter of indigo. [INDIGO + –IN.]

In·di·o (ĭn′dē-ō′). A city of southeast California east of Santa Ana. It is a resort and processing center. Population, 21,611.

in·di·rect (ĭn′dĭ-rĕkt′, -dī-) *adj.* **1.** Diverging from a direct course; roundabout. **2. a.** Not proceeding straight to the point or object. **b.** Not forthright and candid; devious. **3.** Not directly planned for; secondary: *indirect benefits.* **4.** Reporting the exact or approximate words of another with such changes as are necessary to bring the original statement into grammatical conformity with the sentence in which it is included: *indirect discourse.* **5.** *Logic.* Involving, relating to, or being the proof of a statement by the demonstration of the impossibility or absurdity of the statement's negation. **—in′di·rect′ly** *adv.* **—in′di·rect′ness** *n.*

SYNONYMS: *indirect, circuitous, roundabout.* These adjectives mean not leading by a direct or straight line or course to a destination. *Indirect* implies a deviation from the shortest route between starting point and destination: *Sometimes taking the indirect path saves time. Circuitous* suggests a twisting or winding and lengthy course: *We had to take a circuitous route because of an accident on the turnpike. Roundabout* implies taking a course that circles: *I chose a roundabout road to avoid the rush-hour traffic.* In their extended senses the terms are applied to something that is not open and straightforward; they sometimes imply an effort to evade or deceive: *"Persecution is a bad and indirect way to plant religion"* (Thomas Browne). *His explanation was circui-*

ă pat	oi boy
ā pay	ou out
âr care	o͝o took
ä father	o͞o boot
ĕ pet	ŭ cut
ē be	ûr urge
ĭ pit	th thin
ī pie	*th* this
îr pier	hw which
ŏ pot	zh vision
ō toe	ə about, item
ô paw	♦ regionalism

Stress marks: **′** (primary); ′ (secondary), as in **dictionary** (dĭk′shə-nĕr′ē)

tous and puzzling. "I heard in a roundabout way that she's going to marry an old neighbor of theirs" (Arthur S.M. Hutchinson).

---

in·di·rec·tion (ĭn′dĭ-rĕk′shən, -dī-) *n.* **1.** The quality or state of being indirect. **2.a.** Lack of straightforwardness; deviousness: *obtained their goal by subtle indirection.* **b.** A devious act or statement: *wouldn't give us a straight answer, only hints and indirections.* **3.** Lack of direction; aimlessness.

indirect lighting *n.* Illumination by reflected or diffused light.

indirect object *n. Grammar.* An object indirectly affected by the action of a verb, as *me* in *Sing me a song* and *the turtle* in *He feeds the turtle lettuce.*

indirect tax *n.* A tax, such as a sales tax or value-added tax, that is levied on goods or services rather than individuals and is ultimately paid by consumers in the form of higher prices.

in·dis·cern·i·ble (ĭn′dĭ-sûr′nə-bəl, -zûr′-) *adj.* Difficult or impossible to discern or perceive; imperceptible: *an indiscernible increase in temperature.* **—in′dis·cern′i·bly** *adv.*

in·dis·ci·pline (ĭn-dĭs′ə-plĭn) *n.* Lack of discipline or restraint. **—in·dis′ci·plined** *adj.*

in·dis·creet (ĭn′dĭ-skrēt′) *adj.* Lacking discretion; injudicious: *an indiscreet remark.* **—in′dis·creet′ly** *adv.* **—in′dis·creet′ness** *n.*

in·dis·crete (ĭn′dĭ-skrēt′) *adj.* Not divided or divisible into separate parts: *layers that were fused into an indiscrete mass.*

in·dis·cre·tion (ĭn′dĭ-skrĕsh′ən) *n.* **1.** Lack of discretion; injudiciousness. **2.** An indiscreet act or remark.

in·dis·crim·i·nate (ĭn′dĭ-skrĭm′ə-nĭt) *adj.* **1.a.** Not making or based on careful distinctions; unselective: *an indiscriminate shopper; indiscriminate taste in music.* **b.** Widespread; wholesale: *indiscriminate violence; the indiscriminate use of pesticides.* **2.** Random; haphazard: *an indiscriminate assortment of used books for sale.* **3.** Confused; chaotic: *the indiscriminate policies of the previous administration.* **4.** Unrestrained or wanton; profligate: *indiscriminate spending.* **—in′dis·crim′i·nate·ly** *adv.* **—in′dis·crim′i·nate·ness** *n.*

in·dis·crim·i·nat·ing (ĭn′dĭ-skrĭm′ə-nā′tĭng) *adj.* Not discriminating: *an indiscriminating theater audience.*

in·dis·crim·i·na·tion (ĭn′dĭ-skrĭm′ə-nā′shən) *n.* Lack of discrimination or judgment. **—in′dis·crim′i·na′tive** *adj.*

in·dis·pen·sa·ble (ĭn′dĭ-spĕn′sə-bəl) *adj.* **1.** Not to be dispensed with; essential. **2.** Obligatory; unavoidable: *the routine but indispensable ceremonies of state.* **—indispensable** *n.* One that is indispensable. **—in′dis·pen′sa·bil′i·ty, in′dis·pen′sa·ble·ness** *n.* **—in′dis·pen′sa·bly** *adv.*

SYNONYMS: *indispensable, essential, necessary, needful, requisite.* The central meaning shared by these adjectives is "pressingly needed": *foods indispensable to good nutrition; funds essential to the completion of the project; necessary tools and materials; provided them with all things needful; lacking the requisite qualifications for the position.*
ANTONYM: *dispensable.*

---

in·dis·pose (ĭn′dĭ-spōz′) *tr.v.* **-posed, -pos·ing, -pos·es.** **1.** To make averse; disincline. **2.** To cause to be or feel ill; sicken. **3.** To render unfit; disqualify.

in·dis·posed (ĭn′dĭ-spōzd′) *adj.* **1.** Mildly ill. **2.** Averse; disinclined: *was clearly indisposed to grant their request.*

in·dis·po·si·tion (ĭn-dĭs′pə-zĭsh′ən) *n.* **1.** Disinclination; unwillingness. **2.** A minor ailment.

in·dis·put·a·ble (ĭn′dĭ-spyo͞o′tə-bəl) *adj.* Beyond dispute or doubt; undeniable: *indisputable evidence.* **—in′dis·put′a·ble·ness** *n.* **—in′dis·put′a·bly** *adv.*

in·dis·sol·u·ble (ĭn′dĭ-sŏl′yə-bəl) *adj.* **1.** Permanent; binding: *an indissoluble contract; an indissoluble union.* **2.** Impossible to dissolve, disintegrate, or decompose: *an indissoluble compound.* **—in′dis·sol′u·bil′i·ty, in′dis·sol′u·ble·ness** *n.* **—in′dis·sol′u·bly** *adv.*

in·dis·tinct (ĭn′dĭ-stĭngkt′) *adj.* **1.** Not clearly or sharply delineated: *an indistinct pattern; indistinct shapes in the gloom.* **2.** Faint; dim: *indistinct stars.* **3.a.** Hazy, vague: *an indistinct memory; an indistinct notion of how to proceed.* **b.** Difficult to understand or make out: *indistinct speech.* **—in′dis·tinct′ly** *adv.* **—in′dis·tinct′ness** *n.*

in·dis·tinc·tive (ĭn′dĭ-stĭngk′tĭv) *adj.* Lacking distinguishing qualities; not distinctive. **—in′dis·tinc′tive·ly** *adv.* **—in′dis·tinc′tive·ness** *n.*

in·dis·tin·guish·a·ble (ĭn′dĭ-stĭng′gwĭ-shə-bəl) *adj.* **1.** Not distinguishable, especially: **a.** Impossible to differentiate or tell apart: *indistinguishable twins; a moth with markings that make it indistinguishable from its background.* **b.** Impossible to discern; imperceptible: *a sound that was indistinguishable to the human ear.* **2.** Difficult to understand or make out; vague: *indistinguishable speech.* **—in′dis·tin′guish·a·ble·ness, in′dis·tin′guish·a·bil′i·ty** *n.* **—in′dis·tin′guish·a·bly** *adv.*

in·dite (ĭn-dīt′) *tr.v.* **-dit·ed, -dit·ing, -dites.** **1.** To write; compose. **2.** To set down in writing. **3.** *Obsolete.* To dictate. [Middle English *enditen,* from Old French *enditer,* from Vulgar Latin **indictāre* : Latin *in-,* toward; see IN–[2] + Latin *dictāre,* to compose, to say habitually, frequentative of *dīcere,* to say; see **deik-** in Appendix.] **—in·dite′ment** *n.* **—in·dit′er** *n.*

in·di·um (ĭn′dē-əm) *n. Symbol* **In** A soft, malleable, silvery-white metallic element found primarily in ores of zinc and tin, used as a plating over silver in making mirrors, in plating aircraft bearings, and in compounds for making transistors. Atomic number 49; atomic weight 114.82; melting point 156.61°C; boiling point 2,000°C; specific gravity 7.31; valence 1, 2, 3. See table at **element.** [IND(IGO) + –IUM (so called from the indigo-blue lines in its spectrum).]

in·di·vid·u·al (ĭn′də-vĭj′o͞o-əl) *adj.* **1.a.** Of or relating to an individual, especially a single human being: *individual consciousness.* **b.** By or for one person: *individual work; an individual portion.* **2.** Existing as a distinct entity; separate: *individual drops of rain.* **3.a.** Marked by or expressing individuality; distinctive or individualistic: *an individual way of dressing.* **b.** Special; particular: *Each variety of melon has its individual flavor and texture.* **c.** Serving to identify or set apart: *"There was nothing individual about him except a deep scar . . . across his right cheek"* (Rebecca West). **—individual** *n.* **1.a.** A single human being considered apart from a society or community: *the rights of the individual.* **b.** A human being regarded as a unique personality: *always treated her clients as individuals.* **c.** A person distinguished from others by a special quality. **d.** *Usage Problem.* A person. **2.** A single animal or plant as distinguished from a species, community, or group. **3.** A member of a collection or set; a specimen. [Middle English, single, indivisible, from Old French, from Medieval Latin *indīviduālis,* from Latin *indīviduus* : *in-,* not; see IN–[1] + *dīviduus,* divisible (from *dīvidere,* to divide).] **—in′di·vid′u·al·ly** *adv.*

USAGE NOTE: The noun *individual* is used unexceptionably when it refers to an individual person as opposed to a larger social group or as distinguished from others by some special quality: *"This is not only a crisis of individuals, but also of a society"* (Raymond Williams). *She is a real individual.* Since the 19th century, however, there have been numerous critical objections to use of the word to refer simply to "a person" where no larger contrast is implied, as in *Two individuals were placed under arrest* or *The Mayor will make time for any individual who wants to talk to her.* In such contexts the words *person* and *people* will usually do the same semantic job with less affectation.

---

in·di·vid·u·al·ism (ĭn′də-vĭj′o͞o-ə-lĭz′əm) *n.* **1.a.** Belief in the primary importance of the individual and in the virtues of self-reliance and personal independence. **b.** Acts or an act based on this belief. **2.** A doctrine advocating freedom from government regulation in the pursuit of a person's economic or social goals. **3.** The doctrine that the interests of the individual should take precedence over the interests of the state or social group. **4.a.** The quality of being an individual; individuality. **b.** An individual characteristic; a quirk.

in·di·vid·u·al·ist (ĭn′də-vĭj′o͞o-ə-lĭst) *n.* **1.** One that asserts individuality by independence of thought and action. **2.** An advocate of individualism. **—in′di·vid′u·al·is′tic** *adj.* **—in′di·vid′u·al·is′ti·cal·ly** *adv.*

in·di·vid·u·al·i·ty (ĭn′də-vĭj′o͞o-ăl′ĭ-tē) *n., pl.* **-ties. 1.a.** The aggregate of qualities and characteristics that distinguish one person or thing from others; character: *choices that were intended to express his individuality; monotonous towns lacking in individuality.* **b.** An individual or distinguishing feature. **2.** The quality or state of being individual; singularity: *She was so absorbed by the movement that she lost all sense of individuality.* **3.** A single, distinct entity. **4.** *Archaic.* Indivisibility.

in·di·vid·u·al·ize (ĭn′də-vĭj′o͞o-ə-līz′) *tr.v.* **-ized, -iz·ing, -iz·es. 1.** To give individuality to. **2.** To consider or treat individually; particularize. **3.** To modify to suit the wishes or needs of a particular individual: *individualized the work schedules of all the physicians.* **—in′di·vid′u·al·i·za′tion** (-ə-lĭ-zā′shən) *n.*

in·di·vid·u·ate (ĭn′də-vĭj′o͞o-āt′) *tr.v.* **-at·ed, -at·ing, -ates. 1.** To give individuality to; individualize. **2.** To form into a separate, distinct entity.

in·di·vid·u·a·tion (ĭn′də-vĭj′o͞o-ā′shən) *n.* **1.** The act or process of individuating, especially the process by which social individuals become differentiated one from the other. **2.** The condition of being individuated; individuality. **3.** *Philosophy.* **a.** The development of the individual from the general or universal. **b.** The distinction or determination of the individual within the general or universal. **4.** In Jungian psychology, the gradual integration and unification of the self through the resolution of successive layers of psychological conflict. **5.** *Embryology.* Formation of distinct organs or structures through the interaction of adjacent tissues.

in·di·vis·i·ble (ĭn′də-vĭz′ə-bəl) *adj.* **1.** Incapable of undergoing division: *an indivisible union of states.* **2.** *Mathematics.* Incapable of being divided without a remainder: *The number 15 is indivisible by 7.* **—in′di·vis′i·ble·ness, in′di·vis′i·bil′i·ty** *n.* **—in′di·vis′i·bly** *adv.*

indn. *abbr.* Indication.

Indo– *pref.* **1.** India; East Indies: *Indochina.* **2.** Indo-European: *Indo-Hittite.* [Greek, from *Indos,* the Indus River. See INDIGO.]

In·do-Ar·y·an (ĭn′dō-âr′ē-ən, -ăr′-) *adj.* **1.** Of, relating to, or being any of the peoples of the Indian subcontinent who speak an Indo-European language. **2.** Indo-Iranian. **—Indo-Aryan** *n.*

ă pat	oi boy
ā pay	ou out
âr care	o͝o took
ä father	o͞o boot
ĕ pet	ŭ cut
ē be	ûr urge
ĭ pit	th thin
ī pie	*th* this
îr pier	hw which
ŏ pot	zh vision
ō toe	ə about, item
ô paw	♦ regionalism

Stress marks: **′** (primary); ′ (secondary), as in **dictionary** (dĭk′shə-nĕr′ē)

1. A member of any of the Indo-Aryan peoples. **2.** The Indo-Iranian languages.

In·do·chi·na (ĭn′dō-chī′nə). **1.** A peninsula of southeast Asia comprising Vietnam, Laos, Cambodia, Thailand, Burma, and the mainland territory of Malaysia. The area was influenced in early times by India (particularly the Hindu culture) and China. **2.** The former French colonial empire in southeast Asia, including much of the eastern part of the Indochinese peninsula. French influence extended from roughly 1862 to the fall of Dien Bien Phu (1954). **—In′do·chi′nese′** (-nēz′, -nēs′) *adj. & n.*

in·doc·ile (ĭn-dŏs′əl) *adj.* Resistant to authority or discipline; recalcitrant. **—in′do·cil′i·ty** (ĭn′dŏ-sĭl′ĭ-tē, -dō-) *n.*

In·do·cin (ĭn′də-sĭn). A trademark used for a preparation of indomethacin.

in·doc·tri·nate (ĭn-dŏk′trə-nāt′) *tr.v.* **-nat·ed, -nat·ing, -nates. 1.a.** To instruct in a body of doctrine or principles. **b.** To initiate by means of doctrinal instruction: *indoctrinate new members into the party.* **2.** To imbue with a partisan or ideological point of view: *a generation of children who had been indoctrinated against the values of their parents.* **—in·doc′tri·na′tion** *n.*

In·do-Eu·ro·pe·an (ĭn′dō-yo͝or′ə-pē′ən) *n.* **1.a.** A family of languages consisting of most of the languages of Europe as well as those of Iran, the Indian subcontinent, and other parts of Asia. **b.** Proto-Indo-European. Also called *Indo-Germanic.* **2.** A member of any of the peoples speaking an Indo-European language. **—In′do-Eu′ro·pe′an** *adj.*

In·do-Eu·ro·pe·an·ist (ĭn′dō-yo͝or′ə-pē′ə-nĭst) *n.* A student of Indo-European linguistics.

In·do-Ger·man·ic (ĭn′dō-jər-măn′ĭk) *n.* See **Indo-European** (sense 1). **—In′do-Ger·man′ic** *adj.*

In·do-Hit·tite (ĭn′dō-hĭt′īt′) *n.* **1.** A language family that includes Indo-European and Anatolian. **2.** The hypothetical parent language of Indo-European and Anatolian.

In·do-I·ra·ni·an (ĭn′dō-ĭ-rā′nē-ən) *n.* **1.** A subfamily of the Indo-European language family that comprises the Indic and Iranian branches. **2.** A member of any of the peoples speaking an Indo-Iranian language. Also called *Aryan.* **—In′do-I·ra′ni·an** *adj.*

in·dole (ĭn′dōl′) *n.* **1.** A white crystalline compound, C_8H_7N, obtained from coal tar or various plants and produced by the bacterial decomposition of tryptophan in the intestine. It is used in perfumery and as a reagent. **2.** Any of various derivatives of this compound. [IND(IGO) + -OLE.]

in·dole·a·ce·tic acid (ĭn′dō-lə-sē′tĭk) *n. Abbr.* **IAA** A plant hormone, $C_{10}H_9NO_2$, that stimulates growth.

in·dole·am·ine (ĭn′dō-lăm′ēn, ĭn′dō-lə-mēn′) *n.* Any of various derivatives of indole, such as serotonin, containing an amine group.

in·dole·bu·tyr·ic acid (ĭn′dōl-byo͞o-tĭr′ĭk) *n.* A synthetic compound, $C_{12}H_{13}NO_2$, used to regulate plant growth and development.

in·do·lence (ĭn′də-ləns) *n.* Habitual laziness; sloth.

in·do·lent (ĭn′də-lənt) *adj.* **1.a.** Disinclined to exert oneself; habitually lazy. See Synonyms at **lazy. b.** Conducive to inactivity or laziness; lethargic: *humid, indolent weather.* **2.a.** Causing little or no pain: *an indolent tumor.* **b.** Slow to heal, grow, or develop; inactive: *an indolent ulcer.* [Late Latin *indolēns, indolent-,* painless : Latin *in-,* not; see IN-[1] + Latin *dolēns,* present participle of *dolēre,* to feel pain.] **—in′do·lent·ly** *adv.*

in·do·meth·a·cin (ĭn′dō-mĕth′ə-sĭn) *n.* A nonsteroidal anti-inflammatory, antipyretic, and analgesic drug, $C_{19}H_{16}ClNO_4$, used especially in the treatment of some forms of arthritis. [IN-DO(LE) + METH- + AC(ETIC ACID) + -IN.]

in·dom·i·ta·ble (ĭn-dŏm′ĭ-tə-bəl) *adj.* Incapable of being overcome, subdued, or vanquished; unconquerable. [Late Latin *indomitābilis* : Latin *in-,* not; see IN-[1] + Latin *domitāre,* to tame, frequentative of *domāre,* to subdue; see **demə-** in Appendix.] **—in·dom′i·ta·bil′i·ty, in·dom′i·ta·ble·ness** *n.* **—in·dom′i·ta·bly** *adv.*

In·do·ne·sia (ĭn′də-nē′zhə, -shə, -dō-). Formerly **Dutch East In·dies** (dŭch; ĭn′dēz). A country of southeast Asia in the Malay Archipelago comprising Sumatra, Java, Sulawesi, the Moluccas, parts of Borneo, New Guinea, and Timor, and many smaller islands. First visited by Dutch navigators in 1595–1596, Indonesia was dominated by the Dutch East Indies Company from 1602 to 1798, when authority was turned over to the government of the Netherlands. In 1945 the territory declared its independence, which was finally achieved in 1949. Jakarta, on Java, is the capital and the largest city. Population, 147,490,298.

In·do·ne·sian (ĭn′də-nē′zhən, -shən) *n. Abbr.* **Indon. 1.** A native or inhabitant of Indonesia. **2.** A native or inhabitant of the Malay Archipelago. **3.** A subfamily of Austronesian that includes Malay, Tagalog, and the languages of Indonesia. **4.** A dialect of Malay that is the official language of Indonesia. In this sense, also called *Bahasa Indonesia.* **—Indonesian** *adj.* Of or relating to Indonesia, the Indonesians, or their languages or cultures.

in·door (ĭn′dôr′, -dōr′) *adj.* **1.** Of, situated in, or intended for use in the interior of a building: *an indoor pool; indoor paint.* **2.** Carried on within doors: *an indoor party; indoor gardening.*

in·door-out·door (ĭn′dôr′out′dôr′, ĭn′dōr′out′dōr′) *adj.* Designed or suitable for either indoor or outdoor use: *indoor-outdoor furniture; indoor-outdoor carpeting.*

in·doors (ĭn-dôrz′, -dōrz′) *adv.* In or into a house or building.

in·do·phen·ol (ĭn′dō-fē′nôl, -nōl, -nŏl) *n.* Any of various synthetic blue or green dyes. [IND(IGO) + PHENOL.]

In·dore (ĭn-dôr′, -dōr′). A city of west-central India north-northeast of Bombay. Founded in 1715, it is a commercial and industrial center. Population, 829,327.

in·dorse (ĭn-dôrs′) *v.* Variant of **endorse.**

In·dra (ĭn′drə) *n. Hinduism.* A principal Vedic deity associated with rain and thunder.

in·draft (ĭn′drăft′) *n.* **1.** An inward flow or current, as of air. **2.** A pulling or drawing inward.

in·drawn (ĭn′drôn′) *adj.* **1.** Drawn in: *an indrawn gasp.* **2.** Emotionally unresponsive or reserved; withdrawn: *"Her psychiatrist had pronounced her too tense and indrawn to endure a strange teacher"* (Louis Auchincloss).

in·dri (ĭn′drē) *n.* A large arboreal lemur *(Indri indri)* of Madagascar, having large eyes and a rudimentary tail. [Probably ultimately of Malagasy origin.]

in·du·bi·ta·ble (ĭn-do͞o′bĭ-tə-bəl, -dyo͞o′-) *adj.* Too apparent to be doubted; unquestionable. **—in·du′bi·ta·bly** *adv.*

in·duce (ĭn-do͞os′, -dyo͞os′) *tr.v.* **-duced, -duc·ing, -duc·es. 1.** To lead or move, as to a course of action, by influence or persuasion. See Synonyms at **persuade. 2.** To bring about or stimulate the occurrence of; cause: *a drug used to induce labor.* **3.** To infer by inductive reasoning. **4.** *Physics.* **a.** To produce (an electric current or a magnetic charge) by induction. **b.** To produce (radioactivity, for example) artificially by bombardment of a substance with neutrons, gamma rays, and other particles. **5.** *Biochemistry.* To initiate or increase the production of (an enzyme or other protein) at the level of genetic transcription. [Middle English *inducen,* from Old French *inducer,* from Latin *indūcere* : *in-,* in; see IN-[2] + *dūcere,* to lead; see **deuk-** in Appendix.] **—in·duc′i·ble** *adj.*

in·duce·ment (ĭn-do͞os′mənt, -dyo͞os′-) *n.* **1.** Something that helps bring about an action or a desired result; an incentive: *tax breaks intended as an inducement to greater reinvestment.* **2.** The act or process of inducing: *inducement of sleep.* **3.** *Law.* An introductory or background statement explaining the main allegations in a proceeding.

in·duc·er (ĭn-do͞o′sər, -dyo͞o′-) *n.* **1.** One that induces, especially a substance that is capable of activating specific genes within a cell. **2.** A part or structure in an embryo that influences the differentiation of another part.

in·duct (ĭn-dŭkt′) *tr.v.* **-duct·ed, -duct·ing, -ducts. 1.** To place ceremoniously or formally in an office or a position; install: *a service to induct the new president of the university.* **2.a.** To admit as a member; receive. **b.** To admit to military service: *a draftee waiting to be inducted into the army.* **c.** To introduce, as to new experience or knowledge; initiate: *She was inducted into the ways of the legal profession.* **3.** *Physics.* To induce. [Middle English *inducten,* from Latin *indūcere, induct-.* See INDUCE.]

in·duc·tance (ĭn-dŭk′təns) *n.* **1.** The property of an electric circuit by which an electromotive force is induced in it or in a nearby circuit by a change of current in either circuit. **2.** A circuit element, typically a conducting coil, in which electromotive force is generated by electromagnetic induction.

in·duct·ee (ĭn′dŭk-tē′) *n.* One who is inducted, especially a person newly admitted to military service.

in·duc·tion (ĭn-dŭk′shən) *n.* **1.a.** The act or an instance of inducting. **b.** A ceremony or formal act by which a person is inducted, as into office or military service. **2.** *Electricity.* **a.** The generation of electromotive force in a closed circuit by a varying magnetic flux through the circuit. **b.** The charging of an isolated conducting object by momentarily grounding it while a charged body is nearby. **3.** *Logic.* **a.** The process of deriving general principles from particular facts or instances. **b.** A conclusion reached by this process. **4.** *Mathematics.* A two-part method of proving a theorem involving a positive integral variable. First the theorem is verified for the smallest admissible value of the integer. Then it is proven that if the theorem is true for any value of the integer, it is true for the next greater value. The final proof contains the two parts. **5.** The act of inducing: *induction of sleep.* **6.** Presentation of material, such as facts or evidence, in support of an argument or a proposition. **7.** A preface or prologue, as to a literary composition, especially an early English play. **8.** *Biochemistry.* The process of initiating or increasing the production of an enzyme or other protein at the level of genetic transcription. **9.** *Embryology.* The change in form or shape caused by the action of one tissue of an embryo on adjacent tissues or parts, as by the diffusion of hormones or chemicals.

induction coil *n.* A transformer, often used in automotive ignition systems, in which an interrupted, low-voltage direct current in the primary is converted into an intermittent, high-voltage current in the secondary.

in·duc·tive (ĭn-dŭk′tĭv) *adj.* **1.** Of, relating to, or using logical induction: *inductive reasoning.* **2.** *Electricity.* Of or arising from inductance: *inductive reactance.* **3.** Causing or influencing; inducing. **4.** Introductory. **—in·duc′tive·ly** *adv.* **—in·duc′tive·ness** *n.*

inductive statistics *n. (used with a sing. verb).* The branch of statistics that deals with generalizations, predictions, estimations, and decisions from data initially presented.

in·duc·tor (ĭn-dŭk′tər) *n.* One that inducts, especially a device

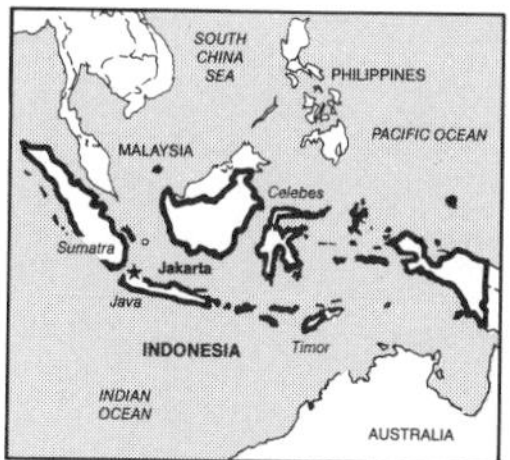

Indonesia

Indra
Riding his white elephant, Airavata

that functions by or introduces inductance into a circuit.

in·due (ĭn-do͞o′, -dyo͞o′) *v.* Variant of **endue.**

in·dulge (ĭn-dŭlj′) *v.* **-dulged, -dulg·ing, -dulg·es.** —*tr.* **1.** To yield to the desires and whims of, especially to an excessive degree; humor. **2.a.** To yield to; gratify: *indulge a craving for chocolate.* **b.** To allow (oneself) unrestrained gratification: *indulged herself with idle daydreams.* See Synonyms at **pamper. 3.** To grant an ecclesiastical indulgence or dispensation to. —*intr.* **1.** To indulge oneself. **2.** To engage or take part, especially freely or avidly: *indulged in outrageous behavior; indulged in all the latest fads.* [Latin *indulgēre.*] —**in·dulg′er** *n.*

in·dul·gence (ĭn-dŭl′jəns) *n.* **1.a.** The act or an instance of indulging; gratification: *indulgence of every whim.* **b.** The state of being indulgent. **2.a.** The act of indulging in something: *indulgence in irresponsible behavior.* **b.** Something indulged in: *Sports cars are an expensive indulgence.* **3.** Liberal or lenient treatment; tolerance: *treated their grandchildren with fond indulgence.* **4.** Self-indulgence: *a life of wealth and indulgence.* **5.a.** Something granted as a favor or privilege. **b.** Permission to extend the time of payment or performance. **c.** Patient attention: *I beg your indulgence for just a few minutes.* **6.** *Roman Catholic Church.* The remission of temporal punishment still due for a sin that has been sacramentally absolved. —**indulgence** *tr.v.* **-genced, -genc·ing, -genc·es.** *Roman Catholic Church.* To attach an indulgence to.

in·dul·gent (ĭn-dŭl′jənt) *adj.* Showing, characterized by, or given to indulgence; lenient: *indulgent grandparents.* —**in·dul′gent·ly** *adv.*

in·dult (ĭn-dŭlt′) *n.* *Roman Catholic Church.* A faculty granted by the pope to deviate from the common law of the Church. [Middle English, from Medieval Latin *indultum,* from Late Latin, concession, gift, from Latin *indultum,* neuter past participle of *indulgēre,* to be kind.]

in·du·ment (ĭn′də-mənt, -dyə-) also **in·du·men·tum** (ĭn′do͞o-mĕn′təm, -dyo͞o-) *n.* A covering of fine hairs or scales. [Latin, garment, from *induere,* to put a garment on, from *indu-,* in. See INDUSTRY.]

in·du·pli·cate (ĭn-do͞o′plĭ-kĭt, -dyo͞o′-) *adj.* *Botany.* Having the edges folded or turned inward.

in·du·rate (ĭn′də-rāt′, -dyə-) *v.* **-rat·ed, -rat·ing, -rates.** —*tr.* **1.** To make hard; harden: *soil that had been indurated by extremes of climate.* **2.** To inure, as to hardship or ridicule. **3.** To make callous or obdurate: *"It is the curse of revolutionary calamities to indurate the heart"* (Helen Maria Williams). —*intr.* **1.** To grow hard; harden. **2.** To become firmly fixed or established. —**indurate** (ĭn′do͞o-rĭt, -dyə-) *adj.* Hardened; obstinate; unfeeling. [Latin *indūrāre, indūrāt-* : *in-,* intensive pref.; see IN–[2] + *dūrus,* hard; see **deru-** in Appendix.] —**in′du·ra′tive** *adj.*

in·du·ra·tion (ĭn′də-rā′shən, -dyə-) *n.* **1.** The quality or condition of being hardened. **2.** The act or process of becoming hardened. **3.** *Pathology.* The hardening of a normally soft tissue or organ, especially the skin, because of inflammation, infiltration of a neoplasm, or an accumulation of blood.

In·dus[1] (ĭn′dəs). A river of south-central Asia rising in southwest Tibet and flowing about 3,057 km (1,900 mi) northwest through northern India and southwest through Pakistan to the Arabian Sea. Its valley was the site of an advanced civilization lasting c. 2500 to 1500 B.C.

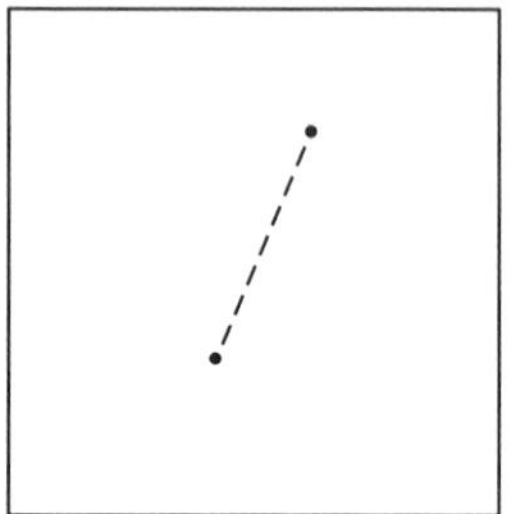

Indus[2]

In·dus[2] (ĭn′dəs) *n.* A constellation in the Southern Hemisphere near Tucana and Pavo. Also called *Indian.* [Latin *Indus,* an Indian, from Greek *Indos,* the Indus River, an Indian. See INDIGO.]

indus. *abbr.* Industrial; industry.

in·du·si·um (ĭn-do͞o′zē-əm, -zhē-, -dyo͞o′-) *n., pl.* **-si·a** (-zē-ə, -zhē-ə). An enclosing membrane, as that covering the sorus of a fern. [Latin, tunic, perhaps alteration of Greek *endusis,* dress, from *enduein,* sink into, to put on : *en-,* in; see EN–[2] + *duein,* to sink.]

in·dus·tri·al (ĭn-dŭs′trē-əl) *adj.* *Abbr.* **indus., ind. 1.** Of, relating to, or resulting from industry: *industrial development; industrial pollution.* **2.** Having highly developed industries: *an industrial nation.* **3.** Employed, required, or used in industry: *industrial workers; industrial diamonds.* —**industrial** *n.* **1.** A firm engaged in industry. **2.** A stock or bond issued by an industrial enterprise. **3.** A person employed in industry. —**in·dus′tri·al·ly** *adv.*

industrial action *n.* *Chiefly British.* A job action.

industrial arts *n.* *(used with a sing. verb).* A subject of study aimed at developing the manual and technical skills required to work with tools and machinery.

industrial disease *n.* Occupational disease.

industrial engineering *n.* *Abbr.* **IE, I.E.** The branch of engineering that is concerned with the efficient production of industrial goods as affected by elements such as plant and procedural design, the management of materials and energy, and the integration of workers within the overall system. —**industrial engineer** *n.*

in·dus·tri·al·ism (ĭn-dŭs′trē-ə-lĭz′əm) *n.* An economic and social system based on the development of large-scale industries and marked by the production of large quantities of inexpensive manufactured goods and the concentration of employment in urban factories.

in·dus·tri·al·ist (ĭ-dŭs′trē-ə-lĭst) *n.* One who owns, directs, or has a substantial financial interest in an industrial enterprise.

in·dus·tri·al·ize (ĭn-dŭs′trē-ə-līz′) *v.* **-ized, -iz·ing, -iz·es.** —*tr.* **1.** To develop industry in (a country or society, for example). **2.** To organize (the production of something) as an industry. —*intr.* To become industrial. —**in·dus′tri·al·i·za′tion** (-ə-lĭ-zā′shən) *n.*

industrial park *n.* An area usually located on the outskirts of a city and zoned for a group of industries and businesses.

industrial psychology *n.* The branch of applied psychology that is concerned with efficient management of an industrial labor force and especially with problems encountered by workers in a mechanized environment. —**industrial psychologist** *n.*

industrial relations *pl.n.* Relations between the management of an industrial enterprise and its employees.

industrial revolution also **Industrial Revolution** *n.* The complex of radical socioeconomic changes, such as the ones that took place in England in the late 18th century, which are brought about when extensive mechanization of production systems results in a shift from home-based hand manufacturing to large-scale factory production.

industrial union *n.* A labor union to which all the workers of a particular industry can belong regardless of their occupation or trade.

in·dus·tri·ous (ĭn-dŭs′trē-əs) *adj.* **1.** Assiduous in work or study; diligent. See Synonyms at **busy. 2.** *Obsolete.* Skillful; clever. —**in·dus′tri·ous·ly** *adv.* —**in·dus′tri·ous·ness** *n.*

in·dus·try (ĭn′də-strē) *n., pl.* **-tries.** *Abbr.* **indus., ind. 1.** Commercial production and sale of goods. **2.** A specific branch of manufacture and trade: *the textile industry.* See Synonyms at **business. 3.** The sector of an economy made up of manufacturing enterprises: *government regulation of industry.* **4.** Industrial management. **5.** Energetic devotion to a task or an endeavor; diligence: *demonstrated great intelligence and industry as a prosecutor.* **6.** Ongoing work or study associated with a specified subject or figure: *the Civil War industry; the Hemingway industry.* [Middle English *industrie,* skill, from Old French, from Latin *industria,* diligence, from feminine of *industrius,* diligent. See **ster-**[2] in Appendix.]

WORD HISTORY: A clear indication of the way in which human effort has been harnessed as a force for the commercial production of goods and services is the change in meaning of the word *industry.* Coming from the Latin word *industria,* meaning "diligent activity directed to some purpose," and its descendant, Old French *industrie,* with the senses "activity," "ability," and "a trade or occupation," our word (first recorded in 1475) originally meant "skill," "a device," and "diligence" as well as "a trade." As more and more human effort over the course of the Industrial Revolution became involved in producing goods and services for sale, the last sense of *industry* as well as the slightly newer sense "systematic work or habitual employment" grew in importance, to a large extent taking over the word. We can even speak now of the Shakespeare industry, rather like the garment industry. The sense "diligence, assiduity," lives on, however, perhaps even to survive industry itself.

in·dus·try·wide (ĭn′də-strē-wīd′) *adv. & adj.* Throughout an entire industry: *sales that have decreased industrywide; industrywide cooperation.*

in·dwell (ĭn-dwĕl′) *v.* **-dwelt** (-dwĕlt′), **-dwell·ing, -dwells.** —*intr.* **1.** To exist as an animating or divine inner spirit, force, or principle. **2.** To be located or implanted inside something. —*tr.* To inhabit or reside within as such a spirit, force, or principle. —**in′dwell′er** *n.*

In·dy (ăn′dē, ăN-dē′), **(Paul Marie Théodore) Vincent d′.** 1851–1931. French composer who was a founder (1894) and director of the Schola Cantorum in Paris.

–ine[1] *suff.* **1.** Of or relating to: *Benedictine.* **2.** Made of; resembling: *opaline.* [Middle English *-in, -ine,* from Old French, from Latin *-īnus, -īna,* adj. suff., and from Latin *-inus* (from Greek *-inos,* adj. suff.).]

–ine[2] *suff.* **1.** Also **-in.** A chemical substance, especially: **a.** Halogen: *bromine.* **b.** Basic compound: *amine.* **c.** Alkaloid: *quinine.* **2.** Amino acid: *glycine.* **3.** A mixture of compounds: *gasoline.* **4.** Commercial material: *glassine.* [Ultimately from Latin *-īnus* and *-inus,* adj. suffixes; see –INE[1].]

in·e·bri·ant (ĭn-ē′brē-ənt) *adj.* Serving to intoxicate. —**inebriant** *n.* An intoxicant.

in·e·bri·ate (ĭn-ē′brē-āt′) *tr.v.* **-at·ed, -at·ing, -ates. 1.** To make drunk; intoxicate. **2.** To exhilarate or stupefy as if with alcohol. —**inebriate** (-ĭt) *adj.* Intoxicated. —**inebriate** (-ĭt) *n.* An intoxicated person. [Latin *inēbriāre, inēbriāt-* : *in-,* intensive pref.; see IN–[2] + *ēbriāre,* to intoxicate (from *ēbrius,* drunk; see **ēgʷh-** in Appendix).] —**in·e′bri·a′tion** *n.*

in·e·bri·at·ed (ĭn-ē′brē-ā′tĭd) *adj.* Exhilarated or stupefied by or as if by alcohol; intoxicated.

in·e·bri·e·ty (ĭn′ĭ-brī′ĭ-tē) *n.* Intoxication; drunkenness.

in·ed·i·ble (ĭn-ĕd′ə-bəl) *adj.* Unfit to be eaten; not edible. —**in·ed′i·bil′i·ty** *n.* —**in·ed′i·bly** *adv.*

in·ed·it·ed (ĭn-ĕd′ĭ-tĭd) *adj.* **1.** Not edited. **2.** Not published.

in·ed·u·ca·ble (ĭn-ĕj′ə-kə-bəl) *adj.* Incapable of being educated. —**in·ed′u·ca·bil′i·ty** *n.*

in·ef·fa·ble (ĭn-ĕf′ə-bəl) *adj.* **1.** Incapable of being expressed; indescribable or unutterable. See Synonyms at **unspeak-**

able. 2. Not to be uttered; taboo: *the ineffable name of the Deity.* [Middle English, from Old French, from Latin *ineffābilis* : *in-*, not; see IN–[1] + *effābilis*, utterable (from *effārī*, to utter : *ex-*, ex- + *fārī*, to speak; see **bhā-**[2] in Appendix).] **—in·ef′fa·bil′i·ty, in·ef′fa·ble·ness** *n.* **—in·ef′fa·bly** *adv.*

in·ef·face·a·ble (ĭn′ĭ-fā′sə-bəl) *adj.* Impossible to efface; indelible. **—in′ef·face′a·bil′i·ty** *n.* **—in′ef·face′a·bly** *adv.*

in·ef·fec·tive (ĭn′ĭ-fĕk′tĭv) *adj.* **1.** Not producing an intended effect; ineffectual: *an ineffective plea.* **2.** Inadequate; incompetent: *an ineffective teacher.* **—in′ef·fec′tive·ly** *adv.* **—in′ef·fec′tive·ness** *n.*

in·ef·fec·tu·al (ĭn′ĭ-fĕk′cho͞o-əl) *adj.* **1.a.** Insufficient to produce a desired effect: *an ineffectual effort to block the legislation.* **b.** Useless; worthless: *an ineffectual treatment for cancer.* **2.** Lacking forcefulness or effectiveness; weak: *an ineffectual ruler.* **—in′ef·fec′tu·al′i·ty** (-ăl′ĭ-tē), **in′ef·fec′tu·al·ness** *n.* **—in′ef·fec′tu·al·ly** *adv.*

in·ef·fi·ca·cious (ĭn-ĕf′ĭ-kā′shəs) *adj.* Not capable of producing a desired effect or result; ineffective. **—in·ef′fi·ca′cious·ly** *adv.* **—in·ef′fi·ca′cious·ness** *n.*

in·ef·fi·ca·cy (ĭn-ĕf′ĭ-kə-sē) *n.* The state or quality of being incapable of producing a desired effect or result.

in·ef·fi·cien·cy (ĭn′ĭ-fĭsh′ən-sē) *n., pl.* **-cies. 1.** The quality, condition, or fact of being inefficient. **2.** An inefficient act, design, or procedure: *pointed out certain inefficiencies in the shipping operation.*

in·ef·fi·cient (ĭn′ĭ-fĭsh′ənt) *adj.* **1.** Not efficient, as: **a.** Lacking the ability or skill to perform effectively; incompetent: *an inefficient worker.* **b.** Not producing the intended result; ineffective: *an inefficient campaign against illegal drugs.* **2.** Wasteful of time, energy, or materials: *an inefficient design; outdated and inefficient methods.* **—in′ef·fi′cient·ly** *adv.*

in·e·gal·i·tar·i·an (ĭn′ĭ-găl′ĭ-târ′ē-ən) *adj.* Marked by or accepting of social, economic, or political inequality.

in·e·las·tic (ĭn′ĭ-lăs′tĭk) *adj.* Lacking elasticity; unyielding or unadaptable. See Synonyms at **stiff. —in′e·las·tic′i·ty** (-ĭ-lă-stĭs′ĭ-tē) *n.*

inelastic collision *n.* A collision between two particles in which part of their kinetic energy is transformed to another form of energy. The total amount of energy remains the same.

inelastic scattering *n.* The scattering of particles resulting from inelastic collision.

in·el·e·gance (ĭn-ĕl′ĭ-gəns) *n.* Lack of refinement or polish.

in·el·e·gant (ĭn-ĕl′ĭ-gənt) *adj.* Lacking refinement or polish; not elegant. **—in·el′e·gant·ly** *adv.*

in·el·i·gi·ble (ĭn-ĕl′ĭ-jə-bəl) *adj.* **1.** Disqualified by law, rule, or provision: *ineligible to run for office; ineligible for retirement benefits.* **2.** Unworthy of being chosen; unfit: *considered her ineligible for the job.* **—ineligible** *n.* One that is not eligible. **—in·el′i·gi·bil′i·ty** *n.* **—in·el′i·gi·bly** *adv.*

in·el·o·quent (ĭn-ĕl′ə-kwənt) *adj.* Lacking or displaying a lack of eloquence. **—in·el′o·quence** *n.* **—in·el′o·quent·ly** *adv.*

in·e·luc·ta·ble (ĭn′ĭ-lŭk′tə-bəl) *adj.* Not to be avoided or escaped; inevitable: *"Those war plans rested on a belief in the ineluctable superiority of the offense over the defense"* (Jack Beatty). [Latin *inēluctābilis* : *in-*, not; see IN–[1] + *ēluctābilis*, penetrable (from *ēluctārī*, to struggle out of : *ex-*, ex- + *luctārī*, to struggle).] **—in′e·luc′ta·bil′i·ty** *n.* **—in′e·luc′ta·bly** *adv.*

in·ept (ĭn-ĕpt′) *adj.* **1.** Not apt or fitting; inappropriate. See Synonyms at **awkward. 2.a.** Displaying a lack of judgment, sense, or reason; foolish: *an inept remark.* **b.** Bungling or clumsy; incompetent: *inept handling of the account.* [Latin *ineptus* : *in-*, not; see IN–[1] + *aptus*, suitable; see APT.] **—in·ept′ly** *adv.* **—in·ept′ness, in·ep′ti·tude′** (-ĕp′tĭ-to͞od′, -tyo͞od′) *n.*

in·e·qual·i·ty (ĭn′ĭ-kwŏl′ĭ-tē) *n., pl.* **-ties. 1.a.** The condition of being unequal. **b.** An instance of being unequal. **2.a.** Lack of equality, as of opportunity, treatment, or status. **b.** Social or economic disparity: *the growing inequality between rich and poor.* **3.** Lack of smoothness or regularity; unevenness. **4.** Variability; changeability. **5.** *Mathematics.* An algebraic expression showing that a quantity is greater than or less than another quantity.

in·eq·ui·ta·ble (ĭn-ĕk′wĭ-tə-bəl) *adj.* Not equitable; unfair. **—in·eq′ui·ta·bly** *adv.*

in·eq·ui·ty (ĭn-ĕk′wĭ-tē) *n., pl.* **-ties. 1.** Injustice; unfairness. **2.** An instance of injustice or unfairness: *discerned some inequities in the criminal justice system.*

in·e·rad·i·ca·ble (ĭn′ĭ-răd′ĭ-kə-bəl) *adj.* Impossible to eradicate or be eradicated: *ineradicable stains.* **—in′e·rad′i·ca·bly** *adv.*

in·er·ran·cy (ĭn-ĕr′ən-sē) *n.* Freedom from error or untruths; infallibility: *belief in the inerrancy of the Scriptures.*

in·er·rant (ĭn-ĕr′ənt) *adj.* **1.** Incapable of erring; infallible. **2.** Containing no errors.

in·er·ran·tism (ĭn-ĕr′ən-tiz′əm) *n.* Belief in the inerrancy or literal truth of a particular writing or document. **—in·er′ran·tist′** *adj. & n.*

in·ert (ĭn-ûrt′) *adj.* **1.** Unable to move or act. **2.** Sluggish in action or motion; lethargic. See Synonyms at **inactive. 3.** *Chemistry.* Not readily reactive with other elements; forming few or no compounds. [Latin *iners*, *inert-* : *in-*, not; see IN–[1] + *ars*, skill; see **ar-** in Appendix.] **—in·ert′ly** *adv.* **—in·ert′ness** *n.*

inert gas *n.* See **noble gas.**

in·er·tia (ĭ-nûr′shə) *n.* **1.** *Physics.* The tendency of a body to resist acceleration; the tendency of a body at rest to remain at rest or of a body in motion to stay in motion in a straight line unless acted on by an outside force. **2.** Resistance or disinclination to motion, action, or change: *the inertia of an entrenched bureaucracy.* [Latin, idleness, from *iners*, *inert-*, inert. See INERT.] **—in·er′tial** *adj.* **—in·er′tial·ly** *adv.*

inertial frame *n.* A coordinate system in which the Newtonian law of motion is valid, specifically one in which a mass m subjected to a force F moves in accordance with the equation $F = ma$, where a is the acceleration.

inertial guidance *n.* Guidance of an aircraft or a spacecraft in which gyroscopic and accelerometer data are used by a computer to maintain a predetermined course.

inertial platform *n.* The sensing devices used in inertial guidance and the platform on which they are mounted.

in·es·cap·a·ble (ĭn′ĭ-skā′pə-bəl) *adj.* Impossible to escape or avoid; inevitable: *inescapable consequences.* See Synonyms at **certain. —in′es·cap′a·bly** *adv.*

in·es·sen·tial (ĭn′ĭ-sĕn′shəl) *adj.* **1.** Not essential; unessential. **2.** Without essence. **—inessential** *n.* Something that is not essential. **—in′es·sen′ti·al′i·ty** (-shē-ăl′ĭ-tē) *n.*

in·es·ti·ma·ble (ĭn-ĕs′tə-mə-bəl) *adj.* **1.** Impossible to estimate or compute: *inestimable damage.* See Synonyms at **incalculable. 2.** Of immeasurable value or worth; invaluable: *"shared all the inestimable advantages of being wealthy, good-looking, confident and intelligent"* (Doris Kearns Goodwin). **—in·es′ti·ma·bly** *adv.*

in·ev·i·ta·ble (ĭn-ĕv′ĭ-tə-bəl) *adj.* **1.** Impossible to avoid or prevent. See Synonyms at **certain. 2.** Invariably occurring or appearing; predictable: *the inevitable changes of the seasons.* **—in·ev′i·ta·bil′i·ty** *n.* **—in·ev′i·ta·bly** *adv.*

in·ex·act (ĭn′ĭg-zăkt′) *adj.* **1.** Not strictly accurate or precise; not exact: *an inexact quotation; an inexact description of what had taken place.* **2.** Not rigorous or meticulous: *an inexact mind; an inexact method.* **—in′ex·act′ly** *adv.* **—in′ex·act′ness** *n.*

in·ex·act·i·tude (ĭn′ĭg-zăk′tĭ-to͞od′, -tyo͞od′) *n.* Lack of exactitude; inexactness.

in·ex·cus·a·ble (ĭn′ĭk-skyo͞o′zə-bəl) *adj.* Impossible to excuse or justify; unpardonable: *inexcusable behavior.* **—in′ex·cus′a·ble·ness** *n.* **—in′ex·cus′a·bly** *adv.*

in·ex·haust·i·ble (ĭn′ĭg-zô′stə-bəl) *adj.* **1.** That cannot be entirely consumed or used up: *an inexhaustible supply of coal.* **2.** Never wearying; tireless: *an inexhaustible campaigner.* **—in′ex·haust′i·bil′i·ty, in′ex·haust′i·ble·ness** *n.* **—in′ex·haust′i·bly** *adv.*

in·ex·is·tent (ĭn′ĭg-zĭs′tənt) *adj.* Having no existence; nonexistent. **—in′ex·is′tence** *n.*

in·ex·o·ra·ble (ĭn-ĕk′sər-ə-bəl) *adj.* Not capable of being persuaded by entreaty; relentless: *an inexorable opponent; a feeling of inexorable doom.* See Synonyms at **inflexible.** [Latin *inexōrābilis* : *in-*, not; see IN–[1] + *exōrābilis*, pliant (from *exōrāre*, to prevail upon : *ex-*, intensive pref.; see EX– + *ōrāre*, to argue).] **—in·ex′o·ra·bil′i·ty, in·ex′o·ra·ble·ness** *n.* **—in·ex′o·ra·bly** *adv.*

in·ex·pe·di·ent (ĭn′ĭk-spē′dē-ənt) *adj.* Not expedient; inadvisable: *an inexpedient tactic.* **—in′ex·pe′di·ence, in′ex·pe′di·en·cy** *n.* **—in′ex·pe′di·ent·ly** *adv.*

in·ex·pen·sive (ĭn′ĭk-spĕn′sĭv) *adj.* Not high in price; cheap. **—in′ex·pen′sive·ly** *adv.* **—in′ex·pen′sive·ness** *n.*

in·ex·pe·ri·ence (ĭn′ĭk-spîr′ē-əns) *n.* **1.** Lack of experience. **2.** Lack of the knowledge gained from experience. **—in′ex·pe′ri·enced** *adj.*

in·ex·pert (ĭn-ĕk′spûrt′) *adj.* Not expert; unskilled. **—in·ex′pert′ly** *adv.* **—in·ex′pert′ness** *n.*

in·ex·pi·a·ble (ĭn-ĕk′spē-ə-bəl) *adj.* **1.** Impossible to expiate or atone for: *inexpiable crimes.* **2.** *Obsolete.* Implacable. **—in·ex′pi·a·bly** *adv.*

in·ex·plain·a·ble (ĭn′ĭk-splā′nə-bəl) *adj.* Difficult or impossible to explain; inexplicable. **—in′ex·plain′a·bly** *adv.*

in·ex·pli·ca·ble (ĭn-ĕk′splĭ-kə-bəl, ĭn′ĭk-splĭk′ə-bəl) *adj.* Difficult or impossible to explain or account for: *left the house at three in the morning for inexplicable reasons.* **—in·ex′pli·ca·bil′i·ty, in·ex′pli·ca·ble·ness** *n.* **—in·ex′pli·ca·bly** *adv.*

in·ex·plic·it (ĭn′ĭk-splĭs′ĭt) *adj.* Not explicit; indefinite.

in·ex·press·i·ble (ĭn′ĭk-sprĕs′ə-bəl) *adj.* Impossible to express; indescribable: *inexpressible grief.* See Synonyms at **unspeakable. —in′ex·press′i·bil′i·ty, in′ex·press′i·ble·ness** *n.* **—in′ex·press′i·bly** *adv.*

in·ex·pres·sive (ĭn′ĭk-sprĕs′ĭv) *adj.* **1.** Lacking expression; blank: *an inexpressive stare.* **2.** Devoid of emotion or style; flat or dull: *an inexpressive performance of the aria.* **—in′ex·pres′sive·ly** *adv.* **—in′ex·pres′sive·ness** *n.*

in·ex·pug·na·ble (ĭn′ĭk-spŭg′nə-bəl, -spyo͞o′nə-) *adj.* **1.** Impossible to overcome or overthrow by force. **2.** Impossible to put aside or drive away: *inexpugnable dislike.* [Middle English, from Old French, from Latin *inexpugnābilis* : *in-*, not; see IN–[1] + *expugnābilis*, capable of being overcome (from *expugnāre* : *ex-*, completely; see EX– + *pugnāre*, to fight; see IMPUGN).] **—in′ex·pug′na·bil′i·ty** *n.* **—in′ex·pug′na·bly** *adv.*

ă pat	oi boy
ā pay	ou out
âr care	o͝o took
ä father	o͞o boot
ĕ pet	ŭ cut
ē be	ûr urge
ĭ pit	th thin
ī pie	*th* this
îr pier	hw which
ŏ pot	zh vision
ō toe	ə about, item
ô paw	♦ regionalism

Stress marks: ′ (primary); ′ (secondary), as in **dictionary** (dĭk′shə-nĕr′ē)

in·ex·ten·si·ble (ĭn′ĭk-stĕn′sə-bəl) *adj.* Not extensible: *an inextensible antenna.*

in ex·ten·so (ĭn ĕk-stĕn′sō) *adv.* At full length: *an article reprinted in extenso in a later collection.* [Latin : *in,* at + *extēnsō,* ablative of *extēnsus,* stretch.]

in·ex·tin·guish·a·ble (ĭn′ĭk-stĭng′gwĭ-shə-bəl) *adj.* Difficult or impossible to extinguish: *an inextinguishable flame; an inextinguishable faith.* **—in′ex·tin′guish·a·bly** *adv.*

in·ex·tir·pa·ble (ĭn′ĭk-stûr′pə-bəl) *adj.* Difficult or impossible to eradicate or destroy.

in ex·tre·mis (ĭn ĕk-strē′mĭs) *adv.* **1.** At the point of death. **2.** In grave or extreme circumstances. [Latin : *in,* in + *extrēmīs,* ablative pl. of *extrēmus,* extreme.]

in·ex·tri·ca·ble (ĭn-ĕk′strĭ-kə-bəl, ĭn′ĭk-strĭk′ə-bəl) *adj.* **1.a.** So intricate or entangled as to make escape impossible: *an inextricable maze; an inextricable web of deceit.* **b.** Difficult or impossible to disentangle or untie: *an inextricable tangle of threads.* **c.** Too involved or complicated to solve: *an inextricable problem.* **2.** Unavoidable; inescapable: *bound together by an inextricable fate.* **—in·ex′tri·ca·bil′i·ty, in·ex′tri·ca·ble·ness** *n.* **—in·ex′tri·ca·bly** *adv.*

INF *abbr.* Intermediate-range nuclear forces.

inf. *abbr.* **1.** Also **Inf.** Infantry. **2.** Inferior. **3.** Infinitive. **4.** Infinity. **5.** Information.

in·fal·li·ble (ĭn-făl′ə-bəl) *adj.* **1.** Incapable of erring: *an infallible guide; an infallible source of information.* **2.** Incapable of failing; certain: *an infallible antidote; an infallible rule.* **3.** *Roman Catholic Church.* Incapable of error in expounding doctrine on faith or morals. [Middle English, from Medieval Latin *īnfallibilis* : Latin *in-,* not; see IN–[1] + Medieval Latin *fallibilis,* fallible; see FALLIBLE.] **—in·fal′li·bil′i·ty, in·fal′li·ble·ness** *n.* **—in·fal′li·bly** *adv.*

in·fa·mous (ĭn′fə-məs) *adj.* **1.** Having an exceedingly bad reputation; notorious. **2.** Causing or deserving infamy; heinous: *an infamous deed.* **3.** *Law.* **a.** Punishable by severe measures, such as death, long imprisonment, or loss of civil rights. **b.** Convicted of a crime, such as treason or felony, that carries such a punishment. [Middle English *infamis,* from Latin *īnfāmis* : *in-,* not; see IN–[1] + *fāma,* renown, fame; see **bhā-**[2] in Appendix.] **—in′fa·mous·ly** *adv.* **—in′fa·mous·ness** *n.*

in·fa·my (ĭn′fə-mē) *n., pl.* **-mies. 1.** Evil fame or reputation. **2.** The condition of being infamous. See Synonyms at **disgrace. 3.** An evil or criminal act that is publicly known. [Middle English *infamie,* dishonor, from Old French, from Latin *īnfāmia,* from *īnfāmis,* infamous. See INFAMOUS.]

in·fan·cy (ĭn′fən-sē) *n., pl.* **-cies. 1.** The earliest period of childhood, especially before the ability to walk has been acquired. **2.** The state of being an infant. **3.** An early stage of existence: *Space exploration is still in its infancy.* **4.** *Law.* The state or period of being a minor.

in·fant (ĭn′fənt) *n.* **1.** A child in the earliest period of life, especially before he or she can walk. **2.** *Law.* A person under the legal age of majority; a minor. **—infant** *adj.* **1.** Of or being in infancy. **2.** Intended for infants or young children. **3.** Newly begun or formed: *an infant enterprise.* [Middle English, from Old French *enfant,* from Latin *īnfāns, īnfant-,* from *īnfāns,* not able to speak, young : *in-,* not; see IN–[1] + *fāns,* present participle of *fārī,* to speak; see **bhā-**[2] in Appendix.]

WORD HISTORY: Anyone who has ever responded to the cries of a howling infant may find it difficult to believe the etymology of the word *infant.* The source of our word is the Latin word *īnfāns* (stem form, or form to which inflections are added, *īnfant–*), meaning "a little child; strictly, one who does not yet speak." The noun is from the adjective *īnfāns,* meaning "not having the power of speech" and "newly born" and made up of the negative prefix *in–* and the present participle *fāns,* "speaking," of the verb *fārī,* "to speak." Latin *īnfāns* and its Old French descendant *enfant* could both be used to refer to a speaking child, and the earliest recorded use (around 1384) of their Middle English descendant *infaunte,* the ancestor of our word, is in the sense "child." This use gave rise to our legal sense of *infant,* "a minor," thus reminding us of individuals who can be very talkative indeed.

infanta
The Infanta Margarita,
c. 1653, by Velázquez

in·fan·ta (ĭn-făn′tə, -fän′-) *n.* A daughter of a Spanish or Portuguese king. [Spanish and Portuguese, feminine of *infante,* infante. See INFANTE.]

in·fan·te (ĭn-făn′tē, -fän′tā) *n.* A son of a Spanish or Portuguese king other than the heir to the throne. [Spanish and Portuguese, both from Latin *īnfāns, īnfant-,* infant. See INFANT.]

in·fan·ti·cide (ĭn-făn′tĭ-sīd′) *n.* **1.** The act of killing an infant. **2.** The practice of killing newborn infants. **3.** One who kills an infant. [Late Latin *īnfanticīdium,* the killing of a child and *īnfanticīda,* killer of a child : Latin *īnfāns, īnfant-,* infant; see INFANT + Latin *-cīdium* and *-cīda,* -cide.] **—in·fan′ti·cid′al** (-sīd′l) *adj.*

in·fan·tile (ĭn′fən-tīl′, -tĭl) *adj.* **1.** Of or relating to infants or infancy. **2.** Displaying or suggesting a lack of maturity; extremely childish: *infantile behavior; an infantile remark.* [Middle English *infantil,* from Latin *īnfantīlis,* from *īnfāns, īnfant-,* infant. See INFANT.]

infantile autism *n. Psychology.* A severe disorder of childhood characterized by withdrawal, preoccupation with fantasy, language impairment, and abnormal behavior, such as ritualistic acts and excessive object attachment.

infantile paralysis *n.* See **poliomyelitis.**

in·fan·til·ism (ĭn′fən-tl-ĭz′əm, ĭn-făn′tl-) *n.* **1.** A state of arrested development in an adult, characterized by retention of infantile mentality, accompanied by stunted growth and sexual immaturity, and often by dwarfism. **2.a.** Extreme immaturity, as in behavior or character: *"infantilism, which is the subtext of so much American cinema and culture"* (John Simon). **b.** An infantile act or remark.

in·fan·til·ize (ĭn′fən-tl-īz′, ĭn-făn′-) *tr.v.* **-ized, -iz·ing, -iz·es. 1.** To reduce to an infantile state or condition: *"It creates a crisis that infantilizes them—causes grown men to squabble like kids about trivial things"* (New Yorker). **2.** To treat or condescend to as if still a young child: *"The Victorian physician infantilized his patient"* (Judith Moore). **—in·fan′til·i·za′tion** (-ĭ-zā′shən) *n.*

in·fan·tine (ĭn′fən-tīn′, -tĭn) *adj.* Infantile; childish.

in·fan·try (ĭn′fən-trē) *n., pl.* **-tries.** *Abbr.* **inf., Inf.** The combat arm made up of units trained to fight on foot. [French *infanterie,* from Old French, from Old Italian *infanteria,* from *infante,* youth, foot soldier, from Latin *īnfāns, īnfant-,* infant. See INFANT.]

in·fan·try·man (ĭn′fən-trē-mən) *n.* A soldier in the infantry.

infant school *n. Chiefly British.* A kindergarten.

in·farct (ĭn′färkt′, ĭn-färkt′) *n. Pathology.* An area of tissue that undergoes necrosis as a result of obstruction of local blood supply, as by a thrombus or an embolus. [From Latin *īnfarctus,* past participle of *īnfarcīre,* to cram : *in-,* in; see IN–[2] + *farcīre,* to stuff.] **—in·farct′ed** *adj.*

in·farc·tion (ĭn-färk′shən) *n.* **1.** The formation or development of an infarct. **2.** An infarct.

in·fat·u·ate (ĭn-făch′o͞o-āt′) *tr.v.* **-at·ed, -at·ing, -ates. 1.** To inspire with unreasoning love or attachment. **2.** To cause to behave foolishly. **—infatuate** (-ĭt, -āt′) *adj.* Infatuated. [Latin *īnfatuāre, īnfatuāt-* : *in-,* causative pref.; see IN–[2] + *fatuus,* foolish.]

in·fat·u·at·ed (ĭn-făch′o͞o-ā′tĭd) *adj.* Possessed by an unreasoning passion or attraction. **—in·fat′u·at′ed·ly** *adv.*

in·fat·u·a·tion (ĭ-făch′o͞o-ā′shən) *n.* **1.** A foolish, unreasoning, or extravagant passion or attraction. See Synonyms at **love. 2.** An object of extravagant, short-lived passion.

in·fau·na (ĭn′fô′nə) *n.* Aquatic animals that live in the substrate of a body of water, especially in a soft sea bottom. [IN–[2] + FAUNA.]

in·fea·si·ble (ĭn-fē′zə-bəl) *adj.* Not feasible; impracticable: *a plan that turned out to be infeasible.*

in·fect (ĭn-fĕkt′) *tr.v.* **-fect·ed, -fect·ing, -fects. 1.** To contaminate with a pathogenic microorganism or agent. **2.** To communicate a pathogen or disease to. **3.** To invade and produce infection in. **4.** To contaminate or corrupt: *envy that infected their thoughts; a society that was infected by racism.* **5.** To affect in a contagious way: *"His fear infected me, and . . . I followed as fast as I could"* (W.H. Hudson). [Middle English *infecten,* to afflict with disease, from Latin *īnficere, īnfect-,* to stain, infect: *in-,* in; see IN–[2] + *facere,* to do; see **dhē-** in Appendix.]

in·fec·tion (ĭn-fĕk′shən) *n.* **1.a.** Invasion by and multiplication of pathogenic microorganisms in a bodily part or tissue, which may produce subsequent tissue injury and progress to overt disease through a variety of cellular or toxic mechanisms. **b.** An instance of being infected. **c.** An agent or a contaminated substance responsible for one's becoming infected. **d.** The pathological state resulting from having been infected. **2.** An infectious disease. **3.a.** Moral contamination or corruption. **b.** Ready communication of an emotion or attitude by contact or example.

in·fec·tious (ĭn-fĕk′shəs) *adj.* **1.** Capable of causing infection. **2.** Caused by or capable of being transmitted by infection. **3.** Caused by a pathogenic microorganism or agent. **4.** Easily or readily communicated: *an infectious laugh.* **—in·fec′tious·ly** *adv.* **—in·fec′tious·ness** *n.*

infectious enterohepatitis *n.* See **blackhead** (sense 2).

infectious hepatitis *n.* See **hepatitis A.**

infectious mononucleosis *n.* A common, acute, infectious disease, usually affecting young people, caused by Epstein-Barr virus and characterized by fever, swollen lymph nodes, sore throat, and lymphocyte abnormalities. Also called *glandular fever.*

in·fec·tive (ĭn-fĕk′tĭv) *adj.* Capable of producing infection; infectious. **—in·fec′tive·ness, in′fec·tiv′i·ty** *n.*

in·fe·lic·i·tous (ĭn′fĭ-lĭs′ĭ-təs) *adj.* **1.** Inappropriate; ill-chosen: *an infelicitous remark.* **2.** Not happy; unfortunate. **—in′fe·lic′i·tous·ly** *adv.*

in·fe·lic·i·ty (ĭn′fĭ-lĭs′ĭ-tē) *n., pl.* **-ties. 1.** The quality or condition of being infelicitous. **2.** Something inappropriate or unpleasing. [Middle English *infelicite,* from Latin *īnfēlīcitās,* from *īnfēlīx, īnfēlīc-,* unhappy : *in-,* not; see IN–[1] + *fēlīx,* happy; see **dhē(i)-** in Appendix.]

in·fer (ĭn-fûr′) *v.* **-ferred, -fer·ring, -fers.** —*tr.* **1.** To conclude from evidence or premises. See Synonyms at **conjecture. 2.** To reason from circumstance; surmise: *We can infer that his motive in publishing the diary was less than honorable.* **3.** To lead to as a consequence or conclusion: *"Socrates argued that a statue inferred the existence of a sculptor"* (Academy). **4.** To hint; imply. —*intr.* To draw inferences. See Synonyms at **conjecture.**

[Latin *īnferre*, to bring in, adduce : *in-*, in; see IN–[2] + *ferre*, to bear; see **bher-**[1] in Appendix.] **—in·fer′a·ble** *adj.* **—in·fer′a·bly** *adv.* **—in·fer′rer** *n.*

USAGE NOTE: *Infer* is sometimes confused with *imply,* but the distinction is a useful one. When we say that a speaker or sentence implies something, we mean that it is conveyed or suggested without being stated outright: *When the mayor said that she would not rule out a business tax increase, she implied* (not *inferred*) *that some taxes might be raised.* Inference, on the other hand, is the activity performed by a reader or interpreter in deriving conclusions that are not explicit in what is said: *When the mayor said that she would not rule out a tax increase, we inferred that she had been consulting with some new financial advisers, since her old advisers were in favor of tax reductions.*

in·fer·ence (ĭn′fər-əns) *n.* **1.a.** The act or process of deriving logical conclusions from premises known or assumed to be true. **b.** The act of reasoning from factual knowledge or evidence. **2.a.** Something inferred. **b.** *Usage Problem.* A hint or suggestion: *The editorial contained an inference of foul play in the awarding of the contract.*

in·fer·en·tial (ĭn′fə-rĕn′shəl) *adj.* **1.** Of, relating to, or involving inference. **2.** Derived or capable of being derived by inference. **—in′fer·en′tial·ly** *adv.*

in·fe·ri·or (ĭn-fîr′ē-ər) *adj. Abbr.* **inf. 1.** Low or lower in order, degree, or rank: *Captain is an inferior rank to major.* **2.a.** Low or lower in quality, value, or estimation: *inferior craft; felt inferior to his older sibling.* **b.** Second-rate; poor: *an inferior student.* **3.** Situated under or beneath. **4.** *Botany.* Located below the perianth and other floral parts. Used of an ovary. **5.** *Anatomy.* Located beneath or directed downward. **6.** *Printing.* Set below the normal line of type; subscript. **7.** *Astronomy.* **a.** Orbiting between the earth and the sun: *Mercury is an inferior planet.* **b.** Lying below the horizon. **—inferior** *n. Abbr.* **inf. 1.** A person lower in rank, status, or accomplishment than another. **2.** *Printing.* An inferior character, such as the number 2 in CO_2. [Middle English, from Latin, comparative of *īnferus,* low. See **ndher-** in Appendix.] **—in·fe′ri·or′i·ty** (-ôr′ĭ-tē, -ŏr′-) *n.*

inferiority complex *n.* A persistent sense of inadequacy or a tendency to self-diminishment, sometimes resulting in excessive aggressiveness through overcompensation.

in·fer·nal (ĭn-fûr′nəl) *adj.* **1.a.** Of or relating to a lower world of the dead. **b.** Of or relating to hell: *infernal punishments; infernal powers.* **2.** Fiendish; diabolical: *infernal instruments of war.* **3.** Abominable; awful: *the infernal racket of the jackhammers.* [Middle English, from Old French, from Late Latin *īnfernālis,* from *īnfernus,* hell, from Latin, lower, underground. See **ndher-** in Appendix.] **—in·fer′nal·ly** *adv.*

infernal machine *n. Law.* An explosive device maliciously designed to harm or destroy.

in·fer·no (ĭn-fûr′nō) *n., pl.* **-nos. 1.** A place or condition suggestive of hell, especially with respect to human suffering or death: *the inferno of battle.* **2.** A place of fiery heat or destruction. [Italian, hell, from Late Latin *īnfernus.* See INFERNAL.]

in·fer·tile (ĭn-fûr′tl) *adj.* **1.** Not fertile; unproductive or barren. See Synonyms at **sterile. 2.** *Biology.* Incapable of producing offspring; sterile.

in·fer·til·i·ty (ĭn′fər-tĭl′ĭ-tē) *n.* **1.** Absent or diminished fertility. **2.** The persistent inability to conceive a child.

in·fest (ĭn-fĕst′) *tr.v.* **-fest·ed, -fest·ing, -fests. 1.** To inhabit or overrun in numbers large enough to be harmful, threatening, or obnoxious: *rats infesting the sewers; streets that were infested with drugs.* **2.** To live as a parasite in or on tissues or organs or on the skin and its appendages: *livestock that were infested with tapeworms.* [Middle English *infesten,* to distress, from Old French *infester,* from Latin *īnfestāre,* from *īnfestus,* hostile. See **gʷhedh-** in Appendix.] **—in′fes·ta′tion** *n.* **—in·fest′er** *n.*

in·fi·del (ĭn′fĭ-dəl, -dĕl′) *n.* **1.** An unbeliever with respect to a particular religion, especially Christianity or Islam. **2.** One who has no religious beliefs. **3.** One who doubts or rejects a particular doctrine, system, or principle: *an infidel to the prohibitionist cause.* [Middle English *infidele,* from Old French, from Latin *īnfidēlis,* disloyal : *in-,* not; see IN–[1] + *fidēlis,* faithful (from *fidēs,* faith; see **bheidh-** in Appendix).]

in·fi·del·i·ty (ĭn′fĭ-dĕl′ĭ-tē) *n., pl.* **-ties. 1.a.** Unfaithfulness to a sexual partner, especially a spouse. **b.** An act of sexual unfaithfulness. **2.** Lack of fidelity or loyalty: *infidelity to the family tradition; infidelity to the principles of the revolution.* **3.** Lack of religious belief.

in·field (ĭn′fēld′) *n.* **1.** *Baseball.* **a.** The area of the field bounded by home plate and first, second, and third bases. **b.** The defensive positions of first base, second base, third base, and shortstop considered as a unit. **2.** *Sports.* The area inside a racetrack or running track. **3.** A field located near a farmhouse.

in·field·er (ĭn′fēl′dər) *n. Baseball.* A player assigned to the infield.

in·fight·ing (ĭn′fī′tĭng) *n.* **1.** Contentious rivalry or disagreement among members or groups within an organization: *behind-the-scenes infighting on the President's staff.* **2.** *Sports.* Fighting or boxing at close range. **—in′fight′er** *n.*

in·fill (ĭn′fĭl′) *n.* **1.** The use of vacant land and property within a built-up area for further construction or development, especially as part of a neighborhood preservation or limited growth program. **2.** A substance or material used to fill in: *a steel structure with an infill of redwood sheathing.*

in·fil·trate (ĭn-fĭl′trāt′, ĭn′fĭl-) *v.* **-trat·ed, -trat·ing, -trates.** —*tr.* **1.a.** To pass (troops, for example) surreptitiously into enemy-held territory. **b.** To penetrate with hostile intent: *infiltrate enemy lines; a team of terrorists that had infiltrated the country.* **2.** To enter or take up positions in gradually or surreptitiously, as for purposes of espionage or takeover: *tried to infiltrate key government agencies with spies.* **3.** To cause (a liquid, for example) to permeate a substance by passing through its interstices or pores. **4.** To permeate (a porous substance) with a liquid or gas. —*intr.* To gain entrance gradually or surreptitiously. **—infiltrate** *n.* One that infiltrates, especially an abnormal substance that accumulates gradually in cells or body tissues. **—in·fil′tra·tor** *n.*

in·fil·tra·tion (ĭn′fĭl-trā′shən) *n.* **1.** The act or process of infiltrating. **2.** The state of being infiltrated. **3.** Something that infiltrates. **—in·fil′tra·tive** (-trə-tĭv) *adj.*

infin. *abbr.* Infinitive.

in·fi·nite (ĭn′fə-nĭt) *adj.* **1.** Having no boundaries or limits. **2.** Immeasurably great or large; boundless: *infinite importance.* **3.** *Mathematics.* **a.** Existing beyond or being greater than any arbitrarily large value. **b.** Unlimited in spatial extent. **c.** Of or relating to a set capable of being put into one-to-one correspondence with a proper subset of itself. **—infinite** *n.* Something infinite. [Middle English *infinit,* from Old French, from Latin *īnfīnītus* : *in-,* not; see IN–[1] + *fīnītus,* finite, from past participle of *fīnīre,* to limit; see FINITE.] **—in′fi·nite·ly** *adv.* **—in′fi·nite·ness** *n.*

SYNONYMS: *infinite, boundless, eternal, illimitable, sempiternal.* The central meaning shared by these adjectives is "being without beginning or end": *infinite wisdom; boundless ambition; eternal beauty; illimitable space; sempiternal truth.* See also Synonyms at **incalculable.**

ANTONYM: *finite.*

USAGE NOTE: *Infinite* is sometimes grouped with absolute terms such as *unique, absolute,* and *omnipotent,* since in its strict mathematical sense it allows no degree modification or comparison; one quantity cannot be more infinite than another (though technically one infinite set can be larger than another). Unlike other absolute terms, however, *infinite* also does not permit modification by adverbs such as *nearly* and *almost;* mathematically, infinity is not approached by degrees. In nontechnical usage, of course, *infinite* is often used metaphorically to refer simply to an unimaginably large degree or amount, and here the comparison of the word is unexceptionable: *Listening to the late quartets on that little gramophone, I experienced the most infinite musical joy that I have ever known.* See Usage Note at **unique.**

in·fin·i·tes·i·mal (ĭn′fĭn-ĭ-tĕs′ə-məl) *adj.* **1.** Immeasurably or incalculably minute. **2.** *Mathematics.* Capable of having values approaching zero as a limit. **—infinitesimal** *n.* **1.** An immeasurably or incalculably minute amount or quantity. **2.** *Mathematics.* A function or variable continuously approaching zero as a limit. [From New Latin *īnfīnītēsimus,* infinite in rank, from Latin *īnfīnītus,* infinite. See INFINITE.] **—in′fin·i·tes′i·mal·ly** *adv.*

infinitesimal calculus *n. Mathematics.* Differential and integral calculus.

in·fin·i·ti·val (ĭn′fĭn-ĭ-tī′vəl) *adj.* Relating to the infinitive.

in·fin·i·tive (ĭn-fĭn′ĭ-tĭv) *n. Abbr.* **inf., infin.** A verb form that functions as a substantive while retaining certain verbal characteristics, such as modification by adverbs, and that in English may be preceded by *to,* as in *To go willingly is to show strength* or *We want him to work harder,* or may also occur without *to,* as in *She had them read the letter* or *We may finish today.* See Usage Note at **split infinitive.** [From Middle English *infinitif,* of an infinitive, from Old French, from Late Latin *īnfīnītīvus,* unlimited, indefinite, infinitive, from Latin *īnfīnītus,* infinite. See INFINITE.]

in·fin·i·tude (ĭn-fĭn′ĭ-to͞od′, -tyo͞od′) *n.* **1.** The state or quality of being infinite. **2.** An immeasurably large quantity, number, or extent: "[His designs contain] *an infinitude of forest shadings for the scenes with animals*" (Alan Rich).

in·fin·i·ty (ĭn-fĭn′ĭ-tē) *n., pl.* **-ties.** *Abbr.* **inf. 1.** The quality or condition of being infinite. **2.** Unbounded space, time, or quantity. **3.** An indefinitely large number or amount. **4.** *Mathematics.* The limit that a function f is said to approach at $x = a$ when for x close to a, $f(x)$ is larger than any preassigned number. **5.a.** A range in relation to an optical system, such as a camera lens, representing distances great enough that light rays reflected from objects within the range may be regarded as parallel. **b.** A distance setting, as on a camera, beyond which the entire field is in focus.

in·firm (ĭn-fûrm′) *adj.* **1.** Weak in body, especially from old age or disease; feeble. See Synonyms at **weak. 2.** Lacking firmness of will, character, or purpose; irresolute. **3.** Not strong or stable; shaky: *an infirm support.* [Middle English *infirme,* from Old French, from Latin *īnfirmus* : *in-,* not; see IN–[1] + *firmus,* strong, firm; see **dher-** in Appendix.] **—in·firm′ly** *adv.*

in·fir·ma·ry (ĭn-fûr′mə-rē) *n., pl.* **-ries.** A place for the care of the infirm, sick, or injured, especially a small hospital or dispensary in an institution. [Middle English *infirmarie,* from Medieval Latin *īnfirmāria,* from Latin *īnfirmus,* infirm. See INFIRM.]

ă pat	oi boy
ā pay	ou out
âr care	o͝o took
ä father	o͞o boot
ĕ pet	ŭ cut
ē be	ûr urge
ĭ pit	th thin
ī pie	*th* this
îr pier	hw which
ŏ pot	zh vision
ō toe	ə about, item
ô paw	♦ regionalism

Stress marks: **′** (primary); ′ (secondary), as in **dictionary** (dĭk′shə-nĕr′ē)

inflatable
In Macy's Thanksgiving Parade, New York City

in·fir·mi·ty (ĭn-fûr′mĭ-tē) *n., pl.* **-ties. 1.** A bodily ailment or weakness, especially one brought on by old age. **2.** Frailty; feebleness. **3.** A condition or disease producing weakness. **4.** A failing or defect in a person's character.

in·fix (ĭn-fĭks′) *tr.v.* **-fixed, -fix·ing, -fix·es. 1.** To fix in the mind; instill. **2.** *Linguistics.* To insert (a morphological element) into the body of a word. **—infix** (ĭn′fĭks′) *n.* An inflectional or derivational element appearing in the body of a word. In the Tagalog word *sinulat,* "written," the infix *-in-* appears as the marker of a passive form that contrasts with the active form *sulat,* "write." [Back-formation from Middle English *infixed,* stuck in, from Latin *īnfīxus,* past participle of *īnfīgere,* to fasten in : *in-,* in; see IN–[2] + *fīgere,* to fasten; see **dhīgʷ-** in Appendix.]

infl. *abbr.* **1.** Influence **2.** Influenced.

in·flame (ĭn-flām′) *v.* **-flamed, -flam·ing, -flames.** —*tr.* **1.** To arouse to passionate feeling or action: *crimes that inflamed the entire community.* **2.** To make more violent; intensify: *"inflamed to madness an already savage nature"* (Robert Graves). **3.a.** To cause (the skin) to redden or grow hot, as from strong emotion or stimulants. **b.** To turn red or make glow: *Great bonfires inflamed the night.* **4.** To produce inflammation in (a tissue or an organ). **5.** To set on fire; kindle. —*intr.* **1.** To become excited or aroused. **2.** To be affected by inflammation. **3.** To catch fire. [Middle English *enflaumen,* from Old French *enflammer,* from Latin *īnflammāre* : *in-,* intensive pref.; see IN–[2] + *flammāre,* to set on fire (from *flamma,* flame; see **bhel-**[1] in Appendix).] **—in·flam′er** *n.*

in·flam·ma·ble (ĭn-flăm′ə-bəl) *adj.* **1.** Easily ignited and capable of burning rapidly; flammable. See Usage Note at **flammable. 2.** Quickly or easily aroused to strong emotion; excitable. [Middle English, liable to inflammation, from Medieval Latin *īnflammābilis,* from Latin *īnflammāre,* to inflame. See INFLAME.] **—in·flam′ma·bil′i·ty** *n.* **—in·flam′ma·ble** *n.* **—in·flam′ma·bly** *adv.*

in·flam·ma·tion (ĭn′flə-mā′shən) *n.* **1.** The act of inflaming or the state of being inflamed. **2.** A localized protective reaction of tissue to irritation, injury, or infection, characterized by pain, redness, swelling, and sometimes loss of function.

in·flam·ma·to·ry (ĭn-flăm′ə-tôr′ē, -tōr′ē) *adj.* **1.** Arousing passion or strong emotion, especially anger, belligerence, or desire. **2.** Characterized or caused by inflammation. **—in·flam′ma·to′ri·ly** *adv.*

in·flat·a·ble (ĭn-flā′tə-bəl) *adj.* Designed to be filled with air or gas before use: *an inflatable mattress.* **—inflatable** *n.* An object or a device that can be filled with air or gas, especially: **a.** A small rubber boat or raft filled with air. **b.** A large helium or hot-air balloon constructed so as to resemble a figure or an object when inflated.

in·flate (ĭn-flāt′) *v.* **-flat·ed, -flat·ing, -flates.** —*tr.* **1.** To fill (something) with air or gas so as to make it swell. **2.a.** To enlarge or amplify unduly or improperly; aggrandize. **b.** To raise or expand abnormally or improperly. See Synonyms at **exaggerate. 3.** To cause (a currency or an economy) to undergo inflation. —*intr.* To become inflated. [Middle English *inflaten,* from Latin *īnflāre, īnflāt-* : *in-,* in; see IN–[2] + *flāre,* to blow; see **bhlē-** in Appendix.] **—in·fla′tor, in·flat′er** *n.*

in·flat·ed (ĭn-flā′tĭd) *adj.* **1.** Filled or expanded by or as if by gas or air. **2.** Unduly enlarged or aggrandized; swollen: *an inflated estimate; an inflated ego.* **3.** Full of empty or pretentious language; bombastic. **4.** Raised or expanded to abnormal levels: *an inflated economy; inflated wages.* **5.** Hollow and enlarged: *an inflated calyx.*

in·fla·tion (ĭn-flā′shən) *n.* **1.** The act of inflating or the state of being inflated. **2.** A persistent increase in the level of consumer prices or a persistent decline in the purchasing power of money, caused by an increase in available currency and credit beyond the proportion of available goods and services.

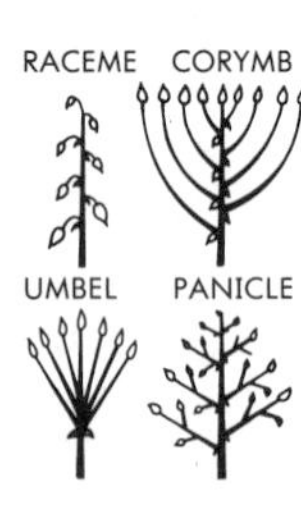

inflorescence

in·fla·tion·ar·y (ĭn-flā′shə-nĕr′ē) *adj.* Of, associated with, or tending to cause inflation: *inflationary policies.*

inflationary spiral *n.* A trend toward ever higher levels of inflation primarily as a result of continuing interactive increases in wages and prices.

in·fla·tion·ist (ĭn-flā′shə-nĭst) *n.* An advocate of the policy of deliberate inflation achieved by increasing the supply of available currency and credit. **—in·fla′tion·ism** *n.* **—in·fla′tion·ist** *adj.*

in·flect (ĭn-flĕkt′) *v.* **-flect·ed, -flect·ing, -flects.** —*tr.* **1.** To alter (the voice) in tone or pitch; modulate. **2.** *Grammar.* To alter (a word) by inflection. **3.** To turn from a course or a specified alignment; bend. —*intr. Grammar.* **1.** To be modified by inflection. **2.** To give all of the inflected forms of a word; to provide a paradigm. [Middle English *inflecten,* to bend down, from Latin *īnflectere* : *in-,* in; see IN–[2] + *flectere,* to bend.] **—in·flec′tive** *adj.* **—in·flec′tor** *n.*

in·flec·tion (ĭn-flĕk′shən) *n.* **1.** The act of inflecting or the state of being inflected. **2.** Alteration in pitch or tone of the voice. **3.** *Grammar.* **a.** An alternation of the form of a word by adding affixes, as in English *dogs* from *dog,* or by changing the form of a base, as in English *spoke* from *speak,* that indicates grammatical features such as number, person, mood, or tense. **b.** The paradigm of a word. **c.** A pattern of forming paradigms, such as noun inflection or verb inflection. **4.** A turning or bending away from a course or position of alignment. **—in·flec′tion·al** *adj.* **—in·flec′tion·al·ly** *adv.*

in·flexed (ĭn-flĕkst′) *adj.* Bent or curved inward or downward, as petals or sepals. [From Latin *īnflexus,* past participle of *īnflectere,* to bend. See INFLECT.]

in·flex·i·ble (ĭn-flĕk′sə-bəl) *adj.* **1.** Not easily bent; stiff or rigid. **2.** Incapable of being changed; unalterable. **3.** Unyielding in purpose, principle, or temper; immovable. **—in·flex′i·bil′i·ty, in·flex′i·ble·ness** *n.* **—in·flex′i·bly** *adv.*

SYNONYMS: *inflexible, inexorable, adamant, obdurate.* These adjectives mean not capable of being swayed or diverted from a course. *Inflexible* implies unyielding adherence to rigidly fixed principles or purposes: *Polite but inflexible, she would not be deflected from her intention. Inexorable* implies lack of susceptibility to persuasion or entreaty: *"Cynthia was inexorable—she would have none of him"* (Winston Churchill). The term also describes things, such as fate and law, that are inevitable, relentless, and often severe in effect: *"Russia's final hour, it seemed, approached with inexorable certainty"* (W. Bruce Lincoln). *Adamant* usually implies imperviousness to pleas or appeals: *He is adamant in his refusal to change his mind. Obdurate* adds to *adamant* the implication of hard, unfeeling resistance to tender feelings: *The child's misery would move even the most obdurate heart.* See also Synonyms at **stiff.**

in·flex·ion (ĭn-flĕk′shən) *n. Chiefly British.* Variant of **inflection.**

in·flict (ĭn-flĭkt′) *tr.v.* **-flict·ed, -flict·ing, -flicts. 1.** To deal or mete out (something punishing or burdensome); impose: *inflicted heavy losses on the enemy; a storm that inflicted widespread damage.* **2.** To afflict. [Latin *īnflīgere, īnflīct-* : *in-,* on; see IN–[2] + *flīgere,* to strike.] **—in·flict′er, in·flic′tor** *n.* **—in·flic′tive** *adj.*

in·flic·tion (ĭn-flĭk′shən) *n.* **1.** The act or process of imposing or meting out something unpleasant. **2.** Something, such as punishment, that is imposed.

in-flight (ĭn′flīt′) *adj.* **1.** Occurring, carried out, or present while in flight: *in-flight refueling; an in-flight emergency.* **2.** Provided or offered during a flight: *in-flight meals.*

in·flo·res·cence (ĭn′flə-rĕs′əns) *n.* **1.a.** A characteristic arrangement of flowers on a stem. **b.** A flower cluster. **2.** A flowering. [New Latin *īnflōrēscentia,* from Late Latin *īnflōrēscēns, īnflōrēscent-,* present participle of *īnflōrēscere,* to begin to flower : Latin *in-,* intensive pref.; see IN–[2] + Latin *flōrēscere,* to begin to blossom; see FLORESCENCE.] **—in′flo·res′cent** *adj.*

in·flow (ĭn′flō′) *n.* **1.** The act or process of flowing in or into: *an inflow of water; an inflow of information.* **2.** Something that flows in or into: *a lake fed by a freshwater inflow.*

in·flu·ence (ĭn′flo͞o-əns) *n. Abbr.* **infl. 1.** A power affecting a person, thing, or course of events, especially one that operates without any direct or apparent effort: *relaxed under the influence of the music; the influence of television on modern life.* **2.a.** Power to sway or affect based on prestige, wealth, ability, or position: *used her parent's influence to get the job.* **b.** One exercising such power: *My parents considered my friend to be a bad influence on me.* **c.** An effect or change produced by such power. **3.a.** A determining factor believed by some to affect individual tendencies and characteristics understood to be caused by the positions of the stars and planets at the time of one's birth. **b.** Factors believed to be caused by the changing positions of the stars and planets in relation to those positions at the time of one's birth. **—influence** *tr.v.* **-enced, -enc·ing, -enc·es. 1.** To produce an effect on by imperceptible or intangible means; sway. **2.** To affect the nature, development, or condition of; modify. See Synonyms at **affect**[1]. **—*idiom.* under the influence.** Intoxicated, especially with alcohol. [Middle English, from Old French, from Medieval Latin *īnfluentia,* influx, from Latin *īnfluēns, īnfluent-,* present participle of *īnfluere,* to flow in : *in-,* in; see IN–[2] + *fluere,* to flow; see **bhleu-** in Appendix.] **—in′flu·ence·a·ble** *adj.* **—in′flu·enc·er** *n.*

influence ped·dling (pĕd′lĭng) *n.* The practice of using one's influence with persons in authority to obtain favors or preferential treatment for another, usually in return for payment. **—influence peddler** *n.*

in·flu·ent (ĭn′flo͞o-ənt, ĭn-flo͞o′-) *adj.* Flowing in or into. **—influent** *n.* **1.** An inflow, especially a tributary. **2.** *Ecology.* A nondominant organism in a community that exerts an important modifying effect. [Middle English, from Latin *īnfluēns, īnfluent-,* present participle of *īnfluere,* to flow in. See INFLUENCE.]

in·flu·en·tial (ĭn′flo͞o-ĕn′shəl) *adj.* Having or exercising influence. **—influential** *n.* One that is of considerable importance or influence: *a select group of media influentials.* **—in′flu·en′tial·ly** *adv.*

in·flu·en·za (ĭn′flo͞o-ĕn′zə) *n.* **1.** An acute contagious viral infection characterized by inflammation of the respiratory tract and by fever, chills, muscular pain, and prostration. Also called *grippe.* **2.** Any of various viral infections of domestic animals characterized generally by fever and respiratory involvement. [Italian, from Medieval Latin *īnfluentia,* influence (so called apparently from the belief that epidemics were due to the influence of the stars). See INFLUENCE.] **—in′flu·en′zal** *adj.*

in·flux (ĭn′flŭks′) *n.* **1.** A flowing in: *an influx of foreign capital.* **2.** A mass arrival or incoming: *an influx of visitors to the city; large influxes of refugees.* [Late Latin *īnfluxus,* from Latin, past participle of *īnfluere,* to flow in. See INFLUENCE.]

in·fo (ĭn′fō) *n. Informal.* Information.

in·fold (ĭn-fōld′) *v.* **-fold·ed, -fold·ing, -folds.** —*intr.* To fold inward. —*tr.* To enfold. —**in·fold′ment** *n.*

in·fo·mer·cial (ĭn′fə-mûr′shəl, -fō-) *n.* Variant of **informercial.**

in·form (ĭn-fôrm′) *v.* **-formed, -form·ing, -forms.** —*tr.* **1.a.** To impart information to; make aware of something: *We were informed by mail of the change in plans. The nurse informed me that visiting hours were over.* **b.** To acquaint (oneself) with knowledge of a subject. **2.** To give form or character to; imbue with a quality or an essence: *"A society's strength is measured by . . . its ability to inform a future generation with its moral standards"* (Vanity Fair). **3.** To be a pervasive presence in; animate: *"It is this brash, backroom sensibility that informs his work as a novelist"* (Jeff Shear). **4.** *Obsolete.* To form (the mind or character) by teaching or training. —*intr.* **1.** To give or provide information. **2.** To disclose confidential or incriminating information to an authority: *The defendant informed against the other members of the ring.* [Middle English *enfourmen, informen,* from Old French *enfourmer,* from Latin *īnfōrmāre* : *in-,* in; see IN–[2] + *fōrmāre,* to fashion (from *fōrma,* form).]

in·for·mal (ĭn-fôr′məl) *adj.* **1.** Not formal or ceremonious; casual: *an informal gathering of friends; a relaxed, informal manner.* **2.** Not being in accord with prescribed regulations or forms; unofficial: *an informal agreement.* **3.** Suited for everyday wear or use: *informal clothes.* **4.** Being more appropriate for use in the spoken language than in the written language. —**in·for′mal·ly** *adv.*

in·for·mal·i·ty (ĭn′fôr-măl′ĭ-tē) *n., pl.* **-ties. 1.** The state or quality of being informal. **2.** An informal act.

in·form·ant (ĭn-fôr′mənt) *n.* **1.a.** One that gives information. **b.** One who informs against others; an informer. **2.** One who furnishes linguistic or cultural information to a researcher.

in·for·mat·ics (ĭn′fər-măt′ĭks) *n. (used with a sing. verb). Chiefly British.* Information science. [INFORMAT(ION) + –ICS.]

in·for·ma·tion (ĭn′fər-mā′shən) *n. Abbr.* **inf. 1.** Knowledge derived from study, experience, or instruction. **2.** Knowledge of a specific event or situation; intelligence. See Synonyms at **knowledge. 3.** A collection of facts or data: *statistical information.* **4.** The act of informing or the condition of being informed; communication of knowledge: *Safety instructions are provided for the information of our passengers.* **5.** *Computer Science.* A nonaccidental signal or character used as an input to a computer or communications system. **6.** A numerical measure of the uncertainty of an experimental outcome. **7.** *Law.* A formal accusation of a crime made by a public officer rather than by grand jury indictment. —**in′for·ma′tion·al** *adj.*

information retrieval *n. Computer Science.* The process of searching for and recovering specific data from large quantities of information stored in a computer.

information science *n.* The science that is concerned with the gathering, manipulation, classification, storage, and retrieval of recorded knowledge.

information theory *n.* The theory of the probability of transmission of messages with specified accuracy when the bits of information constituting the messages are subject, with certain probabilities, to transmission failure, distortion, and accidental additions.

in·form·a·tive (ĭn-fôr′mə-tĭv) *adj.* Serving to inform; providing or disclosing information; instructive. —**in·form′a·tive·ly** *adv.* —**in·form′a·tive·ness** *n.*

in·form·a·to·ry (ĭn-fôr′mə-tôr′ē, -tōr′ē) *adj.* Informative.

in·formed (ĭn-fôrmd′) *adj.* **1.** Possessing, displaying, or based on reliable information: *informed sources; an informed opinion.* **2.** Knowledgeable; educated: *the informed consumer.*

informed consent *n.* Consent by a patient to a surgical or medical procedure or participation in a clinical study after achieving an understanding of the relevant medical facts and the risks involved.

in·form·er (ĭn-fôr′mər) *n.* An informant, especially one who informs against others, often for compensation.

in·for·mer·cial (ĭn′fər-mûr′shəl, -fə-) also **in·fo·mer·cial** (ĭn′fə-mûr′shəl, -fō-) *n.* A commercial television program or relatively long commercial segment offering consumer information, such as educational or instructional material, related to the sponsor's product or service. [INFOR(MATION) + (COM)MERCIAL.]

in·fo·tain·ment (ĭn′fə-tān′mənt) *n.* A television program with a mixture of news and entertainment features, such as interviews, commentaries, and reviews. Also called *docutainment.* [INFO(RMATION) + (ENTER)TAINMENT.]

infra– *pref.* Inferior to, below, or beneath: *infrasonic.* [From Latin *īnfrā,* below. See **n̥dher-** in Appendix.]

in·fra·class (ĭn′frə-klăs′) *n.* A taxonomic category of related organisms ranking below a subclass and above an order.

in·fract (ĭn-frăkt′) *tr.v.* **-fract·ed, -fract·ing, -fracts.** To infringe; violate. [Latin *īnfringere, īnfrāct-,* to destroy. See INFRINGE.] —**in·frac′tor** *n.*

in·frac·tion (ĭn-frăk′shən) *n.* The act or an instance of infringing; a violation. See Synonyms at **breach.**

in·fra dig (ĭn′frə dĭg′) *adj.* Beneath one's dignity. [Short for Latin *īnfrā dignitātem* : *īnfrā,* below + *dignitātem,* accusative of *dignitās,* dignity.]

in·fra·hu·man (ĭ′frə-hyōō′mən) *adj.* Of a lower order than human beings; subhuman. —**in′fra·hu′man** *n.*

in·fran·gi·ble (ĭn-frăn′jə-bəl) *adj.* **1.** Difficult or impossible to break or separate into parts. **2.** Inviolable: *infrangible human rights.* [Late Latin *īnfrangibilis* : Latin *in-,* not; see IN–[1] + Latin *frangere,* to break; see **bhreg-** in Appendix.] —**in·fran′gi·bil′i·ty** *n.* —**in·fran′gi·bly** *adv.*

in·fra·red (ĭn′frə-rĕd′) *adj. Abbr.* **IR 1.** Of or relating to the range of invisible radiation wavelengths from about 750 nanometers, just longer than red in the visible spectrum, to 1 millimeter, on the border of the microwave region. **2.** Generating, using, or sensitive to infrared radiation. —**infrared** *n.* Infrared light or the infrared part of the spectrum.

in·fra·son·ic (ĭn′frə-sŏn′ĭk) *adj.* Generating or using waves or vibrations with frequencies below that of audible sound.

in·fra·sound (ĭn′frə-sound′) *n.* A wave phenomenon sharing the physical nature of sound but with a range of frequencies below that of human hearing.

in·fra·struc·ture (ĭn′frə-strŭk′chər) *n.* **1.** An underlying base or foundation especially for an organization or a system. **2.** The basic facilities, services, and installations needed for the functioning of a community or society, such as transportation and communications systems, water and power lines, and public institutions including schools, post offices, and prisons.

in·fre·quent (ĭn-frē′kwənt) *adj.* **1.** Not occurring regularly; occasional or rare: *an infrequent guest.* **2.** Situated or placed at rather wide intervals, as in time or space: *infrequent oases in the desert.* —**in·fre′quence, in·fre′quen·cy** *n.* —**in·fre′quent·ly** *adv.*

in·fringe (ĭn-frĭnj′) *v.* **-fringed, -fring·ing, -fring·es.** —*tr.* **1.** To transgress or exceed the limits of; violate: *infringe a contract; infringe a patent.* **2.** *Obsolete.* To defeat; invalidate. —*intr.* To encroach on someone or something; engage in trespassing: *an increased workload that infringed on his personal life.* [Latin *īnfringere,* to destroy : *in-,* intensive pref.; see IN–[2] + *frangere,* to break; see **bhreg-** in Appendix.] —**in·fring′er** *n.*

in·fringe·ment (ĭn-frĭnj′mənt) *n.* **1.** A violation, as of a law, a regulation, or an agreement; a breach. **2.** An encroachment, as of a right or privilege. See Synonyms at **breach.**

in·fruc·tes·cence (ĭn′frŭk-tĕs′əns) *n.* The fruiting stage of an inflorescence. [French : Latin *in-,* in; see IN–[2] + Latin *frūctus,* fruit; see FRUIT.]

in·fun·dib·u·la (ĭn′fən-dĭb′yə-lə) *n.* Plural of **infundibulum.**

in·fun·dib·u·li·form (ĭn′fən-dĭb′yə-lə-fôrm′) *adj.* Shaped like a funnel.

in·fun·dib·u·lum (ĭn′fən-dĭb′yə-ləm) *n., pl.* **-la** (-lə). *Anatomy.* Any of various funnel-shaped bodily passages, openings, structures, or parts, especially: **a.** The stalk of the pituitary gland. **b.** The calyx of a kidney. **c.** The ovarian opening of a fallopian tube. [Latin, funnel, from *īnfundere,* to pour in. See INFUSE.] —**in′fun·dib′u·lar** (-lər), **in′fun·dib′u·late′** (-lāt′, -lĭt) *adj.*

in·fu·ri·ate (ĭn-fyŏŏr′ē-āt′) *tr.v.* **-at·ed, -at·ing, -ates.** To make furious; enrage. —**infuriate** (ĭn-fyŏŏr′ē-ĭt) *adj. Archaic.* Furious. [Medieval Latin *īnfuriāre, īnfuriāt-* : Latin *in-,* intensive pref.; see IN–[2] + Latin *furiāre,* to enrage (from *furia,* fury; see FURY).] —**in·fu′ri·at′ing·ly** *adv.* —**in·fu′ri·a′tion** *n.*

in·fuse (ĭn-fyōōz′) *tr.v.* **-fused, -fus·ing, -fus·es. 1.** To put into or introduce as if by pouring: *infused new vigor into the movement.* **2.** To fill or cause to be filled with something: *infused them with a love of the land.* **3.** *Chemistry.* To steep or soak without boiling in order to extract soluble elements or active principles. **4.** To introduce (a solution) into the body through a vein for therapeutic purposes. [Middle English *infusen,* from Old French *infuser,* from Latin *īnfundere, īnfūs-* : *in-,* in; see IN–[2] + *fundere,* to pour; see **gheu-** in Appendix.] —**in·fus′er** *n.*

in·fus·i·ble (ĭn-fyōō′zəbəl) *adj.* Suitable for infusion; capable of being infused. —**in·fus′i·bil′i·ty, in·fus′i·ble·ness** *n.*

in·fu·sion (ĭn-fyōō′zhən) *n.* **1.** The act or process of infusing. **2.** Something infused or introduced: *an economy in need of regular capital infusions.* **3.** The liquid product obtained by infusing: *prepared an infusion of medicinal herbs.* **4.a.** Introduction of a solution into the body through a vein for therapeutic purposes. **b.** The solution so introduced: *a sucrose infusion.*

–ing[1] *suff.* **1.** Used to form the present participle of verbs: *seeing.* **2.** Used to form adjectives resembling present participles but not derived from verbs: *swashbuckling.* [Middle English, alteration (influenced by *-inge,* noun or gerund suff.; see –ING[2]) of *-ende, -inde,* from Old English *-ende,* present participle suff.]

–ing[2] *suff.* **1.a.** Action, process, or art: *dancing.* **b.** An instance of an action, a process, or an act: *a gathering.* **2.** An action or a process connected with a specified thing: *berrying.* **3.a.** Something necessary to perform an action or a process: *mooring.* **b.** The result of an action or a process: *a drawing.* **c.** Something connected with a specified thing or concept: *siding; offing.* [Middle English, from Old English *-ung, -ing.*]

–ing[3] *suff.* One having a specified quality or nature: *wilding.* [Middle English, from Old English, belonging to, descended from.]

in·gath·er (ĭn′găth′ər) *v.* **-ered, -er·ing, -ers.** —*tr.* To gather in; collect. —*intr.* To come together in a central place.

Inge (ĭnj), **William.** 1913–1973. American playwright whose dramas explored the hopes and fears of small-town Midwesterners. His play *Picnic* (1953) won a Pulitzer Prize.

Inge (ĭng), **William Ralph.** 1860–1954. British prelate and writ-

William Inge

ă pat	oi boy
ā pay	ou out
âr care	ŏŏ took
ä father	ōō boot
ĕ pet	ŭ cut
ē be	ûr urge
ĭ pit	th thin
ī pie	*th* this
îr pier	hw which
ŏ pot	zh vision
ō toe	ə about, item
ô paw	♦ regionalism

Stress marks: **′** (primary); ′ (secondary), as in **dictionary** (dĭk′shə-nĕr′ē)

er whose pessimistic sermons and articles won him the nickname "the Gloomy Dean."

in·gen·ious (ĭn-jēn′yəs) *adj.* **1.** Marked by inventive skill and imagination. **2.** Having or arising from an inventive or cunning mind; clever: *an ingenious scheme.* See Synonyms at **clever. 3.** *Obsolete.* Having genius; brilliant. [Middle English, from Old French *ingenios,* from Latin *ingeniōsus,* from *ingenium,* inborn talent. See **gena-** in Appendix.] **—in·gen′ious·ly** *adv.* **—in·gen′ious·ness** *n.*

in·gé·nue (ăn′zhə-no͞o′) *n.* **1.** An artless, innocent girl or young woman. **2. a.** The role of an artless, innocent girl or young woman in a dramatic production. **b.** An actress playing such a role. [French, feminine of *ingénu,* guileless, from Latin *ingenuus,* ingenuous. See INGENUOUS.]

in·ge·nu·i·ty (ĭn′jə-no͞o′ĭ-tē, -nyo͞o′-) *n., pl.* **-ties. 1.** Inventive skill or imagination; cleverness. **2.** Imaginative and clever design or construction: *a narrative plot of great ingenuity.* **3.** An ingenious or imaginative contrivance. **4.** *Obsolete.* Ingenuousness. [Latin *ingenuitās,* frankness (influenced by INGENIOUS), from *ingenuus,* ingenuous. See INGENUOUS.]

in·gen·u·ous (ĭn-jĕn′yo͞o-əs) *adj.* **1.** Lacking in sophistication or worldliness; artless. **2.** Openly straightforward or frank; candid. See Synonyms at **naive. 3.** *Obsolete.* Ingenious. [Latin *ingenuus,* honest, freeborn. See **gena-** in Appendix.] **—in·gen′u·ous·ly** *adv.* **—in·gen′u·ous·ness** *n.*

In·ger·soll (ĭng′gər-sôl′, -sŏl′, -səl), **Robert Green.** 1833–1899. American politician and lecturer known for his adamant support of scientific and humanistic rationalism.

in·gest (ĭn-jĕst′) *tr.v.* **-gest·ed, -gest·ing, -gests.** To take into the body by the mouth for digestion or absorption. See Synonyms at **eat.** [Latin *ingerere, ingest-* : *in-,* in; see IN–^{2} + *gerere,* to carry.] **—in·ges′tion** *n.* **—in·ges′tive** *adj.*

in·ges·ta (ĭn-jĕs′tə) *pl.n.* Ingested matter, especially food taken into the body through the mouth. [New Latin, from neuter pl. of Latin *ingestus,* past participle of *ingerere,* to carry in. See INGEST.]

in·gle (ĭng′gəl) *n.* **1.** An open fire in a fireplace. **2.** A fireplace. [Perhaps Scottish Gaelic *aingeal,* fire, light.]

in·gle·nook (ĭng′gəl-no͝ok′) *n.* **1.** A nook or corner beside an open fireplace. **2.** A bench, especially either of two facing benches, placed in a nook or corner beside a fireplace. [INGLE + NOOK.]

In·gle·wood (ĭng′gəl-wo͝od′). A city of southern California, a suburb of Los Angeles. Population, 94,245.

in·glo·ri·ous (ĭn-glôr′ē-əs, -glōr′-) *adj.* **1.** Ignominious; disgraceful: *Napoleon's inglorious end.* **2.** Not famous or renowned; obscure: *an inglorious young writer.* **—in·glo′ri·ous·ly** *adv.* **—in·glo′ri·ous·ness** *n.*

in·go·ing (ĭn′gō′ĭng) *adj.* **1.** Going in; entering: *the ingoing administration; ingoing data.* **2.** Initial; opening: *an ingoing negotiating position.*

In·gol·stadt (ĭng′gəl-shtät′, -gôl-). A city of southeast Germany on the Danube River north of Munich. Chartered c. 1250, it is a commercial and industrial center. Population, 90,763.

in·got (ĭng′gət) *n.* **1.** A mass of metal, such as a bar or block, that is cast in a standard shape for convenient storage or shipment. **2.** A casting mold for metal. [Middle English, mold for casting metal : probably *in-,* in; see IN–^{2} + Old English *goten,* past participle of *geotan,* to pour, or perhaps from Old French *lingot,* metal ingot (as if *l'ingot* : *le,* definite article + **ingot,* ingot).]

ingot iron *n.* A bar of iron that contains small quantities of other elements.

Jean Auguste Dominique Ingres
After a self-portrait originally painted in 1804 and reworked in 1850

in·grain (ĭn-grān′) *tr.v.* **-grained, -grain·ing, -grains. 1.** To fix deeply or indelibly, as in the mind: *"A system that had been ingrained for generations could not be easily undone by change from the top"* (Doris Kearns Goodwin). **2.** *Archaic.* To dye or stain into the fiber of. **—ingrain** (ĭn′grān′) *adj.* **1.** Deep-seated; ingrained. **2.** Made of predyed fibers; thoroughly dyed: *ingrain yarn.* **3.** Made of fiber or yarn dyed before weaving. Used especially of rugs. **—ingrain** (ĭn′grān′) *n.* **1.** Yarn or fiber dyed before manufacture. **2.** An ingrain rug or carpet. [Variant of ENGRAIN.]

in·grained (ĭn-grānd′) *adj.* **1.** Firmly established; deep-seated: *ingrained prejudice; the ingrained habits of a lifetime.* **2.** Worked deeply into the texture or fiber: *a carpet disfigured by ingrained dirt.*

in·grate (ĭn′grāt′) *n.* An ungrateful person. [From Middle English *ingrat,* ungrateful, from Old French *ingrat,* from Latin *ingrātus* : *in-,* not; see IN–^{1} + *grātus,* pleasing, thankful; see **g^{w}era-^{2}** in Appendix.]

in·gra·ti·ate (ĭn-grā′shē-āt′) *tr.v.* **-at·ed, -at·ing, -ates.** To bring (oneself, for example) into the favor or good graces of another, especially by deliberate effort: *She quickly sought to ingratiate herself with the new administration.* [Perhaps from Italian *ingraziare,* from *in grazia,* into favor, from Latin *in grātiam* : *in,* in; see IN–^{2} + *grātiam,* accusative of *grātia,* favor (from *grātus,* pleasing; see **g^{w}era-^{2}** in Appendix).] **—in·gra′ti·a′tion** *n.* **—in·gra′ti·a·to′ry** (-shē-ə-tôr′ē, -tōr′ē) *adj.*

in·gra·ti·at·ing (ĭn-grā′shē-ā′tĭng) *adj.* **1.** Pleasing; agreeable: *"Reading requires an effort. . . . Print is not as ingratiating as television"* (Robert MacNeil). **2.** Calculated to please or win favor: *an unctuous, ingratiating manner.* **—in·gra′ti·at′ing·ly** *adv.*

inhaler

in·grat·i·tude (ĭn-grăt′ĭ-to͞od′, -tyo͞od′) *n.* Lack of gratitude; ungratefulness.

in·gre·di·ent (ĭn-grē′dē-ənt) *n.* An element in a mixture or compound; a constituent. See Synonyms at **element.** [Middle English, from Latin *ingrediēns, ingredient-,* present participle of *ingredī,* to enter. See INGRESS.]

In·gres (ăN′grə), **Jean Auguste Dominique.** 1780–1867. French painter and leader of the French classical school who is remembered for his historical and mythological works.

in·gress (ĭn′grĕs′) *n.* **1.** Also **in·gres·sion** (ĭn-grĕsh′ən). A going in or entering. **2.** Right or permission to enter. **3.** A means or place of entering. [Middle English *ingresse,* from Latin *ingressus,* from past participle of *ingredī,* to enter : *in-,* in; see IN–^{2} + *gradī,* to step; see **ghredh-** in Appendix.]

in·gres·sive (ĭn-grĕs′ĭv) *adj.* **1.** Of, relating to, or involving ingress. **2.** *Grammar.* Inchoative. **3.** *Linguistics.* Of, designating, or being a speech sound produced with an inhalation of breath. **—in·gres′sive** *n.* **—in·gres′sive·ness** *n.*

in-group (ĭn′gro͞op′) *n.* A group of people united by common beliefs, attitudes, or interests and characteristically excluding outsiders; a clique.

in·grow·ing (ĭn′grō′ĭng) *adj.* Growing inward or into, especially into the flesh.

in·grown (ĭn′grōn′) *adj.* **1.** Grown abnormally into the flesh: *an ingrown toenail.* **2.** Inbred; innate: *ingrown habits.* **3.** Insular; self-contained: *"the small, ingrown world of lower Manhattan"* (Forbes).

in·growth (ĭn′grōth′) *n.* **1.** The act of growing inward or into. **2.** Something that grows inward or into.

in·gui·nal (ĭng′gwə-nəl) *adj.* Of, relating to, or located in the groin. [Latin *inguinālis,* from *inguen, inguin-,* groin.]

in·gur·gi·tate (ĭn-gûr′jĭ-tāt′) *tr.v.* **-tat·ed, -tat·ing, -tates.** To swallow greedily or in excessive amounts; gulp. [Latin *ingurgitāre, ingurgitāt-* : *in-,* in; see IN–^{2} + *gurges, gurgit-,* throat, whirlpool.] **—in·gur′gi·ta′tion** *n.*

INH A trademark used for the drug isoniazid.

in·hab·it (ĭn-hăb′ĭt) *v.* **-it·ed, -it·ing, -its.** *—tr.* **1.** To live or reside in. **2.** To be present in; fill: *Old childhood memories inhabited the attic.* *—intr. Archaic.* To dwell. [Middle English *enhabiten,* from Old French *enhabiter,* from Latin *inhabitāre* : *in-,* in; see IN–^{2} + *habitāre,* to dwell, frequentative of *habēre,* to have; see **ghabh-** in Appendix.] **—in·hab′it·a·bil′i·ty** *n.* **—in·hab′it·a·ble** *adj.* **—in·hab′i·ta′tion** *n.* **—in·hab′it·er** *n.*

in·hab·i·tan·cy (ĭn-hăb′ĭ-tən-sē) *n., pl.* **-cies.** Occupancy.

in·hab·i·tant (ĭn-hăb′ĭ-tənt) *n.* One that inhabits a place, especially as a permanent resident: *the inhabitants of a fishing village; snakes, lizards, and other inhabitants of the desert.*

in·hab·it·ed (ĭn-hăb′ĭ-tĭd) *adj.* Having inhabitants; lived in: *a sparsely inhabited plain.*

in·ha·lant (ĭn-hā′lənt) *adj.* Used in or for inhaling. **—inhalant** *n.* **1.** Something inhaled. **2.** A medication, an anesthetic, or another compound in vapor or aerosol form, taken by inhalation.

in·ha·la·tion (ĭn′hə-lā′shən) *n.* **1.** The act or an instance of inhaling. **2.** An inhalant.

in·ha·la·tor (ĭn′hə-lā′tər) *n.* **1.** See **respirator** (sense 1). **2.** See **inhaler** (sense 2).

in·hale (ĭn-hāl′) *v.* **-haled, -hal·ing, -hales.** *—tr.* **1.** To draw (air or smoke, for example) into the lungs by breathing; inspire. **2.** *Informal.* To take in rapidly or eagerly; devour: *inhaled lunch and then rushed off to the meeting.* *—intr.* **1.** To breathe in; inspire. **2.** To draw smoke into the lungs; puff. [Latin *inhālāre,* to breathe upon (meaning influenced by contrast with EXHALE) : *in-,* in; see IN–^{2} + *hālāre,* to breathe.]

in·hal·er (ĭn-hā′lər) *n.* **1.** One that inhales: *an avid inhaler of aromatic pipe smoke.* **2.** A device that produces a vapor to ease breathing or is used to medicate by inhalation, especially a small nasal applicator containing a volatile medicament. In this sense, also called *inhalator.*

in·har·mon·ic (ĭn′här-mŏn′ĭk) *adj.* Not harmonic; discordant.

in·har·mo·ni·ous (ĭn′här-mō′nē-əs) *adj.* **1.** Not in harmony; discordant. **2.** Not in accord or agreement. **—in′har·mo′ni·ous·ly** *adv.* **—in′har·mo′ni·ous·ness** *n.*

in·har·mo·ny (ĭn-här′mə-nē) *n., pl.* **-nies. 1.** Lack of harmony; discord. **2.** An instance of such discord.

in·here (ĭn-hîr′) *intr.v.* **-hered, -her·ing, -heres.** To be inherent or innate. [Latin *inhaerēre* : *in-,* in; see IN–^{2} + *haerēre,* to stick.] **—in·her′ence** (-hîr′əns, -hĕr′-), **in·her′en·cy** *n.*

in·her·ent (ĭn-hîr′ənt, -hĕr′-) *adj.* Existing as an essential constituent or characteristic; intrinsic. [Latin *inhaerēns, inhaerent-,* present participle of *inhaerēre,* to inhere. See INHERE.] **—in·her′ent·ly** *adv.*

in·her·it (ĭn-hĕr′ĭt) *v.* **-it·ed, -it·ing, -its.** *—tr.* **1. a.** To receive (property or a title, for example) from an ancestor by legal succession or will. **b.** To receive by bequest or as a legacy. **2.** To receive or take over from a predecessor: *The new administration inherited the economic problems of the last four years.* **3.** *Biology.* To receive (a characteristic) from one's parents by genetic transmission. **4.** To gain (something) as one's right or portion. *—intr.* To hold or take possession of an inheritance. [Middle English *enheriten,* from Old French *enheriter,* to make heir to, from Late Latin *inhērēditāre,* to inherit : Latin *in-,* in; see IN–^{2} + Late Latin *hērēditāre,* to inherit (from Latin *hērēs, hērēd-,* heir; see **ghē-** in Appendix).] —**in·her′i·tor** *n.*

in·her·it·a·ble (ĭn-hĕr′ĭ-tə-bəl) *adj.* **1.** That can be inherited: *inheritable traits; inheritable property.* **2.** Having the right to inherit or the capability of inheriting: *an inheritable heir.* —**in·her′it·a·bil′i·ty** *n.*

in·her·i·tance (ĭn-hĕr′ĭ-təns) *n.* **1.a.** The act of inheriting. **b.** Something inherited or to be inherited. **2.** Something regarded as a heritage: *the cultural inheritance of Rome.* See Synonyms at **heritage. 3.** *Biology.* **a.** The process of genetic transmission of characteristics from parents to offspring. **b.** A characteristic so inherited. **c.** The sum of characteristics genetically transmitted from parents to offspring.

inheritance tax *n.* A tax imposed on the privilege of receiving property by inheritance or legal succession and assessed on the value of the property received. Also called *death tax.*

in·hib·in (ĭn-hĭb′ĭn) *n.* A peptide that acts to inhibit follicle-stimulating hormonal secretion from the pituitary gland.

in·hib·it (ĭn-hĭb′ĭt) *tr.v.* **-it·ed, -it·ing, -its. 1.** To hold back; restrain. See Synonyms at **restrain. 2.** To prohibit; forbid. **3.** *Psychology.* To suppress or restrain (behavior, an impulse, or a desire) consciously or unconsciously. **4.a.** *Chemistry.* To prevent or decrease the rate of (a reaction). **b.** *Biology.* To decrease, limit, or block the action or function of (an enzyme or organ, for example). [Middle English *inhibiten,* to forbid, from Latin *inhibēre, inhibit-,* to restrain, forbid : *in-,* in; see IN–^{2} + *habēre,* to hold; see **ghabh-** in Appendix.] —**in·hib′it·a·ble** *adj.* —**in·hib′i·tive, in·hib′i·to′ry** (-tôr′ē, -tōr′ē) *adj.*

in·hib·it·er (ĭn-hĭb′ĭ-tər) *n.* Variant of **inhibitor.**

in·hi·bi·tion (ĭn′hə-bĭsh′ən, ĭn′ə-) *n.* **1.** The act of inhibiting or the state of being inhibited. **2.** Something that restrains, blocks, or suppresses. **3.** *Psychology.* Conscious or unconscious restraint of a behavioral process, a desire, or an impulse. **4.a.** *Chemistry.* The condition in which or the process by which a reaction is inhibited. **b.** *Biology.* The condition in which or the process by which an enzyme, for example, is inhibited.

in·hib·i·tor also **in·hib·it·er** (ĭn-hĭb′ĭ-tər) *n.* One that inhibits, as a substance that retards or stops a chemical reaction.

in·hold·ing (ĭn′hōl′dĭng) *n.* A privately owned parcel of land within the boundaries of a federal preserve, especially within a national park or national seashore. —**in′hold′er** *n.*

in-home (ĭn′hōm′) *adj.* Operating in or provided at the home of the customer or patient: *in-home shopping services; an in-home nursing program.*

in·ho·mo·ge·ne·i·ty (ĭn-hō′mə-jə-nē′ĭ-tē, -nā′-, hŏm′ə-) *n., pl.* **-ties. 1.** Lack of homogeneity. **2.** Something that is not homogeneous or uniform.

in·hos·pi·ta·ble (ĭn-hŏs′pĭ-tə-bəl, ĭn′hŏ-spĭt′ə-bəl) *adj.* **1.** Displaying no hospitality; unfriendly. **2.** Unfavorable to life or growth; hostile: *the barren, inhospitable desert.* —**in·hos′pi·ta·ble·ness** *n.* —**in·hos′pi·ta·bly** *adv.*

in·hos·pi·tal·i·ty (ĭn′hŏs-pĭ-tăl′ĭ-tē) *n.* Lack of hospitality or friendliness.

in-house (ĭn′hous′) *adj.* Conducted within, coming from, or being within an organization or group: *an in-house computer system; an in-house newsletter.* —**in′-house′** *adv.*

in·hu·man (ĭn-hyo͞o′mən) *adj.* **1.a.** Lacking kindness, pity, or compassion; cruel. See Synonyms at **cruel. b.** Deficient in emotional warmth; cold. **2.** Not suited for human needs: *an inhuman environment.* **3.** Not of ordinary human form; monstrous. —**in·hu′man·ly** *adv.* —**in·hu′man·ness** *n.*

in·hu·mane (ĭn′hyo͞o-mān′) *adj.* Lacking pity or compassion. —**in′hu·mane′ly** *adv.*

in·hu·man·i·ty (ĭn′hyo͞o-măn′ĭ-tē) *n., pl.* **-ties. 1.** Lack of pity or compassion. **2.** An inhuman or cruel act.

in·hume (ĭn-hyo͞om′) *tr.v.* **-humed, -hum·ing, -humes.** To place in a grave; bury. [French *inhumer,* from Old French, from Latin *inhumāre* : *in-,* in; see IN–^{2} + *humus,* earth; see **dhghem-** in Appendix.] —**in′hu·ma′tion** *n.* —**in·hum′er** *n.*

in·im·i·cal (ĭ-nĭm′ĭ-kəl) *adj.* **1.** Injurious or harmful in effect; adverse: *habits inimical to good health.* **2.** Unfriendly; hostile: *a cold, inimical voice.* [Late Latin *inimīcālis,* from Latin *inimīcus,* enemy. See ENEMY.] —**in·im′i·cal·ly** *adv.*

in·im·i·ta·ble (ĭ-nĭm′ĭ-tə-bəl) *adj.* Defying imitation; matchless. [Middle English, from Latin *inimitābilis* : *in-,* not; see IN–^{1} + *imitābilis,* imitable (from *imitārī,* to imitate).] —**in·im′i·ta·bil′i·ty, in·im′i·ta·ble·ness** *n.* —**in·im′i·ta·bly** *adv.*

in·i·on (ĭn′ē-ən) *n.* The most prominent projecting point of the occipital bone at the base of the skull. [Greek, occipital bone, from *is, in-,* sinew, fiber. See **wei-** in Appendix.]

in·iq·ui·tous (ĭ-nĭk′wĭ-təs) *adj.* Characterized by iniquity; wicked. —**in·iq′ui·tous·ly** *adv.* —**in·iq′ui·tous·ness** *n.*

in·iq·ui·ty (ĭ-nĭk′wĭ-tē) *n., pl.* **-ties. 1.** Gross immorality or injustice; wickedness. **2.** A grossly immoral act; a sin. [Middle English *iniquite,* from Old French, from Latin *inīquitās,* from *inīquus,* unjust, harmful : *in-,* not; see IN–^{1} + *aequus,* equal.]

in·i·tial (ĭ-nĭsh′əl) *adj.* **1.** Of, relating to, or occurring at the beginning; first: *took the initial step toward reconciliation.* **2.** Designating the first letter or letters of a word. —**initial** *n.* **1.a.** The first letter of a proper name. **b. initials.** The first letter of each word of a person's complete name considered as a unit: *stationery monogrammed with her initials.* **2.** The first letter of a word. **3.** A large, often highly decorated letter set at the beginning of a chapter, verse, or paragraph. —**initial** *tr.v.* **-tialed, -tial·ing, -tials** also **-tialled, -tial·ling, -tials.** To mark or sign with initials, especially for purposes of authorization or approval. [Latin *initiālis,* from *initium,* beginning. See **ei-** in Appendix.] —**in·i′tial·ly** *adv.* —**in·i′tial·ness** *n.*

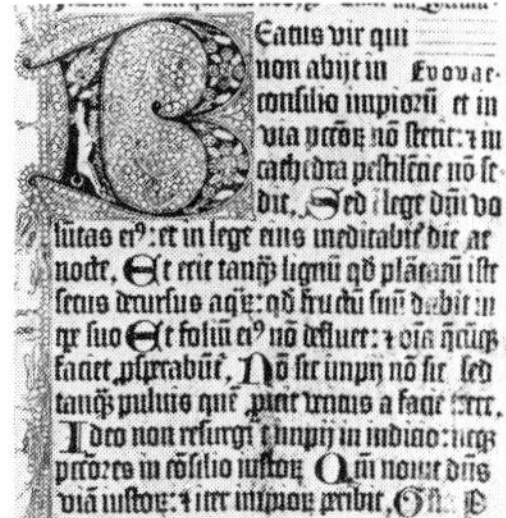

initial

in·i·tial·ize (ĭ-nĭsh′ə-līz′) *tr.v.* **-ized, -iz·ing, -iz·es.** *Computer Science.* To set to a starting position or value. —**in·i′tial·i·za′tion** (-shə-lĭ-zā′shən) *n.* —**in·i′tial·iz′er** *n.*

initial rhyme *n.* See **beginning rhyme** (sense 1).

initial teaching alphabet *n. Abbr.* **ITA, I.T.A.** An alphabet with 44 symbols, each of which represents a single sound that is used to teach beginning reading of English.

in·i·ti·ate (ĭ-nĭsh′ē-āt′) *tr.v.* **-at·ed, -at·ing, -ates. 1.** To set going by taking the first step; begin: *initiated trade with developing nations.* See Synonyms at **begin. 2.** To introduce to a new field, interest, skill, or activity. **3.** To admit into membership, as with ceremonies or ritual. —**initiate** (-ĭt) *adj.* **1.** Initiated or admitted, as to membership or a position of authority. **2.a.** Instructed in esoteric knowledge. **b.** Introduced to something new. —**initiate** (-ĭt) *n.* **1.** One who is being or has been initiated. **2.** One who has been introduced to or has attained knowledge in a particular field. [Latin *initiāre, initiāt-,* from *initium,* beginning. See **ei-** in Appendix.] —**in·i′ti·a′tor** *n.*

in·i·ti·a·tion (ĭ-nĭsh′ē-ā′shən) *n.* **1.a.** The act or an instance of initiating. **b.** The process of being initiated. **c.** The condition of being initiated. **2.** A ceremony, ritual, test, or period of instruction with which a new member is admitted to an organization or office or to knowledge. **3.** The condition of being knowledgeable.

in·i·tia·tive (ĭ-nĭsh′ə-tĭv) *n.* **1.** The power or ability to begin or to follow through energetically with a plan or task; enterprise and determination. **2.** A beginning or introductory step; an opening move: *took the initiative in trying to solve the problem.* **3.a.** The power or right to introduce a new legislative measure. **b.** The right and procedure by which citizens can propose a law by petition and ensure its submission to the electorate. —**initiative** *adj.* **1.** Of or relating to initiation. **2.** Used to initiate; initiatory. —***idiom.* on (one's) own initiative.** Without prompting or direction from others; on one's own. —**in·i′tia·tive·ly** *adv.*

in·i·ti·a·to·ry (ĭ-nĭsh′ē-ə-tôr′ē, -tōr′ē) *adj.* **1.** Introductory; initial. **2.** Tending or used to initiate.

inj. *abbr.* Injection.

in·ject (ĭn-jĕkt′) *tr.v.* **-ject·ed, -ject·ing, -jects. 1.** To force or drive (a fluid) into something: *inject fuel into an engine cylinder; inject air into a liquid mixture.* **2.a.** *Medicine.* To introduce (a drug or vaccine, for example) into a body part. **b.** To treat by means of injection: *injected the patient with digitalis.* **3.** To introduce into conversation or consideration: *tried to inject a note of humor into the negotiations.* **4.** To place into an orbit, a trajectory, or a stream. [Latin *inicere, iniect-,* to throw in : *in-,* in; see IN–^{2} + *iacere,* to throw; see **yē-** in Appendix.] —**in·jec′tor** *n.*

in·ject·a·ble (ĭn-jĕk′tə-bəl) *adj.* That can be injected. Used of a drug. —**injectable** *n.* A drug or medicine that can be injected.

in·jec·tant (ĭn-jĕk′tənt) *n.* A substance injected, as into the skin.

in·jec·tion (ĭn-jĕk′shən) *n. Abbr.* **inj. 1.** The act of injecting. **2.** Something that is injected, especially a dose of liquid medicine injected into the body.

in-joke (ĭn′jōk′) *n. Informal.* A joke originated or appreciated by the members of a particular group.

in·ju·di·cious (ĭn′jo͞o-dĭsh′əs) *adj.* Lacking or showing a lack of judgment or discretion; unwise. —**in′ju·di′cious·ly** *adv.* —**in′ju·di′cious·ness** *n.*

in·junc·tion (ĭn-jŭngk′shən) *n.* **1.** The act or an instance of enjoining; a command, a directive, or an order. **2.** *Law.* A court order prohibiting a party from a specific course of action. [Middle English *injunccion,* from Late Latin *iniūnctiō, iniūnctiōn-,* from Latin *iniūnctus,* past participle of *iniungere,* to enjoin : *in-,* in; see IN–^{2} + *iungere,* to join; see **yeug-** in Appendix.] —**in·junc′tive** *adj.*

in·jure (ĭn′jər) *tr.v.* **-jured, -jur·ing, -jures. 1.** To cause physical harm to; hurt. **2.** To cause damage to; impair. **3.** To cause distress to; wound: *injured their feelings.* **4.** To commit an injustice or offense against; wrong. [Middle English *injuren,* to wrong, dishonor, from Old French *injurier,* from Latin *iniūriārī,* from *iniūria,* a wrong. See INJURY.] —**in′jur·er** *n.*

SYNONYMS: *injure, harm, hurt, damage, impair, mar, spoil.* These verbs mean to affect detrimentally. *Injure* can refer to acts that have an adverse effect on health, appearance, prospects, or well-being: *She was badly injured in an accident. Malicious gossip could injure his chances of success.* It can also mean to treat another unjustly or wrongfully: *"Those that are not favored will think themselves injured"* (Samuel Johnson). *Harm* and *hurt* refer principally to what causes pain, distress, diminution, or loss: *Gypsy moths harm foliage. Failure to pay his bills has harmed his credit. A hailstorm hurt the apple crop. My feelings are hurt. Damage* usually implies injury that decreases value, usefulness, desirability, or effectiveness: *A falling tree damaged the roof. The scandal seriously damaged the senator's reputation. Impair* refers to what diminishes, as in quality: *The patient's intelligence has been impaired by a brain injury.* To *mar* is to impair by or as if by

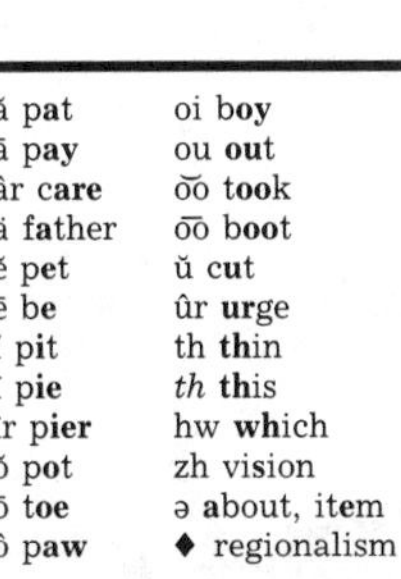

ă pat	oi boy
ā pay	ou out
âr care	o͝o took
ä father	o͞o boot
ĕ pet	ŭ cut
ē be	ûr urge
ĭ pit	th thin
ī pie	*th* this
îr pier	hw which
ŏ pot	zh vision
ō toe	ə about, item
ô paw	♦ regionalism

Stress marks: **′** (primary); ′ (secondary), as in **dictionary** (dĭk′shə-nĕr′ē)

inkstand

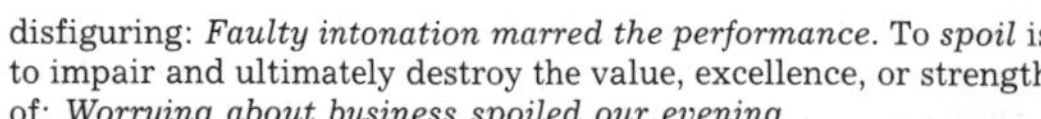

disfiguring: *Faulty intonation marred the performance.* To *spoil* is to impair and ultimately destroy the value, excellence, or strength of: *Worrying about business spoiled our evening.*

in·ju·ri·ous (ĭn-jo͝or′ē-əs) *adj.* **1.** Causing or tending to cause injury; harmful: *eating habits that are injurious to one's health.* **2.** Slanderous; libelous: *made injurious statements about his rival.* **—in·ju′ri·ous·ly** *adv.* **—in·ju′ri·ous·ness** *n.*

in·ju·ry (ĭn′jə-rē) *n., pl.* **-ries. 1.** Damage or harm done to or suffered by a person or thing: *escaped from the accident without injury; a scandal that did considerable injury to the campaign.* **2.** A particular form of hurt, damage, or loss: *a leg injury.* **3.** *Law.* Violation of the rights of another party for which legal redress is available. See Synonyms at **injustice. 4.** *Obsolete.* An insult. [Middle English *injurie,* from Anglo-Norman, from Latin *iniūria,* a wrong, injustice, from feminine of *iniūrius,* unjust : *in-,* not; see IN–[1] + *iūs, iūr-,* law; see **yewes-** in Appendix.]

in·jus·tice (ĭn-jŭs′tĭs) *n.* **1.** Violation of another's rights or of what is right; lack of justice. **2.** A specific unjust act; a wrong. [Middle English, from Old French, from Latin *iniūstitia,* from *iniūstus,* unjust : *in-,* not; see IN–[1] + *iūstus,* just; see JUST[1].]

SYNONYMS: *injustice, injury, wrong, grievance.* These nouns denote acts or conditions that cause people to suffer hardship or loss undeservedly. An *injustice* is a violation of a person's rights; the term can also refer to unfair treatment of another or others: *"Injustice anywhere is a threat to justice everywhere"* (Martin Luther King, Jr.). An *injury* is an injustice for which legal redress is available: *"Private wrongs . . . are an infringement or privation of the private or civil rights belonging to individuals . . . and are thereupon frequently termed civil injuries"* (William Blackstone). *Wrong* in a legal sense refers to what violates the rights of an individual or adversely affects the public welfare; in a more general sense, however, the word is similar in meaning to but more emphatic than *injustice: "The age of chivalry is never past, so long as there is a wrong left unredressed on earth"* (Charles Kingsley). A *grievance* is an act or a condition that is regarded by those involved as a wrong that affords cause for complaint: *A committee of inmates presented a list of grievances to the prison warden.*

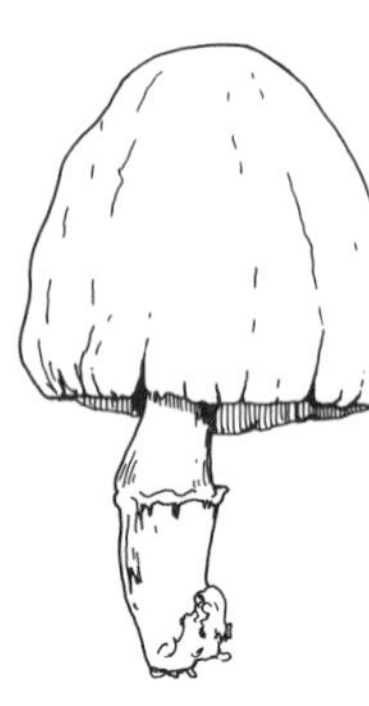

inky cap
Coprinus atramentarius

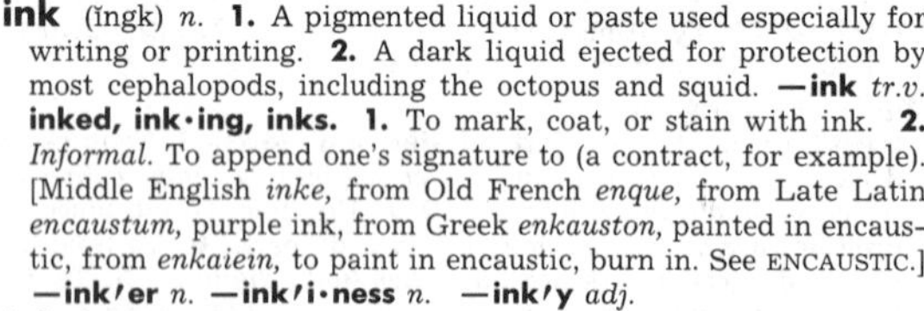

ink (ĭngk) *n.* **1.** A pigmented liquid or paste used especially for writing or printing. **2.** A dark liquid ejected for protection by most cephalopods, including the octopus and squid. **—ink** *tr.v.* **inked, ink·ing, inks. 1.** To mark, coat, or stain with ink. **2.** *Informal.* To append one's signature to (a contract, for example). [Middle English *inke,* from Old French *enque,* from Late Latin *encaustum,* purple ink, from Greek *enkauston,* painted in encaustic, from *enkaiein,* to paint in encaustic, burn in. See ENCAUSTIC.] **—ink′er** *n.* **—ink′i·ness** *n.* **—ink′y** *adj.*

ink·ber·ry (ĭngk′bĕr′ē) *n.* **1.** A shrub *(Ilex glabra)* of eastern North America, having black, berrylike fruit. **2.** The fruit of an inkberry.

ink·blot (ĭngk′blŏt′) *n.* **1.** A blotted pattern of spilled ink. **2.** A pattern resembling an inkblot that is used in inkblot tests, such as the Rorschach test.

inkblot test *n. Psychology.* A projective test in which a subject's interpretation of inkblots is analyzed.

ink·horn (ĭngk′hôrn′) *n.* A small container made of horn or a similar material, formerly used to hold ink for writing. **—inkhorn** *adj.* Affectedly learned; pedantic: *inkhorn words.*

in-kind (ĭn′kīnd′) *adj.* **1.** Given in goods, commodities, or services rather than money: *cash and in-kind benefits.* **2.** Returning something equivalent to that received: *required to make a 30 percent in-kind contribution.*

in·kle (ĭng′kəl) *n.* **1.** A colored linen tape woven on a simple, narrow loom and used for trimmings. **2.** The yarn or thread used in making this tape. [Origin unknown.]

in·kling (ĭng′klĭng) *n.* **1.** A slight hint or indication. **2.** A slight understanding or vague idea or notion. [Probably alteration of Middle English *(a) ningkiling,* (a) hint, suggestion, possibly alteration of *nikking,* from *nikken,* to mark a text for correction, from *nik,* notch, tally, perhaps from variant of Old French *niche,* niche. See NICHE.]

WORD HISTORY: One of the more fascinating journeys in the histories of words is the one that links *nest* and *inkling.* We begin this journey with the Indo-European root *nizdo–,* which by way of Germanic **nist–* will give us *nest* but also leads to Latin *nīdus,* "nest." From Latin *nīdus* may come Old French (and modern French) *niche,* meaning "niche." It is possible that in Old French a variant form existed that was borrowed into Middle English as *nik,* meaning "a notch, tally." This word seems related to the Middle English word *nikken,* which may mean "to mark a text for correction," and *nikking,* "a hint, slight indication," or possibly "a whisper, mention." The word *nikking* appears only once, in a Middle English text composed around 1400, as does the word *ningkiling,* found in another copy of the same text. It is possible that *ningkiling* is from *nikking.* Furthermore, it is probable that people divided *a ninkling* incorrectly and got *an inkling,* just as they did with *a napron,* getting *an apron.* If all this has indeed happened, *inkling* has come a long way from the nest.

ink sac *n.* An ink-containing organ located near the rectum in most cephalopods, including the octopus, squid, and cuttlefish.

inlay

ink·stand (ĭngk′stănd′) *n.* **1.** A tray or rack for pens and bottles of ink. **2.** See **inkwell.**

Ink·ster (ĭngk′stər). A city of southeast Michigan, a residential suburb of Detroit. Population, 35,190.

ink·well (ĭngk′wĕl′) *n.* A small reservoir for ink. Also called *inkstand.*

inky cap *n.* Any of various mushrooms of the genus *Coprinus,* having gills that dissolve into a dark liquid after maturation of the spores.

in·lace (ĭn-lās′) *v.* Variant of **enlace.**

in·laid (ĭn′lād′) *v.* Past tense and past participle of **inlay. —inlaid** *adj.* **1.** Set into a surface in a decorative pattern: *a mahogany dresser with an inlaid teak design.* **2.** Decorated with a pattern set into a surface: *inlaid antique furniture.*

in·land (ĭn′lənd) *adj.* **1.** Of, relating to, or located in the interior part of a country or region. **2.** *Chiefly British.* Operating or applying within the borders of a country or region; domestic: *inland tariffs.* **—inland** *adv.* In, toward, or into the interior of a country or region. **—inland** (-lănd′, -lənd) *n.* The interior of a country or region. **—in′land′er** *n.*

In·land Empire (ĭn′lənd, -lănd′). A region of the northwest United States between the Cascade Range and the Rocky Mountains, comprising eastern Washington, eastern Oregon, northern Idaho, and western Montana. Farming, lumbering, livestock raising, and mining are important to the area.

Inland Passage. See **Inside Passage.**

Inland Sea. An arm of the Pacific Ocean in southern Japan between Honshu, Shikoku, and Kyushu. Linked to the Sea of Japan by a narrow channel, the sea is famous for its scenic beauty.

in-law (ĭn′lô′) *n.* A relative by marriage. [Back-formation from such compounds as *mother-in-law.*]

in-law rental *n.* See **accessory apartment.**

in·lay (ĭn′lā′, ĭn-lā′) *tr.v.* **-laid** (-lād′), **-lay·ing, -lays. 1.a.** To set (pieces of wood or ivory, for example) into a surface, usually at the same level, to form a design. **b.** To decorate by setting in such designs. **2.** To insert (a photograph, for example) within a mat in a book. **—inlay** *n.* **1.a.** Contrasting material set into a surface in pieces to form a design. **b.** A design, pattern, or decoration made by inlaying. **2.** *Dentistry.* A solid filling, as of gold or porcelain, fitted to a cavity in a tooth and cemented into place. **—in·lay′er** *n.*

in·let (ĭn′lĕt′, -lĭt) *n.* **1.a.** A recess, such as a bay or cove, along a coast. **b.** A stream or bay leading inland, as from the ocean; an estuary. **c.** A narrow passage of water, as between two islands. **d.** A drainage passage, as to a culvert. **2.** An opening providing a means of entrance or intake.

in·li·er (ĭn′lī′ər) *n.* An area or a formation of older rocks completely surrounded by younger layers. [IN[1] + (OUT)LIER.]

in lo·co pa·ren·tis (ĭn lō′kō pə-rĕn′tĭs) *adv.* In the position or place of a parent. [Latin *in locō parentis* : *in,* in + *locō,* ablative of *locus,* place + *parentis,* genitive of *parēns,* parent.]

in·ly (ĭn′lē) *adv.* **1.** In an inward manner; inwardly. **2.** With thorough knowledge or understanding.

in·ly·ing (ĭn′lī′ĭng) *adj.* Located farther in: *navigated the river and its inlying tributaries.*

in·mate (ĭn′māt′) *n.* A resident of a dwelling that houses a number of occupants, especially a person confined to an institution, such as a prison or hospital.

in me·di·as res (ĭn mē′dē-əs rās′) *adv.* In or into the middle of a sequence of events, as in a literary narrative. [Latin *in mediās rēs* : *in,* into + *mediās,* accusative pl. feminine of *medius,* in the middle of + *rēs,* accusative pl. of *rēs,* thing.]

in me·mo·ri·am (ĭn′ mə-môr′ē-əm, -mōr′-) *prep.* In memory of; as a memorial to. Used especially in epitaphs. [From Latin *in memoriam,* to the memory (of) : *in,* in, into + *memoriam,* accusative of *memoria,* memory.]

in-mi·grant (ĭn′mī′grənt) *n.* One that in-migrates.

in-mi·grate (ĭn′mī′grāt) *intr.v.* **-grat·ed, -grat·ing, -grates.** To move into a different region of the same country or territory. **—in′-mi·gra′tion** *n.*

in·most (ĭn′mōst′) *adj.* Farthest within; innermost.

inn (ĭn) *n.* **1.** A public lodging house serving food and drink to travelers; a hotel. **2.** A tavern or restaurant. **3.** *Chiefly British.* Formerly, a residence hall for students, especially law students, in London. [Middle English, from Old English. See **en** in Appendix.]

Inn (ĭn). A river of eastern Switzerland, western Austria, and southeast Germany flowing about 515 km (320 mi) to the Danube River.

in·nards (ĭn′ərdz) *pl.n. Informal.* **1.** Internal bodily organs; viscera. **2.** The inner parts, as of a machine. [Alteration of *inwards,* pl. of INWARD.]

in·nate (ĭ-nāt′, ĭn′āt′) *adj.* **1.** Possessed at birth; inborn. **2.** Possessed as an essential characteristic; inherent. **3.** Of or produced by the mind rather than learned through experience: *an innate knowledge of right and wrong.* [Middle English *innat,* from Latin *innātus,* past participle of *innāscī,* to be born in : *in-,* in; see IN–[2] + *nāscī,* to be born; see **gene-** in Appendix.] **—in·nate′ly** *adv.* **—in·nate′ness** *n.*

SYNONYMS: *innate, inborn, inbred, congenital, hereditary.* These adjectives mean existing in a person or thing from birth or origin. *Innate, inborn,* and *inbred* are often used interchangeably. *Inborn,* however, is strongest in implying that something has been present since birth: *inborn intelligence; an inborn sense of the appropriate.* What is *inbred* has either existed from birth or been ingrained through earliest training or associations: *an inbred love of music; inbred superiority.* Something that is *innate* seems essential to the nature, character, or constitution: *innate honesty; innate common sense. Congenital* is applied principally to characteristics, especially defects, acquired during fetal development: *a congenital disease. Hereditary* refers to what is transmitted by biological heredity (*a hereditary heart anomaly*) or by tradition: *"that ignorance and superstitiousness hereditary to all sailors"* (Herman Melville).

---

in·ner (ĭn′ər) *adj.* **1.** Located or occurring farther inside: *an inner room; an inner layer of warm clothing.* **2.** Less apparent; deeper: *the inner meaning of a poem.* **3.** Of or relating to the mind or spirit: *"Beethoven's manuscript looks like a bloody record of a tremendous inner battle"* (Leonard Bernstein). **4.** More exclusive, influential, or important: *the inner circles of government.* [Middle English, from Old English *innera.* See **en** in Appendix.] **—in′ner** *n.* **—in′ner·ly** *adv. & adj.* **—in′ner·ness** *n.*

inner city *n.* The usually older, central part of a city, especially when characterized by crowded neighborhoods in which low-income, often minority groups predominate. **—in′ner-cit′y** (ĭn′ər-sĭt′ē) *adj.*

in·ner-di·rect·ed (ĭn′ər-dĭ-rĕk′tĭd, -dī-) *adj.* Guided in thought and behavior by one's own set of values rather than societal standards or norms.

inner ear *n.* The portion of the ear located within the temporal bone that is involved in both hearing and balance and includes the semicircular canals, vestibule, and cochlea. Also called *internal ear, labyrinth.*

In·ner Heb·ri·des (ĭn′ər hĕb′rĭ-dēz′). See **Hebrides.**

Inner Light *n.* In Quaker doctrine, a divine presence believed to be an enlightening and guiding force in the human soul.

Inner Mon·go·li·a (mŏng-gō′lē-ə, -gōl′yə, mŏn-). See **Nei Monggol.**

in·ner·most (ĭn′ər-mōst′) *adj.* **1.** Situated or occurring farthest within: *the innermost chamber.* **2.** Most intimate: *one's innermost feelings.* **—innermost** *n.* The part situated farthest in.

inner planet *n.* Any of the four planets, Mercury, Venus, Earth, and Mars, whose orbits are closest to the sun.

inner product *n. Mathematics.* See **scalar product.**

in·ner·sole (ĭn′ər-sōl′) *n.* See **insole.**

in·ner·spring (ĭn′ər-sprĭng′) *adj.* Having numerous coil springs enclosed by a padded cover: *an innerspring mattress.*

inner tube *n.* A flexible, airtight hollow ring, usually made of rubber, that is inserted into the casing of a pneumatic tire for holding compressed air.

in·ner·vate (ĭ-nûr′vāt′, ĭn′ər-) *tr.v.* **-vat·ed, -vat·ing, -vates. 1.** To supply (an organ or a body part) with nerves. **2.** To stimulate (a nerve, muscle, or body part) to action. **—in′ner·va′tion** *n.* **—in′ner·va′tion·al** (-vā′shə-nəl) *adj.*

in·nerve (ĭ-nûrv′) *tr.v.* **-nerved, -nerv·ing, -nerves.** To give nervous energy to; stimulate.

in·ner·wear (ĭn′ər-wâr′) *n.* Clothing, such as lingerie, designed to be worn next to the skin.

In·ness (ĭn′ĭs), **George.** 1825–1894. American landscape painter whose principal works include *Rainbow after a Storm* (1869) and *The Afterglow* (1878).

in·ning (ĭn′ĭng) *n.* **1.a.** *Baseball.* One of nine divisions or periods of a regulation game, in which each team has a turn at bat as limited by three outs. **b. innings.** *(used with a sing. verb). Sports.* The division or period of a cricket game during which one team is at bat. **2.** Often **innings.** *(used with a sing. or pl. verb).* An opportunity to act or speak out; a chance for accomplishment. **3.** The reclamation of flooded or marshy land. [Middle English *innynge,* a getting in, from Old English *innung,* gerund of *innian,* to put in, from *in,* in. See IN[1].]

inn·keep·er (ĭn′kē′pər) *n.* One that owns or manages an inn or hotel.

in·no·cence (ĭn′ə-səns) *n.* **1.** The state, quality, or virtue of being innocent, as: **a.** Freedom from sin, moral wrong, or guilt through lack of knowledge of evil. **b.** Guiltlessness of a specific legal crime or offense. **c.** Freedom from guile, cunning, or deceit; simplicity or artlessness. **d.** Lack of worldliness or sophistication; naiveté. **e.** Lack of knowledge or understanding; ignorance. **f.** Freedom from harmfulness; inoffensiveness. **2.** One that is innocent. **3.** *Botany.* See **blue-eyed Mary.**

in·no·cen·cy (ĭn′ə-sən-sē) *n., pl.* **-cies. 1.** Innocence. **2.** An innocent quality or action.

in·no·cent (ĭn′ə-sənt) *adj.* **1.** Uncorrupted by evil, malice, or wrongdoing; sinless: *an innocent child.* **2.a.** Not guilty of a specific crime or offense; legally blameless: *was innocent of all charges.* **b.** Within, allowed by, or sanctioned by the law; lawful. **3.a.** Not dangerous or harmful; innocuous: *an innocent prank.* **b.** Candid; straightforward: *a child's innocent stare.* **4.a.** Not experienced or worldly; naive. **b.** Betraying or suggesting no deception or guile; artless. **5.a.** Not exposed to or familiar with something specified; ignorant: *American tourists wholly innocent of French.* **b.** Unaware: *She remained innocent of the complications she had caused.* **6.** Lacking, deprived, or devoid of something: *a novel innocent of literary merit.* **—innocent** *n.* **1.** A person, especially a child, who is free of evil or sin. **2.** A simple, guileless, inexperienced, or unsophisticated person. **3.** A very young child. [Middle English, from Old French, from Latin *innocēns, innocent-* : *in-,* not; see IN–[1] + *nocēns,* present participle of *nocēre,* to harm; see **nek-[1]** in Appendix.] **—in′no·cent·ly** *adv.*

In·no·cent III (ĭn′ə-sənt). Originally Lotario di Segni. 1161–1216. Pope (1198–1216) whose reign was marked by the Fourth Crusade and papal intervention in European politics.

Innocent III
13th-century mosaic

in·noc·u·ous (ĭ-nŏk′yo͞o-əs) *adj.* **1.** Having no adverse effect; harmless. **2.** Not likely to offend or provoke to strong emotion; insipid. [From Latin *innocuus* : *in-,* not; see IN–[1] + *nocuus,* harmful (from *nocēre,* to harm; see **nek-[1]** in Appendix).] **—in·noc′u·ous·ly** *adv.* **—in·noc′u·ous·ness** *n.*

in·nom·i·nate (ĭ-nŏm′ə-nĭt) *adj.* **1.** Having no name. **2.** Anonymous. [Late Latin *innōminātus* : Latin *in-,* not; see IN–[1] + Latin *nōminātus,* past participle of *nōmināre,* to name; see NOMINATE.]

innominate artery *n.* An artery that arises from the arch of the aorta and divides into the right subclavian and right carotid arteries. Also called *brachiocephalic artery, brachiocephalic trunk.*

innominate bone *n.* See **hipbone.**

innominate vein *n.* Either of a pair of veins in the neck, each formed by the union of the internal jugular and subclavian veins, that join to form the superior vena cava. Also called *brachiocephalic vein.*

in·no·vate (ĭn′ə-vāt′) *v.* **-vat·ed, -vat·ing, -vates.** —*tr.* To begin or introduce (something new) for or as if for the first time. —*intr.* To begin or introduce something new. [French *innover,* from Old French, from Latin *innovāre, innovāt-,* to renew : *in-,* intensive pref.; see IN–[2] + *novāre,* to make new (from *novus,* new; see **newo-** in Appendix).] **—in′no·va′tor** *n.* **—in′no·va·to′ry** (-və-tôr′ē, -tōr′ē) *adj.*

in·no·va·tion (ĭn′ə-vā′shən) *n.* **1.** The act of introducing something new. **2.** Something newly introduced. **—in′no·va′tion·al** *adj.*

in·no·va·tive (ĭn′ə-vā′tĭv) *adj.* Marked by or given to innovations. **—in′no·va′tive·ness** *n.*

Inns·bruck (ĭnz′bro͝ok′, ĭns′-). A city of southwest Austria west-southwest of Salzburg. Established as a fortified town c. 1180, it is an industrial, commercial, and transportation center famed as a summer and winter resort. Population, 117,287.

Inns of Court (ĭnz) *pl.n. Law.* **1.** The four legal societies in England founded about the beginning of the 14th century and having the exclusive right to confer the title of barrister on law students. **2.** The buildings housing the Inns of Court.

in·nu·en·do (ĭn′yo͞o-ĕn′dō) *n., pl.* **-does. 1.** An indirect or subtle, usually derogatory implication in expression; an insinuation. **2.** *Law.* **a.** A plaintiff's interpretation in a libel suit of allegedly libelous or slanderous material. **b.** A parenthetic explanation of a word or charge in a legal document. [From Latin *innuendō,* by hinting, ablative of *innuendum,* gerund of *innuere,* to nod to : *in-,* to, toward; see IN–[2] + *-nuere,* to nod.]

In·nu·it (ĭn′yo͞o-ĭt) *n.* Variant of **Inuit.**

in·nu·mer·a·ble (ĭ-no͞o′mər-ə-bəl, ĭ-nyo͞o′-) *adj.* Too numerous to be counted; numberless. See Synonyms at **incalculable.** [Middle English, from Latin *innumerābilis* : *in-,* not; see IN–[1] + *numerābilis,* countable; see NUMERABLE.] **—in·nu′mer·a·ble·ness** *n.* **—in·nu′mer·a·bly** *adv.*

in·nu·mer·ate (ĭ-no͞o′mər-ĭt, ĭ-nyo͞o′-) *adj.* Unfamiliar with mathematical concepts and methods. **—innumerate** *n.* A person who is unfamiliar with mathematical concepts and methods. **—in·nu′mer·a·cy** *n.*

in·nu·mer·ous (ĭ-no͞o′mər-əs) *adj.* Innumerable. [From Latin *innumerus* : *in-,* not; see IN–[1] + *numerus,* number; see NUMBER.]

in·nu·tri·tion (ĭn′no͞o-trĭsh′ən, -nyo͞o-) *n.* Poor nourishment; lack of good nutrition. **—in′nu·tri′tious** *adj.*

in·ob·ser·vance (ĭn′əb-zûr′vəns) *n.* **1.** Lack of heed or attention; disregard. **2.** Nonobservance, as of a law or custom. **—in′ob·ser′vant** *adj.*

in·ob·tru·sive (ĭn′əb-tro͞o′sĭv) *adj.* Not noticeable; unobtrusive.

in·oc·u·la·ble (ĭ-nŏk′yə-lə-bəl) *adj.* **1.** Susceptible to a disease transmitted by inoculation. **2.** That can be used in an inoculation. **3.** Transmissible by inoculation. **—in·oc′u·la·bil′i·ty** *n.*

in·oc·u·lant (ĭ-nŏk′yə-lənt) *n.* See **inoculum.**

in·oc·u·late (ĭ-nŏk′yə-lāt′) *tr.v.* **-lat·ed, -lat·ing, -lates. 1.** To introduce a serum, a vaccine, or an antigenic substance into (the body of a person or an animal), especially to produce or boost immunity to a specific disease. **2.** To communicate a disease to (a living organism) by transferring its causative agent into the organism. **3.** To implant microorganisms or infectious material into (a culture medium). **4.** To safeguard as if by inoculation; protect. **5.** To introduce an idea or attitude into the mind of. [Middle English *inoculaten,* to graft a scion, from Latin *inoculāre, inoculāt-* : *in-,* in; see IN–[2] + *oculus,* eye, bud; see **okʷ-** in Appendix.] **—in·oc′u·la′tive** *adj.* **—in·oc′u·la′tor** *n.*

in·oc·u·la·tion (ĭ-nŏk′yə-lā′shən) *n.* **1.** The act or an instance of inoculating, especially the introduction of an antigenic substance or vaccine into the body to produce immunity to a specific disease. **2.** *Informal.* A preemptive advertising tactic in

ă pat	oi boy
ā pay	ou out
âr care	o͝o took
ä father	o͞o boot
ĕ pet	ŭ cut
ē be	ûr urge
ĭ pit	th thin
ī pie	*th* this
îr pier	hw which
ŏ pot	zh vision
ō toe	ə about, item
ô paw	♦ regionalism

Stress marks: ′ (primary); ′ (secondary), as in **dictionary** (dĭk′shə-nĕr′ē)

which one party attempts to foresee and neutralize potentially damaging criticism from another party by being the first to confront troublesome issues.

in·oc·u·lum (ĭ-nŏk′yə-ləm) *n., pl.* **-la** (-lə) or **-lums.** The material used in an inoculation. Also called *inoculant.* [New Latin, from Latin *inoculāre,* to graft a scion. See INOCULATE.]

in·o·dor·ous (ĭn-ō′dər-əs) *adj.* Having no odor.

in·of·fen·sive (ĭn′ə-fĕn′sĭv) *adj.* **1.** Giving no offense; unobjectionable. **2.** Causing no harm; harmless. **—in′of·fen′sive·ly** *adv.* **—in′of·fen′sive·ness** *n.*

in·of·fi·cious (ĭn′ə-fĭsh′əs) *adj. Law.* Contrary to natural affection or moral duty. Used of a will in which the testator disinherits the rightful heirs with insufficient reason. [Latin *inofficiōsus,* undutiful : *in-,* not; see IN–[1] + *officiōsus,* dutiful; see OFFICIOUS.]

Ismet Inönü

I·nö·nü (ĭn′ə-no͞o′, ĭ-nœ-nü′), **Ismet.** 1884–1973. Turkish army officer and politician who served as president (1938–1950) and kept Turkey neutral during World War II.

in·op·er·a·ble (ĭn-ŏp′ər-ə-bəl, -ŏp′rə-) *adj.* **1.** Not functioning; inoperative. **2.** Unsuitable for a surgical procedure: *an inoperable tumor.* **—in·op′er·a·bly** *adv.*

in·op·er·a·tive (ĭn-ŏp′ər-ə-tĭv, -ŏp′rə-) *adj.* **1.** Not working or functioning. **2.** No longer in force, countermanded: *declared the previous instructions inoperative.* **—in·op′er·a·tive·ness** *n.*

in·o·per·cu·late (ĭn′ō-pûr′kyə-lĭt) *adj. Biology.* Lacking an operculum. **—in′o·per′cu·late** *n.*

in·op·por·tune (ĭn-ŏp′ər-to͞on′, -tyo͞on′) *adj.* Inappropriate or ill-timed; not opportune. **—in·op′por·tune′ly** *adv.* **—in·op′por·tune′ness** *n.*

in·or·di·nate (ĭn-ôr′dn-ĭt) *adj.* **1.** Exceeding reasonable limits; immoderate. See Synonyms at **excessive. 2.** Not regulated; disorderly. [Middle English *inordinat,* from Latin *inōrdinātus,* disordered : *in-,* not; see IN–[1] + *ōrdinātus,* past participle of *ōrdināre,* to set in order (from *ōrdō, ōrdin-,* order; see **ar-** in Appendix).] **—in·or′di·na·cy, in·or′di·nate·ness** *n.* **—in·or′di·nate·ly** *adv.*

in·or·gan·ic (ĭn′ôr-găn′ĭk) *adj. Abbr.* **inorg. 1.a.** Involving neither organic life nor the products of organic life. **b.** Not composed of organic matter. **2.** *Chemistry.* Of or relating to compounds not containing hydrocarbon groups. **3.** Not arising in normal growth; artificial. **4.** Lacking system or structure. **—in′or·gan′i·cal·ly** *adv.*

in·os·cu·late (ĭn-ŏs′kyə-lāt′) *v.* **-lat·ed, -lat·ing, -lates.** —*tr.* **1.** To unite (blood vessels, nerve fibers, or ducts) by small openings. **2.** To make continuous; blend. —*intr.* **1.** To open into one another. **2.** To unite so as to be continuous; blend. [IN–[2] + Latin *ōsculāre, ōsculāt-,* to provide with an opening (from *ōsculum,* diminutive of *ōs,* mouth; see **ōs-** in Appendix).] **—in·os′cu·la′tion** *n.*

in·o·si·tol (ĭ-nō′sĭ-tôl′, -tōl′, ī-nō′-) *n.* Any of nine isomeric alcohols, $C_6H_{12}O_6{\cdot}2H_2O$, especially one found in plant and animal tissue and classified as a member of the vitamin B complex. [Greek *inos,* genitive of *is,* sinew; see **wei-** in Appendix + –IT(E)[2] + –OL[1].]

in·o·tro·pic (ē′nə-trō′pĭk, -trŏp′ĭk, ī′nə-) *adj.* Affecting the contraction of muscle, especially heart muscle: *an inotropic drug.* [Greek *is, in-,* tendon, sinew; see **wei-** in Appendix + –TROPIC.]

INP *abbr.* International News Photo.

in·pa·tient (ĭn′pā′shənt) *n.* A patient who is admitted to a hospital or clinic for treatment that requires at least one overnight stay. —*attributive.* Often used to modify another noun: *an inpatient procedure; an inpatient facility.*

in per·so·nam (ĭn′ pər-sō′nəm) *adv. & adj. Law.* Against a person rather than against property. Used of an action or a judgment. [Late Latin : Latin *in,* onto, against + Latin *persōnam,* accusative of *persōna,* person.]

in pet·to (ĭn pĕt′ō) *adv. & adj. Roman Catholic Church.* In secret or private. Used of appointments of cardinals by the pope undisclosed in consistory. [Italian : *in,* in + *petto,* breast.]

in·phase (ĭn′fāz′) *adj.* Having the same electrical phase.

in pos·se (ĭn pŏs′ē) *adv. & adj.* In potential but not in actuality. [Medieval Latin : Latin *in,* in + Latin *posse,* to be able.]

in pro·pri·a per·so·na (ĭn prō′prē-ə pər-sō′nə) *adv. Law.* In one's own person, especially without representation by an attorney. [Medieval Latin *in propriā persōnā* : Latin *in,* in + Latin *propriā,* ablative of *proprius,* one's own + Latin *persōnā,* ablative of *persōna,* person.]

in·put (ĭn′po͝ot′) *n.* **1.** Something put into a system or expended in its operation to achieve output or a result, especially: **a.** Energy, work, or power used to drive a machine. **b.** Current, electromotive force, or power supplied to an electric circuit, network, or device. **c.** *Computer Science.* Information put into a communications system for transmission or into a computer system for processing. **d.** *Computer Science.* A position, terminal, or station at which input enters a system. **e.** Any of the items, including materials, equipment, and funds, required for production. **2.a.** The act of putting in; infusion: *a steady input of fuel.* **b.** An amount put in. **3.** *Usage Problem.* **a.** Contribution of information or a comment or viewpoint: *a discussion with input from all members of the group.* **b.** Information in general. **—input** *tr.v.* **-put·ted** or **-put, -put·ting, -puts.** *Computer Science.* To enter (data or a program) into a computer.

USAGE NOTE: The noun *input* has been used as a technical term for about a century in fields such as physics and electrical engineering, but its recent popularity grows out of its use in computer science, where it refers to data or signals entered into a system for processing or transmission. In general discourse *input* is now widely used to refer to the transmission of information and opinion, as in *The report questioned whether a President thus shielded had access to a sufficiently varied input to have a realistic picture of the nation* or *The nominee herself had no input on housing policy.* In this last sentence the meaning of the term is uncertain: it may mean either that the nominee provided no opinions to the policymakers or that she received no information about housing policy. This vagueness in the nontechnical use of *input* may be one reason that some critics have objected to it (including, in an earlier survey, a majority of the Usage Panel). Though the usage is well established, care should be taken not to use the word merely as a way of pretending to a scientific precision unwarranted by the facts of the case.

inq. *abbr.* Inquiry.

in·quest (ĭn′kwĕst′) *n.* **1.** *Law.* **a.** A judicial inquiry into a matter usually held before a jury, especially an inquiry into the cause of a death. **b.** A jury making such an inquiry. **c.** The finding based on such an inquiry. **2.** An investigation or inquiry. See Synonyms at **inquiry.** [Middle English *enqueste,* from Old French, from Vulgar Latin **inquæsīta,* thing inquired into, alteration of Latin *inquīsīta,* feminine past participle of *inquīrere,* to inquire into. See INQUIRE.]

in·qui·e·tude (ĭn-kwī′ĭ-to͞od′, -tyo͞od′) *n.* A state of restlessness or uneasiness; disquietude. [Middle English, disturbance, from Late Latin *inquiētūdō,* restlessness, from Latin *inquiētus,* restless : *in-,* not; see IN–[1] + *quiētus,* quiet; see QUIET.]

in·qui·line (ĭn′kwə-līn′, -lĭn, ĭng′-) *n.* An animal that characteristically lives commensally in the nest, burrow, or dwelling place of an animal of another species. **—inquiline** *adj.* Being or living as an inquiline. [Latin *inquilīnus,* lodger, tenant : *in-,* in; see IN–[2] + *colere,* to inhabit; see **k^wel-[1]** in Appendix.] **—in′qui·lin·ism** (-lə-nĭz′əm), **in′qui·lin′i·ty** (-lĭn′ĭ-tē) *n.* **—in′qui·lin′ous** (-lī′nəs) *adj.*

in·quire (ĭn-kwīr′) also **en·quire** (ĕn-) *v.* **-quired, -quir·ing, -quires.** —*intr.* **1.** To seek information by asking a question: *inquired about prices.* **2.** To make an inquiry or investigation: *inquire into the extent of the corruption.* —*tr.* **1.** To ask about. **2.** To ask: *"I am free to inquire what a work of art means to me"* (Bernard Berenson). See Synonyms at **ask.** ***—phrasal verb.*** **inquire after.** To ask about the health or condition of. [Middle English *enquiren,* from Old French *enquerre,* from Vulgar Latin **inquaerere,* alteration of Latin *inquīrere* : *in-,* into; see IN–[2] + *quaerere,* to seek.] **—in·quir′er** *n.* **—in·quir′ing·ly** *adv.*

in·quir·y (ĭn-kwīr′ē, ĭn′kwīr′ē, ĭn′kwə-rē, ĭng′-) also **en·quir·y** (ĕn-kwīr′ē, ĕn′kwə-rē) *n., pl.* **-ies.** *Abbr.* **inq. 1.** The act of inquiring. **2.** A question; a query. **3.** A close examination of a matter in a search for information or truth.

SYNONYMS: *inquiry, inquest, inquisition, investigation, probe, research.* The central meaning shared by these nouns is "a quest for knowledge, data, or truth": *filed an inquiry about the lost shipment; holding an inquest to determine whether the dead man had been murdered; refused to cooperate with the inquisition into her political activities; a criminal investigation; a probe into alleged police corruption; scientific research.*

in·qui·si·tion (ĭn′kwĭ-zĭsh′ən, ĭng′-) *n.* **1.** The act of inquiring into a matter; an investigation. See Synonyms at **inquiry. 2.** *Law.* **a.** An inquest. **b.** The verdict of a judicial inquiry. **3.a. Inquisition.** A tribunal formerly held in the Roman Catholic Church and directed at the suppression of heresy. **b.** An investigation that violates the privacy or rights of individuals. **c.** A rigorous, harsh interrogation. [Middle English *inquisicioun,* from Old French *inquisicion,* from Latin *inquīsītiō, inquīsītiōn-,* from *inquīsītus,* past participle of *inquīrere,* to inquire. See INQUIRE.] **—in′qui·si′tion·al** *adj.*

in·quis·i·tive (ĭn-kwĭz′ĭ-tĭv) *adj.* **1.** Unduly curious and inquiring. See Synonyms at **curious. 2.** Inclined to investigate; eager for knowledge. [Middle English *inquisitif,* from Old French, from Late Latin *inquīsītīvus,* from Latin *inquīsītus,* past participle of *inquīrere,* to inquire. See INQUIRE.] **—in·quis′i·tive·ly** *adv.* **—in·quis′i·tive·ness** *n.*

in·quis·i·tor (ĭn-kwĭz′ĭ-tər) *n.* One who inquires or makes an inquisition, especially a questioner who is excessively rigorous or harsh. [Middle English *inquisitour,* from Latin *inquīsītor,* from *inquīsītus,* past participle of *inquīrere,* to inquire into. See INQUIRE.]

in·quis·i·to·ri·al (ĭn-kwĭz′ĭ-tôr′ē-əl, -tōr′-) *adj.* **1.** Of, relating to, or having the function of an inquisitor. **2.** *Law.* **a.** Relating to a trial in which one party acts as both prosecutor and judge. **b.** Relating to a criminal proceeding conducted in secrecy. **—in·quis′i·to′ri·al·ly** *adv.*

in re (ĭn rā′, rē′) *prep. Law.* In the matter or case of; in regard to. [Latin *in rē* : *in,* in + *rē,* ablative of *rēs,* thing, matter.]

in rem (ĭn rĕm′) *adv. & adj. Law.* Against a thing, such as property, status, or a right, rather than against a person. Used of an action or a judgment. [Late Latin : Latin *in,* against + Latin *rem,* accusative of *rēs,* thing, matter.]

in-res·i·dence (ĭn-rĕz′ĭ-dəns) *adj.* Associated in an official, specified position with an organization such as a university or college. Often used in combination: *artist-in-residence.*

I.N.R.I. *abbr. Latin.* Iesus Nazarenus Rex Iudaeorum (Jesus of Nazareth, King of the Jews).

in·ro (ĭn′rō) *n., pl.* **inro.** A small, usually ornamented box that is hung from the waist sash of a Japanese kimono and has compartments for holding small objects such as cosmetics, perfumes, or medicines. [Japanese.]

in·road (ĭn′rōd′) *n.* **1.** A hostile invasion; a raid. **2.** An advance, especially at another's expense; an encroachment. Often used in the plural: *Foreign products have made inroads into the American economy.* [IN[1] + ROAD, riding, raid (obsolete).]

in·rush (ĭn′rŭsh′) *n.* A sudden rushing in; an influx.

INS *abbr.* **1.** Immigration and Naturalization Service. **2.** International News Service.

ins. *abbr.* **1.** Inches. **2.** Inspector. **3.** Insulation. **4.** Insurance.

in·sal·i·vate (ĭn-săl′ə-vāt′) *tr.v.* **-vat·ed, -vat·ing, -vates.** To mix (food) with saliva in chewing. **—in·sal′i·va′tion** *n.*

in·sa·lu·bri·ous (ĭn′sə-lo͞o′brē-əs) *adj.* Not promoting health; unwholesome: *an insalubrious environment.* **—in′sa·lu′bri·ous·ly** *adv.* **—in′sa·lu′bri·ty** *n.*

ins and outs (ĭnz; outs) *pl.n.* **1.** The intricate details of a situation, decision, or process. **2.** The windings of a road or path.

in·sane (ĭn-sān′) *adj.* **1.a.** Of, exhibiting, or afflicted with insanity. **b.** Characteristic of or associated with persons afflicted with insanity: *an insane laugh; insane babbling.* **c.** Intended for use by such persons: *an insane asylum.* **2.** Immoderate; wild: *insane jealousy.* **3.** Very foolish; absurd: *took insane risks behind the wheel.* [Latin *īnsānus* : *in-,* not; see IN–[1] + *sānus,* sane, healthy.] **—in·sane′ly** *adv.* **—in·sane′ness** *n.*

in·san·i·tar·y (ĭn-săn′ĭ-tĕr′ē) *adj.* So unclean as to be a likely cause of disease: *insanitary conditions in the restaurant.*

in·san·i·ty (ĭn-săn′ĭ-tē) *n., pl.* **-ties. 1.** Persistent mental disorder or derangement. **2.** *Law.* **a.** Unsoundness of mind sufficient in the judgment of a civil court to render a person unfit to maintain a contractual or other legal relationship or to warrant commitment to a mental health facility. **b.** In most criminal jurisdictions, a degree of mental malfunctioning sufficient to relieve the accused of legal responsibility for the act committed. **3.a.** Extreme foolishness; folly. **b.** Something extremely foolish.

SYNONYMS: *insanity, lunacy, madness, mania, dementia.* These nouns denote conditions of serious mental disability. *Insanity* is a grave, often prolonged condition of mental disorder that prevents a person from being held legally responsible for his or her actions: *was judged not guilty for reasons of insanity. Lunacy* often denotes derangement relieved intermittently by periods of clear-mindedness: *tried to jump out of the fortieth-floor window in a moment of utter lunacy. Madness,* a more general term, often stresses the violent aspect of mental illness: *delusions that progressed to a form of madness. Mania* refers principally to the excited phase of manic-depressive psychosis: *prescribed drugs to control the patient's periods of mania. Dementia* implies mental deterioration brought on by organic brain disorder: *underwent progressive stages of dementia.*

in·sa·tia·ble (ĭn-sā′shə-bəl, -shē-ə-) *adj.* Impossible to satiate or satisfy: *an insatiable appetite; an insatiable hunger for knowledge.* [Middle English *insaciable,* from Old French, from Latin *īnsatiābilis* : *in-,* not; see IN–[1] + *satiāre,* to fill; see SATIATE.] **—in·sa′tia·bil′i·ty, in·sa′tia·ble·ness** *n.* **—in·sa′tia·bly** *adv.*

in·sa·ti·ate (ĭn-sā′shē-ĭt) *adj.* Insatiable. [Latin *īnsatiātus* : *in-,* not; see IN–[1] + *satiātus,* past participle of *satiāre,* to satisfy; see SATIATE.] **—in·sa′ti·ate·ly** *adv.* **—in·sa′ti·ate·ness** *n.*

in·scape (ĭn′skāp′) *n.* The essential, distinctive, and revelatory quality of a thing: *"Here is the inscape, the epiphany, the moment of truth. That stubborn spot has become an image of the agony of human life and death"* (Madison Bell).

in·scribe (ĭn-skrīb′) *tr.v.* **-scribed, -scrib·ing, -scribes. 1.a.** To write, print, carve, or engrave (words or letters) on or in a surface. **b.** To mark or engrave (a surface) with words or letters. **2.** To enter (a name) on a list or in a register. **3.a.** To sign one's name or write a brief message in or on (a gift book or photograph, for example). **b.** To dedicate to someone. **4.** *Mathematics.* To draw (one figure) within another figure so that every vertex of the enclosed figure touches the outer figure. [Latin *īnscrībere* : *in-,* in, on; see IN–[2] + *scrībere,* to write; see **skrībh-** in Appendix.] **—in·scrib′er** *n.*

in·scrip·tion (ĭn-skrĭp′shən) *n.* **1.** The act or an instance of inscribing. **2.** Something, such as the wording on a coin, medal, monument, or seal, that is inscribed. **3.** An enrollment or a registration of names. **4.a.** A short, signed message in a book or on a photograph given as a gift. **b.** The usually informal dedication of a book or an artistic work. [Middle English *inscripcioun,* statement giving the author or title of a book, from Latin *īnscrīptiō, īnscrīptiōn-,* from *īnscrīptus,* past participle of *īnscrībere,* to inscribe. See INSCRIBE.] **—in·scrip′tion·al, in·scrip′tive** *adj.* **—in·scrip′tive·ly** *adv.*

in·scru·ta·ble (ĭn-skro͞o′tə-bəl) *adj.* Difficult to fathom or understand; impenetrable. See Synonyms at **mysterious.** [Middle English, from Old French, from Late Latin *īnscrūtābilis* : *in-,* not; see IN–[1] + *scrūtārī,* to scrutinize; see SCRUTINY.] **—in·scru′ta·bil′i·ty, in·scru′ta·ble·ness** *n.* **—in·scru′ta·bly** *adv.*

in·seam (ĭn′sēm′) *n.* **1.** The inside seam of a pant leg. **2.** The length or measurement of such a seam.

in·sect (ĭn′sĕkt′) *n.* **1.a.** Any of numerous usually small arthropod animals of the class Insecta, having an adult stage characterized by three pairs of legs and a body segmented into head, thorax, and abdomen and usually having two pairs of wings. Insects include the flies, crickets, mosquitoes, beetles, butterflies, and bees. **b.** Any of various similar arthropod animals, such as spiders, centipedes, or ticks. **2.** An insignificant or contemptible person. [Latin *īnsectum,* from neuter past participle of *īnsecāre,* to cut up (translation of Greek *entomon,* segmented, cut up, insect; see ENTOMO–) : *in-,* in; see IN–[2] + *secāre,* to cut; see **sek-** in Appendix.] **—in′sect′** *adj.* **—in′sec·ti′val** (ĭn′sĕk-tī′vəl) *adj.*

in·sec·tar·y (ĭn′sĕk′tə-rē, ĭn-sĕk′-) or **in·sec·tar·i·um** (ĭn′sĕk-târ′ē-əm) *n., pl.* **-tar·ies** or **-tar·i·a** (-târ′ē-ə). A place for keeping, breeding, or observing living insects.

in·sec·ti·cide (ĭn-sĕk′tĭ-sīd′) *n.* A chemical substance used to kill insects. **—in·sec′ti·cid′al** (-sīd′l) *adj.* **—in·sec′ti·cid′al·ly** *adv.*

in·sec·ti·vore (ĭn-sĕk′tə-vôr′, -vōr′) *n.* **1.** Any of various small, principally nocturnal mammals of the order Insectivora, characteristically feeding chiefly on insects and including the shrews, moles, and hedgehogs. **2.** An organism that feeds mainly on insects. [New Latin *Īnsectivora,* order name : Latin *īnsectum,* insect; see INSECT + Latin *-vora,* neuter pl. of *-vorus,* -vorous.]

in·sec·tiv·o·rous (ĭn′sĕk-tĭv′ər-əs) *adj.* **1.** Feeding on insects. **2.** *Botany.* Capable of trapping and absorbing insects, as the pitcher plant.

in·se·cure (ĭn′sĭ-kyo͝or′) *adj.* **1.** Not sure or certain; doubtful: *unemployed and facing an insecure future.* **2.** Inadequately guarded or protected; unsafe: *A shortage of military police made the air base insecure.* **3.** Not firm or fixed; unsteady: *an insecure foothold.* **4.a.** Lacking emotional stability; not well-adjusted: *an insecure relationship.* **b.** Lacking self-confidence; plagued by anxiety: *had always felt insecure at parties.* **—in′se·cure′ly** *adv.* **—in′se·cure′ness** *n.* **—in′se·cu′ri·ty** (-kyo͝or′ĭ-tē) *n.*

in·sem·i·nate (ĭn-sĕm′ə-nāt′) *tr.v.* **-nat·ed, -nat·ing, -nates. 1.** To introduce or inject semen into the reproductive tract of (a female). **2.** To sow seed in. [Latin *īnsēmināre, īnsēmināt-,* to implant, impregnate : *in-,* in; see IN–[2] + *sēmināre,* to plant (from *sēmen, sēmin-,* seed; see SEMEN).] **—in·sem′i·na′tion** *n.* **—in·sem′i·na′tor** *n.*

in·sen·sate (ĭn-sĕn′sāt′, -sĭt) *adj.* **1.a.** Lacking sensation or awareness; inanimate. **b.** Unconscious. **2.** Lacking sensibility; unfeeling: *"a predatory, insensate society in which innocence and decency can prove fatal"* (Peter S. Prescott). **3.a.** Lacking sense or the power to reason. **b.** Foolish; witless. [Latin *īnsēnsātus* : *in-,* not; see IN–[1] + *sēnsus,* understanding, reason; see SENSE.] **—in·sen′sate′ly** *adv.* **—in·sen′sate′ness** *n.*

in·sen·si·ble (ĭn-sĕn′sə-bəl) *adj.* **1.a.** Imperceptible; inappreciable: *an insensible change in temperature.* **b.** Very small or gradual: *insensible movement.* **2.a.** Having lost consciousness, especially temporarily; unconscious: *lay insensible where he had fallen.* **b.** Not invested with sensation; inanimate: *insensible clay.* **c.** Devoid of physical sensation or the power to react, as to pain or cold; numb. **3.a.** Unaware; unmindful: *I am not insensible of your concern.* **b.** Not emotionally responsive; indifferent: *insensible to criticism.* **4.** Lacking meaning; unintelligible. [Middle English, from Old French, from Latin *īnsēnsibilis,* imperceivable : *in-,* not; see IN–[1] + *sēnsibilis,* perceptible; see SENSIBLE.] **—in·sen′si·bil′i·ty, in·sen′si·ble·ness** *n.* **—in·sen′si·bly** *adv.*

in·sen·si·tive (ĭn-sĕn′sĭ-tĭv) *adj.* **1.** Not physically sensitive; numb. **2.a.** Lacking in sensitivity to the feelings or circumstances of others; unfeeling. **b.** Lacking in responsiveness: *insensitive to the needs of the customers.* **—in·sen′si·tive·ly** *adv.* **—in·sen′si·tiv′i·ty, in·sen′si·tive·ness** *n.*

in·sen·tient (ĭn-sĕn′shənt) *adj.* Devoid of sensation or consciousness; inanimate. **—in·sen′tience** *n.*

in·sep·a·ra·ble (ĭn-sĕp′ər-ə-bəl, -sĕp′rə-) *adj.* **1.** Impossible to separate or part: *inseparable pieces of rock.* **2.** Very closely associated; constant: *inseparable companions.* **—in·sep′a·ra·bil′i·ty, in·sep′a·ra·ble·ness** *n.* **—in·sep′a·ra·ble** *n.* **—in·sep′a·ra·bly** *adv.*

in·sert (ĭn-sûrt′) *tr.v.* **-sert·ed, -sert·ing, -serts. 1.** To put or set into, between, or among: *inserted the key in the lock.* See Synonyms at **introduce. 2.** To put or introduce into the body of something; interpolate: *insert an illustration into a text.* **3.** To place into an orbit, a trajectory, or a stream. **—insert** (ĭn′sûrt′) *n.* Something inserted or intended for insertion, as a picture or chart into written material. [Latin *īnserere, īnsert-* : *in-,* in; see IN–[2] + *serere,* to join; see **ser-**[2] in Appendix.] **—in·sert′er** *n.*

in·ser·tion (ĭn-sûr′shən) *n.* **1.** The act or process of inserting. **2.** Something inserted, as an ornamental strip of lace or embroidery inserted between pieces of fabric. **3.** *Anatomy.* The point or mode of attachment of a skeletal muscle to the bone or other body part that it moves. **4.** *Genetics.* The addition, as by mutation, of one or more nucleotides to a chromosome. **—in·ser′tion·al** *adj.*

in-serv·ice (ĭn′sûr′vĭs) *adj.* **1.** Of, relating to, or being a full-time employee: *in-service teachers.* **2.** Taking place or continuing while one is a full-time employee: *in-service training workshops.*

in·ses·so·ri·al (ĭn′sĕ-sôr′ē-əl, -sōr′-) *adj.* Perching or

inro
19th-century black lacquer inro

ă pat	oi boy
ā pay	ou out
âr care	o͝o took
ä father	o͞o boot
ĕ pet	ŭ cut
ē be	ûr urge
ĭ pit	th thin
ī pie	*th* this
îr pier	hw which
ŏ pot	zh vision
ō toe	ə about, item
ô paw	♦ regionalism

Stress marks: ′ (primary); ′ (secondary), as in **dictionary** (dĭk′shə-nĕr′ē)

adapted for perching: *insessorial claws.* [From New Latin *Īnsessores,* the perching birds, from Latin *īnsessus,* past participle of *īnsidēre,* to sit upon. See INSIDIOUS.]

in·set (ĭn′sĕt′, ĭn-sĕt′) *tr.v.* **-set, -set·ting, -sets. 1.** To set in; insert. **2.** To furnish with an inset. **—inset** (ĭn′sĕt′) *n.* **1.** Something set in, as: **a.** A small map or illustration set within a larger one. **b.** A leaf or group of pages inserted into a publication. **c.** A piece of material set into a garment as decoration or trim. **2. a.** An inflow, as of water. **b.** A channel.

in·shore (ĭn′shôr′, -shōr′) *adv. & adj.* **1.** Close to a shore. **2.** Toward or coming toward a shore.

in·shrine (ĭn-shrīn′) *v.* Variant of **enshrine.**

in·side (ĭn-sīd′, ĭn′sīd′) *n.* **1. a.** An inner or interior part. **b.** Inward character, perceptions, or feelings: *felt good on the inside about volunteering to help.* **2.** An inner side or surface. **3.** The part away from the edge; the middle part. **4. insides.** *Informal.* **a.** The inner organs; entrails. **b.** The inner parts or workings: *the insides of a TV set.* **5.** *Slang.* Confidential or secret information. **—inside** *adj.* **1.** Inner; interior. **2.** Relating to, known to, or coming from an exclusive group: *inside information; an inside joke.* **3.** *Baseball.* Passing on the side of home plate nearer the batter. Used of a pitch. **—inside** *adv.* **1.** Into or in the interior; within. **2.** On the inner side. **3.** *Slang.* In prison. **—inside** *prep.* **1.** Within: *We'll be there inside an hour.* **2. a.** On the inner side or part of: *inside the package.* **b.** Into the interior of: *going inside the house.* **—*idioms.* inside of.** *Usage Problem.* Within: *inside of an hour.* **inside out. 1.** With the inner surface turned out; reversed: *wore the sweatshirt inside out.* **2.** *Informal.* As completely as possible; thoroughly: *knew the city inside out.* **on the inside.** In a position of confidence or influence.

USAGE NOTE: The construction *inside of* has sometimes been criticized as redundant or colloquial. But *inside of* is well established in formal writing, particularly in reference to periods of time: *They usually return the manuscript inside of* (or *inside*) *a month.*

inside job *n. Slang.* A crime perpetrated by, or with the help of, a person working for or trusted by the victim.

In·side Passage (ĭn′sīd′) also **In·land Passage** (ĭn′lənd). A natural protected waterway extending about 1,529 km (950 mi) from Puget Sound to Skagway, Alaska. It is known for its snow-capped mountains, waterfalls, and glaciers.

in·sid·er (ĭn-sī′dər) *n.* **1.** An accepted member of a group. **2.** One who has special knowledge or access to confidential information.

inside track *n.* **1.** *Informal.* An advantageous position, as in a competition. **2.** *Sports.* The path next to the inner rail in a curved racetrack.

in·sid·i·ous (ĭn-sĭd′ē-əs) *adj.* **1.** Working or spreading harmfully in a subtle or stealthy manner: *insidious rumors; an insidious disease.* **2.** Intended to entrap; treacherous: *insidious misinformation.* **3.** Beguiling but harmful; alluring: *insidious pleasures.* [From Latin *īnsidiōsus,* from *īnsidiae,* ambush, from *īnsidēre,* to sit upon, lie in wait for : *in-,* in, on; see IN–[2] + *sedēre,* to sit; see **sed-** in Appendix.] **—in·sid′i·ous·ly** *adv.* **—in·sid′i·ous·ness** *n.*

in·sight (ĭn′sīt′) *n.* **1.** The capacity to discern the true nature of a situation; penetration. **2.** The act or outcome of grasping the inward or hidden nature of things or of perceiving in an intuitive manner.

in·sight·ful (ĭn′sīt′fəl, ĭn-sīt′-) *adj.* Showing or having insight; perceptive: *"The major contribution of this new biography . . . is its insightful discussion of the Christian dimension of Dostoyevsky's life and art"* (Maria Carlson). **—in′sight′ful·ly** *adv.* **—in·sight′ful·ness** *n.*

in·sig·ni·a (ĭn-sĭg′nē-ə) also **in·sig·ne** (-nē) *n., pl.* **insignia** or **-ni·as. 1.** A badge of office, rank, membership, or nationality; an emblem. **2.** A distinguishing sign. [Latin *īnsignia,* pl. of *īnsigne,* badge of office, mark, from neuter of *īnsignis,* distinguished, marked : *in-,* in; see IN–[2] + *signum,* sign; see **sekʷ-**[1] in Appendix.]

USAGE NOTE: *Insignia* in Latin is the plural form of *insigne,* but it has long been used in English as both a singular and a plural form: *The insignia was visible on the wingtip. There are five insignia on various parts of the plane.* From the singular use of *insignia* comes the plural *insignias,* which is also common in reputable writing. The Latin singular *insigne* is rare and may strike some readers as pedantic.

in·sig·nif·i·cance (ĭn′sĭg-nĭf′ĭ-kəns) *n.* The quality or state of being insignificant.

in·sig·nif·i·can·cy (ĭn′sĭg-nĭf′ĭ-kən-sē) *n., pl.* **-cies. 1.** Insignificance. **2.** One that is insignificant.

in·sig·nif·i·cant (ĭn′sĭg-nĭf′ĭ-kənt) *adj.* **1.** Not significant, especially: **a.** Lacking in importance; trivial. **b.** Lacking power, position, or value. **c.** Small in size or amount. **2.** Having little or no meaning. **—in′sig·nif′i·cant·ly** *adv.*

in·sin·cere (ĭn′sĭn-sîr′) *adj.* Not sincere; hypocritical. **—in′sin·cere′ly** *adv.* **—in′sin·cer′i·ty** (-sĕr′ĭ-tē) *n.*

in·sin·u·ate (ĭn-sĭn′yo͞o-āt′) *v.* **-at·ed, -at·ing, -ates.** *—tr.* **1.** To introduce or otherwise convey (a thought, for example) gradually and insidiously. See Synonyms at **suggest. 2.** To introduce or insert (oneself) by subtle and artful means. *—intr.* To make insinuations. [Latin *īnsinuāre, īnsinuāt-* : *in-,* in; see IN–[2] + *sinuāre,* to curve (from *sinus,* curve).] **—in·sin′u·a′tive** *adj.* **—in·sin′u·a′tor** *n.* **—in·sin′u·a·tor′y** (-yo͞o-ə-tôr′ē, -tōr′ē) *adj.*

in·sin·u·at·ing (ĭn-sĭn′yo͞o-ā′tĭng) *adj.* **1.** Provoking gradual doubt or suspicion; suggestive: *insinuating remarks.* **2.** Artfully contrived to gain favor or confidence; ingratiating. **—in·sin′u·at′ing·ly** *adv.*

in·sin·u·a·tion (ĭn-sĭn′yo͞o-ā′shən) *n.* **1.** The act, process, or practice of insinuating. **2.** Something insinuated, especially an artfully indirect, often derogatory suggestion.

in·sip·id (ĭn-sĭp′ĭd) *adj.* **1.** Lacking flavor or zest; not tasty. **2.** Lacking excitement, stimulation, or interest; dull. [French *insipide,* from Late Latin *īnsipidus* : Latin *in-,* not; see IN–[1] + Latin *sapidus,* savory (from *sapere,* to taste; see **sep-** in Appendix).] **—in′si·pid′i·ty** (ĭn′sĭ-pĭd′ĭ-tē), **in·sip′id·ness** *n.* **—in·sip′id·ly** *adv.*

in·sip·i·ence (ĭn-sĭp′ē-əns) *n. Archaic.* Lack of wisdom. [Middle English, from Old French, from Latin *īnsipientia,* from *īnsipiēns, insipient-,* not wise : *in-,* not; see IN–[1] + *sapiēns,* wise; see SAPIENT.]

in·sist (ĭn-sĭst′) *v.* **-sist·ed, -sist·ing, -sists.** *—intr.* To be firm in a demand or course; refuse to yield: *insisted on giving me a second helping.* *—tr.* To assert or demand (something) vehemently and persistently: *We insist that you accept these gifts.* [Latin *īnsistere,* to persist : *in-,* on; see IN–[2] + *sistere,* to stand; see **stā-** in Appendix.] **—in·sis′tence, in·sis′ten·cy** *n.* **—in·sist′er** *n.* **—in·sist′ing·ly** *adv.*

in·sis·tent (ĭn-sĭs′tənt) *adj.* **1.** Firm in asserting a demand or an opinion; unyielding. **2.** Demanding notice: *insistent hunger.* **3.** Repetitive and persistent: *the jay's insistent cry.* **—in·sis′tent·ly** *adv.*

in si·tu (ĭn sī′to͞o, sē′-) *adv. & adj.* In the original position. [Latin *in sitū* : *in,* in + *sitū,* ablative of *situs,* place.]

in·snare (ĭn-snâr′) *v.* Variant of **ensnare.**

in·so·bri·e·ty (ĭn′sə-brī′ĭ-tē) *n.* Lack of sobriety; intemperance, especially in drinking.

in·so·cia·ble (ĭn-sō′shə-bəl) *adj.* Not sociable. **—in·so′cia·bil′i·ty** *n.* **—in·so′cia·bly** *adv.*

in·so·far (ĭn′sō-fär′) *adv.* To such an extent.

insofar as *conj.* To the extent that.

insol. *abbr.* Insoluble.

in·so·late (ĭn′sō-lāt′, ĭn-sō′-) *tr.v.* **-lat·ed, -lat·ing, -lates.** To expose to sunlight. [Latin *īnsōlāre, īnsōlāt-* : *in-,* in; see IN–[2] + *sōl,* sun; see **sāwel-** in Appendix.]

in·so·la·tion (ĭn′sō-lā′shən) *n.* **1. a.** The act or an instance of exposing to sunlight. **b.** Therapeutic exposure to sunlight. **2.** See **sunstroke. 3. a.** The solar radiation striking Earth or another planet. **b.** The rate of delivery of solar radiation per unit of horizontal surface.

in·sole (ĭn′sōl′) *n.* **1.** The inner sole of a shoe or boot. **2.** An extra strip of material put inside a shoe for comfort or protection. Also called *innersole.*

in·so·lence (ĭn′sə-ləns) *n.* **1.** The quality or condition of being insolent. **2.** An instance of insolent behavior, treatment, or speech.

in·so·lent (ĭn′sə-lənt) *adj.* **1.** Presumptuous and insulting in manner or speech; arrogant. **2.** Audaciously rude or disrespectful; impertinent. [Middle English, from Latin *insolēns, īnsolent-,* immoderate, arrogant : *in-,* not; see IN–[1] + *solēns,* present participle of *solēre,* to be accustomed.] **—in′so·lent** *n.* **—in′so·lent·ly** *adv.*

in·sol·u·ble (ĭn-sŏl′yə-bəl) *adj.* **1.** *Abbr.* **insol.** That cannot be dissolved: *insoluble matter.* **2.** Difficult or impossible to solve or explain; insolvable: *insoluble riddles.* [Middle English *insolible,* from Latin *īnsolūbilis* : *in-,* not; see IN–[1] + *solvere,* to loosen; see SOLUBLE.] **—in·sol′u·bil′i·ty, in·sol′u·ble·ness** *n.* **—in·sol′u·ble** *n.* **—in·sol′u·bly** *adv.*

in·solv·a·ble (ĭn-sŏl′və-bəl) *adj.* Impossible to solve; having no solution: *a seemingly insolvable problem.* **—in·solv′a·bil′i·ty** *n.* **—in·solv′a·bly** *adv.*

in·sol·ven·cy (ĭn-sŏl′vən-sē) *n., pl.* **-cies. 1.** The condition of being insolvent. **2.** An instance of being insolvent.

in·sol·vent (ĭn-sŏl′vənt) *adj.* **1. a.** Unable to meet debts or discharge liabilities; bankrupt. **b.** Insufficient to meet all debts, as an estate or a fund. **2.** Of or relating to bankrupt persons or entities. **—insolvent** *n.* A bankrupt.

in·som·ni·a (ĭn-sŏm′nē-ə) *n.* Chronic inability to fall asleep or remain asleep for an adequate length of time. [Latin, from *īnsomnis,* sleepless : *in-,* not; see IN–[1] + *somnus,* sleep; see **swep-** in Appendix.]

in·som·ni·ac (ĭn-sŏm′nē-ăk′) *n.* One who suffers from insomnia. **—insomniac** *adj.* Having or causing insomnia.

in·so·much as (ĭn′sō-mŭch′) *conj.* **1.** To such extent or degree as. **2.** Inasmuch as; since.

insomuch that *conj.* With the result that; so.

in·sou·ci·ance (ĭn-so͞o′sē-əns, ăɴ′so͞o-syäɴs′) *n.* Blithe lack of concern; nonchalance.

in·sou·ci·ant (ĭn-so͞o′sē-ənt, ăɴ′so͞o-syäɴ′) *adj.* Marked by blithe unconcern; nonchalant. [French : *in-,* not (from Old French; see IN–[1]) + *souciant,* present participle of *soucier,* to trouble (from Old French, from Vulgar Latin **sollicitāre,* alteration of Latin *sollicitāre,* to vex; see SOLICIT).] **—in·sou′ci·ant·ly** *adv.*

in·soul (ĭn-sōl′) *v.* Variant of **ensoul.**

insp. *abbr.* **1.** Inspected. **2.** Inspector.

in·spect (ĭn-spĕkt′) *tr.v.* **-spect·ed, -spect·ing, -spects. 1.** To examine carefully and critically, especially for flaws. **2.** To review or examine officially: *The commander inspected the troops.* [From Latin *īnspicere, īnspect-* : *in-*, intensive pref.; see IN−[2] + *specere,* to look at; see **spek-** in Appendix.] **—in·spec′tive** *adj.*

in·spec·tion (ĭn-spĕk′shən) *n.* **1.** The act of inspecting. **2.** Official examination or review, as of barracks or troops. **—in·spec′tion·al** *adj.*

in·spec·tor (ĭn-spĕk′tər) *n. Abbr.* **ins., insp. 1.** One who is appointed or employed to inspect something. **2.** A police officer ranking next below superintendent. **—in·spec′to·ral, in′spec·to′ri·al** (-tôr′ē-əl, -tōr′-) *adj.* **—in·spec′tor·ship′** *n.*

in·spec·tor·ate (ĭn-spĕk′tər-ĭt) *n.* **1.** The office or duties of an inspector. **2.** A staff of inspectors. **3.** An inspector's district.

inspector general *n., pl.* **inspectors general.** *Abbr.* **IG, I.G.** An officer with general investigative powers within a civil, military, or other organization.

in·sphere (ĭn-sfîr′) *v.* Variant of **ensphere.**

in·spi·ra·tion (ĭn′spə-rā′shən) *n.* **1.a.** Stimulation of the mind or emotions to a high level of feeling or activity. **b.** The condition of being so stimulated. **2.** An agency, such as a person or work of art, that moves the intellect or emotions or prompts action or invention. **3.** Something, such as a sudden creative act or idea, that is inspired. **4.** The quality of inspiring or exalting: *a painting full of inspiration.* **5.** *Theology.* Divine guidance or influence exerted on the mind and soul of humankind. **6.** The act of drawing in, especially the inhalation of air into the lungs.

in·spi·ra·tion·al (ĭn′spə-rā′shə-nəl) *adj.* **1.** Of or relating to inspiration. **2.** Providing or intended to convey inspiration. **3.** Resulting from inspiration. **—in′spi·ra′tion·al·ly** *adv.*

in·spi·ra·tor (ĭn′spə-rā′tər) *n.* A device, such as a respirator or an inhaler, by which a gas, vapor, or air is drawn in. [Latin *īnspīrāre,* to breathe into; see INSPIRE + −ATOR.]

in·spir·a·to·ry (ĭn-spīr′ə-tôr′ē, -tōr′ē) *adj.* Of, relating to, or used for the drawing in of air.

in·spire (ĭn-spīr′) *v.* **-spired, -spir·ing, -spires.** —*tr.* **1.** To affect, guide, or arouse by divine influence. **2.** To fill with enlivening or exalting emotion: *hymns that inspire the congregation; an artist who was inspired by Impressionism.* **3.a.** To stimulate to action; motivate: *a sales force that was inspired by the prospect of a bonus.* **b.** To affect or touch: *The falling leaves inspired her with sadness.* **4.** To draw forth; elicit or arouse: *a teacher who inspired admiration and respect.* **5.** To be the cause or source of; bring about: *an invention that inspired many imitations.* **6.** To draw in (air) by inhaling. **7.** *Archaic.* **a.** To breathe on. **b.** To breathe life into. —*intr.* **1.** To stimulate energies, ideals, or reverence: *a leader who inspires by example.* **2.** To inhale. [Middle English *enspiren,* from Old French *enspirer,* from Latin *īnspīrāre* : *in-*, into; see IN−[2] + *spīrāre,* to breathe.] **—in·spir′er** *n.*

in·spired (ĭn-spīrd′) *adj.* Of such surpassing brilliance or excellence as to suggest divine inspiration: *an inspired performance.* **—in·spir′ed·ly** (-spī′rĭd-lē, -spīrd′lē) *adv.*

in·spir·ing (ĭn-spīr′ĭng) *adj.* Tending to arouse or exalt: *an inspiring eulogy.* **—in·spir′ing·ly** *adv.*

in·spir·it (ĭn-spĭr′ĭt) *tr.v.* **-it·ed, -it·ing, -its.** To instill courage or life into; animate. See Synonyms at **encourage. —in·spir′it·ing·ly** *adv.*

in·spis·sate (ĭn-spĭs′āt′, ĭn′spĭ-sāt′) *intr. & tr.v.* **-sat·ed, -sat·ing, -sates.** To undergo thickening or cause to thicken, as by boiling or evaporation; condense. [From Late Latin *īnspissāre, īnspissāt-*, to thicken : Latin *in-*, causative pref.; see IN−[2] + Latin *spissus,* thick.] **—in′spis·sa′tion** *n.* **—in·spis′sa′tor** *n.*

inst. *abbr.* **1.** Instant. **2.** Or **Inst.** Institute; institution. **3.** Institutional.

in·sta·bil·i·ty (ĭn′stə-bĭl′ĭ-tē) *n., pl.* **-ties. 1.** Lack of physical stability; unsteadiness. **2.** The quality or condition of being erratic or undependable: *emotional instability.*

in·stall also **in·stal** (ĭn-stôl′) *tr.v.* **-stalled, -stall·ing, -stalls** also **-stals. 1.** To set in position and connect or adjust for use: *installed the new furnace.* **2.** To induct into an office, a rank, or a position: *a ceremony to install the new governor.* **3.** To settle in an indicated place or condition; establish: *installed myself in the spare room.* [Middle English *installen,* to place in office, from Old French *installer,* from Medieval Latin *installāre* : *in-*, in (from Latin; see IN−[2]) + *stallum,* stall, place; see **stel-** in Appendix.] **—in·stall′er** *n.*

in·stal·la·tion (ĭn′stə-lā′shən) *n.* **1.a.** The act of installing. **b.** The state of being installed. Also called *installment.* **2.** A system of machinery or other apparatus set up for use. **3.** A permanent military base.

in·stall·ment[1] also **in·stal·ment** (ĭn-stôl′mənt) *n.* **1.** One of a number of successive payments in settlement of a debt. **2.a.** A portion of something, such as a publication, issued at intervals. **b.** A chapter or part of a literary work presented serially. [Alteration of obsolete *estallment,* from Anglo-Norman, from Old French *estaler,* to place, fix, from *estal,* place, of Germanic origin. See **stel-** in Appendix.]

in·stall·ment[2] also **in·stal·ment** (ĭn-stôl′mənt) *n.* See **installation** (sense 1).

installment plan *n.* A credit system by which payment for merchandise is made in installments over a fixed period of time.

in·stance (ĭn′stəns) *n.* **1.a.** An example that is cited to prove or invalidate a contention or illustrate a point. See Synonyms at **example. b.** A case or an occurrence: *In all such instances, let conscience be your guide.* **2.** *Law.* A legal proceeding or process; a suit. **3.** A step in a process or series of events: *You should apply in the first instance to the personnel manager.* **4.a.** A suggestion or request: *called at the instance of his attorney.* **b.** *Archaic.* Urgent solicitation. **5.** *Obsolete.* An impelling motive. **—instance** *tr.v.* **-stanced, -stanc·ing, -stanc·es. 1.** To offer as an example; cite. **2.** To demonstrate or show by an example; exemplify. ***—idiom.*** **for instance.** As an example; for example. [Middle English *instaunce,* from Old French *instance,* request, instant, and from Medieval Latin *īnstantia,* example, both from Latin, presence, from *īnstāns, īnstant-*, present. See INSTANT.]

in·stan·cy (ĭn′stən-sē) *n., pl.* **-cies. 1.** The quality or condition of being insistent; urgency. **2.** Immediacy of occurrence; instantaneousness.

in·stant (ĭn′stənt) *n. Abbr.* **inst. 1.** An almost imperceptible space of time. See Synonyms at **moment. 2.** A particular time: *Tell me the instant they arrive.* **3.** The current month: *your letter of the 15th instant.* **4.** A food or beverage designed for quick preparation. **—instant** *adj. Abbr.* **inst. 1.** Occurring at once; immediate: *instant gratification.* **2.** Imperative; urgent: *an instant need.* **3.** Now under consideration; present. **4.a.** Commercially prepared or processed for quick and easy final preparation: *an instant cake mix.* **b.** Readily soluble in water: *instant coffee; instant powdered milk.* **c.** Appearing, done, or taking place with or as if with maximum quickness and ease: *"She had the gift of instant intimacy"* (Sylvia Jukes Morris). **—instant** *adv.* At once; instantly. [Middle English, from Old French, from Latin *īnstāns, īnstant-*, present, present participle of *īnstāre,* to approach : *in-*, on; see IN−[2] + *stāre,* to stand; see **stā-** in Appendix.] **—in′stant·ness** *n.*

in·stan·ta·ne·ous (ĭn′stən-tā′nē-əs) *adj.* **1.** Occurring or completed without perceptible delay: *Relief was instantaneous.* **2.** Done or made as quickly or directly as possible: *an instantaneous reply to my letter.* **3.** Present or occurring at a specific instant: *instantaneous velocity; instantaneous pressure.* [From Medieval Latin *īnstantāneus,* from Latin *īnstāns, īnstant-*, present. See INSTANT.] **—in·stan′ta·ne′i·ty** (ĭn-stăn′tə-nē′ĭ-tē, ĭn′stən) *n.* **—in′stan·ta′ne·ous·ly** *adv.* **—in′stan·ta′ne·ous·ness** *n.*

in·stan·ter (ĭn-stăn′tər) *adv.* Without delay; instantly. [Medieval Latin, from Latin, urgently, from *īnstāns, īnstant-*, present. See INSTANT.]

in·stant·ly (ĭn′stənt-lē) *adv.* **1.** At once. **2.** With insistence; urgently. **—instantly** *conj. Chiefly British.* As soon as.

instant replay *n.* **1.a.** The recording and immediate playback of part of a live television broadcast, as of a sports play. **b.** The part so recorded and replayed. **2.** *Informal.* Something repeated directly or soon after its original occurrence.

in·star[1] (ĭn-stär′) *tr.v.* **-starred, -star·ring, -stars.** To stud with or as if with stars.

in·star[2] (ĭn′stär′) *n.* A stage of an insect or other arthropod between molts. [New Latin, from Latin, image, form.]

in·state (ĭn-stāt′) *tr.v.* **-stat·ed, -stat·ing, -states.** To establish in office; install.

in·stau·ra·tion (ĭn′stô-rā′shən) *n.* **1.** Renovation; restoration. **2.** The institution or establishment of something. [Latin *īnstaurātiō, īnstaurātiōn-*, from *īnstaurātus,* past participle of *īnstaurāre,* to renew. See **stā-** in Appendix.]

in·stead (ĭn-stĕd′) *adv.* **1.** In the place of something previously mentioned; as a substitute or an equivalent: *Having planned to drive, we walked instead.* **2.** In preference; as an alternative: *yearned instead for a home and family.* [Middle English *in sted of,* in place of : *in,* in; see IN[1] + *stede,* place; see STEAD + *of,* of; see OF.]

instead of *prep.* In place of; rather than: *ordered chicken instead of fish.*

in·step (ĭn′stĕp′) *n.* **1.** The arched middle part of the human foot between the toes and the ankle. **2.** The part of a shoe or stocking covering the instep. [Middle English.]

in·sti·gate (ĭn′stĭ-gāt′) *tr.v.* **-gat·ed, -gat·ing, -gates. 1.** To urge on; goad. **2.** To stir up; foment. See Synonyms at **incite.** [Latin *īnstīgāre, īnstīgāt-*. See **steig-** in Appendix.] **—in′sti·ga′tion** *n.* **—in′sti·ga′tive** *adj.* **—in′sti·ga′tor** *n.*

in·still also **in·stil** (ĭn-stĭl′) *tr.v.* **-stilled, -still·ing, -stills** also **-stils. 1.** To introduce by gradual, persistent efforts; implant: *"Morality . . . may be instilled into their minds"* (Thomas Jefferson). **2.** To pour in (medicine, for example) drop by drop. [Middle English *instillen,* from Latin *īnstīllāre* : *in-*, into; see IN−[2] + *stīllāre,* to drip, drop (from *stīlla,* drop).] **—in′stil·la′tion** (ĭn′stə-lā′shən) *n.* **—in·still′er** *n.* **—in·still′ment** *n.*

in·stinct (ĭn′stĭngkt′) *n.* **1.** An inborn pattern of behavior that is characteristic of a species and is often a response to specific environmental stimuli: *the spawning instinct in salmon; altruistic instincts in social animals.* **2.** A powerful motivation or impulse. **3.** An innate capability or aptitude: *an instinct for tact and diplomacy.* **—instinct** (ĭn-stĭngkt′) *adj.* **1.** Deeply filled or im-

ă pat	oi boy
ā pay	ou out
âr care	ŏŏ took
ä father	ōō boot
ĕ pet	ŭ cut
ē be	ûr urge
ĭ pit	th thin
ī pie	*th* this
îr pier	hw which
ŏ pot	zh vision
ō toe	ə about, item
ô paw	♦ regionalism

Stress marks: ′ (primary); ′ (secondary), as in **dictionary** (dĭk′shə-nĕr′ē)

bued: *words instinct with love.* **2.** *Obsolete.* Impelled from within. [Middle English, from Latin *īnstīnctus,* impulse, from past participle of *īnstinguere,* to incite : *in-,* intensive pref.; see IN–² + *stinguere,* to prick; see **steig-** in Appendix.]

in·stinc·tive (ĭn-stĭngk′tĭv) *adj.* **1.** Of, relating to, or prompted by instinct. **2.** Arising from impulse; spontaneous and unthinking: *an instinctive mistrust of bureaucrats.* **—in·stinc′tive·ly** *adv.*

SYNONYMS: *instinctive, instinctual, intuitive, visceral.* The central meaning shared by these adjectives is "derived from or prompted by a natural tendency or impulse": *an instinctive fear of snakes; instinctual behavior; an intuitive perception; visceral revulsion.* See also Synonyms at **spontaneous.**

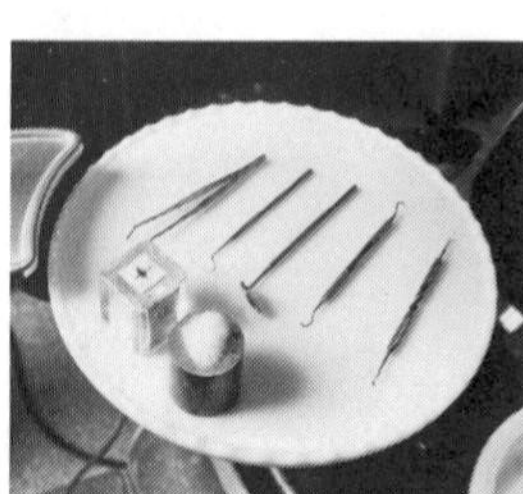
instrument
Dental instruments

in·stinc·tu·al (ĭn-stĭngk′cho͞o-əl) *adj.* Of, relating to, or derived from instinct. See Synonyms at **instinctive.** **—in·stinc′tu·al·ly** *adv.*

in·sti·tute (ĭn′stĭ-to͞ot′, -tyo͞ot′) *tr.v.* **-tut·ed, -tut·ing, -tutes. 1.a.** To establish, organize, and set in operation. **b.** To initiate; begin. See Synonyms at **found¹. 2.** To establish or invest in an office or a position. **—institute** *n.* **1.a.** Something instituted, especially an authoritative rule or precedent. **b. institutes.** A digest of the principles or rudiments of a particular subject, especially a legal abstract. **2.** *Abbr.* **inst., Inst.** An organization founded to promote a cause: *a cancer research institute.* **3.** *Abbr.* **I, Inst. a.** An educational institution, especially one for the instruction of technical subjects. **b.** The building or buildings housing such an institution. **4.** A usually short, intensive workshop or seminar on a specific subject. [Middle English *instituten,* from Latin *īnstituere, īnstitūt-,* to establish : *in-,* in; see IN–² + *statuere,* to set up (from *stāre,* to stand; see **stā-** in Appendix).] **—in′sti·tut′er, in′sti·tu′tor** *n.*

in·sti·tu·tion (ĭn′stĭ-to͞o′shən, -tyo͞o′-) *n.* **1.** The act of instituting. **2.a.** A custom, practice, relationship, or behavioral pattern of importance in the life of a community or society: *the institutions of marriage and the family.* **b.** *Informal.* One long associated with a specified place, position, or function. **3.** *Abbr.* **inst., Inst. a.** An established organization or foundation, especially one dedicated to education, public service, or culture. **b.** The building or buildings housing such an organization. **c.** A place for the care of persons who are destitute, disabled, or mentally ill.

in·sti·tu·tion·al (ĭn′stĭ-to͞o′shə-nəl, -tyo͞o′-) *adj.* **1.** Of or relating to an institution or institutions. **2.** Organized as or forming an institution: *institutional religion.* **3.** Characteristic or suggestive of an institution, especially in being uniform, dull, or unimaginative: *institutional furniture; a pale institutional green.* **4.** Of or relating to the principles or institutes of a subject such as law. **—in′sti·tu′tion·al·ly** *adv.*

in·sti·tu·tion·al·ism (ĭn′stĭ-to͞o′shə-nə-lĭz′əm, -tyo͞o′-) *n.* **1.** Adherence to or belief in established forms, especially belief in organized religion. **2.** Use of public institutions for the care of people who are physically or mentally disabled, criminally delinquent, or incapable of independent living. **—in′sti·tu′tion·al·ist** *n.*

in·sti·tu·tion·al·ize (ĭn′stĭ-to͞o′shə-nə-līz′, -tyo͞o′-) *tr.v.* **-ized, -iz·ing, -iz·es. 1.a.** To make into an institution or give the character of an institution to. **b.** To make part of a structured and usually well-established system: *a society that has institutionalized injustice.* **2.** To place (a person) in the care of an institution. **—in′sti·tu′tion·al·i·za′tion** (-shə-nə-lĭ-zā′shən) *n.*

instr. *abbr.* **1.** Instruction. **2.** Instructor. **3.** Instrument.

in·stroke (ĭn′strōk′) *n.* An inward stroke, especially a piston stroke moving away from the crankshaft.

in·struct (ĭn-strŭkt′) *v.* **-struct·ed, -struct·ing, -structs.** *—tr.* **1.** To provide with knowledge, especially in a methodical way. See Synonyms at **teach. 2.** To give orders to; direct. *—intr.* To serve as an instructor. [Middle English *instructen,* from Latin *īnstruere, īnstrūct-,* to prepare, instruct : *in-,* on; see IN–² + *struere,* to build; see **ster-²** in Appendix.]

in·struc·tion (ĭn-strŭk′shən) *n. Abbr.* **instr. 1.** The act, practice, or profession of instructing. **2.a.** Imparted knowledge. **b.** An imparted or acquired item of knowledge; a lesson. **3.** *Computer Science.* A machine code telling a computer to perform a particular operation. **4.a.** Often **instructions.** An authoritative direction to be obeyed; an order: *had instructions to be home by midnight.* **b. instructions.** Detailed directions on procedure: *read the instructions for assembly.* **—in·struc′tion·al** *adj.*

instrument panel
In an airplane cockpit

in·struc·tive (ĭn-strŭk′tĭv) *adj.* Conveying knowledge or information; enlightening. **—in·struc′tive·ly** *adv.* **—in·struc′tive·ness** *n.*

in·struc·tor (ĭn-strŭk′tər) *n. Abbr.* **instr. 1.** One who instructs; a teacher. **2.** A college or university teacher who ranks below an assistant professor. **—in·struc′tor·ship′** *n.*

in·stru·ment (ĭn′strə-mənt) *n. Abbr.* **instr. 1.** A means by which something is done; an agency. **2.** One used by another to accomplish a purpose; a dupe. **3.** An implement used to facilitate work. See Synonyms at **tool. 4.** A device for recording, measuring, or controlling, especially such a device functioning as part of a control system. **5.** *Music.* A device for playing or producing music: *a percussion instrument; a keyboard instrument.* **6.** A legal document. **—instrument** (-mĕnt′) *tr.v.* **-ment·ed, -ment·ing, -ments. 1.** To provide or equip with instruments. **2.** *Music.* To compose or arrange for performance. **3.** To address a legal document to. [Middle English, from Old French, from Latin *īnstrūmentum,* tool, implement, from *īnstruere,* to prepare. See INSTRUCT.]

in·stru·men·tal (ĭn′strə-mĕn′tl) *adj.* **1.** Serving as a means or an agency; implemental: *was instrumental in solving the crime.* **2.** Of, relating to, or accomplished with an instrument or a tool. **3.** *Music.* Performed on or written for an instrument. **4.** *Grammar.* Of or designating a case used typically to express means, agency, or accompaniment. **5.** Of or relating to instrumentalism. **—instrumental** *n.* **1.a.** *Grammar.* The instrumental case. **b.** A word in the instrumental case. **2.** *Music.* A composition for one or more instruments, usually without vocal accompaniment. **—in′stru·men′tal·ly** *adv.*

in·stru·men·tal·ism (ĭn′strə-mĕn′tl-ĭz′əm) *n.* A pragmatic theory that ideas are instruments that function as guides of action, their validity being determined by the success of the action.

in·stru·men·tal·ist (ĭn′-strə-mĕn′tl-ĭst) *n.* **1.** *Music.* One who plays an instrument. **2.** An advocate or a student of instrumentalism. **—instrumentalist** *adj.* Of, relating to, or advocating instrumentalism.

in·stru·men·tal·i·ty (ĭn′strə-mĕn-tăl′ĭ-tē) *n., pl.* **-ties. 1.** The state or quality of being instrumental. **2.** A means; an agency. **3.** A subsidiary branch, as of a government, by means of which functions or policies are carried out.

in·stru·men·ta·tion (ĭn′strə-mĕn-tā′shən) *n.* **1.** The application or use of instruments. **2.** *Music.* **a.** The study and practice of arranging music for instruments. **b.** The arrangement or orchestration resulting from such practice. **c.** A list of instruments used in an orchestration. **3.a.** The study, development, and manufacture of instruments, as for scientific or industrial use. **b.** Instruments for a specific purpose. **4.** Instrumentality.

instrument board *n.* See **instrument panel.**

instrument flying *n.* Aircraft navigation by reference to instruments only.

instrument landing *n.* An aircraft landing made by means of instruments and ground-based radio equipment only.

instrument panel *n.* A mounted array of instruments used to operate a machine, especially the dashboard of an automotive vehicle, an aircraft, or a motorboat. Also called *instrument board.*

in·sub·or·di·nate (ĭn′sə-bôr′dn-ĭt) *adj.* Not submissive to authority: *has a history of insubordinate behavior.* **—in′sub·or′di·nate** *n.* **—in′sub·or′di·nate·ly** *adv.* **—in′sub·or′di·na′tion** *n.*

SYNONYMS: *insubordinate, rebellious, mutinous, factious, seditious.* These adjectives mean in opposition to and usually in defiance of established authority. *Insubordinate* implies failure or refusal to recognize or submit to the authority of a superior: *To be insubordinate is to invite dismissal from a corporation. Rebellious* implies open defiance of authority or resistance to control: *Rebellious students stubbornly demanded that the CIA be prevented from recruiting on campus. Mutinous* pertains to revolt against constituted authority, especially that of a naval or military command: *"The men became mutinous and insubordinate"* (Walter Besant). *Factious* implies the promotion or existence of divisiveness, dissension, or disunity within a group or an organization: *"The army has been embroiled in a standoff battle against a* [hornets'] *nest of factious groups, including opium warlords"* (Time). *Seditious* applies principally to the treasonous stirring up of resistance or rebellion against a government: *Thomas Paine's* Common Sense *must have seemed seditious to colonial Tories.*

in·sub·stan·tial (ĭn′səb-stăn′shəl) *adj.* **1.** Lacking substance or reality. See Synonyms at **immaterial. 2.a.** Not firm or solid; flimsy. **b.** Delicate; fine. **—in′sub·stan′ti·al′i·ty** (-shē-ăl′ĭ-tē) *n.*

in·suf·fer·a·ble (ĭn-sŭf′ər-ə-bəl, -sŭf′rə-) *adj.* Difficult or impossible to endure; intolerable. **—in·suf′fer·a·ble·ness** *n.* **—in·suf′fer·a·bly** *adv.*

in·suf·fi·cien·cy (ĭn′sə-fĭsh′ən-sē) *n., pl.* **-cies. 1.** The quality or state of being insufficient, especially: **a.** Moral or mental incompetence. **b.** Inadequate supply: *an insufficiency of funds.* **c.** Inability of a bodily part or an organ to function normally: *cardiac insufficiency.* **2.** A failing; an inadequacy: *pointed out the insufficiencies in my report.*

in·suf·fi·cient (ĭn′sə-fĭsh′ənt) *adj.* Not sufficient; inadequate. **—in′suf·fi′cient·ly** *adv.*

in·suf·flate (ĭn′sə-flāt′, ĭn-sŭf′lāt′) *tr.v.* **-flat·ed, -flat·ing, -flates. 1.** To blow or breathe into or on. **2.** *Medicine.* To treat medically by blowing a powder, gas, or vapor into a bodily cavity. [Latin *īnsufflāre, īnsufflāt-* : *in-,* into; see IN–² + *sufflāre,* to inflate; see SOUFFLÉ.] **—in′suf·fla′tor** *n.*

in·suf·fla·tion (ĭn′sə-flā′shən) *n.* **1.** The act or an instance of insufflating. **2.** *Ecclesiastical.* A ritual act of breathing on baptismal water or on the one being baptized.

in·su·lant (ĭn′sə-lənt, ĭns′yə-) *n.* A material used for insulation; an insulator.

in·su·lar (ĭn′sə-lər, ĭns′yə-) *adj.* **1.a.** Of, relating to, or constituting an island. **b.** Living or located on an island. **2.a.** Suggestive of the isolated life of an island: *"He is an exceedingly insular man, so deeply private as to seem inaccessible to the scrutiny of a novelist"* (Leonard Michaels). **b.** Circumscribed and detached in outlook and experience; narrow or provincial. **3.** *Anatomy.* Of or relating to isolated tissue or an island of tissue. [French *insulaire,* from Late Latin *īnsulāris,* from Latin *īnsula,* island.] **—in′su·lar·ism, in′su·lar′i·ty** (-lăr′ĭ-tē) *n.* **—in′su·lar·ly** *adv.*

in·su·late (ĭn′sə-lāt′, ĭns′yə-) *tr.v.* **-lat·ed, -lat·ing, -lates. 1.** To cause to be in a detached or isolated position. See Synonyms at **isolate. 2.** To prevent the passage of heat, electricity, or sound into or out of, especially by surrounding with a nonconducting material. [Latin *īnsula,* island + –ATE^1.]

in·su·la·tion (ĭn′sə-lā′shən, ĭns′yə-) *n. Abbr.* **ins. 1.** The act of insulating or the state of being insulated. **2.** A material or substance used in insulating: *soundproof cork insulation; a layer of trapped air that serves as insulation.*

in·su·la·tive (ĭn′-sə-lā′tĭv, ĭns′yə-) *adj.* Serving to insulate or keep safe: *the insulative value of an animal's fur; insulative packing materials.*

in·su·la·tor (ĭn′sə-lā′tər, ĭns′yə-) *n.* **1.** A material that insulates, especially a nonconductor of sound, heat, or electricity. **2.** A device that insulates.

in·su·lin (ĭn′sə-lĭn) *n.* **1.** A polypeptide hormone secreted by the islets of Langerhans and functioning in the regulation of the metabolism of carbohydrates and fats, especially the conversion of glucose to glycogen, which lowers the blood glucose level. **2.** Any of various pharmaceutical preparations containing this hormone that are derived from the pancreas of certain animals or produced through genetic engineering and are used in the medical treatment and management of diabetes mellitus (type I). [New Latin *īnsula,* island (of Langerhans) (from Latin, island) + –IN.]

in·su·lin-de·pend·ent diabetes (ĭn′sə-lĭn-dĭ-pĕn′dənt) *n.* See **diabetes mellitus** (sense 1).

insulin pump *n.* A portable device for people with diabetes that injects insulin at programmed intervals in order to regulate blood sugar levels.

insulin shock *n.* Acute hypoglycemia usually resulting from an overdose of insulin and characterized by sweating, trembling, dizziness, and, if left untreated, convulsions and coma.

in·sult (ĭn-sŭlt′) *v.* **-sult·ed, -sult·ing, -sults.** *—tr.* **1.a.** To treat with gross insensitivity, insolence, or contemptuous rudeness. See Synonyms at **offend. b.** To affront or demean: *an absurd speech that insulted the intelligence of the audience.* **2.** *Obsolete.* To make an attack on. *—intr. Archaic.* **1.** To behave arrogantly. **2.** To give offense; offend: *a speech that was intended to insult.* **—insult** (ĭn′sŭlt′) *n.* **1.** An offensive action or remark. **2.** *Medicine.* A bodily injury, irritation, or trauma. [French *insulter,* from Old French, to assault, from Latin *īnsultāre,* to leap at, insult, frequentative of *īnsilīre,* to leap upon : *in-,* on; see IN–^{2} + *salīre,* to leap; see **sel-** in Appendix.] **—in·sult′er** *n.* **—in·sult′ing·ly** *adv.*

in·su·per·a·ble (ĭn-so͞o′pər-ə-bəl) *adj.* Impossible to overcome; insurmountable: *insuperable odds.* [Middle English, from Old French, from Latin *īnsuperābilis* : *in-,* not; see IN–^{1} + *superābilis,* superable; see SUPERABLE.] **—in·su′per·a·bil′i·ty, in·su′per·a·ble·ness** *n.* **—in·su′per·a·bly** *adv.*

in·sup·port·a·ble (ĭn′sə-pôr′tə-bəl, -pōr′-) *adj.* **1.** Not endurable; intolerable: *insupportable mental anguish.* **2.** Lacking grounds or defense; unjustifiable: *an insupportable claim.* **—in′sup·port′a·ble·ness** *n.* **—in′sup·port′a·bly** *adv.*

in·sup·press·i·ble (ĭn′sə-prĕs′ə-bəl) *adj.* Impossible to suppress or control; irrepressible. **—in′sup·press′i·bly** *adv.*

in·sur·ance (ĭn-sho͝or′əns) *n. Abbr.* **ins. 1.a.** The act, business, or system of insuring. **b.** The state of being insured. **c.** A means of being insured. **2.a.** Coverage by a contract binding a party to indemnify another against specified loss in return for premiums paid. **b.** The sum or rate for which such a contract insures something. **c.** The periodic premium paid for this coverage. **3.** A protective measure: *biking helmets that provide insurance against an accident.* **—insurance** *adj. Sports.* Of, relating to, or being a score that increases a team's lead enough to prevent the opposing team from tying the game with one more score: *an insurance run.*

in·sure (ĭn-sho͝or′) *v.* **-sured, -sur·ing, -sures.** *—tr.* **1.** To cover with insurance. **2.** To make sure, certain, or secure. See Usage Note at **assure.** *—intr.* To buy or sell insurance. [Middle English *ensuren,* to assure, from Old French *enseurer,* possibly variant of *assurer.* See ASSURE.] **—in·sur′a·bil′i·ty** *n.* **—in·sur′a·ble** *adj.*

in·sured (ĭn-sho͝ord′) *n., pl.* **insured** or **-sureds. 1.** The party who stands to benefit from an insurance policy. **2.** The party insured. Also called *assured.*

in·sur·er (ĭn-sho͝or′ər) *n.* One that insures, especially an insurance underwriter.

in·sur·gence (ĭn-sûr′jəns) *n.* The action or an instance of rebellion; an insurrection.

in·sur·gen·cy (ĭn-sûr′jən-sē) *n., pl.* **-cies. 1.** The quality or circumstance of being rebellious. **2.** An instance of rebellion; an insurgence.

in·sur·gent (ĭn-sûr′jənt) *adj.* Rising in revolt against civil authority or a government in power; rebellious. **—insurgent** *n.* **1.** One that revolts against civil authority. **2.** A member of a political party who rebels against its leadership. [Latin *īnsurgēns, īnsurgent-,* present participle of *īnsurgere,* to rise up : *in-,* intensive pref.; see IN–^{2} + *surgere,* to rise; see SURGE.] **—in·sur′gent·ly** *adv.*

in·sur·mount·a·ble (ĭn′sər-moun′tə-bəl) *adj.* Impossible to surmount; insuperable: *insurmountable difficulties.* **—in′sur·mount′a·bil′i·ty, in′sur·mount′a·ble·ness** *n.* **—in′sur·mount′a·bly** *adv.*

in·sur·rec·tion (ĭn′sə-rĕk′shən) *n.* The act or an instance of open revolt against civil authority or a constituted government. See Synonyms at **rebellion.** [Middle English, from Old French, from Late Latin *īnsurrēctiō, īnsurrēctiōn-,* from Latin *īnsurrēctus,* past participle of *īnsurgere,* to rise up. See INSURGENT.] **—in′sur·rec′tion·al** *adj.* **—in′sur·rec′tion·ar′y** (-shə-nĕr′ē) *adj. & n.* **—in′sur·rec′tion·ism** *n.* **—in′sur·rec′tion·ist** *n.*

in·sus·cep·ti·ble (ĭn′sə-sĕp′tə-bəl) *adj.* Not susceptible: *insusceptible to bribery.* **—in·sus·cep′ti·bil′i·ty** *n.* **—in′sus·cep′ti·bly** *adv.*

int. *abbr.* **1.** Intelligence. **2.** Intercept. **3.** Interest. **4.** Interim. **5.** Interior. **6.** *Grammar.* Interjection. **7.** Intermediate. **8.** Internal. **9.** International. **10.** Intersection. **11.** Interval. **12.** Interview. **13.** *Grammar.* Intransitive.

in·tact (ĭn-tăkt′) *adj.* **1.** Remaining sound, entire, or uninjured; not impaired in any way. **2.** Having all physical parts, especially: **a.** Having the hymen unbroken. **b.** Not castrated. [Middle English, from Latin *intāctus* : *in-,* not; see IN–^{1} + *tāctus,* past participle of *tangere,* to touch; see **tag-** in Appendix.] **—in·tact′ly** *adv.* **—in·tact′ness** *n.*

intaglio
Agate locket depicting
Mars embracing Venus

in·ta·glio (ĭn-tăl′yō, -täl′-) *n., pl.* **-glios. 1.a.** A figure or design carved into or beneath the surface of hard metal or stone. **b.** The art or process of carving a design in this manner. **2.** A gemstone carved in intaglio. **3.** Printing done with a plate bearing an image in intaglio. **4.** A die incised so as to produce a design in relief. [Italian, from *intagliare,* to engrave : *in-,* in (from Latin; see IN–^{2}) + *tagliare,* to cut (from Vulgar Latin **talliāre;* see TAILOR).]

in·take (ĭn′tāk′) *n.* **1.** An opening by which a fluid is admitted into a container or conduit. **2.a.** The act of taking in. **b.** The quantity taken in. **c.** Something, especially energy, taken in.

in·tan·gi·ble (ĭn-tăn′jə-bəl) *adj.* **1.** Incapable of being perceived by the senses. **2.** Incapable of being realized or defined. **—intangible** *n.* Something intangible, especially an asset that cannot be perceived by the senses. Often used in the plural: *intangibles such as goodwill and dedication.* **—in·tan′gi·bil′i·ty, in·tan′gi·ble·ness** *n.* **—in·tan′gi·bly** *adv.*

in·tar·si·a (ĭn-tär′sē-ə) *n.* **1.** A decorative inlaid pattern in a surface, especially a mosaic worked in wood. **2.** The art or practice of making such a pattern. [German, from Italian *intarsio,* from *intarsiare,* to inlay : *in-,* in (from Latin; see EN–^{1}) + *tarsia,* inlaid mosaic work (from Arabic *tarṣī'*).]

intarsia

in·te·ger (ĭn′tĭ-jər) *n. Mathematics.* **1.** A member of the set of positive whole numbers (1, 2, 3, . . .), negative whole numbers (−1, −2, −3, . . .), and zero (0). **2.** A complete unit or entity. [From Latin, whole, complete. See **tag-** in Appendix.]

in·te·gra·ble (ĭn′tĭ-grə-bəl) *adj. Mathematics.* Capable of undergoing integration or of being integrated. **—in′te·gra·bil′i·ty** *n.*

in·te·gral (ĭn′tĭ-grəl, ĭn-tĕg′rəl) *adj.* **1.** Essential or necessary for completeness; constituent: *The kitchen is an integral part of a house.* **2.** Possessing everything essential; entire. **3.** (ĭn′tĭ-grəl). *Mathematics.* **a.** Expressed or expressible as or in terms of integers. **b.** Expressed as or involving integrals. **—integral** *n.* **1.** A complete unit; a whole. **2.** (ĭn′tĭ-grəl). *Mathematics.* **a.** A definite integral. **b.** An indefinite integral. [Middle English, from Old French, from Medieval Latin *integrālis,* making up a whole, from Latin *integer,* complete. See INTEGER.] **—in′te·gral′i·ty** (-grăl′ĭ-tē) *n.* **—in′te·gral·ly** *adv.*

integral calculus *n. Mathematics.* The study of integration and its use in finding volumes, areas, and solutions of differential equations.

integral domain *n. Mathematics.* A commutative ring with unity having no proper divisors of zero, that is, where the product of nonzero elements cannot be zero.

in·te·grand (ĭn′tĭ-grănd′) *n. Mathematics.* A function or an equation to be integrated. [From Latin *integrandus,* gerundive of *integrāre,* to integrate. See INTEGRATE.]

in·te·grant (ĭn′tĭ-grənt) *adj.* Constituting part of a whole; integral.

in·te·grate (ĭn′tĭ-grāt′) *v.* **-grat·ed, -grat·ing, -grates.** *—tr.* **1.** To make into a whole by bringing all parts together; unify. **2.a.** To join with something else; unite. **b.** To make part of a larger unit: *integrated the new procedures into the work routine.* **3.** To open to people of all races or ethnic groups without restriction; desegregate. **4.** *Mathematics.* **a.** To calculate the integral of. **b.** To perform integration on. **5.** *Psychology.* To bring about the integration of (personality traits). *—intr.* To become integrated or undergo integration. [From Middle English, intact, from Latin *integrātus,* past participle of *integrāre,* to make whole, from *integer,* complete. See **tag-** in Appendix.] **—in′te·gra′tive** *adj.*

in·te·grat·ed circuit (ĭn′tĭ-grā′tĭd) *n. Abbr.* **IC** A tiny slice or chip of material on which is etched or imprinted a complex of electronic components and their interconnections. **—integrated circuitry** *n.*

in·te·gra·tion (ĭn′tĭ-grā′shən) *n.* **1.a.** The act or process of

ă pat	oi boy
ā pay	ou out
âr care	o͝o took
ä father	o͞o boot
ĕ pet	ŭ cut
ē be	ûr urge
ĭ pit	th thin
ī pie	*th* this
îr pier	hw which
ŏ pot	zh vision
ō toe	ə about, item
ô paw	♦ regionalism

Stress marks: ′ (primary); ′ (secondary), as in **dictionary** (dĭk′shə-nĕr′ē)

integrating. **b.** The state of becoming integrated. **2.** The bringing of people of different racial or ethnic groups into unrestricted and equal association, as in society or an organization; desegregation. **3.** *Psychology.* The organization of the psychological or social traits and tendencies of a personality into a harmonious whole. **4.** *Mathematics.* The process of finding the equation or function of which a given quantity or function is the derivative.

in·te·gra·tion·ist (ĭn′tĭ-grā′shə-nĭst) *n.* One who advocates or works for social integration. **—in′te·gra′tion·ist** *adj.*

in·te·gra·tor (ĭn′tĭ-grā′tər) *n.* **1.** One that integrates. **2.** An instrument for mechanically calculating definite integrals.

in·teg·ri·ty (ĭn-tĕg′rĭ-tē) *n.* **1.** Steadfast adherence to a strict moral or ethical code. See Synonyms at **honesty. 2.** The state of being unimpaired; soundness. **3.** The quality or condition of being whole or undivided; completeness. [Middle English *integrite,* from Old French, from Latin *integritās,* soundness, from *integer,* whole, complete. See **tag-** in Appendix.]

in·teg·u·ment (ĭn-tĕg′yo͞o-mənt) *n.* **1.** A natural outer covering or coat, such as the skin of an animal or the membrane enclosing an organ. **2.** *Botany.* The envelope of an ovule. [Latin *integumentum,* from *integere,* to cover : *in-,* on; see IN−[2] + *tegere,* to cover; see **(s)teg-** in Appendix.] **—in·teg′u·men′ta·ry** (-mĕn′tə-rē, -mĕn′trē) *adj.*

in·tel·lect (ĭn′tl-ĕkt′) *n.* **1.a.** The ability to learn and reason; the capacity for knowledge and understanding. **b.** The ability to think abstractly or profoundly. See Synonyms at **mind. 2.** A person of great intellectual ability. [Middle English, from Old French *intellecte,* from Latin *intellēctus,* perception, from past participle of *intellegere,* to perceive. See INTELLIGENT.]

in·tel·lec·tion (ĭn′tl-ĕk′shən) *n.* **1.** The act or process of using the intellect; thinking or reasoning. **2.** A thought or an idea. [Middle English *intelleccioun,* understanding, from Latin *intellēctiō, intellēctiōn-,* synecdoche, from *intellēctus,* intellect. See INTELLECT.]

in·tel·lec·tive (ĭn′tl-ĕk′tĭv) *adj.* Of, relating to, or generated by the intellect. **—in′tel·lec′tive·ly** *adv.*

in·tel·lec·tron·ics (ĭn′tl-ĕk-trŏn′ĭks) *n.* *(used with a sing. verb).* The use of electronic devices to extend human intellect. [Blend of INTELLECT and ELECTRONICS.]

in·tel·lec·tu·al (ĭn′tl-ĕk′cho͞o-əl) *adj.* **1.a.** Of or relating to the intellect. **b.** Rational rather than emotional. **2.** Appealing to or engaging the intellect: *an intellectual book; an intellectual problem.* **3.a.** Having or showing intellect, especially to a high degree. See Synonyms at **intelligent. b.** Given to exercise of the intellect; inclined toward abstract thinking about aesthetic or philosophical subjects. **—intellectual** *n.* An intellectual person. [Middle English, from Old French *intellectuel,* from Late Latin *intellēctuālis,* from Latin *intellēctus,* intellect. See INTELLECT.] **—in′tel·lec′tu·al′i·ty** (-ăl′ĭ-tē) *n.* **—in′tel·lec′tu·al·ly** *adv.*

in·tel·lec·tu·al·ism (ĭn′tl-ĕk′cho͞o-ə-lĭz′əm) *n.* **1.** Exercise or application of the intellect. **2.** Devotion to exercise or development of the intellect. **—in′tel·lec′tu·al·ist** *n.* **—in′tel·lec′tu·al·is′tic** *adj.*

in·tel·lec·tu·al·i·za·tion (ĭn′tl-ĕk′cho͞o-ə-lĭ-zā′shən) *n.* *Psychology.* **1.** The act or process of intellectualizing. **2.** An unconscious means of protecting oneself from the emotional stress and anxiety associated with confronting painful personal fears or problems by excessive reasoning.

in·tel·lec·tu·al·ize (ĭn′tl-ĕk′cho͞o-ə-līz′) *tr.v.* **-ized, -iz·ing, -iz·es. 1.** To furnish a rational structure or meaning for. **2.** To avoid psychological insight into (an emotional problem) by performing an intellectual analysis. **—in′tel·lec′tu·al·iz′er** *n.*

in·tel·li·gence (ĭn-tĕl′ə-jəns) *n.* *Abbr.* **int., I 1.a.** The capacity to acquire and apply knowledge. **b.** The faculty of thought and reason. **c.** Superior powers of mind. See Synonyms at **mind. 2.a.** *Theology.* An intelligent, incorporeal being, especially an angel. **b. Intelligence.** *Christian Science.* The primal, eternal quality of God. **3.** Information; news. See Synonyms at **news. 4.a.** Secret information, especially about an actual or potential enemy. **b.** An agency or an office that gathers such information. **c.** Espionage agents, organizations, and activities considered as a group: *"Intelligence is nothing if not an institutionalized black market in perishable commodities"* (John le Carré).

intelligence quotient *n.* *Abbr.* **IQ, I.Q.** The ratio of tested mental age to chronological age, usually expressed as a quotient multiplied by 100.

in·tel·li·genc·er (ĭn-tĕl′ə-jən-sər, -jĕn′-) *n.* **1.** One who conveys news or information. **2.** A secret agent, an informer, or a spy.

intelligence test *n.* A standardized test used to establish an intelligence level rating by measuring a subject's ability to form concepts, solve problems, acquire information, reason, and perform other intellectual operations.

in·tel·li·gent (ĭn-tĕl′ə-jənt) *adj.* **1.** Having intelligence. **2.** Having a high degree of intelligence; mentally acute. **3.** Showing sound judgment and rationality: *an intelligent decision; an intelligent solution to the budget problem.* **4.** Appealing to the intellect; intellectual: *a film with witty and intelligent dialogue.* **5.** *Computer Science.* Having certain data storage and processing capabilities: *an intelligent terminal; intelligent peripherals.* [Latin *intelligēns, intelligent-,* present participle of *intellegere, intelligere,* to perceive : *inter-,* inter- + *legere,* to choose; see **leg-** in Appendix.] **—in·tel′li·gen′tial** (-jĕn′shəl) *adj.* **—in·tel′li·gent·ly** *adv.*

SYNONYMS: *intelligent, bright, brilliant, knowing, quick-witted, smart, intellectual.* These adjectives mean having or showing mental keenness. *Intelligent* usually implies the ability to cope with demands arising from novel situations and new problems and to use the power of reasoning and inference effectively: *The most intelligent students do additional reading to supplement the material in the textbook. Bright* implies quickness or ease in learning: *Some children are brighter in one subject than in another. Brilliant* suggests unusually impressive mental acuteness: *"The dullard's envy of brilliant men is always assuaged by the suspicion that they will come to a bad end"* (Max Beerbohm). *Knowing* implies the possession of knowledge, information, or understanding: *Knowing furniture collectors bought American antiques before the prices soared. Quick-witted* suggests mental alertness and prompt response: *We were successful not because we were quick-witted but because we persevered. Smart* refers to quick intelligence and often a ready capability for taking care of one's own interests: *The smartest lawyers avoid the appearance of manipulating juries. Intellectual* stresses the working of the intellect and especially implies the capacity to grasp difficult or abstract concepts: *The scholar's interest in the intellectual and analytical aspect of music didn't prevent her from enjoying concerts.*

in·tel·li·gent·si·a (ĭn-tĕl′ə-jĕnt′sē-ə, -gĕnt′-) *n.* The intellectual elite of a society. [Russian *intelligentsiya,* from Latin *intelligentia,* intelligence, from *intelligēns, intelligent-,* intelligent. See INTELLIGENT.]

in·tel·li·gi·ble (ĭn-tĕl′ĭ-jə-bəl) *adj.* **1.** Capable of being understood: *an intelligible set of directions.* **2.** Capable of being apprehended by the intellect alone. [Middle English, from Old French, from Latin *intellegibilis, intelligibilis,* from *intellegere,* to perceive. See INTELLIGENT.] **—in·tel′li·gi·bil′i·ty, in·tel′li·gi·ble·ness** *n.* **—in·tel′li·gi·bly** *adv.*

in·tem·per·ance (ĭn-tĕm′pər-əns, -prəns) *n.* **1.** Lack of temperance, as in the indulgence of an appetite or a passion. **2.** Excessive use of alcoholic beverages.

in·tem·per·ate (ĭn-tĕm′pər-ĭt, -prĭt) *adj.* Not temperate or moderate; excessive, especially in the use of alcoholic beverages. **—in·tem′per·ate·ly** *adv.* **—in·tem′per·ate·ness** *n.*

in·tend (ĭn-tĕnd′) *v.* **-tend·ed, -tend·ing, -tends.** —*tr.* **1.** To have in mind; plan: *We intend to go. They intend going. You intended that she go.* **2.a.** To design for a specific purpose. **b.** To have in mind for a particular use. **3.** To signify or mean. —*intr.* To have a design or purpose in mind. [Middle English *entenden,* from Old French *entendre,* from Latin *intendere* : *in-,* toward; see IN−[2] + *tendere,* to stretch; see **ten-** in Appendix.]

in·ten·dance (ĭn-tĕn′dəns) *n.* **1.** The function of an intendant; management. **2.** An administrative office or district.

in·ten·dan·cy (ĭn-tĕn′dən-sē) *n., pl.* **-cies. 1.** The position or function of an intendant. **2.** Intendants considered as a group. **3.** The district supervised by an intendant, as in Latin America.

in·ten·dant (ĭn-tĕn′dənt) *n.* **1.** An administrative official serving a French, Spanish, or Portuguese monarch. **2.** A district administrator in some countries of Latin America. [French, from Old French, administrator, from Latin *intendēns, intendent-,* present participle of *intendere,* to intend. See INTEND.]

in·tend·ed (ĭn-tĕn′dĭd) *adj.* **1.** Deliberate; intentional: *"The only option is whether these will be purposeful, intended policies or whether they will be . . . concealed ones"* (Daniel Patrick Moynihan). **2.** Prospective; future: *an intended trip abroad next month.* **—intended** *n.* *Informal.* A person who is engaged to be married: *our daughter and her intended.* **—in·tend′ed·ly** *adv.*

in·tend·ing (ĭn-tĕn′dĭng) *adj.* Purposing to become or be; prospective: *intending lawyers; an intending contributor.*

in·tend·ment (ĭn-tĕnd′mənt) *n.* The true meaning or intention of something, especially of a law.

in·ten·er·ate (ĭn-tĕn′ə-rāt′) *tr.v.* **-at·ed, -at·ing, -ates.** To make tender; soften. [IN−[2] + Latin *tener,* tender; see TENDER[1] + −ATE[1].] **—in·ten′er·a′tion** *n.*

in·tense (ĭn-tĕns′) *adj.* **-tens·er, -tens·est. 1.** Possessing or displaying a distinctive feature to an extreme degree: *the intense sun of the tropics.* **2.** Extreme in degree, strength, or size: *intense heat.* **3.** Involving or showing strain or extreme effort: *intense concentration.* **4.a.** Deeply felt; profound: *intense emotion.* **b.** Tending to feel deeply: *an intense writer.* [Middle English, from Old French, from Latin *intēnsus,* stretched, intent, from past participle of *intendere,* to stretch, intend. See INTEND.] **—in·tense′ly** *adv.* **—in·tense′ness** *n.*

SYNONYMS: *intense, fierce, vehement, violent.* The central meaning shared by these adjectives is "of an extreme kind": *intense emotions; fierce loyalty; vehement dislike; violent rage.*

USAGE NOTE: The meanings of *intense* and *intensive* overlap considerably, but the two are often subtly distinct. When used to describe human feeling or activity, *intense* often suggests a strength or concentration that arises from inner dispositions and is particularly appropriate when used to describe emotional states: *intense pleasure, dislike, loyalty,* and so forth. *Intensive* is more frequently applied when the strength or concentration of an activity is imposed from without: *intensive bombing, training, marketing.* Thus a reference to *Mark's intense study of German* suggests that Mark himself was responsible for the concentrated activity, whereas *Mark's intensive study of German* suggests that the program in which Mark was studying was designed to cover a great deal of material in a brief period.

in·ten·si·fi·er (ĭn-tĕnʹsə-fīʹər) *n. Grammar.* See **intensive.**

in·ten·si·fy (ĭn-tĕnʹsə-fīʹ) *v.* **-fied, -fy·ing, -fies.** —*tr.* **1.** To make intense or more intense: *The press has intensified its scrutiny of the candidate's background.* **2.** To increase the contrast of (a photographic image). —*intr.* To become intense or more intense: *The search intensified as dusk approached.* **—in·ten'si·fi·ca'tion** (-fĭ-kāʹshən) *n.*

in·ten·sion (ĭn-tĕnʹshən) *n.* **1.** The state or quality of being intense; intensity. **2.** The act of becoming intense or more intense; intensification. **3.** *Logic.* The sum of the attributes contained in a term. [Latin *intēnsiō, intēnsiōn-,* from *intēnsus,* stretched. See INTENSE.] **—in·ten'sion·al** *adj.*

in·ten·si·ty (ĭn-tĕnʹsĭ-tē) *n., pl.* **-ties. 1.** Exceptionally great concentration, power, or force. **2.** *Physics.* The amount or degree of strength of electricity, light, heat, or sound per unit area or volume. **3.** *Color.* **a.** The strength of a color, especially the degree to which it lacks its complementary color. **b.** See **saturation** (sense 5).

in·ten·sive (ĭn-tĕnʹsĭv) *adj.* **1.** Of, relating to, or characterized by intensity: *intensive training.* See Usage Note at **intense. 2.** *Grammar.* Tending to emphasize or intensify: *an intensive adverb.* **3.** Possessing or requiring to a high degree. Often used in combination: *research-intensive; labor-intensive.* **4.** Relating to or being a method especially of land cultivation intended to increase the productivity of a fixed area by means of an increase in capital and labor. **5.** *Physics.* Having the same value for any subdivision of a thermodynamic system: *intensive pressure.* **—intensive** *n. Grammar.* A linguistic element, such as the adverb *extremely* or *awfully,* that provides force or emphasis. Also called *intensifier.* **—in·ten'sive·ly** *adv.* **—in·ten'sive·ness** *n.*

intensive care *n.* Continuous and closely monitored health care that is provided to critically ill patients.

intensive care unit *n. Abbr.* **ICU** A specialized section of a hospital containing the equipment, medical and nursing staff, and monitoring devices necessary to provide intensive care.

in·tent (ĭn-tĕntʹ) *n.* **1.** Something that is intended; an aim or a purpose. See Synonyms at **intention. 2.** *Law.* The state of one's mind at the time one carries out an action. **3.** Meaning; purport. **—intent** *adj.* **1.** Firmly fixed; concentrated: *an intent gaze.* **2.** Having the attention applied; engrossed: *The students, intent upon their books, did not hear me enter the room.* **3.** Having the mind and will focused on a specific purpose: *was intent on leaving within the hour; are intent upon being recognized.* **—*idiom.* for** (or **to**) **all intents and purposes.** In every practical sense; practically: *To all intents and purposes the case is closed.* [Middle English *entent,* from Old French, from Medieval Latin *intentus,* from Latin, an extending, from *intentus,* attentive to, strained, from past participle of *intendere,* to direct attention. See INTEND.] **—in·tent'ly** *adv.* **—in·tent'ness** *n.*

in·ten·tion (ĭn-tĕnʹshən) *n.* **1.** A course of action that one intends to follow. **2. a.** An aim that guides action; an objective. **b. intentions.** Purpose with respect to marriage: *honorable intentions.* **3.** *Philosophy.* A concept arising from directing the attention toward an object. **4.** *Medicine.* The process by which or the manner in which a wound heals. **5.** *Archaic.* Import; meaning. [Middle English *entencioun,* from Old French *intention,* from Latin *intentiō, intentiōn-,* from *intentus,* intent, from past participle of *intendere,* to direct attention. See INTEND.]

SYNONYMS: *intention, intent, purpose, goal, end, aim, object, objective.* These nouns refer to what one intends to do or achieve. *Intention* simply signifies a course of action that one proposes to follow: *It is not my intention to argue with you. Intent* more strongly implies deliberateness: *The executor tried to comply with the intent of the testator. Purpose* strengthens the idea of resolution or determination: *"His purpose was to discover how long these guests intended to stay"* (Joseph Conrad). *Goal* may suggest an idealistic or even a remote purpose: *"Black Power . . . is a call for black people to begin to define their own goals"* (Stokely Carmichael and Charles V. Hamilton). *End* suggests a long-range goal: *It has been said that the end justifies the means. Aim* stresses the direction one's efforts take in pursuit of an end: *The aim of every performing artist is to achieve perfection of execution.* An *object* is an end that one tries to carry out: *"The chief object of the English was to establish . . . a great empire on the Continent"* (Macaulay). *Objective* often implies that the end or goal can be reached: *"A major objective* [of political liberalism] *is the protection of the economic weak"* (Wayne Morse).

in·ten·tion·al (ĭn-tĕnʹshə-nəl) *adj.* **1.** Done deliberately; intended: *an intentional slight.* See Synonyms at **voluntary. 2.** Having to do with intention. **—in·ten'tion·al'i·ty** (-nălʹĭ-tē) *n.* **—in·ten'tion·al·ly** *adv.*

intentional community *n.* A small, localized, often rural community of persons or families pursuing common interests or concentrating on certain basic values.

in·ter (ĭn-tûrʹ) *tr.v.* **-terred, -ter·ring, -ters.** To place in a grave or tomb; bury. [Middle English *enteren,* from Old French *enterrer,* from Medieval Latin *interrāre* : Latin *in-,* in; see IN–[2] + Latin *terra,* earth; see **ters-** in Appendix.]

inter. *abbr.* Intermediate.

inter– *pref.* **1.** Between; among: *international.* **2.** In the midst of; within: *intertropical.* **3.** Mutual; mutually: *interrelate.* **4.** Reciprocal; reciprocally: *intermingle.* [Middle English *entre-, inter-,* from Old French *entre-,* from Latin *inter-,* from *inter,* between, among. See **en** in Appendix.]

in·ter·a·bang (ĭn-tĕrʹə-băngʹ) *n.* Variant of **interrobang.**

in·ter·act (ĭnʹtər-ăktʹ) *intr.v.* **-act·ed, -act·ing, -acts.** To act on each other: *"More than a dozen variable factors could interact, with their permutations running into the thousands"* (Tom Clancy).

in·ter·ac·tion (ĭnʹtər-ăkʹshən) *n.* **1. a.** The act or process of interacting. **b.** The state of undergoing interaction. **2.** *Physics.* Any of four fundamental ways in which elementary particles and bodies can influence each other, classified as strong, weak, electromagnetic, and gravitational.

in·ter·ac·tive (ĭnʹtər-ăkʹtĭv) *adj.* **1.** Acting or capable of acting on each other. **2.** *Computer Science.* Of or relating to a two-way electronic or communications system in which response is direct and continual. **3.** Of, relating to, or being a form of television entertainment in which the signal activates electronic apparatus in the viewer's home or the viewer uses the apparatus to affect events on the screen, or both. **—in'ter·ac'tive·ly** *adv.*

interactive terminal *n. Computer Science.* A computer or data-processing terminal capable of providing a two-way communication with the system to which it is connected.

in·ter·a·gen·cy (ĭnʹtər-āʹjən-sē) *adj.* Involving or representing two or more agencies, especially government agencies.

in·ter a·li·a (ĭnʹtər āʹlē-ə, äʹlē-ə) *adv.* Among other things. [Latin : *inter,* among + *alia,* neuter accusative pl. of *alius,* other.]

inter a·li·os (āʹlē-ōsʹ, äʹlē-ōsʹ) *adv.* Among other persons. [Latin : *inter,* among + *aliōs,* masculine accusative pl. of *alius.*]

in·ter·a·tom·ic (ĭnʹtər-ə-tŏmʹĭk) *adj.* Occurring, operating, or situated between atoms.

in·ter·bank (ĭnʹtər-băngkʹ) *adj.* Relating to, involving, or connecting two or more banks: *interbank borrowing; an interbank network of automated teller machines.*

in·ter·brain (ĭnʹtər-brānʹ) *n.* See **diencephalon.**

in·ter·breed (ĭnʹtər-brēdʹ) *v.* **-bred** (-brĕdʹ), **-breed·ing, -breeds.** —*intr.* **1.** To breed with another kind or species; hybridize. **2.** To breed within a narrow range or with closely related types or individuals; inbreed. —*tr.* To cause to interbreed.

in·ter·ca·lar·y (ĭn-tûrʹkə-lĕrʹē, ĭnʹtər-kălʹə-rē) *adj.* **1. a.** Inserted in the calendar to make the calendar year correspond to the solar year. Used of a day or month. **b.** Having such a day or month inserted. Used of a year. **2.** Inserted between other elements or parts; interpolated. [Latin *intercalārius, intercalāris,* from *intercalāre,* to intercalate. See INTERCALATE.]

in·ter·ca·late (ĭn-tûrʹkə-lātʹ) *tr.v.* **-lat·ed, -lat·ing, -lates. 1.** To insert (a day or month) in a calendar. **2.** To insert, interpose, or interpolate. [Latin *intercalāre, intercalāt-* : *inter-,* inter- + *calāre,* to proclaim; see **kele-**[2] in Appendix.] **—in·ter'ca·la'tion** *n.* **—in·ter'ca·la'tive** *adj.*

in·ter·cede (ĭnʹtər-sēdʹ) *intr.v.* **-ced·ed, -ced·ing, -cedes. 1.** To plead on another's behalf. **2.** To act as mediator in a dispute. [Latin *intercēdere,* to intervene : *inter-,* inter- + *cēdere,* to go; see **ked-** in Appendix.] **—in'ter·ced'er** *n.*

in·ter·cel·lu·lar (ĭnʹtər-sĕlʹyə-lər) *adj. Biology.* Located among or between cells: *intercellular fluid.*

in·ter·cept (ĭnʹtər-sĕptʹ) *tr.v.* **-cept·ed, -cept·ing, -cepts. 1. a.** To stop, deflect, or interrupt the progress or intended course of: *intercepted me with a message as I was leaving.* **b.** *Sports.* To take possession of by catching (an opponent's ball), especially in football. **2.** *Mathematics.* To include or bound (a part of a space or curve) between two points or lines. **3.** *Archaic.* To prevent. **4.** *Obsolete.* To cut off from access or communication. **—intercept** (ĭnʹtər-sĕptʹ) *n. Abbr.* **int. 1.** *Mathematics.* The distance from the origin to the point at which a line, curve, or surface intersects a coordinate axis. **2. a.** The interception of a missile by another missile or an aircraft by another aircraft. **b.** Interception of a radio transmission. **3.** An interceptor. [Middle English *intercepten,* from Latin *intercipere, intercept-* : *inter-,* inter- + *capere,* to seize; see **kap-** in Appendix.] **—in'ter·cep'tive** *adj.*

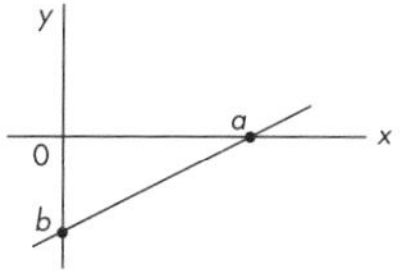

intercept
Intercept form of the equation of a line:
$\frac{x}{a}+\frac{y}{b}=1$

in·ter·cept·er (ĭnʹtər-sĕpʹtər) *n.* Variant of **interceptor.**

in·ter·cep·tion (ĭnʹtər-sĕpʹshən) *n.* **1.** The act of intercepting or the state of being intercepted. **2.** Something, such as a missile, an aircraft, or a radio transmission, that is intercepted. **3.** *Sports.* A pass that is intercepted, especially a forward pass in football.

in·ter·cep·tor also **in·ter·cept·er** (ĭnʹtər-sĕpʹtər) *n.* One that intercepts, specifically a fast-climbing, highly maneuverable fighter plane designed to intercept enemy aircraft or a guided missile designed to intercept enemy missiles and spacecraft.

in·ter·ces·sion (ĭnʹtər-sĕshʹən) *n.* **1.** Entreaty in favor of another, especially a prayer or petition to God in behalf of another. **2.** Mediation in a dispute. [Middle English, from Old French, from Latin *intercessiō, intercessiōn-,* intervention, from *intercessus,* past participle of *intercēdere,* to intervene. See INTERCEDE.] **—in'ter·ces'sion·al** *adj.* **—in'ter·ces'sor** (-sĕsʹər) *n.* **—in'ter·ces'so·ry** *adj.*

in·ter·change (ĭnʹtər-chānjʹ) *v.* **-changed, -chang·ing, -chang·es.** —*tr.* **1.** To switch each of (two things) into the place of the other. **2.** To give and receive mutually; exchange. **3.** To cause to succeed each other in a series or pattern; alternate: *in-*

ă pat	oi boy
ā pay	ou out
âr care	ŏŏ took
ä father	ōō boot
ĕ pet	ŭ cut
ē be	ûr urge
ĭ pit	th thin
ī pie	*th* this
îr pier	hw which
ŏ pot	zh vision
ō toe	ə about, item
ô paw	♦ regionalism

Stress marks: ʹ (primary); ʹ (secondary), as in **dictionary** (dĭkʹshə-nĕrʹē)

terchanged gold and silver beads in the bracelet. —*intr.* **1.** To change places with each other. **2.** To succeed each other; alternate. —**interchange** (ĭn′tər-chānj′) *n.* **1.** The act or process of interchanging. **2.** A highway intersection designed to permit traffic to move freely from one road to another without crossing another line of traffic. [Middle English *enterchaungen,* from Old French *entrechangier,* to change : *entre-,* between (from Latin *inter-;* see INTER–) + *changier,* to change; see CHANGE.] —**in′ter·chang′er** *n.*

in·ter·change·a·ble (ĭn′tər-chān′jə-bəl) *adj.* That can be interchanged: *interchangeable items of clothing; interchangeable automotive parts.* —**in′ter·change′a·bil′i·ty, in′ter·change′a·ble·ness** *n.* —**in′ter·change′a·bly** *adv.*

in·ter·cit·y (ĭn′tər-sĭt′ē) *adj.* Relating to, involving, or connecting two or more cities: *intercity rivalry; an intercity bus.*

in·ter·clav·i·cle (ĭn′tər-klăv′ĭ-kəl) *n.* A bone located in front of the sternum and between the clavicles in certain vertebrates, such as reptiles and amphibians. —**in′ter·cla·vic′u·lar** (-klə-vĭk′yə-lər) *adj.*

in·ter·coast·al (ĭn′tər-kōs′təl) *adj.* Relating to, involving, or connecting two or more coastlines: *intercoastal trade.*

in·ter·col·le·giate (ĭn′tər-kə-lē′jĭt, -jē-ĭt) *adj.* Involving or representing two or more colleges.

in·ter·co·lum·ni·a·tion (ĭn′tər-kə-lŭm′nē-ā′shən) *n.* **1.** The open spaces between the columns in a colonnade. **2.** The system by which the columns in a colonnade are spaced.

in·ter·com (ĭn′tər-kŏm′) *n.* An electronic intercommunication system, as between two or more rooms. [Short for INTERCOMMUNICATION.]

in·ter·com·mu·nal (ĭn′tər-kə-myōō′nəl) *adj.* Existing or occurring between communities: *intercommunal strife; intercommunal negotiations.*

in·ter·com·mu·ni·cate (ĭn′tər-kə-myōō′nĭ-kāt′) *intr.v.* **-cat·ed, -cat·ing, -cates. 1.** To communicate with each other. **2.** To be connected or adjoined, as rooms or passages. —**in′ter·com·mu′ni·ca′tion** *n.* —**in′ter·com·mu′ni·ca′tive** (-kā′tĭv, -kə-tĭv) *adj.*

in·ter·com·mun·ion (ĭn′tər-kə-myōōn′yən) *n.* **1.** Communion, relationship, or association between persons or groups. **2.** The practice by which members of different Christian denominations can receive Communion at one another's Eucharistic services or at a common service.

in·ter·con·nect (ĭn′tər-kə-nĕkt′) *v.* **-nect·ed, -nect·ing, -nects.** —*intr.* To be connected with each other: *The two buildings interconnect.* —*tr.* To connect reciprocally: *tried to interconnect the two theories.* —**in′ter·con·nect′ed·ness** *n.* —**in′ter·con·nect′i·ble, in′ter·con·nect′a·ble** *adj.* —**in′ter·con·nec′tion** *n.*

in·ter·con·ti·nen·tal (ĭn′tər-kŏn′tə-nĕn′tl) *adj.* **1.** Extending or taking place between or among continents: *intercontinental exploration; intercontinental cooperation.* **2.** Having the capability of traveling from one continent to another: *an intercontinental ballistic missile; an intercontinental airline.*

in·ter·con·ver·sion (ĭn′tər-kən-vûr′zhən, -shən) *n.* Mutual conversion. —**in′ter·con·vert′** *v.* —**in′ter·con·vert′i·bil′i·ty** *n.* —**in′ter·con·vert′i·ble** *adj.*

in·ter·cool·er (ĭn′tər-kōō′lər) *n.* A device for cooling a fluid between successive heating stages. —**in′ter·cool′** *v.*

in·ter·cos·tal (ĭn′tər-kŏs′təl) *adj.* Located or occurring between the ribs. —**intercostal** *n.* A space, muscle, or part situated between the ribs. [New Latin *intercostālis* : INTER– + Latin *costa,* rib; see **kost-** in Appendix.]

in·ter·course (ĭn′tər-kôrs′, -kōrs′) *n.* **1.** Dealings or communications between persons or groups. **2.** Sexual intercourse. [Middle English *entercours,* commercial dealings, from Old French *entrecours,* from Latin *intercursus,* a running between, interposition, from past participle of *intercurrere,* to mingle with : *inter-,* inter- + *currere,* to run; see **kers-** in Appendix.]

in·ter·crop (ĭn′tər-krŏp′) *v.* **-cropped, -crop·ping, -crops.** —*intr.* To grow more than one crop in the same field, especially in alternating rows. —*tr.* To plant (a crop) in the same field with another. —**in′ter·crop′** *n.*

in·ter·cul·tur·al (ĭn′tər-kŭl′chər-əl) *adj.* Of, relating to, involving, or representing different cultures: *an intercultural marriage; intercultural exchange in the arts.*

in·ter·cur·rent (ĭn′tər-kûr′ənt, -kŭr′-) *adj. Pathology.* Occurring at the same time as and usually altering the course of another disease. [Latin *intercurrēns, intercurrent-,* present participle of *intercurrere,* to mingle with. See INTERCOURSE.]

in·ter·cut (ĭn′tər-kŭt′) *tr.v.* **-cut, -cut·ting, -cuts.** To insert or alternate (scenes or camera shots) in a film sequence to achieve dramatic contrast or follow two or more actions taking place simultaneously. —**in′ter·cut′** *adj.*

in·ter·de·nom·i·na·tion·al (ĭn′tər-də-nŏm′ə-nā′shə-nəl) *adj.* Of or involving different religious denominations.

in·ter·den·tal (ĭn′tər-dĕn′tl) *adj.* **1.** Located or made for use between the teeth. **2.** *Linguistics.* Pronounced with the tip of the tongue between the teeth, as (*th*) in *that* or (th) in *thumb.* —**interdental** *n. Linguistics.* An interdental consonant.

in·ter·de·part·men·tal (ĭn′tər-dē′pärt-mĕn′tl) *adj.* Involving or representing different departments, as of a business, an academic institution, or a government: *"the petty interdepartmental squabbling that surrounds the making of . . . foreign policy"* (Morton A. Reichek).

in·ter·de·pend·ent (ĭn′tər-dĭ-pĕn′dənt) *adj.* Mutually dependent: *"The mission of one institution can be accomplished only by recognizing that it lives in an interdependent world with conflicts and overlapping interests"* (Jacqueline Grennan Wexler). —**in′ter·de·pend′ence, in′ter·de·pend′en·cy** *n.*

in·ter·dict (ĭn′tər-dĭkt′) *tr.v.* **-dict·ed, -dict·ing, -dicts. 1.** To prohibit or place under an ecclesiastical or legal sanction. **2.** To forbid or debar, especially authoritatively. See Synonyms at **forbid. 3.a.** To cut or destroy (a line of communication) by firepower so as to halt an enemy's advance. **b.** To confront and halt the activities, advance, or entry of: *"the role of the FBI in interdicting spies attempting to pass US secrets to the Soviet Union"* (Christian Science Monitor). —**interdict** (ĭn′tər-dĭkt′) *n.* **1.** *Law.* A prohibition by court order. **2.** *Roman Catholic Church.* An ecclesiastical censure that excludes a person or district from participation in most sacraments and from Christian burial. [Alteration of Middle English *enterditen,* to place under a church ban, from Old French *entredit,* past participle of *entredire,* to forbid, from Latin *interdīcere, interdict-* : *inter-,* inter- + *dīcere,* to say; see **deik-** in Appendix.] —**in′ter·dic′tion** *n.* —**in′ter·dic′tive, in′ter·dic′to·ry** (-dĭk′tə-rē) *adj.* —**in′ter·dic′tive·ly** *adv.* —**in′ter·dic′tor** *n.*

in·ter·dis·ci·pli·nar·y (ĭn′tər-dĭs′ə-plə-nĕr′ē) *adj.* Of, relating to, or involving two or more academic disciplines that are usually considered distinct.

in·ter·est (ĭn′trĭst, -tər-ĭst, -trĕst′) *n. Abbr.* **i., int. 1.a.** A state of curiosity or concern about or attention to something: *an interest in sports.* **b.** Something, such as a quality, a subject, or an activity, that evokes this mental state: *counts the theater among his interests.* **2.** Often **interests.** Regard for one's own benefit or advantage; self-interest: *It is in your best interest to cooperate. She kept her own interests in mind.* **3.a.** A right, claim, or legal share: *an interest in the new company.* **b.** Something in which such a right, claim, or share is held: *has interests overseas.* **c.** A person or group of persons holding such a right, claim, or share: *a petroleum interest.* **4.** Involvement with or participation in something: *She has an interest in the quality of her education.* **5.a.** A charge for a loan, usually a percentage of the amount loaned. **b.** An excess or a bonus beyond what is expected or due. **6.a.** An interest group. **b.** The particular cause supported by an interest group. —**interest** *tr.v.* **-est·ed, -est·ing, -ests. 1.** To arouse the curiosity or hold the attention of: *Your opinions interest me.* **2.** To cause to become involved or concerned with: *tried to interest her in taking a walk.* **3.** *Obsolete.* To concern or affect. —***idiom.* in the interest** (or **interests**) **of.** To the advantage of; for the sake of: *thinking in the interest of the whole family; ate breakfast on the train in the interest of time.* [Middle English, from Old French, from Latin, it is of importance, 3rd person sing. present tense of *interesse,* to be between, take part in : *inter-,* inter- + *esse,* to be; see **es-** in Appendix.]

in·ter·est·ed (ĭn′trĭ-stĭd, -tər-ĭ-stĭd, -tə-rĕs′tĭd) *adj.* **1.** Having or showing curiosity, fascination, or concern: *I'm interested to hear about your family.* **2.** Possessing a right, claim, or stake: *an interested party in the estate.* See Usage Note at **disinterested.** —**in′ter·est·ed·ly** *adv.* —**in′ter·est·ed·ness** *n.*

interest group *n.* A group of persons working on behalf of or strongly supporting a particular cause, such as an item of legislation, an industry, or a special segment of society. —**in′ter·est-group′** (ĭn′trĭst-group′, -tər-ĭst, -trĕst-) *adj.*

in·ter·est·ing (ĭn′trĭ-stĭng, -tər-ĭ-stĭng, -tə-rĕs′tĭng) *adj.* Arousing or holding the attention; absorbing. —**in′ter·est·ing·ly** *adv.*

in·ter·face (ĭn′tər-fās′) *n.* **1.** A surface forming a common boundary between adjacent regions, bodies, substances, or phases. **2.** A point at which independent systems or diverse groups interact: *"the interface between crime and politics where much of our reality is to be found"* (Jack Kroll). **3.** *Computer Science.* The point of interaction or communication between a computer and any other entity, such as a printer or human operator. —**interface** (ĭn′tər-fās′) *v.* **-faced, -fac·ing, -fac·es.** —*tr.* **1.** To join by means of an interface. **2.** To serve as an interface for. —*intr.* **1.** To serve as an interface or become interfaced. **2.** To interact or coordinate smoothly: *"Theatergoers were lured out of their seats and interfaced with the scenery"* (New York Times). —**in′ter·fa′cial** *adj.*

in·ter·fac·ing (ĭn′tər-fā′sĭng) *n.* A piece of firm fabric or other material inserted and usually sewn between the layers of a garment to thicken or stiffen it.

in·ter·faith (ĭn′tər-fāth′) *adj.* Of, relating to, or involving persons of different religious faiths: *an interfaith marriage; an interfaith forum.*

in·ter·fas·cic·u·lar cambium (ĭn′tər-fə-sĭk′yə-lər) *n. Botany.* The cambium arising between the vascular bundles.

in·ter·fere (ĭn′tər-fîr′) *intr.v.* **-fered, -fer·ing, -feres. 1.** To come between so as to be a hindrance or an obstacle: *loud talking that interfered with the other patrons' conversations; assistance that only interfered.* **2.** *Sports.* To perform an act of interference. **3.** To intervene or intrude in the affairs of others; meddle. **4.** To strike one hoof against the opposite hoof or leg while moving. Used of a horse. **5.** *Physics & Electronics.* To cause interference. [Middle English *enterferen,* from Old French *s'entreferer,* to strike one another : *entre-,* between (from Latin *inter-;* see INTER–) +

ferir, to strike (from Latin *ferīre*).] **—in′ter·fer′er** *n.* **—in′ter·fer′ing·ly** *adv.*

SYNONYMS: *interfere, meddle, tamper.* These verbs are compared as they mean to put oneself forward and intervene in the affairs of others when unasked to do so and often in an impudent or indiscreet manner. *Interfere* and *meddle* are sometimes interchangeable. *Meddle,* however, is the stronger in implying unwanted, unwarranted, or unnecessary intrusion: *"wholly unacquainted with the world in which they are so fond of meddling"* (Edmund Burke). It is somewhat weaker than *interfere* in implying action that seriously hampers, hinders, or frustrates: *"It was his peculiar doctrine that a man has a perfect right to interfere by force with the slaveholder, in order to rescue the slave"* (Henry David Thoreau). To *tamper* is to interfere by making unsought, unwelcome, often destructive changes or by trying to influence another in an improper way: *"a large number of persons accused of . . . tampering with ballot boxes"* (James Bryce). *"He began another practice, to tamper with the justices"* (John Strype).

in·ter·fer·ence (ĭn′tər-fîr′əns) *n.* **1.a.** The act or an instance of hindering, obstructing, or impeding. **b.** Something that hinders, obstructs, or impedes. **2.a.** *Sports.* Illegal obstruction or hindrance of the ball or of an opposing player, especially hindrance of a receiver in football. **b.** *Football.* The legal blocking of defensive tacklers to protect and make way for the ball carrier. **3.** *Physics.* The variation of wave amplitude that occurs when waves of the same or nearly the same frequency come together. **4.** *Electronics.* **a.** The inhibition or prevention of clear reception of broadcast signals. **b.** The distorted portion of a received signal. **—in′ter·fer·en′tial** (-fə-rĕn′shəl) *adj.*

in·ter·fe·rom·e·ter (ĭn′tər-fə-rŏm′ĭ-tər) *n.* Any of several optical, acoustic, or radio frequency instruments that use interference phenomena between a reference wave and an experimental wave or between two parts of an experimental wave to determine wavelengths and wave velocities, measure very small distances and thicknesses, and measure indices of refraction. **—in′ter·fer′o·met′ric** (-fîr′ə-mĕt′rĭk) *adj.* **—in′ter·fer′o·met′ri·cal·ly** *adv.* **—in′ter·fe·rom′e·try** *n.*

in·ter·fer·on (ĭn′tər-fîr′ŏn′) *n.* Any of a group of glycoproteins produced by cells in response to infection by a virus that act to prevent viral replication and have the ability to induce resistance to viral antigens. [INTERFER(E) + -ON[3].]

in·ter·fer·tile (ĭn′tər-fûr′tl) *adj.* Capable of interbreeding. **—in′ter·fer·til′i·ty** (-fûr-tĭl′ĭ-tē) *n.*

in·ter·fluve (ĭn′tər-flo͞ov′) *n.* The region of higher land between two rivers that are in the same drainage system. [Back-formation from INTERFLUVIAL.] **—in′ter·flu′vi·al** *adj.*

in·ter·ga·lac·tic (ĭn′tər-gə-lăk′tĭk) *adj.* Being or occurring between galaxies: *intergalactic space.* **—in′ter·ga·lac′ti·cal·ly** *adv.*

in·ter·gen·er·a·tion·al (ĭn′tər-jĕn′ə-rā′shə-nəl) *adj.* Being or occurring between generations: *"These social-insurance programs are intergenerational and all Americans benefit from their success"* (Claude D. Pepper).

in·ter·gla·cial (ĭn′tər-glā′shəl) *adj.* Occurring between glacial epochs. **—interglacial** *n.* A comparatively short period of warmth during an overall period of glaciation.

in·ter·gov·ern·men·tal (ĭn′tər-gŭv′ərn-mĕn′tl) *adj.* Being or occurring between two or more governments or divisions of a government. **—in′ter·gov′ern·men′tal·ly** *adv.*

in·ter·grade (ĭn′tər-grād′) *intr.v.* **-grad·ed, -grad·ing, -grades.** To merge into each other in a series of stages, forms, or types. **—intergrade** (ĭn′tər-grād′) *n.* A transitional stage, form, or type. **—in′ter·gra·da′tion** (-grā-dā′shən) *n.*

in·ter·group (ĭn′tər-gro͞op′) *adj.* Being or occurring between two or more social groups: *intergroup relations.*

in·ter·im (ĭn′tər-ĭm) *n. Abbr.* **int.** An interval of time between one event, process, or period and another. **—interim** *adj.* Belonging to, serving during, or taking place during an intermediate interval of time; temporary: *an interim agreement.* See Synonyms at **temporary.** [From Latin, in the meantime. See **en** in Appendix.]

in·ter·i·on·ic (ĭn′tər-ī-ŏn′ĭk) *adj. Physics & Chemistry.* Located or occurring between ions.

in·te·ri·or (ĭn-tîr′ē-ər) *adj. Abbr.* **int. 1.** Of, relating to, or located on the inside; inner. **2.** Of or relating to one's mental or spiritual being: *"She thinks she has no soul, no interior life, but the truth is that she has no access to it"* (David Denby). **3.** Situated away from a coast or border; inland. **—interior** *n. Abbr.* **int. 1.** The internal portion or area. **2.** One's mental or spiritual life. **3.** The inland part of a political or geographic entity. **4.** The internal affairs of a country or nation. **5.** A representation of the inside of a building or room, as in a photograph. [Ultimately Latin, comparative adj. of *inter,* between. See **en** in Appendix.] **—in·te′ri·or′i·ty** (-ôr′ĭ-tē, -ŏr′-) *n.* **—in·te′ri·or·ly** *adv.*

interior angle *n. Mathematics.* **1.** Any of the four angles formed between two straight lines intersected by a third straight line. **2.** The angle formed inside a polygon by two adjacent sides.

interior decoration *n.* The planning and execution of the layout, decoration, and furnishing of an architectural interior. Also called *interior design.* **—interior decorator** *n.*

in·te·ri·or·ize (ĭn-tîr′ē-ə-rīz′) *tr.v.* **-ized, -iz·ing, -iz·es.** To cause (feelings, for example) to become an interior or internal part of one's mental or spiritual being; internalize: *"In a number of earlier movies, [he] interiorized emotion so much that he became inexpressive"* (Pauline Kael).

interior monologue *n.* A passage of writing presenting a character's inner thoughts and emotions in a direct, sometimes disjointed or fragmentary manner.

In·te·ri·or Salish (ĭn-tîr′ē-ər) *n.* A group of Salish-speaking Native American peoples inhabiting parts of British Columbia, northern Washington, northern Idaho, and western Montana. Also called *Flathead.*

in·ter·is·land (ĭn′tər-ī′lənd) *adj.* Relating to, involving, or connecting two or more islands: *interisland competition; interisland ferries.*

interj. *abbr.* Interjection.

in·ter·ject (ĭn′tər-jĕkt′) *tr.v.* **-ject·ed, -ject·ing, -jects.** To insert between other elements; interpose. See Synonyms at **introduce.** [Latin *interiicere, interiect-* : *inter-,* inter- + *iacere,* to throw; see **yē-** in Appendix.] **—in·ter·jec′tor** *n.* **—in′ter·jec′to·ry** (-jĕk′tə-rē) *adj.*

in·ter·jec·tion (ĭn′tər-jĕk′shən) *n.* **1.** A sudden, short utterance; an ejaculation. **2.** *Abbr.* **interj., int.** A part of speech usually expressing emotion and capable of standing alone, such as *Ugh!* or *Wow!* **—in′ter·jec′tion·al** *adj.* **—in′ter·jec′tion·al·ly** *adv.*

in·ter·lace (ĭn′tər-lās′) *v.* **-laced, -lac·ing, -lac·es.** *—tr.* **1.** To connect by or as if by lacing together; interweave. **2.** To intersperse; intermix: *interlaced the testimony with half-truths.* *—intr.* To intertwine: *"As the earth thaws, numberless little streams are formed to overlap and interlace with one another"* (Joyce Carol Oates). **—in′ter·lace′ment** *n.*

In·ter·la·ken (ĭn′tər-lä′kən, ĭn′tər-lä′-). A town of west-central Switzerland southeast of Bern. It is a popular resort in the Bernese Alps. Population, 4,852.

in·ter·lam·i·nate (ĭn′tər-lăm′ə-nāt′) *tr.v.* **-nat·ed, -nat·ing, -nates. 1.** To insert between layers. **2.** To arrange in alternating layers. **—in′ter·lam′i·na′tion** *n.*

in·ter·lan·guage (ĭn′tər-lăng′gwĭj) *n.* **1.** The type of language produced by nonnative speakers in the process of learning a second language or foreign language. **2.** A lingua franca.

in·ter·lard (ĭn′tər-lärd′) *tr.v.* **-lard·ed, -lard·ing, -lards.** To insert something foreign into: *interlarded the narrative with witty remarks.* See Synonyms at **introduce.** [Middle English *interlarden,* to mix fat into, from Old French *entrelarder* : *entre-,* between (from Latin *inter-;* see INTER-) + *larder,* to lard (from *lard,* lard; see LARD).]

in·ter·leaf (ĭn′tər-lēf′) *n., pl.* **-leaves** (-lēvz′). *Printing.* A blank leaf inserted between the regular pages of a book.

in·ter·leave (ĭn′tər-lēv′) *tr.v.* **-leaved, -leav·ing, -leaves.** *Printing.* To provide with interleaves or an interleaf.

in·ter·leu·kin-1 (ĭn′tər-lo͞o′kĭn-wŭn′) *n. Abbr.* **IL-1** Any of a group of protein substances, released by macrophages and other cells, that induce the production of interleukin-2 by helper T cells and stimulate the inflammatory response. [INTER- + Greek *leukos,* white; see LEUKO- + -IN.]

in·ter·leu·kin-2 (ĭn′tər-lo͞o′kĭn-to͞o′) *n. Abbr.* **IL-2** A lymphokine that is released by helper T cells in response to an antigen and interleukin-1 and stimulates the proliferation of helper T cells. It has been used experimentally to treat cancer.

in·ter·li·brar·y (ĭn′tər-lī′brĕr′ē) *adj.* Existing or occurring between or involving two or more libraries: *an interlibrary loan; an interlibrary network.*

in·ter·line[1] (ĭn′tər-līn′) *tr.v.* **-lined, -lin·ing, -lines.** To insert between printed or written lines. **—in′ter·lin′e·a′tion** (-lĭn′ē-ā′shən) *n.*

in·ter·line[2] (ĭn′tər-līn′) *tr.v.* **-lined, -lin·ing, -lines.** To fit (a garment) with an interlining.

in·ter·lin·e·ar (ĭn′tər-lĭn′ē-ər) *adj. Printing.* **1.** Inserted between the lines of a text. **2.** Written or printed with different languages or versions in alternating lines.

In·ter·lin·gua (ĭn′tər-lĭng′gwə) *n.* An artificial language developed between 1924 and 1951, based mainly on the Romance languages and intended as a medium of international communication among scientists. [INTER- + Latin *lingua,* language; see LINGUA.]

in·ter·lin·ing (ĭn′tər-lī′nĭng) *n.* An extra lining between the outer fabric and regular lining of a garment.

in·ter·link (ĭn′tər-lĭngk′) *tr.v.* **-linked, -link·ing, -links.** To link together or join (one) with another: *The policies, though distinct, are interlinked.*

in·ter·lock (ĭn′tər-lŏk′) *v.* **-locked, -lock·ing, -locks.** *—tr.* **1.** To unite or join closely as by hooking or dovetailing. **2.** To connect together (parts of a mechanism, for example) so that the motion or operation of individual parts affect each other. *—intr.* To become united or joined closely, as by hooking or dovetailing. **—interlock** *n. Computer Science.* (ĭn′tər-lŏk′). A device or an instruction that coordinates two or more processes and prevents one operation from interfering with another.

in·ter·lo·cu·tion (ĭn′tər-lō-kyo͞o′shən) *n.* Speech between two or more persons; conversation. [Latin *interlocūtiō, interlocūtiōn-,* from *interlocūtus,* past participle of *interloquī,* to interrupt : *inter-,* inter- + *loquī,* to speak; see **tolkʷ-** in Appendix.]

in·ter·loc·u·tor (ĭn′tər-lŏk′yə-tər) *n.* **1.** Someone who takes part in a conversation, often formally or officially. **2.** The per-

ă pat	oi boy
ā pay	ou out
âr care	o͝o took
ä father	o͞o boot
ĕ pet	ŭ cut
ē be	ûr urge
ĭ pit	th thin
ī pie	*th* this
îr pier	hw which
ŏ pot	zh vision
ō toe	ə about, item
ô paw	♦ regionalism

Stress marks: ′ (primary); ′ (secondary), as in **dictionary** (dĭk′shə-nĕr′ē)

former in a minstrel show who is placed midway between the end men and engages in banter with them.

in·ter·loc·u·to·ry (ĭn′tər-lŏk′yə-tôr′ē, -tōr′ē) *adj. Law.* Pronounced or decided during the course of an action or a suit and temporary or provisional in nature: *an interlocutory decree.*

in·ter·lop·er (ĭn′tər-lō′pər) *n.* **1.** One that interferes with the affairs of others, often for selfish reasons; a meddler. **2.** *Archaic.* **a.** One that trespasses on a trade monopoly, as by conducting unauthorized trade in an area designated to a chartered company. **b.** A ship or other vessel used in such trade. [INTER– + probably Middle Dutch *loper,* runner (from *loopen,* to run).] **—in′ter·lope′** *v.*

WORD HISTORY: The word *interloper* comes to us from the days when England was embarking on the course that would lead to the British Empire. *Interloper,* first recorded in connection with the Muscovy Company, which was the earliest major English trading company (chartered in 1555), was soon being used as well in regard to the East India Company (chartered in 1600). Since these companies were monopolies, independent traders called *interlopers* were not wanted. The term is probably partly derived from Dutch, the language of one of the great trade rivals of the English at that time. The *inter–* is simply a use of the prefix *inter–,* which English has borrowed from Latin, meaning "between, among." The element *–loper* is probably related to the same element in *landloper,* "vagabond," a word adopted from Dutch *landlooper,* with the same sense and composed of *land,* "land," and *lōper,* from *lōpen,* "to run, leap." The word *interloper,* first recorded around 1590, was too useful in a world of busybodies to be restricted to its original specialized sense and came to be used in the extended sense "busybody" in the 17th century.

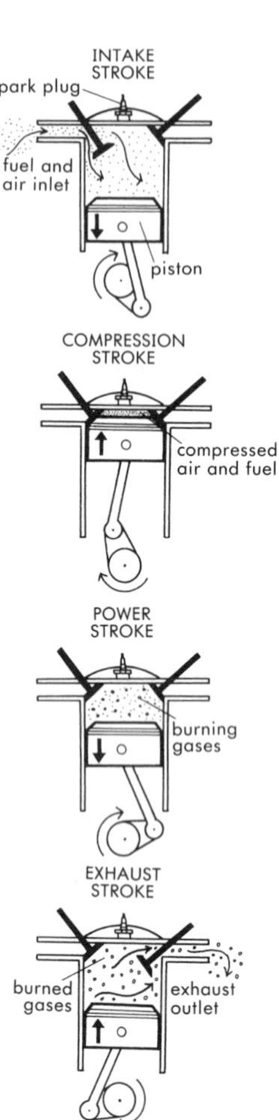

internal-combustion engine

in·ter·lude (ĭn′tər-lo͞od′) *n.* **1.** An intervening episode, feature, or period of time: *"Kerensky has a place in history, of a brief interlude between despotisms"* (William Safire). **2.a.** A short farcical entertainment performed between the acts of a medieval mystery or morality play. **b.** A 16th-century genre of comedy derived from this. **c.** An entertainment between the acts of a play. **3.** *Music.* A short piece inserted between the parts of a longer composition. [Middle English *enterlude,* a dramatic entertainment, from Old French *entrelude,* from Medieval Latin *interlūdium* : Latin *inter-,* inter- + Latin *lūdus,* play; see **leid-** in Appendix.]

in·ter·lu·nar (ĭn′tər-lo͞o′nər) *adj.* Of or relating to the four-day period between the old and new moon when the moon is not visible.

in·ter·mar·ry (ĭn′tər-măr′ē) *intr.v.* **-ried, -ry·ing, -ries. 1.** To marry a member of another group. **2.** To be bound together by the marriages of members. **3.** To marry within one's family, tribe, or clan. **—in′ter·mar′riage** (-măr′ĭj) *n.*

in·ter·med·dle (ĭn′tər-mĕd′l) *intr.v.* **-dled, -dling, -dles.** To interfere in the affairs of others, often officiously; meddle. [Middle English *entermedlen,* from Old French *entremedler* : *entre-,* between (from Latin *inter-;* see INTER–) + *medler,* to mix; see MEDDLE.] **—in′ter·med′dler** *n.*

in·ter·me·di·ar·y (ĭn′tər-mē′dē-ĕr′ē) *adj.* **1.** Existing or occurring between; intermediate. **2.** Acting as a mediator or an agent between persons or things. **—intermediary** *n., pl.* **-ies. 1.** One that acts as a mediator. **2.** One that acts as an agent between persons or things; a means. **3.** An intermediate state or stage. [Probably French *intermédiaire,* from Late Latin *intermedius,* intermediate. See INTERMEDIATE.]

in·ter·me·di·ate (ĭn′tər-mē′dē-ĭt) *adj. Abbr.* **inter., int.** Lying or occurring between two extremes or in a middle position or state: *an aircraft having an intermediate range; an intermediate school.* **—intermediate** *n. Abbr.* **inter., int. 1.** One that is in a middle position or state. **2.** An intermediary. **3.** *Chemistry.* A substance formed as a necessary stage in the manufacture of a desired end product. **4.** An automobile that is smaller than a full-sized model but larger than a compact. **—intermediate** (-āt′) *intr.v.* **-at·ed, -at·ing, -ates. 1.** To act as an intermediary; mediate. **2.** To intervene. [Middle English, from Medieval Latin *intermediātus,* from Latin *intermedius* : Latin *inter-,* inter- + Latin *medius,* middle; see **medhyo-** in Appendix.] **—in′ter·me′di·a·cy** *n.* **—in′ter·me′di·ate·ly** *adv.* **—in′ter·me′di·ate·ness** *n.* **—in′ter·me′di·a′tion** *n.* **—in′ter·me′di·a′tor** *n.*

in·ter·me·din (ĭn′tər-mēd′n) *n.* See **melanocyte-stimulating hormone.** [New Latin *(pars) intermed(ia),* middle part of the hypophysis, from Latin, feminine of *intermedius;* see INTERMEDIATE + –IN.]

in·ter·ment (ĭn-tûr′mənt) *n.* The act or ritual of interring or burying.

in·ter·mez·zo (ĭn′tər-mĕt′sō, -mĕd′zō) *n., pl.* **-zos** or **-zi** (-sē, -zē). **1.** A brief entertainment between two acts of a play; an entr'acte. **2.** *Music.* **a.** A short movement separating the major sections of a lengthy composition or work. **b.** An independent instrumental composition having the character of such a movement. [Italian, from Latin *intermedius,* intermediate. See INTERMEDIATE.]

in·ter·mi·na·ble (ĭn-tûr′mə-nə-bəl) *adj.* **1.** Being or seeming to be without an end; endless. See Synonyms at **continual. 2.** Tiresomely long; wearisome. **—in·ter′mi·na·bil′i·ty** *n.* **—in·ter′mi·na·bly** *adv.*

in·ter·min·gle (ĭn′tər-mĭng′gəl) *tr. & intr.v.* **-gled, -gling, -gles.** To mix or become mixed together.

in·ter·mis·sion (ĭn′tər-mĭsh′ən) *n.* **1.** The act of intermitting or the state of being intermitted. **2.** A respite or recess. **3.** The period between the acts of a theatrical or musical performance. See Synonyms at **pause.** [Middle English *intermissioun,* from Old French *intermission,* from Latin *intermissiō, intermissiōn-,* from *intermissus,* past participle of *intermittere,* to interrupt. See INTERMIT.]

in·ter·mit (ĭn′tər-mĭt′) *intr. & tr.v.* **-mit·ted, -mit·ting, -mits.** To suspend or cause to suspend activity temporarily or periodically. [Latin *intermittere* : *inter-,* inter- + *mittere,* to let go.] **—in′ter·mit′ter** *n.*

in·ter·mit·tent (ĭn′tər-mĭt′nt) *adj.* **1.** Stopping and starting at intervals. See Synonyms at **periodic. 2.** Alternately containing and empty of water: *an intermittent lake.* **—in′ter·mit′tence** *n.* **—in′ter·mit′tent·ly** *adv.*

intermittent current *n.* A periodically interrupted unidirectional electric current.

in·ter·mix (ĭn′tər-mĭks′) *tr. & intr.v.* **-mixed, -mix·ing, -mix·es.** To mix or become mixed together. [Back-formation from *intermixt* (obsolete variant of INTERMIXED), from Latin *intermīxtus,* past participle of *intermīscēre,* to mix together : *inter-,* inter- + *mīscēre,* to mix; see MIX.]

in·tern also **in·terne** (ĭn′tûrn′) *—n.* **1.** An advanced student or a recent graduate undergoing supervised practical training. **2.** One who is interned; an internee. *—v.* **-terned, -tern·ing, -terns.** *—intr.* To train or serve as an intern. *—tr.* (*also* ĭn-tûrn′). To confine, especially in wartime. *—adj.* (ĭn-tûrn′). *Archaic.* Internal. [French *interne,* from Latin *internus,* internal. See INTERNAL.] **—in′tern·ship′** *n.*

in·ter·nal (ĭn-tûr′nəl) *adj. Abbr.* **int. 1.** Of, relating to, or located within the limits or surface; inner. **2.** Residing in or dependent on essential nature; intrinsic: *the internal contradictions of the theory.* **3.** Located, acting, or effective within the body. **4.** Of or relating to mental or spiritual nature: *"An internal sense of righteousness dwindles into an external concern for reputation"* (A.R. Gurney, Jr.). **5.** Of or relating to the domestic affairs of a nation, group, or business. [Middle English *internall,* from Old French *internel,* from Medieval Latin *internālis,* from Latin *internus,* from *inter,* within. See **en** in Appendix.] **—in′ter·nal′i·ty** (-năl′ĭ-tē) *n.* **—in·ter′nal·ly** *adv.*

in·ter·nal-com·bus·tion engine (ĭn-tûr′nəl-kəm-bŭs′chən) *n. Abbr.* **ICE** An engine, such as an automotive gasoline piston engine or a diesel, in which fuel is burned within the engine proper rather than in an external furnace, as in a steam engine.

internal ear *n.* See **inner ear.**

internal energy *n. Symbol* **U** The total kinetic and potential energy associated with the motions and relative positions of the molecules of an object, excluding the kinetic or potential energy of the object as a whole. An increase in internal energy results in a rise in temperature or a change in phase.

in·ter·nal·ize (ĭn-tûr′nə-līz′) *tr.v.* **-ized, -iz·ing, -iz·es. 1.** To make internal, personal, or subjective: *"Protean man internalizes the longing for immortality through an ongoing process of death and rebirth within himself"* (Henry S. Resnik). **2.** To take in and make an integral part of one's attitudes or beliefs: *had internalized the cultural values of the Italians after three years of living in Rome.* **—in·ter′nal·i·za′tion** (-nə-lĭ-zā′shən) *n.*

internal medicine *n.* The branch of medicine that deals with the diagnosis and nonsurgical treatment of diseases affecting the internal organs of the body, especially in adults.

internal respiration *n.* The metabolic process by which living cells absorb oxygen and release carbon dioxide.

internal rhyme *n.* Rhyme that occurs within a line of verse, as in *"the grains beyond age, the dark veins of her mother"* (Dylan Thomas).

internal secretion *n.* A secretion that is produced by an endocrine gland and discharged directly into the bloodstream; a hormone.

in·ter·na·tion·al (ĭn′tər-năsh′ə-nəl) *adj. Abbr.* **int., intl. 1.** Of, relating to, or involving two or more nations: *an international commission; international affairs.* **2.** Extending across or transcending national boundaries: *international fame.* **—International** *n.* Any of several socialist organizations of international scope formed during the late 19th and early 20th centuries. **—in′ter·na′tion·al′i·ty** (-shə-năl′ĭ-tē) *n.* **—in′ter·na′tion·al·ly** *adv.*

international candle *n. Physics.* See **candle** (sense 2a).

International Date Line *n.* An imaginary line through the Pacific Ocean roughly corresponding to 180° longitude, to the east of which, by international agreement, the calendar date is one day earlier than to the west.

in·ter·na·tion·al·ism (ĭn′tər-năsh′ə-nə-lĭz′əm) *n.* **1.** The condition or quality of being international in character, principles, concern, or attitude. **2.** A policy or practice of cooperation among nations, especially in politics and economic matters. **—in′ter·na′tion·al·ist** *n.*

in·ter·na·tion·al·ize (ĭn′tər-năsh′ə-nə-līz′) *tr.v.* **-ized, -iz·ing, -iz·es. 1.** To make international. **2.** To put under international control. **—in′ter·na′tion·al·i·za′tion** (-năsh′ə-nə-lĭ-zā′shən) *n.*

international law *n. Law.* A set of rules generally regarded and accepted as binding in relations between states and nations. Also called *law of nations.*

international Morse code *n.* See **continental code.**

International Phonetic Alphabet *n. Abbr.* **IPA, I.P.A.** A phonetic alphabet and diacritic modifiers sponsored by the International Phonetic Association to provide a uniform and universally understood system for transcribing the speech sounds of all languages.

international pitch *n. Music.* A sound wave frequency of 440 cycles per second, assigned to the A above middle C. Also called *concert pitch.*

international relations *pl.n.* **1.** *(used with a sing. verb).* The branch of political science that is concerned with the foreign affairs of and relations among countries. **2.** *(used with a pl. verb).* Foreign affairs; relations among countries.

International style or **International Style** *n.* An influential modernist style in architecture that developed in Europe and the United States in the 1920's and 1930's, characterized chiefly by regular, unadorned geometric forms, open interiors, and the use of glass, steel, and reinforced concrete.

International System *n.* A complete, coherent system of units used for scientific work, in which the fundamental quantities are length, time, electric current, temperature, luminous intensity, and amount of substance.

international unit *n. Abbr.* **IU** **1.** The quantity of a biologically active substance, such as a hormone or vitamin, required to produce a specific response. **2.** A unit of potency for similarly active substances, based on this quantity and accepted as an international standard.

in•terne (ĭn′tûrn′, ĭn-tûrn′) *n., v., & adj.* Variant of **intern.**

in•ter•nec•ine (ĭn′tər-nĕs′ēn′, -ĭn, -nē′sīn′) *adj.* **1.** Of or relating to struggle within a nation, an organization, or a group. **2.** Mutually destructive; ruinous or fatal to both sides. **3.** Characterized by bloodshed or carnage. [Latin *internecīvus, internecīnus,* destructive, from *internecāre,* to slaughter : *inter-,* intensive pref.; see INTER– + *nex, nec-,* death; see **nek-**[1] in Appendix.]

WORD HISTORY: In the first edition of the *American Heritage Dictionary* 91 percent of the Usage Panel approved the use of *internecine* relating to internal struggle within a nation or organization that did not necessarily imply fatal or destructive conflict. The objection that had been overcome for most of the Panel was that *internecine* should imply such destruction because it came from the Latin word *internecīnus,* a variant of *internecīvus,* "fought to the death, murderous," ultimately derived from *necāre,* "to kill." *Inter–* in this compound is simply an intensive, supplying the notion of "all the way to" in the sense "fought to the death." *Internecine* in English, first recorded in 1663, indeed meant "deadly, destructive," but Samuel Johnson, inserting the word in his dictionary of 1755, thought that *inter–* meant "mutual" and so defined it as "endeavoring mutual destruction." This definition set the word incorrectly on its present course, and when *internecine* was further extended simply to mean "relating to internal struggle," the original error was compounded. However, the point is that the meaning of words can be changed by mistakes and that mistaken meanings adhere to words. Only an occasional etymologist points out that the emperor's new clothes are patched.

in•tern•ee (ĭn′tûr-nē′) *n.* One who is interned or confined, especially in wartime.

in•ter•neu•ron (ĭn′tər-no͝or′ŏn′, -nyo͝or′-) *n.* A nerve cell found entirely within the central nervous system that acts as a link between sensory neurons and motor neurons. **—in′ter•neu′ro•nal** (-no͝or′ə-nəl, -nyo͝or′-, -no͞o-rō′-, -nyo͞o-) *adj.*

in•ter•nist (ĭn-tûr′nĭst) *n.* A physician specializing in internal medicine. [INTERN(AL MEDICINE) + –IST.]

in•tern•ment (ĭn-tûrn′mənt) *n.* **1.** The act of interning or confining, especially in wartime. **2.** The state of being interned; confinement.

in•ter•node (ĭn′tər-nōd′) *n.* A section or part between two nodes, as of a nerve or stem. **—in′ter•nod′al** (-nōd′l) *adj.*

in•ter nos (ĭn′tər nōs′) *adv. & adj.* Between ourselves. [Latin : *inter,* among + *nos,* us.]

in•ter•nu•cle•ar (ĭn′tər-no͞o′klē-ər, -nyo͞o′-) *adj. Physics & Chemistry.* Located or occurring between nuclei.

in•ter•nun•cial (ĭn′tər-nŭn′shəl, -sē-əl) *adj.* Linking two neurons in a neuronal pathway. [INTERNUNCI(O) + –AL[1].] **—in′ter•nun′cial•ly** *adv.*

in•ter•nun•ci•o (ĭn′tər-nŭn′sē-ō′, -no͝on′-) *n., pl.* **-os. 1.** A Vatican diplomatic envoy or representative ranking just beneath a nuncio. **2.** A messenger or an agent; a go-between. [Italian *internunzio,* from Latin *internūntius,* mediator : *inter-,* inter- + *nūntius,* messenger; see NUNCIO.]

in•ter•o•cep•tor (ĭn′tər-ō-sĕp′tər) *n.* A specialized sensory nerve receptor that receives and responds to stimuli originating from within the body. [INTER(IOR) + (RE)CEPTOR.] **—in′ter•o•cep′tive** *adj.*

in•ter•of•fice (ĭn′tər-ô′fĭs, -ŏf′ĭs) *adj.* Transmitted or taking place between offices, especially those of a single organization: *an interoffice memo; interoffice conferences.*

interp. *abbr.* Interpreter.

in•ter•per•son•al (ĭn′tər-pûr′sə-nəl) *adj.* Relating to, occurring among, or involving several people. **—in′ter•per′son•al•ly** *adv.*

in•ter•phase (ĭn′tər-fāz′) *n.* The stage of a cell between two successive mitotic or meiotic divisions. **—in′ter•phase′** *v.*

in•ter•plan•e•tar•y (ĭn′tər-plăn′ĭ-tĕr′ē) *adj.* Existing or occurring between planets.

in•ter•play (ĭn′tər-plā′) *n.* Reciprocal action and reaction; interaction. **—interplay** *intr.v.* **-played, -play•ing, -plays.** To act or react on each other; interact.

in•ter•plead (ĭn′tər-plēd′) *intr.v.* **-plead•ed, -plead•ing, -pleads.** *Law.* To submit one's claim to the process of interpleader. [Middle English *enterpleden,* from Anglo-Norman *enterpleder* : *enter-,* between (from Latin *inter-;* see INTER–) + *pleder,* to plead (variant of Old French *plaidier;* see PLEAD).]

in•ter•plead•er (ĭn′tər-plē′dər) *n. Law.* A procedure to determine which of two parties making the same claim against a third party is the rightful claimant. [Anglo-Norman *enterpleder,* to interplead, interpleader. See INTERPLEAD.]

in•ter•po•late (ĭn-tûr′pə-lāt′) *v.* **-lat•ed, -lat•ing, -lates.** *—tr.* **1.** To insert or introduce between other elements or parts. **2.a.** To insert (material) into a text. **b.** To insert into a conversation. See Synonyms at **introduce. 3.** To change or falsify (a text) by introducing new or incorrect material. **4.** *Mathematics.* To estimate a value of (a function or series) between two known values. *—intr.* To make insertions or additions. [Latin *interpolāre, interpolāt-,* to touch up, refurbish, from *interpolis,* refurbished. See **pel-**[5] in Appendix.] **—in•ter′po•la′tion** *n.* **—in•ter′po•la′tive** *adj.* **—in•ter′po•la′tor** *n.*

in•ter•pose (ĭn′tər-pōz′) *v.* **-posed, -pos•ing, -pos•es.** *—tr.* **1.a.** To insert or introduce between parts. **b.** To place (oneself) between. **2.** To introduce or interject (a comment, for example) during discourse or a conversation. See Synonyms at **introduce. 3.** To exert (influence or authority) in order to interfere or intervene: *interpose one's veto. —intr.* **1.** To come between. **2.** To come between the parties in a dispute; intervene. **3.** To insert a remark, a question, or an argument. [French, from Old French *interposer,* to intervene, alteration (influenced by *poser,* to put, place; see POSE[1]) of Latin *interpōnere,* to put between : *inter-,* inter- + *pōnere,* to put; see **apo-** in Appendix.] **—in′ter•pos′al** *n.* **—in′ter•pos′er** *n.* **—in′ter•po•si′tion** (-pə-zĭsh′ən) *n.*

in•ter•pret (ĭn-tûr′prĭt) *v.* **-pret•ed, -pret•ing, -prets.** *—tr.* **1.** To explain the meaning of: *interpreted the ambassador's remarks.* See Synonyms at **explain. 2.** To conceive the significance of; construe: *interpreted his smile to be an agreement; interpreted the open door as an invitation.* **3.** To present or conceptualize the meaning of by means of art or criticism. **4.** To translate orally. *—intr.* **1.** To offer an explanation. **2.** To serve as an interpreter for speakers of different languages. [Middle English *interpreten,* from Old French *interpreter,* from Latin *interpretārī,* from *interpres, interpret-,* negotiator, explainer. See **per-**[5] in Appendix.] **—in•ter′pret•a•bil′i•ty, in•ter′pret•a•ble•ness** *n.* **—in•ter′pret•a•ble** *adj.*

in•ter•pre•ta•tion (ĭn-tûr′prĭ-tā′shən) *n.* **1.** The act or process of interpreting. **2.** A result of interpreting. **a.** An explanation or a conceptualization by a critic of a work of literature, painting, music, or other art form; an exegesis. **b.** A performer's distinctive personal version of a song, dance, piece of music, or role; a rendering. **—in•ter′pre•ta′tion•al** *adj.*

in•ter•pre•ta•tive (ĭn-tûr′prĭ-tā′tĭv) *adj.* Variant of **interpretive. —in•ter′pre•ta′tive•ly** *adv.*

in•ter•pret•er (ĭn-tûr′prĭ-tər) *n. Abbr.* **interp. 1.** One who translates orally from one language into another. **2.** One who gives or expounds an interpretation: *"An actor is an interpreter of other men's words, often a soul which wishes to reveal itself to the world"* (Alec Guinness). **3.** *Computer Science.* A program that translates an instruction into a machine language and executes it before proceeding to the next instruction.

in•ter•pre•tive (ĭn-tûr′prĭ-tĭv) also **in•ter•pre•ta•tive** (-tā′tĭv) *adj.* Relating to or marked by interpretation; explanatory. **—in•ter′pre•tive•ly** *adv.*

in•ter•pu•pil•lar•y (ĭn′tər-pyo͞o′pə-lĕr′ē) *adj.* Occurring between the pupils of the eyes: *interpupillary distance.*

in•ter•ra•cial (ĭn′tər-rā′shəl) *adj.* Relating to, involving, or representing different races: *interracial fellowship; an interracial neighborhood.*

in•ter•re•gion•al (ĭn′tər-rē′jə-nəl) *adj.* Relating to, involving, or connecting two or more regions: *interregional migration; interregional banking.*

in•ter•reg•num (ĭn′tər-rĕg′nəm) *n., pl.* **-nums** or **-na** (-nə). **1.** The interval of time between the end of a sovereign's reign and the accession of a successor. **2.** A period of temporary suspension of the usual functions of government or control. **3.** A gap in continuity. [Latin : *inter-,* inter- + *rēgnum,* reign; see REIGN.] **—in′ter•reg′nal** (-nəl) *adj.*

in•ter•re•late (ĭn′tər-rĭ-lāt′) *tr. & intr.v.* **-lat•ed, -lat•ing, -lates.** To place in or come into mutual relationship. **—in′ter•re•lat′ed•ness** *n.* **—in′ter•re•la′tion•ship′** *n.*

in•ter•ro•bang also **in•ter•a•bang** (ĭn-tĕr′ə-băng′) *n.* A punctuation mark used especially to end a simultaneous question and exclamation. [INTERRO(GATION POINT) + BANG[1], exclamation point (printers' slang).]

interrog. *abbr.* Interrogative.

ă pat	oi boy
ā pay	ou out
âr care	o͝o took
ä father	o͞o boot
ĕ pet	ŭ cut
ē be	ûr urge
ĭ pit	th thin
ī pie	*th* this
îr pier	hw which
ŏ pot	zh vision
ō toe	ə about, item
ô paw	♦ regionalism

Stress marks: ′ (primary); ′ (secondary), as in **dictionary** (dĭk′shə-nĕr′ē)

in·ter·ro·gate (ĭn-tĕr′ə-gāt′) *tr.v.* **-gat·ed, -gat·ing, -gates. 1.** To examine by questioning formally or officially. See Synonyms at **ask. 2.** *Computer Science.* To transmit a signal for setting off an appropriate response. [Middle English *enterrogate,* from Latin *interrogāre, interrogāt-* : *inter-,* in the presence of; see INTER– + *rogāre,* to ask; see **reg-** in Appendix.] **—in·ter′ro·ga′tion** *n.* **—in·ter′ro·ga′tion·al** *adj.* **—in·ter′ro·ga′tor** *n.*

interrogation point *n.* See **question mark.**

in·ter·rog·a·tive (ĭn′tə-rŏg′ə-tĭv) *adj. Abbr.* **interrog. 1.** Asking a question or being of the nature of a question: *an interrogative raising of the eyebrows.* **2.** Of, relating to, or being an element or construction used to ask a question: *an interrogative adverb; an interrogative particle.* **—interrogative** *n.* **1.** A word or form used to ask a question. **2.** A sentence or an expression that asks a question. **—in′ter·rog′a·tive·ly** *adv.*

in·ter·rog·a·to·ry (ĭn′tə-rŏg′ə-tôr′ē, -tōr′ē) *adj.* Asking a question; of the nature of a question; interrogative. **—interrogatory** *n., pl.* **-ries.** *Law.* A formal or written question, as to a witness, usually requiring an answer under oath. **—in′ter·rog′a·to′ri·ly** *adv.*

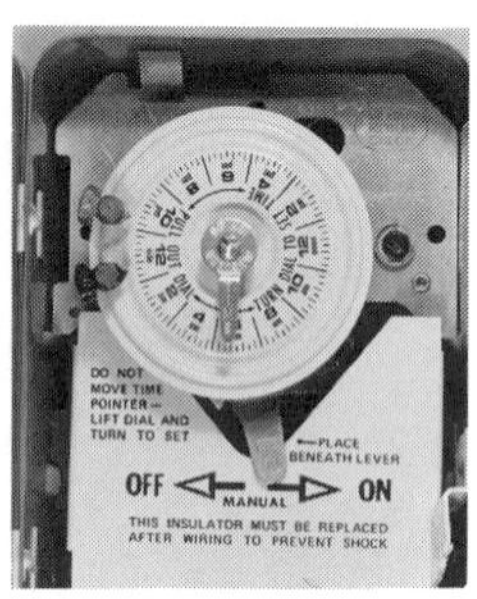

interrupter

in·ter·rupt (ĭn′tə-rŭpt′) *v.* **-rupt·ed, -rupt·ing, -rupts.** *—tr.* **1.** To break the continuity or uniformity of: *Rain interrupted our baseball game.* **2.** To hinder or stop the action or discourse of (someone) by breaking in on: *The baby interrupted me while I was on the phone.* *—intr.* To break in on an action or discourse. **—interrupt** *n. Computer Science.* **1.** A signal to a computer that stops the execution of a running program so that another action can be performed. **2.** A circuit that conveys a signal stopping the execution of a running program. [Middle English *interrupten,* from Old French *interrupte,* interrupted, from Latin *interruptus,* past participle of *interrumpere,* to break off : *inter-,* inter- + *rumpere,* to break; see **reup-** in Appendix.] **—in′ter·rupt′i·ble** *adj.* **—in′ter·rup′tion** *n.* **—in′ter·rup′tive** *adj.*

in·ter·rupt·er (ĭn′tə-rŭp′tər) *n.* **1.** One that interrupts: *an inveterate interrupter of other people's conversations.* **2.** *Electronics.* A device that periodically and automatically opens and closes an electric circuit, producing pulses.

in·ter·scho·las·tic (ĭn′tər-skə-lăs′tĭk) *adj.* Existing or conducted between or among schools. **—in′ter·scho·las′ti·cal·ly** *adv.*

in·ter se (ĭn′tər sē′, sā′) *adv. & adj.* Between or among themselves. [Latin : *inter,* between + *sē,* themselves.]

in·ter·sect (ĭn′tər-sĕkt′) *v.* **-sect·ed, -sect·ing, -sects.** *—tr.* **1.** To cut across or through: *The path intersects the park.* **2.** To form an intersection with; cross: *The road intersects the highway a mile from here.* *—intr.* **1.** To cut across or overlap each other: *circles intersecting on a graph.* **2.** To form an intersection; cross: *These two fences intersect at the creek.* [Latin *intersecāre, intersect-* : *inter-,* inter- + *secāre,* to cut; see **sek-** in Appendix.]

in·ter·sec·tion (ĭn′tər-sĕk′shən) *n. Abbr.* **int. 1.** The act, process, or result of intersecting. **2.** (*also* ĭn′tər-sĕk′-). A place where things intersect, especially a place where two or more roads cross. **3.** *Mathematics.* **a.** The point or locus of points where one line, surface, or solid crosses another. **b.** A set that contains elements shared by two or more given sets.

in·ter·ses·sion (ĭn′tər-sĕsh′ən) *n.* The time between two academic sessions or semesters. **—in′ter·ses′sion·al** *adj.*

in·ter·sex (ĭn′tər-sĕks′) *n. Biology.* An intersexual individual.

in·ter·sex·u·al (ĭn′tər-sĕk′shōō-əl) *adj.* **1.** Existing or occurring between the sexes. **2.** *Biology.* Having sexual characteristics intermediate between those of a typical male and a typical female. **—in′ter·sex′u·al′i·ty** (-ăl′ĭ-tē) *n.* **—in′ter·sex′u·al·ly** *adv.*

in·ter·space (ĭn′tər-spās′) *tr.v.* **-spaced, -spac·ing, -spac·es.** To make or occupy a space between. **—interspace** (ĭn′tər-spās′) *n.* A space between two things; an interval. **—in′ter·spa′tial** (-spā′shəl) *adj.*

in·ter·spe·cif·ic (ĭn′tər-spĭ-sĭf′ĭk) *adj.* Arising or occurring between species.

in·ter·sperse (ĭn′tər-spûrs′) *tr.v.* **-spersed, -spers·ing, -spers·es. 1.** To distribute among other things at intervals: *interspersed red and blue tiles on the walls; intersperse praise with constructive criticism.* **2.** To supply or diversify with things distributed at intervals: *interspersed lamp fixtures on the large ceiling; a newspaper section that was interspersed with advertisements.* [From Latin *interspergere, interspers-* : *inter-,* inter- + *spargere,* to scatter.] **—in′ter·spers′ed·ly** (-spûr′sĭd-lē) *adv.* **—in′ter·sper′sion** (-spûr′zhən, -shən) *n.*

in·ter·state (ĭn′tər-stāt′) *adj.* Involving, existing between, or connecting two or more states. **—interstate** *n. Abbr.* **I** One of a system of highways extending between and connecting the major cities of the 48 contiguous United States.

in·ter·stel·lar (ĭn′tər-stĕl′ər) *adj.* Between or among the stars: *interstellar gases.*

in·ter·stice (ĭn-tûr′stĭs) *n., pl.* **-stic·es** (-stĭ-sēz′, -sĭz). A space, especially a small or narrow one, between things or parts: *"There is a gleam of luminous gold, where the sinking western sun has found a first direct interstice in the clouds"* (John Fowles). [Middle English, from Old French, from Latin *interstitium,* from **interstitus,* past participle of *intersistere,* to pause, make a break : *inter-,* inter- + *sistere,* to cause to stand, set up; see **stā-** in Appendix.]

in·ter·sti·tial (ĭn′tər-stĭsh′əl) *adj.* **1.** Relating to, occurring in, or affecting interstices. **2.** *Anatomy.* Relating to or situated in the small, narrow spaces between tissues or parts of an organ: *interstitial cells; interstitial fluid.* **—in′ter·sti′tial·ly** *adv.*

in·ter·tex·ture (ĭn′tər-tĕks′chər) *n.* **1.** The act of interweaving or the state of being interwoven. **2.** Something interwoven. [From Latin *intertextus,* past participle of *intertexere,* to interweave : *inter,* inter- + *texere,* to weave; see TEXT.]

in·ter·tid·al (ĭn′tər-tīd′l) *adj.* Of, relating to, or being the region between the high tide mark and the low tide mark. **—in′ter·tid′al·ly** *adv.*

in·ter·tri·bal (ĭn′tər-trī′bəl) *adj.* Existing or occurring between tribes.

in·ter·trop·i·cal (ĭn′tər-trŏp′ĭ-kəl) *adj.* **1.** Between or within the tropics. **2.** Of or relating to the tropics.

in·ter·twine (ĭn′tər-twīn′) *tr. & intr.v.* **-twined, -twin·ing, -twines.** To join or become joined by twining together. **—in′ter·twine′ment** *n.*

in·ter·twist (ĭn′tər-twĭst′) *tr. & intr.v.* **-twist·ed, -twist·ing, -twists.** To intertwine.

in·ter·ur·ban (ĭn′tər-ûr′bən) *adj.* Relating to or connecting urban areas: *an interurban railroad.*

in·ter·val (ĭn′tər-vəl) *n. Abbr.* **int. 1.** A space between two objects, points, or units. **2.** The amount of time between two specified instants, events, or states. **3.** *Mathematics.* A set of numbers consisting of all the numbers between a pair of given numbers. **4.** *Mathematics.* A set of numbers consisting of all the numbers between a pair of given numbers and including the endpoints. Also called *closed interval.* **5.** *Mathematics.* A set of numbers consisting of all the numbers between a pair of given numbers but not including the endpoints. Also called *open interval.* **6.** *Mathematics.* A line segment representing all the numbers between a pair of given numbers and including one, both, or neither of the endpoints. **7.** *Chiefly British.* An intermission, as between acts of a play. **8.** *Music.* The difference in pitch between two tones. [Middle English *intervalle,* from Old French, from Latin *intervallum* : *inter-,* inter- + *vallum,* rampart.] **—in′ter·val′ic, in′ter·val′lic** (-văl′ĭk) *adj.*

♦ **in·ter·vale** (ĭn′tər-vəl) *n. New England.* A tract of low-lying land, especially along a river. [Variant (influenced by VALE[1]) of INTERVAL.]

♦ ***REGIONAL NOTE:*** *Intervale* is among the distinctive New England terms mapped by Hans Kurath in the *Linguistic Atlas of New England* in the 1940's. However, by the time the *Dictionary of American Regional English* surveyed the New England states 20 years later, says Craig M. Carver, author of *American Regional Dialects,* only three of the dozens of New England informants used the word *intervale* to indicate a "tract of low-lying land, especially along a river." The word was common in New England at one time because so many settlements were made along the rivers, where the land was more fertile and the towns were accessible by water.

in·ter·vene (ĭn′tər-vēn′) *intr.v.* **-vened, -ven·ing, -venes. 1.** To come, appear, or lie between two things: *You can't see the lake from there because the house intervenes.* **2.** To come or occur between two periods or points of time: *A year intervened between the two dynasties.* **3.** To occur as an extraneous or unplanned circumstance: *He would have his degree by now if his laziness hadn't intervened.* **4. a.** To come in or between so as to hinder or alter an action: *intervened to prevent a fight.* **b.** To interfere, usually through force or threat of force, in the affairs of another nation. **5.** *Law.* To enter into a suit as a third party for one's own interests. [Latin *intervenīre* : *inter-,* inter- + *venīre,* to come; see **gʷā-** in Appendix.] **—in′ter·ve′nor, in′ter·ven′er** *n.* **—in′ter·ven′tion** (-vĕn′shən) *n.* **—in′ter·ven′tion·al** *adj.*

in·ter·ven·tion·ism (ĭn′tər-vĕn′shə-nĭz′əm) *n.* The policy or practice of intervening in the affairs of another sovereign state. **—in′ter·ven′tion·ist** *n.*

in·ter·ver·te·bral (ĭn′tər-vûr′tə-brəl, -vûr-tē′-) *adj.* Located between vertebrae. **—in′ter·ver′te·bral·ly** *adv.*

intervertebral disk *n.* A broad disk of fibrocartilage situated between adjacent vertebrae of the spinal column.

in·ter·view (ĭn′tər-vyōō′) *n. Abbr.* **int. 1.** A formal meeting in person, especially one arranged for the assessment of the qualifications of an applicant. **2. a.** A conversation, such as one conducted by a reporter, in which facts or statements are elicited from another. **b.** An account or a reproduction of such a conversation. **3.** *Informal.* An interviewee: *"I had been warned that* [he] *was a tough interview—that he doled out flip answers . . . to questions he was tired of being asked"* (David Roberts). **—interview** *v.* **-viewed, -view·ing, -views.** *—tr.* To obtain an interview from. *—intr.* To have an interview: *interviewed with a publishing company.* [French *entrevue,* from Old French, from feminine past participle of *entrevoir,* to see : *entre-,* between (from Latin *inter-;* see INTER–) + *voir,* to see (from Latin *vidēre;* see **weid-** in Appendix).] **—in′ter·view′a·ble** *adj.* **—in′ter·view·ee′** *n.* **—in′ter·view′er** *n.*

in·ter vi·vos (ĭn′tər vē′vōs′, vī′-) *adj. Law.* Between living persons: *an inter vivos trust.* [Latin : *inter,* among + *vivōs,* pl. of *vivus,* a living being.]

in·ter·vo·cal·ic (ĭn′tər-vō-kăl′ĭk) *adj.* Occurring between vowels.

in·ter·weave (ĭn′tər-wēv′) *v.* **-wove** (-wōv′), **-wo·ven** (-wō′vən), **-weav·ing, -weaves.** —*tr.* **1.** To weave together. **2.** To blend together; intermix. —*intr.* To intertwine.

in·tes·tate (ĭn-tĕs′tāt′, -tĭt) *Law. adj.* **1.** Having made no legal will: *an intestate parent.* **2.** Not disposed of by a legal will: *intestate lands.* **—intestate** *n.* One who dies without a legal will. [Middle English, from Old French *intestat,* from Latin *intestātus* : *in-,* not; see IN–[1] + *testātus,* testate, from past participle of *testārī,* to make a will; see TESTAMENT.] **—in·tes′ta·cy** (-tə-sē) *n.*

in·tes·ti·nal (ĭn-tĕs′tə-nəl) *adj.* Of, relating to, or constituting the intestine: *the intestinal wall; intestinal bacteria.* **—in·tes′ti·nal·ly** *adv.*

intestinal fortitude *n.* Courage; endurance.

in·tes·tine (ĭn-tĕs′tĭn) *n.* The portion of the alimentary canal extending from the stomach to the anus and, in human beings and other mammals, consisting of two segments, the small intestine and the large intestine. Often used in the plural. **—intestine** *adj.* Internal; civil: *the intestine affairs of the nation.* [Middle English, from Old French *intestin,* from Latin *intestīna,* intestines, from neuter pl. of *intestīnus,* internal, from *intus,* within. See **en** in Appendix.]

in·thrall (ĭn-thrôl′) *v.* Variant of **enthrall.**

in·throne (ĭn-thrōn′) *v.* Variant of **enthrone.**

in·ti (ĭn′tē) *n.* See table at **currency.** [American Spanish, from Quechua, sun.]

in·ti·ma (ĭn′tə-mə) *n., pl.* **-mae** (-mē′) or **-mas.** *Anatomy.* The innermost membrane of an organ or a part, especially the inner lining of a lymphatic vessel, an artery, or a vein. [Latin, from feminine of *intimus,* innermost. See **en** in Appendix.] **—in′ti·mal** *adj.*

in·ti·ma·cy (ĭn′tə-mə-sē) *n., pl.* **-cies. 1.** The condition of being intimate. **2.** An instance of being intimate.

in·ti·mae (ĭn′tə-mē′) *n. Anatomy.* A plural of **intima.**

in·ti·mate[1] (ĭn′tə-mĭt) *adj.* **1.** Marked by close acquaintance, association, or familiarity. See Synonyms at **familiar. 2.** Relating to or indicative of one's deepest nature: *intimate prayers.* **3.** Essential; innermost: *the intimate structure of matter.* **4.** Marked by informality and privacy: *an intimate nightclub.* **5.** Very personal; private: *an intimate letter.* **6.** Of or involved in a sexual relationship. **—intimate** *n.* A close friend or confidant. [Latin *intimātus,* past participle of *intimāre,* to make familiar with. See INTIMATE[2].] **—in′ti·mate·ly** *adv.* **—in′ti·mate·ness** *n.*

in·ti·mate[2] (ĭn′tə-māt′) *tr.v.* **-mat·ed, -mat·ing, -mates. 1.** To make known subtly and indirectly; hint. See Synonyms at **suggest. 2.** To announce; proclaim. [Latin *intimāre, intimāt-,* to make known, from *intimus,* innermost. See **en** in Appendix.] **—in′ti·mat′er** *n.* **—in′ti·ma′tion** *n.*

in·time (ăN-tēm′) *adj.* Intimate; private: *an intime dining corner.* [French, from Old French, from Latin *intimus,* innermost. See INTIMATE[2].]

in·tim·i·date (ĭn-tĭm′ĭ-dāt′) *tr.v.* **-dat·ed, -dat·ing, -dates. 1.** To make timid; fill with fear. **2.** To coerce or inhibit by or as if by threats. [Medieval Latin *intimidāre, intimidāt-* : Latin *in-,* in, into; see IN–[2] + Medieval Latin *timidāre,* to be timorous, to frighten (from Latin *timidus,* timid; see TIMID).] **—in·tim′i·dat′ing·ly** *adv.* **—in·tim′i·da′tion** *n.* **—in·tim′i·da′tor** *n.*

SYNONYMS: *intimidate, browbeat, bulldoze, cow, bully, bludgeon.* These verbs all mean to frighten into submission, compliance, or acquiescence. *Intimidate* implies the presence or operation of a fear-inspiring force that compels one to or keeps one from action: *felt intimidated by his opponent's power and prestige. "It* [atomic energy] *may intimidate the human race into bringing order into its international affairs, which, without the pressure of fear, it would not do"* (Albert Einstein). *Browbeat* suggests the persistent application of highhanded, disdainful, or imperious tactics: *refused to be browbeaten and insulted; browbeating a witness. Bulldoze* connotes the leveling of all spirit of opposition, as through the use of threats: *couldn't be bulldozed into hiring a less than acceptable candidate for the job. Cow* implies treatment that brings about an abject state of timorousness and often demoralization: *submissive children can be cowed by a look of disapproval.* To *bully* is to intimidate through blustering, domineering, or threatening behavior: *The strikers were bullied into dropping their demands. Bludgeon* suggests the use of grossly aggressive or combative methods: *had to be bludgeoned into fulfilling his responsibilities.* See also Synonyms at **threaten.**

in·tinc·tion (ĭn-tĭngk′shən) *n. Ecclesiastical.* The administration of the Eucharist by dipping the host into the wine and thus offering both simultaneously to the communicant. [Late Latin *intīnctiō, intīnctiōn-,* a dipping in, from Latin *intīnctus,* past participle of *intingere,* to dip in : *in-,* in; see IN–[2] + *tingere,* to moisten.]

in·tine (ĭn′tēn′) *n.* The innermost wall of a spore or pollen grain. Also called *endosporium.* [German, from Latin *intus,* within. See **en** in Appendix.]

in·tit·ule (ĭn-tĭch′o͞ol) *tr.v.* **-uled, -ul·ing, -ules.** *Chiefly British.* To give a designation or title to (a legislative act, for example). [Middle English *entitelen, intitulen,* from Old French *intituler,* from Late Latin *intitulāre* : Latin *in-,* in; see IN–[2] + Late Latin *titulāre,* to entitle (from Latin *titulus,* title).]

intl. *abbr.* International.

in·to (ĭn′to͞o) *prep.* **1.** To the inside or interior of: *went into the house.* **2.a.** To the activity or occupation of: *recent college graduates who go into banking.* **b.** To the condition, state, or form of: *dishes breaking into pieces; changed into a butterfly.* **c.** So as to be in or be included in: *parties entering into an agreement; wrote a new character into the play.* **d.** *Informal.* Interested in or involved with: *They are into vegetarianism.* **3.** To a point within the limits of a period of time or extent of space: *well into the week.* **4.** In the direction of; toward: *looked into the distance; pointed into the sky.* **5.** Against: *crashed into a tree.* **6.** As a divisor of: *The number 3 goes into 9 three times.*

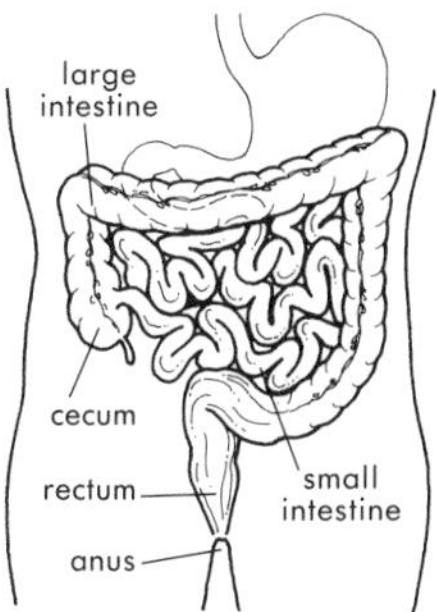

intestine

in·tol·er·a·ble (ĭn-tŏl′ər-ə-bəl) *adj.* Impossible to tolerate or endure; unbearable: *intolerable agony.* **—in·tol′er·a·bil′i·ty, in·tol′er·a·ble·ness** *n.* **—in·tol′er·a·bly** *adv.*

in·tol·er·ance (ĭn-tŏl′ər-əns) *n.* **1.** The quality or condition of being intolerant; lack of tolerance. **2.** *Medicine.* Extreme sensitivity or allergy to a drug, food, or other substance: *lactose intolerance.*

in·tol·er·ant (ĭn-tŏl′ər-ənt) *adj.* Not tolerant, especially: **a.** Unwilling to tolerate differences in opinions or beliefs, especially religious beliefs. **b.** Unable or unwilling to endure or support: *intolerant of interruptions.* **—in·tol′er·ant·ly** *adv.*

in·to·nate (ĭn′tə-nāt′) *tr.v.* **-nat·ed, -nat·ing, -nates. 1.** To intone. **2.** To utter with a particular tone of voice: *pleas that were intonated with desperation.* [Medieval Latin *intonāre, intonāt-.* See INTONE.]

in·to·na·tion (ĭn′tə-nā′shən, -tō-) *n.* **1.a.** The act of intoning or chanting. **b.** An intoned utterance. **2.** A manner of producing or uttering tones, especially with regard to accuracy of pitch. **3.** *Linguistics.* The use of changing pitch to convey syntactic information: *a questioning intonation.* **4.** A use of pitch characteristic of a speaker or dialect: *"He could hear authority, the old parish intonation coming back into his voice"* (Graham Greene). **5.** *Music.* The opening phrase of a plainsong composition sung as a solo part. **—in′to·na′tion·al** *adj.*

in·tone (ĭn-tōn′) *v.* **-toned, -ton·ing, -tones.** —*tr.* **1.** To recite in a singing tone. **2.** To utter in a monotone. —*intr.* **1.** To speak with a singing tone or with a particular intonation. **2.** *Music.* To sing a plainsong intonation. [Middle English *entonen,* from Old French *entoner,* from Medieval Latin *intonāre* : Latin *in-,* in; see IN–[2] + Latin *tonus,* tone; see TONE.] **—in·tone′ment** *n.* **—in·ton′er** *n.*

in to·to (ĭn tō′tō) *adv.* Totally; altogether: *recommendations that were adopted in toto.* [Latin : *in,* in + *tōtō,* ablative of *tōtus,* all.]

in·tox·i·cant (ĭn-tŏk′sĭ-kənt) *n.* An agent that intoxicates, especially an alcoholic beverage. **—in·tox′i·cant** *adj.*

in·tox·i·cate (ĭn-tŏk′sĭ-kāt′) *v.* **-cat·ed, -cat·ing, -cates.** —*tr.* **1.** To stupefy or excite, as by the action of a chemical substance such as alcohol. **2.** To stimulate or excite: *"a man whom life intoxicates, who has no need of wine"* (Anaïs Nin). **3.** To poison. —*intr.* To cause stupefaction, stimulation, or excitement by or as if by use of a chemical substance: *"The notion of Holy War is showing that it has not yet lost all its power to intoxicate and to inflame"* (Conor Cruise O'Brien). [Middle English, to poison, from Medieval Latin *intoxicāre, intoxicāt-* : Latin *in-,* in; see IN–[2] + Late Latin *toxicāre,* to smear with poison (from Latin *toxicum,* poison; see TOXIC).] **—in·tox′i·cat′ing·ly** *adv.* **—in·tox′i·ca′tion** *n.* **—in·tox′i·ca′tive** *adj.* **—in·tox′i·ca′tor** *n.*

intr. *abbr. Abbr.* **Grammar** Intransitive.

intra– *pref.* Within: *intraocular.* [Late Latin *intrā-,* from Latin *intrā.* See **en** in Appendix.]

in·tra-ar·te·ri·al (ĭn′trə-är-tîr′ē-əl) *adj.* Within arteries or an artery: *an intra-arterial injection.* **—in′tra-ar·te′ri·al·ly** *adv.*

in·tra-a·tom·ic (ĭn′trə-ə-tŏm′ĭk) *adj.* Within an atom.

in·tra·car·di·ac (ĭn′trə-kär′dē-ăk′) *adj.* Within the heart.

in·tra·cel·lu·lar (ĭn′trə-sĕl′yə-lər) *adj.* Occurring or situated within a cell or cells: *intracellular fluid.* **—in′tra·cel′lu·lar·ly** *adv.*

In·tra·coas·tal Waterway (ĭn′trə-kōs′təl). A system of artificial and natural channels and canals along the Atlantic and Gulf coasts of the eastern and southeast United States. It includes the Atlantic Intracoastal Waterway and the Gulf Intracoastal Waterway and affords sheltered passage for commercial and pleasure craft.

in·tra·cer·e·bral (ĭn′trə-sə-rē′brəl, -sĕr′ə-) *adj.* Occurring or situated within the cerebrum: *an intracerebral hemorrhage.* **—in′tra·cer·e′bral·ly** *adv.*

in·tra·cra·ni·al (ĭn′trə-krā′nē-əl) *adj.* Occurring or situated within the cranium. **—in′tra·cra′ni·al·ly** *adv.*

in·trac·ta·ble (ĭn-trăk′tə-bəl) *adj.* **1.** Difficult to manage or govern; stubborn. See Synonyms at **unruly. 2.** Difficult to mold or manipulate: *intractable materials.* **3.** Difficult to alleviate, remedy, or cure: *intractable pain.* **—in·trac′ta·bil′i·ty, in·trac′ta·ble·ness** *n.* **—in·trac′ta·bly** *adv.*

in·tra·cu·ta·ne·ous (ĭn′trə-kyo͞o-tā′nē-əs) *adj.* Within the skin; intradermal. **—in′tra·cu·ta′ne·ous·ly** *adv.*

in·tra·day (ĭn′trə-dā′) *adj.* Occurring within a single day.

in·tra·der·mal (ĭn′trə-dûr′məl) *adj.* Within or between the layers of the skin: *an intradermal injection.* **—in′tra·der′mal·ly** *adv.*

intradermal test *n.* A test for hypersensitivity or allergy in

ă pat	oi boy
ā pay	ou out
âr care	o͝o took
ä father	o͞o boot
ĕ pet	ŭ cut
ē be	ûr urge
ĭ pit	th thin
ī pie	*th* this
îr pier	hw which
ŏ pot	zh vision
ō toe	ə about, item
ô paw	♦ regionalism

Stress marks: ′ (primary); ′ (secondary), as in **dictionary** (dĭk′shə-nĕr′ē)

which a small amount of the suspected allergen is injected into the skin.

in·tra·dos (ĭn′trə-dŏs′, -dō′, ĭn-trā′dŏs′, -dōs′) *n., pl.* **-dos** (-dōz′) or **-dos·es** (-dŏs′ĭz). *Architecture.* The inner curve of an arch. [French : *intra-*, within (from Late Latin *intrā-;* see INTRA–) + *dos,* back (from Old French, from Latin *dorsum*).]

in·tra·ga·lac·tic (ĭn′trə-gə-lăk′tĭk) *adj.* Occurring or situated within the space of a galaxy.

in·tra·lin·gual (ĭn′trə-lĭng′gwəl) *adj.* Of or relating to a single language.

in·tra·mo·lec·u·lar (ĭn′trə-mə-lĕk′yə-lər) *adj.* Within a molecule. **—in′tra·mo·lec′u·lar·ly** *adv.*

in·tra·mu·ral (ĭn′trə-myŏŏr′əl) *adj.* **1.** Existing or carried on within the bounds of an institution, especially a school: *intramural athletics.* **2.** *Anatomy.* Occurring or situated within the wall of a cavity or an organ. **—in′tra·mu′ral·ly** *adv.*

in·tra·mus·cu·lar (ĭn′trə-mŭs′kyə-lər) *adj.* Within a muscle: *an intramuscular injection.* **—in′tra·mus′cu·lar·ly** *adv.*

in·tra·na·sal (ĭn′trə-nā′zəl) *adj.* Within the nose. **—in′tra·na′sal·ly** *adv.*

in·tran·si·gent also **in·tran·si·geant** (ĭn-trăn′sə-jənt, -zə-) *adj.* Refusing to moderate a position, especially an extreme position; uncompromising. [French *intransigeant,* from Spanish *intransigente* : *in-*, not (from Latin; see IN–[1]) + *transigente,* present participle of *transigir,* to compromise (from Latin *trānsigere,* to come to an agreement : *trāns-*, trans- + *agere,* to drive; see **ag-** in Appendix).] **—in·tran′si·gence, in·tran′si·gen·cy** *n.* **—in·tran′si·gent** *n.* **—in·tran′si·gent·ly** *adv.*

in·tran·si·tive (ĭn-trăn′sĭ-tĭv, -zĭ-) *Grammar. adj. Abbr.* **intr., int., i.** Designating a verb or verb construction that does not require or cannot take a direct object, as *drive* or *sleep.* **—intransitive** *n.* An intransitive verb. **—in·tran′si·tive·ly** *adv.* **—in·tran′si·tive·ness** *n.*

in·tra·nu·cle·ar (ĭn′trə-nōō′klē-ər, -nyōō′-) *adj.* Situated or occurring within the nucleus of an atom or a cell.

in·tra·oc·u·lar (ĭn′trə-ŏk′yə-lər) *adj.* Situated or occurring within the eyeball: *intraocular pressure.*

in·tra·per·son·al (ĭn′trə-pûr′sə-nəl) *adj.* Existing or occurring within the individual self or mind. **—in′tra·per′son·al·ly** *adv.*

in·tra·pre·neur (ĭn′trə-prə-nûr′) *n.* A person within a large corporation who takes direct responsibility for turning an idea into a profitable finished product through assertive risk-taking and innovation. [*intra(corporate)* + (ENTRE)PRENEUR.] **—in′tra·pre·neur′i·al** *adj.* **—in′tra·pre·neur′i·al·ism** *n.* **—in′tra·pre·neur′i·al·ly** *adv.*

WORD HISTORY: The word *entrepreneur* is more than 150 years old, having come into English from French in 1828. But it is not until very recently that we find its intracorporate counterpart, *intrapreneur,* meaning "a person within a large corporation who takes direct responsibility for turning an idea into a profitable finished product through assertive risk-taking and innovation." This coinage is generally attributed to management consultant Gifford Pinchot, author of the 1985 book entitled *Intrapreneuring;* others insist its true originator was Norman Macrae, deputy editor of the *Economist,* although Macrae himself denies it. Still, whatever its exact source, in the scant number of years since its inception the term *intrapreneur* has gained currency very quickly. It has also given rise to various derivatives, such as the aforementioned gerund *intrapreneuring,* the noun *intrapreneurship* (as in a September 30, 1985, interview with Stephen Jobs in *Newsweek:* "The Macintosh team was what is commonly known as intrapreneurship—only a few years before the term was coined—a group of people going in essence back to the garage, but in a large company"), the adjective *intrapreneurial,* and another noun, *intrapreneurialism* ("what has become known as intrapreneurialism, where people within the corporation acquire more adventurous small business outlooks," by Ian Hamilton-Fazy in "An Uneasy Co-existence," *Financial Times,* October 23, 1984). Broad use of a word and the development of numerous derivatives are strong signals predicting staying power within the language. *Intrapreneur* and its spinoffs are of particular interest to etymologists and lexicographers because they illustrate the constant changes inherent in a living language.

in·tra·psy·chic (ĭn′trə-sī′kĭk) *adj.* Existing or taking place within the mind or psyche: *intrapsychic conflict.* **—in′tra·psy′chi·cal·ly** *adv.*

in·tra·spe·cif·ic (ĭn′trə-spĭ-sĭf′ĭk) also **in·tra·spe·cies** (-spē′shēz, -sēz) *adj.* Arising or occurring within a species: *intraspecific competition.*

in·tra·state (ĭn′trə-stāt′) *adj.* Relating to or existing within the boundaries of a state.

in·tra·u·ter·ine (ĭn′trə-yōō′tər-ĭn, -tə-rīn′) *adj.* Occurring or situated within the uterus.

intrauterine device *n. Abbr.* **IUD** A birth control device, such as a plastic or metallic loop, ring, or spiral, that is inserted into the uterus to prevent implantation.

in·tra·va·sa·tion (ĭn-trăv′ə-sā′shən) *n. Pathology.* Entry of foreign matter into a blood vessel. [INTRA– + (EXTRA)VASATION.]

in·tra·vas·cu·lar (ĭn′trə-văs′kyə-lər) *adj.* Within blood vessels or a blood vessel. **—in′tra·vas′cu·lar·ly** *adv.*

in·tra·ve·nous (ĭn′trə-vē′nəs) *adj. Abbr.* **IV** Within or administered into a vein. **—intravenous** *n.* A drug, nutrient solution, or other substance administered into a vein. **—in′tra·ve′nous·ly** *adv.*

in·tra·vi·tal (ĭn′trə-vīt′l) *adj.* Occurring in or performed on a living organism: *intravital staining techniques.* **—in′tra·vi′tal·ly** *adv.*

in·treat (ĭn-trēt′) *v.* Variant of **entreat.**

in·trench (ĭn-trĕnch′) *v.* Variant of **entrench.**

in·trep·id (ĭn-trĕp′ĭd) *adj.* Resolutely courageous; fearless. See Synonyms at **brave.** [Latin *intrepidus* : *in-*, not; see IN–[1] + *trepidus,* alarmed.] **—in′tre·pid′i·ty** (-trə-pĭd′ĭ-tē), **in·trep′id·ness** *n.* **—in·trep′id·ly** *adv.*

in·tri·ca·cy (ĭn′trĭ-kə-sē) *n., pl.* **-cies. 1.** The condition or quality of being intricate; complexity. **2.** Something intricate: *the intricacies of a census form.*

in·tri·cate (ĭn′trĭ-kĭt) *adj.* **1.** Having many complexly arranged elements; elaborate. See Synonyms at **elaborate. 2.** Solvable or comprehensible only with painstaking effort. See Synonyms at **complex.** [Middle English, from Latin *intrīcātus,* past participle of *intrīcāre,* to entangle, perplex : *in-*, in; see IN–[2] + *trīcae,* perplexities, wiles.] **—in′tri·cate·ly** *adv.* **—in′tri·cate·ness** *n.*

in·trigue (ĭn′trēg′, ĭn-trēg′) *n.* **1.a.** A secret or underhand scheme; a plot. **b.** The practice of or involvement in such schemes. See Synonyms at **conspiracy. 2.** A clandestine love affair. **—intrigue** (ĭn-trēg′) *v.* **-trigued, -trigu·ing, -trigues.** *—intr.* To engage in secret or underhand schemes; plot. *—tr.* **1.** To effect by secret scheming or plotting. **2.** To arouse the interest or curiosity of: *Hibernation has long intrigued biologists.* [Probably from French *intriguer,* to plot, from Italian *intrigare,* to plot, from Latin *intrīcāre,* to entangle. See INTRICATE.] **—in·trigu′er** *n.* **—in′trigu′ing·ly** *adv.*

USAGE NOTE: The introduction of the verb *intrigue* to mean "to arouse the interest or curiosity of" was initially resisted by writers on usage as an unneeded French substitute for available English words such as *interest, fascinate,* or *puzzle,* but it now appears to be well established. Seventy-eight percent of the Usage Panel accepts it in the sentence *The special-quota idea intrigues some legislators, who have asked a Washington think tank to evaluate it,* whereas only 52 percent accepted it in a 1968 survey.

in·trin·sic (ĭn-trĭn′zĭk, -sĭk) *adj.* **1.** Of or relating to the essential nature of a thing; inherent. **2.** *Anatomy.* Situated within or belonging solely to the organ or body part on which it acts. Used of certain nerves and muscles. [Middle English *intrinsique,* inner, from Old French *intrinseque,* from Late Latin *intrīnsecus,* inward, from Latin, inwardly. See **en** in Appendix.] **—in·trin′si·cal·ly** *adv.*

intrinsic factor *n.* A substance that is secreted by the gastric mucous membrane and is essential for the absorption of vitamin B_{12} in the intestines.

in·tro (ĭn′trō′) *n., pl.* **-tros.** *Informal.* An introduction.

intro. *abbr.* Introductory.

intro– *pref.* **1.** In; into: *introjection.* **2.** Inward: *introvert.* [Latin, from *intrō,* to the inside. See **en** in Appendix.]

in·tro·duce (ĭn′trə-dōōs′, -dyōōs′) *tr.v.* **-duced, -duc·ing, -duc·es. 1.a.** To present (someone) by name to another in order to establish an acquaintance. **b.** To present (a performer, for example) to the public for the first time. **2.** To bring forward (a plan, for example) for consideration. **3.** To provide (someone) with a beginning knowledge or first experience of something: *introduced me to weightlifting.* **4.a.** To bring in and establish in a new place or environment: *exotic plants that had been introduced from the jungle.* **b.** To bring into currency, use, or practice; originate: *introduced the new product in several test markets; introduced the tango into their circle of friends.* **5.** To put inside or into; insert or inject. **6.** To open or begin; preface: *introduced the slide show with an orienting talk.* [Middle English *introducen,* to bring into, from Latin *intrōdūcere* : *intrō-*, within; see **en** in Appendix + *dūcere,* to lead; see **deuk-** in Appendix.] **—in′tro·duc′er** *n.* **—in′tro·duc′i·ble** *adj.*

SYNONYMS: *introduce, insert, interject, interlard, interpolate, interpose.* The central meaning shared by these verbs is "to put or set a person or thing into, between, or among others": *introduce suspense into a novel; insert a letter into an envelope; interject a comment into a conversation; interlarded her thesis with Latin expressions; interpolated a transitional passage into the text; interposed himself between the scrapping boys.* See also Synonyms at **broach**[1].

in·tro·duc·tion (ĭn′trə-dŭk′shən) *n.* **1.** The act or process of introducing or the state of being introduced. **2.** A means, such as a personal letter, of presenting one person to another. **3.** Something recently introduced; an innovation: *"He loathed a fork; it is a modern introduction which has still scarcely reached common people"* (D.H. Lawrence). **4.** Something spoken, written, or otherwise presented in beginning or introducing something, especially: **a.** A preface, as to a book. **b.** *Music.* A short preliminary movement in a larger work. **c.** A basic introductory text or course of study. [Middle English *introduccioun,* from Old French *introduction,* from Latin *intrōductiō, intrōductiōn-,* from *intrōductus,* past participle of *intrōdūcere,* to bring in. See INTRODUCE.]

in·tro·duc·to·ry (ĭn′trə-dŭk′tə-rē) *adj. Abbr.* **intro. 1.** Of or constituting an introduction. **2.** Serving to introduce. See Synonyms at **preliminary.** —**in′tro·duc′to·ri·ly** *adv.*

in·tro·gres·sion (ĭn′trə-grĕsh′ən) *n.* Infiltration of the genes of one species into the gene pool of another through repeated backcrossing of an interspecific hybrid with one of its parents. [From Latin *intrōgressus,* past participle of *intrōgredī,* to step in : *intrō-,* intro- + *gradī,* to step; see INGRESS.] —**in′tro·gres′sive** (-grĕs′ĭv) *adj.*

in·tro·it also **In·tro·it** (ĭn′trō′ĭt, -troit′, ĭn-trō′ĭt) *n.* **1.** A hymn or psalm sung when the ministers enter at the opening of a service, especially in the Anglican Church. **2.** *Roman Catholic Church.* The beginning of the Mass, usually consisting of a psalm verse, an antiphon, and the Gloria Patri. [Middle English, introit of the Mass, from Old French *introite,* from Medieval Latin *introitus,* sung passage at entrance of celebrant, from Latin *introitus,* entrance, from past participle of *introīre,* to enter : *intrō-,* in; see **en** in Appendix + *īre,* to go; see **ei-** in Appendix.]

in·tro·ject (ĭn′trə-jekt′) *tr.v. Psychiatry.* To incorporate (characteristics of a person or an object) into one's own psyche unconsciously. [Back-formation from INTROJECTION, from German *Introjektion* : Latin *intrō-,* intro- + Latin *-iectiō, -iectiōn-,* throwing (from *iactus,* past participle of *iacere,* to throw; see INJECT).] —**in′tro·jec′tion** *n.*

in·tro·mis·sion (ĭn′trə-mĭsh′ən) *n.* The act or process of intromitting; introduction or admission. [Medieval Latin *intrōmissiō, intrōmissiōn-,* usurpation, from Latin *intrōmissus,* past participle of *intrōmittere,* to intromit. See INTROMIT.] —**in′tro·mis′sive** (-mĭs′ĭv) *adj.*

in·tro·mit (ĭn′trə-mĭt′) *tr.v.* **-mit·ted, -mit·ting, -mits.** To cause or permit to enter; introduce or admit. [Middle English *intromitten,* to deal illegally with others, from Latin *intrōmittere,* to send in, let into : *intrō-,* in; see **en** in Appendix + *mittere,* to send.] —**in′tro·mit′tent** *adj.* —**in′tro·mit′ter** *n.*

in·tron (ĭn′trŏn) *n.* A segment of a gene situated between axons that does not function in coding for protein synthesis. [*intragenic,* occurring within a gene (INTRA– + GENIC) + –ON[1].]

in·trorse (ĭn′trôrs′) *adj. Botany.* Facing inward; turned toward the axis. Used especially of anthers. [Latin *intrōrsus,* contraction of *intrōversus,* inwards : *intrō-,* to the inside; see **en** in Appendix + *versus,* past participle of *vertere,* to turn; see **wer-**[2] in Appendix.]

in·tro·spect (ĭn′trə-spĕkt′, ĭn′trə-spĕkt′) *intr.v.* **-spect·ed, -spect·ing, -spects.** To engage in introspection. [Latin *intrōspicere, intrōspect-,* to look into : *intrō-,* within; see **en** in Appendix + *specere,* to look at; see **spek-** in Appendix.] —**in′tro·spec′tive** *adj.* —**in′tro·spec′tive·ly** *adv.* —**in′tro·spec′tive·ness** *n.*

in·tro·spec·tion (ĭn′trə-spĕk′shən) *n.* Contemplation of one's own thoughts, feelings, and sensations; self-examination. —**in′tro·spec′tion·al** *adj.*

in·tro·ver·sion (ĭn′trə-vûr′zhən, -shən) *n.* **1.** The act or process of introverting or the condition of being introverted. **2.** *Psychology.* The direction of or tendency to direct one's thoughts and feelings toward oneself. —**in′tro·ver′sive** (-vûr′sĭv) *adj.*

in·tro·vert (ĭn′trə-vûrt′, ĭn′trə-vûrt′) *tr.v.* **-vert·ed, -vert·ing, -verts. 1.** To turn or direct inward. **2.** *Psychology.* To concentrate (one's interests) upon oneself. **3.** *Medicine.* To turn (a tubular organ or part) inward upon itself. —**introvert** (ĭn′trə-vûrt′) *n.* **1.** *Psychology.* One whose thoughts and feelings are directed toward oneself. **2.** *Medicine.* An anatomical structure that is capable of being introverted. [INTRO– + Latin *vertere,* to turn; see **wer-**[2] in Appendix.]

in·trude (ĭn-trōōd′) *v.* **-trud·ed, -trud·ing, -trudes.** —*tr.* **1.** To put or force in inappropriately, especially without invitation, fitness, or permission: *intruded opinion into a factual report.* **2.** *Geology.* To thrust (molten rock) into preexisting rock. —*intr.* To come in rudely or inappropriately; enter as an improper or unwanted element: *"The flute would be intruding here like a delicate lady at a club smoker"* (Leonard Bernstein). [Middle English *intruden,* from Latin *intrūdere, intrūs-,* to thrust in : *in-,* in; see IN–[2] + *trūdere,* to thrust; see **treud-** in Appendix.] —**in·trud′er** *n.*

SYNONYMS: *intrude, obtrude.* These verbs mean to force oneself or something upon another or others without consent or approval. *Intrude* implies thrusting or coming in without permission, warrant, or welcome; it often suggests violation of another's privacy: *You had no right to intrude your opinions on the rest of us. You look busy—I hope I'm not intruding.* To *obtrude* is to push forward, as into consideration or sight: *"He wouldn't obtrude his assistance, if it were declined"* (John Lothrop Motley). *"The remembrance that our poor captain was lying dead in the cabin was constantly obtruding"* (Frederick Marryat).

in·tru·sion (ĭn-trōō′zhən) *n.* **1.** The act of intruding or the condition of being intruded on. **2.** An inappropriate or unwelcome addition. **3.** *Law.* Illegal entry upon or appropriation of the property of another. **4.** *Geology.* **a.** The forcing of molten rock into an earlier formation. **b.** The rock mass produced by an intrusive process.

in·tru·sive (ĭn-trōō′sĭv, -zĭv) *adj.* **1.** Intruding or tending to intrude. **2.** *Geology.* Of or relating to igneous rock forced while molten into cracks or between other layers of rock. **3.** *Linguistics.* Epenthetic. —**in·tru′sive·ly** *adv.* —**in·tru′sive·ness** *n.*

in·trust (ĭn-trŭst′) *v.* Variant of **entrust.**

in·tu·bate (ĭn′tōō-bāt′, -tyōō-) *tr.v.* **-bat·ed, -bat·ing, -bates.** *Medicine.* To insert a tube into (a hollow organ or body passage). —**in′tu·ba′tion** *n.* —**in′tu·ba′tion·al** *adj.* —**in′tu·ba′tion·al·ly** *adv.*

in·tu·it (ĭn-tōō′ĭt, -tyōō′-) *tr.v.* **-it·ed, -it·ing, -its.** *Usage Problem.* To know intuitively. [Back-formation from INTUITION.]

USAGE NOTE: The verb *intuit* is well established in reputable writing, but some critics have objected to it. Only 34 percent of the Usage Panel accepts it in the sentence *Claude often intuits my feelings about things long before I am really aware of them myself.* This lack of acceptance is often attributed to the verb's status as a back-formation from *intuition,* but in fact the verb has existed as long as other back-formations, such as *diagnose* and *donate,* that are now wholly acceptable. The source of the objections most likely lies in the fact that the verb is often used in reference to more trivial sorts of insight than would be permitted by a full appreciation of the traditional meaning of *intuition.* In this connection, a somewhat greater percentage of the Panel, 46 percent, does accept *intuit* in the sentence *Mathematicians sometimes intuit the truth of a theorem long before they are able to prove it.* See Usage Note at **enthuse.**

in·tu·i·tion (ĭn′tōō-ĭsh′ən, -tyōō-) *n.* **1.a.** The act or faculty of knowing or sensing without the use of rational processes; immediate cognition. See Synonyms at **reason. b.** Knowledge gained by the use of this faculty; a perceptive insight. **2.** A sense of something not evident or deducible; an impression. [Middle English *intuicioun,* insight, from Late Latin *intuitiō, intuitiōn-,* a looking at, from Latin *intuitus,* a look, from past participle of *intuērī,* to look at, contemplate : *in-,* on; see IN–[2] + *tuērī,* to look at.] —**in′tu·i′tion·al** *adj.* —**in′tu·i′tion·al·ly** *adv.*

in·tu·i·tion·ism (ĭn′tōō-ĭsh′ə-nĭz′əm, -tyōō-) *n. Philosophy.* **1.** The theory that truth or certain truths are known by intuition rather than reason. **2.** The theory that external objects of perception are immediately known to be real by intuition. **3.** The theory that ethical principles are known to be valid and universal through intuition. —**in′tu·i′tion·ist** *n.*

in·tu·i·tive (ĭn-tōō′ĭ-tĭv, -tyōō′-) *adj.* **1.** Of, relating to, or arising from intuition. **2.** Known or perceived through intuition. See Synonyms at **instinctive. 3.** Possessing or demonstrating intuition. —**in·tu′i·tive·ly** *adv.* —**in·tu′i·tive·ness** *n.*

in·tu·mesce (ĭn′tōō-mĕs′, -tyōō-) *intr.v.* **-mesced, -mesc·ing, -mesc·es. 1.** To swell or expand; enlarge. **2.** To bubble up, especially from the effect of heating. [Latin *intumēscere* : *in-,* intensive pref.; see IN–[2] + *tumēscere,* to begin to swell, inchoative of *tumēre,* to swell; see **teuə-** in Appendix.]

in·tu·mes·cence (ĭn′tōō-mĕs′əns, -tyōō-) *n.* **1.** The act or process of swelling or the condition of being swollen. **2.** A swollen organ or body part. —**in′tu·mes′cent** *adj.*

in·tus·sus·cept (ĭn′tə-sə-sĕpt′) *tr.v.* **-cept·ed, -cept·ing, -cepts.** To take within, as in telescoping one part of the intestine into another; invaginate. [Probably back-formation from INTUSSUSCEPTION.] —**in′tus·sus·cep′tive** *adj.*

in·tus·sus·cep·tion (ĭn′tə-sə-sĕp′shən) *n.* **1.** *Medicine.* Invagination, especially an infolding of one part of the intestine into another. **2.** *Biology.* Assimilation of new substances into the existing components of living tissue. [Medieval Latin *intussusceptiō, intussusceptiōn-,* a taking in, admission, from *intussusceptus,* past participle of *intussuscipere,* to take in : Latin *intus,* within; see **en** in Appendix + Latin *suscipere,* to take up (*sub,* sub- + *capere,* to take; see **kap-** in Appendix).]

in·twine (ĭn-twīn′) *v.* Variant of **entwine.**

in·twist (ĭn-twĭst′) *v.* Variant of **entwist.**

In·u·it also **In·nu·it** (ĭn′yōō-ĭt) *n., pl.* **Inuit** or **-its** also **Innuit** or **-its. 1.** A member of any of the Eskimo peoples of North America and especially of Arctic Canada and Greenland. **2.** Any or all of the Eskimo languages of the Inuit. [Eastern Eskimo, people.]

in·u·lase (ĭn′yə-lās′) *n.* An enzyme that catalyzes the conversion of inulin to fructose. [INUL(IN) + –ASE.]

in·u·lin (ĭn′yə-lĭn) *n.* A polysaccharide with the general formula $(C_6H_{10}O_5)_n$ that is found in the roots of various composite plants and yields fructose when hydrolyzed. [New Latin *Inula,* plant genus (from Latin *inula,* elecampane, from Greek *helenion;* see **wel-**[2] in Appendix) + –IN.]

in·unc·tion (ĭn-ŭngk′shən) *n.* **1.** The process of applying and rubbing in an ointment. **2.** The act of anointing, as in a religious ceremony. [Middle English, anointing, from Latin *inūnctiō, inūnctiōn-,* from *inūnctus,* past participle of *inunguere,* to anoint : *in-,* on; see IN–[2] + *unguere,* to smear.]

in·un·date (ĭn′ŭn-dāt′, ĭn′ən-) *tr.v.* **-dat·ed, -dat·ing, -dates. 1.** To cover with water, especially floodwaters; overflow. **2.** To overwhelm as if with a flood; swamp: *The theater was inundated with requests for tickets.* [Latin *inundāre, inundāt-* : *in-,* in; see IN–[2] + *undāre,* to surge (from *unda,* wave; see **wed-**[1] in

ă pat	oi boy
ā pay	ou out
âr care	ŏŏ took
ä father	ōō boot
ĕ pet	ŭ cut
ē be	ûr urge
ĭ pit	th thin
ī pie	*th* this
îr pier	hw which
ŏ pot	zh vision
ō toe	ə about, item
ô paw	♦ regionalism

Stress marks: ′ (primary); ′ (secondary), as in **dictionary** (dĭk′shə-nĕr′ē)

Appendix).] —**in′un·da′tion** *n.* —**in′un·da′tor** *n.* —**in·un′da·to′ry** (-də-tôr′ē, -tōr′ē) *adj.*

in·ure also **en·ure** (ĭn-yo͝or′) *tr.v.* **-ured, -ur·ing, -ures.** To habituate to something undesirable, especially by prolonged subjection; accustom: *"Though the food became no more palatable, he soon became sufficiently inured to it"* (John Barth). [Middle English, back-formation from *enured,* customary, from *in ure* : *in,* in; see IN[1] + *ure,* use (from Old French *euvre, uevre,* work, from Latin *opera,* activity associated with work; see **op-** in Appendix).] —**in·ure′ment** *n.*

in·urn (ĭn-ûrn′) *tr.v.* **-urned, -urn·ing, -urns. 1.** To put in an urn: *inurned the ashes of the deceased.* **2.** To bury or entomb; inter.

in u·ter·o (ĭn yo͞o′tə-rō) *adv. & adj.* In the uterus. [New Latin *in uterō* : Latin *in,* in + Latin *uterō,* ablative of *uterus,* uterus.]

in·u·tile (ĭn-yo͞ot′l, -yo͞o′tīl′) *adj.* Lacking in utility or serviceability; not useful. [Middle English, from Old French, from Latin *inūtilis* : *in-,* not; see IN–[1] + *ūtilis,* useful; see UTILE.] —**in·u′tile·ly** *adv.* —**in′u·til′i·ty** (ĭn′yo͞o-tĭl′ĭ-tē) *n.*

I·nu·vik (ĭ-no͞o′vĭk). A region of northwest Northwest Territories, Canada. It is crossed by the Mackenzie River.

inv. *abbr.* **1.** Invented; inventor. **2.** Invention. **3.** Invoice.

in vac·u·o (ĭn văk′yo͞o-ō′) *adv.* **1.** In a vacuum. **2.** In isolation; without reference to related evidence. [New Latin *in vacuō* : Latin *in,* in + Latin *vacuō,* ablative of *vacuus,* empty.]

in·vade (ĭn-vād′) *v.* **-vad·ed, -vad·ing, -vades.** —*tr.* **1.** To enter by force in order to conquer or pillage. **2.** To encroach or intrude on; violate: *"The principal of the trusts could not be invaded without trustee approval"* (Barbara Goldsmith). **3.** To overrun as if by invading; infest: *"About 1917 the shipworm invaded the harbor of San Francisco"* (Rachel Carson). **4.** To enter and permeate, especially harmfully. —*intr.* To make an invasion: *"The X-rays showed that the cancer, which had invaded deeply into the chest cavity, was retreating"* (Zach Rosen). [Middle English, from Old French *invader,* from Latin *invādere* : *in-,* in; see IN–[2] + *vādere,* to go.] —**in·vad′er** *n.*

in·vag·i·nate (ĭn-văj′ə-nāt′) *v.* **-nat·ed, -nat·ing, -nates.** —**invaginate** *tr. & intr.v.* **1.** To enclose or become enclosed in or as if in a sheath. **2.** To turn or become turned inward. **3.** To infold or become infolded so as to form a hollow space within a previously solid structure, as in the formation of a gastrula from a blastula. [Medieval Latin *invāgīnāre, invāgīnāt-* : Latin *in-,* in; see IN–[2] + Latin *vāgīna,* sheath.]

in·vag·i·na·tion (ĭn-văj′ə-nā′shən) *n.* **1.** The act or process of invaginating or the condition of being invaginated. **2.** An invaginated organ or part. **3.** *Embryology.* The infolding of a portion of the outer layer of a blastula in the formation of a gastrula.

in·va·lid[1] (ĭn′və-lĭd) *n.* One who is incapacitated by a chronic illness or disability. —**invalid** *adj.* **1.** Incapacitated by illness or injury. **2.** Of, relating to, or intended for chronically ill or disabled people. —**invalid** *tr.v.* **-lid·ed, -lid·ing, -lids. 1.** To incapacitate physically. **2.** *Chiefly British.* To release or exempt from duty because of ill health: *"I was not quite sick enough to be invalided out, even though I was of no more use"* (Mary Lee Settle). [From INVALID[2] (influenced by French *invalide,* sickly, infirm, from Latin *invalidus*).]

inverness
Edward VII
wearing an inverness coat

in·val·id[2] (ĭn-văl′ĭd) *adj.* **1.** Not legally or factually valid; null: *an invalid license.* **2.** Falsely based or reasoned; faulty: *an invalid argument.* [Latin *invalidus,* weak : *in-,* not; see IN–[1] + *validus,* strong (from *valēre,* to be strong; see **wal-** in Appendix).] —**in′va·lid′i·ty** (-və-lĭd′ĭ-tē) *n.* —**in·val′id·ly** *adv.*

in·val·i·date (ĭn-văl′ĭ-dāt′) *tr.v.* **-dat·ed, -dat·ing, -dates.** To make invalid; nullify. —**in·val′i·da′tion** *n.* —**in·val′i·da′tor** *n.*

in·va·lid·ism (ĭn′və-lĭ-dĭz′əm) *n.* The condition of being chronically ill or disabled.

in·val·u·a·ble (ĭn-văl′yo͞o-ə-bəl) *adj.* Of inestimable value; priceless: *invaluable paintings; invaluable help.* —**in·val′u·a·ble·ness** *n.* —**in·val′u·a·bly** *adv.*

in·var·i·a·ble (ĭn-vâr′ē-ə-bəl) *adj.* Not changing or subject to change; constant. —**in·var′i·a·bil′i·ty, in·var′i·a·ble·ness** *n.* —**in·var′i·a·bly** *adv.*

in·var·i·ant (ĭn-vâr′ē-ənt) *adj.* **1.** Not varying; constant. **2.** *Mathematics.* Unaffected by a designated operation, as a transformation of coordinates. —**invariant** *n.* An invariant quantity, function, configuration, or system. —**in·var′i·ance** *n.*

in·va·sion (ĭn-vā′zhən) *n.* **1.** The act of invading, especially the entrance of an armed force into a territory to conquer. **2.** A large-scale onset of something injurious or harmful, such as a disease. **3.** An intrusion or encroachment. [Middle English *invasioun,* from Old French *invasion,* from Late Latin *invāsiō, invāsiōn-,* from *invāsus,* past participle of *invādere,* to invade. See INVADE.]

in·va·sive (ĭn-vā′sĭv) *adj.* **1.** Of, engaging in, or given to armed aggression: *an invasive military force.* **2.** Marked by the tendency to spread, especially into healthy tissue: *an invasive carcinoma.* **3.** Of or relating to a medical procedure in which a part of the body is entered, as by puncture or incision. **4.** Tending to intrude or encroach, as upon privacy. [Middle English, from Old French *invasif,* from Medieval Latin *invāsīvus,* from Latin *invāsus,* past participle of *invādere,* to invade. See INVADE.] —**in·va′sive·ly** *adv.* —**in·va′sive·ness** *n.*

in·vec·tive (ĭn-vĕk′tĭv) *n.* **1.** Denunciatory or abusive language; vituperation. **2.** Denunciatory or abusive expression or discourse. —**invective** *adj.* Of, relating to, or characterized by denunciatory or abusive language. [From Middle English *invectif,* denunciatory, from Old French, from Late Latin *invectīvus,* reproachful, abusive, from Latin *invectus,* past participle of *invehī,* to inveigh against. See INVEIGH.] —**in·vec′tive·ly** *adv.* —**in·vec′tive·ness** *n.*

in·veigh (ĭn-vā′) *intr.v.* **-veighed, -veigh·ing, -veighs.** To give vent to angry disapproval; protest vehemently. [Latin *invehī,* to attack with words, inveigh against, passive of *invehere,* to carry in : *in-,* in; see IN–[2] + *vehere,* to carry; see **wegh-** in Appendix.] —**in·veigh′er** *n.*

in·vei·gle (ĭn-vā′gəl, -vē′-) *tr.v.* **-gled, -gling, -gles. 1.** To win over by coaxing, flattery, or artful talk. See Synonyms at **lure. 2.** To obtain by cajolery: *inveigle a free pass to the screening of the new film.* [Middle English *envegle,* alteration of Old French *aveugler,* to blind, from *aveugle,* blind, from Vulgar Latin **aboculus* : Latin *ab–,* away from; see AB–[1] + Latin *oculus,* eye; see **ok^w-** in Appendix.] —**in·vei′gle·ment** *n.* —**in·vei′gler** *n.*

in·vent (ĭn-vĕnt′) *tr.v.* **-vent·ed, -vent·ing, -vents. 1.** To produce or contrive (something previously unknown) by the use of ingenuity or imagination. **2.** To make up; fabricate: *invent a likely excuse.* [Latin *invenīre, invent-,* to find : *in-,* on, upon; see IN–[2] + *venīre,* to come; see **g^{w}ā-** in Appendix.] —**in·vent′i·ble** *adj.* —**in·ven′tor** *n.*

in·ven·tion (ĭn-vĕn′shən) *n. Abbr.* **inv. 1.** The act or process of inventing: *used a technique of her own invention.* **2.** A new device, method, or process developed from study and experimentation: *the phonograph, an invention attributed to Thomas Edison.* **3.** A mental fabrication, especially a falsehood. **4.** Skill in inventing; inventiveness: *"the invention and sweep of the staging"* (John Simon). **5.** *Music.* A short composition developing a single theme contrapuntally. **6.** A discovery; a finding. [Middle English *invencioun,* scheme, plan, from Old French *invencion,* a finding out, from Latin *inventiō, inventiōn-,* inventiveness, from *inventus,* past participle of *invenīre,* to find. See INVENT.] —**in·ven′tion·al** *adj.*

in·ven·tive (ĭn-vĕn′tĭv) *adj.* **1.** Of, relating to, or characterized by invention. **2.** Adept or skillful at inventing; creative. —**in·ven′tive·ly** *adv.* —**in·ven′tive·ness** *n.*

in·ven·to·ry (ĭn′vən-tôr′ē, -tōr′ē) *n., pl.* **-ries. 1.a.** A detailed, itemized list, report, or record of things in one's possession, especially a periodic survey of all goods and materials in stock. **b.** The process of making such a list, report, or record. **c.** The items listed in such a report or record. **d.** The quantity of goods and materials on hand; stock. **2.** An evaluation or a survey, as of abilities, assets, or resources. —**inventory** *tr.v.* **-ried, -ry·ing, -ries. 1.** To make an itemized report or record of. **2.** To include in an itemized report or record. [Middle English *inventorie,* from Medieval Latin *inventōrium,* alteration of Late Latin *inventārium,* from Latin *inventus,* past participle of *invenīre,* to find. See INVENT.] —**in′ven·to′ri·al** *adj.* —**in′ven·to′ri·al·ly** *adv.*

in·ve·rac·i·ty (ĭn′və-răs′ĭ-tē) *n., pl.* **-ties. 1.** Lack of veracity; untruthfulness. **2.** An untruth; a falsehood.

In·ver Grove Heights (ĭn′vər). A city of southeast Minnesota, a residential suburb of St. Paul. Population, 17,171.

in·ver·ness also **In·ver·ness** (ĭn′vər-nĕs′) *n.* **1.** A long, loose overcoat with a detachable cape having a round collar. **2.** The cape of such an overcoat. [After INVERNESS.]

In·ver·ness (ĭn′vər-nĕs′). A burgh of northern Scotland on the Moray Firth at the terminus of the Caledonian Canal. Thought to have been a Pict stronghold, it was chartered c. 1200. Population, 39,700.

in·verse (ĭn-vûrs′, ĭn′vûrs′) *adj.* **1.** Reversed in order, nature, or effect. **2.** *Mathematics.* Of or relating to an inverse or an inverse function. **3.** *Archaic.* Turned upside down; inverted. —**inverse** (ĭn′vûrs′, ĭn-vûrs′) *n.* **1.** Something that is opposite, as in sequence or character; the reverse. **2.** *Mathematics.* One of a pair of elements in a set whose result under the operation of the set is the identity element, especially: **a.** The reciprocal of a designated quantity. Also called *multiplicative inverse.* **b.** The negative of a designated quantity. Also called *additive inverse.* [Middle English, from Latin *inversus,* past participle of *invertere,* to invert. See INVERT.] —**in·verse′ly** *adv.*

inverse function *n. Mathematics.* A function that replaces another function's independent variable with a value of its dependent value.

in·ver·sion (ĭn-vûr′zhən, -shən) *n.* **1.a.** The act of inverting. **b.** The state of being inverted. **2.** An interchange of position of adjacent objects in a sequence, especially: **a.** A change in normal word order, such as the placement of a verb before its subject. **b.** *Music.* A rearrangement or result of the rearrangement of tones in which upper and lower voices are transposed, as in counterpoint, or in which each interval in a single melody is applied in the opposite direction. **3.** *Psychology.* **a.** The taking on of the gender role of the opposite sex. **b.** Used as a term for homosexuality. **4.** *Chemistry.* Conversion of a substance in which the direction of optical rotation is reversed, from the dextrorotatory to the levorotatory or from the levorotatory to the dextrorotatory form. **5.** *Meteorology.* An atmospheric condition in which the air temperature rises with increasing altitude, holding surface air down and preventing dispersion of pollutants. **6.** *Genetics.* A chromosomal defect in which a segment of the chromosome breaks off and reattaches in the reverse direction. [Latin *inversiō, inversiōn-,* from *inversus,* past participle of *invertere,* to invert. See INVERT.]

in•vert (ĭn-vûrt′) *v.* **-vert•ed, -vert•ing, -verts.** —*tr.* **1.** To turn inside out or upside down: *invert an hourglass.* **2.** To reverse the position, order, or condition of: *invert the subject and predicate of a sentence.* **3.** To subject to inversion. See Synonyms at **reverse.** —*intr.* To be subjected to inversion. —**invert** (ĭn′vûrt′) *n.* **1.** Something inverted. **2.** *Psychology.* **a.** One who takes on the gender role of the opposite sex. **b.** Used as a term for a homosexual person. [Latin *invertere* : *in-,* in; see IN–[2] + *vertere,* to turn; see **wer-**[2] in Appendix.] —**in•vert′i•ble** *adj.*

in•ver•tase (ĭn-vûr′tās′, ĭn′vər-tās′, -tāz′) *n.* An enzyme that catalyzes the hydrolysis of sucrose into glucose and fructose. Also called *saccharase, sucrase.*

in•ver•te•brate (ĭn-vûr′tə-brĭt, -brāt′) *adj.* **1.** Lacking a backbone or spinal column; not vertebrate. **2.** Of or relating to invertebrates: *invertebrate zoology.* —**invertebrate** *n.* An animal, such as an insect or a mollusk, that lacks a backbone or spinal column.

in•vert•ed comma (ĭn-vûr′tĭd) *n. Chiefly British.* A quotation mark.

inverted mordent *n. Music.* See **pralltriller.**

in•vert•er (ĭn-vûr′tər) *n.* **1.** One that inverts or produces inversion. **2.** A device used to convert direct current into alternating current.

invert sugar *n.* A mixture of equal parts of glucose and fructose resulting from the hydrolysis of sucrose. It is found naturally in fruits and honey and produced artificially for use in the food industry.

in•vest (ĭn-vĕst′) *v.* **-vest•ed, -vest•ing, -vests.** —*tr.* **1.** To commit (money or capital) in order to gain a financial return: *invested their savings in stocks and bonds.* **2. a.** To spend or devote for future advantage or benefit: *invested much time and energy in getting a good education.* **b.** To devote morally or psychologically, as to a purpose; commit: *"Men of our generation are invested in what they* do, *women in what we* are" (Shana Alexander). **3.** To endow with authority or power. **4.** To install in office with ceremony: *invest a new emperor.* **5.** To endow with an enveloping or pervasive quality: *"A charm invests a face/ Imperfectly beheld"* (Emily Dickinson). **6.** To clothe; adorn. **7.** To cover completely; envelop. **8.** To surround with troops or ships; besiege. See Synonyms at **besiege.** —*intr.* To make investments or an investment: *invest in real estate.* [From Italian *investire* and from French *investir,* both from Latin *investīre,* to clothe, surround : *in-,* in; see IN–[2] + *vestīre,* to clothe (from *vestis,* clothes; see **wes-**[2] in Appendix).] —**in•vest′a•ble** *adj.* —**in•ves′tor** *n.*

in•ves•ti•gate (ĭn-vĕs′tĭ-gāt′) *v.* **-gat•ed, -gat•ing, -gates.** —*tr.* To observe or inquire into in detail; examine systematically. —*intr.* To make a detailed inquiry or systematic examination. [Latin *investīgāre, investīgāt-* : *in-,* in; see IN–[2] + *vestīgāre,* to track (from *vestīgium,* footprint).] —**in•ves′ti•ga•ble** (-gə-bəl) *adj.* —**in•ves′ti•ga•to′ry** (-gə-tôr′ē, -tōr′ē) *adj.*

in•ves•ti•ga•tion (ĭn-vĕs′tĭ-gā′shən) *n.* **1.** The act or process of investigating. **2.** A detailed inquiry or systematic examination. See Synonyms at **inquiry.** —**in•ves′ti•ga′tion•al** *adj.*

in•ves•ti•ga•tive (ĭn-vĕs′tĭ-gā′tĭv) *adj.* **1.** Of or relating to investigation: *investigative methods.* **2.** Characterized by or engaged in investigation; specializing in uncovering and reporting hidden information: *investigative journalism.*

in•ves•ti•ga•tor (ĭn-vĕs′tĭ-gā′tər) *n.* One, especially a detective, who investigates. —**in•ves′ti•ga•to′ri•al** (-gə-tôr′ē-əl, -tōr′-) *adj.*

in•ves•ti•ture (ĭn-vĕs′tə-cho͝or′, -chər) *n.* **1.** The act or formal ceremony of conferring the authority and symbols of a high office. **2.** An adornment or a cover. [Middle English, from Medieval Latin *investītūra,* from Latin *investīre,* to clothe. See INVEST.]

in•vest•ment (ĭn-vĕst′mənt) *n.* **1.** The act of investing. **2.** An amount invested. **3.** Property or another possession acquired for future financial return or benefit. **4.** A commitment, as of time or support. **5.** A military siege. **6.** *Archaic.* **a.** A garment; a vestment. **b.** An outer covering or layer. —*attributive.* Often used to modify another noun: *investment dollars.*

in•vet•er•ate (ĭn-vĕt′ər-ĭt) *adj.* **1.** Firmly and long established; deep-rooted: *inveterate preferences.* **2.** Persisting in an ingrained habit; habitual: *an inveterate liar.* See Synonyms at **chronic.** [Middle English, from Latin *inveterātus,* past participle of *inveterārī,* to grow old, endure : *in-,* causative pref.; see IN–[2] + *vetus, veter-,* old; see **wet-**[2] in Appendix.] —**in•vet′er•a•cy** (-ər-ə-sē), **in•vet′er•ate•ness** *n.* —**in•vet′er•ate•ly** *adv.*

in•vi•a•ble (ĭn-vī′ə-bəl) *adj.* Unable to survive or develop normally: *an inviable newborn calf.* —**in•vi•a•bil′i•ty** *n.*

in•vid•i•ous (ĭn-vĭd′ē-əs) *adj.* **1.** Tending to rouse ill will, animosity, or resentment: *invidious accusations.* **2.** Containing or implying a slight; discriminatory: *invidious distinctions.* **3.** Envious. [From Latin *invidiōsus,* envious, hostile, from *invidia,* envy. See ENVY.] —**in•vid′i•ous•ly** *adv.*

in•vig•or•ate (ĭn-vĭg′ə-rāt′) *tr.v.* **-at•ed, -at•ing, -ates.** To impart vigor, strength, or vitality to; animate: *"A few whiffs of the raw, strong scent of phlox invigorated her"* (D.H. Lawrence). [Possibly obsolete *invigor* (from French *envigorer,* from Old French *envigourer* : *en-,* in; see IN–[2] + *vigour,* vigor; see VIGOR) + –ATE[1].] —**in•vig′or•at′ing•ly** *adv.* —**in•vig′or•a′tion** *n.* —**in•vig′or•a′tor** *n.*

in•vin•ci•ble (ĭn-vĭn′sə-bəl) *adj.* Incapable of being overcome or defeated; unconquerable. [Middle English, from Old French, from Latin *invincibilis* : *in-,* not; see IN–[1] + *vincibilis,* conquerable; see VINCIBLE.] —**in•vin′ci•bil′i•ty, in•vin′ci•ble•ness** *n.* —**in•vin′ci•bly** *adv.*

in•vi•o•la•ble (ĭn-vī′ə-lə-bəl) *adj.* **1.** Secure from violation or profanation: *an inviolable reliquary deep beneath the altar.* **2.** Impregnable to assault or trespass; invincible: *fortifications that made the frontier inviolable.* [Middle English, from Old French, from Latin *inviolābilis* : *in-,* not; see IN–[1] + *violāre,* to violate; see VIOLATE.] —**in•vi′o•la•bil′i•ty, in•vi′o•la•ble•ness** *n.* —**in•vi′o•la•bly** *adv.*

in•vi•o•late (ĭn-vī′ə-lĭt) *adj.* Not violated or profaned; intact: *"The great inviolate place had an ancient permanence which the sea cannot claim"* (Thomas Hardy). [Middle English, from Latin *inviolātus* : *in-,* not; see IN–[1] + *violātus,* past participle of *violāre,* to violate; see VIOLATE.] —**in•vi′o•la•cy** (-lə-sē), **in•vi′o•late•ness** *n.* —**in•vi′o•late•ly** *adv.*

in•vis•cid (ĭn-vĭs′ĭd) *adj.* **1.** Having no viscosity. **2.** *Physics & Chemistry.* Of or relating to a fluid with no viscosity.

in•vis•i•ble (ĭn-vĭz′ə-bəl) *adj.* **1.** Impossible to see; not visible: *invisible writing.* **2.** Not accessible to view; hidden: *mountain peaks invisible in the fog.* **3.** Not easily noticed or detected; inconspicuous: *"The poor are politically invisible"* (Michael Harrington). **4.** Not published in financial statements: *an invisible asset.* —**invisible** *n.* One that is invisible. —**in•vis′i•bil′i•ty, in•vis′i•ble•ness** *n.* —**in•vis′i•bly** *adv.*

invisible ink *n.* Ink that is colorless and invisible until treated by a chemical, heat, or special light. Also called *sympathetic ink.*

♦ **in•vi•ta•tion** (ĭn′vĭ-tā′shən) *n.* **1.** The act of inviting. **2.** A spoken or written request for someone's presence or participation. **3.** An allurement, enticement, or attraction. **4.** *Chiefly Southern U.S.* See **altar call.**

in•vi•ta•tion•al (ĭn′vĭ-tā′shə-nəl) *adj.* Restricted to invited participants: *an invitational golf tournament.* —**invitational** *n.* An event, especially a sports tournament, restricted to invited participants.

in•vi•ta•to•ry (ĭn-vī′tə-tôr′ē, -tōr′ē) *n.* **-ries.** *pl.* A psalm or other piece sung as an invitation to prayer in church services. —**invitatory** *adj.* Constituting or containing an invitation. [Middle English *invitatorie,* from Medieval Latin *invītātōrium,* from Late Latin *invītātōrius,* inviting, from Latin *invītātus,* past participle of *invītāre,* to invite.]

in•vite (ĭn-vīt′) *tr.v.* **-vit•ed, -vit•ing, -vites.** **1.** To ask for the presence or participation of: *invite friends to dinner; invite writers to a conference.* **2.** To request formally: *invited us to be seated.* **3.** To welcome; encourage: *invite questions from the audience.* **4.** To tend to bring on; provoke: *"Divisions at home would invite dangers from abroad"* (John Jay). **5.** To entice; tempt. —**invite** (ĭn′vīt′) *n. Informal.* An invitation. [French *inviter,* from Old French, from Latin *invītāre.*]

in•vi•tee (ĭn′vī-tē′) *n.* One that is invited.

in•vit•ing (ĭn-vī′tĭng) *adj.* Attractive; tempting: *an inviting dessert.* —**in•vit′ing•ly** *adv.*

in vi•tro (ĭn vē′trō) *adv. & adj.* In an artificial environment outside the living organism: *an egg fertilized in vitro; in vitro fertilization.* [New Latin *in vitrō* : Latin *in,* in + Latin *vitrō,* ablative of *vitrum,* glass.]

in vi•vo (vē′vō) *adv. & adj.* Within a living organism: *metabolic studies conducted in vivo; in vivo techniques.* [New Latin *in vīvō* : Latin *in,* in + Latin *vīvō,* ablative of *vīvus,* living, a living body.]

in•vo•cate (ĭn′və-kāt′) *tr.v.* **-cat•ed, -cat•ing, -cates.** *Archaic.* To invoke. [Latin *invocāre, invocāt-,* to invoke. See INVOKE.]

in•vo•ca•tion (ĭn′və-kā′shən) *n.* **1.** The act or an instance of invoking, especially an appeal to a higher power for assistance. **2.** A prayer or other formula used in invoking, as at the opening of a religious service. **3. a.** The act of conjuring up a spirit by incantation. **b.** An incantation used in conjuring. [Middle English *invocacion,* from Old French, from Latin *invocātiō, invocātiōn-,* from *invocātus,* past participle of *invocāre,* to invoke. See INVOKE.] —**in′vo•ca′tion•al** *adj.*

in•voc•a•to•ry (ĭn-vŏk′ə-tôr′ē, -tōr′ē) *adj.* Of or having the nature of an invocation.

in•voice (ĭn′vois′) *n. Abbr.* **inv.** **1.** A detailed list of goods shipped or services rendered, with an account of all costs; an itemized bill. **2.** The goods or services itemized in an invoice. —**invoice** *tr.v.* **-voiced, -voic•ing, -voic•es.** **1.** To make an invoice of (goods or services). **2.** To send an invoice to; bill. [Alteration of obsolete *invoyes,* pl. of *invoy,* invoice, from French *envoi,* a sending, shipment, from *envoyer,* to send. See ENVOY[1].]

in•voke (ĭn-vōk′) *tr.v.* **-voked, -vok•ing, -vokes.** **1.** To call on (a higher power) for assistance, support, or inspiration: *"Stretching out her hands she had the air of a Greek woman who invoked a deity"* (Ford Madox Ford). **2.** To appeal to or cite in support or justification. **3.** To call for earnestly; solicit: *invoked the help of a passing motorist.* **4.** To summon with incantations; conjure. **5.** To resort to; use or apply: *"Shamelessly, he invokes coincidence to achieve ironic effect"* (Newsweek). See Synonyms at **enforce.** [Middle English *envoken,* from Old French *invoquer,* from Latin *invocāre* : *in-,* in; see IN–[2] + *vocāre,* to call; see **wek^w-** in Appendix.] —**in•vok′er** *n.*

in•vol•u•cel (ĭn-vŏl′yə-sĕl′) *n. Botany.* A secondary involu-

ă pat	oi boy
ā pay	ou out
âr care	o͝o took
ä father	o͞o boot
ĕ pet	ŭ cut
ē be	ûr urge
ĭ pit	th thin
ī pie	*th* this
îr pier	hw which
ŏ pot	zh vision
ō toe	ə about, item
ô paw	♦ regionalism

Stress marks: ′ (primary); ′ (secondary), as in **dictionary** (dĭk′shə-nĕr′ē)

cre, as at the base of an umbel within a compound umbel. [New Latin *involūcellum,* diminutive of *involūcrum,* involucre. See INVOLUCRUM.]

in•vo•lu•cra (ĭn′və-lo͞o′krə) *n.* Plural of **involucrum.**

in•vo•lu•cre (ĭn′və-lo͞o′kər) *n.* A series of bracts beneath or around a flower or flower cluster. [French, from Latin *involūcrum,* wrapper, envelope. See INVOLUCRUM.] **—in′vo•lu′cral** (-krəl), **in′vo•lu′crate** (-krĭt, -krāt′) *adj.*

in•vo•lu•crum (ĭn′və-lo͞o′krəm) *n., pl.* **-cra** (-krə). An enveloping sheath or envelope. [New Latin, from Latin, wrapper, envelope, from *involvere,* to enwrap. See INVOLVE.]

in•vol•un•tar•y (ĭn-vŏl′ən-tĕr′ē, -tĕr′-) *adj.* **1.** Acting or done without or against one's will: *an involuntary participant in what turned out to be an argument.* **2.** Not subject to control of the volition: *gave an involuntary start.* See Synonyms at **spontaneous.** **—in•vol′un•tar′i•ly** (-târ′ə-lē) *adv.* **—in•vol′un•tar′i•ness** *n.*

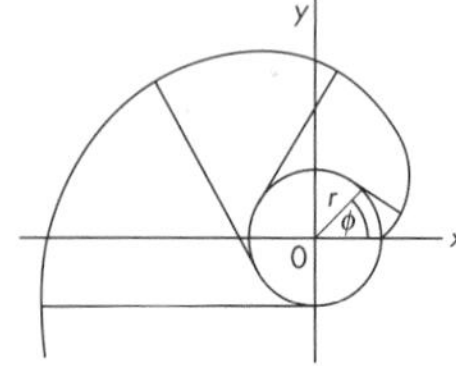

involute
Involute of a circle:
$x = r\cos\phi + r\phi\sin\phi$
$y = r\sin\phi - r\phi\cos\phi$

in•vo•lute (ĭn′və-lo͞ot′) *adj.* **1.** Intricate; complex. **2.** *Botany.* **a.** Having the margins rolled inward. **b.** Having whorls that obscure the axis or other volutions, as the shell of a cowrie. **—involute** *intr.v.* **-lut•ed, -lut•ing, -lutes. 1.** To curl inward. **2.** To return to a normal or former condition. **—involute** *n.* The curve traced by a point on a taut, inextensible string as it unwinds from another curve. [Latin *involūtus,* past participle of *involvere,* to enwrap. See INVOLVE.] **—in′vo•lute′ly** *adv.*

in•vo•lu•tion (ĭn′və-lo͞o′shən) *n.* **1.a.** The act of involving. **b.** The state of being involved. **2.** Intricacy; complexity. **3.** Something, such as a long grammatical construction, that is intricate or complex. **4.** *Mathematics.* The multiplying of a quantity by itself a specified number of times; the raising to a power. **5.** *Embryology.* The ingrowth and curling inward of a group of cells, as in the formation of a gastrula from a blastula. **6.** *Medicine.* **a.** A decrease in size of an organ, as of the uterus following childbirth. **b.** A progressive decline or degeneration of normal physiological functioning occurring as a result of the aging process. [Latin *involūtiō, involūtiōn-,* from *involūtus,* past participle of *involvere,* to enwrap. See INVOLVE.] **—in′vo•lu′tion•al** *adj.*

in•volve (ĭn-vŏlv′) *tr.v.* **-volved, -volv•ing, -volves. 1.** To contain as a part; include. **2.** To have as a necessary feature or consequence; entail: *was told that the job would involve travel.* See Synonyms at **include. 3.** To engage as a participant; embroil: *involved the bystanders in his dispute with the police.* **4.a.** To connect closely and often incriminatingly; implicate: *evidence that involved the governor in the scandal.* **b.** To influence or affect: *The matter is serious because it involves your reputation.* **5.** To occupy or engage the interest of: *a story that completely involved me for the rest of the evening.* **6.** To make complex or intricate; complicate. **7.** To wrap; envelop: *a castle that was involved in mist.* **8.** *Archaic.* To wind or coil about. [Middle English *involven,* from Latin *involvere,* to enwrap : *in-,* in; see IN–[2] + *volvere,* to roll, turn; see **wel-**[2] in Appendix.] **—in•volve′ment** *n.* **—in•volv′er** *n.*

io moth
Automeris io

in•volved (ĭn-vŏlvd′) *adj.* **1.** Complicated; intricate: *the involved procedure of getting a license.* See Synonyms at **complex. 2.** Curled inward; coiled or involute. **3.** Confused; tangled. **4.** Connected by participation or association: *involved in a conspiracy.* **5.a.** Emotionally committed: *He joined their organization but never really got involved.* **b.** Having a sexual relationship: *They see a lot of each other but aren't involved.* **—in•volv′ed•ly** (-vŏl′vĭd-lē) *adv.*

Eugène Ionesco
Receiving an honorary degree at Brown University in 1984

in•vul•ner•a•ble (ĭn-vŭl′nər-ə-bəl) *adj.* **1.** Immune to attack; impregnable. **2.** Impossible to damage, injure, or wound. [French *invulnérable,* from Old French, from Latin *invulnerābilis* : *in-,* not; see IN–[1] + *vulnerāre,* to wound (from *vulnus, vulner-,* wound; see VULNERABLE).] **—in•vul′ner•a•bil′i•ty, in•vul′ner•a•ble•ness** *n.* **—in•vul′ner•a•bly** *adv.*

in•ward (ĭn′wərd) *adj.* **1.** Located inside; inner. **2.** Directed or moving toward the interior: *an inward flow.* **3.** Of, relating to, or existing in the thoughts or mind: *inward doubts.* **4.** Intimate; familiar: *is inward with the right people.* **—inward** *adv.* **1.** Toward the inside, center, or interior. **2.** Toward the mind or the self: *thoughts turned inward.* **—inward** *n.* **1.** An inner or a central part. **2.** An inner essence or spirit. **3. inwards.** Entrails; innards. [Middle English, from Old English *inweard.* See **wer-**[2] in Appendix.] **—in′wards** *adv.*

in•ward•ly (ĭn′wərd-lē) *adv.* **1.** On or in the inside; within: *a window opening flared inwardly.* **2.** Privately; to oneself: *"kept his lips closed with the expression of a man inwardly laughing"* (T.S. Stribling).

in•ward•ness (ĭn′wərd-nĭs) *n.* **1.** Intimacy; familiarity. **2.** Preoccupation with one's own thoughts or feelings; introspection.

in•weave (ĭn-wēv′) *tr.v.* **-wove** (-wōv′), **-wo•ven** (-wō′vən), **-weav•ing, -weaves.** To weave into a fabric or design.

in•wind (ĭn-wīnd′) *v.* Variant of **enwind.**

in•wove (ĭ-wōv′) *v.* Past tense of **inweave.**

in•wo•ven (ĭn-wō′vən) *v.* Past participle of **inweave.**

in•wrap (ĭn-răp′) *v.* Variant of **enwrap.**

in•wreathe (ĭn-rēth′) *v.* Variant of **enwreathe.**

in•wrought (ĭn-rôt′, ĭn′rôt′) *adj.* **1.** Worked or woven in: *an inwrought design.* **2.** Having a decorative pattern worked or woven in.

Ionic order

I•o (ī′ō, ē′ō) *n.* **1.** *Greek Mythology.* A maiden who was loved by Zeus and transformed by Hera into a heifer. **2.** One of the four brightest satellites of Jupiter and the ninth in distance from the planet. It was first sighted by Galileo. [Latin *Īō,* from Greek.]

I/O *abbr.* Input/output.

IOC *abbr.* International Olympic Committee.

iod– *pref.* Variant of **iodo–.**

i•o•date (ī′ə-dāt′) *tr.v.* **-dat•ed, -dat•ing, -dates.** To combine, impregnate, or treat with iodine. **—iodate** (-dāt′, -dĭt) *n.* A salt of iodic acid. **—i′o•da′tion** *n.*

i•od•ic acid (ī-ŏd′ĭk) *n.* A colorless or white crystalline powder, HIO_3, used as an astringent and a disinfectant. [French *iodique,* from *iode,* iodine. See IODINE.]

i•o•dide (ī′ə-dīd′) *n.* A compound of iodine with a more electropositive element or group.

i•o•dine (ī′ə-dīn′, -dĭn, -dēn′) *n. Symbol* **I 1.** A lustrous, grayish-black, corrosive, poisonous halogen element having radioactive isotopes, especially I 131, used as a medical tracer and in thyroid disease diagnosis and therapy. Iodine compounds are used as germicides, antiseptics, and dyes. Atomic number 53; atomic weight 126.9044; melting point 113.5°C; boiling point 184.35°C; specific gravity (solid, at 20°C) 4.93; valence 1, 3, 5, 7. See table at **element. 2.** A liquid containing iodine dissolved in ethyl alcohol, used as an antiseptic for wounds. [French *iode,* iodine (from Greek *ioeidēs,* violet-colored : *ion,* violet + *-oeidēs,* -oid) + –INE[2].]

i•o•dize (ī′ə-dīz′) *tr.v.* **-dized, -diz•ing, -diz•es.** To treat or combine with iodine or an iodide: *iodize salt.* **—i′o•di•za′tion** (-dĭ-zā′shən) *n.*

iodo– or **iod–** *pref.* Iodine: *iodoform.* [From French *iode,* iodine. See IODINE.]

i•o•do•form (ī-ō′də-fôrm′, ī-ŏd′ə-) *n.* A yellowish crystalline iodine compound, CHI_3, used as an antiseptic. [IODO– + FORM(YL).]

i•o•do•phor (ī-ō′də-fôr′) *n.* A substance consisting of iodine and a solubilizing agent that releases free iodine when in solution. [IODO– + –PHOR(E).]

i•o•dop•sin (ī′ə-dŏp′sĭn) *n.* A violet, light-sensitive pigment found in the retinal cones of the eye.

i•o moth (ī′ō, ē′ō) *n.* A large, yellowish North American moth *(Automeris io)* having a prominent eyelike spot on each hind wing. [After Io, who was tormented by gadflies sent by Hera as a punishment (from the stinging spines of its larvae).]

i•on (ī′ən, ī′ŏn′) *n.* An atom or a group of atoms that has acquired a net electric charge by gaining or losing one or more electrons. [Greek *ion,* something that goes, neuter present participle of *ienai,* to go. See **ei-** in Appendix.]

Ion. *abbr.* Ionic.

–ion *suff.* **1.a.** Action or process: *completion.* **b.** Result of an action or process: *indention.* **2.** State or condition: *dehydration.* [Middle English, from Old French, from Latin *-iō, -iōn-,* n. suff.]

I•o•na (ī-ō′nə). An island of western Scotland in the southern Inner Hebrides. An early center of Celtic Christianity, the island is a popular tourist site.

ion engine *n.* A rocket engine that develops thrust by expelling ions rather than gaseous combustion products. Also called *ion rocket.*

Io•nes•co (ē′ə-nĕs′kō, yə-), **Eugène.** Born 1912. Romanian-born French dramatist whose plays *The Bald Soprano* (1956) and *Rhinoceros* (1959) are classics of the Theater of the Absurd.

ion exchange *n.* A reversible chemical reaction between an insoluble solid and a solution during which ions may be interchanged, used in water softening and in the separation of radioactive isotopes.

I•o•ni•a (ī-ō′nē-ə). An ancient region of western Asia Minor along the coast of the Aegean Sea. Greek settlers established colonies here before 1000 B.C.

I•o•ni•an (ī-ō′nē-ən) *n.* **1.** A native or inhabitant of Ionia. **2.** One of a Hellenic people of Mycenaean origin that inhabited Attica, the Peloponnesus along the Saronic Gulf, Euboea, the Cyclades, and Ionia. **—I•o′ni•an** *adj.*

Ionian Islands. A chain of islands of western Greece in the Ionian Sea. Colonized by the ancient Greeks, the islands subsequently came under the rule of Rome, Byzantium, Venice, France, Russia, and Great Britain before being ceded to Greece in 1864.

Ionian Sea. An arm of the Mediterranean Sea between western Greece and southern Italy. It is linked with the Adriatic Sea by the Strait of Otranto.

i•on•ic (ī-ŏn′ĭk) *adj.* Of, containing, or involving ions.

I•on•ic (ī-ŏn′ĭk) *adj.* **1.** Of or relating to Ionia or the Ionians. **2.** *Architecture.* Of or belonging to the Ionic order. **—Ionic** *n. Abbr.* **Ion.** The ancient Greek dialect of Ionia.

ionic bond *n.* A chemical bond between two ions with opposite charges, characteristic of salts. Also called *electrovalent bond.*

Ionic order *n. Architecture.* An order of classical Greek architecture characterized by two opposed volutes in the capital.

ionic propulsion *n.* Propulsion by the reactive thrust of a high-speed beam of similarly charged ions ejected by an ion engine. Also called *ion propulsion.*

i•on•i•za•tion (ī′ə-nĭ-zā′shən) *n.* **1.** The formation of or separation into ions by heat, electrical discharge, radiation, or chemical reaction. **2.** The state of being ionized.

ionization chamber *n.* A gas-filled enclosure containing positive and negative electrodes that measures the amount of radiation passing through the enclosure according to the degree of ionization caused by the radiation.

ionization potential *n.* The energy required to remove completely an electron from its atom.

i·on·ize (ī′ə-nīz′) *tr. & intr.v.* **-ized, -iz·ing, -iz·es.** To convert or be converted totally or partly into ions. **—i′on·iz′er** *n.*

i·on·iz·ing radiation (ī′ə-nī′zĭng) *n.* High-energy radiation capable of producing ionization in substances through which it passes. It includes energetic charged particles, such as alpha and beta rays; nonparticulate radiation, such as x-rays; and neutrons.

ion microscope *n.* A field-ion microscope.

i·o·none (ī′ə-nōn′) *n.* A colorless to yellowish liquid, $C_{13}H_{20}O$, having a strong odor of violets and used in perfumes. [Formerly a trademark.]

i·on·o·phore (ī-ŏn′ə-fôr, -fōr′) *n.* Any of a group of organic compounds that facilitate the transport of ions across the cell membrane.

i·on·o·sphere (ī-ŏn′ə-sfîr′) *n.* A region of the earth's atmosphere where ionization caused by incoming solar radiation affects the transmission of radio waves. It extends from a height of 50 kilometers (30 miles) to 400 kilometers (250 miles) above the surface. **—i·on′o·spher′ic** (-sfîr′ĭk, -sfĕr′-) *adj.*

ion propulsion *n.* See **ionic propulsion.**

ion rocket *n.* **1.** A rocket using ionic propulsion. **2.** See **ion engine.**

ion trap *n.* A device, such as a magnet, used to prevent ions in an electron beam from striking other apparatus.

IOOF *abbr.* Independent Order of Odd Fellows.

i·o·ta (ī-ō′tə) *n.* **1.** The ninth letter of the Greek alphabet. See table at **alphabet. 2.** A very small amount; a bit: *not an iota of truth to that tale.* [Latin *iōta,* from Greek, of Phoenician origin; akin to Hebrew *yôd,* yod.]

i·o·ta·cism (ī-ō′tə-sĭz′əm) *n.* The conversion of other vowel sounds in Greek, such as eta or upsilon, to the sound of iota. [Late Latin *iōtacismus,* from Greek *iōtakismos,* from *iōta,* iota. See IOTA.]

IOU (ī′ō-yo͞o′) *n., pl.* **IOU's** or **IOUs.** A promise to pay a debt, especially a signed paper stating the specific amount owed and often bearing the letters IOU. [From the pronunciation of *I owe you.*]

-ious *suff.* Having; having the qualities of; full of: *bilious.* [Middle English, partly from Latin *-ius* and partly from Old French *-ieus, -ieux,* -ieux, from Latin *-iōsus.*]

I·o·wa¹ (ī′ə-wə) *n., pl.* **Iowa** or **-was. 1.a.** A Native American people formerly inhabiting parts of Iowa and southwest Minnesota, with present-day descendants in Nebraska, Kansas, and Oklahoma. **b.** A member of this people. **2.** The Siouan language of the Iowa. [From French *ayoés,* ultimately from Dakota *ayúxba.*] **—I′o·wa** *adj.*

I·o·wa² (ī′ə-wə). *Abbr.* **IA, Ia.** A state of the north-central United States. It was admitted as the 29th state in 1846. Part of the Louisiana Purchase of 1803, Iowa was organized as a separate territory in 1838. Des Moines is the capital and the largest city. Population, 2,913,808. **—I′o·wan** *adj. & n.*

Iowa City. A city of eastern Iowa on the Iowa River south-southeast of Cedar Rapids. It is the seat of the University of Iowa (established 1847). Population, 50,508.

Iowa River. A river rising in northern Iowa and flowing about 529 km (329 mi) southeast to the Mississippi River.

IPA *abbr.* **1.** Also **I.P.A.** International Phonetic Alphabet. **2.** International Phonetic Association. **3.** Isopropyl alcohol.

ip·e·cac (ĭp′ĭ-kăk′) also **ip·e·cac·u·an·ha** (ĭp′ĭ-kăk′yo͞o-ăn′ə) *n.* **1.a.** A low-growing tropical American shrub *(Cephaelis ipecacuanha)* having roots and rhizomes that yield emetine. **b.** The dried roots and rhizomes of this shrub. **2.** A medicinal preparation made from the dried roots and rhizomes of this shrub that is used to induce vomiting, particularly in cases of poisoning and drug overdose. [Short for Portuguese *ipecacuanha,* from Tupi *ipekaaguéne* : *ipeh,* low + *kaá,* leaves + *guéne,* vomit.]

Iph·i·ge·ni·a (ĭf′ə-jə-nī′ə, -nē′ə) *n. Greek Mythology.* The daughter of Clytemnestra and Agamemnon, who was offered as a sacrifice by Agamemnon but rescued by Artemis. She later became a priestess.

ipm *abbr.* Inches per minute.

I·poh (ē′pō). A city of western Malaysia north-northwest of Kuala Lumpur. It is a commercial center in a tin-mining area. Population, 300,325.

i·pro·ni·a·zid (ī′prə-nī′ə-zĭd) *n.* A compound, $C_9H_{13}N_3O$, used as an antidepressant and formerly used to treat tuberculosis. [I(SO)PRO(PYL ALCOHOL) + NI(COTINE) + AZ- + -ID.]

ips or **i.p.s.** *abbr.* Inches per second.

ip·se dix·it (ĭp′sē dĭk′sĭt) *n.* An unsupported assertion, usually by a person of standing; a dictum. [Latin *ipse dīxit,* he himself said (it) : *ipse,* he himself + *dīxit,* third person sing. perfect tense of *dīcere,* to say.]

ip·si·lat·er·al (ĭp′sə-lăt′ər-əl) *adj.* Located on or affecting the same side of the body. [Alteration of Latin *ipse,* self + LATERAL.] **—ip′si·lat′er·al·ly** *adv.*

ip·sis·si·ma ver·ba (ĭp-sĭs′ə-mə vûr′bə) *pl.n.* The very words. [New Latin : Latin *ipsissima,* the very, neuter pl. superlative of *ipse,* self + Latin *verba,* pl. of *verbum,* word.]

ip·so fac·to (ĭp′sō făk′tō) *adv.* By the fact itself; by that very fact: *An alien, ipso facto, has no right to a U.S. passport.* [New Latin *ipsō factō* : Latin *ipsō,* ablative of *ipse,* itself + Latin *factō,* ablative of *factum,* fact.]

ipso ju·re (jo͝or′ē) *adv. Law.* By the law itself. [New Latin *ipsō iūre* : Latin *ipsō,* ablative of *ipse,* itself + Latin *iūre,* ablative of *iūs,* law.]

Ips·wich (ĭp′swĭch′). A borough of eastern England near the North Sea northeast of London. It was a commercial and pottery-making center from the 7th to the 12th century and was later (16th century) important in the woolen trade. Population, 118,900.

IQ or **I.Q.** *abbr.* Intelligence quotient.

i.q. *abbr. Latin.* Idem quod (the same as).

I·qui·que (ĭ-kē′kĕ). A city of northwest Chile on the Pacific Ocean south of the Peruvian border. Founded in the 16th century, it was ceded to Chile by Peru in 1883. Population, 110,153.

I·qui·tos (ĭ-kē′tōs, ē-kē′tôs). A city of northeast Peru on the Amazon River northeast of Lima. It grew after a boom in wild rubber in the early 20th century. Population, 178,738.

Ir The symbol for the element **iridium.**

IR *abbr.* **1.** Information retrieval. **2.** Infrared.

Ir. *abbr.* Irish.

ir-¹ *pref.* Variant of **in-¹.**

ir-² *pref.* Variant of **in-².**

IRA *abbr.* **1.** Individual Retirement Account. **2.** Individual Retirement Arrangement. **3.** Also **I.R.A.** Irish Republican Army.

I·rá·kli·on (ĭ-rä′klē-ôn′) also **Can·di·a** (kăn′dē-ə). A city of southern Greece on the northern coast of Crete. It was founded by Saracens in the ninth century and passed to the Byzantines, Venetians, and Ottoman Turks before becoming part of Crete in 1913. Population, 102,398.

I·ran (ĭ-răn′, ĭ-rän′, ī-răn′). Formerly **Per·sia** (pûr′zhə, -shə). A country of southwest Asia. First inhabited c. 4000 B.C., the region was overrun (c. 2000) by Aryans, who later split into two groups, the Medes and the Persians. The Persian Empire was founded c. 550 B.C. by Cyrus the Great and dominated the surrounding area until the time of Alexander the Great. In World War II Russia and Great Britain occupied the country and installed Mohammed Reza Pahlevi as shah (1941). He was overthrown (1979) by a revolution led by the Ayatollah Khomeini. The name of the country was officially changed to Iran in 1935. Tehran is the capital and the largest city. Population, 40,777,000.

Iran

I·ra·ni·an (ĭ-rā′nē-ən, ĭ-rä′-, ī-rā′-) *adj.* Of or relating to Iran or its people, language, or culture. **—Iranian** *n.* **1.** A native or inhabitant of Iran. **2.** A branch of the Indo-European language family that includes Persian, Kurdish, Pashto, and other languages of Iran, Afghanistan, and western Pakistan.

I·ra·pua·to (îr′ə-pwä′tō, ē′rä-). A city of central Mexico east of Guadalajara. It is the commercial center of a mining and agricultural area. Population, 170,138.

I·raq (ĭ-răk′, ĭ-räk′). A country of southwest Asia. Site of a number of flourishing ancient Mesopotamian civilizations, Iraq fell to the Arabs (7th century) and later to the Ottoman Turks (16th century). It was established as an independent kingdom in 1921 and became a republic after the assassination (1958) of Faisal II. Baghdad is the capital and largest city. Population, 15,584,987.

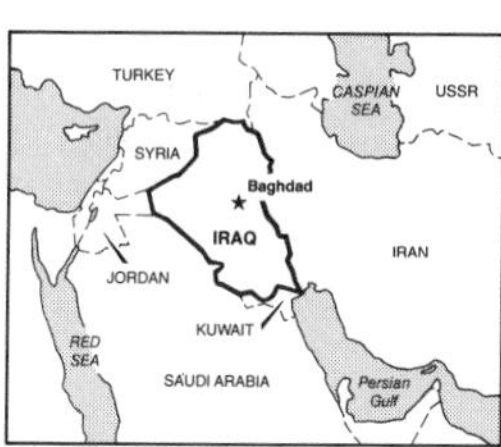

Iraq

I·ra·qi (ĭ-răk′ē, ĭ-rä′kē) *adj.* Of or relating to Iraq or its people, language, or culture. **—Iraqi** *n., pl.* **-qis. 1.** A native or inhabitant of Iraq. **2.** The modern dialect of Arabic spoken in Iraq.

i·ras·ci·ble (ĭ-răs′ə-bəl, ī-răs′-) *adj.* **1.** Prone to outbursts of temper; easily angered. **2.** Characterized by or resulting from anger. [Middle English, from Old French, from Late Latin *īrāscibilis,* from Latin *īrāscī,* to be angry, from *īra,* anger. See **eis-** in Appendix.] **—i·ras′ci·bil′i·ty, i·ras′ci·ble·ness** *n.* **—i·ras′ci·bly** *adv.*

i·rate (ī-rāt′, ī′rāt′) *adj.* **1.** Extremely angry; enraged. See Synonyms at **angry. 2.** Characterized or occasioned by anger: *an irate phone call.* [Latin *īrātus,* past participle of *īrāscī,* to be angry, from *īra,* anger. See **eis-** in Appendix.] **—i·rate′ly** *adv.* **—i·rate′ness** *n.*

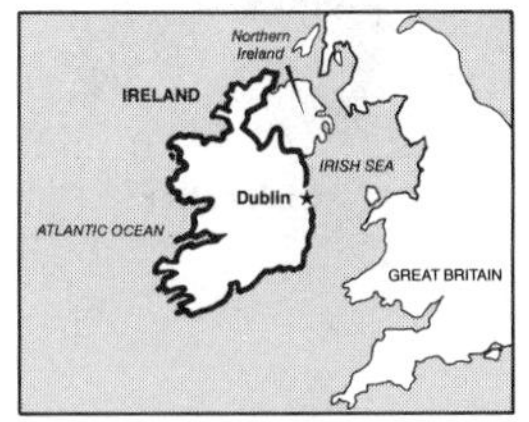

Ireland²

Ir·bil (îr′bĭl) also **Er·bil** (îr′bĭl, ĕr′-). A city of northern Iraq north of Baghdad. Built on the site of ancient Arbela, it is a trade center. Population, 333,903.

IRBM *abbr.* Intermediate-range ballistic missile.

ire (īr) *n.* Anger; wrath. See Synonyms at **anger.** [Middle English, from Old French, from Latin *īra.* See **eis-** in Appendix.]

Ire. *abbr.* Ireland.

Ire·dell (îr′dĕl′), **James.** 1751–1799. American jurist who served as an associate justice of the U.S. Supreme Court (1790–1799).

ire·ful (īr′fəl) *adj.* Full of ire; wrathful. See Synonyms at **angry. —ire′ful·ly** *adv.*

Ire·land¹ (īr′lənd). An island in the northern Atlantic Ocean west of Great Britain. The island was invaded by Celts c. 500 B.C. and converted to Christianity by Saint Patrick in the fifth century A.D. It joined Great Britain in 1801 but after the Easter Rebellion (1916) and a civil war (1919–1921) the island was split into the independent Irish Free State (now Ireland) and Northern Ireland, which is still allied with Great Britain.

Ire·land² (īr′lənd). Formerly **I·rish Free State** (ī′rĭsh) also

ă pat	oi boy
ā pay	ou out
âr care	o͝o took
ä father	o͞o boot
ĕ pet	ŭ cut
ē be	ûr urge
ĭ pit	th thin
ī pie	*th* this
îr pier	hw which
ŏ pot	zh vision
ō toe	ə about, item
ô paw	♦ regionalism

Stress marks: ′ (primary); ′ (secondary), as in **dictionary** (dĭk′shə-nĕr′ē)

iris

Irish moss
Chondrus crispus

Irish setter

Irish wolfhound

Eir·e (âr′ə, ī′rə, âr′ē, ī′rē). *Abbr.* **Ire.** A country occupying most of the island of Ireland. Established as the Irish Free State in 1922, Ireland officially became the sovereign state of Eire in 1937. The Republic of Ireland was proclaimed on Easter Monday (April 18), 1949. Dublin is the capital and the largest city. Population, 3,443,405.

Ireland, Northern. See **Northern Ireland.**

i·ren·ic (ī-rĕn′ĭk, ī-rē′nĭk) also **i·ren·i·cal** (-ĭ-kəl, -nĭ-kəl) *adj.* Promoting peace; conciliatory. [Greek *eirēnikos,* from *eirēnē,* peace.] **—i·ren′i·cal·ly** *adv.*

irid. *abbr.* Iridescent.

irid– *pref.* Variant of **irido–.**

ir·i·da·ceous (ĭr′ĭ-dā′shəs) *adj.* Of or belonging to the iris family. [From New Latin *Īridācea,* iris family, from *Īris, Īrid-,* type genus, from Latin *īris,* iris. See IRIS.]

ir·i·dec·to·my (ĭr′ĭ-dĕk′tə-mē, ī′rĭ-) *n., pl.* **-mies.** Surgical removal of part of the iris of the eye.

i·ri·des (ī′rĭ-dēz′, ĭr′ĭ-) *n.* A plural of **iris.**

ir·i·des·cence (ĭr′ĭ-dĕs′əns) *n.* The quality or state of being iridescent.

ir·i·des·cent (ĭr′ĭ-dĕs′ənt) *adj. Abbr.* **irid. 1.** Producing a display of lustrous, rainbowlike colors: *an iridescent oil slick; iridescent plumage.* **2.** Brilliant, lustrous, or colorful in effect or appearance: *"The prelude was as iridescent as a prism in a morning room"* (Carson McCullers). **—ir′i·des′cent·ly** *adv.*

i·rid·ic (ĭ-rĭd′ĭk, ī-rĭd′-) *adj.* Of or relating to the iris of the eye.

i·rid·i·um (ĭ-rĭd′ē-əm) *n. Symbol* **Ir** A very hard and brittle, exceptionally corrosion-resistant, whitish-yellow metallic element occurring in platinum ores and used principally to harden platinum and in high-temperature materials, electrical contacts, and wear-resistant bearings. Atomic number 77; atomic weight 192.2; melting point 2,410°C; boiling point 4,130°C; specific gravity 22.42 (at 17°C); valence 3, 4. See table at **element.** [Latin *īris, īrid-,* rainbow (from the colors produced by dissolving it in hydrochloric acid); see IRIDO– + –IUM.]

irido– or **irid–** *pref.* **1.** Rainbow: *iridescent.* **2.** Iris of the eye: *iridectomy.* **3.** Iridium: *iridosmine.* [Latin *īris, īrid-,* rainbow, from Greek *iris.* See **wei-** in Appendix.]

ir·i·dol·o·gy (ĭr′ĭ-dŏl′ə-jē, ī′rĭ-) *n.* The study of the iris of the eye, especially with regard to disease. **—ir′i·dol′o·gist** *n.*

ir·i·dos·mine (ĭr′ĭ-dŏz′mēn) *n.* See **osmiridium.** [IRID(O)– + OSM(IUM) + –INE².]

i·ris (ī′rĭs) *n., pl.* **i·ris·es** or **i·ri·des** (ī′rĭ-dēz′, ĭr′ĭ-). **1.** The pigmented, round, contractile membrane of the eye, suspended between the cornea and lens and perforated by the pupil. It regulates the amount of light entering the eye. **2.** Any of numerous plants of the genus *Iris,* having narrow sword-shaped leaves and showy, variously colored flowers. **3.** A rainbow or rainbowlike display of colors. [Middle English, rainbow, from Latin *īris, īrid-,* from Greek, rainbow, iris of the eye. See **wei-** in Appendix.]

I·ris (ī′rĭs) *n. Greek Mythology.* The goddess of the rainbow and messenger of the gods. [Latin *Īris,* from Greek. See **wei-** in Appendix.]

iris diaphragm *n.* A circular device with a variable diameter, commonly used on cameras to regulate the amount of light admitted to a lens.

I·rish (ī′rĭsh) *adj. Abbr.* **Ir.** Of or relating to Ireland or its people, language, or culture. **—Irish** *n. Abbr.* **Ir. 1.** The people of Ireland. **2.a.** See **Irish Gaelic. b.** See **Irish English. 3.** *Informal.* Fieriness of temper or passion; high spirit. [Middle English, from Old English *Īras,* the Irish. See **peie-** in Appendix.]

Irish bull *n.* A statement containing an incongruity or a logical absurdity, usually unbeknown to the speaker. "With a pistol in each hand and a sword in the other" is an Irish bull.

Irish coffee *n.* A beverage of sweetened hot coffee and Irish whiskey, topped with whipped cream.

Irish elk *n.* A large extinct European deer of the genus *Megaceros* of the Pliocene Epoch and the Pleistocene Epoch, having very large palmate antlers.

Irish English *n.* English as spoken by the Irish. Also called *Anglo-Irish, Hiberno-English, Irish.*

Irish Free State. See **Ireland².**

Irish Gaelic *n.* The Goidelic language of Ireland. Also called *Erse, Irish.*

I·rish·ism (ī′rĭsh-ĭz′əm) *n.* An Irish idiom or custom.

I·rish·man (ī′rĭsh-mən) *n.* A man of Irish birth or ancestry.

Irish moss *n.* An edible North Atlantic seaweed *(Chondrus crispus)* that yields a mucilaginous substance used medicinally and in preparing jellies. Also called *carrageen.*

I·rish·ry (ī′rĭsh-rē) *n., pl.* **-ries. 1.** The Irish people, especially those of Celtic descent. **2.a.** Irish character. **b.** An Irish trait, custom, or locution; an Irishism.

Irish Sea. An arm of the northern Atlantic Ocean between Ireland and Great Britain.

Irish setter *n.* Any of a breed of setters having a silky reddish-brown coat.

Irish stew *n.* A stew of meat and vegetables.

Irish terrier *n.* Any of a breed of terriers having a wiry reddish-brown coat.

Irish whiskey *n.* Whiskey made by the distillation of barley.

Irish wolfhound *n.* Any of an ancient breed of large powerful dogs having a rough, shaggy coat.

I·rish·wom·an (ī′rĭsh-wo͝om′ən) *n.* A woman of Irish birth or ancestry.

i·ri·tis (ī-rī′tĭs) *n.* Inflammation of the iris of the eye. [IR(IS) + –ITIS.] **—i·rit′ic** (ī-rĭt′ĭk) *adj.*

irk (ûrk) *tr.v.* **irked, irk·ing, irks.** To be irritating, wearisome, or vexing to. See Synonyms at **annoy.** [Middle English *irken,* to weary, possibly from Old Norse *yrkja,* to work, make verses, harangue. See **werg-** in Appendix.]

irk·some (ûrk′səm) *adj.* Causing annoyance, weariness, or vexation; tedious: *irksome restrictions.* See Synonyms at **boring. —irk′some·ly** *adv.* **—irk′some·ness** *n.*

Ir·kutsk (ĭr-ko͞otsk′). A city of south-central Russia near the southern end of Lake Baikal. It is an industrial center and a major stop on the Trans-Siberian Railroad. Population, 597,000.

IRO *abbr.* International Refugee Organization.

i·ron (ī′ərn) *n.* **1.** *Symbol* **Fe** A silvery-white, lustrous, malleable, ductile, magnetic or magnetizable, metallic element occurring abundantly in combined forms, notably in hematite, limonite, magnetite, and taconite, and used alloyed in a wide range of important structural materials. Atomic number 26; atomic weight 55.847; melting point 1,535°C; boiling point 2,750°C; specific gravity 7.874 (at 20°C); valence 2, 3, 4, 6. See table at **element. 2.** An implement made of iron alloy or similar metal, especially a bar heated for use in branding, curling hair, or cauterizing. **3.** Great hardness or strength; firmness: *a will of iron.* **4.** *Sports.* A golf club with a metal head, numbered from one to nine in order of increasing loft. **5.** A metal appliance with a handle and a weighted flat bottom, used when heated to press wrinkles from fabric. **6.** A harpoon. **7. irons.** Fetters; shackles. **8.** A tonic, pill, or other medication containing iron and taken as a dietary supplement. **—iron** *adj.* **1.** Made of or containing iron: *iron bars; an iron alloy.* **2.** Very hard and strong: *an iron fist.* **3.** Hardy; robust: *an iron constitution.* **4.** Inflexible; unyielding: *iron resolve.* **—iron** *v.* **i·roned, i·ron·ing, i·rons.** *—tr.* **1.a.** To press and smooth with a heated iron: *iron clothes.* **b.** To remove (creases) by pressing. **2.** To put into irons; fetter. **3.** To fit or clad with iron. *—intr.* To iron clothes. ***—phrasal verb.* iron out.** To settle through discussion or compromise; work out. ***—idiom.* iron in the fire.** An undertaking or project in progress: *has many irons in the fire this year.* [Middle English *iren,* from Old English *īren.* See **eis-** in Appendix.]

I·ron Age (ī′ərn) *n.* The period in human cultural development succeeding the Bronze Age, characterized by the introduction of iron metallurgy and in Europe beginning around the eighth century B.C.

iron blue *n.* Any of various light-resistant and heat-resistant, semitransparent blue pigments of powerful tinctorial strength, used chiefly in permanent industrial finishes, printing inks, and artists' colors. Also called *Prussian blue.*

i·ron·bound (ī′ərn-bound′) *adj.* **1.** Bound with iron. **2.** Rigid and unyielding: *an ironbound moral code.* **3.** Bound with rocks and cliffs: *ironbound coasts.*

i·ron·clad (ī′ərn-klăd′) *adj.* **1.** Sheathed with iron plates for protection. **2.** Rigid; fixed: *an ironclad rule.* **—ironclad** *n. Nautical.* A 19th-century warship having sides armored with metal plates.

iron curtain *n.* **1.** Often **Iron Curtain.** The military, political, and ideological barrier established between the Soviet bloc and western Europe after World War II. **2.** A barrier that prevents free exchange of ideas and information: *"That department and the editorial department are separated by an almost impenetrable iron curtain"* (Brendan Gill).

I·ron·de·quoit (ĭ-rŏn′dĭ-kwoit′, -kwŏt′). A town of western New York west of Rochester. It was settled in 1791. Population, 57,648.

Iron Gate. A narrow gorge of the Danube River on the border of Yugoslavia and Romania. Created by a gap between the Carpathian and Balkan mountains, the gorge is bypassed by a ship canal (opened in 1896) to allow navigation by large river craft.

iron gray *n. Color.* A dark gray with a slightly greenish tinge.

iron hand *n.* Rigorous or despotic control: *ruled the nation with an iron hand.* **—i′ron·hand′ed** (ī′ərn-hăn′dĭd) *adj.* **—i′ron·hand′ed·ness** *n.*

iron horse *n. Informal.* A railroad locomotive.

i·ron·ic (ī-rŏn′ĭk) also **i·ron·i·cal** (ī-rŏn′ĭ-kəl) *adj.* **1.** Characterized by or constituting irony. **2.** Given to the use of irony. See Synonyms at **sarcastic. 3.** Poignantly contrary to what was expected or intended: *madness, an ironic fate for such a clear thinker.* **—i·ron′i·cal·ly** *adv.* **—i·ron′i·cal·ness** *n.*

USAGE NOTE: The words *ironic, irony,* and *ironically* are sometimes used of events and circumstances that might better be described as simply "coincidental" or "improbable," in that they suggest no particular lessons about human vanity or folly. Thus 78 percent of the Usage Panel rejects the use of *ironically* in the sentence *In 1969 Susie moved from Ithaca to California where she met her husband-to-be, who, ironically, also came from upstate New York* (though some Panelists noted that this particular usage might be acceptable if Susie had in fact moved to California in order to find a husband, in which case the story could be taken as exemplifying the folly of supposing that we can know what fate has in store for us). By contrast, 73 percent accepted the sentence

Ironically, even as the government was fulminating against American policy, American jeans and videocassettes were the hottest items in the stalls of the market, where the incongruity can be seen as an example of human inconsistency.

---

i·ron·ing (ī′ər-nĭng) *n.* **1.** The act or process of pressing clothes with a heated iron. **2.** The clothing pressed or to be pressed with a heated iron.

ironing board *n.* A long, narrow padded board, often with collapsible supporting legs, used as a working surface for ironing.

i·ro·nist (ī′rə-nĭst) *n.* A notable user of irony, especially a writer.

iron lung *n.* An airtight metal tank that encloses all of the body except the head and forces the lungs to inhale and exhale through regulated changes in air pressure.

iron maiden *n.* A medieval instrument of torture consisting of an iron frame in the form of a person in which the victim was enclosed and impaled on interior spikes.

i·ron·mon·ger (ī′ərn-mŭng′gər, -mŏng′-) *n. Chiefly British.* A hardware merchant.

i·ron·mon·ger·y (ī′ərn-mŭng′gə-rē, -mŏng′-) *n., pl.* **-ies.** *Chiefly British.* **1.** Ironware. **2.** The shop or business of an ironmonger.

iron oxide *n.* Any of various oxides of iron, such as ferric oxide or ferrous oxide.

iron pyrites *n.* See **pyrite.**

i·ron·smith (ī′ərn-smĭth′) *n.* One that makes iron articles; a blacksmith.

i·ron·stone (ī′ərn-stōn′) *n.* **1.** A hard white pottery. **2.** A rock containing enough iron to permit commercial extraction; an iron ore.

i·ron·ware (ī′ərn-wâr′) *n.* Iron utensils and other products made of iron.

i·ron·weed (ī′ərn-wēd′) *n.* Any of various plants of the genus *Vernonia,* having alternate leaves and clusters of purplish flower heads.

i·ron·wood (ī′ərn-wo͝od′) *n.* **1.** Any of numerous trees, such as the hornbeam and the hop hornbeam, that have very hard wood. **2.** The wood of any of these trees.

i·ron·work (ī′ərn-wûrk′) *n.* Work in iron, such as gratings and rails.

i·ron·work·er (ī′ərn-wûr′kər) *n.* **1.** A construction worker who builds steel structures. **2.** One who is employed in an ironworks. **3.** One who makes iron articles.

i·ron·works (ī′ərn-wûrks′) *pl.n.* *(used with a sing. or pl. verb).* A building or an establishment where iron is smelted or where heavy iron products are made.

i·ro·ny (ī′rə-nē, ī′ər-) *n., pl.* **-nies. 1.a.** The use of words to express something different from and often opposite to their literal meaning. **b.** An expression or utterance marked by a deliberate contrast between apparent and intended meaning. **c.** A literary style employing such contrasts for humorous or rhetorical effect. See Synonyms at **wit[1]**. **2.a.** Incongruity between what might be expected and what actually occurs: *"Hyde noted the irony of Ireland's copying the nation she most hated"* (Richard Kain). **b.** An occurrence, a result, or a circumstance notable for such incongruity. See Usage Note at **ironic. 3.** Dramatic irony. **4.** Socratic irony. [French *ironie,* from Old French, from Latin *īrōnīa,* from Greek *eirōneia,* feigned ignorance, from *eirōn,* dissembler, probably from *eirein,* to say. See **wer-[5]** in Appendix.]

Ir·o·quoi·an (ĭr′ə-kwoi′ən) *n.* **1.** A family of North American Indian languages of the eastern part of Canada and the United States that includes Cayuga, Mohawk, Oneida, Onondaga, Seneca, Tuscarora, Cherokee, Erie, Huron, and Wyandot. **2.** A member of an Iroquoian-speaking people. **—Iroquoian** *adj.* Of or constituting the Iroquoian language family.

Ir·o·quois (ĭr′ə-kwoi′) *n., pl.* **Iroquois** (-kwoi′, -kwoiz′). **1.a.** A Native American confederacy inhabiting New York State and originally composed of the Mohawk, Oneida, Onondaga, Cayuga, and Seneca peoples, known as the Five Nations. After 1722 the confederacy was joined by the Tuscaroras to form the Six Nations. Also called *Iroquois League.* **b.** A member of this confederacy or of any of its peoples. **2.** Any or all of the languages of the Iroquois. [Origin unknown.] **—Ir′o·quois′** *adj.*

ir·ra·di·ant (ĭ-rā′dē-ənt) *adj.* Sending forth radiant light. [Latin *irradiāns, irradiant-,* present participle of *irradiāre,* to shine forth. See IRRADIATE.] **—ir·ra′di·ance, ir·ra′di·an·cy** *n.*

ir·ra·di·ate (ĭ-rā′dē-āt′) *v.* **-at·ed, -at·ing, -ates.** *—tr.* **1.a.** To expose to radiation. **b.** To treat with radiation: *irradiate farm produce so as to destroy bacteria.* **2.** To shed light on; illuminate. **3.** To manifest in a manner suggesting the emission of light; radiate: *irradiate goodness.* *—intr. Archaic.* **1.** To send forth rays; radiate. **2.** To become radiant. [Latin *irradiāre, irradiāt-,* to illuminate : *in-,* on; see IN–[2] + *radiāre,* to shine; see RADIATE.] **—ir·ra′di·a′tive** *adj.* **—ir·ra′di·a′tor** *n.*

ir·ra·di·a·tion (ĭ-rā′dē-ā′shən) *n.* **1.** The act of exposing to radiation or the condition of being so exposed. **2.** Therapy or treatment by exposure to radiation.

ir·rad·i·ca·ble (ĭ-răd′ĭ-kə-bəl) *adj.* Impossible to uproot or destroy; ineradicable: *irradicable weeds; irradicable prejudices.* [Medieval Latin *irrādīcābilis* : Latin *in-,* not; see IN–[1] + Latin *rādīx, rādīc-,* root; see ERADICATE.] **—ir·rad′i·ca·bly** *adv.*

ir·ra·tion·al (ĭ-răsh′ə-nəl) *adj.* **1.a.** Not endowed with reason. **b.** Affected by loss of usual or normal mental clarity; incoherent, as from shock. **c.** Marked by a lack of accord with reason or sound judgment: *an irrational dislike.* See Synonyms at **meaningless, unreasonable. 2.a.** Being a syllable in Greek and Latin prosody whose length does not fit the metric pattern. **b.** Being a metric foot containing such a syllable. **3.** *Mathematics.* Of or relating to an irrational number. **—ir·ra′tion·al·ly** *adv.* **—ir·ra′tion·al·ness** *n.*

ir·ra·tion·al·ism (ĭ-răsh′ə-nə-lĭz′əm) *n.* **1.** Irrational thought, expression, or behavior; irrationality. **2.** Belief in feeling, instinct, or other nonrational forces rather than reason.

ir·ra·tion·al·i·ty (ĭ-răsh′ə-năl′ĭ-tē) *n., pl.* **-ties. 1.** The state or quality of being irrational. **2.** An irrational idea, expression, or act.

irrational number *n.* Any real number that cannot be expressed as an integer or as a ratio between two integers.

Ir·ra·wad·dy (ĭr′ə-wŏd′ē, -wô′dē). A river of Burma flowing about 1,609 km (1,000 mi) southward to the Bay of Bengal and the Andaman Sea. It is the chief river of the country.

ir·re·claim·a·ble (ĭr′ĭ-klā′mə-bəl) *adj.* Impossible to reclaim; being such that reclamation is precluded: *irreclaimable wasteland.* **—ir′re·claim′a·bil′i·ty, ir′re·claim′a·ble·ness** *n.* **—ir′re·claim′a·bly** *adv.*

ir·rec·on·cil·a·ble (ĭ-rĕk′ən-sī′lə-bəl, ĭ-rĕk′ən-sī′-) *adj.* Impossible to reconcile: *irreconcilable differences.* **—irreconcilable** *n.* **1.** A person, especially a member of a group, who will not compromise, adjust, or submit. **2.** One of two or more conflicting ideas or beliefs that cannot be brought into harmony. **—ir·rec′on·cil′a·bil′i·ty** *n.* **—ir·rec′on·cil′a·bly** *adv.*

ir·re·cov·er·a·ble (ĭr′ĭ-kŭv′ər-ə-bəl) *adj.* Impossible to recover; irreparable: *irrecoverable losses.* **—ir′re·cov′er·a·ble·ness** *n.* **—ir′re·cov′er·a·bly** *adv.*

ir·re·cu·sa·ble (ĭr′ĭ-kyo͞o′zə-bəl) *adj.* Not subject to challenge or objection: *an irrecusable premise.* [French *irrécusable,* from Late Latin *irrecūsābilis* : Latin *in-,* not; see IN–[1] + *recūsābilis,* deserving of rejection (from Latin *recūsāre,* to refuse; see RECUSE).] **—ir′re·cu′sa·bly** *adv.*

ir·re·deem·a·ble (ĭr′ĭ-dē′mə-bəl) *adj.* **1.** That cannot be bought back or paid off: *an irredeemable annuity.* **2.** Not convertible into coin. **3.** Impossible to remedy: *irredeemable losses.* **4.** Impossible to redeem or reform: *an irredeemable evil.* **—ir′re·deem′a·bly** *adv.*

ir·re·den·tist (ĭr′ĭ-dĕn′tĭst) *n.* One who advocates the recovery of territory culturally or historically related to one's nation but now subject to a foreign government. [Italian *irredentista,* from *(Italia) irredenta,* unredeemed (Italy), Italian-speaking areas subject to other countries, feminine of *irredento* : *in-,* not (from Latin *in-;* see IN–[1]) + *redento,* redeemed (from Latin *redemptus,* past participle of *redimere,* to redeem; see REDEEM).] **—ir′re·den′tism** *n.* **—ir′re·den′tist** *adj.*

ir·re·duc·i·ble (ĭr′ĭ-do͞o′sə-bəl, -dyo͞o′-) *adj.* Impossible to reduce to a desired, simpler, or smaller form or amount: *irreducible burdens.* **—ir′re·duc′i·bil′i·ty, ir′re·duc′i·ble·ness** *n.* **—ir′re·duc′i·bly** *adv.*

ir·ref·ra·ga·ble (ĭ-rĕf′rə-gə-bəl) *adj.* Impossible to refute or controvert; indisputable: *irrefragable evidence.* [Late Latin *irrefrāgābilis* : Latin *in-,* not; see IN–[1] + Latin *refrāgārī,* to oppose, resist; see **bhreg-** in Appendix.] **—ir·ref′ra·ga·bil′i·ty** *n.* **—ir·ref′ra·ga·bly** *adv.*

ir·re·fran·gi·ble (ĭr′ĭ-frăn′jə-bəl) *adj.* **1.** Impossible to break; indestructible: *irrefrangible cooking ware.* **2.** *Physics.* That cannot be refracted. **—ir′re·fran′gi·bly** *adv.*

ir·ref·u·ta·ble (ĭ-rĕf′yə-tə-bəl, ĭr′ĭ-fyo͞o′-) *adj.* Impossible to refute or disprove; incontrovertible: *irrefutable arguments; irrefutable evidence of guilt.* **—ir·ref′u·ta·bil′i·ty** *n.* **—ir·ref′u·ta·bly** *adv.*

irreg. *abbr.* Irregular.

ir·re·gard·less (ĭr′ĭ-gärd′lĭs) *adv. Non-Standard.* Regardless. [Perhaps from IR(RESPECTIVE) + REGARDLESS.]

USAGE NOTE: The label *Non-Standard* does only approximate justice to the status of *irregardless.* More precisely, it is a form that many people mistakenly believe to be a correct usage in formal style but that in fact has no legitimate antecedents in either standard or nonstandard varieties. (The word was likely coined from a blend of *irrespective* and *regardless.*) Perhaps this is why critics have sometimes insisted that there is "no such word" as *irregardless,* a charge they would not level at a bona fide nonstandard word such as *ain't,* which has an ancient genealogy.

---

ir·reg·u·lar (ĭ-rĕg′yə-lər) *adj. Abbr.* **irreg. 1.** Contrary to rule, accepted order, or general practice: *irregular hiring practices.* **2.** Not conforming to legality, moral law, or social convention: *an irregular marriage.* **3.** Not straight, uniform, or symmetrical: *irregular facial features.* **4.** Of uneven rate, occurrence, or duration: *an irregular heartbeat.* **5.** Deviating from a type; atypical. **6.** *Botany.* Having differing floral parts, as of a zygomorphic or asymmetrical flower. **7.** Falling below the manufacturer's standard or usual specifications; imperfect. **8.** *Grammar.* Departing from the usual pattern of inflection, derivation, or word formation, as the present forms of the verb *be* or the plural noun *children.* **9.** Not belonging to a permanent, organized military force: *irregular troops.* **—irregular** *n.* **1.** One, such as an item of merchandise, that is irregular. **2.** A soldier, such as a guerrilla,

ironwork
Window grille

ă pat	oi boy
ā pay	ou out
âr care	o͝o took
ä father	o͞o boot
ĕ pet	ŭ cut
ē be	ûr urge
ĭ pit	th thin
ī pie	*th* this
îr pier	hw which
ŏ pot	zh vision
ō toe	ə about, item
ô paw	♦ regionalism

Stress marks: ′ (primary); ′ (secondary), as in **dictionary** (dĭk′shə-nĕr′ē)

who is not a member of a regular military force. **—ir·reg′u·lar·ly** *adv.*

ir·reg·u·lar·i·ty (ĭ-rĕg′yə-lăr′ĭ-tē) *n., pl.* **-ties. 1.** The quality or state of being irregular. **2.** Something irregular: *found the firm's books riddled with irregularities.* **3.** Constipation.

ir·rel·a·tive (ĭ-rĕl′ə-tĭv) *adj.* **1.** Having no correlative relationship; unconnected. **2.** Irrelevant. **—ir·rel′a·tive·ly** *adv.*

ir·rel·e·vance (ĭ-rĕl′ə-vəns) *n.* **1.** The quality or state of being unrelated to the matter at hand. **2.** Something unrelated to the matter at hand.

ir·rel·e·van·cy (ĭ-rĕl′ə-vən-sē) *n., pl.* **-cies.** Irrelevance.

ir·rel·e·vant (ĭ-rĕl′ə-vənt) *adj.* Unrelated to the matter at hand. **—ir·rel′e·vant·ly** *adv.*

SYNONYMS: *irrelevant, extraneous, immaterial, impertinent.* The central meaning shared by these adjectives is "not pertinent to the subject under consideration": *an irrelevant comment; a question extraneous to the discussion; an objection that is immaterial after the fact; mentioned several impertinent facts before finally coming to the point.*
ANTONYM: *relevant.*

irrigate
Irrigation of a barley field in Wyoming

ir·re·lig·ion (ĭr′ĭ-lĭj′ən) *n.* Hostility or indifference to religion.

ir·re·lig·ious (ĭr′ĭ-lĭj′əs) *adj.* Hostile or indifferent to religion; ungodly. **—ir′re·lig′ious·ly** *adv.* **—ir′re·lig′ious·ness** *n.*

ir·re·me·a·ble (ĭ-rē′mē-ə-bəl) *adj. Archaic.* Affording no possibility of return. [Latin *irremeābilis* : *in-*, not; see IN–[1] + *remeāre*, to return (*re-*, re- + *meāre*, to go; see **mei-**[1] in Appendix).]

ir·re·me·di·a·ble (ĭr′ĭ-mē′dē-ə-bəl) *adj.* Impossible to remedy, correct, or repair; incurable or irreparable: *irremediable errors in judgment.* **—ir′re·me′di·a·bly** *adv.*

ir·re·mis·si·ble (ĭr′ĭ-mĭs′ə-bəl) *adj.* Not remissible; unpardonable: *irremissible sins.* **—ir′re·mis′si·bil′i·ty** *n.* **—ir′re·mis′si·bly** *adv.*

ir·re·mov·a·ble (ĭr′ĭ-mo͞o′və-bəl) *adj.* Impossible to remove: *irremovable boulders; irremovable obstacles.* **—ir′re·mov′a·bil′i·ty** *n.* **—ir′re·mov′a·bly** *adv.*

ir·rep·a·ra·ble (ĭ-rĕp′ər-ə-bəl) *adj.* Impossible to repair, rectify, or amend: *irreparable harm; irreparable damages.* [Middle English, from Old French, from Latin *irreparābilis* : *in-*, not; see IN–[1] + *reparābilis*, reparable; see REPARABLE.] **—ir·rep′a·ra·bil′i·ty, ir·rep′a·ra·ble·ness** *n.* **—ir·rep′a·ra·bly** *adv.*

ir·re·peal·a·ble (ĭr′ĭ-pē′lə-bəl) *adj.* Impossible to repeal: *irrepealable laws.*

ir·re·place·a·ble (ĭr′ĭ-plā′sə-bəl) *adj.* Impossible to replace: *irreplaceable antiques.* **—ir′re·place′a·bil′i·ty, ir′re·place′a·ble·ness** *n.* **—ir′re·place′a·bly** *adv.*

ir·re·press·i·ble (ĭr′ĭ-prĕs′ə-bəl) *adj.* Difficult or impossible to control or restrain: *irrepressible laughter.* **—ir′re·press′i·bil′i·ty, ir′re·press′i·ble·ness** *n.* **—ir′re·press′i·bly** *adv.*

ir·re·proach·a·ble (ĭr′ĭ-prō′chə-bəl) *adj.* Perfect or blameless in every respect; faultless: *irreproachable conduct.* **—ir′re·proach′a·bil′i·ty, ir′re·proach′a·ble·ness** *n.* **—ir′re·proach′a·bly** *adv.*

Washington Irving
1832 engraving by Hatch (1805?–1867) and Smillie (1807–1885)

ir·re·sis·ti·ble (ĭr′ĭ-zĭs′tə-bəl) *adj.* **1.** Impossible to resist: *an irresistible impulse to sneeze.* **2.** Having an overpowering appeal: *irresistible beauty.* **—ir′re·sis′ti·bil′i·ty, ir′re·sis′ti·ble·ness** *n.* **—ir′re·sis′ti·bly** *adv.*

ir·re·sol·u·ble (ĭr′ĭ-zŏl′yə-bəl) *adj.* Impossible to resolve: *irresoluble conflicts.* [Latin *irresolūbilis* : *in-*, not; see IN–[1] + *resolvere, resolūt-*, to untie; see RESOLVE.]

ir·res·o·lute (ĭ-rĕz′ə-lo͞ot′) *adj.* **1.** Unsure of how to act or proceed; undecided. **2.** Lacking in resolution; indecisive. **—ir·res′o·lute′ly** *adv.* **—ir·res′o·lute′ness, ir·res′o·lu′tion** *n.*

ir·re·solv·a·ble (ĭr′ĭ-zŏl′və-bəl) *adj.* **1.** Irresoluble. **2.** Impossible to separate into component parts; irreducible.

ir·re·spec·tive (ĭr′ĭ-spĕk′tĭv) *adj. Archaic.* Characterized by disregard; heedless. **—ir′re·spec′tive·ly** *adv.*

irrespective of *prep.* Without consideration of; regardless of.

ir·res·pi·ra·ble (ĭ-rĕs′pər-ə-bəl, ĭr′ĭ-spīr′-) *adj.* Not fit for breathing; not respirable.

ir·re·spon·si·ble (ĭr′ĭ-spŏn′sə-bəl) *adj.* **1.** Marked by a lack of responsibility: *irresponsible accusations.* **2.** Lacking a sense of responsibility; unreliable or untrustworthy. **3.** *Law.* Not mentally or financially fit to assume responsibility. **4.** Not liable to be called to account by a higher authority. **—irresponsible** *n.* **1.** One who has no sense of responsibility. **2.** *Law.* One who is mentally or financially unfit to assume responsibility for one's actions. **3.** One who is unlikely to be called to account by a higher authority. **—ir′re·spon′si·bil′i·ty, ir′re·spon′si·ble·ness** *n.* **—ir′re·spon′si·bly** *adv.*

ir·re·spon·sive (ĭr′ĭ-spŏn′sĭv) *adj.* **1.** Not responsive, as to treatment or stimuli. **2.** Not responding or answering readily. **—ir′re·spon′sive·ly** *adv.* **—ir′re·spon′sive·ness** *n.*

Isabella I

ir·re·triev·a·ble (ĭr′ĭ-trē′və-bəl) *adj.* Difficult or impossible to retrieve or recover: *When the diamond fell into the lake, it was virtually irretrievable.* **—ir′re·triev′a·ble·ness, ir′re·triev′a·bil′i·ty** *n.* **—ir′re·triev′a·bly** *adv.*

ir·rev·er·ence (ĭ-rĕv′ər-əns) *n.* **1.** Lack of reverence or due respect. **2.** A disrespectful act or remark.

ir·rev·er·ent (ĭ-rĕv′ər-ənt) *adj.* **1.** Lacking or exhibiting a lack of reverence; disrespectful. **2.** Critical of what is generally accepted or respected; satirical: *irreverent humor.* **—ir·rev′er·ent·ly** *adv.*

ir·re·vers·i·ble (ĭr′ĭ-vûr′sə-bəl) *adj.* Impossible to reverse: *an irreversible momentum toward revolution.* **—ir′re·vers′i·bil′i·ty, ir′re·vers′i·ble·ness** *n.* **—ir′re·vers′i·bly** *adv.*

ir·rev·o·ca·ble (ĭ-rĕv′ə-kə-bəl) *adj.* Impossible to retract or revoke: *an irrevocable decision.* **—ir·rev′o·ca·bil′i·ty, ir·rev′o·ca·ble·ness** *n.* **—ir·rev′o·ca·bly** *adv.*

ir·ri·ga·ble (ĭr′ĭ-gə-bəl) *adj.* That can be irrigated: *irrigable desert.*

ir·ri·gate (ĭr′ĭ-gāt′) *v.* **-gat·ed, -gat·ing, -gates.** *—tr.* **1.** To supply (dry land) with water by means of ditches, pipes, or streams; water artificially. **2.** To wash out (a body cavity or wound) with water or a medicated fluid. **3.** To make fertile or vital as if by watering. *—intr.* To supply land with water artificially. [Latin *irrigāre, irrigāt-* : *in-*, in; see IN–[2] + *rigāre*, to water.] **—ir′ri·ga′tion** *n.* **—ir′ri·ga′tion·al** *adj.* **—ir′ri·ga′tor** *n.*

ir·ri·ta·bil·i·ty (ĭr′ĭ-tə-bĭl′ĭ-tē) *n., pl.* **-ties. 1.** The quality or state of being irritable; testiness or petulance. **2.** *Pathology.* Abnormal or excessive sensitivity of a body organ or part to a stimulus. **3.** *Physiology.* The capacity to respond to stimuli.

ir·ri·ta·ble (ĭr′ĭ-tə-bəl) *adj.* **1.** Easily irritated or annoyed. **2.** *Pathology.* Abnormally sensitive to a stimulus. **3.** *Physiology.* Capable of responding to stimuli. [French *irritable*, from Latin *irrītābilis*, from *irrītāre*, to irritate.] **—ir′ri·ta·ble·ness** *n.* **—ir′ri·ta·bly** *adv.*

ir·ri·tant (ĭr′ĭ-tənt) *adj.* Causing irritation, especially physical irritation. **—irritant** *n.* A source of irritation: *tobacco smoke, a common eye irritant.* [French, from Latin *irrītāns, irrītant-*, present participle of *irrītāre*, to irritate.]

ir·ri·tate (ĭr′ĭ-tāt′) *v.* **-tat·ed, -tat·ing, -tates.** *—tr.* **1.** To rouse to impatience or anger; annoy: *a loud bossy voice that irritates listeners.* See Synonyms at **annoy. 2.** To chafe or inflame. *—intr.* To be a cause of impatience or anger. [Latin *irrītāre, irrītāt-*.] **—ir′ri·tat′ing·ly** *adv.* **—ir′ri·ta′tor** *n.*

ir·ri·ta·tion (ĭr′ĭ-tā′shən) *n.* **1.a.** The act of irritating. **b.** The condition of being irritated; vexation: *honked the horn with irritation at the delay.* **2.** A source of irritation. **3.** *Pathology.* A condition of inflammation, soreness, or irritability of a bodily organ or part.

ir·ri·ta·tive (ĭr′ĭ-tā′tĭv) *adj.* Involving irritation.

ir·ro·ta·tion·al (ĭr′ō-tā′shə-nəl) *adj.* Not rotating or involving rotation.

ir·rupt (ĭ-rŭpt′) *intr.v.* **-rupt·ed, -rupt·ing, -rupts. 1.** To break or burst in. **2.** *Ecology.* To increase rapidly and irregularly in number: *In the absence of predators, the island's rodent population irrupted.* [Latin *irrumpere, irrupt-* : *in-*, in; see IN–[2] + *rumpere*, to break; see **reup-** in Appendix.] **—ir·rup′tion** *n.*

ir·rup·tive (ĭ-rŭp′tĭv) *adj.* **1.** Irrupting or tending to irrupt. **2.** *Geology.* Intrusive.

IRS *abbr.* Internal Revenue Service.

Ir·tysh or **Ir·tish** (ĭr-tĭsh′). A river of northwest China, eastern Kazakhstan, and central Russia flowing about 4,264 km (2,650 mi) generally northwest to the Ob River.

Ir·vine (ûr′vīn′). A city of southern California southeast of Santa Ana. A branch of the University of California (opened 1965) is here. Population, 62,134.

Ir·ving (ûr′vĭng). A town of northeast Texas, an industrial suburb of Dallas. Population, 109,943.

Irving, Sir **Henry.** 1838–1905. British Shakespearean actor whose productions won him the first knighthood awarded to a member of his profession (1895).

Irving, John. Born 1942. American writer. His darkly humorous novels include *The World According to Garp* (1978).

Irving, Washington. 1783–1859. American writer remembered for the stories "Rip Van Winkle" and "The Legend of Sleepy Hollow," contained in *The Sketch Book* (1819–1820).

Ir·ving·ton (ûr′vĭng-tən). A town of northeast New Jersey, a residential and industrial suburb of Newark. It was settled in 1692 as Camptown and renamed in 1852 in honor of Washington Irving. Population, 61,493.

is (ĭz) *v.* Third person singular present indicative of **be.** [Middle English, from Old English. See **es-** in Appendix.]

is. or **Is.** *abbr.* Island.

Is. *abbr. Bible.* Isaiah.

is– *pref.* Variant of **iso–.**

Isa. *abbr. Bible.* Isaiah.

I·saac (ī′zək). In the Old Testament, the son of Abraham who was offered as a sacrifice to God. The sacrifice was prevented at the last moment by divine intervention.

Is·a·bel·la I (ĭz′ə-bĕl′ə). Known as "Isabella the Catholic." 1451–1504. Queen of Castile (1474–1504). Her marriage in 1469 to Ferdinand V of Castile and León (later Ferdinand II of Aragon) marked the beginning of a unified Spanish state. Isabella sponsored the voyages of Christopher Columbus.

I·sa·iah (ī-zā′ə, ī-zī′ə) *n. Bible.* **1.** A Hebrew prophet of the eighth century B.C. **2.** *Abbr.* **Isa., Is.** See table at **Bible.**

i·sal·lo·bar (ī-săl′ə-bär′) *n.* A line on a weather map connecting places having equal changes in atmospheric pressure within a given period of time. [ɪs(o)– + ALLO– + Greek *baros,* weight; see **gʷerə-**[1] in Appendix.]

–i·sa·tion *suff.* Variant of **–ization.**

ISBN *abbr.* International Standard Book Number.

is·che·mi·a (ĭ-skē′mē-ə) *n.* A decrease in the blood supply to a bodily organ, tissue, or part caused by constriction or obstruction of the blood vessels. [New Latin *ischaemia,* from Greek *iskhaimos,* a stopping of the blood : *iskhein,* to keep back; see **segh-** in Appendix + *haima,* blood.] **—i·sche′mic** *adj.*

is·chi·a (ĭs′kē-ə) *n.* Plural of **ischium.**

Is·chi·a (ĭs′kē-ə, ē′skyä). An island of southern Italy in the Tyrrhenian Sea at the entrance to the Bay of Naples.

is·chi·um (ĭs′kē-əm) *n., pl.* **-chi·a** (-kē-ə). The lowest of the three major bones that constitute each half of the pelvis. [Latin, hip joint, from Greek *iskhion.*] **—is′chi·al** (-əl) *adj.*

–ise *suff.* Variant of **–ize.**

I·se Bay (ē′sā, ē′sĕ′). An arm of the Pacific Ocean on the south-central coast of Honshu, Japan. The city of **Ise,** near the entrance to the bay, has several ancient Shinto shrines built in a distinctive archaic style of architecture. Population, 105,455.

Ise·lin (ĭz′lĭn). A community of east-central New Jersey northwest of Perth Amboy. Population, 16,500.

is·en·tro·pic (ī′sən-trō′pĭk, -trŏp′ĭk) *adj.* Without change in entropy; at constant entropy. [ɪs(o)– + ENTROP(Y) + –IC.] **—is′en·tro′pi·cal·ly** *adv.*

I·sère (ē-zâr′). A river, about 290 km (180 mi) long, of southeast France rising in the Graian Alps near the Italian border and flowing west and southwest to the Rhone River.

I·ser·lohn (ē′zər-lōn′, ē′zər-lōn′). A city of west-central Germany northeast of Cologne. Founded in the 13th century, it is a manufacturing center. Population, 89,951.

I·seult (ĭ-so͞olt′) also **I·sol·de** (ĭ-sōl′də, ĭ-zōl′-) *n.* In Arthurian legend, an Irish princess who married the king of Cornwall and had a love affair with his knight Tristan.

Is·fa·han (ĭs′fə-hän′) or **Es·fa·han** (ĕs′-). A city of central Iran south of Tehran. An ancient town and capital of Persia from 1598 to 1722, it was long noted for its fine carpets and silver filigree. Today it has textile and steel mills. Population, 927,000.

–ish *suff.* **1.** Of, relating to, or being: *Swedish.* **2.a.** Characteristic of: *girlish.* **b.** Having the usually undesirable qualities of: *childish.* **3.** Approximately; somewhat: *greenish.* **4.** Tending toward; preoccupied with: *selfish.* [Middle English, from Old English *-isc.*]

Ish·er·wood (ĭsh′ər-wo͝od′), **Christopher William Bradshaw.** 1904–1986. British-born American writer best known for his portrayals of Berlin in the early 1930's in works such as *Goodbye to Berlin* (1939).

I·shi·ka·ri Bay (ĭsh′ĭ-kär′ē). An inlet of the Sea of Japan on the western coast of Hokkaido, Japan. The **Ishikari River,** about 443 km (275 mi) long, flows generally southwest from the mountainous interior of the island into the bay.

I·shim (ĭ-shĭm′). A river, about 1,818 km (1,130 mi) long, rising in the steppe region of Kazakhstan and flowing northwest then northeast to the Irtysh River in south-central Russia.

Ish·ma·el[1] (ĭsh′mē-əl, -mā-). In the Old Testament, the son of Abraham who was cast out after the birth of Isaac. He is traditionally considered to be the forebear of the Arabs.

Ish·ma·el[2] (ĭsh′mē-əl, -mā-) *n.* An outcast.

Ish·ma·el·ite (ĭsh′mē-ə-līt′, -mā-) *n.* **1.** A descendant of Ishmael. **2.** An outcast. **—Ish′ma·el·it′ism** *n.*

Ish·tar (ĭsh′tär′) *n. Mythology.* The ancient Assyrian and Babylonian goddess of love, fertility, and war.

Is·i·dore of Se·ville (ĭz′ĭ-dôr′, -dōr′; sə-vĭl′), Saint. 560?–636. Spanish scholar and ecclesiastic. He wrote the encyclopedia *Etymologiae,* an important medieval reference work.

i·sin·glass (ī′zən-glăs′, ī′zĭng-) *n.* **1.** A transparent, almost pure gelatin prepared from the air bladder of the sturgeon and certain other fishes and used as an adhesive and a clarifying agent. **2.** Mica in thin, transparent sheets. [By folk etymology (influenced by GLASS) from obsolete Dutch *huizenblas,* from Middle Dutch *huusblase* : *huus,* sturgeon + *blase,* bladder; see **bhlē-** in Appendix.]

I·sis[1] (ī′sĭs) *n. Mythology.* An ancient Egyptian goddess of fertility, the sister and wife of Osiris.

I·sis[2] (ī′sĭs). The upper Thames River in south-central England in the vicinity of Oxford. The name is used locally and in literature.

Is·ken·de·run (ĭs-kĕn′də-ro͞on′, -kĕn′dĕ-ro͞on′). Formerly **Al·ex·an·dret·ta** (ăl′ĭg-zăn-drĕt′ə). A city of southern Turkey on an inlet of the eastern Mediterranean Sea. Founded by Alexander the Great, it is Turkey's chief port on the Mediterranean. Population, 124,824.

isl. *abbr.* Island.

Is·lam (ĭs-läm′, ĭz-, ĭs′läm′, ĭz′-) *n.* **1.** A monotheistic religion characterized by the acceptance of the doctrine of submission to God and Mohammed as the chief and last prophet of God. **2.a.** The people or nations that practice Islam; the Moslem world. **b.** The civilization based on Islam. [Arabic *'islām,* submission, from *'aslama,* to surrender, resign oneself, from Syriac *'ašlem.*] **—Is·lam′ic** *adj.*

Is·lam·a·bad (ĭs-lä′mə-bäd′, ĭz-lăm′ə-băd′). The capital of Pakistan, in the northeast part of the country northeast of Rawalpindi. Construction began on the city in 1960, and it replaced Karachi as the capital in 1967. Population, 201,000.

Is·lam·ism (ĭs′lə-mĭz′əm, ĭz′-) *n. Offensive.* The religious faith, principles, or cause of Islam. **—Is·lam′ist** (-lä′mĭst) *n.*

Is·lam·ize (ĭs′lə-mīz′, ĭz′-) *tr.v.* **-ized, -iz·ing, -iz·es. 1.** To convert to Islam. **2.** To cause to conform to Islamic law or precepts. **—Is′lam·i·za′tion** (-lə-mĭ-zā′shən) *n.*

is·land (ī′lənd) *n.* **1.** *Abbr.* **is., i., Is., I., isl.** A land mass, especially one smaller than a continent, entirely surrounded by water. **2.** Something resembling an island, especially in being isolated or surrounded: *a counter forming an island in the middle of the kitchen; islands of people living on the empty prairie.* **3.** The superstructure, as of an aircraft carrier. **4.** *Anatomy.* A cluster of cells differing in structure or function from the cells constituting the surrounding tissue. **—island** *tr.v.* **-land·ed, -land·ing, -lands.** To make into or as if into an island; insulate: *a secluded mansion, islanded by shrubbery and fences.* [Alteration (influenced by ISLE) of Middle English *ilond,* from Old English *īegland* : *īg, īeg;* see **akʷ-ā-** in Appendix + *land,* land; see **lendh-** in Appendix.]

is·land·er (ī′lən-dər) *n.* An inhabitant of an island.

is·lands of Lang·er·hans (ī′ləndz; läng′ər-häns′) *pl.n.* See **islets of Langerhans.**

Is·la Vis·ta (ī′lə vĭs′tə). A community of southern California on the Pacific Ocean west of Santa Barbara. Population, 16,700.

Is·lay (ī′lā, ī′lə). An island of the southern Inner Hebrides of western Scotland. Farming, fishing, and distilling are important to its economy.

isle (īl) *n. Abbr.* **i., I.** An island, especially a small one. [Middle English *ile,* from Old French *isle,* from Latin *īnsula.*]

Isle of (īl). For names of actual isles, see the specific element of the name; for example, **Wight, Isle of.**

Isle Roy·ale (roi′əl). An island of northern Michigan in Lake Superior near the coast of Ontario. French fur traders named the island in 1671. Native Americans mined the island's copper for centuries before ceding the island to the United States in 1843.

is·let (ī′lĭt) *n.* A very small island: *rocky islets off the coast.*

islets of Lang·er·hans (läng′ər-häns′) *pl.n.* Irregular clusters of endocrine cells scattered throughout the tissue of the pancreas that secrete insulin and glucagon. Also called *islands of Langerhans.* [After Paul *Langerhans* (1847–1888), German pathologist.]

ism (ĭz′əm) *n. Informal.* A distinctive doctrine, system, or theory: *"Formalism, by being an 'ism,' kills form by hugging it to death"* (Peter Viereck). [From –ISM.]

–ism *suff.* **1.** Action, process; practice: *terrorism.* **2.** Characteristic behavior or quality: *heroism.* **3.a.** State; condition; quality: *pauperism.* **b.** State or condition resulting from an excess of something specified: *strychninism.* **4.** Distinctive or characteristic trait: *Latinism.* **5.a.** Doctrine; theory; system of principles: *pacifism.* **b.** An attitude of prejudice against a given group: *racism.* [Middle English *-isme,* from Old French, from Latin *-ismus,* from Greek *-ismos,* n. suff.]

Is·ma·i·li (ĭs′mä-ē′lē) also **Is·ma·i·li·an** (-ē′lē-ən) *n.* A member of a branch of Shiism that follows a living imam and is noted for esoteric philosophy. [Arabic *Isma'īlīy,* after *Isma'īl* (died 760), son of the sixth imam, Jafar (700?–765).]

Is·ma·i·li·a (ĭz′mā-ə-lē′ə, ĭs′-). A city of northeast Egypt on the Suez Canal. It was founded in 1863 by Ferdinand de Lesseps as a base of operations during the building of the canal. Population, 191,700.

Is·ma·i·li·an (ĭs′mä-ē′lē-ən) *n.* Variant of **Ismaili.**

Is·ma·il Pa·sha (ĭs-mä′ēl pä′shə). 1830–1895. Egyptian viceroy (1863–1879). The Suez Canal was completed during his reign (1869).

is·n't (ĭz′ənt). Is not.

iso– or **is–** *pref.* **1.** Equal; uniform: *isobar.* **2.** Isomeric: *isopropyl.* [Greek, from *isos,* equal.]

i·so·ag·glu·ti·na·tion (ī′sō-ə-glo͞ot′n-ā′shən) *n.* The agglutination of the red blood cells of an individual by antibodies in the serum of another individual of the same species.

i·so·ag·glu·ti·nin (ī′sō-ə-glo͞ot′n-ĭn) *n.* An isoantibody normally present in the serum of an individual that causes the agglutination of the red blood cells of another individual of the same species.

i·so·ag·glu·tin·o·gen (ī′sō-ăg′lo͞o-tĭn′ə-jən) *n.* An isoantigen that on exposure to its corresponding isoantibody causes agglutination of the red blood cells to which it is attached. [ISO- AGGLUTIN(IN) + –GEN.]

i·so·an·ti·bod·y (ī′sō-ăn′tē-bŏd′ē) *n., pl.* **-ies.** An antibody produced by or derived from the same species as the antigen with which it reacts. Also called *alloantibody.*

i·so·an·ti·gen (ī′sō-ăn′tĭ-jən) *n.* A protein or other antigenic substance present in only some members of a species and therefore able to stimulate antibody production in those members that lack it. Also called *alloantigen.* **—i′so·an′ti·gen′ic** (-jĕn′ĭk) *adj.* **—i′so·an′ti·ge·nic′i·ty** (-jə-nĭs′ĭ-tē) *n.*

i·so·bar (ī′sə-bär′) *n.* **1.** A line on a weather map connecting points of equal atmospheric pressure. Also called *isopiestic.* **2.** Any of two or more kinds of atoms having the same atomic mass but different atomic numbers. [ISO– + Greek *baros,* weight; see **gʷerə-**[1] in Appendix.] **—i′so·bar′ic** (-bär′ĭk, -băr′-) *adj.*

Christopher Isherwood
Photographed in 1979

Isis[1]

ă pat	oi boy
ā pay	ou out
âr care	o͝o took
ä father	o͞o boot
ĕ pet	ŭ cut
ē be	ûr urge
ĭ pit	th thin
ī pie	*th* this
îr pier	hw which
ŏ pot	zh vision
ō toe	ə about, item
ô paw	♦ regionalism

Stress marks: ′ (primary); ′ (secondary), as in **dictionary** (dĭk′shə-nĕr′ē)

i·so·car·box·a·zid (ī′sō-kär-bŏk′sə-zĭd) *n.* A compound, $C_{12}H_{13}N_3O_2$, used as an antidepressant. [Contraction and alteration of *isoxazolylcarbonyl,* one of its components + (HYDR)AZ(INE) + –ID.]

i·so·chro·mat·ic (ī′sə-krō-măt′ĭk) *adj.* **1.** Having the same color or wavelength. Used of light. **2.** Orthochromatic.

i·soch·ro·nal (ī-sŏk′rə-nəl) or **i·soch·ro·nous** (-nəs) *adj.* **1.** Equal in duration. **2.** Characterized by or occurring at equal intervals of time. [From New Latin *isochronus,* from Greek *isokhronos* : *iso-,* iso- + *khronos,* time.] **—i·soch′ro·nal·ly** *adv.* **—i·soch′ro·nism** *n.*

i·soch·ro·nize (ī-sŏk′rə-nīz′) *tr.v.* **-nized, -niz·ing, -niz·es.** To make isochronal.

i·soch·ro·nous (ī-sŏk′rə-nəs) *adj.* Variant of **isochronal.** **—i·soch′ro·nous·ly** *adv.*

i·soch·ro·ous (ī-sŏk′rō-əs) *adj.* Having the same color throughout. [Greek *isokhroos* : *iso-,* iso- + *khrōs,* flesh, color.]

i·so·cli·nal (ī′sə-klī′nəl) or **i·so·clin·ic** (-klĭn′ĭk) *—adj.* Having the same magnetic inclination or dip. *—n.* See **isoclinic line.** **—i′so·cli′nal·ly** *adv.*

i·so·cline (ī′sə-klīn′) *n. Geology.* An anticline or a syncline so tightly folded that the rock beds of the two sides are nearly parallel.

i·so·clin·ic (ī′sə-klĭn′ĭk) *adj. & n.* Variant of **isoclinal.** **—i′so·clin′i·cal·ly** *adv.*

isoclinic line *n.* A line on a map connecting points of equal magnetic dip. Also called *isoclinal.*

I·soc·ra·tes (ī-sŏk′rə-tēz′). 436–338 B.C. Athenian orator and rhetorician whose letters and pamphlets are a valuable source of ancient Greek political thought.

i·so·di·a·met·ric (ī′sō-dī′ə-mĕt′rĭk) *adj.* Having equal diameters or axes.

i·so·di·mor·phism (ī′sō-dī-môr′fĭz′əm) *n.* Isomorphism between crystalline forms of two dimorphic substances.

i·so·dy·nam·ic (ī′sō-dī-năm′ĭk) *adj.* **1.** Having equal force or strength. **2.** Connecting points of equal magnetic intensity.

i·so·e·lec·tric (ī′sō-ĭ-lĕk′trĭk) *adj.* Having equal electric potential.

i·so·e·lec·tron·ic (ī′sō-ĭ-lĕk-trŏn′ĭk, -ē′lĕk-) *adj.* Having equal numbers of electrons or the same electronic configuration.

i·so·en·zyme (ī′sō-ĕn′zīm′) *n.* Any of the chemically distinct forms of an enzyme that perform the same biochemical function. **—i′so·en·zy′mic** *adj.*

i·so·ga·mete (ī′sō-găm′ēt′, -gə-mēt′) *n.* A gamete that has the same size and structure as the one with which it unites. **—i′so·ga·met′ic** (-gə-mĕt′ĭk) *adj.*

i·sog·a·my (ī-sŏg′ə-mē) *n., pl.* **-mies.** Reproduction by the fusion or conjugation of isogametes, as in certain algae and fungi. **—i·sog′a·mous** *adj.*

i·sog·e·nous (ī-sŏj′ə-nəs) *adj.* Having the same or similar origin, as organs or parts derived from the same embryonic tissue. **—i·sog′e·ny** *n.*

i·so·gloss (ī′sə-glôs′, -glŏs′) *n.* A geographic boundary line delimiting the area in which a given linguistic feature occurs. [ISO– + Greek *glōssa,* language, tongue.] **—i′so·gloss′al** *adj.*

i·so·gon (ī′sə-gŏn′) *n.* A polygon whose angles are equal.

i·so·gon·ic (ī′sə-gŏn′ĭk) also **i·sog·o·nal** (ī-sŏg′ə-nəl) *adj.* Having equal angles.

isogonic line *n.* A line on a map connecting points of equal magnetic declination.

i·so·graft (ī′sə-grăft) *n.* A graft of tissue that is obtained from a donor genetically identical to the recipient.

i·so·gram (ī′sə-grăm′) *n.* See **isoline.**

i·so·hel (ī′sō-hĕl′) *n.* A line drawn on a map connecting points that receive equal amounts of sunlight. [ISO– + Greek *hēlios,* sun; see **sāwel-** in Appendix.]

i·so·hy·et (ī′sō-hī′ĭt) *n.* A line drawn on a map connecting points that receive equal amounts of rainfall. [ISO– + Greek *huetos,* rain; see **seuə-²** in Appendix.]

i·so·ki·net·ic exercise (ī′sō-kĭ-nĕt′ĭk, -kī-) *n.* Exercise performed with a specialized apparatus that provides variable resistance to a movement, so that no matter how much effort is exerted, the movement takes place at a constant speed. Such exercise is used to test and improve muscular strength and endurance, especially after injury.

i·so·la·ble (ī′sə-lə-bəl) also **i·so·lat·a·ble** (-lā′tə-bəl) *adj.* Possible to isolate: *isolable viruses.*

i·so·late (ī′sə-lāt′) *tr.v.* **-lat·ed, -lat·ing, -lates. 1.** To set apart or cut off from others. **2.** To place in quarantine. **3.** *Chemistry.* To separate (a substance) out of a combined mixture. **4.** To render free of external influence; insulate. **5.** *Microbiology.* To separate (a pure strain) from a mixed bacterial or fungal culture. **—isolate** (-lĭt, -lāt′) *adj.* Solitary; alone. **—isolate** *n. Microbiology.* A bacterial or fungal strain that has been isolated. [Back-formation from ISOLATED.] **—i′so·la′tor** *n.*

SYNONYMS: *isolate, insulate, seclude, segregate, sequester.* The central meaning shared by these verbs is "to separate from others": *a mountain village that is isolated from all other communities; trying to insulate herself from the chaos surrounding her; a famous actor who was secluded from public scrutiny; characteristics that segregate leaders from followers; sequestering a jury during its deliberations.*

i·so·lat·ed (ī′sə-lā′tĭd) *adj.* Separated from others; solitary or singular: *Reporters in the field observed isolated instances of rebellion.* [From French *isolé,* from Italian *isolato,* from Latin *īnsulātus,* made into an island, from Latin *īnsula,* island.]

i·so·la·tion (ī′sə-lā′shən) *n.* **1.** The act of isolating. **2.** The quality or condition of being isolated. See Synonyms at **solitude.**

i·so·la·tion·ism (ī′sə-lā′shə-nĭz′əm) *n.* A national policy of abstaining from political or economic relations with other countries. **—i′so·la′tion·ist** *n.*

I·sol·de (ĭ-sōl′də, ĭ-zōl′-) *n.* Variant of **Iseult.**

i·so·lec·i·thal (ī′sə-lĕs′ə-thəl) *adj. Embryology.* Having the yolk evenly distributed throughout the egg. [ISO– + LECITH(IN) + –AL[1].]

i·so·leu·cine (ī′sə-lo͞o′sēn′) *n.* An essential amino acid, $C_6H_{13}NO_2$, that is isomeric with leucine.

i·so·line (ī′sə-līn′) *n.* A line on a map, chart, or graph connecting points of equal value. Also called *isogram.*

i·so·mag·net·ic (ī′sō-măg-nĕt′ĭk) *adj.* Of, relating to, or being lines connecting points of equal magnetic force.

i·so·mer (ī′sə-mər) *n.* **1.** *Chemistry.* Any of two or more substances that are composed of the same elements in the same proportions but differ in properties because of differences in the arrangement of atoms. **2.** *Physics.* Any of two or more nuclei with the same mass number and atomic number that have different radioactive properties and can exist in any of several energy states for a measurable period of time. **—i′so·mer′ic** (-mĕr′ĭk) *adj.*

i·som·er·ase (ī-sŏm′ə-rās′) *n.* One of a group of enzymes that catalyzes the conversion of one isomer into another.

i·som·er·ism (ī-sŏm′ə-rĭz′əm) *n.* **1.** The phenomenon of the existence of isomers. **2.** The complex of chemical and physical phenomena characteristic of or attributable to isomers. **3.** The state or condition of being an isomer.

i·som·er·ize (ī-sŏm′ə-rīz′) *v.* **-ized, -iz·ing, -iz·es.** *—tr.* To cause to change into an isomeric form. *—intr.* To become changed into an isomeric form. **—i·som′er·i·za′tion** (-ər-ĭ-zā′shən) *n.*

i·som·er·ous (ī-sŏm′ər-əs) *adj.* **1.** Having an equal number of parts, as organs or markings. **2.** Having or designating floral whorls with equal numbers of parts: *the isomerous flower of the tulip.*

i·so·met·ric (ī′sə-mĕt′rĭk) also **i·so·met·ri·cal** (-rĭ-kəl) *—adj.* **1.** Of or exhibiting equality in dimensions or measurements. **2.** Of or being a crystal system of three equal axes lying at right angles to each other. **3.** *Physiology.* Of or involving muscular contraction against resistance in which the length of the muscle remains the same. *—n.* A line connecting isometric points. [From Greek *isometros,* of equal measure : *iso-,* iso- + *metron,* measure; see **mē-²** in Appendix.]

i·so·met·rics (ī′sə-mĕt′rĭks) *n.* (*used with a sing. or pl. verb*). Exercise or a system of exercises in which isometric muscular contraction is used to strengthen and tone muscles, performed by the exertion of effort against resistance, usually of a stationary object.

i·so·me·tro·pi·a (ī′sō-mĭ-trō′pē-ə) *n.* Equality of refraction in both eyes. [Greek *isometros,* isometric + –OPIA.]

i·som·e·try (ī-sŏm′ĭ-trē) *n.* **1.** Equality of measure. **2.** Equality of elevation above sea level.

i·so·morph (ī′sə-môrf′) *n.* An object, an organism, or a substance exhibiting isomorphism.

i·so·mor·phic (ī′sə-môr′fĭk) *adj.* **1.** *Biology.* Having a similar structure or appearance but being of different ancestry. **2.** Related by an isomorphism.

i·so·mor·phism (ī′sə-môr′fĭz′əm) *n.* **1.** *Biology.* Similarity in form, as in organisms of different ancestry. **2.** *Mathematics.* A one-to-one correspondence between the elements of two sets such that the result of an operation on elements of one set corresponds to the result of the analogous operation on their images in the other set. **3.** A close similarity in the crystalline structure of two or more substances of similar chemical composition. **—i′so·mor′phous** *adj.*

i·so·ni·a·zid (ī′sə-nī′ə-zĭd) *n.* A crystalline antibacterial compound, $C_6H_7N_3O$, used in the treatment of tuberculosis. [*isoni(cotinic acid),* isomer of nicotinic acid (ISO– + NICOTINIC ACID) + *(hydr)azid(e)* (HYDR(O)– + AZ(O)– + –IDE).]

i·so·oc·tane (ī′sō-ŏk′tān′) *n.* A flammable liquid, $(CH_3)_2CHCH_2C(CH_3)_3$, used to determine the octane ratings of fuels.

i·so·pi·es·tic (ī′sō-pī-ĕs′tĭk, -pē-) *adj.* Marked by or indicating equal pressure; isobaric. **—isopiestic** *n.* See **isobar** (sense 1). [ISO– + Greek *piestos,* able to be compressed (from *piezein,* to press tight; see **sed-** in Appendix) + –IC.]

i·so·pod (ī′sə-pŏd′) *n.* Any of numerous crustaceans of the order Isopoda, characterized by a flattened body bearing seven pairs of legs and including the sow bugs and gribbles. **—isopod** *adj.* Of or belonging to the order Isopoda. [From New Latin *Isopoda,* order name : ISO– + New Latin *-poda,* -pod.]

i·so·prene (ī′sə-prēn′) *n.* A colorless volatile liquid, C_5H_8, used chiefly to make synthetic rubber. [ISO– + PR(OPYL)ENE.]

i·so·pro·pyl alcohol (ī′sə-prō′pəl) *n. Abbr.* **IPA** A clear, colorless, flammable, mobile liquid, $(CH_3)_2CHOH$, used in antifreeze compounds, in lotions and cosmetics, and as a solvent for gums, shellac, and essential oils.

i·sos·ce·les (ī-sŏs′ə-lēz′) *adj.* *Mathematics.* Having two equal sides: *an isosceles triangle.* [Late Latin *īsoscelēs,* from Greek *isoskelēs* : *iso-,* iso- + *skelos,* leg.]

i·so·seis·mic (ī′sə-sīz′mĭk) also **i·so·seis·mal** (-məl) *adj.* Of, relating to, or exhibiting equal intensity of earthquake shock.

i·sos·mot·ic (ī′sŏz-mŏt′ĭk, -sŏs-) *adj.* Of or exhibiting equal osmotic pressure.

i·so·spin (ī′sə-spĭn′) *n.* *Abbr.* **I** A quantum number related to the number of charge states of a baryon or meson. [ISO(TOPIC) + SPIN.]

i·sos·ta·sy (ī-sŏs′tə-sē) *n.* Equilibrium in the earth's crust such that the forces tending to elevate land masses balance the forces tending to depress land masses. [ISO– + Greek *stasis,* a standstill; see **stā-** in Appendix + –Y[2].]

i·so·therm (ī′sə-thûrm′) *n.* A line drawn on a weather map or chart linking all points of equal or constant temperature. [From French *isotherme,* having the same temperature : Greek *iso-,* iso- + Greek *thermē,* heat; see –THERM.]

i·so·ther·mal (ī′sə-thûr′məl) *adj.* **1.** Of, relating to, or indicating equal or constant temperatures. **2.** Of or designating changes of pressure and volume at constant temperature. **3.** Of or relating to an isotherm. **—isothermal** *n.* An isotherm.

i·so·tone (ī′sə-tōn′) *n.* One of two or more atoms whose nuclei have the same number of neutrons but different numbers of protons. [Alteration of ISOTOPE (with *n* for *neutron* replacing *p* for *proton*).]

i·so·ton·ic (ī′sə-tŏn′ĭk) *adj.* **1.** Of equal tension. **2.** Isosmotic. **3.** Having the same concentration of solutes as the blood: *an isotonic saline solution.* **4.** *Physiology.* Of or involving muscular contraction in which the muscle remains under relatively constant tension while its length changes. [ISO– + Greek *tonos,* tension; see TONE + –IC.] **—i′so·ton′i·cal·ly** *adv.* **—i′so·to·nic′i·ty** (-tə-nĭs′ĭ-tē) *n.*

isotonic exercise *n.* Exercise in which isotonic muscular contraction is used to strengthen muscles and improve joint mobility.

i·so·tope (ī′sə-tōp′) *n.* One of two or more atoms having the same atomic number but different mass numbers. [ISO– + Greek *topos,* place (so called because the isotopes of a chemical element occupy the same position in the periodic table of elements).] **—i′so·top′ic** (-tŏp′ĭk) *adj.* **—i′so·top′i·cal·ly** *adv.*

isotopic spin *n.* An isospin.

i·so·tre·tin·o·in (ī′sō-trĭ-tĭn′ō-ĭn, -tĭn′oin) *n.* A chemical compound, $C_{20}H_{28}O_2$, used in the treatment of severe forms of acne. [ISO– + *tretinoin,* name for retinoic acid.]

i·so·tro·pic (ī′sə-trō′pĭk, -trŏp′ĭk) *adj.* Identical in all directions; invariant with respect to direction. **—i·sot′ro·py** (ī-sŏt′rə-pē), **i·sot′ro·pism** (-pĭz′əm) *n.*

i·so·zyme (ī′sə-zīm′) *n.* An isoenzyme. [ISO– + (EN)ZYME.] **—i′so·zy′mic** *adj.*

Isr. *abbr.* Israel; Israeli.

Is·ra·el[1] (ĭz′rē-əl) *n.* **1.** *Bible.* **a.** In the Old Testament, Jacob. **b.** The descendants of Jacob. **2.** *Judaism.* The Hebrew people, past, present, and future, regarded as the chosen people of God by virtue of the covenant of Jacob. [Middle English, from Old English, from Latin, from Greek *Israēl,* from Hebrew *yiśrā'ēl.*]

Is·ra·el[2] (ĭz′rē-əl). **1.** An ancient kingdom of Palestine founded by Saul c. 1025 B.C. After 933 it split into the Northern Kingdom, or kingdom of Israel, and the kingdom of Judah to the south. Israel was overthrown by the Assyrians in 721. **2.** *Abbr.* **Isr.** A country of southwest Asia on the eastern Mediterranean Sea. It was created in 1948 on recommendation of the United Nations. Discord with its Arab neighbors has led to a number of wars, notably in 1956–1957 and 1967. Israel has occupied the Gaza Strip and the West Bank (the area west of the Jordan River) since 1967. Jerusalem is the capital and Tel Aviv–Jaffa the largest city. Population, 4,141,400.

Is·rae·li (ĭz-rā′lē) *adj.* *Abbr.* **Isr.** Of or relating to modern-day Israel or its people. **—Israeli** *n., pl.* **-lis.** A native or inhabitant of modern-day Israel.

Is·ra·el·ite (ĭz′rē-ə-līt′) *n.* **1.** A native or inhabitant of the ancient Northern Kingdom of Israel. **2.** A descendant of Jacob; a Jew. **3.** A member of a people regarded as the chosen people of God. **—Israelite** *adj.* also **Is·ra·el·it·ic** (ĭz′rē-ə-lĭt′ĭk). Of or relating to Israel, the Israelites, or their culture.

Is·sa·char (ĭs′ə-kär′). In the Old Testament, a son of Jacob and Leah and the forebear of one of the tribes of Israel.

is·sei (ēs′sā′) *n., pl.* **issei** or **-seis.** A Japanese immigrant, especially one to the United States. [Japanese : *is,* first + *sei,* generation.]

ISSN *abbr.* International Standard Serial Number.

is·su·a·ble (ĭsh′o͞o-ə-bəl) *adj.* **1.** Authorized for issue or to be issued: *issuable currency; issuable securities.* **2.** Open to debate or litigation: *issuable matters of probate.* **3.** That can be accrued: *a corporation's issuable profits.*

is·su·ance (ĭsh′o͞o-əns) *n.* **1.** The act of issuing. **2.** An issue.

is·su·ant (ĭsh′o͞o-ənt) *adj.* **1.** *Heraldry.* Designating an animal with only the upper part depicted. **2.** *Archaic.* Emerging.

is·sue (ĭsh′o͞o) *n.* **1.a.** The act or an instance of flowing, passing, or giving out. **b.** The act of circulating, distributing, or publishing by an office or official group: *government issue of new bonds.* **2.** Something produced, published, or offered, as: **a.** An item or set of items, as stamps or coins, made available at one time by an office or bureau. **b.** A single copy of a periodical: *the March issue of the magazine.* **c.** A distinct set of copies of an edition of a book distinguished from others of that edition by variations in the printed matter. **d.** A final result or conclusion, as a solution to a problem. **e.** Proceeds from estates or fines. **f.** Something proceeding from a specified source: *suspicions that were the issue of a deranged mind.* **3.** Offspring; progeny: *died without issue.* **4.a.** A point or matter of discussion, debate, or dispute: *legal and moral issues.* **b.** A matter of public concern: *refused to address the economic issues.* **c.** The essential point; crux: *the issue of how to provide adequate child care.* **d.** A culminating point leading to a decision: *bring a case to an issue.* **5.** A place of egress; an outlet: *a lake with no issue to the sea.* **6.** *Pathology.* **a.** A discharge, as of blood or pus. **b.** A lesion, a wound, or an ulcer producing such a discharge. **7.** *Archaic.* Termination; close. **—issue** *v.* **-sued, -su·ing, -sues.** —*intr.* **1.** To go or come out. See Synonyms at **appear. 2.** To accrue as proceeds or profit: *Little money issued from the stocks.* **3.** To be born or be descended. **4.** To be circulated or published. **5.** To spring or proceed from a source. See Synonyms at **stem**[1]. **6.** To terminate or result. —*tr.* **1.** To cause to flow out; emit. **2.** To circulate or distribute in an official capacity: *issued uniforms to the players.* **3.** To publish: *issued periodic statements.* **—*idioms.* at issue. 1.** In question; in dispute: *"Many people fail to grasp what is really at issue here"* (Gail Sheehy). **2.** At variance; in disagreement. **join issue. 1.** To enter into controversy. **2.** *Law.* To submit an issue for decision. **take issue.** To take an opposing point of view; disagree. [Middle English, from Old French *eissue, issue,* from Vulgar Latin **exūta,* alteration of Latin *exita,* feminine past participle of *exīre,* to go out : *ex-,* ex- + *īre,* to go; see **ei-** in Appendix.] **—is′su·er** *n.* **—is′sue·less** *adj.*

Is·sus (ĭs′əs). An ancient town of southeast Asia Minor near modern-day Iskenderun, Turkey. Alexander the Great defeated Darius III of Persia here in 333 B.C.

Is·syk-Kul (ĭs′ĭk-ko͝ol′, ē-sĭ′ko͞ol′). A lake of northeast Kirghiz in the Tien Shan near the Chinese border.

IST *abbr.* Insulin shock therapy.

-ist *suff.* **1.a.** One that performs a specified action: *lobbyist.* **b.** One that produces, makes, operates, plays, or is connected with a specified thing: *novelist.* **2.** A specialist in a specified art, science, or skill: *biologist.* **3.** An adherent or advocate of a specified doctrine, theory, or school of thought: *anarchist.* **4.** One that is characterized by a specified trait or quality: *romanticist.* [Middle English *-iste,* from Old French, from Latin *-istēs, -ista,* from Greek *-istēs,* agent n. suff.]

Is·tan·bul (ĭs′tăn-bo͞ol′, -tän-, ī-stän′bo͞ol). Formerly **Con·stan·ti·no·ple** (kŏn′stăn-tə-nō′pəl). The largest city of Turkey, in the northwest part of the country on both sides of the Bosporus at its entrance into the Sea of Marmara. Founded c. 660 B.C. as Byzantium, it was renamed Constantinople in A.D. 330 by Constantine the Great, who made it the capital of the Eastern Roman, or Byzantine, Empire. The city was sacked by Crusaders in 1204 and taken by the Turks in 1453. Istanbul was chosen as the official name in 1930. Population, 2,772,708.

isth. *abbr.* Isthmus.

isth·mi (ĭs′mī′) *n.* A plural of **isthmus.**

isth·mi·an (ĭs′mē-ən) *adj.* **1.** Of, relating to, or forming an isthmus. **2.** Of or relating to the Isthmus of Corinth, especially with regard to the biennial Pan-Hellenic games held there in antiquity.

isth·mus (ĭs′məs) *n., pl.* **-mus·es** or **-mi** (-mī′). *Abbr.* **isth. 1.** A narrow strip of land connecting two larger masses of land. **2.** *Anatomy.* **a.** A narrow strip of tissue joining two larger organs or parts of an organ. **b.** A narrow passage connecting two larger cavities. [Latin, from Greek *isthmos.*]

is·tle also **ix·tle** (ĭs′lē, ĭst′-) *n.* See **pita**[2] (sense 1). [American Spanish *ixtle,* from Nahuatl *ixtli,* fibrous stem.]

Is·tri·a (ĭs′trē-ə). A peninsula of northwest Yugoslavia projecting into the northeast Adriatic Sea. The original Istrian inhabitants were overthrown by the Romans in the second century A.D. Istria was subsequently occupied by Austria, Venice, and Italy. All but the area surrounding Trieste was awarded to Yugoslavia in 1946. **—Is′tri·an** *adj. & n.*

ISV *abbr.* International Scientific Vocabulary.

it (ĭt) *pron.* **1.** Used to refer to that one previously mentioned. Used of a nonhuman entity; an animate being whose sex is unspecified, unknown, or irrelevant; a group of objects or individuals; or an abstraction: *polished the table until it shone; couldn't find out who it was; opened the meeting by calling it to order.* **2.** Used as the subject of an impersonal verb: *It is snowing.* **3.a.** Used as an anticipatory subject or object: *Is it certain that they will win?* **b.** Used as an anticipatory subject to emphasize a term that is not itself a subject: *It was on Friday that all the snow fell.* **4.** Used to refer to a general condition or state of affairs: *She couldn't stand it.* **5.** *Informal.* Used to refer to something that is the best, the most desirable, or without equal: *He thinks he's it. That steak was really it!* **—it** *n.* **1.** *Games.* A player, as in tag, who attempts to find or catch the other players. **2.** An animal that has been neutered: *The cat is an it.* [Middle English, from Old English *hit.* See **ko-** in Appendix.]

It. *abbr.* Italian; Italy.

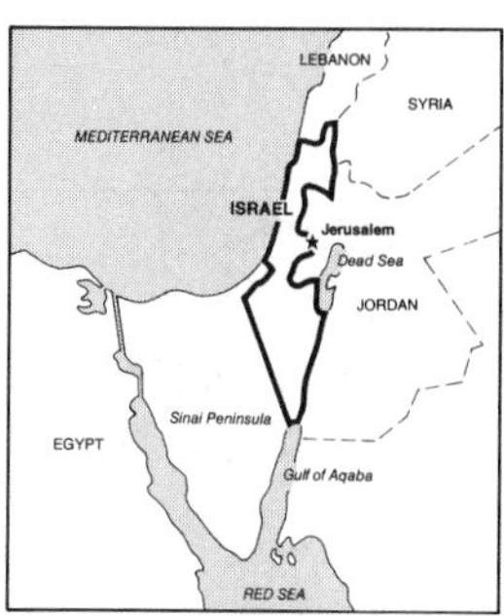

Israel[2]

issuant

ă pat	oi boy
ā pay	ou out
âr care	o͝o took
ä father	o͞o boot
ĕ pet	ŭ cut
ē be	ûr urge
ĭ pit	th thin
ī pie	*th* this
îr pier	hw which
ŏ pot	zh vision
ō toe	ə about, item
ô paw	♦ regionalism

Stress marks: **′** (primary); ′ (secondary), as in **dictionary** (dĭk′shə-nĕr′ē)

Italy

Ivan the Great

Ivan the Terrible

ITA or **I.T.A.** *abbr.* Initial teaching alphabet.

it·a·col·u·mite (ĭt′ə-kŏl′yə-mīt′) *n.* A variety of sandstone that is flexible when cut into thin slabs. [After *Itacolumi* (Itacolomi), a mountain of east-central Brazil.]

ital. *abbr.* **1.** Italic. **2.** Italics.

Ital. *abbr.* Italian.

♦**I·tal·ian** (ĭ-tăl′yən) *adj.* *Abbr.* **It., Ital.** Of or relating to Italy or its people, language, or culture. **—Italian** *n.* **1.a.** A native or inhabitant of Italy. **b.** A person of Italian descent. **2.** The Romance language of the Italians and an official language of Switzerland. **3.** *Midland U.S.* See **submarine** (sense 2). See Regional Note at **submarine.** [Middle English, from Latin *Italiānus,* from *Italia,* Italy.]

I·tal·ian·ate (ĭ-tăl′yə-nāt′, -nĭt) *adj.* Italian in character: *Italianate buildings.*

Italian East Af·ri·ca (ăf′rĭ-kə). A former federation of Italian-held territories in eastern Africa, including Ethiopia and part of present-day Somalia. It was formed in 1936 and lasted until the British World War II invasion of 1941.

I·tal·ian·ism (ĭ-tăl′yə-nĭz′əm) *n.* **1.** An Italian idiom or custom. **2.** A quality characteristic of Italy or its people.

I·tal·ian·ize (ĭ-tăl′yə-nīz′) *v.* **-ized, -iz·ing, -iz·es.** *—tr.* To give an Italian aspect to. *—intr.* To adopt Italian speech, manners, or customs. **—I·tal′ian·i·za′tion** (-yə-nĭ-zā′shən) *n.*

♦**Italian sandwich** *n.* *Chiefly Maine.* See **submarine** (sense 2).

Italian So·ma·li·land (sō-mä′lē-lănd′, sə-). A former Italian colony of eastern Africa. It became part of Italian East Africa in 1936 and was invaded by British troops in 1941.

Italian sonnet *n.* See **Petrarchan sonnet.**

I·tal·ic (ĭ-tăl′ĭk, ī-tăl′-) *adj.* **1.** Of or relating to ancient Italy or its peoples or cultures. **2.** Of or relating to Italic. **3. italic.** *Abbr.* **ital.** Of or being a style of printing type patterned on a Renaissance script with the letters slanting to the right: *This sentence is printed in italic type.* **—Italic** *n.* **1.** A branch of the Indo-European language family that includes Latin, Faliscan, Oscan, Umbrian, and other languages or dialects. **2.** Often **italics.** *Abbr.* **ital.** Italic print or typeface. [Latin *Italicus,* from Greek *Italikos,* from *Italia,* Italy, from Latin.]

I·tal·i·cism (ĭ-tăl′ĭ-sĭz′əm) *n.* An Italianism, especially a word or an idiom borrowed from or suggestive of the Italian language.

i·tal·i·cize (ĭ-tăl′ĭ-sīz′, ī-tăl′-) *tr.v.* **-cized, -ciz·ing, -ciz·es.** **1.** To print in italic type. **2.** To underscore (written matter) with a single line to indicate italics. **3.** To emphasize: *"italicizing the upper extremity of the pitch spectrum with flute or piccolo"* (Arthur Berger). **—i·tal′i·ci·za′tion** (-sĭ-zā′shən) *n.*

I·tal·o·phile (ĭ-tăl′ə-fīl′) *n.* An admirer of Italy or of its people, language, or culture. **—I·tal′o·phil′i·a** (-fĭl′ē-ə) *n.*

I·tal·o·phobe (ĭ-tăl′əfōb′) *n.* One who fears or dislikes Italy or its people or culture. **—I·tal′o·pho′bi·a** (-fō′bē-ə) *n.*

It·a·ly (ĭt′l-ē). **1.** A peninsula of southern Europe projecting into the Mediterranean Sea between the Tyrrhenian and Adriatic seas. **2.** *Abbr.* **It.** A country of southern Europe comprising the peninsula of Italy, Sardinia, Sicily, and several smaller islands. It was settled by Ligurian peoples and later by Etruscans (before 800 B.C.), who were supplanted by the Latin Romans by 270 B.C. After the fall of the empire (A.D. 476), Italy was ruled by various barbarian tribes, local families, and popes. The country was finally unified under Victor Emmanuel II in 1870. Rome is the capital and the largest city. Population, 56,243,935.

I·tas·ca (ī-tăs′kə). A lake of northwest Minnesota. It was identified in 1832 as the source of the Mississippi River.

itch (ĭch) *n.* **1.** An irritating skin sensation causing a desire to scratch. **2.** Any of various skin disorders, such as scabies, marked by intense irritation and itching. **3.** A restless desire or craving for something: *an itch to travel.* **—itch** *v.* **itched, itch·ing, itch·es.** *—intr.* **1.a.** To feel, have, or produce an itch. **b.** To have a desire to scratch. **2.** To have a persistent, restless craving. *—tr.* **1.** To cause to itch. **2.** To scratch an itch. [Middle English *yicche,* from Old English *gicce,* from *giccan,* to itch.]

itch mite *n.* A parasitic mite *(Sarcoptes scabiei)* that burrows into the skin and causes scabies.

itch·y (ĭch′ē) *adj.* **-i·er, -i·est.** **1.** Having or causing an itching sensation. **2.** Restless or nervous. **—itch′i·ness** *n.*

it'd (ĭt′əd). **1.** It would. **2.** It had.

–ite[1] *suff.* **1.** Native or resident of: *New Jerseyite.* **2.a.** Descendant of: *Levite.* **b.** Adherent or follower of: *Luddite.* **3.** A part of an organ, body, or bodily part: *somite.* **4.a.** Rock; mineral: *graphite.* **b.** Fossil: *trilobite.* **5.a.** Product: *metabolite.* **b.** A commercial product: *ebonite.* [Middle English, from Old French, from Latin *-ītēs, -īta,* from Greek *-ītēs.*]

–ite[2] *suff.* A salt or ester of an acid named with an adjective ending in *-ous: sulfite.* [Alteration of –ATE[2].]

i·tem (ī′təm) *n.* **1.** A single article or unit in a collection, an enumeration, or a series. **2.** A clause of a document, such as a bill or charter. **3.** An entry in an account. **4.a.** A bit of information; a detail. **b.** A short piece in a newspaper or magazine. **—item** *adv.* Also; likewise. Used to introduce each article in an enumeration or a list. **—item** *tr.v.* **i·temed, i·tem·ing, i·tems.** *Archaic.* To compute. [From Middle English, also, moreover, from Latin. See **i-** in Appendix.]

SYNONYMS: *item, detail, particular.* The central meaning shared by these nouns is "an individual, often specialized element of a whole": *a shopping list with numerous items; discussed all the details of their trip; furnished the particulars of the accident.*

WORD HISTORY: The word *item* seems to us to be very much a noun, whether it refers to an article in a collection or a bit of information. But it began its life in English (first recorded before 1398) as an adverb meaning "moreover, also, in addition." *Item* was typically used in front of each object listed in an inventory, as we might put *also.* This use in English simply reflects a meaning of the word in Latin. However, it is easy to see how *item* could be taken to stand for the thing that it preceded, and so we get, for example, the sense "an article included in an enumeration." The first such usages are found in the 16th century, while the sense "a bit of information" is not found until the 19th century.

i·tem·ize (ī′tə-mīz′) *v.* **-ized, -iz·ing, -iz·es.** *—tr.* To set down item by item; list. *—intr.* To list deductions from taxable income on a tax return: *This benefit is available only to taxpayers who itemize.* **—i′tem·i·za′tion** (ī′tə-mĭ-zā′shən) *n.* **—i′tem·iz′er** *n.*

item veto *n.* Authority, as of a state governor, to reject provisions of a bill individually. Also called *selective veto.*

it·er·ance (ĭt′ər-əns) *n.* Iteration.

it·er·ant (ĭt′ər-ənt) *adj.* Marked by iteration; repeating.

it·er·ate (ĭt′ə-rāt′) *tr.v.* **-at·ed, -at·ing, -ates.** To say or perform again; repeat. See Synonyms at **repeat.** [Latin *iterāre, iterāt-,* from *iterum,* again. See **i-** in Appendix.]

it·er·a·tion (ĭt′ə-rā′shən) *n.* **1.** The act or an instance of iterating; repetition. **2.** *Mathematics.* A computational procedure in which the desired result is approached through a repeated cycle of operations, each of which more closely approximates the desired result. **3.** *Computer Science.* The process of repeating a set of instructions a specified number of times or until a specific result is achieved.

it·er·a·tive (ĭt′ə-rā′tĭv, -ər-ə-tĭv) *adj.* **1.** Characterized by or involving repetition, recurrence, reiteration, or repetitiousness. **2.** *Grammar.* Frequentative.

Ith·a·ca (ĭth′ə-kə). **1.** A city of southwest-central New York on Cayuga Lake south-southwest of Syracuse. It is the seat of Cornell University (chartered 1865). Population, 28,732. **2.** See **Itháki.**

I·thá·ki (ē-thä′kē) also **Ith·a·ca** (ĭth′ə-kə). An island of western Greece in the Ionian Islands. According to tradition, it was the home of Odysseus, the hero of Homer's *Odyssey.*

ith·y·phal·lic (ĭth′ə-făl′ĭk) *adj.* **1.** Of or relating to the phallus carried in the ancient festival of Bacchus. **2.** Having the penis erect. Used of graphic and sculptural representations. **3.** Lascivious; salacious. [Late Latin *ithyphallicus,* from Greek *ithuphallikos,* from *ithuphallos,* erect phallus : *ithus,* straight + *phallos,* phallus; see **bhel-**[2] in Appendix.]

i·tin·er·an·cy (ī-tĭn′ər-ən-sē, ĭ-tĭn′-) also **i·tin·er·a·cy** (-ə-sē) *n., pl.* **-cies.** A state or system of itinerating, especially in the role or office of public speaker, minister, or judge.

i·tin·er·ant (ī-tĭn′ər-ənt, ĭ-tĭn′-) *adj.* Traveling from place to place, especially to perform work or a duty: *an itinerant judge; itinerant labor.* **—itinerant** *n.* One who travels from place to place. [Late Latin *itinerāns, itinerant-,* present participle of *itinerārī,* to travel, from Latin *iter, itiner-,* journey. See **ei-** in Appendix.]

i·tin·er·ar·y (ī-tĭn′ə-rĕr′ē, ĭ-tĭn′-) *n., pl.* **-ies.** **1.** A route or proposed route of a journey. **2.** An account or a record of a journey. **3.** A guidebook for travelers. **—itinerary** *adj.* **1.** Of or relating to a journey or route. **2.** Traveling from place to place; itinerant. [Middle English *itinerarie,* from Late Latin *itinerārium,* account of a journey, from neuter of *itinerārius,* of traveling, from Latin *iter, itiner-,* journey. See **ei-** in Appendix.]

i·tin·er·ate (ī-tĭn′ə-rāt′, ĭ-tĭn′-) *intr.v.* **-at·ed, -at·ing, -ates.** To travel from place to place. [Late Latin *itinerārī, itinerāt-,* from Latin *iter, itiner-,* journey. See ITINERARY.] **—i·tin′er·a′tion** *n.*

–itis *suff.* **1.** Inflammation or disease of: *laryngitis.* **2.** Excessive preoccupation with, indulgence in, reliance on, or possession of the qualities of: *televisionitis.* [Greek, n. suff.]

it'll (ĭt′l). **1.** It will. **2.** It shall.

I·to (ē′tō′), Prince **Hirobumi.** 1841–1909. Japanese politician who helped draft the constitution of 1889 and served as prime minister (1885–1888, 1892–1896, 1898, and 1900–1901).

ITO *abbr.* International Trade Organization.

its (ĭts) *adj.* The possessive form of **it.** Used as a modifier before a noun: *The airline cancelled its early flight to New York.* [Alteration of *it's* : IT + –'S.]

USAGE NOTE: *Its,* the possessive form of the pronoun *it,* is never written with an apostrophe. The contraction *it's* (for *it is* or *it has*) is always written with an apostrophe.

it's (ĭts). **1.** It is. **2.** It has. See Usage Note at **its.**

it·self (ĭt-sĕlf′) *pron.* **1.** That one identical with it: **a.** Used reflexively as the direct or indirect object of a verb or the object of a preposition: *The cat scratched itself.* **b.** Used for emphasis: *The trouble is in the machine itself.* **c.** Used in an absolute construction: *Itself no great poem, it still reveals talent.* **2.** Its normal

ă pat	oi boy
ā pay	ou out
âr care	ŏŏ took
ä father	ōō boot
ĕ pet	ŭ cut
ē be	ûr urge
ĭ pit	th thin
ī pie	*th* this
îr pier	hw which
ŏ pot	zh vision
ō toe	ə about, item
ô paw	♦ regionalism

Stress marks: ′ (primary); ′ (secondary), as in **dictionary** (dĭk′shə-nĕr′ē)

or healthy condition or state: *The car is acting itself again since we changed the oil.*

I·tsu·ku·shi·ma (ĭt′so͞o-ko͞o′shĭ-mə). An island of southwest Japan in the Inland Sea southwest of Hiroshima.

it·ty-bit·ty (ĭt′ē-bĭt′ē) also **it·sy-bit·sy** (ĭt′sē-bĭt′sē) *adj. Informal.* Very small. [Probably alteration of *little bit.*]

It·u·rae·a (ĭch′ə-rē′ə). An ancient country of northeast Palestine. The area was first inhabited by Arabians and later passed to Judea and Rome. **—It′u·rae′an** *adj. & n.*

I·tur·bi·de (ē′to͝or-bē′dā, ē-to͝or′vē-*th*ĕ), **Agustín de.** 1783–1824. Mexican revolutionary leader who established Mexican independence from Spain (1821) and served as emperor of Mexico from 1822 to 1823.

–ity *suff.* State; quality: *abnormality.* [Middle English *-itie,* from Old French *-ite,* from Latin *-itās,* variant of *-tās,* -ty.]

IU *abbr.* International unit.

IUD *abbr.* Intrauterine device.

–ium *suff.* Chemical element or group: *californium.* [Alteration of *-um,* neuter suff.]

IV *abbr.* **1.** Intravenous. **2.** Intravenously.

I·van III Va·sil·ie·vich (ī′vən, ē-vän′; və-sĭl′yə-vĭch′). Known as "Ivan the Great." 1440–1505. Grand duke of Muscovy (1462–1505). His victories against the Tartars laid the foundations for eventual Russian unity.

Ivan IV Vasilievich. Known as "Ivan the Terrible." 1530–1584. The first czar of Russia (1547–1584). He conducted unsuccessful wars against Sweden and Livonia and terrorized the Russian aristocracy.

I·va·no-Fran·kovsk (ĭ-vä′nō-fräng-kôfsk′, ē-vä′nə-frŭn-). A city of southwest Ukraine southwest of Kiev. Chartered in 1662 as Stanislov, it passed to Austria in 1772 and to Poland in 1919. The city was incorporated into the Ukraine in 1939. Population, 210,000.

I·va·no·vo (ĭ-vä′nə-və). A city of west-central Russia northeast of Moscow. It has long been a textile-producing center. Population, 474,000.

–ive *suff.* Performing or tending toward a specified action: *demonstrative.* [Middle English, from Old French, from Latin *-īvus,* adj. suff.]

I've (īv). I have.

Ives (īvz), **Charles Edward.** 1874–1954. American composer whose works anticipated those of later 20th-century musicians in their abandonment of conventional tonality.

Ives, James Merritt. 1824–1895. American lithographer who with his partner Nathaniel Currier produced more than 7,000 popular prints depicting scenes from American life.

i·vied (ī′vēd) *adj.* Overgrown or cloaked with ivy: *"Harvard's ivied edifices"* (Joseph P. Kahn).

I·vi·za (ē-bē′sə, ē-vē′thä). See **Ibiza.**

i·vo·ry (ī′və-rē, īv′rē) *n., pl.* **-ries. 1.a.** A hard, smooth, yellowish-white substance composed primarily of dentin that forms the tusks of the elephant. **b.** A similar substance forming the tusks or teeth of certain other mammals, such as the walrus. **2.** A tusk, especially an elephant's tusk. **3.** An article made of ivory. **4.** A substance resembling ivory. **5.** *Color.* A pale or grayish yellow to yellowish white. **6.** Often **ivories. a.** *Music.* Piano keys. **b.** *Games.* Dice. **c.** *Slang.* The teeth. **—ivory** *adj.* **1.** Composed or constructed of ivory. **2.** *Color.* Of a pale or grayish yellow to yellowish white. [Middle English *ivorie,* from Old French *ivoire, ivurie,* from Latin *eboreus,* of ivory, from *ebur, ebor-,* ivory, from Coptic *ebou,* elephant, from Egyptian *'bw.*]

i·vo·ry·bill (ī′və-rē-bĭl′, īv′rē-) *n.* See **ivory-billed woodpecker.**

i·vo·ry-billed woodpecker (ī′və-rē-bĭld′, īv′rē-) *n.* A large, nearly extinct woodpecker *(Campephilus principalis)* of the southern United States and Cuba, having black plumage, white wing patches, an ivory-colored bill, and a bright red crest in the male. Also called *ivorybill.*

ivory black *n.* A black pigment prepared from charred ivory.

I·vo·ry Coast (ī′və-rē, īv′rē). A country of western Africa on the Gulf of Guinea. A former French colony, it became independent in 1960. Abidjan is the current capital and the largest city. Yamoussoukro was designated the new capital in 1983. Population, 7,920,000. **—I·vo′ri·an** (ī-vôr′ē-ən, ī-vōr′-), **I·voir′i·an** (ē-vwär′ē-ən) *adj. & n.*

ivory nut *n.* The seed of the ivory palm, having bony endosperm that is used as a substitute for true ivory.

i·vor·y-nut palm (ī′və-rē-nŭt′, īv′rē-) *n.* An ivory palm.

ivory palm *n.* A stemless, unarmed dioecious palm *(Phytelephas macrocarpa)* native to Brazil and Peru and having hard seeds that yield an ivorylike substance.

ivory tower *n.* A place or an attitude of retreat, especially preoccupation with lofty, remote, or intellectual considerations rather than practical everyday life. [Translation of French *tour d'ivoire* : *tour,* tower + *d',* of + *ivoire,* ivory.]

i·vy (ī′vē) *n., pl.* **i·vies.** Any of several woody, climbing or trailing evergreen plants of the genus *Hedera* native to the Old World, especially *H. helix,* having palmately lobed leaves, root-bearing young stems, and small green flowers grouped in umbels. [Middle English *ivi,* from Old English *īfig.*]

I·vy League (ī′vē) *n.* An association of eight universities and colleges in the northeast United States, comprising Brown, Columbia, Cornell, Dartmouth, Harvard, Princeton, the University of Pennsylvania, and Yale. **—Ivy League** *adj.* Of or resembling the traditions of the Ivy League. [So called because of the ivy that covers the older college buildings.] **—Ivy Leaguer** *n.*

IW *abbr.* **1.** Index word. **2.** Isotopic weight.

i.w. *abbr.* Inside width.

I·wa·ki (ĭ-wä′kē). A city of eastern Honshu, Japan, on the Pacific Ocean north-northeast of Tokyo. It is a port and an industrial center. Population, 350,566.

i·wis also **y·wis** (ĭ-wĭs′) *adv. Archaic.* Certainly; assuredly. [Middle English, from Old English *gewis,* certain. See **weid-** in Appendix.]

I·wo (ē′wō). A city of southwest Nigeria east-northeast of Ibadan. It was the capital of a Yoruba kingdom from the 17th to the 19th century. Population, 255,100.

I·wo Ji·ma (ē′wə jē′mə, ē′wō). The largest of the Volcano Islands of Japan in the northwest Pacific Ocean east of Taiwan. The island was the scene of severe fighting during World War II.

IWW *abbr.* Industrial Workers of the World.

Ix·elles (ēk-sĕl′). A city of central Belgium, an industrial suburb of Brussels. Population, 76,146.

Ix·i·on (ĭk-sī′ən, ĭk′sē-ŏn′) *n. Greek Mythology.* A king of Thessaly whom Zeus punished for his temerity in seeking Hera's love by having him bound to a perpetually revolving wheel in Hades.

ix·tle (ĭs′lē, ĭst′-) *n.* Variant of **istle.**

I·yar also **Iy·yar** (ē-yär′, ē′yär′) *n.* The eighth month of the year in the Jewish calendar. See table at **calendar.** [Hebrew *'iyār.*]

I·zal·co (ĭ-zăl′kō, ē-säl′-). An active volcano, about 2,388 m (7,828 ft) high and still increasing in height, of western El Salvador. It is sometimes called "the Lighthouse of the Pacific."

iz·ar (ĭ-zär′) *n.* A long cotton outer garment, usually white, traditionally worn by Moslem women. [Arabic *'izār, 'izr,* veil, covering, izar.]

–ization or **–isation** *suff.* Action, process, or result of doing or making: *colonization.* [–IZ(E) + –ATION.]

–ize or **–ise** *suff.* **1.a.** To cause to be or to become: *dramatize.* **b.** To cause to conform to or resemble: *Hellenize.* **c.** To treat as: *idolize.* **2.a.** To treat or affect with: *anesthetize.* **b.** To subject to: *tyrannize.* **3.** To treat according to or practice the method of: *pasteurize.* **4.** To become; become like: *materialize.* **5.** To perform, engage in, or produce: *botanize.* [Middle English *-isen,* from Old French *-iser,* from Late Latin *-izāre,* from Greek *-izein,* v. suff.]

USAGE NOTE: The suffix *–ize* is a productive means of turning nouns or adjectives into verbs, as in well-established forms such as *formalize, criticize, jeopardize,* and *hospitalize.* But the semantic versatility of the suffix can cause ambiguity, since the nature of the activity denoted by a verb formed in this way often depends on the context. Thus *computerize* may mean "to furnish with computers," as in *The entire office has been computerized,* or "to enter on a computer," as in *The records are not yet computerized.* And the sentence *Earthquake relief requirements must be prioritized* may mean that all relief requirements must be assigned a high priority or that the relative priority among requirements must be determined. The meanings of verbs such as these may be obscure to people who lack the relevant background information and will naturally tend to regard them as jargon. This is one reason that so many words formed with *–ize* met with critical resistance when they were first introduced, among them being *Americanize, nationalize,* and *jeopardize,* all of which are now acceptable. Although some recent words of this type are unobjectionable, for example, *computerize, institutionalize,* and *radicalize,* many others are associated with bureaucratic and corporate jargon, for example, *accessorize, incentivize, prioritize, privatize,* and in particular *finalize,* which despite its wide usage was judged unacceptable by 71 percent of the Usage Panel. Coinages of this sort should be used with caution until they have passed the tests of manifest utility and acceptance by reputable writers. See Usage Notes at **finalize, prioritize.**

I·zhevsk (ē-zhĕfsk′, ē-zhĭfsk′). Formerly **U·sti·nov** (o͞o-stĭn′ôf). A city of west-central Russia northeast of Kazan. Its ironworks date to 1760. Population, 611,000.

Iz·mir (ĭz-mîr′). Formerly **Smyr·na** (smûr′nə). A city of western Turkey on the **Gulf of Izmir,** an inlet of the Aegean Sea. Settled during the Bronze Age, Izmir is now a major port and an industrial center. Population, 757,854.

ivory
Nigerian belt mask of ivory, metal, and stone

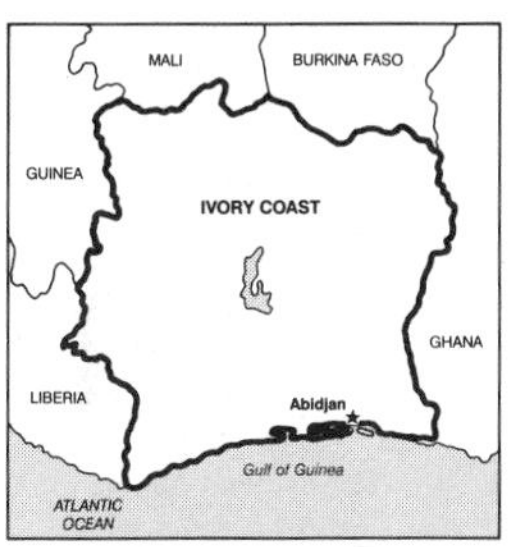

Ivory Coast

ivy

izar
Worn by Javanese women

Phoenician
The seventh letter of the Phoenician alphabet stood for the consonantal sound at the beginning of *yōdh,* "arm."

Early Greek
In adapting the Phoenician alphabet to their own language the Greeks applied this letter, which they called *iōta,* to the related vowel *i.*

I

Roman
The Romans used it for both sounds, *i* and *y*, the second of which came to be pronounced like English *j* by the 6th century. It was not until the 16th century that the medieval cursive variant J was used systematically to distinguish the consonant from the vowel.

jack

jackal

j[1] or **J** (jā) *n., pl.* **j's** or **J's.** **1.** The tenth letter of the modern English alphabet. **2.** Any of the speech sounds represented by the letter *j.* **3.** The tenth in a series. **4.** Something shaped like the letter J.

j[2] or **J** *Electricity.* The symbol for **current density** (sense 1).

j[3] or **J** *abbr.* Joule.

J *abbr. Games.* Jack.

J. *abbr.* **1.** Japanese. **2.** Or **j.** Journal. **3.** Or **j.** *Law.* Judge. **4.** Or **j.** *Law.* Justice.

JA *abbr.* **1.** Joint account. **2.** Also **J.A.** *Law.* Judge advocate.

jab (jăb) *v.* **jabbed, jab·bing, jabs.** —*tr.* **1.** To poke or thrust abruptly, especially with something sharp. **2.** To stab or pierce. **3.** To thrust into or against with a rough, abrupt movement: *"He laughed and jabbed his spectacles back on his nose"* (John Barth). **4.** To punch with short blows. —*intr.* **1.** To make an abrupt poking or thrusting motion. **2.** To deliver a quick punch. —**jab** *n.* **1.** A quick stab or blow. **2.** *Sports.* A short straight punch in boxing. [Variant of JOB[2].]

Jab·al·pur (jŭb′əl-po͝or′) also **Jub·bul·pore** (-pôr′, -pōr′). A city of central India south-southeast of Delhi. It is a manufacturing center and rail junction. Population, 614,162.

jab·ber (jăb′ər) *v.* **-bered, -ber·ing, -bers.** —*intr.* To talk rapidly, unintelligibly, or idly. —*tr.* To utter rapidly or unintelligibly. —**jabber** *n.* Rapid or babbling talk. [Middle English *javeren,* of imitative origin.] —**jab′ber·er** *n.*

jab·ber·wock·y (jăb′ər-wŏk′ē) *n.* Nonsensical speech or writing. [From *"Jabberwocky,"* a poem by Lewis Carroll.]

Ja·bir (jā′bər, jä′bîr). See **Geber.**

jab·i·ru (jăb′ə-ro͞o′) *n.* A large tropical American stork *(Jabiru mycteria)* having white plumage with a pink band at the neck and a naked head. [Portuguese and American Spanish *jabirú.*]

jab·o·ran·di (jăb′ə-răn-dē′, -răn′dē) *n., pl.* **-dis.** **1.** Either of two tropical American shrubs *(Pilocarpus jaborandi* or *P. microphyllus)* whose dried leaves yield the medicinal alkaloid pilocarpine. **2.** The dried leaves of these plants. [Portuguese and American Spanish.]

ja·bot (zhă-bō′, jăb′ō) *n.* An ornamental cascade of ruffles or frills down the front of a shirt, blouse, or dress. [French, crop of a bird, jabot; akin to Old French dialectal **gave,* throat, gullet, from Romance **gab-,* perhaps of Celtic origin.]

ja·cal (hä-käl′) *n., pl.* **-ca·les** (-kä′lās) or **-cals.** A thatch-roofed hut made of wattle and daub found in Mexico and the southwest United States. [American Spanish, from Nahuatl *xacalli* : *xamitl,* adobe + *calli,* house.]

jac·a·mar (jăk′ə-mär′) *n.* Any of various tropical American birds of the family Galbulidae, having iridescent plumage and a long bill. [French, possibly of Tupian origin.]

ja·ça·na (zhä′sə-nä′) also **ja·ca·na** (-kə-nä′) *n.* Any of several tropical water birds of the family Jacanidae, having long toes adapted for walking on floating vegetation. Also called *lily-trotter.* [Portuguese *jaçanã.*]

jac·a·ran·da (jăk′ə-răn′də) *n.* **1.** Any of several tropical American trees or shrubs of the genus *Jacaranda,* having pinnately compound, opposite leaves and panicles of pale purple flowers with funnel-shaped corollas. **2.** The wood of this tree or a wood similar to it. [Portuguese and American Spanish.]

ja·cinth (jā′sĭnth, jăs′ĭnth) *n.* See **hyacinth** (sense 1a). [Middle English *jacinte,* from Old French *jacinte* or from Medieval Latin *jacintus,* both from Latin *hyacinthus.* See HYACINTH.]

jack (jăk) *n.* **1.** Often **Jack.** *Informal.* A man; a fellow. **2. a.** One who does odd or heavy jobs; a laborer. **b.** One who works in a specified manual trade. Often used in combination: *a lumberjack; a steeplejack.* **c. Jack.** A sailor; a tar. **3.** *Abbr.* **J** *Games.* A playing card showing the figure of a servant or soldier and ranking below a queen. Also called *knave.* **4.** *Games.* **a. jacks** *(used with a sing. or pl. verb).* A game played with a set of small six-pointed metal pieces and a small ball, the object being to pick up the pieces in various combinations. **b.** One of the metal pieces so used. **5.** *Sports.* A pin used in some games of bowling. **6. a.** A usually portable device for raising heavy objects by means of force applied with a lever, screw, or hydraulic press. **b.** A wooden wedge for cleaving rock. **7.** *Nautical.* **a.** A support or brace, especially the iron crosstree on a topgallant masthead. **b.** A small flag flown at the bow of a ship, usually to indicate nationality. **8.** The male of certain animals, especially the ass. **9.** Any of several food and game fishes of the family Carangidae, found in tropical and temperate seas. **10.** A jackrabbit. **11.** A socket that accepts a plug at one end and attaches to electric circuitry at the other. **12.** *Slang.* Money. **13.** Applejack. —**jack** *v.* **jacked, jack·ing, jacks.** —*tr.* **1.** To hunt or fish for with a jacklight: *hunters illegally jacking deer.* **2. a.** To hoist with a jack: *jacked the rear of the car to replace the tire.* **b.** To raise (something) to a higher level, as in cost: *"Foreign producers jacked up the price on some steels by over 100"* (Forbes). —*intr.* To hunt or fish for quarry by using a jacklight. —***phrasal verb.* jack off.** *Vulgar Slang.* To masturbate. [From the name *Jack,* from Middle English *Jakke,* possibly from Old French *Jacques,* from Latin *Iacōbus,* from Greek *Iakōb,* from Hebrew *Ya'ăqōb.*] —**jack′er** *n.*

jack·al (jăk′əl, -ôl′) *n.* **1.** Any of several doglike mammals of the genus *Canis* of Africa and southern Asia that are mainly foragers feeding on plants, small animals, and occasionally carrion. **2. a.** An accomplice or a lackey who aids in the commission of base or disreputable acts. **b.** One who performs menial tasks for another. [Turkish *chakāl,* from Persian *shaghāl,* from Middle Indic *shagāl,* from Sanskrit *śṛgālaḥ.*]

jack·a·napes (jăk′ə-nāps′) *n.* **1.** A conceited or impudent person. **2.** A mischievous child. **3.** *Archaic.* A monkey or an ape. [From Middle English *Jack Napis,* nickname of William de la Pole, Fourth Earl and First Duke of Suffolk (1396–1450).]

jack·ass (jăk′ăs′) *n.* **1.** A male ass or donkey. **2.** A foolish or stupid person; a blockhead: *"You've acted like an irrational jackass and it's time you stopped"* (Margaret Truman).

jackass rig *n. Nautical.* A nonstandard combination of square rig and fore-and-aft rig on a sailing ship that has two or more masts. Also called *hermaphrodite rig.*

jack bean *n.* A tropical American annual plant *(Canavalia ensiformis)* having clusters of purple flowers and long pods with edible seeds.

jack·boot also **jack-boot** (jăk′bo͞ot′) *n.* **1.** A stout military boot that extends above the knee. **2.** A person who uses bullying tactics, especially to force compliance. **3.** The spirit sustaining and motivating a militaristic, highly aggressive, or totalitarian regime or system.

jack·boot·ed also **jack-boot·ed** (jăk′bo͞o′tĭd) *adj.* **1.** Wearing jackboots. **2.** Cruelly and violently oppressive: *"a revival of the aggressive, jack-booted militarism of the Thirties and Forties"* (Saturday Review).

jack·daw (jăk′dô′) *n.* A Eurasian crow *(Corvus monedula).*

jack·et (jăk′ĭt) *n.* **1.** A short coat usually extending to the hips. **2.** An outer covering or casing, especially: **a.** The skin of a potato. **b.** The dust jacket of a book. **c.** An insulation covering for a steam pipe, wire, boiler, or similar part. **d.** A paper or thin cardboard envelope for a phonograph record. **e.** An open envelope or folder for filing papers. **f.** *Computer Science.* The plastic or cardboard container that holds a floppy disk. **g.** The outer metal shell or case of a bullet. —**jacket** *tr.v.* **-et·ed, -et·ing, -ets.** To supply or cover with a jacket. [Middle English *jaket,* from Old French *jaquet,* diminutive of *jaque,* short jacket, tunic, from *jacques,* nickname for French peasants (from the name *Jacques;* see JACK) or from Catalan (from Arabic *šakk,* mailcoat, breastplate).] —**jack′et·ed** *adj.*

Jack Frost *n.* Frost or cold weather personified.

jack·fruit (jăk′fro͞ot′) *n.* **1.** A tropical Asian tree *(Artocarpus heterophyllus)* having large edible fruits, unisexual flowers, and fine-grained durable wood. **2.** The fruit of this tree. [Portuguese *jaca* (from Malayalam *cakkai*) + FRUIT.]

jack·ham·mer (jăk′hăm′ər) *n.* A hand-held machine for drilling rock and breaking up pavement, operated by compressed air. —**jack′ham′mer** *v.*

jack-in-the-box (jăk′ĭn-*thə*-bŏks′) *n., pl.* **jack-in-the-box·es** or **jacks-in-the-box** (jăks′-). A toy consisting of a clownlike puppet that springs out of a box when the lid is activated.

♦ **jack-in-the-pul·pit** (jăk′ĭn-*th*ə-po͝ol′pĭt, -pŭl′-) *n., pl.* **jack-in-the-pulpits.** An eastern North American tuberous herb *(Arisaema triphyllum)* having a striped, leaflike spathe with a bent blade and three-lobed leaves. Also called *Indian turnip.*

jack·knife (jăk′nīf′) *n.* **1.** A large clasp knife. **2.** *Sports.* A dive executed by jumping headfirst, bending the body at the waist, and, with the legs straight, touching the feet with the hands before straightening out to enter the water hands first. —**jackknife** *v.* **-knifed, -knif·ing, -knifes.** —*tr.* **1.** To fold or double (something or oneself) like a jackknife. **2.** To cut or stab with a jackknife. —*intr.* **1.** To bend or fold up like a jackknife: *A truck that had jackknifed was blocking the road.* **2.** To form a 90° angle.

jack·leg (jăk′lĕg′) *n.* A strikebreaker. [Perhaps JACK + (BLACK)LEG.]

jack·light (jăk′līt′) *n.* A light used as a lure in night hunting or fishing. —**jacklight** *intr.v.* **-light·ed, -light·ing, -lights.** To hunt or fish with a jacklight.

jack mackerel or **jack·mack·er·el** (jăk′măk′ər-əl, -măk′rəl) *n.* A common food and game fish *(Trachurus symmetricus)* of Pacific coastal waters. Also called *saurel.*

jack-of-all-trades (jăk′əv-ôl′trādz′) *n., pl.* **jacks-of-all-trades** (jăks′-). A person who can do many different kinds of work.

jack-o'-lan·tern (jăk′ə-lăn′tərn) *n., pl.* **jack-o'-lanterns.** **1.** A lantern made from a hollowed pumpkin with a carved face, usually displayed on Halloween. **2.** A phosphorescent light over marshy ground; ignis fatuus.

jack pine *n.* An evergreen tree *(Pinus banksiana)* of northern North America, having soft wood and short, twisted needles grouped in fascicles of two. Also called *scrub pine.*

jack·plane (jăk′plān′) *n.* A bench plane for rough surfacing, usually slightly over one foot in length.

jack·pot (jăk′pŏt′) *n.* **1.** *Games.* **a.** The accumulated stakes in a kind of poker that require one to hold a pair of jacks or better in order to open the betting. **b.** A cumulative pool in competitions and various other games. **2.** A top prize or reward.

jack·rab·bit (jăk′ răb′ĭt) or **jack rabbit** *n.* Any of several large, long-eared, long-legged hares of the genus *Lepus.* —**jackrabbit** *intr.v.* **-bit·ed, -bit·ing, -bits.** To move or begin to move rapidly or suddenly: *"A rear tire blew out and the car jackrabbited out of control"* (Sonny Kleinfield). —**jackrabbit** *adj.* Moving or beginning to move in a sudden, rapid manner: *won the race with a jackrabbit start.* [JACK(ASS) (from its long ears) + RABBIT.]

jack·screw (jăk′skro͞o′) *n.* A jack operated by a screw. Also called *screw jack.*

jack·shaft (jăk′shăft′) *n.* A short shaft that transmits motion from a motor to a machine, especially in an automobile.

jacks-in-the-box (jăks′ĭn-*th*ə-bŏks′) *n.* A plural of **jack-in-the-box.**

jack·snipe (jăk′snīp′) *n., pl.* **jacksnipe** or **-snipes.** **1.** An Old World wading bird *(Limnocryptes minima)* having brownish plumage and a long bill. **2.** Any of several similar New World wading birds.

jacks-of-all-trades (jăks′əv-ôl′trādz′) *n.* Plural of **jack-of-all-trades.**

Jack·son (jăk′sən). **1.** A city of south-central Michigan on the Grand River south of Lansing. It is an industrial and commercial center. Population, 39,739. **2.** The capital and largest city of Mississippi, in the west-central part of the state. Originally a small trading post, it was chosen as capital in 1821 and named in honor of Andrew Jackson. Population, 202,895. **3.** A city of western Tennessee northeast of Memphis. Settled in 1819, it is a processing and educational center. Population, 49,131.

Jackson, Andrew. Known as "Old Hickory." 1767–1845. The seventh President of the United States (1829–1837), who as a general in the War of 1812 defeated the British at New Orleans (1815). As president he opposed the Bank of America and increased the presidential powers.

Jackson, Helen (Maria Fiske) Hunt. 1830–1885. American writer known for *Ramona* (1884), a romantic novel concerning the injustices suffered by Native Americans.

Jackson, Howell Edmunds. 1832–1895. American jurist who served as an associate justice of the U.S. Supreme Court (1893–1895).

Jackson, Jesse Louis. Born 1941. American civil rights leader and politician. A Baptist minister, he directed national antidiscrimination efforts (1966–1977) and sought the 1984 and 1988 Democratic presidential nominations.

Jackson, Mahalia. 1911–1972. American singer whose powerful performances and recordings, such as "Move on up a Little Higher" (1945), did much to popularize gospel music.

Jackson, Robert Houghwout. 1892–1954. American jurist who served as an associate justice of the U.S. Supreme Court (1941–1954).

Jackson, Thomas Jonathan. Known as "Stonewall." 1824–1863. American Confederate general who commanded troops at both battles of Bull Run (1861 and 1862) and directed the Shenandoah Valley campaign (1862). He was accidentally killed by his own troops at Chancellorsville (1863).

Jackson Hole. A fertile valley of northwest Wyoming in the Rocky Mountains east of the Teton Range.

Jack·so·ni·an (jăk-sō′nē-ən) *adj.* Of or relating to Andrew Jackson, his concepts of popular government, or his presidency. —**Jack·so′ni·an** *n.* —**Jack·so′ni·an·ism** *n.*

Jack·son·ville (jăk′sən-vĭl′). **1.** A city of central Arkansas northeast of Little Rock. Population, 27,589. **2.** A city of northeast Florida on the St. Johns River near the Atlantic Ocean and the Georgia border. Settled in 1816, it is the largest city in Florida. Population, 540,920. **3.** A city of west-central Illinois west of Springfield. Laid out in 1825, it has varied industries. Population, 20,284. **4.** A city of eastern North Carolina near the Atlantic Ocean north-northeast of Wilmington. Population, 18,237.

jack·stay (jăk′stā′) *n.* *Nautical.* **1.** A stay for racing or cruising vessels used to steady the mast against the strain of the gaff. **2.** A rope, rod, or batten along the upper side of a yard, gaff, or boom to which a sail is fastened. **3.** A rope or rod running vertically on the forward side of the mast on which the yard moves.

jack·stone (jăk′stōn′) *n.* *Games.* **1. jackstones** *(used with a sing. verb).* The game of jacks. **2.** One of the pieces used in playing jacks.

jack·straw (jăk′strô′) *n.* *Games.* **1. jackstraws** *(used with a sing. verb).* A game played with a pile of straws or thin sticks, with the players attempting in turn to remove a single stick without disturbing the others. **2.** One of the straws or sticks used in this game.

jack-tar also **Jack-tar** (jăk′tär′) *n.* A sailor.

Ja·cob (jā′kəb). In the Old Testament, the son of Isaac and grandson of Abraham. His 12 sons became the progenitors of the 12 tribes of Israel.

Jac·o·be·an (jăk′ə-bē′ən) *adj.* Of or having to do with the reign of James I of England or his times. —**Jacobean** *n.* A prominent figure during this period. [From New Latin *Jacobaeus,* from Latin *Iacōbus,* James, Jacob. See JACK.]

Jac·o·bin (jăk′ə-bĭn) *n.* **1.** A radical or extreme leftist. **2.** A radical republican during the French Revolution. **3.** A Dominican friar. [French, after the *Jacobin* friars, in whose convent the Jacobins first met.] —**Jac′o·bin′ic, Jac′o·bin′i·cal** *adj.* —**Jac′o·bin·ism** *n.* —**Jac′o·bin·ize′** (-bĭ-nīz′) *v.*

Jac·o·bite (jăk′ə-bīt′) *n.* A supporter of James II of England or of the Stuart pretenders after 1688. [From New Latin *Jacobus,* James, from Latin *Iacōbus.* See JACK.] —**Jac′o·bit′i·cal** (-bĭt′ĭ-kəl) *adj.* —**Jac′o·bit·ism** (-bī-tĭz′əm) *n.*

Ja·cobs (jā′kəbz), **Aletta.** 1854–1929. Dutch physician who opened the world's first birth control clinic in Amsterdam in 1882.

Jacobs, Jane. Born 1916. American writer whose works, including *The Death and Life of Cities* (1961), challenge traditional theories and methods of urban planning.

Ja·cob's ladder (jā′kəbz) *n.* **1.** *Nautical.* A rope or chain ladder with rigid rungs. **2.** Any of various plants of the genus *Polemonium,* especially *P. caeruleum,* having blue flowers and alternate, pinnately compound leaves with numerous leaflets. [From the ladder seen by the biblical patriarch Jacob in a dream (Genesis 28:12).]

jac·o·net (jăk′ə-nĕt′) *n.* A lightweight cotton cloth resembling lawn used for clothing and bandages. [From Urdu *jagannāthī,* after *Jagannath* (Puri), a town of eastern India.]

jac·quard also **Jac·quard** (jăk′ärd′, jə-kärd′) *n.* **1.** A fabric with an intricately woven pattern. **2.** A special loom or the method employed in the weaving of a figured fabric. [After Joseph Marie JACQUARD.] —**jac′quard′** *adj.*

Jac·quard (jăk′ärd′, jə-kärd′, zhä-kär′), **Joseph Marie.** 1752–1834. French inventor of the jacquard loom (1801), the first automatic loom able to weave complex patterns.

Jac·que·rie (zhä-krē′) *n.* **1.** The uprising of the French peasants against the nobility in 1358. **2. jacquerie.** A peasant revolt, especially a very bloody one. [French, from Old French *jacquerie,* peasantry, from *jacques,* peasant. See JACKET.]

jac·ti·ta·tion (jăk′tĭ-tā′shən) *n.* **1.** A false boasting or claim, especially one detrimental to the interests of another. **2.** *Pathology.* Extreme restlessness or tossing in bed, as can occur with some forms of acute disease. [Medieval Latin *iactitātiō, iactitātiōn-,* false declaration, from Latin *iactitātus,* past participle of *iactitāre,* to utter, frequentative of *iactāre,* to boast, frequentative of *iacere,* to throw. See **yē-** in Appendix.]

Ja·cuz·zi (jə-ko͞o′zē, jă-). A trademark used for a whirlpool bath or a device that swirls water in a bath.

jade¹ (jād) *n.* Either of two distinct minerals, nephrite and jadeite, that are generally pale green or white and are used mainly as gemstones or in carving. [French *(le) jade,* (the) jade, alteration of *(l')ejade,* from Spanish *(piedra de) ijada,* flank (stone) (from the belief that it cured renal colic), from Vulgar Latin **īliāta,* from Latin *īlia,* pl. of *īlium,* flank.] —**jade** *adj.*

jade² (jād) *v.* **jad·ed, jad·ing, jades.** —*tr.* To wear out, as by overuse or overindulgence. See Synonyms at **tire¹.** —*intr.* To become weary or spiritless. —**jade** *n.* **1.** A broken-down or useless horse; a nag. **2.** A woman regarded as disreputable or shrewish. [Middle English *iade;* akin to Swedish dialectal *jälda,* mare, possibly of Finno-Ugric origin.]

jad·ed (jā′dĭd) *adj.* **1.** Worn out; wearied: *"My father's words had left me jaded and depressed"* (William Styron). **2.** Dulled by surfeit; sated: *"the sickeningly sweet life of the amoral, jaded, bored upper classes"* (John Simon). **3.** Cynically or pretentiously callous. —**jad′ed·ly** *adv.* —**jad′ed·ness** *n.*

jade·ite (jā′dīt′) *n.* A rare, usually emerald to light green but sometimes white, auburn, buff, or violet mineral, $NaAlSi_2O_6$, used

jackhammer

Andrew Jackson

Jesse Jackson
Photographed in 1988

ă pat	oi boy
ā pay	ou out
âr care	o͝o took
ä father	o͞o boot
ĕ pet	ŭ cut
ē be	ûr urge
ĭ pit	th thin
ī pie	*th* this
îr pier	hw which
ŏ pot	zh vision
ō toe	ə about, item
ô paw	♦ regionalism

Stress marks: ′ (primary); ′ (secondary), as in **dictionary** (dĭk′shə-nĕr′ē)

jaguar
Panthera onca

Jahangir
Detail of *Jahangir Entertains Shah Abbas,* c. 1618

jai alai

jalousie
Window shutters

as a gem and for ornamental carvings. It is the tougher and more highly valued form of jade.

jae·ger (yā′gər) *n.* **1.** (*also* jā′gər). Any of several Arctic and Boreal sea birds of the genus *Stercorarius* that harass smaller birds and snatch the food they drop. Also called *skua.* **2.** A huntsman or hunting attendant. [German *Jäger,* hunter, jaeger, from Middle High German *jeger,* from Old High German *jagāri,* from *jagōn,* to hunt.]

Ja·én (hä-ĕn′). A city of southern Spain north-northwest of Granada. It is a distribution center. Population, 102,262.

Jaf·fa (jă′fə, yäf′ə). A former city of west-central Israel on the Mediterranean Sea. An ancient Phoenician city, it was taken by the Israelites in the 6th century A.D. and later fell to the Arabs (636), Crusaders (12th century), and Ottoman Turks (16th century). Jaffa was inhabited mainly by Arabs until the state of Israel was proclaimed in 1948. Since 1950 the city has been part of Tel Aviv–Jaffa.

Jaff·na (jäf′nə). A city of extreme northern Sri Lanka on Palk Strait. It was the center of an ancient Tamil culture until the Portuguese conquest of 1617. Population, 118,215.

jag¹ (jăg) *n.* **1.** A sharp projection; a barb. **2. a.** A hanging flap along the edge of a garment. **b.** A slash or slit in a garment exposing material of a different color. —**jag** *tr.v.* **jagged, jag·ging, jags. 1.** To cut jags in; notch. **2.** To cut unevenly. **3.** *Scots.* To jab sharply; prick. [Middle English *jagge.*] —**jag′ger** *n.* —**jag′less** *adj.*

jag² (jăg) *n.* **1.** *Slang.* **a.** A bout of drinking or drug use. **b.** A period of overindulgence in an activity; a spree: *a shopping jag; a crying jag.* See Synonyms at **binge. 2.** A small load or portion. [Origin unknown.]

J.A.G. also **JAG** *abbr. Law.* Judge advocate general.

Jag·a·tai (jăg′ə-tī′) or **Chag·a·tai** (chăg′-). Died 1242. Mongol ruler who succeeded his father, Genghis Khan.

jag·ged (jăg′ĭd) *adj.* **1.** Marked by irregular projections and indentations on the edge or surface. See Synonyms at **rough. 2.** Having a rough or harsh quality: *"not a stutter exactly but a jagged sound, as if the words were being broken-off from some other, stronger current of words deep inside"* (Anne Tyler). —**jag′ged·ly** *adv.* —**jag′ged·ness** *n.*

jag·ger·y (jăg′ə-rē) *n.* Unrefined sugar made from palm sap. [Portuguese dialectal *jagara,* ultimately from Dravidian *carucarai,* to be rough.]

jag·gy (jăg′ē) *adj.* **-gi·er, -gi·est.** Jagged or serrated.

jag·uar (jăg′wär′, jăg′yo͞o-är′) *n.* A large feline mammal *(Panthera onca)* of Central and South America, closely related to the leopard and having a tawny coat spotted with black rosettes. [Spanish and Portuguese, from Guarani *jaguá, yaguar,* dog.]

jag·ua·run·di also **jag·ua·ron·di** (jăg′wə-rŭn′dē) *n., pl.* **-dis.** A long-tailed, grayish-brown wildcat *(Felis yagouaroundi)* of tropical America. [Spanish and Portuguese, from Guarani *jaguarundi, yaguarundi,* variant of *jaguá, yaguar,* dog.]

Ja·han·gir (jə-hän′gîr). Called "Conqueror of the World." 1569–1627. Mogul emperor (1605–1627) who succeeded his father, Akbar, and continued his expansionist policies.

Jah·veh (yä′vā, vĕ) or **Jah·weh** (-wā, -wĕ) *n.* Variants of **Yahweh.**

jai a·lai (hī′ lī′, hī′ ə-lī′, hī′ ə-lī′) *n. Sports.* An extremely fast court game in which players use a long hand-shaped basket strapped to the wrist to propel the ball against a wall. [Spanish, from Basque : *jai,* festival + *alai,* joyous.]

jail (jāl) *n.* **1.** A place for the confinement of persons in lawful detention; a prison. **2.** Detention in a jail. —*attributive.* Often used to modify another noun: *a jail population; jail conditions.* —**jail** *tr.v.* **jailed, jail·ing, jails.** To detain in custody; imprison. [From Middle English *jaiole* (from Old French) and from Middle English *gaiol, gaol* (from Old North French *gaiole*), both from Vulgar Latin **gaviola,* from Latin **caveola,* diminutive of *cavea,* cage, hollow.]

jail·bait (jāl′bāt′) *n. Slang.* A person below the age of consent with whom sexual intercourse can constitute statutory rape.

jail·bird (jāl′bûrd′) *n. Informal.* A prisoner or an ex-convict.

jail·break (jāl′brāk′) *n.* An escape from jail.

jail·er also **jail·or** (jā′lər) *n.* One whose responsibility is keeping a jail.

jail·house (jāl′hous′) *n.* A place for incarcerating prisoners; a jail.

jailhouse lawyer *n. Slang.* A prison inmate who is usually self-taught in the law and offers legal consultation within a prison or corrections system.

jail·or (jā′lər) *n.* Variant of **jailer.**

Jain (jīn) also **Jai·na** (jī′nə) *n.* A believer or follower of Jainism. [Hindi *jaina,* from Sanskrit *jaina-,* relating to the saints, from *jinaḥ,* saint, victor, from *jayati,* he conquers.]

Jain·ism (jī′nĭz′əm) *n.* An ascetic religion of India, founded in the sixth century B.C., that teaches the immortality and transmigration of the soul and denies the existence of a perfect or supreme being.

Jai·pur (jī′po͝or′). A city of northwest India south-southwest of Delhi. The center of a former state established in the 12th century, Jaipur was founded in 1728. Population, 977,165.

Ja·kar·ta or **Dja·kar·ta** (jə-kär′tə). Formerly **Ba·ta·vi·a** (bə-tā′vē-ə). The capital and largest city of Indonesia, on the northeast coast of Java. Founded c. 1619 by the Dutch, it became an important center of the Dutch East India Company and was renamed Jakarta after Indonesia became independent in 1949. Population, 6,503,449.

jake (jāk) *adj. Slang.* Suitable or satisfactory; fine. [Origin unknown.]

jakes (jāks) *pl.n. (used with a sing. or pl. verb). Chiefly British.* A latrine; a privy. [Perhaps from French *Jacques,* James, Jack. See JACK.]

Ja·kob-Creutz·feldt disease (yä′kôp-kroits′fĕlt) *n.* See **Creutzfeldt-Jakob disease.**

jal·ap (jăl′əp, jä′ləp) *n.* **1.** A twining, eastern Mexican vine *(Exogonium purga)* having tuberous roots that are dried, powdered, and used medicinally as a cathartic. **2.** Any of several similar or related plants. **3.** The dried tuberous roots of these plants. [French, from American Spanish *jalapa,* short for *(purga de) Jalapa,* (purgative of) Jalapa, after JALAPA.]

Ja·la·pa (hə-lä′pə, hä-lä′pä) also **Jalapa En·rí·quez** (ĕn-rē′kĕs). A city of east-central Mexico east of Mexico City. Built on the site of a pre-Columbian city, Jalapa was captured by Cortés in 1519. Population, 204,594.

ja·la·pe·ño (hä′lə-pān′yō) *n., pl.* **-ños.** A cultivar of the tropical pepper *(Capsicum annuum)* having a very pungent green or red fruit used in cooking. [American Spanish *(chile) jalapeño,* (chile of) Jalapa, after JALAPA.]

ja·lop·y (jə-lŏp′ē) *n., pl.* **-ies.** *Informal.* An old, dilapidated motor vehicle, especially an automobile. [Origin unknown.]

jal·ou·sie (jăl′ə-sē) *n.* A blind or shutter having adjustable horizontal slats for regulating the passage of air and light. [French, from *jalousie,* jealousy, from Old French *gelosie,* from *gelos,* jealous. See JEALOUS.]

jam¹ (jăm) *v.* **jammed, jam·ming, jams.** —*tr.* **1.** To drive or wedge forcibly into a tight position: *jammed the cork in the bottle.* **2.** To activate or apply suddenly: *jam the brakes on.* **3.** To cause (moving parts, for example) to lock into an unworkable position: *jammed the typewriter keys.* **4. a.** To pack (items, for example) to excess; cram: *jammed my clothes into the suitcase.* **b.** To fill (something) to excess: *a suitcase that had been jammed with clothes.* **5.** To block, congest, or clog: *a drain that was jammed by debris.* **6.** To crush or bruise: *jam a finger.* **7.** *Electronics.* To interfere with or prevent the clear reception of (broadcast signals) by electronic means. —*intr.* **1.** To become wedged or stuck. **2.** To become inoperable: *a typewriter keyboard that had jammed.* **3.** To force one's way into or through a limited space. **4.** *Music.* To play improvisations. —**jam** *n.* **1.** The act of jamming or the condition of being jammed. **2.** A crush or congestion of people or things in a limited space: *a traffic jam.* **3.** A trying situation; a predicament. See Synonyms at **predicament.** [Origin unknown.] —**jam′ma·ble** *adj.* —**jam′mer** *n.*

jam² (jăm) *n.* A preserve made from whole fruit boiled to a pulp with sugar. [Possibly from JAM¹.] —**jam′my** *adj.*

Ja·mai·ca (jə-mā′kə). *Abbr.* **Jam.** An island country in the Caribbean Sea south of Cuba. It was settled in 1509 by the Spanish and ceded to Great Britain in 1670. The country became independent in 1962. Kingston is the capital and the largest city. Population, 2,190,357. —**Ja·mai′can** *adj. & n.*

jamb also **jambe** (jăm) *n.* **1.** One of a pair of vertical posts or pieces that together form the sides of a door, window frame, or fireplace, for example. **2.** A projecting mass or columnar part. [Middle English *jambe,* from Old French, leg, jamb, from Late Latin *gamba,* horse's hock, leg. See GAMBOL.]

jam·ba·lay·a (jŭm′bə-lī′ə) *n.* A Creole dish consisting of rice that has been cooked with shrimp, oysters, ham, or chicken and seasoned with spices and herbs. [Louisiana French, from Provençal *jambalaia.*]

jambe (jăm) *n.* Variant of **jamb.**

jam·beau (jăm′bō) *n., pl.* **-beaux** (-bōz). A piece of armor for the leg below the knee. [Middle English, probably from Old North French **jambeau,* from Old French *jambe,* leg. See JAMB.]

jam·bo·ree (jăm′bə-rē′) *n.* **1.** A noisy celebration. **2.** A large assembly, often international, especially of Boy Scouts or Girl Scouts. **3.** A mass gathering or assembly, as of a political party or association. [Origin unknown.]

James (jāmz) *n. Abbr.* **Jm.** *Bible.* See table at **Bible.**

James¹, Saint. Known as "the Great." Died A.D. 44. One of the 12 Apostles. The son of Zebedee and brother of John, he preached in Spain and was martyred on his return to Judea.

James², Saint. Known as "the Less." Died c. A.D. 62. Traditionally regarded as the brother of Jesus, the author of the Epistle of James in the New Testament, and the first bishop of Jerusalem.

James³, Saint. fl. first century A.D. One of the 12 Apostles.

James I. 1566–1625. King of England (1603–1625) and of Scotland as James VI (1567–1625). The son of Mary Queen of Scots, he succeeded Elizabeth I as the first Stuart king of England. His belief in the divine right of kings and attempts to keep peace with Spain led to the English Civil War.

James II. 1633–1701. King of England, Scotland, and Ireland (1685–1688). The last Stuart king to rule both England and Scotland, he was overthrown by his son-in-law William of Orange.

James, Henry. 1843–1916. American writer and critic whose works generally concern the confrontation of American and European culture. He wrote numerous novels, including *The Bostonians* (1886) and *The Golden Bowl* (1904).

James, **Jesse.** 1847–1882. American outlaw. After fighting in the Civil War as a Confederate guerrilla, he led a group of armed brigands that for 15 years robbed banks and trains in the West. He was murdered by a member of his own gang.

James, **William.** 1842–1910. American psychologist and philosopher. A founder of pragmatism and the psychological movement of functionalism, he developed an approach to intellectual issues that greatly influenced American thought.

James Bay. The southern arm of Hudson Bay, in Northwest Territories, Canada, between northeast Ontario and western Quebec. It was first sighted by Henry Hudson in 1610.

James·i·an (jām′zē-ən) *adj.* **1.** Of, relating to, or characteristic of William James, his philosophy, or his teachings. **2.** Of, relating to, or characteristic of Henry James or his writings.

James River. **1.** A river rising in central North Dakota and flowing about 1,142 km (710 mi) generally south across South Dakota to the Missouri River. **2.** A river, about 547 km (340 mi) long, rising in central Virginia and flowing eastward to Chesapeake Bay. The river is navigable to Richmond for large craft.

James·town (jāmz′toun′). **1.** The capital of St. Helena in the southern Atlantic Ocean. Population, 1,516. **2.** A city of western New York on Chautauqua Lake near the Pennsylvania border. It is the trade center of a farming and grape-producing region. Population, 35,775. **3.** A city of southeast-central North Dakota on the James River east of Bismarck. Settled in 1872 when Fort Seward was established nearby, it is an agricultural market center. Population, 16,280. **4.** A former village of southeast Virginia, the first permanent English settlement in America. It was founded in May 1607 and named for James I. Jamestown became the capital of Virginia after 1619 but was almost entirely destroyed during Bacon's Rebellion (1676) and further declined after the removal of the capital to Williamsburg (1698–1700).

Ja·mi·son (jā′mĭ-sən), **Judith.** Born 1944. American dancer and choreographer who became director of the Alvin Ailey American Dance Theater in 1989.

jam·mies (jăm′ēz) *pl.n.* *Informal.* Pajamas. [By shortening and alteration.]

Jam·mu (jŭm′o͞o). A city of northern India near the Pakistan border south of Srinagar. Formerly the seat of a Rajput dynasty, it was later captured by the Sikhs. Population, 206,135.

Jammu and Kash·mir (kăsh′mîr′, kăsh-mîr′). A former princely state of northern India and Pakistan. Part of the Mogul Empire after 1587, it was annexed by British India in 1846 and partitioned between India and Pakistan after fierce fighting (1947–1949).

Jam·na·gar (jäm-nŭg′ər). A city of western India on the Gulf of Kutch southwest of Ahmadabad. Founded in 1540, it is noted for its silk, embroidery, and marble. Population, 277,615.

jam-pack (jăm′păk′) *tr.v.* **-packed, -pack·ing, -packs.** *Informal.* To crowd to capacity: *a road jam-packed with cars.*

jam session *n.* **1.** *Music.* An impromptu gathering of musicians to play improvisations. **2.** *Informal.* An impromptu discussion.

Jam·shed·pur (jäm′shĕd-po͝or′). A city of eastern India west-northwest of Calcutta. It developed as a steel-producing center after 1911. Population, 438,385.

jam-up (jăm′ŭp′) *n.* A congested situation; a jam.

Jan. *abbr.* January.

Ja·ná·ček (yä′nə-chĕk′), **Leoš.** 1854–1928. Czechoslovakian composer whose works, such as the operas *Jenůfa* (1904) and *Katya Kabanová* (1921), draw themes from his nation's folk music.

Jane Doe (jān′ dō′) *n.* **1.** Used as a name in legal proceedings to designate a fictitious or unidentified woman or girl. **2.** An average, undistinguished woman.

Janes·ville (jānz′vĭl′). A city of southern Wisconsin north of Beloit. It is an industrial center. Population, 51,071.

jan·gle (jăng′gəl) *v.* **-gled, -gling, -gles.** —*intr.* To make a harsh, metallic sound: *The spurs jangled noisily.* —*tr.* **1.** To cause to make a harsh, discordant sound. **2.** To grate on or jar (the nerves). —**jangle** *n.* A harsh, metallic sound. [Middle English *janglen,* to chatter, from Old French *jangler,* probably of Germanic origin.] —**jan′gler** *n.*

jan·is·sar·y (jăn′ĭ-sĕr′ē) also **jan·i·zar·y** (-zĕr′ē) *n., pl.* **-ies.** **1.** A member of a group of elite, highly loyal supporters. **2.** A soldier in an elite Turkish guard organized in the 14th century and abolished in 1826. [French *janissaire,* from Old French *jehanicere,* from Old Italian *giannizero,* from Ottoman Turkish *yanī cheri,* new army : *yanī,* new + *cheri,* special troops (from Middle Persian *chērīh,* bravery, victory, from *chēr,* brave, victorious, from Avestan *chairya-,* vigorous, brave).]

jan·i·tor (jăn′ĭ-tər) *n.* **1.** One who attends to the maintenance or cleaning of a building. **2.** A doorman. [Latin *iānitor,* doorkeeper, from *iānua,* door, from *iānus,* archway. See **ei-** in Appendix.] —**jan′i·to′ri·al** (-tôr′ē-əl, -tōr′-) *adj.*

WORD HISTORY: A holiday for janitors ought to take place in January, for both words are linked. In Latin *iānus* was the word for "archway, gateway, or covered passage" and also for the god of gates, doorways, and beginnings in general. As many schoolchildren know, our month January—a month of beginnings—is named for the god. Latin *iānitor,* the source of our word *janitor* and ultimately also from *iānus,* meant "doorkeeper or gatekeeper." Probably because *iānitor* was common in Latin records and documents, it was adopted into English, first being recorded in the sense "doorkeeper" around 1567 in a Scots text. In an early quotation Saint Peter is called "the Janitor of heaven." The term can still mean "doorkeeper," but in Scots usage *janitor* also referred to a minor school official. Apparently this position at times involved maintenance duties and doorkeeping, and the maintenance duties took over the more exalted tasks, giving us the position of janitor as we know it today.

jan·i·zar·y (jăn′ĭ-zĕr′ē) *n.* Variant of **janissary.**

Jan May·en Island (yän mī′ən). An island of Norway in the Greenland Sea between northern Norway and Greenland.

Jan·sen (jăn′sən, yän′-), **Cornelis.** 1585–1638. Dutch theologian whose teachings were deemed heretical by Pope Urban VIII (1642) and influenced Jean Racine and Blaise Pascal.

Jan·sen·ism (jăn′sə-nĭz′əm) *n.* The theological principles of Cornelis Jansen, which emphasize predestination, deny free will, and maintain that human nature is incapable of good and were condemned as heretical by the Roman Catholic Church. —**Jan′sen·ist** *n.* —**Jan′sen·is′tic** *adj.*

Jan·u·ar·y (jăn′yo͞o-ĕr′ē) *n., pl.* **-ies.** *Abbr.* **Jan., Jan** The first month of the year in the Gregorian calendar. See table at **calendar.** [Middle English *Januarie, Jenever,* from Old North French *Jenever,* from Latin *Iānuārius (mēnsis),* (month) of Janus, from *Iānus,* Janus. See **ei-** in Appendix.]

Ja·nus (jā′nəs) *n.* *Roman Mythology.* **1.** The god of gates and doorways, depicted with two faces looking in opposite directions. **2.** The satellite of Saturn that is fourth in distance from the planet. [Latin *Iānus.* See **ei-** in Appendix.]

Ja·nus-faced (jā′nəs-fāst′) *adj.* Hypocritical.

Jap (jăp) *n.* *Offensive Slang.* Used as a disparaging term for a Japanese.

ja·pan (jə-păn′) *n.* **1.** A black enamel or lacquer used to produce a durable glossy finish. **2.** An object decorated with this substance. —**japan** *tr.v.* **-panned, -pan·ning, -pans.** **1.** To decorate with a black enamel or lacquer. **2.** To coat with a glossy finish. [After JAPAN.]

Ja·pan (jə-păn′). A country of Asia on an archipelago off the northeast coast of the mainland. Traditionally settled c. 660 B.C., Japan's written history began in the 5th century A.D. During the feudal period (12th–19th century) real power was held by the shoguns, local warriors whose dominance was finally ended by the restoration of the emperor Mutsuhito in 1868. At about the same time the country was opened to Western trade and industrial technology. Expansionist policies led to Japan's participation in World War II, which ended after atomic bombs were dropped on Hiroshima and Nagasaki (August 1945). Today the country is highly industrialized and noted for its advanced technology. Tokyo is the capital and the largest city. Population, 121,047,196.

Japan, **Sea of.** An enclosed arm of the western Pacific Ocean between Japan and the Asian mainland. It is connected with the East China Sea, the Pacific Ocean, and the Sea of Okhotsk by several straits.

Japan clover *n.* An annual plant *(Lespedeza striata)* native to China and Japan, having compound leaves with many leaflets and small pink axillary flowers. Cultivated as a forage plant and for soil improvement, it is widely naturalized in the southeast United States. Also called *Japanese clover.*

Japan Current *n.* A warm ocean current flowing northeast from the Philippine Sea past southeast Japan to the North Pacific. Also called *Kuroshio Current.*

Jap·a·nese (jăp′ə-nēz′, -nēs′) *adj.* Of or relating to Japan or its people, language, or culture. —**Japanese** *n., pl.* **Japanese.** **1.a.** A native or inhabitant of Japan. **b.** A person of Japanese ancestry. **2.** *Abbr.* **J.** The language of the Japanese, written in kana mixed with Chinese characters.

Japanese andromeda *n.* An ornamental shrub *(Pieris japonica)* native to Japan and having small, early-blooming white flowers.

Japanese beetle *n.* A metallic-green and brown beetle *(Popillia japonica)* native to eastern Asia, the larvae and adults of which feed on and damage various crop plants in North America.

Japanese cedar *n.* An eastern Asian coniferous evergreen tree *(Cryptomeria japonica)* having curved, spirally arranged leaves and cultivated as an ornamental and timber tree. Also called *cryptomeria.*

Japanese clover *n.* See **Japan clover.**

Japanese iris *n.* A Japanese ornamental plant *(Iris kaempferi)* widely grown for its numerous cultivars, which have large, variously colored, showy flowers.

Japanese ivy *n.* See **Boston ivy.**

Japanese maple *n.* An eastern Asian shrub or small tree *(Acer palmatum)* widely cultivated for its decorative, deeply and palmately lobed, often reddish foliage.

Japanese persimmon *n.* See **kaki.**

Japanese quail *n.* See **coturnix.**

Japanese quince *n.* A Chinese ornamental shrub *(Chaenomeles speciosa)* having spiny branches, sharply serrate leaves, and red or white flowers.

Japanese radish *n.* See **daikon.**

Japanese river fever *n.* See **scrub typhus.**

Japanese spurge *n.* See **pachysandra.**

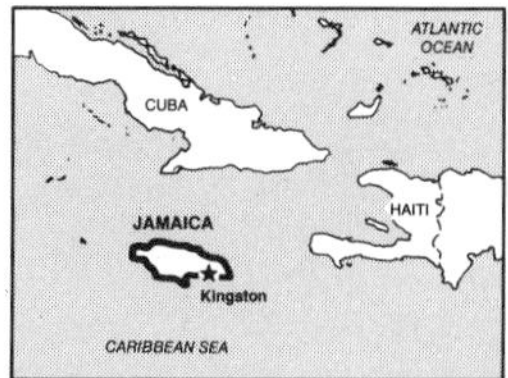

Jamaica

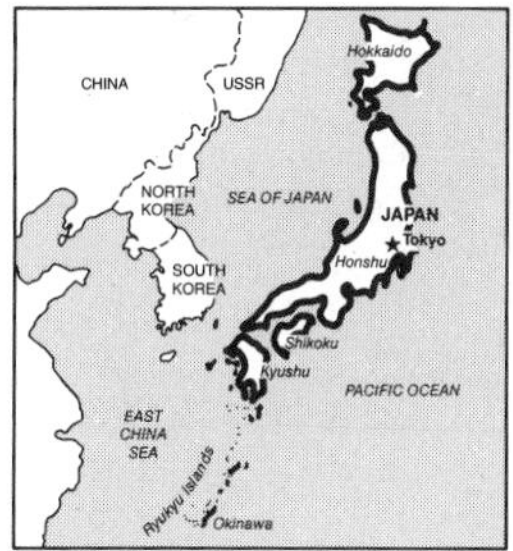

Japan

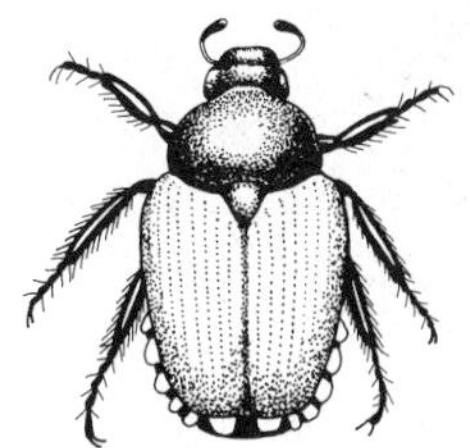
Japanese beetle
Popillia japonica

ă pat	oi boy
ā pay	ou out
âr care	o͝o took
ä father	o͞o boot
ĕ pet	ŭ cut
ē be	ûr urge
ĭ pit	th thin
ī pie	*th* this
îr pier	hw which
ŏ pot	zh vision
ō toe	ə about, item
ô paw	♦ regionalism

Stress marks: **′** (primary); ′ (secondary), as in **dictionary** (dĭk′shə-nĕr′ē)

Jap·a·nize (jăp′ə-nīz′) *tr. & intr.v.* **-nized, -niz·ing, -niz·es.** To make or become Japanese in form, idiom, style, or character. **—Jap′a·ni·za′tion** (-nĭ-zā′shən) *n.*

Japan Trench. A depression in the floor of the northern Pacific Ocean off northeast Japan. It extends from the Bonin to the Kuril islands and reaches depths of more than 9,000 m (30,000 ft).

Japan wax *n.* A pale yellow solid wax obtained from the berries of certain plant species of the genus *Rhus* and used in wax matches, soaps, and food packaging.

jape (jāp) *v.* **japed, jap·ing, japes.** *—intr.* To joke or quip. *—tr.* To make sport of. **—jape** *n.* A joke or quip. [Middle English *japen,* probably from Old French *japer,* to yap, chatter, nag, of imitative origin.] **—jap′er** *n.* **—jap′er·y** *n.*

Ja·pheth (jā′fĭth′, jăf′ĭth). In the Old Testament, a son of Noah and the brother of Shem and Ham.

Ja·phet·ic (jə-fĕt′ĭk) *adj.* **1.** Of or relating to Japheth or his descendants. **2.** Of or relating to a discredited linguistic grouping that attempted to associate Basque, Etruscan, and sometimes Sumerian and Elamite with the Caucasian languages.

jasmine
Common white jasmine
Jasminum officinale

Jap·lish (jăp′lĭsh) *n.* **1.** Japanese characterized by numerous borrowings from English. **2.** English affected by Japanese pronunciation, vocabulary, or syntax. [JAP(ANESE) + (ENG)LISH.]

ja·pon·i·ca (jə-pŏn′ĭ-kə) *n.* An ornamental shrub *(Chaenomeles japonica)* that is native to Japan and cultivated for its red flowers. [New Latin, species name, from *Japonia,* Japan.]

Jap·o·nism (jăp′ə-nĭz′əm) *n.* Something characteristically Japanese. [French *japonisme,* from *Japon,* Japan.]

Ja·pu·rá (zhä′po͞o-rä′). A river rising in the Andes of southwest Colombia and flowing about 2,816 km (1,750 mi) southeast across northwest Brazil to the Amazon River.

Jaques-Dal·croze (zhäk′däl-krōz′), **Émile.** 1865–1950. Swiss composer and educator who developed eurythmics.

jar¹ (jär) *n.* **1.** A cylindrical glass or earthenware vessel with a wide mouth and usually no handles. **2.** The amount that a jar can hold. **3.** *Chiefly British.* A glass of beer. **—jar** *tr.v.* **jarred, jar·ring, jars.** To put into a jar. [Middle English *jarre,* a liquid measure, from Old French (from Provençal *jarra)* and from Medieval Latin *jarra,* both from Arabic *jarrah,* earthen jar.] **—jar′ful′** *n.*

jar² (jär) *v.* **jarred, jar·ring, jars.** *—intr.* **1.** To make or utter a harsh sound. **2.** To be disturbing or irritating; grate: *The incessant talking jarred on my nerves.* **3.** To shake or shiver from impact. **4.** To clash or conflict: *"We ourselves . . . often jar with the landscape"* (Isak Dinesen). *—tr.* **1.** To bump or cause to move or shake from impact. **2.** To startle or unsettle; shock. **—jar** *n.* **1.** A jolt; a shock. See Synonyms at **collision. 2.** Harsh or grating sound; discord. [Perhaps of imitative origin.] **—jar′ring·ly** *adv.*

jar·di·nière (jär′dn-îr′, zhär′dn-yâr′) *n.* **1.** A large decorative stand or pot for plants or flowers. **2.** Diced, cooked vegetables served as a garnish with meat. [French, from feminine of *jardinier,* gardener, from Old French, from *jardin,* garden. See GARDEN.]

jar·gon (jär′gən) *n.* **1.** Nonsensical, incoherent, or meaningless talk. **2.** A hybrid language or dialect; a pidgin. **3.** The specialized or technical language of a trade, profession, or similar group. See Synonyms at **dialect. —jargon** *intr.v.* **-goned, -gon·ing, -gons.** To speak in or use jargon. [Middle English *jargoun,* from Old French *jargon,* probably of imitative origin.] **—jar′gon·ist, jar′gon·eer′** *n.* **—jar′gon·is′tic** *adj.*

jar·gon·ize (jär′gə-nīz′) *v.* **-ized, -iz·ing, -iz·es.** *—tr.* To translate into jargon. *—intr.* To talk or write jargon.

jar·head (jär′hĕd′) *n. Slang.* A U.S. Marine. [Perhaps from the shape of the hat the Marines once wore.]

jarl (yärl) *n.* A great medieval Scandinavian chieftain or nobleman. [Old Norse.]

Jarls·berg (yärlz′bûrg′). A trademark used for a mild, pale-yellow, hard Norwegian cheese with large holes.

javelin

jar·rah (jăr′ə) *n.* An Australian tree *(Eucalyptus marginata)* widely grown for its hard red-brown wood. [Nyungar (Aboriginal language of southwest Australia) *jarily.*]

Jar·rell (jə-rĕl′), **Randall.** 1914–1965. American poet whose works concern war, loneliness, and art.

jas·mine (jăz′mĭn) also **jes·sa·mine** (jĕs′ə-mĭn) *n.* **1.a.** Any of several vines or shrubs of the genus *Jasminum,* native chiefly to Asia and having usually compound leaves and white or yellow flowers. **b.** The perfume obtained from these plants. **2.** See **Carolina jasmine. 3.** Any of several plants or shrubs having fragrant flowers. **4.** *Color.* A light to brilliant yellow. [French *jasmin,* from Old French *jassemin,* from Arabic *yasmīn,* from Persian *yasmīn, yāsman.*]

Ja·son (jā′sən) *n. Greek Mythology.* The husband of Medea and leader of the Argonauts who went in quest of the Golden Fleece.

jas·per (jăs′pər) *n.* An opaque cryptocrystalline variety of quartz that may be red, yellow, or brown. [Middle English *jaspre,* from Anglo-Norman, from Latin *iaspis, iaspid-,* from Greek *iaspis,* from Persian *yašm,* from Arabic *yašb,* from Hebrew *yāšpê,* from Akkadian *ašpū.*]

Jas·pers (yäs′pərs), **Karl Theodor.** 1883–1969. German psychiatrist and philosopher. His works include *Man and the Modern World* (1931) and *The Future of Mankind* (1957).

jasper ware or **jas·per·ware** (jăs′pər-wâr′) *n.* A fine white stoneware originally produced by Josiah Wedgwood, often colored by metallic oxides with raised designs remaining white.

Jat (jät) *n.* A member of a peasant caste residing in the Punjab and other areas of northern India and Pakistan, comprising Moslem, Hindu, and Sikh groups. [Hindi *jāṭ.*]

ja·to (jā′tō) *n., pl.* **-tos. 1.** An aircraft takeoff aided by an auxiliary jet or rocket. **2.** An auxiliary jet-producing unit providing additional thrust for a takeoff. [*j(et-)a(ssisted) t(ake)o(ff).*]

jaun·dice (jôn′dĭs, jän′-) *n.* Yellowish discoloration of the whites of the eyes, skin, and mucous membranes caused by deposition of bile salts in these tissues. It occurs as a symptom of various diseases, such as hepatitis, that affect the processing of bile. Also called *icterus.* **—jaundice** *tr.v.* **-diced, -dic·ing, -dic·es. 1.** To affect with jaundice. **2.** To affect with envy, jealousy, prejudice, or hostility. See Synonyms at **bias.** [Middle English *jaundis, jaunis,* from Old French *jaunice,* yellowness, jaundice, from *jaune, jalne,* yellow, from Latin *galbinus,* yellowish.]

jaun·diced (jôn′dĭst, jän′-) *adj.* **1.** Affected with jaundice. **2.** Yellow or yellowish. **3.** Affected by or exhibiting envy, prejudice, or hostility.

jaunt (jônt, jänt) *n.* A short trip or excursion, usually for pleasure; an outing. **—jaunt** *intr.v.* **jaunt·ed, jaunt·ing, jaunts.** To make a short journey. [Origin unknown.]

jaun·ty (jôn′tē, jän′-) *adj.* **-ti·er, -ti·est. 1.** Having a buoyant or self-confident air; brisk. **2.** Crisp and dapper in appearance; natty. **3.** *Archaic.* **a.** Stylish. **b.** Genteel. [French *gentil,* nice, from Old French, noble. See GENTLE.] **—jaun′ti·ly** *adv.* **—jaun′ti·ness** *n.*

Jau·rès (zhô-rĕs′), **Jean.** 1859–1914. French journalist and leader of the French Socialist Party before World War II.

Jav. *abbr.* Javanese.

ja·va (jăv′ə, jä′və) *n. Informal.* Brewed coffee. [After JAVA.]

Ja·va (jä′və, jăv′ə). An island of Indonesia separated from Borneo by the **Java Sea,** an arm of the western Pacific Ocean. Center of an early Hindu-Javanese civilization, Java was converted to Islam before the arrival of the Europeans (mainly the Dutch) in the late 16th century.

Java man *n.* Pithecanthropus.

Jav·a·nese (jăv′ə-nēz′, -nēs′, jä′və-) *adj. Abbr.* **Jav.** Of or relating to Java or its people, language, or culture. **—Javanese** *n., pl.* **Javanese.** *Abbr.* **Jav. 1.** A native or inhabitant of Java, especially a member of the Javanese-speaking majority population. **2.** The Austronesian language of the principal ethnic group of Java. [JAVA + *-nese* (as in *Japanese*).]

Ja·va·rí (zhä′və-rē′). A river rising in eastern Peru and flowing about 965 km (600 mi) northeast along the Peru-Brazil border to the Amazon River.

Java sparrow *n.* A small grayish bird *(Padda oryzivora)* native to tropical Asia and often kept as a cage bird.

jave·lin (jăv′lĭn, jăv′ə-) *n.* **1.** A light spear thrown with the hand and used as a weapon. **2.** *Sports.* **a.** A metal or metal-tipped spear, about 2.5 meters (8¼ feet) in length, used in contests of distance throwing. **b.** The athletic field event in which a javelin is thrown. [Middle English, from Old French *javeline,* diminutive of *javelot,* of Celtic origin.]

ja·ve·li·na (hä′və-lē′nə) *n.* See **collared peccary.** [Alteration of Spanish *jabalina,* feminine of *jabalí, jabalín,* wild boar, from Arabic *(ḫinzīr) jabalī,* mountain (swine), from *jabal,* mountain.]

Ja·velle water also **Ja·vel water** (zhə-vĕl′) *n.* An aqueous solution of potassium or sodium hypochlorite, used as a disinfectant and bleaching agent. [Translation of French *eau de Javel,* after *Javel,* a former town of north-central France, now a section of Paris.]

jaw (jô) *n.* **1.a.** Either of two bony or cartilaginous structures that in most vertebrates form the framework of the mouth and hold the teeth. **b.** The mandible or maxilla or the part of the face covering these bones. **2.** Either of two opposed hinged parts in a mechanical device. **3. jaws.** The walls of a pass, canyon, or cavern. **4. jaws.** A dangerous situation or confrontation: *the jaws of death.* **5.** *Slang.* **a.** Impudent argument or back talk: *Don't give me any jaw.* **b.** A conversation or chat. **—jaw** *intr.v.* **jawed, jaw·ing, jaws.** *Slang.* **1.** To talk vociferously; jabber. **2.** To talk; converse. [Middle English *jawe, jowe,* perhaps from Old French *joue,* cheek.] **—jaw′less** *adj.*

jaw·bone (jô′bōn′) *n.* A bone of the jaw, especially the bone of the lower jaw. **—jawbone** *v.* **-boned, -bon·ing, -bones.** *Slang.* *—tr.* To try to influence or pressure through strong persuasion, especially to urge to comply voluntarily. *—intr.* To urge voluntary compliance with official wishes or guidelines. **—jaw′bon′er** *n.* **—jaw′bon′ing** *n.*

jaw·break·er (jô′brā′kər) *n.* **1.** A very hard candy. **2.** *Slang.* A word that is difficult to pronounce. **3.** A machine that crushes rock or ore. **—jaw′break′ing** *adj.* **—jaw′break′ing·ly** *adv.*

jawless fish (jô′lĭs) *n.* Any of several eellike marine and freshwater fishes lacking a jaw and paired appendages that constitute the subphylum Agnatha. The only present-day jawless fish are the hagfish and lampreys.

Jaws of Life (jôz). A trademark used for a pneumatic tool consisting of a pincerlike metal device that is inserted into the body of a severely damaged vehicle and opened to provide access to people trapped inside. This trademark sometimes occurs in print in lowercase: *"Firefighters used the jaws of life to remove* [the operator and the passenger]*"* (Boston Globe).

jay¹ (jā) *n.* The letter *j.*

jay² (jā) *n.* **1.** Any of various often crested birds of the genera *Garrulus, Cyanocitta, Aphelocoma,* and related genera within the family Corvidae, often having a loud, harsh call. Also called *jaybird.* **2.** An over talkative person; a chatterbox. [Middle English *jai,* from Old French, from Late Latin *gāius, gāia,* perhaps from Latin *Gāius,* personal name.]

Jay (jā), **John.** 1745–1829. American diplomat and jurist who served in both Continental Congresses and helped negotiate peace with Great Britain (1782–1783). He was the first chief justice of the U.S. Supreme Court (1789–1795) and negotiated a second agreement with Great Britain, Jay's Treaty (1794–1795).

jay·bird (jā′bûrd′) *n.* See **jay²** (sense 1).

Jay·cee (jā′sē′) *n.* A member of a junior chamber of commerce. [Pronunciation of the initial letters in *Junior Chamber (of Commerce).*]

jay·hawk·er (jā′hô′kər) *n.* **1.** One of the free-soil guerrillas in Kansas and Missouri during the border disputes of 1854 to 1859. **2.** A Unionist guerrilla. **3. Jayhawker.** *Informal.* A native or resident of Kansas. [From *jayhawk,* a fictitious bird.]

jay·vee (jā′vē′) *n. Sports.* **1.** Junior varsity. **2.** A member of a junior varsity. [Pronunciation of the initial letters in J(UNIOR) V(ARSITY).] **—jay′vee′** *adj.*

jay·walk (jā′wôk′) *intr.v.* **-walked, -walk·ing, -walks.** To cross a street illegally or in a reckless manner. [From JAY², inexperienced person.] **—jay′walk′er** *n.*

jazz (jăz) *n.* **1.** *Music.* **a.** A style of music, native to America, characterized by a strong but flexible rhythmic understructure with solo and ensemble improvisations on basic tunes and chord patterns and, more recently, a highly sophisticated harmonic idiom. **b.** Big band dance music. **2.** *Slang.* **a.** Animation; enthusiasm. **b.** Nonsense. **c.** Miscellaneous, unspecified things: *brought the food and all the jazz to go with it.* **—jazz** *v.* **jazzed, jazz·ing, jazz·es.** *—tr.* **1.** *Music.* To play in a jazz style. **2.** *Slang.* To exaggerate or lie to: *Don't jazz me.* *—intr. Slang.* To exaggerate or lie. ***—phrasal verb.*** **jazz up.** *Slang.* To make more interesting; enliven: *jazzed up the living area with beaded curtains.* [Origin unknown.] **—jazz′er** *n.* **—jazz′ish** *adj.*

jazz-fu·sion (jăz-fyo͞o′zhən) *n. Music.* See **jazz-rock.**

jazz·man (jăz′măn′, -mən) *n.* A jazz musician or composer.

jazz-rock (jăz′rŏk′) *n. Music.* Music that blends jazz elements and the heavy repetitive rhythms of rock. Also called *jazz-fusion.*

jazz·y (jăz′ē) *adj.* **-i·er, -i·est.** **1.** Resembling jazz in form or nature; rhythmical. **2.** *Slang.* Showy; flashy: *a jazzy car.* **—jazz′i·ly** *adv.* **—jazz′i·ness** *n.*

Jb. *abbr. Bible.* Job.

J-bar (jā′bär′) *n. Sports.* A J-shaped bar, suspended from a system of overhead cables, by which a skier is towed uphill.

J.C.D. *abbr. Latin.* Juris Canonici Doctor (Doctor of Canon Law).

JCL *n., pl.* **JCLs.** *Computer Science.* The common language of a computer operating system, used to tell the computer what to do. [J(OB) C(ONTROL) L(ANGUAGE).]

J.C.S. or **JCS** *abbr.* Joint Chiefs of Staff.

jct. *abbr.* Junction.

JD *abbr.* **1.** Or **J.D.** Juris doctor. **2.** Justice Department. **3.** Also **J.D.** Juvenile delinquent.

Jdt. *abbr. Bible.* Judith.

jeal·ous (jĕl′əs) *adj.* **1.** Fearful or wary of being supplanted; apprehensive of losing affection or position. **2.a.** Resentful or bitter in rivalry; envious: *jealous of the success of others.* **b.** Inclined to suspect rivalry. **3.** Having to do with or arising from feelings of envy, apprehension, or bitterness: *jealous thoughts.* **4.** Vigilant in guarding something: *We are jealous of our good name.* **5.** Intolerant of disloyalty or infidelity; autocratic: *a jealous God.* [Middle English *jelous,* from Old French *gelos,* jealous, zealous, from Vulgar Latin **zēlōsus,* from Late Latin *zēlus,* zeal. See ZEAL.] **—jeal′ous·ly** *adv.* **—jeal′ous·ness** *n.*

SYNONYMS: *jealous, covetous, envious.* The central meaning shared by these adjectives is "resentfully or painfully desirous of another's advantages": *jealous of her friend's success; covetous of his neighbor's possessions; envious of their art collection.*

jeal·ous·y (jĕl′ə-sē) *n., pl.* **-ies.** **1.** A jealous attitude or disposition. **2.** Close vigilance.

jean (jēn) *n.* **1.** A heavy, strong, twilled cotton, used in making uniforms and work clothes. **2. jeans.** Pants made of jean, denim, or another durable fabric. [Short for obsolete *jene (fustian),* Genoan (fustian), from Middle English *jene, gene,* from Old French *Genes,* Genoa.]

Jeanne d'Arc (zhän därk′). See **Joan of Arc.**

Jeans (jēnz), Sir **James Hopwood.** 1877–1946. British astronomer, physicist, and mathematician noted for his work on the kinetic theory of gases.

Je·bel Mu·sa also **Ge·bel Mu·sa** (jĕb′əl mo͞o′sə, -sä). A mountain, 851 m (2,790 ft) high, of northern Morocco on the Strait of Gibraltar. With Gibraltar it forms the so-called Pillars of Hercules.

Jebel Toub·kal (to͝ob-käl′). A mountain, 4,167.8 m (13,665 ft) high, of central Morocco in the Atlas Mountains.

jee (jē) *interj.* Variant of **gee³.**

jeep (jēp) *n.* A small, durable, general-purpose motor vehicle with four-wheel drive and a quarter-ton capacity, used by the U.S. Army during and after World War II. [Probably pronunciation of the letters *GP,* designation for this vehicle in the manufacturer's parts numbering system : *G(overnment)* + *P,* designator for 80-inch wheelbase reconnaissance car.]

Jeep (jēp). A trademark used for a civilian motor vehicle.

jeep·ney (jēp′nē) *n., pl.* **-neys.** A jitney bus used in the Philippines for public transportation. [JEEP + (JIT)NEY.]

jeer (jîr) *v.* **jeered, jeer·ing, jeers.** *—intr.* To speak or shout derisively; mock. *—tr.* To abuse vocally; taunt: *jeered the speaker off the stage.* **—jeer** *n.* A scoffing or taunting remark or shout. [Origin unknown.] **—jeer′er** *n.* **—jeer′ing·ly** *adv.*

jeez (jēz) *interj.* Used to express surprise or annoyance. [Alteration of JESUS.]

Jef·fers (jĕf′ərz), **(John) Robinson.** 1887–1962. American poet many of whose works are set in California. His collections include *Tamar and Other Poems* (1924).

Jef·fer·son (jĕf′ər-sən), **Thomas.** 1743–1826. The third President of the United States (1801–1809). A member of the second Continental Congress, he drafted the Declaration of Independence (1776). His presidency was marked by the purchase of the Louisiana Territory from France (1803) and the Tripolitan War (1801–1805). Jefferson designed his own estate, Monticello, and buildings for the University of Virginia.

Jefferson City. The capital of Missouri, in the central part of the state on the Missouri River. It was chosen as the capital when Missouri was admitted to the Union in 1821. Population, 33,619.

Jef·fer·so·ni·an (jĕf′ər-sō′nē-ən) *adj.* Of, relating to, or characteristic of Thomas Jefferson or his political attitudes and theories. **—Jeffersonian** *n.* A follower of Thomas Jefferson or a proponent of his politics. **—Jef′fer·so′ni·an·ism** *n.*

Jefferson River. A river, about 402 km (250 mi) long, of southwest Montana. It is a headwater of the Missouri River.

Jef·fer·son·ville (jĕf′ər-sən-vĭl′). A city of southern Indiana on the Ohio River opposite Louisville, Kentucky. It was founded in 1802 on the site of a frontier fort. Population, 21,220.

Jef·frey (jĕf′rē), **Francis.** Lord Jeffrey. 1773–1850. Scottish literary critic and jurist who cofounded (1802) and edited (1803–1829) the *Edinburgh Review.*

je·had (jĭ-häd′) *n.* Variant of **jihad.**

Je·hosh·a·phat (jə-hŏsh′ə-făt′, -hŏs′-). Ninth century B.C. King of Judah who formed an alliance with the kingdom of Israel.

Je·ho·vah (jĭ-hō′və) *n.* God, especially in Christian translations of the Old Testament. [Alteration of Hebrew *Yahweh,* Yahweh.]

Je·ho·vah's Witness (jĭ-hō′vəz) *n.* A member of a religious denomination founded in the United States during the late 19th century in which active evangelism is practiced, the imminent approach of the millennium is preached, and war and organized governmental authority in matters of conscience are strongly opposed.

Je·hu (jē′hyo͞o). Ninth century B.C. Israeli king who, according to the Old Testament, slew Ahab, Jezebel, and the prophets of Baal. He is proverbially known for his swift chariot driving.

je·ju·na (jə-jo͞o′nə) *n.* Plural of **jejunum.**

je·june (jə-jo͞on′) *adj.* **1.** Not interesting; dull: *"and there pour forth jejune words and useless empty phrases"* (Anthony Trollope). **2.** Lacking maturity; childish: *surprised by their jejune responses to our problems.* **3.** Lacking in nutrition: *a jejune diet.* [From Latin *iēiūnus,* meager, dry, fasting.] **—je·june′ly** *adv.* **—je·june′ness** *n.*

je·ju·num (jə-jo͞o′nəm) *n., pl.* **-na** (-nə). The section of the small intestine between the duodenum and the ileum. [Middle English, from Medieval Latin *iēiūnum (intestīnum),* fasting (intestine) (so called because in dissection it was always found empty), neuter of Latin *iēiūnus.*]

Je·kyll and Hyde (jĕk′əl, jē′kəl; hīd′) *n. Informal.* One who has a dual personality that alternates between phases of good and evil behavior. [After *The Strange Case of Dr. Jekyll and Mr. Hyde* by Robert Louis Stevenson.]

jell (jĕl) *v.* **jelled, jell·ing, jells.** *—intr.* **1.** To become firm or gelatinous; congeal. See Synonyms at **coagulate.** **2.** To take shape or fall into place; crystallize: *A plan of action finally jelled in my mind.* *—tr.* **1.** To cause to become firm or gelatinous. **2.** To cause to take shape; make clear and definite; crystallize. [Probably back-formation from JELLY.]

jel·la·ba (jə-lä′bə) *n.* Variant of **djellaba.**

Jel·li·coe (jĕl′ĭ-kō′), **John Rushworth.** First Earl Jellicoe. 1859–1935. British naval officer who commanded the fleet that fought the Germans at Jutland (1916).

jel·lied (jĕl′ēd) *adj.* **1.** Chilled or otherwise congealed into jelly. **2.** Coated with jelly. **3.** Prepared or cooked in or with jelly.

jel·li·fy (jĕl′ə-fī′) *intr. & tr.v.* **-fied, -fy·ing, -fies.** To become or make into jelly.

Jell-O (jĕl′ō). A trademark used for a gelatin dessert. This trademark often occurs in print without a hyphen and in figurative contexts: *"For many, cooking became a matter of opening cans, heating frozen dinners and making Jello molds"* (Chicago Trib-

J-bar

Thomas Jefferson

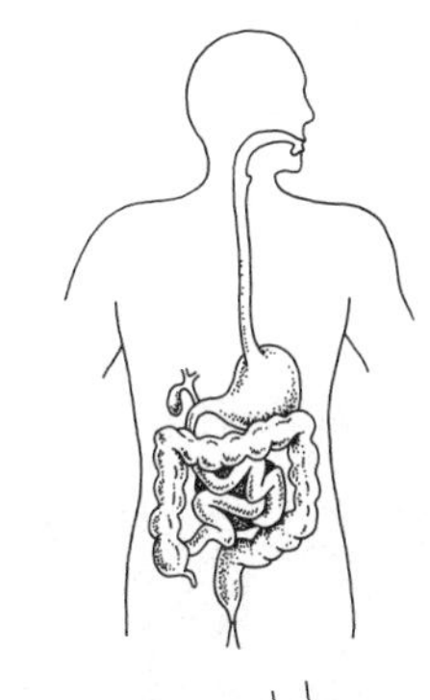

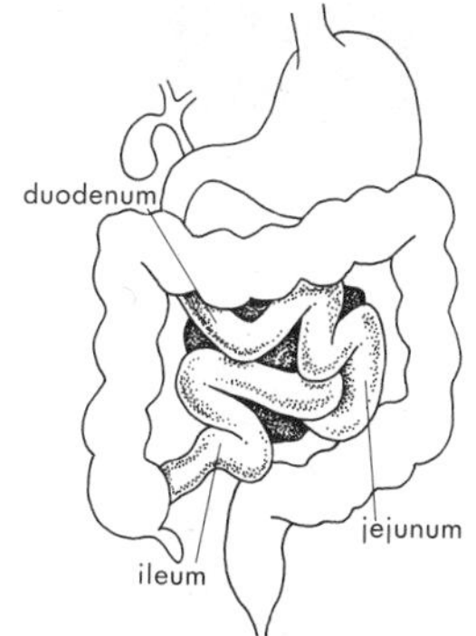

jejunum

ă pat	oi boy
ā pay	ou out
âr care	o͝o took
ä father	o͞o boot
ĕ pet	ŭ cut
ē be	ûr urge
ĭ pit	th thin
ī pie	*th* this
îr pier	hw which
ŏ pot	zh vision
ō toe	ə about, item
ô paw	♦ regionalism

Stress marks: **′** (primary); ′ (secondary), as in **dictionary** (dĭk′shə-nĕr′ē)

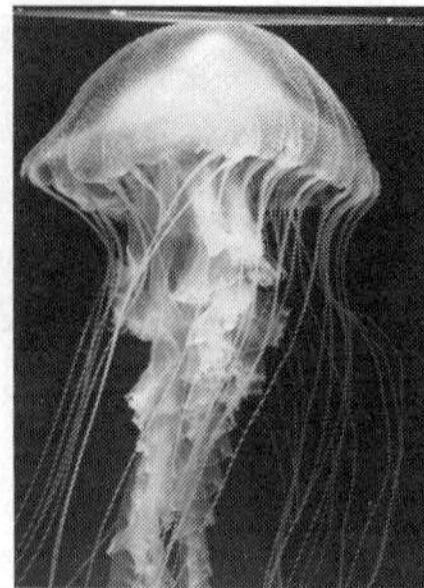
jellyfish
Sea nettle
Chrysaora quinquecirrha

jellyroll

Jersey
Jersey cow

Jerusalem artichoke
Helianthus tuberosus

une). *"But you can't protect some dummies from themselves. So if they want to turn their heads into Jello, that's their lookout"* (Mike Royko). "[His nerves] *surely must have felt like Jell-O in a high wind"* (Washington Post).

jel·ly (jĕl′ē) *n., pl.* **-lies. a.** A soft, semisolid food substance with a resilient consistency, made by the setting of a liquid containing pectin or gelatin or by the addition of gelatin to a liquid, especially such a substance made of fruit juice containing pectin boiled with sugar. **b.** Something, such as a petroleum ointment, having the consistency of a soft, semisolid food substance. **—jelly** *v.* **-lied, -ly·ing, -lies.** *—tr.* To cause to have the consistency of jelly. *—intr.* To acquire the consistency of jelly. See Synonyms at **coagulate.** [Middle English *gelee,* from Old French, from Vulgar Latin **gelāta,* from Latin, feminine past participle of *gelāre,* to freeze. See **gel-** in Appendix.]

jel·ly·bean (jĕl′ē-bēn′) *n.* A small ovoid candy with a hardened sugar coating over a chewy center.

jel·ly·fish (jĕl′ē-fĭsh′) *n., pl.* **jellyfish** or **-fish·es. 1.a.** Any of numerous usually free-swimming marine coelenterates of the class Scyphozoa, characteristically having a gelatinous, tentacled, often bell-shaped medusoid stage as the dominant phase of its life cycle. **b.** Any of various similar or related coelenterates. **2.** *Informal.* One who lacks force of character; a weakling.

jel·ly·roll (jĕl′ē-rōl′) *n.* A thin sheet of sponge cake layered with jelly and then rolled up.

jem·my (jĕm′ē) *n. & v. Chiefly British.* Variant of **jimmy.**

Je·na (yā′nə). A city of central Germany southwest of Leipzig. Napoleon I decisively defeated the Prussians here on October 14, 1806. Population, 106,555.

je ne sais quoi (zhə′ nə sā kwä′, sē) *n.* A quality or an attribute that is difficult to describe or express: *"Fishing has lacked a certain je ne sais quoi in terms of its public image, as all activities must that involve beer, worms and one-size-fits-all gimme caps"* (Charles Leerhsen). [French : *je,* I + *ne,* not + *sais,* first person present indicative of *savoir,* to know + *quoi,* what.]

Jen·ghis Khan or **Jen·ghiz Khan** (jĕn′gĭz kän′, -gĭs, jĕng′-). See **Genghis Khan.**

Jen·ner (jĕn′ər), **Edward.** 1749–1823. British physician and vaccination pioneer. He found that smallpox could be prevented by inoculation with the substance from cowpox lesions.

jen·net also **gen·et** (jĕn′ĭt) *n.* A small Spanish saddle horse. [Middle English *genet,* from Old French, from Catalan *ginet,* from Arabic *zinētī,* from colloquial Arabic *Zenetī,* a Berber tribe famed for horsemanship.]

Jen·nings (jĕn′ĭngz). A city of eastern Missouri, a residential suburb of St. Louis. Population, 17,026.

jen·ny (jĕn′ē) *n., pl.* **-nies. 1.** The female of certain animals, especially the donkey and the wren. **2.** A spinning jenny. [From the name *Jenny.*]

Jen·sen (yĕn′sən, jĕn′-), **Johannes Vilhelm.** 1873–1950. Danish writer of modernistic novels, poetry, and essays. He won the 1944 Nobel Prize for literature.

jeop·ard·ize (jĕp′ər-dīz′) *tr.v.* **-ized, -iz·ing, -iz·es.** To expose to loss or injury; imperil. See Synonyms at **endanger.**

jeop·ard·y (jĕp′ər-dē) *n., pl.* **-ies. 1.** Risk of loss or injury; peril or danger. **2.** *Law.* A defendant's risk or danger of conviction when put on trial. [Middle English *juperti,* from Old French *jeu parti,* even game, uncertainty : *jeu,* game (from Latin *iocus,* joke, game; see **yek-** in Appendix) + *parti,* past participle of *partir,* to divide (from Latin *partīre,* from *pars, part-,* part; see PART).]

Je·qui·tin·hon·ha (zhə-kēt′n-yōn′yə, zhĭ-kwē′tĭ-nyô′nyä). A river, about 805 km (500 mi) long, of eastern Brazil flowing northeast and east to the Atlantic Ocean.

Jer. *abbr. Bible.* Jeremiah.

jer·bo·a (jər-bō′ə) *n.* Any of various small, nocturnal, leaping rodents of the family Dipodidae of Asia and northern Africa, having long hind legs and a long, tufted tail. [Medieval Latin *jerbōa,* from Arabic *jarbū',* flesh of the loins.]

jer·e·mi·ad (jĕr′ə-mī′əd) *n.* A literary work or speech expressing a bitter lament or a righteous prophecy of doom. [French *jérémiade,* after *Jérémie,* Jeremiah, author of *The Lamentations,* from Late Latin *Ieremiās,* from Hebrew *Yirmĕyāhû.*]

Jer·e·mi·ah (jĕr′ə-mī′ə) *n. Bible.* **1.** A Hebrew prophet of the seventh and sixth centuries B.C. **2.** *Abbr.* **Jer., Jr** See table at **Bible.** [Hebrew *Yirmĕyāhû.*]

Je·rez (hĕ-rĕs′, -rĕth′) also **Jerez de la Fron·te·ra** (də lä frŭn-tĕr′ə, *thĕ* lä frôn-tĕ′rä). A city of southwest Spain northeast of Cádiz. It was held by the Moors from 711 to 1264. Population, 138,700.

Jer·i·cho (jĕr′ĭ-kō′). An ancient city of Palestine near the northwest shore of the Dead Sea. A stronghold commanding the valley of the lower Jordan River, it was, according to the Old Testament, captured and destroyed by Joshua.

jerk[1] (jûrk) *v.* **jerked, jerk·ing, jerks.** *—tr.* **1.** To give a sudden quick thrust, push, pull, or twist to. **2.** To throw or toss with a quick abrupt motion. **3.** To utter abruptly or sharply: *jerked out the answer.* **4.** To make and serve (ice-cream sodas, for example) at a soda fountain. *—intr.* **1.** To move in sudden abrupt motions; jolt: *The train jerked ahead.* **2.** To make spasmodic motions: *My legs jerked from fatigue.* **—jerk** *n.* **1.** A sudden abrupt motion, such as a yank or twist. **2.** A jolting or lurching motion. **3.** *Physiology.* A sudden reflexive or spasmodic muscular movement. **4. jerks.** Involuntary convulsive twitching often resulting from excitement. Often used with *the.* **5.** *Slang.* A dull, stupid, or fatuous person. **6.** *Sports.* A lift in which the weight is heaved overhead from shoulder height with a quick motion. ***—phrasal verb.* jerk off.** *Vulgar Slang.* To masturbate. [Origin unknown.] **—jerk′er** *n.* **—jerk′ing·ly** *adv.*

SYNONYMS: *jerk, snap, twitch, wrench, yank.* The central meaning shared by these verbs is "to move with a sudden short, quick motion": *jerked the rope and broke it; a lock snapping shut; her mouth twitching with suppressed amusement; wrenched the stick out of his hand; yanked the door open.*

jerk[2] (jûrk) *tr.v.* **jerked, jerk·ing, jerks.** To cut (meat) into long strips and dry in the sun or cure by exposing to smoke. [Back-formation from JERKY[2].]

jerk[3] (jûrk) *adj.* Being or relating to a method of barbecuing meat that has been seasoned and wrapped in leaves of the allspice tree: *jerk chicken; jerk pork.* [From JERKY[2].]

jer·kin (jûr′kĭn) *n.* **1.** A close-fitting, hip-length, collarless jacket having no sleeves but often extended shoulders, belted and worn over a doublet by men especially in the 16th century. **2.** A short, close-fitting, often sleeveless coat or jacket, usually of leather. [Origin unknown.]

jerk·wa·ter (jûrk′wô′tər, -wŏt′ər) *adj. Informal.* **1.** Remote, small, and insignificant: *a jerkwater town.* **2.** Contemptibly trivial: *jerkwater notions.* [From *jerkwater,* a branch-line train, so called because its small boiler had to be refilled often, requiring train crews to "jerk" or draw water from streams.]

jerk·y[1] (jûr′kē) *adj.* **-i·er, -i·est. 1.** Characterized by jerks or jerking: *a jerky train ride.* **2.** *Slang.* Foolish; silly: *jerky ideas about saving money.* **—jerk′i·ly** *adv.* **—jerk′i·ness** *n.*

jerk·y[2] (jûr′kē) *n.* Meat cured by jerking. Also called *charqui.* [Alteration of CHARQUI.]

jer·o·bo·am (jĕr′ə-bō′əm) *n.* A wine bottle holding ⅘ of a gallon (3.03 liters). [After *Jeroboam I* (died c. 901 B.C.), king of northern Israel.]

Je·rome (jə-rōm′), Saint. Originally Sophronius Eusebius Hieronymus. 340?–420? Latin scholar who produced the *Vulgate,* the first authentic Latin translation of the Bible from Hebrew.

Jer·ry (jĕr′ē) *n., pl.* **-ries.** *Chiefly British.* A German, especially a German soldier. [Alteration of GERMAN.]

jer·ry-build (jĕr′ē-bĭld′) *tr.v.* **-built** (-bĭlt′), **-build·ing, -builds.** To build shoddily, flimsily, and cheaply. [From dialectal *jerry,* defective, perhaps from the name *Jerry.*] **—jer′ry·build′er** *n.*

jer·ry can (jĕr′ē) *n.* A flat-sided can for storing or transporting liquids, especially gasoline, having a capacity of 5 gallons (19 liters). [From JERRY.]

jer·sey (jûr′zē) *n., pl.* **-seys. 1.a.** A soft, plain-knitted fabric used for clothing. **b.** A garment made of this fabric. **2.** A close-fitting knitted pullover shirt, jacket, or sweater. **3.** Often **Jersey.** Any of a breed of fawn-colored dairy cattle developed on the island of Jersey and producing milk that is rich in butterfat. [After JERSEY.]

Jersey. The largest of the Channel Islands in the English Channel. It was annexed by the Normans in 933, and French influence has persisted since autonomy was granted in 1204.

Jersey barrier *n.* A protective concrete barrier used as a highway divider and a means of preventing access to a prohibited area. [From the fact that they were first used on the NEW JERSEY Turnpike.]

Jersey City. A city of northeast New Jersey on the Hudson River opposite Lower Manhattan. Settled before 1650 by the Dutch, it came under English control in 1664 and is today a port of entry and major distribution center. Population, 223,532.

Je·ru·sa·lem (jə-rōō′sə-ləm, -zə-). The capital of Israel, in the east-central part of the country in the West Bank. Of immense religious and historical importance, the city was occupied as far back as the fourth millennium B.C. and became the capital of King David c. 1000 B.C. Destroyed by Nebuchadnezzar in the sixth century B.C., it was later ruled by Greeks, Romans, Persians, Arabs, Crusaders, and Turks and by Great Britain under a League of Nations mandate. Israeli forces took control of the city in 1967. Jerusalem is considered a holy city to Jews, Moslems, and Christians. Population, 446,500.

Jerusalem artichoke *n.* **1.** A North American sunflower *(Helianthus tuberosus)* having yellow, rayed flower heads and edible tubers. **2.** The tuber of this plant, eaten as a vegetable. Also called *girasol.* [By folk etymology from obsolete Italian *girasole,* sunflower. See GIRASOL.]

Jerusalem cherry *n.* An Old World ornamental shrub *(Solanum pseudocapsicum)* having inedible scarlet or yellow fruit and grown as a houseplant.

Jerusalem oak *n.* A sticky Old World weed *(Chenopodium botrys)* naturalized in North America and having lobed leaves and an odor suggestive of turpentine.

Jerusalem thorn *n.* A spiny tropical American tree *(Parkinsonia aculeata)* having clusters of yellow flowers, green branches, and bipinnately compound leaves.

Jes·per·sen (yĕs′pər-sən), **(Jens) Otto (Harry).** 1860–1943. Danish philologist noted for his contributions to phonetics and the teaching of languages.

jess (jĕs) *n.* A short strap fastened around the leg of a hawk or other bird used in falconry, to which a leash may be fastened. **—jess** *tr.v.* **jessed, jess·ing, jess·es.** To put jesses or a jess on (a hawk, for example). [Middle English *ges,* from Old French, pl. of *jet,* something thrown, from Vulgar Latin **iectus,* alteration of Latin *iactus,* past participle of *iacere,* to throw. See **yē-** in Appendix.]

jes·sa·mine (jĕs′ə-mĭn) *n.* Variant of **jasmine.**

Jes·se (jĕs′ē). In the Old Testament, King David's father and the progenitor of the line of Jesus.

jest (jĕst) *n.* **1.** A playful or amusing act; a prank. See Synonyms at **joke. 2.** A frolicsome or frivolous mood: *spoken in jest.* **3.** An object of ridicule; a laughingstock. **4.** A witty remark. **—jest** *v.* **jest·ed, jest·ing, jests.** —*intr.* **1.** To act or speak playfully. **2.** To make witty remarks. **3.** To utter scoffs; gibe. —*tr.* To make fun of; ridicule. [Middle English *geste,* tale, from Old French, from Latin *gesta,* deeds, from neuter pl. past participle of *gerere,* to perform.] **—jest′ing·ly** *adv.*

jest·er (jĕs′tər) *n.* **1.** One given to jesting. **2.** A fool or buffoon at medieval courts.

Jes·u·it (jĕzh′o͞o-ĭt, jĕz′o͞o-, -yo͞o-) *n.* **1.** *Roman Catholic Church.* A member of the Society of Jesus, an order founded by Saint Ignatius of Loyola in 1534. **2.** Often **jesuit.** One given to subtle casuistry. [French *Jésuite,* from *Jésus,* Jesus, from Late Latin *Iēsus.* See JESUS.] **—Jes′u·it′i·cal** *adj.*

Jes·u·it's bark (jĕzh′o͞o-ĭts, jĕz′o͞o-, -yo͞o-) *n.* See **cinchona** (sense 2). [So called because it was first known to Europeans through Jesuit missions in Peru.]

Je·sus (jē′zəs) *n.* **1.** A teacher and prophet who lived in the first century of this era and whose life and teachings form the basis of Christianity. Christians believe Jesus to be Son of God and the Christ. **2.** *Christian Science.* "The highest human corporeal concept of the divine idea" (Mary Baker Eddy). [Middle English, from Late Latin *Iēsus,* from Greek *Iēsous,* from Hebrew *Yēšûa‘,* from *Yĕhôšûa‘,* Joshua.]

Jesus freak *n. Slang.* A member of a movement among young Christians adapting traditional evangelicalism to pop culture.

jet¹ (jĕt) *n.* **1.** A dense black coal that takes a high polish and is used for jewelry. **2.** *Color.* A deep black. **—jet** *adj.* **1.** Made of or resembling a dense, black, highly polished coal. **2.** Black as coal: *jet hair.* [Middle English, from Anglo-Norman *geet,* from Latin *gagātēs,* from Greek *gagātēs,* after *Gagas,* a town of Lycia.]

jet² (jĕt) *n.* **1.a.** A high-velocity fluid stream forced under pressure out of a small-diameter opening or nozzle. **b.** An outlet, such as a nozzle, used for emitting such a stream. **c.** Something emitted in or as if in a high-velocity fluid stream: *"such myriad and such vivid jets of images"* (Henry Roth). **2.a.** A jet-propelled vehicle, especially a jet-propelled aircraft. **b.** A jet engine. **—jet** *v.* **jet·ted, jet·ting, jets.** —*intr.* **1.** To travel by jet aircraft: *jetted from Houston to Los Angeles.* **2.** To move very quickly. —*tr.* To propel outward or squirt, as under pressure: *"Any man might . . . hang around . . . jetting tobacco juice"* (Ross Lockridge, Jr.). [French, from Old French, from *jeter,* to spout forth, throw, from Vulgar Latin **iectāre,* alteration of Latin *iactāre,* frequentative of *iacere,* to throw. See **yē-** in Appendix.] **—jet′ful′** *n.*

jet·a·va·tor (jĕt′ə-vā′tər) *n.* A control surface that may be moved into the propulsion stream of a rocket in order to change the direction of thrust. [JET² + (ELE)VATOR.]

jet boat *n. Nautical.* A boat propelled by a powerful jet of water created by a specially designed engine.

je·té (zhə-tā′) *n.* A leap in ballet in which one leg is extended forward and the other backward. [French, from past participle of *jeter,* to throw, from Old French. See JET².]

jet engine *n.* **1.** An engine that develops thrust by ejecting a jet, especially a jet of gaseous combustion products. **2.** An engine that obtains the oxygen needed from the atmosphere, used especially to propel aircraft and distinguished from rocket engines having self-contained fuel-oxidizer systems.

jet·fight·er or **jet fighter** (jĕt′fī′tər) *n.* A jet-propelled fighter aircraft.

jet·foil (jĕt′foil′) *n. Nautical.* A passenger-carrying hydrofoil that is propelled by a jet engine. [JET² + (HYDRO)FOIL.]

jet lag also **jet·lag** (jĕt′lăg′) *n.* A temporary disruption of bodily rhythms caused by high-speed travel across several time zones typically in a jet aircraft. **—jet′-lagged′** *adj.*

jet·lin·er (jĕt′lī′nər) *n.* A large passenger jet airplane.

jet·pack (jĕt′păk′) *n.* A backpack that is maneuvered by jets and permits an astronaut to move about alone in space away from a spacecraft.

jet·port (jĕt′pôrt′, -pōrt′) *n.* An airport for jet aircraft.

jet-pro·pelled (jĕt′prə-pĕld′) *adj.* Driven by jet propulsion.

jet propulsion *n.* Propulsion derived from the rearward expulsion of matter in a jet stream, especially propulsion by jet engines.

jet·sam (jĕt′səm) *n.* **1.** Cargo or equipment thrown overboard to lighten a ship in distress. **2.** Discarded cargo or equipment found washed ashore. See Usage Note at **flotsam. 3.** Discarded odds and ends. [From earlier *jetson,* alteration of Middle English *jetteson,* a throwing overboard. See JETTISON.]

jet set *n.* An international social set made up of wealthy people who travel from one fashionable place to another. **—jet′-set′** (jĕt′sĕt′), **jet′-set′ting** (-sĕt′ĭng) *adj.* **—jet setter** *n.*

Jet Ski (jĕt). A trademark used for a jet-propelled recreational watercraft for one or two persons. This trademark often appears in print in lowercase: *"The second rider aimed the nose of his jet ski through the wave like a football fullback diving for the goal line"* (Newsday). It also has given rise to a number of derived forms, among them being *jet skier: "He'll probably become a professional jet skier next spring"* (Los Angeles Times).

jet stream *n.* **1.** A high-speed, meandering wind current, generally moving from a westerly direction at speeds often exceeding 400 kilometers (250 miles) per hour at altitudes of 15 to 25 kilometers (10 to 15 miles). **2.** A high-speed stream; a jet.

jet·ti·son (jĕt′ĭ-sən, -zən) *tr.v.* **-soned, -son·ing, -sons. 1.** To cast overboard or off: *a ship jettisoning wastes; a pilot jettisoning aircraft fuel.* **2.** *Informal.* To discard (something) as unwanted or burdensome: *jettisoned the whole marketing plan.* **—jettison** *n.* **1.** The act of discarding or casting overboard. **2.** Jetsam. [From Middle English *jetteson,* a throwing overboard of goods to lighten ship, from Anglo-Norman *getteson,* from Vulgar Latin **iectātiō, iectātiōn-,* from **iectātus,* past participle of **iectāre,* to throw. See JET².]

jet·ty¹ (jĕt′ē) *n., pl.* **-ties. 1.** A structure, such as a pier, that projects into a body of water to influence the current or tide or to protect a harbor or shoreline from storms or erosion. **2.** A wharf. [Middle English *getti, jettie,* from Old French *jetee,* from feminine past participle of *jeter,* to project, throw. See JET².]

jet·ty² (jĕt′ē) *adj.* **1.** Resembling jet, as in texture. **2.** Of the color jet; black: *jetty tresses.* **—jet′ti·ness** *n.*

Jet·way (jĕt′wā′). A trademark used for a telescoping corridor that extends from an airport terminal to an aircraft, for the boarding and disembarkation of passengers. This trademark often occurs in print in lowercase: *"At least 15 . . . jetways were damaged as well"* (Aviation Week & Space Technology). *"It would invest more than $100 million in the terminal, expanding and adding jetways"* (New York Times). *"It has all the amenities—Jetways, spacious terminal areas, etc."* (Air Transport World).

jeu·nesse do·rée (zhœ-nĕs′ dô-rā′) *n.* Fashionable and wealthy young people. [French : *jeunesse,* youth + *dorée,* gilded.]

Jev·ons (jĕv′ənz), **William Stanley.** 1835–1882. British economist and logician who codeveloped the marginal utility theory (published 1886), which explains the value of goods and services in terms of the subjective valuation of consumers.

Jew (jo͞o) *n.* **1.** An adherent of Judaism as a religion or culture. **2.** A member of the widely dispersed people originally descended from the ancient Hebrews and sharing an ethnic heritage based on Judaism. **3.** A native or inhabitant of the ancient kingdom of Judah. [Middle English *Jeu,* from Old French *giu,* from Latin *Iūdaeus,* from Greek *Ioudaios,* from Aramaic *yĕhûdāy,* from Hebrew *yĕhûdî,* after *yĕhûdâ,* Judah, son of Jacob and Leah.]

USAGE NOTE: It is widely recognized that the attributive use of the noun *Jew,* in phrases such as *Jew lawyer* or *Jew ethics,* is both offensive and vulgar. In such contexts *Jewish* is the only acceptable possibility. But some people have become so wary of this construction that they have overgeneralized the anathema to any use of the noun, a practice that carries risks of its own. In a sentence such as *There are now several Jews on the council,* which is unexceptionable, the substitution of a circumlocution like *Jewish people* or *persons of Jewish background* may unwittingly suggest an unwarranted and hence suspect delicacy.

jew·el (jo͞o′əl) *n.* **1.a.** A precious stone; a gem. **b.** A small natural or artificial gem used as a bearing in a watch. **2.** A costly ornament of precious metal or gems. **3.** One that is treasured or esteemed. **—jewel** *tr.v.* **-eled, -el·ing, -els** or **-elled, -el·ling, -els. 1.** To adorn with jewels. **2.** To fit with jewels. [Middle English *juel,* from Anglo-Norman, perhaps from Vulgar Latin **iocāle,* from neuter of **iocālis,* of play, from Latin *iocus,* joke. See **yek-** in Appendix.]

jew·el·er also **jew·el·ler** (jo͞o′ə-lər) *n. Abbr.* **jwlr.** One that makes, repairs, or deals in jewelry.

jew·el·fish (jo͞o′əl-fĭsh′) *n., pl.* **jewelfish** or **-fish·es.** A small, brilliantly colored freshwater fish *(Hemichromis bimaculatus)* of tropical Africa, popular in home aquariums.

jew·el·ler (jo͞o′ə-lər) *n.* Variant of **jeweler.**

jew·el·ry (jo͞o′əl-rē) *n.* Ornaments, such as bracelets, necklaces, or rings, made of precious metals set with gems or imitation gems.

jew·el·weed (jo͞o′əl-wēd′) *n.* Any of several plants of the genus *Impatiens* having yellowish, spurred flowers and seed pods that dehisce into five valves when mature. Also called *balsam, touch-me-not.*

Jew·ess (jo͞o′ĭs) *n. Offensive.* A Jewish woman or girl.

USAGE NOTE: Like the feminine forms of other ethnic terms, such as *Negress,* the word *Jewess* has come to be widely regarded as offensive, since it seems to imply that the conjunction of Jewishness and female sex is sufficient to establish a distinct racial or social category. Where reference to gender is relevant, the phrase *Jewish woman* can be used: *As a Jewish woman, Rosa Luxemburg was doubly sensitive to the discrimination that underlay social attitudes in late 19th-century Europe.* See Usage Note at **Negress.**

Jew·ett (jo͞o′ĭt), **Sarah Orne.** 1849–1909. American writer noted for novels and stories concerning her native Maine.

jew·fish (jo͞o′fĭsh′) *n., pl.* **jewfish** or **-fish·es.** Any of several

Jesus
Byzantine mosaic

jet²

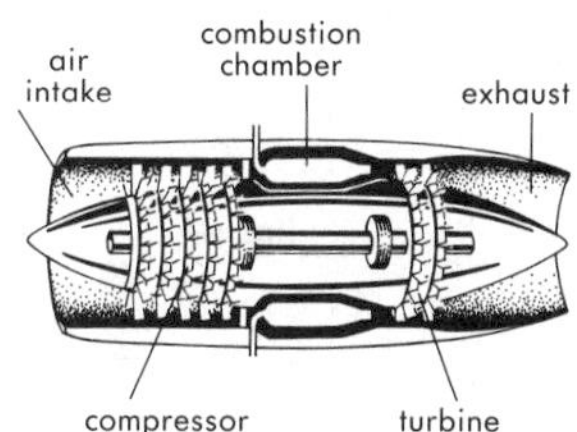

jet engine
Cutaway view of a turbojet engine

jetpack

ă pat	oi boy
ā pay	ou out
âr care	o͝o took
ä father	o͞o boot
ĕ pet	ŭ cut
ē be	ûr urge
ĭ pit	th thin
ī pie	*th* this
îr pier	hw which
ŏ pot	zh vision
ō toe	ə about, item
ô paw	♦ regionalism

Stress marks: ′ (primary); ′ (secondary), as in **dictionary** (dĭk′shə-nĕr′ē)

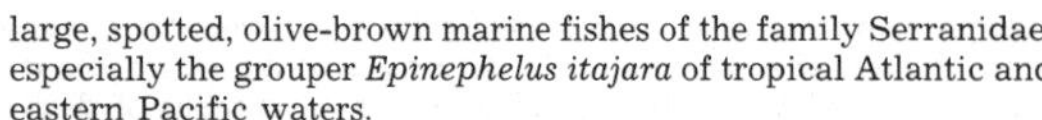

mast
battens
mainsail
jib
boom
tiller
hull
centerboard
rudder

jib[1]
Bermuda-rigged sloop

large, spotted, olive-brown marine fishes of the family Serranidae, especially the grouper *Epinephelus itajara* of tropical Atlantic and eastern Pacific waters.

Jew·ish (jo͞o′ĭsh) *adj.* Of or relating to the Jews or their culture or religion. See Usage Note at **Jew.** —**Jew′ish·ness** *n.*

Jewish calendar *n.* The lunisolar calendar used to mark the events of the Jewish year, dating the creation of the world at 3761 B.C. See table at **calendar.**

Jew·ry (jo͞o′rē) *n.* **1.** The Jewish people. **2.** A section of a medieval city inhabited by Jews; a ghetto.

jew's-harp also **jews'-harp** (jo͞oz′härp′) *n. Music.* A small instrument consisting of a lyre-shaped metal frame that is held between the teeth and a projecting steel tongue that is plucked to produce a soft, twanging sound.

jez·e·bel (jĕz′ə-bĕl′, -bəl) *n.* A woman who is regarded as evil and scheming.

Jez·e·bel (jĕz′ə-bĕl′). fl. ninth century B.C. Phoenician princess and queen of Israel as the wife of Ahab. According to the Old Testament, she encouraged idolatry and was killed by Jehu.

jg *abbr.* Junior grade.

Jg. *abbr. Bible.* Judges.

Jhan·si (jän′sē). A city of north-central India south-southeast of Delhi. The city grew around a walled Mogul fort built in 1613. Population, 246,172.

Jhe·lum (jā′ləm). A river, about 772 km (480 mi) long, of northern India and northeast Pakistan. It is the westernmost of the five rivers of the Punjab.

JHVH or **JHWH** (yo͝od′hā′väv′hā′, yä′wā, yä′wĕ) *n.* Variants of **YHWH.**

Jia·ling also **Chia-ling** (jyä′lĭng′), or **Kia·ling** (kyä′-, jyä′-). A river, about 965 km (600 mi) long, of central China flowing east and south to the Chang Jiang (Yangtze River).

Jia·mu·si (jyä′mo͞o′sē′, -mü′-) also **Chia·mus·su** (-mo͞o′-so͞o′) or **Kia·mu·sze** (kyä′mo͞o′so͞o′). A city of extreme northeast China east-northeast of Harbin. It is an industrial center and a river port. Population, 350,000.

Jiang·su (jyäng′so͞o′, -sü′) also **Kiang·su** (kyäng′-). A province of eastern China bordering on the Yellow Sea. Densely populated and highly industrialized, it became a separate province in the 18th century. Nanjing is the capital. Population, 62,130,000.

Jiang·xi (jyäng′shē′) also **Kiang·si** (kyäng′-). A province of southeast China. In early times it served as a corridor for north-south migration and communications. Nanchang is the capital. Population, 34,600,000.

jiao (jyou) also **chiao** (chyou) *n., pl.* **jiao** also **chiao.** See table at **currency.** [Chinese *jiăo,* one tenth of a dollar.]

jib[1] (jĭb) *n.* **1.** *Nautical.* A triangular sail stretching from the foretopmast head to the jib boom and in small craft to the bowsprit or the bow. **2.a.** The arm of a mechanical crane. **b.** The boom of a derrick. [Origin unknown.]

jib[2] (jĭb) *intr.v.* **jibbed, jib·bing, jibs.** To stop short and turn restively from side to side; balk. [Origin unknown.] —**jib′ber** *n.*

ji·ba·ro (hē′vä-rō′) *n., pl.* **-ros. 1.** A rural inhabitant of Puerto Rico. **2.** *Music.* The country music of Puerto Rico. [American Spanish *jíbaro,* possibly from Taino *siba,* stone.]

jib boom *n. Nautical.* A spar forming a continuation of the bowsprit.

jibe[1] also **gybe** (jīb) *Nautical. v.* **jibed, jib·ing, jibes** also **gybed, gyb·ing, gybes.** —*intr.* To shift a fore-and-aft sail from one side of a vessel to the other while sailing before the wind so as to sail on the opposite tack. —*tr.* To cause (a sail) to jibe. —*n.* The act of jibing. [Alteration (perhaps influenced by JIB[1]) of *gybe,* from obsolete Dutch *gijben.*]

jibe[2] (jīb) *intr.v.* **jibed, jib·ing, jibes.** *Informal.* To be in accord; agree: *Your figures jibe with mine.* [Origin unknown.]

jibe[3] (jīb) *v. & n.* Variant of **gibe.**

ji·ca·ma (hē′kə-mə, hĭk′ə-) *n.* A crisp, sweet turnip-shaped root vegetable used raw in salads and as crudités or cooked in stews. [American Spanish *jícama,* from Nahuatl *xīcamatl.*]

Ji·ca·ril·la (hē′kə-rē′yə, -rēl′yə) *n., pl.* **Jicarilla** or **-las. 1.** An Apache tribe formerly inhabiting southeast Colorado and northern New Mexico and ranging eastward to the Great Plains, with a present-day population in northern New Mexico. **2.** A member of this tribe. [American Spanish *(Apaches de la) Jicarilla,* (Apaches of the) Jicarilla, probably diminutive of *jícara,* chocolate-cup (from the shape of a local hill), perhaps from Nahuatl *xicalli,* gourd, drinking vessel.]

Jid·da (jĭd′ə). A city of west-central Saudi Arabia on the Red Sea. Ruled by the Turks until 1916, Jidda has long been used as a port by Moslem pilgrims making the journey to Mecca. Population, 1,300,000.

jiff (jĭf) *n. Informal.* A jiffy.

jif·fy (jĭf′ē) *n., pl.* **jif·fies.** *Informal.* A short space of time; a moment. See Synonyms at **moment.** [Origin unknown.]

jig (jĭg) *n.* **1.a.** Any of various lively dances in triple time. **b.** The music for such a dance. Also called *gigue.* **2.** A joke or trick. **3.** A typically metal fishing lure with one or more hooks, usually deployed with a jiggling motion on or near the bottom. **4.** An apparatus for cleaning or separating crushed ore by agitation in water. **5.** A device for guiding a tool or for holding machine work in place. —**jig** *v.* **jigged, jig·ging, jigs.** —*intr.* **1.** To dance or play a jig. **2.** To move or bob up and down jerkily and rapidly. **3.** To operate a jig. —*tr.* **1.** To bob or jerk (something) up and down or to and fro. **2.** To machine (an object) with the aid of a jig. **3.** To separate or clean (ore) by shaking a jig. [Origin unknown.]

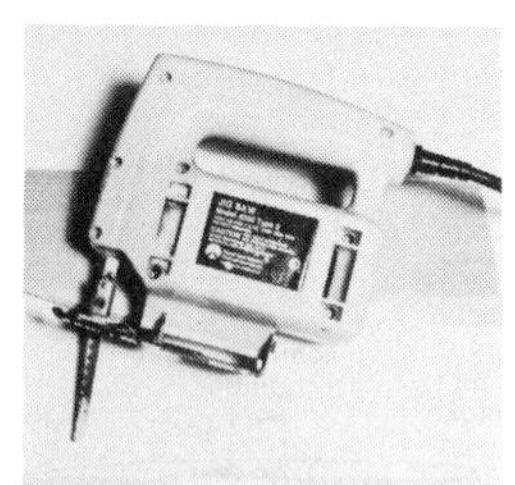

jigsaw

jig·ger[1] (jĭg′ər) *n.* **1.** A person who jigs or operates a jig. **2.a.** A small measure for liquor, usually holding 1½ ounces. **b.** This amount of liquor. **3.** A device, such as a drill, that operates with a jerking or jolting motion. **4.** *Nautical.* **a.** A light all-purpose tackle. **b.** A small sail set in the stern of a yawl or similar boat. **c.** A boat having such a sail. **d.** A jigger mast. **5.** *Informal.* An article or a device, the name of which eludes one.

jig·ger[2] (jĭg′ər) *n.* **1.** See **chigger** (sense 1). **2.** See **chigoe** (sense 1). [Variant of CHIGGER.]

jigger mast *n. Nautical.* **1.** The short after mast from which the jigger sail is set on a ketch or yawl. **2.** The fourth mast aft on a four-masted ship. In this sense, also called *mizzenmast.*

jig·ger·y-pok·er·y (jĭg′ə-rē-pō′kə-rē) *n.* Underhand scheming or behavior; trickery: *"By some legal—or perhaps illegal—jiggery-pokery, he could declare the election void"* (John Hughes). [Alteration of *joukery-pawkery* : from Scots *jouk,* to dodge (probably from DUCK[2]) + Scots *pawk,* trick.]

jig·gle (jĭg′əl) *v.* **-gled, -gling, -gles.** —*intr.* To move or rock lightly up and down or to and fro in an unsteady, jerky manner. —*tr.* To cause to jiggle. —**jiggle** *n.* A jiggling motion. [Frequentative of JIG.] —**jig′gly** *adj.*

jig·saw (jĭg′sô′) *n.* A usually power-driven saw with a narrow vertical blade, used to cut sharp curves.

jigsaw puzzle *n. Games.* A puzzle consisting of a mass of irregularly shaped pieces of cardboard, plastic, or wood that form a picture when fitted together. Also called *picture puzzle.*

ji·had also **je·had** (jĭ-häd′) *n.* **1.** A Moslem holy war or spiritual struggle against infidels. **2.** A crusade or struggle: *"The war against smoking is turning into a jihad against people who smoke"* (Fortune). [Arabic *jihād.*]

Ji·lin also **Chi·lin** (jē′lĭn′) or **Ki·rin** (kē′rĭn′). **1.** A province of northeast China bordering on North Korea. Extensive timberlands have long been important to the province's economy. Changchun is the capital. Population, 22,980,000. **2.** A city of northeast China east of Changchun. Founded in 1673, it is now a commercial and industrial center. Population, 882,700.

jill (jĭl) *n.* Variant of **gill**[4]**.**

jil·lion (jĭl′yən) *n.* An indeterminately huge number. [On the model of *million, billion,* etc.] —**jil′lion·aire′** (jĭl′yə-nâr′) *n.* —**jil′lionth** *adj. n.*

jilt (jĭlt) *tr.v.* **jilt·ed, jilt·ing, jilts.** To deceive or drop (a lover) suddenly or callously. —**jilt** *n.* One who discards a lover. [Possibly from obsolete *jilt,* harlot, alteration of *gillot,* diminutive of *gille,* woman, girl, from Middle English. See GILL[4].]

Jim Crow or **jim crow** (jĭm′ krō′) *Slang. n.* The systematic practice of discriminating against and suppressing Black people. —*adj.* **1.** Upholding or practicing discrimination against and suppression of Black people: *Jim Crow laws; a Jim Crow town.* **2.** Reserved for a racial or ethnic group that is to be discriminated against: *"I told them I wouldn't take a Jim Crow job"* (Ralph Bunche). [From obsolete *Jim Crow,* derogatory name for a Black person, ultimately from the title of a 19th-century minstrel song, from CROW[1].] —**Jim′-Crow′ism** (jĭm′krō′ĭz′əm) *n.*

jim-dan·dy (jĭm′dăn′dē) *n., pl.* **-dies.** *Informal.* One that is very pleasing or excellent of its kind. [*Jim* (nickname for *James*) + DANDY.] —**jim′-dan′dy** *adj.*

Ji·mé·nez (hē-mĕ′nĕs, -nĕth), **Juan Ramón.** 1881–1958. Spanish poet who introduced modernism to Spanish verse. He won the 1956 Nobel Prize for literature.

Jiménez de Cis·ne·ros (dĕ sēs-nĕ′rôs, *th*ĕ thēs-), **Francisco.** 1436–1517. Spanish prelate and political leader. The confessor of Isabella I, he imposed conversion to Christianity on the Moors of Granada, leading to an uprising (1499–1500), and was appointed grand inquisitor (1507).

jim-jams (jĭm′jămz′) *pl.n. Slang.* **1.** The jitters. **2.** Delirium tremens. [Expressive of the trembling associated with delirium tremens.]

jim·mies (jĭm′ēz) *pl.n.* Small particles of chocolate or flavored candy sprinkled on ice cream as a topping. [Origin unknown.]

jim·my (jĭm′ē) *n., pl.* **-mies.** A short crowbar with curved ends. —**jimmy** *tr.v.* **-mied, -my·ing, -mies.** To pry (something) open with or as if with a jimmy: *jimmy a door.* [Probably from the name *Jimmy,* nickname for *James.*]

jimsonweed
Datura stramonium

jim·son·weed (jĭm′sən-wēd′) *n.* A coarse, poisonous plant *(Datura stramonium)* having large, trumpet-shaped white or purplish flowers and prickly capsules. Also called *stramonium.* [Alteration of *Jamestown weed,* after JAMESTOWN, Virginia.]

Jin also **Chin** (jĭn). The name of four Chinese dynasties, including **Western Jin** (A.D. 265–316), **Eastern Jin** (317–420), **Later Jin** (936–946), and **Jin** (1115–1234).

Ji·nan also **Tsi·nan** (jē′nän′). A city of eastern China on the Huang He (Yellow River) south of Tianjin. Opened to foreign commerce in 1904, it is the capital of Shandong province. Population, 1,430,000.

Jing·de·zhen (jĭng′də′jœn′) also **King·teh·chen** (kĭng′-tə′chœn′). A city of southeast China southwest of Shanghai. Established in the sixth century A.D., it has an important pottery industry. Population, 400,000.

jin·gle (jĭng′gəl) *v.* **-gled, -gling, -gles.** —*intr.* **1.** To make a tinkling or ringing metallic sound. **2.** To have the catchy sound of a simple, repetitious rhyme or doggerel. —*tr.* To cause to make a tinkling or ringing metallic sound. —**jingle** *n.* **1.** The sound produced by or as if by bits of metal striking together. **2.** A piece of light singsong verse or rhyme. **3.** A catchy, often musical advertising slogan. [Middle English *ginglen,* of imitative origin.] —**jin′gly** *adj.*

jingle shell *n.* The thin, translucent, rounded, yellowish or grayish shell of any of several marine bivalve mollusks of the genus *Anomia.*

jin·go (jĭng′gō) *n., pl.* **-goes.** One who vociferously supports one's country, especially one who supports a belligerent foreign policy; a chauvinistic patriot. —**jingo** *adj.* **1.** Of or relating to a chauvinistic patriot. **2.** Characterized by chauvinistic patriotism. —**jingo** *interj.* Used for emphasis or to express surprise: *By jingo, I'm leaving here in spite of the blizzard.* [From the phrase *by jingo,* used in the refrain of a bellicose 19th-century English music-hall song, from alteration of JESUS.] —**jin′go·ish** *adj.*

jin·go·ism (jĭng′gō-ĭz′əm) *n.* Extreme nationalism characterized especially by a belligerent foreign policy; chauvinistic patriotism. —**jin′go·ist** *n.* —**jin′go·is′tic** *adj.*

jink (jĭngk) *v.* **jinked, jink·ing, jinks.** —*intr.* To make a quick, evasive turn: *"He jinked every five seconds, and now brought his tank left again"* (Tom Clancy). —*tr.* To cause (a vehicle or an aircraft, for example) to make a quick, evasive turn. —**jink** *n.* **1.** A quick, evasive turn. **2. jinks.** Rambunctious play; frolic. [Origin unknown.]

Jin·men (jĭn′mœn′). See **Quemoy.**

jinn (jĭn) *n.* Plural of **jinni.**

Jin·nah (jĭn′ə), **Mohammed Ali.** 1876–1948. Founder and first governor-general (1947–1948) of Pakistan. When India's independence from Britain was imminent, he feared the Moslem minority would be oppressed by the Hindus and insisted on a Moslem homeland, founded in 1947 as Pakistan.

jin·ni or **jin·nee** also **djin·ni** or **djin·ny** (jĭn′ē, jĭ-nē′) *n., pl.* **jinn** also **djinn** (jĭn). In Moslem legend, a spirit capable of assuming human or animal form and exercising supernatural influence over people. [Arabic *jinnī.*]

jin·rik·sha or **jin·rick·sha** also **jin·riki·sha** (jĭn-rĭk′shô′) *n.* A small, two-wheeled carriage drawn by one or two persons; a ricksha. [Japanese *jinrikisha* : *jin,* person + *riki,* strength + *sha,* vehicle.]

jinx (jĭngks) *Informal. n.* **1.** A person or thing that is believed to bring bad luck. **2.** A condition or period of bad luck that appears to have been caused by a specific person or thing. —**jinx** *tr.v.* **jinxed, jinx·ing, jinx·es.** To bring bad luck to. [Possibly from *jynx,* wryneck (from its use in witchcraft), from Latin *iynx,* from Greek *iunx,* perhaps from *iuzein,* to call, cry.]

Jin·zhou also **Chin·chow** (jĭn′jō′). A city of northern China east-northeast of Beijing. It is a commercial center. Population, 584,800.

ji·pi·ja·pa (hē′pē-hä′pə) *n.* A stemless palmlike plant *(Carludovica palmata)* of Central and South America, having long-stalked, fanlike leaves that are used to make Panama hats. [American Spanish, after *Jipijapa,* a city of western Ecuador.]

jit·ney (jĭt′nē) *n., pl.* **-neys.** **1.** A small motor vehicle, such as a bus or van, that transports passengers on a route for a small fare. **2.** *Archaic.* A nickel. [Origin unknown.]

jit·ter (jĭt′ər) *intr.v.* **-tered, -ter·ing, -ters.** To be nervous or uneasy; fidget. —**jitter** *n.* **1.** A jittering movement; a tic. **2. jitters.** A fit of nervousness. Often used with *the.* [Perhaps alteration of CHITTER.]

jit·ter·bug (jĭt′ər-bŭg′) *n.* **1.** A strenuous dance performed to quick-tempo swing or jazz music and consisting of various two-step patterns embellished with twirls and sometimes acrobatic maneuvers. **2.** One who performs this dance. —**jitterbug** *intr.v.* **-bugged, -bug·ging, -bugs.** To perform this dance. [From *jitterbug,* heavy drinker who suffers from the jitters, from JITTER.]

jit·ter·y (jĭt′ə-rē) *adj.* **-i·er, -i·est.** **1.** Having or feeling nervous unease: *a jittery vigil in the dark.* **2.** Marked by jittering movements: *a jittery ride over rough terrain.* —**jit′ter·i·ness** *n.*

jiu·jit·su (jo͞o-jĭt′so͞o) *n.* Variant of **jujitsu.**

Ji·va·ro (hē′və-rō′) *n., pl.* **Jivaro** or **-ros.** **1.** A member of a South American Indian people of eastern Ecuador and northeast Peru. **2.** The language of this people.

jive (jīv) *n.* **1.** *Music.* **a.** Jazz or swing music. **b.** The jargon of jazz musicians and enthusiasts. **2.** *Slang.* Deceptive, nonsensical, or glib talk: *"the sexist, locker-room jive of men boasting and bonding"* (Trip Gabriel). —**jive** *v.* **jived, jiv·ing, jives.** —*intr.* **1.** *Music.* To play or dance to jive music. **2.** *Slang.* **a.** To talk nonsense; kid. **b.** To talk or chat: *"You just jive in one big group, putting each other on, trying to top the last line"* (Time). —*tr. Slang.* To cajole or mislead. —**jive** *adj. Slang.* Misleading; phony. [Origin unknown.] —**jiv′er** *n.* —**jiv′ey, jiv′y** *adj.*

Ji·xi (jē′shē′) also **Ki·si** (kē′sē′, -shē′). A city of northeast China east of Harbin. Population, 626,300.

JJ *abbr.* **1.** *Bible.* Judges. **2.** *Law.* Judges; justices.

Jl. *abbr. Bible.* Joel.

Jm. *abbr. Bible.* James.

Jn. *abbr. Bible.* John.

jnr. *abbr.* Junior.

jnt. *abbr.* Joint.

Joan of Arc (jōn; ärk), Saint. French name **Jeanne d'Arc** (zhän därk′). 1412?–1431. French military leader and heroine. Inspired and directed by religious visions, she organized the French resistance that forced the English to end their siege of Orléans (1429). The same year she led an army of 12,000 to Rheims and had the dauphin crowned Charles VII. Captured and sold to the English by the Burgundians (1430), she was later tried for heresy and sorcery and was burned at the stake in Rouen.

João Pes·so·a (zhwouN′ pə-sō′ə). A city of northeast Brazil near the Atlantic Ocean north of Recife. Founded in 1585, it has excellent examples of colonial architecture. Population, 290,247.

job¹ (jŏb) *n.* **1.** A regular activity performed in exchange for payment, especially as one's trade, occupation, or profession. **2.** A position in which one is employed. **3. a.** A task that must be done: *Washing the windows is not my job.* **b.** A specified duty or responsibility. See Synonyms at **task.** **4. a.** A specific piece of work to be done for a set fee: *an expensive repair job.* **b.** The object to be worked on. **c.** Something resulting from or produced by work. **5.** *Computer Science.* A program application that may consist of several steps but is performed as a single logical unit. **6.** *Informal.* A difficult or strenuous task: *It was a real job to convince them to drop the charges.* **7.** *Informal.* A bad or unsatisfactory piece of work: *The stylist did a real job on my hair.* **8.** *Informal.* A state of affairs: *Their marriage was a bad job right from the start. It's a good job that we left early to avoid the traffic.* **9.** *Informal.* A criminal act, especially a robbery: *a bank job.* —**job** *v.* **jobbed, job·bing, jobs.** —*intr.* **1.** To work at odd jobs. **2.** To work by the piece. **3.** To act as a jobber. —*tr.* **1.** To purchase (merchandise) from manufacturers and sell it to retailers. **2.** To arrange for (contracted work) to be done in portions by others; subcontract. **3.** To transact (official business) dishonestly for private profit. —***idiom.* on the job.** Paying close attention; on the alert. [Perhaps from obsolete *jobbe,* piece, alteration of Middle English *gobbe,* lump. See GOB¹.]

job² (jŏb) *Archaic. tr. & intr.v.* **jobbed, job·bing, jobs.** To jab or make a jab. —**job** *n.* A jab. [Middle English *jobben.*]

Job (jōb) *n. Bible.* **1.** In the Old Testament, an upright man whose faith in God survived the test of repeated calamities. **2.** *Abbr.* **Jb.** See table at **Bible.** [Hebrew *'iyôb.*]

job action *n.* A temporary action, such as a strike or slowdown, by workers to make demands or protest a company or managerial decision.

job·ber (jŏb′ər) *n.* **1.** One that buys merchandise from manufacturers and sells it to retailers. **2.** One that works by the piece or at odd jobs. **3.** *Chiefly British.* A middleman in the exchange of stocks and securities among brokers.

job·ber·y (jŏb′ə-rē) *n.* Corruption among public officials. [From JOB¹.]

job control language *n. Computer Science.* JCL.

job·hold·er (jŏb′hōl′dər) *n.* One who has a regular job.

job-hop (jŏb′hŏp′) *intr.v.* **-hopped, -hop·ping, -hops.** *Informal.* To change jobs frequently. —**job′-hop′per** *n.*

job-hop·ping (jŏb′hŏp′ĭng) *n. Informal.* The practice of changing jobs frequently, especially as a means of quick financial gain or career advancement.

job-hunt (jŏb′hŭnt′) *intr.v.* **-hunt·ed, -hunt·ing, -hunts.** To look actively for suitable employment. —**job hunter** *n.*

job·less (jŏb′lĭs) *adj.* **1.** Having no job. **2.** Of or relating to those who have no jobs. —**jobless** *n. (used with a pl. verb).* Unemployed people considered as a group. Used with *the.* —**job′less·ness** *n.*

job lot *n.* **1.** Miscellaneous merchandise sold in one lot. **2.** A collection of cheap items.

job printer *n.* A printer that does miscellaneous work such as circulars and cards.

Job's comforter (jōbz) *n.* One who is discouraging or saddening while seemingly offering sympathy or comfort. [After JOB, whose friends pretended to comfort but actually found fault with him.]

job seeker also **job·seek·er** (jŏb′sē′kər) *n.* One who seeks employment.

job-shar·ing (jŏb′shâr′ĭng) *n.* A practice whereby the responsibility for one job is shared between two or more alternating part-time workers. —**job′shar′er** *n.*

Job's tears *pl.n.* **1.** *(used with a sing. or pl. verb).* A tropical Asian grass *(Coix lacryma-jobi)* having white, beadlike grains. **2.** *(used with a pl. verb).* The grains of this plant, eaten or often used as ornamental beads.

job stick *n. Printing.* See **composing stick.**

Jo·cas·ta (jō-kăs′tə) *n. Greek Mythology.* A queen of Thebes who unknowingly married her own son, Oedipus.

jock¹ (jŏk) *n.* **1.** *Sports.* A jockey. **2.** A disc jockey. [Short for JOCKEY.]

jock² (jŏk) *n.* **1.** An athletic supporter. **2.** *Sports.* An athlete, especially in college. **3.** *Slang.* One characterized by excessive concern for machismo. [Short for JOCKSTRAP.]

jock·ey (jŏk′ē) *n., pl.* **-eys.** **1.** *Sports.* One who rides horses in races, especially as a profession. **2.** *Slang.* One who operates a specified vehicle, machine, or device: *a bus jockey; a computer jockey; a jet jockey.* —**jockey** *v.* **-eyed, -ey·ing, -eys.** —*tr.* **1.** *Sports.* To ride (a horse) as jockey. **2.** To direct or maneuver by cleverness or skill: *jockeyed the car into a tight space.* **3.** To trick; cheat. —*intr.* **1.** *Sports.* To ride a horse in a race. **2.** To

jinriksha
In Hong Kong

Joan of Arc
Detail from a 15th-century illuminated manuscript

jockey
Patrick Valenzuela racing Sunday Silence in the 1989 Kentucky Derby

ă pat	oi boy
ā pay	ou out
âr care	o͝o took
ä father	o͞o boot
ĕ pet	ŭ cut
ē be	ûr urge
ĭ pit	th thin
ī pie	*th* this
îr pier	hw which
ŏ pot	zh vision
ō toe	ə about, item
ô paw	♦ regionalism

Stress marks: ′ (primary); ′ (secondary), as in **dictionary** (dĭk′shə-nĕr′ē)

maneuver for a certain position or advantage: *jockeying for a promotion.* **3.** To employ trickery. [Diminutive of Scots *Jock,* variant of *Jack,* nickname for *John.*]

jock itch *n.* See **tinea cruris.**

jock·strap also **jock strap** (jŏk′străp′) *n.* An athletic supporter. [*jock,* male genitals + STRAP.]

jo·cose (jō-kōs′) *adj.* **1.** Given to joking; merry. **2.** Characterized by joking; humorous. [Latin *iocōsus,* from *iocus,* joke. See **yek-** in Appendix.] **—jo·cose′ly** *adv.* **—jo·cose′ness, jo·cos′i·ty** (-kŏs′ĭ-tē) *n.*

joc·u·lar (jŏk′yə-lər) *adj.* **1.** Characterized by joking. **2.** Given to joking. [Latin *ioculāris,* droll, from *ioculus,* diminutive of *iocus,* joke. See **yek-** in Appendix.] **—joc′u·lar′i·ty** (-lăr′ĭ-tē) *n.* **—joc′u·lar·ly** *adv.*

joc·und (jŏk′ənd, jō′kənd) *adj.* Sprightly and lighthearted in disposition, character, or quality. See Synonyms at **jolly.** [Middle English, from Old French *jocond,* from Latin *iūcundus, iōcundus,* from *iuvāre,* to delight.] **—jo·cun′di·ty** (jō-kŭn′dĭ-tē) *n.* **—joc′und·ly** *adv.*

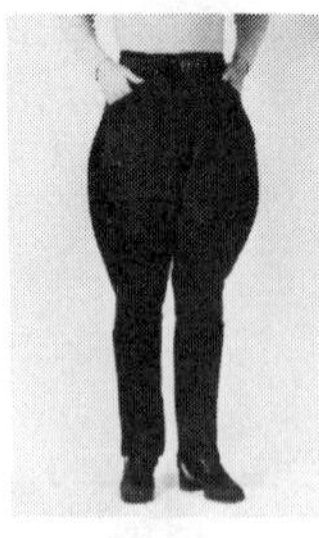
jodhpurs

Jodh·pur (jŏd′pər, jōd′po͝or′). A city of western India southwest of Delhi. Center of a former principality founded in the 13th century, it is an important wool market. Population, 506,345.

jodh·purs (jŏd′pərz) *pl.n.* Wide-hipped riding pants of heavy cloth, fitting tightly from knee to ankle. [After JODHPUR.]

Jo·el (jō′əl) *n. Bible.* **1.** A Hebrew prophet of the sixth century B.C. **2.** *Abbr.* **Jl.** See table at **Bible.**

joe-pye weed (jō′pī′) *n.* Any of several tall North American plants of the genus *Eupatorium,* having whorled leaves and terminal clusters of small pinkish or purplish flower heads. [Origin unknown.]

jo·ey (jō′ē) *n., pl.* **-eys.** *Australian.* A young animal, especially a baby kangaroo. [Origin unknown.]

Jof·fre (zhôf′rə), **Joseph Jacques Césaire.** 1852–1931. French field marshal who commanded the Allied armies in France during World War I.

jog[1] (jŏg) *v.* **jogged, jog·ging, jogs.** *—tr.* **1.** To move by shoving, bumping, or jerking; jar: *a rough wagon ride that jogged the passengers.* **2.** To give a push or shake to; nudge: *jogged her dozing companion with her elbow.* **3.** To rouse or stimulate as if by nudging: *an old photo that might jog your memory.* **4.** To cause (a horse) to move at a leisurely pace. *—intr.* **1.** To move with a jolting rhythm: *The pack jogged against his back as he ran.* **2.a.** To run or ride at a steady slow trot: *jogged out to their positions on the playing field.* **b.** *Sports.* To run in such a way for sport or exercise. **3.a.** To go or travel at a slow or leisurely pace: *The old car jogged along until it reached the hill.* **b.** To proceed in a leisurely manner: *"while his life was thus jogging easily along"* (Duff Cooper). **—jog** *n.* **1.** A slight push or shake; a nudge. **2.** A jogging movement or rhythm. **3.** A slow steady trot. [Perhaps alteration of Middle English *shoggen,* to shake, move with a jerk, perhaps alteration of *shokken,* to move rapidly, from Middle Low German *schocken,* to shake.] **—jog′ger** *n.*

jog[2] (jŏg) *n.* **1.** A protruding or receding part in a surface or line. **2.** An abrupt change in direction: *a jog in the road.* **—jog** *intr.v.* **jogged, jog·ging, jogs.** To turn sharply; veer: *Here the boundary jogs south.* [Variant of JAG[1].]

jog·gle[1] (jŏg′əl) *v.* **-gled, -gling, -gles.** *—tr.* To shake or jar slightly. *—intr.* To move with a shaking or lightly jolting motion. **—joggle** *n.* A shaking or lightly jolting motion. [Perhaps frequentative of JOG[1].]

jog·gle[2] (jŏg′əl) *n.* **1.** A joint between two pieces of building material formed by a notch and a fitted projection. **2.** The notch or the projecting piece used in such a joint. **—joggle** *tr.v.* **-gled, -gling, -gles.** To join or attach by means of a joggle. [Perhaps from JOG[2].]

Jog·ja·kar·ta (jŏg′yə-kär′tə, jôk′jä-) also **Yog·ya·kar·ta** (yŏg′yə-, jôk′jä-) or **Djok·ja·kar·ta** (jŏk′yə-). A city of southern Java, Indonesia, east-southeast of Jakarta. Founded in 1749, it is a major cultural center known for its dance and drama festivals. Population, 398,727.

jog trot *n.* **1.** A slow, steady trot, as of a horse. **2.** A regular, humdrum way of living or of doing.

Jo·han·nes·burg (jō-hăn′ĭs-bûrg′, -hä′nĭs-). The largest city of South Africa, in the northeast part of the country northwest of Durban. Founded in 1886 after the discovery of gold nearby, it is a major industrial center. Population, 703,980.

john (jŏn) *n. Slang.* **1.** A toilet. **2.** A man who is a prostitute's customer. [From the name *John.*]

John[1] (jŏn). Known as John Lackland. 1167?–1216. King of England (1199–1216). The youngest son of Henry II, he schemed against his father and his brother Richard I. During his reign, the English lost most of their possessions in France. The nobility rose against John and forced him to sign the Magna Carta (June 15, 1215), a cornerstone of English freedom.

John[2] (jŏn) *n. Abbr.* **Jn.** *Bible.* See table at **Bible.**

John, Saint. Known as "the Evangelist" or "the Divine." fl. first century A.D. One of the 12 Apostles and the brother of James the Great. He is traditionally considered the author of the fourth Gospel, three epistles, and the Book of Revelation.

John III So·bies·ki (sō-byĕs′kē). 1629–1696. King of Poland (1674–1696) who was a leader in the military expulsion of the Turks from Christian Europe. He formed an alliance with the pope, the Holy Roman emperor, and the rulers of Vienna (1684).

John XXIII. Originally Angelo Giuseppe Roncalli. 1881–1963. Pope (1958–1963) who convoked the Second Vatican Council (1962), the first general council of the Church in almost a century.

John, Augustus Edwin. 1878–1961. British painter whose portraits, as of George Bernard Shaw (1914) and Thomas Hardy (1923), offer unflattering characterizations.

John Bar·ley·corn (bär′lē-kôrn′) *n.* A personification of alcoholic liquor.

john·boat (jŏn′bōt′) *n. Nautical.* A small flat-bottomed boat with square ends, paddled or poled on shallow waterways. [Probably from the name *John.*]

John Bull *n.* **1.** A personification of England or the English. **2.** A typical Englishman. [After *John Bull,* a character in *Law Is a Bottomless Pit* by John Arbuthnot.]

John Day. A river, about 452 km (281 mi) long, of northern Oregon flowing west and north to the Columbia River.

John Doe (jŏn′ dō′) *n.* **1.** Used as a name in legal proceedings to designate a fictitious or unidentified man or boy. **2.** An average, undistinguished man.

John Dory *n.* Either of two North Atlantic fish *(Zeus faber* or *Z. ocellata)* having a laterally compressed body and long spines on the dorsal fin. [The name *John* + DORY[2].]

Joh·ne's disease (yō′nəz) *n.* A chronic disease of domestic animals, especially cattle and sheep, caused by the bacterium *Mycobacterium paratuberculosis* and characterized by persistent diarrhea, gradual loss of weight, and general weakness. [After Heinrich Albert *Johne* (1839–1910), German physician.]

John Han·cock (hăn′kŏk′) *n. Informal.* A person's signature. [After John HANCOCK (from the prominence of his signature on the Declaration of Independence).]

john·ny (jŏn′ē) *n., pl.* **-nies.** A loose short-sleeved gown opening in the back, worn by patients undergoing medical treatment or examination. [From the name *Johnny,* nickname for *John.*]

John·ny Ap·ple·seed (jŏn′ē ăp′əl-sēd′). See John **Chapman.**

♦ **john·ny·cake** also **jon·ny·cake** (jŏn′ē-kāk′) *n. New England.* Cornmeal bread usually shaped into a flat cake and baked or fried on a griddle. Also called ♦*ashcake,* ♦*battercake,* ♦*corn cake,* ♦*cornpone,* ♦*hoecake,* ♦*journey cake,* ♦*mush bread,* ♦*pone,* ♦*Shawnee cake.* [Perhaps by folk etymology from *jonakin.*]

♦ ***REGIONAL NOTE:*** When the Native Americans showed the Pilgrims how to cook with maize, they must have taught them to make *johnnycake,* a dense cornmeal bread whose thick batter is shaped into a flat cake and baked or fried on a griddle. *Johnnycake,* also spelled *jonnycake* and also called *journey cake* and *Shawnee cake,* is still considered a New England specialty, especially in Rhode Island, where it is celebrated by the Society for the Propagation of Johnny Cakes. The Usquepaugh, Rhode Island, Johnnycake Festival features johnnycakes made of white Indian corn called *flint corn.* Outside New England johnnycake is most popular in the South and South Midland states, where it is known as *ashcake, battercake, corn cake, cornpone, hoecake,* or *mush bread.* The color of the cornmeal, the consistency of the batter, the size of the cake, and the cooking method can vary from region to region. For example, an ashcake, according to a Georgia informant, is "made by wrapping cornbread batter in cabbage leaves and burying it gently at the back of the fireplace" (Dudley Clendinen).

John·ny-come-late·ly (jŏn′ē-kŭm-lāt′lē) *n., pl.* **John·ny-come-late·lies** or **John·nies-come-late·ly** (jŏn′ēz-). *Informal.* A newcomer or latecomer, especially a recent adherent to a cause or fashion.

John·ny-jump-up (jŏn′ē-jŭmp′ŭp′) *n., pl.* **Johnny-jump-ups.** Any of various plants of the genus *Viola,* especially a California violet *(V. pedunculata)* or a European pansy *(V. tricolor),* having ovate leaves and variously colored flowers. [From its quick growth.]

John·ny-on-the-spot (jŏn′ē-ŏn′*th*ə-spŏt′, -ôn′-) *n. Informal.* A person who is available and ready to act when needed.

Johnny Reb *n. Informal.* A Confederate soldier.

John of Aus·tri·a (ôs′trē-ə). 1547–1578. Spanish general who commanded the fleet that defeated the Turks at the Battle of Lepanto in the Gulf of Corinth (1571).

John of Gaunt (gônt, gänt). Duke of Lancaster. 1340–1399. English soldier. The fourth son of Edward III, he ruled England during his father's last years and in the beginning of Richard II's reign.

John of Lan·cas·ter (lăng′kə-stər, lăn′-). Duke of Bedford. 1389–1435. English noble who was regent of England and France (1422–1435) during the early reign of Henry VI.

John o'Groat's (ə-grōts′). A location on the northeast coast of Scotland, considered the northernmost point of Great Britain.

John Paul I (pôl, pŏl). Originally Albino Luciani. 1912–1978. Pope (1978). The first pope to assume a double name, he reigned for only 34 days.

John Paul II. Originally Karol Wojtyla. Born 1920. Pope (since 1978). The first Polish-born pope and the first non-Italian pope in 450 years, he has traveled extensively in support of human rights and conservative dogma.

Johns (jŏnz), **Jasper.** Born 1930. American artist and pioneer of

ă pat	oi boy
ā pay	ou out
âr care	o͝o took
ä father	o͞o boot
ĕ pet	ŭ cut
ē be	ûr urge
ĭ pit	th thin
ī pie	*th* this
îr pier	hw which
ŏ pot	zh vision
ō toe	ə about, item
ô paw	♦ regionalism

Stress marks: ′ (primary); ′ (secondary), as in **dictionary** (dĭk′shə-nĕr′ē)

pop art whose works place everyday objects within artistic contexts.

John•son (jŏn′sən), **Andrew.** 1808–1875. The 17th President of the United States (1865–1869). Elected Vice President (1864), he succeeded the assassinated Abraham Lincoln as President. His administration was marked by reconstruction policies in the South and the purchase of Alaska (1867). An attempt to unseat Secretary of War Edwin Stanton led to Johnson's impeachment on purely political charges brought by Republican senators (1868). Johnson was acquitted by one vote.

Johnson, Claudia Alta Taylor. Known as "Lady Bird." Born 1912. First Lady of the United States (1963–1969) as the wife of President Lyndon Johnson. She directed a nationwide beautification project.

Johnson, Eastman. 1824–1906. American painter known for his genre scenes and portraits of notable contemporaries.

John•son (yo͝on′sôn), **Eyvind.** 1900–1976. Swedish writer whose works concern his impoverished youth and sociopolitical issues. He shared the 1974 Nobel Prize for literature.

Johnson, James Weldon. 1871–1938. American writer and educator who was a founder and secretary (1916–1930) of the NAACP.

Johnson, John Arthur. Known as "Jack." 1878–1946. American prizefighter. He was the first Black world heavyweight champion (1908–1915).

Johnson, Lyndon Baines. 1908–1973. The 36th President of the United States (1963–1969), who succeeded to the office after John F. Kennedy was assassinated. He won the 1964 election but faced increasing criticism over the mounting U.S. involvement in Vietnam and did not stand for reelection in 1968.

Johnson, Philip Cortelyou. Born 1906. American architect who designed the New York State Theater at Lincoln Center (1964) in New York City.

Johnson, Richard Mentor. 1780–1850. Vice President of the United States (1837–1841) under Martin Van Buren.

Johnson, Samuel. Known as "Dr. Johnson." 1709–1784. British writer and lexicographer. The leading literary figure in the second half of the 18th century, he wrote *Dictionary of the English Language* (1755) and *Lives of the Poets* (1779–1781).

Johnson, Thomas. 1732–1819. American politician and jurist. He was the first governor of Maryland (1777–1779) and served as an associate justice of the U.S. Supreme Court (1792–1793).

Johnson, William. 1771–1834. American jurist who served as an associate justice of the U.S. Supreme Court (1804–1834).

Johnson, Sir **William.** 1715–1774. British-born American pioneer and public official. In the French and Indian Wars he defeated the French at Lake George (1755).

Johnson City. 1. A village of south-central New York east of Binghamton. It has tanneries and other industries. Population, 17,126. **2.** A city of northest Tennessee east-northeast of Knoxville. Settled in the 1760's, it is a railroad junction and manufacturing center. Population, 39,753.

Johnson grass *n.* A coarse perennial Mediterranean grass *(Sorghum halepense)* cultivated for forage but often a troublesome weed. Also called *Egyptian millet.* [After William *Johnson* (died 1859), American agriculturalist.]

John•so•ni•an (jŏn-sō′nē-ən) *adj.* Of, resembling, or relating to Samuel Johnson or his writings. **—Johnsonian** *n.* An admirer or a student of Samuel Johnson or his work.

Johnson noise *n.* See **thermal noise.** [After John Bertrand *Johnson* (1887–1970), Swedish-born American physicist.]

John•ston (jŏn′stən). A town of north-central Rhode Island, a manufacturing suburb of Providence. Population, 24,907.

Johnston, Albert Sidney. 1803–1862. American Confederate general in the Civil War. He was defeated by Ulysses S. Grant at Shiloh (1862).

Johnston, Joseph Eggleston. 1807–1891. American Confederate general in the Civil War who surrendered to William Tecumseh Sherman in 1865.

Johns•town (jŏnz′toun′). A city of southwest Pennsylvania east of Pittsburgh. A devastating flood on May 31, 1889, killed more than 2,000 people. Population, 35,496.

John the Bap•tist (băp′tĭst), Saint. First century B.C. Jewish prophet who in the New Testament baptized and prepared the way for Jesus. He was executed by Herod Antipas at the behest of Salome.

Jo•hor Ba•ha•ru (jə-hôr′ bə-hä′ro͞o, jə-hōr′) also **Jo•hore Bah•ru** (bä′ro͞o). A city of Malaysia on the southern tip of the Malay Peninsula opposite Singapore Island. The city is connected with Singapore by a causeway across the narrow **Johore Strait.** Population, 249,880.

joie de vi•vre (zhwä′ də vē′vrə) *n.* Hearty or carefree enjoyment of life. [French : *joie,* joy + *de,* of + *vivre,* to live, living.]

join (join) *v.* **joined, join•ing, joins.** *—tr.* **1.** To put or bring together so as to make continuous or form a unit: *join two boards with nails; joined hands in a circle.* **2.** To put or bring into close association or relationship: *were joined by marriage; join forces.* **3.** To connect (points), as with a straight line. **4.** To meet and merge with: *where the creek joins the river.* **5.** To become a part or member of: *join a club.* **6.** To come into the company of: *joined the group in the waiting room.* **7.** To participate with in an act or activity: *The committee joins me in welcoming you.* **8.** To adjoin. **9.** To engage in; enter into: *Opposing armies joined battle on the plain.* *—intr.* **1.** To come together so as to form a connection: *where the two bones join.* **2.** To act together; form an alliance: *The two factions joined to oppose the measure.* **3.** To become a member of a group. **4.** To take part; participate: *joined in the search.* **—join** *n.* A joint; a junction. [Middle English *joinen,* from Old French *joindre, joign-, join-,* from Latin *iungere.* See **yeug-** in Appendix.]

SYNONYMS: *join, combine, unite, link, connect, relate, associate.* These verbs mean to fasten or affix or become fastened or affixed. *Join* applies to the physical contact, connection, or union of at least two separate things and to the coming together of persons, as into a group: *The children joined hands. Join the panels of fabric at the selvages. "Join the union, girls, and together say* Equal Pay for Equal Work" (Susan B. Anthony). *Combine* suggests the mixing or merging of components, often for a specific or shared purpose: *The cook combined whipped cream, sugar, and vanilla to make a topping for the compote. "When bad men combine, the good must associate"* (Edmund Burke). *Unite* stresses the coherence or oneness of the persons or things joined: *Can strips of plastic be united with epoxy? The attack on their country united squabbling political factions in a common purpose. Link* and *connect* imply a firm attachment in which individual components nevertheless retain their identities: *linked poverty and unemployment to the social unrest besetting the city. The chief of police is in no way connected with the scandal. Relate* refers to connection of persons through marriage or kinship (*Though they have the same surname, the two are not even distantly related*) or of things through logical association (*The two events seem to be related*). *Associate* usually implies a relationship of persons as partners or allies: *His daughter is associated with him in the family business.* It can also refer to a relationship of things that are similar or complementary or that have a connection in one's thoughts: *I can forgive his bluntness because it is associated with a basic kindliness of spirit.*

join•der (join′dər) *n.* **1.** The act of joining. **2.** *Law.* **a.** A joining of causes of action or defense in a suit. **b.** A joining of parties in a suit. **c.** Formal acceptance of an issue offered. [From French *joindre,* to join, from Old French. See JOIN.]

join•er (joi′nər) *n.* **1.** A carpenter, especially a cabinetmaker. **2.** *Informal.* A person given to joining groups, organizations, or causes.

join•er•y (joi′nə-rē) *n.* **1.** The art or craft of a joiner; cabinetmaking. **2.** Work done by a joiner; fine woodwork.

joint (joint) *n. Abbr.* **jnt., jt. 1.a.** A place or part at which two or more things are joined. **b.** A way in which two or more things are joined: *a mortise-and-tenon joint; flexible joints.* **2.** *Anatomy.* **a.** A point of articulation between two or more bones, especially such a connection that allows motion. **b.** A point in the exoskeleton of an invertebrate at which moveable parts join, as along the leg of an arthropod. **3.** *Botany.* An articulation on a fruit or stem, such as the node of a grass stem. **4.** *Geology.* A fracture or crack in a rock mass along which no appreciable movement has occurred. **5.** A large cut of meat for roasting. **6.** *Slang.* **a.** A cheap or disreputable gathering place: *"The tavern is . . . just a joint with Formica tables, a vinyl floor, lights over the mirrors"* (Scott Turow). **b.** A building or dwelling. **c.** A prison. Often used with *the.* **7.** *Slang.* A marijuana cigarette. **8.** *Vulgar Slang.* A penis. **—joint** *adj. Abbr.* **jnt., jt. 1.** Shared by or common to two or more: *our joint presence; a joint income-tax return.* **2.** Sharing with another or others: *a joint tenant.* **3.** Formed or characterized by cooperation or united action: *joint military maneuvers.* **4.** Involving both houses of a legislature: *a joint session of Congress.* **5.** *Law.* Regarded as one legal body; united in identity of interest or liability. **6.** *Mathematics.* Involving two or more variables. **—joint** *tr.v.* **joint•ed, joint•ing, joints. 1.** To combine or attach with a joint or joints: *securely jointed the sides of the drawer.* **2.** To provide or construct with joints: *joint a boom on a crane.* **3.** To separate (meat) at the joints. ***—idiom.*** **out of joint. 1.** Dislocated, as a bone. **2.** *Informal.* **a.** Not harmonious; inconsistent. **b.** Out of order; inauspicious or unsatisfactory. **c.** In bad spirits or humor; out of sorts. [Middle English, from Old French, from past participle of *joindre,* to join. See JOIN.]

Joint Chiefs of Staff (joint) *n. Abbr.* **J.C.S., JCS** The principal military advisory group to the President of the United States, composed of the chiefs of the Army, Navy, and Air Force and the commandant of the Marine Corps.

joint•er (join′tər) *n.* **1.** A machine or tool used in making joints. **2.** A tool used to cut grooves indicating the joints in cement. **3.** A triangular attachment to a plow used in covering trash or refuse.

joint•ly (joint′lē) *adv.* In common; together.

joint probability *n.* The probability that two or more specific outcomes will occur in an event.

joint resolution *n.* A resolution passed by both houses of a bicameral legislature and eligible to become a law if signed by the chief executive or passed over the chief executive's veto.

joint stock *n.* Stock or capital funds of a company held jointly or in common by its owners.

joint-stock company (joint′stŏk′) *n.* A business whose capital is held in transferable shares of stock by its joint owners.

join•ture (join′chər) *n.* **1.** *Law.* **a.** An arrangement by which a man sets aside property to be used for the support of his wife after his death. **b.** The property so designated. **2.** The act of

Andrew Johnson
1865 mezzotint after a photograph by John Sartain (1808–1897)

Lady Bird Johnson

Lyndon B. Johnson
Photographed in 1967

John the Baptist
Detail of triptych *The Penitence of Saint Jerome* by Joachim Patinir (1485?–1524)

joining or the state of being joined. [Middle English, from Anglo-Norman, from Latin *iunctūra,* joint. See JUNCTURE.]

joint venture *n.* A partnership or conglomerate, formed often to share risk or expertise: *a joint venture between the film companies to produce TV shows.*

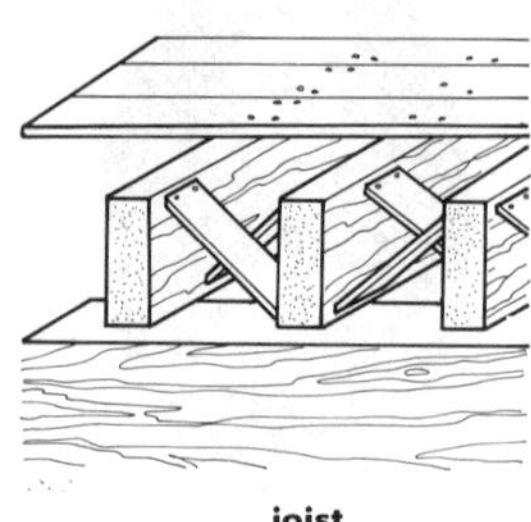
joist

joint·worm (joint′wûrm′) *n.* The larva of certain wasps of the family Eurytomidae, especially of *Harmolita tritici,* that infest grains and cause hard swellings near the first joint of the stems.

Join·vi·le also **Join·vil·le** (zhoiN-vē′lē). A city of southern Brazil north-northeast of Pôrto Alegre. Founded c. 1850 by German immigrants, it is an industrial center. Population, 216,986.

Join·ville (zhwăN-vēl′), **Jean de.** 1224?–1317. French chronicler who wrote *Histoire de Saint Louis* (1309), the principal source on the life of Louis IX.

joist (joist) *n.* Any of the parallel horizontal beams set from wall to wall to support the boards of a floor or ceiling. **—joist** *tr.v.* **joist·ed, joist·ing, joists.** To construct with such parallel horizontal beams. [Middle English *giste, joiste,* from Old French *giste,* from feminine past participle of *gesir,* to lie, lie down, from Latin *iacēre.* See **yē-** in Appendix.]

jo·jo·ba (hə-hō′bə, hō-) *n.* A dioecious shrub *(Simmondsia chinensis)* of the southwest United States and northern Mexico, having opposite, leathery leaves and edible seeds that contain a valuable oil. [American Spanish.]

joke (jōk) *n.* **1.** Something said or done to evoke laughter or amusement, especially an amusing story with a punch line. **2.** A mischievous trick; a prank. **3.** An amusing or ludicrous incident or situation. **4.** *Informal.* **a.** Something not to be taken seriously; a triviality: *The accident was no joke.* **b.** An object of amusement or laughter; a laughingstock: *His preference for loud ties was the joke of the office.* **—joke** *v.* **joked, jok·ing, jokes.** —*intr.* **1.** To tell or play jokes; jest. **2.** To speak in fun; be facetious. —*tr.* To make fun of; tease. [Latin *iocus.* See **yek-** in Appendix.] **—jok′ing·ly** *adv.*

SYNONYMS: *joke, jest, witticism, quip, sally, crack, wisecrack, gag.* These nouns refer to something that is said or done in order to evoke laughter or amusement. *Joke* especially denotes an amusing story with a punch line at the end: *told jokes at the beginning of the show. Jest* suggests frolicsome humor: *All jests aside, we're in big trouble.* A *witticism* is a witty, usually cleverly phrased remark: *a speech that was full of witticisms.* A *quip* is a clever, pointed, often sarcastic remark: *a President who responded to the tough questions with quips. Sally* denotes a sudden quick witticism: *In a sally at the end of the debate the candidate elicited much laughter from the audience. Crack* and *wisecrack* refer less formally to flippant or sarcastic retorts: *He made a crack about my driving ability. Don't give me any more wisecracks. Gag* is principally applicable to a broadly comic remark or to comic byplay in a theatrical routine: *one of the most memorable gags in the history of vaudeville.*

WORD HISTORY: It is hard to imagine the English language without the word *joke,* but *joke* is only first recorded in 1670. Since *joke* was originally considered a slang or informal usage, it was not suitable to all contexts. The change in status of *joke* from then to now provides us with an excellent example of how usage changes. *Joke* has a decent enough heritage at any rate, coming from Latin *iocus,* "jest, sport, laughingstock, trifle." *Iocus* in turn can be traced back to the Indo-European root *yek–,* meaning "to speak," from which also comes the Umbrian word *iuka,* "prayers," and the Welsh word *iaith,* "speech."

Jolly Roger
After the flag of the Colonial pirate Richard Worley

jok·er (jō′kər) *n.* **1. a.** One who tells or plays jokes. **b.** An insolent person who seeks to make a show of cleverness. **c.** *Informal.* A person, especially an annoying or inept one: *Some joker is blocking my driveway.* **2.** *Games.* A playing card, usually printed with a picture of a jester, used in certain games as the highest-ranking card or as a wild card. **3.** A minor clause in a document such as a legislative bill that voids or changes its original or intended purpose. **4.** An unforeseen but important difficulty, fact, or circumstance. **5.** A deceptive means of getting the better of someone.

joke·ster (jōk′stər) *n.* One who tells or plays jokes; a joker.

jok·ey also **jok·y** (jō′kē) *adj.* **-i·er, -i·est.** Characterized by joking or jokes, especially stale or clumsy jokes: *jokey bumper stickers.* **—jok′i·ly** *adv.* **—jok′i·ness** *n.*

Jo·li·et (jō′lē-ĕt′, jō′lē-ĕt′). A city of northeast Illinois southwest of Chicago. It is an industrial center and a river port. Population, 77,956.

Jo·li·et (jō′lē-ĕt′, jō′lē-ĕt′, zhô-lyā′), **Louis.** See Louis **Jolliet.**

jonquil
Narcissus jonquilla

Jo·li·ette (zhō′lē-ĕt′). A city of southern Quebec, Canada, north of Montreal. It was founded in 1841 by descendants of the explorer Louis Jolliet. Population, 16,987.

Jo·li·ot-Cu·rie (zhô-lyō′ kyo͝or′ē, -kyo͞o-rē′, -kü-), **Irène.** 1897–1956. French physicist. She shared a 1935 Nobel Prize with her husband, **Frédéric Joliot-Curie** (1900–1958), for synthesizing new radioactive elements.

Jol·li·et also **Jo·li·et** (jō′lē-ĕt′, jō′lē-ĕt′, zhô-lyā′), **Louis.** 1645–1700. French-Canadian explorer of the upper Mississippi Valley who with Jacques Marquette sighted the Mississippi River on June 17, 1673, and descended it to the mouth of the Arkansas River.

jol·li·fi·ca·tion (jŏl′ə-fĭ-kā′shən) *n.* Festivity; revelry.

jol·li·ty (jŏl′ĭ-tē) *n., pl.* **-ties.** Convivial merriment or celebration. See Synonyms at **mirth.**

jol·ly (jŏl′ē) *adj.* **-li·er, -li·est. 1.** Full of good humor and high spirits. **2.** Exhibiting or occasioning happiness or mirth; cheerful: *a jolly tune.* **3.** Greatly pleasing; enjoyable: *had a jolly time.* **—jolly** *adv. Chiefly British.* To a great extent or degree; extremely. **—jolly** *v.* **-lied, -ly·ing, -lies.** —*tr.* To keep amused or diverted for one's own purposes; humor. —*intr.* To amuse oneself with humorous or teasing banter. **—jolly** *n., pl.* **-lies. 1.** *Chiefly British.* A good or festive time. **2. jollies.** *Slang.* Amusement; kicks: *However you get your jollies is fine with me.* [Middle English *joli,* from Old French, perhaps of Scandinavian origin.] **—jol′li·ly** *adv.* **—jol′li·ness** *n.*

SYNONYMS: *jolly, jovial, merry, blithe, jocund.* These adjectives mean feeling, showing, or marked by good humor and high spirits. *Jolly* and *jovial* are especially associated with hearty, convivial good cheer: *A jolly crowd attended the reunion. Her grandfather is a jovial, ruddy-faced old gentleman. Merry* suggests gaiety, animation, and love of fun: *a peal of merry laughter. Blithe* implies buoyancy and freedom from care: *"His spirit was blithe and its fire unquenchable"* (John Morley). *Jocund* suggests sprightly lightheartedness: *"A poet could not but be gay,/In such a jocund company"* (William Wordsworth).

jol·ly·boat (jŏl′ē-bōt′) *n. Nautical.* A medium-sized ship's boat used for rough work and minor tasks. [Origin unknown.]

Jol·ly Rog·er (jŏl′ē rŏj′ər) *n.* A black flag bearing the emblematic white skull and crossbones of a pirate ship. [Origin unknown.]

Jol·son (jōl′sən), **Al.** 1886–1950. American entertainer who starred in *The Jazz Singer* (1927), the first major film with synchronized sound.

jolt (jōlt) *v.* **jolt·ed, jolt·ing, jolts.** —*tr.* **1.** To move or dislodge with a sudden, hard blow; strike heavily or jarringly: *jolted his opponent with a heavy punch; an impact that jolted the mailbox loose.* **2.** To cause to move jerkily: *stops and starts that jolted the passengers.* **3.** To put into a specified condition by or as if by a blow: *"Now and then he jolted a nodding reader awake by inserting a witty paragraph"* (Walter Blair). **4.** To make suddenly active or effective: *The remark jolted my memory.* **5.** To disturb suddenly and severely; stun: *She was jolted by the betrayal of her trusted friend.* —*intr.* To proceed in an irregular, bumpy, or jerky fashion. **—jolt** *n.* **1.** A sudden jarring or jerking, as from a heavy blow or an abrupt movement. See Synonyms at **collision. 2. a.** A sudden, strong feeling of surprise or disappointment; a shock. **b.** The cause of such a feeling: *The news came as a jolt.* **3.** A brief strong portion: *a jolt of electricity; a jolt of whiskey.* [Origin unknown.] **—jolt′er** *n.* **—jolt′i·ly** *adv.* **—jolt′i·ness** *n.* **—jolt′y** *adj.*

Jo·ma·da (jə-mä′dä) *n.* Variant of **Jumada.**

Jo·nah (jō′nə) *n.* **1.** *Bible.* **a.** In the Old Testament, a prophet who was swallowed by a great fish and disgorged unharmed three days later. **b.** *Abbr.* **Jon., Jon** See table at **Bible. 2.** One thought to bring bad luck.

Jon·a·than[1] (jŏn′ə-thən). In the Old Testament, the eldest son of King Saul of Israel and friend of David.

Jon·a·than[2] (jŏn′ə-thən) *n.* A variety of red, late-ripening apple. [After *Jonathan* Hasbrouck (died 1846), American jurist and gardener.]

jones (jōnz) *n. Slang.* **1.** Heroin. **2.** An addiction, especially to heroin. [Perhaps from the name *Jones.*]

Jones (jōnz), **Inigo.** 1573–1652. English architect who brought the Palladian classical style to England.

Jones, John Luther. Known as "Casey." 1864–1900. American locomotive engineer who died trying to stop his train from crashing into another train. A friend wrote "The Ballad of Casey Jones," a popular song about his heroic death.

Jones, John Paul. 1747–1792. Scottish-born American naval officer. In the American Revolution he raided the British coast and destroyed two warships (1779).

Jones, LeRoi. See Imamu Amiri **Baraka.**

Jones, Mary Harris. Known as "Mother Jones." 1830–1930. Irish-born American labor leader and union organizer. She helped found (1905) the Industrial Workers of the World.

Jones·bor·o (jōnz′bûr′ō, -bûr′ə, -bŭr′ō). A city of northeast Arkansas northeast of Little Rock. It is the seat of Arkansas State University (founded 1909). Population, 31,530.

jon·gleur (zhôN-glœr′) *n.* A wandering minstrel, poet, or entertainer in medieval England and France. [French, from Old French, variant of *jogleor,* from Latin *ioculātor,* jester, from *ioculārī,* to jest. See JUGGLE.]

Jön·kö·ping (yœn′chœ′pĭng). A city of southern Sweden southwest of Stockholm. Chartered in 1284, it was burned by its citizens in 1612 to prevent the Danes from sacking it. Population, 107,031.

♦**jon·ny·cake** (jŏn′ē-kāk′) *n. New England.* Variant of **johnnycake.**

Jon·quière (zhôN-kyĕr′). A city of southern Quebec, Canada, on the Saguenay River north of Quebec City. Population, 60,354.

jon·quil (jŏng′kwəl, jŏn′-) *n.* A widely cultivated ornamental plant *(Narcissus jonquilla)* native chiefly to southern Europe, having long, narrow leaves and short-tubed, fragrant yellow flowers.

[Spanish *junquilla,* from the name *Junquello,* diminutive of *junco,* reed, from Latin *iuncus.*]

Jon·son (jŏn′sən), **Benjamin.** Known as "Ben." 1572–1637. English actor and writer. Among his major plays are *Every Man in His Humour* (1598) and *Volpone* (1606).

♦ **joo·al** (zho͞o-äl′) *n. Chiefly Canadian & Maine.* Variant of **joual.**

Jop·lin (jŏp′lĭn). A city of southwest Missouri near the Kansas border. It was founded in 1839. Population, 39,023.

Joplin, Scott. 1868–1917. American pianist and composer known for his ragtime works, including "Maple Leaf Rag" (1899).

Jor·dan (jôr′dn). Formerly **Trans·jor·dan** (trăns′-, trănz′-). A country of southwest Asia in northwest Arabia. Inhabited since biblical times, the area was held by the Turks from 1516 until World War I. The country became the British mandate of Transjordan in 1923 and gained independence in 1946. Its territory west of the Jordan River was occupied by Israeli forces in the Six-Day War of 1967. Amman is the capital and the largest city. Population, 2,595,100. **—Jor·da′ni·an** (jôr-dā′nē-ən) *adj. & n.*

Jordan almond *n.* **1.** A large variety of almond from Málaga, Spain, used widely in confections. **2.** An almond covered with a hard, colored, and flavored sugar coating. [By folk etymology from Middle English *jardin almaund* : Old French *jardin,* garden; see JARDINIÈRE + *almande,* almond; see ALMOND.]

Jordan curve *n. Mathematics.* See **simple closed curve.** [After Camille *Jordan* (1838–1922), French mathematician.]

Jordan curve theorem *n. Mathematics.* The theorem that states that every simple closed curve divides a plane into two parts and acts as the common boundary between them.

Jordan River. A river of southwest Asia rising in Syria and flowing about 322 km (200 mi) south through the Sea of Galilee to the northern end of the Dead Sea.

jo·rum (jôr′əm, jōr′-) *n.* **1.** A large drinking bowl. **2.** The amount that such a bowl contains. [Perhaps after *Joram,* who brought vessels of silver, gold, and brass to King David (II Samuel 8:10).]

Jos *abbr. Bible.* Joshua.

jo·seph (jō′zəf, -səf) *n.* A long riding coat with a small cape, worn by women in the 18th century. [After JOSEPH[1], who left an outer garment in the hands of Potiphar's wife when he fled her attempt to seduce him (Genesis 39:12).]

Jo·seph[1] (jō′zəf, -səf). In the Old Testament, the older son of Jacob and Rachel and the forebear of one of the tribes of Israel.

Jo·seph[2] (jō′zəf, -səf). Known as "Chief Joseph." 1840?–1904. Nez Percé leader who conducted a skillful but unsuccessful retreat from U.S. forces (1877).

Joseph, Saint. fl. first century A.D. In the New Testament, the husband of Mary, mother of Jesus.

Joseph II. 1741–1790. Holy Roman emperor (1765–1790) and king of Bohemia and Hungary (1780–1790). He instituted a number of social reforms aimed at curbing hereditary privileges.

Jo·se·phine (jō′zə-fēn′, -sə-). See Josephine de **Beauharnais.**

Joseph of Ar·i·ma·the·a (ăr′ə-mə-thē′ə). fl. first century A.D. In the New Testament, the disciple who buried the body of Jesus.

Jo·seph·son (jō′zəf-sən, -səf-), **Brian David.** Born 1940. British physicist. He shared a 1973 Nobel Prize for theoretical advances in the field of solid-state electronics.

Josephson effect *n.* The radiative effect associated with the passage of electron pairs across an insulating barrier separating two superconductors. [After Brian David JOSEPHSON.]

Josephson junction *n.* An insulating barrier separating two superconducting materials and producing the Josephson effect.

Jo·se·phus (jō-sē′fəs), **Flavius.** A.D. 37–100? Jewish general and historian who took part in the Jewish revolt against the Romans. His *History of the Jewish War* is the major source of information about the siege of Masada (72–73).

josh (jŏsh) *v.* **joshed, josh·ing, josh·es.** *—tr.* To tease (someone) good-humoredly. *—intr.* To make or exchange good-humored jokes; banter. See Synonyms at **banter.** **—josh** *n.* A teasing or joking remark. [Origin unknown.] **—josh′er** *n.* **—josh′ing·ly** *adv.*

Josh·u·a (jŏsh′o͞o-ə) *n. Bible.* **1.** In the Old Testament, a Hebrew leader who succeeded Moses as leader of Israel. **2.** *Abbr.* **Josh., Jos** See table at **Bible.**

Joshua tree *n.* A treelike plant *(Yucca brevifolia)* of the southwest United States, having sword-shaped leaves and greenish-white flowers grouped in large panicles. [Probably after JOSHUA, from the resemblance of the tree's greatly extended branches to Joshua's outstretched arm as he pointed with his spear to the city of Ai (Joshua 8:18).]

Jo·si·ah (jō-sī′ə, -zī′ə). Died 609? B.C. King of Judah (640?–609?) who attempted to destroy all forms of idolatry.

joss (jŏs) *n.* A Chinese cult image or idol. [Pidgin English, from Javanese *deyos,* from Portugese *deos,* god, from Latin *deus.* See **deiw-** in Appendix.]

joss house *n.* A Chinese temple or shrine.

joss stick *n.* A stick of incense of the kind burned before a Chinese image, idol, or shrine.

jos·tle (jŏs′əl) *v.* **-tled, -tling, -tles.** *—intr.* **1.** To come in rough contact while moving; push and shove: *jostled against the others on the crowded platform.* **2.** To make one's way by pushing or elbowing: *jostled through the guests to the bar.* **3.** To vie for an advantage or a position. **4.** To be in close proximity. **5.** To pick or try to pick pockets. *—tr.* **1.** To come into rough contact with while moving: *messengers who jostle pedestrians on the sidewalk.* **2.** To force by pushing or elbowing: *jostled my way through the mob.* **3.** To vie with for an advantage or a position. **4.** To be in close proximity with: *"Books written in all languages . . . jostle each other on the shelf"* (Virginia Woolf). **5.** To pick or try to pick the pocket of. **—jostle** *n.* **1.** A rough shove or push. **2.** The condition of being crowded together. [Middle English *justilen,* to have sexual relations with, frequentative of *justen,* to joust, from Old French *juster.* See JOUST.] **—jos′tler** *n.*

jot (jŏt) *n.* The smallest bit; iota. **—jot** *tr.v.* **jot·ted, jot·ting, jots.** To write down briefly or hastily: *jot down an address.* [Middle English *jote,* from Latin *iōta,* iota, from Greek, iota. See IOTA.]

jot·ting (jŏt′ĭng) *n.* A brief note or memorandum.

♦ **jou·al** also **joo·al** (zho͞o-äl′) *n. Chiefly Canadian & Maine.* A dialect of Canadian French characterized by nonstandard pronunciations and grammar and by English vocabulary and syntax. [Canadian French dialectal, variant of French *cheval.* See CHEVALET.]

♦ ***REGIONAL NOTE:*** London has Cockney; Liverpool has Scouse. Certain dialects often become so famous and distinctive that they acquire names. Such is the case with the Canadian French dialect known in Quebec and in Maine as *joual* or *jooal.* The name, derived from a regional dialect pronunciation of the word *cheval,* "horse," is applied to the rural French patois of Quebec. Canadian opinions differ as to whether *joual* is a "language" of its own or merely a regional French characterized by nonstandard grammar and heavy borrowing from English words and word order.

Jou·haux (zho͞o-ō′), **Léon.** 1879–1954. French politician and labor leader. He won the 1951 Nobel Peace Prize for his international efforts on behalf of workers and unions.

joule (jo͞ol, joul) *n. Abbr.* **j, J** **1.** The International System unit of electrical, mechanical, and thermal energy. **2.a.** A unit of electrical energy equal to the work done when a current of 1 ampere is passed through a resistance of 1 ohm for 1 second. **b.** A unit of energy equal to the work done when a force of 1 newton acts through a distance of 1 meter. See table at **measurement.** [After James Prescott JOULE.]

Joule (jo͞ol, joul), **James Prescott.** 1818–1889. British physicist who established the mechanical theory of heat and discovered the first law of thermodynamics.

jounce (jouns) *intr. & tr.v.* **jounced, jounc·ing, jounc·es.** To move or cause to move with bumps and jolts; bounce. **—jounce** *n.* A rough, jolting movement; a jolt. [Middle English *jouncen.*]

jour. *abbr.* **1.** Journal; journalist. **2.** Journeyman.

jour·nal (jûr′nəl) *n. Abbr.* **jour., J., j.** **1.a.** A personal record of occurrences, experiences, and reflections kept on a regular basis; a diary. **b.** An official record of daily proceedings, as of a legislative body. **c.** *Nautical.* A ship's log. **2.** *Accounting.* **a.** A daybook. **b.** A book of original entry in a double-entry system, listing all transactions and indicating the accounts to which they belong. **3.** A newspaper. **4.** A periodical presenting articles on a particular subject: *a medical journal.* **5.** The part of a machine shaft or axle supported by a bearing. [Middle English, breviary, from Old French, daily, breviary, from Late Latin *diurnālis,* daily. See DIURNAL.]

journal box *n.* A housing in a machine enclosing a journal and its bearings.

jour·nal·ese (jûr′nə-lēz′, -lēs′) *n.* The style of writing often held to be characteristic of newspapers and magazines, distinguished by clichés, sensationalism, and triteness of thought.

jour·nal·ism (jûr′nə-lĭz′əm) *n.* **1.** The collecting, writing, editing, and presentation of news or news articles in newspapers and magazines and in radio and television broadcasts. **2.** Material written for publication in a newspaper or magazine or for broadcast. **3.** The style of writing characteristic of material in newspapers and magazines, consisting of direct presentation of facts or occurrences with little attempt at analysis or interpretation. **4.** Newspapers and magazines. **5.** An academic course training students in journalism. **6.** Written material of current interest or wide popular appeal.

jour·nal·ist (jûr′nə-lĭst) *n.* **1.** *Abbr.* **jour.** One whose occupation is journalism. **2.** One who keeps a journal.

jour·nal·is·tic (jûr′nə-lĭs′tĭk) *adj.* Of, relating to, or characteristic of journalism or journalists. **—jour′nal·is′ti·cal·ly** *adv.*

jour·nal·ize (jûr′nə-līz′) *v.* **-ized, -iz·ing, -iz·es.** *—tr.* To record in a journal. *—intr.* To keep a personal or financial journal. **—jour′nal·iz′er** *n.*

jour·ney (jûr′nē) *n., pl.* **-neys.** **1.a.** The act of traveling from one place to another; a trip. **b.** A distance to be traveled or the time required for a trip: *a 2,000-mile journey to the Pacific; the three-day journey home.* **2.** A process or course likened to traveling; a passage: *the journey of life.* **—journey** *v.* **-neyed, -ney·ing, -neys.** *—intr.* To make a journey; travel. *—tr.* To travel over or through. [Middle English *journei,* day, day's travel, journey, from Old French *jornee,* from Vulgar Latin **diurnāta,* from Late Latin *diurnum,* day, from neuter of Latin *diurnus,* of a day, from *diēs,* day. See DIARY.] **—jour′ney·er** *n.*

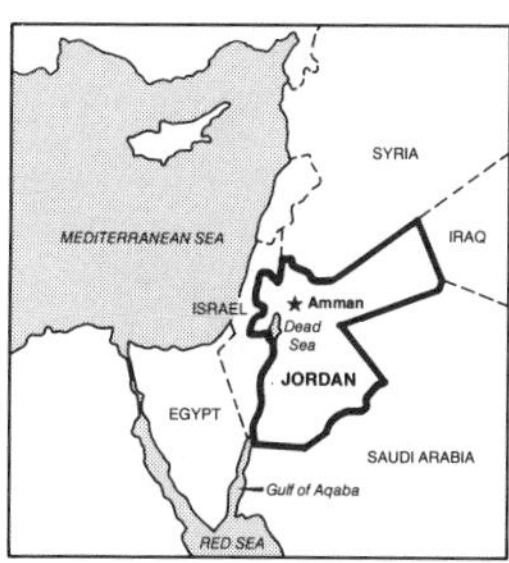

Jordan

Chief Joseph

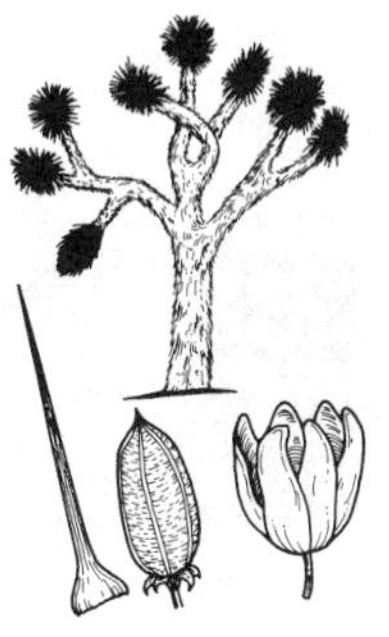

Joshua tree
Yucca brevifolia

ă pat	oi boy
ā pay	ou out
âr care	o͝o took
ä father	o͞o boot
ĕ pet	ŭ cut
ē be	ûr urge
ĭ pit	th thin
ī pie	*th* this
îr pier	hw which
ŏ pot	zh vision
ō toe	ə about, item
ô paw	♦ regionalism

Stress marks: **′** (primary); ′ (secondary), as in **dictionary** (dĭk′shə-nĕr′ē)

♦ **journey cake** *n. New England.* See **johnnycake.** See Regional Note at **johnnycake.** [Perhaps by folk etymology from *jonakin.* See JOHNNYCAKE.]

jour·ney·man (jûr′nē-mən) *n.* **1.** *Abbr.* **jour.** One who has fully served an apprenticeship in a trade or craft and is a qualified worker in another's employ. **2.** An experienced and competent but undistinguished worker. [Middle English *journeiman* : *journei,* a day's work; see JOURNEY + *man,* man; see MAN.]

jour·ney·work (jûr′nē-wûrk′) *n.* The work of a journeyman.

joust (joust, jŭst, jo͞ost) also **just** (jŭst) —*n.* **1.a.** A combat between two mounted knights or men-at-arms using lances; a tilting match. **b. jousts.** A series of tilting matches; a tournament. **2.** A personal competition or combat suggestive of combat with lances: *a politician who relishes a joust with reporters.* —*intr.v.* **joust·ed, joust·ing, jousts** also **just·ed, just·ing, justs. 1.** To engage in mounted combat with lances; tilt. **2.** To engage in a personal combat or competition. [Middle English, from Old French *juste,* from *juster,* to joust, from Vulgar Latin **iuxtāre,* to be next to, from Latin *iuxtā,* close by. See **yeug-** in Appendix.] —**joust′er** *n.*

Jove (jōv) *n. Roman Mythology.* See **Jupiter** (sense 1). —***idiom.*** **by Jove.** Used as a mild oath to express surprise or emphasis. [Middle English, from Old Latin *Iovis* or from Latin *Iov-,* stem of *Iuppiter.* See **deiw-** in Appendix.]

jo·vi·al (jō′vē-əl) *adj.* Marked by hearty conviviality and good cheer: *a jovial host.* See Synonyms at **jolly.** [French, probably from Italian *gioviale,* from Old Italian, of Jupiter (regarded as the source of happiness), from Late Latin *Ioviālis,* from Latin *Iovis,* Jupiter. See **deiw-** in Appendix.] —**jo′vi·al′i·ty** (-ăl′ĭ-tē) *n.* —**jo′vi·al·ly** *adv.*

Jo·vi·an¹ (jō′vē-ən). A.D. 331?–364. Emperor of Rome (363–364). He made peace with the Persians by giving up all Roman territories beyond the Tigris River.

Jo·vi·an² (jō′vē-ən) *adj.* **1.** *Roman Mythology.* Of, relating to, or resembling Jupiter. **2.** Of, relating to, or resembling the planet Jupiter.

Jovian planet *n.* One of the four major planets, Jupiter, Saturn, Uranus, and Neptune, which have very large masses and are farther from the sun than the terrestrial planets.

Jow·ett (jou′ĭt), **Benjamin.** 1817–1893. British classical scholar known for his translations of Plato and Aristotle.

jowl¹ (joul) *n.* **1.** The jaw, especially the lower jaw. **2.** The cheek. [Middle English *chavel, chaule, jaule* (influenced by *joue,* jaw, or *jol,* head) from Old English *ceafl.*]

jowl² (joul) *n.* **1.** The flesh under the lower jaw, especially when plump or flaccid. **2.** A fleshy part similar to a jowl, such as the dewlap of a cow or the wattle of a fowl. [Alteration of Middle English *cholle* (influenced by Middle English *joue,* jaw, or *jol,* head).]

jowl·y (jou′lē) *adj.* **-i·er, -i·est.** Having heavy or sagging jowls. —**jowl′i·ness** *n.*

joy (joi) *n.* **1.a.** Intense and especially ecstatic or exultant happiness. See Synonyms at **pleasure. b.** The expression or manifestation of such feeling. **2.** A source or an object of pleasure or satisfaction: *their only child, their pride and joy.* —**joy** *v.* **joyed, joy·ing, joys.** —*intr.* To take great pleasure; rejoice. —*tr. Archaic.* **1.** To fill with ecstatic happiness, pleasure, or satisfaction. **2.** To enjoy. [Middle English *joie,* from Old French, from Latin *gaudia,* pl. of *gaudium,* joy, from *gaudēre,* to rejoice. See **gāu-** in Appendix.]

James Joyce

Joyce (jois), **James.** 1882–1941. Irish writer whose literary innovations have had a profound influence on modern fiction. His works include *Ulysses* (1922). —**Joyc′e·an** (joi′sē-ən) *adj.*

joy·ful (joi′fəl) *adj.* Feeling, causing, or indicating joy. See Synonyms at **glad¹.** —**joy′ful·ly** *adv.* —**joy′ful·ness** *n.*

joy·less (joi′lĭs) *adj.* Cheerless; dismal. —**joy′less·ly** *adv.* —**joy′less·ness** *n.*

joy·ous (joi′əs) *adj.* Feeling or causing joy; joyful. See Synonyms at **glad¹.** —**joy′ous·ly** *adv.* —**joy′ous·ness** *n.*

joy·pop (joi′pŏp′) *intr.v.* **-popped, -pop·ping, -pops.** *Slang.* To use narcotic drugs, especially heroin, occasionally without becoming addicted. —**joy′pop′per** *n.*

joy ride *n. Slang.* **1.** A ride taken for fun and often for the thrills provided by reckless driving. **2.** A hazardous, reckless, often costly venture. —**joy rider** *n.*

joy·stick (joi′stĭk′) *n. Slang.* **1.** The control stick of an aircraft. **2.** A manual control or cursor device, as one attached to a computer.

J.P. or **JP** *abbr. Law.* Justice of the peace.

J particle *n.* A neutral meson having an unusually large mass (about 6,060 times the mass of an electron) and a long lifetime (about 10^{-20} second). Also called *psi particle.* See table at **subatomic particle.**

Jr *abbr. Bible.* Jeremiah.

jr. or **Jr.** *abbr.* Junior.

JRC *abbr.* Junior Red Cross.

J.S.D. *abbr. Latin.* Juris Scientiae Doctor (Doctor of Juristic Science).

jt. *abbr.* Joint.

Juan Carlos
Receiving an honorary degree from Cambridge University in 1988

Juan Car·los (wän kär′ləs, -lôs, hwän). Born 1938. Spanish king (since 1975) who acceded to the throne on the death of Francisco Franco and helped restore parliamentary democracy.

Juan de Fu·ca (də fo͞o′kə, fyo͞o′-), **Strait of.** A strait between northwest Washington State and Vancouver Island, British Columbia, Canada, linking Puget Sound and the Strait of Georgia with the Pacific Ocean.

Juan Fer·nán·dez Islands (fər-năn′dəs, fĕr-nän′dĕs). An island group belonging to Chile, in the southeast Pacific Ocean west of Valparaiso, Chile. Alexander Selkirk, a Scottish sailor and the inspiration for Defoe's *Robinson Crusoe,* lived on one of the islands from 1704 to 1709.

Juá·rez (wär′ĕz, hwä′rĕs). See **Ciudad Juárez.**

Juárez, Benito Pablo. 1806–1872. Mexican politician who took part in the overthrow of Santa Anna and served as president from 1858 to 1872.

ju·ba (jo͞o′bə) *n.* A group dance, probably of West African origin, characterized by complex rhythmic clapping and body movements and practiced on plantations in the southern United States during the 18th and 19th centuries. [Origin unknown.]

Ju·ba (jo͞o′bə, -bä). A river of southern Ethiopia and southern Somalia flowing about 1,609 km (1,000 mi) to the Indian Ocean.

Ju·bal (jo͞o′bəl). In the Old Testament, a descendant of Cain who is said to have invented musical instruments.

Jub·bul·pore (jŭb′əl-pôr′, -pōr′). See **Jabalpur.**

ju·bi·lant (jo͞o′bə-lənt) *adj.* **1.** Exultingly joyful. **2.** Expressing joy. [Latin *iūbilāns, iūbilant-,* present participle of *iūbilāre,* to raise a shout of joy.] —**ju′bi·lance** *n.* —**ju′bi·lant·ly** *adv.*

ju·bi·late (jo͞o′bə-lāt′) *intr.v.* **-lat·ed, -lat·ing, -lates.** To rejoice; exult. [Latin *iūbilāre, iūbilāt-,* to raise a shout of joy.]

Ju·bi·la·te (yo͞o′bə-lä′tā, -tē, jo͞o′-) *n.* **1.a.** The 100th Psalm in the King James Bible and in most modern Catholic versions or the 99th in the Vulgate. **b.** A musical setting of the Jubilate. **2.** The third Sunday after Easter. **3.** A song or an outburst of joy and triumph. [Middle English, from Latin *iūbilāte,* second person pl. imperative of *iūbilāre,* to raise a shout of joy, the first word of the psalm.]

ju·bi·la·tion (jo͞o′bə-lā′shən) *n.* **1.a.** The act of rejoicing. **b.** The condition or feeling of being jubilant. **2.** A celebration or other expression of joy.

ju·bi·lee (jo͞o′bə-lē′, jo͞o′bə-lē′) *n.* **1.a.** A specially celebrated anniversary, especially a 50th anniversary. **b.** The celebration of such an anniversary. **2.** A season or an occasion of joyful celebration. **3.** Jubilation; rejoicing. **4.** Often **Jubilee.** *Bible.* In the Hebrew Scriptures, a year of rest to be observed by the Israelites every 50th year, during which slaves were to be set free, alienated property restored to the former owners, and the lands left untilled. **5.** Often **Jubilee.** *Roman Catholic Church.* A year during which plenary indulgence may be obtained by the performance of certain pious acts. [Middle English *jubile,* from Old French, from Late Latin *iūbilaeus,* the Jewish year of jubilee, alteration (influenced by *iubilāre,* to raise a shout of joy) of Greek *iōbēlaios,* from *iōbēlos,* from Hebrew *yôbēl.*]

Ju·dae·a (jo͞o-dē′ə, -dā′ə). See **Judea.**

Ju·dah¹ (jo͞o′də). In the Old Testament, a son of Jacob and Leah and the forebear of one of the tribes of Israel.

Ju·dah² (jo͞o′də). An ancient kingdom of southern Palestine between the Mediterranean and the Dead Sea. It lasted from the division of Palestine in 931 B.C. until the destruction of Jerusalem in 586.

Ju·da·ic (jo͞o-dā′ĭk) also **Ju·da·i·cal** (-ĭ-kəl) *adj.* Of, relating to, or characteristic of Jews or Judaism: *Judaic traditions.* [Latin *Iūdaicus,* from Greek *Ioudaikos,* from Greek *Ioudaios,* Jew. See JEW.] —**Ju·da′i·cal·ly** *adv.*

Ju·da·ism (jo͞o′dē-ĭz′əm) *n.* **1.** The monotheistic religion of the Jews, tracing its origins to Abraham and having its spiritual and ethical principles embodied chiefly in the Bible and the Talmud. **2.** Conformity to the traditional ceremonies and rites of the Jewish religion. **3.** The cultural, religious, and social practices and beliefs of the Jews. **4.** The Jews considered as a people or community. [Middle English *Iudaisme,* from Old French *Judaisme,* from Late Latin *Iūdāismus,* from Greek *Ioudaismos,* from *Ioudaios,* Jew. See JEW.]

Ju·da·ize (jo͞o′dē-īz′) *v.* **-ized, -iz·ing, -iz·es.** —*tr.* To bring into conformity with Judaism. —*intr.* To adopt Jewish customs and beliefs. —**Ju′da·i·za′tion** (-ĭ-zā′shən) *n.* —**Ju′da·i′zer** *n.*

Ju·das (jo͞o′dəs) *n.* **1.** One who betrays another under the guise of friendship. **2. judas.** A one-way peephole in a door. [Middle English, from Late Latin *Iūdas,* Judas Iscariot, from Greek *Ioudas,* from Hebrew *yĕhûdâ,* Judah.]

Judas Is·car·i·ot (ĭ-skăr′ē-ət). Died c. A.D. 30. One of the 12 Apostles and the betrayer of Jesus.

Judas tree *n.* See **redbud.** [From the belief that Judas Iscariot hanged himself on such a tree.]

jud·der (jŭd′ər) *intr.v.* **-dered, -der·ing, -ders.** To shake rapidly or spasmodically; vibrate conspicuously: *"Edith would watch her wrestling with words, her thin little body juddering with the effort to unlock them"* (Anita Brookner). —**judder** *n.* A rapid or spasmodic shaking. [Perhaps J(ERK)¹ + (SH)UDDER.]

Jude (jo͞od) *n. Bible.* See table at **Bible.**

Jude, Saint. fl. first century A.D. One of the 12 Apostles. He is invoked in prayer when a situation seems hopeless.

Ju·de·a also **Ju·dae·a** (jo͞o-dē′ə, -dā′ə). An ancient region of southern Palestine comprising present-day southern Israel and southwest Jordan. In the time of Jesus it was a kingdom ruled by the Herods and part of the Roman province of Syria. **—Ju·de′an** *adj. n.*

Ju·de·o-Span·ish (jo͞o-dā′ō-spăn′ĭsh) *n.* See **Ladino** (sense 1). [From Latin *Iūdaeus,* Jewish, from Greek *Ioudaios.* See JUDAIC.]

Judg. *abbr. Bible.* Judges.

judge (jŭj) *v.* **judged, judg·ing, judg·es.** *—tr.* **1.** To form an opinion or estimation of after careful consideration: *judge heights; judging character.* **2. a.** *Law.* To hear and decide on in a court of law; try: *judge a case.* **b.** *Obsolete.* To pass sentence on; condemn. **c.** To act as one appointed to decide the winners of: *judge an essay contest.* **3.** To determine or declare after consideration or deliberation. **4.** *Informal.* To have as an opinion or assumption; suppose: *I judge you're right.* **5.** *Bible.* To govern; rule. Used of an ancient Israelite leader. *—intr.* **1.** To form an opinion or evaluation. **2.** To act or decide as a judge. **—judge** *n.* **1.** One who judges, especially: **a.** One who makes estimates as to worth, quality, or fitness: *a good judge of used cars; a poor judge of character.* **b.** *Abbr.* **J., j.** *Law.* A public official who hears and decides cases brought before a court of law. **c.** *Law.* A bankruptcy referee. **d.** One appointed to decide the winners of a contest or competition. **2.** *Bible.* **a.** A leader of the Israelites during a period of about 400 years between the death of Joshua and the accession of Saul. **b. Judges** *(used with a sing. verb). Abbr.* **Judg., Jg., JJ** See table at **Bible.** [Middle English *jugen,* from Anglo-Norman *juger,* from Latin *iūdicāre,* from *iūdex, iūdic-,* judge. See **deik-** in Appendix.]

SYNONYMS: *judge, arbitrator, arbiter, referee, umpire.* These nouns denote persons who make decisions that determine points at issue. A *judge* is one capable of making rational, dispassionate, and wise decisions: *The members of the jury are the sole judges of what the truth is in this case.* An *arbitrator* works to settle controversies and is either appointed or derives authority from the consent of the disputants, who choose him or her or approve the selection: *The mayor appointed an experienced arbitrator to mediate between the sides and resolve the transit strike.* An *arbiter* is one who may or may not have official status but whose opinion or judgment is recognized as being unassailable or binding: *a critic who considers himself the supreme arbiter of literary taste.* Less often *arbiter* is used interchangeably with *arbitrator.* A *referee* is an attorney appointed by a court to make a determination of a case or to investigate and report on it (*a bankruptcy case handled by a referee*), and an *umpire* is a person appointed to settle an issue that arbitrators are unable to resolve (*umpires studying complex tax cases*). In sports *referee* and *umpire* refer to officials who enforce the rules and settle points at issue.

judge advocate *n., pl.* **judge advocates.** *Abbr.* **JA, J.A.** *Law.* **1.** A commissioned officer in the U.S. Army, Air Force, or Navy assigned to the Judge Advocate General's Corps. **2.** A staff officer serving as legal adviser to a commander. **3.** An officer acting as prosecutor at a court-martial.

judge advocate general *n., pl.* **judge advocates general** or **judge advocate generals.** *Abbr.* **J.A.G., JAG** The chief legal officer of a branch of the U.S. armed forces.

judge·ment (jŭj′mənt) *n.* Variant of **judgment.**

judge·ship (jŭj′shĭp′) *n. Law.* The office or jurisdiction of a judge.

judg·mat·ic (jŭj-măt′ĭk) also **judg·mat·i·cal** (-ĭ-kəl) *adj.* Judicious. [Perhaps JUDG(MENT) + (DOG)MATIC.] **—judg·mat′i·cal·ly** *adv.*

judg·ment also **judge·ment** (jŭj′mənt) *n.* **1.** The act or process of judging; the formation of an opinion after consideration or deliberation. **2. a.** The mental ability to perceive and distinguish relationships; discernment: *Fatigue may affect a pilot's judgment of distances.* **b.** The capacity to form an opinion by distinguishing and evaluating: *His judgment of fine music is impeccable.* **c.** The capacity to assess situations or circumstances and draw sound conclusions; good sense: *She showed good judgment in saving her money.* See Synonyms at **reason. 3.** An opinion or estimate formed after consideration or deliberation, especially a formal or authoritative decision: *awaited the judgment of the umpire.* **4.** *Law.* **a.** A determination of a court of law; a judicial decision. **b.** A court act creating or affirming an obligation, such as a debt. **c.** A writ in witness of such an act. **5.** An assertion of something believed. **6.** A misfortune believed to be sent by God as punishment for sin. **7. Judgment.** In traditional Christian eschatology, God's determination of which human beings shall be sent to heaven and which condemned to hell. [Middle English *jugement,* from Old French, from *jugier,* to judge, from Latin *iūdicāre.* See JUDGE.]

judg·men·tal (jŭj-mĕn′tl) *adj.* **1.** Of, relating to, or dependent on judgment: *a judgmental error.* **2.** Inclined to make judgments, especially moral or personal ones: *a marriage counselor who tries not to be judgmental.* **—judg·men′tal·ly** *adv.*

Judgment Day *n.* **1.** In traditional Christian eschatology, the day at the end of the world when God judges all human beings, sending the saved to heaven and the damned to hell. Also called *Day of Judgment.* **2. judgment day.** A day of reckoning or final judgment.

ju·di·ca·ble (jo͞o′dĭ-kə-bəl) *adj.* **1.** That can be judged: *judicable issues.* **2.** Liable to be judged: *judicable actions and complaints.* [Late Latin *iūdicābilis,* from Latin *iūdicāre,* to judge. See JUDGE.]

ju·di·ca·tor (jo͞o′dĭ-kā′tər) *n.* One that acts as judge. [Late Latin *iūdicātor,* from Latin *iūdicāre,* to judge. See JUDGE.]

ju·di·ca·to·ry (jo͞o′dĭ-kə-tôr′ē, -tōr′ē) *Law. n., pl.* **-ries.** A law court or system of law courts; a judiciary. **—judicatory** *adj.* Of or relating to the administration of justice. [Late Latin *iūdicātōrium,* from neuter of *iūdicātōrius,* judicial, from Latin *iūdicāre,* to judge. See JUDGE.]

ju·di·ca·ture (jo͞o′dĭ-kə-cho͝or′) *n. Law.* **1.** Administration of justice. **2.** The position, function, or authority of a judge. **3.** The jurisdiction of a law court or judge. **4.** A court or system of courts of law. [Medieval Latin *iūdicātūra,* from feminine future participle of Latin *iūdicāre,* to judge. See JUDGE.]

ju·di·cial (jo͞o-dĭsh′əl) *adj.* **1.** *Law.* **a.** Of, relating to, or proper to courts of law or to the administration of justice: *the judicial system.* **b.** Decreed by or proceeding from a court of justice: *a judicial decision.* **c.** Belonging or appropriate to the office of a judge: *in judicial robes.* **2.** Characterized by or expressing judgment: *the judicial function of a literary critic.* **3.** *Theology.* Proceeding from a divine judgment. [Middle English, from Anglo-Norman, from Latin *iūdiciālis,* from *iūdicium,* judgment, from *iūdex, iūdic-,* judge. See **deik-** in Appendix.] **—ju·di′cial·ly** *adv.*

judicial separation *n. Law.* See **legal separation.**

ju·di·ci·ar·y (jo͞o-dĭsh′ē-ĕr′ē, -dĭsh′ə-rē) *n., pl.* **-ies.** *Law.* **1.** The judicial branch of government. **2. a.** A system of courts of law for the administration of justice. **b.** The judges of these courts. [Probably from Latin *iūdiciārius,* of the courts, from *iūdicium,* judgment, from *iūdex, iūdic-,* judge. See JUDGE.]

ju·di·cious (jo͞o-dĭsh′əs) *adj.* Having or exhibiting sound judgment; prudent. [From French *judicieux,* from Latin *iūdicium,* judgment, from *iūdex, iūdic-,* judge. See JUDGE.] **—ju·di′cious·ly** *adv.* **—ju·di′cious·ness** *n.*

Ju·dith (jo͞o′dĭth) *n. Bible.* **1.** In the Old Testament, a Jewish heroine who rescued her people by slaying an Assyrian general. **2.** *Abbr.* **Jdt.** See table at **Bible.**

ju·do (jo͞o′dō) *n.* A sport and method of physical training similar to wrestling, developed in Japan in the late 19th century and using principles of balance and leverage adapted from jujitsu. [Japanese *jūdō* : *jū,* soft + *dō,* way.] **—ju′do·ist** *n.*

judo

Jud·son (jŭd′sən), **Edward Zane Carroll.** Pen name Ned Buntline. 1823–1886. American writer who is remembered for his dime novels and his magazine *Ned Buntline's Own.*

jug (jŭg) *n.* **1. a.** A large, often rounded vessel of earthenware, glass, or metal with a small mouth, a handle, and usually a stopper or cap. **b.** The amount that a jug can hold. **2.** A small pitcher. **3.** *Slang.* A jail. **—jug** *tr.v.* **jugged, jug·ging, jugs. 1.** To stew (a hare, for example) in an earthenware jug or jar. **2.** *Slang.* To put into jail. [Middle English *jugge.*]

ju·ga (jo͞o′gə) *n.* A plural of **jugum.**

ju·gate (jo͞o′gāt′, -gĭt) *adj.* Joined in or forming pairs or a pair. [Latin *iugātus,* past participle of *iugāre,* to join, from Latin *iugum,* yoke. See **yeug-** in Appendix.]

jug band *n. Music.* A group that uses unconventional or improvised instruments, such as jugs, kazoos, and washboards.

jug·ger·naut (jŭg′ər-nôt′) *n.* **1.** Something, such as a belief or an institution, that elicits blind and destructive devotion or to which people are ruthlessly sacrificed. **2.** An overwhelming, advancing force that crushes or seems to crush everything in its path: *"It doesn't assume that people need necessarily remain passive when confronted by what appears to be the juggernaut of history"* (Christopher Lehmann-Haupt). **3. Juggernaut.** Used as a title for the Hindu deity Krishna. [Hindi *jagannāth,* title of Krishna, from Sanskrit *jaganāthaḥ,* lord of the world : *jagat,* moving, the world (from *jigāti,* he goes; see **gʷā-** in Appendix) + *nāthaḥ,* lord. Senses 1 and 2, from the fact that worshipers have thrown themselves under the wheels of a huge car or wagon on which the idol of Krishna was drawn in an annual procession at Puri in east-central India.]

juggle
Juggling Indian clubs

jug·gle (jŭg′əl) *v.* **-gled, -gling, -gles.** *—tr.* **1.** To keep (two or more objects) in the air at one time by alternately tossing and catching them. **2.** To have difficulty holding; balance insecurely: *juggled the ball but finally caught it; shook hands while juggling a cookie and a teacup.* **3.** To keep (more than two activities, for example) in motion or progress at one time: *managed to juggle a full-time job and homemaking.* **4.** To manipulate in order to deceive: *juggle figures in a ledger.* *—intr.* **1.** To juggle objects or perform other tricks of manual dexterity. **2.** To make rapid motions or manipulations: *juggled with the controls on the television to improve the picture.* **3.** To use trickery; practice deception. **—juggle** *n.* **1.** The act of juggling. **2.** Trickery for a dishonest end. [Middle English *jogelen,* to entertain by performing tricks, from Old French *jogler,* from Latin *ioculārī,* to jest, from *ioculus,* diminutive of *iocus,* joke. See **yek-** in Appendix.]

jug·gler (jŭg′lər) *n.* **1.** One that juggles objects or performs other tricks of manual dexterity. **2.** One that uses tricks, deception, or fraud.

jug·gler·y (jŭg′lə-rē) *n., pl.* **-ies. 1.** The skill or performance of a juggler. **2.** Trickery; deception.

jug·u·lar (jŭg′yə-lər) *adj. Anatomy.* Of, relating to, or located in the region of the neck or throat. **—jugular** *n.* **1.** *Anatomy.* A jugular vein. **2.** The most vital part: *a strategic attack aimed at the enemy's jugular.* [Late Latin *iugulāris (vēna),* jugular

ă pat	oi boy
ā pay	ou out
âr care	o͝o took
ä father	o͞o boot
ĕ pet	ŭ cut
ē be	ûr urge
ĭ pit	th thin
ī pie	*th* this
îr pier	hw which
ŏ pot	zh vision
ō toe	ə about, item
ô paw	♦ regionalism

Stress marks: **′** (primary); ′ (secondary), as in **dictionary** (dĭk′shə-nĕr′ē)

(vein), from Latin *iugulum*, collarbone, diminutive of *iugum*, yoke. See **yeug-** in Appendix.]

jugular vein *n. Anatomy.* Any of several large veins of the neck that drain blood from the head.

ju·gum (jo͞o′gəm) *n., pl.* **-ga** (-gə) or **-gums.** A yokelike structure in certain insects that joins the forewings to the hind wings, keeping them together during flight. [Latin *iugum*, yoke. See **yeug-** in Appendix.]

jug wine *n.* Inexpensive table wine sold in large bottles.

juice (jo͞os) *n.* **1.a.** A fluid naturally contained in plant or animal tissue: *fruit juice; meat braised in its own juices.* **b.** A bodily secretion: *digestive juices.* **c.** The liquid contained in something that is chiefly solid. **2.** A substance or quality that imparts identity and vitality; essence. **3.** *Slang.* Vigorous life; vitality. **4.** *Slang.* Political power or influence; clout. **5.** *Slang.* **a.** Electric current. **b.** Fuel for an engine. **6.** *Slang.* Funds; money. **7.** *Slang.* Alcoholic drink; liquor. **8.** *Slang.* Racy or scandalous gossip. —*tr.* **juiced, juic·ing, juic·es.** To extract the juice from. —*intr. Slang.* To drink alcoholic beverages excessively. —***phrasal verb.*** **juice up.** *Slang.* To give energy, spirit, or interest to. [Middle English *jus*, from Old French, from Latin *iūs*.]

juiced (jo͞ost) *adj. Slang.* Intoxicated; drunk.

juice·head (jo͞os′hĕd′) *n. Slang.* A heavy drinker; an alcoholic.

juic·er (jo͞o′sər) *n.* **1.** An appliance that is used to extract juice from fruits and vegetables. **2.** *Slang.* One who drinks liquor or alcoholic beverages habitually or excessively.

juic·y (jo͞o′sē) *adj.* **-i·er, -i·est. 1.** Full of juice; succulent. **2.a.** Richly interesting: *a juicy mystery novel.* **b.** Racy; titillating: *a juicy bit of gossip.* **3.** Yielding profit; rewarding or gratifying: *a juicy raise; a juicy part in a play.* —**juic′i·ly** *adv.* —**juic′i·ness** *n.*

Juiz de Fo·ra (zhwēzh′ də fôr′ə). A city of southeast Brazil north of Rio de Janeiro. It is an industrial and commercial center. Population, 299,432.

ju·jit·su also **ju·jut·su** or **jiu·jit·su** or **jiu·jut·su** (jo͞o-jĭt′so͞o) *n.* An art of weaponless self-defense developed in China and Japan that uses throws, holds, and blows and derives added power from the attacker's own weight and strength. [Japanese *jūjitsu* : *jū*, soft + *jitsu*, arts.]

ju·ju (jo͞o′jo͞o) *n.* **1.** An object used as a fetish, a charm, or an amulet in West Africa. **2.** The supernatural power ascribed to such an object. [Hausa *jūjū*, fetish, evil spirit.] —**ju′ju·ism** *n.*

ju·jube (jo͞o′jo͞ob′) *n.* **1.a.** Any of several Old World trees of the genus *Ziziphus*, especially *Z. jujuba*, having palmately veined leaves, spiny stipules, small yellowish flowers, and dark red fruit. **b.** The fleshy, edible drupe of this tree. Also called *Chinese date.* **2.** (*also* jo͞o′jo͞o-bē′). A fruit-flavored, usually chewy candy or lozenge. [Middle English, jujube fruit, from Old French, from Medieval Latin *jujuba*, from Latin *zizyphum*, from Greek *zizuphon*.]

ju·jut·su (jo͞o-jĭt′so͞o) *n.* Variant of **jujitsu.**

♦**juke¹** (jo͞ok) *Southeastern U.S. n.* A roadside drinking establishment that offers inexpensive drinks, food, and music for dancing. —**juke** *intr.v.* **juked, juk·ing, jukes.** To dance, especially in a roadside drinking establishment or to the music of a jukebox. [Probably from Gullah *juke, joog*, disorderly, wicked, of West African origin; akin to Wolof *dzug*, to live wickedly, Mandingo (Bambara) *dzugu*, wicked.]

♦***REGIONAL NOTE:*** Gullah, the English-based Creole language spoken by Black people off the coast of Georgia and South Carolina, retains a number of words from the West African languages brought over by slaves. One such word is *juke*, "bad, wicked, disorderly," the probable source of the English word *juke*. Used chiefly in the Southeastern states, *juke* (also appearing in the compound *juke joint*) means a roadside drinking establishment that offers cheap drinks, food, and music for dancing and often doubles as a brothel. "To juke" is to dance, particularly at a juke joint or to the music of a jukebox whose name, no longer regional and having lost the connotation of sleaziness, contains the same word.

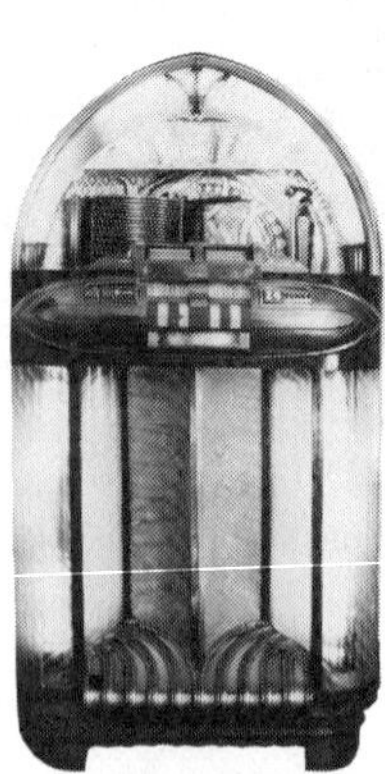
jukebox

juke² (jo͞ok) *Football. v.* —*tr.* To deceive or outmaneuver (a defending opponent) by a feint; fake. —*intr.* To deceive or outmaneuver a defender by a feint. —**juke** *n.* A feint or fake. [Middle English *jowken*, to bend in a supple way.]

♦**juke·box** (jo͞ok′bŏks′) *n.* A coin-operated phonograph, equipped with push buttons for the selection of records. See Regional Note at **juke¹**. —*attributive.* Often used to modify another noun: *the jukebox industry; jukebox music; jukebox hits.*

♦**juke joint** *n. Informal.* A bar, tavern, or roadhouse featuring music played on a jukebox. See Regional Note at **juke¹**.

Jul. or **Jul** *abbr.* July.

ju·lep (jo͞o′lĭp) *n.* **1.** A mint julep. **2.** A sweet syrupy drink, especially one to which medicine can be added. [Middle English, a sugar syrup, from Old French, from Medieval Latin, from Arabic *julāb*, from Persian *gulāb*, rosewater : *gul*, rose (from Middle Persian *vardā*) + *āb*, water (from Middle Persian *āp*, from Old Persian).]

Jul·ian (jo͞ol′yən). A.D. 331?–363. Emperor of Rome (361–363) who attempted to restore the official dominance of paganism.

Ju·li·an·a (jo͞o′lē-ăn′ə). Born 1909. Queen of the Netherlands (1948–1980) who abdicated in favor of her daughter Beatrix.

Julian Alps. A range of the eastern Alps in northwest Yugoslavia and northeast Italy rising to 2,864 m (9,390 ft).

Julian calendar *n.* The solar calendar introduced by Julius Caesar in Rome in 46 B.C., having a year of 12 months and 365 days and a leap year of 366 days every fourth year. It was eventually replaced by the Gregorian calendar.

ju·li·enne (jo͞o′lē-ĕn′, zhü-lyĕn′) *n.* Consommé or broth garnished with long, thin strips of vegetables. —**julienne** *adj.* Cut into long, thin strips: *julienne potatoes.* [French, probably from the name *Julienne*.]

Ju·lius II (jo͞ol′yəs). Originally Giuliano della Rovere. 1443–1513. Pope (1503–1513) who ordered the construction of Saint Peter's in Rome and commissioned Michelangelo to decorate the Sistine Chapel in the Vatican.

Jul·lun·dur (jŭl′ən-dər). A city of northwest India north-northwest of Delhi. It was the capital of an ancient kingdom and came under British jurisdiction in 1846. Population, 408,186.

Ju·ly (jo͞o-lī′) *n. Abbr.* **Jul., Jul** The seventh month of the year in the Gregorian calendar. See table at **calendar.** [Middle English *Julie*, from Old North French, from Latin *Iūlius* (see **deiw-** in Appendix), after Julius CAESAR.]

Ju·ma·da (jo͞o-mä′dä) also **Jo·ma·da** (jə-) *n.* Either the fifth or the sixth month of the year in the Moslem calendar. See table at **calendar.** [Arabic *jumādā*, from *jamada*, to freeze.]

jum·ble (jŭm′bəl) *v.* **-bled, -bling, -bles.** —*tr.* **1.** To mix in a confused way; throw together carelessly: *jumble socks in a heap in the closet.* **2.** To muddle; confuse: *The rapid-fire questioning jumbled the witness's thoughts.* —*intr.* To be mixed in a confused way: *dividers that keep the files from jumbling.* —**jumble** *n.* **1.** A confused or disordered mass: *a jumble of paper scraps in a drawer.* **2.** A disordered state; a muddle: *financial accounts in a jumble.* [Origin unknown.]

jum·bo (jŭm′bō) *n., pl.* **-bos.** An unusually large person, animal, or thing. —**jumbo** *adj.* Unusually large: *jumbo shrimp; a jumbo jet.* [After *Jumbo*, a large elephant exhibited by P.T. Barnum, probably from slang, clumsy person.]

jum·buck (jŭm′bŭk′) *n. Australian.* A sheep. [Australian Pidgin, perhaps of English origin.]

Jum·na (jŭm′nə). A river of northern India rising in the Himalaya Mountains and flowing about 1,384 km (860 mi) generally southeast to the Ganges River at Allahabad.

jump (jŭmp) *v.* **jumped, jump·ing, jumps.** —*intr.* **1.a.** To spring off the ground or other base by a muscular effort of the legs and feet. **b.** To move suddenly and in one motion: *jumped out of bed.* **c.** To move involuntarily, as in surprise: *jumped when the phone rang.* **d.** To parachute from an aircraft. **2.a.** *Informal.* To move quickly; hustle: *Jump when I give you an order.* **b.** To take prompt advantage; respond quickly: *jump at a bargain.* **3.a.** To enter eagerly into an activity; plunge: *jumped into the race for the nomination.* **b.** To begin or start. Often used with *off*: *The project jumped off with great enthusiasm but interest flagged during the summer.* **4.** To form an opinion or a judgment hastily: *jump to conclusions.* **5.** To make a sudden verbal attack; lash out: *jumped at me for being late; jumped on her subordinates for their carelessness.* **6.a.** To undergo a sudden and pronounced increase: *Prices jumped in October.* **b.** To rise suddenly in position or rank: *jumped over two others with more seniority.* **7.** To move discontinuously or change after a short period: *jumps from one subject to another; jumped from one job to another.* **8.a.** To be displaced by a sudden jerk: *The phonograph needle jumped.* **b.** To be displaced vertically or laterally because of improper alignment: *The film jumped during projection.* **9.** *Computer Science.* To move from one set of instructions in a program to another out of sequence. **10.** *Games.* **a.** To move over an opponent's playing piece in a board game. **b.** To make a jump bid in bridge. **11.** *Slang.* To be lively; bustle: *a disco that really jumps.* —*tr.* **1.** To leap over or across: *jump a fence.* **2.** To leap onto: *jump a bus.* **3.** *Slang.* To spring upon in sudden attack; assault or ambush: *Muggers jumped him in the park.* **4.** To move or start prematurely before: *jumped the starting signal.* **5.** To cause to leap: *jump a horse over a fence.* **6.** To cause to increase suddenly: *Unexpected shortages jumped milk prices by several cents a quart.* **7.** To pass over; skip: *The typewriter jumped a space.* **8.** To raise in rank or position; promote. **9.** *Games.* **a.** To move a piece over (an opponent's piece) in a board game, often thereby capturing the opponent's piece. **b.** To raise (a partner's bid) in bridge by more than is necessary. **10.** To jump-start (a motor vehicle). **11.** To leave (a course), especially through mishap: *The train jumped the rails.* **12.** *Slang.* **a.** To leave hastily; skip: *jumped town a step ahead of the police.* **b.** To leave (an organization, for example) suddenly or in violation of an agreement: *jumped the team and signed with a rival club.* **13.** To seize or occupy illegally: *jump a mining claim.* **14.** To forfeit (bail) by failing to appear in court. —**jump** *n.* **1.a.** The act of jumping; a leap. **b.** The distance covered by a jump: *a jump of seven feet.* **c.** An obstacle or a span to be jumped. **2.** A descent from an aircraft by parachute. **3.** *Sports.* Any of several track-and-field events in which contestants jump. **4.** *Informal.* An initial competitive advantage; a head start: *got the jump on the other daily papers.* **5.a.** A sudden pronounced rise, as in price or salary. **b.** An impressive promotion. **6.** A step or level: *managed to stay a jump ahead of the others.* **7.** A sudden or major transition, as from one career or subject to another. **8.a.** A short trip. **b.** One in a series of moves and stopovers, as with a circus or road show. **9.** *Games.* A move in a board game over an opponent's piece. **10.** *Computer Science.* A movement from one set of instructions to another. **11.a.** An involuntary nervous movement; a start. **b. jumps.** A condition of nervousness. Often used with *the.* **12.** A jump-start of a motor vehicle. **—*idiom.* jump the gun.** To start doing something too soon. [Middle English *jumpen,* to jump (sense uncertain).]

jump ball *n. Basketball.* A method of starting play or determining possession in which an official tosses the ball up between two opposing players who jump and try to tap it to a teammate.

jump bid *n. Games.* A bridge bid at a higher level than that required to exceed the preceding bid.

jump cut *n.* A cut to slightly later action in the course of a filmed scene, creating an effect of discontinuity or acceleration.

jump·er¹ (jŭm′pər) *n.* **1.** One that jumps. **2.** A type of coasting sled. **3.** *Electricity.* A short length of wire used temporarily to complete a circuit or to bypass a break in a circuit. **4.** *Basketball.* See **jump shot. 5.** A saddle horse that has been trained to jump over obstacles.

jump·er² (jŭm′pər) *n.* **1.** A sleeveless dress worn over a blouse or sweater. **2.** A loose, protective garment worn over other clothes. **3.** Often **jumpers.** A child's garment consisting of straight-legged pants attached to a biblike bodice. **4.** *Chiefly British.* A pullover sweater. [Probably from *jump,* short coat.]

jump·er cable (jŭm′pər) *n.* See **booster cable.**

jump·ing bean (jŭm′pĭng) *n.* A seed, as of certain Mexican plants of the genera *Sebastiana* and *Sapium,* containing the larva of the moth *Laspeyresia saltitans,* whose movements cause the seed to jerk or roll.

jumping jack *n.* **1.** A toy figure with jointed limbs that can be made to dance by pulling an attached string. **2.** *Sports.* A physical exercise performed by jumping to a position with the legs spread wide and the hands touching overhead and then returning to a position with the feet together and the arms at the sides.

jumping mouse *n.* Any of various small Eurasian and North American rodents of the family Zapodidae, having a very long tail and long hind legs.

jump·ing-off place (jŭm′pĭng-ôf′, -ŏf′) *n.* **1.** A beginning point for a journey or venture. **2.** A very remote spot.

jump jet *n.* A jet aircraft capable of vertical takeoffs and landings.

jump·mas·ter (jŭmp′măs′tər) *n.* One who supervises the jumping of parachutists from an aircraft.

jump-off (jŭmp′ôf′, -ŏf′) *n.* **1.** The commencement of a race or of a planned military attack. **2.** A jumping contest at a horse show, especially a final or tie-breaking round.

jump rope *n.* A rope that is twirled and jumped over in children's games or in conditioning exercises.

jump seat *n.* **1.** A small folding seat, as in an automobile between the front and rear seats. **2.** A small rear seat in a sports car.

jump shooter *n. Basketball.* A player who makes jump shots.

jump shot *n. Basketball.* A shot made by a player at the highest point of a jump. Also called *jumper.*

jump-start (jŭmp′stärt′) *tr.v.* **-start·ed, -start·ing, -starts. 1.** To start (the engine of a motor vehicle) by using a booster cable connected to the battery of another vehicle or by engaging the drive train while the vehicle is rolling downhill or being pushed. **2.** *Informal.* To start or set in motion (an otherwise stalled or sluggish activity, system, or process): *"struggled to jump-start his once front-running . . . presidential campaign"* (Susan Feeney). **—jump-start** *n.* **1.** The act, process, or an instance of starting a motor vehicle by using a booster cable or suddenly releasing the clutch while the vehicle is being pushed. **2.** *Informal.* The act or an instance of starting or setting in motion a stalled or sluggish system or process.

jump suit *n.* **1.** A parachutist's uniform. **2.** Also **jump·suit** (jŭmp′so͞ot′). A one-piece garment consisting of a blouse or shirt with attached slacks or shorts.

jump·y (jŭm′pē) *adj.* **-i·er, -i·est. 1.** Characterized by fitful, jerky movements. **2.** On edge; nervous. **—jump′i·ness** *n.*

jun. or **Jun.** *abbr.* Junior.

Jun. or **Jun** *abbr.* June.

junc. *abbr.* Junction.

jun·co (jŭng′kō) *n., pl.* **-cos** or **-coes.** Any of various small North American birds of the genus *Junco,* having predominantly gray plumage, a gray or black head, and white outer tail feathers. [Spanish, reed, from Latin *iuncus.*]

junc·tion (jŭngk′shən) *n.* **1.** The act or process of joining or the condition of being joined. **2.** *Abbr.* **jct., junc.** A place where two things join or meet, especially a place where two roads or railway routes come together and one terminates. **3.** A transition layer or boundary between two different materials or between physically different regions in a single material, especially: **a.** A connection between conductors or sections of a transmission line. **b.** The interface between two different semiconductor regions in a semiconductor device. **c.** A mechanical or alloyed contact between different metals or other materials, as in a thermocouple. [Latin *iūnctiō, iūnctiōn-,* from *iūnctus,* past participle of *iungere,* to join. See **yeug-** in Appendix.] **—junc′tion·al** *adj.*

junction box *n.* An enclosure within which electric circuits are connected.

Junc·tion City (jŭngk′shən). A city of northeast-central Kansas west of Topeka. It is the rail and trade center of an agricultural and dairy region. Population, 19,305.

junc·ture (jŭngk′chər) *n.* **1.** The act of joining or the condition of being joined. **2.** A place where two things are joined; a junction or joint. **3.** A point in time, especially a critical point. See Synonyms at **crisis. 4.** The transition or mode of transition from one sound to another in speech. [Middle English, from Latin *iūnctūra,* from *iūnctus,* past participle of *iungere,* to join. See **yeug-** in Appendix.]

Jun·dia·í (zho͞on′dyə-ē′). A city of southeast Brazil north-northwest of São Paulo. Population, 221,888.

June (jo͞on) *n. Abbr.* **Jun., Jun** The sixth month of the year in the Gregorian calendar. See table at **calendar.** [Middle English, from Old English *Junius* and from Old French *juin,* both from Latin *(mēnsis) Iūnius,* (month) of June, from *Iūnō,* Juno.]

Ju·neau (jo͞o′nō′). The capital of Alaska, in the Panhandle northeast of Sitka. It was settled by gold miners in 1880 and designated territorial capital in 1900 (effective 1906) and state capital in 1959. Population, 19,528.

June beetle *n.* Any of various large North American scarabaeid beetles of the subfamily Melolonthinae, appearing in late spring and having larvae that are destructive to vegetation. Also called *June bug, May beetle.*

June·ber·ry (jo͞on′bĕr′ē) *n.* See **shadbush.**

June bug *n.* See **June beetle.**

Jung (yo͝ong), **Carl Gustav.** 1875–1961. Swiss psychiatrist who founded analytical psychology. His works include *The Psychology of the Unconscious* (1912).

Jung·frau (yo͝ong′frou′). A mountain, 4,160.8 m (13,642 ft) high, in the Bernese Alps of south-central Switzerland.

Jung·i·an (yo͝ong′ē-ən) *adj.* **1.** Of, relating to, or characteristic of Jung or his theories of psychology. **2.** Maintaining Jung's psychological theories, especially those that stress the contribution of racial and cultural inheritance to the psychology of an individual. **—Jung′i·an** *n.*

jun·gle (jŭng′gəl) *n.* **1.** Land densely overgrown with tropical vegetation. **2.** A dense thicket or growth. **3.** A dense, confused mass; a jumble. **4.** Something made up of many confused elements; a bewildering complex or maze: *sorting through the jungle of regulations.* **5.** A place or milieu characterized by intense, often ruthless competition or struggle for survival: *the corporate jungle.* **6.** *Slang.* A place where hoboes camp. [Ultimately from Sanskrit *jaṅgalam,* desert, wasteland, uncultivated area, from *jaṅgala-,* desert, waste.] **—jun′gly** (-glē) *adj.*

WORD HISTORY: One might be surprised to learn that the word *jungle* is not African in origin nor does it come from a word that only meant "land densely overgrown with tropical vegetation and trees." *Jungle* goes back to the Sanskrit word *jaṅgalam,* meaning "desert, wasteland," and also "any kind of uncultivated area, such as heavily forested land." The Sanskrit word *jaṅgala-* passed into various Indian languages and from one or more of these languages into English. In English *jungle* was used for land overgrown with vegetation, for the vegetation itself, and for such land outside India. The word was also extended figuratively in various ways. We have, for example, asphalt jungles, concrete jungles, blackboard jungles, academic jungles, corporate jungles, and, in a February 1972 issue of the *Guardian,* the government official who "lit up some lurid corners of the taxation jungle."

jungle fever *n.* **1.** Malaria, especially a severe form occurring in the East Indies and other tropical regions. **2.** Any of various diseases native to the tropics.

jungle fowl *n.* Any of several game birds of the genus *Gallus* of southeast Asia, especially *G. gallus,* considered to be the ancestor of the common domestic fowl.

jungle gym *n.* A structure of poles and bars for children to climb and play on. [Originally a trademark.]

jun·ior (jo͞on′yər) *adj.* **1.** *Abbr.* **jr., Jr., Jun., jun., jnr.** Used to distinguish a son from his father when they have the same given name. **2.** Intended for or including youthful persons: *junior fashions; a junior sports league.* **3.** Lower in rank or shorter in length of tenure: *a junior officer; the junior senator from Texas.* **4.** Of, for, or constituting students in the third year of a U.S. high school or college: *the junior class; the junior prom.* **5.** Lesser in scale than the usual. **—junior** *n. Abbr.* **jr., Jr., Jun., jun., jnr. 1.** A person who is younger than another: *a sister four years my junior.* **2.** A person lesser in rank or time of participation or service; subordinate. **3.** A student in the third year of a U.S. high school or college. **4.** A class of clothing sizes for girls and slender women. In this sense, also called *junior miss.* [Middle English, from Latin, comparative of *iuvenis,* young. See **yeu-** in Appendix.]

junior college *n.* An educational institution offering a two-year course that is generally the equivalent of the first two years of a four-year undergraduate course.

junior high school *n.* A school in the U.S. system generally including the seventh, eighth, and sometimes ninth grades.

junior middleweight *n. Sports.* **1.** A professional boxer weighing between 147 and 154 pounds (67–71 kilograms), heavier than a welterweight and lighter than a middleweight. **2.** A contestant in various other sports in a similar weight class.

junior miss *n.* **1.** A teenage girl. **2.** See **junior** (sense 4).

jump ball

jumping jack
c. 1827 American jumping jack of Puss in Boots

Carl Jung

ă pat	oi boy
ā pay	ou out
âr care	o͝o took
ä father	o͞o boot
ĕ pet	ŭ cut
ē be	ûr urge
ĭ pit	th thin
ī pie	*th* this
îr pier	hw which
ŏ pot	zh vision
ō toe	ə about, item
ô paw	♦ regionalism

Stress marks: ′ (primary); ′ (secondary), as in **dictionary** (dĭk′shə-nĕr′ē)

juniper
Eastern red cedar
Juniperus virginiana

junior varsity *n. Abbr.* **JV** *Sports.* A high-school or college team that competes in interschool sports on the level below varsity.

ju·ni·per (jo͞o′nə-pər) *n.* Any of various evergreen trees or shrubs of the genus *Juniperus,* having needlelike or scalelike, often pointed leaves and aromatic, bluish-gray, berrylike, seed-bearing cones. [Middle English, from Latin *iūniperus.*]

juniper oil *n.* An essential oil obtained from the seed-bearing cones of the common juniper, most commonly used for flavoring gin and liqueurs.

juniper tar *n.* A tarry substance obtained from the wood of the European juniper *Juniperus oxcedrus* and used topically to treat various skin ailments. Also called *cade oil.*

junk¹ (jŭngk) *n.* **1.** Discarded material, such as glass, rags, paper, or metal, that may be reused in some form. **2.** *Informal.* **a.** Articles that are worn-out or fit to be discarded: *broken furniture and other junk in the attic.* **b.** Cheap or shoddy material. **c.** Something meaningless, fatuous, or unbelievable: *nothing but junk in the annual report.* **3.** *Slang.* Heroin. **4.** Hard salt beef for consumption on board a ship. **—junk** *tr.v.* **junked, junk·ing, junks.** To throw away or discard as useless; scrap. **—junk** *adj.* **1.** Cheap, shoddy, or worthless: *junk jewelry.* **2.** Having a superficial appeal or utility, but lacking substance: *"the junk issues that have dominated this year's election"* (New Republic). [Middle English *jonk,* an old cable or rope.]

WORD HISTORY: The word *junk* is an example of the change in meaning known as generalization, and very aptly too, since the amount of junk in the world seems to be generalizing and proliferating rapidly. The Middle English word *jonk,* ancestor of *junk,* originally had a very specific meaning restricted to nautical terminology. First recorded in 1353, the word meant "an old cable or rope." On a sailing ship it made little sense to throw away useful material since considerable time might pass before one could get new supplies. Old cable was used in a variety of ways, for example, to make fenders, that is, material hung over the side of the ship to protect it from scraping other ships or wharves. *Junk* came to refer to this old cable as well. The big leap in meaning taken by the word seems to have occurred when *junk* was applied to discarded but useful material in general. This extension may also have taken place in a nautical context, for the earliest, more generalized use of *junk* is found in the compound *junk shop,* referring to a store where old materials from ships were sold. *Junk* has gone on to mean useless waste as well.

junk²
In Victoria harbor, Hong Kong

junk² (jŭngk) *n. Nautical.* A Chinese flat-bottomed ship with a high poop and battened sails. [Portuguese *junco* or Dutch *jonk,* both from Javanese *djong.*]

junk art *n.* Three-dimensional art made from junked materials, such as metal, glass, or wood.

junk bond *n.* A corporate bond having a high yield and high risk.

junker (jŭng′kər) *n. Slang.* A car or truck that is old and in poor repair.

Jun·ker (yo͝ong′kər) *n.* A member of the Prussian landed aristocracy, a class formerly associated with political reaction and militarism. [German, from Middle High German *junchērre,* page, squire, from Old High German *junchērro* : *junc,* young; see **yeu-** in Appendix + *hērro,* lord; see HERR.] **—Jun′ker·dom** *n.*

Jun·kers (yo͝ong′kərz, -kərs), **Hugo.** 1859–1935. German aircraft engineer who designed the first successful all-metal airplane (1915) and helped establish early mail and passenger airlines.

jun·ket (jŭng′kĭt) *n.* **1.** A sweet food made from flavored milk and rennet. **2.** A party, a banquet, or an outing. **3.** A trip or tour, especially: **a.** One taken by an official at public expense. **b.** One taken by a person who is the guest of a business or an agency seeking favor or patronage. **—junket** *v.* **-ket·ed, -ket·ing, -kets.** *—intr.* **1.** To hold a party or banquet. **2.** To go on a junket. *—tr.* To fete at a party or banquet. [Middle English *jonket,* rush basket, a kind of food served on rushes, feast, perhaps from Old North French *jonquette,* rush basket (probably from *jonc,* rush) or from Medieval Latin *iuncāta,* rush basket, both from Latin *iuncus,* rush.] **—jun′ket·er** *n.*

jun·ke·teer (jŭng′kĭ-tîr′) *n.* One who goes on a junket or junkets. **—junketeer** *intr.v.* **-teered, -teer·ing, -teers.** To go on a junket, especially at the expense of a government or a favor-seeking business or agency.

junk food *n.* Any of various prepackaged snack foods high in calories but low in nutritional value.

junk·ie also **junk·y** (jŭng′kē) *n., pl.* **-ies.** *Slang.* **1.** A narcotics addict, especially one using heroin. **2.** One who has an insatiable interest or devotion: *a sports junkie.*

junk mail *n.* Third-class mail, such as advertisements, mailed indiscriminately in large quantities.

junk·y¹ (jŭng′kē) *adj.* **-i·er, -i·est. 1.** Of or related to junk; worthy of being discarded. **2.** Meaningless, fatuous, or unbelievable: *a junky novel.*

junk·y² (jŭng′kē) *n.* Variant of **junkie.**

junk·yard (jŭngk′yärd′) *n.* A yard or lot that is used to store junk, such as scrap metal or resalable car parts.

Ju·no (jo͞o′nō) *n. Roman Mythology.* The principal goddess of the Pantheon, the wife and sister of Jupiter and the patroness primarily of marriage and the well-being of women.

Jupiter
Photographed by Voyager I in 1979 at a distance of 28.4 million kilometers (17.6 million miles)

Ju·no·esque (jo͞o′nō-ĕsk′) *adj.* Having the stately bearing and imposing beauty of the goddess Juno.

jun·ta (ho͝on′tə, jŭn′-) *n.* **1.** A group of military officers ruling a country after seizing power. **2.** A council or small legislative body in a government, especially in Central or South America. **3.** A junto. [Spanish and Portuguese, conference, probably from Latin *iūncta,* feminine past participle of *iungere,* to join. See **yeug-** in Appendix.]

jun·to (jŭn′tō) *n., pl.* **-tos.** A small, usually secret group united for a common interest. [Alteration of JUNTA.]

Ju·pi·ter (jo͞o′pĭ-tər) *n.* **1.** *Roman Mythology.* The supreme god, patron of the Roman state and brother and husband of Juno. Also called *Jove.* **2.** *Astronomy.* The fifth planet from the sun, the largest and most massive in the solar system, having a sidereal period of revolution about the sun of 11.86 years at a mean distance of 777 million kilometers (483 million miles), a mean diameter of approximately 138,000 kilometers (86,000 miles), and a mass approximately 318 times that of Earth. [Latin *Iūpiter.* See **deiw-** in Appendix.]

ju·ral (jo͝or′əl) *adj.* **1.** Of or relating to law. **2.** Of or relating to rights and obligations. [From Latin *iūs, iūr-,* law. See **yewes-** in Appendix.] **—ju′ral·ly** *adv.*

Ju·ra Mountains (jo͝or′ə, zhü-rä′). A range extending about 241 km (150 mi) along the French-Swiss border and rising to 1,723.9 m (5,652 ft).

Ju·ras·sic (jo͞o-răs′ĭk) *adj.* Of, belonging to, or designating the time and deposits of the second period of the Mesozoic Era, characterized by the existence of dinosaurs and the appearance of the earliest mammals and birds. See table at **geologic time.** **—Jurassic** *n.* The Jurassic Period. [French *jurassique,* after the JURA (MOUNTAINS).]

ju·rat (jo͝or′ăt′) *n. Law.* A certification on an affidavit declaring when, where, and before whom it was sworn. [Middle English, informant under oath, member of a ruling body of a city, from Anglo-Norman, member of a ruling body of a city, from Medieval Latin *iūrātus,* juror, from past participle of Latin *iūrāre,* to swear. See JURY¹.]

ju·rid·i·cal (jo͞o-rĭd′ĭ-kəl) also **ju·rid·ic** (-ĭk) *adj. Law.* Of or relating to the law and its administration. [From Latin *iūridicus* : *iūs, iūr-,* law; see **yewes-** in Appendix + *dīcere, dic-,* to say; see **deik-** in Appendix.] **—ju·rid′i·cal·ly** *adv.*

ju·ris·con·sult (jo͝or′ĭs-kŏn′sŭlt′) *n. Law.* A person learned in law; a jurist. [Latin *iūrisconsultus* : *iūris,* genitive of *iūs,* law; see **yewes-** in Appendix + *cōnsultus,* skilled, past participle of *cōnsulere,* to take counsel.]

ju·ris·dic·tion (jo͝or′ĭs-dĭk′shən) *n.* **1.** *Law.* The right and power to interpret and apply the law: *courts having jurisdiction in this district.* **2. a.** Authority or control: *islands under U.S. jurisdiction; a bureau with jurisdiction over Native American affairs.* **b.** The extent of authority or control: *a family matter beyond the school's jurisdiction.* **3.** The territorial range of authority or control. [Middle English *jurisdiccioun,* from Old French *juridicion,* from Latin *iūrisdictiō, iūrisdictiōn-* : *iūris,* genitive of *iūs,* law; see **yewes-** in Appendix + *dictiō, dictiōn-,* declaration (from *dictus,* past participle of *dīcere,* to say; see **deik-** in Appendix).] **—ju′ris·dic′tion·al** *adj.* **—ju′ris·dic′tion·al·ly** *adv.*

ju·ris·pru·dence (jo͝or′ĭs-pro͞od′ns) *n. Law.* **1.** The philosophy or science of law: *"His jurisprudence—his vision of what the rule of law requires—is superficial and inadequate"* (John Bayley). **2.** A division or department of law. [Late Latin *iūrisprūdentia* : Latin *iūris,* genitive of *iūs,* law; see **yewes-** in Appendix + Latin *prūdentia,* knowledge (from *prūdēns, prūdent-,* knowing; see PRUDENT).] **—ju′ris·pru·den′tial** (-pro͞o-dĕn′shəl) *adj.* **—ju′ris·pru·den′tial·ly** *adv.*

ju·ris·pru·dent (jo͝or′ĭs-pro͞od′nt) *Law. adj.* Versed in jurisprudence. **—jurisprudent** *n.* See **jurist.**

ju·rist (jo͝or′ĭst) *n. Law.* One who has thorough knowledge and experience of law, especially an eminent judge, lawyer, or legal scholar. Also called *jurisprudent.* [Middle English, from Old French *juriste,* from Medieval Latin *iurista,* from Latin *iūs, iūr-,* law. See **yewes-** in Appendix.]

ju·ris·tic (jo͞o-rĭs′tĭk) also **ju·ris·ti·cal** (-tĭ-kəl) *adj. Law.* **1.** Of or relating to a jurist or to jurisprudence. **2.** Of or relating to law or legality. **—ju·ris′ti·cal·ly** *adv.*

ju·ror (jo͝or′ər, -ôr′) *n.* **1.** *Law.* **a.** One who serves as a member of a jury. **b.** One who awaits or is called for service on a jury. **2.** One who serves on a deliberative body analogous to a jury. [Middle English *jurour,* from Anglo-Norman, from Latin *iūrātor,* swearer, from *iūrāre,* to swear. See JURY¹.]

Ju·ru·á (zho͞o′ro͞o-ä′). A river of eastern Peru and northwest Brazil flowing about 1,931 km (1,200 mi) northeast to the Amazon River.

ju·ry¹ (jo͝or′ē) *n., pl.* **-ries. 1.** *Law.* A body of persons sworn to judge and give a verdict on a given matter, especially a body of persons summoned by law and sworn to hear and hand down a verdict upon a case presented in court. **2.** A committee, usually of experts, that judges contestants or applicants, as in a competition or an exhibition; a panel of judges. **—jury** *tr.v.* **-ried, -ry·ing, -ries.** To judge or evaluate by a jury: *jurying submitted samples for a crafts fair.* [Middle English *jure,* from Anglo-Norman *juree,* from feminine past participle of *jurer,* to swear, from Latin *iūrāre,* from *iūs, iūr-,* law. See **yewes-** in Appendix.]

ju·ry² (jo͝or′ē) *adj. Nautical.* Intended or designed for temporary use; makeshift: *a jury sail.* [Ultimately from Old French *ajuri,* help, from Latin *adiūtāre,* to help. See AID.]

ju·ry-rig (jo͝or′ē-rĭg′) *tr.v.* **-rigged, -rig·ging, -rigs.** To rig or assemble for temporary emergency use; improvise: *The survivors of the shipwreck jury-rigged some fishing gear.*

jus gen·ti·um (yo͞os gĕn′tē-əm, jŭs jĕn′shē-əm) *n. Law.* The law of nations; international law. [Latin *iūs gentium* : *iūs,* law + *gentium,* genitive pl. of *gēns,* nation.]

jus·sive (jŭs′ĭv) *n. Grammar.* A word, mood, or form used to express command. [From Latin *iussus,* past participle of *iubēre,* to command.] **—jus′sive** *adj.*

just¹ (jŭst) *adj.* **1.** Honorable and fair in one's dealings and actions: *a just ruler.* See Synonyms at **fair¹. 2.** Consistent with what is morally right; righteous: *a just cause.* **3.** Properly due or merited: *just deserts.* **4.** *Law.* Valid within the law; lawful: *just claims.* **5.** Suitable or proper in nature; fitting: *a just touch of solemnity.* **6.** Based on fact or sound reason; well-founded: *a just appraisal.* **—just** (jəst, jĭst; jŭst *when stressed*) *adv.* **1.** Precisely; exactly: *just enough salt.* **2.** Only a moment ago: *He just arrived.* **3.** By a narrow margin; barely: *just missed being hit; just caught the bus before it pulled away.* **4.** At a little distance: *just down the road.* **5.** Merely; only: *just a scratch.* **6.** Simply; certainly: *It's just beautiful!* **7.** Perhaps; possibly: *I just may go.* ***—idioms.*** **just about.** Almost; very nearly: *This job is just about done.* **just now.** Only a moment ago. **just the same.** Nevertheless. [Middle English *juste,* from Old French, from Latin *iūstus.* See **yewes-** in Appendix.] **—just′ly** *adv.* **—just′ness** *n.*

just² (jŭst) *n. & v.* Variant of **joust.**

just-folks (jŭst′fōks′) *adj.* Unpretentious and friendly: *"the essence of this small-town state is a friendly, trusting, just-folks way of dealing with one another"* (T.R. Reid).

jus·tice (jŭs′tĭs) *n.* **1.** The quality of being just; fairness. **2.a.** The principle of moral rightness; equity. **b.** Conformity to moral rightness in action or attitude; righteousness. **3.a.** The upholding of what is just, especially fair treatment and due reward in accordance with honor, standards, or law. **b.** *Law.* The administration and procedure of law. **4.** Conformity to truth, fact, or sound reason: *The overcharged customer was angry, and with justice.* **5.** *Abbr.* **J., j.** *Law.* **a.** A judge. **b.** A justice of the peace. ***—idiom.*** **do justice to.** To treat adequately, fairly, or with full appreciation: *The subject is so complex that I cannot do justice to it in a brief survey.* [Middle English, from Old French, from Latin *iūstitia,* from *iūstus,* just. See JUST¹.]

justice of the peace *n., pl.* **justices of the peace.** *Abbr.* **J.P., JP** *Law.* A magistrate of the lowest level of certain state court systems, having authority to act upon minor offenses, commit cases to a higher court for trial, perform marriages, and administer oaths.

jus·ti·ci·a·ble (jŭ-stĭsh′ə-bəl) *adj. Law.* **1.** Appropriate for or subject to court trial: *a justiciable charge.* **2.** That can be settled by law or a court of law: *justiciable disputes.* [Middle English, from Old French, from Medieval Latin *iūstitiābilis,* from Medieval Latin *iūstitiāre,* to try, from Latin *iūstitia,* justice. See JUSTICE.] **—jus·ti′cia·bil′i·ty** *n.*

jus·ti·ci·ar·y (jŭ-stĭsh′ē-ĕr′ē) also **jus·ti·ci·ar** (-ē-ər) *n., pl.* **-ies** also **-ars.** *Law.* A high judicial officer in medieval England. [Medieval Latin *iūstitiāria,* from feminine of *iūstitiārius,* of the administration of justice, from Latin *iūstitia,* justice. See JUSTICE.]

jus·ti·fi·a·ble (jŭs′tə-fī′ə-bəl, jŭs′tə-fī′-) *adj.* Having sufficient grounds for justification; possible to justify: *justifiable resentment.* **—jus′ti·fi′a·bil′i·ty, jus′ti·fi′a·ble·ness** *n.* **—jus′ti·fi′a·bly** *adv.*

jus·ti·fi·ca·tion (jŭs′tə-fĭ-kā′shən) *n.* **1.a.** The act of justifying. **b.** The condition or fact of being justified. **2.** Something, such as a fact or circumstance, that justifies: *considered misgovernment to be a justification for revolution.* See Synonyms at **apology.**

jus·ti·fi·ca·tive (jŭs′tə-fĭ-kā′tĭv) also **jus·tif·i·ca·to·ry** (jŭ-stĭf′ĭ-kə-tôr′ē, -tōr′ē) *adj.* Serving as justification.

jus·ti·fy (jŭs′tə-fī′) *v.* **-fied, -fy·ing, -fies.** *—tr.* **1.** To demonstrate or prove to be just, right, or valid: *justified each budgetary expense as necessary; anger that is justified by the circumstances.* **2.** To declare free of blame; absolve. **3.** *Theology.* To free (a human being) of the guilt and penalty attached to grievous sin. Used only of God. **4.** *Law.* **a.** To demonstrate sufficient legal reason for (an action taken). **b.** To prove to be qualified as a bondsman. **5.** *Printing.* To adjust the spacing within (lines in a document, for example), so that the lines end evenly at a straight margin. *—intr. Printing.* To be adjusted in spacing so as to end evenly at the margin. [Middle English *justifien,* from Old French *justifier,* from Late Latin *iūstificāre,* from Latin, to act justly toward : *iūstus,* just; see JUST¹ + *-ficāre,* -fy.]

SYNONYMS: *justify, warrant.* The central meaning shared by these verbs is "to be a proper or sufficient reason for": *an angry outburst justified by extreme provocation; drastic measures not warranted by the circumstances.*

Jus·tin (jŭs′tĭn), Saint. A.D. 100?–165. Greek theologian who founded a school of Christian philosophy at Rome and wrote the *Apology* and the *Dialogue.*

Jus·tin·i·an I (jŭ-stĭn′ē-ən). Known as "Justinian the Great." A.D. 483–565. Byzantine emperor (527–565) who held the eastern frontier of his empire against the Persians and reconquered former Roman territories in Africa, Italy, and Spain.

Justinian I
Detail from
Justinian and Attendants,
a sixth-century mosaic in
the Church of San Vitale,
Ravenna, Italy

jut (jŭt) *v.* **jut·ted, jut·ting, juts.** *—intr.* To extend outward or upward beyond the limits of the main body; project: *"He had a sharp crooked nose jutting out of a lean dancer's face"* (Graham Greene). *—tr.* To cause to jut. See Synonyms at **bulge. —jut** *n.* Something that protrudes; a projection. [Middle English *jutten,* from *gete, iutei,* jetty, projecting upper story, from Old French *jetee.* See JETTY¹.]

jute (jo͞ot) *n.* **1.** Either of two Asian plants *(Corchorus capsularis* or *C. olitorius)* yielding a fiber used for sacking and cordage. **2.** The fiber obtained from these plants. [Bengali *jhuṭo,* from Sanskrit *jūṭaḥ,* twisted hair, probably of Dravidian origin.]

Jute (jo͞ot) *n.* A member of a Germanic people who invaded Britain in the fifth and sixth centuries A.D. and settled in the south and southeast and on the Isle of Wight. [From Middle English *Jutes,* the Jutes, from Medieval Latin *Iutae.*]

Jut·land (jŭt′lənd). A peninsula of northern Europe comprising mainland Denmark and northern Germany. The name is usually applied only to the Danish section of the peninsula. The largest naval battle of World War I was fought by British and German fleets off the western coast of Jutland on May 31–June 1, 1916.

juv. *abbr.* Juvenile.

Ju·ve·nal (jo͞o′və-nəl). A.D. 60?–140? Roman satirist whose works denounced the corruption and extravagance of the privileged classes in Rome.

ju·ve·nes·cent (jo͞o′və-nĕs′ənt) *adj.* Becoming young or youthful. [Latin *iuvenēscēns, iuvenēscent-,* present participle of *iuvenēscere,* to reach the age of youth, from *iuvenis,* young. See JUVENILE.] **—ju′ve·nes′cence** *n.*

ju·ve·nile (jo͞o′və-nīl′, -nəl) *adj. Abbr.* **juv. 1.** Not fully grown or developed; young. **2.** Of, relating to, characteristic of, intended for, or appropriate for children or young people: *juvenile fashions.* **3.** Marked by immaturity; childish: *juvenile behavior.* See Synonyms at **young. —juvenile** *n. Abbr.* **juv. 1.a.** A young person; a child. **b.** A young animal that has not reached sexual maturity. **2.** An actor who plays roles of children or young persons. **3.** A children's book. [Latin *iuvenīlis,* from *iuvenis,* young. See **yeu-** in Appendix.] **—ju′ve·nile′ly** *adv.* **—ju′ve·nile′ness** *n.*

juvenile court *n. Law.* A court with jurisdiction over all cases involving children under a specified age, usually 18 years.

juvenile delinquency *n.* Antisocial or criminal behavior by children or adolescents.

juvenile delinquent *n. Abbr.* **JD, J.D.** A juvenile guilty of antisocial or criminal behavior.

juvenile diabetes *n.* Insulin-dependent diabetes mellitus.

juvenile hormone *n.* A hormone in arthropod larvae that inhibits ecdysone, thereby preventing molting and the development of larvae into adults until its level drops.

ju·ve·nil·i·a (jo͞o′və-nĭl′ē-ə, -nĭl′yə) *pl.n.* Works, particularly written or artistic works, produced in an author's or artist's youth. [Latin *iuvenīlia,* neuter pl. of *iuvenīlis,* juvenile. See JUVENILE.]

ju·ve·nil·i·ty (jo͞o′və-nĭl′ĭ-tē) *n., pl.* **-ties. 1.** The quality or condition of being juvenile; youthfulness. **2.a.** Foolishly juvenile behavior or character; immaturity. **b.** An instance of juvenile behavior.

jux·ta·pose (jŭk′stə-pōz′) *tr.v.* **-posed, -pos·ing, -pos·es.** To place side by side, especially for comparison or contrast. [French *juxtaposer* : Latin *iuxtā,* close by; see **yeug-** in Appendix + French *poser,* to place (from Old French; see POSE¹).]

jux·ta·po·si·tion (jŭk′stə-pə-zĭsh′ən) *n.* The act or an instance of juxtaposing or the state of being juxtaposed. **—jux′ta·po·si′tion·al** *adj.*

JV *abbr. Sports.* Junior varsity.

jwlr. *abbr.* Jeweler.

ă pat	oi boy
ā pay	ou out
âr care	o͝o took
ä father	o͞o boot
ĕ pet	ŭ cut
ē be	ûr urge
ĭ pit	th thin
ī pie	*th* this
îr pier	hw which
ŏ pot	zh vision
ō toe	ə about, item
ô paw	♦ regionalism

Stress marks: **′** (primary); ′ (secondary), as in **dictionary** (dĭk′shə-nĕr′ē)

Kk

Phoenician
The Phoenician alphabet used this sign to represent the sound *k* in the Semitic word *kaph,* "hand."

Early Greek
The letter was adopted with little change by the Greeks, who called it *kappa.*

Roman
It was eventually passed on to the Roman alphabet, where it took its modern form. Though it was rarely used in early Roman times, it came into its own to represent the hard *k* sound after the pronunciation of C was softened before *e, i,* and *y* (see C).

k¹ or **K** (kā) *n., pl.* **k's** or **K's. 1.** The 11th letter of the modern English alphabet. **2.** Any of the speech sounds represented by the letter *k.* **3.** The 11th in a series. **4.** Something shaped like the letter K.

k² *abbr.* Karat.

K¹ *n., pl.* **K's.** *Slang.* One thousand dollars. [K(ILO)–.]

K² The symbol for the element **potassium.** [From *kali,* potassium, from Arabic *qily,* alkali, from *qalā,* to bake.]

K³ *abbr.* **1.** Kaon. **2.** Kelvin (temperature scale). **3.** *Computer Science.* Kilobyte. **4.** Kindergarten. **5.** Or **k.** *Games.* King (chess). **6.** *Bible.* Kings. **7.** Or **k.** Knight.

K2 (kā′to͞o′). Also **Mount God·win Aus·ten** (gŏd′wĭn ô′stən). A peak in the Karakoram Range of northern India. At 8,616.3 m (28,250 ft), it is the second-highest mountain in the world.

k. or **K.** *abbr.* **1.** Kopeck. **2.** Krona. **3.** Krone.

ka *abbr.* Cathode.

Kaa·ba (kä′bə) *n.* A Moslem shrine in Mecca toward which the faithful turn to pray. [Arabic *ka'bah,* square building, from *ka'b,* cube.]

kab (kăb) *n.* Variant of **cab².**

kab·a·la or **kab·ba·la** (kăb′ə-lə, kə-bä′lə) *n.* Variants of **cabala.**

ka·bob (kə-bŏb′) *n.* Variant of **kebab.**

ka·bu·ki also **Ka·bu·ki** (kə-bo͞o′kē) *n.* A type of popular Japanese drama, evolved from the older No theater, in which elaborately costumed performers, nowadays men only, use stylized movements, dances, and songs in order to enact tragedies and comedies. [Japanese, art of singing and dancing : *kabu,* singing and dancing + *ki,* art, artist.]

Ka·bul (kä′bo͝ol, kə-bo͞ol′). The capital and largest city of Afghanistan, in the eastern part of the country near the border with Pakistan on the **Kabul River,** about 483 km (300 mi) long. Strategically located and more than 3,000 years old, the city became the capital of Afghanistan in the 1700's. Population, 913,164.

Ka·byle (kə-bīl′) *n., pl.* **Kabyle** or **-byles. 1.** A member of a Berber people of northeast Algeria. **2.** The Berber language of this people. [Arabic *qabā'il,* pl. of *qabīlah,* tribe.]

ka·chi·na (kə-chē′nə) *n.* **1.** Any of numerous deified ancestral spirits of the Pueblo peoples, believed to reside in the pueblo for part of each year. **2.** A masked dancer believed to embody a particular spirit during a religious ceremony. **3.** A carved doll in the costume of a particular spirit, usually presented as a gift to a child. [Hopi *katsina,* supernatural being, masked impersonator of a supernatural being.]

kachina

Ká·dar (kä′där), **János.** 1912–1989. Hungarian politician and first secretary-general of the Hungarian Communist Party (1956–1988).

Kad·da·fi (kə-dä′fē), **Muammar al-.** See Muammar al-**Qaddafi.**

Kad·dish (kä′dĭsh) *n. Judaism.* A prayer that is recited in the daily synagogue services and by mourners after the death of a close relative. [Aramaic *qaddīš.*]

kaf·fee·klatsch (kŏf′ē-klăch′, -kläch′, kô′fē-) *n.* Variant of **coffee klatch.**

kaf·fir also **kaf·ir** (kăf′ər) *n.* A tropical African variety of sorghum *(Sorghum bicolor)* grown in dry regions and in the Great Plains for grain and forage. Also called *kaffir corn.*

Kaf·fir also **Kaf·ir** (kăf′ər) *n., pl.* **Kaffir** or **-firs** also **Kafir** or **-irs. 1.** *Offensive.* A Xhosa. **2.** *Offensive.* Used especially in southern Africa as a disparaging term for a Black person. **3.** Often **Kafir.** See **Nuristani. 4.** Also **kaffir.** *Islam.* An infidel. [Arabic *kāfir,* infidel, present participle of *kafara,* to deny, be skeptical.]

kaffir corn *n.* See **kaffir.**

kaf·fi·yeh (kä-fē′ə) *n.* A cloth headdress fastened by a band around the crown and usually worn by Arab men. [Arabic *kaffīyah.*]

kaf·ir (kăf′ər) *n.* Variant of **kaffir.**

Kaf·ir (kăf′ər) *n.* Variant of **Kaffir.** [Arabic *kāfir,* infidel.]

Kaf·i·ri (kăf′ə-rē, kə-fîr′ē) *n.* The Dardic language of the Nuristani.

Kaf·ka (käf′kə, -kä), **Franz.** 1883–1924. Austrian writer whose stories and novels, including *The Trial* (1925), concern troubled individuals in a nightmarishly impersonal world.

Kaf·ka·esque (käf′kə-ĕsk′) *adj.* **1.** Of, relating to, or characteristic of Franz Kafka or his writings. **2.** Characterized by surreal distortion and usually by a sense of impending danger: *"Kafkaesque fantasies of the impassive interrogation, the false trial . . . haunt his innocence"* (New Yorker).

kaf·tan (kăf′tăn′, -tən, kăf-tăn′) *n.* Variant of **caftan.**

Ka·fu·e (kə-fo͞o′ā). A river rising along the Zambia-Zaire border and meandering about 965 km (600 mi) through central Zambia to the Zambezi River.

Ka·go·shi·ma (kä′gô-shē′mə). A city of southern Kyushu, Japan, on **Kagoshima Bay,** an inlet of the East China Sea. Population, 530,496.

Ka·ho·o·la·we (kä-hō′ō-lä′wē, -wā, -vā). An island of south-central Hawaii southwest of Maui.

kai·ak (kī′ăk′) *n. & v.* Variant of **kayak.**

Kai·e·teur Falls (kī′ĭ-to͝or′). A waterfall, 250.7 m (822 ft) high, in the Potaro River of central Guyana.

Kai·feng (kī′fŭng′). A city of east-central China south-southwest of Beijing. Founded in the third century B.C., it is a commercial and industrial center. Population, 450,000.

Kai·las (kī-läs′). A peak, 6,718.2 m (22,027 ft) high, in the Himalaya Mountains of southwest China. It is the highest elevation of the **Kailas Range** and according to Hindu legend was the dwelling place of the god Shiva.

Kai·lu·a (kī-lo͞o′ə). A city of Hawaii, a suburb of Honolulu on the southeast coast of Oahu on **Kailua Bay,** an inlet of the Pacific Ocean. Population, 35,812.

Kail·yard School (kāl′yärd′) *n.* A group of Scottish writers, including J.M. Barrie, who made considerable use of Scots dialect in their sentimental and romantic works about Scottish life. [Scots *kailyard,* kitchen garden : *kail,* kale (from Middle English *kal;* see KALE) + YARD².]

kai·nite (kī′nīt′, kā′-) *n.* A white, gray, pink, or black mineral, $MgSO_4{\cdot}KCl{\cdot}3H_2O$, used as a fertilizer and a source of potassium compounds. [Greek *kainos,* new; see **ken-** in Appendix + –ITE¹.]

Kai·ser (kī′zər) *n.* **1.** Any of the emperors of the Holy Roman Empire (962–1806), of Austria (1806–1918), or of Germany (1871–1918). **2.** Used as the title for such a man. [German, from Middle High German *keiser,* from Old High German *keisar,* from Latin *Caesar.* See CAESAR.]

Kaiser, Henry John. 1882–1967. American industrialist who oversaw the construction of major highways, bridges, and dams, including the Grand Coulee Dam (1942).

Kai·ser·in (kī′zər-ĭn) *n.* **1.** The wife of a Kaiser. **2.** Used as the title for such a woman. [German, feminine of *Kaiser,* Kaiser. See KAISER.]

Kai·sers·lau·tern (kī′zərs-lou′tərn). A city of southwest Germany southwest of Frankfurt. Population, 98,212.

ka·ka (kä′kə) *n.* A brownish-green New Zealand parrot *(Nestor meridionalis).* [Maori *kākā.*]

ka·ka·po (kä′kə-pō′) *n., pl.* **-pos.** A ground-dwelling New Zealand parrot *(Strigops habroptilus)* with greenish plumage. [Maori *kākāpō* : *kākā,* parrot; see KAKA + *pō,* night, period after death, early epoch.]

ka·ke·mo·no (kä′kə-mō′nō) *n., pl.* **-nos.** A vertical Japanese scroll painting. [Japanese : *kake,* hanging + *mono,* object.]

ka·ki (kä′kē) *n., pl.* **-kis. 1.** A Chinese tree *(Diospyros kaki)* having large, edible, orange to reddish fruit with orange flesh and an enlarged, persistent calyx. **2.** The fruit of this tree. Also called *Japanese persimmon.* [Japanese.]

kak·is·toc·ra·cy (kăk′ĭ-stŏk′rə-sē, kä′kĭ-) *n., pl.* **-cies.** Government by the least qualified or most unprincipled citizens. [Greek *kakistos,* worst, superlative of *kakos,* bad; see CACO– + –CRACY.]

ka·la-a·zar (kä′lə-ə-zär′) *n.* A chronic, often fatal disease occurring chiefly in Asia, caused by a protozoan parasite *(Leishmania donovani)* and characterized by irregular fever, enlargement of the spleen and liver, and emaciation. [Urdu *kālā āzār* : *kālā*, black (from Sanskrit *kāla-*, of Dravidian origin) + *āzār*, disease (from Persian, from Middle Persian, pain, torment).]

Ka·la·ha·ri Desert (kä′lə-här′ē). An arid plateau region of southern Botswana, eastern Namibia, and western South Africa.

Ka·lakh (kä′läKH). See **Calah.**

Kal·a·ma·zoo (kăl′ə-mə-zo͞o′). A city of southwest Michigan south of Grand Rapids. First settled in 1829, it is a manufacturing center. Population, 79,722.

Kalb (kălb, kälp), **Johann.** Known as "Baron de Kalb." 1721–1780. German general in the American Revolution who wintered with George Washington at Valley Forge (1777–1778) and was mortally wounded at the Battle of Camden (1780).

kale (kāl) *n.* **1.** An edible plant *(Brassica oleracea* var. *acephala)* in the mustard family, having spreading, crinkled leaves that do not form a compact head. Also called *borecole, cole, colewort, collard.* **2.** *Slang.* Money. [Middle English *col, kal.* See COLE.]

ka·lei·do·scope (kə-lī′də-skōp′) *n.* **1.** A tube-shaped optical instrument that is rotated to produce a succession of symmetrical designs by means of mirrors reflecting the constantly changing patterns made by bits of colored glass at one end of the tube. **2.** A constantly changing set of colors. **3.** A series of changing phases or events: *a kaleidoscope of illusions.* [Greek *kalos,* beautiful + *eidos,* form; see **weid-** in Appendix + –SCOPE.] —**ka·lei′do·scop′ic** (-skŏp′ĭk), **ka·lei′do·scop′i·cal** *adj.* —**ka·lei′do·scop′i·cal·ly** *adv.*

kal·ends (kăl′əndz, kā′ləndz) *n.* Variant of **calends.**

Kal·gan (käl′gän′). See **Zhangjiakou.**

Kal·goor·lie (kăl-go͝or′lē). A town of southwest Australia east-northeast of Perth. Gold was discovered in the area in the late 1800's. Population, 10,100.

Ka·li·man·tan (kăl′ə-măn′tăn′, kä′lē-män′tän). The Indonesian part of the island of Borneo.

ka·lim·ba (kə-lĭm′bə) *n. Music.* An African instrument in the shape of a wooden box set with metal bars that are plucked with the fingers. [Bantu; akin to Bemba *aka-limba (zanza)* : *aka-,* diminutive pref. + *limba,* xylophone, hand piano.]

Ka·li·nin (kə-lē′nĭn, kəl-yē′-). A city of west-central Russia on the Volga River northwest of Moscow. Settled around a fort established in the 12th century, it was a powerful principality in the 13th and 14th centuries. Population, 438,000.

Kalinin, Mikhail Ivanovich. 1875–1946. Russian politician who was head of state as chairman of the All-Union Central Executive Committee (1919–1938) and the Presidium of the Supreme Soviet (1938–1946).

Ka·li·nin·grad (kə-lē′nĭn-grăd′, -gräd′, -lyĭ-nĭn-grät′). Formerly **Kö·nigs·berg** (kā′nĭgz-bûrg′, kœ′nĭKHs-bĕrk′). A city of extreme western Russia near the Polish border. It was founded in 1255 by the Teutonic Knights and joined the Hanseatic League in 1340. Population, 385,000.

Ka·lisz (kä′lĭsh). A city of central Poland west of Łódź. An ancient settlement dating possibly to the second century A.D., it passed to Prussia in 1793, Russia in 1815, and Poland in 1919. Population, 103,500.

Kal·mar (käl′mär′, käl′-). A city of southeast Sweden on **Kalmar Sound,** an arm of the Baltic Sea between the Swedish mainland and Öland. The city was the site of the Union of Kalmar (1397), which joined Sweden, Denmark, and Norway into a single monarchy that lasted until 1523. Population, 30,300.

Kal·myk[1] (kăl′mĭk, kăl-mĭk′) also **Kal·muck** or **Kal·muk** (kăl′mŭk, kăl-mŭk′) *n., pl.* **Kalmyk** or **-myks** also **Kalmuck** or **-mucks** or **Kalmuk** or **-muks. 1.** A member of a Buddhist Mongol people now located primarily in Kalmyk. **2.** The Mongolian language of this people. [Russian *Kalmyk,* from Kazan Tatar.]

Kal·myk[2] (kăl′mĭk, kăl-mĭk′). A region of southwest Russia on the Caspian Sea. Settled in the early 17th century, it came under Russian control after 1646.

kal·pac (kăl′păk′, kăl-păk′) *n.* Variant of **calpac.**

kal·so·mine (kăl′sə-mīn′) *n. & v.* Variant of **calcimine.**

Ka·lu·ga (kə-lo͞o′gə). A city of west-central Russia southwest of Moscow. Dating to the 14th century, it is an industrial center and a river port. Population, 297,000.

Ka·ma[1] (kä′mə) *n. Hinduism.* The god of love. [Sanskrit *kāmaḥ,* love, desire, Kama. See **kā-** in Appendix.]

Ka·ma[2] (kä′mə). A river of west-central Russia rising in the central Ural Mountains and flowing about 2,031 km (1,262 mi) to the Volga River. It is the chief tributary of the Volga.

ka·ma·la (kä′mə-lə, kăm′ə-) *n.* **1.** An Asian tree *(Mallotus philippinensis)* that bears a hairy, capsular fruit. **2.** A vermifugal powder obtained from the capsules of this tree. [Sanskrit *kamalam,* lotus, pale red, probably of Dravidian origin.]

Ka·ma·su·tra (kä′mə-so͞o′trə) *n.* A Sanskrit treatise setting forth rules for sensuous and sensual pleasure, love, and marriage in accordance with Hindu law. [Sanskrit *kāmasūtram* : *kāmaḥ,* love; see **kā-** in Appendix + *sūtram,* manual, string; see **syū-** in Appendix.]

Kam·chat·ka (kăm-chăt′kə, -chät′-, kəm-chyät′-). A peninsula of eastern Russia between the Sea of Okhotsk and the Bering Sea. It was first explored in the 18th century.

kame (kām) *n.* A short ridge or mound of sand and gravel deposited during the melting of glacial ice. [Dialectal, a low ridge, from Middle English *camb, comb,* comb, from Old English. See **gembh-** in Appendix.]

Ka·me·ha·me·ha I (kə-mā′ə-mā′ə). Known as "Kamehameha the Great." 1758?–1819. King of the Hawaiian Islands (1795–1819) who united all the islands under his rule.

Ka·me·nev (kä′mə-nĕf, -mĭ-nyĭf), **Lev Borisovich.** 1883–1936. Russian Communist leader who ruled with Stalin and Zinoviev after the death of Lenin (1924) but was expelled as a Trotskyite (1927) and was later imprisoned (1934) and executed.

Ka·met (kŭm′āt′). A mountain, 7,761.3 m (25,447 ft) high, in the northwest Himalaya Mountains on the India-China border.

ka·mi·ka·ze (kä′mĭ-kä′zē) *n.* **1.** A Japanese pilot trained in World War II to make a suicidal crash attack, especially upon a ship. **2.** An airplane loaded with explosives to be piloted in a suicide attack. **3.** *Slang.* An extremely reckless person who seems to court death. —**kamikaze** *adj.* **1.** Of or relating to a suicidal air attack: *a kamikaze mission.* **2.** *Slang.* So reckless in behavior or actions as to be suicidal: *kamikaze hot rodders.* [Japanese : *kami,* divine + *kaze,* wind (from legendary name of a typhoon that in 1281 saved Japan by destroying the Mongol navy).]

Kam·loops (kăm′lo͞ops′). A city of southern British Columbia, Canada, northeast of Vancouver. It was founded in the early 1800's as a trading post. Population, 64,048.

Kam·pa·la (käm-pä′lə). The capital and largest city of Uganda, in the southern part of the country on Lake Victoria. It grew around a fort established in 1890. Population, 458,503.

Kam·pu·che·a (kăm′po͞o-chē′ə). See **Cambodia.**

ka·na (kä′nə) *n., pl.* **kana** or **-nas. 1.** Japanese syllabic writing. The characters are simplified kanji and are usually used with kanji primarily to write inflections, particles, and function words and to show the pronunciations of some kanji and of all foreign words. **2.** Any of the characters used in this system. [Japanese, pseudo-characters, kana : *ka,* false (from Chinese *jiǎ*) + *na,* name (from Chinese *míng*).]

Ka·na·ka also **ka·na·ka** (kə-nä′kə, -năk′ə) *n.* **1.** A Hawaiian of Polynesian descent. **2.** A South Sea Islander, especially one brought to Australia as a laborer in the 19th and early 20th centuries. Often used disparagingly. [Hawaiian, human being, Kanaka.]

USAGE NOTE: *Kanaka,* which simply means "human being" in Hawaiian, is mostly found today in historical contexts and is not usually appropriate in ordinary discourse. As with many terms that refer to ethnic identity, *Kanaka* can suggest ethnic pride in some contexts while in others it may be taken as derogatory.

kan·a·my·cin (kăn′ə-mī′sĭn) *n.* A water-soluble broad-spectrum antibiotic, $C_{18}H_{36}O_{11}N_4$, obtained from the soil bacterium *Streptomyces kanamyceticus.* [New Latin *kanamyc(ēticus),* specific epithet of a species of actinomycete (*kana,* of unknown meaning + *mycēticus,* fungus, from *-mycētēs;* see –MYCETE) + –IN.]

Ka·nan·ga (kə-näng′gə). A city of south-central Zaire east-southeast of Kinshasa. Founded in 1884, it is the trade center of an agricultural region. Population, 290,898.

Kan·a·rese (kăn′ə-rēz′, -rēs′) *n., pl.* **Kanarese. 1.** A member of a Kannada-speaking people of southwest India. **2.** See **Kannada.** [After *Kanara,* a historical region of southwest India.] —**Kan′ar·ese′** *adj.*

Ka·na·ta (kə-nä′tä). A city of eastern Ontario, Canada, a suburb of Ottawa on the Ottawa River. Population, 19,728.

Ka·na·za·wa (kä′nä-zä′wə). A city of western Honshu, Japan, on the Sea of Japan north of Nagoya. It was ruled by powerful daimios during the feudal period (16th–19th century). Population, 430,480.

Kan·chen·jun·ga (kŭn′chən-jŭng′gə, -jo͝ong′-, kän′-). A mountain, 8,603.4 m (28,208 ft) high, in the Himalaya Mountains on the Sikkim-Nepal border.

Kan·da·har also **Qan·da·har** (kŭn′də-här′, kän′-). A city of southeast Afghanistan near the Pakistan border southwest of Kabul. Perhaps founded by Alexander the Great in the fourth century B.C., the city has long been important for its strategic location on the trade routes of central Asia. Population, 178,409.

Kan·din·sky or **Kan·din·ski** (kăn-dĭn′skē, kən-dyĭn′-), **Wassily.** 1866–1944. Russian abstract painter who considered form and color capable of expression.

Kan·dy (kăn′dē). A city of central Sri Lanka east-northeast of Colombo. The last capital of the ancient kings of Ceylon, it is a resort and religious center. Population, 97,872.

Ka·ne·o·he (kä′nē-ō′ē, -nā-ō′hā). A city of Hawaii in eastern Oahu on **Kaneohe Bay,** an inlet of the Pacific Ocean. The city is a residential community. Population, 29,919.

kan·ga·roo (kăng′gə-ro͞o′) *n., pl.* **kangaroo** or **-roos.** Any of various herbivorous marsupials of the family Macropodidae of Australia and adjacent islands, having short forelimbs, large hind limbs adapted for leaping, and a long, tapered tail. [Guugu Yimidhirr (Aboriginal language of northeast Australia) *gaŋurru.*]

kangaroo court *n.* **1.** A mock court set up in violation of established legal procedure. **2.** A court characterized by dishonesty or incompetence.

kaffiyeh

kalimba

Kamehameha I

kangaroo
Red kangaroo
Macropus rufus

ă pat	oi boy
ā pay	ou out
âr care	o͝o took
ä father	o͞o boot
ĕ pet	ŭ cut
ē be	ûr urge
ĭ pit	th thin
ī pie	*th* this
îr pier	hw which
ŏ pot	zh vision
ō toe	ə about, item
ô paw	♦ regionalism

Stress marks: **′** (primary); ′ (secondary), as in **dictionary** (dĭk′shə-nĕr′ē)

kangaroo rat

Konstantinos Karamanlis

karate
Side blade kick

kangaroo rat *n.* Any of various long-tailed rodents of the genus *Dipodomys* of arid areas of western North America, with long hind legs adapted for jumping.

kangaroo vine *n.* A climbing or trailing woody vine *(Cissus antarctica)* native to Australia, often grown as a houseplant for its glossy green foliage.

Kan·i·a·pis·kau (kăn′ē-ə-pĭs′kō, -kou). See **Caniapiscau.**

kan·ji (kän′jē) *n., pl.* **kanji** or **-jis. 1.** A Japanese system of writing based on borrowed or modified Chinese characters. **2.** A character used in this system of writing. [Japanese : Chinese (Mandarin) *hàn,* Chinese + Chinese *zì,* characters.]

Kan·ka·kee (kăng′kə-kē′). A city of northeast Illinois south-southwest of Chicago. It is an industrial center. Population, 30,141.

Kan·na·da (kä′nə-də) *n.* The principal Dravidian language of Mysore, a region of southern India. Also called *Kanarese.*

Ka·no (kä′nō). A city of north-central Nigeria northeast of Lagos. A powerful Hausa city-state, particularly in the 17th and 18th centuries, it was taken by the British in 1903. It is now the chief industrial city of northern Nigeria. Population, 475,000.

Kan·pur (kän′po͝or) also **Cawn·pore** (kôn′pôr′, -pōr′). A city of northern India on the Ganges River southeast of Delhi. During the Indian Mutiny, a disgruntled pension-seeker slaughtered the entire British garrison (July 1857). Population, 1,481,879.

Kan River (kän). See **Gan Jiang.**

Kans. *abbr.* Kansas.

Kan·sa (kăn′zə, -sə) *n., pl.* **Kansa** or **-sas. 1.a.** A Native American people formerly inhabiting eastern and central Kansas, with a present-day population in eastern Oklahoma. **b.** A member of this people. **2.** The Siouan language of the Kansa. Also called *Kaw.*

Kan·san (kăn′zən) *adj.* **1.** Of or relating to Kansas or its residents. **2.** *Geology.* Of or relating to the second glacial stage of the Pleistocene in North America. **—Kansan** *n.* A native or resident of Kansas.

Kan·sas[1] (kăn′zəz, -səz) *n.* A plural of **Kansa.**

Kan·sas[2] (kăn′zəs). *Abbr.* **KS, Kans.** A state of the central United States. It was admitted as the 34th state in 1861. Organized as a territory by the Kansas-Nebraska Act of 1854, which provided it would be classified as a free or slave state on the basis of popular sovereignty, it became a virtual battleground, known as Bleeding Kansas, for free and slave factions (1854–1859). Kansas was finally admitted as a free state. Topeka is the capital and Wichita the largest city. Population, 2,364,236.

Kansas City. 1. A city of northeast Kansas on the Missouri River adjacent to Kansas City, Missouri. It is an industrial center. Population, 161,148. **2.** A city of western Missouri on the Missouri River west-northwest of St. Louis. Established as a fur-trading post in the 1820's, it is a commercial, industrial, and cultural center. Population, 448,159.

Kansas River. Locally known as **Kaw River** (kô). A river formed by the confluence of the Republican and Smoky Hill rivers and flowing about 272 km (169 mi) east to the Missouri River.

Kan·su (kän′so͞o′, gän′-). See **Gansu.**

Kant (kănt, känt), **Immanuel.** 1724–1804. German idealist philosopher who argued that reason is the means by which the phenomena of experience are translated into understanding. His classic works include *Critique of Pure Reason* (1781) and *Critique of Practical Reason* (1788). **—Kant′i·an** *adj. & n.*

Ka·nu·ri (kə-no͝or′ē) *n., pl.* **Kanuri** or **-ris. 1.** A member of a Moslem people in the Bornu region west of Lake Chad in northeast Nigeria. **2.** The Nilo-Saharan language of this people.

kan·zu (kăn′zo͞o) *n.* A long, usually white garment worn by men in Africa. [Swahili.]

Kao·hsiung (kou′shyo͝ong′, gou′-). A city of southwest Taiwan on Formosa Strait. It was developed as a manufacturing center by the Japanese and is now the country's leading port. Population, 1,248,175.

ka·o·lin also **ka·o·line** (kā′ə-lĭn) *n.* A fine clay used in ceramics and refractories and as a filler or coating for paper and textiles. [French, from Chinese (Mandarin) *gāo lĭng,* an area of Jiangxi province.]

ka·o·lin·ite (kā′ə-lĭ-nīt′) *n.* A mineral, $Al_2Si_2O_5(OH)_4$, that is the principal constituent of kaolin. **—ka′o·lin·it′ic** (-lĭ-nĭt′ĭk) *adj.*

ka·on (kā′ŏn′) *n. Abbr.* **K** An unstable meson produced either in an electrically charged form with a mass 966 times that of an electron or in a neutral form with a mass 974 times that of an electron as a result of a high-energy particle collision. Also called *K-meson.* See table at **subatomic particle.** [*ka,* pronunciation of the letter *k* + –ON[1].]

Ka·pell·meis·ter (kə-pĕl′mī′stər, kä-) *n. Music.* The leader of a choir or an orchestra. [German : *Kapell,* choir (from Medieval Latin *capella;* see CHAPEL) + *Meister,* master; see MEISTERSINGER.]

kaph (käf, kôf) *n.* The 11th letter of the Hebrew alphabet. See table at **alphabet.** [Hebrew *kap,* from *kap,* hand.]

Ka·pi·tsa (kä′pyĭ-tsə), **Pyotr Leonidovich.** 1894–1984. Russian physicist. He shared a 1978 Nobel Prize for his inventions and discoveries concerning low-temperature physics.

ka·pok (kā′pŏk′) *n.* A silky fiber obtained from the fruit of the silk-cotton tree and used for insulation and as padding in pillows, mattresses, and life preservers. [Malay.]

Ka·po·si's sarcoma (kə-pō′sēz, kăp′ə-) *n.* A cancer characterized by numerous bluish-red nodules on the skin, usually on the lower extremities, that is endemic to equatorial Africa and often occurs in a particularly virulent form in people with AIDS. [After Moritz *Kaposi* (1837–1902), Austrian dermatologist.]

kap·pa (kăp′ə) *n.* The tenth letter of the Greek alphabet. See table at **alphabet.** [Greek, of Phoenician origin; akin to Hebrew *kap.*]

Ka·pu·as (kä′po͞o-äs′). A river, about 1,142 km (710 mi) long, of western Borneo, flowing west to the South China Sea.

ka·put also **ka·putt** (kä-po͞ot′, -po͝ot′, kə-) *adj. Informal.* **1.** Having been destroyed; wrecked. **2.** Having been incapacitated. [German *kaputt,* from French *capot,* not having won a single trick at piquet.]

WORD HISTORY: The games people play can become deadly serious, as exemplified by the word *kaput.* Our word is an adoption of the German word *kaputt,* whose senses are similar to those of the English word. German in turn borrowed this word from the French gaming tables, where *capot* as an adjective meant "not having won a single trick at piquet." Devastating as this might be to a piquet player, it would surprise kibitzers to see how widely the word's range of meaning has been extended in German and English, in which it is first recorded in 1895. For example, one's car can be kaput and so can oneself. As for the ultimate source of French *capot* we cannot be certain, but it seems to go back to a modern Provençal word, of which the first element is *cap,* "head."

kar·a·bi·ner (kăr′ə-bē′nər) *n.* Variant of **carabiner.**

Ka·ra·chi (kə-rä′chē). A city of southern Pakistan on the Arabian Sea. Developed as a trading center in the early 18th century, it passed to the British in 1843 and was the capital of newly independent Pakistan from 1947 until 1959. Population, 4,776,000.

Ka·ra·gan·da (kăr′ə-gən-dä′, kə-rə-). A city of central Kazakhstan north-northeast of Tashkent. Founded in 1857 as a copper-mining settlement, it is now the center of a coal industry. Population, 617,000.

Ka·ra·jan (kär′ə-yän′), **Herbert von.** 1908–1989. Austrian conductor. In 1955 he became conductor for life of the Berlin Philharmonic.

Ka·ra·ko·ram Range also **Ka·ra·ko·rum Range** (kăr′-ə-kôr′əm, -kōr′-, kär′-). A mountain system of northern Pakistan and India and southwest China. An extension of the Hindu Kush, it rises to 8,616.3 m (28,250 ft) at K2.

Ka·ra·ko·rum (kăr′ə-kôr′əm, -kōr′-, kär′-). A ruined ancient Mongol city in central Mongolia. Inhabited by Turkic tribes from the first century A.D., it became Genghis Khan's capital c. 1220 but was abandoned by Kublai Khan in 1267.

Karakorum Range. See **Karakoram Range.**

kar·a·kul also **car·a·cul** (kăr′ə-kəl) *n.* **1.** Any of a breed of Central Asian sheep having a wide tail and wool that is curled and glossy in the young but wiry and coarse in the adult. **2.** Fur made from the pelt of a karakul lamb. Also called *broadtail.* [After *Kara Kul,* a lake of southern Central Asian U.S.S.R.]

Ka·ra Kum (kär′ə ko͞om′). A desert region of Turkmenistan between the Caspian Sea and the Amu Darya.

Ka·ra·man·lis (kä′rə-män′lĭs, -rä-män′lēs), **Konstantinos.** Born 1907. Greek politician who served as prime minister (1955–1963 and 1974–1980) and president (1980–1985).

Kara Sea. A section of the Arctic Ocean between Novaya Zemlya and the Siberian mainland. Icebound much of the year, it is connected with the Barents Sea by **Kara Strait.**

kar·at also **car·at** (kăr′ət) *n. Abbr.* **k, kt.** A unit of measure for the fineness of gold, equal to 1/24 part. Pure gold is 24 karat; gold that is 50 percent pure is 12 karat. [Variant of CARAT.]

ka·ra·te (kə-rä′tē) *n.* A Japanese art of self-defense in which sharp blows and kicks are administered to pressure-sensitive points on the body of an opponent. [Japanese : *kara,* empty + *te,* hand.] **—ka·ra′te·ist** *n.*

Kar·ba·la (kär′bə-lə) also **Ker·be·la** (kûr′-). A city of central Iraq south-southwest of Baghdad. It is a pilgrimage site for Shiite Moslems. Population, 184,574.

Ka·re·li·a (kə-rē′lē-ə, -rēl′yə, -ryĕ′lē-yə). A region of northeast Europe mainly in northwest Russia between the Gulf of Finland and the White Sea. First mentioned in the ninth century, the area was annexed by Russia in 1721.

Ka·re·li·an (kə-rē′lē-ən, -rēl′yən) *adj.* Of or relating to Karelia or its people, language, or culture. **—Karelian** *n.* **1.** A native or inhabitant of Karelia. **2.** The Finnic language spoken in Karelia.

Karelian Isthmus. A land bridge of northwest Russia between Lake Ladoga and the Gulf of Finland.

Ka·ren (kə-rĕn′) *n., pl.* **Karen** or **-rens. 1.** A member of a Thai people inhabiting southern and eastern Burma. **2.** Any of the Tibeto-Burman languages of this people.

Karl·feldt (kärl′fĕlt′), **Erik Axel.** 1864–1931. Swedish poet whose works, written in an archaic style, are based on Swedish custom and folklore. He refused the Nobel Prize for literature in 1918 but won it posthumously in 1931.

Karl-Marx-Stadt (kärl-märk′shtät′). Formerly and officially (since April 1990) **Chem·nitz** (kĕm′nĭts). A city of east-central

ă pat	oi boy
ā pay	ou out
âr care	o͝o took
ä father	o͞o boot
ĕ pet	ŭ cut
ē be	ûr urge
ĭ pit	th thin
ī pie	*th* this
îr pier	hw which
ŏ pot	zh vision
ō toe	ə about, item
ô paw	♦ regionalism

Stress marks: ′ (primary); ′ (secondary), as in **dictionary** (dĭk′shə-nĕr′ē)

Germany southeast of Leipzig. Chartered in 1143, it prospered as a textile center after the late 17th century. Population, 318,917.

Kar·loff (kär′lôf′, -lŏf′), **Boris.** 1887–1969. British-born American actor noted for his portrayals of monsters and other evil characters in a number of films, including *Frankenstein* (1931).

Kar·lo·vy Va·ry (kär′lə-vē vär′ē) also **Carls·bad** or **Karls·bad** (kärlz′băd′, kärls′bät′). A city of northwest Czechoslovakia west of Prague. Chartered in the 14th century, it has long been popular as a spa. Population, 58,541.

Karls·ru·he also **Carls·ru·he** (kärlz′ro͞o′ə, kärls′-). A city of southwest Germany on the Rhine River west-northwest of Stuttgart. Founded in 1715, it was badly damaged in World War II. Population, 269,638.

kar·ma (kär′mə) *n.* **1.** *Hinduism & Buddhism.* The total effect of a person's actions and conduct during the successive phases of the person's existence, regarded as determining the person's destiny. **2.** Fate; destiny. **3.** *Informal.* A distinctive aura, atmosphere, or feeling: *There's bad karma around the house today.* [Sanskrit deed, karma. See **kʷer-** in Appendix.] **—kar′mic** (-mĭk) *adj.*

Kar·nak (kär′năk′). A village of east-central Egypt on the right bank of the Nile River on part of the site of ancient Thebes. Its pharaonic remains include the Great Temple of Amen.

Kar·ok (kə-rŏk′) *n., pl.* **Karok** or **-oks. 1.a.** A Native American people inhabiting northwest California, closely related in culture to the Yurok. **b.** A member of this people. **2.** The Hokan language of the Karok.

ka·roo also **kar·roo** (kə-ro͞o′) *n., pl.* **-roos.** An arid plateau of southern Africa. [Afrikaans, from Khoikhoin (Nama) *!garo-b,* desert.]

Ka·roo (kə-ro͞o′). See **Karroo.**

Kar·rer (kär′ər), **Paul.** 1889–1971. Russian-born Swiss chemist. He shared a 1937 Nobel Prize for his research on carotenoids and flavins.

kar·roo (kə-ro͞o′) *n.* Variant of **karoo.**

Kar·roo also **Ka·roo** (kə-ro͞o′). A semiarid plateau region of southwest South Africa. It is divided into the **North Karroo,** along the Orange River; the **Great,** or **Central, Karroo;** and the **Little Karroo,** near the coast.

Kars (kärs). A city of northeast Turkey near the Armenian border. Capital of an Armenian principality in the 9th and 10th centuries, it was destroyed by Tamerlane c. 1386, rebuilt by Ottoman Turks in the 16th century, and ceded to Russia in 1878. It was returned to Turkey in 1921. Population, 58,799.

Kar·sa·vi·na (kär-sä′və-nə), **Tamara.** 1885–1978. Russian ballerina noted for her partnership (1909–1913) with Nijinsky.

karst (kärst) *n.* An area of irregular limestone in which erosion has produced fissures, sinkholes, underground streams, and caverns. [German, after the *Karst,* a limestone plateau near Trieste.] **—karst′ic** *adj.*

kart (kärt) *n. Sports.* A miniature car used in racing. [Probably from *GoKart,* a trademark.]

kart·ing (kär′tĭng) *n. Sports.* The racing of miniature cars.

Ka·run (kə-ro͞on′, kä-). A river of western Iran flowing about 724 km (450 mi) west and south into the Shatt al Arab.

karyo– or **caryo–** *pref.* **1.** Cell nucleus: *karyogamy.* **2.** Nut; kernel: *caryopsis.* [New Latin, from Greek *karuo-,* nut, from *karuon.* See **kar-** in Appendix.]

kar·y·og·a·my (kăr′ē-ŏg′ə-mē) *n., pl.* **-mies.** The coming together and fusing of cell nuclei, as in fertilization.

kar·y·o·ki·ne·sis (kăr′ē-ō-kə-nē′sĭs) *n.* See **mitosis** (sense 1).

kar·y·o·lymph (kăr′ē-ə-lĭmf′) *n.* The colorless, liquid component of the cell nucleus.

kar·y·o·plasm (kăr′ē-ə-plăz′əm) *n.* See **nucleoplasm.**

kar·y·o·some (kăr′ē-ə-sōm′) *n.* An irregular aggregation of chromatin in the nucleus of a cell not undergoing mitosis. Also called *net knot.*

kar·y·o·type (kăr′ē-ə-tīp′) *n.* **1.** The characterization of the chromosomal complement of an individual or a species, including number, form, and size of the chromosomes. **2.** A photomicrograph of chromosomes arranged according to a standard classification. **—karyotype** *tr.v.* **-typed, -typ·ing, -types.** To classify and array (the chromosome complement of an organism or a species) according to the arrangement, number, size, shape, or other characteristics of the chromosomes. **—kar′y·o·typ′ic** (-tĭp′ĭk), **kar′y·o·typ′i·cal** *adj.*

Ka·sai (kə-sī′). A river of northeast Angola and western Zaire flowing about 1,931 km (1,200 mi) into the Congo River on the Zaire-Congo border.

Kas·bah (kăz′bä′, käz′-) *n.* Variant of **Casbah.**

ka·sha (kä′shə) *n.* Buckwheat groats. [Russian, from Old Russian.]

ka·sher (kä′shər) *adj. & v.* Variant of **kosher.**

Kash·mir also **Cash·mere** (kăsh′mîr′, kăsh-mîr′). A historical region of northwest India and northeast Pakistan. Conquered by Moslems in the 14th century, it was part of the Mogul empire after 1587 and became an independent kingdom in 1751. The British pacified the region in 1846 and installed a Hindu dynasty, which was overthrown by a Moslem revolt in 1947. Continued fighting in the area led to United Nations intervention (1949 and 1965) and the current partition of the region between India and Pakistan.

Kashmir goat *n.* Variant of **Cashmere goat.**

Kash·mir·i (kăsh-mîr′ē, kăzh-) *n., pl.* **Kashmiri** or **-is. 1.** A native or inhabitant of Kashmir. **2.** A Dardic language of Jammu and Kashmir.

kash·rut also **kash·ruth** (käsh′rəth, -rəs, käsh-ro͞ot′) *n.* **1.** The state of being kosher. **2.** The body of Jewish dietary law. [Hebrew *kašrût,* from *kāšēr,* fitting.]

Kas·kas·ki·a (kəs-kăs′kē-ə) *n., pl.* **Kaskaskia** or **-as. 1.** A Native American people forming part of the Illinois confederacy. **2.** A member of this people.

Kaskaskia River. A river, about 483 km (300 mi) long, rising in east-central Illinois and flowing southwest to the Mississippi.

Kas·sel also **Cas·sel** (kăs′əl, kä′səl). A city of central Germany south-southwest of Hanover. Chartered in 1198, it was a munitions center in World War II. Population, 184,997.

Kast·ler (käst′lər), **Alfred.** 1902–1984. French physicist. He won a 1966 Nobel Prize for research on the interior energy of atoms.

kat·a·bat·ic (kăt′ə-băt′ĭk) *adj.* Of or relating to a cold flow of air traveling downward: *a katabatic wind.* [Greek *katabatikos,* pertaining to descent, from *katabatos,* descending : *kata-,* cata- + *batos,* going; see **gʷā-** in Appendix.]

Ka·tah·din (kə-täd′n), **Mount.** A mountain, 1,606.7 m (5,268 ft) high, of north-central Maine. It is the highest elevation in the state and the northern terminus of the Appalachian Trail.

ka·ta·ka·na (kä′tä-kä′nä) *n.* A relatively angular kana used for writing foreign words or official documents, such as telegrams. [Japanese : *kata,* one + *kana,* kana; see KANA.]

Ka·tan·ga (kə-täng′gə, -tăng′-). See **Shaba. —Kat′an·gese′** (kăt′ăng-gēz′, -gēs′, -ăng-) *adj. & n.*

Ka·tha·rev·u·sa (kä′thä-rĕv′o͞o-sä′) *n.* The puristic, archaizing form of Modern Greek, which contains morphological and lexical features borrowed from Koine. [Modern Greek *kathareuousa,* from Greek, feminine present participle of *kathareuein,* to be pure, from *katharos,* pure.]

Ka·thi·a·war (kä′tē-ə-wär′). A peninsula of western India projecting into the Arabian Sea between the Gulfs of Kutch and Cambay.

Kath·man·du (kăt′măn-do͞o′, kät′män-). See **Katmandu.**

Kat·mai (kăt′mī′), **Mount.** An active volcano, about 2,048 m (6,715 ft) high, in the Aleutian Range of southern Alaska at the eastern end of the Alaska Peninsula. It is located in a national monument that includes the Valley of the Ten Thousand Smokes.

Kat·man·du also **Kath·man·du** (kăt′măn-do͞o′, kät′män-). The capital and largest city of Nepal, in the central part of the country in the eastern Himalaya Mountains. It was founded c. 723 and was a Gurkha capital from 1768 until the late 18th century. Population, 235,160.

Ka·to·wi·ce (kä′tə-vēt′sə, -tô-vē′tsĕ). A city of southern Poland west-northwest of Cracow. Chartered in 1865, it is an important mining and industrial center. Population, 363,300.

Kat·te·gat (kăt′ĭ-găt′). A strait of the North Sea between southwest Sweden and eastern Jutland, Denmark. It connects with the North Sea through the Skagerrak.

ka·ty·did (kā′tē-dĭd′) *n.* Any of various green insects of the family Tettigoniidae related to the grasshoppers and the crickets, the male of which produces a shrill sound by rubbing together specialized organs on the forewings. [Imitative of its sound.]

katz·en·jam·mer (kăt′sən-jăm′ər) *n.* **1.** A loud, discordant noise. **2.** A hangover. **3.** A state of depression or bewilderment. [German, hangover : *Katzen,* pl. of *Katze,* cat (from Middle High German *katze,* from Old High German *kazza*; akin to Old English *catt;* see CAT) + *Jammer,* wailing (from Middle High German *jāmer,* from Old High German *jāmar,* misery).]

Kau·ai (kou′ī′, kou-ī′). An island of Hawaii northwest of Oahu. It was an independent royal domain when visited by Capt. James Cook in 1778 and became part of the kingdom of Hawaii in 1810.

Kauff·mann (kouf′män), **Angelica.** 1741–1807. Swiss-born artist known for her historical and allegorical paintings and her portraits of contemporaries.

Kauf·man (kôf′mən), **George Simon.** 1889–1961. American playwright noted for his many collaborations, including *You Can't Take It with You* (1936) with Moss Hart.

Kau·nas (kou′nəs, -näs). A city of central Lithuania on the Neman River northwest of Vilnius. Founded in the 11th century, it was a medieval trading post and a Lithuanian stronghold against the Teutonic Knights. Russia acquired the city in the third partition of Poland (1795). Population, 405,000.

Ka·un·da (kä-o͝on′də), **Kenneth David.** Born 1924. President of Zambia (since 1964). He led Northern Rhodesia to full independence as Zambia (1964).

kau·ri (kou′rē) *n., pl.* **-ris. 1.** Any of several coniferous evergreen trees of the genus *Agathis,* especially *A. australis* of New Zealand, having broad leathery leaves. **2.** The white, close-grained wood of one of these trees. **3.** A resinous copal or a fossilized resin of these trees, used in varnishes and enamels. [Maori *kawri.*]

ka·va (kä′və) *n.* **1.** A dioecious shrub *(Piper methysticum)* native to the Pacific islands, having cordate leaves and minute flow-

Boris Karloff
Top: Photographic portrait
Bottom: As Frankenstein's monster

katydid

Kenneth Kaunda
Photographed in 1984

kayak

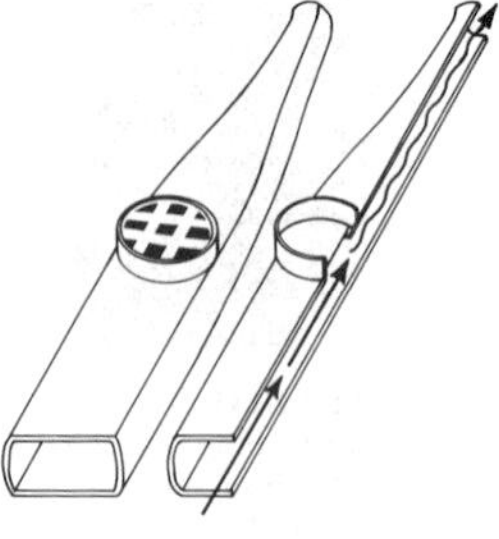
kazoo
Kazoo (*left*) and cross section (*right*) showing airflow through the tube

Buster Keaton
In character for *The General,* 1926

ers clustered in solitary spikes. **2.** The narcotic beverage made from the roots of this plant. [Tongan, acrid, kava.]

Kaw (kô) *n., pl.* **Kaw** or **Kaws.** See **Kansa.**

Ka·wa·ba·ta (kä′wə-bä′tə), **Yasunari.** 1899–1972. Japanese writer whose novels, including *Thousand Cranes* (1959), often concern alienated, lonely individuals in search of beauty and purity. He won the 1968 Nobel Prize for literature.

Ka·wa·gu·chi (kä′wə-go͞o′chē). A city of east-central Honshu, Japan, an industrial suburb of Tokyo. Population, 403,012.

Ka·wa·sa·ki (kä′wə-sä′kē). A city of east-central Honshu, Japan, an industrial suburb of Tokyo on Tokyo Bay. Population, 1,088,611.

Kaw River. See **Kansas River.**

kay (kā) *n.* The letter *k.*

Kay (kā) *n.* In Arthurian legend, the foster brother and steward of King Arthur.

kay·ak also **kai·ak** (kī′ăk′) —*n.* **1.** A watertight Eskimo canoe consisting of a light wooden frame completely covered with skins except for a single or double opening in the center and propelled by a double-bladed paddle. **2.** A lightweight canoe that is similar in construction. —*v.* **-aked, -ak·ing, -aks.** —*intr.* To go, travel, or race in a kayak. —*tr.* To go or travel on (a body of water) by kayak: *kayaked rapids of the Colorado River.* [Canadian and Greenlandic Eskimo *qajaq.*] —**kay′ak′er** *n.*

♦ **Kay·beck·er** (kā-bĕk′ər) *n. Maine.* A French-speaking Canadian lumberjack working in the United States. [From French *québecois,* Québecois. See QUÉBECOIS.]

kay·o (kā-ō′, kā′ō′) *n., pl.* **-os.** *Sports.* A knockout in boxing. —**kayo** *tr.v.* **-oed, -o·ing, -os. 1.** *Sports.* To knock out. **2.** *Slang.* To put out of commission. [Pronunciation of *K.O.,* abbreviation of *knock out.*]

Kay·se·ri (kī′zə-rē′, -sə-). A city of central Turkey southeast of Ankara. The modern city was founded in the fourth century A.D. Population, 281,320.

Ka·zakh also **Ka·zak** (kə-zăk′, -zäk′) *n., pl.* **Kazakh** or **-zakhs** also **Kazak** or **-zaks. 1.** A member of a pastoral Moslem people inhabiting Kazakhstan and parts of Xinjiang Uygur in China. **2.** The Turkic language of this people. [Russian *kazakh,* from Kazakh *qazaq,* from Old Turkic **qazhaq,* a profiteer, from *qazqhanmaq,* to acquire, from *qazmaq,* to dig out.]

Ka·zakh·stan (kə-zăk′stăn′, -zŭkн-stän′). A region south of Russia and northeast of the Caspian Sea. The original Turkic inhabitants were overrun by the Mongols in the 13th century and ruled by various khanates until the Russian conquest of 1730 to 1853. The region was organized as an autonomous republic in 1920 and became a constituent republic in 1936. Alma-Ata is the capital. Population, 15,842,000.

Ka·zan (kə-zăn′, -zän′). A city of west-central Russia on the Volga River east of Moscow. Founded in 1401, the modern city became the capital of a powerful Tartar khanate in 1455 but was conquered by Czar Ivan IV in 1552. Population, 1,047,000.

Ka·zan River (kə-zăn′). A river, about 732 km (455 mi) long, of southeast Northwest Territories, Canada, flowing north-northeast through a series of lakes to Baker Lake.

Ka·zan·tza·kis (kä′zən-zä′kĭs, -zän-dzä′kēs), **Nikos.** 1885–1957. Greek writer whose works, including the novel *Zorba the Greek* (1946), often contrast the sensual and intellectual facets of human nature.

Kaz·bek (käz-bĕk′), **Mount.** An extinct volcano, 5,042.3 m (16,532 ft) high, of northern Georgia in the central Caucasus. It is the subject of many legends.

ka·zoo (kə-zo͞o′) *n., pl.* **-zoos.** *Music.* A toy instrument with a membrane that produces a sound when a player hums or sings into the mouthpiece. [Perhaps imitative of its sound.]

Kaz·vin (kăz-vēn′). See **Qazvin.**

kb or **Kb** *abbr.* Kilobar.

KB *abbr.* **1.** *Computer Science.* Kilobyte. **2.** *Games.* King's bishop.

kc *abbr.* **1.** Also **kC.** Kilocurie. **2.** Kilocycle.

K.C. *abbr.* **1.** King's Counsel. **2.** Knight of Columbus.

kcal *abbr.* Kilocalorie.

kcl *abbr.* Kilocalorie.

KD *abbr.* **1.** Kiln-dried. **2.** Knocked down.

ke·a (kē′ə) *n.* A brownish-green mountain-dwelling New Zealand parrot *(Nestor notabilis)* that usually eats insects but sometimes feeds on carrion and rubbish. [Maori, perhaps imitative of its call.]

Ke·a·la·ke·ku·a Bay (kā-ä′lə-kə-ko͞o′ə). An inlet of the Pacific Ocean on the western coast of Hawaii Island. Capt. James Cook landed here (January 1779) during his second voyage to the islands and was killed (February 14) during a beach fight with the islanders.

Kean (kēn), **Edmund.** 1789?–1833. British actor known for his portrayals of Shakespeare's great tragic characters.

Kear·ney (kär′nē). A city of south-central Nebraska on the Platte River west-southwest of Grand Island. It is a trade and industrial center in an agricultural region. Population, 21,158.

Kear·ny (kär′nē). A town of northeast New Jersey on the Passaic River opposite Newark. It is a port and an industrial center. Population, 35,735.

Kea·ton (kēt′n), **Buster.** 1895–1966. American actor who wrote, directed, and starred in silent film classics, such as *The General* (1926), in which he employed a deadpan expression and acrobatic artistry to great comedic effect.

Keats (kēts), **John.** 1795–1821. British poet considered among the greatest in English. His works, melodic and rich in classical imagery, include "The Eve of St. Agnes," "Ode on a Grecian Urn," and "To Autumn" (all 1819). —**Keats′i·an** *adj.*

ke·bab or **ke·bob** also **ka·bob** (kə-bŏb′) *n.* Shish kebab.

Ke·ble (kē′bəl), **John.** 1792–1866. British cleric and poet whose sermon "National Apostasy" (1833) initiated the Oxford Movement, an effort to reintroduce doctrines that the Church of England had discarded or neglected since the Reformation.

ke·bob (kə-bŏb′) *n.* Variant of **kebab.**

Kech·ua (kĕch′wə, -wä′) *n.* Variant of **Quechua.**

Kecs·ke·mét (kĕch′kĕ-māt′). A city of central Hungary southeast of Budapest. Known since the fourth century A.D., it is a manufacturing center. Population, 81,300.

kedge (kĕj) *Nautical. n.* A light anchor used for warping a vessel. —**kedge** *v.* **kedged, kedg·ing, kedg·es.** —*tr.* To warp (a vessel) by means of a light anchor. —*intr.* To move by means of a light anchor. [From *kedge,* to warp a vessel, perhaps from Middle English *caggen,* to tie, perhaps of Scandinavian origin.]

kedg·er·ee (kĕj′ə-rē′, kĕj′ə-rē′) *n.* A dish consisting of flaked fish, boiled rice, and eggs. [Hindi *khichṛī,* from Sanskrit *khiccā.*]

keek (kēk) *Scots. intr.v.* **keeked, keek·ing, keeks.** To peek; peep. —**keek** *n.* A look, especially a quick one; a peek. [Middle English *kiken, keken,* perhaps from Middle Dutch *kiken.*]

keel[1] (kēl) *n.* **1.** *Nautical.* **a.** The principal structural member of a ship, running lengthwise along the center line from bow to stern, to which the frames are attached. **b.** A ship. **2.** A structure, such as the breastbone of a bird, that resembles a ship's keel in function or shape. **3.** The principal structural member of an aircraft, resembling a ship's keel in shape and function. **4.** A pair of united petals in certain flowers, as those of the pea. —**keel** *intr. & tr.v.* **keeled, keel·ing, keels.** *Nautical.* To capsize or cause to capsize. —***phrasal verb.* keel over.** To collapse or fall into or as if into a faint. [Middle English *kele,* from Old Norse *kjölr.*]

keel[2] (kēl) *n.* **1.** *Nautical.* **a.** A freight barge, especially one for carrying coal on the Tyne River in England. **b.** The load capacity of this barge. **2.** A British unit of weight formerly used for coal, equal to about 21.2 long tons. [Middle English *kele,* from Middle Dutch *kiel.*]

keel[3] (kēl) *tr.v.* **keeled, keel·ing, keels.** *Chiefly British.* To make cool. [Middle English *kelen,* from Old English *cēlan,* to cool. See **gel-** in Appendix.]

keel·boat (kēl′bōt′) *n. Nautical.* A riverboat with a keel but without sails, used for carrying freight.

keel·haul (kēl′hôl′) *tr.v.* **-hauled, -haul·ing, -hauls. 1.** *Nautical.* To discipline by dragging under the keel of a ship. **2.** To rebuke harshly. [Alteration (influenced by KEEL[1] and HAUL) of Dutch *kielhalen* : *kiel,* keel of a ship (from Middle Dutch) + *halen,* to haul (from Middle Dutch); see **kele-**[2] in Appendix.]

Kee·ling Islands (kē′lĭng). See **Cocos Islands.**

keel·son (kĕl′sən, kēl′-) also **kel·son** (kĕl′-) *n. Nautical.* A timber or girder fastened above and parallel to the keel of a ship or boat for additional strength. [Alteration (influenced by KEEL[1]) of Middle English *kelswin,* probably from Old Norse **kjölsvīn* : *kjölr,* keel + *svīn,* swine, timber; see **sū-** in Appendix.]

Kee·lung (kē′lo͝ong′) also **Chi·lung** (jē′-, chē′-). A city of northern Taiwan on the East China Sea. It is a port for the capital city of Taipei. Population, 349,686.

keen[1] (kēn) *adj.* **keen·er, keen·est. 1.** Having a fine, sharp cutting edge or point. **2.** Having or marked by intellectual quickness and acuity. See Synonyms at **sharp. 3.** Acutely sensitive: *a keen ear.* **4.** Sharp; vivid; strong: *"His entire body hungered for keen sensation, something exciting"* (Richard Wright). **5.** Intense; piercing: *a keen wind.* **6.** Pungent; acrid: *A keen smell of skunk was left behind.* **7. a.** Ardent; enthusiastic: *a keen chess player.* **b.** Eagerly desirous: *keen on going to Europe in the spring.* See Synonyms at **eager**[1]. **8.** *Slang.* Great; splendid; fine: *What a keen day!* [Middle English *kene,* from Old English *cēne,* brave.] —**keen′ly** *adv.* —**keen′ness** *n.*

keen[2] (kēn) *n.* A loud, wailing lament for the dead. —**keen** *intr.v.* **keened, keen·ing, keens.** To wail in lamentation, especially for the dead. See Synonyms at **cry.** [From Irish Gaelic *caoineadh,* from *caoninim,* I lament, from Old Irish *coínim.*] —**keen′er** *n.*

Keene (kēn). A city of southwest New Hampshire west of Manchester. It was first settled in 1736. Population, 21,449.

keep (kēp) *v.* **kept** (kĕpt), **keep·ing, keeps.** —*tr.* **1.** To retain possession of: *kept the change; must keep your equanimity.* **2.** To have as a supply: *keep a cord of wood in the shed.* **3.** To provide (a family, for example) with maintenance and support: *"There's little to earn and many to keep"* (Charles Kingsley). **4.** To put customarily; store: *Where do you keep your saw?* **5. a.** To supply with room and board for a charge: *keep boarders.* **b.** To raise: *keep chickens.* **6.** To maintain for use or service: *a city dweller who didn't keep a car.* **7.** To manage, tend, or have charge of: *Keep the shop while I'm away.* **8.** To preserve (food). **9.** To cause to continue in a state, condition, or course of action:

attempted to keep the patient calm. **10.a.** To maintain records in: *keep a yearly diary.* **b.** To enter (data) in a book: *keep financial records.* **11.a.** To detain: *was kept after school.* **b.** To restrain: *kept the child away from the hot stove; kept the crowd back with barriers.* **c.** To prevent or deter: *tried to keep the ice from melting.* **d.** To refrain from divulging: *keep a secret.* **e.** To save; reserve: *keep extra money for emergencies.* **12.** To maintain: *keep late hours.* **13.** To adhere to; fulfill: *keep one's word; keep a busy schedule.* **14.** To celebrate; observe. —*intr.* **1.** To remain in a state or condition; stay: *keep in line; keep quiet; kept well.* **2.** To continue to do: *keep on talking; keep guessing.* **3.** To remain fresh or unspoiled: *The dessert won't keep.* **—keep** *n.* **1.** Care; charge: *The child is in my keep for the day.* **2.** The means by which one is supported: *earn one's keep.* **3.a.** The stronghold of a castle. **b.** A jail. **—*phrasal verbs.* keep at.** To persevere in work or an action. **keep down.** To prevent from growing, accomplishing, or succeeding: *keep down prices; keep the revolutionaries down.* **keep off.** To stay away from. **keep to.** To adhere to: *keep to the original purpose.* **keep up. 1.** To maintain in good condition: *kept up the property.* **2.** To persevere in; carry on: *We asked her to stop talking, but she kept up.* **3.** To continue at the same level or pace. **4.** To match one's competitors, colleagues, or neighbors in success or lifestyle: *unsuccessfully tried to keep up with his associates.* **—*idioms.* for keeps. 1.** For an indefinitely long period: *gave the ring to me for keeps.* **2.** Seriously and permanently: *We're separating for keeps.* **keep an eye out.** To be watchful. **keep company.** To carry on a courtship: *a couple who kept company but never married.* **keep (one's) chin up.** To be stalwart, courageous, or optimistic in the face of difficulty. **keep (one's) eyes open** (or **peeled**). To be on the lookout. **keep (one's) nose clean.** *Informal.* To stay out of trouble. **keep pace.** To stay even with others, as in a contest. **keep (someone) company.** To accompany or remain with. **keep time.** To indicate the correct time. *Music.* To maintain the tempo or rhythm. **keep to (oneself). 1.** To shun the company of others: *She kept to herself all morning.* **2.** To refrain from divulging: *He kept the news to himself.* [Middle English *kepen,* from Old English *cēpan,* to observe, seize.]

SYNONYMS: *keep, retain, withhold, reserve.* These verbs mean to have and maintain in one's possession or control. *Keep* is the most general: *We received a tempting offer for the house but decided to keep it. I don't know which is more difficult—to earn money or to keep it. Retain* means to continue to hold, especially in the face of possible loss: *"The executor . . . is allowed to pay himself first, by retaining in his hands so much as his debt amounts to"* (William Blackstone). *Withhold* implies reluctance or refusal to give, grant, or allow: *The tenants withheld their rent until the landlord repaired the boiler.* To *reserve* is to hold back for the future or for a special purpose: *I will reserve my questions for the discussion period. The farmer reserved two acres for an orchard.* See also Synonyms at **livelihood, observe.**

keep·er (kē′pər) *n.* **1.** One that keeps, especially: **a.** An attendant, a guard, or a warden. **b.** One that has the charge or care of something: *a lion keeper; the keeper of the budget.* **2.** *Football.* A play made by the quarterback who keeps the ball after it is snapped and then runs with it. **3.** *Informal.* One that is worth keeping, especially a fish large enough to be legally caught.

keep·ing (kē′pĭng) *n.* **1.** The act of holding, guarding, or supporting. **2.** Custody; care. See Synonyms at **care. 3.** Harmony; conformity: *"A facade had been added, in perfect keeping with* [the] *original architecture"* (Nancy Holmes).

keep·sake (kēp′sāk′) *n.* Something given or kept; a memento.

kees·hond (kās′hônt′, -hŏnd′) *n., pl.* **-hon·den** (-hôn′dən) or **-honds.** Any of a breed of dog originating in the Netherlands and having a thick grayish-black coat. [Dutch : probably the name *Kees* (nickname for *Cornelis,* Cornelius) + *hond,* dog (from Middle Dutch; see **kwon-** in Appendix).]

Kee·wa·tin (kē-wāt′n). A region of southeast Northwest Territories, Canada. It includes the eastern section of the mainland and various islands in Hudson Bay.

kef (kĕf, kēf, kāf) *n.* Variant of **kif.**

Ke·fal·li·ní·a (kĕ′fä-lē-nē′ä). See **Cephalonia.**

Ke·fau·ver (kē′fô′vər), **(Carey) Estes.** 1903–1963. American politician. A U.S. representative (1939–1949) and senator (1949–1963) from Tennessee, he directed a highly publicized investigation into organized crime (1950–1951).

ke·fir (kĕ-fîr′) *n.* A creamy drink made of fermented cow's milk. [Russian, probably ultimately from Old Turkic *köpür,* (milk) froth, foam, from *köpürmäk,* to froth, foam.]

Kef·la·vík (kyĕb′lə-vēk′, kĕf′-). A town of southwest Iceland west-southwest of Reykjavík. Its international airport was built by the U.S. military during World War II. Population, 6,907.

keg (kĕg) *n.* **1.a.** A small cask or barrel with a capacity of about 30 gallons (114 liters). **b.** Such a container and its contents. **2.** A unit of weight used for nails, equal to 100 pounds (45.5 kilograms). **—keg** *tr.v.* **kegged, keg·ging, kegs.** To put or store in a small cask or barrel. [Middle English *kag,* from Old Norse *kaggi.*]

keg·ler (kĕg′lər) *n.* *Sports.* A person who bowls; a bowler. [German, from *kegeln,* to bowl, from *Kegel,* bowling pin, from Middle High German *kegel,* from Old High German *kegil,* peg.]

keis·ter (kē′stər) *n.* *Slang.* **1.** The buttocks. **2.** The anus. [Origin unknown.]

Kei·tel (kīt′l), **Wilhelm.** 1882–1946. German general and chief of the supreme command of Nazi forces during World War II.

Kel·ler (kĕl′ər), **Helen Adams.** 1880–1968. American memoirist and lecturer. Blind and deaf since infancy, she learned to read, write, and speak from her teacher Anne Sullivan, was graduated from Radcliffe (1904), and lectured widely on behalf of sightless people. Her books include *Out of the Dark* (1913).

Helen Keller
Photographed in the 1950's

Kel·logg (kĕl′ôg′, -ŏg′), **Frank Billings.** 1856–1937. American public official who as U.S. secretary of state (1925–1929) co-sponsored the Kellogg-Briand Pact (1928), ratified by 62 nations, that renounced war as an instrument of national policy. For this he won the 1929 Nobel Peace Prize.

Kel·ly (kĕl′ē), **Emmett.** 1898–1979. American clown who was famous as "Weary Willie," a sad-faced hobo with the Ringling Brothers and Barnum & Bailey Circus (1942–1956).

Kelly, Grace Patricia. Princess Grace. 1929–1982. American actress whose motion pictures include *High Noon* (1952) and *Country Girl* (1954), for which she won an Academy Award. In 1956 she married Prince Rainier III of Monaco.

kel·ly green (kĕl′ē) *n.* *Color.* A strong yellowish green. [From the name *Kelly.*] **—kel′ly-green′** (kĕl′ē-grēn′) *adj.*

ke·loid also **che·loid** (kē′loid′) *n.* A red, raised formation of fibrous scar tissue caused by excessive tissue repair in response to trauma or surgical incision. [French *kéloïde* : Greek *khēlē,* claw + *-oïde,* resembling (from Greek *-oeidēs;* see -OID).] **—ke·loid′al** (-loid′l) *adj.*

Ke·low·na (kə-lō′nə). A city of southern British Columbia, Canada, on Okanagan Lake east-northeast of Vancouver. It is a tourist resort and trade center. Population, 59,196.

kelp (kĕlp) *n.* **1.** Any of various brown, often very large seaweeds of the order Laminariales. **2.** The ash of these seaweeds, used as a source of potash and iodine. [Middle English *culp.*]

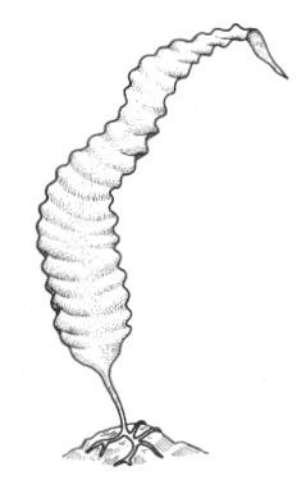
kelp
Common southern kelp
Laminaria agardhii

kel·pie¹ also **kel·py** (kĕl′pē) *n., pl.* **-pies.** A malevolent water spirit of Scottish legend, usually having the shape of a horse and rejoicing in or causing drownings. [Probably of Celtic origin; akin to Scottish Gaelic *colpach,* heifer.]

kel·pie² (kĕl′pē) *n.* Any of a breed of sheepdog originating in Australia. [From *Kelpie,* the name of an early specimen of the breed.]

kel·py (kĕl′pē) *n.* Variant of **kelpie¹.**

kel·son (kĕl′sən) *n.* *Nautical.* Variant of **keelson.**

Kelt (kĕlt) *n.* Variant of **Celt.**

Kelt·ic (kĕl′tĭk) *n. & adj.* Variant of **Celtic.**

kel·vin (kĕl′vĭn) *n.* *Abbr.* **K** A unit of absolute temperature equal to 1/273.16 of the absolute temperature of the triple point of water. This unit is equal to one Celsius degree. See table at **measurement.** [After First Baron KELVIN.]

Kel·vin (kĕl′vĭn), First Baron. Title of William Thomson. 1824–1907. British physicist who developed the Kelvin scale of temperature (1848).

Kelvin scale *n.* An absolute scale of temperature in which each degree equals one kelvin. Water freezes at 273.15 K and boils at 373.15 K.

Ke·mal At·a·türk (kə-mäl′ ăt′ə-tûrk′, kĕ-mäl′ ä-tä-türk′). Originally Mustafa Kemal. 1881–1938. Turkish national leader and founder of modern Turkey. In 1919 he organized the Turkish Nationalist Party and established a rival government to the Ottoman sultan. After a civil war he served as president of the Turkish Republic (1923–1938).

Ke·me·ro·vo (kĕm′ə-rō′və, kyĕ′mər-ə-və). A city of south-central Russia east-northeast of Novosibirsk. It is an industrial center in a coal-mining region. Population, 507,000.

kendo
World Championships, 1985

Kem·pis (kĕm′pĭs), **Thomas à.** See **Thomas à Kempis.**

kempt (kĕmpt) *adj.* Tidy; trim: *a nicely kempt beard.* [Back-formation from UNKEMPT.]

ken (kĕn) *n.* **1.** Perception; understanding: *complex issues well beyond our ken.* **2.a.** Range of vision. **b.** View; sight. **—ken** *v.* **kenned** or **kent** (kĕnt), **ken·ning, kens.** *Scots.* —*tr.* **1.** To know (a person or thing). **2.** To recognize. —*intr.* To have knowledge or an understanding of. [From Middle English *kennen* (influenced by Old Norse *kenna,* to know), from Old English *cennan,* to declare. See **gnō-** in Appendix.]

Ken. *abbr.* Kentucky.

Ke·nai Peninsula (kē′nī′). A peninsula of south-central Alaska between Cook Inlet and the Gulf of Alaska.

Ken·dal green (kĕn′dl) *n.* **1.** A coarse green woolen fabric similar to tweed. **2.** The color of this fabric. [After *Kendal,* a municipal borough of northwest England.]

Ken·dall (kĕn′dl). A community of southeast Florida, a suburb of Miami. Population, 51,000.

ken·do (kĕn′dō) *n.* The Japanese martial art of fencing with bamboo sticks. [Japanese.]

Ken·drew (kĕn′drōō′), Sir **John Cowdery.** Born 1917. British biologist. He shared the 1962 Nobel Prize for chemistry for determining the molecular structure of blood components.

Ken·il·worth (kĕn′əl-wûrth′). An urban district of central England southeast of Birmingham. It is famous for the ruins of Kenilworth Castle, founded c. 1120 and celebrated in Sir Walter Scott's novel *Kenilworth* (1821). Population, 19,315.

Kenilworth ivy *n.* A European creeping herb *(Cymbalaria*

ă pat	oi boy
ā pay	ou out
âr care	ŏŏ took
ä father	ōō boot
ĕ pet	ŭ cut
ē be	ûr urge
ĭ pit	th thin
ī pie	*th* this
îr pier	hw which
ŏ pot	zh vision
ō toe	ə about, item
ô paw	♦ regionalism

Stress marks: **′** (primary); ′ (secondary), as in **dictionary** (dĭk′shə-nĕr′ē)

Jacqueline Kennedy
Photographed January 20, 1961, after the inauguration

John F. Kennedy

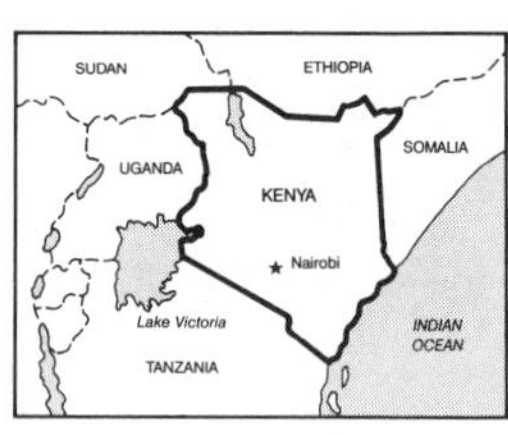

Kenya

kepi

muralis) with palmately lobed leaves and solitary, pale purple flowers. [After *Kenilworth* Castle, Kenilworth.]

Ken·more (kĕn′môr′, -mōr′). A village of western New York on the Niagara River north of Buffalo. It is mainly residential. Population, 18,474.

Ken·nan (kĕn′ən), **George Frost.** Born 1904. American diplomat and historian who recommended the policy of containment toward Soviet aggression. He served as U.S. ambassador to the U.S.S.R. (1952) and Yugoslavia (1961–1963).

Ken·ne·bec (kĕn′ə-bĕk′). A river, about 257 km (160 mi) long, of west-central and southern Maine flowing generally south to the Atlantic Ocean.

Ken·ne·dy (kĕn′ĭ-dē), **Anthony M.** Born 1936. American jurist who was appointed an associate justice of the U.S. Supreme Court in 1988.

Kennedy, Cape. See Cape **Canaveral.**

Kennedy, Edward Moore. Born 1932. American politician. A U.S. senator from Massachusetts (since 1962), he has sponsored national health insurance legislation and been a long-time leader of the Democratic Party.

Kennedy, Jacqueline Lee Bouvier. Former name of Jacqueline Kennedy Onassis. Born 1929. First Lady of the United States (1961–1963) as the wife of President John F. Kennedy. She promoted the arts and supervised the redecoration of the White House. Since 1975 she has worked as an editor in New York.

Kennedy, John Fitzgerald. 1917–1963. The 35th President of the United States (1961–1963). A U.S. representative (1947–1953) and senator (1953–1960) from Massachusetts, he became the youngest man elected to the presidency (1960). Kennedy approved the failed invasion of the Bay of Pigs (1961) and forced Khrushchev to remove Soviet missiles from Cuba (1962). He also established the Peace Corps (1961). Kennedy was assassinated in Dallas, Texas, on November 22, 1963.

Kennedy, Joseph Patrick. 1888–1969. American banker and industrialist who served as ambassador to Great Britain (1937–1940). With his wife, **Rose Fitzgerald Kennedy** (born 1890), he raised nine children, three of whom became prominent politicians.

Kennedy, Robert Francis. 1925–1968. American politician who served as U.S. attorney general (1961–1964) during the presidency of his brother John F. Kennedy. He was elected to the Senate (1964) and was campaigning for the presidency when he was assassinated in Los Angeles.

ken·nel[1] (kĕn′əl) *n.* **1.** A shelter for a dog. **2.** A pack of dogs, especially hounds. See Synonyms at **flock**[1]. **3.** An establishment where dogs are bred, trained, or boarded. **4.** The lair of a wild animal, such as a fox. **—kennel** *v.* **-neled, -nel·ing, -nels** or **-nelled, -nel·ling, -nels.** *—tr.* To place or keep in or as if in a kennel. *—intr.* To take cover or lie in or as if in a kennel. [Middle English *kenel,* from Anglo-Norman **kenil,* from Vulgar Latin **canīle,* from Latin *canis,* dog. See **kwon-** in Appendix.]

ken·nel[2] (kĕn′əl) *n.* A gutter along a street. [Middle English *cannel,* from Old North French *canel,* channel, from Latin *canālis.* See CANAL.]

Ken·nel·ly (kĕn′ə-lē), **Arthur Edwin.** 1861–1939. American electrical engineer who concurrently with Oliver Heaviside predicted the existence of the ionosphere.

Ken·nel·ly-Heav·i·side layer (kĕn′ə-lē-hĕv′ē-sīd′) *n.* See **E layer.** [After Arthur Edwin KENNELLY and Oliver HEAVISIDE.]

Ken·ner (kĕn′ər). A city of southeast Louisiana, an industrial suburb of New Orleans on the Mississippi River. Population, 66,382.

Ken·ne·wick (kĕn′ə-wĭk′). A city of southern Washington on the Columbia River west-northwest of Walla Walla. The Hanford Works, a nuclear plant built during World War II, is nearby. Population, 34,397.

ken·ning (kĕn′ĭng) *n.* A figurative, usually compound expression used in place of a name or noun, especially in Old English and Old Norse poetry; for example, *storm of swords* is a kenning for *battle.* [Old Norse, from *kenna,* to know, to name with a kenning. See **gnō-** in Appendix.]

Ken·ny (kĕn′ē), **Elizabeth.** 1880?–1952. Australian nurse who developed a simple treatment for the paralysis brought on by poliomyelitis.

ke·no (kē′nō) *n. Games.* A game of chance, similar to lotto, that uses balls rather than counters. [French *quine,* set of five winning numbers (from Latin *quīnī,* five each; see **penkʷe** in Appendix) + *-o* (as in LOTTO).]

Ke·no·sha (kə-nō′shə). A city of extreme southeast Wisconsin on Lake Michigan south of Milwaukee. Founded in 1835, it is an industrial center and a port of entry. Population, 77,685.

ke·no·sis (kĭ-nō′sĭs) *n. Theology.* The relinquishment of the form of God by Jesus in becoming man and suffering death. [Late Greek *kenōsis,* from Greek, an emptying, from *kenoun,* to empty, from *kenos,* empty.] **—ke·not′ic** (-nŏt′ĭk) *adj.*

kent (kĕnt) *v. Scots.* A past tense and a past participle of **ken.**

Kent (kĕnt). **1.** A region and former kingdom of southeast England. Jutes settled in the area in the fifth century A.D., displacing the original inhabitants and establishing one of the seven kingdoms of the Anglo-Saxon Heptarchy. **2.** A city of northeast Ohio east-northeast of Akron. Kent State University (founded 1910) is in the city and was the site of a 1970 demonstration against the Vietnam War in which four students were killed by members of the National Guard. Population, 26,164. **3.** A city of west-central Washington south of Seattle. It is a food-processing center with an aerospace industry. Population, 23,152.

Kent, Corita. Known as "Sister Corita." 1918–1986. American artist noted for her prints and for the "Love" postage stamp she designed (1985).

Kent, James. 1763–1847. American jurist who as chief judge of the New York Supreme Court (1804–1823) revived the use of equity in the American legal system.

Kent, Rockwell. 1882–1971. American artist noted for his stark woodcuts, which illustrated published accounts of his travels and special editions of classic literary works.

Kent·ish (kĕn′tĭsh) *adj.* Of or relating to Kent, England, or its inhabitants. **—Kentish** *n.* The dialect of English spoken in Kent.

kent·ledge (kĕnt′lĭj) *n. Nautical.* Pig iron used as permanent ballast. [Origin unknown.]

Ken·tuck·y (kən-tŭk′ē). *Abbr.* **KY, Ken., Ky.** A state of the east-central United States. It was admitted as the 15th state in 1792. Daniel Boone's Transylvania Company made the first permanent settlement in the area in 1775. By the Treaty of Paris (1783) the territory became part of the United States. Frankfort is the capital and Louisville the largest city. Population, 3,660,257. **—Ken·tuck′i·an** *adj. & n.*

Kentucky bluegrass *n.* A perennial rhizomatous grass *(Poa pratensis)* native to Eurasia and North Africa and naturalized throughout the United States. It is commonly cultivated for pasture and lawns.

Kentucky coffee tree *n.* A deciduous North American tree *(Gymnocladus dioica)* having bipinnately compound leaves and flat, pulpy pods with large seeds formerly used as a coffee substitute.

Kentucky River. A river, about 417 km (259 mi) long, of north-central Kentucky flowing northwest to the Ohio River.

Kent·wood (kĕnt′wo͝od′). A city of western Michigan, a suburb of Grand Rapids. Population, 30,438.

Ken·ya (kĕn′yə, kēn′-). A country of east-central Africa bordering on the Indian Ocean. Controlled by the British in the late 19th and early 20th centuries, Kenya became independent in 1963. Nairobi is the capital and the largest city. Population, 15,327,061. **—Ken′yan** *adj. & n.*

Kenya, Mount. An extinct volcano, 5,202.7 m (17,058 ft), in central Kenya. It is the second-highest peak in Africa.

Ken·yat·ta (kĕn-yä′tə), **Jomo.** 1893?–1978. Kenyan nationalist politician and first president of independent Kenya (1964–1978).

Ke·ogh plan (kē′ō) *n.* A retirement plan for the self-employed and their employees. [After Eugene James *Keogh* (born 1907), former U.S. representative from New York.]

Ke·o·kuk (kē′ə-kŭk′). 1790?–1848? American Sauk leader who aided the United States in the Black Hawk War (1832) and negotiated peace between his people and the Sioux (1837).

keph·a·lin (kĕf′ə-lĭn) *n.* Variant of **cephalin.**

ke·pi (kā′pē, kĕp′ē) *n., pl.* **-pis.** A French military cap with a flat, circular top and a visor. [French *képi,* from German dialectal *Käppi,* diminutive of German *Kappe,* cap, from Middle High German *kappe,* cloak, cap, from Old High German *kappa,* cloak, probably from Late Latin *cappa,* head covering.]

Kep·ler (kĕp′lər), **Johannes.** 1571–1630. German astronomer and mathematician. Considered the founder of modern astronomy, he formulated three laws to clarify the theory that the planets revolve around the sun.

kept (kĕpt) *v.* Past tense and past participle of **keep.**

kerat– *pref.* Variant of **kerato–.**

ker·a·tec·to·my (kĕr′ə-tĕk′tə-mē) *n., pl.* **-mies.** Surgical removal of a part of the cornea.

ker·a·tin (kĕr′ə-tĭn) *n.* A tough, insoluble protein substance that is the chief structural constituent of hair, nails, horns, and hoofs. [Greek *keras, kerat-,* horn; see **ker-**[1] in Appendix + –IN.] **—ke·rat′i·nous** (kə-răt′n-əs) *adj.*

ker·a·tin·ize (kĕr′ə-tə-nīz′) *v.* **-ized, -iz·ing, -iz·es.** *—intr.* To produce keratin or become like keratin. *—tr.* To convert (something) into keratin. **—ker′a·tin·i·za′tion** (-tə-nĭ-zā′shən) *n.*

ker·a·ti·tis (kĕr′ə-tī′tĭs) *n., pl.* **-tit·i·des** (-tĭt′ĭ-dēz′). Inflammation of the cornea.

kerato– or **kerat–** also **cerato–** or **cerat–** *pref.* **1.** Horn; horny: *keratosis.* **2.** Cornea: *keratectomy.* [Greek *kerato-,* horn, from *keras, kerat-.* See **ker-**[1] in Appendix.]

ker·a·to·sis (kĕr′ə-tō′sĭs) *n., pl.* **-ses** (-sēz). Excessive growth of horny tissue of the skin. **—ker′a·tot′ic** (-tŏt′ĭk) *adj.*

ker·a·tot·o·my (kĕr′ə-tŏt′ə-mē) *n., pl.* **-mies.** Surgical incision of the cornea.

kerb (kûrb) *n. Chiefly British.* Variant of **curb** (sense 1).

Ker·be·la (kûr′bə-lə). See **Karbala.**

Kerch (kĕrch, kyĕrch). A city of southern Ukraine on **Kerch Strait,** a shallow waterway connecting the Black Sea with the Sea of Azov and bordered on the west by the **Kerch Peninsula.** The city was founded by Greek colonists in the sixth century B.C. Population, 168,000.

ker·chief (kûr′chĭf, -chēf′) *n., pl.* **-chiefs** also **-chieves** (-chĭvz, -chēvz). **1.** A woman's square scarf, often worn as a head covering. **2.** A handkerchief. [Middle English *coverchef, curchef,* from Anglo-Norman *courchief* (variant of Old French *couvrechef*) and from Old French *couvrechef* : *covrir,* to cover (from Latin *cooperīre;* see COVER) + *chef,* head (from Latin *caput;* see **kaput-** in Appendix).]

Ke·ren·sky (kə-rĕn′skē, kĕr′ən-, kyĕr′yĭn-), **Aleksandr Fedorovich.** 1881–1970. Russian revolutionary who was appointed the head of government (July 1917) after the abdication of Nicholas II but was overthrown by the Bolsheviks (October 1917) for his moderate policies.

Ker·e·san (kĕr′ĭ-sən) *n.* Any of a group of languages spoken by certain Pueblo peoples. **—Ker′e·san** *adj.*

kerf (kûrf) *n.* **1.** A groove or notch made by a cutting tool, such as a saw or an ax. **2.** The width of a groove made by a cutting tool. [Middle English, from Old English *cyrf,* a cutting. See **gerbh-** in Appendix.]

Ker·gue·len Islands (kûr′gə-lən, -lĕn′). A French-administered island group in the southern Indian Ocean southeast of South Africa. The largest island, **Kerguelen,** is used mainly as a research station.

Kér·ki·ra (kĕr′kē-rä′). See **Corfu.**

Ker·man (kər-män′, kĕr-). A city of east-central Iran southeast of Tehran. It is famous for its carpets. Population, 239,000.

Ker·man·shah (kĕr-män′-shä′, -shô′). See **Bakhtaran.**

ker·mes (kûr′mēz) *n.* A red dyestuff once prepared from the dried bodies of various female scale insects of the genus *Kermes.* [French *kermès,* short for *alkermès,* from Arabic *al-qirmiz,* probably from Sanskrit *kṛmi-ja-,* (red dye) produced by worms. See **kʷṛmi-** in Appendix.]

ker·mis also **ker·mess** or **kir·mess** (kûr′mĭs) *n.* **1.** An outdoor fair in the Low Countries. **2.** A fund-raising fair or carnival. [Dutch *kermis,* from Middle Dutch *kercmisse,* mass on the anniversary of a church dedication, on which day was held a yearly fair : *kerc,* church (ultimately from Late Greek *kuriakon, kurikon (dōma),* (house) of the lord; see CHURCH) + *misse,* mass (from Late Latin *missa;* see MASS).]

kern¹ also **kerne** (kûrn) *n.* **1.** A medieval Scottish or Irish foot soldier. **2.** A loutish person. [Middle English *kerne,* from Middle Irish *ceithern,* band of soldiers, from Old Irish.]

kern² (kûrn) *Printing. n.* The portion of a typeface that projects beyond the body or shank of a character. **—kern** *tr.v.* **kerned, kern·ing, kerns.** To provide (type) with a kern. [French *carne,* corner, from Old North French, from Latin *cardō, cardin-,* hinge.]

Kern (kûrn), **Jerome David.** 1885–1945. American composer of numerous musicals, including *Show Boat* (1927), and more than a thousand songs, such as "Smoke Gets in Your Eyes."

kerne (kûrn) *n.* Variant of **kern¹.**

ker·nel (kûr′nəl) *n.* **1.** A grain or seed, as of a cereal grass, enclosed in a husk. **2.** The inner, usually edible seed of a nut or fruit stone. **3.** The most material and central part; the core: *"that hard kernel of gaiety that never breaks"* (Evelyn Waugh). [Middle English, from Old English *cyrnel.* See **gr̥-no-** in Appendix.] **—ker′neled** *adj.*

kern·ite (kûr′nīt′) *n.* A colorless to white lustrous crystalline mineral, $Na_2B_4O_7 \cdot 4H_2O$, that is a major source of ore of boron. [After *Kern,* a county of southern California.]

ker·o·gen (kĕr′ə-jən) *n.* A fossilized material in shale and other sedimentary rock that yields oil upon heating. [Greek *kēros,* wax + –GEN.]

ker·o·sene also **ker·o·sine** (kĕr′ə-sēn′, kăr′-, kĕr′ə-sēn′, kăr′-) *n.* A thin oil distilled from petroleum or shale oil, used as a fuel for heating and cooking, in lamps, and as a denaturant for alcohol. Also called *coal oil, lamp oil.* [Greek *kēros,* wax + –ENE.]

Ker·ou·ac (kĕr′o͞o-ăk′), **Jack.** 1922–1969. American writer and leading figure of the beat generation. His primarily autobiographical books include *On the Road* (1957).

Ker·ry (kĕr′ē) *n., pl.* **-ries.** One of a breed of small, black dairy cattle of Irish origin. [After *Kerry,* a county of southwest Ireland.]

Kerry blue terrier *n.* Any of a breed of terriers of Irish origin, having a dense, wavy bluish-gray coat. [After *Kerry,* a county of southwest Ireland.]

ker·sey (kûr′zē) *n., pl.* **-seys. 1.** A twilled woolen fabric, sometimes with a cotton warp, used for coats. **2.** Often **kerseys.** A garment made of this fabric. **3.** A woolen, often ribbed fabric formerly used for hose and trousers. [Middle English *kersei,* after *Kersey,* a village of southeast England.]

ker·sey·mere (kûr′zē-mîr′) *n.* A fine woolen cloth with a fancy twill weave. [KERSEY + (CASSI)MERE.]

Ker·u·len (kĕr′o͞o-lĕn). A river rising in northeast Mongolia and flowing about 1,263 km (785 mi) south then east to a lake in northeast China.

ke·ryg·ma (kə-rĭg′mə) *n. Theology.* The proclamation of religious truths, especially as taught in the Gospels. [Greek *kērugma,* preaching, proclamation, from *kērux, kērug-,* herald.]

Kes·sel·ring (kĕs′əl-rĭng), **Albert.** 1885–1960. German general who was active on virtually all European and North African fronts during World War II.

kes·trel (kĕs′trəl) *n.* Any of various small falcons belonging to the genus *Falco* that are distributed worldwide, especially the American kestrel and the European kestrel. [Probably from obsolete French *cresserelle,* from Old French *cresserele,* probably from *cresselle,* clacker, kestrel.]

ket– *pref.* Variant of **keto–.**

ketch (kĕch) *n. Nautical.* A two-masted fore-and-aft-rigged sailing vessel with a mizzenmast stepped aft of a taller mainmast but forward of the rudder. [Middle English *cache,* from *cacchen,* to catch. See CATCH.]

Ketch·i·kan (kĕch′ĭ-kăn′). A city of southeast Alaska on an island in the Alexander Archipelago. A supply point for miners during the gold rush of the 1890's, it is now a major port and tourist center on the Inside Passage. Population, 7,198.

ketch·up (kĕch′əp, kăch′-) also **catch·up** (kăch′əp, kĕch′-) or **cat·sup** (kăt′səp, kăch′əp, kĕch′-) *n.* A condiment consisting of a thick, smooth-textured, spicy sauce usually made from tomatoes. [Probably Malay *kēchap,* fish sauce, possibly from Chinese (Cantonese) *kē-tsiap.*]

WORD HISTORY: The word *ketchup* exemplifies the types of modifications that can take place in the borrowing process, both in the borrowing of a word and in the borrowing of a substance. The source of our word *ketchup* may be the Malay word *kēchap,* possibly taken into Malay from the Cantonese dialect of Chinese. *Kēchap,* like our word, referred to a kind of sauce, but a sauce without tomatoes; rather, it contained fish brine, herbs, and spices. The sauce seems to have emigrated to Europe by way of sailors, where it was made with locally available ingredients such as the juice of mushrooms or walnuts. At some point, when the juice of tomatoes was first used, ketchup as we know it was born. However, it is important to realize that in the 18th and 19th centuries *ketchup* was a generic term for sauces whose only common ingredient was vinegar. The word is first recorded in English in 1690 in the form *catchup,* in 1711 in the form *ketchup,* and in 1730 in the form *catsup.* These three spelling variants of a foreign borrowing remain current.

ke·tene (kē′tēn′) *n.* A pungent, toxic, colorless gas, C_2H_2O, used chiefly as an acetylation agent.

keto– or **ket–** *pref.* Ketone; ketone group: *ketosis.* [From KETONE.]

ke·to·gen·e·sis (kē′tō-jĕn′ĭ-sĭs) *n.* The formation of ketone bodies, as occurs in diabetes. **—ke′to·gen′ic** *adj.*

ke·tone (kē′tōn′) *n.* Any of a class of organic compounds having a carbonyl group linked to a carbon atom in each of two hydrocarbon radicals and having the general formula R(CO)R′, where R may be the same as R′. [German *Keton,* short for *Aketon,* acetone : Latin *acētum,* vinegar; see ACETUM + *-on,* n. suff. (alteration of *-en,* from Greek *-ēnē*).] **—ke·ton′ic** (-tŏn′ĭk) *adj.*

ketone body *n.* A ketone-containing substance, such as acetoacetic acid, that is an intermediate product of fatty acid metabolism. Ketone bodies tend to accumulate in the blood and are excreted in the urine of individuals affected by starvation or uncontrolled diabetes mellitus. Also called *acetone body.*

ke·tose (kē′tōs′) *n.* Any of various carbohydrates containing a ketone group.

ke·to·sis (kē-tō′sĭs) *n., pl.* **-ses** (-sēz). A pathological increase in the production of ketone bodies. **—ke·tot′ic** (-tŏt′ĭk) *adj.*

ke·to·ste·roid (kē′tō-stîr′oid′, -stĕr′-) *n.* A steroid containing a ketone group.

Ket·ter·ing (kĕt′ər-ĭng). A city of southwest Ohio, an industrial suburb of Dayton. Population, 61,186.

Kettering, Charles Franklin. 1876–1958. American electrical engineer and manufacturer who developed the first electric cash register (1905) and numerous automotive improvements, such as an electric ignition system (1912).

ket·tle (kĕt′l) *n.* **1.** A metal pot, usually with a lid, for boiling or stewing. **2.** A teakettle. **3.** *Music.* A kettledrum. **4.** *Geology.* A depression left in a mass of glacial drift, formed by the melting of an isolated block of glacial ice. **5.** A pothole. [Middle English *ketel,* from Old Norse *ketill* and Old English *cetel,* both from Latin *catīllus,* diminutive of *catīnus,* large bowl.]

ket·tle·drum (kĕt′l-drŭm′) *n. Music.* A large copper or brass hemispherical drum with a parchment head that can be tuned by adjusting the tension.

kettle of fish *n., pl.* **kettles of fish. 1.** A troublesomely awkward or embarrassing situation. **2.** A matter to be reckoned with: *Making money and keeping it are two quite different kettles of fish.*

Keu·ka Lake (kyo͞o′kə, kā-yo͞o′-). A lake of west-central New York, one of the Finger Lakes west of Seneca Lake.

keV *abbr.* Kiloelectron unit.

kev·el (kĕv′əl) *n. Nautical.* A sturdy belaying pin for the heavier cables of a ship. [Middle English *kevil,* from Old French *keville,* wooden peg, from Latin *clāvicula,* diminutive of *clāvis,* key.]

Kew (kyo͞o). A district of western Greater London in southeast England. The famed Royal Botanic Gardens were established in 1759 and presented to the nation in 1841.

kew·pie (kyo͞o′pē) *n.* A small, fat-cheeked, wide-eyed doll with a curl of hair on top of the head. [Originally a trademark.]

key¹ (kē) *n., pl.* **keys. 1.a.** A notched and grooved, usually metal implement that is turned to open or close a lock. **b.** A similar device used for opening or winding: *the key of a clock; a can that has a key attached.* **2.** A means of access, control, or possession. **3.a.** A vital, crucial element. **b.** A set of answers to

Kerry blue terrier

kestrel

kettledrum

ă pat	oi boy
ā pay	ou out
âr care	o͝o took
ä father	o͞o boot
ĕ pet	ŭ cut
ē be	ûr urge
ĭ pit	th thin
ī pie	*th* this
îr pier	hw which
ŏ pot	zh vision
ō toe	ə about, item
ô paw	♦ regionalism

Stress marks: ′ (primary); ′ (secondary), as in **dictionary** (dĭk′shə-nĕr′ē)

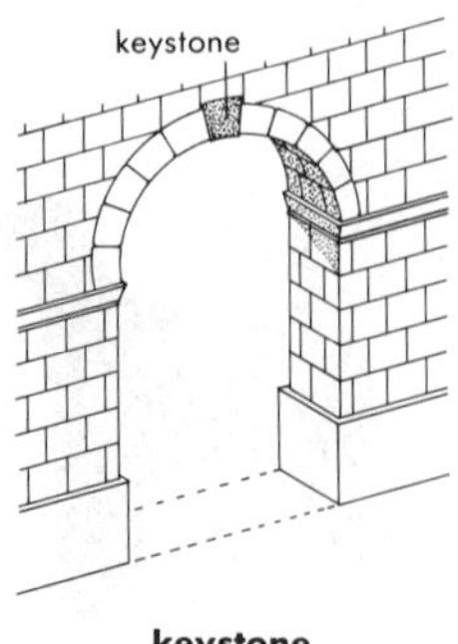

keystone

a test. **c.** A table, gloss, or cipher for decoding or interpreting. **4.** A device, such as a wedge or pin, inserted to lock together mechanical or structural parts. **5.** *Architecture.* The keystone in the crown of an arch. **6. a.** A button or lever that is pressed with the finger to operate a machine. **b.** *Music.* A button or lever that is pressed with the finger to produce or modulate the sound of an instrument, such as a clarinet or piano. **7.** *Music.* **a.** A tonal system consisting of seven tones in fixed relationship to a tonic, having a characteristic key signature and being since the Renaissance the structural foundation of the bulk of Western music; tonality. **b.** The principal tonality of a work: *an etude in the key of E.* **8.** The pitch of a voice or other sound. **9.** A characteristic tone or level of intensity, as of a speech or sales campaign. Often used in combination: *high-key; low-key.* **10.** *Botany.* The key fruit. **11.** An outline of the distinguishing characteristics of a group of organisms, used as a guide in taxonomic identification. **12.** *Basketball.* An area at each end of the court between the base line and the foul line and including the jump-ball circle at the foul line: *a jump shot from the top of the key.* **—key** *adj.* Of crucial importance; significant: *key decisions; the key element of the thesis.* **—key** *tr.v.* **keyed, key·ing, keys. 1.** To lock with or as if with a key. **2.** *Architecture.* To furnish (an arch) with a keystone. **3.** *Music.* To regulate the pitch of. **4.** To bring into harmony; adjust or adapt. **5.** To supply an explanatory key for. **6. a.** To operate (a device), as for typesetting by means of a keyboard. **b.** To enter (data) into a computer by means of a keyboard. **7.** To identify (a biological specimen). ***—phrasal verb.*** **key up.** To make intense, excited, or nervous. ***—idioms.*** **in key.** In consonance with other factors. **out of key.** Not in consonance with other factors. [Middle English *kai, kei,* from Old English *cǣg.*]

key² (kē) *n., pl.* **keys.** A low offshore island or reef, especially in the Gulf of Mexico; a cay. [Alteration (influenced by *key,* variant of QUAY) of Spanish *cayo.* See CAY.]

key³ (kē) *n., pl.* **keys.** *Slang.* A kilogram of marijuana, cocaine, or heroin. [Shortening and alteration of KILOGRAM.]

Key (kē), **Francis Scott.** 1779–1843. American lawyer and poet who wrote "Defense of Fort M'Henry" after witnessing the British attack on Fort McHenry at Baltimore on September 13–14, 1814. The poem was set to the music of an 18th-century tune called "To Anacreon in Heaven," renamed "The Star-Spangled Banner," and in 1931 was adopted by Congress as the national anthem.

key·board (kē′bôrd′, -bōrd′) *n.* **1.** A set of keys, as on a computer terminal, word processor, typewriter, or piano. **2.** *Music.* Any one of various instruments played by means of a set of pianolike keys, often connected to a synthesizer or an amplifier. **—keyboard** *tr.v.* **-board·ed, -board·ing, -boards. 1.** *Printing.* To set (copy) by means of a keyed typesetting machine: *keyboard a manuscript.* **2.** *Music.* To play (a composition) by means of an instrument having a set of pianolike keys. **—key′board′er, key′board′ist** *n.*

key·card (kē′kärd′) *n.* A usually plastic card with a magnetically coded strip that is scanned in order to operate a mechanism such as a door or an automated teller machine.

key club *n.* A private club featuring liquor and entertainment. [From the key to the premises given to each member.]

key fruit *n.* *Botany.* See **samara.** [From the shape of its bunches.]

key·hole (kē′hōl′) *n.* **1.** The hole in a lock into which a key fits. **2.** *Basketball.* The key.

Key Lar·go (lär′gō). A narrow island off southern Florida. It is the largest of the Florida Keys.

key money *n.* Payment made to a landlord as an inducement to assure a rental.

Keynes (kānz), **John Maynard.** First Baron of Tilton. 1883–1946. British economist who proposed that high unemployment, being a result of insufficient consumer spending, could be relieved by government-sponsored programs.

Keynes·i·an (kān′zē-ən) *adj.* Of or relating to the economic theories of John Maynard Keynes, especially those theories advocating government monetary and fiscal programs designed to increase employment and stimulate business activity. **—Keynesian** *n.* A supporter of Keynes's theories. **—Keynes′i·an·ism** *n.*

key·note (kē′nōt′) *n.* **1.** *Music.* The tonic of a musical key. **2.** A prime underlying element or theme: *"The keynote of the revolution settlement was personal freedom under the law"* (G.M. Trevelyan). **—keynote** *tr.v.* **-not·ed, -not·ing, -notes. 1.** To give or set the keynote of. **2.** *Informal.* To give a keynote address at: *keynoted the press luncheon.*

keynote address *n.* An opening address, as at a political convention, that outlines the issues to be considered. Also called *keynote speech.*

key·not·er (kē′nō′tər) *n.* One who gives a keynote address.

keynote speech *n.* See **keynote address.**

key·pad (kē′păd′) *n.* *Computer Science.* An input device, sometimes part of a standard typewriter keyboard, consisting of a separate grid of numerical and function keys arranged for efficient data entry.

key·punch (kē′pŭnch′) *n.* A keyboard machine that is used to punch holes in cards or tapes for data-processing systems. **—keypunch** *intr. & tr.v.* **-punched, -punch·ing, -punch·es.** To process on such a keyboard machine. **—key′punch′er** *n.*

key signature *n.* *Music.* The group of sharps or flats placed to the right of the clef on a staff to identify the key.

ă pat	oi boy
ā pay	ou out
âr care	ŏŏ took
ä father	ōō boot
ĕ pet	ŭ cut
ē be	ûr urge
ĭ pit	th thin
ī pie	*th* this
îr pier	hw which
ŏ pot	zh vision
ō toe	ə about, item
ô paw	♦ regionalism

Stress marks: ′ (primary); ′ (secondary), as in **dictionary** (dĭk′shə-nĕr′ē)

key·stone (kē′stōn′) *n.* **1.** *Architecture.* The central wedge-shaped stone of an arch that locks its parts together. Also called *headstone.* **2.** The central supporting element of a whole.

key·stroke (kē′strōk′) *n.* A stroke of a key, as on a word processor. **—key′stroke′** *v.*

key·way (kē′wā′) *n.* **1.** A slot for a key in the hub or shaft of a wheel. **2.** The keyhole of a cylinder lock.

Key West. A city of extreme southern Florida on the island of **Key West,** the westernmost of the Florida Keys in the Gulf of Mexico. Population, 24,292.

key·word also **key word** (kē′wûrd′) *n.* **1.** A word that serves as a key to a code or cipher. **2.** A significant or descriptive word. **3.** A word used as a reference point for finding other words or information.

kg *abbr.* Kilogram.

kG *abbr.* Kilogauss.

K.G. *abbr.* Knight of the Order of the Garter.

KGB or **K.G.B.** (kā′gē-bē′) *n.* The intelligence and internal security agency of the Soviet Union. [Russian, from *K(omitét) G(osudárstvennoĭ) B(ezopásnosti)* : *komitet,* committee + *gosudarstvennoĭ,* genitive of *gosudar'stvennyĭ,* of the state + *bezopasnosti,* genitive of *bezopasnost',* security.]

kgf *abbr.* Kilogram force.

Kha·ba·rovsk (kə-bär′əfsk, KHə-). A city of southeast Russia on the Amur River near the Chinese border. Located on the site of a fort established in 1652, it prospered after the coming of the railroad in 1905. Population, 576,000.

Kha·cha·tu·ri·an (kä′chä-tŏŏr′ē-ən, kăch′ə-, KHə-chə-tŏŏr-yän′), **Aram Ilich.** 1903–1978. Russian composer of Armenian parentage whose works include concertos for piano and violin, symphonies, and ballets, such as *Gayane* (1942).

Kha·da·fy (kə-dä′fē), **Muammar al-.** See Muammar al-**Qaddafi.**

khak·i (kăk′ē, kä′kē) *n.* **1.** *Color.* A light olive brown to moderate or light yellowish brown. **2. a.** A sturdy cloth of this color. **b. khakis.** A uniform made of this cloth. [Urdu *khākī,* dusty, from Persian, from *khāk,* dust, from Middle Persian.] **—khak′i** *adj.*

Kha·lid (kä-lēd′, KHä-). Full name Khalid ibn Abd al-Aziz Al Saud. 1913–1982. King of Saudi Arabia (1975–1982).

kha·lif (kā′lĭf, kăl′ĭf) *n.* Variant of **caliph.**

Khal·ki·dhi·kí (käl-kē′*th*ē-kē′, KHäl-). See **Chalcidice.**

Khal·kís (käl-kēs′, KHäl-). See **Chalcis.**

kham·sin (kăm-sēn′) *n.* A generally southerly hot wind from the Sahara that blows across Egypt from late March to early May. [Arabic *(rīḥ al-)hamsīn,* (wind of the) 50 (days), khamsin, from *ḥamsūn,* 50.]

khan¹ (kän, kăn) *n.* **1.** A ruler, an official, or an important person in India and some central Asian countries. **2.** A medieval ruler of a Mongol, Tartar, or Turkish tribe. [Middle English *caan,* from Old French *can,* from Turkish *khān* (from Old Turkic *qaghan*) and from Mongolian *qā'ān,* ruler.]

khan² (kän, kăn) *n.* A caravansary in certain Asian countries. [Arabic *ḫān,* inn, from Persian *khān,* house, from Middle Persian.]

khan·ate (kä′nāt′, kăn′āt′) *n.* **1.** The realm of a khan. **2.** The position of a khan.

kha·pra beetle (kä′prə, kăp′rə) *n.* A beetle *(Trogoderma granurium)* accidentally introduced to several places in the United States that is an extremely destructive grain pest. [Hindi *khaprā,* from *khapnā,* to destroy.]

Khar·kov (kär′kôf′, KHär′kəf). A city of northeast Ukraine east of Kiev. Founded in 1656, it was an important 17th-century frontier headquarters of Ukrainian Cossacks who were loyal to the Russian czars. Population, 1,554,000.

Khar·toum also **Khar·tum** (kär-tōōm′). The capital and largest city of Sudan, in the east-central part of the country at the confluence of the Blue Nile and the White Nile. It was founded c. 1821 as an Egyptian army camp and was destroyed by Mahdists in 1885 after a long siege. Population, 476,218.

khat (kät) *n.* **1.** An evergreen shrub *(Catha edulis)* native to tropical East Africa, having dark green opposite leaves that are chewed fresh for their stimulating effects. **2.** A tealike beverage prepared from the leaves of this plant. [Arabic *qatt.*]

Kha·tan·ga (kə-tăng′gə, -tăng′-, KHä-tän′-). A river, about 1,150 km (715 mi) long, of north-central Russia flowing to the **Khatanga Gulf,** an arm of the Laptev Sea.

Khay·yám (kī-yäm′, -ăm′), **Omar.** See **Omar Khayyám.**

khe·dive (kə-dēv′) *n.* One of several Turkish viceroys ruling Egypt from 1867 to 1914. [French *khédive,* from Turkish *hidiv,* from Persian *khidēw,* lord, from Middle Persian *khwadāy,* from Old Iranian *khvadāta-.* See **s(w)e-** in Appendix.]

Kher·son (kĕr-sôn′, KHyĭr-). A city of south-central Ukraine on the Dnieper River near the Black Sea east-northeast of Odessa. It was founded in 1778. Population, 346,000.

khi (kī) *n.* Variant of **chi.**

Khí·os (kē′ôs, KHē′-). See **Chios.**

Khir·bet Qum·ran (kîr′bĕt kŏŏm-rän′). See **Qumran.**

Khmer (kmâr) *n., pl.* **Khmer** or **Khmers. 1.** A member of a people of Cambodia whose civilization reached its height from the 9th to the 15th centuries. **2.** The Mon-Khmer language that is the official language of Cambodia. **—Khmer, Khmer′i·an** *adj.*

Khmer Republic. See **Cambodia.**

Khoi·khoin (koi′koi′ĭn) or **Khoi·khoi** (koi′koi) *n., pl.* **Khoikhoin** or **-khoins** or **Khoikhoi** or **-khois. 1.** A member of a pastoral people of Namibia and South Africa. **2.** Any of the Khoisan languages of the Khoikhoin, including Nama. [Nama *khoi-khoi-n,* the Nama people : *khoi-khoi,* to speak Nama (from *khoi-,* human being) + *-n,* pl. common gender suff.]

Khoi·san (koi′sän′) *n.* A family of languages of southern Africa, including those of the Khoikhoin and the San. [Nama *khoi-khoi-n,* the Nama people; see KHOIKHOIN + *san,* the San people; see SAN.]

Kho·mei·ni (kō-mā′nē, KHō-, KHô′mā-nē′), Ayatollah **Ruholla.** 1900–1989. Iranian Shiite leader and head of state (1979–1989). Arrested (1963) and exiled (1964) for his opposition to Shah Mohammed Reza Pahlavi's regime, he returned to Iran on the shah's downfall (1979) and established a new constitution giving himself supreme powers.

Kho·per (kə-pyôr′, KHŏ-). A river, about 1,006 km (625 mi) long, of southwest Russia flowing south to the Don River.

Kho·ra·na (kō-rä′nə), **Har Gobind.** Born 1922. Indian-born American biochemist. He shared a 1968 Nobel Prize for the study of genetic codes.

khoum (ko͞om, ko͝om) *n.* See table at **currency.** [Native word in Mauritania.]

Khru·shchev (kro͞osh′chĕf, -chôf, KHro͞o-shchyôf′), **Nikita Sergeyevich.** 1894–1971. Soviet politician. A Stalin loyalist in the 1930's, he was appointed first secretary of the Communist Party in 1953. As Soviet premier (1958–1964) he denounced Stalin (1956), thwarted the Hungarian Revolution of 1956, and improved his country's image abroad. He was deposed (1964) for his failure to improve the Soviet economy.

Khu·fu (ko͞o′fo͞o′). See **Cheops.**

Khul·na (ko͞ol′nə). A city of southwest Bangladesh near the Ganges River delta. It is a trade and processing center for a large swampy, forested region. Population, 623,184.

Khwa·riz·mi (kwär′ĭz-mē, KHwär′-), **al-.** Full name Muhammad ibn-Musa al-Khwarizmi. 780?–850? Moslem mathematician whose works introduced Arabic numerals and algebraic concepts to Western mathematics.

Khy·ber Pass (kī′bər). A narrow pass, about 53 km (33 mi) long, through mountains on the border between western Afghanistan and northern Pakistan. It has long been a strategic trade and invasion route.

kHz *abbr.* Kilohertz.

KIA (kā′ī-ā′) *n., pl.* **KIA's** also **KIAs.** A member of the armed services who is reported killed during a combat mission. [*k(illed) i(n) a(ction).*]

Kia·ling (kyä′lĭng′, jyä′-). See **Jialing.**

Kia·mu·sze (kyä′mo͞o′so͞o′). See **Jiamusi.**

ki·ang (kē-äng′) *n.* A large wild ass (*Equus hemionus* subsp. *kiang*) of the mountains of Asia. [Tibetan *rkyan.*]

Kiang·si (kyäng′shē′). See **Jiangxi.**

Kiang·su (kyäng′so͞o′, -sü′). See **Jiangsu.**

kiaugh (kyäKH) *n. Scots.* Trouble; anxiety. [Probably from Scottish Gaelic *cabhag.*]

kib·ble¹ (kĭb′əl) *n.* An iron bucket used in wells or mines for hoisting water, ore, or refuse to the surface. [Probably from German *Kübel,* pail, from Middle High German *kübel,* from Old High German *-chublī* (in *miluhchublī,* milk pail) from Vulgar Latin **cupia,* from Latin *cūpa,* vat.]

kib·ble² (kĭb′əl) *tr.v.* **-bled, -bling, -bles.** To crush or grind (grain, for example) coarsely. **—kibble** *n.* Meal ground by this process and used in the form of pellets especially for pet food. [Origin unknown.]

kib·butz (kĭ-bo͝ots′, -bo͞ots′) *n., pl.* **kib·but·zim** (kĭb′o͝ot-sēm′, -o͞ot-). A collective farm or settlement in modern Israel. [Hebrew *qibbûṣ,* gathering, from *qibbēṣ,* to gather.]

kib·butz·nik (kĭ-bo͝ots′nĭk, -bo͞ots′-) *n.* A member of a kibbutz.

kibe (kīb) *n.* A chapped or inflamed area on the skin, especially on the heel, resulting from exposure to cold; an ulcerated chillblain. [Middle English *kybe.*]

Ki·bei (kē-bā′) *n., pl.* **Kibei** or **-beis.** A person born in the United States of Japanese immigrant parents and educated chiefly in Japan. [Japanese, to go home, return to America, Kibei.]

kib·itz (kĭb′ĭts) *intr.v.* **-itzed, -itz·ing, -itz·es.** *Informal.* **1.** To look on and offer unwanted, usually meddlesome advice to others. **2.** To chat; converse. [Yiddish *kibitsen,* from German *kiebitzen,* from *Kiebitz,* pewit, kibitzer, from Middle High German *gībitz,* pewit, of imitative origin.] **—kib′itz·er** *n.*

kib·lah (kĭb′lə) *n. Islam.* The direction facing the Kaaba, toward which Moslems look when praying. [Arabic *qiblah.*]

ki·bosh (kī′bŏsh′, kĭ-bŏsh′) *n. Informal.* A checking or restraining element: *had to put the kibosh on a poorly conceived plan.* [Origin unknown.]

kick (kĭk) *v.* **kicked, kick·ing, kicks.** *—intr.* **1.** To strike out with the foot or feet. **2.a.** *Sports.* To score or gain ground by kicking a ball. **b.** *Football.* To punt. **3.** To recoil: *The high-powered rifle kicked upon being fired.* **4.** *Informal.* **a.** To express negative feelings vigorously; complain. **b.** To oppose by argument; protest. See Synonyms at **object.** *—tr.* **1.** To strike with the foot. **2.** To propel by striking with the foot. **3.** To spring back against suddenly: *The rifle kicked my shoulder when I fired it.* **4.** *Sports.* To score (a goal or point) by kicking a ball. **—kick** *n.* **1.a.** A vigorous blow with the foot. **b.** *Sports.* The thrusting motion of the legs in swimming. **2.** A jolting recoil: *a rifle with a heavy kick.* **3.** *Slang.* A complaint; a protest. **4.** *Slang.* Power; force: *an old engine that still has lots of kick.* **5.** *Slang.* **a.** A feeling of pleasurable stimulation: *got a kick out of the show.* **b. kicks.** Fun: *Let's go to the show just for kicks.* **6.** *Slang.* Temporary, often obsessive interest: *I'm on a science fiction kick.* **7.** *Slang.* A sudden, striking surprise; a twist. **8.** *Sports.* **a.** The act or an instance of kicking a ball. **b.** A kicked ball. **c.** The distance spanned by a kicked ball. ***—phrasal verbs.*** **kick around.** *Informal.* **1.** To treat badly; abuse. **2.** To move from place to place: *"spent the next three years in Italy, kicking around the country on a motor scooter"* (Charles E. Claffey). **3.** To give consideration or thought to (an idea). **kick back.** To recoil unexpectedly and violently. **1.** *Slang.* To return (stolen items). **2.** *Slang.* To pay a kickback. **kick in. 1.** *Informal.* To contribute (one's share): *kicked in a few dollars for the office party.* **2.** *Slang.* To die. **kick off. 1.** *Sports.* To begin or resume play with a kickoff. **2.** *Informal.* To begin; start: *kicked off the promotional tour with a press conference for the author.* **3.** *Slang.* To die. **kick out.** *Slang.* To throw out; dismiss. **kick over.** To begin to fire: *The engine finally kicked over.* **kick up.** *Informal.* **1.** To increase in amount or force; intensify: *A sandstorm kicked up while we drove through the desert.* **2.** To stir up (trouble): *kicked up a row.* **3.** To show signs of disorder: *His ulcer has kicked up again.* ***—idioms.*** **kick the bucket.** *Slang.* To die. **kick the habit.** *Slang.* To free oneself of an addiction, as to narcotics or cigarettes. **kick up (one's) heels.** *Informal.* To cast off one's inhibitions and have a good time. **kick upstairs.** *Slang.* To promote to a higher yet less desirable position. [Middle English *kiken,* perhaps of Scandinavian origin.]

Kick·a·poo (kĭk′ə-po͞o′) *n., pl.* **Kickapoo** or **-poos. 1.a.** A Native American people formerly inhabiting southern Wisconsin and northern Illinois, with small present-day populations in Kansas, Oklahoma, and northern Mexico. **b.** A member of this people. **2.** The Algonquian language of the Kickapoo.

kick·back (kĭk′băk′) *n.* **1.** A sharp reaction; a repercussion. **2.** *Slang.* A return of a percentage of a sum of money already received, typically as a result of pressure, coercion, or a secret agreement.

kick·box·ing (kĭk′bŏk′sĭng) *n.* The martial art and sport of attack and defense, practiced in a boxing ring and combining many elements of karate and boxing. **—kick′box·er** *n.*

kick·er (kĭk′ər) *n.* **1.** One that kicks: *a soccer player who was an excellent kicker.* **2.** *Informal.* **a.** A sudden, surprising turn of events or ending; a twist. **b.** A tricky or concealed condition; a pitfall: *"The kicker is that the relationship of guide and seeker gets all mixed up with a confusing male-female attachment"* (Gail Sheehy). **3.** A condition that imposes an automatic increase, as in a pension plan.

kick·off (kĭk′ôf′, -ŏf′) *n.* **1.** *Sports.* A place kick in football or soccer with which play is begun. **2.** *Informal.* A beginning: *the kickoff of a charity campaign.*

kick plate *n.* A protective sheet of metal attached to the bottom of a door.

kick·shaw (kĭk′shô′) *n.* **1.** Fancy food; a delicacy. **2.** A trinket; a gewgaw. [By folk etymology from French *quelque chose,* something : *quelque,* some (*quel,* what, from Latin *quālis,* of what kind; see QUALITY + *que,* what, which, who, from Vulgar Latin **que,* from Latin *quid,* what; see QUIDDITY) + *chose,* thing; see CHOSE².]

kick·stand (kĭk′stănd′) *n.* A swiveling metal bar for holding a two-wheeled vehicle, such as a motorcycle, upright when not being ridden.

kick·y (kĭk′ē) *adj.* **-i·er, -i·est.** *Slang.* So unusual or unconventional in character or nature as to provide a thrill.

kid (kĭd) *n.* **1.a.** A young goat. **b.** The young of a similar animal, such as an antelope. **2.a.** The flesh of a young goat. **b.** Leather made from the skin of a young goat; kidskin. **c.** An article made from this leather. **3.** *Informal.* **a.** A child. **b.** A young person. **4.** *Slang.* Pal. Used as a term of familiar address, especially for a young person: *Hi, kid! What's up?* **—kid** *adj.* **1.** Made of kid. **2.** *Informal.* Younger than oneself: *my kid brother.* **—kid** *v.* **kid·ded, kid·ding, kids.** *—tr. Informal.* **1.** To mock playfully; tease. See Synonyms at **banter.** **2.** To deceive in fun; fool. *—intr.* **1.** *Informal.* To engage in teasing or good-humored fooling. **2.** To bear young. Used of a goat or an antelope. [Middle English *kide,* from Old Norse *kidh.*] **—kid′der** *n.* **—kid′ding·ly** *adv.*

Kid (kĭd), **Thomas.** See Thomas **Kyd.**

kid·com (kĭd′kŏm′) *n.* A television or video presentation for children, especially a cartoon. [KID + (SIT)COM.]

Kidd (kĭd), **William.** Known as "Captain Kidd." 1645?–1701. British sea captain who turned to piracy after being hired to protect British ships in the Indian Ocean (1696).

Kid·der·min·ster¹ (kĭd′ər-mĭn′stər). A municipal borough of west-central England west-southwest of Birmingham. Carpets have been manufactured here since 1735. Population, 91,600.

Kid·der·min·ster² (kĭd′ər-mĭn′stər) *n.* An ingrain carpet originally made in Kidderminster.

kid·die or **kid·dy** (kĭd′ē) *n., pl.* **-dies.** *Slang.* A small child.

Ruholla Khomeini

Nikita Khrushchev
Photographed in 1960 at the United Nations

kickboxing

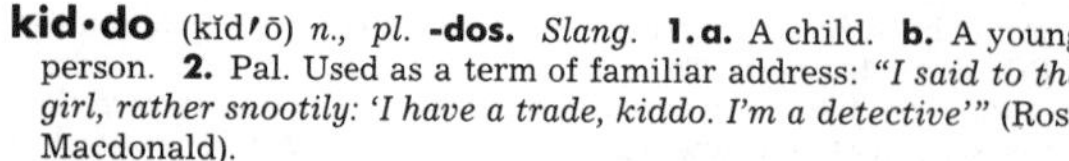

kid·do (kĭd′ō) *n., pl.* **-dos.** *Slang.* **1.a.** A child. **b.** A young person. **2.** Pal. Used as a term of familiar address: *"I said to the girl, rather snootily: 'I have a trade, kiddo. I'm a detective'"* (Ross Macdonald).

Kid·dush (kĭd′əsh, kē-do͞osh′) *n. Judaism.* The traditional blessing and prayer recited over wine on the eve of the Sabbath or a festival. [Hebrew *qiddûš*, from *qāddēš*, to sanctify.]

kid·dy (kĭd′ē) *n. Slang.* Variant of **kiddie.**

kid·e·o (kĭd′ē-ō) *n. Slang.* Kidvid. [KID + (VID)EO.]

Søren Kierkegaard

kid glove *n.* A glove made of fine, soft leather, especially kidskin. **—*idiom.* with kid gloves.** Tactfully and cautiously: *had to handle the temperamental artist with kid gloves.*

kid·nap (kĭd′năp′) *tr.v.* **-napped, -nap·ping, -naps** or **-naped, -nap·ing, -naps.** To seize and detain unlawfully and usually for ransom. [Probably KID + *nap*, to snatch (perhaps variant of NAB, or of Scandinavian origin).] **—kid′nap′** *n.* **—kid′nap′per, kid′nap′er** *n.*

WORD HISTORY: *Kidnapper* seems to have originated appropriately enough among those who perpetrate this crime. We know this because *kid* and *napper,* the two parts of the compound, were slang of the sort that criminals might use. *Kid,* which some still find slangy, was considered low slang when *kidnapper* was formed, and *napper* is obsolete slang for a thief, coming from the verb *nap,* "to seize a person or thing; steal." *Nap* is possibly a variant of *nab,* which still has a slangy ring to it. In 1678, the year in which the word is first recorded, kidnappers plied their trade on behalf of plantations in colonies such as the ones in North America. The term later took on the broader sense that it has today. The verb *kidnap* is recorded later (1682) than the noun and so is possibly a back-formation, that is, people have assumed that a kidnapper kidnaps.

kid·ney (kĭd′nē) *n., pl.* **-neys. 1.** *Anatomy.* Either one of a pair of organs in the dorsal region of the vertebrate abdominal cavity, functioning to maintain proper water and electrolyte balance, regulate acid-base concentration, and filter the blood of metabolic wastes, which are then excreted as urine. **2.** The kidney of certain animals, eaten as food. **3.** An excretory organ of certain invertebrates. **4.** Kind; sort. [Middle English *kidenere, kidenei,* perhaps from Old English **cydenēora* : **cyde,* belly + **nēora,* kidney.]

kidney bean *n.* **1.** An annual plant *(Phaseolus vulgaris)* cultivated in many forms for its edible pods and seeds. **2.** The pod or seed of this plant.

kidney stone *n.* A small hard mass in the kidney that forms from deposits chiefly of phosphates and urates.

kid·skin (kĭd′skĭn′) *n.* Soft leather made from the skin of a young goat.

kid stuff *n. Slang.* **1.** Something suitable only for children. **2.** Something very easy or uncomplicated.

Mount Kilimanjaro

kid·vid (kĭd′vĭd′) *n. Slang.* **1.** Television programs for children. **2.** Home videotapes for children. [KID + VID(EO).]

Kiel (kēl). A city of northern Germany on **Kiel Bay,** an arm of the Baltic Sea. Chartered in 1242, Kiel joined the Hanseatic League in 1284, passed to Denmark in 1773, and was annexed by Prussia in 1866. Population, 245,751.

kiel·ba·sa (kĭl-bä′sə, kēl-) *n.* A spicy, smoked Polish sausage. [Polish *kiełbasa,* from East and West Slavic **kŭlbasa,* from East Turkic *kül bassï,* grilled cutlet, from Turkic *kül bastï* : *kül,* coals, ashes + *bastï,* pressed (meat) (from *basmaq,* to press).]

Kiel Canal also **Nord-Ost·see Ka·nal** (nört-ôst′zā kä-näl′). An artificial waterway, 98.1 km (61 mi) long, of northern Germany connecting the North Sea with the Baltic Sea.

Kiel·ce (kyĕl′tsĕ). A city of southeast-central Poland south of Warsaw. Founded in 1173, it was controlled by Austria (from 1795) and Russia (from 1815) before reverting to Poland in 1919. Population, 200,500.

Kier·ke·gaard (kîr′kĭ-gärd′, -gôr′), **Søren Aaby.** 1813–1855. Danish religious philosopher. A precursor of modern existentialism, he insisted on the need for individual decision and leaps of faith in the search for religious truth.

kie·sel·guhr (kē′zəl-go͝or′) *n.* See **diatomite.** [German *Kieselgur* : *Kiesel,* pebble (from Middle High German *kisel,* from Old High German *chisil*) + *Gur, Guhr,* ferment, earthy deposit from water (from *gären,* to ferment, blend of Middle High German *jësan,* from Old High German, and Middle High German **jern,* to cause to ferment, from Old High German *jerian;* see **yes-** in Appendix).]

kie·ser·ite (kē′zə-rīt′) *n.* A whitish to yellowish hydrous magnesium sulfate mineral, $MgSO_4·H_2O$, found in salt residues. [After Dietrich Georg *Kieser* (1779–1862), German physician.]

killdeer
Charadrius vociferus

Ki·ev (kē′ĕf, -ĕv, kyĕ′yĭf). The capital of Ukraine, in the north-central part of the republic on the Dnieper River. One of the oldest cities in the country, it was the center of the first Russian state and an early seat of Christianity. It is often known as "the Mother of Cities." Population, 2,448,000.

kif (kĭf, kēf) also **kef** (kĕf, kēf, kāf) *n.* **1.** Smoking material, such as Indian hemp, used especially in the Maghreb. **2.** The euphoria caused by smoking this material. [Arabic *kayf, kef,* pleasure, well-being.]

Ki·ga·li (kĭ-gä′lē, kē-). The capital and largest city of Rwanda, in the central part east of Lake Kivu. Population, 156,700.

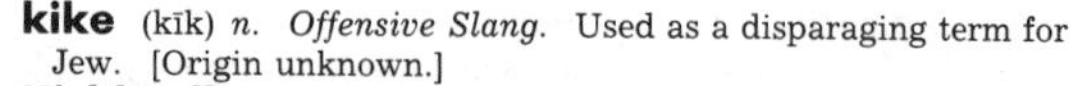

kike (kīk) *n. Offensive Slang.* Used as a disparaging term for a Jew. [Origin unknown.]

Ki·klá·dhes (kē-klä′thĕs). See **Cyclades.**

Ki·kon·go (kē-kŏng′gō) *n.* See **Kongo** (sense 2).

Ki·ku·yu (kĭ-ko͞o′yo͞o) also **Gi·ku·yu** (gĭ-ko͞o′yo͞o) *n., pl.* **Kikuyu** or **-yus** also **Gikuyu** or **-yus. 1.** A member of a people of central and southern Kenya. **2.** The Bantu language of the Kikuyu.

Ki·lau·e·a (kē′lou-ā′ə). An active volcanic crater on the southeast slope of Mauna Loa in south-central Hawaii Island. It is one of the largest and most spectacular craters in the world.

kil·der·kin (kĭl′dər-kĭn) *n.* **1.** A cask. **2.** An obsolete English measure of capacity equal to about 18 gallons (68 liters). [Middle English, alteration of Middle Flemish *kinderkin* (variant of Middle Dutch *kindekijn*) : *quintel, quintlein,* quintal (from Medieval Latin *quintāle;* see QUINTAL) + *-kijn,* diminutive suff.]

ki·lim (kē-lēm′, kĭl′ĭm) *n.* A tapestry-woven Turkish rug or other textile with geometric designs in rich, brilliant colors. [Turkish, from Persian *gilīm.*]

Kil·i·man·ja·ro (kĭl′ə-mən-jär′ō), **Mount.** The highest mountain in Africa, in northeast Tanzania near the Kenya border, rising in two snow-capped peaks to 5,898.7 m (19,340 ft).

kill¹ (kĭl) *v.* **killed, kill·ing, kills.** *—tr.* **1.a.** To put to death. **b.** To deprive of life: *The Black Death was a disease that killed millions.* **2.** To put an end to; extinguish. **3.a.** To destroy a vitally essential quality in: *Too much garlic killed the taste of the meat.* **b.** To cause to cease operating; turn off: *killed the motor.* **c.** To tire out completely; exhaust: *"The trip to work, and the boredom and nervousness of jobs, kills men"* (Jimmy Breslin). **4.** To pass (time) in aimless activity: *killed a few hours before the flight by sightseeing.* **5.** To consume entirely; finish off: *kill a bottle of brandy.* **6.** To cause extreme pain or discomfort to: *My shoes are killing me.* **7.** To mark for deletion; rule out: *killed the story.* **8.** To thwart passage of; veto: *kill a congressional bill.* **9.** *Informal.* To overwhelm with hilarity, pleasure, or admiration: *The outstanding finale killed the audience.* **10.** *Sports.* **a.** To hit (a ball) with great force. **b.** To hit (a ball) with such force as to make a return impossible, especially in a racquet game. *—intr.* **1.** To cause death or extinction; be fatal. **2.** To commit murder. **—kill** *n.* **1.** The act of killing. **2.a.** An animal killed, especially in hunting. **b.** A person killed or to be killed: *"Infantrymen . . . had seen too many kills suddenly get up and run away or shoot at them as they approached"* (Nelson DeMille). **c.** An enemy aircraft, vessel, or missile that has been attacked and destroyed. **3.** *Sports.* A kill shot. *—attributive.* Often used to modify another noun: *kill range; kill probability.* **—*phrasal verb.* kill off.** To destroy in such large numbers as to render extinct. **—*idiom.* in at** (or **on**) **the kill.** Present at the moment of triumph. [Middle English *killen,* perhaps from Old English **cyllan.* See **gʷelə-** in Appendix.]

♦**kill²** (kĭl) *n. New York State.* See **creek** (sense 1). See Regional Notes at **olicook, run.** [Dutch *kil,* from Middle Dutch *kille.*]

Kil·lar·ney (kĭ-lär′nē), **Lakes of.** Three small lakes of southwest Ireland near the market town of **Killarney** (population, 7,693). Studded with islands, the lakes are a popular tourist attraction noted for their scenic beauty.

kill·deer (kĭl′dîr′) *n., pl.* **killdeer** or **-deers.** A New World plover *(Charadrius vociferus)* that has a distinctive noisy cry and two black bands across its breast. [Probably imitative of its call.]

Kil·leen (kĭ-lēn′). A city of central Texas southwest of Waco. Founded in 1882, it has some light industry. Population, 46,296.

kill·er (kĭl′ər) *n.* **1.** One that kills: *a disease that was a killer of thousands; a killer of new ideas.* **2.** *Slang.* Something that is extremely difficult to deal with or withstand: *an exam that was a real killer.*

killer bee *n.* See **Africanized bee.**

killer cell *n.* A large, differentiated T cell that attacks and lyses target cells bearing specific antigens. Also called *cytotoxic T cell, killer T cell.*

kill·er·sat (kĭl′ər-săt′) *n.* An artificial satellite intended to destroy enemy satellites, especially one that contains explosives to be detonated when the satellite is maneuvered into the target's orbit. Also called *killer satellite.*

killer T cell *n.* See **killer cell.**

killer whale *n.* A black and white predatory whale *(Orcinus orca)* that feeds on large fish, squid, and sometimes dolphins and seals. Also called *orca.*

kil·lick also **kil·lock** (kĭl′ĭk) *n. Nautical.* A small anchor, especially one made of a stone in a wooden frame. [Origin unknown.]

kil·lie (kĭl′ē) *n.* A killifish.

kil·li·fish (kĭl′ĭ-fĭsh′) *n., pl.* **killifish** or **-fish·es.** Any of numerous small fishes of the family Cyprinodontidae, including the guppy and mosquito fish, inhabiting chiefly fresh and brackish waters in warm regions. [Perhaps KILL² + FISH.]

kill·ing (kĭl′ĭng) *n.* **1.** Murder; homicide. **2.** A kill; a quarry. **3.** A sudden large profit: *made a killing on the stock market.* **—killing** *adj.* **1.** Intended or apt to kill; fatal. **2.** Thoroughly exhausting. **3.** *Informal.* Hilarious. **—kill′ing·ly** *adv.*

kill·joy (kĭl′joi′) *n.* One who spoils the enthusiasm or fun of others.

kil·lock (kĭl′ĭk) *n. Nautical.* Variant of **killick.**

kill shot *n. Sports.* A shot in various games, especially racquet games, that is so forcefully hit or perfectly placed that it cannot be returned.

Kil·mar·nock (kĭl-mär′nək). A burgh of southwest Scotland south-southwest of Glasgow. It is an industrial town in a mining region. Population, 51,800.

Kil·mer (kĭl′mər), **(Alfred) Joyce.** 1886–1918. American poet whose best known work is "Trees" (1913).

kiln (kĭln, kĭl) *n.* Any of various ovens for hardening, burning, or drying substances such as grain, meal, or clay, especially a brick-lined oven used to bake or fire ceramics. **—kiln** *tr.v.* **kilned, kiln·ing, kilns.** To process in one of these ovens. [Middle English *kilne,* from Old English *cyln,* from Latin *culīna,* kitchen, stove. See **pekʷ-** in Appendix.]

ki·lo (kē′lō) *n., pl.* **-los. 1.** A kilogram. **2.** A kilometer.

kilo– *pref.* One thousand (10^3): *kilowatt.* [French, from Greek *khilioi,* thousand. See **gheslo-** in Appendix.]

kil·o·bit (kĭl′ə-bĭt′) *n. Computer Science.* **1.** A unit of information equal to 1,024 (2^{10}) bits. **2.** One thousand bits.

kil·o·byte (kĭl′ə-bīt′) *n. Abbr.* **K, KB** *Computer Science.* **1.** A unit of measurement of the memory capacity of a computer, equal to 1,024 (2^{10}) bytes. **2.** One thousand bytes.

kil·o·cal·o·rie (kĭl′ə-kăl′ə-rē) *n. Abbr.* **kcal** See **calorie** (sense 3a).

kil·o·cu·rie (kĭl′ə-kyo͝or-ē′, -kyo͝o′rē) *n. Abbr.* **kc, kC** One thousand curies.

kil·o·cy·cle (kĭl′ə-sī′kəl) *n. Abbr.* **kc** Kilohertz.

kil·o·gauss (kĭl′ə-gous′) *n. Abbr.* **kG** A unit of magnetic induction equal to 1,000 (10^3) gauss.

kil·o·gram (kĭl′ə-grăm′) *n. Abbr.* **kg 1.** The base unit of mass in the International System, equal to 1,000 grams (2.2046 pounds). See table at **measurement. 2.** Kilogram force.

kilogram calorie *n.* See **calorie** (sense 3a).

kilogram force *n. Abbr.* **kgf** A force equal to a kilogram weight or a one-kilogram mass times the acceleration of gravity.

kil·o·gram-me·ter (kĭl′ə-grăm-mē′tər) *n.* A unit of energy and work in the meter-kilogram-second system, equal to the work performed by a one-kilogram force acting through a distance of one meter.

kil·o·hertz (kĭl′ə-hûrts′) *n. Abbr.* **kHz** A unit of frequency equal to 1,000 hertz.

kil·o·meg·a·cy·cle (kĭl′ə-mĕg′ə-sī′kəl) *n.* See **gigahertz.**

kil·o·me·ter (kĭ-lŏm′ĭ-tər, kĭl′ə-mē′tər) *n. Abbr.* **km** A metric unit of length equal to 1,000 meters (0.62 mile). See table at **measurement. —kil′o·met′ric** (kĭl′ə-mĕt′rĭk) *adj.*

kil·o·oer·sted (kĭl′ō-ûr′stĕd′) *n.* One thousand oersteds.

kil·o·ton (kĭl′ə-tŭn′) *n. Abbr.* **kt 1.** A unit of weight or capacity equal to 1,000 tons. **2.** An explosive force equivalent to that of 1,000 metric tons of TNT.

kil·o·watt (kĭl′ə-wŏt′) *n. Abbr.* **kW** A unit of power equal to 1,000 watts.

kil·o·watt-hour (kĭl′ə-wŏt-our′) *n. Abbr.* **kWh, kW-hr** A unit of electric power equal to the work done by one kilowatt acting for one hour.

kilt (kĭlt) *n.* **1.** A knee-length skirt with deep pleats, usually of a tartan wool, worn as part of the dress for men in the Scottish Highlands. **2.** A similar skirt worn by women, girls, and boys. **—kilt** *tr.v.* **kilt·ed, kilt·ing, kilts.** To tuck up (something) around the body. [From *kilt,* to tuck up, from Middle English *kilten,* of Scandinavian origin.]

kil·ter (kĭl′tər) *n.* Good condition; proper form: *"policy 'adjustments' designed to bring the . . . country's economy back into kilter with the Western economic system"* (Edward Zuckerman). [Origin unknown.]

Kim·ber·ley (kĭm′bər-lē). A city of central South Africa west-northwest of Bloemfontein. Founded in 1871 after the discovery of a rich trove of diamonds nearby, Kimberley also has some manufacturing industries. Population, 70,920.

kim·ber·lite (kĭm′bər-līt′) *n.* A rock formation in South Africa containing peridotite, in which diamonds are formed. [After KIMBERLEY.] **—kim′ber·lit′ic** (-lĭt′ĭk) *adj.*

Kim·bun·du (kĭm-bo͝on′do͞o) *n.* See **Mbundu** (sense 4).

ki·mo·no (kə-mō′nə, -nō) *n., pl.* **-nos. 1.** A long, wide-sleeved Japanese robelike dress worn with an obi and often elaborately decorated. **2.** A loose robe worn chiefly by women. [Japanese : *ki,* to wear + *mono,* object.]

kin (kĭn) *n.* **1.** *(used with a pl. verb).* One's relatives; family; kinfolk. **2.** A kinsman or kinswoman. **—kin** *adj.* Related; akin. [Middle English, from Old English *cyn.* See **gene-** in Appendix.]

–kin or **–kins** *suff.* Little one: *devilkin.* [Middle English, probably from Middle Dutch *-kijn, -kin.*]

ki·na (kē′nə) *n., pl.* **kina** or **-nas.** See table at **currency.** [Indigenous word in Papua New Guinea.]

ki·nase (kī′nās′, -nāz′, kĭn′ās′, āz′) *n.* Any of various enzymes that catalyze the transfer of a phosphate group from a donor, such as ADP or ATP, to an acceptor. [KIN(ETIC) + –ASE.]

kind¹ (kīnd) *adj.* **kind·er, kind·est. 1.** Of a friendly, generous, or warm-hearted nature. **2.** Showing sympathy or understanding; charitable: *a kind word.* **3.** Humane; considerate: *kind to animals.* **4.** Forbearing; tolerant: *Our neighbor was very kind about the window we broke.* **5.** Generous; liberal: *kind words of praise.* **6.** Agreeable; beneficial: *a dry climate kind to asthmatics.* [Middle English, natural, kind, from Old English *gecynde,* natural. See **gene-** in Appendix.]

SYNONYMS: *kind, kindly, kindhearted, benign, benevolent.* These adjectives apply to persons and their actions and mean having or showing a tender, considerate, and helping nature. *Kind* and *kindly* are the least specific: *is kind to sick patients; thanked her for her kind letter; a kindly gentleman; kindly criticism. Kindhearted* especially suggests an innately kind disposition: *a generous and kindhearted teacher. Benign* implies gentleness and mildness: *a benign smile; benign intentions; a benign ruler of millions. Benevolent* suggests charitableness and a desire to promote the welfare or happiness of others: *has a benevolent nature; a benevolent contributor.*

kind² (kīnd) *n.* **1.** A group of individuals linked by traits held in common. **2.** A particular variety; a sort: *What kind of soap do you like best?* See Synonyms at **type. 3.** Fundamental, underlying character as a determinant of the class to which a thing belongs; nature or essence. **4.** A doubtful or borderline member of a given category: *fashioned a kind of shelter; a kind of bluish color.* **5.** *Archaic.* Manner. ***—idioms.*** **all kinds of.** *Informal.* Plenty of; ample: *We have all kinds of time to finish the job.* **in kind. 1.** With produce or commodities rather than with money: *pay in kind.* **2.** In the same manner or with an equivalent: *returned the slight in kind.* **kind of.** *Informal.* Rather; somewhat: *I'm kind of hungry.* [Middle English, from Old English *gecynd,* race, offspring, kind. See **gene-** in Appendix.]

USAGE NOTE: The use of the plural demonstratives *these* and *those* with *kind* and *sort,* as in *these kind* (or *sort*) *of films,* has been a traditional bugbear of American grammarians. By and large, British grammarians have been more tolerant, and the construction can be found in the works of British writers from Pope to Dickens to Churchill. Grammatically, the question boils down to whether *kind* and *sort* should be treated as head nouns (analogous to *species* or *variety,* for example) or whether they have become semantically weakened to the status of a sort of phrasal quantifier that functions like an adjective, analogous in some ways to *bunch* and *number* in expressions such as *a bunch of friends, a number of reasons.* If *kind* and *sort* are unambiguously nouns, one would expect to see only singular demonstratives and singular verbs accompanying them: *This kind of films is popular* (compare *This species of spider is found only in the New World*). If they are functioning as adjectives, however, the plural demonstrative and plural verb should be acceptable: *These kind of films are popular.* In fact, the *kind of* construction can be plausibly analyzed either way, which is doubtless why writers have mixed and matched the number of demonstratives and verbs in just about every possible combination. We find reputable precedent for *this kind of films are, these kind of films are, this kind of films is, these kind of films is,* and so on. There are only two reliable regularities: when the plural *kinds* is used, the demonstrative and the verb must also be plural: *These* (not *this*) *kinds of films are* (not *is*) *popular.* By the same token, when both *kind* and the noun following it are singular, the verb must be singular: *This kind of film is* (not *are*) *popular.* To this may be added a word of caution to American writers: despite the existence of ample literary precedent for *these kind of films,* the construction has been so thoroughly stigmatized by native grammarians that its use would have to be reckoned indiscreet, if not strictly incorrect.

kin·der·gar·ten (kĭn′dər-gär′tn, -dn) *n. Abbr.* **K** A program or class for four-year-old to six-year-old children that serves as an introduction to school. [German : *Kinder,* genitive pl. of *Kind,* child (from Middle High German *kint,* from Old High German *kind;* see **gene-** in Appendix) + *Garten,* garden (from Middle High German *garte,* from Old High German *garto;* see **gher-¹** in Appendix).]

kin·der·gart·ner also **kin·der·gar·ten·er** (kĭn′dər-gärt′nər, -gärd′-) *n.* **1.** A child who attends kindergarten. **2.** A teacher in a kindergarten. [German *Kindergärtner,* from *Kindergarten,* kindergarten. See KINDERGARTEN.]

kind·heart·ed (kīnd′här′tĭd) *adj.* Having or proceeding from a kind heart. See Synonyms at **kind¹. —kind′heart′ed·ly** *adv.* **—kind′heart′ed·ness** *n.*

kin·dle¹ (kĭn′dl) *v.* **-dled, -dling, -dles.** *—tr.* **1.a.** To build or fuel (a fire). **b.** To set fire to; ignite. **2.** To cause to glow; light up: *The sunset kindled the skies.* **3.** To arouse (an emotion, for example): *"No spark had yet kindled in him an intellectual passion"* (George Eliot). *—intr.* **1.** To catch fire; burst into flame. **2.** To become bright; glow. **3.** To become inflamed. To be stirred up; rise. [Middle English *kindelen* (influenced by *kindelen,* to give birth to, cause; see KINDLE²), probably from Old Norse *kynda.*] **—kin′dler** *n.*

kin·dle² (kĭn′dl) *n.* A brood or litter, especially of kittens. See Synonyms at **flock¹. —kindle** *intr.v.* **-dled, -dling, -dles.** To give birth to young. Used especially of rabbits. [Middle English *kindelen,* from *kindel,* offspring, from Old English *gecynd.* See KIND².]

kind·less (kīnd′lĭs) *adj.* **1.** Exhibiting or feeling no kindness or compassion; heartless: *a kindless refusal of our pleas.* **2.** *Obsolete.* Inhuman.

kind·li·ness (kīnd′lē-nĭs) *n.* **1.** The quality or state of being kindly. **2.** A kindly deed: *Thank you for your many kindlinesses.*

kiln
An intermittent kiln

kilt

kimono

ă pat	oi boy
ā pay	ou out
âr care	o͝o took
ä father	o͞o boot
ĕ pet	ŭ cut
ē be	ûr urge
ĭ pit	th thin
ī pie	*th* this
îr pier	hw which
ŏ pot	zh vision
ō toe	ə about, item
ô paw	♦ regionalism

Stress marks: ′ (primary); ′ (secondary), as in **dictionary** (dĭk′shə-nĕr′ē)

king
Chess piece

Billie Jean King
At Wimbledon, 1983

Martin Luther King, Jr.
Photographed in 1964

♦**kin·dling** (kĭnd′lĭng) *n.* Easily ignited material, such as dry sticks of wood, used to start a fire. Also called ♦*lightwood.* See Regional Note at **lightwood.**

kindling point *n.* See **ignition point.**

kind·ly (kīnd′lē) *adj.* **-li·er, -li·est. 1.** Of a sympathetic, helpful, or benevolent nature: *a kindly interest; a gentle, kindly soul.* See Synonyms at **kind**[1]. **2.** Agreeable; pleasant: *a kindly breeze.* **3. a.** *Archaic.* Within the law; lawful. **b.** *Obsolete.* Natural to its kind. **—kindly** *adv.* **1.** Out of kindness: *She kindly overlooked their mistake.* **2.** In a kind manner: *He spoke kindly to us.* **3.** Pleasantly; agreeably: *The sun shone kindly.* **4.** In an accommodating manner: *Would you kindly fill in your name and address?* **5.** *Obsolete.* In a way or course that is natural; fittingly.

kind·ness (kīnd′nĭs) *n.* **1.** The quality or state of being kind. **2.** An instance of kind behavior: *I will always remember your many kindnesses to me.*

kin·dred (kĭn′drĭd) *n.* **1.** A group of related persons, as a clan or tribe. **2.** *(used with a pl. verb).* A person's relatives; kinfolk. **—kindred** *adj.* **1.** Of the same ancestry or family: *kindred clans.* **2.** Having a similar or related origin, nature, or character: *kindred emotions.* [Middle English *kinrede, kindrede,* from Old English *cynrēde* : *cyn,* kin; see **gene-** in Appendix + *-rēde* (variant of *rǣden,* condition; see **ar-** in Appendix).] **—kin′dred·ness** *n.*

kine (kīn) *n.* *Archaic.* A plural of **cow**[1]. [Middle English *kyn,* from Old English *cȳna,* genitive pl. of *cū,* cow. See COW[1].]

kin·e·mat·ics (kĭn′ə-măt′ĭks) *n. (used with a sing. verb).* The branch of mechanics that studies the motion of a body or a system of bodies without consideration given to its mass or the forces acting on it. [From Greek *kinēma, kinēmat-,* motion, from *kinein,* to move. See **kei-**[2] in Appendix.] **—kin′e·mat′ic, kin′e·mat′i·cal** *adj.* **—kin′e·mat′i·cal·ly** *adv.*

kin·e·scope (kĭn′ĭ-skōp′, kī′nĭ-) *n.* **1.** See **picture tube. 2.** A film of a transmitted television program. **—kinescope** *tr.v.* **-scoped, -scop·ing, -scopes.** To make a film of (a transmitted television program). [Originally a trademark.]

ki·ne·sics (kə-nē′sĭks, -zĭks, kī-) *n. (used with a sing. verb).* The study of nonlinguistic bodily movements, such as gestures and facial expressions, as a systematic mode of communication. [From Greek *kinēsis,* movement, from *kinein,* to move. See **kei-**[2] in Appendix.] **—ki·ne′sic** (-sĭk, -zĭk) *adj.*

ki·ne·si·ol·o·gy (kə-nē′sē-ŏl′ə-jē, -zē-) *n.* The study of muscles, especially the mechanics of human motion. [Greek *kinēsis,* movement (from *kinein,* to move; see **kei-**[2] in Appendix) + -LOGY.] **—ki·ne′si·ol′o·gist** *n.*

-kinesis *suff.* Motion: *photokinesis.* [From Greek *kinēsis,* movement, from *kinein,* to move. See **kei-**[2] in Appendix.]

kin·es·the·sia (kĭn′ĭs-thē′zhə, kī′nĭs-) *n.* The sense that detects bodily position, weight, or movement of the muscles, tendons, and joints. [Greek *kinein,* to move; see **kei-**[2] in Appendix + ESTHESIA.] **—kin′es·thet′ic** (-thĕt′ĭk) *adj.* **—kin′es·thet′i·cal·ly** *adv.*

ki·net·ic (kĭ-nĕt′ĭk, kī-) *adj.* Of, relating to, or produced by motion. [Greek *kinētikos,* from *kinētos,* moving, from *kinein,* to move. See **kei-**[2] in Appendix.] **—ki·net′i·cal·ly** *adv.*

kinetic art *n.* An art form, such as an assemblage or a sculpture, made up of parts designed to be set in motion by an internal mechanism or an external stimulus, such as light or air. **—kinetic artist** *n.*

kinetic energy *n.* The energy possessed by a body because of its motion, equal to one half the mass of the body times the square of its speed.

ki·net·i·cism (kə-nĕt′ĭ-sĭz′əm, kī-) *n.* The theory or practice of kinetic art. **—ki·net′i·cist** *n.*

ki·net·ics (kĭ-nĕt′ĭks, kī-) *n. (used with a sing. verb).* **1.** See **dynamics** (sense 1a). **2.** The branch of chemistry that is concerned with the rates of change in the concentration of reactants in a chemical reaction.

kinetic theory *n.* A theory concerning the thermodynamic behavior of matter, especially the relationships among pressure, volume, and temperature in gases. It is based on the dependence of temperature on the kinetic energy of the rapidly moving particles of a substance. According to the theory, energy and momentum are conserved in all collisions between particles, and the average behavior of the particles can be deduced by statistical analysis.

ki·ne·tin (kī′nə-tĭn) *n.* A plant hormone that promotes cell division.

kineto– *pref.* Movement: *kinetoplast.* [Greek *kinēto-,* from *kinētos,* moving, from *kinein,* to move. See KINETIC.]

ki·net·o·chore (kĭ-nĕt′ə-kôr′, -kōr′, -nē′tə-, kī-) *n.* *Biology.* Either of two submicroscopic attachment points for chromosomal microtubules, present on each centromere during the process of cell division. [KINETO– + Greek *khōros,* place; see –CHORE.]

ki·net·o·plast (kĭ-nĕt′ə-plăst′, -nē′tə-, kī-) *n.* *Microbiology.* An independently replicating structure lying near the base of the flagellum in certain protozoans.

ki·net·o·some (kĭ-nĕt′ə-sōm′, -nē′tə-, kī-) *n.* See **basal body.**

kin·folk (kĭn′fōk′) also **kins·folk** (kĭnz′-) or **kin·folks** (kĭn′fōks′) *pl.n.* Relatives; kindred.

king (kĭng) *n.* **1.** *Abbr.* **k., K.** A male sovereign. **2.** One that is supreme or preeminent in a particular group, category, or sphere. **3. King. a.** The perfect, omniscient, omnipotent being; God. **b.** Jesus. **4.** *Games.* **a.** A playing card bearing the figure of a king, ranking above a queen. **b.** *Abbr.* **K, k.** The principal chess piece, which can move one square in any direction and must be protected against checkmate. **c.** A piece in checkers that has been moved to the last row on the opponent's side of the board and been crowned, thus becoming free to move both forward and backward. **5. Kings.** *(used with a sing. verb). Abbr.* **K** *Bible.* See table at **Bible. —king** *adj.* Principal or chief, as in size or importance. **—king** *tr.v.* **kinged, king·ing, kings.** *Games.* To make (a piece in checkers) into a king; crown. [Middle English, from Old English *cyning.* See **gene-** in Appendix.]

King, Billie Jean Moffitt. Born 1943. American tennis player who won 20 titles at Wimbledon (6 singles, 10 women's doubles, and 4 mixed doubles) and 4 U.S. Open championships (1967, 1971, 1972, and 1974).

King, Coretta Scott. Born 1927. American civil rights leader noted for her work on behalf of the Southern Christian Leadership Conference.

King, Martin Luther, Jr. 1929–1968. American cleric whose eloquence and commitment to nonviolent tactics formed the foundation of the civil rights movement of the 1950's and 1960's. He won the 1964 Nobel Peace Prize, four years before he was assassinated in Memphis, Tennessee.

King, William Lyon Mackenzie. 1874–1950. Canadian politician who three times served as prime minister (1921–1926, 1926–1930, and 1935–1948).

King, William Rufus de Vane. 1786–1853. Vice President of the United States (1853) under Franklin Pierce. He died in office.

king·bird (kĭng′bûrd′) *n.* Any of various American flycatchers of the genus *Tyrannus,* especially *T. tyrannus.*

king·bolt (kĭng′bōlt′) *n.* A vertical bolt that joins the body of a wagon or other vehicle to its front axle and usually acts as a pivot. Also called *kingpin.*

King Charles spaniel *n.* Any of a variety of English toy spaniel with a curly, black and tan coat and long ears. [After *King Charles II.*]

king cobra *n.* A large venomous snake *(Ophiophagus hannah)* of southeast Asia and the Philippines that can grow to a length of 5.5 meters (18 feet). Also called *hamadryad.*

king crab *n.* **1.** A large crab *(Paralithodes camtschatica)* inhabiting the coastal waters of Alaska, Japan, and Siberia and valued commercially for its edible flesh. Also called *Alaskan king crab.* **2.** See **horseshoe crab.**

king·craft (kĭng′krăft′) *n.* The artful exercise of power by a king.

king·cup (kĭng′kŭp′) *n.* *Chiefly British.* **1.** Any of several plants with yellow flowers. **2.** The marsh marigold.

king·dom (kĭng′dəm) *n.* **1.** A political or territorial unit ruled by a sovereign. **2. a.** The eternal spiritual sovereignty of God or Christ. **b.** The realm of this sovereignty. **3.** A realm or sphere in which one thing is dominant: *the kingdom of the imagination.* **4.** One of the three main divisions (animal, vegetable, and mineral) into which natural organisms and objects are classified. **5.** The highest taxonomic classification into which organisms are grouped, based on fundamental similarities and common ancestry. One widely accepted taxonomic system designates five such classifications: animals, plants, fungi, prokaryotes, and protoctists. See table at **taxonomy.** [Middle English, from Old English *cyningdōm* : *cyning,* king; see KING + *-dōm,* -dom.]

kingdom come *n.* *Informal.* **1.** The next world: *a bomb that could blow us to kingdom come.* **2.** The end of time: *You can complain till kingdom come, but it won't help.* [From the phrase *thy kingdom come* in the Lord's Prayer.]

king·fish (kĭng′fĭsh′) *n., pl.* **kingfish** or **-fish·es. 1. a.** Any of several food and game fishes of the drum family, especially of the genus *Menticirrhus,* indigenous to warm Atlantic waters. **b.** Any of several similar or related fishes, indigenous to the Pacific Ocean. **2.** *Informal.* A person in a position of uncontested authority or influence, especially a powerful political leader.

king·fish·er (kĭng′fĭsh′ər) *n.* Any of various birds of the family Alcedinidae, characteristically having a crested head, a long stout beak, a short tail, and brilliant coloration.

King James Bible *n.* *Bible.* An English translation of the Bible from Hebrew and Greek published in 1611. Also called *Authorized Version, King James Version.*

king·let (kĭng′lĭt) *n.* **1.** Any of several small, grayish North American birds of the genus *Regulus,* having a yellowish or reddish patch on the crown of the head. **2.** A king ruling a kingdom considered small or unimportant.

king·ly (kĭng′lē) *adj.* **-li·er, -li·est. 1.** Having the status or rank of king. **2.** Of, like, or befitting a king; majestic and regal. **—kingly** *adv.* In a royal way; royally. **—king′li·ness** *n.*

king mackerel *n.* A food and game fish *(Scomberomorus cavalla)* of warm Atlantic waters. Also called *cavalla.*

king·mak·er (kĭng′mā′kər) *n.* One who has the political power to influence the selection of a candidate for high public office. **—king′mak′ing** *adj. & n.*

king-of-arms (kĭng′əv-ärmz′) *n., pl.* **kings-of-arms** (kĭngz′-). A high-ranking heraldic officer in Great Britain.

King of Prus·sia (prŭsh′ə). A community of southeast Pennsylvania, a suburb of Philadelphia. Population, 18,200.

king·pin (kĭng′pĭn′) *n.* **1.** *Sports.* The foremost or central pin in an arrangement of bowling pins. Also called *head pin.* **2.** The most important person or element in an enterprise or a system. **3.** See **kingbolt.**

king post *n.* *Architecture.* A supporting post extending vertically from a crossbeam to the apex of a triangular truss.

king salmon *n.* See **Chinook salmon.**

King's Bench (kĭngz) *n.* *Law.* A division of the British superior court system that hears criminal and civil cases. Used when the sovereign is a man.

King's Counsel *n.* *Abbr.* **K.C.** *Law.* A barrister appointed as counsel to the British crown. Used when the sovereign is a man.

King's English *n.* English speech or usage that is considered standard or accepted; Received Standard English.

king·ship (kĭng′shĭp′) *n.* **1.** The position, power, or province of a king. **2.** The domain ruled by a king; a kingdom. **3.** The period or tenure of a king; a reign. **4.** Used with *his* as a title for a king. **5.** A monarchy.

kingside (kĭng′sīd′) *n.* *Games.* The side of the chessboard that is nearest to the king's opening position. **—king′side′** *adv. & adj.*

king-size (kĭng′sīz′) or **king-sized** (-sīzd′) *adj.* **1.** Larger or longer than the usual or standard size: *a king-size desk; king-size pretzels.* **2.** Very large in scope or intensity: *a king-size headache.* **3.a.** Measuring about 76 inches by 80 inches (1.9 meters by 2.0 meters). Used of a bed. **b.** Being of a size that will fit such a bed: *king-size fitted sheets.*

king snake *n.* Any of various nonvenomous constricting New World snakes of the genus *Lampropeltis,* having a black or brown body with white, yellow, or reddish markings and feeding principally on rodents.

kings-of-arms (kĭngz′əv-ärmz′) *n.* Plural of **king-of-arms.**

Kings·port (kĭngz′pôrt′, -pōrt′). A city of northeast Tennessee near the Virginia border east-northeast of Knoxville. Its industries include printing and bookbinding. Population, 32,027.

Kings River. A river, about 201 km (125 mi) long, of central California rising in headstreams that flow through the gorges of **Kings Canyon** in the Sierra Nevada.

King·ston (kĭng′stən). **1.** A city of southeast Ontario, Canada, on Lake Ontario near the head of the St. Lawrence River. The present city was founded by Loyalists in 1783 on the site of Fort Frontenac, a crucial defense point in the French and Indian Wars. It was the capital of Canada from 1841 to 1844. Population, 52,616. **2.** The capital of Jamaica, in the southeast part of the island on the Caribbean Sea. It was founded c. 1692 and became the capital in 1872. Population, 586,930. **3.** A city of southeast New York on the Hudson River north of Poughkeepsie. Permanently established in 1652, it was the capital of New York State until the British burned the town in October 1777. Population, 24,481.

King·ston-up·on-Hull (kĭng′stən-ə-pŏn-hŭl′, -pôn-). See **Hull** (sense 2).

Kings·town (kĭngz′toun′). The capital of St. Vincent and the Grenadines in the West Indies, on the southwest coast of St. Vincent Island. Population, 18,378.

Kings·ville (kĭngz′vĭl′, -vəl). A city of southern Texas southwest of Corpus Christi. Population, 28,808.

Kings·wood (kĭngz′wo͝od′). An urban district of southwest England, a residential suburb of Bristol. Population, 84,200.

King·teh·chen (kĭng′tə′chœn′). See **Jingdezhen.**

King Wil·liam Island (wĭl′yəm). An island of central Northwest Territories, Canada, in the Arctic Ocean between Boothia Peninsula and Victoria Island. It was first explored in 1831.

king·wood (kĭng′wo͝od′) *n.* **1.** A South American tree *(Dalbergia cearensis)* with hard, fine-textured, purplish-brown wood used in cabinetmaking. **2.** The wood of this tree.

ki·nin (kī′nĭn) *n.* Any of various structurally related polypeptides, such as bradykinin, that act locally to induce vasodilation and contraction of smooth muscle. [Short for *bradykinin* : BRADY– + Greek *kinein,* to move; see **kei-²** in Appendix + –IN.]

kink (kĭngk) *n.* **1.** A tight curl, twist, or bend in a length of thin material, as one caused by the tensing of a looped section of wire. **2.** A painful muscle spasm, as in the neck or back; a crick. **3.** A difficulty or flaw that is likely to impede operation, as in a plan or system. **4.** A mental peculiarity; a quirk. **5.** An unusual or eccentric idea. **6.** *Slang.* Peculiarity or deviation in sexual behavior or taste. **—kink** *intr. & tr.v.* **kinked, kink·ing, kinks.** To form or cause to form a kink or kinks. [Dutch, twist in a rope.]

kink·a·jou (kĭng′kə-jo͞o′) *n.* An arboreal mammal *(Potos flavus)* of Central and South America, having brownish fur and a long, prehensile tail. Also called *honey bear.* [French *quincajou,* wolverine, probably blend of Ojibwa *gwiingwa'aage* and Montagnais (Cree) *kuàkuàtsheu.*]

kink·y (kĭng′kē) *adj.* **-i·er, -i·est. 1.** Tightly twisted or curled: *kinky hair.* **2.** *Slang.* Showing or appealing to bizarre or deviant tastes, especially of a sexual or erotic nature: *"his appetite for kinky filmmaking, unmitigated by any artistry"* (John Simon). **—kink′i·ly** *adv.* **—kink′i·ness** *n.*

kin·ni·kin·nick also **kin·ni·kin·nic** (kĭn′ĭ-kĭ-nĭk′) *n.* **1.** A preparation made from dried leaves, bark, and sometimes tobacco and smoked especially by certain Native American peoples. **2.** See **bearberry.** [Unami (Delaware language) *kələkkəníikkan,* literally, item for mixing in, kinnikinnick.]

ki·no (kē′nō) *n., pl.* **-nos.** A reddish resin obtained from several Old World trees of the genera *Eucalyptus, Pterocarpus,* and *Butea* and from tropical American trees of the genera *Coccoloba* and *Dipteryx.* [New Latin, of West African origin; akin to Mandingo *keno.*]

–kins *suff.* Variant of **–kin.**

Kin·sey (kĭn′zē), **Alfred Charles.** 1894–1956. American biologist noted for his studies of human sexuality.

kins·folk (kĭnz′fōk′) *pl.n.* Variant of **kinfolk.**

Kin·sha·sa (kĭn-shä′sə). Formerly **Le·o·pold·ville** (lē′ə-pōld-vĭl′, lā′-). The capital and largest city of Zaire, in the western part of the country on the Congo River. Founded in 1881 by the explorer Henry M. Stanley, who named it after his patron, Leopold II of Belgium, it became capital of the Belgian Congo in 1926 and was the scene of the revolt (June 1960) that led to Zaire's independence. In 1966 its name was changed to Kinshasa, after the name of an early village. Population, 2,653,558.

kin·ship (kĭn′shĭp′) *n.* **1.** Connection by blood, marriage, or adoption; family relationship. **2.** Relationship by nature or character; affinity.

kins·man (kĭnz′mən) *n.* **1.** A relative who is a man. **2.** A man sharing the same racial, cultural, or national background as another.

Kin·ston (kĭn′stən). A city of east-central North Carolina southeast of Raleigh. It is a tobacco market. Population, 25,234.

kins·wom·an (kĭnz′wo͝om′ən) *n.* **1.** A relative who is a woman. **2.** A woman sharing the same racial, cultural, or national background as another.

Kin·yar·wan·da (kĭn′yär-wän′də) *n.* A Bantu language of Rwanda, closely related to Kirundi and an official language of Rwanda.

Ki·o·ga or **Ky·o·ga** (kē-ō′gə). **Lake.** An irregularly shaped lake of central Uganda. The shallow lake is noted for its papyrus swamps.

ki·osk (kē′ŏsk′, kē-ŏsk′) *n.* **1.** A small open gazebo or pavilion. **2.** A small structure, often open on one or more sides, used as a newsstand or booth. **3.** A cylindrical structure on which advertisements are posted. [French *kiosque,* from Turkish *köşk,* from Middle Persian *gōshak,* corner, from Avestan **gaoshaka-,* diminutive of *gaosha-,* ear.]

WORD HISTORY: The lowly kiosk where one buys a newspaper or on which one posts advertisements is like a child in a fairy tale who though raised by humble parents is really the descendant of kings. The word *kiosk* was originally taken into English ultimately from Turkish, in which its source *köşk* meant "pavilion." The open structures referred to by the Turkish word were used as pavilions and summerhouses in Turkey and Persia. The first recorded use of *kiosk* in English (1625) has reference to these Middle Eastern structures, which Europeans imitated in their own gardens and parks. In France and Belgium, where the Turkish word had also been borrowed, their word *kiosque* was applied to something lower on the scale, structures resembling these pavilions but used as places to sell newspapers or as bandstands. England borrowed this lowly structure from France and reborrowed the word, which is first recorded in 1865 with reference to a place where newspapers are sold.

Ki·o·wa (kī′ə-wô′, -wä′, -wā′) *n., pl.* **Kiowa** or **-was. 1.a.** A Native American people formerly inhabiting the southern Great Plains, with a present-day population in southwest Oklahoma. The Kiowa migrated onto the plains in the late 17th century from an earlier territory in western Montana. **b.** A member of this people. **2.** The Tanoan language of the Kiowa.

Kiowa Apache *n., pl.* **Kiowa Apache** or **Kiowa Apaches. 1.a.** A Native American people of the southern Great Plains who formed an integral part of the Kiowa tribe and shared its culture and history although speaking an unrelated Athabaskan language. **b.** A member of this people. **2.** The Athabaskan language of the Kiowa Apache.

kip¹ (kĭp) *n., pl.* **kip.** See table at **currency.** [Thai.]

kip² (kĭp) *n.* **1.** The untanned hide of a small or young animal, such as a calf. **2.** A set or bundle of such hides. [Middle English, bundle of animal hides, perhaps from Middle Dutch or Middle Low German.]

kip³ (kĭp) *Chiefly British. n.* **1.** A rooming house. **2.** A place to sleep; a bed. **3.** Sleep. **—kip** *intr.v.* **kipped, kip·ping, kips.** To sleep. [Perhaps from Danish *kippe,* cheap inn; akin to Old Norse *-kippa,* as in *korn-kippa,* seedcorn holder; akin to Low German *kiffe,* hovel.]

kip⁴ (kĭp) *n.* A unit of weight equal to 1,000 pounds (455 kilograms). [KI(LO)– + P(OUND)¹.]

Kip·ling (kĭp′lĭng), **(Joseph) Rudyard.** 1865–1936. British writer whose major works, including *Kim* (1901), are set in British-occupied India. He won the 1907 Nobel Prize for literature.

kip·per (kĭp′ər) *n.* **1.** A male salmon or sea trout during or shortly after the spawning season. **2.** A herring or salmon that has been split, salted, and smoked. **—kipper** *tr.v.* **-pered, -per·ing, -pers.** To prepare (fish) by splitting, salting, and smoking. [Middle English *kipre,* from Old English *cypera,* spawning male salmon, probably from *cyperen,* of copper, from *coper,* copper (be-

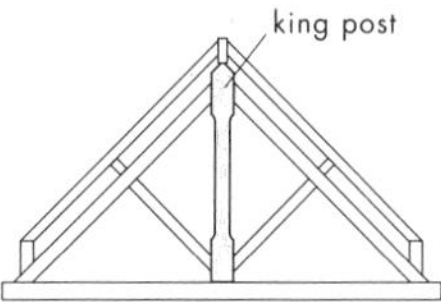

king post

kinkajou
Potos flavus

kiosk

ă pat	oi boy
ā pay	ou out
âr care	o͝o took
ä father	o͞o boot
ĕ pet	ŭ cut
ē be	ûr urge
ĭ pit	th thin
ī pie	*th* this
îr pier	hw which
ŏ pot	zh vision
ō toe	ə about, item
ô paw	♦ regionalism

Stress marks: ′ (primary); ′ (secondary), as in **dictionary** (dĭk′shə-nĕr′ē)

cause of the fish's color during the spawning season). See COPPER[1].]

kir also **Kir** (kîr) *n.* A drink consisting of dry white wine flavored with cassis. [After Canon Félix *Kir* (1876–1968), mayor of Dijon, France.]

Kirch·hoff (kîr′kôf′, kĭrKH′hôf), **Gustav Robert.** 1824–1887. German physicist noted for his research in spectrum analysis, optics, and electricity.

Kirch·ner (kîrk′nər, kîrKH′-), **Ernst Ludwig.** 1880–1938. German expressionist artist whose woodcuts and paintings, such as *The Street* (1913), convey psychological tension and eroticism with sharply contrasting colors and angular forms.

Kir·ghiz[1] or **Kir·giz** (kîr-gēz′) *n., pl.* **Kirghiz** or **-ghiz·es** or **Kirgiz** or **-giz·es. 1.** A member of a traditionally nomadic people living principally in Kirghiz. **2.** The Turkic language of the Kirghiz.

Kir·ghiz[2] or **Kir·giz** (kîr-gēz′, -gyēs′) also **Kir·ghiz·stan** or **Kir·giz·stan** (-gē-stän′, -gyē-), **Kir·ghi·zia** or **Kir·gi·zia** (-gē′zhə, -zhē-ə, -gyē′zĭ-yə). A region in west-central Asia bordering on northwest China. It was probably inhabited before the 13th century by a Turkic-speaking Mongolian people and was annexed by Russia in 1864. Part of a larger autonomous region after 1917, it was reorganized in 1926 and became a constituent republic in 1936. Frunze is the capital. Population, 3,967,000.

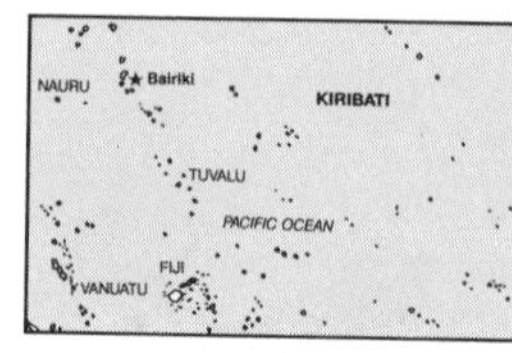

Kiribati

Ki·ri·ba·ti (kēr′ə-bä′tē, kîr′ə-băs′). An island country of the west-central Pacific Ocean near the equator. It includes the former Gilbert Islands, Ocean Island, and the Phoenix and Line islands. The country became independent from Great Britain in 1979. Bairiki, on Tarawa atoll, is the administrative center. Population, 56,213.

kir·i·ga·mi (kîr′ĭ-gä′mē) *n.* The Japanese art of cutting and folding paper into ornamental objects or designs. [Japanese : *kiri,* to cut + *kami,* paper.]

Ki·rin (kē′rĭn′). See **Jilin.**

kirk (kûrk) *n.* **1.** *Scots.* A church. **2. Kirk.** *Chiefly British.* The Presbyterian Church of Scotland. Used with *the.* [Middle English, from Old Norse *kirkja,* from Old English *cirice,* church. See CHURCH.]

Kirk·land (kûrk′lənd). A city of west-central Washington on Lake Washington northeast of Seattle. It is a residential community with some light industry. Population, 18,779.

Kirk·pat·rick (kûrk-păt′rĭk), **Mount.** A mountain, 4,531.1 m (14,856 ft) high, of Antarctica near the edge of the Ross Ice Shelf.

Kirks·ville (kûrks′vĭl′). A city of northern Missouri northwest of Hannibal. It is a manufacturing center. Population, 17,167.

Kir·kuk (kîr-ko͝ok′). A city of northeast Iraq southeast of Mosul. Built on the site of a settlement dating to 3000 B.C., it is an agricultural market. Population, 207,900.

Kirk·wood (kûrk′wo͝od′). A city of eastern Missouri, a commercial and residential suburb of St. Louis. Population, 27,987.

Henry Kissinger

Kir·li·an photography (kîr′lē-ən) *n.* The process of photographing an object by exposing film in a dark room to ultraviolet light that results from electronic and ionic interactions caused by an electric field. The photograph shows a light, glowing band surrounding the outline of the object. [After S.D. and V.K. *Kirlian,* 20th-century Russian electricians.]

Kir·man (kîr-män′, kər-) *n.* A Persian rug with a pastel background, a center medallion, and an ornately patterned border. [After KERMAN.]

kir·mess (kûr′mĭs) *n.* Variant of **kermis.**

Ki·rov (kē′rôf′, kyē′-rəf). A city of west-central Russia east-northeast of Moscow. Founded c. 1174, it became the center of a medieval principality that was conquered by Ivan III in 1489. Population, 411,000.

Ki·ro·va·bad (kĭ-rō′və-băd′, kyĭ′rə-və-bät′). A city of western Azerbaijan southeast of Tbilisi. An important textile and wine center in medieval times, Kirovabad was annexed by Russia in 1804. Population, 261,000.

Ki·ro·vo·grad (kĭ-rō′və-grăd′, kyĭ′rə-va-grät′). A city of central Ukraine south-southeast of Kiev. It is primarily an agricultural trade center. Population, 263,000.

kirsch (kîrsh) *n.* A colorless brandy made from the fermented juice of cherries. [French *kirsch,* short for German *Kirschwasser.* See KIRSCHWASSER.]

kirsch·was·ser (kîrsh′vä′sər) *n.* Kirsch. [German : *Kirsch,* cherry (from Middle High German *kirse,* from Old High German *kirsa,* from Vulgar Latin **ceresia;* see CHERRY) + *Wasser,* water (from Middle High German *wasser,* from Old High German *wassar;* see **wed-**[1] in Appendix).]

kir·tle (kûr′tl) *n. Archaic.* **1.** A man's knee-length tunic or coat. **2.** A woman's dress or skirt. [Middle English *kirtel,* from Old English *cyrtel,* probably ultimately from Latin *curtus,* short. See **sker-**[1] in Appendix.]

Ki·run·di (kē-ro͞on′dē) *n.* A Bantu language of Burundi, closely related to Kinyarwanda and an official language of Burundi.

Ki·san·ga·ni (kē′sän-gä′nē, kĭ-zăng′gä-nē). Formerly **Stan·ley·ville** (stăn′lē-vĭl′). A city of northern Zaire on the Congo River northeast of Kinshasa. It was founded in 1883 by the explorer Henry M. Stanley. Population, 282,650.

Kish (kĭsh). An ancient city of Mesopotamia in the Euphrates River valley of present-day central Iraq. Its extensive ruins have yielded valuable archaeological evidence about Sumerian culture.

Ki·shi·nev (kĭsh′ə-nĕf′, -nôf′, kyĭ′shĭ-nyôf′). The capital of Moldavia, in the southern part of the republic near the Romanian border northwest of Odessa. It was founded as a monastery center in the 15th century. Population, 624,000.

kish·ke also **kish·ka** (kĭsh′kə) *n.* See **derma**[2]. [Yiddish, from Russian *kishka,* intestine. See **(s)keu-** in Appendix.]

Ki·si (kē′sē′, -shē′). See **Jixi.**

Kis·ka Island (kĭs′kə). An island of southwest Alaska near the western end of the Aleutian Islands.

Kis·lev (kĭs′ləv, kēs-lĕv′) *n.* The third month of the year in the Jewish calendar. See table at **calendar.** [Hebrew *kislēw,* from Akkadian *kislimu, kisliwu.*]

kis·met (kĭz′mĕt′, -mĭt) *n.* Fate; fortune. See Synonyms at **fate.** [Turkish, from Persian *qismat,* from Arabic *qismah,* lot, from *qasama,* to divide, allot.]

kiss (kĭs) *v.* **kissed, kiss·ing, kiss·es.** —*tr.* **1.** To touch or caress with the lips as an expression of affection, greeting, respect, or amorousness. **2.** To touch lightly or gently: *flowers that were kissed by dew.* **3.** To strike lightly; brush against: *barely kissed the other car with the bumper.* —*intr.* **1.** To engage in mutual touching or caressing with the lips. **2.** To come into light contact. —**kiss** *n.* **1.** A caress or touch with the lips. **2.** A slight or gentle touch. **3.** A small piece of candy, especially of chocolate. **4.** A drop cookie made of egg whites and sugar. —***phrasal verb.*** **kiss off.** *Slang.* **1.** To dismiss or reject. **2.** To be forced to give up or regard as lost: *He can kiss off that promotion.* **3.** To leave or disappear from notice: *got bad press by telling the reporters to kiss off.* —***idioms.*** **kiss ass.** *Vulgar Slang.* To act submissively or obsequiously in order to gain favor. **kiss good-bye.** *Informal.* To be forced to regard as lost, ruined, or hopeless: *She can kiss her vacation plans good-bye.* [Middle English *kissen,* from Old English *cyssan.*] —**kiss′a·ble** *adj.*

kiss and tell *n.* An article, a book, an interview, or a film containing confidential or embarrassing information based on firsthand knowledge: *"a literature that combines the best of success with the best of kiss and tell"* (Ellen Goodman).

kiss-and-tell (kis′ən-tĕl′) *adj. Informal.* Revealing confidential or embarrassing information that is based on firsthand knowledge: *"upset the CIA with a kiss-and-tell book"* (Sharon Churcher).

kiss·er (kĭs′ər) *n.* **1.** One that kisses: *a politician known as an inveterate kisser of babies.* **2.** *Slang.* The mouth. **3.** *Slang.* The face. See Synonyms at **face.**

kiss·ing bug (kĭs′ĭng) *n.* See **conenose.**

kissing cousin *n.* **1.** A distant relative known well enough to be kissed when greeted. **2.** One of two or more things that are closely akin.

kissing disease *n. Informal.* Infectious mononucleosis.

Kis·sin·ger (kĭs′ĭn-jər), **Henry Alfred.** Born 1923. German-born American diplomat who was national security adviser (1969–1975) and U.S. secretary of state (1973–1977) under Presidents Nixon and Ford. He shared the 1973 Nobel Peace Prize for helping negotiate the Vietnam cease-fire.

kiss of death *n.* Something that is ultimately ruinous, destructive, or fatal: *"Divorce was once a political kiss of death"* (Ellen Goodman). [From the kiss by which Judas betrayed Jesus (Mark 14:44–46).]

kiss-off (kĭs′ôf′, -ŏf′) *n. Slang.* A dismissal, as from a job.

kiss of life *n.* Mouth-to-mouth resuscitation.

kiss of peace *n.* A ceremonial gesture, such as a kiss or handclasp, used as a sign of love and union in some Christian churches during celebration of the Eucharist.

kist (kĭst) *n.* Variant of **cist**[2].

Kist·na (kĭst′nə) or **Krish·na** (krĭsh′-). A river of southern India rising in the Western Ghats and flowing about 1,287 km (800 mi) eastward to the Bay of Bengal.

Ki·swa·hi·li (kē′swä-hē′lē) *n.* See **Swahili** (sense 2).

kit[1] (kĭt) *n.* **1.a.** A set of articles or implements used for a specific purpose: *a survival kit; a shaving kit.* **b.** A container for such a set. **2.** A set of parts or materials to be assembled: *a model airplane kit.* **3.** A packaged set of related materials: *a sales kit.* **4.a.** A collection of clothing and other personal effects used for travel. **b.** A container, such as a bag, valise, or knapsack, for storing or holding such a collection. —***idiom.*** **the (whole) kit and caboodle.** *Informal.* The entire collection or lot. [Middle English *kitte,* wooden tub, probably from Middle Dutch.]

kit[2] (kĭt) *n.* **1.** A kitten. **2.** A young, often undersized furbearing animal. [Short for KITTEN.]

kit[3] (kĭt) *n. Music.* A tiny, narrow violin used by dancing masters in the 17th and 18th centuries. [Origin unknown.]

Ki·ta·kyu·shu (kē-tä′kyo͞o-sho͞o). A city of northern Kyushu, Japan, on the channel connecting the Inland Sea with the Korea Strait. Population, 1,056,400.

kit bag *n.* A traveling bag, such as a knapsack.

Kit Car·son Mountain (kĭt kär′sən). A peak, 4,320.3 m (14,165 ft) high, in the Sangre de Cristo Mountains of south-central Colorado.

kitch·en (kĭch′ən) *n.* **1.** A room or an area equipped for preparing and cooking food. **2.** A style of cooking; cuisine: *a restaurant with a fine French kitchen.* **3.** A staff that prepares, cooks, and serves food. —*attributive.* Often used to modify another noun: *kitchen appliances; kitchen help.* [Middle English *kichene,* from Old English *cycene,* probably from Vulgar Latin

ă pat	oi boy
ā pay	ou out
âr care	o͝o took
ä father	o͞o boot
ĕ pet	ŭ cut
ē be	ûr urge
ĭ pit	th thin
ī pie	*th* this
îr pier	hw which
ŏ pot	zh vision
ō toe	ə about, item
ô paw	♦ regionalism

Stress marks: ′ (primary); ′ (secondary), as in **dictionary** (dĭk′shə-nĕr′ē)

*cocīna, from Late Latin coquīna, from feminine of Latin coquīnus, of cooking, from coquus, cook, from coquere, to cook. See **pekʷ-** in Appendix.]

kitchen cabinet *n.* A group of unofficial advisers to the head of a government. [From the story that President Andrew Jackson met with his unofficial cabinet in the White House kitchen.]

Kitch·e·ner (kĭch′-nər, kĭch′ə-nər). A city of southern Ontario, Canada, west-southwest of Toronto. Settled by Mennonites (1806) and by Germans who named it Berlin in 1825, it was renamed in honor of Lord Kitchener in 1916. Population, 139,734.

Kitchener, Horatio Herbert. First Earl Kitchener of Khartoum and of Broome. 1850–1916. British soldier who brought the Boer War (1899–1902) to a conclusion and served as secretary for war (1914–1916) during World War I.

kitch·en·ette (kĭch′ə-nĕt′) *n.* A small kitchen.

kitchen garden *n.* A garden in which vegetables, fruits, and herbs are grown for household consumption.

kitchen midden *n.* **1.** A mound of kitchen refuse. **2.** *Archaeology.* A mound containing shells, animal bones, and other refuse that indicates the site of a human settlement.

kitchen police *n.* **1.** Enlisted military personnel assigned to work in a kitchen. **2.** Military duty assisting cooks.

kitch·en·ware (kĭch′ən-wâr′) *n.* Utensils, such as pots and pans, for use in a kitchen.

kite (kīt) *n.* **1.** A light framework covered with cloth, plastic, or paper, designed to be flown in the wind at the end of a long string. **2.** *Nautical.* Any of the light sails of a ship that are used only in a light wind. **3.** Any of various predatory birds of the hawk family Accipitridae, having a long, often forked tail and long pointed wings. **4.a.** A piece of negotiable paper representing a fictitious financial transaction and used temporarily to sustain credit or raise money. **b.** A bank check drawn on insufficient funds to take advantage of the time interval required for collection. **c.** A bank check that has been fraudulently altered to show a larger amount. —**kite** *v.* **kit·ed, kit·ing, kites.** —*intr.* **1.** To fly like a kite; soar or glide. **2.** To get money or credit with a kite. —*tr.* **1.** To use (a bad check) to sustain credit or raise money. **2.** To increase the amount of (a check) fraudulently. [Middle English, bird of prey, from Old English *cȳta.*]

kith and kin (kĭth′ ən kĭn′) *pl.n.* **1.** One's acquaintances and relatives. **2.** One's relatives. [Middle English *kith,* from Old English *cȳth,* kinsfolk, neighbors. See **gnō-** in Appendix.]

Kí·thi·ra (kē′thē-rä′). See **Cythera.**

Ki·tik·me·ot (kĭ-tĭk′mē-ŏt′). A region of central Northwest Territories, Canada, including a portion of the northern mainland and Victoria and King William islands.

kitsch (kĭch) *n.* **1.a.** Art or artwork characterized by sentimental, often pretentious bad taste: *"When money tries to buy beauty it tends to purchase a kind of courteous kitsch"* (William H. Gass). **b.** The aesthetic or mentality in which such art is conceived or appreciated: *"a movie that sets out to expose the kitsch of Hollywood fantasy"* (Vincent Canby). **2.** Culture or civilization in a degraded state of sentimentality and vulgarity. —**kitsch** *adj.* Relating to or characterized by kitsch. [German, probably of dialectal origin.] —**kitsch′i·fy′** *v.* —**kitsch′y** *adj.*

kit·ten (kĭt′n) *n.* A young cat. —**kitten** *intr.v.* **-tened, -ten·ing, -tens.** To bear kittens. [Middle English *kitoun,* probably from Old North French **caton,* diminutive of *cat,* cat, from Late Latin *cattus.*]

kit·ten·ish (kĭt′n-ĭsh) *adj.* Playfully coy and frisky. —**kit′ten·ish·ly** *adv.* —**kit′ten·ish·ness** *n.*

kit·ti·wake (kĭt′ē-wāk′) *n.* Either of two cliff-nesting gulls *(Rissa tridactyla* or *R. brevirostris)* of northern regions, having a rudimentary hind toe. [Perhaps imitative of its cry.]

kit·tle (kĭt′l) *Scots. adj.* Touchy; unpredictable. —**kittle** *tr.v.* **-tled, -tling, -tles. 1.** To tickle; arouse. **2.** To puzzle; perplex. [From Middle English *kitillen,* to tickle, probably from Old English **citelian* or from Old Norse *kitla,* to tickle.]

Kit·tredge (kĭt′rĭj), **George Lyman.** 1860–1941. American scholar noted for his expertise on the works of Chaucer and Shakespeare.

kit·ty¹ (kĭt′ē) *n., pl.* **-ties. 1.** *Games.* A fund made up of a portion of each pot in a poker game. **2.** A pool of money, especially one to which a number of people have contributed for a designated purpose. **3.** See **widow** (sense 3). [Probably from KIT¹.]

kit·ty² (kĭt′ē) *n., pl.* **-ties.** A cat, especially a kitten. [Shortening and alteration of KITTEN.]

kit·ty-cor·nered (kĭt′ē-kôr′nərd) or **kit·ty-cor·ner** (-kôr′nər) *adj. & adv.* Variants of **cater-cornered.**

Kit·ty Hawk (kĭt′ē hôk′). A village of northeast North Carolina on a sandy peninsula between Albemarle Sound and the Atlantic Ocean. Nearby is Kill Devil Hill, the site of the Wright brothers' first two successful flights (December 17, 1903).

KIT·TY LIT·TER (kĭt′ē lĭt′ər). A trademark used for granulated clay placed in a box or pan to absorb the waste of a pet.

Ki·twe (kē′twā′). A city of north-central Zambia near the Zaire border. It was founded in 1936. Population, 207,500.

ki·va (kē′və) *n.* An underground or partly underground chamber in a Pueblo village, used by the men especially for ceremonies or councils. [Hopi *kíva.*]

Ki·vu (kē′vo͞o), **Lake.** A lake on the Zaire-Rwanda border north of Lake Tanganyika.

ki·wi (kē′wē) *n., pl.* **-wis. 1.** Any of several flightless birds of the genus *Apteryx* native to New Zealand, having vestigial wings and a long, slender bill. Also called *apteryx.* **2.a.** A woody Chinese vine *(Actinidia chinensis)* having brown, fuzzy, edible fruit with a green, sweet pulp. **b.** The fruit of this plant. Also called *Chinese gooseberry.* [Maori, perhaps of imitative origin.]

Ki·zil Ir·mak also **Ki·zil-Ir·mak** (kĭ-zĭl′ îr-măk′). A river of north-central Turkey flowing about 1,150 km (715 mi) southwest, west, north, and then northeast to the Black Sea.

kJ or **kj** *abbr.* Kilojoule.

KJV *abbr. Bible.* King James Version.

KKK or **K.K.K.** *abbr.* Ku Klux Klan.

KKt *abbr. Games.* King's knight.

kl *abbr.* Kiloliter.

Kla·gen·furt (klä′gən-fo͝ort′). A city of southern Austria southwest of Graz. It was chartered in 1279 and is today a manufacturing center and noted ski resort. Population, 87,321.

Klai·pe·da (klī′pĭ-də, -pĕ-dä). Formerly **Me·mel** (mā′məl). A city of western Lithuania on the Baltic Sea. Founded as a fortress in 1252, it was an important trading town of the Hanseatic League. Population, 195,000.

Klam·ath (klăm′əth) *n., pl.* **Klamath** or **-aths. 1.a.** A Native American people inhabiting an area of the Cascade Range in south-central Oregon and northern California, with close cultural ties to the Modoc. **b.** A member of this people. **2.** The Penutian language of the Klamath.

Klamath Falls. A city of southern Oregon near the California border east-southeast of Medford. It is a resort center in a lumber, livestock, and agriculture area. Population, 16,661.

Klamath River. A river flowing about 423 km (263 mi) generally southwest from Upper Klamath Lake in southwest Oregon through northwest California to the Pacific Ocean.

Klan (klăn) *n.* The Ku Klux Klan.

Klans·man (klănz′mən) *n.* A member of the Ku Klux Klan.

klav·ern (klăv′ərn) *n.* A local organizational unit of the Ku Klux Klan. [KL(AN) + (C)AVERN.]

Klax·on (klăk′sən). A trademark used for a loud electric horn.

Klee (klā), **Paul.** 1879–1940. Swiss artist who combined his expert use of line and color and his theories of abstract art to produce works of whimsy and innocence.

Kleen·ex (klē′nĕks′). A trademark used for a soft facial tissue. This trademark sometimes occurs in print, capitalized or lowercased, with the general meaning "a facial tissue": *"handed out police badges to a platoon of extras and later dispensed Kleenexes to the same extras dressed in funereal black"* (Los Angeles Times). *"'Does somebody have a Kleenex?' she asked"* (New York Times). The trademark is also used in print in figurative extensions as an adjective: *"It's an attitude that comes from looking at countries—and people—as 'dispensable,' the Kleenex school of foreign policy"* (Mary McGrory).

Klein bottle (klīn) *n.* A one-sided topologic surface having no inside or outside, formed by inserting the small open end of a tapered tube through the side of the tube and making it contiguous with the larger open end. [After Felix *Klein* (1849–1925), German mathematician.]

Kleist (klīst), **Heinrich von.** 1777–1811. German writer whose novellas and dramas, including *The Broken Pitcher* (1811), concern characters torn between reason and emotion.

Klem·per·er (klĕm′pər-ər), **Otto.** 1885–1973. German conductor noted for his interpretations of Beethoven and Mahler.

klep·toc·ra·cy (klĕp-tŏk′rə-sē) *n., pl.* **-cies.** A government characterized by rampant greed and corruption. [Greek *kleptein,* to steal + -CRACY.] —**klep′to·crat′ic** (-tə-krăt′ĭk) *adj.*

klep·to·ma·ni·a (klĕp′tə-mā′nē-ə, -mān′yə) *n. Psychiatry.* An obsessive impulse to steal regardless of economic need, usually arising from an unconscious symbolic value associated with the stolen item. [Greek *kleptein,* to steal + -MANIA.] —**klep′to·ma′ni·ac′** (-nē-ăk′) *n.* —**klep′to·ma·ni′a·cal** (-mə-nī′ĭ-kəl) *adj.*

Kle·ve (klā′və) also **Cleves** (klēvz). A city of west-central Germany west-southwest of Münster. It was the seat of a historical duchy and passed subsequently to Brandenburg, Prussia, France, and Prussia again. Population, 44,223.

klez·mer (klĕz′mər) *n., pl.* **klez·mo·rim** (klĕz′mə-rēm′). *Music.* **1.** A traditionally itinerant Jewish folk musician of eastern Europe performing in a small band, as at weddings. **2.** The Jewish folk music played by small, traditionally itinerant bands. —*attributive.* Often used to modify another noun: *klezmer bands; klezmer repertory; klezmer music.* [Yiddish, from Hebrew *kĕlê zemer,* musical instruments.]

klieg light (klēg) *n.* A powerful carbon-arc lamp producing an intense light and used especially in making movies. [After John H. Kliegl (1869–1959) and his brother Anton T. Kliegl (1872–1927), German-born American lighting experts.]

Klimt (klĭmt), **Gustav.** 1862–1918. Austrian painter whose works, in the art nouveau style, include *The Kiss* (1908).

Kline (klīn), **Franz Joseph.** 1910–1962. American abstract expressionist painter many of whose works are characterized by bold, controlled black strokes on a white field.

klip·spring·er (klĭp′sprĭng′ər) *n.* A small, agile African antelope *(Oreotragus oreotragus)* having large ears. [Afrikaans :

kite

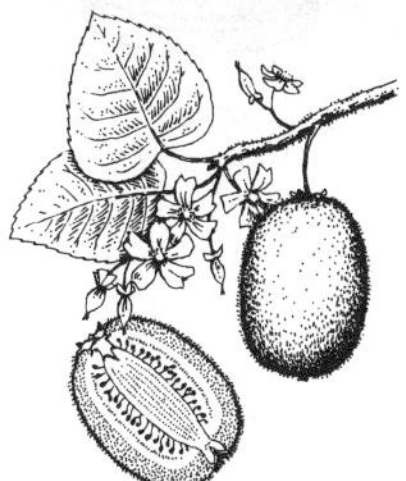

kiwi
Top: Common kiwi
Apteryx australis
Bottom: Actinidia chinensis

Paul Klee

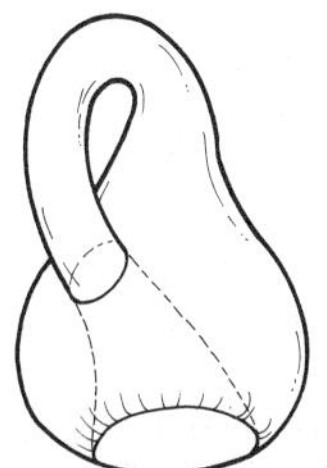

Klein bottle

kneehole
c. 1755-1780 American kneehole bureau table

knight
Chess piece

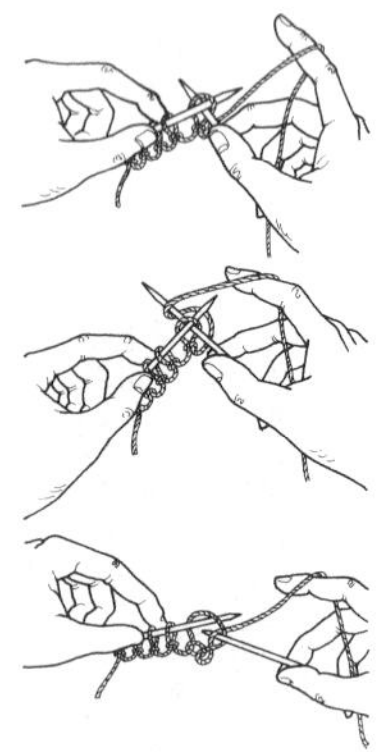
knit
Right-handed English knitting stitch

ă pat	oi boy
ā pay	ou out
âr care	o͝o took
ä father	o͞o boot
ĕ pet	ŭ cut
ē be	ûr urge
ĭ pit	th thin
ī pie	*th* this
îr pier	hw which
ŏ pot	zh vision
ō toe	ə about, item
ô paw	♦ regionalism

Stress marks: **′** (primary); ′ (secondary), as in **dictionary** (dĭk′shə-nĕr′ē)

Dutch *klip,* cliff (from Middle Dutch *klippe*) + Dutch *springer,* jumper (from *springen,* to leap, from Middle Dutch).]

Klon·dike (klŏn′dīk′). A region of Yukon Territory, Canada, just east of Alaska and traversed by the **Klondike River,** about 145 km (90 mi) long. Gold was discovered here in August 1896, leading to the gold rush of 1897–1898 in which more than 25,000 people sought their fortune in the frozen north.

kloof (klo͞of) *n. South African.* A deep ravine. [Afrikaans, from Dutch, from Middle Dutch *clove,* cleft. See **gleubh-** in Appendix.]

Klop·stock (klŏp′stŏk′, klôp′shtôk′), **Friedrich Gottlieb.** 1724–1803. German poet whose unrhymed classically structured works influenced the development of German literature.

kludge or **kluge** (klo͞oj) *n. Slang.* A system, especially a computer system, that is constituted of poorly matched elements or of elements originally intended for other applications. [Origin unknown.] **—kludge** *v.* **—kludg′y** *adj.*

WORD HISTORY: The word *kludge* is not "etymologist-friendly," having many possible origins, none of which can be definitively established. This term, found frequently in the jargon of the engineering and computer professions, denotes a usually workable but makeshift system, modification, solution, or repair. *Kludge* has had a relatively short life (first recorded in 1962 although it is said to have been used as early as 1944 or 1945) for a word with so many possible origins. The proposed sources of the word, German *klug, kluge,* "intelligent, clever," or a blend of *klutz* and *nudge* or *klutz* and *refudge,* do not contain all the necessary sounds to give us the word, correctly pronounced at least. The notions that *kludge* may have been coined by a computer technician or that it might be the last name of a designer of graphics hardware seem belied by the possibility that it is older than such origins would allow. It seems most likely that the word *kludge* originally was formed during the course of a specific situation in which such a device was called for. The makers of the word, if still alive, are no doubt unaware that etymologists need information so they can stop trying to "kludge" an etymology together.

klutz (klŭts) *n. Slang.* **1.** A clumsy person. **2.** A person regarded as stupid. [Yiddish *klots,* from Middle High German *kloz,* block, lump.] **—klutz′i·ness** *n.* **—klutz′y** *adj.*

kly·stron (klī′strŏn′) *n.* An electron tube used to amplify or generate ultrahigh frequency by means of velocity modulation. [Greek *kluzein, klus-,* to wash + –TRON.]

km *abbr.* Kilometer.

K-me·son (kā′mĕz′ŏn, -mē′zŏn, -mĕs′ŏn, -mē′sŏn) *n.* See **kaon.**

kmph *abbr.* Kilometers per hour.

kmps *abbr.* Kilometers per second.

KN *abbr. Games.* King's knight.

kn. *abbr. Nautical.* Knot.

knack (năk) *n.* **1.** A clever, expedient way of doing something. **2.** A specific talent for something, especially one difficult to explain or teach. See Synonyms at **art**[1]. **3.** *Archaic.* **a.** A cleverly designed device. **b.** A knickknack. [Middle English *knakke,* from Middle Dutch *cnacken,* to strike, crack, probably of imitative origin.]

knack·er (năk′ər) *n. Chiefly British.* **1.** A person who buys worn-out or old livestock and slaughters them to sell the meat or hides. **2.** A person who buys discarded structures and dismantles them to sell the materials. [Probably of Scandinavian origin.] **—knack′er·y** (-ə-rē) *n.*

knack·wurst or **knock·wurst** (nŏk′wûrst′, -wo͝orst′) *n.* A short, thick, highly seasoned sausage. [German : *knacken,* to crack (from Middle High German, of imitative origin) + *Wurst,* sausage; see WURST.]

knap (năp) *tr.v.* **knapped, knap·ping, knaps. 1.** To break or chip (stone) with sharp blows, as in shaping flint or obsidian into tools. **2.** *Chiefly British.* **a.** To strike sharply; rap. **b.** To snap at or bite. [Middle English *knappen,* probably of imitative origin.] **—knap′per** *n.*

knap·sack (năp′săk′) *n.* A bag made of sturdy material and furnished with shoulder straps, designed for carrying articles such as camping supplies on the back. [Probably Low German *Knappsack* : *knappen,* to bite (probably of imitative origin) + *Sack,* bag (from Middle Low German *sak,* from Old High German *sac,* from Late Latin *saccus;* see SACK[1]).]

knap·weed (năp′wēd′) *n.* Any of various thistles of the genus *Centaurea,* having variously colored flowers grouped in a head with a spiny involucre. [Middle English *knopwed* : *knop,* knob (from Old English *cnop*) + *wed,* weed; see WEED[1].]

knar also **knaur** (när) *n.* A knot or burl on a tree or in wood. [Middle English *knarre,* probably from Old English **cnear* or from Middle Dutch and Middle Low German *knorre.*]

knave (nāv) *n.* **1.** An unprincipled, crafty fellow. **2. a.** A male servant. **b.** A man of humble birth. **3.** *Games.* See **jack** (sense 3). [Middle English, from Old English *cnafa,* boy, male servant.] **—knav′ish** *adj.* **—knav′ish·ly** *adv.* **—knav′ish·ness** *n.*

knav·er·y (nā′və-rē) *n., pl.* **-ies. 1.** Dishonest or crafty dealing. **2.** An instance of trickery or mischief.

knawel (nôl) also **knawe** (nô) *n.* A low-growing, weedy Eurasian annual *(Scleranthus annuus)* having narrow leaves and inconspicuous green flowers. [German *Knäuel,* from Middle High German *kliuwel, kniuwel,* diminutive of *kliuwe,* ball of yarn, from Old High German *kliuwa.*]

knead (nēd) *tr.v.* **knead·ed, knead·ing, kneads. 1.** To mix and work into a uniform mass, as by folding, pressing, and stretching with the hands: *kneading dough.* **2.** To make or shape by or as if by folding, pressing, and stretching with the hands. **3.** To squeeze, press, or roll with the hands, as in massaging: *kneading a painful calf muscle.* [Middle English *kneden,* from Old English *cnedan.*] **—knead′er** *n.*

knee (nē) *n.* **1. a.** *Anatomy.* The joint between the thigh and the lower leg, formed by the articulation of the femur and the tibia and covered anteriorly by the patella. **b.** The region of the leg that encloses and supports this joint. **2.** An analogous joint or part of a leg of a quadruped vertebrate. **3.** Something resembling the human knee, such as a bent piece of pipe. **4.** The part of a garment, as of trousers, that covers the knee. **5.** An abrupt woody projection arising from the roots of some swamp-growing trees: *cypress knees.* **—knee** *tr.v.* **kneed, knee·ing, knees.** To strike with the knee. [Middle English, from Old English *cnēo.* See **genu-**[1] in Appendix.]

knee action *n.* An automotive front-wheel suspension that permits independent vertical motion of each wheel.

knee·board (nē′bôrd′, -bōrd′) *n.* **1.** *Sports.* A short surfboard ridden in a kneeling position. **2.** A clipboard used especially by pilots during flights for holding maps and checklists. **—kneeboard** *intr.v.* **-board·ed, -board·ing, -boards.** *Sports.* To ride a short surfboard in a kneeling position.

knee breeches *pl.n.* Trousers extending down to or just below the knee.

knee·cap (nē′kăp′) *n.* **1.** See **patella** (sense 1a). **2.** See **kneepad. —kneecap** *tr.v.* **-capped, -cap·ping, -caps.** To cripple by shooting in the legs, especially in the knees.

knee-deep (nē′dēp′) *adj.* **1.** Reaching as high as the knees: *knee-deep floodwaters.* **2.** Submerged to the knees: *was knee-deep in mud.* **3.** Deeply involved: *is knee-deep in work.*

knee-high (nē′hī′) *adj.* Reaching up to the knees: *a knee-high table.* **—knee-high** (nē′hī′) *n.* A sock or stocking that extends just below the knee.

knee·hole (nē′hōl′) *n.* A space or an opening for the knees, as under a desk.

knee jerk *n.* A reflex contraction of the quadriceps muscle resulting in a sudden involuntary extension of the leg, produced by a sharp tap to the tendon below the patella; patellar reflex.

knee-jerk (nē′jûrk′) *adj. Slang.* **1.** Easily predictable; automatic: *"quick, easy laughs and knee-jerk responses"* (New York). **2.** Reacting spontaneously in the expected manner: *a knee-jerk cynic.*

kneel (nēl) *intr.v.* **knelt** (nĕlt), or **kneeled, kneel·ing, kneels.** To go down or rest on one or both knees. [Middle English *knelen,* from Old English *cnēowlian.* See **genu-**[1] in Appendix.]

kneel·er (nē′lər) *n.* **1.** One who kneels, as to pray. **2.** Something, such as a stool, cushion, or board, on which to kneel.

knee·pad (nē′păd′) *n.* A protective covering for the knee. Also called *kneecap.*

knee sock *n.* A sock that reaches just below the knee. Often used in the plural.

knell (nĕl) *v.* **knelled, knell·ing, knells.** *—intr.* **1.** To ring slowly and solemnly, especially for a funeral; toll. **2.** To give forth a mournful or ominous sound. *—tr.* To signal, summon, or proclaim by tolling. **—knell** *n.* **1.** The sound of a bell knelling; a toll. **2.** A signal of disaster or destruction. [Middle English *knellen,* from Old English *cnyllan.*]

Knel·ler (nĕl′ər), Sir **Godfrey.** 1646?–1723. German-born English portrait painter.

knelt (nĕlt) *v.* A past tense and a past participle of **kneel.**

Knes·set (knĕs′ĕt′) *n.* The unicameral parliament of Israel. [Modern Hebrew *Kneset,* from Hebrew (Mishnaic) *kĕneset,* assembly, from *kānas,* to assemble.]

knew (no͞o, nyo͞o) *v.* Past tense of **know.**

Knick·er·bock·er (nĭk′ər-bŏk′ər) *n.* **1. a.** A descendant of the Dutch settlers of New York. **b.** A native or inhabitant of New York. **2. knickerbockers.** Full breeches gathered and banded just below the knee; knickers. [After Diedrich *Knickerbocker,* fictitious author of *History of New York* by Washington Irving.]

knick·ers (nĭk′ərz) *pl.n.* **1. a.** Long bloomers formerly worn as underwear by women and girls. **b.** *Chiefly British.* Panties. **2.** Full breeches gathered and banded just below the knee. [Short for KNICKERBOCKERS.]

knick·knack also **nick·nack** (nĭk′năk′) *n.* A small ornamental article; a trinket. [Reduplication of KNACK.]

knife (nīf) *n., pl.* **knives** (nīvz). **1.** A cutting instrument consisting of a sharp blade attached to a handle. **2.** A cutting edge; a blade. **—knife** *v.* **knifed, knif·ing, knifes.** *—tr.* **1.** To use a knife on, especially to stab; wound with a knife. **2.** *Informal.* To betray or attempt to defeat by underhand means. *—intr.* To cut or slash a way through something with or as if with a knife: *The boat knifed through the waves.* **—*idiom.* under the knife.** *Informal.* Undergoing surgery. [Middle English *knif,* from Old English *cnīf,* from Old Norse *knīfr.*] **—knif′er** *n.*

knife-edge (nīf′ĕj′) *n.* **1.** A sharp cutting edge. **2.** A sharp, narrow edge or border: *"saying lines that teeter on the knife-edge between literature and lunacy"* (Vincent Canby). **3.** A wedge of metal used as a low-friction fulcrum for a beam or lever.

knife·point (nīf′point′) *n.* The sharp end of a knife. **—*idiom.* at knifepoint.** Under threat of being stabbed or cut with a knife: *was mugged at knifepoint.*

knight (nīt) *n.* **1.** *Abbr.* **Knt, kt. a.** A medieval tenant giving military service as a mounted man-at-arms to a feudal landholder. **b.** *Abbr.* **Knt, kt.** A medieval gentleman-soldier, usually highborn, raised by a sovereign to privileged military status after training as a page and squire. **c.** *Abbr.* **K, k.** A man holding a nonhereditary title conferred by a sovereign in recognition of personal merit or service to the country. **2.** *Abbr.* **Knt., kt.** A man belonging to an order or a brotherhood. **3.a.** A defender, champion, or zealous upholder of a cause or principle. **b.** The devoted champion of a lady. **4.** *Abbr.* **Kt, N** *Games.* A chess piece, usually in the shape of a horse's head, that can be moved two squares horizontally and one vertically or two squares vertically and one horizontally. **—knight** *tr.v.* **knight·ed, knight·ing, knights.** To raise (a person) to knighthood. [Middle English, from Old English *cniht.*] **—knight′ly** *adj. & adv.* **—knight′li·ness** *n.*

knight bachelor *n., pl.* **knights bachelors** or **knight bachelors.** An English knight of the lowest rank; a bachelor.

knight-errant (nīt′ĕr′ənt) *n., pl.* **knights-errant** (nīts′-). **1.** A knight, often portrayed in medieval romances, who wanders in search of adventures to prove his chivalry. **2.** One given to adventurous or quixotic conduct. **—knight′-er′rant·ry** (-ĕr′ən-trē) *n.*

knight·head (nīt′hĕd′) *n. Nautical.* Either of two timbers rising from the keel of a sailing ship and supporting the inner end of the bowsprit. [From the fact that it was sometimes decorated with a carving of a man's head.]

knight·hood (nīt′ho͝od′) *n.* **1.** The rank, dignity, or vocation of a knight. **2.** Behavior or qualities befitting a knight; chivalry. **3.** Knights considered as a group.

Knight of Columbus (nīt) *n., pl.* **Knights of Columbus.** *Abbr.* **K of C, K.C.** A member of a benevolent and fraternal society of Roman Catholic men founded in 1882.

Knight of Pythias *n., pl.* **Knights of Pythias.** *Abbr.* **K of P** A member of a secret fraternal order founded in 1864.

knights-errant (nīts′ĕr′ənt) *n.* Plural of **knight-errant.**

Knights of the Round Table (nīts) *pl.n.* In Arthurian legend, the knights of King Arthur's court.

Knight Templar *n., pl.* **Knights Templars** or **Knights Templar. 1.** A member of an order of knights founded about 1118 to protect pilgrims in the Holy Land during the Second Crusade and suppressed in 1312. **2.** A man belonging to a Masonic order in the United States.

knish (kə-nĭsh′) *n.* A piece of dough stuffed with potato, meat, or cheese and baked or fried. [Yiddish, from Ukrainian *knysh,* probably of Turkic origin.]

knit (nĭt) *v.* **knit** or **knit·ted, knit·ting, knits.** *—tr.* **1.** To make (a fabric or garment) by intertwining yarn or thread in a series of connected loops either by hand with knitting needles or on a machine. **2.** To form (yarn or thread) into fabric by intertwining. **3.** To join closely; unite securely. **4.** To draw (the brows) together in wrinkles; furrow. *—intr.* **1.** To make a fabric or garment by knitting. **2.** To become securely joined or mended together closely, as a fractured bone. **3.** To come together in wrinkles or furrows, as the brows. **—knit** *n.* **1.** A fabric or garment made by knitting. **2.** The way in which a fabric has been knit: *a loose knit.* [Middle English *knitten,* to tie in a knot, from Old English *cnyttan.*] **—knit′ter** *n.*

knit·ting (nĭt′ĭng) *n.* **1.** The act or process of producing something knitted. **2.** Material that has been knitted or is in the process of being knitted; knitted work.

knitting needle *n.* A long, thin, pointed rod used in pairs to knit yarn into cloth.

knit·wear (nĭt′wâr′) *n.* Knitted garments.

knives (nīvz) *n.* Plural of **knife.**

knob (nŏb) *n.* **1.** A rounded protuberance. **2.a.** A rounded handle, as on a drawer or door. **b.** A rounded control switch or dial. **3.** A prominent rounded hill or mountain. [Middle English *knobbe.*] **—knobbed** (nŏbd) *adj.* **—knob′by** *adj.*

knob·ker·rie (nŏb′kĕr′ē) *n.* A short club with one knobbed end, used as a weapon by warriors of certain South African peoples. [Afrikaans *knopkierie* : *knop,* knob (from Middle Dutch *cnoppe*) + *kieri,* club (from Khoikhoin *kirri,* stick).]

knock (nŏk) *v.* **knocked, knock·ing, knocks.** *—tr.* **1.** To strike with a hard blow. **2.** To affect in a specified way by striking hard: *knocked the attacker senseless.* **3.** To cause to collide: *I knocked my head on a low beam.* **4.** To produce by hitting or striking: *knocked a hole in the wall.* **5.** To instill with or as if with blows: *We tried to knock some sense into his head.* **6.** *Slang.* To find fault with; criticize: *Don't knock the food; it's free.* *—intr.* **1.** To strike a sharp, audible blow or series of blows, as on a door. **2.** To collide with something: *knocked into the table.* **3.** To make a pounding or clanking noise: *The car engine is knocking.* **—knock** *n.* **1.** An instance of striking or colliding; a blow. **2.** The sound of a sharp tap on a hard surface; a rap. **3.** A pounding or clanking noise made by an engine, often as a result of faulty fuel combustion. Also called *ping.* **4.** *Slang.* A cutting, often petty criticism. **—*phrasal verbs.* knock around** (or **about**). **1.** To be rough or brutal with; maltreat. **2.** To wander from place to place: *knocking around Europe.* **3.** *Informal.* To discuss or consider: *met to knock around some ideas.* **knock back.** *Informal.* To gulp (an alcoholic drink). **knock down. 1.** To bring to the ground with a blow; topple. **2.** To disassemble into parts, as for storage or shipping. **3.** To declare sold at an auction, as by striking a blow with a gavel. **4.** *Informal.* To reduce, as in price: *knocked all the radios down 20 percent.* **5.** *Slang.* To receive as wages; earn: *knocks down $50 an hour.* **knock off. 1.** *Informal.* **a.** To take a break or rest from; stop: *knocked off work at noon.* **b.** To cease work: *It's after five; let's knock off.* **2.** *Informal.* To complete, accomplish, or dispose of hastily or easily; finish: *That author knocks off a book a year.* **3.** *Informal.* To get rid of; eliminate: *knocked off 12 pounds in a month.* **4.** *Slang.* To kill or overcome. **5.** *Slang.* To hold up or rob: *knocked off a bank.* **6.** *Informal.* To copy or imitate, especially without permission: *knocking off someone else's ideas.* **knock out. 1.** To render unconscious. **2.** *Sports.* To defeat (a boxing opponent) by a knockout. **3.** To render useless or inoperative: *The storm knocked out the telephones.* **4.** *Informal.* To exert or exhaust (oneself or another) to the utmost: *knocked herself out to be ready on time.* **knock together.** To make or assemble quickly or carelessly. **knock up. 1.** *Slang.* To make pregnant. **2.** *Chiefly British.* To wake up or summon, as by knocking at the door. **3.** *Chiefly British.* To wear out; exhaust. **—*idioms.* have it knocked.** *Slang.* To be certain of success: *"He knew he had it knocked after he saw a rough cut of* Chinatown" (Time). **knock cold.** To render unconscious; knock out. **knock dead. 1.** To kill with a blow. **2.** *Slang.* To affect strongly and positively: *an amazing performance that knocked the audience dead.* **knock for a loop.** *Slang.* To surprise tremendously; astonish. **knock it off.** *Slang.* Quit it. Used in the imperative: *Knock it off! I'm trying to sleep.* **knock out of the box.** *Baseball.* To force the removal of (an opposing pitcher) by heavy hitting. **knock the** (or **someone's**) **socks off.** *Slang.* To overwhelm or amaze. [Middle English *knokken,* from Old English *cnocian.*]

knock·a·bout (nŏk′ə-bout′) *adj.* **1.** Boisterous; rowdy. **2.** Appropriate for rough wear or use: *a knockabout overcoat.* **—knockabout** *n. Nautical.* A small sloop with a mainsail, jib, and keel but no bowsprit.

knock·down (nŏk′doun′) *n.* **1.a.** The act of knocking down. **b.** The condition of being knocked down. **2.** An overwhelming blow or shock. **3.** Something designed to be easily assembled or disassembled. **—knockdown** *adj.* **1.** Strong enough to knock down or overwhelm; powerful: *a knockdown blow.* **2.** Designed to be easily assembled or disassembled: *knockdown furniture.* **3.** Reduced: *knockdown prices.*

knock·down-drag·out (nŏk′doun′drăg′out′) *adj.* Marked by roughness, violence, and acrimony: *a knockdown-dragout fight.*

knock·er (nŏk′ər) *n.* **1.** A hinged fixture, such as a metal ring or bar, used for knocking on a door. **2.** *Vulgar Slang.* A woman's breast. **3.** A goblin or dwarf said to live under the earth and direct miners to ore by knocking.

knocker
Lion-faced door knocker

knock-knee (nŏk′nē′) *n.* A deformity of the legs in which the knees are abnormally close together and the ankles are spread widely apart. **—knock′-kneed′** *adj.*

knock·off (nŏk′ôf′, -ŏf′) *n. Informal.* An unauthorized copy or imitation, as of designer clothing: *"the place to go for quality knockoffs"* (Women's Wear Daily).

knock·out (nŏk′out′) *n.* **1.a.** The act of knocking out. **b.** The state of being knocked out. **c.** A blow that knocks out an opponent. **2.** *Sports.* **a.** A victory in boxing in which one's opponent is unable to rise from the canvas within a specified time after being knocked down. **b.** The act of winning a boxing match in this way: *won the fight by a knockout.* **3.** *Slang.* A strikingly attractive or impressive person or thing. **—knockout** *adj.* Capable of knocking out: *a knockout punch.*

knockout drops *pl.n. Slang.* A solution, usually of chloral hydrate in alcohol, put into a drink surreptitiously in order to render the drinker unconscious.

knock·wurst (nŏk′wûrst′, -wo͝orst′) *n.* Variant of **knackwurst.**

knoll¹ (nōl) *n.* A small rounded hill or mound; a hillock. [Middle English *knol,* from Old English *cnoll.*]

knoll² (nōl) *Archaic. v. —intr.* **knolled, knoll·ing, knolls.** To ring mournfully; knell. *—tr.* To ring or sound (a bell, for example) mournfully; knell. **—knoll** *n.* A knell. [Middle English *knollen,* probably alteration of *knellen,* to knell, from Old English *cnyllan.*]

knop (nŏp) *n.* A small decorative knob or boss. [Middle English *knoppe,* from Old English *cnop.*]

Knos·sos also **Cnos·sos** or **Cnos·sus** (nŏs′əs). An ancient city of northern Crete near present-day Iráklion. The center of a Bronze Age culture that probably flourished from c. 2000 to 1400 B.C., it is the traditional site of the labyrinth of Daedalus and the palace of King Minos.

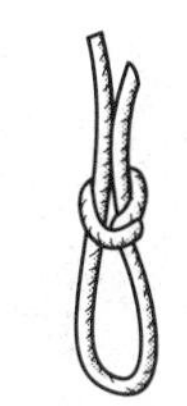

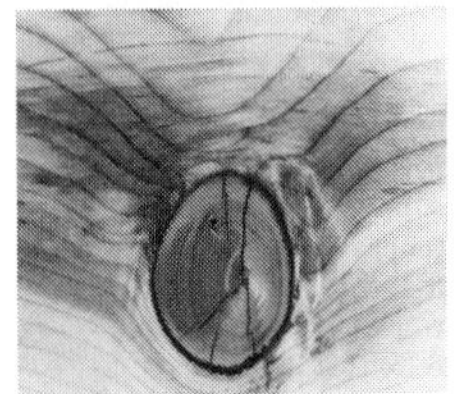

knot¹
Top: Slipknot (*above*), square knot (*center*), and barrel knot (*below*)
Bottom: Cross section of cut lumber

knot¹ (nŏt) *n.* **1.a.** A compact intersection of interlaced material, such as cord, ribbon, or rope. **b.** A fastening made by tying together lengths of material, such as rope, in a prescribed way. **2.** A decorative bow of ribbon, fabric, or braid. **3.** A unifying bond, especially a marriage bond. **4.** A tight cluster of persons or things: *a knot of onlookers.* **5.** A feeling of tightness: *a knot of fear in my stomach.* **6.** A complex problem. **7.a.** A hard place or lump, especially on a tree, at a point from which a stem or branch grows. **b.** The round, often darker cross section of such a

John Knox

lump as it appears on a piece of cut lumber. Also called *node.* **8.** A protuberant growth or swelling in a tissue: *a knot in a gland.* **9. a.** A division on a log line used to measure the speed of a ship. **b.** *Abbr.* **kn., kt.** A unit of speed, one nautical mile per hour, approximately 1.85 kilometers (1.15 statute miles) per hour. **c.** A distance of one nautical mile. **—knot** *v.* **knot·ted, knot·ting, knots.** —*tr.* **1.** To tie in or fasten with a knot or knots. **2.** To snarl or entangle. **3.** To cause to form a knot or knots. —*intr.* **1.** To form a knot or knots. **2.** To become snarled or entangled. [Middle English, from Old English *cnotta.*]

USAGE NOTE: In nautical usage *knot* is a unit of speed, not of distance, and has a built-in meaning of "per hour." Therefore, a ship would strictly be said to travel at ten knots (not ten knots per hour).

knot² (nŏt) *n.* Either of two migratory sandpipers *(Calidris canutus* or *C. tenuirostris)* that breed in Arctic regions. [Middle English, of Scandinavian origin.]

knot·grass (nŏt′grăs′) *n.* **1.** A low-growing, weedy grass *(Paspalum distichum)* with spikelets arranged in two rows along the rachis. **2.** Any of several weedy plants of the genus *Polygonum* that have stems with nodes.

knot·hole (nŏt′hōl′) *n.* A hole in a piece of lumber where a knot has dropped out or been removed.

knot·ty (nŏt′ē) *adj.* **-ti·er, -ti·est. 1.** Tied or snarled in knots. **2.** Covered with knots or knobs; gnarled. **3.** Difficult to understand or solve; puzzlingly intricate. See Synonyms at **complex. —knot′ti·ness** *n.*

knotty pine *n.* Pine wood with a large number of knots, used especially for paneling and furniture.

knot·weed (nŏt′wēd′) *n.* Any of several plants of the genus *Polygonum,* with jointed stems and inconspicuous flowers.

knout (nout) *n.* A leather scourge used for flogging. **—knout** *tr.v.* **knout·ed, knout·ing, knouts.** To flog with a leather scourge. [French, from Russian *knut,* from Old Russian *knutŭ,* from Old Norse *knūtr,* knot in cord.]

know (nō) *v.* **knew** (no͞o, nyo͞o), **known** (nōn), **know·ing, knows.** —*tr.* **1.** To perceive directly; grasp in the mind with clarity or certainty. **2.** To regard as true beyond doubt: *I know she won't fail.* **3.** To have a practical understanding of, as through experience; be skilled in: *knows how to cook.* **4.** To have fixed in the mind: *knows her Latin verbs.* **5.** To have experience of: *"a black stubble that had known no razor"* (William Faulkner). **6. a.** To perceive as familiar; recognize: *I know that face.* **b.** To be acquainted with: *He doesn't know his neighbors.* **7.** To be able to distinguish; recognize as distinct: *knows right from wrong.* **8.** To discern the character or nature of: *knew him for a liar.* **9.** *Archaic.* To have sexual intercourse with. —*intr.* **1.** To possess knowledge, understanding, or information. **2.** To be cognizant or aware. **—*idioms.* in the know.** *Informal.* Possessing special or secret information. **you know.** *Informal.* Used parenthetically in conversation, as to fill pauses or educe the listener's agreement or sympathy: *Please try to be, you know, a little quieter. How were we supposed to make camp in a storm like that, you know?* [Middle English *knowen,* from Old English *cnāwan.* See **gnō-** in Appendix.] **—know′a·ble** *adj.* **—know′er** *n.*

know-how (nō′hou′) *n.* The knowledge and skill required to do something correctly. See Synonyms at **art¹.**

know·ing (nō′ĭng) *adj.* **1.** Possessing knowledge, information, or understanding. See Synonyms at **intelligent. 2.** Showing clever awareness and resourcefulness; shrewd. **3.** Suggestive of secret or private knowledge: *a knowing glance.* **4.** Deliberate; conscious: *a knowing attempt to defraud.* **—know′ing·ly** *adv.*

know-it-all (nō′ĭt-ôl′) *n. Informal.* One who claims to know everything and rejects advice or information from others. **—know′-it-all′** *adj.*

knowl·edge (nŏl′ĭj) *n.* **1.** The state or fact of knowing. **2.** Familiarity, awareness, or understanding gained through experience or study. **3.** The sum or range of what has been perceived, discovered, or learned. **4.** Learning; erudition: *teachers of great knowledge.* **5.** Specific information about something. **6.** Carnal knowledge. [Middle English *knowlech* : *knowen,* to know; see KNOW + *-leche,* n. suff.]

SYNONYMS: *knowledge, information, learning, erudition, lore, scholarship.* These nouns refer to what is known, as by having been acquired through study or experience. *Knowledge* is the broadest; it includes facts and ideas, understanding, and the totality of what is known: *"A knowledge of Greek thought and life, and of the arts in which the Greeks expressed their thought and sentiment, is essential to high culture"* (Charles Eliot Norton). *"Science is organized knowledge"* (Herbert Spencer). *Information* is usually construed as being narrower in scope than *knowledge;* it often implies a collection of facts and data: *"Obviously, a man's judgment cannot be better than the information on which he has based it"* (Arthur Hays Sulzberger). *Learning* usually refers to knowledge that is gained by schooling and study: *"Learning is not attained by chance, it must be sought for with ardor and attended to with diligence"* (Abigail Adams). *Erudition* implies profound knowledge, often in a specialized area: *"Some have criticized his poetry as elitist, unnecessarily impervious to readers who do not share his erudition"* (Elizabeth Kastor). *Lore* is usually applied to knowledge about a particular subject that is gained through tradition or anecdote: *Early peoples passed on plant and animal lore*

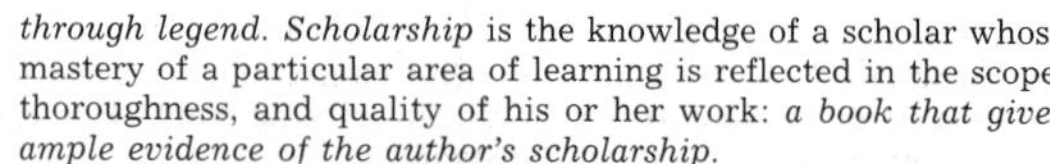

through legend. Scholarship is the knowledge of a scholar whose mastery of a particular area of learning is reflected in the scope, thoroughness, and quality of his or her work: *a book that gives ample evidence of the author's scholarship.*

knowl·edge·a·ble (nŏl′ĭ-jə-bəl) *adj.* Possessing or showing knowledge or intelligence; perceptive and well-informed. **—knowl′edge·a·bil′i·ty, knowl′edge·a·ble·ness** *n.* **—knowl′edge·ably** *adv.*

knowledge base *n.* **1.** *Computer Science.* The part of an expert system that contains the facts and rules needed to solve problems in a specified domain. **2.** A collection of facts and rules for problem solving.

knowledge engineer *n. Computer Science.* A programmer who constructs expert systems. **—knowledge engineering** *n.*

known (nōn) *v.* Past participle of **know. —known** *adj.* Proved or generally recognized: *the only known case; a known authority.* **—known** *n.* Something that is known: *In this instance, the only known is our actual profit margin.*

know-noth·ing (nō′nŭth′ĭng) *n.* **1.** A totally ignorant person; an ignoramus. **2.** An anti-intellectual. **3.** An agnostic. **4. Know-Nothing.** A member of a political party in the United States during the 1850's that was antagonistic toward recent immigrants and Roman Catholics. **—know′-noth′ing·ism** *n.*

Knox (nŏks), **Henry.** 1750–1806. American Revolutionary soldier who transported 55 captured British cannon from Fort Ticonderoga, New York, to Boston, where George Washington used them to force the British to evacuate the city (1776).

Knox, John. 1514?–1572. Scottish religious reformer and founder of Scottish Presbyterianism.

Knox·ville (nŏks′vĭl′, -vəl). A city of eastern Tennessee on the Tennessee River northeast of Chattanooga. Settled c. 1785, it twice served as the state capital (1796–1812 and 1817–1819). Population, 175,045.

Knt *abbr.* Knight.

knuck·le (nŭk′əl) *n.* **1.** *Anatomy.* **a.** The prominence of the dorsal aspect of a joint of a finger, especially of one of the joints connecting the fingers to the hand. **b.** A rounded protuberance formed by the bones in a joint. **2.** A cut of meat centering on the carpal or tarsal joint, as of a pig. **3.** The part of a hinge through which the pin passes. **4. knuckles.** Brass knuckles. **—knuckle** *tr.v.* **-led, -ling, -les. 1.** To press, rub, or hit with the knuckles. **2.** *Games.* To shoot (a marble) with the thumb over the bent forefinger. **—*phrasal verbs.* knuckle down.** To apply oneself earnestly to a task. **knuckle under.** To yield to pressure; give in. [Middle English *knokel.*]

knuckle ball or **knuck·le·ball** (nŭk′əl-bôl′) *n. Baseball.* A slow, randomly fluttering pitch thrown by gripping the ball with the tips or nails of two or three fingers. **—knuck′le·ball′er** *n.*

knuck·le·bone (nŭk′əl-bōn′) *n.* A knobbed bone, as of a knuckle or joint.

knuck·le-dust·er (nŭk′əl-dŭs′tər) *n. Slang.* Brass knuckles.

knuck·le·head (nŭk′əl-hĕd′) *n. Informal.* A stupid person; a blockhead.

knuckle joint *n.* A hinged joint in which a pin fastens the ends of two rods, one of which has an eye that fits between the two perforated projections of the other.

knuck·ler (nŭk′lər) *n. Baseball.* A knuckle ball.

knuckle sandwich *n. Slang.* A punch in the mouth.

knur (nûr) *n.* A bump or knot, as on a tree trunk; a gnarl. [Middle English *knarre, knor.* See KNAR.]

knurl (nûrl) *n.* **1.** A knob, knot, or other small protuberance. **2.** One of a series of small ridges or grooves on the surface or edge of a metal object, such as a thumbscrew, to aid in gripping. **—knurl** *tr.v.* **knurled, knurl·ing, knurls.** To provide with knurls; mill. [Probably diminutive of KNUR.] **—knurled** (nûrld) *adj.* **—knurl′y** *adj.*

Knut (kə-no͞ot′, -nyo͞ot′). See **Canute.**

KO (kā′ō′) *Slang. tr.v.* **KO'd, KO'ing, KO's.** To knock out, as in boxing. **—KO** (kā-ō′, kā′ō′) *n., pl.* **KO's.** A knockout, as in boxing.

ko·a·la (kō-ä′lə) *n.* An arboreal Australian marsupial *(Phascolarctos cinereus)* that has dense grayish fur, large ears, and sharp claws and feeds chiefly on the leaves of eucalyptus trees. [Dharuk (Aboriginal language of southeast Australia) *gulawaŋ.*]

ko·an (kō′än′) *n.* A riddle in the form of a paradox used in Zen Buddhism as an aid to meditation and a means of gaining intuitive knowledge. [Japanese : *ko,* public + *an,* matter.]

kob (kŏb, kōb) *n.* An orange-brown antelope *(Kobus kob)* of southeast Africa. [Of African origin.]

Ko·be (kō′bē′, -bā′). A city of southern Honshu, Japan, on Osaka Bay south-southwest of Kyoto. A port and manufacturing center, it was rebuilt after World War II. Population, 1,410,843.

Ko·blenz also **Co·blenz** (kō′blĕnts′). A city of west-central Germany at the confluence of the Rhine and Moselle rivers southeast of Bonn. Founded as a Roman frontier station, the city was prominent during Carolingian times as a residence of Frankish kings. Population, 111,235.

ko·bo (kô′bô′) *n., pl.* **kobo.** See table at **currency.** [Possibly Yoruba *kọbọ,* from English COPPER¹, penny.]

koala
Adult female and young koala
Phascolarctos cinereus

ă pat	oi boy
ā pay	ou out
âr care	o͝o took
ä father	o͞o boot
ĕ pet	ŭ cut
ē be	ûr urge
ĭ pit	th thin
ī pie	*th* this
îr pier	hw which
ŏ pot	zh vision
ō toe	ə about, item
ô paw	♦ regionalism

Stress marks: ′ (primary); ′ (secondary), as in **dictionary** (dĭk′shə-nĕr′ē)

ko•bold (kō′bôld′) *n.* **1.** An often mischievous household elf in German folklore. **2.** A gnome that haunts underground places in German folklore. [German, from Middle High German *kobolt.* See COBALT.]

Koch (kôk, kôKH), **Robert.** 1843–1910. German bacteriologist who discovered the cholera bacillus and the bacterial cause of anthrax. He won a 1905 Nobel Prize for developing tuberculin.

Ko•chi (kō′chē). A city of southern Shikoku, Japan, on an inlet of the Pacific Ocean. It is a port and fish-processing center. Population, 312,253.

Ko•dak (kō′dăk′). A trademark used for a hand-held camera and camera film.

Ko•dál•y (kō′dī′, kô′dä-yə), **Zoltán.** 1882–1967. Hungarian composer whose works include the opera *Háry János* (1926).

Ko•di•ak bear (kō′dē-ăk′) *n.* A brown bear inhabiting islands and coastal areas of Alaska and sometimes considered a separate species *(Ursus middendorffi).* [After KODIAK (ISLAND).]

Kodiak Island. An island of southern Alaska in the Gulf of Alaska east of the Alaska Peninsula. The island was the site of the first permanent Russian settlement in the area (1784).

Koest•ler (kĕst′lər, kĕs′-), **Arthur.** 1905–1983. Hungarian-born writer whose novel *Darkness at Noon* (1941) portrays his disillusionment with Communism.

K of C *abbr.* Knight of Columbus.

K of P *abbr.* Knight of Pythias.

Ko•fu (kō′fo͞o). A city of central Honshu, Japan, west of Tokyo. The seat of several powerful lords during the feudal era, it is now an industrial center. Population, 202,405.

kohl (kōl) *n.* A cosmetic preparation, such as powdered antimony sulfide, used especially in Middle Eastern countries to darken the rims of the eyelids. [Arabic *kuḥl,* powder of antimony, kohl.]

kohl•ra•bi (kōl-rä′bē, -răb′ē) *n., pl.* **-bies.** A plant *(Brassica oleracea* var. *gongylodes)* in the mustard family, having a thick basal part of the stem that is eaten as a vegetable. Also called *turnip cabbage.* [German, partial translation (with German *Kohl,* cabbage, ultimately from Latin *caulis)* of Italian *cavoli rape,* pl. of *cavolo rapa* : *cavolo,* cabbage (from Latin *caulis)* + *rapa,* turnip (from Latin *rāpa).*]

Koi•ne (koi-nā′, koi′nā′) *n.* **1.** A dialect of Greek that developed primarily from Attic and became the common language of the Hellenistic world, from which later stages of Greek are descended. **2. koine.** A lingua franca. **3. koine.** A regional dialect or language that becomes the standard language over a wider area, losing its most extreme local features. [From Greek *(hē) koinē (dialektos),* common (language), feminine of *koinos,* common. See **kom** in Appendix.]

Ko•kand (kō-kănd′). A city of eastern Uzbekistan southeast of Tashkent. It was the center of a powerful khanate in the 18th century and was finally conquered by Russia in 1876. Population, 166,000.

Ko•ko•mo (kō′kə-mō′). A city of central Indiana north of Indianapolis. Founded in the 1840's, it is a manufacturing center. Population, 47,808.

Ko•ko Nor (kō′kō′ nôr′, nōr′). See **Qinghai Hu.**

Ko•kosch•ka (kə-kôsh′kə), **Oskar.** 1886–1980. Austrian expressionist painter noted for his portraits and landscapes.

kok-sa•ghyz (kōk′sə-gēz′) *n.* A central Asian dandelion *(Taraxacum koksaghyz)* having fleshy roots that yield a form of rubber. [Russian, from Turkish *kok-sagïz* : *kok,* root + *sagïz,* rubber.]

ko•la (kō′lə) *n.* Variant of **cola**[4].

ko•lac•ky (kə-lä′chē, -läch′kē) *n., pl.* **kolacky** or **-la•che** (-lä′chē). A square, sweet bun with a fruit or poppy seed filling. [Czech *koláče,* wheel-shaped cake, pl. of *koláč,* from Old Church Slavonic, wheel. See **k^{w}el-**[1] in Appendix.]

Ko•la Peninsula (kō′lə). A peninsula of northwest Russia projecting eastward from Scandinavia between the White Sea and the Barents Sea.

Kol•ha•pur (kō′lə-po͝or′). A city of southwest India south-southeast of Bombay. It was formerly the center of an important Deccan state. Population, 340,625.

ko•lin•sky (kə-lĭn′skē) *n., pl.* **-skies. 1.** A northern Eurasian mink *(Mustela siberica)* having a dark brown coat with tawny markings. **2.** The tawny fur of this animal. [Russian *kolinskiĭ,* of Kola, from KOLA (PENINSULA).]

kol•khoz (kŏl-kôz′, kŭl-KHôs′) *n.* A collective farm in the Soviet Union. [Russian, from *kol(lektivnoe) khoz(yaĭstvo)* : *kollektivnoe,* neuter of *kollektivnyĭ,* collective + *khozyaĭstvo,* economy, farm.]

Kol•lon•tai (kŏl′ən-tī′), **Aleksandra Mikhailovna.** 1872–1952. Russian revolutionary and writer. After the October Revolution (1917) she advocated sweeping reforms in traditional customs and institutions.

Koll•witz (kōl′wĭts′, kôl′vĭts′), **Käthe** or **Kaethe.** 1867–1945. German artist whose sculptures and prints express her abhorrence of war and poverty.

Kol•mar (kōl′mär, kôl-mär′). See **Colmar.**

Köln (kœln). See **Cologne.**

Kol Nid•re (kōl nĭd′rā, -rə, kôl nē-drā′) *n. Judaism.* The opening prayer recited on the eve of Yom Kippur, declaring the annulment of all personal vows made to God in the preceding year. [Aramaic *kol nidhrê,* all vows (the opening words of the prayer) : *kol,* all + *nidhrê,* vows.]

Ko•ly•ma (kə-lē′mə, kə-lē-mä′). A river of northeast Russia rising in the Kolyma Mountains and flowing about 2,148 km (1,335 mi) generally north and northeast to the East Siberian Sea. Its upper course crosses rich gold fields.

Kolyma Mountains. A range of northeast Russia extending about 1,126 km (700 mi) north and south to the east of the Kolyma River.

Ko•man•dor•ski Islands (kŏm′ən-dôr′skē) also **Ko•man•dor•ski•ye Islands** (-skē-yĕ). An island group of northeast Russia in the Bering Sea east of the Kamchatka Peninsula.

Ko•ma•ti (kə-mä′tē). A river flowing about 805 km (500 mi) through northeast South Africa, northern Swaziland, and southern Mozambique to an inlet of the Indian Ocean.

Kom•bu (kŏm′bo͞o) *n.* A food derived from seaweed. [Origin unknown.]

Ko•mo•do dragon (kə-mō′dō) *n.* A large monitor lizard *(Varanus komodoensis)* native to Indonesia. It is the largest living lizard, sometimes growing to a length of 3 meters (10 feet). [After *Komodo,* an island of south-central Indonesia.]

Kom•so•molsk (kŏm′sə-môlsk′). A city of southeast Russia north of Vladivostok. It was laid out and settled in 1932 by members of Komsomol, the Communist youth organization. Population, 300,000.

Kon•go (kŏng′gō) *n., pl.* Kongo or **-gos. 1.** A member of a people living in west-central Africa along the lower Congo River. **2.** A Bantu language of the Kongo used as a lingua franca in southern Congo, western Zaire, and northern Angola. In this sense, also called *Kikongo.*

Kon•ia (kôn-yä′). See **Konya.**

Kö•nigs•berg (kā′nĭgz-bûrg′, kœ′nĭKHs-bĕrk′). See **Kaliningrad.**

Ko•no•ye (kə-nō′ā, kô′nô-yĕ′), Prince **Fumimaro.** 1891–1946. Japanese political leader who as premier (1937–1939 and 1940–1941) outlined Japan's expansionist policies, sought to avoid American intervention in the Sino-Japanese War, and formed an alliance with Germany and Italy (1941).

Kon•stanz (kôn′stänts′) also **Con•stance** (kŏn′stəns). A city of southwest Germany on the Lake of Constance south of Stuttgart. Thought to have been founded c. A.D. 300, it is a tourist center with varied industries. Population, 68,605.

Kon•ya also **Kon•ia** (kôn-yä′). A city of southwest-central Turkey south of Ankara. Built on the site of an ancient Phrygian city, Konya was a powerful Seljuk sultanate from the 11th to the 13th century. Population, 329,139.

koo•doo (ko͞o′do͞o) *n.* Variant of **kudu.**

kook (ko͝ok) *n. Slang.* A person regarded as strange, eccentric, or crazy. [Possibly from CUCKOO.]

kook•a•bur•ra (ko͝ok′ə-bûr′ə, -bŭr′ə) *n.* A large kingfisher *(Dacelo gigas)* native to Australia, with a call that resembles raucous laughter. Also called *laughing jackass.* [Wiradhuri (Aboriginal language of southeast Australia) *gugubarra.*]

kook•y also **kook•ie** (ko͞o′kē) *adj.* **-i•er, -i•est.** *Slang.* Characteristic of a kook; strange or crazy. **—kook′i•ness** *n.*

Koop•mans (ko͞op′mənz), **Tjalling Charles.** Born 1910. Dutch-born American economist. He shared a 1975 Nobel Prize for developing the theory of optimum allocation of resources.

Koo•te•nay River also **Koo•te•nai River** (ko͞ot′n-ā′). A river, about 655 km (407 mi) long, flowing from southeast British Columbia, Canada, south through northwest Montana, northwest through northern Idaho, and then north again into British Columbia, where it widens to form **Kootenay Lake** before joining the Columbia River.

ko•peck or **ko•pek** also **co•peck** (kō′pĕk) *n. Abbr.* **k., K.** See table at **currency.** [Russian *kopeĭka,* from Middle Russian *kopeika,* from *kopie,* spear (from the image of a rider with a spear on the coins minted by Moscow after the capture of Novgorod in 1478).]

kor (kôr, kōr) *n.* See **homer**[2]. [Hebrew *kôr.*]

Kor. *abbr.* Korea; Korean.

Ko•ran or **Qur•'an** (kə-răn′, -rän′, kô-, kō-) *n.* The sacred text of Islam, considered by Moslems to contain the revelations of God to Mohammed. Also called *Alcoran.* [Arabic *qur'ān,* reading, recitation, Koran, from *qara'a,* to read, recite.] **—Ko•ran′ic** *adj.*

Kor•do•fan•i•an (kôr′də-făn′ē-ən) *n.* A small group of related languages spoken in Sudan and forming part of the Niger-Kordofanian language family.

Ko•re•a (kə-rē′ə, kô-, kō-). *Abbr.* **Kor.** A peninsula and former country of eastern Asia between the Yellow Sea and the Sea of Japan. Site of an ancient civilization dating to the 12th century B.C., the peninsula was united as a kingdom in the 7th century A.D. and despite a Mongol invasion (13th century) remained unified until the Japanese occupation of 1910 to 1945. After World War II the Soviet- and U.S.-occupied territories formed separate republics, and a Soviet-backed invasion of the south led to the Korean War (1950–1953). The peninsula is now divided between North Korea and South Korea.

Korea Bay. An inlet of the Yellow Sea between northeast China and western North Korea.

Ko•re•an (kə-rē′ən, kô-, kō-) *n. Abbr.* **Kor. 1.** A native or

kohl

kookaburra
Dacelo gigas

inhabitant of Korea. **2.** The language of the Koreans, possibly in the Altaic family. —**Korean** *adj. Abbr.* **Kor.** Of or relating to Korea or its people, language, or culture.

Korean War *n.* A conflict that lasted from 1950 to 1953 between North Korea, aided by China, and South Korea, aided by United Nations forces consisting primarily of U.S. troops.

Korea Strait. A channel between southeast South Korea and southwest Japan. It connects the East China Sea with the Sea of Japan.

Kó•rin•thos (kôʹrĭn-thôsʹ). See **Corinth.**

Ko•ri•ya•ma (kôr′ē-äʹmə, -yäʹmä). A city of north-central Honshu, Japan, north of Tokyo. It is a major commercial and communications center. Population, 301,672.

Korn•berg (kôrnʹbûrg′), **Arthur.** Born 1918. American biochemist. He shared a 1959 Nobel Prize for work on the biological synthesis of nucleic acids.

Kor•sa•koff's syndrome (kôrʹsə-kôfs′, -kŏfs′) *n. Psychiatry.* A syndrome of severe mental impairment characterized by multiple neuritis, confusion, disorientation, and amnesia in which memory of recent events is especially impaired, often causing the patient to attempt to compensate through confabulation. Also called *Korsakoff's psychosis.* [After Sergei S. *Korsakoff* (1854–1900), Russian neurologist.]

Kort•rijk (kôrtʹrīk′) also **Cour•trai** (ko͝or-trāʹ, ko͝or-). A city of western Belgium west of Brussels. It was the most important cloth-manufacturing town of medieval Flanders and is still a textile center. Population, 75,587.

ko•ru•na (kôrʹə-nä′) *n.* See table at **currency.**

Kor•zyb•ski (kôr-zĭpʹskē, kô-zhĭpʹ-), **Alfred Habdank Skarbek.** 1879–1950. Polish-born American semanticist who proposed his theories in *Science and Sanity: An Introduction to Non-Aristotelian Systems and General Semantics* (1933).

Kos also **Cos** (kŏs, kôs). An island of southeast Greece in the northern Dodecanese Islands at the entrance to the **Gulf of Kos,** an inlet of the Aegean Sea on the southwest coast of Turkey. Kos became part of modern Greece in 1947.

Kos•ci•us•ko (kŏs′ē-ŭsʹkō, kŏs′kē-), **Mount.** The highest mountain of Australia, in the southeast part of the country in the Australian Alps. It rises to 2,231.4 m (7,316 ft).

Kos•ci•us•ko (kŏs′ē-ŭsʹkō, kŏs′kē-, kôsh-cho͞oshʹkō), **Thaddeus.** 1746–1817. Polish general and patriot who fought with the colonists in the American Revolution and was a leader in Poland's struggle for independence from Russia.

ko•sher (kōʹshər) also **ka•sher** (käʹ-) —*adj.* **1.** *Judaism.* **a.** Conforming to dietary laws; ritually pure: *kosher meat.* **b.** Selling or serving food prepared in accordance with dietary laws: *a kosher restaurant.* **2.** *Slang.* **a.** Legitimate; permissible: *"consolidating noneditorial functions of the papers, which is kosher"* (Christian Science Monitor). **b.** Genuine; authentic. —*tr.v.* **-shered, -sher•ing, -shers.** To make proper or ritually pure. [Yiddish *kósher,* from Hebrew *kāšēr,* proper.]

Ko•ši•ce (kôʹshĭtsĕ). A city of eastern Czechoslovakia northeast of Budapest, Hungary. Chartered in 1241, it was an important trade center during the Middle Ages. Population, 218,238.

koto

Kos•suth (kŏsʹo͞oth′, kôʹsho͝ot′), **Lajos.** 1802–1894. Hungarian revolutionary leader who sought Hungary's independence from Austria. Declaring the Hapsburg dynasty invalid, he briefly led a provisional government (1849) until Russia interceded on Austria's behalf.

Kos•tro•ma (kŏs′trə-mäʹ). A city of northwest Russia on the Volga River northeast of Moscow. Founded in 1152, it was annexed by Moscow in 1364. Population, 269,000.

Ko•sy•gin (kə-sēʹgən, -gyĭn), **Aleksei Nikolayevich.** 1904–1980. Soviet premier (1964–1980) who succeeded Nikita Khrushchev but was often overshadowed by party secretary Leonid Brezhnev.

Ko•ta (kōʹtə). A city of northwest India south-southwest of Delhi. Enclosed by a massive wall, it is an agricultural market and has many fine temples. Population, 358,241.

ko•to (kōʹtō) *n., pl.* **-tos.** *Music.* A Japanese instrument similar to a zither, having 7 to 13 silk strings stretched over an oblong box. [Japanese.]

Kott•bus (kŏtʹbəs, kôtʹbo͝os′). See **Cottbus.**

Kot•ze•bue Sound (kŏtʹsə-byo͞o′). An inlet of the Chukchi Sea in northwest Alaska north of Seward Peninsula.

kou•miss (ko͞o-mĭsʹ, ko͞oʹmĭs) *n.* Variant of **kumiss.**

Kous•se•vitz•ky (ko͞o′sə-vĭtʹskē), **Sergei Aleksandrovich.** Known as "Serge." 1874–1951. Russian-born American conductor of the Boston Symphony Orchestra (1924–1949) noted for his support of contemporary composers.

Kov•a•lev•sky (kŏv′ə-lĕvʹskē, -lĕfʹ-), **Sonya.** 1850–1891. Russian mathematician known for her work on partial differential equations and equations of rotatory motion.

Kow•loon (kouʹlo͞onʹ). A city of Hong Kong on the southeast coast of China on **Kowloon Peninsula** opposite Hong Kong Island. The city was ceded to the British in 1860. Population, 799,123.

kow•tow (kou-touʹ, kouʹtou′) *intr.v.* **-towed, -tow•ing, -tows.** **1.** To kneel and touch the forehead to the ground in expression of deep respect, worship, or submission, as formerly done in China. **2.** To show servile deference; fawn. See Synonyms at **fawn**[1]. —**kowtow** *n.* **1.** The act of kneeling and touching the forehead to the ground. **2.** An obsequious act. [From Chinese (Mandarin) *kòu tóu,* a kowtow : *kòu,* to knock + *tóu,* head.]

Koy•u•kuk (kīʹə-ko͝ok′). A river, about 805 km (500 mi) long, of northern Alaska flowing generally southwest from the Brooks Range to the Yukon River.

Ko•zhi•kode (kōʹzhĭ-kōd′). See **Calicut.**

KP[1] (kāʹpēʹ) *n.* Kitchen police. [K(ITCHEN) P(OLICE).]

KP[2] *abbr. Games.* King's pawn.

Kr The symbol for the element **krypton.**

KR *abbr. Games.* King's rook.

kr. *abbr.* **1.** Krona. **2.** Krone.

Kra (krä), **Isthmus of.** A strip of land, about 64 km (40 mi) wide at its narrowest point, linking the Malay Peninsula with the Asian mainland.

kraal (krôl, kräl) *n. South African.* **1.** A rural village, typically consisting of huts surrounded by a stockade. **2.** An enclosure for livestock. [Afrikaans, from Portuguese *curral,* pen, perhaps from Vulgar Latin **currāle,* enclosure for carts. See CORRAL.]

Krafft-E•bing (krăftʹĕb′ĭng, kräftʹāʹbĭng), Baron **Richard von.** 1840–1902. German physician and neurologist particularly known for his studies of sexual deviance and the published collection of case histories *Psychopathia Sexualis* (1886).

kraft (krăft) *n.* A tough, usually brown paper made from wood pulp treated with a solution of sodium sulfate, used chiefly for bags and wrapping paper. [Short for Swedish *kraftpapper* : *kraft* (from Old Swedish *krapt*) + *papper,* paper.]

krait (krīt) *n.* Any of several brightly banded, highly venomous snakes of the genus *Bungarus* of southeast Asia and adjacent islands. [Hindi *karait.*]

Kra•ka•tau (krăk′ə-touʹ, kräʹkə-) or **Kra•ka•to•a** (-tōʹə). A volcanic island of Indonesia between Sumatra and Java. A violent explosion in August 1883 blew the island apart and caused a tidal wave that killed more than 36,000 people.

kra•ken (kräʹkən) *n.* A huge sea monster in Norwegian legend. [Norwegian dialectal : *krake,* kraken + Norwegian *-n,* suffixed definite article.]

Kra•ków (krăkʹou, kräʹkou, -ko͝of). See **Cracow.**

Kra•ma•torsk (kräʹmə-tôrsk′, krə-). A city of eastern Ukraine in the Donets Basin south-southeast of Kharkov. It is an iron and steel center. Population, 192,000.

Kras•ner (krăzʹnər), **Lee.** 1908–1984. American artist known for her spontaneous, gestural approach to painting. She was a founder of the New York School of abstract expressionism.

Kras•no•dar (krăsʹnə-där′, krə-snə-därʹ). A city of southwest Russia in the northern Caucasus south of Rostov. Founded by Cossacks on orders from Catherine II in 1794, it is now an industrial center. Population, 609,000.

Kras•no•yarsk (krăsʹnə-yärsk′, krə-snə-). A city of south-central Russia on the upper Yenisei River east of Novosibirsk. It was founded in 1628. Population, 872,000.

kra•ter or **cra•ter** (krāʹtər) *n.* A wide, two-handled bowl used in ancient Greece and Rome for mixing wine and water. [Greek *kratēr.* See CRATER.]

K ration *n.* An emergency field ration for U.S. armed forces in World War II, consisting of a single packaged meal. [After Ancel Benjamin *Keys* (born 1904), American physiologist.]

kraut (krout) *n.* **1.** Sauerkraut. **2.** Often **Kraut.** *Offensive Slang.* Used as a disparaging term for a German. [German. See SAUERKRAUT.]

Krebs (krĕbz, krĕps), Sir **Hans Adolf.** 1900–1981. German-born British biochemist who discovered the Krebs cycle (1936). He shared a 1953 Nobel Prize for investigations into metabolic processes.

Krebs cycle (krĕbz) *n. Biochemistry.* A series of enzymatic reactions in aerobic organisms involving oxidative metabolism of acetyl units and producing high-energy phosphate compounds, which serve as the main source of cellular energy. Also called *citric acid cycle, tricarboxylic acid cycle.* [After Sir Hans Adolf *Krebs.*]

Kre•feld (krāʹfĕld′, -fĕlt′). A city of west-central Germany on the Rhine River north-northwest of Cologne. Chartered in 1373, it has long been important as a textile center. Population 217,276.

Krei•sler (krīʹslər), **Fritz.** 1875–1962. Austrian-born American violinist and composer of violin works and the operetta *Apple Blossoms* (1919).

Kre•men•chug (krĕm′ən-cho͞okʹ, -cho͞ogʹ, kryĭʹmĭn-cho͞okʹ). A city of east-central Ukraine on the Dnieper River southeast of Kiev. It was founded as a fortress in 1571. Population, 224,000.

Krem•lin (krĕmʹlĭn) *n.* **1.** The citadel of Moscow, housing the offices of the Soviet government. The outer walls of the compound date to the 15th century. **2.** The government of the Soviet Union. **3. kremlin.** The citadel of a Russian city. [Obsolete German *Kremelin,* from Old Russian **kremlĭnŭ,* separate, from *kremlĭ,* a separate place.]

Krem•lin•ol•o•gy (krĕm′lə-nŏlʹə-jē) *n.* The study of the policies of the Soviet government. —**Krem′lin•o•log′i•cal** (-lə-nə-lŏjʹĭ-kəl) *adj.* —**Krem′lin•ol′o•gist** *n.*

krep•lach (krĕpʹləKH, -läKH) *pl.n.* Small pockets of noodle dough filled with ground meat or cheese, usually boiled and served in soups. [Yiddish *kreplech,* pl. of *krepel,* from German dialectal *Kräppel,* fried pastry, variant of German *Krapfen,* from

Middle High German *krapfe,* from Old High German *krapfo,* hook (from their hooklike shape).]

kreu·zer or **kreut·zer** (kroit′sər) *n.* Any of several small coins of low value formerly used in Austria and Germany. [German, from Middle High German *kriuzer,* from *kriuze,* cross (originally stamped with a cross), from Old High German *krūzi,* from Latin *crux, cruc-.*]

♦ **krewe** (kro͞o) *n. New Orleans.* Any of several groups with hereditary membership whose members organize and participate as costumed paraders in the annual Mardi Gras carnival: *"They . . . watched a parade of bands and New Orleans-style floats run by krewes throwing necklaces of colored beads"* (Robert Reinhold). See Regional Note at **beignet.** [Alteration of CREW[1].]

♦ ***REGIONAL NOTE:*** In order to organize and stage the enormous Mardi Gras carnival every year, many New Orleans families have belonged for generations to *krewes,* groups that create elaborate costumes and floats for the many Mardi Gras parades in the two weeks leading up to "Fat Tuesday." Not only do the krewes participate in the parades, but, as leaders of New Orleans society, they also hold balls and other elaborate events during the carnival season, which lasts from Christmas up to Mardi Gras itself. The krewes are responsible for electing Rex, the annual king of the carnival, whose parade is the climax of Mardi Gras. While masked paraders had long been a part of Mardi Gras, the first carnival group organized as such was the Mystick Krewe of Comus in 1857. *Krewe* is only a fanciful spelling of *crew* in its standard meaning, but the word, thanks to its association with Mardi Gras and New Orleans high society, has taken on some of the mystique of the carnival.

Kriem·hild (krēm′hĭld′, -hĭlt′) also **Kriem·hil·de** (krēm-hĭl′də) *n.* The wife of Siegfried and sister of Gunther in the *Nibelungenlied.*

krill (krĭl) *n., pl.* **krill.** The collection of small marine crustaceans of the order Euphausiacea that are the principal food of baleen whales. [Norwegian *kril,* young fry of fish.]

krim·mer (krĭm′ər) *n.* Gray, curly fur made from the pelts of lambs of the Crimean region. [German, from *Krim,* Crimea.]

kris also **creese** (krēs) *n.* A Malayan dagger with a wavy double-edged blade. [Malay *kĕris.*]

Krish·na[1] (krĭsh′nə) *n. Hinduism.* The eighth and principal avatar of Vishnu, often depicted as a handsome young man playing a flute. **—Krish′na·ism** *n.*

Krish·na[2] (krĭsh′nə). See **Kistna.**

Kriss Krin·gle (krĭs′ krĭng′gəl) *n.* Santa Claus. [Alteration of German dialectal *Christkindl,* Christmas present, the Christ child : German *Christ,* Christ (from Middle High German *Krist,* from Old High German *Krīst,* from Latin *Chrīstus;* see CHRIST) + *Kindl* (diminutive of German *Kind,* child, from Middle High German *kint,* from Old High German *kind;* see **gene-** in Appendix).]

Kris·tian·sand (krĭs′chən-sănd′, krĭs′tyän-sän′). A city of extreme southern Norway on the Skagerrak southwest of Oslo. Founded in 1641, it is a commercial port. Population, 61,834.

Kri·voi Rog or **Kri·voy Rog** (krĭ-voi′ rôg′, rôk′). A city of south-central Ukraine northeast of Odessa. Located in a rich iron-producing region, it is highly industrialized. Population, 684,000.

Kroe·ber (krō′bər), **Alfred Louis.** 1876–1960. American anthropologist noted for his inquiry into the nature of culture.

Kroe·neck·er delta (krō′nĕk-ər) *n. Mathematics.* A function of two variables that is equal to zero when the variables have different values and equal to one when the variables have the same value. [After Leopold *Kronecker* (1823–1891), German mathematician.]

Krogh (krôg, krôKH), **(Schack) August Steenberg.** 1874–1949. Danish physiologist. He won a 1920 Nobel Prize for the discovery of the regulation of the capillaries' motor mechanism.

kro·na[1] (krō′nə) *n., pl.* **-nur** (-nər). *Abbr.* **kr., k., K.** See table at **currency.** [Icelandic *króna,* from Old Norse *krūna,* from Middle Low German *krūne, krōne,* ultimately from Latin *corōna,* wreath, crown (from the crown printed on the coin). See CROWN.]

kro·na[2] (krō′nə) *n., pl.* **-nor** (-nôr′, -nər). *Abbr.* **kr., k., K.** See table at **currency.** [Swedish, from Old Swedish *krōna,* from Middle Low German *krūne, krōne.* See KRONA[1].]

kro·ne[1] (krō′nə) *n., pl.* **-ner** (-nər). *Abbr.* **kr., k., K.** See table at **currency.** [Norwegian, from Old Norse *krūna.* See KRONA[1].]

kro·ne[2] (krō′nə) *n., pl.* **-ner** (-nər). See table at **currency.** [Danish *krone,* from Old Norse *krūna.* See KRONA[1].]

kro·ner[1] (krō′nər) *n.* Plural of **krone[1].**

kro·ner[2] (krō′nər) *n.* Plural of **krone[2].**

kro·nor (krō′nôr′, -nər) *n.* Plural of **krona[2].**

kro·nur (krō′nər) *n.* Plural of **krona[1].**

Kro·pot·kin (krə-pŏt′kĭn, krō-), Prince **Pyotr Alekseyevich.** 1842–1921. Russian anarchist and political philosopher who maintained that cooperation, not competition, was the means to bettering the human condition.

Kru·ger (kro͞o′gər, krü′-), **Stephanus Johannes Paulus.** Known as "Oom Paul." 1825–1904. South African politician. A founder (1852) and president (1883–1900) of Transvaal, he instituted nationalist policies that led to the Boer War (1899–1902).

Kru·ger·rand (kro͞o′gə-rănd′, -ränd′) *n.* A one-ounce gold coin of the Republic of South Africa. [Afrikaans : after Stephanus Johannes Paulus KRUGER + *rand,* rand; see RAND.]

krumm·horn or **crum·horn** (krŭm′hôrn′) *n. Music.* A wind instrument of the Renaissance with a curving tube and a double reed. [German : *krumm,* crooked (from Middle High German *krump, krum,* from Old High German *krump*) + *Horn,* horn; see ALPENHORN.]

♦ **krumm·kake** (kro͝om′kä′kə, krŭm′kāk′) *n. Upper Midwest.* A large, thin cookie made from batter poured into an embossed mold with hinged plates. [Norwegian *krumkake* : *krum,* curved, crooked (from Middle Low German *krum,* from Old High German *krump*) + *kake,* cake (from Old Norse *kaka*).]

♦ ***REGIONAL NOTE:*** The Upper Midwest received a great influx of Scandinavian immigrants in the 19th century, and the English that these people learned was augmented by Scandinavian words for their native food and customs. Thus we have *krummkake,* the name of a large, light, very thin Norwegian cookie made from an egg-based batter poured into an embossed hinged iron similar to a waffle iron. Peeled off the iron while warm and pliable, each krummkake is then rolled around a cone-shaped metal tube so that it hardens in that shape and is filled with sweetened whipped cream. Krummkake is best known in the Upper Midwest, but the term is familiar elsewhere thanks to the inclusion of the recipe in nationally used cookbooks.

Krung Thep (gro͝ong tĕp′). See **Bangkok.**

Krupp (kro͞op, krŭp). German family of steel and munitions manufacturers, including **Friedrich** (1787–1826), who founded the Krupp Works in Essen (1811), and his son **Alfred** (1812–1887), who there began the production of ordnance (c. 1847). Alfred's granddaughter **Bertha** (1886–1957) and her husband **Gustav Krupp von Bohlen und Halbach** (1870–1950) were important in the secret rearming of Germany after World War I.

Krup·ska·ya (kro͞op′skə-yə), **Nadezhda Konstantinovna.** 1869–1939. Russian revolutionary and wife of Vladimir Lenin. She held numerous political posts before and after the October Revolution (1917) and wrote *Memories of Lenin* (1930).

kryp·ton (krĭp′tŏn′) *n. Symbol* **Kr** A whitish, inert gaseous element used chiefly in gas discharge lamps and fluorescent lamps. Atomic number 36; atomic weight 83.80; melting point −156.6°C; boiling point −152.30°C; density 3.73 grams per liter (0°C). See table at **element.** [Greek *krupton,* neuter of *kruptos,* hidden, from *kruptein,* to hide.]

KS *abbr.* Kansas.

K selection *n.* A form of selection that occurs in an environment at or near carrying capacity, favoring a reproductive strategy in which few offspring are produced. [From *K,* the constant for carrying capacity in the equation for population growth.]

Ksha·tri·ya (kə-shăt′rē-ə, -chăt′-) *n.* **1.** The second of the four Hindu classes, responsible for upholding justice and social harmony. In ancient India this was the royal or warrior class; in modern India, the professional, governing, or military class. **2.** A member of this class. [Sanskrit *kṣatriyaḥ,* from *kṣatram,* rule, power.]

kt *abbr.* Kiloton.

Kt *abbr. Games.* Knight.

kt. also **kt** *abbr.* **1.** Karat. **2.** Knight. **3.** *Nautical.* Knot.

Kua·la Lum·pur (kwä′lə lo͝om-po͝or′). The capital and largest city of Malaysia, on the southwest Malay Peninsula northwest of Singapore. Founded by tin miners in 1857, it is the commercial and industrial hub of the country. Population 937,817.

Ku·ban (ko͞o-băn′, -bän′). A river of southwest Russia flowing about 917 km (570 mi) generally north and west to the Sea of Azov.

Ku·blai Khan (ko͞o′blī kän′) **Ku·bla Khan** (-blə). 1215–1294. Mongol emperor (1260–1294) and founder of the Mongol dynasty in China. A grandson of Genghis Khan, he conquered the Song dynasty (1279) and established a great capital, now Beijing, where he received Marco Polo (1275–1292).

Kublai Khan

ku·chen (ko͞o′kən, -KHən) *n.* A coffeecake raised with yeast, often containing fruit and nuts. [German, from Middle High German *kuoche,* cake, from Old High German *kuocho.*]

ku·dos (ko͞o′dōz′, -dōs′, -dŏs′, kyo͞o′-) *n.* Acclaim or praise for exceptional achievement. [Greek, magical glory.]

USAGE NOTE: *Kudos* is one of those words like *congeries* that look like plurals but are etymologically singular: correctness requires *Kudos is* (not *are*) *due her for her brilliant work on the score.* Some writers have tried to defend the use of *kudos* with a plural verb, or even the introduction of a new singular form of *kudo,* on the grounds that these innovations follow the pattern whereby the English words *pea* and *cherry* were re-formed from nouns ending in *–s* that were thought to be plural. Perhaps the singular *kudo* would have to be acknowledged as a legitimate formation if it came to be widely adopted in the popular language in the way that *cherry* and *pea* have. But at present *kudos* is still regarded as a slightly pretentious variant for *praise* and can scarcely claim to be part of the linguistic folkways of the community. When writers reach for an unfamiliar Greek word for the sake of elegance, it is fair to ask that they get it right. Still, it is worth noting that even people who are careful to treat the word syntactically as a singular often pronounce it as if it were a plural:

ă pat	oi boy
ā pay	ou out
âr care	o͝o took
ä father	o͞o boot
ĕ pet	ŭ cut
ē be	ûr urge
ĭ pit	th thin
ī pie	*th* this
îr pier	hw which
ŏ pot	zh vision
ō toe	ə about, item
ô paw	♦ regionalism

Stress marks: **′** (primary); ′ (secondary), as in **dictionary** (dĭk′shə-nĕr′ē)

etymology would require that the final consonant be pronounced as a voiceless (s), rather than as a voiced (z).

ku·du also **koo·doo** (ko͞o′do͞o) *n., pl.* **kudu** or **-dus** also **koodoo** or **-doos.** Either of two large African antelopes *(Tragelaphus strepsiceros* or *T. imberbis)* having a brownish coat with narrow, white vertical stripes and, in the male, long, spirally curved horns. [Afrikaans *koedoe,* from Nguni (Xhosa) *i-quda, i-qudu,* possibly of Khoikhoin (Nama) origin.]

kud·zu (ko͝od′zo͞o) *n.* An eastern Asian vine *(Pueraria lobata)* having compound leaves and clusters of reddish-purple flowers. It is grown for fodder, forage, and root starch. [Japanese *kuzu.*]

kudzu
Pueraria lobata

Ku·fic also **Cu·fic** (ko͞o′fĭk, kyo͞o′-) *adj.* Relating to or being an angular form of the Arabic alphabet used in making fine copies of the Koran. [After Al *Kufa,* a town of south-central Iraq.]

Kuhn (ko͞on), **Richard.** 1900–1967. Austrian chemist. He won a 1938 Nobel Prize for research on carotenoids and vitamins but declined the award by order of the Nazi government.

Kui·by·shev or **Kuy·by·shev** (kwē′bə-shĕf′, -shĕv′, ko͞o′ē-bə-shĭf). A city of western Russia on the Volga River east-southeast of Moscow. It was founded in 1586. Population, 1,257,000.

Ku Klux·er (ko͞o klŭk′sər, kyo͞o) *n.* A member of the Ku Klux Klan. **—Ku Klux′ism** *n.*

Ku Klux Klan (ko͞o′ klŭks klăn′, kyo͞o′) *n. Abbr.* **KKK, K.K.K. 1.** A secret society organized in the South after the Civil War to reassert white supremacy by means of terrorism. **2.** A secret fraternal organization of similar intent founded in Georgia in 1915. [Perhaps alteration of Greek *kuklos,* circle; see CYCLE + alteration of *clan.*]

WORD HISTORY: The name of a group that has done so much to prevent the spread of openness in society should be suitably mysterious, and certainly the etymology of *Ku Klux Klan* is not easily penetrated. The most widely accepted theory is that *Ku Klux* is an illiterate misspelling of the Greek word *kuklos,* meaning "ring, circle," and *Klan* is the word *clan* spelled with a *k.* Why this name, first recorded in 1867, was chosen is not exactly known. Certainly the name fits, because the groups or clans that have used the name have drawn a circle around those who can and cannot be considered as United States citizens with full rights to life, liberty, and the pursuit of happiness. Recalling the violent habits of the Klan, others have derived the word from the sounds made in the cocking of a gun, but it seems far more likely that the ignorance of those who espoused the principles of such a group was also responsible for the illiterate transcription of the Greek word *kuklos.*

ku·lak (ko͞o-lăk′, ko͞o′lăk′, -läk′) *n.* A prosperous landed peasant in czarist Russia, characterized by the Communists during the October Revolution as an exploiter. [Russian, fist, kulak, probably of Turkic origin.]

Kul·tur (ko͝ol-to͝or′) *n.* **1.** Culture; civilization. **2.** German culture and civilization as idealized by the exponents of German imperialism during the Hohenzollern and Nazi regimes. [German, from Latin *cultūra,* cultivation, care. See CULTURE.]

Kul·tur·kampf (ko͝ol-to͝or′kämpf′) *n.* **1.** The struggle (1871–1883) between the Roman Catholic Church and the German government under Bismarck for control over school and ecclesiastical appointments and civil marriage. **2.** A conflict between secular and religious authorities: *"The 1920's proved to be the focal decade in the Kulturkampf of American Protestantism"* (Richard Hofstadter). [German : *Kultur,* Kultur; see KULTUR + *Kampf,* struggle (from Middle High German *kampf,* from Old High German *kamph,* probably ultimately from Latin *campus,* field).]

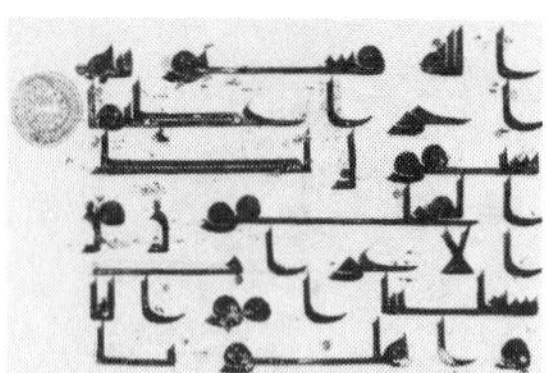
Kufic

Ku·ma·mo·to (ko͞o′mə-mō′tō). A city of western Kyushu, Japan, east of Nagasaki. It was an important castle town during the feudal period. Population, 555,722.

Ku·ma·si (ko͞o-mä′sē). A city of south-central Ghana northwest of Accra. Founded c. 1700, it is a commercial and transportation center in a cocoa-producing region. Population, 348,880.

ku·miss also **kou·miss** (ko͞o-mĭs′, ko͞o′mĭs) *n.* The fermented milk of a mare or camel, used as a beverage by certain peoples of western and central Asia. [Russian *kumys,* from Old Russian *komyzŭ,* from Old Turkic *qïmïz,* from *qammaq,* to shake.]

küm·mel (kĭm′əl, kü′məl) *n.* A colorless liqueur flavored chiefly with caraway seeds. [German, from Middle High German *kümel,* cumin seed, from Old High German *kumīn, kumil,* ultimately from Latin *cumīnum.* See CUMIN.]

♦ **küm·mel·weck** (kĭm′əl-vĕk′) *n. Buffalo.* A hard roll containing caraway seeds and coated with salt. Also called *weck.* [German *Kümmel,* cumin; see KÜMMEL + German dialectal *Weck,* roll; see WECK.]

kum·quat also **cum·quat** (kŭm′kwŏt′) *n.* **1.** Any of several trees or shrubs of the genus *Fortunella,* having small, edible, orangelike fruit. **2.** The fruit of these plants, having an acid pulp and a thin, edible rind. It is the smallest of the citrus fruits. [Chinese (Cantonese) *kam kwat* : *kêm,* gold + *kwêt,* orange.]

kumquat

Kun (ko͞on), **Béla.** 1886–1939? Hungarian politician who founded the Hungarian Communist Party (1918) and organized the revolution in Budapest (1919). He briefly served as premier but fled the country during a counterrevolution (1919).

kun·da·li·ni (ko͞on′də-lē′nē) *n. Hinduism.* Energy that lies dormant at the base of the spine until it is activated, as by the practice of yoga, and channeled upward through the chakras in the process of spiritual perfection. [Sanskrit *kuṇḍalinī,* from feminine sing. of *kuṇḍalin-,* coiled, spiral, from *kuṇḍalam,* ring, coil.]

Ku·ne·ne (ko͞o-nā′nə). See **Cunene.**

Kung (ko͝ong, go͝ong), Prince. 1833–1898. Chinese leader who as prime minister and coregent (1862–1873) suppressed the Taiping rebellion (1864).

Küng (ko͝ong, küng), **Hans.** Born 1928. Swiss Roman Catholic theologian. An adviser (1962–1965) during Vatican II, he was later censored (1979) for his rejection of papal infallibility.

kung fu (kŭng′ fo͞o′, ko͝ong′, go͝ong′) *Sports. n.* The Chinese martial arts, especially those forms that are similar to karate. *—attributive.* Often used to modify another noun: *kung fu movies; kung fu exercises.* [Chinese (Cantonese) *kung fu.*]

Kun·lun (ko͞on′lo͞on′). A mountain system of western China extending from the Karakoram Range eastward along the northern edge of the Xizang (Tibet) plateau. Its highest point is 7,729 m (25,341 ft).

Kun·ming (ko͞on′mĭng′). A city of southern China southwest of Chongqing. The Chinese terminus of the Burma Road during World War II, Kunming is the capital of Yunnan province. Population, 1,080,000.

kunz·ite (ko͝ont′sīt′) *n.* A lilac-colored spodumene used as a gemstone. [After George Frederick *Kunz* (1856–1932), American gemologist.]

Kuo·pio (kwô′py-ô′). A city of south-central Finland north-northeast of Helsinki. Chartered in 1782, it is a winter sports center in a lumbering area. Population, 77,371.

Kuo·yu (kwô′yo͞o′) *n.* Variant of **Guoyu.**

Ku·ra (ko͞o-rä′). A river of northeast Turkey and southern Azerbaijan flowing about 1,514 km (941 mi) generally northeast and southeast to the Caspian Sea south of Baku.

Ku·ra·shi·ki (ko͞o-rä′shē-kē). A city of western Honshu, Japan, an industrial suburb of Okayama on the Inland Sea. Population, 413,644.

kur·cha·tov·i·um (kûr′chə-tō′vē-əm) *n.* Element 104. [After Igor Vasilyevich *Kurchatov* (1903–1960), Soviet nuclear physicist.]

Kurd (kûrd, ko͝ord) *n.* A member of a pastoral and agricultural people inhabiting the transnational region of Kurdistan.

Kurd·ish (kûr′dĭsh, ko͝or′-) *adj.* Of or relating to the Kurds or their language or culture. **—Kurdish** *n.* The Iranian language of the Kurds.

Kurd·i·stan (kûr′dĭ-stăn′, ko͝or′dĭ-stän′). An extensive plateau region of southwest Asia. Since the dissolution of the Ottoman Empire after World War I, it has been divided among southeast Turkey, northeast Iraq, and northwest Iran, with smaller sections in Syria and Armenia.

Ku·re (ko͞o′rĕ′). A city of southwest Honshu, Japan, on an arm of the Inland Sea southeast of Hiroshima. It is a naval base and major port. Population, 226,489.

kur·gan (ko͝or-gän′, -găn′) *n.* **1.** A type of tumulus or barrow characteristic of a culture located on the steppes of southern Russia about 5000 B.C. and later spreading to the Danube, northern Europe, and northern Iran from around 3500 B.C. **2. Kurgan. a.** The culture that produced these tumuli or barrows. **b.** A member of the people or peoples sharing this culture. The earliest Kurgans are considered by some to be speakers of Proto-Indo-European. [Russian, fortified place, grave mound, from Old Turkic *kurghan,* fortified place.] **—Kur·gan′** *adj.*

Kur·gan (ko͝or-gän′). A city of western Russia southeast of Sverdlovsk. Founded in the 17th century, it is a trade center in a rich agricultural area. Population, 343,000.

Ku·ril Islands also **Ku·rile Islands** (ko͝or′ĭl, ko͞o-rēl′). An island chain of extreme eastern Russia extending about 1,207 km (750 mi) in the Pacific Ocean between Kamchatka Peninsula and northern Hokkaido, Japan. The islands were held by Japan from 1875 to 1945. **—Ku·ril′i·an** *adj. & n.*

Kur·land (ko͝or′lənd). See **Courland.**

Ku·ro·sa·wa (ko͝or′ə-sä′wə, ko͞o′rō-sä′wä), **Akira.** Born 1910. Japanese filmmaker whose internationally acclaimed works, including *Rashomon* (1950), *The Seven Samurai* (1954), and *Ran* (1985), often concern traditional Japanese institutions.

Ku·ro·shi·o Current (ko͞o-rō′shē-ō′) *n.* See **Japan Current.**

kur·ra·jong (kûr′ə-jông′, -jŏng′, kŭr′-) *n.* An Australian evergreen tree *(Brachychiton populneus)* having palmately lobed leaves, yellowish or reddish flowers, and long-stalked follicles. [Dharuk (Aboriginal language of southeast Australia) *garajuŋ.*]

Kursk (ko͝orsk). A city of western Russia southwest of Moscow. First mentioned in 1095, it was destroyed by the Mongols in 1240 and rebuilt as a fortress in 1586. Population, 420,000.

kur·to·sis (kər-tō′sĭs) *n., pl.* **-ses** (-sēz′). The general form or a quantity indicative of the general form of a statistical frequency curve near the mean of the distribution. [Greek *kurtōsis,* curvature, from *kurtos,* bent. See **sker-**[2] in Appendix.]

ku·ru (ko͝or′o͞o) *n.* A fatal progressive, degenerative neurological disease caused by a slow-acting virus, found in certain peoples of New Guinea and transmitted by cannibalism. [Indigenous word in Papua New Guinea.]

ku·rus (kə-ro͞osh′, ko͞o-) *n., pl.* **kurus.** See table at **currency.**

[Turkish *kuruş,* ultimately from Latin *(dēnārius) grossus,* thick (denarius). See GROSZ.]

Kush (kŭsh, ko͝osh). See **Cush²**.

Kus·ko·kwim (kŭs′kə-kwĭm′). A river of southwest Alaska flowing about 965 km (600 mi) southwest to **Kuskokwim Bay,** an inlet of the Bering Sea.

Ku·ta·i·si (ko͞o-tī′sē, ko͞o′tə-yē′syĭ). A city of western Georgia west-northwest of Tbilisi. The capital of ancient Colchis in the eighth century, it was taken by the Russians after 1773. Population, 214,000.

Kutch (kŭch). See **Rann of Kutch.**

Kutch, Gulf of. An inlet of the Arabian Sea in western India adjoining the Rann of Kutch.

Ku·te·nai (ko͞ot′n-ā′, -n-ē′) *n., pl.* **Kutenai** or **-nais. 1.a.** A Native American people inhabiting parts of southeast British Columbia, northeast Washington, and northern Idaho. **b.** A member of this people. **2.** The language of the Kutenai.

Ku·tu·zov (ko͞o-to͞o′zôf, -zəf), **Mikhail Ilarionovich.** Prince of Smolensk. 1745–1813. Russian field marshal who distinguished himself in the wars against Turkey (1770–1774 and 1787–1791) and commanded (1805–1812) the Russian opposition to Napoleon.

Ku·wait (ko͞o-wāt′). **1.** A country of the northeast Arabian Peninsula at the head of the Persian Gulf. With its major oil reserves, discovered in 1938, it has one of the highest per capita incomes in the world. The country was a British protectorate from 1897 to 1961. It was briefly occupied by Iraq (1990–1991). The city of Kuwait is its capital. Population, 1,355,827. **2.** The capital of Kuwait, in the east-central part of the country on the Persian Gulf. Population, 60,365. **—Ku·wait′i** (-wā′tē) *adj. & n.*

Kuy·by·shev (kwē′bə-shĕf′, -shĕv′, ko͞o′ē-bə-shĭf). See **Kuibyshev.**

Kuz·nets (ko͝oz′nĕts′, ko͝oz′nĭts), **Simon.** 1901–1985. Russian-born American economist. He won a 1971 Nobel Prize for developing a method of using a country's gross national product to determine its economic growth.

Kuz·netsk Basin (ko͝oz-nĕtsk′, -nyĕtsk′). A coal-producing region of west-central Russia extending from Tomsk southward to Novokuznetsk. The area's mineral resources were first exploited in the mid-19th century.

kV or **kv** *abbr.* Kilovolt.

kvass (kväs) *n.* A Russian fermented beverage similar to beer, made from rye or barley. [Russian *kvas,* from Old Russian *kvasŭ.*]

kvetch (kvĕch) *Slang. intr.v.* **kvetched, kvetch·ing, kvetch·es.** To complain persistently and whiningly. **—kvetch** *n.* **1.** A chronic, whining complainer. **2.** A nagging complaint: *"a rambling kvetch against the system"* (Leonard Ross). [Yiddish *kvetshn,* to squeeze, complain, from Middle High German *quetzen, quetschen,* to squeeze.]

kW *abbr.* Kilowatt.

Kwa (kwä) *n.* Any of several West African languages belonging to the South Central Niger-Congo language family, including Efik, Ewe, Ibibio, Ibo, and Yoruba. **—Kwa** *adj.*

kwa·cha (kwä′chə) *n.* See table at **currency.** [Bemba and Chewa, dawn : *kw-,* infinitive pref. + *-acha,* to dawn.]

Kwa·ja·lein (kwä′jə-lən, -lān′). An atoll in the Marshall Islands of the western Pacific Ocean. It was used as a Japanese air and naval base during World War II.

Kwa·ki·u·tl (kwä′kē-o͞ot′l) *n., pl.* **Kwakiutl** or **-tls. 1.a.** A Native American people inhabiting parts of coastal British Columbia and northern Vancouver Island. **b.** A member of this people. **2.** The Wakashan language of the Kwakiutl.

Kwan·do (kwän′dō). A river rising in central Angola and flowing about 965 km (600 mi) generally southeast and east to the Zambezi River.

Kwang·chow (kwäng′chō′). See **Guangzhou.**

Kwang·ju (kwäng′jo͞o′, gwäng′-). A city of southwest South Korea south-southeast of Seoul. It is an agricultural market and a commercial center. Population, 843,000.

Kwang·si Chuang (kwäng′sē′ chwäng′). See **Guangxi Zhuangzu.**

Kwang·tung (kwäng′to͝ong′, gwäng′do͝ong′). See **Guangdong.**

Kwan·tung (kwän′to͝ong′, gwän′do͝ong′). A former coastal territory of northeast China in southern Manchuria. It was leased to Russia in 1898 and controlled by Japan from 1905 to 1945.

kwan·za (kwän′zə) *n., pl.* **kwanza** or **-zas.** See table at **currency.** [Bantu, possibly from *Kwanza* (Cuanza), a river of Angola or from Swahili *kwanza,* first or from *kuanza,* to begin.]

Kwan·za¹ (kwän′zə). See **Cuanza.**

Kwan·za² (kwän′zə) *n.* An African-American cultural festival, celebrated from December 26 to January 1. [Possibly from Swahili *kwanzaa,* first fruit of the harvest.]

kwa·shi·or·kor (kwä′shē-ôr′kôr′) *n.* Severe protein malnutrition, especially in children after weaning, characterized by lethargy, growth retardation, anemia, edema, potbelly, depigmentation of the skin, and loss of hair or change in hair color. [Gã (Niger-Congo language of Ghana) *kwashiɔkɔ.*]

Kwei·chow (kwā′chō′). See **Guizhou.**

Kwei·lin (kwā′lĭn′). See **Guilin.**

Kwei·yang (kwā′yäng′). See **Guiyang.**

kWh *abbr.* Kilowatt-hour.

kW-hr *abbr. Kilowatt-hour.*

KY or **Ky.** *abbr.* Kentucky.

ky·ack (kī′ăk′) *n.* A packsack that hangs on either side of a packsaddle. [Probably from KAYAK.]

ky·a·nite (kī′ə-nīt′) also **cy·a·nite** (sī′ə-) *n.* A bluish-green to colorless mineral, Al_2SiO_5, used as a refractory. [Greek *kuanos,* dark blue enamel + –ITE¹.]

kyat (chät) *n.* See table at **currency.** [Burmese.]

Kyd or **Kid** (kĭd), **Thomas.** 1558–1594. English dramatist who wrote *The Spanish Tragedy* (c. 1584), is thought to have contributed to Shakespeare's *Titus Andronicus* and *Henry VI,* and may have written a version of *Hamlet.*

ky·lix (kī′lĭks, kĭl′ĭks) *n., pl.* **ky·li·kes** (kī′lĭ-kēz′, kĭl′ĭ-). A shallow, stemmed, two-handled drinking cup used in ancient Greece. [Greek *kulix.*]

ky·mo·gram (kī′mə-grăm′) *n.* A graph or record made by a kymograph. [Greek *kuma,* something swollen; see CYMA + –GRAM.]

ky·mo·graph (kī′mə-grăf′) *n. Physiology.* An instrument for recording variations in pressure, as of the blood, or in tension, as of a muscle, by means of a pen or stylus that marks a rotating drum. [Greek *kuma,* something swollen; see CYMA + –GRAPH.] **—ky′mo·graph′ic** *adj.*

Ky·o·ga (kē-ō′gə), **Lake.** See Lake **Kioga.**

Kyo·to (kē-ō′tō, kyō′-). A city of west-central Honshu, Japan, north-northeast of Osaka. Founded in the eighth century, it has long been a cultural, artistic, and religious center. Kyoto was Japan's capital from 794 until 1869. Population, 1,479,125.

ky·pho·sis (kī-fō′sĭs) *n.* Abnormal rearward curvature of the spine, resulting in protuberance of the upper back; hunchback. [Greek *kuphōsis,* from *kuphos,* bent.] **—ky·phot′ic** (-fŏt′ĭk) *adj.*

Kyr·i·e (kîr′ē-ā′) *n.* **1.** A brief petition and response used in various liturgies of several Christian churches, beginning with or composed of the words "Lord, have mercy." **2.** A musical setting of this petition and response, usually forming the first movement of a Mass. [Late Latin, from Greek *Kurie eleēson,* Lord, have mercy : *Kurie,* vocative of *kurios,* lord, master; see **keuə-** in Appendix + *eleēson,* aorist imperative of *elein,* to show mercy (from *eleos,* mercy).]

Kyrie e·le·i·son (ĭ-lā′ĭ-sŏn′, -sən) *n.* The Kyrie. [Late Latin. See KYRIE.]

Kyu·shu (kē-o͞o′sho͞o, kyo͞o′-). The southernmost of the major islands of Japan, in the southwest on the East China Sea and the Pacific Ocean.

Ky·zyl-Kum (kĭ-zĭl′ko͞om′). A desert of north-central Uzbekistan and south-central Kazakhstan southeast of the Aral Sea between the Amu Darya and the Syr Darya.

Kuwait

kylix

ă pat	oi boy
ā pay	ou out
âr care	o͝o took
ä father	o͞o boot
ĕ pet	ŭ cut
ē be	ûr urge
ĭ pit	th thin
ī pie	*th* this
îr pier	hw which
ŏ pot	zh vision
ō toe	ə about, item
ô paw	♦ regionalism

Stress marks: **′** (primary); ′ (secondary), as in **dictionary** (dĭk′shə-nĕr′ē)

Ll

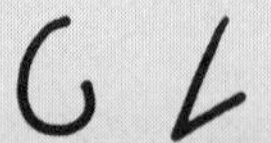

Phoenician
The sign for the sound *l* was called *lāmedh* in Phoenician.

Early Greek
It was modified slightly in the Greek alphabet, where it was named *lambda.*

L

Roman
The Romans gave L the upright shape it has today.

l[1] or **L** (ĕl) *n., pl.* **l's** or **L's. 1.** The 12th letter of the modern English alphabet. **2.** Any of the speech sounds represented by the letter *l.* **3.** The 12th in a series. **4.** Something shaped like the letter L.

l[2] *abbr.* Liter.

L[1] also **l** The symbol for the Roman numeral 50.

L[2] *abbr.* **1.** Lambert. **2.** Also **L.** Large.

l. *abbr.* **1.** Also **L.** Lake. **2.** Land. **3.** Late. **4.** Left. **5.** Length. **6.** Line. **7.** Lira.

L. *abbr.* **1.** Latin. **2.** Licentiate (in titles). **3.** Linnaean. **4.** Lodge (society).

la[1] (lä) *n. Music.* The sixth tone of the diatonic scale in solfeggio. [Middle English, from Medieval Latin. See GAMUT.]

la[2] (lä) *interj.* Used to express emphasis or indicate surprise.

La The symbol for the element **lanthanum.**

LA or **La.** *abbr.* Louisiana.

L.A. *abbr.* **1.** Legislative Assembly. **2.** Local agent. **3.** Also **LA.** Los Angeles.

laa·ger (lä′gər) *n.* A defensive encampment encircled by armored vehicles or wagons. **—laager** *intr.v.* **-gered, -ger·ing, -gers.** To camp in a defensive encirclement. [Alteration of Obsolete Afrikaans *lager,* probably from German *Lager,* camp, lair, from Middle High German *lĕger,* bed, lair, from Old High German *legar.* See **legh-** in Appendix.]

lab (lăb) *n.* A laboratory.

Lab. *abbr.* Labrador.

La Baie (lä bā′). A city of south-central Quebec, Canada, on the Saguenay River southeast of Chicoutimi. Population, 20,935.

La·ba·no·ta·tion (lä′bə-nō-tā′shen) *n.* A system of movement notation for dance that employs various symbols to record the points of a dancer's body, the direction of a dancer's movement, the tempo, and the dynamics: *"Labanotation is specific enough to record the flutter of an eyelid"* (Joseph Menosky). [After Rudolph *Laban* (1879–1958), Hungarian choreographer.]

lab·a·rum (lăb′ər-əm) *n., pl.* **-a·ra** (-ər-ə). **1.** An ecclesiastical banner, especially one carried in processions. **2.** The banner adopted by Constantine I after his conversion to Christianity. [Latin.]

lab·da·num (lăb′də-nəm) also **lad·a·num** (lăd′n-əm) *n.* A resin of certain Old World plants of the genus *Cistus,* yielding a fragrant essential oil used in flavorings and perfumes. [Middle English, from Medieval Latin *lapdanum, labdanum,* alteration of Latin *lādanum,* from Greek *lēdanon,* from *lēdon,* rockrose, of Semitic origin; akin to Akkadian *ladunu.*]

la·bel (lā′bəl) *n.* **1.** An item that functions as a means of identification, especially a small piece of paper or cloth attached to an article to designate its origin, owner, contents, use, or destination. **2.** A descriptive term; an epithet. **3.** A distinctive name or trademark identifying a product or manufacturer, especially a recording company. **4.** *Computer Science.* A symbol or set of symbols identifying the contents of a file, memory, tape, or record. **5.** *Architecture.* A molding over a door or window; a dripstone. **6.** *Heraldry.* A figure in a field consisting of a narrow horizontal bar with several pendants. **7.** *Chemistry.* See **tracer** (sense 4). **—label** *tr.v.* **-beled, -bel·ing, -bels** or **-belled, -bel·ling, -bels. 1.** To attach a label to. **2.** To identify or designate with a label; describe or classify: *labeled them Yuppies.* See Synonyms at **mark**[1]. **3.** *Chemistry.* To add a tracer to (a compound). [Middle English, ornamental strip of cloth, from Old French, probably of Germanic origin.] **—la′bel·er, la′bel·ler** *n.*

la·bel·lum (lə-bĕl′əm) *n., pl.* **-bel·la** (-bĕl′ə). **1.** The often enlarged petal of an orchid flower. **2.** A liplike part, such as the tip of the proboscis of various insects, used for lapping up liquids. [Latin, diminutive of *labrum,* lip. See **leb-** in Appendix.] **—la·bel′late** (-ĭt) *adj.*

la·bi·a (lā′bē-ə) *n.* Plural of **labium.**

la·bi·al (lā′bē-əl) *adj.* **1.** Of or relating to the lips or labia. **2.** *Linguistics.* Articulated mainly by closing or partly closing the lips, as the sounds (b), (m), or (w). **—labial** *n.* **1.** *Linguistics.* A labial consonant. **2.** *Music.* See **flue**[1] (sense 2a). [Medieval Latin *labiālis,* from Latin *labium,* lip. See **leb-** in Appendix.] **—la′bi·al·ly** *adv.*

la·bi·al·ize (lā′bē-ə-līz′) *tr.v.* **-ized, -iz·ing, -iz·es.** *Linguistics.* To round (a vowel); make labial. **—la′bi·al·i·za′tion** (-ə-lĭ-zā′shən) *n.*

labia ma·jo·ra (mə-jôr′ə, -jōr′ə) *pl.n.* The two outer rounded folds of adipose tissue that lie on either side of the vaginal opening and form the external lateral boundaries of the vulva. [New Latin *labia mājōra* : Latin *labia,* pl. of *labium,* lip + Latin *māiōra,* neuter pl. of *māior,* larger.]

labia mi·no·ra (mə-nôr′ə, -nōr′ə) *pl.n.* The two thin inner folds of skin within the vestibule of the vagina enclosed within the cleft of the labia majora; nymphae. [New Latin *labia minōra* : Latin *labia,* pl. of *labium,* lip + Latin *minōra,* neuter pl. of *minor,* smaller.]

la·bi·ate (lā′bē-ĭt, -āt′) *adj.* **1.** Having lips or liplike parts. **2.** *Botany.* **a.** Having or characterizing flowers with the corolla divided into two liplike parts, as in the snapdragon. **b.** Of or belonging to the mint family Labiatae. **—labiate** *n.* A plant belonging to the Labiatae. [Latin *labium,* lip; see LABIUM + –ATE[1].]

la·bile (lā′bĭl′, -bəl) *adj.* **1.** Open to change; adaptable: *an emotionally labile person.* **2.** *Chemistry.* Constantly undergoing or likely to undergo change; unstable: *a labile compound.* [Middle English *labil,* forgetful, wandering, from Old French *labile,* from Late Latin *lābilis,* apt to slip, from *lābī,* to slip.] **—la·bil′i·ty** (-bĭl′ĭ-tē) *n.*

labio– *pref.* Labial: *labiovelar.* [From Latin *labium,* lip. See LABIUM.]

la·bi·o·den·tal (lā′bē-ō-dĕn′tl) *Linguistics. adj.* Articulated with the lower lip and upper teeth, as the sounds (f) and (v). **—labiodental** *n.* A labiodental sound.

la·bi·o·na·sal (lā′bē-ō-nā′zəl) *Linguistics. adj.* Simultaneously labial and velar. **—labionasal** *n.* A labionasal sound.

la·bi·o·ve·lar (lā′bē-ō-vē′lər) *Linguistics. adj.* Simultaneously labial and velar, as (kw) in *quick.* **—labiovelar** *n.* A labiovelar sound.

la·bi·um (lā′bē-əm) *n., pl.* **-bi·a** (-bē-ə). **1.** *Anatomy.* Any of four folds of tissue of the female external genitalia. **2.** *Zoology.* **a.** A liplike structure, such as that forming the floor of the mouth of certain invertebrates, especially insects. **b.** The inner margin of the opening of a gastropod shell. **3.** *Botany.* One of the liplike divisions of a labiate corolla. [Latin, lip. See **leb-** in Appendix.]

lab·lab (lăb′lăb′) *n.* See **hyacinth bean.** [Arabic *lablāb.*]

la·bor (lā′bər) *n.* **1.a.** Physical or mental exertion, especially when difficult or exhausting; work. See Synonyms at **work. b.** Something produced by work. **2.** A specific task. **3.** A particular form of work or method of working: *manual labor.* **4.** Work for wages. **5.a.** Workers considered as a group. **b.** The trade union movement, especially its officials. **6. Labor.** A political party representing the interests of workers, especially in Great Britain. **7.** The physical efforts of childbirth; parturition. **—labor** *v.* **-bored, -bor·ing, -bors.** *—intr.* **1.** To work; toil: *labored in the fields.* **2.** To strive painstakingly: *labored over the needlepoint.* **3.a.** To proceed with great effort; plod: *labored up the hill.* **b.** *Nautical.* To pitch and roll. **4.** To suffer from distress or a disadvantage: *labored under the misconception that others were cooperating.* **5.** To undergo the efforts of childbirth. *—tr.* **1.** To deal with in exhaustive or excessive detail; belabor: *labor a point in the argument.* **2.** To distress; burden: *I will not labor you with trivial matters.* **—labor** *adj.* **1.** Of or relating to labor. **2. Labor.** Of or relating to a political party representing the interests of the working class. [Middle English, from Old French *labour,* from Latin *labor.*] **—la′bor·er** *n.*

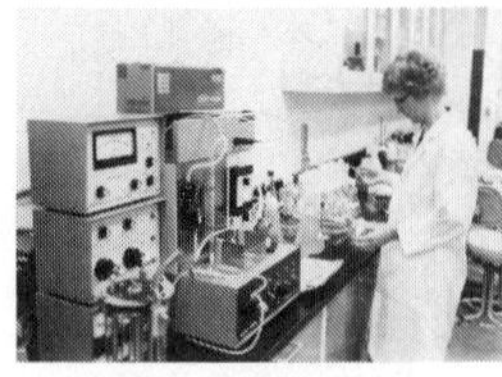

laboratory

lab·o·ra·to·ry (lăb′rə-tôr′ē, -tōr′ē) *n., pl.* **-ries. 1.a.** A room or building equipped for scientific experimentation or research. **b.** An academic period devoted to work or study in such a place. **2.** A place where drugs and chemicals are manufactured. **3.** A place for practice, observation, or testing. [Medieval Latin *labōrātōrium,* from Latin *labōrāre,* to labor, from *labor,* labor.]

Labor Day *n.* The first Monday in September, observed as a holiday in the United States and Canada in honor of working people.

la·bored (lā′bərd) *adj.* **1.** Produced or done with effort: *the labored breathing of a very ill person.* **2.** Lacking natural ease; strained: *a labored style of debating.*

la·bor-in·ten·sive (lā′bər-ĭn-tĕn′sĭv) *adj.* Requiring or having a large expenditure of labor in comparison to capital: *"Intrigue and subversion are labor-intensive undertakings"* (George F. Kennan).

la·bo·ri·ous (lə-bôr′ē-əs, -bōr′-) *adj.* **1.** Marked by or requiring long, hard work: *spent many laborious hours on the project.* **2.** Hard-working; industrious. [Middle English, from Old French *laborieux,* from Latin *labōriōsus,* from *labor,* labor.] **—la·bo′ri·ous·ly** *adv.* **—la·bo′ri·ous·ness** *n.*

la·bor·ite (lā′bə-rīt′) *n.* **1.** A member or supporter of a labor movement or union. **2. Laborite.** A member of a political party representing labor.

la·bor·sav·ing (lā′bər-sā′vĭng) *adj.* Designed to conserve human energy in performing work or to decrease the amount of human labor needed.

labor union *n.* An organization of wage earners formed for the purpose of serving the members' interests with respect to wages and working conditions.

la·bour (lā′bər) *n., v., & adj. Chiefly British.* Variant of **labor.**

la·bra (lā′brə) *n.* Plural of **labrum.**

Lab·ra·dor (lăb′rə-dôr′). *Abbr.* **Lab.** The mainland territory of Newfoundland, Canada, on the northeast portion of the Labrador Peninsula. Its coastline was visited by Norse seamen as early as the tenth century. The area was awarded to Newfoundland in 1927. **—Lab′ra·dor′e·an, Lab′ra·dor′i·an** *adj. & n.*

Labrador Current *n.* A cold ocean current flowing southward from Baffin Bay along the coast of Labrador and turning east after intersecting with the Gulf Stream.

lab·ra·dor·ite (lăb′rə-dôr′īt′, -dô-rīt′) *n.* A variety of plagioclase feldspar found in igneous rocks and characterized by brilliant colors in some specimens. [After the LABRADOR (PENINSULA).]

Labrador Peninsula. A peninsula of eastern Canada between Hudson Bay and the Atlantic Ocean. It is divided between Quebec and Newfoundland provinces.

Labrador retriever *n.* Any of a breed of dog originating in Newfoundland, having a short, dense, yellow, black, or brown coat and a tapering tail and used in hunting to retrieve felled game. [After LABRADOR.]

Labrador Sea. An arm of the northern Atlantic Ocean between eastern Canada and southwest Greenland.

la·bret (lā′brĭt) *n.* An ornament inserted into a perforation in the lip. [Latin *labrum,* lip; see **leb-** in Appendix + –ET.]

la·brum (lā′brəm) *n., pl.* **-bra** (-brə). **1.** A lip or liplike structure, such as the one forming the roof of the mouth in insects. **2.** The outer margin of the opening of a gastropod shell. [Latin, lip. See **leb-** in Appendix.]

La Bru·yère (lä bro͞o-yĕr′, brē-, brü-), **Jean de.** 1645–1696. French moralist and satirist. His works provide a critical account of 17th-century Paris.

La·bu·an (lə-bo͞o′ən, lä′bo͞o-än′). An island of Malaysia off the northeast coast of Borneo. At one time a British crown colony (after 1848), it became part of Malaysia in 1963.

la·bur·num (lə-bûr′nəm) *n.* Any of several trees or shrubs of the genus *Laburnum,* especially *L. anagyroides,* which is cultivated for its drooping clusters of yellow flowers. [New Latin *Laburnum,* genus name, from Latin *laburnum,* broad-leaved bean-trefoil, perhaps of Etruscan origin.]

lab·y·rinth (lăb′ə-rĭnth′) *n.* **1.a.** An intricate structure of interconnecting passages through which it is difficult to find one's way; a maze. **b. Labyrinth.** *Greek Mythology.* The maze in which the Minotaur was confined. **2.** Something highly intricate or convoluted in character, composition, or construction: *a labyrinth of rules and regulations.* **3.** *Anatomy.* **a.** A group of complex interconnecting anatomical cavities. **b.** See **inner ear.** [Middle English *laberinthe,* from Latin *labyrinthus,* from Greek *laburinthos;* possibly akin to *labrus,* double-headed axe, of Lydian origin.]

lab·y·rin·thine (lăb′ə-rĭn′thĭn, -thēn′) **lab·y·rin·thi·an** (-thē-ən) *adj.* Of, relating to, resembling, or constituting a labyrinth: *"the labyrinthine corridors and alleys of bureaucratic red tape"* (William H. Hallahan).

labyrinthine fluid *n.* The fluid separating the osseous and the membranous labyrinths of the inner ear.

lab·y·rin·tho·dont (lăb′ə-rĭn′thə-dŏnt′) *n.* **1.** Having teeth with a labyrinthine internal structure. **2.** Of or relating to the superorder Labyrinthodontia, an extinct group of amphibians resembling crocodiles and having a labyrinthine tooth structure.

lac (lăk) *n.* A resinous secretion of the lac insect deposited on trees and used in making shellac. [Dutch *lac* or French *laque* (from Old French *lacce,* from Medieval Latin *lacca,* from Arabic *lakk,* from Persian *lak*), both from Hindi *lākh,* from Prakrit *lakkha,* from Sanskrit *lākṣā,* red dye, resin, alteration of *rākṣā.*]

Lac·ca·dive Islands (lăk′ə-dīv′, lä′kə-dēv′). A group of islands and coral reefs in the Arabian Sea off the southwest coast of India. The islands are now part of the region of Lakshadweep.

lac·co·lith (lăk′ə-lĭth′) *n.* A mass of igneous rock intruded between layers of sedimentary rock, resulting in uplift. [Greek *lakkos,* cistern + –LITH.]

lace (lās) *n.* **1.** A cord or ribbon used to draw and tie together two opposite edges, as of a shoe. **2.** A delicate fabric made of yarn or thread in an open weblike pattern. **3.** Gold or silver braid ornamenting an officer's uniform. **—lace** *v.* **laced, lac·ing, lac·es.** *—tr.* **1.** To thread a cord through the eyelets or around the hooks of. **2.a.** To draw together and tie the laces of. **b.** To restrain or constrict by tightening laces, especially of a corset. **3.** To pull or pass through; intertwine: *lace garlands through a trellis.* **4.** To trim or decorate with or as if with lace. **5.a.** To add a touch of liquor to: *laced the eggnog with rum and brandy.* **b.** To add a touch of flavor or a dash of zest to, so as to make more effective, for example: *"Quacks now lace their pitch with scientific terms that may sound authentic to the uninformed"* (Jane E. Brody). **6.** To streak with color. **7.** To give a beating to; thrash: *laced his opponent in the second round.* *—intr.* To be fastened or tied with laces or a lace. ***—phrasal verb.*** **lace into.** *Informal.* To attack; assail: *laced into me for arriving so late.* [Middle English, from Old French *las,* noose, string, from Vulgar Latin **laceum,* from Latin *laqueus,* noose; probably akin to *lacere,* to entice, ensnare.] **—lace′less** *adj.* **—lac′er** *n.*

lace bug *n.* Any of several insects of the family Tingidae, predominantly grayish and rectangular, with a lacelike pattern of ridges on the thorax, head, and wings.

lace-cur·tain (lās′kûr′tn) *adj.* Aspiring to or emulating the middle class.

Lac·e·dae·mon (lăs′ĭ-dē′mən). See **Sparta.** **—Lac′e·dae·mo′ni·an** (-də-mō′nē-ən) *adj. & n.*

lac·er·ate (lăs′ə-rāt′) *tr.v.* **-at·ed, -at·ing, -ates. 1.** To rip, cut, or tear. **2.** To cause deep emotional pain to; distress. **—lacerate** (-rĭt, -rāt′) *adj.* **1.** Torn; mangled. **2.** Wounded. **3.** Having jagged, deeply cut edges: *lacerate leaves.* [Middle English *laceraten,* from Latin *lacerāre, lacerāt-,* from *lacer,* torn.]

lac·er·a·tion (lăs′ə-rā′shən) *n.* A jagged wound or cut.

La·cer·ta (lə-sûr′tə) *n.* A constellation in the Northern Hemisphere near Cygnus and Andromeda. [Latin *lacerta,* lizard.]

lac·er·til·i·an (lăs′ər-tĭl′ē-ən) *adj.* Of, relating to, or characteristic of lizards and closely related reptiles; Saurian. [From New Latin *Lacertilia,* former suborder name, from Latin *lacerta,* lizard.]

lace·wing (lās′wĭng′) *n.* Any of various insects of the superfamily Hemerobioidea, having four gauzy wings, threadlike antennae, and larvae that feed on insect pests such as aphids.

La·chaise (lə-shāz′, lä-shĕz′), **Gaston.** 1882–1935. French-born American sculptor known for his large nude figures, including *Standing Woman.*

Lach·e·sis (lăk′ĭ-sĭs, lăch′-) *n. Greek Mythology.* One of the three Fates, the measurer of the thread of destiny.

La·chine (lə-shēn′, lä-). A city of southern Quebec, Canada, on Montreal Island and the St. Lawrence River. It was first settled as an estate by Sieur La Salle in 1668. Population, 37,521.

La·chish (lā′kĭsh). An ancient city of southern Palestine southwest of Jerusalem. It was probably inhabited as early as 3200 B.C.

Lach·lan (läk′lən). A river, about 1,483 km (922 mi) long, of southeast Australia flowing northwest then southwest to the Murrumbidgee River.

lach·ry·mal also **lac·ri·mal** (lăk′rə-məl) *adj.* **1.** Of or relating to tears. **2.** Of, relating to, or constituting the glands that produce tears. [Middle English *lacrimale,* from Old French *lacrymal,* from Medieval Latin *lachrymālis,* from Latin *lacrima,* tear. See **dakru-** in Appendix.]

lach·ry·ma·tion (lăk′rə-mā′shən) *n.* Variant of **lacrimation.**

lach·ry·ma·tor also **lac·ri·ma·tor** (lăk′rə-mā′tər) *n.* Tear gas. [Latin *lacrimāre, lacrimātus,* to cry (from *lacrima,* tear; see LACHRYMAL) + –ATOR.]

lach·ry·mose (lăk′rə-mōs′) *adj.* **1.** Weeping or inclined to weep; tearful. **2.** Causing or tending to cause tears. [Latin *lacrimōsus,* from *lacrima,* tear. See LACHRYMAL.] **—lach′ry·mose′ly** *adv.* **—lach′ry·mos′i·ty** (-mŏs′ĭ-tē) *n.*

lac·ing (lā′sĭng) *n.* **1.** Something that laces; a lace. **2.** A touch of liquor added to a beverage or food. **3.** *Informal.* A beating or thrashing.

la·cin·i·a (lə-sĭn′ē-ə) *n.* **1.** A slash, as in a leaf or petal. **2.** The apex of the insect maxilla. [Latin, fringe, hem.]

la·cin·i·ate (lə-sĭn′ē-ĭt, -āt′) *adj.* **1.** Having a fringe; fringed. **2.** Shaped or formed like a fringe, as a ligament. **3.** Slashed into narrow, pointed lobes: *a laciniate leaf.* [Latin *lacinia,* fringe, hem + –ATE[1].] **—la·cin′i·a′tion** *n.*

lac insect *n.* Any of various insects of the subfamily Lacciferinae, especially *Laccifer lacca* of southern Asia, the female of which secretes lac.

lack (lăk) *n.* **1.** A deficiency or an absence: *a lack of money.* **2.** Something needed or wanted. **—lack** *v.* **lacked, lack·ing, lacks.** *—tr.* **1.** To be entirely without or have very little of. **2.** To be in need of. *—intr.* **1.** To be wanting or deficient: *You will not be lacking in support from me.* **2.** To be in need of something: *I lacked for nothing.* [Middle English, perhaps from Middle Dutch *lac,* deficiency, fault.]

SYNONYMS: *lack, want, need.* These verbs mean to be without something, especially something that is necessary or desirable.

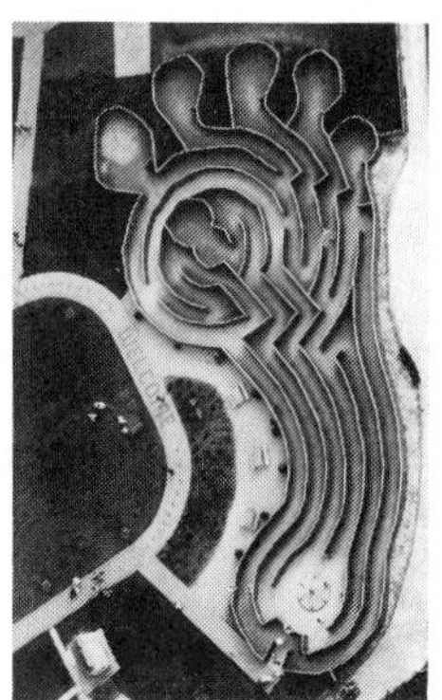

labyrinth

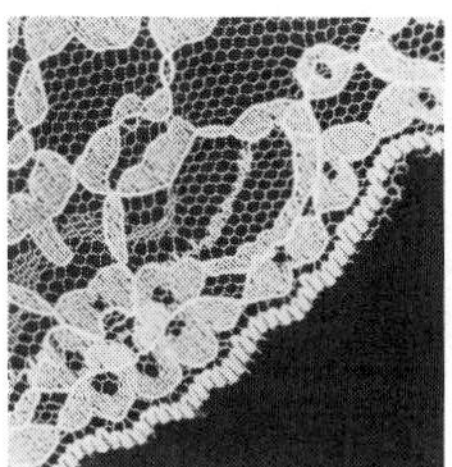

lace

ă pat	oi boy
ā pay	ou out
âr care	o͝o took
ä father	o͞o boot
ĕ pet	ŭ cut
ē be	ûr urge
ĭ pit	th thin
ī pie	*th* this
îr pier	hw which
ŏ pot	zh vision
ō toe	ə about, item
ô paw	♦ regionalism

Stress marks: **′** (primary); ′ (secondary), as in **dictionary** (dĭk′shə-nĕr′ē)

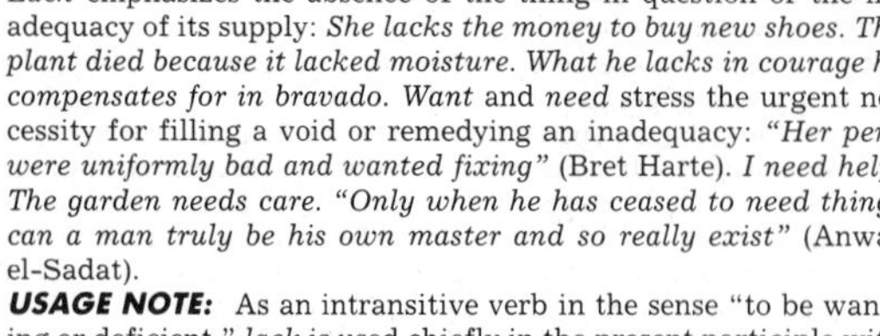
Lack emphasizes the absence of the thing in question or the inadequacy of its supply: *She lacks the money to buy new shoes. The plant died because it lacked moisture. What he lacks in courage he compensates for in bravado. Want* and *need* stress the urgent necessity for filling a void or remedying an inadequacy: *"Her pens were uniformly bad and wanted fixing"* (Bret Harte). *I need help. The garden needs care. "Only when he has ceased to need things can a man truly be his own master and so really exist"* (Anwar el-Sadat).

USAGE NOTE: As an intransitive verb in the sense "to be wanting or deficient," *lack* is used chiefly in the present participle with *in: You will not be lacking in support from me.* In the sense "to be in need of something" it is often used with *for: "In the terrible, beautiful age of my prime,/I lacked for sweet linen but never for time"* (E.B. White).

lacrosse

lack·a·dai·si·cal (lăk′ə-dā′zĭ-kəl) *adj.* Lacking spirit, liveliness, or interest; languid: *"There'll be no time to correct lackadaisical driving techniques after trouble develops"* (William J. Hampton). [From *lackadaisy,* alteration of LACKADAY.] **—lack′a·dai′si·cal·ly** *adv.* **—lack′a·dai′si·cal·ness** *n.*

lack·a·day (lăk′ə-dā′) *interj. Archaic.* Used to express regret or disapproval. [Alteration of *alack the day.*]

Lack·a·wan·na (lăk′ə-wŏn′ə). A city of western New York on Lake Erie south of Buffalo. Population, 22,701.

lack·ey (lăk′ē) *n., pl.* **-eys. 1.** A liveried male servant; a footman. **2.** A servile follower; a toady. **—lackey** *v.* **-eyed, -ey·ing, -eys.** *—tr.* To wait on as a footman; attend. *—intr.* To act in a servile manner; fawn. [French *laquais,* from Old French.]

lack·lus·ter (lăk′lŭs′tər) *adj.* Lacking brightness, luster, or vitality; dull. See Synonyms at **dull.**

La·co·ni·a (lə-kō′nē-ə). An ancient region of southern Greece in the southeast Peloponnesus. It was dominated by Sparta until the rise of the second Achaean League in the third and second centuries B.C.

la·con·ic (lə-kŏn′ĭk) *adj.* Using or marked by the use of few words; terse or concise. [Latin *Lacōnicus,* Spartan, from Greek *Lakōnikos,* from *Lakōn,* a Spartan (from the reputation of the Spartans for brevity of speech).] **—la·con′i·cal·ly** *adv.*

WORD HISTORY: As the study of the classics has disappeared from the curriculum, so has the ready understanding that terms such as *laconic* once possessed. *Laconic,* which comes to us via Latin from Greek *Lakōnikos,* is first recorded in 1583 with the sense "of or relating to Laconia or its inhabitants." *Lakōnikos* is derived from *Lakōn,* "a Laconian, a person from Lakedaimon," the name for the region of Greece of which Sparta was the capital. The Spartans, noted for being warlike and disciplined, were also known for the brevity of their speech, and it is this quality that English writers still denote by the use of the adjective *laconic,* which is first found in this sense in 1589.

ladder-back
18th-century English ladder-back chair

lac·o·nism (lăk′ə-nĭz′əm) *n.* Terseness or succinctness of style or expression.

La Co·ru·ña (lä′ kə-ro͞on′yə, kô-ro͞o′nyä). A city of northwest Spain on the Atlantic Ocean west of Oviedo. Perhaps predating Roman times, it was the point of departure for the Spanish Armada (1588). Population, 240,463.

lac·quer (lăk′ər) *n.* **1.** Any of various clear or colored synthetic coatings made by dissolving nitrocellulose or other cellulose derivatives together with plasticizers and pigments in a mixture of volatile solvents and used to impart a high gloss to surfaces. **2.** A glossy, resinous material, such as the exudation of the lacquer tree, used as a surface coating. **3.** A finish that is baked onto the inside of food and beverage cans. **—lacquer** *tr.v.* **-quered, -quer·ing, -quers. 1.** To coat with lacquer. **2.** To give a sleek, glossy finish to. [Obsolete French *lacre,* sealing wax, from Portuguese, from *lacca,* resin of the lac insect, from Arabic *lakk.* See LAC.] **—lac′quer·er** *n.*

lacquer tree *n.* A poisonous, eastern Asian tree *(Rhus verniciflua)* having pinnately compound leaves and a toxic exudation from which a black lacquer is obtained.

lac·ri·mal (lăk′rə-məl) *adj.* Variant of **lachrymal.**

lac·ri·ma·tion also **lach·ry·ma·tion** (lăk′rə-mā′shən) *n.* Secretion of tears, especially in excess.

lac·ri·ma·tor (lăk′rə-mā′tər) *n.* Variant of **lachrymator.**

la·crosse (lə-krôs′, -krŏs′) *n. Sports.* A game of Native American origin that is played on a field by two teams of ten players each, in which participants use a long-handled stick with a webbed pouch to maneuver a ball into the opposing team's goal. [Canadian French *la crosse,* from French *(jeu de) la crosse,* (game of) the hooked stick, from Old French *croce, crosse,* crosier, of Germanic origin.]

La Crosse (lə krôs′, krŏs′). A city of western Wisconsin on the Mississippi River northwest of Madison. It was founded on the site of a French fur-trading post established in the late 18th century. Population, 48,347.

lact– *pref.* Variant of **lacto–.**

lac·tal·bu·min (lăk′tăl-byo͞o′mĭn) *n.* The albumin contained in milk and obtained from whey.

lac·tase (lăk′tās′) *n.* An enzyme occurring in certain yeasts and in the intestinal juices of mammals that is capable of splitting lactose into glucose and galactose.

lac·tate[1] (lăk′tāt′) *intr.v.* **-tat·ed, -tat·ing, -tates.** To secrete or produce milk. [Latin *lactāre, lactāt-,* from *lac, lact-,* milk. See LACTO–.]

lac·tate[2] (lăk′tāt′) *n.* A salt or an ester of lactic acid.

lactate dehydrogenase *n.* Any of a class of enzymes found in the liver, kidneys, striated muscle, and heart muscle that catalyze the reversible interconversion of pyruvate and lactate.

lac·ta·tion (lăk-tā′shən) *n.* **1.** Secretion or formation of milk by the mammary glands. **2.** The period during which the mammary glands secrete milk. **—lac·ta′tion·al** *adj.*

lac·te·al (lăk′tē-əl) *adj.* **1.** Of, relating to, or resembling milk. **2.** *Anatomy.* Of or relating to any of numerous minute intestinal lymph-carrying vessels that convey chyle from the intestine to lymphatic circulation and thereby to the thoracic duct. **—lacteal** *n. Anatomy.* A lacteal vessel. [From Latin *lacteus,* from *lac, lact-,* milk. See **melg-** in Appendix.] **—lac′te·al·ly** *adv.*

lac·tes·cent (lăk-tĕs′ənt) *adj.* **1.** Becoming milky. **2.** Milky. **3.** *Biology.* Secreting or yielding a milky juice, as certain plants and insects. [Latin *lactēscēns, lactēscent-,* present participle of *lactēscere,* inchoative of *lactēre,* to be milky, from *lac, lact-,* milk. See **melg-** in Appendix.] **—lac·tes′cence** *n.*

lac·tic (lăk′tĭk) *adj.* Of, relating to, or derived from milk.

lactic acid *n.* A syrupy, water-soluble liquid, $C_3H_6O_3$, produced as a result of anaerobic glucose metabolism and present in sour milk, molasses, various fruits, and wines. A synthetic form of the compound is used in foods and beverages as a flavoring and preservative, in dyeing and textile printing, and in pharmaceuticals.

lac·tif·er·ous (lăk-tĭf′ər-əs) *adj.* **1.** Producing, secreting, or conveying milk. **2.** *Botany.* Yielding latex. **—lac·tif′er·ous·ness** *n.*

lacto– or **lact–** *pref.* **1.** Milk: *lactoprotein.* **2.** Lactose: *lactase.* **3.** Lactic acid: *lactate.* [From Latin *lac, lact-,* milk. See **melg-** in Appendix.]

lac·to·ba·cil·lus (lăk′tō-bə-sĭl′əs) *n., pl.* **-cil·li** (-sĭl′ī′). Any of various rod-shaped, nonmotile aerobic bacteria of the genus *Lactobacillus* that ferment lactic acid from sugars and are the causative agents in the souring of milk.

lac·to·fla·vin (lăk′tə-flā′vĭn, lăk′tə-flā′-) *n.* See **riboflavin.**

lac·to·gen·ic (lăk′tə-jĕn′ĭk) *adj.* Inducing lactation.

lac·tom·e·ter (lăk-tŏm′ĭ-tər) *n.* A device used to measure the specific gravity, and therefore the richness, of milk.

lac·tone (lăk′tōn′) *n.* An anhydride formed by the removal of a water molecule from the hydroxyl and carboxyl radicals of hydroxy acids. [LACT(O)– + –ONE.] **—lac·ton′ic** (-tŏn′ĭk) *adj.*

lac·to·pro·tein (lăk′tō-prō′tēn′, -tē-ən) *n.* A protein normally present in milk.

lac·tose (lăk′tōs′) *n.* **1.** A disaccharide, $C_{12}H_{22}O_{11}$, found in milk, that may be hydrolyzed to yield glucose and galactose. **2.** A white crystalline substance obtained from whey and used in infant foods, bakery products, confections, and pharmaceuticals as a diluent and excipient. Also called *milk sugar.*

la·cu·na (lə-kyo͞o′nə) *n., pl.* **-nae** (-nē) or **-nas. 1.** An empty space or a missing part; a gap: *"self-centered in opinion, with curious lacunae of astounding ignorance"* (Frank Norris). **2.** *Anatomy.* A cavity, space, or depression, especially in a bone, containing cartilage or bone cells. [Latin *lacūna.* See LAGOON.] **—la·cu′nal** *adj.*

la·cu·nar (lə-kyo͞o′nər) *n.* **1.** A ceiling constructed with recessed panels. **2.** *pl.* **lac·u·nar·i·a** (lăk′yə-nâr′ē-ə) A recessed panel in such a ceiling. [Latin *lacūnar,* from *lacūna,* hole. See LAGOON.]

la·cus·trine (lə-kŭs′trĭn) *adj.* **1.** Of or relating to lakes. **2.** Living or growing in or along the edges of lakes. [French or Italian *lacustre* (from Latin *lacus,* lake) + –INE[1].]

lac·y (lā′sē) *adj.* **-i·er, -i·est.** Of, relating to, or resembling lace. **—lac′i·ness** *n.*

lad (lăd) *n.* **1.** A young man; a youth. **2.** *Informal.* A man of any age; a fellow. [Middle English *ladde,* perhaps of Scandinavian origin.]

lad·a·num (lăd′n-əm) *n.* Variant of **labdanum.**

lad·der (lăd′ər) *n.* **1.a.** An often portable structure consisting of two long sides crossed by parallel rungs, used to climb up and down. **b.** Something that resembles this device, especially a run in a stocking. **2.a.** A means of ascent and descent: *ascending the social ladder.* **b.** A series of ranked stages or levels: *high on the executive ladder.* **—ladder** *intr.v.* **-dered, -der·ing, -ders.** To run, as a stocking does. [Middle English, from Old English *hlǣder.* See **klei-** in Appendix.]

lad·der-back (lăd′ər-băk′) *n.* **1.** A chair back consisting of two upright posts connected by horizontal slats. **2.** A chair with such a back. **—lad′der-back′** *adj.*

lad·die (lăd′ē) *n.* A boy or young man; a lad.

lade (lād) *v.* **lad·ed, lad·en** (lād′n) or **lad·ed, lad·ing, lades.** *—tr.* **1.a.** To load with or as if with cargo. **b.** To place (something) as a load for or as if for shipment. **2.** To burden or oppress; weigh down. **3.** To take up or remove (water) with a ladle or dipper. *—intr.* **1.** To take on cargo. **2.** To ladle a liquid. [Middle English *laden,* from Old English *hladan.*]

la-de-da (lä′dē-dä′) *adj. Informal.* Variant of **la-di-da.**

lad·en (lăd′n) *v.* A past participle of **lade. —laden** *adj.* **1.** Weighed down with a load; heavy: *"the warmish air, laden with*

ă pat	oi boy
ā pay	ou out
âr care	o͝o took
ä father	o͞o boot
ĕ pet	ŭ cut
ē be	ûr urge
ĭ pit	th thin
ī pie	*th* this
îr pier	hw which
ŏ pot	zh vision
ō toe	ə about, item
ô paw	♦ regionalism

Stress marks: ′ (primary); ′ (secondary), as in **dictionary** (dĭk′shə-nĕr′ē)

the rains of those thousands of miles of western sea" (Hilaire Belloc). **2.** Oppressed; burdened: *laden with grief.*

la-di-da also **la-de-da** (lä′dē-dä′) *adj. Informal.* Affectedly genteel; pretentious. [Perhaps imitative of affected speech.]

la·dies' man (lā′dēz) *n.* Variant of **lady's man.**

ladies' room *n.* A restroom for women.

ladies' tress·es also **lady's tresses** *pl.n. (used with a sing. or pl. verb).* Any of various orchids of the genus *Spiranthes,* having a spike or raceme of small flowers usually arranged in a spiral.

La·din (lə-dēn′) *n.* **1.** See **Romansch. 2.** A person who is a native speaker of Ladin. [Rhaeto-Romanic, from Latin *Latīnus,* Latin. See LATIN.]

lad·ing (lā′dĭng) *n.* **1.** The act of loading. **2.** Cargo; freight.

La·di·no (lə-dē′nō) *n., pl.* **-nos. 1.** A Romance language with elements borrowed from Hebrew that is spoken by Sephardic Jews especially in the Balkans. Also called *Judeo-Spanish.* **2.** Also **ladino.** In Central America, a Spanish-speaking or acculturated Indian; a mestizo. [Spanish *ladino,* from Latin *Latīnus,* Latin. See LATIN.]

la·dle (lād′l) *n.* A long-handled spoon with a deep bowl for serving liquids. **—ladle** *tr.v.* **-dled, -dling, -dles.** To lift out or serve with a long-handled spoon. [Middle English, from Old English *hlædel,* from *hladan,* to draw out, lade.] **—la′dler** *n.*

Lad·o·ga (lä′də-gə), **Lake.** A lake of northwest Russia northeast of St. Petersburg. It is the largest lake in Europe.

la·dy (lā′dē) *n., pl.* **-dies. 1.** A well-mannered and considerate woman with high standards of proper behavior. **2.a.** A woman regarded as proper and virtuous. **b.** A well-behaved young girl. **3.** A woman who is the head of a household. **4.** A woman, especially when spoken of or to in a polite way. **5.a.** A woman to whom a man is romantically attached. **b.** *Informal.* A wife. **6. Lady.** *Chiefly British.* A general feminine title of nobility and other rank, specifically: **a.** Used as the title for the wife or widow of a knight or baronet. **b.** Used as a form of address for a marchioness, countess, viscountess, baroness, or baronetess. **c.** Used as a form of address for the wife or widow of a baron. **d.** Used as a courtesy title for the daughter of a duke, a marquis, or an earl. **e.** Used as a courtesy title for the wife of a younger son of a duke or marquis. **7.** The Virgin Mary. Often used with *Our.* **8.** *Slang.* Cocaine. [Middle English, mistress of a household, from Old English *hlǣfdige.* See **dheigh-** in Appendix.]

USAGE NOTE: *Lady,* a social term, is properly used as a parallel to *gentleman* in order to emphasize norms expected in civil society or in situations requiring civil courtesies: *She is too much of a lady to tell your secrets to her friends. I believe the lady in front of the cheese counter was here before me.* Used attributively together with the name of an occupational role, as in *lady doctor,* the word is widely regarded as condescending because of its implication that the usual person in that role is a man. When the gender of the referent is relevant, the preferred term is *woman.*

lady beetle also **la·dy·bee·tle** (lā′dē-bēt′l) *n.* See **ladybug.**

la·dy·bird (lā′dē-bûrd′) *n.* See **ladybug.**

la·dy·bug (lā′dē-bŭg′) *n.* Any of numerous small, rounded, usually brightly colored beetles of the family Coccinellidae, often reddish with black spots and feeding primarily on insect pests, such as scale insects and aphids. Also called *lady beetle, ladybird.*

Lady Chapel also **lady chapel** *n.* A chapel, as in a cathedral or church, usually located behind the sanctuary and dedicated to the Virgin Mary.

Lady Day *n. Chiefly British.* Annunciation, celebrated on March 25.

la·dy·fin·ger (lā′dē-fĭng′gər) also **la·dys·fin·ger** (lā′dēz-) *n.* A small oval sponge cake shaped like a human finger.

la·dy·fish (lā′dē-fĭsh′) *n., pl.* **ladyfish** or **-fish·es.** Any of several marine fishes, especially the tarpon *Elops saurus,* a game fish of tropical seas. Also called *tenpounder.*

lady in waiting *n., pl.* **ladies in waiting.** A lady of a court appointed to serve or attend a queen, princess, or royal duchess.

la·dy-kill·er (lā′dē-kĭl′ər) *n. Slang.* A man reputed to be exceptionally attractive to and often ruthless with women.

la·dy·like (lā′dē-līk′) *adj.* **1.** Characteristic of a lady; wellbred. **2.** Appropriate for or becoming to a lady. See Synonyms at **feminine. 3.** Unduly sensitive to matters of propriety or decorum. **4.** Lacking virility or strength. **—la′dy·like′ness** *n.*

la·dy·love (lā′dē-lŭv′) *n.* A woman or girl who is someone's sweetheart.

la·dys·fin·ger (lā′dēz-fĭng′gər) *n.* Variant of **ladyfinger.**

la·dy·ship also **La·dy·ship** (lā′dē-shĭp′) *n.* Used with *Your, Her,* or *Their* as a title and form of address for a woman or women holding the rank of lady.

la·dy's man also **la·dies' man** (lā′dēz) *n.* A man who enjoys and attracts the company of women.

lady's slipper *n., pl.* **lady's slippers.** Any of various orchids of the genus *Cypripedium,* having variously colored flowers with an inflated, pouchlike lip. Also called *moccasin flower.*

lady's smock *n., pl.* **lady's smocks.** See **cuckooflower** (sense 1).

lady's thumb *n., pl.* **lady's thumbs.** A European perennial weed *(Polygonum persicaria)* having clusters of very small pinkish flowers.

lady's tresses *pl.n. (used with a sing. or pl. verb).* Variant of **ladies' tresses.**

lady tulip *n.* A central Asian tulip *(Tulipa clusiana)* having red outer perianth segments with white margins.

La·er·tes (lā-ûr′tēz, -âr′-) *n. Greek Mythology.* The father of Odysseus.

la·e·trile (lā′ĭ-trĭl′, -trəl) *n.* A drug derived from amygdalin and purported to have antineoplastic properties.

La Farge (lə färzh′, färj′), **John.** 1835–1910. American artist known for his murals and stained-glass designs and for his art criticism.

La Farge, Oliver Hazard Perry. 1901–1963. American writer. His novels, including *Laughing Boy* (1929), concern Native American culture.

La·fa·yette (lăf′ē-ĕt′, lä′fē-, -fä-). **1.** A city of western California, a residential suburb in the San Francisco Bay area. Population, 20,879. **2.** A city of west-central Indiana on the Wabash River northwest of Indianapolis. It is the seat of Purdue University (founded 1869). Population, 43,011. **3.** A city of south-central Louisiana west-southwest of Baton Rouge. Settled by Acadians, it is a commercial and shipping center. Population, 81,961.

Lafayette, Marquis **Marie Joseph Paul Yves Roch Gilbert du Motier de.** 1757–1834. French soldier and politician who served on George Washington's staff in the American Revolution. In France he also took part in the 1789 and 1830 revolutions.

Laf·fer curve or **Laf·fer Curve** (lăf′ər) *n.* A curved graph that illustrates a relationship between tax rates and government revenues. As tax rates increase from zero, revenues increase until an optimum is reached. But if tax rates are further increased, they are supposed to discourage government spending and business investment, thereby reducing revenues. [After Arthur *Laffer* (born 1940), American economist.]

Laf·fite or **La·fitte** (lə-fēt′, lä-), **Jean.** 1780?–1826? French pirate leader who aided U.S. troops in the War of 1812 in return for an official pardon for his crimes.

La Flesche (lä flĕsh′, lə), **Susette.** Originally Inshta Theumba ("Bright Eyes"). 1854–1903. Native American writer and lecturer whose work helped bring about more favorable U.S. government policies toward her people.

La Fol·lette (lə fŏl′ət), **Robert Marion.** 1855–1925. American politician and reformer who served as a U.S. senator from Wisconsin (1906–1925). In 1924 he ran unsuccessfully for President on the Progressive Party ticket.

La·fon·taine (lə-fŏn-tān′, lä-fôN-tĕn′), **Henri Marie.** 1854–1943. Belgian politician and pacifist who was awarded the Nobel Peace Prize in 1913.

La Fon·taine (lə fŏn-tān′, lä fôN-tĕn′), **Jean de.** 1621–1695. French writer who collected the stories of Aesop and others in his *Fables* (1668–1694).

lag¹ (lăg) *v.* **lagged, lag·ging, lags.** *—intr.* **1.** To fail to keep up a pace; straggle. **2.** To proceed or develop with comparative slowness: *The electric current lags behind the voltage.* **3.** To fail, weaken, or slacken gradually; flag. **4.** *Games.* To determine the order of play in billiards by successively hitting the cue ball against the end rail, the ball rebounding closest to the head rail indicating the player to shoot first. *—tr.* **1.** To cause to hang back or fall behind. **2.** To shoot, throw, or pitch (a coin, for example) at a mark. **—lag** *n.* **1.** The act, process, or condition of lagging. **2.** One that lags. **3.** A condition of slowness or retardation. **4.a.** The extent or duration of lagging: *"He wondered darkly at how great a lag there was between his thinking and his actions"* (Thomas Wolfe). **b.** An interval between events or phenomena considered together. [From earlier *lag,* last person, from Middle English *lag-,* last, perhaps of Scandinavian origin.] **—lag′ger** *n.*

lag² (lăg) *n.* **1.** A barrel stave. **2.** A strip, as of wood, that forms a part of the covering for a cylindrical object. **—lag** *tr.v.* **lagged, lag·ging, lags.** To furnish or cover with lags. [Probably of Scandinavian origin; akin to Swedish *lagg.* See **leu-** in Appendix.]

lag³ (lăg) *Chiefly British. tr.v.* **lagged, lag·ging, lags. 1.** To arrest. **2.** To send to prison. **—lag** *n.* **1.a.** A convict. **b.** An ex-convict. **2.** A period of imprisonment; a sentence. [Origin unknown.]

lag·an (lăg′ən) also **li·gan** (lī′gən) or **lag·end** (lăg′ənd) *n. Nautical.* Cargo or equipment thrown into the sea but attached to a float or buoy so that it can be recovered. [French, from Old French, perhaps of Scandinavian origin. See **legh-** in Appendix.]

La·gash (lā′găsh). An ancient city of Sumer in southern Mesopotamia. It flourished c. 2400 B.C. and after the fall of Akkad (2180) enjoyed a revival noted for its sculpture and literature.

Lag b'O·mer (läg′ bō′mər, läg′ bə-ō′mĕr) *n.* A Jewish feast celebrated on the 33rd day of the Omer (the 18th day of Iyar). [Hebrew : *lag,* 33rd + *bā,* in, of + *'ōmer,* the Omer (period from the second day of Passover to the first day of Shavuoth).]

lag·end (lăg′ənd) *n. Nautical.* Variant of **lagan.**

la·ger (lä′gər) *n.* A type of beer, originally brewed in Germany, that contains a relatively small amount of hops and is aged from six weeks to six months to allow sedimentation. Also called *lager beer.* [German, short for *Lagerbier* : *Lager,* storehouse, cellar (from Middle High German *leger,* from Old High German *legar,* bed, lair; see **legh-** in Appendix) + *Bier,* beer.]

La·ger·kvist (lä′gər-kfĭst′), **Pär Fabian.** 1891–1974. Swed-

ladies' tresses
Nodding ladies' tresses
Spiranthes cernua

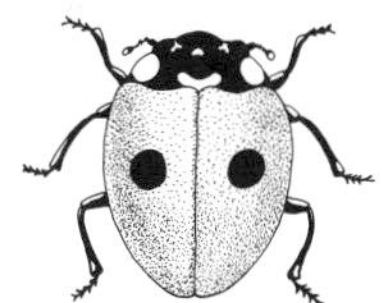

ladybug
Two-spotted ladybug
Adalia bipunctata

Marquis de Lafayette
Etching by Charles François Gabriel Levachez and son (fl. 1760–1820) tinted by Jean Duplessi-Bertaux (1747–1819)

ish writer whose novels explore morality and the search for belief. He won the 1951 Nobel Prize for literature.

La·ger·löf (lä′gər-ləv, -lœf), **Selma Ottiliana Lovisa.** 1858–1940. Swedish writer whose novels include *Gösta Berlings Saga* (1891). In 1909 she became the first woman to win the Nobel Prize for literature.

lag·gard (lăg′ərd) *n.* One that lags; a straggler. **—laggard** *adj.* Hanging back or falling behind; dilatory. See Synonyms at **slow.** **—lag′gard·ly** *adv.* **—lag′gard·ness** *n.*

lag·ging (lăg′ĭng) *n.* **1.** Insulation used to prevent heat diffusion, as from a steam pipe. **2.** A wooden frame built especially to support the sides of an arch until the keystone is positioned. [From LAG[2].]

lag screw

♦la·gniappe (lăn-yăp′, lăn′yăp′) *n. Chiefly Southern Louisiana.* **1.** A small gift presented by a storeowner to a customer with the customer's purchase. **2.** An extra or unexpected gift or benefit. Also called ♦*boot.* See Regional Note at **beignet.** [Louisiana French, from American Spanish *(la) ñapa,* (the) gift, from Quechua *yapa,* from *yapay,* to give more.]

♦ *REGIONAL NOTE:* *Lagniappe* derives from New World Spanish *la ñapa,* "the gift," and perhaps ultimately from Quechua *yapay,* "to give more." The word came into the rich Creole dialect mixture of New Orleans and there acquired a French spelling. It is still used chiefly in southern Louisiana to denote a little bonus that a friendly shopkeeper might add to a purchase. By extension, it may mean "an extra or unexpected gift or benefit."

lag·o·morph (lăg′ə-môrf′) *n.* Any of various plant-eating mammals having fully furred feet and two pairs of upper incisors and belonging to the order Lagomorpha, which includes the rabbits, hares, and pikas. [From New Latin *Lagomorpha,* order name : Greek *lagōs,* hare; see **slēg-** in Appendix + Greek *morphē,* shape.] **—lag′o·mor′phic** (-fĭk), **lag′o·mor′phous** (-fəs) *adj.*

la·goon (lə-go͞on′) *n.* **1.** A shallow body of water, especially one separated from a sea by sandbars or coral reefs. **2.** A shallow body of liquid waste material, as one in a dump. [French *lagune* and Italian *laguna,* both from Latin *lacūna,* pool, hollow, gap, from *lacus,* lake.]

La·gos (lā′gŏs′, lä′gōs). The capital and largest city of Nigeria, in the southwest part of the country on the Gulf of Guinea. An old Yoruba town, it was the center of the nationalist movement before independence was achieved in 1960. Abuja was designated the new capital in 1982, but Lagos remains the economic and commercial center. Population, 1,404,000.

La·grange (lə-grānj′, lä-gräNzh′), Comte **Joseph Louis.** 1736–1813. French mathematician and astronomer. He developed the calculus of variations (1755).

La Grange (lə grānj′). A city of western Georgia north of Columbus. Incorporated in 1828, it is an industrial center. Population, 24,204.

lag screw *n.* A heavy wood screw having a square bolt head. [From LAG[2] (From its original use in securing barrel staves).]

La Guar·di·a (lə gwär′dē-ə), **Fiorello Henry.** Known as "the Little Flower." 1882–1947. American politician who was a U.S. representative from New York (1917–1921 and 1923–1933) and mayor of New York City (1934–1945).

La·gu·na Beach (lə-go͞o′nə). A city of southern California southeast of Long Beach. It is a seaside resort with a noted art colony. Population, 17,860.

Laguna Hills. A city of southern California southeast of Santa Ana. Population, 16,400.

La Ha·bra (lə hä′brə). A city of southern California, a suburb of Los Angeles. Population, 45,232.

la·har (lä′här′) *n.* **1.** A landslide or mudflow of volcanic fragments on the flanks of a volcano. **2.** The deposit produced by such a landslide. [Javanese, lava.]

La·hon·tan (lə-hŏn′tən), **Lake.** An extinct lake with surviving remnants in western Nevada and northeast California.

La·hore (lə-hôr′, -hōr′). A city of northeast Pakistan near the Indian border southeast of Rawalpindi. The city reached the height of its grandeur as a Mogul capital in the 16th century and retains many splendid architectural examples from that period. Population, 2,685,000.

Lah·ti (lä′tē, läKH′-). A city of southern Finland north-northeast of Helsinki. It is a lake port with woodworking industries. Population, 94,347.

la·ic (lā′ĭk) also **la·i·cal** (-ĭ-kəl) *—adj.* Of or relating to the laity; secular. *—n.* A layperson. [Late Latin *lāicus.* See LAY[2].] **—la′i·cal·ly** *adv.*

la·i·cize (lā′ĭ-sīz′) *tr.v.* **-cized, -ciz·ing, -ciz·es. 1.** To free from ecclesiastical control; give over to laypeople. **2.** To change to lay status; secularize. **—la′i·ci·za′tion** (-sĭ-zā′shən) *n.*

laid (lād) *v.* Past tense and past participle of **lay[1].**

laid-back (lād′băk′) *adj. Informal.* Having a relaxed or casual atmosphere or character; easygoing: *"laid-back, untroubled people"* (New Yorker). **—laid′-back′ness** *n.*

laid paper *n.* A paper made on wire molds that give it a characteristic watermark of close thin lines.

lain (lān) *v.* Past participle of **lie[1].**

Laing (lăng), **R(onald) D(avid).** 1927–1989. British writer and psychiatrist. His works explore psychosis as a reaction to a dehumanized, irrational society.

lair (lâr) *n.* **1.** The den or dwelling of a wild animal. **2.** A den or hideaway. **3.** *Obsolete.* A resting place; a couch. [Middle English, from Old English *leger.* See **legh-** in Appendix.]

laird (lârd) *n. Scots.* The owner of a landed estate. [Scots, from Middle English *lard, lavered,* variant of *lord,* owner, master. See LORD.]

lais·sez faire also **lais·ser faire** (lĕs′ā fâr′) *n.* **1.** An economic doctrine that opposes governmental regulation of or interference in commerce beyond the minimum necessary for a free-enterprise system to operate according to its own economic laws. **2.** Noninterference in the affairs of others. [French : *laissez,* second person pl. imperative of *laisser,* to let, allow + *faire,* to do.] **—lais′sez-faire′** *adj.*

lais·sez-pas·ser (lĕs′ā-pä-sā′) *n.* A pass, especially one used in lieu of a passport. [French : *laissez,* second person pl. imperative of *laisser,* to let + *passer,* to pass.]

la·i·ty (lā′ĭ-tē) *n.* **1.** Laypeople considered as a group. **2.** All those persons who are not members of a given profession or other specialized field. [Middle English *laite,* from *lay,* of the laity. See LAY[2].]

La·ius (lā′əs) *n. Greek Mythology.* A king of Thebes who was mistakenly killed by his own son, Oedipus.

LAK cell (lăk) *n.* A white blood cell produced by cultivation of peripheral lymphocytes with interleukin-2 and used experimentally to shrink malignant tumors. [*l(ymphokine-)a(ctivated) k(iller cell).*]

lake[1] (lāk) *n. Abbr.* **l., L. 1.** A large inland body of fresh water or salt water. **2.** A scenic pond, as in a park. **3.** A large pool of liquid: *a lake of spilled coffee on my desk.* [Middle English, from Old French *lac* and from Old English *lacu,* both from Latin *lacus.*]

lake[2] (lāk) *n.* **1.** A pigment consisting of organic coloring matter with an inorganic, usually metallic base or carrier, used in dyes, inks, and paints. **2.** *Color.* A deep red. [From French *laque.* See LAC.]

Lake or **Lake of** (lāk) or **Loch** (lŏk, lôKH). For the names of actual lakes, see the specific element of the name; for example, **Erie, Lake; Lucerne, Lake of; Lomond, Loch.**

lake·bed (lāk′bĕd′) *n.* The floor of a lake.

Lake Charles (chärlz). A city of southwest Louisiana east of Beaumont, Texas. It is a deep-water port and the center of a petrochemical industry. Population, 75,051.

Lake District. A scenic area of northwest England including the Cumbrian Mountains and some 15 lakes. It is a popular tourist attraction for its associations with the 19th-century Lake Poets, notably Wordsworth, Coleridge, and Southey.

lake dwelling *n.* A dwelling, especially a prehistoric dwelling, built on piles in a shallow lake.

lake effect *n.* The effect of any lake, especially the Great Lakes, in modifying the weather in nearby areas.

lake·front (lāk′frŭnt′) *n.* The land along the edge of a lake. *—attributive.* Often used to modify another noun: *lakefront property; a lakefront house.*

Lake Hav·a·su City (hăv′ə-so͞o′). A city of west-central Arizona on the California border. London Bridge, transported from England, is a popular tourist attraction. Population, 15,737.

lake herring *n.* A food fish, especially the trout *Coregonus artedii* of the Great Lakes region, related to the whitefishes.

Lake·hurst (lāk′hûrst). A borough of east-central New Jersey south of Freehold. The dirigible *Hindenburg* was destroyed by fire at the naval air station here (May 6, 1937). Population, 2,908.

Lake Jack·son (jăk′sən). A city of southeast Texas southwest of Galveston. It is mainly residential. Population, 19,102.

Lake·land (lāk′lənd). A city of central Florida east-northeast of Tampa. Population, 50,455.

Lakeland terrier *n.* Any of a breed of small, straight-legged, slender dogs, originally bred in England for hunting foxes. [After *Lakeland,* a region of northwest England.]

Lake Os·we·go (ŏs-wē′gō). A city of northwest Oregon, a residential suburb of Portland. Population, 22,527.

Lake Plac·id (plăs′ĭd). A village of northeast New York in the Adirondack Mountains southwest of Plattsburg. A popular year-round resort, it was the site of the Winter Olympics in 1932 and 1980. Population, 2,490.

lak·er (lā′kər) *n.* **1.** A fish, such as the lake trout, that lives in a lake. **2.** *Nautical.* A ship used on lakes.

lake·shore (lāk′shôr′, -shōr′) *n.* Land by a lake. Also called *lakeside. —attributive.* Often used to modify another noun: *lakeshore condominiums; a lakeshore road.*

lake·side (lāk′sīd′) *n.* See **lakeshore.** *—attributive.* Often used to modify another noun: *lakeside shops; lakeside paths.*

Lake·side (lāk′sīd′). **1.** A community of southern California, a residential and resort suburb of San Diego. Population, 23,921. **2.** A community of east-central Virginia, a suburb of Richmond. Population, 29,400.

Lake Suc·cess (sək-sĕs′). An unincorporated village of southeast New York on northwest Long Island northwest of Mineola. It was the temporary headquarters of the United Nations from 1946 to 1951.

lake trout *n.* A freshwater food and game fish *(Salvelinus na-*

maycush) of the Great Lakes. Also called *Mackinaw trout, namaycush, togue.*

Lake•wood (lāk′wo͝od′). **1.** A city of southern California, a residential and industrial suburb of Long Beach. Population, 74,654. **2.** A city of north-central Colorado, a residential suburb of Denver. Population, 113,808. **3.** A city of northeast Ohio, a suburb of Cleveland on Lake Erie. Population, 61,963.

Lakewood Center. A community of west-central Washington, a suburb of Tacoma. Population, 51,300.

Lake Worth (wûrth). A city of southeast Florida south of West Palm Beach. It is a resort center. Population, 27,048.

La•ko•ta (lə-kō′tə) *n., pl.* **Lakota** or **-tas.** See **Teton.**

Lak•shad•weep (lək-shäd′wēp′, lŭk′shə-dwēp′). A region of southwest India comprising the Laccadive, Minicoy, and Amindivi islands.

lal•a•pa•loo•za (lŏl′ə-pə-lo͞o′zə) *n. Slang.* Variant of **lollapalooza.**

La Lí•ne•a (lä lē′nē-ə). A city of southwest Spain on the Bay of Gibraltar southeast of Cadíz. There is a military garrison in the city. Population, 58,945.

Lal•lan (lăl′ən) also **Lal•lans** (-ənz) *n. Scots.* **1.** The Lowlands of Scotland. **2.** Scots as spoken in southern and eastern Scotland. [Scots, alteration of LOWLAND.] **—Lal′lan** *adj.*

lal•la•pa•loo•za (lŏl′ə-pə-lo͞o′zə) *n. Slang.* Variant of **lollapalooza.**

lal•la•tion (lă-lā′shən) *n. Linguistics.* The substitution of the phoneme /l/ for /r/ or the mispronunciation of (l). [Latin *lallāre, lallāt-,* to sing a lullaby + –ATION.]

Lal•ly (lă′lē). A trademark used for a concrete-filled steel cylinder utilized as a supporting member in a building.

lal•ly•gag (lăl′ē-găg′) *v.* Variant of **lollygag.**

La Lou•vière (lä lo͞o-vyĕr′). A city of southwest Belgium south of Brussels. It is a manufacturing commune. Population, 76,534.

lam[1] (lăm) *v.* **lammed, lam•ming, lams.** *Slang.* *—tr.* To give a thorough beating to; thrash. *—intr.* To strike; wallop. [Probably of Scandinavian origin; akin to Old Norse *lemja,* to cripple by beating, flog.]

lam[2] (lăm) *Slang. intr.v.* **lammed, lam•ming, lams.** To escape, as from prison. **—lam** *n.* Flight, especially from the law: *escaped convicts on the lam.* [Origin unknown.]

lam. *abbr.* Laminated.

Lam. *abbr. Bible.* Lamentations.

la•ma (lä′mə) *n.* A Buddhist monk of Tibet or Mongolia. [Tibetan *bla-ma,* from *bla,* superior.]

La•ma•ism (lä′mə-ĭz′əm) *n.* Tibetan Buddhism. **—La′ma•ist** *n.* **—La′ma•is′tic** *adj.*

La Man•cha (lä män′chə). A region of south-central Spain. The high, mostly barren plateau is famous as the setting for Cervantes's *Don Quixote.*

La•mar (lə-mär′), **Joseph Rucker.** 1857–1916. American jurist who served as an associate justice of the U.S. Supreme Court (1911–1916).

Lamar, Lucius Quintus Cincinnatus. 1825–1893. American politician and jurist who served as an associate justice of the U.S. Supreme Court (1888–1893).

La•marck (lə-märk′, lä-), Chevalier de **Jean Baptiste Pierre Antoine de Monet.** 1744–1829. French naturalist whose ideas about evolution influenced Darwin's theory.

La•marck•i•an (lə-mär′kē-ən) *adj.* Of or relating to Lamarckism. **—Lamarckian** *n.* A supporter of Lamarckism.

La•marck•ism (lə-mär′kĭz′əm) also **La•marck•i•an•ism** (-kē-ə-nĭz′əm) *n.* A theory of biological evolution holding that species evolve by the inheritance of traits acquired or modified through the use or disuse of body parts. [After Chevalier de Jean Baptiste Pierre Antoine de Monet LAMARCK.]

La•mar•tine (lä-mär-tēn′), **Alphonse Marie Louis de Prat de.** 1790–1869. French romantic poet who served briefly as minister of foreign affairs (1848).

la•ma•ser•y (lä′mə-sĕr′ē) *n., pl.* **-ies.** A monastery of lamas. [French *lamaserie* : *lama,* lama (from Tibetan *bla-ma;* see LAMA) + *-serie,* dwelling (probably from Persian *sarāī,* inn, palace).]

La•maze (lə-mäz′) *adj.* Relating to or being a method of childbirth in which the expectant mother is prepared psychologically and physically to give birth without the use of drugs. [After Fernand *Lamaze* (1890–1957), French physician.]

lamb (lăm) *n.* **1.a.** A young sheep, especially one that is not yet weaned. **b.** The flesh of a young sheep used as meat. **c.** Lambskin. **2.** A sweet, mild-mannered person; a dear. **3.** One who can be duped or cheated especially in financial matters. **4. Lamb.** Jesus. **—lamb** *intr.v.* **lambed, lamb•ing, lambs.** To give birth to a young sheep. [Middle English, from Old English.]

Lamb, Charles. Known as "Elia." 1775–1834. British critic and essayist. With his sister **Mary Ann Lamb** (1764–1847) he wrote the children's book *Tales from Shakespeare* (1807).

Lamb, William. Second Viscount Melbourne. 1779–1848. British prime minister (1834 and 1835–1841) and adviser to Queen Victoria.

Lamb, Willis Eugene, Jr. Born 1913. American physicist. He shared a 1955 Nobel Prize for advances in atomic measurement.

lam•baste (lăm-bāst′) *tr.v.* **-bast•ed, -bast•ing, -bastes.** *Informal.* **1.** To give a thrashing to; beat. See Synonyms at **beat.** **2.** To scold sharply; berate. [Perhaps LAM[1] + BASTE[3].]

lamb•da (lăm′də) *n.* **1.** The 11th letter of the Greek alphabet. See table at **alphabet.** **2.** A lambda hyperon. [Greek, of Phoenician origin,; akin to Hebrew *lāmed,* lamed.]

lambda hyperon *n.* An electrically neutral baryon having a mass 2,183 times that of the electron and a mean lifetime of approximately 2.6×10^{-10} second. Also called *lambda particle.* See table at **subatomic particle.**

lambda point *n.* The temperature at which the transition from helium I to superfluid helium II occurs, approximately 2.19°K.

lamb•doid (lăm′doid′) *adj.* **1.** Having the shape of the Greek letter lambda. **2.** *Anatomy.* Relating to the deeply serrated suture in the skull between the parietal bones and the occipital bone.

lam•bent (lăm′bənt) *adj.* **1.** Flickering lightly over or on a surface: *lambent moonlight.* **2.** Effortlessly light or brilliant: *lambent wit.* **3.** Having a gentle glow; luminous. See Synonyms at **bright.** [Latin *lambēns, lambent-,* present participle of *lambere,* to lick.] **—lam′ben•cy** *n.* **—lam′bent•ly** *adv.*

lam•bert (lăm′bərt) *n. Abbr.* **L** The unit of brightness in the centimeter-gram-second system, equivalent to the brightness of a perfectly diffusing surface that emits or reflects one lumen per square centimeter. [After Johann Heinrich *Lambert* (1728–1777), German physicist and astronomer.]

lamb•kill (lăm′kĭl′) *n.* See **sheep laurel.** [From its poisonous effect on sheep.]

Lamb of God *n.* Jesus.

lam•bre•quin (lăm′bər-kĭn, -brə-kĭn) *n.* **1.** A short ornamental drapery for the top of a window or door or the edge of a shelf. **2.** A heavy protective cloth worn over a helmet in medieval times. [French, probably from Dutch **lamperkijn,* diminutive of Middle Dutch *lamper,* veil.]

lamb•skin (lăm′skĭn′) *n.* **1.** The hide of a lamb, especially when dressed without removing the fleece, as for a garment. **2.** Leather made from the dressed hide of a lamb. **3.** Parchment made from such hide.

lamb's lettuce (lămz′) *n.* See **corn salad.**

lamb's quarters *pl.n. (used with a sing. or pl. verb).* See **pigweed** (sense 1).

lamb's wool *n.* **1.** Wool shorn from a lamb. **2.** A fabric or yarn made from this wool.

lame[1] (lām) *adj.* **lam•er, lam•est.** **1.** Disabled so that movement, especially walking, is difficult or impossible: *Lame from the accident, he walked with a cane. A lame wing kept the bird from flying.* **2.** Marked by pain or rigidness: *a lame back.* **3.** Weak and ineffectual; unsatisfactory: *a lame attempt to apologize; lame excuses for not arriving on time.* **—lame** *tr.v.* **lamed, lam•ing, lames.** To cause to become lame; cripple. [Middle English, from Old English *lama.*] **—lame′ly** *adv.* **—lame′ness** *n.*

lame[2] (lām) *n.* A thin metal plate, especially one of the overlapping steel plates in medieval armor. [French, from Old French, from Latin *lāmina,* thin plate.]

la•mé (lă-mā′) *n.* A brocaded fabric woven with metallic threads, often of gold or silver. [French, spangled, laminated, lamé, from Old French *lame,* thin metal plate. See LAME[2].]

lame•brain (lām′brān′) *n. Informal.* A person regarded as stupid. **—lame′brained′** (-brānd′) *adj.*

la•medh (lä′mĭd, -mĕd′) *n.* The 12th letter of the Hebrew alphabet. See table at **alphabet.** [Hebrew *lāmed.*]

lame duck *n.* **1.** An elected officeholder or group continuing in office during the period between failure to win an election and the inauguration of a successor. **2.** An ineffective person; a weakling. **—lame′-duck′** (lām′dŭk′) *adj.*

lamell– *pref.* Variant of **lamelli–.**

la•mel•la (lə-mĕl′ə) *n., pl.* **-mel•lae** (-mĕl′ē′) or **-mel•las.** A thin scale, plate, or layer of bone or tissue, as in the gills of a bivalve mollusk or around the minute vascular canals in bone. [Latin *lāmella,* small thin plate, diminutive of *lāmina,* thin plate.] **—la•mel′lar** *adj.* **—la•mel′lar•ly** *adv.*

la•mel•late (lə-mĕl′āt′, lăm′ə-lāt′) *adj.* **1.** Having, composed of, or arranged in lamellae. **2.** Resembling a lamella. **—lam′el•la′ted** *adj.* **—lam′el•la′tion** *n.*

lamelli– or **lamell–** *pref.* Lamella: *lamelliform.* [From LAMELLA.]

la•mel•li•branch (lə-mĕl′ə-brănk′) *n.* Any of the bivalve mollusks of the class Lamellibranchia, including the clams, scallops, and oysters. Also called *pelecypod.* **—lamellibranch** *adj.* Of or relating to lamellibranchs. [From New Latin *Lāmellibranchia,* class name : LAMELLI– + Latin *branchia,* gill; see BRANCHIA.]

la•mel•li•corn (lə-mĕl′ĭ-kôrn′) *adj.* Of or belonging to the superfamily Lamellicornia, which includes the scarabs and other beetles that have club-shaped, lamellate antennae. **—lamellicorn** *n.* A lamellicorn beetle. [From New Latin *Lāmellicornia,* superfamily name : LAMELLI– + Latin *cornū,* horn; see **ker-**[1] in Appendix.]

la•mel•li•form (lə-mĕl′ə-fôrm′) *adj.* Having the form of a thin plate or lamella.

la•ment (lə-mĕnt′) *v.* **-ment•ed, -ment•ing, -ments.** *—tr.* **1.** To express grief for or about; mourn: *lament a death.* **2.** To regret deeply; deplore: *He lamented his thoughtless acts.* *—intr.* **1.** To grieve audibly; wail. **2.** To express sorrow or regret. See Syn-

lamb

ă pat	oi boy
ā pay	ou out
âr care	o͝o took
ä father	o͞o boot
ĕ pet	ŭ cut
ē be	ûr urge
ĭ pit	th thin
ī pie	*th* this
îr pier	hw which
ŏ pot	zh vision
ō toe	ə about, item
ô paw	♦ regionalism

Stress marks: ′ (primary); ′ (secondary), as in **dictionary** (dĭk′shə-nĕr′ē)

lammergeier
Gypaetus barbatus

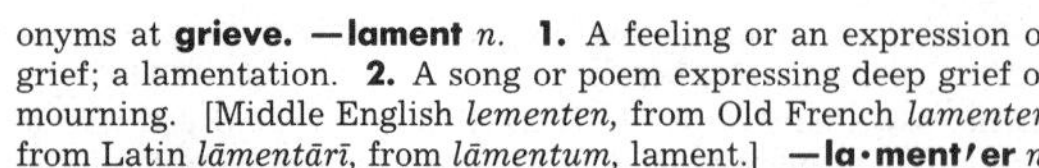

onyms at **grieve.** —**lament** *n.* **1.** A feeling or an expression of grief; a lamentation. **2.** A song or poem expressing deep grief or mourning. [Middle English *lementen,* from Old French *lamenter,* from Latin *lāmentārī,* from *lāmentum,* lament.] —**la·ment′er** *n.*

la·men·ta·ble (lə-mĕn′tə-bəl, lăm′ən-) *adj.* Inspiring or deserving of lament or regret; deplorable or pitiable. See Synonyms at **pathetic.** —**lam′en·ta·bly** *adv.*

lam·en·ta·tion (lăm′ən-tā′shən) *n.* **1.** The act of lamenting. **2.** A lament. **3. Lamentations** *(used with a sing. verb). Abbr.* **Lam., Lm** *Bible.* See table at **Bible.**

la·ment·ed (lə-mĕn′tĭd) *adj.* Mourned for: *our late lamented president.* —**la·ment′ed·ly** *adv.*

La Me·sa (lə mā′sə). A city of southern California, a residential suburb of San Diego. Population, 50,342.

la·mi·a (lā′mē-ə) *n., pl.* **-mi·as** or **-mi·ae** (-mē-ē′). **1.** *Greek Mythology.* A monster represented as a serpent with the head and breasts of a woman and reputed to prey on human beings and suck the blood of children. **2.** A female vampire. [Middle English, from Latin, from Greek.]

La·mi·a (lə-mē′ə, lä-mē′ä). A city of east-central Greece northwest of Athens. Founded c. fifth century B.C., it was the site of the Lamian War (323–322 B.C.) between the confederated Greeks and the Macedonian general Antipater, who was besieged in the city for several months before his ultimate victory. Population, 41,667. —**La·mi′an** *adj. & n.*

la·mi·ae (lā′mē-ē′) *n.* A plural of **lamia.**

lam·i·na (lăm′ə-nə) *n., pl.* **-nae** (-nē′) or **-nas. 1.** A thin plate, sheet, or layer. **2.** *Botany.* The expanded area of a leaf or petal; a blade. **3.** A thin layer of bone, membrane, or other tissue. **4.** *Zoology.* A thin scalelike or platelike structure, as one of the thin layers of sensitive vascular tissue in the hoof of a horse. **5.** *Geology.* A narrow bed of rock. [Latin *lāmina.*] —**lam′i·nar, lam′i·nal** *adj.*

lamina pro·pri·a (prō′prē-ə) *n.* A thin vascular layer of connective tissue beneath the epithelium of an organ. [New Latin *lāmina propria* : Latin *lāmina,* lamina + Latin *propria,* feminine of *proprius,* proper.]

laminar flow *n.* Nonturbulent flow of a viscous fluid in layers near a boundary, as that of lubricating oil in bearings.

lam·i·nar·in (lăm′ə-nâr′ĭn) *n.* A polymer of glucose that is the principal storage product of brown algae. [New Latin *Lāmināria,* kelp genus (from Latin *lāmina,* thin plate) + –IN.]

lam·i·nate (lăm′ə-nāt′) *v.* **-nat·ed, -nat·ing, -nates.** —*tr.* **1.** To beat or compress into a thin plate or sheet. **2.** To divide into thin layers. **3.** To make by uniting several layers. **4.** To cover with thin sheets. —*intr.* To split into thin layers or sheets. —**laminate** (-nĭt, -nāt′) *adj.* Consisting of, arranged in, or covered with laminae. —**laminate** (-nāt′, -nĭt) *n.* A laminated product, such as plywood. —**lam′i·na′tor** *n.*

lam·i·nat·ed (lăm′ə-nā′tĭd) *adj. Abbr.* **lam. 1.** Composed of layers bonded together. **2.** Arranged in laminae; laminate.

lam·i·na·tion (lăm′ə-nā′shən) *n.* **1. a.** The act or process of laminating. **b.** The state of being laminated. **2.** Something laminated. **3.** A lamina.

lam·i·nec·to·my (lăm′ə-nĕk′tə-mē) *n., pl.* **-mies.** Surgical removal of the posterior arch of a vertebra.

lam·i·ni·tis (lăm′ə-nī′tĭs) *n.* Inflammation of the sensitive laminae of the hoof, especially in horses. Also called *founder.*

La Mi·ra·da (lä′ mə-rä′də). A city of southern California southeast of Los Angeles. Population, 40,986.

Lam·mas (lăm′əs) *n.* **1. a.** A feast formerly celebrated in England, during which bread from the season's first wheat was consecrated at Mass in thanksgiving for the harvest. **b.** A feast formerly celebrated in commemoration of Saint Peter's deliverance from prison. **2.** August 1, the day on which these feasts were celebrated. [Middle English *Lammasse,* from Old English *hlāfmæsse* : *hlāf,* loaf + *mæsse,* Mass; see MASS.]

lam·mer·gei·er also **lam·mer·gey·er** (lăm′ər-gī′ər) *n.* A large predatory bird *(Gypaetus barbatus)* of the vulture family, ranging from the mountainous regions of southern Europe to China and having a wide wingspan and black plumage. Also called *bearded vulture, ossifrage.* [German *Lämmergeier* : *Lämmer,* genitive pl. of *Lamm,* lamb (from Middle High German *lamp,* from Old High German *lamb*) + *Geier,* vulture (from Middle High German *gīr,* from Old High German).]

lamp (lămp) *n.* **1. a.** A device that generates light, heat, or therapeutic radiation. **b.** A vessel containing oil or alcohol burned through a wick for illumination. **2.** A celestial body that gives off or reflects light. **3.** Something that illumines the mind or soul. [Middle English *lampe,* from Old French, from Latin *lampas,* from Greek, from *lampein,* to shine.]

lamp·black (lămp′blăk′) *n.* Fine soot collected from incompletely burned carbonaceous materials, used as a pigment and in matches, explosives, lubricants, and fertilizers. Also called *blacking.*

lamp·brush chromosome (lămp′brŭsh′) *n.* A large chromosome found especially in the immature eggs of amphibians, consisting of two long strands that form many brushlike loops along the main axis of the chromosome.

lam·per eel (lăm′pər) *n.* See **lamprey.** [Alteration of LAMPREY.]

lam·pi·on (lăm′pē-ən) *n.* An oil-burning lamp, often of colored glass, for outdoor use. [French, from Italian *lampione,* augmentative of *lampa,* lamp, from Old French *lampe.* See LAMP.]

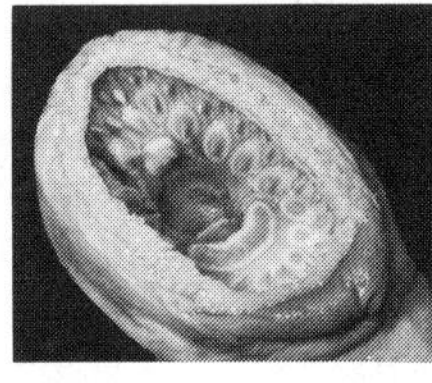

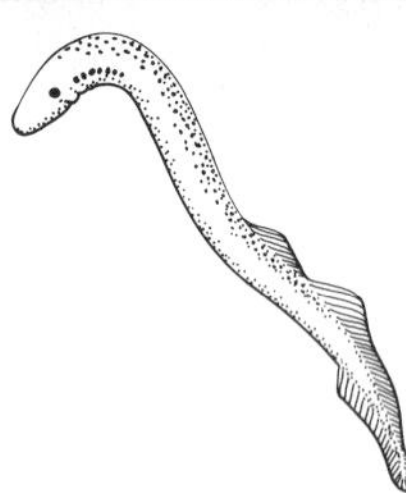

lamprey
Top: Close-up of mouth
Bottom: Full-length view

lamp·light (lămp′līt′) *n.* The light shed by a lamp.

lamp·light·er (lămp′lī′tər) *n.* One that lights lamps.

lamp oil *n.* See **kerosene.**

lam·poon (lăm-po͞on′) *n.* **1.** A broad satirical piece that uses ridicule to attack a person or group. See Synonyms at **caricature. 2.** A light, good-humored satire. —**lampoon** *tr.v.* **-pooned, -poon·ing, -poons.** To ridicule or satirize in or as if in a lampoon. [French *lampon,* perhaps from *lampons,* let us drink (from a common refrain in drinking songs), first person pl. imperative of *lamper,* to gulp down, of Germanic origin.] —**lam·poon′er, lam·poon′ist** *n.* —**lam·poon′er·y** *n.*

lamp·post (lămp′pōst′) *n.* A post supporting a street lamp.

lam·prey (lăm′prē) *n., pl.* **-preys.** Any of various primitive elongated freshwater or anadromous fishes of the family Petromyzontidae, characteristically having a jawless sucking mouth with rasping teeth. Also called *lamper eel.* [Middle English *lamprei,* from Old French *lampreie,* from Medieval Latin *lampreda.*]

lam·pro·phyre (lăm′prə-fīr′) *n.* Any of several intermediate igneous rocks constituting feldspar and ferromagnesium minerals that occur as dikes and minor intrusions. [German *Lamprophyr* : Greek *lampros,* clear (from *lampein,* to shine) + French *porphyre,* porphyry (from Old French *porfire,* from Medieval Latin *porphyrium;* see PORPHYRY).]

lamp·shade (lămp′shād′) *n.* Any of various protective or ornamental coverings used to screen a light bulb.

lamp·shell (lămp′shĕl′) *n.* See **brachiopod.**

lamp·work·ing (lămp′wûr′kĭng) *n.* The process of sculpting glass by twirling thin rods of colored glass over a gas-oxygen burner.

lampworking

LAN (lăn) *n. Computer Science.* A system that links together electronic office equipment, such as computers, terminals, and word processors, and forms a network within an office or a building. [*l(ocal) a(rea) n(etwork).*]

la·nai (lə-nī′, lä-) *n., pl.* **-nais.** A veranda or roofed patio. [Hawaiian.]

La·nai (lə-nī′). An island of central Hawaii west of Maui. It developed as a pineapple-growing area after 1922.

la·nate (lā′nāt′) *adj.* Having or consisting of woolly hairs. [Latin *lānātus,* from *lāna,* wool.]

Lan·ca·shire (lăng′kə-shîr′, -shər). A historical region of northwest England on the Irish Sea. It was part of the kingdom of Northumbria in Anglo-Saxon times and became a county palatine in 1351. Long noted for its textiles, the area grew rapidly after the Industrial Revolution.

Lan·cas·ter[1] (lăng′kə-stər, -lăn′-). English royal house that from 1399 to 1461 produced three kings of England—Henry IV, Henry V, and Henry VI. During the Wars of the Roses its symbol was a red rose. —**Lan·cas′tri·an** (lăng-kăs′trē-ən) *adj. & n.*

Lan·cas·ter[2] (lăng′kə-stər, -kăs′tər, lăn′-). **1.** A municipal borough of northwest England north of Liverpool. Chartered in 1193, it was built on the site of a Roman frontier station. Population, 47,900. **2.** A city of south-central Ohio southeast of Columbus. The birthplace of William Tecumseh Sherman has been preserved. Population, 34,952. **3.** A city of southeast Pennsylvania west of Philadelphia. A trade center in a rich farming region, it was settled by German Mennonites c. 1709. Population, 54,725.

lance (lăns) *n.* **1. a.** A thrusting weapon with a long wooden shaft and a sharp metal head. **b.** A similar implement for spearing fish. **2.** A cavalry lancer. **3.** *Medicine.* See **lancet** (sense 1). —**lance** *tr.v.* **lanced, lanc·ing, lanc·es. 1.** To pierce with a lance. **2.** *Medicine.* To make a surgical incision in; cut into: *lance a boil.* [Middle English, from Old French, from Latin *lancea,* probably of Celtic origin.]

lance corporal *n. Abbr.* **L.Cpl. 1.** A noncommissioned rank in the U.S. Marine Corps that is above private first class and below corporal. **2.** One who holds this rank. [From *lancepesade,* from obsolete French *lancepessade,* from Italian *lancia spezzata,* superior soldier : *lancia,* lance (from Latin *lancea;* see LANCE) + *spezzata,* feminine past participle of *spezzare,* to break to pieces (Latin *dis-,* apart; see DIS– + *pezza,* piece, from Medieval Latin *pecia,* piece).]

lance·let (lăns′lĭt) *n.* Any of various small, flattened marine organisms of the subphylum Cephalochordata, structurally similar to the vertebrates but having a notochord rather than a true vertebral column. Also called *amphioxus.*

Lan·ce·lot (lăn′sə-lət, -lŏt′, län′-) *n.* In Arthurian legend, a Knight of the Round Table whose love affair with Queen Guinevere resulted in a war with King Arthur.

lan·ce·o·late (lăn′sē-ə-lāt′) *adj.* Tapering from a rounded base toward an apex; lance-shaped: *lanceolate leaves.* [Late Latin *lanceolātus,* from Latin *lanceola,* diminutive of Latin *lancea,* lance.] —**lan′ce·o·late′ly** *adv.*

lanc·er (lăn′sər) *n.* **1.** A cavalryman armed with a lance. **2.** A member of a regiment originally armed with lances. **3. lancers** *(used with a sing. verb).* **a.** A form of quadrille. **b.** The music for this dance. [French *lancier,* from Old French, maker of lances, from *lance,* lance. See LANCE.]

lan·cet (lăn′sĭt) *n.* **1.** *Medicine.* A surgical knife with a short, wide, pointed double-edged blade, used especially for making punctures and small incisions. Also called *lance.* **2.** *Architecture.* A lancet arch. —**lancet** *adj.* A lancet window. [Middle English, from Old French, diminutive of *lance,* lance. See LANCE.]

lancet arch *n. Architecture.* An arch that is narrow and pointed like the head of a spear.

lancet fish *n.* Either of two large, elongated marine fishes *(Alepisaurus ferox* or *A. brevirostris)* having long sharp teeth, a large dorsal fin, and no scales.

lancet window *n. Architecture.* A tall, narrow window set in a lancet arch.

lance•wood (lăns′wo͝od′) *n.* **1.** Any of several tropical American trees, especially *Calycophyllum candidissimum,* having hard, durable, uniformly grained wood. **2.** The wood of this tree, used for construction and cabinet work.

Lan•chow (län′jō′). See **Lanzhou.**

lan•ci•nat•ing (lăn′sə-nā′tĭng) *adj.* Characterized by a sensation of cutting, piercing, or stabbing. [From *lancinate,* to stab, from Latin *lancināre, lancināt-,* to lacerate.]

land (lănd) *n. Abbr.* **l. 1.** The solid ground of the earth. **2. a.** Ground or soil: *tilled the land.* **b.** A topographically or functionally distinct tract: *desert land; prime building land.* **3. a.** A nation; a country. **b.** The people of a nation, district, or region. **c. lands.** Territorial possessions or property. **4.** Public or private landed property; real estate. **5.** An area or a realm: *the land of make-believe; the land of television.* **6.** *Law.* **a.** A tract that may be owned, together with everything growing or constructed on it. **b.** A landed estate. **7.** The raised portion of a grooved surface, as on a phonograph record. **—land** *v.* **land•ed, land•ing, lands.** *—tr.* **1. a.** To bring to and unload on land: *land cargo.* **b.** To set (a vehicle) down on land or another surface: *land an airplane smoothly; land a seaplane on a lake.* **2.** *Informal.* To cause to arrive in a place or condition: *Civil disobedience will land you in jail.* **3. a.** To catch and pull in (a fish): *landed a big catfish.* **b.** *Informal.* To win; secure: *land a big contract.* **4.** *Informal.* To deliver: *landed a blow on his opponent's head.* *—intr.* **1. a.** To come to shore: *landed against the current with great difficulty.* **b.** To disembark: *landed at a crowded dock.* **2.** To descend toward and settle onto the ground or another surface: *The helicopter has landed.* **3.** *Informal.* To arrive in a place or condition: *landed at the theater too late for the opening curtain.* **4.** To come to rest in a certain way or place: *land on one's feet.* [Middle English, from Old English. See **lendh-** in Appendix.]

Land (lănd), **Edwin Herbert.** 1909–1991. American inventor who developed (1932) the light-polarizing plastic film called Polaroid and incorporated it into lenses for cameras and sunglasses. He also invented the one-step photographic process (1947).

lan•dau (lăn′dô′, -dou′) *n.* **1.** A four-wheeled carriage with front and back passenger seats that face each other and a roof in two sections that can be lowered or detached. **2.** A style of automobile with a similar roof. [After *Landau,* a city of southwest Germany.]

Lan•dau (lăn-dou′), **Lev Davidovich.** 1908–1968. Soviet physicist. He won a 1962 Nobel Prize for his contributions to low-temperature physics.

land bank *n.* A bank that issues long-term loans on real estate in return for mortgages.

land breeze *n.* A breeze that blows from the land toward open water.

land bridge *n.* A neck of land that connects two landmasses; an isthmus.

land crab *n.* A terrestrial crab of the tropical family Gecarinidae, having a large square body.

land•ed (lăn′dĭd) *adj.* **1.** Owning land: *the landed gentry.* **2.** Consisting of land or real estate: *landed property.*

land•er (lăn′dər) *n.* A space vehicle designed to land on a celestial body, such as the moon or a planet.

land•fall (lănd′fôl′) *n.* **1.** The act or an instance of sighting or reaching land after a voyage or flight. **2.** The land sighted or reached after a voyage or flight.

land•fill (lănd′fĭl′) *n.* **1.** A method of solid waste disposal in which refuse is buried between layers of dirt so as to fill in or reclaim low-lying ground. **2.** A site used for or reclaimed by such disposal. **—landfill** *v.* **-filled, -fill•ing, -fills.** *—tr.* **1.** To dispose of (waste material) in a landfill. **2.** To fill in or reclaim (land) by this method. *—intr.* To dispose of refuse or reclaim land by filling in low-lying ground.

land•form (lănd′fôrm′) *n.* One of the features that make up the earth's surface, such as a plain, mountain, or valley.

land grant *n.* A government grant of public land for a railroad, highway, or state college.

land•grave (lănd′grāv′) *n.* **1.** A man in medieval Germany who had jurisdiction over a particular territory. **2.** Used as the title for such a nobleman. [From Middle Low German : *lant,* land; see **lendh-** in Appendix + *grave,* count.]

land•gra•vi•ate (lănd-grā′vē-ĭt, -āt′) *n.* The rank and office of a landgrave or landgravine.

land•gra•vine (lănd′grə-vēn′) *n.* **1.** A woman holding the title to a landgraviate. **2.** The wife or widow of a landgrave. **3.** Used as the title for such a noblewoman. [From Middle Low German *landgravin,* feminine of *landgrave,* landgrave. See LANDGRAVE.]

land•hold•er (lănd′hōl′dər) *n.* One that owns land. **—land′hold′ing** *n.*

land•ing (lăn′dĭng) *n. Abbr.* **ldg. 1. a.** The act or process of coming to land or rest, especially after a voyage or flight. **b.** A termination, especially of a voyage or flight. **2.** A site for loading and unloading passengers and cargo. **3. a.** An intermediate platform on a flight of stairs. **b.** The area at the top or bottom of a staircase.

landing craft *n. Abbr.* **LC** A naval craft designed to convey troops and equipment from ship to shore.

landing field *n.* A tract of land used by aircraft for landing and taking off.

landing gear *n.* The components of an aircraft or a spacecraft that support the weight of the craft and its load and give it mobility on ground or water.

landing strip *n.* An aircraft runway without airport facilities. Also called *airstrip.*

land•la•dy (lănd′lā′dē) *n.* **1.** A woman who owns and rents land, buildings, or dwelling units. **2.** A woman who runs a rooming house or an inn; an innkeeper.

land•less (lănd′lĭs) *adj.* Owning or having no land. **—land′less•ness** *n.*

land•line (lănd′līn′) *n.* A communications cable, as one used to transmit telephone or telegraph signals.

land•locked (lănd′lŏkt′) *adj.* **1.** Entirely or almost entirely surrounded by land: *a landlocked country.* **2.** Confined to inland waters, as certain salmon.

land•lord (lănd′lôrd′) *n.* **1.** A person who owns and rents land, buildings, or dwelling units. **2.** A man who runs a rooming house or an inn; an innkeeper.

land•lub•ber (lănd′lŭb′ər) *n.* A person unfamiliar with the sea or seamanship. **—land′lub′ber•ly** *adj.*

land•mark (lănd′märk′) *n.* **1.** A prominent identifying feature of a landscape. **2.** A fixed marker, such as a concrete block, that indicates a boundary line. **3.** An event marking an important stage of development or a turning point in history. **4.** A building or site that has historical significance, especially one that is marked for preservation by a municipal or national government. **—landmark** *adj.* Having great import or significance: *a landmark court ruling; a landmark decision.*

land•mass (lănd′măs′) *n.* A large unbroken area of land.

land mile *n.* See **mile** (sense 1).

land mine *n.* **1.** An explosive mine laid usually just below the surface of the ground. **2.** *Informal.* A concealed yet incipient crisis.

land office *n.* A government office that handles and keeps records of the sale or transfer of public land.

land-of•fice business (lănd′ô′fĭs, -ŏf′ĭs) *n.* A thriving, extensive, or rapidly moving volume of trade.

Land of Oz *n.* See **Oz.**

Lan•don (lăn′dən), **Alfred Mossman.** Known as "Alf." 1887–1987. American politician who served as governor of Kansas (1933–1937) and ran unsuccessfully for President in 1936.

Lan•dor (lăn′dôr, -dər), **Walter Savage.** 1775–1864. British writer who is best known for his *Imaginary Conversations of Literary Men and Statesmen* (1824–1829).

land•own•er (lănd′ō′nər) *n.* One that owns land. **—land′own′er•ship′** *n.* **—land′own′ing** *adj. & n.*

Lan•dow•ska (lăn-dôf′skə, län-dôf′skä), **Wanda.** 1879?–1959. Polish-born harpsichordist who was largely responsible for the modern revival of interest in the harpsichord.

land-poor (lănd′po͝or′) *adj.* Owning much unprofitable land but lacking the capital to improve or maintain it.

land reform *n.* Measures, such as the division of large properties into smaller ones, that are taken to bring about a more equitable apportionment of agricultural land. **—land′-re•form′** (lănd′rĭ-fôrm′) *adj.*

land•scape (lănd′skāp′) *n.* **1.** An expanse of scenery that can be seen in a single view: *a desert landscape.* **2.** A picture depicting an expanse of scenery. **3.** The branch of art dealing with the representation of natural scenery. **4.** The aspect of the land characteristic of a particular region: *a bleak New England winter landscape.* **5.** An extensive mental view; an interior prospect: *"They occupy the whole landscape of my thought"* (James Thurber). **—landscape** *v.* **-scaped, -scap•ing, -scapes.** *—tr.* To adorn or improve (a section of ground) by contouring and by planting flowers, shrubs, or trees. *—intr.* To arrange grounds artistically as a profession. [Dutch *landschap,* from Middle Dutch *landscap,* region : *land,* land; see **lendh-** in Appendix + *-scap,* state, condition (collective suff.).] **—land′scap′er** *n.*

WORD HISTORY: It would seem that in the case of the word *landscape* we have an example of nature imitating art, insofar as sense development is concerned. *Landscape,* first recorded in 1598, was borrowed as a painters' term from Dutch during the 16th century, when Dutch artists were on the verge of becoming masters of the landscape genre. The Dutch word *landschap* had earlier meant simply "region, tract of land," but had acquired the artistic sense, which it brought over into English, of "a picture depicting scenery on land." The fascinating thing is that 34 years pass after the first recorded use of *landscape* in English before the word is used of a view or vista of natural scenery. This delay suggests that people were first introduced to landscapes in paintings and then saw landscapes in real life.

landscape architect *n.* One whose profession is the decorative and functional alteration and planting of grounds, especially

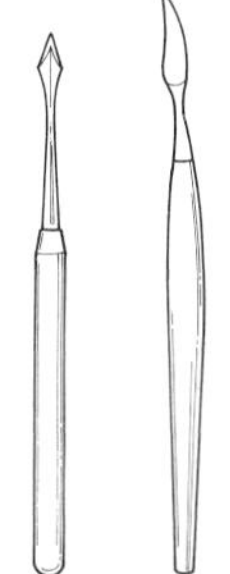

lancet
Left: Dissecting
Right: Dental

lancet window

landau
With lowered roof

ă pat	oi boy
ā pay	ou out
âr care	o͝o took
ä father	o͞o boot
ĕ pet	ŭ cut
ē be	ûr urge
ĭ pit	th thin
ī pie	*th* this
îr pier	hw which
ŏ pot	zh vision
ō toe	ə about, item
ô paw	♦ regionalism

Stress marks: ′ (primary); ′ (secondary), as in **dictionary** (dĭk′shə-nĕr′ē)

at or around a building site. **—landscape architecture** *n.*

landscape gardener *n.* One whose occupation is the decoration of land by planting trees and shrubs and designing gardens. **—landscape gardening** *n.*

land·scap·ist (lănd′skā′pĭst) *n.* A painter of landscapes.

Land·seer (lănd′sîr′), Sir **Edwin Henry.** 1802–1873. British painter known for his sentimental paintings of animals.

Land's End or **Lands End** (lăndz′ ĕnd′). A peninsula of southwest England on the coast of Cornwall. It is the westernmost point of the country.

land·side (lănd′sīd′) *n.* The flat side of a plow opposite the furrow.

lands·leit (länts′līt′) *n.* Plural of **landsman²**. [Yiddish *landslayt*, from Middle High German *lantsliute*, natives, compatriots : Old High German *lant*, land; see LANDSMAN² + Old High German *liuti*, pl. of *liut*, person, people; see **leudh-** in Appendix.]

land·slide (lănd′slīd′) *n.* **1.a.** The downward sliding of a relatively dry mass of earth and rock. **b.** The mass that slides. Also called *landslip.* **2.a.** An overwhelming majority of votes for a political party or candidate. **b.** An election that sweeps a party or candidate into office. **3.** A great victory.

land·slip (lănd′slĭp′) *n.* See **landslide** (sense 1).

Lands·mål (länts′môl′) *n.* See **New Norwegian.** [Norwegian : *land*, country (from Old Norse; see **lendh-** in Appendix) + *mål*, speech (from Old Norse *mál*).]

lands·man¹ (lăndz′mən) *n.* One who lives and works on land.

lands·man² (länts′mən) *n., pl.* **lands·leit** (-līt′). A fellow Jew who comes from the same district or town, especially in Eastern Europe. [Yiddish, from Middle High German *lantsman*, countryman : Old High German *lant*, land; see **lendh-** in Appendix + Old High German *man*, man; see **man-¹** in Appendix.]

Land·stei·ner (lănd′stī′nər, länt′-shtī′-), **Karl.** 1868–1943. Austrian-born American pathologist. He won a 1930 Nobel Prize for the discovery of human blood groups.

Land·tag (länt′täk′) *n.* **1.** A legislative assembly of a West German state. **2.** A diet or an assembly in some German states in the 19th century. [German : *Land*, country (from Middle High German *lant*, from Old High German; see LANDSMAN²) + *Tag*, day, diet, assembly (from Middle High German, from Old High German, influenced by Medieval Latin *diēta*, diet; see **agh-** in Appendix).]

land·ward (lănd′wərd) *adv. & adj.* To or toward land: *sailing landward; the landward side of a coastal fortification.* **—land′wards** *adv.*

lane (lān) *n.* **1.a.** A narrow country road. **b.** A narrow way or passage between walls, hedges, or fences. **2.** A narrow passage, course, or track, especially: **a.** A prescribed course for ships or aircraft. **b.** A strip delineated on a street or highway to accommodate a single line of vehicles: *a breakdown lane; an express lane.* **c.** *Sports.* One of a set of parallel courses marking the bounds for contestants in a race, especially in swimming or track. **d.** *Sports.* A wood-surfaced passageway or alley along which a bowling ball is rolled. [Middle English, from Old English.]

Lillie Langtry

La·ney (lā′nē), **Lucy Craft.** 1854–1933. American educator. She founded one of the first private schools for Black students, in Augusta, Georgia, in 1886.

lang (lăng) *adj. Scots.* Long.

Lang (lăng), **Andrew.** 1844–1912. British writer and anthropologist who is best known for his fairy tales.

Lang, Fritz. 1890–1976. Austrian-born American filmmaker. He made *Metropolis* (1927), *M* (1931), and a number of other expressionist films before fleeing to Hollywood from Nazi Germany. His American films include *The Ministry of Fear* (1944).

lang. *abbr.* Language.

lang·bein·ite (lăng′bī-nīt′, läng′-) *n.* An evaporite mineral, $K_2Mg_2(SO_4)_3$, used as a source of potassium sulfate for fertilizer. [After A. *Langbein*, 19th-century German chemist.]

Lang·e (läng′ə), **Christian Louis.** 1869–1938. Norwegian pacifist and historian. He shared the 1921 Nobel Peace Prize for his work as secretary-general of the Inter-Parliamentary Union (1909–1933).

Lange (lăng), **Dorothea.** 1895–1965. American photographer remembered for her documentary portraits of rural workers during the Depression.

Lang·er (lăng′ər), **Susanne Knauth.** 1895–1985. American educator. Her major work is *Philosophy in a New Key: A Study of the Symbolism of Reason, Rite, and Art* (1942).

Lang·land (lăng′lənd), **William.** 1332?–1400. English poet who is credited with the authorship of *The Vision of William Concerning Piers the Plowman*, a medieval religious allegory.

lang·lauf (läng′louf′) *n. Sports.* A cross-country ski run. [German : *lang*, long (from Old High German; see **del-¹** in Appendix) + *Lauf*, race (from Middle High German *louf*, from Old High German *hlouf*).] **—lang′lauf′er** *n.*

lang·ley (lăng′lē) *n., pl.* **-leys.** A unit equal to one gram calorie per square centimeter of irradiated surface, used to measure solar radiation. [After Samuel Pierpoint LANGLEY.]

Lang·ley (lăng′lē). A city of southern British Columbia, Canada, near the Washington border east-southeast of Vancouver. It is in a diversified farming area. Population, 15,124.

Langley, Mount. A peak, 4,227.9 m (14,026 ft) high, in the Sierra Nevada of southern California.

Langley, Samuel Pierpoint. 1834–1906. American astronomer and aviation pioneer who built the first successful heavier-than-air flying machines.

Lang·muir (lăng′myo͝or′), **Irving.** 1881–1957. American chemist. He won a 1932 Nobel Prize for his work in surface chemistry.

Lan·go·bard (lăng′gə-bärd′) *n.* See **Lombard¹** (sense 1). [Latin *Langobardus.* See LOMBARD¹.] **—Lan′go·bar′dic** *adj.*

lan·gouste (läɴ-go͞ost′) *n.* See **spiny lobster.** [French, from Old French, from Old Provençal *langosta*, from Vulgar Latin **lacusta*, from Latin *locusta*, lobster, locust.]

lan·gous·tine (lăng′gə-stēn′) *n.* A large, edible prawn. [French, diminutive of *langouste*, langouste. See LANGOUSTE.]

lan·grage (lăng′grĭj) *n.* A type of shot consisting of scrap iron loaded into a case and formerly used in naval warfare to damage sails and rigging. [Origin unknown.]

lang·syne also **lang syne** (lăng-zīn′) *Scots.* —*adv.* Long ago; long since. —*n.* Time long past; times past. [Scots *lang syne*, from Middle English *lang sine* : *long, lang*, long; see LONG¹ + *sine*, since (contraction of *sithen, sithens;* see SINCE).]

Lang·ton (lăng′tən), **Stephen.** 1150?–1228. English prelate who as archbishop of Canterbury (1207–1228) sided with the nobility in their struggle with King John and was a signer of the Magna Carta (1215).

Lang·try (lăng′trē), **Lillie.** Known as "the Jersey Lily." 1853–1929. British actress famous for her great beauty and her love affair with Edward VII.

lan·guage (lăng′gwĭj) *n. Abbr.* **lang. 1.a.** The use by human beings of voice sounds, and often written symbols representing these sounds, in organized combinations and patterns in order to express and communicate thoughts and feelings. **b.** A system of words formed from such combinations and patterns, used by the people of a particular country or by a group of people with a shared history or set of traditions. **2.a.** A nonverbal method of communicating ideas, as by a system of signs, symbols, gestures, or rules: *the language of algebra.* **b.** *Computer Science.* A system of symbols and rules used for communication with or between computers. **3.** Body language; kinesics. **4.** The special vocabulary and usages of a scientific, professional, or other group: *"his total mastery of screen language—camera placement, editing—and his handling of actors"* (Jack Kroll). **5.** A characteristic style of speech or writing: *Shakespearean language.* **6.a.** Abusive, violent, or profane utterance: *"language that would make your hair curl"* (W.S. Gilbert). **b.** A particular manner of utterance: *gentle language.* **7.** The manner or means of communication between living creatures other than human beings: *the language of dolphins.* **8.** Verbal communication as a subject of study. **9.** The wording of a legal document or statute as distinct from the spirit. [Middle English, from Old French *langage*, from *langue*, tongue, language, from Latin *lingua.* See **dn̥ghū-** in Appendix.]

language laboratory *n.* A room designed for learning foreign languages in which students use equipment such as tape recorders connected to monitoring devices enabling the instructor to listen and speak to the students individually or as a group.

langue (läng, läɴg) *n. Linguistics.* Language viewed as a system including vocabulary, grammar, and pronunciation of a particular community. [French, from Old French. See LANGUAGE.]

Lan·gue·doc (läng-dôk′, läɴg-). A historical region and former province of south-central France on an arm of the Mediterranean Sea west of the Rhone River. Named after the Romance language of its inhabitants, it was incorporated into the French royal domain in 1271.

langue d'oc (dôk′) *n.* The Romance language spoken in and around Provence and Roussillon, surviving in Provençal. [French, from Old French : *langue*, language + *de*, of + Old Provençal *oc*, yes.]

langue d'o·ïl (doil′, doi′, dô-ēl′) *n.* The Romance language of Gaul north of the Loire River, on which modern French is based. [French, from Old French : *langue*, language + *de*, of + *oil*, yes.]

lan·guet (lăng′gwĭt, lăng-gwĕt′) *n.* A tongue-shaped thing, part, or process. [Middle English, from Old French *languete*, diminutive of *langue*, tongue, from Latin *lingua.* See **dn̥ghū-** in Appendix.]

lan·guid (lăng′gwĭd) *adj.* **1.** Lacking energy or vitality; weak: *a languid wave of the hand.* **2.** Showing little or no spirit or animation; listless: *a languid mood.* **3.** Lacking vigor or force; slow: *languid breezes.* [French *languide*, from Latin *languidus*, from *languēre*, to be languid. See LANGUISH.] **—lan′guid·ly** *adv.* **—lan′guid·ness** *n.*

lan·guish (lăng′gwĭsh) *intr.v.* **-guished, -guish·ing, -guish·es. 1.** To be or become weak or feeble; lose strength or vigor. **2.** To exist or continue in miserable or disheartening conditions. **3.** To remain unattended or be neglected: *legislation that continued to languish in committee.* **4.** To become downcast; pine: *languish for home and family.* **5.** To affect a wistful or languid air, especially in order to gain sympathy. [Middle English *languishen*, from Old French *languir, languiss-*, from Latin *languēre*, to be languid. See **slēg-** in Appendix.] **—lan′guish·er** *n.* **—lan′guish·ing·ly** *adv.* **—lan′guish·ment** *n.*

lan·guor (lăng′gər, lăng′ər) *n.* **1.** Lack of physical or mental

ă pat	oi boy
ā pay	ou out
âr care	o͝o took
ä father	o͞o boot
ĕ pet	ŭ cut
ē be	ûr urge
ĭ pit	th thin
ī pie	*th* this
îr pier	hw which
ŏ pot	zh vision
ō toe	ə about, item
ô paw	♦ regionalism

Stress marks: ′ (primary); ′ (secondary), as in **dictionary** (dĭk′shə-nĕr′ē)

energy; listlessness. See Synonyms at **lethargy. 2.** A dreamy, lazy mood or quality: *"It was hot, yet with a sweet languor about it"* (Theodore Dreiser). **3.** Oppressive quiet or stillness. [Middle English, from Old French, from Latin, from *languēre,* to be languid. See LANGUISH.] **—lan′guor·ous** *adj.* **—lan′guor·ous·ly** *adv.* **—lan′guor·ous·ness** *n.*

lan·gur (läng-gŏŏr′) *n.* Any of various slender, long-tailed Asian monkeys of the genus *Presbytis* and related genera that eat leaves, fruits, and seeds and have a chin tuft and bushy eyebrows. [Hindi *laṅgūr,* perhaps from Sanskrit *lāṅgūlam,* tail.]

lan·iard (lăn′yərd) *n.* Variant of **lanyard.**

La·nier (lə-nîr′), **Sidney.** 1842–1881. American writer and musician noted for his melodic poems, including "The Marshes of Glynn" (1878).

la·nif·er·ous (lə-nĭf′ər-əs) *adj.* Having wool or woollike hair. [Latin *lānifer* (*lāna,* wool + *-fer,* -fer) + –OUS.]

lank (lăngk) *adj.* **lank·er, lank·est. 1.** Long and lean. See Synonyms at **lean². 2.** Long, straight, and limp: *lank and floppy hair.* [Middle English, from Old English *hlanc.*] **—lank′ly** *adv.* **—lank′ness** *n.*

lank·y (lăng′kē) *adj.* **-i·er, -i·est.** Tall, thin, and ungainly. See Synonyms at **lean². —lank′i·ly** *adv.* **—lank′i·ness** *n.*

lan·ner (lăn′ər) *n.* **1.** A falcon *(Falco biarmicus)* of Africa, the Mediterranean, and southern Asia. **2.** A female of this species, used in falconry. [Middle English *laner,* from Old French *lanier,* woolweaver, coward, from Latin *lānārius,* woolworker, from *lāna,* wool.]

lan·ner·et (lăn′ə-rĕt′) *n.* A male lanner, smaller than the female, used in falconry. [Middle English *laneret,* from Old French, diminutive of *lanier,* lanner. See LANNER.]

lan·o·lin (lăn′ə-lĭn) *n.* A fatty substance obtained from wool and used in soaps, cosmetics, and ointments. Also called *wool fat.* [German : from Latin *lāna,* wool + Latin *oleum,* oil.]

la·nose (lā′nōs′) *adj.* Woolly. [Latin *lānōsus,* from *lāna,* wool.] **—la·nos′i·ty** (-nŏs′ĭ-tē) *n.*

Lans·dale (lănz′dāl′). A borough of southeast Pennsylvania north of Philadelphia. It has varied industries. Population, 16,526.

Lan·sing (lăn′sĭng). **1.** A village of northeast Illinois, a suburb of Chicago near the Indiana border. Population, 29,039. **2.** The capital of Michigan, in the south-central part of the state northwest of Detroit. It is an automobile-manufacturing center and became the state capital in 1847. Population, 130,414.

Lansing, Robert. 1864–1928. American public official who as U.S. secretary of state (1915–1920) arranged the purchase of the Virgin Islands (1917).

lan·ta·na (lăn-tä′nə, -tăn′ə) *n.* Any of various aromatic, chiefly tropical shrubs of the genus *Lantana,* having dense spikes or heads and small colorful flowers. [New Latin *Lantana,* genus name, from Italian dialectal *lantana,* wayfaring tree, viburnum.]

lan·tern (lăn′tərn) *n.* **1.a.** An often portable case with transparent or translucent sides for holding and protecting a light. **b.** A decorative casing for a light, often of paper. **c.** A light and its protective or decorative case. **2.a.** The room at the top of a lighthouse where the light is located. **b.** *Obsolete.* A lighthouse. **3.** A structure built on top of a roof with open or windowed walls to admit light and air. [Middle English, from Old French *lanterne,* from Latin *lanterna,* from Greek *lamptēr,* from *lampein,* to shine.]

lantern fish *n.* Any of numerous small deep-sea fishes of the family Myctophidae that have distinguishing phosphorescent light organs along each body wall and that often swim to the surface at night.

lantern fly *n.* Any of various chiefly tropical insects of the family Fulgoridae that have an enlarged, elongated head, once thought to be luminescent.

lantern jaw *n.* **1.** A lower jaw that protrudes beyond the upper jaw. **2.** A long, thin jaw that gives the face a gaunt appearance. **—lan′tern-jawed′** (lăn′tərn-jôd′) *adj.*

lantern wheel *n.* A small pinion consisting of circular disks connected by cylindrical bars that serve as teeth. Also called *lantern pinion.*

lan·tha·nide (lăn′thə-nīd′) *n.* See **rare-earth element.** [LANTHAN(UM) + –IDE.]

lanthanide series *n.* The set of chemically related elements with properties similar to those of lanthanum, with atomic numbers from 57 to 71; the rare-earth elements.

lan·tha·num (lăn′thə-nəm) *n.* *Symbol* **La.** A soft, silvery-white, malleable, ductile, metallic rare-earth element, obtained chiefly from monazite and bastnaesite and used in glass manufacture and with other rare earths in carbon lights for movie and television studio lighting. Atomic number 57; atomic weight 138.91; melting point 920°C; boiling point 3,469°C; specific gravity 5.98 to 6.186; valence 3. See table at **element.** [New Latin, from Greek *lanthanein,* to escape notice (from the finding of the element hidden in oxide of cerium).]

lant·horn (lănt′hôrn′, lăn′tərn) *n.* *Chiefly British.* A lantern. [Alteration (influenced by HORN, of which the sides were once made) of LANTERN.]

la·nu·gi·nous (lə-nōō′jə-nəs, -nyōō′-) also **la·nu·gi·nose** (-nōs′) *adj.* Covered with soft, short hair; downy. [From Latin *lānūginōsus,* from *lānūgō, lānūgin-,* lanugo. See LANUGO.] **—la·nu′gi·nous·ness** *n.*

la·nu·go (lə-nōō′gō, -nyōō′-) *n., pl.* **-gos.** A covering of fine, soft hair, as on a leaf, an insect, or a newborn child. [Middle English, pith, from Latin *lānūgō,* down, from *lana,* wool.]

lan·yard also **lan·iard** (lăn′yərd) *n.* **1.** *Nautical.* A short rope or gasket used for fastening something or securing rigging. **2.** A cord worn around the neck for carrying something, such as a knife or whistle. **3.** A cord with a hook at one end used to fire a cannon. [Perhaps alteration (influenced by YARD¹, spar) of Middle English *lainere,* strap, from Old French *laniere,* from *lasne,* perhaps alteration (influenced by *las,* string; see LACE) of **nasle,* lace, of Germanic origin.]

Lan·zhou also **Lan·chow** (län′jō′). A city of central China on the Huang He (Yellow River) north of Chengdu. A major oil-refining center, it is the capital of Gansu province. Population, 1,060,000.

Lao (lou) *n., pl.* **Lao** or **Laos** (louz). **1.** A member of a Buddhist people inhabiting the area of the Mekong River in Laos and Thailand. **2.** The Tai language of the Lao. **—Lao** *adj.* Of or relating to the Lao or their language or culture.

La·oc·o·ön (lā-ŏk′ō-ŏn′) *n.* *Greek Mythology.* A Trojan priest of Apollo who was killed along with his two sons by two sea serpents for having warned his people of the Trojan horse.

La·od·i·ce·a (lā-ŏd′ĭ-sē′ə, lā′ə-dĭ-). An ancient city of western Asia Minor in present-day western Turkey. Built by the Seleucids in the third century B.C., it was a prosperous Roman market town and an early center of Christianity.

La·od·i·ce·an (lā-ŏd′ĭ-sē′ən) *adj.* **1.** Of or relating to Laodicea. **2.** Indifferent or lukewarm especially in matters of religion. **—Laodicean** *n.* A native or inhabitant of Laodicea. [Adj., sense 2, in reference to Revelation 3:14–16.]

La·om·e·don (lā-ŏm′ĭ-dŏn′) *n.* *Greek Mythology.* The founder and first king of Troy and father of Priam.

La·os (lous, lā′ŏs′). A country of southeast Asia. Mainly united as a kingdom by 1353, it became part of French Indochina in 1893 and finally gained its independence in 1953. It has long been the scene of bitter guerrilla warfare. Vientiane is the capital and the largest city. Population, 3,811,000.

La·o·tian (lā-ō′shən, lou′shen) *adj.* **1.** Of or relating to Laos or its people, language, or culture. **2.** Of or relating to the Lao people. **—Laotian** *n.* **1.** A native or inhabitant of Laos. **2.** A Lao.

Lao-tzu (lou′dzŭ′) also **Lao-tse** or **Lao·zi** (-dzə′). fl. sixth century B.C. Chinese philosopher who is traditionally regarded as the founder of Taoism.

lap¹ (lăp) *n.* **1.a.** The front area from the waist to the knees of a seated person. **b.** The portion of a garment that covers the lap. **2.** A hanging or flaplike part, especially of a garment. **3.** An area of responsibility, interest, or control: *an opportunity that dropped in his lap.* ***—idiom.*** **the lap of luxury.** Conditions of great affluence or material comfort: *an heiress living in the lap of luxury.* [Middle English *lappe,* lappet, lap, from Old English *læppa,* lappet.] **—lap′ful′** *n.*

lap² (lăp) *v.* **lapped, lap·ping, laps.** *—tr.* **1.a.** To place or lay (something) so as to overlap another: *roof tiles that were lapped so that water will run off.* **b.** To lie partly over or on: *each shingle lapping the next; shadows that lapped the wall.* **2.** To fold (something) over onto itself: *a cloth edge that had been lapped and sewn to make a hem.* **3.** To wrap or wind around (something); encircle. **4.** To envelop in something; swathe: *models who were lapped in expensive furs.* **5.** To join (pieces, as of wood) by means of a scarf or lap joint. **6.** To get ahead of (an opponent) in a race by one or more complete circuits of the course. **7.** To convert (cotton or other fibers) into a sheet or layer. **8.a.** To polish (a surface) until smooth. **b.** To hone (two mating parts) against each other until closely fitted. *—intr.* **1.** To lie partly on or over something; overlap. **2.** To form a lap or fold. **3.** To wind around or enfold something. **—lap** *n.* **1.a.** A part that overlaps. **b.** The amount by which one part overlaps another. **2.a.** One complete round or circuit, especially of a racetrack. **b.** One complete length of a straight course, as of a swimming pool. **3.** A segment or stage, as of a trip. **4.a.** A length, as of rope, required to make one complete turn around something. **b.** The act of lapping or encircling. **5.** A continuous band or layer of cotton, flax, or other fiber. **6.** A wheel, disk, or slab of leather or metal, either stationary or rotating, used for polishing and smoothing. [Middle English *lappen,* from *lappe,* lap, lappet. See LAP¹.]

lap³ (lăp) *v.* **lapped, lap·ping, laps.** *—tr.* **1.** To take in (a liquid or food) by lifting it with the tongue. **2.** To wash or slap against with soft liquid sounds: *waves lapping the side of the boat.* *—intr.* **1.** To take in a liquid or food with the tongue. **2.** To wash against something with soft liquid sounds. **—lap** *n.* **1.a.** The act or an instance of lapping. **b.** The amount taken in by lapping. **2.** The sound of lapping. **3.** A watery food or drink. ***—phrasal verb.*** **lap up.** To receive eagerly or greedily: *lapping up praise.* [Middle English *lapen,* from Old English *lapian.*]

lap·a·ro·scope (lăp′ər-ə-skōp′) *n.* A slender, tubular endoscope that is inserted through an incision in the abdominal wall to examine or perform minor surgery within the abdominal or pelvic cavities. [Greek *lapara,* flank (from *laparos,* soft) + –SCOPE.]

lap·a·ros·co·py (lăp′ə-rŏs′kə-pē) *n., pl.* **-pies.** An operation in which a laparoscope is used, as in an examination of the liver or the surgical treatment of endometriosis. [Greek *lapara,* flank; see LAPAROSCOPE + –SCOPY.] **—lap′a·ro·scop′ic** (-ər-ə-skŏp′ĭk) *adj.* **—lap′a·ros′co·pist** *n.*

lap·a·rot·o·my (lăp′ə-rŏt′ə-mē) *n., pl.* **-mies.** Surgical in-

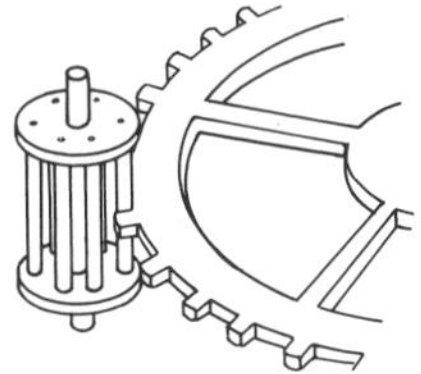

lantern wheel

Laocoön
Attributed to Agesander, Athenodorus, and Polydorus of Rhodes (first century B.C.)

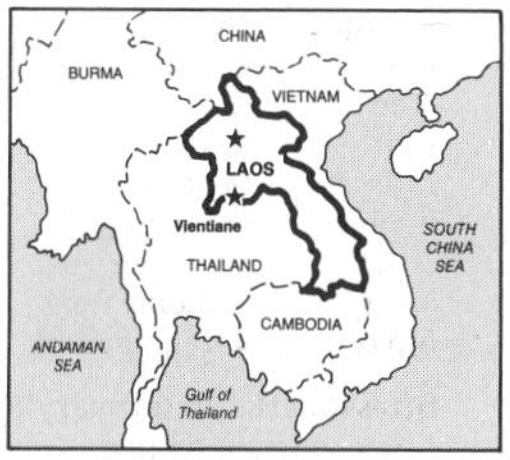

Laos

cision into the abdominal wall, especially into the flank. [Greek *lapara,* flank; see LAPAROSCOPE + -TOMY.]

La Paz (lə päz′, lä päs′). The administrative capital and largest city of Bolivia, in the western part of the country near Lake Titicaca. Built on the site of an Inca village, it is the highest capital in the world, lying at an altitude of about 3,660 m (12,000 ft) above sea level. Population, 992,592.

lap belt *n.* A seat belt that fastens across the lap.

lap·board (lăp′bôrd′, -bōrd′) *n.* A flat board held on the lap as a substitute for a table or desk.

lap dissolve *n.* See **dissolve.**

lap dog *n.* **1.** A small dog kept as a pet. **2.** *Informal.* One that is eager to do another's bidding, especially so as to maintain a position of privilege or favor: *"a bunch of intellectual lap dogs for anybody who holds a big job in government"* (Mike Barnicle).

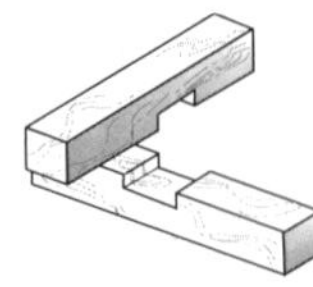

lap joint

la·pel (lə-pĕl′) *n.* The part of a garment, such as a coat or jacket, that is an extension of the collar and folds back against the breast. [From LAP[1].] **—la·peled′, la·pelled′** *adj.*

La Pé·rouse (lä pā-ro͞oz′), Comte de. Title of Jean François de Galaup. 1741–1788? French explorer who led an expedition to the western Pacific Ocean (1785–1788).

La Pérouse Strait. A channel of the western Pacific Ocean between Sakhalin Island and northern Hokkaido, Japan, connecting the Sea of Okhotsk with the Sea of Japan.

lap·i·dar·i·an (lăp′ĭ-dâr′ē-ən) *adj.* Of or relating to the working of stone or gems; lapidary. [From Latin *lapidārius,* stonecutter. See LAPIDARY.]

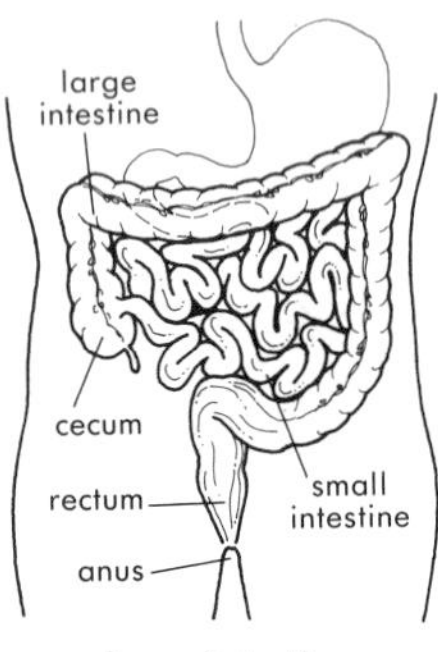

large intestine

lap·i·dar·y (lăp′ĭ-dĕr′ē) *n., pl.* **-ies. 1.** One who cuts, polishes, or engraves gems. **2.** A dealer in precious or semiprecious stones. **—lapidary** *adj.* **1.** Of or relating to precious stones or the art of working with them. **2.a.** Engraved in stone. **b.** Marked by conciseness, precision, or refinement of expression: *lapidary prose.* **c.** Sharply or finely delineated: *a face with lapidary features.* [Middle English *lapidarie,* from Old French *lapidaire,* from Latin *lapidārius,* from *lapis, lapid-,* stone.]

la·pil·lus (lə-pĭl′əs) *n., pl.* **-pil·li** (-pĭl′ī′). A small, solidified fragment of lava. [Latin, diminutive of *lapis,* stone.]

lap·in (lăp′ĭn, lä-păN′) *n.* Rabbit fur, especially when dyed to imitate a more expensive fur. [French, from Old French *lapriel.*]

lap·is laz·u·li (lăp′ĭs lăz′ə-lē, -yə-, lăzh′ə-) *n.* An opaque to translucent blue, violet-blue, or greenish-blue semiprecious gemstone composed mainly of lazurite and calcite. [Middle English, from Old French, from Medieval Latin *lapis lazulī* : Latin *lapis,* stone + Medieval Latin *lazulī,* genitive of *lazulum,* lapis lazuli (from Arabic *lāzaward,* from Persian *lajward*).]

Lap·ith (lăp′ĭth) *n. Greek Mythology.* One of a Thessalian tribe who at the disastrous wedding of their king defeated the drunken centaurs.

lap joint *n.* A joint, as between two boards or metal parts, in which the ends or edges are overlapped and fastened together, usually so as to produce a flush or continuous surface.

La·place or **La Place** (lə-pläs′). A village of southeast Louisiana on the Mississippi River west-northwest of New Orleans. It is a trade center. Population, 16,112.

La·place (lə-pläs′, lä-), Marquis **Pierre Simon de.** 1749–1827. French mathematician and astronomer noted for his theory of a nebular origin of the solar system and his investigations into gravity and the stability of planetary motion.

largemouth bass
Micropterus salmoides

Lap·land (lăp′lănd′, -lənd). A region of extreme northern Europe including northern Norway, Sweden, and Finland and the Kola Peninsula of northwest Russia. **—Lap′land·er** *n.*

La Pla·ta (lä plä′tä). A city of east-central Argentina southeast of Buenos Aires. Founded in 1882, it is an industrial center. Population, 454,884.

La Pla·ta Peak (lə plä′tə). A mountain, 4,380.1 m (14,361 ft) high, in the Sawatch Range of the Rocky Mountains in central Colorado.

La Porte (lə pôrt′, pōrt′). **1.** A city of northwest Indiana west-southwest of South Bend. Settled in 1832, it is a manufacturing center. Population, 21,796. **2.** A city of southeast Texas on Galveston Bay east of Houston. It is a popular summer resort. Population, 16,836.

Lapp (lăp) *n.* **1.** A member of a people of nomadic herding tradition inhabiting Lapland. Also called *Sami.* **2.** Any of the Finnic languages of the Lapps. [Swedish, from Old Swedish *lapper,* piece, perhaps of Finnish origin.] **—Lapp′ish** (lăp′ĭsh) *adj.*

lap·pet (lăp′ĭt) *n.* **1.** A decorative flap or loose fold on a garment or headdress. **2.** A flaplike structure, such as the wattle of a bird or the lobe of the ear.

lap robe *n.* A blanket or fur piece for covering the lap, legs, and feet, as of a passenger in an unheated car or carriage.

lapse (lăps) *v.* **lapsed, laps·ing, laps·es.** *—intr.* **1.a.** To fall from a previous level or standard, as of accomplishment, quality, or conduct: *lapse into bad habits; a team that lapsed into mediocrity halfway through the season.* **b.** To deviate from a prescribed or accepted way: *lapse into heresy.* **c.** To pass gradually or smoothly; slip: *lapse into reverie.* **2.a.** To come to an end, especially gradually or temporarily: *He realized that his attention had lapsed and he hadn't heard the assignment.* **b.** To be no longer valid or active; expire: *She allowed her membership to lapse after the first year.* **3.** *Law.* To pass to another through neglect or omission. Used of a right or privilege, a benefice, or an estate. **4.** To go by; elapse: *Years had lapsed since we last met.* *—tr.* To allow to lapse. **—lapse** *n.* **1.** The act or an instance of lapsing, as: **a.** A usually minor or temporary failure; a slip: *a lapse of memory; a lapse in judgment.* **b.** A deterioration or decline: *a lapse into barbarism.* **c.** A moral fall: *a lapse from grace.* **2.** A break in continuity; a pause: *a lapse in the conversation.* **3.** A period of time; an interval: *a lapse of several years between the two revolutions.* **4.** *Law.* The termination of a right or privilege through disuse, neglect, or death. [Middle English *lapsen,* to deviate from the normal, from *laps,* lapse of time, sin (from Old French, lapse of time, from Latin *lāpsus,* from past participle of *lābī,* to lapse) and from Latin *lāpsāre,* frequentative of *lābī,* Latin *lābī, lāps-,* to lapse.] **—laps′er** *n.*

ă pat	oi boy
ā pay	ou out
âr care	o͝o took
ä father	o͞o boot
ĕ pet	ŭ cut
ē be	ûr urge
ĭ pit	th thin
ī pie	*th* this
îr pier	hw which
ŏ pot	zh vision
ō toe	ə about, item
ô paw	♦ regionalism

Stress marks: ′ (primary); ′ (secondary), as in **dictionary** (dĭk′shə-nĕr′ē)

lapsed (lăpst) *adj.* No longer active or practicing: *a lapsed Catholic; a lapsed club member.*

lapse rate *n.* The rate of decrease of atmospheric temperature with increase in altitude.

lap·strake (lăp′strāk′) also **lap·streak** (-strēk′) *adj. Nautical.* Clinker-built.

Lap·tev Sea (lăp′tĕf′, -tĕv′, läp′tyĭf). A section of the Arctic Ocean north of eastern Russia between the Taimyr Peninsula and the New Siberian Islands.

lap·top (lăp′tŏp′) *n. Computer Science.* A microcomputer small enough to use on one's lap.

La Pu·en·te (lä′ po͞o-ĕn′tē, pwĕn′tā). A city of southern California, a residential suburb of Los Angeles. Population, 30,882.

La·pu·tan (lə-pyo͞ot′n) *adj.* Absurdly impractical or visionary, especially to the neglect of more useful activity. [After the flying island of *Laputa* in *Gulliver's Travels* by Jonathan Swift, where absurd projects are pursued and useful pursuits neglected.] **—La·pu′tan** *n.*

lap·wing (lăp′wĭng′) *n.* Any of several Old World birds of the genus *Vanellus* related to the plovers, especially *V. vanellus,* having a narrow crest and erratic flight behavior. Also called *green plover, pewit.* [Middle English, by folk etymology (perhaps influenced by *lapen,* to lap; see LAP[3], and *wing,* wing; see WING) from Old English *hlēapewince* : *hlēapan,* to leap + *-wince,* to waver.]

L'A·qui·la (lăk′wə-lə, lä′kwē-lä) also **A·qui·la** (ăk′wə-lə, ä′kwē-lä). A city of central Italy northeast of Rome. It is a trade and industrial center. Population, 63,465.

Lar (lär) *n., pl.* **Lar·es** (lâr′ēz, lär′-). A tutelary deity or spirit of an ancient Roman household. [Latin *Lār,* probably of Etruscan origin.]

Lar·a·mie (lăr′ə-mē). A city of southeast Wyoming west-northwest of Cheyenne. Settled in 1868 with the coming of the railroad, it is the seat of the University of Wyoming (founded 1886). Population, 24,410.

lar·board (lär′bərd) *Nautical. n.* See **port².** **—larboard** *adj.* On the port side. [Alteration (influenced by *starboard*) of Middle English *laddebord* : perhaps *ladde,* past participle of *leden,* to lead; see LEAD[1] + *borde,* side of a ship (from the fact that this side of the ship was guided by the steering apparatus on the other side of the ship); see STARBOARD.]

lar·ce·nist (lär′sə-nĭst) also **lar·ce·ner** (-nər) *n.* One who commits larceny.

lar·ce·nous (lär′sə-nəs) *adj.* **1.** Of, relating to, or involving larceny: *a larcenous scheme; with larcenous intent.* **2.** Guilty of or given to larceny. **—lar′ce·nous·ly** *adv.*

lar·ce·ny (lär′sə-nē) *n., pl.* **-nies.** *Law.* The unlawful taking and removing of another's personal property with the intent of permanently depriving the owner; theft. [Middle English, from Anglo-Norman *larcin,* theft, from Latin *latrōcinium,* robbery, from *latrō,* robber, mercenary, utimately from Greek *latron,* pay, hire.]

larch (lärch) *n.* **1.** Any of several deciduous, coniferous trees of the genus *Larix,* having needlelike leaves clustered on short shoots and heavy, durable wood. **2.** The wood of these trees. [German *Lärche,* from Middle High German *larche,* from Latin *larix, laric-.*]

Larch River (lärch). A river, about 434 km (270 mi) long, of northern Quebec, Canada, flowing northeast to join the Caniapiscau River.

lard (lärd) *n.* The white solid or semisolid rendered fat of a hog. *—tr.* **lard·ed, lard·ing, lards. 1.** To cover or coat with lard or a similar fat. **2.** To insert strips of fat or bacon in (meat) before cooking. **3.a.** To enrich or lace heavily with extra material; embellish: *larded the report with quotations.* **b.** To fill throughout; inject: *"The history of Sicily was larded with treachery"* (Mario Puzo). [Middle English, from Old French *larde,* from Latin *lārdum.*] **—lard′y** *adj.*

lar·der (lär′dər) *n.* **1.** A place, such as a pantry or cellar, where food is stored. **2.** A supply of food. [Middle English, from Anglo-Norman, from Medieval Latin *lārdārium,* from Latin *lārdum,* bacon.]

Lard·ner (lärd′nər), **Ringgold Wilmer.** Known as "Ring." 1885–1933. American humorist and writer whose satirical short stories were published in collections, including *You Know Me, Al* (1916) and *How to Write Short Stories (with Samples)* (1924).

La·re·do (lə-rā′dō). A city of southern Texas on the Rio Grande south-southwest of San Antonio. Established by Spanish settlers in 1755, it is a major port of entry. Population, 91,449.

lar·ee (lâr′ē) *n.* See table at **currency.** [Ultimately from Persian *lārī.*]

Lar•es (lâr′ēz) *n.* Plural of **Lar.**

lar•es and penates (lâr′ēz, lär′-) *pl.n.* Treasured household possessions. [Translation of Latin *Larēs et Penātēs* : *Larēs*, pl. of *Lār*, Lar + *et*, and + *Penātēs*, Penates.]

large (lärj) *adj.* **larg•er, larg•est.** *Abbr.* **L, L., lg., lge. 1.** Of greater than average size, extent, quantity, or amount; big. **2.** Of greater than average scope, breadth, or capacity; comprehensive. **3.** Important; significant: *had a large role in the negotiations; a large producer of paper goods.* **4.a.** Understanding and tolerant; liberal: *a large and generous spirit.* **b.** Of great magnitude or intensity; grand: *"a rigid resistance to the large emotions"* (Stephen Koch). **5.a.** Pretentious; boastful. Used of speech or manners. **b.** *Obsolete.* Gross; coarse. Used of speech or language. **6.** *Nautical.* Favorable. Used of a wind. **—*idiom.* at large. 1.** Not in confinement or captivity; at liberty: *a convict still at large.* **2.** As a whole; in general: *the country at large.* **3.** Representing a nation, state, or district as a whole. Often used in combination: *councilor-at-large.* **4.** Not assigned to a particular country. Often used in combination: *ambassador-at-large.* **5.** At length; copiously. [Middle English, from Old French, from Latin *largus*, generous.] **—large′ness** *n.*

SYNONYMS: *large, big, great.* The central meaning shared by these adjectives is "being notably above the average in size or magnitude": *a large city; a large sum of money; a big brown barn; a big sweep of open lawn; a great old oak tree; a great ocean liner.* ***ANTONYM:*** *small.*

large calorie *n.* See **calorie** (sense 3a).

large-heart•ed (lärj′här′tĭd) *adj.* Having a generous disposition; sympathetic. **—large′-heart′ed•ness** *n.*

large intestine *n.* The portion of the intestine that extends from the ileum to the anus, forming an arch around the convolutions of the small intestine and including the cecum, colon, rectum, and anal canal.

large•ly (lärj′lē) *adv.* **1.** For the most part; mainly. **2.** On a large scale; amply.

large-mind•ed (lärj′mīn′dĭd) *adj.* Marked by breadth or tolerance of views; broad-minded. **—large′-mind′ed•ly** *adv.* **—large′-mind′ed•ness** *n.*

large•mouth bass (lärj′mouth′) *n.* A North American freshwater food and game fish *(Micropterus salmoides),* mostly grayish black with a dark irregular stripe along each side and a large upper jaw extending past the eye.

larg•er than life (lär′jər) *adj.* So impressive or imposing as to exceed most others of a class: *"This is a person of surpassing integrity; a man of the utmost sincerity; somewhat larger than life"* (Joyce Carol Oates).

large-scale (lärj′skāl′) *adj.* **1.** Large in scope or extent. **2.** Drawn or made large to show detail.

large-scale integration *n.* *Abbr.* **LSI** The technology for placing more than 100 integrated circuits on a single chip.

lar•gess also **lar•gesse** (lär-zhĕs′, -jĕs′, lär′jĕs′) *n.* **1.a.** Liberality in bestowing gifts, especially in a lofty or condescending manner. **b.** Money or gifts bestowed. **2.** Generosity of spirit or attitude. [Middle English *largesse*, from Old French, from *large*, generous, from Latin *largus*.]

large-toothed aspen (lärj′tōōtht′, -tōōthd′) *n.* An eastern North American deciduous tree *(Populus grandidentata)* having ovate leaves with coarsely toothed margins.

lar•ghet•to (lär-gĕt′ō) *Music. adv. & adj.* In a dignified style and slow tempo, usually considered to be slightly faster than largo but slower than adagio. Used chiefly as a direction. **—larghetto** *n., pl.* **-tos.** A larghetto passage or movement. [Italian, diminutive of *largo*, largo. See LARGO.]

larg•ish (lär′jĭsh) *adj.* Fairly large.

lar•go (lär′gō) *Music. adv. & adj.* In a very slow tempo, usually considered to be slower than adagio, and with great dignity. Used chiefly as a direction. **—largo** *n., pl.* **-gos.** A largo passage or movement. [Italian, from Latin *largus*, generous.]

Lar•go (lär′gō). A city of western Florida on the Gulf of Mexico northwest of St. Petersburg. It is a resort and processing center in a citrus-growing area. Population, 58,977.

lar•i•at (lăr′ē-ət) *n.* **1.** See **lasso. 2.** A rope for picketing grazing horses or mules. [Spanish *la reata* : *la*, the (from Latin *illa*; see ALERT) + *reatar*, to tie again (*re-*, again, from Latin; see RE– + *atar*, to tie, from Latin *aptāre*, to join, from *aptus*, past participle of *apere*, to tie).]

Lá•ri•sa (lä′rē-sä) or **La•ris•sa** (lə-rĭs′ə). A city of eastern Greece near the Aegean Sea. The chief city of ancient Thessaly, it was later part of the Byzantine Empire, Serbia, and Ottoman Turkey (until 1881). Population, 102,048.

lark[1] (lärk) *n.* **1.** Any of various chiefly Old World birds of the family Alaudidae, especially the skylark, having a sustained, melodious song. **2.** Any of several similar birds, such as the meadowlark. [Middle English *laveroc, larke*, from Old English *lāwerce*.]

lark[2] (lärk) *n.* **1.** A carefree or spirited adventure. **2.** A harmless prank. **—lark** *intr.v.* **larked, lark•ing, larks.** To engage in spirited fun or merry pranks. [Perhaps short for SKYLARK, to frolic, and possibly alteration of dialectal *lake*, play (from Middle English *leik, laik*, from Old Norse *leikr*).] **—lark′ish** *adj.*

lark•spur (lärk′spûr′) *n.* See **delphinium.**

lark•y (lär′kē) *adj.* **lark•i•er, lark•i•est. 1.** High-spirited; zestful: *"It's a very larky Nureyev whom we see—a buoyant imp who . . . cavorts in various disguises"* (Arlene Croce). **2.** Silly; zany: *"The filmmakers replace characterization with larky pop-culture references and associations"* (David Denby). **—lark′i•ness** *n.*

lark[1]
Horned lark
Eremophila alpestris;
horns, as in this
photograph, are not
always evident

La Roche•fou•cauld (lä rōsh-fōō-kō′, -rôsh-), Duc **François de.** 1613–1680. French writer of moralistic aphorisms, published as *Maxims* (1665).

La Ro•chelle (lä′ rə-shĕl′, rô-). A city of western France on the Bay of Biscay southwest of Tours. It was a Huguenot stronghold in the 16th century. Population, 75,840.

La•rousse (lä-rōōs′), **Pierre Athanase.** 1817–1875. French lexicographer, grammarian, and encyclopedist who compiled the *Grand Dictionnaire Universel du XIXe Siècle* (1866–1876).

lar•ri•gan also **lar•ri•gan** (lăr′ĭ-gən) *n.* A moccasin with knee-high leggings made of oiled leather. [Origin unknown.]

lar•rup (lăr′əp) *tr.v.* **-ruped, -rup•ing, -rups.** To beat, flog, or thrash. **—larrup** *n.* A blow. [Perhaps from Dutch *larpen*, to slap, thrash, from *larp*, rod, whip.]

lar•um (lăr′əm) *n.* An alarm. [Middle English *larum-*, as in *larumbelle*, short for *alarum*. See ALARUM.]

lar•va (lär′və) *n., pl.* **-vae** (-vē) or **-vas. 1.** The newly hatched, wingless, often wormlike form of many insects before metamorphosis. **2.** The newly hatched, earliest stage of any of various animals that undergo metamorphosis, differing markedly in form and appearance from the adult. **3.** *Roman Mythology.* A malevolent spirit of the dead; a lemur. [Latin *lārva*, specter, mask (because it acts as a specter of or a mask for the adult form).] **—lar′val** *adj.*

WORD HISTORY: The word *larva* referring to the newly hatched form of insects before they undergo metamorphosis comes from the Latin word *lārva*, meaning "evil spirit, demon, devil." To understand why this should be so, we need to know that the Latin word also was used for a terrifying mask, and it is this sense of the word that has come down to us. In Medieval Latin *larva* could mean "mask or visor." *Larva* is therefore an appropriate term for that stage of an insect's life during which its final form was still hidden or masked, and New Latin *lārva* was thus applied by Carolus Linnaeus, the Swedish botanist who originated our system of classifying plants and animals. The word *larva* is first recorded in English in its scientific sense in 1768, although it had been used in its "spirit" sense in 1651 and in a way that foreshadowed the usage by Linnaeus in 1691.

lar•vi•cide (lär′vĭ-sīd′) *n.* An insecticide designed to kill larval pests. **—lar′vi•cid′al** (-sīd′l) *adj.*

laryng– *pref.* **laryngo–.**

la•ryn•ge•al (lə-rĭn′jē-əl, -jəl, lăr′ən-jē′əl) also **la•ryn•gal** (lə-rĭng′gəl) *—adj.* **1.** Of, relating to, affecting, or near the larynx. **2.** Produced in or with the larynx; glottal. *—n.* **1.** A laryngeal sound. **2.** Any of a set of *h*-like sounds reconstructed for early Proto-Indo-European and partially preserved in Anatolian. [From New Latin *laryngeus*, from Greek *larunx, larung-*, larynx.]

lar•yn•gec•to•my (lăr′ən-jĕk′tə-mē) *n., pl.* **-mies.** Surgical removal of part or all of the larynx.

la•ryn•ges (lə-rĭn′jēz) *n.* A plural of **larynx.**

lar•yn•gi•tis (lăr′ən-jī′tĭs) *n.* Inflammation of the larynx. **—lar′yn•git′ic** (-jĭt′ĭk) *adj.*

laryngo– or **laryng–** *pref.* Larynx: *laryngoscope.* [New Latin, from Greek *larungo-*, from *larunx, larung-*, larynx.]

lar•yn•gol•o•gy (lăr′ən-gŏl′ə-jē) *n.* The branch of medicine that studies and treats the larynx, pharynx, and fauces. **—lar′yn•gol′o•gist** *n.*

la•ryn•go•phar•ynx (lə-rĭng′gō-făr′ĭngks) *n.* The portion of the pharynx just above the larynx.

la•ryn•go•scope (lə-rĭng′gə-skōp′, -rĭn′jə-) *n.* A tubular endoscope that is inserted into the larynx through the mouth and used for observing the interior of the larynx. **—la•ryn′go•scop′ic** (-skŏp′ĭk), **la•ryn′go•scop′i•cal** *adj.* **—la•ryn′go•scop′i•cal•ly** *adv.* **—lar′yn•gos′co•py** (lăr′ən-gŏs′kə-pē) *n.*

lar•ynx (lăr′ĭngks) *n., pl.* **la•ryn•ges** (lə-rĭn′jēz) or **lar•ynx•es.** The part of the respiratory tract between the pharynx and the trachea, having walls of cartilage and muscle and containing the vocal cords enveloped in folds of mucous membrane. [New Latin, from Greek *larunx*.]

la•sa•gna also **la•sa•gne** (lə-zän′yə) *n.* **1.** Flat, wide strips of pasta. **2.** A dish made by baking such pasta with layers of tomato sauce and fillings such as cheese or ground meat. [Italian, possibly from Vulgar Latin **lasania*, from Latin *lasanum*, chamber pot, cooking pot, from Greek *lasanon*.]

La Salle (lə săl′, lä). A city of southern Quebec, Canada, on Montreal Island and the St. Lawrence River. It is a residential suburb of Montreal. Population, 76,299.

La Salle, Sieur de. Title of Robert Cavelier. 1643–1687. French explorer in North America who claimed Louisiana for France (1682).

La Salle

las•car (lăs′kər) *n.* An East Indian sailor, army servant, or artillery trooper. [Urdu *lashkar*, army, from Persian, from Arabic *al-'askar*, the army : *al*, the + *'askar*, army.]

Las Ca•sas (läs kä′səs, -säs), **Bartolomé de.** Known as "Apos-

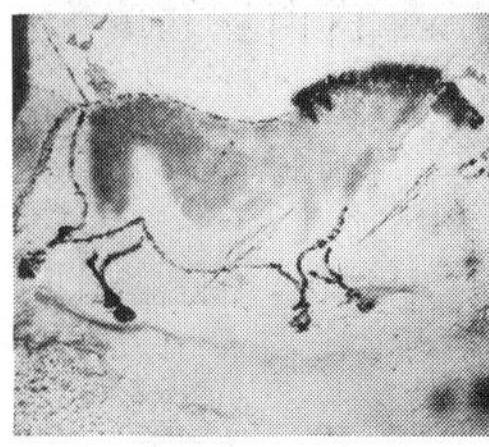
Lascaux
Bister and black horse with arrows in the Painted Gallery

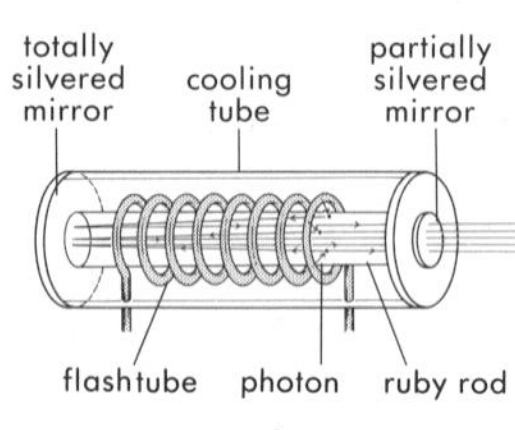

laser
Ruby laser

lasso

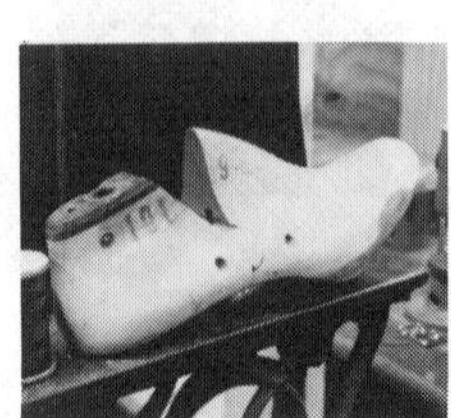
last³

tle of the Indies." 1474–1566. Spanish missionary and historian who sought to abolish the oppression and enslavement of the native peoples in the Americas.

Las•caux (lă-skō′). A cave of southwest France in the Dordogne River valley. The cave, discovered in 1940 and now closed to the public, contains important Paleolithic paintings.

las•civ•i•ous (lə-sĭv′ē-əs) *adj.* **1.** Given to or expressing lust; lecherous. **2.** Exciting sexual desires; salacious. [Middle English, from Late Latin *lascīviōsus,* from Latin *lascīvia,* lewdness, playfulness, from *lascīvus,* lustful, playful. See **las-** in Appendix.] **—las•civ′i•ous•ly** *adv.* **—las•civ′i•ous•ness** *n.*

Las Cru•ces (läs krōō′sĭs). A city of southern New Mexico on the Rio Grande north-northwest of El Paso, Texas. Irrigated farming and the nearby White Sands Missile Range are important to its economy. Population, 45,086.

lase (lāz) *intr.v.* **lased, las•ing, las•es.** To function as a laser; emit coherent radiation by the action of a laser. [Back-formation from LASER.]

la•ser (lā′zər) *n.* **1.** Any of several devices that convert incident electromagnetic radiation of mixed frequencies to one or more discrete frequencies of highly amplified and coherent ultraviolet, visible, or infrared radiation. **2.** A device whose output is in an invisible region of the electromagnetic spectrum. [*l(ight) a(mplification by) s(timulated) e(mission of) r(adiation).*]

laser disk *n.* See **optical disk.**

laser printer *n.* A printer that uses a laser to produce an image on a rotating drum before electrostatically transferring the image to paper.

lash¹ (lăsh) *n.* **1.a.** A stroke or blow with or as if with a whip. **b.** A whip. **c.** The flexible portion of a whip, such as a plait or thong. **2.** Punishment administered with a whip. **3.a.** A lacerating presence or power: *the lash of conscience.* **b.** A caustic verbal attack. **4.** An eyelash. **—lash** *v.* **lashed, lash•ing, lash•es.** *—tr.* **1.** To strike with or as if with a whip. **2.** To strike against with force or violence: *sleet lashing the roof.* **3.** To beat or swing rapidly: *The alligator lashed its tail in the water.* **4.** To make a scathing oral or written attack against. **5.** To drive or goad; sting: *words that lashed them into action.* *—intr.* **1.** To move swiftly or violently; thrash: *heard the snake lashing about in the leaves.* **2.a.** To aim a sudden blow; strike: *The mule lashed out with its hind legs.* **b.** To beat; flail: *waves lashing at the shore.* **3.** To make a scathing verbal or written attack: *lashed out at her critics during the interview.* [Middle English, probably from *lashen,* to deal a blow, perhaps of imitative origin.]

lash² (lăsh) *tr.v.* **lashed, lash•ing, lash•es.** To secure or bind, as with a rope, cord, or chain. [Middle English *lashen, lasen,* to lace, from Old French *lachier, lacier,* from Vulgar Latin **laceāre,* from Latin *laqueāre,* to ensnare, from *laqueus,* snare. See LACE.]

lash•er¹ (lăsh′ər) *n.* One that lashes, as with a whip.

lash•er² (lăsh′ər) *n.* One who lashes so as to secure or bind, as with a rope.

lash•ing (lăsh′ĭng) *n.* Something used for securing or binding.

lash•ings (lăsh′ĭngz) *pl.n. Chiefly British.* Lavish quantities. [From LASH¹, to lavish (obsolete).]

Las•ki (lăs′kē), **Harold Joseph.** 1893–1950. British political scientist and member of the Fabian Society who led the British Labor Party (1945–1946).

Las Pal•mas (läs päl′mäs). The chief city of the Canary Islands of Spain, on the northeast coast of Grand Canary Island. It was founded in the late 15th century. Population, 377,353.

La Spe•zia (lä spĕt′sē-ə, spĕ′tsyä). A city of northwest Italy east-southeast of Genoa on the **Gulf of La Spezia,** an arm of the Ligurian Sea. The city is a major seaport and year-round resort. Population, 115,215.

lass (lăs) *n.* **1.** A girl or young woman. **2.** A sweetheart. [Middle English *las,* probably of Scandinavian origin.]

Las•sa fever (lä′sə, lăs′ə) *n.* An acute, often fatal viral disease endemic to West Africa and characterized by high fever, headache, ulcers of the mucous membranes, and disturbances of the gastrointestinal tract. [After *Lassa,* a village of northeast Nigeria.]

Las•salle (lə-săl′, lä-säl′), **Ferdinand.** 1825–1864. German politician who promoted the political involvement of the working class.

Las•sen Peak (lăs′ən). An active volcano, 3,188.2 m (10,453 ft) high, in the Cascade Range of northern California.

las•sie (lăs′ē) *n.* A lass.

las•si•tude (lăs′ĭ-tōōd′, -tyōōd′) *n.* A state or feeling of weariness, diminished energy, or listlessness. See Synonyms at **lethargy.** [Middle English, from Old French, from Latin *lassitūdō,* from *lassus,* weary. See **lē-** in Appendix.]

las•so (lăs′ō, lă-sōō′) *n., pl.* **-sos** or **-soes.** A long rope with a running noose at one end, used especially to catch horses and cattle. Also called *lariat.* **—lasso** *tr.v.* **-soed, -so•ing, -sos** or **-soes.** To catch with or as if with such a rope. [Spanish *lazo,* from Vulgar Latin **laceum,* noose. See LACE.] **—las′so•er** *n.*

last¹ (lăst) *adj.* **1.** Being, coming, or placed after all others; final: *the last game of the season.* **2.** Being the only one left: *his last nickel; as a last resort.* **3.** Just past; most recent: *last year; the last time I checked.* **4.** Most up-to-date; newest: *the last thing in swimwear.* **5.** Highest in extent or degree; utmost: *to the last measure of human endurance.* **6.** Most valid, authoritative, or conclusive: *The arbiter will have the last say in resolving this dispute.* **7.a.** Least likely or expected: *the last person we would have suspected.* **b.** The least desirable or suitable: *the last man for the job.* **8.** Being the latest possible: *waited until the last second before boarding the train.* **9.** Lowest in rank or importance: *last prize; last place.* **10.** Used as an intensive: *Every last dollar was donated to charity.* **11.a.** Of or relating to a terminal period or stage, as of life: *the last days of the dinosaurs.* **b.** Administered just before death: *the last sacraments.* **—last** *adv.* **1.** After all others in chronology or sequence: *arrived last.* **2.** Most recently: *a fashion last popular in the 1940's.* **3.** At the end; finally: *Add the butter last.* **—last** *n.* **1.** One that is at the end or last: *the last to be chosen; on every page but the last.* **2.** The end: *held out until the last.* **3.** The final mention or appearance: *haven't seen the last of our troubles.* **—*idioms.* at last.** After a considerable length of time; finally. **at long last.** After a lengthy or troublesome wait or delay: *At long last the winter was over.* [Middle English, from Old English *latost,* superlative of *læt,* late. See **lē-** in Appendix.] **—last′ly** *adv.*

SYNONYMS: *last, final, terminal, eventual, ultimate.* These adjectives mean coming after all others in chronology or sequence. *Last* applies to what comes at the end of a series, as of like things: *the last day of the month; the last piece of candy. The last time I saw them they were fine.* Something *final* comes at the end of a progression or process; the term stresses the definitiveness and decisiveness of the conclusion: *This is our final offer. The decision of the board of trustees will be final. "I believe that unarmed truth and unconditional love will have the final word in reality"* (Martin Luther King, Jr.). *Terminal* applies to what marks or forms a limit or boundary, as in space, time, or development: *In order to increase its freight revenues the railroad chose as its terminal city a town with a large harbor.* Something *eventual* will inevitably come about as a result of a particular circumstance or contingency: *If prices continue to spiral out of control, it is reasonable to expect the eventual collapse of the stock market. Ultimate* applies to what concludes a series, process, or progression, to what constitutes a final result or objective, and to what is most distant or remote, as in time: *the ultimate sonata of that opus; our ultimate goal; the ultimate effect; an ultimate authority. "I know no safe depository of the ultimate powers of the society but the people themselves"* (Thomas Jefferson).

last² (lăst) *v.* **last•ed, last•ing, lasts.** *—intr.* **1.a.** To continue in time; go on: *The war lasted four years.* **b.** To continue; survive: *The patient is not expected to last much longer.* **2.a.** To remain in good or usable condition: *Produce lasts longer if it is refrigerated. I wanted a car that would last.* **b.** To continue in force or practice: *wondered if the marriage would last.* **3.** To remain in adequate supply: *Will our water last?* *—tr.* **1.** To keep adequately supplied: *left enough bread to last the family for the weekend.* **2.** To persist or endure for the entire length of; survive: *hoped to last the season without injuring her leg again.* [Middle English *lasten,* from Old English *lǣstan.* See **leis-¹** in Appendix.]

last³ (lăst) *n.* A block or form shaped like a human foot and used in making or repairing shoes. **—last** *tr.v.* **last•ed, last•ing, lasts.** To mold or shape on a last. [Middle English *leste, laste,* from Old English *lǣste,* from *lǣst, lāst,* sole of the foot. See **leis-¹** in Appendix.]

last⁴ (lăst) *n. Chiefly British.* A unit of volume or weight varying for different commodities and in different districts, equal to about 80 bushels, 640 gallons, or 2 tons. [Middle English, load, a kind of measure, from Old English *hlæst,* load.]

last-born or **last•born** (lăst′bôrn′) *—adj.* Last in order of birth; youngest. *—n.* One that is born last, as a youngest child.

last-ditch (lăst′dĭch′) *adj.* Done or made as a final recourse, especially to prevent a crisis or disaster: *a last-ditch effort to avert the threatened strike.*

Las•tex (lăs′tĕks′). A trademark used for a yarn having a core of elastic rubber wound with rayon, nylon, silk, or cotton threads.

last hurrah *n.* A final appearance or effort, especially at the end of a career: *a reelection campaign that was expected to be her last hurrah.* [After *The Last Hurrah,* a novel by Edwin O'Connor (1918–1968), American writer.]

last-in, first-out (lăst′ĭn′ fûrst′out′) *n. Accounting.* A method of inventory accounting in which the most recently acquired items are assumed to have been the first sold. In a period of rising prices, this method yields a lower ending inventory, a higher cost of goods sold, a lower gross profit (assuming constant price), and a lower taxable income. Also called *LIFO.*

last•ing (lăs′tĭng) *adj.* Continuing or remaining for a long time; enduring: *a lasting peace.* **—lasting** *n.* A sturdy twilled fabric. **—last′ing•ly** *adv.* **—last′ing•ness** *n.*

Last Judgment (lăst) *n.* The final judgment by God of all humankind, especially as envisioned in Christian, Jewish, and Islamic scriptures.

last laugh *n.* Ultimate success or victory, achieved after an apparent failure or loss: *After all was said and done, our competitors had the last laugh: they cornered the market.*

last minute *n.* The period just before a significant or awaited moment such as a deadline, due date, or scheduled event: *always waits until the last minute to do his holiday shopping.* **—last′-min′ute** (lăst′mĭn′ĭt) *adj.*

last rites *pl.n.* **1.** Rites performed in connection with a death or burial. **2.** A rite or sacrament administered to a dying person.

last straw *n.* The last of a series of annoyances or disappointments that leads one to a final loss of patience, temper, trust, or hope. [From the proverb "It's the last straw that breaks the camel's back."]

Last Supper *n.* Jesus's supper with his disciples on the night before his crucifixion, at which he instituted the Eucharist. Also called *Lord's Supper.*

last word *n.* **1.** The final statement in a verbal argument. **2. a.** A conclusive or authoritative statement or treatment: *The report was considered to be the last word on the hazards of smoking.* **b.** Power or authority of ultimate decision: *The treasurer has the last word in all financial matters.* **3.** *Informal.* The newest or most fashionable example of its kind; the latest thing: *a food processor that is the last word in kitchen equipment.*

Las Ve•gas (läs vā′gəs). A city of southeast Nevada near the California and Arizona borders. It is a major tourist center known for its casinos. Population, 164,674.

lat. *abbr.* Latitude.

Lat. *abbr.* **1.** Latin. **2.** Latvia; Latvian.

latch (lăch) *n.* **1.** A fastening, as for a door or gate, typically consisting of a bar that fits into a notch or slot and is lifted from either side by a lever or string. **2.** A spring lock, as for a door, that is opened from the outside by a key. **—latch** *v.* **latched, latch•ing, latch•es.** *—tr.* To close or lock with or as if with a latch. *—intr.* **1.** To have or be closed with a latch. **2.** To shut tightly so that the latch is engaged: *a door too warped to latch.* ***—idiom.*** **latch on to** (or **onto**). To get hold of; obtain: *latched on to a fortune in the fur trade.* [Middle English *latche,* from *lacchen,* to seize, from Old English *læccan.*]

latch•et (lăch′ĭt) *n.* A leather thong or strap used to fasten a shoe or sandal on the foot. [Middle English *lachet,* from Old French *lacet, lachet,* from *lace,* lace. See LACE.]

latch•key (lăch′kē′) *n.* A key for opening a latch or lock, especially one on an outside door.

latchkey child *n.* A usually school-age child who regularly spends part of the day unsupervised at home while the parents are at work.

latch•string (lăch′strĭng′) *n.* A cord attached to a latch and often passed through a hole in the door to allow lifting of the latch from the outside.

late (lāt) *adj.* **lat•er, lat•est.** *Abbr.* **l. 1.** Coming, occurring, or remaining after the correct, usual, or expected time; delayed: *The bus is late.* See Synonyms at **tardy. 2. a.** Beginning after or continuing past the usual or expected hour: *a late breakfast; a late meeting.* **b.** Occurring at an advanced hour, especially well into the evening or night: *a late movie on television; the late flight to Denver.* **3.** Of or toward the end or more advanced part, as of a period or stage: *the late 19th century; a later symptom of the disease.* **4. a.** Having begun or occurred just previous to the present time; recent: *a late development.* **b.** Contemporary; up-to-date: *the latest fashion.* **5. a.** Having recently occupied a position or place: *the company's late president gave the address.* **b.** Dead, especially if only recently deceased: *in memory of the late explorer.* **—late** *adv.* **later, latest. 1.** After the expected, usual, or proper time: *a train that arrived late; woke late and had to skip breakfast.* **2. a.** At or until an advanced hour: *talked late into the evening.* **b.** At or into an advanced period or stage: *a project undertaken late in her career.* **3.** Recently: *As late as last week he was still in town.* ***—idiom.*** **of late.** Recently; lately: *was feeling better of late.* [Middle English, from Old English *læt.* See **lē-** in Appendix.] **—late′ness** *n.*

USAGE NOTE: It is technically correct to use a phrase such as *our late treasurer* to refer to a person who is still alive but who no longer holds the relevant post, but the use of *former* in this context will ensure that no embarrassing misunderstanding is created.

late blight *n.* A disease of potato plants caused by the fungus *Phytophthora infestans* and characterized by decay of the foliage and tubers.

late•com•er (lāt′kŭm′ər) *n.* **1.** One that arrives late: *waited for the latecomers to be seated.* **2.** A recent arrival, participant, or convert: *a company that was a latecomer to the video-game market.*

lat•ed (lā′tĭd) *adj.* Belated. [From LATE.]

la•teen (lə-tēn′, lă-) *Nautical. adj.* Being, relating to, or rigged with a triangular sail hung on a long yard that is attached at an angle to the top of a short mast. **—lateen** *n.* **1.** A lateen-rigged boat. **2.** A lateen sail. [French *(voile) latine,* lateen (sail), feminine of *latin,* Latin (from its use in the Mediterranean), from Old French. See LATIN.]

Late Greek (lāt) *n.* The Greek language as used from the fourth to the ninth century A.D.

Late Hebrew *n.* The Hebrew language as used from the 12th to the 18th century.

Late Latin *n.* The Latin language as used from the third to the seventh century A.D.

late•ly (lāt′lē) *adv.* Not long ago; recently.

lat•en (lāt′n) *tr. & intr.v.* **-ened, -en•ing, -ens.** To make or grow late.

la•ten•cy (lāt′n-sē) *n., pl.* **-cies. 1.** The state or quality of being latent. **2.** The psychoanalytic stage of development, from about five years to puberty, during which a child represses sexual urges and prefers to associate with members of the same sex.

La Tène (lä tĕn′) *adj.* Of or relating to an Iron Age European civilization dating from the fifth to the first century B.C. [After *La Tène,* a district at the eastern end of the Lake of Neuchâtel in Switzerland.]

la•tent (lāt′nt) *adj.* **1.** Present or potential but not evident or active: *latent talent.* **2.** *Pathology.* In a dormant or hidden stage: *a latent infection.* **3.** *Biology.* Undeveloped but capable of normal growth under the proper conditions: *a latent bud.* **4.** *Psychology.* Present in the unconscious mind but not consciously expressed. **—latent** *n.* A fingerprint that is not apparent to the eye but can be made sufficiently visible, as by dusting or fuming, for use in identification. [Middle English, from Old French, from Latin *latēns, latent-,* present participle of *latēre,* to lie hidden.] **—la′tent•ly** *adv.*

lateen

SYNONYMS: *latent, dormant, quiescent.* These adjectives mean present or in existence but not active or manifest. What is *latent* is present but not visible or apparent: *latent energy; latent ability. His critical remark immediately awakened all her latent hostility. Dormant* evokes the idea of sleep; the term applies to what is inactive or in suspended animation: *a dormant volcano. Her enormous talents were dormant.* Persons or things are *quiescent* when they cease to be active; sometimes—but not always—the term suggests temporary inactivity: *"How for nine years you could be patient and quiescent under any treatment . . . I can never comprehend"* (Charlotte Brontë). *"For a time, he* [the whale] *lay quiescent"* (Herman Melville).

latent heat *n.* The quantity of heat absorbed or released by a substance undergoing a change of state, such as ice changing to water or water to steam, at constant temperature and pressure. Also called *heat of transformation.*

latent period *n.* **1.** The interval between exposure to an infectious organism or a carcinogen and the clinical appearance of disease. **2.** The interval between stimulus and response.

lat•er•al (lăt′ər-əl) *adj.* **1.** Of, relating to, or situated at or on the side. **2.** Of or constituting a change within an organization or a hierarchy to a position at a similar level, as in salary or responsibility, to the one being left: *made a lateral move within the company.* **3.** *Linguistics.* Of, relating to, or being a sound produced by breath passing along one or both sides of the tongue. **—lateral** *n.* **1.** A lateral part, projection, passage, or appendage. **2.** *Football.* A lateral pass. **3.** *Linguistics.* A lateral sound, such as (l). **—lateral** *v.* **-aled, -al•ing, -als** also **-alled, -al•ling, -als.** *Football. —intr.* To execute a lateral pass. *—tr.* To pass (the ball) sideways or backward. [Middle English, from Old French, from Latin *laterālis,* from *latus, later-,* side.] **—lat′er•al•ly** *adv.*

lateral bud *n.* A bud located on the side of the stem, usually in a leaf axil.

lat•er•al•i•za•tion (lăt′ər-ə-lĭ-zā′shən) *n.* Localization of function attributed to either the right or left side of the brain.

lateral line *n.* A series of sensory pores along the head and sides of fish and some amphibians by which water currents, vibrations, and pressure changes are detected.

lateral pass *n.* *Football.* A usually underhand pass that is thrown sideways or somewhat backward with respect to downfield.

lat•er•ite (lăt′ə-rīt′) *n.* A red residual soil in humid tropical and subtropical regions that is leached of soluble minerals, aluminum hydroxides, and silica but still contains concentrations of iron oxides and iron hydroxides. [Latin *later,* brick + -ITE[1].] **—lat′er•it′ic** (-rĭt′ĭk) *adj.*

lat•est (lā′tĭst) *adj.* Superlative of **late. —latest** *n.* Something that is the most recent or current of its kind: *the latest in electronic gadgetry.* ***—idiom.*** **at the latest.** No later than: *Have it done by Tuesday at the latest.*

la•tex (lā′tĕks′) *n., pl.* **la•ti•ces** (lā′tĭ-sēz′, lăt′ĭ-) or **la•tex•es. 1.** The colorless or milky sap of certain plants, such as the poinsettia or milkweed, that coagulates on exposure to air. **2.** An emulsion of rubber or plastic globules in water, used in paints, adhesives, and various synthetic rubber products. **3.** Latex paint. [Latin, fluid.] **—la′tex′** *adj.*

lathe
Working wood

latex paint *n.* A paint having a latex binder. Also called *rubber-base paint.*

lath (lăth) *n., pl.* **laths** (lăthz, lăths). **1. a.** A thin strip of wood or metal, usually nailed in rows to framing supports as a substructure for plaster, shingles, slates, or tiles. **b.** A building material, such as a sheet of metal mesh, used for similar purposes. **2. a.** A quantity of laths; lathing. **b.** Work made with or from lath. **—lath** *tr.v.* **lathed, lath•ing, laths.** To build, cover, or line with laths. [Middle English *latthe,* probably alteration (influenced by Welsh *llath,* rod) of Old English *lætt.*]

lathe (lāth) *n.* A machine for shaping a piece of material, such as wood or metal, by rotating it rapidly along its axis while pressing against a fixed cutting or abrading tool. **—lathe** *tr.v.* **lathed, lath•ing, lathes.** To cut or shape on a lathe. [Middle English, a device used by coopers, perhaps a turning lathe, probably of Scandinavian origin.]

lath•er (lăth′ər) *n.* **1.** A foam formed by soap or detergent agitated in water, as in washing or shaving. **2.** Froth formed by profuse sweating, as on a horse. **3.** *Informal.* A condition of anxious or heated discomposure; agitation: *The students were in a lather over the proposed restrictions.* **—lather** *v.* **-ered, -er•ing,**

ă pat	oi boy
ā pay	ou out
âr care	o͝o took
ä father	o͞o boot
ĕ pet	ŭ cut
ē be	ûr urge
ĭ pit	th thin
ī pie	*th* this
îr pier	hw which
ŏ pot	zh vision
ō toe	ə about, item
ô paw	♦ regionalism

Stress marks: **′** (primary); ′ (secondary), as in **dictionary** (dĭk′shə-nĕr′ē)

-ers. —*tr.* **1.** To spread with or as if with lather. **2.** *Informal.* To give a beating to; whip. —*intr.* **1.** To produce lather; foam. **2.** To become coated with lather. [Probably from Middle English *latheren,* to wash or soak clothes, from Old English *lēthran,* to cover with lather. See **leu(ə)-** in Appendix.] —**lath′er·y** *adj.*

lath·ing (lăth′ĭng, lăth′-) *n.* **1.** The act or process of building with laths. **2.** Work made of laths. **3.** A quantity of laths.

lath·y·rism (lăth′ə-rĭz′əm) *n.* A disease of human beings and animals caused by eating legumes of the genus *Lathyrus* and characterized by spastic paralysis, hyperesthesia, and paresthesia. [From New Latin *Lathyrus,* genus name, from Greek *lathuros,* a type of pea.]

la·ti·ces (lā′tĭ-sēz′, lăt′ĭ-) *n.* A plural of **latex.**

la·tic·i·fer (lā-tĭs′ə-fər) *n.* A plant duct containing latex. [Latin *latex, latic-,* fluid; see LATEX + -FER.]

lat·i·cif·er·ous (lăt′ĭ-sĭf′ər-əs) *adj.* Producing or containing latex.

lat·i·fun·di·um (lăt′ə-fŭn′dē-əm) *n., pl.* **-di·a** (-dē-ə). A great landed estate, especially of the ancient Romans. [Latin *lātifundium* : *lātus,* broad + *fundus,* estate, base.]

Lat·i·mer (lăt′ə-mər), **Hugh.** 1485?–1555. English prelate who refused to recant his Protestantism after the accession of Mary I, a Catholic, and was executed for heresy.

Latin cross

Lat·in (lăt′n). *Abbr.* **Lat., L.** *n.* **1.a.** The Indo-European language of the ancient Latins and Romans. Latin, the most important member of the Italic branch of Indo-European, is divided into several historical periods and social dialects and was the most important cultural language of western Europe until the end of the 17th century. **b.** The Latin language and literature from the end of the third century B.C. to the end of the second century A.D. **2.** A member of a Latin people, especially a native or inhabitant of Latin America. **3.** A native or resident of ancient Latium. —**Latin** *adj.* **1.** Of, relating to, or composed in Latin: *a Latin scholar; Latin verse.* **2.a.** Of or relating to ancient Rome, its people, or its culture. **b.** Of or relating to Latium, its people, or its culture. **3.a.** Of or relating to the languages that developed from Latin, such as Italian, French, Spanish, and Portuguese, or to the peoples that speak them. **b.** Of or relating to the peoples, countries, or cultures of Latin America. **4.** Of or relating to the Roman Catholic Church. [Middle English, from Old French and from Old English *Lātīn,* both from Latin *Latīnus,* from *Latium,* an ancient country of west-central Italy.]

La·ti·na[1] (lə-tē′nə, lă-) *n.* A Latino woman or girl. [Spanish, Latin, from Latin *Latīna,* feminine of *Latīnus.* See LATIN.]

La·ti·na[2] (lə-tē′nə, lä-tē′nä). A city of west-central Italy southeast of Rome. Population, 81,000.

Latin alphabet *n.* The Roman alphabet adopted from the Greek by way of the Etruscan alphabet, consisting of 23 letters upon which the modern western European alphabets are founded. Also called *Roman alphabet.*

Latin A·mer·i·ca (ə-mĕr′ĭ-kə). The countries of the Western Hemisphere south of the United States, especially those speaking Spanish, Portuguese, or French.

Latin American *n.* **1.** A native or inhabitant of Latin America. **2.** A person of Latin-American descent. —**Lat′in-A·mer′i·can** (lăt′n-ə-mĕr′ĭ-kən) *adj.*

Lat·in·ate (lăt′n-āt′) *adj.* Of, derived from, or suggestive of Latin: *a Latinate word; a formal, Latinate prose style.*

Latin Church *n.* The Roman Catholic Church.

Latin cross *n.* A cross with a shorter horizontal bar intersecting a longer vertical bar above the midpoint.

Lat·in·ism (lăt′n-ĭz′əm) *n.* An idiom, a structure, or a word derived from or suggestive of Latin.

Lat·in·ist (lăt′n-ĭst) *n.* A specialist in Latin.

lattice
Pattern on a trellis

La·tin·i·ty (lə-tĭn′ĭ-tē) *n.* The manner in which Latin is used in speaking or writing.

Lat·in·ize (lăt′n-īz′) *v.* **-ized, -iz·ing, -iz·es.** —*tr.* **1.a.** To translate into Latin. **b.** To transliterate into the Latin alphabet; Romanize. **2.** To cause to adopt or acquire Latin characteristics or customs. **3.** To cause to follow or resemble the Roman Catholic Church in dogma or practices. —*intr.* To use Latinisms. —**Lat′in·i·za′tion** (-ĭ-zā′shən) *n.* —**Lat′in·iz′er** *n.*

La·ti·no (lə-tē′nō, lă-) *n., pl.* **-nos.** **1.** A Latin American. **2.** A person of Hispanic, especially Latin-American, descent. See Usage Note at **Hispanic.** [Spanish, Latin, from Latin *Latīnus.* See LATIN.]

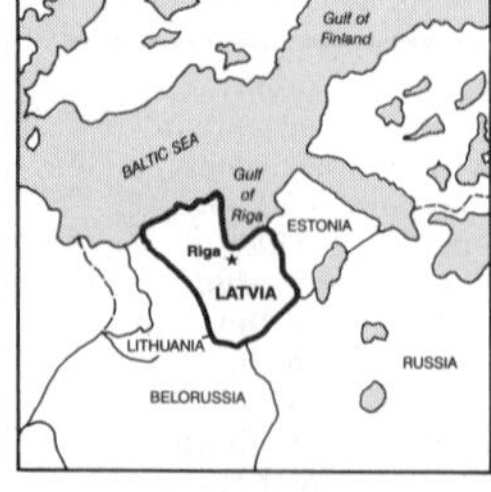

Latvia

Latin Quar·ter (kwôr′tər). A section of Paris on the southern bank of the Seine River. Centered around the Sorbonne, it has attracted students for many centuries.

lat·ish (lā′tĭsh) *adv. & adj.* Fairly late.

la·tis·si·mus dor·si (lə-tĭs′ə-məs dôr′sī) *n., pl.* **la·tis·si·mi dorsi** (lə-tĭs′ə-mī′ dôr′sī). Either of two broad, flat, triangular muscles running from the vertebral column to the humerus. [New Latin *lātissimus dorsī* : Latin *lātissimus,* superlative of *lātus,* wide + Latin *dorsī,* genitive of *dorsum,* back.]

lat·i·tude (lăt′ĭ-to͞od′, -tyo͞od′) *n. Abbr.* **lat.** **1.a.** The angular distance north or south of the earth's equator, measured in degrees along a meridian, as on a map or globe. **b.** A region of the earth considered in relation to its distance from the equator: *temperate latitudes.* **2.** *Astronomy.* The angular distance of a celestial body north or south of the ecliptic. **3.** Freedom from normal restraints, limitations, or regulations. See Synonyms at **room.** **4.** A range of values or conditions, especially the range of exposures over which a photographic film yields usable images. **5.** Extent; breadth. [Middle English, geographical latitude, from Old French, width, from Latin *lātitūdō,* width, geographical latitude, from *lātus,* wide.] —**lat′i·tu′din·al** (-to͞od′n-əl, -tyo͞od′-) *adj.* —**lat′i·tu′di·nal·ly** *adv.*

lat·i·tu·di·nar·i·an (lăt′ĭ-to͞od′n-âr′ē-ən, -tyo͞od′-) *adj.* Holding or expressing broad or tolerant views, especially in religious matters. [Latin *lātitūdō, lātitūdin-,* latitude; see LATITUDE + -ARIAN.] —**lat′i·tu′di·nar′i·an** *n.* —**lat′i·tu′di·nar′i·an·ism** *n.*

La·ti·um (lā′shē-əm, -shəm). An ancient country of west-central Italy bordering on the Tyrrhenian Sea. It was dominated by Rome after the third century B.C.

lat·ke (lät′kə) *n.* A pancake, especially one made of grated potato. [Yiddish, from Ukrainian *oladka,* from Old Russian, diminutive of *olad'ya,* from Greek *eladia,* pl. of *eladion,* little oily thing, diminutive of *elaion,* olive oil.]

lat·o·sol (lăt′ə-sôl′, -sŏl′) *n.* Soil that is rich in iron, alumina, or silica and formed in tropical woodlands under very humid climate with relatively high temperature. [LAT(ERITE) + *-sol,* soil (from Latin *solum*).]

La Tour (lə to͝or′, lä to͝or′), **Georges de.** 1593–1652. French painter of religious subjects and genre scenes. Many of his works are dramatically lit nocturnal scenes.

la·trine (lə-trēn′) *n.* A communal toilet of a type often used in a camp or barracks. [From French *latrines,* privies, from Old French, from Latin *lātrīna,* from *lavātrīna,* bath, privy. See **leu(ə)-** in Appendix.]

La·trobe (lə-trōb′), **Benjamin Henry.** 1764–1820. British-born American engineer and the first professional American architect. His works include the Baltimore Cathedral (1805–1818) and the chambers of the U.S. Congress and Supreme Court.

-latry *suff.* Worship: *bibliolatry.* [From Greek *latreia,* service, worship.]

lat·ten (lăt′n) *n.* **1.** Brass or an alloy resembling brass, hammered thin and formerly used in the manufacture of church vessels. **2.** A thin sheet of metal, especially of tin. [Middle English *laton,* from Old French, from Arabic *lātūn,* probably from Old Turkic *altun,* gold; akin to Mongolian *altan.*]

lat·ter (lăt′ər) *adj.* **1.** Being the second of two persons or things mentioned: *Between captain and major, the latter is the higher rank.* See Usage Note at **former**[2]. **2.** Near or nearer to the end: *the latter part of the book.* **3.** Further advanced in time or sequence; later: *a style that has been revived in latter times.* [Middle English, later, from Old English *lætra.* See **lē-** in Appendix.] —**lat′ter·ly** *adv.*

lat·ter-day (lăt′ər-dā′) *adj.* Belonging to present or recent times; modern.

Lat·ter-day Saint (lăt′ər-dā′) *n.* See **Mormon** (sense 2).

lat·tice (lăt′ĭs) *n.* **1.a.** An open framework made of strips of metal, wood, or similar material overlapped or overlaid in a regular, usually crisscross pattern. **b.** A structure, such as a window, screen, or trellis, made of or containing such a framework. **2.** Something, such as a decorative motif or heraldic bearing, that resembles an open, patterned framework. **3.** *Physics.* **a.** A regular, periodic configuration of points, particles, or objects throughout an area or a space, especially the arrangement of ions or molecules in a crystalline solid. **b.** The spatial arrangement of fissionable and nonfissionable materials in a nuclear reactor. —**lattice** *tr.v.* **-ticed, -tic·ing, -tic·es.** To construct or furnish with a lattice or latticework. [Middle English *latis,* from Old French *lattis,* from *latte,* lath, of Germanic origin.] —**lat′ticed** *adj.*

lat·tice·work (lăt′ĭs-wûrk′) *n.* **1.** A lattice or latticelike structure. **2.** An open, crisscross pattern or weave.

Lat·vi·a (lăt′vē-ə). *Abbr.* **Lat.** A country of northern Europe on the Baltic Sea. Conquered and Christianized by the Livonian Brothers of the Sword in the 13th century, Latvia passed under Russian control in the 18th century. It became independent after World War I but was annexed by the U.S.S.R. in 1940. It officially became a constituent republic in August 1940. Latvia made a formal declaration of independence in March 1990 and was admitted to the United Nations in September 1991. Riga is the capital. Population, 2,604,000.

Lat·vi·an (lăt′vē-ən) *adj. Abbr.* **Lat.** Of or relating to Latvia or its people, language, or culture. —**Latvian** *n. Abbr.* **Lat.** **1.** A native or inhabitant of Latvia. **2.** The Baltic language of the Latvians. In this sense, also called *Lettish.*

laud (lôd) *tr.v.* **laud·ed, laud·ing, lauds.** To give praise to; glorify. See Synonyms at **praise.** —**laud** *n.* **1.** Praise; glorification. **2.** A hymn or song of praise. **3.** Often **Lauds** *(used with a sing. or pl. verb).* **a.** The service of prayers following the matins and constituting with them the first of the seven canonical hours. **b.** The time appointed for this service. [Middle English *lauden,* from Old French *lauder,* from Latin *laudāre,* from *laus, laud-,* praise.] —**laud′er** *n.*

Laud (lôd), **William.** 1573–1645. English prelate who as archbishop of Canterbury (1633–1645) was a strident supporter of Charles I and absolutism in church and state. His attempts to impose High Church doctrine led to his imprisonment and execution for treason by Parliament.

laud·a·ble (lô′də-bəl) *adj.* Deserving commendation; praiseworthy. **—laud′a·bil′i·ty, laud′a·ble·ness** *n.* **—laud′a·bly** *adv.*

lau·da·num (lôd′n-əm) *n.* A tincture of opium, formerly used as a drug. [New Latin, perhaps alteration of Medieval Latin *labdanum,* labdanum. See LABDANUM.]

laud·a·tion (lô-dā′shən) *n.* The act of lauding; praise.

laud·a·tive (lô′də-tĭv) *adj.* Laudatory.

laud·a·to·ry (lô′də-tôr′ē, -tōr′ē) *adj.* Expressing or conferring praise: *a laudatory review of the new play.*

Lau·der (lô′dər), Sir **Harry MacLennan.** 1870–1950. British singer noted for his comic stage persona, a wry and nostalgic Highlander.

Lau·der·dale Lakes (lô′dər-dāl′). A city of southeast Florida, a residential suburb of Fort Lauderdale. Population, 25,426.

Lau·der·hill (lô′dər-hĭl′). A city of southeast Florida, a residential suburb of Fort Lauderdale. Population 37,271.

laugh (lăf, läf) *v.* **laughed, laugh·ing, laughs.** —*intr.* **1.** To express certain emotions, especially mirth, delight, or derision, by a series of spontaneous, usually unarticulated sounds often accompanied by corresponding facial and bodily movements. **2.** To show or feel amusement or good humor: *laughed to herself at the memory; an experience we would laugh about later on.* **3.a.** To feel or express derision or contempt; mock: *We used to laugh at their provincial manners. I had to laugh when I saw who my opponent was.* **b.** To feel a triumphant or exultant sense of well-being: *You won't be laughing when the truth comes out.* **4.** To produce sounds resembling laughter: *parrots laughing and chattering in the trees.* —*tr.* **1.** To affect or influence by laughter: *laughed the speaker off the stage; laughed the proposal down.* **2.** To say with a laugh: *He laughed his delight at the victory.* **—laugh** *n.* **1.a.** The act of laughing. **b.** The sound of laughing; laughter. **2.** *Informal.* Something amusing, absurd, or contemptible; a joke: *The solution they recommended was a laugh.* **3.** Often **laughs.** *Informal.* Fun; amusement: *decided to go along just for laughs.* **—*phrasal verbs.* laugh at.** To treat lightly; scoff at: *a daredevil who laughed at danger.* **laugh off** (or **away**). To dismiss as ridiculously or laughably trivial: *laughed off any suggestion that her career was over.* **—*idiom.* laugh up** (or **in**) **(one's) sleeve.** To rejoice or exult in secret, as at another's error or defeat. [Middle English *laughen,* from Old English *hlæhhan,* probably ultimately of imitative origin.] **—laugh′er** *n.* **—laugh′ing·ly** *adv.*

laugh·a·ble (lăf′ə-bəl, lä′fə-) *adj.* Causing or deserving laughter or derision. **—laugh′a·bly** *adv.*

laugh·ing gas (lăf′ĭng, lä′fĭng) *n.* Nitrous oxide, especially as used as an anesthetic.

laughing jackass *n.* See **kookaburra.**

laugh·ing·stock (lăf′ĭng-stŏk′, lä′fĭng-) *n.* An object of jokes or ridicule; a butt.

laugh·ter (lăf′tər, läf′-) *n.* **1.** The act of laughing. **2.** The sound produced by laughing. **3.** *Archaic.* A cause or subject for laughter. [Middle English, from Old English *hleahtor,* probably ultimately of imitative origin.]

Laugh·ton (lôt′n), **Charles.** 1899–1962. British-born American actor whose many motion-picture roles include that of Captain Bligh in *Mutiny on the Bounty* (1935).

laugh track *n.* Recorded laughter added to a soundtrack, as of a television or radio show.

launce (lăns, läns, lôns) *n.* See **sand lance.** [Perhaps alteration of LANCE.]

launch¹ (lônch, länch) *v.* **launched, launch·ing, launch·es.** —*tr.* **1.a.** To throw or propel with force; hurl: *launch a spear.* **b.** To set or thrust (a self-propelled craft or projectile) in motion: *launch a rocket; launch a torpedo.* **2.** *Nautical.* To put (a boat) into the water in readiness for use. **3.** To set going; initiate: *launch a career; launch a business venture.* **4.** To introduce to the public or to a market: *launched the new perfume with prime-time commercials on the major networks.* **5.** To give (someone) a start, as in a career or vocation. —*intr.* **1.** To begin a new venture or phase; embark: *launch forth on a dangerous mission; launched out on her own after college.* **2.** To enter enthusiastically into something; plunge: *launched into a description of the movie.* **—launch** *n.* The act of launching. [Middle English *launchen,* from Old North French *lancher,* from Latin *lanceāre,* to wield a lance, from *lancea,* lance. See LANCE.]

launch² (lônch, länch) *n.* *Nautical.* **1.** A large ship's boat. **2.** A large, open motorboat. [Probably alteration (probably influenced by LAUNCH¹) of Malay *lancha.*]

launch·er (lôn′chər, län′-) *n.* One that launches, as: **a.** A rifle attachment for firing grenades. **b.** A device, such as an attached tube or a portable unit, for firing rockets. **c.** An aircraft catapult.

launch·ing pad (lôn′chĭng, län′-) *n.* A launch pad.

launch pad *n.* **1.** The base or platform from which a rocket or space vehicle is launched. **2.** A foundation or starting point.

launch vehicle *n.* A rocket used to launch a spacecraft or satellite into an orbit or a trajectory.

launch window *n.* A brief, specific period of time during which a spacecraft or projectile must be launched so that a desired mission or effect can be achieved.

laun·der (lôn′dər, län′-) *v.* **-dered, -der·ing, -ders.** —*tr.* **1.a.** To wash (clothes, for example). **b.** To wash, fold, and iron: *shirts that were neatly laundered by the hotel staff.* **2.** To disguise the source or nature of (illegal funds, for example) by channeling through an intermediate agent. **3.** To make more acceptable or presentable, sanitize: *"The transcripts are, of course, laundered . . . unidentified larger chunks of conversation are reported missing throughout"* (Eliot Fremont-Smith). —*intr.* **1.** To undergo washing in a specified way: *This material launders well.* **2.** To wash or prepare laundry. **—launder** *n.* A trough or flume used in washing ore. [From Middle English *launder, lavender,* launderer, from Old French *lavandier,* from Vulgar Latin **lavandārius,* from Latin *lavandāria,* things to be washed, from *lavanda,* neuter pl. gerundive of *lavāre,* to wash. See LAVE.]

laun·der·ette (lôn′də-rĕt′, län′-) *n.* A self-service laundry. [LAUNDER + -ETTE.]

laun·dress (lôn′drĭs, län′-) *n.* A woman employed to launder clothes or linens.

Laun·dro·mat (lôn′drə-măt′, län′-). A service mark used for a commercial establishment equipped with washing machines and dryers, usually coin-operated and self-service. This service mark often occurs in print in lowercase: *"pointed to a laundromat and a restaurant as viable businesses"* (Alaska Business Monthly). *"A car veered out of control and hit him and his mother as they left a Brooklyn laundromat"* (New York Times).

laun·dry (lôn′drē, län′-) *n., pl.* **-dries. 1.** Soiled or laundered clothes and linens; wash. **2.a.** A commercial establishment for laundering clothes or linens. **b.** A room or an area, as in a house, for doing the wash. [Middle English *lavendrye, laundry,* from Old French *lavanderie,* from *lavandier.* See LAUNDER.]

laundry list *n.* *Informal.* An item-by-item enumeration.

Laur·a·sia (lô-rā′zhə, -shə) *n.* The protocontinent of the Northern Hemisphere, a hypothetical landmass that according to the theory of plate tectonics broke up into North America, Europe, and Asia. [New Latin *Laur(entia),* geologic precursor of North America (after the SAINT LAWRENCE RIVER) + (EUR)ASIA.]

lau·re·ate (lôr′ē-ĭt, lŏr′-) *adj.* **1.** Worthy of the greatest honor or distinction: *"The nation's pediatrician laureate is preparing to lay down his black bag"* (James Traub). **2.** Crowned or decked with laurel as a mark of honor. **3.** *Archaic.* Made of laurel sprigs, as a wreath or crown. **—laureate** *n.* **1.** One honored or awarded a prize for great achievements especially in the arts or sciences: *a Nobel laureate.* **2.** A poet laureate. [Middle English, from Latin *laureātus,* adorned with laurel, from *laurea,* crown of laurel, from feminine of *laureus,* of laurel, from *laurus,* laurel.] **—lau′re·ate·ship′** *n.*

lau·rel (lôr′əl, lŏr′-) *n.* **1.** A Mediterranean evergreen tree *(Laurus nobilis)* having aromatic, simple leaves and small blackish berries. Also called *bay, bay laurel, sweet bay.* **2.** A shrub or tree, such as the mountain laurel, having a similar aroma or leaf shape. **3.** Often **laurels. a.** A wreath of laurel conferred as a mark of honor in ancient times upon poets, heroes, and victors in athletic contests. **b.** Honor and glory won for great achievement. **—laurel** *tr.v.* **-reled, -rel·ing, -rels** also **-relled, -rel·ling, -rels. 1.** To crown with laurel. **2.** To honor, especially with an award or a prize. [Middle English, from Old French *laureole,* from Latin *laureola,* diminutive of *laurea,* laurel tree. See LAUREATE.]

Lau·rel (lôr′əl, lŏr′-). A city of southeast Mississippi southwest of Meridian. Population, 21,897.

Laurel, Arthur Stanley Jefferson. Known as "Stan." 1890–1965. British-born American comedian who with Oliver Hardy formed the first great comedy team of talking films. Their works include *The Music Box* (1932) and *A Chump at Oxford* (1940).

Lau·ren·cin (lô-räN-săN′), **Marie.** 1885–1956. French artist noted for her soft, pastel technique in portraiture.

Lau·rens (lôr′ənz, lŏr′-), **Henry.** 1724–1792. American Revolutionary leader. A member (1777–1779) and president (1777–1778) of the Continental Congress, he was captured by the British while en route to Holland to obtain aid for the colonists (1780). Exchanged for Cornwallis (1782), he also helped negotiate the Treaty of Paris (1782–1784).

Lau·ren·tian (lô-rĕn′shən) *adj.* **1.** Of, relating to, or being in the vicinity of the St. Lawrence River. **2.** *Geology.* Of or relating to the Precambrian gneissic granite of the Lake Superior area. [From Latin *Laurentius,* Lawrence.]

Laurentian Mountains. A range of southern Quebec, Canada, north of the St. Lawrence and Ottawa rivers. Rising to 960.8 m (3,150 ft), the mountains are a year-round recreational area.

Laurentian Plateau or **Laurentian Highlands** also **Ca·na·di·an Shield** (kə-nā′dē-ən). A plateau region of eastern Canada extending from the Great Lakes and the St. Lawrence River northward to the Arctic Ocean. The highland formation also covers much of Greenland and forms the Adirondack Mountains in the United States.

lau·ric acid (lôr′ĭk, lŏr′-) *n.* A fatty acid, $CH_3(CH_2)_{10}COOH$, obtained chiefly from coconut and laurel oils and used in making soaps, cosmetics, esters, and lauryl alcohol. [Latin *laurus,* laurel + -IC.]

Lau·ri·er (lôr′ē-ā′, lŏr′-), Sir **Wilfrid.** 1841–1919. Canadian politician who served as prime minister (1896–1911).

lau·ryl alcohol (lôr′əl, lŏr′-) *n.* A colorless solid alcohol, $CH_3(CH_2)_{11}OH$, used in synthetic detergents and pharmaceuticals. [LAUR(EL) + -YL.]

Lau·sanne (lō-zăn′, -zän′). A city of western Switzerland on

launch pad
Apollo 15 prior to launching on July 26, 1971

laurels
White marble low relief of Papinian (A.D. 140?–212?) wearing crown of laurels, by Laura Gardin Fraser (1889–1966)

ă pat	oi boy
ā pay	ou out
âr care	ŏŏ took
ä father	ōō boot
ĕ pet	ŭ cut
ē be	ûr urge
ĭ pit	th thin
ī pie	*th* this
îr pier	hw which
ŏ pot	zh vision
ō toe	ə about, item
ô paw	♦ regionalism

Stress marks: **′** (primary); ′ (secondary), as in **dictionary** (dĭk′shə-nĕr′ē)

lava
Encroaching on a roadway

the northern shore of Lake Geneva. Originally a Celtic settlement, Lausanne became a center of Calvinism after the 1530's. Population, 126,200.

lav. *abbr.* Lavatory.

la·va (lä′və, lăv′ə) *n.* **1.** Molten rock that reaches the earth's surface through a volcano or fissure. **2.** The rock formed by the cooling and solidifying of molten rock. [Italian, perhaps from Latin *lābēs,* fall, from Latin *lābī,* to fall.]

WORD HISTORY: Lava was appropriately named by people living near Mount Vesuvius. The only active volcano on the European mainland, Vesuvius has erupted frequently since Pompeii and Herculaneum were buried by it in A.D. 79. The Neapolitans who lived in the vicinity took a word in Italian, *lava,* meaning "a stream caused suddenly by rain," and applied it to the streams of molten rock coming down the sides of Vesuvius. The term was then taken into Standard Italian, where it came to mean the rock in both its molten and its solidified states. The Italian word in all its senses was borrowed into English around the middle of the 18th century (1750 being the earliest date of record).

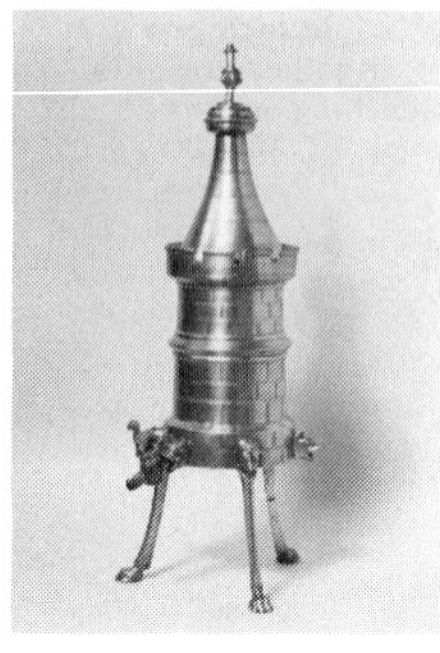

laver¹
14th- to 15th-century bronze turret-shaped laver

la·va·bo (lə-vā′bō, -vä′-) *n., pl.* **-boes. 1.** Often **Lavabo.** The ceremonial washing of the hands and recitation from the Psalms by the celebrant before the Eucharist in the Roman Catholic and Anglican churches. **2.** A washbowl that is attached to a wall and filled from a water tank fastened above. [Latin *lavābō,* I shall wash (opening word of the recited portion of Psalm 26), first person future indicative of *lavāre,* to wash. See LAVE.]

lav·age (lăv′ĭj, lä-väzh′) *n.* A washing, especially of a hollow organ, such as the stomach or lower bowel, with repeated injections of water. [French, from Old French, from *laver,* to wash, from Latin *lavāre.* See LAVE.]

La·val (lə-văl′, lä-väl′). A city of southern Quebec, Canada, on an island opposite Montreal, of which it is a residential suburb. Population, 268,335.

Laval, Pierre. 1883–1945. French politician who twice served as prime minister (1931–1932 and 1935–1936) and became head of the Vichy government (1942) after the surrender of France.

la·va-la·va (lä′və-lä′və) *n.* A Polynesian, especially Samoan, garment consisting of a rectangular piece of printed cotton tied loosely around the waist. [Samoan.]

lav·a·liere (lăv′ə-lîr′) also **la·val·lière** (lä′vä-lyâr′) *n.* A pendant worn on a chain around the neck. [French *lavallière,* type of necktie, after Duchesse de LA VALLIÈRE.]

La Val·lière (lä vəl-yĕr′, vä-lyâr′), Duchesse de. Title of Françoise Louise de la Baume Le Blanc. 1644–1710. French noblewoman. The lover of Louis XIV, she had four children with him.

la·va·tion (lă-vā′shən, lā-) *n.* The process of washing; a cleansing. [Latin *lavātiō, lavātiōn-,* from *lavātus,* past participle of *lavāre,* to wash. See LAVE.]

lav·a·to·ry (lăv′ə-tôr′ē, -tōr′ē) *n., pl.* **-ries.** *Abbr.* **lav. 1.** A room equipped with washing and often toilet facilities; a bathroom. **2.** A washbowl or basin, especially one permanently installed with running water. **3.** A flush toilet. [Middle English, piscina, from Late Latin *lavātōrium,* from *lavātor,* launderer, from *lavāre,* to wash. See LAVE.]

Antoine Lavoisier
Detail from *Antoine Laurent Lavoisier and his Wife* by Jacques Louis David

lave (lāv) *v.* **laved, lav·ing, laves.** —*tr.* **1.** To wash; bathe. **2.** To lap or wash against. **3.** To refresh or soothe as if by washing: *"The quiet and the cool laved her"* (Edna Ferber). —*intr. Archaic.* To wash oneself. [Middle English *laven,* from Old English *gelafian* and from Old French *laver,* both from Latin *lavāre.* See **leu(ə)-** in Appendix.]

lav·en·der (lăv′ən-dər) *n.* **1.a.** Any of various aromatic Old World plants of the genus *Lavandula,* especially *L. angustifolia,* having clusters of small purplish flowers that yield an oil used in perfumery. **b.** The fragrant dried leaves, stems, and flowers of this plant. **2.** *Color.* A pale to light purple to very light or very pale violet. [Middle English *lavendre,* from Anglo-Norman, from Medieval Latin *livendula, lavendula,* perhaps from Latin *līvidus,* bluish. See LIVID.] —**lav′en·der** *adj.*

la·ver¹ (lā′vər) *n.* **1.** A large basin used in the ancient Jewish Temple by a priest for ablutions before making a sacrificial offering. **2.** *Archaic.* A vessel, stone basin, or trough used for washing. [Middle English, water pitcher, from Old French *laveoir,* probably from Late Latin *lavātōrium.* See LAVATORY.]

la·ver² (lā′vər) *n.* Any of several dried, edible seaweeds of the genera *Porphyra* (the red algae) and *Ulva* (the green algae). [Middle English, a water plant, from Old English *læfer,* from Latin.]

lawn mower

La Vé·ren·drye (lä vā-räN-drē′), Sieur de. Title of Pierre Gaultier de Varennes. 1685–1749. French-Canadian explorer who established a chain of trading posts in New France, thus breaking Britain's economic stronghold on the region.

La Verne (lə vûrn′). A city of southern California east of Los Angeles. It is mainly residential. Population, 23,508.

lav·ish (lăv′ĭsh) *adj.* **1.** Characterized by or produced with extravagance and profusion: *a lavish buffet.* See Synonyms at **profuse. 2.** Immoderate in giving or bestowing; unstinting: *The critics were lavish with their praise.* —**lavish** *tr.v.* **-ished, -ish·ing, -ish·es.** To give or bestow in abundance; shower: *lavished attention on his customers.* [Middle English *laves,* probably from Old French *lavasse,* downpour, from *laver,* to wash, from Latin *lavāre.* See LAVE.] —**lav′ish·er** *n.* —**lav′ish·ly** *adv.* —**lav′ish·ness** *n.*

La·voi·sier (lə-vwä′zē-ā′, lä-vwä-zyā′), **Antoine Laurent.** 1743–1794. French chemist who is regarded as the founder of modern chemistry. He isolated the major components of air and organized the classification of compounds.

law (lô) *n.* **1.** A rule of conduct or procedure established by custom, agreement, or authority. **2.a.** The body of rules and principles governing the affairs of a community and enforced by a political authority; a legal system: *international law.* **b.** The condition of social order and justice created by adherence to such a system: *a breakdown of law and civilized behavior.* **3.** A set of rules or principles dealing with a specific area of a legal system: *tax law; criminal law.* **4.** A piece of enacted legislation. **5.a.** The system of judicial administration giving effect to the laws of a community: *All citizens are equal before the law.* **b.** Legal action or proceedings; litigation: *submit a dispute to law.* **c.** An impromptu or extralegal system of justice substituted for established judicial procedure: *frontier law.* **6.a.** An agency or agent responsible for enforcing the law. Often used with *the*: *"The law . . . stormed out of the woods as the vessel was being relieved of her cargo"* (Sid Moody). **b.** *Informal.* A police officer. Often used with *the.* **7.a.** The science and study of law; jurisprudence. **b.** Knowledge of law. **c.** The profession of an attorney. **8.** Something, such as an order or a dictum, having absolute or unquestioned authority: *The commander's word was law.* **9. Law. a.** The body of principles or precepts held to express the divine will, especially as revealed in the Bible: *Mosaic Law.* **b.** The first five books of the Hebrew Scriptures. **10.** A code of principles based on morality, conscience, or nature. **11.a.** A rule or custom generally established in a particular domain: *the unwritten laws of good sportsmanship.* **b.** A way of life: *the law of the jungle.* **12.a.** A formulation describing a relationship observed to be invariable between or among phenomena for all cases in which the specified conditions are met: *the law of gravity.* **b.** A generalization based on consistent experience or results: *the law of supply and demand; the law of averages.* **13.** *Mathematics.* A general principle or rule that is assumed or that has been proven to hold between expressions. **14.** A principle of organization, procedure, or technique: *the laws of grammar; the laws of visual perspective.* —**law** *intr.v.* **lawed, law·ing, laws.** To go to law; litigate. —***idioms.* a law unto (oneself).** A totally independent operator: *An executive who is a law unto herself.* **take the law into (one's) own hands.** To mete out justice as one sees fit without due recourse to law enforcement agencies or the courts. [Middle English, from Old English *lagu,* from Old Norse **lagu,* sing. of *lög,* pl. of *lag,* that which is laid down. See **legh-** in Appendix.]

Law, (Andrew) Bonar. 1858–1923. Canadian-born British politician who served as prime minister (1922–1923).

Law, John. 1671–1729. Scottish financier active in France, where he engaged in highly profitable speculation on the development of Louisiana. The investment scheme ultimately collapsed, and he fled the country in ruin (1720).

law-a·bid·ing (lô′ə-bī′dĭng) *adj.* Adhering to the law.

law-and-or·der (lô′ən-ôr′dər) *adj.* Advocating and following the established social order and the statutes written to enforce such order: *running for election as the law-and-order candidate.*

law·break·er (lô′brā′kər) *n.* One that breaks the law.

law clerk *n.* A person, typically an attorney, employed as an assistant to a judge or another attorney, especially in order to gain legal experience.

law·ful (lô′fəl) *adj.* **1.** Being within the law; allowed by law: *lawful methods of dissent.* **2.** Established, sanctioned, or recognized by the law: *the lawful heir.* **3.** Obeying the law; law-abiding. —**law′ful·ly** *adv.* —**law′ful·ness** *n.*

law·giv·er (lô′gĭv′ər) *n.* **1.** One who gives a code of laws to a people. **2.** See **lawmaker.**

law·less (lô′lĭs) *adj.* **1.** Unrestrained by law; unruly: *a lawless mob.* **2.** Contrary to the law; unlawful: *the lawless slaughter of protected species.* **3.** Not governed by law: *the lawless frontier.* —**law′less·ly** *adv.* —**law′less·ness** *n.*

law·mak·er (lô′mā′kər) *n.* One who makes or enacts laws; a legislator. Also called *lawgiver.* —**law′mak′ing** *n.*

law·man (lô′măn′, -mən) *n.* A law officer, such as a sheriff or marshal.

law merchant *n., pl.* **laws merchant.** A body of principles and regulations applied to commercial transactions and deriving from the established customs of merchants and traders rather than the jurisprudence of a particular nation or state.

lawn¹ (lôn) *n.* A plot of grass, usually tended or mowed, as one around a residence or in a park or an estate. [Alteration of Middle English *launde,* glade, from Old French *launde,* heath, pasture, wooded area. See **lendh-** in Appendix.]

lawn² (lôn) *n.* A light cotton or linen fabric of very fine weave. [Middle English *laun,* after *Laon,* a city of northern France.]

lawn bowling *n. Sports & Games.* A game played on a level lawn in which players roll biased wooden balls as close as possible to a smaller target ball. Also called *bowls.*

Lawn·dale (lôn′dāl′). A city of southern California southwest of Los Angeles near the Pacific Ocean. Population, 23,460.

lawn mower also **lawn·mow·er** (lôn′mō′ər) *n.* A machine with a rotating blade for cutting grass.

lawn tennis *n. Sports.* See **tennis** (sense 1).

law of averages *n.* The principle holding that probability will influence all occurrences in the long term.

law of diminishing returns *n.* The tendency for a continuing application of effort or skill toward a particular project or goal to decline in effectiveness after a certain level of result has been achieved.

law of independent assortment *n.* See **Mendel's law** (sense 2).

law of large numbers *n. Statistics.* The rule or theorem that a large number of items chosen at random from a population will, on the average, have the characteristics of the population. Also called *Bernoulli's law.*

Law of Moses *n.* See **Mosaic Law.**

law of nations *n.* See **international law.**

law of parsimony *n.* See **Ockham's razor.**

law of segregation *n.* See **Mendel's law** (sense 1).

Law·rence (lôr′əns, lŏr′-). **1.** A city of central Indiana, a residential suburb of Indianapolis. Population, 25,591. **2.** A city of northeast Kansas on the Kansas River east-southeast of Topeka. It was founded in 1854 by the New England Emigrant Aid Society and was the scene of a proslavery raid (1856) that sparked retaliatory killings by the abolitionist John Brown. Population, 52,738. **3.** A city of northeast Massachusetts on the Merrimack River north-northeast of Lowell. Laid out as an industrial town in 1845, it soon became one of the world's greatest centers for woolen textiles. Population, 63,175.

Lawrence, Abbott. 1792–1855. American merchant and politician who was a central figure in the development of the textile industry in New England.

Lawrence, D(avid) H(erbert). 1885–1930. British writer whose novels include *Sons and Lovers* (1913), *Women in Love* (1920), and *Lady Chatterley's Lover* (1928).

Lawrence, Ernest Orlando. 1901–1958. American physicist. He won a 1939 Nobel Prize for the development of the cyclotron.

Lawrence, Gertrude. 1898–1952. British actress remembered for her performances in the plays *Private Lives* (1930) and *Lady in the Dark* (1940) as well as the film *The King and I* (1951).

Lawrence, Sir **Thomas.** 1769–1830. British painter remembered for his portrait series (1814–1818) of the leaders of the alliance against Napoleon.

Lawrence, T(homas) E(dward). Known as "Lawrence of Arabia." 1888–1935. Welsh-born British soldier, adventurer, and writer who led the Arab revolt against the Turks (1916–1918) and later wrote an account of his adventures, *The Seven Pillars of Wisdom* (1926).

law·ren·ci·um (lô-rĕn′sē-əm, lō-) *n. Symbol* **Lr** A short-lived, radioactive synthetic transuranic element produced from californium and having isotopes with mass numbers 255 through 260 and half-lives of a few seconds to three minutes; atomic number 103. See table at **element.** [After Ernest Orlando LAWRENCE.]

law·suit (lô′so͞ot′) *n.* An action or a suit brought before a court, as to recover a right or redress a grievance.

Law·ton (lôt′n). A city of southwest Oklahoma southwest of Oklahoma City. It is a trade center. Population, 80,054.

law·yer (lô′yər) *n.* One whose profession is to give legal advice and assistance to clients and represent them in court or in other legal matters. [Middle English *lauier,* from *law,* law. See LAW.] **—law′yer·ly** *adv.*

SYNONYMS: *lawyer, attorney, counselor, counsel, barrister, solicitor.* These nouns denote persons who practice law. *Lawyer* is the general and most comprehensive term for one authorized to give legal advice to clients and to plead cases in a court of law: *called her lawyer after the automobile accident. Attorney* is often used interchangeably with *lawyer,* but in a narrower sense it denotes a legal agent for a client in the transaction of business: *Corporate attorneys negotiated the new contract. Counselor* and *counsel* are terms for persons who give legal advice and serve as trial lawyers; *counsel* also applies to a team of lawyers employed in conducting a case: *Ms. Barnes is counselor for the defense. A table has been reserved for the defense counsel during the trial. Barrister* refers principally to a British trial lawyer: *The defense is represented by a barrister from Leeds.* In England a *solicitor* is a lawyer whose practice is devoted largely to serving as a legal agent, representing clients in lower courts, and preparing cases for barristers to try in superior courts; in the United States the term denotes the chief law officer of a city, town, or governmental department: *Solicitors for the squire handled the sale of his extensive lands. The case will be presented by the Solicitor General.*

law·yer·ing (lô′yər-ĭng) *n.* The profession or work of practicing law: *"Thousands of individual practitioners and small firms do most of the lawyering in this country"* (Newsweek).

lax (lăks) *adj.* **lax·er, lax·est. 1.** Lacking in rigor, strictness, or firmness. See Synonyms at **negligent. 2.** Not taut, firm, or compact; slack. See Synonyms at **loose. 3.** Loose and not easily retained or controlled. Used of bowel movements. **4.** *Linguistics.* Pronounced with the muscles of the tongue and jaw relatively relaxed, as the vowel *e* in *let.* [Middle English, from Latin *laxus,* loose, lax. See **slēg-** in Appendix.] **—lax·a′tion** *n.* **—lax′ly** *adv.* **—lax′ness** *n.*

lax·a·tive (lăk′sə-tĭv) *n.* A food or drug that stimulates evacuation of the bowels. **—laxative** *adj.* **1.** Stimulating evacuation of the bowels. **2.** Causing looseness or relaxation, especially of the bowels. [Middle English, from Old French *laxatif,* from Medieval Latin *laxātīvus,* preventing constipation, from Late Latin, assuaging, from Latin *laxātus,* past participle of *laxāre,* to relax, from *laxus,* loose. See LAX.]

lax·i·ty (lăk′sĭ-tē) *n.* The state or quality of being lax.

Lax·ness (läks′nĕs′), **Halldór Kiljan.** Born 1902. Icelandic novelist whose works include *Iceland's Bell* (1943–1946). He won the 1955 Nobel Prize for literature.

lay¹ (lā) *v.* **laid** (lād), **lay·ing, lays.** *—tr.* **1.** To cause to lie down: *lay a child in its crib.* **2.a.** To place in or bring to a particular state or position. **b.** To bury. **3.** To put or set down: *lay new railroad track.* **4.** To produce and deposit: *lay eggs.* **5.** To cause to subside; calm or allay: *"chas'd the clouds . . . and laid the winds"* (John Milton). **6.** To put up to or against: *lay an ear to the door.* **7.** To put forward as a reproach or an accusation: *They laid the blame on us.* **8.** To put or set in order or readiness for use: *lay the table for lunch.* **9.** To devise; contrive: *lay plans.* **10.** To spread over a surface: *lay paint on a canvas.* **11.** To place or give (importance): *lay stress on clarity of expression.* **12.** To impose as a burden or punishment: *lay a penalty upon the offender.* **13.** To present for examination: *lay a case before a committee.* **14.** To put forward as a demand or an assertion: *laid claim to the estate.* **15.** *Games.* To place (a bet); wager. **16.** To aim (a gun or cannon). **17.a.** To place together (strands) to be twisted into rope. **b.** To make in this manner: *lay up cable.* **18.** *Vulgar Slang.* To have sexual intercourse with. *—intr.* **1.** To produce and deposit eggs. **2.** To bet; wager. **3.** *Non-Standard.* To lie. **4.** To engage energetically in an action. **5.** *Nautical.* To put oneself into the position indicated. **—lay** *n.* **1.a.** The direction the strands of a rope or cable are twisted in: *a left lay.* **b.** The amount of such twist. **2.** The state of one that lays eggs: *a hen coming into lay.* **3.** *Vulgar Slang.* **a.** Sexual intercourse. **b.** A partner in sexual intercourse. ***—phrasal verbs.*** **lay about.** To strike blows on all sides. **lay aside. 1.** To give up; abandon: *lay aside all hope of rescue.* **2.** To save for the future. **lay away. 1.** To reserve for the future; save. **2.** To put aside and hold for future delivery. **lay by.** To save for future use. **lay down. 1.** To give up and surrender: *laid down their arms.* **2.** To specify: *laid down the rules.* **3.** To store for the future. **4.** *Non-Standard.* To lie down. **lay for.** *Informal.* To be waiting to attack: *Muggers lay for the unsuspecting pedestrian in the dark alley.* **lay in.** To store for future use: *lay in supplies for an Arctic winter.* **lay into.** *Slang.* **1.** To scold sharply. **2.** To attack physically; beat up. **lay off. 1.** To terminate the employment of (a worker), especially temporarily. **2.** To mark off: *lay off an area for a garden.* **3.** *Slang.* To stop doing something; quit. **4.** *Games.* To place all or a part of an accepted bet with another bookie in order to reduce the risk. **lay on. 1.** To apply (something) by or as if by spreading (it) onto a flat surface: *laid on a thick Southern accent.* **2.** To prepare, usually in an elaborate fashion; arrange: *laid on cocktails for 50 at the last minute.* **3.** *Slang.* To present or reveal to; confront with: *"went around talking to people about anything until he could lay his standard question on them"* (John Vinocur). **lay out. 1.** To make a detailed plan for. **2.** To clothe and prepare (a corpse) for burial. **3.** To rebuke harshly: *She laid me out for breaking the vase.* **4.** To knock to the ground or unconscious. **5.** To expend; spend: *lay out a fortune on jewelry.* **6.** To display: *lay out merchandise; lay the merchandise out.* **lay over.** To make a stopover in the course of a journey. **lay to.** *Nautical.* **1.** To bring (a ship) to a stop in open water. **2.** To remain stationary and face into the wind. **lay up. 1.** To stock for future use: *lay up supplies for a long journey.* **2.** *Informal.* To confine with an illness or injury: *was laid up for a month.* **3.** *Nautical.* To put (a ship) in dock, as for repairs. ***—idioms.*** **lay down the law.** To assert positively and often arrogantly. **lay it on thick.** *Informal.* **1.** To exaggerate; overstate. **2.** To flatter effusively. **lay of the land.** The nature, arrangement, or disposition of something. **lay rubber.** *Slang.* To accelerate suddenly a motor vehicle from a halt to a high speed, thereby spinning the wheels and depositing on the road a thin film of burned rubber from the rear tire or tires. **lay waste.** To ravage: *Rebel troops laid waste the town.* [Middle English *leien,* from Old English *lecgan.* See **legh-** in Appendix.]

USAGE NOTE: *Lay* ("to put, place, or prepare") and *lie* ("to recline or be situated") are frequently confused. *Lay* is a transitive verb and takes an object. *Lay* and its principal parts (*laid, laying*) are correctly used in the following examples: *He laid* (not *lay*) *the newspaper on the table. The table was laid for four. Lie* is an intransitive verb and does not take an object. *Lie* and its principal parts (*lay, lain, lying*) are correctly used in the following examples: *She often lies* (not *lays*) *down after lunch. When I lay* (not *laid*) *down, I fell asleep. The rubbish had lain* (not *laid*) *there a week. I was lying* (not *laying*) *in bed when he called.* There are a few exceptions to these rules. The phrasal verb *lay for* and the nautical use of *lay,* as in *lay at anchor,* though intransitive, are well established.

lay² (lā) *adj.* **1.** Of, relating to, or involving the laity: *a lay preacher.* **2.** Not of or belonging to a particular profession; nonprofessional: *a lay opinion as to the seriousness of the disease.* [Middle English, from Old French *lai,* from Late Latin *lāicus,* from Greek *laikos,* of the people, from *laos,* the people.]

lay³ (lā) *n.* **1.** A narrative poem, such as one sung by medieval minstrels; a ballad. **2.** A song; a tune. [Middle English, from Old French *lai.*]

lay⁴ (lā) *v.* Past tense of **lie¹.**

lay·a·bout (lā′ə-bout′) *n.* A lazy or idle person; a loafer.

T.E. Lawrence

ă pat	oi boy
ā pay	ou out
âr care	o͝o took
ä father	o͞o boot
ĕ pet	ŭ cut
ē be	ûr urge
ĭ pit	th thin
ī pie	*th* this
îr pier	hw which
ŏ pot	zh vision
ō toe	ə about, item
ô paw	♦ regionalism

Stress marks: ′ (primary); ′ (secondary), as in **dictionary** (dĭk′shə-nĕr′ē)

layback
Debi Thomas at the World Figure Skating Championship, Budapest, 1988

Lay·a·mon (lā′ə-mən, lī′-). fl. 13th century. English poet who wrote *The Brut* (c. 1205), the first account in English of King Arthur and his knights.

lay·a·way (lā′ə-wā′) *n.* **1.** A payment plan in which a buyer reserves an article of merchandise by placing a deposit with the retailer until the balance is paid in full: *bought a suit on layaway.* **2.** An article reserved under such a plan.

lay·back (lā′băk′) *n. Sports.* A spin in figure skating in which the skater's upper body is arched backward.

lay·er (lā′ər) *n.* **1.a.** One that lays: *a tile layer.* **b.** A hen kept for laying eggs. **2.a.** A single thickness of a material covering a surface or forming an overlying part or segment: *a layer of dust on the windowsill; a cake with four layers.* **b.** A usually horizontal deposit or expanse; a stratum: *layers of sedimentary rock; a layer of warm air.* **c.** A depth or level: *a poem with several layers of meaning.* **3.** *Botany.* A stem that is covered with soil for rooting while still part of the living plant. **—layer** *v.* **-ered, -er·ing, -ers.** *—tr.* **1.** To divide or form into layers: *layered gravel and charcoal to make a filter.* **2.** To cut (hair) into different, usually overlapping lengths. **3.** *Botany.* To propagate (a plant) by means of a layer. *—intr.* **1.** To form or come apart as layers. **2.** *Botany.* To take root as a result of layering.

lay·er·ing (lā′ər-ĭng) also **lay·er·age** (-ĭj) *n.* The process of rooting branches, twigs, or stems that are still attached to a parent plant, as by placing a specially treated part in moist soil.

lay·ette (lā-ĕt′) *n.* Clothing and other equipment for a newborn child. [French, from Old French, chest of drawers, diminutive of *laie,* box, from Middle Dutch *laeye.*]

lay figure *n.* **1.** See **mannequin** (sense 2). **2.** A subservient or insignificant person. [From obsolete *layman,* from Dutch *leeman,* variant of *ledenman* : obsolete Dutch *led,* limb (from Middle Dutch *lit*) + *man,* man (from Middle Dutch; see MANIKIN).]

lay·man (lā′mən) *n.* **1.** A man who is not a cleric. **2.** A man who is a nonprofessional: *His is just the layman's view of medicine.* See Usage Note at **man.**

lay·off (lā′ôf′, -ŏf′) *n.* **1.** Suspension or dismissal of employees, especially for lack of work. **2.** A period of temporary inactivity or rest.

lay·out (lā′out′) *n.* **1.** The act or an instance of laying out. **2.** An arrangement or a plan, especially the schematic arrangement of parts or areas: *the layout of a factory; the layout of a printed circuit.* **3.** *Printing.* **a.** The art or process of arranging printed or graphic matter on a page. **b.** The overall design of a page, spread, or book, including elements such as page and type size, typeface, and the arrangement of titles and page numbers. **c.** A page or set of pages marked to indicate this design. **4.** *Informal.* An establishment or property, especially a large residence or estate: "[Her] *show horses . . . were kept on the couple's one-and-a-half acre Malibu layout*" (People).

lay·o·ver (lā′ō′vər) *n.* A short stop or break in a journey, usually imposed by scheduling requirements.

lay·peo·ple or **lay people** (lā′pē′pəl) *pl.n.* Laymen and laywomen considered as a group.

lay·per·son (lā′pûr′sən) *n.* A layman or a laywoman.

lay reader *n.* A layperson in the Anglican or Roman Catholic church authorized by a bishop to read some parts of the service.

Lay·san Island (lī′sän′). An island of Hawaii in the Leeward Islands northwest of the main islands.

Lay·ton (lāt′n). A city of northern Utah south of Ogden. It is a processing center. Population, 26,393.

lay-up (lā′ŭp′) *n.* **1.** *Basketball.* A usually one-handed, banked shot made close to the basket after driving in. **2.** The act or an instance of laying up: *budget cuts that forced the lay-up of several ships.*

lay·wom·an (lā′wo͝om′ən) *n.* **1.** A woman who is not a cleric. **2.** A woman who is a nonprofessional: "[a program] *to educate laywomen in the ways of political campaigns*" (New York).

la·zar (lā′zər, lăz′ər) *n. Archaic.* A diseased person; a leper. [Middle English, from Old French *lazre,* from Late Latin *Lazarus,* Lazarus, the beggar full of sores in a New Testament parable (Luke 16:20).]

lazy Susan

laz·a·ret·to (lăz′ə-rĕt′ō) also **laz·a·ret** or **laz·a·rette** (lăz′ə-rĕt′) *n., pl.* **-tos** also **-rets** or **-rettes.** **1.** A hospital treating contagious diseases. **2.** A building or ship used as a quarantine station. **3.** Often **lazaret.** *Nautical.* A storage space between the decks of a ship. [Italian *lazzaretto* : *lazzaro,* lazar (from Late Latin *Lazarus;* see LAZAR) + Italian dialectal *Nazareto,* popular name for a hospital maintained in Venice by the Church of Santa Maria di Nazaret.]

Laz·a·rus (lăz′ər-əs). In the New Testament, the brother of Mary and Martha.

Lazarus, Emma. 1849–1887. American writer. Her poem "The New Colossus" is inscribed on the base of the Statue of Liberty.

laze (lāz) *v.* **lazed, laz·ing, laz·es.** *—intr.* To be lazy; loaf: *laze around the house.* *—tr.* To spend (time) in loafing: *lazed the afternoon away in a hammock.* [Back-formation from LAZY.]

laz·u·lite (lăz′yo͝o-līt′, lăz′ə-, lăzh′ə-) *n.* A relatively rare blue mineral, (Mg, Fe)$Al_2(PO_4)_2(OH)_2$, with a vitreous luster. [Medieval Latin *lazulum,* lapis lazuli; see LAPIS LAZULI + –ITE¹.]

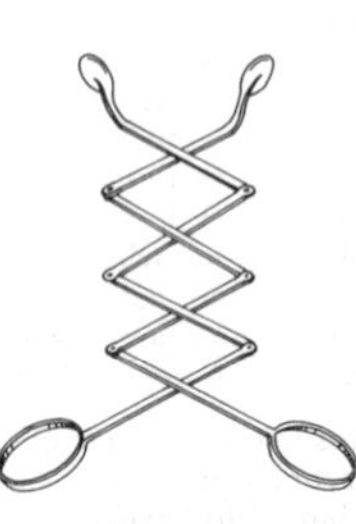

lazy tongs

laz·u·rite (lăz′yo͝o-rīt′, lăz′ə-, lăzh′ə-) *n.* A relatively rare blue, violet-blue, or greenish-blue translucent mineral, $Na_{4-5}Al_3Si_3O_{12}S$, the chief component of lapis lazuli. [Medieval Latin *lāzur,* lapis lazuli (from Arabic *lāzaward;* see LAPIS LAZULI) + –ITE¹.]

la·zy (lā′zē) *adj.* **-zi·er, -zi·est.** **1.** Resistant to work or exertion; disposed to idleness. **2.** Slow-moving; sluggish: *a lazy river.* **3.** Conducive to idleness or indolence: *a lazy summer day.* **4.** Depicted as reclining or lying on its side. Used of a brand on livestock. [Probably of Low German origin.] **—la′zi·ly** *adv.* **—la′zi·ness** *n.*

SYNONYMS: *lazy, fainéant, idle, indolent, slothful.* The central meaning shared by these adjectives is "not disposed to exertion, work, or activity": *too lazy to wash the breakfast dishes; fainéant aristocrats; an idle drifter; a good-natured but indolent hanger-on; slothful employees.*

la·zy·bones (lā′zē-bōnz′) *pl.n.* *(used with a sing. verb). Informal.* A lazy person.

lazy eye *n.* See **amblyopia.**

lazy Su·san (so͞o′zən) *n.* A revolving tray for condiments or food.

lazy tongs *pl.n.* *(used with a sing. or pl. verb).* Tongs having a jointed extensible framework operated by scissorslike handles, used for grasping an object at a distance.

lb. *abbr.* **1.** Libra (ancient Roman weight). **2.** Pound (modern weight).

LBO *abbr.* Leveraged buyout.

lc also **l.c.** *abbr.* Lowercase.

LC *abbr.* **1.** Landing craft. **2.** Also **L.C.** Library of Congress.

L/C *abbr.* Letter of credit.

l.c.d. *abbr. Mathematics.* Least common denominator.

LCD *abbr.* Liquid-crystal display.

LCL *abbr.* Less-than-carload lot.

l.c.m. *abbr. Mathematics.* Least common multiple.

LCM *abbr.* Landing craft, mechanized.

L.Cpl. *abbr.* Lance corporal.

LCS *abbr.* Landing craft, support.

LCT *abbr.* **1.** Land conservation trust. **2.** Landing craft, tank. **3.** Local civil time.

LD *abbr.* **1.** Learning disability; learning-disabled. **2.** Lethal dose.

ld. *abbr.* **1.** *Printing.* Lead. **2.** Load.

Ld. *abbr.* **1.a.** Limited. **b.** Limited company. **2.** Lord.

LDC *abbr.* Less-developed country.

ldg. *abbr.* **1.** Landing. **2.** Loading.

LDL *abbr.* Low-density lipoprotein.

L-do·pa (ĕl-dō′pə) *n.* The levorotatory form of dopa, used to treat Parkinson's disease. Also called *levodopa.* [L(EVOROTATORY) + DOPA.]

lea (lē, lā) also **ley** (lā, lē) *n.* A grassland; a meadow. [Middle English *leie,* from Old English *lēah.* See **leuk-** in Appendix.]

lea. *abbr.* League (measurement).

leach (lēch) *v.* **leached, leach·ing, leach·es.** *—tr.* **1.** To remove soluble or other constituents from by the action of a percolating liquid. **2.** To empty; drain: *"a world leached of pleasure, voided of meaning"* (Marilynne Robinson). *—intr.* To be dissolved or passed out by a percolating liquid. **—leach** *n.* **1.** The act or process of leaching. **2.** A porous, perforated, or sievelike vessel that holds material to be leached. **3.** The substance through which a liquid is leached. [From Middle English *leche,* leachate, from Old English **lece,* muddy stream; akin to *leccan,* to moisten.] **—leach′a·bil′i·ty** *n.* **—leach′a·ble** *adj.*

leach·ate (lē′chāt) *n.* A product or solution formed by leaching, especially a solution containing contaminants picked up through the leaching of soil.

Lea·cock (lē′kŏk′), **Stephen Butler.** 1869–1944. Canadian economist who is best remembered for his humorous writing, contained in volumes such as *Nonsense Novels* (1911).

lead¹ (lēd) *v.* **led** (lĕd), **lead·ing, leads.** *—tr.* **1.** To show the way to by going in advance. **2.** To guide or direct in a course: *lead a horse by the halter.* See Synonyms at **guide. 3.a.** To serve as a route for; take: *The path led them to a cemetery.* **b.** To be a channel or conduit for (water or electricity, for example). **4.** To guide the behavior or opinion of; induce: *led us to believe otherwise.* **5.a.** To direct the performance or activities of: *lead an orchestra.* **b.** To inspire the conduct of: *led the nation in its crisis.* **6.** To play a principal or guiding role in: *lead a discussion; led the antiwar movement.* **7.a.** To go or be at the head of: *The queen led the procession. My name led the list.* **b.** To be ahead of: *led the runner-up by three strides.* **c.** To be foremost in or among: *led the field in nuclear research; led her teammates in free throws.* **8.** To pass or go through; live: *lead an independent life.* **9.** To begin or open with, as in games: *led an ace.* **10.** To guide (a partner) in dancing. **11.** To aim in front of (a moving target). *—intr.* **1.** To be first; be ahead. **2.** To go first as a guide. **3.** To act as commander, director, or guide. **4.** To afford a passage, course, or route: *a road that leads over the mountains; a door leading to the pantry.* **5.** To tend toward a certain goal or result: *a remark that led to further discussion; policies that led to disaster.* **6.** To make the initial play, as in a game or contest. **7.** To begin a presentation or an account in a given way: *The announcer led with the day's top stories.* **8.a.** To guide a dance partner. **b.** To start a dance step on a specified foot. **9.** *Baseball.* To advance a few paces away from one's base toward the next while the pitcher is in the delivery. Used of a base runner. **10.** *Sports.* To begin an attack in boxing with a specified hand or punch: *led with a right to the body.* **—lead** *n.* **1. a.** The first or foremost position. **b.** One occupying such a position; a leader. **c.** The initiative: *took the lead in setting the pace of the project.* **2.** The margin by which one holds a position of advantage or superiority: *held a lead of nine points at the half.* **3. a.** Information pointing toward a possible solution; a clue: *followed a promising lead in the murder case.* **b.** An indication of potential opportunity; a tip: *a good lead for a job.* **4.** Command; leadership: *took over the lead of the company.* **5.** An example; a precedent: *followed his sister's lead in running for office.* **6. a.** The principal role in a dramatic production. **b.** The person playing such a role. **7. a.** The introductory portion of a news story. **b.** An important, usually prominently displayed news story. **8.** *Games.* **a.** The first play. **b.** The prerogative or turn to make the first play: *The lead passes to the player on the left.* **c.** A card played first in a round. **9.** *Baseball.* A position taken by a base runner away from one base in the direction of the next. **10.** A leash. **11.** *Geology.* **a.** A deposit of gold ore in an old riverbed. **b.** See **lode** (sense 1). **12.** *Electronics.* A conductor by which one circuit element is electrically connected to another. **13.** *Nautical.* The direction in which a rope runs. **14.** The distance aimed in front of a moving target. ***—phrasal verbs.*** **lead off. 1.** To begin; start. **2.** *Baseball.* To be the first batter in an inning. **lead on. 1.** To keep in a state of expectation or hope; entice. **2.** To mislead; deceive. ***—idiom.*** **lead up to. 1.** To result in by a series of steps: *events leading up to the coup.* **2.** To proceed toward (a main topic) with preliminary remarks. [Middle English *leden,* from Old English *lǣdan.* See **leit-** in Appendix.]

lead[2] (lĕd) *n.* **1.** *Symbol* **Pb** A soft, malleable, ductile, bluish-white, dense metallic element, extracted chiefly from galena and used in containers and pipes for corrosives, solder and type metal, bullets, radiation shielding, paints, and antiknock compounds. Atomic number 82; atomic weight 207.19; melting point 327.5°C; boiling point 1,744°C; specific gravity 11.35; valence 2, 4. See table at **element. 2.** A lead weight suspended by a line, used to make soundings. **3.** Bullets from or for firearms; shot: *pumped the target full of lead.* **4. leads.** Strips of lead used to hold the panes of a window. **5.** *Abbr.* **ld.** *Printing.* A thin strip of metal used to separate lines of type. **6. leads.** *Chiefly British.* A flat roof covered with sheets of lead. **7. a.** Any of various, often graphitic compositions used as the writing substance in pencils. **b.** A thin stick of such material. *—tr.* **lead·ed, lead·ing, leads. 1.** To cover, line, weight, or fill with lead. **2.** *Printing.* To provide space between (lines of type) with leads. **3.** To secure (window glass) with leads. **4.** To treat with lead or a lead compound: *leaded gasoline; leaded paint.* ***—idiom.*** **get the lead out.** *Informal.* To start moving or move more rapidly. [Middle English *led,* from Old English *lēad,* probably of Celtic origin.] **—lead** *adj.*

lead acetate (lĕd) *n.* A poisonous white crystalline compound, $Pb(C_2H_3O_2)_2 \cdot 3H_2O$, used in hair dyes, waterproofing compounds, and varnishes. Also called *sugar of lead.*

lead arsenate (lĕd) *n.* A poisonous white crystalline compound, $Pb_3(AsO_4)_2$, used in insecticides and herbicides.

lead carbonate (lĕd) *n.* A poisonous white amorphous powder, $PbCO_3$, used as a paint pigment.

lead chromate (lĕd) *n.* A poisonous yellow crystalline compound, $PbCrO_4$, used as a paint pigment.

lead colic (lĕd) *n.* See **painter's colic.**

lead dioxide (lĕd) *n.* A poisonous brown crystalline compound, PbO_2, used as an oxidizing agent in electrodes, batteries, and explosives.

lead·en (lĕd′n) *adj.* **1.** Made of or containing lead. **2. a.** Heavy and inert. **b.** Listless; sluggish. **3.** Lacking liveliness or sparkle; dull: *a leaden conversation.* **4.** Downcast; depressed: *leaden spirits.* **5.** Dull, dark gray in color: *drizzle from a leaden sky.* **—lead′en·ly** *adv.* **—lead′en·ness** *n.*

lead·er (lē′dər) *n.* **1.** One that leads or guides. **2.** One who is in charge or in command of others. **3. a.** One who heads a political party or organization. **b.** One who has influence or power, especially of a political nature. **4.** *Music.* **a.** A conductor, especially of an orchestra, a band, or a choral group. **b.** The principal performer in an orchestral section or a group. **5.** The foremost animal, such as a horse or dog, in a harnessed team. **6.** A loss leader. **7.** *Chiefly British.* The main editorial in a newspaper. **8. leaders.** *Printing.* Dots or dashes in a row leading the eye across a page, as in an index entry. **9.** A pipe for conducting liquid. **10.** A short length of gut, wire, or similar material by which a hook is attached to a fishing line. **11.** A blank strip at the end of a film or tape used in threading or winding. **12.** *Botany.* The growing apex or main shoot of a shrub or tree. **13.** An economic indicator.

lead·er·ship (lē′dər-shĭp′) *n.* **1.** The position or office of a leader: *ascended to the leadership of the party.* **2.** Capacity or ability to lead: *showed strong leadership during her first term in office.* **3.** A group of leaders: *met with the leadership of the nation's top unions.* **4.** Guidance; direction: *The business prospered under the leadership of the new president.*

lead glass (lĕd) *n.* See **flint glass.**

lead-in (lēd′ĭn′) *n.* **1.** Opening or introductory matter: *The joke served as a lead-in to a discussion of more serious matters.* **2.** A program, as on television, scheduled to precede another. **3.** The wire that connects an outdoor antenna to an electronic transmitter or receiver.

lead·ing[1] (lē′dĭng) *adj.* **1.** Having a position in the lead; foremost: *the leading candidate.* **2.** Chief; principal: *the leading cause of inflation.* **3.** Of or performing a lead in a theatrical production: *a leading role.* **4.** Formulated so as to elicit a desired response: *a leading question.* **—lead′ing·ly** *adv.*

lead·ing[2] (lĕd′ĭng) *n.* **1.** A border or rim of lead, as around a windowpane. **2.** *Printing.* The spacing between lines, usually measured in points.

lead·ing economic indicator (lē′dĭng) *n.* An economic or a financial variable that tends to move ahead of and in the same direction as general economic activity.

lead·ing edge (lē′dĭng) *n.* **1.** *Nautical.* The edge of a sail that faces the wind. **2.** The front edge of an airplane propeller blade or wing. **3. a.** The foremost position in a trend or movement; the vanguard: *"a company on the leading edge of machine-tool technology"* (Christian Science Monitor). **b.** Someone or something occupying such a position: *"Together they are the leading edge of a new wing of historians known as cliometricians"* (Timothy Foote). **—lead′ing-edge′** (lē′dĭng-ĕj′) *adj.*

lead·ing tone (lē′dĭng) *n.* *Music.* The seventh tone or degree of a scale that is a half tone below the tonic; a subtonic. [From its tendency to lead into or rise to the tonic.]

lead line (lĕd) *n.* *Nautical.* See **sounding line.** [From the use of lead weights for making soundings.]

lead monoxide (lĕd) *n.* See **litharge.**

lead·off (lēd′ôf′, -ŏf′) *n.* **1.** An opening play or move. **2.** One that leads off. **—lead′off′** *adj.*

lead-out (lēd′out′) *n.* A program, as on television, scheduled to follow another: "[Viewers] *also stay around for the 11:30 movie lead-out"* (Edwin Diamond).

lead pencil (lĕd) *n.* A pencil that uses graphite as its marking substance.

lead·plant (lĕd′plănt′) *n.* A deciduous shrub *(Amorpha canescens)* of central North America, having pinnately compound leaves covered with whitish hairs.

lead poisoning (lĕd) *n.* Acute or chronic poisoning by lead or any of its salts, with the acute form causing severe gastroenteritis and encephalopathy and the chronic form causing anemia and damage to the gastrointestinal tract and nervous system. Also called *saturnism.*

leads·man (lĕdz′mən) *n.* *Nautical.* The person using the lead line in taking soundings.

lead tetraethyl (lĕd) *n.* Tetraethyl lead.

lead-time (lēd′tīm′) *n.* The time between the initial stage of a project or policy and the appearance of results: *a long lead-time in oil production because of the need for new exploration.*

lead·wort (lĕd′wûrt′, -wôrt′) *n.* **1.** Any of various chiefly tropical plants of the genus *Plumbago,* having clusters of variously colored flowers. **2.** Any of several similar plants. [From the hue of some of its flowers.]

leaf (lēf) *n., pl.* **leaves** (lēvz). **1.** A usually green, flattened, lateral structure attached to a stem and functioning as a principal organ of photosynthesis and transpiration in most plants. **2.** A leaflike organ or structure. **3. a.** Leaves considered as a group; foliage. **b.** The state or time of having or showing leaves: *trees in full leaf.* **4.** The leaves of a plant used or processed for a specific purpose: *large supplies of tobacco leaf.* **5.** Any of the sheets of paper bound in a book, each side of which constitutes a page. **6.** A very thin sheet of material, especially metal: *silver leaf.* **7.** A hinged or removable section for a table top. **8.** A hinged or otherwise movable section of a folding door, shutter, or gate. **9.** One of several metal strips forming a leaf spring. **—leaf** *v.* **leafed, leaf·ing, leafs.** *—intr.* **1.** To produce leaves; put forth foliage: *trees just beginning to leaf.* **2.** To turn pages, as in searching or browsing: *leafed through the catalog.* *—tr.* To turn through the pages of. [Middle English, from Old English *lēaf.*]

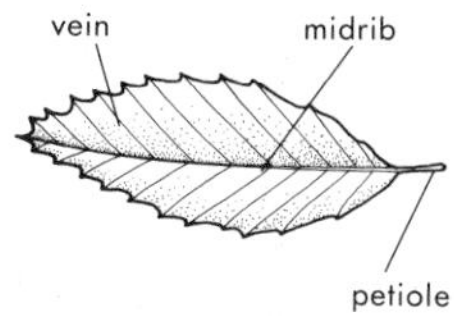

leaf
Simple leaf

leaf·age (lē′fĭj) *n.* Foliage.

leaf butterfly *n.* Any of several butterflies of the genus *Kallima,* having wings that resemble leaves.

leaf fat *n.* Layered fat that encloses the kidneys of a hog, used in making lard.

leaf gap *n.* A break in the vascular tissue of a stem above the point of attachment of a leaf trace.

leaf·hop·per (lēf′hŏp′ər) *n.* Any of numerous insects of the family Cicadellidae that suck juices from plants, often damaging crops.

leaf insect *n.* Any of various chiefly Asian insects of the family Phyllidae that resemble leaves in color and form. Also called *walking leaf.*

leaf lard *n.* High-grade lard made from leaf fat.

leaf·let (lē′flĭt) *n.* **1.** One of the segments of a compound leaf. **2.** A small leaf or leaflike part. **3.** A printed, usually folded handbill or flier intended for free distribution. **—leaflet** *v.* **-let·ed, -let·ing, -lets** also **-let·ted, -let·ting, -lets.** *—intr.* To hand out leaflets. *—tr.* To hand out leaflets to or in: *leafleted the morning commuters; leaflet a neighborhood.*

leaf miner *n.* Any of numerous small flies and moths that in the larval stage dig into and feed on leaf tissue.

leaf mold *n.* Humus or compost consisting of decomposed leaves and other organic material.

ă pat	oi boy
ā pay	ou out
âr care	o͝o took
ä father	o͞o boot
ĕ pet	ŭ cut
ē be	ûr urge
ĭ pit	th thin
ī pie	*th* this
îr pier	hw which
ŏ pot	zh vision
ō toe	ə about, item
ô paw	♦ regionalism

Stress marks: ′ (primary); ′ (secondary), as in **dictionary** (dĭk′shə-nĕr′ē)

leaf spring

leaf primordium *n.* A lateral outgrowth from the apical meristem that develops into a leaf.

leaf roller *n.* Any of several moths of the family Tortricidae whose larvae make nests of rolled leaves and silk.

leaf scar *n.* The mark left on a twig after a leaf falls.

leaf spot *n.* Any of various plant diseases resulting in well-defined necrotic areas on the leaves.

leaf spring *n.* A composite spring, used especially in automotive suspensions, consisting of several layers of flexible metallic strips joined to act as a single unit.

leaf·stalk or **leaf stalk** (lēf′stôk′) *n.* See **petiole** (sense 1).

leaf trace *n.* A strand of vascular tissue that extends between the vascular bundle of a stem and a leaf.

leaf·y (lē′fē) *adj.* **-i·er, -i·est. 1.** Covered with or having leaves. **2.** Consisting of leaves: *Spinach is a leafy green vegetable.* **3.** Similar to or resembling a leaf. **—leaf′i·ness** *n.*

league[1] (lēg) *n.* **1.** An association of states, organizations, or individuals for common action; an alliance. **2.** *Sports.* An association of teams or clubs that compete chiefly among themselves. Also called *loop.* **3.** A class or level of competition: *The ski jump was out of his league.* **—league** *v.* **leagued, leagu·ing, leagues.** *—intr.* To come together in or as if in a league. *—tr.* To bring together in or as if in a league. [Alteration (influenced by Italian *lega*) of Middle English *liege,* from Old French *ligue,* from Medieval Latin *liga* and from Old Italian *lega, liga* (from *legare,* to bind), both from Latin *ligāre.* See **leig-** in Appendix.]

league[2] (lēg) *n. Abbr.* **lea. 1.a.** A unit of distance equal to 3.0 statute miles (4.8 kilometers). **b.** Any of various other units of about the same length. **2.** A square league. [Middle English *lege,* from Old French *liue, leguee,* from Latin *leuga,* a measure of distance, of Celtic origin.]

League City (lēg). A city of southeast Texas southeast of Houston. The aeronautics industry is important to its economy. Population, 16,578.

League of Nations. A world organization established in 1920 to promote international cooperation and peace. It was first proposed in 1918 by President Woodrow Wilson, although the United States never joined the League. Essentially powerless, it was officially dissolved in 1946.

lea·guer[1] (lē′gər) *n.* **1.** A siege. **2.** The camp especially of a besieging army. **—leaguer** *tr.v.* **-guered, -guer·ing, -guers.** *Archaic.* To besiege; beleaguer. [Dutch *leger,* lair, camp, from Middle Dutch *lēgher,* lair, camp, siege. See **legh-** in Appendix.]

leagu·er[2] (lē′gər) *n.* One that belongs to a league.

Le·ah (lē′ə). In the Old Testament, the first wife of Jacob.

Lea·hy (lā′hē), **William Daniel.** 1875–1959. American naval officer who became Admiral of the Fleet in 1944.

leak (lēk) *v.* **leaked, leak·ing, leaks.** *—intr.* **1.** To permit the escape, entry, or passage of something through a breach or flaw: *rusted pipes that were beginning to leak; a boat leaking at the seams.* **2.** To escape or pass through a breach or flaw: *helium leaking slowly from the balloon.* **3.** *Informal.* To become publicly known through a breach of secrecy: *The news has leaked.* *—tr.* **1.** To permit (a substance) to escape or pass through a breach or flaw: *a damaged reactor leaking radioactivity into the atmosphere.* **2.** *Informal.* To disclose without authorization or official sanction: *leaked classified information to a reporter.* **—leak** *n.* **1.** A crack or flaw that permits something to escape from or enter a container or conduit: *fixed the leak in the roof.* **2.a.** The act or instance of leaking. **b.** An amount leaked: *equipment used in cleaning up oil leaks.* **3.** *Informal.* An unauthorized or a deliberate disclosure of confidential information: *"Sometimes we can't respond to stories based on leaks"* (Ronald Reagan). **4.a.** Loss of electric current as a result of faulty insulation. **b.** The path or place at which this loss takes place. ***—idiom.*** **take a leak.** *Vulgar Slang.* To urinate. [Middle English *leken,* probably from Middle Dutch.] **—leak′er** *n.*

leak·age (lē′kĭj) *n.* **1.** The act or an instance of leaking. **2.** Something that escapes by leaking. **3.** An amount lost as the result of leaking.

Lea·key (lē′kē), **Louis Seymour Bazett.** 1903–1972. British anthropologist and archaeologist. He influenced evolutionary theory with his account and analysis of the discovery, by his wife, **Mary Leakey** (born 1913), of the 1.75-million-year-old Zinjanthropus skull in Tanzania. Mary Leakey and their son **Richard Leakey** (born 1944) have continued his research.

leak·proof (lēk′pro͞of′) *adj.* So constructed or contrived as to prevent leaks or leakage.

leak·y (lē′kē) *adj.* **-i·er, -i·est.** Permitting leaks or leakage: *a leaky roof; a leaky defense system.*

Leal·man (lēl′mən). A community of west-central Florida, a suburb of St. Petersburg. Population, 19,875.

Leam·ing·ton (lĕm′ĭng-tən). Officially Royal Leamington Spa. A municipal borough of central England northeast of Warwick. It is a health resort. Population, 42,953.

lean[1]
Leaning Tower,
Pisa, Italy

lean[1] (lēn) *v.* **leaned, lean·ing, leans.** *—intr.* **1.** To bend or slant away from the vertical. **2.** To incline the weight of the body so as to be supported: *leaning against the railing.* See Synonyms at **slant. 3.** To rely for assistance or support: *Lean on me for help.* **4.** To have a tendency or preference: *a government that leans toward fascism.* **5.** *Informal.* To exert pressure: *The boss is leaning on us to meet the deadline.* *—tr.* **1.** To set or place so as to be resting or supported. **2.** To cause to incline. **—lean** *n.* A tilt or an inclination away from the vertical. [Middle English *lenen,* from Old English *hleonian.* See **klei-** in Appendix.]

lean[2] (lēn) *adj.* **lean·er, lean·est. 1.** Not fleshy or fat; thin. **2.** Containing little or no fat. **3.a.** Not productive or prosperous; meager: *lean years.* **b.** Containing little excess or waste; spare: *a lean budget.* **c.** Thrifty in management; economical: *"Company leaders know their industries must be lean to survive"* (Christian Science Monitor). **4.** *Metallurgy.* Low in mineral contents: *lean ore.* *Chemistry.* Lacking in combustible material: *lean fuel.* **—lean** *n.* Meat with little or no fat. [Middle English *lene,* from Old English *hlǣne.*] **—lean′ly** *adv.* **—lean′ness** *n.*

SYNONYMS: *lean, spare, skinny, scrawny, lank, lanky, rawboned, gaunt.* These adjectives mean lacking excess flesh. *Lean* emphasizes absence of fat: *The farmer tried to fatten the lean cattle for market. Spare* sometimes suggests trimness and good muscle tone: *"an old man, very tall and spare, with an ascetic aspect"* (William H. Mallock). *She has the spare figure of a marathon runner. Skinny* and *scrawny* imply unattractive thinness, as that associated with undernourishment: *The child has skinny, freckled legs with prominent knees. "He* [had] *a long, scrawny neck that rose out of a very low collar"* (Winston Churchill). *Lank* describes one who is thin and tall, and *lanky* one who is thin, tall, and ungraceful: *"He was . . . exceedingly lank, with narrow shoulders"* (Washington Irving). *She was transformed from a lanky adolescent into a willowy young woman. Rawboned* suggests a thin, bony, gangling build: *a rawboned cowhand with a weather-beaten, tanned face. Gaunt* implies thinness and boniness and a haggard appearance; it may suggest illness or hardship: *a white-haired pioneer, her face gaunt from overwork and worry.*

Le·an·der (lē-ăn′dər) *n. Greek Mythology.* A youth who loved Hero and drowned during one of his nightly swims across the Hellespont to be with her.

lean·ing (lē′nĭng) *n.* An inclination, a tendency, or a preference. See Synonyms at **predilection.**

leant (lĕnt) *v. Chiefly British.* A past tense and a past participle of **lean**[1]**.**

lean-to (lēn′to͞o′) *adj.* Having or characterized by a single slope or pitch: *a lean-to roof; lean-to construction.* **—lean-to** *n., pl.* **-tos. 1.** A structure with a single-pitch roof that is attached to the side of a building as a wing or an extension. **2.** A shelter or shed having a roof with a single slope or pitch.

leap (lēp) *v.* **leaped** or **leapt** (lĕpt, lēpt), **leap·ing, leaps.** *—intr.* **1.** To spring or bound upward from or as if from the ground; jump: *leaped over the wall; salmon leaping upriver.* **2.a.** To move quickly or abruptly from one condition or subject to another: *always leaping to conclusions.* **b.** To act impulsively: *leaped at the opportunity to travel.* *—tr.* **1.** To jump over: *couldn't leap the brook.* **2.** To cause to leap: *leap a horse over a hurdle.* **—leap** *n.* **1.a.** The act of leaping; a jump. **b.** A place jumped over or from. **c.** The distance cleared in a leap. **2.** An abrupt or precipitous passage, shift, or transition: *a leap from rags to riches.* ***—idioms.*** **by leaps and bounds.** Very quickly: *growing by leaps and bounds.* **leap in the dark.** An act whose consequences cannot be predicted. **leap of faith.** The act or an instance of believing or trusting in something intangible or incapable of being proved. [Middle English *lepen,* from Old English *hlēapan.*] **—leap′er** *n.*

leap·frog (lēp′frôg′, -frŏg′) *n. Games.* A game in which one player kneels or bends over while the next in line leaps over him or her. **—leapfrog** *v.* **-frogged, -frog·ging, -frogs.** *—tr.* **1.** To jump over in or as if in leapfrog. **2.** To advance (two military units) by engaging one with the enemy while moving the other to a position forward of the first unit. **3.** To avoid by or as if by a roundabout route. *—intr.* To move forward or progress in or as if in leapfrog.

leapfrog test *n. Computer Science.* A method of checking the internal operations of a computer by performing arithmetic or logical operations on one section of storage, transferring the new information to another section, repeating the operations, and crosschecking the results.

leap second *n.* A second of time, as measured by an atomic clock, added to or omitted from official timekeeping systems annually to compensate for changes in the rotation of Earth.

leapt (lĕpt, lēpt) *v.* A past tense and a past participle of **leap.**

leap year *n.* **1.** A year in the Gregorian calendar having 366 days, with the extra day, February 29, intercalated to compensate for the quarter-day difference between an ordinary year and the astronomical year. **2.** An intercalary year in a calendar.

Lear (lîr) *n.* The protagonist in Shakespeare's tragedy *King Lear,* based on a legendary king of Britain.

Lear, Edward. 1812–1888. British artist and writer of nonsense verse, included in such works as his first *Book of Nonsense* (1846).

learn (lûrn) *v.* **learned** also **learnt** (lûrnt), **learn·ing, learns.** *—tr.* **1.** To gain knowledge, comprehension, or mastery of through experience or study. **2.** To fix in the mind or memory; memorize: *learned the speech in a few hours.* **3.a.** To acquire experience of or an ability or a skill in: *learn tolerance; learned how to whistle.* **b.** To become aware: *learned that it was best not to argue.* **4.** To become informed of; find out. See Synonyms at **discover. 5.** *Non-Standard.* To cause to acquire knowledge; teach. **6.** *Obsolete.* To give information to. *—intr.* To gain knowledge, information, comprehension, or skill: *learns quickly; learned about computers; learned of the job through friends.*

[Middle English *lernen*, from Old English *leornian*. See **leis-**[1] in Appendix.] **—learn′a·ble** *adj.* **—learn′er** *n.*

learn·ed (lûr′nĭd) *adj.* **1.** Possessing or demonstrating profound, often systematic knowledge; erudite. **2.** Directed toward scholars: *a learned journal.* **3.** (lûrnd). Acquired by learning or experience: *learned behavior; a learned response.* [Middle English *lerned*, educated, past participle of *lernen*, to learn, teach. See LEARN.] **—learn′ed·ly** *adv.* **—learn′ed·ness** *n.*

SYNONYMS: *learned, erudite, scholarly.* The central meaning shared by these adjectives is "having or showing profound knowledge": *a learned jurist; an erudite professor; a scholarly treatise.*

learn·ing (lûr′nĭng) *n.* **1.** The act, process, or experience of gaining knowledge or skill. **2.** Knowledge or skill gained through schooling or study. See Synonyms at **knowledge. 3.** Behavioral modification especially through experience or conditioning.

learning curve *n.* A graph that depicts rate of learning, especially a graph of progress in the mastery of a skill against the time required for such mastery.

learning disability *n. Abbr.* **LD** Difficulty in understanding or using spoken or written language, affecting a person of normal intelligence and not arising from emotional disturbance or impairment of sight or hearing.

learn·ing-dis·a·bled (lûr′nĭng-dĭs-ā′bəld) *adj. Abbr.* **LD** Having a learning disability: *special help for learning-disabled students.*

learnt (lûrnt) *v.* A past tense and a past participle of **learn.**

lease (lēs) *n.* **1.a.** A contract granting use or occupation of property during a specified period in exchange for a specified rent. **b.** The term or duration of such a contract. **2.** Property used or occupied under the terms of such a contract. *—tr.* **leased, leas·ing, leas·es. 1.** To grant use or occupation of under the terms of a contract. **2.** To get or hold by such a contract. ***—idiom.* a new lease on life.** An opportunity to improve one's circumstances or outlook. [Middle English *les*, from Anglo-Norman, from *lesser*, to lease, variant of Old French *laissier*, to let go, from Latin *laxāre*, to loosen, from *laxus*, loose. See LAX.] **—leas′a·ble** *adj.* **—leas′er** *n.*

lease·back (lēs′băk′) *n.* A business arrangement whereby property is simultaneously sold and leased back to the seller for usually long-term continued use. Also called *sale and leaseback, sale-leaseback.*

lease·hold (lēs′hōld′) *n.* **1.** The fact of holding property by lease. **2.** Property held by lease. **—lease′hold′er** *n.*

leash (lēsh) *n.* **1.** A chain, rope, or strap attached to the collar or harness of an animal, especially a dog, and used to lead it or hold it in check. **2.** Control or restraint: *emotions kept in leash.* **3.a.** A set of three animals, such as hounds. **b.** A set of three. **—leash** *tr.v.* **leashed, leash·ing, leash·es.** To restrain with or as if with a leash. [Middle English *lees, lesh*, from Old French *laisse*, from *laissier*, to let go. See LEASE.]

leash law *n.* An ordinance requiring that dogs be kept on a leash when not restricted to their owners' property.

leas·ing (lē′sĭng) *n. Archaic.* **1.** The act of lying. **2.** A lie; a falsehood. [Middle English *lesing*, from Old English *lēasung*, from *lēasian*, to lie, from *lēas*, untrue. See **leu-** in Appendix.]

least (lēst) *adj.* A superlative of **little. 1.** Lowest in importance or rank. **2.a.** Smallest in magnitude or degree. **b.** Slightest or tiniest: *didn't care the least bit.* **—least** *adv.* Superlative of **little.** To or in the lowest or smallest degree. **—least** *n.* One that is the lowest or smallest in importance, rank, magnitude, or degree: *The dinner menu is the least of my worries tonight. The least you can do is to be polite.* ***—idioms.* at least. 1.** According to the lowest possible assessment; not less than: *waited at least an hour.* **2.** In any event; anyway: *You might at least answer.* **in the least.** At all: *I don't mind in the least.* **least of all.** Particularly not: *Nobody cared, least of all the manager.* [Middle English, from Old English *lǣst*. See **leis-**[2] in Appendix.]

least common denominator *n. Abbr.* **l.c.d.** *Mathematics.* The least common multiple of the denominators of a set of fractions: *The least common denominator of ⅓ and ¼ is 12.* Also called *lowest common denominator.*

least common multiple *n. Abbr.* **l.c.m.** *Mathematics.* The smallest quantity that is divisible by two or more given quantities without a remainder: *12 is the least common multiple of 2, 3, 4, and 6.* Also called *lowest common multiple.*

least flycatcher *n.* A small grayish bird *(Empidonax minimus)* commonly inhabiting fields and groves of eastern North America. Also called *chebec.*

least squares *pl.n. Statistics.* A method of determining the curve that best describes the relationship between expected and observed sets of data by minimizing the sums of the squares of deviation between observed and expected values.

♦**least·ways** (lēst′wāz′) *adv. Chiefly Southern U.S.* At least.

least·wise (lēst′wīz′) *adv. Informal.* In any event; at least.

leath·er (lĕth′ər) *n.* **1.** The dressed or tanned hide of an animal, usually with the hair removed. **2.** Any of various articles or parts made of dressed or tanned hide, such as a boot or strap. **3.** The flap of a dog's ear. **—leather** *tr.v.* **-ered, -er·ing, -ers. 1.** To cover wholly or in part with the dressed or tanned hide of an animal. **2.** *Informal.* To beat with a strap made of hide. **—leather** *adj.* **1.** Made of, relating to, or resembling dressed or tanned animal hide. **2.** *Slang.* Of, relating to, or patronized by people who dress in leather clothing primarily to indicate a preference for sadomasochistic sex: *leather types; a leather bar.* [Middle English *lether*, from Old English *lether-*.]

leath·er·back (lĕth′ər-băk′) *n.* The largest living sea turtle *(Dermochelys coriacea)*, found in tropical waters and having a tough, leathery carapace with seven longitudinal ridges.

leath·er·ette (lĕth′ə-rĕt′) *n.* Imitation leather. [Originally a trademark.]

leath·er·head (lĕth′ər-hĕd′) *n.* See **friarbird.**

leath·er·jack·et (lĕth′ər-jăk′ĭt) *n.* **1.** A silvery blue fish *(Oligoplites saurus)* of Atlantic waters, having leathery skin, yellow fins, and five spines on the anal fin. **2.** A fish of the family Balistidae of warm-temperate and tropical waters, including the filefishes and triggerfishes.

leath·ern (lĕth′ərn) *adj.* Made of, covered with, or resembling leather. [Middle English *lethern*, from Old English.]

leath·er·neck (lĕth′ər-nĕk′) *n. Slang.* A member of the U.S. Marine Corps. [From the leather neckband that was once part of the uniform.]

leath·er·wear (lĕth′ər-wâr′) *n.* Clothing made of leather.

leath·er·wood (lĕth′ər-wo͝od′) *n.* **1.** A deciduous shrub *(Dirca palustris)* of eastern North America, having tough flexible branches, pliable bark, and small yellow flowers. Also called *moosewood, wicopy.* **2.** See **titi**[1] (sense 1).

leath·er·work (lĕth′ər-wûrk′) *n.* **1.** Decorative work crafted in leather. **2.** Articles made of leather. **—leath′er·work′er** *n.* **—leath′er·work′ing** *n.*

leath·er·y (lĕth′ə-rē) *adj.* Having the texture or appearance of leather: *a leathery face.* **—leath′er·i·ness** *n.*

leave[1] (lēv) *v.* **left** (lĕft), **leav·ing, leaves.** *—tr.* **1.** To go out of or away from: *not allowed to leave the room.* **2.a.** To go without taking or removing: *left my book on the bus.* **b.** To omit or exclude: *left out the funniest part of the story.* **3.** To have as a result, consequence, or remainder: *The car left a trail of exhaust fumes. Two from eight leaves six.* **4.** To cause or allow to be or remain in a specified state: *left the lights on.* **5.a.** To have remaining after death: *left a young son.* **b.** To bequeath: *left her money to charity.* **6.** To give over to another to control or act on: *Leave all the details to us.* **7.a.** To abandon or forsake: *leave home; left her husband.* **b.** To remove oneself from association with or participation in: *left the navy for civilian life.* **8.a.** To give or deposit, as for use or information, upon one's departure or in one's absence: *He left a note for you. Leave your name and address.* **b.** To cause or permit to be or remain attainable: *left myself plenty of time.* **9.** *Non-Standard.* To allow or permit; let. *—intr.* To set out or depart; go: *When can you leave?* ***—phrasal verbs.* leave alone.** To refrain from disturbing or interfering. **leave off. 1.** To stop; cease. **2.** To stop doing or using. [Middle English *leaven*, from Old English *lǣfan*. See **leip-** in Appendix.] **—leav′er** *n.*

USAGE NOTE: *Leave alone* is acceptable as a substitute for *let alone* in the sense "to refrain from disturbing or interfering." The following examples were approved by a majority of the Usage Panel in an earlier survey: *Leave him alone and he will produce. Left alone, he was quite productive.* Those who do not accept these examples generally feel that *leave alone* should mean simply "to depart from one who remains in solitude": *They were left alone in the wilderness.* • In formal writing *leave* is not an acceptable substitute for *let* in the sense "to allow or permit." Only *let* is acceptable in the following examples: *Let me be. Let him go. Let us not quarrel. Let it lie.*

leave[2] (lēv) *n. Abbr.* **lv. 1.** Permission to do something. See Synonyms at **permission. 2.a.** Official permission to be absent from work or duty, as that granted to military or corporate personnel. **b.** The period of time granted by such permission. Also called *leave of absence.* **3.** An act of departing; a farewell: *took leave of her sadly.* [Middle English *leve*, from Old English *lēafe*, dative and accusative of *lēaf*. See **leubh-** in Appendix.]

leave[3] (lēv) *intr.v.* **leaved, leav·ing, leaves.** To put forth foliage; leaf. [Middle English *leaven*, from *leaf*, leaf. See LEAF.]

leaved (lēvd) *adj.* **1.** Having or bearing a leaf or leaves. **2.** Having a specified number or kind of leaves. Often used in combination: *three-leaved; wide-leaved.*

leav·en (lĕv′ən) *n.* **1.** An agent, such as yeast, that causes batter or dough to rise, especially by fermentation. **2.** An element, influence, or agent that works subtly to lighten, enliven, or modify a whole. See Synonyms at **catalyst. —leaven** *tr.v.* **-ened, -en·ing, -ens. 1.** To add a rising agent to. **2.** To cause to rise, especially by fermentation. **3.** To pervade with a lightening, enlivening, or modifying influence. [Middle English, from Old French *levain*, from Vulgar Latin **levāmen*, from Latin *levāre*, to raise. See **legʷh-** in Appendix.]

leav·en·ing (lĕv′ə-nĭng) *n.* An agent that causes rising, fermentation, or ferment; leaven. See Synonyms at **catalyst.**

Leav·en·worth (lĕv′ən-wûrth′). A city of northeast Kansas on the Missouri River northwest of Kansas City. Settled in 1854 by proslavery partisans from Missouri, it is near Fort Leavenworth, the site of a federal penitentiary. Population, 33,656.

leave of absence *n., pl.* **leaves of absence.** See **leave**[2] (sense 2).

leaves (lēvz) *n.* Plural of **leaf.**

least flycatcher
Empidonax minimus

leatherback
Dermochelys coriacea

ă pat	oi boy
ā pay	ou out
âr care	o͝o took
ä father	o͞o boot
ĕ pet	ŭ cut
ē be	ûr urge
ĭ pit	th thin
ī pie	*th* this
îr pier	hw which
ŏ pot	zh vision
ō toe	ə about, item
ô paw	♦ regionalism

Stress marks: **′** (primary); ′ (secondary), as in **dictionary** (dĭk′shə-nĕr′ē)

Lebanon

lectern
Franciscan friar reading at lectern

Leda
Leda and the Swan, 1654, by Michel Anguier (1613?–1686)

lederhosen
Traditional Tyrolean attire

leave-tak·ing (lēv′tā′kĭng) *n.* A departure or farewell.

leav·ings (lē′vĭngz) *pl.n.* Scraps or remains; residue. See Synonyms at **remainder.**

Leb·a·nese (lĕb′ə-nēz′, -nēs′) *adj. Abbr.* **Leb.** Of or relating to Lebanon, its people, or their culture. **—Lebanese** *n., pl.* **Lebanese.** *Abbr.* **Leb.** A native or inhabitant of Lebanon.

Leb·a·non (lĕb′ə-nən, -nŏn′). **1.** *Abbr.* **Leb.** A country of southwest Asia on the Mediterranean Sea. Occupied by Canaanites in ancient times, Lebanon has long been torn by civil and religious strife. It proclaimed its independence in 1941, but full self-government was not achieved until 1945. Beirut is the capital and the largest city. Population, 2,637,000. **2.** A city of southeast Pennsylvania east-northeast of Harrisburg. It is an industrial center in the Pennsylvania Dutch farm country. Population, 25,711.

Lebanon Mountains. A range of Lebanon extending about 161 km (100 mi) parallel to the Mediterranean coast and rising to 3,090 m (10,131 ft).

le·bens·raum (lā′bəns-roum′) *n.* **1.** Additional territory deemed necessary to a nation, especially Nazi Germany, for its continued existence or economic well-being. **2.** Adequate space in which to live, develop, or function. [German : *Lebens,* genitive sing. of *Leben,* life (from Middle High German, from Old High German *lebēn;* see **leip-** in Appendix) + *Raum,* space (from Middle High German *roum,* from Old High German *rūm;* see **reuə-** in Appendix).]

leb·ku·chen (lāb′ko͞o′kən, lāp′ko͞o′KHən) *n., pl.* **lebkuchen.** A chewy, usually honey-flavored Christmas cookie containing nuts and candied fruits. [German, from Middle High German *lebekuoche* : *lebe,* loaf (from Old High German *leip*) + *kuoche,* kuchen; see KUCHEN.]

Le·brun (lə-brœN′), **Albert.** 1871–1950. French politician who was the last president of the Third Republic (1932–1940).

Lebrun, Charles. 1619–1690. French painter, designer, and courtier. As head of the French Royal Academy, he had a major influence on the development of the Louis Quatorze style.

le Car·ré (lə kă-rā′), **John.** Pen name of David John Moore Cornwell. Born 1931. British writer of popular espionage novels, including *The Spy Who Came in from the Cold* (1963).

Lec·ce (lĕch′ā, lĕt′chĕ). A city of extreme southeast Italy east of Taranto. Lecce was a semi-independent county from 1053 to 1463. Population, 91,625.

lech[1] (lĕch) *Slang. n.* **1.** A lecher: *"a coke-snorting arbitrageur who's an irrepressible lech"* (Pauline Kael). **2.** A lecherous desire. **—lech** *intr.v.* **leched, lech·ing, lech·es.** To behave in a lecherous manner. [Short for LECHER.]

lech[2] (lĕch) *n.* Variant of **letch.**

Lech (lĕk, lĕKH). A river rising in western Austria and flowing about 249 km (155 mi) generally north to the Danube River in southern Germany.

lech·er (lĕch′ər) *n.* A man given to lechery. [Middle English, from Old French *lecheor,* from *lechier,* to lick, to live in debauchery, of Germanic origin. See **leigh-** in Appendix.]

lech·er·ous (lĕch′ər-əs) *adj.* Given to, characterized by, or eliciting lechery. **—lech′er·ous·ly** *adv.* **—lech′er·ous·ness** *n.*

lech·er·y (lĕch′ə-rē) *n., pl.* **-ies. 1.** Excessive indulgence in sexual activity; lewdness. **2.** A lecherous act.

lec·i·thin (lĕs′ə-thĭn) *n.* Any of a group of phospholipids found in egg yolks and the plasma membrane of plant and animal cells, used as an emulsifier in a wide range of commercial products, including foods, cosmetics, paints, and plastics. [French *lécithine* : Greek *lekithos,* egg yolk + *-ine,* -in.]

lec·i·thin·ase (lĕs′ə-thə-nās′, -nāz′) *n.* Any of several enzymes that hydrolyze lecithin.

Leck·y (lĕk′ē), **William Edward Hartpole.** 1838–1903. Irish historian who wrote *Democracy and Liberty* (1896).

Le·conte de Lisle (lə- kôNt′ də lēl′), **Charles Marie.** 1818–1894. French poet and a leading Parnassian. His works include *Poèmes Antiques* (1852) and *Poèmes Barbares* (1862).

Le Cor·bu·sier (lə kôr-bo͞o-zyā′, -bü-). Pseudonym of Charles Édouard Jeanneret. 1887–1965. Swiss-born French architect and writer. The most powerful advocate of the modernist school, he designed numerous high-rise residential complexes.

lect. *abbr.* Lecture.

lec·tern (lĕk′tərn) *n.* **1.** A reading desk with a slanted top holding the books from which scriptural passages are read during a church service. **2.** A stand that serves as a support for the notes or books of a speaker. [Middle English *lettorne, lectorn,* from Old French *lettrun,* from Medieval Latin *lēctrīnum,* from Late Latin *lēctrum,* from Latin *lēctus,* past participle of *legere,* to read. See **leg-** in Appendix.]

lec·tin (lĕk′tĭn) *n.* Any of several plant glycoproteins that bind to specific carbohydrate groups on the plasma membrane of cells, used in the laboratory to stimulate proliferation of lymphocytes and to agglutinate red blood cells. [Latin *lēctus,* past participle of *legere,* to select; see SELECT + –IN.]

lec·tion (lĕk′shən) *n.* **1.** A variant reading or transcription of a text or copy. **2.** A reading from Scripture that forms a part of a church service. [Latin *lēctiō, lēctiōn-,* a reading. See LESSON.]

lec·tion·ar·y (lĕk′shə-nĕr′ē) *n., pl.* **-ies.** A book or list of lections to be read at church services during the year. [Medieval Latin *lēctiōnārium,* from Latin *lēctiō, lēctiōn-,* a reading. See LESSON.]

lec·tor (lĕk′tər) *n.* **1.** A person who reads aloud certain of the scriptural passages used in a church service. **2.** A public lecturer or reader in certain universities. [Middle English, from Late Latin *lēctor,* from Latin, reader, from *lēctus,* past participle of *legere,* to read. See LECTURE.]

lectr. *abbr.* Lecturer.

lec·ture (lĕk′chər) *n. Abbr.* **lect. 1.** An exposition of a given subject delivered before an audience or a class, as for the purpose of instruction. **2.** An earnest admonition or reproof; a reprimand. **—lecture** *v.* **-tured, -tur·ing, -tures.** *—intr.* To deliver a lecture or series of lectures. *—tr.* **1.** To deliver a lecture to (a class or an audience). **2.** To admonish or reprove earnestly, often at length: *always lecturing me about my manners.* [Middle English, a reading, from Old French, from Medieval Latin *lēctūra,* from Latin *lēctus,* past participle of *legere,* to read. See **leg-** in Appendix.]

lec·tur·er (lĕk′chər-ər) *n. Abbr.* **lectr. 1.** One who delivers lectures, especially professionally. **2.a.** A member of the faculty of a college or university usually having qualified status without rank or tenure. **b.** A faculty member ranking below an assistant professor. **c.** The academic rank held by such a faculty member. **3.** *Chiefly British.* A university teacher, especially one ranking next below a reader.

lec·ture·ship (lĕk′chər-shĭp′) *n.* **1.** The status or position of a lecturer. **2.** An endowment or a foundation supporting a series or course of lectures. [Alteration of *lecturership.*]

led (lĕd) *v.* Past tense and past participle of **lead[1].**

LED (ĕl′ē-dē′, lĕd) *n.* A semiconductor diode that converts applied voltage to light and is used in digital displays, as of a calculator. [*l(ight-)e(mitting) d(iode).*]

Le·da (lē′də) *n.* **1.** *Greek Mythology.* A queen of Sparta and the mother, by Zeus in the form of a swan, of Helen and Pollux and, by her husband Tyndareus, of Castor and Clytemnestra. **2.** The tenth satellite of the planet Jupiter.

Led·bet·ter (lĕd′bĕt′ər), **Huddie.** Known as "Leadbelly." 1885?–1949. American folk and blues musician.

Led·er·berg (lĕd′ər-bûrg′, lā′dər-), **Joshua.** Born 1925. American geneticist. He shared a 1958 Nobel Prize for work with genetic mechanisms.

le·der·ho·sen (lā′dər-hō′zən) *pl.n.* Leather shorts, often with suspenders, worn by men and boys, especially in Bavaria. [German, from Middle High German *lederhose* : *leder,* leather (from Old High German *ledar*) + *hose,* trousers (from Old High German *hosa;* see **(s)keu-** in Appendix).]

ledge (lĕj) *n.* **1.** A horizontal projection forming a narrow shelf on a wall. **2.** A cut or projection forming a shelf on a cliff or rock wall. **3.** An underwater ridge or rock shelf. **4.** A level of rock-bearing ore; a vein. [Middle English, crossbar, probably from *leggen,* to lay, from Old English *lecgan.* See **legh-** in Appendix.] **—ledg′y** *adj.*

ledg·er (lĕj′ər) *n.* **1.a.** A book in which the monetary transactions of a business are posted in the form of debits and credits. **b.** A book to which the record of accounts is transferred as final entry from original postings. **2.** A slab of stone laid flat over a grave. **3.** A horizontal timber in a scaffold, attached to the uprights and supporting the putlogs. [Middle English *legger,* breviary, probably from *leggen,* to lay. See LEDGE.]

ledger board *n.* **1.** The top railing of a fence or balustrade. **2.** A narrow horizontal board attached to a row of studs to support the ends of floor or ceiling joists. In this sense, also called *ribbon.*

ledger line *n. Music.* A short line placed above or below a staff to accommodate notes higher or lower than the range of the staff.

Le Duc Tho (lā′ dŭk′ tō′). 1911–1990. Vietnamese political leader who negotiated the North Vietnamese–U.S. cease-fire (1973) with Henry Kissinger. Both were awarded the Nobel Peace Prize (1973), but Le Duc Tho refused it on the grounds that peace was not yet established in South Vietnam.

lee (lē) *n.* **1.** *Nautical.* The side away from the direction from which the wind blows; the side sheltered from the wind. **2.** Cover; shelter. **—lee** *adj.* **1.** *Nautical.* Of or relating to the side sheltered from the wind: *the lee gunwale.* **2.** Located in or facing the path of an oncoming glacier. Used of a geologic formation. [Middle English *le,* from Old English *hlēo,* shelter, protection. See **kele-[1]** in Appendix.]

Lee (lē), **Ann.** Known as "Mother Ann." 1736–1784. British religious leader and founder (1776) of the Shakers in America.

Lee, Charles. 1731–1782. British-born American Revolutionary general whose performance at the Battle of Monmouth (1778) brought about his court-martial and dismissal.

Lee, Henry. Known as "Lighthorse Harry." 1756–1818. American Revolutionary politician and soldier. He served in the Virginia legislature (1785–1788 and 1789–1791) and as governor of Virginia (1792–1795).

Lee, (Nelle) Harper. Born 1926. American writer. Her novel *To Kill a Mockingbird* (1960), dealing with racial injustice in the South, won a Pulitzer Prize.

Lee, Richard Henry. 1732–1794. American Revolutionary leader who proposed the resolution calling for the independence of the American colonies from England (1776).

Lee, Robert Edward. 1807–1870. American Confederate general in the Civil War. He won victories at Bull Run (1862), Fredericksburg (1862), and Chancellorsville (1863) before surrendering to Gen. Ulysses S. Grant at Appomattox (1865).

Lee, Sir **Sidney.** 1859–1926. British biographer who edited the *Dictionary of National Biography* from 1891 to 1917.

Lee, Tsung Dao. Born 1926. Chinese-born American physicist. He shared a 1957 Nobel Prize for disproving the principle of conservation of parity.

lee·board (lē′bôrd′, -bōrd′) *n. Nautical.* One of a pair of movable boards or plates attached to the hull of a sailing vessel to reduce downwind drift.

leech¹ (lēch) *n.* **1.** Any of various chiefly aquatic bloodsucking or carnivorous annelid worms of the class Hirudinea, of which one species *(Hirudo medicinalis)* was formerly used by physicians to bleed patients. **2.** One that preys on or clings to another; a parasite. **3.** *Archaic.* A physician. **—leech** *v.* **leeched, leech·ing, leech·es.** *—tr.* **1.** To bleed with leeches. **2.** To drain the essence or exhaust the resources of. *—intr.* To attach oneself to another in the manner of a leech. [Middle English *leche,* physician, leech, from Old English *lǣce.* See **leg-** in Appendix.]

leech² (lēch) *n. Nautical.* **1.** Either vertical edge of a square sail. **2.** The after edge of a fore-and-aft sail. [Middle English *leche,* probably from Middle Low German *līk,* leech line. See **leig-** in Appendix.]

Leeds (lēdz). A borough of north-central England northeast of Manchester. Incorporated in 1626, it is a major commercial, transportation, and industrial center. Population, 718,100.

leek (lēk) *n.* An edible plant *(Allium porrum)* related to the onion and having a white, slender bulb and flat, dark-green leaves. [Middle English *lek,* from Old English *lēac.*]

leer (lîr) *intr.v.* **leered, leer·ing, leers.** To look with a sidelong glance, indicative especially of sexual desire or sly and malicious intent. **—leer** *n.* A desirous, sly, or knowing look. [Probably from obsolete *leer,* cheek, from Middle English *ler,* from Old English *hlēor.* See **kleu-** in Appendix.] **—leer′ing·ly** *adv.*

leer·y (lîr′ē) *adj.* **-i·er, -i·est.** Suspicious or distrustful; wary: *was leery of aggressive salespeople.* **—leer′i·ly** *adv.* **—leer′i·ness** *n.*

lees (lēz) *pl.n.* Sediment settling during fermentation, especially in wine; dregs. [Middle English *lies,* pl. of *lie,* from Old French, from Medieval Latin *lia,* probably of Celtic origin. See **legh-** in Appendix.]

lee shore *n. Nautical.* A shore toward which the wind blows and toward which a ship is likely to be driven.

Lee's Summit (lēz). A city of western Missouri southeast of Kansas City. It is a manufacturing center within the Kansas City metropolitan area. Population, 28,741.

Leeu·war·den (lā′vär-dn, lā′ü-wär′dn). A city of northern Netherlands northeast of the Ijsselmeer. Chartered in 1435, it was noted for its manufacture of gold and silver articles from the 16th to the 18th century. Population, 85,435.

Leeu·wen·hoek or **Leu·wen·hoek** (lā′vən-ho͝ok′, lā′ü-wən-ho͝ok′), **Anton van.** 1632–1723. Dutch microscopy pioneer and naturalist who formulated early descriptions of bacteria and spermatozoa.

lee·ward (lē′wərd, lo͞o′ərd) *Nautical. adv. & adj.* On or toward the side to which the wind is blowing. **—leeward** *n.* The lee side or quarter.

Lee·ward Islands (lē′wərd). **1.** The northern group of the Lesser Antilles in the West Indies, extending from the Virgin Islands southeast to Guadeloupe. The islands were hotly contested by the Spanish, French, and British in the 17th and 18th centuries. **2.** A chain of small islets of Hawaii in the central Pacific Ocean west-northwest of the main islands.

lee·way (lē′wā′) *n.* **1.** *Nautical.* The drift of a ship or an aircraft to leeward of the course being steered. **2.** A margin of freedom or variation, as of activity, time, or expenditure; latitude. See Synonyms at **room.**

left¹ (lĕft) *adj. Abbr.* **l. 1.a.** Of, belonging to, located on, or being the side of the body to the north when the subject is facing east. **b.** Of, relating to, directed toward, or located on the left side. **c.** Located on the left side of a person facing downstream: *the left bank of a river.* **2.** Often **Left.** Of or belonging to the political or intellectual left. **—left** *n.* **1.a.** The direction or position on the left side. **b.** The left side. **c.** The left hand. **d.** A turn in the direction of the left hand or side. **2.** Often **Left. a.** The people and groups who advocate liberal, often radical measures to effect change in the established order, especially in politics, usually to achieve the equality, freedom, and well-being of the common citizens of a state. Also called *left wing.* **b.** The opinion of those advocating such measures. **3.** *Sports.* A blow delivered by a boxer's left hand. **4.** *Baseball.* Left field. **—left** *adv.* Toward or on the left. [Middle English, from Old English *lyft-,* weak, useless (in *lyftādl,* paralysis).]

left² (lĕft) *v.* Past tense and past participle of **leave¹.**

left atrioventricular valve *n.* See **mitral valve.**

Left Bank. A district of Paris on the southern, or left, bank of the Seine River. It has long been noted for its artistic and bohemian atmosphere.

left-brain (lĕft′brān′) *n.* The cerebral hemisphere to the left of the corpus callosum, controlling the right side of the body.

left face *n.* A military command to turn 90 degrees to the left.

left field *n.* **1.** *Abbr.* **LF** *Baseball.* **a.** The third of the outfield that is to the left, looking from home plate. **b.** The position played by the left fielder. **2.** *Informal.* A position far from the center or mainstream, as of opinion or reason: *opinions that are out in left field.*

left fielder *n. Abbr.* **LF** *Baseball.* The player who defends left field.

left-hand (lĕft′hănd′) *adj.* **1.** Of, relating to, or located on the left. **2.** Relating to, designed for, or done with the left hand.

left-hand·ed (lĕft′hăn′dĭd) *adj.* **1.a.** Using the left hand more skillfully or easily than the right. **b.** *Sports.* Swinging from left to right: *a left-handed batter; a left-handed golfer.* **2.a.** Done with the left hand. **b.** Intended for wear on or use by the left hand: *left-handed scissors.* **3.** Awkward; maladroit. **4.** Of doubtful sincerity; dubious: *left-handed flattery; a left-handed compliment.* **5.** Of, relating to, or born of a morganatic marriage. **6.** Turning or spiraling from right to left; counterclockwise. **—left-handed** *adv.* **1.** With the left hand. **2.** *Sports.* From the left to the right: *swings left-handed.* **—left′-hand′ed·ly** *adv.* **—left′-hand′ed·ness** *n.*

left-hand·er (lĕft′hăn′dər) *n.* One who is left-handed.

left·ish (lĕf′tĭsh) *adj.* Tending toward the political left.

left·ism also **Left·ism** (lĕf′tĭz′əm) *n.* **1.** The ideology of the political left. **2.** Belief in or support of the tenets of the political left. **—left′ist** *adj. & n.*

left·most (lĕft′mōst′) *adj.* Farthest to the left: *in the leftmost lane of traffic.*

left·o·ver (lĕft′ō′vər) *adj.* Remaining as an unused portion or amount. **—leftover** *n.* **1.** A remnant or an unused portion. **2. leftovers.** A dish made of food remaining from a previous meal.

left·ward (lĕft′wərd) *adv. & adj.* To or on the left.

left wing also **Left Wing** *n.* **1.** The liberal or radical faction of a group. **2.** See **left¹** (sense 2a). **—left′-wing′** (lĕft′wĭng′) *adj.* **—left′-wing′er** *n.*

left·y (lĕf′tē) *Informal. n., pl.* **-ies. 1.** A left-handed person. **2.** An advocate or a member of the political left. **—lefty** *adv.* With the left hand or in a left-handed manner: *bats lefty.*

leg (lĕg) *n.* **1.a.** A limb or an appendage of an animal, used for locomotion or support. **b.** One of the lower or hind limbs in human beings and primates. **c.** The part of the limb between the knee and foot in vertebrates. **d.** The back part of the hindquarter of a meat animal. **2.** A supporting part resembling a leg in shape or function. **3.** One of the branches of a forked or jointed object. **4.** The part of a garment, especially of a pair of trousers, that covers the leg. **5.** *Mathematics.* Either side of a right triangle that is not the hypotenuse. **6.** A stage of a journey or course, especially: **a.** *Nautical.* The distance traveled by a sailing vessel on a single tack. **b.** The part of an air route or a flight pattern that is between two successive stops, positions, or changes in direction. **c.** One of several contests that must be successfully completed in order to determine the winner of a competition. **d.** *Sports.* One stretch of a relay race. **7. legs.** The narrow streams of swirled wine that run slowly down along the inside of a glass, often believed to indicate that the wine is full-bodied. **—leg** *intr.v.* **legged, leg·ging, legs.** *Informal.* To go on foot; walk or run. Often used with the indefinite *it: Because we missed the bus, we had to leg it across town.* ***—idioms.*** **a leg to stand on.** *Slang.* A justifiable or logical basis for defense; support: *He doesn't have a leg to stand on in this debate.* **a leg up.** *Slang.* **1.** The act or an instance of assisting; a boost. **2.** A position of advantage; an edge: *We have a leg up on the competition.* **on (one's) last legs.** At the end of one's strength or resources; ready to collapse, fail, or die. [Middle English, from Old Norse *leggr.*]

leg. *abbr.* **1.** Legal. **2.** Legate. **3.** *Music.* Legato. **4.** Legislation; legislative; legislature.

leg·a·cy (lĕg′ə-sē) *n., pl.* **-cies. 1.** Money or property bequeathed to another by will. **2.** Something handed down from an ancestor or a predecessor or from the past: *a legacy of religious freedom.* See Synonyms at **heritage.** [Middle English *legacie,* office of a deputy, from Old French, from Medieval Latin *lēgātia,* from Latin *lēgātus,* past participle of *lēgāre,* to depute, bequeath. See **leg-** in Appendix.]

le·gal (lē′gəl) *adj. Abbr.* **leg. 1.** Of, relating to, or concerned with law: *legal papers.* **2.a.** Authorized by or based on law: *a legal right.* **b.** Established by law; statutory: *the legal owner.* **3.** In conformity with or permitted by law: *legal business operations.* **4.** Recognized or enforced by law rather than by equity. **5.** In terms of or created by the law: *a legal offense.* **6.** Applicable to or characteristic of attorneys or their profession. **—legal** *n.* **1.** One that is in accord with certain rules or laws. **2. legals.** Investments that may be legally made by fiduciaries and certain institutions, such as savings banks and insurance companies. In this sense, also called *legal list.* [Middle English, from Old French, from Latin *lēgālis,* from *lēx, lēg-,* law. See **leg-** in Appendix.] **—le′gal·ly** *adv.*

legal age *n.* The age at which a person may by law assume the rights and responsibilities of an adult.

legal aid *n.* Legal assistance provided, as by a specially established organization, for those unable to afford an attorney.

legal cap *n.* Ruled writing paper in tablet form, measuring 8½ by 13 to 16 inches and generally used by attorneys.

le·gal·ese (lē′gə-lēz′, -lēs′) *n.* The specialized vocabulary of

Le Duc Tho
Photographed in 1972

Robert E. Lee
Photographed in 1865 by Mathew Brady

leeboard

ă pat	oi boy
ā pay	ou out
âr care	o͝o took
ä father	o͞o boot
ĕ pet	ŭ cut
ē be	ûr urge
ĭ pit	th thin
ī pie	*th* this
îr pier	hw which
ŏ pot	zh vision
ō toe	ə about, item
ô paw	♦ regionalism

Stress marks: **′** (primary); ′ (secondary), as in **dictionary** (dĭk′shə-nĕr′ē)

the legal profession, especially when considered to be complex or abstruse.

legal holiday *n.* A holiday authorized by law and characterized by a limit or ban on work or official business.

le·gal·ism (lē′gə-lĭz′əm) *n.* **1.** Strict, literal adherence to the law or to a particular code, as of religion or morality. **2.** A legal word, expression, or rule. **—le′gal·ist** *n.* **—le′gal·is′tic** *adj.* **—le′gal·is′ti·cal·ly** *adv.*

le·gal·i·ty (lē-găl′ĭ-tē) *n., pl.* **-ties. 1.** The state or quality of being legal; lawfulness. **2.** Adherence to or observance of the law. **3.** A requirement enjoined by law. Often used in the plural.

le·gal·ize (lē′gə-līz′) *tr.v.* **-ized, -iz·ing, -iz·es.** To make legal or lawful; authorize or sanction by law. **—le′gal·i·za′tion** (-gə-lĭ-zā′shən) *n.*

Le Gal·lienne (lə găl′yən, găl-yĕn′), **Eva.** 1899–1991. British-born American actress who founded (1926) and directed (1926–1934) the Civic Repertory Theatre in New York City.

legal list *n.* See **legal** (sense 2).

legal pad *n.* A pad of ruled, usually yellow writing paper that measures 8½ by 14 inches.

legal reserve *n.* The sum of money that a bank or an insurance company is required by law to set aside as security.

legal separation *n. Law.* A court decree recognizing that a married couple is living apart and regulating the couple's mutual rights and liabilities. Also called *judicial separation.*

le·gal-size (lē′gəl-sīz′) *adj.* **1.** Being a sheet of paper that measures approximately 8½ by 14 inches. **2.** Designed to hold such sheets of paper: *a legal-size envelope.*

legal tender *n.* Legally valid currency that may be offered in payment of a debt and that a creditor must accept.

Le·ga·nés (lĕ′gä-nĕs′). A city of central Spain, an industrial and residential suburb of Madrid. Population, 168,984.

leg·ate (lĕg′ĭt) *n. Abbr.* **leg.** An official emissary, especially an official representative of the pope. [Middle English, from Old French *legat,* from Medieval Latin *lēgātus,* from Latin, past participle of *lēgāre,* to depute. See **leg-** in Appendix.] **—leg′ate·ship′** *n.*

leg·a·tee (lĕg′ə-tē′) *n.* The inheritor of a legacy. [From *legate,* to bequeath, from Latin *lēgāre, lēgāt-.* See LEGACY.]

leg·a·tine (lĕg′ə-tĭn, -tīn′) *adj.* Of, directed by, or authorized by a legate.

le·ga·tion (lĭ-gā′shən) *n.* **1.** The act of sending a legate. **2. a.** A diplomatic mission in a foreign country ranking below an embassy. **b.** The diplomatic minister and staff of such a mission. **c.** The premises occupied by such a mission.

le·ga·to (lĭ-gä′tō) *Music. adv. & adj. Abbr.* **leg.** In a smooth, even style. Used chiefly as a direction. **—legato** *n., pl.* **-tos.** A legato passage or movement. [Italian, past participle of *legare,* to bind, tie together, from Latin *ligāre.* See **leig-** in Appendix.]

le·ga·tor (lĭ-gā′tər) *n.* One that makes a will; a testator. [Latin *lēgātor,* from *lēgāre,* to bequeath. See LEGACY.]

leg·end (lĕj′ənd) *n.* **1. a.** An unverified story handed down from earlier times, especially one popularly believed to be historical. **b.** A body or collection of such stories. **c.** A romanticized or popularized myth of modern times. **2.** One that inspires legends or achieves legendary fame. **3. a.** An inscription or a title on an object, such as a coin. **b.** An explanatory caption accompanying an illustration. **c.** An explanatory table or list of the symbols appearing on a map or chart. [Middle English, from Old French *legende,* from Medieval Latin *(lectiō) legenda,* (lesson) to be read, from Latin, feminine gerundive of *legere,* to read. See **leg-** in Appendix.]

USAGE NOTE: The words *legend* and *legendary* have come to be used in recent years to refer to any person or achievement whose fame promises to be particularly enduring, even if its renown is created more by the media than by oral tradition. Strictly speaking, there is nothing *legendary* about the accomplishments of a major-league baseball star or the voice of a famous opera singer, since their accomplishments are documented in an extensive public record. But this new usage is common journalistic hyperbole and is acceptable to 55 percent of the Usage Panel.

leg·en·dar·y (lĕj′ən-dĕr′ē) *adj.* **1.** Of, constituting, based on, or of the nature of a legend. **2. a.** Celebrated in legend. **b.** Extremely well known; famous or renowned. See Usage Note at **legend. —leg′en·dar′i·ly** *adv.*

Le·gen·dre (lə-zhän′drə, -zhäɴ′-), **Adrien Marie.** 1752–1833. French mathematician who is best remembered for his work on number theory and elliptic integrals.

leg·end·ry (lĕj′ən-drē) *n., pl.* **-ries.** A collection or body of legends.

Lé·ger (lā-zhā′), **Alexis Saint-Léger.** Pseudonym Saint-John Perse. 1887–1975. French poet and diplomat who won the 1960 Nobel Prize for literature.

Léger, Fernand. 1881–1955. French artist. An early cubist who worked in bright flat colors, Léger incorporated industrial and mechanical images into his work.

leg·er·de·main (lĕj′ər-də-mān′) *n.* **1.** Sleight of hand. **2.** A show of skill or deceitful cleverness: *financial legerdemain.* [Middle English *legerdemayn,* from Old French *leger de main* : *leger,* light (from Vulgar Latin **leviārius,* from Latin *levis;* see **legʷh-** in Appendix) + *de,* of (from Latin *dē;* see DE–) + *main,* hand; see MORTMAIN.]

le·ger·i·ty (lə-jĕr′ĭ-tē) *n.* Quickness or agility of mind or body. [French *légèreté,* from Old French *legerete,* from *leger,* light. See LEGERDEMAIN.]

le·ges (lē′jēz′) *n.* Plural of **lex.**

leg·ged (lĕg′ĭd, lĕgd) *adj.* Having a specified kind or number of legs. Often used in combination: *long-legged; four-legged.*

leg·ging (lĕg′ĭng) *n.* **1.** A leg covering usually extending from the ankle to the knee and often made of material such as leather or canvas, worn especially by soldiers and workers. **2. leggings. a.** Close-fitting usually knit trousers, often worn under a skirt for warmth. **b.** Warm outerwear trousers for children.

leg·gy (lĕg′ē) *adj.* **-gi·er, -gi·est. 1.** Having disproportionately long legs: *a leggy colt.* **2.** *Informal.* Having attractively long, slender legs: *a leggy dancer.* **3.** Having long, spindly, often leafless stems: *a leggy houseplant.* **—leg′gi·ness** *n.*

leg·horn (lĕg′hôrn′, -ərn) *n.* **1. a.** The dried and bleached straw of an Italian variety of wheat. **b.** A plaited fabric made from this straw. **c.** A hat made from this fabric. **2.** Often **Leghorn.** Any of a breed of small, hardy domestic fowl of Mediterranean origin, noted for prolific production of eggs. [After LEGHORN.]

Leghorn or **Li·vor·no** (lē-vōr′nō). A city of northwest Italy on the Ligurian Sea southeast of Genoa. A fortified town in the Middle Ages, Leghorn was developed into a flourishing community by the Medici. Population, 175,371.

leg·i·ble (lĕj′ə-bəl) *adj.* **1.** Possible to read or decipher. **2.** Plainly discernible; apparent: *legible weaknesses in character and disposition.* [Middle English, from Late Latin *legibilis,* from Latin *legere,* to read. See **leg-** in Appendix.] **—leg′i·bil′i·ty, leg′i·ble·ness** *n.* **—leg′i·bly** *adv.*

le·gion (lē′jən) *n.* **1.** The major unit of the Roman army consisting of 3,000 to 6,000 infantry troops and 100 to 200 cavalry troops. **2.** A large military unit trained for combat; an army. **3.** A large number; a multitude. See Synonyms at **multitude. 4.** Often **Legion.** A national organization of former members of the armed forces. **—legion** *adj.* Constituting a large number; multitudinous: *Her admirers were legion. His mistakes were legion.* [Middle English *legioun,* from Old French *legion,* from Latin *legiō, legiōn-,* from *legere,* to gather. See **leg-** in Appendix.]

le·gion·ar·y (lē′jə-nĕr′ē) *adj.* Of, relating to, or constituting a legion. **—legionary** *n., pl.* **-ies.** A soldier of a legion.

legionary ant *n.* See **army ant.**

le·gion·naire (lē′jə-nâr′) *n.* A member of a legion. [French *légionnaire,* from Old French, from *legion,* legion. See LEGION.]

Le·gion·naires' disease (lē′jə-nârz′) *n.* An acute, sometimes fatal respiratory disease caused by a bacterium of the genus *Legionella,* especially *L. pneumophila,* and characterized by severe pneumonia, headache, and a dry cough. [So called because it was first recognized when an outbreak occurred during an American Legion Convention in Philadelphia in 1976.]

Legion of Honor *n.* A high French civilian and military decoration, instituted in 1802. [Translation of French *Légion d'honneur.*]

Legion of Merit *n. Abbr.* **LM** A U.S. military decoration awarded for exceptionally meritorious conduct in the performance of outstanding services.

legis. *abbr.* Legislation; legislative; legislature.

leg·is·late (lĕj′ĭ-slāt′) *v.* **-lat·ed, -lat·ing, -lates.** *—intr.* To create or pass laws. *—tr.* To create or bring about by or as if by legislation. [Back-formation from LEGISLATOR.]

leg·is·la·tion (lĕj′ĭ-slā′shən) *n. Abbr.* **leg., legis. 1.** The act or process of legislating; lawmaking. **2.** A proposed or enacted law or group of laws.

leg·is·la·tive (lĕj′ĭ-slā′tĭv) *adj. Abbr.* **leg., legis. 1.** Of or relating to the enactment of laws. **2.** Resulting from or decided by legislation. **3.** Having the power to create laws; intended to legislate. **4.** Of or relating to a legislature. **—legislative** *n.* The legislative body of a government; a legislature. **—leg′is·la′tive·ly** *adv.*

leg·is·la·tor (lĕj′ĭ-slā′tər) *n.* One that creates or enacts laws, especially a member of a legislative body. [French *législateur,* from Old French, from Latin *lēgis lātor* : *lēgis,* genitive of *lēx,* law; see **leg-** in Appendix + *lātor,* proposer, bearer (from *lātus,* past participle of *ferre,* to propose, bear; see **tele-** in Appendix).] **—leg′is·la·to′ri·al** (-lə-tôr′ē-əl, -tōr′-) *adj.* **—leg′is·la′tor·ship′** *n.*

leg·is·la·ture (lĕj′ĭ-slā′chər) *n. Abbr.* **leg., legis.** An officially elected or otherwise selected body of people vested with the responsibility and power to make laws for a political unit, such as a state or nation.

le·gist (lē′jĭst) *n.* A specialist in law. [Middle English *legiste,* from Old French, from Medieval Latin *lēgista,* from Latin *lēx, lēg-,* law. See **leg-** in Appendix.]

le·git (lə-jĭt′) *adj. Slang.* Legitimate.

le·git·i·ma·cy (lə-jĭt′ə-mə-sē) *n.* The quality or fact of being legitimate.

le·git·i·mate (lə-jĭt′ə-mĭt) *adj.* **1.** Being in compliance with the law; lawful: *a legitimate business.* **2.** Being in accordance with established or accepted patterns and standards: *legitimate advertising practices.* **3.** Based on logical reasoning; reasonable: *a legitimate solution to the problem.* **4.** Authentic; genuine: *a*

leg-of-mutton

ă pat	oi boy
ā pay	ou out
âr care	ŏŏ took
ä father	ōō boot
ĕ pet	ŭ cut
ē be	ûr urge
ĭ pit	th thin
ī pie	*th* this
îr pier	hw which
ŏ pot	zh vision
ō toe	ə about, item
ô paw	♦ regionalism

Stress marks: ′ (primary); ′ (secondary), as in **dictionary** (dĭk′shə-nĕr′ē)

legitimate complaint. **5.** Born of legally married parents: *legitimate issue.* **6.** Of, relating to, or ruling by hereditary right: *a legitimate monarch.* **7.** Of or relating to drama of high professional quality that excludes burlesque, vaudeville, and some forms of musical comedy: *the legitimate theater.* **—legitimate** (-māt′) *tr.v.* **-mat·ed, -mat·ing, -mates.** To make legitimate, as: **a.** To give legal force or status to; make lawful. **b.** To establish (a child born out of wedlock) as legitimate by legal means. **c.** To sanction formally or officially; authorize. **d.** To demonstrate or declare to be justified. [Middle English *legitimat,* born in wedlock, from Medieval Latin *lēgitimātus,* past participle of *lēgitimāre,* to make lawful, from Latin *lēgitimus,* legitimate, from *lēx, lēg-,* law. See **leg-** in Appendix.] **—le·git′i·mate·ly** *adv.* **—le·git′i·mate·ness** *n.* **—le·git′i·ma′tion** *n.* **—le·git′i·mat′or** (-māt′ər) *n.*

le·git·i·ma·tize (lə-jĭt′ə-mə-tīz′) *tr.v.* **-tized, -tiz·ing, -tiz·es.** To legitimate.

le·git·i·mist (lə-jĭt′ə-mĭst) *n.* One that believes in or advocates rule by hereditary right. **—le·git′i·mism** *n.* **—le·git′i·mist** *adj.*

le·git·i·mize (lə-jĭt′ə-mīz′) *tr.v.* **-mized, -miz·ing, -miz·es.** To legitimate. **—le·git′i·mi·za′tion** (-mĭ-zā′shən) *n.* **—le·git′i·miz′er** *n.*

leg·man (lĕg′măn′, -mən) *n. Informal.* **1.** A reporter whose job is to gather information at the scene of an event or by visiting various news sources. **2.** An assistant, as in an office, who performs tasks such as gathering information or running errands especially outside the workplace.

Leg·ni·ca (lĕg-nēt′sə). A city of southwest Poland west of Wrocław. Chartered in 1252, it was acquired by Prussia in 1742 and was the site of Frederick the Great's victory over the Austrians (August 15, 1760). Population, 97,700.

leg-of-mut·ton (lĕg′ə-mŭt′n, lĕg′əv-) or **leg-o′-mut·ton** (lĕg′ə-) *adj.* Resembling a leg of mutton in shape; tapering sharply from one large end to a point or smaller end, as a sleeve or sail.

leg-pull (lĕg′po͝ol′) *n.* A comical hoax or practical joke. **—leg′-pull′er** *n.*

leg·room (lĕg′ro͞om′, -ro͝om′) *n.* Room in which to stretch the legs while seated.

leg·ume (lĕg′yo͞om′, lə-gyo͞om′) *n.* **1.a.** A pod, such as that of a pea or bean, that splits into two valves with the seeds attached to one edge of the valves. **b.** Such a pod or seed used as food. **2.** A plant of the pea family. [French *légume,* from Latin *legūmen,* bean.]

legume family *n.* The pea family.

le·gu·mi·nous (lə-gyo͞o′mə-nəs) *adj.* **1.** Of, belonging to, or characteristic of the family Leguminosae, which includes peas, beans, clover, alfalfa, and other plants. **2.** Resembling a legume. [From Middle English and from French *légumineux,* both from Latin *legūminosus,* from *legūmen, legūmin-,* bean.]

leg warmer also **leg·warm·er** (lĕg′wôr′mər) *n.* A knitted covering for the leg, resembling a stocking but without a foot, usually worn over tights or pants, as by dancers.

leg·work (lĕg′wûrk′) *n. Informal.* Work, such as collecting information or doing research in preparation for a project, that involves much walking or traveling about.

Le·hár (lā′här), **Franz.** 1870–1948. Hungarian composer of light operas, most notably *The Merry Widow* (1905).

Le Ha·vre (lə hä′vrə, häv′). A city of northern France on the English Channel west-northwest of Paris. It has been a major port since the 16th century. Population, 199,388.

Le·high River (lē′hī′). A river, about 166 km (103 mi) long, of eastern Pennsylvania flowing southeast to the Delaware River.

le·hu·a (lā-ho͞o′ə) *n.* An ornamental evergreen shrub or tree *(Metrosideros collinus)* of Hawaii and other Pacific islands, having showy red flowers. [Hawaiian.]

lei[1] (lā, lā′ē) *n., pl.* **leis.** A garland of flowers, especially one worn around the neck. [Hawaiian.]

lei[2] (lā) *n.* Plural of **leu.**

Leib·nitz or **Leib·niz** (līb′nĭts, līp′-), Baron **Gottfried Wilhelm von.** 1646–1716. German philosopher and mathematician. He invented differential and integral calculus independently of Newton and proposed the metaphysical theory that we live in "the best of all possible worlds."

Leices·ter[1] (lĕs′tər). A borough of central England east-northeast of Birmingham. Built on the site of a Roman settlement, it is an important industrial center. Population, 283,000.

Leices·ter[2] (lĕs′tər) *n.* **1.** Any of a breed of large, white-faced sheep having long coarse wool, developed in Leicestershire, a county of central England. **2.** A hard cheese similar to Cheddar and usually orange.

Leicester, First Earl of. Title of Robert Dudley. 1532?–1588. English courtier who was privy councilor to Elizabeth I and the captain general of her armies from 1587.

Lei·den also **Ley·den** (līd′n). A city of southwest Netherlands northeast of The Hague. Dating from Roman times, Leiden has had an important textile industry since the 16th century. Its university was founded in 1575. Population, 104,261.

Leigh (lē), **Vivien.** 1913–1967. British actress who won the Academy Award as best actress for her roles in *Gone With the Wind* (1939) and in *A Streetcar Named Desire* (1951).

Lein·ster (lĕn′stər). A historical region of southeast Ireland. Its wealth and accessibility made it an early prey to Danish and Anglo-Saxon invasions.

Leip·zig (līp′sĭg, -sĭk, -tsĭk). A city of east-central Germany south-southwest of Berlin. Originally a Slavic settlement called Lipsk, it developed by the early Middle Ages into a major commercial and cultural center. Population, 558,994.

leish·man·i·a·sis (lēsh′mə-nī′ə-sĭs) *n.* **1.** An infection caused by any of the flagellate protozoans of the genus *Leishmania,* transmitted to human beings and animals by bloodsucking sand flies. **2.** A disease, such as kala-azar or either of two clinically distinct ulcerative skin diseases, caused by flagellate protozoans of the genus *Leishmania.* [From New Latin *Leishmania,* genus of protozoans, after Sir William Boog *Leishman* (1865–1926), British medical officer.]

leis·ter (lē′stər) *n.* A three-pronged spear used in fishing. **—leister** *tr.v.* **-tered, -ter·ing, -ters.** To spear (a fish) with a leister. [Of Scandinavian origin.]

lei·sure (lē′zhər, lĕzh′ər) *n.* Freedom from time-consuming duties, responsibilities, or activities. See Synonyms at **rest**[1]. *—attributive.* Often used to modify another noun: *leisure time; leisure travel.* **—*idiom.* at (one's) leisure.** When one has free time; at one's convenience: *I'll return the call at my leisure.* [Middle English, from Norman French *leisour,* from Old French *leisir,* to be permitted, from Latin *licēre.*]

lei·sure·ly (lē′zhər-lē, lĕzh′ər-) *adj.* Acting, proceeding, or done without haste; unhurried. See Synonyms at **slow. —leisurely** *adv.* In an unhurried manner; slowly. **—lei′sure·li·ness** *n.*

leisure suit *n.* A man's suit for informal wear, consisting of a shirtlike jacket and matching slacks.

lei·sure·wear (lēzh′ər-wâr′, lĕzh′ər-) *n.* Informal, comfortable clothing designed for wear during times of relaxation.

Leith (lēth). A district of Edinburgh, Scotland, on the southern shore of the Firth of Forth. It is a noted seaport.

leit·mo·tif also **leit·mo·tiv** (līt′mō-tēf′) *n.* **1.** *Music.* A melodic passage or phrase, especially in Wagnerian opera, associated with a specific character or situation. **2.** A dominant and recurring theme, as in a novel. [German *Leitmotiv* : *leiten,* to lead (from Middle High German, from Old High German *leitan;* see **leit-** in Appendix) + *Motiv,* motif (from French *motif;* see MOTIF).]

Lei·zhou Peninsula (lā′jō′) also **Lui·chow Peninsula** (lwē′jō′). A peninsula of southern China between the Gulf of Tonkin and the South China Sea.

lek (lĕk) *n.* See table at **currency.** [Albanian, after *Lek* Dukagjin, Albanian feudal lord and lawgiver.]

lek·var (lĕk′vär) *n.* A sweet spread or pastry filling made of prunes or apricots. [Hungarian *lekvár,* jam, from Slovak, from Czech *lektvar,* electuary, from Middle High German *lactwārje, latwērge,* from Old French *leituaire,* from Late Latin *ēlēctuārium,* electuary. See ELECTUARY.]

Le·land (lē′lənd) or **Ley·land** (lā′-), **John.** 1506?–1552. English antiquarian who made a tour (1533–1545) of Britain to collect historical documents and relics.

Le·ly (lē′lē, lā′-), Sir **Peter.** 1618–1680. Dutch painter in England. He was principal painter to Charles II.

LEM (lĕm) *n., pl.* **LEMs.** A lunar excursion module. [L(UNAR) E(XCURSION) M(ODULE).]

Le·maî·tre (lə-mĕt′rə), **Georges Henri** or **Édouard.** 1894–1966. Belgian astrophysicist who proposed the big bang theory of the origin of the universe (1927).

lem·an (lĕm′ən, lē′mən) *n. Archaic.* **1.** A sweetheart; a lover. **2.** A mistress. [Middle English *leofman, lemman* : *leof,* dear (from Old English *lēof;* see **leubh-** in Appendix) + *man,* man; see MAN.]

Le·man (lē′mən, lə-măn′), **Lake.** See Lake **Geneva.**

Le Mans (lə mäɴ′). A city of northwest France west-southwest of Paris. Settled in pre-Roman times, it is famous for its annual (since 1906) 24-hour sports car races. Population, 147,697.

Le·may (lə-mā′, lē-). A community of east-central Missouri, a suburb on the southern border of St. Louis. Population, 35,424.

lem·ma[1] (lĕm′ə) *n., pl.* **lem·mas** or **lem·ma·ta** (lĕm′ə-tə). **1.** A subsidiary proposition assumed to be valid and used to demonstrate a principal proposition. **2.** A theme, an argument, or a subject indicated in a title. **3.** A word or phrase treated in a glossary or similar listing. [Latin *lēmma,* from Greek, from *lambanein,* to take.]

lem·ma[2] (lĕm′ə) *n. Botany.* The outer or lower of the two bracts that enclose the flower in a grass spikelet. [Greek, husk, from *lepein,* to peel.]

lem·ma·ta (lĕm′ə-tə) *n.* A plural of **lemma**[1].

lem·ming (lĕm′ĭng) *n.* Any of various small, thickset rodents, especially of the genus *Lemmus,* inhabiting northern regions and known for periodic mass migrations that sometimes end in drowning. [Norwegian.]

lem·nis·cus (lĕm-nĭs′kəs) *n., pl.* **-nis·ci** (-nĭs′ī′, -nĭs′kī′, -nĭs′kē). *Anatomy.* A bundle or band of sensory nerve fibers. [Latin *lēmniscus,* ribbon, from Greek *lēmniskos.*]

Lem·nos (lĕm′nŏs, -nōs, lēm′nôs) also **Lím·nos** (lēm′nôs). An island of northeast Greece in the Aegean Sea off the coast of Turkey northwest of Lesbos. Occupied in ancient times by Greeks, the island was later held by Persians, Romans, Byzantines, and Ottoman Turks. It became part of modern Greece in 1913.

lem·on (lĕm′ən) *n.* **1.a.** A spiny, Asian evergreen tree *(Citrus*

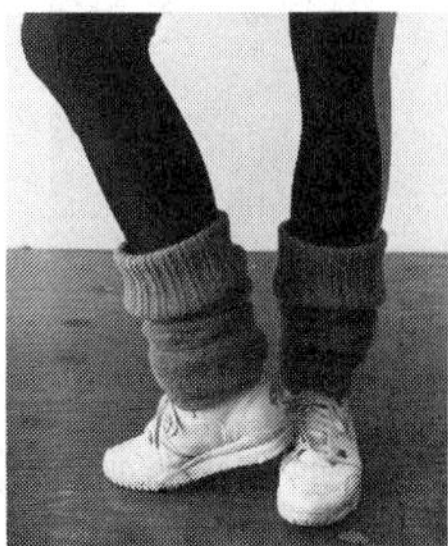

leg warmer
Pair of leg warmers

lemming

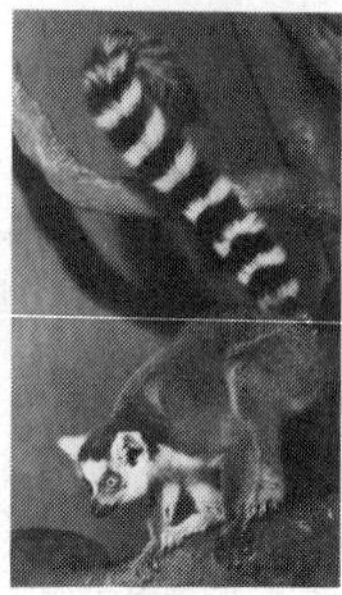

lemur
Ring-tailed lemur
Lemur catta

limon) widely cultivated for its yellow, egg-shaped fruit. **b.** The fruit of this tree, having a yellow aromatic rind and juicy, acid pulp. **2.** *Color.* Lemon yellow. **3.** *Informal.* One that is unsatisfactory or defective: *Their new car turned out to be a lemon.* **—lemon** *adj.* **1.** *Color.* Lemon-yellow. **2. a.** Made from lemons. **b.** Tasting or smelling like lemons. [Middle English *limon,* from Old French, from Old Italian *limone,* from Arabic *laymūn, līmūn,* from Persian *līmūn.*]

WORD HISTORY: Although we know neither where the lemon was first grown nor when it first came to Europe, we do know from its name alone that it came to us from the Middle East, because we can trace its etymological path. One of the earliest if not the earliest occurrences of our word is found in a Middle English customs document of 1420–1421. The Middle English word, which was of the form *limon,* goes back to Old French *limon,* showing that yet another delicacy passed into England through France. The Old French word probably came from Italian *limone,* another step on the route that leads back to the Arabic word *laymūn* or *līmūn,* which comes from the Persian word *līmūn.*

lem·on·ade (lĕm′ə-nād′) *n.* A drink made of lemon juice, water, and sugar.

lemonade berry *n.* An evergreen shrub or tree *(Rhus integrifolia)* native to southern California and Baja California, having opposite leaves, dark red fruit, and white flowers clustered in a panicle.

Vladimir Lenin

lemon balm *n.* See **balm** (sense 1a).

lem·on·grass also **lemon grass** (lĕm′ən-grăs′) *n.* A tropical grass *(Cymbopogon citratus)* native to southern India and Sri Lanka, yielding an aromatic oil used as flavoring and in perfumery and medicine.

lemon law *n.* A law obligating manufacturers or sellers to repair, replace, or refund the price of motor vehicles that prove to be defective.

♦ **lemon stick** *n. Baltimore.* A lemon half garnished with a peppermint stick through which the lemon juice is sucked: *"Who but a Baltimorean would know how to eat a lemon stick?"* (Marian Burros).

lemon verbena *n.* An aromatic shrub *(Aloysia triphylla)* native to Argentina and Chile, cultivated for its fragrant foliage and flowers.

lem·on·y (lĕm′ə-nē) *adj.* Having the characteristic odor, flavor, or color of lemons.

John Lennon
Photographed in 1969

lemon yellow *n. Color.* A moderate to brilliant vivid yellow. **—lem′on-yel′low** (lĕm′ən-yĕl′ō) *adj.*

lem·pi·ra (lĕm-pîr′ə) *n.* See table at **currency.** [American Spanish, after *Lempira* (1497–1537), Honduran Indian leader who resisted the Spanish conquistadors.]

le·mur (lē′mər) *n.* Any of several small arboreal, mostly nocturnal primates chiefly of the family Lemuridae of Madagascar and adjacent islands, having large eyes, a long slim muzzle, and a long tail. [New Latin *Lemur,* genus name, from Latin *lemurēs,* lemures (from their ghostly appearance and their nocturnal habits).]

lem·u·res (lĕm′ə-rās′, lĕm′yə-rēz′) *pl.n.* The spirits of the dead considered in ancient Rome as frightening specters and often exorcised from the homes in religious rituals. [Latin *Lemurēs.*]

Le·na (lē′nə, lyĕ′-). A river of eastern Russia rising near Lake Baikal and flowing about 4,296 km (2,670 mi) northeast and north to the Laptev Sea.

Len·a·pe (lĕn′ə-pē) *n., pl.* **Lenape** or **-pes.** See **Delaware**[1] (sense 1).

Le·nard (lā′närd, -närt), **Philipp.** 1862–1947. German physicist. He won a 1905 Nobel Prize for his work on cathode rays.

Len·clos or **L'En·clos** (läɴ-klō′), **Anne.** 1620–1705. French courtesan. Her salon was a meeting place for many prominent literary and political figures.

lend (lĕnd) *v.* **lent** (lĕnt), **lend·ing, lends.** *—tr.* **1. a.** To give or allow the use of temporarily on the condition that the same or its equivalent will be returned. **b.** To provide (money) temporarily on condition that the amount borrowed be returned, usually with an interest fee. **2.** To contribute or impart: *Books and a fireplace lent a feeling of warmth to the room.* **3.** To accommodate or offer (itself) to; be suitable for: *The Bible lends itself to various interpretations.* *—intr.* To make a loan. See Usage Note at **loan.** ***—idiom.*** **lend a helping hand.** To be of assistance. [Middle English *lenden,* from Old English *lǣnan.* See **leikʷ-** in Appendix.] **—lend′er** *n.*

lend·a·ble (lĕn′də-bəl) *adj.* Available for lending: *lendable funds; lendable resources.*

lend·ing library (lĕn′dĭng) *n.* A library from which books may be borrowed or rented for a minimal fee. Also called *circulating library.*

Le·nex·a (lə-nĕk′sə). A city of eastern Kansas, a suburb of Kansas City. Population, 18,639.

L'En·fant (län-fänt′, läɴ-fäɴ′), **Pierre Charles.** 1754–1825. French-born architect who designed the basic city plan for Washington, D.C.

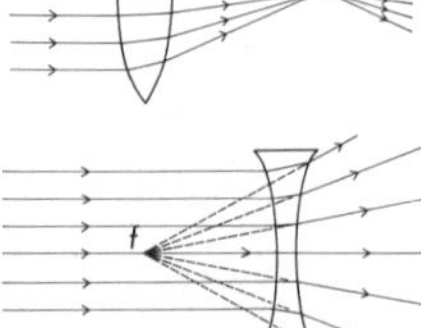

lens
Light passing through a double-convex lens (*top*) and a double-concave lens (*bottom*); *f* indicates the focus

length (lĕngkth, lĕngth) *n. Abbr.* **l.** **1.** The state, quality, or fact of being long. **2.** The measurement of the extent of something along its greatest dimension: *the length of the boat.* **3.** A piece, often of a standard size, that is normally measured along its greatest dimension: *a length of cloth.* **4.** A measure used as a unit to estimate distances: *won the race by a length.* **5.** Extent or distance from beginning to end: *the length of a novel; the length of a journey.* **6.** The amount of time between specified moments; the duration: *the length of a meeting.* **7.** Often **lengths.** Extent or degree to which an action or a policy is carried: *went to great lengths to prove his point.* **8.** *Linguistics.* **a.** The duration of a vowel. **b.** The duration of a syllable. **9.** The vertical extent of a garment. Often used in combination: *knee-length; floor-length.* ***—idiom.*** **at length. 1.** After some time; eventually: *At length we arrived at our destination.* **2.** For a considerable time; fully: *spoke at length about the court ruling.* [Middle English, from Old English *lengthu.* See **del-**[1] in Appendix.]

length·en (lĕngk′thən, lĕng′-) *tr. & intr.v.* **-ened, -en·ing, -ens.** To make or become longer. **—length′en·er** *n.*

length·ways (lĕngkth′wāz′, lĕngth′-) *adv.* Lengthwise.

length·wise (lĕngkth′wīz′, lĕngth′-) *adv. & adj.* Of, along, or in reference to the direction of the length; longitudinally.

length·y (lĕngk′thē, lĕng′-) *adj.* **-i·er, -i·est. 1.** Of considerable length, especially in time; extended: *a lengthy convalescence.* **2.** Tediously long; drawn-out: *a lengthy explanation.* **—length′i·ly** *adv.* **—length′i·ness** *n.*

le·ni·ence (lē′nē-əns, lēn′yəns) *n.* Leniency.

le·ni·en·cy (lē′nē-ən-sē, lēn′yən-) *n., pl.* **-cies. 1.** The condition or quality of being lenient. See Synonyms at **mercy. 2.** A lenient act.

le·ni·ent (lē′nē-ənt, lēn′yənt) *adj.* Inclined not to be harsh or strict; merciful, generous, or indulgent: *lenient parents; lenient rules.* [Obsolete French, from Latin *lēniēns, lēnient-,* present participle of *lēnīre,* to pacify, from *lēnis,* soft. See **lē-** in Appendix.] **—le′ni·ent·ly** *adv.*

Len·i Len·a·pe (lĕn′ē lĕn′ə-pē) *n.* Variant of **Lenni Lenape.**

Le·nin (lĕn′ĭn, lyĕ′nyĭn), **Vladimir Ilich.** Known as "Nikolai Lenin." 1870–1924. Russian founder of the Bolsheviks, leader of the Russian Revolution (1917), and first head of the U.S.S.R. (1917–1924).

Le·nin·a·bad (lĕn′ĭ-nə-băd′, lyĭ-nĭ-nəbät′). A city of northwest Tadzhikistan on the Syr Darya River south of Tashkent. One of the oldest towns of central Asia, it marked the farthest eastward expansion of Alexander the Great. Russia annexed the city in 1866. Population, 150,000.

Le·nin·a·kan (lĕn′ĭ-nə-kän′, lyĭ-nĭ-). A city of northwest Armenia south-southeast of Tbilisi. It was founded on the site of a Turkish fortress. Population, 223,000.

Len·in·grad (lĕn′ĭn-grăd′, lyĭ-nĭn-grät′). Officially (since 1991) **Saint Pe·ters·burg** (sānt pē′tərz-bûrg′) also **Pet·ro·grad** (pĕt′rə-grăd′, pyĭ-trə-grät′). A city of northwest Russia on the Neva River at the head of the Gulf of Finland. Founded by Peter the Great in 1703 as St. Petersburg, it soon flourished as his "window on Europe" and became the capital of Russia in 1712. The city was called Petrograd from 1914 to 1924. Moscow replaced it as capital in 1918. Population, 4,329,000.

Len·in·ism (lĕn′ə-nĭz′əm) *n.* The theory and practice of proletarian revolution as developed by Lenin. **—Len′in·ist** *adj. & n.* **—Len′in·ite′** (lĕn′ə-nīt′) *adj. & n.*

Lenin Peak. A mountain, 7,138.5 m (23,405 ft) high, in the Trans Alai on the Kirghiz-Tadzhikistan border.

le·nis (lē′nĭs, lā′-) *adj. Linguistics.* Articulated with relatively low pressure of the airstream below the glottis, as English (b) and (d) compared with (p) and (t). [Latin *lēnis,* soft. See **lē-** in Appendix.]

len·i·tive (lĕn′ĭ-tĭv) *adj.* Capable of easing pain or discomfort. **—lenitive** *n.* A lenitive medicine. [Middle English *lenitif,* from Old French, from Medieval Latin *lēnitīvus,* from Latin *lēnitus,* past participle of *lēnīre,* to soothe, from *lēnis,* soft. See **lē-** in Appendix.] **—len′i·tive·ly** *adv.*

len·i·ty (lĕn′ĭ-tē) *n.* The condition or quality of being lenient; leniency. See Synonyms at **mercy.** [Latin *lēnitās,* from *lēnis,* soft. See **lē-** in Appendix.]

Len·ni Len·a·pe or **Len·i Len·a·pe** (lĕn′ē lĕn′ə-pē) *n.* See **Delaware**[1] (sense 1).

Len·non (lĕn′ən), **John.** 1940–1980. British musician and composer who was a member of the Beatles. With Paul McCartney he wrote many of the group's songs, including "Yesterday."

le·no (lē′nō) *n., pl.* **-nos. 1.** Weaving in which the warp yarns are paired and twisted. **2.** A fabric having such a weave. [Perhaps from French *linon,* linen fabric, from *lin,* flax, from Old French, from Latin *līnum.* See LINEN.]

lens (lĕnz) *n., pl.* **lens·es. 1.** A ground or molded piece of glass, plastic, or other transparent material with opposite surfaces either or both of which are curved, by means of which light rays are refracted so that they converge or diverge to form an image. **2.** A combination of two or more such pieces, sometimes with other optical devices such as prisms, used to form an image for viewing or photographing. Also called *compound lens.* **3.** A device that causes radiation other than light to converge or diverge by an action analogous to that of an optical lens. **4.** A transparent, biconvex body of the eye between the iris and the vitreous humor that focuses light rays entering through the pupil to form an image on the retina. **—lens** *tr.v.* **lensed, lens·ing, lens·es.** *Informal.* To make a photograph or movie of. [New Latin *lēns,* from Latin, lentil (from the shape of a double convex lens).] **—lensed** *adj.*

lent (lĕnt) *v.* Past tense and past participle of **lend.**

Lent (lĕnt) *n.* The 40 weekdays from Ash Wednesday until Easter observed by Christians as a season of fasting and penitence in preparation for Easter. [Middle English *lenten, lente,* spring, Lent, from Old English *lencten.* See **del-**[1] in Appendix.]

len·ta·men·te (lĕn′tə-mĕn′tā) *adv. & adj. Music.* Lento. [Italian, from *lento,* slow. See LENTO.]

len·tan·do (lĕn-tän′dō) *adv. & adj. Music.* Slowing gradually. Used chiefly as a direction. [Italian, present participle of *lentare,* to make slow, from *lento,* slow. See LENTO.]

Lent·en (lĕn′tən) *adj.* **1.** Of or relating to Lent: *Lenten observances.* **2.** Characteristic of or appropriate to Lent; meager: *Lenten meals.*

len·ti·cel (lĕn′tĭ-sĕl′) *n.* One of the small, corky pores or narrow lines on the surface of the stems of woody plants that allow the interchange of gases between the interior tissue and the surrounding air. [New Latin *lenticella,* diminutive of *lēns, lent-,* lens. See LENS.] **—len′ti·cel′late** (-sĕl′ĭt) *adj.*

len·tic·u·lar (lĕn-tĭk′yə-lər) *adj.* **1.** Shaped like a biconvex lens. **2.** Of or relating to a lens. [Latin *lenticulāris,* lentil-shaped, from *lenticula,* lentil. See LENTIL.]

len·ti·go (lĕn-tī′gō) *n., pl.* **-tig·i·nes** (-tĭj′ə-nēz′). A small, flat, pigmented spot on the skin. [Latin *lentīgō, lentīgin-,* from *lēns, lent-,* lentil.] **—len·tig′i·nous** (-tĭj′ə-nəs), **len·tig′i·nose′** (-nōs′) *adj.*

len·til (lĕn′təl) *n.* **1.** A leguminous plant *(Lens culinaris)* native to southwest Asia, having flat pods containing lens-shaped, edible seeds. **2.** The round, flattened seed of this plant. [Middle English, from Old French *lentille,* from Vulgar Latin **lentīcula,* from Latin *lenticula,* diminutive of *lēns, lent-,* lentil.]

len·tisk (lĕn′tĭsk′) *n.* See **mastic tree.** [Middle English *lentiske,* from Latin *lentiscus.*]

len·tis·si·mo (lĕn-tĭs′ĭ-mō′, -tē′sē-) *adv. & adj. Music.* Very slowly. Used chiefly as a direction. [Italian, superlative of *lento,* slow. See LENTO.]

len·ti·vi·rus (lĕn′tə-vī′rəs) *n., pl.* **-rus·es.** See **slow virus.** [New Latin *Lentivirus,* genus name : Latin *lentus,* slow + VIRUS.]

len·to (lĕn′tō) *Music. adv. & adj.* In a slow tempo. Used chiefly as a direction. **—lento** *n., pl.* **-tos.** A lento passage or movement. [Italian, from Latin *lentus,* slow.]

Len·ya (lān′yə, lĕn′-), **Lotte.** 1898–1981. Austrian singer and actress who popularized the music of her husband, Kurt Weill, and appeared in a number of plays by Bertolt Brecht.

Le·o (lē′ō) *n.* **1.** A constellation in the Northern Hemisphere near Cancer and Virgo, containing the bright stars Regulus and Denebola. **2.a.** The fifth sign of the zodiac in astrology. **b.** One who is born under this sign. Also called *Lion.* [Latin *Leō,* from *leō,* lion. See LION.]

Leo I, Saint. Known as "Leo the Great." A.D. 400?–461. Pope (440–461). His negotiations with Attila (452) and Genseric the Vandal (455) saved Rome from barbarian invasion.

Leo III, Saint. Died 816. Pope (795–816) who crowned Charlemagne emperor (800), causing the division between the Eastern and Western empires.

Leo X. Originally Giovanni de Medici. 1475–1521. Pope (1513–1521). During his reign the Reformation began and Martin Luther was excommunicated (1521).

Leo Minor *n.* A constellation in the Northern Hemisphere near Leo and Ursa Major. [New Latin *Leō Minor* : Latin *leō,* lion; see LION + Latin *minor,* lesser; see MINOR.]

Leom·in·ster (lĕm′ĭn-stər). A city of north-central Massachusetts south-southeast of Fitchburg. Population, 34,508.

Le·ón (lā-ōn′). **1.** A historical region and former kingdom of northwest Spain. United first with Asturias (eighth–ninth century), it was conquered by Castile in 1037, became independent in 1157, and was rejoined with Castile in 1230. **2.** A city of central Mexico east-northeast of Guadalajara. It was founded in the 1570's. Population, 593,002. **3.** A city of western Nicaragua northwest of Managua. Founded in 1524 on Lake Managua, it was moved to its present site in 1610. Population, 92,764. **4.** A city of northwest Spain at the foot of the Cantabrian Mountains south-southeast of Oviedo. Reconquered from the Moors in 882, it is now a tourist center. Population, 133,658.

Le·o·nar·do da Vin·ci (lē′ə-när′dō də vĭn′chē, dä, lā′-). 1452–1519. Italian painter, engineer, musician, and scientist. The most versatile genius of the Renaissance, Leonardo filled notebooks with engineering and scientific observations that were centuries ahead of their time. As a painter he is best known for *The Last Supper* (c. 1495) and *Mona Lisa* (c. 1503).

Le·on·ca·val·lo (lā′ōn-kə-vä′lō, -kä-väl′-), **Ruggiero.** 1858–1919. Italian composer who wrote *Pagliacci* (1892).

le·one (lē-ōn′) *n.* See table at **currency.** [After SIERRA LEONE.]

Le·o·nid (lē′ə-nĭd) *n., pl.* **Le·o·nids** or **Le·on·i·des** (lē-ŏn′ĭ-dēz′). One of the falling stars of the meteor shower recurring annually in mid-November. [From Latin *Leō, Leōn-,* Leo. See LEO.]

Le·on·i·das I (lē-ŏn′ĭ-dəs). Died 480 B.C. Spartan king (490–480) who led a small force against a huge Persian army at the pass of Thermopylae (480). All of the Spartans were killed.

le·o·nine (lē′ə-nīn′) *adj.* Of, relating to, or characteristic of a lion. [Middle English, from Old French *leonin,* from Latin *leōnīnus,* from *leō, leōn-,* lion. See LION.]

leonine rhyme *n.* A form of internal rhyme in which the word preceding the caesure rhymes with the final word in the line, as in: *"For the moon never beams without bringing me dreams"* (Edgar Allan Poe). [Probably after *Leo* or *Leonius,* name of an unknown medieval poet.]

Le·on·tief (lē-ôn′tyĕf, -ŏn′-), **Wassily.** Born 1906. Russian-born American economist. He won a 1973 Nobel Prize for devising the input-output technique of economic analysis.

leop·ard (lĕp′ərd) *n.* **1.a.** A large, ferocious cat *(Panthera pardus)* of Africa and southern Asia, having either tawny fur with dark rosettelike markings or black fur. **b.** Any of several felines, such as the cheetah or the snow leopard. **c.** The pelt or fur of this animal. **2.** *Heraldry.* A lion in side view, having one forepaw raised and the head facing the observer. [Middle English, from Old French *leupart,* from Late Latin *leopardus,* from Greek *leopardos* : Greek *leōn,* lion; see LION + Greek *pardos,* pard; see PARD.]

leop·ard·ess (lĕp′ər-dĭs) *n.* A female leopard.

leopard flower *n.* See **blackberry lily.**

leopard lily *n.* A tall plant *(Lilium pardalinum)* native to California and southwest Oregon, having nodding, dark-spotted, orange-red flowers.

leopard moth *n.* A large moth *(Zeuzera pyrina)* having white wings with black spots and larvae that damage trees by boring into the wood.

leop·ard's bane (lĕp′ərdz) *n.* **1.** Any of several widely cultivated ornamental plants of the genus *Doronicum* native to Eurasia, having rayed, yellow flower heads borne on long stalks. **2.** Any of several similar or related plants.

Le·o·pold I (lē′ə-pōld′). 1640–1705. King of Hungary (1655–1705) and Bohemia (1656–1705) and Holy Roman emperor (1658–1705). He fought with the Turks and the French for most of his reign and consolidated his authority in the empire.

Leopold II. 1835–1909. King of Belgium (1865–1909) who also reigned in the Congo Free State (now Zaire) from 1876 to 1904, when he was forced to abdicate because of his harsh treatment of the native population.

Le·o·pold·ville (lē′ə-pōld-vĭl′, lā′-). See **Kinshasa.**

le·o·tard (lē′ə-tärd′) *n.* **1.** A snugly fitting, stretchable one-piece garment with or without sleeves that covers the torso, worn especially by dancers, gymnasts, acrobats, and those engaging in exercise workouts. **2. leotards.** Tights. [After Jules *Léotard* (1830–1870), French aerialist.] **—le′o·tard′ed** *adj.*

Le·pan·to (lĭ-păn′tō, lĕ′pän-tô), **Gulf of.** See Gulf of **Corinth.**

Lep·cha (lĕp′chə) *n., pl.* **Lepcha** or **-chas. 1.** A member of a Buddhist people living in Sikkim. **2.** The Tibeto-Burman language of the Lepcha.

lep·er (lĕp′ər) *n.* **1.** A person affected by leprosy. **2.** A person who is avoided by others; a pariah. [Middle English, from *lepre,* leprosy, from Old French, from Late Latin *lepra,* from Greek *lepros,* scaly, from *lepis, lepos,* scale.]

lepido– *pref.* Scale; flake: *lepidopteran.* [Greek, from *lepis, lepid-.*]

le·pid·o·lite (lĭ-pĭd′l-īt′) *n.* A lilac or pink to gray mineral of the mica group, $K(Li,Al)_3(Si,Al)_4O_{10}(F,OH)_2$, used as lithium ore and in ceramic production. [LEPIDO– + –LITE.]

lep·i·dop·ter·an (lĕp′ĭ-dŏp′tər-ən) *n.* An insect belonging to the large order Lepidoptera, which includes the butterflies and moths, characterized by four membranous wings covered with small scales. **—lepidopteran** *adj.* Lepidopterous. [From New Latin *Lepidoptera,* order name : LEPIDO– + Greek *ptera,* pl. of *pteron,* wing, winged creature; see –PTER.]

lep·i·dop·ter·ist (lĕp′ĭ-dŏp′tər-ĭst) *n.* An entomologist specializing in the study of butterflies and moths.

lep·i·dop·ter·ous (lĕp′ĭ-dŏp′tər-əs) *adj.* Of or belonging to the order Lepidoptera, which includes insects such as the butterflies and moths.

lep·i·dote (lĕp′ĭ-dōt′) *adj.* Covered with small, scurfy scales. [Greek *lepidōtos,* scaly, from *lepis, lepid-,* scale.]

Lep·i·dus (lĕp′ĭ-dəs), **Marcus Aemilius.** Died 13 B.C. Roman leader. He was a member of the triumvirate with Augustus and Mark Antony (43–36 B.C.).

Le·pon·tic (lĭ-pŏn′tĭk) *n.* An ancient Indo-European language of northeast Italy and southern Switzerland, known from inscriptions dated from the third century B.C. [From Latin *Lēpontiī,* a people of Cisalpine Gaul.] **—Le·pon′tic** *adj.*

Le·pon·tine Alps (lĭ-pŏn′tīn′). A range of the central Alps in southern Switzerland and along the Swiss-Italian border rising to 3,563.3 m (11,683 ft).

lep·o·rine (lĕp′ə-rīn′, -ər-ĭn) *adj.* Of or characteristic of rabbits or hares. [Latin *leporīnus,* from *lepus, lepor-,* hare.]

lep·re·chaun (lĕp′rĭ-kŏn′, -kôn′) *n.* One of a race of elves in Irish folklore who can reveal hidden treasure to someone who catches him. [Irish Gaelic *luprachán,* alteration of Middle Irish *luchrupán,* from Old Irish *luchorpān* : *luchorp* (*lū-,* small; see **legʷh-** in Appendix + *corp,* body, from Latin *corpus;* see **kʷrep-** in Appendix) + *-ān,* diminutive suff.] **—lep′re·chaun′ish** *adj.*

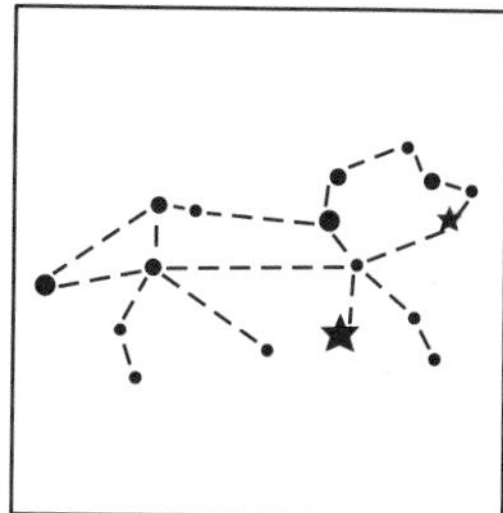

Leo

Leonardo da Vinci
c. 1512 self-portrait

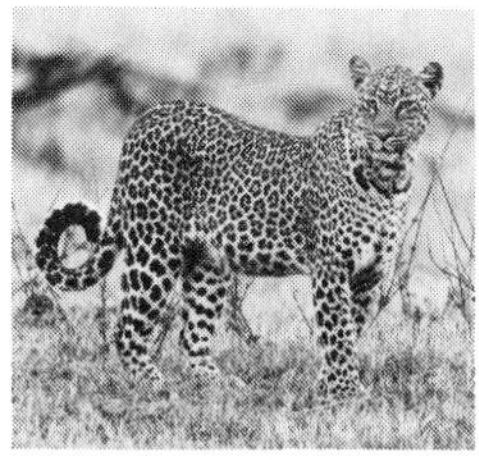

leopard
North African leopard
Panthera pardus

leopard moth
Zeuzera pyrina

ă pat	oi boy
ā pay	ou out
âr care	ŏŏ took
ä father	ōō boot
ĕ pet	ŭ cut
ē be	ûr urge
ĭ pit	th thin
ī pie	*th* this
îr pier	hw which
ŏ pot	zh vision
ō toe	ə about, item
ô paw	♦ regionalism

Stress marks: **′** (primary); ′ (secondary), as in **dictionary** (dĭk′shə-nĕr′ē)

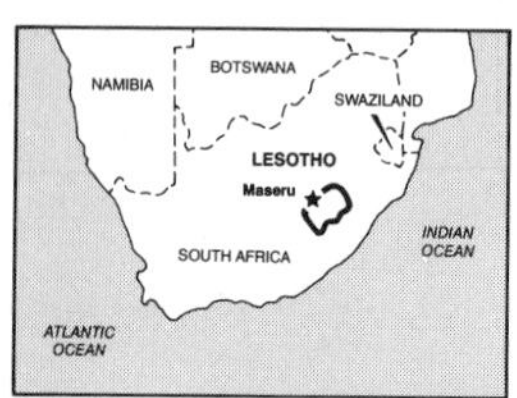

Lesotho

WORD HISTORY: Nothing seems more Irish than the leprechaun; yet, hiding within the word *leprechaun* is a word from another language entirely. If we look back beyond Modern Irish Gaelic *luprachán* and Middle Irish *luchrupán* to Old Irish *luchorpān*, we can see the connection. *Luchorpān* is a compound of Old Irish *lū*, meaning "small," and the Old Irish word *corp*, "body." *Corp* is borrowed from Latin *corpus* (which we know from *habeas corpus*). Here is a piece of evidence attesting to the deep influence of Church Latin on the Irish language. Although the word is old in Irish it is fairly new in English, being first recorded in 1604.

lep·ro·sar·i·um (lĕp′rə-sâr′ē-əm) *n., pl.* **-i·ums** or **-i·a** (-ē-ə). A hospital for the treatment of leprosy. [Medieval Latin *leprōsārium*, from Late Latin *leprōsus*, leprous. See LEPROUS.]

lep·rose (lĕp′rōs′) *adj.* Scurfy or scaly; leprous. [Late Latin *leprōsus.* See LEPROUS.]

lep·ro·sy (lĕp′rə-sē) *n.* A chronic, mildly contagious granulomatous disease of tropical and subtropical regions, caused by the bacillus *Mycobacterium leprae*, characterized by ulcers of the skin, bone, and viscera and leading to loss of sensation, paralysis, gangrene, and deformation. [Middle English *lepruse*, from *leprus*, leprous. See LEPROUS.] **—lep·rot′ic** (lĕ-prŏt′ĭk) *adj.*

lep·rous (lĕp′rəs) *adj.* **1.** Having leprosy. **2.** Of, relating to, or resembling leprosy. **3.** *Biology.* Having or consisting of loose, scurfy scales. [Middle English *leprus*, from Old French *lepros*, from Late Latin *leprōsus*, from *lepra*, leprosy. See LEPER.] **—lep′rous·ly** *adv.* **—lep′rous·ness** *n.*

–lepsy *suff.* Fit; seizure: *narcolepsy.* [New Latin *-lēpsia*, from Greek, from *lēpsis*, seizure, from *lambanein, lēp-*, to take, seize.]

lept– *pref.* Variant of **lepto–.**

lep·ta (lĕp′tə) *n.* Plural of **lepton[1].**

Lep·tis Mag·na (lĕp′tĭs măg′nə). An ancient city of northern Africa in present-day Libya east of Tripoli. Founded by Phoenicians, it flourished as a port during Roman times.

lepto– or **lept–** *pref.* Slender; thin; fine: *leptocephalus.* [Greek, from *leptos*, fine, thin, from *lepein*, to peel.]

lep·to·ceph·a·lus (lĕp′tə-sĕf′ə-ləs) *n., pl.* **-li** (-lī′). One of the small, flat, transparent larvae of eels and certain other fishes, characterized by a long, narrow head. [New Latin : LEPTO– + *cephalus*, head (from Greek *-kephalos*, -headed); see –CEPHALOUS.]

lep·ton[1] (lĕp′tŏn′) *n., pl.* **-ta** (-tə). See table at **currency.** [Modern Greek, from Greek, small coin, from neuter of *leptos*, fine, small. See LEPTO–.]

lep·ton[2] (lĕp′tŏn′) *n.* Any of a family of elementary particles that participate in the weak interaction, including the electron, the muon, and their associated neutrinos. See table at **subatomic particle.** [LEPTO– + –ON[1].] **—lep·ton′ic** (-tŏn′ĭk) *adj.*

lep·to·some (lĕp′tə-sōm′) *n.* A person with a slender, thin, or frail body. **—lep′to·so·mat′ic** (-sō-măt′ĭk) *adj.*

lep·to·spi·ro·sis (lĕp′tō-spī-rō′sĭs) *n.* An infectious disease of domestic animals, especially cattle, swine, and dogs, caused by spirochetes of the genus *Leptospira* and characterized by jaundice and fever. Also called *swamp fever.* [New Latin *Leptospīra*, genus name (LEPTO– + Latin *spīra*, coil; see SPIRAL) + –OSIS.]

Le·pus (lē′pəs) *n.* A constellation in the Southern Hemisphere near Orion and Columba. [Latin, from *lepus*, hare.]

Lé·ri·da (lā′rĭ-də, lĕ′rē-*th*ä). A city of northeast Spain west of Barcelona. Julius Caesar defeated Pompey's generals here in 49 B.C. Population, 87,800.

Ler·mon·tov (lĕr′mən-tôf′, lyĕr′mən-təf), **Mikhail Yurievich.** 1814–1841. Russian writer who is remembered for the novel *A Hero of Our Time* (1840) and his many poems.

Ler·ner (lûr′nər), **Alan Jay.** 1918–1986. American playwright and lyricist. He wrote a number of musicals with the composer Frederick Loewe, including *My Fair Lady* (1956).

Le·sage (lə-säzh′), **Alain René.** 1668–1747. French writer. His novel *Gil Blas* (1715–1735) had a major influence on modern realistic fiction.

lesser celandine
Ranunculus ficaria

les·bi·an (lĕz′bē-ən) *n.* A gay or homosexual woman. **—lesbian** *adj.* Of, relating to, or being a lesbian. [From the putative homosexuality of Sappho, lyric poet of Lesbos.]

Les·bi·an (lĕz′bē-ən) *n.* **1.** A native or inhabitant of Lesbos. **2.** The ancient Greek dialect of Lesbos. **—Lesbian** *adj.* Of or relating to Lesbos. [From Latin *Lesbius*, from Greek *Lesbios*, from LESBOS.]

les·bi·an·ism (lĕz′bē-ə-nĭz′əm) *n.* Sexual orientation of women to other women.

Les·bos (lĕz′bŏs, -bōs) also **Lés·vos** (-vôs). An island of eastern Greece in the Aegean Sea near the northwest coast of Turkey. An important Aeolian settlement, Lesbos was noted for its lyric poets, including Sappho, in the seventh century B.C. The island was annexed by Greece in 1913.

lese maj·es·ty also **lèse ma·jes·té** (lēz′ măj′ĭ-stē) *n., pl.* **lese maj·es·ties** or **lèse ma·jes·tés. 1.** An offense or a crime committed against the ruler or supreme power of a state. **2.** An affront to another's dignity. [Partial translation of French *lèse-majesté*, from Latin *(crimen) laesae māiestātis*, (the crime) of injured majesty : *laesae*, feminine genitive of *laesus*, past participle of *laedere*, to injure + *māiestātis*, genitive of *māiestās*, majesty.]

le·sion (lē′zhən) *n.* **1.** A wound or an injury. **2.** A localized pathological change in a bodily organ or tissue. **3.** An infected or diseased patch of skin. [Middle English *lesioun*, from Old French *lesion*, from Latin *laesiō, laesiōn-*, from *laesus*, past participle of *laedere*, to injure.]

Le·so·tho (lə-sō′tō, -so͞o′to͞o). Formerly **Ba·su·to·land** (bə-so͞o′tō-lănd′). A country of southern Africa forming an enclave within east-central South Africa. It became a British protectorate in 1868 and achieved its independence in 1966. Maseru is the capital. Population, 1,213,960.

les·pe·de·za (lĕs′pĭ-dē′zə) *n.* See **bush clover.** [New Latin *Lespedeza*, genus name, after V.M. de *Céspedez* (misread as *Léspedez*; fl. 1785), Spanish governor of Florida.]

less (lĕs) *adj.* A comparative of **little. 1.** Not as great in amount or quantity: *had less time to spend with the family.* **2.** Lower in importance, esteem, or rank: *no less a person than the ambassador.* **3.** Consisting of a smaller number. See Usage Note at **few. —less** *prep.* With the deduction of; minus: *Five less two is three.* **—less** *adv.* Comparative of **little.** To a smaller extent, degree, or frequency: *less happy; less expensive.* **—less** *n.* **1.** A smaller amount: *She received less than she asked for.* **2.** Something not as important as something else: *People have been punished for less.* ***—idioms.*** **less than.** Not at all: *He had a less than favorable view of the matter.* **much** (or **still**) **less.** Certainly not: *I'm not blaming anyone, much less you.* [Middle English *lesse*, from Old English *lǣssa* (adj.) and *lǣs* (adv.); see **leis-[2]** in Appendix.]

–less *suff.* **1.** Without; lacking: *blameless.* **2.** Unable to act or be acted on in a specified way: *dauntless.* [Middle English *-lesse*, from Old English *-lēas*, from *lēas*, without. See **leu-** in Appendix.]

les·see (lĕ-sē′) *n.* One that holds a lease. [Middle English, from Anglo-Norman, from past participle of *lesser*, to let out, lease. See LEASE.]

less·en (lĕs′ən) *v.* **-ened, -en·ing, -ens.** *—tr.* **1.** To make less; reduce. **2.** *Archaic.* To make little of; belittle. *—intr.* To become less; decrease. See Synonyms at **decrease.** [Middle English *lessen, lessenen*, from *lesse*, less. See LESS.]

Les·seps (lĕs′əps, lĕ-sĕps′), Vicomte **Ferdinand Marie de.** 1805–1894. French diplomat and engineer who supervised the construction of the Suez Canal (1859–1869).

less·er (lĕs′ər) *adj.* A comparative of **little. 1.** Smaller in amount, value, or importance, especially in a comparison between two things: *chose the lesser evil.* **2.** Of a smaller size than other, similar forms: *the lesser anteater.* [Middle English, from *lesse*, less. See LESS.]

Less·er An·til·les (lĕs′ər ăn-tĭl′ēz). An island group of the eastern West Indies extending in an arc from Curaçao to the Virgin Islands.

lesser celandine *n.* A Eurasian plant *(Ranunculus ficaria)* having heart-shaped leaves, solitary yellow flowers, and tuberous roots.

lesser omentum *n. Anatomy.* A fold of the peritoneum joining parts of the stomach and duodenum to the liver.

lesser panda *n.* See **panda** (sense 2).

Lesser Slave Lake (slāv). A lake of central Alberta, Canada, drained by the **Lesser Slave River,** a tributary of the Athabasca River.

Lesser Sun·da Islands (sŭn′də, so͞on′-). See **Sunda Islands.**

Les·sing (lĕs′ĭng), **Doris.** Born 1919. British writer known for her five-volume series *Children of Violence* (1952–1969).

Lessing, Gotthold Ephraim. 1729–1781. German playwright and critic. A leader of the Enlightenment, he wrote the plays *Minna von Barnheim* (1763) and *Nathan the Wise* (1779).

les·son (lĕs′ən) *n.* **1.** Something to be learned: *lessons from observing nature.* **2. a.** A period of instruction; a class. **b.** An assignment or exercise in which something is to be learned. **c.** The act or an instance of instructing; teaching. **3. a.** An experience, example, or observation that imparts beneficial new knowledge or wisdom. **b.** The knowledge or wisdom so acquired. **4.** A rebuke or reprimand. **5.** Often **Lesson.** A reading from the Bible or other sacred text as part of a religious service. **—lesson** *tr.v.* **-soned, -son·ing, -sons. 1.** To teach a lesson to; instruct. **2.** To rebuke or reprimand. [Middle English *lessoun*, from Old French *leson*, from Latin *lēctiō, lēctiōn-*, a reading, from *lēctus*, past participle of *legere*, to read. See **leg-** in Appendix.]

les·sor (lĕs′ôr′, lĕ-sôr′) *n.* One that lets property under a lease. [Middle English *lessour*, from Anglo-Norman, from *lesser*, to let out, lease. See LEASE.]

lest (lĕst) *conj.* For fear that: *tiptoed lest the guard should hear her; anxious lest he become ill.* [Middle English, from Old English *thӯ lǣs the*, so that not, from *lǣs*, less. See LESS.]

Lés·vos (lĕz′vôs). See **Lesbos.**

let[1] (lĕt) *v.* **let, let·ting, lets.** *—tr.* **1.** To give permission or opportunity to; allow: *I let them borrow the car. The inheritance let us finally buy a house.* See Usage Note at **leave[1]. 2.** To cause to; make: *Let the news be known.* **3. a.** Used as an auxiliary in the imperative to express a command, request, or proposal: *Let's finish the job! Let x equal y.* **b.** Used as an auxiliary in the imperative to express a warning or threat: *Just let her try!* **4.** To permit to enter, proceed, or depart: *let the dog in.* **5.** To release from or as if from confinement: *let the air out of the balloon; let out a yelp.* **6.** To rent or lease: *let rooms.* **7.** To award, especially after bids have been submitted: *let the construction job to a new firm.* *—intr.* **1.** To become rented or leased. **2.** To be or become assigned, as to a contractor. ***—phrasal verbs.*** **let down. 1.** To cause to come down gradually; lower: *let down the sails.* **2.a.** To withdraw support from; forsake. **b.** To fail to meet the expectations of; disappoint. **let on. 1.** To allow to be known; admit: *Don't let on that you know me.* **2.** To pretend. **let out. 1.** To come to a close; end: *School let out early. The play let out at 11 P.M.* **2.** To make known; reveal: *Who let that story out?* **3.** To increase the size of (a garment, for example): *let out a coat.* **let up. 1.** To slow down; diminish: *didn't let up in their efforts.* **2.** To come to a stop; cease: *The rain let up.* **—idioms. let alone.** Not to mention; much less: *"Their ancestors had been dirt poor and never saw royalty, let alone hung around with them"* (Garrison Keillor). **let go.** To cease to employ; dismiss: *had to let 20 workers go.* **let off on.** *Informal.* To cause to diminish, as in pressure; ease up on: *Let off on the gas so that we do not exceed the speed limit.* **let (one's) hair down.** To drop one's reserve or inhibitions. **let up on.** To be or become more lenient with: *Why don't you let up on the poor child?* [Middle English *leten,* from Old English *lǣtan.* See **lē-** in Appendix.]

let² (lĕt) *n.* **1.** Something that hinders; an obstacle: *free to investigate without let or hindrance.* **2.** *Sports.* An invalid stroke in tennis and other net games that must be repeated. **—let** *tr.v.* **let·ted** or **let, let·ting, lets.** *Archaic.* To hinder or obstruct. [Middle English *lette,* from *letten,* to hinder, from Old English *lettan.* See **lē-** in Appendix.]

–let *suff.* **1.** Small one: *craterlet.* **2.** Something worn on: *armlet.* [Middle English, from Old French *-elet,* diminutive suff.: *-el* (from Latin *-ellus*) + *-et,* -et.]

letch also **lech** (lĕch) *n.* **1.** A strong, especially sexual desire or craving. **2.** A lecher. [Perhaps back-formation from obsolete *letcher,* variant of LECHER.]

let·down (lĕt′doun′) *n.* **1.** A decrease, decline, or relaxation, as of effort or energy. **2.** A disappointment: *The cancellation of the game was a real letdown.* **3.** The descent made by an aircraft in order to land.

le·thal (lē′thəl) *adj.* **1.** Capable of causing death. **2.** Of, relating to, or causing death. See Synonyms at **fatal. 3.** Extremely harmful; devastating: *accusations lethal to the candidate's image.* [Late Latin *lēthālis,* alteration (probably influenced by *Lēthē,* Lethe) of Latin *lētālis,* from *lētum,* death.] **—le·thal′i·ty** (lē-thăl′ĭ-tē) *n.* **—le′thal·ly** *adv.*

lethal gene *n.* A gene whose expression results in the death of the organism.

le·thar·gic (lə-thär′jĭk) *adj.* Of, causing, or characterized by lethargy. **—le·thar′gi·cal·ly** *adv.*

leth·ar·gy (lĕth′ər-jē) *n., pl.* **-gies. 1.** A state of sluggishness, inactivity, and apathy. **2.** A state of unconsciousness resembling deep sleep. [Middle English *letargie,* from Old French, from Late Latin *lēthārgia,* from Greek *lēthargia,* from *lēthargos,* forgetful : *lēthē,* forgetfulness + *argos,* idle (*a-,* without; see A–¹ + *ergon,* work; see ERG).]

SYNONYMS: *lethargy, lassitude, torpor, torpidity, stupor, languor.* These nouns refer to a deficiency in mental and physical alertness and activity. *Lethargy,* a state of sluggishness and inactivity, may be caused by factors such as illness, fatigue, or overwork, but it manifests itself in drowsy dullness or apathy: *A surprise military attack roused the nation from its lethargy. Lassitude* implies weariness or diminished energy such as might result from physical or mental strain: *"His anger had evaporated; he felt nothing but utter lassitude"* (John Galsworthy). *Torpor* and *torpidity* suggest the suspension of activity characteristic of an animal in hibernation; they imply lethargy or inertia: *"My calmness was the torpor of despair"* (Charles Brockden Brown). *Nothing could dispel the torpidity of the indifferent audience. Stupor,* which is marked by cessation or great decrease of mental activity or feeling, is often produced by sleepiness, illness, or the effects of alcohol or narcotics; it suggests a benumbed or dazed state: *"The huge height of the buildings . . . the hubbub and endless stir . . . struck me into a kind of stupor of surprise"* (Robert Louis Stevenson). *Languor* is the lack of energy or spirit typical of one who is indolent or satiated by a life of luxury or pleasure: *"But for the criminal . . . languor which characterized that commander's movements . . . the honor of France might still have been saved"* (John Lothrop Motley).

Leth·bridge (lĕth′brĭj′). A city of southern Alberta, Canada, south-southeast of Calgary. It is a commercial center in an irrigated farming region. Population, 54,072.

le·the (lē′thē) *n.* **1. Lethe.** *Greek Mythology.* The river of forgetfulness, one of the five rivers in Hades. **2.** A condition of forgetfulness; oblivion. [Greek *Lēthē.*] **—le′the·an** *adj.*

Le·to (lē′tō) *n.* *Greek Mythology.* A consort of Zeus and the mother of Apollo and Artemis.

let-out (lĕt′out′) *n.* *Chiefly British.* A means of evasion or avoidance.

let's (lĕts). Let us.

Lett (lĕt) *n.* A member of a Baltic people constituting the main population of Latvia. [German *Lette,* from Latvian *Latvi.*]

let·ter (lĕt′ər) *n.* **1.** A written symbol or character representing a speech sound and being a component of an alphabet. **2.** A written or printed communication directed to a person or an organization. **3.** Often **letters.** A certified document granting rights to its bearer. **4.** Literal meaning: *had to adhere to the letter of the law.* **5. letters** *(used with a sing. verb).* **a.** Literary culture; belles-lettres. **b.** Learning or knowledge, especially of literature. **c.** Literature or writing as a profession. **6.** *Printing.* **a.** A piece of type that prints a single character. **b.** A specific style of type. **c.** The characters in one style of type. **7.** An emblem in the shape of the initial of a school awarded for outstanding performance, especially in varsity athletics. **—letter** *v.* **-tered, -ter·ing, -ters.** *—tr.* **1.** To write letters on. **2.** To write in letters. *—intr.* **1.** To write or form letters. **2.** To earn a school letter, as for outstanding athletic achievement: *She lettered in three collegiate sports.* **—idiom. to the letter.** To the last detail; exactly: *followed instructions to the letter.* [Middle English, from Old French *lettre,* from Latin *littera,* perhaps from Etruscan, from Greek *diphthera,* hide, leather, writing surface.] **—let′ter·er** *n.*

SYNONYMS: *letter, epistle, missive, note.* The central meaning shared by these nouns is "a written communication directed to another": *received a letter of complaint; the Epistles of the New Testament; a missive of condolence; a thank-you note.*

letter bomb *n.* An explosive mailed in an envelope to a designated victim.

let·ter·box (lĕt′ər-bŏks′) *n.* See **mailbox** (sense 2).

letter carrier *n.* A person, especially a postal worker, who delivers mail. Also called *mail carrier.*

let·tered (lĕt′ərd) *adj.* **1.a.** Educated to read and write; literate. **b.** Highly educated; learned. **2.** Of or relating to literacy or learning. **3.** Inscribed or marked with or as if with letters.

let·ter·form (lĕt′ər-fôrm′) *n.* The development or design of the shape of an alphabet letter.

let·ter·head (lĕt′ər-hĕd′) *n.* **1.** The heading at the top of a sheet of letter paper, usually consisting of a name and an address. **2.** Stationery imprinted with such a heading.

let·ter·ing (lĕt′ər-ĭng) *n.* **1.** The act, process, or art of forming letters. **2.** Letters inscribed, as on a sign.

let·ter·man (lĕt′ər-măn′, -mən) *n.* A secondary or college student who has earned a letter in a particular activity, especially a varsity sport.

letter of credence *n.* An official document conveying the credentials of a diplomatic envoy to a foreign government. Also called *letters of credence.*

letter of credit *n., pl.* **letters of credit.** *Abbr.* **L/C** A letter issued by a bank authorizing the bearer to draw a stated amount of money from the issuing bank, its branches, or other associated banks or agencies.

letter of intent *n., pl.* **letters of intent.** A written statement expressing the intention of the undersigned to enter into a formal agreement, especially a business arrangement or transaction.

letter of marque *n.* See **letters of marque.**

let·ter-per·fect (lĕt′ər-pûr′fĭkt) *adj.* Correct to the last detail, especially being in or following the exact words.

let·ter·press (lĕt′ər-prĕs′) *n.* **1.a.** The process of printing from a raised inked surface. **b.** Something printed in this fashion. **2.** *Chiefly British.* The text, as of a book, distinct from illustrations or other ornamentation.

let·ter-qual·i·ty (lĕt′ər-kwŏl′ĭ-tē) *adj.* Of or producing printed characters similar in clarity to those produced by a conventional typewriter: *a letter-quality computer printer; letter-quality output.*

let·ters of administration (lĕt′ərz) *pl.n.* A legal document entrusting an individual with the administration of the estate of a deceased person.

letters of credence *pl.n.* See **letter of credence.**

letters of marque *pl.n.* **1.** A document issued by a nation allowing a private citizen to seize citizens or goods of another nation. **2.** A document issued by a nation allowing a private citizen to equip a ship with arms in order to attack enemy ships. Also called *letter of marque.* [Middle English *letters of mark,* from Old French *marque,* mark, seizure, reprisal. See MARQUETRY.]

letters patent *pl.n.* A document issued by a government to a patentee granting an exclusive right to the enjoyment or possession of an invention.

letters testamentary *pl.n.* A document issued by a probate court or officer informing an executor of a will of his or her appointment and empowering the executor to discharge the appointed responsibilities.

Let·tish (lĕt′ĭsh) *adj.* Of or relating to the Letts or their language or culture. **—Lettish** *n.* See **Latvian** (sense 2).

let·tuce (lĕt′əs) *n.* **1.a.** Any of various plants of the genus *Lactuca,* especially *L. sativa,* cultivated for their edible leaves. **b.** The leaves of *L. sativa,* used especially in salads. **2.** *Slang.* Paper money. [Middle English *lettuse,* from Old French *laitues,* pl. of *laitue,* from Latin *lactūca,* from *lac, lact-,* milk (from its milky juice). See **melg-** in Appendix.]

let·up (lĕt′ŭp′) *n.* **1.** A reduction in pace, force, or intensity; a slowdown. **2.** A temporary stop; a pause.

le·u (lĕ′o͞o) *n., pl.* **lei** (lā). See table at **currency.** [Rumanian, from Latin *leō,* lion (from the image of a lion on a coin used in the late Ottoman Empire). See LION.]

leuc– *pref.* Variant of **leuko–.**

leu·cine (lo͞o′sēn′) *n.* An essential amino acid, $C_4H_9CH(NH_2)COOH$, derived from the hydrolysis of protein by pancreatic enzymes during digestion and necessary for optimal growth in in-

ă pat	oi boy
ā pay	ou out
âr care	o͝o took
ä father	o͞o boot
ĕ pet	ŭ cut
ē be	ûr urge
ĭ pit	th thin
ī pie	*th* this
îr pier	hw which
ŏ pot	zh vision
ō toe	ə about, item
ô paw	♦ regionalism

Stress marks: **′** (primary); ′ (secondary), as in **dictionary** (dĭk′shə-nĕr′ē)

levee[1]

fants and children and for the maintenance of nitrogen balance in adults. [LEUC(O)– + –INE[2].]

leu·cite (lo͞o′sīt′) *n.* A white or gray mineral of potassium aluminum silicate, $KAlSi_2O_6$. —**leu·cit′ic** (-sĭt′ĭk) *adj.*

leuco– *pref.* Variant of **leuko–.**

leu·co·cyte (lo͞o′kə-sīt′) *n.* Variant of **leukocyte.**

leu·co·cy·to·sis (lo͞o′kə-sī-tō′sĭs) *n.* Variant of **leukocytosis.**

leu·co·der·ma (lo͞o′kə-dûr′mə) *n.* Variant of **leukoderma.**

leu·co·pe·ni·a (lo͞o′kə-pē′nē-ə) *n.* Variant of **leukopenia.**

leu·co·plast (lo͞o′kə-plăst′) also **leu·co·plas·tid** (lo͞o′kə-plăs′tĭd) *n.* A colorless plastid in the cytoplasm of plant cells around which starch collects.

leu·cor·rhe·a (lo͞o′kə-rē′ə) *n.* Variant of **leukorrhea.**

leu·cot·o·my (lo͞o-kŏt′əmē) *n.* Variant of **leukotomy.**

Leuc·tra (lo͞ok′trə). A village of ancient Greece southwest of Thebes. It was the site of a major Spartan defeat by the Thebans (371 B.C.).

leuk– *pref.* Variant of **leuko–.**

leu·ke·mi·a (lo͞o-kē′mē-ə) *n.* Any of various acute or chronic neoplastic diseases of the bone marrow in which unrestrained proliferation of white blood cells occurs, usually accompanied by anemia, impaired blood clotting, and enlargement of the lymph nodes, liver, and spleen. —**leu·ke′mic** *adj. & n.*

leuko– or **leuk–** also **leuco–** or **leuc–** *pref.* **1.** White; colorless: *leukoderma.* **2.** Leukocyte: *leukopenia.* [Greek, from *leukos,* clear, white. See **leuk-** in Appendix.]

leu·ko·cyte also **leu·co·cyte** (lo͞o′kə-sīt′) *n.* See **white blood cell.** —**leu′ko·cyt′ic** (-sĭt′ĭk) *adj.* —**leu′ko·cy′toid′** *adj.*

leu·ko·cy·to·sis also **leu·co·cy·to·sis** (lo͞o′kə-sī-tō′sĭs) *n., pl.* **-ses** (-sēz). An abnormally large increase in the number of white blood cells in the blood, often occurring during an acute infection or inflammation. —**leu′ko·cy·tot′ic** (-tŏt′ĭk) *adj.*

leu·ko·der·ma also **leu·co·der·ma** (lo͞o′kə-dûr′mə) *n.* Partial or total loss of skin pigmentation, often occurring in patches. Also called *vitiligo.* —**leu′ko·der′mal, leu′ko·der′mic** *adj.*

leu·ko·pe·ni·a also **leu·co·pe·ni·a** (lo͞o′kə-pē′nē-ə) *n.* An abnormally low number of leukocytes in the circulating blood. —**leu′ko·pe′nic** *adj.*

leu·ko·pla·ki·a (lo͞o′kə-plā′kē-ə) *n.* An abnormal condition characterized by white spots or patches on mucous membranes, especially of the mouth and vulva. Also called *leukoplasia.* [New Latin : LEUKO– + Greek *plax, plak-,* flat area; see **plāk-**[1] in Appendix + –IA[1].]

leuk·o·pla·sia (lo͞o′kə-plā′zhə, -zhē-ə, -zē-ə) *n.* See **leukoplakia.**

leu·kor·rhe·a also **leu·cor·rhe·a** (lo͞o′kə-rē′ə) *n.* A thick, whitish discharge from the vagina or cervical canal. —**leu′kor·rhe′al** *adj.*

leu·kot·o·my also **leu·cot·o·my** (lo͞o-kŏt′ə-mē) *n., pl.* **-mies.** *Chiefly British.* A prefrontal lobotomy. [LEUKO– (referring to the white matter of the brain) + –TOMY.]

leu·ko·tri·ene (lo͞o′kə-trī′ēn) *n.* Any of several lipid compounds that contain 20 carbon atoms, are related to prostaglandins, and mediate the inflammatory response. [LEUKO(CYTE) + *triene,* a compound containing three double bonds (TRI– + –ENE).]

Leu·ven (lœ′vən). See **Louvain.**

Leu·wen·hoek (lā′vən-ho͝ok′, lā′ü-wən-ho͝ok′), **Anton van.** See Anton van **Leeuwenhoek.**

lev (lĕf) *n., pl.* **lev·a** (lĕv′ə). See table at **currency.** [Bulgarian, lion, lev, from Old Church Slavonic *lĭvŭ,* lion, probably from Old High German *lewo,* from Latin *leō.* See LION.]

lev– *pref.* Variant of **levo–.**

Lev. *abbr. Bible.* Leviticus.

lev·a (lĕv′ə) *n.* Plural of **lev.**

Lev·al·loi·si·an (lĕv′ə-loi′zē-ən) *adj.* Of or relating to a western European stage in lower Paleolithic culture, characterized by a distinctive method of striking off flake tools from pieces of flint. [After LEVALLOIS(-PERRET).]

Le·val·lois-Per·ret (lə-väl-wä′pĕ-rā′). A city of north-central France, a residential and industrial suburb of Paris on the Seine River. Population, 53,500.

le·vant (lə-vănt′) *intr.v.* **-vant·ed, -vant·ing, -vants.** *Chiefly British.* To leave hurriedly or in secret to avoid unpaid debts. [Possibly from Spanish *levantar (el campo),* to lift, break (camp), from Vulgar Latin **levantāre,* from Latin *levāns, levant-,* present participle of *levāre,* to raise. See LEVER.]

Le·vant[1] (lə-vănt′). The countries bordering on the eastern Mediterranean Sea from Turkey to Egypt. —**Le′van·tine′** (lĕv′ən-tīn′, -tēn′, lə-văn′-) *adj. & n.*

Le·vant[2] (lə-vănt′) *n.* A heavy, coarse-grained morocco leather often used in bookbinding. Also called *Levant morocco.* [After LEVANT[1].]

le·vant·er (lə-văn′tər) *n.* **1.** A strong easterly wind of the Mediterranean area. **2. Levanter.** A native or inhabitant of the Levant.

Levant morocco *n.* See **Levant**[2]**.**

le·va·tor (lə-vā′tər) *n., pl.* **lev·a·to·res** (lĕv′ə-tôr′ēz, -tōr′-). **1.** *Anatomy.* A muscle that raises a bodily part. **2.** A surgical instrument for lifting the depressed fragments of a fractured skull. [New Latin, from Medieval Latin *levātor,* one that raises, from Latin *levāre,* to raise. See LEVER.]

lev·ee[1] (lĕv′ē) *n.* **1.** An embankment raised to prevent a river from overflowing. **2.** A small ridge or raised area bordering an irrigated field. **3.** A landing place on a river; a pier. —**levee** *tr.v.* **lev·eed, lev·ee·ing, lev·ees.** To provide with a levee. [French *levée,* from Old French *levee,* from feminine past participle of *lever,* to raise. See LEVER.]

lev·ee[2] (lĕv′ē, lə-vē′, -vā′) *n.* **1.** A reception held, as by royalty, upon arising from bed. **2.** A formal reception, as at a royal court. [From French *lever,* a rising, from Old French, from *lever,* to raise, rise. See LEVER.]

lev·el (lĕv′əl) *n.* **1.a.** Relative position or rank on a scale: *the local level of government; studying at the graduate level.* **b.** A relative degree, as of achievement, intensity, or concentration: *an unsafe level of toxicity; a high level of frustration.* **2.** A natural or proper position, place, or stage: *I finally found my own level in the business world.* **3.** Position along a vertical axis; height or depth: *a platform at knee level.* **4.a.** A horizontal line or plane at right angles to the plumb. **b.** The position or height of such a line or plane. **5.** A flat, horizontal surface. **6.** A land area of uniform elevation. **7.a.** An instrument for ascertaining whether a surface is horizontal, vertical, or at a 45° angle, consisting essentially of an encased, liquid-filled tube containing an air bubble that moves to a center window when the instrument is set on an even plane. Also called *spirit level.* **b.** Such a device combined with a telescope and used in surveying. **c.** A computation of the difference in elevation between two points by using such a device. **8.** *Computer Science.* A bit, an element, a channel, or a row of information. —**level** *adj.* **1.** Having a flat, smooth surface. **2.** Being on a horizontal plane. **3.a.** Being at the same height or position as another; even. **b.** Being at the same degree of rank, standing, or advantage as another; equal. **4.** Exhibiting no abrupt variations; steady: *spoke in a level tone.* **5.** Rational and balanced; sensible: *came to a level appraisal of the situation; keeps a level head in an emergency.* **6.** Filled evenly to the top: *a level tablespoon of cough medicine.* —**level** *v.* **-eled, -el·ing, -els** or **-elled, -el·ling, -els.** —*tr.* **1.** To make horizontal, flat, or even: *leveled the driveway with a roller; leveled off the hedges with the clippers.* **2.** To tear down; raze. **3.** To knock down with or as if with a blow: *The challenger leveled the champion with a mighty uppercut.* **4.** To place on the same level; equalize. **5.** To aim along a horizontal plane: *leveled the gun at the target.* **6.** To direct emphatically or forcefully toward someone: *leveled charges of dishonesty.* **7.** To measure the different elevations of (a tract of land) with a level. —*intr.* **1.** To bring persons or things to an equal level; equalize. **2.** To aim a weapon horizontally. **3.** *Informal.* To be frank and open: *advised the suspect to level with the authorities.* —**level** *adv.* Along a flat or even line or plane. —***phrasal verb.* level off. 1.** To move toward stability or consistency: *Prices leveled off.* **2.** To maneuver an aircraft into a flight attitude that is parallel to the surface of the earth after gaining or losing altitude. —***idioms.* (one's) level best.** The best one can do in an earnest attempt: *I did my level best in math class.* **on the level.** *Informal.* Without deception; honest. [Middle English, an instrument to check that a surface is horizontal, from Old French *livel,* from Vulgar Latin **lībellum,* from Latin *lībella,* diminutive of *lībra,* balance.] —**lev′el·ly** *adv.* —**lev′el·ness** *n.*

SYNONYMS: *level, flat, even, plane, smooth, flush.* These adjectives are applicable to surfaces without irregularities in the form of elevations or depressions. *Level* implies being parallel with the line of the horizon: *acres of level farmland. Flat* applies to surfaces without curves, protuberances, or indentations: *a flat desk; flat country; a flat rock. Even* refers to flat surfaces in which no part is higher or lower than another: *The water in the pool is as even as a mirror. Plane* is principally a mathematical term and refers to a surface containing all the straight lines connecting any two points on it: *a plane figure. Smooth* describes a surface on which the absence of even slight irregularities can be established by sight or touch: *smooth marble; a smooth skin. Flush* applies to a surface that is on an exact level with an adjoining one, forming a continuous surface: *a door that is flush with the wall.* See also Synonyms at **aim.**

level compensator *n. Electronics.* An automatic gain control device used in the receiving equipment of telegraphic circuits.

level crossing *n. Chiefly British.* A grade crossing.

lev·el·er also **lev·el·ler** (lĕv′ə-lər) *n.* **1.** One that levels: *a leveler of boards.* **2.a.** One who advocates the abolition of social inequities. **b. Leveller.** A member of an English radical political movement arising in the Parliamentarian forces of the 1640's and advocating universal male suffrage, equality before the law, parliamentary democracy, and religious tolerance.

lev·el·head·ed (lĕv′əl-hĕd′ĭd) *adj.* Characteristically self-composed and sensible. —**lev′el·head′ed·ness** *n.*

lev·el·ing rod (lĕv′ə-lĭng) *n.* A graduated pole or stick with a movable marker, used with a surveyor's level to measure differences in elevation. Also called *leveling pole, leveling staff.*

lev·el·ler (lĕv′ə-lər) *n.* Variant of **leveler.**

level of significance *n., pl.* **levels of significance.** *Statistics.* The probability of a false rejection of the null hypothesis in a statistical test. Also called *significance level.*

level
Carpenter's level

lev·er (lĕvʹər, lēʹvər) *n.* **1.** A simple machine consisting of a rigid bar pivoted on a fixed point and used to transmit force, as in raising or moving a weight at one end by pushing down on the other. **2.** A projecting handle used to adjust or operate a mechanism. **3.** A means of accomplishing; a tool: *used friendship as a lever to obtain advancement.* **—lever** *tr.v.* **-ered, -er·ing, -ers.** To move or lift with or as if with a lever. [Middle English, from Old French *levier,* from *lever,* to raise, from Latin *levāre,* from *levis,* light. See **legʷh-** in Appendix.]

lev·er·age (lĕvʹər-ĭj, lēʹvər-) *n.* **1.a.** The action of a lever. **b.** The mechanical advantage of a lever. **2.** Positional advantage; power to act effectively: *"started his . . . career with far more social leverage than his father had enjoyed"* (Doris Kearns Goodwin). **3.** The use of credit or borrowed funds to improve one's speculative capacity and increase the rate of return from an investment, as in buying securities on margin. **—leverage** *tr.v.* **-aged, -ag·ing, -ag·es. 1.** To provide (a company) with leverage. **2.** To supplement (money, for example) with leverage. To affect as if by leverage: *a lifestyle that was leveraged by business responsibilities.*

lev·er·aged buyout (lĕvʹər-ĭjd, lēʹvər-ĭjd) *n. Abbr.* **LBO** The use of a target company's asset value to finance the debt incurred in acquiring the company.

lev·er·et (lĕvʹər-ĭt) *n.* A young hare, especially one less than a year old. [Middle English, from Anglo-Norman, diminutive of *levere,* hare, from Latin *lepus, lepor-.*]

Le·ver·ku·sen (lāʹvər-ko͞oʹzən). A city of west-central Germany on the Rhine River north of Cologne. Population, 155,411.

Lé·vesque (lə-vĕkʹ), **René.** 1922–1987. Canadian politician who cofounded (1967) the Parti Québecois to further the cause of French-Canadian separatism. He served as premier of Quebec (1976–1985).

Le·vi (lēʹvīʹ). In the Old Testament, a son of Jacob and Leah and the forebear of one of the tribes of Israel.

Le·vi (lāʹvē), **Carlo.** 1902–1975. Italian writer best known for his novel *Christ Stopped at Eboli* (1945).

lev·i·a·ble (lĕvʹē-ə-bəl) *adj.* **1.** That can be levied: *leviable taxes.* **2.** Liable to be taxed: *leviable imports.*

le·vi·a·than (lə-vīʹə-thən) *n.* **1.** Something unusually large of its kind, especially a ship. **2.** A very large animal, especially a whale. **3.** *Bible.* A monstrous sea creature mentioned in the Old Testament. [Middle English, huge biblical sea creature, from Late Latin, from Hebrew *liwyātān*; akin to Canaanite *ltn,* Lotan, the Hydra.]

lev·i·gate (lĕvʹĭ-gātʹ) *tr.v.* **-gat·ed, -gat·ing, -gates. 1.a.** To make into a smooth, fine powder or paste, as by grinding when moist. **b.** To separate fine particles from coarse by grinding in water. **2.** To suspend in a liquid. **3.** To make smooth; polish. **—levigate** (-gātʹ, -gĭt) *adj.* Smooth. [Latin *lēvigāre, lēvigāt-* : *lēvis,* smooth; see **lei-** in Appendix + *agere,* to make, do; see **ag-** in Appendix.] **—levʹi·gaʹtion** *n.*

lev·in (lĕvʹĭn) *n. Archaic.* Lightning. [Middle English *levene, levin.* See **leuk-** in Appendix.]

lev·i·rate (lĕvʹər-ĭt, -ə-rātʹ, lēʹvər-ĭt, -və-rātʹ) *n.* The practice of marrying the widow of one's brother to maintain his line, as required by ancient Hebrew law. [From Latin *lēvir,* husband's brother. See **daiwer-** in Appendix.] **—levʹi·ratʹic** (-rătʹĭk), **levʹi·ratʹi·cal** *adj.*

Le·vi's (lēʹvīzʹ). A trademark used for close-fitting trousers of heavy denim.

Lé·vis (lēʹvĭs, lā-vēʹ). A city of southern Quebec, Canada, on the St. Lawrence River opposite Quebec City. Settled in the mid-17th century, it is a port and shipbuilding center. Population, 17,895.

Lé·vi-Strauss (lāʹvē-strousʹ), **Claude.** Born 1908. French social anthropologist and leading exponent of the theory of structuralism. His works include *Structural Anthropology* (1958).

Levit. *abbr. Bible.* Leviticus.

lev·i·tate (lĕvʹĭ-tātʹ) *intr. & tr.v.* **-tat·ed, -tat·ing, -tates.** To rise or cause to rise into the air and float in apparent defiance of gravity. [From Latin *levis,* light (on the model of GRAVITATE). See LEVITY.] **—levʹi·taʹtion** *n.* **—levʹi·taʹtion·al** *adj.* **—levʹi·taʹtor** *n.*

Le·vite (lēʹvītʹ) *n. Bible.* A member of the tribe of Levi but not descended from Aaron, chosen to assist the Temple priests. [Middle English, from Late Latin *Lēvītēs, Lēvīta,* from Greek *Leuitēs,* from *Leui,* Levi, from Hebrew *Lēwî.*]

Le·vit·i·cal (lə-vĭtʹĭ-kəl) also **Le·vit·ic** (-vĭtʹĭk) *adj. Bible.* **1.** Of or relating to the Levites. **2.** Of or relating to Leviticus.

Le·vit·i·cus (lə-vĭtʹĭ-kəs) *n. Abbr.* **Lev., Levit., Lv** *Bible.* See table at **Bible.** [Middle English, from Late Latin *Levīticus,* from Greek *Leuitikos,* Levitical, from *Leuitēs,* Levite. See LEVITE.]

Lev·it·town (lĕvʹĭt-tounʹ). **1.** An unincorporated community of southeast New York on western Long Island east-southeast of Mineola. It was founded in 1947 as a low-cost housing development for World War II veterans. Population 65,400. **2.** A community of southeast Pennsylvania near the Delaware River northeast of Philadelphia. Population, 17,420.

lev·i·ty (lĕvʹĭ-tē) *n., pl.* **-ties. 1.** Lightness of manner or speech, especially when inappropriate; frivolity. **2.** Inconstancy; changeableness. **3.** The state or quality of being light; buoyancy. [Latin *levitās,* from *levis,* light. See **legʷh-** in Appendix.]

le·vo (lēʹvō) *adj.* Levorotatory.

levo– or **lev–** *pref.* **1.** To the left: *levorotatory.* **2.** Levorotatory: *levulose.* [French *lévo-,* from Latin *laevus,* left.]

le·vo·do·pa (lēʹvə-dōʹpə) *n.* See **L-dopa.**

le·vo·ro·ta·ry (lēʹvə-rōʹtə-rē) *adj.* Variant of **levorotatory.**

le·vo·ro·ta·tion (lēʹvə-rō-tāʹshən) *n.* A counterclockwise rotation, especially of the plane of polarized light.

le·vo·ro·ta·to·ry (lēʹvə-rōʹtə-tôrʹē, -tōrʹē) also **le·vo·ro·ta·ry** (-tə-rē) *adj.* **1.** Turning or rotating the plane of polarization of light to the left, or counterclockwise. **2.** Of or relating to a chemical solution that rotates the plane of polarized light to the left, or counterclockwise.

lev·u·lose (lĕvʹyə-lōsʹ, -lōzʹ) *n.* See **fructose.** [LEV(O)– + –UL(E) + –OSE[2].]

lev·y (lĕvʹē) *v.* **-ied, -y·ing, -ies.** —*tr.* **1.** To impose or collect (a tax, for example). **2.** To draft into military service. **3.** To declare and wage (a war). —*intr.* To confiscate property, especially in accordance with a legal judgment. **—levy** *n., pl.* **-ies. 1.** The act or process of levying. **2.** Money, property, or troops levied. [Middle English *levien,* from *leve,* levy, tax, from Old French *levee,* from feminine past participle of *lever,* to raise. See LEVER.] **—levʹi·er** *n.*

lewd (lo͞od) *adj.* **lewd·er, lewd·est. 1.a.** Preoccupied with sex and sexual desire; lustful. **b.** Obscene; indecent. **2.** *Obsolete.* Wicked. [Middle English *leued,* unlearned, lay, lascivious, from Old English *lǣwede,* ignorant, lay.] **—lewdʹly** *adv.* **—lewdʹness** *n.*

Lew·es (lo͞oʹĭs), **George Henry.** 1817–1878. British philosopher and critic who was the first editor (1865–1866) of the *Fortnightly Review.*

Lewes River. The upper course of the Yukon River above its junction with the Pelly River in southern Yukon Territory, Canada. It is about 544 km (338 mi) long.

lew·is (lo͞oʹĭs) *n.* A dovetailed iron tenon made of several parts and designed to fit into a dovetail mortise in a large stone so that it can be lifted by a hoisting apparatus. Also called *lewisson.* [Perhaps from the name *Lewis.*]

Lew·is (lo͞oʹĭs), **Cecil Day.** See Cecil **Day Lewis.**

Lewis, C(live) S(taples). 1898–1963. British writer and critic. His works include *The Allegory of Love* (1936) and a series of books for children known as *The Chronicles of Narnia* (1950–1956).

Lewis, (Harry) Sinclair. 1885–1951. American novelist who satirized middle-class America in his 22 works, including *Babbitt* (1922) and *Elmer Gantry* (1927). He was the first American to receive (1930) a Nobel Prize for literature.

Lewis, John Llewellyn. 1880–1969. American labor leader who was president of the United Mine Workers of America (1920–1960) and the Congress of Industrial Organizations (1935–1940).

Lewis, Matthew Gregory. 1775–1818. British gothic writer who is remembered for the novel *The Monk* (1796), for which he was known as "Monk Lewis."

Lewis, Meriwether. 1774–1809. American soldier and explorer who led the Lewis and Clark expedition (1803–1806) from St. Louis to the mouth of the Columbia River and served as governor of the Louisiana Territory (1806–1809).

Lewis, (Percy) Wyndham. 1884–1957. British writer and artist. He wrote the novels *The Apes of God* (1930) and *Revenge for Love* (1937) and painted portraits of T.S. Eliot and Ezra Pound.

lew·is·ite (lo͞oʹĭ-sītʹ) *n.* An oily, colorless to violet or brown liquid, $C_2H_2AsCl_3$, used to make a highly toxic gas weapon. [After Winford Lee *Lewis* (1878–1943), American chemist.]

lew·is·son (lo͞oʹĭ-sən) *n.* See **lewis.** [From LEWIS.]

Lew·is·ton (lo͞oʹĭ-stən). **1.** A city of northwest Idaho on the border south-southeast of Spokane, Washington. A commercial and industrial center in a timber, grain, and livestock region, it was the first capital (1863–1864) of the Idaho Territory. Population, 27,986. **2.** A city of southwest Maine on the Androscoggin River north of Portland. Settled in 1770, it became a textile center in the early 19th century. Population, 40,481.

Lew·is·ville (lo͞oʹĭs-vĭlʹ, lo͞oʹē-). A city of northeast Texas, an industrial and residential suburb in the Dallas–Fort Worth metropolitan area. Population, 24,273.

Lewis with Har·ris (hărʹĭs). An island of northwest Scotland. The largest and northernmost of the Outer Hebrides, it is noted for its tweeds.

lex (lĕks) *n., pl.* **le·ges** (lēʹjēzʹ). Law. [Latin *lēx.* See **leg-** in Appendix.]

lex. *abbr.* Lexicon.

lex·eme (lĕkʹsēmʹ) *n.* The fundamental unit of the lexicon of a language. *Find, found,* and *finding* are members of the English lexeme *find.* [LEX(ICON) + –EME.]

lex·i·ca (lĕkʹsĭ-kə) *n.* A plural of **lexicon.**

lex·i·cal (lĕkʹsĭ-kəl) *adj.* **1.** Of or relating to the vocabulary, words, or morphemes of a language. **2.** Of or relating to lexicography or a lexicon. [LEXIC(ON) + –AL[1].] **—lexʹi·calʹi·ty** (-kălʹĭ-tē) *n.* **—lexʹi·cal·ly** *adv.*

lex·i·cog·ra·phy (lĕkʹsĭ-kŏgʹrə-fē) *n.* The process or work of writing or compiling a dictionary. **—lexʹi·cogʹra·pher** *n.* **—lexʹi·co·graphʹic** (-kə-grăfʹĭk), **lexʹi·co·graphʹi·cal** (-ĭ-kəl) *adj.* **—lexʹi·co·graphʹi·cal·ly** *adv.*

lex·i·col·o·gy (lĕkʹsĭ-kŏlʹə-jē) *n.* The branch of linguistics that deals with the lexical component of language. **—lexʹi·co·**

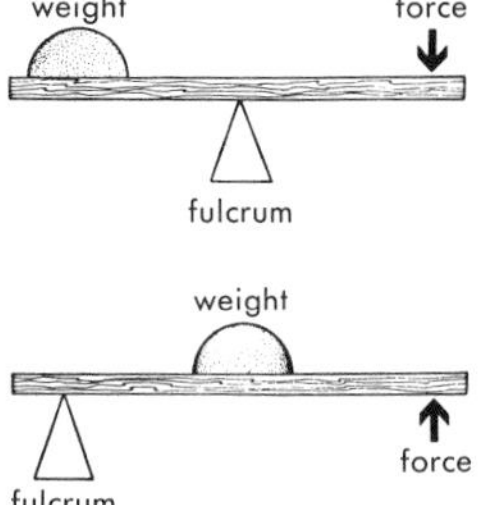

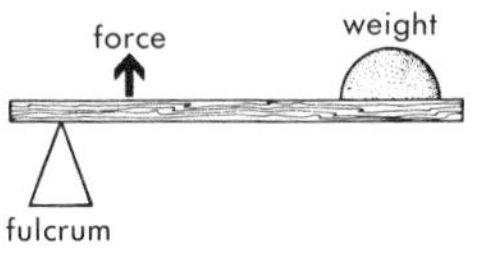

lever
Top: First-class lever, with fulcrum between weight and force
Center: Second-class lever, with weight between fulcrum and force
Bottom: Third-class lever, with force between fulcrum and weight

Meriwether Lewis

ă pat	oi boy
ā pay	ou out
âr care	o͝o took
ä father	o͞o boot
ĕ pet	ŭ cut
ē be	ûr urge
ĭ pit	th thin
ī pie	*th* this
îr pier	hw which
ŏ pot	zh vision
ō toe	ə about, item
ô paw	♦ regionalism

Stress marks: ʹ (primary); ʹ (secondary), as in **dictionary** (dĭkʹshə-nĕrʹē)

log′i·cal (-kə-lŏj′ĭ-kəl) *adj.* **—lex′i·co·log′i·cal·ly** *adv.* **—lex′i·col′o·gist** *n.*

lex·i·con (lĕk′sĭ-kŏn′) *n., pl.* **-cons** or **-ca** (-kə). *Abbr.* **lex.** **1.** A dictionary. **2.** A stock of terms used in a particular profession, subject, or style; a vocabulary: *the lexicon of surrealist art.* **3.** *Linguistics.* The morphemes of a language considered as a group. [Medieval Latin, from Greek *lexikon (biblion),* word-(book), from neuter of *lexikos,* of words, from *lexis,* word, from *legein,* to speak. See **leg-** in Appendix.]

Lex·ing·ton (lĕk′sĭng-tən). **1.** A city of northeast-central Kentucky east-southeast of Louisville. A noted center for the raising of thoroughbred horses, it was named in 1775 after the Battle of Lexington. Population, 204,165. **2.** A town of northeast Massachusetts, a residential suburb of Boston. The Battle of Lexington (April 19, 1775) marked the beginning of the American Revolution. Population, 29,479.

lex·is (lĕk′sĭs) *n.* The total set of words in a language as distinct from morphology; vocabulary. [Greek, speech, word. See LEXICON.]

ley (lā, lē) *n.* Variant of **lea.**

Ley·den (līd′n). See **Leiden.**

Leyden jar *n.* An early form of capacitor consisting of a glass jar lined inside and out with tinfoil and having a conducting rod connected to the inner foil lining and passing out of the jar through an insulated stopper. [After *Leyden* (Leiden).]

Ley·land (lā′lənd). An urban district of northwest England north-northeast of Liverpool. Population, 97,700.

Leyland, John. See John **Leland.**

Ley·ster (lī′stər), **Judith.** 1609–1660. Dutch painter known for her portraits and genre paintings.

Ley·te (lā′tē, -tĕ). An island of the east-central Philippines in the Visayan group north of Mindanao.

Leyte Gulf. An inlet of the western Pacific Ocean in the Philippines south of Samar and east of Leyte. An invasion force led by Gen. Douglas MacArthur decisively defeated the Japanese here on October 25–26, 1944.

lf *abbr.* *Printing.* Lightface.

LF **1.** *Baseball.* Left field; left fielder. **2.** Or **lf.** Low frequency.

lg. *abbr.* **1.** Large. **2.** Long.

lge. *abbr.* Large.

LH *abbr.* Luteinizing hormone.

Lha·sa (lä′sə, lăs′ə). A city of southwest China, the capital of Xizang (Tibet). Because of its remoteness and exclusivity as the center of Tibetan Buddhism, Lhasa was long closed to foreign visitors and known as "the Forbidden City." Population, 105,897.

Lha·sa ap·so (ăp′sō) *n., pl.* **-sos.** Any of a breed of small dog originating in Tibet and having a long, straight coat. [LHASA + Tibetan *apso,* Lhasa apso.]

Lho·tse (lō′tsĕ′). A peak, 8,506.5 m (27,890 ft) high, of the central Himalaya Mountains on the Nepal-Tibet border.

LHRH *abbr.* Luteinizing hormone releasing hormone.

li[1] (lē) *n., pl.* **li.** A traditional Chinese measure of distance, today standardized at 500 meters (547 yards). [Chinese (Mandarin) *lĭ.*]

li[2] *abbr.* Link.

Li The symbol for the element **lithium.**

L.I. *abbr.* Long Island.

li·a·bil·i·ty (lī′ə-bĭl′ĭ-tē) *n., pl.* **-ties.** **1.** The state of being liable. **2.a.** Something for which one is liable; an obligation, a responsibility, or a debt. **b. liabilities.** The financial obligations entered in the balance sheet of a business enterprise. **3.** Something that holds one back; a handicap. **4.** Likelihood.

li·a·ble (lī′ə-bəl) *adj.* **1.** Legally obligated; responsible: *liable for military service.* See Synonyms at **responsible. 2.** At risk of or subject to experiencing or suffering something unpleasant. Used with *to: liable to criminal charges; liable to diabetes.* **3.** Often used with reference to an unfavorable outcome: *In a depression banks are liable to fail.* [Middle English, probably from Old French *lier,* to bind, from Latin *ligāre.* See **leig-** in Appendix.]

USAGE NOTE: *Liable, apt,* and *likely* are often used interchangeably in constructions with following infinitives, as in *John is liable to lose, John is apt to lose,* and *John is likely to lose.* The three words are distinct in meaning. A widely repeated rule holds that *liable* should only be used if the subject would be adversely affected by the outcome expressed by the infinitive. The rule therefore permits *John is liable to fall out of his chair if he doesn't sit up straight* but not *The chair is liable to be slippery,* though constructions of the latter type have long been common in reputable writing. *Apt* usually suggests that the subject has a natural tendency enhancing the probability of an outcome, and that the speaker is in some way apprehensive about the outcome. Thus *apt* is more naturally used in a sentence like *The fuel pump is apt to give out at any minute* than in *Even the clearest instructions are apt to be misinterpreted by those idiots* (since the instructions are not at fault) or in *The fuel pump is apt to give you no problems for the life of the car* (since there is no reason that the speaker should regard such an outcome as unfortunate). *Likely* is more general than either *liable* or *apt.* It ascribes no particular property to the subject that enhances the probability of the outcome: while *John is apt to lose the election* may suggest that the loss will result from something John does or fails to do, *John is likely to lose the election* does not. Nor does it suggest anything about the desirability of the outcome from the point of view of either the speaker or the subject. A football coach who says *We are apt to win* may be suspected of sarcasm, and one who says *We are liable to win* may be suspected of having bet on the opposition; only *We are likely to win* is consistent with the expression of an unambivalent expectation of victory. See Usage Note at **likely.**

li·aise (lē-āz′) *intr.v.* **-aised, -ais·ing, -ais·es. 1.** To effect or establish a liaison. **2.** To act or serve as a liaison officer. [Back-formation from LIAISON.]

li·ai·son (lē′ā-zŏn′, lē-ā′-) *n.* **1.a.** An instance or a means of communication between different groups or units of an organization, especially in the armed forces. **b.** One that maintains communication: *served as the President's liaison with Congress.* **2.a.** A close relationship, connection, or link. **b.** An adulterous relationship; an affair. **3.** *Linguistics.* Pronunciation of the usually silent final consonant of a word when followed by a word beginning with a vowel, especially in French. [French, from Old French, from Latin *ligātiō, ligātiōn-,* from *ligātus,* past participle of *ligāre,* to bind. See LIGATE.]

li·an·a (lē-ä′nə, -ăn′ə) also **li·ane** (-än′, -ăn′) *n.* Any climbing, woody, usually tropical vine. [Alteration of French *liane,* probably from *lier,* to bind. See LIABLE.]

Liang (lyäng′). The name of two Chinese dynasties, the Earlier Liang (502–557) and the Later Liang (907–923).

Lian·yun·gang (lyän′yo͞on′gäng′, -yœn′-) also **Lien·yün·kang** (lyŭn′yün′käng′). A city of eastern China near the Yellow Sea south-southwest of Qingdao. Population, 275,000.

Liao (lyou′). A Chinese dynasty that ruled from 916 to 1125.

Liao·dong (lyou′dŭng′) also **Liao·tung** (-to͝ong′). **Gulf of.** The northern part of the Gulf of Bo Hai in northeast China. It borders on the **Liaodong Peninsula,** a land area projecting southwest into the Yellow Sea.

Liao He (hə′). A river of northeast China flowing about 1,448 km (900 mi) northeast and southwest to the Gulf of Liaodong.

Liao·ning (lyou′nĭng′). A province of northeast China on the Gulf of Bo Hai and Korea Bay. It was under Japanese control from 1932 until 1945. Shenyang is the capital. Population, 36,860,000.

Liao·tung (lyou′to͝ong′), **Gulf of.** See Gulf of **Liaodong.**

Liao·yang (lyou′yäng′). A city of northeast China south-southwest of Shenyang. One of the oldest cities in Manchuria, it was the site of a Russian victory (August–September 1904) in the Russo-Japanese War. Population, 275,000.

Liao·yu·an (lyou′yo͞o′än′, -yüän′). A city of northeast China south of Changchun. It is a coal-mining center with iron and steel works. Population, 300,000.

li·ar (lī′ər) *n.* One that tells lies.

Li·ard (lē′ərd, lē-ärd′). A river rising in southeast Yukon Territory, Canada, and flowing about 1,215 km (755 mi) southeast into northern British Columbia then northeast to the Mackenzie River in southwest Northwest Territories.

lib (lĭb) *n.* *Informal.* A movement that seeks to achieve equal rights for a group; liberation.

lib. *abbr.* **1.** Or **Lib.** Liberal; Liberalism. **2.** Librarian. **3.** Library.

li·ba·tion (lī-bā′shən) *n.* **1.a.** The pouring of a liquid offering as a religious ritual. **b.** The liquid so poured. **2.** *Informal.* **a.** A beverage, especially an intoxicating beverage. **b.** The act of drinking an intoxicating beverage. [Middle English *libacioun,* from Latin *lībātiō, lībātiōn-,* from *lībātus,* past participle of *lībāre,* to pour out as an offering.] **—li·ba′tion·ar′y** (-shə-nĕr′ē) *adj.*

lib·ber (lĭb′ər) *n.* *Informal.* A proponent of liberation for a group.

Lib·by (lĭb′ē), **Willard Frank.** 1908–1980. American chemist. He won a 1960 Nobel Prize for developing the method of radiocarbon dating.

li·bel (lī′bəl) *Law. n.* **1.a.** A false publication in writing, printing, or typewriting or in signs or pictures that maliciously damages a person's reputation. **b.** The act or an instance of presenting such a statement to the public. **2.** The written claims presented by a plaintiff in an action at admiralty law or to an ecclesiastical court. **—libel** *tr.v.* **-beled, -bel·ing, -bels** or **-belled, -bel·ling, -bels.** To communicate a false statement about in writing or by means of signs or pictures. See Synonyms at **malign.** [Middle English, litigant's written complaint, from Old French, from Latin *libellus,* diminutive of *liber,* book.] **—li′bel·er, li′bel·ist** *n.*

li·bel·ant also **li·bel·lant** (lī′bə-lənt) *n.* *Law.* The plaintiff in a case of ecclesiastical or admiralty libel.

li·bel·ee also **li·bel·lee** (lī′bə-lē′) *n.* *Law.* The defendant in a case of ecclesiastical or admiralty libel.

li·bel·ous also **li·bel·lous** (lī′bə-ləs) *adj.* *Law.* Involving or constituting a libel; defamatory. **—li′bel·ous·ly** *adv.*

Lib·er·a·ce (lĭb′ə-rä′chē), **(Wladziu).** 1919–1987. American pianist and entertainer who is remembered for his virtuosity and flamboyant style.

lib·er·al (lĭb′ər-əl, lĭb′rəl) *adj.* *Abbr.* **lib. 1.a.** Not limited to or by established, traditional, orthodox, or authoritarian attitudes, views, or dogmas; free from bigotry. **b.** Favoring proposals for reform, open to new ideas for progress, and tolerant of the ideas and behavior of others; broad-minded. **c.** Of, relating to, or characteristic of liberalism. **d. Liberal.** *Abbr.* **Lib.** Of, designating, or characteristic of a political party founded on or associated with principles of social and political liberalism, especially in

ă pat	oi boy
ā pay	ou out
âr care	o͝o took
ä father	o͞o boot
ĕ pet	ŭ cut
ē be	ûr urge
ĭ pit	th thin
ī pie	*th* this
îr pier	hw which
ŏ pot	zh vision
ō toe	ə about, item
ô paw	♦ regionalism

Stress marks: ′ (primary); ′ (secondary), as in **dictionary** (dĭk′shə-nĕr′ē)

Great Britain, Canada, and the United States. **2.a.** Tending to give freely; generous: *a liberal benefactor.* **b.** Generous in amount; ample: *a liberal serving of potatoes.* **3.** Not strict or literal; loose or approximate: *a liberal translation.* **4.** Of, relating to, or based on the traditional arts and sciences of a college or university curriculum: *a liberal education.* **5.a.** *Archaic.* Permissible or appropriate for a person of free birth; befitting a lady or gentleman. **b.** *Obsolete.* Morally unrestrained; licentious. **—liberal** *n.* **1.** A person with liberal ideas or opinions. **2. Liberal.** *Abbr.* **Lib.** A member of a Liberal political party. [Middle English, generous, from Old French, from Latin *līberālis,* from *līber,* free. See **leudh-** in Appendix.] **—lib′er·al·ly** *adv.*

SYNONYMS: *liberal, bounteous, bountiful, freehanded, generous, handsome, munificent, openhanded.* The central meaning shared by these adjectives is "willing or marked by a willingness to give unstintingly": *a liberal backer of the arts; a bounteous feast; bountiful compliments; a freehanded host; a generous donation; a handsome offer; a munificent gift; a fond and openhanded grandfather.* See also Synonyms at **broad-minded.**
ANTONYM: *stingy.*

liberal arts *pl.n.* **1.** Academic disciplines, such as languages, literature, history, philosophy, mathematics, and science, that provide information of general cultural concern: *"The term 'liberal arts' connotes a certain elevation above utilitarian concerns. Yet liberal education is intensely useful"* (George F. Will). **2.** The disciplines comprising the trivium and quadrivium. [Middle English, translation of Medieval Latin *artēs līberālēs,* the trivium and quadrivium : Latin *artēs,* pl. of Latin *ars, art-,* subject of study + *līberālēs,* pl. of *līberālis,* proper to free persons.]

lib·er·al·ism (lĭb′ər-ə-lĭz′əm, lĭb′rə-) *n.* *Abbr.* **lib. 1.** The state or quality of being liberal. **2.a.** A political theory founded on the natural goodness of human beings and the autonomy of the individual and favoring civil and political liberties, government by law with the consent of the governed, and protection from arbitrary authority. **b.** Often **Liberalism.** *Abbr.* **Lib.** The tenets or policies of a Liberal party. **3.** An economic theory in favor of laissez-faire, the free market, and the gold standard. **4.a.** A 19th-century Protestant movement that favored free intellectual inquiry, stressed the ethical and humanitarian content of Christianity, and de-emphasized dogmatic theology. **b.** A 19th-century Roman Catholic movement that favored political democracy and ecclesiastical reform but was theologically orthodox. **—lib′er·al·ist** *n.* **—lib′er·al·is′tic** (-lĭs′tĭk) *adj.*

lib·er·al·i·ty (lĭb′ə-răl′ĭ-tē) *n., pl.* **-ties. 1.** The quality or state of being liberal or generous. **2.** An instance of being liberal.

lib·er·al·ize (lĭb′ər-ə-līz′, lĭb′rə-) *v.* **-ized, -iz·ing, -iz·es.** *—tr.* To make liberal or more liberal: *"Our standards of private conduct have been greatly liberalized . . . over recent years"* (Meg Greenfield). *—intr.* To become liberal or more liberal. **—lib′er·al·i·za′tion** (-lĭ-zā′shən) *n.* **—lib′er·al·iz′er** *n.*

lib·er·ate (lĭb′ə-rāt′) *tr.v.* **-at·ed, -at·ing, -ates. 1.** To set free, as from oppression, confinement, or foreign control. **2.** *Chemistry.* To release (a gas, for example) from combination. **3.** *Slang.* To obtain by illegal means, as by looting: *some fine brandy we had liberated from the Germans during World War II.* [Latin *līberāre, līberāt-,* from *līber,* free. See **leudh-** in Appendix.] **—lib′er·at′ing·ly** *adv.* **—lib′er·a′tor** *n.*

lib·er·a·tion (lĭb′ə-rā′shən) *n.* **1.** The act of liberating or the state of being liberated. **2.** The act or process of trying to achieve equal rights and status. **—lib′er·a′tion·ist** *n.*

liberation theology *n.* A school of theology, especially prevalent in the Roman Catholic Church in Latin America, that finds in the Gospel a call to free people from political, social, and material oppression. **—liberation theologian** *n.*

Li·be·rec (lĭb′ə-rĕts′). A city of northwest Czechoslovakia north-northeast of Prague. Founded c. 1350, it has been a textile center since the 16th century. Population, 100,048.

Li·be·ri·a (lī-bîr′ē-ə). A country of western Africa on the Atlantic Ocean. It was founded (1821) through the efforts of the American Colonization Society and settled mainly by freed slaves from 1822 to the 1860's. Liberia is the oldest independent country in Africa (established 1847). Monrovia is the capital and the largest city. Population, 1,911,000. **—Li·be′ri·an** *adj. & n.*

lib·er·tar·i·an (lĭb′ər-târ′ē-ən) *n.* **1.** One who believes in freedom of action and thought. **2.** One who believes in free will. [From LIBERTY.] **—lib′er·tar′i·an·ism** *n.*

lib·er·tin·age (lĭb′ər-tē′nĭj) *n.* Libertinism.

lib·er·tine (lĭb′ər-tēn′) *n.* **1.** One who acts without moral restraint; a dissolute person. **2.** One who defies established religious precepts; a freethinker. **—libertine** *adj.* Morally unrestrained. [Middle English, freedman, from Latin *lībertīnus,* from *lībertus,* from *līber,* free. See **leudh-** in Appendix.]

lib·er·tin·ism (lĭb′ər-tē-nĭz′əm) *n.* **1.** The state or quality of being libertine. **2.** The behavior characteristic of a libertine; promiscuity.

lib·er·ty (lĭb′ər-tē) *n., pl.* **-ties. 1.a.** The condition of being free from restriction or control. **b.** The right and power to act, believe, or express oneself in a manner of one's own choosing. **c.** The condition of being physically and legally free from confinement, servitude, or forced labor. See Synonyms at **freedom. 2.** Freedom from unjust or undue governmental control. **3.** A right and power to engage in certain actions without control or interference: *the liberties protected by the Bill of Rights.* **4.** Often **liberties. a.** A breach or overstepping of propriety or social convention. **b.** A statement, an attitude, or an action not warranted by conditions or actualities: *a historical novel that takes liberties with chronology.* **c.** An unwarranted risk; a chance: *took foolish liberties on the ski slopes.* **5.** A period, usually short, during which a sailor is authorized to go ashore. ***—idiom.* at liberty. 1.** Not in confinement or under constraint; free. **2.** Not employed, occupied, or in use. [Middle English *liberte,* from Old French, from Latin *lībertās,* from *līber,* free. See **leudh-** in Appendix.]

Lib·er·ty (lĭb′ər-tē). A city of western Missouri, an industrial suburb of Kansas City. Population, 16,251.

liberty cap *n.* A brimless, limp, conical cap fitting snugly around the head and given to a slave in ancient Rome upon manumission. It was used as a symbol of liberty by the French revolutionaries and was also worn in the United States before 1800. Also called *Phrygian cap.*

Liberia

Liberty Island. Formerly **Bed·loe's Island** (bĕd′lōz). An island of southeast New York in Upper New York Bay southwest of Manhattan. The Statue of Liberty was placed on the island in 1885, using the star-shaped Fort Wood (built in 1841) as a base. Congress officially renamed the island in 1956.

Lib·er·ty·ville (lĭb′ər-tē-vĭl′). A village of northeast Illinois southwest of Waukegan. Population, 16,520.

li·bid·i·nous (lĭ-bĭd′n-əs) *adj.* Having or exhibiting lustful desires; lascivious. [Middle English, from Old French *libidineux,* from Latin *libīdinōsus,* from *libīdō, libīdin-,* lust, desire. See LIBIDO.] **—li·bid′i·nous·ly** *adv.* **—li·bid′i·nous·ness** *n.*

li·bi·do (lĭ-bē′dō, -bī′-) *n., pl.* **-dos. 1.** The psychic and emotional energy associated with instinctual biological drives. **2.a.** Sexual desire. **b.** Manifestation of the sexual drive. [Latin, desire. See **leubh-** in Appendix.] **—li·bid′i·nal** (-bĭd′n-əl) *adj.* **—li·bid′i·nal·ly** *adv.*

Li Bo (lē′ bō′). See **Li Po.**

li·bra (lē′brə) *n., pl.* **-brae** (-brē′). *Abbr.* **lb.** A unit of weight in ancient Rome equivalent to about 12 ounces. [Middle English, from Latin *lībra.*]

Li·bra (lē′brə, lī′-) *n.* **1.** A constellation in the Southern Hemisphere near Scorpius and Virgo. Also called *Balance, Scales.* **2.a.** The seventh sign of the zodiac in astrology. Also called *Balance, Scales.* **b.** One who is born under this sign. [Middle English, from Latin *lībra,* balance, the constellation Libra.]

li·brae (lē′brē′) *n.* Plural of **libra.**

Li·bran (lē′brən, lī′-) *n.* One who is born under the sign of Libra.

li·brar·i·an (lī-brâr′ē-ən) *n.* *Abbr.* **lib. 1.** A person who is a specialist in library work. **2.** *Computer Science.* A program used in maintaining a library, especially that of an operating system. **—li·brar′i·an·ship′** *n.*

li·brar·y (lī′brĕr′ē) *n., pl.* **-ies.** *Abbr.* **lib. 1.a.** A place in which literary and artistic materials, such as books, periodicals, newspapers, pamphlets, prints, records, and tapes, are kept for reading, reference, or lending. **b.** A collection of such materials, especially when systematically arranged. **c.** A room in a private home for such a collection. **d.** An institution or a foundation maintaining such a collection. **2.** A commercial establishment that lends books for a fee. **3.** A series or set of books issued by a publisher. **4.** A collection of recorded data or tapes arranged for ease of use. **5.** *Computer Science.* A collection of standard programs, routines, or subroutines, often related to a specific application, that are available for general use. [Middle English *librarie,* from Anglo-Norman, from Latin *librārium,* bookcase, from neuter of *librārius,* of books, from *liber, libr-,* book.]

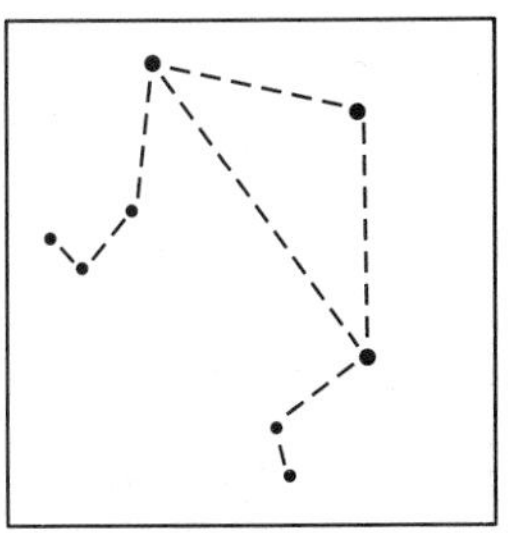
Libra

library science *n.* The principles, practice, or study of library administration.

li·bra·tion (lī-brā′shən) *n.* A very slow oscillation, real or apparent, of a satellite as viewed from the larger celestial body around which it revolves. [Latin *lībrātio, lībrātiōn-,* oscillation, from *lībrātus,* past participle of *lībrāre,* to balance, from *lībra,* balance.] **—li·bra′tion·al** *adj.* **—li′bra·to′ry** (-brə-tôr′ē, -tōr′ē) *adj.*

li·bret·ti (lĭ-brĕt′ē) *n.* *Music.* A plural of **libretto.**

li·bret·tist (lĭ-brĕt′ĭst) *n.* *Music.* The author of a libretto.

li·bret·to (lĭ-brĕt′ō) *n., pl.* **-bret·tos** or **-bret·ti** (-brĕt′ē). *Music.* **1.** The text of a dramatic musical work, such as an opera. **2.** A book containing such a text. [Italian, diminutive of *libro,* book, from Latin *liber, libr-.*]

Li·bre·ville (lē′brə-vĭl′, -vēl′). The capital and largest city of Gabon, in the northwest part of the country on the Gulf of Guinea. Founded as a French trading post in 1843, it was named Libreville after freed slaves settled here (1848). Population, 235,700.

Lib·ri·um (lĭb′rē-əm). A trademark used for preparations of chlordiazepoxide hydrochloride.

Lib·y·a (lĭb′ē-ə). A country of northern Africa on the Mediterranean Sea. It achieved independence in 1951 and became an important oil producer during the 1960's. Libya has been ruled by Muammar al-Qaddafi since 1969. Tripoli is the capital and the largest city. Population, 3,096,000.

Lib·y·an (lĭb′ē-ən) *adj.* Of or relating to Libya or its people, language, or culture. **—Libyan** *n.* **1.** A native or inhabitant of Libya. **2.** A Berber language of ancient northern Africa.

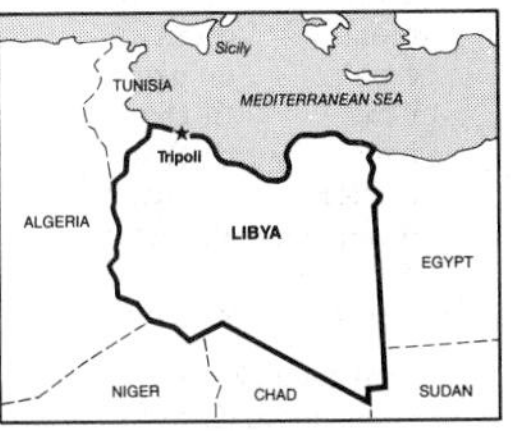

Libya

Libyan Desert. A desert of northeast Africa in Egypt, Libya,

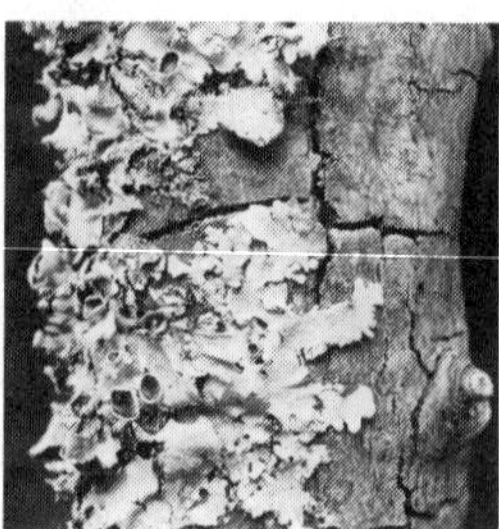

lichen
Growing on a tree limb

Liechtenstein

ă pat	oi boy
ā pay	ou out
âr care	o͝o took
ä father	o͞o boot
ĕ pet	ŭ cut
ē be	ûr urge
ĭ pit	th thin
ī pie	*th* this
îr pier	hw which
ŏ pot	zh vision
ō toe	ə about, item
ô paw	♦ regionalism

Stress marks: **ʹ** (primary); ʹ (secondary), as in **dictionary** (dĭkʹshə-nĕrʹē)

and Sudan. It is the northeast section of the Sahara Desert.

lice (līs) *n.* Plural of **louse** (sense 1).

li·cence (līʹsəns) *n. & v. Chiefly British.* Variant of **license.**

li·cense (līʹsəns) *n.* **1.a.** Official or legal permission to do or own a specified thing. See Synonyms at **permission. b.** Proof of permission granted, usually in the form of a document, card, plate, or tag: *a driver's license.* **2.** Deviation from normal rules, practices, or methods in order to achieve a certain end or effect: *poetic license.* **3.** Latitude of action, especially in behavior or speech. See Synonyms at **freedom. 4.a.** Lack of due restraint; excessive freedom: *"When liberty becomes license, dictatorship is near"* (Will Durant). **b.** Heedlessness for the precepts of proper behavior; licentiousness. **—license** *tr.v.* **-censed, -cens·ing, -cens·es. 1.** To give or yield permission to or for. **2.** To grant a license to or for; authorize. See Synonyms at **authorize.** [Middle English *licence,* from Old French, from Medieval Latin *licentia,* authorization, from Latin, freedom, from *licēns, licent-,* present participle of *licēre,* to be permitted.] **—liʹcens·a·ble** *adj.* **—liʹcens·er, liʹcen·sorʹ** (-sən-sôrʹ) *n.*

li·censed practical nurse (līʹsənst) *n. Abbr.* **LPN, L.P.N.** A nurse who has completed a practical nursing program and is licensed by a state to provide routine patient care under the direction of a registered nurse or a physician.

licensed vocational nurse *n. Abbr.* **LVN, L.V.N.** A licensed practical nurse who is permitted by license to practice in California or Texas.

li·cens·ee (līʹsən-sēʹ) *n.* One to whom or to which a license is granted.

li·cen·sure (līʹsən-shər, -sho͝orʹ) *n.* The act or an instance of granting a license, usually to practice a profession.

li·cen·ti·ate (lī-sĕnʹshē-ĭt) *n. Abbr.* **L. 1.** One who is granted a license by an authorized body to practice a specified profession. **2.a.** A degree from certain European universities ranking just below that of a doctor. **b.** One holding such a degree. [Middle English, from Medieval Latin *licentiātus,* from past participle of *licentiāre,* to allow, from *licentia,* authorization. See LICENSE.]

li·cen·tious (lī-sĕnʹshəs) *adj.* **1.** Lacking moral discipline or ignoring legal restraint, especially in sexual conduct. **2.** Having no regard for accepted rules or standards. [Latin *licentiōsus,* from *licentia,* freedom, license. See LICENSE.] **—li·cenʹtious·ly** *adv.* **—li·cenʹtious·ness** *n.*

li·chee (lēʹchē) *n.* Variant of **litchi.**

li·chen (līʹkən) *n.* **1.** A fungus, usually of the class Ascomycetes, that grows symbiotically with algae, resulting in a composite organism that characteristically forms a crustlike or branching growth on rocks or tree trunks. **2.** *Pathology.* Any of various skin diseases characterized by patchy eruptions of small, firm papules. **—lichen** *tr.v.* **-chened, -chen·ing, -chens.** To cover with lichens. [Latin *līchēn,* a kind of plant, from Greek *leikhēn,* from *leikhein,* to lick. See **leigh-** in Appendix.] **—liʹchen·ous** *adj.*

li·chen·ol·o·gy (līʹkə-nŏlʹə-jē) *n.* The branch of biology that deals with the study of lichens. **—liʹchen·olʹo·gist** *n.*

Lich·field (lĭchʹfēldʹ). A municipal borough of west-central England north-northeast of Birmingham. Samuel Johnson was born here in 1709. Population, 25,800.

lich gate (lĭch) *n.* Variant of **lych-gate.**

Lich·ten·stein (lĭkʹtən-stīnʹ, -stēnʹ), **Roy.** Born 1923. American pop artist who is best known for his large-scale depictions of comic book panels.

lic·it (lĭsʹĭt) *adj.* Permitted by law; legal. [Middle English, from Old French *licite,* from Latin *licitus,* past participle of *licēre,* to be permitted.] **—licʹit·ly** *adv.* **—licʹit·ness** *n.*

lick (lĭk) *v.* **licked, lick·ing, licks.** *—tr.* **1.** To pass the tongue over or along: *lick a stamp.* **2.** To lap up. **3.** To lap or flicker at like a tongue: *The waves licked the sides of the boat.* **4.** *Slang.* To punish with a beating; thrash. **5.** *Slang.* To get the better of; defeat: *licked her weight problem.* *—intr.* To pass or lap quickly and rapidly: *The flames licked at our feet.* **—lick** *n.* **1.** The act or process of licking. **2.** A small quantity; a bit: *hasn't got a lick of common sense.* **3.** A deposit of exposed natural salt that is licked by passing animals. **4.** A sudden hard stroke; a blow. **5.** *Informal.* Speed; pace: *moving along at a good lick.* **6.** *Music.* A phrase improvised by a soloist, especially on the guitar or banjo. ***—idioms.*** **lick and a promise.** A superficial effort made without care or enthusiasm. **lick into shape.** *Informal.* To bring into satisfactory condition or appearance. **lick (one's) chops.** To anticipate delightedly. **lick (one's) wounds.** To recuperate after a defeat. [Middle English *licken,* from Old English *liccian.* See **leigh-** in Appendix.] **—lickʹer** *n.*

lick·er·ish (lĭkʹər-ĭsh) *adj.* **1.** Lascivious; lecherous. **2.** Greedy; desirous. **3.a.** *Archaic.* Relishing good food. **b.** *Obsolete.* Arousing hunger; appetizing. [Middle English *likerous,* perhaps from Old French *lecheor, lekier.* See LECHER.] **—lickʹer·ish·ness** *n.*

lick·e·ty-split (lĭkʹĭ-tē-splĭtʹ) *adv. Informal.* With great speed. [*lickety,* very fast, alteration of LICK, fast (dialectal) + SPLIT.]

lick·ing (lĭkʹĭng) *n. Slang.* **1.** A beating, thrashing, or spanking. **2.** A severe loss or defeat.

Lick·ing River (lĭkʹĭng). A river of northeast Kentucky flowing about 515 km (320 mi) northwest to the Ohio River at Covington.

lick·spit·tle (lĭkʹspĭtʹl) *n.* A fawning underling; a toady.

lic·o·rice (lĭkʹər-ĭs, -ĭsh) *n.* **1.a.** A Mediterranean perennial plant *(Glycyrrhiza glabra)* having blue flowers, pinnately compound leaves, and a sweet, distinctively flavored root. **b.** The root of this plant, used as a flavoring in candy, liqueurs, tobacco, and medicines. **c.** A confection made from or flavored with the licorice root. **2.** Any of various similar plants. [Middle English, from Old French, from Late Latin *liquirītia,* alteration (influenced by Latin *liquēre,* to flow) of Latin *glycyrrhīza,* root of licorice, from Greek *glukurrhiza* : *glukus,* sweet + *rhiza,* root; see **wrād-** in Appendix.]

lic·tor (lĭkʹtər) *n.* A Roman functionary who carried fasces when attending a magistrate in public appearances. [From Middle English *littoures,* lictors, from Latin *lictōrēs,* pl. of *lictor.* See **leig-** in Appendix.]

lid (lĭd) *n.* **1.** A removable or hinged cover for a hollow receptacle or box. **2.** An eyelid. **3.** *Biology.* A flaplike covering, such as an operculum. **4.** A curb, restraint, or limit: *approved a new lid on corporate spending.* **5.** *Informal.* An act of concealment; a cover: *told us to keep a lid on the report until the campaign was over.* **6.** *Slang.* A hat. **7.** *Slang.* An ounce of marijuana. **—lid** *tr.v.* **lid·ded, lid·ding, lids.** To cover with or as if with a lid. [Middle English, from Old English *hlid.* See **klei-** in Appendix.]

Li·di·ce (lĭdʹĭ-sē, -chāʹ, lyĭʹdĭ-tsĕ). A village of northwest Czechoslovakia west-northwest of Prague. In reprisal for the murder of a Nazi official, German forces killed its male population, deported the women and children to concentration camps, and burned the village to the ground (June 9–10, 1942).

lid·less (lĭdʹlĭs) *adj.* Having no lid or lids.

Li·do (lēʹdō). An island reef of northeast Italy separating the lagoon of Venice from the Adriatic Sea. The town of **Lido,** at the northern end of the island, is a fashionable resort.

li·do·caine (līʹdə-kānʹ) *n.* A synthetic amide, $C_{14}H_{22}N_2O$, used chiefly in the form of its hydrochloride as a local anesthetic and antiarrhythmic agent. [(ACETANI)LID(E) + -CAINE.]

lie[1] (lī) *intr.v.* **lay** (lā), **lain** (lān), **ly·ing** (līʹĭng), **lies. 1.** To be or place oneself at rest in a flat, horizontal, or recumbent position; recline: *lay under a tree to sleep.* **2.** To be placed on or supported by a surface that is usually horizontal: *Dirty dishes lay on the table.* See Usage Note at **lay[1]. 3.** To be or remain in a specified condition: *The dust has lain undisturbed for years. He lay sick in bed.* **4.** To exist; be inherent: *The solution lies in research.* **5.** To occupy a position or place: *The lake lies beyond this hill.* **6.** To extend: *Our land lies between these trees and the river.* **7.** *Law.* To be admissible or maintainable. **8.** *Archaic.* To stay for a night or short while. **—lie** *n.* **1.** The manner or position in which something is situated. **2.** A haunt or hiding place of an animal. **3.** *Sports.* The position of a golf ball that has come to a stop. ***—phrasal verbs.*** **lie down.** To do little or nothing: *He's lying down on the job.* **lie in.** To be in confinement for childbirth. **lie to.** *Nautical.* To remain stationary while facing the wind. **lie with. 1.** To be decided by, dependent on, or up to: *The choice lies with you.* **2.** *Archaic.* To have sexual intercourse with. ***—idiom.*** **lie** (or **lay**) **low. 1.** To keep oneself or one's plans hidden. **2.** To bide one's time but remain ready for action. [Middle English *lien,* from Old English *licgan.* See **legh-** in Appendix.]

lie[2] (lī) *n.* **1.** A false statement deliberately presented as being true; a falsehood. **2.** Something meant to deceive or give a wrong impression. **—lie** *v.* **lied, ly·ing** (līʹĭng), **lies.** *—intr.* **1.** To present false information with the intention of deceiving. **2.** To convey a false image or impression: *Appearances often lie.* *—tr.* To cause to be in a specific condition or affect in a specific way by telling falsehoods: *You have lied yourself into trouble.* [Middle English, from Old English *lyge.* See **leugh-** in Appendix.]

SYNONYMS: *lie, equivocate, fib, palter, prevaricate.* The central meaning shared by these verbs is "to evade or depart from the truth": *a witness who lied under oath; didn't equivocate about her real purpose in coming; fibbed to escape being scolded; paltering with an irate customer; didn't prevaricate but answered forthrightly and honestly.*

Lie (lē), **Trygve Halvden.** 1896–1968. Norwegian politician and first secretary-general of the United Nations (1946–1953).

Lie·big (lēʹbĭg, -bĭκн), Baron **Justus von.** 1803–1873. German chemist who made a number of contributions to organic chemistry and pioneered laboratory-based scientific education (1826).

Lieb·knecht (lēpʹknĕktʹ, -knĕκнtʹ), **Karl.** 1871–1919. German journalist and politician who founded (1918) the Spartacus Party, the precursor of the German Communist Party. He was arrested and murdered after a Spartacist uprising in 1919.

Liech·ten·stein (lĭkʹtən-stīnʹ, lĭκнʹtən-shtīnʹ). *Abbr.* **Liech.** A small Alpine principality in central Europe between Austria and Switzerland. The principality was created in 1719 and became independent in 1866. Vaduz is the capital. Population, 27,076.

lied (lēt) *n., pl.* **lie·der** (lēʹdər). *Music.* A German art song in the style of a ballad for solo voice and piano. [German *Lied,* from Middle High German *liet,* from Old High German *liod.*]

Lie·der·kranz (lēʹdər-kränts', -krăntsʹ). A trademark for a soft cheese resembling a mild Limburger.

lie detector *n.* A polygraph used to detect possible deception during an interrogation.

lief (lēf) *adv.* **lief·er, lief·est.** Readily; willingly: *I would as lief go now as later.* **—lief** *adj.* **liefer, liefest.** *Archaic.* **1.** Beloved; dear. **2.** Ready or willing. [Middle English *leve, lef,* dear, willingly, from Old English *lēof,* dear. See **leubh-** in Appendix.]

liege (lēj) *n.* **1.** A lord or sovereign to whom allegiance and service are due according to feudal law. **2.** A vassal or subject owing allegiance and services to a lord or sovereign under feudal law. **3.** A loyal subject to a monarch. **—liege** *adj.* **1. a.** Entitled to the loyalty and services of vassals or subjects: *a liege lord.* **b.** Bound to give such allegiance and services to a lord or monarch. **2.** Loyal; faithful. [Middle English, from Old French, entitled to feudal allegiance, from Late Latin *læticus,* being a semifree colonist in Gaul, from *lætus,* a semifree colonist, of Germanic origin. See **lē-** in Appendix.]

Li·ège (lē-āzh′, lyĕzh). A city of eastern Belgium near the Dutch and German borders. First mentioned in 558, it was a noted intellectual center in the Middle Ages. Population, 207,496.

liege·man (lēj′mən) *n.* **1.** A feudal vassal or subject. **2.** A loyal supporter, follower, or subject.

lien (lēn, lē′ən) *n. Law.* The right to take and hold or sell the property of a debtor as security or payment for a debt or duty. [French, tie, bond, from Old French, constraint, from Latin *ligāmen,* bond, from *ligāre,* to bind. See **leig-** in Appendix.]

Lien·yün·kang (lyŭn′yün′käng′). See **Lianyungang.**

Lie·pa·ja (lē-ĕp′ə-yə, lyĕ′pä-yä). A city of southwest Latvia on the Baltic Sea southwest of Riga. Founded by the Teutonic Knights in 1263, it passed to Russia in 1795, was briefly the capital of the Latvian provisional government (1918), and was annexed by the U.S.S.R. after World War II. Population, 112,000.

li·erne (lē-ûrn′) *n. Architecture.* A reinforcing rib used in Gothic vaulting to connect the intersections and bosses of the primary ribs. [French, from *lier,* to bind, from Old French. See LIABLE.]

lieu (lo͞o) *n. Archaic.* Place; stead. **—*idiom.* in lieu of.** In place of; instead of. [French, from Old French, from Latin *locus.*]

lieu·ten·ant (lo͞o-tĕn′ənt) *n.* **1. a.** *Abbr.* **Lt.** A commissioned rank in the U.S. Navy or Coast Guard that is above lieutenant junior grade and below lieutenant commander. **b.** A first lieutenant. **c.** A second lieutenant. **d.** One who holds the rank of lieutenant, first lieutenant, or second lieutenant. **2.** (lĕf-tĕn′ənt). A commissioned officer in the British and Canadian navies ranking just below a lieutenant commander. **3.** An officer in a police or fire department ranking below a captain. **4.** One who acts in place of or represents a superior; an assistant or a deputy: *the organized crime figure and his lieutenants.* See Synonyms at **assistant.** [Middle English, deputy, from Old French : *lieu,* lieu; see LIEU + *tenant,* present participle of *tenir,* to hold (from Latin *tenēre;* see **ten-** in Appendix).] **—lieu·ten′an·cy** *n.*

WORD HISTORY: What is the connection between a lieutenant governor and a lieutenant in the army? In the etymology of the word *lieutenant,* at least, the connection lies in their holding a place; that is, the word *lieutenant* is from an Old French compound made up of *lieu,* "place," and *tenant,* "holding," the present participle of the verb *tenir,* "to hold." The word in Old French and the borrowed Middle English word *lieutenant,* first recorded near the end of the 14th century, referred to a person who acted for another as a deputy. This usage has survived, for example, in our term *lieutenant governor,* the deputy of the governor and the one who replaces the governor if need be. In military parlance *lieutenant* appears by itself as well as in compounds such as *first lieutenant* and *second lieutenant,* which muddy the water a bit, but the original notion of the word in military usage was that the officer it referred to ranked below the next one up and could replace him if need be. A lieutenant in the U.S. Army could thus step into the shoes of a captain.

lieutenant colonel *n. Abbr.* **Lt. Col., LTC** **1.** A commissioned rank in the U.S. Army, Air Force, or Marine Corps that is above major and below colonel. **2.** One who holds this rank.

lieutenant commander *n. Abbr.* **Lt. Comdr.** **1.** A commissioned rank in the U.S. Navy or Coast Guard that is above lieutenant and below commander. **2.** One who holds this rank.

lieutenant general *n. Abbr.* **Lt. Gen., LTG** **1.** A commissioned rank in the U.S. Army, Air Force, or Marine Corps that is above major general and below general. **2.** One who holds this rank.

lieutenant governor *n. Abbr.* **Lt. Gov.** **1.** An elected official ranking just below the governor of a state in the United States. **2.** The nonelective chief of government of a Canadian province. **—lieutenant governorship** *n.*

lieutenant junior grade *n., pl.* **lieutenants junior grade.** *Abbr.* **LTJG** **1.** A commissioned rank in the U.S. Navy or Coast Guard that is above ensign and below lieutenant. **2.** One who holds this rank.

life (līf) *n., pl.* **lives** (līvz). **1.** *Biology.* **a.** The property or quality that distinguishes living organisms from dead organisms and inanimate matter, manifested in functions such as metabolism, growth, reproduction, and response to stimuli or adaptation to the environment originating from within the organism. **b.** The characteristic state or condition of a living organism. **2.** Living organisms considered as a group: *plant life; marine life.* **3.** A living being, especially a person: *an earthquake that claimed hundreds of lives.* **4.** The physical, mental, and spiritual experiences that constitute existence: *the artistic life of a writer.* **5. a.** The interval of time between birth and death: *She led a good, long life.* **b.** The interval of time between one's birth and the present: *has had hay fever all his life.* **c.** A particular segment of one's life: *my adolescent life.* **d.** The period from an occurrence until death: *elected for life; paralyzed for life.* **e.** *Slang.* A sentence of imprisonment lasting till death. **6.** The time for which something exists or functions: *the useful life of a car.* **7.** A spiritual state regarded as a transcending of corporeal death. **8.** An account of a person's life; a biography. **9.** Human existence, relationships, or activity in general: *real life; everyday life.* **10. a.** A manner of living: *led a hard life.* **b.** A specific, characteristic manner of existence. Used of inanimate objects: *"Great institutions seem to have a life of their own, independent of those who run them"* (New Republic). **c.** The activities and interests of a particular area or realm: *musical life in New York.* **11. a.** A source of vitality; an animating force: *She's the life of the show.* **b.** Liveliness or vitality; animation: *a face that is full of life.* **12. a.** Something that actually exists regarded as a subject for an artist: *painted from life.* **b.** Actual environment or reality; nature. **13.** *Christian Science.* God. **—*idioms.* as big as life.** **1.** Life-size. **2.** Actually present. **bring to life.** **1.** To cause to regain consciousness. **2.** To put spirit into; to animate. **3.** To make lifelike. **come to life.** To become animated; grow excited. **for dear life.** Desperately or urgently: *I ran for dear life when I saw the tiger.* **for life.** Till the end of one's life. **for the life of (one).** Though trying hard: *For the life of me I couldn't remember his name.* **not on your life.** *Informal.* Absolutely not; not for any reason whatsoever. **take (one's) life.** To commit suicide. **take (someone's) life.** To commit murder. **the good life.** A wealthy, luxurious way of living. **the life of Riley.** *Informal.* An easy life. **the life of the party.** *Informal.* An animated, amusing person who is the center of attention at a social gathering. **to save (one's) life.** No matter how hard one tries: *He can't ski to save his life.* **true to life.** Conforming to reality. [Middle English, from Old English *līf.* See **leip-** in Appendix.]

lierne

life-and-death (līf′ən-dĕth′) or **life-or-death** (līf′ər-) *adj.* **1.** Involving or ending in life or death: *a mongoose in a life-and-death battle with a cobra.* **2.** Vitally important: *a life-and-death struggle between union and management.*

life belt *n.* A life preserver worn like a belt.

life·blood (līf′blŭd′) *n.* **1.** Blood regarded as essential for life. **2.** An indispensable or vital part: *Capable workers are the lifeblood of the business.*

life·boat (līf′bōt′) *n. Nautical.* **1.** A boat carried on a ship for use if the ship has to be abandoned. **2.** A boat used for rescue service.

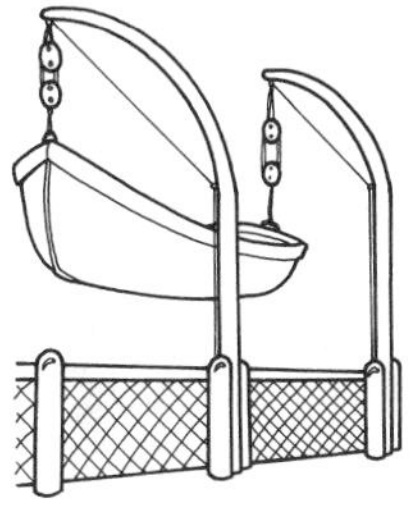
lifeboat

life buoy *n.* A buoyant device, such as a cork or polystyrene ring, for keeping a person afloat in water.

life cycle *n.* **1.** The course of developmental changes through which an organism passes from its inception as a fertilized zygote to the mature state in which another zygote may be produced. **2.** A progression through a series of differing stages of development.

life expectancy *n.* The number of years that an individual is expected to live as determined by statistics.

life force *n.* See **élan vital.**

life form *n.* The characteristic morphology of a mature organism.

life·guard (līf′gärd′) *n.* An expert swimmer trained and employed to watch over other swimmers, as at a beach or swimming pool. Also called *lifesaver.* **—lifeguard** *intr.v.* **-guard·ed, -guard·ing, -guards.** To work or serve as a lifeguard.

life history *n.* **1.** The history of changes undergone by an organism from inception or conception to death. **2.** The developmental history of an individual or a group in society.

life insurance *n.* Insurance that guarantees a specific sum of money to a designated beneficiary upon the death of the insured or to the insured if he or she lives beyond a certain age.

life jacket

life jacket *n.* A life preserver in the form of a sleeveless jacket or vest.

life·less (līf′lĭs) *adj.* **1.** Having no life; inanimate. **2.** Having lost life; dead. See Synonyms at **dead.** **3.** Not inhabited by living beings; not capable of sustaining life. **4.** Lacking vitality or animation; dull: *a lifeless party.* **—life′less·ly** *adv.* **—life′less·ness** *n.*

life·like (līf′līk′) *adj.* Accurately representing real life: *a lifelike statue.* See Synonyms at **graphic.** **—life′like′ness** *n.*

life·line (līf′līn′) *n.* **1. a.** An anchored line thrown as a support to someone falling or drowning. **b.** *Nautical.* A line shot to a ship in distress. **c.** A line used to raise and lower deep-sea divers. **2. a.** A means or route by which necessary supplies are transported. **b.** One that is or is regarded as a source of salvation in a crisis. **3.** A diagonal line crossing the palm of the hand and believed to indicate the length and major events of one's life.

life list *n.* A cumulative record of the species seen and identified by a naturalist, especially a bird watcher.

life·long (līf′lông′, -lŏng′) *adj.* Continuing for a lifetime.

life-or-death (līf′ər-dĕth′) *adj.* Variant of **life-and-death.**

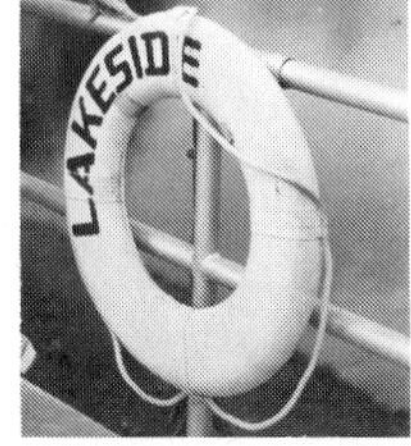

life preserver

life preserver *n.* **1.** A buoyant device, usually in the shape of a ring, belt, or jacket, designed to keep a person afloat in the water. **2.** *Chiefly British.* A weapon, such as a blackjack.

lif·er (lī′fər) *n. Slang.* **1. a.** A prisoner serving a life sentence. **b.** One who makes a career in one of the armed forces. **2.** A right-to-lifer.

life raft *n. Nautical.* A raft usually made of inflatable material or wood and used in an emergency at sea.

life·sav·er (līf′sā′vər) *n.* **1.** One that saves a life. **2.** See

lifeguard. **3.** One that provides help in a crisis or emergency. **4.** A life preserver shaped like a ring. **—life′sav′ing** *n.*

life science *n.* Any of several branches of science, such as biology, medicine, anthropology, or ecology, that deal with living organisms and their organization, life processes, and relationships to each other and their environment. Also called *bioscience.*

life-size (līf′sīz′) also **life-sized** (-sīzd′) *adj.* Being of the same size as an original: *a life-size statue.*

life span *n.* **1.** A lifetime. **2.** The average or maximum length of time an organism, a material, or an object can be expected to survive or last.

life•style also **life-style** or **life style** (līf′stīl′) *n.* A way of life or style of living that reflects the attitudes and values of a person or group: *"It was a millionaire's lifestyle on the pocketbook of a hairdresser"* (People).

USAGE NOTE: When *lifestyle* began to gain wide currency a generation ago, a number of critics objected to it as voguish and superficial, perhaps because it appeared to elevate habits of consumption, dress, and recreation to a primary basis of social classification. Nonetheless, the word has proved durable and useful, if only because such categories do in fact figure importantly in the schemes that Americans commonly invoke in explaining social values and social behavior, whether appropriately or not, as in Rachel Brownstein's remark that *"an anticonventional lifestyle is no sure sign of feminist politics, or indeed, of any politics at all."* As such, the word has won the occasionally grudging acceptance of the Usage Panel. Fifty-three percent of the Panelists accepts the word in the sentence *Bohemian attitudes toward conventional society have been outstripped and outdated by the lifestyles of millions of young people,* and fully 70 percent accepts the word in the sentence *Salaries in the Bay Area may be higher, but it may cost employees as much as 30 percent more to maintain their lifestyles,* where the economic context makes more apparent the need for a word that denotes categories based on consumption practices.

ligature
Opening notes of "The Star-Spangled Banner"

life-sup•port system (līf′sə-pôrt′, -pōrt′) *n.* **1.** Equipment that creates a viable environment under conditions otherwise incompatible with life. **2.** Medical equipment that augments or substitutes for an essential bodily function, such as respiration or excretion, enabling a patient who otherwise might not survive to live.

life•time (līf′tīm′) *n.* **1.** The period of time during which an individual is alive. **2.** The period of time during which property, an object, a process, or a phenomenon exists or functions. *—attributive.* Often used to modify another noun: *a lifetime guarantee; lifetime membership.*

life•work (līf′wûrk′) *n.* The chief or entire work of a person's lifetime.

life zone *n. Ecology.* A geographic region or area defined by its characteristic life forms.

LIFO (lī′fō) *n. Accounting.* See **last-in, first-out.**

lift (lĭft) *v.* **lift•ed, lift•ing, lifts.** *—tr.* **1.a.** To direct or carry from a lower to a higher position; raise: *lift one's eyes; lifted the suitcase.* **b.** To transport by air: *The helicopter lifted the entire team to the meet.* **2.a.** To revoke by taking back; rescind: *lifted the embargo.* **b.** To bring an end to (a blockade or siege) by removing forces. **3.** To cease (artillery fire) in an area. **4.a.** To raise in condition, rank, or esteem. **b.** To uplift; elate: *Your telephone call really lifted my spirits.* **5.** To remove (plants) from the ground for transplanting. **6.** To project or sound in loud, clear tones: *lifted their voices in song.* **7.** *Informal.* To steal; pilfer: *A thief lifted my wallet.* **8.** *Informal.* To copy from something already published; plagiarize: *lifted whole paragraphs from the encyclopedia.* **9.** To pay off or clear (a debt or mortgage, for example). **10.** To perform cosmetic surgery on (the face), especially in order to remove wrinkles or sagging skin. **11.a.** *Sports.* To hit (a golf ball) very high into the air. **b.** To pick up (a golf ball) to place it in a better lie. *—intr.* **1.a.** To rise; ascend. **b.** To yield to upward pressure: *These windows lift easily.* **2.a.** To disappear or disperse by or as if by rising: *By afternoon the smog had lifted.* **b.** To stop temporarily: *The rain lifted by morning.* **3.** To become elevated; soar: *Their spirits lifted when help came.* **—lift** *n.* **1.** The act or process of rising or raising to a higher position. **2.** Power or force available for raising: *the lift of a pump.* **3.** An amount or a weight raised or capable of being raised at one time; a load. **4.a.** The extent or height to which something is raised or rises; the amount of elevation. **b.** The distance or space through which something is raised or rises. **5.** A rise or an elevation in the level of the ground. **6.** An elevation of the spirits: *The good news gave us a lift.* **7.** A raised, high, or erect position, as of a part of the body: *the lift of his chin.* **8.** A machine or device designed to pick up, raise, or carry something. **9.** One of the layers of leather, rubber, or other material making up the heel of a shoe. **10.** *Chiefly British.* A passenger or cargo elevator. **11.** A ride in a vehicle given to help someone reach a destination: *gave my friend a lift into town.* **12.** Assistance or help: *gave her a lift with her heavy packages.* **13.** A set of pumps used in a mine. **14.** The component of the total aerodynamic force acting on an airfoil or on an entire aircraft or winged missile perpendicular to the relative wind and normally exerted in an upward direction, opposing the pull of gravity. ***—phrasal verb.*** **lift off.** To begin flight: *The spacecraft lifted off at noon.* ***—idiom.*** **lift fire.** To increase the range of artillery fire by elevating the muzzle of a piece. [Middle English *liften,* from Old Norse *lypta.*] **—lift′a•ble** *adj.*

SYNONYMS: *lift, raise, rear, elevate, hoist, heave, boost.* These verbs mean to move something from a lower to a higher level or position. *Lift* sometimes stresses the expenditure of effort: *a trunk too heavy to lift; requires three men to lift the piano. Raise* often implies movement to an approximately vertical position: *raised the window slightly; raising a monument to the war dead. Rear* is frequently interchangeable with *raise: rear a ladder; rear a flagpole. "Her family reared a sumptuous mausoleum over her remains"* (Macaulay). *Elevate* is sometimes synonymous with the preceding terms (*used two pillows to keep his head elevated*), but it more often suggests exalting, ennobling, or raising morally or intellectually: *"A generous and elevated mind is distinguished by nothing more certainly than an eminent degree of curiosity"* (Samuel Johnson). *Hoist* is applied principally to the lifting of heavy objects, often by mechanical means: *hoist a sunken ship; uses a crane to hoist the construction beams.* To *heave* is to lift or raise with great effort or force: *heaved the pack onto his back. Boost* suggests upward movement effected by or as if by pushing from below: *boosted the child into the saddle; boost sales; boost morale.* See also Synonyms at **steal.**

lift•ing body (lĭf′tĭng) *n.* An aircraft or a spacecraft that has no wings and gains lift by the action of aerodynamic forces on its body.

lift•off (lĭft′ôf′, -ŏf′) *n.* The initial movement by which or the instant in which a rocket or other such craft commences flight.

lig•a•ment (lĭg′ə-mənt) *n.* **1.** *Anatomy.* A sheet or band of tough, fibrous tissue connecting bones or cartilages at a joint or supporting an organ. **2.** A unifying or connecting tie or bond. [Middle English, from Medieval Latin *ligāmentum,* from Latin, bandage, from *ligāre,* to bind. See LIEN.] **—lig′a•ment′al** (-mĕn′tl), **lig′a•men′ta•ry** (-mĕn′tə-rē, -mĕn′trē), **lig′a•men′tous** *adj.*

li•gan (lī′gən) *n.* Variant of **lagan.**

li•gand (lī′gənd, lĭg′ənd) *n.* An ion, a molecule, or a molecular group that binds to another chemical entity to form a larger complex. [From Latin *ligandus,* gerundive of *ligāre,* to bind. See LIGATE.]

li•gase (lī′gās′, -gāz′) *n.* Any of a class of enzymes, including the carboxylases, that catalyze the linkage of two molecules, generally utilizing ATP as the energy donor. Also called *synthetase.* [Latin *ligāre,* to bind; see **leig-** in Appendix + -ASE.]

li•gate (lī′gāt′) *tr.v.* **-gat•ed, -gat•ing, -gates.** To tie or bind with a ligature. [Latin *ligāre, ligāt-.* See **leig-** in Appendix.]

li•ga•tion (lī-gā′shən) *n.* **1.a.** The act of binding or of applying a ligature. **b.** The state of being bound. **2.** Something that binds; a ligature.

lig•a•ture (lĭg′ə-cho͝or′, -chər) *n.* **1.** The act of tying or binding. **2.** A cord, wire, or bandage used for tying or binding. **3.** A thread, wire, or cord used in surgery to close vessels or tie off ducts. **4.** Something that unites; a bond. **5.** A character, letter, or type, such as æ, combining two or more letters. **6.** *Music.* **a.** A group of notes intended to be played or sung as one phrase. **b.** A curved line indicating such a phrase; a slur. **—ligature** *tr.v.* **-tured, -tur•ing, -tures.** To ligate. [Middle English, from Old French, from Late Latin *ligātūra,* from Latin *ligātus,* past participle of *ligāre,* to bind. See **leig-** in Appendix.]

li•ger (lī′gər) *n.* The product of crossbreeding between a male lion and a female tiger, having features of both but generally being larger than either. [LI(ON) + (TI)GER.]

light¹ (līt) *n.* **1.** *Physics.* **a.** Electromagnetic radiation that has a wavelength in the range from about 4,000 (violet) to about 7,700 (red) angstroms and may be perceived by the normal unaided human eye. **b.** Electromagnetic radiation of any wavelength. **2.** The sensation of perceiving light; brightness: *a sudden light that made me blink.* **3.a.** A source of light, especially a lamp, a lantern, or an electric lighting fixture: *Turn out the lights when you leave.* **b.** The illumination derived from a source of light: *by the light of the moon.* **c.** The particular quantity or quality of such illumination: *moved the lamp closer to get better light.* **d.** The pathway or route of such illumination to a person: *You're standing in his light.* **4.** A mechanical device that uses illumination as a signal or warning, especially a beacon or traffic signal. **5.a.** Daylight. **b.** Dawn; daybreak. **6.** Something, such as a window, that admits illumination. **7.** A source of fire, such as a match or cigarette lighter. **8.** Spiritual awareness; illumination. **9.a.** Something that provides information or clarification: *threw some light on the question.* **b.** A state of awareness or understanding, especially as derived from a particular source: *in the light of experience.* **10.** Public attention; general knowledge: *brought the scandal to light.* **11.** A way of looking at or considering a matter; an aspect: *saw the situation in a different light.* **12.** *Archaic.* Eyesight. **13. lights.** One's individual opinions, choices, or standards: *acted according to their own lights.* **14.** A person who inspires or is adored by another: *My daughter is the light of my life.* **15.** A prominent or distinguished person; a luminary: *one of the leading lights of the theater.* **16.** An expression of the eyes: *a strange light in her eyes.* **17. Light.** In Quaker doctrine, the guiding spirit or divine presence in each person. **18.** The representation of light in art. **—light** *v.* **light•ed** or **lit** (lĭt), **light•ing, lights.** *—tr.* **1.** To set on fire; ignite or kindle. **2.** To cause to give out light; make luminous: *lit a lamp.* **3.** To provide, cover, or fill with light; illuminate: *fireworks lighting the sky.* **4.** To signal, direct, or guide with or as if with illumination. **5.** To enliven or animate: *A smile lit her face.* —*intr.* **1.** To start to burn; be ignited or kindled: *Green wood does not light easily.* **2.** To emit light; be lighted: *Wait until the indicator lights up.* —**light** *adj.* **light·er, light·est. 1.** *Color.* **a.** Having a greater rather than lesser degree of lightness. **b.** Of or being an additive primary color. **2.** Characterized by or filled with light; bright: *a room that is light when the shutters are open.* **3.** Not dark in color; fair: *light hair and skin.* **4.** Served with milk or cream. Used of coffee. —***phrasal verb.* light up. 1.** To become or cause to become animated or cheerful. **2.** To start smoking a cigarette, cigar, or pipe. —***idiom.* in (the) light of.** In consideration of; in relationship to. [Middle English, from Old English *lēoht, līht.* See **leuk-** in Appendix.]

USAGE NOTE: *Lighted* and *lit* are equally acceptable as past tense and past participle of *light.* Both forms are well established as adjectives also: *a lighted* (or *lit*) *cigarette.*

light² (līt) *adj.* **light·er, light·est. 1.a.** Of relatively little weight; not heavy: *a light load.* **b.** Of relatively little weight for its size or bulk: *Balsa is a light wood.* **c.** Of less than the correct, standard, or legal weight: *a light pound.* **2.** Exerting little force or impact; gentle: *a light pat.* **3.a.** Of little quantity; scanty: *light snow.* **b.** Consuming or using relatively moderate amounts; abstemious: *a light eater; a light smoker.* **c.** Not harsh or severe: *gave the offender a light sentence.* **4.** Demanding little exertion or effort; not burdensome: *light household tasks.* See Synonyms at **easy. 5.** Having little importance; insignificant: *light, idle chatter.* **6.** Intended primarily as entertainment; not serious or profound: *a light comedy.* **7.** Free from worries or troubles; blithe: *a light heart.* **8.** Characterized by frivolity; silly or trivial. **9.** Liable to change; fickle. **10.** Mildly dizzy or faint: *felt light in the head.* **11.** Lacking in ethical discrimination. **12.** Moving easily and quickly; nimble: *The dancer was light and graceful.* **13.** Designed for ease and quickness of movement; having a relatively slim structure and little weight: *light aircraft.* **14.** Designed to carry relatively little weight: *a light truck.* **15.** Carrying little equipment or armament: *light cavalry; light tanks.* **16.** Requiring relatively little equipment and using relatively simple processes to produce consumer goods: *light industry.* **17.** Easily awakened or disturbed: *a light sleeper.* **18.a.** Easily digested: *a light supper.* **b.** Having a spongy or flaky texture; well-leavened: *light pastries.* **19.** Having a loose, porous consistency: *light soil.* **20.** Containing a relatively small amount of a potentially harmful ingredient, such as alcohol, fat, or sodium: *light beer; light mayonnaise.* **21.** *Linguistics.* **a.** Of, relating to, or being a syllable ending in a short vowel or a short vowel plus a consonant. **b.** Of, relating to, or being a vowel or syllable pronounced with little or no stress. —**light** *adv.* **lighter, lightest. 1.** In a light manner; lightly. **2.** With little weight and few burdens: *traveling light.* —**light** *intr.v.* **light·ed** or **lit** (lĭt), **light·ing, lights. 1.** To get down, as from a vehicle or horse; dismount. **2.** To descend to the ground after flight; land. **3.** To come upon one unexpectedly: *Misfortune lighted upon him.* **4.** To come upon by chance or accident. Used with *on* or *upon*: *lit on the perfect solution to the problem.* —***phrasal verbs.* light into.** *Informal.* To attack verbally or physically; assail. **light out.** *Informal.* To leave hastily; run off. —***idiom.* go light on.** To treat casually or gingerly. [Middle English, from Old English *lēoht, līht.* See **legʷh-** in Appendix.]

light adaptation *n.* The process, chiefly involving constriction of the pupil, by which the eye adapts to an increase in illumination. —**light′-a·dapt′ed** (līt′ə-dăp′tĭd) *adj.*

light air *n. Meteorology.* A wind with a speed of from 1 to 3 miles (2 to 5 kilometers) per hour, according to the Beaufort scale.

♦ **light bread** *n. Chiefly Southern U.S.* See **white bread.**

light breeze *n. Meteorology.* A wind with a speed of from 4 to 7 miles (6 to 11 kilometers) per hour, according to the Beaufort scale.

light bulb *n.* An electric light in which a filament is heated to incandescence by an electric current.

light-e·mit·ting diode (līt′ĭ-mĭt′ĭng) *n.* LED.

light·en¹ (līt′n) *v.* **-ened, -en·ing, -ens.** —*tr.* **1.a.** To make light or lighter; illuminate or brighten. **b.** To make (a color) lighter. **2.** *Archaic.* To enlighten. —*intr.* **1.** To become lighter; brighten. **2.** To be luminous; shine. **3.** To give off flashes of lightning.

light·en² (līt′n) *v.* **-ened, -en·ing, -ens.** —*tr.* **1.** To make less heavy. **2.** To lessen the oppressiveness, trouble, or severity of. See Synonyms at **relieve. 3.** To relieve of cares or worries; gladden. —*intr.* **1.** To become less in weight. **2.** To become less oppressive, troublesome, or severe. **3.** To become cheerful.

light·er¹ (lī′tər) *n.* **1.** One that ignites or kindles. **2.** A mechanical device for lighting a cigarette, cigar, or pipe.

light·er² (lī′tər) *Nautical. n.* A large flat-bottomed barge, especially one used to deliver or unload goods to or from a cargo ship or transport goods over short distances. —**lighter** *tr.v.* **-ered, -er·ing, -ers.** To convey (cargo) in a lighter. [Middle English, perhaps from *lighten,* to make less heavy, from Old English *līhtan.* See **legʷh-** in Appendix.]

light·er·age (lī′tər-ĭj) *n. Nautical.* **1.** Transportation of goods on a lighter. **2.** The fee charged for lightering.

light·er-than-air (lī′tər-*th*ən-âr′) *adj.* Having a weight less than that of the air displaced. Used of certain aircraft.

light·face (līt′fās′) *n. Abbr.* **lf** *Printing.* A typeface or font of characters having relatively thin, light lines. —**light′faced′** *adj.*

light-fin·gered (līt′fĭng′gərd) *adj.* **1.** Having quick and nimble fingers. **2.** Skilled at or given to petty thievery. —**light′-fin′gered·ness** *n.*

light-foot·ed (līt′fo͝ot′ĭd) also **light·foot** (-fo͝ot′) *adj.* Treading with light and nimble ease. —**light′-foot′ed·ly** *adv.* —**light′-foot′ed·ness** *n.*

light-hand·ed (līt′hăn′dĭd) *adj.* Having a light, delicate touch. —**light′-hand′ed·ly** *adv.* —**light′-hand′ed·ness** *n.*

light·head·ed (līt′hĕd′ĭd) *adj.* **1.** Faint, giddy, or delirious: *lightheaded with wine.* **2.** Given to frivolity; silly. —**light′head′ed·ly** *adv.* —**light′head′ed·ness** *n.*

light·heart·ed (līt′här′tĭd) *adj.* Not being burdened by trouble, worry, or care; happy and carefree. See Synonyms at **glad¹.** —**light′heart′ed·ly** *adv.* —**light′heart′ed·ness** *n.*

light heavyweight *n. Sports.* **1.** A professional boxer weighing more than 160 and not more than 175 pounds (approximately 72.5–79.5 kilograms), heavier than a middleweight and lighter than a heavyweight. **2.** A contestant in various other sports in a similar weight class.

light·house (līt′hous′) *n. Nautical.* A tall structure topped by a powerful light used as a beacon or signal to aid marine navigation.

light·ing (lī′tĭng) *n.* **1.** The state of being lighted; illumination. **2.a.** The method or equipment used to provide artificial illumination. **b.** The illumination so provided. **3.** The act or process of igniting.

light·ly (līt′lē) *adv.* **1.** With little weight or force; gently. **2.** To a slight extent or amount: *apply paint lightly.* **3.a.** With little difficulty; easily. **b.** With agility and grace; nimbly. **4.a.** In a carefree manner; cheerfully: *took the news lightly.* **b.** Without sufficient care or consideration; indifferently: *treated the situation much too lightly.*

light machine gun *n.* An air-cooled machine gun not greater than .30 caliber.

light meter *n.* See **exposure meter.**

light-mind·ed (līt′mīn′dĭd) *adj.* Frivolous, silly, or inanely giddy. —**light′-mind′ed·ly** *adv.* —**light′-mind′ed·ness** *n.*

light·ness¹ (līt′nĭs) *n.* **1.** The quality or condition of being illuminated. **2.** *Color.* The dimension of the color of an object by which the object appears to reflect or transmit more or less of the incident light, varying from black to white for surface colors and from black to colorless for transparent volume colors.

light·ness² (līt′nĭs) *n.* **1.** The state or quality of having little weight or force. **2.** Ease or quickness of movement; agility. **3.** Ease or cheerfulness in manner or style. **4.** Freedom from worry or trouble. **5.** Lack of appropriate seriousness; levity. **6.** Delicacy or subtlety in craft, performance, or effect.

light·ning (līt′nĭng) *n.* **1.a.** An abrupt, discontinuous natural electric discharge in the atmosphere. **b.** The visible flash of light accompanying such a discharge. **2.** *Informal.* A sudden, usually improbable stroke of fortune. —**lightning** *intr.v.* **-ninged** (-nĭngd), **-ning, -nings.** To discharge a flash of lightning. —**lightning** *adj.* Moving or occurring with remarkable speed or suddenness. [Middle English, gerund of *lightnen,* to illuminate, and *lighten* (*lightnen,* from *lighten*) from Old English *līhtan.* See **leuk-** in Appendix.]

lightning arrester *n.* A protective device for electrical equipment that reduces excessive voltage resulting from lightning to a safe level by grounding the discharge.

lightning bug *n.* See **firefly.**

lightning rod *n.* **1.** A grounded metal rod placed high on a structure to prevent damage by conducting lightning to the ground. **2.** One that attracts and absorbs powerful, typically negative feelings and reactions, thereby diverting interest from other issues: "[His] *business dealings have become a lightning rod for criticism*" (Walter Shapiro).

light opera *n. Music.* See **operetta.**

light pen *n. Computer Science.* A small, photosensitive device connected to a computer and moved by hand over an output display in order to manipulate information in the computer. Also called *electronic stylus, light stylus.*

light·proof (līt′pro͞of′) *adj.* Impenetrable by light: *film stored in lightproof containers.*

light reaction *n.* The first stage of photosynthesis, occurring only in the presence of light, during which energy captured from light drives the production of ATP.

light reflex *n.* Contraction of the pupil of the eye in response to an increase in light.

lights (līts) *pl.n.* The lungs, especially the lungs of an animal slaughtered for food. [Middle English *lightes,* from *light,* light in weight (from the lightness of the lungs compared to other organs). See LIGHT².]

light·ship (līt′shĭp′) *n. Nautical.* A ship with a powerful light or warning signals that is anchored in dangerous waters to alert other vessels.

light show *n.* A display of colored lights in shifting patterns, often accompanied by slides and film loops.

light·some¹ (līt′səm) *adj.* **1.** Providing light; luminous. **2.** Covered with or full of light; bright. —**light′some·ly** *adv.* —**light′some·ness** *n.*

light·some² (līt′səm) *adj.* **1.** Light, nimble, or graceful in

lighthouse
West Quoddy lighthouse, Lubec, Maine

lightning

ă pat	oi boy
ā pay	ou out
âr care	o͝o took
ä father	o͞o boot
ĕ pet	ŭ cut
ē be	ûr urge
ĭ pit	th thin
ī pie	*th* this
îr pier	hw which
ŏ pot	zh vision
ō toe	ə about, item
ô paw	♦ regionalism

Stress marks: ′ (primary); ′ (secondary), as in **dictionary** (dĭk′shə-nĕr′ē)

movement. **2.** Free from worry or care; cheerful. **3.** Frivolous; silly. **—light′some·ly** *adv.* **—light′some·ness** *n.*

lights out *n.* **1.** A signal or command to extinguish lights for the night. **2.** Bedtime.

light-struck (līt′strŭk′) *adj.* Fogged by accidental exposure. Used of photosensitive materials.

light stylus *n. Computer Science.* See **light pen.**

light water *n. Physics & Chemistry.* Ordinary water, H_2O.

light·weight (līt′wāt′) *n.* **1.** One that weighs relatively little or less than average. **2.** *Sports.* **a.** A professional boxer weighing more than 126 and not more than 135 pounds (approximately 57–61 kilograms), heavier than a featherweight and lighter than a welterweight. **b.** A contestant in various other sports in a similar weight class. **3.** A person of little ability, intelligence, influence, or importance. **—lightweight** *adj.* **1.** Weighing relatively little; not heavy: *lightweight clothing; a lightweight wood.* **2.** *Sports.* Of, relating to, or characteristic of a lightweight: *the lightweight title.* **3.** Having no significance or influence: *a lightweight intellect.*

♦**light·wood** (līt′wo͝od′) *n. Chiefly Southern U.S.* See **kindling.**

♦ ***REGIONAL NOTE:*** There are a number of regional equivalents for small pieces of easily ignited wood used to start a fire, what Standard English calls *kindling. Lightwood,* derived from the verb *to light (a fire),* probably originated in Virginia, according to Craig M. Carver in *American Regional Dialects,* and is now used throughout the South Midland. *Fat pine, fatwood,* and *rich pine* all refer to the resinous pine native to the Gulf States. The resin makes even a small sliver of the wood easily kindled.

light-year also **light year** (līt′yîr′) *n.* **1.** The distance that light travels in a vacuum in one year, approximately 9.46 trillion (9.46×10^{12}) kilometers or 5.88 trillion (5.88×10^{12}) miles. **2.** Often **light-years.** *Informal.* A long way: *a small town light-years away from the action of the capital.*

lign– *pref.* Variant of **ligni–.**

lig·ne·ous (lĭg′nē-əs) *adj.* Consisting of or having the texture or appearance of wood; woody. [From Latin *ligneus,* from *lignum,* wood. See **leg-** in Appendix.]

ligni– or **ligno–** or **lign–** *pref.* Wood: *lignocellulose.* [From Latin *lignum,* wood. See **leg-** in Appendix.]

lig·ni·fy (lĭg′nə-fī′) *v.* **-fied, -fy·ing, -fies.** —*intr.* To turn into wood or become woody through the formation and deposit of lignin in cell walls. —*tr.* To make woody or woodlike by the deposit of lignin. **—lig′ni·fi·ca′tion** (-fĭ-kā′shən) *n.*

lig·nin (lĭg′nĭn) *n.* A complex polymer, the chief noncarbohydrate constituent of wood, that binds to cellulose fibers and hardens and strengthens the cell walls of plants.

lig·nite (lĭg′nīt′) *n.* A soft, brownish-black coal in which the alteration of vegetable matter has proceeded further than in peat but not as far as in bituminous coal. Also called *brown coal.* **—lig·nit′ic** (-nĭt′ĭk) *adj.*

ligno– *pref.* Variant of **ligni–.**

lig·no·cel·lu·lose (lĭg′nō-sĕl′yə-lōs′) *n.* A combination of lignin and cellulose that strengthens woody plant cells.

lig·num vi·tae (lĭg′nəm vī′tē) *n., pl.* **lignum vitaes. 1.** Either of two tropical American trees *(Guaiacum officinale* or *G. sanctum)* having evergreen leaves and very heavy, durable, resinous wood. **2.** The wood of either of these trees, the hardest of commercial woods. [New Latin *lignum vītae* : Latin *lignum,* wood + Latin *vītae,* genitive of *vīta,* life.]

lig·ro·in (lĭg′rō-ĭn) *n.* A volatile, flammable fraction of petroleum, obtained by distillation and used as a solvent. [Origin unknown.]

lig·u·la (lĭg′yə-lə) *n., pl.* **-lae** (-lē′) or **-las.** A strap-shaped or tonguelike structure, especially a mouth part in certain insects. [Latin, diminutive of *lingua,* tongue. See **dn̥ghū-** in Appendix.]

lig·u·late (lĭg′yə-lĭt, -lāt′) *adj.* **1.** Strap-shaped. **2.** Having a ligule.

lig·ule (lĭg′yo͞ol) *n.* A straplike structure, such as the corolla of a ray flower or a membranous or hairy appendage between the sheaf and blade of a grass leaf. [Latin *ligula,* diminutive of *lingua,* tongue. See **dn̥ghū-** in Appendix.]

lig·ure (lĭg′yo͝or′) *n.* A precious stone of ancient Israel. [Middle English *liguri,* from Late Latin *ligūrius,* from Greek *ligurion,* diminutive of *liguros,* clear, from *ligus.*]

Li·gu·ri·a (lĭ-gyo͝or′ē-ə). A region of northwest Italy on the **Ligurian Sea,** an arm of the Mediterranean Sea between northwest Italy and Corsica. Named for an ancient pre-Indo-European people, the Ligurii, the region was subdued by the Romans in the 2nd century B.C. and was later (16th–19th century) controlled by Genoa. A small section of the coastline formed the **Ligurian Republic** from 1797 until 1815. **—Li·gu′ri·an** *adj. & n.*

lik·a·ble also **like·a·ble** (lī′kə-bəl) *adj.* Pleasing; attractive. **—lik′a·ble·ness, like′a·ble·ness** *n.*

like[1] (līk) *v.* **liked, lik·ing, likes.** —*tr.* **1.** To find pleasant or attractive; enjoy. **2.** To want to have: *would like some coffee.* **3.** To feel about; regard: *How do you like her nerve!* **4.** *Archaic.* To be pleasing to. —*intr.* **1.** To have an inclination or a preference: *If you like, we can meet you there.* **2.** *Scots.* To be pleased. **—like** *n.* Something that is liked; a preference: *made a list of his likes and dislikes.* [Middle English *liken,* from Old English *līcian,* to please. See **līk-** in Appendix.]

SYNONYMS: *like, love, enjoy, relish, fancy, dote.* These verbs mean to be attracted to or to find agreeable. *Like,* the least forceful, suggests mere interest, approval, or favor: *"I may* like *him well enough; but you don't* love *your servants"* (Harriet Beecher Stowe). *Love* implies a strong attachment or intense affection and deep involvement on an emotional level: *"All his faults are such that one loves him still the better for them"* (Oliver Goldsmith). *Enjoy* is applied to what gives personal satisfaction or pleasure: *"There are two things to aim at in life: first, to get what you want; and after that, to enjoy it"* (Logan Pearsall Smith). *Relish* applies to what moves one to keen or zestful appreciation: *"Every great and original writer . . . must himself create the taste by which he is to be relished"* (William Wordsworth). One *fancies* what appeals to one's taste, inclination, imagination, or notion of what a person or thing should be: *She fancies elegant clothes and jewelry. Caviar is a delicacy, but few children fancy it. Dote* implies foolish, extravagant attachment: *He dotes on his grandchildren and indulges their every whim.*

like[2] (līk) *prep.* **1.** Possessing the characteristics of; resembling closely; similar to. **2. a.** In the typical manner of: *It's not like you to take offense.* **b.** In the same way as: *lived like royalty.* **3.** Inclined or disposed to: *felt like running away.* **4.** As if the probability exists for: *looks like a bad year for farmers.* **5.** Such as; for example: *saved things like old newspapers and pieces of string.* **—like** *adj.* **1.** Possessing the same or almost the same characteristics; similar: *on this and like occasions.* **2.** Alike: *They are as like as two siblings.* **3.** Having equivalent value or quality. Usually used in negative sentences: *There's nothing like a good night's sleep.* **—like** *adv.* **1.** In the manner of being; as if. Used as an intensifier of action: *worked like hell; ran like crazy.* **2.** *Informal.* Probably; likely: *Like as not she'll change her mind.* **3.** *Non-Standard.* Used to provide emphasis or a pause: *Like let's get going.* **—like** *n.* **1.** One similar to or like another. Used with *the*: *was subject to coughs, asthma, and the like.* **2.** Often **likes.** *Informal.* An equivalent or similar person or thing; an equal or match: *I've never seen the likes of this before. We'll never see his like again.* **—like** *conj. Usage Problem.* **1.** In the same way that; as: *To dance like she does requires great discipline.* **2.** As if: *It looks like we'll finish on time.* [Middle English, from *like,* similar (from Old English *gelīc,* and Old Norse *līkr*) and from *like,* similarly (from Old English *gelīce,* from *gelīc,* similar; see **līk-** in Appendix).]

USAGE NOTE: Writers since Chaucer's time have used *like* as a conjunction, but 19th-century and 20th-century critics have been so vehement in their condemnations of this usage that a writer who uses the construction in formal style risks being accused of illiteracy or worse. Prudence requires *The dogs howled as* (not *like) we expected them to. Like* is more acceptably used as a conjunction in informal style with verbs such as *feel, look, seem, sound,* and *taste,* as in *It looks like we are in for a rough winter.* But here too *as if* is to be preferred in formal writing. There can be no objection to the use of *like* as a conjunction when the following verb is not expressed, as in *He took to politics like a duck to water.* See Usage Notes at **as**[1]**, together.**

♦**like**[3] (līk) also **liked** (līkt) *aux.v. Chiefly Southern U.S.* To be just on the point of; be or come near to: *I like to have killed him when he said that.* [Middle English *liken,* to compare, from *like,* similar. See LIKE[2].]

–like *suff.* Resembling or characteristic of: *ladylike.* [Middle English, from *like,* similar. See LIKE[2].]

like·a·ble (lī′kə-bəl) *adj.* Variant of **likable.**

like·li·hood (līk′lē-ho͝od′) *n.* **1.** The state of being probable; probability. **2.** Something probable.

like·ly (līk′lē) *adj.* **-li·er, -li·est. 1.** Possessing or displaying the qualities or characteristics that make something probable: *They are likely to become angry with him.* **2.** Within the realm of credibility; plausible: *not a very likely excuse.* **3.** Apparently appropriate or suitable: *There were several likely candidates for the job.* **4.** Apt to achieve success or yield a desired outcome; promising: *a likely topic for investigation.* **5.** Attractive; pleasant: *found a likely spot under a shady tree for the picnic.* **—likely** *adv. Usage Problem.* Probably. [Middle English *likly,* from Old English *gelīclīc* (from *gelīc,* similar) and from Old Norse *līkligr* (from *līkr,* similar; see **līk-** in Appendix).]

USAGE NOTE: Used as an adverb *likely* is most commonly preceded by a qualifier such as *very* or *quite*: *He will quite likely require some help with his classes.* But the unmodified use of *likely* is common enough in educated writing, and though it might be better avoided in highly formal style, it should not be regarded as incorrect: *They'll likely buy a new car this year.* See Usage Note at **liable.**

like-mind·ed (līk′mīn′dĭd) *adj.* Of the same turn of mind.

lik·en (lī′kən) *tr.v.* **-ened, -en·ing, -ens.** To see, mention, or show as similar; compare. [Middle English *liknen,* from *like,* similar. See LIKE[2].]

like·ness (līk′nĭs) *n.* **1.** The state, quality, or fact of being like; resemblance. **2.** An imitative appearance; a semblance. **3.** A pictorial, graphic, or sculptured representation of something.

SYNONYMS: *likeness, similarity, similitude, resemblance, analogy, affinity.* These nouns denote agreement or conformity, as in character, nature, or appearance between persons or things. *Likeness* implies close agreement: *"There is a devil haunts thee in the likeness of a fat old man"* (Shakespeare). *It was your uncanny likeness to my sister that made me stare at you. Similarity* and *similitude* suggest agreement only in some respects or to some degree: *They were drawn to each other by similarity of interests. "A striking similitude between the brother and sister now first arrested my attention"* (Edgar Allan Poe). *Resemblance* refers to similarity in appearance or in external or superficial details: *"The child . . . bore a remarkable resemblance to her grandfather"* (Lytton Strachey). *Analogy* is similarity, as of properties or functions, between unlike things that are otherwise not comparable: *The operation of a computer presents an interesting analogy to the working of the human brain. Affinity* is likeness deriving from kinship or from the possession of shared or compatible properties, characteristics, or sympathies: *There is a discernible stylistic affinity between the compositions of Brahms and those of Dvořák.*

like•wise (līk′wīz′) *adv.* **1.** In the same way; similarly: *"Some have little power to do good, and have likewise little strength to resist evil"* (Samuel Johnson). **2.** As well; also. See Synonyms at **also.**

lik•ing (lī′kĭng) *n.* **1.** A feeling of attraction or love; fondness. **2.** Preference or taste.

li•ku•ta (lē-ko͞o′tä) *n., pl.* **ma•ku•ta** (mä-ko͞o′tä). See table at **currency.** [Alteration of Portuguese *macuta,* an old West African unit of currency consisting originally of a piece of cloth : Bantu *li-,* sing. n. pref. + Kimbundu and Kongo *kuta,* cloth.]

li•lac (lī′lək, -lŏk, -läk) *n.* **1.** Any of various shrubs of the genus *Syringa,* especially *S. vulgaris,* widely cultivated for its clusters of fragrant purplish or white flowers. **2.** *Color.* A pale to light or moderate purple. [Obsolete French, from Arabic *līlak,* from Middle Persian *nīlak,* from *nīl,* indigo, from Sanskrit *nīlī,* from *nīla-,* dark blue.] **—li′lac** *adj.*

li•lan•ge•ni (lĭ-läng′gĕ-nē) *n., pl.* **em•a•lan•ge•ni** (ĕm′ə-läng-gĕn′ē). See table at **currency.** [Nguni (Siswati) : *li-,* sing. n. pref. + *langeni,* money.]

Lil•ith (lĭl′ĭth) *n.* **1.** An evil female spirit in ancient Semitic legend, alleged to haunt deserted places and attack children. **2.** The first wife of Adam in Hebrew folklore, believed to have been in existence before the creation of Eve.

Li•li•u•o•ka•la•ni (lə-lē′ə-ō-kə-lä′nē, lē-lē′o͞o-ō-kä-lä′nē), **Lydia Kamekeha Paki.** 1838–1917. Queen of the Hawaiian Islands (1891–1893).

Lille (lēl). A city of northern France north-northeast of Paris near the Belgian border. Founded c. 1030, it was the medieval capital of Flanders. Population, 168,424.

Lil•lie (lĭl′ē), **Beatrice.** Lady Peel. 1898–1989. Canadian-born British comedienne who appeared on stage in such productions as *Auntie Mame* (1958) and *High Spirits* (1964).

Lil•li•pu•tian also **lil•li•pu•tian** (lĭl′ə-pyo͞o′shən) *—n.* A very small person or being. *—adj.* **1.** Very small; diminutive. **2.** Trivial; petty. [After the *Lilliputians,* a people in *Gulliver's Travels* by Jonathan Swift.]

Li•long•we (lĭ-lông′wā). The capital of Malawi, in the south-central part of the country. It was founded in the 1940's as an agricultural market town. Population, 103,000.

lilt (lĭlt) *n.* **1.** A cheerful or lively manner of speaking, in which the pitch of the voice varies pleasantly. **2.** A light, happy tune or song. **3.** A light or resilient manner of moving or walking. **—lilt** *v.* **lilt•ed, lilt•ing, lilts.** *—tr.* To say, sing, or play (something) in a cheerful, rhythmic manner. *—intr.* **1.** To speak, sing, or play with liveliness or rhythm. **2.** To move with lightness and buoyancy. [From Middle English *lulten, lilten,* to sound an alarm.]

lil•y (lĭl′ē) *n., pl.* **-ies. 1.** Any of various plants of the genus *Lilium,* having variously colored, often trumpet-shaped flowers. **2.** Any of various similar or related plants, such as the day lily or the water lily. **3.** The flower of any of these plants. [Middle English *lilie,* from Old English, from Latin *līlium.*]

lily family *n.* A large family of plants, the Liliaceae, characterized by showy flowers with six perianth segments, six stamens, and a superior ovary and usually producing bulbs or rhizomes.

lil•y-liv•ered (lĭl′ē-lĭv′ərd) *adj.* Cowardly; timid.

lily of the Nile *n., pl.* **lilies of the Nile.** See **African lily.**

lily of the valley *n., pl.* **lilies of the valley.** A widely cultivated ornamental European plant *(Convallaria majalis)* having one-sided racemes of fragrant, bell-shaped white flowers.

lily pad *n.* One of the floating leaves of a water lily.

lil•y-trot•ter (lĭl′ē-trŏt′ər) *n.* See **jacana.**

lil•y-white (lĭl′ē-hwīt′, -wīt′) *adj.* **1.** White as a lily. **2.** Beyond reproach; blameless. **3.** *Informal.* Excluding or seeking to exclude Black people.

lim. *abbr.* Limit.

Li•ma. 1. (lē′mə). The capital and largest city of Peru, in the west-central part of the country near the Pacific Ocean. Founded by Francisco Pizarro in 1535, it was the capital of Spain's New World empire until the 19th century. The city was largely rebuilt after earthquakes in 1687 and 1746. Population, 371,122. **2.** (lī′mə). A city of northwest Ohio south-southwest of Toledo. It is a processing and marketing center for a rich farm area. Population, 47,381.

♦**li•ma bean** (lī′mə) *n.* **1.** Any of several varieties of a tropical American plant *(Phaseolus limensis)* having flat pods containing large, light green, edible seeds. **2.** The seed of this plant. Also called ♦*butter bean.* [After LIMA, Peru.]

lim•a•cine (lĭm′ə-sēn′, lī′mə-) *adj.* Of, relating to, or resembling a slug. [From Latin *līmāx, līmāc-,* slug, snail; akin to *līmus,* slime. See **lei-** in Appendix.]

limb¹ (lĭm) *n.* **1.** One of the larger branches of a tree. **2.** One of the jointed appendages of an animal, such as an arm, a leg, a wing, or a flipper, used for locomotion or grasping. **3.** An extension or a projecting part, as of a building or mountain range. **4.** One that is considered to be an extension, a member, or a representative of a larger body or group. **5.** *Informal.* An impish child. **—limb** *tr.v.* **limbed, limb•ing, limbs.** To dismember. ***—idiom.*** **(out) on a limb.** *Informal.* In a difficult, awkward, or vulnerable position. [Alteration (probably influenced by LIMB²) of Middle English *lim,* from Old English.]

limb² (lĭm) *n.* **1.** *Astronomy.* The circumferential edge of the apparent disk of a celestial body. **2.** *Mathematics.* The edge of a graduated arc or circle used in an instrument to measure angles. **3.** *Botany.* The expanded tip of a plant organ, such as a petal or corolla lobe. [Middle English, graduated edge of an astronomical instrument, from Old French *limbe,* from Latin *limbus,* border.]

lim•bate (lĭm′bāt′) *adj. Botany.* Having an edge or a margin of a different color. [Late Latin *limbātus,* bordered, from Latin *limbus,* border.]

lim•ber¹ (lĭm′bər) *adj.* **1.** Bending or flexing readily; pliable. **2.** Capable of moving, bending, or contorting easily; supple. **—limber** *v.* **-bered, -ber•ing, -bers.** *—tr.* To make limber: *limbered up his legs. —intr.* To make oneself limber: *players limbering up before the game.* [Origin unknown.] **—lim′ber•ly** *adv.* **—lim′ber•ness** *n.*

lim•ber² (lĭm′bər) *n.* A two-wheeled, horse-drawn vehicle used to tow a field gun or a caisson. [Alteration of Middle English *limour,* shaft of a cart, perhaps from *limon,* from Old French.]

lim•bers (lĭm′bərz) *pl.n. Nautical.* Gutters or channels on each side of a ship's keelson that drain bilge water into the pump well. [Probably alteration of French *lumière,* one of the limbers, from Old French *lumiere,* opening, light, from Late Latin *lūmināria,* pl. of *lūmināre,* window, from Latin, lamp. See LUMINARY.]

lim•bi (lĭm′bī′) *n. Biology.* Plural of **limbus.**

lim•bic (lĭm′bĭk) *adj.* **1.** Of, relating to, or characterized by a limbus. **2.** Of or relating to the limbic system. [French *limbique,* from *limbe,* edge, from Old French, graduated edge of an astronomical instrument. See LIMB².]

limbic system *n.* A group of interconnected deep brain structures, common to all mammals, and involved in olfaction, emotion, motivation, behavior, and various autonomic functions.

lim•bo¹ (lĭm′bō) *n., pl.* **-bos. 1.** Often **Limbo.** *Theology.* The abode of just or innocent souls excluded from the beatific vision but not condemned to further punishment. **2.** A region or condition of oblivion or neglect: *Management kept her promotion in limbo for months.* **3.** A state or place of confinement. **4.** An intermediate place or state. [Middle English, from Medieval Latin *(in) limbō,* (in) Limbo, ablative of *limbus,* Limbo, from Latin, border.]

WORD HISTORY: Our use of the word *limbo* to refer to states of oblivion, confinement, or transition is derived from the theological sense of *Limbo* as a place where souls remain that cannot enter heaven, for example, unbaptized infants. *Limbo* in Roman Catholic theology is located on the border of Hell, which explains the name chosen for it. The Latin word *limbus,* having meanings such as "an ornamental border to a fringe" and "a band or girdle," was chosen by Christian theologians of the Middle Ages to denote this border region. English borrowed the word *limbus* directly, but the form *limbo* that caught on in English, first recorded in a work composed around 1378, is from the ablative form of *limbus,* the form used in expressions such as *in limbō,* "in Limbo."

lim•bo² (lĭm′bō) *n., pl.* **-bos.** A West Indian dance in which the dancers keep bending over backward and passing under a pole that is lowered slightly each time. [Probably ultimately of African origin.]

Lim•burg (lĭm′bûrg′, -bœrKH′). A former duchy of northwest Europe. Founded in the 11th century, it was incorporated into the Netherlands in 1815 and divided into the Dutch and Belgian provinces of Limburg in 1839.

Lim•burg•er (lĭm′bûr′gər) *n.* A soft white cheese with a very strong odor and flavor. [Flemish, one from Limburg, after *Limburg,* a province of northeast Belgium.]

lim•bus (lĭm′bəs) *n., pl.* **-bi** (-bī′). *Biology.* A distinctive border or edge, such as the junction between the cornea and sclera of the eyeball. [Latin, border.]

lime¹ (līm) *n.* **1.** A spiny evergreen shrub or tree *(Citrus aurantifolia),* native to Asia and having leathery leaves, fragrant white flowers, and edible fruit. **2.** The egg-shaped fruit of this plant, having a green rind and acid juice used as flavoring. [Probably French, from Spanish *lima,* from Arabic *līmah, līm,* probably from *līmūn,* lemon. See LEMON.]

lime² (līm) *n.* See **linden.** [Alteration of Middle English *lind, line,* from Old English *lind.*]

Liliuokalani
c. 1891 photograph by
Menzies Dickson
(1840?–1891)

lily

lily pad

ă pat	oi boy
ā pay	ou out
âr care	o͝o took
ä father	o͞o boot
ĕ pet	ŭ cut
ē be	ûr urge
ĭ pit	th thin
ī pie	*th* this
îr pier	hw which
ŏ pot	zh vision
ō toe	ə about, item
ô paw	♦ regionalism

Stress marks: ′ (primary); ′ (secondary), as in **dictionary** (dĭk′shə-nĕr′ē)

limousine
Used by
President George Bush
in the inaugural parade
of January 20, 1989

lime³ (līm) *n.* **1.a.** See **calcium oxide. b.** Any of various mineral and industrial forms of calcium oxide differing chiefly in water content and percentage of constituents such as silica, alumina, and iron. Also called *quicklime.* **2.** Birdlime. **—lime** *tr.v.* **limed, lim·ing, limes. 1.** To treat with lime. **2.** To smear with birdlime. **3.** To catch or snare with or as if with birdlime. [Middle English *lim,* from Old English *līm,* birdlime. See **lei-** in Appendix.] **—lim′y** *adj.*

lime·ade (lī-mād′) *n.* A sweetened beverage of lime juice and plain or carbonated water.

lime·kiln (līm′kĭl′, -kĭln′) *n.* A furnace used to reduce naturally occurring forms of calcium carbonate to lime.

lime·light (līm′līt′) *n.* **1.** A focus of public attention. **2.a.** An early type of stage light in which lime was heated to incandescence producing brilliant illumination. **b.** The brilliant white light so produced. In this sense, also called *calcium light.*

li·men (lī′mən) *n., pl.* **li·mens** or **lim·i·na** (lĭm′ə-nə). The threshold of a physiological or psychological response. [Latin, threshold.] **—lim′i·nal** (lĭm′ə-nəl) *adj.*

lim·er·ick (lĭm′ər-ĭk) *n.* A light humorous, nonsensical, or bawdy verse of five anapestic lines usually with the rhyme scheme *aabba.* [After LIMERICK.]

WORD HISTORY: Etymologies can sometimes be a bit disappointing, as, for example, when one is told that *limerick* is named after a city or county in Ireland without being told why it is so named. Unfortunately, we run into a difficulty here that is not uncommonly faced by etymologists, namely, that no one is precisely sure why this piece of humorous verse was so named. One theory is that it was named for a group of poets who wrote in Limerick in the 18th century; another, that it came from a custom at parties of making up a nonsense verse and following it with a chorus of "Will you come up to Limerick." In any case, the first limericks appeared in books published in 1820 and 1821, and the form was popularized by Edward Lear in a collection published in 1846. The word itself, however, is not recorded until 1896. Let us sum up by saying: "There once was a verse form named limerick./ No one can account for the name of it./Some think from a game/ Or from poets it came./If you know please come up to Limerick."

Lim·er·ick (lĭm′ər-ĭk, lĭm′rĭk). A borough of southwest Ireland on the Shannon River estuary. It was an important Norse settlement in the 9th and 10th centuries and was taken by the English in the late 12th century. Population, 60,736.

li·mes (lī′mēz) *n., pl.* **lim·i·tes** (lĭm′ĭ-tēz′). A fortified boundary or border, especially of the Roman Empire. [Latin *līmes.*]

lime·stone (līm′stōn′) *n.* A common sedimentary rock consisting mostly of calcium carbonate, $CaCO_3$, used as a building stone and in the manufacture of lime, carbon dioxide, and cement. *—attributive.* Often used to modify another noun: *limestone cliffs; limestone walls.*

lime·wa·ter (līm′wô′tər, -wŏt′ər) *n.* A clear colorless alkaline aqueous solution of calcium hydroxide, used in calamine lotion and other skin preparations and sometimes as an antacid.

lim·ey (lī′mē) *n., pl.* **-eys.** *Slang.* **1.** A British sailor. **2.** An English person. [Short for *lime juicer* (from the use of lime juice on British warships in order to prevent scurvy).]

li·mic·o·line (lī-mĭk′ə-līn′, -lĭn) *adj.* Of or relating to shore birds, especially the plovers, sandpipers, and phalaropes. [From New Latin *Līmicolae,* group name, from pl. of Late Latin *līmicola,* living in mud : Latin *līmus,* slime; see **lei-** in Appendix + Latin *-cola,* inhabitant; see -COLOUS.]

li·mic·o·lous (lī-mĭk′ə-ləs) *adj.* Living in mud. [From Late Latin *līmicola.* See LIMICOLINE.]

lim·i·na (lĭm′ə-nə) *n.* A plural of **limen.**

lim·it (lĭm′ĭt) *n. Abbr.* **lim. 1.** The point, edge, or line beyond which something cannot or may not proceed. **2. limits.** The boundary surrounding a specific area; bounds: *within the city limits.* **3.** A confining or restricting object, agent, or influence. **4.** The greatest or least amount, number, or extent allowed or possible: *a withdrawal limit of $200.* **5.** *Games.* The largest amount which may be bet at one time in games of chance. **6.** *Mathematics.* A number or point *k* that is approached by a function *f(x)* as *x* approaches *a* if, for every positive number ϵ, there exists a number δ such that $|f(x)-k| < \epsilon$ if $0 < |x-a| < \delta$. Also called *limit point, point of accumulation.* **7.** *Informal.* One that approaches or exceeds certain limits, as of credibility, forbearance, or acceptability: *He is the limit of irresponsibility.* **—limit** *tr.v.* **-it·ed, -it·ing, -its. 1.** To confine or restrict within a boundary or bounds. **2.** To fix definitely; to specify. [Middle English *limite,* from Old French, border, from Latin *līmes, līmit-,* border, limit.] **—lim′it·a·ble** *adj.*

SYNONYMS: *limit, restrict, confine, circumscribe.* These verbs mean to establish or keep within specified bounds. *Limit* refers principally to the establishment of a maximum, as of quantity, degree, or time, beyond which a person or thing cannot or may not go: *The Constitution limits the President's term of office to four years. "Liberty, too, must be limited in order to be possessed"* (Edmund Burke). To *restrict* is to keep within prescribed limits, as of choice or action: *"a pardon, so restricted that none were likely to be forgiven save those who had done no wrong"* (John Lothrop Motley). *The sale of alcoholic beverages is restricted to those over 21. Confine* suggests limits that imprison, restrain, or impede: *All prisoners will be confined to their cells. Interest in Asia is no longer confined to scholars. Circumscribe* connotes an encircling or surrounding line that confines and especially that confines narrowly: *"A man . . . should not circumscribe his activity by any inflexible fence of rigid rules"* (John Stuart Blackie). See also Synonyms at **boundary.**

lim·i·tar·y (lĭm′ĭ-tĕr′ē) *adj. Archaic.* **1.a.** Of or relating to a limit or boundary. **b.** Limiting; restrictive. **2.** Limited.

lim·i·ta·tion (lĭm′ĭ-tā′shən) *n.* **1.** The act of limiting or the state of being limited. **2.** A restriction. **3.** A shortcoming or defect. **4.** *Law.* A specified period during which, by statute, an action may be brought.

lim·it·ed (lĭm′ĭ-tĭd) *adj.* **1.** Confined or restricted within certain limits: *has only limited experience.* **2.a.** Not attaining the highest goals or achievement: *a limited success.* **b.** Having only mediocre talent or range of ability: *a popular but limited actor.* **3.** Having governmental or ruling powers restricted by enforceable limitations, as a constitution or a legislative body: *limited monarchy.* **4.** *Abbr.* **ltd., Ltd., Ld.** Of, relating to, or being a limited company. **5.** *Abbr.* **ltd., Ltd., Ld.** Of, relating to, or being transportation facilities, such as trains or buses, that make few stops and carry relatively few passengers. **—limited** *n. Abbr.* **ltd., Ltd., Ld.** A limited train or bus. **—lim′i·ted·ness** *n.*

limited company *n. Abbr.* **ltd., Ltd., Ld.** A firm, usually associated with British registration, that is organized in such a way as to give its owners limited liability.

limited edition *n.* An edition, as of a book or print, restricted to a specified number of copies.

limited liability *n.* The liability of a firm's owners for no more capital than they have invested in the business.

limited war *n.* A war whose objective is of smaller scope than total defeat of the enemy.

lim·it·er (lĭm′ĭt-ər) *n.* **1.** One that limits: *a limiter of choices.* **2.** *Electronics.* A circuit that prevents the amplitude of a waveform from exceeding a specified value. In this sense, also called *clipper.*

lim·i·tes (lĭm′ĭ-tēz′) *n.* Plural of **limes.**

lim·it·ing (lĭm′ĭ-tĭng) *adj.* **1.** Acting as a limit. **2.** *Grammar.* Restricting the range of application of the noun modified.

lim·it·less (lĭm′ĭt-lĭs) *adj.* Having no limit or limits; unrestricted: *limitless authority; the limitless reaches of outer space.* **—lim′it·less·ly** *adv.* **—lim′it·less·ness** *n.*

limit point *n. Mathematics.* See **limit** (sense 6).

limn (lĭm) *tr.v.* **limned, limn·ing** (lĭm′nĭng), **limns. 1.** To describe. **2.** To depict by painting or drawing. See Synonyms at **represent.** [Middle English *limnen,* to illuminate (a manuscript), probably alteration (influenced by *limnour,* illustrator, from Anglo-Norman *lymnour*) of *luminen,* from Old French *luminer,* from Latin *lūmināre,* to illuminate, adorn, from *lūmen, lūmin-,* light. See **leuk-** in Appendix.] **—limn′er** (lĭm′nər) *n.*

lim·net·ic (lĭm-nĕt′ĭk) *adj.* Of or occurring in the deeper, open waters of lakes or ponds. [From Greek *limnētēs,* marsh-dwelling, from Greek *limnē,* lake.]

lim·nol·o·gy (lĭm-nŏl′ə-jē) *n.* The scientific study of the life and phenomena of fresh water, especially lakes and ponds. [Greek *limnē,* lake + -LOGY.] **—lim′no·log′i·cal** (-nə-lŏj′ĭ-kəl) *adj.* **—lim′no·log′i·cal·ly** *adv.* **—lim·nol′o·gist** *n.*

Lím·nos (lēm′nôs). See **Lemnos.**

lim·o (lĭm′ō) *n., pl.* **lim·os.** *Informal.* A limousine.

Li·moges (lē-mōzh′). A city of west-central France northeast of Bordeaux. Its ceramic industry dates to the 18th century. Population, 140,400.

lim·o·nene (lĭm′ə-nēn′) *n.* A liquid, $C_{10}H_{16}$, with a characteristic lemonlike fragrance, used as a solvent, wetting agent, and dispersing agent and in the manufacture of resins. [French *limonène,* from French *limon,* lemon (obsolete), from Old French. See LEMON.]

li·mo·nite (lī′mə-nīt′) *n.* Any of a group of widely occurring yellowish-brown to black iron oxide minerals, essentially $FeO(OH){\cdot}nH_2O$, used as a minor ore of iron. [German *Limonit,* from Greek *leimōn,* meadow.] **—li′mo·nit′ic** (-nĭt′ĭk) *adj.*

Li·mou·sin (lē-mōō-zăN′). A historical region and former province of central France west of the Auvergne Mountains. It was included in the dowry given by Eleanor of Aquitaine to Henry II of England in 1152 and was eventually reconquered by France (1370–1374).

lim·ou·sine (lĭm′ə-zēn′, lĭm′ə-zēn′) *n.* Any of various large passenger vehicles, especially a luxurious automobile usually driven by a chauffeur and sometimes having a partition separating the passenger compartment from the driver's seat. [French, perhaps after LIMOUSIN.]

limp (lĭmp) *intr.v.* **limped, limp·ing, limps. 1.** To walk lamely, especially with irregularity, as if favoring one leg. **2.** To move or proceed haltingly or unsteadily: *The project limped along with half its previous funding.* **—limp** *n.* An irregular, jerky, or awkward gait. **—limp** *adj.* **limp·er, limp·est. 1.** Lacking or having lost rigidity, as of structure or substance. **2.** Lacking strength or firmness; weak or spiritless; *a limp handshake.* [Probably from obsolete *lymphault,* lame, from Old English *lemphealt* : *lemp-,* hanging loosely + *-healt,* lame, limping.] **—limp′ly** *adv.*

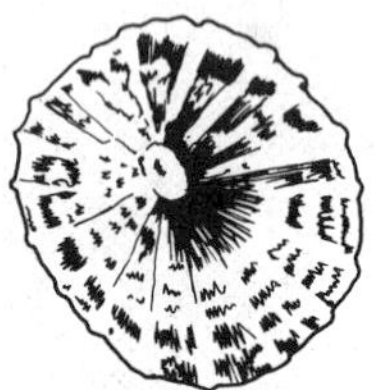

limpet
Top: Overhead view
Bottom: Profile

ă pat	oi boy
ā pay	ou out
âr care	ŏŏ took
ä father	ōō boot
ĕ pet	ŭ cut
ē be	ûr urge
ĭ pit	th thin
ī pie	*th* this
îr pier	hw which
ŏ pot	zh vision
ō toe	ə about, item
ô paw	♦ regionalism

Stress marks: ′ (primary); ′ (secondary), as in **dictionary** (dĭk′shə-nĕr′ē)

SYNONYMS: *limp, flabby, flaccid, floppy.* The central meaning shared by these adjectives is "lacking in stiffness or firmness": *a limp shirt collar; flabby, wrinkled flesh; flaccid cheeks; a floppy hat brim.*
ANTONYM: *firm.*

lim·pet (lĭm′pĭt) *n.* **1.** Any of numerous marine gastropod mollusks, as of the families Acmaeidae and Patellidae, characteristically having a conical shell and adhering to rocks of tidal areas. **2.** One that clings persistently. **3.** A type of explosive designed to cling to the hull of a ship and detonate on contact or signal. [Possibly Middle English *lempet,* European limpet (sense uncertain).]

lim·pid (lĭm′pĭd) *adj.* **1.** Characterized by transparent clearness; pellucid. See Synonyms at **clear. 2.** Easily intelligible; clear: *writes in a limpid style.* **3.** Calm and untroubled; serene. [Latin *limpidus.*] **—lim·pid′i·ty, lim′pid·ness** *n.*

limp·kin (lĭmp′kĭn) *n.* A large brownish wading bird *(Aramus guarauna)* of warm, swampy regions of the New World, having long legs, a drooping bill, and a distinctive wailing call. Also called *courlan.* [From its gait.]

Lim·po·po (lĭm-pō′pō) also **Croc·o·dile River** (krŏk′ə-dīl′). A river of southeast Africa rising near Johannesburg in northeast South Africa and flowing about 1,770 km (1,100 mi) to the Indian Ocean in southern Mozambique.

lim·u·lus (lĭm′yə-ləs) *n., pl.* **-li** (-lī, -lē). See **horseshoe crab.** [Latin *līmulus,* sidelong (from its motion), diminutive of *līmus.*]

Lin (lĭn), **Maya.** Born 1959. American sculptor and architect whose public works include the Vietnam Veterans Memorial in Washington, D.C. (1982).

lin. *abbr.* **1.** Lineal. **2.** Linear.

lin·ac (lĭn′ăk′) *n.* See **linear accelerator.** [LIN(EAR) AC(CELERATOR).]

lin·age also **line·age** (lī′nĭj) *n.* **1.** The number of lines of printed or written material. **2.** Payment for written work at a specified amount per line.

lin·al·o·ol (lĭ-năl′ō-ôl′, -ōl′, -ŏl′) *n.* A colorless, fragrant liquid, $(CH_3)_2CCH(CH_2)_2CCH_3OCOCH_3CHCH_2$, distilled from the oils of rosewood, bergamot, and other plants and trees and used in perfume manufacture. [Spanish *lináloe,* aloe (from Late Latin *lignum aloēs,* wood of the aloe : Latin *lignum,* wood; see LIGNI– + Latin *aloēs,* genitive of *aloē,* aloe; see ALOE) + –OL¹.]

Lin Biao (lĭn′ byou′) or **Lin Piao** (pyou′, byou′). 1907–1971. Chinese political leader. He fought to achieve a Communist takeover in China (1949) and became minister of defense (1959). Lin Biao compiled *Quotations from Chairman Mao Tse-tung,* the well-known "Little Red Book."

linch·pin or **lynch·pin** (lĭnch′pĭn′) *n.* **1.** A locking pin inserted in the end of a shaft, as in an axle, to prevent a wheel from slipping off. **2.** A central cohesive element: *Reduced spending is the linchpin of their economic program.* [Middle English *linspin* : *lins,* linchpin (from Old English *lynis*) + *pin,* pin (from Old English *pinn;* see PIN).]

Lin·coln¹ (lĭng′kən). **1.** A borough of eastern England northeast of Nottingham. Located on the site of Roman, Saxon, and Danish settlements, it was first chartered in 1157. Population, 75,900. **2.** A city of central Illinois north-northeast of Springfield. It was platted (1853) with the aid of Abraham Lincoln, who practiced law here from 1847 to 1859. Population, 16,327. **3.** The capital of Nebraska, in the southeast part of the state southwest of Omaha. Founded in 1864 as Lancaster, it was renamed when it was chosen as the state capital in 1867. Population, 171,932.

Lin·coln² (lĭng′kən) *n.* Any of a breed of sheep with long wool, developed in Lincolnshire, a county of eastern England.

Lincoln, Abraham. 1809–1865. The 16th President of the United States (1861–1865), who led the Union during the Civil War and emancipated slaves in the South (1863). He was assassinated shortly after the end of the war by John Wilkes Booth.

Lincoln, Mary Todd. 1818–1882. First Lady of the United States (1861–1865) as the wife of President Abraham Lincoln. Born in the South, she was criticized during the Civil War for allegedly having Confederate sympathies.

Lincoln, Mount. A peak, 4,357.2 m (14,286 ft) high, in the Rocky Mountains of central Colorado.

Lin·coln·esque (lĭng′kə-nĕsk′) *adj.* Suggestive of Abraham Lincoln.

Lincoln Park. A city of southeast Michigan, a residential suburb of Detroit. Population, 45,105.

lin·co·my·cin (lĭng′kə-mī′sĭn) *n.* An antibiotic derived from cultures of the bacterium *Streptomyces lincolnensis,* used in the treatment of certain penicillin-resistant infections. [*lincolnensis,* specific epithet + –MYCIN.]

Lind (lĭnd), **Jenny.** Known as "the Swedish Nightingale." 1820–1887. Swedish soprano who toured the United States (1850–1852) under the management of P.T. Barnum.

lin·dane (lĭn′dān) *n.* A white crystalline powder, $C_6H_6Cl_6$, used chiefly as an agricultural pesticide but also used topically in the treatment of scabies and pediculosis. [After Teunis van der *Linden,* 20th-century Dutch chemist.]

Lind·bergh (lĭnd′bûrg′, lĭn′-), **Anne Spencer Morrow.** Born 1906. American aviator and writer. She accompanied her husband, Charles Lindbergh, on many of his flights and wrote *North to the Orient* (1935) and *Listen! the Wind* (1938).

Lindbergh, Charles Augustus. Known as "Lucky Lindy." 1902–1974. American aviator who made the first solo transatlantic flight (May 20–21, 1927). His books include *We* (1936) and an autobiography, *The Spirit of St. Louis* (1953).

lin·den (lĭn′dən) *n.* Any of various deciduous shade trees of the genus *Tilia* having heart-shaped leaves, drooping cymose clusters of yellowish, often fragrant flowers, and peduncles united into a large lingulate bract. Also called *basswood, lime.* [Middle English, made of linden wood, from Old English, from *lind,* linden.]

Lin·den (lĭn′dən). A city of northeast New Jersey, an industrial center adjacent to Elizabeth. Population, 37,836.

Lin·den·hurst (lĭn′dən-hûrst′). A village of southeast New York on southern Long Island near Babylon. It is mainly residential. Population, 26,919.

Lin·den·wold (lĭn′dən-wōld′). A borough of southwest New Jersey southeast of Camden. It was settled in 1742. Population, 18,196.

Lin·dis·farne (lĭn′dĭs-färn′). See **Holy Island.**

Lind·ley (lĭnd′lē, lĭn′-), **John.** 1799–1865. British botanist and horticulturist who wrote *The Vegetable Kingdom* (1846).

Lind·say (lĭn′zē), **Howard.** 1889–1968. American playwright and producer who collaborated with Russel Crouse on a number of musical comedies, including *State of the Union* (1946).

Lindsay, (Nicholas) Vachel. 1879–1931. American poet who traveled the United States exchanging poems for room and board. His volumes include *General William Booth Enters Heaven and Other Poems* (1913) and *The Congo and Other Poems* (1914).

lin·dy or **Lin·dy** (lĭn′dē) *n., pl.* **-dies.** A lively swing dance for couples. Also called *lindy hop.* [After the name *Lindy,* nickname of Charles Augustus LINDBERGH.]

line¹ (līn) *n. Abbr.* **l. 1.** The path traced by a moving point. **2.a.** A thin continuous mark, as that made by a pen, pencil, or brush applied to a surface. **b.** A similar mark cut or scratched into a surface. **c.** A crease in the skin, especially on the face; a wrinkle. **3.a.** A real or imaginary mark positioned in relation to fixed points of reference. **b.** A degree or circle of longitude or latitude drawn on a map or globe. **c.** The equator. Used with *the.* **4.a.** A border or boundary: *the county line.* **b.** A demarcation: *a line of darker water beyond the reef.* **c.** A contour or an outline: *the line of the hills against the evening sky.* **5.a.** A mark used to define a shape or represent a contour. **b.** Any of the marks that make up the formal design of a picture. **6.a.** A cable, rope, string, cord or wire. **b.** *Nautical.* A rope used aboard a ship. **c.** A fishing line. **d.** A clothesline. **e.** A cord or tape used, as by builders or surveyors, for measuring, leveling, or straightening. **7.** A pipe or system of pipes for conveying a fluid: *gas lines.* **8.** An electric-power transmission cable. **9.a.** A wire or system of wires connecting telephone or telegraph systems. **b.** An open or functioning telephone connection: *tried to get a free line.* **10.a.** A passenger or cargo system of public or private transportation, as by ship, aircraft, or bus, usually over a definite route. **b.** A company owning or managing such a system. **11.a.** A railway track or system of tracks. **b.** A particular section of a railway network: *the Philadelphia–Trenton line.* **12.** A course of progress or movement; a route: *a line of flight.* **13.a.** A general method, manner, or course of procedure: *different lines of thought; took a hard line on defense.* **b.** A manner or course of procedure determined by a specified factor: *development along socialist lines.* **c.** An official or prescribed policy: *the party line.* **14.** Often **lines.** A general concept or model: *a trilogy along the lines of the* Oresteia. **15.** A condition of agreement; alignment: *brought the front wheels into line; a wage agreement in line with current inflation.* **16.a.** One's trade, occupation, or field of interest: *What line of work are you in?* **b.** Range of competence: *not in my line.* **17.** Merchandise or services of a similar or related nature: *carries a complete line of small tools.* **18.** A group of persons or things arranged in a row or series: *long lines at the box office; a line of stones.* **19.a.** Ancestry or lineage. **b.** A series of persons, especially from one family, who succeed each other: *a line of monarchs; comes from a long line of bankers.* **c.** A strain, as of livestock or plants, developed and maintained by selective breeding. **20.a.** A sequence of related things that leads to a certain ending: *a line of argument.* **b.** An ordered system of operations that allows a sequential manufacture or assembly of goods at all or various stages of production. **c.** The personnel of an organization or a business who actually make a product or perform a service. **21.a.** A horizontal row of printed or written words or symbols. **b.** One of the horizontal scans forming a television image. **22.** A brief letter; a note: *I'll drop you a line.* **23.a.** A unit of verse ending in a visual or typographic break and generally characterized by its length and meter: *a line of iambic pentameter.* **b.** Often **lines.** The dialogue of a theatrical presentation, such as a play: *spent the weekend learning her lines.* **24.** *Informal.* Glib or insincere talk, usually intended to deceive or impress: *He kept on handing me a line about how busy he is.* **25.** Abbr. **lines.** *Chiefly British.* **a.** A marriage certificate. **b.** A usually specified number of lines of prose or verse to be written out by a pupil as punishment. **26.** *Games.* A horizontal demarcation on a scorecard in bridge dividing the honor score from the trick score. **27.a.** A source of information. **b.** The information itself: *got a line on the computer project.* **28.a.** *Music.* One of the five parallel marks constituting a staff. **b.** A sustained melodic or harmonic part in a piece: *a rock song with a driving bass line.* **29.a.** A formation

Abraham Lincoln
1863 photograph by Alexander Gardner (1821–1882)

Mary Todd Lincoln
c. 1863-1865 photograph attributed to Mathew Brady

Charles Lindbergh
Photographed in 1927

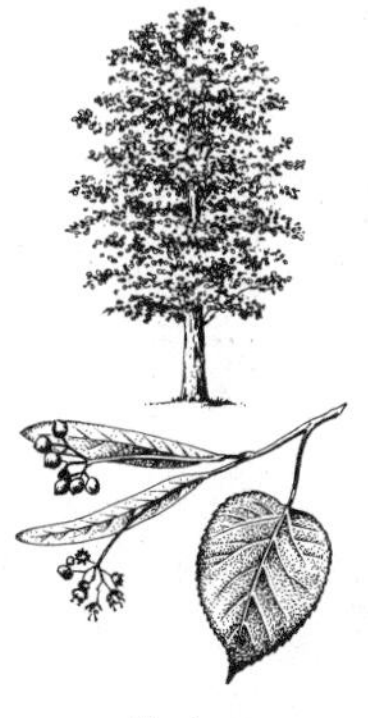
linden
American linden
Tilia americana

in which elements, such as troops, tanks, or ships, are arranged abreast of one another. **b.** The battle area closest to the enemy; the front. **c.** The combat troops or warships at the front, arrayed for defense or offense. **d.** The regular forces of an army or a navy, in contrast to staff and support personnel. **e.** The class of officers in direct command of warships or of army combat units. **f.** A bulwark or trench. **g.** An extended system of such fortifications or defenses: *the Siegfried line.* **30.** *Sports.* **a.** A foul line. **b.** A real or imaginary mark demarcating a specified section of a playing area or field. **c.** A real or imaginary mark or point at which a race begins or ends. **d.** The center and two wings making up a hockey team's offensive unit. **31. a.** A line of scrimmage. **b.** The linemen considered as a group. **32.** *Informal.* The odds a bookmaker gives, especially for sports events. **33. a.** A kind of coverage available in insurance. **b.** The proportion of an insurance risk assumed by a particular underwriter or company. **34.** *Slang.* A small amount of cocaine arranged in a thin, usually tightly rolled strip for sniffing. **35.** *Archaic.* One's lot or position in life. **—line** *v.* **lined, lin·ing, lines.** *—tr.* **1.** To mark, incise, or cover with a line or lines. **2.** To represent with lines. **3.** To place in a series or row. **4.** To form a bordering line along: *Small stalls lined the alley.* **5.** *Baseball. To hit (a ball) sharply, usually in a straight line.* *—intr.* *Baseball.* To hit a line drive: *lined out to shortstop.* ***—phrasal verb.*** **line up. 1.** To arrange in or form a line. **2.** To organize and make ready: *lined up considerable support for the bill.* ***—idioms.*** **all along the line. 1.** In every place. **2.** At every stage or moment. **down the line. 1.** All the way; throughout: *Errors are to be found down the line.* **2.** At a point or an end in the future. **in line for.** Next in order for: *in line for the presidency.* **on the line. 1.** Ready or available for immediate payment. **2.** So as to be risked; in jeopardy: *"Careers were on the line once again"* (Seymour M. Hersh). **out of line. 1.** Uncalled-for; improper. **2.** Unruly and out of control. [Middle English, from Old English *līne* and from Old French *ligne,* both from Latin *līnea,* feminine sing. of *līneus,* of linen, from *līnum,* thread, linen. See **līno-** in Appendix.]

line² (līn) *tr.v.* **lined, lin·ing, lines. 1.** To fit a covering to the inside surface of: *a coat lined with fur.* **2.** To cover the inner surface of: *Moisture lined the walls of the cave.* **3.** To fill plentifully, as with money or food. [Middle English *linen,* from *line,* flax, linen cloth, from Old English *līn,* from Latin *līnum.* See **līno-** in Appendix.]

lin·e·age¹ (lĭn′ē-ĭj) *n.* **1. a.** Direct descent from a particular ancestor; ancestry. **b.** Derivation. **2.** The descendants of a common ancestor considered to be the founder of the line. [Middle English *linage, lineage,* from Old French *lignage,* from *ligne,* line. See LINE¹.]

line·age² (lī′nĭj) *n.* Variant of **linage.**

lin·e·al (lĭn′ē-əl) *adj.* *Abbr.* **lin. 1.** Belonging to or being in the direct line of descent from an ancestor. **2.** Derived from or relating to a particular line of descent; hereditary. **3.** Linear. [Middle English, from Old French, from Late Latin *līneālis,* consisting of lines, from Latin *līnea,* line. See LINE¹.] **—lin′e·al·ly** *adv.*

lin·e·a·ment (lĭn′ē-ə-mənt) *n.* **1.** A distinctive shape, contour, or line, especially of the face. **2.** Often **lineaments.** A definitive or characteristic feature. [Middle English *liniament,* from Latin *līneāmentum,* from *līnea,* line. See LINE¹.]

lin·e·ar (lĭn′ē-ər) *adj.* *Abbr.* **lin. 1.** Of, relating to, or resembling a line; straight. **2. a.** In, of, describing, described by, or related to a straight line. **b.** Having only one dimension. **3.** Characterized by, composed of, or emphasizing drawn lines rather than painterly effects. **4.** *Botany.* Narrow and elongated with nearly parallel margins: *a linear leaf.* [Latin *līneāris,* from *līnea,* line. See LINE¹.] **—lin′e·ar·ly** *adv.*

Lin·e·ar A (lĭn′ē-ər) *n.* An undeciphered writing system used in Crete from the 18th to the 15th century B.C.

linear accelerator *n.* An electron, a proton, or a heavy-ion accelerator in which the paths of the particles accelerated are essentially straight lines rather than circles or spirals. Also called *linac.*

linear algebra *n.* *Mathematics.* **1.** The branch of mathematics that deals with the theory of systems of linear equations, matrices, vector spaces, determinants, and linear transformations. **2.** A mathematical ring and vector space with scalars from an associated field, the multiplication of which is of the form $(a\mathbf{A})(b\mathbf{B}) = (ab)(\mathbf{AB})$, where a and b are scalars and $\mathbf{A}$ and $\mathbf{B}$ are vectors.

Linear B *n.* A syllabic script used in Mycenaean Greek documents chiefly from Crete and Pylos, mostly from the 14th to the 12th century B.C.

linear combination *n.* *Mathematics.* An expression of first order, composed of the sums and differences of elements with non-zero coefficients.

linear dependence *n.* *Mathematics.* The property of a set with the coefficients of another set of having at least one linear combination equal to zero when at least one of the coefficients is not equal to zero.

linear equation *n.* *Mathematics.* An algebraic equation, such as $y = 2x + 7$, in which the highest degree term in the variable or variables is of the first degree. The graph of such an equation is a straight line.

linear independence *n.* *Mathematics.* The property of a set with the coefficients of another set of having no linear combinations equal to zero unless all of the coefficients are equal to zero.

lin·e·ar·ize (lĭn′ē-ə-rīz′) *tr.v.* **-ized, -iz·ing, -iz·es.** To put in linear form. **—lin′e·ar·i·za′tion** (-ər-ĭ-zā′shən) *n.*

linear measure *n.* **1.** The measurement of length. **2.** A unit or system of units for measuring length. Also called *long measure.*

linear momentum *n.* See **momentum** (sense 1).

linear perspective *n.* A form of perspective in drawing and painting in which parallel lines are represented as converging so as to give the illusion of depth and distance.

lin·e·a·tion (lĭn′ē-ā′shən) *n.* **1.** The act of marking or outlining with lines. **2.** An outline. **3.** An arrangement of lines. [Middle English *lineacioun,* from Latin *līneātiō, līneātiōn-,* from *līneātus,* past participle of *līneāre,* to make straight, from *līnea,* thread, line. See LINE¹.]

line·back·er (līn′băk′ər) *n.* *Football.* Any of the defensive players forming a second line of defense behind the ends and tackles. **—line′back′ing** *n.*

line breeding *n.* Selective inbreeding to perpetuate certain desired qualities or characteristics in a strain of livestock.

line cut *n.* A letterpress printing plate made from a line drawing by a photoengraving process. Also called *line engraving.*

line drawing *n.* A drawing made with lines only, especially one used as copy for a line cut.

line drive *n.* *Baseball.* A batted ball hit sharply so that its path roughly describes a straight line.

line engraving *n.* **1. a.** A metal plate, used in intaglio printing, on the surface of which design lines have been engraved by hand. **b.** The process of making such an engraving. **c.** A print made from such an engraving. **2.** See **line cut.**

Line Islands (līn). A group of islands in the central Pacific Ocean south of Hawaii and astride the equator. First visited in 1798 by American sailors, the islands are now part of Kiribati.

line item *n.* A single item, especially of a legislative appropriations bill: *Most governors have the power to veto line items of the proposed state budget.* **—line′-i′tem** (līn′ī′təm) *adj.*

line·man (līn′mən) *n.* **1.** A person employed to install or repair telephone, telegraph, or electric power lines. Also called *linesman.* **2.** A man employed to inspect and repair railroad tracks. **3.** *Football.* A player positioned on the forward line.

lin·en (lĭn′ən) *n.* **1. a.** Thread made from fibers of the flax plant. **b.** Cloth woven from this thread. **2.** Also **linens.** Articles or garments made from linen or a similar cloth, such as cotton; bed sheets and tablecloths. **3.** Paper made from flax fibers or having a linenlike luster. **—linen** *adj.* **1.** Made of flax or linen. **2.** Resembling linen. [Middle English, from Old English *līnen,* made of flax, from Germanic **līnin-,* from **līnam,* flax, probably from Latin *līnum.* See **līno-** in Appendix.]

line of credit *n., pl.* **lines of credit.** See **credit line** (sense 2).

line officer *n.* A commissioned officer in the armed forces who is assigned to the line for duty.

line of force *n., pl.* **lines of force.** A theoretical line in a field of force, such that a tangent at any point gives the direction of the field at that point.

line of scrimmage *n., pl.* **lines of scrimmage.** *Abbr.* **LOS** *Football.* An imaginary line across the field on which the ball rests and at which the teams line up for a new play.

line of sight *n., pl.* **lines of sight.** *Abbr.* **LOS 1.** An imaginary line from the eye to a perceived object. **2.** An unobstructed path between sending and receiving antennas.

lin·e·o·late (lĭn′ē-ə-lāt′) *adj.* Marked with fine lines. [New Latin *līneolātus,* from Latin *līneola,* diminutive of *līnea,* thread, line. See LINE¹.]

line printer *n.* A high-speed printing device, primarily used in data processing, that prints an entire line of type as a unit instead of printing each character individually.

lin·er¹ (lī′nər) *n.* **1.** One that draws or makes lines. **2.** A large commercial ship or airplane, especially one carrying passengers on a regular route. **3.** *Baseball.* A line drive.

lin·er² (lī′nər) *n.* **1.** One that makes or puts in linings. **2. a.** A lining. **b.** Material used as a lining. **3.** A jacket for a phonograph record.

lin·er·board (lī′nər-bôrd′, -bōrd′) *n.* A type of paperboard used in making corrugated cartons.

line score *n.* *Sports.* A summary of the scoring by period in a game displayed in the form of a horizontal table, especially an inning-by-inning record of the runs scored in a baseball game followed by the total of each team's runs, hits, and errors.

lines·man (līnz′mən) *n.* **1. a.** *Football.* An official who marks the downs and the position of the ball and watches for certain violations from the sidelines. **b.** *Sports.* A man in various court games whose chief duty is to call shots that fall out of bounds. **2.** See **lineman** (sense 1).

line spectrum *n.* A spectrum produced by a luminous gas or vapor and appearing as distinct lines characteristic of the various elements constituting the gas.

line squall *n.* A squall or a series of squalls occurring along a narrow band of thunderstorms.

line storm *n.* A violent storm or a series of storms of rain and wind believed to take place during the equinoxes.

lines·wom·an (līnz′wo͝om′ən) *n.* *Sports.* A woman in various court games whose chief duty is to call shots that fall out of bounds.

line·up also **line-up** (līn′ŭp′) *n.* **1.** A line of people that is formed for inspection or identification. **2.** *Sports.* **a.** The members of a team chosen to start a game. **b.** A list of such players. **3.** A group of people or organizations enlisted or arrayed for a purpose: *a candidate with an impressive lineup of endorsements.*

ling¹ (lĭng) *n., pl.* **ling** or **lings.** Any of various marine food fishes related to or resembling the cod, especially *Molva molva* of northern European waters. [Middle English, possibly of Low German origin. See **del-¹** in Appendix.]

ling² (lĭng) *n.* See **heather** (sense 1). [Middle English, from Old Norse *lyng.*]

ling. *abbr.* Linguistics.

–ling¹ *suff.* **1.** One connected with: *worldling.* **2.** One having a specified quality: *underling.* **3.** One that is young, small, or inferior: *duckling.* [Middle English, from Old English.]

–ling² *suff.* In a specified direction, manner, way, or condition: *darkling.* [Middle English, from Old English.]

lin·ga (lĭn′gə) *n. Hinduism.* Variant of **lingam.**

Lin·ga·la (lĭng-gä′lə) *n.* A creole based on Bantu, widely spoken as a lingua franca in Zaire.

lin·gam (lĭng′gəm) also **lin·ga** (lĭn′-gə) *n. Hinduism.* A stylized phallus worshiped as a symbol of the god Shiva. [Sanskrit *liṅgam,* mark, penis.]

Lin·ga·yen Gulf (lĭng′gä-yĕn′). An inlet of the South China Sea on the western coast of Luzon, Philippines. It was captured by the Japanese in December 1941 and retaken by American forces in January 1945.

ling·ber·ry (lĭng′bĕr′ē) *n.* See **cowberry.** [Variant of LINGONBERRY.]

ling·cod (lĭng′kŏd′) *n., pl.* **lingcod** or **-cods.** A large, northern Pacific food fish *(Ophiodon elongatus)* related to the greenling.

lin·ger (lĭng′gər) *v.* **-gered, -ger·ing, -gers.** —*intr.* **1.** To be slow in leaving, especially out of reluctance; tarry. See Synonyms at **stay¹.** **2.** To remain feebly alive for some time before dying. **3.** To persist: *an aftertaste that lingers.* **4.** To proceed slowly; saunter. **5.** To be tardy in acting; procrastinate. —*tr.* To pass (a period of time) in a leisurely or aimless manner. [Middle English *lengeren,* frequentative of *lengen,* to prolong, from Old English *lengan.* See **del-¹** in Appendix.] —**lin′ger·er** *n.* —**lin′ger·ing·ly** *adv.*

lin·ge·rie (län′zhə-rā′, län′zhə-rē, lăN-zhə-rē′) *n.* **1.** Women's underclothes. **2.** *Archaic.* Linen articles, especially garments. [French, from Old French, from *linge,* linen, from Latin *līneus,* made of linen, from *līnum,* flax. See **līno-** in Appendix.]

lin·go (lĭng′gō) *n., pl.* **-goes.** **1.** Language that is unintelligible or unfamiliar. **2.** The specialized vocabulary of a particular field or discipline: *spoke to me in the lingo of fundamentalism.* See Synonyms at **dialect.** [Probably from Portuguese *lingoa,* from Latin *lingua,* language. See **dn̥ghū-** in Appendix.]

WORD HISTORY: A look at the Indo-European roots entry for *dn̥ghū-* will show that the words *tongue, language,* and *lingo* are related, all going back to the Indo-European root *dn̥ghū-,* "tongue." The relationship between *language* and *lingo* is not particularly surprising given their related meanings and common root, but one might be curious as to the routes by which these two words came into English. *Language,* as did so many of our important borrowings from Latin, passed through French into English during the Middle Ages, the forms involved being Latin *lingua,* "language," its descendant, Old French *langue,* and its derivative, *langage. Lingo,* on the other hand, entered English after the end of the Middle Ages when Europe had opened itself to the larger world. We have probably borrowed *lingo* from *lingoa,* a Portuguese descendant of Latin *lingua.* The Portuguese were great traders before the English were, and it is not unlikely that the sense "foreign language" was strengthened as the Portuguese traveled around the world. Interestingly enough, the first recorded instance of *lingo* in English is in the New World (1660) in a reference to the "Dutch lingo." The development in sense to "unintelligible language" and "specialized language" is an obvious one.

lin·gon·ber·ry (lĭng′ən-bĕr′ē) *n.* See **cowberry.** [Swedish *lingon,* a kind of berry + BERRY.]

lin·gua (lĭng′gwə) *n., pl.* **-guae** (-gwē′). A tongue or tonguelike organ. [Latin, tongue, language. See **dn̥ghū-** in Appendix.]

lingua fran·ca (frăng′kə) *n., pl.* **lingua fran·cas** (-kəz) also **linguae fran·cae** (-kē). **1.** A medium of communication between peoples of different languages. **2.** A mixture of Italian with Provençal, French, Spanish, Arabic, Greek, and Turkish, formerly spoken on the eastern Mediterranean coast. [Italian : *lingua,* language + *franca,* Frankish (that is, European).]

lin·gual (lĭng′gwəl) *adj.* **1.** Of, relating to, or situated near the tongue or a tonguelike organ. **2.** *Linguistics.* Pronounced with the tongue in conjunction with other organs of speech. **3.** Of languages; linguistic: *lingual diversity.* —**lingual** *n. Linguistics.* A sound, such as (t), (l), and (n), that is pronounced with the tongue and other organs of speech. —**lin′gual·ly** *adv.*

lin·gui·ne also **lin·gui·ni** (lĭng-gwē′nē) *n.* Pasta in the form of long, flat, thin strands. [Italian, pl. of *linguina,* diminutive of *lingua,* tongue, from Latin. See LINGUA.]

lin·guist (lĭng′gwĭst) *n.* **1.** A person who speaks several languages fluently. **2.** A specialist in linguistics. [Latin *lingua,* language; see **dn̥ghū-** in Appendix + -IST.]

lin·guis·tic (lĭng-gwĭs′tĭk) *adj.* Of or relating to language or linguistics. —**lin·guis′ti·cal·ly** *adv.*

linguistic atlas *n.* A set of maps recording the geographic distribution of variations in speech. Also called *dialect atlas.*

linguistic form *n.* A meaningful unit of speech, such as an affix, a word, a phrase, or a sentence.

linguistic geography *n.* The branch of linguistics that involves the study of regional variations of speech forms. Also called *dialect geography.* —**linguistic geographer** *n.*

lin·guis·tics (lĭng-gwĭs′tĭks) *n. (used with a sing. verb). Abbr.* **ling.** The study of the nature and structure of human speech.

lin·gu·late (lĭng′gyə-lāt′) *adj.* Shaped like a tongue: *lingulate antennae.* [Latin *lingulātus,* from *lingula,* diminutive of *lingua.* See LINGUA.]

lin·i·ment (lĭn′ə-mənt) *n.* A medicinal fluid rubbed into the skin to soothe pain or relieve stiffness. [Middle English, from Late Latin *linīmentum,* from Latin *linere, linīre,* to rub over, anoint. See **lei-** in Appendix.]

li·nin (lī′nĭn) *n.* The filamentous, achromatic material in the nucleus of a cell that interconnects chromatin granules. [Latin *līnum,* thread; see **līno-** in Appendix + -IN.]

lin·ing (lī′nĭng) *n.* **1.** A covering or coating for an inside surface: *The jacket had a patterned lining.* **2.** Material used for such covering or coating.

link¹ (lĭngk) *n.* **1.** One of the rings or loops forming a chain. **2.a.** A unit in a connected series of units: *links of sausage; one link in a molecular chain.* **b.** A unit in a transportation or communications system. **c.** A connecting element; a tie or bond: *grandparents, our link with the past.* **3.a.** An association; a relationship: *The Alumnae Association is my link to the school's present administration.* **b.** A causal, parallel, or reciprocal relationship; a correlation: *Researchers have detected a link between smoking and heart disease.* **4.** A cuff link. **5.** *Abbr.* **li.** A unit of length used in surveying, equal to 0.01 chain, 7.92 inches, or about 20.12 centimeters. **6.** A rod or lever transmitting motion in a machine. **7.** *Computer Science.* An identifying term attached to an element in a system to facilitate connection to other identified elements. —**link** *tr. & intr.v.* **linked, link·ing, links.** To connect or become connected with or as if with a link. See Synonyms at **join.** [Middle English *linke,* of Scandinavian origin; akin to Old Norse *hlekkr,* *hlenkr.] —**link′er** *n.*

link² (lĭngk) *n.* A torch formerly used for lighting one's way in the streets. [Possibly from Medieval Latin *linchinus, lichnus,* candle, from Latin *lychnus,* from Greek *lukhnos,* lamp. See **leuk-** in Appendix.]

link·age (lĭng′kĭj) *n.* **1.a.** The act or process of linking. **b.** The condition of being linked. **2.** A connection or relation; an association. **3.** A negotiating policy of making agreement on one issue dependent on progress toward another objective. **4.** A system of interconnected machine elements, such as rods, springs, and pivots, used to transmit power or motion. **5.** *Electricity.* A measure of the induced voltage in a circuit caused by a magnetic flux and equal to the flux times the number of turns in the coil that surrounds it. **6.** *Genetics.* An association between two or more genes such that the traits they control tend to be inherited together.

linkage group *n.* A pair or set of genes on a chromosome that tend to be transmitted together.

linked (lĭngkt) *adj.* **1.** Connected, especially by or as if by links. **2.** *Genetics.* Exhibiting linkage. **3.** *Computer Science.* Provided with links.

link·ing verb (lĭng′kĭng) *n.* See **copula** (sense 1).

Lin·kö·ping (lĭn′chœ′pĭng). A city of southeast Sweden southwest of Stockholm. It was a noted intellectual and religious center during the Middle Ages. Population, 115,600.

links (lĭngks) *pl.n.* **1.** *Sports.* A golf course. **2.** *Scots.* Relatively flat or undulating sandy turf-covered ground usually along a seashore. [From Middle English *link,* ridge of land, hill, from Old English *hlinc,* ridge.]

link·up (lĭngk′ŭp′) *n.* **1.** The act of linking or connecting: *a linkup of two orbiting spacecraft.* **2.** Something that serves to link or join; a connection. **3.** A set of linked elements that forms a functioning system: *a closed-circuit TV linkup.*

linn (lĭn) *n. Scots.* **1.** A waterfall. **2.** A steep ravine. [Scottish Gaelic *linne,* pool, waterfall.]

Lin·nae·an also **Lin·ne·an** (lĭ-nē′ən) *adj. Abbr.* **L.** Of or relating to Carolus Linnaeus or to the system of taxonomic classification and binomial nomenclature that he originated.

Lin·nae·us (lĭ-nē′əs, -nā′-), **Carolus.** Known as "Karl Linné." 1707–1778. Swedish botanist and founder of the modern classification system for plants and animals.

lin·net (lĭn′ĭt) *n.* **1.** A small Old World finch *(Carduelis cannabina)* having brownish plumage. **2.** A similar bird *(Carpodacus mexicanus)* of Mexico and the western United States. In this sense, also called *house finch.* [Obsolete French *linette,* from Old French, from *lin,* flax (from its feeding on flax seed), from Latin *līnum.* See **līno-** in Appendix.]

Linn·he (lĭn′ē), **Loch.** An inlet of the Atlantic Ocean on the western coast of Scotland.

lin·o·le·ic acid (lĭn′ə-lē′ĭk) *n.* An unsaturated fatty acid,

ă pat	oi boy
ā pay	ou out
âr care	ŏŏ took
ä father	ōō boot
ĕ pet	ŭ cut
ē be	ûr urge
ĭ pit	th thin
ī pie	*th* this
îr pier	hw which
ŏ pot	zh vision
ō toe	ə about, item
ô paw	♦ regionalism

Stress marks: ′ (primary); ′ (secondary), as in **dictionary** (dĭk′shə-nĕr′ē)

$C_{17}H_{31}COOH$, considered essential to the human diet, that is an important component of drying oils, such as linseed oil. [Greek *linon,* flax; see **līno-** in Appendix + OLEIC ACID.]

lin·o·len·ic acid (lĭn′ə-lĕn′ĭk) *n.* An unsaturated fatty acid, $C_{17}H_{29}COOH$, considered essential to the human diet, that is an important component of natural drying oils. [Blend of LINOLEIC ACID and -ENE.]

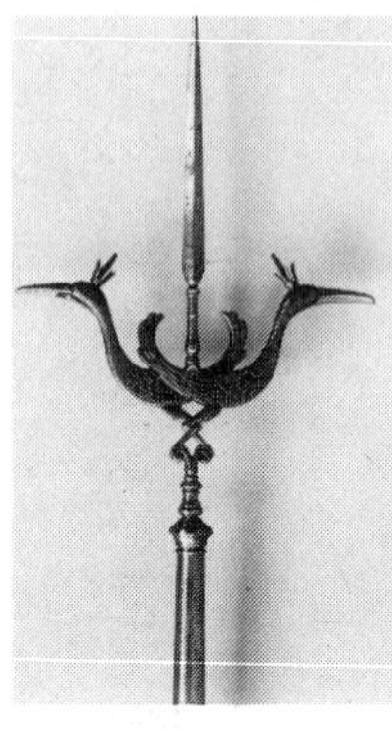

linstock
17th-century linstock head

li·no·le·um (lĭ-nō′lē-əm) *n.* A durable, washable material made in sheets by pressing a mixture of heated linseed oil, rosin, powdered cork, and pigments onto a burlap or canvas backing. Linoleum is used as a covering especially for floors. [Originally a trademark.]

Li·no·type (lī′nə-tīp′). A trademark used for a machine that sets type on a metal slug, operated by a keyboard.

Lin Piao (lĭn′ pyou′, byou′). See **Lin Biao.**

lin·sang (lĭn′săng′) *n.* Any of several Asian or African catlike carnivorous mammals of the genera *Poiana* or *Prionodon,* having a spotted coat and a long banded tail. [Malay.]

lin·seed (lĭn′sēd′) *n.* The seed of flax, especially when used as the source of linseed oil; flaxseed. [Middle English *linsed,* from Old English *līnsǣd* : *līn,* flax (from Latin *līnum;* see **līno-** in Appendix) + *sǣd,* seed; see SEED.]

linseed oil *n.* A yellowish oil extracted from the seeds of flax and used as a drying oil in paints and varnishes and in linoleum, printing inks, and synthetic resins.

lin·sey-wool·sey (lĭn′zē-wo͝ol′zē) *n., pl.* **-seys.** A coarse, woven fabric of wool and cotton or of wool and linen. [Middle English *linsiwolsie* : alteration of *linen,* linen; see LINEN + *wolle,* wool; see WOOL.]

lin·stock (lĭn′stŏk′) *n.* A long forked stick for holding a match, formerly used to fire cannon. [Obsolete *lyntstock,* alteration (possibly influenced by LINT, used for tinder) of Dutch *lontstok* : *lont,* match + *stok,* stick (from Middle Dutch *stoc*).]

lint (lĭnt) *n.* **1.** Clinging bits of fiber and fluff; fuzz. **2.** Downy material obtained by scraping linen cloth and used for dressing wounds. **3.** The mass of soft fibers surrounding the seeds of unginned cotton. [Middle English, variant of *linet* (from Old French *linette,* grain of flax, diminutive of *lin,* flax) or from Medieval Latin *linteum,* lint (from Latin, linen cloth), both from Latin *līnum,* flax. See **līno-** in Appendix.] **—lint′less** *adj.* **—lint′y** *adj.*

lin·tel (lĭn′tl) *n.* The horizontal beam that forms the upper member of a window or door frame and supports the structure above it. [Middle English, from Old French, probably alteration of *lintier,* from Vulgar Latin **līmitāris,* of a threshold (meaning influenced by Latin *līmen,* threshold), from Latin, on a border, from *līmes, līmit-,* boundary.]

lint·er (lĭn′tər) *n.* **1.** Often **linters.** The short fibers that cling to cottonseeds after the first ginning. **2.** A machine that removes these short fibers from the seeds of cotton.

lint·white (lĭnt′hwīt′, -wīt′) *n.* A linnet. [By folk etymology from Middle English *linkwhitte,* alteration of Old English *līnetwige* : *līn,* flax; see LINSEED + *-twige,* plucker, eater.]

lin·u·ron (lĭn′yə-rŏn′) *n.* A herbicide, $C_9H_{10}Cl_2N_2O_2$, used to kill weeds selectively. [Origin unknown.]

Lin Yu·tang (lĭn′ yo͞o′täng′). 1895–1976. Chinese-born American philologist who wrote a number of books on China, including *My Country and My People* (1936).

Linz (lĭnts). A city of northern Austria on the Danube River west of Vienna. Originally a Roman settlement, it was a provincial capital of the Holy Roman Empire in the late 15th century. Population, 199,910.

li·on (lī′ən) *n.* **1.** A large, carnivorous, feline mammal *(Panthera leo)* of Africa and northwest India, having a short tawny coat, a tufted tail, and, in the male, a long heavy mane around the neck and shoulders. **2.** Any of several large wildcats related to or resembling the lion. **3. a.** A very brave person. **b.** A person regarded as fierce or ferocious. **c.** An eminent person; a celebrity: *a literary lion.* **—*idiom.* lion's share.** The greatest or best part. [Middle English, from Old French, from Latin *leō, leōn-,* from Greek *leōn,* of Semitic origin; akin to Hebrew *lābî'.*]

Li·on (lī′ən) *n.* See **Leo.**

li·on·ess (lī′ə-nĭs) *n.* A female lion.

li·on·fish (lī′ən-fĭsh′) *n., pl.* **lionfish** or **-fish·es.** Any of various brightly colored tropical Pacific scorpion fishes of the genus *Pterois,* having venomous spines in the dorsal fin.

li·on·heart·ed (lī′ən-här′tĭd) *adj.* Extraordinarily courageous.

li·on·ize (lī′ə-nīz′) *tr.v.* **-ized, -iz·ing, -iz·es.** To look on or treat (a person) as a celebrity. **—li′on·i·za′tion** (lī′ə-nĭ-zā′shən) *n.* **—li′on·iz′er** *n.*

Li·ons (lī′ənz), **Gulf of.** A wide inlet of the Mediterranean Sea on the southern coast of France.

lion
Female and male lions
Panthera leo

lip (lĭp) *n.* **1.** *Anatomy.* Either of two fleshy folds that surround the opening of the mouth. **2.** A structure or part that encircles or bounds an orifice, as: **a.** *Anatomy.* A labium. **b.** The margin of flesh around a wound. **c.** Either of the margins of the aperture of a gastropod shell. **d.** A rim, as of a vessel, bell, or crater. **3.** *Botany.* One of the two divisions of bilabiate corolla or calyx, as in the snapdragon, or the modified upper petal of an orchid flower. **4.** The tip of a pouring spout, as on a pitcher. **5.** *Slang.* Insolent talk. **—lip** *tr.v.* **lipped, lip·ping, lips. 1. a.** To touch the lips to. **b.** To kiss. **2.** To utter. **3.** To lap or splash against. **4.** *Sports.* To hit a golf ball so that it touches the edge of (the hole) without dropping in. [Middle English, from Old English *lippa.* See **leb-** in Appendix.] **—lip′less** *adj.*

lip– *pref.* Variant of **lipo–.**

Li·pan (lĭ-pän′) *n., pl.* **Lipan** or **-pans. 1. a.** An Apache tribe formerly inhabiting western Texas, with a present-day population in southern New Mexico. **b.** A member of this tribe. **2.** The Apachean language of this tribe.

Lip·a·ri Islands (lĭp′ə-rē, lē′pä-). Formerly **Ae·o·li·an Islands** (ē-ō′lē-ən). A group of volcanic islands of Italy off the northeast coast of Sicily in the Tyrrhenian Sea.

lip·ase (lĭp′ās′, lī′pās′) *n.* Any of a group of enzymes that catalyze the hydrolysis of fats into glycerol and fatty acids.

Lip·chitz (lĭp′shĭts), **Jacques.** 1891–1973. Russian-born French sculptor who was associated with the cubists.

lip·ec·to·my (lĭ-pĕk′tə-mē, lī-) *n., pl.* **-mies.** Surgical excision of subcutaneous fatty tissue.

Li·petsk (lē′pĕtsk′, lyĕ′pyĭtsk). A city of west-central Russia south-southeast of Moscow. Originally founded in the 13th century, it was rebuilt in 1707 as a metallurgical center by orders of Peter the Great. Population, 447,000.

lip-gloss (lĭp′glôs′, -glŏs′) *n.* A cosmetic that gives shine or gloss to the lips.

lip·id (lĭp′ĭd, lī′pĭd) also **lip·ide** (lĭp′īd′, lī′pīd′) *n.* Any of a group of organic compounds, including the fats, oils, waxes, sterols, and triglycerides, that are insoluble in water but soluble in common organic solvents, are oily to the touch, and together with carbohydrates and proteins constitute the principal structural material of living cells. [French *lipide* : Greek *lipos,* fat; see LIPO– + French *-ide,* -ide.] **—lip·id′ic** *adj.*

Lip·mann (lĭp′mən), **Fritz Albert.** 1899–1986. German-born American biochemist. He shared a 1953 Nobel Prize for studies of metabolic processes.

Li Po (lē′ pō′, bō′) or **Li Bo** (bō′). Died c. 762. Chinese poet.

lipo– or **lip–** *pref.* Fat; fatty; fatty tissue: *lipolysis.* [From Greek *lipos,* fat. See **leip-** in Appendix.]

lip·oid (lĭp′oid′, lī′poid′) *n.* **1.** A lipid. **2.** Any of various substances, such as lecithin, that resemble fat. **—lipoid** also **li·poi·dal** (lĭ-poid′l, lī-) *adj.* Resembling fat; fatty.

li·pol·y·sis (lĭ-pŏl′ĭ-sĭs, lī-) *n., pl.* **-ses** (-sēz′). The hydrolysis of lipids. **—lip′o·lyt′ic** (lĭp′ə-lĭt′ĭk, lī′pə-) *adj.*

li·po·ma (lĭ-pō′mə, lī-) *n., pl.* **-ma·ta** (-mə-tə) or **-mas.** A benign tumor composed chiefly of fat cells. **—li·pom′a·tous** (-pŏm′ə-təs) *adj.*

lip·o·phil·ic (lĭp′ə-fĭl′ĭk, lī′pə-) *adj.* Having an affinity for, tending to combine with, or capable of dissolving in lipids.

lip·o·pol·y·sac·cha·ride (lĭp′ō-pŏl′ē-săk′ə-rīd′, lī′pō-) *n.* Any of a group of polysaccharides in which a lipid constitutes a portion of the molecule.

lip·o·pro·tein (lĭp′ō-prō′tēn′, -tē-ĭn, lī′pō-) *n.* Any of a group of conjugated proteins in which at least one of the components is a lipid. Lipoproteins, classified according to their densities and chemical qualities, are the principal means by which lipids are transported in the blood.

lip·o·some (lĭp′ə-sōm′, lī′pə-) *n.* An artificial microscopic vesicle consisting of an aqueous core enclosed in one or more phospholipid layers, used to convey vaccines, drugs, enzymes, or other substances to target cells or organs. **—lip′o·so′mal** *adj.*

lip·o·suc·tion (lĭp′ō-sŭk′shən, lī′pō-) *n.* A usually cosmetic surgical procedure in which excess fatty tissue is removed from a specific area of the body, such as the thighs or abdomen, by means of suction. Also called *suction lipectomy.*

lip·o·trop·ic (lĭp′ō-trŏp′ĭk, -trō′pĭk, lī′pō-) *adj.* **1.** Preventing abnormal or excessive accumulation of fat in the liver. **2.** Having an affinity for lipids. **—li·pot′ro·py** (lĭ-pŏt′rə-pē, lī-), **li·pot′ro·pism** *n.*

lip·o·tro·pin (lĭp′ə-trō′pĭn, lī′pə-) *n.* A hormone produced by the anterior pituitary gland that promotes the utilization of fat by the body and is a precursor to the endorphins. [LIPOTROP(IC) + -IN.]

Lip·pi (lĭp′ē), **Filippino.** 1457?–1504? Italian painter who completed Masaccio's frescoes in the Brancacci Chapel, Florence.

Lippi, Fra **Filippo.** 1406?–1469? Italian Renaissance painter whose works display a bold three-dimensional style.

Lipp·mann (lēp-män′), **Gabriel.** 1845–1921. French physicist. He won a 1908 Nobel Prize for developing a method of reproducing colors by photography.

Lipp·mann (lĭp′mən), **Walter.** 1889–1974. American journalist. He cofounded (1914) the weekly *New Republic.*

lip-read (lĭp′rēd′) *v.* **-read** (-rĕd′), **-read·ing, -reads.** *—tr.* To interpret (utterances) by lip reading. *—intr.* To interpret utterances by lip reading.

lip reading *n.* A technique for understanding unheard speech by interpreting the lip and facial movements of the speaker. **—lip reader** *n.*

Lip·scomb (lĭp′skəm), **William Nunn, Jr.** Born 1919. American chemist. He won a 1976 Nobel Prize for his contributions to the theory of molecular structure.

lip service *n.* Verbal expression of agreement or allegiance, unsupported by real conviction or action; hypocritical respect: *"Lip service continues to be paid to resolving regional conflicts, but there is no sense of urgency"* (Henry A. Kissinger).

lip•stick (lĭp′stĭk′) *n.* A small stick of waxy lip coloring enclosed in a cylindrical case.

lipstick tree *n.* See **annatto** (sense 1).

lip-synch also **lip-sync** (lĭp′sĭngk′) *—v.* **-synched, -synch•ing, -synchs** also **-synced, -sync•ing, -syncs.** *—intr.* To move the lips in synchronization with recorded speech or song. *—tr.* To move the lips in synchronization with (recorded speech or song): *She lip-synched the songs for the movie.*

Lip•tau•er (lĭp′tou′ər) *n.* **1.** A soft cheese originating in Hungary. **2.** A spread made of Liptauer or a cream cheese substitute and seasonings. [German, after *Liptau* (Liptó), Hungary.]

Lip•ton (lĭp′tən), Sir **Thomas Johnstone.** 1850–1931. British merchant who established tea processing factories in England and the United States.

liq. *abbr.* **1.** Liquid. **2.** Liquor.

li•quate (lī′kwāt′) *tr.v.* **-quat•ed, -quat•ing, -quates.** To separate (the metals in an alloy) by melting the more fusible constituents while leaving the less fusible ones solid. [Latin *liquāre, liquāt-,* to melt.] **—li•qua′tion** *n.*

liq•ue•fac•tion (lĭk′wə-făk′shən) *n.* **1.** The process of liquefying. **2.** The state of being liquefied. [Middle English *liquefaccion,* from Old French *liquefacion,* from Late Latin *liquefactiō, liquefactiōn-,* from Latin *liquefactus,* past participle of *liquefacere,* to make liquid. See LIQUEFY.]

liq•ue•fy also **liq•ui•fy** (lĭk′wə-fī′) *—v.* **-fied, -fy•ing, -fies.** *—tr.* To cause to become liquid, especially: **a.** To melt (a solid) by heating. **b.** To condense (a gas) by cooling. *—intr.* To become liquid. See Synonyms at **melt.** [Middle English *liquefien,* from Old French *liquefier,* from Latin *liquefacere* : *liquēre,* to be liquid + *facere,* to make; see FACT.] **—liq′ue•fi′er** *n.*

li•ques•cent (lĭ-kwĕs′ənt) *adj.* Becoming or tending to become liquid; melting. [Latin *liquēscēns, liquēscent-,* present participle of *liquēscere,* to become liquid, inchoative of *liquēre,* to be liquid.] **—li•ques′cence, li•ques′cen•cy** *n.*

li•queur (lĭ-kûr′, -kyo͝or′) *n.* Any of various strongly flavored alcoholic beverages typically served in small quantities after dinner. [French, from Old French *licour,* a liquid. See LIQUOR.]

liq•uid (lĭk′wĭd) *n. Abbr.* **liq. 1.a.** The state of matter in which a substance exhibits a characteristic readiness to flow, little or no tendency to disperse, and relatively high incompressibility. **b.** Matter or a specific body of matter in this state. **2.** *Linguistics.* A consonant articulated without friction and capable of being prolonged like a vowel, such as English *l* and *r.* **—liquid** *adj. Abbr.* **liq. 1.** Of or being a liquid. **2.** Having been liquefied, especially: **a.** Melted by heating: *liquid wax.* **b.** Condensed by cooling: *liquid oxygen.* **3.** Flowing readily; fluid: *added milk to make the batter more liquid.* **4.** Having a flowing quality without harshness or abrupt breaks: *liquid prose; the liquid movements of a Balinese dancer.* **5.** *Linguistics.* Articulated without friction and capable of being prolonged like a vowel. **6.** Clear and shining: *the liquid brown eyes of a spaniel.* **7.** Readily convertible into cash: *liquid assets.* [From Middle English, of a liquid, from Old French *liquide,* from Latin *liquidus,* from *liquēre,* to be liquid.] **—liq′uid•ly** *adv.* **—liq′uid•ness** *n.*

liquid air *n.* Air in its liquid state, intensely cold and bluish, obtained by cooling and compression.

liq•uid•am•bar (lĭk′wĭd-ăm′bər) *n.* Any of several deciduous trees of the genus *Liquidambar,* such as the sweet gum. [New Latin, genus name : Latin *liquidus,* liquid; see LIQUID + Medieval Latin *ambar,* amber; see AMBER.]

liq•ui•date (lĭk′wĭ-dāt′) *v.* **-dat•ed, -dat•ing, -dates.** *—tr.* **1.a.** To pay off (a debt, a claim, or an obligation); settle. **b.** To settle the affairs of (a business firm, for example) by determining the liabilities and applying the assets to their discharge. **2.** To convert (assets) into cash. **3.** To put an end to; abolish. **4.** To put to death; kill. *—intr.* **1.** To settle a debt, a claim, or an obligation. **2.** To settle the affairs of a business or an estate by disposing of its assets and liabilities. See Synonyms at **eliminate.** [Late Latin *liquidāre, liquidāt-,* to melt, from Latin *liquidus,* liquid. See LIQUID.] **—liq′ui•da′tion** *n.* **—liq′ui•da′tor** *n.*

liquid crystal *n.* Any of various liquids in which the atoms or molecules are regularly arrayed in either one dimension or two dimensions, the order giving rise to optical properties, such as anisotropic scattering, associated with the crystals.

liq•uid-crys•tal display (lĭk′wĭd-krĭs′təl) *n. Abbr.* **LCD** An alphanumeric display on calculators and digital watches, made up of a liquid sandwiched between layers of glass or plastic, that becomes opaque when an electric current is passed through it. The contrast between the opaque and transparent areas forms visible characters.

li•quid•i•ty (lĭ-kwĭd′ĭ-tē) *n.* **1.** The state of being liquid. **2.** The quality of being readily convertible into cash: *an investment with high liquidity.* **3.** Available cash or the capacity to obtain it on demand: *a bank that is increasing its liquidity by shortening the average term of its loans.*

liquid measure *n.* **1.** The measurement of liquid capacity. **2.** A unit or system of units of liquid capacity.

liq•ui•fy (lĭk′wə-fī′) *v.* Variant of **liquefy.**

liq•uor (lĭk′ər) *n. Abbr.* **liq. 1.** An alcoholic beverage made by distillation rather than by fermentation. **2.** A liquid substance, such as broth, produced in cooking. **3.** An aqueous solution of a nonvolatile substance. **4.** A solution, an emulsion, or a suspension for industrial use. **—liquor** *tr.v.* **-uored, -uor•ing, -uors. 1.** To steep (malt, for example). **2.** *Slang.* To make drunk with alcoholic liquor. Often used with *up*: *was all liquored up.* [Middle English *licour,* a liquid, from Old French, from Latin *liquor,* from *liquēre,* to be liquid.]

li•quo•rice (lĭk′ər-ĭs, -ĭsh) *n. Chiefly British.* Variant of **licorice.**

li•ra (lîr′ə, lē′rä) *n., pl.* **li•re** (lîr′ā, lē′rĕ) or **li•ras.** *Abbr.* **l.** See table at **currency.** [Italian, from Old Italian, from Old Provençal *liura,* from Latin *lībra,* a unit of weight, pound.]

lir•i•pipe (lîr′ə-pīp′) *n.* A long scarf or cord attached to and hanging from a hood. [Medieval Latin *liripipium.*]

Lis•bon (lĭz′bən). The capital and largest city of Portugal, in the western part of the country on the Tagus River estuary. An ancient Iberian settlement, it was held by the Phoenicians and Carthaginians, taken by the Romans in 205 B.C., and conquered by the Moors c. A.D. 714. Reconquered by the Portuguese in 1147, it flourished in the 16th century during the heyday of colonial expansion in Africa and India. Population, 807,167.

li•sen•te (lē-sĕn′tā) *n.* Plural of **sente.**

lisle (līl) *n.* **1.** A fine, smooth, tightly twisted thread spun from long-stapled cotton. **2.** Fabric knitted of this thread, used especially for hosiery and underwear. [After *Lisle* (Lille), France.]

lisp (lĭsp) *n.* **1.** A speech defect or mannerism characterized by mispronunciation of the sounds (s) and (z) as (th) and (*th*). **2.** A sound of or like a lisp: *"The carpenter['s] . . . plane whistles its wild ascending lisp"* (Walt Whitman). **—lisp** *v.* **lisped, lisp•ing, lisps.** *—intr.* **1.** To speak with a lisp. **2.** To speak imperfectly, as a child does. *—tr.* To pronounce with a lisp. [From Middle English *lispen,* to lisp, from Old English *-wlispian,* from *wlisp,* lisping.] **—lisp′er** *n.*

LISP (lĭsp) *n. Computer Science.* A programming language designed to process data consisting of lists. It is widely used in artificial intelligence research. [*lis(t) p(rocessing).*]

lis•some also **lis•som** (lĭs′əm) *adj.* **1.** Easily bent; supple. **2.** Having the ability to move with ease; limber. [Alteration of LITHESOME.] **—lis′some•ly** *adv.* **—lis′some•ness** *n.*

list¹ (lĭst) *n.* **1.** A series of names, words, or other items written, printed, or imagined one after the other: *a shopping list; a guest list; a list of things to do.* **2.** A considerable number; a long series: *recited a list of dates memorized.* **—list** *v.* **list•ed, list•ing, lists.** *—tr.* **1.** To make a list of; itemize: *listed his previous jobs.* **2.** To enter in a list; register: *listed each item received.* **3.** To put (oneself) in a specific category: *lists herself as an artist.* **4.** *Archaic.* To recruit. *—intr.* **1.** To have a stated list price: *a radio that lists for ten dollars over the sale price.* **2.** *Archaic.* To enlist in the armed forces. [French *liste,* from Old French, from Old Italian *lista,* of Germanic origin.] **—list′er** *n.*

list² (lĭst) *n.* **1.a.** A narrow strip, especially of wood. **b.** *Architecture.* See **listel. c.** A border or selvage of cloth. **2.** A stripe or band of color. **3.** Often **lists. a.** An arena for jousting tournaments or other contests. **b.** A place of combat. **c.** An area of controversy. **4.** A ridge thrown up between two furrows by a lister in plowing. **5.** *Obsolete.* A boundary; a border. **—list** *tr.v.* **list•ed, list•ing, lists. 1.** To cover, line, or edge with list. **2.** To cut a thin strip from the edge of. **3.** To furrow or plant (land) with a lister. [Middle English, from Old English *līste.*]

list³ (lĭst) *n.* An inclination to one side, as of a ship; a tilt. **—list** *intr. & tr.v.* **list•ed, list•ing, lists.** To lean or cause to lean to the side: *The damaged ship listed badly to starboard. Erosion first listed, then toppled the spruce tree.* [Origin unknown.]

list⁴ (lĭst) *intr. & tr.v.* **list•ed, list•ing, lists.** *Archaic.* To listen or listen to. [Middle English *listen,* from Old English *hlystan.* See **kleu-** in Appendix.]

list⁵ (lĭst) *Archaic. v.* **list•ed, list•ing, lists.** *—tr.* To be pleasing to; suit. *—intr.* To be disposed; choose. **—list** *n.* A desire or an inclination. [Middle English *listen,* to desire, please, from Old English *lystan.* See **las-** in Appendix.]

lis•tel (lĭs′təl) *n. Architecture.* A narrow border, molding, or fillet. Also called *list.* [French, from Italian *listello,* diminutive of *lista,* border, of Germanic origin.]

lis•ten (lĭs′ən) *intr.v.* **-tened, -ten•ing, -tens. 1.** To make an effort to hear something: *listen to the radio; listening for the bell.* **2.** To pay attention; heed: *"She encouraged me to listen carefully to what country people called mother wit"* (Maya Angelou). **—*phrasal verb.* listen in. 1.** To listen to a conversation between others; eavesdrop. **2.** To tune in and listen to a broadcast. [Middle English *listenen,* alteration (influenced by *listen,* see LIST⁴) of Old English *hlysnan.* See **kleu-** in Appendix.]

lis•ten•a•ble (lĭs′ə-nə-bəl) *adj.* Being such that listening is pleasurable: *an undistinguished but listenable soundtrack.* **—lis′ten•a•bil′i•ty** *n.*

lis•ten•er•ship (lĭs′ə-nər-shĭp′, lĭs′nər-) *n.* The people who listen to a radio program or station.

list•er (lĭs′tər) *n.* A plow equipped with a double moldboard that turns up the soil on each side of the furrow, often having an attached drill for seed planting. [From LIST².]

Lis•ter (lĭs′tər), **Joseph.** First Baron Lister. 1827–1912. British surgeon. He demonstrated in 1865 that carbolic acid was an effective antiseptic agent.

lis•te•ri•a (lĭ-stîr′ē-ə) *n.* Any of various rod-shaped, gram-positive bacteria of the genus *Listeria,* which includes the causative agent of listeriosis. [New Latin *Listeria,* genus name, after Joseph LISTER.]

lionfish

ă pat	oi boy
ā pay	ou out
âr care	o͝o took
ä father	o͞o boot
ĕ pet	ŭ cut
ē be	ûr urge
ĭ pit	th thin
ī pie	*th* this
îr pier	hw which
ŏ pot	zh vision
ō toe	ə about, item
ô paw	♦ regionalism

Stress marks: **′** (primary); ′ (secondary), as in **dictionary** (dĭk′shə-nĕr′ē)

Franz Liszt

lis·te·ri·o·sis (lĭ-stîr′ē-ō′sĭs) *n.* A bacterial disease caused by *Listeria monocytogenes,* affecting wild and domestic animals and occasionally human beings and characterized by fever, meningitis, and encephalitis.

list·ing (lĭs′tĭng) *n.* **1.** An entry in a list or directory: *the first listing in the telephone book.* **2.** A list: *a listing of physicians.* **3.** *Computer Science.* A printout of a program or data set.

list·less (lĭst′lĭs) *adj.* Lacking energy or disinclined to exert effort; lethargic: *reacted to the latest crisis with listless resignation.* [Middle English *listles* : probably from *liste,* desire (from *listen,* to desire; see LIST[5]) + *-les, -lesse,* -less.] **—list′less·ly** *adv.* **—list′less·ness** *n.*

list price *n.* A basic published or advertised price, often subject to discount. Also called *sticker price.*

Liszt (lĭst), **Franz.** 1811–1886. Hungarian composer who achieved fame in his lifetime as a piano virtuoso. His best-known compositions include the *Faust Symphony* (1853–1861).

lit[1] (lĭt) *v.* A past tense and a past participle of **light**[1]**.** See Usage Note at **light**[1]**.**

lit[2] (lĭt) *v.* A past tense and a past participle of **light**[2]**.**

lit. *abbr.* **1.** Liter. **2.a.** Literal. **b.** Literally. **3.** Literary. **4.** Literature.

lit·a·ny (lĭt′n-ē) *n., pl.* **-nies. 1.** A liturgical prayer consisting of a series of petitions recited by a leader alternating with fixed responses by the congregation. **2.** A repetitive or incantatory recital: *a litany of praise for the new professor.* [Middle English *letanie,* from Old French, from Medieval Latin *letanīa,* from Late Latin *litanīa,* from Late Greek *litaneia,* from Greek, entreaty, from *litaneuein,* to entreat, from *litanos,* entreating, from *litē,* supplication.]

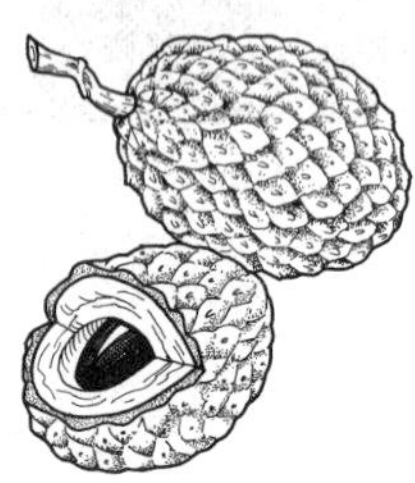
litchi
Litchi chinensis

Lit.B. *abbr. Latin.* Litterarum Baccalaureus (Bachelor of Letters; Bachelor of Literature).

li·tchi also **li·chee** or **ly·chee** (lē′chē) *n.* **1.** A Chinese tree *(Litchi chinensis)* that bears bright red fruits, each of which has a large single seed with a white, fleshy, edible aril. **2.** The nutlike fruit of this tree. In this sense, also called *litchi nut.* [Chinese (Mandarin) *lì zhī.*]

Lit.D. *abbr. Latin.* Litterarum Doctor (Doctor of Letters; Doctor of Literature).

lite (lĭt) *adj. Slang.* Having less substance or weight or fewer calories than something else: *"lite music, shimmering on the surface and squishy soft at the core"* (Mother Jones). [Alteration of LIGHT[2].]

–lite *suff.* Stone; mineral; fossil: *coprolite.* [French, alteration of *-lithe,* from Greek *lithos,* stone.]

li·ter (lē′tər) *n. Abbr.* **l, lit.** A metric unit of volume equal to approximately 1.056 liquid quarts, 0.908 dry quart, or 0.264 gallon. See table at **measurement.** [French *litre,* from obsolete *litron,* measure of capacity, from Medieval Latin *lītra,* from Greek *litra,* unit of weight.]

lit·er·a·cy (lĭt′ər-ə-sē) *n.* The condition or quality of being literate, especially the ability to read and write. See Usage Note at **literate.**

lit·er·al (lĭt′ər-əl) *adj. Abbr.* **lit. 1.** Being in accordance with, conforming to, or upholding the exact or primary meaning of a word or words. **2.** Word for word; verbatim: *a literal translation.* **3.** Avoiding exaggeration, metaphor, or embellishment; factual; prosaic: *a literal description; a literal mind.* **4.** Consisting of, using, or expressed by letters: *literal notation.* **—literal** *n. Computer Science.* A letter or symbol that represents a particular constant or number, known or unknown, and is not programmer-defined. [Middle English, from Old French, from Late Latin *litterālis,* of letters, from Latin *littera,* letter.] **—lit′er·al·ness** *n.*

lit·er·al·ism (lĭt′ər-ə-lĭz′əm) *n.* **1.** Adherence to the explicit sense of a given text or doctrine. **2.** Literal portrayal; realism. **—lit′er·al·ist** *n.* **—lit′er·al·is′tic** *adj.*

lit·er·al·ize (lĭt′ər-ə-līz′) *tr.v.* **-ized, -iz·ing, -iz·es.** To make literal.

lit·er·al·ly (lĭt′ər-ə-lē) *adv.* **1.** In a literal manner; word for word: *translated the Greek passage literally.* **2.** *Abbr.* **lit.** In a literal or strict sense: *Don't take my remarks literally.* **3.** *Usage Problem.* **4.a.** Really; actually: *"There are people in the world who literally do not know how to boil water"* (Craig Claiborne). **b.** Used as an intensive before a figurative expression.

USAGE NOTE: For more than a hundred years, critics have remarked on the incoherency of using *literally* in a way that suggests the exact opposite of its primary sense of "in a manner that accords with the literal sense of the words." In 1926, for example, H.W. Fowler cited the example *"The 300,000 Unionists . . . will be literally thrown to the wolves."* The practice does not stem from a change in the meaning of *literally* itself—if it did, the word would long since have come to mean "virtually" or "figuratively"—but from a natural tendency to use the word as a general intensive meaning "without exaggeration," as in *They had literally no help from the government on the project,* where no contrast with the figurative sense of the words is intended. This looser use of the word *literally* does not usually create problems, but it can lead to an inadvertently comic effect when the word is used together with an idiomatic expression that has its source in a frozen figure of speech, such as in *I literally died laughing.*

lit·er·ar·y (lĭt′ə-rĕr′ē) *adj. Abbr.* **lit. 1.** Of, relating to, or dealing with literature: *literary criticism.* **2.** Of or relating to writers or the profession of literature: *literary circles.* **3.** Versed in or fond of literature or learning. **4.a.** Appropriate to literature rather than everyday speech or writing. **b.** Bookish; pedantic. [Latin *litterārius,* of reading and writing, from *littera,* letter. See LETTER.] **—lit′er·ar′i·ly** (-râr′ə-lē) *adv.* **—lit′er·ar′i·ness** *n.*

lit·er·ate (lĭt′ər-ĭt) *adj.* **1.a.** Able to read and write. **b.** Knowledgeable or educated in several fields or a particular field. **2.** Familiar with literature; literary. **3.** Well-written; polished: *a literate essay.* **—literate** *n.* **1.** One who can read and write. **2.** A well-informed, educated person. [Middle English *litterate,* from Latin *litterātus,* from *littera,* letter. See LETTER.] **—lit′er·ate·ly** *adv.* **—lit′er·ate·ness** *n.*

USAGE NOTE: For most of its long history in English, *literate* has meant only "familiar with literature," or more generally, "well-educated, learned"; it is only during the last hundred years that it has also come to refer to the basic ability to read and write. Its antonym *illiterate* has an equally broad range of meanings: an *illiterate* person may be incapable of reading a shopping list or perhaps may only be unable to grasp an allusion to Shakespeare or Keats. The term *functional illiterate* is often used to describe a person who can read or write to some degree, but below a minimum level required to function in even a limited social situation or job setting. More recently, the meanings of the words *literacy* and *illiteracy* have been extended from their original connection with reading and literature to any body of knowledge. For example, "geographic illiterates" cannot identify the countries on a map, and "computer illiterates" are unable to use a word-processing system. None of these uses of *literacy* or *illiteracy* are incorrect, but it might be preferable to use another word in instances where the context does not make the meaning clear.

lit·er·a·ti (lĭt′ə-rä′tē) *pl.n.* The literary intelligentsia. [Latin *litterātī, līterātī,* pl. of *litterātus,* literate. See LITERATE.]

lit·er·a·tim (lĭt′ə-rā′tĭm, -rä′-) *adv.* Letter for letter: *a word transcribed literatim.* [Medieval Latin *līterātim, litterātim,* from Latin *littera,* letter. See LETTER.]

lit·er·a·ture (lĭt′ər-ə-cho͝or′, -chər) *n. Abbr.* **lit. 1.** A body of writings in prose or verse. **2.** Imaginative or creative writing, especially of recognized artistic value: *"Literature must be an analysis of experience and a synthesis of the findings into a unity"* (Rebecca West). **3.** The art or occupation of a literary writer. **4.** The body of written work produced by scholars or researchers in a given field: *medical literature.* **5.** Printed material: *collected all the available literature on the subject.* **6.** *Music.* All the compositions of a certain kind or for a specific instrument or ensemble: *the symphonic literature.* [Middle English, book learning, from Old French *litterature,* from Latin *litterātūra,* from *litterātus,* lettered. See LITERATE.]

lith. *abbr.* **1.** Lithograph; lithography. **2.** Lithographic.

Lith. *abbr.* Lithuania; Lithuanian.

lith– *pref.* Variant of **litho–.**

–lith *suff.* **1.** Rock; stone: *xenolith.* **2.** Stone implement or structure: *megalith.* **3.** Mineral concretion; calculus: *cystolith.* [From Greek *lithos,* stone.]

lith·arge (lĭth′ärj′, lĭ-thärj′) *n.* A yellow lead oxide, PbO, used in storage batteries and glass and as a pigment. Also called *lead monoxide.* [Middle English *litarge,* from Old French, alteration of *litargire,* from Latin *lithargyrus,* from Greek *litharguros* : *lithos,* stone + *arguros,* silver; see **arg-** in Appendix.]

lithe (līth) *adj.* **lith·er, lith·est. 1.** Readily bent; supple: *lithe birch branches.* **2.** Marked by effortless grace: *a lithe ballet dancer.* [Middle English, from Old English *līthe,* flexible, mild.] **—lithe′ly** *adv.* **—lithe′ness** *n.*

lithe·some (līth′səm) *adj.* Lithe; lissome.

lith·i·a (lĭth′ē-ə) *n.* See **lithium oxide.** [New Latin, from *lithion,* from Greek *lithos,* stone.]

li·thi·a·sis (lĭ-thī′ə-sĭs) *n., pl.* **-ses** (-sēz′). Pathological formation of mineral concretions in the body.

lithia water *n.* Mineral water containing lithium salts.

lith·ic[1] (lĭth′ĭk) *adj.* Consisting of or relating to stone or rock.

lith·ic[2] (lĭth′ĭk) *adj.* Of or relating to lithium.

–lithic *suff.* Relating to or characteristic of a specified stage in the use of stone by human beings: *Eolithic.* [From LITHIC[1].]

lith·i·um (lĭth′ē-əm) *n. Symbol* **Li** A soft, silvery, highly reactive metallic element that is used as a heat transfer medium, in thermonuclear weapons, and in various alloys, ceramics, and optical forms of glass. Atomic number 3; atomic weight 6.939; melting point 179°C; boiling point 1,317°C; specific gravity 0.534; valence 1. See table at **element.** [From LITHIA.]

lithium carbonate *n.* A white, granular powder, $LiCO_3$, used in the manufacture of glass and ceramics and in the treatment of depression and manic-depressive illness.

lithium oxide *n.* A strongly alkaline white powder, Li_2O, used in ceramics and glass. Also called *lithia.*

litho. *abbr.* **1.** Lithograph; lithography. **2.** Lithographic.

litho– or **lith–** *pref.* **1.** Stone: *lithosphere.* **2.** Lithium: *lithic.* **3.** Mineral concretion; calculus: *lithotomy.* [Greek, from *lithos,* stone.]

lithog. *abbr.* **1.** Lithograph; lithography. **2.** Lithographic.

lith·o·graph (lĭth′ə-grăf′) *n. Abbr.* **lith., litho., lithog.** A print produced by lithography. **—lithograph** *tr.v.* **-graphed,**

-graph·ing, -graphs. To produce by lithography. [Back-formation from LITHOGRAPHY.] **—li·thog′raph·er** (lĭ-thŏg′rə-fər) *n.* **—lith′o·graph′ic, lith′o·graph′i·cal** *adj.* **—lith′o·graph′i·cal·ly** *adv.*

li·thog·ra·phy (lĭ-thŏg′rə-fē) *n. Abbr.* **lith., litho., lithog.** A printing process in which the image to be printed is rendered on a flat surface, as on sheet zinc or aluminum, and treated to retain ink while the nonimage areas are treated to repel ink.

li·thol·o·gy (lĭ-thŏl′ə-jē) *n.* **1.** The gross physical character of a rock or rock formation. **2.** The microscopic study, description, and classification of rock. **—lith′o·log′ic** (lĭth′ə-lŏj′ĭk), **lith′o·log′i·cal** *adj.* **—lith′o·log′i·cal·ly** *adv.* **—li·thol′o·gist** *n.*

lith·o·phyte (lĭth′ə-fīt′) *n.* **1.** *Botany.* A plant that grows on rock and derives its nourishment chiefly from the atmosphere. **2.** *Zoology.* An organism, such as coral, that has a stony structure. **—lith′o·phyt′ic** (-fĭt′ĭk) *adj.*

lith·o·pone (lĭth′ə-pōn′) *n.* A white pigment consisting of a mixture of zinc sulfide, zinc oxide, and barium sulfate. [LITHO– + Greek *ponos,* toil, product; see **(s)pen-** in Appendix.]

lith·o·sphere (lĭth′ə-sfîr′) *n.* **1.** The solid part of the earth. **2.** The rocky crust of the earth.

lith·o·stra·tig·ra·phy (lĭth′ō-strə-tĭg′rə-fē) *n.* **1.** Stratigraphy based on the physical and petrographic properties of rocks. **2.** Interpretation of the physical characters of sedimentary rocks. **—lith′o·strat′i·graph′ic** (-străt′ĭ-grăf′ĭk) *adj.*

li·thot·o·my (lĭ-thŏt′ə-mē) *n., pl.* **-mies.** Surgical removal of a stone or stones from the urinary tract.

lith·o·trip·sy (lĭth′ə-trĭp′sē) *n., pl.* **-sies.** Pulverization of kidney stones by means of a lithotripter. [LITHO– + Greek *tripsis,* a rubbing, pounding (from *tribein,* to rub, pound; see LITHOTRIPTER) + –Y[2].]

lith·o·trip·ter (lĭth′ə-trĭp′tər) *n.* A device that pulverizes kidney stones by passing shock waves through a water-filled tub in which the patient sits. The device creates stone fragments small enough to be expelled in the urine. [Alteration of obsolete *lithotriptor, lithontriptor,* from *lithontriptic,* breaking up kidney stones, from New Latin *lithontripticus,* alteration (influenced by Greek *tribein, trip-,* to rub, pound; see TRYPSIN) of *lithonthrypticus,* from Greek *(pharmaka tōn en nephrōis) lithōn thruptika,* (drugs) crushing stones (in the kidneys) : *lithōn,* accusative pl. of *lithos,* stone + *thruptikos,* crushing (from *thruptein,* to crush; see **dhreu-** in Appendix).]

li·thot·ri·ty (lĭ-thŏt′rĭ-tē) *n., pl.* **-ties.** A surgical procedure to pulverize stones in the urinary bladder or urethra so that they can be passed out of the body in the urine. [From *lithotritor,* lithotripter, alteration (influenced by Latin *trītor,* pounder, grinder; see TRITURATE) of obsolete *lithotriptor.* See LITHOTRIPTER.]

Lith·u·a·ni·a (lĭth′o͞o-ā′nē-ə). *Abbr.* **Lith.** A country of northern Europe on the Baltic Sea. Perhaps settled as early as 1500 B.C., the area was formed into a strong unified state in the 13th century and became one of the largest territories of medieval Europe. Lithuania merged with Poland in 1569 but was absorbed into Russia by three partitions of Poland (1772, 1793, and 1795). The independent country of Lithuania (1918–1940) was officially proclaimed a constituent republic of the U.S.S.R. in August 1940. Lithuania declared its independence in March 1990 and was formally admitted to the United Nations in September 1991. Vilnius is the capital. Population, 3,570,000.

Lith·u·a·ni·an (lĭth′o͞o-ā′nē-ən) *adj. Abbr.* **Lith.** Of or relating to Lithuania or its people, language, or culture. **—Lithuanian** *n. Abbr.* **Lith. 1.a.** A native or inhabitant of Lithuania. **b.** A person of Lithuanian ancestry. **2.** The Baltic language of the Lithuanians.

lit·i·gant (lĭt′ĭ-gənt) *Law. n.* A party engaged in a lawsuit. **—litigant** *adj.* Engaged in a lawsuit. [French, from Old French, from Latin *lītigāns, lītigant-,* a disputant, from present participle of *lītigāre,* to bring suit. See LITIGATE.]

lit·i·gate (lĭt′ĭ-gāt′) *v.* **-gat·ed, -gat·ing, -gates.** *Law.* —*tr.* To subject to legal proceedings. —*intr.* To engage in legal proceedings. [Latin *lītigāre, lītigāt-* : *līs, līt-,* lawsuit + *agere,* to drive; see **ag-** in Appendix.] **—lit′i·ga·ble** (-gə-bəl) *adj.* **—lit′i·ga′tion** *n.* **—lit′i·ga′tor** *n.*

li·ti·gious (lĭ-tĭj′əs) *adj. Law.* **1.** Of, relating to, or characterized by litigation. **2.** Tending to engage in lawsuits. [Middle English, from Old French, from Latin *lītigiōsus,* from *lītigium,* dispute, from *lītigāre,* to quarrel. See LITIGATE.] **—li·ti′gious·ly** *adv.* **—li·ti′gious·ness** *n.*

lit·mus (lĭt′məs) *n.* A water-soluble blue powder derived from certain lichens that changes to red with increasing acidity and to blue with increasing basicity. [Middle English *litmose,* of Scandinavian origin; akin to Old Norse *litmosi,* dyer's herbs : *litr,* color, dye + *mosi,* bog, moss.]

litmus paper *n.* An unsized white paper impregnated with litmus and used as a pH or acid-base indicator.

litmus test *n.* **1.** A test for chemical acidity or basicity using litmus paper. **2.** A test that uses a single indicator to prompt a decision: *"The word 'hopefully' has become the litmus test to determine whether one is a language snob or a language slob"* (William Safire).

li·to·tes (lī′tə-tēz′, lĭt′ə-, lī-tō′tēz) *n., pl.* **litotes.** A figure of speech consisting of an understatement in which an affirmative is expressed by negating its opposite, as in *This is no small problem.* [Greek *litotēs,* from *litos,* plain. See **lei-** in Appendix.]

li·tre (lē′tər) *n. Chiefly British.* Variant of **liter.**

Litt.B. *abbr. Latin.* Litterarum Baccalaureus (Bachelor of Letters; Bachelor of Literature).

Litt.D. *abbr. Latin.* Litterarum Doctor (Doctor of Letters; Doctor of Literature).

lit·ter (lĭt′ər) *n.* **1.a.** A disorderly accumulation of objects; a pile. **b.** Carelessly discarded refuse, such as wastepaper: *the litter in the streets after a parade.* **2.** The offspring produced at one birth by a multiparous mammal. See Synonyms at **flock**[1]. **3.a.** Material, such as straw, used as bedding for animals. **b.** An absorbent material, such as granulated clay, for covering the floor of an animal's cage or excretory box. **4.** An enclosed or curtained couch mounted on shafts and used to carry a single passenger. **5.** A flat supporting framework, such as a piece of canvas stretched between parallel shafts, for carrying a disabled or dead person; a stretcher. **6.** The uppermost layer of the forest floor consisting chiefly of fallen leaves and other decaying organic matter. **—litter** *v.* **-tered, -ter·ing, -ters.** —*tr.* **1.** To give birth to (a litter). **2.** To make untidy by discarding rubbish carelessly: *Selfish picnickers litter the beach with food wrappers.* **3.** To scatter about: *littered towels all over the locker room.* **4.** To supply (animals) with litter for bedding. —*intr.* **1.** To give birth to a litter. **2.** To scatter litter. [Middle English, from Anglo-Norman *litere,* from Medieval Latin *lectāria* (influenced by Old French *lit,* bed), from Latin *lectus,* bed. See **legh-** in Appendix.] **—lit′ter·er** *n.*

Lithuania

lit·té·ra·teur also **lit·ter·a·teur** (lĭt′ər-ə-tûr′, lĭt′rə-) *n.* One who is devoted to the study or writing of literature. [French, from Latin *litterātor,* critic, lettered person, from *littera,* letter. See LETTER.]

lit·ter·bag (lĭt′ər-băg′) *n.* A bag used, as in an automobile, for disposal of trash.

lit·ter·bug (lĭt′ər-bŭg′) *n. Informal.* One who litters public areas with waste materials.

lit·ter·mate (lĭt′ər-māt′) *n.* One member of a given litter of animal offspring.

lit·tle (lĭt′l) *adj.* **lit·tler, lit·tlest** or **less, least. 1.** Small in size: *a little dining room.* See Synonyms at **small. 2.** Short in extent or duration; brief: *There is little time left.* **3.** Small in quantity or degree: *little money.* **4.** Unimportant; trivial: *a little matter.* **5.** Narrow; petty: *mean little comments; a little mind consumed with trivia.* **6.** Without much power or influence; of minor status. **7.** Being at an early stage of growth; young: *a little child.* **—little** *adv.* **less, least. 1.** Not much; scarcely: *works long hours, sleeping little.* **2.** Not in the least; not at all: *They little expected such a generous gift.* **—little** *n.* **1.** A small quantity or amount: *Give me a little.* **2.** Something much less than all: *I know little of their history.* **3.** A short distance or time: *a little down the road; waited a little.* **—*idioms.* a little.** Somewhat; a bit: *felt a little better.* **little by little.** By small degrees or increments; gradually. [Middle English, from Old English *lȳtel.*] **—lit′tle·ness** *n.*

litter
Italian greyhounds

Lit·tle Al·föld (lĭt′l ôl′fəld). See **Alföld.**

Little A·mer·i·ca (ə-mĕr′ĭ-kə). A U.S. base for explorations in Antarctica on the Ross Ice Shelf.

little auk *n.* See **dovekie.**

Little Bear *n.* See **Ursa Minor.**

Little Big·horn River (bĭg′hôrn′). A river, about 145 km (90 mi) long, rising in the Bighorn Mountains of northern Wyoming and flowing north to the Bighorn River in southern Montana. Sioux and Cheyenne warriors defeated the forces of Gen. George A. Custer in the Little Bighorn valley on June 25, 1876.

Little Cay·man (kā-măn′, kā′mən). See **Cayman Islands.**

Little Col·o·ra·do River (kŏl′ə-răd′ō, -rä′dō). A river of northeast Arizona flowing about 507 km (315 mi) northwest to the Colorado River just above the Grand Canyon.

Little Di·o·mede Island (dī′ə-mēd′). See **Diomede Islands.**

Little Dipper *n.* The seven bright stars that form the constellation Ursa Minor.

little finger *n.* The smallest finger of the human hand; the last finger as counted from the thumb.

Little Kar·roo (kə-ro͞o′). See **Karroo.**

little magazine *n.* A literary magazine that publishes the work of relatively unknown writers.

Little Minch (mĭnch). See **Minch.**

Little Mis·sou·ri River (mĭ-zo͝or′ē, -zo͝or′ə). A river of the northern United States rising in northeast Wyoming and flowing about 901 km (560 mi) through southeast Montana and northwest South Dakota to the Missouri River in western North Dakota.

Little Na·ma·qua·land (nə-mä′kwə-lănd′). See **Namaqualand.**

lit·tle·neck (lĭt′l-nĕk′) *n.* The quahog clam when small and suitable for eating raw. Also called *littleneck clam.* [After *Little Neck* Bay, off western Long Island, New York.]

little owl *n.* A small European owl *(Athene noctua)* having streaked brownish plumage.

Little Pee Dee River (pē′ dē′). A river, about 169 km (105 mi) long, of southern North Carolina and northern South Carolina flowing south then southeast to the Pee Dee River.

Little Rock. The capital and largest city of Arkansas, in the

ă pat	oi boy
ā pay	ou out
âr care	o͝o took
ä father	o͞o boot
ĕ pet	ŭ cut
ē be	ûr urge
ĭ pit	th thin
ī pie	*th* this
îr pier	hw which
ŏ pot	zh vision
ō toe	ə about, item
ô paw	♦ regionalism

Stress marks: ′ (primary); **′** (secondary), as in **dictionary** (dĭk′shə-nĕr′ē)

live oak
Quercus virginiana

central part of the state on the Arkansas River. It became territorial capital in 1821 and state capital in 1836. Federal troops were sent to the city in 1957 to enforce a 1954 U.S. Supreme Court ruling against segregation in the public schools. Population, 153,831.

Little Saint Ber·nard Pass (sănt′ bər-närd′). A mountain pass through the Savoy Alps between Italy and France south of Mont Blanc. It rises to 2,189.9 m (7,180 ft).

Little Sark (särk). See **Sark.**

little slam *n. Games.* The winning of all but one of the tricks during the play of one hand of bridge.

Little Ten·nes·see River (tĕn′ĭ-sē′). A river, about 217 km (135 mi) long, of northeast Georgia, southwest North Carolina, and eastern Tennessee, where it joins the Tennessee River.

little theater *n.* A small theater usually for a community, collegiate, or experimental drama group.

little toe *n.* The smallest and outermost toe of the human foot.

Lit·tle·ton (lĭt′l-tən). A city of north-central Colorado, a residential and industrial suburb of Denver. Population, 28,349.

lit·to·ral (lĭt′ər-əl) *adj.* Of or on a shore, especially a seashore: *a littoral property; the littoral biogeographic zone.* **—littoral** *n.* A coastal region; a shore. [Latin *lītorālis,* from *lītus, lītor-,* shore. N., from Italian *littorale,* from Latin *lītorālis.*]

Lit·tré (lĭ-trā′, lē-), **Maximilien Paul Émile.** 1801–1881. French philosopher and lexicographer whose chief work is the *Dictionnaire de la Langue Française* (1863–1872).

li·tur·gi·cal (lĭ-tûr′jĭ-kəl) also **li·tur·gic** (-tûr′jĭk) *adj.* **1.** Of, relating to, or in accordance with liturgy: *a book of liturgical forms.* **2.** Using or used in liturgy. **—li·tur′gi·cal·ly** *adv.*

li·tur·gics (lĭ-tûr′jĭks) *n. (used with a sing. verb).* The study of liturgies. Also called *liturgiology.*

li·tur·gi·ol·o·gy (lĭ-tûr′jē-ŏl′ə-jē) *n.* See **liturgics.** **—li·tur′gi·ol′o·gist** *n.*

lit·ur·gist (lĭt′ər-jĭst) *n.* **1.** One who uses or advocates the use of liturgical forms. **2.** A scholar in liturgics.

lit·ur·gy (lĭt′ər-jē) *n., pl.* **-gies. 1.** A prescribed form or set of forms for public Christian ceremonies; ritual. **2.** Often **Liturgy.** The sacrament of the Eucharist. [Late Latin *lītūrgia,* from Greek *leitourgia,* public service, from *leitourgos,* public servant : *lēos, leit-,* people (variant of *laos*) + *ergon,* work; see **werg-** in Appendix.]

Liu·zhou (lyo͞o′jō′) also **Liu·chow** (-chō′). A city of southern China north-northeast of Nanning. It is an industrial and transportation center with a large integrated iron and steel complex. Population, 375,000.

liv·a·ble also **live·a·ble** (lĭv′ə-bəl) *adj.* **1.** Suitable to live in; habitable: *a livable dwelling.* **2.** Possible to bear; endurable: *livable trials and tribulations.* **—liv′a·ble·ness** *n.*

live¹ (lĭv) *v.* **lived, liv·ing, lives.** —*intr.* **1.** To be alive; exist. **2.** To continue to be alive: *lived through a bad accident.* **3.** To support oneself; subsist: *living on rice and fish; lives on a small inheritance.* **4.** To reside; dwell: *lives on a farm.* **5.** To conduct one's life in a particular manner: *lived frugally.* **6.** To pursue a positive, satisfying existence; enjoy life: *those who truly live.* **7.** To remain in human memory: *an event that lives on in our minds.* —*tr.* **1.** To spend or pass (one's life). **2.** To go through; experience: *lived a nightmare.* **3.** To practice in one's life: *live one's beliefs.* See Synonyms at **be.** ***—phrasal verbs.*** **live down.** To overcome or reduce the shame of (a misdeed, for example) over a period of time. **live in.** To reside in the place where one is employed: *household servants who live in.* **live out.** To live outside one's place of domestic employment: *household servants who live out.* **live with.** To put up with; resign oneself to: *disliked the situation but had to live with it.* ***—idioms.*** **live it up.** *Slang.* To engage in festive pleasures or extravagances. **live up to. 1.** To live or act in accordance with: *lived up to their parents' ideals.* **2.** To prove equal to: *a new technology that did not live up to our expectations.* **3.** To carry out; fulfill: *lived up to her end of the bargain.* [Middle English *liven,* from Old English *libban, lifian.* See **leip-** in Appendix.]

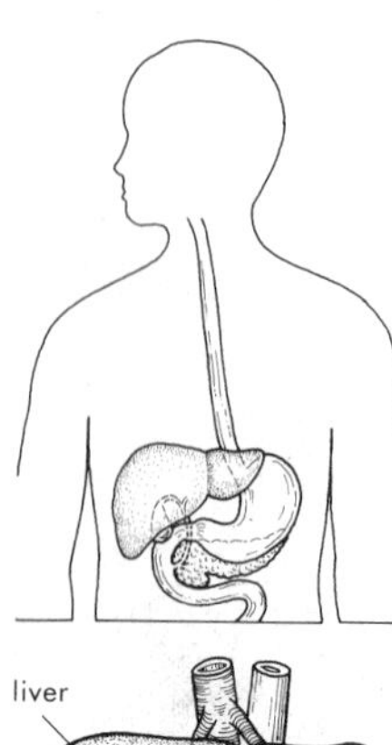

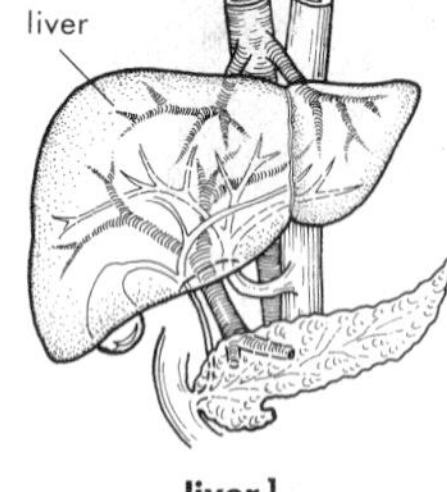

liver¹

live² (līv) *adj.* **1.** Having life; alive: *live animals.* See Synonyms at **living. 2.** Of current interest or relevance: *a live topic; still a live option.* **3.** Glowing; burning: *live coals.* **4.** Not yet exploded but capable of being fired: *live ammunition.* **5.** *Electricity.* Carrying an electric current or energized with electricity. **6.** Not mined or quarried; in the natural state: *live ore.* **7. a.** Broadcast while actually being performed; not taped, filmed, or recorded: *a live television program.* **b.** Involving performers or spectators who are physically present: *live entertainment.* **8.** *Printing.* Not yet set into type: *live copy.* **9.** *Sports.* In play: *a live ball.* **—live** *adv.* At, during, or from the time of actual occurrence or performance: *The landing on the moon was telecast live.* [Short for ALIVE.] **—live′ness** *n.*

live·a·ble (lĭv′ə-bəl) *adj.* Variant of **livable.**

live·bear·er (līv′bâr′ər) *n.* A fish, especially of the family Poeciliidae, that bears live young rather than depositing eggs. **—live′-bear′ing** *adj.*

live-for·ev·er (lĭv′fər-ĕv′ər) *n.* **1.** See **orpine. 2.** See **houseleek.**

live-in (lĭv′ĭn′) *adj.* **1.** Residing in the place where one is employed: *a live-in cook.* **2.** Residing together with another, especially in sexual intimacy.

live·li·hood (līv′lē-ho͝od′) *n.* Means of support; subsistence. [Middle English *livelyhed,* alteration (influenced by *liflihed,* energy, vigor, from *lifli,* lively) of *livelode,* from Old English *līflād* : *līf,* life; see LIFE + *lād,* course; see **leit-** in Appendix.]

SYNONYMS: *livelihood, living, subsistence, sustenance, maintenance, support, keep.* These nouns denote the means needed to provide the necessities of life. *Livelihood* and *living* are often interchangeable, but *livelihood* may specify the occupation by means of which one earns an income: *Painting is her livelihood. He earns a precarious living as a window washer. Subsistence* is sometimes equivalent to *living: "The principal part of our subsistence was to be had by our guns"* (Daniel Defoe). Very often, however, it suggests resources barely sufficient to support life: *"They* [the Pilgrims] *fell upon an ungenial climate . . . that called out* [their] *best energies . . . to get a mere subsistence out of the soil"* (Ulysses S. Grant). *Sustenance* applies to what is necessary to sustain life and especially to the food needed for health and comfort: *The urban homeless are often in desperate need of sustenance. Maintenance, support,* and *keep* are usually reckoned as the equivalent in money of what is needed to supply necessities such as food, lodging, and clothing: *Both parents contribute to the maintenance of their children. He lives in an opulent apartment but has no visible means of support. "Long before they reached their teens they were earning their keep"* (J.M. Barrie). *Support* also applies to one that provides the means or funds to sustain others: *Her earnings are the only support of her aged parents.*

live load (līv) *n.* A moving, variable weight added to the dead load or intrinsic weight of a structure or vehicle.

live·long (lĭv′lông′, -lŏng′) *adj.* Complete; whole: *the livelong day.* [Middle English : *leve, lefe,* dear, used as an intensive (from Old English *lēof,* dear; see **leubh-** in Appendix) + *long,* long; see LONG¹.]

live·ly (līv′lē) *adj.* **-li·er, -li·est. 1.** Full of life and energy; vigorous: *a lively baby.* **2.** Full of spirit; gay and animated: *a lively tune.* **3.** Marked by animated intelligence: *a lively discussion.* **4.** Invigorating; refreshing. **5.** Effervescent; sparkling. **6.** Keen; brisk: *gave the kitchen floor a lively sweeping.* **7.** Rebounding readily upon impact; resilient: *a lively tennis ball.* See Synonyms at **active. —lively** *adv.* With energy or vigor; briskly: *Step lively!* [Middle English *lifli,* from Old English *līflīc,* from *līf,* life. See **leip-** in Appendix.] **—live′li·ly** *adv.* **—live′li·ness** *n.*

li·ven (lī′vən) *tr. & intr.v.* **-vened, -ven·ing, -vens.** To make or become lively: *liven up a party; a discussion that livened up.*

live oak (līv) *n.* Any of several American evergreen oaks, such as *Quercus virginiana* of Mexico and the southeast United States or *Q. agrifolia* of California. Also called *encina.*

liv·er¹ (lĭv′ər) *n.* **1.** *Anatomy.* A large, reddish-brown, glandular vertebrate organ located in the upper right portion of the abdominal cavity that secretes bile and is active in the formation of certain blood proteins and in the metabolism of carbohydrates, fats, and proteins. **2.** An organ in invertebrates that is similar to the vertebrate liver. **3.** The bile-secreting organ of an animal, used as food. **4.** *Color.* A dark reddish brown. **—liver** *adj.* **1.** Made of or flavored with liver: *liver pâté; liver sandwiches.* **2.** Of a dark reddish brown. [Middle English, from Old English *lifer.* See **leip-** in Appendix.]

liv·er² (lĭv′ər) *n.* One who lives in a specified manner: *a high liver.*

liver extract *n.* A dry, brownish powder containing the soluble thermolabile fraction of mammalian livers that is capable of stimulating the production of red blood cells.

liver fluke *n.* **1.** Any of several parasitic trematode worms, especially *Clonorchis sinensis,* that infest the liver of various animals, including human beings. **2.** Infestation with such parasitic worms. In this sense, also called *rot.*

liv·er·ied (lĭv′ə-rēd, lĭv′rēd) *adj.* Wearing livery: *Liveried footmen stood on the palace steps.*

liv·er·ish (lĭv′ər-ĭsh) *adj.* **1.** Resembling liver, especially in color. **2.** Having a liver disorder; bilious. **3.** Having a disagreeable disposition; irritable. **—liv′er·ish·ness** *n.*

liv·er·leaf (lĭv′ər-lēf′) *n.* See **hepatica.**

Liv·er·more (lĭv′ər-môr′, -mōr′). A city of western California east-southeast of Oakland. Population, 48,349.

Livermore, Mary Ashton Rice. 1820–1905. American suffragist, reformer, and lecturer. She founded (1869) *The Agitator.*

Liv·er·pool (lĭv′ər-po͞ol′). A borough of northwest England on the Mersey River near its mouth on the Irish Sea. First colonized by Norsemen in the late eighth century, Liverpool received a charter from King John in 1207. Population, 518,900.

liver spot *n.* A benign, localized brownish patch on the skin, often occurring in old age and in people with sun-damaged skin.

liv·er·wort (lĭv′ər-wûrt′, -wôrt′) *n.* Any of numerous small, green, nonvascular plants of the class Hepaticae within the division Bryophyta.

liv·er·wurst (lĭv′ər-wûrst′, -wo͝orst′) *n.* A sausage made of or containing ground liver. [Partial translation of German *Leberwurst* : *Leber,* liver + *Wurst,* sausage; see WURST.]

liv·er·y (lĭv′ə-rē, lĭv′rē) *n., pl.* **-ies. 1.** A distinctive uniform worn by the male servants of a household. **2.** The distinctive dress worn by the members of a particular group; uniform: *ushers in livery.* **3.** The costume or insignia worn by the retainers of a feudal lord. **4. a.** The boarding and care of horses for a fee. **b.** The hiring out of horses and carriages. **c.** A livery stable. **5.** A business that offers vehicles, such as automobiles or boats, for hire. **6.** *Law.* Official delivery of property, especially land, to a new owner. [Middle English *liveri,* from Old French *livree,* delivery, from feminine past participle of *livrer,* to deliver, from Latin *līberāre,* to free, from *līber,* free. See **leudh-** in Appendix.]

liv·er·y·man (lĭv′ə-rē-mən, lĭv′rē-) *n.* A man who is employed in or keeps a livery stable.

livery stable *n.* A stable that boards horses and keeps horses and carriages for hire.

lives (līvz) *n.* Plural of **life.**

live steam (līv) *n.* Steam coming from a boiler at full pressure.

live·stock (līv′stŏk′) *n.* Domestic animals, such as cattle or horses, raised for home use or for profit, especially on a farm. —*attributive.* Often used to modify another noun: *livestock prices; a livestock auction.*

live wire (līv) *n.* **1.** A wire carrying electric current. **2.** *Informal.* A vivacious, alert, or energetic person.

liv·id (lĭv′ĭd) *adj.* **1.** Discolored, as from a bruise; black-and-blue. **2.** Ashen or pallid: *a face livid with shock.* **3.** Extremely angry; furious. [Middle English *livide,* from Old French, from Latin *līvidus,* from *līvēre,* to be bluish. See **slī-** in Appendix.] **—li·vid′i·ty, liv′id·ness** *n.* **—liv′id·ly** *adv.*

liv·ing (lĭv′ĭng) *adj.* **1.** Possessing life: *famous living painters; transplanted living tissue.* **2.** In active function or use: *a living language.* **3.** Of persons who are alive: *events within living memory.* **4.** Full of life, interest, or vitality: *made history a living subject.* **5.** True to life; realistic: *the living image of her mother.* **6.** *Informal.* Used as an intensive: *beat the living hell out of his opponent in the boxing match.* **—living** *n.* **1.** The condition or action of maintaining life: *the high cost of living.* **2.** A manner or style of life: *preferred plain living.* **3.** A means of maintaining life; livelihood: *made their living by hunting.* **4.** *Chiefly British.* A church benefice, including the revenue attached to it.

SYNONYMS: *living, alive, live, animate, animated, vital.* These adjectives mean possessed of or exhibiting life. *Living, alive,* and *live* refer principally to organisms that are not dead but continue to live: *living plants and animals; the happiest woman alive; a live canary. Animate* applies to living animal as distinct from living plant life: *early peoples worshiping animate and inanimate objects. Animated* suggests renewed life, vigor, or spirit: *became very animated when he heard the good news. Vital* refers to what is characteristic of or necessary to the continuation of life: *eating to maintain vital energy.* See also Synonyms at **livelihood.**

living death *n.* A situation or period of time characterized by unremitting pain and suffering.

living fossil *n.* An organism, such as a coelacanth or the ginkgo, that is the sole surviving member of an otherwise extinct taxonomic group.

living room *n.* *Abbr.* **LR** A room in a private residence intended for social and leisure activities. Also called *front room.*

Liv·ing·ston (lĭv′ĭng-stən). A community of northeast New Jersey northwest of Newark. It is in a truck-farming area. Population, 28,040.

Livingston, Henry Brockholst. 1757–1823. American jurist who served as an associate justice of the U.S. Supreme Court (1806–1823).

Livingston, Robert R. 1746–1813. American Revolutionary leader and diplomat who served in the Continental Congress (1775–1781) and as minister to France (1801–1804).

Liv·ing·stone (lĭv′ĭng-stən), **David.** 1813–1873. Scottish missionary and African explorer. He discovered the Zambezi River (1851) and Victoria Falls (1855). Henry M. Stanley found him in Tanzania (1871), and together they attempted to find the source of the Nile.

living unit *n.* A dwelling for use by one family.

living wage *n.* A wage sufficient to provide minimally satisfactory living conditions. Also called *minimum wage.*

living will *n.* A will in which the signer requests not to be kept alive by medical life-support systems in the event of a terminal illness.

Li·vo·ni·a (lĭ-vō′nē-ə, -vōn′yə). **1.** A region comprising southern Latvia and northern Estonia. The Livonian Brothers of the Sword conquered the area in the 13th century and converted the inhabitants to Christianity. After the dissolution of the order (1561), Livonia was contested by Poland, Russia, and Sweden, finally passing to Russia in 1721. **2.** A city of southeast Michigan, an industrial suburb of Detroit. Population, 104,814.

Li·vo·ni·an (lĭ-vō′nē-ən) *adj.* Of or relating to the region of Livonia or its people or culture. **—Livonian** *n.* A native or inhabitant of the region of Livonia.

Li·vor·no (lē-vôr′nō). See **Leghorn.**

li·vre (lē′vər, lē′vrə) *n.* *Abbr.* **lv.** A money of account formerly used in France and originally worth a pound of silver. [French, from Old French, from Latin *lībra,* a unit of weight, pound.]

Liv·y (lĭv′ē). 59 B.C.–A.D.17. Roman historian. His history of Rome consisted of 142 volumes, of which only 35 survive.

lix·iv·i·ate (lĭk-sĭv′ē-āt′) *tr.v.* **-at·ed, -at·ing, -ates.** To wash or percolate the soluble matter from. [Late Latin *lixīvium,* lye (from Latin *lixīvius,* of lye, from *lix,* lye) + –ATE[1].] **—lix·iv′i·a′tion** *n.*

liz·ard (lĭz′ərd) *n.* **1.** Any of numerous reptiles of the suborder Sauria or Lacertilia, characteristically having a scaly elongated body, movable eyelids, four legs, and a tapering tail. **2.** Leather made from the skin of one of these reptiles. [Middle English, from Old French *lesarde,* from Latin *lacertus, lacerta.*]

liz·ard·fish (lĭz′ərd-fĭsh′) *n., pl.* **lizardfish** or **-fish·es.** Any of various bottom-dwelling, large-mouthed fishes of the family Synodontidae of warm seas, having a lizardlike head.

Liz·ard Point or **Liz·ard Head** (lĭz′ərd). A cape of southwest England at the southern tip of **The Lizard,** a peninsula extending southward into the English Channel. It is the southernmost point of Great Britain.

Lju·blja·na (lo͞o′blē-ä′nə, lyo͞o′blyä-nä). A city of northwest Yugoslavia on the Sava River west-northwest of Zagreb. Founded by Augustus in 34 B.C., it came under Hapsburg rule in A.D. 1277 and passed to Yugoslavia in 1919. Population, 205,600.

Lk *abbr.* *Bible.* Luke.

ll or **ll.** *abbr.* Lines.

'll Shall; will: *We'll arrive later.*

lla·ma (lä′mə) *n.* **1.** A domesticated South American ruminant mammal *(Lama glama)* related to the camel, raised for its soft, fleecy wool and used as a beast of burden. **2.** Any of various other mammals of the genus *Lama,* such as the alpaca and guanaco. [Spanish, from Quechua.]

llama
Lama glama

lla·no (lä′nō, lăn′ō) *n., pl.* **-nos.** A large, grassy, almost treeless plain, especially one in Latin America. [Spanish, plain, from Latin *plānum,* from neuter of *plānus,* level. See **pelə-**[2] in Appendix.]

Lla·no Es·ta·ca·do (lăn′ō ĕs′tə-kä′dō, lä′nō). An extensive, semiarid plateau region of the southern Great Plains in southeast New Mexico, western Texas, and northwest Oklahoma.

LL.B. *abbr.* *Latin.* Legum Baccalaureus (Bachelor of Laws).

LL.D. *abbr.* *Latin.* Legum Doctor (Doctor of Laws).

Llew·el·lyn (lo͞o-ĕl′ĭn), **Richard.** 1906–1983. Welsh-born British writer noted for his novel *How Green Was My Valley* (1940), a portrait of life in a Welsh mining village.

LL.M. *abbr.* *Latin.* Legum Magister (Master of Laws).

Lloyd (loid), **Harold Clayton.** 1894–1971. American silent film actor. His most famous stunt was hanging from a clock face at the top of a building in *Safety Last* (1923).

Lloyd George (jôrj′), **David.** First Earl of Dwyfor. 1863–1945. British politician who served as prime minister from 1916 to 1922.

Llu·llai·lla·co (yo͞o′yī-yä′kō). A volcano, 6,727.4 m (22,057 ft) high, in the Andes of northern Chile near the Argentine border.

lm *abbr.* *Physics.* Lumen.

Lm *abbr.* *Bible.* Lamentations.

LM *abbr.* **1.** Legion of Merit. **2.** Lunar module.

LMT *abbr.* Local mean time.

ln The symbol for **natural logarithm.**

LNG *abbr.* Liquefied natural gas.

lo (lō) *interj.* Used to attract attention or to show surprise. [Middle English, from Old English *lā.*]

loach (lōch) *n.* Any of various Eurasian and African freshwater fishes of the family Cobitidae, having barbels around the mouth. [Middle English *loche,* from Old French, perhaps from Vulgar Latin **laukka,* fish, slug, possibly of Celtic origin.]

load (lōd) *n.* *Abbr.* **ld.** **1.a.** A weight or mass that is supported: *the load on an arch.* **b.** The overall force to which a structure is subjected in supporting a weight or mass or in resisting externally applied forces. **2.a.** Something that is carried, as by a vehicle, a person, or an animal: *a load of firewood.* **b.** The quantity that is or can be carried at one time. **3.a.** The share of work allocated to or required of a person, a machine, a group, or an organization. **b.** The demand for services or performance made on a machine or system. **4.** The amount of material that can be inserted into a device or machine at one time: *The camera has a full load of film.* **5.** A single charge of ammunition for a firearm. **6.a.** A mental weight or burden: *Good news took a load off my mind.* **b.** A responsibility regarded as oppressive. **7.** The external mechanical resistance against which a machine acts. **8.** *Electricity.* **a.** The power output of a generator or power plant. **b.** A device or the resistance of a device to which power is delivered. **9.** A front-end load. **10.** Often **loads.** *Informal.* A great number or amount: *loads of parties during the holiday season.* **11.** *Slang.* A satisfying view; an eyeful: *Get a load of that new car!* **12.** Genetic load. **—load** *v.* **load·ed, load·ing, loads.** —*tr.* **1.a.** To put (something) into or onto a structure, device, or conveyance: *loading grain onto a train.* **b.** To put something into or onto (a structure, device, or conveyance): *loaded the tanker with crude oil.* **2.** To provide or fill nearly to overflowing; heap: *loaded the table with food.* **3.** To weigh down; burden: *was loaded with worries.* **4.** To charge (a firearm) with ammunition. **5.** To insert a necessary material into: *loaded tape into the recorder.* **6.** *Games.* To make (dice) heavier on one side by adding weight. **7.** To charge with additional meanings, implications, or emotional import: *loaded the question to trick the witness.* **8.** To dilute, adulterate, or doctor. See Synonyms at **adulterate.** **9.** To raise the power demand in (an electrical circuit), as by adding resistance. **10.** To increase (an insurance premium or a mutual fund share price) by adding expenses or sale costs. **11.** *Baseball.* To have or put runners on (all three bases). **12.** *Computer Science.* **a.** To transfer (data) from a storage device into a computer's memory. **b.** To mount (a

ă pat	oi boy
ā pay	ou out
âr care	o͝o took
ä father	o͞o boot
ĕ pet	ŭ cut
ē be	ûr urge
ĭ pit	th thin
ī pie	*th* this
îr pier	hw which
ŏ pot	zh vision
ō toe	ə about, item
ô paw	♦ regionalism

Stress marks: **′** (primary); ′ (secondary), as in **dictionary** (dĭk′shə-nĕr′ē)

loblolly pine
Pinus taeda

lobster

lobster pot

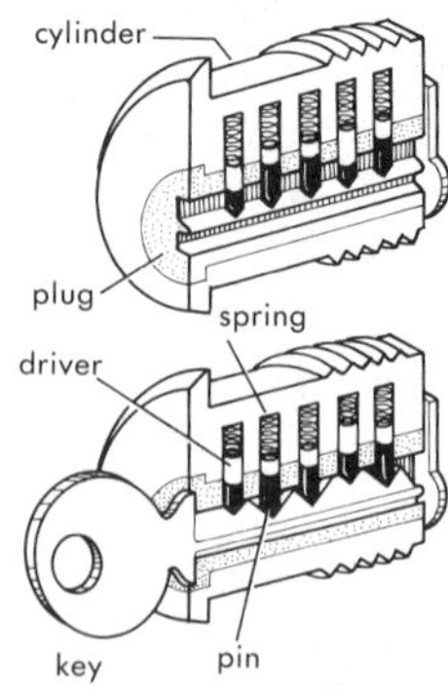

lock[1]
Top: Pin-tumbler cylinder lock
Bottom: River lock near Heidelberg, Germany

diskette) onto a floppy disk drive. **c.** To mount (a magnetic tape) onto a tape drive. —*intr.* **1.** To receive a load: *Container ships can load rapidly.* **2.** To charge a firearm with ammunition. **3.** To put or place a load into or onto a structure, device, or conveyance. [Middle English *lode,* alteration (influenced by *laden,* to load; see LADE) of *lade,* course, way, from Old English *lād.* See **leit-** in Appendix.]

load·ed (lō′dĭd) *adj.* **1.** Carrying a load. **2.** Heavy with meaning or emotional import: *The psychoanalyst specialized in asking loaded questions.* **3.** *Slang.* Intoxicated; drunk. **4.** *Slang.* Having a great deal of money. See Synonyms at **rich.**

load·er (lō′dər) *n.* *Computer Science.* A program that transfers data from off-line memory into internal storage.

load·ing (lō′dĭng) *n.* *Abbr.* **ldg. 1.** A weight placed on something else; a burden. **2.** A substance added to something else; a filler. **3.** An addition to an insurance premium. **4.** *Electricity.* The addition of inductance to a transmission line to improve its transmission characteristics.

loading program *n.* *Computer Science.* A sequence of instructions that starts the processing of a program entered by means of an automatic input device.

load line *n.* *Nautical.* See **Plimsoll mark.**

load·mas·ter (lōd′măs′tər) *n.* An aircraft crew member in charge of loading and unloading cargo or heavy weapons.

load·star (lōd′stär′) *n.* Variant of **lodestar.**

load·stone (lōd′stōn′) *n.* Variant of **lodestone.**

loaf[1] (lōf) *n., pl.* **loaves** (lōvz). **1.** A shaped mass of bread baked in one piece. **2.** A shaped, usually rounded or oblong, mass of food: *veal loaf.* [Middle English *lof,* from Old English *hlāf.*]

loaf[2] (lōf) *intr.v.* **loafed, loaf·ing, loafs.** To pass time at leisure; idle. [Probably back-formation from LOAFER.]

loaf·er (lō′fər) *n.* One who is habitually idle: *disliked loafers on the job.* [Short for obsolete *land-loafer,* vagabond, idler, possibly partial translation of obsolete German *Landläufer,* from Middle High German *landlöufer* : *land,* land + *löufer,* runner (from *loufen,* to run, from Old High German *hlouffan*).]

Loaf·er (lō′fər). A trademark used for a low leather step-in shoe with an upper resembling a moccasin but with a broad, flat heel. This trademark often occurs in print in lowercase: *"Under the . . . private label, there is a simple black patent loafer for $175"* (New York Times). *"Popular looks for men include: knee-length shorts worn with a blazer, white socks and loafers; or turtlenecks, often white"* (San Francisco Chronicle). *"The groom wore jeans, loafers and no socks"* (Sports Illustrated).

loam (lōm) *n.* **1.** Soil composed of a mixture of sand, clay, silt, and organic matter. **2.** A mixture of moist clay and sand, together with straw, used especially in making bricks and foundry molds. —**loam** *tr.v.* **loamed, loam·ing, loams.** To fill, cover, or coat with loam. [Middle English *lam, lom,* clay, from Old English *lām.* See **lei-** in Appendix.] —**loam′y** *adj.*

loan (lōn) *n.* **1.a.** Something lent for temporary use. **b.** A sum of money lent at interest. **2.** An act of lending; a grant for temporary use: *asked for the loan of a garden hose.* **3.** A temporary transfer to a duty or place away from a regular job: *an efficiency expert on loan from the main office.* —**loan** *tr.v.* **loaned, loan·ing, loans.** *Usage Problem.* To lend. [Middle English *lan, lon,* from Old Norse *lān.* See **leikʷ-** in Appendix.] —**loan′er** *n.*

USAGE NOTE: The verb *loan* is well established in American usage and cannot be considered incorrect. The frequent objections to the form by American grammarians may have originated from a provincial deference to British critics, who long ago labeled the usage a typical Americanism. But *loan* is used only to describe physical transactions, as of money or goods. For figurative transactions, *lend* is the only possible form: *Distance lends enchantment. The allusions lend the work a classical tone. Lend* is also required in fixed expressions such as *lend-lease* and *moneylender.*

Lo·an·da (lō-än′də). See **Luanda.**

loan shark *n.* *Informal.* One who lends money at exorbitant interest rates, especially one financed and supported by an organized crime network.

loan·shark·ing (lōn′shär′kĭng) *n.* *Informal.* The practice of lending money at usurious, often illegal interest rates.

loan translation *n.* A form of borrowing from one language to another whereby the semantic components of a given term are literally translated into their equivalents in the borrowing language. English *superman,* for example, is a loan translation from German *Übermensch.* Also called *calque.*

loan word or **loan·word** (lōn′wûrd′) *n.* A word adopted from another language and completely or partially naturalized, as *very* and *hors d'oeuvre,* both from French.

loath also **loth** (lōth, lōth) *adj.* Unwilling or reluctant; disinclined: *I am loath to go on such short notice.* [Middle English *loth,* displeasing, loath, from Old English *lāth,* hateful, loathsome.]

loathe (lōth) *tr.v.* **loathed, loath·ing, loathes.** To dislike (someone or something) greatly; abhor. [Middle English *lothen,* from Old English *lāthian.*] —**loath′er** *n.*

loath·ing (lō′thĭng) *n.* Great dislike; abhorrence. —**loath′ing·ly** *adv.*

loath·ly (lōth′lē, lōth′-) *adj.* Loathsome. [Middle English *lothly,* from Old English *lāthlīc* : *lāth,* hateful + *-līc,* like; see -LY[1].]

loath·some (lōth′səm, lōth′-) *adj.* Arousing loathing; abhorrent. See Synonyms at **offensive.** [Middle English *lothsome* : *loth,* hateful; see LOATH + *-som,* adj. suff.; see -SOME[1].] —**loath′some·ly** *adv.* —**loath′some·ness** *n.*

loaves (lōvz) *n.* Plural of **loaf**[1].

lob (lŏb) *v.* **lobbed, lob·bing, lobs.** —*tr.* To hit, throw, or propel in a high arc: *lob a beach ball; lob a tennis shot over an opponent's head.* —*intr.* **1.** To hit a ball in a high arc. **2.** To move heavily or clumsily. —**lob** *n.* **1.** A ball hit, thrown, or propelled in a high arc. **2.** *Chiefly British.* A clumsy dull person; a lout. [From Middle English, pollack, lout, probably of Low German origin.] —**lob′ber** *n.*

Lo·ba·chev·ski (lō′bə-chĕf′skē, lə-bə-chyĕf′-), **Nikolai Ivanovich.** 1792–1856. Russian mathematician who developed (1826) hyperbolic geometry.

lo·bar (lō′bər, -bär′) *adj.* Of or relating to a lobe or lobes, as of the lungs: *lobar pneumonia.*

lo·bate (lō′bāt′) also **lo·bat·ed** (-bā′tĭd) *adj.* **1.** Having lobes; lobed. **2.** Shaped like a lobe. **3.** Having separate toes, each bordered by a weblike lobe. Used of the feet of certain birds. —**lo′bate′ly** *adv.*

lo·ba·tion (lō-bā′shən) *n.* **1.** The state of being lobed. **2.** A structure or part resembling a lobe. **3.** A lobe.

lob·by (lŏb′ē) *n., pl.* **-bies. 1.** A hall, foyer, or waiting room at or near the entrance to a building, such as a hotel or theater. **2.** A public room next to the assembly chamber of a legislative body. **3.** A group of persons engaged in trying to influence legislators or other public officials in favor of a specific cause: *the banking lobby; the labor lobby.* —**lobby** *v.* **-bied, -by·ing, -bies.** —*intr.* To try to influence the thinking of legislators or other public officials for or against a specific cause: *lobbying for stronger environmental safeguards; lobbied against the proliferation of nuclear arms.* —*tr.* **1.** To try to influence public officials on behalf of or against (proposed legislation, for example): *lobbied the bill through Congress; lobbied the bill to a negative vote.* **2.** To try to influence (an official) to take a desired action. [Medieval Latin *lobia,* monastic cloister, of Germanic origin.] —**lob′by·er, lob′by·ist** *n.* —**lob′by·ism** *n.*

lobe (lōb) *n.* **1.** A rounded projection, especially a rounded, projecting anatomical part: *the lobe of an ear.* **2.** A subdivision of a bodily organ or part bounded by fissures, connective tissue, or other structural boundaries. [Middle English, from Old French, from Late Latin *lobus,* hull, pod, from Greek *lobos,* lobe, pod.]

lo·bec·to·my (lō-bĕk′tə-mē) *n., pl.* **-mies.** Surgical excision of a lobe, as of the lung.

lobed (lōbd) *adj.* Having a lobe or lobes: *lobed leaves.*

lobe·fin (lōb′fĭn′) *n.* Any of various mostly extinct bony fishes of the subclass Crossopterygii, of which the coelacanth is a living representative. —**lobe′finned′** *adj.*

lo·be·li·a (lō-bē′lē-ə, -bēl′yə) *n.* Any of numerous plants of the genus *Lobelia,* having terminal racemes of variously colored flowers with a bilabiate corolla. [New Latin *Lobelia,* genus name, after Matthias de *Lobel* (1538–1616), Flemish botanist and physician.]

Lo·bi·to (lō-bē′tō). A city of west-central Angola on **Lobito Bay,** an inlet of the Atlantic Ocean. It is the country's chief port. Population, 120,000.

♦**lob·lol·ly** (lŏb′lŏl′ē) *n., pl.* **-lies. 1.** *Chiefly Southern U.S.* A mudhole; a mire. **2.** The loblolly pine. [Perhaps dialectal *lob,* to bubble + *lolly,* broth.]

♦***REGIONAL NOTE:*** *Loblolly* is a combination of *lob,* probably an onomatopoeia for the thick, heavy bubbling of cooking porridge, and *lolly,* an old British dialect word for "broth, soup, or any other food boiled in a pot." Thus, *loblolly* originally denoted thick porridge or gruel, especially that eaten by sailors on board ship. In the southern United States, the word is used to mean "a mudhole; a mire," a sense derived from an allusion to the consistency of porridge. The name *loblolly* has become associated with several varieties of trees as well, all of which favor wet bottomlands or swamps in the Gulf and South Atlantic states.

loblolly pine *n.* A pine *(Pinus taeda)* of the southeast United States, having needles in fascicles of three, oblong cones, and strong wood used as lumber and for paper pulp.

♦**lo·bo** (lō′bō) *n., pl.* **-bos.** *Western U.S.* The gray wolf. [Spanish, wolf, from Latin *lupus.* See **wl̥kʷo-** in Appendix.]

lo·bo·la (lō′bə-lə) *n.* A set amount paid by a prospective husband to the bride's family among certain peoples in southern Africa.

lo·bot·o·mize (lə-bŏt′ə-mīz′, lō-) *tr.v.* **-mized, -miz·ing, -miz·es. 1.** To perform a lobotomy on (a patient). **2.** To deprive (a person) of energy or vitality.

lo·bot·o·my (lə-bŏt′ə-mē, lō-) *n., pl.* **-mies.** Surgical incision into the frontal lobe of the brain to sever one or more nerve tracts, a technique formerly used to treat certain mental disorders but now rarely performed. [LOBE + -TOMY.]

lob·scouse (lŏb′skous′) *n.* A sailor's stew made of meat, vegetables, and hardtack. [Perhaps dialectal *lob,* to bubble + *scouse,* of unknown origin.]

lob·ster (lŏb′stər) *n.* **1.** Any of several edible marine crustaceans of the family Homaridae, especially of the genus *Homarus,* having stalked eyes, long antennae, and five pairs of legs, the first pair of which is modified into large pincers. **2.** Any of several crustaceans, such as the spiny lobster, that are related to the lobsters. **3.** The flesh of a lobster used as food. —*attributive.* Often used to modify another noun: *a lobster dinner; lobster boats.* **—lobster** *intr.v.* **-stered, -ster·ing, -sters.** To search for and catch lobsters. [Middle English *lopster, lobstere,* from Old English *loppestre,* alteration (perhaps influenced by *loppe, lobbe,* spider) of Latin *locusta.*] **—lob′ster·er** *n.*

WORD HISTORY: A lobster and a locust may share a common source for their name, that is, the Latin word *locusta,* which was used for the locust and also for a crustacean that was probably a kind of lobster. We can see that *locusta* would be the source of *locust,* but it looks like an unlikely candidate as the source of *lobster.* It is thought, however, that Old English *loppestre,* the ancestor of *lobster,* was formed from *locusta* and the suffix *-estre* used to make agent nouns (our *-ster*). The change from Latin *locusta* to Old English *loppestre* may have been influenced by Old English *loppe,* meaning "spider."

lob·ster·man (lŏb′stər-mən) *n.* **1.** A man whose occupation is catching lobsters. **2.** *Nautical.* A ship used in locating and catching lobsters.

lobster pot *n.* A slatted cage with an opening covered by a funnel-shaped net, used for trapping lobsters.

lobster ther·mi·dor (thûr′mĭ-dôr′) *n.* A dish consisting of cooked lobster meat mixed with a cream sauce, put into a lobster shell, sprinkled with cheese, and browned. [After French *Thermidor,* the 11th month of the calendar used during the French Revolution : Greek *thermē,* heat; see THERM + Greek *dōron,* gift; see **dō-** in Appendix.]

lob·u·late (lŏb′yə-lāt′) also **lob·u·lat·ed** (-lā′tĭd) *adj.* Having or consisting of lobules. **—lob′u·la′tion** *n.*

lob·ule (lŏb′yo͞ol) *n.* **1.** A small lobe. **2.** A section or subdivision of a lobe. **—lob′u·lar** (-yə-lər), **lob′u·lose′** (-yə-lōs′) *adj.* **—lob′u·lar·ly** *adv.*

lob·worm (lŏb′wûrm′) *n.* See **lugworm.** [Alteration (influenced by LOB, lump, something hanging) of LUGWORM.]

lo·cal (lō′kəl) *adj.* **1.a.** Of, relating to, or characteristic of a particular place: *a local custom; the local slang.* **b.** Of or relating to a city, town, or district rather than a larger area: *state and local government.* **2.** Not broad or general; not widespread: *local outbreaks of flu.* **3.** *Medicine.* Of or affecting a specific part of the body: *a local infection.* **4.** Making all possible or scheduled stops on a route; not express: *a local train.* **—local** *n.* **1.** A public conveyance that makes several intermediate stops before the final destination is reached: *changed trains to a local.* **2.** A local chapter or branch of an organization, especially of a labor union. **3.** *Informal.* A person from a particular locality. [Middle English, from Old French, from Late Latin *locālis,* from Latin *locus,* place.] **—lo′cal·ly** *adv.* **—lo′cal·ness** *n.*

local anesthetic *n.* An anesthetic that induces loss of sensation only on and around the point where it is applied or injected.

local area network *n.* LAN.

local color *n.* **1.** The interest or flavor of a locality imparted by the customs and sights peculiar to it. **2.** The use of regional detail in a literary or an artistic work.

lo·cale (lō-kăl′) *n.* **1.** A place, especially with reference to a particular event: *the locale of a crime.* **2.** The scene or setting, as of a novel. [From French *local,* local, locale, from Old French. See LOCAL.]

lo·cal·ism (lō′kə-lĭz′əm) *n.* **1.a.** A local linguistic feature. **b.** A local custom or peculiarity. **2.** Devotion to local interests and customs. **—lo′cal·ist** *n.*

lo·cal·i·ty (lō-kăl′ĭ-tē) *n., pl.* **-ties. 1.** A particular neighborhood, place, or district: *"Localities, even individual villages, developed their own languages"* (Wall Street Journal). See Synonyms at **area. 2.** The fact or quality of having position in space. [French *localité,* from Late Latin *locālitās,* from *locālis,* local. See LOCAL.]

lo·cal·ize (lō′kə-līz′) *v.* **-ized, -iz·ing, -iz·es.** —*tr.* **1.** To make local: *decentralize and localize political authority.* **2.** To confine or restrict to a particular locality: *localized the infection.* **3.** To attribute to a particular locality: *sought to localize the origin of the rumor.* —*intr.* To become local, especially to become fixed in one area. **—lo′cal·i·za′tion** (-kə-lĭ-zā′shən) *n.*

local option *n.* The power granted to a local political subdivision to decide whether to apply a law, such as a ban on liquor sales, within its jurisdiction.

Lo·car·no (lō-kär′nō). A town of southern Switzerland at the northern end of Lake Maggiore. First mentioned in 749, it passed to Milan in 1342 and was taken by the Swiss in 1512. The Locarno Pact between Germany and various European powers was signed here on December 1, 1925, in an effort to promote peace and maintain existing territorial borders. Population, 14,300.

lo·cate (lō′kāt′, lō-kāt′) *v.* **-cat·ed, -cat·ing, -cates.** —*tr.* **1.** To determine or specify the position or limits of: *locate Albany on the map; managed to locate the site of the old artists' colony.* **2.** To find by searching, examining, or experimenting: *locate the source of error.* **3.** To place at a certain location; station or situate: *locate an agent in Rochester.* —*intr.* To become established; settle. [Latin *locāre, locāt-,* to place, from *locus,* place.] **—lo′cat′a·ble** *adj.* **—lo′cat′er** *n.*

lo·ca·tion (lō-kā′shən) *n.* **1.** The act or process of locating. **2.** A place where something is or could be located; a site. **3.** A site away from a studio at which part or all of a movie is shot: *filming a Western on location in the Mexican desert.* **4.** A tract of land that has been surveyed and marked off. [Latin *locātiō, locātiōn-,* a placing, from *locātus,* past participle of *locāre,* to place. See LOCATE.] **—lo·ca′tion·al** *adj.*

loc·a·tive (lŏk′ə-tĭv) *adj.* Of, relating to, or being a grammatical case in certain inflected languages that indicates place in or on which or time at which, as in Latin *domī,* "at home." **—locative** *n.* **1.** The locative case. **2.** A word in the locative case. [New Latin *locātīvus,* from Latin *locātus,* past participle of *locāre,* to place. See LOCATE.]

lo·ca·tor (lō′kā′tər) *n.* One that locates, as a person who fixes the boundaries of mining claims.

loc. cit. *abbr. Latin.* Loco citato (in the place cited).

loch (lŏKH, lŏk) *n. Scots.* **1.** A lake. **2.** An arm of the sea similar to a fjord. [Middle English *louch,* from Scottish Gaelic *loch,* from Old Irish.]

Loch (lŏk, lôKH). See **Lake.**

lo·chi·a (lō′kē-ə, lŏk′ē-ə) *pl.n. Medicine.* The normal uterine discharge of blood, tissue, and mucus from the vagina after childbirth. [Greek *lokhia,* from neuter pl. of *lokhios,* of childbirth, from *lokhos,* childbirth. See **legh-** in Appendix.] **—lo′chi·al** *adj.*

lo·ci (lō′sī′, -kē, -kī′) *n.* Plural of **locus.**

lock¹ (lŏk) *n.* **1.** A device operated by a key, combination, or keycard and used, as on a door, for holding, closing, or securing. **2.** A section of a waterway, such as a canal, closed off with gates, in which vessels in transit are raised or lowered by raising or lowering the water level of that section. **3.** A mechanism in a firearm for exploding the charge. **4.** An interlocking or entanglement of elements or parts. **5.a.** *Sports.* A hold in wrestling or self-defense that is secured on a part of an opponent's body. **b.** A secure hold or grip: *The distributor has a lock on most of the market.* **—lock** *v.* **locked, lock·ing, locks.** —*tr.* **1.a.** To fasten the lock of: *close and lock a drawer.* **b.** To shut or make secure with or as if with locks: *locked the house.* **2.** To confine or exclude by or as if by means of a lock: *locked the dog in for the night; locked the criminal up in a cell.* **3.** To fix in place so that movement or escape is impossible; hold fast: *The ship was locked in the ice through the winter. She felt that she had become locked into a binding agreement.* **4.a.** To sight and follow (a moving target) automatically: *locked the enemy fighter in the gun sights.* **b.** To aim (a weapon or other device) at a moving target so as to follow it automatically: *"The pilot had locked his targeting radar on the slow-moving frigate"* (Ed Magnuson). **5.** To engage and interlock securely so as to be immobile. **6.** To clasp or link firmly; intertwine: *locked arms and walked away.* **7.** To bind in close struggle or battle: *The two dogs were locked in combat.* **8.a.** To equip (a waterway) with locks. **b.** To pass (a vessel) through a lock. **9.** *Printing.* **a.** To secure (letterpress type) in a chase or press bed by tightening the quoins. **b.** To fasten (a curved plate) to the cylinder of a rotary press. **10.** To invest (funds) in such a way that they cannot easily be converted into cash. **11.** *Computer Science.* To end the processing of (a magnetic tape or disk) in such a way as to deny access to its contents. —*intr.* **1.** To become fastened by or as if by means of a lock: *We tried the door, but it was locked.* **2.** To become entangled; interlock. **3.** To become rigid or immobile: *The mechanism tends to lock in cold weather.* **4.** To pass through a lock or locks in a waterway. ***—phrasal verb.* lock out.** To withhold work from (employees) during a labor dispute. ***—idioms.* lock horns.** To become embroiled in conflict. **lock, stock, and barrel.** To the greatest or most complete extent; wholly: *an estate that was auctioned off lock, stock, and barrel.* [Middle English, from Old English *loc,* bolt, bar.] **—lock′a·ble** *adj.*

lock² (lŏk) *n.* **1.a.** A length or curl of hair; a tress. **b.** Often **locks.** The hair of the head. **2.** A small wisp or tuft, as of wool or cotton. [Middle English, from Old English *locc.*]

lock·age (lŏk′ĭj) *n.* **1.** The passage of a ship through a lock. **2.** A toll paid for the use of a lock. **3.** A system of locks.

Locke (lŏk), **Alain LeRoy.** 1886–1954. American educator and writer who was a leader of the Harlem Renaissance.

Locke, David Ross. Pseudonym Petroleum V. Nasby. 1833–1888. American satirist who edited the *Toledo Blade* (1865–1871).

Locke, John. 1632–1704. English philosopher. In *An Essay Concerning Human Understanding* (1690) he set out the principles of empiricism.

lock·er (lŏk′ər) *n.* **1.** One that locks: *a locker of windows and doors.* **2.** A small, usually metal compartment that can be locked, especially one at a gymnasium or public place for the safekeeping of clothing and valuables. **3.** A flat trunk for storage. **4.** A heavily insulated refrigerated cabinet, compartment, or room for storing frozen foods.

locker room *n.* A room furnished with lockers, as in a gymnasium, school, or workplace, used as a place in which to change clothes and store equipment.

lock·er-room (lŏk′ər-ro͞om′, -ro͝om′) *adj.* Relating to, found in, or appropriate for a locker room: *locker-room interviews; locker-room stories that could not be told in mixed company.*

lock·et (lŏk′ĭt) *n.* A small ornamental case for a picture or

John Locke

locket

ă pat	oi boy
ā pay	ou out
âr care	o͝o took
ä father	o͞o boot
ĕ pet	ŭ cut
ē be	ûr urge
ĭ pit	th thin
ī pie	*th* this
îr pier	hw which
ŏ pot	zh vision
ō toe	ə about, item
ô paw	♦ regionalism

Stress marks: ′ (primary); ′ (secondary), as in **dictionary** (dĭk′shə-nĕr′ē)

keepsake, usually worn as a pendant. [Middle English *loket*, crossbar, from Old French *loquet*, latch, diminutive of *loc*, lock, of Germanic origin.]

lock·jaw (lŏk′jô′) *n.* **1.** See **tetanus** (sense 1). **2.** An early sign of tetanus, in which the jaw is locked closed because of a tonic spasm of the muscles of mastication. Also called *trismus.*

lock·keep·er (lŏk′kē′pər) *n.* One who is in charge of a lock on a waterway. Also called *lockmaster.*

lock·mas·ter (lŏk′măs′tər) *n.* See **lockkeeper.**

lock·nut also **lock nut** (lŏk′nŭt′) *n.* **1.** A usually thin nut screwed down on another nut to prevent it from loosening. **2.** A self-locking nut.

lock-on (lŏk′ŏn′, -ôn′) *n.* The start of the automatic tracking of a target, as by a missile.

lock·out (lŏk′out′) *n.* The withholding of work from employees and closing down of a workplace by an employer during a labor dispute. Also called *shutout.*

Lock·port (lŏk′pôrt′, -pōrt′). A city of western New York north-northeast of Buffalo. An industrial center, the city was built around a series of locks on the Erie Canal. Population, 24,844.

locomotive
Diesel locomotive

lock·set (lŏk′sĕt′) *n.* A set of hardware for shutting or locking a door.

lock·smith (lŏk′smĭth′) *n.* One that makes or repairs locks.

lock step or **lock·step** (lŏk′stĕp′) *n.* **1.** A way of marching in which the marchers follow each other as closely as possible. **2.** A standardized procedure that is closely, often mindlessly followed.

lock stitch *n.* A stitch made on a sewing machine by the interlocking of the upper thread and the bobbin thread.

lock·up (lŏk′ŭp′) *n.* **1.** *Informal.* A jail, especially one in which offenders are held while awaiting a court hearing. **2. a.** The act or an instance of locking. **b.** The state of being locked.

Lock·wood (lŏk′wo͝od′), **Belva Ann Bennett.** 1830–1917. American lawyer and suffragist. She was the first woman admitted to practice before the U.S. Supreme Court (1879).

Lock·yer (lŏk′yər), Sir **Joseph Norman.** 1836–1920. British astronomer who founded and was the first editor (1869–1919) of *Nature* magazine.

lo·co¹ (lō′kō) *adj. Slang.* Mad; insane. **—loco** *n., pl.* **-cos. 1.** See **locoweed. 2.** See **loco disease. —loco** *tr.v.* **-coed, -co·ing, -cos. 1.** To poison with locoweed. **2.** *Slang.* To make insane; craze. [Spanish, crazy, possibly from Arabic *lawqā*, foolish, from *'alwaq*, stupid.]

lo·co² (lō′kō) *adv. & adj. Music.* At the pitch written. Used chiefly as a direction. [From Italian *loco*, from Latin *locō*, ablative of *locus*, place.]

loco disease *n.* A disease of livestock caused by locoweed poisoning and characterized by weakness, lack of coordination, trembling, and partial paralysis. Also called *loco, locoism.*

lo·co·ism (lō′kō-ĭz′əm) *n.* See **loco disease.**

lo·co·mo·tion (lō′kə-mō′shən) *n.* **1.** The act of moving from place to place. **2.** The ability to move from place to place. [Latin *locō*, from a place, ablative of *locus*, place + MOTION.]

lo·co·mo·tive (lō′kə-mō′tĭv) *n.* **1.** A self-propelled vehicle, usually electric or diesel-powered, for pulling or pushing freight or passenger cars on railroad tracks. **2.** A driving or pulling force; an impetus: *"The US could no longer serve as the locomotive for the world economy"* (George Soros). **—locomotive** *adj.* **1. a.** Of, relating to, or involved in locomotion. **b.** Serving to put into motion or propel forward: *"It may be that the founding fathers overestimated the locomotive force of the collective and mutual self-interest"* (Ian Davidson). **2.** Able to move independently from place to place. **3.** Of or relating to a self-propelled locomotive. **4.** Of or relating to travel. [Latin *locō*, from a place, ablative of *locus*, place + Medieval Latin *mōtīvus*, causing motion; see MOTIVE.]

lo·co·mo·tor (lō′kə-mō′tər) *adj.* Of or relating to locomotion; locomotive. [Latin *locō*, from a place, ablative of *locus*, place + MOTOR.]

locomotor ataxia *n.* See **tabes dorsalis.**

lo·co·weed (lō′kō-wēd′) *n.* Any of several plants of the genera *Oxytropis* and *Astragalus* in the pea family, which are widespread in the western and central United States and cause severe poisoning when eaten by livestock. Also called *crazyweed, loco.*

loc·u·lar (lŏk′yə-lər) also **loc·u·late** (-lāt′, -lĭt) or **loc·u·lat·ed** (-lā′tĭd) *adj.* Having or divided into small cavities or compartments. [LOCUL(US) + -AR.] **—loc′u·la′tion** *n.*

loc·ule (lŏk′yo͞ol) or **loc·u·lus** (-yə-ləs) *n., pl.* **-ules** or **-li** (-lī′). A small cavity or compartment within an organ or a part of an animal or a plant, as any of the cavities within a plant ovary. [Latin *loculus*, little place, diminutive of *locus*, place.]

loc·u·li·cid·al (lŏk′yə-lə-sīd′l) *adj. Botany.* Longitudinally dehiscent along the capsule wall between the partitions of the locule, as in the fruits of irises and lilies. [LOCUL(US) + Latin *-cīda*, one who cuts; see -CID(E) + -AL¹.]

loc·u·lus (lŏk′yə-ləs) *n.* Variant of **locule.** [Latin, little place, diminutive of *locus*, place.]

locust
Top: Desert locusts
Schistocerca gregaria
Bottom: Black locust
Robinia pseudoacacia

lo·cum te·nens (lō′kəm tē′nĕnz′, tĕn′ənz) *n., pl.* **locum te·nen·tes** (tə-nĕn′tēz). A person, especially a physician or cleric, who substitutes temporarily for another. [Medieval Latin *locum tenēns* : Latin *locum*, accusative of *locus*, place + Latin *tenēns*, present participle of *tenēre*, to hold.]

lo·cus (lō′kəs) *n., pl.* **-ci** (-sī′, -kē, -kī′). **1.** A locality; a place. **2.** A center or focus of great activity or intense concentration: *"the cunning exploitation of loci of power; the insulation from normal American society"* (Clifton Fadiman). **3.** *Mathematics.* The set or configuration of all points whose coordinates satisfy a single equation or one or more algebraic conditions. **4.** The position that a given gene occupies on a chromosome. [Latin.]

locus clas·si·cus (klăs′ĭ-kəs) *n., pl.* **loci clas·si·ci** (klăs′ĭ-sī′, -kī′). A passage from a classic or standard work that is cited as an illustration or instance. [New Latin : Latin *locus*, place + Latin *classicus*, belonging to the highest class.]

lo·cust (lō′kəst) *n.* **1.** Any of numerous grasshoppers of the family Acrididae, often migrating in immense swarms that devour vegetation and crops. **2.** The seventeen-year locust. **3. a.** Any of several North American deciduous trees of the genus *Robinia*, especially *R. pseudoacacia*, having compound leaves, drooping clusters of fragrant white flowers, and durable hard wood. **b.** Any of several similar or related trees, such as the honey locust or the carob. **c.** The wood of one of these trees. [Middle English, from Old French *locuste*, from Latin *locusta*. Sense 3a, probably from the resemblance of its fruit to a locust.]

lo·cu·tion (lō-kyo͞o′shən) *n.* **1.** A particular word, phrase, or expression, especially one that is used by a particular person or group. **2.** Style of speaking; phraseology. [Middle English *locucion*, from Old French *locution*, from Latin *locūtiō*, *locūtiōn-*, from *locūtus*, past participle of *loquī*, to speak. See **tolkʷ-** in Appendix.]

lode (lōd) *n.* **1. a.** The metalliferous ore that fills a fissure in a rock formation. **b.** A vein of mineral ore deposited between clearly demarcated layers of rock. Also called *lead.* **2.** A rich source or supply. [Middle English *lode*, way, load, from Old English *lād*, way. See **leit-** in Appendix.]

lode·star also **load·star** (lōd′stär′) *n.* **1.** A star, especially Polaris, that is used as a point of reference. **2.** A guiding principle, interest, or ambition. [Middle English *lodesterre* : *lode*, way; see LODE + *sterre*, star; see STAR.]

lode·stone also **load·stone** (lōd′stōn′) *n.* **1.** A piece of magnetite that has magnetic properties and attracts iron or steel. **2.** One that attracts strongly. [Middle English *lode*, way; see LODE + STONE (from its use by sailors to show the way).]

lodge (lŏj) *n.* **1. a.** A cottage or cabin, often rustic, used as a temporary abode or shelter: *a ski lodge.* **b.** A small house on the grounds of an estate or a park, used by a caretaker or gatekeeper. **c.** An inn. **2. a.** Any of various Native American dwellings, such as a hogan, wigwam, or longhouse. **b.** The group living in such a dwelling. **3.** *Abbr.* **L. a.** A local chapter of certain fraternal organizations. **b.** The meeting hall of such a chapter. **c.** The members of such a chapter. **4.** The den of certain animals, such as the dome-shaped structure built by beavers. **—lodge** *v.* **lodged, lodg·ing, lodg·es.** —*tr.* **1. a.** To provide with temporary quarters, especially for sleeping: *lodges travelers in the shed.* **b.** To rent a room to. **c.** To place or establish in quarters: *lodged the children with relatives after the fire.* **2.** To serve as a depository for; contain: *This cabinet lodges our oldest wines.* **3.** To place, leave, or deposit, as for safety: *documents lodged with a trusted associate.* **4.** To fix, force, or implant: *lodge a bullet in a wall.* **5.** To register (a charge or complaint, for example) before an authority, such as a court; file. **6.** To vest (authority, for example). **7.** To beat (crops) down flat: *rye lodged by the cyclone.* —*intr.* **1. a.** To live in a place temporarily. **b.** To rent accommodations, especially for sleeping. **2.** To be or become embedded: *The ball lodged in the fence.* [Middle English, from Old French *loge*, of Germanic origin.]

Lodge (lŏj), **Henry Cabot.** 1850–1924. American politician. As Senate majority leader (1918–1924) and head of the foreign relations committee (1918–1924) he successfully opposed United States membership in the League of Nations.

Lodge, Henry Cabot, Jr. 1902–1985. American politician and diplomat. He was ambassador to South Vietnam (1963–1967).

Lodge, Thomas. 1558?–1625. English writer. His pastoral romance *Rosalynde* (c. 1584) provided the plot for Shakespeare's play *As You Like It.*

lodge·ment (lŏj′mənt) *n.* Variant of **lodgment.**

lodge·pole pine (lŏj′pōl′) *n.* A pine *(Pinus contorta* var. *latifolia)* of western North America, having light wood used in construction.

lodg·er (lŏj′ər) *n.* One that lodges, especially one who rents and lives in a furnished room.

lodg·ing (lŏj′ĭng) *n.* **1.** A place to live: *found lodging near her new job.* **2.** Often **lodgings.** Sleeping accommodations: *We found the lodgings on the tour rather primitive.* **3. lodgings.** Furnished rooms in another's house rented for accommodation.

lodg·ment also **lodge·ment** (lŏj′mənt) *n.* **1. a.** The act of lodging. **b.** The state of being lodged. **2.** A place for lodging. **3.** An accumulation or a deposit. **4.** A foothold or beachhead gained by troops in enemy or neutral territory.

Lo·di (lō′dī′). **1.** A city of central California north of Stockton. It is a processing center in a rich farming area. Population, 35,221. **2.** A borough of northeast New Jersey northeast of Passaic. The city has varied industries. Population, 23,956.

lod·i·cule (lŏd′ĭ-kyo͞ol′) *n.* One of two or three small scales at the base of the ovary in a grass flower, believed to be a rudimentary perianth. [Latin *lōdīcula*, small blanket, diminutive of *lōdīx*, *lōdīc-*, blanket.]

Lódź (lo͞oj, lŏdz, wo͝oj). A city of central Poland west-southwest of Warsaw. Chartered in 1423, it passed to Prussia in 1793 and to Russia in 1815. It became part of Poland after World War I. Population, 849,400.

Loeb (lōb), **Jacques.** 1859–1924. German-born American physiologist noted for his work on parthenogenesis.

lo·ess (lō′əs, lĕs, lŭs) *n.* A buff to gray windblown deposit of fine-grained, calcareous silt or clay. [German *Löss,* from German dialectal *Lösch,* from *lösch,* loose. See **leu-** in Appendix.] **—lo·es′si·al** (lō-ĕs′ē-əl, lĕs′ē-əl, lŭs′-) *adj.*

Loewe (lō), **Frederick.** 1901–1987. Austrian-born American composer who collaborated with Alan Jay Lerner on a number of musicals, including *My Fair Lady* (1956).

Loe·wy (lō′ē), **Raymond Fernand.** 1893–1986. French-born American industrial designer. His practical designs include a 1934 Sears refrigerator and the interiors of NASA spacecraft.

loft (lôft, lŏft) *n.* **1.a.** A large, usually unpartitioned floor over a factory, warehouse, or other commercial or industrial space. **b.** Such a floor converted into an apartment or artist's studio. **2.** An open space under a roof; an attic or a garret. **3.** A gallery or balcony, as in a church. **4.** A hayloft. **5.** *Sports.* **a.** The backward slant of the face of a golf club head, designed to drive the ball in a high arc. **b.** A golf stroke that drives the ball in a high arc. **c.** The upward course of a ball driven in a high arc. **6.a.** The thickness of a fabric or yarn. **b.** The thickness of an item, such as a down comforter, that is filled with compressible insulating material. **—loft** *tr.v.* **loft·ed, loft·ing, lofts. 1.** To put, store, or keep in a loft. **2.** To propel in a high arc: *lofted the ball into the outfield.* **3.** *Nautical.* To lay out a full-size drawing of (the parts of a ship's hull, for example). *—intr.* **1.** To propel something, especially a ball, in a high arc. **2.** To rise high into the air. [Middle English, sky, upstairs room, from Old English, air, from Old Norse *lopt,* upstairs room, sky, air.]

loft·y (lôf′tē, lŏf′-) *adj.* **-i·er, -i·est. 1.** Of imposing height. **2.** Elevated in character; exalted. See Synonyms at **high. 3.** Affecting grandness; pompous. **4.** Arrogant; haughty. [Middle English, noble, from *loft,* upstairs room, sky. See LOFT.] **—loft′i·ly** *adv.* **—loft′i·ness** *n.*

log¹ (lôg, lŏg) *n.* **1.a.** A usually large section of a trunk or limb of a fallen or felled tree. **b.** A long, thick section of trimmed, unhewn timber. **2.** *Nautical.* **a.** A device trailed from a ship to determine its speed through the water. **b.** A record of a ship's speed, its progress, and any shipboard events of navigational importance. **c.** The book in which this record is kept. **3.** A record of a vehicle's performance, as the flight record of an aircraft. **4.** A record, as of the performance of a machine or the progress of an undertaking: *a computer log; a trip log.* **—log** *v.* **logged, log·ging, logs.** *—tr.* **1.a.** To cut down, trim, and haul the timber of (a piece of land). **b.** To cut (timber) into unhewn sections. **2.** To enter in a record, as of a ship or an aircraft. **3.** To travel (a specified distance, time, or speed): *logged 30,000 air miles in April.* **4.** To spend or accumulate (time): *had logged 25 years with the company.* *—intr.* To cut down, trim, and haul timber. ***—phrasal verbs.*** **log in** (or **on**). *Computer Science.* To enter into a computer the information required to begin a session. **log out** (or **off**). *Computer Science.* To enter into a computer the command to end a session. [Middle English *logge.*]

log² (lôg, lŏg) *n. Mathematics.* A logarithm.

log. *abbr.* Logic.

log– *pref.* Variant of **logo–.**

–log *suff.* Variant of **–logue.**

Lo·gan (lō′gən). A city of northern Utah north of Ogden. Settled in the 1850's, it is the seat of Utah State University (chartered 1888). Population, 26,844.

Logan, Mount. A peak, 5,954.8 m (19,524 ft) high, of the St. Elias Mountains in southwest Yukon Territory, Canada, near the Alaska border. It is the highest elevation in Canada.

lo·gan·ber·ry (lō′gən-bĕr′ē) *n.* **1.** A trailing, prickly plant *(Rubus ursinus* var. *loganobaccus)* native to Oregon and south to Baja California, cultivated for its acid, edible fruit. **2.** The red fruit of this plant. [After James Harvey *Logan* (1841–1928), American jurist and horticulturist.]

Lo·gans·port (lō′gənz-pôrt′, -pōrt′). A city of north-central Indiana north-northwest of Kokomo. Population, 17,899.

log·a·rithm (lô′gə-rĭth′əm, lŏg′ə-) *n. Mathematics.* The power to which a base, usually 10, must be raised to produce a given number. If $n^x = a$, the logarithm of a, with n as the base, is x; symbolically, $\log_n a = x$. For example, $10^3 = 1{,}000$; therefore, $\log_{10} 1{,}000 = 3$. The kinds most often used are the common logarithm and the natural logarithm. [New Latin *logarithmus* : Greek *logos,* reason, proportion; see **leg-** in Appendix + Greek *arithmos,* number; see **ar-** in Appendix.] **—log′a·rith′mic** (-rĭth′mĭk), **log′a·rith′mi·cal** (-mĭ-kəl) *adj.* **—log′a·rith′mi·cal·ly** *adv.*

log·book (lôg′bo͝ok′, lŏg′-) *n.* **1.** The official record book of a ship or an aircraft. **2.** A record book with periodic entries.

loge (lōzh) *n.* **1.** A small compartment, especially a box in a theater. **2.** The front rows of the mezzanine in a theater. [French, from Old French, covered walk, lodge. See LODGE.]

log·ger (lô′gər, lŏg′ər) *n.* **1.a.** One who logs trees; a lumberjack. **b.** One engaged in the logging business. **2.** A machine, such as a crane or tractor, that is used for hauling or loading logs.

log·ger·head (lô′gər-hĕd′, lŏg′ər-) *n.* **1.** A loggerhead turtle. **2.** An iron tool consisting of a long handle with a bulbous end, used when heated to melt tar or warm liquids. **3.** *Nautical.* A post on a whaleboat used to secure the harpoon rope. **4.** *Informal.* **a.** A blockhead; a dolt. **b.** A disproportionately large head. ***—idiom.*** **at loggerheads.** Engaged in a dispute: *The question of car privileges put Sam and his parents at loggerheads.* [Probably dialectal *logger,* wooden block (probably from LOG¹) + HEAD.]

loganberry
Rubus ursinus

loggerhead shrike *n.* A common North American bird *(Lanius ludovicianus)* having gray, black, and white plumage, a black facial mask, and a hooked beak. [From its large head.]

loggerhead turtle *n.* A very large marine turtle *(Caretta caretta)* inhabiting warm ocean waters and having a beaked head.

log·gi·a (lô′jē-ə, lŏj′ē-ə) *n.* **1.** An open-sided, roofed gallery or arcade along the front or side of a building, often at an upper level. **2.** An open balcony in a theater. [Italian, from Old Italian, from Old French *loge.* See LOGE.]

log·ging (lô′gĭng, lŏg′ĭng) *n.* The work or business of felling and trimming trees and transporting the logs to a mill.

lo·gi·a (lō′gē-ə) *n. Bible.* Plural of **logion.**

log·ic (lŏj′ĭk) *n. Abbr.* **log. 1.** The study of the principles of reasoning, especially of the structure of propositions as distinguished from their content and of method and validity in deductive reasoning. **2.a.** A system of reasoning: *Aristotle's logic.* **b.** A mode of reasoning: *By that logic, we should sell the company tomorrow.* **c.** The formal, guiding principles of a discipline, school, or science. **3.** Valid reasoning: *Your paper lacks the logic to prove your thesis.* **4.** The relationship between elements and between an element and the whole in a set of objects, individuals, principles, or events: *There's a certain logic to the motion of rush-hour traffic.* **5.** *Computer Science.* **a.** The nonarithmetic operations performed by a computer, such as sorting, comparing, and matching, that involve yes-no decisions. **b.** Computer circuitry. **c.** Graphic representation of computer circuitry. [Middle English, from Old French *logique,* from Latin *logica,* from Greek *logikē (tekhnē),* (art) of reasoning, logic, feminine of *logikos,* of reasoning, from *logos,* reason. See **leg-** in Appendix.]

log·i·cal (lŏj′ĭ-kəl) *adj.* **1.** Of, relating to, in accordance with, or of the nature of logic. **2.** Based on earlier or otherwise known statements, events, or conditions; reasonable: *Rain was a logical expectation, given the time of year.* **3.** Reasoning or capable of reasoning in a clear and consistent manner. **—log′i·cal′i·ty** (-kăl′ĭ-tē), **log′i·cal·ness** *n.* **—log′i·cal·ly** *adv.*

SYNONYMS: *logical, analytic, ratiocinative, rational.* The central meaning shared by these adjectives is "capable of or reflecting the capability for correct and valid reasoning": *a logical mind; an analytic thinker; the ratiocinative process; a rational being.*
ANTONYM: *illogical.*

logical atomism *n.* A philosophy asserting that knowledge consists in awareness of individual facts and in an understanding of the logical relations among them.

logical positivism *n.* A philosophy asserting the primacy of observation in assessing the truth of statements of fact and holding that metaphysical and subjective arguments not based on observable data are meaningless. Also called *logical empiricism.*

logic circuit *n. Computer Science.* A computer switching circuit that performs problem-solving functions.

lo·gi·cian (lō-jĭsh′ən) *n.* **1.** A practitioner of a system of logic. **2.** A student or scholar of logic.

logic operator *n. Computer Science.* An instruction in a program in which the quantity being operated on and the result of the operation each can have one of two values. Logic operators include AND, OR, NAND, EXCLUSIVE OR, and NOR.

loggia
Loggia dei Lanzi,
Florence, Italy

lo·gi·on (lō′gē-ŏn′) *n., pl.* **-gi·a** (-gē-ə). *Bible.* One of the sayings of Jesus not recorded in the Gospels but supposed to have belonged to the source material from which they were compiled. [Greek, oracle, from *legein,* to speak. See **leg-** in Appendix.]

lo·gis·tic (lō-jĭs′tĭk) also **lo·gis·ti·cal** (-tĭ-kəl) *adj.* **1.** Of or relating to symbolic logic. **2.** Of or relating to logistics. [Medieval Latin *logisticus,* of calculation, from Greek *logistikos,* skilled in calculating, from *logistēs,* calculator, from *logizesthai,* to calculate, from *logos,* reckoning, reason. See **leg-** in Appendix.] **—lo·gis′ti·cal·ly** *adv.* **—lo′gis·ti′cian** (-jĭ-stĭsh′ən) *n.*

lo·gis·tics (lō-jĭs′tĭks, lə-) *n. (used with a sing. or pl. verb).* **1.** The branch of military operations that deals with the procurement, distribution, maintenance, and replacement of materiel and personnel. **2.** The management of the details of an operation. [French *logistiques,* from *logistique,* logic (perhaps influenced by *loger,* to quarter), from Medieval Latin *logisticus,* of calculation. See LOGISTIC.]

log·jam (lôg′jăm′, lŏg′-) *n.* **1.** An immovable mass of floating logs crowded together. **2.** A deadlock, as in negotiations; an impasse.

log line *n. Nautical.* The line by which the log is trailed from a ship to determine its speed.

log·nor·mal (lôg-nôr′məl, lŏg-) *adj. Mathematics.* Of, relating to, or being a logarithmic function with a normal distribution. **—log′nor·mal′i·ty** (-măl′ĭ-tē) *n.* **—log·nor′mal·ly** *adv.*

lo·go (lō′gō′) *n., pl.* **-gos.** A name, symbol, or trademark designed for easy and definite recognition, especially one borne on a single printing plate or piece of type. [Short for LOGOGRAM and LOGOTYPE.]

ă pat	oi boy
ā pay	ou out
âr care	o͝o took
ä father	o͞o boot
ĕ pet	ŭ cut
ē be	ûr urge
ĭ pit	th thin
ī pie	*th* this
îr pier	hw which
ŏ pot	zh vision
ō toe	ə about, item
ô paw	♦ regionalism

Stress marks: **′** (primary); ′ (secondary), as in **dictionary** (dĭk′shə-nĕr′ē)

Lombardy poplar
Populus nigra

LO·GO (lō′gō) *n. Computer Science.* A programming language developed for teaching young children. Elementary exercises involve drawing geometric shapes. [Alteration of Greek *logos,* word. See LOGOS.]

logo– or **log–** *pref.* Word; speech: *logogram.* [Greek, from *logos,* word, speech. See **leg-** in Appendix.]

log·o·gram (lô′gə-grăm′, lŏg′ə-) *n.* A written symbol representing an entire spoken word without expressing its pronunciation; for example, for 4 read "four" in English, "quattro" in Italian. Also called *ideogram, logograph.* **—log′o·gram·mat′ic** (-grə-măt′ĭk) *adj.* **—log′o·gram·mat′i·cal·ly** *adv.*

log·o·graph (lô′gə-grăf′, lŏg′ə-) *n.* See **logogram.** **—log′o·graph′ic** *adj.* **—log′o·graph′i·cal·ly** *adv.*

lo·gog·ra·phy (lō-gŏg′rə-fē) *n.* The use of logotypes in design and printing.

log·o·griph (lô′gə-grĭf′, lŏg′ə-) *n. Games.* A word puzzle, such as an anagram or one in which clues are given in a set of verses. [LOGO– + Greek *griphos,* fishing basket, riddle.]

lo·gom·a·chy (lə-gŏm′ə-kē) *n., pl.* **-chies. 1.** A dispute about words. **2.** A dispute carried on in words only; a battle of words. [Greek *logomakhia,* from *logomakhein,* to fight about words : *logo-,* logo- + *makhē,* battle.]

log·or·rhe·a (lô′gə-rē′ə, lŏg′ə-) *n.* Excessive use of words. **—log′or·rhe′ic** *adj.*

Lo·gos (lō′gŏs′, lŏg′ŏs′) *n.* **1.** *Philosophy.* **a.** In pre-Socratic philosophy, the principle governing the cosmos, the source of this principle, or human reasoning about the cosmos. **b.** Among the Sophists, the topics of rational argument or the arguments themselves. **c.** In Stoicism, the active, material, rational principle of the cosmos; nous. Identified with God, it is the source of all activity and generation and is the power of reason residing in the human soul. **2.** *Judaism.* **a.** In biblical Judaism, the word of God, which itself has creative power and is God's medium of communication with the human race. **b.** In Hellenistic Judaism, a hypostasis associated with divine wisdom. **3.** *Theology.* In Saint John's Gospel, especially in the prologue (1:1–14), the creative word of God, which is itself God and incarnate in Jesus. In this sense, also called *Word.* [Greek. See **leg-** in Appendix.]

lo·go·type (lô′gə-tīp′, lŏg′ə-) *n.* **1.** *Printing.* A single piece of type bearing two or more usually separate elements. **2.** A logo.

log·roll (lôg′rōl′, lŏg′-) *v.* **-rolled, -roll·ing, -rolls.** *—tr.* To work toward the passage of (legislation) by logrolling. *—intr.* To engage in political logrolling.

log·roll·ing (lôg′rō′lĭng, lŏg′-) *n.* **1.** The exchanging of political favors, especially the trading of influence or votes among legislators to achieve passage of projects that are of interest to one another. **2.** The exchanging of favors or praise, as among artists, critics, or academics. **3.** See **birling.** [From the early American practice of neighbors gathering to help clear land by rolling off and burning felled timber.] **—log′roll′er** *n.*

Lo·gro·ño (lə-grōn′yə, lô-grô′nyô). A city of northern Spain on the Ebro River north-northeast of Madrid. Wood products, textiles, and wine are important to its economy. Population, 113,576.

–logue or **–log** *suff.* Speech; discourse: *travelogue.* [French, from Greek *-logos,* from *legein,* to speak. See **leg-** in Appendix.]

log·wood (lôg′wo͝od′, lŏg′-) *n.* **1.** A spiny tropical American tree *(Haematoxylon campechianum)* in the pea family, having dark heartwood from which a dyestuff is obtained. **2.** The heartwood of this tree. **3.** The purplish-red dye obtained from the heartwood of this tree.

lo·gy (lō′gē) *adj.* **-gi·er, -gi·est.** Characterized by lethargy; sluggish. [Perhaps from Dutch *log,* heavy or variant of English *loggy,* heavy, sluggish, from LOG[1].]

–logy *suff.* **1.** Discourse; expression: *phraseology.* **2.** Science; theory; study: *dermatology.* [Middle English *-logie,* from Old French, from Latin *-logia,* from Greek (from *logos,* word, speech; see **leg-** in Appendix) and from *-logos,* one who deals with (from *legein,* to speak; see **leg-** in Appendix).]

loin (loin) *n.* **1.** The part of the body of a human being or quadruped on either side of the backbone and between the ribs and hips. **2.** One of several cuts of meat, such as tenderloin, taken from this part of an animal's body, typically including the vertebrae of the segment from which it is taken. **3. loins. a.** The region of the hips, groin, and lower abdomen. **b.** The reproductive organs. [Middle English *loine,* from Old French *loigne,* from Vulgar Latin **lumbea (carō),* loin (meat), feminine of **lumbeus,* of the loin, from Latin *lumbus.*]

loin·cloth (loin′klôth′, -klŏth′) *n.* A strip of cloth worn around the loins.

Loir (lwär). A river, about 311 km (193 mi) long, of northwest France flowing generally westward to the Sarthe River.

Loire (lwär). The longest river of France, rising in the Cévennes and flowing about 1,014 km (630 mi) north, northwest, and west to the Bay of Biscay.

loi·ter (loi′tər) *intr.v.* **-tered, -ter·ing, -ters. 1.** To stand idly about; linger aimlessly. **2.** To proceed slowly or with many stops: *loitered all the way home.* **3.** To delay or dawdle: *loiter over a job.* [Middle English *loitren,* probably from Middle Dutch *loteren,* to totter, be loose.] **—loi′ter·er** *n.*

Lo·ki (lō′kē) *n. Mythology.* A Norse god who created discord, especially among his fellow gods.

Lo·li·ta (lō-lē′tə) *n.* A seductive adolescent girl. [After *Lolita,* the heroine of *Lolita,* a novel by Vladimir Nabokov.]

loll (lŏl) *v.* **lolled, loll·ing, lolls.** *—intr.* **1.** To move, stand, or recline in an indolent or relaxed manner. **2.** To hang or droop laxly: *a pennant lolling from the mast.* *—tr.* To permit to hang or droop laxly: *lolled his head on the armrest.* **—loll** *n. Archaic.* An act or attitude of lolling. [Middle English *lollen,* probably from Middle Dutch, to doze.] **—loll′er** *n.* **—loll′ing·ly** *adv.*

Lol·land (lŏl′ənd, lô′län). An island of southeast Denmark in the Baltic Sea south of Sjaelland.

lol·la·pa·loo·za also **lal·a·pa·loo·za** or **lal·la·pa·loo·za** (lŏl′ə-pə-lo͞o′zə) *n. Slang.* Something outstanding of its kind. [Origin unknown.]

Lol·lard (lŏl′ərd) *n.* A member of a sect of religious reformers in England who were followers of John Wycliffe in the 14th and 15th centuries. [Middle English, from Middle Dutch *Lollaerd,* mumbler, mutterer, heretic, from *lollen,* doze, to mumble.]

lol·li·pop also **lol·ly·pop** (lŏl′ē-pŏp′) *n.* A confection consisting of a piece of hard candy attached to the end of a small stick. [Perhaps dialectal *lolly,* tongue (from LOLL, to dangle the tongue) + POP[1].]

lol·lop (lŏl′əp) *intr.v.* **-loped, -lop·ing, -lops. 1.** To move with a bobbing motion. **2.** *Chiefly British.* To lounge about; loll. [Alteration of LOLL.] **—lol′lop·y** *adj.*

lol·ly (lŏl′ē) *n., pl.* **-lies.** *Chiefly British.* **1. a.** A piece of candy, especially hard candy. **b.** A lollipop. **2.** Money. [Short for LOLLIPOP.]

lol·ly·gag (lŏl′ē-găg′) also **lal·ly·gag** (lăl′ē-) *intr.v.* **-gagged, -gag·ging, -gags.** To waste time by puttering aimlessly; dawdle. [Origin unknown.]

lol·ly·pop (lŏl′ē-pŏp′) *n.* Variant of **lollipop.**

Lo·ma·mi (lō-mä′mē). A river of Zaire flowing about 1,448 km (900 mi) northward to the Congo River.

Lo·mas de Za·mo·ra (lō′mäs də zə-môr′ə, -mōr′ə, *thĕ* sä-mô′rä). A city of eastern Argentina, an industrial suburb of Buenos Aires. Population, 508,620.

Lo·max (lō′măks′), **John Avery.** 1867–1948. American folklorist and musicologist. With his son **Alan Lomax** (born 1915) he toured the country recording blues and folk musicians for the Library of Congress and various record companies.

Lom·bard[1] (lŏm′bərd, -bärd′, lŭm′-) *n.* **1.** A member of a Germanic people that invaded northern Italy in the sixth century A.D. and established a kingdom in the Po River valley. Also called *Langobard.* **2.** A native or inhabitant of Lombardy. **3.** A banker or moneylender. [Middle English *Lumbarde,* from Old French *lombard,* from Old Italian *lombardo,* from Medieval Latin *lombardus,* from Latin *Langobardus, Longobardus.* See **del-[1]** in Appendix. Sense 3, from the prominence of Lombards in 13th-century banking.] **—Lom·bar′dic** (-bär′dĭk) *adj.*

Lom·bard[2] (lŏm′bärd′). A village of northeast Illinois, a residential suburb of Chicago. Population, 37,295.

Lombard, Peter. 1100?–1160? Italian theologian whose *Sententiarum Libri IV* (1148–1151) had an important influence on official Catholic doctrine concerning the sacraments.

Lom·bar·dy (lŏm′bər-dē, lŭm′-). A region of northern Italy bordering on Switzerland. First inhabited by a Gallic people, it became the center of the kingdom of the Lombards in the sixth century A.D. and part of Charlemagne's empire in 774. The Lombard League of cities defeated Emperor Frederick I in 1176.

Lombardy poplar *n.* A deciduous tree *(Populus nigra* var. *italica)* having upward-pointing branches that form a slender, columnar outline. [After LOMBARDY.]

Lom·bok (lŏm-bŏk′). An island of south-central Indonesia in the Lesser Sundas Islands east of Bali, from which it is separated by the **Lombok Strait.** The island was first visited by the Dutch in 1674.

Lom·bro·so (lôm-brō′sō), **Cesare.** 1836–1909. Italian criminologist who suggested that some individuals are born with criminal dispositions and can be identified by certain physical characteristics.

Lo·mé (lō-mā′). The capital and largest city of Togo, in the southern part of the country on the Gulf of Guinea. It is Togo's administrative and transportation center. Population, 369,926.

lo·ment (lō′mĕnt′) *n.* An indehiscent legume, as of the tick trefoil, usually constricted between the seeds and separating at maturity into one-seeded segments. [Latin *lōmentum,* skin conditioner made of bean meal, from *lavere,* to wash. See **leu(ə)-** in Appendix.]

Lo·mi·ta (lō-mē′tə). A city of southern California, a residential suburb of Los Angeles. Population, 18,807.

Lo·mond (lō′mənd), **Loch.** A lake in south-central Scotland. Surrounded by mountains, it is the largest lake in Scotland and a popular tourist region for its associations with the 18th-century outlaw Rob Roy.

Lom·poc (lŏm′pŏk′). A city of southern California west-northwest of Santa Barbara. Population, 26,267.

Lon·don (lŭn′dən). **1.** A city of southeast Ontario, Canada, southwest of Toronto. Settled in 1826, it is an industrial city. Population, 254,280. **2.** The capital and largest city of the United Kingdom, on the Thames River in southeast England. Greater London consists of 32 boroughs surrounding the City of London, built on the site of a Roman outpost named Londinium. Its growth as an important trade center dates from 886, under the rule of Alfred the Great. Population, 6,851,400.

London, John Griffith. Pen name Jack London. 1876–1916.

ă pat	oi boy
ā pay	ou out
âr care	o͝o took
ä father	o͞o boot
ĕ pet	ŭ cut
ē be	ûr urge
ĭ pit	th thin
ī pie	*th* this
îr pier	hw which
ŏ pot	zh vision
ō toe	ə about, item
ô paw	♦ regionalism

Stress marks: **′** (primary); ′ (secondary), as in **dictionary** (dĭk′shə-nĕr′ē)

American writer of rugged adventure novels, including *The Call of the Wild* (1903) and *The Sea Wolf* (1904).

London broil *n.* Broiled flank steak cut into thin slices. [After LONDON, England.]

Lon·don·der·ry (lŭn′dən-dĕr′ē, lŭn′dən-dĕr′ē) also **Der·ry** (dĕr′ē). A borough of northwest Northern Ireland northwest of Belfast. Built on the site of an abbey founded by Saint Columba in 546, it is a port and manufacturing center. Population, 68,000.

lone (lōn) *adj.* **1.a.** Without accompaniment; solitary: *a lone skier on the mountain.* **b.** Without companionship; isolated or lonely. **2.** Being the only one; sole: *the lone doctor in the county.* See Synonyms at **single. 3.** Situated by itself: *a lone tree on the prairie; a lone blue tile in a white floor.* [Middle English, short for *alone.* See ALONE.]

lone hand *n.* **1.** *Games.* **a.** A hand played without help from a partner's hand. **b.** A card player without a partner. **2.** See **lone wolf.**

lone·ly (lōn′lē) *adj.* **-li·er, -li·est. 1.a.** Without companions; lone. **b.** Characterized by aloneness; solitary. **2.** Unfrequented by people; desolate: *a lonely crossroads.* **3.a.** Dejected by the awareness of being alone. See Synonyms at **alone. b.** Producing such dejection: *the loneliest night of the week.* **—lone′li·ly** *adv.* **—lone′li·ness** *n.*

WORD HISTORY: Henry Bradley, one of the four editors of the *Oxford English Dictionary,* said "It is a truth often overlooked, but not unimportant, that every addition to the resources of a language must in the first instance have been due to an act (though not necessarily to a voluntary or conscious act) of some one person." In many cases this one person may have been an author, since the first recorded instance of a word is often found in an author's work. Of course, as Bradley warns, this is the first *recorded* instance; it is possible that a given author picked up the word or sense somewhere else or that these reside undiscovered in an earlier work. In any case it might be a minor relief of our condition the next time we feel lonely to know that the first recorded instance of the word *lonely* occurs in the works of Shakespeare. The passage appears in *Coriolanus* (1607–1608) in a speech by Coriolanus to his mother Volumnia: "My mother, you wot [know] well/My hazards still have been your solace, and/ Believe't not lightly—though I go alone,/Like to a *lonely* dragon, that his fen/Makes fear'd and talk'd of more than seen—your son/ Will or exceed the common or be caught/With cautelous [crafty] baits and practice." *Lonely* here, of course, has the sense "solitary." The dragon does not feel dejected, or if he does, he does not seem to know how to reach out to others effectively.

lone·ly-hearts or **lone·ly·hearts** (lōn′lē-härts′) *adj.* Of or relating to people who are looking for companions or marriage partners: *a lonely-hearts column in the newspaper.*

lon·er (lō′nər) *n.* One who avoids the company of other people.

lone·some (lōn′səm) *adj.* **1.a.** Dejected because of a lack of companionship. See Synonyms at **alone. b.** Producing such dejection: *a lonesome hour at the bar.* **2.** Deserted; unfrequented: *a lonesome valley.* **3.** Solitary; lone: *a lonesome pine.* **—lonesome** *n. Informal.* Self: *He ate the meal all by his lonesome.* **—lone′some·ly** *adv.* **—lone′some·ness** *n.*

lone wolf *n.* One who prefers to go without the company or assistance of others. Also called *lone hand.*

long¹ (lông, lŏng) *adj.* **long·er, long·est.** *Abbr.* **lg. 1.a.** Extending a relatively great distance. **b.** Having relatively great height; tall. **c.** Having the greater length of two or the greatest length of several: *the long edge of the door.* **2.** Of relatively great duration: *a long time.* **3.** Of a specified linear extent or duration: *a mile long; an hour long.* **4.** Made up of many members or items: *a long shopping list.* **5.** Extending beyond an average or a standard: *a long game.* **6.** Tediously protracted; lengthy: *a long speech.* **7.** Concerned with distant issues; far-reaching: *took a long view of the geopolitical issues.* **8.** Involving substantial chance; risky: *long odds.* **9.** Having an abundance or excess of: *"politicians whose résumés are long on competence"* (Margaret Garrard Warner). **10.** Having a holding of a commodity or security in expectation of a rise in price: *long on soybeans.* **11.** *Linguistics.* **a.** Having a comparatively great duration. Used of a vowel or consonant. **b.** Of, relating to, or being a vowel sound in English, such as the vowel sound in *mate* or *feet,* that is historically descended from a long vowel. **12.a.** Stressed or accented. Used of a syllable in accentual prosody. **b.** Being of relatively great duration. Used of a syllable in quantitative prosody. **—long** *adv.* **1.** During or for an extended period of time: *The promotion was long due.* **2.** At or to a considerable distance; far: *She walked long past the end of the trail.* **3.** For or throughout a specified period: *They talked all night long.* **4.** At a point of time distant from that referred to: *That event took place long before we were born.* **5.** Into or in a long position, as of a commodity market. **—long** *n.* **1.** A long time: *This won't take long.* **2.** *Linguistics.* A long syllable, vowel, or consonant. **3.** One who acquires holdings in a security or commodity in expectation of a rise in price. **4.a.** A garment size for a tall person. **b. longs.** Trousers extending to the feet or ankles. ***—idioms.* any longer.** For more time: *can't wait any longer.* **as** (or **so**) **long as. 1.** During the time that: *I'll stay as long as I can.* **2.** Inasmuch as; since: *As long as you're up, get me a drink.* **3.** Under the condition that; provided that: *"So long as we don't understand it too well, every other language is poetry"* (Anatole Broyard). **before long.** Soon. **long ago. 1.** At a time or during a period well before the present: *I read that book long ago.* **2.** A time well before the present: *heroes of long ago.* **long in the tooth.** Growing old. **no longer.** Not now as formerly: *He no longer smokes.* **not long for.** Unlikely to remain for much more time in: *not long for this world.* **the long and the short of it.** The substance or gist: *You can look on the front page of the paper for the long and the short of it.* [Middle English, from Old English *lang.* See **del-¹** in Appendix.]

long² (lông, lŏng) *intr.v.* **longed, long·ing, longs.** To have an earnest, heartfelt desire, especially for something beyond reach. See Synonyms at **yearn.** [Middle English *longen,* from Old English *langian.* See **del-¹** in Appendix.]

Long (lông, lŏng), **Crawford Williamson.** 1815–1878. American surgeon and pioneer anesthetist who was among the first (1842) to use ether as an anesthetic.

Long, Huey Pierce. Called "the Kingfish." 1893–1935. American politician. As governor of Louisiana (1928–1932) and U.S. senator (1930–1935) he established dictatorial control over the state.

long. *abbr.* Longitude.

lon·gan (lŏng′gən, lông′-) *n.* **1.** An Indian evergreen tree *(Euphoria longan)* having yellowish-brown drupes with white, juicy, edible flesh. **2.** The fruit of this plant. [New Latin *longanum,* specific epithet, from Chinese (Mandarin) *lóng yǎn* : *lóng,* dragon + *yǎn,* eye.]

lon·ga·nim·i·ty (lŏng′gə-nĭm′ĭ-tē, lông′-) *n.* Calmness in the face of suffering and adversity; forbearance. [Middle English *longanimite,* from Old French, from Late Latin *longanimitās,* from *longanimis,* patient : Latin *longus,* long; see LONGITUDE + Latin *animus,* mind, reason; see **ane-** in Appendix.]

Long Beach. 1. A city of southern California on an arm of the Pacific Ocean southeast of Los Angeles. It is a thriving port and year-round resort and convention center. Population, 361,334. **2.** A city of southeast New York on an island off southern Long Island. It is a residential community. Population, 34,073.

long·boat (lông′bōt′, lŏng′-) *n. Nautical.* The longest boat carried by a sailing ship, especially by a merchant ship.

long bone *n.* Any of several elongated bones of vertebrate limbs that have a roughly cylindrical shaft containing marrow.

long·bow (lông′bō′, lŏng′-) *n.* A long, hand-drawn bow, such as that used in medieval England, which sometimes exceeded 6 feet (1.8 meters) in length.

Long Branch. A city of east-central New Jersey on the Atlantic Ocean north of Asbury Park. It has been a popular ocean resort since the 19th century. Population, 29,819.

long distance *n.* **1.** An operator or a system that places long-distance telephone calls. **2.** A long-distance telephone call.

long-dis·tance (lông′dĭs′təns, lŏng′-) *adj.* **1.** Covering a long distance: *a long-distance runner; operating under long-distance supervision.* **2.** Of, relating to, or being telephone communication to a distant station: *a long-distance call.* **—long′dis′tance** *adv.*

long division *n. Mathematics.* A process of division in arithmetic, usually used when the divisor is a large number, in which each step of the division is written out.

long dozen *n.* A baker's dozen; thirteen.

long-drawn-out (lông′drôn′out′, lŏng′-) *adj.* Greatly extended or protracted; prolonged: *a long-drawn-out speech.*

lon·ge·ron (lŏn′jər-ən) *n.* A major structural member of an aircraft fuselage, running from front to rear. [French, from Old French, beam, from *long,* long, from Latin *longus.* See **del-¹** in Appendix.]

lon·gev·i·ty (lŏn-jĕv′ĭ-tē, lôn-) *n., pl.* **-ties. 1.a.** Long life; great duration of life: *His longevity vexed his heirs.* **b.** Length or duration of life: *comparing the longevities of the two peoples.* **2.** Long duration or continuance, as in an occupation: *had unusual longevity in the company; her longevity as a star.* [Late Latin *longaevitās,* from Latin *longaevus,* ancient : *longus,* long; see **del-¹** in Appendix + *aevum,* age; see **aiw-** in Appendix.] **—lon·ge′vous** (-jē′vəs) *adj.*

long face *n.* A discontented or sullen facial expression.

Long·fel·low (lông′fĕl′ō, lŏng′-), **Henry Wadsworth.** 1807–1882. American writer. The best-known 19th-century poet in the United States, he wrote *The Song of Hiawatha* (1855) and a translation (1865–1867) of *Dante's Divine Comedy.*

Henry Wadsworth Longfellow
1870 photograph by George K. Warren (1824–1884)

long green *n. Slang.* Paper money.

long·hair (lông′hâr′, lŏng′-) *n. Informal.* **1.** One dedicated to the arts and especially to classical music. **2.** One whose taste in the arts is considered to be overrefined. **3.** A person with long hair, especially a hippie. **—long′hair′, long′haired′** *adj.*

long·hand (lông′hănd′, lŏng′-) *n.* Cursive writing.

long haul *n. Informal.* **1.** A long distance: *It is a long haul from New York to Los Angeles.* **2.** A long period of time: *Over the long haul the candidates performed well.* **—long′-haul′** (lông′hôl′, lŏng′-) *adj.*

long·head (lông′hĕd′, lŏng′-) *n. Anthropology.* **1.** A head having a cephalic index less than 76. **2.** A person having such a head.

long·head·ed also **long-head·ed** (lông′hĕd′ĭd, lŏng′-) *adj.* **1.** *Anthropology.* Dolichocephalic. **2.** Foresighted; wise.

long·horn (lông′hôrn′, lŏng′-) *n.* **1.** Any of a breed of cattle with long horns, formerly bred in great numbers in the southwest

longhorn

long jump

United States. **2.** A variety of Cheddar cheese molded into a long cylinder.

long-horned beetle (lông′hôrnd′, lŏng′-) *n.* Any of numerous beetles of the family Cerambycidae, having long antennae. Also called *longicorn.*

long-horned grasshopper *n.* Any of various large, usually greenish insects of the family Tettigoniidae, having very long, slender antennae.

long·house or **long house** (lông′hous′) *n.* A long communal dwelling, especially of the Iroquois, typically built of poles and bark and having a central corridor with family compartments on either side.

lon·gi·corn (lŏn′jĭ-kôrn′) *n.* See **long-horned beetle.** **—longicorn** *adj.* **1.** Having long antennae. **2.** Of or belonging to the family Cerambycidae, which includes the long-horned beetles. [From New Latin *Longicornia,* former group name : Latin *longus,* long; see LONGITUDE + Latin *cornū,* horn; see **ker-**[1] in Appendix.]

long·ing (lông′ĭng, lŏng′-) *n.* A strong persistent yearning or desire, especially one that cannot be fulfilled. **—long′ing·ly** *adv.*

Lon·gi·nus (lŏn-jī′nəs), **Dionysius Cassius.** A.D. 210?–273. Greek philosopher. The volume of literary criticism *On The Sublime* is attributed to him.

Long Island. *Abbr.* **L.I.** A long, narrow island of southeast New York bordered on the south by the Atlantic Ocean. **Long Island Sound,** an arm of the Atlantic, separates it from Connecticut on the north. The western part of Long Island includes two boroughs of New York City.

lon·gi·tude (lŏn′jĭ-to͞od′, -tyo͞od′, lôn′-) *n. Abbr.* **long. 1.** Angular distance on the earth's surface, measured east or west from the prime meridian at Greenwich, England, to the meridian passing through a position, expressed in degrees (or hours), minutes, and seconds. **2.** Celestial longitude. [Middle English, length, a measured length, from Old French, from Latin *longitūdō, longitūdin-,* from *longus,* long. See **del-**[1] in Appendix.]

lon·gi·tu·di·nal (lŏn′jĭ-to͞od′n-əl, -tyo͞od′-, lôn′-) *adj.* **1.a.** Of or relating to longitude or length: *a longitudinal reckoning by the navigator; made longitudinal measurements of the hull.* **b.** Concerned with the development of persons or groups over time: *a longitudinal study of twins.* **2.** Placed or running lengthwise: *longitudinal stripes.* **—lon′gi·tu′di·nal·ly** *adv.*

long johns *pl.n. Informal.* Long, warm underwear. [From the name *John.*]

long jump *n. Sports.* A jump in track and field that is made for distance rather than height, performed either from a stationary position or a moving start. Also called *broad jump.*

long·leaf pine (lông′lēf′, lŏng′-) *n.* An evergreen tree *(Pinus palustris)* of the southeast United States, having long needles and heavy, tough, resinous wood valued as a source of timber, pulp, and turpentine. Also called *yellow pine.*

long-lived (lông′lĭvd′, -līvd′, lŏng′-) *adj.* **1.** Having a long life: *a long-lived aunt.* **2.** Lasting a long time; persistent: *a long-lived rumor.* **3.** Functioning a long time; durable: *a long-lived light bulb.* **—long′-lived′ness** *n.*

Long·mea·dow (lông′mĕd′ō, lŏng′-). A town of southwest Massachusetts, a residential suburb of Springfield on the Connecticut River. Population, 16,301.

long measure *n.* **1.** See **linear measure. 2.** See **long meter.**

long meter *n.* A quatrain in iambic tetrameter, rhyming in the second and fourth lines and often in the first and third. Also called *long measure.*

Long·mont (lông′mŏnt′, lŏng′-). A city of north-central Colorado north-northeast of Boulder. It is a trade and processing center for an irrigated farming region. Population, 42,942.

♦ **long·neck** (lông′nĕk′, lŏng′-) *n. Texas.* A glass beer bottle with an elongated neck.

long-play·ing (lông′plā′ĭng, lŏng′-) *adj.* Relating to or being a phonograph record that turns at 33⅓ revolutions per minute.

long-range (lông′rānj′, lŏng′-) *adj.* **1.** Of, suitable for, or reaching long distances: *long-range missiles.* **2.** Requiring or involving an extended span of time: *long-range planning.*

long run *n.* A rather lengthy period of time: *We expect a substantial increase in sales of the book in the long run. The paint must not deteriorate in quality over the long run.*

long·shore (lông′shôr′, -shōr′, lŏng′-) *adj.* Occurring, living, or working along a seacoast. [Short for ALONGSHORE.]

long·shore·man (lông′shôr′mən, -shōr′-, lŏng′-) *n.* A dock worker who loads and unloads ships.

long shot *n.* **1.** *Sports & Games.* An entry, as in a horserace, with only a slight chance of winning. **2.a.** A bet made at great odds. **b.** A venture that offers a great reward if successful but has very little chance of success. **3.** A photograph or a film or television shot taken at relatively long range. ***—idiom.*** **by a long shot.** *Informal.* By any means. Usually used in negative sentences: *She doesn't do her share of the work by a long shot.*

long-sight·ed (lông′sī′tĭd, lŏng′-) *adj.* Farsighted. **—long′-sight′ed·ly** *adv.* **—long′-sight′ed·ness** *n.*

long·some (lông′səm, lŏng′-) *adj.* Tiresomely long.

Longs Peak (lôngz, lŏngz). A mountain, 4,347.8 m (14,255 ft) high, in the Front Range of the Rocky Mountains in north-central Colorado. It was discovered in 1820.

long·spur (lông′spûr′, lŏng′-) *n.* Any of several birds, especially of the genus *Calcarius* of the northern United States, Canada, and the Arctic, having brownish plumage and long-clawed hind toes.

long-stand·ing (lông′stăn′dĭng, lŏng′-) *adj.* Of long duration or existence: *a long-standing friendship.*

Long·street (lông′strēt′, lŏng′-), **James.** 1821–1904. American Confederate general. His delay in carrying out Gen. Robert E. Lee's orders contributed to the defeat at Gettysburg (1863).

long-suf·fer·ing (lông′sŭf′ər-ĭng, lŏng′-) *adj.* Patiently enduring wrongs or difficulties. **—long-suffering** *n.* Patient endurance. See Synonyms at **patience. —long′-suf′fer·ing·ly** *adv.*

long suit *n.* **1.** *Games.* The suit in which a player holds the most cards in a given hand. **2.** The personal quality or talent that is one's strongest asset.

long-tailed duck (lông′tāld′, lŏng′-) *n.* See **oldsquaw.**

long-term (lông′tûrm′, lŏng′-) *adj.* Involving, maturing after, or being in effect for a long time: *a long-term investment.*

long-time or **long·time** (lông′tīm′, lŏng′-) *adj.* Having existed or persisted for a long time.

long ton *n.* See **ton** (sense 2).

Lon·gueil (lông-gāl′). A city of southern Quebec, Canada, on the St. Lawrence River opposite Montreal. Population, 124,320.

lon·gueur (lông-gûr′, lŏng-) *n.* A tedious passage in a work of literature or performing art: *"longueurs and passages of meretricious vulgarity"* (Stephen Schiff). [French, from Old French *longor,* a protracted discussion, from *long,* long, from Latin *longus.* See LONGITUDE.]

Long·view (lông′vyo͞o′, lŏng′-). **1.** A city of northeast Texas west of Shreveport, Louisiana. The city produces varied manufactures. Population, 62,762. **2.** A city of southwest Washington on the Columbia River north of Vancouver. Population, 31,052.

long-wind·ed (lông′wĭn′dĭd, lŏng′-) *adj.* **1.** Wearisomely verbose: *a long-winded speaker.* See Synonyms at **wordy. 2.** Able to maintain breathing power during exertion: *a long-winded swimmer.* **—long′-wind′ed·ly** *adv.* **—long′-wind′ed·ness** *n.*

long·wise (lông′wīz′, lŏng′-) *adv. & adj.* Lengthwise.

Long·worth (lông′wûrth′, lŏng′-), **Alice Roosevelt.** 1884–1980. American socialite. The daughter of Theodore Roosevelt, she was a favorite subject of the press because of her active social life and her caustic wit.

lon·gyi (lŏng′gē, lo͝ong′-) *n.* Variant of **lungi.**

loo[1] (lo͞o) *n., pl.* **loos.** *Games.* A card game in which each player contributes stakes to a pool. [Short for obsolete *lanterloo,* from French *lanturlu,* a meaningless refrain, loo.]

loo[2] (lo͞o) *n., pl.* **loos.** *Chiefly British.* A toilet. [Origin unknown.]

loo·fa or **loo·fah** (lo͞o′fə) also **luf·fa** (lo͞o′fə, lŭf′ə) *n.* **1.** Any of several Old World tropical vines of the genus *Luffa,* having cylindrical fruit with a fibrous, spongelike interior. **2.** The dried, fibrous part of the loofa fruit, used as a washing sponge or as a filter. In this sense, also called *dishcloth gourd, vegetable sponge.* [Arabic *lūf, lūfah.*]

look (lo͝ok) *v.* **looked, look·ing, looks.** *—intr.* **1.a.** To employ one's sight, especially in a given direction or on a given object: *looking out the window; looked at the floor.* **b.** To search: *We looked all afternoon but could not find it.* **2.a.** To turn one's glance or gaze: *looked to the right.* **b.** To turn one's attention; attend: *looked to his neglected guitar during vacation.* **c.** To turn one's expectations: *looked to us for a solution.* **3.** To seem or appear to be: *look morose.* See Synonyms at **seem. 4.** To face in a specified direction: *The cottage looks on the river.* *—tr.* **1.** To turn one's eyes on: *looked him in the eye.* **2.** To convey by one's expression: *looked annoyance at the judge; looked his devotion to me.* **3.a.** To have an appearance of conformity with: *He looks his age. She dressed up to look the part.* **b.** To appear to be: *looked the fool in one version of the story.* **—look** *n.* **1.a.** The act or instance of looking: *I took just one look and I was sure.* **b.** A gaze or glance expressive of something: *gave her a mournful look.* **2.a.** Appearance or aspect: *a look of great age.* **b. looks.** Physical appearance, especially when pleasing. **c.** A distinctive, unified manner of dress or fashion: *the preferred look for this fall.* ***—phrasal verbs.*** **look after.** To take care of: *looked after his younger brother.* **look for. 1.** To search for; seek: *looking for my gloves.* **2.** To expect: *Look for a change of weather in March.* **look on** (or **upon**)**.** To regard in a certain way: *looked on them as incompetents.* **look out.** To be watchful or careful; take care: *If you don't look out, you may fall on the ice. We looked out for each other on the trip.* **look to. 1.** To expect: *He looked to hear from her.* **2.** To seem about to; promise to: *"an 'Action Program,' which . . . looked to reduce tariffs on over 1,800 items"* (Alan D. Romberg). **look up. 1.** To search for and find, as in a reference book. **2.** To visit: *look up an old friend.* **3.** To become better; improve: *Things are at last looking up.* ***—idioms.*** **look a gift horse in the mouth.** *Informal.* To be critical or suspicious of something one has received without expense. **look alive** (or **sharp**)**.** *Informal.* To act or respond quickly: *Look alive! We leave in five minutes.* **look down on** (or **upon**)**.** To regard with contempt or condescension. **look down (one's) nose at** (or **on**)**.** To regard with contempt or condescension. **look forward to.** To think of (a future event) with pleasurable, eager anticipation:

ă pat	oi boy
ā pay	ou out
âr care	o͝o took
ä father	o͞o boot
ĕ pet	ŭ cut
ē be	ûr urge
ĭ pit	th thin
ī pie	*th* this
îr pier	hw which
ŏ pot	zh vision
ō toe	ə about, item
ô paw	♦ regionalism

Stress marks: ′ (primary); ′ (secondary), as in **dictionary** (dĭk′shə-nĕr′ē)

looking forward to graduation. **look up to.** To admire. [Middle English *loken,* from Old English *lōcian.*]

look·a·like (lo͝ok′ə-līk′) *n.* One that closely resembles another; a double. —*attributive.* Often used to modify another noun: *look-alike computers; look-alike cars.*

look·down (lo͝ok′doun′) *n.* An iridescent, silvery marine fish *(Selene vomer)* of Atlantic waters, having a compressed body and a steep frontal profile.

look·er (lo͝ok′ər) *n.* **1.** One that looks, especially a spectator or an onlooker. **2.** *Slang.* A very attractive person.

look·er-on (lo͝ok′ər-ŏn′, -ôn′) *n., pl.* **look·ers-on** (lo͝ok′ərz-). A spectator; an onlooker.

look-in (lo͝ok′ĭn′) *n.* **1.** A short visit. **2.** A quick glance.

look·ing glass (lo͝ok′ĭng) *n.* See **mirror** (sense 1).

look·out (lo͝ok′out′) *n.* **1.** The act of observing or keeping watch. **2.** A high place or structure commanding a wide view, used for observation. **3.** One who keeps watch. **4.** Outlook; view. **5.** An object of concern or worry. See Synonyms at **affair.**

Look·out (lo͝ok′out′), **Cape.** A point on a sandy reef off eastern North Carolina southwest of Cape Hatteras.

look-see (lo͝ok′sē′) *n. Informal.* A quick survey or glance.

look-up (lo͝ok′ŭp′) *n. Computer Science.* A procedure in which a table of values stored in a computer is searched until a specified value is found.

loom[1] (lo͞om) *intr.v.* **loomed, loom·ing, looms. 1.** To come into view as a massive, distorted, or indistinct image. See Synonyms at **appear. 2.** To appear to the mind in a magnified and threatening form: *"Stalin looms over the whole human tragedy of 1930–1933"* (Robert Conquest). **3.** To seem imminent; impend: *Revolution loomed but the aristocrats paid no heed.* —**loom** *n.* A distorted, threatening appearance of something, as through fog or darkness. [Perhaps of Scandinavian origin.]

loom[2] (lo͞om) *n.* An apparatus for making thread or yarn into cloth by weaving strands together at right angles. [Middle English *lome,* from Old English *gelōma,* tool : *ge-,* collective pref.; see YCLEPT + *-lōma,* tool, as in *andlōman,* tools.]

loon[1] (lo͞on) *n.* Any of several fish-eating, diving birds of the genus *Gavia* of northern regions, having a short tail, webbed feet, and a laughlike cry. [Of Scandinavian origin.]

loon[2] (lo͞on) *n. Informal.* One who is crazy or deranged. [Middle English *louen,* rogue.]

loon·y or **loon·ey** also **lun·y** (lo͞o′nē) *Informal.* —*adj.* **-i·er, -i·est. 1.** Extremely foolish or silly. **2.** Crazy; insane. —*n., pl.* **-ies** also **-eys.** A foolish or crazy person. [Shortening and alteration (probably influenced by LOON[1]) of LUNATIC.] —**loon′i·ly** *adv.* —**loon′i·ness** *n.*

loony bin *n. Offensive Slang.* A mental health facility.

loop[1] (lo͞op) *n.* **1.a.** A length of line, thread, ribbon, or other thin material that is curved or doubled over making an opening. **b.** The opening formed by such a doubled line. **2.** Something having a shape, order, or path of motion that is circular or curved over on itself. **3.** *Electricity.* A closed circuit. **4.** *Computer Science.* A sequence of instructions that repeats either a specified number of times or until a particular condition prevails. **5.** A type of loop-shaped intrauterine device. **6.** A flight maneuver in which an aircraft flies a circular path in a vertical plane with the lateral axis of the aircraft remaining horizontal. **7.** *Sports.* See **league**[1] (sense 2). —**loop** *v.* **looped, loop·ing, loops.** —*tr.* **1.** To form into a loop. **2.** To fasten, join, or encircle with loops or a loop. **3.** To fly (an aircraft) in a loop. **4.** To move in a loop or an arc. **5.** *Electricity.* To join (conductors) so as to complete a circuit. **6.** To add or substitute (words) in a film by altering the sound track. —*intr.* **1.** To form a loop. **2.** To move in a loop: *"The couple looped constantly around the international social circuit"* (Walter Isaacson). **3.** To make a loop in an aircraft. [Middle English *loupe,* probably from Middle Irish *lúb* (perhaps influenced by Middle English *lep,* basket).]

loop[2] (lo͞op) *n. Archaic.* A loophole through which small arms may be fired. [Middle English *loupe.*]

Loop (lo͞op). The central business district of Chicago, Illinois. The Loop was originally named for a loop in the elevated railroad tracks.

looped (lo͞opt) *adj.* **1.** Formed into or having a loop or loops. **2.** *Slang.* Intoxicated; drunk.

loop·er (lo͞o′pər) *n.* **1.** One that makes loops. **2.** See **measuring worm.**

loop·hole (lo͞op′hōl′) *n.* **1.** A way of escaping a difficulty, especially an omission or ambiguity in the wording of a contract or law that provides a means of evading compliance. **2.** A small hole or slit in a wall, especially one through which small arms may be fired.

loop of Hen·le (hĕn′lē) *n.* The segment of the nephron of a vertebrate kidney that is situated between the proximal and distal convoluted tubules. It plays a role in the transport of ions and water and the concentrating of urine. [After Friedrich Gustav Jacob *Henle* (1809–1885), German pathologist.]

loop·y (lo͞o′pē) *adj.* **-i·er, -i·est. 1.** Consisting of or covered with loops. **2.** Offbeat; crazy: *"the loopy energy of Harpo Marx"* (Michael Wood).

Loos (lo͞os), **Anita.** 1893?–1981. American writer who is best known for her novel *Gentlemen Prefer Blondes* (1925).

loose (lo͞os) *adj.* **loos·er, loos·est. 1.** Not fastened, restrained, or contained: *loose bricks.* **2.** Not taut, fixed, or rigid: *a loose anchor line; a loose chair leg.* **3.** Free from confinement or imprisonment; unfettered: *criminals who were loose in the neighborhood; dogs that are loose on the streets.* **4.** Not tight-fitting or tightly fitted: *loose shoes.* **5.** Not bound, bundled, stapled, or gathered together: *loose papers.* **6.** Not compact or dense in arrangement or structure: *loose gravel.* **7.** Lacking a sense of restraint or responsibility; idle: *loose talk.* **8.** Lacking conventional moral restraint in sexual behavior. **9.** Not literal or exact: *a loose translation.* **10.** Characterized by a free movement of fluids in the body: *a loose cough; loose bowels.* —**loose** *adv.* In a loose manner. —**loose** *v.* **loosed, loos·ing, loos·es.** —*tr.* **1.** To let loose; release: *loosed the dogs.* **2.** To make loose; undo: *loosed his belt.* **3.** To cast loose; detach: *hikers loosing their packs at camp.* **4.** To let fly; discharge: *loosed an arrow.* **5.** To release pressure or obligation from; absolve: *loosed her from the responsibility.* **6.** To make less strict; relax: *a leader's strong authority that was loosed by easy times.* —*intr.* **1.** To become loose. **2.** To discharge a missile; fire. —***idiom.* on the loose. 1.** At large; free. **2.** Acting in an uninhibited fashion. [Middle English *louse, los,* from Old Norse *lauss.* See **leu-** in Appendix.] —**loose′ly** *adv.* —**loose′ness** *n.*

loom[2]

SYNONYMS: *loose, lax, slack.* The central meaning shared by these adjectives is "not tautly bound, held, or fastened": *loose reins; a lax rope; slack sails.*
ANTONYM: *tight.*

loose cannon *n. Slang.* One that is uncontrolled and therefore poses danger: "[His] *bloopers in the White House seem to make him . . . a political loose cannon"* (Tom Morgenthau). [From the threat posed by loose cannon rolling about a warship under sail.]

loose end *n.* A minor unresolved problem or difficulty, especially a final detail preceding the completion of something. Often used in the plural.

loose-joint·ed (lo͞os′join′tĭd) *adj.* **1.** Having freely articulated, highly mobile joints. **2.** Limber or agile in movement. —**loose′-joint′ed·ness** *n.*

loose-leaf (lo͞os′lēf′) *adj.* Relating to, having, or being leaves that can be easily removed, rearranged, or replaced: *a loose-leaf notebook; loose-leaf paper.*

loon[1]

loos·en (lo͞o′sən) *v.* **-ened, -en·ing, -ens.** —*tr.* **1.** To untie or make looser. **2.** To free from restraint, pressure, or strictness. **3.** To free (the bowels) from constipation. —*intr.* To become loose or looser. [Middle English *lousnen, losnen,* from *losen,* from *los,* loose. See LOOSE.]

loose·strife (lo͞os′strīf′) *n.* **1.** Any of various plants of the genus *Lysimachia,* having usually yellow flowers. **2.** Any of various plants of the genus *Lythrum,* having purple or white flowers. [Mistranslation of Latin *lȳsimachīa* (as if from Greek *lusis,* loosening, and Greek *makhē,* battle), from Greek *lusimakheios,* perhaps after *Lusimakhos,* Lysimachos, Greek physician of the fifth or fourth century B.C.]

loot (lo͞ot) *n.* **1.** Valuables pillaged in time of war; spoils. **2.** Stolen goods. **3.** *Informal.* Goods illicitly obtained, as by bribery. **4.** *Informal.* Things of value, such as gifts, received on one occasion. **5.** *Slang.* Money. —**loot** *v.* **loot·ed, loot·ing, loots.** —*tr.* **1.** To pillage; spoil. **2.** To take as spoils; steal. —*intr.* To engage in pillaging. [Hindi *lūṭ,* from Sanskrit *loptram, lotram,* plunder. See **reup-** in Appendix.] —**loot′er** *n.*

lop[1] (lŏp) *tr.v.* **lopped, lop·ping, lops. 1.** To cut off (a part) from; trim: *lopped her long curls.* **2.** To cut off from a tree or shrub: *lopped dead branches.* **3.** To eliminate or excise as superfluous: *lopped him from the payroll.* [Perhaps from Middle English *loppe,* small branches and twigs.] —**lop′per** *n.*

lop[2] (lŏp) *intr. & tr.v.* **lopped, lop·ping, lops.** To hang or let hang loosely; droop. [Origin unknown.]

lope (lōp) *intr.v.* **loped, lop·ing, lopes.** To run or ride with a steady, easy gait. —**lope** *n.* A steady, easy gait. [Middle English *lopen,* to leap, from Old Norse *hlaupa.*] —**lop′er** *n.*

loosestrife

lop-eared (lŏp′îrd′) *adj.* Having bent or drooping ears: *a lop-eared hound.*

Lop Nur (lŏp′ no͝or′) also **Lop Nor** (nôr′). A marshy depression of northwest China. Once a large salt lake, the area has been used since 1964 for nuclear testing.

lop·py (lŏp′ē) *adj.* **-pi·er, -pi·est.** Hanging limp; pendulous.

lop·sid·ed (lŏp′sī′dĭd) *adj.* **1.** Heavier, larger, or higher on one side than on the other. **2.** Sagging or leaning to one side. —**lop′sid′ed·ly** *adv.* —**lop′sid′ed·ness** *n.*

loq. *abbr. Latin.* Loquitur (speaks).

lo·qua·cious (lō-kwā′shəs) *adj.* Very talkative; garrulous. See Synonyms at **talkative.** [From Latin *loquāx, loquāc-,* from *loquī,* to speak. See **tolkʷ-** in Appendix.] —**lo·qua′cious·ly** *adv.* —**lo·qua′cious·ness, lo·quac′i·ty** (lō-kwăs′ĭ-tē) *n.*

lo·quat (lō′kwŏt′, -kwăt′) *n.* **1.** A small evergreen tree *(Eriobotrya japonica)* native to China and Japan, having fragrant white flowers and pear-shaped yellow fruit with large seeds. **2.** The edible fruit of this plant. [Chinese (Cantonese) *lo kwat* : *lo,* kind of tree + *kwăt,* an orange.]

Lo·rain (lə-rān′, lō-). A city of northern Ohio on Lake Erie west of Cleveland. Settled in 1807, it is now highly industrialized. Population, 75,416.

lo·ran (lôr′ăn′, lōr′-) *n.* A long-range navigational system in which position is determined by an analysis involving the time

loquat
Eriobotrya japonica

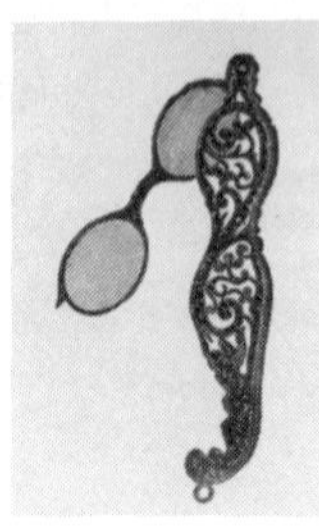

lorgnette

intervals between pulsed radio signals from two or more pairs of ground stations of known position. [*lo(ng-)ra(nge) n(avigation).*]

Lor·ca (lôr′kə, -kä), **Federico García.** See Federico **García Lorca.**

lord (lôrd) *n.* **1.** A man of high rank in a feudal society or in one that retains feudal forms and institutions, especially: **a.** A king. **b.** A territorial magnate. **c.** The proprietor of a manor. **2. Lords.** See **House of Lords. 3. Lord.** *Abbr.* **Ld.** *Chiefly British.* The general masculine title of nobility and other rank: **a.** Used as a form of address for a marquis, an earl, or a viscount. **b.** Used as the usual style for a baron. **c.** Used as a courtesy title for a younger son of a duke or marquis. **d.** Used as a title for certain high officials and dignitaries. **e.** Used as a title for a bishop. **4. Lord. a.** God. **b.** Jesus. **c.** A man of renowned power or authority. **d.** A man who has mastery in a given field or activity. **e.** *Archaic.* The male head of a household. **f.** *Archaic.* A husband. —**lord** *intr.v.* **lord·ed, lord·ing, lords.** To act like a lord; domineer. Often used with the indefinite *it: lorded it over their subordinates.* [Middle English, from Old English *hlāford* : *hlāf,* bread + *weard,* guardian; see **wer-**[3] in Appendix.]

Lord Chancellor *n., pl.* **Lords Chancellor.** The presiding officer of the House of Lords.

lord·ing (lôr′dĭng) *n.* **1.** *Archaic.* Used as a form of address for a lord. **2.** *Obsolete.* A lordling.

lord·ling (lôrd′lĭng) *n.* A lord regarded as immature or insignificant.

lord·ly (lôrd′lē) *adj.* **-li·er, -li·est. 1.** Of, relating to, or characteristic of a lord. **2.** Very dignified and noble: *a lordly and charitable enterprise.* **3.** Pretentiously arrogant and overbearing. —**lordly** *adv.* **1.** In a dignified, noble fashion befitting or characteristic of a lord. **2.** In a pretentiously arrogant and overbearing manner. —**lord′li·ness** *n.*

Lord of Misrule *n., pl.* **Lords of Misrule.** One who presided at traditional Christmas revelry in England during the 15th and 16th centuries.

lor·do·sis (lôr-dō′sĭs) *n., pl.* **-ses** (-sēz). An abnormal forward curvature of the spine in the lumbar region. [Greek *lordōsis,* from *lordos,* bent backward.] —**lor·dot′ic** (-dŏt′ĭk) *adj.*

lords-and-la·dies (lôrdz′ən-lā′dēz) *pl.n. (used with a sing. or pl. verb).* See **cuckoopint.** [From its dark (lords) and light (ladies) spadices.]

Lord's Day or **Lord's day** (lôrdz) *n.* The Christian Sabbath; Sunday.

lord·ship (lôrd′shĭp′) *n.* **1.** Often **Lordship.** Used with *Your, His,* or *Their* as a title and form of address for a man or men holding the rank of lord. **2.** The position or authority of a lord. **3.** The territory belonging to a feudal lord.

Lord's Prayer (prâr) *n.* The prayer taught by Jesus to his disciples. Also called *Our Father.*

Lord's Supper *n.* **1.** See **Last Supper. 2.** The sacrament of the Eucharist.

Lord's Table *n.* The table or altar used by Christians to celebrate the Eucharist.

lore[1] (lôr, lōr) *n.* **1.** Accumulated facts, traditions, or beliefs about a particular subject. See Synonyms at **knowledge. 2.** Knowledge acquired through education or experience. **3.** *Archaic.* Material taught or learned. [Middle English, from Old English *lār.* See **leis-**[1] in Appendix.]

lore[2] (lôr, lōr) *n.* The space between the eye and the base of the bill of a bird or between the eye and nostril of a snake. [Latin *lōrum,* thong.]

Lo·re·lei (lôr′ə-lī′, lō′rə-) *n.* A siren of Germanic legend whose singing lures sailors to shipwreck.

Lo·rentz (lôr′ənts, lōr′-, lō′rĕnts), **Hendrik.** 1853–1928. Dutch physicist. He shared a 1902 Nobel Prize for researching the influence of magnetism on radiation.

Lorentz contraction *n.* See **Lorentz-Fitzgerald contraction.**

Lo·rentz-Fitz·ger·ald contraction (lôr′ənts-fĭts-jĕr′ld, lōr′-) *n.* The contraction in length of a moving body as it approaches the speed of light, as measured by an observer at rest with respect to the body. Also called *Lorentz contraction.* [After Hendrik LORENTZ and George Francis FITZGERALD.]

Lo·renz (lō′rĕnts′), **Konrad Zacharias.** 1903–1989. Austrian psychologist. He shared a 1973 Nobel Prize for studies of individual and social behavior patterns.

lor·gnette (lôrn-yĕt′) *n.* A pair of eyeglasses or opera glasses with a short handle. [French, from *lorgner,* to peer at, from Old French, from *lorgne,* squinting, of Germanic origin.]

lo·ri·ca (lô-rī′kə, lō-) *n., pl.* **-cae** (-sē). **1.** *Zoology.* A protective external shell or case, as of a rotifer or any of certain other microscopic animals. **2.** A cuirass or corselet worn by Roman soldiers. [Latin *lōrīca,* leather cuirass, perhaps from *lōrum,* thong.] —**lor′i·cate′** (lôr′ĭ-kāt′, lŏr′-), **lor′i·ca′ted** (-kā′tĭd) *adj.*

Lo·rient (lô-ryäN′). A city of northwest France on the Bay of Biscay southeast of Brest. Established in the 17th century, it was developed as a naval base by Napoleon I. Population, 62,554.

lor·i·keet (lôr′ĭ-kēt′, lŏr′-) *n.* Any of several small, often brilliantly colored Australasian parrots that feed primarily on soft fruits or the nectar and pollen of flowers and blooming trees. [LOR(Y) + (PARA)KEET.]

lo·ris (lôr′ĭs, lōr′-) *n.* Any of several small, slow-moving, nocturnal prosimian primates of the genera *Loris* and *Nycticebus* of tropical Asia, having dense woolly fur, large eyes, and a vestigial tail. [French, possibly from obsolete Dutch *loeris,* simpleton, from *loer,* from Old French *lourt,* from Latin *lūridus,* pale. See LURID.]

lorn (lôrn) *adj.* Bereft; forlorn. [Middle English, from Old English *-loren,* past participle of *-lēosan,* to lose, as in *forlēosan.* See **leu-** in Appendix.]

Lorne also **Lorn** (lôrn), **Firth of.** An inlet of the Atlantic Ocean on the western coast of Scotland between Mull Island and the mainland.

Lor·rain (lō-rān′, lô-răN′), **Claude.** 1600–1682. French painter known especially for his skill in depicting light in his landscapes and seascapes.

Lor·raine (lô-rān′, lō-, lō-rĕn′). A historical region and former province of northeast France. Originally part of a kingdom belonging to Charlemagne's grandson Lothair I, the region passed to France in 1766 but was ceded with Alsace to Germany after the Franco-Prussian War (1871). The area was returned to France by the Treaty of Versailles (1919).

Lor·re (lôr′ē), **Peter.** 1904–1964. Czechoslovakian-born American actor. In the German film *M* (1931) he portrayed a psychotic killer, establishing his trademark role as a sinister villain. His other films include *Casablanca* (1942).

lor·ry (lôr′ē, lŏr′ē) *n., pl.* **-ries.** *Chiefly British.* A motor truck. [Perhaps akin to dialectal *lurry,* to lug, haul.]

lo·ry (lôr′ē, lōr′ē) *n., pl.* **-ries.** Any of various brightly colored Australasian parrots having a tongue with a brushlike tip that is used to feed on nectar and pollen. [Malay *luri.*]

LOS *abbr.* **1.** Length of stay. **2.** *Football.* Line of scrimmage. **3.** Line of sight.

Los Al·a·mos (lôs ăl′ə-mōs′, lŏs). An unincorporated community of north-central New Mexico northwest of Santa Fe. It was chosen in 1942 as a nuclear research site to produce the first atomic bombs. Population, 11,039.

Los Al·tos (ăl′təs, -tōs). A city of western California south of Palo Alto. It is mainly residential. Population, 25,769.

Los An·ge·les (ăn′jə-ləs, -lēz′, ăng′gə-ləs). *Abbr.* **L.A., LA.** A city of southern California on the Pacific Ocean in a widespread metropolitan area. The so-called City of the Angels was founded by the Spanish in 1781 and served several times as a colonial capital. Population, 2,966,763.

lose (lo͞oz) *v.* **lost** (lôst, lŏst), **los·ing, los·es.** —*tr.* **1.** To be unsuccessful in retaining possession of; mislay: *He's always losing his keys on the way out the door.* **2. a.** To come to be deprived of the ownership, care, or control of (something one has had), as by negligence, accident, or theft: *I've lost three umbrellas this year. Britain lost its American colonies in a revolution.* **b.** To be deprived of (something one has had): *lost their lives; lost her youth through hardship.* **c.** To be bereaved of: *lost his wife.* **d.** To be unable to keep alive: *a doctor who has lost very few patients.* **3.** To be unable to maintain, sustain, or keep: *lost everything in the stock market crash; is losing supporters by changing his mind.* **4.** To fail to win; fail in: *lost the game; lost the court case.* **5.** To fail to use or take advantage of: *Don't lose a chance to improve your position.* **6.** To fail to hear, see, or understand: *We lost the plane in the fog. I lost her when she started speaking about thermodynamics.* **7. a.** To let (oneself) become unable to find the way. **b.** To remove (oneself), as from everyday reality into a fantasy world. **8.** To rid oneself of: *lost five pounds.* **9.** To consume aimlessly; waste: *lost a week in idle occupations.* **10.** To stray or wander from: *lose one's way.* **11. a.** To elude or outdistance: *lost their pursuers.* **b.** To be outdistanced by: *chased the thieves but lost them.* **12.** To become slow by (a specified amount of time). Used of a timepiece. **13.** To cause or result in the loss of: *Failure to reply to the advertisement lost her the job.* **14.** To cause to be destroyed. Usually used in the passive: *Both planes were lost in the crash.* **15.** To cause to be damned. —*intr.* **1.** To suffer loss. **2.** To be defeated. **3.** To operate or run slow. Used of a timepiece. —***phrasal verb.*** **lose out.** To fail to achieve or receive an expected gain. —***idioms.*** **lose out on.** To miss (an opportunity, for example). **lose time. 1.** To operate too slowly. Used of a timepiece. **2.** To delay advancement. [Middle English *losen,* from Old English *losian,* to perish, from *los,* loss. See **leu-** in Appendix.]

lo·sel (lō′zəl, lo͞o′-, lŏz′əl) *n.* One that is worthless. [Middle English, from *lōsen,* past participle of *lēsen,* to lose, from Old English *-lēosan.* See LORN.]

los·er (lo͞o′zər) *n.* **1. a.** One that fails to win: *the losers of the game.* **b.** One who takes loss in a specified way: *a graceful loser; a poor loser.* **2. a.** One that fails consistently, especially a person with bad luck or poor skills: *"losers at home seeking wealth and glory in undeveloped countries"* (Arthur M. Schlesinger, Jr.). **b.** One that is bad in quality: *That book is a real loser.*

Los Ga·tos (lôs găt′əs, lŏs). A city of western California, a residential suburb of San Jose. Population, 26,593.

los·ing (lo͞o′zĭng) *adj.* **1.** Failing to win, as in a sport or game: *a losing team; a losing lottery ticket.* **2.** Of or relating to one that fails to win: *a losing season; a losing battle.* —**losing** *n.* **1.** The act of one that loses; loss. **2.** Often **losings.** Something lost, such as money at gambling.

los·ing·est (lo͞o′zĭng-ĭst) *adj. Slang.* Less successful or losing more often than any others of its kind: *"help turn around one of the network's losingest nights of the week"* (Washington Post).

Los Mo·chis (lôs mō′chĭs, mô′chēs). A city of northwest Mex-

ă pat	oi boy
ā pay	ou out
âr care	o͝o took
ä father	o͞o boot
ĕ pet	ŭ cut
ē be	ûr urge
ĭ pit	th thin
ī pie	*th* this
îr pier	hw which
ŏ pot	zh vision
ō toe	ə about, item
ô paw	♦ regionalism

Stress marks: ′ (primary); ′ (secondary), as in **dictionary** (dĭk′shə-nĕr′ē)

ico near the Gulf of California south-southeast of Hermosillo. It is a resort in a farming area. Population, 122,531.

loss (lôs, lŏs) *n.* **1.** The act or an instance of losing: *nine losses during the football season.* **2.a.** One that is lost: *wrote their flooded house off as a loss.* **b.** The condition of being deprived or bereaved of something or someone: *mourning their loss.* **c.** The amount of something lost: *selling at a 50 percent loss.* **3.** The harm or suffering caused by losing or being lost. **4. losses.** People lost in wartime; casualties. **5.** Destruction: *The war caused incalculable loss.* **6.** *Electricity.* The power decrease caused by resistance in a circuit, circuit element, or device. **7.** The amount of a claim on an insurer by an insured. **—*idiom.* at a loss. 1.** Below cost: *sold the merchandise at a loss.* **2.** Perplexed; puzzled: *I am at a loss to understand those remarks.* [Middle English *los,* from Old English. See LOSE.]

loss leader *n.* A commodity offered especially by a retail store at cost or below cost to attract customers.

loss ratio *n.* The ratio between the premiums paid to an insurance company and the claims settled by the company.

lost (lôst, lŏst) *v.* Past tense and past participle of **lose. —lost** *adj.* **1.** Unable to find one's way: *a lost child.* **2.a.** No longer in the possession, care, or control of someone or something: *a lost pen.* **b.** No longer known or practiced: *a lost art.* **3.** Unable to function, act, or make progress. **4.** Spiritually or physically destroyed. **5.** Completely involved or absorbed; rapt: *lost in thought.*

lost and found or **lost-and-found** (lôst′ən-found′, lŏst′-) *n.* A repository in a public place, as in a school or theater, where found items are kept for reclaiming by their owners.

Lost River Range (lôst, lŏst). A chain of mountains in east-central Idaho rising to 3,861.9 m (12,662 ft).

lot (lŏt) *n.* **1.** An object used in making a determination or choice at random: *casting lots.* **2.a.** The use of objects in making a determination or choice at random: *chosen by lot.* **b.** The determination or choice so made. **3.** Something that befalls one because of or as if because of determination by lot. **4.** One's fortune in life; fate. See Synonyms at **fate. 5.** A number of associated people or things: *placating an angry lot of tenants; kids who made a noisy lot.* **6.** Kind; type: *That dog is a contented lot.* **7.** Miscellaneous articles sold as one unit. **8.** *Informal.* A large extent, amount, or number: *is in a lot of trouble; made lots of new friends.* Often used adverbially with *a* or in the plural: *felt a lot better; ran lots faster.* **9.a.** A piece of land having specific boundaries, especially one constituting a part of a city, town, or block. **b.** A piece of land used for a given purpose: *a parking lot.* **c.** A film studio. **—lot** *tr.v.* **lot·ted, lot·ting, lots. 1.** To apportion by lots; allot. **2.** To divide (land) into lots. [Middle English, from Old English *hlot.*]

Lot[1] (lŏt). In the Old Testament, Abraham's nephew, whose wife was turned into a pillar of salt when she looked back as they fled Sodom.

Lot[2] (lŏt, lôt). A river of southern France rising in the Cévennes and flowing about 483 km (300 mi) to the Garonne River.

loth (lōth, lōth) *adj.* Variant of **loath.**

Lo·thair I (lō-thâr′, -târ′). 795?–855. Holy Roman emperor (840–855). In the Treaty of Verdun (843) the empire was divided into three parts, and Lothair received the Middle Kingdom.

Lothair II. 1070?–1137. King of Germany (1125–1137) and Holy Roman emperor (1133–1137). He invaded Italy in 1136.

Lo·thar·i·o also **lo·thar·i·o** (lō-thâr′ē-ō) *n., pl.* **-os.** A man who seduces women. [After *Lothario,* a character in *The Fair Penitent,* a play by Nicholas Rowe.]

lo·ti (lō′tē) *n., pl.* **ma·lo·ti** (mä-). See table at **currency.** [Sotho, from *Maloti,* a range of mountains in Lesotho.]

Lo·ti (lō-tē′, lô-), **Pierre.** 1850–1923. French writer whose novels, including *Aziyadé* (1879), are noted for their exotic settings.

lo·tic (lō′tĭk) *adj.* Of, relating to, or living in moving water. [From Latin *lōtus,* past participle of *lavere,* to wash. See LOTION.]

lo·tion (lō′shən) *n.* **1.** A medicated liquid for external application. **2.** Any of various externally applied cosmetic liquids. [Middle English *locion,* from Old French *lotion,* from Latin *lōtiō, lōtiōn-,* a washing, from *lōtus,* past participle of *lavere,* to wash. See **leu(ə)-** in Appendix.]

lo·tos (lō′təs) *n.* Variant of **lotus.**

lot·ter·y (lŏt′ə-rē) *n., pl.* **-ies. 1.** *Games.* A contest in which tokens are distributed or sold, the winning token or tokens being secretly predetermined or ultimately selected in a random drawing. **2.** A selection made by lot from a number of applicants or competitors: *The state uses a lottery to assign spaces in the campground.* **3.** An activity or event regarded as having an outcome depending on fate: *They considered combat duty a lottery.* [French *loterie,* probably from Dutch *loterije,* from Middle Dutch, from *lot,* lot.]

lot·to (lŏt′ō) *n., pl.* **-tos.** *Games.* **1.** A game of chance similar to bingo. **2.** A lottery, typically with an accumulating jackpot, in which participants play numbers of their choice in a random drawing. [Italian and French *loto,* both from French *lot,* lot, from Old French, from Frankish **lot.*]

lo·tus also **lo·tos** (lō′təs) *n.* **1.a.** An aquatic plant *(Nelumbo nucifera)* native to southern Asia and Australia, having large leaves, fragrant, pinkish flowers, a broad, rounded, perforated seedpod, and fleshy rhizomes. **b.** The edible seed, leaf, or rhizome of this plant. **c.** Any of several similar or related plants, such as the water lilies *Nymphaea caerula* or *N. lotus.* **2.** A representation of any of various lotuses or similar or related plants in Egyptian or classical sculpture, architecture, or art. **3.** Any of several leguminous plants of the genus *Lotus.* **4.** *Greek Mythology.* **a.** A small Mediterranean tree or shrub whose fruit was eaten by the lotus-eaters. **b.** The fruit of this plant. [Latin *lōtus,* name of several plants, from Greek *lōtos,* perhaps of Semitic origin.]

lotus

lo·tus-eat·er (lō′təs-ē′tər) *n.* **1.** *Greek Mythology.* One of a people described in the *Odyssey* who fed on the lotus and hence lived in a drugged, indolent state. **2.** A lazy person devoted to pleasure and luxury.

lotus land *n. Informal.* A place or condition of irresponsibility and luxury.

lotus position *n.* A cross-legged sitting position used in yoga. [From its resemblance to a lotus.]

louche (lo͞osh) *adj.* Of questionable taste or morality: *a louche night club; a louche painting.* [French, from Old French *losche,* squint-eyed, feminine of *lois,* from Latin *luscus,* blind in one eye.]

loud (loud) *adj.* **loud·er, loud·est. 1.** Characterized by high volume and intensity. Used of sound. **2.** Producing sound of high volume and intensity. **3.** Clamorous and insistent: *loud denials.* **4.a.** Having offensively bright colors: *a loud necktie.* **b.** Having an offensively strong odor. **c.** Offensive in manner. **—loud** *adv.* **louder, loudest.** In a loud manner. [Middle English, from Old English *hlūd.* See **kleu-** in Appendix.] **—loud′ly** *adv.*

SYNONYMS: *loud, earsplitting, stentorian, strident.* The central meaning shared by these adjectives is "marked by or producing great volume and often disagreeable intensity of sound": *loud trumpets; earsplitting shrieks; stentorian tones; strident, screeching brakes.* See also Synonyms at **gaudy[1].**
ANTONYM: *soft.*

---

loud·en (loud′n) *tr. & intr.v.* **-ened, -en·ing, -ens.** To make or become louder.

loud·mouth (loud′mouth′) *n. Informal.* One given to loud, irritating, or indiscreet talk. **—loud′mouthed′** (-mouthd′, -moutht′) *adj.*

loud pedal *n. Music.* See **sustaining pedal.**

loud·speak·er (loud′spē′kər) *n.* A device that converts electric signals to audible sound.

lotus position

Lou Gehrig's disease (lo͞o′ gĕr′ĭgz) *n.* See **amyotrophic lateral sclerosis.** [After Henry Louis ("Lou") GEHRIG.]

lough (lŏKH, lŏk) *n. Irish.* **1.** A lake. **2.** A bay or an inlet of the sea. [Middle English, from Old English *luh,* ultimately from Old Irish *loch.*]

Lou·is VII (lo͞o′ē, lo͞o-ē′). 1120?–1180. King of France (1137–1180) who led the unsuccessful Second Crusade (1147–1149) and frequently fought against Henry II of England.

Louis IX. Known as "Saint Louis." 1214–1270. King of France (1226–1270) who led the Seventh Crusade (1248–1254) and died in a subsequent crusade to Tunisia.

Louis XIII. 1601–1643. King of France (1610–1643) who relied heavily on his political adviser Cardinal Richelieu to overcome familial insurgence and war with Spain and the Hapsburgs.

Louis XIV. Known as "Louis the Great" and "the Sun King." 1638–1715. King of France (1643–1715). His reign, the longest in French history, was characterized by a magnificent court and the expansion of French influence in Europe.

Louis XV. 1710–1774. King of France (1715–1774) who led France into the War of the Austrian Succession (1740–1748) and the Seven Years' War (1756–1763).

Louis XVI. 1754–1793. King of France (1774–1792). In 1789 he summoned the Estates-General, but he did not grant the reforms that were demanded and revolution followed. Louis and his queen, Marie Antoinette, were executed in 1793.

Louis XVIII. 1755–1824. King of France (1814–1824). His reign was interrupted by Napoleon (1815), but he returned to power after Napoleon's defeat at Waterloo in the same year.

Lou·is (lo͞o′ĭs), **Joe.** 1914–1981. American prizefighter who held the heavyweight title for nearly 12 years (1937–1949), successfully defending it for a record 25 times.

Lou·is·burg or **Lou·is·bourg** (lo͞o′ĭs-bûrg′). A town of Nova Scotia, Canada, on eastern Cape Breton Island. It is near the site of the fortress of Louisbourg, built c. 1712–1740 by the French to guard the entrance to the Gulf of St. Lawrence.

Lou·ise (lo͞o-ēz′), **Lake.** A lake of southwest Alberta, Canada, in the Rocky Mountains near Banff. Surrounded by high peaks and glaciers, it is noted for its scenic beauty.

Lou·i·si·an·a (lo͞o-ē′zē-ăn′ə, lo͞o′zē-). *Abbr.* **LA, La.** A state of the southern United States on the Gulf of Mexico. It was admitted as the 18th state in 1812. Part of the vast region claimed by La Salle for France in 1682, it was first successfully settled in 1718 with the foundation of New Orleans. Control of the area passed to the United States in 1803, and the Territory of Orleans was created in 1804 when the northern part was split off to form the District of Louisiana (later the Territory of Louisiana and the Missouri Territory). Baton Rouge is the capital and New Orleans the largest city. Population, 4,206,098.

Louisiana French *n.* French as spoken by the descendants of the original French settlers of Louisiana.

Louisiana Purchase. A territory of the western United States extending from the Mississippi River to the Rocky Moun-

Louis XIV
1701 portrait by Hyacinthe Rigaud (1659–1743)

tains between the Gulf of Mexico and the Canadian border. It was purchased from France in 1803 for $15 million and officially explored by the Lewis and Clark expedition (1804–1806).

Lou·is Na·po·le·on (lo͞o′ē nə-pō′lē-ən). See **Napoleon III.**

Lou·is Phi·lippe (lo͞o′ē fĭ-lēp′, lo͞o-ē′ fē-lēp′). Known as "the Citizen King." 1773–1850. King of France (1830–1848). He ruled after the overthrow of the Bourbons in the July Revolution (1830) and abdicated during the Revolution of 1848.

Louis Qua·torze (kă-tôrz′) *adj.* Of, relating to, or characteristic of the baroque style in architecture, furniture, and decoration of the reign of Louis XIV. [French.]

Louis Quinze (kăNz′) *adj.* Of, relating to, or characteristic of the rococo style in architecture, furniture, and decoration of the reign of Louis XV. [French.]

Louis Seize (sĕz′) *adj.* Of, relating to, or characteristic of the neoclassic style in architecture, furniture, and decoration of the reign of Louis XVI. [French.]

Louis Treize (trĕz′) *adj.* Of, relating to, or characteristic of the heavy late-Renaissance style in architecture, furniture, and decoration of the reign of Louis XIII. [French.]

Lou·is·ville (lo͞o′ē-vĭl′, -ə-vəl). The largest city of Kentucky, in the north-central part of the state on the Ohio River west of Lexington. On the site of a fort built by George Rogers Clark in 1778, it is a port of entry. Population, 298,451.

lounge (lounj) *v.* **lounged, loung·ing, loung·es.** —*intr.* **1.** To move or act in a lazy, relaxed way; loll: *lounging on the sofa; lounged around in pajamas.* **2.** To pass time idly: *lounged in Venice till June.* —*tr.* To pass (time) in a lazy, relaxed, or idle way: *lounged the day away.* —**lounge** *n.* **1.** A public waiting room, as in a hotel or an air terminal, often having smoking or lavatory facilities. **2.** An establishment or a room in an establishment, as in a hotel or restaurant, where cocktails are served. **3.a.** A living room. **b.** A lobby. **4.** A long couch, especially one having no back and a headrest at one end. [Possibly from French *s'allonger,* to stretch out, from Old French *alongier,* to lengthen, from Medieval Latin *allongāre* : Latin *ad-,* ad- + Latin *longus,* long; see LONG[1].] —**loung′er** *n.*

lounge car *n.* See **club car.**

lounge lizard *n. Slang.* **1.** A generally idle man who haunts establishments or gatherings frequented by the rich or fashionable; a social parasite. **2.** A habitué of cocktail lounges.

lounge·wear (lounj′wâr′) *n.* Clothing suitable for relaxing.

loupe

loupe (lo͞op) *n.* A small magnifying glass usually set in an eyepiece and used chiefly by watchmakers and jewelers. [French, from Old French, flawed gem, probably of Germanic origin.]

loup-ga·rou (lo͞o′gə-ro͞o′, -gä-) *n., pl.* **loups-ga·rous** (lo͞o′gə-ro͞oz′, -gä-ro͞o′). A werewolf. [French, from Old French *leu garoul* : *leu,* wolf (from Latin *lupus;* see **wlkʷo-** in Appendix) + *garoul,* werewolf (of Germanic origin; see **wi-ro-** in Appendix).]

loup·ing ill (lou′pĭng, lō′-) *n.* See **tremble** (sense 3a). [From Scots *loup,* to leap, from Middle English *loupen.* See LOPE.]

Loup River (lo͞op). A river of east-central Nebraska rising in three branches and flowing a total length of about 451 km (280 mi) eastward to the Platte River.

louver

loups-ga·rous (lo͞o′gə-ro͞oz′, -gä-ro͞o′) *n.* Plural of **loup-garou.**

lour (lour) *v. & n.* Variant of **lower[1].**

Lourdes (lo͝ord, lo͝ordz). A town of southwest France at the foot of the Pyrenees. It is noted for its Roman Catholic shrine marking the site where the Virgin Mary is said to have appeared to Saint Bernadette in 1858. Population, 17,425.

Lou·ren·ço Mar·ques (lə-rĕn′sō mär′kĕs, lô-rĕN′so͞o mär′kĕsh). See **Maputo.**

lou·ry (lour′ē) *adj.* Variant of **lowery.**

louse (lous) *n.* **1.** *pl.* **lice** (līs). Any of numerous small, flat-bodied, wingless biting or sucking insects of the orders Mallophaga or Anoplura, many of which are external parasites on various animals, including human beings. **2.** *pl.* **lous·es.** *Slang.* A mean or despicable person. —**louse** *tr.v.* **loused, lous·ing, lous·es.** *Slang.* To bungle: *loused the project; louse up a deal.* [Middle English, from Old English *lūs.* See **lūs-** in Appendix.]

louse·wort (lous′wûrt′, -wôrt′) *n.* Any of numerous plants of the genus *Pedicularis,* having clusters of irregular, variously colored flowers. Also called *wood betony.* [From the belief that sheep feeding on it were prone to lice.]

lous·y (lou′zē) *adj.* **-i·er, -i·est. 1.** Infested with lice. **2.** Extremely contemptible; nasty: *a lousy trick.* **3.** Very painful or unpleasant: *a lousy headache.* **4.** Inferior or worthless: *a lousy play.* **5.** *Slang.* Abundantly supplied: *lousy with money.* —**lous′i·ly** *adv.* —**lous′i·ness** *n.*

lout[1] (lout) *n.* A person regarded as awkward and stupid; an oaf. See Synonyms at **boor.** [Possibly from LOUT[2].]

lout[2] (lout) *intr.v.* **lout·ed, lout·ing, louts. 1.** To bow or curtsy. **2.** To bend or stoop. [Middle English *louten,* from Old English *lūtan.*]

lout·ish (lou′tĭsh) *adj.* Having the characteristics of a lout; awkward, stupid, and boorish. —**lout′ish·ness** *n.*

Lou·vain (lo͞o-văN′) also **Leu·ven** (lœ′vən). A city of central Belgium east of Brussels. First mentioned in the 9th century, it was a center of the wool trade in the Middle Ages but declined in the late 14th century because of civil strife. Its famed university dates from the 15th century. Population, 85,068.

lou·ver also **lou·vre** (lo͞o′vər) *n.* **1.a.** A framed opening, as in a wall, door, or window, fitted with fixed or movable horizontal slats for admitting air and light and shedding rain. **b.** One of the slats used in such an opening. **c.** One of the narrow openings formed by such slats. **2.** A slatted, ventilating opening, as on the hood of a motor vehicle. **3.** A lantern-shaped cupola on the roof of a medieval building for admitting air and providing for the escape of smoke. [Middle English *lover,* skylight, chimney, from Old French, from Middle Dutch *love,* gallery, from Middle High German *lauble.*] —**lou′vered** *adj.*

Lou·ÿs (lo͞o-ē′, lwē), **Pierre.** 1870–1925. French writer whose novels include *Aphrodite* (1896) and *Woman and Puppet* (1908).

lov·a·ble also **love·a·ble** (lŭv′ə-bəl) *adj.* Having characteristics that attract love or affection. —**lov′a·bil′i·ty, lov′a·ble·ness** *n.* —**lov′a·bly** *adv.*

lov·age (lŭv′ĭj) *n.* A Mediterranean perennial plant *(Levisticum officinale)* having small, aromatic, seedlike fruit used as seasoning. [Middle English, from Anglo-Norman *luvesche,* from Old English *lufestice,* from Medieval Latin *levistica,* from Late Latin *levisticum,* alteration of Latin *ligusticum,* from neuter of *ligusticus,* Ligurian.]

love (lŭv) *n.* **1.** A deep, tender, ineffable feeling of affection and solicitude toward a person, such as that arising from kinship, recognition of attractive qualities, or a sense of underlying oneness. **2.** A feeling of intense desire and attraction toward a person with whom one is disposed to make a pair; the emotion of sex and romance. **3.a.** Sexual passion. **b.** Sexual intercourse. **c.** A love affair. **4.** An intense emotional attachment, as for a pet or treasured object. **5.** A person who is the object of deep or intense affection or attraction; beloved. Often used as a term of endearment. **6.** An expression of one's affection: *Send him my love.* **7.a.** A strong predilection or enthusiasm: *a love of language.* **b.** The object of such an enthusiasm: *The outdoors is her greatest love.* **8. Love.** *Mythology.* Eros or Cupid. **9.** Often **Love.** *Theology.* Charity. **10. Love.** *Christian Science.* God. **11.** *Sports.* A zero score in tennis. —**love** *v.* **loved, lov·ing, loves.** —*tr.* **1.** To have a deep, tender, ineffable feeling of affection and solicitude toward (a person): *We love our parents. I love my friends.* **2.** To have a feeling of intense desire and attraction toward (a person). **3.** To have an intense emotional attachment to: *loves his house.* **4.a.** To embrace or caress. **b.** To have sexual intercourse with. **5.** To like or desire enthusiastically: *loves swimming.* **6.** *Theology.* To have charity for. **7.** To thrive on; need: *The cactus loves hot, dry air.* —*intr.* To experience deep affection or intense desire for another. —***idioms.*** **for love.** Out of compassion; with no thought for a reward: *She volunteers at the hospital for love.* **for love or money.** Under any circumstances. Usually used in negative sentences: *I would not do that for love or money.* **for the love of.** For the sake of; in consideration for: *did it all for the love of praise.* **no love lost.** No affection; animosity: *There's no love lost between them.* [Middle English, from Old English *lufu.* See **leubh-** in Appendix.]

SYNONYMS: *love, affection, devotion, fondness, infatuation.* These nouns denote feelings of warm personal attachment or strong attraction to another person. *Love* suggests a more intense feeling than that associated with the other words of this group: *married for love. Affection* is a less ardent and more unvarying feeling of tender regard: *parental affection. Devotion* is earnest, affectionate dedication; it implies a more selfless, often more abiding feeling than *love: The devotion of the aged couple is inspiring. Fondness* is strong liking or affection: *showed their fondness for their grandchildren by financing their education. Infatuation* is foolish or extravagant attraction, often of short duration: *Their infatuation blinded them to the fundamental differences in their points of view.* See also Synonyms at **like[1].**

love·a·ble (lŭv′ə-bəl) *adj.* Variant of **lovable.**

love affair *n.* **1.** An intimate sexual relationship or episode between lovers. **2.** A strong enthusiasm: *America's love affair with the automobile.*

love apple *n.* A tomato. [Probably translation of French *pomme d'amour* (from the former belief in the tomato's aphrodisiacal powers) : *pomme,* apple + *de,* of + *amour,* love.]

love beads *pl.n.* Small beads on a necklace, especially ones worn by hippies.

love·bird (lŭv′bûrd′) *n.* **1.** Any of various small Old World parrots, especially of the genus *Agapornis,* often kept as cage birds and noted for the apparent affection between mates. **2. lovebirds.** *Informal.* A couple who are openly affectionate or demonstrative with each other, especially in public.

love child *n.* A child born of parents who are not married to each other.

Love·craft (lŭv′krăft′), **H(oward) P(hillips).** 1890–1937. American writer of fantasy and horror tales. His works were collected in *The Outsider and Others* (1939), *Beyond the Wall of Sleep* (1943), and *Marginalia* (1944).

love feast *n.* **1.a.** A meal shared among early Christians as a symbol of love. **b.** A similar symbolic meal among certain modern Christian sects. **2.** A gathering intended to promote goodwill among the participants.

love handle *n. Slang.* A deposit of fat at the waistline. Often used in the plural.

love-in (lŭv′ĭn′) *n. Slang.* A gathering to engender and pro-

ă pat	oi boy
ā pay	ou out
âr care	o͝o took
ä father	o͞o boot
ĕ pet	ŭ cut
ē be	ûr urge
ĭ pit	th thin
ī pie	*th* this
îr pier	hw which
ŏ pot	zh vision
ō toe	ə about, item
ô paw	♦ regionalism

Stress marks: ′ (primary); ′ (secondary), as in **dictionary** (dĭk′shə-nĕr′ē)

mote love, as for the satisfaction of the participants or as a form of social activism.

love-in-a-mist (lŭv′ĭn-ə-mĭst′) *n.* A Mediterranean plant *(Nigella damascena)* having blue or whitish flowers surrounded by numerous threadlike bracts.

love knot *n.* A stylized knot regarded as a symbol of the constancy of two lovers. Also called *lovers' knot, true lovers' knot.*

Love•lace (lŭv′lās′), **Richard.** 1618–1657? English Cavalier poet who is noted especially for the lyrics "To Althea, from Prison" and "To Lucasta, Going to the Wars."

Love•land (lŭv′lənd). A city of northern Colorado south of Fort Collins. It is a food-processing center. Population, 30,244.

love•less (lŭv′lĭs) *adj.* **1.** Characterized by an absence of love: *a loveless marriage.* **2.** Exhibiting or feeling no love; unloving: *a loveless glance.* **3.** Receiving no love; unloved: *a loveless child.*

love-lies-bleed•ing (lŭv′līz-blē′dĭng) *n.* A tropical Indian plant *(Amaranthus caudatus)* having clusters of small red flowers.

Lov•ell (lŭv′əl), Sir **(Alfred Charles) Bernard.** Born 1913. British radio astronomer who founded and directed (1951–1981) the Jodrell Bank Experimental Station.

love life *n.* The aspect of one's life including amatory or sexual relationships with others.

love•lock (lŭv′lŏk′) *n.* A lock of hair hanging separately from the rest of the hair, as one tied with ribbon and worn by courtiers during the 17th and 18th centuries.

love•lorn (lŭv′lôrn′) *adj.* Bereft of love or one's lover.

love•ly (lŭv′lē) *adj.* **-li•er, -li•est. 1.** Full of love; loving. **2.** Inspiring love or affection. **3.** Having beauty that appeals to the emotions as well as to the eye. See Synonyms at **beautiful. 4.** Enjoyable; delightful. **—lovely** *n., pl.* **-lies. 1.** A beautiful person, especially a woman. **2.** A lovely object. **—love′li•ness** *n.* **—love′ly** *adv.*

love•mak•ing (lŭv′mā′kĭng) *n.* **1.** Sexual activity, especially sexual intercourse. **2.** Courtship; wooing.

lov•er (lŭv′ər) *n.* **1.** One who loves another, especially one who feels sexual love. **2. lovers.** A couple in love with each other. **3. a.** A paramour. **b.** A sexual partner. **4.** One who is fond of or devoted to something: *a lover of art.* **—lov′er•ly** *adv. & adj.*

lov•ers' knot (lŭv′ərz) *n.* See **love knot.**

love seat or **love•seat** (lŭv′sēt′) *n.* A small sofa or double chair that seats two people.

love•sick (lŭv′sĭk′) *adj.* **1.** So deeply affected by love as to be unable to act normally. **2.** Exhibiting a lover's yearning. **—love′sick′ness** *n.*

lov•ey-dov•ey (lŭv′ē-dŭv′ē) *adj. Informal.* Expressing affection in an extravagantly sentimental way; mushy.

lov•ing (lŭv′ĭng) *adj.* **1.** Feeling love; affectionate. **2.** Indicative of or exhibiting love.

loving cup *n.* **1.** A large ornamental wine vessel, usually made of silver and having two or more handles. **2.** A large ornamental vessel given as an award in modern sporting contests and similar events.

low¹ (lō) *adj.* **low•er, low•est. 1. a.** Having little relative height; not high or tall. **b.** Rising only slightly above surrounding surfaces. **c.** Situated or placed below normal height: *a low lighting fixture.* **d.** Situated below the surrounding surfaces: *water standing in low spots.* **e.** Dead and buried. **f.** Cut to show the wearer's neck and chest; décolleté: *a low neckline.* **2.** Near or at the horizon: *The sun is low in the sky.* **3.** *Linguistics.* Produced with part or all of the tongue depressed, as *a,* pronounced (ä), in *father.* Used of vowels. **4.** Of less than usual or average depth; shallow: *The river is low.* **5.** Humble in status or character. **6.** *Biology.* Of relatively simple structure in the scale of living organisms. **7.** Unrefined; coarse: *low humor.* **8.** Violating standards of morality or decency; base: *a low stunt to pull.* See Synonyms at **mean². 9. a.** Lacking strength or vigor; weak. **b.** Emotionally or mentally depressed. **10. a.** Below average in degree, intensity, or amount: *a low temperature.* **b.** Below an average or a standard: *low wages; a low level of communication.* **c.** Ranked near the beginning of an ascending series or scale: *a low number; a low grade of oil.* **d.** Relating to or being latitudes nearest to the equator. **e.** Relatively small. Used of a cost, price, or other value: *a low fee; a low income.* **f.** Characterized by a small degree, intensity, or amount of a specified attribute: *a low cholesterol diet.* **11.** Having a pitch corresponding to a relatively small number of sound-wave cycles per second. **12.** Not loud; soft: *a low murmur.* **13.** Being near total depletion: *My savings account is low.* **14.** Not adequately provided or equipped; short: *low on supplies.* **15.** Depreciatory; disparaging: *a low opinion of his qualities.* **16.** Brought down or reduced in health or wealth: *in a low state.* **17.** Of, relating to, or being the gear configuration or setting, as in an automotive transmission, that produces the least vehicular speed with respect to engine speed. **—low** *adv.* **1. a.** In or to a low position, level, or space: *aimed low; bent low.* **b.** In or to a low condition or rank; humbly: *thought low of himself.* **2.** In or to a reduced, humbled, or degraded condition: *brought low by business reverses.* **3.** Softly; quietly: *speak low.* **4.** With a deep pitch: *sang low.* **5.** At a small price: *bought low and sold high.* **—low** *n.* **1.** A low level, position, or degree: *The stock market fell to a new low.* **2.** *Meteorology.* A region of atmospheric pressure that is below normal. **3.** The low gear configuration of a transmission. [Middle English *loue,* from Old Norse *lāgr.* See **legh-** in Appendix.] **—low′ness** *n.*

low² (lō) *n.* The characteristic sound uttered by cattle; a moo. **—low** *intr.v.* **lowed, low•ing, lows.** To utter the sound made by cattle; moo. [From Middle English *lowen,* to moo, from Old English *hlōwan.* See **kelə-²** in Appendix.]

Low (lō), Sir **David Alexander Cecil.** 1891–1963. British political cartoonist who created the pompous Colonel Blimp.

Low, Juliette Magill Kinzie Gordon. 1860–1927. American founder of the Girl Scouts (1912).

low-ball or **low•ball** (lō′bôl′) *v.* **-balled, -bal•ling, -balls.** *Slang.* —*tr.* To underestimate or understate (a cost) deliberately: *"He often took illegal cash payments from developers in return for . . . low-balling the cost of construction and renovation work"* (Boston Globe). —*intr.* To engage in the deliberate understatement of cost. [From the card game of the same name.] **—low′-ball** *adj.*

low beam *n.* The beam of a vehicle's headlight that provides short-range illumination.

low blow *n.* An unscrupulous attack; an insult.

low•born (lō′bôrn′) *adj.* Of humble birth.

low•boy (lō′boi′) *n.* A low tablelike chest of drawers.

low•bred (lō′brĕd′) *adj.* Coarse; vulgar.

low•brow (lō′brou′) *n.* One having uncultivated tastes. **—lowbrow** also **low•browed** (-broud′) *adj.* Uncultivated; vulgar. [LOW¹ + (HIGH)BROW.]

Low Church *n.* A group in the Anglican Church that minimizes the episcopacy, priesthood, and sacraments and favors evangelical doctrines, polity, and usages. **—Low′-Church′** (lō′chûrch′) *adj.*

low comedy *n.* Comedy characterized by slapstick, burlesque, and horseplay.

Low Countries. A region of northeast Europe comprising Belgium, the Netherlands, and Luxembourg.

low-den•si•ty (lō′dĕn′sĭ-tē) *adj.* Having a low concentration: *low-density urban areas.*

low-density lipoprotein *n. Abbr.* **LDL** A complex of lipids and proteins that functions as a transporter of cholesterol in the blood. High levels are associated with an increased risk of atherosclerosis and coronary heart disease.

low•down (lō′doun′) *n. Slang.* The whole truth: *gave us the lowdown on what happened at the party.*

low-down (lō′doun′) *adj.* **1.** Despicable; base. **2.** Emotionally depressed.

Low•ell (lō′əl). A city of northeast Massachusetts on the Merrimack River northwest of Boston. Settled in 1653, it was once a major textile center. Population, 92,418.

Lowell, Abbott Lawrence. 1856–1943. American educator and president (1909–1933) of Harvard University.

Lowell, Amy. 1874–1925. American poet. A leader of the imagists, she wrote several volumes of poetry, including *Sword Blades and Poppy Seed* (1914).

Lowell, James Russell. 1819–1891. American editor and diplomat. He edited the *Atlantic Monthly* (1857–1861) and served as minister to Spain (1877–1880) and Great Britain (1880–1885).

Lowell, Percival. 1855–1916. American astronomer. He founded the Lowell Observatory in Arizona (1894), where his studies of Mars led him to believe that the planet was inhabited.

Lowell, Robert Traill Spence, Jr. 1917–1977. American poet whose works include *Life Studies* (1959) and *The Dolphin* (1973).

low-end (lō′ĕnd′) *adj.* **1.** Cheapest in a line of merchandise: *low-end subcompact cars.* **2.** *Informal.* **a.** Appealing to unsophisticated and undiscerning customers: *a low-end department store; low-end video equipment.* **b.** Unsophisticated and undiscerning: *books targeted to the low-end consumer.*

low•er¹ (lou′ər, lour) also **lour** (lour) —*intr.v.* **low•ered, low•er•ing, low•ers** also **loured, lour•ing, lours. 1.** To look angry, sullen, or threatening. See Synonyms at **frown. 2.** To appear dark or threatening, such as the sky. —*n.* **1.** A threatening, sullen, or angry look. **2.** A dark and ominous look: *the lower of thunderheads.* [Middle English *louren.*] **—low′er•ing•ly** *adv.*

low•er² (lō′ər) *adj.* Comparative of **low¹. 1.** Below another in rank, position, or authority. **2.** Physically situated below a similar or comparable thing: *a lower shelf.* **3. Lower.** *Geology & Archaeology.* Relating to or being an earlier or older division of the period named. **4.** *Biology.* Less advanced in organization or evolutionary development. **5.** Denoting the larger and usually more representative house of a bicameral legislature. **—lower** *v.* **-ered, -er•ing, -ers.** —*tr.* **1.** To let, bring, or move down to a lower level. **2.** To reduce in value, degree, or quality. **3.** To weaken; undermine: *lower one's energy.* **4.** To reduce in standing or respect. —*intr.* **1.** To move down: *Her hand lowered.* **2.** To become less; diminish: *The temperature has lowered gradually this month.*

low•er bound (lō′ər) *n. Mathematics.* A number less than or equal to any number in a set.

Low•er Cal•i•for•nia (lō′ər kăl′ĭ-fôr′nyə, -fôr′nē-ə). See **Baja California.**

Lower Can•a•da (kăn′ə-də). The southern, mainly French-speaking portion of Quebec, Canada, from 1791 until 1841, when it was reunited with Upper Quebec to form the present-day province of Quebec.

Lower Carboniferous *n.* See **Mississippian** (sense 2).

low•er•case or **low•er-case** (lō′ər-kās′) *Printing.* —*adj.*

loving cup
1897 American silver loving cup by Wilcox and Evertsen (1892–1898)

Juliette Low

lowboy

low relief
16th-century cast of a 1446 Italian portrait medal of Sigismondo Pandolfo Malatesta (1417–1468) by Matteo de' Pasti (fl. 1446–1477)

Abbr. **lc** Of, relating to, or being lowercase letters. —*tr.v.* **-cased, -cas•ing, -cas•es.** To put (type or text) in lowercase letters. —**low′er•case′** *n.*

lowercase letter *n. Printing.* A letter written or printed in a size smaller than and often in a form differing from its corresponding capital letter. [From their storage in the lower of two trays used by compositors.]

low•er class (lō′ər) *n.* The class or classes of lower than middle rank in a society. —**low′er-class′** (lō′ər-klăs′) *adj.*

low•er•class•man (lō′ər-klăs′mən) *n.* See **underclassman.**

low•er criticism (lō′ər) *n.* Critical study, especially of the Bible, that attends chiefly to the words of the work being examined, exploring their meaning and seeking to establish an accurate text. [As against HIGHER CRITICISM.]

Lower East Side. See **East Side.**

Lower E•gypt (ē′jĭpt). The part of ancient Egypt comprising the Nile River delta. It was united with Upper Egypt c. 3100 B.C.

Lower En•ga•dine (ĕng′gə-dēn′). See **Engadine.**

Lower Mich•i•gan (mĭsh′ĭ-gən). See **Lower Peninsula.**

low•er•most (lō′ər-mōst′) *adj.* Lowest.

Lower New York Bay (no͞o yôrk′, nyo͞o). See **New York Bay.**

Lower Pa•lat•i•nate (pə-lăt′n-ĭt). See **Palatinate.**

Lower Peninsula also **Lower Mich•i•gan** (mĭsh′ĭ-gən). The section of Michigan between Lakes Michigan and Huron and south of the Straits of Mackinac.

Lower Tun•gus•ka (to͝ong-go͞o′skə, to͞on-). See **Tunguska.**

low•er world (lō′ər) *n. Mythology.* The abode of the dead, considered to be beneath the surface of the earth.

low•er•y (lou′ə-rē) also **lour•y** (lour′ē) *adj.* Overcast; threatening.

Lowes (lōz), **John Livingston.** 1867–1945. American educator and literary critic who wrote *The Road to Xanadu* (1927).

low•est common denominator (lō′ĭst) *n.* **1.** *Mathematics.* See **least common denominator. 2.** That which is understood, believed, or accepted by a majority of people: *"The press can resist the standard of the lowest common denominator, the rationalization that all news is fit to print that has appeared anywhere else"* (Edward M. Kennedy).

lowest common multiple *n. Mathematics.* See **least common multiple.**

Lowes•toft (lō′stəf, -stôft′, -stŏft′). A municipal borough of extreme eastern England on the North Sea east-southeast of Norwich. A seaside resort, it is famous for the fine bone china produced here in the 18th century. Population, 55,800.

lowest terms *pl.n. Mathematics.* The numerator and denominator of a fraction that have had all common factors but 1 factored out and canceled.

low frequency *n. Abbr.* **LF, lf** A radio frequency in the range from 30 to 300 kilohertz.

low gear *n.* **1.** The low gear configuration of a transmission. **2.** A state of minimum activity, energy, or force: *The project went into low gear during summer vacation.*

Low German *n.* **1.** The German dialects of northern Germany. Also called *Plattdeutsch.* **2.** The continental West Germanic languages except High German. [Translation of German *Plattdeutsch* : *platt,* flat (from the terrain of northern Germany) + *Deutsch,* German.]

low-grade (lō′grād′) *adj.* **1.** Of inferior grade or quality: *low-grade merchandise.* **2.** Reduced in degree or intensity: *a low-grade fever.*

low-in•come (lō′ĭn′kŭm) *adj.* Of or relating to individuals or households supported by an average or slightly below average income.

low-key (lō′kē′) also **low-keyed** (-kēd′) *adj.* **1.** Having low intensity; restrained, as in style or quality; subdued. **2.** Having or producing uniformly dark tones with little contrast, as in a photograph.

low•land (lō′lənd) *n.* An area of land that is low in relation to the surrounding country. —**lowland** *adj.* Relating to or characteristic of low, usually level land.

low•land•er (lō′lən-dər) *n.* A native or inhabitant of a lowland.

Low•lands (lō′ləndz). A region of Scotland lying south of the Highlands. —**Low′land** *adj.* —**Low′land•er** *n.*

low-lev•el (lō′lĕv′əl) *adj.* **1.** Relating to or being of low rank or importance: *a low-level job.* **2.** Situated in or occurring at a low level: *low-level radiation.* **3.** *Computer Science.* Of or relating to a computer language, such as an assembly language, in which each instruction corresponds to an instruction in machine language.

low•life also **low-life** (lō′līf′) *n., pl.* **-lifes** also **-lives** (-līvz′). A person of low social status or moral character: *"explores a world of London lowlifes in sinister prosperity"* (Times Literary Supplement). —**low′life** *adj.*

low•ly (lō′lē) *adj.* **-li•er, -li•est. 1.** Having or suited for a low rank or position. **2.** Humble or meek in manner. **3.** Plain or prosaic in nature. —**lowly** *adv.* **1.** In a low manner, condition, or position. **2.** In a meek or humble manner. **3.** Low in sound. —**low′li•ness** *n.*

low-ly•ing (lō′lī′ĭng) *adj.* **1.** Lying close to water or ground level: *low-lying coastal areas.* **2.** Situated below the normal height or altitude: *low-lying deserts of central Arizona.*

Low Mass *n.* A Mass of simple ceremony that was recited rather than sung by the priest. No longer in official use.

low-mind•ed (lō′mīn′dĭd) *adj.* Exhibiting a coarse, vulgar character. —**low′-mind′ed•ly** *adv.* —**low′-mind′ed•ness** *n.*

low-necked (lō′nĕkt′) also **low-neck** (-nĕk′) *adj.* Having a low-cut neckline; décolleté.

low-pitched (lō′pĭcht′) *adj.* **1.** Low in tone or tonal range. **2.** Having a moderate slope: *a low-pitched roof.*

low-pres•sure (lō′prĕsh′ər) *adj.* **1.** Having, working under, or exerting little pressure. **2.** Relaxed in attitude, nature, or style; easygoing: *a low-pressure lifestyle; a low-pressure personality.*

low profile *n.* Behavior or activity carried out with deliberate restraint or modesty so as not to attract attention: *keep a low profile.* —**low′-pro′file′** (lō′prō′fīl′) *adj.*

low relief *n.* Sculptural relief that projects very little from the background. Also called *bas-relief, basso-relievo.*

low-res (lō′rĕz′) *adj.* Low-resolution.

low-res•o•lu•tion (lō′rĕz′ə-lo͞o′shən) *adj.* **1.** Of or relating to an image that lacks fine detail. **2.** *Computer Science.* Of or relating to an output device, such as a printer, whose images do not contain a large number of pixels and therefore lack sharpness and may have jagged edges.

♦ **low rider** or **low-rid•er** (lō′rī′dər) *n. Chiefly Southwestern U.S.* **1.** A customized car whose springs have been shortened so that the chassis rides close to the ground, often equipped with hydraulic lifts that can be controlled by the driver: *"a 1964 Chevrolet Impala low rider belonging to Clemente Fuentes, who can make the car rock and wobble like a conga dancer"* (Edmund Newton). **2.** A person who drives such a car. —**low rid′er** *adj.*

low-rise (lō′rīz′) *adj.* Of or relating to a building having few stories and often no elevators: *a low-rise apartment house.* [LOW[1] + (HIGH)-RISE.]

low road *n.* Behavior or practice that is deceitful or immoral: *He spent much of the campaign on the low road, making scurrilous and unsubstantiated remarks about the incumbent's past.*

Low•ry (lou′rē), **(Clarence) Malcolm.** 1909–1957. British writer. His novel *Under the Volcano* (1947) is recognized as a masterpiece of modern fiction.

low-spir•it•ed (lō′spĭr′ĭ-tĭd) *adj.* Being in low spirits; depressed. —**low′-spir′it•ed•ly** *adv.* —**low′-spir′it•ed•ness** *n.*

Low Sunday *n.* The first Sunday after Easter.

low-tech (lō′tĕk′) *adj.* Of or relating to low technology.

low technology *n.* Technology that does not involve highly advanced or specialized systems or devices. —**low′-tech•nol′o•gy** (lō′tĕk-nŏl′ə-jē) *adj.*

low-ten•sion (lō′tĕn′shən) *adj.* **1.** Of or at low potential or voltage. **2.** Operating at low voltage.

low-test (lō′tĕst′) *adj.* Having low volatility and a high boiling point. Used of gasoline. [LOW[1] + (HIGH)-TEST.]

low-tick•et (lō′tĭk′ĭt) *adj. Informal.* Fairly inexpensive: *low-ticket merchandise.*

low tide *n.* **1.** The lowest level of the tide. **2.** The time at which the tide is lowest. Also called *low water.* —*attributive.* Often used to modify another noun: *a low tide mark; a low tide departure.*

low water *n. Abbr.* **LW 1.** The lowest level of water in a body of water, such as a river, lake, or reservoir. **2.** See **low tide.**

lox[1] (lŏks) *n., pl.* **lox** or **lox•es.** Smoked salmon. [Yiddish *laks,* from Middle High German *lahs,* salmon, from Old High German. See **laks-** in Appendix.]

lox[2] (lŏks) *n.* Liquid oxygen, especially when used as a rocket fuel oxidizer. [L(IQUID) + OX(YGEN).]

lox•o•drom•ic (lŏk′sə-drŏm′ĭk) also **lox•o•drom•i•cal** (-ĭ-kəl) *adj. Nautical.* Relating to sailing on a rhumb line. [Greek *loxos,* slanting + Greek *dromos,* course.] —**lox′o•drom′i•cal•ly** *adv.*

loxodromic curve *n. Nautical.* See **rhumb line.**

loy•al (loi′əl) *adj.* **1.** Steadfast in allegiance to one's homeland, government, or sovereign. **2.** Faithful to a person, an ideal, a custom, a cause, or a duty. **3.** Of, relating to, or marked by loyalty. See Synonyms at **faithful.** [French, from Old French *leial, loial,* from Latin *lēgālis,* legal, from *lēx, lēg-,* law. See **leg-** in Appendix.] —**loy′al•ly** *adv.*

loy•al•ist (loi′ə-lĭst) *n.* **1.** One who maintains loyalty to an established government, political party, or sovereign, especially during war or revolutionary change. **2. Loyalist.** See **Tory** (sense 2). **3. Loyalist.** One who supported the established government of Spain during the Spanish Civil War. —**loy′al•ism** *n.*

loy•al•ty (loi′əl-tē) *n., pl.* **-ties. 1.** The state or quality of being loyal. See Synonyms at **fidelity. 2. loyalties.** Feelings of devoted attachment and affection: *My loyalties lie with my family.*

Lo•yang (lō′yăng′). See **Luoyang.**

Loy•o•la (loi-ō′lə), Saint **Ignatius of.** See Saint **Ignatius of Loyola.**

loz•enge (lŏz′ĭnj) *n.* **1.** A small, medicated candy intended to be dissolved slowly in the mouth to lubricate and soothe irritated tissues of the throat. **2. a.** A four-sided planar figure with a diamondlike shape; a rhombus that is not a square. **b.** Something having this shape, especially a heraldic device. [Middle English, rhombus, from Old French *losenge,* perhaps of Celtic origin.]

Lo·zi·er (lō′zē-ər), **Clemence Sophia Harned.** 1813–1888. American physician and feminist. She founded (1863) the New York Medical College and Hospital for Women.

LP (ĕl′pē′) *n., pl.* **LP's** or **LPs.** A long-playing phonograph record. [Originally a trademark.]

LPG *abbr.* Liquefied petroleum gas.

LPM or **lpm** *abbr.* Lines per minute.

LPN or **L.P.N.** *abbr.* Licensed practical nurse.

Lr The symbol for the element **lawrencium.**

LR *abbr.* Living room.

L/R *abbr.* Left/right.

L.S. *abbr. Latin.* Locus sigilli (the place of the seal).

LSAT *abbr.* Law School Admissions Test.

LSD[1] (ĕl′ĕs-dē′) *n.* A crystalline compound, $C_{20}H_{25}N_3O$, derived from lysergic acid and used as a powerful hallucinogenic drug. Also called *acid, lysergic acid diethylamide.* [L(Y)S(ERGIC ACID) D(IETHYLAMIDE).]

LSD[2] *abbr.* Least significant digit.

LSI *abbr.* Large-scale integration.

lt. *abbr.* Light.

Lt. *abbr.* Lieutenant.

l.t. or **LT** *abbr.* Local time.

Lt. Col. or **LTC** *abbr.* Lieutenant colonel.

Lt. Comdr. *abbr.* Lieutenant commander.

ltd. or **Ltd.** *abbr.* **1.** Limited. **2.** Limited company.

Lt. Gen. or **LTG** *abbr.* Lieutenant general.

Lt. Gov. *abbr.* Lieutenant governor.

LTJG *abbr.* Lieutenant junior grade.

Lu The symbol for the element **lutetium.**

Lu·an·da (lo͞o-ăn′də) **Lo·an·da** (lō-ăn′də). The capital and largest city of Angola, in the northwest part of the country on the Atlantic Ocean. Founded by the Portuguese in 1575, it has a fine natural harbor and diversified industries. Population, 1,200,000.

Lu·ang·wa (lo͞o-äng′wä). A river, about 805 km (500 mi) long, of eastern Zambia flowing south-southwest to the Zambezi River.

lu·au (lo͞o-ou′, lo͞o′ou′) *n.* A traditional, elaborate Hawaiian feast. [Hawaiian *lu'au.*]

Lu·ba (lo͞o′bə) *n., pl.* **Luba** or **-bas. 1.** A member of a Bantu people inhabiting southeast Zaire. **2.** The Bantu language of this people. In this sense, also called *Tshiluba.*

Lu·ba·vitch·er (lo͞o-bä′vĭ-chər, lo͞o′bə-vĭch′ər) *n.* A member of a Hasidic community founded in Russia in the late 18th century that stresses the importance of religious study. **—Lubavitcher** *adj.* Of or relating to this movement and its followers. [Yiddish *Libavitsher,* from *Libavitsh,* Jewish town in Russia where the movement originated.]

lub·ber (lŭb′ər) *n.* **1.** A clumsy person. **2.** *Nautical.* An inexperienced sailor; a landlubber. [Middle English *lobur,* lazy lout; akin to *lob,* lout. See LOB.] **—lub′ber·ly** *adv. & adj.*

lubber line also **lub·ber's line** (lŭb′ərz) *n.* A line or mark on a compass or cathode-ray indicator that represents the heading of a ship or an aircraft.

lubber's hole *n. Nautical.* A hole through the platform surrounding the upper part of a ship's mast, through which one may climb to go aloft.

Lub·bock (lŭb′ək). A city of northwest Texas south of Amarillo. Settled in 1879, it is an industrial center in an agricultural region. Population, 173,979.

lube (lo͞ob) *Informal. tr.v.* **lubed, lub·ing, lubes.** To lubricate (a car's joints, for example). **—lube** *n.* A lubricant, especially one applied to machinery: *silicone lube.* —*attributive.* Often used to modify another noun: *a lube job; a lube rack.*

Lü·beck (lo͞o′bĕk′, lü′-). A city of north-central Germany northeast of Hamburg. A major Baltic port and industrial center, the present city dates from 1143 and was the leading town of the Hanseatic League after its designation as a free city in 1226. It retained that status until 1937. Population, 211,707.

Lu·bitsch (lo͞o′bĭch), **Ernst.** 1892–1947. German filmmaker whose sophisticated comedies include *Ninotchka* (1939).

Lu·blin (lo͞o′blən, -blĕn′). A city of eastern Poland southeast of Warsaw. Chartered in 1317, it passed to Austria in 1795 and Russia in 1815. Population, 324,100.

lu·bri·cant (lo͞o′brĭ-kənt) *n.* **1.** A substance, such as grease or oil, that reduces friction when applied as a surface coating to moving parts. **2.** One that helps reduce difficulty or conflict. **—lu′bri·cant** *adj.*

lu·bri·cate (lo͞o′brĭ-kāt′) *v.* **-cat·ed, -cat·ing, -cates.** —*tr.* **1.** To apply a lubricant to. **2.** To make slippery or smooth. —*intr.* To act as a lubricant. [Latin *lūbricāre, lūbricāt-,* from *lūbricus,* slippery. See **sleubh-** in Appendix.] **—lu′bri·ca′tion** *n.* **—lu′bri·ca′tive** *adj.*

lu·bri·ca·tor (lo͞o′brĭ-kā′tər) *n.* **1.** One that lubricates, especially a lubricant. **2.** A device for applying a lubricant.

lu·bri·cious (lo͞o-brĭsh′əs) also **lu·bri·cous** (lo͞o′brĭ-kəs) *adj.* **1.** Having a slippery or smooth quality. **2.** Shifty or tricky. **3. a.** Lewd; wanton. **b.** Sexually stimulating; salacious. [Alteration of *lubricous,* from Latin *lūbricus,* slippery. See **sleubh-** in Appendix.] **—lu·bri′cious·ly** *adv.* **—lu·bri′cious·ness** *n.*

lu·bric·i·ty (lo͞o-brĭs′ĭ-tē) *n.* The quality or condition of being lubricious. [Late Latin *lūbricitās,* slipperiness, from Latin *lūbricus,* slippery. See **sleubh-** in Appendix.]

lu·bri·cous (lo͞o′brĭ-kəs) *adj.* Variant of **lubricious.**

Lu·bum·ba·shi (lo͞o′bo͝om-bä′shē). Formerly **E·lis·a·beth·ville** (ĭ-lĭz′ə-bəth-vĭl′). A city of southeast Zaire near the Zambia border. Founded in 1910, it was the center of a secessionist state during the civil war in Zaire (1960–1963). Population, 543,268.

Lu·can (lo͞o′kən). A.D. 39–65. Roman poet who wrote the *Pharsalia,* an epic account of the civil war between Caesar and Pompey.

Lu·ca·ni·a (lo͞o-kā′nē-ə, -kān′yə), **Mount.** A peak, 5,229.8 m (17,147 ft) high, of the St. Elias Mountains in southwest Yukon Territory, Canada, near the Alaskan border.

lu·carne (lo͞o-kärn′) *n.* A dormer window. [French, from Old French, alteration (influenced by *luiserne,* light, from Latin *lūcerna,* lamp; see LUCERNE) of Old Provençal *lucana,* possibly of Germanic origin.]

Luc·ca (lo͞o′kə). A city of northwest Italy west of Florence. On the site of an ancient Ligurian settlement and a Roman colony, it became a free commune in the 12th century and was later an independent republic. Population, 91,097.

Luce (lo͞os), **Clare Boothe.** 1902–1987. American writer and public official. She wrote several plays, including *The Women* (1936), and served as ambassador to Italy (1953–1956).

Luce, Henry Robinson. 1898–1967. American editor and publisher who cofounded *Time* (1923) and founded *Fortune* (1930), *Life* (1936), and *Sports Illustrated* (1954).

lu·cent (lo͞o′sənt) *adj.* **1.** Giving off light; luminous. **2.** Translucent; clear. [Latin *lūcēns, lūcent-,* present participle of *lūcēre,* to shine. See **leuk-** in Appendix.] **—lu′cen·cy** *n.*

lu·cerne (lo͞o-sûrn′) *n. Chiefly British.* Alfalfa. [French *luzerne,* from Provençal *luzerno,* glowworm (perhaps from its shiny seeds), from Latin *lūcerna,* lamp, from *lūcēre,* to shine. See LUCID.]

Lu·cerne (lo͞o-sûrn′, lü-sĕrn′). A city of central Switzerland on the northern shore of the **Lake of Lucerne,** an irregularly shaped lake surrounded by mountains. The city developed around a monastery founded in the eighth century. Population, 61,000.

lu·ces (lo͞o′sēz) *n.* A plural of **lux.**

Lu·cian (lo͞o′shən). fl. second century A.D. Greek satirist. His two major works, *Dialogues of the Gods* and *Dialogues of the Dead,* ridicule Greek philosophy and mythology.

lu·cid (lo͞o′sĭd) *adj.* **1.** Easily understood; intelligible. **2.** Mentally sound; sane or rational. **3.** Translucent or transparent. See Synonyms at **clear.** [Latin *lūcidus,* from *lūcēre,* to shine. See **leuk-** in Appendix.] **—lu·cid′i·ty, lu′cid·ness** *n.*

Lu·ci·fer (lo͞o′sə-fər) *n.* **1.** The archangel cast from heaven for leading the revolt of the angels; Satan. **2.** The planet Venus in its appearance as the morning star. **3. lucifer.** A friction match. [Middle English, from Old English, morning star, Lucifer, from Late Latin *Lūcifer,* from Latin, morning star, light-bringer : *lūx, lūc-,* light; see **leuk-** in Appendix + *-fer,* -fer.]

lu·cif·er·ase (lo͞o-sĭf′ə-rās′, -rāz′) *n.* An enzyme present in the cells of bioluminescent organisms that catalyzes the oxidation of luciferin.

lu·cif·er·in (lo͞o-sĭf′ər-ĭn) *n.* A chemical substance present in the cells of bioluminescent organisms, such as fireflies, that produces an almost heatless, bluish-green light when oxidized under the catalytic effects of luciferase. [Latin *lūcifer,* light-bringing; see LUCIFER + –IN.]

Lu·ci·na (lo͞o-sī′nə) *n. Archaic.* A midwife. [Latin *Lūcīna,* goddess of childbirth, from feminine of *lūcīnus,* light-bringing, from *lūx, lūc-,* light. See **leuk-** in Appendix.]

Lu·cite (lo͞o′sīt′). A trademark used for a transparent thermoplastic acrylic resin employed in paints, enamels, and primers.

luck (lŭk) *n.* **1.** The chance happening of fortunate or adverse events; fortune: *as luck would have it.* **2.** Good fortune or prosperity; success: *We wish you luck.* **3.** One's personal fate or lot: *It's just my luck.* **—luck** *intr.v.* **lucked, luck·ing, lucks.** *Informal.* To gain success or something desirable by chance: *lucked into a good apartment; lucked out in finding that rare book.* ***—idioms.*** **in luck.** Enjoying success; fortunate. **out of luck.** Lacking good fortune. **push (one's) luck.** To risk one's good fortune, often by acting overconfidently. **try (one's) luck.** To attempt something without knowing if one will be successful. [Middle English *lucke,* from Middle Dutch *luc,* short for *gheluc.*]

luck·i·ly (lŭk′ə-lē) *adv.* With or by favorable chance: *Luckily, the police came right away.*

luck·less (lŭk′lĭs) *adj.* Marked by, suffering, or promising lack of luck; unlucky. See Synonyms at **unfortunate.**

Luck·now (lŭk′nou). A city of north-central India east-southeast of Delhi. Once the capital of the kingdom of Oudh (1775–1856), it was besieged for five months during the Indian Mutiny of 1857. Population, 895,721.

luck·y (lŭk′ē) *adj.* **-i·er, -i·est. 1.** Having or attended by good luck. See Synonyms at **happy. 2.** Occurring by chance; fortuitous. **3.** Believed to bring good luck: *hoped to draw a lucky number.* **—luck′i·ness** *n.*

lu·cra·tive (lo͞o′krə-tĭv) *adj.* Producing wealth; profitable: *a lucrative income; a lucrative marketing strategy.* [Middle English *lucratif,* from Old French, from Latin *lucrātīvus,* from *lucrātus,* past participle of *lucrārī,* to profit, from *lucrum,* profit. See **lau-** in Appendix.]

Clare Boothe Luce
Photographed in 1956

Henry Luce
Photographed in 1966

ă pat	oi boy
ā pay	ou out
âr care	o͝o took
ä father	o͞o boot
ĕ pet	ŭ cut
ē be	ûr urge
ĭ pit	th thin
ī pie	*th* this
îr pier	hw which
ŏ pot	zh vision
ō toe	ə about, item
ô paw	♦ regionalism

Stress marks: ′ (primary); ′ (secondary), as in **dictionary** (dĭk′shə-nĕr′ē)

lu·cre (lo͞o′kər) *n.* Money or profits. [Middle English, from Latin *lucrum.* See **lau-** in Appendix.]

WORD HISTORY: When William Tyndale translated *aiskhron kerdos,* "shameful gain" (Titus 1:11), as *filthy lucre* in his edition of the Bible, he was tarring the word *lucre* for the rest of its existence. But we cannot lay the pejorative sense of *lucre* completely at Tyndale's door. He was merely a link, albeit a strong one, in a process that had begun long before with respect to the ancestor of our word, the Latin word *lucrum,* "material gain, profit." This process was probably controlled by the inevitable conjunction of profit, especially monetary profit, with evils such as greed. In Latin *lucrum* also meant "avarice," and in Middle English *lucre,* besides meaning "monetary gain, profit," meant "illicit gain." Furthermore, many of the contexts in which the neutral sense of the word appeared were not that neutral, as in "It is a wofull thyng . . . ffor lucre of goode . . . A man to fals his othe [it is a sad thing for a man to betray his oath for monetary gain]." Tyndale thus merely helped the process along when he gave us the phrase *filthy lucre.*

Lu·cre·tius (lo͞o-krē′shəs, -shē-əs). 96?–55? B.C. Roman philosopher and poet who is famous for *De Rerum Natura* (*On the Nature of Things*), a long poem that attempts to explain the universe in scientific terms. **—Lu·cre′tian** (-shən) *adj.*

lu·cu·brate (lo͞o′kyo͞o-brāt′) *intr.v.* **-brat·ed, -brat·ing, -brates.** To write in a scholarly fashion; produce scholarship. [Latin *lūcubrāre, lūcubrāt-,* to work at night by lamplight. See **leuk-** in Appendix.]

lu·cu·bra·tion (lo͞o′kyo͞o-brā′shən) *n.* **1.** Laborious study or meditation. **2.** Often **lucubrations.** Writing produced by laborious effort or study, especially pedantic or pretentious writing.

lu·cu·lent (lo͞o′kyo͞o-lənt) *adj.* Easily understood; clear or lucid. [Middle English, shiny, from Latin *lūculentus,* from *lūx, lūc-,* light. See **leuk-** in Appendix.]

Lu·cul·lan (lo͞o-kŭl′ən) *adj.* **1.** Lavish; luxurious. **2.** Of or relating to Lucullus or his luxurious banquets. [After Lucius Licinius LUCULLUS.]

Lu·cul·lus (lo͞o-kŭl′əs), **Lucius Licinius.** 110?–57? B.C. Roman general and consul noted for his self-indulgence.

Lü·da also **Lü·ta** (lo͞o′dä′, lü′-). An industrial conurbation of northeast China on Korea Bay at the southern end of the Liaodong Peninsula. It includes the cities of Lushun and Dalian. Population, 1,380,000.

Lud·dite (lŭd′īt) *n.* **1.** Any of a group of British workers who between 1811 and 1816 rioted and destroyed laborsaving textile machinery in the belief that such machinery would diminish employment. **2.** One who opposes technical or technological change. [After Ned *Ludd,* an English laborer who was supposed to have destroyed weaving machinery around 1779.] **—Lud′dism** *n.*

lude (lo͞od) *n. Slang.* A pill or tablet containing methaqualone. [Short for QUAALUDE.]

Lu·den·dorff (lo͞od′n-dôrf′), **Erich Friedrich Wilhelm von.** 1865–1937. German general and politician. He was chief of staff in the east during World War I.

Lü·den·scheid (lo͞od′n-shīt′, lüd′-). A city of west-central Germany east of Düsseldorf. Chartered in 1287, it is an industrial center. Population, 73,496.

Lu·dhi·a·na (lo͞o′dē-ä′nə). A city of northwest India north-northwest of Delhi. Population, 607,502.

lu·dic (lo͞o′dĭk) *adj.* Of, relating to, or connoting play or playfulness: *"Fiction . . . now makes* [language] *the center of its reflexive concern, and explodes in ludic, parodic, ironic forms"* (Ihab Hassan). [French *ludique,* from Latin *lūdus,* play. See **leid-** in Appendix.]

lu·di·crous (lo͞o′dĭ-krəs) *adj.* Laughable or hilarious because of obvious absurdity or incongruity. See Synonyms at **foolish.** [From Latin *lūdicrus,* sportive, from *lūdus,* game. See **leid-** in Appendix.] **—lu′di·crous·ly** *adv.* **—lu′di·crous·ness** *n.*

Lud·low (lŭd′lō). A town of southwest Massachusetts, an industrial suburb of Springfield. Population, 18,150.

Lud·wigs·burg (lo͝od′vĭgz-bûrg′, lo͞ot′vĭkhs-bo͝ork′). A city of southwest Germany north of Stuttgart. It grew around a baroque 18th-century castle built in imitation of Versailles. Population, 77,054.

Lud·wigs·ha·fen (lo͝od′vĭgz-hä′fən, lo͞ot′vĭkhs-). A city of southwest Germany on the Rhine River opposite Mannheim. Founded as a fortress in the early 17th century, it is now a leading center of the country's chemical industry. Population, 155,311.

lu·es (lo͞o′ēz) *n., pl.* **lues.** Syphilis. [New Latin *luēs,* from Latin, plague. See **leu-** in Appendix.] **—lu·et′ic** (-ĕt′ĭk) *adj.* **—lu·et′i·cal·ly** *adv.*

luff (lŭf) *n.* **1.** *Nautical.* **a.** The act of sailing closer into the wind. **b.** The forward side of a fore-and-aft sail. **2.** *Archaic.* The fullest part of the bow of a ship. **—luff** *v.* **luffed, luff·ing, luffs.** *—intr. Nautical.* **1.** To steer a sailing vessel closer into the wind, especially with the sails flapping. **2.** To flap while losing wind. Used of a sail. *—tr.* **1.** *Nautical.* To sail (a vessel, such as a yacht) closer into the wind during a race so as to prevent an opponent's craft from passing on the windward side. **2.** To raise or lower (the boom of a crane or derrick). [Middle English *lof,* spar holding out the windward tack of a square sail, from Old French, probably of Germanic origin.]

luf·fa (lo͞o′fə, lŭf′ə) *n.* Variant of **loofa.**

Luf·kin (lŭf′kĭn). A city of eastern Texas north-northeast of Houston. It is a commercial center. Population, 28,562.

Luft·waf·fe (lo͝oft′väf′ə) *n.* The German air force before and during World War II. [German : *Luft,* air (from Middle High German, from Old High German) + *Waffe,* weapon (from Middle High German *wāfen,* from Old High German *waffan*).]

lug¹ (lŭg) *n.* **1.** A handle or projection used as a hold or support. **2.** A lug nut. **3.** *Nautical.* A lugsail. **4.** A projecting part of a larger piece that helps to provide traction, as on a tire or the sole of a boot. **5.** A copper or brass fitting to which electrical wires can be soldered or otherwise connected. **6.** *Slang.* A clumsy fool; a blockhead. [Middle English *lugge,* earflap, probably of Scandinavian origin.]

lug² (lŭg) *v.* **lugged, lug·ging, lugs.** *—tr.* **1.** To drag or haul (an object) laboriously. **2.** To pull or drag with short jerks. **3.** To cause (an engine, for example) to run poorly or hesitate: *If you drive too slowly in third gear, you'll lug the engine. —intr.* **1.** To pull something with difficulty; tug. **2.** To move along by jerks or as if under a heavy burden. **3.** To run poorly or hesitate because of strain. Used of an engine: *The motor lugged as they drove up the hill.* **—lug** *n.* **1.** *Archaic.* **a.** The act of lugging. **b.** Something lugged. **2.** A box for shipping fruit or vegetables. [Middle English *luggen,* of Scandinavian origin.]

luge (lo͞ozh) *n. Sports.* **1.** A racing sled for one or two people that is ridden with the rider or riders lying supine. **2.** A competition in which these sleds race against a clock. [French dialectal, from Medieval Latin *sludia,* perhaps of Celtic origin.] **—luge** *v.* **—lug′er** *n.*

lug·gage (lŭg′ĭj) *n.* **1.** Containers for a traveler's belongings. **2.** The cases and belongings of a traveler. [Probably LUG² + (BAG)GAGE.]

lug·ger (lŭg′ər) *n. Nautical.* A small boat used for fishing, sailing, or coasting and having two or three masts, each with a lugsail, and two or three jibs set on the bowsprit. [From LUGSAIL.]

lug nut *n.* A heavy, rounded nut that fits over a bolt, used especially to attach an automotive vehicle's wheel to its axle.

Lu·go·si (lo͞o-gō′sē, lə-), **Bela.** 1884–1956. Hungarian-born American actor known for portraying monsters in a number of films, including *Dracula* (1931) and *The Wolf Man* (1941).

lug·sail (lŭg′səl) *n. Nautical.* A quadrilateral sail that lacks a boom, has the foot larger than the head, and is bent to a yard hanging obliquely on the mast. [Possibly from LUG¹.]

lu·gu·bri·ous (lo͞o-go͞o′brē-əs, -gyo͞o′-) *adj.* Mournful, dismal, or gloomy, especially to an exaggerated or ludicrous degree. [From Latin *lūgubris,* from *lūgēre,* to mourn.] **—lu·gu′bri·ous·ly** *adv.* **—lu·gu′bri·ous·ness** *n.*

lug·worm (lŭg′wûrm′) *n.* Any of various segmented, burrowing marine worms of the genus *Arenicola,* especially *A. marina,* often used as fishing bait. Also called *lobworm.* [Origin unknown.]

Lui·chow Peninsula (lwē′jō′). See **Leizhou Peninsula.**

Lui·se·ño (lwē-sān′yō) *n., pl.* **Luiseño** or **-ños. 1.a.** A Native American people inhabiting the coastal area of California south of Los Angeles, associated during Spanish times with the missions of San Luis Rey and San Juan Capistrano. **b.** A member of this people. **2.** The Uto-Aztecan language of the Luiseño. [American Spanish, from San *Luis* Rey de Francia, a mission in southern California.]

Luke (lo͞ok) *n. Abbr.* **Lk** *Bible.* See table at **Bible.**

Luke, Saint. First century A.D. Companion of Saint Paul and author of the third Gospel of the New Testament.

luke·warm (lo͞ok′wôrm′) *adj.* **1.** Mildly warm; tepid. **2.** Lacking conviction or enthusiasm; indifferent: *gave only lukewarm support to the incumbent candidate.* [Middle English *leukwarm* : *leuk, luke* (possibly variant of *leu,* from Old English *-hlēow;* see **kelə-¹** in Appendix) + *warm,* warm; see WARM.] **—luke′warm′ly** *adv.* **—luke′warm′ness** *n.*

Luks (lŭks), **George.** 1867–1933. American painter known for his studies of urban life, including *The Spielers* (1905).

Lu·le·å (lo͞o′lĕ-ô′, lü′-). A city of northeast Sweden on the Gulf of Bothnia. Chartered in 1621, it was rebuilt after a devastating fire in 1887. Population, 66,811.

Lu·le·älv (lo͞o′lĕ-ôlv′, lü′lə-ĕlv′). A river, about 443 km (275 mi) long, of northern Sweden flowing southeast to the Gulf of Bothnia.

lull (lŭl) *v.* **lulled, lull·ing, lulls.** *—tr.* **1.** To cause to sleep or rest; soothe or calm. **2.** To deceive into trustfulness: *"that honeyed charm that he used so effectively to lull his victims"* (S.J. Perelman). *—intr.* To become calm. **—lull** *n.* **1.** A relatively calm interval, as in a storm. **2.** An interval of lessened activity: *a lull in sales.* [Middle English *lullen,* possibly of Low German origin.]

lull·a·by (lŭl′ə-bī′) *n., pl.* **-bies.** *Music.* A soothing song with which to lull a child to sleep. **—lullaby** *tr.v.* **-bied, -bying, -bies.** To quiet with or as if with a lullaby. [Obsolete *lulla,* word used in lullabies (from Middle English *lullai,* from *lullen,* to lull; see LULL) + *by, bye* (as in GOOD-BYE).]

Lul·ly (lo͞o-lē′, lŭ-), **Jean Baptiste.** 1632–1687. Italian-born French composer. He was court composer to Louis XIV, founding the national French opera.

Lul·ly (lŭl′ē), **Raymond.** 1235?–1316. Spanish philosopher and mystic who attempted to identify the common elements shared by Christianity, Islam, and Judaism.

lu·lu (lo͞o′lo͞o) *n. Slang.* A remarkable person, object, or idea. [Alteration (probably influenced by the nickname *Lulu*) of obsolete *looly.*]

lum·ba·go (lŭm-bā′gō) *n.* A painful condition of the lower back, as one resulting from muscle strain or a slipped disk. [Late Latin *lumbāgō,* from Latin *lumbus,* loin.]

lum·bar (lŭm′bər, -bär′) *adj.* Of, near, or situated in the part of the back and sides between the lowest ribs and the pelvis. **—lumbar** *n.* A lumbar artery, nerve, vertebra, or part. [New Latin *lumbāris,* from Latin *lumbus,* loin.]

lumbar puncture *n.* The insertion of a hollow needle beneath the arachnoid membrane of the spinal cord in the lumbar region to withdraw cerebrospinal fluid for diagnostic purposes or to administer medication.

lum·ber¹ (lŭm′bər) *n.* **1.** Timber sawed into boards, planks, or other structural members of standard or specified length. **2.** Something useless or cumbersome. **3.** *Chiefly British.* Miscellaneous stored articles. **—lumber** *v.* **-bered, -ber·ing, -bers.** *—tr.* **1.a.** To cut down (trees) and prepare as marketable timber. **b.** To cut down the timber of. **2.** *Chiefly British.* To clutter with or as if with unused articles. *—intr.* To cut and prepare timber for marketing. [Perhaps from LUMBER².] **—lum′ber** *adj.* **—lum′ber·er** *n.*

lum·ber² (lŭm′bər) *intr.v.* **-bered, -ber·ing, -bers. 1.** To walk or move with heavy clumsiness. See Synonyms at **blunder. 2.** To move with a rumbling noise. [Middle English *lomeren,* possibly of Scandinavian origin; akin to Swedish dialectal *loma,* to move heavily.] **—lum′ber·ing·ly** *adv.*

lum·ber·jack (lŭm′bər-jăk′) *n.* **1.** One who fells trees and transports the timber to a mill; a logger. **2.** A short, warm outer jacket. Also called *lumber jacket.*

Lum·ber·ton (lŭm′bər-tən) A city of southern North Carolina south of Fayetteville. It is a tobacco market with lumber and textile mills. Population, 18,340.

lum·ber·yard (lŭm′bər-yärd′) *n.* An establishment that sells lumber and other building materials from a yard.

lum·bri·coid (lŭm′brĭ-koid′) *adj.* Of or resembling an earthworm. [From New Latin *lumbrīcoidēs,* species of intestinal parasitic roundworm : Latin *lumbrīcus,* earthworm + –OID.]

lu·men (lo͞o′mən) *n., pl.* **-mens** or **-mi·na** (-mə-nə). **1.** *Anatomy.* The inner open space or cavity of a tubular organ, as of a blood vessel or an intestine. **2.** *Abbr.* **lm** *Physics.* The unit of luminous flux in the International System, equal to the amount of light given out through a solid angle by a source of one candela intensity radiating equally in all directions. See table at **measurement. 3.** *Botany.* The cavity bounded by a plant cell wall. [Latin, an opening, light. See **leuk-** in Appendix.] **—lu′men·al, lu′min·al** *adj.*

Lu·mière (lo͞o-myĕr′, lü-), **Auguste Marie Louis Nicolas.** 1862–1954. French chemist, inventor, and cinematography pioneer. With his brother **Louis Jean Lumière** (1864–1948) he gave the first public showing of a cinematic film (1895).

lu·mi·nance (lo͞o′mə-nəns) *n.* **1.** The condition or quality of being luminous. **2.** *Physics.* The intensity of light per unit area of its source.

♦**lu·mi·nar·i·a** (lo͞o′mə-nâr′ē-ə) *n.* **1.** *Southwestern U.S.* A votive candle set into a small, decorative paper bag weighted with sand and placed in a row with others along a walkway, driveway, or rooftop as a holiday decoration. Also called ♦*farolito.* **2.** *New Mexico.* A bonfire built in front of each house in a pueblo to celebrate Christmas Eve. [Spanish, from Latin *lūmināria,* pl. of *lūmināre,* lamp. See LUMINARY.]

♦***REGIONAL NOTE:*** In recent years it has become commonplace to see entire American neighborhoods decorated during holiday seasons with *luminarias* lining driveways, sidewalks, or rooftops. A luminaria is a votive candle set inside a small decorative paper bag weighted with sand. The bags are usually colored and often perforated with designs through which the candle inside shows as bright pinpricks of light. The custom of luminarias comes from Mexico and is associated especially with the southwest United States. The same word is used for a similar holiday custom of the Pueblo peoples in New Mexico. On Christmas Eve they build a bonfire, called a *luminaria,* outside each house in the pueblo.

lu·mi·nar·y (lo͞o′mə-nĕr′ē) *n., pl.* **-ies. 1.** An object, such as a celestial body, that gives light. **2.** A person who is an inspiration to others. **3.** A person who has achieved eminence in a specific field. See Synonyms at **celebrity.** [Middle English, from Old French *luminarie,* from Latin *lūmināre* to shine, from *lūmen, lūmin-,* light. See **leuk-** in Appendix.] **—lu′mi·nar′y** *adj.*

lu·mi·nesce (lo͞o′mə-nĕs′) *intr.v.* **-nesced, -nesc·ing, -nesc·es.** To be or become luminescent. [Back-formation from LUMINESCENCE.]

lu·mi·nes·cence (lo͞o′mə-nĕs′əns) *n.* **1.** The emission of light that does not derive energy from the temperature of the emitting body, as in phosphorescence, fluorescence, and bioluminescence. Luminescence is caused by chemical, biochemical, or crystallographic changes, the motions of subatomic particles, or radiation-induced excitation of an atomic system. **2.** The light so emitted.

lu·mi·nes·cent (lo͞o′mə-nĕs′ənt) *adj.* Capable of, suitable for, or exhibiting luminescence. [Latin *lūmen, lūmin-,* light; see LUMEN + –ESCENT.]

lu·mi·nif·er·ous (lo͞o′mə-nĭf′ər-əs) *adj.* Generating, yielding, or transmitting light. [Latin *lūmen, lūmin-,* light; see LUMEN + –FEROUS.]

lu·mi·nism also **Lu·mi·nism** (lo͞o′mə-nĭz′əm) *n.* A style of 19th-century American painting concerned especially with the precise, realistic rendering of atmospheric light and the perceived effects of that light on depicted objects. [Latin *lūmen, lūmin-,* light; see LUMEN + –ISM.] **—lu′mi·nist** *adj. & n.*

lu·mi·nos·i·ty (lo͞o′mə-nŏs′ĭ-tē) *n., pl.* **-ties. 1.** The condition or quality of being luminous. **2.** Something luminous. **3.** The ratio of luminous flux at a specific wavelength to the radiant flux at the same wavelength. In this sense, also called *luminosity factor.*

lu·mi·nous (lo͞o′mə-nəs) *adj.* **1.** Emitting light, especially emitting self-generated light. **2.** Full of light; illuminated. See Synonyms at **bright. 3.a.** Easily comprehended; clear: *luminous prose.* **b.** Enlightened and intelligent; inspiring: *luminous ideas.* [Middle English, from Old French *lumineux,* from Latin *lūminōsus,* from *lūmen, lūmin-,* light. See **leuk-** in Appendix.] **—lu′mi·nous·ly** *adv.* **—lu′mi·nous·ness** *n.*

luminous efficiency *n.* The ratio of the total luminous flux to the total radiant flux of an emitting source.

luminous energy *n.* The radiant energy of electromagnetic waves in the visible portion of the electromagnetic spectrum.

luminous flux *n.* The rate of flow of light per unit of time, especially the flux of visible light expressed in lumens.

luminous intensity *n.* The luminous flux density per solid angle as measured in a given direction relative to the emitting source.

lum·mox (lŭm′əks) *n. Informal.* A person regarded as clumsy or stupid. [Origin unknown.]

lump¹ (lŭmp) *n.* **1.** An irregularly shaped mass or piece. **2.** A small cube of sugar. **3.** *Pathology.* A swelling or small palpable mass. **4.** A collection or totality; an aggregate. **5.** A person regarded as ungainly or dull witted. **6. lumps.** *Informal.* **a.** Severe punishment or treatment, as a beating or an unsparing criticism: *take one's lumps.* **b.** One's just deserts; comeuppance: *get one's lumps.* **—lump** *adj.* **1.** Formed into lumps: *lump sugar.* **2.** Not broken or divided into parts: *a lump payment.* **—lump** *v.* **lumped, lump·ing, lumps.** *—tr.* **1.** To put together in a single group without discrimination. **2.** To move with heavy clumsiness. **3.** To make into lumps. *—intr.* **1.** To become lumpy. **2.** To move heavily. ***—idiom.* lump in (one's) throat.** A feeling of constriction in the throat caused by emotion. [Middle English *lumpe,* of Low German origin; akin to obsolete Dutch *lompe.*]

lump² (lŭmp) *tr.v.* **lumped, lump·ing, lumps.** *Informal.* To tolerate (what must be endured): *like it or lump it.* [Perhaps from dialectal *lump,* to look sullen.]

lump·ec·to·my (lŭm-pĕk′tə-mē) *n., pl.* **-mies.** Surgical excision of a tumor from the breast with the removal of a minimal amount of surrounding tissue.

lum·pen (lŭm′pən, lo͝om′-) *adj.* **1.** Of or relating to dispossessed, often displaced people who have been cut off from the socioeconomic class with which they would ordinarily be identified: *lumpen intellectuals unable to find work in their fields.* **2.** Of or relating to the lumpenproletariat. **3.** Boorish or unenlightened: *Her music found no audience among the lumpen bourgeoisie.* [From German *Lumpenproletariat,* the lowest section of the proletariat. See LUMPENPROLETARIAT.]

lum·pen·pro·le·tar·i·at (lŭm′pən-prō′lĭ-târ′ē-ət, lo͝om′-) *n.* **1.** The lowest, most degraded stratum of the proletariat. Used originally in Marxist theory to describe those members of the proletariat, especially criminals, vagrants, and the unemployed, who lacked class consciousness. **2.** The underclass of a human population. [German : *Lumpen,* pl. of *Lump,* ragamuffin (from Middle High German *lumpe,* rag) + *Proletariat,* proletariat (from French *prolétariat;* see PROLETARIAT).]

lump·fish (lŭmp′fĭsh′) *n., pl.* **lumpfish** or **-fishes.** Any of various fishes of the family Cyclopteridae, especially *Cyclopterus lumpus* of North Atlantic waters, having pelvic fins united to form a suction disk and a body bearing prominent tubercles. [Obsolete *lump,* lumpfish (perhaps from Dutch *lomp,* blenny, loach, from Middle Dutch *lompe,* cod) + FISH.]

lump·ish (lŭm′pĭsh) *adj.* **1.** Stupid or dull. **2.** Clumsy or cumbersome. **—lump′ish·ly** *adv.* **—lump′ish·ness** *n.*

lump sum *n.* A single sum of money that serves as complete payment. **—lump′-sum′** (lŭmp′sŭm′) *adj.*

lump·y (lŭm′pē) *adj.* **-i·er, -i·est. 1.** Covered or filled with lumps. **2.** Thickset or cumbersome. **3.** Exhibiting short, jumbled waves, as a tidal rip. **—lump′i·ly** *adv.* **—lump′i·ness** *n.*

lumpy jaw *n.* See **actinomycosis.**

Lu·mum·ba (lo͞o-mo͝om′bə), **Patrice Emergy.** 1925–1961. First prime minister (1960–1961) of the Congo (now Zaire).

Lu·na (lo͞o′nə) *n. Roman Mythology.* The goddess of the moon. [Latin *Lūna,* from *lūna,* moon. See **leuk-** in Appendix.]

lu·na·cy (lo͞o′nə-sē) *n., pl.* **-cies. 1.** Insanity, especially insanity relieved intermittently by periods of clear-mindedness. See Synonyms at **insanity. 2.a.** Great foolishness. **b.** A wildly foolish act. **3.** *Archaic.* Intermittent mental derangement associated with the changing phases of the moon. [From LUNATIC.]

lu·na moth (lo͞o′nə) *n.* A large, pale-green North American

luna moth
Actias luna

ă pat	oi boy
ā pay	ou out
âr care	o͝o took
ä father	o͞o boot
ĕ pet	ŭ cut
ē be	ûr urge
ĭ pit	th thin
ī pie	*th* this
îr pier	hw which
ŏ pot	zh vision
ō toe	ə about, item
ô paw	♦ regionalism

Stress marks: **′** (primary); ′ (secondary), as in **dictionary** (dĭk′shə-nĕr′ē)

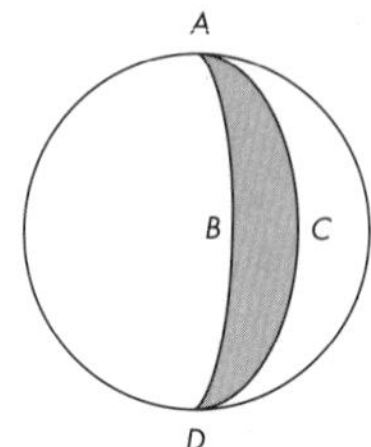

lune
Lune of a sphere bounded by arcs ABD and ACD

moth *(Actias luna)* having elongated, taillike hind wings. [New Latin *lūna,* species name, from Latin, moon. See LUNAR.]

lu·nar (lo͞o′nər) *adj.* **1.** Of, involving, caused by, or affecting the moon. **2.** Measured by the revolution of the moon. **3.** Of or relating to silver. [Middle English, crescent-shaped, from Old French *lunaire,* from Latin *lūnāris,* of the moon, from *lūna,* moon. See **leuk-** in Appendix.]

lunar caustic *n.* Silver nitrate in the form of sticks used in cauterization.

lunar excursion module *n.* A spacecraft designed to transport astronauts from a command module orbiting the moon to the lunar surface and back. Also called *lunar module.*

lunar month *n.* The average time between successive new or full moons, equal to 29 days 12 hours 44 minutes. Also called *synodic month.*

lu·nar·scape (lo͞o′nər-skāp′) *n.* **1.** A picture or other representation of the moon's surface. **2.** A landscape reminiscent of the moon's surface: *The sandstone formations transformed the land into a barren lunarscape.*

lunar year *n.* An interval of 12 lunar months.

lu·nate (lo͞o′nāt′) also **lu·nat·ed** (-nā′tĭd) —*adj.* Shaped like a crescent. —*n. Archaeology.* A small stone artifact, probably an arrowhead, with a blunt straight edge and a sharpened, crescent-shaped back, especially characteristic of the Mesolithic Age. [Latin *lūnātus,* past participle of *lūnāre,* to bend like a crescent, from *lūna,* moon. See **leuk-** in Appendix.]

lunate bone *n.* The second of three bones forming the proximal row of bones in the wrist. Also called *semilunar bone.*

lu·na·tic (lo͞o′nə-tĭk) *adj.* **1.** Suffering from lunacy; insane. **2.** Of or for the insane. **3.** Wildly or giddily foolish: *a lunatic decision.* **4.** Characterized by lunacy or eccentricity. [Middle English *lunatik,* from Old French *lunatique,* from Latin *lūnāticus,* from *lūna,* moon. See **leuk-** in Appendix.] —**lu′na·tic** *n.*

lunatic fringe *n.* The fanatical, extremist, or irrational members of a society or group.

lu·na·tion (lo͞o-nā′shən) *n.* The time that elapses between successive new moons, averaging 29 days, 12 hours, 44 minutes; a lunar month. [Middle English *lunacioun,* from Medieval Latin *lūnātiō, lūnātiōn-,* from Latin *lūna.* See LUNAR.]

lunch (lŭnch) *n.* **1.** A meal eaten at midday. **2.** The food provided for a midday meal. —*attributive.* Often used to modify another noun: *a lunch date; a lunch box.* —**lunch** *intr.v.* **lunched, lunch·ing, lunch·es.** To eat a midday meal. —***idiom.* out to lunch.** *Slang.* Not in touch with the real world; crazy. [Short for LUNCHEON.] —**lunch′er** *n.*

lunch·eon (lŭn′chən) *n.* **1.** A lunch, especially a formal one. **2.** An afternoon party at which a light meal is served. [Probably alteration (influenced by dialectal *lunch,* hunk of cheese or bread) of obsolete *nuncheon,* light snack, from Middle English *nonschench* : *none,* noon; see NOON + *schench,* drink (from Old English *scenc,* from *scencan,* to pour out).]

lunch·eon·ette (lŭn′chə-nĕt′) *n.* A small restaurant that serves simple, easily prepared meals.

luncheon meat *n.* Processed, prepackaged meat, often molded into a loaf and served sliced for use in sandwiches or salads. Also called *lunchmeat.*

lunch·meat (lŭnch′mēt′) *n.* See **luncheon meat.**

lunch·room (lŭnch′ro͞om′, -ro͝om′) *n.* **1.** A luncheonette. **2.** A room in a facility, such as a school, in which lunches may be purchased or those brought from home may be eaten.

lunch·time (lŭnch′tīm′) *n.* The time during which lunch is usually eaten.

Lund (lŭnd). A city of southern Sweden north of Malmö. It is an educational center. Population, 81,199.

Lun·dy (lŭn′dē), **Benjamin.** 1789–1839. American abolitionist who founded the *Genius of Universal Emancipation* (1821), one of the earliest antislavery newspapers.

lune (lo͞on) *n.* A crescent-shaped portion of a plane or sphere bounded by two arcs of circles. [Latin *lūna,* moon. See **leuk-** in Appendix.]

Lü·nen (lo͞o′nən, lü′-). A city of west-central Germany east-northeast of Essen. It is an industrial center in a coal-mining region. Population, 84,084.

lu·nette (lo͞o-nĕt′) *n.* **1.** *Architecture.* **a.** A small, circular or crescent-shaped opening in a vaulted roof. **b.** A crescent-shaped or semicircular space, usually over a door or window, that may contain another window, a sculpture, or a mural. **2.** A fortification that has two projecting faces and two parallel flanks. **3.** A broad, low-lying, typically crescent-shaped mound of sandy or loamy matter that is formed by the wind, especially along the windward side of a lake basin. [French, from Old French *lunete,* moon-shaped object, diminutive of *lune,* moon, from Latin *lūna,* moon. See LUNE.]

lungi

lung (lŭng) *n.* **1.** Either of two spongy, saclike respiratory organs in most vertebrates, occupying the chest cavity together with the heart and functioning to remove carbon dioxide from the blood and provide it with oxygen. **2.** A similar organ in some invertebrates, including spiders and terrestrial snails. —***idiom.* at the top of (one's) lungs.** As loudly as possible. [Middle English *lunge,* from Old English *lungen,* lungs. See **legʷh-** in Appendix.]

lunge (lŭnj) *n.* **1.** A sudden thrust or pass, as with a sword. **2.** A sudden forward movement or plunge. —**lunge** *v.* **lunged, lung·ing, lung·es.** —*intr.* **1.** To make a sudden thrust or pass. **2.** To move with a sudden thrust. —*tr.* To cause (someone) to lunge. [From alteration of obsolete *allonge,* to thrust, from French *allonger,* from Old French *alongier,* to lengthen : *a,* to (from Latin *ad;* see AD–) + *long,* long (from Latin *longus;* see **del-¹** in Appendix).]

lung·er (lŭn′jər) *n.* One that lunges.

lung·fish (lŭng′fĭsh′) *n., pl.* **lungfish** or **-fish·es.** Any of several elongated freshwater fishes of the Amazon, western and central Africa, and Australia that have lunglike organs as well as gills and are able to breathe air, allowing certain species to survive periods of drought inside a mucus-lined cocoon in the mud.

lun·gi or **lun·gyi** (lo͝ong′gē) also **lon·gyi** (lŏng′gē, lo͝ong′-) *n., pl.* **lun·gis** or **lun·gyis** also **lon·gyis.** A cloth, often of brightly colored silk or cotton, that is used as a piece of clothing, especially the traditional skirtlike garment of India, Pakistan, and Burma. [Urdu *lungī,* from Persian, variant of *lung.*]

lung·worm (lŭng′wûrm′) *n.* Any of various nematode worms, especially of the family Metastrongylidae, that are parasitic in the lungs of mammals.

lung·wort (lŭng′wûrt′, -wôrt′) *n.* **1.** Any of various plants of the genus *Mertensia,* such as the Virginia cowslip, having drooping clusters of tubular, usually blue flowers. **2.** Any of several European plants of the genus *Pulmonaria,* having long-stalked leaves and coiled clusters of blue or purple flowers and formerly used in treating respiratory disorders.

lun·gyi (lo͝ong′gē) *n.* Variant of **lungi.**

lu·ni·so·lar (lo͞o′nĭ-sō′lər) *adj.* Of or caused by both the sun and the moon. [Latin *lūna,* moon; see LUNAR + SOLAR.]

lu·ni·ti·dal (lo͞o′nĭ-tīd′l) *adj.* Of or relating to tidal phenomena caused by the moon. [Latin *lūna,* moon; see LUNAR + TIDAL.]

lunitidal interval *n.* The time elapsing between the moon's transit of a particular meridian and the next high tide at that meridian.

lunk·er (lŭng′kər) *n. Informal.* Something, especially a game fish, that is large for its kind. [Origin unknown.]

lunk·head (lŭngk′hĕd′) *n. Slang.* A person regarded as stupid. [Probably alteration of LUMP¹ + HEAD.] —**lunk′head′ed** *adj.*

Lunt (lŭnt), **Alfred.** 1893–1977. American actor who performed with his wife Lynn Fontanne in many stage productions, including *Pygmalion* (1926) and *Quadrille* (1952–1955).

lu·nu·la (lo͞on′yə-lə) *n., pl.* **-lae** (-lē′). A small crescent-shaped structure or marking, especially the white area at the base of a fingernail that resembles a half-moon. [New Latin *lūnula,* from Latin, crescent-shaped ornament, diminutive of *lūna,* moon. See **leuk-** in Appendix.]

lu·nu·lar (lo͞on′yə-lər) *adj.* Shaped like a crescent.

lu·nu·late (lo͞on′yə-lāt′, -lĭt) also **lu·nu·lat·ed** (-lā′tĭd) *adj.* **1.** Small and lunular. **2.** Having crescent-shaped markings.

lu·nule (lo͞on′yo͞ol) *n.* A lunula.

lun·y (lo͞o′nē) *adj. Informal.* Variant of **loony.**

Luo·yang (lwō′yäng′) also **Lo·yang** (lō′-). A city of east-central China east-northeast of Xi'an. A cultural and industrial center, it was the capital of several ancient dynasties, including the Han and Tang. Population, 624,000.

Lu·per·ca·li·a (lo͞o′pər-kā′lē-ə, -kāl′yə) *n.* A fertility festival in ancient Rome, celebrated on February 15 in honor of the pastoral god Lupercus. [Latin *Lupercālia,* from *Lupercus,* Roman god of flocks.] —**Lu′per·ca′li·an** *adj.*

lu·pine¹ also **lu·pin** (lo͞o′pən) *n.* Any of numerous plants of the genus *Lupinus* in the pea family, having palmately compound leaves and variously colored flowers grouped in spikes or racemes. [Middle English, from Old French *lupin,* from Latin *lupīnum,* from neuter of *lupīnus,* wolflike. See LUPINE².]

lu·pine² (lo͞o′pīn′) *adj.* **1.** Characteristic of or resembling a wolf. **2.** Rapacious; ravenous. [French, from Latin *lupīnus,* from *lupus,* wolf. See **wl̥kʷo-** in Appendix.]

lu·pu·lin (lo͞op′yə-lən) *n.* Minute yellowish-brown hairs obtained from the strobili of the hop plant, formerly used in medicine as a sedative. [New Latin *lupulus,* hop species (diminutive of Latin *lupus,* hop plant, from *lupus,* wolf; see LUPINE²) + –IN.]

lu·pus (lo͞o′pəs) *n.* Any of several diseases, especially systemic lupus erythematosus, that principally affect the skin and joints but often also involve other systems of the body. [Medieval Latin, from Latin, wolf. See **wl̥kʷo-** in Appendix.]

Lu·pus (lo͞o′pəs) *n.* A constellation of stars in the Southern Hemisphere near Centaurus and Scorpius. [Latin, from *lupus,* wolf. See LUPUS.]

lupus er·y·the·ma·to·sus (ĕr′ə-thē′mə-tō′səs, -thĕm′ə-) *n.* **1.** A chronic disease of unknown origin characterized by the appearance of red, scaly lesions or patches on the face and upper portion of the trunk. **2.** Systemic lupus erythematosus. [New Latin *lupus erythēmatōsus* : *lupus,* lupus + *erythēmatōsus,* erythematous.]

lupus vul·gar·is (vŭl-gâr′ĭs) *n.* A cutaneous form of tuberculosis characterized by reddish-brown ulcerating nodules, usually appearing on the face, that heal slowly and produce deep scars. [New Latin *lupus vulgāris,* common lupus : LUPUS + Latin *vulgāris,* common.]

lurch¹ (lûrch) *intr.v.* **lurched, lurch·ing, lurch·es. 1.** To stagger. See Synonyms at **blunder. 2.** To roll or pitch suddenly or erratically: *The ship lurched in the storm. The car gave a start and then lurched forward.* **—lurch** *n.* **1.** A staggering or tottering movement or gait. **2.** An abrupt rolling or pitching. [Origin unknown.] **—lurch′ing·ly** *adv.*

lurch² (lûrch) *n. Games.* The losing position of a cribbage player who scores 30 points or less to the winner's 61. ***—idiom.* in the lurch.** In a difficult or embarrassing position. [Perhaps back-formation from Middle English *lurching,* a total victory at *lorche,* from *lorche,* a kind of game; perhaps akin to *lurken,* to lurk. See LURK.]

lurch·er (lûr′chər) *n.* **1.** *Chiefly British.* A crossbred dog used by poachers. **2.** *Archaic.* A sneak thief. [Middle English, from *lorchen,* to lurk, perhaps from *lurken.* See LURK.]

lure (lo͝or) *n.* **1.a.** Something that tempts or attracts with the promise of pleasure or reward. **b.** An attraction or appeal. **2.** A decoy used in catching animals, especially an artificial bait used in catching fish. **3.** A bunch of feathers attached to a long cord, used in falconry to recall the hawk. **—lure** *tr.v.* **lured, lur·ing, lures. 1.** To attract by wiles or temptation; entice. **2.** To recall (a falcon) with a lure. [Middle English, from Anglo-Norman, of Germanic origin.] **—lur′er** *n.* **—lur′ing·ly** *adv.*

SYNONYMS: *lure, entice, inveigle, decoy, tempt, seduce.* These verbs mean to lead or attempt to lead into a wrong or foolish course, as of action. *Lure* suggests the use of something that attracts like bait: *Industry often seeks to lure scientists from universities by offering them huge salaries.* To *entice* is to draw on skillfully, as by arousing hopes or desires: *The teacher opened the door and, showing the tot the toys on the shelves, tried to entice him into the classroom. Inveigle* implies winning over by coaxing, flattery, or artful talk: *With tact and perseverance he inveigled her into becoming his law partner.* To *decoy* is to trap or ensnare by cunning or deception: *Partisans dressed as simple farmers selling produce decoyed the soldiers into blistering crossfire. Tempt* implies the operation of an attraction that disposes or invites one to do something, especially something immoral, unwise, or contrary to one's better judgment: *I'm tempted to tell him what I really think of him.* To *seduce* is to entice away, as from duty, accepted principles, or proper conduct; it usually suggests the overcoming of moral resistance: *"The French King attempted by splendid offers to seduce him from the cause of the Republic"* (Macaulay).

Lur·ex (lo͝or′ĕks). A trademark used for a yarn made of plastic-coated aluminum filaments. This trademark often occurs in print in uppercase and lowercase as an attributive: *"The Lurex sock became the signature leg fashion for glitter rockers"* (Women's Wear Daily). It can also occur in figurative extensions: *"The videos range from loud, lurex pop nonsense . . . through acid house psychedelia"* (Time Out).

lu·rid (lo͝or′ĭd) *adj.* **1.** Causing shock or horror; gruesome. **2.** Marked by sensationalism: *a lurid account of the crime.* See Synonyms at **ghastly. 3.** Glowing or shining with the glare of fire through a haze: *lurid flames.* **4.** Sallow or pallid in color. [Latin *lūridus,* pale, from *lūror,* paleness.] **—lu′rid·ly** *adv.* **—lu′rid·ness** *n.*

lurk (lûrk) *intr.v.* **lurked, lurk·ing, lurks. 1.** To lie in wait, as in ambush. **2.** To move furtively; sneak. **3.** To exist unobserved or unsuspected: *danger lurking around every bend.* [Middle English *lurken,* possibly of Scandinavian origin.] **—lurk′ing·ly** *adv.*

Lur·ton (lûr′tn), **Horace Harmon.** 1844–1914. American jurist who served as an associate justice of the U.S. Supreme Court (1910–1914).

Lu·sa·ka (lo͞o-sä′kə). The capital and largest city of Zambia, in the south-central part of the country. It was founded by Europeans in 1905. Population, 535,830.

Lu·sa·ti·a (lo͞o-sā′shē-ə, -shə). A region of central Europe in eastern Germany and southwest Poland. Settled by descendants of the Wends, a Slavic people, it changed hands frequently before passing to Prussia in 1815. **—Lu·sa′tian** *adj. & n.*

lus·cious (lŭsh′əs) *adj.* **1.** Sweet and pleasant to taste or smell: *a luscious melon.* See Synonyms at **delicious. 2.** Having strong sensual or sexual appeal; seductive. **3.** Richly appealing to the senses or the mind: *a luscious, vivid description.* **4.** *Archaic.* Excessively sweet; cloying. [Middle English *lucius,* alteration of *licious,* perhaps short for *delicious,* delicious. See DELICIOUS.] **—lus′cious·ly** *adv.* **—lus′cious·ness** *n.*

lush¹ (lŭsh) *adj.* **lush·er, lush·est. 1.a.** Having or characterized by luxuriant vegetation. **b.** Abundant; plentiful. See Synonyms at **profuse. c.** Extremely productive; thriving. **2.a.** Luxurious; opulent: *the lush décor of a grand hotel.* **b.** Extremely pleasing to the senses: *a lush scent; lush fruit; the lush sounds of an orchestra.* **c.** Voluptuous or sensual. **3.** Overelaborate or extravagant: *lush rhetoric.* [Middle English *lush,* relaxed, soft, probably alteration of *lache,* loose, weak, from Old French, soft, succulent, from *laschier,* to loosen, from Late Latin *laxicāre,* to become shaky, frequentative of Latin *laxāre,* to open, relax, from *laxus,* loose. See LAX.] **—lush′ly** *adv.* **—lush′ness** *n.*

lush² (lŭsh) *Slang. n.* A drunkard. **—lush** *intr.v.* **lushed, lush·ing, lush·es.** To drink liquor to excess. [Origin unknown.]

Lü·shun (lo͞o′sho͞on′, lü′-). A city of northeast China at the tip of the Liaodong Peninsula. A major port and naval base, it is part of the conurbation of Lüda. Population, 40,752.

Lu·si·ta·ni·a (lo͞o′sĭ-tā′nē-ə). An ancient region and Roman province of the Iberian Peninsula. It corresponded roughly to modern-day Portugal. **—Lu′si·ta′ni·an** *adj. & n.*

lust (lŭst) *n.* **1.** Intense or unrestrained sexual craving. **2.a.** An overwhelming desire or craving: *a lust for power.* **b.** Intense eagerness or enthusiasm: *a lust for life.* **3.** *Obsolete.* Pleasure; relish. **—lust** *intr.v.* **lust·ed, lust·ing, lusts.** To have an intense or obsessive desire, especially one that is sexual. [Middle English, from Old English, desire. See **las-** in Appendix.]

lus·ter (lŭs′tər) *n.* **1.** Soft reflected light; sheen. **2.** Brilliance or radiance of light; brightness. **3.** Glory, radiance, distinction, or splendor, as of achievement, reputation, or beauty. **4.** A glass pendant, especially on a chandelier. **5.** A decorative object, such as a chandelier, that gives off light. **6.** Any of various substances, such as wax or glaze, used to give an object a gloss or polish. **7.** The surface glossiness of ceramic ware after glazing, especially the metallic sheen of lusterware. **8.** A fabric, such as alpaca, having a glossy surface. **9.** The appearance of a mineral surface judged by its brilliance and ability to reflect light. **—luster** *v.* **-tered, -ter·ing, -ters.** *—tr.* **1.** To give a gloss, glaze, or sheen to. **2.** To give or add glory, radiance, distinction, or splendor to. *—intr.* To be or become lustrous. [French *lustre,* from Old French, from Old Italian *lustro,* from *lustrare,* to make bright, from Latin *lūstrāre,* from *lūstrum,* purification. See **leuk-** in Appendix.]

luster
Late 19th-century English

lus·ter·less (lŭs′tər-lĭs) *adj.* Lacking distinction, radiance, or vitality; dull: *a lusterless performance; lusterless hair.*

lus·ter·ware (lŭs′tər-wâr′) *n.* Pottery or porcelain having a metallic sheen produced when metallic oxides are added to the glaze.

lust·ful (lŭst′fəl) *adj.* Excited or driven by lust. **—lust′ful·ly** *adv.* **—lust′ful·ness** *n.*

lus·tra (lŭs′trə) *n.* A plural of **lustrum.**

lus·tral (lŭs′trəl) *adj.* Of or used in a rite of purification. [Latin *lūstrālis,* from *lūstrum,* purification. See LUSTER.]

lus·trate (lŭs′trāt′) *tr.v.* **lus·trat·ed, lus·trat·ing, lus·trates.** To purify by means of ceremony. [Latin *lūstrāre, lūstrāt-,* to purify, make bright. See LUSTER.] **—lus·tra′tion** *n.* **—lus′tra·tive** (-trə-tĭv) *adj.*

lus·tre (lŭs′tər) *n. & v. Chiefly British.* Variant of **luster.**

lus·trous (lŭs′trəs) *adj.* **1.** Having a sheen or glow. **2.** Gleaming with or as if with brilliant light; radiant. See Synonyms at **bright. —lus′trous·ly** *adv.* **—lus′trous·ness** *n.*

lus·trum (lŭs′trəm) *n., pl.* **-trums** or **-tra** (-trə). **1.** A ceremonial purification of the entire ancient Roman population after the census every five years. **2.** A period of five years. [Latin *lūstrum.* See LUSTER.]

lust·y (lŭs′tē) *adj.* **-i·er, -i·est. 1.** Full of vigor or vitality; robust. **2.** Powerful; strong: *a lusty cry.* **3.** Lustful. **4.** Merry; joyous. **—lust′i·ly** *adv.* **—lust′i·ness** *n.*

lu·sus na·tu·rae (lo͞o′səs nə-to͝or′ē, -tyo͝or′ē) *n.* A freak or sport of nature. [New Latin *lūsus nātūrae* : Latin *lūsus,* sport, play + Latin *nātūrae,* genitive of *nātūra,* nature.]

Lü·ta (lo͞o′dä′, lü′-). See **Lüda.**

lu·ta·nist (lo͞ot′n-ĭst) *n. Music.* Variant of **lutenist.**

lute¹ (lo͞ot) *n. Music.* A stringed instrument having a body shaped like a pear sliced lengthwise and a neck with a fretted fingerboard that is usually bent just below the tuning pegs. [Middle English, from Old French *lut,* from Old Provençal *laut,* from Arabic *al-'ud* : *al,* the + *'ūd,* lute.]

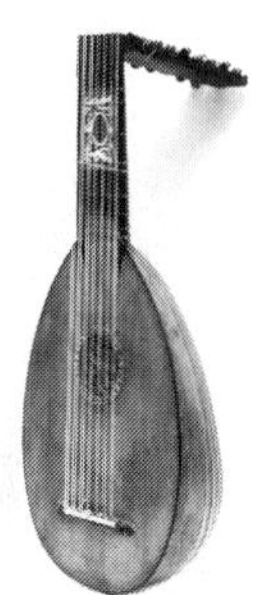

lute¹
17th-century Italian

lute² (lo͞ot) *n.* A substance, such as dried clay or cement, used to pack and seal pipe joints and other connections or coat a porous surface in order to make it tight. Also called *luting.* **—lute** *tr.v.* **lut·ed, lut·ing, lutes.** To coat, pack, or seal with lute. [Middle English, from Old French *lut,* from Latin *lutum,* potter's clay.]

lu·te·al (lo͞o′tē-əl) *adj.* Of, relating to, or involving the corpus luteum.

lu·te·ci·um (lo͞o-tē′shē-əm) *n.* Variant of **lutetium.**

lu·te·fisk (lo͞o′tə-fĭsk′) also **lut·fisk** (lo͞ot′fĭsk′) *n.* A traditional Scandinavian dish prepared by soaking air-dried cod in a lye solution for several weeks before skinning, boning, and boiling it, a process that gives the dish its characteristic gelatinous consistency. [Norwegian : *lut,* lye + *fisk,* fish (from Old Norse *fiskr*).]

lu·te·in (lo͞o′tē-ĭn, -tēn′) *n.* **1.** A yellow carotenoid pigment, $C_{40}H_{56}O_2$, found widely in nature, first isolated in corpus luteum but later discovered in body fats, egg yolk, and green plants; xanthophyll. **2.** A dried preparation of corpus luteum. [Latin *lūteum,* yellow, egg yolk, from neuter of *lūteus,* yellow (from *lūtum,* yellowweed) + -IN.]

lu·te·in·ize (lo͞o′tē-ə-nīz′) *v.* **-ized, -iz·ing, -iz·es.** *—tr.* To cause the production of a corpus luteum in. *—intr.* To develop into or become part of the corpus luteum. **—lu′te·in·i·za′tion** (-ə-nĭ-zā′shən) *n.*

lu·te·in·iz·ing hormone (lo͞o′tē-ə-nī′zĭng) *n. Abbr.* **LH** A hormone produced by the anterior lobe of the pituitary gland that stimulates ovulation and the development of the corpus luteum in the female and the production of testosterone by the interstitial cells of the testis in the male.

luteinizing hor·mone-re·leas·ing hormone (hôr′mōn-rĭ-lē′sĭng) *n. Abbr.* **LHRH** See **gonadotropin-releasing hormone.**

lu·te·nist also **lu·ta·nist** (lo͞ot′n-ĭst) *n. Music.* A lute player. Also called *lutist.* [Medieval Latin *lūtānista,* from *lūtāna,* lute, possibly from Old French *lut.* See LUTE¹.]

ă pat	oi boy
ā pay	ou out
âr care	o͝o took
ä father	o͞o boot
ĕ pet	ŭ cut
ē be	ûr urge
ĭ pit	th thin
ī pie	*th* this
îr pier	hw which
ŏ pot	zh vision
ō toe	ə about, item
ô paw	♦ regionalism

Stress marks: ′ (primary); ′ (secondary), as in **dictionary** (dĭk′shə-nĕr′ē)

Martin Luther
Portrait by Lucas Cranach

lu·te·ous (lo͞o′tē-əs) *adj. Color.* Of a light or moderate greenish yellow. [From Latin *lūteus,* yellow. See LUTEIN.]

lu·te·ti·um also **lu·te·ci·um** (lo͞o-tē′shē-əm) *n. Symbol* **Lu** A silvery-white rare-earth element that is exceptionally difficult to separate from the other rare-earth elements, used in nuclear technology. Atomic number 71; atomic weight 174.97; melting point 1,663°C; boiling point 3,395°C; specific gravity 9.840 (at 25°C); valence 3. See table at **element.** [Latin *Lutetia,* ancient name of Paris, France + –IUM.]

lut·fisk (lo͞ot′fĭsk′) *n.* Variant of **lutefisk.**

Lu·ther (lo͞o′thər), **Martin.** 1483–1546. German theologian and leader of the Reformation. His opposition to the wealth and corruption of the papacy and his belief that salvation would be granted on the basis of faith alone rather than by works caused his excommunication from the Catholic Church (1521). Luther confirmed the Augsburg Confession in 1530, effectively establishing the Lutheran Church.

Lu·ther·an (lo͞o′thər-ən) *adj. Abbr.* **Luth. 1.** Of or relating to Luther or his religious teachings and especially to the doctrine of justification by faith alone. **2.** Of or relating to the branch of the Protestant Church adhering to the views of Luther. —**Lutheran** *n. Abbr.* **Luth.** A member of the Lutheran Church. —**Lu′ther·an·ism, Lu′ther·ism** *n.*

lu·thi·er (lo͞o′tē-ər) *n. Music.* One that makes or repairs stringed instruments, such as violins. [French, from *luth,* lute, from Old French *lut.* See LUTE[1].]

Lu·thu·li (lo͞o-to͞o′lē, -tyo͞o′-), **Albert John.** 1898–1967. Zulu leader who advocated nonviolent resistance against apartheid. He won the 1960 Nobel Peace Prize.

lut·ing (lo͞o′tĭng) *n.* See **lute**[2].

lut·ist (lo͞o′tĭst) *n. Music.* **1.** A maker of lutes. **2.** See **lutenist.**

Lu·ton (lo͞ot′n). A borough of southeast England north-northwest of London. A millinery industry was established here during the reign of James I. Population, 164,200.

Lutsk (lo͞otsk). A city of west-central Ukraine on the Styr River northeast of Lvov. First mentioned in 1085, it was the capital of an independent principality during the 12th century. Population, 172,000.

Lutz also **lutz** (lŭts) *n. Sports.* A jump in figure skating in which the skater takes off from the back outer edge of one skate and makes one full rotation before landing on the back outer edge of the other skate. [Perhaps after Gustave *Lussi,* 20th-century Swiss figure skater.]

Lu·wi·an (lo͞o′ē-ən) *n.* **1.** An Indo-European language of the Anatolian family, attested in documents from the second millennium B.C. and now extinct. **2.** A speaker of Luwian. —**Luwian** *adj.* Of or relating to the Luwians, their culture, or their language.

lux (lŭks) *n., pl.* **lux·es** or **lu·ces** (lo͞o′sēz). *Abbr.* **lx** The International System unit of illumination, equal to one lumen per square meter. See table at **measurement.** [Latin *lūx,* light. See **leuk-** in Appendix.]

Lux. *abbr.* Luxembourg.

lux·ate (lŭk′sāt′) *tr.v.* **-at·ed, -at·ing, -ates.** To put out of joint; dislocate. [Latin *luxāre, luxāt-,* from *luxus,* dislocated.] —**lux·a′tion** *n.*

luxe (lo͝oks, lŭks) *n.* **1.** The condition of being elegantly sumptuous. **2.** Something luxurious; a luxury. [French, luxury, from Latin *luxus.*] —**luxe** *adj.*

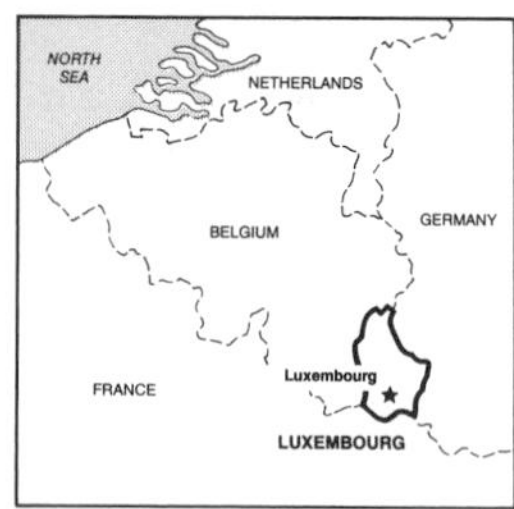

Luxembourg

Lux·em·bourg also **Lux·em·burg** (lŭk′səm-bûrg′). **1.** *Abbr.* **Lux.** A country of northwest Europe. Created as a duchy in 1354, it was ruled from 1443 to 1839 by Burgundy, Spain, Austria, France, and the Netherlands successively. In 1867 the European powers declared Luxembourg a neutral territory. Luxembourg is the capital. Population, 364,606. **2.** Also **Luxembourg City.** The capital of Luxembourg, in the southern part of the country. It developed around a heavily fortified tenth-century castle. Population, 78,924.

Lux·em·burg (lŭk′səm-bûrg′, lo͝ok′səm-bo͝ork′), **Rosa.** 1870–1919. German socialist leader who cofounded (1918) the Spartacus Party, which became the German Communist Party. She was arrested after the Sparticist uprising in 1919 and subsequently murdered.

Lux·or (lŭk′sôr′, lo͝ok′-). A city of central Egypt on the eastern bank of the Nile River. Built partially on the site of ancient Thebes, it includes the Temple of Luxor built in the reign of Amenhotep III and added to significantly by Rameses II, who had colossal statues of himself erected at the complex. Population, 137,300.

lux·u·ri·ant (lŭg-zho͝or′ē-ənt, lŭk-sho͝or′-) *adj.* **1.a.** Characterized by rich or profuse growth. **b.** Producing or yielding in abundance. See Synonyms at **profuse. 2.** Excessively florid or elaborate. **3.** Marked by or displaying luxury; luxurious. [Latin *luxuriāns, luxuriant-,* present participle of *luxuriāre,* to be luxuriant. See LUXURIATE.] —**lux·u′ri·ance** *n.* —**lux·u′ri·ant·ly** *adv.*

lux·u·ri·ate (lŭg-zho͝or′ē-āt′, lŭk-sho͝or′-) *intr.v.* **-at·ed, -at·ing, -ates. 1.** To take luxurious pleasure; indulge oneself. **2.** To proliferate. **3.** To grow profusely; thrive. [Latin *luxuriāre, luxuriāt-,* to be luxuriant, from *luxuria,* luxury. See LUXURY.]

lux·u·ri·ous (lŭg-zho͝or′ē-əs, lŭk-sho͝or′-) *adj.* **1.** Fond of or given to luxury. **2.** Marked by or contributing to luxury. **3.** Of a sumptuous, costly, or rich variety. See Synonyms at **sensuous.** —**lux·u′ri·ous·ness** *n.* —**lux·u′ri·ous·ly** *adv.*

lux·u·ry (lŭg′zhə-rē, lŭk′shə-) *n., pl.* **-ries. 1.** Something inessential but conducive to pleasure and comfort. **2.** Something expensive or hard to obtain. **3.** Sumptuous living or surroundings: *lives in luxury.* —*attributive.* Often used to modify another noun: *a luxury condominium; luxury accommodations.* [Middle English *luxurie,* lust, from Old French, from Latin *luxuria,* excess, luxury, from *luxus.*]

SYNONYMS: *luxury, extravagance, frill.* The central meaning shared by these nouns is "something desirable that is not a necessity": *a fur coat that is a real luxury; antique porcelain, an extravagance we should have resisted; caviar, smoked salmon, and other culinary frills.*
ANTONYM: *necessity.*

Lu·zon (lo͞o-zŏn′). An island of the northwest Philippines. It is the largest and most important island in the archipelago.

Lv *abbr. Bible.* Leviticus.

lv. *abbr.* **1.** Leave. **2.** Livre.

LVN or **L.V.N.** *abbr.* Licensed vocational nurse.

Lvov (lvôf). A city of west-central Ukraine near the Polish border. Founded in 1256, it was captured by Poland in 1340, passed to Austria in 1772, and was retaken by Poland in 1918. The city was formally ceded to the U.S.S.R. in 1945 and is now an industrial center and railroad junction. Population, 742,000.

LW *abbr.* Low water.

lwei (lwā) *n., pl.* **lwei.** See table at **currency.** [Of Bantu origin.]

LWM *abbr.* Low-water mark.

LWV *abbr.* League of Women Voters.

lx *abbr.* Lux.

–ly[1] *suff.* **1.** Like; resembling; having the characteristics of: *sisterly.* **2.** Recurring at a specified interval of time: *hourly.* [Middle English *-li,* from Old English *-līc* (influenced by Old Norse *-ligr*). See **līk-** in Appendix.]

–ly[2] *suff.* **1.** In a specified manner; in the manner of: *gradually.* **2.** At a specified interval of time: *weekly.* **3.** With respect to: *partly.* [Middle English *-li,* from Old English *-līce* (influenced by Old Norse *-liga*), from *-līc,* adj. suff. See **līk-** in Appendix.]

Ly·all·pur (lī′əl-po͝or′). See **Faisalabad.**

ly·ase (lī′ās′) *n.* Any of a group of enzymes that catalyze the formation of double bonds by removing chemical groups from a substrate without hydrolysis or catalyze the addition of chemical groups to double bonds. [Greek *luein,* to loosen; see **leu-** in Appendix + –ASE.]

ly·can·thrope (lī′kən-thrōp′, lī-kăn′-) *n.* A werewolf. [Greek *lukanthrōpos* : *lukos,* wolf; see **wḷkʷo-** in Appendix + *anthrōpos,* man.]

ly·can·thro·py (lī-kăn′thrə-pē) *n.* In folklore, the magical ability to assume the form and characteristics of a wolf.

ly·cée (lē-sā′) *n.* A French public secondary school. [French, from Old French, lyceum, from Latin *Lycēum.* See LYCEUM.]

ly·ce·um (lī-sē′əm) *n.* **1.** A hall in which public lectures, concerts, and similar programs are presented. **2.** An organization sponsoring public programs and entertainment. **3.** A lycée. [Latin *Lycēum,* from Greek *Lukeion,* the school outside Athens where Aristotle taught (335–323 B.C.).]

ly·chee (lē′chē) *n.* Variant of **litchi.**

lych-gate (lĭch′gāt′) or **lych gate** also **lich gate** (lĭch) *n.* A roofed gateway to a churchyard used originally as a resting place for a bier before burial. [Middle English *lycheyate* : *lyche,* corpse, body (from Old English *līc;* see **līk-** in Appendix) + *gate, yate,* gate; see GATE[1].]

lych·nis (lĭk′nĭs) *n.* Any of various plants of the genus *Lychnis,* which includes the campions. [New Latin *Lychnis,* genus name, from Latin *lychnis,* a red flower, from Greek *lukhnis;* akin to *lukhnos,* lamp. See **leuk-** in Appendix.]

Lyc·i·a (lĭsh′ē-ə, lĭsh′ə). An ancient country and Roman province of southwest Asia Minor on the Aegean Sea. Ruled from early times by Persia and Syria, it was annexed by Rome in the first century A.D.

Ly·ci·an (lĭsh′ē-ən, lĭsh′ən) *adj.* Of or relating to Lycia or its people, language, or culture. —**Lycian** *n.* **1.** A language of the extinct Anatolian branch of Indo-European, found in inscriptions down to the beginning of the third century B.C. in southwest Turkey. **2.** A speaker of Lycian.

ly·co·po·di·um (lī′kə-pō′dē-əm) *n.* **1.** A plant of the genus *Lycopodium,* which includes the club mosses. **2.** The yellowish powdery spores of certain club mosses, especially *Lycopodium clavatum,* used in fireworks and explosives and as a covering for pills. [New Latin *Lycopodium,* genus name : Greek *lukos,* wolf; see **wḷkʷo-** in Appendix + Greek *podion,* diminutive of *pous,* foot; see **ped-** in Appendix.]

Ly·cra (lī′krə). A trademark used for a brand of spandex.

Ly·cur·gus (lī-kûr′gəs). fl. ninth century B.C. Spartan lawmaker who is considered the founder of the Spartan constitution.

lyd·dite (lĭd′īt′) *n.* An explosive consisting chiefly of picric acid. [After *Lydd,* a municipal borough of southeast England.]

Lyd·gate (lĭd′gāt′, -gət), **John.** 1370?–1451? English poet who is best known for his long narrative works.

Lyd·i·a (lĭd′ē-ə). An ancient country of west-central Asia Minor on the Aegean Sea in present-day northwest Turkey. Noted for its wealth, it may have been the earliest kingdom to use minted coins (seventh century B.C.).

Lyd·i·an (lĭd′ē-ən) *adj.* Of or relating to Lydia or its people, language, or culture. **—Lydian** *n.* **1.** A language of the extinct Anatolian branch of Indo-European, found in inscriptions of the fourth century B.C. in western Turkey. **2.** A speaker of Lydian.

lye (lī) *n.* **1.** The liquid obtained by leaching wood ashes. **2.** See **potassium hydroxide. 3.** See **sodium hydroxide.** [Middle English *lie,* from Old English *lēag.* See **leu(ə)-** in Appendix.]

Ly·ell (lī′əl), Sir **Charles.** 1797–1875. British geologist. His *Principles of Geology* (1830–1833) opposed the catastrophic theory of geologic change.

ly·gus bug (lī′gəs) *n.* Any of various North American bugs of the genus *Lygus,* including certain species that are destructive to plants. [New Latin *Lygus,* genus name, from Greek *lugaios,* murky.]

ly·ing¹ (lī′ĭng) *v.* Present participle of **lie¹.**

ly·ing² (lī′ĭng) *v.* Present participle of **lie².** **—lying** *adj.* Disposed to or characterized by untruth: *a lying witness.* See Synonyms at **dishonest.**

ly·ing-in (lī′ĭng-ĭn′) *n., pl.* **ly·ings-in** (lī′ĭngz-) or **ly·ing-ins.** The confinement of a woman in childbirth. **—lying-in** *adj.* Of or intended for use during childbirth: *a lying-in hospital.*

Lyl·y (lĭl′ē), **John.** 1554?–1606. English playwright and novelist whose comedies influenced English drama.

Lyme disease (līm) *n.* An inflammatory disease caused by a spirochete *(Borrelia burgdorferi)* that is transmitted by ticks, usually characterized initially by a rash followed by flulike symptoms including fever, joint pain, and headache. If left untreated, the disease can result in chronic arthritis and nerve and heart dysfunction. [After *Lyme,* a town of southeast Connecticut.]

lymph (lĭmf) *n.* **1.** A clear, watery, sometimes faintly yellowish fluid derived from body tissues that contains white blood cells and circulates throughout the lymphatic system, returning to the venous bloodstream through the thoracic duct. Lymph acts to remove bacteria and certain proteins from the tissues, transport fat from the small intestine, and supply mature lymphocytes to the blood. **2.** *Archaic.* A spring or stream of pure, clear water. [Latin *lympha,* water, from Greek *numphē,* water spirit.]

lymph– *pref.* Variant of **lympho–.**

lym·phad·e·ni·tis (lĭm-făd′n-ī′tĭs, lĭm′fə-də-nī′-) *n.* Inflammation of one or more lymph nodes. [LYMPH + ADEN(O)– + –ITIS.]

lym·phad·e·nop·a·thy (lĭm-făd′n-ŏp′ə-thē, lĭm′fə-dn-) *n., pl.* **-thies.** A chronic, abnormal enlargement of the lymph nodes, usually associated with disease. [LYMPH + ADENO– + –PATHY.]

lym·phan·gi·og·ra·phy (lĭm-făn′jē-ŏg′rə-fē) *n., pl.* **-phies.** Examination of the lymph nodes and lymphatic vessels following the injection of a radiopaque substance. Also called *lymphography.* **—lym·phan′gi·o·gram′** (-ə-grăm′) *n.*

lym·phat·ic (lĭm-făt′ĭk) *adj.* **1.** Of or relating to lymph, a lymph vessel, or a lymph node. **2.** Lacking energy or vitality; sluggish. **—lymphatic** *n.* A vessel that conveys lymph. [New Latin *lymphaticus,* from *lympha,* lymph. See LYMPH.] **—lym·phat′i·cal·ly** *adv.*

lymphatic system *n.* The interconnected system of spaces and vessels between body tissues and organs by which lymph circulates throughout the body.

lymph node *n.* Any of the small, oval or round bodies, located along the lymphatic vessels, that supply lymphocytes to the bloodstream and remove bacteria and foreign particles from the lymph. Also called *lymph gland.*

lympho– or **lymph–** *pref.* Lymphatic system; lymph: *lymphocyte.* [From LYMPH.]

lym·pho·blast (lĭm′fə-blăst′) *n.* A cell that gives rise to a mature lymphocyte. **—lym′pho·blas′tic** *adj.*

lym·pho·cyte (lĭm′fə-sīt′) *n.* Any of the nearly colorless cells formed in lymphoid tissue, as in the lymph nodes, spleen, thymus, and tonsils, constituting between 22 and 28 percent of all white blood cells in the blood of a normal adult human being. They function in the development of immunity and include two specific types, B cells and T cells. **—lym′pho·cyt′ic** (-sĭt′ĭk) *adj.*

lym·pho·cy·to·sis (lĭm′fō-sī-tō′sĭs) *n.* A condition marked by an abnormal increase in the number of lymphocytes in the bloodstream, usually resulting from infection or inflammation. **—lym′pho·cy·tot′ic** (-tŏt′ĭk) *adj.*

lym·pho·gran·u·lo·ma ve·ne·re·um (lĭm′fə-grăn′yə-lō′mə və-nîr′rē-əm) *n.* A sexually transmitted disease caused by a bacterium *(Chlamydia trachomatis)* and characterized initially by a genital lesion followed by enlargement of the lymph nodes in the groin area. [New Latin : LYMPHO– + GRANULOMA + Latin *venereum,* neuter of *venereus,* venereal.]

lym·phog·ra·phy (lĭm-fŏg′rə-fē) *n.* See **lymphangiography.**

lym·phoid (lĭm′foid′) *adj.* Of or relating to lymph or the lymphatic tissue where lymphocytes are formed.

lym·pho·kine (lĭm′fə-kīn′) *n.* Any of various substances released by T cells that have been activated by antigens. They function in the immune response through a variety of actions, including stimulating the production of nonsensitized lymphocytes and activating macrophages. [LYMPHO– + Greek *kinein,* to move; see KININ.]

lym·pho·ma (lĭm-fō′mə) *n., pl.* **-ma·ta** (-mə-tə) or **-mas.** Any of various usually malignant tumors that arise in the lymph nodes or in other lymphoid tissue. **—lym·pho′ma·toid′, lym·phom′a·tous** (-fŏm′ə-təs) *adj.*

lym·pho·poi·e·sis (lĭm′fō-poi-ē′sĭs) *n., pl.* **-ses** (-sēz′). The formation of lymphocytes. **—lym′pho·poi·et′ic** (-ĕt′ĭk) *adj.*

lym·pho·tox·in (lĭm′fə-tŏk′sĭn) *n.* A lymphokine that is toxic to certain susceptible target cells.

Lyn·brook (lĭn′bro͝ok′). A village of southeast New York on southwest Long Island east of Queens. Population, 20,431.

lynch (lĭnch) *tr.v.* **lynched, lynch·ing, lynch·es.** To execute without due process of law, especially to hang, as by a mob. [Short for LYNCH LAW.] **—lynch′er** *n.* **—lynch′ing** *n.*

Lynch (lĭnch), **John.** Known as "Jack." Born 1917. Irish political leader who served as prime minister of Ireland (1966–1973 and 1977–1979).

Lynch·burg (lĭnch′bûrg′). An independent city of southwest-central Virgina east-northeast of Roanoke. Located in the foothills of the Blue Ridge, it is an educational center. Population, 66,743.

lynch law *n.* The punishment of persons suspected of crime without due process of law. [After William *Lynch* (died 1820).]

WORD HISTORY: "Whereas, many of the inhabitants of Pittsylvania . . . have sustained great and intolerable losses by a set of lawless men . . . that . . . have hitherto escaped the civil power with impunity . . . we, the subscribers, being determined to put a stop to the iniquitous practices of those unlawful and abandoned wretches, do enter into the following association . . . upon hearing or having sufficient reason to believe that any . . . species of villany [has] been committed within our neighborhood, we will forthwith . . . repair immediately to the person or persons suspected . . . and if they will not desist from their evil practices, we will inflict such corporeal punishment on him or them, as to us shall seem adequate to the crime committed or the damage sustained . . . In witness whereof we have hereunto set our hands, this 22nd day of September 1780." These are the words of a compact drawn up by Captain William Lynch and a group of his neighbors. At the time, Pittsylvania County, Virginia, was troubled by its "set of lawless men." The courts were too distant to deal with them, so it was agreed to punish criminals without due process of law. Both the practice and the punishment came to be called *lynch law* after Captain Lynch. Although lynch law and lynching are mainly associated with hanging, other, less severe punishments were used. William Lynch died in 1820, and the inscription on his grave notes that "he followed virtue as his truest guide." But the good captain, who certainly hadn't invented vigilante justice, yet had tried to justify it, was sentenced to the disgrace of having given his name to the terrible practice of lynching.

lynch·pin (lĭnch′pĭn′) *n.* Variant of **linchpin.**

Lynd (lĭnd), **Robert Staughton.** 1892–1970. American sociologist. With his wife, **Helen Merrell Lynd** (1896–1982), he wrote the pioneering sociological study *Middletown: A Study in Contemporary American Culture* (1929).

Lynd·hurst (lĭnd′hûrst′). A city of northeast Ohio, a residential suburb of Cleveland. Population, 18,092.

Lynn (lĭn). A city of northeast Massachusetts, a residential and industrial suburb of Boston. It was formerly an important shoe-making center. Population, 78,471.

Lynn Canal. An inlet of the Pacific Ocean in southeast Alaska connecting Skagway with Juneau. It was a major route to the goldfields during the Alaskan gold rush (1896–1898).

Lynn·wood (lĭn′wo͝od′). A city of west-central Washington, an industrial suburb of Seattle. Population, 21,937.

Lyn·wood (lĭn′wo͝od′). A city of southern California, an industrial suburb of Los Angeles. Population, 48,548.

lynx

lynx (lĭngks) *n., pl.* **lynx** or **lynx·es.** Any of several wildcats of the genus *Lynx,* especially *L. canadensis* of northern North America or *L. lynx* of Eurasia, having soft thick fur, a black-tipped short tail, and tufted ears. [Middle English, from Latin, from Greek *lunx.* See **leuk-** in Appendix.]

lynx-eyed (lĭngks′īd′) *adj.* Keen of vision.

lyo– *pref.* Dispersion; dissolution: *lyophilic.* [From Greek *luein,* to loosen, dissolve. See **leu-** in Appendix.]

Ly·on (lē-ôN′, lyôN). See **Lyons.**

Ly·on (lī′ən), **Mary Mason.** 1797–1849. American educator who founded (1837) Mount Holyoke College, the first American institution of higher learning for women.

Ly·on·nais (lē-ô-nĕ′). A historical region and former province of east-central France. It was a county during medieval times and became part of the French royal domain in the 14th century.

ly·on·naise (lī′ə-nāz′, lē′ə-nĕz′) *adj.* Cooked with onions: *lyonnaise potatoes; potatoes lyonnaise.* [From French *(à la) Lyonnaise,* (in the manner) of Lyons, from LYONS.]

Ly·ons or **Ly·on** (lē-ôN′, lyôN). A city of east-central France at the confluence of the Rhone and Saône rivers south of Mâcon. Founded in 43 B.C. as a Roman colony, it was the principal city of Gaul and an important religious center after the introduction of Christianity. Population, 413,095.

ă pat	oi boy
ā pay	ou out
âr care	o͝o took
ä father	o͞o boot
ĕ pet	ŭ cut
ē be	ûr urge
ĭ pit	th thin
ī pie	*th* this
îr pier	hw which
ŏ pot	zh vision
ō toe	ə about, item
ô paw	♦ regionalism

Stress marks: ′ (primary); ′ (secondary), as in **dictionary** (dĭk′shə-nĕr′ē)

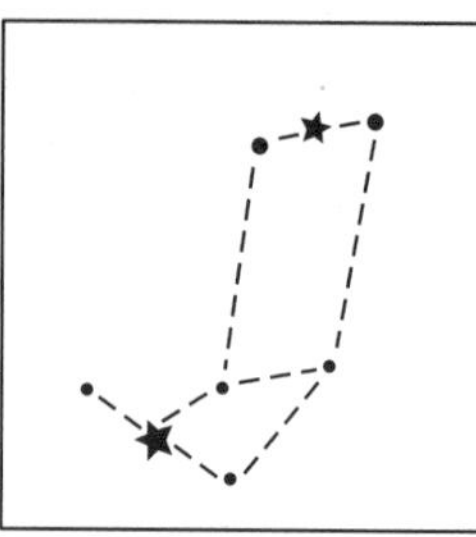

Lyra

lyre
c. 470 B.C. Etruscan painted terra-cotta plaque

lyrebird
Superb lyrebird
Menura novaehollandiae

ă pat	oi boy
ā pay	ou out
âr care	o͝o took
ä father	o͞o boot
ĕ pet	ŭ cut
ē be	ûr urge
ĭ pit	th thin
ī pie	*th* this
îr pier	hw which
ŏ pot	zh vision
ō toe	ə about, item
ô paw	♦ regionalism

Stress marks: **ʹ** (primary); ʹ (secondary), as in **dictionary** (dĭkʹshə-nĕrʹē)

ly•o•phil•ic (līʹə-fĭlʹĭk) *adj.* Characterized by strong attraction between the colloid medium and the dispersion medium of a colloidal system.

ly•oph•i•lize (lī-ŏfʹə-līzʹ) *tr.v.* **-lized, -liz•ing, -liz•es.** To freeze-dry (blood plasma or other biological substances). [LYOPHIL(IC) + -IZE.] **—ly•ophʹi•li•zaʹtion** (-lĭ-zāʹshən) *n.* **—ly•ophʹi•lizʹer** *n.*

ly•o•pho•bic (līʹə-fōʹbĭk) *adj.* Characterized by a lack of attraction between the colloid medium and the dispersion medium of a colloidal system.

lyr. *abbr.* Lyric.

Ly•ra (līʹrə) *n.* A constellation in the Northern Hemisphere near Cygnus and Hercules and containing Vega. [Latin, from *lyra,* lyre. See LYRE.]

ly•rate (līʹrātʹ, -rĭt) *adj.* **1.** Having a form or curvature suggestive of a lyre. **2.** *Botany.* Having a pinnately divided leaf with an enlarged terminal lobe and smaller lateral lobes.

lyre (līr) *n.* *Music.* A stringed instrument of the harp family used to accompany a singer or reader of poetry, especially in ancient Greece. [Middle English *lire,* from Old French, from Latin *lyra,* from Greek *lura.*]

lyre•bird (līrʹbûrdʹ) *n.* Either of two Australian birds of the genus *Menura,* the male of which has long tail feathers that are spread in a lyre-shaped display during courtship.

lyr•ic (lĭrʹĭk) *adj.* *Abbr.* **lyr. 1.a.** Of or relating to a category of poetry that expresses subjective thoughts and feelings, often in a songlike style or form. **b.** Relating to or constituting a poem in this category, such as a sonnet or an ode. **c.** Of or relating to a writer of poems in this category. **2.** Lyrical. **3.** *Music.* **a.** Having a singing voice of light volume and modest range. **b.** Of, relating to, or being musical drama, especially opera: *the lyric stage.* **c.** Of or relating to the lyre or harp. **d.** Appropriate for accompaniment by the lyre. **—lyric** *n.* **1.** A lyric poem. **2.** Often **lyrics.** *Music.* The words of a song. [French *lyrique,* of a lyre, from Old French, from Latin *lyricus,* from Greek *lurikos,* from *lura,* lyre.]

lyr•i•cal (lĭrʹĭ-kəl) *adj.* **1.a.** Expressing deep personal emotion or observations: *a dancer's lyrical performance; a lyrical passage in his autobiography.* **b.** Highly enthusiastic; rhapsodic: *gave a lyrical description of her experiences in the South Seas.* **2.** Lyric. **—lyrʹi•cal•ly** *adv.* **—lyrʹi•cal•ness** *n.*

lyr•i•cism (lĭrʹĭ-sĭzʹəm) *n.* **1.a.** The character or quality of subjectivity and sensuality of expression, especially in the arts. **b.** *Music.* The quality or state of being melodious; melodiousness. **2.** An intense outpouring of exuberant emotion.

lyr•i•cist (lĭrʹĭ-sĭst) *n.* *Music.* A writer of song lyrics. Also called *lyrist.*

lyr•i•cize (lĭrʹĭ-sīzʹ) *v.* **-ciz•ed, -ciz•ing, -ciz•es.** *—intr.* **1.** *Music.* To write or sing lyrics. **2.** To write lyrically or in a lyric style. *—tr.* To treat (something) lyrically; put into lyric style.

lyr•ism (lĭrʹĭzʹəm) *n.* Lyricism. [French *lyrisme,* from Greek *lurismos,* played on the lyre, from *lura,* lyre.]

lyr•ist (lĭrʹĭst) *n.* **1.** *Music.* See **lyricist. 2.** (līrʹĭst). *Music.* One who plays a lyre. **3.** A lyric poet. [Latin *lyristēs,* lyre player, from Greek *luristēs,* from *lura,* lyre.]

Lys (lēs). A river rising in northern France and flowing about 217 km (135 mi) northeast along the French-Belgian border to the Scheldt River.

lys– *pref.* Variant of **lyso–.**

Ly•san•der (lī-sănʹdər). Died 395 B.C. Spartan military leader who won the final victory over Athens (404) in the Peloponnesian War.

lyse (līs, līz) *intr. & tr.v.* **lysed, lys•ing, lys•es.** To undergo or cause to undergo lysis. [Back-formation from LYSIS.]

Ly•sen•ko (lĭ-sĕngʹkō, -syĕnʹkə), **Trofim Denisovich.** 1898–1976. Soviet biologist and agronomist. As director of the Institute of Genetics of the Soviet Academy of Sciences (1940–1964), he had an adverse effect on Soviet agricultural development because of his belief in the genetic theory that acquired characteristics can be inherited.

Ly•sen•ko•ism (lĭ-sĕngʹkō-ĭzʹəm) *n.* A biological doctrine developed by Trofim Lysenko that maintains the possibility of inheriting environmentally acquired characteristics.

ly•ser•gic acid (lĭ-sûrʹjĭk, lī-) *n.* A crystalline alkaloid, $C_{16}H_{16}N_2O_2$, derived from ergot and used in medical research as a psychotomimetic agent. [LYS(O)– + ERG(OT) + –IC.]

lysergic acid di•eth•yl•am•ide (dīʹĕth-əl-ămʹīdʹ) *n.* See **LSD[1].**

ly•ses (līʹsēz) *n.* Plural of **lysis.**

lysi– *pref.* Variant of **lyso–.**

Ly•sim•a•chus (lī-sĭmʹə-kəs). 361?–281 B.C. Macedonian general under Alexander the Great. He ruled Macedonia from 287 to 286.

ly•sin (līʹsĭn) *n.* An antibody that is capable of causing the destruction or dissolution of red blood cells, bacteria, or other cellular elements.

ly•sine (līʹsēn, -sĭn) *n.* An essential amino acid, $C_6H_{14}N_2O_2$, derived from the hydrolysis of proteins and required by the body for optimum growth.

Ly•sip•pus (lī-sĭpʹəs). fl. fourth century B.C. Greek sculptor who was active during the reign of Alexander the Great. He created figures that were more lifelike than traditional forms.

ly•sis (līʹsĭs) *n., pl.* **-ses** (-sēz). **1.** *Biochemistry.* The dissolution or destruction of cells, such as blood cells or bacteria, as by the action of a specific lysin. **2.** *Medicine.* The gradual subsiding of the symptoms of an acute disease. [New Latin, from Latin, a loosening, from Greek *lusis,* from *luein,* to loosen. See **leu-** in Appendix.]

–lysis *suff.* Decomposition; dissolving; disintegration: *hydrolysis.* [New Latin, from Greek *lusis,* a loosening. See LYSIS.]

Ly•sith•e•a (lī-sĭthʹē-ə) *n.* The satellite of Jupiter that is 12th in distance from the planet. [Probably from Greek *Lusithoē,* daughter of Oceanus and mother of Herakles.]

lyso– or **lysi–** or **lys–** *pref.* Lysis: *lysin.* [From Greek *lusis,* a loosening, from *luein,* to loosen. See **leu-** in Appendix.]

ly•so•gen (līʹsə-jən) *n.* A bacterium or bacterial strain that carries a prophage.

ly•so•gen•ic (līʹsə-jĕnʹĭk) *adj.* Carrying a prophage within the cell. Used of a bacterium.

ly•sog•e•nize (lī-sŏjʹĭ-nīzʹ) *tr.v.* **-nized, -niz•ing, -niz•es.** To make lysogenic. **—ly•sogʹe•ni•zaʹtion** (-nĭ-zāʹshən) *n.*

ly•sog•e•ny (lī-sŏjʹə-nē) *n.* The fusion of the nucleic acid of a bacteriophage with that of a host bacterium so that the potential exists for the newly integrated genetic material to be transmitted to daughter cells at each subsequent cell division.

ly•so•some (līʹsə-sōmʹ) *n.* A membrane-bound organelle in the cytoplasm of most cells containing various hydrolytic enzymes that function in intracellular digestion. **—lyʹso•soʹmal** *adj.*

ly•so•zyme (līʹsə-zīmʹ) *n.* An enzyme occurring naturally in egg white, human tears, saliva, and other body fluids, capable of destroying the cell walls of certain bacteria and thereby acting as a mild antiseptic.

–lyte *suff.* A substance that can be decomposed by a specified process: *electrolyte.* [From Greek *lutos,* soluble, from *luein,* to loosen. See **leu-** in Appendix.]

lyt•ic (lĭtʹĭk) *adj.* **1.** Of, relating to, or causing lysis: *a lytic enzyme.* **2.** Of or relating to a lysin. [Greek *lutikos,* able to loosen. See –LYTIC.]

–lytic *suff.* Of, relating to, or causing a specified kind of decomposition: *cellulolytic.* [From Greek *lutikos,* able to loosen, from *luein,* to loosen. See **leu-** in Appendix.]

lyt•ta (lĭtʹə) *n., pl.* **lyt•tae** (lĭtʹēʹ). A thin cartilaginous strip on the underside of the tongue of certain carnivorous mammals, such as dogs. [Latin, worm under a dog's tongue (said to cause madness), from Greek *lussa, lutta,* madness, rabies. See **wĺkʷo-** in Appendix.]

Lyt•ton (lĭtʹn), First Baron. See Edward George Earle Lytton **Bulwer-Lytton.**

Lytton, First Earl of. Title of Edward Robert Bulwer-Lytton. 1831–1891. British politician and diplomat who served as viceroy of India (1875–1880) and ambassador to Paris (1887–1891).

–lyze *suff.* To cause or undergo lysis: *pyrolyze.* [From –LYSIS.]

LZ *abbr.* Landing zone.

Mm

m¹ or **M** (ĕm) *n., pl.* **m's** or **M's.** **1.** The 13th letter of the modern English alphabet. **2.** Any of the speech sounds represented by the letter *m.* **3.** The 13th in a series.

m² *abbr.* **1.** Also **M.** *Printing.* Em. **2.** *Physics.* Mass. **3.** Meter (measurement). **4.** Also **M.** *Physics.* Modulus.

M¹ also **m** The symbol for the Roman numeral 1,000.

M² *abbr.* **1.** *Bible.* Maccabees. **2.** Mach number. **3.** Metal. **4.** *Logic.* Middle term. **5.** *Chemistry.* Molar; molarity. **6.** *Physics.* Moment. **7.** *Physics.* Mutual inductance.

m. *abbr.* **1.** Or **M.** Male. **2.** Manual. **3.** Married. **4.** Or **M.** *Grammar.* Masculine. **5.** Or **M.** Medium. **6.** Or **M.** *Latin.* Merides (noon). **7.** Or **M.** Meridian. **8.** Mile. **9.** Month. **10.** Morning.

M. *abbr.* **1.** Majesty. **2.** Mark (currency). **3.** Master. **4.** Medieval. **5.** Member. **6.** Mill (currency). **7.** Minim. **8.** Monday. **9.** Monsieur.

'm Am: *I'm feeling fine.*

ma (mä, mô) *n. Informal.* Mother. [Short for MAMA.]

mA *abbr.* Milliampere.

MA *abbr.* **1.** Maritime Administration. **2.** Massachusetts. **3.** Also **M.A.** Mental age.

M.A. or **MA** *abbr. Latin.* Magister Artium (Master of Arts).

ma'am (măm) *n.* Used as a form of polite address for a woman: *Will that be cash or charge, ma'am?*

maar (mär) *n.* A flat-bottomed, roughly circular volcanic crater of explosive origin that is often filled with water. [German, from Vulgar Latin **mara,* standing water, lake, from Latin *mare,* sea. See MARE².]

Maas (mäs). A section of the Meuse River flowing westward through the southern Netherlands to the Rhine River.

Maa·sai (mä-sī′, mä′sī) *n., pl.* **Maasai** or **-sais.** Variant of **Masai** (sense 2).

Maas·tricht (mäs′trĭkt′, -trĭKHt′). A city of extreme southeast Netherlands near the Belgian border. Founded on the site of a Roman settlement, it has long been a strategic frontier outpost. Population, 113,277.

M.A.B.E. *abbr.* Master of Agricultural Business and Economics.

Ma·ble·ton (mā′bəl-tən). A community of northwest Georgia, a suburb of Atlanta. Population, 20,200.

mac (măk) *n. Chiefly British.* A mackintosh.

Mac (măk) *n. Slang.* Used as a form of address for a man whose name is unknown. [From *Mac-,* a common prefix in Scottish and Irish surnames.]

Mac. *abbr. Bible.* Maccabees.

ma·ca·bre (mə-kä′brə, mə-käb′, -kä′bər) *adj.* **1.** Suggesting the horror of death and decay; gruesome: *macabre tales of war and plague in the Middle Ages.* See Synonyms at **ghastly. 2.** Constituting or including a representation of death. [Ultimately from Old French *(Danse) Macabre,* (dance) of death, perhaps alteration of *Macabe,* Maccabee, from Latin *Maccabaeus,* from Greek *Makkabios.*] **—ma·ca′bre·ly** *adv.*

WORD HISTORY: The word *macabre* is an excellent example of a word formed with reference to a specific context that has long since disappeared for everyone but scholars. *Macabre* is first recorded in the phrase *Macabrees daunce* in a work written around 1430 by John Lydgate. Lydgate expressed it so because he thought *Macabree* was a French author, although he was actually dealing with the Old French phrase *Danse Macabre,* "the Dance of Death," a subject of art and literature. In this dance, Death leads people of all classes and walks of life to the same final end. The *macabre* element is thought by some to be an alteration of *Macabe,* "a Maccabee." The Maccabees were Jewish martyrs who were honored by a feast throughout the Western Church, and reverence for them was linked to reverence for the dead. One of the biblical books of Maccabees also contains a passage (II Maccabees 12:43–45) mentioning sacrifices for the dead and their future resurrection, which has been used to defend the doctrine of Purgatory. Today *macabre* has no connection with the Maccabees and little connection with the Dance of Death, but it still has to do with death.

ma·ca·co (mə-kä′kō) *n., pl.* **-cos.** Any of various lemurs, especially the species *Lemur macaco.* [Portuguese, of Bantu origin; akin to Kongo *ma-kako,* monkeys : *ma-,* pl. n. pref. + *kako,* monkey.]

mac·ad·am (mə-kăd′əm) *n.* Pavement made of layers of compacted broken stone, now usually bound with tar or asphalt. [After John Loudon *McAdam* (1756–1836), Scottish civil engineer.]

mac·a·da·mi·a nut (măk′ə-dā′mē-ə) *n.* The round, hard-shelled nut or the edible seed of the Australian tree *Macadamia ternifolia,* now cultivated in Hawaii. [New Latin *Macadamia,* genus name, after John *Macadam* (1827–1865), Scottish-born Australian chemist.]

mac·ad·am·ize (mə-kăd′ə-mīz′) *tr.v.* **-ized, -iz·ing, -iz·es.** To construct or pave (a road) with macadam. **—mac·ad′am·i·za′tion** (-ə-mĭ-zā′shən) *n.* **—mac·ad′am·iz′er** *n.*

Ma·cao also **Ma·cau** (mə-kou′). A Portuguese overseas province comprising **Macao Peninsula** and two offshore islands in the South China Sea west of Hong Kong. A Portuguese trading post was established here in 1557 and became a free port in 1849. The province will come under Chinese control in 1999. The city of **Macao** is the capital. Population, 350,000.

ma·caque (mə-kăk′, -käk′) *n.* Any of several short-tailed monkeys of the genus *Macaca* of southeast Asia, Japan, Gibraltar, and northern Africa. [French, from Portuguese *macaco.* See MACACO.]

mac·a·ro·ni (măk′ə-rō′nē) *n.* **1.** *pl.* **macaroni.** A paste or pasta of wheat flour pressed into hollow tubes or other shapes, dried, and prepared for eating by boiling. **2.** *pl.* **macaroni** or **-nies a.** A well-traveled young Englishman of the 18th and 19th centuries who affected foreign customs. **b.** A fop. [Italian dialectal *maccaroni,* pl. of *maccarone,* dumpling, macaroni.]

mac·a·ron·ic (măk′ə-rŏn′ĭk) *adj.* **1.** Of or containing a mixture of vernacular words with Latin words or with vernacular words given Latinate endings: *macaronic verse.* **2.** Of or involving a mixture of two or more languages. [New Latin *macaronicus,* from Italian dialectal *maccarone,* dumpling, macaroni (perhaps from the way macaroni is heaped on a plate and mixed with sauce).] **—mac′a·ron′ic** *n.*

mac·a·roon (măk′ə-ro͞on′) *n.* A chewy cookie made with sugar, egg whites, and almond paste or coconut. [French *macaron,* from Italian dialectal *maccarone,* dumpling, macaroni.]

Mac·Ar·thur (mĭk-är′thər), **Charles.** 1895–1956. American playwright noted for *The Front Page* (1928), which he cowrote with Ben Hecht.

MacArthur, Douglas. 1880–1964. American general who served as U.S. chief of staff (1930–1935) and commanded Allied forces in the South Pacific during World War II. After losing the Philippines to the Japanese (1942), he regained the islands (1944) and accepted the surrender of Japan (1945). He commanded the United Nations forces in Korea (1950–1951) until a conflict in strategies led to his dismissal by President Harry S. Truman.

Ma·cau (mə-kou′). See **Macao.**

Ma·cau·lay (mə-kô′lē), Dame **Rose.** 1881–1958. British writer whose novels include *The World My Wilderness* (1950).

Macaulay, Thomas Babington. First Baron Macaulay. 1800–1859. British historian, writer, and politician whose works include the popular *History of England* (1849–1861) and numerous essays for the *Edinburgh Review.*

ma·caw (mə-kô′) *n.* Any of various parrots of the genera *Ara* and *Anodorhynchus* of Central and South America, including the largest parrots and characterized by long saber-shaped tails, curved powerful bills, and usually brilliant plumage. [Portuguese *macaú,* from *macaúba,* kind of palm tree, from Tupi *macahuba,* palm tree : *maca,* palm + *ybá,* tree.]

Mac·beth (mək-bĕth′). Died 1057. King of Scotland (1040–1057) who ascended the throne after killing his cousin King Duncan (died 1040) in battle. Legends of his rise to power and reign are the basis of Shakespeare's tragedy *Macbeth.*

Mac·Bride (mĭk-brīd′), **Sean.** 1904–1988. Irish politician who was active in a number of international human rights organizations. He shared the 1974 Nobel Peace Prize.

Phoenician
The Phoenician alphabet used this symbol to represent the *m* in *mēm,* "water."

Early Greek
It was adopted with little change by the Greeks, who called it simply *mu* to rhyme with *nu* (see N).

Roman
The Romans simplified it somewhat to arrive at the modern form M.

Douglas MacArthur
Photographed in 1945

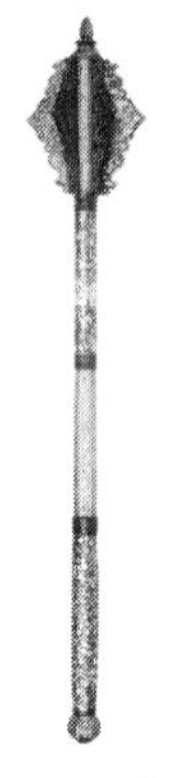
mace[1]
c. 1550 French damascene parade mace

Macc. *abbr. Bible.* Maccabees.

Mac·ca·bae·us (măk′ə-bē′əs), **Judas.** See Judas **Maccabeus.**

Mac·ca·bees (măk′ə-bēz′) *pl.n. Bible.* **1.** A family of Jewish patriots of the second and first centuries B.C., active in the liberation of Judea from Syrian rule. **2.** *Abbr.* **M, Mac., Macc.** See table at **Bible.** —**Mac′ca·be′an** *adj.*

Mac·ca·be·us also **Mac·ca·bae·us** (măk′ə-bē′əs), **Judas** or **Judah.** Died 160 B.C. Jewish patriot and most famous member of the Maccabees family. His rededication of the Temple at Jerusalem (164 B.C.) is commemorated by the feast of Hanukkah.

Mac·Diar·mid (mək-dûr′mĭd), **Hugh.** Pen name of Christopher Murray Grieve. 1892–1978. Scottish poet whose works sparked a revival of modern Scottish literature.

Mac·don·ald (mĭk-dŏn′əld), **George.** 1824–1905. Scottish writer known primarily for his allegorical children's books.

Macdonald, Sir **John Alexander.** 1815–1891. Canadian politician and the first prime minister of the Dominion of Canada (1867–1873 and 1878–1891). He is considered the organizer of the Canadian confederation, established in 1867.

Mac·Don·ald (mĭk-dŏn′əld), **(James) Ramsay.** 1866–1937. British politician who served as prime minister (1924 and 1929–1935).

Mac·Dow·ell (mĭk-dou′əl), **Edward Alexander.** 1861–1908. American composer whose works include the piano sonatas *Woodland Sketches* (1896) and *Sea Pieces* (1898).

mace[1] (mās) *n.* **1.** A ceremonial staff borne or displayed as the symbol of authority of a legislative body. **2.** A macebearer. **3.** A heavy medieval war club with a spiked or flanged metal head, used to crush armor. [Middle English, from Old French, from Vulgar Latin *mattea, from Latin *mateola,* mallet.]

mace[2] (mās) *n.* An aromatic spice made from the dried, waxy, scarlet or yellowish covering that partly encloses the kernel of the nutmeg. [Middle English, from Old French, from Medieval Latin *macis,* alteration of Latin *macir,* fragrant ailanthus resin, from Greek *makir.*]

Niccolò Machiavelli
Detail of a portrait by Santi di Tito (1536–1603)

Mace (mās). An alternate trademark used for Chemical Mace, an aerosol used to immobilize an attacker temporarily.

mace·bear·er (mās′bâr′ər) *n.* An official who carries a mace of office.

Maced. *abbr.* Macedonian.

mac·é·doine (măs′ə-dwän′) *n.* **1.** A mixture of finely cut vegetables or fruits, sometimes jellied, and served as a salad, a dessert, or an appetizer. **2.** A mixture; a medley. [French, from *Macédoine,* Macedonia (perhaps from the variety of races there).]

Mac·e·do·ni·a (măs′ĭ-dō′nē-ə, -dōn′yə). **1.** Also **Mac·e·don** (-dən, -dŏn′). An ancient kingdom of northern Greece. It was a powerful empire under Philip II and his son Alexander the Great (fourth century B.C.) and contributed significantly to the spread of Hellenistic civilization. The Romans annexed it as a province in 148 B.C. **2.** A region of southeast Europe on the Balkan Peninsula including parts of modern-day Greece, Bulgaria, and Yugoslavia. After the fall of the Alexandrian empire, it was held by Romans, Byzantines, Bulgars, Serbs, and Turks.

Mac·e·do·ni·an (măs′ĭ-dō′nē-ən) *adj. Abbr.* **Maced.** Of or relating to ancient or modern Macedonia or its peoples, languages, or cultures. —**Macedonian** *n. Abbr.* **Maced. 1.** A native or inhabitant of ancient or modern Macedonia. **2.** The language of ancient Macedonia, of uncertain affiliation within Indo-European. **3.** The Slavic language of modern Macedonia, closely related to Bulgarian.

Ma·cei·ó (măs′ā-ō′, mä′sā-). A city of northeast Brazil on the Atlantic Ocean south-southwest of Recife. It is a commercial and distribution center. Population, 375,771.

mac·er (mā′sər) *n.* A macebearer.

mac·er·ate (măs′ə-rāt′) *v.* **-at·ed, -at·ing, -ates.** —*tr.* **1.** To make soft by soaking or steeping in a liquid. **2.** To separate into constituents by soaking. **3.** To cause to become lean, usually by starvation; emaciate. —*intr.* To become soft or separated into constituents by soaking. —**macerate** (-ĭt) *n.* A substance prepared or produced by macerating. [Latin *mācerāre, mācerāt-.* See **mag-** in Appendix.] —**mac′er·a′tion** *n.* —**mac′er·a′tor, mac′er·at′er** *n.*

Mach also **mach** (mäk) *n.* Mach number.

Mach (mäk, mäKH), **Ernst.** 1838–1916. Austrian physicist and philosopher whose concept of knowledge as the organization of sensory experience greatly influenced modern science.

mach. *abbr.* Machine; machinery; machinist.

mache also **mâche** (mäsh) *n.* See **corn salad.** [French *mâche,* from dialectal *pomache,* from Vulgar Latin **pōmasca,* from Latin *pōmum,* fruit (perhaps because of its slightly sweet taste).]

ma·chet·e (mə-shĕt′ē, -chĕt′ē) *n.* A large, heavy knife with a broad blade, used as a weapon and an implement for cutting vegetation. [Spanish, diminutive of *macho,* sledge hammer, alteration of *mazo,* club, probably from *maza,* mallet, from Vulgar Latin **mattea,* mace. See MACE[1].]

machicolation

Mach·i·a·vel·li (măk′ē-ə-vĕl′ē, mä′kyä-), **Niccolò.** 1469–1527. Italian political theorist whose book *The Prince* (1513) describes the achievement and maintenance of power by a determined ruler indifferent to moral considerations.

Mach·i·a·vel·li·an (măk′ē-ə-vĕl′ē-ən) *adj.* **1.** Of or relating to Machiavelli or Machiavellianism. **2.** Suggestive of or characterized by expediency, deceit, and cunning. —**Mach′i·a·vel′li·an, Mach′i·a·vel′list** *n.*

Mach·i·a·vel·li·an·ism (măk′ē-ə-vĕl′ē-ə-nĭz′əm) also **Mach·i·a·vel·lism** (-vĕl′ĭz′əm) *n.* The political doctrine of Machiavelli, which denies the relevance of morality in political affairs and holds that craft and deceit are justified in pursuing and maintaining political power.

ma·chic·o·late (mə-chĭk′ə-lāt′) *tr.v.* **-lat·ed, -lat·ing, -lates.** To provide or furnish with machicolations. [Medieval Latin *machicolāre, machicolāt-,* from Old French *machicoller,* from *machicoleis,* machicolation, from Old Provençal *machacol* : *macar,* to crush (from Vulgar Latin **maccāre*) + *col,* neck (from Latin *collum;* see **kʷel-**[1] in Appendix).]

ma·chic·o·la·tion (mə-chĭk′ə-lā′shən) *n.* **1.a.** A projecting gallery at the top of a castle wall, supported by a row of corbeled arches and having openings in the floor through which stones and boiling liquids could be dropped on attackers. **b.** One of these openings. **2.** A row of small corbeled arches used as an ornamental architectural feature.

Ma·chi·da (mə-chē′də, mä-chē′dä). A city of east-central Honshu, Japan, a suburb of Tokyo. Population, 321,182.

mach·i·nate (măk′ə-nāt′, măsh′-) *v.* **-nat·ed, -nat·ing, -nates.** —*tr.* To devise (a plot). —*intr.* To engage in plotting. [Latin *māchinārī, māchināt-,* to design, contrive, from *māchina,* device. See MACHINE.] —**mach′i·na′tor** *n.*

mach·i·na·tion (măk′ə-nā′shən, măsh′-) *n.* **1.** The act of plotting. **2.** A crafty scheme or cunning design for the accomplishment of a sinister end. See Synonyms at **conspiracy.**

ma·chine (mə-shēn′) *n. Abbr.* **mach. 1.a.** A device consisting of fixed and moving parts that modifies mechanical energy and transmits it in a more useful form. **b.** A simple device, such as a lever, a pulley, or an inclined plane, that alters the magnitude or direction, or both, of an applied force; a simple machine. **2.** A system or device for doing work, as an automobile or a jackhammer, together with its power source and auxiliary equipment. **3.** A system or device, such as a computer, that performs or assists in the performance of a human task: *The machine is down.* **4.** An intricate natural system or organism, such as the human body. **5.** A person who acts in a rigid, mechanical, or unconscious manner. **6.** An organized group of people whose members are or appear to be under the control of one or more leaders: *a political machine.* **7.a.** A device used to produce a stage effect, especially a mechanical means of lowering an actor onto the stage. **b.** A literary device used to produce an effect, especially the introduction of a supernatural being to resolve a plot. —**machine** *adj.* Of, relating to, or felt to resemble a machine: *machine repairs; machine politics.* —**machine** *v.* **-chined, -chin·ing, -chines.** —*tr.* To cut, shape, or finish by machine. —*intr.* To be cut, shaped, or finished by machine: *This metal machines easily.* [French, from Old French, from Latin *māchina,* from Greek *mēkhanē, makhana.* See **magh-** in Appendix.] —**ma·chin′a·ble** *adj.*

machine bolt *n.* A bolt with a square or hexagonal head.

machine code *n. Computer Science.* See **machine language.**

machine finish *n.* See **mill finish.**

machine gun *n. Abbr.* **MG** A gun that fires rapidly and repeatedly.

ma·chine-gun (mə-shēn′gŭn′) *tr.v.* **-gunned, -gun·ning, -guns.** To fire at or kill with a machine gun. —**machine-gun** *adj.* Fast and staccato: *a machine-gun style of speaking.* —**machine gunner** *n.*

machine language *n. Computer Science.* A set of instructions coded so that the computer can use it directly without further translation. Also called *machine code.*

machine pistol *n.* A lightweight automatic or semiautomatic submachine gun designed to be fired one-handed like a pistol.

ma·chine-read·a·ble (mə-shēn′rē′də-bəl) *adj. Computer Science.* Easy to feed directly into a computer, as data that have been stored magnetically.

ma·chin·er·y (mə-shē′nə-rē, -shēn′rē) *n., pl.* **-ies.** *Abbr.* **mach. 1.** Machines or machine parts considered as a group. **2.** The working parts of a particular machine. **3.** A system of related elements that operate in a definable manner: *diplomatic and political machinery.* **4.a.** A device or means of achieving or effecting a result. **b.** A literary device for bringing about an effect, such as a happy ending.

machine screw *n.* A screw with a thread along the entire length of the shaft.

machine shop *n.* A workshop where power-driven tools are used for making, finishing, or repairing machines or machine parts.

machine tool *n.* A power-driven tool, such as a lathe or milling machine, used for machining. —**ma·chine′-tooled′** (mə-shēn′to͞old′) *adj.*

machine translation *n.* Automatic translation, as by computer, from one language to another.

ma·chine-wash (mə-shēn′wŏsh′, -wôsh′) *tr. & intr.v.* **-washed, -wash·ing, -wash·es.** To wash or undergo washing in a washing machine.

ma·chin·ist (mə-shē′nĭst) *n. Abbr.* **mach. 1.** One who is skilled in operating machine tools. **2.** One who makes, operates, or repairs machines. **3.** A warrant officer who assists the engineering officer in the engine room of a naval vessel. **4.** *Archaic.* A person in charge of stage machinery.

ma·chis·mo (mä-chēz′mō) *n.* A strong, sometimes exaggerated sense of masculinity stressing attributes such as physical courage, virility, domination of women, and aggressiveness; manliness: *"He might seem during the interview to relish his machismo—why else the karate kick that opens the apartment-house gate?"* (New York). [Spanish, from *macho,* male. See MACHO.]

Mach·me·ter (mäk′mē′tər) *n.* An aircraft instrument that indicates speed in Mach numbers.

Mach number also **mach number** (mäk) *n. Abbr.* **M** The ratio of the speed of an object to the speed of sound in the surrounding medium. For example, an aircraft moving twice as fast as the speed of sound is said to be traveling at Mach 2. [After Ernst MACH.]

ma·cho (mä′chō) *adj.* Characterized or motivated by machismo: *"He was a mindless activist, a war lover, who found macho relish in danger and felt driven to prove manhood by confrontation"* (Arthur M. Schlesinger, Jr.). **—macho** *n., pl.* **-chos. 1.** Machismo. **2.** A person characterized by or exhibiting machismo. [Spanish, male, from Latin *masculus.* See MASCULINE.] **—ma′cho·ism** *n.*

Ma·chu Pic·chu (mä′cho͞o pēk′cho͞o, pē′-). An ancient Inca fortress city in the Andes northwest of Cuzco, Peru. Its extensive ruins, including elaborate terraces, were discovered in 1911.

mach·zor (mäKH′zôr′, -zər, mäKH-zōr′) *n.* Variant of **mahzor.**

mac·in·tosh (măk′ĭn-tŏsh′) *n.* Variant of **mackintosh.**

Mac·Kaye (mə-kī′), **(James Morrison) Steele.** 1842–1894. American actor, playwright, and producer who founded America's first school of drama (1873). Of his sons, **Percy** (1875–1956) was a noted poet and playwright and **Benton** (1879–1975) was a regional planner who proposed the Appalachian Trail (1921).

Ma·cke (mä′kə), **August.** 1887–1914. German painter whose works, such as *Lady in a Green Jacket* (1913), display brilliant use of color.

Mac·ken·zie (mə-kĕn′zē), **Alexander.** 1822–1892. British-born Canadian politician who was the first Liberal prime minister of Canada (1873–1878).

Mackenzie, Sir **Alexander.** 1764–1820. British-born Canadian explorer who navigated the Mackenzie River (1789) and was the first to cross North America by land north of Mexico (1793).

Mackenzie, William Lyon. 1795–1861. British-born Canadian member of Parliament (1828–1836 and 1851–1858) who led an armed insurrection in Toronto (1837) to protest colonial rule.

Mackenzie District. A former district of western and central Northwest Territories, Canada, now divided mainly between Inuvik and Fort Smith districts.

Mackenzie Mountains. A range of the northern Rocky Mountains in eastern Yukon Territory and western Northwest Territories, Canada, rising to 2,973.8 m (9,750 ft).

Mackenzie River. A river of northwest Canada rising in Great Slave Lake in southern Northwest Territories and flowing about 1,802 km (1,120 mi) generally northwest to a vast delta on **Mackenzie Bay,** an arm of the Beaufort Sea.

mack·er·el (măk′ər-əl, măk′rəl) *n., pl.* **mackerel** or **-els. 1.** Any of several widely distributed marine fishes of the family Scombridae, especially the Atlantic mackerel *(Scomber scombrus),* an important food fish having dark, wavy bars on the back and a silvery belly. **2.** Any of the smaller fishes of the suborder Scombroidea, such as the Spanish mackerel. **3.** Any of various similar fishes. [Middle English *makerel,* from Old French *maquerel.*]

mackerel shark *n.* Any of various sharks of the family Lamnidae, including the great white shark, mako, and porbeagle, having a pointed snout, a nearly symmetrical tail, and a reputation for aggressiveness.

♦ **mackerel sky** *n. Northeastern U.S.* A sky covered with many small cirrocumulus or altocumulus clouds, giving an overall effect of the markings to be found on a mackerel. Also called ♦*buttermilk sky.*

Mack·i·nac Island (măk′ə-nô′). An island of northern Michigan in the **Straits of Mackinac,** a passage connecting Lakes Huron and Michigan between the Upper and Lower peninsulas.

mack·i·naw (măk′ə-nô′) *n.* **1.** A short, double-breasted coat of heavy, usually plaid, woolen material. **2.** The cloth from which such a coat is made, usually of wool, often with a heavy nap. **3.** *Nautical.* A flat-bottomed boat with a pointed bow and square stern, once used on the upper Great Lakes. [After Old *Mackinac,* a fort on the site of present-day *Mackinaw City* in northern Michigan.]

Mack·i·naw blanket (măk′ə-nô′) *n.* A thick blanket in solid colors or stripes, formerly used in northern and western North America by traders, trappers, and Native Americans.

Mackinaw trout *n.* See **lake trout.**

mack·in·tosh also **mac·in·tosh** (măk′ĭn-tŏsh′) *n. Chiefly British.* **1.** A raincoat. **2.** A lightweight, waterproof fabric that was originally of rubberized cotton. [After Charles *Macintosh* (1766–1843), Scottish inventor.]

mack·le (măk′əl) also **mac·ule** (măk′yo͞ol′) *—n.* A blurred or double impression in printing. *—v.* **-led, -ling, -les** also **-uled, -ul·ing, -ules.** *—tr.* To blur or double (a printed impression). *—intr.* To become blurred. [Middle English *macule,* spot, from Old French, from Latin *macula.*]

mac·le (măk′əl) *n.* **1.** Chiastolite. **2.** A twinned crystal. **3.** A dark spot or discoloration in a mineral. [French, from Old French, lozenge, from Latin *macula,* mesh.]

Mac·Leish (mĭk-lēsh′), **Archibald.** 1892–1982. American poet who served as Librarian of Congress (1939–1944) and assistant secretary of state (1944–1945).

Mac·Len·nan (mə-klĕn′ən), **Hugh.** Born 1907. Canadian writer whose novels are literary treatments of Canadian political and social concerns.

Mac·leod (mə-kloud′), **John James Rickard.** 1876–1935. British physiologist. He shared a 1923 Nobel Prize for the discovery of insulin.

Mac·mil·lan (mĭk-mĭl′ən), **(Maurice) Harold.** 1894–1986. British politician who joined Churchill in the 1930's in condemning Great Britain's appeasement of Hitler. As prime minister (1957–1963) he sought British entry into the Common Market.

Mac·Mil·lan (mĭk-mĭl′ən), **Donald Baxter.** 1874–1970. American explorer noted for his use of aircraft in several Arctic explorations between 1913 and 1937.

Mac·Neice (mĭk-nēs′), **(Frederick) Louis.** 1907–1963. Irish-born British poet whose works, published in *Blind Fireworks* (1929) and other collections, treat social issues in a detached, often ironic manner.

Ma·comb (mə-kōm′). A city of western Illinois west-southwest of Peoria. It is known for its pottery. Population, 19,632.

Ma·con (mā′kən). A city of central Georgia southeast of Atlanta. Settled in the early 1820's, it is a processing, industrial, and educational center in an extensive farm area. Population, 116,860.

Mâ·con (mä-kôN′). A city of east-central France on the Saône River north of Lyons. A Huguenot stronghold in the 16th century, it is noted for its fine Burgundy wines. Population, 38,404.

Mac·pher·son (mək-fûr′sən), **James.** 1736–1796. Scottish poet who claimed to have translated the works of Ossian, a third-century Gaelic poet and warrior. Although based on unauthenticated original texts, the translations influenced many writers.

Mac·quar·ie (mə-kwär′ē, -kwôr′ē). A river of southeast Australia flowing about 949 km (590 mi) to the Darling River.

macr– *pref.* Variant of **macro–.**

mac·ra·mé (măk′rə-mā′) *n.* Coarse lace work made by weaving and knotting cords into a pattern. *—attributive.* Often used to modify another noun: *macramé holders for plants; macramé work.* [French, from Italian *macramè,* from Turkish *makrama,* towel, from Arabic *miqramah,* embroidered veil.]

mac·ro (măk′rō′) *n., pl.* **-ros.** *Computer Science.* A single instruction in programming language that results in a series of instructions in machine language. [Short for MACROINSTRUCTION.]

macro– or **macr–** *pref.* **1.** Large: *macronucleus.* **2.** Long: *macrobiotics.* **3.** Inclusive: *macroinstruction.* [Greek *makro-,* from *makros,* large. See **māk-** in Appendix.]

mac·ro·bi·ot·ics (măk′rō-bī-ŏt′ĭks) *n. (used with a sing. verb).* The theory or practice of promoting well-being and longevity, principally by means of a diet consisting chiefly of whole grains and beans. **—mac′ro·bi·ot′ic** *adj.*

mac·ro·ceph·a·ly (măk′rō-sĕf′ə-lē) also **mac·ro·ce·pha·li·a** (-sə-fā′lē-ə, -fāl′yə) *n.* Abnormal largeness of the head. Also called *megacephaly, megalocephaly.* **—mac′ro·ce·phal′ic** (-sə-făl′ĭk), **mac′ro·ceph′a·lous** *adj.*

mac·ro·cli·mate (măk′rō-klī′mĭt) *n.* The climate of a large geographic area. **—mac′ro·cli·mat′ic** (-măt′ĭk) *adj.*

mac·ro·code (măk′rə-kōd′) *n. Computer Science.* **1.** A coding system in which single codes generate several sets of instructions. **2.** A single code that represents a set of instructions.

mac·ro·cosm (măk′rə-kŏz′əm) *n.* **1.** The entire world; the universe. **2.** A system reflecting on a large scale one of its component systems or parts. [Medieval Latin *macrocosmus* : Greek *makro-,* macro- + Greek *kosmos,* world.] **—mac′ro·cos′mic** *adj.* **—mac′ro·cos′mic·al·ly** *adv.*

mac·ro·cyte (măk′rō-sīt′) *n.* An abnormally large red blood cell, especially one associated with pernicious anemia. **—mac′ro·cyt′ic** (-sĭt′ĭk) *adj.*

mac·ro·cy·to·sis (măk′rō-sī-tō′sĭs) *n., pl.* **-ses** (-sēz). The presence of macrocytes in the blood. **—mac′ro·cy·tot′ic** (-tŏt′ĭk) *adj.*

mac·ro·ec·o·nom·ics (măk′rō-ĕk′ə-nŏm′ĭks, -ē′kə-) *n. (used with a sing. verb).* The study of the overall aspects and workings of a national economy, such as income, output, and the interrelationship among diverse economic sectors. **—mac′ro·ec′o·nom′ic** *adj.* **—mac′ro·e·con′o·mist** (-ĭ-kŏn′ə-mĭst) *n.*

mac·ro·ev·o·lu·tion (măk′rō-ĕv′ə-lo͞o′shən, -ē′və-) *n.* Large-scale evolution occurring over geologic time that results in the formation of new taxonomic groups. **—mac′ro·ev′o·lu′tion·ar′y** (-shə-nĕr′ē) *adj.*

mac·ro·fos·sil (măk′rō-fŏs′əl) *n.* A fossil large enough to be examined without a microscope.

mac·ro·gam·ete (măk′rō-găm′ēt, -gə-mēt′) *n.* The larger, usually female of two conjugating gametes in a heterogamous organism. Also called *megagamete.*

mac·ro·glob·u·lin (măk′rō-glŏb′yə-lĭn) *n.* A plasma globulin of high molecular weight.

mac·ro·glob·u·lin·e·mi·a (măk′rō-glŏb′yə-lə-nē′mē-ə) *n.* The presence of an abnormally large amount of macroglobulins in the blood serum.

Machu Picchu

mackerel
Atlantic mackerel
Scomber scombrus

mackinaw

ă pat	oi boy
ā pay	ou out
âr care	o͝o took
ä father	o͞o boot
ĕ pet	ŭ cut
ē be	ûr urge
ĭ pit	th thin
ī pie	*th* this
îr pier	hw which
ŏ pot	zh vision
ō toe	ə about, item
ô paw	♦ regionalism

Stress marks: ′ (primary); ′ (secondary), as in **dictionary** (dĭk′shə-nĕr′ē)

mac·ro·graph (măk′rō-grăf′) *n.* A representation of an object that is at least as large as the object.

ma·crog·ra·phy (mə-krŏg′rə-fē) *n.* **1.** Examination of objects with the unaided eye. **2.** Abnormally large handwriting, sometimes indicating a nervous disorder.

mac·ro·in·struc·tion (măk′rō-ĭn-strŭk′shən) *n. Computer Science.* A macro.

mac·ro·mere (măk′rə-mîr′) *n. Embryology.* A large blastomere. [MACRO– + (BLASTO)MERE.]

mac·ro·mol·e·cule (măk′rō-mŏl′ĭ-kyo͞ol′) *n.* A very large molecule, such as a polymer or protein, consisting of many smaller structural units linked together. Also called *supermolecule.* **—mac′ro·mo·lec′u·lar** (-mə-lĕk′yə-lər) *adj.*

ma·cron (mā′krŏn′, -krən, măk′rŏn′) *n.* **1.** A diacritical mark placed above a vowel to indicate a long sound or phonetic value in pronunciation, such as (ā) in the word *make.* **2.** The horizontal mark (¯) used to indicate a stressed or long syllable in a foot of verse. [Greek *makron,* from neuter of *makros,* long. See **māk-** in Appendix.]

mac·ro·nu·cle·us (măk′rō-no͞o′klē-əs, -nyo͞o′-) *n., pl.* **-cle·i** (-klē-ī′). The larger of two nuclei present in ciliate protozoans, which controls nonreproductive functions of the cell, such as metabolism. **—mac′ro·nu′cle·ar** *adj.*

mac·ro·nu·tri·ent (măk′rō-no͞o′trē-ənt, -nyo͞o′-) *n.* An element, such as carbon, hydrogen, oxygen, or nitrogen, required in large proportion for the normal growth and development of a plant.

mac·ro·phage (măk′rə-fāj′) *n.* Any of the large phagocytic cells of the reticuloendothelial system. **—mac′ro·phag′ic** (-făj′ĭk) *adj.*

mac·ro·phys·ics (măk′rō-fĭz′ĭks) *n. (used with a sing. verb).* The branch of physics that deals with objects and phenomena large enough to be measured and observed.

mac·ro·phyte (măk′rə-fīt′) *n.* A macroscopic plant. **—mac′ro·phyt′ic** (-fĭt′ĭk) *adj.*

ma·crop·ter·ous (mə-krŏp′tər-əs) *adj.* Having very large fins or wings. [From Greek *makropteros* : *makro-,* macro- + *-pteros,* winged (from *pteron,* wing; see –PTER).]

mac·ro·scop·ic (măk′rə-skŏp′ĭk) also **mac·ro·scop·i·cal** (-ĭ-kəl) *adj.* **1.** Large enough to be perceived or examined by the unaided eye. **2.** Relating to observations made by the unaided eye. **—mac′ro·scop′i·cal·ly** *adv.*

macroscopic anatomy *n.* See **gross anatomy.**

mac·ro·spo·ran·gi·um (măk′rō-spə-răn′jē-əm) *n., pl.* **-gi·a** (-jē-ə). See **megasporangium.**

mac·ro·spore (măk′rə-spôr′, -spōr′) *n.* See **megaspore.**

mac·u·la (măk′yə-lə) *n., pl.* **-lae** (-lē′) or **-las. 1.** Also **mac·ule** (-yo͞ol′). A spot, stain, or blemish, especially an area of discoloration on the skin caused by excess or lack of pigment. **2.** *Anatomy.* A small area distinguishable from the surrounding tissue. **3.** A sunspot. [Middle English, from Latin.] **—mac′u·lar** *adj.*

macula lu·te·a (lo͞o′tē-ə) *n., pl.* **maculae lu·te·ae** (lo͞o′tē-ē′). A minute yellowish area containing the forea centralis located near the center of the retina of the eye at which visual perception is most acute. Also called *yellow spot.* [New Latin *macula lūtea* : Latin *macula,* spot + Latin *lūtea,* yellow.]

mac·u·late (măk′yə-lāt′) *tr.v.* **-lat·ed, -lat·ing, -lates.** To spot, blemish, or pollute. **—maculate** (-lĭt) *adj.* **1.** Spotted or blotched. **2.** Stained; impure. [Middle English *maculaten,* from Latin *maculāre, maculāt-,* from *macula,* spot.]

mac·u·la·tion (măk′yə-lā′shən) *n.* **1.** The act of spotting or staining or the condition of being spotted or stained. **2.** The spotted markings of a plant or an animal, such as the spots of the leopard.

mac·ule¹ (măk′yo͞ol′) *n. & v.* Variant of **mackle.**

mac·ule² (măk′yo͞ol′) *n.* Variant of **macula** (sense 1).

mad (măd) *adj.* **mad·der, mad·dest. 1.** Angry; resentful. See Synonyms at **angry. 2.** Suffering from a disorder of the mind; insane. **3.** Temporarily or apparently deranged by violent sensations, emotions, or ideas: *mad with jealousy.* **4.** Lacking restraint or reason; foolish: *I was mad to have hired her in the first place.* **5.** Feeling or showing strong liking or enthusiasm: *mad about sports.* **6.** Marked by extreme excitement, confusion, or agitation; frantic: *a mad scramble for the bus.* **7.** Boisterously gay; hilarious: *had a mad time.* **8.** Affected by rabies; rabid. **—mad** *tr. & intr.v.* **mad·ded, mad·ding, mads.** To make or become mad; madden. **—*idioms.* like mad.** *Informal.* **1.** Wildly; impetuously: *drove like mad.* **2.** To an intense degree or great extent: *worked like mad; snowing like mad.* **mad as a hatter.** Crazy; deranged. [Middle English, from Old English *gemǣdde,* past participle of **gemǣdan,* to madden, from *gemād,* insane. See **mei-¹** in Appendix.] **—mad′dish** *adj.*

MAD (măd) *n.* Mutual assured destruction.

Mad·a·gas·car (măd′ə-găs′kər). Formerly **Mal·a·gas·y Republic** (măl′ə-găs′ē). *Abbr.* **Mad., Madag.** An island country in the Indian Ocean off the southeast coast of Africa comprising the island of **Madagascar** and several small islands. The French first established settlements on the island in 1642 and made it a colony in 1896. The country gained full independence as the Malagasy Republic in 1960 and was renamed Madagascar in 1975. Antananarivo is the capital and the largest city. Population, 9,230,000. **—Mad′a·gas′can** *adj. & n.*

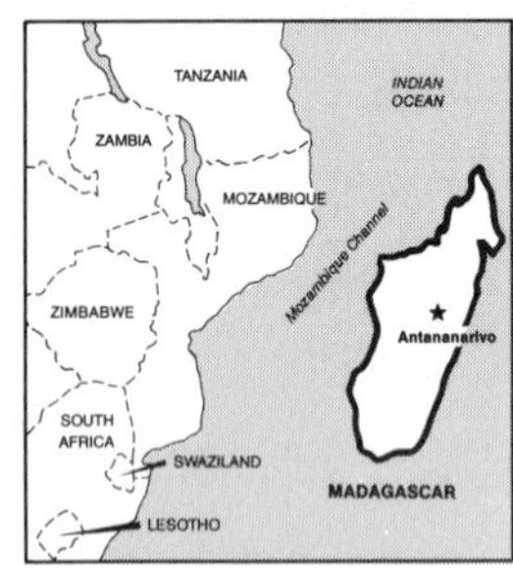

Madagascar

Madagascar periwinkle *n.* A perennial plant *(Catharanthus roseus)* native to Madagascar and India, having pink or white flowers with a salverform corolla and opposite leaves. It is poisonous to domestic animals and is the source of certain substances used in the treatment of cancer. Also called *rose periwinkle.*

Mad·am (măd′əm) *n. Abbr.* **Mdm. 1.** *pl.* **Mes·dames** (mā-dăm′, -däm′) Used formerly as a courtesy title before a woman's given name but now used only before a surname or title indicating rank or office: *Madam Ambassador.* **2.** Used as a salutation in a letter: *Dear Madam or Sir.* **3. madam.** Used as a form of polite address for a woman: *Right this way, madam.* **4. madam.** The mistress of a household. **5. madam.** A woman who manages a brothel. [Middle English *madame,* from Old French *ma dame.* See MADAME.]

Ma·dame (mə-dăm′, măd′əm) *n., pl.* **Mes·dames** or **mes·dames** (mā-dăm′, -däm′). *Abbr.* **Mme. 1.** Used as a courtesy title before the surname or full name of a married woman in a French-speaking area: *Madame Cartier; Madame Jacqueline Cartier.* **2. madame.** Used as a form of polite address for a woman in a French-speaking area. [French, from Old French *ma dame* : *ma,* my (from Latin *mea,* feminine of *meus;* see **me-¹** in Appendix) + *dame,* lady (from Latin *domina,* feminine of *dominus,* lord, master of a household; see **dem-** in Appendix).]

mad·cap (măd′kăp′) *adj.* Behaving or acting impulsively or rashly; wild. [MAD + CAP¹, head.] **—mad′cap′** *n.*

MADD *abbr.* Mothers Against Drunk Driving.

mad·den (măd′n) *v.* **-dened, -den·ing, -dens.** *—tr.* **1.** To make angry; irritate. **2.** To drive insane. *—intr.* To become infuriated.

mad·den·ing (măd′n-ĭng) *adj.* **1.** Tending to anger or irritate: *a maddening delay at the airport.* **2.** Tending to drive insane. **—mad′den·ing·ly** *adv.*

mad·der (măd′ər) *n.* **1.a.** A southwest Asian perennial plant *(Rubia tinctorum)* having small yellow flowers, whorled leaves, and a red root. **b.** The root of this plant, formerly an important source of the dye alizarin. **c.** A red dye obtained from the roots of this plant. **2.** *Color.* A medium to strong red or reddish orange. [Middle English, from Old English *mædere.*]

mad·ding (măd′ĭng) *adj. Archaic.* In a state of frenzy; frenzied: *"far from the madding crowd's ignoble strife"* (Thomas Gray).

mad-dog skullcap (măd′dôg′, -dŏg′) *n.* A North American perennial plant *(Scutellaria lateriflora)* having one-sided clusters of two-lipped blue or white flowers. [So called from its use as an antispasmodic.]

made (mād) *v.* Past tense and past participle of **make. —made** *adj.* **1.** Produced or manufactured by constructing, shaping, or forming. Often used in combination: *handmade lace; ready-made suits.* **2.** Produced or created artificially: *bought some made goods at the local store.* **3.** Having been invented; contrived: *These made excuses of yours just won't wash.* **4.** Assured of success: *a made man.* **—*idiom.* made for.** Perfectly suited for: *They're made for each other.*

Ma·dei·ra¹ (mə-dîr′ə, -dĕr′ə). A river of northwest Brazil rising on the Bolivian border and flowing about 3,315 km (2,060 mi) generally northeast to the Amazon River near Manaus.

Ma·dei·ra² (mə-dîr′ə) *n.* A fortified dessert wine, especially from the island of Madeira.

Madeira Islands. An archipelago of Portugal in the northeast Atlantic Ocean west of Morocco. Only two of the volcanic islands are inhabited. The island of **Madeira** is a tourist center noted for its wine. **—Ma·dei′ran** *adj. & n.*

Madeira vine *n.* A tropical South American ornamental vine *(Anredera cordifolia)* having small, white, fragrant flowers.

mad·e·leine (măd′ə-lĕn′) *n.* A small, rich cake, baked in a shell-shaped mold. [After *Madeleine* Paulmier, 19th-century French pastry cook.]

Mad·e·moi·selle (măd′ə-mə-zĕl′, măd-mwä-zĕl′) *n., pl.* **Mad·e·moi·selles** (-zĕlz) or **Mes·de·moi·selles** (mād′mwä-zĕl′). *Abbr.* **Mlle. 1.** Used as a courtesy title before the surname or full name of a girl or an unmarried woman in a French-speaking area: *Mademoiselle Turot; Mademoiselle Isabelle Turot.* **2. mademoiselle.,** *pl.* **mademoiselles** or **mesdemoiselles** Used as a form of polite address for a girl or young woman in a French-speaking area. **3. mademoiselle.,** *pl.* **mademoiselles.** A French governess. **4. mademoiselle.,** *pl.* **mademoiselle** or **-selles** See **silver perch.** [French, from Old French *ma demoiselle* : *ma,* my; see MADAME + *demoiselle,* young lady (from Old French *damisele,* from Vulgar Latin **dominicella,* diminutive of Latin *domina,* lady, feminine of *dominus,* master of a household; see **dem-** in Appendix).]

Ma·de·ra (mə-dĕr′ə). A city of central California in the San Joaquin Valley northwest of Fresno. Population, 21,732.

Ma·de·ro (mə-dĕr′ō, mä-*thĕ*′rô), **Francisco Indalecio.** 1873–1913. Mexican revolutionary and politician who forced the resignation of Porfirio Díaz and assumed the presidency (1911). He was overthrown and imprisoned (1913) and was killed while reportedly attempting to escape.

made-to-or·der (măd′to͞o-ôr′dər) *adj.* **1.** Made in accordance with particular instructions or requirements; custom-made. **2.** Very suitable: *a made-to-order job.*

made-up (măd′ŭp′) *adj.* **1.** Having been fabricated; invented: *a made-up story.* **2.** Changed or adorned by the application of

ă pat	oi boy
ā pay	ou out
âr care	o͝o took
ä father	o͞o boot
ĕ pet	ŭ cut
ē be	ûr urge
ĭ pit	th thin
ī pie	*th* this
îr pier	hw which
ŏ pot	zh vision
ō toe	ə about, item
ô paw	♦ regionalism

Stress marks: **′** (primary); ′ (secondary), as in **dictionary** (dĭk′shə-nĕr′ē)

cosmetics or makeup: *a made-up actor.* **3.a.** Complete; finished: *a made-up package.* **b.** Put together; arranged: *a made-up page of type.*

mad·house (măd′hous′) *n.* **1.** A mental health facility. **2.** *Informal.* A place of great disorder and confusion.

Mad·i·son (măd′ĭ-sən). The capital of Wisconsin, in the south-central part of the state west of Milwaukee. The main branch of the University of Wisconsin (founded 1848) is here. Population, 170,616.

Madison, Dolley Payne Todd. 1768–1849. First Lady of the United States (1809–1817) as the wife of President James Madison. She earlier served as White House hostess for the widowed Thomas Jefferson. During the British invasion of Washington, D.C. (1814), she heroically carried important government papers and a portrait of George Washington to safety.

Madison, James. 1751–1836. The fourth President of the United States (1809–1817). A member of the Continental Congress (1780–1783) and the Constitutional Convention (1787), he supported ratification of the Constitution and was a contributor to *The Federalist Papers* (1787–1788). His presidency was marked by the War of 1812. **—Mad′i·so′ni·an** (-sō′nē-ən) *adj.*

Madison Avenue *n.* The American advertising industry. **—Madison Avenue** *adj.* Of, relating to, or working in the American advertising industry. [After *Madison Avenue* in New York City, the center of American advertising.]

Madison Heights. A city of southeast Michigan, a suburb of Detroit. Population, 35,375.

Mad·i·son·ville (măd′ĭ-sən-vĭl′). A city of western Kentucky north of Hopkinsville. It is a processing center in a coal and farm area. Population, 16,979.

mad·ly (măd′lē) *adv.* **1.** In a crazy way; insanely. **2.** In a wild manner; frantically. **3.** In a foolish manner; rashly.

mad·man (măd′măn′, -mən) *n.* A man who is or seems to be mentally ill.

mad money *n. Slang.* A small sum of money kept for unlikely contingencies.

mad·ness (măd′nĭs) *n.* **1.** The quality or condition of being insane. See Synonyms at **insanity.** **2.** Great folly: *It was sheer madness to attempt the drive during a blizzard.* **3.** Fury; rage. **4.** Enthusiasm; excitement.

Ma·don·na (mə-dŏn′ə) *n.* **1.** The Virgin Mary. **2.** *Obsolete.* Used as a form of polite address for a married woman in an Italian-speaking area. [Italian : *mia, ma,* my (from Latin *mea;* see MADAME) + *donna,* lady (from Latin *domina,* feminine of *dominus,* master of a household; see **dem-** in Appendix).]

Madonna lily *n.* An eastern Mediterranean plant *(Lilium candidum)* having white, bell-shaped flowers that yield an essential oil used in perfumery. [From its frequent appearance in paintings of the Madonna.]

mad·ras (măd′rəs, mə-drăs′, -dräs′) *n.* **1.** A cotton cloth of fine texture, usually with a plaid, striped, or checked pattern. **2.** A silk, generally striped, cloth. **3.a.** A light cotton cloth used for drapery. **b.** A similar cloth of rayon. **4.** A large handkerchief of brightly colored silk or cotton, often worn as a turban. [After MADRAS.]

Ma·dras (mə-drăs′, -dräs′). A city of southeast India on the Coromandel Coast of the Bay of Bengal. Founded in 1639 as Fort St. George by the British East India Company, Madras was held by the French from 1746 to 1748. Population, 3,276,622.

Ma·dre de Di·os (mä′drā dā dē-ōs′, mä′thrĕ thĕ dyôs′). A river, about 1,126 km (700 mi) long, of southeast Peru and northwest Bolivia flowing northeast from the Andes to the Beni River.

mad·re·pore (măd′rə-pôr′, -pōr′) *n.* Any of various stony corals of the order Madreporaria, which includes the reef builders of tropical seas. [Italian *madrepora* : *madre,* mother (from Latin *māter, mātr-;* see **māter-** in Appendix) + *-pora* (alteration of *poro,* tufa, pore, from Late Latin *porus,* passageway; see PORE[2], or from Latin *pōrus,* calcareous stone, stalactite, from Greek *pōros*).] **—mad′re·po′ri·an** *adj.* **—mad′re·por′ic** *adj.*

mad·re·por·ite (măd′rə-pôr′ĭt, -pōr′-) *n.* A perforated platelike structure in most echinoderms that forms the intake for their water-vascular systems. [So called because the perforations resemble those of a madrepore.]

Ma·drid (mə-drĭd′). The capital and largest city of Spain, on the central plateau north-northeast of Toledo. Built on the site of a Moorish fortress captured in the 10th century, it became the capital in 1561 during the reign of Philip II and grew in importance and magnificence under the Bourbons in the 18th century. Population, 3,200,234.

mad·ri·gal (măd′rĭ-gəl) *n.* **1.a.** *Music.* An unaccompanied vocal composition for two or three voices in simple harmony, following a strict poetic form, developed in Italy in the late 13th and early 14th centuries. **b.** A short poem, often about love, suitable for being set to music. **2.** *Music.* **a.** A typically unaccompanied polyphonic part song using a secular text and intended for four to six voices, developed in Italy in the 16th century and very popular in England in the 16th and early 17th centuries. Sometimes a string accompaniment doubles or replaces one or more of the vocal parts. **b.** A part song. [Italian *madrigale,* probably from dialectal *madregal,* simple, from Late Latin *mātrīcālis,* invented, original, from Latin, of the womb, from *mātrīx, mātrīc-,* womb, from *māter, mātr-,* mother. See MATER.] **—mad′ri·gal·ist** *n.*

ma·dri·lène also **ma·dri·lene** (măd′rĭ-lĕn′) *n.* A consommé flavored with tomato, often served jellied and chilled. [French *(consommé) madrilène,* Madrid (consommé), from Spanish *madrileño,* of Madrid, from MADRID.]

ma·dro·ña (mə-drō′nyə) also **ma·dro·ño** (-drō′nyō) or **ma·dro·ne** (-drō′nə) *n., pl.* **-ñas** also **-ños** or **-nes.** An evergreen tree *(Arbutus menziesii)* native to Pacific North America, having leathery, glossy leaves, white urn-shaped flowers, and orange or red edible berries. The wood has been used for making furniture and the bark for tanning. [American Spanish, from Spanish *madroño,* strawberry tree.]

mad tom *n.* Any of several small freshwater North American catfishes of the genus *Noturus,* having poisonous spines and common in the east-central United States. [MAD + TOM(CAT).]

Ma·du·rai (mä′də-rī′, măd′yo͝o-rī′). A city of southern India south-southwest of Madras. Known as "the City of Festivals and Temples," it is a Hindu pilgrimage site. Population, 820,891.

mad·wom·an (măd′wo͝om′ən) *n.* A woman who is or seems to be mentally ill.

mad·wort (măd′wûrt′, -wôrt′) *n.* **1.** A low-growing Eurasian plant *(Asperugo procumbens)* having rough stems and small blue flowers. **2.** See **alyssum** (sense 2).

M.A.E. *abbr.* **1.** Master of Aeronautical Engineering. **2.** Master of Art Education. **3.** Master of Arts in Education.

Mae·an·der (mē-ăn′dər). An ancient name for the Menderes River of western Turkey.

Mae·ce·nas (mē-sē′nəs, mī-), **Gaius.** 70?–8 B.C. Roman politician and patron of Horace and Virgil.

M.A.Ed. *abbr.* Master of Arts in Education.

mael·strom (māl′strəm) *n.* **1.** A violent or turbulent situation: *caught in the maelstrom of war.* **2.** A whirlpool of extraordinary size or violence. [Obsolete Dutch : Dutch *malen,* to grind, whirl (from Middle Dutch; see **melə-** in Appendix) + Dutch *stroom,* stream (from Middle Dutch; see **sreu-** in Appendix).]

mae·nad (mē′năd′) *n.* **1.** *Greek Mythology.* A woman member of the orgiastic cult of Dionysus. **2.** A frenzied woman. [Latin *Maenas, Maenad-,* from Greek *mainas,* raving, madwoman, Maenad, from *mainesthai,* to be mad. See **men-**[1] in Appendix.]

ma·es·to·so (mä′ĕs-tō′sō, -zō) *adv. & adj. Music.* In a majestic and stately manner. Used chiefly as a direction. [Italian, from *maestà,* majesty, greatness, from Latin *māiestās.* See **meg-** in Appendix.]

maes·tro (mīs′trō) *n., pl.* **-tros** or **-tri** (-trē). A master in an art, especially a composer, conductor, or music teacher. [Italian, from Latin *magister, magistr-,* master. See **meg-** in Appendix.]

Mae·ter·linck (mā′tər-lĭngk′, mĕt′ər-, mä-tĕr-lăN′), Count **Maurice.** 1862–1949. Belgian writer of poetry, a wide variety of essays, and symbolic dramas, including *Pelléas et Mélisande* (1892). He won the 1911 Nobel Prize for literature.

Mae West (mā′ wĕst′) *n.* An inflatable, vestlike life preserver. [After Mae WEST (from its resemblance to her curvaceous torso).]

Maf·e·king (mä′fĭ-kĭng′). Now **Maf·i·keng** (-kĕng′). A town of north-central South Africa west of Pretoria. The relief (May 17, 1900) of a 217-day-long siege of the British garrison here was a celebrated event of the Boer War. Population, 6,500.

maf·fick (măf′ĭk) *intr.v.* **-ficked, -fick·ing, -ficks.** *Chiefly British.* To rejoice or celebrate with boisterous public demonstrations. [After MAFEKING.]

Ma·fi·a (mä′fē-ə) *n.* **1.** A secret terrorist organization in Sicily, operating since the early 19th century in opposition to legal authority: *"Rome they despised, the Mafia they feared, but not to submission"* (Mario Puzo). **2.** An alleged international criminal organization believed active, especially in Italy and the United States, since the late 19th century. **3.** Often **mafia.** *Informal.* A tightly knit group of trusted associates, as of a political leader: *"[He] is one of the personal mafia that* [the chancellor] *brought with him to Bonn"* (Christian Science Monitor). *—attributive.* Often used to modify another noun: *a Mafia overlord; a Mafia organization.* [Italian, perhaps from dialectal *mafia,* bluster, boldness.]

maf·ic (măf′ĭk) *adj.* Containing or relating to a group of dark-colored minerals, composed chiefly of magnesium and iron, that occur in igneous rocks. [MA(GNESIUM) + Latin *ferrum,* iron + -IC.]

Maf·i·keng (mä′fĭ-kĕng′). See **Mafeking.**

Ma·fi·o·so (mä′fē-ō′sō) *n., pl.* **-si** (-sē) or **-sos.** A member of the Mafia. [Italian, from *mafia,* mafia. See MAFIA.]

mag (măg) *n. Slang.* A magazine: *surfing mags.*

mag. *abbr.* **1.** Magnet. **2.** Magnetism. **3.** Magneto. **4.** Magnitude.

Ma·ga·dha (mä′gə-də). An ancient kingdom of northeast India. It was especially powerful from the fourth century B.C. to the fifth century A.D.

mag·a·zine (măg′ə-zēn′, măg′ə-zēn′) *n.* **1.** A periodical containing a collection of articles, stories, pictures, or other features. **2.a.** A place where goods are stored, especially a building in a fort or a storeroom on a warship where ammunition is kept. **b.** The contents of a storehouse, especially a stock of ammunition. **3.a.** A compartment in some types of firearms, often a small detachable box, in which cartridges are held to be fed into the firing chamber. **b.** A compartment in a camera in which rolls or cartridges of film are held for feeding through the exposure mechanism. **c.** Any of various compartments attached to machines, used for storing or supplying necessary material. **—magazine** *adj.* Of

Dolley Madison
Detail of an 1804 portrait by Gilbert Stuart

James Madison

Madonna
The Small Cowper Madonna by Raphael

madroña
Arbutus menziesii

Magen David

16	3	2	13
5	10	11	8
9	6	7	12
4	15	14	1

magic square
After a magic square in Albrecht Dürer's engraving *Melancolia I*

or relating to periodicals: *a magazine story.* [French *magasin,* storehouse, from Old French *magazin* (possibly via Old Italian *magazzino*), from Arabic *maḫāzin,* pl. of *maḫzan,* from *ḫazana,* to store.]

Mag·da·le·na (măg′də-lā′nə, mäg′thä-lĕ′nä). A river rising in the Andes of southwest Colombia and flowing about 1,601 km (1,000 mi) generally northward to the Caribbean Sea.

Mag·da·le·ni·an (măg′də-lē′nē-ən) *adj. Archaeology.* Of or relating to the last upper Paleolithic culture of Europe, succeeding the Aurignacian. [French *magdalénien,* after La *Madeleine,* a prehistoric site of southwest France.]

Mag·de·burg (măg′də-bûrg′, mäg′də-bo͝ork′). A city of central Germany on the Elbe River west-southwest of Berlin. Known as early as 805, it was chartered in the 13th century and one of the chief cities of the Hanseatic League. Population, 289,075.

Ma·gel·lan (mə-jĕl′ən), **Ferdinand.** 1480?–1521. Portuguese navigator. While trying to find a western route to the Moluccas (1519), Magellan and his expedition were blown by storms into the strait that now bears his name (1520). He named and sailed across the Pacific Ocean, reaching the Marianas and the Philippines (1521), where he was killed fighting for a friendly native king. One of his ships returned to Spain (1522), thereby completing the first circumnavigation of the globe.

Magellan, Strait of. A channel separating South America from Tierra del Fuego and other islands south of the continent and connecting the southern Atlantic and Pacific oceans.

Mag·el·lan·ic Clouds (măj′ə-lăn′ĭk) *pl.n.* Two small, irregularly shaped galaxies that are the galaxies closest to the Milky Way and are faintly visible near the south celestial pole. [After Ferdinand MAGELLAN.]

Ma·gen Da·vid also **Mo·gen Da·vid** (mō′gən dô′vĭd, dā′-vĭd, mä-gĕn′ dä-vēd′) *n.* A six-pointed star, the symbol of Judaism, that is formed by placing two triangles together, one inverted over the other or interlaced. Also called *Shield of David, Star of David.* [Hebrew *māgēn dāwid.*]

ma·gen·ta (mə-jĕn′tə) *n.* **1.** See **fuchsin. 2.** *Color.* A moderate to vivid purplish red. [After *Magenta,* a town of northwest Italy.]

Mag·gio·re (mə-jôr′ē, -jōr′ē, mäd-jô′rĕ), **Lake.** A lake of northern Italy and southern Switzerland. Nearly surrounded by peaks of the Lepontine Alps, it is a major resort area.

mag·got (măg′ət) *n.* **1.** The legless, soft-bodied, wormlike larva of any of various flies of the order Diptera, often found in decaying matter. **2.** *Slang.* A despicable person. **3.** An extravagant notion; a whim. [Middle English *magot,* perhaps alteration of *mathek, maddokk,* perhaps from Old English *matha.*] **—mag′got·y** *adj.*

Ma·ghreb or **Ma·ghrib** (mŭg′rəb). A region of northwest Africa comprising the coastlands and the Atlas Mountains of Morocco, Algeria, and Tunisia.

ma·gi (mā′jī′) *n.* Plural of **magus.**

mag·ic (măj′ĭk) *n.* **1.** The art that purports to control or forecast natural events, effects, or forces by invoking the supernatural. **2.a.** The practice of using charms, spells, or rituals to attempt to produce supernatural effects or control events in nature. **b.** The charms, spells, and rituals so used. **3.** The exercise of sleight of hand or conjuring for entertainment. **4.** A mysterious quality of enchantment: *"For me the names of those men breathed the magic of the past"* (Max Beerbohm). **—magic** *adj.* **1.** Of, relating to, or invoking the supernatural: *"stubborn unlaid ghost/ That breaks his magic chains at curfew time"* (John Milton). **2.** Possessing distinctive qualities that produce unaccountable or baffling effects. **—magic** *tr.v.* **-icked, -ick·ing, -ics.** To produce or make by or as if by magic. [Middle English *magik,* from Old French *magique,* from Late Latin *magica,* from Latin *magicē,* from Greek *magikē,* from feminine of *magikos,* Magian, magical, from *magos,* magician, magus. See MAGUS.]

mag·i·cal (măj′ĭ-kəl) *adj.* **1.** Of, relating to, or produced by magic. **2.** Enchanting; bewitching: *a magical performance of the ballet.* **—mag′i·cal·ly** *adv.*

magic bullet *n. Slang.* **1.** A drug, therapy, or preventive therapy that cures or prevents a disease: *"There is no magic bullet against cancer"* (Matt Clark). **2.** Something regarded as a magical solution to a grave problem or as a means of averting a disaster: *"Something new must be tried to discourage drug use. There is clearly no magic bullet"* (Larry Martz).

ma·gi·cian (mə-jĭsh′ən) *n.* **1.** A sorcerer; a wizard. **2.** One who performs magic for entertainment or diversion. **3.** One whose formidable skill or art seems to be magical: *a magician with words.*

magic lantern *n.* An optical device formerly used to project an enlarged image of a picture.

magic number *n. Physics & Chemistry.* **1.** Any of the numbers, 2, 8, 20, 28, 50, 82, or 126, that represent the number of neutrons or protons in strongly bound, exceptionally stable, and abundant atomic nuclei. **2.** *Sports.* The number of wins required in order to capture a division title.

magic square *n.* A square that contains numbers arranged in equal rows and columns in such a way that the sum of each row or column, taken vertically, horizontally, or diagonally, is the same.

Ma·gi·not (măzh′ə-nō′, măj′-, mä-zhē-nō′), **André.** 1877–1932. French politician who as minister of war (1922–1924 and 1929–1932) proposed a line of fortification, called the Maginot Line, along France's border with Germany. Thought to be impregnable, the line was later captured by the Germans (1940).

mag·is·te·ri·al (măj′ĭ-stîr′ē-əl) *adj.* **1.a.** Of, relating to, or characteristic of a master or teacher; authoritative: *a magisterial account of the history of the English language.* **b.** Sedately dignified in appearance or manner: *"She would appear on the porch and reign over the street in magisterial beauty"* (Harper Lee). **2.** Dogmatic; overbearing: *managed the employees in an aloof, magisterial way.* **3.** Of or relating to a magistrate or a magistrate's official functions. [Late Latin *magisteriālis,* from *magisterius,* from Latin *magister,* master, teacher. See **meg-** in Appendix.] **—mag′is·te′ri·al·ly** *adv.*

mag·is·te·ri·um (măj′ĭ-stîr′ē-əm) *n. Roman Catholic Church.* The authority to teach religious doctrine. [Latin, the office of a teacher or other person in authority, from *magister,* master. See MAGISTERIAL.]

mag·is·tra·cy (măj′ĭs-trə-sē) *n., pl.* **-cies. 1.** The position, function, or term of office of a magistrate. **2.** A body of magistrates. **3.** The district under jurisdiction of a magistrate.

mag·is·tral (măj′ĭ-strəl) *adj.* **1.** Of or relating to a magistrate; magisterial. **2.** Prepared as specified by a physician's prescription. Used of medicine. **3.** Principal; main: *the magistral line of fortifications.* [Late Latin *magistrālis,* belonging to a master, from Latin *magister, magistr-,* former chief officer of a college or band of priests. See **meg-** in Appendix.]

mag·is·trate (măj′ĭ-strāt′, -strĭt) *n.* A civil officer with power to administer and enforce law, as: **a.** A local member of the judiciary having limited jurisdiction, especially in criminal cases. **b.** A minor official, such as a justice of the peace, having administrative and limited judicial authority. [Middle English *magistrat,* from Old French, from Latin *magistrātus,* from *magister, magistr-,* master. See **meg-** in Appendix.]

Ma·gle·mo·si·an (mä′glə-mō′zē-ən) *adj. Archaeology.* Of or relating to a Mesolithic forest culture of northern Europe. [After *Maglemose,* a Mesolithic site on the western coast of Sjaelland, Denmark.]

mag·lev or **Mag·lev** (măg′lĕv) *n.* Magnetic levitation.

mag·ma (măg′mə, mäg′-) *n., pl.* **-ma·ta** (-mä′tə) or **-mas. 1.** A mixture of finely divided solids with enough liquid to produce a pasty mass. **2.** *Geology.* The molten rock material under the earth's crust, from which igneous rock is formed by cooling. **3.** *Pharmacology.* A suspension of particles in a liquid, such as milk of magnesia. **4.** The residue of fruits after the juice has been expressed; pomace. [Middle English, sediment, dregs, from Latin, from Greek, unguent, from *massein, mag-,* to knead. See **mag-** in Appendix.] **—mag·mat′ic** (-măt′ĭk) *adj.*

Mag·na Car·ta or **Mag·na Char·ta** (măg′nə kär′tə) *n.* **1.** The charter of English political and civil liberties granted by King John at Runnymede in June 1215. **2.** A document or piece of legislation that is a guarantee of basic rights. [Middle English, from Medieval Latin : Latin *magna,* great + *charta,* charter.]

mag·na cum lau·de (măg′nə ko͝om lou′də) *adv. & adj.* With high honors. Used to express high academic distinction: *graduated magna cum laude; 25 magna cum laude graduates.* [Latin *magnā cum laude,* with great praise : *magnā,* feminine ablative sing. of *magnus,* great + *cum,* with + *laude,* ablative sing. of *laus,* praise.]

Magna Grae·cia (grē′shə). The ancient Greek seaport colonies of southern Italy and Sicily from the eighth to the fourth century B.C. Cumae and Tarantum (modern Taranto) remained significant after the decline of the other colonies.

mag·na·nim·i·ty (măg′nə-nĭm′ĭ-tē) *n., pl.* **-ties. 1.** The quality of being magnanimous. **2.** A magnanimous act.

mag·nan·i·mous (măg-năn′ə-məs) *adj.* **1.** Courageously noble in mind and heart. **2.** Generous in forgiving; eschewing resentment or revenge; unselfish. [From Latin *magnanimus* : *magnus,* great; see **meg-** in Appendix + *animus,* soul, mind; see **ane-** in Appendix.] **—mag·nan′i·mous·ly** *adv.* **—mag·nan′i·mous·ness** *n.*

mag·nate (măg′nāt′, -nĭt) *n.* A powerful or influential person, especially in business or industry: *an oil magnate.* [From Middle English *magnates,* magnates, from Late Latin *magnātēs,* pl. of *magnās,* magnate, from Latin *magnus,* great. See **meg-** in Appendix.]

mag·ne·sia (măg-nē′zhə, -shə) *n.* Magnesium oxide. [Middle English, mineral ingredient of the philosophers' stone, from Medieval Latin *magnēsia,* from Greek *magnēsia,* a kind of ore, from *Magnēsia,* Magnesia, an ancient city of Asia Minor.] **—mag·ne′sian** *adj.*

mag·ne·site (măg′nə-sīt′) *n.* A white, yellowish, or brown mineral, magnesium carbonate, $MgCO_3$, used in the manufacture of magnesium oxide and carbon dioxide.

mag·ne·si·um (măg-nē′zē-əm, -zhəm) *n. Symbol* **Mg** A light, silvery-white, moderately hard metallic element that in ribbon or powder form burns with a brilliant white flame. It is used in structural alloys, pyrotechnics, flash photography, and incendiary bombs. Atomic number 12; atomic weight 24.312; melting point 649°C; boiling point 1,090°C; specific gravity 1.74 (at 20°C); valence 2. See table at **element.** [From MAGNESIA.]

magnesium carbonate *n.* A very light, odorless, white powdery compound, $MgCO_3$, used in a wide variety of manufactured products including inks, glass, dentifrices, and cosmetics.

magnesium hydroxide *n.* A white powder, $Mg(OH)_2$, used as an antacid and a laxative.

magnesium oxide *n.* A white, powdery compound, MgO, having a high melting point (2,800°C), used in high-temperature refractories, electrical insulation, food packaging, cosmetics, and pharmaceuticals.

magnesium sulfate *n.* A colorless, crystalline compound, $MgSO_4$, used in ceramics, matches, explosives, and fertilizers.

mag·net (măg′nĭt) *n. Abbr.* **mag. 1.** An object that is surrounded by a magnetic field and that has the property, either natural or induced, of attracting iron or steel. **2.** An electromagnet. **3.** A person, a place, an object, or a situation that exerts attraction. [Middle English, from Old French *magnete,* from Latin *magnēs, magnēt-,* from Greek *Magnēs (lithos),* Magnesian (stone), magnet, from *Magnēsia,* Magnesia, an ancient city of Asia Minor.]

magnet– *pref.* Variant of **magneto–.**

mag·net·ic (măg-nĕt′ĭk) *adj.* **1.a.** Of or relating to magnetism or magnets. **b.** Having the properties of a magnet. **c.** Capable of being magnetized or attracted by a magnet. **d.** Operating by means of magnetism: *a magnetic recorder.* **2.** Relating to the magnetic poles of the earth: *a magnetic compass bearing.* **3.** Having an unusual power or ability to attract: *a magnetic personality.* **—mag·net′i·cal·ly** *adv.*

magnetic bottle *n.* A magnetic field used to confine plasma, as during nuclear fusion.

magnetic bubble memory *n. Computer Science.* A memory in which data are stored in the form of bubbles, or circular areas, on a thin film of magnetic silicate. Magnetic bubble memory is similar to RAM but does not lose the stored information when the computer is turned off.

magnetic card *n. Computer Science.* A card, such as a bank card for use in an automated teller machine, that has a magnetizable strip or surface on which data can be recorded.

magnetic compass *n.* An instrument that uses a magnetized steel bar to indicate direction relative to the earth's magnetic poles.

magnetic core *n.* See **core** (sense 6b).

magnetic declination *n.* The angle between magnetic north and true north at a particular location. Also called *magnetic variation.*

magnetic dip *n.* The angle that a magnetic needle makes with the horizontal plane at any specific location. Magnetic dip is 0° at the magnetic equator and 90° at each of the magnetic poles. Also called *magnetic inclination.*

magnetic disk *n. Computer Science.* **1.** A memory device covered with a magnetic coating on which information is stored by magnetization of microscopically small needles. **2.** A floppy disk. **3.** A hard disk.

magnetic equator *n.* A line connecting all points on the earth's surface at which a magnetic needle balances horizontally without dipping. Also called *aclinic line.*

magnetic field *n.* A condition found in the region around a magnet or an electric current, characterized by the existence of a detectable magnetic force at every point in the region and by the existence of magnetic poles.

magnetic field strength *n.* **1.** Magnetic intensity. **2.** See **magnetic induction** (sense 1).

magnetic flux *n.* A measure of the quantity of magnetism, being the total number of magnetic lines of force passing through a specified area in a magnetic field.

magnetic flux density *n. Symbol* **B** See **magnetic induction** (sense 1).

magnetic force *n.* **1.** The force exerted between magnetic poles, producing magnetization. **2.** A force that exists between two electrically charged moving particles.

magnetic head *n.* An electromagnet, such as one used in a tape recorder, that converts electrical impulses into variations in the magnetism of a surface for storage and subsequent retrieval.

magnetic inclination *n.* See **magnetic dip.**

magnetic induction *n.* **1.** The amount of magnetic flux in a unit area taken perpendicular to the direction of the magnetic flux. Also called *magnetic field strength, magnetic flux density.* **2.** The process by which a substance, such as iron or steel, becomes magnetized by a magnetic field.

magnetic intensity *n.* A quantity used in describing magnetic phenomena in terms of their magnetic fields and magnetization.

magnetic levitation *n.* A high-speed rail technology by which a train can travel free of friction at speeds of 480 kilometers (300 miles) per hour or more. The train is suspended on a magnetic cushion about half an inch above an elevated magnetic track, whose moving magnetic field alternately attracts and repels magnets mounted on the train, which is pushed and pulled along by this process.

magnetic lines of force *pl.n.* Curved lines used to represent a magnetic field, drawn such that the number of lines is related to the strength of the magnetic field at a given point and the tangent of any curve at a particular point is along the direction of magnetic force at that point.

magnetic meridian *n.* A line passing through both magnetic poles of the earth.

magnetic mine *n.* A marine mine detonated by a mechanism that responds to a mass of magnetic material, such as the steel hull of a ship.

magnetic moment *n.* The product of the pole strength of a magnet and the distance between the poles.

magnetic monopole *n.* A hypothetical particle that has only one pole of magnetic charge instead of the usual two. A magnetic monopole would be a basic unit of magnetic charge.

magnetic needle *n.* A slender bar of magnetized steel usually suspended on a low-friction mounting and used in various instruments, especially in the magnetic compass, to indicate the direction of the earth's magnetic poles.

magnetic north *n. Abbr.* **MN** The direction of the earth's magnetic pole, to which the north-seeking pole of a magnetic needle points when free from local magnetic influence.

magnetic pole *n.* **1.** Either of two limited regions in a magnet at which the magnet's field is most intense, each of which is designated by the approximate geographic direction to which it is attracted. **2.** Either of two variable points on the earth, close to but not coinciding with the geographic poles, where the earth's magnetic field is most intense and toward which a compass needle points.

magnetic pyrites *n.* See **pyrrhotite.**

magnetic recording *n.* **1.** The recording of a signal, such as sound or computer instructions, in the form of a magnetic pattern on a magnetizable surface for storage and subsequent retrieval. **2.** A surface containing a magnetic recording.

magnetic resonance *n.* The phenomenon of absorption of certain frequencies of radio and microwave radiation by atoms placed in a magnetic field. The pattern of absorption reveals molecular structure.

magnetic resonance imaging *n. Abbr.* **MRI** The use of a nuclear magnetic resonance spectrometer to produce electronic images of specific atoms and molecular structures in solids, especially human cells, tissues, and organs.

magnetic storm *n.* A disturbance or fluctuation in the earth's magnetic field, associated with solar flares. Also called *geomagnetic storm.*

magnetic tape *n.* A plastic tape coated with iron oxide for use in magnetic recording.

magnetic variation *n.* **1.** Differences in the earth's magnetic field in time and location. **2.** See **magnetic declination.**

mag·net·ism (măg′nĭ-tĭz′əm) *n. Abbr.* **mag. 1.** The class of phenomena exhibited by a magnetic field. **2.** The study of magnets and their effects. **3.** The force exerted by a magnetic field. **4.** Unusual power to attract, fascinate, or influence: *the magnetism of money.* **5.** Animal magnetism.

mag·net·ite (măg′nĭ-tīt′) *n.* The mineral form of black iron oxide, Fe_3O_4, that often occurs with magnesium, zinc, and manganese and is an important ore of iron.

mag·net·i·za·tion (măg′nĭ-tĭ-zā′shən) *n.* **1.a.** The process of making a substance temporarily or permanently magnetic, as by insertion in a magnetic field. **b.** The extent to which an object is magnetized. **2.** The property of being magnetic.

mag·net·ize (măg′nĭ-tīz′) *tr.v.* **-ized, -iz·ing, -iz·es. 1.** To make magnetic. **2.** To attract, charm, or influence: *a campaign speech that magnetized the crowd.* **—mag′net·iz′a·ble** *adj.* **—mag′net·iz′er** *n.*

mag·ne·to (măg-nē′tō) *n., pl.* **-tos.** *Abbr.* **mag.** A device that produces alternating current for distribution to the spark plugs, used in the ignition systems of some internal-combustion engines. [Short for *magnetoelectric machine.*]

magneto– or **magnet–** *pref.* **1.** Magnetism; magnetic: *magnetoelectric.* **2.** Magnetic field: *magnetometer.* [From MAGNET.]

mag·ne·to·e·lec·tric (măg-nē′tō-ĭ-lĕk′trĭk) *adj.* Of or relating to electricity produced by magnetic means. **—mag·ne′to·e·lec·tric′i·ty** (-ĭ-lĕk-trĭs′ĭ-tē, -ē′lĕk-) *n.*

mag·ne·to·flu·id·dy·nam·ics (măg-nē′tō-flo͞o′ĭd-dī-năm′ĭks) *n. (used with a sing. verb).* Magnetohydrodynamics. **—mag·ne′to·flu′id·dy·nam′ic** *adj.*

mag·ne·to·gas·dy·nam·ics (măg-nē′tō-găs′dī-năm′ĭks) *n. (used with a sing. verb).* Magnetohydrodynamics. **—mag·ne′to·gas′dy·nam′ic** *adj.*

mag·ne·to·graph (măg-nē′tō-grăf′) *n.* A device for detecting and recording variations in the intensity and direction of magnetic fields.

mag·ne·to·hy·dro·dy·nam·ics (măg-nē′tō-hī′drō-dī-năm′ĭks) *n. (used with a sing. verb).* The study of the interaction of magnetic fields and electrically conducting liquids or gases, such as molten metal or plasma. **—mag·ne′to·hy′dro·dy·nam′ic** *adj.*

mag·ne·tom·e·ter (măg′nĭ-tŏm′ĭ-tər) *n.* An instrument for measuring the intensity and direction of a magnetic field. **—mag′ne·to·met′ric** (-tə-mĕt′rĭk) *adj.* **—mag′ne·tom′e·try** *n.*

mag·ne·to·mo·tive force (măg-nē′tō-mō′tĭv) *n. Abbr.* **mmf, m.m.f.** The work that would be required to carry a hypothetical isolated magnetic pole of unit strength completely around a magnetic circuit.

mag·ne·ton (măg′nĭ-tŏn′) *n.* A unit of the magnetic moment of a molecular, atomic, or subatomic particle, especially: **a.** The Bohr magneton, calculated using the mass and charge of the elec-

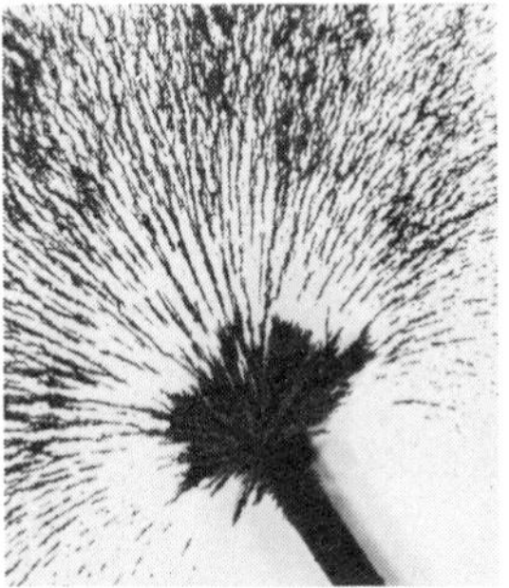

magnetic field
Magnet attracting iron filings

magnetic resonance imaging
Technician with image on screen; patient module in background

ă pat	oi boy
ā pay	ou out
âr care	o͝o took
ä father	o͞o boot
ĕ pet	ŭ cut
ē be	ûr urge
ĭ pit	th thin
ī pie	*th* this
îr pier	hw which
ŏ pot	zh vision
ō toe	ə about, item
ô paw	♦ regionalism

Stress marks: ′ (primary); ′ (secondary), as in **dictionary** (dĭk′shə-nĕr′ē)

tron. **b.** The nuclear magneton, calculated using the mass of the nucleon.

mag·ne·to·pause (măg-nē′tə-pôz′) *n.* The outer boundary of the magnetosphere.

mag·ne·to·plas·ma·dy·nam·ics (măg-nē′tō-plăz′mə-dī-năm′ĭks) *n. (used with a sing. verb).* Magnetohydrodynamics. **—mag·ne′to·plas′ma·dy·nam′ic** *adj.*

mag·ne·to·sphere (măg-nē′tō-sfîr′) *n.* An asymmetrical region surrounding the earth, extending from about one hundred to several thousand kilometers above the surface, in which charged particles are trapped and their behavior is dominated by the earth's magnetic field.

mag·ne·to·stric·tion (măg-nē′tō-strĭk′shən) *n.* Deformation of a ferromagnetic material subjected to a magnetic field. [MAGNETO– + (CON)STRICTION.]

mag·ne·tron (măg′nĭ-trŏn′) *n.* A microwave tube in which electrons generated from a heated cathode are affected by magnetic and electric fields in such a way as to produce microwave radiation used in radar and in microwave ovens. [MAGNE(T) + –TRON.]

magnet school *n.* A public school for students of high academic ability or talent in the visual and performing arts that attracts its student body from all parts of a city, provides a superior education, and serves as a means of desegregation.

mag·nif·ic (măg-nĭf′ĭk) also **mag·nif·i·cal** (-ĭ-kəl) *adj.* **1.** Magnificent. **2.** Imposingly large. **3.** Exalted. **4.** Pompous; grandiloquent. [Middle English *magnifique,* from Old French, from Latin *magnificus* : *magnus,* great; see **meg-** in Appendix + *-ficus,* -fic.] **—mag·nif′i·cal·ly** *adv.*

Mag·nif·i·cat (măg-nĭf′ĭ-kăt′) *n.* **1.a.** The canticle beginning *Magnificat anima mea Dominum* ("My soul doth magnify the Lord"). **b.** A musical setting of this canticle. **2. magnificat.** A hymn or song of praise. [Middle English, from Medieval Latin, from Latin, it magnifies, third person sing. present tense of *magnificāre,* to magnify, extol. See MAGNIFY.]

mag·ni·fi·ca·tion (măg′nə-fĭ-kā′shən) *n.* **1.** The act of magnifying or the state of being magnified. **2.a.** The process of enlarging the size of something, as an optical image. **b.** Something that has been magnified; an enlarged representation, image, or model. **3.** The ratio of the size of an image to the size of an object.

mag·nif·i·cence (măg-nĭf′ĭ-səns) *n.* **1.** Greatness or lavishness of surroundings; splendor. **2.** Grand or imposing beauty.

mag·nif·i·cent (măg-nĭf′ĭ-sənt) *adj.* **1.** Splendid in appearance; grand: *a magnificent palace.* **2.** Grand or noble in thought or deed; exalted. **3.** Outstanding of its kind; superlative: *a magnificent place for sailing.* See Synonyms at **grand.** [Middle English, from Old French, from *magnificence,* splendor, from Latin *magnificentia,* from *magnificus,* magnificent. See MAGNIFIC.] **—mag·nif′i·cent·ly** *adv.*

mag·nif·i·co (măg-nĭf′ĭ-kō′) *n., pl.* **-coes. 1.** A person of distinguished rank, importance, or appearance: *"He is both an old-world and a new-world figure, a feudal magnifico and a modern technocrat"* (Observer). **2.** A nobleman of the Venetian Republic. [Italian, magnificent, magnifico, from Latin *magnificus.* See MAGNIFIC.]

mag·ni·fi·er (măg′nə-fī′ər) *n.* **1.** One that magnifies, especially a magnifying glass. **2.** A system of optical components that magnifies.

mag·ni·fy (măg′nə-fī′) *v.* **-fied, -fy·ing, -fies.** *—tr.* **1.** To make greater in size; enlarge. **2.** To cause to appear greater or seem more important than is in fact the case; exaggerate: *You have grossly magnified a trivial situation.* See Synonyms at **exaggerate. 3.** To increase the apparent size of, especially by means of a lens. **4.** To glorify or praise. *—intr.* To increase or have the power to increase the size or volume of an image or a sound. [Middle English *magnifien,* to extol, from Old French *magnifier,* from Latin *magnificāre,* from *magnificus,* magnificent. See MAGNIFIC.]

magpie
Black-billed magpie
Pica pica

mag·ni·fy·ing glass (măg′nə-fī′ĭng) *n.* A lens or combination of lenses that enlarges the image of an object.

mag·nil·o·quent (măg-nĭl′ə-kwənt) *adj.* Lofty and extravagant in speech; grandiloquent. [From Latin *magniloquentia* : *magnus,* great; see **meg-** in Appendix + *loquēns, loquent-,* present participle of *loquī,* to speak; see **tolkʷ-** in Appendix.] **—mag·nil′o·quence** *n.* **—mag·nil′o·quent·ly** *adv.*

Mag·ni·to·gorsk (măg-nē′tə-gôrsk′, məg-nyĭ-tə-gôrsk′). A city of southwest Russia in the Ural Mountains south-southwest of Chelyabinsk. Population, 422,000.

mag·ni·tude (măg′nĭ-to͞od′, -tyo͞od′) *n. Abbr.* **mag. 1.a.** Greatness of rank or position: *"such duties as were expected of a landowner of his magnitude"* (Anthony Powell). **b.** Greatness in size or extent: *The magnitude of the flood was impossible to comprehend.* **c.** Greatness in significance or influence: *was shocked by the magnitude of the crisis.* **2.** *Astronomy.* The degree of brightness of a celestial body designated on a numerical scale, on which the brightest star has magnitude −1.4 and the faintest visible star has magnitude 6, with the scale rule such that a decrease of one unit represents an increase in apparent brightness by a factor of 2.512. Also called *apparent magnitude.* **3.** *Mathematics.* **a.** A number assigned to a quantity so that it may be compared with other quantities. **b.** A property that can be quantitatively described, such as the volume of a sphere or the length of a vector. **4.** *Geology.* A measure of the amount of energy released by an earthquake, as indicated on the Richter Scale. [Middle English, from Old French, size, from Latin *magnitūdō,* greatness, size, from *magnus,* great. See **meg-** in Appendix.]

mag·no·lia (măg-nōl′yə) *n.* **1.** Any of numerous evergreen or deciduous trees and shrubs of the genus *Magnolia* of the Western Hemisphere and Asia, having aromatic twigs and large showy white, pink, purple, or yellow flowers. **2.** The flower of any of these plants. [New Latin *Magnolia,* genus name, after Pierre *Magnol* (1638–1715), French botanist.]

magnolia warbler *n.* A black-and-yellow songbird *(Dendroica magnolia)* of northern North America that nests in small evergreens.

mag·num (măg′nəm) *n.* **1.** A bottle, holding about two fifths of a gallon (1.5 liters), for wine or liquor. **2.** The amount of liquid that this bottle can hold. [From Latin, neuter of *magnus,* great. See **meg-** in Appendix.]

magnum opus *n.* **1.** A great work, especially a literary or artistic masterpiece. **2.** The greatest single work of an artist, a writer, or a composer. [Latin : *magnum,* neuter of *magnus,* great + *opus,* work.]

mag·nus hitch (măg′nəs) *n.* A clove hitch with one extra turn. [Origin unknown.]

ma·got (mă-gō′, măg′ət) *n.* **1.** See **Barbary ape. 2.** A fanciful, often grotesque figurine in the Japanese or Chinese style rendered in a crouching position. [French, from Old French *magos,* a kind of monkey, from *Magog, Magos,* Magog, name of biblical land (Ezekiel 38–39) and tribe (Revelation 20:8–9), used as an emblem of ugliness in medieval romances.]

mag·pie (măg′pī′) *n.* **1.** Any of various birds of the family Corvidae found worldwide, having a long graduated tail and black, blue, or green plumage with white markings and noted for their chattering call. The species *Pica pica,* the black-billed magpie, is widespread in the Northern Hemisphere. Also called *pie.* **2.** Any of various birds resembling the magpie, such as the Australian bell magpie of the family Cracticidae. **3.** A person who chatters. [*Mag,* a name used in proverbs about chatterers (a nickname for *Margaret*) + PIE².]

M.Agr. *abbr.* Master of Agriculture.

Ma·gritte (mä-grēt′), **René.** 1898–1967. Belgian painter whose surreal works, such as *Steps of Summer* (1938), depict ordinary objects in unexpected or implausible situations.

Mag·say·say (mäg-sī′sī′), **Ramón.** 1907–1957. Philippine politician who served as president (1953–1957).

ma·guey (mə-gā′, măg′wā) *n., pl.* **-gueys. 1.** Any of various American plants of the genus *Agave,* especially the century plant. Also called *mescal.* **2.** Any of various plants of the related genus *Furcraea.* **3.** The fiber obtained from any of these plants. [Spanish, of Cariban origin.]

ma·gus (mā′gəs) *n.* **ma·gi** (mā′jī′). **1.** A member of the Zoroastrian priestly caste of the Medes and Persians. **2. Magus.** One of the three wise men from the East who traveled to Bethlehem to pay homage to the infant Jesus. **3.** A sorcerer; a magician. [From Middle English *magi,* magi, from Latin *magī,* pl. of *magus,* sorcerer, magus, from Greek *magos,* from Old Persian *maguš.* See **magh-** in Appendix.] **—ma′gi·an** (mā′jē-ən) *adj.*

Mag·yar (măg′yär′, mäg′-, mŭd′-) *n.* **1.** A member of the principal ethnic group of Hungary. **2.** See **Hungarian** (sense 2). [Hungarian.] **—Mag′yar** *adj.*

ma·ha·leb (mä′hə-lĕb′) *n.* A small Eurasian ornamental tree *(Prunus mahaleb)* of the rose family, having white flowers and small, ovoid, black drupes with single seeds that are used in Middle Eastern cooking. [Arabic *maḥlab.*]

Ma·hal·la el Ku·bra (mə-hăl′ə ĕl ko͞o′brə). A city of northern Egypt in the Nile River delta north of Cairo. Population, 362,700.

Ma·han (mə-hăn′), **Alfred Thayer.** 1840–1914. American naval officer and historian whose written works, such as *The Influence of Sea Power upon History, 1660–1783* (1890), prompted a worldwide buildup of naval strength prior to World War I.

Ma·ha·na·di (mə-hä′nə-dē). A river of central India flowing about 885 km (550 mi) north and east to the Bay of Bengal.

ma·ha·ra·jah or **ma·ha·ra·ja** (mä′hə-rä′jə, -zhə) *n.* **1.** A king or prince in India ranking above a rajah, especially the sovereign of one of the former native states. **2.** Used as a title for such a king or prince. [Hindi *mahārājā,* from Sanskrit : *mahā-,* great; see **meg-** in Appendix + *rājā,* king; see **reg-** in Appendix.]

ma·ha·ra·ni or **ma·ha·ra·nee** (mä′hə-rä′nē) *n., pl.* **-nis** or **-nees. 1.** The wife of a maharajah. **2.** A princess in India ranking above a rani, especially the sovereign ruler of one of the former native states. **3.** Used as a title for such a woman. [Hindi *mahārānī,* from Sanskrit *mahārājñī* : *mahā-,* great; see **meg-** in Appendix + *rājñī,* queen; see **reg-** in Appendix.]

Ma·ha·rash·tra (mä′hə-răsh′trə). A historical region of west-central India. It was controlled by the Moslem rulers of India from the early 14th to the mid-17th century and incorporated by the British into the province of Bombay in the 19th century.

ma·ha·ri·shi (mä′hə-rē′shē, mə-här′ə-shē) *n., pl.* **-shis.** *Hinduism.* **1.** A teacher of mysticism and spiritual knowledge. **2.** Used as a title for such a person. [Sanskrit *maharṣiḥ* : *mahā-,* great; see **meg-** in Appendix + *ṛṣiḥ,* seer, sage, saint.]

ma·hat·ma (mə-hät′mə, -hăt′-) *n.* **1.** In India and Tibet, one of a class of persons venerated for great knowledge and love of humanity. **2. Mahatma.** *Hinduism.* Used as a title of respect for a person renowned for spirituality and high-mindedness. [Sanskrit *mahātmā* : *mahā-*, great; see **meg-** in Appendix + *ātmā*, life, spirit.]

Ma·ha·ya·na (mä′hə-yä′nə) *n.* One of the major schools of Buddhism, active in Japan, Korea, Nepal, Tibet, Mongolia, and China, which teaches social concern and universal salvation. [Sanskrit *Mahāyānam* : *mahā-*, great; see **meg-** in Appendix + *yānam*, vehicle; see **ei-** in Appendix.] **—Ma′ha·ya′nist** *n.* **—Ma′ha·ya·nis′tic** *adj.*

Mah·di (mä′dē) *n., pl.* **-dis.** *Islam.* **1.** The messiah who, it is believed, will appear at the world's end and establish a reign of peace and righteousness. **2.** A leader who assumes the role of a messiah. [Arabic *mahdī*, rightly guided (one), Mahdi, from *hadā*, to lead.] **—Mah′dism** *n.* **—Mah′dist** *n.*

Mah·fouz (mä-fo͞oz′), **Naguib.** Born 1911. Egyptian writer whose works include the novels *Autumn Quail* (1962) and *The Beggar* (1965). He won the 1988 Nobel Prize for literature.

Ma·hi·can (mə-hē′kən) also **Mo·hi·can** (mō-, mə-) *n., pl.* **Mahican** or **-cans** also **Mohican** or **-cans. 1.a.** A Native American confederacy of subtribes formerly inhabiting the upper Hudson River valley from Albany south to the Catskill Mountains and north to Lake Champlain. Present-day descendants live in Oklahoma and Wisconsin. **b.** A member of this confederacy. **2.** The Algonquian language of the Mahican.

ma·hi-ma·hi also **ma·hi·ma·hi** (mä′hē-mä′hē) *n., pl.* **-his.** A tropical marine food fish *(Coryphaena hippurus)* found worldwide, having an iridescent blue body and a long dorsal fin. [Hawaiian.]

mah-jong also **mah-jongg** (mä′zhŏng′, -zhông′) *n. Games.* A game of Chinese origin usually played by four persons with tiles resembling dominoes and bearing various designs, which are drawn and discarded until one player wins with a hand of four combinations of three tiles each and a pair of matching tiles. [Chinese (Mandarin) *má jiàng* : *má*, spotted + *jiàng*, main piece in Chinese chess.]

Mah·ler (mä′lər), **Gustav.** 1860–1911. Austrian composer and conductor of the Vienna State Opera House (1897–1907) whose works include *Das Lied von der Erde* (1908) and Symphony Number 9 (1909).

mahl·stick (môl′stĭk′) *n.* Variant of **maulstick.**

ma·hog·a·ny (mə-hŏg′ə-nē) *n., pl.* **-nies. 1.a.** Any of various tropical American evergreen trees of the genus *Swietenia*, valued for their hard, reddish-brown wood. **b.** The wood of any of these trees, especially that of *S. mahogani*, used in making furniture. **2.a.** Any of several trees having wood resembling true mahogany. **b.** The wood of any of these trees. **3.** *Color.* A moderate reddish brown. [Obsolete Spanish *mahogani*, perhaps of Mayan origin.]

Ma·hón (mə-hōn′, mä-ôn′). A city of Spain on eastern Minorca. Probably founded by Carthaginians, it was held by the Moors from the 8th to the 13th century. Population, 22,926.

Mah·ra·ti (mə-rä′tē, -răt′ē) *n.* Variant of **Marathi.**

Mah·rat·ta (mə-rä′tə, -răt′ə) *n.* Variant of **Maratha.**

Mah·rat·ti (mə-rä′tē, -răt′ē) *n.* Variant of **Marathi.**

ma·huang (mä-hwäng′) *n.* Any of various Asian shrubs of the genus *Ephedra*, especially *E. sinica*, from which the drug ephedrine is obtained. [Chinese (Mandarin) *má huáng* : *má*, hemp + *huáng*, yellow.]

mah·zor also **mach·zor** (mäкн′zôr′, -zər, mäкн-zōr′) *n., pl.* **-zor·im** (-zôr′ĭm, -zô-rēm′) or **-zors.** The Hebrew prayer book containing rituals prescribed for holidays. [Hebrew *maḥăzôr*, cycle, mahzor.]

Mai·a (mā′ə, mī′ə) *n.* **1.** *Greek Mythology.* A goddess, the eldest of the Pleiades. **2.** The brightest star in the Pleiades. [Latin *Māia*, from Greek, from *maia*, good mother, nurse. See **mā-²** in Appendix.]

maid (mād) *n.* **1.a.** An unmarried girl or woman. **b.** A virgin. **2.** A woman servant. [Middle English *maide*, from Old English *mægden*. See **maghu-** in Appendix.]

maid·en (mād′n) *n.* **1.a.** An unmarried girl or woman. **b.** A virgin. **2.** A machine resembling the guillotine, used in Scotland in the 16th and 17th centuries to behead criminals. **3.** *Sports.* **a.** A racehorse that has never won a race. **b.** A maiden over. **—maiden** *adj.* **1.** Of, relating to, or befitting a maiden: *a maiden blush.* **2.** Being an unmarried girl or woman: *a maiden aunt.* **3.** Inexperienced; untried: *a maiden surfer.* **4.** Being a racehorse that has never won a race. **5.** First or earliest: *a maiden voyage; a maiden speech in the House of Commons.* [Middle English, from Old English *mægden*. See **maghu-** in Appendix.]

maid·en·hair fern (mād′n-hâr′) *n.* Any of various ferns of the genus *Adiantum*, having purplish to black stalks, usually feathery fronds, and delicate fan-shaped leaflets with marginal sori. [From the fineness of its stems.]

maidenhair tree *n.* See **ginkgo.**

maid·en·head (mād′n-hĕd′) *n.* **1.** The condition or quality of being a maiden; virginity. **2.** The hymen. [Middle English *maidenhed* : *maiden*, maid; see MAIDEN + *-hed*, -hood.]

maid·en·hood (mād′n-ho͝od′) *n.* The condition or time of being a maiden.

maid·en·ly (mād′n-lē) *adj.* Of, relating to, or suitable for a maiden. **—maid′en·li·ness** *n.*

maiden name *n.* A woman's family name before she is married.

maiden over *n. Sports.* An over in cricket during which no runs are scored.

maid·hood (mād′ho͝od′) *n.* Maidenhood.

maid in waiting *n., pl.* **maids in waiting.** An unmarried woman attending a queen or princess.

Maid Mar·i·an (mād mâr′ē-ən, măr′-) *n.* Robin Hood's sweetheart.

maid of honor *n., pl.* **maids of honor. 1.** The chief unmarried woman attendant of a bride. **2.** An unmarried noblewoman attendant upon a queen or princess.

maid·ser·vant (mād′sûr′vənt) *n.* A woman servant.

Maid·stone (mād′stən, -stōn′). A municipal borough of southeast England east-southeast of London. First chartered in 1549, it is a papermaking and brewing center. Population, 72,500.

Mai·du (mī′do͞o) *n., pl.* **Maidu** or **-dus. 1.a.** A Native American people inhabiting northeast California south of Lassen Peak. **b.** A member of this people. **2.** The Penutian language of the Maidu. **—Mai′du** *adj.*

ma·ieu·tic (mā-yo͞o′tĭk, mī-) also **ma·ieu·ti·cal** (-tĭ-kəl) *adj.* Of or relating to the aspect of the Socratic method that induces a respondent to formulate latent concepts through a dialectic or logical sequence of questions. [Greek *maieutikos*, from *maieuesthai*, to act as midwife, from *maia*, midwife, nurse. See **mā-²** in Appendix.]

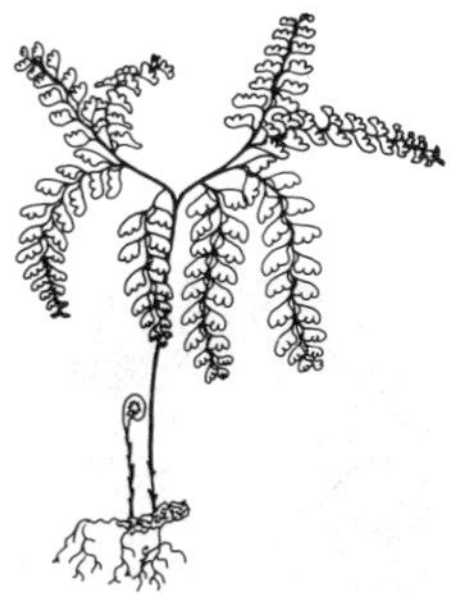

maidenhair fern
Northern maidenhair fern
Adiantum pedatum

mail¹ (māl) *n.* **1.a.** Materials, such as letters and packages, handled in a postal system. **b.** Postal material for a specific person or organization. **c.** Material processed for distribution from a post office at a specified time: *the morning mail.* **2.** Often **mails.** A system by which letters, packages, and other postal materials are transported. Used with *the.* **3.** A vehicle by which mail is transported. **—mail** *v.* **mailed, mail·ing, mails.** —*tr.* To send by mail. —*intr.* To send letters and other postal material by mail. [Middle English *male*, bag, from Old French, of Germanic origin.] **—mail′a·ble** *adj.* **—mail′a·bil′i·ty** *n.*

mail² (māl) *n.* **1.** Flexible armor composed of small overlapping metal rings, loops of chain, or scales. **2.** The protective covering of certain animals, as the shell of a turtle. **—mail** *tr.v.* **mailed, mail·ing, mails.** To cover or armor with mail. [Middle English, from Old French *maile*, from Latin *macula*, blemish, mesh.]

mail³ (māl) *n. Scots.* Rent, payment, or tribute. [Middle English *mol, maile*, from Old Norse *māl*, lawsuit.]

mail·bag (māl′băg′) *n.* **1.** A large canvas sack used for transporting mail. **2.** A bag suspended from the shoulder, used by letter carriers for carrying mail.

mail·box (māl′bŏks′) *n.* **1.** A public container for deposit of outgoing mail. Also called *postbox.* **2.** A private box for incoming mail. Also called *letterbox.*

mail call *n.* Distribution of mail to members of a military unit.

mail carrier *n.* See **letter carrier.**

mail drop *n.* **1.** A receptacle or slot for the delivery of mail. **2.** An address or a place at which a nonresident person receives mail, often of a secret nature.

mailed (māld) *adj.* **1.** Covered with or made of plates of mail: *a mailed sleeve.* **2.** Having a hard covering of scales, spines, or horny plate, as an armadillo or a lobster.

mailed fist *n.* The threat of military force.

mail·er (mā′lər) *n.* **1.** One that uses the mails: *large commercial mailers.* **2.** One who addresses, stamps, or otherwise prepares mail. **3.** A container, such as a cardboard tube, used to hold material to be mailed: *a cardboard book mailer.* **4.** An advertising leaflet included with a letter.

Mail·er (mā′lər), **Norman.** Born 1923. American writer. Acclaimed for his World War II novel *The Naked and the Dead* (1948), he established New Journalism with his accounts of political events in the 1960's.

Mail·gram (māl′grăm′). A trademark used for a telegram transmitted to a post office and delivered to the addressee by the postal service.

mail·ing (mā′lĭng) *n.* **1.** Something sent by mail. **2.** A batch of mail dispatched at one time by a sender.

Mail·lol (mä-yôl′), **Aristide.** 1861–1944. French sculptor noted for his large, classically influenced statues of female nudes.

mail·lot (mä-yō′) *n.* **1.** A coarsely knitted, stretchable jersey fabric. **2.** A pair of tights or a leotard of such fabric, worn for ballet or gymnastics. **3.** A woman's one-piece swimsuit usually cut high on the leg. [French, from Old French, swaddling clothes, from *maille*, mesh, from Latin *macula*.]

mail·man (māl′măn′, -mən) *n.* A man who carries and delivers mail. Also called *postman.*

mail order *n. Abbr.* **m.o., M.O.** An order for goods to be shipped through the mail.

mail-or·der house (māl′ôr′dər) *n.* A business that is organized primarily to promote, receive, and fill requests for merchandise or services through the mail.

mail·room (māl′ro͞om′, -ro͝om′) *n.* A room in which ingoing and outgoing mail is handled for a company or other organization.

maim (mām) *tr.v.* **maimed, maim·ing, maims. 1.** To disable or disfigure, usually by depriving of the use of a limb or other part of the body. See Synonyms at **batter¹. 2.** To make imperfect or defective; impair. [Middle English *maimen*, from Old French *mahaignier*, probably of Germanic origin.] **—maim′er** *n.*

Mai·mon·i·des (mī-mŏn′ĭ-dēz′), **Moses.** Originally Moses

ă pat	oi boy
ā pay	ou out
âr care	o͝o took
ä father	o͞o boot
ĕ pet	ŭ cut
ē be	ûr urge
ĭ pit	th thin
ī pie	*th* this
îr pier	hw which
ŏ pot	zh vision
ō toe	ə about, item
ô paw	♦ regionalism

Stress marks: ′ (primary); ′ (secondary), as in **dictionary** (dĭk′shə-nĕr′ē)

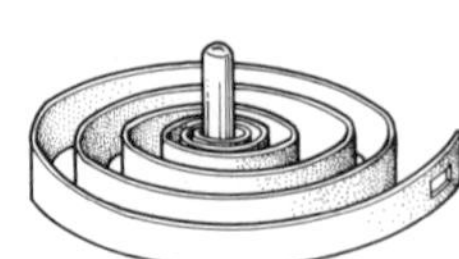
mainspring
Of a watch

Madame de Maintenon
Detail of a portrait by Pierre Mignard (1610?–1695)

maintop

majolica
Early 16th-century Italian plate

Ben Maimon. 1135–1204. Spanish-born Jewish philosopher and physician. The greatest Jewish scholar of the Middle Ages, he codified the Talmud and in *Guide for the Perplexed* (1190) reconciled Aristotelian philosophy with Jewish theology.

main (mān) *adj.* **1.** Most important; principal. **2.** Exerted to the utmost; sheer: *by main strength.* **3.** *Nautical.* Connected to or located near the mainmast: *a main skysail.* **4.** Of, relating to, or being the principal clause or verb of a complex sentence. **5.** *Obsolete.* Of or relating to a continuous area or stretch, as of land or water. **—main** *n.* **1.** The chief or largest part: *His ideas are, in the main, impractical.* **2.** The principal pipe or conduit in a system for conveying water, gas, oil, or other utility. **3.** Physical strength: *fought with might and main.* **4.** A mainland. **5.** The open ocean. **6. a.** A mainsail. **b.** A mainmast. [Middle English, from Old English *mægen,* strength. See **magh-** in Appendix.]

Main (mān, mīn). A river rising in eastern Germany and flowing about 499 km (310 mi) westward to the Rhine River at Mainz.

main chance *n.* One's most advantageous opportunity.

main clause *n. Grammar.* A clause in a complex sentence that contains at least a subject and a verb and can stand alone syntactically as a complete sentence. Also called *independent clause.*

main deck *n. Nautical.* The principal deck of a large vessel.

main drag *n. Slang.* The principal street of a city or town.

Maine (mān). **1.** (*also* mĕn). A historical region and former province of northwest France south of Normandy. United with Anjou in 1126, it passed to England when Henry Plantagenet became king in 1154. Maine reverted to the French crown in 1481. **2.** *Abbr.* **ME, Me.** A state of the northeast United States. It was admitted as the 23rd state in 1820. First explored by Europeans in 1602, the region was annexed by Massachusetts in 1652. Maine's northern boundary with New Brunswick was settled by a treaty with Great Britain in 1842. Augusta is the capital and Portland the largest city. Population, 1,125,030.

main·frame (mān′frām′) *n. Computer Science.* **1.** A large, powerful computer, often serving several connected terminals. **2.** The central processing unit of a computer exclusive of peripheral and remote devices.

main·land (mān′lănd′, -lənd) *n.* The principal landmass of a continent. **—main′land′er** *n.*

main·line (mān′līn′) *v.* **-lined, -lin·ing, -lines.** *Slang.* *—tr.* To inject (a drug, such as heroin) directly into a major vein. *—intr.* To inject a drug intravenously. **—mainline** *adj.* Being in a principal or well-established position: *the mainline churches.* **—main′lin′er** *n.*

main line *n.* **1.** A principal section of a railroad line. **2.** *Slang.* A principal and easily accessible vein, usually in the arm or leg, into which a drug can be injected.

main·ly (mān′lē) *adv.* For the most part; chiefly.

main·mast (mān′məst, -măst′) *n. Nautical.* **1.** The principal mast of a vessel. **2.** The taller mast, whether forward or aft, of a two-masted sailing vessel. **3.** The second mast aft of a sailing ship with three or more masts.

main royalmast *n. Nautical.* The section of the mainmast of a square-rigged vessel above the main topgallantmast.

main·sail (mān′səl, -sāl′) *n. Nautical.* **1.** The principal sail of a vessel. **2.** A quadrilateral or triangular sail set from the after part of the mainmast on a fore-and-aft rigged vessel. **3.** A square sail set from the main yard on a square-rigged vessel.

main sequence *n.* A major grouping of stars that forms a relatively narrow band from the upper left to the lower right when plotted according to luminosity and surface temperature on the Hertzsprung-Russell diagram.

main·sheet (mān′shēt′) *n. Nautical.* The rope that controls the angle at which a mainsail is trimmed and set.

main·spring (mān′spring′) *n.* **1.** The principal spring in a mechanical device, especially a watch or clock, that drives the mechanism by uncoiling. **2.** The chief motivating force: *the mainspring of a reform movement.*

main·stay (mān′stā′) *n.* **1.** A chief support: *Agriculture is a mainstay of the economy.* **2.** *Nautical.* A strong rope that serves to steady and support the mainmast of a sailing vessel.

main·stream (mān′strēm′) *n.* The prevailing current of thought, influence, or actitity: *"You need not accept the nominee's ideology, only be able to locate it in the American mainstream"* (Charles Krauthammer). **—mainstream** *adj.* Representing the prevalent attitudes and values of a society or group: *mainstream morality.* **—mainstream** *tr.v.* **-streamed, -stream·ing, -streams. 1.** To integrate (a physically or intellectually disadvantaged student) into regular school classes. **2.** To incorporate into a prevailing group. **—main′stream′er** *n.*

main street *n.* **1.** The principal street of a small town. **2. Main Street. a.** The inhabitants of small towns considered as a group: *"Main Street may cheer"* (Bernard Kalb). **b.** A place that represents narrowness of view and smug complacency. [Sense 2, after *Main Street,* a novel by Sinclair Lewis.]

main·tain (mān-tān′) *tr.v.* **-tained, -tain·ing, -tains. 1.** To keep up or carry on; continue: *maintain good relations.* **2.** To keep in an existing state; preserve or retain: *maintain one's composure.* **3.** To keep in a condition of good repair or efficiency: *maintain two cars.* **4. a.** To provide for; support: *maintain a family.* **b.** To keep in existence; sustain: *enough food to maintain life.* **5.** To defend or hold against criticism or attack: *maintained his stand on taxes.* **6.** To declare to be true; affirm: *maintained her innocence.* [Middle English *maintainen,* from Old French *maintenir,* from Medieval Latin *manutenēre,* from Latin *manū tenēre,* to hold in the hand : *manū,* ablative of *manus,* hand; see **man-**[2] in Appendix + *tenēre,* to hold; see **ten-** in Appendix.] **—main·tain′a·bil′i·ty** *n.* **—main·tain′a·ble** *adj.* **—main·tain′er** *n.*

main·te·nance (mān′tə-nəns) *n.* **1.** The act of maintaining or the state of being maintained: *the maintenance of family traditions.* **2.** The work of keeping something in proper condition; upkeep. **3. a.** Provision of support or livelihood. **b.** Means of support or livelihood: *an income that barely provided maintenance.* See Synonyms at **livelihood. 4.** *Law.* The unlawful meddling in a suit by providing either party with the means to carry it on. [Middle English *maintenaunce,* from Old French *maintenance,* from *maintenir,* to maintain. See MAINTAIN.]

Main·te·non (măN′tə-nôN′, mănt-nôN′), **Marquise de.** Title of Françoise d'Aubigné. 1635–1719. French consort of Louis XIV. The widow of French writer Paul Scarron, she secretly married the king (c. 1685) after the death of his first wife.

main·top (mān′tŏp′) *n. Nautical.* A platform at the head of the mainmast on a square-rigged vessel.

main topgallant *n. Nautical.* A sail or yard set from the topgallant section of a mainmast.

main top·gal·lant·mast (tə-găl′ənt-məst, tŏp-) *n. Nautical.* The section of the mainmast next above the main topmast on a square-rigged sailing vessel.

main topmast *n. Nautical.* The section of the mainmast on a square-rigged sailing vessel between the lower mast and the main topgallantmast.

main topsail *n. Nautical.* The sail that is set above the mainsail.

main yard *n. Nautical.* The lower yard on a mainmast.

Mainz (mīnts). A city of west-central Germany at the confluence of the Rhine and Main rivers west-southwest of Frankfurt. Built on the site of a Roman camp founded in the 1st century B.C., it is an important industrial city. Population, 187,447.

mai tai (mī′ tī′) *n., pl.* **mai tais.** A cocktail made with rum, curaçao, and fruit juices. [Tahitian *maitai,* good.]

Mait·land (māt′lənd), **Frederic William.** 1850–1906. British jurist noted for his works on the history of English law.

mai·tre d' (mā′trə dē′, mā′tər) *n., pl.* **mai·tre d's** (dēz′). *Informal.* A maitre d'hôtel.

mai·tre d'hô·tel (mā′trə dō-tĕl′) *n., pl.* **mai·tres d'hô·tel** (mā′trə dō-tĕl). **1.** A headwaiter. **2.** A major-domo. **3.** A sauce of melted butter, chopped parsley, lemon juice, salt, and pepper. [French *maître d'hôtel* : *maître,* master + *de,* of + *hôtel,* house.]

maize (māz) *n.* **1.** See **corn**[1] (sense 1). **2.** *Color.* A light yellow to moderate orange yellow. [Spanish *maíz,* from Cariban *mahiz.*] **—maize** *adj.*

Maj. *abbr.* Major.

ma·jes·tic (mə-jĕs′tĭk) also **ma·jes·ti·cal** (-tĭ-kəl) *adj.* Having or showing lofty dignity or nobility; stately. See Synonyms at **grand. —ma·jes′ti·cal·ly** *adv.*

maj·es·ty (măj′ĭ-stē) *n., pl.* **-ties. 1. a.** The greatness and dignity of a sovereign. **b.** The sovereignty and power of God. **2.** Supreme authority or power: *the majesty of the law.* **3. a.** A royal personage. **b. Majesty.** *Abbr.* **M.** Used with *His, Her,* or *Your* as a title and form of address for a sovereign. **4. a.** Royal dignity of bearing or aspect; grandeur. **b.** Stately splendor; magnificence, as of style or character: *the Parthenon in all its majesty.* [Middle English *mageste, maieste,* from Old French *majeste,* from Latin *māiestās.* See **meg-** in Appendix.]

Maj. Gen. *abbr.* Major general.

ma·jol·i·ca (mə-jŏl′ĭ-kə, -yŏl′-) *n.* **1.** Tin-glazed earthenware that is often richly colored and decorated, especially an earthenware of this type produced in Italy. **2.** Pottery made in imitation of this earthenware. [Italian *maiolica,* from Medieval Latin *Māiōlica,* Majorca (where it was made), alteration of Late Latin *Māiōrica.*]

ma·jor (mā′jər) *adj.* **1.** Greater than others in importance or rank: *a major artist.* **2.** Great in scope or effect: *a major improvement.* **3.** Great in number, size, or extent: *the major portion of the population.* **4.** Requiring great attention or concern; very serious: *a major illness.* **5.** *Law.* Having attained full legal age. **6.** Of or relating to the field of academic study in which a student specializes. **7.** *Music.* **a.** Designating a scale or mode having half steps between the third and fourth and the seventh and eighth degrees. **b.** Equivalent to the distance between the tonic note and the second or third or sixth or seventh degrees of a major scale or mode: *a major interval.* **c.** Based on a major scale: *major key.* **—major** *n.* **1.** *Abbr.* **Maj. a.** A comissioned rank in the U.S. Army, Air Force, or Marine Corps that is above captain and below lieutenant colonel. **b.** A similar rank in another military or paramilitary organization. **c.** One who holds this rank. **2.** One that is superior in rank, importance, or ability: *an oil-producing country considered as one of the majors.* **3.** *Law.* One who has reached full legal age. **4. a.** A field of study chosen as an academic specialty. **b.** A student specializing in such studies: *a linguistics major.* **5.** *Logic.* **a.** A major premise. **b.** A major term. **6.** *Music.* A major scale, key, interval, or mode. **7. majors.** *Sports.* The major leagues. **—major** *intr.v.* **-jored, -jor·ing, -jors.** To pursue academic studies in a major: *majoring in mathematics.* [Middle English *majour,* from Latin *māior.* See **meg-** in Appendix.]

major axis *n. Mathematics.* The longer of the two lines about which an ellipse is symmetrical; the axis that passes through both focuses of an ellipse.

Ma·jor·ca (mə-jôrʹkə, -yôrʹ-) also **Mal·lor·ca** (mä-yôrʹkä, -lyôrʹ-). An island of Spain in the western Mediterranean Sea off the east-central coast of the mainland. The largest of the Balearic Islands, it was the center of an independent kingdom from 1276 until 1343. **—Ma·jorʹcan** *adj. & n.*

ma·jor-do·mo (māʹjər-dōʹmō) *n., pl.* **-mos. 1.** The head steward or butler in the household of a sovereign or great noble. **2.** A steward or butler. **3.** One who makes arrangements or directs affairs for another. [Italian *maggiordomo* or Spanish *mayordomo,* both from Medieval Latin *māior domūs* : Latin *māior,* chief; see **meg-** in Appendix + Latin *domūs,* genitive of *domus,* house; see **dem-** in Appendix.]

ma·jor·ette (māʹjə-rětʹ) *n.* A drum majorette. See Usage Note at **-ette.**

major general *n. Abbr.* **Maj. Gen., MG 1.** A commissioned rank in the U.S. Army, Air Force, or Marine Corps that is above brigadier general and below lieutenant general. **2.** One who holds this rank.

ma·jor·i·tar·i·an (mə-jôrʹĭ-târʹē-ən, -jŏrʹ-) *adj.* Based on majority rule: *"a naively uncomplicated premise of simple majoritarian democracy"* (Saturday Review). **—majoritarian** *n.* An advocate of majoritarianism.

ma·jor·i·tar·i·an·ism (mə-jôrʹĭ-târʹē-ə-nĭzʹəm, -jŏrʹ-) *n.* Rule by simple numerical majority in an organized group.

ma·jor·i·ty (mə-jôrʹĭ-tē, -jŏrʹ-) *n., pl.* **-ties. 1.** The greater number or part; a number more than half of the total. **2.** The amount by which the greater number of votes cast, as in an election, exceeds the total number of remaining votes. **3.** The political party, group, or faction having the most power by virtue of its larger representation or electoral strength. **4.** The status of having reached full legal age, with attendant rights and responsibilities. **5.** The military rank, commission, or office of a major. **6.** *Obsolete.* The fact or state of being greater; superiority. [French *majorité,* from Medieval Latin *māiōritās,* from Latin *māior,* greater. See **meg-** in Appendix.]

USAGE NOTE: When *majority* refers to a particular number of votes, it takes a singular verb: *Her majority was five votes. His majority has been growing by 5 percent every year.* When it refers to a group of persons or things that are in the majority, it may take either a singular or plural verb, depending on whether the group is considered as a whole or as a set of people considered individually. So we say *The majority elects* (not *elect*) *the candidate it wants* (not *they want*), since the election is accomplished by the group as a whole; but *The majority of the voters live* (not *lives*) *in the city,* since living in the city is something that each voter does individually. • *Majority* is often preceded by *great* (but not by *greater*) in expressing emphatically the sense of "most of": *The great majority approved.* The phrase *greater majority* is appropriate only when considering two majorities: *He won by a greater majority in this election than in the last.*

majority leader *n.* The leader of the majority party in a legislature, as in the U.S. Senate or House of Representatives.

majority rule *n.* A doctrine by which a numerical majority of an organized group holds the power to make decisions binding on all in the group.

major league *n. Sports.* **1.** Either of the two principal groups of professional baseball teams in the United States. **2.** A league of principal importance in other professional sports, such as basketball, football, or ice hockey.

ma·jor-league (māʹjər-lēgʹ) *adj.* **1.** *Sports.* Of or relating to a major league: *major-league baseball.* **2.** Being in the top rank of its kind: *a major-league ballet company.*

ma·jor-lea·guer (māʹjər-lēʹgər) *n. Sports.* A member of a major-league team, especially a major-league baseball player.

major medical *n.* Insurance that covers all or most of the medical bills engendered by major or prolonged illnesses above a set amount.

major order *n. Ecclesiastical.* See **holy order** (sense 3).

major party *n.* A political party having enough strength to gain control of a government with comparative regularity.

major premise *n. Logic.* The premise containing the major term in a syllogism.

Ma·jor Prophets (māʹjər) *pl.n. Bible.* The Hebrew prophets Isaiah, Jeremiah, and Ezekiel.

major scale *n. Music.* A diatonic scale having half steps between the third and fourth and the seventh and eighth tones and whole steps between the other adjacent tones.

major suit *n. Games.* A suit of superior scoring value, either spades or hearts in bridge.

major term *n. Logic.* The term of a syllogism that forms the predicate of the conclusion.

ma·jus·cule (mə-jŭsʹkyo͞ol, măjʹə-skyo͞olʹ) *n.* A large letter, either capital or uncial, used in writing or printing. [French, from Latin *māiusculus,* somewhat larger, diminutive of *māior,* greater. See **meg-** in Appendix.] **—ma·jusʹcule, ma·jusʹcu·lar** (mə-jŭsʹkyə-lər) *adj.*

Mak·a·lu (mŭkʹə-lo͞o). A mountain, 8,476 m (27,790 ft) high, in the Himalaya Mountains of northeast Nepal.

mak·ar (mäʹkər, māʹ-) *n. Chiefly Scots.* A poet. [Middle English, variant of *maker,* maker, poet.]

Ma·kar·i·os III (mə-kărʹē-əs, -ōsʹ, mä-käʹrē-ôs). 1913–1977. Cypriot prelate and politician. Bishop of the Orthodox Church of Cyprus (1950–1977), he was the first president of independent Cyprus (1959–1977).

Ma·kas·sar or **Ma·ka·sar** (mə-kăsʹər). See **Ujung Pandang.**

Makassar Strait. A strait between Borneo and Celebes connecting the Java Sea with the Celebes Sea.

make (māk) *v.* **made** (mād), **mak·ing, makes.** *—tr.* **1.** To cause to exist or happen; bring about; create: *made problems for him; making a commotion.* **2.** To bring into existence by shaping, modifying, or putting together material; construct: *make a dress; made a wall of stones.* **3.** To form by assembling individuals or constituents: *make a quorum.* **4.** To change from one form or function to another: *make clay into bricks.* **5. a.** To cause to be or become: *made her position clear; a decision that made him happy.* **b.** To cause to assume a specified function or role: *made her treasurer; made Chicago his home.* **6. a.** To cause to act in a specified manner: *Heat makes gases expand.* **b.** To compel: *made him leave.* **7. a.** To form in the mind: *make an estimate.* **b.** To compose: *make verses.* **8. a.** To prepare; fix: *make breakfast.* **b.** To get ready or set in order for use: *made the bed.* **c.** To gather and light the materials for (a fire). **9. a.** To engage in: *make war.* **b.** To carry out; perform: *make a telephone call; make an incision.* **10.** To achieve, produce, or attain: *made peace between the two factions; not making sense; didn't make the quota.* **11. a.** To institute or establish; enact: *make laws.* **b.** To draw up and execute in a suitable form: *make a will.* **12. a.** To arrive at; reach: *made Washington in two hours.* **b.** To reach in time: *just made the plane.* **13. a.** To attain the rank or position of: *She made lieutenant.* **b.** To acquire a place in or on: *made the basketball team; made the morning papers.* **14. a.** To gain or earn, as by working: *make money.* **b.** To behave so as to acquire: *make friends.* **c.** To score or achieve, as in a sport: *made a field goal.* **15. a.** To assure the success of: *A favorable review from him can make a play.* **b.** To favor the development of: *Practice makes a winning team.* **16.** To be suited for: *Oak makes strong furniture.* **17.** To develop into: *She will make a fine doctor.* **18. a.** To draw a conclusion as to the significance or nature of: *don't know what to make of the decision.* **b.** To calculate as being; estimate: *I make the height 20 feet.* **c.** To consider as being: *wasn't the problem some people made it.* **19. a.** To constitute: *Twenty members make a quorum.* **b.** To add up to: *Two and two make four.* **c.** To amount to: *makes no difference.* **20.** To constitute the essence or nature of: *Clothes make the man.* **21.** To cause to be especially enjoyable or rewarding: *You made my day.* **22.** To appear to begin (an action): *She made to leave.* **23.** *Slang.* To persuade to have sexual intercourse. *—intr.* **1.** To act or behave in a specified manner: *make merry; make free.* **2.** To begin or appear to begin an action: *made as if to shake my hand.* **3.** To cause something to be as specified: *make ready; make sure.* **4.** To proceed in a certain direction: *made for home; made after the thief.* **5.** *Slang.* To pretend to be; imitate. Used with *like*: *made like a ballerina.* **6.** To undergo fabrication or manufacture: *This wool makes up into a warm shawl.* **7.** To rise or accumulate: *The tide is making.* **—make** *n.* **1.** The act or process of making; manufacturing. **2.** The style or manner in which a thing is made: *disliked the make of her coat.* **3.** The amount produced, especially the output of a factory. **4.** A specific line of manufactured goods, identified by the manufacturer's name or the registered trademark: *a famous make of shirt.* **5.** The physical or moral nature of a person; character or disposition: *found out what make of man he was.* **6.** *Slang.* Identification of a person or thing, often from information in police records: *Did you get a make on the assailant?* ***—phrasal verbs.*** **make for. 1.** To have or cause to have a particular effect or result: *small details that make for comfort.* **2.** To help promote; further: *makes for better communication.* **make off.** To depart in haste; run away. **make out. 1.** To discern or see, especially with difficulty: *I could barely make out the traffic signs through the rain.* **2.** To understand: *could not make out what she was saying.* **3.** To write out; draw up: *made out the invoices.* **4.** To fill in (a form, for example). **5.** *Informal.* To imply or suggest: *You make me out to be a liar.* **6.** *Informal.* To try to establish or prove: *He made out that he was innocent.* **7.** To get along in a given way; fare: *made out well in business.* **8.** *Slang.* **a.** To neck; pet. **b.** To have sexual intercourse. **make over. 1.** To redo; renovate. **2.** To change or transfer the ownership of, usually by means of a legal document: *made over the property to her son.* **make up. 1.** To put together; construct or compose: *make up a prescription.* **2.** To constitute; form: *One hundred years make up a century.* **3. a.** To alter one's appearance for a role on the stage, as with a costume and cosmetics. **b.** To apply cosmetics. **4.** To devise as a fiction or falsehood; invent: *made up an excuse.* **5. a.** To make good (a deficit or lack): *made up the difference in the bill.* **b.** To compensate for: *make up the lost time.* **6.** To resolve a quarrel: *kissed and made up.* **7.** To make ingratiating or fawning overtures. Used with *to*: *made up to his friend's boss.* **8.** To take (an examination or a course) again or at a later time because of previous absence or failure. **9.** To set in order: *make up a room.* **10.** *Printing.* To select and arrange material for: *made up the front page.* **make with.** *Slang.* **1.** To bring into use: *a flirt making with the eyes.* **2.** To put forth; produce: *always making with the jokes.* ***—idioms.*** **make a clean breast of.** To confess fully. **make a**

major scale

ă pat	oi boy
ā pay	ou out
âr care	o͝o took
ä father	o͞o boot
ĕ pet	ŭ cut
ē be	ûr urge
ĭ pit	th thin
ī pie	*th* this
îr pier	hw which
ŏ pot	zh vision
ō toe	ə about, item
ô paw	♦ regionalism

Stress marks: ʹ (primary); ʹ (secondary), as in **dictionary** (dĭkʹshə-nĕrʹē)

face. To distort the features of the face; grimace. **make a go of.** To achieve success in: *have made a go of the business.* **make away with. 1.** To carry off; steal. **2.** To use up or consume. **3.** To kill or destroy. **make believe.** To pretend. **make bold.** To venture: *I will not make so bold as to criticize such a distinguished scholar.* **make book.** *Games.* To accept bets on a race, game, or contest. **make do.** To manage to get along with the means available: *had to make do on less income.* **make ends meet.** To manage so that one's means are sufficient for one's needs. **make eyes.** To ogle. **make fun of.** To mock; ridicule. **make good. 1.** To carry out successfully: *He made good his escape.* **2.** To fulfill: *She made good her promise.* **3.** To make compensation for; make up for: *made good the loss.* **4.** To succeed: *made good as a writer.* **make hay.** To turn to one's advantage: *The candidate's opponents made hay of the scandal.* **make it. 1.** *Informal.* To be successful: *finally made it as an actor.* **2.** *Slang.* To have sexual intercourse. **make light of.** To treat as unimportant: *He made light of his illness.* **make love. 1.** To engage in amorous caressing. **2.** To engage in sexual intercourse. **make much of.** To treat as of great importance. **make no bones about.** To be forthright and candid about; acknowledge freely: *They make no bones about their dislike for each other.* **make off with.** To snatch or steal: *made off with the profits.* **make sail.** *Nautical.* **1.** To begin a voyage. **2.** To set sail. **make the grade.** To measure up to a given standard. **make the most of.** To use to the greatest advantage. **make the scene.** *Slang.* **1.** To put in an appearance: *made the scene at the party.* **2.** To participate in a specified activity: *made the drug scene.* **make time. 1.** To move or travel fast, as in an attempt to compensate for lost time. **2.** *Slang.* To make progress toward attracting: *He tried to make time with the new neighbor.* **make tracks.** *Slang.* To move or leave in a hurry. **make up (one's) mind.** To decide between alternatives; come to a definite decision or opinion. **make waves.** *Slang.* To cause a disturbance or controversy. **make way. 1.** To give room for passage; move aside. **2.** To make progress. **on the make.** *Slang.* **1.** Aggressively striving for financial or social improvement: *a young executive on the make.* **2.** Eagerly seeking a sexual partner. [Middle English *maken,* from Old English *macian.* See **mag-** in Appendix.] **—mak′a·ble** *adj.*

make-be·lieve (māk′bĭ-lēv′) *n.* Playful or fanciful pretense.

make-do (māk′do͞o′) *n., pl.* **make-do's** or **make-dos** (-do͞oz′). A substitute for something unobtainable at the time; a makeshift. **—make′-do′** *adj.*

make·fast (māk′făst′) *n. Nautical.* An object, such as a buoy, post, or pile, to which a boat is moored.

make-or-break (māk′ər-brāk′) *adj.* Resulting in great success or utter failure: *a make-or-break investment plan.*

make·o·ver (māk′ō′vər) *n.* An overall treatment to improve the appearance or change the image.

mak·er (mā′kər) *n.* **1.** One that makes or manufactures. Often used in combination: *a policymaker; a drugmaker.* **2.** *Law.* A party that signs a promissory note. **3. Maker.** God. Often used with *the* or a possessive adjective. **4.** *Archaic.* A poet.

make-read·y (māk′rĕd′ē) *n. Printing.* The operation of preparing a form for printing by adjusting and leveling the plates to ensure a clear impression.

make·shift (māk′shĭft′) *n.* A temporary or expedient substitute for something else. **—makeshift** *adj.* Suitable as a temporary or expedient substitute: *used a rock as a makeshift hammer.*

SYNONYMS: *makeshift, expedient, resort, stopgap.* The central meaning shared by these nouns is "something used as a substitute when other means fail or are not available": *lacked a cane but used a stick as a makeshift; exhausted every expedient and finally filed suit; will use force only as a last resort; a crate serving as a stopgap for a chair.*

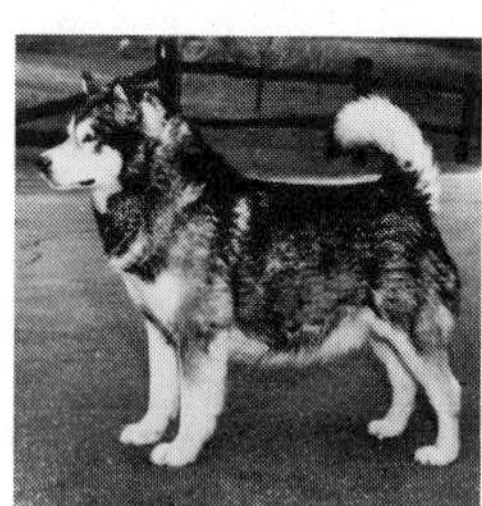

malamute

make·up or **make-up** (māk′ŭp′) *n.* **1.** The way in which something is composed or arranged; composition or construction. **2.** *Printing.* The arrangement or composition, as of type or illustrations, on a page or in a book. **3.** The qualities or temperament that constitute a personality; disposition: *Lying is not in her makeup.* **4.** Cosmetics applied especially to the face. **5.** Materials, such as cosmetics and costumes, that an actor or actress uses in portraying a role. **6.** A special examination for a student who has been absent from or has failed a previous examination.

make·weight (māk′wāt′) *n.* **1.** Something added on a scale in order to meet a required weight. **2.** Something added only to fill a lack. **3.** A counterweight; a counterbalance.

make-work (māk′wûrk′) *n.* Work of little value assigned or taken on only to keep someone from being idle.

Ma·ke·yev·ka (mə-kē′əf-kə, -kyĕ′-). A city of eastern Ukraine northeast of Donetsk. It is a major metallurgical and coal-mining center. Population, 451,000.

Ma·khach·ka·la (mə-kăch′kə-lä′, -KHəch-). A city of southwest Russia on the Caspian Sea. Founded in 1844, it is an oil-refining center. Population, 301,000.

ma·ki·mo·no (mä′kĭ-mō′nō) *n., pl.* **-nos.** A horizontal Japanese decorative scroll featuring pictures or calligraphy. [Japanese, scroll : *maki,* rolled + *mono,* thing.]

mak·ing (mā′kĭng) *n.* **1.a.** The act of one that makes. **b.** The process of coming into being: *trouble in the making.* **2.** The means of gaining success or realizing potential: *That job will be the making of you.* **3.a.** Something made. **b.** The quantity made at one time. **4.** Often **makings. a.** The abilities or qualities needed for development: *She has the makings of a fine teacher.* **b.** The material or ingredients needed for making or doing something: *all the makings for an apple pie.* **5. makings.** *Informal.* The paper and tobacco for rolling a cigarette.

ma·ko (mä′kō) *n., pl.* **-kos.** Either of two mackerel sharks of the genus *Isurus,* characterized by a large heavy body and a nearly symmetrical tail. [Maori *mako.*]

ma·ku·ta (mä-ko͞o′tä) *n.* Plural of **likuta.**

Mal. *abbr.* **1.** *Bible.* Malachi. **2.** Malay.

mal– *pref.* **1.** Bad; badly: *maladminister.* **2.** Abnormal; abnormally: *malformation.* [Middle English, from Old French, from Latin, from *male,* badly and *malus,* bad; see **mel-**[3] in Appendix.]

Mal·a·bar Coast (măl′ə-bär′). A region of southwest India bordering on the Arabian Sea.

Mal·a·bo (măl′ə-bō′, mä-lä′bō). Formerly **San·ta Is·a·bel** (săn′tə ĭz′ə-bĕl′, sän′tä ē-sä-bĕl′). The capital and largest city of Equatorial Guinea, on Bioko in the Gulf of Guinea. It was founded by the British in 1827. Population, 30,710.

mal·ab·sorp·tion (măl′əb-sôrp′shən, -zôrp′-) *n.* Defective or inadequate absorption of nutrients from the intestinal tract.

Ma·lac·ca (mə-lăk′ə, -lä′kə) *n.* The stem of the rattan palm, used for making canes and umbrella handles. [After *Malacca* (now Melaka), a town of western Malaysia.]

Malacca, Strait of. A channel between Sumatra and the Malay Peninsula connecting the Andaman Sea with the South China Sea.

Mal·a·chi (măl′ə-kī′) *n. Bible.* **1.** A Hebrew prophet of the sixth century B.C.. **2.** *Abbr.* **Mal., Ml** See table at **Bible.**

mal·a·chite (măl′ə-kīt′) *n.* A light to dark green carbonate mineral, $Cu_2CO_3(OH)_2$, used as a source of copper and for ornamental stoneware. [Middle English *melochite,* from Latin *molochītes,* from Greek *molokhitis,* from *malakhē, molokhē,* mallow.]

mal·a·col·o·gy (măl′ə-kŏl′ə-jē) *n.* The branch of zoology that deals with mollusks. [French *malacologie,* contraction of *malacozoologie,* from New Latin *Malacozoa,* a classification that includes mollusks : Greek *malakos,* soft; see **mel-**[1] in Appendix + New Latin *-zoa,* pl. of –ZOON.] **—mal′a·co·log′i·cal** (-kə-lŏj′ĭ-kəl) *adj.* **—mal′a·col′o·gist** *n.*

mal·ad·ap·ta·tion (măl′ăd-ăp-tā′shən) *n.* Faulty or inadequate adaptation.

mal·a·dap·ted (măl′ə-dăp′tĭd) *adj.* Poorly suited to a particular function or situation.

mal·a·dap·tive (măl′ə-dăp′tĭv) *adj.* **1.** Marked by faulty or inadequate adaptation. **2.** Not assisting or promoting adaptation.

mal·ad·just·ed (măl′ə-jus′tĭd) *adj.* **1.** Poorly adjusted: *a maladjusted carburetor.* **2.** *Psychology.* Inadequately adjusted to the demands or stresses of daily living.

mal·ad·just·ment (măl′ə-jŭst′mənt) *n.* **1.** Faulty or inadequate adjustment, as in a machine. **2.** *Psychology.* Inability to adjust to the demands of interpersonal relationships and the stresses of daily living.

mal·ad·min·is·ter (măl′əd-mĭn′ĭ-stər) *tr.v.* **-tered, -ter·ing, -ters.** To administer or manage inefficiently or dishonestly. **—mal′ad·min′is·tra′tion** *n.*

mal·a·droit (măl′ə-droit′) *adj.* Marked by a lack of adroitness; inept. See Synonyms at **awkward. —maladroit** *n.* An inept person. [French : *mal-,* mal- + *adroit,* adroit; see ADROIT.] **—mal′a·droit′ly** *adv.* **—mal′a·droit′ness** *n.*

mal·a·dy (măl′ə-dē) *n., pl.* **-dies. 1.** A disease, a disorder, or an ailment. **2.** An unwholesome condition: *the malady of discontent.* [Middle English *maladie,* from Old French, from *malade,* sick, from Latin *male habitus,* in poor condition : *male,* badly; see **mel-**[3] in Appendix + *habitus,* past participle of *habēre,* to hold; see **ghabh-** in Appendix.]

ma·la fi·de (mā′lə fī′dē, mä′lä fē′dĕ) *adv. & adj.* With or in bad faith. [Latin *malā fidē* : *malā,* feminine ablative of *malus,* bad + *fidē,* ablative of *fidēs,* faith.]

Mal·a·ga (măl′ə-gə) *n.* A sweet fortified wine originally from Málaga, Spain.

Má·la·ga (măl′ə-gə, mä′lä-gä′). A city of southern Spain northeast of Gibraltar. Founded by Phoenicians in the 12th century B.C., it was held successively by Carthaginians, Romans, Visigoths, and Moors (after 711). Population, 537,619.

Mal·a·gas·y (măl′ə-găs′ē) *n., pl.* **Malagasy** or **-gas·ies. 1.** A native or inhabitant of Madagascar. **2.** The Austronesian language of the Malagasy. **—Malagasy** *adj.* Of or relating to Madagascar, the Malagasy, or their language or culture.

Malagasy Republic. See **Madagascar.**

ma·la·gue·ña (mä′lə-gā′nyə) *n.* **1.** A dance native to Málaga, Spain, that is a variety of the fandango. **2.** Any of several Spanish folk tunes, especially one native to Málaga that is similar to the fandango. [Spanish, feminine of *malagueño,* of Málaga, from MÁLAGA.]

mal·aise (mă-lāz′, -lĕz′) *n.* **1.** A vague feeling of bodily discomfort, as at the beginning of an illness. **2.** A general sense of depression or unease: *"One year after the crash, the markets remain mired in a deep malaise"* (New York Times). [French, from Old French : *mal-,* mal- + *aise,* ease; see EASE.]

Mal·a·mud (măl′ə-məd), **Bernard.** 1914–1986. American writer whose works include *The Magic Barrel* (1958) and *The Fixer* (1966).

mal·a·mute or **mal·e·mute** (măl′ə-myo͞ot′) *n.* Any of a

ă pat	oi boy
ā pay	ou out
âr care	o͝o took
ä father	o͞o boot
ĕ pet	ŭ cut
ē be	ûr urge
ĭ pit	th thin
ī pie	*th* this
îr pier	hw which
ŏ pot	zh vision
ō toe	ə about, item
ô paw	♦ regionalism

Stress marks: ′ (primary); ′ (secondary), as in **dictionary** (dĭk′shə-nĕr′ē)

breed of powerful dogs developed in Alaska as a sled dog and having a thick gray, black, or white coat. [Short for *malamute dog,* from *Malemute,* an Alaskan Eskimo people, from Inupiaq (Eskimo language of northern Alaska) *malimiut.*]

Ma·lang (mə-läng′). A city of eastern Java, Indonesia, south of Surabaya. Population, 511,780.

mal·a·pert (măl′ə-pûrt′) *adj.* Impudently bold in speech or manner; saucy. **—malapert** *n.* An impudent, saucy person. [Middle English, from Old French : *mal-,* mal- + *apert,* clever, alteration (influenced by *apert,* clever, saucy; see PERT) of Latin *expertus.* See EXPERT.] **—mal′a·pert′ly** *adv.*

mal·ap·por·tioned (măl′ə-pôr′shənd, -pōr′-) *adj.* Characterized by an inappropriate or unfair proportional distribution of representatives to a legislative body. **—mal′ap·por′tion·ment** *n.*

mal·a·prop (măl′ə-prŏp′) *n.* A malapropism. [After Mrs. *Malaprop,* a character in *The Rivals,* a play by Richard Brinsley Sheridan, from MALAPROPOS.]

WORD HISTORY: "She's as headstrong as an allegory on the banks of the Nile" and "He is the very pineapple of politeness" are two of the statements from the mouth of Mrs. Malaprop that helped her name become synonymous with ludicrous misuse of language. Mrs. Malaprop, a character in Richard Brinsley Sheridan's play *The Rivals,* produced in 1775, consistently uses language malapropos, that is, inappropriately. The word *malapropos* comes from the French phrase *mal à propos,* made up of *mal,* "badly," *à,* "to," and *propos,* "purpose, subject," and literally means "badly to the purpose," or "inappropriate." *The Rivals* was a popular play, and Mrs. Malaprop became enshrined in a common noun, first in the form *malaprop* and later in *malapropism,* which is first recorded in 1849. Perhaps that is what Mrs. Malaprop feared when she said "An aspersion upon my parts of speech" and "If I reprehend any thing in this world, it is the use of my oracular tongue, and a nice derangement of epitaphs!"

mal·a·prop·ism (măl′ə-prŏp-ĭz′əm) *n.* **1.** Ludicrous misuse of a word, especially by confusion with one of similar sound. **2.** An example of such misuse. [From MALAPROP.] **—mal′a·prop′i·an** (-prŏp′ē-ən) *adj.*

mal·a·pro·pos (măl′ăp-rə-pō′) *adj.* Out of place; inappropriate. **—malapropos** *adv.* In an inappropriate or inopportune manner. [French *mal à propos* : *mal,* badly + *à propos,* to the purpose.]

ma·lar (mā′lər, -lär′) *adj.* Of or relating to the cheekbone or the cheek. **—malar** *n.* The cheekbone. [New Latin *mālāris,* from *māla,* cheekbone.]

Mä·lar·en (mā′lär′ən). A lake of southeast Sweden. Stockholm is located on both sides of the strait that connects the lake with the Baltic Sea.

ma·lar·i·a (mə-lâr′ē-ə) *n.* **1.** An infectious disease characterized by cycles of chills, fever, and sweating, caused by the parasitic infection of red blood cells by a protozoan of the genus *Plasmodium,* which is transmitted by the bite of an infected female anopheles mosquito. Also called *paludism, swamp fever.* **2.** *Archaic.* Bad or foul air; miasma. [Italian from *mala aria,* bad air : *malo,* bad (from Latin *malus;* see **mel-**[3] in Appendix) + *aria,* air (from Latin *āēr,* from Greek *aēr;* see **wer-**[1] in Appendix).] **—ma·lar′i·al, ma·lar′i·an , ma·lar′i·ous** *adj.*

ma·lar·key also **ma·lar·ky** (mə-lär′kē) *n. Slang.* Exaggerated or foolish talk, usually intended to deceive: *"snookered by a lot of malarkey"* (New Republic). [Origin unknown.]

mal·as·sim·i·la·tion (măl′ə-sĭm′ə-lā′shən) *n.* Incomplete or imperfect assimilation of nutrients by the body.

mal·ate (măl′āt′, mā′lāt′) *n.* A salt or an ester of malic acid. [MAL(IC ACID) + –ATE[2].]

Mal·a·thi·on (măl′ə-thī′ŏn′). A trademark used for the organic compound, $C_{10}H_{19}O_6PS_2$, used as an insecticide.

Ma·la·tya (mä′lə-tyä′). A city of east-central Turkey in the Taurus Mountains. It was the capital of a Hittite kingdom c. 1100 B.C. Population, 179,074.

Ma·la·wi (mə-lä′wē). Formerly **Ny·as·a·land** (nī-ăs′ə-lănd′, nyä′sä-). A country of southeast Africa. Center of the widespread Malawi kingdom from the 15th to the late 18th century, the region became a British protectorate in 1891 and was known as Nyasaland from 1907 until 1964. It joined Northern and Southern Rhodesia (now Zambia and Zimbabwe) in a federation from 1953 to 1963 and became independent as Malawi in 1964. Lilongwe is the capital and Blantyre the largest city. Population, 6,123,000. **—Ma·la′wi·an** *adj. & n.*

Malawi, Lake. See Lake **Nyasa.**

Ma·lay (mə-lā′, mā′lā′) *n. Abbr.* **Mal. 1.** A member of a people inhabiting Malaysia, the northern Malay Peninsula, and parts of the western Malay Archipelago. **2.** The Austronesian language of the Malays. In this sense, also called *Bahasa Malay.* **—Malay** *adj.* **1.** Of, relating to, or characteristic of the Malays or their language. **2.** Of or relating to Malaysia, the Malay Peninsula, or the Malay Archipelago. [Obsolete Dutch *Malayo,* from Malay *Mĕlayu.*] **—Ma·lay′an** (mə-lā′ən) *adj. & n.*

Ma·la·ya (mə-lā′ə, mā-). See **Malay Peninsula.**

Mal·a·ya·lam (măl′ə-yä′ləm) *n.* A Dravidian language spoken in the state of Kerala on the Malabar Coast of India.

Malay Archipelago. An island group of southeast Asia between Australia and the Asian mainland and separating the Indian and Pacific oceans. It includes the islands of Indonesia, the Philippines, and Malaysia.

Ma·lay·o-Pol·y·ne·sian (mə-lā′ō-pŏl′ə-nē′zhən, -shən) *n.* A subgroup of the Austronesian language family. **—Ma·lay′o-Pol′y·ne′sian** *adj.*

Malay Peninsula also **Ma·la·ya** (mə-lā′ə, mā-). A peninsula of southeast Asia comprising southwest Thailand, western Malaysia, and the island of Singapore.

Ma·lay·sia (mə-lā′zhə, -shə). A country of southeast Asia consisting of the southern Malay Peninsula and the northern part of the island of Borneo. First visited by Europeans in the 16th century, it was a union and later federation of British colonies and protectorates from 1946 until independence was achieved in 1963. Kuala Lumpur is the capital and the largest city. Population, 13,486,433. **—Ma·lay′sian** *adj. & n.*

Mal·colm X (măl′kəm ĕks′). Originally Malcolm Little. 1925–1965. American Black activist. A member of the Black Muslims (1952–1963), he advocated separatism and Black pride. After converting to orthodox Islam, he founded the Organization of Afro-American Unity (1964) and was assassinated in Harlem.

mal·con·tent (măl′kən-tĕnt′) *adj.* Dissatisfied with existing conditions. **—malcontent** *n.* **1.** A chronically dissatisfied person. **2.** One who rebels against the established system: *"immature malcontents who have long since sold out to conformity"* (John M. Wilson).

mal de mer (măl′ də mâr′) *n.* Seasickness. [French : *mal,* sickness + *de,* of + *mer,* sea.]

Mal·den (môl′dən). A city of northeast Massachusetts, a residential and manufacturing suburb of Boston. Population, 53,386.

mal·dis·tri·bu·tion (măl′dĭs-trə-byōō′shən) *n.* Faulty distribution or apportionment, as of resources, over an area or among a group.

Mal·dives (môl′dīvz, -dēvz, măl′-). Formerly **Mal·dive Islands** (-dīv, -dēv). An island country in the Indian Ocean southwest of Sri Lanka. The Maldives became a British protectorate in 1887 and achieved independence in 1965. Male is the capital. Population, 181,453. **—Mal·div′i·an** (-dĭv′ē-ən), **Mal·di′van** *adj. & n.*

male (māl) *adj. Abbr.* **m., M. 1.a.** Of, relating to, or designating the sex that has organs to produce spermatozoa for fertilizing ova. **b.** Characteristic of or appropriate to this sex; masculine. **c.** Consisting of members of this sex. **2.** Virile; manly. **3.** *Botany.* **a.** Relating to or designating organs, such as anthers or antheridia, that produce gametes capable of fertilizing those produced by female organs. **b.** Bearing stamens but not pistils; staminate: *male flowers.* **4.** Designating an object, such as an electric plug, configured for insertion into a fitted bore or socket. **—male** *n.* **1.** A member of the sex that begets young by fertilizing ova. **2.** A man or boy. **3.** *Botany.* A plant having only staminate flowers. [Middle English, from Old French, from Latin *māsculus,* diminutive of *mās,* male.] **—male′ness** *n.*

SYNONYMS: *male, masculine, manlike, manly, manful, virile, mannish.* These adjectives mean of, relating to, characteristic of, or appropriate to men. *Male,* like *female,* categorizes by sex; the term is not limited in application to human beings: *a male infant; a male dachshund. Masculine* as the opposite of *feminine* often refers to what is considered characteristic of men: *a masculine appearance; masculine attire. Manlike* usually suggests qualities belonging or held by some to be proper to a man (*manlike physical strength*); often, however, it merely indicates resemblance to a human being (*manlike apes*). *Manly* connotes qualities regarded as becoming to a man: *manly power in combat. Manful* suggests bravery and resoluteness: *We made a manful effort to redress the grievance. Virile* stresses the spirit, strength, vigor, power, or sexual potency of an adult male: *"The virile figure of Theodore Roosevelt swung down the national highway"* (Edward Bok). *Mannish* usually applies to women or their traits, clothing, or actions when they are suggestive of what is deemed by some to be more proper to a man than to a woman: *a mannish cut to the suit.*

Ma·le (mä′lē). The capital of the Maldives, on **Male,** the chief atoll of the island country. Population, 46,334.

ma·le·ate (mā′lē-āt′, mə-lē′ət) *n.* A salt or an ester of maleic acid. [MALE(IC ACID) + –ATE[2].]

Male·branche (măl-bränsh′, măl′ə-), **Nicolas de.** 1638–1715. French philosopher who sought to reconcile the metaphysics of Descartes with the philosophy of Saint Augustine.

male chauvinist *n.* A man whose behavior and attitude toward women indicate a belief that they are innately inferior to men. **—male chauvinism** *n.*

male chauvinist pig *n. Abbr.* **MCP** *Slang.* A particularly aggressive male chauvinist.

Mal·e·cite (măl′ə-sīt′) or **Mal·i·seet** (-sēt′) *n., pl.* **Malecite** or **-cites** or **Maliseet** or **-seets. 1.a.** A Native American people inhabiting the St. John River valley in New Brunswick and northeast Maine. The Malecite helped form the Abenaki confederacy in the mid-18th century. **b.** A member of this people. **2.** The Algonquian language of the Malecite. [From Micmac *malisiit,* one who speaks an incomprehensible language.]

mal·e·dict (măl′ĭ-dĭkt′) *Archaic. adj.* Accursed. **—maledict** *tr.v.* **-dict·ed, -dict·ing, -dicts.** To pronounce a curse against. [Middle English *maladicte,* from Latin *maledictus,* past participle

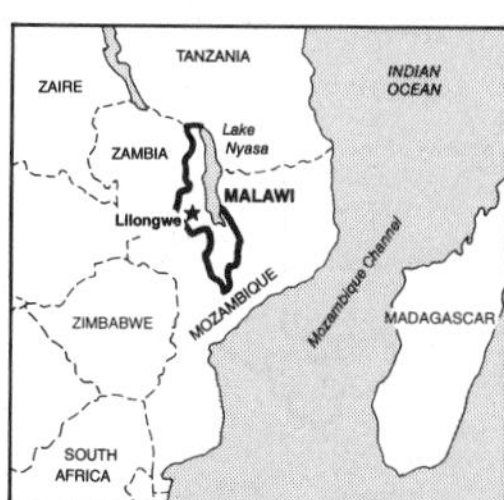

Malawi

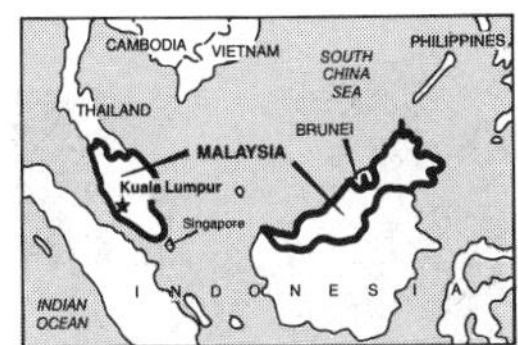

Malaysia

Malcolm X

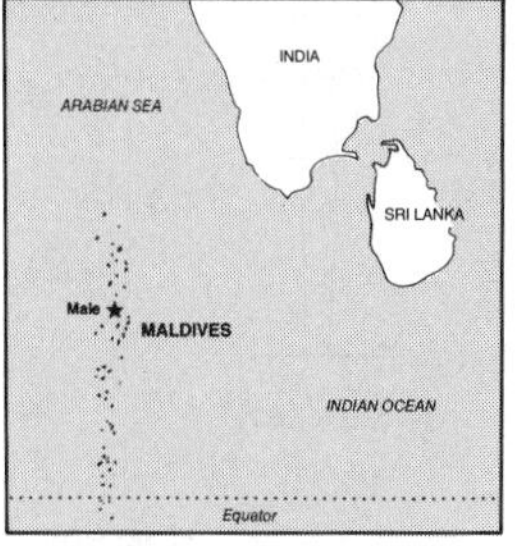

Maldives

Mali

of *maledīcere,* to curse : *male,* ill; see **mel-**[3] in Appendix + *dīcere,* to speak; see **deik-** in Appendix.]

mal•e•dic•tion (măl′ĭ-dĭk′shən) *n.* **1.a.** The calling down of a curse. **b.** A curse. **2.** Slander. **—mal′e•dic′to•ry** (-dĭk′tə-rē) *adj.*

mal•e•fac•tor (măl′ə-făk′tər) *n.* **1.** One that has committed a crime; a criminal. **2.** An evildoer. [Middle English *malefactour,* from Latin *malefactor,* from *malefacere,* to do wrong : *male,* ill; see **mel-**[3] in Appendix + *facere,* to do; see **dhē-** in Appendix.] **—mal′e•fac′tion** (-făk′shən) *n.*

male fern *n.* A fern *(Dryopteris filix-mas)* having rhizomes and stalks that yield an oleoresin used to expel tapeworms.

ma•lef•ic (mə-lĕf′ĭk) *adj.* **1.** Having or exerting a malignant influence. **2.** Evil; malicious. [Latin *maleficus* : *male,* ill; see **mel-**[3] in Appendix + *-ficus,* -fic.]

ma•lef•i•cence (mə-lĕf′ĭ-səns) *n.* **1.** The doing of evil or harm; mischief. **2.** Harmful or evil nature or quality. [Latin *maleficentia,* from *maleficus,* malefic. See MALEFIC.]

ma•lef•i•cent (mə-lĕf′ĭ-sənt) *adj.* Harmful or evil in intent or effect.

ma•le•ic acid (mə-lē′ĭk) *n.* A colorless crystalline acid, $HO_2CCH{:}CHCO_2H$, used in textile processing and as an oil and fat preservative. [From French *acide maléique,* alteration of *acide malique,* malic acid. See MALIC ACID.]

mal•e•mute (măl′ə-myo͞ot′) *n.* Variant of **malamute.**

Ma•len•kov (mə-lĕn′kôf′, mä′lən-, mə-lyĭn-kôf′), **Georgi Maximilianovich.** 1902–1988. Soviet politician who served as deputy premier (1946–1953) and premier (1953–1955).

mall[1]
Washington, D.C.

mal•en•ten•du (măl′ŏn-tŏn-do͞o′) *n.* A misunderstanding. [French, from *mal entendu,* misunderstood : *mal,* badly (from Latin *male;* see **mel-**[3] in Appendix) + *entendu,* past participle of *entendre,* to understand (from Old French; see INTEND).]

ma•lev•o•lence (mə-lĕv′ə-ləns) *n.* **1.** The quality or state of being malevolent. **2.** Malicious behavior. [Middle English, from Old French *malivolence,* from Latin *malevolentia,* from *malevolēns, malevolent-,* malevolent : *male,* badly; see **mel-**[3] in Appendix + *volēns,* present participle of *velle,* to want; see **wel-**[1] in Appendix.]

ma•lev•o•lent (mə-lĕv′ə-lənt) *adj.* **1.** Having or exhibiting ill will; wishing harm to others; malicious. **2.** Having an evil or harmful influence: *malevolent stars.* [Latin *malevolēns, malevolent-.* See MALEVOLENCE.] **—ma•lev′o•lent•ly** *adv.*

mal•fea•sance (măl-fē′zəns) *n. Law.* Misconduct or wrongdoing, especially by a public official. [Anglo-Norman *malfaisance,* from Old French *malfaisant,* malfeasant, present participle of *malfaire,* to do evil, from Latin *malefacere.* See MALEFACTOR.] **—mal•fea′sant** *adj. & n.*

mal•for•ma•tion (măl′fôr-mā′shən) *n.* Abnormal or anomalous formation or structure; deformity.

mal•formed (măl-fôrmd′) *adj.* Abnormally or faultily formed.

mal•func•tion (măl-fŭngk′shən) *intr.v.* **-tioned, -tion•ing, -tions. 1.** To fail to function. **2.** To function improperly. **—malfunction** *n.* **1.** Failure to function. **2.** Faulty or abnormal functioning.

Ma•li (mä′lē). A country of western Africa. A powerful empire from the 14th to the 16th century, Mali became part of French West Africa in the late 19th century and achieved independence in 1960. Bamako is the capital and the largest city. Population, 6,982,000. **—Ma′li•an** *adj. & n.*

mallard
Male mallard
Anas platyrhynchos

mal•ic acid (măl′ĭk, mā′lĭk) *n.* A colorless, crystalline compound, $COOH{\cdot}CH_2{\cdot}CHOH{\cdot}COOH$, that occurs naturally in a wide variety of unripe fruit, including apples, cherries, and tomatoes, and is used as a flavoring and in the aging of wine. [French *(acide) malique,* from Latin *mālum,* apple, from Greek *mēlon, malon.*]

mal•ice (măl′ĭs) *n.* **1.** A desire to harm others or to see others suffer; extreme ill will or spite. **2.** *Law.* The intent, without just cause or reason, to commit a wrongful act that will result in harm to another. [Middle English, from Old French, from Latin *malitia,* from *malus,* bad. See **mel-**[3] in Appendix.]

ma•li•cious (mə-lĭsh′əs) *adj.* Having the nature of or resulting from malice; deliberately harmful; spiteful: *malicious gossip.* **—ma•li′cious•ly** *adv.* **—ma•li′cious•ness** *n.*

malicious mischief *n. Law.* Willful or wanton destruction of another's property.

ma•lign (mə-līn′) *tr.v.* **-ligned, -lign•ing, -ligns.** To make evil, harmful, and often untrue statements about; speak evil of. **—malign** *adj.* **1.** Evil in disposition, nature, or intent. **2.** Evil in influence; injurious. **3.** Having or showing malice or ill will; malevolent. [Middle English *malignen,* to attack, from Old French *malignier,* from Late Latin *malignārī,* from Latin *malignus,* malign. See **gene-** in Appendix. Adj., from Middle English, from Old French, from Latin *malignus.*] **—ma•lign′er** *n.*

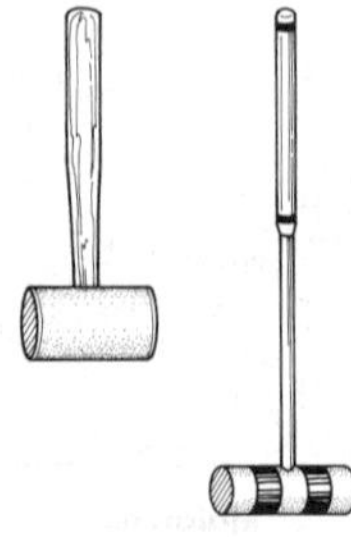
mallet
Carpenter's and croquet mallets

SYNONYMS: *malign, defame, traduce, vilify, asperse, slander, calumniate, libel.* These verbs mean to make evil, harmful, often untrue statements about another. *Malign* stresses malicious intent: *"Have I not taken your part when you were maligned?"* (Thackeray). *Defame* connotes damage to reputation, character, or good name brought about by misrepresentation: *The judge ruled that the plaintiff had been defamed and had legitimate grounds for a lawsuit. Traduce* implies malicious and false statements resulting in humiliation or disgrace: *"My character was traduced by Captain Hawkins . . . so much so, that even the ship's company cried out shame"* (Frederick Marryat). *Vilify* pertains to open, deliberate, vicious defamation or denigration: *"One who belongs to the most vilified and persecuted minority in history is not likely to be insensible to the freedoms guaranteed by our Constitution"* (Felix Frankfurter). To *asperse* is to spread unfavorable charges or insinuations against: *"a libel tending to asperse or vilify the house of Commons"* (Letters of Junius). *Slander* and *calumniate* apply to malicious, false, and defamatory oral expression: *slandered his political opponent; calumniated and ridiculed the President in whose cabinet he had once served. Libel* involves the communication of written or pictorial material injurious to the reputation of another: *The ensuing publicity caused the entertainer to regret having sued the newspaper for libeling his character.* See also Synonyms at **sinister.**

ma•lig•nan•cy (mə-lĭg′nən-sē) *n., pl.* **-cies. 1.** Also **ma•lig•nance** (-nəns). The state or quality of being malignant. **2.** *Pathology.* A malignant tumor.

ma•lig•nant (mə-lĭg′nənt) *adj.* **1.** Showing great malevolence; disposed to do evil. **2.** Highly injurious; pernicious. **3.** *Pathology.* **a.** Threatening to life; virulent: *a malignant disease.* **b.** Tending to metastasize; cancerous. Used of a tumor. **—ma•lig′nant•ly** *adv.*

ma•lig•ni•ty (mə-lĭg′nĭ-tē) *n., pl.* **-ties. 1.a.** Intense ill will or hatred; great malice. **b.** An act or a feeling of great malice. **2.** The condition or quality of being highly dangerous or injurious; deadliness.

ma•li•hi•ni (mä′lĭ-hē′nē) *n., pl.* **-nis.** A newcomer to Hawaii. [Hawaiian.]

ma•lines (mə-lēn′) *n.* **1.** Also **ma•line** (-lēn′). A thin, stiff net woven in a hexagonal pattern and used in dressmaking. **2.** See **Mechlin**[2]. [French, after *Malines* (Mechlin), Belgium.]

Ma•lines (mə-lēnz′, mä-lēn′). See **Mechlin**[1].

ma•lin•ger (mə-lĭng′gər) *intr.v.* **-gered, -ger•ing, -gers.** To feign illness or other incapacity in order to avoid duty or work. [From French *malingre,* sickly.] **—ma•lin′ger•er** *n.*

Ma•lin•ke (mə-lĭng′kē) *n., pl.* **Malinke** or **-kes. 1.** A member of a Mandingo people of Senegal and Gambia. **2.** The Mandingo language of this people.

Mal•i•now•ski (măl′ə-nôf′skē, mä′lĭ-), **Bronislaw Kasper.** 1884–1942. Polish-born British anthropologist who maintained that customs and beliefs have specific social functions.

Mal•i•seet (măl′ə-sēt′) *n.* Variant of **Malecite.**

mal•i•son (măl′ĭ-sən, -zən) *n. Archaic.* A curse. [Middle English *malisoun,* from Old French *maleiçon,* from Latin *maledictiō, maledictiōn-,* from *maledictus,* past participle of *maledīcere,* to speak ill, curse. See MALEDICT.]

♦ **mall**[1] (môl, măl) *n.* **1.** A large, often enclosed shopping complex containing various stores, businesses, and restaurants usually accessible by common passageways. **2.** A street lined with shops and closed to vehicles. **3.** A shady public walk or promenade. **4.** *Upstate New York.* See **median strip.** See Regional Note at **neutral ground.** [After *The Mall* in London, England, originally a pall-mall alley.]

mall[2] (môl) *n. & v.* Variant of **maul.**

mal•lard (măl′ərd) *n., pl.* **mallard** or **-lards.** A wild duck *(Anas platyrhynchos)* of which the male has a green head and neck. Most domestic ducks descend from the mallard. [Middle English *malarde,* from Old French *mallart* : perhaps from *male,* male; see MALE + *-ard,* -ard, or possibly of Germanic origin.]

Mal•lar•mé (măl′är-mā′), **Stéphane.** 1842–1898. French poet and a founder of the symbolist school.

mal•le•a•ble (măl′ē-ə-bəl) *adj.* **1.** Capable of being shaped or formed, as by hammering or pressure: *a malleable metal.* **2.** Easily controlled or influenced; tractable. **3.** Able to adjust to changing circumstances; adaptable: *the malleable mind of the pragmatist.* [Middle English, from Old French, from Medieval Latin *malleābilis,* from *malleāre,* to hammer, from Latin *malleus,* hammer. See **mele-** in Appendix.] **—mal′le•a•bil′i•ty, mal′le•a•ble•ness** *n.* **—mal′le•a•bly** *adv.*

SYNONYMS: *malleable, ductile, plastic, pliable, pliant.* The central meaning shared by these adjectives is "capable of being shaped, bent, or drawn out": *malleable metals such as gold; ductile copper; plastic substances such as wax; soaked the leather to make it pliable; pliant molten glass.*

mal•lee (măl′ē) *n.* **1.** Any of several west Australian evergreen shrubs or trees of the genus *Eucalyptus.* **2.** A thicket or growth of these plants. [Wuywurung (Aboriginal language of southeast Australia) *mali.*]

mal•le•i (măl′ē-ī′) *n. Anatomy.* Plural of **malleus.**

mal•le•muck (măl′ə-mŭk′) *n.* Any of several sea birds, such as the fulmar, albatross, or shearwater. [Dutch *mallemok,* fulmar : *mal,* silly (from Middle Dutch) + *mok,* gull.]

mal•let (măl′ĭt) *n.* **1.a.** A short-handled hammer, usually with a cylindrical head of wood, used chiefly to drive a chisel or wedge. **b.** A tool with a large head, used to strike a surface without damaging it. **2.** *Sports.* A long-handled implement used to strike a ball, as in croquet and polo. **3.** *Music.* A light hammer with a rounded head for striking a percussion instrument. [Middle English, from Old French *maillet,* diminutive of *mail,* maul. See MAUL.]

mal·le·us (măl′ē-əs) *n., pl.* **mal·le·i** (măl′ē-ī′). *Anatomy.* The hammer-shaped bone that is the outermost of the three small bones in the mammalian middle ear. Also called *hammer.* [Latin, hammer. See **mela-** in Appendix.]

Mal·lon (măl′ən), **Mary.** Known as "Typhoid Mary." 1870?–1938. American cook and immune carrier of typhoid fever who infected more than 50 people with the disease.

Mal·lor·ca (mä-yôr′kä, -lyôr′-). See **Majorca.**

mal·low (măl′ō) *n.* **1.** Any of various plants of the genus *Malva,* having pink or white axillary flowers, palmate leaves, and disklike schizocarpic fruits. **2.** Any of various related plants, such as the rose mallow. [Middle English *malwe,* from Old English *mealwe* and from Old French *malve,* both from Latin *malva.*]

Mal·mö (măl′mō, mäl′mœ). A city of southern Sweden on the Oresund opposite Copenhagen. An important trade and shipping center during the Hanseatic period, it passed from Denmark to Sweden in 1658. Population, 229,107.

malm·sey (mäm′zē) *n., pl.* **-seys.** A sweet fortified wine originally made in Greece and now produced mainly in Madeira. Also called *malvasia, malvoisie.* [Middle English, ultimately from Medieval Latin *malvasia, malmasia,* alteration of Medieval Greek *Monemvasia* (Malvasia), a village of southern Greece.]

mal·nour·ished (măl-nûr′ĭsht, -nŭr′-) *adj.* Affected by improper nutrition or an insufficient diet.

mal·nour·ish·ment (măl′nûr′ĭsh-mənt, -nŭr′-) *n.* Malnutrition.

mal·nu·tri·tion (măl′no͞o-trĭsh′ən, -nyo͞o-) *n.* Poor nutrition because of an insufficient or poorly balanced diet or faulty digestion or utilization of foods.

mal·oc·clu·sion (măl′ə-klo͞o′zhən) *n.* Faulty contact between the upper and lower teeth when the jaw is closed.

mal·o·dor (măl-ō′dər) *n.* A bad odor; a stench. See Synonyms at **stench.**

mal·o·dor·ous (măl-ō′dər-əs) *adj.* Having a bad odor; foul. **—mal·o′dor·ous·ly** *adv.* **—mal·o′dor·ous·ness** *n.*

Ma·lone (mə-lōn′), **Edmund** or **Edmond.** 1741–1812. British scholar noted for his chronology of Shakespeare's plays and his editions of Shakespeare (1790) and Dryden (1800).

ma·lo·nic acid (mə-lō′nĭk, -lŏn′ik) *n.* A white crystalline acid, $CH_2(COOH)_2$, derived from malic acid and used in making barbiturates. [French *(acide) malonique,* alteration of *malique,* malic (acid). See MALIC ACID.]

Mal·o·ry (măl′ə-rē), Sir **Thomas.** fl. 1470. English writer of *Le Morte d'Arthur,* a collection of Arthurian romances adapted from French sources and published by William Caxton in 1485.

ma·lo·ti (mä-lō′tē) *n.* Plural of **loti.**

Mal·pi·ghi (măl-pē′gē, mäl-), **Marcello.** 1628–1694. Italian anatomist who was the first to use a microscope in the study of anatomy and discovered the capillary system.

Mal·pigh·i·an corpuscle (măl-pĭg′ē-ən) *n. Anatomy.* **1.** A mass of arterial capillaries enveloped in a capsule and attached to a tubule in the kidney. Also called *Malpighian body, renal corpuscle.* **2.** A nodule of lymphatic tissue surrounding the smaller arteries in the spleen. [After Marcello MALPIGHI.]

Malpighian layer *n. Anatomy.* The deepest layer of the epidermis, from which the outer layers develop. [After Marcello MALPIGHI.]

Malpighian tube *n.* Any of the excretory tubules leading from the posterior portion of the alimentary canal of insects and other arthropods. Also called *Malpighian tubule.* [After Marcello MALPIGHI.]

mal·po·si·tion (măl′pə-zĭsh′ən) *n.* An abnormal position, as of an organ or a body part.

mal·prac·tice (măl-prăk′tĭs) *n.* **1.** Improper or negligent treatment of a patient, as by a physician, resulting in injury, damage, or loss. **2.** Improper or unethical conduct by the holder of a professional or official position. **3.** The act or an instance of improper practice. **—mal′prac·ti′tion·er** (-tĭsh′ə-nər) *n.*

Mal·raux (măl-rō′, mäl-), **André.** 1901–1976. French writer and politician. A member of the French resistance during World War II, he served as minister of culture (1959–1969) under Charles de Gaulle.

M.A.L.S. *abbr.* Master of Library Science.

malt (môlt) *n.* **1.** Grain, usually barley, that has been allowed to sprout, used chiefly in brewing and distilling. **2.** An alcoholic beverage, such as beer or ale, brewed from malt. **3.** See **malted milk** (sense 2). **—malt** *v.* **malt·ed, malt·ing, malts.** *—tr.* **1.** To process (grain) into malt. **2.** To treat or mix with malt or a malt extract. *—intr.* To become malt. [Middle English, from Old English *mealt.* See **mel-**[1] in Appendix.]

Mal·ta (môl′tə). An island country in the Mediterranean Sea south of Sicily, comprising the island of **Malta** and two smaller islands. Occupied successively by Phoenicians, Greeks, Carthaginians, Romans, Saracens, and Normans, Malta was granted to the Knights Hospitalers in 1530 and passed to France in 1798 and Great Britain in 1800. The country became independent in 1964. Valletta, on Malta Island, is the capital. Population, 331,997.

Malta fever *n.* See **brucellosis** (sense 1).

mal·tase (môl′tās′, -tāz′) *n.* An enzyme that catalyzes the hydrolysis of maltose to glucose.

malt·ed milk (môl′tĭd) *n.* **1.** A soluble powder made of dried milk, malted barley, and wheat flour. **2.** A beverage made by mixing milk with this powder and adding ice cream and flavoring. In this sense, also called *malt, malted.*

Mal·tese (môl-tēz′, -tēs′) *adj.* Of or relating to Malta or its people, language, or culture. **—Maltese** *n., pl.* **Maltese. 1.** A native or inhabitant of Malta. **2.** The Semitic language of the people of Malta. **3.** Any of a breed of toy dogs having a long, silky white coat. **4.** A Maltese cat.

Maltese cat *n.* A short-haired domestic cat having a silky, bluish-gray coat.

Maltese cross *n.* A cross having four equal arms resembling arrowheads joined at the points.

mal·tha (măl′thə) *n.* A black, viscous natural bitumen. [Middle English *malthe,* from Latin *maltha,* from Greek, a mixture of wax and pitch. See **mel-**[1] in Appendix.]

Mal·thus (măl′thəs), **Thomas Robert.** 1766–1834. British economist who wrote *An Essay on the Principle of Population* (1798), arguing that population tends to increase faster than food supply unless the increase is checked by moral restraints or by war, famine, and disease. **—Mal·thu′sian** (-tho͞o′zhən, -zē-ən) *adj. & n.* **—Mal·thu′sian·ism** *n.*

malt liquor *n.* A fermented liquor, such as beer or ale, made with malt.

mal·tose (môl′tōs′, -tōz′) *n.* A white crystalline sugar, $C_{12}H_{22}O_{11}{\cdot}H_2O$, formed during the digestion of starch. Also called *malt sugar.* [French, from English MALT.]

mal·treat (măl-trēt′) *tr.v.* **-treat·ed, -treat·ing, -treats.** To treat in a rough or cruel way; abuse. See Synonyms at **abuse.** **—mal·treat′ment** *n.*

malt sugar *n.* See **maltose.**

mal·va·si·a (măl′və-zē′ə) *n.* **1.** A grape from which malmsey wine is made. **2.** See **malmsey.** [Italian, from Medieval Latin *malvasia.* See MALMSEY.]

Mal·vern Hills (môl′vərn, mô′). A range of hills of west-central England rising to 425.5 m (1,395 ft).

mal·ver·sa·tion (măl′vər-sā′shən) *n.* Misconduct in public office. [French, from *malverser,* to misbehave, from Old French, from Latin *male versārī* : *male,* badly; see **mel-**[3] in Appendix + *versārī,* to behave; see **wer-**[2] in Appendix.]

mal·voi·sie (măl′vwə-zē′) *n.* See **malmsey.** [Middle English *malvesie,* from Old French, from Medieval Latin *malvesia, malvasia.* See MALMSEY.]

ma·ma or **mam·ma** also **mom·ma** (mä′mə) *n.* **1.** (*also* mə-mä′). *Informal.* Mother. **2.** *Slang.* **a.** A woman. **b.** A wife. [Of baby-talk origin. See **mā-**[2] in Appendix.]

Ma·mar·o·neck (mə-măr′ə-nĕk′). A village of southeast New York, a suburb of New York City. Population, 17,616.

mam·ba (mäm′bə) *n.* Any of several venomous arboreal snakes of the genus *Dendroaspis* of tropical Africa, especially *D. angusticeps,* a green or black tree snake having an often fatal bite. [Nguni (Zulu) *í-mâmbà.*]

Mam·be·ra·mo (măm′bə-rä′mō). A river, about 805 km (500 mi) long, of western New Guinea flowing northwest into the Pacific Ocean.

mam·bo (mäm′bō) *n., pl.* **-bos. 1.** A dance of Latin American origin, resembling the rumba. **2.** The syncopated music for this dance in 4/4 time. **—mambo** *intr.v.* **-boed, -bo·ing, -bos.** To perform this dance. [American Spanish, from *mamboo,* wooden cane, percussion instrument.]

Mam·e·luke (măm′ə-lo͞ok′) *n.* A member of a former military caste, originally composed of slaves from Turkey, that held the Egyptian throne from about 1250 until 1517 and remained powerful until 1811. [French *mameluk,* from Arabic *mamlūk,* slave, Mameluke, from *malaka,* to possess.]

Mam·et (măm′ĭt), **David.** Born 1947. American playwright whose works include *Glengarry Glen Ross* (1984).

ma·mey (mä-mā′, -mē′) *n., pl.* **-meys. 1.** A West Indian tree *(Mammea americana)* having glossy leaves, white fragrant flowers, and large edible drupes. **2.** The fruit of this tree, having firm juicy flesh and toxic seeds. Also called *mammee apple.* [Spanish, from Arawak or Taino.]

mam·ma[1] (mä′mə) *n.* Variant of **mama.**

mam·ma[2] (măm′ə) *n., pl.* **mam·mae** (măm′ē). An organ of female mammals that contains milk-producing glands; a mammary gland. [Latin. See **mā-**[2] in Appendix.] **—mam′mate′** (măm′āt′) *adj.*

mam·mal (măm′əl) *n.* Any of various warm-blooded vertebrate animals of the class Mammalia, including human beings, characterized by a covering of hair on the skin and, in the female, milk-producing mammary glands for nourishing the young. [From Late Latin *mammālis,* of the breast, from Latin *mamma,* breast. See **mā-**[2] in Appendix.] **—mam·ma′li·an** (mă-mā′lē-ən) *adj. & n.*

mam·mal·o·gy (mă-măl′ə-jē, -mŏl′-) *n.* The branch of zoology that deals with mammals. [MAMMA(L) + -LOGY.] **—mam′ma·log′i·cal** (măm′ə-lŏj′ĭ-kəl) *adj.* **—mam·mal′o·gist** *n.*

mam·ma·plas·ty or **mam·mo·plas·ty** (măm′ə-plăs′tē) *n., pl.* **-ties.** Reconstructive or cosmetic plastic surgery to alter the size or shape of the breast or breasts.

mam·ma·ry (măm′ə-rē) *adj.* Of or relating to a breast or mamma.

mammary gland *n.* Any of the milk-producing glands in fe-

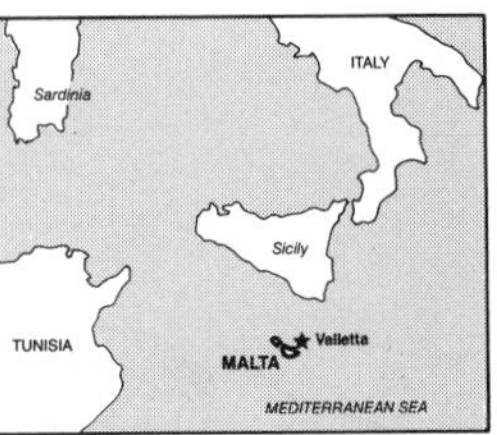

Malta

Maltese cross

ă pat	oi boy
ā pay	ou out
âr care	o͝o took
ä father	o͞o boot
ĕ pet	ŭ cut
ē be	ûr urge
ĭ pit	th thin
ī pie	*th* this
îr pier	hw which
ŏ pot	zh vision
ō toe	ə about, item
ô paw	♦ regionalism

Stress marks: **′** (primary); ′ (secondary), as in **dictionary** (dĭk′shə-nĕr′ē)

male mammals, consisting of lobes containing clusters of alveoli with a system of ducts to convey the milk to an external nipple or teat. These glands typically occur in pairs and begin secreting milk when young are born.

mam·mee apple (mä-mā′, -mē′) *n.* See **mamey.**

mam·mif·er·ous (mă-mĭf′ər-əs) *adj.* Having mammary glands.

mam·mil·la (mă-mĭl′ə) *n., pl.* **-mil·lae** (-mĭl′ē). **1.** A nipple or teat. **2.** A nipple-shaped protuberance. [Latin, diminutive of *mamma,* breast. See **mā-²** in Appendix.] **—mam′mil·lar′y** (măm′ə-lĕr′ē) *adj.*

mam·mil·late (măm′ə-lāt′) also **mam·mil·lat·ed** (-lā′tĭd) *adj.* **1.** Having nipples or mammillae. **2.** Shaped like a nipple or mammilla. **—mam′mil·la′tion** *n.*

mam·mo·gram (măm′ə-grăm′) *n.* An x-ray image of the breast produced by mammography.

mam·mog·ra·phy (mă-mŏg′rə-fē) *n., pl.* **-phies.** X-ray examination of the breasts for detection of tumors.

Mam·mon (măm′ən) *n.* **1.** *Bible.* Riches, avarice, and worldly gain personified as a false god in the New Testament. **2.** Often **mammon.** Material wealth regarded as having an evil influence. [Middle English, from Late Latin *mammon,* from Greek *mamōnas,* from Aramaic *māmōnā,* riches.]

mam·mo·plas·ty (măm′ə-plăs′tē) *n., pl.* **-ties.** Variant of **mammaplasty.**

mammoth
Woolly mammoth
Mammuthus primigenius

mam·moth (măm′əth) *n.* **1.** Any of various large, hairy, extinct elephants of the genus *Mammuthus,* especially the woolly mammoth *(M. primigenius),* once widespread in the Northern Hemisphere. **2.** Something of great size. **—mammoth** *adj.* Of enormous size; huge. See Synonyms at **enormous.** [Obsolete Russian *mamut, mamot.*]

WORD HISTORY: The mammoth was introduced to the English-speaking world after mammoth skeletons were discovered in Siberia, so it is no surprise that this creature's name is taken from Russian, even though the animal roamed over Eurasia and North America. The Russian word, now *mamant'* but formerly *mamot* as well, was borrowed into English in variant spellings. It was first recorded in 1706 in the form *Mammuth,* but in 1763 we find the form *mammon.* It is said that the Russian word is a borrowing of an Ostyak word (the Ostyak people live in western Siberia), but this has not been proved.

mam·my (măm′ē) *n., pl.* **-mies. 1.** Mother. **2.** *Offensive.* A Black nursemaid, especially one formerly in the southern United States. [From dialectal *mam,* variant of MAMA.]

Ma·mo·ré (mä-mə-rā′). A river, about 965 km (600 mi) long, of northern Bolivia flowing partly along the Brazilian border to join the Beni River and form the Madeira River.

Manchester terrier

man (măn) *n., pl.* **men** (mĕn). **1.** An adult male human being. **2.** A human being regardless of sex or age; a person. **3.** A human being or an adult male human being belonging to a specific occupation, group, nationality, or other category. Often used in combination: *a milkman; a congressman; a freeman.* **4.** The human race; mankind: *man's quest for peace.* **5.** *Zoology.* A member of the genus *Homo,* family Hominidae, order Primates, class Mammalia, characterized by erect posture and an opposable thumb, especially a member of the only extant species, *Homo sapiens,* distinguished by a highly developed brain, the capacity for abstract reasoning, and the ability to communicate by means of organized speech and record information in a variety of symbolic systems. **6.** A male human being endowed with qualities, such as strength, considered characteristic of manhood. **7.** *Theology.* In Christianity and Judaism, a being composed of a body and a soul or spirit. **8.** *Informal.* **a.** A husband. **b.** A lover or sweetheart. **9. men. a.** Workers. **b.** Enlisted personnel of the armed forces: *officers and men.* **10.** A male representative, as of a country or company: *our man in Tokyo.* **11.** A male servant or subordinate. **12.** *Informal.* Used as a familiar form of address for a man: *See here, my good man!* **13.** One who swore allegiance to a lord in the Middle Ages; a vassal. **14.** *Games.* Any of the pieces used in a board game, such as chess or checkers. **15.** *Nautical.* A ship. Often used in combination: *a merchantman; a man-of-war.* **16.** Often **Man.** *Slang.* A person or group felt to be in a position of power or authority. Used with *the: "Their writing mainly concerns the street life—the pimp, the junky, the forces of drug addiction, exploitation at the hands of 'the man'"* (Black World). **—man** *tr.v.* **manned, man·ning, mans. 1.** To supply with men, as for defense or service: *man a ship.* **2.** To take stations at, as to defend or operate: *manned the guns.* **3.** To fortify or brace: *manned himself for the battle ahead.* **—man** *interj.* Used as an expletive to indicate intense feeling: *Man! That was close.* **—*idioms.* as one man. 1.** In complete agreement; unanimously. **2.** With no exception: *They objected as one man.* **one's own man.** Independent in judgment and action. **to a man.** Without exception: *All were lost, to a man.* [Middle English, from Old English *mann.* See **man-¹** in Appendix.]

manchineel
Hippomane mancinella

USAGE NOTE: Traditionally, *man* and words derived from it have been used generically to designate any or all of the human race irrespective of sex. In Old English this was the principal sense of *man,* which meant "a human being" regardless of sex; the words *wer* and *wyf* (or *wæpman* and *wifman*) were used to refer to "a male human being" and "a female human being" respectively. But in Middle English *man* displaced *wer* as the term for "a male human being," while *wyfman* (which evolved into present-day *woman*) was retained for "a female human being." The result of these changes was an assymetrical arrangement that many criticize as sexist. Many writers have revised some of their practices accordingly. But the precise implications of the usage vary according to the context and the particular use of *man* or its derivatives. • *Man* sometimes appears to have the sense of "person" or "people" when it is used as a count noun, as in *A man is known by the company he keeps* and *Men have long yearned to unlock the secrets of the atom,* and in phrases like *the common man* and *the man in the street.* Here the generic interpretation arises indirectly: if a man is known by the company he keeps, then so, by implication, is a woman. For this reason the generic interpretation of these uses of *man* is not possible where the applicability of the predicate varies according to the sex of the individual. Thus it would be inappropriate to say that *Men are the only animals that can conceive at any time,* since the sentence literally asserts that the ability to conceive applies to male human beings. This usage presumes that males can be taken as representatives of the species. In almost all cases, however, the words *person* and *people* can be substituted for *man* and *men,* often with a gain in clarity. • By contrast, *man* functions more as a generic when it is used without an article in the singular to refer to the human race, as in sentences like *The capacity for language is unique to man* or in phrases like *man's inhumanity to man.* But this use of *man* is also ambiguous, since it can refer exclusively to male members of the human race. In most contexts words such as *humanity* or *humankind* will convey the generic sense of this use of *man.* • On the whole, the Usage Panel accepts the generic use of *man,* the women members significantly less than the men. The sentence *If early man suffered from a lack of information, modern man is tyrannized by an excess of it* was acceptable to 81 percent of the Panel (including 58 percent of the women and 92 percent of the men). The Panel also accepted compound words derived from generic *man.* The sentence *The Great Wall is the only man-made structure visible from space* was acceptable to 86 percent (including 76 percent of the women and 91 percent of the men). The sentence *"The history of language is the history of mankind"* (James Bradstreet Greenough and George Lyman Kittredge) was acceptable to 76 percent (including 63 percent of the women and 82 percent of the men). Such compounds were acceptable even when the context required that they be applied chiefly to women. Thus, 66 percent of the Panel (including 57 percent of the women and 71 percent of the men) accepts the word *manpower* in the sentence *Countries that do not permit women to participate in the work force are at a disadvantage in competing with those that do avail themselves of that extra source of manpower.* • A related set of problems is raised by the use of *man* in forming the names of occupational and social roles such as *businessman, chairman, spokesman, layman,* and *freshman,* as well as in analogous formations such as *unsportsmanlike* and *showmanship.* Some condemn this use categorically; however, these words remained acceptable to a majority of the Usage Panel when they were used to refer to a role or class in the abstract but were rejected when they were used to refer to a woman. Thus the general use of *chairman* was acceptable to 67 percent of the Panel (including 52 percent of the women and 76 percent of the men) in the sentence *The chairman will be appointed by the Faculty Senate.* But only 48 percent (including 43 percent of the women and 50 percent of the men) accepted the use of the word in *Emily Owen, chairman of the Mayor's Task Force, issued a statement assuring residents that their views would be solicited,* where it is applied to a woman. • Several strategies have been suggested for replacing the categorical use of compounds formed with *man.* Parallel terms like *businesswoman, spokeswoman,* and *chairwoman* are increasingly used to refer to women. Also in use are common-gender terms coined with *person,* such as *businessperson, spokesperson,* and *chairperson.* For occupational titles ending in *man,* new standards of official usage have been established by the U.S. Department of Labor and other government agencies. In official contexts terms such as *firefighter* and *police officer* are now generally used in place of *fireman* and *policeman.* • A majority of the Panelists rejected the verb *man* when it was used to refer to an activity performed by women. The sentence *Members of the League of Women Voters will be manning the registration desk* was unacceptable to 56 percent of the Panel (including 61 percent of the women and 54 percent of the men). See Usage Notes at **-ess, people.**

Man, Isle of. An island of Great Britain in the Irish Sea off the northwest coast of England. Occupied in the 9th century by Vikings, it passed from Norway to Scotland in 1266. Parliament purchased the island in 1765, and it remains an autonomous possession of the British crown.

man. *abbr.* Manual.

Man. *abbr.* Manitoba.

ma·na (mä′nə) *n.* **1.** A supernatural force believed to dwell in a person or sacred object. **2.** Power; authority. [Maori.]

man about town *n., pl.* **men about town.** A sophisticated, socially active man who frequents fashionable places.

man·a·cle (măn′ə-kəl) *n.* **1.** A device for confining the hands, usually consisting of a set of two metal rings that are fastened about the wrists and joined by a metal chain. **2.** Something that confines or restrains. **—manacle** *tr.v.* **-cled, -cling, -cles.** To confine or restrain with or as if with manacles; fetter. See Synonyms at **hamper¹.** [Middle English, from Old French *manicle,* from Latin *manicula,* diminutive of *manus,* hand. See **man-**[2] in Appendix.]

man·age (măn′ĭj) *v.* **-aged, -ag·ing, -ag·es.** —*tr.* **1.** To direct or control the use of; handle: *manage a complex machine tool.* **2.a.** To exert control over: *"Managing the news . . . is the oldest game in town"* (James Reston). *"A major crisis to be managed loomed on the horizon"* (Time). **b.** To make submissive to one's authority, discipline, or persuasion. **3.** To direct the affairs or interests of: *manage a company; an agency that manages performers.* **4.** To succeed in accomplishing or achieving, especially with difficulty; contrive or arrange: *managed to get a promotion.* —*intr.* **1.** To direct or conduct business affairs. **2.** To continue to get along; carry on: *learning how to manage on my own.* [Italian *maneggiare,* from Vulgar Latin **manidiāre,* from Latin *manus,* hand. See **man-**[2] in Appendix.]

man·age·a·ble (măn′ĭ-jə-bəl) *adj.* That can be managed or controlled: *manageable problems.* —**man′age·a·bil′i·ty, man′age·a·ble·ness** *n.* —**man′age·a·bly** *adv.*

man·age·ment (măn′ĭj-mənt) *n. Abbr.* **mgt., mgmt. 1.** The act, manner, or practice of managing; handling, supervision, or control: *management of a crisis; management of factory workers.* **2.** The person or persons who control or direct a business or other enterprise. **3.** Skill in managing; executive ability.

management information system *n. Abbr.* **MIS** *Computer Science.* A computer system designed to help managers plan and direct business and organizational operations.

man·ag·er (măn′ĭ-jər) *n. Abbr.* **mgr., mngr. 1.** One who handles, controls, or directs, especially: **a.** One who directs a business or other enterprise. **b.** One who controls resources and expenditures, as of a household. **2.** One who is in charge of the business affairs of an entertainer. **3.** *Sports.* **a.** One who is in charge of the training and performance of an athlete or a team. **b.** A student who is in charge of the equipment and records of a school or college team. —**man′ag·er·ship′** *n.*

man·a·ge·ri·al (măn′ĭ-jîr′ē-əl) *adj.* Of or characteristic of a manager or management. —**man′a·ge′ri·al·ly** *adv.*

man·ag·ing editor (măn′ĭ-jĭng) *n.* An editor who supervises and coordinates the editorial activities of a publishing house or publication, such as a newspaper.

Ma·na·gua (mə-näg′wə, mä-nä′gwä). The capital and largest city of Nicaragua, in the western part of the country on the southern shore of **Lake Managua.** The city, designated as the capital in the 1850's, has frequently been damaged by earthquakes. Population, 644,588. —**Ma·na′guan** *adj. & n.*

man·a·kin (măn′ə-kĭn) *n.* Any of various small colorful birds of the family Pipridae, found in forests of Central and South America. [Alteration of MANIKIN.]

Ma·na·ma (mə-năm′ə, mă-) or **Al Ma·na·mah** (ăl mə-năm′ə, mă-). The capital and largest city of Bahrain, on the Persian Gulf. Population, 108,684.

ma·ña·na (mä-nyä′nə) *adv.* **1.** Tomorrow. **2.** At an unspecified future time. —**mañana** *n.* An indefinite time in the future. [Spanish, from Vulgar Latin **(crās) māneāna,* early (tomorrow), from Latin *māne,* morning. See **mā-**[1] in Appendix.]

Ma·nas·sas (mə-năs′əs). An independent city of northeast Virginia west of Alexandria. The Civil War Battles of Bull Run (called the Battles of Manassas by the Confederates) were fought nearby in July 1861 and August 1862. Population, 15,438.

Ma·nas·seh (mə-năs′ə). In the Old Testament, the eldest son of Joseph and the forebear of one of the tribes of Israel.

man-at-arms (măn′ət-ärmz′) *n., pl.* **men-at-arms** (mĕn′-). A soldier, especially a medieval cavalryman supplied with heavy arms.

man·a·tee (măn′ə-tē′) *n.* Any of various herbivorous aquatic mammals of the genus *Trichechus,* having paddlelike front flippers and a horizontally flattened tail and found in warm coastal waters of Florida, northern South America, West Africa, and the Caribbean. [Spanish *manatí,* from Cariban, breast.]

Ma·naus (mə-nous′, mä-). A city of northwest Brazil on the Rio Negro near its junction with the Amazon River. Founded in the 1660's, Manaus was a prosperous center of the wild-rubber trade in the late 19th century. Population, 611,763.

Man·ches·ter (măn′chĕs′tər, -chĭ-stər). **1.** A borough of northwest England east-northeast of Liverpool. Founded on the site of Celtic and Roman settlements, it was first chartered in 1301. Greater Manchester is densely populated and highly industrialized. The **Manchester Ship Canal** (completed in 1894) affords access for oceangoing vessels. Population, 464,200. **2.** A town of north-central Connecticut east of Hartford. Population, 49,761. **3.** The largest city of New Hampshire, in the southeast part of the state on the Merrimack River north of Nashua. Incorporated as Derryfield in 1751 and renamed in 1810, it was an important textile center until the 1930's. Population, 90,936.

Manchester terrier *n.* Any of various short-haired, black-and-tan dogs of a breed that originated in Manchester, England. Also called *black-and-tan terrier.*

man-child (măn′chīd′) *n., pl.* **men-chil·dren** (mĕn′chĭl′drən). A male child; a boy; a son.

man·chi·neel (măn′chĭ-nēl′) *n.* A tropical American tree *(Hippomane mancinella)* having poisonous fruit and a milky sap that causes skin blisters on contact. [French *mancenille,* from Spanish *manzanilla,* diminutive of *manzana,* apple, from Old Spanish, from Latin *(māla) Matiāna,* (apples) of Matius, possibly after Caius *Matius* Calvena (fl. first century B.C.), Roman author of a cookbook.]

Man·chu (măn′cho͞o, măn-cho͞o′) *n., pl.* **Manchu** or **-chus. 1.** A member of a people native to Manchuria who ruled China during the Qing dynasty. **2.** The Tungusic language of the Manchu. —**Manchu** *adj.* Of or relating to the Manchu or their language or culture. [Manchu *manju.*]

Man·chu·kuo (măn′cho͞o′kwō′) also **Man·chu·guo** (-gwō′). A former state of eastern Asia in Manchuria and eastern Nei Monggol (Inner Mongolia). It was established as a puppet state (1932) after the Japanese invaded Manchuria in 1931 and was returned to Chinese sovereignty in 1945.

Man·chu·ri·a (măn-cho͝or′ē-ə). A region of northeast China comprising the modern-day provinces of Heilongjiang, Jilin, and Liaoning. It was the homeland of the Manchu people who conquered China in the 17th century and was hotly contested by the Russians and the Japanese in the late 19th and early 20th centuries. —**Man·chu′ri·an** *adj. & n.*

Man·chu-Tun·gus (măn′cho͞o-to͝ong-go͞oz′, -tŭn-, măn-cho͞o′-) *n.* See **Tungusic.** —**Man′chu-Tun·gus′ic** *adj.*

Man·cu·ni·an (măn-kyo͞o′nē-ən, -kyo͞on′yən) *adj.* Of or relating to Manchester, England. —**Mancunian** *n.* A native or inhabitant of Manchester, England. [From Latin *Mancunium,* Manchester, of Celtic origin.]

-mancy *suff.* Divination: *bibliomancy.* [Middle English, from Old French *-mancie,* from Late Latin *-mantīa,* from Greek *manteia, -manteia,* from *manteuesthai,* to prophesy, from *mantis,* prophet. See **men-**[1] in Appendix.]

Man·dae·an (măn-dē′ən) *n.* Variant of **Mandean.**

man·da·la (mŭn′də-lə) *n.* Any of various ritualistic geometric designs symbolic of the universe, used in Hinduism and Buddhism as an aid to meditation. [Sanskrit *maṇḍalam,* circle, perhaps from Tamil *muṭalai,* ball.] —**man·dal′ic** (mŭn-dăl′ĭk) *adj.*

Man·da·lay (măn′dl-ā′, măn′dl-ā′). A city of central Burma on the Irrawaddy River north of Rangoon. Capital of the kingdom of Burma from 1860 to 1885, when it was annexed by the British, it was heavily damaged in World War II. Population, 532,895.

man·da·mus (măn-dā′məs) *Law. n.* A writ issued by a superior court ordering a public official or body or a lower court to perform a specified duty. —**mandamus** *tr.v.* **-mused, -mus·ing, -mus·es.** To serve or compel with such a writ. [Latin *mandāmus,* we order, first person pl. of *mandāre,* to order. See **man-**[2] in Appendix.]

Man·dan[1] (măn′dăn′) *n., pl.* **Mandan** or **-dans. 1.a.** A Native American people formerly living in villages along the Missouri River in south-central North Dakota, with present-day descendants on Lake Sakakawea in west-central North Dakota. **b.** A member of this people. **2.** The Siouan language of the Mandan. [French *Mandane,* probably from Dakota *mawátaNna.*]

Man·dan[2] (măn′dən, -dăn). A city of south-central North Dakota across the Missouri River from Bismarck. It is a distribution and manufacturing center. Population, 15,513.

man·da·rin (măn′də-rĭn) *n.* **1.** A member of any of the nine ranks of high public officials in the Chinese Empire. **2.** A high government official or bureaucrat. **3.** A member of an elite group, especially a person having influence or high status in intellectual or cultural circles. **4. Mandarin.** The official national standard spoken language of China, which is based on the principal dialect spoken in and around Beijing. Also called *Guoyo, Putonghua.* **5.** A mandarin orange; a tangerine. —**mandarin** *adj.* **1.** Of, relating to, or resembling a mandarin. **2.** Marked by elaborate and refined language or literary style. [From Spanish *mandarín,* from Portuguese *mandarim,* from Malay *mĕntĕri,* from Sanskrit *mantrī, mantrin-,* counselor, from *mantraḥ,* counsel. See **men-**[1] in Appendix.]

mandarin collar *n.* A narrow upright collar usually divided in front.

mandarin duck *n.* An Asian duck *(Aix galericulata)* having brightly colored plumage and a crested head.

mandarin orange *n.* See **tangerine** (sense 2). [French *mandarine,* from Spanish *mandarina,* feminine of *mandarín,* mandarin. See MANDARIN.]

man·da·tar·y (măn′də-tĕr′ē) *n., pl.* **-ies.** A person or nation receiving a mandate.

man·date (măn′dāt′) *n.* **1.** An authoritative command or instruction. **2.** A command or an authorization given by a political electorate to its representative. **3.a.** A commission from the League of Nations authorizing a member nation to administer a territory. **b.** A region under such administration. **4.** *Law.* **a.** An order issued by a superior court or an official to a lower court. **b.** A contract by which one party agrees to perform services for another without payment. —**mandate** *tr.v.* **-dat·ed, -dat·ing, -dates. 1.** To assign (a colony or territory) to a specified nation under a mandate. **2.** To make mandatory, as by law; decree or require: *mandated desegregation of public schools.* [Latin *mandātum,* from neuter past participle of *mandāre,* to order. See **man-**[2] in Appendix.] —**man′da′tor** *n.*

man·da·to·ry (măn′də-tôr′ē, -tōr′ē) *adj.* **1.** Required or commanded by authority; obligatory: *Attendance at the meeting is mandatory.* **2.** Of, having the nature of, or containing a mandate. **3.** Holding a League of Nations mandate over a territory. —**mandatory** *n., pl.* **-ries.** A mandatary.

mandala
Earliest dated Hindu mandala known to exist, by Tejarama (fl. early 15th century)

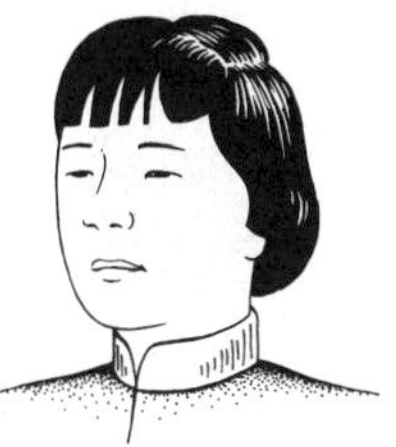

mandarin collar

mandarin duck
Male mandarin duck
Aix galericulata

ă pat	oi boy
ā pay	ou out
âr care	o͝o took
ä father	o͞o boot
ĕ pet	ŭ cut
ē be	ûr urge
ĭ pit	th thin
ī pie	*th* this
îr pier	hw which
ŏ pot	zh vision
ō toe	ə about, item
ô paw	♦ regionalism

Stress marks: ′ (primary); ′ (secondary), as in **dictionary** (dĭk′shə-nĕr′ē)

Nelson Mandela
Photographed in Soweto, South Africa, in 1990

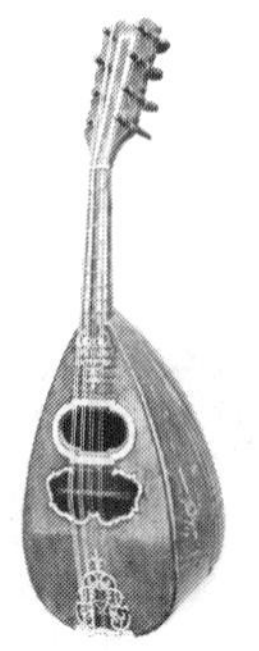
mandolin
Late 18th-century Italian

Edouard Manet
Photographed in 1875

mangle²

man-day (măn′dā′) *n.* An industrial unit of production equal to the work one person can produce in a day.

Man·de (män′dā′) *n., pl.* **Mande** or **-des. 1.** A branch of the Niger-Congo language family, spoken in the upper Niger River valley. **2.** A member of a Mande-speaking people. [Mandingo *mandi, mande,* diminutive of *ma,* mother.]

Man·de·an also **Man·dae·an** (măn-dē′ən) *n.* **1.** A member of a Gnostic sect originating in Jordan and still existing in Iraq. **2.** A form of Aramaic used by the Mandeans. [Mandean *mandaya,* having knowledge, from *manda,* knowledge.] **—Man·de′an** *adj.*

Man·de·kan (măn-dē′kən, män-dā′-) *n.* See **Mandingo** (sense 2).

Man·de·la (măn-dĕl′ə), **Nelson Rolihlahla.** Born 1918. South African Black political leader imprisoned for nearly 30 years for his anti-apartheid activities. He was released in February 1990. His wife, **Winnie** (born c. 1936), maintained strong leadership of the movement during Mandela's imprisonment.

Man·de·ville (măn′də-vĭl′), **Bernard.** 1670?–1733. Dutch-born British physician, philosopher, and satirist whose major work is *The Fable of the Bees* (1714).

Mandeville, Sir **John.** Pen name of the unknown compiler of *The Voyage and Travels of Sir John Mandeville, Knight* (c. 1371), a description of fantastic journeys through the East.

man·di·ble (măn′də-bəl) *n.* **1.** The lower jaw of a vertebrate animal. **2.** Either the upper or lower part of the beak in birds. **3.** Any of various mouth organs of invertebrates used for seizing and biting food, especially either of a pair of such organs in insects and other arthropods. [Middle English, from Old French, from Late Latin *mandibula,* from *mandere,* to chew.] **—man·dib′u·lar** (-dĭb′yə-lər) *adj.*

man·dib·u·late (măn-dĭb′yə-lĭt, -lāt′) *adj.* Having a mandible or mandibles. **—mandibulate** *n.* An insect having mandibles.

Man·din·go (măn-dĭng′gō) *n., pl.* **-gos** or **-goes. 1.** A member of any of various peoples inhabiting a large area of the upper Niger River valley of western Africa. **2.** A group of closely related Mande languages including Bambara, Malinke, and Maninka, widely spoken in western Africa. In this sense, also called *Mandekan.* [Mandingo, from *mandi,* Mande. See MANDE.]

man·do·lin (măn′də-lĭn′, măn′dl-ĭn) *n. Music.* An instrument with a usually pear-shaped body and a fretted neck over which several pairs of strings are stretched. [French *mandoline,* from Italian *mandolino,* diminutive of *mandola,* lute, from French *mandore,* from Late Latin *pandūra,* three-string lute, from Greek *pandoura.*] **—man′do·lin′ist** *n.*

man·drag·o·ra (măn-drăg′ər-ə) *n.* See **mandrake** (sense 1). [Middle English, from Latin *mandragorās.* See MANDRAKE.]

man·drake (măn′drāk′) *n.* **1.a.** A southern European plant *(Mandragora officinarum)* having greenish-yellow flowers and a branched root. This plant was once believed to have magical powers because its root resembles the human body. **b.** The root of this plant, which contains the poisonous alkaloid hyoscyamine. Also called *mandragora.* **2.** See **May apple.** [Middle English, alteration (influenced by *drake,* dragon; see DRAKE²) of *mandragora,* from Old English, from Latin *mandragorās,* from Greek.]

man·drel or **man·dril** (măn′drəl) *n.* **1.** A spindle or an axle used to secure or support material being machined or milled. **2.** A metal rod or bar around which material, such as metal or glass, may be shaped. **3.** A shaft on which a working tool is mounted, as in a dental drill. [Possibly alteration of French *mandrin,* lathe, from Provençal *mandre,* axle, crank, from Old Provençal, beam of a balance, from Latin *mamphur,* bow-drill, perhaps from Oscan.]

man·drill (măn′drəl) *n.* A large, fierce baboon *(Papio sphinx)* of western Africa, having a beard, crest, and mane and brilliant blue, purple, and scarlet facial markings in the adult male. [MAN + DRILL⁴.]

mane (mān) *n.* **1.** The long hair along the top and sides of the neck of certain mammals, such as the horse and the male lion. **2.** A long thick growth of hair on a person's head. [Middle English, from Old English *manu.*]

man-eat·er (măn′ē′tər) *n.* **1.** An animal, such as a tiger, that eats or is reputed to eat human flesh. **2.** A cannibal. **3.** *Slang.* A woman who is considered dangerous or threatening to men. **—man′-eat′ing** *adj.*

ma·nège also **ma·nege** (mă-nĕzh′) *n.* **1.** The art of training and riding horses. **2.** The movements and paces of a trained horse. **3.** A school at which equestrianship is taught and horses are trained. [French, from Italian *maneggio,* from *maneggiare,* to manage. See MANAGE.]

ma·nes or **Ma·nes** (mā′nēz′, mä′nās′) *pl.n.* **1.** The spirits of the dead, regarded as minor supernatural powers in ancient Roman religion. **2.** *(used with a sing. verb).* The revered spirit of one who has died. [Middle English, from Latin *mānēs,* perhaps from *mānis,* good. See **mā-¹** in Appendix.]

Ma·nes (mā′nēz) also **Ma·ni** (mä′nē). A.D. 216?–276? Persian prophet and founder of Manichaeism.

Ma·net (mə-nā′, mă-), **Edouard.** 1832–1883. French painter and forerunner of impressionism whose works include *Le Déjeuner sur l'Herbe (Luncheon on the Grass,* 1862).

ma·neu·ver (mə-no͞o′vər, -nyo͞o′-) *n.* **1.a.** A strategic or tactical military or naval movement. **b.** *Often* **maneuvers.** A large-scale tactical exercise carried out under simulated conditions of war. **2.** A controlled change in movement or direction of a moving vehicle or vessel, as in the flight path of an aircraft. **3.** A movement or procedure involving skill and dexterity. **4.a.** A strategic action undertaken to gain an end. **b.** Artful handling of affairs that is often marked by scheming and deceit. See Synonyms at **artifice. —maneuver** *v.* **-vered, -ver·ing, -vers.** *—intr.* **1.** To carry out a military or naval maneuver. **2.** To make a controlled series of changes in movement or direction toward an objective: *maneuvered to get closer to the stage.* **3.** To shift ground; change tactics: *The opposition had no room in which to maneuver.* **4.** To use stratagems in gaining an end. *—tr.* **1.** To alter the tactical placement of (troops or warships). **2.** To direct through a series of movements or changes in course: *maneuvered the car through traffic.* **3.** To manipulate into a desired position or toward a predetermined goal: *maneuvered him into signing the contract.* See Synonyms at **manipulate.** [French *manoeuvre,* from Old French *maneuvre,* manual work, from Medieval Latin *manuopera,* from Latin *manū operārī,* to work by hand : *manū,* ablative of *manus,* hand; see **man-²** in Appendix + *operārī,* to work; see **op-** in Appendix.] **—ma·neu′ver·a·bil′i·ty** *n.* **—ma·neu′ver·a·ble** *adj.* **—ma·neu′ver·er** *n.*

man Friday *n., pl.* **men Friday** or **men Fridays.** An efficient, faithful male aide or employee. [After *Man Friday,* a character in *Robinson Crusoe,* a novel by Daniel Defoe.]

man·ful (măn′fəl) *adj.* Having or showing the bravery and resoluteness considered characteristic of a man. See Synonyms at **male. —man′ful·ly** *adv.* **—man′ful·ness** *n.*

man·ga·bey (măng′gə-bā′, -bē′) *n., pl.* **-beys.** Any of various forest-dwelling monkeys of the genus *Cercocebus* of central Africa, having a long tail and a slender body. [After *Mangabey,* a region of Madagascar.]

mangan– *pref.* Variant of **mangano–.**

man·ga·nate (măng′gə-nāt′) *n.* A salt containing manganese in its anion, especially a salt containing the MnO_4 radical.

man·ga·nese (măng′gə-nēz′, -nēs′) *n. Symbol* **Mn** A gray-white or silvery brittle metallic element, occurring in several allotropic forms, found worldwide, especially in the ores pyrolusite and rhodochrosite and in nodules on the ocean floor. It is alloyed with steel to increase strength, hardness, wear resistance, and other properties and with other metals to form highly ferromagnetic materials. Atomic number 25; atomic weight 54.9380; melting point 1,244°C; boiling point 1,962°C; specific gravity 7.21 to 7.44; valence 1, 2, 3, 4, 6, 7. See table at **element.** [French *manganèse,* from Italian *manganese,* from Medieval Latin *magnēsia.* See MAGNESIA.] **—man′ga·ne′sian** (-nē′zhən, -shən) *adj.*

manganese dioxide *n.* A black crystalline compound, MnO_2, used as a depolarizer of dry-cell batteries and in textile dyeing.

man·gan·ic (măn-găn′ĭk, măng-) *adj.* Containing manganese, especially with a valence of three or six.

man·ga·nite (măng′gə-nīt′) *n.* A steel-gray to black mineral, MnO(OH), found in North America and Europe; manganese oxide.

mangano– or **mangan–** *pref.* Manganese: *manganite.*

man·ga·nous (măng′gə-nəs) *adj.* Relating to bivalent manganese or to a compound containing bivalent manganese.

mange (mānj) *n.* Any of several chronic skin diseases of mammals caused by parasitic mites and characterized by skin lesions, itching, and loss of hair. [Middle English *manjeue,* from Old French *manjue,* from *mangier,* to eat. See MANGER.]

man·gel-wur·zel (măng′gəl-wûr′zəl) *n.* A variety of the common beet having a large yellowish root, used chiefly as cattle feed. [German, alteration (influenced by *Mangel,* scarcity) of *Mangoldwurzel* : *Mangold,* beet (from Middle High German *mānegolt*) + *Wurzel,* root; see **wrād-** in Appendix.]

man·ger (mān′jər) *n.* A trough or an open box in which feed for livestock is placed. [Middle English, from Old French *mangeoire,* from *mangier,* to eat, from Latin *mandūcāre,* from *mandūcō,* glutton, from *mandere,* to chew.]

man·gle¹ (măng′gəl) *tr.v.* **-gled, -gling, -gles. 1.** To mutilate or disfigure by battering, hacking, cutting, or tearing. See Synonyms at **batter¹. 2.** To ruin or spoil through ineptitude or ignorance: *mangle a speech.* [Middle English *manglen,* from Anglo-Norman *mangler,* frequentative of Old French *mangoner,* to cut to bits; possibly akin to *mahaignier,* to maim. See MAIM.] **—man′gler** *n.*

man·gle² (măng′gəl) *n.* **1.** A machine for pressing fabrics by means of heated rollers. **2.** *Chiefly British.* A clothes wringer. **—mangle** *tr.v.* **-gled, -gling, -gles.** To press with a mangle. [Dutch *mangel,* from German, from Middle High German, diminutive of *mange,* mangonel, from Late Latin *manganum,* catapult. See MANGONEL.]

man·go (măng′gō) *n., pl.* **-goes** or **-gos. 1.a.** A tropical Asian evergreen tree *(Mangifera indica)* cultivated for its edible fruit. **b.** The ovoid fruit of this tree, having a smooth rind, sweet juicy flesh, and a flat one-seeded stone. It is eaten ripe or pickled when green. **2.** Any of various types of pickle, especially a pickled stuffed sweet pepper. [From Portuguese *manga,* fruit of the mango tree, from Malay *mangā,* from Tamil *mānkāy* : *mān,* mango tree + *kāy,* fruit.]

man·go·nel (măng′gə-nĕl′) *n.* A military engine used during the Middle Ages for hurling stones and other missiles. [Middle English, from Old French, from Medieval Latin *mangonellus,* diminutive of Late Latin *manganum,* catapult, from Greek *manganon,* war machine.]

man·go·steen (măng′gə-stēn′) *n.* **1.** A Malaysian evergreen tree *(Garcinia mangostana)* having thick leathery leaves and large edible berries. **2.** The berry of this tree, having a hard rind and five to seven seeds with a sweet juicy aril. [Malay *manggista, mangustan.*]

man·grove (măn′grōv′, măng′-) *n.* **1.** Any of several tropical evergreen trees or shrubs of the genus *Rhizophora,* having stiltlike roots and stems and forming dense thickets along tidal shores. **2.** Any of various similar shrubs or trees, especially of the genus *Avicennia.* [Probably Portuguese *mangue* (from Taino) + GROVE.]

mang·y (mān′jē) *adj.* **-i·er, -i·est. 1.** Affected with, caused by, or resembling mange. **2.** Having many worn spots; shabby: *a mangy old fur coat.* **3.** Rundown and filthy; squalid: *mangy tenements.* **4.** Mean; contemptible. **—mang′i·ly** *adv.* **—mang′i·ness** *n.*

man·han·dle (măn′hăn′dəl) *tr.v.* **-dled, -dling, -dles. 1.** To handle roughly. **2.** To move or handle by manpower alone.

Man·hat·tan¹ (măn-hăt′n). **1.** A city of northeast Kansas west of Topeka. It is a processing and educational center. Population, 32,644. **2.** A borough of New York City in southeast New York, mainly on **Manhattan Island** at the north end of New York Bay. Peter Minuit of the Dutch West Indies Company bought the island in 1626 from the Manhattan Indians, supposedly for some $24 worth of merchandise. Population, 1,427,533. **—Man·hat′tan·ite′** (-īt′) *n.*

Man·hat·tan² (măn-hăt′n, mən-) also **man·hat·tan** *n.* A cocktail made of sweet vermouth, whiskey, and a dash of bitters. [After MANHATTAN¹, a borough of New York City.]

Manhattan Beach. A city of southern California, a residential and industrial suburb of Los Angeles. Population, 31,542.

Manhattan clam chowder *n.* A soup made with clams, tomatoes and other vegetables, and seasonings. [After MANHATTAN¹, a borough of New York City.]

Man·hat·tan·ize (măn-hăt′n-īz′) *tr.v.* **-ized, -iz·ing, -iz·es.** To transform the appearance and character of (a city) by constructing tall and densely situated buildings. **—Man·hat′tan·i·za′tion** (-ĭ-zā′shən) *n.*

man·hole (măn′hōl′) *n.* A hole, usually with a cover, through which a person may enter a sewer, drain, or similar structure.

man·hood (măn′ho͝od′) *n.* **1.** The state or time of being an adult male human being. **2.** The composite of qualities, such as courage, determination, and vigor, often thought to be appropriate to a man. **3.** Adult males considered as a group; men. **4.** The state of being human.

man-hour (măn′our′) *n.* An industrial unit of production equal to the work one person can produce in an hour.

man·hunt (măn′hŭnt′) *n.* An organized, extensive search for a person, usually a fugitive criminal.

Ma·ni (mä′nē). See **Manes.**

ma·ni·a (mā′nē-ə, mān′yə) *n.* **1.** An excessively intense enthusiasm, interest, or desire; a craze: *a mania for neatness.* **2.** *Psychiatry.* A manifestation of manic-depressive illness, characterized by profuse and rapidly changing ideas, exaggerated gaiety, and excessive physical activity. **3.** Violent abnormal behavior. See Synonyms at **insanity.** [Middle English, madness, from Late Latin, from Greek. See **men-¹** in Appendix.]

-mania *suff.* An exaggerated desire or enthusiasm for: *balletomania.* [From MANIA.]

ma·ni·ac (mā′nē-ăk′) *n.* **1.** An insane person. **2.** A person who has an excessive enthusiasm or desire for something: *a sports maniac.* **3.** A person who acts in a wildly irresponsible way: *maniacs on the highway.* **—maniac** *adj.* Variant of **maniacal.** [From Late Latin *maniacus,* maniacal, from Greek *maniakos,* from *mania,* madness. See **men-¹** in Appendix.]

ma·ni·a·cal (mə-nī′ə-kəl) also **ma·ni·ac** (mā′nē-ăk′) *adj.* **1.** Suggestive of or afflicted with insanity: *a maniacal frenzy.* **2.** Characterized by excessive enthusiasm or excitement: *a maniacal interest in gambling.* **—ma·ni′a·cal·ly** *adv.*

man·ic (măn′ĭk) *adj.* *Psychiatry.* Relating to, affected by, or resembling mania. [Greek *manikos,* mad, from *mania,* madness. See **men-¹** in Appendix.]

man·ic-de·pres·sive (măn′ĭk-dĭ-prĕs′ĭv) *Psychiatry. adj.* Of, relating to, or affected by manic-depressive illness. **—manic-depressive** *n.* A person afflicted with manic-depressive illness.

manic-depressive illness *n.* *Psychiatry.* An affective disorder marked by alternating episodes of mania and depression. Also called *bipolar disorder, bipolar illness.*

Man·i·chae·an or **Man·i·che·an** (măn′ĭ-kē′ən) also **Man·i·chee** (măn′ĭ-kē′) *—n.* A believer in Manichaeism. *—adj.* Of or relating to Manichaeism; dualistic. [From Middle English *Maniche,* from Late Latin *Manichaeus,* from Late Greek *Manikhaios,* from *Manikhaios,* Manes, the founder of the philosophy.]

Man·i·chae·ism (măn′ĭ-kē′ĭz′əm) also **Man·i·chae·an·ism** (-kē′ə-nĭz′əm) *n.* **1.** The syncretic, dualistic religious philosophy taught by the Persian prophet Manes, combining elements of Zoroastrian, Christian, and Gnostic thought and opposed by the imperial Roman government, Neo-Platonist philosophers, and orthodox Christians. **2.** A dualistic philosophy dividing the world between good and evil principles or regarding matter as intrinsically evil and mind as intrinsically good.

Man·i·che·an (măn′ĭ-kē′ən) also **Man·i·chee** (măn′ĭ-kē′) *n. & adj.* Variants of **Manichaean.**

man·i·cot·ti (măn′ĭ-kŏt′ē) *n.* An Italian dish consisting of pasta tubes stuffed with chopped meat or ricotta cheese, usually served hot with a tomato sauce. [Italian, pl. of *manicotto,* muff, from *manica,* sleeve, from Latin *manicae,* sleeves, from *manus,* hand. See **man-²** in Appendix.]

man·i·cure (măn′ĭ-kyo͝or′) *n.* A cosmetic treatment of the fingernails, including shaping and polishing. **—manicure** *tr.v.* **-cured, -cur·ing, -cures. 1.** To trim, clean, and polish (the fingernails). **2.** To clip or trim evenly and closely: *manicure a hedge.* [French : Latin *manus,* hand; see **man-²** in Appendix + Latin *cūra,* care; see CURE.]

man·i·cur·ist (măn′ĭ-kyo͝or′ĭst) *n.* One who gives manicures.

man·i·fest (măn′ə-fĕst′) *adj.* Clearly apparent to the sight or understanding; obvious. See Synonyms at **apparent. —manifest** *tr.v.* **-fest·ed, -fest·ing, -fests. 1.** To show or demonstrate plainly; reveal: *"Mercedes . . . manifested the chaotic abandonment of hysteria"* (Jack London). **2.** To be evidence of; prove. **3.a.** To record in a ship's manifest. **b.** To display or present a manifest of (cargo). **—manifest** *n.* **1.** A list of cargo or passengers carried on a ship or plane. **2.** An invoice of goods carried on a truck or train. **3.** A list of railroad cars according to owner and location. [Middle English *manifeste,* from Old French, from Latin *manufestus, manifestus,* caught in the act, blatant, obvious. See **gʷhedh-** in Appendix.] **—man′i·fest′ly** *adv.*

man·i·fes·tant (măn′ə-fĕs′tənt) *n.* A participant in a public demonstration.

man·i·fes·ta·tion (măn′ə-fĕ-stā′shən) *n.* **1.a.** The act of manifesting. **b.** The state of being manifested. **2.** An indication of the existence, reality, or presence of something: *A high fever is an early manifestation of the disease.* **3.a.** One of the forms in which someone or something, such as a person, a divine being, or an idea, is revealed. **b.** The materialized form of a spirit. **4.** A public demonstration, usually of a political nature.

manifest destiny *n.* **1.** A policy of imperialistic expansion defended as necessary or benevolent. **2.** Often **Manifest Destiny.** The 19th-century doctrine that the United States had the right and duty to expand throughout the North American continent.

man·i·fes·to (măn′ə-fĕs′tō) *n.* **-toes** or **-tos.** *pl.* A public declaration of principles, policies, or intentions, especially of a political nature. **—manifesto** *intr.v.* **-toed, -to·ing, -toes.** To issue such a declaration. [Italian, from Latin *manifestus,* clear, evident. See MANIFEST.]

man·i·fold (măn′ə-fōld′) *adj.* **1.** Many and varied; of many kinds; multiple: *our manifold failings.* **2.** Having many features or forms: *manifold intelligence.* **3.** Being such for a variety of reasons: *a manifold traitor.* **4.** Consisting of or operating several devices of one kind at the same time. **—manifold** *n.* **1.** A whole composed of diverse elements. **2.** One of several copies. **3.** A pipe or chamber having multiple apertures for making connections. **4.** *Mathematics.* A topologic space or surface. **—manifold** *tr.v.* **-fold·ed, -fold·ing, -folds. 1.** To make several copies of, as with carbon paper. **2.** To make manifold; multiply. [Middle English, from Old English *manigfeald* : *manig,* many; see MANY + *-feald, -fald,* -fold.] **—man′i·fold′ly** *adv.*

man·i·kin or **man·ni·kin** (măn′ĭ-kĭn) *n.* **1.** A man short in stature. **2.** A mannequin. **3.** An anatomical model of the human body for use in teaching. [Dutch *mannekijn,* from Middle Dutch, diminutive of *man,* man. See **man-¹** in Appendix.]

ma·nil·a or **ma·nil·la** (mə-nĭl′ə) *n.* **1.** Often **Manila** or **Manilla.** A cheroot made in Manila. **2.** See **abaca** (sense 2). **3.** Manila paper. **4.** *Color.* A light yellow brown.

Manila. The capital and largest city of the Philippines, on southwest Luzon Island and **Manilla Bay,** an inlet of the South China Sea. Founded in 1571, the city was controlled by Spain until it was seized by U.S. troops in 1898 during the Spanish-American War. Population, 1,630,485.

Manila hemp *n.* See **abaca** (sense 2).

Manila paper *n.* A strong paper or thin cardboard with a smooth finish, usually buff in color, made from Manila hemp or wood fibers similar to it.

ma·nil·la (mə-nĭl′ə) *n.* Variant of **manila.**

Ma·nin·ka (mə-nĭng′kä, -kē) *n.* **1.** A member of a Mandingo people inhabiting Senegal and Mali. **2.** The Mandingo language of this people.

man in the street *n., pl.* **men in the street.** The ordinary citizen.

man·i·oc (măn′ē-ŏk′) also **man·i·o·ca** (măn′ē-ō′kə) *n.* See **cassava.** [French, from Tupi *mandioca, manioca.*]

man·i·ple (măn′ə-pəl) *n.* **1.** An ornamental silk band hung as an ecclesiastical vestment on the left arm near the wrist. **2.** A subdivision of an ancient Roman legion, containing 60 or 120 men. [Middle English, from Old French, from Latin *manipulus,* handful, from *manus,* hand. See **man-²** in Appendix.]

ma·nip·u·la·ble (mə-nĭp′yə-lə-bəl) *adj.* Possible to manipulate: *a manipulable lever; a manipulable populace.* **—ma·nip′u·la·bil′i·ty** *n.*

ma·nip·u·lar (mə-nĭp′yə-lər) *adj.* **1.** Of or relating to an ancient Roman maniple. **2.** Of or relating to manipulation. **—manipular** *n.* A soldier in a Roman maniple.

ma·nip·u·late (mə-nĭp′yə-lāt′) *tr.v.* **-lat·ed, -lat·ing, -lates. 1.** To operate or control by skilled use of the hands; handle: *She manipulated the lights to get just the effect she wanted.* **2.** To influence or manage shrewdly or deviously: *He manipulated*

manhole

ă pat	oi boy
ā pay	ou out
âr care	o͝o took
ä father	o͞o boot
ĕ pet	ŭ cut
ē be	ûr urge
ĭ pit	th thin
ī pie	*th* this
îr pier	hw which
ŏ pot	zh vision
ō toe	ə about, item
ô paw	♦ regionalism

Stress marks: ′ (primary); ′ (secondary), as in **dictionary** (dĭk′shə-nĕr′ē)

public opinion in his favor. **3.** To tamper with or falsify for personal gain: *tried to manipulate stock prices.* **4.** *Medicine.* To handle and move in an examination or for therapeutic purposes: *manipulate a joint; manipulate the position of a fetus during delivery.* [Back-formation from MANIPULATION.] **—ma·nip′u·la·bil′i·ty** *n.* **—ma·nip′u·lat′a·ble** *adj.* **—ma·nip′u·la′tive** *adj.* **—ma·nip′u·la′tive·ly** *adv.* **—ma·nip′u·la′tive·ness** *n.* **—ma·nip′u·la′tor** *n.* **—ma·nip′u·la·to′ry** (-lə-tôr′ē, -tōr′ē) *adj.*

SYNONYMS: *manipulate, exploit, maneuver.* The central meaning shared by these verbs is "to influence, manage, use, or control to one's advantage by artful or indirect means": *manipulates people into helping him; exploiting her friends; maneuvering to gain an edge over their corporate competitors.* See also Synonyms at **handle.**

mannequin

ma·nip·u·la·tion (mə-nĭp′yə-lā′shən) *n.* **1.a.** The act or practice of manipulating. **b.** The state of being manipulated. **2.** Shrewd or devious management, especially for one's own advantage. [French, from *manipule,* handful, as of grain, from Latin *manipulus,* sheaf, handful : *manus,* hand; see **man-**[2] in Appendix + *-pulus,* of uncertain sense; perhaps akin to *plēre,* to fill; see COMPLETE.]

Man·i·to·ba (măn′ĭ-tō′bə). *Abbr.* **MB, Man.** A province of south-central Canada. It was admitted to the confederation in 1870. Originally part of a 1670 grant to the Hudson's Bay Company, it was largely settled by immigrants in the late 19th and early 20th centuries. Winnipeg is the capital and the largest city. Population, 1,026,241. **—Man′i·to′ban** *adj. & n.*

Manitoba, Lake. A lake of southern Manitoba, Canada. It is a remnant of the glacial age Lake Agassiz.

man·i·tou or **man·i·tu** (măn′ĭ-to͞o′) also **man·i·to** (-tō′) *n., pl.* **-tous** or **-tus** also **-tos. 1.** In Algonquian religious belief, a supernatural power that permeates the world, possessed in varying degrees by both spiritual and human beings. **2.** A deity or spirit. [French, from Ojibwa *manitoo.*]

Man·i·tou·lin Islands (măn′ĭ-to͞o′lĭn). A group of islands of southern Ontario, Canada, in northern Lake Huron. The principal island, **Manitoulin,** is the largest lake island in the world.

Man·i·to·woc (măn′ĭ-tə-wŏk′). A city of eastern Wisconsin on Lake Michigan north of Sheboygan. Population, 32,547.

Ma·ni·za·les (măn′ĭ-zä′lĭs, -zăl′ĭs, mä′nē-sä′lĕs). A city of west-central Colombia west of Bogotá. It is a commercial center in an important coffee-producing region. Population, 275,220.

Man·ka·to (măn-kā′tō). A city of southern Minnesota south-southwest of Minneapolis. Population, 28,651.

man·kind (măn′kīnd′) *n.* **1.** The human race; humankind. **2.** Men as opposed to women.

man·like (măn′līk′) *adj.* **1.** Resembling a human being. **2.** Belonging to or befitting a man. See Synonyms at **male.**

man·ly (măn′lē) *adj.* **-li·er, -li·est. 1.** Having qualities traditionally attributed to a man. **2.** Belonging to or befitting a man; masculine. See Synonyms at **male. —manly** *adv.* In a manly manner. **—man′li·ness** *n.*

man-made or **man·made** (măn′mād′) *adj.* Made by human beings rather than occurring in nature; synthetic: *man-made fibers; a manmade lake.*

Mann (măn), **Horace.** 1796–1859. American educator who as the first secretary of the Massachusetts Board of Education (1837–1848) introduced reforms and regulations that greatly influenced American public education.

Mann (măn, män), **Thomas.** 1875–1955. German writer whose works include *Death in Venice* (1912) and *The Magic Mountain* (1924). He won the 1929 Nobel Prize for literature.

man·na (măn′ə) *n.* **1.** *Bible.* In the Old Testament, the food miraculously provided for the Israelites in the wilderness during their flight from Egypt. **2.** Spiritual nourishment of divine origin. **3.** Something of value that a person receives unexpectedly. **4.** The dried exudate of certain plants, as that of the Mediterranean ash tree, formerly used as a laxative. **5.** A sweet granular substance excreted on the leaves of plants by certain insects, especially aphids, and often harvested by ants. [Middle English, from Old English, from Late Latin, from Greek, from Aramaic *mannâ,* from Hebrew *mān.*]

man·nan (măn′ăn′, -ən) *n.* Any of a group of plant polysaccharides that are polymers of mannose. [MANN(OSE) + -AN[2].]

Man·nar (mə-när′), **Gulf of.** An inlet of the Indian Ocean between southern India and Sri Lanka.

manned (mănd) *adj.* Transporting, operated by, or performed by a human being: *a manned spacecraft; several manned lunar landings.*

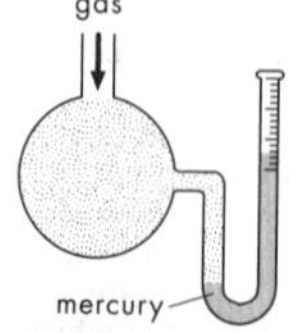

manometer
Measuring high gas pressure

man·ne·quin (măn′ĭ-kĭn) *n.* **1.** A life-size full or partial representation of the human body, used for the fitting or displaying of clothes; a dummy. **2.** A jointed model of the human body used by artists, especially to demonstrate the arrangement of drapery. Also called *lay figure.* **3.** One who models clothes; a model. [French, from Old French, little man, figurine, from Middle Dutch *mannekijn.* See MANIKIN.]

WORD HISTORY: A department store mannequin is often not a man and often not little, yet *mannequin* goes back to the Middle Dutch word *mannekijn,* the diminutive form of *man.* Of course we must consider the fact that *man* in Dutch, as in English, has often been used to mean "person." As for the size of a mannequin, the Middle Dutch word could mean "dwarf" but in Modern Dutch developed the specialized sense of "an artist's jointed model." This was the sense in which we adopted the word (first recorded in 1570), another term like *easel* and *landscape* that was taken over from the terminology of Dutch painters of the time. The word borrowed from Dutch now has the form *manikin.* We later adopted the French version of the Dutch word as well, giving English *mannequin. Mannequin* is considered to be first recorded in a dictionary published from 1730 to 1736 or in 1902, depending on whether one regards early forms showing French influence as variants of *manikin* or as representations of a new word. In any event, *mannequin* is now the form most commonly encountered and the one commonly used for a department store dummy as well as a live model.

man·ner (măn′ər) *n.* **1.** A way of doing something or the way in which a thing is done or happens. See Synonyms at **method. 2.** A way of acting; bearing or behavior. See Synonyms at **bearing. 3. manners. a.** The socially correct way of acting; etiquette. **b.** The prevailing customs, social conduct, and norms of a specific society, period, or group, especially as the subject of a literary work. **4.** Practice, style, execution, or method in the arts: *This fresco is typical of the painter's early manner.* **5.a.** Kind; sort: *What manner of person is she?* **b.** Kinds; sorts: *saw all manner of people at the mall.* **—*idioms.* in a manner of speaking.** In a way; so to speak. **to the manner born.** Accustomed to a position, custom, or lifestyle from or as if from birth. [Middle English *manere,* from Old French *maniere,* from feminine of *manier,* handmade, skilful, from Vulgar Latin **manuārius,* convenient, handy, from Latin, of the hand, from *manus,* hand. See **man-**[2] in Appendix.]

man·nered (măn′ərd) *adj.* **1.** Having manners of a specific kind: *ill-mannered children.* **2.a.** Having or showing a certain manner: *a mild-mannered supervisor.* **b.** Artificial or affected: *mannered speech.* **3.** Of, relating to, or exhibiting mannerisms.

man·ner·ism (măn′ə-rĭz′əm) *n.* **1.** A distinctive behavioral trait; an idiosyncrasy. **2.** Exaggerated or affected style or habit, as in dress or speech. See Synonyms at **affectation. 3. Mannerism.** An artistic style of the late 16th century characterized by distortion of elements such as scale and perspective. **—man′ner·ist** *n.* **—man′ner·is′tic** *adj.*

man·ner·ly (măn′ər-lē) *adj.* Having or showing good manners. See Synonyms at **polite. —mannerly** *adv.* With good manners; politely. **—man′ner·li·ness** *n.*

Mann·heim (măn′hīm′, män′-). A city of southwest Germany at the confluence of the Rhine and Neckar rivers north-northwest of Stuttgart. First mentioned in the 8th century, it was chartered in 1607. Population, 295,178.

man·ni·kin (măn′ĭ-kĭn) *n.* Variant of **manikin.**

man·nish (măn′ĭsh) *adj.* **1.** Of, characteristic of, or natural to a man. **2.** Resembling, imitative of, or suggestive of a man rather than a woman: *a mannish stride.* See Synonyms at **male. —man′nish·ly** *adv.* **—man′nish·ness** *n.*

man·nite (măn′īt′) *n.* Mannitol. [MANN(A) + -ITE[1].]

man·ni·tol (măn′ĭ-tôl′, -tōl′, -tŏl′) *n.* A white, crystalline, water-soluble, slightly sweet alcohol, $C_6H_8(OH)_6$, used as a dietary supplement and dietetic sweetener and in medical tests of renal function. [*mannit(e)* + -OL[1].]

man·nose (măn′ōs′) *n.* A monosaccharide, $C_6H_{12}O_6$, obtained from mannan or by the oxidation of mannitol. [MANN(A) + -OSE[2].]

ma·no (mä′nō) *n., pl.* **-nos.** A hand-held stone or roller for grinding corn or other grains on a metate. [Spanish *mano,* from Latin *manus,* hand. See MANNER.]

ma·no a ma·no (mä′nō ä mä′nō) *n., pl.* **ma·nos a ma·nos** (mä′nōs ä mä′nōs). **1.** A bullfight in which two rival matadors take turns fighting several bulls each. **2.** A face-to-face confrontation or competitive struggle: *a mano a mano between the presidential candidates.* **—mano a mano** *adj.* Being or suggestive of a face-to-face encounter or contest: *a mano a mano duel between golf pros.* **—mano a mano** *adv.* In direct competition: *an industry gearing up to go mano a mano with a rival.* [Spanish : *mano,* hand + *a,* to + *mano,* hand.]

ma·noeu·vre (mə-no͞o′vər, -nyo͞o′-) *n. & v. Chiefly British.* Variant of **maneuver.**

man of God *n., pl.* **men of God.** A clergyman.

man of letters *n., pl.* **men of letters.** A man who is devoted to literary or scholarly pursuits.

man of the cloth *n., pl.* **men of the cloth.** A clergyman.

man of the house *n., pl.* **men of the house.** The primary male member of a household.

man of the world *n., pl.* **men of the world.** A sophisticated, worldly man.

man-of-war (măn′ə-wôr′) *n., pl.* **men-of-war** (mĕn′-). **1.** See **warship. 2.** A Portuguese man-of-war.

ma·nom·e·ter (mă-nŏm′ĭ-tər) *n.* **1.** An instrument used for measuring the pressure of liquids and gases. **2.** A sphygmomanometer. [Greek *manos,* sparse; see **men-**[4] in Appendix + -METER.] **—man′o·met′ric** (măn′ə-mĕt′rĭk), **man′o·met′ri·cal** *adj.* **—man′o·met′ri·cal·ly** *adv.* **—ma·nom′e·try** *n.*

man on horseback *n., pl.* **men on horseback. 1.** A man, usually a military leader, whose popular influence and power may afford him the position of dictator, as in a time of political crisis. **2.** A dictator.

man·or (măn′ər) *n.* **1.a.** A landed estate. **b.** The main house on an estate; a mansion. **2.** A tract of land in certain North American colonies with hereditary rights granted to the proprietor by royal charter. **3.a.** The district over which a lord had domain and could exercise certain rights and privileges in medieval western Europe. **b.** The lord's residence in such a district. [Middle English, from Old French *maneir, manoir,* to dwell, manor, from Latin *manēre,* to remain. See **men-**[3] in Appendix.] **—ma·no′ri·al** (mə-nôr′ē-əl, -nōr′-) *adj.*

manor house *n.* **1.** The main house on an estate. **2.** The house of the lord of a manor.

ma·no·ri·al·ism (mə-nôr′ē-ə-lĭz′əm, -nōr′-) *n.* The medieval manorial system or its precepts and practices.

man-o'-war bird (măn′ə-wôr′) *n.* See **frigate bird.**

man·pow·er (măn′pou′ər) *n.* **1.** The power of human physical strength. **2.** Power in terms of the workers available to a particular group or required for a particular task.

man·qué (mäɴ-kā′) *adj.* Unfulfilled or frustrated in the realization of one's ambitions or capabilities: *an artist manqué; a writer manqué.* [French, from past participle of *manquer,* to fail, from Old French, from Old Italian *mancare,* from *manco,* lacking, from Latin *mancus,* maimed, infirm. See **man-**[2] in Appendix.]

man·rope (măn′rōp′) *n. Nautical.* A rope rigged as a handrail on a gangplank or ladder.

man·sard (măn′särd′) *n.* **1.** A roof having two slopes on all four sides, with the lower slope almost vertical and the upper almost horizontal. **2.** The upper story formed by the lower slope of a mansard roof. [French *mansarde,* after François *Mansart* (1598–1666), French architect.] **—man′sard′ed** *adj.*

manse (măns) *n.* **1.** A cleric's house and land, especially the residence of a Presbyterian minister. **2.** A large, stately residence. **3.** *Archaic.* The dwellings belonging to a householder. [Middle English *manss,* a manor house, from Medieval Latin *mānsa,* a dwelling, from Latin, feminine past participle of *manēre,* to dwell, remain. See **men-**[3] in Appendix.]

man·ser·vant (măn′sûr′vənt) *n., pl.* **men·ser·vants** (mĕn′sûr′vənts). A male servant, especially a valet.

Mans·field (mănz′fēld′). **1.** A municipal borough of central England north of Nottingham. It is an industrial center in a coal-mining region. Population, 99,900. **2.** A town of northeast Connecticut east-northeast of Hartford. It is an agricultural and manufacturing community. Population, 20,634. **3.** A city of north-central Ohio west-southwest of Akron. Population, 53,927.

Mansfield, Katherine. 1888–1923. New Zealand-born British writer known for her short stories. Her collections include *Bliss* (1920) and *The Dove's Nest* (1923).

Mansfield, Mount. The highest peak, 1,339.9 m (4,393 ft), of the Green Mountains in north-central Vermont.

man·sion (măn′shən) *n.* **1.** A large, stately house. **2.** A manor house. **3.** *Archaic.* **a.** A dwelling; an abode. **b. mansions.** A separate dwelling in a large house or structure. **4.a.** See **house** (sense 10). **b.** Any one of the 28 divisions of the moon's monthly path. [Middle English, a dwelling, from Old French, from Latin *mānsiō, mānsiōn-,* from *mānsus,* past participle of *manēre,* to dwell, remain. See **men-**[3] in Appendix.]

man-sized (măn′sīzd′) also **man-size** (-sīz′) *adj.* **1.** *Informal.* Very large: *a man-sized piece of pie.* **2.** Calling for the strength traditionally attributed to a man: *a man-sized job.*

man·slaugh·ter (măn′slô′tər) *n. Law.* The unlawful killing of one human being by another without express or implied intent to do injury.

man·slay·er (măn′slā′ər) *n.* One, such as a person or an animal, that kills a human being.

man·sue·tude (măn′swĭ-to͞od′, -tyo͞od′) *n.* Gentleness of manner; mildness. [Middle English, from Old French, from Latin *mānsuētūdō,* from *mānsuētus,* past participle of *mānsuēscere,* to tame : *manus,* hand; see **man-**[2] in Appendix + *suēscere,* to accustom; see **s(w)e-** in Appendix.]

Man·sur (măn-so͝or′), **al-.** 712?–775. Arab caliph (754–775) who founded Baghdad in 764.

man·ta (măn′tə) *n.* **1.** A rough-textured cotton fabric or blanket made and used in Spanish America and the southwest United States. **2.** Any of several rays of the family Mobulidae, inhabiting tropical and subtropical seas and having a large flattened body, winglike pectoral fins, a whiplike tail, and two hornlike fins that project forward from the head. In this sense, also called *devilfish, manta ray, sea devil.* [Spanish, blanket, manta (from its blanketlike shape), alteration of *manto,* cloak, perhaps from Latin *mantellum, mantēlum.*]

man-tai·lored (măn′tā′lərd) *adj.* Tailored in the traditionally simple, unadorned style of men's clothing: *man-tailored women's apparel.*

manta ray *n.* See **manta** (sense 2).

man·teau (măn-tō′) *n., pl.* **-teaus** (-tōz′) or **-teaux** (-tō′). A loose cloak or mantle. [French, from Old French *mantel.* See MANTLE.]

Man·te·ca (măn-tē′kə). A city of central California south of Stockton. It is a processing center. Population, 24,925.

Man·te·gna (män-tān′yə, -tĕ′nyä), **Andrea.** 1431–1506. Italian painter and engraver who was a pioneer in the Renaissance style. Among his works is the altarpiece for the Church of San Zeno in Verona (1456–1459).

♦**man·tel** also **man·tle** (măn′tl) *n.* **1.** An ornamental facing around a fireplace. **2.** The protruding shelf over a fireplace. In this sense, also called ♦*fireboard,* ♦*mantelpiece,* ♦*mantelshelf.* [Middle English *mantel,* as in *mantiltre,* beam over fireplace opening. See MANTELTREE.]

man·tel·et (măn′tl-ĭt, mănt′lĭt) *n.* **1.** A short cape. **2.** Also **mant·let** (mănt′lĭt). A mobile screen or shield formerly used to protect besieging soldiers. [Middle English, from Old French, diminutive of *mantel,* mantle. See MANTLE.]

man·tel·let·ta (măn′tə-lĕt′ə) *n.* A knee-length, sleeveless vestment worn by Roman Catholic prelates. [Italian, probably from Medieval Latin *mantellētum,* diminutive of Latin *mantellum,* mantle.]

man·tel·piece (măn′tl-pēs′) *n.* See **mantel** (sense 2).

man·tel·shelf (măn′tl-shĕlf′) *n.* See **mantel** (sense 2).

man·tel·tree (măn′tl-trē′) *n.* A beam, a stone, or an arch that functions as a lintel on a fireplace, supporting the masonry above. [Middle English *mantiltre* : *mantle,* mantle; see MANTLE + *tre,* beam; see TREE.]

man·tes (măn′tēz) *n.* A plural of **mantis.**

man·tic (măn′tĭk) *adj.* Of, relating to, or having the power of divination; prophetic. [Greek *mantikos,* from *mantis,* seer. See **men-**[1] in Appendix.] **—man′tic·al·ly** *adv.*

man·ti·core (măn′tĭ-kôr′, -kōr′) *n.* A legendary monster having the head of a man, the body of a lion, and the tail of a dragon or scorpion. [Middle English *manticores,* from Latin *mantichōra,* from Greek *mantikhōras,* variant of *martiokhōras,* from Old Iranian **martiya-khvāra-,* man-eater : **martiya-,* man; akin to Old Persian *martiya-,* man; see **mer-** in Appendix + **-khvāra-,* eater; akin to Avestan *khvar-,* to eat; see **swel-** in Appendix.]

man·tid (măn′tĭd) *n.* See **mantis.** [From New Latin *Mantidae,* family name, from *Mantis,* type genus, from Greek *mantis,* seer. See MANTIS.]

man·til·la (măn-tē′yə, -tĭl′ə) *n.* **1.** A lightweight lace or silk scarf worn over the head and shoulders, often over a high comb, by women in Spain and Latin America. **2.** A short cloak or cape. [Spanish, diminutive of *manta,* cape. See MANTA.]

Man·ti·ne·a (măn′tə-nē′ə). An ancient city of southern Greece in the eastern Peloponnesus. Thebes defeated Sparta here in 362 B.C.

man·tis (măn′tĭs) *n., pl.* **-tis·es** or **-tes** (-tēz). Any of various predatory insects of the family Mantidae, primarily tropical but including a few Temperate Zone species, usually pale green and having two pairs of walking legs and powerful, grasping forelimbs. The mantis feeds on live insects, including others of its own kind. Also called *mantid.* [Greek *mantis,* seer. See **men-**[1] in Appendix.]

WORD HISTORY: The female mantis has the habit of eating the male after mating. In spite of such behavior the mantis is graced with a religious name. *Mantis* is from the Greek word *mantis,* meaning "prophet, seer." The Greeks, who made the connection between the upraised front legs of a mantis waiting for its prey and the hands of a prophet in prayer, used the name *mantis* to mean "the praying mantis." This word and sense were picked up in Modern Latin and from there came into English, being first recorded in 1658. Once we know the origin of the term *mantis,* we realize that the species names *praying mantis* and *Mantis religiosa* are a bit redundant. Two other names of this sort that have been used for mantises are *praying locust* and *orator mantis.* To understand the latter, we must keep in mind the obsolete sense of *orator,* "one who makes a prayer or petition."

mantis crab *n.* See **squilla.**

man·tis·sa (măn-tĭs′ə) *n. Mathematics.* The decimal part of a logarithm. In the logarithm 2.95424, the mantissa is 0.95424. [Latin, makeweight, perhaps of Etruscan origin.]

mantis shrimp *n.* See **squilla.**

man·tle (măn′tl) *n.* **1.** A loose, sleeveless coat worn over outer garments; a cloak. **2.** Something that covers, envelops, or conceals: *"On a summer night . . . a mantle of dust hangs over the gravel roads"* (John Dollard). **3.** Variant of **mantel. 4.** The outer covering of a wall. **5.** A zone of hot gases around a flame. **6.** A device in gas lamps consisting of a sheath of threads that gives off brilliant illumination when heated by the flame. **7.** *Anatomy.* The cerebral cortex. **8.** *Geology.* The layer of the earth between the crust and the core. **9.** The outer wall and casing of a blast furnace above the hearth. **10.** The wings, shoulder feathers, and back of a bird when differently colored from the rest of the body. **11.** *Zoology.* **a.** A fold or pair of folds of the body wall that lines the shell and secretes the substance that forms the shell in mollusks and brachiopods. **b.** The soft outer wall lining the shell of a tunicate or barnacle. **—mantle** *v.* **-tled, -tling, -tles.** *—tr.* To cover with or as if with a mantle; conceal. See Synonyms at **clothe.** *—intr.* **1.** To spread or become extended over a surface. **2.** To become covered with a coating, as scum or froth on the surface of a liquid. **3.** To be overspread by blushes or colors: *a face that was mantled in joy.* [Middle English, from Old English *mentel* and from Old French *mantel,* both from Latin *mantellum.*]

Man·tle (măn′tl), **Mickey Charles.** Born 1931. American baseball player. One of the greatest sluggers of the game, he played center field for the New York Yankees (1951–1968).

mansard

mantel

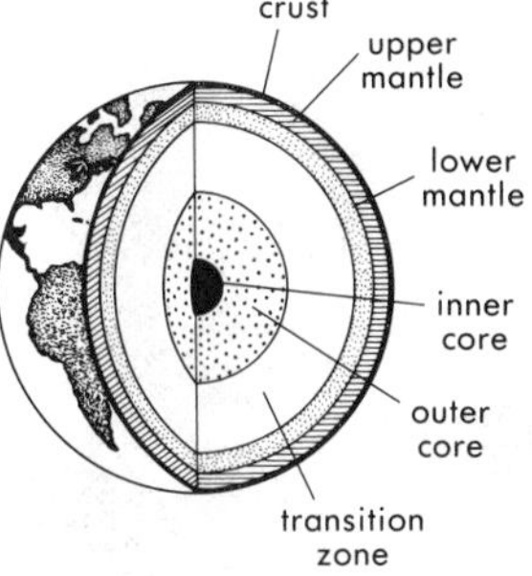

mantle
Cutaway view of Earth

ă pat	oi boy
ā pay	ou out
âr care	o͝o took
ä father	o͞o boot
ĕ pet	ŭ cut
ē be	ûr urge
ĭ pit	th thin
ī pie	*th* this
îr pier	hw which
ŏ pot	zh vision
ō toe	ə about, item
ô paw	♦ regionalism

Stress marks: ′ (primary); ′ (secondary), as in **dictionary** (dĭk′shə-nĕr′ē)

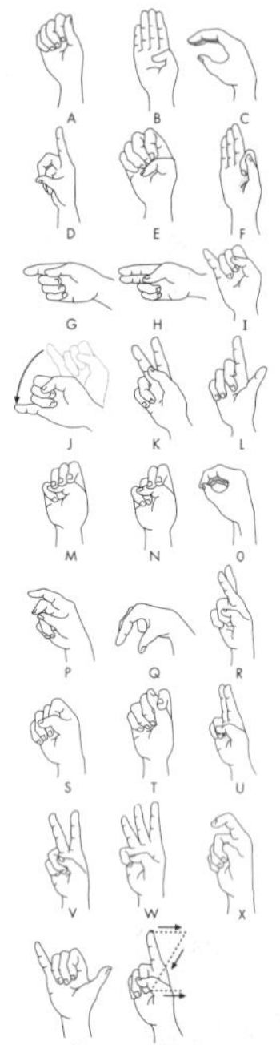

manual alphabet

Manx cat

Mao Zedong

ă pat	oi boy
ā pay	ou out
âr care	o͝o took
ä father	o͞o boot
ĕ pet	ŭ cut
ē be	ûr urge
ĭ pit	th thin
ī pie	*th* this
îr pier	hw which
ŏ pot	zh vision
ō toe	ə about, item
ô paw	♦ regionalism

Stress marks: **′** (primary); ′ (secondary), as in **dictionary** (dĭk′shə-nĕr′ē)

mantle rock *n.* See **regolith.**

mant·let (mănt′lĭt) *n.* Variant of **mantelet** (sense 2).

man-to-man (măn′tə-măn′) *adj.* **1.** Marked by forthrightness and honesty: *had a man-to-man talk about the facts of life.* **2.** *Sports.* Of, relating to, or being a system of defense in which a defensive player guards a specific offensive player.

Man·toux test (măn′to͞o′, män-to͞o′) *n.* A tuberculin test in which a small amount of tuberculin is injected under the skin. [After Charles *Mantoux* (1877–1947), French physician.]

man·tra (măn′trə, mŭn′-) *n.* *Hinduism.* A sacred verbal formula repeated in prayer, meditation, or incantation, such as an invocation of a god, a magic spell, or a syllable or portion of scripture containing mystical potentialities. [Sanskrit *mantraḥ.* See **men-**[1] in Appendix.] **—man′tric** *adj.*

man·trap (măn′trăp′) *n.* **1.** A trap set to catch trespassers or poachers. **2.** *Slang.* A woman considered dangerously seductive and scheming.

man·tu·a (măn′cho͞o-ə, -to͞o-ə) *n.* A loose gown, open in front to reveal an underskirt, worn by European women in the 17th and 18th centuries. [Alteration (influenced by MANTUA) of MANTEAU.]

Man·tu·a (măn′cho͞o-ə, -to͞o-ə). A city of northern Italy south-southwest of Verona. Originally an Etruscan settlement, it was ceded to Austria in 1714 and was finally returned to Italy in 1866. Population, 60,932. **—Man′tu·an** *adj. & n.*

man·u·al (măn′yo͞o-əl) *adj.* **1.a.** Of or relating to the hands: *manual skill.* **b.** Done by, used by, or operated with the hands. **c.** Employing human rather than mechanical energy: *manual labor.* **2.** Of, relating to, or resembling a small reference book. **—manual** *n.* *Abbr.* **m., man. 1.** A small reference book, especially one giving instructions. **2.** *Music.* A keyboard of an organ played with the hands. **3.** A machine operated by hand. **4.** Prescribed movements in the handling of a weapon, especially a rifle: *the manual of arms.* [Middle English, from Old French *manuel,* from Latin *manuālis,* from *manus,* hand. See MANUS.] **—man′u·al·ly** *adv.*

manual alphabet *n.* An alphabet used for communication by hearing-impaired people in which finger positions represent the letters.

manual training *n.* A course of training to develop manual dexterity in practical arts, such as woodworking or handcrafts.

ma·nu·bri·um (mə-no͞o′brē-əm, -nyo͞o′-) *n., pl.* **-bri·a** (-brē-ə). **1.** A body part or process shaped like a handle. Also called *presternum.* **2.a.** The broad upper division of the sternum with which the clavicle and first two ribs articulate. **b.** The long tapering process of the malleus attached to the central portion of the eardrum. [Latin, handle, from *manus,* hand. See **man-**[2] in Appendix.]

manuf. *abbr.* Manufacture.

manufac. *abbr.* Manufacture.

man·u·fac·to·ry (măn′yə-făk′tə-rē) *n., pl.* **-ries.** A factory or manufacturing plant. [Probably MANUFACT(URE) + –ORY.]

man·u·fac·ture (măn′yə-făk′chər) *v.* **-tured, -tur·ing, -tures.** —*tr.* **1.a.** To make or process (a raw material) into a finished product, especially by means of a large-scale industrial operation. **b.** To make or process (a product), especially with the use of industrial machines. **2.** To create, produce, or turn out in a mechanical manner: *"His books seem to have been manufactured rather than composed"* (Dwight Macdonald). **3.** To concoct or invent; fabricate: *manufacture an excuse.* —*intr.* To make or process goods, especially in large quantities and by means of industrial machines. **—manufacture** *n.* *Abbr.* **manuf., manufac., mfg., mfr. 1.a.** The act, craft, or process of manufacturing products, especially on a large scale. **b.** An industry in which mechanical power and machinery are employed. **2.** A product that is manufactured. **3.** The making or producing of something. [From French, manufacture, from Old French, from Medieval Latin **manūfactūra* : Latin *manū,* ablative of *manus,* hand; see **man-**[2] in Appendix + Latin *factūra,* working of a metal, from *factus,* past participle of *facere,* to make. See **dhē-** in Appendix.] **—man′u·fac′tur·a·ble** *adj.* **—man′u·fac′tur·al** *adj.* **—man′u·fac′tur·ing** *n.*

man·u·fac·tured gas (măn′yə-făk′chərd) *n.* A gaseous fuel made from soft coal or various petroleum products.

manufactured home *n.* **1.** A prefabricated house that is put together in standardized sections. **2.** See **mobile home.**

manufactured housing *n.* Manufactured homes considered as a group.

man·u·fac·tur·er (măn′yə-făk′chər-ər) *n.* *Abbr.* **mfr.** A person, an enterprise, or an entity that manufactures something.

man·u·mit (măn′yə-mĭt′) *tr.v.* **-mit·ted, -mit·ting, -mits.** To free from slavery or bondage; emancipate. [Middle English *manumitten,* from Old French *manumitter,* from Latin *manūmittere* : *manū,* ablative of *manus,* hand; see **man-**[2] in Appendix + *mittere,* to send from.] **—man′u·mis′sion** (-mĭsh′ən) *n.* **—man′u·mit′ter** *n.*

ma·nure (mə-no͝or′, -nyo͝or′) *n.* Material, especially barnyard or stable dung, often with discarded animal bedding, used to fertilize soil. **—manure** *tr.v.* **-nured, -nur·ing, -nures.** To fertilize (soil) by applying material such as barnyard dung. [From Middle English *manuren,* to cultivate land, from Anglo-Norman *mainouverer,* from Vulgar Latin **manūoperāre,* to work with the hands : Latin *manū,* ablative of *manus,* hand; see **man-**[2] in Appendix + Latin *operārī,* to work; see **op-** in Appendix.] **—ma·nur′er** *n.* **—ma·nu′ri·al** *adj.*

ma·nus (mā′nəs, mä′-) *n., pl.* **manus.** The distal part of the forelimb of a vertebrate, including the wrist and hand or the carpus and forefoot. [Latin, hand. See **man-**[2] in Appendix.]

man·u·script (măn′yə-skrĭpt′) *n.* *Abbr.* **MS., MS, ms., ms 1.** A book, document, or other composition written by hand. **2.** A typewritten or handwritten version of a book, an article, a document, or other work, especially the author's own copy, prepared and submitted for publication in print. **3.** Handwriting. —*attributive.* Often used to modify another noun: *manuscript delivery; manuscript editing.* [From Medieval Latin *manūscrīptum,* from neuter of *manūscrīptus,* handwritten : Latin *manū,* ablative of *manus,* hand; see **man-**[2] in Appendix + Latin *scrīptus,* past participle of *scrībere,* to write; see **skrībh-** in Appendix.]

Ma·nu·tius (mə-no͞o′shəs, -shē-əs, -nyo͞o′-), **Aldus.** 1450–1515. Italian scholar and printer who established (c. 1498) the Aldine Press in Venice to publish Greek and Latin classics.

man·ward (măn′wərd) *adv. & adj.* Of, at, or toward humankind. **—man′wards** *adv.*

man·wise (măn′wīz′) *adv.* In a manner characteristic of human beings.

Manx (măngks) *adj.* Of or relating to the Isle of Man or its people, language, or culture. **—Manx** *n., pl.* **Manx. 1.** The people of the Isle of Man. **2.** The extinct Goidelic language of the Manx. **3.** A Manx cat. [Alteration of Old Norse **Mansk,* from *Mon, Man-,* Isle of Man.]

Manx cat (măngks) or **manx cat** *n.* Any of a breed of the domestic cat having short hair, usually solid color, and an internal vestigial tail.

Manx·man (măngks′mən) *n.* A man who is a native or inhabitant of the Isle of Man.

Manx·wo·man (măngks′wo͝om′-ən) *n.* A woman who is a native or inhabitant of the Isle of Man.

man·y (mĕn′ē) *adj.* **more** (môr, mōr), **most** (mōst). **1.** Being one of a large, indefinite number; numerous: *many a child; many another day.* **2.** Amounting to or consisting of a large, indefinite number: *many friends.* **—many** *n. (used with a pl. verb).* **1.** A large, indefinite number: *A good many of the workers had the flu.* **2.** The majority of the people; the masses: *"The many fail, the one succeeds"* (Tennyson). **—many** *pron. (used with a pl. verb).* A large number of persons or things: *"For many are called, but few are chosen"* (Matthew 22:14). **—*idiom.* as many.** The same number of: *moved three times in as many years.* [Middle English, from Old English *manig.* See **menegh-** in Appendix.]

man-year (măn′yîr′) *n.* A unit measuring the work of one person in a year, based on a standard number of man-days.

man·y·fold (mĕn′ē-fōld′) *adv.* By many times: *The state's population has increased manyfold.*

man·y·plies (mĕn′ī-plīz′) *n.* See **omasum.**

man·y-sid·ed (mĕn′ē-sī′dĭd) *adj.* **1.** Having many sides. **2.** Having many aspects, talents, or interests. See Synonyms at **versatile.** **—man′y-sid′ed·ness** *n.*

Man·za·nil·la (măn′zə-nē′yə, -nĭl′ə) *n.* A pale, very dry sherry from Spain. [Spanish, diminutive of *manzana,* apple. See MANCHINEEL.]

man·za·ni·ta (măn′zə-nē′tə) *n.* Any of several evergreen shrubs or small trees of the genus *Arctostaphylos* of the Pacific coast of North America, especially *A. manzanita,* bearing white or pink flowers in drooping panicles and producing red berrylike drupes. [Spanish, diminutive of *manzana,* apple. See MANCHINEEL.]

Man·zo·ni (män-zō′nē, -dzô′-), **Alessandro.** 1785–1873. Italian writer best known for his romantic novel *The Betrothed* (1825–1827).

MAO *abbr.* Monoamine oxidase.

MAOI *abbr.* Monoamine oxidase inhibitor.

Mao·ism (mou′ĭz′əm) *n.* Marxism-Leninism developed in China chiefly by Mao Zedong. **—Mao′ist** *adj. & n.*

Mao jacket (mou) *n.* A plain, high-collared, shirtlike jacket customarily worn by Mao Zedong and the people of China during his regime.

Mao·ri (mou′rē) *n., pl.* **Maori** or **-ris. 1.** A member of a people of New Zealand, of Polynesian-Melanesian descent. **2.** The Austronesian language of the Maori. **—Maori** *adj.* Of or relating to the Maori or their language or culture.

Mao suit *n.* An outfit consisting of a Mao jacket and loose trousers, worn especially in China.

mao-tai (mou′tī′) *n.* A clear, very strong Chinese liquor distilled from sorghum. [After *Mao-Tai,* a town of Guizhou province, China.]

Mao Ze·dong (mou′ dzə′dŏng′) also **Mao Tse-tung** (tsə′to͝ong′). 1893–1976. Chinese Communist leader and theorist. A founder of the Chinese Communist Party (1921), he led the Long March (1934–1935) and proclaimed the People's Republic of China in 1949. As party chairman and the country's first head of state (1949–1959) he initiated the Great Leap Forward and the founding of communes. He continued as party chairman after 1959 and was a leading figure in the Cultural Revolution (1966–1969).

map (măp) *n.* **1.a.** A representation, usually on a plane surface, of a region of the earth or heavens. **b.** Something that suggests such a representation, as in clarity of representation. **2.** *Mathematics.* The correspondence of one or more elements in one set to one or more elements in the same set or another set. **3.** *Slang.* The human face. **4.** *Genetics.* A genetic map. **—map** *tr.v.* ***mapped, map·ping, maps.*** **1.a.** To make a map of. **b.** To depict as if on a map: *Grief was mapped on his face.* **2.** To explore or make a survey of (a region) for the purpose of making a map. **3.** To plan or delineate, especially in detail; arrange: *mapping out her future.* **4.** *Genetics.* To locate (a gene or DNA sequence) in a specific region of a chromosome in relation to known genes or DNA sequences. **5.** *Mathematics.* To establish a mapping of (an element or a set). ***—idioms.*** **put on the map.** To make well-known, prominent, or famous. **wipe off the map.** To destroy completely; annihilate. [From Middle English *mapemounde,* from Old French *mapemond,* from Medieval Latin *mappa (mundī),* map (of the world), from Latin, napkin, cloth (on which maps were drawn), perhaps of Carthaginian origin.] **—map′pa·ble** *adj.* **—map′per** *n.*

MAP *abbr.* Modified American plan.

ma·ple (mā′pəl) *n.* **1.** Any of numerous deciduous trees or shrubs of the genus *Acer* of the North Temperate Zone, having opposite, usually palmate leaves and long-winged fruits borne in pairs. **2.** The wood of any of these trees, especially the hard, close-grained wood of the sugar maple, often used for furniture and flooring. **3.** The flavor of the concentrated sap of the sugar maple. [Middle English, from Old English *mapul-,* as in *mapultrēo.*]

Ma·ple Grove (mā′pəl). A city of southeast Minnesota, a suburb of Minneapolis. Population, 20,525.

Maple Heights. A city of northeast Ohio, a residential suburb of Cleveland. Population, 29,735.

Maple Shade. A community of south-central New Jersey east of Camden. It is a manufacturing center. Population, 20,525.

maple sugar *n.* A sugar made by boiling down maple syrup.

maple syrup *n.* **1.** A sweet syrup made from the sap of the sugar maple. **2.** Syrup made from various sugars and flavored with maple syrup or artificial maple flavoring.

Ma·ple·wood (mā′pəl-wo͝od′). **1.** A city of southeast Minnesota, a residential suburb of St. Paul. Population, 26,990. **2.** A community of northeast New Jersey east of Newark. It is mainly residential. Population, 22,950.

map·mak·er (măp′mā′kər) *n.* A person who makes maps; a cartographer. **—map′mak·ing** (-mā′kĭng) *n.*

map·ping (măp′ĭng) *n.* **1.** The act or process of making a map. **2.** *Mathematics.* A rule of correspondence established between sets that associates each element of a set with an element in the same or another set.

Ma·pu·to (mə-po͞o′tō). Formerly **Lou·ren·ço Mar·ques** (lə-rĕn′sō mär′kĕs, lô-rĕN′so͞o mär′kĕsh). The capital and largest city of Mozambique, in the extreme southern part of the country on the Indian Ocean. Founded in the late 18th century, it was renamed (1976) after the country gained its independence (1975). Population, 755,300.

ma·quette (mă-kĕt′) *n.* A usually small model of an intended work, such as a sculpture or piece of architecture. [French, from Italian *macchietta,* sketch, diminutive of *macchia,* spot, from Latin *macula.*]

ma·qui (mä′kē) *n., pl.* **-quis.** **1.** A Chilean evergreen shrub *(Aristotelia chilensis)* bearing edible purple berries. **2.** A Chilean wine made from the fruit of this plant. [Spanish, of Araucanian origin.]

ma·qui·la (mə-kē′lə, mä-kē′lä) *n.* A maquiladora.

ma·qui·la·do·ra (mä-kē′lä-dô′rä) *n.* An assembly plant in Mexico, especially one along the border between the United States and Mexico, to which foreign materials and parts are shipped and from which the finished product is returned to the original market. [American Spanish, place where the miller's fee is paid, maquiladora, from Spanish *maquila,* portion received by the miller in return for milling one's grain, from Old Spanish, from Arabic *makīla,* measure, from *kāla,* to measure.]

ma·quil·lage (mä′kē-äzh′) *n.* Cosmetic or theatrical makeup. [French, from *maquiller,* to apply makeup, from Old French *macquiller,* to work, from Old North French *maquier,* from Middle Dutch *maken,* to make. See **mag-** in Appendix.]

ma·quis (mă-kē′) *n., pl.* **maquis.** **1.** A dense growth of small trees and shrubs in the Mediterranean area. **2. Maquis. a.** A member of the French underground organization that fought against the German occupation forces during World War II; a member of the Resistance. Also called *Maquisard.* **b.** This French underground organization. [French, from Italian *macchie,* pl. of *macchia,* thicket, spot, from Latin *macula,* spot.]

Ma·qui·sard (măk′ē-zärd′, -zär′) *n.* See **maquis** (sense 2a). [French, from *maquis,* the French underground. See MAQUIS.]

mar (mär) *tr.v.* **marred, mar·ring, mars.** **1.** To inflict damage, especially disfiguring damage, on. **2.** To impair the soundness, perfection, or integrity of; spoil. See Synonyms at **injure.** **—mar** *n.* A disfiguring mark; a blemish. [Middle English *merren,* from Old English *mierran, merran,* to impede.]

mar. *abbr.* **1.** Maritime. **2.** Married.

Mar. or **Mar** *abbr.* March.

ma·ra (mə-rä′) *n.* Any of various long-eared and long-legged cavies of the genus *Dolichotis,* inhabiting the scrub desert and grasslands of Argentina. Also called *Patagonian hare.* [American Spanish *mará,* perhaps of Araucanian origin.]

mar·a·bou also **mar·a·bout** (măr′ə-bo͞o′) *n.* **1.** Any of several large African storks of the genus *Leptoptilos* that scavenge for carrion and that have a soft white down on the underside. Also called *adjutant, adjutant stork.* **2.a.** The down of one of these storks or an imitation of it made from other bird feathers. **b.** A hat or garment trimmed with the down of a stork or an imitation of it. **3.a.** A raw silk that can be dyed without being separated from the gum. **b.** A fabric or an article of apparel made from such silk. [French *marabout,* Moslem hermit, marabout. See MARABOUT[1].]

mar·a·bout[1] (măr′ə-bo͞o′, -bo͞ot′) *n.* **1.** A Moslem hermit or saint, especially in northern Africa. **2.** The tomb of such a hermit or saint. [French *marabout,* from Portuguese *marabuto,* from Arabic *murābiṭ.*]

mar·a·bout[2] (măr′ə-bo͞o′) *n.* Variant of **marabou.**

ma·ra·ca (mə-rä′kə) *n. Music.* A percussion instrument consisting of a hollow-gourd rattle containing pebbles or beans and often played in pairs. [Portuguese *maracá,* probably from Tupi.]

Ma·ra·cai·bo (măr′ə-kī′bō, mä′rä-kī′vô). A city of northwest Venezuela south of the Gulf of Venezuela at the outlet of **Lake Maracaibo,** the largest lake of South America. Founded in 1571, the city is a major port on a dredged channel allowing access for oceangoing vessels. Population, 929,000.

Ma·ra·cay (mär′ə-kī′). A city of northern Venezuela west-southwest of Caracas. It is a cattle center. Population, 355,000.

Mar·a·jó (măr′ə-zhō′, mä′rä-). An island of northern Brazil in the Amazon delta between the Amazon and Pará rivers. It is noted for its prehistoric mounds.

Ma·ra·ñón (mär′ən-yōn′, mä′rä-nyôn′). A river flowing about 1,609 km (1,000 mi) from west-central to northeast Peru, where it joins the Ucayali River to form the Amazon.

ma·ran·ta (mə-răn′tə) *n.* **1.** Any of several tropical American plants of the genus *Maranta,* including the arrowroot, having thin, ovate, usually spotted leaves and irregular flowers. **2.** An edible starch made from these plants. [After Bartolomeo *Maranta* (died 1571), Italian herbalist.]

ma·ras·ca (mə-răs′kə) *n.* A European cultivar of the sour cherry tree *(Prunus cerasus)* bearing bitter red fruit from which maraschino is made. [Italian. See MARASCHINO.]

mar·a·schi·no (măr′ə-skē′nō, -shē′-) *n., pl.* **-nos.** A cordial made from the fermented juice and crushed pits of the marasca cherry. [Italian, from *marasca,* marasca, from *amarasca,* from *amaro,* bitter, from Latin *amārus.*]

maraschino cherry *n.* A cherry preserved in a syrup flavored with real or imitation maraschino.

ma·ras·mus (mə-răz′məs) *n. Pathology.* A progressive wasting of the body, occurring chiefly in young children and associated with insufficient intake or malabsorption of food. [New Latin, from Greek *marasmos,* from *marainein,* to waste away. See **mer-** in Appendix.] **—ma·ras′mic** *adj.*

Ma·rat (mə-rä′, mä-), **Jean Paul.** 1743–1793. Swiss-born French revolutionary who founded (1789) *L'Ami du Peuple,* which supported the French Revolution. He was elected to the National Convention in 1792 but was assassinated in the following year by a Girondist.

Ma·ra·tha also **Mah·rat·ta** (mə-rä′tə, -răt′ə) *n., pl.* **Maratha** or **-thas** also **Mahratta** or **-tas.** A member of a Hindu people inhabiting Maharashtra in west-central India. [Marathi *Marāṭhā,* from Sanskrit *Mahārāṣṭraḥ,* Maharashtra.]

Ma·ra·thi also **Mah·ra·ti** or **Mah·rat·ti** (mə-rä′tē, -răt′ē) *n.* The principal Indic language of Maharashtra. [Marathi *Marāṭhī,* from Sanskrit *Mahārāṣṭrī,* from *Mahārāṣṭraḥ,* Maharashtra.]

mar·a·thon (măr′ə-thŏn′) *n.* **1.** *Sports.* **a.** A cross-country footrace of 26 miles, 385 yards (41.3 kilometers). **b.** A long-distance race other than a footrace: *a swimming marathon.* **2.a.** A contest of endurance: *a dance marathon.* **b.** An event or activity that requires prolonged effort or endurance. [After MARATHON (so called because a messenger ran from there to Athens to announce a victory over the Persians in 490 B.C.).]

Mar·a·thon (măr′ə-thŏn′). A village and plain of ancient Greece northeast of Athens. It was the site of a major victory over the Persians in 490 B.C.

mar·a·thon·er (măr′ə-thŏn′ər) *n.* One that participates in a marathon, especially a marathon runner. **—mar′a·thon′ing** *n.*

ma·raud (mə-rôd′) *v.* **-raud·ed, -raud·ing, -rauds.** *—intr.* To rove and raid in search of booty. *—tr.* To raid or pillage for plunder. [French *marauder,* from *maraud,* tomcat, vagabond.] **—ma·raud′er** *n.*

mar·ble (mär′bəl) *n.* **1.a.** A metamorphic rock formed by alteration of limestone or dolomite, often irregularly colored by impurities, and used especially in architecture and sculpture. **b.** A piece of this rock. **c.** A sculpture made from this rock. **2.** Something resembling or suggesting metamorphic rock, as in being very hard, smooth, or cold: *a heart of marble; a brow of marble.* **3.** *Games.* **a.** A small hard ball, usually of glass, used in children's games. **b. marbles.** *(used with a sing. verb).* Any of various games played with marbles. **4. marbles.** *(used with a sing. verb). Slang.* Common sense; sanity: *completely lost his marbles after the stock market crash.* **5.** Marbling. **—marble** *tr.v.* **-bled, -bling, -bles.** To mottle and streak (paper, for example) with colors and veins in imitation of marble. **—marble** *adj.* **1.** Composed of metamorphic rock: *a marble hearth.* **2.** Resembling metamorphic rock in consistency, texture, venation, color, or coldness. [Middle

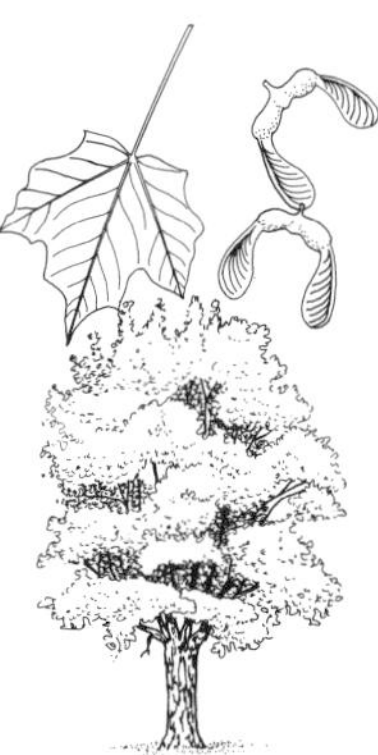

maple
Sugar maple
Acer saccharum

marabou
Leptoptilos crumeniferus

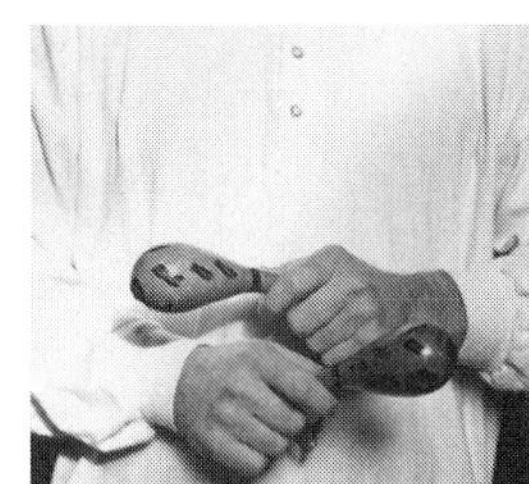

maraca
A pair of maracas

Jean Paul Marat
1793 portrait by
Joseph Boze
(1744–1826)

English, from Old French *marbre,* from Latin *marmor,* from Greek *marmaros.*] **—mar′bly** *adj.*

marble cake *n.* A cake with a streaked or mottled appearance achieved by mixing light and dark batter.

mar·bled (mär′bəld) *adj.* **1.** Made of or covered with marble: *a marbled façade.* **2.** Having a mix of fat and lean: *a well-marbled roast of beef.*

Mar·ble·head (mär′bəl-hĕd′, mär′bəl-hĕd′). A town of northeast Massachusetts northeast of Boston. Founded in the 17th century, it is a boating center and resort. Population, 20,126.

mar·ble·ize (mär′bə-līz′) *tr.v.* **-ized, -iz·ing, -iz·es.** To marble.

mar·ble·wood (mär′bəl-wo͝od′) *n.* An Asian tree *(Diospyros kurzii)* having mottled gray wood used in cabinetwork.

mar·bling (mär′blĭng) *n.* **1.** A mottling or streaking that resembles marble. **2.** The process or operation of giving something the surface appearance of marble. **3.** The decorative imitation of marble patterns printed on page edges and endpapers of books. **4.** Flecks or thin strips of fat, especially when evenly distributed in a cut of meat.

Mar·burg (mär′bûrg′, -bo͝ork′). A city of west-central Germany north of Frankfurt. Europe's first Protestant university was founded here in 1527. Population, 76,260.

marc (märk) *n.* **1.** The pulpy residue left after the juice has been pressed from grapes, apples, or other fruits. **2.** Brandy distilled from grape or apple residue. [French, from Old French *march,* from Old French *marchier,* to trample, of Germanic origin. See **merg-** in Appendix.]

mar·ca·site (mär′kə-sīt′, -zīt′) *n.* **1.** A mineral with the same composition as pyrite, FeS_2, but differing in crystal structure. Also called *white iron pyrites.* **2.** An ornament of pyrite, polished steel, or white metal. [Middle English, from Medieval Latin *marcasīta,* from Arabic *marqašītā,* from Aramaic *marqēšītā,* perhaps from Assyrian *marḫašītu,* of Markhashi, from *Markhashi,* region of perhaps northeast Persia.] **—mar′ca·sit′i·cal** (-sĭt′ĭ-kəl) *adj.*

mar·ca·to (mär-kä′tō) *Music. adv. & adj.* With strong accentuation. Used chiefly as a direction. **—marcato** *n., pl.* **-tos.** A marcato passage or movement. [Italian, past participle of *marcare,* to mark, accent, from Old Italian. See DEMARCATION.]

Marcel Marceau
As *Bip* in 1957

Mar·ceau (mär-sō′), **Marcel.** Born 1923. French mime whose most famous character is Bip, a sad-faced clown.

mar·cel (mär-sĕl′) *n.* A hairstyle characterized by deep, regular waves made by a heated curling iron. **—marcel** *v.* **-celled, -cell·ing, -cels.** *—tr.* To style (the hair) with deep, regular waves, using a curling iron. *—intr.* To make such a hairstyle. [After *Marcel* Grateau (1852–1936), French hairdresser.]

Mar·cel·lus (mär-sĕl′əs), **Marcus Claudius.** 268?–208 B.C. Roman general who in the Second Punic War took Syracuse (212) and Capua (211).

mar·ces·cent (mär-sĕs′ənt) *adj. Botany.* Withering but not falling off, as a blossom that persists on a twig after flowering. [Latin *marcēscēns, marcēscent-,* past participle of *marcēscere,* inchoative of *marcēre,* to wither.]

march¹ (märch) *v.* **marched, march·ing, march·es.** *—intr.* **1.a.** To walk steadily and rhythmically forward in step with others. **b.** To begin to move in such a manner: *The troops will march at dawn.* **2.a.** To proceed directly and purposefully: *marched in and demanded to see the manager.* **b.** To progress steadily onward; advance: *Time marches on.* **3.** To be arranged in an orderly fashion that suggests steady, rhythmical progression. **4.** To participate in an organized walk, as for a public cause. *—tr.* **1.** To cause to move or otherwise progress in a steady, rhythmical manner: *march soldiers into battle; marched us off to the dentist.* **2.** To traverse by progressing steadily and rhythmically: *They marched the route in a day.* **—march** *n.* **1.** The act of marching, especially: **a.** The steady forward movement of a body of troops. **b.** A long tiring journey on foot. **2.** Steady forward movement or progression: *the march of time.* **3.** A regulated pace: *quick march; slow march.* **4.** The distance covered within a certain period of time by moving or progressing steadily and rhythmically: *a week's march away.* **5.** *Music.* A composition in regularly accented, usually duple meter that is appropriate to accompany marching. **6.** An organized walk or procession by a group of people for a specific cause or issue. ***—idioms.* on the march.** Advancing steadily; progressing: *Technology is on the march.* **steal a march on.** To get ahead of, especially by quiet enterprise. [Middle English *marchen,* from Old French *marchier,* from Frankish **markōn,* to mark out. See **merg-** in Appendix.]

march² (märch) *n.* **1.** The border or boundary of a country or an area of land; a frontier. **2.** A tract of land bordering on two countries and claimed by both. **—march** *intr.v.* **marched, march·ing, march·es.** To have a common boundary: *England marches with Scotland.* [Middle English, from Old French *marche,* of Germanic origin. See **merg-** in Appendix.]

March (märch) *n. Abbr.* **Mar., Mar** The third month of the year in the Gregorian calendar. See table at **calendar.** [Middle English, from Anglo-Norman, from Latin *Mārtius (mēnsis),* (month) of Mars, from *Mārs, Mārt-,* Mars.]

March. *abbr.* Marchioness.

mar·chand de vin sauce (mär-shäɴ′ də văɴ′) *n.* A rich, buttery sauce made with onions, brown gravy, and red wine and served especially with steaks and roasts. [French : *marchand,* merchant + *de,* of + *vin,* wine.]

Marche¹ (märsh). A historical region and former province of central France. So called because of its location as a northern border fief of the duchy of Aquitaine, it became part of the French crown lands in 1531.

Mar·che² (mär′kā) or **Mar·ches** (-chĭz). A region of east-central Italy extending from the eastern slopes of the Apennines to the Adriatic Sea. Colonized by Rome in the 3rd century B.C., it was under papal control from the 16th to the 19th century.

Mär·chen (mĕr′ᴋʜən) *n., pl.* **Märchen.** A folk tale or fairy story. [German, from Middle High German *merechyn,* short verse narrative, diminutive of *mære,* narrative, from Old High German *māri,* famous, narrative. See **mē-³** in Appendix.]

march·er¹ (mär′chər) *n.* One that marches, especially for a specific cause: *a protest marcher; a peace marcher.*

march·er² (mär′chər) *n.* One who lives in a border district.

Mar·ches (mär′chĭz). See **Marche².**

mar·che·sa (mär-kā′zə, -kĕ′zä) *n., pl.* **-se** (-zā, -zĕ). **1.** The wife or widow of a marchese. **2.** An Italian noblewoman ranking above a countess and below a princess. **3.** Used as the title for such a noblewoman. [Italian, feminine of *marchese,* marchese. See MARCHESE.]

mar·che·se (mär-kā′zā, -kĕ′zĕ) *n., pl.* **-si** (-zē). **1.** An Italian nobleman ranking above a count and below a prince. **2.** Used as the title for such a nobleman. [Italian, from Medieval Latin *(comēs) marcēnsis,* (count) of the border, from *marca,* border region, of Germanic origin. See **merg-** in Appendix.]

march·ing orders (mär′chĭng) *pl.n.* Orders to move on or depart.

mar·chio·ness (mär′shə-nĭs, mär′shə-nĕs′) *n. Abbr.* **March. 1.** The wife or widow of a marquis. **2.** A noblewoman ranking above a countess and below a duchess. Also called *marquise.* **3.** Used as a title for such a noblewoman. [Medieval Latin *marchionissa,* feminine of *marchiō, marchiōn-,* marquis, from *marca,* boundary, of Germanic origin. See **merg-** in Appendix.]

march·land (märch′lănd′) *n.* A borderland.

march·pane (märch′pān′) *n. Archaic.* Marzipan. [Perhaps obsolete French *marcepain,* from Italian *marzapane,* marzipan. See MARZIPAN.]

march-past (märch′păst′) *n.* A procession or parade, especially of troops being reviewed.

Mar·ci·a·no (mär′sē-ä′nō), **Rocco.** Known as "Rocky." 1924–1969. American boxer who won the world heavyweight championship in 1952 and defended it six times.

Mar·cion·ism (mär′shə-nĭz′əm) *n.* A Christian heresy of the second and third centuries A.D. that rejected the Old Testament and denied the incarnation of God in Jesus as a human being. [After *Marcion* (died c. A.D. 160), Pontic merchant and heretic in Rome.] **—Mar′cion·ite′** (-shə-nīt′) *n.*

Mar·co·ni (mär-kō′nē), **Guglielmo.** 1874–1937. Italian engineer and inventor who in 1901 transmitted long-wave radio signals across the Atlantic Ocean. He shared the 1909 Nobel Prize in physics.

Marconi rig *n. Nautical.* See **Bermuda rig.** [After Guglielmo MARCONI (probably from its resemblance to the early antennas used by him for his wireless telegraphy).]

Mar·co Po·lo (mär′kō pō′lō). See Marco **Polo.**

Mar·cos (mär′kōs), **Ferdinand Edralin.** 1917–1989. Philippine president (1965–1986) who maintained close ties with the United States and exercised dictatorial control over his country. After a fraudulent presidential election against Corazon Aquino (1986) he fled the Philippines with his wife, **Imelda** (born 1930).

Mar·cus Au·re·li·us An·to·ni·nus (mär′kəs ô-rē′lē-əs ăn′tə-nī′nəs). A.D. 121–180. Philosopher and emperor of Rome (161–180) who wrote *Meditations,* a classic work of stoicism.

Mar·cu·se (mär-ko͞o′zə), **Herbert.** 1898–1979. German-born American political philosopher whose works of social criticism include *One-Dimensional Man* (1964).

Mar del Pla·ta (mär′ dĕl plä′tə, *th*ĕl plätä). A city of east-central Argentina on the Atlantic Ocean south-southeast of Buenos Aires. It is a popular resort. Population, 414,696.

Mar·di gras or **Mar·di Gras** (mär′dē grä′) *n.* **1.a.** The day before Ash Wednesday, celebrated as a holiday in many places with carnivals, masquerade balls, and parades of costumed merrymakers. **b.** A carnival period coming to a climax on this day. **2.** An occasion of great festivity and merrymaking. [French : *Mardi,* Tuesday + *gras,* fat (from the feasting on Mardi gras before Lenten fasting).]

Mar·duk (mär′do͝ok) *n. Mythology.* The chief Babylonian god.

mare¹ (mâr) *n.* A female horse or the female of other equine species. [Middle English, alteration of Old English *mere* (influenced by forms of *mearh,* horse). See **marko-** in Appendix.]

ma·re² (mä′rā) *n., pl.* **-ri·a** (-rē-ə). *Astronomy.* Any of the large dark areas on the moon or on Mars or other planets. [Latin *mare,* sea. See **mori-** in Appendix.]

ma·re clau·sum (mä′rā klou′səm, klō′-) *n.* A navigable body of water, such as a sea, that is under the jurisdiction of one nation and closed to all others. [New Latin : Latin *mare,* sea + Latin *clausum,* closed.]

ma·re li·be·rum (mä′rā lē′bə-ro͞om′) *n.* A navigable body

ă pat | oi boy
ā pay | ou out
âr care | o͝o took
ä father | o͞o boot
ĕ pet | ŭ cut
ē be | ûr urge
ĭ pit | th thin
ī pie | *th* this
îr pier | hw which
ŏ pot | zh vision
ō toe | ə about, item
ô paw | ♦ regionalism

Stress marks: ′ (primary); ′ (secondary), as in **dictionary** (dĭk′shə-nĕr′ē)

of water, such as a sea, that is open to navigation by vessels of all nations. [New Latin *mare līberum* : Latin *mare,* sea + Latin *līberum,* free.]

Ma•ren•go (mə-rĕng′gō) *adj.* Browned in oil and sautéed in a sauce of tomatoes, mushrooms, garlic, onion, and white wine: *chicken Marengo; veal Marengo.* [After *Marengo,* a village of northwest Italy (probably from the chicken dish served to Napoleon following his victory over the Austrians here on June 14, 1800).]

ma•re nos•trum (mä′rā nō′strəm) *n.* A navigable body of water, such as a sea, that is under the jurisdiction of one nation or that is shared by two or more nations. [Latin, the Mediterranean : *mare,* sea + *nostrum,* our.]

mare's nest (mârz) *n., pl.* **mare's nests** or **mares' nests. 1.** A hoax or fraud. **2.** An extraordinarily complicated situation.

mare's-tail (mârz′tāl′) *n., pl.* **mare's-tails** or **mares'-tails** (mârz′tālz′). **1.** A cosmopolitan aquatic herb *(Hippuris vulgaris)* having minute flowers and linear whorled leaves. **2.** A long, narrow cirrus cloud with a flowing appearance.

Mar•fan syndrome (mär′făn) *n.* A hereditary disorder principally affecting the connective tissues of the body, manifested in varying degrees by excessive bone elongation and joint flexibility and by abnormalities of the eye and cardiovascular system. [After Antonin Bernard Jean *Marfan* (1858–1942), French pediatrician.]

marg. *abbr.* Margin.

Mar•gar•et of An•jou (mär′gə-rət, -grət; ăn-jo͞o′, äɴ-zho͞o′). 1430–1482. Queen of Henry VI of England. She led the Lancastrians in the Wars of the Roses and was captured (1471) and ransomed to France (1476).

Margaret of Na•varre (nə-vär′, nä-). 1492–1549. Queen of Navarre (1527–1549) who wrote the *Heptameron,* an unfinished collection of stories modeled on Boccaccio's *Decameron.*

Margaret of Val•ois (văl-wä′). 1553–1615. Queen consort whose marriage (1572) to Henry of Navarre, later Henry IV of France, was dissolved in 1599.

Margaret Rose (rōz), Princess. Born 1930. Princess of Great Britain, the sister of Elizabeth II.

mar•gar•ic (mär-găr′ĭk) *adj.* Resembling pearl; pearly. [From Greek *margaron,* pearl.]

margaric acid *n.* A synthetic crystalline fatty acid, $CH_3(CH_2)_{15}CO_2H$.

mar•ga•rine also **mar•ga•rin** (mär′jər-ĭn) *n.* A fatty solid butter substitute consisting of a blend of hydrogenated vegetable oils mixed with emulsifiers, vitamins, coloring matter, and other ingredients. [French, from Greek *margaron,* pearl.]

mar•ga•ri•ta (mär′gə-rē′tə) *n.* A cocktail made with tequila, an orange-flavored liqueur, and lemon or lime juice, often served with salt encrusted on the rim of the glass. [Spanish, from the name *Margarita,* Margaret.]

mar•ga•rite (mär′gə-rīt′) *n.* **1.** A rock formation that resembles beads, found in glassy igneous rocks. **2.** *Archaic.* A pearl. [Ultimately from Greek *margaritēs,* pearl.]

Mar•gate (mär′gāt′). **1.** (*also* -gət). A municipal borough of southeast England east of London. A popular seaside resort, it also has light industries. Population, 121,900. **2.** A city of southeast Florida northwest of Fort Lauderdale. It is a resort community. Population, 36,044.

mar•gay (mär′gā′, mär-gā′) *n., pl.* **-gays.** A spotted Central and South American wildcat *(Felis wiedi)* resembling a long-tailed ocelot. [French, from Portuguese *maracajá,* from Tupi.]

mar•gin (mär′jĭn) *n. Abbr.* **marg. 1.** An edge and the area immediately adjacent to it; a border. See Synonyms at **border. 2.** The blank space bordering the written or printed area on a page. **3.** A limit in a condition or process, beyond or below which something is no longer possible or acceptable: *the margin of reality; has crossed the margin of civilized behavior.* **4.** An amount allowed beyond what is needed: *a small margin of safety.* See Synonyms at **room. 5.** A measure, quantity, or degree of difference: *a margin of 500 votes.* **6.** *Economics.* **a.** The minimum return that an enterprise may earn and still pay for itself. **b.** The difference between the cost and the selling price of securities or commodities. **c.** The difference between the market value of collateral and the face value of a loan. **7.** An amount in money, or represented by securities, deposited by a customer with a broker as a provision against loss on transactions made on account. **8.** *Botany.* The border of a leaf. **—margin** *tr.v.* **-gined, -gin•ing, -gins. 1.** To provide with a margin. **2.** To be a margin to; border. **3.** To inscribe or enter in the margin of a page. **4.** *Economics.* **a.** To add margin to: *margin up a brokerage account.* **b.** To deposit margin for: *margin a transaction.* **c.** To buy or hold (securities) by depositing or adding to a margin. [Middle English, from Old French, from Latin *margō, margin-.* See **merg-** in Appendix.] **—mar′gined** *adj.*

mar•gin•al (mär′jə-nəl) *adj.* **1.** Of, relating to, located at, or constituting a margin, a border, or an edge: *the marginal strip of beach; a marginal issue that had no bearing on the election results.* **2.** Being adjacent geographically: *states marginal to Canada.* **3.** Written or printed in the margin of a book: *marginal notes.* **4.** Barely within a lower standard or limit of quality: *marginal writing ability; eked out a marginal existence.* **5.** *Economics.* **a.** Having to do with enterprises that produce goods or are capable of producing goods at a rate that barely covers production costs. **b.** Relating to commodities thus manufactured and sold. **6.** *Psychology.* Relating to or located at the fringe of consciousness. **—marginal** *n.* One that is considered to be at a lower or outer limit, as of social acceptability: *"is fascinated by marginals, by people who live on the edge of society"* (Dan Yakir). **—mar′gin•al′i•ty** (-jə-năl′ĭ-tē) *n.* **—mar′gin•al•ly** *adv.*

mar•gi•na•li•a (mär′jə-nā′lē-ə) *pl.n.* Notes in the margin or margins of a book. [New Latin, neuter pl. of Medieval Latin *marginālis,* marginal, from Latin *margō, margin-,* margin. See MARGIN.]

mar•gin•al•ize (mär′jə-nə-līz′) *tr.v.* **-ized, -iz•ing, -iz•es.** To relegate or confine to a lower or outer limit or edge, as of social standing. **—mar′gin•al•i•za′tion** (-jə-nə-lĭ-zā′shən) *n.*

mar•gin•ate (mär′jə-nāt′) *tr.v.* **-at•ed, -at•ing, -ates. 1.** To provide with or be a margin to; border. **2.** To add margin to (a stock portfolio). **—marginate** also **mar•gin•at•ed** (-nā′tĭd) (-nĭt, -nāt) *adj. Biology.* Having a border or an edge of distinctive color or pattern. **—mar′gin•a′tion** *n.*

mar•gra•vate (mär′grə-vāt′) *n.* Variant of **margraviate.**

mar•grave (mär′grāv′) *n.* **1.** The lord or military governor of a medieval German border province. **2.** Used as a hereditary title for certain princes in the Holy Roman Empire. [Probably Middle Dutch *marcgrāve* : *marc,* march, border; see **merg-** in Appendix + *grāve,* count.] **—mar•gra′vi•al** (-grā′vē-əl) *adj.*

mar•gra•vi•ate (mär-grā′vē-ĭt, -āt′) also **mar•gra•vate** (mär′grə-vāt′) *n.* The territory governed by a margrave.

mar•gra•vine (mär′grə-vēn′) *n.* **1.** The wife or widow of a margrave. **2.** Used as a title for such a woman. [Probably Middle Dutch *marcgravinne,* feminine of *marcgrāve,* margrave. See MARGRAVE.]

Mar•gre•the II (mär-grā′tə). Born 1940. Queen of Denmark who inherited the throne from her father in 1972 after the Danish constitution was amended to permit the accession of a woman.

Margrethe II

mar•gue•rite (mär′gə-rēt′, -gyə-) *n.* **1.** Either of two plants, *Chrysanthemum frutescens* of the Canary Islands, or *C. leucanthemum* of Eurasia, having white or pale yellow flowers that resemble those of the common American daisy. Also called *Paris daisy.* **2.** Any of several similar or related plants having daisylike flowers. [French, from Old French *margarite,* daisy, pearl, from Latin *margarīta,* pearl, from Greek *margaritēs.*]

ma•ri•a (mä′rē-ə) *n. Astronomy.* Plural of **mare**[2].

ma•ri•a•chi (mä′rē-ä′chē) *n., pl.* **-chis.** *Music.* **1.** A street band in Mexico. **2. a.** The music performed by such a band. **b.** A musician belonging to such a band. [American Spanish, perhaps from French *mariage,* marriage (so called because the music may have originated at weddings in Jalisco, a state of west-central Mexico). See MARRIAGE.]

mariachi

Mar•i•an[1] (mâr′ē-ən, măr′-) *adj.* **1.** Of or relating to the Virgin Mary, her cult, or her theology. **2.** Of or relating to Mary I of England or Mary Queen of Scots.

Mar•i•an[2] (mâr′ē-ən, măr′-) *adj.* Of or relating to Gaius Marius: *the Marian reforms of the legions.*

Mar•i•an•a Islands (măr′ē-ăn′ə, mâr′-, mä′rē-ä′nä). An island group and U.S. commonwealth in the western Pacific Ocean east of the Philippines. Guam, the largest island of the group, is independent of the commonwealth, known as the **Northern Mariana Islands,** which gained official status in 1986. The Marianas were held by Spain until 1898. They were sold to Germany in 1899 (when Guam was ceded to the United States) and later became a Japanese mandate (1919–1944). Population, 16,780.

Mar•i•an•as Trench (măr′ē-ăn′əz, mâr′-, mä′rē-ä′näs). A depression with a maximum depth of 11,040.4 m (36,198 ft) in the floor of the western Pacific Ocean south and east of Guam.

Ma•ri•a The•re•sa (mə-rē′ə tə-rā′sə, -zə). 1717–1780. Queen of Hungary and Bohemia (1740–1780) whose reign was marked by the War of the Austrian Succession (1740–1748) and the Seven Years' War (1756–1763).

Ma•ri•bor (mär′ĭ-bôr′). A city of northwest Yugoslavia on the Drava River near the Austrian border. Population, 105,100.

Marie Antoinette
c. 1770 portrait attributed to Peter Adolf Hall (1739–1793)

Mar•i•co•pa (măr′ĭ-kō′pə) *n., pl.* **Maricopa** or **-pas. 1. a.** A Native American people sharing reservation lands with the Pima in south-central Arizona. **b.** A member of this people. **2.** The Yuman language of the Maricopa.

mar•i•cul•ture (măr′ĭ-kŭl′chər) *n.* Cultivation of marine organisms in their natural habitats, usually for commercial purposes. [Latin *mare, mari-,* sea; see **mori-** in Appendix + CULTURE.] **—mar′i•cul′tur•al** *adj.*

Ma•rie (mə-rē′). 1875–1938. Queen of Romania (1914–1927) noted for her work with the Red Cross.

Marie An•toi•nette (ăn′twə-nĕt′). 1755–1793. Queen of France (1774–1793) as the wife of Louis XVI. Unpopular because of her extravagance and insensitivity toward the masses, she was tried by the Revolutionary Tribunal and executed.

Marie Byrd Land (bûrd′). A region of western Antarctica east of the Amundsen Sea. It was discovered and claimed for the United States by Richard E. Byrd in 1929.

Marie de Mé•di•cis (də mā′dē-sēs′). 1573–1642. Queen of France as the wife (1600–1610) of Henry IV and regent (1610–1617) for her son Louis XIII.

Marie Lou•ise (lo͞o-ēz′). 1791–1847. Austrian archduchess who was empress of the French as the second wife of Napoleon I.

Mar•i•et•ta (măr′ē-ĕt′ə, mâr′-). **1.** A city of northwest Geor-

Marie de Médicis

marigold

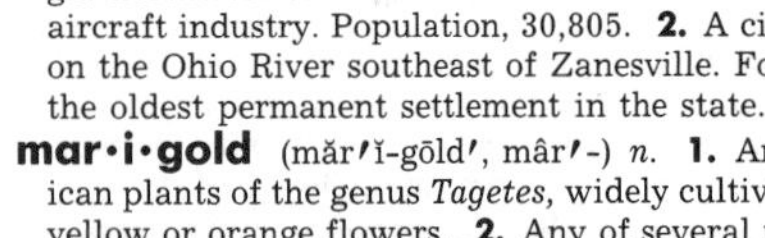

gia northwest of Atlanta. It is a residential community with an aircraft industry. Population, 30,805. **2.** A city of southeast Ohio on the Ohio River southeast of Zanesville. Founded in 1788, it is the oldest permanent settlement in the state. Population, 16,467.

mar·i·gold (mărʹĭ-gōldʹ, mârʹ-) *n.* **1.** Any of various American plants of the genus *Tagetes,* widely cultivated for their showy yellow or orange flowers. **2.** Any of several plants related to the marigold or having similar flowers, such as the marsh marigold. [Middle English : *Mari,* Mary, ultimately from Greek *Maria;* see MARIONETTE + *golde,* marigold (from Old English *golde;* probably akin to GOLD).]

mar·i·jua·na or **mar·i·hua·na** (mărʹə-wäʹnə) *n.* **1.** The cannabis plant. **2.** A preparation made from the dried flower clusters and leaves of the cannibis plant, usually smoked or eaten to induce euphoria. [Spanish *mariguana.*]

ma·rim·ba (mə-rĭmʹbə) *n. Music.* A large wooden percussion instrument with resonators, resembling a xylophone. [Portuguese, of Bantu origin; akin to Kimbundu *ma-rimba* : *ma-,* pl. n. pref. + *rimba,* xylophone, hand piano.]

Mar·in (mărʹĭn), **John.** 1870–1953. American painter noted for his expressionist watercolors, including *Brooklyn Bridge.*

ma·ri·na (mə-rēʹnə) *n.* A boat basin that has docks, moorings, supplies, and other facilities for small boats. [Italian and Spanish, seashore, from feminine of *marino,* belonging to the sea, from Latin *marīnus.* See MARINE.]

marina

Ma·ri·na (mə-rēʹnə). A city of western California on Monterey Bay west of Salinas. It is a resort community. Population, 20,647.

mar·i·nade (mărʹə-nādʹ) *n.* A liquid mixture, usually of vinegar or wine and oil with various spices and herbs, in which meat, fowl, fish, and vegetables are soaked before cooking. —**marinade** (mărʹə-nādʹ) *tr.v.* **-nad·ed, -nad·ing, -nades.** To soak (food) in such a mixture; marinate. [French, probably from Italian *marinare,* to marinate, from Latin *(aqua) marīna,* sea(water), brine, pickle, from feminine of *marīnus,* of the sea. See MARINE.]

ma·ri·na·ra (mărʹə-närʹə, märʹə-närʹə) *adj.* Being or served with a sauce made of tomatoes, onions, garlic, and spices: *spaghetti marinara; mussels marinara.* —**marinara** *n.* Marinara sauce. [Italian *(alla) marinara,* in sailor style, feminine of *marinaro,* of the sea, sailor, from *marino,* marine. See MARINA.]

mar·i·nate (mărʹə-nātʹ) *v.* **-nat·ed, -nat·ing, -nates.** —*tr.* To soak (meat, for example) in a marinade. —*intr.* To become marinated. [Probably from Italian *marinato,* past participle of *marinare,* to marinate, from *marino,* marine. See MARINA.] —**marʹi·naʹtion** *n.*

ma·rine (mə-rēnʹ) *adj.* **1.a.** Of or relating to the sea: *marine exploration.* **b.** Native to, inhabiting, or formed by the sea: *marine animals.* **2.** Of or relating to shipping or maritime affairs. **3.** Of or relating to sea navigation; nautical: *a marine chart.* See Synonyms at **nautical. 4.** Of or relating to troops that serve at sea as well as on land, specifically the U.S. Marine Corps. —**marine** *n.* **1.a.** A soldier serving on a ship or at a naval installation. **b. Marine.** A member of the U.S. Marine Corps. **2.** The mercantile or naval ships or shipping fleet of a country. **3.** The governmental department in charge of naval affairs in some nations. **4.** A painting or photograph of the sea. [Middle English *marin, marine,* from Old French, from Latin *marīnus,* from *mare,* sea. See **mori-** in Appendix.]

Marine Corps *n.* A branch of the U.S. armed forces composed chiefly of amphibious troops under the authority of the Secretary of the Navy.

mar·i·ner (mărʹə-nər) *n. Nautical.* One who navigates or assists in navigating a ship. [Middle English, from Old French *marinier,* from Old French *marin,* marine. See MARINE.]

Ma·ri·net·ti (mărʹə-nĕtʹē, măʹrē-nĕtʹtē), **Emilio Filippo Tommaso.** 1876–1944. Italian writer who founded futurism with the publication of his 1909 manifesto. Among his works are *The Bleeding Mummy* (1904) and *Mafarka the Futurist* (1910).

Ma·ri·ni (mə-rēʹnē, mä-) or **Ma·ri·no** (-nō), **Giambattista.** 1569–1625. Italian poet noted for his elaborate style in works such as the epic *Adonis* (1623).

Mar·i·ol·a·try (mârʹē-ŏlʹə-trē) *n.* Excessive veneration or worship of the Virgin Mary. —**Marʹi·olʹa·ter** *n.* —**Marʹi·olʹa·trous** *adj.*

Mar·i·ol·o·gy also **Mar·y·ol·o·gy** (mârʹē-ŏlʹə-jē) *n.* The body of belief or dogma or the systematic study of the Virgin Mary and her role in the Incarnation. —**Marʹi·o·logʹi·cal** *adj.*

Mar·i·on (mărʹē-ən, mârʹ-). **1.** A city of northeast-central Indiana northwest of Muncie. It is a trade, processing, and industrial center. Population, 35,874. **2.** A city of east-central Iowa, a residential suburb of Cedar Rapids. Population, 19,474. **3.** A city of central Ohio north of Columbus. The home and burial place of President Warren G. Harding, it is a manufacturing center. Population, 37,040.

Marion, Francis. Called "the Swamp Fox." 1732?–1795. American Revolutionary soldier known for his guerrilla tactics against the British in South Carolina.

mar·i·o·nette (mărʹē-ə-nĕtʹ) *n.* A jointed puppet manipulated from above by strings or wires attached to its limbs. [French *marionnette,* from Old French, musical instrument, diminutive of *mariole,* the Virgin Mary, from diminutive of *Marie,* Mary (influenced by the name *Marion*), from Late Latin *Maria,* from Greek, from Hebrew *Miryām.*]

marionette
c. 1950 American

mar·i·po·sa lily (mărʹə-pōʹzə, -sə) *n.* Any of several bulbous plants of the genus *Calochortus* of western North America, having variously colored, tuliplike flowers. Also called *mariposa tulip.* [Probably from American Spanish *mariposa,* from Spanish, butterfly : *mari-,* frequentative pref. + *posar,* to perch (from Late Latin *pausāre,* to pause, from Latin *pausa,* pause).]

Mar·ist (mârʹĭst, mărʹ-) *n.* **1.** A member of the Society of Mary, a congregation of Roman Catholic missionary priests founded in 1824. **2.** A member of the Little Brothers of Mary, a Roman Catholic teaching congregation founded in 1817. [French *Mariste,* from *Marie,* the Virgin Mary, from Late Latin *Maria.* See MARIONETTE.]

Ma·ri·tain (mărʹĭ-tăNʹ, mä-rē-), **Jacques.** 1882–1973. French philosopher and critic noted for his interpretations of Saint Thomas Aquinas. His works include *Art and Scholasticism* (1920).

mar·i·tal (mărʹĭ-tl) *adj.* **1.** Of or relating to marriage: *marital status; marital problems.* **2.** Of or relating to a husband. [Latin *marītālis,* from *marītus,* married.] —**marʹi·tal·ly** *adv.*

mar·i·time (mărʹĭ-tīmʹ) *adj. Abbr.* **mar. 1.** Of, relating to, or adjacent to the sea. **2.** Of or relating to marine shipping or navigation. See Synonyms at **nautical. 3.** Of or resembling a mariner. [Latin *maritimus,* from *mare, mari-,* sea. See **mori-** in Appendix.]

Mar·i·time Alps (mărʹĭ-tīmʹ). A range of the southwest Alps on the French-Italian border near the Mediterranean Sea. The highest elevation is 3,299.2 m (10,817 ft).

Maritime Provinces. The Canadian provinces of Nova Scotia, New Brunswick, and Prince Edward Island, bordering on the Atlantic Ocean. —**Marʹi·timʹer** *n.*

Ma·ri·tsa (mə-rētʹsə). A river of western Bulgaria and western Turkey flowing about 483 km (300 mi) to the Aegean Sea.

Mar·i·us (mârʹē-əs, mărʹ-), **Gaius.** 155?–86 B.C. Roman general and politician. Elected consul seven times, he reformed the military and lost a disastrous civil war (88) to his rival Sulla.

Ma·ri·vaux (mărʹə-vōʹ, mä-rē-), **Pierre Carlet de Chamblain de.** 1688–1763. French writer noted for his sophisticated romantic comedies, including *La Vie de Marianne* (1731–1741).

mar·jo·ram (märʹjər-əm) *n.* Any of several aromatic Eurasian or Mediterranean plants of the genus *Origanum,* especially *O. majorana* or *O. vulgare,* having small, purplish to white flowers and opposite leaves used as seasoning. Also called *sweet marjoram, wild marjoram.* [Middle English *majorane,* from Old French, from Medieval Latin *maiorana.*]

mark¹ (märk) *n. Abbr.* **mk. 1.** A visible trace or impression, such as a line or spot. **2.** A sign, such as a cross, made in lieu of a signature. **3.** A written or printed symbol used for punctuation; a punctuation mark. **4.a.** A number, letter, or symbol used to indicate various grades of academic achievement: *got a mark of 95 instead of 100.* **b.** *Often* **marks.** An appraisal; a rating: *earned high marks from her superiors.* **5.a.** An inscription, name, stamp, label, or seal placed on an article to signify ownership, quality, manufacture, or origin. **b.** A notch in an animal's ear or hide indicating ownership. **6.** *Nautical.* **a.** A knot or piece of material placed at various measured lengths on a lead line to indicate the depth of the water. **b.** A Plimsoll mark. **7.a.** A distinctive trait or property: *Good manners are the mark of a civilized person.* **b.** A lasting effect: *The experience had left its mark.* **c. Mark.** A particular mode, brand, size, or quality of a product, especially a weapon or machine. **8.** A recognized standard of quality: *schoolwork that is not up to the mark.* **9.a.** Importance; prominence: *"a fellow of no mark nor likelihood"* (Shakespeare). **b.** Notice; attention: *a matter unworthy of mark.* **10.** A target: *"A mounted officer would be a conspicuous mark"* (Ambrose Bierce). **11.** Something that one wishes to achieve; a goal. **12.** An object or a point that serves as a guide. **13.** *Slang.* A person who is the intended victim of a swindler; a dupe. **14.a.** *Sports.* The place from which racers begin and sometimes end their contest. **b.** A point reached or gained: *the halfway mark of the race.* **c.** A record: *set a new mark in the long jump.* **15.** *Sports.* **a.** A strike or spare in bowling. **b.** A stationary ball in lawn bowling; a jack. **16.** A boundary between countries. **17.** A tract of land in medieval England and Germany held in common by a community. **18.** *Computer Science.* A character or feature in a file or record used to locate a specific point or condition. —**mark** *v.* **marked, mark·ing, marks.** —*tr.* **1.a.** To make a visible trace or impression on, as with a spot, line, or dent. **b.** To form, make, or depict by making a mark: *marked a square on the board.* **c.** To supply with natural markings: *gray fur that is marked with stripes.* **2.a.** To single out or indicate by or as if by a mark: *marked the spot where the treasure was buried; a career marked for glory.* **b.** To distinguish or characterize: *the exuberance that marks her writings; marked the occasion with celebrations.* **c.** To make conspicuous: *a concert marking the composer's 60th birthday.* **3.** To set off or separate by or as if by a line or boundary: *marked off the limits of our property.* **4.** To attach or affix identification, such as a price tag or maker's label, to. **5.** To evaluate (academic work) according to a scale of letters and numbers. **6.a.** To give attention to; notice: *Mark her expression of discontent. Mark my words: they are asking for trouble.* **b.** To take note of in writing; write down: *marked the appointment on my calendar.* **c.** *Sports & Games.* To record (the score) in various games. —*intr.* **1.** To make a visible impression: *This pen will mark under water.* **2.** To receive a visible impression: *The floor marks easily.* **3.** *Sports & Games.* To keep score. **4.** To determine academic grades: *a teacher who marks strictly.* **5.** *Archaic.* To pay attention; notice. —***phrasal verbs.* mark down.** To mark for sale at a lower price. **mark up. 1.** To deface by covering with marks. **2.** To mark for sale at a higher price. ***—idioms.* beside the mark.** Beside the point; irrelevant. **mark time. 1.** To move the feet alternately in the rhythm of a marching step without advancing. **2.** To suspend progress for the time being; wait in readiness. **3.** To function in an apathetic or ineffective manner. [Middle English, from Old English *mearc.* See **merg-** in Appendix.]

SYNONYMS: *mark, brand, label, tag, ticket.* The central meaning shared by these verbs is "to place a mark of identification on": *marked the furs with their place of origin; brand cattle; labeled the boxes on the shelf; tagging suitcases; ticketed the new merchandise.* See also Synonyms at **sign.**

mark² (märk) *n. Abbr.* **M. 1.** An English and Scottish monetary unit that was equal to 13 shillings and 4 pence. **2.** Any of several European units of weight that were equal to about 8 ounces (227 grams), used especially for weighing gold and silver. [Middle English, from Old English *marc.* See **merg-** in Appendix.]

Mark *n. Abbr.* **Mk 1.** *Bible.* See table at **Bible. 2.** In Arthurian legend, a king of Cornwall who was the husband of Iseult and the uncle of her lover Tristan.

Mark, Saint. Author of the second Gospel in the New Testament and disciple of Saint Peter.

Mark An·to·ny (ăn′tə-nē) or **Mark An·tho·ny** (ăn′thə-nē). 83?–30 B.C. Roman orator, politician, and soldier. His love affair with Cleopatra split the triumverate he had formed with Octavian and Lepidus and led to war. In 31 B.C. the forces of Antony and Cleopatra were defeated by Octavian at Actium.

mark·down (märk′doun′) *n.* **1.** A reduction in price. **2.** The amount by which a price is reduced.

marked (märkt) *adj.* **1.** Having one or more distinguishing marks. **2.** Clearly defined and evident; noticeable: *has a marked limp.* See Synonyms at **noticeable. 3.** Singled out, especially for a dire fate: *a marked man.* **—mark′ed·ly** (mär′kĭd-lē) *adv.* **—mark′ed·ness** *n.*

mark·er (mär′kər) *n.* **1.** One that marks or serves as a mark, as: **a.** A bookmark. **b.** A tombstone. **c.** A milestone. **2.** An implement, especially a felt-tipped pen, used for marking or writing. **3.** One who marks objects, especially for industrial purposes. **4.** One who grades student papers. **5.** *Sports.* A device, such as a line, stake, or flag, set on a playing field and showing the playing or scoring position. **6.** *Games.* **a.** One that keeps score in various games. **b.** A score in a game. **7.** *Slang.* A written, signed promissory note. **8.** A genetic marker. **9.** *Medicine.* A physiological substance, such as human chorionic gonadotropin or alpha-fetoprotein, that when present in abnormal amounts in the serum may indicate the presence of disease, as that caused by a malignancy. Also called *biomarker.* **10.** *Linguistics.* An element that indicates grammatical class or function; a derivational or inflectional morpheme.

mar·ket (mär′kĭt) *n. Abbr.* **mkt. 1.** A public gathering held for buying and selling merchandise. **2.** A place where goods are offered for sale. **3.** A store or shop that sells a particular type of merchandise: *a meat market.* **4.a.** The business of buying and selling a specified commodity: *the soybean market.* **b.** A market price. **c.** A geographic region considered as a place for sales: *grain for the foreign market; the West Coast market.* **d.** A subdivision of a population considered as buyers: *cosmetics for the upscale market.* **5.** The opportunity to buy or sell; extent of demand for merchandise: *a big market for gourmet foods.* **6.a.** An exchange for buying and selling stocks or commodities: *securities sold on the New York market.* **b.** The entire enterprise of buying and selling commodities and securities: *The market has been slow recently.* **—market** *v.* **-ket·ed, -ket·ing, -kets.** *—tr.* **1.** To offer for sale. **2.** To sell. *—intr.* **1.** To deal in a market. **2.** To buy household supplies: *We marketed for a special Sunday dinner.* ***—idioms.* in the market.** Interested in buying: *We are in the market for a used car.* **on the market. 1.** Available for buying: *Many kinds of seasonal flowers are on the market.* **2.** Up for sale: *They put the family business on the market.* [Middle English, from Old North French, from Vulgar Latin **marcātus,* from Latin *mercātus,* from past participle of *mercārī,* to buy, from *merx, merc-,* merchandise.]

mar·ket·a·ble (mär′kĭ-tə-bəl) *adj.* **1.** Fit to be offered for sale, as in a market: *marketable produce.* **2.** In demand by buyers or employers; salable: *a marketable product; marketable skills.* **—mar′ket·a·bil′i·ty** *n.*

market basket *n.* **1.** A grocery cart. **2.** A selection of foods needed for a statistical household of 3.2 persons or for a family of 4, considered in terms of its fluctuating cost.

mar·ket·er (mär′kĭ-tər) also **mar·ket·eer** (-kĭ-tîr′) *n.* One that sells goods or services in or to a market, especially one that markets a specified commodity: *a major wine marketer.*

market garden *n.* A garden in which vegetables are grown for sale in a market. **—market gardening** *n.*

mar·ket·ing (mär′kĭ-tĭng) *n. Abbr.* **mktg. 1.** The act or process of buying and selling in a market. **2.** The commercial functions involved in transferring goods from producer to consumer.

market maker *n.* One that buys and sells securities on a continuous basis for one's own account by setting the prices at which the securities will be bought and sold.

market order *n.* An order to buy or sell stocks or commodities at the prevailing market price.

mar·ket·place also **market place** (mär′kĭt-plās′) *n.* **1.** An open area or square in a town where a public market or sale is set up. **2.** The world of business and commerce. **3.** A situation or place in which values, opinions, and ideas are put forward for debate or recognition: *a marketplace for new ideas; the literary marketplace.*

market price *n.* The prevailing price at which merchandise, securities, or commodities are sold.

market research *n.* The gathering and evaluation of data regarding consumers' preferences for products and services.

market value *n.* The amount that a seller may expect to obtain for merchandise, services, or securities in the open market.

Mark·ham (mär′kəm). A town of southern Ontario, Canada, north-northeast of Toronto. Population, 77,037.

Markham, Beryl. 1903–1986. British aviation pioneer who was the first person to fly solo across the Atlantic Ocean from east to west (1936).

Markham, (Charles) Edwin. 1852–1940. American poet known for "The Man with the Hoe" (1899).

Markham, Mount. A peak, 4,353 m (14,272 ft) high, of Victoria Land, Antarctica. It was discovered in 1902.

mar·khor (mär′kôr) *n., pl.* **markhor** or **-khors.** A large, wild Himalayan goat *(Capra falconeri)* having a reddish-brown coat, spirally curved horns, and a long mane in the male. [Persian *mārkhōr* : *mār,* snake (from Avestan *mairya-,* treacherous) + *-khōr,* eater (from Old Iranian **-khvāra-;* see MANTICORE).]

markhor
Male and female markhor
Capra falconeri

mark·ing (mär′kĭng) *n.* **1.a.** A making or giving of a mark. **b.** A mark or marks made. **2.** The characteristic pattern of coloration of a plant or an animal.

mark·ka (mär′kä′) *n., pl.* **-kaa** (-kä′). *Abbr.* **mk.** See table at **currency.** [Finnish, from Swedish *mark,* a mark of money. See **merg-** in Appendix.]

Mar·ko·va (mär-kō′və, mär′kə-və), Dame **Alicia.** Born 1910. British ballerina known especially for her performance in *Giselle.*

marks·man (märks′mən) *n.* **1.** A man skilled in shooting at a target. **2.a.** A classification in the U.S. Army and Marine Corps for the lowest of three ratings of rifle proficiency. **b.** One who holds this rating. **—marks′man·ship′** *n.*

marks·wo·man (märks′wo͝om′ən) *n.* A woman skilled in shooting at a target.

mark·up (märk′ŭp′) *n.* **1.** A raise in the price of an item for sale. **2.** An amount added to a cost price in calculating a selling price, especially an amount that takes into account overhead and profit. **3.** A session of a U.S. congressional committee at which a legislative bill is put into final form. **4.** Detailed stylistic instructions written on a manuscript that is to be typeset.

marl (märl) *n.* A crumbly mixture of clays, calcium and magnesium carbonates, and remnants of shells, used as fertilizer for lime-deficient soils. **—marl** *tr.v.* **marled, marl·ing, marls.** To fertilize with such a mixture. [Middle English *marle,* from Old French, from Medieval Latin *margila, marla,* diminutive of Latin *marga,* marl, of Celtic origin.] **—marl′y** *adj.*

Marl (märl). A city of west-central Germany in the Ruhr Valley north of Essen. First mentioned in the ninth century, it is now highly industrialized. Population, 87,231.

Marl·bor·ough or **Marl·bo·ro** (märl′bûr′ō, -bər-ə, -bŭr′-ō). A city of east-central Massachusetts east-northeast of Worcester. Settled in 1657, it was nearly destroyed in 1676 during King Philip's War. Population, 30,617.

Marl·bor·ough (märl′bər-ə, -brə, môl′-), First Duke of. See John **Churchill.**

mar·lin¹ (mär′lĭn) *n.* Any of several large game fishes of the genera *Makaira* and *Tetrapturus* of the Atlantic and Pacific oceans, having an elongated, spearlike upper jaw. [Short for MARLINESPIKE (from the pointed shape of its snout).]

mar·lin² (mär′lĭn) *n. Nautical.* Variant of **marline.**

mar·line also **mar·lin** (mär′lĭn) *n. Nautical.* A light rope made of two loosely twisted strands. [Middle English.]

mar·line·spike also **mar·lin·spike** (mär′lĭn-spīk′) or **mar·ling·spike** (-lĭng-spīk′) *n. Nautical.* A pointed metal spike, used to separate strands of rope in splicing.

mar·lite (mär′līt′) *n.* Marlstone. **—mar·lit′ic** (-lĭt′ĭk) *adj.*

Mar·lowe (mär′lō), **Christopher.** 1564–1593. English playwright and poet whose plays include *Tamburlaine the Great* (c. 1587) and *Edward II* (c. 1592).

marl·stone (märl′stōn′) *n.* A rock containing clay materials and calcium and magnesium carbonates, with approximately the same composition as marl.

mar·ma·lade (mär′mə-lād′) *n.* A clear, jellylike preserve made from the pulp and rind of fruits, especially citrus fruits. [French *marmelade,* from Portuguese *marmelada,* from *marmelo,* quince, alteration of Latin *melimēlum,* a kind of sweet apple, from Greek *melimēlon* : *meli,* honey; see **melit-** in Appendix + *mēlon,* apple.]

marmalade box *n.* See **genipap** (sense 2).

marmalade plum *n.* See **sapote.**

Mar·ma·ra (mär′mər-ə), **Sea of.** A sea of northwest Turkey between Europe and Asia. It is connected to the Black Sea through the Bosporus and to the Aegean Sea through the Dardanelles.

mar·mite (mär′mīt, mär-mēt′) *n.* **1.a.** A large, covered earthenware or metal cooking pot. **b.** A small, covered earthenware

ă pat	oi boy
ā pay	ou out
âr care	o͝o took
ä father	o͞o boot
ĕ pet	ŭ cut
ē be	ûr urge
ĭ pit	th thin
ī pie	*th* this
îr pier	hw which
ŏ pot	zh vision
ō toe	ə about, item
ô paw	♦ regionalism

Stress marks: **′** (primary); ′ (secondary), as in **dictionary** (dĭk′shə-nĕr′ē)

casserole designed to hold an individual serving. **2.** A petite marmite. [French, from Old French, hypocritical, marmite (possibly because the food is hidden inside) : *marm-*; akin to *marmouser,* to murmur + *mite,* cat (of imitative origin).]

Mar·mo·la·da (mär′mə-lä′də, -mô-lä′dä). A peak, 3,344.3 m (10,965 ft) high, in the Dolomite Alps of northeast Italy. It is the highest elevation in the range.

mar·mo·re·al (mär-môr′ē-əl, -mōr′-) also **mar·mo·re·an** (-ē-ən) *adj.* Resembling marble, as in smoothness, whiteness, or hardness. [From Latin *marmoreus,* from *marmor,* marble.] **—mar·mo′re·al·ly** *adv.*

mar·mo·set (mär′mə-sĕt′, -zĕt′) *n.* Any of various small, clawed monkeys of the genera *Callithrix* and *Cebuella,* found in tropical forests of the Americas and having soft, dense fur, tufted ears, and long tails. [Middle English *marmusette,* a kind of small monkey, from Old French *marmouset,* grotesque figurine, alteration (influenced by *marmouser,* to murmur) of *marmotte,* marmot. See MARMOT.]

mar·mot (mär′mət) *n.* Any of various stocky, coarse-furred, burrowing rodents of the genus *Marmota,* having short legs and ears and short bushy tails and found throughout the Northern Hemisphere. [French *marmotte,* probably from *marmotter,* to mumble, probably of imitative origin.]

marmot

Marne (märn). A river, about 523 km (325 mi) long, of northeast France flowing in an arc generally northwest to the Seine River near Paris. It was the scene of heavy fighting in World War I (1914 and 1918) and World War II (1944).

Mar·o·nite (măr′ə-nīt′) *n.* A member of a Christian Uniat church, chiefly of Lebanon, the liturgy of which is conducted in Syriac. [Medieval Latin *marōnīta,* after *Maro,* fourth-century A.D. Syrian religious leader.] **—Mar′o·nite′** *adj.*

ma·roon¹ (mə-ro͞on′) *tr.v.* **-rooned, -roon·ing, -roons. 1.** To put ashore on a deserted island or coast and intentionally abandon. **2.** To abandon or isolate with little hope of ready rescue or escape: *The travelers were marooned by the blizzard.* **—maroon** *n.* **1.** Often **Maroon. a.** A fugitive Black slave in the West Indies in the 17th and 18th centuries. **b.** A descendant of such a slave. **2.** A person who is marooned, as on an island. [From French *marron,* fugitive slave, from American Spanish *cimarrón,* wild, runaway, perhaps from *cima,* summit, from Latin *cȳma,* sprout. See CYMA.]

WORD HISTORY: The history of the word *maroon,* which we associate with desert islands, takes us back to the days of slavery, when the noun *maroon* was a term in English for a Black person who lived in the mountains and forests of Dutch Guiana (Suriname) and the West Indies, a term that is still used in parts of the Caribbean. These were plantation slaves who had run away to live free in uncultivated parts. The English word is taken from the French word *marron,* "runaway Black slave," which in turn was an alteration of American Spanish *cimarrón,* meaning "runaway slave." *Cimarrón* is perhaps from *cima,* "summit." Having come into English (first recorded in 1666), *maroon* took on a life of its own and came to be used as a verb meaning "to be lost in the wilds," from which our sense "to put ashore on a deserted island or coast" evolved.

marquee

ma·roon² (mə-ro͞on′) *n. Color.* A dark reddish brown to dark purplish red. [French *marron,* chestnut, from Italian *marrone.*]

Ma·roon Peak (mə-ro͞on′). A mountain, 4,317.6 m (14,156 ft) high, in the Elk Mountains of west-central Colorado.

mar·plot (mär′plŏt′) *n.* A stupid, officious meddler whose interference compromises the success of an undertaking. [After *Marplot,* a character in *The Busy Body,* a play by Susannah Centlivre (1669–1723).]

Mar·quand (mär-kwŏnd′), **John Phillips.** 1893–1960. American writer who created the Japanese sleuth Mr. Moto and wrote comic novels about rich New England families, including *The Late George Apley* (1937).

marque (märk) *n.* A model or brand of a manufactured product, especially an automobile. [French, from Old French. See MARQUETRY.]

mar·quee (mär-kē′) *n.* **1.** A large tent with open sides, used chiefly for outdoor entertainment. **2.** A rooflike structure, often bearing a signboard, projecting over an entrance, as to a theater or hotel. In this sense, also called *marquise.* [French *marquise,* marquise, marquee. See MARQUISE.]

Mar·que·san (mär-kā′zən, -sən) *n.* **1.** A native or inhabitant of the Marquesas Islands. **2.** The Austronesian language of the Marquesans. **—Marquesan** *adj.* Of or relating to the Marquesas Islands or their people, language, or culture.

Mar·que·sas Islands (mär-kā′zəz, -səz, -səs). A volcanic archipelago in the southern Pacific Ocean, part of French Polynesia. France took possession of the islands in 1842.

mar·quess (mär′kwĭs) *n.* Variant of **marquis.**

mar·que·try also **mar·que·terie** (mär′kĭ-trē) *n., pl.* **-tries** also **-teries.** Material, such as wood or ivory, inlaid piece by piece into a wood surface in an intricate design and veneered to another surface, especially of furniture, for decoration. [French *marqueterie,* from Old French, from *marqueter,* to checker, from *marque,* mark, ultimately from Old Norse *merki,* mark. See **merg-** in Appendix.]

marquetry

Mar·quette (mäar-kĕt′). A city of northwest Michigan on the Upper Peninsula and Lake Superior. Population, 23,288.

Marquette, Père **Jacques.** 1637–1675. French missionary who in 1673 accompanied Louis Jolliet on an extensive exploration of the Wisconsin, Mississippi, and Illinois rivers.

mar·quis (mär′kwĭs, mär-kē′) or **mar·quess** (mär′kwĭs) *n., pl.* **-quis·es** (-kwĭ-sĭz) or **mar·quis** (mär-kēz′) or **-quess·es** (-kwĭ-sĭz). **1.** A nobleman ranking below a duke and above an earl or a count. **2.** Used as a title for such a nobleman. [Middle English *marques,* from Old French *marchis, marquis,* from *marche,* border country, of Germanic origin. See **merg-** in Appendix.]

Mar·quis (mär′kwĭs), **Donald Robert Perry.** 1878–1937. American journalist who created the characters *archy* the literary cockroach and *mehitabel* the cat.

mar·quis·ate (mär′kwĭ-zĭt, -sĭt) *n.* The rank or territory of a marquis.

mar·quise (mär-kēz′) *n.* **1.** See **marchioness** (sense 2). **2.** See **marquee** (sense 2). **3. a.** A finger ring set with a pointed oval stone or cluster of pointed oval stones. **b.** A pointed oval shape of a gem. [French, feminine of *marquis,* marquis. See MARQUIS.]

mar·qui·sette (mär′kĭ-zĕt′, -kwĭ-) *n.* A sheer fabric of cotton, rayon, silk, or nylon, used for clothing, curtains, and mosquito nets.

Mar·quis of Queens·ber·ry rules (mär′kwĭs, mär-kē′; kwēnz′bĕr′ē, -bə-rē) *pl.n. Sports.* A set of rules in modern boxing calling for the use of gloves, the division of matches into rounds, and the ten-second count for a knockout, among other provisions. [After Eighth Marquis of QUEENSBERRY.]

Mar·ra·kesh or **Mar·ra·kech** (măr′ə-kĕsh′, mə-rä′kĕsh). A city of west-central Morocco in the foothills of the Atlas Mountains. Founded in 1062, it is a commercial center and a popular resort noted for its leatherwork. Population, 439,728.

mar·ram (măr′əm) *n.* See **beach grass.** [Of Scandinavian origin. See **mori-** in Appendix.]

Mar·ra·no (mə-rä′nō) *n., pl.* **-nos.** A Spanish or Portuguese Jew who was forcibly converted to Christianity in the late Middle Ages but who continued to practice Judaism in secret. [Spanish, pig, Marrano (from the Jewish prohibition against eating pork), probably from Arabic *maḥram,* something forbidden.]

Mar·re·ro (mə-răr′ō, -rĕr′ō). A community of southeast Louisiana, a suburb of New Orleans on the Mississippi River. Population, 36,548.

mar·riage (măr′ĭj) *n.* **1. a.** The legal union of a man and woman as husband and wife. **b.** Wedlock. **2.** A wedding. **3.** A close union: *"the most successful marriage of beauty and blood in mainstream comics"* (Lloyd Rose). **4.** *Games.* The combination of the king and queen of the same suit, as in pinochle. [Middle English *mariage,* from Old French, from *marier,* to marry. See MARRY¹.]

mar·riage·a·ble (măr′ĭ-jə-bəl) *adj.* Suitable for marriage: *of marriageable age.* **—mar′riage·a·bil′i·ty, mar′riage·a·ble·ness** *n.*

marriage of convenience *n., pl.* **marriages of convenience.** A marriage or joint undertaking arranged for political, economic, or social benefit rather than from personal attachment.

mar·ried (măr′ēd) *adj. Abbr.* **mar., m. 1. a.** Having a spouse: *a married woman; a married man.* **b.** United in matrimony: *a married couple.* **2. a.** Of or relating to the state of marriage: *married bliss.* **b.** Acquired through marriage: *her married name.* **3.** Closely connected; united. **—married** *n., pl.* **marrieds** or **married.** A married person: *young marrieds.*

mar·ron (măr′ən, mă-rôN′) *n.* See **Spanish chestnut.** [French. See MAROON².]

mar·rons gla·cés (mă-rôN′ glă-sā′) *pl.n.* Chestnuts glazed with sugar or preserved in vanilla-flavored syrup. [French : *marrons,* marrons + *glacés,* glazed.]

mar·row (măr′ō) *n.* **1.** Bone marrow. **2. a.** Spinal marrow. **b.** The spinal cord. **3. a.** The inmost, choicest, or essential part; the pith. **b.** Strength or vigor; vitality. [Middle English *marow,* from Old English *mearg.*]

mar·row·bone (măr′ō-bōn′) *n.* **1.** A bone for flavoring soup. **2. marrowbones.** *Informal.* The knees.

mar·row·fat (măr′ō-făt′) *n.* One of several varieties of pea that produces large seeds. Also called *marrow pea.*

marrow squash *n.* An edible squash having very large, elongated greenish fruit.

mar·ry¹ (măr′ē) *v.* **-ried, -ry·ing, -ries.** *—tr.* **1. a.** To join as spouses by exchanging vows. **b.** To take as a spouse. **c.** To give in marriage. **2.** To perform a marriage ceremony for: *The rabbi married the couple.* **3.** To obtain by marriage: *marry money.* **4.** *Nautical.* To join (two ropes) end to end by interweaving their strands. **5.** To unite in a close, usually permanent way: *"His material marries the domestic and the exotic"* (Clifton Fadiman). *—intr.* **1.** To take a husband or wife; wed: *They married in their twenties.* **2.** To combine or blend agreeably: *Let the flavors marry overnight.* [Middle English *marien,* from Old French *marier,* from Latin *marītāre,* from *marītus,* married.]

mar·ry² (măr′ē) *interj. Archaic.* Used as an exclamation of surprise or emphasis. [Middle English *Marie,* the Virgin Mary, ultimately from Greek *Maria.* See MARIONETTE.]

Mars (märz) *n.* **1.** *Roman Mythology.* The god of war. **2.** The fourth planet from the sun, having a sidereal period of revolution about the sun of 687 days at a mean distance of 227.8 million kilometers (141.6 million miles) and a mean diameter of approximately 6,726 kilometers (4,180 miles). [Middle English, from Latin *Mārs*.]

Mar·sa·la¹ (mär-sä′lə). A city of western Sicily on the Mediterranean Sea. Founded by the Carthaginians c. 397 B.C., it is noted for its wine. Population, 46,300.

Mar·sa·la² (mär-sä′lə) *n.* A sweet or dry fortified wine of Sicilian origin. **—Marsala** *adj.* Cooked or flavored with Marsala: *veal Marsala.* [Italian, after MARSALA¹.]

mar·seille (mär-sāl′) also **mar·seilles** (-sālz′) *n.* A heavy cotton fabric with a raised pattern of stripes or figures. [After MARSEILLES.]

Mar·seilles also **Mar·seille** (mär-sā′). A city of southeast France on an arm of the Mediterranean Sea west-northwest of Toulon. The oldest city of France, it was founded c. 600 B.C. by Greeks from Asia Minor and overrun by barbarian tribes in the 5th and 6th centuries A.D. Marseilles became independent in the 13th century and passed to France in 1481. Population, 874,436.

marsh (märsh) *n.* An area of soft, wet, low-lying land, characterized by grassy vegetation and often forming a transition zone between water and land. [Middle English, from Old English *mersc.* See **mori-** in Appendix.]

Marsh (Märsh), **Ngaio.** 1899–1982. New Zealand writer known for her detective novels, including *A Man Lay Dead* (1934).

Marsh, Reginald. 1898–1954. American painter whose works, such as *The Bowery* (1930), depict life in New York City.

mar·shal (mär′shəl) *n.* **1.a.** A military officer of the highest rank in some countries. **b.** A field marshal. **2.a.** A U.S. federal officer of a judicial district who carries out court orders and discharges duties similar to those of a sheriff. **b.** A city law enforcement officer in the United States who carries out court orders. **c.** The head, especially of a fire department in the United States. **d.** A fire marshal. **3.** A person in charge of a parade or ceremony. **4.** A high official in a royal court, especially one aiding the sovereign in military affairs. **—marshal** *v.* **-shaled, -shal·ing, -shals** also **-shalled, marshal·ling, -shals.** —*tr.* **1.** To arrange or place (troops, for example) in line for a parade, maneuver, or review. **2.** To arrange, place, or set in methodical order: *marshal facts in preparation for an exam.* See Synonyms at **arrange. 3.** To enlist and organize: *trying to marshal public support.* **4.** To guide ceremoniously; conduct or usher. —*intr.* **1.** To take up positions in or as if in a military formation. **2.** To take form or order: *facts marshaling as research progressed.* [Middle English, from Old French *mareschal,* of Germanic origin.] **—mar′shal·cy, mar′shal·ship′** *n.*

WORD HISTORY: Hard-riding marshals of the Wild West in pursuit of criminals reemphasize the relationship of the word *marshal* with horses. The Germanic ancestor of our word *marshal* is a compound made up of **marhaz,* "horse" (related to the source of our word *mare*), and **skalkaz,* "servant," meaning as a whole literally "horse servant," hence "groom." The Frankish descendant of this Germanic word, **marahskalk,* starting from these humble beginnings, came to designate a high royal official and also a high military commander, not surprisingly so, given the importance of the horse in medieval warfare. The word passed into the period (beginning in 800) in which we speak of Old French, after the Franks and their Germanic language had been fused with the surrounding culture descended from Roman Gaul. When the Normans established a French-speaking official class in England, the Old French word came with them. The Middle English source of our word is first recorded as a surname in 1218 (and the surname Marshal, now spelled Marshall, has been held by some famous people), but it is first recorded as a common noun with the sense "high officer of the royal court" in the first English language proclamation (1258) by an English king, Henry III, after the Norman Conquest. *Marshal* was applied to this high royal official's deputies, who were officers of courts of law, and the word continued to designate various officials involved with courts of law and law enforcement, including the horseback-riding marshals we are familiar with in the United States.

Mar·shall (mär′shəl). A city of northeast Texas west of Shreveport, Louisiana. Population, 24,921.

Marshall, George Catlett. 1880–1959. American soldier, diplomat, and politician. As U.S. secretary of state (1947–1949) he organized the European Recovery Program, often called the Marshall Plan, for which he received the 1953 Nobel Peace Prize.

Marshall, John. 1755–1835. American jurist and politician who served as the chief justice of the U.S. Supreme Court (1801–1835) and helped establish the practice of judicial review.

Marshall, Thomas Riley. 1854–1925. Vice President of the United States (1913–1921) under Woodrow Wilson.

Marshall, Thurgood. Born 1908. American jurist who served as an associate justice of the U.S. Supreme Court (1967–1991).

Marshall Islands. A self-governing island group in the central Pacific Ocean. First sighted by Spanish explorers in the early 16th century, they were governed by Spain and Germany until 1920, when they became a Japanese mandate. From 1947 until 1979 they were part of the U.S. Trust Territory of the Pacific Islands. In 1986 the islands became a republic. Population, 30,873.

Mar·shall·town (mär′shəl-toun′). A city of central Iowa northeast of Des Moines. Population, 26,938.

marsh elder *n.* Any of several herbs or shrubs of the genus *Iva* of eastern and central North America, often growing in salt marshes and having nodding, greenish flower heads with unisexual flowers.

Marsh·field (märsh′fēld′). **1.** A town of southeast Massachusetts on Massachusetts Bay southeast of Boston. The burial place of Daniel Webster, it is now a resort community. Population, 20,916. **2.** A city of central Wisconsin southwest of Wausau. It is a processing center in a dairy region. Population, 18,290.

marsh gas *n.* Methane.

marsh hawk *n.* See **northern harrier.**

marsh hen *n.* Any of various marsh birds of the family Rallidae, which includes the gallinules, coots, and rails.

marsh·land (märsh′lănd′) *n.* A marshy tract of land.

marsh·mal·low (märsh′mĕl′ō, -măl′ō) *n.* **1.a.** A light, spongy, very sweet confection made of corn syrup, gelatin, sugar, and starch and dusted with powdered sugar. **b.** A confection of sweetened paste, formerly made from the root of the marshmallow plant. **2.** Often **marsh mallow.** *Botany.* A perennial plant *(Althaea officinalis)* native to Europe and naturalized in marshes of eastern North America, having showy pink flowers and a mucilaginous root occasionally used as a demulcent and in confectionery. **3.** *Slang.* A timid, cowardly, or ineffective person. **—marsh′mal′low·y** *adj.*

marsh marigold *n.* Any of several plants of the genus *Caltha,* especially *C. palustris,* growing in swampy places and having bright yellow flowers. Also called *cowslip.*

marsh·y (mär′shē) *adj.* **-i·er, -i·est. 1.** Of, resembling, or characterized by a marsh or marshes; boggy. **2.** Growing in marshes. **—marsh′i·ness** *n.*

Mar·sil·i·us of Pad·u·a (mär-sĭl′ē-əs; păj′o͞o-ə, păd′yo͞o-ə). 1280?–1343? Italian philosopher who wrote *Defender of the Peace,* a work that denied the secular authority of the pope.

Mar·ston (mär′stən), **John.** 1575?–1634. English playwright whose works include *The Malcontent* (1604).

Marston Moor. A site in northern England west of York. The first Parliamentarian victory of the English Civil War occurred here on July 2, 1644.

mar·su·pi·a (mär-so͞o′-pē-ə) *n.* Plural of **marsupium.**

mar·su·pi·al (mär-so͞o′pē-əl) *n.* Any of various nonplacental mammals of the order Marsupialia, including kangaroos, opossums, bandicoots, and wombats, found principally in Australia and the Americas. **—marsupial** *adj.* **1.** Of or belonging to the order Marsupialia. **2.** Of or relating to a marsupium. [From MARSUPIUM.]

mar·su·pi·um (mär-so͞o′pē-əm) *n., pl.* **-pi·a** (-pē-ə). **1.** An external pouch or fold on the abdomen of most female marsupials, containing the mammary glands and in which the young continue to develop after leaving the uterus. **2.** A temporary egg pouch in various fishes and crustaceans. [Late Latin *marsūpium,* pouch, from Latin *marsīpium, marsuppium,* from Greek *marsippion, marsipion,* diminutive of *marsippos, marsuppos,* purse, perhaps of Iranian origin; akin to Avestan *marsū-,* belly, paunch.]

mart (märt) *n.* **1.** A trading center; a market. **2.** *Archaic.* A fair. [Middle English, probably from Middle Flemish, from Vulgar Latin **marcātus.* See MARKET.]

Mart. *abbr.* Martinique.

Mar·ta·ban (mär′tə-băn′, -bän′), **Gulf of.** An arm of the Andaman Sea off southern Burma.

mar·ta·gon (mär′tə-gən) *n.* A Eurasian lily *(Lilium martagon)* usually having pinkish-purple, spotted flowers. Also called *Turk's-cap lily.* [Middle English, from Old French, from Old Spanish, from Ottoman Turkish *mārtağān,* a kind of turban.]

Mar·tel (mär-tĕl′), **Charles.** See **Charles Martel.**

mar·ten (mär′tn) *n., pl.* **marten** or **-tens. 1.** Any of several principally arboreal carnivorous mammals of the genus *Martes,* related to the weasel, mainly inhabiting northern forests, and having a slender body, bushy tail, and soft fur. **2.** The fur of one of these carnivorous mammals. [Middle English *martrin, marten,* from Old French *martrine,* from feminine of *martrin,* pertaining to the marten (from *martre,* marten) and from Medieval Latin *martrīna,* both of Germanic origin.]

mar·ten·site (mär′tn-zīt′) *n.* A solid solution of iron and up to 1 percent of carbon, the chief constituent of hardened carbon tool steels. [After Adolf *Martens* (1850–1914), German metallurgist.] **—mar′ten·sit′ic** (-zĭt′ĭk) *adj.*

Mar·tha (mär′thə). In the New Testament, the sister of Lazarus and Mary and a friend of Jesus.

Mar·tha's Vine·yard (mär′thəz vĭn′yərd). An island of southeast Massachusetts off the southwest coast of Cape Cod. Settled in 1642, it was a whaling and fishing center in the 18th and early 19th centuries and is now a popular resort area.

Mar·tí (mär-tē′), **José Julian.** 1853–1895. Cuban revolutionary leader and poet who was killed while fighting for Cuban independence from Spain.

mar·tial (mär′shəl) *adj.* **1.** Of, relating to, or suggestive of war. **2.** Relating to or connected with the armed forces or the profession of arms. **3.** Characteristic of or befitting a warrior. [Middle English, from Latin *Mārtiālis,* from *Mārs, Mārt-,* Mars.] **—mar′tial·ism** *n.* **—mar′tial·ist** *n.* **—mar′tial·ly** *adv.*

Mar·tial (mär′shəl). fl. first century B.C. Roman poet known for his books of epigrams.

martial art *n.* Any of several Oriental arts of combat or self-

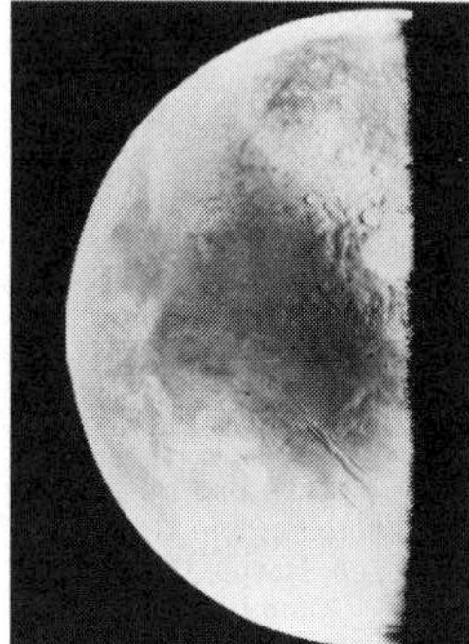

Mars
Photograph of the planet taken by Viking I on June 18, 1976

ă pat	oi boy
ā pay	ou out
âr care	o͝o took
ä father	o͞o boot
ĕ pet	ŭ cut
ē be	ûr urge
ĭ pit	th thin
ī pie	*th* this
îr pier	hw which
ŏ pot	zh vision
ō toe	ə about, item
ô paw	♦ regionalism

Stress marks: ′ (primary); ′ (secondary), as in **dictionary** (dĭk′shə-nĕr′ē)

martlet

Marx Brothers
Top to bottom: Groucho, Zeppo, Harpo, Chico, and Gummo (Milton, 1894–1977)

Mary Queen of Scots
Shown with her son, the future James I, in the Duff-Ogilvy portrait by an unknown artist

defense, such as aikido, karate, judo, or tae kwon do, usually practiced as sport. Often used in the plural.

martial law *n.* **1.** Temporary rule by military authorities, imposed on a civilian population especially in time of war or when civil authority has broken down. **2.** The law imposed on an occupied territory by occupying military forces.

Mar·tian (mär′shən) *adj.* Of or relating to the planet Mars or its hypothetical inhabitants. **—Martian** *n.* A hypothetical inhabitant of the planet Mars, especially as a stock fictional character. [Middle English *marcien,* from Latin *Mārtius,* from *Mārs, Mārt-,* Mars.]

mar·tin (mär′tn) *n.* Any of various swallows, such as the house martin or the purple martin. [Middle English *martoune,* probably from the name *Martin,* Martin.]

Mar·tin I (mär′tn), Saint. Died 655. Pope (649–655) who was banished by Emperor Constans II (630–668) because of disagreements concerning the nature of Christ.

Martin V. Originally Oddo Colonna. 1366–1431. Pope (1417–1431) who restored the authority of the Church in the Papal States.

Martin, Archer John Porter. Born 1910. British chemist. He shared a 1952 Nobel Prize for the development of partition chromatography.

Martin, Homer Dodge. 1836–1897. American painter whose landscapes include *The Harp of the Winds* (1895).

Martin, Mary. 1913–1990. American actress who has appeared in numerous Broadway hits, including *Peter Pan* (1954) and *The Sound of Music* (1959–1960).

Mar·tin Du Gard (mär-tăɴ′ dü gär′), **Roger.** 1881–1958. French writer whose novels include the series *The Thibaults* (1922–1940). He won the 1937 Nobel Prize for literature.

Mar·ti·neau (mär′tn-ō), **Harriet.** 1802–1876. British writer whose *Illustrations of Political Economy* (1832–1834) explained the economic theories of Malthus, Mill, and Ricardo.

mar·ti·net (mär′tn-ĕt′) *n.* **1.** A rigid military disciplinarian. **2.** One who demands absolute adherence to forms and rules. [After Jean *Martinet* (died 1672), French army officer.]

Mar·ti·nez (mär-tē′nəs). **1.** A city of western California northeast of Oakland. It is a manufacturing and processing center. Population, 22,582. **2.** A community of eastern Georgia, a suburb of Augusta. Population, 16,472.

mar·tin·gale (mär′tn-găl′) also **mar·tin·gal** (-găl′) *n.* **1.** The strap of a horse's harness that connects the girth to the nose band and is designed to prevent the horse from throwing back its head. **2.** *Nautical.* Any of several parts of standing rigging strengthening the bowsprit and jib boom against the force of the head stays. **3.** *Games.* A method of gambling in which one doubles the stakes after each loss. **4.** A loose half belt or strap placed on the back of a garment, such as a coat or jacket. [French, perhaps alteration of Spanish *almártaga, almártiga,* rein, harness, of Arabic origin.]

mar·ti·ni (mär-tē′nē) *n., pl.* **-nis.** A cocktail made of gin or vodka and dry vermouth. [Origin unknown.]

Mar·ti·nique (mär′tĭ-nēk′, -tn-ēk′). *Abbr.* **Mart.** An island and overseas department of France in the Windward Islands of the West Indies. Discovered by Columbus in 1502, it was colonized by French settlers after 1635. Fort-de-France is the capital. Population, 328,566.

Martin Luther King Day *n.* The third Monday in January, observed in the United States in commemoration of the birthday of Martin Luther King, Jr.

Mar·tin·mas (mär′tn-məs) *n.* **1.** A Christian feast observed in commemoration of the death and burial of Saint Martin of Tours. **2.** November 11, the day on which this feast is observed. [Middle English *martinmesse* : *Martin,* Saint Martin of Tours + *messe, masse,* Mass; see MASS.]

Mar·tin of Tours (mär′tn, mär-tăɴ′; to͝or, to͞or), Saint. A.D. 316?–397? French prelate considered the patron saint of France.

Mar·tin·son (mär′tn-sôn′, -tēn-), **Harry Edmund.** 1904–1978. Swedish writer whose works include the proletarian novel *The Road* (1948) and *Aniara* (1956), an epic poem about space travel. He shared the 1974 Nobel Prize for literature.

Mar·tins·ville (mär′tnz-vĭl′). An independent city of southern Virginia in the foothills of the Blue Ridge near the North Carolina border. It was founded in 1793. Population, 18,149.

mart·let (märt′lĭt) *n.* **1.** See **house martin. 2.** *Heraldry.* A representation of a bird without feet, used as a crest or bearing to indicate a fourth son. [French *martelet,* from *Martin,* Saint Martin of Tours.]

mar·tyr (mär′tər) *n.* **1.** One who chooses to suffer death rather than renounce religious principles. **2.** One who makes great sacrifices or suffers much in order to further a belief, cause, or principle. **3.a.** One who endures great suffering: *a martyr to arthritis.* **b.** One who makes a great show of suffering in order to arouse sympathy. **—martyr** *tr.v.* **-tyred, -tyr·ing, -tyrs. 1.** To make a martyr of, especially to put to death for devotion to religious beliefs. **2.** To inflict great pain on; torment. [Middle English, from Old English, from Late Latin, from Late Greek *martur,* from Greek *martus, martur-,* witness.]

mar·tyr·dom (mär′tər-dəm) *n.* **1.a.** The state of being a martyr. **b.** The suffering of death by a martyr. **2.** Extreme suffering of any kind.

mar·tyr·ize (mär′tə-rīz′) *tr.v.* **-ized, -iz·ing, -iz·es.** To martyr. **—mar′tyr·i·za′tion** (-tər-ĭ-zā′shən) *n.*

mar·tyr·ol·o·gy (mär′tə-rŏl′ə-jē) *n., pl.* **-gies. 1.** An official list or catalog of religious martyrs, especially of Christian martyrs. **2.a.** An account of the life and manner of death of a martyr. **b.** The branch of ecclesiastical history or hagiography that deals with martyrs. **—mar′tyr·ol′o·gist** *n.*

mar·vel (mär′vəl) *n.* **1.** One that evokes surprise, admiration, or wonder. See Synonyms at **wonder. 2.** Strong surprise; astonishment. **—marvel** *v.* **-veled, -vel·ing, -vels** also **-velled, -vel·ling, -vels.** —*intr.* To become filled with wonder or astonishment. —*tr.* To feel amazement or bewilderment at or about: *We marveled that they walked away unhurt from the car accident.* [Middle English *marvail,* from Old French *merveille,* from Vulgar Latin **mīribilia,* alteration of Latin *mīrābilia,* wonderful things, from neuter pl. of *mīrābilis,* wonderful, from *mīrārī,* to wonder, from *mīrus,* wonderful. See **smei-** in Appendix.]

Mar·vell (mär′vəl), **Andrew.** 1621–1678. English metaphysical poet whose frequently satirical work includes the poems "To His Coy Mistress" (1650) and "The Definition of Love" (1681).

mar·vel·ous also **mar·vel·lous** (mär′və-ləs) *adj.* **1.** Causing wonder or astonishment. **2.** Miraculous; supernatural. **3.** Of the highest or best kind or quality; first-rate: *has a marvelous collection of rare books.* **—mar′vel·ous·ly** *adv.* **—mar′vel·ous·ness** *n.*

Marx (märks). Family of American comedians, including the brothers **Julius** (1890–1977), known as "Groucho"; **Leonard** (1891–1961), known as "Chico"; **Arthur** (1893–1964), known as "Harpo"; and **Herbert** (1901–1979), known as "Zeppo." Some of their many popular motion pictures include *Horse Feathers* (1932) and *Duck Soup* (1933).

Marx, Karl. 1818–1883. German philosopher, economist, and revolutionary. With the help and support of Friedrich Engels he wrote *The Communist Manifesto* (1848) and *Das Kapital* (1867–1894). These works explain historical development in terms of the interaction of contradictory economic forces and have had a profound influence on the social sciences.

Marx·i·an (märk′sē-ən) *n.* One that studies, advocates, or makes use of Karl Marx's philosophical or socioeconomic concepts as a method of analysis and interpretation, as in political economy or historical or literary criticism. **—Marx′i·an** *adj.* **—Marx′i·an·ism** *n.*

Marx·ism (märk′sĭz′əm) *n.* The political and economic ideas of Karl Marx and Friedrich Engels, specifically a system of thought in which the concept of class struggle plays a primary role in analyzing Western society in general and in understanding its allegedly inevitable development from bourgeois oppression under capitalism to a socialist society and thence to Communism.

Marx·ism-Len·in·ism (märk′sĭz′əm-lĕn′ĭ-nĭz′əm) *n.* The expansion of Marxism to include both Lenin's concept of imperialism as the final form of capitalism and a shift in the focus of struggle from the developed to the underdeveloped countries.

Marx·ist (märk′sĭst) *n.* One that believes in or follows the ideas of Marx and Engels, especially a militant Communist. **—Marx′ist** *adj.*

Mar·y[1] (mâr′ē). In the New Testament, the mother of Jesus and the principal saint of many Christian churches.

Mar·y[2] (mâr′ē). In the New Testament, a sister of Lazarus and Martha and a friend of Jesus.

Mar·y[3] (mâr′ē) also **Mary of Teck** (tĕk). 1867–1953. Queen of George V of Great Britain and the mother of Edward VIII and George VI.

Mary I or **Mary Tu·dor** (to͞o′dər, tyo͞o′-). 1516–1558. Queen of England and Ireland (1553–1558) who reestablished Roman Catholicism (1555). Her persecution of Protestants earned her the nickname "Bloody Mary."

Mary II. 1662–1694. Queen of England, Scotland, and Ireland (1689–1694). The eldest daughter of James II, she ruled jointly with her husband, William III, the former William of Orange, at the behest of the Protestant opponents of her father.

Mary Jane (jān′) *n. Slang.* Marijuana. [Possibly translation of Spanish *María Juana,* Mary Jane, by folk etymology from *mariguana,* marijuana. See MARIJUANA.]

Mar·y·land (mĕr′ə-lənd). *Abbr.* **MD, Md.** A state of the east-central United States. It was admitted as one of the original Thirteen Colonies in 1788. The colony was founded by Lord Baltimore in 1634 as a refuge for English Roman Catholics. Annapolis is the capital and Baltimore the largest city. Population, 4,216,941. **—Mar′y·land·er** *n.*

Mary Mag·da·lene (măg′də-lən, -lēn′). In the New Testament, a woman whom Jesus cured of evil spirits. She is also identified with the repentent prostitute who washed the feet of Jesus.

Mary of Teck (tĕk). See **Mary**[3].

Mar·y·ol·o·gy (mâr′ē-ŏl′ə-jē) *n.* Variant of **Mariology.**

Mary Queen of Scots (skŏts). also **Mary Stu·art** (sto͞o′ərt, styo͞o′-). 1542–1587. Queen of Scotland (1542–1567). The Catholic monarch during the bitter Scottish Reformation, she was forced to abdicate in favor of her son, the future James I of England. After fleeing to England (1568), she was imprisoned by Elizabeth I. Catholic supporters plotted to place her on the English throne, resulting in her trial and execution for sedition.

Mary Tu·dor (to͞o′dər, tyo͞o′-). See **Mary I.**

Mar·y·ville (mâr′ē-vĭl′, mĕr′ĭ-vəl, -vĭl′). A city of eastern Tennessee south of Knoxville. Population, 17,480.

mar·zi·pan (mär′zə-păn′, märt′sə-pän′) *n.* A confection made of ground almonds or almond paste, egg whites, and sugar, often molded into decorative shapes. [German, from Italian *marzapane,* container of a standard size, marzipan, from obsolete, fine box for comfits or originally rare coins, from Arabic *mawṭabān,* king on the throne, Byzantine coin with enthroned Christ figure.]

Ma·sac·cio (mə-sä′chē-ō, mä-sät′chô). 1401–1428. Italian painter of the Florentine school whose revolutionary use of linear perspective and mastery of light and shade profoundly influenced Renaissance painting.

Ma·sa·da (mə-sä′də, -tsä-dä′). An ancient mountaintop fortress in southeast Israel on the southwest shore of the Dead Sea. In A.D. 73, after a two-year siege, members of the Zealot Jewish sect committed mass suicide rather than surrender to the Romans.

Ma·sai (mä-sī′, mä′sī) *n., pl.* **Masai** or **-sais. 1.** A member of a chiefly pastoral people of Kenya and parts of Tanzania. **2.** Also **Maa·sai.** The Nilotic language of this people. **—Ma·sai′** *adj.*

Ma·san (mä′sän′). A city of southeast South Korea west of Pusan. Its port was opened to foreign trade in 1899. Population, 424,000.

Mas·a·ryk (măs′ə-rĭk, mä′sä-), **Tomáš Garrigue.** 1850–1937. Czechoslovakian politician who served as the first president of independent Czechoslovakia (1918–1935). His son **Jan Garrigue Masaryk** (1886–1948) was the foreign minister of the provisional government in London (1940–1945) and the restored government in Prague (1945–1948).

Mas·ba·te (mäs-bä′tē, -tĕ). An island of the central Philippines south of Luzon.

masc. *abbr. Grammar.* Masculine.

mas·car·a (mă-skăr′ə) *n.* A cosmetic applied to darken the eyelashes. **—mascara** *tr.v.* **-car·aed, -car·a·ing, -car·as.** To apply mascara to. [Probably Spanish *máscara,* mask; akin to Italian *maschera.* See MASK.]

Mas·ca·rene Islands (măs′kə-rēn′). A group of islands in the Indian Ocean east of Madagascar. Mauritius and the French island of Réunion are in the group.

mas·car·po·ne (mäs′kär-pō′nĕ, -pōn′) *n.* A fresh, soft Italian cheese with a high butterfat content, made from cow's milk enriched with cream. [Italian, augmentative of dialectal *mascarpa,* whey cheese.]

mas·con (măs′kŏn′) *n.* A mare on the moon having rock of greater density than that of the surrounding area, thus exerting a slightly higher gravitational force. [MAS(S) + CON(CENTRATION).]

mas·cot (măs′kŏt′, -kət) *n.* A person, an animal, or an object believed to bring good luck, especially one kept as the symbol of an organization such as a sports team. [French *mascotte,* sorcerer's charm, mascot, from Provençal *mascoto,* sorcery, fetish, from *masco,* witch, ultimately from Late Latin, mask, specter, witch.]

WORD HISTORY: The word *mascot,* which usually denotes something or someone that brings good luck, enjoys a positive meaning that is a distinct improvement over the meanings of some of its ancestors. *Mascot* came into English as a borrowing of the French word *mascotte,* meaning "mascot, charm." The English word is first recorded in 1881 shortly after the French word, itself first recorded in 1867, was popularized by the opera *La Mascotte,* performed in December 1880. The French word in turn came from the Modern Provençal word *mascoto,* "piece of witchcraft, charm, amulet," a feminine diminutive of *masco,* "witch." This word can probably be traced back to Late Latin *masca,* "witch, specter." Perhaps a mascot is as powerful as people think; fortunately, it is now in our corner.

Mas·couche (mä-sko͞osh′). A city of southern Quebec, Canada, a suburb of Montreal on the upper bank of the St. Lawrence River. Population, 20,345.

mas·cu·line (măs′kyə-lĭn) *adj.* **1.** Of or relating to men or boys; male. **2.** Suggestive or characteristic of a man; mannish. See Synonyms at **male. 3.** *Abbr.* **masc., m., M.** *Grammar.* Relating or belonging to the gender of words or grammatical forms that refer chiefly to males or to things classified as male. **4.** *Music.* Ending on an accented beat: *a masculine cadence.* **—masculine** *n.* **1.** *Abbr.* **masc., m., M.** *Grammar.* **a.** The masculine gender. **b.** A word or word form of the masculine gender. **2.** A male person. [Middle English *masculin,* from Old French, from Latin *māsculīnus,* from *māsculus,* male, diminutive of *mās.*] **—mas′cu·line·ly** *adv.* **—mas′cu·line·ness** *n.*

masculine ending *n.* **1.** A stressed syllable that ends a line of verse. **2.** *Grammar.* A final syllable or termination that marks or forms words in the masculine gender.

masculine rhyme *n.* A rhyme made on a single stressed syllable, as in *sky/fly.*

mas·cu·lin·i·ty (măs′kyə-lin′ĭ-tē) *n., pl.* **-ties. 1.** The quality or condition of being masculine. **2.** Something traditionally considered to be characteristic of a male.

mas·cu·lin·ize (măs′kyə-lə-nīz′) *tr.v.* **-ized, -iz·ing, -iz·es. 1.** To give a masculine appearance or character to. **2.** To cause (a female) to assume masculine characteristics, as through hormonal imbalance or male hormone therapy. **—mas′cu·lin·i·za′tion** (-lə-nĭ-zā′shən) *n.*

Mase·field (măs′fēld′), **John.** 1878–1967. British writer primarily known for his poetry, including the colloquial *Everlasting Mercy* (1911) and the Chaucerian *Reynard the Fox* (1919).

ma·ser (mā′zər) *n.* Any of several devices that amplify or generate electromagnetic waves, especially microwaves. [*m(icrowave) a(mplification by) s(timulated) e(mission of) r(adiation).*]

Mas·er·u (măz′ə-ro͞o′, mä′sə-ro͞o′). The capital of Lesotho, in the western part of the country. It was founded in 1869. Population, 14,686.

mash (măsh) *n.* **1.** A fermentable starchy mixture from which alcohol or spirits can be distilled. **2.** A mixture of ground grain and nutrients fed to livestock and fowl. **3.** A soft, pulpy mixture or mass. **4.** A crushing or grinding. **—mash** *tr.v.* **mashed, mash·ing, mash·es. 1.** To convert (malt or grain) into mash. **2.** To convert into a soft, pulpy mixture: *mash potatoes.* **3.** To crush or grind. See Synonyms at **crush. 4.** *Slang.* To flirt with or make sexual advances to. [Middle English *mash,* as in *mashfat,* mash tub, from Old English **māsc, *mǣsc, *māx-,* in *māxwyrt,* wort. See **meik-** in Appendix. V., sense 4, perhaps from Romany *mash,* to entice.]

MASH *abbr.* Mobile Army Surgical Hospital.

mash·er (măsh′ər) *n.* **1.** A kitchen utensil for mashing vegetables or fruit. **2.** *Slang.* A man who attempts to force his attentions on a woman.

Ma·sher·brum (mŭsh′ər-bro͞om′). A peak, 7,826.3 m (25,660 ft) high, in the Karakoram Range of the Himalaya Mountains in northern India. It was first scaled in 1960.

mash·gi·ah or **mash·gi·ach** (mäsh-gē′äkн) *n., pl.* **-gi·him** or **-gi·chim** (-gē′kнĭm, -gē-kнēm′). An Orthodox rabbi, or a person appointed or approved by such a rabbi, whose responsibility is to prevent violations of Jewish dietary laws by inspection of slaughterhouses, meat markets, and restaurants where food assumed to be kosher is prepared for the public. [Hebrew *mašgīaḥ.*]

Mash·had (mə-shăd′, mäsh-häd′). See **Meshed.**

mash·ie also **mash·y** (măsh′ē) *n., pl.* **-ies.** *Sports.* A five iron used in golf. [Perhaps from French *massue,* club, from Old French, from Vulgar Latin **matteūca,* from **mattea,* mace. See MACE[1].]

mashie niblick *n. Sports.* A six iron used in golf.

mas·jid (mŭs′jĭd) *n.* A mosque. [Arabic, from *sajada,* to worship.]

mask (măsk) *n.* **1.** A covering worn on the face to conceal one's identity, as: **a.** A covering, as of cloth, that has openings for the eyes, entirely or partly conceals the face, and is worn especially at a masquerade ball. **b.** A grotesque or comical representation of a face, worn especially to frighten or amuse, as at Halloween. **c.** A facial covering worn for ritual. **d.** A figure of a head worn by actors in Greek and Roman drama to identify a character or trait and to amplify the voice. **2. a.** A protective covering for the face or head. **b.** A gas mask. **c.** A covering for the nose and mouth that is used for inhaling oxygen or an anesthetic. **d.** A covering worn over the nose and mouth, as by a surgeon or dentist, to prevent infection. **3. a.** A mold of a person's face, often made after death. **b.** An often grotesque representation of a head and face, used for ornamentation. **4.** The face or facial markings of certain animals, such as foxes or dogs. **5.** A face having a blank, fixed, or enigmatic expression. **6.** Something, often a trait, that disguises or conceals: *"If ever I saw misery under a mask, it was on her face"* (Erskine Childers). **7.** A natural or artificial feature of terrain that conceals and protects military forces or installations. **8. a.** An opaque border or pattern placed between a source of light and a photosensitive surface to prevent exposure of specified portions of the surface. **b.** The translucent border framing a television picture tube and screen. **9.** *Computer Science.* A pattern of characters, bits, or bytes used to control the elimination or retention of another pattern of characters, bits, or bytes. **10.** A cosmetic preparation that is applied to the face and allowed to dry before being removed, used especially for cleansing and tightening the skin. **11.** Variant of **masque. 12.** A person wearing a mask. **—mask** *v.* **masked, mask·ing, masks.** —*tr.* **1.** To cover with a decorative or protective mask. **2.** To make indistinct or blurred to the senses: *spices that mask the strong flavor of the meat.* **3.** To cover in order to conceal, protect, or disguise. See Synonyms at **disguise. 4.** To block the view of: *Undergrowth masked the entrance to the cave.* **5.** To cover (a part of a photographic film) by the application of an opaque border. **6.** *Chemistry.* To prevent (an atom or a group of atoms) from taking part in a normal reaction. —*intr.* **1.** To put on a mask, especially for a masquerade ball. **2.** To conceal one's real personality, character, or intentions. [French *masque,* from Italian *maschera,* from Late Latin *masca,* specter, witch, mask.] **—mask′a·ble** *adj.*

masked (măskt) *adj.* **1.** Wearing a mask. **2.** Disguised or concealed as if by a mask: *very cleverly masked emotions.* **3.** Latent or hidden, as a symptom or disease. **4.** *Botany.* Personate. **5.** *Zoology.* **a.** Having masklike markings on the head or face. **b.** Having the anatomy of the next developmental form outlined beneath the integument, as in certain insect pupae.

masked ball *n.* A ball at which masks are worn.

mas·keg (măs′kĕg′) *n.* Variant of **muskeg.**

mask·er also **mas·quer** (măs′kər) *n.* One who wears a mask, especially a participant in a masquerade or masque.

mask
19th-century frontlet mask from the Chilkat people of Alaska

ă pat	oi boy
ā pay	ou out
âr care	o͝o took
ä father	o͞o boot
ĕ pet	ŭ cut
ē be	ûr urge
ĭ pit	th thin
ī pie	*th* this
îr pier	hw which
ŏ pot	zh vision
ō toe	ə about, item
ô paw	♦ regionalism

Stress marks: ′ (primary); ′ (secondary), as in **dictionary** (dĭk′shə-nĕr′ē)

mask·ing (măs′kĭng) *n.* **1.** *Physiology.* The concealment or screening of one sensory process or sensation by another. **2.** A piece of theatrical scenery used to conceal a part of the stage from the audience.

masking tape *n.* An adhesive tape used to cover and protect a surface that is not to be painted.

mas·och·ism (măs′ə-kĭz′əm) *n.* **1.a.** The act or an instance of deriving sexual gratification from being physically or emotionally abused. **b.** A psychological disorder in which sexual gratification is derived from being physically or emotionally abused. **2.a.** The act or an instance of deriving pleasure from being offended, dominated, or mistreated. **b.** The tendency to seek such mistreatment. **3.** The turning of destructive tendencies upon oneself. [After Leopold von Sacher-*Masoch* (1836–1895), Austrian novelist.] **—mas′o·chist** *n.* **—mas′och·is′tic** *adj.* **—mas′och·is′ti·cal·ly** *adv.*

ma·son (mā′sən) *n.* **1.** One who builds or works with stone or brick. **2. Mason.** A Freemason. **—mason** *tr.v.* **-soned, -son·ing, -sons.** To build of or strengthen with masonry. [Middle English, from Old French *maçon, masson,* of Germanic origin. See **mag-** in Appendix.]

mast[1]
Six-masted schooner, the *Mertie B. Crowley*

Mason, George. 1725–1792. American Revolutionary politician from Virginia. A member of the Constitutional Convention (1787), he voiced criticism that resulted in the drafting of the Bill of Rights. His grandson **James Murray Mason** (1798–1871) was a Confederate diplomat to Great Britain and France.

Mason, Lowell. 1792–1872. American musician who composed several hymns, including "Nearer, My God, to Thee."

mason bee *n.* Any of various solitary bees of the family Megachilidae, found worldwide, that build clay nests.

Mason City. A city of north-central Iowa north-northeast of Des Moines. It is a trade and industrial center in an agricultural region. Population, 30,144.

Ma·son-Dix·on Line (mā′sən-dĭk′sən). The boundary between Pennsylvania and Maryland, regarded as the division between free and slave states before the Civil War. It was established between 1763 and 1767 by the British surveyors Charles Mason (1730–1787) and Jeremiah Dixon (died 1777).

Ma·son·ic (mə-sŏn′ĭk) *adj.* Of or relating to Freemasons or Freemasonry.

Ma·son·ite (mā′sə-nīt′). A trademark used for a type of fiberboard employed for insulation, paneling, or partitions. This trademark sometimes occurs in print in lowercase: *"Portions of the archways were reconstructed in masonite"* (Chicago Tribune). *"Four pieces of masonite . . . lace together like shoelaces"* (New York Times).

Mason jar *n.* A wide-mouthed glass jar with a screw top, used for canning and preserving food. [After John L. *Mason* (1832–1902), American inventor.]

ma·son·ry (mā′sən-rē) *n., pl.* **-ries. 1.a.** The trade of a mason. **b.** Work done by a mason. **c.** Stonework or brickwork. **2. Masonry.** Freemasonry.

masonry cement *n.* Cement used in the mortar of block and brick masonry.

mason wasp *n.* Any of various solitary wasps, especially of the subfamily Eumeninae, that build nests of mud.

Ma·so·ra also **Ma·so·rah** (mə-sôr′ə, -sōr′ə) *n.* **1.** The body of Judaic tradition relating to correct textual reading of the Hebrew scriptures. **2.** The critical notes made on manuscripts of the Hebrew scriptures before the tenth century, which embody this tradition. [Hebrew *māsôrâ,* from *māsar,* to hand over.] **—Mas′o·ret′ic** (măs′ə-rĕt′ĭk) *adj.*

masque also **mask** (măsk) *n.* **1.** A dramatic entertainment, usually performed by masked players representing mythological or allegorical figures, that was popular in England in the 16th and early 17th centuries. **2.** A dramatic verse composition written for such an entertainment. **3.** See **masquerade** (sense 1a). [French. See MASK.]

mas·quer (măs′kər) *n.* Variant of **masker.**

mas·quer·ade (măs′kə-rād′) *n.* **1.a.** A costume party at which masks are worn; a masked ball. Also called *masque.* **b.** A costume for such a party or ball. **2.a.** A disguise or false outward show; a pretense: *a masquerade of humility.* **b.** An involved scheme; a charade. **—masquerade** *intr.v.* **-ad·ed, -ad·ing, -ades. 1.** To wear a mask or disguise, as at a masquerade: *She masqueraded as a shepherd.* **2.** To go about as if in disguise; have or put on a deceptive appearance: *The stowaway masqueraded as a crew member.* [French *mascarade,* from Italian *mascarata,* variant of *mascherata,* from Old Italian *maschera,* mask. See MASK.] **—mas′quer·ad′er** *n.*

mass (măs) *n.* **1.** A unified body of matter with no specific shape: *a mass of clay.* **2.** A grouping of individual parts or elements that compose a unified body of unspecified size or quantity: *"Take mankind in mass, and for the most part, they seem a mob of unnecessary duplicates"* (Herman Melville). **3.** A large but nonspecific amount or number: *a mass of bruises.* **4.** The principal part; the majority: *the mass of the continent.* **5.** The physical volume or bulk of a solid body. **6.** *Abbr.* **m** *Physics.* The measure of the quantity of matter that a body or an object contains. The mass of the body is not dependent on gravity and therefore is different from but proportional to its weight. **7.** An area of unified light, shade, or color in a painting. **8.** *Pharmacology.* A thick, pasty mixture containing drugs from which pills are formed. **9. masses.** The body of common people or people of low socioeconomic status. Used with *the.* **—mass** *tr. & intr.v.* **massed, mass·ing, mass·es.** To gather or be gathered into a mass. **—mass** *adj.* **1.** Of, relating to, characteristic of, directed at, or attended by a large number of people: *mass education; mass communication.* **2.** Done or carried out on a large scale: *mass production.* **3.** Total; complete: *The mass result is impressive.* [Middle English *masse,* from Old French, from Latin *massa,* from Greek *maza.* See **mag-** in Appendix.]

Mass also **mass** (măs) *n.* **1.a.** Public celebration of the Eucharist in the Roman Catholic Church and some Protestant churches. **b.** The sacrament of the Eucharist. **2.** A musical setting of certain parts of the Mass, especially the Kyrie, Gloria, Credo, Sanctus, Benedictus, and Agnus Dei. [Middle English *masse,* from Old English *mæsse,* from Vulgar Latin **messa,* from Late Latin *missa,* from Latin, feminine past participle of *mittere,* to send away, dismiss.]

Mass. *abbr.* Massachusetts.

Mas·sa (mä′sə). A city of north-central Italy near the Ligurian Sea north of Leghorn. It was the capital of an independent principality and duchy from the 15th to the 19th century. Population, 65,726.

Mas·sa·chu·sett also **Mas·sa·chu·set** (măs′ə-cho͞o′sĭt, -zĭt) *n., pl.* **Massachusett** or **-setts** also **Massachuset** or **-sets. 1.a.** A Native American people formerly located along Massachusetts Bay from Plymouth north to Salem. Reduced by epidemics, the Massachusett ceased to exist as a people during the 17th century. **b.** A member of this people. **2.** The Algonquian language of the Massachusett. [From the Massachusett name of Great Blue Hill south of Boston.]

Mas·sa·chu·setts (măs′ə-cho͞o′sĭts). *Abbr.* **MA, Mass.** A state of the northeast United States. It was admitted as one of the original Thirteen Colonies in 1788. The first settlement was made by the Pilgrims of the *Mayflower* in 1620. Governed by the Massachusetts Bay Company from 1629 until 1684, the colony was a leader in the move for independence from Great Britain and the site of the first battles of the Revolutionary War in 1775. Boston is the capital and the largest city. Population, 5,737,081.

Massachusetts Bay. An inlet of the Atlantic Ocean off eastern Massachusetts extending from Cape Ann in the north to Cape Cod in the south.

mas·sa·cre (măs′ə-kər) *n.* **1.** The act or an instance of killing a large number of human beings indiscriminately and cruelly. **2.** The slaughter of a large number of animals. **3.** *Informal.* A severe defeat, as in a sports event. **—massacre** *tr.v.* **-cred** (-kərd), **-cring** (-krĭng, -kər-ĭng), **-cres. 1.** To kill indiscriminately and wantonly; slaughter. **2.** *Informal.* To defeat decisively. [French, from Old French *macecle, macecre,* butchery, shambles.] **—mas′sa·crer** (-kər-ər, -krər) *n.*

mas·sage (mə-säzh′ -säj′) *n.* The rubbing or kneading of parts of the body to aid circulation or relax the muscles. **—massage** *tr.v.* **-saged, -sag·ing, -sag·es. 1.** To give a massage to. **2.** To treat by means of a massage. **3.** To coddle or cajole. **4.** To manipulate (data, for example): *Pollsters massaged the numbers to favor their candidate.* [French, from *masser,* to massage, from Arabic *masaḥa,* to stroke, anoint or *massa,* to touch.] **—mas·sag′er** *n.*

massage parlor *n.* **1.** An establishment that offers therapeutic massage. **2.** An establishment that offers illicit sexual services under the guise of therapeutic massage.

mas·sa·sau·ga (măs′ə-sô′gə) *n.* A small, variably colored rattlesnake *(Sistrurus catenatus)* found in parts of the United States, Canada, and Mexico. [After the *Mississagi,* a river of southeast Ontario, Canada.]

Mas·sa·soit (măs′ə-soit′). 1580?–1661. Wampanoag leader who aided the Pilgrim colonists and signed a peace treaty with them at Plymouth.

Mass card *n.* *Roman Catholic Church.* A card sent to a bereaved person or family indicating that the sender has arranged for a Mass to be said in memory of the deceased.

mass·cult (măs′kŭlt′) *n.* Culture as popularized by the mass media. [MASS + CULT(URE).]

mass defect *n.* The amount by which the mass of an atomic nucleus is less than the sum of the masses of its constituent particles. Also called *mass deficiency.*

mas·sé (mă-sā′) *n.* *Games.* A stroke in billiards made by striking the cue ball off center with the cue held nearly vertically, so that the cue ball moves in a curve around one ball before hitting another ball. [French, from past participle of *masser,* to make a massé shot, from *masse,* mace (an early form of billiard cue), from Old French, club. See MACE[1].]

mass-en·er·gy equivalence (măs′ĕn′ər-jē) *n.* The physical principle that a measured quantity of energy is equivalent to a measured quantity of mass. The equivalence is expressed by Einstein's equation, $E = mc^2$, where E represents energy, m the equivalent mass, and c the speed of light.

Mas·se·net (măs′ə-nā′, măs-nā′), **Jules Émile Frédéric.** 1842–1912. French composer whose works include more than 20 operas, including *Manon* (1884) and *Thaïs* (1894).

mas·se·ter (mə-sē′tər, mă-) *n.* A thick muscle in the cheek that closes the jaws during chewing. [New Latin, from Greek *masētēr,* from *masasthai,* to chew.] **—mas′se·ter′ic** (măs′ĭ-tĕr′ĭk) *adj.*

mas·seur (mă-sûr′, mə-) *n.* A man who gives massages professionally. [French, from *masser,* to massage. See MASSAGE.]

mas·seuse (mă-sœz′) *n.* A woman who gives massages professionally. [French, feminine of *masseur,* masseur. See MASSEUR.]

Mas·sey (măs′ē), **(Charles) Vincent.** 1887–1967. Canadian politician who served as high commissioner for Canada in Great Britain (1935–1946) and as governor-general (1952–1959).

mas·si·cot (măs′ĭ-kŏt′, -kō′) *n.* **1.** The mineral form of lead monoxide, PbO. **2.** A yellow powder, PbO, used as a pigment. [Middle English *masticot,* from Old French, perhaps from Old Italian *marzacotto,* potter's glaze (perhaps from Spanish *mazacote,* mortar), possibly from Arabic *mashaqūnīyā,* perhaps of Greek origin.]

mas·sif (mă-sēf′) *n.* **1.** A large mountain mass or compact group of connected mountains forming an independent portion of a range. **2.** A large section or block of the earth's crust that is more rigid than the surrounding rock and has been moved or displaced as a unit. [French, massive, massif, from Old French. See MASSIVE.]

Mas·sif Cen·tral (mă-sēf′ sĕn-träl′, săɴ-). A mountainous plateau of south-central France. It includes the Cévennes and the Auvergne Mountains, which rise to the plateau's highest point, 1,887.3 m (6,188 ft).

Mas·sil·lon (măs′ə-lən, -lŏn′). A city of northeast Ohio west of Canton. It is an industrial center. Population, 30,557.

Mas·sine (mä-sēn′), **Léonide.** 1896–1979. Russian-born American dancer who choreographed more than 100 ballets, including *Parade* (1917), the first cubist ballet.

Mas·sin·ger (măs′ĭn-jər), **Philip.** 1583–1640. English playwright known for his satirical comedies, most notably *A New Way to Pay Old Debts* (c. 1625).

mas·sive (măs′ĭv) *adj.* **1.** Consisting of or making up a large mass; bulky, heavy, and solid: *a massive piece of furniture.* **2.** Large or imposing, as in quantity, scope, degree, intensity, or scale: *"Local defense must be reinforced by the further deterrent of massive retaliatory power"* (John Foster Dulles). See Synonyms at **heavy. 3.** Large in comparison with the usual amount: *a massive dose.* **4.** *Pathology.* Affecting a large area of bodily tissue; widespread and severe: *massive gangrene.* **5.** *Mineralogy.* Lacking internal crystalline structure; amorphous. **6.** *Geology.* Without internal structure or layers and homogeneous in composition. Used of a rock. [Middle English *massif,* from Old French, from *masse,* mass. See MASS.] **—mas′sive·ly** *adv.* **—mas′sive·ness** *n.*

Mas·sive (măs′ĭv), **Mount.** A peak, 4,398.4 m (14,421 ft), in the Sawatch Range of the Rocky Mountains in central Colorado.

mass·less (măs′lĭs) *adj.* Having a mass of zero.

mass-mar·ket (măs′mär′kĭt) *adj.* Of, relating to, or produced for consumption by large numbers of people. Used especially of inexpensive paperback books.

mass medium *n., pl.* **mass media.** A means of public communication reaching a large audience.

mass noun *n.* A noun, such as *sand, oil,* or *honesty,* that denotes a substance or concept indivisible into countable units and is preceded in English indefinite constructions by modifiers such as *some* or *much* rather than *a* or *one.*

mass number *n.* The sum of the number of neutrons and protons in an atomic nucleus. Also called *nucleon number.*

mass-pro·duce (măs′prə-do͞os′, -dyo͞os′) *tr.v.* **-duced, -duc·ing, -duc·es.** To manufacture in large quantities often by or as if by assembly-line techniques.

mass production *n.* The manufacture of goods in large quantities, often using standardized designs and assembly-line techniques.

mass spectrograph *n.* An instrument used to determine the masses of atoms or molecules, in which a beam of charged particles is passed through an electromagnetic field that separates particles of different masses. The resulting distribution or spectrum of masses is recorded on a photographic plate.

mass·y (măs′ē) *adj.* **-i·er, -i·est.** Having great mass or bulk; massive.

mast¹ (măst) *n.* **1.** *Nautical.* A tall vertical spar, sometimes sectioned, that rises from the keel or deck of a sailing vessel to support the sails and running rigging. **2. a.** A vertical pole. **b.** A tall vertical antenna, as for a radio. **3.** A captain's mast. [Middle English, from Old English *mæst.*]

mast² (măst) *n.* The nuts of forest trees accumulated on the ground, used especially as food for swine. [Middle English, from Old English *mæst.*]

mast– *pref.* Variant of **masto–.**

mas·ta·ba also **mas·ta·bah** (măs′tə-bə) *n.* An ancient Egyptian tomb with a rectangular base, sloping sides, and a flat roof. [Arabic *maṣṭabah,* stone bench.]

mast cell *n.* A cell in connective tissue that contains numerous basophilic granules and releases substances such as heparin and histamine in response to injury or inflammation of bodily tissues. [Partial translation of German *Mastzelle* : *Mast,* food, mast (from Middle High German, from Old High German) + *Zelle,* cell.]

mas·tec·to·my (mă-stĕk′tə-mē) *n., pl.* **-mies.** Surgical removal of all or part of a breast, sometimes including excision of the underlying pectoral muscles and regional lymph nodes, usually performed as a treatment for cancer.

mas·ter (măs′tər) *n. Abbr.* **M. 1.** One that has control over another or others. **2.** The owner of a slave or an animal. **3.** One who has control over or ownership of something: *the master of a large tea plantation.* **4.** The captain of a merchant ship. Also called *master mariner.* **5.** An employer. **6.** The man who serves as the head of a household. **7.** One who defeats another; a victor. **8. a.** One whose teachings or doctrines are accepted by followers. **b. Master.** Jesus. **9.** A male teacher, schoolmaster, or tutor. **10.** One who holds a master's degree. **11. a.** An artist or a performer of great and exemplary skill. **b.** An old master. **12.** A worker qualified to teach apprentices and carry on the craft independently. **13.** An expert: *a master of three languages.* **14. a.** Used formerly as a title for a man holding a naval office ranking next below a lieutenant on a warship. **b.** Used as a title for a man who serves as the head or presiding officer of certain societies, clubs, orders, or institutions. **c.** *Chiefly British.* Used as a title for any of various male law court officers. **d. Master.** Used as a title for any of various male officers having specified duties concerning the management of the British royal household. **e. Master.** Used as a courtesy title before the given or full name of a boy not considered old enough to be addressed as Mister. **f.** *Archaic.* Used as a form of address for a man; mister. **15. Master.** A man who owns a pack of hounds or is the chief officer of a hunt. **16.** An original, especially an original audio recording, from which copies can be made. **—master** *adj.* **1.** Of, relating to, or characteristic of a master. **2.** Principal or predominant: *a master plot.* **3.** Controlling all other parts of a mechanism: *a master switch.* **4.** Highly skilled or proficient: *a master thief.* **5.** Being an original from which copies are made. **—master** *tr.v.* **-tered, -ter·ing, -ters. 1.** To act as or be the master of. **2.** To make oneself a master of: *mastered the language in a year's study.* **3.** To overcome or defeat: *He finally mastered his addiction to drugs.* **4.** To reduce to subjugation; break or tame (an animal, for example). **5.** To produce a master audio recording for. **6.** To season or age (dyed goods). [Middle English, from Old English *māgister, mægister* and Old French *maistre,* both from Latin *magister.* See **meg-** in Appendix.] **—mas′ter·dom** *n.*

mas·ter-at-arms (măs′tər-ət-ärmz′) *n., pl.* **mas·ters-at-arms** (măs′tərz-). A petty officer assigned to maintain order.

master bedroom *n.* A main bedroom in a house.

master chief petty officer *n. Abbr.* **MCPO, CPOM 1.** The highest noncommissioned rank in the U.S. Navy or Coast Guard. **2.** One who holds this rank.

mas·ter·ful (măs′tər-fəl) *adj.* **1.** Given to playing the master; imperious or domineering. **2.** Fit to command. **3.** Revealing mastery or skill; expert: *a masterful technique; masterful moviemaking.* **—mas′ter·ful·ly** *adv.* **—mas′ter·ful·ness** *n.*

USAGE NOTE: According to a widely repeated dictum, *masterful* should be reserved for the sense "imperious, domineering," as in *a masterful tone of voice,* whereas *masterly* should be the choice when the intended sense is "having the skill of a master," as in *a masterly performance of the sonata.* The distinction is a nicety that some writers will want to continue to observe. But the use of *masterful* in the latter sense has long been common in reputable writing and cannot be regarded as incorrect.

master gunnery sergeant *n. Abbr.* **MGy Sgt 1.** A noncommissioned rank in the U.S. Marine Corps that is above master sergeant and equivalent to the position of sergeant major. **2.** One who holds this rank.

master key *n.* A key that opens every one of a given set of locks. Also called *passkey.*

mas·ter·ly (măs′tər-lē) *adj.* Having the knowledge or skill of a master. See Usage Note at **masterful. —masterly** *adv.* With the skill of a master. **—mas′ter·li·ness** *n.*

master mariner *n.* See **master** (sense 4).

master mason *n.* **1.** An expert mason. **2. Master Mason.** The third degree of Freemasonry.

mas·ter·mind (măs′tər-mīnd′) *n.* A highly intelligent person, especially one who plans and directs a complex or difficult project: *the mastermind of a robbery.* **—mastermind** *tr.v.* **-mind·ed, -mind·ing, -minds.** To direct, plan, or supervise (a project or an activity).

master of ceremonies *n., pl.* **masters of ceremonies. 1.** A person who acts as host at a formal event, making the welcoming speech and introducing other speakers. **2.** A performer who conducts a program of varied entertainment by introducing other performers to the audience.

mas·ter·piece (măs′tər-pēs′) *n.* **1.** An outstanding work of art or craft. **2.** The greatest work, as of an artist. Also called *masterwork.* **3.** Something superlative of its kind: *a masterpiece of political ingenuity.* [Probably translation of Dutch *meesterstuk* or German *Meisterstück* : Dutch *meester* and German *Meister,* master + Dutch *stuk* and German *Stück,* piece of work.]

master plan *n.* A plan giving comprehensive guidance or instruction.

master race *n.* A people who consider themselves to be superior to other races and therefore suited to rule over them.

Mas·ters (măs′tərz), **Edgar Lee.** 1869–1950. American poet whose *Spoon River Anthology* (1915), a collection of free verse epitaphs of the citizens of a small Midwestern town, was acclaimed for its directness and simplicity.

master's degree (măs′tərz) *n.* An academic degree con-

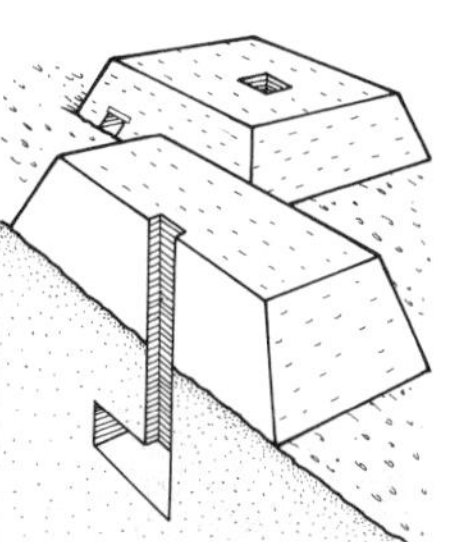

mastaba
Cutaway view in foreground

ă pat	oi boy
ā pay	ou out
âr care	o͝o took
ä father	o͞o boot
ĕ pet	ŭ cut
ē be	ûr urge
ĭ pit	th thin
ī pie	*th* this
îr pier	hw which
ŏ pot	zh vision
ō toe	ə about, item
ô paw	♦ regionalism

Stress marks: ′ (primary); ′ (secondary), as in **dictionary** (dĭk′shə-nĕr′ē)

ferred by a college or university upon those who complete at least one year of prescribed study beyond the bachelor's degree.

mas·ters-at-arms (măs′tərz-ət-ärmz′) *n.* Plural of **master-at-arms.**

master sergeant *n. Abbr.* **M.Sgt., MSGT** **1.a.** A noncommissioned rank in the U.S. Army that is above sergeant first class and below the position of sergeant major. **b.** A noncommissioned rank in the U.S. Air Force that is above technical sergeant and below senior master sergeant. **c.** A noncommissioned rank in the U.S. Marine Corps that is above gunnery sergeant and below the position of sergeant major. **2.** One who holds the rank of master sergeant.

mas·ter·ship (măs′tər-shĭp′) *n.* **1.** The office, function, or authority of a master. **2.** The skill or dexterity of a master.

mas·ter·sing·er (măs′tər-sĭng′ər) *n.* See **Meistersinger.**

Mas·ter·son (măs′tər-sən), **William Barclay.** Known as "Bat." 1853–1921. American frontier marshal and journalist. Famed for his exploits as an army scout, gambler, and law enforcer in towns such as Dodge City and Tombstone, he was later a sports writer for the *New York Morning Telegraph* (1902–1921).

mastiff

mas·ter·stroke (măs′tər-strōk′) *n.* An achievement or action revealing consummate skill or mastery: *a masterstroke of diplomacy.* See Synonyms at **feat[1].**

mas·ter·work (măs′tər-wûrk′) *n.* See **masterpiece** (sense 2).

mas·ter·y (măs′tə-rē) *n., pl.* **-ies.** **1.** Possession of consummate skill. **2.** The status of master or ruler; control: *mastery of the seas.* **3.** Full command of a subject of study: *Her mastery of economic theory impressed the professors.*

mast·head (măst′hĕd′) *n.* **1.** *Nautical.* The top of a mast. **2.** The listing in a newspaper or periodical of information about its staff, operation, and circulation. **3.** The title of a newspaper or periodical as it appears across the first page, front cover, or title page of each issue. In this sense, also called *nameplate.*

mas·tic (măs′tĭk) *n.* **1.** The mastic tree. **2.** The aromatic resin of the mastic tree, used especially in varnishes, lacquers, adhesives, and condiments and as an astringent. **3.** A pastelike cement used in highway construction, especially one made with powdered lime or brick and tar. [Middle English, mastic resin, from Old French *mastich,* from Latin *mastichum, mastichē,* from Greek *mastikhē,* chewing gum, mastic, from *mastikhan,* to grind the teeth.]

mas·ti·cate (măs′tĭ-kāt′) *v.* **-cat·ed, -cat·ing, -cates.** —*tr.* **1.** To chew (food). **2.** To grind and knead (rubber, for example) into a pulp. —*intr.* To chew food. [Late Latin *masticāre, masticāt-,* to masticate, from Greek *mastikhan,* to grind the teeth.] **—mas′ti·ca′tion** *n.* **—mas′ti·ca′tor** *n.*

mas·ti·ca·to·ry (măs′tĭ-kə-tôr′ē, -tōr′ē) *adj.* **1.** Of, relating to, or used in mastication: *masticatory muscles.* **2.** Adapted for chewing. **—masticatory** *n., pl.* **-ries.** A medicinal substance chewed to increase salivation.

mastic tree *n.* A small evergreen shrub *(Pistacia lentiscus)* of the Mediterranean, cultivated for its resin. Also called *lentisk.*

mas·tiff (măs′tĭf) *n.* Any of an ancient breed of large, strong dogs, probably originating in Asia and having a short, often fawn-colored coat. [Middle English *mastif,* alteration of Old French *mastin,* from Vulgar Latin **(canis) mānsuētīnus,* tame (dog), from Latin *mānsuētus,* past participle of *mānsuēscere,* to tame : *manus,* hand; see **man-[2]** in Appendix + *suēscere,* to accustom; see **s(w)e-** in Appendix.]

WORD HISTORY: The mastiff, which was at one time used in bullbaiting and bearbaiting as well as in dogfights, is ultimately named not for its fierceness but for its tameness. To find this tameness we must look back to the ultimate source of *mastiff* in the Latin word *mānsuētus,* "tame, domesticated," itself derived from the past participle of *manusuēscere,* "to tame," made up of the root *man-* found in the word *manus,* "hand," and the verb *suēscere,* "to become accustomed to." Tame beasts are accustomed to the hand. To explain how *mānsuēscere* became *mastiff,* we must follow it through its Vulgar Latin development, **mānsuētīnus,* "domesticated," and the later Old French development, *mastin,* "mastiff." While being borrowed into English, *mastin* was probably blended with the Old French word *mestif,* "mongrel," and was possibly influenced by the Medieval Latin word *mastīvus,* "mastiff," probably itself an error for *mastīnus,* which came from the same Vulgar Latin source as the Old French word. *Mastiff* is first recorded in Middle English (as *mastif*) in a work written before 1387.

mastiff bat *n.* Any of various snub-nosed bats of the family Molossidae, found in warm regions of most parts of the world and having narrow wings and brown, gray, or black fur.

mas·ti·goph·o·ran (măs′tĭ-gŏf′ər-ən) *n.* Any of various protozoans of the class Mastigophora, all of which possess one or more flagella. **—mastigophoran** *adj.* Of or belonging to the class Mastigophora. [From New Latin *Mastigophora,* class name : Greek *mastix, mastig-,* whip + New Latin *-phora* (from Greek, neuter pl. of *-phoros,* -phore).]

mas·ti·tis (mă-stī′tĭs) *n.* Inflammation of the breast or udder. **—mas·tit′ic** (-tĭt′ĭk) *adj.*

masto– or **mast–** *pref.* Breast; mammary gland; nipple: *mastectomy.* [From Greek *mastos,* breast.]

mas·to·don (măs′tə-dŏn′) *n.* Any of several very large, extinct proboscidian mammals of the genus *Mammut* (sometimes *Mastodon*), resembling the elephant but having molar teeth of a different structure. [New Latin *Mastodōn,* genus name : Greek *mastos,* nipple + Greek *odōn, odont-,* tooth; see **dent-** in Appendix.] **—mas′to·don′ic** *adj.*

mas·to·dont (măs′tə-dŏnt′) *adj.* Of, relating to, or characteristic of a mastodon. [From New Latin *Mastodōn,* genus name. See MASTODON.]

mas·toid (măs′toid′) *n.* The mastoid process. **—mastoid** *adj.* **1.** Of or relating to the mastoid process. **2.** Shaped like a breast or nipple. [New Latin *mastoidēs,* nipple-like, mastoid (from its shape), from Greek *mastoeidēs* : *mastos,* breast + *-oeidēs,* -oid.]

mastoid bone *n.* See **mastoid process.**

mastoid cell *n.* Any of numerous air-filled spaces of various sizes in the mastoid process.

mas·toid·ec·to·my (măs′toi-dĕk′tə-mē) *n., pl.* **-mies.** Surgical removal of mastoid cells or part or all of the mastoid process.

mas·toid·i·tis (măs′toid-ī′tĭs) *n.* Inflammation of the mastoid process and mastoid cells.

mastoid process *n.* A conical protuberance of the posterior portion of the temporal bone that is situated behind the ear in human beings and many other vertebrates and serves as a site of muscle attachment. Also called *mastoid bone.*

mas·tur·bate (măs′tər-bāt′) *v.* **-bat·ed, -bat·ing, -bates.** —*intr.* To perform an act of masturbation. —*tr.* To perform an act of masturbation on. [Latin *masturbārī, masturbāt-.*]

mas·tur·ba·tion (măs′tər-bā′shən) *n.* Excitation of one's own or another's genital organs, usually to orgasm, by manual contact or means other than sexual intercourse. **—mas′tur·ba′tion·al, mas′tur·ba·to′ry** (-bə-tôr′ē, -tōr′ē) *adj.* **—mas′tur·ba′tor** *n.*

Ma·su·ri·a (mə-zo͝or′ē-ə). A historical region of northeast Poland. Ruled by the Teutonic Knights after the 14th century and later part of East Prussia, it was assigned to Poland by the Potsdam Conference of 1945. **—Ma·su′ri·an** *adj.*

mat[1] (măt) *n.* **1.** A flat piece of coarse fabric or other material used for wiping one's shoes or feet, or in various other forms as a floor covering. **2.** A small, flat piece of decorated material placed under a lamp, dish of food, or other object. **3.** *Sports.* A floor pad to protect athletes, as in wrestling or gymnastics. **4.** A densely woven or thickly tangled mass: *a mat of hair.* **5.** The solid part of a lace design. **6.** A heavy woven net of rope or wire cable placed over a blasting site to keep debris from scattering. **—mat** *v.* **mat·ted, mat·ting, mats.** —*tr.* **1.** To cover, protect, or decorate with mats or a mat. **2.** To pack or interweave into a thick mass: *High winds matted the leaves against the base of the fence.* —*intr.* To be packed or interwoven into a thick mass; become entangled. [Middle English, from Old English *matte,* from Late Latin *matta,* possibly from Phoenician (Punic) *maṭṭā;* akin to Hebrew *miṭṭa,* bed, couch.]

mat[2] (măt) *n.* **1.** A decorative border placed around a picture to serve as a frame or provide contrast between the picture and the frame. **2.** Also **matte. a.** A dull, often rough finish, as of paint, glass, metal, or paper. **b.** A special tool for producing such a surface or finish. **3.** *Printing.* See **matrix** (sense 10a). **—mat** *tr.v.* **mat·ted, mat·ting, mats. 1.** To put a mat around (a picture). **2.** To produce a dull finish on. **—mat** also **matte** *adj.* Having a dull finish. [From French, dull, from Old French, defeated, withered, perhaps from Latin *mattus,* stupefied, senseless, possibly from **maditus,* past participle of *madēre,* to be wet.]

mat. *abbr.* Matinee.

M.A.T. *abbr.* Master of Arts in Teaching.

Mat·a·be·le (mä′tä-bĕl′ā) *n., pl.* **Matabele** or **-les.** See **Ndebele.**

Mat·a·be·le·land (mä′tə-bĕl′ā-lănd′). A region of western Zimbabwe. Inhabited by the Ndebele people after 1827, it came under the control of the British South Africa Company in 1889.

mat·a·dor (măt′ə-dôr′) *n.* **1.** A bullfighter who performs the final passes and kills the bull. **2.** *Games.* One of the highest trumps in certain card games. [Spanish, from *matar,* to kill, possibly from Vulgar Latin **mattāre,* to beat senseless, perhaps from Latin *mattus,* stupefied. See MAT[2].]

Mat·a·gor·da Bay (măt′ə-gôr′də). An inlet of southeast Texas separated from the Gulf of Mexico by the **Matagorda Peninsula,** a narrow sand spit.

Ma·ta Ha·ri (mä′tə här′ē, măt′ə hăr′ē). Originally Margaretha Geertruida Zelle. 1876–1917. Dutch spy. A professional dancer in Paris after 1905, she apparently spied for Germany during World War I and was arrested and executed by the French.

Ma·ta·mo·ros (măt′ə-môr′əs, -mōr′-, mä′tä-mô′rôs). A city of northeast Mexico near the mouth of the Rio Grande opposite Brownsville, Texas. Population, 188,745.

Ma·tan·zas (mə-tăn′zəs, mä-tän′säs). A city of northwest-central Cuba east of Havana. Founded in 1693, it was once a haven for pirates. Population, 100,367.

Mat·a·pan (măt′ə-păn′), **Cape.** See Cape **Taínaron.**

match[1] (măch) *n.* **1.a.** One that is exactly like another; a counterpart. **b.** One that is like another in one or more specified qualities: *He is John's match for bravery.* **2.** One that is able to compete equally with another: *The boxer had met his match.* **3.a.** One that closely resembles or harmonizes with another: *The napkins were a nice match for the tablecloth.* **b.** A pair, each one of which resembles or harmonizes with the other: *The colors were a close match.* **4.** *Sports.* **a.** A game or contest in which two or more persons, animals, or teams oppose and compete with each other: *a soccer match.* **b.** A tennis contest won by the player or side that wins a specified number of sets, usually two out of three or three out of five. **5.** A marriage or an arrangement of marriage: *a royal match.* **6.** A person viewed as a prospective marriage partner. **—match** *v.* **matched, match·ing, match·es.** —*tr.* **1.a.** To be exactly like; correspond exactly. **b.** To be like with respect to specified qualities. **2.** To resemble or harmonize with: *The coat matches the dress.* **3.** To adapt or suit so that a balanced or harmonious result is achieved; cause to correspond: *You should match your deeds to your beliefs.* **4.** To find or produce a counterpart to: *It's difficult to match the color of old paint.* **5.** To fit together or cause to fit together. **6.** To join or give in marriage. **7.** To place in opposition or competition; pit: *She matched her skill against all comers.* **8.** To provide with an adversary or a competitor. **9.** To do as well as or better than in competition; equal. **10.** To set in comparison; compare: *beauty that could never be matched.* **11.** To provide funds so as to equal or complement: *The government will match all private donations to the museum.* **12.** To flip or toss (coins) and compare the sides that land face up. **13.** To couple (electric circuits) by means of a transformer. —*intr.* To be a close counterpart; correspond. [Middle English *macche,* from Old English *gemæcca,* companion, mate. See **mag-** in Appendix.] **—match′er** *n.*

match² (măch) *n.* **1.** A narrow piece, usually of wood or cardboard, coated on one end with a compound that ignites when scratched against a rough or chemically treated surface. **2.** An easily ignited cord or wick, formerly used to detonate powder charges or to fire cannons and muzzle-loading firearms. [Middle English *matche,* lamp wick, from Old French *mesche,* from Vulgar Latin **micca,* from Latin *myxa,* a lamp's nozzle, from Greek *muxa,* mucus, lamp wick.]

match·a·ble (măch′ə-bəl) *adj.* That can be matched: *matchable colors.* **—match′a·bil′i·ty** *n.*

match·board (măch′bôrd′, -bōrd′) *n.* A board cut with a tongue on one side and a matching groove on the other to fit with other boards of similar cut.

match·book (măch′bo͝ok′) *n.* A small cardboard folder containing safety matches and having a striking surface along the bottom.

match·box (măch′bŏks′) *n.* A box in which to keep matches.

match·less (măch′lĭs) *adj.* Having no match or equal; unsurpassed: *matchless virtuosity at the keyboard.* **—match′less·ly** *adv.* **—match′less·ness** *n.*

match·lock (măch′lŏk′) *n.* **1.** A gunlock in which powder is ignited by a match. **2.** A musket having such a gunlock.

match·mak·er (măch′mā′kər) *n.* **1.** One who arranges or tries to arrange marriages. **2.** *Sports.* One who arranges athletic competitions. **—match′mak′ing** *n.*

match play *n.* *Sports.* A method of scoring golf games by counting only the number of holes won by each side rather than the number of strokes taken.

match point *n.* *Sports.* The final point needed to win a sports match, especially in tennis.

match·stick (măch′stĭk′) *n.* **1.** A short, slender piece of wood from which a match is made. **2.** Something similar to a matchstick, as in slenderness or strength. **—matchstick** *adj.* Short, narrow, and slender: *matchstick arms; matchstick slices of potato.*

match·up (măch′ŭp′) *n.* The pairing of two people or things, as for athletic competition or for comparison.

match·wood (măch′wo͝od′) *n.* **1.** Wood in small pieces or splinters suitable especially for making matches. **2.** Splinters: *The vessel was beaten to matchwood on the rocks.*

mate¹ (māt) *n.* **1.** One of a matched pair: *the mate to this glove.* **2.** A spouse. **3.a.** Either of a pair of animals or birds that associate in order to propagate. **b.** Either of a pair of animals brought together for breeding. **4.a.** A person with whom one is in close association; an associate. **b.** A good friend or companion. **5.** A deck officer on a merchant ship ranking below the master. **6.** A U.S. Navy petty officer who is an assistant to a warrant officer. **—mate** *v.* **mat·ed, mat·ing, mates.** —*tr.* **1.** To join closely; pair. **2.** To unite in marriage. **3.** To pair (animals) for breeding. —*intr.* **1.** To become joined in marriage. **2.a.** To be paired for reproducing; breed. **b.** To copulate. [Middle English, from Middle Low German *māte, gemate,* messmate.]

mate² (māt) *Games. n.* A checkmate. **—mate** *tr. & intr.v.* **mat·ed, mat·ing, mates.** To checkmate or achieve a checkmate. [Middle English, from Old French *mat,* checkmated, from Arabic *māt,* dead. See CHECKMATE.]

ma·té (mä′tā, mä-tā′) *n.* **1.** A South American evergreen tree *(Ilex paraguariensis)* widely cultivated for its leaves, which are used to prepare a tealike beverage. **2.** A tealike beverage, popular in South America, made from the dried leaves of this plant. In this sense, also called *Paraguay tea, yerba maté.* [American Spanish, from Quechua *mate,* hollow gourd used as a bowl or container for brewing yerba maté.]

mat·e·lote (măt′l-ōt′, mä-tə-lōt′) also **mat·e·lotte** (-l-ŏt′, -lŏt′) *n.* A fish stew that is cooked in a wine sauce. [French, from *matelot,* sailor, from Old French *matenot,* sailor, bunkmate (from the practice of sharing a berth with someone on an alternate watch), possibly from Middle Dutch *mattenoot* (perhaps from *matte,* bed, from Late Latin *matta;* see MAT¹ + *noot,* fellow) or from Old Norse *mötunautr,* messmate (*mata,* food, mess + *nautr,* companion).]

ma·ter (mā′tər) *n.* *Chiefly British.* Mother. [Latin *māter.* See **māter-** in Appendix.]

ma·ter·fa·mil·i·as (mā′tər-fə-mĭl′ē-əs) *n.* A woman who is the head of a household or the mother of a family. [Latin *māterfamiliās : māter,* mother; see MATER + *familiās,* archaic genitive of *familia,* household; see FAMILY.]

ma·te·ri·al (mə-tîr′ē-əl) *n.* **1.** The substance or substances out of which a thing is or can be made. **2.** Something, such as an idea or information, that is to be refined and made or incorporated into a finished effort: *material for a comedy.* **3. materials.** Tools or apparatus for the performance of a given task: *writing materials.* **4.** Yard goods or cloth. **5.** A person who is qualified or suited for a position or activity: *The members of the board felt that she was vice-presidential material.* **—material** *adj.* **1.** Of, relating to, or composed of matter. **2.** Of, relating to, or affecting physical well-being; bodily: *"the moral and material welfare of all good citizens"* (Theodore Roosevelt). **3.** Of or concerned with the physical as distinct from the intellectual or spiritual: *"Great men are they who see that spiritual is stronger than any material force, that thoughts rule the world"* (Ralph Waldo Emerson). **4.** Being both relevant and consequential; crucial: *testimony material to the inquiry.* See Synonyms at **relevant. 5.** *Philosophy.* Of or relating to the matter of reasoning, rather than the form. [Middle English, consisting of matter, material, from Old French, from Late Latin *māteriālis,* from Latin *māteria,* matter. See **māter-** in Appendix.] **—ma·te′ri·al·ness** *n.*

ma·te·ri·al·ism (mə-tîr′ē-ə-lĭz′əm) *n.* **1.** *Philosophy.* The theory that physical matter is the only reality and that everything, including thought, feeling, mind, and will, can be explained in terms of matter and physical phenomena. **2.** The theory or doctrine that physical well-being and worldly possessions constitute the greatest good and highest value in life. **3.** A great or excessive regard for worldly concerns. **—ma·te′ri·al·ist** *n.* **—ma·te′ri·al·is′tic** *adj.* **—ma·te′ri·al·is′ti·cal·ly** *adv.*

ma·te·ri·al·i·ty (mə-tîr′ē-ăl′ĭ-tē) *n., pl.* **-ties. 1.** The state or quality of being material. **2.** Physical substance; matter.

ma·te·ri·al·ize (mə-tîr′ē-ə-līz′) *v.* **-ized, -iz·ing, -iz·es.** —*tr.* **1.** To cause to become real or actual: *By building the house, we materialized a dream.* **2.** To cause to become materialistic: *"Inequality has the natural and necessary effect . . . of materializing our upper class, vulgarizing our middle class, and brutalizing our lower class"* (Matthew Arnold). —*intr.* **1.** To assume material or effective form: *Their support on the eastern flank did not materialize.* **2.** To take physical form or shape. **3.** To appear, especially suddenly. See Synonyms at **appear. —ma·te′ri·al·i·za′tion** (-ə-lĭ-zā′shən) *n.* **—ma·te′ri·al·iz′er** *n.*

USAGE NOTE: In its original senses *materialize* is used intransitively to mean "to assume material form," as in *Marley's ghost materialized before Scrooge's eyes,* or transitively to mean "to cause to assume material form," as in *Disney materialized his dream in a plot of orchard land in Orange County.* But these uses are probably less common nowadays than two extended senses of the intransitive sense of the verb. In the first the meaning is roughly "to appear suddenly," as in *No sooner had we set the menu down than a waiter materialized at our table.* Some critics have labeled this use incorrect, but the criticism may suggest an overliteralism; used in this way, the verb has the sense "to appear as if by magic." *Materialize* also means "to take effective shape, come into existence," particularly as applied to things or events that have been foreseen or anticipated: *The promised subsidies never materialized. It was thought the community would oppose the measure, but no new objections materialized.* This usage has been criticized, but it is well established in reputable writing and follows a familiar pattern of metaphoric extension. The same logic that allows us to say *The plans did not materialize* allows us to use equivalent and unobjectionable paraphrases with expressions such as *take form* and *take shape.*

ma·te·ri·al·ly (mə-tîr′ē-ə-lē) *adv.* **1.** With regard to the physical world. **2.** With regard to matter as distinguished from form. **3.** To a significant extent or degree; substantially.

ma·te·ri·als science (mə-tîr′ē-əlz) *n.* The study of the characteristics and uses of the various materials, such as metals, ceramics, and plastics, employed in science and technology.

ma·te·ri·a med·i·ca (mə-tîr′ē-ə mĕd′ĭ-kə) *n.* *Medicine.* **1.** The scientific study of medicinal drugs and their sources, preparation, and use. **2.** Substances used in the preparation of medicinal drugs. [New Latin *māteria medica* (translation of Greek *hulē iatrikē*) : Latin *māteria,* material + Latin *medica,* medical.]

ma·te·ri·el or **ma·té·ri·el** (mə-tîr′ē-ĕl′) *n.* The equipment, apparatus, and supplies of a military force or other organization. See Synonyms at **equipment.** [French *matériel,* consisting of matter, materiel, from Old French *material.* See MATERIAL.]

ma·ter·nal (mə-tûr′nəl) *adj.* **1.** Relating to or characteristic of a mother or motherhood or motherly: *maternal instinct.* **2.** Inherited from one's mother: *a maternal trait.* **3.** Related through one's mother: *my maternal uncle.* [Middle English, from Old French *maternel,* from Medieval Latin *māternālis,* from Latin *māternus,* from *māter,* mother. See **māter-** in Appendix.] **—ma·ter′nal·ism** *n.* **—ma·ter′nal·ly** *adv.*

ma·ter·ni·ty (mə-tûr′nĭ-tē) *n., pl.* **-ties. 1.** The state of being a mother; motherhood. **2.** The feelings or characteristics as-

ă pat	oi boy
ā pay	ou out
âr care	o͝o took
ä father	o͞o boot
ĕ pet	ŭ cut
ē be	ûr urge
ĭ pit	th thin
ī pie	*th* this
îr pier	hw which
ŏ pot	zh vision
ō toe	ə about, item
ô paw	♦ regionalism

Stress marks: ′ (primary); ′ (secondary), as in **dictionary** (dĭk′shə-nĕr′ē)

sociated with being a mother; motherliness. **3.** A maternity ward. **—maternity** *adj.* Relating to or effective during pregnancy, childbirth, or the first months of motherhood: *a maternity dress; maternity leave.* [French *maternité,* from Medieval Latin *māternitās,* from Latin *māternus,* maternal, from *māter,* mother. See **māter-** in Appendix.]

maternity ward *n.* The department of a hospital that provides care for women during pregnancy and childbirth as well as for newborn infants.

mat•ey (mā′tē) *adj. Chiefly British.* Sociable; friendly.

math (măth) *n.* Mathematics.

math. *abbr.* **1.** Mathematical. **2.** Mathematician.

math•e•mat•i•cal (măth′ə-măt′ĭ-kəl) also **math•e•mat•ic** (-ĭk) *adj. Abbr.* **math. 1.** Of or relating to mathematics. **2.a.** Precise; exact. **b.** Absolute; certain. **3.** Possible according to mathematics but highly improbable: *The team has only a mathematical chance to win the championship.* [Middle English, from Medieval Latin *mathēmaticālis,* from Latin *mathēmaticus,* from Greek *mathēmatikos,* from *mathēma, mathēmat-,* science, learning, from *manthanein,* to learn. See **mendh-** in Appendix.] **—math′e•mat′i•cal•ly** *adv.*

matilija poppy
Romneya coulteri

mathematical induction *n. Mathematics.* Induction.

mathematical logic *n.* See **symbolic logic.**

math•e•ma•ti•cian (măth′ə-mə-tĭsh′ən) *n. Abbr.* **math.** A person skilled or learned in mathematics.

math•e•mat•ics (măth′ə-măt′ĭks) *n. (used with a sing. verb).* The study of the measurement, properties, and relationships of quantities, using numbers and symbols. [From Middle English *mathematik,* from Old French *mathematique,* from Latin *mathēmatica,* from Greek *mathēmatikē (tekhnē),* mathematical (science), feminine of *mathēmatikos,* mathematical. See MATHEMATICAL.]

math•e•ma•tize (măth′ə-mə-tīz′) *tr.v.* **-tized, -tiz•ing, -tiz•es.** To reduce to or as if to mathematical formulas. **—math′e•ma•ti•za′tion** (-tĭ-zā′shən) *n.*

Math•er (măth′ər), **Increase.** 1639–1723. American clergyman and writer. He and his son **Cotton** (1663–1728) exerted great theological and political influence on the colony of Massachusetts through their staunch Puritanism and prolific writing.

Ma•thi•as (mə-thī′əs), **Robert Bruce.** Known as "Bob." Born 1930. American athlete who won two consecutive Olympic gold medals in the decathlon (1948 and 1952).

maths (măths) *n. (used with a sing. verb). Chiefly British.* Mathematics.

Ma•thu•ra (mŭt′ər-ə) also **Mut•tra** (mŭt′rə). A city of north-central India northwest of Agra. An important repository of ancient Indian art, it is a Hindu pilgrimage site revered as the reputed birthplace of Krishna. Population, 147,493.

Ma•til•da (mə-tĭl′də). Known as "Empress Maud." 1102–1167. English princess as the daughter of Henry I. After her first husband, Emperor Henry V, died, she married Geoffrey, Count of Anjou (died 1151), in 1128 and by him bore Henry II.

ma•til•i•ja poppy (mə-tĭl′ē-hä′) *n.* A perennial herb *(Romneya coulteri)* of California and Baja California, having very large, solitary white flowers. [After *Matilija* Canyon in southwest California.]

mat•in (măt′n) also **mat•in•al** (-əl) *adj.* Of or relating to matins or to the early part of the day. [Middle English, from Old French, sing. of *matines,* matins. See MATINS.]

Henri Matisse

mat•i•nee or **mat•i•née** (măt′n-ā′) *n. Abbr.* **mat.** An entertainment, such as a dramatic or musical performance, given in the daytime, usually in the afternoon. [French *matinée,* from *matin,* morning, from Old French *matines,* matins. See MATINS.]

mat•ins (măt′nz) *n. (used with a sing. or pl. verb).* **1.a.** *Ecclesiastical.* The office that formerly constituted the first of the seven canonical hours. **b.** The time of day appointed for this service, traditionally midnight or 2 A.M. but often sunrise. **2.** Often **Matins.** See **Morning Prayer.** [Middle English *matines,* from Old French, from Medieval Latin *(vigiliae) mātūtīnae,* morning (vigils), feminine pl. of Latin *mātūtīnus,* of the morning, from *Mātūta,* goddess of dawn. See **mā-**[1] in Appendix.]

Ma•tisse (mə-tēs′, mä-), **Henri.** 1869–1954. French artist. A leading fauvist, he employed pure color, simple shapes, and an exquisite sense of design to produce paintings, such as *The Dance* (1930–1932), and collages.

mat•jes herring (mät′yĭs) *n.* Herring that have not spawned, filleted and prepared with salt, vinegar, sugar, and spices. [Partial translation of Dutch *maatjesharing* : *maatjes* (alteration of *maeghdekins,* genitive of *maeghdekin,* maiden, diminutive of *maagd,* maid; see **maghu-** in Appendix) + *haring,* herring.]

matri– or **matro–** or **matr–** *pref.* Mother; maternal: *matrilineal.* [Latin *mātri-,* from *māter, mātr-,* mother. See MATER.]

ma•tri•arch (mā′trē-ärk′) *n.* **1.** A woman who rules a family, clan, or tribe. **2.** A woman who dominates a group or an activity. **3.** A highly respected woman who is a mother. **—ma′tri•ar′chal** (-är′kəl), **ma′tri•ar′chic** (-är′kĭk) *adj.* **—ma′tri•ar′chal•ism** *n.*

ma•tri•ar•chate (mā′trē-är′kĭt, -kāt′) *n.* **1.** See **matriarchy. 2.** A hypothetical stage in the evolution of a society in which authority is held by women.

ma•tri•ar•chy (mā′trē-är′kē) *n., pl.* **-chies. 1.** A social system in which the mother is head of the family and descent is traced through the mother's side of the family. **2.** A family, community, or society based on this system or governed by women. Also called *matriarchate.*

ma•tri•ces (mā′trĭ-sēz′, măt′rĭ-) *n.* A plural of **matrix.**

mat•ri•cide (măt′rĭ-sīd′) *n.* **1.** The act of killing one's mother. **2.** One who kills one's mother. **—mat′ri•ci′dal** (-sīd′l) *adj.*

mat•ri•cli•nous (măt′rĭ-klī′nəs) *adj.* Having predominantly maternal hereditary traits. [MATRI– + Greek *klinein,* to lean; see **klei-** in Appendix + –OUS.]

ma•tric•u•lant (mə-trĭk′yə-lənt) *n.* One who matriculates or is a candidate for matriculation.

ma•tric•u•late (mə-trĭk′yə-lāt′) *tr. & intr.v.* **-lat•ed, -lat•ing, -lates.** To admit or be admitted into a group, especially a college or university. **—matriculate** (-lĭt, -lāt′) *n.* One who is so admitted. [From Medieval Latin *mātrīculāre, mātrīculāt-,* from Late Latin *mātrīcula,* list, diminutive of *mātrīx, mātrīc-.* See MATRIX.] **—ma•tric′u•la′tion** *n.*

mat•ri•lin•e•age (măt′rə-lĭn′ē-ĭj) *n.* Line of descent as traced through the maternal side of a family.

mat•ri•lin•e•al (măt′rə-lĭn′ē-əl) *adj.* Relating to, based on, or tracing ancestral descent through the maternal line. **—mat′ri•lin′e•al•ly** *adv.*

mat•ri•lo•cal (măt′rə-lō′kəl) *adj. Anthropology.* Of or relating to the residence of a wife's kin group or clan. **—mat′ri•lo′cal•ly** *adv.*

mat•ri•mo•ny (măt′rə-mō′nē) *n., pl.* **-nies.** The act or state of being married; marriage. [Middle English, from Old French *matrimoine,* from Latin *mātrimōnium,* from *māter, mātr-,* mother. See **māter-** in Appendix.] **—mat′ri•mo′ni•al** *adj.* **—mat′ri•mo′ni•al•ly** *adv.*

matrimony vine *n.* Any of various often thorny shrubs of the genus *Lycium,* some species of which are cultivated for their purplish flowers and brightly colored berries. Also called *boxthorn.*

ma•trix (mā′trĭks) *n., pl.* **ma•tri•ces** (mā′trĭ-sēz′, măt′rĭ-) or **ma•trix•es. 1.** A situation or surrounding substance within which something else originates, develops, or is contained: *"Freedom of expression is the matrix, the indispensable condition, of nearly every form of freedom"* (Benjamin N. Cardozo). **2.** The womb. **3.** *Anatomy.* **a.** The formative cells or tissue of a fingernail, toenail, or tooth. **b.** See **ground substance** (sense 1). **4.** *Geology.* **a.** The solid matter in which a fossil or crystal is embedded. **b.** Groundmass. **5.** A mold or die. **6.** The principal metal in an alloy, as the iron in steel. **7.** A binding substance, as cement in concrete. **8.a.** *Mathematics.* A rectangular array of numeric or algebraic quantities subject to mathematical operations. **b.** Something resembling such an array, as in the regular formation of elements into columns and rows. **9.** *Computer Science.* The network of intersections between input and output leads in a computer, functioning as an encoder or a decoder. **10.** *Printing.* **a.** A mold used in stereotyping and designed to receive positive impressions of type or illustrations from which metal plates can be cast. Also called *mat.* **b.** A metal plate used for casting typefaces. **11.** An electroplated impression of a phonograph record used to make duplicate records. [Middle English *matrice,* from Old French, from Late Latin *mātrīx, mātrīc-,* from Latin, breeding-animal, from *māter, mātr-,* mother. See **māter-** in Appendix.]

matro– *pref.* Variant of **matri–.**

ma•tron (mā′trən) *n.* **1.** A married woman or a widow, especially a mother of dignity, mature age, and established social position. **2.** A woman who acts as a supervisor or monitor in a public institution, such as a school, hospital, or prison. [Middle English *matrone,* from Old French, from Latin *mātrōna,* from *māter, mātr-,* mother. See **māter-** in Appendix.] **—ma′tron•al** *adj.* **—ma′tron•li•ness** *n.* **—ma′tron•ly** *adv. & adj.*

matron of honor *n., pl.* **matrons of honor.** A married woman serving as chief attendant of the bride at a wedding.

mat•ro•nym•ic (măt′rə-nĭm′ĭk) *adj. & n.* Variant of **metronymic.**

Mat•su (măt′so͞o′). An island in the East China Sea off the southeast coast of mainland China. It remained a Nationalist stronghold after the Chinese Communist revolution of 1949 and is now administered by Taiwan.

Ma•tsu•do (mä-tso͞o′dō). A city of east-central Honshu, Japan, a suburb of Tokyo. Population, 427,479.

Ma•tsu•ya•ma (mä′tso͞o-yä′mä). A city of western Shikoku, Japan, on the Inland Sea. It was an important fortress town during the feudal period. Population, 426,646.

Matt. *abbr. Bible.* Matthew.

Mat•tag•a•mi (mə-tăg′ə-mē). A river, about 443 km (275 mi) long, of eastern Ontario, Canada, rising in **Mattagami Lake** and flowing north to the Moose River.

matte[1] (măt) *n.* Variant of **mat**[2] (sense 2). **—matte** *adj.* Variant of **mat**[2].

matte[2] (măt) *n.* A mixture of a metal with its sulfides, produced by smelting the sulfide ores of copper, lead, or nickel. [French.]

mat•ted (măt′ĭd) *adj.* **1.** Covered with or made from mats. **2.** Tangled in a dense mass: *tried to push through the matted undergrowth.*

mat•ter (măt′ər) *n.* **1.a.** Something that occupies space and can be perceived by one or more senses; a physical body, a physical substance, or the universe as a whole. **b.** *Physics.* Something that has mass and exists as a solid, liquid, or gas. **2.** A specific type of substance: *inorganic matter.* **3.** Discharge or waste, such

ă pat	oi boy
ā pay	ou out
âr care	o͝o took
ä father	o͞o boot
ĕ pet	ŭ cut
ē be	ûr urge
ĭ pit	th thin
ī pie	*th* this
îr pier	hw which
ŏ pot	zh vision
ō toe	ə about, item
ô paw	♦ regionalism

Stress marks: ′ (primary); ′ (secondary), as in **dictionary** (dĭk′shə-nĕr′ē)

as pus or feces, from a living organism. **4.** *Philosophy.* In Aristotelian and Scholastic use, that which is in itself undifferentiated and formless and which, as the subject of change and development, receives form and becomes substance and experience. **5.** *Christian Science.* "Spirit is the real and eternal; matter is the unreal and temporal" (Mary Baker Eddy). **6.** The substance of thought or expression as opposed to the manner in which it is stated or conveyed. **7.** A subject of concern, feeling, or action: *matters of foreign policy; a personal matter.* See Synonyms at **subject. 8.** Trouble or difficulty: *What's the matter with your car?* **9.** An approximated quantity, amount, or extent: *The construction will last a matter of years.* **10.** Something printed or otherwise set down in writing: *reading matter.* **11.** Something sent by mail. **12.** *Printing.* **a.** Composed type. **b.** Material to be set in type. **—matter** *intr.v.* **-tered, -ter·ing, -ters.** To be of importance: *"Love is most nearly itself/When here and now cease to matter"* (T.S. Eliot). See Synonyms at **count[1]**. **—*idioms.* as a matter of fact.** In fact; actually. **for that matter.** So far as that is concerned; as for that. **no matter.** Regardless of: *"Yet there isn't a train I wouldn't take,/No matter where it's going"* (Edna St. Vincent Millay). [Middle English, from Old French *matere,* from Latin *māteria.* See **māter-** in Appendix.]

Mat·ter·horn (măt′ər-hôrn′, mä′tər-). A mountain, 4,481.1 m (14,692 ft) high, in the Pennine Alps on the Italian-Swiss border.

matter of course *n.* A natural or logical outcome.

mat·ter-of-fact (măt′ər-əv-făkt′) *adj.* **c.** Relating or adhering to facts; literal. **d.** Straightforward or unemotional: *"the matter-of-fact tones in which the local guides describe the history of the various places"* (New York Times). **—mat′ter-of-fact′ly** *adv.* **—mat′ter-of-fact′ness** *n.*

Mat·thew (măth′yo͞o) *n. Abbr.* **Matt., Mt** *Bible.* See table at **Bible.**

Matthew, Saint. First century A.D. One of the 12 Apostles and the traditionally accepted author of the first Gospel of the New Testament.

Mat·thews (măth′yo͞oz), **Stanley.** 1824–1889. American jurist who served as an associate justice of the U.S. Supreme Court (1881–1889).

mat·ting[1] (măt′ĭng) *n.* **1.a.** Material formed into or considered as a mat: *The forest floor had a thick matting of pine needles.* **b.** A coarsely woven fabric used for covering floors and similar purposes. **2.** The activity of making mats.

mat·ting[2] (măt′ĭng) *n.* **1.** A dull surface or finish. **2.** The process of dulling a surface, as of metal.

mat·tins (măt′nz) *n. (used with a sing. or pl. verb). Chiefly British.* Variant of **matins.**

mat·tock (măt′ək) *n.* A digging tool with a flat blade set at right angles to the handle. [Middle English, from Old English *mattuc,* perhaps from Vulgar Latin **matteūca,* club; akin to **mattea.* See MACE[1].]

Mat·toon (mə-to͞on′). A city of east-central Illinois southeast of Decatur. It is a processing center. Population, 19,787.

mat·tress (măt′rĭs) *n.* **1.a.** A usually rectangular pad of heavy cloth filled with soft material or an arrangement of coiled springs, used as or on a bed. **b.** An airtight inflatable pad used as or on a bed or as a cushion. **2.** A closely woven mat of brush and poles used to protect an embankment, a dike, or a dam from erosion. [Middle English *mattresse,* from Old French *materas,* from Old Italian *materasso* and from Medieval Latin *matracium,* both from Arabic *maṭraḥ,* place where something is thrown, mat, cushion, from *ṭaraḥa,* to throw.]

WORD HISTORY: The history of the word *mattress* is a small lesson in the way amenities have come to Europe from the Middle East. During the earlier part of the Middle Ages, Arabic culture was more advanced than that of Europe. One of the amenities of life enjoyed by the Arabs was sleeping on cushions thrown on the floor. Derived from the Arabic word *ṭaraḥa,* "to throw," the word *maṭraḥ* meant "place where something is thrown" and "mat, cushion." This kind of sleeping surface was adopted by the Europeans during the Crusades, and the Arabic word was taken into Italian (*materasso*) and then into Old French (*materas*), from which comes the Middle English word *materas,* first recorded in a work written around 1300. The Arabic word also became Medieval Latin *matracium,* another source of our word.

mat·u·rate (măch′ə-rāt′) *v.* **-rat·ed, -rat·ing, -rates.** *—intr.* **1.** To mature, ripen, or develop. **2.** To suppurate. *—tr.* To cause to suppurate. [Latin *mātūrāre, mātūrāt-,* from *mātūrus,* mature. See MATURE.] **—mat′u·ra′tive** *adj.*

mat·u·ra·tion (măch′ə-rā′shən) *n.* **1.** The process of becoming mature. **2.** Production or discharge of pus. **3.** *Biology.* **a.** The processes by which gametes are formed, including the reduction of chromosomes in a germ cell from the diploid number to the haploid number by meiosis. **b.** The final differentiation processes in biological systems, such as the final ripening of a seed or the attainment of full functional capacity by a cell, a tissue, or an organ. **—mat′u·ra′tion·al** *adj.*

maturation division *n.* Either of the two successive cell divisions of meiosis, with only one duplication of the chromosomes, that results in the formation of haploid gametes.

ma·ture (mə-tyo͝or′, -to͝or′, -cho͝or′) *adj.* **-tur·er, -tur·est. 1.a.** Having reached full natural growth or development: *a mature cell.* **b.** Having reached a desired or final condition; ripe: *a mature cheese.* **2.** Of, relating to, or characteristic of full development, either mental or physical: *mature for her age.* **3.a.** Suitable or intended for adults: *mature subject matter.* **b.** Composed of adults: *a mature audience.* **4.** Worked out fully by the mind; considered: *a mature plan of action.* **5.** Having reached the limit of its time; due: *a mature bond.* **6.** No longer subject to great expansion or development. Used of an industry, a market, or a product. **7.** *Geology.* Having reached maximum development of form. Used of streams and landforms. **—mature** *v.* **-tured, -tur·ing, -tures.** *—tr.* **1.** To bring to full development; ripen. **2.** To work out fully in the mind: *"able to digest and mature my thoughts for my own mind only"* (John Stuart Mill). *—intr.* **1.** To evolve toward or reach full development: *The child's judgment matures as she grows older.* **2.** To become due. Used of notes and bonds. [Middle English, from Old French, from Latin *mātūrus.* See **mā-[1]** in Appendix.] **—ma·ture′ly** *adv.* **—ma·ture′ness** *n.*

SYNONYMS: *mature, age, develop, ripen.* The central meaning shared by these verbs is "to bring or come to full development or maximum excellence": *maturing the wines in vats; aged the brandy for 100 years; developed the flavor slowly; fruits that were ripened on the vine.*

Matterhorn

ma·ture-on·set diabetes (mə-tyo͝or′ŏn′sĕt′, -ôn′, -to͝or′-, -cho͝or′-) *n.* Non-insulin-dependent diabetes mellitus.

ma·tur·i·ty (mə-tyo͝or′ĭ-tē, -to͝or′-, -cho͝or′-) *n., pl.* **-ties. 1.a.** The state or quality of being fully grown or developed. **b.** The state or quality of being mature. **2.a.** The time at which a note or bond is due. **b.** The state of a note or bond being due. **3.** *Geology.* A stage in the development of streams or landscapes at which maximum development has been reached or at which the process of erosion is going on with maximum vigor, continuing until about three fourths of the original mass is carried away by erosion. [Middle English *maturite,* from Old French, from Latin *mātūritās,* from *mātūrus,* mature. See MATURE.]

ma·tu·ti·nal (mə-to͞ot′n-əl, -tyo͞ot′-, măch′o͞o-tī′nəl) *adj.* Of, relating to, or occurring in the morning; early. [Late Latin *mātūtīnālis,* from Latin *mātūtīnus.* See MATINS.] **—ma·tu′ti·nal·ly** *adv.*

mat·zo also **mat·zoh** (mät′sə, -sô, mät-sä′) *—n., pl.* **-zos** also **-zohs** (-səz, -sōs′) or **-zot** or **-zoth** (-sôt′). A brittle, flat piece of unleavened bread, eaten especially during Passover. *—attributive.* Often used to modify another noun: *matzo meal.* [Yiddish *matse,* from Hebrew *maṣṣâ.*]

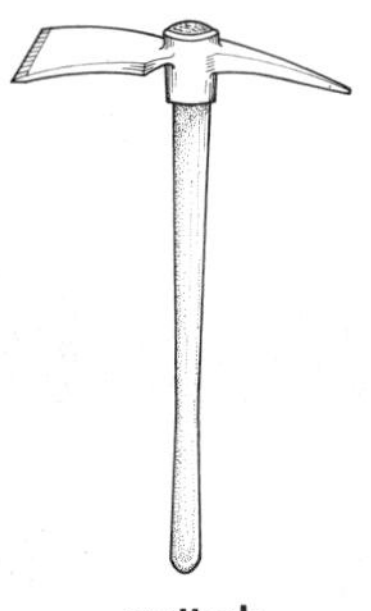

mattock

matzo ball *n.* A small dumpling made from matzo meal.

mat·zoh (mät′sə, -sô, mät-sä′) *n.* Variant of **matzo.**

mat·zot or **mat·zoth** (mät-sôt′) *n.* Plurals of **matzo.**

maud·lin (môd′lĭn) *adj.* Effusively or tearfully sentimental: *"displayed an almost maudlin concern for the welfare of animals"* (Aldous Huxley). See Synonyms at **sentimental.** [Alteration of (MARY) MAGDALENE, who was frequently depicted as a tearful penitent.] **—maud′lin·ly** *adv.* **—maud′lin·ness** *n.*

Maugham (môm), **W(illiam) Somerset.** 1874–1965. British writer whose short stories, such as "Miss Thompson" (1921), and novels, including *Of Human Bondage* (1915), illustrate his economy of expression and masterly storytelling.

mau·gre (mô′gər) *prep. Archaic.* Notwithstanding; in spite of. [Middle English, from Old French : *mal-, mau-,* bad; see MAL- + *gre,* liking, pleasure (from Latin *grātum,* from neuter of *grātus,* pleasing; see **gʷerə-[2]** in Appendix).]

Mau·i (mou′ē). An island of Hawaii northwest of Hawaii Island. It is the second-largest island in the state, with an economy based chiefly on sugar cane, pineapples, and tourism.

matzo

maul also **mall** (môl) *—n.* **1.** A heavy, long-handled hammer used especially to drive stakes, piles, or wedges. **2.** A heavy hammer having a wedge-shaped head and used for splitting logs. *—tr.v.* **mauled, maul·ing, mauls** also **malled, mall·ing, malls. 1.** To injure by or as if by beating: *The boxer mauled the other fighter. The critics mauled the novelist's first effort.* See Synonyms at **batter[1]**. **2.** To handle roughly: *The package was mauled by the careless messenger.* **3.** To split (wood) with a maul and wedge. [Middle English *malle,* from Old French *mail,* from Latin *malleus.* See **mele-** in Appendix.] **—maul′er** *n.*

Maul·din (môl′dĭn), **William Henry.** Known as "Bill." Born 1921. American editorial cartoonist noted for his realistic, bitterly comic drawings of front-line soldiers.

maul·stick also **mahl·stick** (môl′stĭk′) *n.* A long wooden stick used by painters as a support to keep the hand that holds the brush from touching the painting surface. [Partial translation of Dutch *maalstok* : *maalen,* to paint (from Middle Dutch *malen*) + *stok,* stick.]

Mau·na Ke·a (mou′nə kā′ə, mô′nə kē′ə). An active volcano, about 4,208 m (13,796 ft) high, of north-central Hawaii Island. It is the highest peak in the islands.

Mauna Lo·a (lō′ə). An active volcano, 4,172.4 m (13,680 ft) high, of south-central Hawaii Island.

maund (mônd) *n.* A unit of weight varying in different countries of Asia from 11.2 to 37.4 kilograms (24.8 to 82.6 pounds) avoirdupois, the latter being the official maund in India. [Hindi *mān,* from Sanskrit *mānam,* measure.]

maun·der (môn′dər, măn′-) *intr.v.* **-dered, -der·ing, -ders. 1.** To talk incoherently or aimlessly. **2.** To move or act aimlessly or vaguely; wander. [Origin unknown.]

Maun·dy Thursday (môn′dē, măn′-) *n.* The Thursday be-

Somerset Maugham
Photographed in 1952

Mauritania

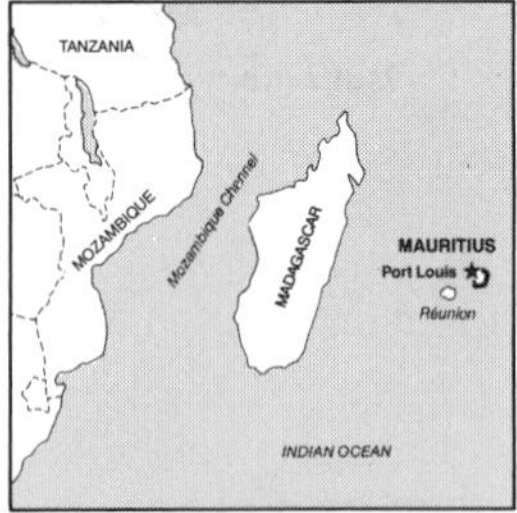

Mauritius

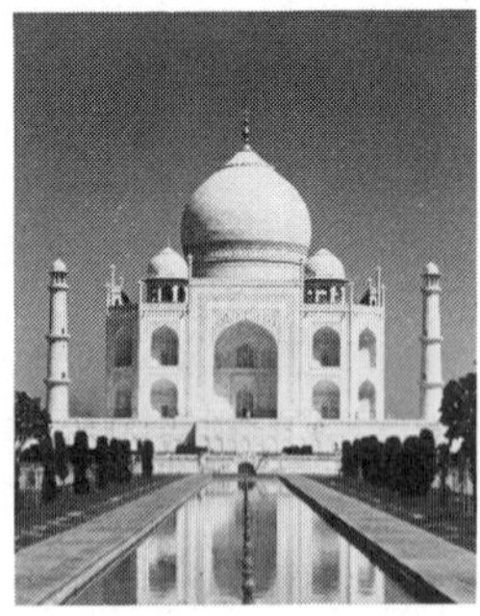

mausoleum
The Taj Mahal,
Agra, India

Maximilian

ă pat	oi boy
ā pay	ou out
âr care	ŏŏ took
ä father	ōō boot
ĕ pet	ŭ cut
ē be	ûr urge
ĭ pit	th thin
ī pie	*th* this
îr pier	hw which
ŏ pot	zh vision
ō toe	ə about, item
ô paw	♦ regionalism

Stress marks: **ʹ** (primary); ʹ (secondary), as in **dictionary** (dĭkʹshə-nĕrʹē)

fore Easter, observed in commemoration of the Last Supper of Jesus. Also called *Holy Thursday.* [From Middle English *maunde,* ceremony of washing the feet of the poor on this day, from Old French *mande,* from Latin *(novum) mandātum,* (new) commandment (from Jesus's words to the Apostles after washing their feet, John 13:34). See MANDATE.]

Mau·pas·sant (mōʹpə-säntʹ, mō-pă-säNʹ), **(Henri René Albert) Guy de.** 1850–1893. French writer whose works, mainly realistic short stories such as "The Necklace," examine hypocrisy, madness, Parisian society, and peasant life in Normandy.

Mau·re·ta·ni·a (môrʹĭ-tāʹnē-ə, -tānʹyə, märʹ-). An ancient district of the Roman Empire in present-day Morocco and Algeria. Settled by a Berber people, it was ruled by Rome from c. 100 B.C. to the fifth century A.D. **—Mauʹre·taʹni·an** *adj. & n.*

Mau·riac (môrʹē-äkʹ, môr-yäkʹ), **François.** 1885–1970. French writer many of whose novels, notably *Thérèse Desqueyroux* (1927), are psychological studies of temptation, sin, and redemption. He won the 1952 Nobel Prize for literature.

Mau·rice of Nas·sau (môrʹĭs, mŏrʹ-; năsʹô) Prince of Orange. 1567–1625. Dutch general and politician whose strategic and material improvements to the Dutch army led to the repulsion of Spanish forces from Dutch territory (1590–1609).

Mau·ri·ta·ni·a (môrʹĭ-tāʹnē-ə, -tānʹyə, märʹ-). A country of northwest Africa bordering on the Atlantic Ocean. Settled by Berbers c. 1000, the area was visited by European traders after the 15th century. French influence over the region lasted from the early 1800's until independence was achieved in 1960. Nouakchott is the capital and the largest city. Population, 1,727,000. **—Mauʹri·taʹni·an** *adj. & n.*

Mau·ri·tius (mô-rĭshʹəs, -ē-əs). An island country in the southwest Indian Ocean comprising the island of **Mauritius** and several dependencies in the Mascarene Islands. Mauritius was controlled by the Dutch (1598–1710), the French (1715–1810), and the British (after 1814) before independence was achieved in 1968. Port Louis is the capital and the largest city. Population, 1,023,934. **—Mau·riʹtian** *adj. & n.*

Mau·rois (môr-wäʹ), **André.** Pen name of Émile Herzog. 1885–1967. French writer noted for his essays, biographies, and novels, including *The Family Circle* (1932).

Mau·ry (môrʹē), **Matthew Fontaine.** 1806–1873. American naval officer and oceanographer who charted the currents and winds of the Atlantic, Pacific, and Indian oceans.

Mau·ser (mouʹzər). A trademark used for a repeating rifle or pistol.

Mauser, Peter Paul. 1838–1914. German weapons manufacturer who with his brother **Wilhelm** (1834–1882) invented a breechloading rifle and a repeating pistol and rifle.

mau·so·le·um (môʹsə-lēʹəm, -zə-) *n., pl.* **-le·ums** or **-le·a** (-lēʹə). **1.** A large, stately tomb or a building housing such a tomb or several tombs. **2.** A gloomy, usually large room or building. [Middle English, from Latin *Mausōlēum,* from Greek *Mausōleion,* from *Mausōlos,* Mausolus (died c. 353 B.C.), Persian satrap of Caria.] **—mauʹso·leʹan** *adj.*

mauve (mōv) *n. Color.* A moderate grayish violet to moderate reddish purple. [French, from Old French *mallow,* from Latin *malva.*] **—mauve** *adj.*

ma·ven also **ma·vin** (māʹvən) *n.* A person who has special knowledge or experience; an expert. [Yiddish *meyvn,* from Hebrew *mēbîn.*]

mav·er·ick (măvʹər-ĭk, măvʹrĭk) *n.* **1.** An unbranded range animal, especially a calf that has become separated from its mother, traditionally considered the property of the first person who brands it. **2.** One that refuses to abide by the dictates of or resists adherence to a group; a dissenter. **—maverick** *adj.* Being independent in thought and action or exhibiting such independence: *maverick politicians; a maverick decision.* [Possibly after Samuel Augustus *Maverick* (1803–1870), American cattleman, or perhaps after Samuel *Maverick* (1602?–1676?), English-born colonist.]

ma·vin (māʹvən) *n.* Variant of **maven.**

ma·vis (māʹvĭs) *n.* See **song thrush.** [Middle English, from Old French *mauvis,* probably from *mauve,* seagull, mew.]

ma·vour·neen also **ma·vour·nin** (mə-vŏŏrʹnēnʹ) *n. Irish.* My darling. [Irish Gaelic *mo mhuirnín* : *mo,* my (from Old Irish; see **me-¹** in Appendix) + *muirnín,* darling, diminutive of *muirn,* delight (from Old Irish, tumult, revels).]

maw (mô) *n.* **1.** The mouth, stomach, jaws, or gullet of a voracious animal, especially a carnivore. **2.** The opening into something felt to be insatiable: *"I saw the opening maw of hell"* (Herman Melville). [Middle English *mawe,* from Old English *maga.*]

mawk·ish (môʹkĭsh) *adj.* **1.** Excessively and objectionably sentimental. See Synonyms at **sentimental. 2.** Sickening or insipid. [From Middle English *mawke,* maggot, variant of *magot.* See MAGGOT.] **—mawkʹish·ly** *adv.* **—mawkʹish·ness** *n.*

max (măks) *Slang. n.* The maximum: *The car can seat five adults, but that's the max. The movie was boring to the max.* **—max** *adj.* Maximal. **—max** *adv.* Maximally: *We'll pay $250 max.* **—max** *intr.v.* **maxed, max·ing, max·es. 1.** To reach one's limit, as of endurance or capability: *The weight lifter maxed out at 180 kilograms.* **2.** To reach a point from which no additional growth, improvement, or benefit is possible: *The salary for this position maxes at $45,000.*

max. *abbr.* Maximum.

max·i (măkʹsē) *n., pl.* **max·is.** A long skirt, coat, or dress that usually extends to or just past the ankles. [From MAXIMUM.]

max·il·la (măk-sĭlʹə) *n., pl.* **max·il·lae** (măk-sĭlʹē) or **max·il·las. 1.** *Anatomy.* Either of a pair of bones of the human skull fusing in the midline and forming the upper jaw. **2.** A homologous bone of the skull in other vertebrates. **3.** Either of two laterally moving appendages situated behind the mandibles in insects and most other arthropods. [Latin, jawbone.]

max·il·lar·y (măkʹsə-lĕrʹē) *adj.* Of or relating to a jaw or jawbone, especially the upper one. **—maxillary** *n., pl.* **-ies.** A maxillary bone; a jawbone.

max·il·li·ped (măk-sĭlʹə-pĕdʹ) *n.* One of the three pairs of crustacean head appendages located just posterior to the maxillae and used in feeding. [MAXILL(A) + –PED.]

max·il·lo·fa·cial (măk-sĭlʹō-fāʹshəl) *adj. Anatomy.* Relating to or involving the maxilla and the face: *a maxillofacial prosthesis.* [MAXILL(A) + FACIAL.]

max·im (măkʹsĭm) *n.* A succinct formulation of a fundamental principle, general truth, or rule of conduct. See Synonyms at **saying.** [Middle English *maxime,* from Old French, from Medieval Latin *maxima,* from *maxima (prōpositiō),* greatest (premise), feminine of Latin *maximus,* greatest. See **meg-** in Appendix.]

Max·im (măkʹsĭm), Sir **Hiram Stevens.** 1840–1916. American-born British inventor of an automatic, recoil-operated machine gun (1884), which was widely used during World War I. His brother **Hudson** (1853–1927) invented smokeless gun powder, and his son **Hiram Percy** (1896–1936) developed a silencer for firearms.

max·i·ma (măkʹsə-mə) *n.* A plural of **maximum.**

max·i·mal (măkʹsə-məl) *adj.* **1.** Of, relating to, or consisting of a maximum. **2.** Being the greatest or highest possible. **—maximal** *n. Mathematics.* An element in an ordered set that is followed by no other. **—maxʹi·mal·ly** *adv.*

max·i·mal·ist (măkʹsə-mə-lĭst) *n.* One who advocates direct or radical action to secure a social or political goal in its entirety: *"the maximalists . . . who want the undivided land"* (Arthur Hertzberg). [Russian *maksimalist,* name applied in 1906 to an extreme splinter group of the Russian Socialist Revolutionary Party, ultimately from Latin *maximum,* maximum. See MAXIMUM.] **—maxʹi·mal·ist** *adj.*

Maxim gun *n.* An early, single-barreled, water-cooled machine gun. [After Sir Hiram Stevens MAXIM.]

Max·i·mil·ian (măkʹsə-mĭlʹyən). 1832–1867. Austrian archduke and emperor of Mexico (1864–1867). Appointed emperor by the French, who had recently captured Mexico, he lacked popular support and was captured and executed by Mexican republicans when France withdrew from the country.

Maximilian I. 1459–1519. King of Germany (1486–1519) and Holy Roman emperor (1493–1519) who through arranged marriages added greatly to the territory and power of the Hapsburgs.

Maximilian II. 1527–1576. Holy Roman emperor (1564–1576) who was tolerant of Lutheranism and supported Catholic reform.

max·i·mize (măkʹsə-mīzʹ) *tr.v.* **-mized, -miz·ing, -miz·es. 1.** To increase or make as great as possible: *"the ideal of maximizing opportunity through the equalizing of educational opportunity"* (Robert J. Havighurst). **2.** To assign the highest possible importance to. **3.** *Mathematics.* To find the largest value of (a function). **—maxʹi·mi·zaʹtion** (-mĭ-zāʹshən) *n.* **—maxʹi·mizʹer** *n.*

max·i·mum (măkʹsə-məm) *n.* **-mums** or **-ma** (-mə). *Abbr.* **max.** *pl.* **1. a.** The greatest possible quantity or degree. **b.** The greatest quantity or degree reached or recorded; the upper limit of variation. **c.** The time or period during which the highest point or degree is attained. **2.** An upper limit permitted by law or other authority. **3.** *Astronomy.* **a.** The moment when a variable star is most brilliant. **b.** The magnitude of the star at such a moment. **4.** *Mathematics.* **a.** The greatest value assumed by a function over a given interval. **b.** The largest number in a set. **—maximum** *adj. Abbr.* **max. 1.** Having or being the greatest quantity or the highest degree that has been or can be attained: *maximum temperature.* **2.** Of, relating to, or making up a maximum: *a maximum number in a series.* [Latin, from neuter of *maximus,* greatest. See **meg-** in Appendix.]

max·i·mum-se·cu·ri·ty (măkʹsə-məm-sĭ-kyŏŏrʹĭ-tē) *adj.* Having more restrictions than others of its kind: *a maximum-security prison; a maximum-security air force base.*

max·well (măksʹwĕlʹ, -wəl) *n. Abbr.* **Mx** The unit of magnetic flux in the centimeter-gram-second system, equal to the flux perpendicularly intersecting an area of one square centimeter in a region where the magnetic intensity is one gauss. [After James Clerk MAXWELL.]

Max·well (măksʹwĕlʹ, -wəl), **James Clerk.** 1831–1879. British physicist who made fundamental contributions to electromagnetic theory and the kinetic theory of gases.

may¹ (mā) *aux.v.* Past tense **might** (mīt). **1.** To be allowed or permitted to: *May I take a swim? Yes, you may.* **2.** Used to indicate a certain measure of likelihood or possibility: *It may rain this afternoon.* **3.** Used to express a desire or fervent wish: *Long may he live!* **4.** Used to express contingency, purpose, or result in clauses introduced by *that* or *so that*: *expressing ideas so that the average person may understand.* **5.** To be obliged; must. Used in statutes, deeds, and other legal documents. See Usage Note at **can¹.** [Middle English, to be able, from Old English *mæg,* first and third person sing. of *magan,* to be strong, be able. See **magh-** in Appendix.]

may² (mā) *n. Chiefly British.* The blossoms of the hawthorn. [French *mai,* hawthorn, from *Mai,* May (so called because it blooms in May). See MAY.]

May (mā) *n.* **1.** The fifth month of the year in the Gregorian calendar. See table at **calendar. 2.** The springtime of life; youth. **3.** The celebration of May Day. [Middle English, from Old French *Mai,* from Latin *Maius (mēnsis),* (the month) of Maia, from *Maia,* an Italic goddess. See **meg-** in Appendix.]

May, Cape. A peninsula of southern New Jersey between the Atlantic Ocean and Delaware Bay. The southern tip forms **Cape May Point.**

ma·ya (mä′yə) *n. Hinduism.* **1.** The power of a god or demon to transform a concept into an element of the sensible world. **2.** The transitory, manifold appearance of the sensible world, which obscures the undifferentiated spiritual reality from which it originates; the illusory appearance of the sensible world. [Sanskrit *māyā.*]

Ma·ya (mä′yə) *n., pl.* **Maya** or **-yas. 1.a.** A member of a Mesoamerican Indian people inhabiting southeast Mexico, Guatemala, and Belize, whose civilization reached its height around A.D. 300–900. The Maya are noted for their architecture and city planning, their mathematics and calendar, and their hieroglyphic writing system. **b.** A modern-day descendant of this people. **2.** Any of the Mayan languages, especially Quiché and Yucatec. [Spanish.] **—Ma′ya** *adj.*

Ma·ya·güez (mī′ə-gwĕz′, mä′yä-gwĕs′). A city of western Puerto Rico west-southwest of San Juan. It is a port of entry and manufacturing center. Population, 82,968.

Ma·ya·kov·ski (mä′yə-kôf′skē, mə-), **Vladimir Vladimirovich.** 1893–1930. Soviet poet and leader of futurism in Russian literature.

Ma·yan (mä′yən) *adj.* Of or relating to the Maya, their culture, their languages, or the language group to which it belongs. **—Mayan** *n.* **1.** A Maya. **2.** A linguistic stock of Central America that includes Quiché and Yucatec.

May apple *n.* **1.** A rhizomatous plant *(Podophyllum peltatum)* of eastern North America, having a single, nodding white flower and oval yellow fruit. Although the pulp of the ripe fruit is edible, the roots, leaves, and seeds of the plant are poisonous. **2.** The fruit of this plant. Also called *mandrake.*

may·be (mā′bē) *adv.* Perhaps; possibly. **—maybe** *n. Informal.* **1.** An uncertainty: *There are so many maybes involved in playing the stock market.* **2.** An uncertain reply: *It's better to receive a fast and honest no than a drawn-out maybe.*

May beetle *n.* See **June beetle.**

may·day (mā′dā′) *n.* An international radiotelephone signal word used by aircraft and ships in distress. [From French *m'aidez,* help me!]

WORD HISTORY: "Mayday, mayday!" comes the international distress signal over the radio, and nobody stops to ask why the first of May is being mentioned at a time of crisis. *Mayday,* in fact, has nothing to do with the first of May. Instead, it is a spelling that represents the pronunciation of French *m'aidez,* "help me," or the latter part of the phrase *venez m'aider,* "come help me," either of which are quite appropriate at such a critical juncture.

May Day *n.* **1.** May 1, observed in the United States, Canada, and parts of Western Europe in celebration of the coming of spring. **2.** May 1, observed as a holiday especially in socialist countries in honor of labor and labor organizations.

May·er (mā′ər), **Louis Burt.** 1885–1957. Russian-born American motion-picture producer who formed a film company (1918) and merged with Samuel Goldwyn to form Metro-Goldwyn-Mayer (1924).

May·er (mī′ər), **Marie Goeppert.** 1906–1972. German-born American physicist. She shared a 1963 Nobel Prize for research on the structure of the atom and its nucleus.

may·est (mā′ĭst) or **mayst** (māst) *aux.v. Archaic.* Second person singular present tense of **may¹.**

May·fair (mā′fâr′). A fashionable district in the West End of London, England. It was named after an annual fair held in the district until 1708.

May·field Heights (mā′fēld′). A city of northeast Ohio, a residential suburb of Cleveland. Population, 21,550.

may·flow·er (mā′flou′ər) *n.* **1.** Any of various plants that bloom in May. **2.** See **trailing arbutus.**

may·fly (mā′flī′) *n.* Any of various fragile winged insects of the order Ephemeroptera that develop from aquatic nymphs and live in the adult stage no longer than a few days. Also called *dayfly, shadfly.*

may·hap (mā′hăp′, mā-hăp′) *adv.* Perhaps; perchance. [From the phrase *it may hap.*]

may·hem (mā′hĕm′, mā′əm) *n.* **1.** *Law.* The offense of willfully maiming or crippling a person. **2.** Infliction of violent injury on a person or thing; wanton destruction: *children committing mayhem in the flower beds.* **3.** A state of violent disorder or riotous confusion; havoc. [Middle English *maim, mayhem,* from Anglo-Norman *maihem,* from Old French *mahaigne,* injury, from *mahaignier,* to maim, from Vulgar Latin **mahanāre,* probably of Germanic origin.]

may·ing or **May·ing** (mā′ĭng) *n.* The celebration of May Day, especially by the gathering of spring flowers.

may·n't (mā′ənt, mānt). May not. See Usage Note at **can¹.**

may·o (mā′ō) *n. Informal.* Mayonnaise.

Ma·yo (mā′ō), **William James.** 1861–1939. American surgeon who with his brother **Charles Horace Mayo** (1865–1939) founded the Mayo Clinic in Rochester, Minnesota.

Ma·yon (mä-yōn′), **Mount.** An active volcano, 2,461.4 m (8,070 ft) high, of southeast Luzon, Philippines. It is considered one of the world's most perfect cones.

may·on·naise (mā′ə-nāz′, mā′ə-nāz′) *n.* A dressing made of beaten raw egg yolk, oil, lemon juice or vinegar, and seasonings. [French *mahonnaise, mayonnaise,* possibly from MAHÓN, captured by Louis François Armand de Vignerot du Plessis, Duc de Richelieu (1696–1788), in 1756 (the duke's chef is said to have introduced mayonnaise in honor of this victory).]

may·or (mā′ər, mâr) *n.* The head of government of a city, town, borough, or municipal corporation. [Middle English *maire,* from Old French, from Medieval Latin *māior,* from Latin, greater, superior. See **meg-** in Appendix.] **—may′or·al** *adj.* **—may′or·ship′** *n.*

may·or·al·ty (mā′ər-əl-tē, mâr′əl-) *n., pl.* **-ties. 1.** The office of a mayor. **2.** The term of office of a mayor. [Middle English *mairalte,* from Anglo-Norman, from Old French *maire,* mayor. See MAYOR.]

may·or·ess (mā′ər-ĭs, mâr′ĭs) *n.* **1.** A woman serving as the head of government of a city, town, borough, or municipal corporation. **2.** The wife of a mayor.

Ma·yotte (mä-yôt′). An island of the eastern Comoros in the Mozambique Channel. It remained a French territory after the other islands declared their independence in 1975.

May·pole also **may·pole** (mā′pōl′) *n.* A pole decorated with streamers that those celebrating May Day hold while dancing.

may·pop (mā′pŏp′) *n.* **1.** A vine *(Passiflora incarnata)* of the southeast United States having purple and white flowers, three-lobed leaves, and edible yellow fruit. **2.** The fruit of this plant. [Alteration of *maycock,* from earlier *maracock,* perhaps of Virginia Algonquian origin.]

Mays (māz), **Willie Howard, Jr.** Known as "the Say Hey Kid." Born 1931. American baseball player. An exciting outfielder and base runner, he hit 660 home runs.

mayst (māst) *aux.v.* Variant of **mayest.**

may tree *n. Chiefly British.* The hawthorn.

may·weed (mā′wēd′) *n.* A widespread weed *(Anthemis cotula)* having rank-smelling, bipinnately divided leaves and white-rayed flower heads. Also called *stinking chamomile.* [Middle English *maythe weed, mayyen wed,* alteration (influenced by *May* and *maiden*) of *maithe,* from Old English *mægtha.*]

May wine *n.* **1.** A still white wine with woodruff flavoring, often containing orange or pineapple slices. **2.** A punch of champagne, claret, and Moselle or Rhine wine, flavored with woodruff. [Translation of German *Maiwein.*]

May·wood (mā′wo͝od′). **1.** A city of southern California, a residential and industrial suburb of Los Angeles. Population, 21,810. **2.** A village of northeast Illinois, a residential suburb of Chicago. Population, 27,998.

ma·zae·di·um (mə-zē′dē-əm) *n., pl.* **-di·a** (-dē-ə). A fruiting body of some lichens in which the spores lie freely in a powdery mass that is enclosed in a peridium. [New Latin : Greek *maza,* lump; see **mag-** in Appendix + Latin *aedēs,* house.]

ma·zal tov (mä′zəl tôf′, tôv′, tōv′) *interj.* Variant of **mazel tov.**

Maz·a·rin (măz′ə-răɴ′), **Jules.** 1602–1661. Italian-born French cardinal who excercised great political influence as the tutor and chief minister to Louis XIV.

Ma·za·tlán (mä′sət-län′). A city of western Mexico on the Pacific Ocean northwest of Guadalajara. It is a seaport and tourist center. Population, 199,830.

Maz·da·ism also **Maz·de·ism** (măz′də-ĭz′əm) *n.* Zoroastrianism. [From Avestan *mazdā,* the good principle, from *mazdā-,* wise. See AHURA MAZDA.]

♦**maze** (māz) *n.* **1.a.** An intricate, usually confusing network of interconnecting pathways, as in a garden; a labyrinth. **b.** A physical situation in which it is easy to get lost: *a maze of bureaucratic divisions.* **2.** A graphic puzzle, the solution of which is an uninterrupted path through an intricate pattern of line segments from a starting point to a goal. **3.** Something made up of many confused or conflicting elements; a tangle: *a maze of government regulations.* **—maze** *tr.v.* **mazed, maz·ing, maz·es.** *Chiefly Southern U.S.* **1.** To bewilder or astonish. **2.** To stupefy; daze. See Regional Note at **possum.** [Middle English *mase,* confusion, maze, from *masen,* to confuse, daze, from Old English *āmasian,* to confound.]

ma·zel tov also **ma·zal tov** (mä′zəl tôf′, tôv′, tōv′) *interj.* Used to express congratulations or best wishes. [Late Hebrew *mazzālṭôb* : *mazzāl,* luck + *ṭôb,* good.]

ma·zer (mā′zər) *n.* A large drinking bowl or goblet made of metal or hard wood. [Middle English, from Old French *masere,* kind of wood, maple burl, of Germanic origin.]

ma·zour·ka (mə-zûr′kə, -zo͝or′-) *n.* Variant of **mazurka.**

ma·zu·ma (mə-zo͞o′mə) *n. Slang.* Money; cash. [Yiddish *mazume, mezumen,* cash, from *binzumen,* in cash, from Medieval

Mayan
Temple pyramid of Quetzalcoatl, Chichén Itzá, Mexico

May apple
Podophyllum peltatum

Maypole
c. 1900

Willie Mays

mazer

Hebrew *bimĕzummān,* in fixed currency, from Mishnaic Hebrew *mĕzummān,* fixed.]

ma·zur·ka also **ma·zour·ka** (mə-zûr′kə, -zo͝or′-) *n.* **1.** A lively Polish dance resembling the polka, frequently adopted as a ballet form. **2.** A piece of music for such a dance, written in 3/4 or 3/8 time with the second beat heavily accented. [Russian, possibly from Polish *(tańczyć) mazurka,* (to dance) the mazurka, accusative of *mazurek,* Mazovian dance from diminutive of *Mazur,* person from Mazovia, a historical region of eastern Poland.]

maz·y (mā′zē) *adj.* **-i·er, -i·est.** Resembling a maze, as in design or complexity; labyrinthine. **—maz′i·ly** *adv.* **—maz′i·ness** *n.*

maz·zard (măz′ərd) *n.* A wild sweet cherry *(Prunus avium)* often used as grafting stock. [Perhaps alteration of Middle English *mazer,* goblet, hard wood. See MAZER.]

Maz·zi·ni (mät-sē′nē), **Giuseppe.** 1805–1872. Italian patriot who spurred the movement for an independent, unified Italy with his political writings.

Paul McCartney
Photographed in 1989

mb *abbr.* Millibar.

MB *abbr.* **1.** Bachelor of medicine. **2.** Manitoba. **3.** Megabyte.

M.B.A. or **MBA** *abbr.* Master of Business Administration.

Mba·bane (əm-bä-bän′, -bä′nē). The capital of Swaziland, in the northwest part of the country. It is a commercial center for an agricultural region. Population, 33,000.

mbd *abbr.* Million barrels per day.

mbi·ra (ĕm-bîr′ə, əm-) *n. Music.* An African instrument consisting of a hollow gourd or wooden resonator and a number of usually metal strips that vibrate when plucked. [Of Bantu origin; akin to Shona *mbira.*]

Mbu·ji Ma·yi (əm-bo͞o′jē mä′yē). A city of south-central Zaire east of Kinshasa. It is a commercial center in a diamond-mining region. Population, 423,363.

Mbun·du (əm-bo͞on′do͞o) *n., pl.* **Mbundu** or **-dus. 1.** A member of a Bantu people inhabiting southern and central Angola. Also called *Ovimbundu.* **2.** The Bantu language of this people. Also called *Umbundu.* **3.** A member of a Bantu people inhabiting northern Angola. Also called *Ndongo.* **4.** The Bantu language of this people. Also called *Kimbundu.*

mc *abbr.* Millicurie.

Mc *abbr.* Megacycle.

MC¹ (ĕm′sē′) *n.* A master of ceremonies.

MC² *abbr.* **1.** Marine Corps. **2.** Medical Corps. **3. M.C.** Member of Congress.

Mc·Al·es·ter (mĭ-kăl′ĭ-stər). A city of southeast Oklahoma southeast of Oklahoma City. Population, 17,255.

Mc·Al·len (mĭ-kăl′ən). A city of southern Texas on the Rio Grande west-northwest of Brownsville. It is a processing and shipping center for a citrus-growing region. Population, 67,042.

MCAT *abbr.* Medical College Admissions Test.

Mc·Car·thy (mə-kär′thē), **Joseph Raymond.** 1908–1957. American politician. A U.S. senator from Wisconsin (1947–1957), he presided over the permanent subcommittee on investigations and held public hearings in which he accused army officials, members of the media, and public figures of being Communists. He was censured by the Senate in 1954.

McCarthy, Mary Therese. 1912–1989. American writer noted for her sharp literary criticism and satirical fiction, including the novels *The Groves of Academe* (1952) and *The Group* (1963).

William McKinley

Mc·Car·thy·ism (mə-kär′thē-ĭz′əm) *n.* **1.** The practice of publicizing accusations of political disloyalty or subversion with insufficient regard to evidence. **2.** The use of unfair investigatory or accusatory methods in order to suppress opposition. [After Joseph Raymond MCCARTHY.] **—Mc·Car′thy·ist** *n.*

Mc·Cart·ney (mə-kärt′nē), **(James) Paul.** Born 1942. British musician who as a member of the Beatles, a popular music group (1960–1971), wrote many notable songs with John Lennon, including *Love Me Do* (1962) and *A Day in the Life* (1967).

Mc·Cau·ley (mə-kô′lē), **Mary Ludwig Hays.** Known as "Molly Pitcher." 1754–1832. American Revolutionary heroine who carried water to the soldiers during the Battle of Monmouth (June 28, 1778) and took over the gun of her husband after he was overcome with heat.

Mc·Clel·lan (mə-klĕl′ən), **George Brinton.** 1826–1885. American general and commander of the Union Army (1861–1862) whose overcautious tactics prompted President Abraham Lincoln to relieve him of duty.

Mc·Clin·tock (mə-klĭn′tək, -tŏk′), **Barbara.** Born 1902. American botanist. She won a 1983 Nobel Prize for discovering that genes are mobile within the chromosomes of a plant cell.

Mc·Clos·key (mə-klŏs-kē), **John.** 1810–1885. American religious leader who became the first American Roman Catholic cardinal (1875).

Mc·Clure (mə-klo͝or′), **Samuel Sidney.** 1857–1949. Irish-born American editor who founded *McClure's Magazine* (1893).

McClure Strait. An arm of the Beaufort Sea in western Northwest Territories, Canada, between Banks Island and Melville Island. Icebreakers cut through the strait for the first time in 1954.

Mc·Cor·mack (mə-kôr′mək, -mĭk), **John.** 1884–1945. Irish-born American operatic tenor whose notable roles included Rodolpho in *La Boheme* and Pinkerton in *Madame Butterfly.*

Mc·Cor·mick (mə-kôr′mĭk), **Anne Elizabeth O'Hare.** 1882–1954. British-born American journalist. A foreign correspondent for the *New York Times* (1922–1954), she was the first woman to receive a Pulitzer Prize for journalism (1937).

McCormick, Cyrus Hall. 1809–1884. American inventor and manufacturer who developed a mechanical harvester (1831).

Mc·Coy (mə-koi′) *n. Informal.* The authentic thing or quality; something that is not an imitation or substitute: *This gem is the real McCoy.* [Origin unknown.]

Mc·Crae (mə-krā′), **John.** 1872–1918. Canadian poet noted for "In Flanders Fields" (1915), which he wrote while serving in France during World War I.

Mc·Cul·lers (mə-kŭl′ərz), **Carson Smith.** 1917–1967. American writer whose novels include *The Heart is a Lonely Hunter* (1940) and *The Member of the Wedding* (1946).

Mc·Dow·ell (mĭk-dou′əl), **Ephraim.** 1771–1830. American surgeon who performed the first recorded ovarian surgery in America (1809).

mcf *abbr.* Thousand cubic feet.

Mc·Gil·li·vray (mə-gĭl′ə-vrā′), **Alexander.** 1759?–1793. Creek leader who sided with the British during the American Revolution, accepted Spanish aid in resisting U.S. expansion, and signed a peace treaty with the United States (1790).

Mc·Gov·ern (mə-gŭv′ərn), **George Stanley.** Born 1922. American politician. A U.S. senator from South Dakota (1963–1981), he opposed the Vietnam War and was defeated as the 1972 Democratic candidate for President.

Mc·Graw (mə-grô′), **John Joseph.** Called "Little Napoleon." 1873–1934. American baseball player (1891–1900) and manager (1902–1932) of the New York Giants, which he led to 2,840 victories, including 10 pennants and 3 World Series championships (1905, 1921, and 1922).

Mc·Guf·fey (mə-gŭf′ē), **William Holmes.** 1800–1873. American educator who compiled the *McGuffey Eclectic Readers* (1836–1857), schoolbooks that combined reading lessons with moralistic teachings.

mCi *abbr.* Millicurie.

Mc·In·tosh (măk′ĭn-tŏsh′) *n.* A variety of red eating apple, grown commercially in the northern United States. [After John *McIntosh* (fl. 1796), Canadian farmer.]

Mc·Kay (mə-kā′), **Claude.** 1890–1948. Jamaican-born American writer who figured prominently in the Harlem Renaissance of the 1920's.

Mc·Kees·port (mĭ-kēz′pôrt′, -pōrt′). A city of southwest Pennsylvania east-southeast of Pittsburgh. Population, 31,012.

Mc·Ken·na (mə-kĕn′ə), **Joseph.** 1843–1926. American jurist who served as an associate justice of the U.S. Supreme Court (1898–1925).

Mc·Kim (mə-kĭm′), **Charles Follen.** 1847–1909. American architect who was a leading proponent of the neoclassic revival. His designs include the Boston Public Library (1887).

Mc·Kin·ley (mə-kĭn′lē), **John.** 1780–1852. American jurist who served as an associate justice of the U.S. Supreme Court (1837–1852).

McKinley, Mount. Also **De·na·li** (də-nä′lē). A peak, 6,197.6 m (20,320 ft) high, in the Alaska Range of south-central Alaska. The highest point in North America, it was first scaled in 1913.

McKinley, William. 1843–1901. The 25th President of the United States (1897–1901). His presidency was marked by the Spanish-American War (1898), the annexation of Cuba and the Philippines, and the passage of the Gold Standard Act (1900). He was assassinated by an anarchist in Buffalo, New York.

Mc·Kin·ney (mə-kĭn′ē). A city of northeast Texas north-northeast of Dallas. Population, 16,249.

M.C.L. *abbr.* **1.** Master of Civil Law. **2.** Master of Comparative Law.

Mc·Lean (mə-klān′, -klēn′). A community of northern Virginia, a suburb in the Washington, D.C., area. Population, 22,000.

Mc·Lean (mə-klēn′), **John.** 1785–1861. American jurist who served as an associate justice of the U.S. Supreme Court (1830–1861).

Mc·Lu·han (mə-klo͞o′ən), **(Herbert) Marshall.** 1911–1980. Canadian cultural critic and communications theorist who maintained that the method of communicating information has more influence on the public than the information itself.

Mc·Mas·ter (mĭk-măs′tər), **John Bach.** 1852–1932. American historian noted for his nine-volume *History of the People of the United States* (1883–1927).

Mc·Mil·lan (mĭk-mĭl′ən), **Edwin Mattison.** 1907–1991. American physicist and chemist. He shared a 1951 Nobel Prize for the discovery of neptunium (1940).

Mc·Mur·do Sound (mĭk-mûr′dō). An inlet of the Ross Sea in Antarctica off the coast of Victoria Land. A U.S. research and exploration base is here.

Mc·Pher·son (mĭk-fûr′sən), **Aimee Semple.** 1890–1944. Canadian-born American evangelist who founded the International Church of the Foursquare Gospel (1927) and was known for her flamboyant preaching and extravagant religious services.

MCP *abbr.* Male chauvinist pig.

MCPO *abbr.* Master chief petty officer.

Mc·Rey·nolds (mĭk-rĕn′əldz), **James Clark.** 1862–1946. American jurist who served as an associate justice of the U.S. Supreme Court (1914–1941).

Md The symbol for the element **mendelevium.**

MD *abbr.* **1.** Also **Md.** Maryland. **2.** Medical department. **3.** Also **M.D.** *Latin.* Medicinae Doctor (Doctor of Medicine). **4.** Muscular dystrophy.

m/d *abbr.* Month after date.

M-day (ĕm′dā′) *n.* The day on which national mobilization for war is ordered; mobilization day.

Mde·wa·kan·ton (əm-dē-wô′kən-tōn′, mĕd′ē-wô′-) *n., pl.* **Mdewakanton** or **-tons. 1.** A Sioux people of the Santee division. **2.** A member of this people.

M.Div. *abbr.* Master of Divinity.

Mdm. *abbr.* Madam.

M.D.S. *abbr.* Master of Dental Surgery.

mdse. *abbr.* Merchandise.

MDT *abbr.* Mountain Daylight Time.

me (mē) *pron.* The objective case of **I. 1.** Used as the direct object of a verb: *He assisted me.* **2.** Used as the indirect object of a verb: *They offered me a ride.* **3.** Used as the object of a preposition: *This letter is addressed to me.* **4.** *Informal.* Used as a predicate nominative: *It's me.* See Usage Notes at **be, but, I¹.** [Middle English, from Old English *mē.* See **me-¹** in Appendix.]

ME *abbr.* **1.** Also **Me.** Maine. **2.a.** Mechanical engineering. **b.** Mechanical engineer. **3.** Medical examiner. **4.** Or **M.E.** Middle English.

me·a cul·pa (mā′ə ko͝ol′pə, mē′ə) *n.* An acknowledgment of a personal error or fault. [Latin *meā culpā,* through my fault : *meā,* feminine ablative of *meus,* my + *culpā,* ablative of *culpa,* fault.]

mead¹ (mēd) *n.* An alcoholic beverage made from fermented honey and water. [Middle English, from Old English *meodu.* See **medhu-** in Appendix.]

mead² (mēd) *n. Archaic.* A meadow. [Middle English *mede,* from Old English *mǣd.* See **mē-⁴** in Appendix.]

Mead (mēd), **George Herbert.** 1863–1931. American philosopher who was a leader of the American pragmatists and contributed greatly to the development of social psychology.

Mead, Lake. A reservoir of southeast Nevada and northwest Arizona formed by Hoover Dam on the Colorado River. It is the center of a large recreational area.

Mead, Margaret. 1901–1978. American anthropologist noted for her landmark studies of adolescence and sexual behavior in primitive cultures.

Meade (mēd), **George Gordon.** 1815–1872. American Union general who commanded the costly victory at Gettysburg (1863).

Meade, James Edward. Born 1907. British economist. He shared a 1977 Nobel Prize for contributions to theories of international trade and finance.

mead·ow (mĕd′ō) *n.* A tract of grassland, either in its natural state or used as pasture or for growing hay. [Middle English *medwe, medoue,* from Old English *mǣdwe,* from *mǣd,* meadow. See **mē-⁴** in Appendix.] **—mead′ow·y** *adj.*

meadow beauty *n.* Any of several North American plants of the genus *Rhexia,* growing in wet ground and having opposite leaves and showy purple flowers. Also called *deer grass.*

meadow fern *n.* See **sweet gale.**

meadow fescue *n.* A grass *(Festuca eliator)* grown for hay.

mead·ow·land (mĕd′ō-lănd′) *n.* A tract of land having the characteristics of or used for a meadow.

mead·ow·lark (mĕd′ō-lärk′) *n.* Any of various songbirds of the genus *Sturnella* of North America, especially *S. magna,* the eastern meadowlark, and *S. neglecta,* the western meadowlark, having brownish plumage, a yellow breast, and a black crescent-shaped marking beneath the throat.

meadow mouse *n.* See **field mouse.**

meadow mushroom *n.* An edible mushroom *(Agaricus campestris)* that thrives in moist soil and is cultivated for food.

meadow nematode *n.* Any of various nematodes of the genus *Pratylenchus* that are parasitic on the roots of plants.

meadow rue *n.* Any of various plants of the genus *Thalictrum,* having compound leaves and clusters of small white, yellowish, or purplish apetalous flowers.

meadow saffron *n.* See **autumn crocus.**

mead·ow·sweet (mĕd′ō-swēt′) *n.* **1.** Either of two North American shrubs *(Spiraea alba* or *S. latifolia)* having umbel-shaped clusters of white flowers. **2.** Any of various perennial herbs of the genus *Filipendula* in the rose family.

mea·ger also **mea·gre** (mē′gər) *adj.* **1.** Deficient in quantity, fullness, or extent; scanty. **2.** Deficient in richness, fertility, or vigor; feeble: *the meager soil of an eroded plain.* **3.** Having little flesh; lean. [Middle English *megre,* thin, from Old French, from Latin *macer.* See **māk-** in Appendix.] **—mea′ger·ly** *adv.* **—mea′ger·ness** *n.*

SYNONYMS: *meager, spare, sparse, skimpy, scanty, scant.* These adjectives mean lacking in quantity, fullness, or extent. *Meager* suggests leanness (*a small, meager woman*); in a less specific sense it implies an insufficiency of what is needed for completeness or richness: *meager fare; meager resources. "The report that first reached us through the newspapers was meager and contradictory"* (Thomas B. Aldrich). *Spare* implies bare sufficiency without excess: *The library had a spare but efficient look about it. The author's style is spare and elegant. Sparse* indicates a lack of density and a thin distribution of units: *a sparse hedge; sparse hair; "a party which as yet was . . . an unorganized mob–thick in one place, sparse in another"* (Walter Besant). *Skimpy* implies inadequacy, as in length or fullness, such as might result from frugality or stinginess: *a skimpy dress; a skimpy allowance. The skimpy rug barely covers the floor. Scanty* implies a lack of sufficiency, as in extent, quantity, or degree: *His knowledge of mathematics is superficial and scanty. The farmer's financial difficulties were caused by a scanty harvest. Scant* applies to what is barely enough (*gave us scant respect*) or to what falls short of an expected or desired amount (*The movers gave me a scant hour's notice of their arrival*).

meal¹ (mēl) *n.* **1.** The edible whole or coarsely ground grains of a cereal grass. **2.** A granular substance produced by grinding. [Middle English *mele,* from Old English *melu.* See **melə-** in Appendix.]

meal² (mēl) *n.* **1.** The food served and eaten in one sitting. **2.** A customary time or occasion of eating food. [Middle English *mele,* from Old English *mǣl.* See **mē-²** in Appendix.]

meal·ie (mē′lē) *n. South African.* **1.** An ear of corn. **2. mealies.** Corn; maize. [Afrikaans *mielie,* from Portuguese *milho,* millet, from Latin *milium.* See **melə-** in Appendix.]

meal ticket *n.* **1.** A card or ticket entitling the holder to a meal or meals. **2.** *Informal.* A person or thing depended on as a source of financial support.

meal·time (mēl′tīm′) *n.* The usual time for eating a meal.

meal·worm (mēl′wûrm′) *n.* The larva of various beetles of the genus *Tenebrio* that infest flour and other grain products and are often raised for bird feed.

meal·y (mē′lē) *adj.* **-i·er, -i·est. 1.** Resembling meal in texture or consistency; granular: *mealy potatoes.* **2.a.** Made of or containing meal. **b.** Sprinkled or covered with meal or a similar granular substance. **3.** Flecked with spots; mottled. **4.** Lacking healthy coloring; pale: *"I only know two sorts of boys. Mealy boys, and beef-faced boys"* (Charles Dickens). **5.** Mealy-mouthed. **—meal′i·ness** *n.*

meal·y·bug (mē′lē-bŭg′) *n.* Any of various homopterous insects, especially of the family Pseudococcidae, some of which are destructive to citrus trees and other plants. [So called because it is covered with a white powdery substance.]

meal·y-mouthed (mē′lē-mouthd′, -moutht′) *adj.* Unwilling to state facts or opinions simply and directly.

WORD HISTORY: One does not hear the word *mealy-mouthed* today as much as one could, since the unwillingness to state facts or opinions directly seems a perennial condition of leaders and their underlings in all walks of life. It would be singularly appropriate if a man who was noted for not being mealy-mouthed had helped give us this word. The term does perhaps come to us from an expression such as German *Mehl im Maule behalten,* "to carry meal in the mouth, that is, not to be direct in speech." The expression occurs in the writings of Martin Luther, who was willing to speak his mind. In English we find recorded the terms *mealmouth* (1546) and *meal-mouthed* (1576) around the same time that we find *mealymouthed* (around 1572), but only *mealy-mouthed* has survived, fortunately for us, as it seems there will always be a need for it.

mean¹ (mēn) *v.* **meant** (mĕnt), **mean·ing, means.** *—tr.* **1.a.** To be used to convey; denote: *"'The question is,' said Alice, 'whether you can make words mean so many different things'"* (Lewis Carroll). **b.** To act as a symbol of; signify or represent: *In this poem, the budding flower means youth.* **2.** To intend to convey or indicate: *"No one means all he says, and yet very few say all they mean, for words are slippery and thought is viscous"* (Henry Adams). **3.** To have as a purpose or an intention; intend: *I meant to go running this morning, but I overslept.* **4.** To design, intend, or destine for a certain purpose or end: *a building that was meant for storage; a student who was meant to be a scientist.* **5.** To have as a consequence; bring about: *Friction means heat.* **6.** To have the importance or value of: *The opinions of the critics meant nothing to him. She meant so much to me. —intr.* To have intentions of a specified kind; be disposed: *She means well, despite her blunders.* ***—idiom.*** **mean business.** *Informal.* To be in earnest. [Middle English *menen,* from Old English *mǣnan,* to tell of. See **mei-no-** in Appendix.]

SYNONYMS: *mean, denote, import, signify.* The central meaning shared by these verbs is "to convey a particular idea": *what does the word serendipity mean? The prefix* pro- *may denote "earlier" or "anterior." Philadelphia is the city of brotherly love; that is what its name imports. A crown signifies royal power.*

mean² (mēn) *adj.* **mean·er, mean·est. 1.a.** Selfish in a petty way; unkind. **b.** Cruel, spiteful, or malicious. **2.** Ignoble; base: *a mean motive.* **3.** Miserly; stingy. **4.a.** Low in quality or grade; inferior. **b.** Low in value or amount; paltry: *paid no mean amount for the new shoes.* **5.** Common or poor in appearance; shabby: *"The rowhouses had been darkened by the rain and looked meaner and grimmer than ever"* (Anne Tyler). **6.** Low in social status; of humble origins. **7.** Humiliated or ashamed. **8.** In poor physical condition; sick or debilitated. **9.** Extremely unpleasant or disagreeable: *The meanest storm in years.* **10.** *Informal.* Ill-tempered. **11.** *Slang.* **a.** Hard to cope with; difficult or troublesome: *He throws a mean fast ball.* **b.** Excellent; skillful:

Margaret Mead

meadowlark
Western meadowlark
Sturnella neglecta

ă pat	oi boy
ā pay	ou out
âr care	o͝o took
ä father	o͞o boot
ĕ pet	ŭ cut
ē be	ûr urge
ĭ pit	th thin
ī pie	*th* this
îr pier	hw which
ŏ pot	zh vision
ō toe	ə about, item
ô paw	♦ regionalism

Stress marks: **′** (primary); ′ (secondary), as in **dictionary** (dĭk′shə-nĕr′ē)

She plays a mean game of bridge. [Middle English, from Old English *gemǣne,* common. See **mei-¹** in Appendix.] **—mean′ly** *adv.*

SYNONYMS: *mean, low, base, abject, ignoble, sordid.* These adjectives mean lacking in the elevation or dignity or falling short of the standards befitting human beings. *Mean* suggests pettiness; it may also connote traits such as spite or niggardliness: *"chok'd with ambition of the meaner sort"* (Shakespeare). *"Never ascribe to an opponent motives meaner than your own"* (J.M. Barrie). Something *low* violates standards of morality, ethics, or propriety: *low cunning; a low trick. Base* suggests a contemptible, mean-spirited, or selfish lack of human decency: *"that liberal obedience, without which your army would be a base rabble"* (Edmund Burke). *Abject* means brought low in condition; it often indicates starkness or hopelessness: *abject submission; abject poverty. Ignoble* means lacking those qualities, such as elevated moral character, that give human beings distinction of mind and soul: *"For my part I think it a less evil that some criminals should escape than that the government should play an ignoble part"* (Oliver Wendell Holmes, Jr.). *Sordid* suggests foul, repulsive degradation: *"It is through art . . . that we can shield ourselves from the sordid perils of actual existence"* (Oscar Wilde).

meander
White River, South Dakota

mean³ (mēn) *n.* **1.** Something having a position, quality, or condition midway between extremes; a medium. **2.** *Mathematics.* **a.** A number that typifies a set of numbers, such as a geometric mean or an arithmetic mean. **b.** The average value of a set of numbers. **3.** *Logic.* The middle term in a syllogism. **4. means** *(used with a sing. or pl. verb).* A method, a course of action, or an instrument by which an act can be accomplished or an end achieved. **5. means** *(used with a pl. verb).* **a.** Money, property, or other wealth: *You ought to live within your means.* **b.** Great wealth: *a woman of means.* **—mean** *adj.* **1.** Occupying a middle or intermediate position between two extremes. **2.** Intermediate in size, extent, quality, time, or degree; medium. ***—idioms.*** **by all means.** Without fail; certainly. **by any means.** In any way possible; in any case: *not by any means an easy opponent.* **by means of.** With the use of; owing to: *They succeeded by means of patience and sacrifice.* **by no means.** In no sense; certainly not: *This remark by no means should be taken lightly.* [Middle English *mene,* middle, from Old French *meien,* from Latin *mediānus,* from *medius.* See **medhyo-** in Appendix.]

USAGE NOTE: In the sense of "financial resources" *means* takes a plural verb: *His means are more than adequate.* In the sense of "a way to an end" *means* may be treated as either a singular or plural. It is singular when referring to a particular strategy or method: *The best means of securing the cooperation of the builders is to appeal to their self-interest.* It is plural when it refers to a group of strategies or methods: *The most effective means for dealing with the drug problem have generally been those suggested by the affected communities.* • *Means* is most often followed by *of: a means of noise reduction.* But *for, to,* and *toward* are also used: *a means for transmitting signals; a means to an end; a means toward achieving social equality.*

mean calorie *n.* See **calorie** (sense 2).

me·an·der (mē-ăn′dər) *intr.v.* **-dered, -der·ing, -ders. 1.** To follow a winding and turning course: *Streams tend to meander through level land.* **2.** To move aimlessly and idly without fixed direction: *vagabonds meandering through life.* See Synonyms at **wander. —meander** *n.* **1. meanders.** Circuitous windings or sinuosities, as of a stream or path. **2.** Often **meanders.** A circuitous journey or excursion; ramble. **3.** The Greek fret or key pattern, used in art and architecture. [From Latin *maeander,* circuitous windings, from Greek *maiandros,* after the MAEANDER River in Phrygia.] **—me·an′der·er** *n.* **—me·an′der·ing·ly** *adv.* **—me·an′drous** (-drəs) *adj.*

mean deviation *n.* In a statistical distribution, the average of the absolute values of the differences between individual numbers and their mean.

mean·ie (mē′nē) *n. Informal.* A malicious or petty person.

mean·ing (mē′nĭng) *n.* **1.** Something that is conveyed or signified; sense or significance. **2.** Something that one wishes to convey, especially by language: *The writer's meaning was obscured by his convoluted prose.* **3.** An interpreted goal, intent, or end: *"The central meaning of his pontificate is to restore papal authority"* (Conor Cruise O'Brien). **4.** Inner significance: *"But who can comprehend the meaning of the voice of the city?"* (O. Henry). **—meaning** *adj.* **1.** Full of meaning; expressive. **2.** Disposed or intended in a specified manner. Often used in combination: *a well-meaning fellow; ill-meaning intentions.*

measure
From "Roses of the South," a waltz by Johann Strauss the Younger

SYNONYMS: *meaning, acceptation, import, sense, significance, signification.* The central meaning shared by these nouns is "the idea that is conveyed by something, such as a word, an action, a gesture, or a situation": *Synonyms are words that have the same or approximately the same meaning. In one of its acceptations value is a technical term in music. The import of his statement is ambiguous. The term* anthropomorphism *has only one sense. The significance of a green traffic light is generally understood. Scientists have been unable to determine the signification of most Etruscan inscriptions.*

mean·ing·ful (mē′nĭng-fəl) *adj.* **1.** Having meaning, function, or purpose. **2.** Fraught with meaning; significant: *A meaningful glance.* See Synonyms at **expressive. —mean′ing·ful·ly** *adv.* **—mean′ing·ful·ness** *n.*

mean·ing·less (mē′nĭng-lĭs) *adj.* Having no meaning or significance. **—mean′ing·less·ly** *adv.* **—mean′ing·less·ness** *n.*

SYNONYMS: *meaningless, senseless, mindless, irrational, pointless, purposeless.* These adjectives mean lacking import, direction, or purpose. *Meaningless* and *senseless* emphasize absence of meaning, significance, or motivation: *a verbose but meaningless explanation; senseless violence. Mindless* applies to that which lacks the will and thinking capacity characteristic of a conscious being: *"the shrieking of the mindless wind"* (John Greenleaf Whittier). *"We must dare to think about 'unthinkable things' because when things become unthinkable, thinking stops and action becomes mindless"* (J. William Fulbright). *Irrational* implies a lack of accord with or a lack of reason or sound judgment: *"It is the function of speech to free men from the bondage of irrational fears"* (Louis D. Brandeis). *Pointless* and *purposeless* stress the absence of an aim or end: *The host bored his guests with a long and pointless anecdote. She feels that her life is purposeless and empty.*

mean·ly (mēn′lē) *adv.* In a poor, lowly, or base manner.

mean·ness (mēn′nĭs) *n.* **1.** The state of being inferior in quality, character, or value; commonness. **2.** The quality or state of being selfish or stingy. **3.** A spiteful or malicious act.

mean solar day *n.* The period of time between two successive transits of the mean sun; the standard for the 24-hour day measured from midnight to midnight.

mean-spir·it·ed or **mean spir·it·ed** (mēn′spĭr′ĭ-tĭd) *adj.* Having or characterized by a malicious or petty spirit. **—mean′-spir′it·ed·ly** *adv.* **—mean′-spir′it·ed·ness** *n.*

mean square *n. Mathematics.* The average of the squares of a set of numbers.

means test (mēnz) *n.* An investigation into the financial well-being of a person to determine the person's eligibility for financial assistance.

mean sun *n.* A hypothetical sun defined as moving at a uniform rate along the celestial equator at the mean speed with which the real sun apparently moves along the ecliptic, used in computing the mean solar day.

meant (mĕnt) *v.* Past tense and past participle of **mean¹.**

mean·time (mēn′tīm′) *n.* The time between one occurrence and another; an interval. **—meantime** *adv.* During a period of intervening time; meanwhile.

USAGE NOTE: *Meantime* is more common than *meanwhile* as a noun: *In the meantime we waited.* As an adverb *meantime* is less common than *meanwhile: Meanwhile we waited.* All of these uses are standard, however.

mean time *n.* Time measured with reference to the mean sun, giving equal 24-hour days throughout the year.

mean·while (mēn′hwīl′, -wīl′) *n.* The intervening time. **—meanwhile** *adv.* **1.** During or in the intervening time: *Meanwhile, life goes on.* **2.** At the same time: *The court is deliberating; meanwhile, we must be patient.* See Usage Note at **meantime.**

Mea·ny (mē′nē), **George.** 1894–1980. American labor leader who exerted great political influence as the first president of the American Federation of Labor and the Congress of Industrial Organizations (1955–1979).

meas. *abbr.* Measurable; measure.

mea·sles (mē′zəlz) *n. (used with a sing. or pl. verb).* **1. a.** An acute, contagious viral disease, usually occurring in childhood and characterized by eruption of red spots on the skin, fever, and catarrhal symptoms. Also called *rubeola.* **b.** Black measles. **c.** Any of several other diseases, especially German measles, that cause similar but milder symptoms. **2.** A disease of cattle and swine caused by tapeworm larvae. **3.** A plant disease, usually caused by fungi, that produces minute spots on leaves and stems. [Middle English *maseles, mesels,* pl. of *masel,* measles-spot, of Middle Low German origin.]

mea·sly (mēz′lē) *adj.* **-sli·er, -sli·est. 1.** *Slang.* Contemptibly small; meager: *gave the parking attendant a measly tip.* **2.** Infected with measles.

meas·ur·a·ble (mĕzh′ər-ə-bəl) *adj. Abbr.* **meas. 1.** Possible to be measured: *measurable depths.* **2.** Of distinguished importance; significant: *a measurable figure in literature.* **—meas′ur·a·bil′i·ty** *n.* **—meas′ur·a·bly** *adv.*

meas·ure (mĕzh′ər) *n. Abbr.* **meas. 1.** Dimensions, quantity, or capacity as ascertained by comparison with a standard. **2.** A reference standard or sample used for the quantitative comparison of properties: *The standard kilogram is maintained as a measure of mass.* **3.** A unit specified by a scale, such as an inch, or by variable conditions, such as a day's march. **4.** A system of measurement, such as the metric system. **5.** A device used for measuring. **6.** The act of measuring. **7.** An evaluation or a basis of comparison: *"the final measure of the worth of a society"* (Joseph Wood Krutch). See Synonyms at **standard. 8.** Extent or degree: *The problem was in large measure caused by his carelessness.* **9.** A definite quantity that has been measured out: *a measure of wine.* **10.** A fitting amount: *a measure of recognition.* **11.** A limited amount or degree: *a measure of good-will.* **12.** Limit; bounds: *generosity knowing no measure.* **13.** Appropriate restraint; moderation: *"The union of . . . fervor with measure, passion with correctness, this surely is the ideal"* (William James). **14.** Often **measures.** An action taken as a means to an end; an expedient: *desperate measures.* **15.** A legislative bill or enactment. **16.** Poetic meter. **17.** *Music.* The metric unit between two bars on the staff; a bar. **—measure** *v.* **-ured, -ur·ing, -ures.** *—tr.* **1.** To ascertain the dimensions, quantity, or capacity of: *measured the height of the ceiling.* **2.** To mark, lay out, or establish dimensions for by measuring: *measure off an area.* **3.** To estimate by evaluation or comparison: *"I gave them an account . . . of the situation as far as I could measure it"* (Winston S. Churchill). **4.** To bring into comparison: *She measured her power with that of a dangerous adversary.* **5.a.** To mark off or apportion, usually with reference to a given unit of measurement: *measure out a pint of milk.* **b.** To allot or distribute as if by measuring; mete: *The revolutionary tribunal measured out harsh justice.* **6.** To serve as a measure of: *The inch measures length.* **7.** To consider or choose with care; weigh: *He measures his words with caution.* **8.** *Archaic.* To travel over: *"We must measure twenty miles today"* (Shakespeare). *—intr.* **1.** To have a measurement of: *The room measures 12 by 20 feet.* **2.** To take a measurement. **3.** To allow of measurement: *White sugar measures more easily than brown.* ***—phrasal verb.*** **measure up. 1.** To be the equal of. **2.** To have the necessary qualifications: *a candidate who just didn't measure up.* ***—idioms.*** **beyond measure. 1.** In excess. **2.** Without limit. **for good measure.** In addition to the required amount. **in a** (or **some**) **measure.** To a degree: *The new law was in a measure harmful.* [Middle English, from Old French *mesure,* from Latin *mēnsūra,* from *mēnsus,* past participle of *mētīrī,* to measure. See **mē-[2]** in Appendix.] **—meas′ur·er** *n.*

meas·ured (mĕzh′ərd) *adj.* **1.** Determined by measurement: *The measured distance was less than a mile.* **2.** Careful; restrained: *spoke in measured words.* **3.** Calculated; deliberate: *with measured irony.* **4.** Regular in rhythm and number: *"A clock struck slowly in the house with a measured, solemn chime"* (Thomas Wolfe). **5.** Slow and stately. **6.** Written in meter. **7.** *Music.* Mensural. **—meas′ured·ly** *adv.* **—meas′ured·ness** *n.*

meas·ure·less (mĕzh′ər-lĭs) *adj.* Too great to be measured; immeasurable: *measureless happiness.* See Synonyms at **incalculable. —meas′ure·less·ly** *adv.* **—meas′ure·less·ness** *n.*

meas·ure·ment (mĕzh′ər-mənt) *n.* **1.** The act of measuring or the process of being measured. **2.** A system of measuring: *measurement in miles.* **3.** The dimension, quantity, or capacity determined by measuring: *the measurements of a room.*

meas·ur·ing worm (mĕzh′ə-rĭng) *n.* A geometrid caterpillar that moves in alternate contractions and expansions suggestive of measuring. Also called *inchworm, looper, spanworm.*

meat (mēt) *n.* **1.** The edible flesh of animals, especially that of mammals as opposed to that of fish or poultry. **2.** The edible part, as a piece of fruit or a nut. **3.** The essence, substance, or gist: *the meat of the editorial.* **4.** *Slang.* Something that one enjoys or excels in; a forte: *Tennis is his meat.* **5.** Nourishment; food: *"Love is not all: it is not meat nor drink"* (Edna St. Vincent Millay). *—attributive.* Often used to modify another noun: *meat products; a meat market.* [Middle English *mete,* from Old English, food.]

meat and potatoes *pl.n.* *(used with a sing. or pl. verb). Informal.* The fundamental parts or part; the basis.

meat-and-po·ta·toes (mēt′n-pə-tā′tōz, -təz) *adj. Informal.* Fundamental; basic.

meat·ball (mēt′bôl′) *n.* **1.** A small ball of ground meat variously seasoned and cooked. **2.** *Slang.* A stupid, clumsy, or dull person.

meat·head (mēt′hĕd′) *n.* *Slang.* A stupid or dull person.

meat hook *n.* **1.** A hook used to hang the carcasses of slaughtered animals or large pieces of meat. **2. meat hooks.** *Slang.* The hands or fists.

meat·less (mēt′lĭs) *adj.* **1.** Lacking meat. **2.** Being or relating to a time when meat is not to be eaten: *meatless days.*

meat loaf or **meat·loaf** (mēt′lōf′) *n.* A mounded or molded dish, usually baked, of ground beef or a combination of various meats and other ingredients.

meat·pack·ing (mēt′păk′ĭng) *n.* The business or activity of slaughtering animals and preparing the meat for sale. **—meat′pack·er** *n.*

me·a·tus (mē-ā′təs) *n., pl.* **-tus·es** or **meatus.** A body opening or passage, such as the opening of the ear or the urethral canal. [Latin *meātus,* passage, from past participle of *meāre,* to pass. See **mei-[1]** in Appendix.]

meat·y (mē′tē) *adj.* **-i·er, -i·est. 1.a.** Of or relating to meat. **b.** Having the flavor or smell of meat. **c.** Full of or containing meat. **2.** Heavily fleshed. **3.** Prompting considerable thought: *a meaty theme for study and debate.* **—meat′i·ness** *n.*

mec·ca (mĕk′ə) *n.* **1.a.** A place that is regarded as the center of an activity or interest. **b.** A goal to which adherents of a religious faith or practice fervently aspire. **2.** A place visited by many people: *a mecca for tourists.* [After MECCA (from its being a place of pilgrimage).]

Mec·ca (mĕk′ə). A city of western Saudi Arabia near the coast of the Red Sea. The birthplace of Mohammed, it is the holiest city of Islam and a pilgrimage site for all devout believers of the faith. Population, 550,000.

mech. *abbr.* **1.** Mechanical; mechanics. **2.** Mechanism.

mechan– *pref.* Variant of **mechano–.**

me·chan·ic (mĭ-kăn′ĭk) *n.* A worker skilled in making, using, or repairing machines, vehicles, and tools. [From Middle English, mechanical, from Old French *mecanique,* from Latin *mēchanicus,* from Greek *mēkhanikos,* from *mēkhanē,* machine, device. See **magh-** in Appendix.] **—me·chan′ic** *adj.*

me·chan·i·cal (mĭ-kăn′ĭ-kəl) *adj. Abbr.* **mech. 1.** Of or relating to machines or tools: *mechanical skill.* **2.** Operated or produced by a mechanism or machine: *a mechanical toy dog.* **3.** Of, relating to, or governed by mechanics. **4.** Performed or performing in an impersonal or machinelike manner; automatic: *a droning, mechanical delivery of the speech.* **5.** Relating to, produced by, or dominated by physical forces: *the mechanical aspect of trumpet playing.* **6.** *Philosophy.* Interpreting and explaining the phenomena of the universe by referring to causally determined material forces; mechanistic. **7.** Of or relating to manual labor, its tools, and its skills. **—mechanical** *n.* *Printing.* A layout consisting of type proofs, artwork, or both, exactly positioned and prepared for making an offset or other printing plate. **—me·chan′i·cal·ly** *adv.* **—me·chan′i·cal·ness** *n.*

mechanical advantage *n.* The ratio of the output force produced by a machine to the applied input force.

mechanical drawing *n.* **1.** Drafting. **2.** A drawing, such as an architect's plans, that enables measurements to be interpreted.

mechanical engineering *n. Abbr.* **ME** The branch of engineering that encompasses the generation and application of heat and mechanical power and the design, production, and use of machines and tools. **—mechanical engineer** *n.*

me·chan·ics (mĭ-kăn′ĭks) *n. Abbr.* **mech. 1.** *(used with a sing. verb).* The branch of physics that is concerned with the analysis of the action of forces on matter or material systems. **2.** *(used with a sing. or pl. verb).* Design, construction, and use of machinery or mechanical structures. **3.** *(used with a pl. verb).* The functional and technical aspects of an activity: *The mechanics of football are learned with practice.*

mech·a·nism (mĕk′ə-nĭz′əm) *n. Abbr.* **mech. 1.a.** A machine or mechanical appliance. **b.** The arrangement of connected parts in a machine. **2.** A system of parts that operate or interact like those of a machine: *the mechanism of the solar system.* **3.** An instrument or a process, physical or mental, by which something is done or comes into being: *"The mechanism of oral learning is largely that of continuous repetition"* (T.G.E. Powell). **4.** A habitual manner of acting to achieve an end. **5.** *Biology.* The involuntary and consistent response of an organism to a given stimulus. **6.** *Psychology.* A usually unconscious mental and emotional pattern that dominates behavior in a given situation or environment: *a defense mechanism.* **7.** The sequence of steps in a chemical reaction. **8.** *Philosophy.* The doctrine that all natural phenomena are explicable by material causes and mechanical principles. [New Latin *mēchanismus,* from Late Latin *mēchanisma,* from Greek *mēkhanē,* machine. See MECHANIC.]

mech·a·nist (mĕk′ə-nĭst) *n.* *Philosophy.* One who believes in the doctrine of mechanism.

mech·a·nis·tic (mĕk′ə-nĭs′tĭk) *adj.* **1.** Mechanically determined. **2.** *Philosophy.* Of or relating to the philosophy of mechanism, especially tending to explain phenomena only by reference to physical or biological causes. **3.** Automatic and impersonal; mechanical. **—mech′a·nis′ti·cal·ly** *adv.*

mech·a·nize (mĕk′ə-nīz′) *tr.v.* **-nized, -niz·ing, -niz·es. 1.** To equip with machinery: *mechanize a factory.* **2.** To equip (a military unit) with motor vehicles, such as tanks and trucks. **3.** To make automatic or unspontaneous; render routine or monotonous. **4.** To produce by or as if by machines. **—mech′a·ni·za′tion** (-nĭ-zā′shən) *n.* **—mech′a·niz′er** *n.*

mechano– or **mechan–** *pref.* **1.** Machine; machinery: *mechanize.* **2.** Mechanical: *mechanotherapy.* [Greek *mēkhano-,* from *mēkhanē,* machine. See MACHINE.]

mech·a·no·chem·i·cal (mĕk′ə-nō-kĕm′ĭ-kəl) *adj.* Of or relating to conversion of chemical energy into mechanical work.

mech·a·no·re·cep·tor (mĕk′ə-nō-rĭ-sĕp′tər) *n.* *Physiology.* A specialized sensory end organ that responds to mechanical stimuli such as tension, pressure, or displacement. **—mech′a·no·re·cep′tion** *n.* **—mech′a·no·re·cep′tive** *adj.*

mech·a·no·ther·a·py (mĕk′ə-nō-thĕr′ə-pē) *n., pl.* **-pies.** Medical treatment by mechanical methods, such as massage. **—mech′a·no·ther′a·pist** *n.*

Mech·lin[1] (mĕk′lĭn) also **Mech·e·len** (mĕk′ə-lən, mĕkн′-) or **Ma·lines** (mə-lēnz′, mä-lēn′). A city of north-central Belgium north-northeast of Brussels. Founded in the early Middle Ages, it enjoyed its greatest prosperity during the 15th and early 16th centuries. Population, 77,010.

Mech·lin[2] (mĕk′lĭn) *n.* A lace in which the pattern details are defined by a flat thread. Also called *malines.* [After MECHLIN[1].]

Meck·len·burg (mĕk′lən-bûrg′, -bŏŏrk′). A historical region of northeast Germany on the Baltic Sea. It was originally occupied c. sixth century A.D. by Slavic peoples who were then displaced by Germanic settlements. After 1621 Mecklenburg was divided into two duchies, which joined the German Confederation in 1867.

mec·li·zine (mĕk′lĭ-zēn′) *n.* A whitish crystalline powder, $C_{25}H_{27}ClN_2$, used to treat nausea and motion sickness. [ME(TH-YLBENZENE) + C(H)L(ORO–) + (PIPERA)ZINE.]

me·co·ni·um (mĭ-kō′nē-əm) *n.* A dark green fecal material that accumulates in the fetal intestines and is discharged at or

Mecca
In the courtyard of the Great Mosque

ă pat	oi boy
ā pay	ou out
âr care	ŏŏ took
ä father	ōō boot
ĕ pet	ŭ cut
ē be	ûr urge
ĭ pit	th thin
ī pie	*th* this
îr pier	hw which
ŏ pot	zh vision
ō toe	ə about, item
ô paw	♦ regionalism

Stress marks: **′** (primary); **′** (secondary), as in **dictionary** (dĭk′shə-nĕr′ē)

CONVERSION BETWEEN METRIC AND U.S. CUSTOMARY UNITS

FROM U.S. CUSTOMARY TO METRIC

WHEN YOU KNOW	MULTIPLY BY	TO FIND
inches	25.4	millimeters
	2.54	centimeters
feet	30.48	centimeters
yards	0.91	meters
miles	1.61	kilometers
teaspoons	4.93	milliliters
tablespoons	14.79	milliliters
fluid ounces	29.57	milliliters
cups	0.24	liters
pints	0.47	liters
quarts	0.95	liters
gallons	3.79	liters
cubic feet	0.028	cubic meters
cubic yards	0.76	cubic meters
ounces	28.35	grams
pounds	0.45	kilograms
short tons (2,000 lbs)	0.91	metric tons
square inches	6.45	square centimeters
square feet	0.09	square meters
square yards	0.84	square meters
square miles	2.60	square kilometers
acres	0.40	hectares

FROM METRIC TO U.S. CUSTOMARY

WHEN YOU KNOW	MULTIPLY BY	TO FIND
millimeters	0.04	inches
centimeters	0.39	inches
meters	3.28	feet
	1.09	yards
kilometers	0.62	miles
milliliters	0.20	teaspoons
	0.06	tablespoons
	0.03	fluid ounces
liters	1.06	quarts
	0.26	gallons
	4.23	cups
	2.12	pints
cubic meters	35.32	cubic feet
	1.35	cubic yards
grams	0.035	ounces
kilograms	2.21	pounds
metric ton (1,000 kg)	1.10	short ton
square centimeters	0.16	square inches
square meters	1.20	square yards
square kilometers	0.39	square miles
hectares	2.47	acres

TEMPERATURE CONVERSION BETWEEN CELSIUS AND FAHRENHEIT

°C = (°F − 32) ÷ 1.8

CONDITION	FAHRENHEIT	CELSIUS
Boiling point of water	212°	100°
A very hot day	104°	40°
Normal body temperature	98.6°	37°
A warm day	86°	30°
A mild day	68°	20°

°F = (°C × 1.8) + 32

CONDITION	FAHRENHEIT	CELSIUS
A cool day	50°	10°
Freezing point of water	32°	0°
Lowest temperature Gabriel Fahrenheit could obtain by mixing salt and ice	0°	−17.8°

U.S. CUSTOMARY SYSTEM

UNIT	RELATION TO OTHER U.S. CUSTOMARY UNITS	METRIC EQUIVALENT
LENGTH		
inch	1/12 foot	2.54 centimeters
foot	12 inches or 1/3 yard	0.3048 meter
yard	36 inches or 3 feet	0.9144 meter
rod	16½ feet or 5½ yards	5.0292 meters
furlong	220 yards or 1/8 mile	0.2012 kilometer
mile (statute)	5,280 feet or 1,760 yards	1.6093 kilometers
mile (nautical)	6,076 feet or 2,025 yards	1.852 kilometers
VOLUME OR CAPACITY (LIQUID MEASURE)		
ounce	1/16 pint	29.574 milliliters
gill	4 ounces	0.1183 liter
pint	16 ounces	0.4732 liter
quart	2 pints or ¼ gallon	0.9463 liter
gallon	128 ounces or 8 pints	3.7853 liters
barrel		
(wine)	31½ gallons	119.24 liters
(beer)	36 gallons	136.27 liters
(oil)	42 gallons	158.98 liters
VOLUME OR CAPACITY (DRY MEASURE)		
pint	½ quart	0.5506 liter
quart	2 pints	1.1012 liters
peck	8 quarts or ¼ bushel	8.8098 liters
bucket	2 pecks	17.620 liters
bushel	2 buckets or 4 pecks	35.239 liters
WEIGHT		
grain	1/7000 pound	64.799 milligrams
dram	1/16 ounce	1.7718 grams
ounce	16 drams	28.350 grams
pound	16 ounces	453.6 grams
ton (short)	2,000 pounds	907.18 kilograms
ton (long)	2,240 pounds	1,016.0 kilograms
GEOGRAPHIC AREA		
acre	4,840 square yards	4,047 square meters

COOKING MEASURES

UNIT	RELATION TO OTHER COOKING MEASURES	CONVERSION TO METRIC UNITS
drop	1/76 teaspoon	0.0649 milliliter
teaspoon	76 drops or 1/3 tablespoon	4.9288 milliliters
tablespoon	3 teaspoons	14.786 milliliters
cup	16 tablespoons or ½ pint	0.2366 liter
pint	2 cups	0.4732 liters
quart	4 cups or 2 pints	0.9463 liter

BRITISH IMPERIAL SYSTEM

UNIT	RELATION TO OTHER BRITISH IMPERIAL UNITS	CONVERSION TO U.S. CUSTOMARY UNITS	CONVERSION TO METRIC UNITS
VOLUME OR CAPACITY (LIQUID MEASURE)			
pint	½ quart	1.201 pints	0.5683 liter
quart	2 pints ¼ gallon	1.201 quarts	1.137 liters
gallon	8 pints 4 quarts	1.201 gallons	4.546 liters
VOLUME OR CAPACITY (DRY MEASURE)			
peck	¼ bushel	1.0314 pecks	9.087 liters
bushel	4 pecks	1.0320 bushels	36.369 liters

APOTHECARY WEIGHTS

UNIT	RELATION TO OTHER APOTHECARY UNITS	CONVERSION TO U.S. CUSTOMARY UNITS	CONVERSION TO METRIC UNITS
grain	1/60 dram 1/5760 pound	equal to the U.S. Customary grain	64.799 milligrams
dram	60 grains 1/8 ounce	2.1943 drams	3.8879 grams
ounce	8 drams	1.0971 ounces	31.1035 grams
pound	12 ounces 96 drams	0.8232 pound	373.242 grams

UNITS OF THE INTERNATIONAL SYSTEM

The **International System** (abbreviated **SI,** for Systeme International, the French name for the system) was adopted in 1960 by the 11th General Conference on Weights and Measures. An expanded and modified version of the metric system, the International System addresses the needs of modern science for additional and more accurate units of measurement. The key features of the International System are decimalization, a system of prefixes, and a standard defined in terms of an invariable physical measure.

BASE UNITS

The International System has base units from which all others in the system are derived. The standards for the base units, except for the kilogram, are defined by unchanging and reproducible physical occurrences. For example, the meter is defined as the distance traveled by light in a vacuum in 1/299,792,458 of a second. The standard for the kilogram is a platinum-iridium cylinder kept at the International Bureau of Weights and Standards in Sèvres, France.

UNIT	QUANTITY	SYMBOL
meter	length	m
kilogram	mass	kg
second	time	s
ampere	electric current	A
kelvin	temperature	K
mole	amount of matter	mol
candela	luminous intensity	cd

SUPPLEMENTARY UNITS

The International System uses two supplementary units that are based on abstract geometrical concepts rather than physical standards.

UNIT	QUANTITY	SYMBOL
radian	plane angles	rad
steradian	solid angles	sr

PREFIXES

A multiple of a unit in the International System is formed by adding a prefix to the name of that unit. The prefixes change the magnitude of the unit by orders of ten from 10^{18} to 10^{-18}.

PREFIX	SYMBOL	MULTIPLYING FACTOR
exa-	E	10^{18} = 1,000,000,000,000,000,000
peta-	P	10^{15} = 1,000,000,000,000,000
tera-	T	10^{12} = 1,000,000,000,000
giga-	G	10^{9} = 1,000,000,000
mega-	M	10^{6} = 1,000,000
kilo-	K	10^{3} = 1,000
hecto-	h	10^{2} = 100
deca-	da	10 = 10
deci-	d	10^{-1} = 0.1
centi-	c	10^{-2} = 0.01
milli-	m	10^{-3} = 0.001
micro-	μ	10^{-6} = 0.000,001
nano-	n	10^{-9} = 0.000,000,001
pico-	p	10^{-12} = 0.000,000,000,001
femto-	f	10^{-15} = 0.000,000,000,000,001
atto-	a	10^{-18} = 0.000,000,000,000,000,001

ADDITIONAL UNITS

Listed below are a few of the non-SI units that are commonly used with the International System.

UNIT	QUANTITY	SYMBOL
angstrom (= 10^{-10}m)	length	Å
electron-volt (= 0.160 aJ)	energy	eV
hectare (= 10,000 m^2)	land area	ha
liter (= 1.0 dm^3)	volume or capacity	l
standard atmosphere (= 101.3 kPa)	pressure	atm

DERIVED UNITS

Most of the units in the International System are derived units, that is units defined in terms of base units and supplementary units. Derived units can be divided into two groups—those that have a special name and symbol, and those that do not.

WITHOUT NAMES AND SYMBOLS

MEASURE OF	DERIVATION
acceleration	m/s^2
angular acceleration	rad/s^2
angular velocity	rad/s
density	kg/m^3
electric field strength	V/m
luminance	cd/m^2
magnetic field strength	A/m
velocity	m/s

WITH NAMES AND SYMBOLS

UNIT	MEASURE OF	SYMBOL	DERIVATION
coulomb	electric charge	C	A · s
farad	electric capacitance	F	A · s/V
henry	inductance	H	V · s/A
hertz	frequency	Hz	cycles/s
joule	quantity of energy	J	N · m
lumen	flux of light	lm	cd · sr
lux	illumination	lx	lm/m^2
newton	force	N	kg · m/s^2
ohm	electric resistance	Ω	V/A
pascal	pressure	Pa	N/m^2
tesla	magnetic flux density	T	Wb/m^2
volt	voltage	V	W/A
watt	power	W	J/s
weber	magnetic flux	Wb	V · s

near the time of birth. [Latin *mēcōnium,* from Greek *mēkōnion,* from *mēkōn,* poppy.]

me·cop·ter·an (mĭ-kŏp′tər-ən) *n.* Any of various carnivorous insects of the order Mecoptera, which includes the scorpion flies, characterized by long membranous wings and an elongated beaklike head having chewing mouthparts at the tip. [From New Latin *Mecoptera,* order name : Greek *mēkos,* length; see **māk-** in Appendix + Greek *ptera,* pl. of *pteron,* wing; see **pet-** in Appendix.] —**me·cop′ter·ous** *adj.*

med (mĕd) *adj. Informal.* Medical: *med schools; med students.*

med. *abbr.* **1.** Medicine. **2.** Medieval. **3.** Medium.

M.Ed. *abbr.* Master of Education.

mé·dail·lon (mā-dä-yôɴ′, mə-dăl′yən) *n., pl.* **-lons** (-yôɴ′, -yənz). A circular portion of food; a medallion. [French. See MEDALLION.]

me·da·ka (mĭ-dä′kə) *n.* A small Japanese fish *(Oryzias latipes)* commonly found in rice fields and often used in biological research or in stocking aquariums. [Japanese, killifish : *me,* eye + *daka,* high.]

med·al (mĕd′l) *n.* **1.** A flat piece of metal stamped with a design or an inscription commemorating an event or a person, often given as an award. **2.** A piece of metal stamped with a religious device, used as an object of veneration or commemoration. —**medal** *v.* **-aled, -al·ing, -als** also **-alled, -al·ling, -als.** *Informal.* —*intr.* To win a medal, as in a sports contest: *"We were the first Americans to medal"* (Jill Watson). —*tr.* To award a medal to. [French *médaille,* from Old French, from Italian *medaglia,* coin worth half a denarius, medal, from Vulgar Latin **medālia,* coins worth half a denarius, from Late Latin *mediālia,* little halves, from neuter pl. of *mediālis,* of the middle, medial. See MEDIAL.] —**me·dal′lic** (mə-dăl′ĭk) *adj.*

Med·al for Merit (mĕd′əl) *n.* A decoration awarded by the United States to civilians for outstanding service in peace or war.

med·al·ist (mĕd′l-ĭst) *n.* **1.** One who has received a medal. **2.** *Sports.* The winner at medal play in a golf tournament. **3.** One who designs, makes, or collects medals.

me·dal·lion (mĭ-dăl′yən) *n.* **1.** A large medal. **2.** An emblem of registration for a taxicab. **3.** Any of various large ancient Greek coins. **4.** Something resembling a large medal, as: **a.** An oval or circular design used as decoration. **b.** A painting or an engraving set in an oval or circular frame. **c.** A circular portion of food, especially a boneless cut of meat: *medallions of veal.* [French *médaillon,* from Italian *medaglione,* augmentative of *medaglia,* medal, from Old Italian. See MEDAL.]

med·al·list (mĕd′l-ĭst) *n. Chiefly British.* Variant of **medalist.**

Medal of Freedom *n.* A decoration awarded by the United States to civilians for outstanding achievement in various fields of endeavor.

Medal of Honor *n. Abbr.* **MH** The Congressional Medal of Honor.

medal

medal play *n. Sports.* Golf competition in which the total number of strokes taken is the basis of the score.

Me•dan (mā-dän′). A city of Indonesia on northern Sumatra north-northwest of Padang. Population, 1,378,955.

Med•a•war (mĕd′ə-wər), Sir **Peter Brian.** 1915–1987. Brazilian-born British biologist. He shared a 1960 Nobel Prize for his work on acquired immunological tolerance.

med•dle (mĕd′l) *intr.v.* **-dled, -dling, -dles. 1.** To intrude into other people's affairs or business; interfere. See Synonyms at **interfere. 2.** To handle something idly or ignorantly; tamper. [Middle English *medlen,* from Anglo-Norman *medler,* variant of Old French *mesler,* from Vulgar Latin **misculāre,* to mix thoroughly, from Latin *miscēre,* to mix. See **meik-** in Appendix.] **—med′dler** (mĕd′lər, mĕd′l-ər) *n.*

med•dle•some (mĕd′l-səm) *adj.* Inclined to meddle or interfere. **—med′dle•some•ly** *adv.* **—med′dle•some•ness** *n.*

Mede (mēd) *n.* A member of an Iranian people, closely related to the Persians, inhabiting ancient Media. [Ultimately from Greek *Mēdos,* from Old Persian *Māda.*]

Me•de•a (mĭ-dē′ə) *n. Greek Mythology.* A princess and sorceress of Colchis who helped Jason obtain the Golden Fleece, lived as his consort, and killed their children as revenge for his infidelity.

me decade *n.* The 1970's, viewed as being distinguished by self-centered attitudes and self-indulgent behavior.

Me•del•lín (mĕd′l-ēn′, mĕ′thĕ-yēn′). A city of northwest-central Colombia northwest of Bogotá. Founded in 1675, it is a coffee market in a mining region. Population, 1,473,351.

medevac

med•e•vac (mĕd′ĭ-văk′) *n.* **1.** Air transport of persons to a place where they can receive medical or surgical care; medical evacuation. **2.** A helicopter or other aircraft used for such transport. *—attributive.* Often used to modify another noun: *a medevac chopper; a medevac mission.* **—medevac** *tr.v.* **-vaced, -vac•ing, -vacs.** To transport (a patient) to a place where medical care is available. [MED(ICAL) + EVAC(UATION).]

Med•fly also **med•fly** (mĕd′flī′) *n. Informal.* The Mediterranean fruit fly.

Med•ford (mĕd′fərd). **1.** A city of northeast Massachusetts, a residential and industrial suburb of Boston. Settled in 1630, it is the seat of Tufts University (chartered 1852). Population, 58,076. **2.** A city of southwest Oregon west of Klamath Falls. It is a summer resort and processing center. Population, 39,603.

Med. Gr. *abbr.* Medieval Greek.

me•di•a¹ (mē′dē-ə) *n.* A plural of **medium.** See Usage Note at **medium.**

me•di•a² (mē′dē-ə) *n.* **1.** *Linguistics.* See **medial** (sense 1). **2.** The middle, often muscular layer of the wall of a blood vessel. [Late Latin, from Latin, feminine of Latin *medius,* middle. See MEDIUM.]

Me•di•a (mē′dē-ə). An ancient country of southwest Asia in present-day northwest Iran. Settled by an Indo-European people, it became part of the Assyrian Empire and was conquered c. 550 B.C. by Cyrus the Great. **—Me′di•an** *adj. & n.*

me•di•a•cy (mē′dē-ə-sē) *n.* The state or quality of being mediate.

me•di•ae•val (mē′dē-ē′vəl, mĕd′ē-) *adj.* Variant of **medieval.**

me•di•ae•val•ism (mē′dē-ē′və-lĭz′əm, mĕd′ē-) *n.* Variant of **medievalism.**

me•di•ae•val•ist (mē′dē-ē′və-lĭst, mĕd-ē-) *n.* Variant of **medievalist.**

media event *n.* **1.** An occasion that attracts prominent coverage by news organizations: *"It was a media event with flowing blood and absurdist overtones"* (Lance Morrow). **2.** *Informal.* The central figure of such an occasion: *"The . . . decision turned the startled author into a media event"* (William Zinsser).

me•di•a•gen•ic (mē′dē-ə-jĕn′ĭk) *adj.* Attractive as a subject for reporting by news media: *"a minor leaguer of bumptious manner and mediagenic good looks"* (Larry Martz).

me•di•al (mē′dē-əl) *adj.* **1.** Relating to, situated in, or extending toward the middle; median. **2.** *Linguistics.* Being a sound, syllable, or letter occurring between the initial and final positions in a word or morpheme. **3.** *Mathematics.* Being or relating to an average or a mean. **4.** Average; ordinary. **—medial** *n. Linguistics.* **1.** A voiced stop, such as (b), (d), or (g). Also called *media.* **2.** A sound, letter, or form of a letter that is neither initial nor final. [Late Latin *mediālis,* from Latin *medius,* middle. See **medhyo-** in Appendix.] **—me′di•al•ly** *adv.*

♦**medial strip** *n. Pennsylvania.* See **median strip.** See Regional Note at **neutral ground.**

♦**me•di•an** (mē′dē-ən) *adj.* **1.** Relating to, located in, or extending toward the middle. **2.** *Anatomy.* Of, relating to, or situated in or near the plane that divides a bilaterally symmetrical animal into right and left halves; mesial. **3.** *Statistics.* Relating to or constituting the middle value in a distribution. **—median** *n.* **1.a.** A median point, plane, line, or part. **b.** See **median strip.** See Regional Note at **neutral ground. 2.** *Statistics.* The middle value in a distribution, above and below which lie an equal number of values. **3.** *Mathematics.* **a.** A line that joins a vertex of a triangle to the midpoint of the opposite side. **b.** The line that joins the midpoints of the nonparallel sides of a trapezoid. [Latin *mediānus,* from *medius,* middle. See **medhyo-** in Appendix.] **—me′di•an•ly** *adv.*

median plane *n.* A plane dividing a bilaterally symmetrical animal into right and left halves.

median point *n. Mathematics.* The intersection of the medians of a triangle.

♦**median strip** *n.* The dividing area, either paved or landscaped, between opposing lanes of traffic on some highways. Also called ♦*boulevard,* ♦*boulevard strip,* ♦*mall,* ♦*medial strip,* ♦*median,* ♦*meridian,* ♦*neutral ground.* See Regional Note at **neutral ground.**

me•di•ant (mē′dē-ənt) *n. Music.* The third tone in a diatonic musical scale, determining the major or minor quality of the tonic chord. [Italian *mediante,* from Late Latin *mediāns, mediant-,* present participle of *mediāre,* to be in the middle, from *medius,* middle. See MEDIUM.]

me•di•as•ti•num (mē′dē-ə-stī′nəm) *n., pl.* **-na** (-nə). *Anatomy.* The region in mammals between the pleural sacs, containing the heart and all of the thoracic viscera except the lungs. [New Latin, from neuter of Medieval Latin *mediastīnus,* medial, alteration (influenced by Latin *mediastīnus,* inferior servant, drudge, probably from *medius,* middle, intermediary) of *medius,* middle. See **medhyo-** in Appendix.] **—me′di•as•ti′nal** (-nəl) *adj.*

me•di•ate (mē′dē-āt′) *v.* **-at•ed, -at•ing, -ates.** *—tr.* **1.** To resolve or settle (differences) by working with all the conflicting parties: *mediate a labor-management dispute.* **2.** To bring about (a settlement, for example) by working with all the conflicting parties. **3.** To effect or convey as an intermediate agent or mechanism. *—intr.* **1.** To intervene between two or more disputants in order to bring about an agreement, a settlement, or a compromise. **2.** To settle or reconcile differences. **3.** To have a relation to two differing persons or things. **—mediate** (-ĭt) *adj.* **1.** Acting through, involving, or dependent on an intervening agency. **2.** Being in a middle position. [Late Latin *mediāre, mediāt-,* to be in the middle, from Latin *medius,* middle. See **medhyo-** in Appendix.] **—me′di•ate•ly** (-ĭt-lē) *adv.*

me•di•a•tion (mē′dē-ā′shən) *n.* **1.** The act of mediating; intervention. **2.** The state of being mediated. **3.** *Law.* An attempt to bring about a peaceful settlement or compromise between disputants through the objective intervention of a neutral party. **—me′di•a′tive, me′di•a•to′ry** (mē′dē-ə-tôr′ē, -tōr′ē) *adj.*

me•di•a•tize (mē′dē-ə-tīz′) *tr.v.* **-tized, -tiz•ing, -tiz•es.** To annex (a lesser state) to a greater state as a means of permitting the ruler of the lesser state to retain title and partial authority. [Probably French *médiatiser,* from *médiat,* dependent, from Old French, back-formation from *immediat,* independent, from Late Latin *immediātus.* See IMMEDIATE.] **—me′di•a•ti•za′tion** (-tĭ-zā′shən) *n.*

me•di•a•tor (mē′dē-ā′tər) *n.* **1.** One that mediates, especially one that reconciles differences between disputants. **2.** *Physiology.* A substance or structure that mediates a specific response in a bodily tissue.

med•ic¹ or **med•ick** (mĕd′ĭk) *n.* Any of several Old World herbs of the genus *Medicago* in the pea family, having clusters of small, usually yellow flowers and compound leaves with three leaflets. Several species are important for fodder and green manure. [Middle English *medike,* from Latin *Mēdica,* from Greek *Mēdikē,* from feminine of *Mēdikos,* of Media, from *Mēdos,* a Mede. See MEDE.]

med•ic² (mĕd′ĭk) *n.* **1.** A member of a military medical corps. **2.** A physician or surgeon. **3.** A medical student or intern. [Latin *medicus,* physician. See MEDICAL.]

med•i•ca•ble (mĕd′ĭ-kə-bəl) *adj.* Potentially responsive to treatment with medicine; curable: *medicable conditions; a medicable complaint.*

Med•i•caid also **med•i•caid** (mĕd′ĭ-kād′) *n.* A program in the United States, jointly funded by the states and the federal government, that reimburses hospitals and physicians for providing care to qualifying people who cannot finance their own medical expenses. [MEDIC(AL) + AID.]

med•i•cal (mĕd′ĭ-kəl) *adj.* **1.** Of or relating to the study or practice of medicine. **2.** Requiring treatment by medicine. **—medical** *n. Informal.* A thorough physical examination. [Medieval Latin *medicālis,* from Latin *medicus,* physician, from *medērī,* to heal. See **med-** in Appendix.]

medical examiner *n.* **1.** *Abbr.* **ME** A physician officially authorized by a governmental unit to ascertain causes of deaths, especially those not occurring under natural circumstances. **2.** A physician who examines employees of a particular firm or applicants for life insurance.

medical jurisprudence *n.* See **forensic medicine.**

medical law *n.* The branch of law that deals with the application of medical knowledge to legal problems.

me•dic•a•ment (mĭ-dĭk′ə-mənt, mĕd′ĭ-kə-) *n.* An agent that promotes recovery from injury or ailment; a medicine. [Latin *medicāmentum,* from *medicāre,* to cure. See MEDICATE.]

Med•i•care also **med•i•care** (mĕd′ĭ-kâr′) *n.* A program under the U.S. Social Security Administration that reimburses hospitals and physicians for medical care provided to qualifying people over 65 years old. [MEDI(CAL) + CARE.]

med•i•cate (mĕd′ĭ-kāt′) *tr.v.* **-cat•ed, -cat•ing, -cates. 1.** To treat with medicine. **2.** To tincture or permeate with a medicinal substance. [Latin *medicāre, medicāt-,* from *medicus,* doctor, from *medērī,* to heal. See **med-** in Appendix.] **—med′i·ca′-tive** *adj.*

med·i·ca·tion (mĕd′ĭ-kā′shən) *n.* **1.** A medicine; a medicament. **2.** The act or process of treating with medicine. **3.** Administration of medicine.

Med·i·ci (mĕd′ə-chē′, mĕ′dē-). Italian noble family that produced three popes (Leo X, Clement VII, and Leo XI) and two queens of France (Catherine de Médicis and Marie de Médicis). **Cosimo** "the Elder" (1389–1464) was the first of the family to rule Florence. **Lorenzo** "the Magnificent" (1449–1492) was an outstanding patron of learning and the arts, whose clients included Michelangelo. **—Med′i·ce′an** (-chē′ən, -sē′-) *adj.*

me·dic·i·nal (mĭ-dĭs′ə-nəl) *adj.* **1.** Of, relating to, or having the properties of medicine. **2.** Having an unappealing, bitter flavor. **—me·dic′i·nal·ly** *adv.*

med·i·cine (mĕd′ĭ-sĭn) *n. Abbr.* **med. 1.a.** The science of diagnosing, treating, or preventing disease and other damage to the body or mind. **b.** The branch of this science encompassing treatment by drugs, diet, exercise, and other nonsurgical means. **2.** The practice of medicine. **3.** An agent, such as a drug, used to treat disease or injury. **4.** Something, such as corrective discipline or punishment, that is unpleasant but necessary or unavoidable. **5.a.** Shamanistic practices or beliefs, especially among Native Americans. **b.** Something, such as a ritual practice or sacred object, believed to control natural or supernatural powers or serve as a preventive or remedy. *—attributive.* Often used to modify another noun: *a medicine cabinet; medicine bottles.* [Middle English, from Old French, from Latin *medicīna,* from feminine of *medicīnus,* of a doctor, from *medicus,* physician. See MEDICAL.]

medicine ball *n. Sports.* A large, heavy stuffed ball used in conditioning exercises.

Med·i·cine Bow Mountains (mĕd′ĭ-sĭn bō′). A range of the eastern Rocky Mountains in southeast Wyoming and northern Colorado. It rises to 3,664 m (12,013 ft) at **Medicine Bow Peak** in south-central Wyoming.

medicine bundle *n.* A covered or wrapped parcel containing items of personal or tribal religious significance, used by certain Native American peoples.

medicine dance *n.* A ritual dance performed by some Native American peoples to obtain supernatural assistance, as in healing or crop control.

Medicine Hat (hăt). A city of southeast Alberta, Canada, near the Saskatchewan border southeast of Calgary. Founded in 1883, it is a trade center. Population, 40,380.

medicine lodge *n.* A building or structure used by some Native American peoples for ceremonies.

medicine man *n.* **1.** A shaman, especially a Native American shaman. **2.** A hawker of brews and potions among the audience in a medicine show.

medicine show *n.* A traveling show, popular especially in the 19th century, that offered varied entertainment, between the acts of which medicines were peddled.

med·ick (mĕd′ĭk) *n.* Variant of **medic**[1].

med·i·co (mĕd′ĭ-kō′) *n., pl.* **-cos.** *Informal.* **1.** A physician. **2.** A medical student. [Italian *medico* or Spanish *médico,* both from Latin *medicus.* See MEDICAL.]

med·i·co·le·gal (mĕd′ĭ-kō-lē′gəl) *adj.* Of, relating to, or concerned with medicine and law. [Latin *medicus,* physician; see MEDICAL + LEGAL.]

me·di·e·val also **me·di·ae·val** (mē′dē-ē′vəl, mĕd′ē-) *adj. Abbr.* **med., M. 1.** Relating or belonging to the Middle Ages. **2.** *Informal.* Old-fashioned; unenlightened: *parents with a medieval attitude toward dating.* [From New Latin *medium aevum,* the middle age : Latin, neuter of *medius,* middle; see **medhyo-** in Appendix + Latin *aevum,* age; see **aiw-** in Appendix.] **—me′-di·e′val·ly** *adv.*

Me·di·e·val Greek (mē′dē-ē′vəl, mĕd′ē-) *n. Abbr.* **Med. Gr.** The Greek language as used from about 800 to about 1500.

me·di·e·val·ism also **me·di·ae·val·ism** (mē′dē-ē′və-lĭz′əm, mĕd′ē-) *n.* **1.** The spirit or the body of beliefs, customs, or practices of the Middle Ages. **2.** Devotion to or acceptance of the ideas of the Middle Ages. **3.** Study of the Middle Ages.

me·di·e·val·ist also **me·di·ae·val·ist** (mē′dē-ē′və-lĭst, mĕd-ē-) *n.* **1.** A specialist in the study of the Middle Ages. **2.** A connoisseur of medieval culture.

Medieval Latin *n. Abbr.* **Med. Lat.** The Latin language as used from about 700 to about 1500.

Me·dill (mə-dĭl′), **Joseph.** 1823–1899. American newspaperman who was a founder of the Republican Party (1854).

me·di·na (mĭ-dē′nə) *n.* The old section of an Arab city in North Africa. [Arabic *madīna,* city.]

Me·di·na (mĭ-dē′nə). A city of western Saudi Arabia north of Mecca. Mohammed lived here after fleeing from Mecca in 622. The Mosque of the Prophet, containing Mohammed's tomb, is a holy site for Moslem pilgrims. Population, 290,000.

Me·di·na-Si·do·nia (mə-dē′nə-sĭ-dōn′yə, mĕ-*thē*′nä-sē-*thô*′nyä), Seventh Duke of. Title of Alonso Pérez de Guzmán. 1550–1619. Spanish naval officer who led the Spanish Armada to utter defeat by English forces (1588).

me·di·o·cre (mē′dē-ō′kər) *adj.* Moderate to inferior in quality; ordinary. See Synonyms at **average.** [French *médiocre,* from Latin *mediocris* : *medius,* middle; see **medhyo-** in Appendix + *ocris,* a rugged mountain; see **ak-** in Appendix.]

me·di·oc·ri·ty (mē′dē-ŏk′rĭ-tē) *n., pl.* **-ties. 1.** The state or quality of being mediocre. **2.** Mediocre ability, achievement, or performance. **3.** One that displays mediocre qualities. **—me·di·oc′ri·tize′** (-tīz′) *v.* **—me·di·oc′ri·ti·za′tion** *n.*

Medit. *abbr.* Mediterranean.

med·i·tate (mĕd′ĭ-tāt′) *v.* **-tat·ed, -tat·ing, -tates.** *—tr.* **1.** To reflect on; contemplate. **2.** To plan in the mind; intend: *meditated a visit to her daughter.* *—intr.* **1.** To consider or reflect at length. **2.** To engage in contemplation, especially of a spiritual or devotional nature. See Synonyms at **ponder.** [Latin *meditārī, meditāt-.* See **med-** in Appendix.] **—med′i·ta′tor** *n.*

med·i·ta·tion (mĕd′ĭ-tā′shən) *n.* **1.a.** The act or process of meditating. **b.** A devotional exercise of or leading to contemplation. **2.** A contemplative discourse, usually on a religious or philosophical subject. **—med′i·ta′tion·al** *adj.*

med·i·ta·tive (mĕd′ĭ-tā′tĭv) *adj.* Characterized by or prone to meditation. See Synonyms at **pensive.** **—med′i·ta′tive·ly** *adv.* **—med′i·ta′tive·ness** *n.*

med·i·ter·ra·ne·an (mĕd′ĭ-tə-rā′nē-ən, -rān′yən) *adj.* Surrounded nearly or completely by dry land. Used of large bodies of water, such as lakes or seas. [Latin *mediterrāneus,* inland : *medius,* middle; see **medhyo-** in Appendix + *terra,* land; see **ters-** in Appendix.]

WORD HISTORY: When one hears the word *mediterranean,* one thinks of a specific place and perhaps of the great cultures that have surrounded it. But the word can also apply to any large body of water that is surrounded completely or almost completely by dry land. This usage goes back to the use in Late Latin of the Latin word *mediterrāneus,* the source of our word, as part of the name *Mediterrāneum mare* for the mostly landlocked Mediterranean Sea. But Latin *mediterrāneus,* which is derived from *medius,* "the middle of, the heart of," and *terra,* "land," in Classical Latin actually meant "remote from the coast, inland." In Late Latin, in referring to the sea, *mediterrāneus* probably meant originally "in the middle of the earth" rather than "surrounded by land," for to the Mediterranean cultures without knowledge of much of the earth, the Mediterranean Sea was in the center of the world. Our word *mediterranean* is first recorded in English in 1594 as the name of the sea.

Med·i·ter·ra·ne·an (mĕd′ĭ-tə-rā′nē-ən). *Abbr.* **Medit.** The region surrounding the Mediterranean Sea. Some of the most ancient civilizations flourished in the region, which was dominated for millenniums by Phoenicia, Carthage, Greece, Sicily, and Rome. **—Med′i·ter·ra′ne·an** *adj. & n.*

Mediterranean fever *n.* See **brucellosis** (sense 1).

Mediterranean flour moth *n.* A small, pale gray moth *(Anagasta kuehniella)* now found worldwide, the larvae of which destroy flour and other stored grain products.

Mediterranean fruit fly *n.* A black and white two-winged fly *(Ceratitis capitata)* found in many warm regions of the world, the larvae of which destroy citrus and other fruit crops.

Mediterranean Sea. An inland sea surrounded by Europe, Asia, Asia Minor, the Near East, and Africa. It connects with the Atlantic Ocean through the Strait of Gibraltar; with the Black Sea through the Dardanelles, the Sea of Marmara, and the Bosporus; and with the Red Sea through the Suez Canal.

me·di·um (mē′dē-əm) *n., pl.* **-di·a** (-dē-ə) or **-di·ums.** *Abbr.* **med., m., M. 1.** Something, such as an intermediate course of action, that occupies a position or represents a condition midway between extremes. **2.** An intervening substance through which something else is transmitted or carried on. **3.** An agency by which something is accomplished, conveyed, or transferred: *The train was the usual medium of transportation in those days.* **4.** *pl.* **media.** *Usage Problem.* **a.** A means of mass communication, such as newpapers, magazines, radio, or television. **b. media** *(used with a sing. or pl. verb).* The group of journalists and others who constitute the communications industry and profession. **5.** *pl.* **mediums.** A person thought to have the power to communicate with the spirits of the dead or with agents of another world or dimension. Also called *psychic.* **6.** *pl.* **media. a.** A surrounding environment in which something functions and thrives. **b.** The substance in which a specific organism lives and thrives. **c.** A culture medium. **7.a.** A specific kind of artistic technique or means of expression as determined by the materials used or the creative methods involved: *the medium of lithography.* **b.** The materials used in a specific artistic technique: *oils as a medium.* **8.** A solvent with which paint is thinned to the proper consistency. **9.** *Chemistry.* A filtering substance, such as filter paper. **10.** A size of paper, usually 18 × 23 inches or 17½ × 22 inches. **—medium** *adj. Abbr.* **med., m., M.** Occurring or being between two degrees, amounts, or quantities; intermediate: *broil a medium steak.* See Synonyms at **average.** [Latin, from neuter of *medius,* middle. See **medhyo-** in Appendix.]

USAGE NOTE: The etymologically plural form *media* is often used as a singular to refer to a particular means of communication, as in *This is the most exciting new media since television.* This usage is widely regarded as incorrect; *medium* is preferred. A stronger case can be made in defense of the use of *media* as a collective term, as in *The media has not shown much interest in covering the issue.* As with the analogous words *data* and *agenda,* the originally plural form has begun to acquire a sense that departs from that of the singular: used as a collective term, *media*

Lorenzo de Medici
c. 1485 terra-cotta bust by Andrea del Verrocchio

ă pat	oi boy
ā pay	ou out
âr care	ŏŏ took
ä father	ōō boot
ĕ pet	ŭ cut
ē be	ûr urge
ĭ pit	th thin
ī pie	*th* this
îr pier	hw which
ŏ pot	zh vision
ō toe	ə about, item
ô paw	♦ regionalism

Stress marks: ′ (primary); ′ (secondary), as in **dictionary** (dĭk′shə-nĕr′ē)

medlar
Mespilus germanica

denotes an industry or community. Thus the example sentence given here would not be appropriately paraphrased as *No medium has shown much interest in covering the issue,* which suggests that the disinclination abides in the means of communication itself rather than in its practitioners. If *media* follows the pattern of *data* and *agenda,* this singular use may become entirely acceptable someday. But despite its utility, many people still regard it as a grammatical error.

---

medium frequency *n. Abbr.* **mf** A radio frequency or radio-frequency band in the range 300 to 3,000 kilohertz.

medium of exchange *n., pl.* **media of exchange** or **mediums of exchange.** Something, such as a precious metal, that is commonly used in a specific area or among a certain group of people as money.

med·lar (mĕd′lər) *n.* **1.** A deciduous European tree *(Mespilus germanica)* having white flowers and edible apple-shaped fruit. **2.** The fruit of this plant, eaten fresh or made into preserves. [Middle English *medler,* from Old French *meslier, medler,* from *mesle, medle,* fruit of the medlar, from Late Latin *mespila,* from Greek *mespilē.*]

Med. Lat. *abbr.* Medieval Latin.

med·ley (mĕd′lē) *n., pl.* **-leys. 1.** An often jumbled assortment; a mixture: *"That night he dreamed he was traveling in a foreign country, only it seemed to be a medley of all the countries he'd ever been to and even some he hadn't"* (Anne Tyler). **2.** *Music.* An arrangement made from a series of melodies, often from various sources. [Middle English *medlee,* from Anglo-Norman *medlee,* meddling, from past participle of *medler,* to meddle. See MEDDLE.]

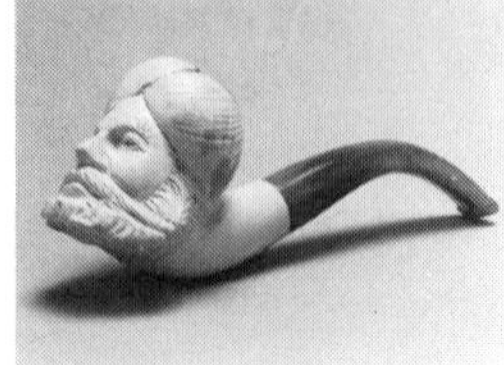

meerschaum

Mé·doc[1] (mā-dŏk′, -dôk′). A region of southwest France north of Bordeaux between the Bay of Biscay and the Gironde River.

Mé·doc[2] (mā-dôk′, -dŏk′) *n.* A red Bordeaux wine. [After MÉDOC[1].]

me·dul·la (mĭ-dŭl′ə) *n., pl.* **-dul·las** or **-dul·lae** (-dŭl′ē). **1.** The inner core of certain organs or body structures, such as the marrow of bone. **2.** The medulla oblongata. **3.** See **myelin. 4.** *Botany.* **a.** The pith in the stems or roots of certain plants. **b.** The central portion of a thallus in certain lichens and red or brown algae. [Middle English, from Latin, perhaps alteration (influenced by *medius,* middle; see MEDIAL) of *merulla.] **—me·dul′lar, med′ul·lar′y** (mĕd′l-ĕr′ē, mə-dŭl′ə-rē) *adj.*

medulla ob·lon·ga·ta (ŏb′lông-gä′tə) *n., pl.* **-ga·tas** or **-ga·tae** (-gä′tē). The lowermost portion of the vertebrate brain, continuous with the spinal cord, responsible for the control of respiration, circulation, and certain other bodily functions. [New Latin : Latin *medulla,* medulla + New Latin *oblongata,* oblong.]

medullary sheath *n.* See **myelin sheath.**

med·ul·lat·ed (mĕd′l-ā′tĭd) *adj.* **1.** Myelinated. **2.** *Anatomy.* Having a medulla.

med·ul·li·za·tion (mĕd′l-ĭ-zā′shən) *n.* Replacement of bone tissue by marrow, as in inflammatory bone disease.

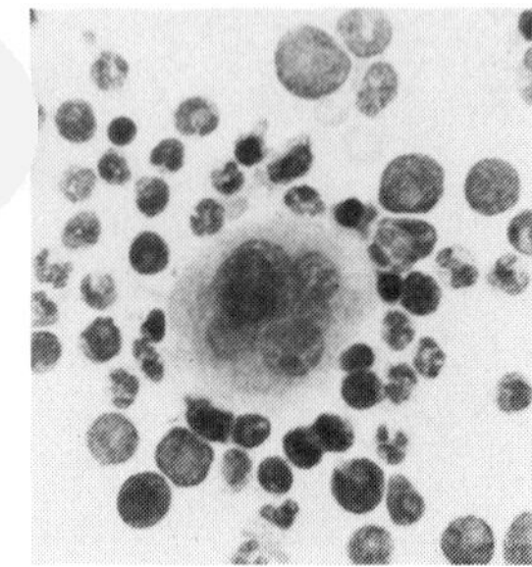

megakaryocyte
Bone marrow smear from a guinea pig (magnified 1,000 times)

me·du·sa (mĭ-do͞o′sə, -zə, -dyo͞o′-) *n., pl.* **-sas** or **-sae** (-sē, -zē). The tentacled, usually bell-shaped, free-swimming sexual stage in the life cycle of a coelenterate, such as a jellyfish. [Latin *Medūsa,* Medusa (from the Medusa's snaky locks). See MEDUSA.]

Me·dus·a (mĭ-do͞o′sə,-zə, -dyo͞o′-) *n., pl.* **-sas** or **-sae** (-sē, -zē). *Greek Mythology.* The Gorgon who was killed by Perseus. [Middle English *Meduse,* from Latin *Medūsa,* from Greek *Medousa,* from feminine present participle of *medein,* to protect, rule over. See **med-** in Appendix.]

me·du·soid (mĭ-do͞o′soid′, -zoid′, -dyo͞o′-) *n.* **1.** A shape resembling a jellyfish. **2.** A jellyfish. **—me·du′soid′** *adj.*

meed (mēd) *n.* **1.** A fitting recompense. **2.** *Archaic.* A merited gift or wage. [Middle English *mede,* from Old English *mēd.*]

meek (mēk) *adj.* **meek·er, meek·est. 1.** Showing patience and humility; gentle. **2.** Easily imposed on; submissive. [Middle English *meke,* of Scandinavian origin; akin to Old Norse *mjūkr,* soft.] **—meek′ly** *adv.*

meer·schaum (mîr′shəm, -shôm′) *n.* **1.** A fine, compact, usually white claylike mineral of hydrous magnesium silicate, $H_4Mg_2Si_3O_{10}$, found in the Mediterranean area and used in fashioning tobacco pipes and as a building stone. Also called *sepiolite.* **2.** A tobacco pipe with a bowl made of this mineral. [German : *Meer,* sea (from Middle High German *mer,* from Old High German *mari;* see **mori-** in Appendix) + *Schaum,* foam (from Middle High German *schūm,* from Old High German *scūm;* see **(s)keu-** in Appendix).]

Mee·rut (mā′rət, mîr′ət). A city of north-central India northeast of Delhi. A Mogul city after the 14th century, it was the site of the first uprising (May 1857) against the British in the Indian Mutiny. Population, 417,395.

megaphone

meet[1] (mēt) *v.* **met** (mĕt), **meet·ing, meets.** *—tr.* **1.** To come upon by chance or arrangement. **2.** To be present at the arrival of: *met the train.* **3.** To be introduced to. **4.** To come into conjunction with; join: *where the sea meets the sky.* **5.** To come into the company or presence of, as for a conference. **6.** To come to the notice of (the senses): *There is more here than meets the eye.* **7.** To experience; undergo: *met his fate with courage.* **8.** To deal with; oppose: *"We have met the enemy and they are ours"* (Oliver Hazard Perry). **9.** To cope or contend effectively with: *meet each problem as it arises.* **10.** To come into conformity with the views, wishes, or opinions of: *The firm has done its best to meet us on that point.* **11.** To satisfy (a need, for example); fulfill: *meet all the conditions in the contract.* See Synonyms at **satisfy. 12.** To pay; settle: *enough money to meet expenses.* *—intr.* **1.** To come together: *Let's meet tonight.* **2.** To come into conjunction; be joined: *"East is East, and West is West, and never the twain shall meet"* (Rudyard Kipling). **3.** To come together as opponents; contend. **4.** To become introduced. **5.** To assemble. **6.** To experience or undergo. Used with *with: The housing bill met with approval.* **7.** To occur together, especially in one person or entity: *"The hopes and fears of all the years/Are met in thee tonight"* (Phillips Brooks). **—meet** *n.* A meeting or contest, especially an athletic competition. **—*idiom.* meet (someone) halfway.** To make a compromise with. [Middle English *meten,* from Old English *mētan.*]

meet[2] (mēt) *adj.* Fitting; proper: *"It seems not meet, nor wholesome to my place"* (Shakespeare). See Synonyms at **fit[1].** [Middle English *mete,* from Old English *gemǣte.* See **med-** in Appendix.] **—meet′ly** *adv.*

meet·ing (mē′tĭng) *n. Abbr.* **mtg. 1.** The act or process or an instance of coming together; an encounter. **2.** An assembly or a gathering of people, as for a business, social, or religious purpose. **—*idiom.* meeting of the minds.** Agreement; concord.

meet·ing·house (mē′tĭng-hous′) *n.* A building used for public meetings and especially for Protestant or Quaker religious services.

mef·e·nam·ic acid (mĕf′ə-năm′ĭk) *n.* A crystalline compound, $C_{15}H_{15}NO_2$, used as an anti-inflammatory drug and as an analgesic. [(DI)ME(THYL) + *fen* (alteration of PHENYL) + AM(INOBENZO)IC ACID.]

mega– *pref.* **1.** Large: *megadose.* **2.** One million (10^6): *megahertz.* [Greek, from *megas,* great. See **meg-** in Appendix.]

meg·a·bit (mĕg′ə-bĭt′) *n. Computer Science.* **1.** A unit of storage capacity equal to 1,048,576 (220) bits. **2.** One million bits.

meg·a·buck (mĕg′ə-bŭk′) *n. Slang.* One million dollars.

meg·a·byte (mĕg′ə-bīt′) *n. Abbr.* **MB** *Computer Science.* **1.** A unit of storage capacity equal to 1,048,576 (2^{20}) bytes. **2.** One million bytes.

meg·a·ceph·a·ly (mĕg′ə-sĕf′ə-lē) *n., pl.* **-lies.** See **macrocephaly. —meg′a·ce·phal′ic** (-sə-făl′ĭk), **meg′a·ceph′a·lous** (-sĕf′ə-lĕs) *adj.*

meg·a·cy·cle (mĕg′ə-sī′kəl) *n. Abbr.* **Mc** See **megahertz.**

me·ga·death (mĕg′ə-dĕth′) *n.* One million deaths. Used as a unit in reference to nuclear warfare.

meg·a·dose (mĕg′ə-dōs′) *n.* An exceptionally large dose, as of a drug or vitamin.

Me·gae·ra (mə-jîr′ə) *n. Greek Mythology.* One of the Furies.

meg·a·gam·ete (mĕg′ə-găm′ēt′, -gə-mēt′) *n.* See **macrogamete.**

meg·a·ga·me·to·phyte (mĕg′ə-gə-mē′tə-fīt′) *n.* The female gametophyte that arises from a megaspore of a heterosporous plant.

meg·a·hertz (mĕg′ə-hûrts′) *n., pl.* **megahertz.** *Abbr.* **MHz** One million cycles per second. Used especially as a radio-frequency unit. Also called *megacycle.*

meg·a·kar·y·o·cyte (mĕg′ə-kăr′ē-ō-sīt′, -ə-sīt′) *n.* A large bone marrow cell with a lobulate nucleus that gives rise to blood platelets.

megal– *pref.* Variant of **megalo–.**

meg·a·lith (mĕg′ə-lĭth′) *n.* A very large stone used in various prehistoric architectures or monumental styles, notably in western Europe during the second millennium B.C. **—meg′a·lith′ic** *adj.*

megalo– or **megal–** *pref.* Large; of exaggerated size or greatness: *megalocephaly.* [Greek, from *megas, megal-,* great. See **meg-** in Appendix.]

meg·a·lo·blast (mĕg′ə-lō-blăst′) *n.* An abnormally large nucleated red blood cell found especially in people having pernicious anemia or certain vitamin deficiencies. **—meg′a·lo·blas′tic** *adj.*

meg·a·lo·car·di·a (mĕg′ə-lō-kär′dē-ə) *n.* See **cardiomegaly.** [MEGALO– + Greek *kardia,* heart; see **kerd-** in Appendix.]

meg·a·lo·ceph·a·ly (mĕg′ə-lō-sĕf′ə-lē) *n., pl.* **-lies.** See **macrocephaly. —meg′a·lo·ce·phal′ic** (-sə-făl′ĭk), **meg′a·lo·ceph′a·lous** (-sĕf′ə-ləs) *adj.*

meg·a·lo·ma·ni·a (mĕg′ə-lō-mā′nē-ə, -mān′yə) *n.* **1.** A psychopathological condition in which delusional fantasies of wealth, power, or omnipotence predominate. **2.** An obsession with grandiose or extravagant things or actions. **—meg′a·lo·ma′ni·ac′** *n.* **—meg′a·lo·ma·ni′a·cal** (-mə-nī′ə-kəl), **meg′a·lo·man′ic** (-măn′ĭk) *adj.*

meg·a·lop·o·lis (mĕg′ə-lŏp′ə-lĭs) also **me·gap·o·lis** (mĭ-găp′ə-lĭs, mĕ-) *n.* A region made up of several large cities and their surrounding areas in sufficient proximity to be considered a single urban complex. [MEGALO– + Greek *polis,* city; see **pele-[3]** in Appendix.] **—meg′a·lop·o·lis′tic** *adj.* **—meg′a·lo·pol′i·tan** (-lō-pŏl′ĭ-tən) *adj.*

meg·a·lo·saur (mĕg′ə-lə-sôr′) *n.* A gigantic carnivorous dinosaur of the genus *Megalosaurus* of the Jurassic Period. [New Latin *Megalosaurus,* genus name : MEGALO– + Greek *sauros,* lizard.] **—meg′a·lo·sau′ri·an** *adj. & n.*

meg·a·phone (mĕg′ə-fōn′) *n.* A funnel-shaped device used to direct and amplify the voice. **—megaphone** *tr. & intr.v.* **-phoned, -phon·ing, -phones.** To transmit (a message) or speak through or as if through a funnel-shaped voice amplification device. **—meg′a·phon′ic** (-fŏn′ĭk) *adj.* **—meg′a·phon′i·cal·ly** *adv.*

meg·a·pode (mĕg′ə-pōd′) *n.* Any of various large-footed, ground-dwelling birds of the family Megapodiidae, found in Australia and many South Pacific islands, that build mounds or burrows of earth and compost in which to incubate their eggs. Also called *moundbird, mound builder, scrub fowl.* [From *Megapodius,* type genus : MEGA– + New Latin *-podius,* masculine of *-podium,* -pod.]

me·gap·o·lis (mĭ-găp′ə-lĭs, mĕ-) *n.* Variant of **megalopolis.**

Meg·a·ra (mĕg′ər-ə). An ancient city of east-central Greece. It was the capital of Megaris, a small Dorian state between the Saronic Gulf and the Gulf of Corinth. Megara flourished as a maritime center from the eighth to the fifth century B.C.

meg·a·ron (mĕg′ə-rŏn′) *n., pl.* **-a·ra** (-ər-ə). The main hall or central room of a palace or house, especially of Mycenaean Greece, having a pillared porch and a more or less central hearth. [Greek.]

meg·a·scop·ic (mĕg′ə-skŏp′ĭk) *adj.* Macroscopic. **—meg′a·scop′i·cal·ly** *adv.*

meg·a·spo·ran·gi·um (mĕg′ə-spə-răn′jē-əm) *n., pl.* **-gi·a** (-jē-ə). A structure that produces one or more megaspores. Also called *macrosporangium.*

meg·a·spore (mĕg′ə-spôr′, -spōr′) *n.* The larger of two types of spores that give rise to a female gametophyte. Also called *macrospore.* **—meg′a·spor′ic** *adj.*

megaspore mother cell *n. Botany.* A cell that undergoes meiosis to produce four megaspores. Also called *megasporocyte.*

meg·a·spo·ro·cyte (mĕg′ə-spôr′ə-sīt′, -spōr′-) *n.* See **megaspore mother cell.**

meg·a·spo·ro·gen·e·sis (mĕg′ə-spôr′ə-jĕn′ĭ-sĭs, -spōr′-) *n., pl.* **-ses** (-sēz). The formation of megaspores.

meg·a·spo·ro·phyll (mĕg′ə-spôr′ə-fĭl′, -spōr′-) *n.* A leaflike structure that bears megasporangia.

meg·a·struc·ture (mĕg′ə-strŭk′chər) *n.* An extremely large, tall building.

meg·a·there (mĕg′ə-thîr′) *n.* A large extinct ground sloth of the family Megatheriidae of the Miocene Epoch through the Pleistocene Epoch. [From New Latin *Megatherium,* type genus : MEGA– + Greek *thēr,* beast; see THEROPOD.] **—meg′a·the′ri·an** *adj.*

meg·a·ton (mĕg′ə-tŭn′) *n. Abbr.* **MT** A unit of explosive force equal to that of one million metric tons of TNT. **—meg′a·ton′nage** (-tŭn′ĭj) *n.*

meg·a·vi·ta·min (mĕg′ə-vī′tə-mĭn) *n.* A dose of a vitamin greatly exceeding the amount required to maintain health.

meg·a·volt (mĕg′ə-vōlt′) *n. Abbr.* **MV** One million volts. **—meg′a·volt′age** *n.*

meg·a·watt (mĕg′ə-wŏt′) *n. Abbr.* **MW** One million watts. **—meg′a·watt′age** *n.*

me generation *n.* The younger people of the 1970's, viewed as self-centered and self-indulgent.

Me·gid·do (mĭ-gĭd′ō). An ancient city of northwest Palestine on the southern edge of the Plain of Esdraelon. It was the scene of many battles throughout early history because of its strategic position on the route connecting Egypt with Mesopotamia.

Me·gil·lah (mə-gĭl′ə) *n.* **1.** *Judaism.* The scroll containing the biblical narrative of the Book of Esther, traditionally read in synagogues to celebrate the festival of Purim. **2. megillah.** *Slang.* A tediously detailed or embroidered account: *told us the whole megillah.* [Hebrew *megillâ,* scroll, from *gālal,* to roll.]

Me·grez (mē′grĕz′) *n.* A star in the Big Dipper. [Short for Arabic *maġriz aḏ-ḏanab ad-dubb al-Akbar,* the root of the tail of the greater bear.]

me·grim (mē′grĭm) *n.* **1.** See **migraine. 2.** Often **megrims.** A caprice or fancy. **3. megrims.** Depression or unhappiness: *"If these megrims are the effect of Love, thank Heaven, I never knew what it was"* (Samuel Richardson). [Middle English *migrem,* variant of *migraine.* See MIGRAINE.]

Me·he·met A·li (mĭ-hĕm′ĕt ä-lē′, mā′mĕt). See **Mohammed Ali.**

Meigh·en (mē′ən), **Arthur.** 1874–1960. Canadian politician who served as prime minister (1920–1921 and 1926).

Mei·ji (mā′jē′). See **Mutsuhito.**

mei·o·sis (mī-ō′sĭs) *n., pl.* **-ses** (-sēz′). **1.** *Genetics.* The process of cell division in sexually reproducing organisms that reduces the number of chromosomes in reproductive cells, leading to the production of gametes in animals and spores in plants. **2.** Rhetorical understatement. [Greek *meiōsis,* diminution, from *meioun,* to diminish, from *meiōn,* less. See **mei-**[2] in Appendix.] **—mei·ot′ic** (-ŏt′ĭk) *adj.* **—mei·ot′i·cal·ly** *adv.*

Me·ir (mĭ′ər, mā-ēr′), **Golda.** 1898–1978. Russian-born Israeli politician. After living in the United States (1906–1921), she moved to Palestine and later served as minister of labor (1949–1956) and prime minister (1969–1974) of Israel.

Meis·sen[1] (mī′sən). A city of east-central Germany on the Elbe River northwest of Dresden. Its porcelain industry dates to the early 18th century. Population, 38,710.

Meis·sen[2] (mī′sən) *n.* A delicate porcelain ware originally made in Meissen, Germany.

Meis·so·nier (mā′sən-yā′, -sôn-), **Jean Louis Ernest.** 1815–1891. French painter noted for his genre and military scenes.

Meis·ter·sing·er (mīs′tər-sĭng′ər) *n., pl.* **Meistersinger** or **-ers.** A member of one of the guilds organized in the principal cities of Germany in the 14th, 15th, and 16th centuries to establish competitive standards for the composition and performance of music and poetry. Also called *mastersinger.* [German, from Middle High German : *meister,* master (from Old High German *meistar,* from Latin *magister;* see MASTER) + *singer,* singer (from *singen,* to sing, from Old High German *singan;* see **sengʷh-** in Appendix).]

Meit·ner (mīt′nər), **Lise.** 1878–1968. Austrian-born Swedish physicist and pioneer in the study of nuclear fission.

Mek·nes (mĕk-nĕs′). A city of northern Morocco west-southwest of Fez. A capital of Moroccan sultans after c. 1672, it was once known as "the Versailles of Morocco" for its palatial buildings and splendid gardens. Population, 319,783.

Me·kong (mā′kông′, -kŏng′). A river of southeast Asia flowing about 4,183 km (2,600 mi) from southeast China to the South China Sea through a vast delta in southern Vietnam.

mel·a·mine (mĕl′ə-mēn′) *n.* **1.** A white crystalline compound, $C_3H_6N_6$, used in making melamine resins and for tanning leather. **2.** A plastic made from such resin. [*Melam,* distillate of ammonium thiocyanate + AMINE.]

melamine resin *n.* A thermosetting resin used for molded products, adhesives, and surface coatings.

melan– *pref.* Variant of **melano–.**

mel·an·cho·li·a (mĕl′ən-kō′lē-ə) *n. Psychiatry.* A mental disorder characterized by severe depression, apathy, and withdrawal. [Late Latin, melancholy. See MELANCHOLY.] **—mel′an·cho′li·ac** (-lē-ăk′) *adj. & n.*

mel·an·chol·ic (mĕl′ən-kŏl′ĭk) *adj.* **1.** Affected with or subject to melancholy. **2.** Of or relating to melancholia. **—mel′an·chol′ic** *n.* **—mel′an·chol′i·cal·ly** *adv.*

mel·an·chol·y (mĕl′ən-kŏl′ē) *n.* **1.** Sadness or depression of the spirits; gloom: *"There is melancholy in the wind and sorrow in the grass"* (Charles Kuralt). **2.** Pensive reflection or contemplation. **3.** *Archaic.* **a.** Black bile. **b.** An emotional state characterized by sullenness and outbreaks of violent anger, believed to arise from black bile. **—melancholy** *adj.* **1.** Affected with or marked by depression of the spirits; sad. See Synonyms at **sad. 2.** Tending to promote sadness or gloom: *a letter with some melancholy news.* **3.** Pensive; thoughtful. [Middle English *melancolie,* from Old French, from Late Latin *melancholia,* from Greek *melankholia* : *melas, melan-,* black + *kholē,* bile; see **ghel-**[2] in Appendix.] **—mel′an·chol′i·ly** *adv.* **—mel′an·chol′i·ness** *n.*

Me·lanch·thon (mə-lăngk′thən, mā-länkн′tôn), **Philipp.** 1497–1560. German theologian and a leader of the German Reformation. A friend of Martin Luther, he wrote *Loci Communes* (1521), the first extensive treatise on Protestant doctrine.

Mel·a·ne·sia (mĕl′ə-nē′zhə, -shə). A division of Oceania in the southwest Pacific Ocean comprising the islands northeast of Australia and south of the equator. It includes the Solomon Islands, New Hebrides, New Caledonia, the Bismarck Archipelago, various other island groups, and sometimes New Guinea.

Mel·a·ne·sian (mĕl′ə-nē′zhən, -shən) *adj.* Of or relating to Melanesia or its peoples, languages, or cultures. **—Melanesian** *n.* **1.** A member of any of the indigenous peoples of Melanesia. **2.** A subfamily of the Austronesian languages that includes the languages of Melanesia.

mé·lange also **me·lange** (mā-länzh′) *n.* A mixture: "[a] *building crowned with a mélange of antennae and satellite dishes"* (Howard Kaplan). [French, from Old French *meslance,* from *mesler,* to mix. See MEDDLE.]

me·lan·ic (mə-lăn′ĭk) *adj.* **1.** Of, relating to, or exhibiting melanism. **2.** Of or affected with melanosis; melanotic.

mel·a·nin (mĕl′ə-nĭn) *n.* Any of a group of naturally occurring dark pigments, especially the pigment found in skin, hair, fur, and feathers.

mel·a·nism (mĕl′ə-nĭz′əm) *n.* **1.** See **melanosis. 2.** Dark coloration of the skin, hair, fur, or feathers because of a high concentration of melanin. **—mel′a·nis′tic** *adj.*

mel·a·nite (mĕl′ə-nīt′) *n.* A black variety of garnet. **—mel′a·nit′ic** (-nĭt′ĭk) *adj.*

melano– or **melan–** *pref.* Black; dark: *melanin.* [Greek, from *melas, melan-,* black.]

mel·a·no·blast (mĕl′ə-nō-blăst′, mə-lăn′ə-) *n.* A precursor cell of a melanocyte or melanophore. **—mel′a·no·blas′tic** *adj.*

mel·a·no·cyte (mĕl′ə-nō-sīt′) *n.* An epidermal cell capable of synthesizing melanin.

mel·a·no·cyte-stim·u·lat·ing hormone (mĕl′ə-nō-sīt′stĭm′yə-lā′tĭng, mə-lăn′ə-) *n. Abbr.* **MSH** A hormone secreted by the pituitary gland that regulates skin color in human beings and other vertebrates by stimulating melanin synthesis in melanocytes and melanin granule dispersal in melanophores. Also called *intermedin.*

mel·a·noid (mĕl′ə-noid′) *adj.* **1.** Of or related to melanin; black-pigmented. **2.** Of or affected with melanosis. **—mel′a·noid′** *n.*

mel·a·no·ma (mĕl′ə-nō′mə) *n., pl.* **-mas** or **-ma·ta** (-mə-tə). *Pathology.* A dark-pigmented, usually malignant tumor arising from a melanocyte and occurring most commonly in the skin.

mel·a·no·phore (mĕl′ə-nə-fôr′, -fōr′, mə-lăn′ə-) *n.* A pig-

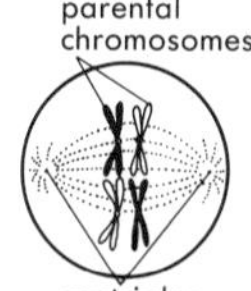

FIRST DIVISION

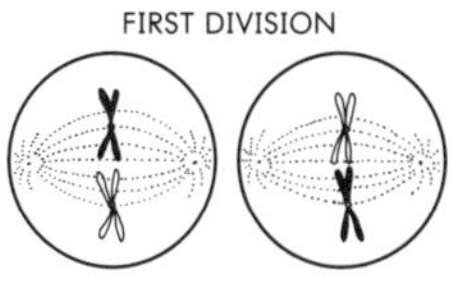

SECOND DIVISION

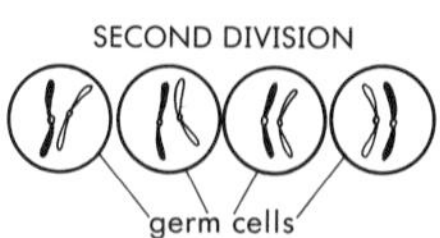

meiosis

Golda Meir

ă pat	oi boy
ā pay	ou out
âr care	ŏŏ took
ä father	ōō boot
ĕ pet	ŭ cut
ē be	ûr urge
ĭ pit	th thin
ī pie	*th* this
îr pier	hw which
ŏ pot	zh vision
ō toe	ə about, item
ô paw	♦ regionalism

Stress marks: **′** (primary); ′ (secondary), as in **dictionary** (dĭk′shə-nĕr′ē)

ment cell that contains melanin, especially as found in the skin of amphibians and reptiles.

mel•a•no•sis (mĕl′ə-nō′sĭs) *n., pl.* **-ses** (-sēz). Abnormally dark pigmentation of the skin or other tissues, resulting from a disorder of pigment metabolism. Also called *melanism.* **—mel′a•not′ic** (-nŏt′ĭk) *adj.*

mel•a•nous (mĕl′ə-nəs) *adj.* Having a swarthy or black complexion and black hair. **—mel′a•nos′i•ty** (-nŏs′ĭ-tē) *n.*

mel•a•phyre (mĕl′ə-fīr′) *n.* A dark igneous porphyry embedded with feldspar crystals. [French *mélaphyre* : Greek *melas,* black + French *porphyre,* porphyry (from Medieval Latin *porphyrium;* see PORPHYRY).]

mel•a•to•nin (mĕl′ə-tō′nĭn) *n.* A hormone derived from serotonin and produced by the pineal gland that stimulates color change in the epidermis of amphibians and reptiles but whose function in mammals is not clear. [Greek *melas,* black + TONE + –IN.]

Mel•ba (mĕl′bə), Dame **Nellie.** Originally Helen Porter Mitchell. 1861–1931. Australian soprano primarily with London's Covent Garden (1889–1926) and the Metropolitan Opera in New York City (1893–1911).

Melba toast *n.* Very thinly sliced crisp toast. [After Dame Nellie MELBA.]

WORD HISTORY: One might think that Helen Porter Mitchell has nothing named after her until one learns that Mitchell's stage name was Dame Nellie Melba, her last name being an allusion to her native city, Melbourne, Australia. This famous opera singer of the late 19th and early 20th century inspired others to honor her by naming things, such as "soaps and sauces, ribbons and ruffles," after her. Perhaps the most well known of such honors are Melba toast and peach Melba. Auguste Escoffier, the famous chef, is thought to have had a hand in both. *Melba toast* is said to be derived from the crisp toast that was part of her diet during the year 1897, a year in which she was very ill. It was supposedly named *toast Melba* by César Ritz, the hotel proprietor, in a conversation with Escoffier. *Pêche Melba* was supposedly created by Escoffier in 1892 for a party honoring her at the Savoy Hotel in London, although neither Escoffier nor Melba agrees with this version. *Peach Melba* is first recorded in English in 1905 (in the form *Pêches à la Melba* and *Melba toast)* in 1925.

Mel•bourne (mĕl′bərn). **1.** A city of southeast Australia southwest of Canberra. Settled in 1835, it was the seat of the Australian federal government from 1901 to 1927. Metropolitan area population, 2,722,817. **2.** A city of east-central Florida on Indian River south of Cocoa Beach. It is a winter resort with varied light industries. Population, 45,536.

Melbourne, Second Viscount. Title of William Lamb. 1779–1848. British politician who served as prime minister (1834 and 1835–1841) during the early reign of Victoria.

Mel•chi•or (mĕl′kē-ôr′). In the New Testament, one of the three wise men from the East who came bearing gifts for the infant Jesus, guided by the Star of Bethlehem.

Melchior, Lauritz Lebrecht Hommel. 1890–1973. Danish-born American operatic tenor noted for his Wagnerian roles.

Mel•chite (mĕl′kīt) *n.* Variant of **Melkite.**

Mel•chiz•e•dek[1] (mĕl-kĭz′ĭ-dĕk′). In the Old Testament, the high priest and king of Salem who blessed Abraham.

Mel•chiz•e•dek[2] (mĕl-kĭz′ĭ-dĕk′) *n. Mormon Church.* The higher order of priesthood. [After MELCHIZEDEK[1].] **—Mel•chiz′e•dek′** *adj.*

meld[1] (mĕld) *Games. v.* **meld•ed, meld•ing, melds.** *—tr.* To declare or display (a card or combination of cards in a hand) for inclusion in one's score in various card games, such as pinochle. *—intr.* To present a meld. **—meld** *n.* A combination of cards to be declared for a score. [Probably German *melden,* to announce, from Middle High German, from Old High German *meldōn.*]

meld[2] (mĕld) *v.* **meld•ed, meld•ing, melds.** *—tr.* To cause to merge: *"a professional position that seemed to meld all his training"* (Art Jahnke). *—intr.* To become merged. **—meld** *n.* A blend or merger: *"a meld of diverse ethnic stocks"* (Kenneth L. Woodward). [Perhaps blend of MELT and WELD[2].]

me•lee (mā′lā′, mā-lā′) also **mê•lée** (mĕ-lā′) *n.* **1.a.** Confused, hand-to-hand fighting in a pitched battle. **b.** A violent free-for-all. See Synonyms at **brawl. 2.** A confused, tumultuous mingling, as of a crowd: *the rush-hour melee.* [French *mêlée,* from Old French *meslee,* past participle of *mesler,* to mix. See MEDDLE.]

me•le•na (mə-lē′nə) *n.* A condition marked by black, tarry stool or vomit composed largely of blood that has been acted on by gastric juices, resulting from a hemorrhage along the digestive tract. [New Latin *melēna,* from Greek *melaina,* feminine of *melas,* black.]

mel•ic (mĕl′ĭk) *adj.* Of or relating to verse that is intended to be sung, especially Greek lyric verse of the seventh to fifth century B.C. [Greek *melikos,* from *melos,* song.]

Me•lil•la (mā-lēl′yä). A Spanish city on the Mediterranean coast of northeast Morocco. Conquered by Spain c. 1496, it was the site of the army revolt that triggered the Spanish Civil War in 1936. Population, 56,247.

mel•i•lot (mĕl′ə-lŏt′) *n.* Any of several Old World plants of the genus *Melilotus* in the pea family, having compound leaves with three leaflets and narrow racemes of small white or yellow flowers. Also called *sweet clover.* [Middle English *melilote,* from Old French, from Latin *melilōtos,* from Greek : *meli,* honey; see **melit-** in Appendix + *lōtos,* lotus.]

mel•io•rate (mēl′yə-rāt′, mē′lē-ə-) *v.* **-rat•ed, -rat•ing, -rates.** *—tr.* To make better; improve. *—intr.* To grow better. [Latin *meliōrāre, meliōrāt-,* from *melior,* better. See **mel-[2]** in Appendix.] **—mel′io•ra•ble** (-rə-bəl) *adj.* **—mel′io•ra′tive** *adj. & n.* **—mel′io•ra′tor** *n.*

mel•io•ra•tion (mēl′yə-rā′shən, mē′lē-ə-) *n.* **1.a.** The act or process of improving something or the state of being improved. **b.** An improvement. **2.** The linguistic process by which a word over a period of time grows more elevated in meaning or more positive in connotation.

mel•io•rism (mēl′yə-rĭz′əm, mē′lē-ə-) *n.* The belief that society has an innate tendency toward improvement and that this tendency may be furthered through conscious human effort. [Latin *melior,* better; see **mel-[2]** in Appendix + –ISM.] **—mel′io•rist** *n.* **—mel′io•ris′tic** *adj.*

me•lis•ma (mə-lĭz′mə) *n., pl.* **-ma•ta** (-mə-tə) or **-mas.** *Music.* A decorative passage of several notes sung to one syllable of text, as in Gregorian chant. [Greek, melody, from *melizein,* to sing, from *melos,* song.] **—mel′is•mat′ic** (mĕl′ĭz-măt′ĭk) *adj.*

Mel•kite or **Mel•chite** (mĕl′kīt) *n.* **1.** A member of the Christian churches in Egypt and Syria that accepted the Council of Chalcedon. **2.** A member of a Christian church using the Byzantine rite and belonging to the patriarchates of Alexandria, Antioch, or Jerusalem, especially a Uniat Christian. [New Latin *Melchītae,* Melkites, from Medieval Greek *Melkhitai,* from Syriac *malkāyê,* royalists, pl. of *malkā,* king.]

mel•lif•er•ous (mə-lĭf′ər-əs) also **mel•lif•ic** (-lĭf′ĭk) *adj.* Forming or bearing honey. [From Latin *mellifer* : *mel, mell-,* honey; see **melit-** in Appendix + *-fer,* -fer.]

mel•lif•lu•ent (mə-lĭf′lo͞o-ənt) *adj.* Mellifluous. **—mel•lif′lu•ent•ly** *adv.*

mel•lif•lu•ous (mə-lĭf′lo͞o-əs) *adj.* **1.** Flowing with sweetness or honey. **2.** Smooth and sweet: *"polite and cordial, with a mellifluous, well-educated voice"* (H.W. Crocker III). [Middle English, from Late Latin *mellifluus* : Latin *mel, mell-,* honey; see **melit-** in Appendix + Latin *-fluus,* flowing; see **bhleu-** in Appendix.] **—mel•lif′lu•ous•ly** *adv.* **—mel•lif′lu•ous•ness** *n.*

Mel•lon (mĕl′ən), **Andrew William.** 1855–1937. American financier and public official who served as U.S. secretary of the treasury (1921–1932).

mel•lo•phone (mĕl′ō-fōn′) *n. Music.* A brass wind instrument, similar to the French horn, often used in military or marching bands. [MELLO(W) + –PHONE.]

mel•low (mĕl′ō) *adj.* **-er, -est. 1.a.** Soft, sweet, juicy, and full-flavored because of ripeness: *a mellow fruit.* **b.** Suggesting softness or sweetness: *"The mellow air brought in the feel of imminent autumn"* (Thomas Hardy). **2.** Rich and soft in quality: *a mellow sound; a mellow wine.* **3.** Having the gentleness, wisdom, or tolerance often characteristic of maturity. **4.** Relaxed and unhurried; easygoing: *a mellow friend; a mellow conversation.* **5.** *Slang.* **a.** Slightly and pleasantly intoxicated. **b.** Pleasantly high from a drug, especially from smoking marijuana. **6.** Moist, rich, soft, and loamy. Used of soil. **—mellow** *tr. & intr.v.* **-lowed, -low•ing, -lows.** To make or become mellow. ***—phrasal verb.*** **mellow out.** *Slang.* To become genial and pleasant; relax: *"The cowboy mellowed out when they read him a sweet letter from his wife"* (Bobbie Ann Mason). [Middle English *melwe,* perhaps from *melowe,* variant of *mele,* ground grain, meal. See MEAL[1].] **—mel′low•ly** *adv.* **—mel′low•ness** *n.*

me•lo•de•on (mə-lō′dē-ən) *n. Music.* A small reed organ. [Probably alteration of *melodium,* from MELODY.]

me•lod•ic (mə-lŏd′ĭk) *adj. Music.* Of, relating to, or containing melody. **—me•lod′i•cal•ly** *adv.*

me•lo•di•ous (mə-lō′dē-əs) *adj.* **1.** Of, relating to, or containing a pleasing succession of sounds; tuneful. **2.** Agreeable to hear: *a melodious voice; the melodious song of a bird.* **—me•lo′di•ous•ly** *adv.* **—me•lo′di•ous•ness** *n.*

mel•o•dize (mĕl′ə-dīz′) *v.* **-dized, -diz•ing, -diz•es.** *Music. —tr.* **1.** To write a melody for (a song lyric). **2.** To make melodious. *—intr.* To compose a melody. **—mel′o•diz′er, mel′o•dist** *n.*

mel•o•dra•ma (mĕl′ə-drä′mə, -drăm′ə) *n.* **1.a.** A drama, such as a play, film, or television program, characterized by exaggerated emotions, stereotypical characters, and interpersonal conflicts. **b.** The dramatic genre characterized by this treatment. **2.** Behavior or occurrences having melodramatic characteristics. [Alteration of *melodrame,* from French *mélodrame,* spoken drama that includes some musical accompaniment, melodrama : Greek *melos,* song + French *drame,* drama (from Late Latin *drāma;* see DRAMA).]

mel•o•dra•mat•ic (mĕl′ə-drə-măt′ĭk) *adj.* **1.** Having the excitement and emotional appeal of melodrama: *"a melodramatic account of two perilous days spent among the planters"* (Frank O. Gatell). **2.** Exaggeratedly emotional or sentimental; histrionic: *"Accuse me, if you will, of melodramatic embroidery"* (Erskine Childers). See Synonyms at **dramatic. 3.** Characterized by false pathos and sentiment. **—mel′o•dra•mat′i•cal•ly** *adv.*

mel•o•dra•mat•ics (mĕl′ə-drə-măt′ĭks) *n.* **1.** *(used with a sing. verb).* Melodramatic theatrical performance. **2.** *(used with a pl. verb).* Exaggeratedly emotional behavior; histrionics.

mel•o•dy (mĕl′ə-dē) *n., pl.* **-dies. 1.** A pleasing succession or arrangement of sounds. **2.** Musical quality: *the melody of verse.* **3.** *Music.* **a.** A rhythmically organized sequence of single tones so related to one another as to make up a particular phrase or idea. **b.** Structure with respect to the arrangement of single notes in succession. **c.** The leading part or the air in a harmonic composition. **4.** A poem suitable for setting to music or singing. [Middle English *melodie,* from Old French, from Late Latin *melōdia,* from Greek *melōidia,* singing choral song : *melos,* tune + *aoidē,* song; see **wed-**[2] in Appendix.]

mel•oid (mĕl′oid′, mĕl′ō-ĭd) *n.* See **blister beetle. —meloid** *adj.* Of or relating to blister beetles. [From New Latin *Meloidae,* family name, from *Meloe,* type genus.]

mel•on (mĕl′ən) *n.* **1.** Any of several varieties of two related vines *(Cucumis melo* or *Citrullus lanatus)* widely cultivated for their edible fruit. **2.** The fruit of any of these plants, having a hard rind and juicy flesh. [Middle English, from Old French, from Late Latin *mēlō, mēlōn-,* short for Latin *mēlopepō,* from Greek *mēlopepōn* : *mēlon,* apple + *pepōn,* gourd.]

mel•on•gene (mĕl′ən-jēn′) *n.* See **eggplant** (sense 1). [French *mélongène,* from Old French *melanjan, melonge,* from Medieval Latin *melongēna,* from Old Italian *melanzana, melongiane,* from Medieval Greek *melintzana, melanzana,* alteration (influenced by Greek *melas,* dark) of Arabic *bāḏinjān,* from Persian *bādingān.*]

Me•los (mē′lôs). See **Milos.**

Mel•pom•e•ne (mĕl-pŏm′ə-nē′) *n.* *Greek Mythology.* The Muse of tragedy.

Mel•rose (mĕl′rōz′). A city of northeast Massachusetts, a residential suburb of Boston. Population, 30,005.

Melrose Park. A village of northeast Illinois, an industrial suburb of Chicago. Population, 20,735.

melt (mĕlt) *v.* **melt•ed, melt•ing, melts.** —*intr.* **1.** To be changed from a solid to a liquid state by application of heat or pressure or both. **2.** To dissolve: *Sugar melts in water.* **3.** To disappear or vanish gradually as if by dissolving: *The crowd melted away after the rally.* **4.** To pass or merge imperceptibly into something else: *Sea melted into sky along the horizon.* **5.** To become softened in feeling: *Our hearts melted at the child's tears.* **6.** *Obsolete.* To be overcome or crushed, as by grief, dismay, or fear. —*tr.* **1.** To change (a solid) to a liquid state by the application of heat or pressure or both. **2.** To dissolve: *The tide melted our sand castle away.* **3.** To cause to disappear gradually; disperse. **4.** To cause (units) to blend: *"Here individuals of all races are melted into a new race of men"* (Michel Guillaume Jean de Crèvecoeur). **5.** To soften (someone's feelings); make gentle or tender. **—melt** *n.* **1.** A melted solid; a fused mass. **2.** The state of being melted. **3. a.** The act or operation of melting. **b.** The quantity melted at a single operation or in one period. **4.** A usually open sandwich topped with melted cheese: *a tuna melt.* —*attributive.* Often used to modify another noun: *glacial melt water; the summer melt season.* [Middle English *melten,* from Old English *meltan.* See **mel-**[1] in Appendix.] **—melt′a•bil′i•ty** *n.* **—melt′a•ble** *adj.* **—melt′er** *n.* **—melt′ing•ly** *adv.* **—melt′y** *adj.*

SYNONYMS: *melt, fuse, liquefy, thaw, deliquesce.* These verbs mean to change or cause to change into a liquid. *Melt* implies liquefaction caused principally by heat: *The candle softened and melted in the sun. I melted the butter in a saucepan.* Figuratively the term suggests gradual dispersion, dissipation, and disappearance: *"They melt like mist, the solid lands"* (Tennyson). *"The usual reserve of their manner . . . has . . . melted away"* (Thomas De Quincey). *Melt* can also mean to become softened in feeling, as through pity, sympathy, or love: *His heart melted at the sight of the injured child. Fuse* primarily suggests the union of different constituents, such as two minerals, by or as if by heating: *"It is the most formidable kind of faith—the kind that is emotionally fused with national pride"* (Conor Cruise O'Brien). *Liquefy,* unlike the other terms in this group, is restricted to physical processes but is used of both gases and solids: *a process that is used to liquefy nitrogen. Thaw* applies to the partial or complete melting of something, such as ice, that is frozen; figuratively it suggests the softening or dissolution of something, as of formality or reserve, likened to a frozen substance: *"The short, shy manner of their white-haired host thawed under the influence of Mrs. Elsmere's racy, unaffected ways"* (Mrs. Humphry Ward). To *deliquesce* is to become liquid, usually gradually, through absorption of moisture from the air: *"Pure chloride of sodium is not liable to deliquesce"* (David Page).

melt•age (mĕl′tĭj) *n.* **1.** The substance or quantity of a substance produced by a melting process. **2.** The act or process of melting.

melt•down (mĕlt′doun′) *n.* **1.** Severe overheating of a nuclear reactor core, resulting in melting of the core and escape of radiation. **2.** *Informal.* A situation likened to the melting of a nuclear reactor core: *"After several corporate meltdowns, only two reporters remain in* [the] *bureau"* (David Fitzpatrick).

melt•ing point (mĕl′tĭng) *n.* *Abbr.* **mp, m.p.** *Chemistry.* **1.** The temperature at which a solid becomes a liquid at standard atmospheric pressure. **2.** The temperature at which a solid and its liquid are in equilibrium, at any fixed pressure.

melting pot *n.* **1.** A container in which a substance is melted. **2.** A place where immigrants of different cultures or races form an integrated society: *"Canadians . . . liked to think of their country as a mosaic rather than a melting pot"* (Kenneth McNaught).

mel•ton (mĕl′tən) *n.* A heavy woolen cloth used chiefly for making overcoats and hunting jackets. [After *Melton* Mowbray, an urban district of central England.]

Mel•ville (mĕl′vĭl), **Herman.** 1819–1891. American writer whose experiences at sea provided the factual basis of his allegorical masterpiece *Moby Dick* (1851), considered among the greatest American novels. **—Mel•vil′le•an** (-vĭl′ē-ən) *adj.*

Melville, Lake. A saltwater lake of Newfoundland, Canada, in southeast Labrador. It receives the Churchill River in Goose Bay, its southwest arm.

Melville Island. 1. An island of northern Australia in the Timor Sea. **2.** An island of northern Northwest Territories, Canada, in the Queen Elizabeth Islands north of Victoria Island.

Melville Peninsula. A peninsula of eastern Northwest Territories, Canada, between Foxe Basin and an arm of the Gulf of Boothia. It is separated from Baffin Island by a narrow strait.

melon

mem (mĕm) *n.* The 13th letter of the Hebrew alphabet. See table at **alphabet.** [Hebrew, perhaps from *mayīm,* water.]

mem. *abbr.* **1.** Member. **2.** Memoir. **3.** Memorandum. **4.** Memorial.

mem•ber (mĕm′bər) *n.* *Abbr.* **mem. 1.** A distinct part of a whole, especially: **a.** *Linguistics.* A syntactic unit of a sentence; a clause. **b.** *Logic.* A proposition of a syllogism. **c.** *Mathematics.* An element in a set. **2.** A part or an organ of a human or animal body, as: **a.** A limb, such as an arm or a leg. **b.** The penis. **3.** A part of a plant. **4.** One that belongs to a group or an organization: *a club member; a bank that is a member of the FDIC.* **5.** *Mathematics.* The expression on either side of an equality sign. **6.** A structural unit, such as a beam or wall. [Middle English *membre,* from Old French, from Latin *membrum.*]

member firm *n.* A securities firm with officers or partners who are members of an organized exchange.

mem•ber•ship (mĕm′bər-shĭp′) *n.* **1.** The state of being a member. **2.** The total number of members in a group: *an organization with a growing membership.*

mem•brane (mĕm′brān′) *n.* **1.** *Biology.* **a.** A thin, pliable layer of tissue covering surfaces or separating or connecting regions, structures, or organs of an animal or a plant. **b.** Cell membrane. **2.** A piece of parchment. **3.** *Chemistry.* A thin sheet of natural or synthetic material that is permeable to substances in solution. [Latin *membrāna,* skin, from *membrum,* member of the body.] **—mem′bra•nal** (-brə-nəl) *adj.*

membrane bone *n.* A bone that forms directly in membranous connective tissue, as some cranial bones, instead of developing from cartilage.

mem•bra•nous (mĕm′brə-nəs) *adj.* **1.** Relating to, made of, or similar to a membrane. **2.** *Pathology.* Characterized by the formation of a membrane or a layer similar to a membrane.

membranous labyrinth *n.* The fluid-filled membranous sacs of the inner ear that are associated with the senses of hearing and balance.

Me•mel (mā′məl). See **Klaipeda.**

me•men•to (mə-mĕn′tō) *n., pl.* **-tos** or **-toes.** A reminder of the past; a keepsake. [Middle English, commemoration of the living or the dead in the Canon of the Mass, from Latin *mementō,* imperative of *meminisse,* to remember. See **men-**[1] in Appendix.]

memento mo•ri (môr′ē) *n., pl.* **memento mori. 1.** A reminder of death or mortality, especially a death's-head. **2.** A reminder of human failures or errors. [Medieval Latin **mementō morī,* be mindful of dying : Latin *mementō,* imperative of *meminisse,* to remember + Latin *morī,* to die.]

Mem•ling (mĕm′lĭng) also **Mem•linc** (-lĭngk), **Hans.** 1430?–1494. Flemish painter of portraits and, more notably, religious works, such as the triptych *Adoration of the Magi* (1479).

Herman Melville

Mem•non (mĕm′nŏn′) *n.* *Greek Mythology.* An Ethiopian king killed by Achilles and made immortal by Zeus.

mem•o (mĕm′ō) *n., pl.* **-os.** *Informal.* A memorandum.

mem•oir (mĕm′wär′, -wôr′) *n.* *Abbr.* **mem. 1.** An account of the personal experiences of an author. **2.** Often **memoirs.** An autobiography. **3.** A biography or biographical sketch. **4.** A report, especially on a scientific or scholarly topic. **5. memoirs.** The report of the proceedings of a learned society. [French *mémoire,* from Old French *memoire,* memory. See MEMORY.] **—mem′oir•ist** *n.*

mem•o•ra•bil•i•a (mĕm′ər-ə-bĭl′ē-ə, -bĭl′yə) *pl.n.* **1.** Objects valued for their connection with historical events, culture, or entertainment: *posters, publicity photographs, and other movie memorabilia.* **2.** Events or experiences worthy of remembrance: *memorabilia of a life in the theater.* [Latin *memorābilia,* neuter pl. of *memorābilis,* memorable. See MEMORABLE.]

mem•o•ra•ble (mĕm′ər-ə-bəl) *adj.* Worth being remembered or noted: *"memoirs of people who never had a memorable thought"* (George F. Will). [Middle English, from Old French, from Latin *memorābilis,* from *memorāre,* to bring to remembrance, from *memor,* mindful. See **(s)mer-**[1] in Appendix.] **—mem′o•ra•bil′i•ty, mem′o•ra•ble•ness** *n.* **—mem′o•ra•bly** *adv.*

mem•o•ran•dum (mĕm′ə-răn′dəm) *n., pl.* **-dums** or **-da** (-də). *Abbr.* **mem. 1.** A short note written as a reminder. **2.** A written record or communication, as in a business office. **3.** *Law.*

ă pat	oi **boy**
ā pay	ou **out**
âr **care**	ŏŏ **took**
ä father	ōō **boot**
ĕ pet	ŭ cut
ē be	ûr **urge**
ĭ pit	th **thin**
ī **pie**	*th* **this**
îr **pier**	hw **which**
ŏ pot	zh vision
ō **toe**	ə about, item
ô paw	♦ regionalism

Stress marks: ′ (primary); ′ (secondary), as in **dictionary** (dĭk′shə-nĕr′ē)

memorial
Vietnam Veterans Memorial by Maya Yang Lin

A short written statement outlining the terms of an agreement, a transaction, or a contract. **4.** A business statement made by a consignor about a shipment of goods that may be returned. **5.** A brief, unsigned diplomatic communication. [Middle English, to be remembered: used as a manuscript notation, from Latin, neuter sing. gerundive of *memorāre,* to bring to remembrance. See MEMORABLE.]

me·mo·ri·al (mə-môr′ē-əl, -mōr′-) *n. Abbr.* **mem. 1.** Something, such as a monument or holiday, intended to celebrate or honor the memory of a person or an event. **2.** A written statement of facts or a petition presented to a legislative body or an executive. **—memorial** *adj.* **1.** Serving as a remembrance of a person or an event; commemorative. **2.** Of, relating to, or being in memory. [Middle English, from Old French, from Late Latin *memoriāle,* from neuter of Latin *memoriālis,* belonging to memory, from *memoria,* memory. See MEMORY.] **—me·mo′ri·al·ly** *adv.*

Me·mo·ri·al Day (mə-môr′ē-əl, -mōr′-) *n.* May 30, observed in the United States in commemoration of those members of the armed forces killed in war. It is officially observed on the last Monday in May. Also called *Decoration Day.*

me·mo·ri·al·ist (mə-môr′ē-ə-lĭst, -mōr′-) *n.* **1.** A person who writes memoirs. **2.** A person who writes or signs a memorial.

me·mo·ri·al·ize (mə-môr′ē-ə-līz′, mə-mōr′-) *tr.v.* **-ized, -iz·ing, -iz·es. 1.** To provide a memorial for; commemorate. **2.** To present a memorial to; petition. **—me·mo′ri·al·i·za′tion** (-ə-lĭ-zā′shən) *n.* **—me·mo′ri·al·iz′er** *n.*

memorial park *n.* A cemetery.

mem·o·rize (mĕm′ə-rīz′) *tr.v.* **-rized, -riz·ing, -riz·es. 1.** To commit to memory; learn by heart. **2.** *Computer Science.* To store in memory: *"Some programmable phones can now memorize up to 100 numbers"* (Time). **—mem′o·riz′a·ble** *adj.* **—mem′o·ri·za′tion** (-rĭ-zā′shən) *n.* **—mem′o·riz′er** *n.*

mem·o·ry (mĕm′ə-rē) *n., pl.* **-ries. 1.** The mental faculty of retaining and recalling past experience. **2.** The act or an instance of remembering; recollection: *spent the afternoon lost in memory.* **3.** All that a person can remember: *It hasn't happened in my memory.* **4.** Something remembered: *pleasant childhood memories.* **5.** The fact of being remembered; remembrance: *dedicated to their grandparents' memory.* **6.** The period of time covered by the remembrance or recollection of a person or group of persons: *within the memory of humankind.* **7.** *Biology.* Persistent modification of behavior resulting from an animal's experience. **8.** *Computer Science.* **a.** A unit of a computer that preserves data for retrieval. **b.** Capacity for storing information: *two million bytes of memory.* **9.** *Statistics.* The set of past events affecting a given event in a stochastic process. **10.** The capacity of a material, such as plastic or metal, to return to a previous shape after deformation. [Middle English *memorie,* from Anglo-French, from Latin *memoria,* from *memor,* mindful. See **(s)mer-**[1] in Appendix.]

SYNONYMS: *memory, remembrance, recollection, reminiscence.* These nouns denote the act or an instance of remembering, or something remembered. *Memory* is the faculty of retaining and reviving impressions or recalling past experiences: *He has a bad memory for facts and figures. "Even memory is not necessary for love"* (Thornton Wilder). The word also applies to something recalled to the mind, a sense in which it often suggests a personal, cherished quality: *"My earliest memories were connected with the South"* (Thomas B. Aldrich). *Remembrance* most often denotes the process or act of recalling: *The remembrance of his humiliation was almost too painful to bear. Recollection* is sometimes interchangeable with *memory*: *My recollection of the incident differs from yours.* Often, though, the term suggests a deliberate, concentrated effort to remember: *After a few minutes' recollection she produced the answer. Reminiscence* is the act or process of recollecting past experiences or events within one's personal knowledge: *"Her mind seemed wholly taken up with reminiscences of past gaiety"* (Charlotte Brontë). When the word refers to what is remembered, it may involve the sharing of the recollection with another or others: *They spent some time in reminiscence before turning to the business that had brought them together.*

memory engram *n.* An engram.

memory trace *n.* An engram.

Mem·phis (mĕm′fĭs). **1.** An ancient city of Egypt south of Cairo. Reputedly founded by Menes, the first king of united Egypt, it retained its primacy until the conquest of Egypt by Alexander the Great. **2.** A city of southwest Tennessee on the Mississippi River near the Mississippi border. Established and named (1819) by Andrew Jackson on the site of a fort built in 1797, it was an important Union base after its capture by federal troops in 1862 during the Civil War. Population, 646,356.

mem·sa·hib (mĕm′sä′ĭb) *n.* Used formerly as a form of respectful address for a European woman in colonial India. [MA'AM + SAHIB.]

men (mĕn) *n.* Plural of **man.**

men– *pref.* Variant of **meno–.**

men·ace (mĕn′ĭs) *n.* **1.a.** A possible danger; a threat: *the menace of nuclear war.* **b.** The act of threatening. **2.** A troublesome or annoying person: *a toddler who was a menace in a shop full of crystal.* **—menace** *v.* **-aced, -ac·ing, -ac·es.** *—tr.* **1.** To utter threats against. **2.** To constitute a threat to; endanger. See Synonyms at **threaten.** *—intr.* To make threats. [Middle English, from Old French, from Vulgar Latin **mināciа,* sing. of Latin *mināciæ,* threats, menaces, from *mināx, mindruc-,* threatening, from *minārī,* to threaten, from *minae,* threats. See **men-**[2] in Appendix.] **—men′ac·er** *n.* **—men′ac·ing·ly** *adv.*

men·a·di·one (mĕn′ə-dī′ōn′) *n.* A yellow crystalline powder, $C_{11}H_8O_2$, used in medicine as a vitamin K supplement. [ME(THYL) + NA(PHTHALENE) + DI–[1] + –ONE.]

mé·nage (mā-näzh′) *n.* **1.** People living together as a unit; a household. **2.** The management of a household. [French, from Old French, from *maneir,* to stay, from Latin *manēre,* to remain. See REMAIN.]

ménage à trois (ä trwä′) *n.* A relationship wherein three people, such as a married couple and a lover, live together. [French : *ménage,* household + *à,* for + *trois,* three.]

me·nag·er·ie (mə-năj′ə-rē, -năzh′-) *n.* **1.a.** A collection of live wild animals on exhibition. **b.** An enclosure in which wild animals are kept. **2.** A diverse or miscellaneous group. [French *ménagerie,* from Old French *menage,* ménage. See MÉNAGE.]

Me·nan·der (mə-năn′dər). 342–292 B.C. Greek dramatist whose works were influential in the development of comedy.

me·nar·che (mə-när′kē) *n.* The first menstrual period, usually occurring during puberty. [MEN(O)– + Greek *arkhē,* beginning (from *arkhein,* to begin).] **—me·nar′che·al** *adj.*

men-at-arms (mĕn′ət-ärmz′) *n.* Plural of **man-at-arms.**

men·a·zon (mĕn′ə-zŏn′) *n.* A colorless crystalline compound, $C_6H_8N_5O_2PS_2$, used as an insecticide against aphids. [(DI)ME(THYL) + (DIAMI)N(E) + (TRI)AZ(INE) + *(thi)on(ate),* salt or ester of a thionic acid (THION– + –ATE[2]).]

men·chil·dren (mĕn′ chĭl′drən) *n.* Plural of **man-child.**

Men·ci·us (mĕn′shē-əs). Originally **Meng·zi** (mœng′zē′). Fourth century B.C. Chinese Confucian philosopher who taught that man is innately good and that one's nature can be enhanced or perverted by one's environment.

Menck·en (mĕng′kən), **H(enry) L(ouis).** 1880–1956. American editor and critic. A founder and editor (1924–1933) of the *American Mercury,* he wrote essays of vitriolic social criticism. **—Menck·e′ni·an** (mĕng-kē′nē-ən) *adj.*

mend (mĕnd) *v.* **mend·ed, mend·ing, mends.** *—tr.* **1.** To make repairs or restoration to; fix. **2.** To reform or correct: *mend one's ways.* *—intr.* **1.a.** To improve in health or condition: *The patient is mending well.* **b.** To heal: *The bone mended in a month.* **2.** To make repairs or corrections. **—mend** *n.* **1.** The act of mending: *did a neat mend on the sock.* **2.** A mended place: *You can't tell where the mend is.* **—*idioms.* mend fences.** To improve poor relations, especially in politics: *"Whatever thoughts he may have entertained about mending some fences with* [them] *were banished"* (Conor Cruise O'Brien). **on the mend.** Improving, especially in health. [Middle English *menden,* short for *amenden,* to amend. See AMEND.] **—mend′a·ble** *adj.* **—mend′er** *n.*

men·da·cious (mĕn-dā′shəs) *adj.* **1.** Lying; untruthful: *a mendacious child.* **2.** False; untrue: *a mendacious statement.* See Synonyms at **dishonest.** [From Latin *mendācium,* lie, from *mendāx, mendāc-,* mendacious.] **—men·da′cious·ly** *adv.*

men·dac·i·ty (mĕn-dăs′ĭ-tē) *n., pl.* **-ties. 1.** The condition of being mendacious; untruthfulness. **2.** A lie; a falsehood.

Men·del (mĕn′dl), **Gregor Johann.** 1822–1884. Austrian botanist and founder of the science of genetics. Through years of experiments with plants, chiefly garden peas, he discovered the principle of the inheritance of characteristics through the combination of genes from parent cells.

Men·de·le·ev (mĕn′də-lā′əf, myĭn-dĭ-lĕ′yĕf), **Dmitri Ivanovich.** 1834–1907. Russian chemist who first devised and published the periodic table of the elements (1869).

men·de·le·vi·um (mĕn′də-lē′vē-əm) *n. Symbol* **Md** A synthetic radioactive transuranium element of the actinide series. Atomic number 101; mass numbers 255 and 256; half-lives approximately 30 minutes (Md 255) and 1.5 hours (Md 256). See table at **element.** [After Dmitri Ivanovich MENDELEEV.]

Men·de·li·an (mĕn-dē′lē-ən, -dēl′yən) *adj.* Of, relating to, or designating Gregor Mendel or his theories of genetics.

Men·del·ism (mĕn′dl-ĭz′əm) also **Men·de·li·an·ism** (mĕn-dē′lē-ə-nĭz′əm) *n.* The theoretical principles of heredity formulated by Gregor Mendel; Mendel's laws.

Men·del's law (mĕn′dlz) *n.* **1.** One of two principles of heredity first formulated by Gregor Mendel, founded on his experiments with pea plants and stating that the members of a pair of homologous chromosomes segregate during meiosis and are distributed to different gametes. Also called *law of segregation.* **2.** The second of these two principles, stating that each member of a pair of homologous chromosomes segregates during meiosis independently of the members of other pairs, so that alleles carried on different chromosomes are distributed randomly to the gametes. Also called *law of independent assortment.*

Men·dels·sohn (mĕn′dl-sən, -zōn′), **Felix.** Full name Jakob Ludwig Felix Mendelssohn-Bartholdy. 1809–1847. German conductor, pianist, and composer whose works include the *Reformation* (1830) and *Scotch* (1842) symphonies.

Mendelssohn, Moses. 1729–1786. German philosopher noted for his writings on the inborn ability of human beings to recognize beauty, truth, and goodness.

Men·de·res (mĕn′də-rĕs′). A river of western Turkey flowing about 402 km (250 mi) southwest and west to the Aegean Sea. In ancient times it was called the Maeander and was legendary for its winding course.

ă pat	oi boy
ā pay	ou out
âr care	o͝o took
ä father	o͞o boot
ĕ pet	ŭ cut
ē be	ûr urge
ĭ pit	th thin
ī pie	*th* this
îr pier	hw which
ŏ pot	zh vision
ō toe	ə about, item
ô paw	♦ regionalism

Stress marks: ′ (primary); ′ (secondary), as in **dictionary** (dĭk′shə-nĕr′ē)

Men·dès-France (mĕn′dĭs-frăns′, mäN-dĕs-fräNs′), **Pierre.** 1907–1982. French politician who as prime minister (1954–1955) negotiated the withdrawal of France from Indochina.

men·di·cant (mĕn′dĭ-kənt) *adj.* Depending on alms for a living. —**mendicant** *n.* **1.** A beggar. **2.** A member of an order of friars forbidden to own property in common, who work or beg for their living. [Middle English, from Old French, from Latin *mendīcāns, mendīcant-*, present participle of *mendīcāre*, to beg, from *mendīcus*, needy, beggar, from *mendum*, physical defect.] —**men′di·can·cy, men·dic′i·ty** (-dĭs′ĭ-tē) *n.*

mend·ing (mĕn′dĭng) *n.* Clothes and other articles that must be repaired: *We let the mending accumulate until Wednesday.*

Men·do·ci·no (mĕn′də-sē′nō), **Cape.** A promontory of northwest California south-southwest of Eureka. It is the westernmost extremity of the state.

Men·do·za (mĕn-dō′zə, -dô′sä). A city of western Argentina east-northeast of Santiago, Chile. Founded c. 1560, it was part of Chile until 1776. Population, 118,427.

men·eer (mə-nîr′) *n.* Variant of **mynheer.**

Men·e·la·us (mĕn′ə-lā′əs) *n. Greek Mythology.* The king of Sparta at the time of the Trojan War; husband of Helen and brother of Agamemnon.

Men·e·lik II (mĕn′ə-lĭk). 1844–1913. Ethiopian emperor (1889–1913) who established independence from Italy and expanded Ethiopia's borders through military conquests.

Me·nén·dez de A·vi·lés (mə-nĕn′dəs dā ä′və-lās′, mĕ-nĕn′dĕth *thĕ* ä′vē-lĕs′), **Pedro.** 1519–1574. Spanish colonizer who founded the city of St. Augustine, Florida (1565).

Me·nes (mē′nēz). fl. 3000 B.C. King of Egypt who founded the first dynasty uniting Upper and Lower Egypt.

men·folk (mĕn′fōk′) or **men·folks** (-fōks′) *pl.n.* **1.** Men considered as a group. **2.** The male members of a community or family.

Meng·zi (mœng′zē′). See **Mencius.**

men·ha·den (mĕn-hăd′n) *n., pl.* **menhaden** or **-dens.** Any of several species of fish of the genus *Brevoortia*, especially *B. tyrannus* of American Atlantic and Gulf waters, used as a source of fish oil, fertilizer, and bait. Also called *mossbunker, pogy.* [Probably blend of Narragansett *munnawhatteaûg* and English dialectal *poghaden* (probably of Algonquian origin).]

men·hir (mĕn′hîr′) *n.* A prehistoric monument of a class found chiefly in the British Isles and northern France, consisting of a single tall, upright megalith. [French, from Breton : *men*, stone (from Middle Breton) + *hir*, long (from Middle Breton).]

me·ni·al (mē′nē-əl, mēn′yəl) *adj.* **1.** Of or relating to work or a job regarded as servile. **2.** Of, relating to, or appropriate for a servant. —**menial** *n.* **1.** A servant, especially a domestic servant. **2.** A person who has a servile or low nature. [Middle English *meinial*, belonging to a household, from Anglo-Norman *meignial*, from *meignee*, household, from Vulgar Latin **mānsiōnāta*, from Latin *mānsiō, mānsiōn-*, house. See MANSION.] —**me′ni·al·ly** *adv.*

Mé·nière's disease (mān-yârz′) *n.* A pathological condition of the inner ear characterized by dizziness, ringing in the ears, and progressive loss of hearing. Also called *Ménière's syndrome.* [After Prosper *Ménière* (1799–1862), French physician.]

mening– *pref.* Variant of **meningo–.**

me·nin·ge·al (mə-nĭn′jē-əl) *adj.* Of, relating to, or affecting the meninges.

me·nin·ges (mə-nĭn′jēz) *n.* Plural of **meninx.**

meningi– *pref.* Variant of **meningo–.**

me·nin·gi·o·ma (mə-nĭn′jē-ō′mə) *n., pl.* **-mas** or **-ma·ta** (-mə-tə). A slow-growing tumor of the meninges, occurring most often in adults. [Short for *meningothelioma* : MENINGO– + (EN-DO)THELIOMA.]

men·in·gi·tis (mĕn′ĭn-jī′tĭs) *n.* Inflammation of the meninges of the brain and the spinal cord, most often caused by a bacterial or viral infection and characterized by fever, vomiting, intense headache, and stiff neck. —**men′in·git′ic** (-jĭt′ĭk) *adj.*

meningo– or **meningi–** or **mening–** *pref.* Meninges: *meningococcus.* [From Greek *mēninx, mēning-*, meninx.]

me·nin·go·coc·cus (mə-nĭng′gə-kŏk′əs, -nĭn′jə-) *n., pl.* **-coc·ci** (-kŏk′sī, -kī). A bacterium *(Neisseria meningitidis)* that causes cerebrospinal meningitis. —**me·nin′go·coc′cal** (-kŏk′əl), **me·nin′go·coc′cic** (-kŏk′sĭk) *adj.*

me·nin·go·en·ceph·a·li·tis (mə-nĭng′gō-ĕn-sĕf′ə-lī′tĭs) *n.* Inflammation of the brain and meninges. —**me·nin′go·en·ceph′a·lit′ic** (-lĭt′ĭk) *adj.*

me·ninx (mē′nĭngks) *n., pl.* **me·nin·ges** (mə-nĭn′jēz). A membrane, especially one of the three membranes enclosing the brain and spinal cord in vertebrates. [Greek *mēninx.*]

me·nis·cus (mə-nĭs′kəs) *n., pl.* **-nis·ci** (-nĭs′ī, -kī, -kē) or **-nis·cus·es. 1.** A crescent-shaped body. **2.** A concavo-convex lens. **3.** The curved upper surface of a nonturbulent liquid in a container that is concave if the liquid wets the container walls and convex if it does not. **4.** *Anatomy.* A cartilage disk that acts as a cushion between the ends of bones that meet in a joint. [New Latin, from Greek *mēniskos*, diminutive of *mēnē*, moon, month. See **mē-**[2] in Appendix.] —**me·nis′cal** (-kəl), **me·nis′cate′** (-kāt′), **me·nis′coid′** (-koid′), **men′is·coi′dal** (mĕn′ĭs-koid′l) *adj.*

Men·lo Park (mĕn′lō). **1.** A city of western California southeast of San Francisco. Population, 25,673. **2.** An unincorporated community of central New Jersey north of New Brunswick. A memorial tower marks the site of the laboratory where Thomas Edison perfected the incandescent light bulb in 1879.

Men·ning·er (mĕn′ĭn-jər). Family of American psychiatrists, including **Charles Frederick** (1862–1953) and his sons **Karl Augustus** (1893–1990) and **William Claire** (1899–1966). The family founded the Menninger Clinic in Topeka, Kansas (1920), and the Menninger Foundation (1941), both dedicated to psychiatric treatment, research, training, and public education.

Men·non·ite (mĕn′ə-nīt′) *n.* A member of an Anabaptist church characterized particularly by simplicity of life, pacifism, and nonresistance. [German *Mennonit*, after *Menno* Simons (1492–1559), Frisian religious leader.]

meno– or **men–** *pref.* **1.** Menstruation: *menarche.* **2.** Menses: *menorrhagia.* [Greek, from *mēn*, month. See **mē-**[2] in Appendix.]

men-of-war (mĕn′ə-wôr′) *n.* Plural of **man-of-war.**

Me·nom·i·nee (mə-nŏm′ə-nē) *n., pl.* **Menominee** or **-nees. 1.a.** A Native American people formerly inhabiting an area along the Menominee River, with a present-day population in northeast Wisconsin. **b.** A member of this people. **2.** The Algonquian language of the Menominee.

Menominee River. A river rising in the Upper Peninsula of northwest Michigan and flowing about 190 km (118 mi) southeast along the Michigan-Wisconsin border to Green Bay.

Me·nom·o·nee Falls (mə-nŏm′ə-nē). A village of southeast Wisconsin, a suburb of Milwaukee. Population, 27,845.

me·no mos·so (mā′nō môs′sō, mĕ′nō) *adv. & adj. Music.* At a lower speed. Used chiefly as a direction. [Italian : *meno*, less + *mosso*, agitated.]

men·o·pause (mĕn′ə-pôz′) *n.* The period marked by the natural and permanent cessation of menstruation, occurring usually between the ages of 45 and 55. [New Latin *mēnopausis* : MENO– + Greek *pausis*, pause; see PAUSE.] —**men′o·paus′al** *adj.*

me·no·rah (mə-nôr′ə, -nōr′ə) *n. Judaism.* **1.** A nine-branched candelabrum used in celebration of Hanukkah. **2.** Often **Menorah.** A ceremonial seven-branched candelabrum of the Jewish Temple symbolizing the seven days of the Creation. [Hebrew *mĕnôrâ.*]

Me·nor·ca (mə-nôr′kə, mĕ-nôr′kä). See **Minorca**[1].

men·or·rha·gi·a (mĕn′ə-rā′jē-ə) *n.* Abnormally heavy or extended menstrual flow. —**men′or·rha′gic** (-jĭk) *adj.*

Me·not·ti (mə-nŏt′ē), **Gian Carlo.** Born 1911. Italian-born American composer and librettist whose operas include *The Medium* (1946) and *The Consul* (1950).

Men·sa (mĕn′sə) *n.* A southern constellation between Hydrus and Volans. [Latin *mēnsa*, table.]

men·sal (mĕn′səl) *adj.* Used at the table. [Middle English, from Late Latin *mēnsālis*, from Latin *mēnsa*, table.]

mensch or **mensh** (mĕnsh) *n., pl.* **mensch·en** (mĕn′shən) or **mensch·es.** *Informal.* A person having admirable characteristics, such as fortitude and firmness of purpose: *"He radiates the kind of fundamental decency that has a name in Yiddish; he's a mensch"* (James Atlas). [Yiddish, human being, mensch, from Middle High German, human being, from Old High German *mennisco.* See **man-**[1] in Appendix.]

men·ses (mĕn′sēz) *pl.n. (used with a sing. or pl. verb).* The monthly flow of blood and cellular debris from the uterus that begins at puberty in women and the females of other primates. In women, menses ceases at menopause. Also called *catamenia.* [Latin *mēnsēs*, pl. of *mēnsis*, month. See **mē-**[2] in Appendix.]

mensh (mĕnsh) *n.* **mensch.**

Men·she·vik (mĕn′shə-vĭk) *n., pl.* **-viks** or **-vi·ki** (-vē′kē). A member of the liberal minority faction of the Social Democratic Party that struggled against the Bolsheviks before and during the Russian Revolution. [Russian *men'shevik*, from *men'she*, less (from their minority status). See **mei-**[2] in Appendix.] —**Men′she·vism** *n.* —**Men′she·vist** *n.*

men's room (mĕnz) *n.* A restroom for men.

men·stru·a (mĕn′stro͞o-ə) *n.* A plural of **menstruum.**

men·stru·al (mĕn′stro͞o-əl) also **men·stru·ous** (-əs) *adj.* **1.** Of or relating to menstruation. **2.a.** Taking place on a monthly basis. **b.** Lasting for one month. [Middle English, from Old French *menstruel*, from Latin *mēnstruālis*, from *mēnstruus*, menstrual, from *mēnsis*, month. See **mē-**[2] in Appendix.]

men·stru·ate (mĕn′stro͞o-āt′) *intr.v.* **-at·ed, -at·ing, -ates.** To undergo menstruation. [Late Latin *mēnstruāre, mēnstruāt-*, from Latin *mēnstrua*, menses, from neuter pl. of *mēnstruus*, menstrual. See MENSTRUAL.]

men·stru·a·tion (mĕn′stro͞o-ā′shən) *n.* The process or an instance of discharging the menses.

men·stru·ous (mĕn′stro͞o-əs) *adj.* Variant of **menstrual.**

men·stru·um (mĕn′stro͞o-əm) *n., pl.* **-stru·ums** or **-stru·a** (-stro͞o-ə). A solvent, especially one used in extracting compounds from plant and animal tissues and preparing drugs. [Middle English, menstruation, from Medieval Latin, sing. of Latin *mēnstrua*, menses. See MENSTRUATE.]

men·su·ra·ble (mĕn′sər-ə-bəl, -shər-) *adj.* **1.** That can be measured: *mensurable results in employee performance; a mensurable increase in the cost of oil.* **2.** Having fixed rhythm and measure, as in music; mensural. —**men′su·ra·bil′i·ty, men′su·ra·ble·ness** *n.*

menhir
Menhir of Champ-Dolent, France, standing over 9 meters (30 feet) high

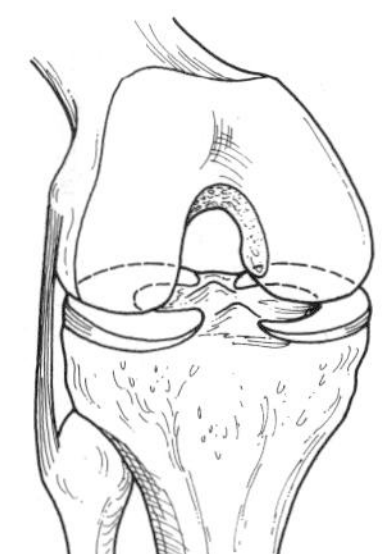

meniscus
View of a flexed knee

menorah

men·su·ral (mĕn′sər-əl, -shər-) *adj.* **1.** Of or relating to measure. **2.** *Music.* Having notes of fixed rhythmic value. [Late Latin *mēnsūrālis,* from Latin *mēnsūra,* measure. See MEASURE.]

men·su·ra·tion (mĕn′sə-rā′shən, -shə-) *n.* **1.** The act, process, or art of measuring. **2.** Measurement of geometric quantities. [Late Latin *mēnsūrātiō, mēnsūrātiōn-,* from *mēnsūrātus,* past participle of *mēnsūrāre,* to measure, from Latin *mēnsūra,* measure. See MEASURE.] **—men′su·ra′tive** *adj.*

mens·wear also **men's wear** (mĕnz′wâr′) *n.* Clothing for men.

–ment *suff.* **1.** Action; process: *appeasement.* **2.** Result of an action or process: *advancement.* **3.** Means, instrument, or agent of an action or process: *adornment.* [Middle English, from Old French, from Latin *-mentum,* n. suff.]

men·tal[1] (mĕn′tl) *adj.* **1.** Of or relating to the mind; intellectual: *mental powers.* **2.** Executed or performed by the mind; existing in the mind: *mental images of happy times.* See Usage Note at **mental telepathy. 3.** Of, relating to, or affected by a disorder of the mind. **4.** Intended for treatment of people affected with disorders of the mind. **5.** Of or relating to telepathy or mind reading. **6.** *Slang.* **a.** Emotionally upset; crazed: *got mental when he saw the dent in his new car.* **b.** *Offensive Slang.* Mentally or psychologically disturbed. [Middle English, from Old French, from Late Latin *mentālis,* from Latin *mēns, ment-,* mind. See **men-[1]** in Appendix.] **—men′tal·ly** *adv.*

men·tal[2] (mĕn′tl) *adj.* Of or relating to the chin. [From Latin *mentum,* chin. See **men-[2]** in Appendix.]

mental age *n. Abbr.* **MA, M.A.** A measure of mental development as determined by intelligence tests, generally restricted to children and expressed as the age at which that level is typically attained.

mental deficiency *n.* See **mental retardation.**

mental hospital *n.* See **psychiatric hospital.**

men·tal·ism (mĕn′tl-ĭz′əm) *n.* **1.** Parapsychological activities, such as telepathy and mind reading. **2.** The belief that some mental phenomena cannot be explained by physical laws. **—men′tal·ist** *n.* **—men′tal·is′tic** *adj.*

men·tal·i·ty (mĕn-tăl′ĭ-tē) *n., pl.* **-ties. 1.** Cast or turn of mind: *a vindictive mentality.* **2.** The sum of a person's intellectual capabilities or endowment.

mental retardation *n.* Subnormal intellectual development or functioning that is the result of congenital causes, brain injury, or disease and is characterized by any of various deficiencies, ranging from impaired learning ability to social and vocational inadequacy. Also called *mental deficiency.*

mental telepathy *n.* Telepathy.

USAGE NOTE: Strictly speaking, the phrase *mental telepathy* ought to be regarded as redundant, but like some other fixed phrases (for example, *hollow tube*), it has become so well established that the objection smacks of nitpicking. See Usage Note at **redundancy.**

men·ta·tion (mĕn-tā′shən) *n.* Mental activity; thinking: *"The heartless hip analysis of crime is . . . a part of my life and my mentation"* (Scott Turow). [From Latin *mēns, ment-,* mind. See MENTAL[1].]

men·thol (mĕn′thôl′) *n.* A white crystalline organic compound, $CH_3C_6H_9(C_3H_7)OH$, obtained from peppermint oil or synthesized. It is used in perfumes, in cigarettes, as a mild topical anesthetic, and as a mint flavoring. [German, from Latin *mentha,* mint.] **—men′tho·lat′ed** *adj.*

men·tion (mĕn′shən) *tr.v.* **-tioned, -tion·ing, -tions.** To refer to, especially incidentally. See Synonyms at **refer. —mention** *n.* **1. a.** The act of referring to something briefly or casually. **b.** An incidental reference or allusion. **2.** Honorable mention. [From Middle English *mencioun,* reference, from Old French, from Latin *mentiō, mentiōn-.* See **men-[1]** in Appendix.] **—men′tion·a·ble** *adj.*

men·tor (mĕn′tôr′, -tər) *n.* **1.** A wise and trusted counselor or teacher. **2. Mentor.** *Greek Mythology.* Odysseus's trusted counselor, under whose disguise Athena became the guardian and teacher of Telemachus. **—mentor** *v.* **-tored, -tor·ing, -tors.** *Informal.* —*intr.* To serve as a trusted counselor or teacher, especially in occupational settings. —*tr.* To serve as a trusted counselor or teacher to (another person). [French *Mentor,* Mentor, from Latin *Mentōr,* from Greek. See **men-[1]** in Appendix.]

WORD HISTORY: The word *mentor* is an example of the way in which the great works of literature live on without our knowing it. The word has recently gained currency in the professional world, where it is thought to be a good idea to have a mentor, a wise and trusted counselor, guiding one's career, preferably in the upper reaches of the organization. We owe this word to the more heroic age of Homer, in whose *Odyssey* Mentor is the trusted friend of Odysseus left in charge of the household during Odysseus's absence. More important for our usage of the word *mentor,* Athena disguised as Mentor guides Odysseus's son Telemachus in his search for his father. Fénelon in his romance *Télémaque* (1699) emphasized Mentor as a character, and so it was that in French (1749) and English (1750) *mentor,* going back through Latin to a Greek name, became a common noun meaning "wise counselor," first recorded in 1750. *Mentor* is an appropriate name for such a person because it probably meant "adviser" in Greek and comes from the Indo-European root *men-[1],* meaning "to think."

Men·tor (mĕn′tər). A city of northeast Ohio, a residential suburb of Cleveland on Lake Erie. Population, 42,065.

men·u (mĕn′yo͞o, mā′nyo͞o) *n.* **1.** A list of the dishes to be served or available for a meal. **2.** The dishes served or available at a meal. **3. a.** *Computer Science.* A list, displayed on a monitor, of options available to a computer user. **b.** A similar list of options: *a menu of professional opportunities.* [French, small, minute, menu, from Old French *menut,* small, from Latin *minūtus,* past participle of *minuere,* to diminish. See **mei-[2]** in Appendix.]

WORD HISTORY: An enormous menu might be considered an oxymoron if one were to restrict the word etymologically. *Menu* can be traced back to the Latin word *minūtus,* meaning "small in size, amount, or degree" and also "possessing or involving minute knowledge." Latin *minūtus* became Old French *menut* and Modern French *menu,* "small, fine, trifling, minute." The French adjective came to be used as a noun with the sense of "detail, details collectively," and "detailed list." As such, it was used in the phrase *menu de repas,* "list of items of a meal," which was shortened to *menu.* This word was borrowed into English, being first recorded in 1837. The French word had been borrowed before, perhaps only briefly, as a shortening of the French phrase *menu peuple,* "the common people." This usage, however, is recorded in only one text, in 1658.

Men·u·hin (mĕn′yo͞o-ĭn), **Yehudi.** Born 1916. American violinist considered among the great virtuosos of his time.

Men·zies (mĕn′zēz), Sir **Robert Gordon.** 1894–1978. Australian politician who twice served as prime minister (1939–1941 and 1949–1966).

Me·o (mē-ou′) *n.* Variant of **Miao.**

me·ow (mē-ou′) *n.* **1.** The cry of a cat. **2.** *Informal.* A malicious, spiteful comment. **—meow** *intr.v.* **-owed, -ow·ing, -ows.** To make the crying sound of a cat. [Imitative.]

mep or **m.e.p.** *abbr.* Mean effective pressure.

me·per·i·dine (mə-pĕr′ĭ-dēn′) *n.* A synthetic narcotic compound, $C_{15}H_{21}NO_2$, used in its hydrochloride form as an analgesic and a sedative. [ME(THYL) + (PI)PERIDINE.]

Meph·i·stoph·e·les (mĕf′ĭ-stŏf′ə-lēz′) *n.* The devil in the Faust legend to whom Faust sold his soul. **—Me·phis′to·phe′le·an, Me·phis′to·phe′li·an** (mə-fĭs′tō-fē′lē-ən, -fēl′yən, mĕf′ĭ-stō-) *adj.*

me·phit·ic (mə-fĭt′ĭk) also **me·phit·i·cal** (-ĭ-kəl) *adj.* Of, relating to, or resembling mephitis; poisonous or foul-smelling. See Synonyms at **poisonous. —me·phit′i·cal·ly** *adv.*

me·phi·tis (mə-fī′tĭs) *n.* **1.** An offensive smell; a stench. **2.** A poisonous or foul-smelling gas emitted from the earth. [Latin *mephītis.*]

mep·ro·bam·ate (mĕp′rō-băm′āt′, mĕ-prō′bə-) *n.* A bitter white powder, $C_9H_{18}N_2O_4$, used as a tranquilizer, a muscle relaxant, and an anticonvulsant. [ME(THYL) + PRO(PYL) + (CAR)BAMATE.]

Meq·uon (mĕk′wŏn′). A city of southeast Wisconsin, a suburb of Milwaukee. Population, 16,193.

mer. *abbr.* Meridian.

mer– *pref.* Variant of **mero–.**

–mer *suff.* Variant of **–mere.**

mer·bro·min (mər-brō′mĭn) *n.* A green crystalline organic compound, $C_{20}H_8Br_2HgNa_2O_6$, that forms a red aqueous solution, used as a germicide and an antiseptic. [MER(CURIC) + (ACETATE) + (DI)BROM(IDE) + (FLUORESCE)IN.]

mer·can·tile (mûr′kən-tēl′, -tīl′, -tĭl) *adj.* **1.** Of or relating to merchants or trade. **2.** Of or relating to mercantilism. [French, from Italian, from *mercante,* merchant, from Latin *mercāns, mercant-,* from present participle of *mercārī,* to trade, from *merx, merc-,* merchandise, goods.]

mer·can·til·ism (mûr′kən-tē-lĭz′əm, -tĭ-) *n.* **1.** The theory and system of political economy prevailing in Europe after the decline of feudalism, based on national policies of accumulating bullion, establishing colonies and a merchant marine, and developing industry and mining to attain a favorable balance of trade. **2.** The practice, methods, or spirit of merchants; commercialism. [MERCANTIL(E) + –ISM.] **—mer′can·til·ist** *adj. & n.* **—mer′can·til·is′tic** *adj.*

mer·cap·tan (mər-kăp′tăn′) *n.* A sulfur-containing organic compound with the general formula RSH where R is any radical, especially ethyl mercaptan, C_2H_5SH. Also called *thiol.* [German, from Danish, from Medieval Latin *(corpus) mercurium captāns,* (a substance) seizing mercury : *mercurium,* accusative of *mercurius,* mercury (from Latin *Mercurius,* the god Mercury) + Latin *captāns,* present participle of *captāre,* frequentative of *capere,* to seize; see CAPTURE.]

mercapto– *pref.* Containing the univalent radical –SH: *mercaptopurine.* [From MERCAPTAN.]

mer·cap·to·pu·rine (mər-kăp′tō-pyo͝or′ēn) *n.* A purine analogue, $C_5H_4N_4S$, that acts as an antimetabolite by interfering with purine synthesis, used primarily in the treatment of acute leukemia.

Mer·ca·tor (mər-kā′tər, mĕr-kä′tôr), **Gerhardus.** Originally

Gerhard Kremer. 1512–1594. Flemish cartographer who developed the Mercator projection (1568).

Mercator projection *n.* A cylindrical map projection in which the meridians and parallels of latitude appear as lines crossing at right angles and in which areas appear greater farther from the equator. [After Gerhardus MERCATOR.]

Mer·ced (mər-sĕd′). A city of central California in the San Joaquin Valley northwest of Fresno. It is a trade and tourist center in a farm and dairy region. Population, 36,499.

Mer·ce·da·rio (mĕr′sə-där′ē-ō, -sĕ-*thä*′ryô). A mountain, 6,774.4 m (22,211 ft) high, in the Andes of western Argentina on the border with Chile.

mer·ce·nar·y (mûr′sə-nĕr′ē) *adj.* **1.** Motivated solely by a desire for monetary or material gain. **2.** Hired for service in a foreign army. **—mercenary** *n., pl.* **-ies. 1.** One who serves or works merely for monetary gain; a hireling. **2.** A professional soldier hired for service in a foreign army. [Middle English *mercenarie,* a mercenary, from Old French *mercenaire,* from Latin *mercēnārius,* from *mercēs,* wages, price.] **—mer′ce·nar′i·ly** *adv.* **—mer′ce·nar′i·ness** *n.*

mer·cer (mûr′sər) *n. Chiefly British.* A dealer in textiles, especially silks. [Middle English, from Old French *mercier,* trader, from *merz,* merchandise, from Latin *merx, merc-,* merchandise.]

Mer·cer Island (mûr′sər). A city of west-central Washington, coextensive with **Mercer Island** in Lake Washington near Seattle. It is primarily residential. Population, 21,522.

mer·cer·ize (mûr′sə-rīz′) *tr.v.* **-ized, -iz·ing, -iz·es.** To treat (cotton thread) with sodium hydroxide so as to shrink the fiber and increase its luster and affinity for dye. [After John *Mercer* (1791–1866), British calico printer.]

mer·chan·dise (mûr′chən-dīz′, -dīs′) *n. Abbr.* **mdse.** Goods bought and sold in business; commercial wares. **—merchandise** also **mer·chan·dize** (-dīz′) *v.* **-dised, -dis·ing, -dis·es** also **-dized, -diz·ing, -diz·es.** *—tr.* **1.** To buy and sell (goods). **2.** To promote the sale of, as by advertising or display: *merchandised a new product. —intr.* To buy and sell goods; trade commercially. [Middle English *merchaundise,* from Old French *marchandise,* trade, from *marcheant, marchand,* merchant. See MERCHANT.] **—mer′chan·dis′a·ble** *adj.* **—mer′chan·dis′er** *n.*

mer·chan·dis·ing also **mer·chan·diz·ing** (mûr′chən-dī′zĭng) *n.* The promotion of merchandise sales, as by coordinating production and marketing and developing advertising, display, and sales strategies.

mer·chant (mûr′chənt) *n.* **1.** One whose occupation is the wholesale purchase and retail sale of goods for profit. **2.** One who runs a retail business; a shopkeeper. **—merchant** *adj.* **1.** Of or relating to merchants, merchandise, or commercial trade: *a merchant guild.* **2.** Of or relating to the merchant marine: *merchant ships.* [Middle English *merchaunt,* from Old French *marcheant,* from Vulgar Latin **mercātāns,* present participle of **mercātāre,* frequentative of Latin *mercārī,* to trade, from *merx, merc-,* merchandise.]

mer·chant·a·ble (mûr′chənt-ə-bəl) *adj.* Suitable for buying and selling; marketable. **—mer′chant·a·bil′i·ty** *n.*

mer·chant·man (mûr′chənt-mən) *n.* **1.** *Nautical.* A ship used in commerce. **2.** *Archaic.* A merchant.

merchant marine *n.* **1.** A nation's commercial ships. **2.** The personnel of a nation's commercial ships.

Mer·ci·a (mûr′shē-ə, -shə). An Anglo-Saxon kingdom of central England. It was settled by Angles c. A.D. 500 and enjoyed its greatest influence during the rule (757–796) of Offa. In 874 the kingdom was overrun by the Danes and split between Wessex and the Danelaw.

Mer·ci·an (mûr′shē-ən, -shən) *adj.* Of or relating to Mercia or its people, dialect, or culture. **—Mercian** *n.* **1.** A native or inhabitant of Mercia. **2.** The Old English dialect of Mercia.

mer·ci·ful (mûr′sĭ-fəl) *adj.* Full of mercy; compassionate: *sought merciful treatment for the captives.* See Synonyms at **humane. —mer′ci·ful·ly** *adv.* **—mer′ci·ful·ness** *n.*

mer·ci·less (mûr′sĭ-lĭs) *adj.* Having no mercy; cruel. **—mer′ci·less·ly** *adv.* **—mer′ci·less·ness** *n.*

mercur– *pref.* Variant of **mercuro–.**

mer·cu·rate (mûr′kyə-rāt′) *tr.v.* **-rat·ed, -rat·ing, -rates.** To treat or combine with mercury or a mercury compound. **—mer′cu·ra′tion** *n.*

mer·cu·ri·al (mər-kyo͝or′ē-əl) *adj.* **1.** Often **Mercurial. a.** *Roman Mythology.* Of or relating to the god Mercury. **b.** *Astronomy.* Of or relating to the planet Mercury. **2.** Having the characteristics of eloquence, shrewdness, swiftness, and thievishness attributed to the god Mercury. **3.** Containing or caused by the action of the element mercury. **4.** Quick and changeable in temperament; volatile: *a mercurial nature.* **—mercurial** *n.* A pharmacological or chemical preparation containing mercury. [Middle English, of the planet Mercury, from Latin *mercuriālis,* of the god or planet Mercury, from *Mercurius,* Mercury.] **—mer·cu′ri·al·ly** *adv.*

mer·cu·ri·al·ism (mər-kyo͝or′ē-ə-lĭz′əm) *n. Pathology.* Poisoning caused by mercury or a compound containing mercury.

mer·cu·ric (mər-kyo͝or′ĭk) *adj.* Relating to or containing mercury, especially with valence 2.

mercuric chloride *n.* A poisonous white crystalline compound, $HgCl_2$, used as an antiseptic and a disinfectant, in insecticides, preservatives, and batteries, and in metallurgy and photography. Also called *corrosive sublimate.*

mercuric sulfide *n.* A poisonous compound, HgS, having two forms: **a.** Black mercuric sulfide, a black powder obtained from mercury salts or by the reaction of mercury with sulfur, used as a pigment. **b.** Red mercuric sulfide, a bright scarlet powder derived from heating mercury with sulfur, used as a pigment.

mercuro– or **mercur–** *pref.* Mercury: *mercurous.* [From MERCURY.]

Mer·cu·ro·chrome (mər-kyo͝or′ə-krōm′). A trademark used for a solution of merbromin.

mer·cu·rous (mər-kyo͝or′əs, mûr′kyər-əs) *adj.* Relating to or containing mercury, especially with valence 1.

mercurous chloride *n.* See **calomel.**

mer·cu·ry (mûr′kyə-rē) *n.* **1.** *Symbol* **Hg** A silvery-white poisonous metallic element, liquid at room temperature and used in thermometers, barometers, vapor lamps, and batteries and in the preparation of chemical pesticides. Atomic number 80; atomic weight 200.59; melting point −38.87°C; boiling point 356.58°C; specific gravity 13.546 (at 20°C); valence 1, 2. Also called *quicksilver.* See table at **element. 2.** Temperature: *The mercury had fallen rapidly by morning.* **3.** Any of several weedy plants of the genera *Mercurialis* or *Acalypha.* [Middle English *mercurie,* from Medieval Latin *mercurius,* from Latin *Mercurius,* Mercury.]

Mer·cu·ry (mûr′kyə-rē) *n.* **1.** *Roman Mythology.* A god that served as messenger to the other gods and was himself the god of commerce, travel, and thievery. **2.** The smallest of the planets and the one nearest the sun, having a sidereal period of revolution about the sun of 88.0 days at a mean distance of 58.3 million kilometers (36.2 million miles) and a mean radius of approximately 2,414 kilometers (1,500 miles). [Middle English *Mercurie,* from Old French, from Latin *Mercurius.*]

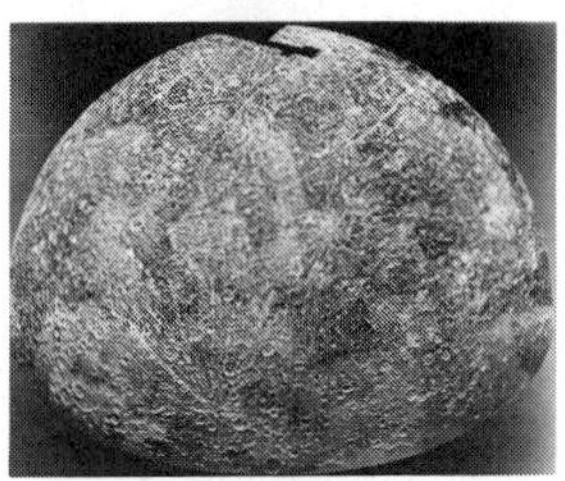

Mercury
Top: 1793 American post office sign
Bottom: Mercury's South Pole, photographed by Mariner 10 on December 1, 1975

mer·cu·ry-va·por lamp (mûr′kyə-rē-vā′pər) *n.* A lamp in which ultraviolet and yellowish-green to blue visible light is produced by an electric discharge through mercury vapor.

mer·cy (mûr′sē) *n., pl.* **-cies. 1.** Compassionate treatment, especially of those under one's power; clemency. **2.** A disposition to be kind and forgiving: *a heart full of mercy.* **3.** Something for which to be thankful; a blessing: *It was a mercy that no one was hurt.* **4.** Alleviation of distress; relief: *Distributing food among the homeless was an act of mercy.* **—*idiom.* at the mercy of.** Without any protection against: *drifting in an open boat, at the mercy of the elements.* [Middle English, from Old French *merci,* from Medieval Latin *mercēs,* from Latin, reward.]

SYNONYMS: *mercy, leniency, lenity, clemency, charity.* These nouns mean kind, forgiving, or sympathetic and humane treatment of or disposition toward others. *Mercy* is compassionate forbearance: *"We hand folks over to God's mercy, and show none ourselves"* (George Eliot). *Leniency* and *lenity* imply mildness, gentleness, and often a tendency to reduce the severity or harshness of punishment: *"When you have gone too far to recede, do not sue* [appeal] *to me for leniency"* (Charles Dickens). *"His Majesty gave many marks of his great lenity, often . . . endeavoring to extenuate your crimes"* (Jonathan Swift). *Clemency* is mercy shown by one in a position of authority or power and especially by one charged with administering justice: *The judge believed in clemency for youthful offenders. Charity* is goodwill and benevolence, especially as it manifests itself in kindly forbearance in judging others: *"But how shall we expect charity towards others, when we are uncharitable to ourselves?"* (Thomas Browne).

mercy killing *n.* Euthanasia.

mercy seat *n.* **1.** The golden covering of the ark of the covenant, regarded as the resting place of God. **2.** The throne of God.

mere[1] (mîr) *adj.* Superlative **mer·est. 1.** Being nothing more than what is specified: *a mere child; a mere 50 cents an hour.* **2.** Considered apart from anything else: *shocked by the mere idea.* **3.** Small; slight: *could detect only the merest whisper.* **4.** *Obsolete.* Pure; unadulterated. [Middle English, absolute, pure, from Old French *mier,* pure, from Latin *merus.*]

mere[2] (mîr) *n.* A small lake, pond, or marsh: *"Sometimes on lonely mountain meres/I find a magic bark"* (Tennyson). [Middle English, from Old English. See **mori-** in Appendix.]

mere[3] (mîr) *n. Archaic.* A boundary. [Middle English, from Old English *mǣre.*]

–mere or **–mer** *suff.* Part; segment: *blastomere.* [French *-mère,* from Greek *meros,* part. See **(s)mer-**[2] in Appendix.]

Mer·e·dith (mĕr′ĭ-dĭth), **George.** 1828–1909. British writer of novels, such as *The Ordeal of Richard Feverel* (1859), and poetic works, including*Modern Love* (1862).

Meredith, James Howard. Born 1933. American civil rights advocate whose registration (1963) at the traditionally segregated University of Mississippi prompted a riot, which was spurred by state officials who defied federal pleas for peaceful integration.

mere·ly (mîr′lē) *adv.* And nothing else or more; only: *merely a flesh wound.*

me·ren·gue (mə-rĕng′gā) *n.* **1.** A ballroom dance of Dominican and Haitian folk origin, characterized by a sliding step. **2.** Music for this dance, in rapid 2/4 time. [American Spanish, from Spanish, meringue, from French *méringue.*]

mer·e·tri·cious (mĕr′ĭ-trĭsh′əs) *adj.* **1.a.** Attracting attention in a vulgar manner: *meretricious ornamentation.* See Syn-

ă pat	oi boy
ā pay	ou out
âr care	o͝o took
ä father	o͞o boot
ĕ pet	ŭ cut
ē be	ûr urge
ĭ pit	th thin
ī pie	*th* this
îr pier	hw which
ŏ pot	zh vision
ō toe	ə about, item
ô paw	♦ regionalism

Stress marks: **′** (primary); ′ (secondary), as in **dictionary** (dĭk′shə-nĕr′ē)

merganser
Male hooded merganser
Mergus cucullatus

onyms at **gaudy**[1]. **b.** Plausible but false or insincere; specious: *a meretricious argument.* **2.** Of or relating to prostitutes or prostitution: *meretricious relationships.* [Latin *meretrīcius,* of prostitutes, from *meretrīx, meretrīc-,* prostitute, from *merēre,* to earn money. See **(s)mer-**[2] in Appendix.] **—mer′e·tri′cious·ly** *adv.* **—mer′e·tri′cious·ness** *n.*

mer·gan·ser (mər-găn′sər) *n.* Any of various fish-eating diving ducks of the genus *Mergus* or related genera, having a slim, hooked bill. Also called *sheldrake.* [New Latin : Latin *mergus,* diver (from *mergere,* to plunge) + Latin *ānser,* goose; see **ghans-** in Appendix.]

merge (mûrj) *v.* **merged, merg·ing, merg·es.** *—tr.* **1.** To cause to be absorbed, especially in gradual stages. **2.** To combine or unite. *—intr.* **1.** To blend together, especially in gradual stages. **2.** To become combined or united. See Synonyms at **mix.** [Latin *mergere,* to plunge.] **—mer′gence** *n.*

Mer·gen·thal·er (mûr′gən-thô′lər, mĕr′gən-tä′-), **Ottmar.** 1854–1899. German-born American inventor of the Linotype typesetting machine (patented 1884).

merg·er (mûr′jər) *n.* **1.** The act or an instance of merging; union. **2.** The union of two or more commercial interests or corporations. **3.** *Law.* The absorption of a lesser estate, liability, right, action, or offense into a greater one.

Mé·ri·da (mĕr′ĭ-də, mĕ′rē-*thä*). A city of southeast Mexico on the Yucatán Peninsula. It was founded in 1542 on the site of a ruined Mayan city. Population, 400,142.

Mer·i·den (mĕr′ĭ-dən). A city of south-central Connecticut north-northeast of New Haven. Settled in 1661, it is known for its silver industry. Population, 57,118.

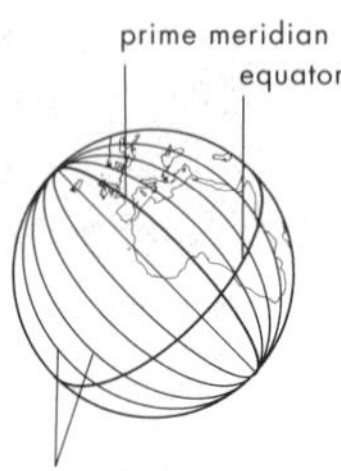

meridian
Terrestrial meridians

♦**me·rid·i·an** (mə-rĭd′ē-ən) *n.* *Abbr.* **m., M., mer. 1.a.** An imaginary great circle on the earth's surface passing through the North and South geographic poles. All points on the same meridian have the same longitude. **b.** Either half of such a great circle from pole to pole. **2.** *Astronomy.* A great circle passing through the two poles of the celestial sphere and the zenith of a given observer. **3.** *Mathematics.* **a.** A curve on a surface of revolution, formed by the intersection of the surface with a plane containing the axis of revolution. **b.** A plane section of a surface of revolution containing the axis of revolution. **4.** Any of the longitudinal lines or pathways on the body along which the acupuncture points are distributed. **5.** *Archaic.* **a.** The highest point in the sky reached by the sun or another celestial body; a zenith. **b.** Noon. **6.** The highest point or stage of development; peak: *"Men come to their meridian at various periods of their lives"* (John Henry Newman). **7.** *Upper Midwest.* See **median strip.** See Regional Note at **neutral ground. —meridian** *adj.* **1.** Of or relating to a meridian; meridional. **2.** Of or at midday: *the meridian hour.* **3.** Of, relating to, or constituting the highest point, as of development or power: *the empire in its meridian period.* [Middle English, from Old French, midday, from Latin *merīdiānus,* of midday, from *merīdiēs,* midday, from *merīdiē,* at midday, from Old Latin **mediei diē* : **mediei,* dative (locative) of *medius,* middle; see **medhyo-** in Appendix + *diē,* dative of *diēs,* day; see **deiw-** in Appendix.]

Me·rid·i·an (mə-rĭd′ē-ən). A city of eastern Mississippi near the Alabama border east of Jackson. Population, 46,577.

me·rid·i·o·nal (mə-rĭd′ē-ə-nəl) *adj.* **1.** Of or relating to meridians or a meridian. **2.** Located in the south; southern. **3.** Of or characteristic of southern areas or people. **—meridional** *n.* An inhabitant of a southern region, especially the south of France. [Middle English, pertaining to the sun's position at noon, from Old French *meridionel,* southern, from Late Latin *merīdiōnālis,* from Latin *merīdiānus,* of midday, southern. See MERIDIAN.]

merlon

Mé·ri·mée (mĕr′ə-mā′, mā-rē-mā′), **Prosper.** 1803–1870. French writer of romantic stories and novels, such as *Carmen* (1846), on which Bizet's opera is based.

me·ringue (mə-răng′) *n.* **1.** A topping for pastry or pies made of a mixture of egg whites and sugar beaten until stiff and often baked until brown. **2.** A small pastry shell or cake made of stiffly beaten, baked egg whites and sugar, often containing fruit or nutmeats. [French *méringue.*]

me·ri·no (mə-rē′nō) *n., pl.* **-nos. 1.a.** Any of a breed of sheep, originally from Spain, having long, fine wool. **b.** The wool of this sheep. **2.** A soft, lightweight fabric made originally of merino wool but now of any fine wool. **3.a.** A fine wool and cotton yarn used especially for knitting underwear and hosiery. **b.** A knitted fabric made from this yarn. [Spanish, perhaps from Berber *Benī Merīn,* name of the tribe that developed the breed or from Spanish *merino,* local magistrate (from Latin *māiōrīnus,* larger, from *māior;* see MAJOR).] **—me·ri′no** *adj.*

mermaid
Sculpture at Copenhagen, Denmark

mer·i·stem (mĕr′ĭ-stĕm′) *n.* The undifferentiated plant tissue from which new cells are formed, as that at the tip of a stem or root. [Greek *meristos,* divided (from *merizein,* to divide, from *meris,* division; see **(s)mer-**[2] in Appendix) + *-em* (as in *xylem,* and *phloem*).] **—mer′i·ste·mat′ic** (-stə-măt′ĭk) *adj.* **—mer′i·ste·mat′i·cal·ly** *adv.*

me·ris·tic (mə-rĭs′tĭk) *adj.* *Biology.* **1.** Having or composed of segments; segmented. **2.** Relating to a change in the number or placement of body parts or segments: *meristic variation.* [From Greek *meristos,* divided. See MERISTEM.] **—me·ris′ti·cal·ly** *adv.*

mer·it (mĕr′ĭt) *n.* **1.a.** Superior quality or worth; excellence: *a proposal of some merit; an ill-advised plan without merit.* **b.** A quality deserving praise or approval; virtue: *a store having the merit of being open late.* **2.** Demonstrated ability or achievement: *promotions based on merit alone.* **3.** Often **merits.** An aspect of character or behavior deserving approval or disapproval: *judging people according to their merits.* **4.** *Theology.* Spiritual credit granted for good works. **5. merits. a.** *Law.* A party's strict legal rights, excluding jurisdictional, personal, or technical aspects. **b.** The factual content of a matter, apart from emotional, contextual, or formal considerations. **—merit** *v.* **-it·ed, -it·ing, -its.** *—tr.* To earn; deserve. See Synonyms at **earn**[1]. *—intr.* To be worthy or deserving: *Pupils are rewarded or corrected, as they merit.* [Middle English, from Old French *merite,* reward or punishment, from Latin *meritum,* from neuter past participle of *merēre,* to deserve. See **(s)mer-**[2] in Appendix.] **—mer′it·less** *adj.*

mer·i·toc·ra·cy (mĕr′ĭ-tŏk′rə-sē) *n., pl.* **-cies. 1.** A system in which advancement is based on individual ability or achievement. **2.a.** A group selected on the basis of individual ability or achievement. **b.** Leadership by such a group. **—mer′it·o·crat′** (-ĭ-tə-krăt′) *n.* **—mer′it·o·crat′ic** *adj.*

mer·i·to·ri·ous (mĕr′ĭ-tôr′ē-əs, -tōr′-) *adj.* Deserving reward or praise. [Middle English, from Latin *meritōrius,* earning money, from *meritus,* past participle of *merēre,* to earn. See MERIT.] **—mer′i·to′ri·ous·ly** *adv.* **—mer′i·to′ri·ous·ness** *n.*

merit pay *n.* Extra pay awarded to an employee, especially a schoolteacher, for past performance.

merit system *n.* The system of appointing and promoting civil service personnel on the basis of merit rather than on political affiliation or loyalty.

merle also **merl** (mûrl) *n.* See **blackbird** (sense 2). [Middle English, from Old French, from Latin *merulus, merula.*]

mer·lin (mûr′lĭn) *n.* A small falcon *(Falco columbarius)* of northern regions, having predominantly dark plumage and a black-striped tail. Also called *pigeon hawk.* [Middle English, from Anglo-Norman *merilun,* from Old French *esmerillon,* diminutive of *esmeril,* of Germanic origin.]

Mer·lin (mûr′lĭn) *n.* In Arthurian legend, a magician and prophet who served as counselor to King Arthur.

Mer·lo (mĕr′lō). A city of eastern Argentina, a suburb of Buenos Aires. Population, 293,059.

mer·lon (mûr′lən) *n.* A solid portion of a crenelated wall between two open spaces. [French, from Italian *merlone,* augmentative of *merlo,* battlement, perhaps from Medieval Latin *merulus,* from Latin, merle (from their imagined similarity to blackbirds sitting on a wall).]

mer·lot or **Mer·lot** (mər-lō′, mĕr-) *n.* A dry red wine made from a grape originating in southern France and Italy and introduced into California and Oregon. [French, young blackbird, merlot, diminutive of *merle,* blackbird (probably from the color of the grape), from Old French. See MERLE.]

mer·maid (mûr′mād′) *n.* A legendary sea creature having the head and upper body of a woman and the tail of a fish. [Middle English : *mere,* sea, lake; see MERE[2] + *maid,* maid; see MAID.]

mer·man (mûr′măn′, -mən) *n.* A legendary sea creature having the head and upper body of a man and the tail of a fish. [MER(MAID) + MAN.]

Mer·man (mûr′mən), **Ethel.** 1909–1984. American musical comedy actress noted for her powerful voice. She appeared in *Annie Get Your Gun* (1946) and many other productions.

mero– or **mer–** *pref.* **1.** Part; segment: *merozoite.* **2.** Partial; partially: *meropia.* [From Greek *meros,* part. See **(s)mer-**[2] in Appendix.]

mer·o·blas·tic (mĕr′ə-blăs′tĭk) *adj.* *Embryology.* Undergoing partial cleavage. Used of a fertilized egg. **—mer′o·blas′ti·cal·ly** *adv.*

mer·o·crine (mĕr′ə-krĭn, -krīn′, -krēn′) *adj.* Of or relating to a gland whose secretory cells remain undamaged during secretion. [MERO– + Greek *krinein,* to separate; see ENDOCRINE.]

Mer·o·ë also **Mer·o·we** (mĕr′ō-ē′). An ancient city of northern Sudan on the Nile River north of Khartoum. It was the capital of a Cush dynasty from 530 B.C. to A.D. 350.

mer·o·my·o·sin (mĕr′ə-mī′ə-sĭn) *n.* Either of two protein subunits of a myosin molecule, obtained especially through the digestive action of trypsin.

Mer·o·pe (mĕr′ə-pē′) *n.* **1.** *Greek Mythology.* One of the Pleiades, who hid her face in shame after marrying a mortal. **2.** One of the six stars in the Pleiades cluster, faintly visible to the unaided eye. [Greek *Meropē.*]

me·ro·pi·a (mə-rō′pē-ə) *n.* Partial blindness. **—me·ro′pic** (-rō′pĭk, -rŏp′ĭk) *adj.*

mer·o·plank·ton (mĕr′ə-plăngk′tən) *n.* Any of various organisms that spend part of their life cycle, usually the larval or egg stages, as plankton. **—mer′o·plank·ton′ic** (-tŏn′ĭk) *adj.*

–merous *suff.* Having a specified kind or number of parts: *isomerous.* [From New Latin *-merus,* from Greek *-meros,* from *meros,* part. See **(s)mer-**[2] in Appendix.]

Mer·o·vin·gi·an (mĕr′ə-vĭn′jē-ən, -jən). A Frankish ruling dynasty (c. A.D.450–751) founded by Merovech (fl. fifth century) and brought to prominence by Clovis I. **—Mer′o·vin′gi·an** *adj.*

Mer·o·we (mĕr′ō-ē′). See **Meroë.**

mer·o·zo·ite (mĕr′ə-zō′īt) *n.* A protozoan cell that arises from the schizogony of a parent sporozoan and may enter either the asexual or sexual phase of the life cycle.

Mer·rill·ville (mĕr′əl-vĭl′). A town of northwest Indiana, a suburb of Gary. Population, 27,677.

Mer·ri·mack River (mĕr′ə-măk′). A river rising in south-central New Hampshire and flowing about 177 km (110 mi) south into northeast Massachusetts then northeast to the Atlantic Ocean. It was long used as a source of power for textile mills.

mer·ri·ment (mĕr′ĭ-mənt) *n.* High-spirited fun and enjoyment; hilarity. See Synonyms at **mirth.**

Mer·ritt Island (mĕr′ĭt). A city of east-central Florida on **Merritt Island** between the mainland and Cape Canaveral. Population, 30,708.

mer·ry (mĕr′ē) *adj.* **-ri·er, -ri·est. 1.** Full of high-spirited gaiety; jolly. See Synonyms at **jolly. 2.** Marked by or offering fun and gaiety; festive: *a merry evening.* **3.** *Archaic.* Delightful; entertaining. **4.** Brisk: *a merry pace.* [Middle English *merri,* from Old English *mirige,* pleasant. See **mregh-u-** in Appendix.] **—mer′ri·ly** *adv.* **—mer′ri·ness** *n.*

mer·ry-an·drew (mĕr′ē-ăn′dro͞o) *n.* A clown; a buffoon. [MERRY + the name *Andrew.*]

mer·ry-bells (mĕr′ē-bĕlz′) *pl.n. (used with a sing. or pl. verb).* See **bellwort.**

mer·ry-go-round (mĕr′ē-gō-round′) *n.* **1.** A revolving circular platform fitted with seats, often in the form of animals, ridden for amusement. **2.** A piece of playground equipment consisting of a small circular platform that revolves when pushed or pedaled. **3.** A busy round; a whirl: *a merry-go-round of parties.*

mer·ry·mak·ing (mĕr′ē-mā′kĭng) *n.* **1.** Participation in festive activities. **2.a.** A festivity; a revelry. **b.** Festive activities. **—mer′ry·mak′er** *n.*

mer·ry·thought (mĕr′ē-thôt′) *n. Chiefly British.* A wishbone.

Mer·sey (mûr′zē). A river of northwest England flowing about 113 km (70 mi) generally westward to the Irish Sea at Liverpool.

Mer·sin (mĕr-sēn′). A city of southern Turkey on the Mediterranean Sea west-southwest of Adana. Population, 216,308.

Mer·thi·o·late (mər-thī′ə-lāt′). A trademark used for thimerosal.

Mer·thyr Tyd·fil (mûr′thər tĭd′vĭl). A borough of southern Wales north-northwest of Cardiff. It is a manufacturing center in a coal-mining region. Population, 60,200.

Mer·ton (mûr′tn), **Robert King.** Born 1910. American sociologist who proposed that deviant behavior results when a society offers no acceptable means of achieving acceptable goals.

Merton, Thomas. 1915–1968. American religious and writer of works on contemporary spiritual and secular life, including *The Seven Story Mountain* (1948) and *No Man Is an Island* (1955).

mes– *pref.* Variant of **meso–.**

me·sa (mā′sə) *n.* A broad, flat-topped elevation with one or more clifflike sides, common in the southwest United States. [Spanish, table, mesa, from Old Spanish, table, from Latin *mēnsa.*]

Me·sa (mā′sə). A city of south-central Arizona east of Phoenix. It is a winter resort and trade center. Population, 152,453.

Me·sa·bi Range (mə-sä′bē). A series of low hills in northeast Minnesota. Iron ore deposits were discovered here in 1887.

mé·sal·li·ance (mā-zăl′ē-əns, mā′ză-lyäns′) *n.* A marriage with a person of inferior social position. [French : *més-,* bad (from Old French *mes-;* see MIS–[1]) + *alliance,* alliance (from Old French *aliance;* see ALLIANCE).]

mes·arch (mĕz′ärk′, mĕs′-, mē′zärk′, -särk′) *adj. Ecology.* Originating in a moderately moist habitat. Used of a sere. [MES(O)– + Greek *arkhē,* beginning.]

mes·cal (mĕs-kăl′) *n.* **1.** See **peyote** (sense 1). **2.a.** A Mexican liquor distilled from the fermented juice of certain species of agave. **b.** A food prepared by cooking the fleshy leaf base and trunk of certain agaves. **3.** See **maguey** (sense 1). [American Spanish, from Nahuatl *mexcalli,* mescal liquor, from *metl,* maguey plant.]

mescal button *n.* The fresh or dried buttonlike tubercles of peyote, chewed as a drug by certain Native American peoples. Also called *peyote.*

Mes·ca·le·ro (mĕs′kə-lâr′ō) *n., pl.* **Mescalero** or **-ros. 1.** An Apache tribe formerly inhabiting southern New Mexico, western Texas, and north-central Mexico, with a present-day population in southern New Mexico. **2.** A member of this tribe.

mes·ca·line (mĕs′kə-lēn′, -lĭn) *n.* An alkaloid drug, $(CH_3O)_3C_6H_2CH_2CH_2NH_2$, obtained from mescal buttons, which produces hallucinations. Also called *peyote.*

Mes·dames[1] (mā-däm′, -dăm′) *n. Abbr.* **Mmes.** Plural of **Madam** (sense 1).

Mes·dames[2] also **mes·dames** (mā-dăm′, -däm′) *n. Abbr.* **Mmes.** Plural of **Madame.**

Mes·de·moi·selles also **mes·de·moi·selles** (mād′mwä-zĕl′) *n. Abbr.* **Mlles.** Plural of **Mademoiselle.**

me·seems (mē-sēmz′) *intr.v.* Past tense **-seemed.** *Archaic.* It seems to me. [Middle English *me semeth* : *me,* to me; see ME + *semeth,* third person sing. present tense of *semen,* to seem; see SEEM.]

mes·en·ceph·a·lon (mĕz′ĕn-sĕf′ə-lŏn′, mĕs′-) *n.* The portion of the vertebrate brain that develops from the middle section of the embryonic brain. Also called *midbrain.* **—mes′en·ce·phal′ic** (-sə-făl′ĭk) *adj.*

mes·en·chyme (mĕz′ən-kīm′, mĕs′-) *n.* The part of the embryonic mesoderm, consisting of loosely packed, unspecialized cells set in a gelatinous ground substance, from which connective tissue, bone, cartilage, and the circulatory and lymphatic systems develop. [MES(O)– + –ENCHYMA.] **—mes·en′chy·mal, mes′en·chym′a·tous** (-kī′mə-təs) *adj.*

mes·en·ter·i·tis (mĕz-ĕn′tə-rī′tĭs, mĕs-) *n.* Inflammation of the mesentery.

mes·en·ter·on (mĕz-ĕn′tə-rŏn′, mĕs-) *n.* See **midgut** (sense 1). **—mes·en′ter·on′ic** *adj.*

mes·en·ter·y (mĕz′ən-tĕr′ē, mĕs′-) *n., pl.* **-ies.** Any of several folds of the peritoneum that connect the intestines to the dorsal abdominal wall, especially such a fold that envelops the jejunum and ileum. [Middle English *mesenterie,* from Medieval Latin *mesenterium,* from Greek *mesenterion* : *meso-,* meso- + *enterion,* diminutive of *enteron,* entrails; see **en** in Appendix.] **—mes′en·ter′ic** *adj.*

mesh (mĕsh) *n.* **1.a.** Any of the open spaces in a net or network; an interstice. **b.** Often **meshes.** The cords, threads, or wires surrounding these spaces. **2.** An openwork fabric or structure; a net or network: *a screen made of wire mesh.* **3.** Often **meshes.** Something that snares or entraps: *"Arabia had become entangled in the meshes of . . . politics"* (W. Montgomery Watt). **4.a.** The engagement of gear teeth. **b.** The state of being so engaged: *gear teeth in mesh.* **—mesh** *v.* **meshed, mesh·ing, mesh·es.** *—tr.* **1.** To catch in or as if in a net; ensnare. **2.** To cause (gear teeth) to become engaged. **3.** To cause to work closely together; coordinate. *—intr.* **1.** To become entangled. **2.** To become engaged or interlocked: *gears that are not meshing properly.* **3.a.** To fit together effectively; be coordinated. **b.** To accord with another or each other; harmonize. [Middle English *mesch,* probably from Middle Dutch *maesche.*] **—mesh′y** *adj.*

Me·shach (mē′shăk). In the Old Testament, a young man who with Abednego and Shadrach emerged unharmed from the fiery furnace of Babylon.

Me·shed (mĕ-shĕd′) also **Mash·had** (mə-shăd′, mäsh-häd′). A city of northeast Iran near the Turkmenistan and Afghanistan borders. It was long an important trade center on caravan routes from Tehran to India. Population, 1,130,000.

me·shu·ga also **me·shug·ga** (mə-sho͝og′ə) *adj. Slang.* Crazy; senseless. [Yiddish *meshuge,* from Hebrew *məšuggāʿ.*]

me·shu·gaas or **mish·e·gaas** or **mish·e·goss** (mĭsh′ə-gäs′) *n. Slang.* Crazy or senseless activity or behavior; craziness. [Yiddish *meshegas,* from Hebrew *məšuggāʿ.*]

me·shug·ga (mə-sho͝og′ə) *adj.* Variant of **meshuga.**

mesh·work (mĕsh′wûrk′) *n.* Meshed material; network.

me·si·al (mē′zē-əl, -zhəl) *adj.* **1.** Of, in, near, or toward the middle. **2.** *Dentistry.* Situated toward the middle of the front of the jaw along the curve of the dental arch. **—me′si·al·ly** *adv.*

mes·ic (mĕz′ĭk, mĕs′-, mē′zĭk, -sĭk) *adj. Ecology.* Of, characterized by, or adapted to a moderately moist habitat.

me·sit·y·lene (mə-sĭt′l-ēn′) *n.* A hydrocarbon, $C_6H_3(CH_3)_3$, occurring in petroleum and coal tar or synthesized from acetone and used as a solvent. [MESITYL (OXIDE) + –ENE.]

mes·i·tyl oxide (mĕs′ĭ-tĭl) *n.* An oily liquid, $(CH_3)_2C{:}CHCOCH_3$, obtained from acetones and used as a solvent and in lacquers, paints, and varnishes. [Greek *mesitēs,* mediator (from its use as an intermediate in organic synthesis) (from *mesos,* middle; see MESO–) + –YL.]

Mes·mer (mĕz′mər, mĕs′-), **Franz** or **Friedrich Anton.** 1734–1815. Austrian physician who sought to treat disease through animal magnetism, an early therapeutic application of hypnotism.

mes·mer·ism (mĕz′mə-rĭz′əm, mĕs′-) *n.* **1.** A strong or spellbinding appeal; fascination. **2.** Hypnotic induction believed to involve animal magnetism. **3.** Hypnotism. [After Franz MESMER.] **—mes·mer′ic** (-mĕr′ĭk) *adj.* **—mes·mer′i·cal·ly** *adv.* **—mes′mer·ist** *n.*

WORD HISTORY: When the members of an audience sit mesmerized by a speaker, their reactions do not take the form of dancing, sleeping, or falling into convulsions. But if Franz Anton Mesmer were addressing the audience, such behavior could be expected. Mesmer, a visionary 18th-century physician, believed cures could be effected by having patients do things such as sit with their feet in a fountain of magnetized water while holding cables attached to magnetized trees. Mesmer then came to believe that magnetic powers resided in himself, and during highly fashionable curative sessions in Paris he caused his patients to have reactions ranging from sleeping or dancing to convulsions. These reactions were actually brought about by hypnotic powers that Mesmer was unaware he possessed. One of his pupils, named Puységur, then used the term *mesmerism* (first recorded in English in 1802) for Mesmer's practices. The related word *mesmerize* (first recorded in English in 1829), having shed its reference to the hypnotic doctor, lives on in the sense "to enthrall."

mes·mer·ize (mĕz′mə-rīz′, mĕs′-) *tr.v.* **-ized, -iz·ing, -iz·es. 1.** To spellbind; enthrall: *"He could mesmerize an audience by the sheer force of his presence"* (Justin Kaplan). **2.** To hypnotize. **—mes′mer·i·za′tion** (-mər-ĭ-zā′shən) *n.* **—mes′mer·iz′er** *n.*

meso– or **mes–** *pref.* **1.** In the middle; middle: *mesoderm.* **2.** Intermediate: *mesophyte.* [Greek, from *mesos,* middle. See **medhyo-** in Appendix.]

Mes·o·a·mer·i·ca (mĕz′ō-ə-mĕr′ĭ-kə, mĕs′-). A region extending south and east from central Mexico to include parts of Guatemala, Belize, Honduras, and Nicaragua. In pre-Columbian

mesa
Monument Valley, Utah

ă pat	oi boy
ā pay	ou out
âr care	o͝o took
ä father	o͞o boot
ĕ pet	ŭ cut
ē be	ûr urge
ĭ pit	th thin
ī pie	*th* this
îr pier	hw which
ŏ pot	zh vision
ō toe	ə about, item
ô paw	♦ regionalism

Stress marks: ′ (primary); ′ (secondary), as in **dictionary** (dĭk′shə-nĕr′ē)

times it was inhabited by diverse civilizations, including the Mayan and the Olmec. **—Mes′o·a·mer′i·can** *adj. & n.*

mes·o·blast (mĕz′ə-blăst′, mĕs′-) *n.* The middle germinal layer of an early embryo, consisting of undifferentiated cells destined to become the mesoderm. **—mes′o·blas′tic** *adj.*

mes·o·carp (mĕz′ə-kärp′, mĕs′-) *n. Botany.* The middle, usually fleshy layer of a fruit wall.

mes·o·ce·phal·ic (mĕz′ō-sə-făl′ĭk, mĕs′-) *adj.* Having a head of medium breadth, with a cephalic index between 76 and 80. **—mes′o·ceph′al·ly** (-ə-sĕf′ə-lē) *n.*

mes·o·derm (mĕz′ə-dûrm′, mĕs′-) *n.* The middle embryonic germ layer, lying between the ectoderm and the endoderm, from which connective tissue, muscle, bone, and the urogenital and circulatory systems develop. **—mes′o·der′mal, mes′o·der′mic** *adj.*

mes·o·gas·tri·um (mĕz′ə-găs′trē-əm, mĕs′-) *n., pl.* **-tri·a** (-trē-ə). **1.** The portion of the embryonic mesentery that is attached to the early stomach. **2.** The region of the abdomen surrounding the navel. **—mes′o·gas′tric** *adj.*

mes·o·gle·a also **mes·o·gloe·a** (mĕz′ə-glē′ə, mĕs′-, mē′-zə-, -sə-) *n.* The layer of gelatinous material that separates the inner and outer cell layers of a coelenterate. [New Latin *mesogloea* : MESO– + Medieval Greek *gloia, glia,* glue; see ZOOGLEA.] **—mes′o·gle′al** *adj.*

Mes·o·lith·ic (mĕz′ə-lĭth′ĭk, mĕs′-) *adj.* Of, relating to, or being the cultural period of the Stone Age between the Paleolithic and Neolithic ages, marked by the appearance of the bow and cutting tools. **—Mesolithic** *n.* The Mesolithic Age.

mes·o·mere (mĕz′ə-mîr′, mĕs′-) *n.* **1.** A blastomere of intermediate size, larger than a micromere but smaller than a macromere. **2.** The middle zone of the mesoderm of a chordate vertebrate embryo, from which excretory tissue develops.

mes·o·morph (mĕz′ə-môrf′, mĕs′-) *n. Anatomy.* A mesomorphic person. [MESO(DERM) + –MORPH.]

mes·o·mor·phic (mĕz′ə-môr′fĭk, mĕs′-) *adj.* **1.** Also **mes·o·mor·phous** (-môr′fəs). Of, relating to, or existing in a state of matter intermediate between liquid and crystal. **2.** *Anatomy.* Having or characterized by a robust, muscular body build caused by the predominance of structures developed from the embryonic mesodermal layer. **—mes′o·mor′phism, mes′o·mor′phy** *n.*

mes·on (mĕz′ŏn′, mĕs′-, mē′zŏn′, -sŏn′) *n.* Any of a family of subatomic particles that participate in strong interactions, are composed of a quark and an antiquark, and have masses generally intermediate between leptons and baryons. See table at **subatomic particle.** **—me·son′ic** (mĕ-zŏn′ĭk, -sŏn′, mē-) *adj.*

mes·o·neph·ros (mĕz′ə-nĕf′rəs, -rŏs′, mĕs′-) *n. Biology.* The second of the three excretory organs that develop in a vertebrate embryo, becoming the functioning kidney in fish and amphibians but replaced by the metanephros in higher vertebrates. Also called *Wolffian body.* [MESO– + Greek *nephros,* kidney.] **—mes′o·neph′ric** *adj.*

mes·o·pause (mĕz′ə-pôz′, mĕs′-) *n.* An atmospheric area about 80 kilometers (50 miles) above the earth's surface, forming the upper boundary of the mesosphere.

mes·o·pe·lag·ic (mĕz′ə-pə-lăj′ik, mĕs′-) *adj.* Of, relating to, or living at ocean depths between about 180 and 900 meters (600 and 3000 feet): *mesopelagic organisms.*

mes·o·phyll (mĕz′ə-fĭl′, mĕs′-) *n.* The photosynthetic tissue of a leaf, located between the upper and lower epidermis. **—mes′o·phyl′lic, mes′o·phyl′lous** *adj.*

mes·o·phyte (mĕz′ə-fīt′, mĕs′-) *n.* A land plant that grows in an environment having a moderate amount of moisture. **—mes′o·phyt′ic** (-fĭt′ĭk) *adj.*

Mes·o·po·ta·mi·a (mĕs′ə-pə-tā′mē-ə). An ancient region of southwest Asia between the Tigris and Euphrates rivers in modern-day Iraq. Probably settled before 5000 B.C., the area was the home of numerous early civilizations, including Sumer, Akkad, Babylonia, and Assyria. **—Mes′o·po·ta′mi·an** *adj. & n.*

mes·o·some (mĕz′ə-sōm′, mĕs′-, mē′zə-, -sə-) *n.* A convoluted invagination of the cytoplasmic membrane in some bacterial cells.

mes·o·sphere (mĕz′ə-sfîr′, mĕs′-) *n.* The portion of the atmosphere from about 30 to 80 kilometers (20 to 50 miles) above the earth's surface, characterized by temperatures that decrease from 10°C to −90°C (50°F to −130°F) with increasing altitude. **—mes′o·spher′ic** (-sfîr′ĭk, -sfĕr′-) *adj.*

mes·o·the·li·a (mĕz′ə-thē′lē-ə, mĕs′-) *n.* Plural of **mesothelium.**

mes·o·the·li·o·ma (mĕz′ə-thē′lē-ō′mə, mĕs′-, mē′zə-, -sə-) *n., pl.* **-ma·ta** (-mə-tə) or **-mas.** A usually malignant tumor of mesothelial tissue, especially that of the pleura or peritoneum.

mes·o·the·li·um (mĕz′ə-thē′lē-əm, mĕs′-) *n., pl.* **-li·a** (-lē-ə). The layer of flat cells of mesodermal origin that lines the embryonic body cavity and gives rise to the squamous cells of the peritoneum, pericardium, and pleura. [MESO– + (EPI)THELIUM.] **—mes′o·the′li·al** *adj.*

mes·o·tho·rax (mĕz′ə-thôr′ăks′, -thōr′-, mĕs′-) *n., pl.* **-tho·rax·es** or **-tho·ra·ces** (-thôr′ə-sēz′, -thōr′-). The middle of the three divisions of the thorax of an insect, bearing the middle pair of legs and the first pair of wings. **—mes′o·tho·rac′ic** (-thô-răs′ĭk, -thō-) *adj.*

mes·o·tho·ri·um (mĕz′ə-thôr′ē-əm, -thōr′-, mĕs′-) *n.* Either of two decay products of thorium, mesothorium I, an isotope of radium, or mesothorium II, an isotope of actinium.

Mes·o·zo·ic (mĕz′ə-zō′ĭk, mĕs′-) *adj.* Of, relating to, or being the third era of geologic time, including the Triassic Period, the Jurassic Period, and the Cretaceous Period and characterized by the development of flying reptiles, birds, and flowering plants and the appearance and extinction of dinosaurs. See table at **geologic time.** **—Mesozoic** *n.* The Mesozoic Era.

mes·quite (mĕ-skēt′, mə-) *n.* Any of several small spiny trees or shrubs of the genus *Prosopis* in the pea family, native to hot, dry regions of the New World and important as plants for bees and forage for cattle, especially: **a.** *P. glandulosa,* native to the southwest United States and northern Mexico. Also called *honey mesquite, western honey mesquite.* **b.** *P. juliflora,* native to the Gulf Coast and Caribbean islands from Mexico to Venezuela. Also called *algarroba.* [Spanish *mezquite,* from Nahuatl *mizquitl.*]

Mes·quite (mə-skēt′, mĕ-). A city of northeast Texas, an industrial and residential suburb of Dallas. Population, 67,053.

mess (mĕs) *n.* **1.** A disorderly or dirty accumulation, heap, or jumble: *left a mess in the yard.* **2. a.** A cluttered, untidy, usually dirty condition: *The kitchen was in a mess.* **b.** A confused, troubling, or embarrassing condition; a muddle: *With divorce and bankruptcy proceedings pending, his personal life was in a mess.* **c.** One that is in such a condition: *clothes that were a mess after painting the ceiling; made a mess of their marriage.* **3. a.** An amount of food, as for a meal, course, or dish: *cooked up a mess of fish.* **b.** A serving of soft, semiliquid food: *a mess of porridge.* **4. a.** A group of people, usually soldiers or sailors, who regularly eat meals together. **b.** Food or a meal served to such a group: *took mess with the enlistees.* **c.** A mess hall. **—mess** *v.* **messed, mess·ing, mess·es.** *—tr.* **1.** To make disorderly or soiled; clutter or foul: *a puppy that still messes the floor.* **2.** To botch; bungle. *—intr.* **1.** To cause or make a mess. **2.** To use or handle something carelessly; fiddle: *messed with the blender until he broke it.* **3.** To intrude; interfere: *messing in the neighbors' affairs.* **4.** To take a meal in a military mess. ***—phrasal verbs.*** **mess around.** *Informal.* **1.** To pass time in aimless puttering. **2.** To associate casually or playfully: *liked to mess around with pals on days off.* **mess up. 1.** *Informal.* To make a mistake, especially from nervousness or confusion: *messed up and dropped the ball.* **2.** *Slang.* To beat up; manhandle: *got messed up in a brawl.* [Middle English *mes,* course of a meal, food, group of people eating together, from Old French, from Late Latin *missus,* from Latin, past participle of *mittere,* to place.]

mes·sage (mĕs′ĭj) *n. Abbr.* **msg. 1. a.** A usually short communication transmitted by words, signals, or other means from one person, station, or group to another. **b.** The substance of such a communication; the point or points conveyed: *gestured to a waiter, who got the message and brought the bill.* **2.** A statement made or read before a gathering: *a retiring executive's farewell message.* **3.** A basic thesis or lesson; a moral: *a play with a message.* *—tr.* **-saged, -sag·ing, -sag·es. 1.** To send a message to. **2.** To send as a message: *messaged the instruction by cable.* *—intr.* To send a message; communicate. [Middle English, from Old French, from Medieval Latin *missāticum,* from Latin *missus,* past participle of *mittere,* to send.]

Mes·sa·li·na (mĕs′ə-lī′nə), **Valeria.** Died A.D. 48. Roman empress as the third wife of Claudius I. She was executed after Claudius discovered that she had married a lover in his absence.

mes·sa·line (mĕs′ə-lēn′) *n.* A lightweight, soft, shiny silk cloth with a twilled or satin weave. [French.]

Mes·sei·gneurs (mā-sĕ-nyœr′) *n.* Plural of **Monseigneur.**

Mes·se·ne (mĭ-sē′nē). An ancient Greek city in the southwest Peloponnesus. It was founded c. 369 B.C.

mes·sen·ger (mĕs′ən-jər) *n.* **1.** One that carries messages or performs errands, as: **a.** A person employed to carry telegrams, letters, or parcels. **b.** A military or official courier. **c.** An envoy to another person, party, or government. **2.** A bearer of news. **3.** A forerunner; a harbinger: *the crocus and other messengers of spring.* **4.** A prophet: *the messenger of Allah.* **5.** *Nautical.* A chain or rope used for hauling in a cable. In this sense, also called *messenger line.* **—messenger** *tr.v.* **-gered, -ger·ing, -gers.** To send by messenger. [Middle English *messanger,* from Old French *messagier,* from *message,* message. See MESSAGE.]

messenger RNA *n. Abbr.* **mRNA** The form of RNA that mediates the transfer of genetic information from the cell nucleus to ribosomes in the cytoplasm, where it serves as a template for protein synthesis. It is synthesized from a DNA template during the process of transcription.

Mes·se·ni·a (mĭ-sē′nē-ə, -sēn′yə). An ancient region of southwest Greece in the Peloponnesus on the Ionian Sea. It fought a series of wars against Sparta c. 736 to 371 B.C. The Romans conquered the area in 146 B.C. **—Mes·sen′i·an** *adj. & n.*

mess hall *n.* A building or room used for serving and eating meals, as on an army post.

Mes·si·ah (mĭ-sī′ə) *n.* **1.** Also **Mes·si·as** (mĭ-sī′əs). The anticipated deliverer and king of the Jews. **2.** Also **Messias.** Jesus. **3. messiah.** A leader who is regarded as or professes to be a savior or liberator. [Middle English *Messias, Messie,* from Old French *Messie,* from Late Latin *Messīās,* from Greek, from Aramaic *məšîḥā* or Hebrew *māšîaḥ,* the anointed, messiah.]

mes·si·an·ic also **Mes·si·an·ic** (mĕs′ē-ăn′ĭk) *adj.* **1.** Of or relating to a messiah: *messianic hopes.* **2.** Of or characterized by messianism: *messianic nationalism.* [New Latin *messiānicus,* from Late Latin *messīās,* Messiah. See MESSIAH.]

mes·si·a·nism (mĕs′ē-ə-nĭz′əm, mĭ-sī′-) *n.* **1.** Belief in a messiah. **2.** Belief that a particular cause or movement is destined to triumph or save the world. **3.** Zealous devotion to a leader, cause, or movement. **—mes′si·a·nist** *n.*

Mes·si·as (mĭ-sī′əs) *n.* Variant of **Messiah** (senses 1, 2).

Mes·sieurs (mā-syœ′, mĕs′ərz) *n. Abbr.* **Messrs., M.M.** Plural of **Monsieur.**

Mes·si·na (mĭ-sē′nə, mĕ-). A city of northeast Sicily, Italy, on the **Strait of Messina,** a channel separating Sicily from mainland Italy. Founded in the eighth century B.C. by Greek colonists. Messina was decimated by the plague in 1743 and suffered severe earthquakes in 1783 and 1908. The strait's rocks, currents, and whirlpools may have been the inspiration for the legend of Scylla and Charybdis. Population, 255,890.

mess jacket *n.* A waist-length fitted jacket, worn chiefly as part of a uniform on formal occasions. Also called *monkey jacket, shell jacket.*

mess kit *n.* A set of cooking and eating utensils compactly arranged in a kit, used by soldiers and campers.

mess·mate (mĕs′māt′) *n.* A person with whom one eats regularly, as in a military mess.

Messrs.[1] (mĕs′ərz) *n.* Plural of **Mr.**

Messrs.[2] *abbr.* Messieurs.

mess·y (mĕs′ē) *adj.* **-i·er, -i·est. 1.** Disorderly and dirty: *a messy bedroom.* **2.** Exhibiting or demonstrating carelessness: *messy reasoning.* **3.** Unpleasantly difficult to settle or resolve: *a messy court case.* **—mess′i·ly** *adv.* **—mess′i·ness** *n.*

mes·ti·za (mĕs-tē′zə) *n.* A woman of mixed racial ancestry, especially of mixed European and Native American ancestry. [Spanish, feminine of *mestizo.* See MESTIZO.]

mes·ti·zo (mĕs-tē′zō) *n., pl.* **-zos** or **-zoes.** A person of mixed racial ancestry, especially of mixed European and Native American ancestry. [Spanish, mixed, mestizo, from Old Spanish, mixed, from Late Latin *mixtīcius,* from Latin *mixtus,* past participle of *miscēre,* to mix. See **meik-** in Appendix.]

mes·tra·nol (mĕs′trə-nôl′, -nōl′, -nŏl′) *n.* A synthetic estrogen, $C_{21}H_{26}O_2$, used in combination with a progestin in oral contraceptive preparations. [Alteration of *ethynyl methoxy estratriene,* one of its chemical names.]

Meš·tro·vić (mĕsh′trə-vĭch′, -trô-), **Ivan.** 1883–1962. Yugoslavian-born American sculptor of religious, mythological, and Slavic folklore subjects.

met (mĕt) *v.* Past tense and past participle of **meet**[1].

met. *abbr.* **1.a.** Metaphor. **b.** Metaphoric. **2.** Metaphysics. **3.a.** Meteorological. **b.** Meteorology. **4.** Metropolitan.

met– *pref.* Variant of **meta–.**

Me·ta (mā′tə, mĕ′tä). A river, about 1,102 km (685 mi) long, of northeast Colombia flowing along the border with Venezuela.

meta– or **met–** *pref.* **1.a.** Later in time: *metestrus.* **b.** At a later stage of development: *metanephros.* **2.** Situated behind: *metacarpus.* **3.a.** Change; transformation: *metachromatism.* **b.** Alternation: *metagenesis.* **4.a.** Beyond; transcending; more comprehensive: *metalinguistics.* **b.** At a higher state of development: *metazoan.* **5.** Having undergone metamorphosis: *metasomatic.* **6.a.** Derivative or related chemical substance: *metaprotein.* **b.** Of or relating to one of three possible isomers of a benzene ring with two attached chemical groups, in which the carbon atoms with attached groups are separated by one unsubstituted carbon atom: meta-*dibromobenzene.* [Greek, from *meta,* beside, after. See **me-**[2] in Appendix.]

met·a·bol·ic (mĕt′ə-bŏl′ĭk) *adj. Biology.* Of, relating to, or resulting from metabolism. [Greek *metabolikos,* changeable, from *metabolē,* change. See METABOLISM.] **—met′a·bol′i·cal·ly** *adv.*

me·tab·o·lism (mĭ-tăb′ə-lĭz′əm) *n. Biology.* **1.** The complex of physical and chemical processes occurring within a living cell or organism that are necessary for the maintenance of life. In metabolism some substances are broken down to yield energy for vital processes while other substances, necessary for life, are synthesized. **2.** The functioning of a specific substance within the living body: *water metabolism; iodine metabolism.* [From Greek *metabolē,* change, from *metaballein,* to change : *meta-,* meta- + *ballein,* to throw; see **g**ʷ**elə-** in Appendix.]

me·tab·o·lite (mĭ-tăb′ə-līt′) *n.* **1.** A substance produced by metabolism. **2.** A substance necessary for or taking part in a particular metabolic process. [METABOL(ISM) + –ITE[1].]

me·tab·o·lize (mĭ-tăb′ə-līz′) *v.* **-lized, -liz·ing, -liz·es.** —*tr.* **1.** To subject (a substance) to metabolism. **2.** To produce (a substance) by metabolism. —*intr.* To undergo change by metabolism. **—me·tab′o·liz′a·ble** *adj.*

met·a·car·pal (mĕt′ə-kär′pəl) *adj.* Of or relating to the metacarpus. **—metacarpal** *n.* Any of the bones of the metacarpus. **—met′a·car′pal·ly** *adv.*

met·a·car·pus (mĕt′ə-kär′pəs) *n., pl.* **-pi** (-pī). **1.** The part of the human hand that includes the five bones between the fingers and the wrist. **2.** The corresponding part of the forefoot of a quadruped.

met·a·cen·ter (mĕt′ə-sĕn′tər) *n.* The intersection of vertical lines through the center of buoyancy of a floating body when it is at equilibrium and when it is floating at an angle. The location of the metacenter is an indication of the stability of a floating body.

met·a·cen·tric (mĕt′ə-sĕn′trĭk) *adj.* **1.** Of or relating to a metacenter. **2.** *Genetics.* Having the centromere in the median position so that the arms are of equal length. Used of a chromosome. **—metacentric** *n.* A metacentric chromosome. **—met′a·cen·tric′i·ty** (-sĕn-trĭs′ĭ-tē) *n.*

met·a·chro·ma·tism (mĕt′ə-krō′mə-tĭz′əm) *n.* A change in color caused by variation of the physical conditions to which a body is subjected, especially such a change caused by variation in temperature. **—met′a·chro·mat′ic** (-măt′ĭk) *adj.*

met·a·eth·ics (mĕt′ə-ĕth′ĭks) *n. (used with a sing. verb).* The study of the meaning and nature of ethical terms, judgments, and arguments. **—met′a·eth′i·cal** *adj.*

met·a·fic·tion (mĕt′ə-fĭk′shən) *n.* Fiction that deals, often playfully and self-referentially, with the writing of fiction or its conventions. **—met′a·fic′tion·al** *adj.* **—met′a·fic′tion·ist** *n.*

met·a·gal·ax·y (mĕt′ə-găl′ək-sē) *n., pl.* **-ies.** The assemblage of all galaxies; the entire physical universe.

met·a·gen·e·sis (mĕt′ə-jĕn′ĭ-sĭs) *n. Biology.* See **alternation of generations. —met′a·ge·net′ic** (-jə-nĕt′ĭk) *adj.*

me·tag·na·thous (mĭ-tăg′nə-thəs) *adj.* Having a bill in which the tips of the mandibles cross. Used of a bird. **—me·tag′na·thism** *n.*

Met·ai·rie (mĕt′ə-rē). A community of southeast Louisiana, a suburb of New Orleans. Population, 164,160.

met·al (mĕt′l) *n.* **1.** *Abbr.* **M** Any of a category of electropositive elements that usually have a shiny surface, are generally good conductors of heat and electricity, and can be melted or fused, hammered into thin sheets, or drawn into wires. Typical metals form salts with nonmetals, basic oxides with oxygen, and alloys with one another. **2.** An alloy of two or more metallic elements. **3.** An object made of metal. **4.** Basic character; mettle. **5.** Broken stones used for road surfaces or railroad beds. **6.** Molten glass, especially when used in glassmaking. **7.** Molten cast iron. **8.** *Printing.* Type made of metal. **—metal** *tr.v.* **-aled, -al·ing, -als** also **-alled, -al·ling, -als.** To cover or surface (a roadbed, for example) with broken stones. [Middle English, from Old French, from Latin *metallum,* from Greek *metallon,* mine, mineral, metal.]

metal. *abbr.* **1.** Metallurgic. **2.** Metallurgy.

met·a·lin·guis·tics (mĕt′ə-lĭng-gwĭs′tĭks) *n. (used with a sing. verb).* The study of the interrelationship between language and other cultural behavior.

metall. *abbr.* **1.** Metallurgic. **2.** Metallurgy.

metall– or **metalli–** *pref.* Variants of **metallo–.**

me·tal·lic (mə-tăl′ĭk) *adj.* **1.** Of, relating to, or having the characteristics of a metal. **2.** Containing a metal: *a metallic compound.* **3.** Having a quality suggesting or associated with metal, especially: **a.** Lustrous; sparkling: *metallic colors.* **b.** Sharp-tasting: *an unpleasant, metallic flavor.* **4.** Harshly resonant: *"the strange metallic note of the meadow lark, suggesting the clash of vibrant blades"* (Ambrose Bierce). **—metallic** *n.* **1.** A yarn or fiber made of or containing metal. **2.** A fabric, typically shiny or iridescent, made of such yarn or fiber. **—me·tal′li·cal·ly** *adv.*

metallic bond *n.* The chemical bond characteristic of metals, in which mobile valence electrons are shared among atoms in a usually stable crystalline structure.

met·al·lif·er·ous (mĕt′l-ĭf′ər-əs) *adj.* Containing metal. Used of a mineral deposit or an ore. [From Latin *metallifer* : *metallum,* metal; see METAL + *-fer,* -fer.]

met·al·line (mĕt′l-ĭn, -īn′) *adj.* **1.** Of, resembling, or having the properties of a metal. **2.** Containing metal ions.

metallo– or **metall–** or **metalli–** *pref.* Metal: *metallography.* [From Latin *metallum,* metal. See METAL.]

met·al·log·ra·phy (mĕt′l-ŏg′rə-fē) *n.* The study of the structure of metals and alloys, especially by optical and electron microscopy and x-ray diffraction. **—met′al·log′ra·pher** *n.* **—me·tal′lo·graph′ic** (mə-tăl′ə-grăf′ĭk) *adj.* **—me·tal′lo·graph′i·cal·ly** *adv.*

met·al·loid (mĕt′l-oid′) *n.* **1.** A nonmetallic element, such as arsenic, that has some of the chemical properties of a metal. **2.** A nonmetallic element, such as carbon, that can form an alloy with metals. **—metalloid** also **met·al·loi·dal** (mĕt′l-oid′l) *adj.* **1.** Relating to or having the properties of a metalloid. **2.** Having the appearance of a metal.

me·tal·lo·phone (mə-tăl′ə-fōn′) *n. Music.* A percussion instrument consisting of a graduated series of metal bars struck with either hand-held or keyboard-controlled hammers.

met·al·lur·gy (mĕt′l-ûr′jē) *n. Abbr.* **metal., metall. 1.** The science that deals with procedures used in extracting metals from their ores, purifying and alloying metals, and creating useful objects from metals. **2.** The study of metals and their properties in bulk and at the atomic level. [New Latin *metallurgia,* from Greek *metallourgos,* miner, worker in metals : *metallon,* a mine, metal + *-ourgos,* -worker (from *ergon,* work; see **werg-** in Appendix).] **—met′al·lur′gic, met′al·lur′gi·cal** *adj.* **—met′al·lur′gi·cal·ly** *adv.* **—met′al·lur′gist** *n.*

met·al·mark (mĕt′l-märk′) *n.* Any of several small, darkly colored butterflies of the family Riodinidae, occurring mainly in tropical regions and having iridescent lines or spots on the wings.

met·al·work (mĕt′l-wûrk′) *n.* Work done in metal.

met·al·work·ing (mĕt′l-wûr′kĭng) *n.* The process or art of shaping things out of metal. **—met′al·work′er** *n.*

met·a·math·e·mat·ics (mĕt′ə-măth′ə-măt′ĭks) *n. (used*

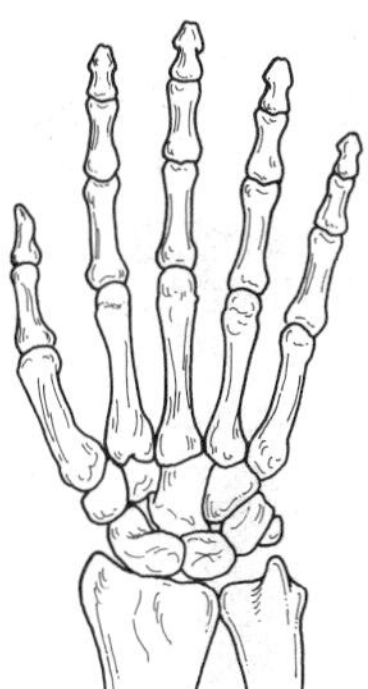

metacarpus

ă pat	oi boy
ā pay	ou out
âr care	ŏŏ took
ä father	ōō boot
ĕ pet	ŭ cut
ē be	ûr urge
ĭ pit	th thin
ī pie	*th* this
îr pier	hw which
ŏ pot	zh vision
ō toe	ə about, item
ô paw	♦ regionalism

Stress marks: **′** (primary); ′ (secondary), as in **dictionary** (dĭk′shə-nĕr′ē)

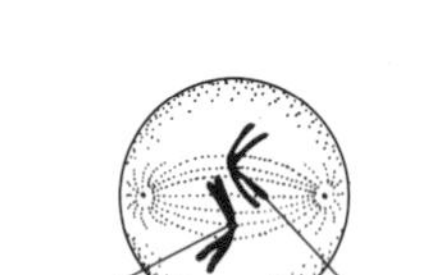

metaphase
Of mitosis

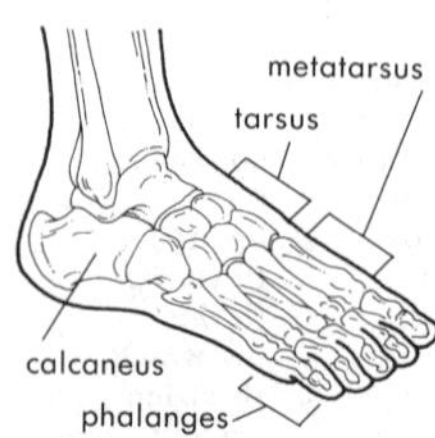

metatarsus

with a sing. verb). The branch of mathematics that deals with the logic and consistency of mathematical proofs, formulas, and equations. **—met′a·math′e·mat′i·cal** *adj.* **—met′a·math′e·ma·ti′cian** (-mə-tĭsh′ən) *n.*

met·a·mere (mĕt′ə-mîr′) *n. Zoology.* Any of the homologous segments, lying in a longitudinal series, that compose the body of certain animals, such as earthworms and lobsters. Also called *somite.* **—met′a·mer′ic** (-mĕr′ĭk, -mîr′-) *adj.* **—met′a·mer′i·cal·ly** *adv.*

me·tam·er·ism (mə-tăm′ə-rĭz′əm) *n.* The condition of having the body divided into metameres, exhibited in most animals only in the early embryonic stages of development.

met·a·mor·phic (mĕt′ə-môr′fĭk) *adj.* **1.** Also **met·a·mor·phous** (-fəs). Of, relating to, or characterized by metamorphosis. **2.** *Geology.* Changed in structure or composition as a result of metamorphism. Used of rock. [METAMORPH(OSIS) + –IC.]

met·a·mor·phism (mĕt′ə-môr′fĭz′əm) *n. Geology.* The process by which rocks are altered in composition, texture, or internal structure by extreme heat, pressure, and the introduction of new chemical substances. [METAMORPH(IC) + –ISM.]

met·a·mor·phose (mĕt′ə-môr′fōz′, -fōs′) *v.* **-phosed, -phos·ing, -phos·es.** *—tr.* **1.** To change into a wholly different form or appearance; transform: *"His eyes turned bloodshot, and he was metamorphosed into a raging fiend"* (Jack London). **2.** To subject to metamorphosis or metamorphism. *—intr.* To be changed or transformed by or as if by metamorphosis or metamorphism. See Synonyms at **convert.** [French *métamorphoser,* from Old French, from *metamorphose,* metamorphosis, from Latin *metamorphōsis.* See METAMORPHOSIS.]

met·a·mor·pho·sis (mĕt′ə-môr′fə-sĭs) *n., pl.* **-ses** (-sēz′). **1.** A transformation, as by magic or sorcery. **2.** A marked change in appearance, character, condition, or function. **3.** *Biology.* A change in the form and often habits of an animal during normal development after the embryonic stage. Metamorphosis includes, in insects, the transformation of a maggot into an adult fly and a caterpillar into a butterfly and, in amphibians, the changing of a tadpole into a frog. **4.** *Pathology.* A usually degenerative change in the structure of a particular body tissue. [Latin *metamorphōsis,* from Greek, from *metamorphoun,* to transform : *meta-,* meta- + *morphē,* form.]

metamorphosis
Of a monarch butterfly
Danaus plexippus

met·a·mor·phous (mĕt′ə-môr′fəs) *adj.* Variant of **metamorphic** (sense 1).

met·a·neph·ros (mĕt′ə-nĕf′rŏs′) *n.* The third and final excretory organ that develops in a vertebrate embryo. In birds, reptiles, and mammals it replaces the mesonephros as the functional excretory organ and develops into the adult kidney. [META– + Greek *nephros,* kidney.]

metaph. *abbr.* **1.** Metaphor. **2.** Metaphoric. **3.** Metaphysics.

met·a·phase (mĕt′ə-fāz′) *n.* The stage of mitosis and meiosis, following prophase and preceding anaphase, during which the chromosomes are aligned along the metaphase plate.

metaphase plate *n.* An imaginary plane perpendicular to the spindle fibers of a dividing cell, along which chromosomes align during metaphase.

met·a·phor (mĕt′ə-fôr′, -fər) *n.* **1.** *Abbr.* **met., metaph.** A figure of speech in which a word or phrase that ordinarily designates one thing is used to designate another, thus making an implicit comparison, as in *"a sea of troubles"* or *"All the world's a stage"* (Shakespeare). **2.** One thing conceived as representing another; a symbol: *"The high-rise garbage repository is a metaphor for both accomplishment and failure"* (Richard Sever). [Middle English *methaphor,* from Old French *metaphore,* from Latin *metaphora,* from Greek, transference, metaphor, from *metapherein,* to transfer : *meta-,* meta- + *pherein,* to carry; see **bher-**[1] in Appendix.] **—met′a·phor′ic** (-fôr′ĭk, -fŏr′-), **met′a·phor′i·cal** *adj.* **—met′a·phor′i·cal·ly** *adv.*

met·a·phos·phate (mĕt′ə-fŏs′fāt′) *n.* A salt or an ester of metaphosphoric acid.

met·a·phos·phor·ic acid (mĕt′ə-fŏs-fôr′ĭk, -fŏr′-) *n.* An inorganic compound, HPO_3, used as a dehydrating agent and in dental cements.

met·a·phrase (mĕt′ə-frāz′) *n.* A word-for-word translation. **—metaphrase** *tr.v.* **-phrased, -phras·ing, -phras·es. 1.** To translate, especially literally. **2.** To alter the wording of (a text). [New Latin *metaphrasis,* from Greek, translation, paraphrase, from *metaphrazein,* to translate : *meta-,* meta- + *phrazein,* tell, show; see **gʷhren-** in Appendix.] **—met′a·phras′tic** (-frăs′tĭk) *adj.*

met·a·phrast (mĕt′ə-frăst′) *n.* One who renders a text into a different form, as by recasting prose in verse. [Medieval Greek *metaphrastēs,* from Greek *metaphrazein,* to translate. See METAPHRASE.]

met·a·phys·ic (mĕt′ə-fĭz′ĭk) *n.* **1.a.** Metaphysics. **b.** A system of metaphysics. **2.** An underlying philosophical or theoretical principle: *a belief in luck, the metaphysic of the gambler.* [Middle English *methaphisik, metaphisik.* See METAPHYSICS.]

met·a·phys·i·cal (mĕt′ə-fĭz′ĭ-kəl) *adj.* **1.** Of or relating to metaphysics. **2.** Based on speculative or abstract reasoning. **3.** Highly abstract or theoretical; abstruse. **4.a.** Immaterial; incorporeal. See Synonyms at **immaterial. b.** Supernatural. **5.** Often **Metaphysical.** Of or relating to the poetry of a group of 17th-century English poets whose verse is characterized by an intellectually challenging style and extended metaphors comparing very dissimilar things. [Middle English *metaphisicalle,* from Medieval Latin *metaphysicālis,* from *metaphysica,* metaphysics. See METAPHYSICS.] **—met′a·phys′i·cal·ly** *adv.*

met·a·phy·si·cian (mĕt′ə-fĭ-zĭsh′ən) *n.* One who specializes or is skilled in metaphysics.

met·a·phys·ics (mĕt′ə-fĭz′ĭks) *n. Abbr.* **met., metaph. 1.** *(used with a sing. verb). Philosophy.* The branch of philosophy that examines the nature of reality, including the relationship between mind and matter, substance and attribute, fact and value. **2.** *(used with a pl. verb).* The theoretical or first principles of a particular discipline: *the metaphysics of law.* **3.** *(used with a sing. verb).* A priori speculation upon questions that are unanswerable to scientific observation, analysis, or experiment. **4.** *(used with a sing. verb).* Excessively subtle reasoning. [Pl. of Middle English *methaphisik,* from Medieval Latin *metaphysica,* from Medieval Greek *(ta) metaphusika,* Greek *(Ta) meta (ta) phusika,* (the things) after the physics, the title of Aristotle's treatise on first principles (so called because it followed his work on physics) : *meta,* after; see META– + *phusika,* physics; see PHYSICS.]

met·a·pla·sia (mĕt′ə-plā′zhə, -zhē-ə) *n.* **1.** Normal transformation of tissue from one type to another, as in the ossification of cartilage to form bone. **2.** Transformation of cells from a normal to an abnormal state. **—met′a·plas′tic** (-plăs′tĭk) *adj.*

met·a·plasm[1] (mĕt′ə-plăz′əm) *n. Grammar.* Alteration of a word by the addition, omission, or transposition of sounds or syllables or the letters that represent them. [Middle English *metaplasmus,* from Latin, from Greek *metaplasmos,* remodeling, from *metaplassein,* to remold : *meta-,* meta- + *plassein,* to mold; see **pelə-**[2] in Appendix.] **—met′a·plas′tic** (-plăs′tĭk), **met′a·plas′mic** (-plăz′mĭk) *adj.*

met·a·plasm[2] (mĕt′ə-plăz′əm) *n. Biology.* Nonliving material in the protoplasm of a cell, such as pigment granules or nutritive substances. **—met′a·plas′mic** (-plăz′mĭk) *adj.*

Met·a·pon·tum (mĕt′ə-pŏn′təm). An ancient city of southeast Italy on the Gulf of Taranto. It was settled by Greeks c. 700 B.C. Pythagoras taught here in the sixth century.

met·a·pro·tein (mĕt′ə-prō′tēn′, -prō′tē-ĭn) *n.* Any of various organic compounds that result from a reaction between an acid or alkali and a protein and are soluble in weak acids or alkalis and insoluble in neutral solutions.

met·a·psy·chol·o·gy (mĕt′ə-sī-kŏl′ə-jē) *n.* Philosophical inquiry supplementing the empirical science of psychology. Metapsychology deals with aspects of the mind that cannot be evaluated on the basis of objective or empirical evidence.

met·a·so·ma·tism (mĕt′ə-sō′mə-tĭz′əm) also **met·a·so·ma·to·sis** (-sō′mə-tō′sĭs) *n.* The process by which the chemical composition of a rock is changed by interaction with fluids; replacement of one mineral by another without melting. **—met′a·so·mat′ic** (-măt′ĭk) *adj.* **—met′a·so·mat′i·cal·ly** *adv.*

met·a·sta·ble (mĕt′ə-stā′bəl) *adj.* Of, relating to, or being a relatively unstable and transient but significant state of a chemical or physical system, as of a supersaturated solution or an excited atom. **—met′a·sta·bil′i·ty** (-stə-bĭl′ĭ-tē) *n.*

me·tas·ta·sis (mə-tăs′tə-sĭs) *n., pl.* **-ses** (-sēz′). **1.** *Pathology.* Transmission of pathogenic microorganisms or cancerous cells from an original site to one or more sites elsewhere in the body, usually by way of the blood vessels or lymphatics. **2.** A secondary cancerous growth formed by transmission of cancerous cells from a primary growth located elsewhere in the body. [Greek, from *methistanai,* to change : *meta-,* meta- + *histanai,* to cause to stand, place; see **stā-** in Appendix.] **—met′a·stat′ic** (mĕt′ə-stăt′ĭk) *adj.* **—met′a·stat′i·cal·ly** *adv.*

me·tas·ta·size (mə-tăs′tə-sīz′) *intr.v.* **-sized, -siz·ing, -siz·es.** To be transmitted or transferred by or as if by metastasis.

met·a·tar·sal (mĕt′ə-tär′səl) *adj.* Of or relating to the metatarsus. **—metatarsal** *n.* Any of the bones of the metatarsus. **—met′a·tar′sal·ly** *adv.*

met·a·tar·sus (mĕt′ə-tär′səs) *n., pl.* **-si** (-sī, -sē). **1.** The middle part of the human foot that forms the instep and includes the five bones between the toes and the ankle. **2.** The corresponding part of the hind foot in quadrupeds or of the foot in birds.

me·ta·te (mə-tä′tē, mĕ-tä′tĕ) *n.* A stone block with a shallow concave surface, used with a mano for grinding corn or other grains. [American Spanish, from Nahuatl *metlatl.*]

me·tath·e·sis (mĭ-tăth′ĭ-sĭs) *n., pl.* **-ses** (-sēz′). **1.** *Linguistics.* Transposition within a word of letters, sounds, or syllables, as in the change from Old English *brid* to modern English *bird* or in the confusion of *modren* for *modern.* **2.** *Chemistry.* Double decomposition. [Late Latin, from Greek, from *metatithenai,* to transpose : *meta-,* meta- + *tithenai,* to place; see **dhē-** in Appendix.] **—met′a·thet′ic** (mĕt′ə-thĕt′ĭk), **met·a·thet′i·cal** *adj.* **—met′a·thet′i·cal·ly** *adv.*

me·tath·e·size (mĭ-tăth′ĭ-sīz′) *tr. & intr.v.* **-sized, -siz·ing, -siz·es.** To subject to or undergo metathesis.

met·a·tho·rax (mĕt′ə-thôr′ăks′, -thōr′-) *n., pl.* **-tho·rax·es** or **-tho·ra·ces** (-thôr′ə-sēz′, -thōr′-). The hindmost of the three divisions of the thorax of an insect, bearing the third pair of legs and the second pair of wings. **—met′a·tho·rac′ic** (-thô-răs′ĭk, -thō-) *adj.*

met·a·xy·lem (mĕt′ə-zī′ləm) *n. Botany.* The part of the primary xylem that differentiates after the protoxylem and is characterized by broader vessels and tracheids.

met·a·zo·an (mĕt′ə-zō′ən) *n.* A multicellular animal of the subkingdom Metazoa, a division of the animal kingdom in traditional two-kingdom classification systems. [New Latin *Metazoa,* a subdivision of the animal kingdom : META– + *-zoa,* pl. of *-zoon,* animal; see –ZOON.] **—met′a·zo′al, met′a·zo′an, met′a·zo′ic** *adj.*

Metch·ni·koff also **Metch·ni·kov** (mĕch′nĭ-kôf′, myĕch′nĭ-kəf), **Élie.** 1845–1916. Russian zoologist. He shared a 1908 Nobel Prize for discoveries and advances in immunology.

mete[1] (mēt) *tr.v.* **met·ed, met·ing, metes. 1.** To distribute by or as if by measure; allot: *mete out punishment.* **2.** *Archaic.* To measure. [Middle English *meten,* from Old English *metan.* See **med-** in Appendix.]

mete[2] (mēt) *n.* A boundary line; a limit: *metes and bounds.* [Middle English, from Anglo-Norman, from Latin *mēta,* turning post, boundary.]

me·tem·psy·cho·sis (mə-tĕm′sĭ-kō′sĭs, mĕt′əm-sī-) *n., pl.* **-ses** (-sēz). Reincarnation. [Late Latin *metempsȳchōsis,* from Greek *metempsukhōsis,* from *metempsukhousthai,* to transmigrate : *meta-,* meta- + *empsukhos,* animate (*en,* in; see EN–[2] + *psukhē,* soul; see **bhes-** in Appendix).]

met·en·ceph·a·lon (mĕt′ĕn-sĕf′ə-lŏn′) *n., pl.* **-la** (-lə). The anterior part of the embryonic hindbrain, which gives rise to the cerebellum and pons. **—met′en·ce·phal′ic** (-sə-făl′ĭk) *adj.*

me·te·or (mē′tē-ər, -ôr′) *n.* A bright trail or streak that appears in the sky when a meteoroid is heated to incandescence by friction with the earth's atmosphere. Also called *falling star, shooting star.* [Middle English *metheour,* atmospheric phenomenon, from Old French *meteore,* from Medieval Latin *meteōrum,* from Greek *meteōron,* astronomical phenomenon, from neuter of *meteōros,* high in the air : *meta-,* meta- + *-aoros,* lifted; akin to *aeirein,* to lift up; see AORTA.]

meteor. *abbr.* **1.** Meteorological. **2.** Meteorology.

me·te·or·ic (mē′tē-ôr′ĭk, -ŏr′-) *adj.* **1.** Of, relating to, or formed by a meteoroid. **2.** Of or relating to the earth's atmosphere. **3.** Similar to a meteor in speed, brilliance, or brevity: *a meteoric rise to fame.* **—me′te·or′i·cal·ly** *adv.*

me·te·or·ite (mē′tē-ə-rīt′) *n.* A stony or metallic mass of matter that has fallen to the earth's surface from outer space. **—me′te·or·it′ic** (-ə-rĭt′ĭk), **me′te·or·it′i·cal** *adj.*

me·te·or·o·graph (mē′tē-ôr′ə-grăf′, -ŏr′-) *n.* An instrument that records simultaneously several meteorological conditions, such as temperature, pressure, and humidity.

me·te·or·oid (mē′tē-ə-roid′) *n.* A solid body, moving in space, that is smaller than an asteroid and at least as large as a speck of dust.

me·te·or·ol·o·gist (mē′tē-ə-rŏl′ə-jĭst) *n.* **1.** One who studies meteorology. **2.** One who reports and forecasts weather conditions, as on television.

me·te·or·ol·o·gy (mē′tē-ə-rŏl′ə-jē) *n. Abbr.* **meteor., meteorol., met.** The science that deals with the phenomena of the atmosphere, especially weather and weather conditions. [French *météorologie,* from Greek *meteōrologia,* discussion of astronomical phenomena : *meteōron,* astronomical phenomenon; see METEOR + *-logia,* -logy.] **—me′te·or·o·log′i·cal** (-ər-ə-lŏj′ĭ-kəl), **me′te·or·o·log′ic** *adj.* **—me′te·or·o·log′i·cal·ly** *adv.*

meteor shower *n.* A large number of meteors that appear together and seem to come from the same area in the sky.

me·ter[1] (mē′tər) *n.* **1.a.** The measured arrangement of words in poetry, as by accentual rhythm, syllabic quantity, or the number of syllables in a line. **b.** A particular arrangement of words in poetry, such as iambic pentameter, determined by the kind and number of metrical units in a line. **c.** The rhythmic pattern of a stanza, determined by the kind and number of lines. **2.** *Music.* **a.** Division into measures or bars. **b.** A specific rhythm determined by the number of beats and the time value assigned to each note in a measure. See Synonyms at **rhythm.** [Middle English, from Old English *meter* and from Old French *metre,* both from Latin *metrum,* from Greek *metron,* measure, poetic meter. See **mē-**[2] in Appendix.]

me·ter[2] (mē′tər) *n. Abbr.* **m** The international standard unit of length, approximately equivalent to 39.37 inches. It was redefined in 1983 as the distance traveled by light in a vacuum in 1/299,792,458 of a second. See table at **measurement.** [French *mètre,* from Greek *metron,* measure. See **mē-**[2] in Appendix.]

me·ter[3] (mē′tər) *n.* **1.** Any of various devices designed to measure time, distance, speed, or intensity or indicate and record or regulate the amount or volume, as of the flow of a gas or an electric current. **2.** A postage meter. **3.** A parking meter. **—meter** *tr.v.* **-tered, -ter·ing, -ters. 1.** To measure with a meter: *meter a flow of water.* **2.** To supply in a measured or regulated amount: *metered the allotted gasoline to each vehicle.* **3.** To imprint with postage or other revenue stamps by means of a postage meter or similar device: *metering bulk mail.* **4.** To provide with a parking meter or parking meters: *meter parking spaces.* [From –METER.]

–meter *suff.* Measuring device: *anemometer.* [French *-mètre,* from Greek *metron,* measure. See **mē-**[2] in Appendix.]

me·ter-kil·o·gram-sec·ond (mē′tər-kĭl′ə-grăm-sĕk′ənd) *adj. Abbr.* **mks, MKS** Of, relating to, or being a system of units for mechanics, using the meter, the kilogram, and the second as basic units of length, mass, and time.

me·ter-kil·o·gram-sec·ond-am·pere (mē′tər-kĭl′ə-grăm-sĕk′ənd-ăm′pîr) *adj. Abbr.* **mksA** Of, relating to, or being a system of units using the meter, kilogram, second, and ampere as basic units of length, mass, time, and electric current.

meter maid *n.* A woman member of a police traffic control department who issues tickets for parking violations.

me·tes·trus (mĕ-tĕs′trəs) *n.* The period of sexual inactivity that follows estrus. **—me·tes′trous** (-trəs) *adj.*

meth (mĕth) *n. Slang.* Methamphetamine.

meth– *pref.* Methyl: *methane.* [From METHYL.]

meth·ac·ry·late (mĕth-ăk′rə-lāt′) *n.* **1.** An ester of methacrylic acid, CH_2:C(CH_3)COOR, R being an organic radical. It is used in the manufacture of plastics. **2.** A resin derived from methacrylic acid. [METH– + ACRYL(IC) + –ATE[2].]

meth·a·cryl·ic acid (mĕth′ə-krĭl′ĭk) *n.* A colorless liquid, CH_2:C(CH_3)COOH, used in the manufacture of resins and plastics.

meth·a·done (mĕth′ə-dōn′) *n.* A potent synthetic narcotic drug, $C_{21}H_{27}NO$, that is less addictive than morphine or heroin and is used as a substitute for these drugs in addiction treatment programs. [Short for *methadone hydrochloride* : (DI)METH(YL) + A(MINO) + D(IPHENYL) + *(heptan)one,* a ketone.]

meth·am·phet·a·mine (mĕth′ăm-fĕt′ə-mēn′, -mĭn) *n.* An amine derivative of amphetamine, $C_{10}H_{15}N$, used in the form of its crystalline hydrochloride as a stimulant.

meth·ane (mĕth′ān′) *n.* An odorless, colorless, flammable gas, CH_4, the major constituent of natural gas, that is used as a fuel and is an important source of hydrogen and a wide variety of organic compounds.

methane series *n. Chemistry.* See **alkane series.**

meth·a·nol (mĕth′ə-nôl′, -nōl′, -nŏl′) *n.* A colorless, toxic, flammable liquid, CH_3OH, used as an antifreeze, a general solvent, a fuel, and a denaturant for ethyl alcohol. Also called *carbinol, methyl alcohol, wood alcohol, wood spirits.* [METHAN(E) + –OL[1].]

meth·a·qua·lone (mĕth′ə-kwā′lōn′) *n.* A potentially habit-forming drug, $C_{16}H_{14}N_2O$, used as a sedative and hypnotic. [Blend of METH– and *quinazolinon,* a derivative of quinoline.]

Meth·e·drine (mĕth′ĭ-drēn′, -drĭn). A trademark used for methamphetamine.

me·theg·lin (mə-thĕg′lĭn) *n.* A beverage typically made of fermented honey and water; mead. [Welsh *meddyglyn* : *meddyg,* medicinal (from Latin *medicus,* from *medērī,* to heal; see **med-** in Appendix) + *llyn,* liquor.]

met·he·mo·glo·bin (mĕt-hē′mə-glō′bĭn) *n.* A brownish-red crystalline organic compound formed in the blood when hemoglobin is oxidated either by decomposition of the blood or by the action of various oxidizing drugs or toxic agents. It contains iron in the ferric state and cannot function as an oxygen carrier. [MET(A)– + HEMOGLOBIN.]

me·the·na·mine (mə-thē′nə-mēn′, -mĭn) *n.* An organic compound, $(CH_2)_6N_4$, used as a urinary tract antiseptic and in rubber vulcanizing. Also called *hexamethylenetetramine.* [METH– + –EN(E) + AMINE.]

meth·i·cil·lin (mĕth′ĭ-sĭl′ĭn) *n.* A synthetic antibiotic, $C_{17}H_{19}N_2O_6NaS$, related to penicillin and most commonly used in treatment of infections caused by penicillinase-producing staphylococci. [METH– + (PEN)ICILLIN.]

me·thinks (mĭ-thĭngks′) *intr.v.* Past tense **me·thought** (-thôt′). *Archaic.* It seems to me. [Middle English *me thinkes,* from Old English *mē thyncth* : *mē,* to me; see ME + *thyncth,* it seems; see **tong-** in Appendix.]

me·thi·o·nine (mə-thī′ə-nēn′) *n.* A sulfur-containing essential amino acid, $C_5H_{11}NO_2S$, obtained from various proteins or prepared synthetically and used as a dietary supplement and in pharmaceuticals. [ME(TH)– + THION– + –INE[2].]

meth·od (mĕth′əd) *n.* **1.** A means or manner of procedure, especially a regular and systematic way of accomplishing something: *a simple method for making a pie crust; mediation as a method of solving disputes.* See Usage Note at **methodology. 2.** Orderly arrangement of parts or steps to accomplish an end: *random efforts that lack method.* **3.** The procedures and techniques characteristic of a particular discipline or field of knowledge: *This field course gives an overview of archaeological method.* **4. Method.** A technique of acting in which the actor recalls emotions and reactions from past experience and uses them in identifying with and individualizing the character being portrayed. [Middle English, medical procedure, from Latin *methodus,* method, from Greek *methodos,* pursuit, method : *meta-,* beyond, after; see META– + *hodos,* way, journey.]

SYNONYMS: *method, system, routine, manner, mode, fashion, way.* These nouns refer to the plans or procedures followed to accomplish a task or attain a goal. *Method* implies a detailed, logically ordered plan: *"The convention system has its faults, of course, but I do not know of a better method for choosing a presidential nominee"* (Harry S. Truman). *System* suggests order, regularity, and coordination of methods, often affecting all parts of a whole: *"Of generalship, of strategic system . . . there was little or none"* (John Morley). A *routine* is a habitual, often tiresome meth-

metate
Grinding meal

meter[3]

ă pat   oi boy
ā pay   ou out
âr care   ŏŏ took
ä father   ōō boot
ĕ pet   ŭ cut
ē be   ûr urge
ĭ pit   th thin
ī pie   *th* this
îr pier   hw which
ŏ pot   zh vision
ō toe   ə about, item
ô paw   ♦ regionalism

Stress marks: ′ (primary); ′ (secondary), as in **dictionary** (dĭk′shə-nĕr′ē)

od: *"The common business of the nation . . . is carried on in a constant routine by the clerks of the different offices"* (Tobias Smollett). *Manner* emphasizes a personal or distinctive method of action or procedure: *She has a precise, clearly articulated manner of speaking. The basset, in the manner of hunting dogs, dashed across the field, nose to the ground. Mode* often denotes a manner influenced by or arising from tradition or custom: *A nomadic mode of life was typical of many peoples of the Great Plains. Fashion* is often synonymous with *manner* and *mode;* it sometimes suggests highly personal, even idiosyncratic behavior: *The chief of staff issued a series of orders in an arbitrary and abrasive fashion. She sang, in her own inimitable fashion. Way* is the least specific of these terms: *"It is absurd to think that the only way to tell if a poem is lasting is to wait and see if it lasts"* (Robert Frost). *"For she and I were long acquainted/And I knew all her ways"* (A.E. Housman).

me·thod·i·cal (mə-thŏd′ĭ-kəl) also **me·thod·ic** (-ĭk) *adj.* **1.** Arranged or proceeding in regular, systematic order. **2.** Characterized by ordered and systematic habits or behavior. See Synonyms at **orderly.** —**me·thod′i·cal·ly** *adv.* —**me·thod′i·cal·ness** *n.*

Meth·od·ism (mĕth′ə-dĭz′əm) *n.* **1.** The beliefs, worship, and system of organization of the Methodists. **2. methodism.** Emphasis on systematic procedure.

Meth·od·ist (mĕth′ə-dĭst) *n.* **1.** A member of an evangelical Protestant church founded on the principles of John and Charles Wesley in England in the early 18th century and characterized by active concern with social welfare and public morals. **2. methodist.** One who emphasizes or insists on systematic procedure. —**Meth′od·is′tic** *adj.*

Me·tho·di·us (mĭ-thō′dē-əs), Saint. See Saint **Cyril.**

meth·od·ize (mĕth′ə-dīz′) *tr.v.* **-ized, -iz·ing, -iz·es.** To reduce to or organize according to a method; systematize. —**meth′od·i·za′tion** (-ə-dĭ-zā′shən) *n.* —**meth′od·iz′er** *n.*

meth·od·ol·o·gist (mĕth′ə-dŏl′ə-jĭst) *n.* One who studies methodology.

meth·od·ol·o·gy (mĕth′ə-dŏl′ə-jē) *n., pl.* **-gies. 1.a.** A body of practices, procedures, and rules used by those who work in a discipline or engage in an inquiry; a set of working methods: *the methodology of genetic studies; an opinion poll marred by faulty methodology.* **b.** The study or theoretical analysis of such working methods. **2.** The branch of logic that deals with the general principles of the formation of knowledge. **3.** *Usage Problem.* Means, technique, or procedure; method. —**meth′od·o·log′i·cal** (mĕth′ə-də-lŏj′ĭ-kəl) *adj.* —**meth′od·o·log′i·cal·ly** *adv.*

USAGE NOTE: *Methodology* can properly refer to the theoretical analysis of the methods appropriate to a field of study or to the body of methods and principles particular to a branch of knowledge. In this sense, one may speak of *objections to the methodology of a geographic survey* (i.e., objections dealing with the appropriateness of the methods used) or of the *methodology of modern cognitive psychology* (i.e., the principles and practices that underlie research in the field). In recent years, however, *methodology* has been increasingly used as a pretentious substitute for *method* in scientific and technical contexts, as in *The oil company has not yet decided on a methodology for restoring the beaches.* This usage may have been fostered in part by the tendency to use the adjective *methodological* to mean "pertaining to methods," inasmuch as the regularly formed adjective *methodical* has been preempted to mean "orderly, systematic." But the misuse of *methodology* obscures an important conceptual distinction between the tools of scientific investigation (properly *methods*) and the principles that determine how such tools are deployed and interpreted—a distinction that the scientific and scholarly communities, if not the wider public, should be expected to maintain.

meth·o·trex·ate (mĕth′ə-trĕk′sāt) *n.* A toxic antimetabolite, $C_{20}H_{22}N_8O_5$, that acts as a folic acid antagonist to interfere with cellular reproduction and is used in the treatment of psoriasis and certain cancers. [METH– + *trex-* (of unknown origin) + –ATE[2].]

me·thought (mĭ-thôt′) *v. Archaic.* Past tense of **methinks.**

me·thox·y·chlor (mə-thŏk′sĭ-klôr′, -klōr′) *n.* A white crystalline compound, $Cl_3CCH(C_6H_4OCH_3)_2$, used as an insecticide. [METH– + OXY– + *(tri)chlor(oethane),* a chemical compound used in pesticides.]

Me·thu·en (mə-thōō′ən, -thyōō′-). A town of northeast Massachusetts on the New Hampshire border northeast of Lowell. It was settled c. 1642. Population, 36,701.

Me·thu·se·lah[1] (mə-thōō′zə-lə). A biblical patriarch said to have lived 969 years.

Me·thu·se·lah[2] (mə-thōō′zə-lə) *n.* An extremely old man.

meth·yl (mĕth′əl) *n.* The univalent hydrocarbon radical, CH_3^-, derived from methane and occurring in many important organic compounds. [French *méthyle,* back-formation from *méthylène,* methylene. See METHYLENE.] —**me·thyl′ic** (mə-thĭl′ĭk) *adj.*

methyl acetate *n.* An organic compound, $CH_3CO_2CH_3I$, used as a paint remover and general solvent and in the manufacture of perfumes.

meth·yl·al (mĕth′ə-lăl′) *n.* A colorless flammable liquid, $CH_3OCH_2OCH_3$, used as a solvent and in the manufacture of perfumes, adhesives, and protective coatings. [METHYL + –AL[3].]

methyl alcohol *n.* See **methanol.**

meth·yl·a·mine (mĕth′ə-lə-mēn′, -lăm′ēn, mə-thĭl′ə-mēn′) *n.* A toxic flammable gas, CH_3NH_2, produced by the decomposition of organic matter and synthesized for use as a solvent and in the manufacture of many products, such as dyes.

meth·yl·ate (mĕth′ə-lāt′) *n.* An organic compound in which the hydrogen of the hydroxyl group of methyl alcohol is replaced by a metal. —**methylate** *tr.v.* **-at·ed, -at·ing, -ates. 1.** To mix or combine with methyl alcohol. **2.** To combine with the methyl radical. —**meth′yl·a′tion** *n.* —**meth′yl·a′tor** *n.*

meth·yl·at·ed spirit (mĕth′ə-lā′tĭd) *n.* A denatured alcohol consisting of a mixture of ethyl alcohol and methyl alcohol. Often used in the plural.

meth·yl·ben·zene (mĕth′əl-bĕn′zēn, -bĕn-zēn′) *n.* See **toluene.**

methyl bromide *n.* A toxic gas, CH_3Br, used as a fumigant.

meth·yl·cel·lu·lose (mĕth′əl-sĕl′yə-lōs′, -lōz′) *n.* A powdery substance prepared synthetically by the methylation of natural cellulose and used as a food additive, a bulk-forming laxative, an emulsifier, and a thickener.

methyl chloride *n.* An explosive gas, CH_3Cl, used in organic synthesis and polymerization as a refrigerant and an anesthetic.

meth·yl·do·pa (mĕth′əl-dō′pə) *n.* A drug, $C_{10}H_{13}NO_4$, used in the treatment of high blood pressure.

meth·yl·ene (mĕth′ə-lēn′) *n.* A bivalent hydrocarbon radical, CH_2^-, a component of unsaturated hydrocarbons. [French *méthylène* : Greek *methu,* wine; see **medhu-** in Appendix + Greek *hulē,* wood, substance.]

methylene blue *n.* A basic aniline dye, $C_{16}H_{18}N_3SCl{\cdot}3H_2O$, that forms a deep blue solution when dissolved in water. It is used as an antidote for cyanide poisoning and a bacteriological stain.

methyl ethyl ketone *n.* See **butanone.**

methyl isocyanate *n.* A crystalline compound, C_2H_3NS, used as a pesticide.

methyl methacrylate *n.* A colorless liquid, $CH_2C(CH_3)COOCH_3$, used as a monomer in plastics.

meth·yl·naph·tha·lene (mĕth′əl-năf′thə-lēn′, -năp′thə-) *n.* An organic compound, $C_{10}H_7CH_3$, obtained from coal tar in two isomeric forms, one a liquid, the other a solid.

meth·yl·phen·i·date (mĕth′əl-fĕn′ĭ-dāt′, -fē′nĭ-) *n.* A drug, $C_{14}H_{19}NO_2$, chemically related to amphetamine, that acts as a mild stimulant of the central nervous system and is used especially in the form of its hydrochloride for the treatment of narcolepsy in adults and hyperkinetic disorders in children. [METHYL + PHEN(YL) + (PIPER)ID(INE) + (ACET)ATE.]

met·i·cal (mĕt′ĭ-kăl′, mĕt′ĭ-kăl′) *n.* See table at **currency.** [Portuguese, from Arabic *miṯqāl, mitqāl,* a unit of weight, from *ṯaqula,* to be heavy.]

me·tic·u·lous (mĭ-tĭk′yə-ləs) *adj.* **1.** Extremely careful and precise. **2.** Extremely or excessively concerned with details. [From Latin *metīculōsus,* timid, from *metus,* fear.] —**me·tic′u·los′i·ty** (-lŏs′ĭ-tē), **me·tic′u·lous·ness** *n.* —**me·tic′u·lous·ly** *adv.*

SYNONYMS: *meticulous, careful, painstaking, scrupulous, fastidious, punctilious.* These adjectives mean showing or marked by attentiveness to all aspects or details. *Meticulous* stresses extreme, sometimes exaggerated care for small details: *"He had throughout been almost worryingly meticulous in his business formalities"* (Arnold Bennett). *Careful* suggests the exercise of attention, circumspection, and solicitude: *A careful examination of the antique bronze showed it to be a forgery. Painstaking* means extremely careful: *The skillful repair of fine lace entails slow and painstaking work. Scrupulous* suggests care prompted by conscience: *"Cynthia was scrupulous in her efforts to give no trouble"* (Winston Churchill). *Fastidious* implies concern, often excessive, for the requirements of taste: *"Your true lover of literature is never fastidious"* (Robert Southey). *Punctilious* specifically applies to strict, exact attention to minute details of conduct: *"The more unpopular an opinion is, the more necessary is it that the holder should be somewhat punctilious in his observance of conventionalities generally"* (Samuel Butler).

mé·tier (mĕ-tyā′, mā-) *n.* **1.** An occupation, a trade, or a profession. **2.** Work or activity for which a person is particularly suited; one's specialty. See Synonyms at **forte[1].** [French, from Old French *mestier,* from Vulgar Latin **misterium,* from Latin *ministerium.* See MINISTRY.]

mé·tis (mā-tēs′) *n., pl.* **métis. 1.** A mestizo. **2.** Often **Métis.** A person of Native American and French-Canadian ancestry. **3.** A crossbred animal. [Canadian French, from Old French *metis,* of mixed race, from Late Latin *mixtīcius,* mixed. See MESTIZO.]

Me·tis (mē′tĭs) *n.* The satellite of Jupiter that is second in distance from the planet. [After *Mētis,* consort of Zeus (Jupiter), from Greek *mētis,* wisdom. See **mē-[2]** in Appendix.]

Me·ton·ic cycle (mĭ-tŏn′ĭk) *n.* A period of 235 lunar months, or about 19 years in the Julian calendar, at the end of which the phases of the moon recur in the same order and on the same days as in the preceding cycle. [After *Meton* (fl. fifth century B.C.), Athenian astronomer.]

met·o·nym (mĕt′ə-nĭm′) *n.* A word used in metonymy. [Back-formation from METONYMY.]

me·ton·y·my (mə-tŏn′ə-mē) *n., pl.* **-mies.** A figure of speech in which one word or phrase is substituted for another with which it is closely associated, as in the use of *Washington* for *the United States government.* [Late Latin *metōnymia,* from Greek *metōnumia* : *meta-,* meta- + *onuma,* name; see **nō-men-** in Appendix.] **—met′o·nym′ic** (mĕt′ə-nĭm′ĭk), **met′o·nym′i·cal** *adj.* **—met′o·nym′i·cal·ly** *adv.*

me·too or **me-too** (mē′to͞o′) *adj. Informal.* Using principles, practices, or designs copied from and closely similar to those of a rival: *"Ready availability of inexpensive components has created an age of metoo hardware in everything from mainframes to personal computers"* (Business Week). **—me′too′** *n.* **—me′-too′er** *n.* **—me′-too′ism** *n.*

met·o·pe (mĕt′ə-pē) *n. Architecture.* Any of the spaces between two triglyphs on a Doric frieze. [Greek *metopē* : *meta,* between; see META– + *opē,* opening; see **okʷ-** in Appendix.]

me·top·ic (mə-tŏp′ĭk) *adj.* Of or relating to the forehead. [Greek *metōpikos,* from *metōpon,* forehead : *meta,* between; see META– + *ōps,* eye; see **okʷ-** in Appendix.]

met·o·pon (mĕt′ə-pŏn′) *n.* A narcotic drug, $C_{18}H_{21}NO_3$, derived from morphine and used in the form of its hydrochloride as an analgesic. [*met(hyldihydr)o(mor)p(hin)on(e).*]

metr– *pref.* Variant of **metro–.**

me·tral·gi·a (mĭ-trăl′jē-ə) *n.* Pain in the uterus.

me·tre¹ (mē′tər) *n. Chiefly British.* Variant of **meter¹.**

me·tre² (mē′tər) *n. Chiefly British.* Variant of **meter².**

met·ric¹ (mĕt′rĭk) *adj.* Of or relating to the meter or the metric system: *U.S. Customary units and their metric equivalents.* [French *métrique,* from *mètre,* meter. See METER².]

met·ric² (mĕt′rĭk) *n.* **1.** A standard of measurement. **2.** *Mathematics.* A geometric function defined for a coordinate system such that the distance between any two points in that system may be determined from their coordinates. **—metric** *adj.* Of or relating to distance. [From Latin *metricus,* relating to measurement. See METRICAL.]

met·ric³ (mĕt′rĭk) *n.* Poetic meter. [Greek *(hē) metrikē (tekhnē),* (the art) of meter, feminine of *metrikos,* relating to measurement. See METRICAL.]

–metric *suff.* Of or relating to measurement: *volumetric.* [Latin *metricus.* See METRICAL.]

met·ri·cal (mĕt′rĭ-kəl) *adj.* **1.** Of, relating to, or composed in poetic meter: *metrical verse; five metrical units in a line.* **2.** Of or relating to measurement. [Middle English, from Latin *metricus,* from Greek *metrikos,* from *metron,* measure, poetic meter. See **mē-²** in Appendix.] **—met′ri·cal·ly** *adv.*

met·ri·ca·tion (mĕt′rĭ-kā′shən) *n.* Conversion to the metric system of weights and measures; metrification.

met·rics (mĕt′rĭks) *n. (used with a sing. verb).* The use or study of metrical structures in verse; prosody.

–metrics *suff.* The application of statistics and mathematical analysis to a specified field of study: *econometrics.* [From METRIC².]

metric system *n.* A decimal system of units based on the meter as a unit length, the kilogram as a unit mass, and the second as a unit time. See table at **measurement.**

metric ton *n. Abbr.* **m.t., M.T.** A unit of mass equal to 1,000 kilograms (2,205 pounds).

met·ri·fy¹ (mĕt′rə-fī′) *tr.v.* **-fied, -fy·ing, -fies.** To put into or compose in poetic meter; versify. [French *métrifier,* from Old French, from Medieval Latin *metrificāre* : Latin *metrum,* measure; see METER¹ + Latin *-ficāre,* -fy.] **—met′ri·fi·ca′tion** (-fĭ-kā′shən) *n.*

met·ri·fy² (mĕt′rə-fī′) *tr. & intr.v.* **-fied, -fy·ing, -fies.** To convert into or adopt the metric system.

me·tri·tis (mĭ-trī′tĭs) *n.* Inflammation of the uterus.

met·ro¹ (mĕt′rō) *n., pl.* **met·ros.** A subway system. [French *métro,* short for *(chemin de fer) métropolitain,* metropolitan (railway), from Late Latin *mētropolītānus.* See METROPOLITAN.]

met·ro² (mĕt′rō) *Informal. adj.* Metropolitan. **—metro** *n., pl.* **met·ros.** A metropolitan area: *"This metro ranks number one in unemployment"* (American Demographics).

metro– or **metr–** *pref.* Uterus: *metritis.* [From Greek *mētra,* uterus, from *mētēr, mētr-,* mother. See **māter-** in Appendix.]

me·trol·o·gy (mĕ-trŏl′ə-jē) *n., pl.* **-gies. 1.** The science that deals with measurement. **2.** A system of measurement. [French *métrologie,* from Greek *metrologia,* theory of ratios : *metron,* measure; see **mē-²** in Appendix + *-logia,* -logy.] **—met′ro·log′i·cal** (mĕt′rə-lŏj′ĭ-kəl) *adj.* **—met′ro·log′i·cal·ly** *adv.* **—me·trol′o·gist** *n.*

me·tro·ni·da·zole (mĕt′rə-nī′də-zōl′) *n.* A synthetic antimicrobial drug, $C_6H_9N_3O_3$, used in the treatment of vaginal trichomoniasis and intestinal amebiasis. [ME(THYL) + *-tron-* (alteration of NITRO–) + (IM)ID(E) + AZOLE.]

met·ro·nome (mĕt′rə-nōm′) *n. Music.* A device used to mark time by means of regularly recurring ticks or flashes at adjustable intervals. [Greek *metron,* measure; see **mē-²** in Appendix + Greek *nomos,* rule, division; see **nem-** in Appendix.]

met·ro·nom·ic (mĕt′rə-nŏm′ĭk) also **met·ro·nom·i·cal** (-ĭ-kəl) *adj.* **1.** *Music.* Of or relating to a metronome. **2.** Mechanically or unvaryingly regular in rhythm: *a strict metronomic tempo.* **—met′ro·nom′i·cal·ly** *adv.*

me·tro·nym·ic (mē′trə-nĭm′ĭk, mĕt′rə-) also **mat·ro·nym·ic** (măt′-) *—adj.* Of, relating to, or derived from the name of one's mother or maternal ancestor. *—n.* A name so derived. [Greek *mētrōnumikos* : from *mētēr, mētr-,* mother; see METRO– + *onuma,* name; see **nō-men-** in Appendix.]

met·ro·plex also **Metroplex** (mĕt′rə-plĕks′) *n.* A large metropolitan region, especially one encompassing two or more cities and their surrounding suburbs. [Probably METRO(POLITAN) + (COM)PLEX.]

me·trop·o·lis (mĭ-trŏp′ə-lĭs) *n.* **1.** A major city, especially the chief city of a country or region: *Chicago, the metropolis of the Midwest.* **2.** A city or an urban area regarded as the center of a specific activity: *a great cultural metropolis.* **3.** *Ecclesiastical.* The chief see of a metropolitan bishop. **4.** The mother city or country of an overseas colony, especially in ancient Greece. [Middle English *metropol,* from Late Latin *mētropolis,* mother-city, from Greek : *mētēr, mētr-,* mother; see **māter-** in Appendix + *polis,* city; see **pelə-³** in Appendix.]

met·ro·pol·i·tan (mĕt′rə-pŏl′ĭ-tən) *adj. Abbr.* **met. 1.a.** Of, relating to, or characteristic of a major city: *crowded metropolitan streets; a metropolitan newspaper.* **b.** Of or constituting a large city or urbanized area, including adjacent suburbs and towns: *the Dallas–Fort Worth metropolitan area; a metropolitan county.* **2.** Of, relating to, or constituting the home territory of an imperial or colonial state. **3.** Of or relating to an ecclesiastical metropolitan. **—metropolitan** *n.* **1.** A citizen of a metropolis, especially one who displays urbane characteristics, attitudes, and values. **2.a.** In the Western Christian churches, a bishop with provincial powers, with some authority over suffragan bishops. **b.** *Eastern Orthodox Church.* A bishop who is head of an ecclesiastical province and ranks next below the patriarch. [Middle English, of a metropolitan bishop, from Late Latin *mētropolītānus,* metropolitan, from Greek *mētropolītēs,* citizen of a metropolis, from *mētropolis,* mother city. See METROPOLIS.]

me·tror·rha·gi·a (mē′trə-rā′jē-ə, -jə) *n.* Bleeding from the uterus that is not associated with menstruation. **—me′tror·rha′gic** (-rā′jĭk) *adj.*

–metry *suff.* Process or science of measuring: *isometry.* [Greek *-metria,* from *metron,* measure. See **mē-²** in Appendix.]

Met·ter·nich (mĕt′ər-nĭk, -nĭKH), Prince **Klemens Wenzel Nepomuk Lothar von.** 1773–1859. Austrian politician who helped form the Quadruple Alliance that defeated Napoleon I.

met·tle (mĕt′l) *n.* **1.** Courage and fortitude; spirit: *troops who showed their mettle in combat.* **2.** Inherent quality of character and temperament. **—*idiom.* on (one's) mettle.** Prepared to accept a challenge and do one's best. [Variant of METAL.]

met·tle·some (mĕt′l-səm) *adj.* Full of mettle; spirited and plucky. See Synonyms at **brave.**

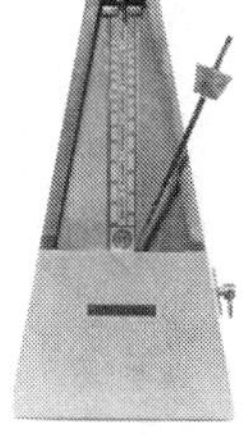

metronome

Metz (mĕts, mĕs). A city of northeast France on the Moselle River north of Nancy. Settled before Roman times, it was annexed by France in 1552 and ruled by Germany from 1871 to 1918. Population, 114,232.

meu·nière (mən-yâr′) *adj.* Rolled in flour and fried in butter, usually with lemon juice and chopped parsley sprinkled on top. Used of fish. [French, from *(à la) meunière,* (in the style of) a miller's wife, from Old French *munoiere,* feminine of *mounier,* miller, from Late Latin *molīnārius,* from *molīna,* mill. See MILL¹.]

Meuse (myo͞oz, mœz). A river of western Europe flowing about 901 km (560 mi) from northeast France through southern Belgium and the southeast Netherlands to the North Sea.

mev or **Mev** or **MeV** *abbr.* Million electron volts.

mew¹ (myo͞o) *n.* **1.** A cage for hawks, especially when molting. **2.** A secret place; a hideaway. **3. mews** *(used with a sing. or pl. verb).* **a.** A group of buildings originally containing private stables, often converted into residential apartments. **b.** A small street, alley, or courtyard on which such buildings stand. **—mew** *v.* **mewed, mew·ing, mews.** *—tr.* To confine in or as if in a cage. *—intr.* To molt. Used of a hawk. [Middle English *meue,* from Old French *mue,* from *muer,* to molt, from Latin *mūtāre,* to change. See **mei-¹** in Appendix.]

mew² (myo͞o) *intr.v.* **mewed, mew·ing, mews.** To make the high-pitched, crying sound of a cat; meow. **—mew** *n.* The crying sound of a cat. [Middle English *meuen,* of imitative origin.]

mew³ (myo͞o) *n.* A seagull *(Larus canus)* of northern Eurasia and northwest North America. [Middle English *meue,* from Old English *mǣw, mēu.*]

mews

mewl (myo͞ol) *intr.v.* **mewled, mewl·ing, mewls.** To cry weakly; whimper. [Perhaps imitative or perhaps French *mouiller (les yeux),* to wet (the eyes), cry, from Old French *moillier,* from Vulgar Latin **molliāre,* to make soggy, from Latin *mollis,* soft, mild. See MOIL.]

Mex. *abbr.* **1.** Mexican. **2.** Mexico.

Mex·i·cal·i (mĕk′sĭ-kăl′ē, mĕ′hē-kä′lē). A city of northwest Mexico near the California border east of Tijuana. It is a distribution and processing center. Population, 341,559.

Mex·i·can (mĕk′sĭ-kən) *n.* A native or inhabitant of Mexico. **—Mexican** *adj. Abbr.* **Mex.** Of or relating to Mexico or its people, language, or culture.

Mexican bean beetle *n.* A spotted ladybug *(Epilachna varivestis)* of the southern United States and Mexico that feeds on the leaves of the bean plant.

Mexican hairless *n.* Any of a breed of small dog of unknown origin, found in Mexico and having a smooth hairless body except for tufts on the head and tail.

Mexican ivy vine *n.* See **cup-and-saucer plant.**

ă pat	oi boy
ā pay	ou out
âr care	o͝o took
ä father	o͞o boot
ĕ pet	ŭ cut
ē be	ûr urge
ĭ pit	th thin
ī pie	*th* this
îr pier	hw which
ŏ pot	zh vision
ō toe	ə about, item
ô paw	♦ regionalism

Stress marks: **′** (primary); ′ (secondary), as in **dictionary** (dĭk′shə-nĕr′ē)

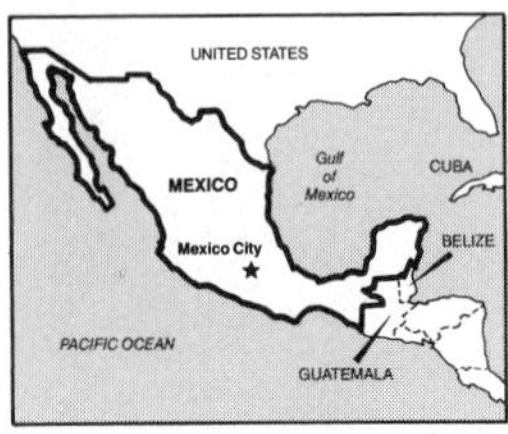

Mexico

Mexican Spanish *n.* Spanish as used in Mexico.

Mex·i·co (mĕk′sĭ-kō′). *Abbr.* **Mex.** A country of south-central North America. Inhabited in pre-Columbian times by the Aztecs and Maya among others, Mexico was conquered by Cortés in 1521 and held by the Spanish until 1821. The Treaty of Guadelupe Hidalgo that ended the Mexican War (1846–1848) awarded all lands north of the Rio Grande to the United States. Mexico City is the capital and the largest city. Population, 67,395,826.

Mexico, Gulf of. An arm of the Atlantic Ocean in southeast North America bordering on eastern Mexico, the southeast United States, and Cuba.

Mexico City. The capital and largest city of Mexico, at the southern end of the central plateau. Situated at an altitude of 2,379 m (7,800 ft), it was founded on the site of an ancient Aztec capital destroyed by Cortés in 1521. Population, 8,831,079.

Mey·er (mī′ər), **Annie Florance Nathan.** 1867–1951. American writer and a founder of Barnard College at Columbia University (1889).

Mey·er·beer (mī′ər-bîr′), **Giacomo.** 1791–1864. German composer of French operas, notably *Les Huguenots* (1836).

me·ze·re·on (mə-zîr′ē-ən) or **me·ze·re·um** (-əm) *n.* **1.** A poisonous Eurasian ornamental shrub *(Daphne mezereum)* having fragrant lilac-purple flowers and small scarlet fruit. **2.** The dried bark of this plant, formerly used externally as a vesicant and internally for arthritis. [Middle English *mizerion,* from Medieval Latin *mezereon,* from Arabic *māzaryūn,* of Persian origin.]

me·zu·zah also **me·zu·za** (mə-zo͝oz′ə, -zo͞o-zä′) *n., pl.* **-zu·zahs** also **-zu·zas** (-zo͝oz′əz) or **-zu·zot** (-zo͞o-zôt′). A small piece of parchment inscribed with the biblical passages Deuteronomy 6:4–9 and 11:13–21 and marked with the word *Shaddai,* a name of the Almighty, that is rolled up in a container and affixed by many Jewish households to their door frames in conformity with Jewish law and as a sign of their faith. [Hebrew *mĕzûzâ,* doorpost, mezuzah.]

mez·za·nine (mĕz′ə-nēn′, mĕz′ə-nēn′) *n.* **1.** A partial story between two main stories of a building. **2.** The lowest balcony in a theater or the first few rows of that balcony. [French, from Italian *mezzanino,* diminutive of *mezzano,* middle, from Latin *mediānus,* in the middle. See MEDIAN.]

mez·za vo·ce (mĕt′sə vō′chā, mĕd′zə, mĕz′ə) *adv. & adj. Music.* With moderate volume or in a subdued tone. Used chiefly as a direction. [Italian : *mezza,* half + *voce,* voice.]

mez·zo (mĕt′sō, mĕd′zō, mĕz′ō) *n., pl.* **-zos.** *Music.* A mezzo-soprano.

mezzo for·te (fôr′tā) *adv. & adj. Abbr.* **mf, m.f.** *Music.* Moderately loud. Used chiefly as a direction. [Italian : *mezzo,* half + *forte,* loud.]

mezzo pi·a·no (pē-ä′nō) *adv. & adj. Abbr.* **mp, m.p.** *Music.* Moderately soft. Used chiefly as a direction. [Italian : *mezzo,* half + *piano,* soft.]

mez·zo-re·lie·vo (mĕt′sō-rĭ-lē′vō, -rĕl-yä′vō, mĕd′zō-, mĕz′ō-) *n., pl.* **-vos.** See **half relief.** [Italian *mezzorilievo* : *mezzo,* half (from Latin *medius;* see MEDIUM) + *rilievo,* relief; see RELIEVO.]

mez·zo-so·pran·o (mĕt′sō-sə-prăn′ō, -prä′nō, mĕd′zō-, mĕz′ō-) *n., pl.* **-nos.** *Music.* **1.a.** A voice having a range between soprano and contralto. **b.** A vocal part calling for a voice having such a range. **2.** A woman having a mezzo-soprano voice. [Italian : *mezzo,* half (from Latin *medius;* see MEDIUM) + *soprano,* soprano; see SOPRANO.]

mez·zo·tint (mĕt′sō-tĭnt′, mĕd′zō-, mĕz′ō-) *n.* **1.** A method of engraving a copper or steel plate by scraping and burnishing areas to produce effects of light and shadow. **2.** A print made from a plate engraved by mezzotint. [Alteration of Italian *mezzotinta,* halftone : *mezza,* feminine of *mezzo,* half (from Latin *medius;* see MEDIUM) + *tinta,* tint, from feminine past participle of *tingere* (from Latin, to dye).]

mf *abbr.* **1.** Medium frequency. **2.** Also **m.f.** *Music.* Mezzo forte. **3.** Also **mF.** Millifarad.

M.F.A. *abbr.* Master of Fine Arts.

mfd. *abbr.* Manufactured.

mfg. *abbr.* **1.a.** Manufacture. **b.** Manufacturing. **2.** Manufactured.

MFN *abbr.* Most-favored nation.

MFP *abbr.* Mean free path.

mfr. *abbr.* Manufacture; manufacturer.

mg *abbr.* Milligram.

Mg The symbol for the element **magnesium.**

MG *abbr.* **1.** Machine gun. **2.** Major general. **3.** Military government.

mgd *abbr.* Million gallons per day.

mgmt. *abbr.* Management.

mgr. *abbr.* Manager.

Mgr. *abbr.* Monseigneur; Monsignor.

mgt. *abbr.* Management.

MGySgt *abbr.* Master gunnery sergeant.

mh also **mH** *abbr.* Millihenry.

MH *abbr.* **1.** Medal of Honor. **2.** Mental health.

MHC *abbr.* Major histocompatibility complex.

MHD *abbr.* Magnetohydrodynamic.

M.H.L. *abbr.* Master of Hebrew Literature.

Michelangelo
Portrait by Daniele de Volterra (1509–1566)

mho (mō) *n., pl.* **mhos.** A siemens. [Backward spelling of OHM.]

MHW *abbr.* Mean high water.

MHz *abbr.* Megahertz.

mi (mē) *n. Music.* The third tone of the diatonic scale in solfeggio. [Middle English, from Medieval Latin. See GAMUT.]

Mi *abbr. Bible.* Micah.

MI *abbr.* **1.** Michigan. **2.** Military intelligence. **3.** Myocardial infarction.

mi. *abbr.* **1.** Mile. **2.** Mill.

MIA (ĕm′ī-ā′) *n., pl.* **MIA's** also **MIAs.** A member of the armed services who is reported missing following a combat mission and whose status as to injury, capture, or death is unknown. [*m(issing) i(n) a(ction).*]

Mi·am·i[1] (mī-ăm′ē, -ăm′ə) *n., pl.* **Miami** or **-is. 1.a.** A Native American people originally of the Green Bay area of Wisconsin, with various groups later inhabiting parts of southern Michigan and northern Ohio, Indiana, and Illinois. Present-day populations are in northern Indiana and northeast Oklahoma. **b.** A member of this people. **2.** The variety of Illinois spoken by the Miami.

Mi·am·i[2] (mī-ăm′ē, -ăm′ə). A city of southeast Florida on Biscayne Bay south of Fort Lauderdale. Settled in the 1870's near the site of a fort built in 1836, it expanded greatly during the land boom of the 1920's and again after World War II. Today it is an important resort and cruise center. Population, 346,931.

Miami Beach. A city of southeast Florida across from Miami on an island between Biscayne Bay and the Atlantic Ocean. It was long famous for its gold coast strip of fashionable hotels, palatial estates, and recreational facilities. Population, 96,298.

Miami River or **Great Miami River.** A river rising in western Ohio and flowing about 257 km (160 mi) generally southwest to the Ohio River at the Indiana border.

Miao (myou′) also **Me·o** (mē-ou′) *n., pl.* **Miao** or **Miaos** also **Meo** or **Me·os.** See **Hmong.**

Miao-Yao (myou′ you′) *n.* A small group of languages of uncertain affinity, including Hmong and Yao, spoken in southern China, northern Laos, Thailand, and Vietnam.

mi·as·ma (mī-ăz′mə, mē-) *n., pl.* **-mas** or **-ma·ta** (-mə-tə). **1.** A noxious atmosphere or influence: *"The family affection, the family expectations, seemed to permeate the atmosphere . . . like a coiling miasma"* (Louis Auchincloss). **2.a.** A poisonous atmosphere formerly thought to rise from swamps and putrid matter and cause disease. **b.** A thick, vaporous atmosphere or emanation: *wreathed in a miasma of cigarette smoke.* [Greek, pollution, stain, from *miainein,* to pollute.] **—mi·as′mal, mi′as·mat′ic** (mī′əz-măt′ĭk) , **mi·as′mic** (-mĭk) *adj.*

Mic *abbr. Bible.* Micah.

mi·ca (mī′kə) *n.* Any of a group of chemically and physically related aluminum silicate minerals, common in igneous and metamorphic rocks, characteristically splitting into flexible sheets used in insulation and electrical equipment. [Latin, grain (perhaps influenced by Latin *micāre,* to flash).] **—mi·ca′ceous** (-kā′shəs) *adj.*

Mi·cah (mī′kə) also **Mi·che·as** (mī-kē′əs) *n. Bible.* **1.** A Hebrew prophet of the eighth century B.C. **2.** *Abbr.* **Mi, Mic** See table at **Bible.**

Mic·co·su·kee (mĭk′ə-so͞o′kē) *n.* Variant of **Mikasuki.**

mice (mīs) *n.* Plural of **mouse.**

mi·celle (mī-sĕl′) *n.* **1.** A submicroscopic aggregation of molecules, as a droplet in a colloidal system. **2.** An organic particle of colloidal size found in coal. **3.** A coherent strand or structure in natural or synthetic fibers. **4.** A submicroscopic structural unit of protoplasm, composed of a cluster of molecules. [New Latin *mīcella,* from Latin *mīca,* grain.] **—mi·cel′lar** (-sĕl′ər) *adj.*

Mich. *abbr.* Michigan.

Mi·chael (mī′kəl) *n.* The guardian archangel of the Jews in the Old Testament.

Michael I. Born 1921. King of Romania (1927–1930 and 1940–1947). He was forced to abdicate in 1947 by the newly formed Communist government.

Mich·ael·mas (mĭk′əl-məs) *n.* **1.** A Christian feast observed in honor of the archangel Michael. **2.** September 29, the day on which this feast is observed. [Middle English *mychelmesse,* from Old English *(Sanct) Michaeles mæsse,* (Saint) Michael's mass : *Michaeles,* genitive of *Michael,* the archangel Michael + *mæsse,* Mass; see MASS.]

Michaelmas daisy *n.* Any of several North American species of asters that have leafy stems and flower in the fall.

Mi·che·as (mī-kē′əs) *n. Bible.* Variant of **Micah.**

Mi·chel·an·ge·lo Buo·nar·ro·ti (mī′kəl-ăn′jə-lō′ bwôn′ə-rô′tē, mĭk′əl-, mē′kĕl-än′jĕ-lô). 1475–1564. Italian sculptor, painter, architect, and poet who created some of the greatest works of art of all time, including the marble sculpture *David* (1501), the paintings on the ceiling of the Sistine Chapel (1508–1512), and the plans for Saint Peter's Church in Rome.

Mi·che·let (mēsh-ə-lā′, mēsh-lā′), **Jules.** 1798–1874. French historian noted for his 17-volume *Histoire de France* (1833–1867).

Mi·chel·son (mī′kəl-sən), **Albert Abraham.** 1852–1931. German-born American physicist who with Edward Morley disproved the existence of ether, the hypothetical medium of electromagnetic waves. He won a 1907 Nobel Prize for his spectroscopic and metrological investigations.

Mich·i·gan (mĭsh′ĭ-gən). *Abbr.* **MI, Mich.** A state of the north-central United States. It was admitted as the 26th state in 1837. French explorers first visited the area in 1618, and the French retained nominal control until the end of the French and Indian Wars (1763), when the region passed to Great Britain. It was ceded to the United States in 1783, although the British held some areas until 1796. The Michigan Territory was organized in 1805 with Detroit as its capital. Lansing is the state capital (since 1847) and Detroit the largest city. Population, 9,262,070. **—Mich′i·gan′der** (-găn′dər) *adj. & n.*

Michigan, Lake. The third largest of the Great Lakes, between Wisconsin and Michigan. It is the only one of the lakes entirely within the United States. Lake Michigan is connected with the Mississippi River by the Illinois Waterway and with Lake Huron through the Straits of Mackinac. The St. Lawrence Seaway links it with the Atlantic Ocean.

Michigan City. A city of northwest Indiana on Lake Michigan northeast of Gary. Population, 36,850.

mick (mĭk) *n. Offensive Slang.* Used as a disparaging term for an Irish person. [Probably the name *Mick,* nickname for *Michael.*]

mick·ey (mĭk′ē) *n., pl.* **-eys. 1.** *Informal.* A roasted potato. **2.** *Canadian.* A small bottle of liquor, shaped to fit in a pocket. **3.** *Chiefly British.* Self-assurance. [Perhaps from MICK.]

Mick·ey Finn (mĭk′ē fĭn′) *n. Slang.* An alcoholic beverage that is surreptitiously altered to induce diarrhea or stupefy, render unconscious, or otherwise incapacitate the person who drinks it. [Origin unknown.]

Mickey Mouse *adj.* **1.a.** *Slang.* Unimportant; trivial: *"It's a Mickey Mouse operation compared to what goes on in Lyons or Paris"* (Jack Higgins). **b.** *Slang.* Irritatingly petty: *the school's Mickey Mouse requirements for graduation.* **2.** *Slang.* Intellectually unchallenging; simple: *His Mickey Mouse assignments soon bored the students.* **3.** *Music.* **a.** Blandly sentimental. Used of popular compositions and performers. **b.** Relating to a soundtrack that accompanies the action in an unsubtle, melodramatic way suggestive of music written for animated films. [After the cartoon character *Mickey Mouse,* created by Walt Disney.]

mick·le (mĭk′əl) *Scots. adj.* Great. **—mickle** *adv.* Greatly. [Middle English *mikel,* from Old English *micel* and from Old Norse *mikill;* see **meg-** in Appendix.]

Mic·mac (mĭk′măk′) *n., pl.* **Micmac** or **-macs. 1.a.** A Native American people inhabiting Nova Scotia, New Brunswick, Prince Edward Island, and the Gaspé Peninsula of Quebec. **b.** A member of this people. **2.** The Algonquian language of the Micmac.

MICR *abbr.* Magnetic ink character recognition.

micr– *pref.* Variant of **micro–.**

mi·cra (mī′krə) *n.* A plural of **micron.**

mi·cro (mī′krō) *adj.* Basic or small-scale: *the economy's performance at the micro level.* **—micro** *n., pl.* **-cros. 1.** *Computer Science.* **a.** A microcomputer. **b.** A microprocessor. **2.** A microwave oven. [From MICRO–.]

micro– or **micr–** *pref.* **1.a.** Small: *microcircuit.* **b.** Abnormally small: *microcephaly.* **c.** Requiring or involving microscopy: *microsurgery.* **2.** One-millionth (10^{-6}): *microampere.* [Greek *mikro-,* from *mikros,* small.]

mi·cro·am·pere (mī′krō-ăm′pîr) *n.* A unit of electric current equal to one millionth of an ampere.

mi·cro·a·nal·y·sis (mī′krō-ə-năl′ĭ-sĭs) *n.* The chemical identification and analysis of extremely small quantities of matter. **—mi′cro·an′a·lyst** (-ăn′ə-lĭst) *n.* **—mi′cro·an′a·lyt′ic** (-ăn′ə-lĭt′ĭk), **mi′cro·an′a·lyt′i·cal** *adj.*

mi·cro·a·nat·o·my (mī′krō-ə-năt′ə-mē) *n.* Histology. **—mi′cro·an′a·tom′i·cal** (-ăn′ə-tŏm′ĭ-kəl) *adj.*

mi·cro·bal·ance (mī′krō-băl′əns) *n.* A balance designed to weigh very small loads, up to 0.1 gram.

mi·cro·bar (mī′krō-bär′) *n.* A unit of pressure equal to one millionth of a bar.

mic·ro·bar·o·graph (mī′krō-băr′ə-grăf′) *n.* An instrument used to record very small changes in atmospheric pressure.

mi·crobe (mī′krōb′) *n.* A minute life form; a microorganism, especially a bacterium that causes disease. Not in technical use. [French : Greek *mikro-,* micro- + Greek *bios,* life; see **gʷei-** in Appendix.] **—mi·cro′bi·al** (mī-krō′bē-əl), **mi·cro′bic** (-krō′bĭk) *adj.*

mi·cro·bi·ol·o·gy (mī′krō-bī-ŏl′ə-jē) *n.* The branch of biology that deals with microorganisms and their effects on other living organisms. **—mi′cro·bi′o·log′i·cal** (-bī′ə-lŏj′ĭ-kəl), **mi′cro·bi′o·log′ic** *adj.* **—mi′cro·bi′o·log′i·cal·ly** *adv.* **—mi′cro·bi·ol′o·gist** *n.*

mi·cro·brew·er·y (mī′krō-bro͞o′ə-rē, -bro͝or′ē) *n., pl.* **-ies.** A small brewery, generally producing fewer than 10,000 barrels of beer and ale a year and frequently selling its products on the premises. Also called *boutique brewery, brewpub.* **—mi′cro·brew′er** *n.*

mi·cro·burst (mī′krō-bûrst′) *n.* A sudden, violent downdraft of air over a small area. Microbursts are difficult to detect and predict with standard weather instruments and are especially hazardous to airplanes during landing or taking off.

mi·cro·bus (mī′krō-bŭs′) *n., pl.* **-bus·es** or **-bus·ses.** A station wagon in the shape of a small bus.

mi·cro·cap·sule (mī′krō-kăp′səl, -so͞ol) *n.* A small, sometimes microscopic capsule designed to release its contents when broken by pressure, dissolved, or melted.

mi·cro·ceph·a·ly (mī′krō-sĕf′ə-lē) *n., pl.* **-lies.** Abnormal smallness of the head. **—mi′cro·ce·phal′ic** (-sə-făl′ĭk) *adj. & n.* **—mi′cro·ceph′a·lous** (-sĕf′ə-ləs) *adj.*

mi·cro·chem·is·try (mī′krō-kĕm′ĭ-strē) *n.* Chemistry that deals with minute quantities of materials, frequently less than one milligram in mass or one milliliter in volume. **—mi′cro·chem′i·cal** (-ĭ-kəl) *adj.* **—mi′cro·chem′ist** *n.*

mi·cro·chip (mī′krə-chĭp′) *n. Computer Science.* See **chip**[1] (sense 4a).

mi·cro·cir·cuit (mī′krō-sûr′kĭt) *n.* An electric circuit consisting of miniaturized components. **—mi′cro·cir′cuit·ry** (-kĭ-trē) *n.*

mi·cro·cir·cu·la·tion (mī′krō-sûr-kyə-lā′shən) *n.* The flow of blood or lymph through the smallest vessels of the body, as the venules, capillaries, and arterioles. **—mi′cro·cir′cu·la·to′ry** (-lə-tôr′ē, -tōr′ē) *adj.*

mi·cro·cli·mate (mī′krō-klī′mĭt) *n.* The climate of a small, specific place within an area as contrasted with the climate of the entire area. **—mi′cro·cli·mat′ic** (-măt′ĭk) *adj.* **—mi′cro·cli′ma·to·log′ic** (-mə-tə-lŏj′ĭk), **mi′cro·cli′ma·to·log′i·cal** *adj.* **—mi′cro·cli′ma·tol′o·gy** (-tŏl′ə-jē) *n.*

mi·cro·cline (mī′krō-klīn′) *n.* A mineral of the feldspar group, chiefly $KAlSi_3O_8$, used in making glass, porcelain, and enamel. [Greek *mikro-,* micro- (from the fact that its cleavage angle is not exactly equal to 90°) + Greek *klinein,* to lean; see CLINE.]

mi·cro·coc·cus (mī′krō-kŏk′əs) *n., pl.* **-coc·ci** (-kŏk′sī′, -kŏk′ī′). A spherical, aerobic, gram-positive bacterium of the genus *Micrococcus,* usually occurring in irregular clusters. **—mi′cro·coc′cal** (-kŏk′əl) *adj.*

mi·cro·com·put·er (mī′krō-kəm-pyo͞o′tər) *n. Computer Science.* A very small computer, such as a laptop or personal computer, built around a microprocessor and designed to be used by one person at a time.

mi·cro·cop·y (mī′krō-kŏp′ē) *n., pl.* **-ies.** A greatly reduced photographic copy, usually reproduced by projection.

mi·cro·cosm (mī′krə-kŏz′əm) *n.* A small, representative system having analogies to a larger system in constitution, configuration, or development: *"He sees the auto industry as a microcosm of the U.S. itself"* (William J. Hampton). [Middle English *microcosme,* man as a little world, from Old French, from Late Latin *mīcrocosmus,* from Greek *mikros kosmos* : *mikros,* small + *kosmos,* world, order.] **—mi′cro·cos′mic** (-kŏz′mĭk), **mi′cro·cos′mi·cal** (-mĭ-kəl) *adj.* **—mi′cro·cos′mi·cal·ly** *adv.*

microcosmic salt *n.* A white crystalline salt of phosphorus, $HNaNH_4PO_4{\cdot}4H_2O$, used in blowpipe analysis of minerals to test for the presence of certain metals.

mi·cro·crys·tal·line (mī′krō-krĭs′tə-lĭn) *adj.* Having a crystalline structure visible only under a microscope. **—mi′cro·crys′tal** *n.*

mi·cro·cyte (mī′krə-sīt′) *n.* An abnormally small red blood cell that is less than five microns in diameter and may occur in certain forms of anemia. [MICRO– + (ERYTHRO)CYTE.] **—mi′cro·cyt′ic** (-sĭt′ĭk) *adj.*

mi·cro·den·si·tom·e·ter (mī′krō-dĕn′sĭ-tŏm′ĭ-tər) *n.* An extremely sensitive densitometer used to detect on a film or photographic plate spectrum lines too faint to be seen by the human eye.

mi·cro·dot (mī′krə-dŏt′) *n.* A copy or photograph that has been reduced to an extremely small size for ease of transport and purposes of security.

mi·cro·ec·o·nom·ics (mī′krō-ĕk′ə-nŏm′ĭks, -ē′kə-) *n. (used with a sing. verb).* The study of the operations of the components of a national economy, such as individual firms, households, and consumers. **—mi′cro·ec′o·nom′ic** *adj.*

mi·cro·e·lec·trode (mī′krō-ĭ-lĕk′trōd′) *n.* A very small electrode, often used to study electrical characteristics of living cells and tissues.

mi·cro·e·lec·tron·ics (mī′krō-ĭ-lĕk-trŏn′ĭks) *n. (used with a sing. verb).* The branch of electronics that deals with miniature components. **—mi′cro·e·lec·tron′ic** *adj.*

mi·cro·el·e·ment (mī′krō-ĕl′ə-mənt) *n.* A trace element.

mi·cro·en·cap·su·late (mī′krō-ĕn-kăp′sə-lāt′) *tr.v.* **-lat·ed, -lat·ing, -lates.** To enclose in microcapsules. **—mi′cro·en·cap′su·la′tion** *n.*

mi·cro·en·vi·ron·ment (mī′krō-ĕn-vī′rən-mənt, -vī′ərn-) *n.* The environment of a very small, specific area.

mi·cro·ev·o·lu·tion (mī′krō-ĕv′ə-lo͞o′shən, -ē′və-) *n.* Evolution resulting from a succession of relatively small genetic variations that often cause the formation of new subspecies. **—mi′cro·ev′o·lu′tion·ar′y** *adj.*

mi·cro·far·ad (mī′krō-făr′əd, -ăd) *n.* A unit of capacitance equal to one millionth (10^{-6}) of a farad.

mi·cro·fiche (mī′krō-fēsh′) *n., pl.* **microfiche** or **-fich·es.** A card or sheet of microfilm capable of accommodating and preserving a considerable number of pages, as of printed text, in reduced form. *—attributive.* Often used to modify another noun: *microfiche data; a microfiche collection.* [French : Greek *mikro-,* micro- + *fiche,* peg, slip of paper, index card (from Old French,

microbus

ă pat	oi boy
ā pay	ou out
âr care	o͝o took
ä father	o͞o boot
ĕ pet	ŭ cut
ē be	ûr urge
ĭ pit	th thin
ī pie	*th* this
îr pier	hw which
ŏ pot	zh vision
ō toe	ə about, item
ô paw	♦ regionalism

Stress marks: **′** (primary); ′ (secondary), as in **dictionary** (dĭk′shə-nĕr′ē)

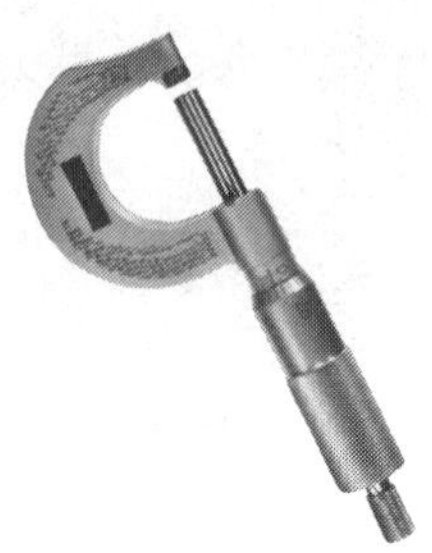
micrometer[1]

peg, from *fichier,* to drive in, fasten, from Vulgar Latin **fīgicāre,* from Latin *fīgere;* see **dhīgʷ-** in Appendix).]

mi·cro·fil·a·ment (mī′krō-fĭl′ə-mənt) *n.* Any of the minute fibers located throughout the cytoplasm of cells, composed of actin and functioning primarily in maintaining the structural integrity of a cell. **—mi′cro·fil′a·men′tous** (-mĕn′təs) *adj.*

mi·cro·fi·lar·i·a (mī′krə-fə-lâr′ē-ə) *n., pl.* **-i·ae** (-ē-ē′). The minute larval form of a filarial worm. **—mi′cro·fi·lar′i·al** *adj.*

mi·cro·film (mī′krə-fĭlm′) *n.* **1.** A film on which printed materials are photographed at greatly reduced size for ease of storage. **2.** A reproduction on this kind of film. **—microfilm** *tr.v.* **-filmed, -film·ing, -films.** To reproduce (documents, for example) on microfilm.

mi·cro·flop·py (mī′krō-flŏp′ē) *n., pl.* **-pies.** *Computer Science.* A computer disk 3½ inches in diameter and encased in a hard protective covering.

mi·cro·form (mī′krə-fôrm′) *n.* An arrangement of images reduced in size, as on microfilm or microfiche.

mi·cro·fos·sil (mī′krō-fŏs′əl) *n.* A microscopic fossil, as of a pollen grain or unicellular organism.

mi·cro·gam·ete (mī′krō-găm′ēt′, -gə-mēt′) *n.* The smaller of a pair of conjugating gametes, usually the male, in an organism that reproduces by heterogamy.

mi·cro·ga·me·to·cyte (mī′krō-gə-mē′tə-sīt′) *n.* A gametocyte that gives rise to microgametes.

mi·cro·graph (mī′krə-grăf′) *n.* **1.** A drawing or photographic reproduction of an object as viewed through a microscope. **2.** An instrument used to make tiny writing or engraving. **—mi′cro·graph′ic** *adj.* **—mi·crog′ra·phy** (mī-krŏg′rə-fē) *n.*

microphone

mi·cro·hab·i·tat (mī′krō-hăb′ĭ-tăt′) *n.* A very small, specialized habitat, such as a clump of grass or a space between rocks.

mi·cro·in·jec·tion (mī′krō-ĭn-jĕk′shən) *n.* Injection of minute amounts of a substance into a microscopic structure, such as a single cell. **—mi′cro·in·ject′** (-jĕkt′) *v.*

mi·cro·in·struc·tion (mī′krō-ĭn-strŭk′shən) *n. Computer Science.* A small, specific instruction, used in series to make up a high-level machine instruction.

mi·cro·ma·nip·u·la·tor (mī′krō-mə-nĭp′yə-lā′tər) *n.* A device for manipulating minute instruments and needles under a microscope in order to perform delicate procedures, such as microsurgery. **—mi′cro·ma·nip′u·la′tion** *n.* **—mi′cro·ma·nip′u·la′tive** *adj.*

mi·cro·mere (mī′krō-mîr′) *n.* A very small blastomere. [MICRO– + (BLASTO)MERE.]

mi·cro·me·te·or·ite (mī′krō-mē′tē-ə-rīt′) *n.* A tiny particle of meteoric dust, especially one of many that fall to the surface of the earth or moon.

mi·cro·me·te·or·oid (mī′krō-mē′tē-ə-roid′) *n.* A very small, often dust-sized meteoroid.

mi·cro·me·te·or·ol·o·gy (mī′krō-mē′tē-ə-rŏl′ə-jē) *n.* The study of weather conditions in a very small area, such as the area immediately around the trunk of a tree, that can affect meteorological conditions. **—mi′cro·me′te·or′o·log′i·cal** (-ôr′ə-lŏj′ĭ-kəl, -ər-ə-) *adj.* **—mi′cro·me′te·or·ol′o·gist** *n.*

microreader

mi·crom·e·ter¹ (mī-krŏm′ĭ-tər) *n.* A device for measuring very small distances, objects, or angles, especially one based on the rotation of a finely threaded screw, as in relation to a microscope.

mi·cro·me·ter² (mī′krō-mē′tər) *n.* A unit of length equal to one thousandth (10^{-3}) of a millimeter or one millionth (10^{-6}) of a meter.

mi·crom·e·try (mī-krŏm′ĭ-trē) *n.* Measurement of minute objects with a micrometer. **—mi′cro·met′ric** (mī′krō-mĕt′rĭk), **mi′cro·met′ri·cal** (-rĭ-kəl) *adj.* **—mi′cro·met′ri·cal·ly** *adv.*

mi·cro·min·i·a·tur·ize (mī′krō-mĭn′ē-chə-rīz′, -mĭn′ə-) *tr.v.* **-ized, -iz·ing, -iz·es.** To construct devices on an extremely small scale. Used especially of electronic circuitry.

mi·cro·mole (mī′krō-mōl′) *n.* One millionth (10^{-6}) of a mole.

mi·cron also **mi·kron** (mī′krŏn′) *n., pl.* **-crons** or **-cra** (-krə) also **-krons** or **-kra** (-krə). A unit of length equal to one millionth (10^{-6}) of a meter. No longer in technical use. [Greek *mikron,* neuter of *mikros,* small.]

Mi·cro·ne·si·a (mī′krō-nē′zhə, -shə). A division of Oceania in the western Pacific Ocean comprising the islands east of the Philippines and north of the equator.

Micronesia, Federated States of. A group of associated islands in the Caroline Islands of the western Pacific Ocean. They were administered as part of the U.S. Trust Territory of the Pacific Islands from 1947 to 1986 and are now self-governing under a compact of free association with the United States. Kolonia, on Pohnpei (Ponape) Island, is the capital. Population, 73,160.

Mi·cro·ne·sian (mī′krə-nē′zhən, -shən) *adj.* Of or relating to Micronesia or its peoples, languages, or cultures. **—Micronesian** *n.* **1.** A member of any of the peoples inhabiting Micronesia. **2.** A subfamily of the Austronesian language family that includes the languages of Micronesia.

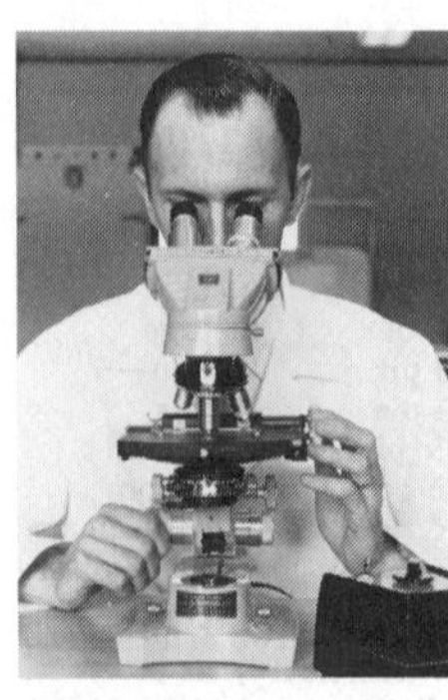
microscope

mi·cron·ize (mī′krə-nīz′) *tr.v.* **-ized, -iz·ing, -iz·es.** To reduce to particles that are only a few microns in diameter.

mi·cro·nu·cle·us (mī′krō-nōō′klē-əs, -nyōō′-) *n., pl.* **-cle·i** (-klē-ī′) or **-cle·us·es.** The smaller of two nuclei in ciliate protozoans that contains genetic material and functions in reproduction. **—mi′cro·nu′cle·ar** *adj.*

mi·cro·nu·tri·ent (mī′krō-nōō′trē-ənt, -nyōō′-) *n.* A substance, such as a vitamin, that is essential in minute amounts for the proper growth and metabolism of a living organism.

mi·cro·or·gan·ism (mī′krō-ôr′gə-nĭz′əm) *n.* An organism of microscopic or submicroscopic size, especially a bacterium or protozoan.

mi·cro·pa·le·on·tol·o·gy (mī′krō-pā′lē-ŏn-tŏl′ə-jē, -ən-) *n.* The branch of paleontology that deals with microfossils. **—mi′cro·pa′le·on′to·log′ic** (-ŏn′tl-ŏj′ĭk), **mi′cro·pa′le·on′to·log′i·cal** *adj.* **—mi′cro·pa′le·on·tol′o·gist** *n.*

mi·cro·phage (mī′krə-fāj′) *n.* A small phagocyte. **—mi′cro·phag′ic** *adj.*

mi·cro·phone (mī′krə-fōn′) *n.* An instrument that converts sound waves into an electric current, usually fed into an amplifier, a recorder, or a broadcast transmitter. **—mi′cro·phon′ic** (-fŏn′ĭk) *adj.*

mi·cro·pho·to·graph (mī′krō-fō′tə-grăf′) *n.* **1.** A photograph requiring magnification for viewing. **2.** A photograph on microfilm. **3.** See **photomicrograph.** **—mi′cro·pho′to·graph′ic** *adj.* **—mi′cro·pho·tog′ra·pher** (-fə-tŏg′rə-fər) *n.* **—mi′cro·pho·tog′ra·phy** (-rə-fē) *n.*

mi·cro·phys·ics (mī′krō-fĭz′ĭks) *n. (used with a sing. verb).* The physics of molecular, atomic, nuclear, and subnuclear systems. **—mi′cro·phys′i·cal** (-fĭz′ĭ-kəl) *adj.* **—mi′cro·phys′i·cal·ly** *adv.* **—mi′cro·phys′i·cist** (-fĭz′ĭ-sĭst) *n.*

mi·cro·phyte (mī′krə-fīt′) *n.* A plant of microscopic size. **—mi′cro·phyt′ic** (-fĭt′ĭk) *adj.*

mi·cro·pi·pette (mī′krō-pī-pĕt′) *n.* **1.** A very small pipette used in microinjection. **2.** A pipette used to measure very small volumes of liquids.

mi·cro·print (mī′krə-prĭnt′) *n.* The printed or positive reproduction of a microphotograph.

mi·cro·proc·es·sor (mī′krō-prŏs′ĕs-ər) *n. Computer Science.* An integrated circuit that contains the entire central processing unit of a computer on a single chip.

mi·cro·pro·gram·ming (mī′krō-prō′grăm-ĭng, -grə-mĭng) *n. Computer Science.* A method of operating the control unit of a computer by breaking down the control instructions into a sequence of small steps.

mi·cro·pub·lish·ing (mī′krō-pŭb′lĭ-shĭng) *n.* Publishing by microform. **—mi′cro·pub′lish·er** *n.*

mi·cro·pyle (mī′krə-pīl′) *n.* **1.** *Botany.* A minute opening in the ovule of a seed plant through which the pollen tube usually enters. **2.** *Zoology.* A pore in the membrane covering the ovum of some animals through which a spermatozoon can enter. [MICRO– + Greek *pulē,* gate.] **—mi′cro·py′lar** *adj.*

mi·cro·ra·di·o·graph (mī′krō-rā′dē-ō-grăf′) *n.* An enlarged x-ray photograph, used to study small details. **—mi′cro·ra′di·og′ra·phy** (-ŏg′rə-fē) *n.*

mi·cro·read·er (mī′krō-rē′dər) *n.* A device for reading materials in microform, such as microfilm and microfiche.

mi·cro·scope (mī′krə-skōp′) *n.* **1.** An optical instrument that uses a lens or a combination of lenses to form magnified images of objects, especially of objects too small to be seen by the unaided eye. **2.** An instrument, such as an electron microscope, that uses electronic or other processes to magnify objects.

mi·cro·scop·ic (mī′krə-skŏp′ĭk) also **mi·cro·scop·i·cal** (-ĭ-kəl) *adj.* **1.a.** Too small to be seen by the unaided eye but large enough to be studied under a microscope. **b.** Of, relating to, or concerned with a microscope. **2.** Exceedingly small; minute: *"The activities of men . . . were reduced to a microscopic scale"* (John Hersey). **3.** Characterized by or done with extreme attention to detail. **—mi′cro·scop′i·cal·ly** *adv.*

Mi·cro·sco·pi·um (mī′krə-skō′pē-əm) *n.* A constellation in the Southern Hemisphere. [New Latin *Mīcroscopium,* microscope, Microscopium : MICRO– + *-scopium,* -scope.]

mi·cros·co·py (mī-krŏs′kə-pē) *n., pl.* **-pies. 1.a.** The study of microscopes. **b.** The use of microscopes. **2.** Investigation employing a microscope. **—mi·cros′co·pist** *n.*

mi·cro·seism (mī′krə-sī′zəm) *n.* A faint earth tremor caused by natural phenomena, such as winds and strong ocean waves. **—mi′cro·seis′mic** (-sīz′mĭk, -sīs′-) *adj.*

mi·cro·some (mī′krə-sōm′) *n.* A small particle in the cytoplasm of a cell, typically consisting of fragmented endoplasmic reticulum to which ribosomes are attached. **—mi′cro·so′mal** (-sō′məl), **mi′cro·so′mic** (-sō′mĭk) *adj.*

mi·cro·spo·ran·gi·um (mī′krō-spə-răn′jē-əm) *n., pl.* **-gi·a** (-jē-ə). *Botany.* A structure in which microspores are formed. **—mi′cro·spo·ran′gi·ate** (-jē-ĭt) *adj.*

mi·cro·spore (mī′krə-spôr′, -spōr′) *n. Botany.* The smaller of two types of spores that give rise to a male gametophyte. **—mi′cro·spo′ric, mi′cro·spo′rous** (mī′krə-spôr′əs, -spōr′-, mī-krŏs′pər-əs) *adj.*

microspore mother cell *n. Botany.* A cell that undergoes meiosis to produce four microspores. Also called *microsporocyte.*

mi·cro·spo·ro·cyte (mī′krə-spôr′ə-sīt′, -spōr′-) *n.* See **microspore mother cell.**

mi·cro·spo·ro·phyll (mī′krə-spôr′ə-fĭl′, -spōr′-) *n. Botany.* A leaflike structure that bears microsporangia.

mi·cro·state (mī′krō-stāt′) *n.* An independent country that is very small in area and population. Also called *ministate.*

mi·cro·struc·ture (mī′krō-strŭk′chər) *n.* The structure of an object as revealed through microscopic examination.

mi·cro·sur·ger·y (mī′krō-sûr′jə-rē) *n., pl.* **-ies.** Surgery on minute body structures or cells performed with the aid of a microscope and other specialized instruments, such as a micromanipulator. **—mi′cro·sur′gi·cal** (-jĭ-kəl) *adj.*

mi·cro·teach·ing (mī′krə-tē′chĭng) *n.* A method of practice teaching in which a videotape of a small segment of a student's classroom teaching is made and later evaluated.

mi·cro·tome (mī′krə-tōm′) *n.* An instrument used to cut a specimen, as of organic tissue, into thin sections for microscopic examination.

mi·crot·o·my (mī-krŏt′ə-mē) *n., pl.* **-mies.** The preparation of specimens with a microtome. **—mi′cro·tom′ic** (mī′krə-tŏm′ĭk) *adj.*

mi·cro·tone (mī′krə-tōn′) *n. Music.* An interval smaller than a semitone. **—mi′cro·ton′al** (-tō′nəl) *adj.* **—mi′cro·to·nal′i·ty** (-tō-năl′ĭ-tē) *n.* **—mi′cro·ton′al·ly** *adv.*

mi·cro·tu·bule (mī′krō-to͞o′byo͞ol, -tyo͞o-) *n.* Any of the proteinaceous cylindrical hollow structures that are distributed throughout the cytoplasm of eukaryotic cells, providing structural support and assisting in cellular locomotion and transport. **—mi′cro·tu′bu·lar** *adj.*

mi·cro·vas·cu·la·ture (mī′krō-văs′kyə-lə-cho͝or′, -chər) *n.* The portion of the circulatory system composed of the smallest vessels, such as the capillaries, arterioles, and venules. **—mi′cro·vas′cu·lar** (-kyə-lər) *adj.*

mi·cro·vil·lus (mī′krō-vĭl′əs) *n., pl.* **-vil·li** (-vĭl′ī′). Any of the minute hairlike structures projecting from the surface of certain types of epithelial cells, especially those of the small intestine. **—mi′cro·vil′lar** (-lər) *adj.*

mi·cro·volt (mī′krə-vōlt′) *n.* A unit of electric potential equal to one millionth (10^{-6}) of a volt.

mi·cro·watt (mī′krō-wŏt′) *n.* A unit of power equal to one millionth (10^{-6}) of a watt.

mi·cro·wave (mī′krə-wāv′, -krō-) *n.* **1.** A high-frequency electromagnetic wave, one millimeter to one meter in wavelength, intermediate between infrared and short-wave radio wavelengths. **2.** *Informal.* A microwave oven. **—microwave** *tr.v.* **-waved, -wav·ing, -waves.** To cook or heat (food) in a microwave oven. **—mi′cro·wav′a·ble, mi′cro·wave′a·ble** *adj.*

microwave oven *n.* An oven in which microwaves cook the food.

mic·tu·rate (mĭk′chə-rāt′, mĭk′tə-) *intr.v.* **-rat·ed, -rat·ing, -rates.** To urinate. [From Latin *micturīre,* to want to urinate, desiderative of *mēiere,* to urinate. See **meigh-** in Appendix.] **—mic′tu·ri′tion** (-rĭsh′ən) *n.*

mid[1] (mĭd) *adj.* **1.** Middle; central. **2.** Being the part in the middle or center: *in the mid Pacific.* **3.** *Linguistics.* Of, relating to, or being a vowel produced with the tongue in a position approximately intermediate between high and low, as the vowel in *but.* [Middle English, from Old English *midd.* See **medhyo-** in Appendix.]

mid[2] (mĭd) *prep.* Surrounded by; amid: *mid smoke and flame.* [Middle English. See MIDWIFE.]

mid. *abbr.* Middle.

mid– *pref.* Middle: *midsummer.* [Middle English, from *mid,* middle. See MID[1].]

USAGE NOTE: Many compounds other than those entered here may be formed with *mid–*. In forming compounds, *mid–* is normally joined to the following word or element without a space or hyphen: *midpoint.* However, if the second element begins with a capital letter, it is always separated with a hyphen: *mid-May.* It is always acceptable to separate the elements with a hyphen to prevent possible confusion with another form, as, for example, to distinguish *mid-den* (the middle of a den) from the word *midden.* Note that the adjective *mid*[1] is a separate word, though, as is the case with any adjective, it may be joined to another word with a hyphen when used as a unit modifier: *in the mid Pacific* but *a mid-Pacific island.*

mid·air (mĭd′âr′) *n.* **1.** A point or region in the air. **2.** *Informal.* A collision involving two or more aircraft while fully airborne. *—attributive.* Often used to modify another noun: *a midair hijacking; a midair emergency.*

Mi·das (mī′dəs) *n.* The fabled king of Phrygia to whom Dionysus gave the power of turning to gold all that he touched. [Latin *Midās,* from Greek.]

Midas touch *n.* The ability to make, manage, and keep huge amounts of money: *"Today's market has convinced dozens of kids barely out of college that they've got the Midas touch"* (Business Week). [After MIDAS.]

Mid-At·lan·tic States (mĭd′ăt-lăn′tĭk). See **Middle Atlantic States.**

mid·brain (mĭd′brān′) *n.* See **mesencephalon.**

mid·course (mĭd′kôrs′, -kōrs′) *n.* **1.** The part of a missile flight between the end of the launching phase and reentry, during which corrective maneuvers are made. **2.** The middle point of a course or a course of action. *—attributive.* Often used to modify another noun: *a midcourse personnel shakeup; a midcourse change in policy.*

mid·cult (mĭd′kŭlt′) *n.* A form of intellectual and artistic culture that has qualities of high culture and mass culture without being either. [MID(DLEBROW) + CULT(URE).]

mid·day (mĭd′dā′) *n.* The middle of the day; noon. *—attributive.* Often used to modify another noun: *a midday snack; midday meals.*

mid·den (mĭd′n) *n.* **1.** A dunghill or refuse heap. **2.** A kitchen midden. [Middle English *midding,* of Scandinavian origin.]

mid·dle (mĭd′l) *adj. Abbr.* **mid. 1.** Equally distant from extremes or limits; central: *the middle point on a line.* **2.** Being at neither one extreme nor the other; intermediate. **3.a.** Intervening between an earlier and a later period of time; being an intermediate part of a sequence or series: *the middle years.* **b. Middle.** *Geology.* Of or relating to a division of geologic time between an earlier and a later division: *the Middle Paleozoic.* **4. Middle.** Of or relating to a stage in the development of a language or literature between earlier and later stages: *Middle Swedish.* **5.** *Grammar.* Of a verb form or voice in which the subject both performs and is affected by the action specified. **—middle** *n.* **1.** An area or a point equidistant between extremes; a center: *the middle of a circle.* **2.** Something intermediate between extremes; a mean. **3.** The interior portion: *the middle of a chain.* **4.** The middle part of the human body; the waist. **5.** *Logic.* A middle term. **—middle** *tr.v.* **-dled, -dling, -dles. 1.** To place in the middle. **2.** *Nautical.* To fold in the middle: *middle the sail.* [Middle English *middel,* from Old English. See **medhyo-** in Appendix.]

middle age *n.* The time of human life between youth and old age, usually reckoned as the years between 40 and 60. Also called *midlife.*

mid·dle-aged (mĭd′l-ājd′) *adj.* Of or relating to middle age: *middle-aged parents; middle-aged interests.*

Middle Ages *pl.n.* The period in European history between antiquity and the Renaissance, often dated from A.D. 476 to 1453.

Middle A·mer·i·ca[1] (ə-mĕr′ĭ-kə). A region of southern North America comprising Mexico, Central America, and sometimes the West Indies. **—Middle A·mer′i·can** *adj. & n.*

Middle A·mer·i·ca[2] (ə-mĕr′ĭ-kə) *n.* **1.** That part of the U.S. middle class thought of as being average in income and education and moderately conservative in values and attitudes. **2.** The American heartland thought of as being made up of small towns, small cities, and suburbs.

Middle At·lan·tic States (ăt-lăn′tĭk) also **Mid-At·lan·tic States** (mĭd′ăt-lăn′tĭk). The U.S. states of New York, Pennsylvania, New Jersey, and usually Delaware and Maryland.

Mid·dle·bor·ough or **Mid·dle·bor·o** (mĭd′l-bûr′ō, -bŭr′ō). A town of southeast Massachusetts north of New Bedford. Population, 16,404.

mid·dle·brow (mĭd′l-brou′) *n. Informal.* One who is somewhat cultured; one who is neither highbrow nor lowbrow. [MIDDLE + (HIGH)BROW and (LOW)BROW.] **—mid′dle·brow′** *adj.*

Mid·dle·burg Heights (mĭd′l-bûrg′). A city of northeast Ohio, a suburb of Cleveland. Population, 16,218.

middle C *n. Music.* The tone represented by a note on the first ledger line below a treble clef or the first ledger line above a bass clef. It is the first C below international pitch.

middle class *n.* The members of society occupying a socioeconomic position intermediate between those of the lower working classes and the wealthy.

middle distance *n.* **1.** The area between the foreground and background in a painting, drawing, or photograph. Also called *middle ground.* **2.** *Sports.* A division of competition in racing with events usually ranging from 400 meters to 1,500 meters or from 440 yards to 1 mile.

Middle Dutch *n.* The Dutch language from the middle of the 12th through the 15th century.

middle ear *n.* The space between the eardrum and the inner ear that contains the three auditory ossicles, which convey vibrations to the cochlea. Also called *tympanum.*

Middle East also **Mid·east** (mĭd-ēst′). An area comprising the countries of southwest Asia and northeast Africa. **—Middle East′ern** *adj.* **—Middle East′ern·er** *n.*

Middle English *n. Abbr.* **ME, M.E.** The English language from about 1100 to 1500.

middle ground *n.* **1.** See **middle distance** (sense 1). **2.** A point of view midway between extremes: *"the middle ground between news and amusement"* (Roderick Anscombe).

Middle High German *n.* High German from the 11th through the 15th century.

mid·dle-in·come (mĭd′l-ĭn′kŭm) *adj.* Of or relating to people or groups whose income falls in the middle of the range for an overall population.

Middle Irish *n.* Irish from the 10th through the 13th century.

middle lamella *n. Botany.* The pectin-rich intercellular material cementing together the primary walls of adjacent plant cells.

Middle Loup (lo͞op). A river rising in central Nebraska and flowing about 354 km (220 mi) east and southeast to join the North Loup and South Loup rivers and form the Loup River.

Middle Low German *n.* Low German from the middle of the 13th through the 15th century.

mid·dle·man (mĭd′l-măn′) *n.* **1.** A trader who buys from

ă pat	oi boy
ā pay	ou out
âr care	o͝o took
ä father	o͞o boot
ĕ pet	ŭ cut
ē be	ûr urge
ĭ pit	th thin
ī pie	*th* this
îr pier	hw which
ŏ pot	zh vision
ō toe	ə about, item
ô paw	♦ regionalism

Stress marks: ′ (primary); ′ (secondary), as in **dictionary** (dĭk′shə-nĕr′ē)

producers and sells to retailers or consumers. **2.** An intermediary; a go-between.

middle management *n.* A group of persons occupying managerial positions intermediate between lower and higher executives. **—middle manager** *n.*

mid·dle·most (mĭd′l-mōst′) *adj.* Midmost.

mid·dle-of-the-road (mĭd′l-əv-thə-rōd′) *adj.* **1.** Pursuing a course of action midway between extremes, especially following a course in politics that is neither liberal nor conservative. **2.** *Abbr.* **MOR** Of, relating to, or being a type of entertainment, especially popular music, that appeals to a wide audience. **—mid′dle-of-the-road′er** *n.*

Middle Pal·i·sade (păl′ĭ-sād′). A mountain, 4,273.7 m (14,012 ft) high, of the Sierra Nevada in east-central California.

Middle River. A community of northern Maryland, an industrial suburb of Baltimore. Population, 26,756.

Mid·dles·brough (mĭd′lz-brə). A borough of northeast England at the mouth of the Tees River. Population, 150,600.

middle school *n.* A school at a level between elementary and high school, typically including grades five through eight.

middle term *n. Abbr.* **M** *Logic.* The term in a syllogism presented in both premises but not appearing in the conclusion.

Mid·dle·ton (mĭd′l-tən), **Thomas.** 1570?–1627. English playwright whose comedies include *A Chaste Maid in Cheapside.*

Mid·dle·town (mĭd′l-toun′). **1.** A city of central Connecticut on the Connecticut River south of Hartford. It is an industrial center and the seat of Wesleyan University (chartered 1831). Population, 39,040. **2.** A community of eastern New Jersey northwest of Red Bank. It was settled in 1665. Population, 61,615. **3.** A city of southeast New York west-southwest of Newburgh. Population, 21,454. **4.** A city of southwest Ohio north-northeast of Cincinnati. Founded in 1802, it has a steel industry. Population, 43,719. **5.** A town of southeast Rhode Island on Narragansett Bay north of Newport. Population, 17,216.

mid·dle·weight (mĭd′l-wāt′) *n. Sports.* **1.** A professional boxer weighing between 147 and 160 pounds (approximately 66.5–72.5 kilograms), heavier than a welterweight and lighter than a light heavyweight. **2.** A contestant in various other sports in a similar weight class.

Middle Welsh *n.* Welsh from the 12th through the 15th century.

Middle West. See **Midwest.** **—Middle West′ern** *adj.* **—Middle West′ern·er** *n.*

♦ **mid·dling** (mĭd′lĭng, -lĭn) *adj.* **1.** Of medium size, position, or quality. **2.** Mediocre. See Synonyms at **average.** **—middling** *n.* **1.** Often **middlings.** *Chiefly Southern U.S.* **a.** Pork or bacon cut from between the ham and shoulder of a pig. **b.** Salt pork. Also called *middling meat.* **2. middlings.** Any of various products, such as partially refined petroleum or ore, that are intermediate in quality, size, price, or grade. **3. middlings** *(used with a sing. or pl. verb).* Coarsely ground wheat mixed with bran. **—middling** *adv. Informal.* Fairly; moderately: *"a middling nice cake"* (Hatfield MA Valley Advocate). [Probably Middle English *midlin* : *mid,* mid; see MID[1] + *-ling,* having a quality; see –LING[1].] **—mid′dling·ly** *adv.*

mid·dy (mĭd′ē) *n., pl.* **-dies. 1.** *Informal.* A midshipman. **2.** A middy blouse.

middy blouse *n.* A woman's or child's loose blouse with a sailor collar.

Mid·east (mĭd-ēst′). See **Middle East.** **—Mid·east′ern** *adj.* **—Mid·east′ern·er** *n.*

mid·field (mĭd′fēld′) *n. Sports.* **1.** The section of a playing field midway between goals. **2.** Players whose usual positions are in the midfield. **—mid′field′er** *n.*

Mid·gard (mĭd′gärd′) *n.* The part of the world inhabited by people, imagined as a fortress encircled by a huge serpent and built by the Norse gods around the middle region of the universe. [Old Norse *Midhgardhr.* See **medhyo-** in Appendix.]

midge (mĭj) *n.* **1.** Any of various gnatlike flies of the family Chironomidae, found worldwide and frequently occurring in swarms near ponds and lakes. **2.** Any of various similar dipteran insects, such as the biting midges of the family Ceratopogonidae. **3.** A little person. [Middle English, from Old English *mycg.*]

midg·et (mĭj′ĭt) *n.* **1.** *Offensive.* An extremely little person who is otherwise normally proportioned. **2.** A small or miniature version of something. **3.** A class of small objects, as a class of very small sailboats or racing cars. **—midget** *adj.* **1.** Miniature; diminutive. **2.** Belonging to a type or class much smaller than what is considered standard: *a midget automobile.* [Diminutive of MIDGE.]

mid·gut (mĭd′gŭt′) *n.* **1.** The middle section of the digestive tract in a vertebrate embryo from which the ileum, jejunum, and portions of the duodenum and colon develop. Also called *mesenteron.* **2.** The middle portion of the digestive tract of certain invertebrates, such as arthropods, lined with an enzyme-secreting tissue and serving as the main site of digestion and absorption.

mid·i (mĭd′ē) *n., pl.* **mid·is.** A skirt or coat of mid-calf length. [Short for *midiskirt* : MID[1] + (MIN)ISKIRT.]

Mi·di (mē-dē′). The south of France.

Mid·i·an·ite (mĭd′ē-ə-nīt′) *n.* A member of an ancient tribe of Midian in northwest Arabia. **—Mid′i·an·ite′** *adj.*

mid·i·ron (mĭd′ī′ərn) *n. Sports.* An iron golf club that has more loft than a driver and less than a three iron, used for medium fairway shots and long approach shots; a two iron.

mid·land (mĭd′lənd) *n.* The middle or interior part of a country or region. **—midland** *adj.* Of or in a midland.

Mid·land (mĭd′lənd). **1.** A city of central Michigan west of Bay City. Chemical industries are important to its economy. Population, 37,250. **2.** A city of west-central Texas west-southwest of Abilene. It is an industrial center. Population, 70,525.

Mid·lands (mĭd′ləndz). A region of central England. It roughly corresponds with the Anglo-Saxon kingdom of Mercia and is today a highly industrialized area.

mid·lev·el (mĭd′lĕv′əl) *n.* The middle stage or level, as in a series, course of action, or career. *—attributive.* Often used to modify another noun: *midlevel managers; a midlevel crisis team.*

mid·life (mĭd′līf′) *n., pl.* **-lives** (-līvz′). See **middle age.** **—midlife** *adj.* Of, relating to, or characteristic of middle age: *"a midlife lull when it was feared he was finished"* (Curtis Wilkie).

midlife crisis *n.* A period of psychological doubt and anxiety that some people experience in middle age.

mid·line (mĭd′līn′) *n.* A medial line, especially the medial line or plane of the body.

Mid·lo·thi·an (mĭd-lō′thē-ən). A region of southeast Scotland on the Firth of Forth surrounding Edinburgh. "The Heart of Midlothian" was a popular name for the former Tolbooth Prison in Edinburgh and was used by Sir Walter Scott as the title of his 1818 novel.

mid·morn·ing (mĭd′môr′nĭng) *n.* The middle of the morning. *—attributive.* Often used to modify another noun: *midmorning coffee; a midmorning appointment.*

mid·most (mĭd′mōst′) *adj.* **1.** Situated in the very middle; middlemost. **2.** Situated nearest the middle. **—midmost** *adv.* In the middle.

Midn. *abbr.* Midshipman.

mid·night (mĭd′nīt′) *n.* **1.** The middle of the night, specifically 12 o'clock at night. **2. a.** Intense darkness or gloom. **b.** A period of darkness and gloom. *—attributive.* Often used to modify another noun: *a midnight swim; a midnight meeting.*

midnight sun *n.* The sun as seen at midnight during the summer within the Arctic and Antarctic regions.

mid-o·cean ridge (mĭd′ō′shən) *n.* A series of mountain ranges on the ocean floor, more than 84,000 kilometers (52,000 miles) in length, extending through the North and South Atlantic, the Indian Ocean, and the South Pacific. According to the plate tectonics theory, volcanic rock is added to the sea floor as the mid-ocean ridge spreads apart.

mid·point (mĭd′point′) *n.* **1.** *Mathematics.* The point of a line segment or curvilinear arc that divides it into two parts of the same length. **2.** A position midway between two extremes.

mid·range or **mid-range** (mĭd′rānj′) *—n.* **1.** The middle part of an audio frequency. **2.** The middle part of a series, a progression, or an array: *prices in the midrange.* *—attributive.* Often used to modify another noun: *midrange ballistic missiles; midrange torque.*

Mid·rash (mĭd′răsh′) *n., pl.* **Mid·rash·im** (mĭd-rô′shĭm, mĭd′rä-shēm′). Any of a group of Jewish commentaries on the Hebrew Scriptures compiled between A.D. 400 and 1200 and based on exegesis, parable, and haggadic legend. [Late Hebrew *midrāš,* commentary, explanation, Midrash, from *dāraš,* to interpret.]

mid·rib (mĭd′rĭb′) *n.* The central or principal vein of a leaf.

mid·riff (mĭd′rĭf) *n.* **1.** See **diaphragm** (sense 1). **2.** The middle outer portion of the front of the human body, extending roughly from just below the breast to the waistline. [Middle English *midrif,* from Old English *midhrif* : *midd,* mid; see MID[1] + *hrif,* belly; see **k**ʷ**rep-** in Appendix.] **—mid′riff** *adj.*

mid-rise (mĭd′rīz′) *adj.* Moderately tall: *a mid-rise office building.* **—mid-rise** *n.* A moderately tall building.

mid·sec·tion (mĭd′sĕk′shən) *n.* A middle section, especially the midriff of the human body.

mid·ship (mĭd′shĭp′) *adj. Nautical.* Of, relating to, or located in the middle of a ship.

mid·ship·man (mĭd′shĭp′mən, mĭd-shĭp′mən) *n.* **1.** *Abbr.* **Midn.** A student training to be a commissioned naval officer, especially a student at a naval academy. **2.** Any of various fishes of the genus *Porichthys,* having several rows of light-producing organs along their bodies.

mid·ships (mĭd′shĭps′) *adv. Nautical.* **1.** Amidships. **2.** In the center position. Used of the helm. [Probably short for AMIDSHIPS.]

mid·size or **mid-size** (mĭd′sīz′) *adj.* Of intermediate size. Used especially of motor vehicles, such as cars.

midst (mĭdst, mĭtst) *n.* **1.** The middle position or part; the center: *in the midst of the desert.* **2.** A position of proximity to others: *a stranger in our midst.* **3.** The condition of being surrounded or beset by something: *in the midst of all of our problems.* **4.** A period of time approximately in the middle of a continuing condition or act: *in the midst of the war.* **—midst** *prep.* Among; amid. [Middle English *middest,* alteration of *middes* : *mid,* middle; see MID[1] + *-es,* adv. suff.; see –S[3].]

mid·stream (mĭd′strēm′) *n.* **1.** The middle part of a stream. **2.** The part of a course that is neither at the beginning nor at the end: *the midstream of life.*

mid·sum·mer (mĭd′sŭm′ər) *n.* **1.** The middle of the summer.

2. The summer solstice, about June 21. —*attributive.* Often used to modify another noun: *a midsummer night; midsummer rain.*

Mid·sum·mer Day (mĭd**′**sŭm**′**ər) *n.* **1.** June 24, observed in Europe, Latin America, and Scandinavian communities in the United States in commemoration of the summer solstice. **2.** June 24, observed in many Christian churches in commemoration of the birth of Saint John the Baptist.

Midsummer Eve *n.* **1.** June 23, the day before Midsummer Day, celebrated in Europe, Latin America, and Scandinavian communities in the United States by merrymaking. **2.** June 23, the day before Midsummer Day, celebrated in many Christian churches by feasting. In this sense, also called *Saint John's Eve.*

mid·term (mĭd**′**tûrm**′**) *n.* **1.** The middle of an academic term or a political term of office. **2.a.** An examination given at the middle of a school or college term. **b. midterms.** A series of such examinations. —*attributive.* Often used to modify another noun: *midterm examinations; a midterm break.*

mid·town (mĭd**′**toun**′**) *n.* A central portion of a city, between uptown and downtown. —*attributive.* Often used to modify another noun: *midtown traffic; midtown shops.*

mid-Vic·to·ri·an (mĭd**′**vĭk-tôr**′**ē-ən, -tōr**′**-) *adj.* Relating to, occurring in, or characteristic of the middle period of the reign of Queen Victoria in Great Britain (1837–1901), a period known for rigid social standards. **—mid-Victorian** *n.* **1.** A person living in this period: *"The mid-Victorians had moral zeal but no religion"* (Keith Thomas). **2.** A person having rigid social standards.

mid·way (mĭd**′**wā**′**) *n.* **1.** The area of a fair, a carnival, a circus, or an exposition where sideshows and other amusements are located. **2.** *Obsolete.* **a.** The middle of a way or distance. **b.** A middle course of action or thought. **—midway** *adv.* In the middle of a way or distance; halfway: *midway through the second quarter of the football game.* **—mid′way′** *adj.*

Mid·way Islands (mĭd**′**wā**′**). Two small islands and a surrounding coral atoll in the central Pacific Ocean northwest of Honolulu. They were annexed by the United States in 1867 and remain a U.S. territory with an important naval base. A decisive World War II Allied victory in the Battle of Midway (June 3–6, 1942) was a major turning point in the war in the Pacific.

mid·week (mĭd**′**wēk**′**) *n.* **1.** The middle of the week. **2. Midweek.** Wednesday. —*attributive.* Often used to modify another noun: *a midweek appointment; midweek travel.* **—mid′week′ly** *adj. & adv.*

Mid·west (mĭd-wĕst**′**) or **Middle West.** A region of the north-central United States around the Great Lakes and the upper Mississippi Valley. It is generally considered to include Ohio, Indiana, Illinois, Michigan, Wisconsin, Minnesota, Iowa, Missouri, Kansas, and Nebraska. **—Mid·west′ern** *adj.* **—Mid·west′ern·er** *n.*

Midwest City. A city of central Oklahoma, a residential suburb of Oklahoma City. Population, 49,559.

♦**mid·wife** (mĭd**′**wīf**′**) *n., pl.* **-wives** (-wīvz**′**). **1.** A person, usually a woman, who is trained to assist women in childbirth. Also called ♦*granny.* **2.** One who assists in or takes a part in bringing about a result: *"In the Renaissance, artists and writers start to serve as midwives of fame"* (Carlin Romano). **—midwife** *tr.v.* **-wifed, -wif·ing, -wifes** or **-wived, -wiv·ing, -wives. 1.** To assist in the birth of (a baby). **2.** To assist in bringing forth or about: *"Washington's efforts to midwife a Mideast settlement"* (Newsweek). [Middle English *midwif* : probably *mid,* with (from Old English; see **me-**[2] in Appendix) + *wif,* woman (from Old English *wīf*).]

WORD HISTORY: The word *midwife* is the sort of word whose etymology is perfectly clear until one tries to figure it out. *Wife* would seem to refer to the woman giving birth, who is usually a wife, but *mid*? A knowledge of older senses of words helps us with this puzzle. *Wife* in its earlier history meant "woman," as it still did when the compound *midwife* was formed in Middle English (first recorded around 1300). *Mid* is probably a preposition, meaning "together with." Thus a *midwife* was literally a "with woman" or "a woman who assists other women in childbirth." Even though obstetrics has been rather resistant to midwifery until fairly recently, the etymology of *obstetric* is rather similar, going back to the Latin word *obstetrīx,* "a midwife," from the verb *obstāre,* "to stand in front of," and the feminine suffix *-trix;* the *obstetrīx* would thus literally stand in front of the baby.

mid·wife·ry (mĭd-wīf**′**ə-rē, mĭd**′**wīf**′**rē, -wī**′**fə-rē) *n.* The techniques and practice of a midwife.

mid·win·ter (mĭd**′**wĭn**′**tər) *n.* **1.** The middle of the winter. **2.** The period of the winter solstice, about December 22. —*attributive.* Often used to modify another noun: *a midwinter day; midwinter storms.*

mid·year (mĭd**′**yîr**′**) *n.* **1.** The middle of the calendar or academic year. **2.a.** An examination given in the middle of a school year. **b. midyears.** A series of such examinations. —*attributive.* Often used to modify another noun: *midyear examinations; a midyear break.*

mien (mēn) *n.* **1.** Bearing or manner, especially as it reveals an inner state of mind: *"He was a Vietnam veteran with a haunted mien"* (James Traub). See Synonyms at **bearing. 2.** An appearance or aspect. [Alteration (influenced by French *mine,* appearance; see MINAUDIÈRE) of Middle English *demeine,* demeanor, from Old French, from *demener,* to behave. See DEMEAN[1].]

Mies Van Der Ro·he (mēz**′** văn dər rō**′**ə, rō**′**, fän, mēs**′**), **Ludwig.** 1886–1969. German-born American architect considered a founder of the International Style. His steel-frame and glass buildings include the Seagram Building in New York City (1956–1959). **—Mies′i·an** (mē**′**sē-ən) *adj.*

miff (mĭf) *n.* **1.** A petulant, bad-tempered mood; a huff. **2.** A petty quarrel or argument; a tiff. **—miff** *tr.v.* **miffed, miff·ing, miffs.** To cause to become offended or annoyed. [Possibly expressive of disgust.]

mif·fy (mĭf**′**ē) *adj.* **-fi·er, -fi·est. 1.** *Informal.* Easily offended; oversensitive. **2.** *Botany.* Difficult to raise except under perfect conditions. Used of certain plants. **—mif′fi·ness** *n.*

might[1] (mīt) *n.* **1.** The power, force, or influence held by a person or group. **2.** Physical strength. **3.** Strength or ability to do something. See Synonyms at **strength.** See Regional Note at **powerful.** [Middle English, from Old English *meaht, miht.* See **magh-** in Appendix.]

might[2] (mīt) *aux.v.* Past tense of **may**[1]. **1.a.** Used to indicate a condition or state contrary to fact: *She might help if she knew the truth.* **b.** Used to indicate a possibility or probability that is weaker than *may*: *We might discover a pot of gold at the end of the rainbow.* **2.** Used to express possibility or probability or permission in the past: *She told him yesterday he might not go on the trip.* **3.** Used to express a higher degree of deference or politeness than *may, ought,* or *should*: *Might I express my opinion?* [Middle English, from Old English *meahte, mihte,* first and third person sing. past tense of *magan,* to be able. See MAY[1].]

USAGE NOTE: In many Southern varieties of English, *might* is used in the "double modal" construction with *could,* as in *We might could park over there.* Less frequently, one hears *may can* and *might should.* These constructions are not familiar to the majority of Americans and are best avoided in formal writing.

might-have-been (mīt**′**əv-bĭn**′**) *n., pl.* **might-have-beens** (-bĭnz**′**). An event that could have but never did occur: *"This is one of the great might-have-beens of modern history"* (Arthur M. Schlesinger, Jr.).

might·i·ly (mīt**′**l-ē) *adv.* **1.** In a mighty manner; powerfully. **2.** To a great degree; greatly.

might·n't (mīt**′**nt). Might not.

♦**might·y** (mī**′**tē) *adj.* **-i·er, -i·est. 1.** Having or showing great power, skill, strength, or force: *a mighty orator; a mighty blow.* **2.** Imposing or awesome in size, degree, or extent: *a mighty stone fortress.* **—mighty** *adv. Chiefly Upper Southern U.S.* To a great degree; extremely. Used as an intensive: *mighty fine; mighty tired.* See Regional Note at **powerful. —might′i·ness** *n.*

mi·gnon·ette (mĭn**′**yə-nĕt**′**) *n.* Any of several Mediterranean plants of the genus *Reseda,* especially *R. odorata,* widely cultivated for its terminal, dense, spikelike clusters of very fragrant but inconspicuous greenish flowers. [French, from feminine of *mignonnet,* dainty, pretty, from Old French, diminutive of *mignon,* lover, dainty. See MINION.]

mi·graine (mī**′**grān**′**) *n.* A severe, recurring headache, usually affecting only one side of the head, characterized by sharp pain and often accompanied by nausea, vomiting, and visual disturbances. Also called *megrim.* [Middle English, from Old French, from Late Latin *hēmicrānia,* from Greek *hēmikrania* : *hēmi-,* hemi- + *kranion,* head; see **ker-**[1] in Appendix.] **—mi·grain′ous** *adj.*

mi·grant (mī**′**grənt) *n.* **1.** One that moves from one region to another by chance, instinct, or plan. **2.** An itinerant worker who travels from one area to another in search of work. **—migrant** *adj.* Migratory. [Latin *migrāns, migrant-,* present participle of *migrāre,* to migrate. See MIGRATE.]

mi·grate (mī**′**grāt**′**) *intr.v.* **-grat·ed, -grat·ing, -grates. 1.** To move from one country or region and settle in another. **2.** To change location periodically, especially by moving seasonally from one region to another. [Latin *migrāre, migrāt-.* See **mei-**[1] in Appendix.] **—mi′gra′tor** *n.*

USAGE NOTE: *Migrate,* which is used of people and animals, sometimes implies a lack of permanent settlement, especially as a result of seasonal or periodic movement. *Emigrate* and *immigrate* are used only of people and imply a permanent move, generally across a political boundary. *Emigrate* describes the move relative to the point of departure: *After the Nazis came to power in Germany, many scientists emigrated* (that is, left Germany). By contrast, *immigrate* describes the move relative to the destination: *The promise of prosperity in the United States encouraged many people to immigrate* (that is, move to the United States).

mi·gra·tion (mī-grā**′**shən) *n.* **1.** The act or an instance of migrating. **2.** A group migrating together. **3.** *Chemistry & Physics.* **a.** The movement of one atom or more from one position to another within a molecule. **b.** The movement of ions between electrodes during electrolysis. **—mi·gra′tion·al** *adj.*

mi·gra·to·ry (mī**′**grə-tôr**′**ē, -tōr**′**ē) *adj.* **1.** Characterized by migration; undergoing periodic migration: *migratory birds.* **2.** Of or relating to a migration. **3.** Roving; nomadic.

mih·rab (mîr**′**əb) *n. Islam.* **1.** A niche in the wall of a mosque or a room in the mosque that indicates the direction of Mecca. **2.** An undecorated oblong space in the middle of a Moslem prayer rug, pointed toward Mecca during worship. [Arabic *miḥrāb.*]

mihrab

ă pat	oi boy
ā pay	ou out
âr care	o͝o took
ä father	o͞o boot
ĕ pet	ŭ cut
ē be	ûr urge
ĭ pit	th thin
ī pie	*th* this
îr pier	hw which
ŏ pot	zh vision
ō toe	ə about, item
ô paw	♦ regionalism

Stress marks: **′** (primary); ′ (secondary), as in **dictionary** (dĭk**′**shə-nĕr′ē)

milestone

mi·ka·do (mĭ-kä′dō) *n., pl.* **-dos.** An emperor of Japan. [Japanese : *mi,* honorific pref. + *kado,* gate.]

Mik·a·su·ki also **Mic·co·su·kee** (mĭk′ə-so͞o′kē) *n., pl.* **Mikasuki** or **-kis** also **Miccosukee** or **-kees. 1.a.** A Native American people formerly inhabiting northwest Florida, now forming part of the Seminole people of southern Florida. **b.** A member of this people. **2.** The Muskogean language of the Mikasuki.

♦ **mike** (mīk) *Informal. n.* **1.** A microphone. **2.** See Regional Note at **igg.** **—mike** *tr.v.* **miked, mik·ing, mikes.** To supply with or transmit through a microphone.

mike fright *n. Informal.* Fear of performing or appearing on radio.

Mí·ko·nos (mē′kô-nôs′). See **Mykonos.**

Mi·koy·an (mē′kō-yän′, myĭ-kə-), **Anastas Ivanovich.** 1895–1978. Soviet politician who was chairman of the presidium of the Supreme Soviet (1964–1965).

mi·kron (mī′krŏn′) *n.* Variant of **micron.**

mik·vah (mĭk′və, mĕk-vä′) *n., pl.* **-voth** or **-vot** (-vōt′) or **-vos** (-vōs). **1.** A ritual purification bath taken by Jews on certain occasions, as before the Sabbath or after menstruation or ejaculation. **2.** A building, room, or fixture in which this bath takes place. [Hebrew *miqwāh.*]

mil (mĭl) *n.* **1.** A unit of length equal to one thousandth (10^{-3}) of an inch (0.0254 millimeter), used, for example, to specify the diameter of wire or the thickness of materials sold in sheets. **2.** A milliliter; one cubic centimeter. **3.** A unit of angular measurement used in artillery and equal to 1/6400 of a complete revolution. [Short for Latin *millēsimus,* thousandth, from Latin *mille,* thousand. See **gheslo-** in Appendix.]

mil. *abbr.* Military; militia.

mi·la·dy (mĭ-lā′dē) *n., pl.* **-dies. 1.** An English noblewoman or gentlewoman. **2.** Used as a form of address for such a woman. **3.** A chic or fashionable woman. [French, from English, my lady.]

mil·age (mī′lĭj) *n.* Variant of **mileage.**

Mi·lan (mĭ-lăn′, -län′). A city of northern Italy northeast of Genoa. Probably of Celtic origin, it was taken by the Romans in 222 B.C. and has been an important commercial and cultural center since medieval times. Population, 1,634,638. **—Mil′a·nese′** (mĭl′ə-nēz′, -nēs′) *adj. & n.*

milch (mĭlch) *adj.* Giving milk: *a milch cow.* [Middle English *milche,* from Old English *-milce,* in *thrīmilce,* May (when cows can be milked thrice in a day). See **melg-** in Appendix.]

mil·chig (mĭl′KHĭk) *adj.* Derived from or made of milk or dairy products. [Yiddish *milkhik,* from *milkh,* milk, from Middle High German, from Old High German *miluh.* See **melg-** in Appendix.]

mild (mīld) *adj.* **mild·er, mild·est. 1.** Gentle or kind in disposition, manners, or behavior. **2.a.** Moderate in type, degree, effect, or force: *a mild pipe tobacco; a mild sedative.* **b.** Not extreme: *a mild winter storm.* **c.** Warm and full of sunshine; pleasant: *a mild spring day; mild weather in June.* **3.** Not severe or acute: *a mild fever.* **4.** Easily molded, shaped, or worked; malleable: *mild steel.* [Middle English, from Old English *milde.* See **mel-**[1] in Appendix.] **—mild′ly** *adv.* **—mild′ness** *n.*

mil·dew (mĭl′do͞o′, -dyo͞o′) *n.* **1.** Any of various fungi that form a superficial, usually whitish growth on plants and various organic materials. **2.** A superficial coating or discoloration of organic materials, such as cloth, paper, or leather, caused by fungi, especially under damp conditions. **3.** A plant disease caused by such fungi. **—mildew** *tr. & intr.v.* **-dewed, -dew·ing, -dews.** To affect or become affected with mildew. [Middle English, from Old English *mildēaw,* honeydew, nectar. See **melit-** in Appendix.]

mile (mīl) *n. Abbr.* **mi., m. 1.** A unit of length equal to 5,280 feet or 1,760 yards (1,609 meters), used in the United States and other English-speaking countries. Also called *land mile, statute mile.* See table at **measurement. 2.** A nautical mile. **3.** An air mile. **4.** *Sports.* A race that is one mile long. **5.** A relatively great distance: *had to walk for miles in the airport.* [Middle English, from Old English *mīl,* from Latin *mīlia (passuum),* a thousand (double paces), a Roman mile, pl. of *mīlle,* thousand. See **gheslo-** in Appendix.]

mile·age also **mil·age** (mī′lĭj) *n.* **1.** Total length, extent, or distance measured or expressed in miles. **2.** Total miles covered or traveled in a given time. **3.** The amount of service, use, or wear estimated by miles used or traveled: *This tire will give very good mileage.* **4.** The number of miles traveled by a motor vehicle on a given quantity of fuel. **5.a.** An allowance for travel expenses established at a specified rate per mile. **b.** Expense per mile, as for the use of a car. **6.** *Informal.* The amount of service something has yielded or may yield in the future; usefulness: *a tape player that still has a lot of mileage left.*

mile·post (mīl′pōst′) *n.* A post set up to indicate distance in miles, as along a highway.

mil·er (mī′lər) *n.* One who competes in races one mile long.

mi·les glo·ri·o·sus (mē′lās glôr′ē-ō′səs, glōr′-) *n., pl.* **mi·li·tes glo·ri·o·si** (mē′lĭ-tās glôr′ē-ō′sē, glōr′-). A bragging and often cowardly soldier, especially as a stock character in comedy. [Latin *mīles glōriōsus,* after *Mīles Glōriōsus,* a comedy by Plautus.]

Mi·le·sian[1] (mī-lē′zhən, -shən) *adj.* Of or relating to Miletus or its inhabitants. **—Milesian** *n.* A native or inhabitant of Miletus. [From Latin *Mīlēsius,* from Greek *Milēsios,* from *Milētos,* Miletus.]

Mi·le·sian[2] (mī-lē′zhən, -shən) *n.* **1.** *Mythology.* A member of a people who invaded Ireland and became the ancestors of the Irish. **2.** A native or inhabitant of Ireland. **—Milesian** *adj.* Of or relating to Ireland; Irish. [After *Milesius,* legendary ancestor of the Irish people.]

mile·stone (mīl′stōn′) *n.* **1.** A stone marker set up on a roadside to indicate the distance in miles from a given point. **2.** An important event, as in a person's career, the history of a nation, or the advancement of knowledge in a field; a turning point.

Mi·let·us (mī-lē′təs). An ancient Ionian city of western Asia Minor in present-day Turkey. Occupied by Greeks c. 1000 B.C., it became an important trading and colonizing settlement and also flourished as a center of learning.

mil·foil (mĭl′foil′) *n.* **1.** See **yarrow. 2.** Water milfoil. [Middle English, from Old French, from Latin *mīlifolium* : *mīlle,* thousand; see **gheslo-** in Appendix + *folium,* leaf; see **bhel-**[3] in Appendix.]

Mil·ford (mĭl′fərd). **1.** A city of southwest Connecticut on Long Island Sound southwest of New Haven. Founded in 1639, it was a shipbuilding center until the early 19th century. Population, 50,898. **2.** A city of south-central Massachusetts southeast of Worcester. It is an industrial center. Population, 23,390.

Mil·haud (mē-yō′), **Darius.** 1892–1974. French composer who experimented with polytonality and jazz styles.

mil·i·a (mĭl′ē-ə) *n.* Plural of **milium.**

mil·i·ar·i·a (mĭl′ē-âr′ē-ə) *n.* See **heat rash.** [New Latin *(fēbris) miliāria,* miliary (fever), feminine of Latin *miliārius,* of millet. See MILIARY.] **—mil′i·ar′i·al** *adj.*

mil·i·ar·y (mĭl′ē-ĕr′ē) *adj.* **1.** Having the appearance of millet seeds. **2.** *Pathology.* Characterized by the presence of small skin lesions that have the size and appearance of millet seeds. [From Middle English *miliaris, miliari,* skin disease characterized by miliary eruptions, from Medieval Latin *miliāris,* from Latin *miliārius,* of millet, from *milium,* millet. See MILLET.]

miliary tuberculosis *n.* An acute form of tuberculosis characterized by very small tubercles in various body organs, caused by the spread of tubercle bacilli through the bloodstream.

mi·lieu (mĭl-yo͞o′, mē-lyœ′) *n., pl.* **-lieus** or **-lieux** (-lyœ′). An environment or a setting. [French, from Old French, center : *mi,* middle (from Latin *medius;* see **medhyo-** in Appendix) + *lieu,* place (from Latin *locus*).]

Mi·li·la·ni Town (mē′lē-lä′nē). A community of south-central Oahu, Hawaii, a suburb of Honolulu. Population, 20,351.

mil·i·tant (mĭl′ĭ-tənt) *adj.* **1.** Fighting or warring. **2.** Having a combative character; aggressive, especially in the service of a cause: *a militant political activist.* **—militant** *n.* A fighting, warring, or aggressive person or party. [Middle English, from Old French, from Latin *mīlitāns, mīlitant-,* present participle of *mīlitāre,* to serve as a soldier. See MILITATE.] **—mil′i·tance, mil′i·tan·cy** *n.* **—mil′i·tant·ly** *adv.*

mil·i·tar·i·a (mĭl′ĭ-târ′ē-ə) *pl.n.* Objects, such as weapons, that are connected with warfare or military service and are usually collected for their historical interest. [MILITARY + –IA[2].]

mil·i·ta·rism (mĭl′ĭ-tə-rĭz′əm) *n.* **1.** Glorification of the ideals of a professional military class. **2.** Predominance of the armed forces in the administration or policy of the state. **3.** A policy in which military preparedness is of primary importance to a state. **—mil′i·ta·rist** *n.* **—mil′i·ta·ris′tic** (-rĭs′tĭk) *adj.* **—mil′i·ta·ris′ti·cal·ly** *adv.*

mil·i·ta·rize (mĭl′ĭ-tə-rīz′) *tr.v.* **-rized, -riz·ing, -riz·es. 1.** To equip or train for war. **2.** To imbue with militarism. **3.** To adopt for use by or in the military. **—mil′i·ta·ri·za′tion** (-tər-ĭ-zā′shən) *n.*

mil·i·tar·y (mĭl′ĭ-tĕr′ē) *adj. Abbr.* **mil. 1.** Of, relating to, or characteristic of members of the armed forces: *a military bearing; military attire.* **2.** Performed or supported by the armed forces: *military service.* **3.** Of or relating to war: *military operations.* **4.** Of or relating to land forces. **—military** *n., pl.* **military** also **-ies. 1.** Armed forces: *a country ruled by the military.* **2.** Members, especially officers, of an armed force. [Middle English, from Latin *mīlitāris,* from *mīles, mīlit-,* soldier.] **—mil′i·tar′i·ly** (-târ′ə-lē) *adv.*

military attaché *n.* An officer in the armed forces who is assigned to the official staff of an ambassador, a consul general, or a minister.

military intelligence *n. Abbr.* **MI 1.** Information relating to the armed forces of a foreign country that is significant to the planning and conduct of another country's military doctrine, policy, and operations. **2.** An agency of the armed forces that procures, analyzes, and uses information of tactical and strategic military value.

military law *n.* The statutes, codes, and common traditions relating to and executed by military courts for the discipline, trial, and punishment of military personnel.

military police *n. Abbr.* **MP, M.P.** The branch of an armed force assigned to perform law enforcement duties, as on a military installation.

military science *n.* The principles of military conflict and of warfare.

mil·i·tate (mĭl′ĭ-tāt′) *intr.v.* **-tat·ed, -tat·ing, -tates.** To have force or influence; bring about an effect or a change: *"All these factors militated to a different targeting priority"* (Tom Clancy). *"The chaste banality of his prose . . . militates against the* *stories' becoming literature"* (Anthony Burgess). [Latin *mīlitāre, mīlitāt-*, to serve as a soldier, from *mīles, mīlit-*, soldier.]

mi·li·tes glo·ri·o·si (mē′lĭ-tās glôr′ē-ō′sē, glōr′-) *n.* Plural of **miles gloriosus.**

mi·li·tia (mə-lĭsh′ə) *n. Abbr.* **mil. 1.** An army composed of ordinary citizens rather than professional soldiers. **2.** A military force that is not part of a regular army and is subject to call for service in an emergency. **3.** The whole body of physically fit civilians eligible by law for military service. [Latin *mīlitia*, warfare, military service, from *mīles, mīlit-*, soldier.]

mi·li·tia·man (mə-lĭsh′ə-mən) *n.* A man who is a member of a militia.

mil·i·um (mĭl′ē-əm) *n., pl.* **-i·a** (-ē-ə). A small cystlike mass just below the surface of the skin, caused by retention of the secretion of a sebaceous gland. Also called *whitehead.* [Middle English, millet, from Latin. See **mele-** in Appendix.]

milk (mĭlk) *n.* **1.** A whitish liquid containing proteins, fats, lactose, and various vitamins and minerals that is produced by the mammary glands of all mature female mammals after they have given birth and serves as nourishment for their young. **2.** The milk of cows, goats, or other animals, used as food by human beings. **3.** A liquid, such as coconut milk, milkweed sap, plant latex, or various medical emulsions, that is similar to milk in appearance. *—attributive.* Often used to modify another noun: *milk cows; milk products.* **—milk** *v.* **milked, milk·ing, milks.** *—tr.* **1.a.** To draw milk from the teat or udder of (a female mammal). **b.** To draw or extract a liquid from: *milked the stem for its last drops of sap.* **2.** To press out, drain off, or remove by or as if by milking: *milk venom from a snake.* **3.** *Informal.* **a.** To draw out or extract something from, as if by milking: *milked the witness for information.* **b.** To obtain money or benefits from, in order to achieve personal gain; exploit: *"The dictator and his cronies had milked their country of somewhere between $5 billion and $10 billion"* (Russell Watson). *—intr.* **1.** To yield or supply milk. **2.** To draw milk from a female mammal. [Middle English, from Old English *milc.* See **melg-** in Appendix.] **—milk′er** *n.*

milk adder *n.* See **milk snake.**

milk-and-wa·ter (mĭlk′ən-wô′tər, -wŏt′ər) *adj.* Insipid; weak; wishy-washy.

milk chocolate *n.* Sweetened chocolate made with milk and other ingredients.

milk fever *n.* **1.** A mild fever, usually occurring at the beginning of lactation, associated with infection following childbirth. **2.** A disease affecting dairy cows and occasionally sheep or goats, especially soon after giving birth.

milk·fish (mĭlk′fĭsh′) *n., pl.* **milkfish** or **-fish·es.** A large silvery fish *(Chanos chanos)* of the South Pacific and Indian oceans, widely used for food. [From its color.]

milk glass *n.* An opaque or translucent whitish glass.

milk leg *n.* A painful swelling of the leg occurring in women after childbirth as a result of clotting and inflammation of the femoral veins.

milk·maid (mĭlk′mād′) *n.* A girl or woman who milks cows.

milk·man (mĭlk′măn′) *n.* A man who sells or delivers milk to customers.

milk of magnesia *n.* A milky white aqueous suspension of magnesium hydroxide, $Mg(OH)_2$, used as an antacid and a laxative.

Milk River (mĭlk). A river rising in the Rocky Mountains of northwest Montana and flowing about 1,006 km (625 mi) northward to southern Alberta then east and south back to northern Montana, where it joins the Missouri River.

milk run *n. Slang.* A routine trip involving many stops.

♦ **milk shake** *n.* **1.** A beverage made of milk, flavoring, and ice cream, shaken or whipped until foamy. Also called ♦*cabinet,* ♦*frappé,* ♦*shake,* ♦*velvet.* **2.** *New England.* A beverage made of milk and flavored syrup, whipped until foamy.

♦ ***REGIONAL NOTE:*** To most Americans, a milk shake, that thick, sweet accompaniment to a hamburger and fries, naturally includes ice cream. But speakers in parts of New England make finer distinctions in their ice cream terminology. To a person living in Rhode Island or the adjoining part of Massachussetts, a milk shake consists of milk shaken up with flavored syrup and nothing more; if ice cream is included, the drink is called a *cabinet,* possibly, says food writer John F. Mariani in *The Dictionary of American Food and Drink,* named after the square wooden cabinet in which the mixer was encased. Farther north in New England, the same drink is called a *velvet* or a *frappé* (from French *frapper,* "to ice"). Other ice cream drinks and concoctions are known by different terms in various parts of the country: a banana split is called a *houseboat* in some locales, and a float made of root beer and vanilla ice cream is called a *black cow* in Chicago.

milk sickness *n.* **1.** An acute, now rare disease characterized by trembling, vomiting, and severe intestinal pain that affects individuals who eat dairy products or meat from a cow that has fed on white snakeroot. **2.** See **tremble** (sense 3b).

milk snake *n.* Any of various nonvenomous grayish or tan king snakes of the species *Lampropeltis triangulum* of the southeast and central United States and Mexico, often having red, yellow, and black markings. Also called *house snake, milk adder.* [From the claim that it sucks milk from cows.]

milk·sop (mĭlk′sŏp′) *n.* A man lacking courage and other qualities deemed manly. **—milk′sop′py** *adj.*

milk sugar *n.* See **lactose.**

milk toast *n.* Toast, usually buttered, served in warm milk, often with sugar or seasonings.

milk tooth *n.* Any of the temporary first teeth of a young mammal. Also called *baby tooth, primary tooth.*

milk vetch *n.* Any of various plants of the genus *Astragalus,* having pinnate, compound leaves and clusters of purple, white, or yellowish flowers. [From the belief that it increases the milk yield of goats.]

milk·weed (mĭlk′wēd′) *n.* Any of numerous plants of the genus *Asclepias,* having milky juice, usually opposite leaves, variously colored flowers grouped in umbels, and pods that split open to release seeds with downy tufts. Also called *silkweed.*

milkweed

milkweed butterfly *n.* See **monarch butterfly.**

milk·wort (mĭlk′wûrt′, -wôrt′) *n.* Any of various plants of the genus *Polygala,* having variously colored, irregular flowers with two petaloid sepals. [From the belief that it increases human lactation.]

milk·y (mĭl′kē) *adj.* **-i·er, -i·est. 1.** Resembling milk in color or consistency: *milky glass.* **2.** Filled with, consisting of, or yielding milk or a fluid resembling milk: *a milky kernel of corn.* **3.** Meek; timid. **—milk′i·ness** *n.*

milky disease *n.* A bacterial disease of Japanese beetle larvae and other scarabaeid grubs that eventually turns the grub a milky white color. Also called *milky spore disease.*

Milk·y Way (mĭl′kē) *n.* The galaxy containing the solar system, visible as a broad band of faint light in the night sky. [Middle English, translation of Latin *via lactea* : *via,* way + *lactea,* milky.]

♦ **mill**[1] (mĭl) *n.* **1.a.** A building equipped with machinery for grinding grain into flour or meal. **b.** A device or mechanism that grinds grain. **2.** A machine or device that reduces a solid or coarse substance into pulp or minute grains by crushing, grinding, or pressing: *a pepper mill.* **3.** A machine that releases the juice of fruits and vegetables by pressing or grinding: *a cider mill.* **4.a.** A machine, such as one for stamping coins, that produces something by the repetition of a simple process. **b.** A steel roller bearing a raised design, used for making a die or a printing plate by pressure. **c.** Any of various machines for shaping, cutting, polishing, or dressing metal surfaces. **5.a.** A building or group of buildings equipped with machinery for processing raw materials into finished or industrial products: *a textile mill; a steel mill.* **b.** A building or collection of buildings that has machinery for manufacture; a factory. **6.** A process, an agency, or an institution that operates in a routine way or turns out products in the manner of a factory: *The college was nothing more than a diploma mill.* **7.** A slow or laborious process: *It took three years to get the bill through the legislative mill.* **—mill** *v.* **milled, mill·ing, mills.** *—tr.* **1.** To grind, pulverize, or break down into smaller particles in a mill. **2.** To transform or process mechanically in a mill. **3.** To shape, polish, dress, or finish in a mill or with a milling tool. **4.a.** To produce a ridge around the edge of (a coin). **b.** To groove or flute the rim of (a coin or other metal object). **5.** To agitate or stir until foamy. **6.** *Western U.S.* To halt (a cattle stampede) by turning the lead animals in a wide arc so that they form the center of a gradually tightening spiral. *—intr.* **1.** To move around in churning confusion: *"A crowd of school children milled about on the curb looking scared"* (Anne Tyler). **2.** *Slang.* To fight with the fists; box. **3.** To undergo milling. [Middle English *milne, mille,* from Old English *mylen,* from Late Latin *molīna, molīnum,* from feminine and neuter of *molīnus,* of a mill, from Latin *mola,* millstone, from *molere,* to grind. See **mele-** in Appendix.]

♦ ***REGIONAL NOTE:*** To *mill,* in Western U.S. English, means "to halt a cattle stampede by turning the lead animals." In the *Oxford English Dictionary* we find this 19th-century example of the verb: *"At last the cattle ran with less energy, and it was presently easy to 'mill' them into a circle and to turn them where it seemed most desirable"* (Munsey's Magazine). This usage of *mill* comes from the resemblance of the cattle's circular motion to the action of millstones. A related intransitive sense of the verb is better known in Standard English: *A crowd milled around in the street.* Originally this sense also meant "circular motion"; now it means "to move around in churning confusion" with no pattern in particular.

WORD HISTORY: Industrial mill towns are a far cry from the small water mill grinding grain near an Anglo-Saxon settlement, but the same word *mill* is used in both contexts, showing how the meaning of a word can be generalized. The Old English word *mylen,* "water mill for grinding grain," is itself adopted from Late Latin *molīna* or *molīnum,* "mill," just as the Germanic peoples, such as the Anglo-Saxons, adopted the water mill from the Romans. In Middle English *milne,* the descendant of the Old English word, was generalized to refer to a windmill, any power-driven mill for grinding grain, and a fulling mill. But it was left for the postmedieval, increasingly industrialized world really to generalize the meaning of *mill,* applying it to machines such as pepper mills and cider mills and buildings such as textile mills and steel mills. *Mill town* is first recorded in 1847.

mill[2] (mĭl) *n. Abbr.* **mi., M.** A monetary unit equal to $1/1000$ of a U.S. dollar or $1/10$ of a cent. [Short for Latin *millēsimus,* thousandth. See MIL.]

ă pat	oi boy
ā pay	ou out
âr care	ŏŏ took
ä father	ōō boot
ĕ pet	ŭ cut
ē be	ûr urge
ĭ pit	th thin
ī pie	*th* this
îr pier	hw which
ŏ pot	zh vision
ō toe	ə about, item
ô paw	♦ regionalism

Stress marks: **′** (primary); ′ (secondary), as in **dictionary** (dĭk′shə-nĕr′ē)

Edna Saint Vincent Millay
Photographed in 1933

Glenn Miller
Photographed in 1940

millinery

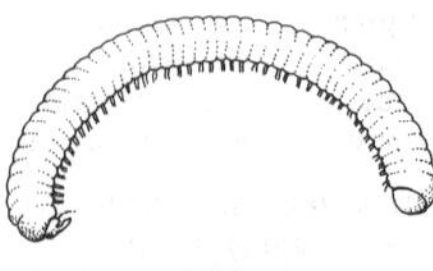
millipede

Mill (mĭl), **James.** 1773–1836. Scottish philosopher, economist, and a founder of utilitarianism.

Mill, John Stuart. 1806–1873. British philosopher and economist known especially for his interpretations of empiricism and utilitarianism. His many works include *Principles of Political Economy* (1848).

mill·age (mĭl′ĭj) *n.* A tax rate on property, expressed in mills per dollar of value of the property.

Mil·lais (mĭ-lā′), Sir **John Everett.** 1829–1896. British painter and founder of the Pre-Raphaelite Brotherhood (1848).

Mil·lay (mĭ-lā′), **Edna Saint Vincent.** 1892–1950. American poet whose volumes include *The Harp Weaver and Other Poems* (1923), for which she won a Pulitzer Prize.

mill·board (mĭl′bôrd′, -bōrd′) *n.* A stiff, heavy paperboard used primarily for book covers. [Alteration of *milled board.*]

Mill·brae (mĭl′brā′). A city of western California south of San Francisco. It is mainly residential. Population, 20,058.

Mill·burn (mĭl′bərn). A community of northeast New Jersey, a residential suburb west of Newark. Population, 19,543.

Mill·creek (mĭl′krēk′). A community of north-central Utah, a suburb of Salt Lake City. Population 24,150.

mill·dam (mĭl′dăm′) *n.* A dam constructed across a stream to raise the water level so that the overflow will have sufficient power to turn a mill wheel.

mil·le·nar·i·an (mĭl′ə-nâr′ē-ən) *adj.* **1.** Of or relating to a thousand, especially to a thousand years. **2.** Of, relating to, or believing in the doctrine of the millennium. —**millenarian** *n.* One who believes the millennium will occur. —**mil′le·nar′i·an·ism** *n.*

mil·le·nar·y (mĭl′ə-nĕr′ē, mə-lĕn′ə-rē) *adj.* **1.** Of or relating to a thousand, especially to a thousand years; millenarian. **2. a.** Of or relating to the doctrine of the millennium; millenarian. **b.** Of or relating to millenarians. —**millenary** *n., pl.* **-ies. 1.** A sum or total of one thousand, especially a thousand years. **2.** A millenarian. [Latin *millēnārius,* from *millēnī,* a thousand each, from *mīlle,* thousand. See **gheslo-** in Appendix.]

mill end *n.* An end portion of a roll of carpeting or fabric.

mil·len·ni·um (mə-lĕn′ē-əm) *n., pl.* **-len·ni·ums** or **-len·ni·a** (-lĕn′ē-ə). **1.** A span of one thousand years. **2.** A thousand-year period of holiness mentioned in Revelation 20, during which Jesus and his faithful followers are to rule on earth. **3.** A hoped-for period of joy, serenity, prosperity, and justice. **4.** A thousandth anniversary. [New Latin : Latin *mīlle,* thousand; see **gheslo-** in Appendix + Latin *annus,* year; see **at-** in Appendix.] —**mil·len′ni·al** (-əl) *adj.* —**mil·len′ni·al·ism** *n.* —**mil·len′ni·al·ist** *n.* —**mil·len′ni·al·ly** *adv.*

mil·le·pede (mĭl′ə-pēd′) *n.* Variant of **millipede.**

mil·le·pore (mĭl′ə-pôr′, -pōr′) *n.* Any of various reef-building hydrocorals of the order Milleporina of tropical marine waters, forming white or yellowish calcareous structures and resembling the true corals of the class Anthozoa. [Italian *millepora* : *mille,* thousand (from Latin *mīlle;* see **gheslo-** in Appendix) + *-pora* (alteration of *poro,* tufa, pore; see MADREPORE).]

mill·er (mĭl′ər) *n.* **1.** One who works in, operates, or owns a mill, especially a grain mill. **2.** A milling machine. **3.** Any of various moths whose wings and bodies have a powdery appearance.

Mil·ler (mĭl′ər), **Alice Duer.** 1874–1942. American writer whose best-known work, the narrative poem *The White Cliffs* (1940), describes Great Britain in the midst of World War II.

Miller, Arthur. Born 1915. American playwright whose works include *Death of a Salesman* (1949) and *The Crucible* (1953).

Miller, Glenn. 1909–1944. American bandleader and composer whose orchestra was one of the most popular groups of the big-band era.

Miller, Henry Valentine. 1891–1980. American writer whose novels *Tropic of Cancer* (1934) and *Tropic of Capricorn* (1939) were banned in the United States because of their sexual content.

Miller, Joaquin. Pseudonym of Cincinnatus Hiner Miller. 1837–1913. American poet whose work is based on his adventures in the West. His collections include *Joaquin et al.* (1869).

Miller, Samuel Freeman. 1816–1890. American jurist who served as an associate justice of the U.S. Supreme Court (1862–1890).

Miller, William. 1782–1849. American religious leader who preached that Christ's Second Coming would take place in 1843. Miller's followers organized the Advent Christian Church (1860).

mil·ler·ite (mĭl′ə-rīt′) *n.* A nickel sulfide mineral, NiS, usually occurring in long hairlike crystals and sometimes used as a nickel ore. [After William Hallowes *Miller* (1801–1880), British mineralogist.]

mill·er's thumb (mĭl′ərz) *n.* Any of several small freshwater sculpins of the genus *Cottus,* especially *C. gobio,* found in Europe and North America and having a large spiny head and spiny fins. [From its stocky, thumblike shape (the phrase *miller's thumb* was originally a folk expression referring to millers who gave short weight by tipping the scales with their thumbs).]

mil·les·i·mal (mə-lĕs′ə-məl) *adj.* **1.** Thousandth. **2.** Consisting of a thousandth. **3.** Relating to thousandths. —**millesimal** *n.* A thousandth. [From Latin *millēsimus,* from *mīlle,* thousand. See **gheslo-** in Appendix.] —**mil·les′i·mal·ly** *adv.*

mil·let (mĭl′ĭt) *n.* **1. a.** An annual grass *(Panicum milaiceum)* cultivated in Eurasia for its grains and in North America for hay. **b.** The white grains of this plant. **2.** Any of several similar or related grasses. [Middle English *milet,* from Old French, diminutive of *mil,* millet, from Latin *milium.* See **melə-** in Appendix.]

Mil·let (mĭ-lā′, mē-), **Jean François.** 1814–1875. French painter whose works, such as *The Gleaners* (1857) and *Winter with Ravens* (1862), portray peasant life and bucolic landscapes.

Mil·lett (mĭl′ĭt), **Kate.** Born 1934. American feminist leader who wrote *Sexual Politics* (1970).

mill finish *n.* A smooth surface made by machine on various papers. Also called *machine finish.*

milli– *pref.* One thousandth (10^{-3}): *millisecond.* [Latin *mīlli-,* from *mīlle,* thousand. See **gheslo-** in Appendix.]

mil·li·am·pere (mĭl′ē-ăm′pîr) *n. Abbr.* **mA** A unit of current equal to one thousandth (10^{-3}) of an ampere.

mil·liard (mĭl′yərd, -yärd′, mĭl′ē-ärd′) *n. Chiefly British.* The cardinal number equal to 10^9. [French, from Old French *milliart,* from *milion,* million. See MILLION.]

mil·li·ar·y (mĭl′ē-ĕr′ē) *adj.* Relating to or marking the distance of an ancient Roman mile, which equaled 1,000 paces. [Latin *mīlliārius,* consisting of a thousand, one mile long, from *mīlle (passuum),* a thousand (double paces), a Roman mile. See **gheslo-** in Appendix.]

mil·li·bar (mĭl′ə-bär′) *n. Abbr.* **mb** A unit of atmospheric pressure equal to one thousandth (10^{-3}) of a bar. Standard atmospheric pressure at sea level is about 1,013 millibars.

mil·li·cur·ie (mĭl′ĭ-kyo͝or′ē, -kyo͝o-rē′) *n. Abbr.* **mCi, mc** A unit of radioactivity equal to one thousandth (10^{-3}) of a curie.

mil·li·far·ad (mĭl′ə-făr′əd, -ăd) *n. Abbr.* **mf, mF** A unit of capacitance equal to one thousandth (10^{-3}) of a farad.

mil·li·gram (mĭl′ĭ-grăm′) *n. Abbr.* **mg** A unit of mass equal to one thousandth (10^{-3}) of a gram. See table at **measurement.**

mil·li·hen·ry (mĭl′ə-hĕn′rē) *n., pl.* **-rys** or **-ries.** *Abbr.* **mh, mH** A unit of inductance equal to one thousandth (10^{-3}) of a henry.

Mil·li·kan (mĭl′ĭ-kən), **Robert Andrews.** 1868–1953. American physicist. He won a 1923 Nobel Prize for his measurement of the electron charge.

mil·li·lam·bert (mĭl′ə-lăm′bərt) *n. Abbr.* **mL** A unit of luminance equal to one thousandth (10^{-3}) of a lambert.

mil·li·li·ter (mĭl′ə-lē′tər) *n. Abbr.* **ml, mL** A unit of volume equal to one thousandth (10^{-3}) of a liter. See table at **measurement.**

mil·li·li·tre (mĭl′ə-lē′tər) *n. Chiefly British.* Variant of **milliliter.**

mil·lime (mĭl′ĭm, -ēm) *n.* See table at **currency.** [French *millième,* thousandth, from Old French *milisme,* from Latin *millēsimus,* thousandth, from *mīlle,* thousand. See **gheslo-** in Appendix.]

mil·li·me·ter (mĭl′ə-mē′tər) *n. Abbr.* **mm** A unit of length equal to one thousandth (10^{-3}) of a meter, or 0.0394 inch. See table at **measurement.**

mil·li·me·tre (mĭl′ə-mē′tər) *n. Chiefly British.* Variant of **millimeter.**

mil·li·mi·cron (mĭl′ə-mī′krŏn) *n.* A unit of length equal to one thousandth (10^{-3}) of a micrometer or one billionth (10^{-9}) of a meter.

mil·li·mole (mĭl′ə-mōl′) *n.* One thousandth (10^{-3}) of a mole.

mil·line (mĭl′līn′) *n.* **1.** A unit of advertising copy equal to one agate line one column wide printed in one million copies of a publication. **2.** The cost of a unit of advertising copy. [MIL(LION) + LINE[1].]

mil·li·ner (mĭl′ə-nər) *n.* One that makes, trims, designs, or sells hats. [Probably alteration of Middle English *Milener,* native of Milan, from MILAN, the source of goods such as bonnets and lace.]

mil·li·ner·y (mĭl′ə-nĕr′ē) *n., pl.* **-ies. 1.** Articles, especially women's hats, sold by a milliner. **2.** The profession or business of a milliner.

mill·ing (mĭl′ĭng) *n.* **1.** The act or process of grinding, especially grinding grain into flour or meal. **2.** The operation of cutting, shaping, finishing, or working products manufactured in a mill. **3.** The ridges cut on the edges of coins.

Mill·ing·ton (mĭl′ĭng-tən). A city of southwest Tennessee north of Memphis. Population, 20,236.

mil·lion (mĭl′yən) *n., pl.* **million** or **-lions. 1.** The cardinal number equal to 10^6. **2.** A million monetary units, such as dollars: *made a million in the stock market.* **3.** Often **millions.** An indefinitely large number: *millions of bicycles on the road.* **4.** Often **millions.** The common people; the masses: *entertainment for the millions.* [Middle English, from Old French *milion,* probably from Old Italian *milione,* augmentative of *mille,* thousand, from Latin *mīlle.* See **gheslo-** in Appendix.] —**mil′lion** *adj.*

mil·lion·aire (mĭl′yə-nâr′) *n.* A person whose wealth amounts to at least a million dollars, pounds, or the equivalent in other currency. [French *millionnaire,* from *million,* million, from Old French *milion.* See MILLION.]

mil·lionth (mĭl′yənth) *n.* **1.** The ordinal number matching the number million in a series. **2.** One of a million equal parts. —**mil′lionth** *adv. & adj.*

mil·li·pede or **mil·le·pede** (mĭl′ə-pēd′) *n.* Any of various crawling, herbivorous myriapods of the class Diplopoda, found worldwide and having a cylindrical, segmented body with two pairs of legs attached to all segments except for the first four in the thoracic region. Also called *diplopod.* [Latin *mīlipeda,* a kind of insect : *mīlle,* thousand; see **gheslo-** in Appendix + *pēs, ped-,* foot; see **ped-** in Appendix.]

mil·li·sec·ond (mĭl′ĭ-sĕk′ənd) *n. Abbr.* **ms, msec** One thousandth (10^{-3}) of a second.

mil·li·volt (mĭl′ə-vōlt′) *n. Abbr.* **mV** A unit of potential difference equal to one thousandth (10^{-3}) of a volt.

mil·li·watt (mĭl′ə-wŏt′) *n. Abbr.* **mW** A unit of power equal to one thousandth (10^{-3}) of a watt.

mill·pond (mĭl′pŏnd′) *n.* A pond formed by a milldam.

mill·race (mĭl′rās′) *n.* **1.** The fast-moving stream of water that drives a mill wheel. **2.** The channel for the water that drives a mill wheel. Also called *millrun.*

mill·run (mĭl′rŭn′) *n.* **1.** See **millrace.** **2.** The output of a sawmill. **3.a.** A test of the mineral quality or content of an ore by milling. **b.** The mineral yielded by this test.

mill-run (mĭl′rŭn′) *adj.* Being in the state in which a product leaves a mill; unsorted and uninspected: *mill-run fabric.*

mill·stone (mĭl′stōn′) *n.* **1.** One of a pair of cylindrical stones used in a mill for grinding grain. **2.** A heavy weight; a burden: *This job is a millstone around my neck.*

mill·stream (mĭl′strēm′) *n.* The rapid stream of water flowing in a millrace.

Mill·ville (mĭl′vĭl′). A city of southern New Jersey west of Atlantic City. Settled in the 18th century, it has varied light industries. Population, 24,815.

mill wheel *n.* A wheel, typically driven by water, that powers a mill.

mill·work (mĭl′wûrk′) *n.* Woodwork, such as doors, window casings, and baseboards, ready-made by a lumber mill.

mill·wright (mĭl′rīt′) *n.* One that designs, builds, or repairs mills or mill machinery.

Milne (mĭln), **A(lan) A(lexander).** 1882–1956. British writer known especially for the children's books *Winnie-the-Pooh* (1926) and *The House at Pooh Corner* (1928).

mi·lo (mī′lō) *n., pl.* **-los.** An early-growing, usually drought-resistant grain sorghum resembling millet. [Possibly from Afrikaans *mealie,* corn, probably from Portuguese *milho,* from Latin *milium,* millet. See MILLET.]

Mi·lo (mē′lō, mī′-). See **Milos.**

mi·lord (mĭ-lôrd′) *n.* **1.** An English nobleman or gentleman. **2.** Used as a form of address for such a man. [French, from English *my lord.*]

Mi·los also **Me·los** (mē′lôs) or **Mi·lo** (mē′lō, mī′-). An island of southeast Greece in the Cyclades Islands of the Aegean Sea. It was a flourishing trade and obsidian-mining center in ancient times but lost importance when bronze replaced obsidian as a material for tools and weapons.

Mi·losz (mē′lŏsh′, -wŏsh′), **Czeslaw.** Born 1911. Polish-born American writer whose poetry, fiction, and essays often explore the role of intellect and ideology in politics. He won the 1980 Nobel Prize for literature.

Mil·pi·tas (mĭl-pē′təs). A city of western California north of San Jose. Population, 37,820.

milque·toast (mĭlk′tōst′) *n.* One who has a meek, timid, unassertive nature. [After Caspar *Milquetoast,* a comic-strip character created by Harold Tucker Webster (1885–1952).] **—milque′toast′y** *adj.*

WORD HISTORY: An indication of the effect on the English language of popular culture such as that found in comic strips is the adoption of names from the strips as English words. Casper Milquetoast, created by Harold Webster in 1924, was a timid and retiring man, whose name was, of course, created from the name of a timid food. The first instance of *milquetoast* as a common noun is found in the mid-1930's. *Milquetoast* thus joins the ranks of other such words, including *sad sack,* from a blundering army private invented by George Baker in 1942, and *Wimpy,* from J. Wellington Wimpy in the *Popeye* comic strip, which became a trade name for a hamburger. If we look to the related world of the animated cartoon, we must of course acknowledge *Mickey Mouse,* which has become a slang term for something that is easy, insignificant, small-time, worthless, or petty.

milt (mĭlt) *n.* **1.a.** Fish sperm, including the seminal fluid. **b.** The reproductive glands of male fishes when filled with this fluid. **2.** The spleen of certain vertebrate animals, such as cows or pigs. **—milt** *tr.v.* **milt·ed, milt·ing, milts.** To fertilize (fish roe) with milt. [Middle English, roe, spleen, partly from Middle Dutch *milte* and partly from Old English *milte,* spleen; see **mel-**[1] in Appendix.]

milt·er (mĭl′tər) *n.* A male fish that is ready to breed.

Mil·ti·a·des (mĭl-tī′ə-dēz′). 540?–489? B.C. Athenian general who defeated the Persians in the Battle of Marathon (490 B.C.).

Mil·ton (mĭl′tən). **1.** A town of southeast Ontario west-southwest of Toronto. It is an industrial center. Population, 28,067. **2.** A town of eastern Massachusetts, a residential suburb of Boston. Population, 25,860.

Milton, John. 1608–1674. English poet and scholar who is best known for the epic poem *Paradise Lost* (1667), an account of humanity's fall from grace.

Milton Keynes (kēnz). A town of south-central England northeast of Oxford. It was designated as a new town in 1967 to alleviate overcrowding in London. Population, 126,500.

Mil·wau·kee (mĭl-wô′kē). A city of southeast Wisconsin on Lake Michigan. Established as a fur-trading post in 1795, it was a major center of German immigration during the last half of the 19th century. Population, 636,212.

Mil·wau·kie (mĭl-wô′kē). A city of northwest Oregon, a suburb of Portland on the Willamette River. Population, 17,931.

Mi·mas (mī′măs, mē′-) *n.* The satellite of Saturn that is sixth in distance from the planet. [After *Mimas,* one of the Giants slain by Hercules.]

Mim·bres (mĭm′brĭs) *n.* The final period of the Mogollon culture, from the 9th to the 13th century, noted for its distinctive pottery bowls painted with black-on-white designs. [Spanish, pl. of *mimbre,* willow, withy, wicker, variant of *vimbre,* from Latin *vīmen, vīmin-.* See **wei-** in Appendix.]

mime (mīm) *n.* **1.a.** A form of ancient Greek and Roman theatrical entertainment in which familiar characters and situations were farcically portrayed on stage, often with coarse dialogue and ludicrous actions. **b.** A performance of or dialogue for such an entertainment. **c.** A performer in a mime. **2.** A modern performer who specializes in comic mimicry. **3.a.** The art of portraying characters and acting out situations or a narrative by gestures and body movement without the use of words; pantomime. **b.** A performance of pantomime. **c.** An actor or actress skilled in pantomime. **—mime** *v.* **mimed, mim·ing, mimes.** *—tr.* **1.** To ridicule by imitation; mimic. **2.** To act out with gestures and body movement. *—intr.* **1.** To act as a mimic. **2.** To portray characters and situations by gesture and body movement. [Latin *mīmus,* from Greek *mimos.*] **—mim′er** *n.*

mim·e·o (mĭm′ē-ō′) *Informal. n., pl.* **-os.** A mimeograph. **—mimeo** *tr.v.* **-oed, -o·ing, -os.** To mimeograph.

mim·e·o·graph (mĭm′ē-ə-grăf′) *n.* **1.** A duplicator that makes copies of written, drawn, or typed material from a stencil that is fitted around an inked drum. **2.** A copy made by this method of duplication. **—mimeograph** *v.* **-graphed, -graph·ing, -graphs.** *—tr.* To make (copies) on a mimeograph. *—intr.* To use a mimeograph. [Originally a trademark.]

mi·me·sis (mĭ-mē′sĭs, mī-) *n.* **1.** The imitation or representation of aspects of the sensible world, especially human actions, in literature and art. **2.** *Biology.* Mimicry. **3.** *Medicine.* The appearance, often caused by hysteria, of symptoms of a disease not actually present. [Greek *mimēsis,* from *mimeisthai,* to imitate, from *mimos,* imitator, mime.]

mi·met·ic (mĭ-mĕt′ĭk, mī-) *adj.* **1.** Relating to, characteristic of, or exhibiting mimicry. **2.a.** Of or relating to an imitation; imitative. **b.** Using imitative means of representation: *a mimetic dance.* [Greek *mimētikos,* from *mimēsis,* mimicry. See MIMESIS.] **—mi·met′i·cal·ly** *adv.*

mim·ic (mĭm′ĭk) *tr.v.* **-icked, -ick·ing, -ics. 1.** To copy or imitate closely, especially in speech, expression, and gesture; ape. **2.** To copy or imitate so as to ridicule; mock: *always mimicking the boss.* See Synonyms at **imitate.** **3.** To resemble closely; simulate: *an insect that mimics a twig.* **4.** To take on the appearance of. **—mimic** *n.* **1.** One who imitates, especially: **a.** An actor or actress in a mime. **b.** One who practices the art of mime. **c.** One who copies or mimics others, as for amusement. **2.** A copy or an imitation. **—mimic** *adj.* **1.** Relating to, acting as, resembling, or characteristic of a mimic or mimicry. **2.a.** Tending to imitate; imitative. **b.** Make-believe; mock: *a mimic battle.* [From Latin *mīmicus,* mimic, from Greek *mimikos,* from *mimos,* imitator, mime.] **—mim′ick·er** *n.*

mim·ic·ry (mĭm′ĭ-krē) *n., pl.* **-ries. 1.a.** The act, practice, or art of mimicking. **b.** An instance of mimicking. **2.** *Biology.* The resemblance of one organism to another or to an object in its surroundings for concealment and protection from predators.

Mi·mir (mē′mîr′) *n. Mythology.* A Norse giant who lived by the roots of Yggdrasil, where he guarded the well of wisdom. [Old Norse. See **(s)mer-**[1] in Appendix.]

mi·mo·sa (mĭ-mō′sə, -zə) *n.* **1.** Any of various mostly tropical herbs, shrubs, and trees of the genus *Mimosa,* having globular heads of small flowers with protruding stamens and usually bipinnate, compound leaves that are often sensitive to touch or light. **2.** See **silk tree.** **3.** A drink consisting of champagne and orange juice. [New Latin *Mimosa,* genus name, from Latin *mīmus,* mime (from the plant's apparent mimicry of animal reactions), from Greek *mimos.*]

min. *abbr.* **1.a.** Mineralogical. **b.** Mineralogy. **2.** Minim. **3.** Minimum. **4.** Mining. **5.** Minister. **6.** Minor. **7.** Also **min.** Minute.

mi·na[1] (mī′nə) *n., pl.* **-nas** or **-nae** (-nē). A varying unit of weight or money used in ancient Greece and Asia. [Latin, from Greek *mna,* from Akkadian *manû,* a unit of weight.]

mi·na[2] (mī′nə) *n.* Variant of **myna.**

min·a·ble or **mine·a·ble** (mī′nə-bəl) *adj.* That can be mined: *a minable seam of gold.*

mi·na·cious (mĭ-nā′shəs) *adj.* Of a menacing or threatening nature; minatory. [Latin *mināx, mināc-* (from *minārī,* to threaten, from *minae,* threats; see **men-**[2] in Appendix) + -IOUS.] **—mi·na′cious·ness, mi·nac′i·ty** (mĭ-năs′ĭ-tē) *n.*

mi·nae (mī′nē) *n.* A plural of **mina**[1].

Min·a·ma·ta disease (mĭn′ə-mä′tə) *n.* A degenerative neurological disorder caused by poisoning with a mercury compound found in seafood obtained from waters contaminated with

ă **pat**	oi **boy**
ā **pay**	ou **out**
âr **care**	o͝o **took**
ä **father**	o͞o **boot**
ĕ **pet**	ŭ **cut**
ē **be**	ûr **urge**
ĭ **pit**	th **thin**
ī **pie**	*th* **this**
îr **pier**	hw **which**
ŏ **pot**	zh **vision**
ō **toe**	ə **about, item**
ô **paw**	♦ **regionalism**

Stress marks: **′** (primary); ′ (secondary), as in **dictionary** (dĭk′shə-nĕr′ē)

minaret
At the Blue Mosque in Istanbul, Turkey, designed for Ahmed I (1590–1617) by Mehmed Aga (fl. late 16th century and early 17th century)

mercury-containing industrial waste. [After *Minamata,* a town of western Kyushu, Japan.]

min·a·ret (mĭn′ə-rĕt′) *n.* A tall, slender tower on a mosque, having one or more projecting balconies from which a muezzin summons the people to prayer. [French, from Turkish *minārat,* from Arabic *manārah,* lamp.]

Mi·nas Basin (mī′nəs). An arm of the Bay of Fundy extending into west-central Nova Scotia, Canada. It is connected with the bay by the **Minas Channel.**

min·a·to·ry (mĭn′ə-tôr′ē, -tōr′ē) also **min·a·to·ri·al** (mĭn′ə-tôr′ē-əl, -tōr′-) *adj.* Of a menacing or threatening nature; minacious. [French *minatoire,* from Late Latin *minātōrius,* from Latin *minātus,* past participle of *minārī,* to threaten. See MINACIOUS.] **—min′a·to′ri·ly** *adv.*

min·au·dière (mē′nō-dyâr′) *n., pl.* **-dières** (-dyârz′, -dyâr′). A small ornamental case for a woman's cosmetics, jewelry, or personal items that is often carried as a handbag. [French, from feminine of *minaudier,* affected, smirking, from *minauder,* to simper, smirk, from *mine,* appearance, countenance, from Old French, probably from Breton *min,* muzzle.]

mince (mĭns) *v.* **minced, minc·ing, minc·es.** *—tr.* **1.a.** To cut or chop into very small pieces. **b.** To subdivide (land, for example) into minute parts. **2.** To pronounce in an affected way, as with studied elegance and refinement. **3.** To moderate or restrain (words) for the sake of politeness and decorum; euphemize: *Don't mince words: say what you mean.* *—intr.* **1.** To walk with very short steps or with exaggerated primness. **2.** To speak in an affected way. **—mince** *n.* Finely chopped food, especially mincemeat. [Middle English *mincen,* from Old French *mincier,* from Vulgar Latin **minūtiāre,* from Latin *minūtia,* smallness. See MINUTIA.] **—minc′er** *n.*

mince·meat (mĭns′mēt′) *n.* **1.** A mixture, as of finely chopped apples, raisins, spices, meat, and sometimes rum or brandy, used especially as a pie filling. **2.** Finely chopped meat. ***—idiom.*** **make mincemeat of.** *Slang.* To destroy utterly: *made mincemeat of the opponent's argument.*

Minch (mĭnch). A channel, divided into **North Minch** and **Little Minch,** separating northwest Scotland from the Outer Hebrides.

minc·ing (mĭn′sĭng) *adj.* Affectedly refined or dainty. **—minc′ing·ly** *adv.*

♦ **mind** (mīnd) *n.* **1.** The human consciousness that originates in the brain and is manifested especially in thought, perception, emotion, will, memory, and imagination. **2.** The collective conscious and unconscious processes in a sentient organism that direct and influence mental and physical behavior. **3.** The principle of intelligence; the spirit of consciousness regarded as an aspect of reality. **4.** The faculty of thinking, reasoning, and applying knowledge: *Follow your mind, not your heart.* **5.** A person of great mental ability: *the great minds of the century.* **6.a.** Individual consciousness, memory, or recollection: *I'll bear the problem in mind.* **b.** A person or group that embodies certain mental qualities: *the medical mind; the public mind.* **c.** The thought processes characteristic of a person or group; psychological makeup: *the criminal mind.* **7.** Opinion or sentiment: *He changed his mind when he heard all the facts.* **8.** Desire or inclination: *She had a mind to spend her vacation in the desert.* **9.** Focus of thought; attention: *I can't keep my mind on work.* **10.** A healthy mental state; sanity: *losing one's mind.* **11. Mind.** *Christian Science.* The Deity regarded as the perfect intelligence ruling over all of divine creation. **—mind** *v.* **mind·ed, mind·ing, minds.** *—tr.* **1.** To bring (an object or idea) to mind; remember. **2.a.** To become aware of; notice. **b.** *Upper Southern U.S.* To have in mind as a goal or purpose; intend. **3.** To heed in order to obey: *The children mind well.* **4.** To attend to: *Mind closely what I tell you.* **5.** To be careful about: *Mind the icy sidewalk!* **6.a.** To care about; be concerned about. **b.** To object to; dislike: *doesn't mind doing the chores.* **7.** To take care or charge of; look after. *—intr.* **1.** To take notice; give heed. **2.** To behave obediently. **3.** To be concerned or troubled; care: *"Not minding about bad food has become a national obsession"* (Times Literary Supplement). **4.** To be cautious or careful. [Middle English *minde,* from Old English *gemynd.* See **men-**[1] in Appendix.] **—mind′er** *n.*

SYNONYMS: *mind, intellect, intelligence, brain, wit, reason.* These nouns denote the faculty of thinking, reasoning, and acquiring and applying knowledge. *Mind,* opposed to *heart, soul,* or *spirit,* refers broadly to the capacities for thought, perception, memory, and decision: *"No passion so effectually robs the mind of all its powers of acting and reasoning as fear"* (Edmund Burke). *Intellect* stresses the capacity for knowing, thinking, and understanding as contrasted with feeling and willing: *"Opinion is ultimately determined by the feelings, and not by the intellect"* (Herbert Spencer). *Intelligence* implies the capacity for solving problems, learning from experience, and reasoning abstractly: *"The world of the future will be an ever more demanding struggle against the limitations of our intelligence"* (Norbert Wiener). *Brain* suggests strength of intellect: *Anyone with a brain knows that overwork leads to decreased efficiency. Many of the most successful people are endowed with brains, talent, and perseverance. Wit* stresses quickness of intelligence or facility of comprehension: *"There is no such whetstone, to sharpen a good wit and encourage a will to learning, as is praise"* (Roger Ascham). *He lacks formal education but is adept at living by his wits. Reason,* the capacity for logical, rational, and analytic thought, embraces comprehending, evaluating, and drawing conclusions: *"I am sure that, since I have had the full use of my reason, nobody has ever heard me laugh"* (Earl of Chesterfield). See also Synonyms at **tend**[2]**.**

mind-al·ter·ing (mīnd′ôl′tər-ĭng) *adj.* Producing mood changes or distorted perceptions: *a mind-altering drug.*

Min·da·na·o (mĭn′də-nä′ō, -nou′). An island of the southern Philippines northeast of Borneo. The **Mindanao Sea** borders the island on the west.

mind-bend·ing (mīnd′bĕn′dĭng) *adj. Informal.* Intensely affecting the mind, especially to the extent of producing hallucinations. **—mind′-bend′er** *n.* **—mind′-bend′ing·ly** *adv.*

mind-blow·ing (mīnd′blō′ĭng) *adj. Informal.* **1.** Producing hallucinatory effects: *mind-blowing drugs.* **2.** Intensely affecting the mind or emotions: *a mind-blowing horror story.* **—mind′-blow′er** *n.*

mind-bog·gling (mīnd′bŏg′lĭng) *adj. Informal.* Intellectually or emotionally overwhelming: *"a mind-boggling bazaar of competing manufacturers and overlapping technologies"* (William D. Marbach). **—mind′-bog′gler** *n.*

mind·ed (mīn′dĭd) *adj.* **1.** Disposed; inclined: *I am not minded to answer any of your questions.* **2.** Having a specified kind of mind. Often used in combination: *fair-minded; evil-minded.* **3.** Directed or oriented toward something specified. Often used in combination: *civic-minded; career-minded.* **—mind′ed·ness** *n.*

Min·den (mĭn′dən). A city of northwest Germany on the Weser River south of Bremen. Settled in Roman times, it was founded c. 800 as a bishopric by Charlemagne. Minden joined the Hanseatic League in the 13th century and passed to Prussia in 1814. Population, 75,419.

mind-ex·pand·ing (mīnd′ĭk-spăn′dĭng) *adj.* **1.** Producing intensified or distorted perceptions; psychedelic. **2.** Producing an increased perceptive awareness: *The trip into the wilderness was a mind-expanding experience.*

mind·ful (mīnd′fəl) *adj.* Attentive; heedful: *always mindful of family responsibilities.* See Synonyms at **careful.** **—mind′ful·ly** *adv.* **—mind′ful·ness** *n.*

mind·less (mīnd′lĭs) *adj.* **1.a.** Lacking intelligence or good sense; foolish. **b.** Having no intelligent purpose, meaning, or direction: *mindless violence.* See Synonyms at **meaningless. 2.** Giving or showing little attention or care; heedless: *mindless of the dangers.* **—mind′less·ly** *adv.* **—mind′less·ness** *n.*

Min·do·ro (mĭn-dôr′ō, -dōr′ō). An island of the west-central Philippines south of Luzon.

mind reading *n.* The faculty of discerning another's thoughts through extrasensory means of communication; telepathy. **—mind reader** *n.*

mind·scape (mīnd′skāp′) *n.* **1.** A mental or psychological scene or area of the imagination: *"mindscapes, in which memories from an American childhood mingle with those from the fantasy world of the films"* (Grace Glueck). **2.** A representation of such a scene or an area, as in a work of art.

mind·set or **mind-set** (mīnd′sĕt′) *n.* **1.** A fixed mental attitude or disposition that predetermines a person's responses to and interpretations of situations. **2.** An inclination or a habit.

mind's eye (mīndz) *n.* **1.** The inherent mental ability to imagine or remember scenes. **2.** The imagination.

mine[1] (mīn) *n.* **1.a.** An excavation in the earth from which ore or minerals can be extracted. **b.** The site of such an excavation, with its surface buildings, elevator shafts, and equipment. **2.** A deposit of ore or minerals in the earth or on its surface. **3.** An abundant supply or source of something valuable: *This guidebook is a mine of information.* **4.a.** A tunnel dug under an enemy emplacement to gain an avenue of attack or to lay explosives. **b.** An explosive device used to destroy enemy personnel, shipping, fortifications, or equipment, often placed in a concealed position and designed to be detonated by contact, proximity, or a time fuse. **5.** A burrow or tunnel made by an insect, especially a corridor on a leaf made by a leaf miner. **—mine** *v.* **mined, min·ing, mines.** *—tr.* **1.a.** To extract (ore or minerals) from the earth. **b.** To dig a mine in (the earth) to obtain ore or minerals. **2.a.** To tunnel under (the earth or a surface feature). **b.** To make (a tunnel) by digging. **3.** To lay explosive mines in or under. **4.** To attack, damage, or destroy by underhand means; subvert. **5.** To delve into and make use of; exploit: *mine the archives for detailed information.* *—intr.* **1.a.** To excavate the earth for the purpose of extracting ore or minerals. **b.** To work in a mine. **2.** To dig a tunnel under the earth, especially under an enemy emplacement or fortification. **3.** To lay explosive mines. [Middle English, from Old French, from Vulgar Latin **mīna,* probably of Celtic origin.]

mine[2] (mīn) *pron. (used with a sing. or pl. verb).* Used to indicate the one or ones belonging to me: *The green gloves are mine. If you can't find your hat, take mine.* **—mine** *adj.* A possessive form of **I**[1]. *Archaic.* Used instead of *my* before an initial vowel or the letter *h.* [Middle English, from Old English *mīn.* See **me-**[1] in Appendix.]

mine·a·ble (mī′nə-bəl) *adj.* Variant of **minable.**

mine detector *n.* An electromagnetic device used to locate explosive mines. **—mine detection** *n.*

mine·field (mīn′fēld′) *n.* An area in which explosive mines have been placed.

mine·lay·er (mīn′lā′ər) *n.* A ship equipped for laying explosive underwater mines.

ă pat	oi boy
ā pay	ou out
âr care	o͝o took
ä father	o͞o boot
ĕ pet	ŭ cut
ē be	ûr urge
ĭ pit	th thin
ī pie	*th* this
îr pier	hw which
ŏ pot	zh vision
ō toe	ə about, item
ô paw	♦ regionalism

Stress marks: **′** (primary); ′ (secondary), as in **dictionary** (dĭk′shə-nĕr′ē)

Min·e·o·la (mĭn′ē-ō′lə). A village of southeast New York on west-central Long Island. Population, 20,757.

min·er (mī′nər) *n.* **1.** One whose work or business it is to extract ore or minerals from the earth. **2.** A machine for the automatic extraction of minerals, especially of coal. **3.** A member of a military unit engaged in laying explosive mines. **4.** *Zoology.* A leaf miner.

min·er·al (mĭn′ər-əl) *n.* **1.** A naturally occurring, homogeneous inorganic solid substance having a definite chemical composition and characteristic crystalline structure, color, and hardness. **2.** Any of various natural substances, as: **a.** An element, such as gold or silver. **b.** An organic derivative, such as coal or petroleum. **c.** A substance, such as stone, sand, salt, or coal, that is extracted or obtained from the ground or water and used in economic activities. **3.** A substance that is neither animal nor vegetable; inorganic matter. **4.** An inorganic element, such as calcium, iron, potassium, sodium, or zinc, that is essential to the nutrition of human beings, animals, and plants. **5.** An ore. **6. minerals.** *Chiefly British.* Mineral water. —**mineral** *adj.* **1.** Of or relating to minerals: *a mineral deposit.* **2.** Impregnated with minerals. [Middle English, from Medieval Latin *minerāle,* from neuter of *minerālis,* pertaining to mines, from Old French *miniere,* mine, from *mine.* See MINE[1].]

min·er·al·ize (mĭn′ər-ə-līz′) *v.* **-ized, -iz·ing, -iz·es.** —*tr.* **1.** To convert to a mineral substance; petrify. **2.** To transform a metal into a mineral by oxidation. **3.** To impregnate with minerals. —*intr.* **1.** To develop or hasten mineral formation. **2.** To collect or study minerals. —**min′er·al·iz′a·ble** *adj.* —**min′er·al·i·za′tion** (-ə-lĭ-zā′shən) *n.* —**min′er·al·iz′er** *n.*

mineral kingdom *n.* The group of natural objects and substances that are composed only of inorganic matter.

min·er·al·o·cor·ti·coid (mĭn′ər-ə-lō-kôr′tĭ-koid′) *n.* Any of a group of steroid hormones, such as aldosterone, that are secreted by the adrenal cortex and regulate the balance of water and electrolytes in the body.

min·er·al·o·gy (mĭn′ə-rŏl′ə-jē, -răl′-) *n., pl.* **-gies.** *Abbr.* **min. 1.** The study of minerals, including their distribution, identification, and properties. **2.** A book or treatise on mineralogy. —**min′er·a·log′i·cal** (-ər-ə-lŏj′ĭ-kəl) *adj.* —**min′er·a·log′i·cal·ly** *adv.* —**min′er·al′o·gist** *n.*

mineral oil *n.* **1.** Any of various light hydrocarbon oils, especially a distillate of petroleum. **2.** A refined distillate of petroleum, used as a laxative.

mineral tar *n.* Maltha.

mineral water *n.* Naturally occurring or prepared water that contains dissolved mineral salts, elements, or gases, often used therapeutically.

mineral wax *n.* Ozocerite.

mineral wool *n.* An inorganic fibrous substance that is produced by steam blasting and cooling molten glass or a similar substance and is used as an insulator and a filtering material. Also called *rock wool.*

min·er's lettuce (mī′nərz) *n.* See **winter purslane.**

Mi·ner·va (mĭ-nûr′və) *n.* *Roman Mythology.* The goddess of wisdom, invention, the arts, and martial prowess. [Latin. See **men-**[1] in Appendix.]

mine·shaft (mīn′shăft′) *n.* A vertical, sloping passageway made in the earth for finding or mining ore and ventilating underground excavations.

min·e·stro·ne (mĭn′ĭ-strō′nē) *n.* A thick soup of Italian origin containing assorted vegetables, beans, pasta such as vermicelli or macaroni, and herbs in a meat or vegetable broth. [Italian, augmentative of *minestra,* dish consisting of pasta, rice, vegetables or beans cooked in water, from Old Italian, from *minestrare,* to dish up, serve this dish, from Latin *ministrāre,* to serve food, from *minister,* servant. See **mei-**[2] in Appendix.]

WORD HISTORY: The thick vegetable soup known as *minestrone* did not come by its name because of its ingredients or their shape but rather because of service, something highly valued by many restaurant patrons. *Minestrone* is from the Italian word of the same form and sense, which in turn is derived from *minestra,* meaning "a dish generally consisting of pasta, rice, beans, or vegetables cooked in water." *Minestra* has been borrowed into English as well, being first recorded in 1750, while *minestrone* is first found in 1891. The Italian word *minestra* is from the verb *minestrare,* meaning "to serve this type of soup" or "dish up," which goes back to the Latin verb *ministrāre,* "to serve food," from Latin *minister,* "servant."

mine·sweep·er (mīn′swē′pər) *n.* A ship equipped for detecting, destroying, removing, or neutralizing explosive marine mines. —**mine′sweep′ing** *n.*

mine·work·er (mīn′wûr′kər) *n.* One who works in a mine; a miner.

Ming (mĭng). A Chinese dynasty (1368–1644) noted for its flourishing foreign trade, achievements in scholarship, and development of the arts, especially in porcelain. —**Ming** *adj.*

min·gle (mĭng′gəl) *v.* **-gled, -gling, -gles.** —*tr.* **1.** To mix or bring together in combination, usually without loss of individual characteristics. See Synonyms at **mix. 2.** To mix so that the components become united; merge. —*intr.* **1.** To be or become mixed or united. **2.** To join or take part with others: *The alumnae mingled with the trustees.* [Middle English *menglen,* frequentative of *mengen,* to mix, from Old English *mengan.* See **mag-** in Appendix.] —**min′gler** *n.*

min·gy (mĭn′jē) *adj.* **-gi·er, -gi·est.** *Informal.* **1.** Small in quantity; meager: *mingy wages.* **2.** Mean and stingy. [Perhaps from M(EAN)[2] + (ST)INGY.]

Mi·nho (mē′nyo͞o) or **Mi·ño** (-nyô). A river flowing about 338 km (210 mi) from northwest Spain south and southwest to the Atlantic Ocean.

min·i (mĭn′ē) *n., pl.* **min·is. 1.** Something, such as a minicomputer, that is distinctively smaller than other members of its type or class. **2.** A miniskirt. —**min′i** *adj.*

mini– *pref.* Small; miniature: *minicar.* [From MINIATURE and MINIMUM.]

min·i·a·ture (mĭn′ē-ə-cho͝or′, -chər, mĭn′ə-) *n.* **1.a.** A copy or model that represents or reproduces something in a greatly reduced size. **b.** Something small of its class. **2.a.** A small painting executed with great detail, often on a surface such as ivory. **b.** A small portrait, picture, or decorative letter on an illuminated manuscript. **c.** The art of painting miniatures. —**miniature** *adj.* Being on a small or greatly reduced scale. See Synonyms at **small.** [Italian *miniatura,* illumination of manuscripts, small painting, from *miniare,* to illuminate, from Latin *miniāre,* to color red, from *minium,* red lead.] —**min′i·a·tur′ist** *n.*

miniature golf *n.* *Games.* A novelty version of golf played with a putter and golf ball on a miniature course and featuring obstacles such as alleys, bridges, and tunnels.

min·i·a·tur·ize (mĭn′ē-ə-chə-rīz′, mĭn′ə-) *tr.v.* **-ized, -iz·ing, -iz·es.** To plan or make on a greatly reduced scale. —**min′i·a·tur′i·za′tion** (-chər-ĭ-zā′shən) *n.*

miniature pinscher *n.* Any of a breed of small dogs resembling the Doberman pinscher but typically reaching a height of only 25–30 centimeters (10–12 inches).

miniature schnauzer *n.* Any of a breed of small schnauzers typically standing 30–35 centimeters (12–14 inches) high.

min·i·bar (mĭn′ē-bär′) *n.* A small refrigerator, as in a hotel room, stocked with liquor and nonalcoholic beverages. Also called *servibar.*

min·i·bike (mĭn′ē-bīk′) *n.* A small motorbike having a low frame, small wheels, and elevated handlebars. [Originally a trademark.] —**min′i·bik′er** *n.*

min·i·bus (mĭn′ē-bŭs′) *n., pl.* **-bus·es** or **-bus·ses.** A small bus typically used for short trips.

min·i·cab (mĭn′ē-kăb′) *n.* A minicar used as a taxicab, especially in England.

min·i·cam (mĭn′ē-kăm′) *n.* A small, portable television camera used especially for on-the-scene videotaping.

min·i·car (mĭn′ē-kär′) *n.* A very small car, especially a subcompact.

min·i·com·put·er (mĭn′ē-kəm-pyo͞o′tər) *n.* *Computer Science.* A small computer, usually fitting within a single cabinet, that has more memory and a higher execution speed than a microcomputer.

Min·i·con·jou also **Min·ne·con·jou** (mĭn′ĭ-kŏn′jo͞o) *n., pl.* **Miniconjou** or **-jous** also **Minneconjou** or **-jous. 1.** A Native American people constituting a subdivision of the Teton Sioux, formerly inhabiting an area from the Black Hills to the Platte River, with a present-day population in west-central South Dakota. **2.** A member of this people.

min·i·con·ven·tion (mĭn′ē-kən-vĕn′shən) *n.* A convention limited in size or extent, especially a political convention preliminary to a larger or national convention.

min·i·course (mĭn′ē-kôrs′, -kōrs′) *n.* A short, usually intensive course on a subject of study.

Mi·ni·coy Island (mĭn′ĭ-koi′). An island in the Arabian Sea off the southwest coast of India. It is part of the region of Lakshadweep.

min·ié ball (mĭn′ē, mĭn′ē-ā′) *n.* A conical rifle bullet used in the 19th century and designed with a hollow base that expanded when fired. [After Claude Étienne Minié (1814?–1879), French army officer.]

min·i·fy (mĭn′ə-fī′) *tr.v.* **-fied, -fy·ing, -fies.** To make smaller or less significant; reduce. [MIN(IMUM) + (MAGN)IFY.]

min·i·kin (mĭn′ĭ-kĭn) *n.* *Archaic.* A very small delicate creature. [Obsolete Dutch *minneken,* darling, from Middle Dutch, diminutive of *minne,* love. See **men-**[1] in Appendix.]

min·im (mĭn′əm) *n.* **1.** *Abbr.* **min., M.** A unit of fluid measure, as: **a.** In the United States, 1/60 of a fluid dram (0.0616 milliliters). **b.** In Great Britain, 1/20 of a scruple (0.0592 milliliters). **2.** *Music.* A half note. **3.** An insignificantly small portion or thing. **4.** A downward vertical stroke in handwriting. [Middle English, half note, from Medieval Latin *minimus,* least, from Latin.]

min·i·ma (mĭn′ə-mə) *n.* A plural of **minimum.**

min·i·mal (mĭn′ə-məl) *adj.* **1.a.** Smallest in amount or degree. **b.** Small in amount or degree. **c.** Only barely adequate. **2.** Often **Minimal.** Of, relating to, or being minimalism. —**min′i·mal′i·ty** (-măl′ĭ-tē) *n.* —**min′i·mal·ly** *adv.*

USAGE NOTE: Etymologically, *minimal* is properly used to refer to the smallest possible amount, as in *The amplifier reduces distortion to the minimal level that can be obtained with present technologies.* In recent years, however, the word has come to be used to refer simply to a small amount, as in *If you would just put*

Minerva

miniature
c. 1590 portrait of George Clifford, Third Earl of Cumberland, by Nicolas Hilliard; approximately 2¾″ × 2³⁄₁₆″

miniature golf

in a minimal amount of time on your homework, I am sure your grades would improve. Critics have often objected to this extension, but it appears to be well established. To determine the acceptability of the newer use, we presented the Usage Panel with the sentence *Alcohol has a particularly unpleasant effect on me when I have a minimal amount of food in my stomach.* Under the strict interpretation of *minimal,* this sentence should mean only "Alcohol has an unpleasant effect when I have eaten nothing." If the looser interpretation is allowed, however, the sentence can also mean " . . . when I have eaten a bit." Presented with the sentence, 29 percent of the Usage Panel said that it could have only the "eaten nothing" (that is, the strict) interpretation; 34 percent said that it could have only the "eaten a bit" (that is, the looser) interpretation; and 37 percent said that it could have either meaning. Thus the looser sense of *minimal* is accepted by 71 percent of the Panel and must be considered acceptable in nontechnical use. • In an analogous shift, the verb *minimize* is often used to mean "to reduce," an extension of its strict etymological sense of "to reduce to the smallest possible level." This looser usage is the result of the imprecision that usually attaches to the use of the verb in most nontechnical contexts. When a manager announces that *The company wants to minimize the risk of accidents to line workers,* we naturally interpret the manager as meaning that the risk is to be reduced to the smallest level consistent with considerations of efficiency and cost, not that risks are to be reduced to the lowest level logically possible. Even when used with allowable imprecision, however, the verb *minimize* should carry some implication that the relevant quantity is reduced as much as could reasonably be expected in the circumstances. Thus *minimize* retains at least an approximately superlative sense and so is inconsistent with modification by adverbs such as *greatly* or *considerably,* which imply that the verb is being used as a simple synonym for *lessen* or *reduce.*

---

minimal art *n.* See **minimalism** (sense 1). **—minimal artist** *n.*

min·i·mal·ism (mĭn′ə-mə-lĭz′əm) *n.* **1.** A school of abstract painting and sculpture that emphasizes extreme simplification of form, as by the use of basic shapes and monochromatic palettes of primary colors, objectivity, and anonymity of style. Also called *ABC art, minimal art, reductivism, rejective art.* **2.** Use of the fewest and barest essentials or elements, as in the arts, literature, or design. **3.** *Music.* A school or mode of contemporary music marked by extreme simplification of rhythms and patterns, prolonged chordal or melodic repetitions, and often the achievement of a throbbing, trancelike effect.

min·i·mal·ist (mĭn′ə-mə-lĭst) *n.* **1.** One who advocates a moderate or conservative approach, action, or policy, as in a political or governmental organization. **2.** A practitioner of minimalism. **—minimalist** *adj.* **1.** Of, relating to, characteristic of, or in the style of minimalism. **2.** Being or providing a bare minimum of what is necessary.

min·i·mal·ize (mĭn′ə-mə-līz′) *tr.v.* **-ized, -iz·ing, -iz·es.** To make minimal. **—min′i·mal·i·za′tion** (-mə-lĭ-zā′shən) *n.*

min·i·max (mĭn′ə-măks′) *adj.* Of or relating to the strategy in game theory that minimizes the maximum risk for a player. [MINI(MUM) + MAX(IMUM).]

min·i·mill (mĭn′ē-mĭl′) *n.* A small mill or plant, especially a steel mill that uses electric furnaces to produce steel from scrap.

min·i·mize (mĭn′ə-mīz′) *tr.v.* **-mized, -miz·ing, -miz·es.** **1.a.** To reduce to the smallest possible amount, extent, size, or degree. **b.** *Usage Problem.* To reduce. See Usage Note at **minimal. 2.** To represent as having the least degree of importance, value, or size: *minimized the magnitude of the crisis.* See Synonyms at **decry.** [From MINIMUM.] **—min′i·mi·za′tion** (-mĭ-zā′shən) *n.* **—min′i·miz′er** *n.*

min·i·mum (mĭn′ə-məm) *n., pl.* **-mums** or **-ma** (-mə). *Abbr.* **min. 1.a.** The least possible quantity or degree. **b.** The lowest degree or amount reached or recorded; the lower limit of variation. **2.** A lower limit permitted by law or other authority. **3.** A sum of money set by a nightclub or restaurant as the least amount each patron must spend on food and drink. **4.** *Mathematics.* **a.** The smallest number in a finite set of numbers. **b.** A value of a function that is less than any other value of the function over a specific interval. **—minimum** *adj.* Of, consisting of, or representing the lowest possible amount or degree permissible or attainable. [Latin, from neuter of *minimus,* least. See **mei-**[2] in Appendix.]

min·i·mum-se·cu·ri·ty (mĭn′ə-məm-sĭ-kyo͝or′ĭ-tē) *adj.* Having fewer restrictions than others of its kind: *a minimum-security prison; a minimum-security air force base.*

minimum wage *n.* **1.** The lowest wage, determined by law or contract, that an employer may pay an employee for a specified job. **2.** See **living wage.**

min·ing (mī′nĭng) *n. Abbr.* **min. 1.** The process or business of extracting ore or minerals from the ground. **2.** The process of laying explosive mines.

min·ion (mĭn′yən) *n.* **1.** An obsequious follower or dependent; a sycophant. **2.** A subordinate official. **3.** One who is highly esteemed or favored; a darling. [French *mignon,* darling, from Old French *mignot, mignon.*]

min·i·park (mĭn′ē-pärk′) *n.* A very small park in a usually large city. Also called *pocket park.*

min·i·school (mĭn′ē-sko͞ol′) *n.* **1.** An alternative school offering specialized or one-on-one instruction. **2.** A small school serving as an addition to or an extension of a larger one.

min·is·cule (mĭn′ĭ-skyo͞ol′) *adj.* Variant of **minuscule.**

min·i·se·ries (mĭn′ē-sîr′ēz) *n., pl.* **miniseries. 1.** A televised dramatic production, as of a novel or film, shown in a number of episodes. **2.** *Sports.* A short series of performances or athletic contests.

min·i·ski (mĭn′ē-skē′) *n., pl.* **-skis.** *Sports.* A short ski used by beginners or skibobbers.

min·i·skirt (mĭn′ē-skûrt′) *n.* A short skirt with a hemline that falls above the knee. **—min′i·skirt′ed** *adj.*

min·i·state (mĭn′ē-stāt′) *n.* See **microstate.**

min·is·ter (mĭn′ĭ-stər) *n. Abbr.* **min. 1.a.** One who is authorized to perform religious functions in a Christian church, especially a Protestant church. **b.** *Roman Catholic Church.* The superior in certain orders. **2.** A high officer of state appointed to head an executive or administrative department of government. **3.** An authorized diplomatic representative of a government, usually ranking next below an ambassador. **4.** A person serving as an agent for another by carrying out specified orders or functions. **—minister** *v.* **-tered, -ter·ing, -ters.** *—intr.* **1.** To attend to the wants and needs of others: *Volunteers ministered to the homeless after the flood.* See Synonyms at **tend**[2]. **2.** To perform the functions of a cleric. *—tr.* To administer or dispense, as a sacrament. [Middle English, from Old French *ministre,* from Latin *minister,* servant. See **mei-**[2] in Appendix.]

min·is·te·ri·al (mĭn′ĭ-stîr′ē-əl) *adj.* **1.** Of, relating to, or characteristic of a minister of religion or of the ministry. **2.** Of or relating to administrative and executive duties and functions of government. **3.** *Law.* Of, relating to, or being a mandatory act or duty admitting of no personal discretion or judgment in its performance. **4.** Acting or serving as an agent; instrumental. **—min′is·te′ri·al·ly** *adv.*

minister plenipotentiary *n., pl.* **ministers plenipotentiary.** A diplomatic representative ranking below an ambassador but having full governmental power and authority; a plenipotentiary.

minister resident *n., pl.* **ministers resident.** A diplomatic agent ranking below a minister plenipotentiary.

min·is·trant (mĭn′ĭ-strənt) *n.* One who ministers. **—ministrant** *adj. Archaic.* Serving attendance on someone. [From Latin *ministrāns, ministrant-,* present participle of *ministrāre,* to serve, from *minister,* servant. See MINISTER.]

min·is·tra·tion (mĭn′ĭ-strā′shən) *n.* **1.** The act or process of serving or aiding. **2.** The act of performing the duties of a cleric. [Middle English, from Old French, from Latin *ministrātiō, ministrātiōn-,* from *ministrātus,* past participle of *ministrāre,* to serve, from *minister,* servant. See MINISTER.] **—min′is·tra′tive** *adj.*

min·i·stroke (mĭn′ē-strōk′) *n.* See **transient ischemic attack.**

min·is·try (mĭn′ĭ-strē) *n., pl.* **-tries. 1.a.** The act of serving; ministration. **b.** One that serves as a means; an instrumentality. **2.a.** The profession, duties, and services of a minister. **b.** The Christian clergy. **c.** The period of service of a minister. **3.a.** A governmental department presided over by a minister. **b.** The building in which such a department is housed. **c.** The duties, functions, or term of a governmental minister. **d.** Often **Ministry.** Governmental ministers considered as a group. [Middle English *ministerie,* from Old French *ministere,* from Latin *ministerium,* from *minister,* servant. See **mei-**[2] in Appendix.]

min·i·track (mĭn′ē-trăk′) *n.* An electronic system designed to follow the course of satellites and rockets and correlate radio signals received by a network of ground stations.

min·i·um (mĭn′ē-əm) *n.* Red lead. [Latin.]

min·i·van (mĭn′ē-văn′) *n.* A small passenger van having a boxlike shape, side and rear windows, and typically removable rear seats for cargo.

min·i·ver (mĭn′ə-vər) *n.* A white or light gray fur used as a trim on medieval robes and on ceremonial robes of state. [Middle English *meniver,* from Old French *menu vair,* small vair : *menu,* small; see MINUET + *vair,* vair; see VAIR.]

mink (mĭngk) *n., pl.* **mink** or **minks. 1.** Any of various semiaquatic carnivores of the genus *Mustela,* especially *M. vison* of North America, resembling the weasel and having short ears, a pointed snout, short legs, and partly webbed toes. **2.a.** The soft, thick, lustrous fur of this animal. **b.** A coat, stole, or hat made of the fur of this animal. [Middle English, mink fur, possibly of Scandinavian origin.]

min·ke whale (mĭng′kē) *n.* See **piked whale.** [Partial translation of Norwegian *minkehval* : *minke* (perhaps after *Meincke,* member of a 19th-century Norwegian whaling crew) + *hval,* whale.]

Minn. *abbr.* Minnesota.

Min·nan (mĭ-nän′) *n.* The dialect of Chinese spoken on most of Taiwan, in southern Fujian province, and in parts of Guangzhou and Hainan. Minnan is the vernacular of most traditional Chinese communities outside China. [Chinese (Mandarin) *mǐn nán* : *mǐn,* Fujian Province + *nán,* south.]

Min·ne·ap·o·lis (mĭn′ē-ăp′ə-lĭs). A city of southeast Minnesota on the Mississippi River adjacent to St. Paul. The largest city in the state, it was a leading lumbering center in the 19th century. Population, 370,951.

Min·ne·con·jou (mĭn′ĭ-kŏn′jo͞o) *n.* Variant of **Miniconjou.**

min·ne·sing·er (mĭn′ĭ-sĭng′ər, -zĭng′-) *n.* One of the German lyric poets and singers in the troubadour tradition who flourished from the 12th to the 14th century. [German, from Middle High German : *minne,* love (from Old High German *minna;* see **men-**[1] in Appendix) + *singer,* singer (from *singen,* to sing, from Old High German *singan;* see **seng**ʷ**h-** in Appendix).]

Min·ne·so·ta (mĭn′ĭ-sō′tə). *Abbr.* **MN, Minn.** A state of the northern United States bordering on Lake Superior and on Manitoba and Ontario, Canada. It was admitted as the 32nd state in 1858. First explored by the French in the mid-17th century, the area became part of the United States through the Treaty of Paris (1783) and the Louisiana Purchase (1803). St. Paul is the capital and Minneapolis the largest city. Population, 4,075,970. **—Min′ne·so′tan** *adj. & n.*

Minnesota River. A river, about 534 km (332 mi) long, of southern Minnesota flowing southeast and northeast to the Mississippi River near St. Paul.

Min·ne·ton·ka (mĭn′ĭ-tŏng′kə). A city of southeast Minnesota, a residential suburb of Minneapolis. Population, 38,683.

Min·ne·wit (mĭn′ə-wĭt), **Peter.** See Peter **Minuit.**

min·now (mĭn′ō) *n., pl.* **minnow** or **-nows. 1.** Any of a large group of small, freshwater fishes of the family Cyprinidae, widely used as live bait. **2.** Any of various other small, often silver-colored fishes. [Middle English *meneu.* See **men-**[4] in Appendix.]

Mi·ño (mē′nyô). See **Minho.**

Mi·no·an (mĭ-nō′ən) *adj.* Of or relating to the advanced Bronze Age culture that flourished in Crete from about 3000 to 1100 B.C. **—Minoan** *n.* A native or inhabitant of ancient Crete. [From Latin *Mīnōus,* of Minos, from Greek *Minōios,* from *Minōs,* Minos.]

mi·nor (mī′nər) *adj. Abbr.* **min. 1.** Lesser or smaller in amount, extent, or size. **2.** Lesser in importance, rank, or stature: *a minor politician.* **3.** Lesser in seriousness or danger: *a minor injury.* **4.** *Law.* Being under legal age; not yet a legal adult. **5.** *Chiefly British.* Relating to or being the junior or younger of two pupils with the same surname. **6.** Of or relating to a secondary area of academic specialization. **7.** *Logic.* Dealing with a more restricted category. **8.** *Music.* **a.** Relating to or being a minor scale. **b.** Less in distance by a half step than the corresponding major interval. **c.** Based on a minor scale: *a minor key.* **—minor** *n.* **1.** One that is lesser in comparison with others of the same class. **2.** *Law.* One who has not reached full legal age. **3. a.** A secondary area of specialized academic study, requiring fewer courses or credits than a major. **b.** One studying in a secondary area of specialization: *She is a chemistry minor.* **4.** *Logic.* **a.** A minor premise. **b.** A minor term. **5.** *Music.* A minor key, scale, or interval. **6. minors.** *Sports.* The minor leagues of a sport, especially baseball. **—minor** *intr.v.* **-nored, -nor·ing, -nors.** To pursue academic studies in a minor field: *minored in literature.* [Middle English, from Latin. See **mei-**[2] in Appendix.]

Mi·nor·ca[1] (mĭ-nôr′kə) also **Me·nor·ca** (mə-nôr′kə, mĕ-nôr′kä). A Spanish island in the Balearics of the western Mediterranean Sea. Held by the British and the French at various times during the 18th century, it was a Loyalist stronghold in the Spanish Civil War. **—Mi·nor′can** *adj. & n.*

Mi·nor·ca[2] (mĭ-nôr′kə) *n.* A domestic fowl of a breed originating in the Mediterranean region and having white or black plumage. [After MINORCA[1].]

Mi·nor·ite (mī′nə-rīt′) *n.* A Franciscan friar. [From Medieval Latin *(Frātrēs) Minōrēs,* minor (friars), from Latin *minōrēs,* pl. of *minor,* lesser. See MINOR.]

mi·nor·i·ty (mə-nôr′ĭ-tē, -nŏr′-, mī-) *n., pl.* **-ties. 1. a.** The smaller in number of two groups forming a whole. **b.** A group or party having fewer than a controlling number of votes. **2. a.** A racial, religious, political, national, or other group regarded as different from the larger group of which it is part. **b.** A member of such a group. See Usage Note at **color. 3.** The state or period of being under legal age: *still in her minority.* —*attributive.* Often used to modify another noun: *the minority vote; minority political concerns.* [French *minorité,* from Medieval Latin *minōritās,* from Latin *minor,* smaller. See MINOR.]

minority leader *n.* The head of the minority party in a legislative body.

minor league *n. Sports.* A league of professional sports clubs, especially baseball, not belonging to the major leagues.

mi·nor-league (mī′nər-lēg′) *adj.* **1.** *Sports.* Relating or belonging to a minor league. **2.** Of subordinate position or importance: *a minor-league politician.*

mi·nor-leagu·er (mī′nər-lē′gər) *n.* A member of a minor-league team, especially a minor-league baseball player.

minor order *n. Ecclesiastical.* One of the lower grades of the priesthood or ministry in some Christian churches, now consisting of lectors and acolytes in the Western church and of lectors and cantors in the Eastern. Often used in the plural.

minor planet *n.* See **asteroid** (sense 1).

minor premise *n. Logic.* The premise in a syllogism containing the minor term, which will form the subject of the conclusion.

Mi·nor Prophets (mī′nər) *pl.n.* The Hebrew prophets Hosea, Joel, Amos, Obadiah, Jonah, Micah, Nahum, Habakkuk, Zephaniah, Haggai, Zechariah, and Malachi.

minor scale *n. Music.* A diatonic scale having an interval of a minor third between the first and third tones and several forms with different intervals above the fifth.

minor suit *n. Games.* The suit of clubs or of diamonds in bridge, both having a lower scoring value.

minor term *n. Logic.* The term in a syllogism that is stated in the minor premise and forms the subject of the conclusion.

Mi·nos (mī′nəs, -nŏs′) *n. Greek Mythology.* A king of Crete, the son of Zeus and Europa, who was made one of the three judges in the underworld after his death.

Mi·not (mī′nŏt′). A city of northwest-central North Dakota north-northwest of Bismarck. Population, 32,843.

Min·o·taur (mĭn′ə-tôr′, mī′nə-) *n. Greek Mythology.* A monster who was half man and half bull, to whom young Athenian men and women were sacrificed in the Cretan labyrinth until Theseus killed him.

Minsk (mĭnsk, myĕnsk). The capital of Belorussia, in the central part of the republic. First mentioned in 1067, Minsk passed to Russia in 1793 and was occupied (1941–1943) by German forces in World War II. Population, 1,472,000.

min·ster (mĭn′stər) *n. Chiefly British.* A monastery church. [Middle English, from Old English *mynster,* from Vulgar Latin **monistērium,* from Late Latin *monastērium,* monastery. See MONASTERY.]

min·strel (mĭn′strəl) *n.* **1.** A medieval entertainer who traveled from place to place, especially to sing and recite poetry. **2. a.** A lyric poet. **b.** A musician. **3. a.** One of a troupe of entertainers made up in blackface and presenting a comic variety show. **b.** A performance of such a show. [Middle English *minstral,* from Old French *menestrel,* servant, entertainer, from Late Latin *ministeriālis,* official in the imperial household, from Latin *ministerium,* ministry. See MINISTRY.]

minstrel show *n.* A comic variety show in which a troupe of actors made up in blackface present jokes, songs, dances, and comic skits.

min·strel·sy (mĭn′strəl-sē) *n., pl.* **-sies. 1.** The art or profession of a minstrel. **2.** A troupe of minstrels. **3.** Ballads and lyrics sung by minstrels. [Middle English *minstralsie,* from Anglo-Norman *menestralsie,* from Old French *menestrel,* entertainer. See MINSTREL.]

mint[1] (mĭnt) *n.* **1.** A place where the coins of a country are manufactured by authority of the government. **2.** A place or source of manufacture or invention. **3.** An abundant amount, especially of money. **—mint** *tr.v.* **mint·ed, mint·ing, mints. 1.** To produce (money) by stamping metal; coin. **2.** To invent or fabricate: *a phrase that was minted for one occasion.* **—mint** *adj.* Undamaged as if freshly minted: *The painting was in mint condition.* [Middle English, from Old English *mynet,* coin, from Latin *monēta.* See MONEY.] **—mint′er** *n.*

mint[2] (mĭnt) *n.* **1.** A member of the mint family. **2. a.** Any of various plants of the genus *Mentha,* characteristically having aromatic foliage and nearly regular flowers. Some plants are cultivated for their aromatic oil and used for flavoring. **b.** The fresh, dried foliage of some of these plants. **3.** Any of various similar or related plants, such as the stone mint. **4.** A candy flavored with mint. [Middle English *minte,* from Old English, from Germanic **minta,* from Latin *menta,* possibly from Greek *minthē.*] **—mint′y** *adj.*

mint·age (mĭn′tĭj) *n.* **1.** The act or process of minting coins. **2.** Coins manufactured in a mint. **3.** The fee paid to a mint by a government. **4.** The impression stamped on a coin.

mint family *n.* A large family of aromatic herbs, the Labiatae (or Lamiaceae), including lavender, mint, rosemary, sage, and thyme and characterized by opposite leaves, square stems, bilaterally symmetrical flowers with united petals, and a four-lobed ovary that produces four one-seeded nutlets.

mint julep *n.* A tall, frosted drink made of bourbon whiskey or sometimes brandy or rum, sugar, crushed mint leaves, and shaved ice.

mint·mark (mĭnt′märk′) *n.* A letter or symbol on a coin that identifies the mint of origin.

Min·ton (mĭn′tən), **Sherman.** 1890–1965. American jurist who served as an associate justice of the U.S. Supreme Court (1949–1956).

min·u·end (mĭn′yo͞o-ĕnd′) *n. Mathematics.* The quantity from which another quantity, the subtrahend, is to be subtracted. In the equation 50 − 16 = 34, the minuend is 50. [Latin *minuendum,* thing to be diminished, neuter gerundive of *minuere,* to lessen. See **mei-**[2] in Appendix.]

min·u·et (mĭn′yo͞o-ĕt′) *n.* **1.** A slow, stately pattern dance in 3/4 time for groups of couples, originating in 17th-century France. **2.** The music for or in the rhythm of the minuet. [French *menuet,* from Old French, small, dainty (from the small steps characteristic of the dance), diminutive of *menu,* small, from Latin *minūtus.* See MINUTE[2].]

Min·u·it (mĭn′yo͞o-ĭt) also **Min·ne·wit** (-ə-wĭt), **Peter.** 1580–1638. Dutch colonial administrator who purchased Manhattan from Native Americans for the equivalent of $24.

mi·nus (mī′nəs) *prep.* **1.** *Mathematics.* Reduced by the subtraction of; less: *Nine minus three is six.* **2.** *Informal.* Without: *I went to work minus my briefcase.* **—minus** *adj.* **1.** *Mathematics.* Negative or on the negative part of a scale: *a minus value; minus five degrees.* **2.** Ranking on the lower end of a designated scale: *a grade of A minus.* **—minus** *n.* **1.** *Mathematics.* **a.** The minus sign (−). **b.** A negative quantity. **2.** A deficiency or defect.

minor scale

Minotaur

ă pat	oi boy
ā pay	ou out
âr care	o͝o took
ä father	o͞o boot
ĕ pet	ŭ cut
ē be	ûr urge
ĭ pit	th thin
ī pie	*th* this
îr pier	hw which
ŏ pot	zh vision
ō toe	ə about, item
ô paw	♦ regionalism

Stress marks: ′ (primary); ′ (secondary), as in **dictionary** (dĭk′shə-nĕr′ē)

[Middle English, from Latin *minus,* comparative of *minor,* less. See **mei-²** in Appendix.]

min·us·cule (mĭn′ə-skyo͞ol′, mĭ-nŭs′kyo͞ol′) also **min·is·cule** (mĭn′ĭ-skyo͞ol′) —*adj.* **1.** Very small; tiny. See Synonyms at **small. 2.** Of, relating to, or written in miniscule. —*n.* **1.** A small, cursive script developed from uncial between the seventh and ninth centuries and used in medieval manuscripts. **2.** A letter written in minuscule. **3.** A lowercase letter. [French, from Latin *minusculus,* rather small, diminutive of *minus,* neuter of *minor,* smaller. See **mei-²** in Appendix.] —**mi·nus′cu·lar** (mĭ-nŭs′kyə-lər) *adj.*

minus sign *n. Mathematics.* The symbol −, as in 4 − 2 = 2, that is used to indicate subtraction or a negative quantity.

min·ute¹ (mĭn′ĭt) *n. Abbr.* **min., min 1.** A unit of time equal to one sixtieth of an hour, or 60 seconds. **2.** A unit of angular measurement equal to one sixtieth of a degree, or 60 seconds. Also called *minute of arc.* **3.** A measure of the distance one can cover in a minute: *lives ten minutes from school.* **4.** A short interval of time; moment. See Synonyms at **moment. 5.** A specific point in time: *Stop that this minute!* **6.** A note or summary covering points to be remembered; a memorandum. **7. minutes.** An official record of the proceedings at a meeting. —**minute** *tr.v.* **-ut·ed, -ut·ing, -utes.** To record in a memorandum or the minutes of a meeting. [Middle English, from Old French, from Medieval Latin *(pars) minūta (prīma),* (first) minute (part), from Latin *minūta,* feminine of *minūtus,* small. See MINUTE².]

minuteman
Statue of Capt. John Parker (1729–1775) in Lexington, Massachusetts, by Henry Kitson (1865–1947)

mi·nute² (mī-no͞ot′, -nyo͞ot′, mĭ-) *adj.* **1.** Exceptionally small; tiny. See Synonyms at **small. 2.** Beneath notice; insignificant. **3.** Characterized by careful scrutiny and close examination: *held a minute inspection of the grounds.* See Synonyms at **detailed.** [Middle English, from Latin *minūtus,* past participle of *minuere,* to lessen. See **mei-²** in Appendix.] —**mi·nute′ness** *n.*

min·ute hand (mĭn′it) *n.* The long hand on a clock or watch that indicates minutes.

mi·nute·ly¹ (mī-no͞ot′lē, -nyo͞ot′-, mĭ-) *adv.* **1.** With attention to small details. **2.** On a small scale. **3.** Into tiny pieces.

min·ute·ly² (mĭn′ĭt-lē) *adj. Archaic.* On a minute-by-minute basis.

min·ute·man (mĭn′ĭt-măn′) *n.* An armed man pledged to be ready to fight on a minute's notice just before and during the Revolutionary War in the United States.

min·ute of arc (mĭn′ĭt) *n.* See **minute¹** (sense 2).

min·ute steak (mĭn′ĭt) *n.* A small thin steak, often scored or cubed, that can be cooked quickly.

mi·nu·ti·a (mĭ-no͞o′shē-ə, -shə, -nyo͞o′-) *n., pl.* **-ti·ae** (-shē-ē′). A small or trivial detail: *"the minutiae of experimental and mathematical procedure"* (Frederick Turner). [From Late Latin *minūtiae,* petty details, from Latin *minūtia,* smallness, from *minūtus,* small. See MINUTE².]

minx (mĭngks) *n.* **1.** A girl or young woman who is considered pert, flirtatious, or impudent. **2.** *Obsolete.* A promiscuous woman. [Origin unknown.] —**minx′ish** *adj.*

min·yan (mĭn′yən, mēn-yän′) *n., pl.* **min·ya·nim** (mēn-yä-nēm′, mĭn-yô′nĭm) or **min·yans** (mĭn′yənz). A minimum of ten Jews or, among the Orthodox, Jewish men required for a communal religious service. [Hebrew *minyān,* number, minyan.]

Mi·o·cene (mī′ə-sēn′) *adj.* Of, belonging to, or characteristic of the geologic time, rock series, and sedimentary deposits of the fourth epoch of the Tertiary Period, characterized by the development of grasses and grazing mammals. See table at **geologic time.** —**Miocene** *n.* **1.** The Miocene Epoch. **2.** The deposits of the Miocene Epoch. [Greek *meiōn,* less; see **mei-²** in Appendix + -CENE.]

mi·o·sis also **my·o·sis** (mī-ō′sĭs) *n., pl.* **-ses** (-sēz). Constriction of the pupil of the eye, resulting from a normal response to an increase in light or caused by certain drugs or pathological conditions. [Greek *muein,* to close the eyes + -OSIS.]

mi·ot·ic (mī-ŏt′ĭk) *n.* A substance that causes constriction of the pupil of the eye. —**miotic** *adj.* Characterized by, involving, or causing miosis. [From MIOSIS.]

MIP *abbr.* Monthly investment plan.

Mi·que·lon (mĭk′ə-lŏn′, mēk-lôN′). A French island in the Atlantic Ocean off the southern coast of Newfoundland, Canada. It is part of the overseas department of St. Pierre and Miquelon.

mirror
Early 19th-century American

mir (mîr) *n.* A village community of peasant farmers in prerevolutionary Russia. [Russian, commune, peace, from Old Church Slavonic *mirŭ,* peace, possibly of Iranian origin.]

Mi·ra·beau (mîr′ə-bō′, mē-rä-bō′), Comte de. Title of Honoré Gabriel Victor Riqueti. 1749–1791. French revolutionist. As a member of the States-General (1789–1791) he attempted to create a constitutional monarchy.

mi·ra·bi·le dic·tu (mĭ-rä′bĭ-lē dĭk′to͞o) *interj.* Wonderful to relate. [Latin *mīrābile dictū* : *mīrābile,* neuter sing. of *mīrābilis,* wonderful + *dictū,* ablative sing. supine of *dīcere,* to say.]

mir·a·cle (mĭr′ə-kəl) *n.* **1.** An event that appears inexplicable by the laws of nature and so is held to be supernatural in origin or an act of God: *"Miracles are spontaneous, they cannot be summoned, but come of themselves"* (Katherine Anne Porter). **2.** One that excites admiring awe. See Synonyms at **wonder. 3.** A miracle play. [Middle English, from Old French, from Latin *mīrāculum,* from *mīrārī,* to wonder at, from *mīrus,* wonderful. See **smei-** in Appendix.]

miracle drug *n.* A usually new drug that proves extraordinarily effective. Also called *wonder drug.*

miracle play *n.* A medieval drama portraying events in the lives of saints and martyrs.

mi·rac·u·lous (mĭ-răk′yə-ləs) *adj.* **1.** Of the nature of a miracle; preternatural. **2.** So astounding as to suggest a miracle; phenomenal: *a miraculous recovery; a miraculous escape.* **3.** Able to work miracles. [Middle English *miraclous,* from Old French *miraculeux,* from Medieval Latin *mīrāculōsus,* from Latin *mīrāculum,* miracle. See MIRACLE.] —**mi·rac′u·lous·ly** *adv.* —**mi·rac′u·lous·ness** *n.*

mir·a·dor (mĭr′ə-dôr′, -dōr′) *n.* A window, balcony, or small tower affording an extensive view. [Catalan, from *mirar,* to view, from Latin *mīrārī,* to wonder at. See MIRAGE.]

mi·rage (mĭ-räzh′) *n.* **1.** An optical phenomenon that creates the illusion of water, often with inverted reflections of distant objects, and results from distortion of light by alternate layers of hot and cool air. Also called *fata morgana.* **2.** Something illusory. [French, from *mirer,* to look at, from Latin *mīrārī,* to wonder at, from *mīrus,* wonderful. See **smei-** in Appendix.]

Mir·a·mar (mîr′ə-mär′). A city of southeast Florida south of Fort Lauderdale. It is a resort community. Population, 32,813.

Mi·ran·da¹ (mə-răn′də) *n.* The satellite of Uranus that is closest to the planet. [After *Miranda,* daughter of the magician Prospero in Shakespeare's *The Tempest.*]

Mi·ran·da² (mə-răn′də) *adj.* Of, relating to, upholding, or being a Supreme Court decision requiring that a person under arrest be informed of his or her rights to remain silent and to have legal counsel. [After Ernesto A. *Miranda,* plaintiff in the case of *Miranda* v. *Arizona* (1966).]

Mi·ran·dize (mə-răn′dīz′) *tr.v.* **-dized, -diz·ing, -diz·es.** *Slang.* To inform (a suspect) of his or her legal rights: "[The police] *Mirandized the . . . kid again, and pinned the Miranda card to his sheet"* (Carsten Stroud).

mire (mīr) *n.* **1.** An area of wet, soggy, muddy ground; a bog. **2.** Deep, slimy soil or mud. **3.** A disadvantageous or difficult condition or situation: *the mire of poverty.* —**mire** *v.* **mired, mir·ing, mires.** —*tr.* **1. a.** To cause to sink or become stuck in or as if in mire. **b.** To hinder, entrap, or entangle as if in mire. **2.** To soil with mud or mire. —*intr.* To sink or become stuck in mire. [Middle English, from Old Norse *mȳrr,* bog.]

mire·poix (mîr-pwä′) *n.* A seasoning composed of finely diced sautéed vegetables and herbs and sometimes diced ham, bacon, or salt pork. [After Charles Pierre Gaston François de Lévis, Duc de *Mirepoix* (1699–1757), French diplomat.]

mi·rex (mī′rĕks′) *n.* An insecticide, $C_{10}Cl_{12}$, used especially against ants. [Perhaps (PIS)MIR(E) + EX(TERMINATE).]

mir·in (mĭr′ĭn) *n.* A sweetened Japanese rice wine used especially in cooking. [Japanese.]

mirk (mûrk) *n. & adj.* Variant of **murk.**

mirk·y (mûr′kē) *adj.* Variant of **murky.**

♦ **mir·li·ton** (mîr′lĭ-tŏn′, mîr-lē-tôN′) *n. Southern Louisiana.* See **chayote.** [Louisiana French, from French, toy reed flute, tube-shaped pastry, perhaps of imitative origin.]

Mi·ró (mē-rō′), **Joan.** 1893–1983. Spanish artist whose abstract and surrealist paintings are characterized by bright colors and simple bold forms.

mir·ror (mĭr′ər) *n.* **1.** A surface capable of reflecting sufficient undiffused light to form a virtual image of an object placed in front of it. Also called *looking glass.* **2.** Something that faithfully reflects or gives a true picture of something else. **3.** Something worthy of imitation. —**mirror** *tr.v.* **-rored, -ror·ing, -rors.** To reflect in or as if in a mirror: *"The city mirrors many of the greatest moments of Western culture"* (Olivier Bernier). [Middle English *mirour,* from Old French *mireor,* from *mirer,* to look at, from Latin *mīrārī,* to wonder at, from *mīrus,* wonderful. See **smei-** in Appendix.]

mirror image *n.* An image that has its parts arranged with a reversal of right and left, as it would appear if seen in a mirror.

mirth (mûrth) *n.* Gladness and gaiety, especially when expressed by laughter. [Middle English, from Old English *myrgth.* See **mregh-u-** in Appendix.]

SYNONYMS: *mirth, merriment, jollity, hilarity, glee.* These nouns denote a state of joyful exuberance. *Mirth* stresses lightheartedness and gaiety; it often suggests easy laughter: *"Again the young friends gave way to their mirth"* (Henry Wadsworth Longfellow). *Merriment* is high-spirited fun and enjoyment: *Her escapades were a subject of merriment in the sorority house. Jollity* applies to convivial merriment or celebration: *"Perhaps* [an English pub is] *a place of rural jollity with log fires crackling and grinning farm lads slurping pints and squaring up to the dart board"* (John Mortimer). *Hilarity* is great, often uproarious merriment: *"Fan the sinking flame of hilarity with the wing of friendship; and pass the rosy wine"* (Charles Dickens). *Glee* applies especially to jubilant delight resulting from a particular circumstance, such as winning a victory (*Her glee knew no bounds when she crossed the finish line first*); it may suggest spiteful pleasure such as that experienced at another's bad fortune (*He laughed with glee when he learned of his opponent's defeat*).

mirth·ful (mûrth′fəl) *adj.* **1.** Full of gladness and gaiety. **2.** Characterized by or expressing gladness and gaiety: *a tender,* *mirthful movie.* **—mirth′ful·ly** *adv.* **—mirth′ful·ness** *n.*

mirth·less (mûrth′lĭs) *adj.* Devoid of gladness and gaiety. **—mirth′less·ly** *adv.* **—mirth′less·ness** *n.*

MIRV (mûrv) *n., pl.* **MIRVs. 1.** An offensive ballistic missile system in which a number of warheads aimed at independent targets can be launched by a single booster rocket. **2.** One of these warheads. **—MIRV** *v.* **MIRVed, MIRV·ing, MIRVs.** *—tr.* To provide with multiple independent warheads. *—intr.* To equip a military force with a missile system of multiple independent warheads. [*m(ultiple) i(ndependently-targeted) r(eentry) v(ehicles).*]

mir·y (mīr′ē) *adj.* **-i·er, -i·est. 1.** Full of or resembling mire; swampy. **2.** Smeared with mire; muddy. **—mir′i·ness** *n.*

MIS *abbr. Computer Science.* Management information system.

mis–[1] *pref.* **1.** Bad; badly; wrong; wrongly: *misconduct.* **2.** Failure; lack: *misfire.* **3.** Used as an intensive: *misdoubt.* [Partly from Middle English *mis-* (from Old English) and partly from Middle English *mes-, mis-* (from Old French); see **mei-**[1] in Appendix.]

mis–[2] *pref.* Variant of **miso–.**

mis·ad·dress (mĭs′ə-drĕs′) *tr.v.* **-dressed, -dress·ing, -dress·es.** To address (a piece of mail) incorrectly.

mis·ad·ven·ture (mĭs′əd-vĕn′chər) *n.* An instance of misfortune; a mishap. [Middle English *misaventure,* from Old French *mesaventure,* from *mesavenir,* to result in misfortune : *mes-,* badly; see MIS–[1] + *avenir,* to turn out (from Latin *advenīre,* to come to; see ADVENT).]

mis·ad·vise (mĭs′əd-vīz′) *tr.v.* **-vised, -vis·ing, -vis·es.** To advise wrongly.

mis·a·ligned (mĭs′ə-līnd′) *adj.* Incorrectly aligned. **—mis′a·lign′ment** (-līn′mənt) *n.*

mis·al·li·ance (mĭs′ə-lī′əns) *n.* **1.** An unsuitable alliance, especially in marriage. **2.** A mésalliance.

mis·al·lo·cate (mĭs-ăl′ə-kāt′) *tr.v.* **-cat·ed, -cat·ing, -cates.** To allocate (resources or capital, for example) wrongly or inappropriately. **—mis′al·lo·ca′tion** *n.*

mis·al·ly (mĭs′ə-lī′) *tr.v.* **-lied, -ly·ing, -lies.** To ally inappropriately.

mis·an·thrope (mĭs′ən-thrōp′, mĭz′-) also **mis·an·thro·pist** (mĭs-ăn′thrə-pĭst, mĭz′-) *n.* One who hates or mistrusts humankind. [French, from Greek *misanthrōpos,* hating mankind : *miso-,* miso- + *anthrōpos,* man.]

mis·an·throp·ic (mĭs′ən-thrŏp′ĭk, mĭz′-) *adj.* **1.** Of, relating to, or characteristic of a misanthrope. **2.** Characterized by a hatred or mistrustful scorn for humankind. **—mis′an·throp′i·cal·ly** *adv.*

mis·an·thro·pist (mĭs-ăn′thrə-pĭst, mĭz-) *n.* Variant of **misanthrope.**

mis·an·thro·py (mĭs-ăn′thrə-pē, mĭz-) *n.* Hatred or mistrust of humankind.

mis·ap·ply (mĭs′ə-plī′) *tr.v.* **-plied, -ply·ing, -plies.** To use or apply wrongly. **—mis·ap′pli·ca′tion** (-ăp′lĭ-kā′shən) *n.*

mis·ap·pre·hend (mĭs-ăp′rĭ-hĕnd′) *tr.v.* **-hend·ed, -hend·ing, -hends.** To apprehend incorrectly; misunderstand. **—mis·ap′pre·hen′sion** (-hĕn′shən) *n.*

mis·ap·pro·pri·ate (mĭs′ə-prō′prē-āt′) *tr.v.* **-at·ed, -at·ing, -ates. 1.a.** To appropriate wrongly: *misappropriating the theories of social science.* **b.** To appropriate dishonestly for one's own use; embezzle. **2.** To use illegally. **—mis′ap·pro′pri·a′tion** *n.*

mis·at·trib·ute (mĭs′ə-trĭb′yo͞ot) *tr.v.* **-ut·ed, -ut·ing, -utes.** To attribute incorrectly: *misattributed the quotation to Dickens.* **—mis′at·tri·bu′tion** (-ă-trĭ-byo͞o′shən) *n.*

mis·be·come (mĭs′bĭ-kŭm′) *tr.v.* **-came** (-kām′), **-come, -com·ing, -comes.** To be unsuitable or inappropriate for.

mis·be·got·ten (mĭs′bĭ-gŏt′n) *adj.* **1.a.** Of, relating to, or being a child or children born to unmarried parents. **b.** Not lawfully obtained: *misbegotten wealth.* **2.** Having an improper basis or origin; ill-conceived: *misbegotten ideas about education.*

mis·be·have (mĭs′bĭ-hāv′) *v.* **-haved, -hav·ing, -haves.** *—intr.* To behave badly. *—tr.* To behave (oneself) in an inappropriate way: *The children misbehaved themselves at dinner.* **—mis′be·hav′er** *n.* **—mis′be·hav′ior** (-hāv′yər) *n.*

mis·be·lief (mĭs′bĭ-lēf′) *n.* **1.** A wrong or faulty belief. **2.** A heretical or unorthodox religious belief.

mis·be·lieve (mĭs′bĭ-lēv′) *intr.v.* **-lieved, -liev·ing, -lieves.** *Obsolete.* To hold a false or erroneous belief or opinion, especially in religious matters. **—mis′be·liev′er** *n.*

mis·brand (mĭs-brănd′) *tr.v.* **-brand·ed, -brand·ing, -brands.** To brand or label misleadingly or fraudulently.

misc. *abbr.* Miscellaneous.

mis·cal·cu·late (mĭs-kăl′kyə-lāt′) *tr. & intr. v.* **-lat·ed, -lat·ing, -lates.** To count or estimate incorrectly. **—mis·cal′cu·la′tion** *n.*

mis·call (mĭs-kôl′) *tr.v.* **-called, -call·ing, -calls.** To call by a wrong name.

mis·car·riage (mĭs′kăr′ĭj, mĭs-kăr′-) *n.* **1.** Premature expulsion of a nonviable fetus from the uterus. Also called *spontaneous abortion.* **2.a.** Bad administration; mismanagement: *a miscarriage of justice.* **b.** Failure to attain the right or desired end: *the miscarriage of a cherished plan.*

mis·car·ry (mĭs′kăr′ē, mĭs-kăr′ē) *intr.v.* **-ried, -ry·ing, -ries. 1.** To have a miscarriage; abort. **2.** To go astray or be lost in transit, as mail or cargo. **3.** To fail to attain an intended goal, as a plan or project.

mis·cast (mĭs-kăst′) *tr.v.* **-cast, -cast·ing, -casts. 1.** To cast in an unsuitable role. **2.** To cast (a role or theatrical production) inappropriately.

mis·ceg·e·na·tion (mĭ-sĕj′ə-nā′shən, mĭs′ĭ-jə-) *n.* **1.** A mixture of different races. **2.** Cohabitation, sexual relations, or marriage involving persons of different races. [Latin *miscēre,* to mix; see **meik-** in Appendix + *genus,* race; see **gene-** in Appendix + -ATION.] **—mis·ceg′e·na′tion·al** *adj.*

mis·cel·la·ne·a (mĭs′ə-lā′nē-ə) *pl.n.* Miscellaneous items or written works collected together. [Latin *miscellānea,* from neuter pl. of *miscellāneus,* miscellaneous. See MISCELLANEOUS.]

mis·cel·la·ne·ous (mĭs′ə-lā′nē-əs) *adj. Abbr.* **misc. 1.** Made up of a variety of parts or ingredients. **2.** Having a variety of characteristics, abilities, or appearances. **3.** Concerned with diverse subjects or aspects. [From Latin *miscellāneus,* from *miscellus,* mixed, from *miscēre,* to mix. See **meik-** in Appendix.] **—mis′cel·la′ne·ous·ly** *adv.* **—mis′cel·la′ne·ous·ness** *n.*

SYNONYMS: *miscellaneous, heterogeneous, motley, mixed, varied, assorted.* These adjectives mean consisting of a number of different kinds. *Miscellaneous* implies a varied, often haphazard combination: *The shop carries suits, coats, shirts, and miscellaneous accessories. "My reading . . . had been extremely miscellaneous"* (William Godwin). *Heterogeneous* emphasizes diversity and dissimilarity: *The population of the United States is vast and heterogeneous. Motley* emphasizes difference to the point of incongruity and discordance and is sometimes used derogatorily: *The audience consisted of a motley crowd of property owners, renters, and drifters. Mixed* suggests a combination of differing but not necessarily conflicting elements: *The orchestra offered a mixed program of baroque and contemporary fare. Varied* stresses absence of uniformity: *"The assembly was large and varied, containing clergy and laity, men and women"* (Nicholas P.S. Wisemen). *Assorted* often suggests the purposeful arrangement of different but complementary elements: *The centerpiece is a luxuriant arrangement of assorted garden flowers.*

mis·cel·la·nist (mĭs′ə-lā′nĭst, mĭ-sĕl′ə-) *n. Chiefly British.* One who compiles, writes, or edits miscellanies.

mis·cel·la·ny (mĭs′ə-lā′nē) *n., pl.* **-nies. 1.** A collection of various items, parts, or ingredients, especially one composed of diverse literary works. **2. miscellanies.** A publication containing various literary works. [Latin *miscellānea,* miscellanea. See MISCELLANEA.]

mis·chance (mĭs-chăns′) *n.* **1.** An unfortunate occurrence; a mishap. **2.** Bad luck. See Synonyms at **misfortune.**

mis·char·ac·ter·ize (mĭs-kăr′ək-tə-rīz′) *tr.v.* **-ized, -iz·ing, -iz·es.** To give a false or misleading character to: *mischaracterized the findings of the study.* **—mis·char′ac·ter·i·za′tion** (-tər-ĭ-zā′shən) *n.*

mis·chief (mĭs′chĭf) *n.* **1.** Behavior that causes discomfiture or annoyance in another. **2.** An inclination or a tendency to play pranks or cause embarrassment. **3.** One that causes minor trouble or disturbance: *The child was a mischief in school.* **4.** Damage, destruction, or injury caused by a specific person or thing: *The broken window was the mischief of vandals.* **5.** The state or quality of being mischievous. [Middle English *mischef,* from Old French *meschief,* misfortune, from *meschever,* to end badly : *mes-,* badly; see MIS–[1] + *chever,* to happen, come to an end (from Vulgar Latin **capāre,* to come to a head, from **capum,* head, from Latin *caput;* see **kaput-** in Appendix).]

mis·chief-mak·er (mĭs′chĭf-mā′kər) *n.* One who causes mischief, especially one who makes trouble by spreading gossip. **—mis′chief-mak′ing** *n.*

mis·chie·vous (mĭs′chə-vəs) *adj.* **1.** Causing mischief. **2.** Playful in a naughty or teasing way. See Synonyms at **playful. 3.** Troublesome; irritating: *a mischievous prank.* **4.** Causing harm, injury, or damage: *mischievous rumors and falsehoods.* [Middle English *mischevous,* from *mischef,* mischief. See MISCHIEF.] **—mis′chie·vous·ly** *adv.* **—mis′chie·vous·ness** *n.*

mis·ci·ble (mĭs′ə-bəl) *adj. Chemistry.* That can be mixed in all proportions. Used of liquids. [Medieval Latin *miscibilis,* from Latin *miscēre,* to mix. See **meik-** in Appendix.] **—mis′ci·bil′i·ty** *n.*

mis·clas·si·fy (mĭs-klăs′ə-fī′) *tr.v.* **-fied, -fy·ing, -fies.** To classify incorrectly. **—mis·clas′si·fi·ca′tion** (-fĭ-kā′shən) *n.*

mis·com·mu·ni·ca·tion (mĭs′kə-myo͞o′nĭ-kā′shən) *n.* **1.** Lack of clear or adequate communication. **2.** An unclear or inadequate communication.

mis·con·ceive (mĭs′kən-sēv′) *tr.v.* **-ceived, -ceiv·ing, -ceives.** To interpret incorrectly; misunderstand. **—mis′con·ceiv′er** *n.*

mis·con·cep·tion (mĭs′kən-sĕp′shən) *n.* A mistaken thought, idea, or notion; a misunderstanding: *had many misconceptions about the new tax program.*

mis·con·duct (mĭs-kŏn′dŭkt) *n.* **1.a.** Behavior not conforming to prevailing standards or laws; impropriety. **b.** The act or an instance of adultery. **2.** Dishonest or bad management, especially by persons entrusted or engaged to act on another's behalf. **3.** Deliberate wrongdoing, especially by government or military officials. **—misconduct** (mĭs′kən-dŭct′) *v.* **—misconduct** *tr.v.*

ă pat	oi boy
ā pay	ou out
âr care	o͝o took
ä father	o͞o boot
ĕ pet	ŭ cut
ē be	ûr urge
ĭ pit	th thin
ī pie	*th* this
îr pier	hw which
ŏ pot	zh vision
ō toe	ə about, item
ô paw	♦ regionalism

Stress marks: ′ (primary); ′ (secondary), as in **dictionary** (dĭk′shə-nĕr′ē)

-duct·ed, -duct·ing, -ducts. 1. To mismanage. **2.** To behave (oneself) improperly.

mis·con·struc·tion (mĭs′kən-strŭk′shən) *n.* **1.** An inaccurate explanation, interpretation, or report; a misunderstanding. **2.** *Grammar.* A faulty construction, especially of a sentence or clause.

mis·con·strue (mĭs′kən-stro͞o′) *tr.v.* **-strued, -stru·ing, -strues.** To mistake the meaning of; misinterpret.

mis·count (mĭs-kount′) *v.* **-count·ed, -count·ing, -counts.** —*tr.* To count (something) incorrectly; miscalculate. —*intr.* To make an incorrect count. —**miscount** (mĭs′kount′) *n.* An inaccurate count.

mis·cre·ant (mĭs′krē-ənt) *n.* **1.** An evildoer; a villain. **2.** An infidel; a heretic. [Middle English *miscreaunt,* heretic, from Old French *mescreant,* present participle of *mescroire,* to disbelieve : *mes-,* wrongly, not; see MIS–[1] + *croire,* to believe (from Latin *crēdere;* see **kerd-** in Appendix).] —**mis′cre·ant** *adj.*

mis·cre·ate (mĭs′krē-āt′) *tr.v.* **-at·ed, -at·ing, -ates.** To make or shape badly. —**miscreate** (mĭs′krē-ĭt, -āt′) *adj.* Formed unnaturally; misshapen. —**mis′cre·a′tion** *n.*

mis·cue (mĭs-kyo͞o′) *n.* **1.** *Games.* A stroke in billiards that misses or just brushes the ball because of a slip of the cue. **2.** A mistake. —**miscue** *intr.v.* **-cued, -cu·ing, -cues. 1.** To make a miscue. **2.** To miss a stage cue.

mis·date (mĭs-dāt′) *tr.v.* **-dat·ed, -dat·ing, -dates.** To date (a document or an event, for example) inaccurately. —**misdate** *n.* An inaccurate date.

mis·deal (mĭs-dēl′) *v.* **-dealt** (-dĕlt′), **-deal·ing, -deals.** *Games.* —*tr.* To deal (cards) incorrectly. —*intr.* To deal cards incorrectly. —**mis′deal′** *n.* —**mis·deal′er** *n.*

mis·deed (mĭs-dēd′) *n.* A wrong or illegal deed; a wrongdoing.

mis·de·mean·ant (mĭs′dĭ-mē′nənt) *n.* *Law.* One who has been convicted of a misdemeanor.

mis·de·mean·or (mĭs′dĭ-mē′nər) *n.* **1.** A misdeed. **2.** *Law.* An offense less serious than a felony.

mis·de·mean·our (mĭs′dĭ-mē′nər) *n.* *Chiefly British.* Variant of **misdemeanor.**

mis·de·scribe (mĭs′dĭ-skrīb′) *tr.v.* **-scribed, -scrib·ing, -scribes.** To describe wrongly or falsely. —**mis′de·scrip′tion** (-skrĭp′shən) *n.*

mis·di·ag·nose (mĭs-dī′əg-nōs′, -nōz′) *tr.v.* **-nosed, -nos·ing, -nos·es.** To diagnose incorrectly.

mis·di·ag·no·sis (mĭs-dī′əg-nō′sĭs) *n., pl.* **-ses** (-sēz). An incorrect diagnosis.

mis·di·al (mĭs-dī′əl) *tr. & intr.v.* **-aled, -al·ing, -als** or **-alled, -al·ling, -als.** To dial or be dialed incorrectly. —**mis′di′al** *n.*

mis·did (mĭs-dĭd′) *v.* Past tense of **misdo.**

mis·di·rect (mĭs′dĭ-rĕkt′, -dī-) *tr.v.* **-rect·ed, -rect·ing, -rects. 1.** To aim (a blow or projectile, for example) badly. **2.** To give wrong instructions or directions to. **3.** To put a wrong address on (a piece of mail).

mis·di·rec·tion (mĭs′dĭ-rĕk′shən, -dī-) *n.* **1.** Inaccurate aim. **2.** Incorrect instructions or directions. **3.** *Law.* An error made by a judge in charging a jury.

mis·do (mĭs-do͞o′) *tr.v.* **-did** (-dĭd′), **-done** (-dŭn′), **-do·ing, -does** (-dŭz′). To do wrongly or awkwardly; botch. —**mis·do′er** *n.* —**mis·do′ing** *n.*

mis·doubt (mĭs-dout′) *tr.v.* **-doubt·ed, -doubt·ing, -doubts.** To feel doubt or distrust about.

mis·ed·u·cate (mĭs-ĕj′ə-kāt′) *tr.v.* **-cat·ed, -cat·ing, -cates.** To educate improperly. —**mis′ed·u·ca′tion** *n.*

mise en scène (mēz′ äɴ sĕn′) *n., pl.* **mise en scènes** (sĕn′). **1.a.** The arrangement of performers and properties on a stage for a theatrical production. **b.** A stage setting. **2.** Physical environment; surroundings. [French, putting on stage : *mise,* putting + *en,* on + *scène,* stage.]

mi·ser (mī′zər) *n.* **1.** One who lives very meagerly in order to hoard money. **2.** A greedy or avaricious person. [From Latin, wretched.]

mis·er·a·ble (mĭz′ər-ə-bəl, mĭz′rə-) *adj.* **1.** Very uncomfortable or unhappy; wretched. **2.** Causing or accompanied by great discomfort or distress: *a miserable climate.* **3.** Mean or shameful; contemptible: *a miserable trick.* **4.** Wretchedly inadequate: *lived in a miserable shack; fed the prisoners miserable rations.* **5.** Of poor quality; inferior: *miserable handicraft.* [Middle English, from Old French, from Latin *miserābilis,* pitiable, from *miserārī,* to pity, from *miser,* wretched.] —**mis′er·a·ble** *n.* —**mis′er·a·ble·ness** *n.* —**mis′er·a·bly** *adv.*

mis·e·re·re (mĭz′ə-râr′ē, -rîr′ē) *n.* **1. Miserere. a.** The 51st Psalm. **b.** A musical setting of this psalm. **2.a.** A prayer for mercy. **b.** An expression of lamentation or complaint. **3.** See **misericord** (sense 2). [Latin, have mercy, the first word of the psalm, imperative sing. of *miserērī,* to feel pity, from *miser,* wretched.]

misericord

mis·er·i·cord or **mis·er·i·corde** (mĭz′ər-ĭ-kôrd′, mĭ-zĕr′-) *n.* **1.a.** Relaxation of monastic rules, as a dispensation from fasting. **b.** The room in a monastery used by monks who have been granted such a dispensation. **2.** A bracket attached to the underside of a hinged seat in a church stall against which a standing person may lean. Also called *miserere.* **3.** A narrow dagger used in medieval times to deliver the death stroke to a seriously wounded knight. [Middle English, pity, from Old French, from Latin *misericordia,* from *misericors, misericord-,* merciful : *miserērī,* to feel pity; see MISERERE + *cor, cord-,* heart; see **kerd-** in Appendix.]

WORD HISTORY: A dagger, a support for someone who is standing, and a special monastic apartment are all called by the same name because, strangely enough, they are all examples of mercy. The word *misericord* goes back to Latin *misericordia,* "mercy," derived from *misericors,* "merciful," which is in turn derived from *miserērī,* "to pity," and *cor,* "heart." In Medieval Latin the word *misericordia* was used to denote various merciful things, and these senses were borrowed into English. *Misericordia* referred to an apartment in a monastery where certain relaxations of the monastic rule were permitted, especially those involving food and drink. The word also designated a projection on the underside of a hinged seat in a choir stall against which a standing person could lean, no doubt a merciful thing during long services. Finally, *misericordia* was used for a dagger with which the death stroke was administered to a seriously wounded knight.

mi·ser·ly (mī′zər-lē) *adj.* Of, relating to, or characteristic of a miser; avaricious, grasping, and penurious. See Synonyms at **stingy.** —**mi′ser·li·ness** *n.*

mis·er·y (mĭz′ə-rē) *n., pl.* **-ies. 1.a.** The state of suffering and want as a result of physical circumstances or extreme poverty. **b.** Mental or emotional unhappiness or distress: *"Our happiness or misery depends on our dispositions, and not on our circumstances"* (Martha Washington). **2.** A cause or source of suffering. **3.** *Informal.* A physical ache or ailment. [Middle English *miserie,* from Old French, from Latin *miseria,* from *miser,* wretched.]

mis·es·teem (mĭs′ə-stēm′) *tr.v.* **-teemed, -teem·ing, -teems.** To fail to regard with deserved esteem.

mis·es·ti·mate (mĭs-ĕs′tə-māt′) *tr.v.* **-mat·ed, -mat·ing, -mates.** To estimate wrongly. —**mis·es′ti·mate** (-mĭt) *n.* —**mis·es′ti·ma′tion** *n.*

mis·fea·sance (mĭs-fē′zəns) *n.* *Law.* Improper and unlawful execution of an act that in itself is lawful and proper. [Anglo-Norman *mesfesaunce,* from *mesfere,* to do wrong : *mes-,* wrongly (from Old French; see MIS–[1]) + *fere,* to do (from Latin *facere;* see **dhē-** in Appendix).]

mis·fea·sor (mĭs-fē′zər) *n.* *Law.* One guilty of misfeasance. [Anglo-Norman *mesfesor,* from *mesfere,* to do wrong. See MISFEASANCE.]

mis·file (mĭs-fīl′) *tr.v.* **-filed, -fil·ing, -files.** To file in the wrong place or order.

mis·fire (mĭs-fīr′) *intr.v.* **-fired, -fir·ing, -fires. 1.** To fail to ignite when expected. Used of an internal-combustion engine. **2.** To fail to discharge. Used of a firearm. **3.** To fail to achieve an anticipated result: *a scheme that misfired.* —**mis′fire′** (mĭs′fīr′, mĭs-fīr′) *n.*

mis·fit (mĭs′fĭt′, mĭs-fĭt′) *n.* **1.** Something of the wrong size or shape for its purpose. **2.** One who is unable to adjust to one's environment or circumstances or is considered to be disturbingly different from others.

mis·for·tune (mĭs-fôr′chən) *n.* **1.a.** Bad fortune or ill luck. **b.** The condition resulting from bad fortune or ill luck: *wanted to help those in misfortune.* **2.** A distressing occurrence: *"Misfortunes are too apt to wear out Friendship"* (Charlotte Charke).

SYNONYMS: *misfortune, adversity, mishap, mischance.* These nouns all refer to a state or an instance of ill fortune or bad luck. *Misfortune,* which applies most broadly, often suggests the operation of distressing circumstances beyond the victim's control: *She had the misfortune to become gravely ill. Adversity* frequently implies continuing hardship or affliction: *debt-ridden farmers struggling with adversity.* Both *mishap* and *mischance* connote slight or negligible incidents or consequences: *They arrived at their destination without any mishaps. By mischance I dialed a wrong number.*

mis·fu·el (mĭs-fyo͞o′əl) *tr.v.* **-eled, -el·ing, -els** or **-elled, -el·ling, -els.** To provide (a motor vehicle) with inappropriate fuel, especially to provide with leaded gas when unleaded gas is required.

mis·give (mĭs-gĭv′) *v.* **-gave** (-gāv′), **-giv·en** (-gĭv′ən), **-giv·ing, -gives.** —*tr.* To arouse suspicion or apprehension in (one's mind or heart, for example). —*intr.* To be suspicious, apprehensive, or doubtful. [MIS–[1] + GIVE, to suggest (obsolete).]

mis·giv·ing (mĭs-gĭv′ĭng) *n.* A feeling of doubt, distrust, or apprehension. See Synonyms at **apprehension, qualm.**

mis·gov·ern (mĭs-gŭv′ərn) *tr.v.* **-erned, -ern·ing, -erns.** To govern inefficiently or badly. —**mis·gov′ern·ment** *n.* —**mis·gov′er·nor** *n.*

mis·guide (mĭs-gīd′) *tr.v.* **-guid·ed, -guid·ing, -guides.** To lead or guide in the wrong direction; lead astray. —**mis·guid′ance** (-gīd′ns) *n.* —**mis·guid′er** *n.*

mis·guid·ed (mĭs-gī′dĭd) *adj.* Based or acting on error; misled: *well-intentioned but misguided efforts; misguided do-gooders.* —**mis·guid′ed·ly** *adv.*

mis·han·dle (mĭs-hăn′dl) *tr.v.* **-dled, -dling, -dles. 1.** To deal with clumsily or inefficiently; mismanage. **2.** To treat roughly; maltreat.

mis·hap (mĭs′hăp′, mĭs-hăp′) *n.* **1.** Bad luck. **2.** An unfortunate accident. See Synonyms at **misfortune.**

Mish·a·wa·ka (mĭsh′ə-wô′kə, -wŏk′ə). A city of northern Indiana, an industrial suburb of South Bend. Population, 40,224.

mis·hear (mĭs-hîr′) *tr. & intr.v.* **-heard** (-hûrd′), **-hear·ing, -hears.** To hear wrongly; misunderstand.

mish·e·gaas or **mish·e·goss** (mĭsh′ə-gäs′) *n. Slang.* Variants of **meshugaas.**

mis·hit (mĭs-hĭt′) *tr.v.* **-hit, -hit·ting, -hits.** To hit (a tennis or cricket ball, for example) incorrectly or badly. **—mis′hit′** *n.*

mish·mash (mĭsh′măsh′, -mäsh′) *n.* A collection or mixture of unrelated things; a hodgepodge. [Middle English *missemasche,* probably reduplication of *mash,* soft mixture. See MASH.]

Mish·nah also **Mish·na** (mĭsh′nə) *n. Judaism.* **1.** The first section of the Talmud, being a collection of early oral interpretations of the scriptures as compiled about A.D. 200. **2.** A paragraph from this section of the Talmud. **3.** The teaching of a rabbi or other noted authority on Jewish laws. [Rabbinical Hebrew *mišnâ,* repetition, instruction, from *šānâ,* to repeat.] **—Mish·na′ic** (mĭsh-nā′ĭk) *adj.*

Mishnaic Hebrew *n.* The Hebrew language as used from the fifth century B.C. to the late seventh century A.D. Also called *Rabbinic Hebrew.*

mis·i·den·ti·fy (mĭs′ī-dĕn′tə-fī′) *tr.v.* **-fied, -fy·ing, -fies.** To identify incorrectly. **—mis′i·den′ti·fi·ca′tion** (-fĭ-kā′shən) *n.*

mis·im·pres·sion (mĭs′ĭm-prĕsh′ən) *n.* A faulty or mistaken impression.

mis·in·form (mĭs′ĭn-fôrm′) *tr.v.* **-formed, -form·ing, -forms.** To provide with incorrect information. **—mis′in·form′ant** (-fôr′mənt), **mis′in·form′er** *n.* **—mis·in′for·ma′tion** *n.*

mis·in·ter·pret (mĭs′ĭn-tûr′prĭt) *tr.v.* **-pret·ed, -pret·ing, -prets. 1.** To interpret inaccurately. **2.** To explain inaccurately. **—mis′in·ter′pre·ta′tion** *n.* **—mis′in·ter′pret·er** *n.*

mis·join·der (mĭs-join′dər) *n. Law.* Improper joining of different causes of action or of different parties to a lawsuit.

mis·judge (mĭs-jŭj′) *v.* **-judged, -judg·ing, -judg·es.** *—tr.* To judge wrongly. *—intr.* To be wrong in judging. **—mis·judg′ment** *n.*

Mis·ki·to (mĭ-skē′tō) *n., pl.* **Miskito** or **-tos. 1.** A member of an American Indian people inhabiting the Caribbean coast of northeast Nicaragua and southeast Honduras. **2.** The language of the Miskito. Also called *Mosquito.*

mis·know (mĭs-nō′) *tr.v.* **-knew** (-nōō′, -nyōō′), **-known** (-nōn′), **-know·ing, -knows.** To misunderstand. **—mis·knowl′edge** (-nŏl′ĭj) *n.*

Mis·kolc (mĭsh′kôlts′). A city of northeast Hungary northeast of Budapest. A major industrial center, it was invaded by Mongols in the 13th century and by German imperial forces in the 17th and 18th centuries. Population, 211,645.

mis·la·bel (mĭs-lā′bəl) *tr.v.* **-beled, -bel·ing, -bels** also **-belled, -bel·ling, -bels.** To label inaccurately.

mis·lay (mĭs-lā′) *tr.v.* **-laid** (-lād′), **-lay·ing, -lays. 1.** To put in a place that is afterward forgotten: *I have mislaid my hat.* **2.** To place or put down incorrectly: *They mislaid the linoleum.* **—mis·lay′er** *n.*

mis·lead (mĭs-lēd′) *tr.v.* **-led** (-lĕd′), **-lead·ing, -leads. 1.** To lead in the wrong direction. **2.** To lead into error of thought or action, especially by intentionally deceiving. See Synonyms at **deceive. —mis·lead′er** *n.*

mis·lead·ing (mĭs-lē′dĭng) *adj.* Tending to mislead. **—mis·lead′ing·ly** *adv.*

***SYNONYMS:** misleading, deceptive, delusive, delusory.* These adjectives describe what leads or tends to lead one into error or wrongdoing. *Misleading,* the least specific, applies to something that inadvertently or deliberately guides one into an erroneous or wrong path: *a misleading similarity.* Something *deceptive* causes one to believe what is not true or fail to believe what is true; the term may or may not imply intentional misrepresentation: *deceptive calm. Delusive* and *delusory* both connote deception, sham, or fallaciousness: *delusive expectations; a delusory pleasure.*

mis·led (mĭs-lĕd′) *v.* Past tense and past participle of **mislead.**

mis·like (mĭs-līk′) *tr.v.* **-liked, -lik·ing, -likes. 1.** To disapprove of; dislike. **2.** *Archaic.* To displease. **—mislike** *n.* Disapproval; dislike. [Middle English *misliken,* from Old English *mislīcian* : *mis-,* ill; see MIS–¹ + *līcian,* to please; see LIKE¹.]

mis·man·age (mĭs-măn′ĭj) *tr.v.* **-aged, -ag·ing, -ag·es.** To manage badly or carelessly. **—mis·man′age·ment** *n.*

mis·match (mĭs-măch′) *tr.v.* **-matched, -match·ing, -match·es.** To match unsuitably or inaccurately. **—mis′match′** (mĭs′măch′, mĭs-măch′) *n.*

mis·mate (mĭs-māt′) *tr.v.* **-mat·ed, -mat·ing, -mates.** To mate or match unsuitably.

mis·name (mĭs-nām′) *tr.v.* **-named, -nam·ing, -names.** To call by a wrong name.

mis·no·mer (mĭs-nō′mər) *n.* **1.** An error in naming a person or place. **2.a.** Application of a wrong name. **b.** A name wrongly or unsuitably applied to a person or an object. [Middle English *misnoumer,* from Old French *mesnomer,* to misname : *mes-,* wrongly; see MIS–¹ + *nommer,* to name (from Latin *nōmināre,* from *nōmen,* name; see **nō-men-** in Appendix).] **—mis·no′mered** *adj.*

mi·so (mē′sō) *n., pl.* **-sos.** A thick fermented paste made by grinding together cooked soybeans, rice or barley, and salt and used especially in making soups and sauces. [Japanese.]

miso– or **mis–** *pref.* Hatred: *misogamy.* [Greek, from *misein,* to hate and *misos,* hatred.]

mi·sog·a·my (mĭ-sŏg′ə-mē) *n.* Hatred of marriage. **—mis′o·gam′ic** (mĭs′ə-găm′ĭk) *adj.* **—mi·sog′a·mist** *n.*

mi·sog·y·nist (mĭ-sŏj′ə-nĭst) *n.* One who hates women. **—misogynist** *adj.* Of or characterized by a hatred of women.

mi·sog·y·nis·tic (mĭ-sŏj′ə-nĭs′tĭk) **mi·sog·y·nous** (-sŏj′ə-nəs) *adj.* Of or characterized by a hatred of women.

mi·sog·y·ny (mĭ-sŏj′ə-nē) *n.* Hatred of women: *"Every organized patriarchal religion works overtime to contribute its own brand of misogyny"* (Robin Morgan). [Greek *misogunia* : *miso-,* miso- + *gunē,* woman; see –GYNY.] **—mis′o·gyn′ic** (mĭs′ə-jĭn′ĭk, -gī′nĭk) *adj.*

mi·sol·o·gy (mĭ-sŏl′ə-jē) *n.* Hatred of reason, argument, or enlightenment. **—mi·sol′o·gist** *n.*

mis·o·ne·ism (mĭs′ə-nē′ĭz′əm) *n.* Hatred or fear of change or innovation. [Italian *misoneismo* : Greek *miso-,* miso- + Greek *neos,* new; see **newo-** in Appendix.] **—mis′o·ne′ist** *n.*

mis·o·ri·ent (mĭs-ôr′ē-ənt, -ĕnt′, -ōr′-) *tr.v.* **-ent·ed, -ent·ing, -ents.** To orient incorrectly or inappropriately. **—mis·o′ri·en·ta′tion** *n.*

mis·per·ceive (mĭs′pər-sēv′) *tr.v.* **-ceived, -ceiv·ing, -ceives.** To perceive incorrectly; misunderstand. **—mis′per·cep′tion** (-sĕp′shən) *n.*

mis·pick·el (mĭs′pĭk′əl) *n.* See **arsenopyrite.** [German.]

mis·place (mĭs-plās′) *tr.v.* **-placed, -plac·ing, -plac·es. 1.a.** To put into a wrong place: *misplace punctuation in a sentence.* **b.** To mislay: *I have misplaced my wallet.* **2.** To bestow (confidence, for example) on an improper, unsuitable, or unworthy person or idea. **—mis·place′ment** *n.*

misplaced modifier (mĭs′plāst′) *n.* A modifying clause or phrase placed so awkwardly as to create ambiguity or misunderstanding. For example, in *Streaking through the sky, we watched the rocket reenter the atmosphere,* the phrase *Streaking through the sky* is misplaced.

mis·play (mĭs-plā′, mĭs′plā′) *n. Sports & Games.* A mistaken play. **—misplay** (mĭs-plā′) *tr.v.* **-played, -play·ing, -plays.** To make a misplay of.

mis·print (mĭs-prĭnt′) *tr.v.* **-print·ed, -print·ing, -prints.** To print incorrectly. **—misprint** (mĭs′prĭnt′, mĭs-prĭnt′) *n.* An error in printing.

mis·pri·sion¹ (mĭs-prĭzh′ən) *n. Law.* **1.** Maladministration of public office. **2.** Neglect in preventing or reporting a felony or treason by one not an accessory. **3.** An act of sedition against a government or the courts. [Middle English, from Anglo-Norman, variant of Old French *mesprison,* from *mespris,* past participle of *mesprendre,* to make a mistake : *mes-,* wrongly; see MIS–¹ + *prendre,* to take, seize (from Latin *prehendere, prendere;* see **ghend-** in Appendix).]

mis·pri·sion² (mĭs-prĭzh′ən) *n.* Contempt; disdain. [*mispris(e)* (variant of MISPRIZE) + –ION.]

mis·prize (mĭs-prīz′) *tr.v.* **-prized, -priz·ing, -priz·es. 1.** To despise. **2.** To undervalue. **—mis·priz′er** *n.*

mis·pro·nounce (mĭs′prə-nouns′) *v.* **-nounced, -nounc·ing, -nounc·es.** *—tr.* To pronounce badly or incorrectly. *—intr.* To make a poor pronunciation. **—mis′pro·nun′ci·a′tion** (-nŭn′sē-ā′shən) *n.*

mis·quote (mĭs-kwōt′) *tr.v.* **-quot·ed, -quot·ing, -quotes.** To quote incorrectly. **—mis′quo·ta′tion** (-kwō-tā′shən) *n.* **—mis·quot′er** *n.*

mis·read (mĭs-rēd′) *tr.v.* **-read** (-rĕd′), **-read·ing, -reads. 1.** To read inaccurately. **2.** To misinterpret or misunderstand: *misread our friendly concern as prying.*

mis·reck·on (mĭs-rĕk′ən) *v.* **-oned, -on·ing, -ons.** *—tr.* To reckon incorrectly; miscalculate. *—intr.* To engage in incorrect reckoning or miscalculation.

mis·re·mem·ber (mĭs′rĭ-mĕm′bər) *tr. v.* **-bered, -ber·ing, -bers.** To remember incorrectly.

mis·re·port (mĭs′rĭ-pôrt′ -pōrt′) *tr.v.* **-port·ed, -port·ing, -ports.** To report mistakenly or falsely. **—misreport** *n.* An inaccurate or wrong report. **—mis′re·port′er** *n.*

mis·rep·re·sent (mĭs-rĕp′rĭ-zĕnt′) *tr.v.* **-sent·ed, -sent·ing, -sents. 1.** To give an incorrect or misleading representation of. **2.** To serve incorrectly or dishonestly as an official representative of. **—mis·rep′re·sen·ta′tion** *n.* **—mis·rep′re·sen′ta·tive** (-zĕn′tə-tĭv) *adj.* **—mis·rep′re·sent′er** *n.*

mis·rule (mĭs-rōōl′) *n.* **1.** Disorder or lawless confusion. **2.** Inept or unwise rule; misgovernment. **—misrule** *tr.v.* **-ruled, -rul·ing, -rules.** To rule ineptly, unjustly, or unwisely.

miss¹ (mĭs) *v.* **missed, miss·ing, miss·es.** *—tr.* **1.** To fail to hit, reach, catch, meet, or otherwise make contact with. **2.** To fail to perceive, understand, or experience: *completely missed the point of the film.* **3.** To fail to accomplish, achieve, or attain (a goal). **4.** To fail to attend or perform: *never missed a day of work.* **5.a.** To leave out; omit. **b.** To let go by; let slip: *miss a chance.* **6.** To escape or avoid: *narrowly missed crashing into the tree.* **7.** To discover the absence or loss of: *I missed my book after getting off the bus without it.* **8.** To feel the lack or loss of: *Do you miss your family? —intr.* **1.** To fail to hit or otherwise make contact

ă pat	oi boy
ā pay	ou out
âr care	ŏŏ took
ä father	ōō boot
ĕ pet	ŭ cut
ē be	ûr urge
ĭ pit	th thin
ī pie	*th* this
îr pier	hw which
ŏ pot	zh vision
ō toe	ə about, item
ô paw	♦ regionalism

Stress marks: **′** (primary); ′ (secondary), as in **dictionary** (dĭk′shə-nĕr′ē)

with something: *fired the final shot and missed again.* **2.a.** To be unsuccessful; fail. **b.** To misfire, as an internal-combustion engine. **—miss** *n.* **1.** A failure to hit, succeed, or find. **2.** The misfiring of an engine. **—*idioms.* miss fire. 1.** To fail to discharge. Used of a firearm. **2.** To fail to achieve the anticipated result. **miss out on.** To lose a chance for: *missed out on the promotion.* **miss the boat.** *Informal.* **1.** To fail to avail oneself of an opportunity. **2.** To fail to understand. [Middle English *missen,* from Old English *missan.* See **mei-**[1] in Appendix.]

miss² (mĭs) *n.* **1. Miss.** Used as a courtesy title before the surname or full name of a girl or single woman. See Usage Note at **Ms. 2.** Used as a form of polite address for a girl or young woman: *I beg your pardon, miss.* **3.** A young unmarried woman. **4. Miss.** Used as a prefix to the name of that which a usually young woman is held to represent: *She's Miss Personality.* **5. mis•ses.** A series of clothing sizes for women and girls of average height and proportions. [Short for MISTRESS.]

Miss. *abbr.* Mississippi.

mis•sa cantata (mĭs′ə) *n.* A Mass in which certain parts are sung but which is ceremonially less elaborate than a High Mass. [New Latin *missa cantāta* : Late Latin *missa,* Mass + Latin *cantāta,* sung.]

mis•sal (mĭs′əl) *n.* **1.** *Roman Catholic Church.* A book containing all the prayers and responses necessary for celebrating the Mass throughout the year. **2.** A prayer book. [Middle English *messel,* from Old French, from Medieval Latin *missāle,* from neuter of *missālis,* of the Mass, from Late Latin *missa,* Mass. See MASS.]

mis•sel thrush (mĭs′əl) *n.* Variant of **mistle thrush.**

mis•sense (mĭs′sĕns′) *n. Genetics.* A section within a strand of messenger RNA containing a codon altered through mutation so that it codes for a different amino acid.

missense mutation *n. Genetics.* A mutation that changes a codon for one amino acid into a codon for a different amino acid. [MIS–[1] + (NON)SENSE.]

mis•shape (mĭs-shāp′) *tr.v.* **-shaped** or **-shap•en** (-shā′pən), **-shap•ing, -shapes.** To shape badly; deform. **—mis•shap′en•ly** *adv.* **—mis•shap′er** *n.*

mis•sile (mĭs′əl, -īl′) *n.* **1.** An object or a weapon that is fired, thrown, dropped, or otherwise projected at a target; a projectile. **2.** A guided missile. **3.** A ballistic missile. *—attributive.* Often used to modify another noun: *missile technology; a missile silo.* [Latin, from neuter of *missilis,* able to be thrown, from *missus,* past participle of *mittere,* to let go, throw.]

mis•sile•ry also **mis•sil•ry** (mĭs′əl-rē) *n.* **1.** The science and technology of making and using guided or ballistic missiles. **2.** Missiles considered as a group.

miss•ing (mĭs′ĭng) *adj.* **1.a.** Not present; absent. **b.** Lost: *a missing person; soldiers missing in action.* **2.** Lacking; wanting: *This book has 12 missing pages.*

missing link *n.* **1.** A theoretical primate postulated to bridge the evolutionary gap between the anthropoid apes and human beings. **2.** Something lacking that is needed to complete a series.

mis•sion (mĭsh′ən) *n.* **1.a.** A body of persons sent to conduct negotiations or establish relations with a foreign country. **b.** The business with which such a body of persons is charged. **c.** A permanent diplomatic office abroad. **d.** A body of experts or dignitaries sent to a foreign country. **2.a.** A body of persons sent to a foreign land by a religious organization, especially a Christian organization, to spread its faith or provide educational, medical, and other assistance. **b.** A mission established abroad. **c.** The district assigned to a mission worker. **d.** A building or compound housing a mission. **e.** An organization for carrying on missionary work in a territory. **f. missions.** Missionary duty or work. **3.** A Christian church or congregation with no cleric of its own that depends for support on a larger religious organization. **4.** A series of special Christian services for purposes of proselytizing. **5.** A welfare or educational organization established for the needy people of a district. **6.a.** A special assignment given to a person or group: *an agent on a secret mission.* **b.** A combat operation assigned to a person or military unit. **c.** An aerospace operation intended to carry out specific program objectives: *a mission to Mars.* **7.** An inner calling to pursue an activity or perform a service; a vocation. **—mission** *tr.v.* **-sioned, -sion•ing, -sions. 1.** To send on a mission. **2.** To organize or establish a religious mission among or in. **—mission** *adj.* **1.** Of or relating to a mission. **2.** Of or relating to a style of architecture or furniture used in the early Spanish missions of California. **3.** Often **Mission.** Of, relating to, or having the distinctive qualities of an early 20th-century style of plain, heavy, dark-stained wood furniture. [French, from Old French, from Latin *missiō, missiōn-,* from *missus,* past participle of *mittere,* to send off.] **—mis′sion•al** *adj.*

mission
San Xavier del Bac Mission, founded in 1700, near Tucson, Arizona

Mission. A city of southern Texas near the Rio Grande west-northwest of Brownsville. Population, 22,589.

mis•sion•ar•y (mĭsh′ə-nĕr′ē) *n., pl.* **-ies. 1.** One who is sent on a mission, especially one sent to do religious or charitable work in a territory or foreign country. **2.** One who attempts to persuade or convert others to a particular program, doctrine, or set of principles; a propagandist. **—missionary** *adj.* **1.** Of or relating to missions or missionaries. **2.** Engaged in the activities of a mission or missionary. **3.** Tending to propagandize or use insistent persuasion: *missionary fervor.*

missionary position *n.* A position for sexual intercourse in which a woman and man lie facing each other, with the woman on the bottom and the man on the top.

Mis•sion•ar•y Ridge (mĭsh′ə-nĕr′ē). A range of hills in southeast Tennessee and northwest Georgia. It was the site of an important Union victory (November 25, 1863) in the Civil War.

mis•sion•er (mĭsh′ə-nər) *n.* A missionary.

mis•sion•ize (mĭsh′ə-nīz′) *v.* **-ized, -iz•ing, -iz•es.** *—intr.* To do missionary work. *—tr.* **1.** To perform missionary work in or among. **2.** To bring under the influence or control of a mission: *"Eastern Apaches in what is now Texas were even missionized—briefly—in the eighteenth century"* (William Brandon).

Mission Vi•e•jo (vē-ā′hō). A community of southern California southeast of Irvine. It is mainly residential. Population, 50,666.

mis•sis or **mis•sus** (mĭs′ĭz, -ĭs) *n. Informal.* **1.** The mistress of a household. **2.** Used as a term of reference by a man of his wife. [Alteration of MISTRESS.]

Mis•sis•sau•ga (mĭs′ĭ-sô′gə). A town of southern Ontario, Canada, a suburb of Toronto. Population, 315,056.

Mis•sis•sip•pi (mĭs′ĭ-sĭp′ē). *Abbr.* **MS, Miss.** A state of the southeast United States. It was admitted as the 20th state in 1817. The first settlers in the region (1699) were French, and the area passed to the British (1763–1779) and then to the Spanish before being ceded to the United States in 1783. Jackson is the capital and the largest city. Population, 2,520,631.

Mis•sis•sip•pi•an (mĭs′ĭ-sĭp′ē-ən) *adj.* **1.** Of or relating to the state or residents of Mississippi or the Mississippi River. **2.** Of, belonging to, or being the geologic time, system of rocks, and sedimentary deposits of the fifth period of the Paleozoic Era, characterized by the submergence of extensive land areas under shallow seas. See table at **geologic time. —Mississippian** *n.* **1.** A native or resident of Mississippi. **2.** The Mississippian Period. Also called *Lower Carboniferous.*

Mississippi River. The chief river of the United States, rising in the lake region of northern Minnesota and flowing about 3,781 km (2,350 mi) generally southward to enter the Gulf of Mexico through a huge delta in southeast Louisiana.

Mississippi Sound. An arm of the Gulf of Mexico bordering on southeast Louisiana, southern Mississippi, southwest Alabama, and a chain of small offshore islands.

mis•sive (mĭs′ĭv) *n.* A written message; a letter. See Synonyms at **letter.** [From Middle English *(letter) missive,* (letter) sent (by superior authority), from Medieval Latin *(littere) missīve,* feminine pl. of *missīvus,* sent, from Latin *missus,* past participle of *mittere,* to send.]

Mis•sou•la (mĭ-zo͞o′lə). A city of western Montana west-northwest of Helena. It is a processing center and the seat of the University of Montana (founded 1893). Population, 33,388.

Mis•sou•ri¹ (mĭ-zo͝or′ē) *n., pl.* **Missouri** or **-ris. 1.a.** A Native American people formerly inhabiting north-central Missouri, with present-day descendants living with the Oto in north-central Oklahoma. **b.** A member of this people. **2.** The Siouan language of the Missouri. [French, from Illinois *ouemessourita,* those that have dugout canoes.]

Mis•sou•ri² (mĭ-zo͝or′ē, -zo͝or′ə). *Abbr.* **MO, Mo.** A state of the central United States. It was admitted as the 24th state in 1821. Under Spanish control from 1762 to 1800, the area passed to the United States through the Louisiana Purchase of 1803. Organized as a territory in 1812, Missouri's application for admission as a slaveholding state in 1817 sparked a bitter controversy over the question of extending slavery into new territories. The Missouri Compromise of 1820 provided for the admission of Maine as a free state and Missouri as a slave state in the following year. Jefferson City is the capital and St. Louis the largest city. Population, 4,916,759. **—Mis•sou′ri•an** *adj. & n.*

Missouri City. A city of southeast Texas, a suburb of Houston. Population, 24,533.

Missouri River. A river of the United States rising in the Rocky Mountains as various headstreams that join to form the Missouri proper in southwest Montana. The longest river in the United States, it flows about 4,127 km (2,565 mi) in a meandering course to the Mississippi River north of St. Louis, Missouri.

mis•speak (mĭs-spēk′) *v.* **-spoke** (-spōk′), **-spo•ken** (-spō′kən), **-speak•ing, -speaks.** *—tr.* To speak or pronounce incorrectly: *The lead actor mispoke his lines.* *—intr.* To speak mistakenly, inappropriately, or rashly.

mis•spell (mĭs-spĕl′) *tr.v.* **-spelled** or **-spelt** (-spĕlt′), **-spell•ing, -spells.** To spell incorrectly.

mis•spell•ing (mĭs-spĕl′ĭng) *n.* **1.** The act or an instance of spelling incorrectly. **2.** A word spelled incorrectly.

mis•spelt (mĭs-spĕlt′) *v.* A past tense and a past participle of **misspell.**

mis•spend (mĭs-spĕnd′) *tr.v.* **-spent** (-spĕnt′), **-spend•ing, -spends.** To spend improperly or extravagantly; squander: *misspent the funds; misspent their youth.*

mis•spoke (mĭs-spōk′) *v.* Past tense of **misspeak.**

mis•spo•ken (mĭs-spō′kən) *v.* Past participle of **misspeak.**

mis•state (mĭs-stāt′) *tr.v.* **-stat•ed, -stat•ing, -states.** To state wrongly or falsely. **—mis•state′ment** *n.*

mis•step (mĭs-stĕp′) *n.* **1.** A misplaced or awkward step. **2.** An instance of wrong or improper conduct; a blunder.

mis•sus (mĭs′ĭz, -ĭs) *n.* Variant of **missis.**

mis·sy (mĭs′ē) *n., pl.* **-sies.** *Informal.* Used as a familiar term of address for a young woman or girl.

mist (mĭst) *n.* **1.** A mass of fine droplets of water in the atmosphere near or in contact with the earth. **2.** Water vapor condensed on and clouding the appearance of a surface. **3.** Fine drops of a liquid, such as water, perfume, or medication, sprayed into the air. **4.** A suspension of fine drops of a liquid in a gas. **5.** Something that dims or conceals. **6.** A haze before the eyes that blurs the vision. **7.** Something that produces or gives the impression of dimness or obscurity: *the mists of the past.* **8.** A drink consisting of a liquor served over cracked ice. **—mist** *v.* **mist·ed, mist·ing, mists.** *—intr.* **1.** To be or become obscured or blurred by or as if by mist. **2.** To rain in a fine shower. *—tr.* **1.** To conceal or veil as if with mist. **2.** To moisturize (plants or dry air, for example) with a fine spray of water. [Middle English, from Old English. See **meigh-** in Appendix.]

mis·tak·a·ble (mĭ-stā′kə-bəl) *adj.* Capable of being mistaken or misunderstood: *mistakable signals.* **—mis·tak′a·bly** *adv.*

mis·take (mĭ-stāk′) *n.* **1.** An error or a fault resulting from defective judgment, deficient knowledge, or carelessness. **2.** A misconception or misunderstanding. See Synonyms at **error.** **—mistake** *v.* **mis·took** (mĭ-stŏŏk′), **mis·tak·en** (mĭ-stā′kən), **mis·tak·ing, mis·takes.** *—tr.* **1.** To understand wrongly; misinterpret: *mistook my politeness for friendliness.* **2.** To identify incorrectly: *He mistook her for her sister.* *—intr.* To make a mistake. [From Middle English *mistaken,* to misunderstand, from Old Norse *mistaka,* to take in error : *mis-,* wrongly; see **mei-**[1] in Appendix + *taka,* to take.] **—mis·tak′er** *n.*

mis·tak·en (mĭ-stā′kən) *v.* Past participle of **mistake.** **—mistaken** *adj.* **1.** Wrong or incorrect in opinion, understanding, or perception. **2.** Based on error; wrong: *a mistaken view of the situation.* **—mis·tak′en·ly** *adv.*

Mis·tas·si·ni (mĭs′tə-sē′nē), **Lake.** A lake of south-central Quebec, Canada, draining westward into James Bay by way of the Rupert River.

Mis·ter (mĭs′tər) *n. Abbr.* **Mr. 1.** Used as a courtesy title before the surname, full name, or professional title of a man, usually written in its abbreviated form: *Mr. Jones; Mr. Secretary.* **2.** Used as the official term of address for certain U.S. military personnel, such as warrant officers. **3. mister.** *Informal.* Used as a form of address for a man: *Watch your step, mister.* **4.** *Informal.* Used as a term of reference by a woman of her husband. [Alteration of MASTER.]

Mister Char·lie (chär′lē) *n. Offensive Slang.* Variant of **Mr. Charlie.**

mist·flow·er (mĭst′flou′ər) *n.* A perennial plant *(Eupatorium coelestinum)* of the southeast and central United States, having corymbs of small blue flowers.

Mis·ti (mē′stē), **El.** See **El Misti.**

mis·time (mĭs-tīm′) *tr.v.* **-timed, -tim·ing, -times.** To time inaccurately or inappropriately; misjudge the timing of: *The basketball team mistimed the final play and lost the game.*

mis·tle thrush also **mis·sel thrush** (mĭs′əl) *n.* A European thrush *(Turdus viscivorus)* that feeds on berries, especially those of mistletoe. [From obsolete *missel,* mistletoe, from Middle English *mistel,* from Old English. See MISTLETOE.]

mis·tle·toe (mĭs′əl-tō′) *n.* **1.** A Eurasian parasitic shrub *(Viscum album)* having leathery evergreen leaves and waxy white berries. **2.** Any of several American parasitic shrubs, such as *Phoradendron flavescens* of eastern North America. **3.** A sprig of mistletoe, often used as a Christmas decoration. [Middle English *mistelto,* back-formation from Old English *misteltān (tān,* taken for pl. of *tā,* toe) : *mistel,* mistletoe; see **meigh-** in Appendix + *tān,* twig.]

mistletoe cactus *n.* A leafless, epiphytic tropical American cactus *(Rhipsalis baccifera).*

mis·took (mĭ-stŏŏk′) *v.* Past tense of **mistake.**

mis·tral (mĭs′trəl, mĭ-sträl′) *n.* A dry, cold northerly wind that blows in squalls toward the Mediterranean coast of southern France. [French, from Provençal *maestral,* from Old Provençal, from Late Latin *magistrālis,* of a master, from *magister,* master. See **meg-** in Appendix.]

Mis·tral (mĭ-sträl′, mē-), **Frédéric.** 1830–1914. French writer and leader in the revival of Provençal as a literary language. He shared the 1904 Nobel Prize for literature.

Mistral, Gabriela. Pen name of Lucila Godoy Alcayaga. 1889–1957. Chilean poet whose works include *Sonnets of Death* (1914) and *Tala* (1938). She won the 1945 Nobel Prize for literature.

mis·trans·late (mĭs′trăns-lāt′, -trănz-, mĭs-trăns′lāt′, -trănz′-) *tr.v.* **-lat·ed, -lat·ing, -lates.** To translate incorrectly. **—mis′trans·la′tion** *n.*

mis·treat (mĭs-trēt′) *tr.v.* **-treat·ed, -treat·ing, -treats.** To treat roughly or wrongly; abuse. See Synonyms at **abuse.** **—mis·treat′ment** *n.*

mis·tress (mĭs′trĭs) *n.* **1.** A woman in a position of authority, control, or ownership, as the head of a household: *"Thirteen years had seen her mistress of Kellynch Hall"* (Jane Austen). **2.** A woman owner of an animal or a slave. **3.** A woman with ultimate control over something: *the mistress of her own mind.* **4.a.** A nation or country that has supremacy over others: *Great Britain, once the mistress of the seas.* **b.** Something personified as female that directs or reigns: *"my mistress . . . the open road"* (Robert Louis Stevenson). **5.** A woman who has mastered a skill or a branch of learning: *a mistress of the culinary art.* **6.** A woman who has a continuing sexual relationship with a usually married man who is not her husband and from whom she generally receives material support. **7. Mistress.** Used formerly as a courtesy title when speaking to or of a woman. **8.** *Chiefly British.* A woman schoolteacher. [Middle English *maistresse,* from Old French, feminine of *maistre,* master, from Latin *magister.* See MASTER.]

mis·tri·al (mĭs-trī′əl, -trīl′) *n. Law.* **1.** A trial that becomes invalid because of basic prejudicial error in procedure. **2.** An inconclusive trial, as one in which the jurors fail to agree on a verdict.

mis·trust (mĭs-trŭst′) *n.* Lack of trust or confidence arising from suspicion. See Synonyms at **uncertainty.** **—mistrust** *v.* **-trust·ed, -trust·ing, -trusts.** *—tr.* To regard without trust or confidence. *—intr.* To be wary, suspicious, or doubtful. **—mis·trust′ful** *adj.* **—mis·trust′ful·ly** *adv.* **—mis·trust′ful·ness** *n.*

mist·y (mĭs′tē) *adj.* **-i·er, -i·est. 1.** Consisting of or marked by mist: *a misty rain; a misty night.* **2.** Obscured or clouded by or as if by mist: *far-off, misty mountains.* **3.a.** Vague; hazy: *a misty recollection of a dream.* **b.** Full of tender emotion; sentimental: *a love story that left us feeling misty and sad.* **—mist′i·ly** *adv.* **—mist′i·ness** *n.*

mist·y-eyed (mĭs′tē-īd′) *adj.* **1.** Having the eyes blurred, as with tears. **2.** Having a sentimental or dreamy quality: *a misty-eyed view of the past.*

mis·un·der·stand (mĭs′-ŭn-dər-stănd′) *tr.v.* **-stood** (-stŏŏd′), **-stand·ing, -stands.** To understand incorrectly; misinterpret.

mis·un·der·stand·ing (mĭs′-ŭn-dər-stăn′dĭng) *n.* **1.** A failure to understand or interpret correctly. **2.** A disagreement or quarrel.

mis·un·der·stood (mĭs′ŭn-dər-stŏŏd′) *v.* Past tense and past participle of **misunderstand.** **—misunderstood** *adj.* **1.** Incorrectly understood or interpreted. **2.** Not appreciated or given sympathetic understanding: *a sorely misunderstood child.*

mis·us·age (mĭs-yōō′sĭj, -zĭj) *n.* **1.** Abusive treatment. **2.** Improper application, as of words.

mis·use (mĭs-yōōs′) *n.* Improper, unlawful, or incorrect use; misapplication. **—misuse** (-yōōz′) *tr.v.* **-used, -us·ing, -us·es. 1.** To use incorrectly. **2.** To mistreat or abuse. See Synonyms at **abuse.**

mis·us·er (mĭs-yōō′-zər) *n.* **1.** One that misuses: *a misuser of school athletic equipment.* **2.** *Law.* Unlawful use of an authorized privilege, right, or form of empowerment, as that of a franchise by a corporation.

mis·val·ue (mĭs-văl′yōō) *tr.v.* **-ued, -u·ing, -ues.** To value or estimate incorrectly, especially to undervalue: *The art critics had misvalued his work for years.*

mis·word (mĭs-wûrd′) *tr.v.* **-word·ed, -word·ing, -words.** To express incorrectly; word improperly.

mis·write (mĭs-rīt′) *tr.v.* **-wrote** (-rōt′), **-writ·ten** (-rĭt′n), **-writ·ing, -writes.** To write incorrectly or carelessly: *miswrite a word; miswrite a historical account.*

Mi·tan·ni (mĭ-tăn′ē, -tä′nē). An ancient kingdom of northwest Mesopotamia extending from the bend in the Euphrates River nearly to the Tigris River. Founded probably by Aryans, the kingdom was established c. 1475 B.C. and lasted until c. 1275, when it fell to the Hittites. **—Mi·tan′ni·an** *adj. & n.*

Mitch·ell (mĭch′əl), **John.** 1870–1919. American labor leader who was president of the United Mine Workers from 1898 to 1908.

Mitchell, Margaret Munnerlyn. 1900–1949. American writer known for her novel *Gone With the Wind* (1936).

Mitchell, Maria. 1818–1889. American astronomer and educator noted for her study of sunspots and nebulae and for the discovery of a comet (1847).

Mitchell, Mount. A peak, 2,038.6 m (6,684 ft) high, in the Appalachian Mountains of western North Carolina. It is the highest point east of the Mississippi River.

Mitchell, William. Known as "Billy." 1879–1936. American soldier and aviation pioneer who was one of the first advocates of military air power.

mite[1] (mīt) *n.* Any of various small or minute arachnids of the order Acarina that are often parasitic on animals and plants, infest stored food products, and in some species transmit disease. [Middle English, from Old French *mite,* from Middle Dutch.]

mite[2] (mīt) *n.* **1.a.** A very small contribution or amount of money. **b.** A widow's mite. **2.** A very small object, creature, or particle. **3.** A coin of very small value, especially an obsolete British coin worth half a farthing. [Middle English, from Middle Dutch and Middle Low German *mīte,* a small Flemish coin, tiny animal.]

mi·ter (mī′tər) *n.* **1.** *Ecclesiastical.* The liturgical headdress and part of the insignia of a Christian bishop. In the Western church it is a tall pointed hat with peaks in front and back, worn at all solemn functions. **2.a.** A thong for binding the hair, worn by women in ancient Greece. **b.** The ceremonial headdress worn by ancient Jewish high priests. **3.a.** A miter joint. **b.** The edge of a piece of material that has been beveled preparatory to making a miter joint. **c.** A miter square. **—miter** *v.* **-tered, -ter·ing, -ters.** *—tr.* **1.** To bestow a miter upon. **2.a.** To make (two pieces or surfaces) join with a miter joint. **b.** To bevel the edges of for joining with a miter joint. *—intr.* To meet in a miter joint. [Middle English *mitre,* from Old French, from Medieval Latin, from

mistletoe

miter
Worn by
Cardinal Bernard Law
of Boston, Massachusetts

ă pat	oi boy
ā pay	ou out
âr care	ŏŏ took
ä father	ōō boot
ĕ pet	ŭ cut
ē be	ûr urge
ĭ pit	th thin
ī pie	*th* this
îr pier	hw which
ŏ pot	zh vision
ō toe	ə about, item
ô paw	♦ regionalism

Stress marks: ′ (primary); ′ (secondary), as in **dictionary** (dĭk′shə-nĕr′ē)

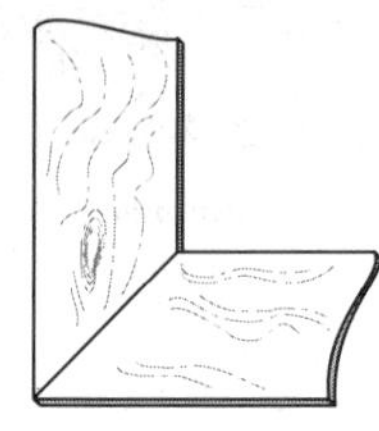

miter joint

PROPHASE

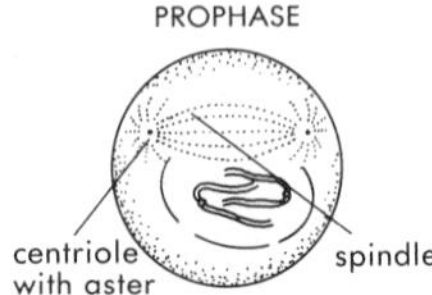

METAPHASE

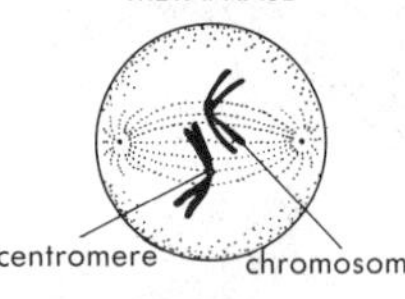

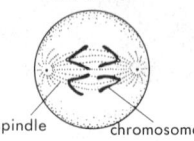

ANAPHASE

spindle chromosome

TELOPHASE

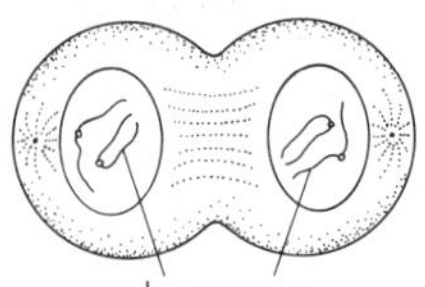

mitosis

François Mitterrand
Photographed in 1981

Latin *mitra,* headdress of the Jewish high priest, from Greek.] **—mi′ter·er** *n.*

miter box *n.* A fixed or adjustable device for guiding handsaws in cutting miter joints or in making crosscuts, especially an open-ended box with slotted sides.

miter joint *n.* A joint made by beveling each of two surfaces to be joined, usually at a 45° angle, to form a corner, usually a 90° angle.

miter square *n.* An instrument with straight edges that are set at a 45° angle or that are adjustable, used for marking the angles of a miter joint.

mi·ter·wort (mī′tər-wûrt′, -wôrt′) *n.* Any of several North American plants of the genus *Mitella,* having heart-shaped leaves and clusters of small white flowers with pinnately divided petals. Also called *bishop's cap.* [From the shape of its capsule.]

Mith·ra·ism (mĭth′rə-ĭz′əm, -rā-) *n.* A religious cult of Persian origin, especially popular among the Roman military, that flourished in the late Roman Empire, rivaling Christianity. **—Mith·ra′ic** (mĭ-thrā′ĭk) *adj.* **—Mith·ra′ist** *n.*

Mith·ras (mĭth′rəs) *n. Mythology.* The ancient Persian god of light and guardian against evil, often identified with the sun.

mith·ri·date (mĭth′rĭ-dāt′) *n.* An antidote against poison, especially a confection formerly held to be an antidote to all poisons. [Medieval Latin *mithridātum,* alteration of Late Latin *mithridātīum,* from Latin, neuter of *Mithridātīus,* of Mithridates, from Greek *mithridateios,* after MITHRIDATES VI, who is said to have acquired tolerance for poison.]

Mith·ri·da·tes VI (mĭth′rĭ-dā′tēz). Known as "Mithridates the Great." 132?–63 B.C. King of Pontus (120–63) who expanded the kingdom through victories over the Romans during the early part of his reign but was later driven from Pontus by Pompey (66).

mith·ri·da·tism (mĭth′rĭ-dā′tĭz′əm) *n.* Tolerance or immunity to a poison acquired by taking gradually larger doses of it. [After MITHRIDATES VI, who is said to have acquired tolerance for poison.] **—mith′ri·dat′ic** (-dăt′ĭk) *adj.*

mi·ti·cide (mī′tĭ-sīd′) *n.* An agent that kills mites. **—mi′ti·cid′al** (-sīd′l) *adj.*

mit·i·gate (mĭt′ĭgāt′) *v.* **-gat·ed, -gat·ing, -gates.** *—tr.* To moderate (a quality or condition) in force or intensity; alleviate. See Synonyms at **relieve.** *—intr.* To become milder. [Middle English *mitigaten,* from Latin *mītigāre, mītigāt-* : *mītis,* soft + *agere,* to drive, do; see ACT.] **—mit′i·ga·ble** (-gə-bəl) *adj.* **—mit′i·ga′tion** *n.* **—mit′i·ga′tive, mit′i·ga·to′ry** (-gə-tôr′ē, -tōr′ē) *adj.* **—mit′i·ga′tor** *n.*

mi·to·chon·dri·on (mī′tə-kŏn′drē-ən) *n., pl.* **-dri·a** (-drē-ə). A spherical or elongated organelle in the cytoplasm of nearly all eukaryotic cells, containing genetic material and many enzymes important for cell metabolism, including those responsible for the conversion of food to usable energy. Also called *chondriosome.* [New Latin : Greek *mitos,* warp thread + Greek *khondrion,* diminutive of *khondros,* grain, granule; see **ghrendh-** in Appendix.] **—mi′to·chon′dri·al** (-drē-əl) *adj.*

mi·to·gen (mī′tə-jən) *n.* An agent that induces mitosis. [MITO(SIS) + -GEN.] **—mi′to·gen′ic** (mī′tə-jĕn′ĭk, mĭt′ə-) *adj.* **—mi′to·ge·nic′i·ty** (-jə-nĭs′ĭ-tē) *n.*

mi·to·my·cin (mī′tə-mī′sĭn) *n.* Any of a group of antibiotics produced by the soil actinomycete *Streptomyces caespitosus* that inhibit DNA synthesis and are used against bacteria and cancerous tumor cells. [Probably MITO(SIS) + -MYCIN.]

mi·to·sis (mī-tō′sĭs) *n., pl.* **-ses** (-sēz). *Biology.* **1.** The process in cell division by which the nucleus divides, typically consisting of four stages, prophase, metaphase, anaphase, and telophase, and normally resulting in two new nuclei, each of which contains a complete copy of the parental chromosomes. Also called *karyokinesis.* **2.** The process of cell division including division of the nucleus and the cytoplasm. [Greek *mitos,* warp thread + -OSIS.] **—mi·tot′ic** (-tŏt′ĭk) *adj.* **—mi·tot′i·cal·ly** *adv.*

mi·tral (mī′trəl) *adj.* **1.** Relating to or resembling a miter worn by certain ecclesiastics. **2.** Relating to a mitral valve.

mitral stenosis *n.* A narrowing of the mitral valve, usually caused by rheumatic fever, resulting in an obstruction to the flow of blood from the left atrium to the left ventricle.

mitral valve *n.* A valve of the heart, composed of two triangular flaps, that is located between the left atrium and left ventricle and regulates blood flow between these chambers. Also called *bicuspid valve, left atrioventricular valve.*

mi·tre (mī′tər) *n. & v. Chiefly British.* Variant of **miter.**

mitt (mĭt) *n.* **1.** A woman's glove that extends over the hand and only partially covers the fingers. **2.** A mitten. **3.** *Baseball.* A large, padded, protective leather glove, usually with one sheath for the thumb and one undivided sheath for the remaining fingers, used by catchers and first basemen. **4.** *Slang.* A hand or fist. [Short for MITTEN.]

mit·ten (mĭt′n) *n.* A covering for the hand that encases the thumb separately and the four fingers together. [Middle English, from Old French *mitaine* (from *mite,* cat's caress, mitten, from *mit,* cat) and from Medieval Latin *mitta,* mitten (possibly from Old French *mite*).]

Mit·ter·rand (mē′tə-ränd′, -räN′), **François Maurice.** Born 1916. French politician who became president of France in 1981 and was reelected in 1988.

mitz·vah (mĭts′və) *n., pl.* **-voth** (-vōt′, -vōs′) or **-vahs. 1.a.** A commandment of the Jewish law. **b.** The fulfillment of such a commandment. **2.** A worthy deed. [Hebrew *miṣwâ,* from *ṣiwwâ,* to command.]

Mi·wok (mē′wŏk) *n., pl.* **Miwok** or **-woks. 1.a.** A Native American people formerly composed of numerous groups inhabiting central California from the Sierra Nevada foothills to the San Francisco Bay area, with a small number of present-day descendants in the same region. **b.** A member of this people. **2.** Any of the Penutian languages of this people.

mix (mĭks) *v.* **mixed, mix·ing, mix·es.** *—tr.* **1.a.** To combine or blend into one mass or mixture. **b.** To create or form by combining ingredients: *mix a drink; mix cement.* **c.** To add (an ingredient or element) to another: *mix an egg into batter.* **2.** To combine or join: *mix joy with sorrow.* **3.** To bring into social contact: *mix boys and girls in the classroom.* **4.** To crossbreed. **5.** *Electronics.* **a.** To combine (two or more audio tracks or channels) to produce a composite audio recording. **b.** To produce (a soundtrack or recording) in this manner. *—intr.* **1.a.** To become mixed or blended together. **b.** To be capable of being blended together: *Oil does not mix with water.* **2.** To associate socially or get along with others: *He does not mix well at parties.* **3.** To be crossbred. **4.** To become involved: *In the case of a family argument, it is better for a friend not to mix in.* **—mix** *n.* **1.** An act of mixing. **2.a.** A mixture, especially of ingredients packaged and sold commercially: *a cake mix.* **b.** A blend of diverse elements; an amalgamation: *"a mix of mean streets and the grandest boulevards—no other place in Paris is as eclectic and eccentric . . . as the 17th"* (Jean Rafferty). **3.** *Electronics.* A recording that is produced by combining and adjusting two or more audio tracks or channels. ***—phrasal verbs.*** **mix down.** *Electronics.* To combine all of the audio components of a recording into a final soundtrack or mix. **mix up. 1.** To confuse; confound: *His explanation just mixed me up more. I always mix up the twins.* **2.** To involve or implicate: *He got himself mixed up with the wrong people.* ***—idiom.*** **mix it up.** *Slang.* To fight. [Back-formation from Middle English *mixt, mixed,* mixed, from Anglo-Norman *mixte,* from Latin *mixtus,* past participle of *miscēre,* to mix. See **meik-** in Appendix.] **—mix′a·ble** *adj.*

SYNONYMS: *mix, blend, mingle, coalesce, merge, amalgamate, fuse.* These verbs mean to put into or come together in one mass so that constituent parts or elements are diffused or commingled. *Mix* is the least specific, implying only components capable of being combined: *mix water and wine; motives that were mixed. Greed and charity don't mix.* To *blend* is to mix intimately and harmoniously so that the components shade into each other, losing some or all of their original definition: *blended mocha and java coffee beans; snow-covered mountains blending into the clouds. Mingle* implies combination without loss of individual characteristics: *"Respect was mingled with surprise"* (Sir Walter Scott). *"His companions mingled freely and joyously with the natives"* (Washington Irving). *Coalesce* involves a union, often slowly achieved, with a distinct new identity: *Indigenous peoples and conquerors gradually coalesced into the present-day population. Merge* implies the absorption of one entity into another with resultant homogeneity: *Tradition and innovation are merged in this new composition. Twilight merged into night. Amalgamate* implies the integration of elements: *"The four sentences of the original are amalgamated into two"* (William Minto). *Fuse* emphasizes an enduring union, as that formed by heating metals, strongly marked by the merging of parts: *"He diffuses a tone and spirit of unity, that blends, and (as it were) fuses, each into each"* (Samuel Taylor Coleridge).

Mix (mĭks), **Thomas Edwin.** Known as "Tom." 1880–1940. American film actor noted for his performances in silent Westerns.

mixed (mĭkst) *adj. Abbr.* **mxd. 1.** Blended together into one unit or mass; intermingled. **2.** Composed of a variety of differing, sometimes conflicting entities: *viewed the change in management with mixed emotions; a closet full of mixed outfits.* See Synonyms at **miscellaneous. 3.** Made up of people of different sex, race, or social class. **4.a.** Descended from two or more races or breeds. **b.** Crossbred.

mixed bag *n.* A collection of dissimilar things; an assortment.

mixed doubles *pl.n. (used with a sing. verb). Sports.* A game of doubles, as in tennis, that is played with each team composed of one man and one woman.

mixed drink *n.* A drink made of one or more kinds of liquor combined with other ingredients, usually shaken or stirred before serving.

mixed economy *n.* An economic system that allows for the simultaneous operation of publicly and privately owned enterprises.

mixed farm·ing (fär′mĭng) *n.* The use of a single farm for multiple purposes, as the growing of cash crops or the raising of livestock.

mixed grill *n.* A single dish consisting of a variety of broiled meats and vegetables.

mixed marriage *n.* Marriage between persons of different races or religions.

mixed media *pl.n. (used with a sing. verb).* **1.** A technique involving the use of two or more artistic media, such as ink and pastel or painting and collage, that are combined in a single composition. **2.** See **multimedia. —mixed′-me′di·a** (mĭkst′-mē′dē-ə) *adj.*

mixed metaphor *n.* A succession of incongruous metaphors, as in *The negotiator played his cards to the hilt.*

mixed nerve *n.* A nerve that contains both sensory and motor fibers.

mixed number *n. Mathematics.* A number, such as 7¼, consisting of an integer and a fraction or decimal.

mixed-up (mĭkst′ŭp′) *adj. Informal.* In a state of confusion; bewildered or muddled: *just a mixed-up kid.*

mixed-use (mĭkst′yo͞os′) *adj.* Containing or zoned for commercial and residential facilities or development: *a 40-story mixed-use tower; a mixed-use parcel of land.*

mix·er (mĭk′sər) *n.* **1.** One that mixes: *a mixer of concrete; a mixer of drinks.* **2.** A sociable person: *She's outgoing and a good mixer.* **3.** An informal dance or party arranged to give members of a group an opportunity to get acquainted. **4.** A device that blends or mixes substances or ingredients, especially by mechanical agitation. **5.** A beverage, such as soda water or ginger ale, used in diluting alcoholic drinks. **6.** *Electronics.* **a.** One who mixes the audio components of a recording. **b.** A device used to combine and adjust sounds from a variety of sources in order to create a final recorded audio product, such as the soundtrack of a movie.

mix·ol·o·gy (mĭk-sŏl′ə-jē) *n.* The study or skill of preparing mixed drinks. **—mix·ol′o·gist** *n.*

mixt (mĭkst) *v. Archaic.* A past tense and a past participle of **mix.**

Mix·tec (mēs′tĕk) *n., pl.* **Mixtec** or **-tecs. 1.a.** A member of a Mesoamerican Indian people of southern Mexico whose civilization was overthrown by the Aztecs in the 16th century. **b.** A modern-day descendant of this people. **2.** The language of this people. [Spanish, from Nahuatl *mixtecatl,* inhabitant of Mixtecapán, a province of the Mexican empire.]

mix·ture (mĭks′chər) *n.* **1.a.** The act or process of mixing: *an alloy made from the mixture of two metals.* **b.** The condition of being mixed: *the inevitable mixtures of urban neighborhoods.* **2.** Something produced by mixing. **3.** One that consists of diverse elements: *The day was a mixture of sun and clouds.* **4.** A fabric made of different kinds of thread or yarn. **5.** *Chemistry.* A composition of two or more substances that are not chemically combined with each other and are capable of being separated. [Middle English, from Old French, from Latin *mixtūra,* from *mixtus,* past participle of *miscēre,* to mix. See **meik-** in Appendix.]

SYNONYMS: *mixture, blend, admixture, compound, composite, amalgam.* These nouns refer to a combination produced by mixing. *Mixture* has the widest application: *a mixture of tea and honey; yarn that is a mixture of nylon and cotton. "He showed a curious mixture of eagerness and terror"* (Francis Parkman). *Blend* denotes an intimate, harmonious mixture in which the original components lose their distinctness: *The novel is a fascinating blend of illusion and reality. Admixture* suggests that one of the components of the mixture is dissimilar to the others: *The essential oil in the perfume contains a large admixture of alcohol.* A *compound* is a combination of elements or parts that together constitute a new and independent entity: *The word* houseboat *is a compound. Creative genius is a compound made up of exceptional intellect and superior imagination.* A *composite* usually lacks the unity of a compound since the components may not wholly lose their identities: *The suite is a composite of themes for various parts of the opera. Amalgam* implies an intimate union of diverse elements likened to an alloy of mercury and another metal: *an amalgam of charming agreeability and indefatigable humor.*

mix-up also **mix·up** (mĭks′ŭp′) *n.* **1.** A state or an instance of confusion; a muddle: *maddening bureaucratic mix-ups.* **2.** *Informal.* A fight or melee.

Mi·ya·za·ki (mē-yä′zä-kē, mē′yä-zä′kē). A city of southeast Kyushu, Japan, southeast of Kumamoto on an arm of the Pacific Ocean. It is an industrial and resort center. Population, 279,118.

Mi·zar (mī′zär′) *n.* The double star in the middle of the handle of the Big Dipper. [Arabic *mi'zar,* cloak, Mizar.]

miz·zen or **miz·en** (mĭz′ən) *n. Nautical.* **1.** A fore-and-aft sail set on the mizzenmast. **2.** A mizzenmast. [Middle English *mesan,* from Old French *misaine,* Old Spanish *mezana* or Old Italian *mezzana,* all ultimately from Latin *mediānus,* of the middle, from *medius,* middle. See **medhyo-** in Appendix.]

miz·zen·mast or **miz·en·mast** (mĭz′ən-məst, -măst′) *n. Nautical.* **1.** The third mast aft on sailing ships carrying three or more masts. **2.** See **jigger mast** (sense 2).

miz·zle[1] (mĭz′əl) *intr.v.* **-zled, -zling, -zles.** To rain in fine, mistlike droplets; drizzle. **—mizzle** *n.* A mistlike rain; a drizzle. [Middle English *misellen*; probably akin to Dutch dialectal *mieselen.* See **meigh-** in Appendix.] **—miz′zly** *adv.*

miz·zle[2] (mĭz′əl) *intr.v.* **-zled, -zling, -zles.** *Chiefly British.* To make a sudden departure. [Origin unknown.]

Mk *abbr. Bible.* Mark.

mk. *abbr.* **1.** Mark (currency). **2.** Markka.

mks or **MKS** *abbr.* Meter-kilogram-second.

mksA *abbr.* Meter-kilogram-second-ampere.

mkt. *abbr.* Market.

mktg. *abbr.* Marketing.

ml or **mL** *abbr.* Milliliter.

mL *abbr.* Millilambert.

Ml *abbr. Bible.* Malachi.

MLA or **M.L.A.** *abbr.* Modern Language Association.

MLD *abbr.* Median lethal dose; minimum lethal dose.

Mlle. *abbr.* Mademoiselle.

Mlles. *abbr.* Mesdemoiselles.

M.L.S. *abbr.* Master of Library Science.

MLW *abbr.* Mean low water.

mm *abbr.* Millimeter.

m.m. *abbr.* Mutatis mutandis.

M.M. *abbr.* Messieurs.

Mme. *abbr.* Madame.

Mmes. *abbr.* Mesdames.

mmf or **m.m.f.** *abbr.* Magnetomotive force.

MMPI *abbr.* Minnesota Multiphasic Personality Inventory.

Mn The symbol for the element **manganese.**

MN *abbr.* **1.** Magnetic north. **2.** Minnesota.

mobcap
Detail of
oil on canvas portrait of
Mrs. Charles S. Gatewood
by Matthew Harris Jouett
(1788?–1827)

mne·mon·ic (nĭ-mŏn′ĭk) *adj.* Relating to, assisting, or intended to assist the memory. **—mnemonic** *n.* A device, such as a formula or rhyme, used as an aid in remembering. [Greek *mnēmonikos,* from *mnēmōn, mnēmon-,* mindful. See **men-**[1] in Appendix.] **—mne·mon′i·cal·ly** *adv.*

mne·mon·ics (nĭ-mŏn′ĭks) *n. (used with a sing. verb).* A system to develop or improve the memory.

Mne·mos·y·ne (nĭ-mŏs′ə-nē, -mŏz′-) *n. Greek Mythology.* The goddess of memory, mother of the Muses.

mngr. *abbr.* Manager.

Mo The symbol for the element **molybdenum.**

MO or **Mo.** *abbr.* Missouri.

mo. *abbr.* Month.

m.o. or **M.O.** *abbr.* **1.** Mail order. **2.** Medical officer. **3.** Modus operandi. **4.** Also **MO.** Money order.

-mo *suff.* Used after numerals to indicate the number of leaves that results from folding a sheet of paper: *twelvemo.* [From (DU-ODECI)MO.]

mo·a (mō′ə) *n.* Any of various flightless ostrichlike birds of the family Dinornithidae, native to New Zealand and extinct for over a century. [Maori.]

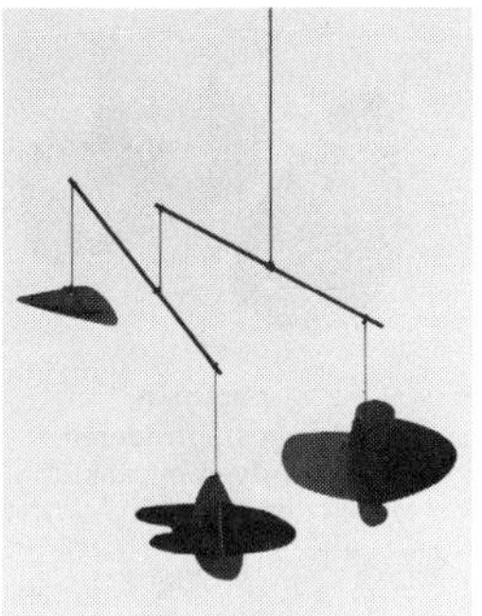

mobile
c. 1934 *Mobile* of sheet metal, metal rods, and cord by Alexander Calder

Mo·ab (mō′ăb). An ancient kingdom east of the Dead Sea in present-day southwest Jordan. According to the Old Testament, its inhabitants were descendants of Lot.

Mo·ab·ite (mō′ə-bīt′) *n.* **1.** A native or inhabitant of Moab. **2.** The Semitic language of Moab. **—Mo′a·bite′, Mo′a·bit′ish** *adj.*

moan (mōn) *n.* **1.a.** A low, sustained, mournful cry, usually indicative of sorrow or pain. **b.** A similar sound: *the eerie moan of the night wind.* **2.** Lamentation. **—moan** *v.* **moaned, moan·ing, moans.** *—intr.* **1.a.** To utter a moan or moans. **b.** To make a sound resembling a moan: *A saxophone moaned in the background.* **2.** To complain, lament, or grieve: *an old man who still moans about his misspent youth.* *—tr.* **1.** To bewail or bemoan: *She moaned her misfortunes to anyone who would listen.* **2.** To utter with moans or a moan. [Middle English *mone,* from Old English **mān.* See **mei-no-** in Appendix.]

moat (mōt) *n.* **a.** A deep, wide ditch, usually filled with water, typically surrounding a fortified medieval town, fortress, or castle as a protection against assault. **b.** A ditch similar to one surrounding a fortification: *A moat separates the animals in the zoo from the spectators.* *—tr.* **moat·ed, moat·ing, moats.** To surround with or as if with a deep, wide ditch. [Middle English *mote,* mound, moat, from Old French, mound, or Medieval Latin *mota.*]

mob (mŏb) *n.* **1.** A large disorderly crowd or throng. See Synonyms at **crowd**[1]. **2.** The mass of common people; the populace. **3.** *Informal.* **a.** An organized gang of criminals; a crime syndicate. **b.** Often **Mob.** Organized crime. Often used with *the: a murder suspect with links to the Mob.* **4.** An indiscriminate or loosely associated group of persons or things: *a mob of boats in the harbor.* **5.** *Australian.* A flock or herd of animals. **—mob** *tr.v.* **mobbed, mob·bing, mobs. 1.** To crowd around and jostle or annoy, especially in anger or excessive enthusiasm: *Eager fans mobbed the popular singer.* **2.** To crowd into: *Visitors mobbed the fairgrounds.* **3.** To attack in large numbers; overwhelm: *The quarterback was mobbed by the defensive line.* [Short for *mobile,* from Latin *mōbile (vulgus),* fickle (crowd), neuter of *mōbilis.* See MOBILE.] **—mob′bish** *adj.* **—mob′bish·ly** *adv.*

mob·cap (mŏb′kăp′) *n.* A large, high, frilly cap with a full crown, worn indoors by women in the 18th and early 19th centuries. [Probably *mob,* mobcap (possibly from Dutch *mopmuts,* cap : obsolete Dutch *mop-,* to cover up + *muts,* cap) + CAP[1].]

mo·bile (mō′bəl, -bēl′, -bīl′) *adj.* **1.** Capable of moving or of being moved readily from place to place: *a mobile organism; a mobile missile system.* **2.a.** Capable of moving or changing quickly from one state or condition to another: *a mobile, expressive face.* **b.** Fluid; unstable: *a mobile situation following the coup.* **3.a.** Marked by the easy intermixing of different social groups: *a mobile community.* **b.** Moving relatively easily from one social class or level to another: *an upwardly mobile generation.* **c.** Tending to travel and relocate frequently: *a restless, mobile society.* **4.** Flowing freely; fluid: *a mobile liquid.* **—mobile** (mō′bēl′) *n.* A type of sculpture consisting of carefully equilibrated parts that move, especially in response to air currents.

ă pat	oi boy
ā pay	ou out
âr care	o͝o took
ä father	o͞o boot
ĕ pet	ŭ cut
ē be	ûr urge
ĭ pit	th thin
ī pie	*th* this
îr pier	hw which
ŏ pot	zh vision
ō toe	ə about, item
ô paw	♦ regionalism

Stress marks: ′ (primary); ′ (secondary), as in **dictionary** (dĭk′shə-nĕr′ē)

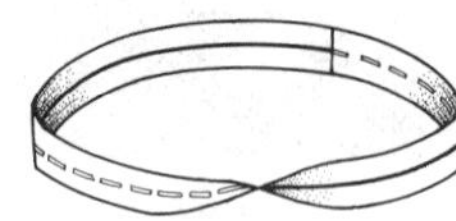
Möbius strip
Half-twist model

moccasin
Huron embroidered black-dyed buckskin moccasins

model
Model of Marina City towers, Chicago, Illinois

[Middle English, from Old French, from Latin *mōbilis*, from **movibilis*, from *movēre*, to move. See **meuə-** in Appendix.]

Mo•bile (mō-bēl′, mō′bēl′). A city of southwest Alabama at the mouth of the **Mobile River**, about 61 km (38 mi) long, on the north shore of **Mobile Bay**, an arm of the Gulf of Mexico. Founded c. 1710, the city was held by the French, British, and Spanish until it was seized by U.S. forces in 1813. Population, 200,452.

mo•bile home (mō′bəl, -bēl′, -bīl′) *n.* A large trailer, fitted with parts for connection to utilities, that can be installed on a relatively permanent site and that is used as a residence. Also called *manufactured home.*

mo•bile telephone (mō′bəl, -bēl′, -bīl′) also **mobile phone** *n.* A portable radiotelephone, especially one mounted in an automobile.

mo•bil•i•ty (mō-bĭl′ĭ-tē) *n.* **1.** The quality or state of being mobile. **2.** The movement of people, as from one social group, class, or level to another: *"There's been . . . restructuring of industry and downward mobility for Americans as a whole"* (Lawrence W. Sherman).

mo•bi•lize (mō′bə-līz′) *v.* **-lized, -liz•ing, -liz•es.** —*tr.* **1.** To make mobile or capable of movement. **2.a.** To assemble, prepare, or put into operation for or as if for war: *mobilize troops; mobilize the snowplows.* **b.** To assemble, marshal, or coordinate for a purpose: *mobilized the country's economic resources.* —*intr.* To become prepared for or as if for war. **—mo′bi•li•za′tion** (-lĭ-zā′shən) *n.*

Mö•bi•us strip (mœ′bē-əs, mā′-, mō′-) *n.* A continuous one-sided surface that can be formed from a rectangular strip by rotating one end 180° and attaching it to the other end. [After August Ferdinand *Möbius* (1790–1868), German mathematician.]

mob•oc•ra•cy (mŏb-ŏk′rə-sē) *n., pl.* **-cies. 1.** Political control by a mob. **2.** The mass of common people as the source of political control. **—mob′o•crat** (mŏb′ə-krăt′) *n.* **—mob′o•crat′ic, mob′o•crat′i•cal** *adj.*

mob•ster (mŏb′stər) *n. Informal.* A member of a criminal gang or crime syndicate.

Mo•bu•to Lake (mō-bōō′tō). See Lake **Albert.**

moc•ca•sin (mŏk′ə-sĭn) *n.* **1.** A soft leather slipper traditionally worn by Native Americans. **2.** Footwear resembling such a slipper. **3.** A water moccasin. [Of Virginia Algonquian origin.]

moccasin flower *n.* See **lady's slipper.**

mo•cha (mō′kə) *n.* **1.** A rich, pungent Arabian coffee. **2.** Coffee of high quality. **3.** A flavoring made of coffee often mixed with chocolate. **4.** A soft, thin, suede-finished glove leather usually made from sheepskin. **5.** *Color.* A dark olive brown. [After *Mocha*, a town of southwest Yemen.] **—mo′cha** *adj.*

Mo•chi•ca (mō-chē′kə) or **Mo•che** (mō′chā, -chĕ) *n.* A pre-Incan civilization that flourished on the northern coast of Peru from about 200 B.C. to A.D. 600, known especially for its pottery vessels modeled into naturalistic human and animal figures.

mock (mŏk) *v.* **mocked, mock•ing, mocks.** —*tr.* **1.** To treat with ridicule or contempt; deride. **2.a.** To mimic, as in sport or derision. See Synonyms at **ridicule. b.** To imitate; counterfeit. **3.** To frustrate the hopes of; disappoint. —*intr.* To express scorn or ridicule; jeer: *They mocked at the idea.* **—mock** *n.* **1.a.** The act of mocking. **b.** Mockery; derision: *said it merely in mock.* **2.** An object of scorn or derision. **3.** An imitation or a counterfeit. **—mock** *adj.* Simulated; false; sham: *a mock battle.* **—mock** *adv.* In an insincere or pretending manner: *mock sorrowful.* [Middle English *mokken*, from Old French *mocquer.*] **—mock′er** *n.* **—mock′ing•ly** *adv.*

mock•er•y (mŏk′ə-rē) *n., pl.* **-ies. 1.** Scornfully contemptuous ridicule; derision. **2.** A specific act of ridicule or derision. **3.** An object of scorn or ridicule: *made a mockery of the rules.* **4.** A false, derisive, or impudent imitation: *The trial was a mockery of justice.* **5.** Something ludicrously futile or unsuitable: *The few packages of food seemed a mockery in the face of such enormous destitution.*

mock-he•ro•ic (mŏk′hĭ-rō′ĭk) *n.* A satirical imitation or burlesque of the heroic manner or style. **—mock′-he•ro′ic** *adj.* **—mock′-he•ro′i•cal•ly** *adv.*

mock•ing•bird (mŏk′ĭng-bûrd′) *n.* Any of several species of New World birds of the family Mimidae, especially *Mimus polyglottos*, a gray and white bird of the southern and eastern United States, noted for the ability to mimic the sounds of other birds. [From its skill in mimicking other birdsongs.]

mock moon *n.* A paraselene.

mock orange *n.* **1.** Any of numerous deciduous shrubs of the genus *Philadelphus*, having opposite, simple leaves and white, usually fragrant flowers with four petals and numerous stamens. **2.** Any of various similar or related shrubs or trees.

mock sun *n.* A parhelion.

mock turtle soup *n.* Soup made from calf's head, veal, or other meat and spiced to taste like green turtle soup.

mock•up also **mock-up** (mŏk′ŭp′) *n.* **1.** A usually full-sized scale model of a structure, used for demonstration, study, or testing. **2.** A layout of printed matter.

mod¹ (mŏd) *n.* An unconventionally modern style of fashionable dress originating in England in the 1960's. **—mod** *adj.* **1.** In or characteristic of this unconventionally modern style. **2.** Fashionably up-to-date, especially in style, design, or dress. [After *the Mods*, name of several gangs of English youths in the 1960's, short for MODERN.]

mod² *abbr. Mathematics.* Modulus.

mod. *abbr.* **1.** Moderate. **2.** *Music.* Moderato. **3.** Modern.

mod•a•cryl•ic (mŏd′ə-krĭl′ĭk) *n.* One of several synthetic, long-chain polymer textile fibers containing 35–85 percent acrylonitrile. [*mod(ified) acrylic.*]

mo•dal (mōd′l) *adj.* **1.** Of, relating to, or characteristic of a mode. **2.** *Grammar.* Of, relating to, or expressing the mood of a verb. **3.** *Music.* Of, relating to, characteristic of, or composed in any of the modes typical of medieval church music. **4.** *Philosophy.* Of or relating to mode without referring to substance. **5.** *Logic.* Expressing or characterized by modality. **6.** *Statistics.* Of or relating to a statistical mode or modes. [Medieval Latin *modālis*, from Latin *modus*, measure. See **med-** in Appendix.] **—mo′dal•ly** *adv.*

modal auxiliary *n.* One of a set of English verbs, including *can, may, must, ought, shall, should, will,* and *would,* that are characteristically used with other verbs to express mood or tense.

mo•dal•i•ty (mō-dăl′ĭ-tē) *n., pl.* **-ties. 1.** The fact, state, or quality of being modal. **2.** A tendency to conform to a general pattern or belong to a particular group or category. **3.** *Logic.* The classification of propositions on the basis of whether they assert or deny the possibility, impossibility, contingency, or necessity of their content. Also called *mode.* **4. modalities.** The ceremonial forms, protocols, or conditions that surround formal agreements or negotiations: "[He] *grew so enthusiastic about our prospects that he began to speculate on the modalities of signing"* (Henry A. Kissinger). **5.** *Medicine.* A therapeutic method or agent, such as surgery, chemotherapy, or electrotherapy, that involves the physical treatment of a disorder. **6.** *Physiology.* Any of the various types of sensation, such as vision or hearing.

mode (mōd) *n.* **1.a.** A manner, way, or method of doing or acting: *modern modes of travel.* See Synonyms at **method. b.** A particular form, variety, or manner: *a mode of expression.* **c.** A given condition of functioning; a status: *The spacecraft was in its recovery mode.* **2.** The current or customary fashion or style. See Synonyms at **fashion. 3.** *Music.* **a.** Any of certain fixed arrangements of the diatonic tones of an octave, as the major and minor scales of Western music. **b.** A patterned arrangement, as the one characteristic of the music of classical Greece or the medieval Christian Church. **4.** *Philosophy.* The particular appearance, form, or manner in which an underlying substance, or a permanent aspect or attribute of it, is manifested. **5.** *Logic.* **a.** See **modality** (sense 3). **b.** The arrangement or order of the propositions in a syllogism according to both quality and quantity. **6.** *Statistics.* The value or item occurring most frequently in a series of observations or statistical data. **7.** *Mathematics.* The number or range of numbers in a set that occurs the most frequently. **8.** *Geology.* The mineral composition of a sample of igneous rock. **9.** *Physics.* Any of numerous patterns of wave motion. **10.** *Grammar.* Mood. [Middle English, tune, from Latin *modus*, manner, tune. Sense 2, French, from Old French, fashion, manner, from Latin *modus*. See **med-** in Appendix.]

mod•el (mŏd′l) *n.* **1.** A small object, usually built to scale, that represents in detail another, often larger object. **2.a.** A preliminary work or construction that serves as a plan from which a final product is to be made: *a clay model ready for casting.* **b.** Such a work or construction used in testing or perfecting a final product: *a test model of a solar-powered vehicle.* **3.** A schematic description of a system, theory, or phenomenon that accounts for its known or inferred properties and may be used for further study of its characteristics: *a model of generative grammar; a model of an atom; an economic model.* **4.** A style or design of an item: *My car is last year's model.* **5.** One serving as an example to be imitated or compared: *a model of decorum.* See Synonyms at **ideal. 6.** One that serves as the subject for an artist, especially a person employed to pose for a painter, sculptor, or photographer. **7.** A person employed to display merchandise, such as clothing or cosmetics. **8.** *Zoology.* An animal whose appearance is copied by a mimic. **—model** *v.* **-eled, -el•ing, -els** also **-elled, -el•ling, -els.** —*tr.* **1.** To make or construct a model of. **2.** To plan, construct, or fashion according to a model. **3.** To make conform to a chosen standard: *He modeled his manners on his father's.* **4.** To make by shaping a plastic substance: *model clay.* **5.** To display by wearing or posing. **6.** In painting, drawing, and photography, to give a three-dimensional appearance to, as by shading or highlighting. —*intr.* **1.** To make a model. **2.** To serve as a model. **—model** *adj.* **1.** Being, serving as, or used as a model. **2.** Worthy of imitation: *a model child.* [French *modèle*, from Italian *modello*, diminutive of *modo*, form, from Latin *modus*, measure, standard. See **med-** in Appendix.] **—mod′el•er** *n.*

mod•el•ing (mŏd′l-ĭng) *n.* **1.** The act or art of sculpturing or forming in a pliable material, such as clay or wax. **2.a.** Representation of depth and solidity in painting, drawing, or photography. **b.** Visual shape and texture of something regarded aesthetically, especially the human face or form. **3.** The act or profession of being a model.

mo•dem (mō′dĕm′) *n. Computer Science.* A device that converts data from one form into another, as from one form usable in data processing to another form usable in telephonic transmission. Also called *data set.* [MO(DULATOR) + DEM(ODULATOR).]

Mo•de•na (mōd′n-ə, mô′dĕ-nä). A city of northern Italy west-northwest of Bologna. An ancient Etruscan settlement and later (after 183 B.C.) a Roman colony, Modena became a free commune in the 12th century A.D. Population, 179,933.

mod·er·ate (mŏd′ər-ĭt) *adj. Abbr.* **mod. 1.** Being within reasonable limits; not excessive or extreme: *a moderate price.* **2.** Not violent or subject to extremes; mild or calm; temperate: *a moderate climate.* **3. a.** Of medium or average quantity or extent. **b.** Of limited or average quality; mediocre. **4.** Opposed to radical or extreme views or measures, especially in politics or religion. **—moderate** *n.* One who holds or champions moderate views or opinions, especially in politics or religion. **—moderate** (mŏd′ə-rāt′) *v.* **-at·ed, -at·ing, -ates.** *—tr.* **1.** To lessen the violence, severity, or extremeness of. **2.** To preside over: *She was chosen to moderate the convention.* *—intr.* **1.** To become less violent, severe, or extreme; abate. **2.** To act as a moderator. [Middle English *moderat,* from Latin *moderātus,* past participle of *moderārī,* to moderate. See **med-** in Appendix.] **—mod′er·ate·ly** *adv.* **—mod′er·ate·ness** *n.* **—mod′er·a′tion** *n.*

SYNONYMS: *moderate, qualify, temper.* The central meaning shared by these verbs is "to make less extreme or intense": *moderated the severity of the rebuke; qualified her criticism; admiration tempered with fear.*
ANTONYM: *intensify.*

moderate breeze *n. Meteorology.* A wind with a speed from 13 to 18 miles (20 to 29 kilometers) per hour, according to the Beaufort scale.

moderate gale *n. Meteorology.* A wind with a speed from 32 to 38 miles (51 to 61 kilometers) per hour, according to the Beaufort scale. Also called *near gale.*

mod·er·ate-in·come (mŏd′ər-ĭt-ĭn′kŭm′) *adj.* Of or relating to people or households supported by an average or slightly below average income: *moderate-income housing.*

mod·e·ra·to (mŏd′ə-rä′tō) *adv. & adj. Abbr.* **mod.** *Music.* In moderate tempo that is slower than allegretto but faster than andante. Used chiefly as a direction. [Italian, from Latin *moderātus,* moderate. See MODERATE.]

mod·er·a·tor (mŏd′ə-rā′tər) *n.* **1.** One that moderates, as: **a.** One that arbitrates or mediates. **b.** One who presides over a meeting, forum, or debate. **2.** The officer who presides over a synod or general assembly of the Presbyterian Church. **3.** *Physics.* A substance, such as water or graphite, that is used in a nuclear reactor to decrease the speed of fast neutrons and increase the likelihood of fission.

mod·ern (mŏd′ərn) *adj. Abbr.* **mod. 1. a.** Of or relating to recent times or the present: *modern history.* **b.** Characteristic or expressive of recent times or the present; contemporary or up-to-date: *a modern lifestyle; a modern way of thinking.* **2. a.** Of or relating to a recently developed or advanced style, technique, or technology: *modern art; modern medicine.* **b.** Avant-garde; experimental. **3. Modern.** *Linguistics.* Of, relating to, or being a living language or group of languages: *Modern Italian; Modern Romance languages.* **—modern** *n.* **1.** One who lives in modern times. **2.** One who has modern ideas, standards, or beliefs. **3.** *Printing.* Any of a variety of typefaces characterized by strongly contrasted heavy and thin parts. [French *moderne,* from Old French, from Late Latin *modernus,* from Latin *modo,* in a certain manner, just now, from *modō,* ablative of *modus,* manner. See **med-** in Appendix.] **—mod′ern·ly** *adv.* **—mod′ern·ness** *n.*

WORD HISTORY: The word *modern,* first recorded in 1585 in the sense "of present or recent times," has traveled through the centuries designating things that inevitably must become old-fashioned as the word itself goes on to the next modern thing. We have now invented the word *postmodern,* as if we could finally fix *modern* in time, but even *postmodern* (first recorded in 1949) will seem fusty in the end, perhaps sooner than *modern* will. Going back to Late Latin *modernus,* "modern," which is derived from *modo* in the sense "just now," the English word *modern* (first recorded at the beginning of the 16th century) was not originally concerned with anything that could be later considered old-fashioned. It simply meant "being at this time, now existing," an obsolete sense today. Beginning in the later 16th century, however, we see the word contrasted with the word *ancient* and also used of technology in a way that is clearly related to our own modern way of using the word. *Modern* was being applied specifically to what pertained to present times and also to what was new and not old-fashioned. Thus in the 19th and 20th centuries the word could be used to designate a movement in art, which is now being followed by postmodernism.

modern dance *n.* A style of theatrical dance that rejects the limitations of classical ballet and favors movement deriving from the expression of inner feeling.

mo·derne (mō-dârn′) *adj.* Striving to be modern in appearance or style but lacking taste or refinement; pretentious. [French, modern, from Old French. See MODERN.]

Modern English *n.* English since about 1500. Also called *New English.*

Modern Greek *n.* Greek since the early 16th century. Also called *New Greek.*

Modern Hebrew *n.* **1.** The Hebrew language as used from 1948 to the present. **2.** See **New Hebrew.**

mod·ern·ism (mŏd′ər-nĭz′əm) *n.* **1. a.** Modern thought, character, or practice. **b.** Sympathy with or conformity to modern ideas, practices, or standards. **2.** A peculiarity of usage or style, as of a word or phrase, that is characteristic of modern times. **3.** Often **Modernism.** The deliberate departure from tradition and the use of innovative forms of expression that distinguish many styles in the arts and literature of the 20th century. **4.** Often **Modernism.** A Roman Catholic movement, officially condemned in 1907, that attempted to examine traditional belief according to contemporary philosophy, criticism, and historiography. **—mod′ern·ist** *n.* **—mod′ern·is′tic** *adj.*

mo·der·ni·ty (mŏ-dûr′nĭ-tē, mō-) *n., pl.* **-ties.** The state or quality of being modern: *"Warriors of the . . . tribe, imposing symbols of a nomadic culture . . . are caught between tradition and modernity"* (Sheila Rule).

mod·ern·ize (mŏd′ər-nīz′) *v.* **-ized, -iz·ing, -iz·es.** *—tr.* To make modern in appearance, style, or character; update. *—intr.* To accept or adopt modern ways, ideas, or style. **—mod′ern·i·za′tion** (-ər-nĭ-zā′shən) *n.* **—mod′ern·iz′er** *n.*

modern pentathlon *n. Sports.* An athletic contest in which each participant competes in five events: running, swimming, horseback riding, fencing, and pistol shooting.

mod·est (mŏd′ĭst) *adj.* **1.** Having or showing a moderate estimation of one's own talents, abilities, and value. **2.** Having or proceeding from a disinclination to call attention to oneself; retiring or diffident. See Synonyms at **shy**[1]. **3.** Observing conventional proprieties in speech, behavior, or dress. **4.** Free from showiness or ostentation; unpretentious. See Synonyms at **plain. 5.** Moderate or limited in size, quantity, or range; not extreme: *a modest price; a newspaper with a modest circulation.* [Latin *modestus.* See **med-** in Appendix.] **—mod′est·ly** *adv.*

Mo·des·to (mə-dĕs′tō). A city of central California southeast of Stockton. Founded in 1870, it is a processing and trade center in the San Joaquin Valley. Population, 106,105.

mod·es·ty (mŏd′ĭ-stē) *n.* **1.** The state or quality of being modest. **2.** Reserve or propriety in speech, dress, or behavior. **3.** Lack of pretentiousness; simplicity.

mod·i·cum (mŏd′ĭ-kəm) *n., pl.* **-cums** or **-ca** (-kə). A small, moderate, or token amount: *"England still expects a modicum of eccentricity in its artists"* (Ian Jack). [Middle English, from Latin, from neuter of *modicus,* moderate, from *modus,* measure. See **med-** in Appendix.]

mod·i·fi·ca·tion (mŏd′ə-fĭ-kā′shən) *n. Abbr.* **modif. 1.** The act of modifying or the condition of being modified. **2.** A result of modifying. **3.** A small alteration, adjustment, or limitation. **4.** *Biology.* Any of the changes in an organism caused by environment or activity and not genetically transmissable to offspring. **5.** *Linguistics.* **a.** A change undergone by a word that is borrowed from another language. **b.** A phonological change undergone by a word or morpheme when it is used in a construction, as the change of *will* to *'ll* in *they'll.* **—mod′i·fi·ca′tor** *n.* **—mod′i·fi·ca′to·ry** (-kā′tə-rē), **mod′i·fi·ca′tive** (-kā′-tĭv) *adj.*

mod·i·fied American plan (mŏd′ə-fīd′) *n. Abbr.* **MAP** A system of hotel management in which guests pay a fixed daily or weekly rate for room, breakfast, and lunch or dinner.

mod·i·fi·er (mŏd′ə-fī′ər) *n. Grammar.* A word, phrase, or clause that limits or qualifies the sense of another word or word group.

mod·i·fy (mŏd′ə-fī′) *v.* **-fied, -fy·ing, -fies.** *—tr.* **1.** To change in form or character; alter. **2.** To make less extreme, severe, or strong: *refused to modify her stand on the issue.* **3.** *Grammar.* To qualify or limit the meaning of. For example, *summer* modifies *day* in the phrase *a summer day.* **4.** *Linguistics.* To change (a vowel) by umlaut. *—intr.* To be or become modified; change. [Middle English *modifien,* from Old French *modifier,* from Latin *modificāre,* to measure, limit : *modus,* measure; see **med-** in Appendix + *-ficāre,* -fy.] **—mod′i·fi′a·bil′i·ty** *n.* **—mod′i·fi′a·ble** *adj.*

Mo·di·glia·ni (mō-dē′lē-ä′nē, mô′dē-lyä′nē), **Amedeo.** 1884–1920. Italian painter and sculptor noted for the graceful, elongated lines of his portraits and nudes.

mo·dil·lion (mō-dĭl′yən) *n. Architecture.* An ornamental bracket used in series under a cornice, especially a cornice of the Corinthian, Composite, or Ionic orders. [Italian *modiglione,* from Vulgar Latin **mutiliō, mutiliōn-,* from Latin *mūtulus,* perhaps of Etruscan origin.]

mo·di·o·lus (mō-dī′ə-ləs) *n., pl.* **-li** (-lī′). The central, conical, bony core of the cochlea. [Latin, socket, hub, diminutive of *modius,* a measure of grain, measuring vessel. See **med-** in Appendix.]

mod·ish (mō′dĭsh) *adj.* Being in or conforming to the prevailing or current fashion; stylish. See Synonyms at **fashionable. —mod′ish·ly** *adv.* **—mod′ish·ness** *n.*

mo·diste (mō-dēst′) *n.* One that produces, designs, or deals in women's fashions. [French, from *mode,* fashion. See MODE.]

Mo·doc (mō′dŏk) *n., pl.* **Modoc** or **-docs. 1. a.** A Native American people inhabiting an area of the Cascade Range in south-central Oregon and northern California. **b.** A member of this people. **2.** The dialect of Klamath spoken by the Modoc.

mod·u·lar (mŏj′ə-lər) *adj.* **1.** Of, relating to, or based on a module or modulus. **2.** Designed with standardized units or dimensions, as for easy assembly and repair or flexible arrangement and use: *modular furniture; modular homes.* **—mod′u·lar** *n.* **—mod′u·lar′i·ty** (-lăr′ĭ-tē) *n.* **—mod′u·lar·ly** *adv.*

modular arithmetic *n. Mathematics.* A form of arithmetic dealing with the remainders after whole numbers are divided by

modular
Habitat housing complex in Montreal, Canada, designed by Moshe Safdie (born 1938)

ă pat	oi boy
ā pay	ou out
âr care	o͝o took
ä father	o͞o boot
ĕ pet	ŭ cut
ē be	ûr urge
ĭ pit	th thin
ī pie	*th* this
îr pier	hw which
ŏ pot	zh vision
ō toe	ə about, item
ô paw	♦ regionalism

Stress marks: **′** (primary); ′ (secondary), as in **dictionary** (dĭk′shə-nĕr′ē)

a modulus: *Clocks use modular arithmetic with modulus 12, so 4 hours after 9 o'clock is 1 o'clock.*

mod·u·lar·ized (mŏj′ə-lə-rīzd′) *adj.* Having or made up of modules: *modularized housing.*

mod·u·late (mŏj′ə-lāt′) *v.* **-lat·ed, -lat·ing, -lates.** —*tr.* **1.** To adjust or adapt to a certain proportion; regulate or temper. **2.** To change or vary the pitch, intensity, or tone of (one's voice or a musical instrument, for example). **3.** *Electronics.* **a.** To vary the frequency, amplitude, phase, or other characteristic of (electromagnetic waves). **b.** To vary (electron velocity) in an electron beam. —*intr. Music.* **1.** To pass from one key or tonality to another by means of a regular melodic or chord progression. **2.** To sing or play with modulation. [Latin *modulārī, modulāt-,* to measure off, to regulate, from *modulus,* diminutive of *modus,* measure. See **med-** in Appendix.] **—mod′u·la·bil′i·ty** *n.* **—mod′u·la′tive, mod′u·la·to′ry** (-lə-tôr′ē, -tōr′ē) *adj.*

mod·u·la·tion (mŏj′ə-lā′shən) *n.* **1.** The act or process of modulating. **2.** The state of being modulated. **3.** *Music.* A passing from one key or tonality to another by means of a regular melodic or chord progression. **4.a.** A change in stress, pitch, loudness, or tone of the voice; an inflection of the voice. **b.** An instance of such a change or an inflection. **5.** The harmonious use of language, as in poetry or prose. **6.** *Electronics.* The variation of a property of an electromagnetic wave or signal, such as its amplitude, frequency, or phase.

mod·u·la·tor (mŏj′ə-lā′tər) *n. Electronics.* A device used to modulate an electromagnetic wave.

mod·ule (mŏj′o͞ol) *n.* **1.** A standard or unit of measurement. **2.** *Architecture.* The dimensions of a structural component, such as the base of a column, used as a unit of measurement or standard for determining the proportions of the rest of the construction. **3.** A standardized, often interchangeable component of a system or construction that is designed for easy assembly or flexible use: *a sofa consisting of two end modules.* **4.** *Electronics.* A self-contained assembly of electronic components and circuitry, such as a stage in a computer, that is installed as a unit. **5.** *Computer Science.* A portion of a program that carries out a specific function and may be used alone or combined with other modules of the same program. **6.** A self-contained unit of a spacecraft that performs a specific task or class of tasks in support of the major function of the craft. **7.** A unit of education or instruction with a relatively high teacher-to-student ratio, in which a single topic or a small section of a broad topic is studied for a given period of time. [Latin *modulus,* diminutive of *modus,* measure. See **med-** in Appendix.]

mod·u·li (mŏj′ə-lī′) *n.* Plural of **modulus.**

mod·u·lo (mŏj′ə-lō) *prep. Mathematics.* With respect to a specified modulus: *18 is congruent to 42 modulo 12 because both 18 and 42 leave 6 as a remainder when divided by 12.* [Latin *modulō,* ablative of *modulus,* diminutive of *modus,* measure. See MODE.]

mod·u·lus (mŏj′ə-ləs) *n., pl.* **-li** (-lī′). *Abbr.* **m, M 1.** *Physics.* A quantity that expresses the degree to which a substance possesses a property, such as elasticity. **2.a.** *Mathematics.* The absolute value of a complex number. **b.** *Abbr.* **mod** A number by which two given numbers can be divided and produce the same remainder. **c.** The number by which a logarithm in one system must be multiplied to obtain the corresponding logarithm in another system. [Latin, diminutive of *modus,* measure. See **med-** in Appendix.]

mo·dus op·er·an·di (mō′dəs ŏp′ə-răn′dē, -dī′) *n., pl.* **mo·di operandi** (mō′dē, -dī). *Abbr.* **m.o., M.O. 1.** A method of operating or functioning. **2.** A person's manner of working. [New Latin *modus operandī* : Latin *modus,* mode + Latin *operandī,* genitive sing. gerund of *operārī,* to work.]

modus vi·ven·di (vĭ-vĕn′dē, -dī′) *n., pl.* **modi vivendi. 1.** A manner of living; a way of life. **2.** A temporary agreement between contending parties pending a final settlement. [New Latin *modus vīvendī* : Latin *modus,* mode + Latin *vīvendī,* genitive sing. gerund of *vīvere,* to live.]

Moers also **Mörs** (mœrs). A city of west-central Germany west of Essen. Chartered in 1300, it is a market and industrial center. Population, 97,753.

Moe·sia (mē′shə, -shē-ə). An ancient region of southeast Europe south of the Danube River in what is now eastern Yugoslavia and northern Bulgaria. Originally inhabited by Thracians, it was conquered by the Romans c. 29 B.C.

Moes·kroen (mo͞os′kro͞on′). See **Mouscron.**

mo·fette also **mof·fette** (mō-fĕt′) *n.* **1.** An opening in the earth from which carbon dioxide and other gases escape, usually marking the last stage of volcanic activity. **2.** The gases escaping from such an opening. [French, gaseous exhalation, from Italian *moffetta,* diminutive of *muffa,* mold, moldy smell, probably of Germanic origin.]

Mog·a·dish·u (mŏg′ə-dĭsh′o͞o, -dē′sho͞o). The capital and largest city of Somalia, on the Indian Ocean. Settled by Arab colonists in the ninth or tenth century, it was occupied in 1871 by the sultan of Zanzibar, who leased it to the Italians in 1892. Population, 400,000.

Mo·gen Da·vid (mŏ′gən dô′vĭd, dā′vĭd, mä-gĕn′ dä-vēd′) *n.* Variant of **Magen David.**

Mo·ghul (mo͞o-gŭl′) *n.* Variant of **Mogul** (sense 1).

Mo·gi·lev (mŏg′ə-lĕf′, mə-gĭ-lyôf′). A city of east-central Belorussia on the Dnieper River east of Minsk. Founded around a castle built in 1267, the city passed to Russia in the First Partition of Poland (1772). Population, 343,000.

Mo·gol·lon (mō′gə-yōn′) *n.* A Native American culture flourishing from the 2nd century B.C. to the 13th century A.D. in southeast Arizona and southwest New Mexico, especially noted for its development of pottery. [After the MOGOLLON (PLATEAU).]

Mogollon Plateau. A tableland, 2,135–2,440 m (7,000–8,000 ft) high, of east-central Arizona. Its southern edge is the rugged escarpment **Mogollon Rim.**

mo·gul (mō′gəl) *n. Sports.* A small hard mound or bump on a ski slope. [Probably of Scandinavian origin; akin to Old Norse *mūgi,* heap.]

Mo·gul (mō′gəl, mō-gŭl′) *n.* **1.** Also **Mo·ghul** (mo͞o-gŭl′). **a.** A member of the force that under Baber conquered India in 1526. **b.** A member of the Moslem dynasty founded by Baber that ruled India until 1857. **2.** A Mongol or Mongolian. **3. mogul.** A very rich or powerful person; a magnate. [Persian and Arabic *muġul,* from Mongolian *Moṅgul.*] **—Mo′gul, mo′gul** *adj.*

mo·hair (mō′hâr′) *n.* **1.** The long, silky hair of the Angora goat. **2.** Fabric made with yarn from this hair. [Alteration (influenced by HAIR) of obsolete Italian *mocaiaro,* from Arabic *muḫayyar.*]

Mo·ham·med (mō-hăm′ĭd, -hä′mĭd, mo͞o-) also **Mu·ham·mad** (mo͞o-). 570?–632. Arab prophet of Islam. At the age of 40 he began to preach as God's prophet of the true religion. Mohammed established a theocratic state at Medina after 622 and began to convert Arabia to Islam.

Mohammed II also **Muhammad II.** 1429?–1481. Sultan of Turkey (1451–1481) and founder of the Ottoman Empire. He conquered Constantinople in 1453 and made it his capital.

Mohammed A·li (ä-lē′) also **Me·he·met Ali** (mĭ-hĕm′ĕt, mā′mĕt). 1769–1849. Turkish soldier and viceroy of Egypt (1805–1848) who wrested control of Egypt from the weakening Ottoman Empire (1811) and established a modern state, over which his family ruled until 1952.

Mo·ham·med·an (mō-hăm′ĭ-dən) also **Mu·ham·mad·an** or **Mu·ham·med·an** (mo͞o-) —*adj.* Of or relating to Mohammed or Islam; Moslem. —*n. Offensive.* A Moslem.

Mo·ham·med·an·ism (mō-hăm′ĭ-də-nĭz′əm) also **Mu·ham·mad·an·ism** (mo͞o-) *n. Offensive.* The religion of Moslems; Islam.

Mo·har·ram (mō-hăr′əm) *n.* Variant of **Muharram.**

Mo·ha·ve also **Mo·ja·ve** (mō-hä′vē) *n., pl.* **Mohave** or **-ves** also **Mojave** or **-ves. 1.a.** A Native American people inhabiting lands along the lower Colorado River on the Arizona-California border. **b.** A member of this people. **2.** The Yuman language of the Mohave. [Mohave *hàmakháav.*]

Mohave Desert. See **Mojave Desert.**

Mo·hawk[1] (mō′hôk′) *n., pl.* **Mohawk** or **-hawks. 1.a.** A Native American people formerly inhabiting northeast New York along the Mohawk and upper Hudson valleys north to the St. Lawrence River, with present-day populations chiefly in southern Ontario and extreme northern New York. The Mohawk were the easternmost member of the Iroquois confederacy. **b.** A member of this people. **2.** The Iroquoian language of the Mohawk. [Narragansett *Mohowaúg.*]

Mo·hawk[2] (mō′hôk′) *n., pl.* **-hawks.** A hairstyle in which the scalp is shaved except for an upright strip of hair that runs across the crown of the head from the forehead to the nape of the neck. [After MOHAWK[1].]

Mohawk River. A river of east-central New York flowing about 225 km (140 mi) south and southeast to the Hudson River.

Mo·he·gan (mō-hē′gən) *n., pl.* **Mohegan** or **-gans. 1.a.** A Native American people formerly inhabiting eastern Connecticut, with present-day descendants in southeast Connecticut and Wisconsin. The Mohegan broke away from the Pequot in the early 17th century under the leadership of Uncas. **b.** A member of this people. **2.** The Algonquian language of the Mohegan. **—Mo·he′gan** *adj.*

Mo·hen·jo-Da·ro (mō-hĕn′jō-där′ō). A ruined prehistoric city of Pakistan in the Indus River valley northeast of Karachi. Its remains date to c. 3000 B.C.

Mo·hi·can (mō-hē′kən, mə-) *n.* Variant of **Mahican.**

Mo·ho (mō′hō′) *n. Geology.* The Mohorovičić discontinuity.

Mo·holy-Nag·y (mə-hō′lē-nŏj′, mō′hoi-nŏd′yə), **Laszlo.** 1895–1946. Hungarian-born American artist and educator known for his artistic experiments with modern technology.

Mo·ho·ro·vi·čić discontinuity (mō′hə-rō′və-chĭch) *n. Geology.* The boundary between the earth's crust and the underlying mantle, averaging 8 kilometers (5 miles) in depth under the oceans and 32 kilometers (20 miles) in depth under the continents. [After Andrija *Mohorovičić* (1857–1936), Croatian geophysicist.]

Mohs scale (mōz) *n.* A scale for classifying minerals based on relative hardness, determined by the ability of harder minerals to scratch softer ones. The scale includes the following minerals, in order from softest to hardest: 1. talc; 2. gypsum; 3. calcite; 4. fluorite; 5. apatite; 6. orthoclase; 7. quartz; 8. topaz; 9. corundum; 10. diamond. [After Friedrich *Mohs* (1773–1839), German mineralogist.]

mo·hur (mō′ər, mə-ho͝or′) *n.* A gold coin, equal to 15 rupees, that was used in British India in the 19th and early 20th centuries. [Hindi *muhr,* gold coin, seal, from Persian.]

moi·dore (moi′dôr′, -dōr′, moi-dôr′, -dōr′) *n.* A former Por-

ă pat	oi boy
ā pay	ou out
âr care	o͝o took
ä father	o͞o boot
ĕ pet	ŭ cut
ē be	ûr urge
ĭ pit	th thin
ī pie	*th* this
îr pier	hw which
ŏ pot	zh vision
ō toe	ə about, item
ô paw	♦ regionalism

Stress marks: **′** (primary); ′ (secondary), as in **dictionary** (dĭk′shə-nĕr′ē)

tuguese or Brazilian gold coin that was also current in England in the early 18th century. [Alteration of Portuguese *moeda d'ouro* : *moeda* (from Latin *monēta,* coin; see MONEY) + *de,* of (from Latin *dē;* see DE–) + *ouro,* gold (from Latin *aurum,* gold).]

moi·e·ty (moiʹĭ-tē) *n., pl.* **-ties. 1.** A half. **2.** A part, portion, or share. **3.** Either of two basic units in cultural anthropology that make up a tribe on the basis of unilateral descent. [Middle English *moite,* from Old French *meitiet, moitie,* from Late Latin *medietās,* from Latin, middle, from *medius,* middle. See **medhyo-** in Appendix.]

moil (moil) *intr.v.* **moiled, moil·ing, moils. 1.** To toil; slave. **2.** To churn about continuously. **—moil** *n.* **1.** Toil; drudgery. **2.** Confusion; turmoil. [Middle English *moillen,* to soften by wetting, from Old French *moillier,* from Vulgar Latin **molliāre,* from Latin *mollia (pānis),* the soft part (of bread), from neuter pl. of *mollis,* soft. See **mel-**[1] in Appendix.] **—moilʹer** *n.* **—moilʹing·ly** *adv.*

moire (mwär, mwä-rāʹ, môr, mô-rāʹ) *n.* A watered or moiré fabric. [French. See MOIRÉ.]

moi·ré (mwä-rāʹ, mô-) *adj.* Having a wavy or rippled surface pattern. Used of fabric. **—moiré** *n.* **1.** Fabric, such as silk or rayon, finished so as to have a wavy or rippled surface pattern. **2.** A similar pattern produced on cloth by engraved rollers. [French, from past participle of *moirer,* to water, from *mouaire, moire,* moiré fabric, probably alteration of English MOHAIR.] **—moi·réʹ** *adj.*

moiré effect *n.* The effect of superimposing a repetitive design, such as a grid, on the same or a different design in order to produce a pattern distinct from its components.

moist (moist) *adj.* **moist·er, moist·est. 1.** Slightly wet; damp or humid. See Synonyms at **wet. 2.** Filled with or characterized by moisture. **3.** Tearful. [Middle English *moiste,* from Old French, alteration (influenced by Latin *musteus,* juicy, from *mustum,* must; see MUST[3]) of Vulgar Latin **muscidus,* alteration of Latin *mūcidus,* moldy, from *mūcus,* mucus.] **—moistʹly** *adv.* **—moistʹness** *n.*

mois·ten (moiʹsən) *tr. & intr.v.* **-tened, -ten·ing, -tens.** To make or become moist. **—moisʹten·er** *n.*

mois·ture (moisʹchər) *n.* **1.** Diffuse wetness that can be felt as vapor in the atmosphere or condensed liquid on the surfaces of objects; dampness. **2.** The state or quality of being damp. [Middle English, from Old French, from *moiste,* moist. See MOIST.]

mois·tur·ize (moisʹchə-rīzʹ) *tr.v.* **-ized, -iz·ing, -iz·es.** To add or restore moisture to: *lotion that moisturizes the face.*

mois·tur·iz·er (moisʹchə-rīʹzər) *n.* A cosmetic lotion or cream applied to the skin to counter dryness.

mo·jar·ra (mō-härʹə) *n., pl.* **mojarra** or **-ras.** Any of several species of small, silvery, mainly tropical American marine fishes of the family Gerridae, having extremely protrusile mouths. [Spanish, knife, a kind of fish found off the coast of Spain, from Arabic *muḥarrab,* pointed, from *ḥarrab,* to sharpen, point.]

Mo·ja·ve (mō-häʹvē) *n.* Variant of **Mohave.**

Mojave Desert also **Mohave Desert.** An arid region of southern California southeast of the Sierra Nevada. Once part of an ancient inland sea, the desert was formed by volcanic action and by materials deposited by the Colorado River.

moke (mōk) *n.* **1.** *Slang.* A dull or boring person. **2.** *Chiefly British.* A donkey. **3.** *Australian.* An old, broken-down horse. [Origin unknown.]

mol (mōl) *n.* Variant of **mole**[5]**.**

MOL *abbr.* Manned Orbital Laboratory.

mol. *abbr.* **1.** Molecular. **2.** Molecule.

mo·la[1] (mōʹlə, -lä) *n., pl.* **-las.** A colorful fabric panel of Central American origin, sewn with a reverse-appliqué technique and used for decorative purposes, as on clothing or furniture or as a wall hanging. [Cuna (Panama Chibchan language), clothing, blouse, mola.]

mo·la[2] (mōʹlə) *n., pl.* **mola** or **-las.** See **ocean sunfish.** [Latin, millstone (from its shape and rough skin). See **mele-** in Appendix.]

mo·lal (mōʹləl) *adj.* Of or designating a solution that contains one mole of solute in 1,000 grams of solvent.

mo·lal·i·ty (mō-lălʹĭ-tē) *n., pl.* **-ties.** The molal concentration of a solute, usually expressed as the number of moles of solute per 1,000 grams of solvent.

mo·lar[1] (mōʹlər) *adj.* **1.** *Abbr.* **M** *Chemistry.* **a.** Relating to or designating a solution that contains one mole of solute per liter of solution. **b.** Containing one mole of a substance. **2.** *Physics.* Of or relating to a body of matter as a whole, perceived apart from molecular or atomic properties. [From MOLE[5].]

mo·lar[2] (mōʹlər) *n.* A tooth with a broad crown used to grind food, located behind the premolars. **—molar** *adj.* **1.** Of or relating to the molars. **2.** Capable of grinding. [From Middle English *molares,* molars, from Latin *molāris,* belonging to a mill, grinder, molar, from *mola,* millstone. See **mele-** in Appendix.]

mo·lar·i·ty (mō-lărʹĭ-tē) *n., pl.* **-ties.** *Abbr.* **M** *Chemistry.* The molar concentration of a solution, usually expressed as the number of moles of solute per liter of solution.

mo·las·ses (mə-lăsʹĭz) *n., pl.* **molasses.** A thick syrup produced in refining raw sugar and ranging from light to dark brown. [Portuguese *melaços,* pl. of *melaço,* from Late Latin *mellāceum,* must, from Latin *mel, mell-,* honey. See **melit-** in Appendix.]

mold[1] (mōld) *n.* **1.** A hollow form or matrix for shaping a fluid or plastic substance. **2.** A frame or model around or on which something is formed or shaped. **3.** Something that is made in or shaped on a mold. **4.** The shape or pattern of a mold. **5.** General shape or form: *the oval mold of her face.* **6.** Distinctive character or type: *a leader in the mold of her predecessors.* **7.** A fixed or restrictive pattern or form: *a method of scientific investigation that broke the mold and led to a new discovery.* **8.** *Architecture.* See **molding** (sense 3). **—mold** *v.* **mold·ed, mold·ing, molds.** *—tr.* **1.** To shape in or on a mold. **2. a.** To form into a particular shape; give shape to. **b.** To guide or determine the growth or development of; influence: *a teacher who helps to mold the minds of his students.* **3.** To fit closely by following the contours of. **4.** To make a mold of or from (molten metal, for example) before casting. **5.** To ornament with moldings. *—intr.* To be shaped in or as if in a mold: *shoes that gradually molded to my feet.* [Middle English *molde,* from Old French *molle, molde,* from Latin *modulus,* diminutive of *modus,* measure. See **med-** in Appendix.] **—moldʹa·ble** *adj.* **—moldʹer** *n.*

mola[1]

mold[2] (mōld) *n.* **1.** Any of various fungi that often cause disintegration of organic matter. **2.** The growth of such fungi. **—mold** *intr.v.* **mold·ed, mold·ing, molds.** To become moldy. [Middle English *moulde,* probably from past participle of *moulen,* to grow moldy, from Old Norse *mygla.*]

mold[3] (mōld) *n.* **1.** Loose, friable soil, rich in humus and fit for planting. **2.** *Chiefly British.* **a.** The earth; the ground. **b.** The earth of the grave. **3.** *Archaic.* Earth as the substance of the human body. [Middle English, from Old English *molde.* See **mele-** in Appendix.]

Mol·da·vi·a (mŏl-dāʹvē-ə, -dāvʹyə). **1.** A historical region of eastern Romania east of Transylvania. Part of the Roman province of Dacia, it became a principality in the 14th century and passed to the Ottoman Empire in 1504, although it was continually attacked and often virtually controlled by numerous other powers. In 1859 Moldavia united with Walachia to form the nucleus of modern Romania. **2.** A republic of eastern Europe bordering on Romania. Acquired by Russia from the Romanian region of Moldavia in the late 18th and early 19th centuries, it became an autonomous republic of the U.S.S.R. in 1924 and a constituent republic in 1940. Kishinev is the capital. Population, 4,111,000. **—Mol·daʹvi·an** *adj. & n.*

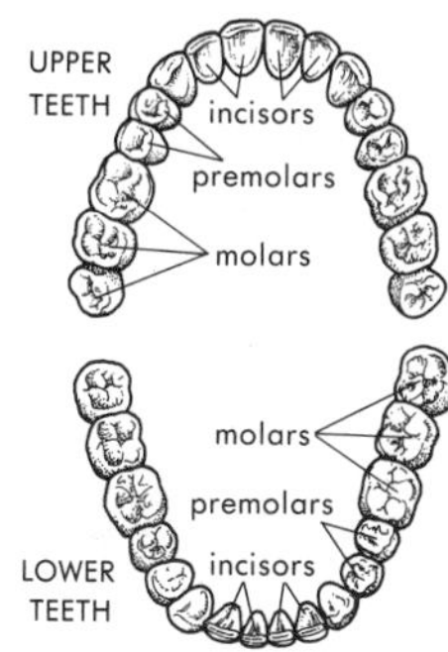

molar[2]

mold·board (mōldʹbôrdʹ, -bōrdʹ) *n.* The curved plate of a plow that turns over the soil. [MOLD[3] + BOARD.]

mold·er (mōlʹdər) *v.* **-ered, -er·ing, -ers.** *—intr.* To crumble to dust; disintegrate. *—tr.* To cause to crumble. See Synonyms at **decay.** [Probably frequentative of MOLD[3].]

mold·ing (mōlʹdĭng) *n.* **1.** The act or process of molding. **2.** Something that is molded. **3.** An embellishment in strip form, made of wood or other structural material, that is used to decorate or finish a surface, such as the wall of a room or the surface of a door or piece of furniture. In this sense, also called *mold.*

mold·y (mōlʹdē) *adj.* **-i·er, -i·est. 1.** Covered with or containing mold: *moldy bread.* **2.** Musty or stale, as from age or decay. **—moldʹi·ness** *n.*

mole[1] (mōl) *n.* A small congenital growth on the human skin, usually slightly raised and dark and sometimes hairy, especially a pigmented nevus. [Middle English, from Old English *māl.*]

mole[2] (mōl) *n.* **1.** Any of various small, insectivorous mammals of the family Talpidae, usually living underground and having thickset bodies with light brown to dark gray silky fur, rudimentary eyes, tough muzzles, and strong forefeet for burrowing. **2.** A machine that bores through hard surfaces, used especially for tunneling through rock. **3.** A spy who operates from within an organization, especially a double agent operating against his or her own government from within its intelligence establishment. [Middle English *molle;* possibly akin to MOLD[3].]

mold[1]

mole[3] (mōl) *n.* **1.** A massive, usually stone wall constructed in the sea, used as a breakwater and built to enclose or protect an anchorage or a harbor. **2.** The anchorage or harbor enclosed by a mole. [French *môle,* from Italian *molo,* from Late Greek *mōlos,* from Latin *mōlēs,* mass, mole.]

mole[4] (mōl) *n.* A fleshy, abnormal mass formed in the uterus by the degeneration or abortive development of an ovum. [French *môle,* from Latin *mola,* millstone, mole. See **mele-** in Appendix.]

mole[5] or **mol** (mōl) *n.* **1.** The amount of a substance that contains as many atoms, molecules, ions, or other elementary units as the number of atoms in 0.012 kilogram of carbon 12. The number is 6.0225×10^{23}, or Avogadro's number. Also called *gram molecule.* **2.** The mass in grams of this amount of a substance, numerically equal to the molecular weight of the substance. Also called *gram-molecular weight.* See table at **measurement.** [German *Mol,* short for *Molekulargewicht,* molecular weight, from *molekular,* molecular, from French *moléculaire,* from *molécule,* molecule. See MOLECULE.]

mo·le[6] (mōʹlāʹ) *n.* A spicy sauce of Mexican origin, made with unsweetened chocolate and a variety of chilies and spices and usually served with meat or poultry. [American Spanish, from Nahuatl *mōlli.*]

mole crab (mōl) *n.* Any of various small crustaceans of the genus *Emerita,* having very long eyestalks and hairy antennae and commonly found burrowing in sand on ocean beaches.

mole cricket (mōl) *n.* Any of various burrowing crickets of the family Gryllotalpidae, having short wings and front legs well adapted for digging and feeding mainly on the roots of plants.

moldboard

moloch
Moloch horridus

mo·lec·u·lar (mə-lĕk′yə-lər) *adj.* **1.** *Abbr.* **mol.** Of, relating to, or consisting of molecules. **2.** Of or relating to simple or basic structure or form. **—mo·lec′u·lar′i·ty** (-lăr′ĭ-tē) *n.* **—mo·lec′u·lar·ly** *adv.*

molecular biology *n.* The branch of biology that deals with the formation, structure, and activity of macromolecules essential to life, such as nucleic acids and proteins, and especially with their role in cell replication and the transmission of genetic information. **—molecular biologist** *n.*

molecular formula *n.* A chemical formula that shows the number and kinds of atoms in a molecule.

molecular genetics *n. (used with a sing. verb).* The branch of genetics that deals with hereditary transmission and variation on the molecular level.

molecular weight *n. Abbr.* **mol wt** The sum of the atomic weights of all the atoms in a molecule. Also called *formula weight.*

mol·e·cule (mŏl′ĭ-kyo͞ol′) *n. Abbr.* **mol. 1.** The smallest particle into which an element or a compound can be divided without changing its chemical and physical properties; a group of like or different atoms held together by chemical forces. **2.** A small particle; a tiny bit. [French *molécule,* from New Latin *mōlēcula,* diminutive of Latin *mōlēs,* mass.]

mole·hill (mōl′hĭl′) *n.* A small mound of loose earth raised by a burrowing mole. ***—idiom.*** **make a mountain out of a molehill.** To exaggerate a minor problem.

mole rat *n.* **1.** Any of several furry, short-limbed, tailless burrowing rodents of the genus *Spalax,* found in eastern Europe and the Middle East. **2.** Any of various similar molelike rodents of the family Bathyergidae and especially of the genus *Bathyergus,* found from South Africa to Kenya.

mole·skin (mōl′skĭn′) *n.* **1.** The short, soft, silky fur of a mole. **2.a.** A heavy-napped cotton twill fabric. **b. moleskins.** Clothing, especially trousers, of this fabric. **3.** A soft material, often with an adhesive backing, used especially on the feet to protect against chafing.

mo·lest (mə-lĕst′) *tr.v.* **-lest·ed, -lest·ing, -lests. 1.** To disturb, interfere with, or annoy. **2.** To subject to unwanted or improper sexual activity. [Middle English *molesten,* from Old French *molester,* from Latin *molestāre,* from *molestus,* troublesome.] **—mo′les·ta′tion** (mō′lĕ-stā′shən) *n.* **—mo·lest′er** *n.*

Mo·lière (mōl-yâr′), **Jean Baptiste Poquelin.** 1622–1673. French playwright whose sophisticated comedies include *Tartuffe* (1664) and *The Misanthrope* (1666).

Mo·line (mō-lēn′). A city of northwest Illinois on the Mississippi River across from Davenport, Iowa. Settled in 1847, it is a transportation and industrial center. Population, 45,709.

Mo·li·se (mô′lĭ-zā′). A region of south-central Italy bordering on the Adriatic Sea. Conquered by the Romans in the 4th century B.C., it was ruled by a Lombard duchy from the 6th to the 11th century A.D.

moll (mŏl) *n. Slang.* **1.** A woman companion of a gunman or gangster. **2.** A prostitute. [Probably from the name *Moll,* nickname for *Mary.*]

mol·lie (mŏl′ē) *n.* Variant of **molly.**

mol·li·fy (mŏl′ə-fī′) *tr.v.* **-fied, -fy·ing, -fies. 1.** To calm in temper or feeling; soothe. See Synonyms at **pacify. 2.** To lessen in intensity; temper. **3.** To reduce the rigidity of; soften. [Middle English *mollifien,* from Old French *mollifier,* from Late Latin *mollificāre* : *mollis,* soft; see **mel-**[1] in Appendix + *-ficāre,* -fy.] **—mol′li·fi′a·ble** *adj.* **—mol′li·fi·ca′tion** (-fĭ-kā′shən) *n.* **—mol′li·fi′er** *n.* **—mol′li·fy′ing·ly** *adv.*

mol·lusc (mŏl′əsk) *n.* Variant of **mollusk.**

mol·lus·ca (mə-lŭs′kə) *n.* Plural of **molluscum.**

mol·lus·can also **mol·lus·kan** (mə-lŭs′kən) *—adj.* Of or relating to the mollusks. *—n.* A mollusk.

mol·lus·ci·cide (mə-lŭs′kĭ-sīd′) *n.* An agent that kills mollusks. **—mol·lus′ci·cid′al** (-sīd′l) *adj.*

mol·lus·coid (mə-lŭs′koid) *adj.* Of, belonging to, or resembling the mollusks.

mol·lus·cum (mə-lŭs′kəm) *n., pl.* **-ca** (-kə). Any of various skin diseases in which soft, spherical tumors form on the face or other part of the body. [Latin, a kind of fungus, from neuter of *molluscus,* soft. See MOLLUSK.]

mol·lusk also **mol·lusc** (mŏl′əsk) *n.* Any of numerous chiefly marine invertebrates of the phylum Mollusca, typically having a soft unsegmented body, a mantle, and a protective calcareous shell and including the edible shellfish and the snails. [French *mollusque,* from New Latin *Mollusca,* phylum name, from neuter pl. of Latin *molluscus,* thin-shelled, from *mollis,* soft. See **mel-**[1] in Appendix.] **—mol·lus′cous** (mə-lŭs′kəs) *adj.*

mol·lus·kan (mə-lŭs′kən) *adj. & n.* Variant of **molluscan.**

mol·ly also **mol·lie** (mŏl′ē) *n., pl.* **-lies.** Any of several tropical and subtropical live-bearing fishes of the genus *Poecilia* or *Mollienesia,* commonly kept in aquariums. [From New Latin *Mollienesia,* former genus name, after Comte François Nicolas Mollien (1758–1850), French politician.]

mol·ly·cod·dle (mŏl′ē-kŏd′l) *v. —tr.* **-dled, -dling, -dles.** To be overprotective and indulgent toward. See Synonyms at **pamper. —mollycoddle** *n.* A person, especially a boy, who is pampered and overly protected. [*molly,* milksop (from the name *Molly,* nickname for *Mary*) + CODDLE.] **—mol′ly·cod′dler** *n.*

Mol·nár (mōl′när′, môl′-), **Ferenc.** 1878–1952. Hungarian writer known particularly for his comedies, including *The Devil* (1907) and *Liliom* (1909).

mo·loch (mō′lŏk′, mŏl′ək) *n.* A lizard *(Moloch horridus)* of the deserts and plains of central and southern Australia, having a head and back covered with large spiny scales. [Late Latin *Moloch,* Semitic deity. See MOLOCH.]

Mo·loch (mō′lŏk′, mŏl′ək) *n.* **1.** *Bible.* In the Old Testament, the god of the Ammonites and Phoenicians to whom children were sacrificed. **2.** Something possessing the power to exact severe sacrifice. [Late Latin *Moloch,* from Greek *Molokh,* from Hebrew *Mōlek.*]

Mo·lo·kai (mŏl′ə-kī′, mō′lə-). An island of central Hawaii between Oahu and Maui. The Belgian missionary Father Damien established a leper colony on the northern coast in 1860.

Mo·lo·po (mə-lō′pō). An intermittent river of South Africa flowing about 965 km (600 mi) westward to the Orange River.

Mo·lo·tov (mŏl′ə-tôf′, môl′-, mō′lə-), **Vyacheslav Mikhailovich.** 1890–1986. Soviet politician who was head of the Council of People's Commissars (1930–1941) and foreign minister (1939–1949 and 1953–1956).

Molotov cocktail *n.* A makeshift bomb made of a breakable container filled with flammable liquid and provided with a usually rag wick that is lighted just before being hurled. [After Vyacheslav Mikhailovich MOLOTOV.]

molt (mōlt) *v.* **molt·ed, molt·ing, molts.** *—intr.* To shed periodically part or all of a coat or an outer covering, such as feathers, cuticle, or skin, which is then replaced by a new growth. *—tr.* To shed or cast off (a bodily covering). **—molt** *n.* **1.** The act or process of molting. **2.** The material cast off during molting. [Alteration of Middle English *mouten,* from Old English *-mūtian* (in *bemūtian,* to exchange for), from Latin *mūtāre,* to change. See **mei-**[1] in Appendix.] **—molt′er** *n.*

mol·ten (mōl′tən) *v. Archaic.* A past participle of **melt. —molten** *adj.* **1.** Made liquid by heat; melted: *molten lead.* **2.** Made by melting and casting in a mold. **3.** Brilliantly glowing, from or as if from intense heat: *"A huge red bed of coals blazed and quivered with molten fury"* (Richard Wright).

mol·to (mōl′tō) *adv. Music.* Very; much. Used chiefly in directions. [Italian, from Latin *multum,* from neuter sing. of *multus,* many, much. See **mel-**[2] in Appendix.]

Mo·luc·cas (mə-lŭk′əz). Formerly **Spice Islands** (spīs). A group of islands of eastern Indonesia between Celebes and New Guinea. The islands were settled by the Portuguese but taken in the 17th century by the Dutch, who used them as the basis for their monopoly of the spice trade. **—Mo·luc′can** *adj. & n.*

mol wt *abbr.* Molecular weight.

mo·ly (mō′lē) *n., pl.* **-lies.** *Greek Mythology.* A magic herb with black roots and white flowers that was given to Odysseus by Hermes to ward off the spells of Circe. [Latin *mōly,* from Greek *mōlu.*]

mo·lyb·de·nite (mə-lĭb′də-nīt′) *n.* A mineral form of molybdenum sulfide, MoS_2, that is the principal ore of molybdenum. [MOLYBDEN(UM) + -ITE[1].]

mo·lyb·de·num (mə-lĭb′də-nəm) *n. Symbol* **Mo** A hard, silvery-white metallic element used to toughen alloy steels and soften tungsten alloy. An essential trace element in plant nutrition, it is used in fertilizers, dyes, enamels, and reagents. Atomic number 42; atomic weight 95.94; melting point 2,617°C; boiling point 4,612°C; specific gravity 10.22 (at 20°C); valence 2, 3, 4, 5. See table at **element.** [New Latin, from earlier *molybdena,* lead one, from Latin *molybdaena,* galena, from Greek *molubdaina,* from *molubdos,* lead.]

mo·lyb·dic (mə-lĭb′dĭk) *adj.* Designating molybdenum or a compound containing molybdenum, especially with a valence of 6.

mo·lyb·dous (mə-lĭb′dəs) *adj.* Designating molybdenum or a compound containing molybdenum, especially with a valence of less than 6.

mom (mŏm) *n. Informal.* Mother. [Shortening and alteration of MAMA.]

m.o.m. *abbr.* Middle of month.

mom-and-pop (mŏm′ən-pŏp′) *adj.* **1.** Of or being a small business that is typically owned and run by members of a family: *a mom-and-pop grocery store.* **2.** Resembling or evocative of the small-scale, homelike, or informal atmosphere of such a business: *"toasted the advantages of mom-and-pop journalism"* (Newsweek).

Mom·ba·sa (mŏm-băs′ə, -bä′sä). A city of southeast Kenya mainly on **Mombasa Island,** in the Indian Ocean north of Zanzibar. Visited by Vasco da Gama on his first voyage to India (1498), the island-city was ruled successively by Portugal, Oman, Zanzibar, and Great Britain until the early 20th century. Population, 341,148.

mo·ment (mō′mənt) *n.* **1.** A brief, indefinite interval of time. **2.** A specific point in time, especially the present time: *He is not here at the moment.* **3.** A particular period of importance, influence, or significance in a series of events or developments: *a great moment in history; waiting for her big moment.* **4.** Outstanding significance or value; importance: *a discovery of great moment.* **5.** A brief period of time that is characterized by a quality, such as excellence, suitability, or distinction: *a lackluster performance that nevertheless had its moments.* **6.** *Philosophy.* **a.** An essential or constituent element, as of a complex idea. **b.** A phase or an aspect of a logically developing process. **7.** *Abbr.* **M** *Physics.*

a. The product of a quantity and its perpendicular distance from a reference point. **b.** The tendency to cause rotation about a point or an axis. **8.** *Statistics.* The expected value of a positive integral power of a random variable. The first moment is the mean of the distribution. [Middle English, from Old French, from Latin *mōmentum,* from **movimentum,* from *movēre,* to move. See **meuə-** in Appendix.]

SYNONYMS: *moment, instant, minute, second, jiffy, flash.* These nouns denote a brief interval of time. A *moment* is an indeterminately short but not insignificant period: I'll be with you in a moment. It took him a moment to answer. Instant is a period of time almost too brief to detect; it implies haste and often urgency: *She hesitated for just an instant. Stop it this instant. Minute* and *second,* used strictly, refer to measured intervals of time; often, though, *minute* is interchangeable with *moment* (*Wait a minute. The plane will be arriving in a minute*), and *second* with *instant* (*I slipped out of the room for a few seconds to turn the oven on*). *Jiffy* and *flash* occur principally in combinations preceded by *in a; in a jiffy* means in a short space of time, while *in a flash* suggests the almost imperceptible duration of a flash of light: *"He was on his stool in a jiffy, driving away with his pen"* (Charles Dickens). *She was on her feet in a flash when the doorbell rang.* See also Synonyms at **importance.**

mo·men·ta (mō-mĕnʹtə) *n.* A plural of **momentum.**

mo·men·tar·i·ly (mōʹmən-târʹə-lē) *adv.* **1.** For a moment or an instant. **2.** *Usage Problem.* In a moment; very soon. **3.** Moment by moment; progressively.

USAGE NOTE: *Momentarily* is widely used in speech to mean "in a moment," as in *The manager is on another line, but she'll be with you momentarily.* This usage rarely leads to ambiguity since the intended sense can usually be determined on the basis of the tense of the verb and the context. Nonetheless, many critics hold that the adverb should be reserved for the senses "for a moment" or "moment by moment," and the extended usage is unacceptable to 59 percent of the Usage Panel.

mo·men·tar·y (mōʹmən-tĕrʹē) *adj.* **1.** Lasting for only a moment. See Synonyms at **transient. 2.** Occurring or present at every moment: *in momentary fear of being exposed.* **3.** Short-lived or ephemeral, as a life. [Middle English *momentare,* from Latin *mōmentārius,* from *mōmentum,* moment. See MOMENT.] **—moʹmen·tarʹi·ness** *n.*

mo·ment·ly (mōʹmənt-lē) *adv.* **1.** From moment to moment. **2.** At any moment. **3.** For a moment.

moment of inertia *n., pl.* **moments of inertia.** A measure of a body's resistance to angular acceleration, equal to: **a.** The product of the mass of a particle and the square of its distance from a reference. **b.** The sum of the products of each mass element of a body multiplied by the square of its distance from an axis. **c.** The sum of the products of each element of an area multiplied by the square of its distance from a coplanar axis.

moment of truth *n., pl.* **moments of truth. 1.** A critical or decisive time on which much depends; a crucial moment. **2.** *Sports.* The point in a bullfight at which the matador makes the kill. [Translation of Spanish *el momento de verdad.*]

mo·men·tous (mō-mĕnʹtəs) *adj.* Of utmost importance; of outstanding significance or consequence: *a momentous occasion; a momentous decision.* **—mo·menʹtous·ly** *adv.* **—mo·menʹtous·ness** *n.*

mo·men·tum (mō-mĕnʹtəm) *n., pl.* **-ta** (-tə) or **-tums. 1.** *Symbol* **p** *Physics.* A measure of the motion of a body equal to the product of its mass and velocity. Also called *linear momentum.* **2.a.** Impetus of a physical object in motion. **b.** Impetus of a nonphysical process, such as an idea or a course of events: *The soaring rise in interest rates finally appeared to be losing momentum.* **3.** *Philosophy.* An essential or constituent element; a moment. [Latin *mōmentum,* movement, short for **movimentum,* from *movēre,* to move. See **meuə-** in Appendix.]

mom·ma (mäʹmə) *n.* Variant of **mama.**

Momm·sen (mŏmʹzən), **Theodor.** 1817–1903. German historian whose best-known work is the three-volume *History of Rome* (1854–1856). He won the 1902 Nobel Prize for literature.

mom·my (mŏmʹē) *n., pl.* **-mies.** *Informal.* Mother. [Alteration of MAMMY.]

Mo·mus (mōʹməs) *n. Greek Mythology.* The god of blame and ridicule.

mon (mŏn) *n. Scots.* Man.

Mon (mōn) *n.* **1.** A member of a Buddhist people inhabiting an area of eastern Burma and adjacent parts of Thailand. **2.** The Mon-Khmer language of the Mon.

mon. *abbr.* **1.** Monastery. **2.** Monetary.

Mon. *abbr.* Monday.

mon– *pref.* Variant of **mono–.**

mon·a·chism (mŏnʹə-kĭzʹəm) *n.* Monasticism. [Medieval Latin *monachismus,* from Late Greek *monakhismos,* from Late Greek *monakhos,* monk. See MONK.]

Mon·a·co (mŏnʹə-kōʹ, mə-näʹkō). A principality on the Mediterranean Sea consisting of an enclave in southeast France. Probably settled by Phoenicians, it has been ruled by the Grimaldi family since the 13th century (first by the Genovese line and, after 1731, by a French line). The village of **Monaco,** or **Monaco-Ville,** is the capital. Population, 27,063. **—Monʹa·can** *adj. & n.*

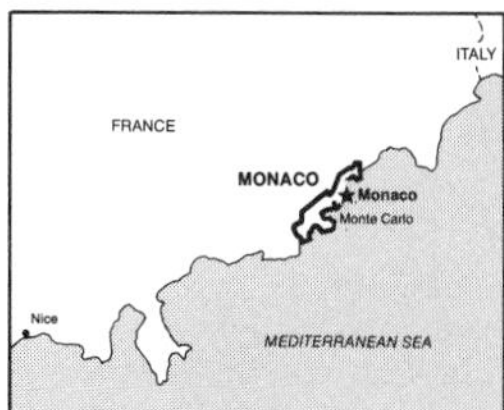

Monaco

mo·nad (mōʹnădʹ) *n.* **1.** *Philosophy.* An indivisible, impenetrable unit of substance viewed as the basic constituent element of physical reality in the metaphysics of Leibnitz. **2.** *Biology.* A single-celled microorganism, especially a flagellate protozoan of the genus *Monas.* **3.** *Chemistry.* An atom or a radical with a valence of 1. [Latin *monas, monad-,* unit, from Greek, from *monos,* single. See **men-**[4] in Appendix.] **—mo·nadʹic** (mə-nădʹĭk), **mo·nadʹi·cal** *adj.* **—mo·nadʹi·cal·ly** *adv.* **—moʹnad·ism** *n.*

mon·a·del·phous (mŏnʹə-dĕlʹfəs, mōʹnə-) *adj. Botany.* Related to or being stamens with all the filaments united into a single tubelike group.

mo·nad·nock (mə-nădʹnŏkʹ) *n.* A mountain or rocky mass that has resisted erosion and stands isolated in an essentially level area. [After Mount *Monadnock,* a peak of southwest New Hampshire.]

mo·nan·drous (mə-nănʹdrəs) *adj.* **1.** *Botany.* Having flowers bearing a single stamen, as in the poinsettia. **2.** Of, relating to, or characterized by monandry.

mo·nan·dry (mə-nănʹdrē) *n.* **1.** The state or practice of having one husband at a time. **2.** *Botany.* The condition of being monandrous.

mo·nan·thous (mə-nănʹthəs) *adj. Botany.* Bearing a single flower.

Mo·na Passage (mōʹnə). A strait between Puerto Rico and the Dominican Republic connecting the northern Atlantic Ocean with the Caribbean Sea.

mon·arch (mŏnʹərk, -ärkʹ) *n.* **1.** One who reigns over a state or territory, usually for life and by hereditary right, especially: **a.** A sole and absolute ruler. **b.** A sovereign, often with constitutionally limited authority: *a constitutional monarch.* **2.** One that commands or rules: *"I am monarch of all I survey"* (William Cowper). **3.** One that surpasses others in power or preeminence: *"Mont Blanc is the monarch of the mountains"* (Byron). **4.** A monarch butterfly. [Middle English *monarke,* from Old French *monarque,* from Late Latin *monarcha,* from Greek *monarkhos* : *mono-,* mono- + *arkhein,* to rule.] **—mo·narʹchal** (mə-närʹkəl), **mo·narʹchic** (-kĭk), **mo·narʹchi·cal** (-kĭ-kəl) *adj.* **—mo·narʹchal·ly, mo·narʹchi·cal·ly** *adv.*

monarch butterfly
Danaus plexippus

monarch butterfly *n.* A large American butterfly *(Danaus plexippus)* having light brown wings with black veins and white-spotted black borders, noted for its long-distance migrations and its brightly striped caterpillars that feed on the milkweed plant. Also called *milkweed butterfly.*

Mon·ar·chi·an·ism (mə-närʹkē-ə-nĭzʹəm) *n.* Any of several Christian heresies of the second and third centuries A.D. that attempted to maintain monotheism and the unity of the Godhead but thereby denied the independent hypostasis of God the Son. [From Latin *Monarchiānī,* the Monarchians, from *monarchia,* monarchy. See MONARCHY.] **—Mo·narʹchi·an** *n.*

mon·ar·chism (mŏnʹər-kĭzʹəm, -ärʹ-) *n.* **1.** The system or principles of monarchy. **2.** Belief in or advocacy of monarchy. **—monʹar·chist** (-kĭst) *n.* **—monʹar·chisʹtic** *adj.*

mon·ar·chy (mŏnʹər-kē, -ärʹ-) *n., pl.* **-chies. 1.** Government by a monarch. **2.** A state ruled or headed by a monarch. [Middle English *monarchie,* from Old French, from Latin *monarchia,* from Greek *monarkhia,* from *monarkhos,* monarch. See MONARCH.] **—mo·narʹchi·al** (mə-närʹkē-əl) *adj.*

mo·nar·da (mə-närʹdə) *n.* Any of various aromatic plants of the genus *Monarda* in the mint family, such as the bee balm. [New Latin *Monarda,* genus name, after Nicolas *Monardes* (1493–1588), Spanish botanist.]

mon·as·ter·y (mŏnʹə-stĕrʹē) *n., pl.* **-ries.** *Abbr.* **mon. 1.** A community of persons, especially monks, bound by vows to a religious life and often living in partial or complete seclusion. **2.** The dwelling place of such a community. [Middle English *monasterie,* from Old French *monastere,* from Late Latin *monastērium,* from Late Greek *monastērion,* from Greek *monazein,* to live alone, from *monos,* alone. See **men-**[4] in Appendix.] **—monʹas·teʹri·al** (mŏnʹə-stîrʹē-əl, -stĕrʹ-) *adj.*

mo·nas·tic (mə-năsʹtĭk) also **mo·nas·ti·cal** (-tĭ-kəl) *adj.* **1.** Of, relating to, or characteristic of a monastery. Used often of monks and nuns. **2.** Resembling life in a monastery in style, structure, or manner, especially: **a.** Secluded and contemplative. **b.** Strictly disciplined or regimented. **c.** Self-abnegating; austere. **—monastic** *n.* A monk. [Middle English *monastik,* from Old French *monastique,* from Late Latin *monasticus,* from Late Greek *monastikos,* from Greek *monazein,* to live alone. See MONASTERY.] **—mo·nasʹti·cal·ly** *adv.*

mo·nas·ti·cism (mə-năsʹtĭ-sĭzʹəm) *n.* The monastic life or system, especially as practiced in a monastery.

mon·a·tom·ic (mŏnʹə-tŏmʹĭk) *adj.* **1.** Occurring as single atoms: *Helium is a monatomic gas.* **2.** Having one replaceable atom or radical. **3.** Univalent. **—monʹa·tomʹic·al·ly** *adv.*

mon·au·ral (mŏn-ôrʹəl) *adj.* **1.** Of, relating to, or designating sound reception by one ear. **2.** *Electronics.* Relating to a system of transmitting, recording, or reproducing sound in which one or more sources are connected to a single channel; monophonic. **—mon·auʹral·ly** *adv.*

mon·ax·i·al (mŏn-ăkʹsē-əl) *adj.* Uniaxial.

mon·a·zite (mŏnʹə-zītʹ) *n.* A reddish-brown phosphate mineral containing rare-earth metals, $(Ce,La,Y,Th)PO_4$, important as

ă pat	oi boy
ā pay	ou out
âr care	ŏŏ took
ä father	ōō boot
ĕ pet	ŭ cut
ē be	ûr urge
ĭ pit	th thin
ī pie	*th* this
îr pier	hw which
ŏ pot	zh vision
ō toe	ə about, item
ô paw	♦ regionalism

Stress marks: **ʹ** (primary); ʹ (secondary), as in **dictionary** (dĭkʹshə-nĕrʹē)

Mongolia

ă pat | oi boy
ā pay | ou out
âr care | ŏŏ took
ä father | ōō boot
ĕ pet | ŭ cut
ē be | ûr urge
ĭ pit | th thin
ī pie | *th* this
îr pier | hw which
ŏ pot | zh vision
ō toe | ə about, item
ô paw | ♦ regionalism

Stress marks: **ʹ** (primary); ʹ (secondary), as in **dictionary** (dĭkʹshə-nĕrʹē)

a source of cerium and thorium. [Greek *monazein,* to live alone; see MONASTERY + –ITE [1].]

Mön·chen·glad·bach (mŭnʹkən-glätʹbäk, mœnʹKHən-glätʹbäKH). A city of west-central Germany west-southwest of Düsseldorf. Established around a Benedictine abbey founded c. 972, the city was chartered in 1336. Population, 255,085.

Monck or **Monk** (mŭngk), **George.** First Duke of Albemarle. 1608–1670. English general who was instrumental in the restoration of Charles II (1660).

Monc·ton (mŭngkʹtən). A city of southeast New Brunswick, Canada, northeast of Saint John. Originally settled by Acadians, it was resettled by Germans in 1763. Population, 54,743.

Mon·dale (mŏnʹdālʹ), **Walter Frederick.** Born 1928. Vice President of the United States (1977–1981) under Jimmy Carter. He earlier served as a U.S. senator from Minnesota (1964–1977) and was the unsuccessful 1984 Democratic nominee for President.

Mon·day (mŭnʹdē, -dāʹ) *n. Abbr.* **M., Mon.** The second day of the week. [Middle English, from Old English *Mōnandæg* (translation of Latin *lūnae diēs,* day of the moon) : *mōnan,* genitive of *mōna,* moon; see MOON + *dæg,* day; see DAY.]

Monday morning quarterback *n. Informal.* One who criticizes or passes judgment from a position of hindsight. **—Monday morning quar·ter·back·ing** (kwôrʹtər-băkʹĭng) *n.*

Mon·dri·an (mônʹdrē-änʹ, mŏnʹ-), **Piet.** 1872–1944. Dutch painter whose works, characterized by intersecting perpendicular lines and planes of primary colors, profoundly influenced the development of abstract art.

mo·ne·cious (mə-nēʹshəs) *adj.* Variant of **monoecious.**

Mo·né·gasque (mô-nā-găskʹ) *n.* A native or inhabitant of Monaco; a Monacan. [French, from Provençal *mounegasc,* from *Mounegue,* Monaco.] **—Mo·né·gasqueʹ** *adj.*

Mo·nel (mō-nĕlʹ). A trademark used for an alloy of nickel, copper, iron, and manganese. This trademark sometimes occurs in print in lowercase: *"Five-way configurations are offered in sizes to 18 in. of ductile iron, carbon steel, various stainless steels, monel, nickel, and a large selection of other alloys"* (Offshore). *"If pure oxygen is involved, or if the plant is near a sea coast with a salt-laden atmosphere, the use of monel may have to be considered"* (Oil & Gas Journal).

mo·nen·sin (mō-nĕnʹsĭn) *n.* A broad-spectrum antibiotic, $C_{36}H_{62}O_{11}$, obtained from the actinomycete *Streptomyces cinnamonensis* and used chiefly as an additive to beef cattle feed. [New Latin *(cinna)mōnēns(is),* species name (from Latin *cinnamon, cinnamōmum,* cinnamon; see CINNAMON) + –IN.]

mo·ne·ran (mə-nîrʹən) *n.* A member of the kingdom Monera (or Prokaryotae), comprising the prokaryotes and including all bacteria. **—moneran** *adj.* Of or relating to the monerans. [From New Latin *Monēra,* kingdom name, from Greek *monērēs,* solitary, from *monos,* single, alone. See MONAD.]

mon·es·trous (mŏn-ĕsʹtrəs) *adj.* Having one estrous cycle per year. Used of certain mammals.

Mo·net (mō-nāʹ, mô-), **Claude.** 1840–1926. French painter and founder of impressionism who captured on canvas his spontaneous reaction to landscapes and outdoor events.

Mo·ne·ta (mō-nāʹtə, mô-nĕʹtä), **Ernesto Teodoro.** 1833–1918. Italian journalist and pacifist who founded societies for the preservation of peace. He shared the 1907 Nobel Peace Prize.

mon·e·ta·rism (mŏnʹĭ-tə-rĭzʹəm, mŭnʹ-) *n.* **1.** A theory holding that economic variations within a given system, such as changing rates of inflation, are most often caused by increases or decreases in the money supply. **2.** A policy that seeks to regulate an economy by altering the domestic money supply, especially by increasing it in a moderate but steady manner. **—monʹe·ta·rist** *adj. & n.*

mon·e·tar·y (mŏnʹĭ-tĕrʹē, mŭnʹ-) *adj. Abbr.* **mon. 1.** Of or relating to money. **2.** Of or relating to a nation's currency. See Synonyms at **financial.** [Late Latin *monētārius,* from Latin *monēta,* money, mint. See MONEY.] **—monʹe·tarʹi·ly** *adv.*

mon·e·tize (mŏnʹĭ-tīzʹ, mŭnʹ-) *tr.v.* **-tized, -tiz·ing, -tiz·es. 1.** To establish as legal tender. **2.** To coin (money). **3.** To convert (government debt) from securities into currency that can be used to purchase goods and services. [From Latin *monēta,* money. See MONEY.] **—monʹe·ti·zaʹtion** (-tĭ-zāʹshən) *n.*

mon·ey (mŭnʹē) *n., pl.* **-eys** or **-ies. 1.** A commodity, such as gold, or an officially issued coin or paper note that is legally established as an exchangeable equivalent of all other commodities, such as goods and services, and is used as a measure of their comparative values on the market. **2.** The official currency, coins, and negotiable paper notes issued by a government. **3.** Assets and property considered in terms of monetary value; wealth. **4. a.** Pecuniary profit or loss; *He made money on the sale of his properties.* **b.** One's salary; pay: *It was a terrible job, but the money was good.* **5.** An amount of cash or credit: *raised the money for the new playground.* **6.** Often **moneys** or **monies.** Sums of money, especially of a specified nature: *state tax moneys; monies set aside for research and development.* **7.** A wealthy person, family, or group: *marry into money.* ***—idioms.*** **for (one's) money.** According to one's opinion, choice, or preference: *For my money, it's not worth the trouble.* **in the money. 1.** *Slang.* Rich; affluent. **2.** Taking first, second, or third place in a contest on which a bet has been placed, such as a horserace. **on the money.** Exact; precise. **put money on.** To place a bet on. **put (one's) money where (one's) mouth is.** *Slang.* To live up to one's words; act according to one's own advice. [Middle English *moneie,* from Old French, from Latin *monēta,* mint, coinage, from *Monēta,* epithet of Juno, temple of Juno of Rome where money was coined.]

mon·ey·bag (mŭnʹē-băgʹ) *n.* **1.** A bag for holding money. **2. moneybags.** *(used with a sing. or pl. verb).* Wealth. **3. moneybags.** *(used with a sing. verb).* A rich, often extravagant person.

mon·ey·chang·er (mŭnʹē-chānʹjər) *n.* **1.** One that exchanges money, as from one currency to another. **2.** A machine that holds and dispenses coins.

mon·eyed also **mon·ied** (mŭnʹēd) *adj.* **1.** Having a great deal of money: *the moneyed classes.* See Synonyms at **rich. 2.** Representing or arising from the possession of money or wealth: *the triumph of moneyed interests over landed interests.*

mon·ey·grub·ber (mŭnʹē-grŭbʹər) *n.* One who is intent on or preoccupied with accumulating money. **—monʹey·grubʹbing** *adj. & n.*

mon·ey·lend·er (mŭnʹē-lĕnʹdər) *n.* One that lends money at an interest rate.

mon·ey·mak·ing (mŭnʹē-māʹkĭng) *n.* Acquisition of money or other wealth. **—moneymaking** *adj.* **1.** Engaged or successful in acquiring wealth. **2.** Actually or potentially profitable: *a moneymaking business proposition.* **—monʹey·makʹer** *n.*

mon·ey·man (mŭnʹē-mănʹ) *n. Informal.* **1.** A man who assesses or advises on economic policies and trends. **2.** A man who manages the financial aspect of a business or an operation.

money market *n. Economics.* **1.** The trade in short-term, low-risk securities, such as certificates of deposit and U.S. Treasury notes. **2.** A mutual fund that sells its shares in order to purchase short-term securities, the income from which is distributed among shareholders in the form of additional shares in the fund. In this sense, also called *money market fund.*

money of account *n.* A monetary unit in which accounts are kept and that may or may not correspond to actual current denominations.

money order *n. Abbr.* **m.o., M.O., MO** An order for the payment of a specified amount of money, usually issued and payable at a bank or post office.

money plant *n.* See **honesty** (sense 4).

money shell *n.* See **butter clam.**

money supply *n.* The amount of money in the economy, measured according to varying methods or principles. One such method incorporates only money that is usually used to purchase goods and services, such as cash and the contents of checking accounts.

mon·ey·wort (mŭnʹē-wûrtʹ, -wôrtʹ) *n.* A European creeping plant *(Lysimachia nummularia)* naturalized in eastern North America, having rounded, opposite leaves and single, axillary yellow flowers. Also called *creeping Charlie, creeping Jennie.* [From the round shape of its leaves.]

mon·ger (mŭngʹgər, mŏngʹ-) *n.* **1.** A dealer in a specific commodity. Often used in combination: *an ironmonger.* **2.** A person promoting something undesirable or discreditable. Often used in combination: *a scandalmonger; a warmonger.* **—monger** *tr.v.* **-gered, -ger·ing, -gers.** To peddle. [Middle English *mongere,* from Old English *mangere,* from Latin *mangō,* probably of Greek origin.]

mon·go (mŏngʹgō) *n., pl.* **mongo.** See table at **currency.** [Mongolian.]

Mon·gol (mŏngʹgəl, -gōlʹ, mŏnʹ-) *n.* **1.** A member of any of the traditionally nomadic peoples of Mongolia. **2.** See **Mongolian** (sense 4). **3.** *Anthropology.* A member of the Mongoloid racial division. No longer in scientific use. **—Mongol** *adj.* **1.** Of or relating to Mongolia, the Mongols, or their language or culture. **2.** *Anthropology.* Of or relating to the Mongoloid racial division. No longer in scientific use. [Mongolian.]

Mon·go·li·a (mŏng-gōʹlē-ə, -gōlʹyə, mŏn-). **1.** An ancient region of east-central Asia comprising modern-day Nei Monggol (Inner Mongolia) and the country of Mongolia. In the 13th century Genghis Khan, leader of the Mongols, united all the tribes of the area and forged a great empire that eventually stretched from China to the Danube River and into Persia. After the 17th century China and Russia contended for control of the area, with the southern part eventually joining China. **2.** Formerly **Out·er Mongolia** (outʹər). A country of north-central Asia between Russia and China. Originally part of the Mongol Empire, the area was under Chinese control from 1691 to 1911 and from 1919 to 1921, when it formed a separate state under the protection of the U.S.S.R. Ulan Bator is the capital and the largest city. Population, 1,866,300.

Mon·go·li·an (mŏng-gōʹlē-ən, -gōlʹyən, mŏn-) *adj.* **1.** Of or relating to Mongolia, the Mongols, or their language or culture. **2.** Also **mongolian.** *Offensive.* Of or relating to Down syndrome. **—Mongolian** *n.* **1.** A native or inhabitant of Mongolia. **2.** A member of the Mongol people. **3.** *Anthropology.* A member of the Mongoloid racial division. No longer in scientific use. **4. a.** A subfamily of the Altaic language family, Mongolian and Kalmyk being the most important members. **b.** Any of the various spoken and written dialects and languages of the Mongols living in Mongolia and China. In this sense, also called *Mongol.*

Mongolian fold *n.* The epicanthic fold.

Mon·gol·ic (mŏng-gŏlʹĭk, mŏn-) *adj. Anthropology.* Of or relating to the Mongoloid racial division. No longer in scientific use.

mon·gol·ism also **Mon·gol·ism** (mŏngʹgə-lĭzʹəm, mŏnʹ-) *n.*

Offensive. Down syndrome. [From MONGOLIAN, term used in a system of classification for mentally retarded people, devised around ethnic lines by John L.H. Down (1828–1896), British physician.]

Mon·gol·oid (mŏng′gə-loid′, mŏn′-) *adj.* **1.** *Anthropology.* Of, relating to, or being a major human racial division traditionally distinguished by physical characteristics such as yellowish-brown skin pigmentation, straight black hair, dark eyes with pronounced epicanthic folds, and prominent cheekbones and including peoples indigenous to central and eastern Asia. No longer in scientific use. **2.** Characteristic of or resembling a Mongol. **3.** Also **mongoloid.** *Offensive.* Of or relating to Down syndrome. **—Mongoloid** *n.* **1.** *Anthropology.* A member of the Mongoloid racial division. No longer in scientific use. **2.** Also **mongoloid.** *Offensive.* A person affected with Down syndrome.

mon·goose (mŏng′go͞os′, mŏn′-) *n., pl.* **-goos·es.** Any of various Old World carnivorous mammals of the genus *Herpestes* and related genera, having a slender agile body and a long tail and noted for the ability to seize and kill venomous snakes. [Marathi *mangūs,* of Dravidian origin.]

mon·grel (mŭng′grəl, mŏng′-) *n.* **1.** An animal or a plant resulting from various interbreedings, especially a dog of mixed or undetermined breed. **2.** A cross between different breeds, groups, or varieties, especially a mixture that is or appears to be incongruous. **—mongrel** *adj.* Of mixed origin. [Probably from Middle English *mong,* mixture, from Old English *gemang.* See **mag-** in Appendix.] **—mon·grel′ism** *n.* **—mon′grel·ly** *adv.*

mon·grel·ize (mŭng′grə-līz′, mŏng′-) *tr.v.* **-ized, -iz·ing, -iz·es.** To make mongrel in race, nature, or character. **—mon′grel·i·za′tion** (-grə-lĭ-zā′shən) *n.*

mon·ick·er (mŏn′ĭ-kər) *n.* Variant of **moniker.**

mon·ied (mŭn′ēd) *adj.* Variant of **moneyed.**

mon·ies (mŭn′ēz) *n.* A plural of **money.**

mon·i·ker or **mon·ick·er** (mŏn′ĭ-kər) *n. Slang.* A personal name or nickname. [Probably from Shelta *munik,* name, possibly alteration of Irish Gaelic *ainm,* from Old Irish. See **nō-men-** in Appendix.]

mo·nil·i·al (mə-nĭl′ē-əl) *adj.* Of, relating to, or caused by a fungus of the genus *Monilia* (or *Candida*): *monilial infections.*

mo·ni·li·a·sis (mō′nə-lī′ə-sĭs, mŏn′ə-) *n.* See **candidiasis.** [New Latin *Monīlia,* type genus (from Latin *monīle,* necklace) + –IASIS.]

mo·nil·i·form (mō-nĭl′ə-fôrm′) *adj.* Resembling a string of beads, as the roots of certain plants or the antennae of certain insects. [Latin *monīle,* necklace + –FORM.] **—mo·nil′i·form′ly** *adv.*

mon·ish (mŏn′ĭsh) *tr.v.* **-ished, -ish·ing, -ish·es.** To admonish; warn. [Middle English *monesten, monishe,* from Old French *monester,* from Vulgar Latin **monestāre,* alteration of Latin *monēre,* to warn. See **men-¹** in Appendix.]

mo·nism (mō′nĭz′əm, mŏn′ĭz′əm) *n. Philosophy.* **1.** The view in metaphysics that reality is a unified whole and that all existing things can be ascribed to or described by a single concept or system. **2.** The doctrine that mind and matter are formed, or reducible to, the same ultimate substance or principle of being. **—mo′nist** *n.* **—mo·nis′tic** (mō-nĭs′tĭk, mŏ-) *adj.* **—mo·nis′ti·cal·ly** *adv.*

mo·ni·tion (mō-nĭsh′ən, mə-) *n.* **1.** A warning or an intimation of something imminent, especially of impending danger. **2.** Cautionary advice or counsel; an admonition. **3.** A formal order from a bishop or an ecclesiastical court to refrain from a specified offense. **4.** A summons or citation in civil or admiralty law. [Middle English *monicioun,* from Old French *monicion,* from Latin *monitiō, monitiōn-,* from *monitus,* past participle of *monēre,* to warn. See **men-¹** in Appendix.]

mon·i·tor (mŏn′ĭ-tər) *n.* **1.** One that admonishes, cautions, or reminds, especially with respect to matters of conduct. **2.** A pupil who assists a teacher in routine duties. **3. a.** A usually electronic device used to record, regulate, or control a process or system. **b.** A receiver, such as a screen or speaker, that is used to check the quality or content of an electronic transmission: *followed the broadcast on the television monitor.* **c.** *Computer Science.* A device that accepts video signals from a computer and displays information on a screen. **4.** *Computer Science.* A program that observes, supervises, or controls the activities of other programs. **5.** An articulated device holding a rotating nozzle with which a jet of water is regulated, used in mining and firefighting. **6. a.** A heavily ironclad warship of the 19th century with a low, flat deck and one or more gun turrets. **b.** A modern warship designed for coastal bombardment. **7.** *Biology.* Any of various tropical carnivorous lizards of the family *Varanidae,* living in the East Indies, southern Asia, Africa, Australia, and New Guinea and ranging in length from several centimeters to 3 meters (10 feet). **—monitor** *v.* **-tored, -tor·ing, -tors.** *—tr.* **1.** To check the quality or content of (an electronic audio or visual signal) by means of a receiver. **2.** To check by means of an electronic receiver for significant content, such as military, political, or illegal activity: *monitor a suspected criminal's phone conversations.* **3.** To keep track of systematically with a view to collecting information: *monitor the bear population of a national park; monitored the political views of the people.* **4. a.** To test or sample on a regular or ongoing basis: *monitored the city's drinking water for impurities.* **b.** To test (air or an object's surface, for example) for radiation intensity. **5.** To keep close watch over; supervise. **6.** To direct. *—intr.* To act as a monitor. [Latin, from *monēre,* to warn. See **men-¹** in Appendix.] **—mon′i·tor·ship′** *n.*

mon·i·to·ri·al (mŏn′ĭ-tôr′ē-əl, -tōr′-) *adj.* **1.** Of, relating to, or performed by monitors. **2.** Monitory. **—mon′i·to′ri·al·ly** *adv.*

mon·i·to·ry (mŏn′ĭ-tôr′ē, -tōr′ē) *adj.* Conveying an admonition or a warning: *a monitory glance.* **—monitory** *n., pl.* **-ries.** A letter of admonition, such as one from a bishop or an ecclesiastical court. [Middle English *monitorie,* letter of admonition, admonitory, from Medieval Latin *monitōria,* admonition, from feminine of Latin *monitōrius,* monitory, from *monitor,* monitor. See MONITOR.]

monk (mŭngk) *n.* A man who is a member of a brotherhood living in a monastery and devoted to a discipline prescribed by his order: *a Carthusian monk; a Buddhist monk.* [Middle English *munk,* from Old English *munuc,* from Late Latin *monachus,* from Late Greek *monakhos,* from Greek, single, from *monos.* See **men-⁴** in Appendix.]

Monk (mŭngk), **George.** See George **Monck.**

Monk, Thelonious Sphere. 1917–1982. American jazz pianist and composer whose spare piano style and unusual harmonic sense made him one of the most influential modern jazz musicians.

Thelonious Monk
Photographed in 1949

monk·er·y (mŭng′kə-rē) *n., pl.* **-ies. 1.** Monastic life or practices. **2.** Monks considered as a group. **3.** A monastery.

mon·key (mŭng′kē) *n., pl.* **-keys. 1.** Any of various long-tailed, medium-sized members of the order Primates, including the macaques, baboons, guenons, capuchins, marmosets, and tamarins and excluding the anthropoid apes and the prosimians. **2.** One that behaves in a way suggestive of a monkey, as a mischievous child or a mimic. **3.** The iron block of a pile driver. **4.** *Slang.* A person who is mocked, duped, or made to appear a fool: *They made a monkey out of him.* **5.** *Slang.* Drug addiction: *have a monkey on one's back.* **—monkey** *v.* **-keyed, -key·ing, -keys.** *—intr. Informal.* **1.** To play, fiddle, trifle, or tamper with something. **2.** To behave in a mischievous or apish manner: *Stop monkeying around!* *—tr.* To imitate or mimic; ape. [Origin unknown.]

monkey
Javan macaque
Macaca irus

monkey bars *pl.n.* A three-dimensional structure of poles and bars on which children can play, as in a playground; a jungle gym.

monkey bread *n.* The hanging, gourdlike fruit of the baobab.

monkey business *n. Slang.* Silly, mischievous, or deceitful acts or behavior.

mon·key-faced owl (mŭng′kē-fāst′) *n.* See **barn owl.**

monkey flower *n.* Any of various herbs or shrubs of the genus *Mimulus,* having variously colored, two-lipped flowers. [From the pattern of spots on its flowers.]

monkey jacket *n.* **1.** A short, tight-fitting jacket, traditionally worn by sailors. **2.** See **mess jacket.** [From its resemblance to the jacket worn by an organ grinder's monkey.]

monkey pot *n.* **1. a.** Any of various tropical American trees of the genus *Lecythis,* having a large, woody, urn-shaped pod that dehisces by a lid. **b.** The fruit of this tree. **2.** A cylindrical or barrel-shaped melting pot used in making flint glass.

mon·key-puz·zle (mŭng′kē-pŭz′əl) *n.* A coniferous evergreen tree *(Araucaria araucana)* native to Chile, having intricately ramifying branches covered with overlapping, leathery, lanceolate, prickle-tipped leaves. [Perhaps from the obstacle its intertwined branches would pose.]

mon·key·shine (mŭng′kē-shīn′) *n. Slang.* A mischievous or playful trick; a prank. Often used in the plural: *laughed at my daughter's monkeyshines.*

monkey wrench *n.* **1.** A hand tool with adjustable jaws for turning nuts of varying sizes. **2.** *Informal.* Something that disrupts: *He threw a monkey wrench into our plans.* [Origin unknown.]

monkey bars

monk·fish (mŭngk′fĭsh′) *n., pl.* **monkfish** or **-fish·es.** See **goosefish.** [Perhaps from the cowled appearance of its head.]

Mon-Khmer (mōn′kmĕr′) *n.* A subfamily of the Austro-Asiatic language family that includes Mon, Khmer, and other languages of southeast Asia.

monk·hood (mŭngk′ho͝od′) *n.* **1.** The character, condition, or profession of a monk; monasticism. **2.** Monks considered as a group.

monk·ish (mŭng′kĭsh) *adj.* **1.** Of, relating to, or characteristic of monks or monasticism. **2.** Inclined to self-denial; ascetic. **—monk′ish·ly** *adv.* **—monk′ish·ness** *n.*

monk's cloth (mŭngks) *n.* A heavy cotton cloth in a coarse basket weave, now used chiefly for draperies.

monks·hood (mŭngks′ho͝od′) *n.* **1.** See **aconite. 2.** A slender, erect, poisonous perennial herb *(Aconitum napellus)* native to northern Europe, having violet flowers and whose dried leaves and roots yield aconite. Also called *wolfsbane.*

Mon·mouth (mŏn′məth), Duke of. Title of James Scott. 1649–1685. English pretender to the throne. The illegitimate son of Charles II, he led a rebellion after the succession of the Catholic James II but was defeated in battle, captured, and beheaded.

Mon·net (mō-nā′), **Jean.** 1888–1979. French economist and politician who laid the plans for the Common Market.

mon·o¹ (mŏn′ō) *n. Informal.* Infectious mononucleosis.

mon·o² (mŏn′ō) *adj. Informal.* Monaural; monophonic. [Short for MONOPHONIC.]

mono– or **mon–** *pref.* **1.** One; single; alone: *monomorphic.*

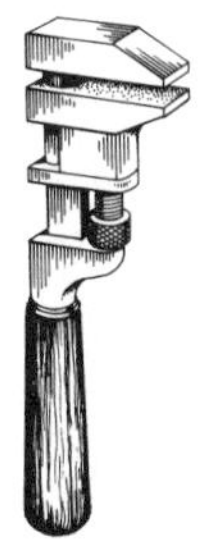
monkey wrench

2. Containing a single atom, radical, or group: *monobasic.* **3.** Monomolecular; monatomic: *monolayer.* [Middle English, from Old French, from Latin, from Greek, from *monos,* single, alone. See **men-**[4] in Appendix.]

mon·o·ac·id (mŏn′ō-ăs′ĭd) *n.* An acid having one replaceable hydrogen atom. **—monoacid** also **mon·o·a·cid·ic** (-ə-sĭd′ĭk) *adj.* Having only one hydroxyl group to react with acids.

mon·o·am·ine (mŏn′ō-ăm′ēn, -ə-mēn′) *n.* An amine compound containing one amino group, especially a compound that functions as a neurotransmitter.

monoamine oxidase *n. Abbr.* **MAO** An enzyme in the cells of most tissues that catalyzes the oxidation of monoamines such as norepinephrine and serotonin.

monoamine oxidase inhibitor *n. Abbr.* **MAOI** Any of a class of antidepressant drugs that block the action of monoamine oxidase in the brain, thereby allowing the accumulation of monoamines such as norepinephrine.

mon·o·ba·sic (mŏn′ə-bā′sĭk) *adj.* **1.** Having only one hydrogen ion to donate to a base in an acid-base reaction; monoprotic. **2.** Having only one metal ion or positive radical.

mon·o·carp (mŏn′ə-kärp′) *n.* A monocarpic plant.

mon·o·car·pel·lar·y (mŏn′ə-kär′pə-lĕr′ē) *adj. Botany.* Consisting of only one carpel.

mon·o·car·pic (mŏn′ə-kär′pĭk) also **mon·o·car·pous** (-kär′pəs) *adj. Botany.* Flowering and bearing fruit only once.

mon·o·ce·phal·ic (mŏn′ō-sə-făl′ĭk) *adj. Botany.* Bearing one flower head, as in the scape of a dandelion.

Mo·noc·er·os (mə-nŏs′ər-əs) *n.* A constellation near Canis Major and Canis Minor. [Middle English, unicorn, from Old French, from Latin, from Greek *monokerōs,* having one horn : *mono-,* mono- + *keras,* horn; see **ker-**[1] in Appendix.]

mon·o·cha·si·um (mŏn′ə-kā′zē-əm, -zhē-) *n., pl.* **-si·a** (-zē-ə, -zhē-ə, -zhə). *Botany.* A cyme having a single flower on each axis. [MONO– + (DI)CHASIUM.] **—mon′o·cha′si·al** *adj.*

mon·o·chord (mŏn′ə-kôrd′) *n. Music.* An acoustical instrument consisting of a sounding box with one string and a movable bridge, used to study musical tones. [Middle English *monocorde,* from Old French, from Medieval Latin *monochordum,* from Greek *monokhordon* : *mono-,* mono- + *khordē,* string; see CORD.]

mon·o·chro·mat (mŏn′ə-krō′măt) *n.* A person with monochromatism.

mon·o·chro·mat·ic (mŏn′ə-krō-măt′ĭk) *adj.* **1.** Having or appearing to have only one color. **2.** Of or composed of radiation of only one wavelength: *monochromatic light.* **3.** Done in monochrome: *monochromatic prints and paintings.* **4.** Of or exhibiting monochromatism. **—mon′o·chro·mat′i·cal·ly** *adv.* **—mon′o·chro′ma·tic′i·ty** (-mə-tĭs′ĭ-tē) *n.*

mon·o·chro·ma·tism (mŏn′ə-krō′mə-tĭz′əm) *n.* The condition of being completely colorblind.

mon·o·chrome (mŏn′ə-krōm′) *n.* **1.a.** A picture, especially a painting, done in different shades of a single color. **b.** The art or technique of executing such a picture. **2.** The state of being in a single color. **3.** A black-and-white image, as in photography or cinematography. [Medieval Latin *monochrōma,* from feminine of Greek *monokhrōmos,* of one color : *mono-,* mono- + *khrōma,* color.] **—mon′o·chrome′, mon′o·chro′mic** (-krō′mĭk) *adj.*

mon·o·cle (mŏn′ə-kəl) *n.* An eyeglass for one eye. [French, from Late Latin *monoculus,* having one eye : Greek *mono-,* mono- + Latin *oculus,* eye; see **okʷ-** in Appendix.] **—mon′o·cled** (-kəld) *adj.*

monocle

mon·o·cline (mŏn′ə-klīn′) *n.* A geologic structure in which all layers are inclined in the same direction. **—mon′o·cli′nal** *adj.*

mon·o·clin·ic (mŏn′ə-klĭn′ĭk) *adj.* Of or relating to three unequal crystal axes, two of which intersect obliquely and are perpendicular to the third.

mon·o·cli·nous (mŏn′ə-klī′nəs) *adj. Botany.* Having pistils and stamens in the same flower. [New Latin *monoclinus* : MONO– + Greek *klinē,* bed; see **klei-** in Appendix.]

mon·o·clo·nal (mŏn′ə-klō′nəl) *adj.* Of, forming, or derived from a single clone: *a monoclonal population of tumor cells.*

monoclonal antibody *n.* Any of a class of highly specific antibodies that are produced by the clones of a single hybrid cell formed in the laboratory by the fusion of a B cell with a tumor cell. Such a hybrid cell and its clones combine the specificity of the B cell with the ability of the tumor cell to reproduce indefinitely. Monoclonal antibodies are used widely in medical and biological research.

mon·o·coque (mŏn′ə-kōk′, -kŏk′) *n.* A metal structure, such as an aircraft, in which the skin absorbs all or most of the stresses to which the body is subjected. [French : *mono-,* mono- + *coque,* shell (from Old French, from Latin *coccum,* berry, from Greek *kokkos*).]

mon·o·cot (mŏn′ə-kŏt′) *n.* A monocotyledon.

mon·o·cot·y·le·don (mŏn′ə-kŏt′l-ēd′n) *n.* Any of various flowering plants, such as grasses, orchids, and lilies, having a single cotyledon in the seed. **—mon′o·cot′y·le′don·ous** *adj.*

mo·noc·ra·cy (mō-nŏk′rə-sē, mə-) *n., pl.* **-cies.** Government or rule by a single person; autocracy. **—mon′o·crat′** (mŏn′ə-krăt′) *n.* **—mon′o·crat′ic** *adj.*

mo·noc·u·lar (mŏ-nŏk′yə-lər, mə-) *adj.* **1.** Having or relating to one eye. **2.** Of, relating to, or intended for use by only one eye: *a monocular microscope.* [From Late Latin *monoculus,* having one eye. See MONOCLE.] **—mo·noc′u·lar·ly** *adv.*

mon·o·cul·ture (mŏn′ə-kŭl′chər) *n.* **1.** The cultivation of a single crop on a farm or in a region or country. **2.** A single, homogeneous culture without diversity or dissension. **—mon′o·cul′tur·al** *adj.*

mon·o·cy·cle (mŏn′ə-sī′kəl) *n.* A unicycle.

mon·o·cy·clic (mŏn′ə-sī′klĭk, -sĭk′lĭk) *adj.* **1.** Having a single cycle, as of activity or development. **2.** *Biology.* Having a single whorl, as certain flowers and the shells of certain invertebrates. **3.** *Chemistry.* Having a molecular structure with only one ring.

mon·o·cyte (mŏn′ə-sīt′) *n.* A large, circulating, phagocytic white blood cell, having a single well-defined nucleus and very fine granulation in the cytoplasm. Monocytes constitute from 3 to 8 percent of the white blood cells in human beings. **—mon′o·cyt′ic** (-sĭt′ĭk), **mon′o·cy′toid′** (-sī′toid′) *adj.*

mon·o·cy·to·sis (mŏn′ə-sī-tō′sĭs) *n., pl.* **-ses** (-sēz). An abnormal increase of monocytes in the blood, occurring in infectious mononucleosis and certain bacterial infections such as tuberculosis.

Mo·nod (mô-nō′), **Jacques Lucien.** 1910–1976. French biochemist. He shared a 1965 Nobel Prize for the study of regulatory activity in body cells.

mon·o·dac·tyl (mŏn′ə-dăk′təl) *n.* An animal having one toe, digit, or claw on each limb. **—mon′o·dac′ty·lous** *adj.*

mon·o·dra·ma (mŏn′ə-drä′mə, -drăm′ə) *n.* A dramatic composition written for one performer. **—mon′o·dra·mat′ic** (-drə-măt′ĭk) *adj.*

mon·o·dy (mŏn′ə-dē) *n., pl.* **-dies.** **1.** An ode for one voice or actor, as in Greek drama. **2.** A poem in which the poet or speaker mourns another's death. **3.** *Music.* **a.** A style of composition having or dominated by a single melodic line; monophony. **b.** A composition in this style. [Late Latin *monōdia,* from Greek *monōidia* : *mono-,* mono- + *ōidē,* song; see **wed-**[2] in Appendix.] **—mo·nod′ic** (mə-nŏd′ĭk), **mo·nod′i·cal** (-ĭ-kəl) *adj.* **—mo·nod′i·cal·ly** *adv.* **—mon′o·dist** (mŏn′ə-dĭst) *n.*

mo·noe·cious also **mo·ne·cious** (mə-nē′shəs) *adj.* **1.** *Botany.* Having unisexual reproductive organs or flowers, with the organs or flowers of both sexes borne on a single plant, as in corn and pines. **2.** *Zoology.* Hermaphroditic. [New Latin *Monoecia,* class name : MONO– + Greek *oikia,* dwelling; see **weik-**[1] in Appendix.] **—mo·noe′cious·ly** *adv.* **—mo·noe′cism** (mə-nē′sĭz′əm) *n.*

mon·o·es·ter (mŏn′ō-ĕs′tər) *n.* An ester having only one ester group.

mon·o·fil·a·ment (mŏn′ə-fĭl′ə-mənt) *n.* A single strand of untwisted synthetic fiber, such as nylon, used especially for fishing line.

mo·nog·a·my (mə-nŏg′ə-mē) *n.* **1.** The practice or condition of being married to only one person at a time. **2.** The practice of marrying only once in a lifetime. **3.** *Zoology.* The condition of having only one mate. **—mo·nog′a·mist** *n.* **—mo·nog′a·mous** *adj.* **—mo·nog′a·mous·ly** *adv.*

mon·o·ge·ne·an (mŏn′ə-jē′nē-ən) *n.* Any of various trematodes of the order Monogenea that typically pass the entire life cycle as ectoparasites on a single fish. [From New Latin *Monogenea,* order name : MONO– + Greek *genea,* race; see GENEALOGY.] **—mon′o·ge′ne·an** *adj.*

mon·o·gen·e·sis (mŏn′ə-jĕn′ĭ-sĭs) *n.* **1.** The theory that all living organisms are descended from a single cell or organism. **2.** Asexual reproduction, as by sporulation. **—mo·nog′e·nous** (mə-nŏj′ə-nəs) *adj.*

mon·o·ge·net·ic (mŏn′ə-jə-nĕt′ĭk) *adj.* **1.** Relating to or exhibiting monogenesis. **2.** Having a single host through the course of the life cycle. **3.** Produced under a single set of continuing conditions. Used of soil.

mon·o·gen·ic (mŏn′ə-jĕn′ĭk) *adj.* **1.a.** Of or relating to monogenesis; monogenetic. **b.** Relating to monogenism. **2.** Of or regulated by one gene or one of a pair of allelic genes. **3.** Producing offspring of only one sex, as some species of aphids. **—mon′o·gen′i·cal·ly** *adv.*

mo·nog·e·nism (mə-nŏj′ə-nĭz′əm) *n.* The theory that all human beings are descended from a single pair of ancestors. **—mo·nog′e·nist** *n.* **—mo·nog′e·nis′tic** *adj.*

mon·o·glot (mŏn′ə-glŏt′) *n.* A person who knows only one language. **—monoglot** *adj.* Knowing only one language; monolingual. [MONO– + (POLY)GLOT.]

mon·o·gram (mŏn′ə-grăm′) *n.* A design composed of one or more letters, typically the initials of a name, used as an identifying mark. **—monogram** *tr.v.* **-grammed, -gram·ming, -grams** also **-gramed, -gram·ing, -grams.** To mark with a design composed of one or more letters. [Late Latin *monogramma,* from Late Greek *monogrammon,* from neuter of *monogrammos,* consisting of a single letter : Greek *mono-,* mono- + Greek *gramma,* letter; see –GRAM.] **—mon′o·gram·mat′ic** (-grə-măt′ĭk) *adj.*

mon·o·graph (mŏn′ə-grăf′) *n.* A scholarly piece of writing of essay or book length on a specific, often limited subject. **—monograph** *tr.v.* **-graphed, -graph·ing, -graphs.** To write a monograph on. **—mo·nog′ra·pher** (mə-nŏg′rə-fər) *n.* **—mon′o·graph′ic** *adj.* **—mon′o·graph′i·cal·ly** *adv.*

mo·nog·y·ny (mə-nŏj′ə-nē) *n.* The practice or condition of having only one wife at a time. **—mo·nog′y·nist** *n.* **—mo·nog′y·nous** *adj.*

mon·o·hy·brid (mŏn′ō-hī′brĭd) *n. Genetics.* The hybrid of parents that differ at only one gene locus, for which each parent is homozygous with a different allele.

mon·o·hy·drate (mŏn′ō-hī′drāt′) *n.* A compound, such as calcium chloride monohydrate, $CaCl_2 \cdot H_2O$, that contains one molecule of water. **—mon′o·hy′drat′ed** *adj.*

mon·o·hy·dric (mŏn′ō-hī′drĭk) *adj.* Containing one replaceable atom of hydrogen.

mo·noi·cous (mə-noi′kəs) *adj. Botany.* Having archegonia and antheridia on the same plant; bisexual. [Alteration of MONOECIOUS.]

mon·o·lay·er (mŏn′ō-lā′ər) *n.* **1.** A film or layer of a compound one molecule thick. **2.** A layer of cells one cell thick, grown in a culture.

mon·o·lin·gual (mŏn′ə-lĭng′gwəl) *adj.* Using or knowing only one language. **—mon′o·lin′gual** *n.* **—mon′o·lin′gual·ism** *n.*

mon·o·lith (mŏn′ə-lĭth′) *n.* **1.** A large block of stone, especially one used in architecture or sculpture. **2.** Something, such as a column or monument, made from one large block of stone. **3.** Something suggestive of a large block of stone, as in immovability, massiveness, or uniformity. [French *monolithe,* from Greek *monolithos,* consisting of a single stone : *mono-,* mono- + *lithos,* stone.]

mon·o·lith·ic (mŏn′ə-lĭth′ĭk) *adj.* **1.** Constituting a monolith: *a monolithic sculpture.* **2.** Massive, solid, and uniform: *the monolithic proportions of Stalinist architecture.* **3.** Constituting or acting as a single, often rigid, uniform whole: *a monolithic worldwide movement.* **—mon′o·lith′i·cal·ly** *adv.*

mon·o·logue also **mon·o·log** (mŏn′ə-lôg′, -lŏg′) *—n.* **1.a.** A dramatic soliloquy. **b.** A literary composition in the form of a soliloquy. **2.** A continuous series of jokes or comic stories delivered by one comedian. **3.** A long speech made by one person, often monopolizing a conversation. *—v.* **-logued, -logu·ing, -logues** also **-logged, -log·ging, -logs.** *—intr.* To give or perform a monologue. *—tr.* To address a monologue to. [French : Greek *mono-,* mono- + Greek *-logos, -logue.*] **—mon′o·log′ic** (-lŏj′ĭk), **mon′o·log′i·cal** (-ĭ-kəl) *adj.* **—mon′o·logu′ist** (mŏn′ə-lôg′ĭst, -lŏg′-), **mo·nol′o·gist** (mə-nŏl′ə-jĭst, mŏn′ə-lôg′ĭst, -lŏg′-) *n.*

mon·o·ma·ni·a (mŏn′ə-mā′nē-ə, -mān′yə) *n.* **1.** Pathological obsession with one idea or subject, as in paranoia. **2.** Intent concentration on or exaggerated enthusiasm for a single subject or idea. **—mon′o·ma′ni·ac′** (-mā′nē-ăk′) *n.* **—mon′o·ma·ni′a·cal** (-mə-nī′ə-kəl) *adj.* **—mon′o·ma·ni′a·cal·ly** *adv.*

mon·o·mer (mŏn′ə-mər) *n.* A molecule that can combine with others to form a polymer. [MONO– + (POLY)MER.] **—mon′o·mer′ic** (-mĕr′ĭk) *adj.*

mon·o·me·tal·lic (mŏn′ō-mə-tăl′ĭk) *adj.* **1.** Consisting of or containing one metal. **2.** Of, advocating, or practicing monometallism.

mon·o·met·al·lism (mŏn′ō-mĕt′l-ĭz′əm) *n.* The economic theory or practice of using only one metal as a monetary standard. **—mon′o·met′al·list** *n.*

mo·nom·e·ter (mə-nŏm′ĭ-tər) *n.* A verse consisting of a single metrical foot or one dipody.

mo·no·mi·al (mŏ-nō′mē-əl, mə-) *n.* **1.** *Mathematics.* An algebraic expression consisting of only one term. **2.** *Biology.* A taxonomic name consisting of a single word. [MON(O)– + (BIN)OMIAL.] **—mo·no′mi·al** *adj.*

mon·o·mo·lec·u·lar (mŏn′ō-mə-lĕk′yə-lər) *adj.* **1.** Of or relating to a single molecule. **2.** Of or consisting of a layer one molecule thick. **—mon′o·mo·lec′u·lar·ly** *adv.*

mon·o·mor·phic (mŏn′ō-môr′fĭk) also **mon·o·mor·phous** (-fəs) *adj.* **1.** *Chemistry.* Having only one form, as one crystal form. **2.** *Zoology.* Having one or the same genotype, form, or structure through a series of developmental changes. **—mon′o·mor′phism** *n.*

Mo·non·ga·he·la River (mə-nŏng′gə-hē′lə). A river rising in northern West Virginia and flowing about 206 km (128 mi) generally north into southwest Pennsylvania, where it joins the Allegheny River at Pittsburgh to form the Ohio River.

mon·o·nu·cle·ar (mŏn′ō-no͞o′klē-ər, -nyo͞o′-) *adj.* **1.** Having only one nucleus: *a mononuclear cell.* **2.** *Chemistry.* Monocyclic.

mon·o·nu·cle·o·sis (mŏn′ō-no͞o′klē-ō′sĭs, -nyo͞o-) *n.* **1.** The presence of an abnormally large number of white blood cells with single nuclei in the bloodstream. **2.** Infectious mononucleosis. [MONO– + NUCLE(US) + –OSIS.]

mon·o·nu·cle·o·tide (mŏn′ō-no͞o′klē-ə-tīd′, -nyo͞o′-) *n.* A nucleotide consisting of one molecule each of a phosphoric acid, a sugar, and either a purine or a pyrimidine base.

mon·o·pet·al·ous (mŏn′ə-pĕt′l-əs) *adj. Botany.* Having the petals united to form one unit; gamopetalous.

mo·noph·a·gous (mə-nŏf′ə-gəs) *adj.* Eating only one kind of food. **—mo·noph′a·gy** (-ə-jē) *n.*

mon·o·pho·bi·a (mŏn′ō-fō′bē-ə) *n.* An abnormal fear of being alone. **—mon′o·pho′bic** (-fō′bĭk) *adj.*

mon·o·phon·ic (mŏn′ə-fŏn′ĭk) *adj.* **1.** *Music.* Having a single melodic line; monodic. **2.** *Electronics.* Monaural. **—mon′o·phon′i·cal·ly** *adv.*

mo·noph·o·ny (mə-nŏf′ə-nē) *n., pl.* **-nies.** *Music.* Music consisting of a single melodic line. [MONO– + (POLY)PHONY.]

mon·oph·thong (mŏn′əf-thông′, -thŏng′) *n. Linguistics.* **1.** A single vowel articulated without change in quality throughout the course of a syllable, as the vowel of English *bed.* **2.** Two written vowels representing a single sound, as *oa* in *boat.* [Late Greek *monophthongos* : Greek *mono-,* mono- + Greek *phthongos,* sound.] **—mon′oph·thon′gal** (-thông′gəl, -thŏng′-) *adj.*

mon·o·phy·let·ic (mŏn′ō-fī-lĕt′ĭk) *adj.* **1.** Of or concerning a single taxon of animals. **2.** Relating to, descended from, or derived from one stock or source. **—mon′o·phy·let′ic·al·ly** *adv.*

Mo·noph·y·site (mə-nŏf′ə-sīt′) *n. Theology.* An adherent of the doctrine that in the person of Jesus there was but a single, divine nature. Coptic and Syrian Christians profess this doctrine. [Late Latin *monophysita,* from Late Greek *monophusitēs* : Greek *mono-,* mono- + Greek *phusis,* nature; see **bheuə-** in Appendix.] **—Mo·noph′y·site, Mo·noph′y·sit′ic** (-sĭt′ĭk) *adj.* **—Mo·noph′y·sit′ism** *n.*

mon·o·plane (mŏn′ə-plān′) *n.* An airplane with only one pair of wings.

mon·o·ple·gi·a (mŏn′ə-plē′jē-ə, -plē′jə) *n.* Paralysis of a single limb, muscle, or muscle group. **—mon′o·ple′gic** (-plē′jĭk) *adj.*

mon·o·ploid (mŏn′ə-ploid′) *adj.* Having a single set of chromosomes; haploid. **—monoploid** *n.* A monoploid cell or organism.

mon·o·pod (mŏn′ə-pŏd′) *n.* A single-legged support for a camera or other hand-held device.

mon·o·pode (mŏn′ə-pōd′) *n.* **1.** A creature having only one foot. **2.** *Botany.* A monopodium. [Late Latin *monopodius,* one-footed. See MONOPODIUM.]

mon·o·po·di·um (mŏn′ə-pō′dē-əm) *n., pl.* **-di·a** (-dē-ə). A main axis of a plant, such as the trunk of a spruce, that maintains a single line of growth, giving off lateral branches. [New Latin, from Late Latin *monopodius,* one-footed, from Greek *monopous* : *mono-,* mono- + *pous, pod-,* foot; see **ped-** in Appendix.] **—mon′o·po′di·al** (-dē-əl) *adj.*

mon·o·pole (mŏn′ə-pōl′) *n.* A magnetic monopole.

mo·nop·o·lize (mə-nŏp′ə-līz′) *tr.v.* **-lized, -liz·ing, -liz·es.** **1.** To acquire or maintain a monopoly of. **2.** To dominate by excluding others: *monopolized the conversation.* **—mo·nop′o·li·za′tion** (-lĭ-zā′shən) *n.* **—mo·nop′o·liz′er** *n.*

SYNONYMS: *monopolize, absorb, consume, engross, preoccupy.* The central meaning shared by these verbs is "to have exclusive possession or control of": *desirable housing monopolized by the wealthy; study that absorbs all her time; was consumed by fear; engrossed herself in her reading; a mind that was preoccupied with financial worries.*

mo·nop·o·ly (mə-nŏp′ə-lē) *n., pl.* **-lies.** **1.** Exclusive control by one group of the means of producing or selling a commodity or service. **2.** *Law.* A right granted by a government giving exclusive control over a specified commercial activity to a single party. **3.a.** A company or group having exclusive control over a commercial activity. **b.** A commodity or service so controlled. **4.a.** Exclusive possession or control: *arrogantly claims to have a monopoly on the truth.* **b.** Something that is exclusively possessed or controlled: *showed that scientific achievement is not a male monopoly.* [Latin *monopōlium,* from Greek *monopōlion* : *mono-,* mono- + *pōlein,* to sell; see **pel-**[4] in Appendix.] **—mo·nop′o·lism** *n.* **—mo·nop′o·list** *n.* **—mo·nop′o·lis′tic** *adj.* **—mo·nop′o·lis′ti·cal·ly** *adv.*

mon·o·pro·pel·lant (mŏn′ō-prə-pĕl′ənt) *n.* A rocket propellant consisting of a single substance or mixture that contains both fuel and oxidizer.

mon·o·pro·tic (mŏn′ə-prō′tĭk) *adj.* Monobasic. [MONO– + PROT(ON) + –IC.]

mo·nop·so·ny (mə-nŏp′sə-nē) *n., pl.* **-nies.** A market in which the product or service of several sellers is sought by only one buyer. [MON(O)– + Greek *opsōnia,* purchase of food; see DUOPSONY.] **—mo·nop′so·nist** *n.* **—mo·nop′so·nis′tic** *adj.*

mon·o·rail (mŏn′ə-rāl′) *n.* **1.** A single rail serving as a track for wheeled vehicles traveling on it or suspended from it. **2.** A railway system using a single rail.

mon·o·sac·cha·ride (mŏn′ə-săk′ə-rīd′, -rĭd) *n.* A carbohydrate that cannot be decomposed by hydrolysis, especially one of the hexoses, having the general formula $C_6H_{12}O_6$. Also called *simple sugar.*

mon·o·sep·al·ous (mŏn′ə-sĕp′ə-ləs) *adj. Botany.* Having the sepals united to form one unit; gamosepalous.

mon·o·so·di·um glu·ta·mate (mŏn′ə-sō′dē-əm glo͞o′tə-māt′) *n. Abbr.* **MSG** A white crystalline compound, $COOH(CH_2)_2CH(NH_2)COONa$, used as a flavor enhancer in foods. [MONO– + SODIUM + GLUTAM(IC ACID) + –ATE[2].]

mon·o·some (mŏn′ə-sōm′) *n.* **1.** A chromosome having no homologue, especially an unpaired X-chromosome. **2.** A single ribosome, especially one combined with a molecule of messenger RNA. **—mon′o·so′mic** (-sō′mĭk) *adj.* **—mon′o·so′my** *n.*

mon·o·sper·mous (mŏn′ə-spûr′məs) also **mon·o·sper·mal** (-məl) *adj. Botany.* Having a single seed.

monolith
Stonehenge, Salisbury Plain, England

ă pat	oi boy
ā pay	ou out
âr care	o͝o took
ä father	o͞o boot
ĕ pet	ŭ cut
ē be	ûr urge
ĭ pit	th thin
ī pie	*th* this
îr pier	hw which
ŏ pot	zh vision
ō toe	ə about, item
ô paw	♦ regionalism

Stress marks: ′ (primary); ′ (secondary), as in **dictionary** (dĭk′shə-nĕr′ē)

James Monroe
Detail of an 1817 portrait by Gilbert Stuart

monstrance
Late 16th- to early 17th-century Spanish

mon•o•stich (mŏn′ə-stĭk′) *n.* **1.** A poem consisting of a single line. **2.** A single line of poetry.

mon•o•stome (mŏn′ə-stōm′) also **mo•nos•to•mous** (mə-nŏs′tə-məs) *adj.* Having only one mouth or oral sucker, as certain flatworms. [From Greek *monostomos* : *mono-*, mono- + *stoma*, mouth.]

mon•o•sty•lous (mŏn′ə-stī′ləs) *adj. Botany.* Having one style.

mon•o•syl•lab•ic (mŏn′ə-sĭ-lăb′ĭk) *adj. Linguistics.* **1.** Having only one syllable. **2.** Characterized by or consisting of monosyllables. **—mon′o•syl•lab′ic•al•ly** *adv.*

mon•o•syl•la•ble (mŏn′ə-sĭl′ə-bəl) *n. Linguistics.* A word or an utterance of one syllable. [From Late Latin *monosyllabon,* from Greek *monosullabon* : *mono-*, mono- + *sullabē,* syllable; see SYLLABLE.]

mon•o•syn•ap•tic (mŏn′ō-sə-năp′tĭk) *adj.* Having one neural synapse. **—mon′o•syn•ap′ti•cal•ly** *adv.*

mon•o•the•ism (mŏn′ə-thē-ĭz′əm) *n.* The doctrine or belief that there is only one God. **—mon′o•the′ist** *n.* **—mon′o•the•is′tic** *adj.* **—mon′o•the•is′ti•cal•ly** *adv.*

mon•o•the•mat•ic (mŏn′ə-thē-măt′ĭk) *adj.* Having only one theme.

mon•o•tint (mŏn′ə-tĭnt′) *n.* A monochrome painting or print.

mon•o•tone (mŏn′ə-tōn′) *n.* **1.** A succession of sounds or words uttered in a single tone of voice. **2.** *Music.* **a.** A single tone repeated with different words or time values, as in plainsong. **b.** A chant in a single tone. **3.** Sameness or dull repetition in sound, style, manner, or color. **—monotone** *adj.* **1.** Characterized by or uttered in a monotone: *a monotone recitation of names.* **2.** Of or having a single color: *a cat with a monotone coat.* **3.** Also **mon•o•ton•ic** (mŏn′ə-tŏn′ĭk). *Mathematics.* Designating sequences, the successive members of which either consistently increase or decrease but do not oscillate in relative value. Each member of a monotone increasing sequence is greater than or equal to the preceding member; each member of a monotone decreasing sequence is less than or equal to the preceding member. [From Greek *monotonos,* monotonous. See MONOTONOUS.] **—mon′o•ton′ic** (-tŏn′ĭk) *adj.* **—mon′o•ton′i•cal•ly** *adv.*

mo•not•o•nous (mə-nŏt′n-əs) *adj.* **1.** Sounded or spoken in an unvarying tone. **2.** Tediously repetitious or lacking in variety. See Synonyms at **boring.** [Greek *monotonos* : *mono-*, mono- + *tonos,* tone; see TONE.] **—mo•not′o•nous•ly** *adv.* **—mo•not′o•nous•ness** *n.*

mo•not•o•ny (mə-nŏt′n-ē) *n., pl.* **-nies. 1.** Uniformity or lack of variation in pitch, intonation, or inflection. **2.** Tedious sameness or repetitiousness: *monotony of routine.* [Greek *monotonia,* from *monotonos,* monotonous. See MONOTONOUS.]

mon•o•treme (mŏn′ə-trēm′) *n.* A member of the Monotremata, an order of primitive egg-laying mammals restricted to Australia and New Guinea and consisting of only the platypus and the echidna. [From New Latin *Monotremata,* order name : MONO– + Greek *trēma,* perforation; see **tera-**[1] in Appendix.] **—mon′o•trem′a•tous** (-trĕm′ə-təs) *adj.*

mo•not•ri•chous (mə-nŏt′rĭ-kəs) also **mon•o•trich•ic** (mŏn′ə-trĭk′ĭk) or **mo•not•ri•chate** (mə-nŏt′rĭ-kĭt) *adj.* Having one flagellum at only one pole or end, as certain bacteria.

mon•o•type (mŏn′ə-tīp′) *n.* **1.** *Biology.* The sole member of its group, such as a single species that constitutes a genus. **2.** A unique print made by pressing paper against a painted or inked surface. **—mon′o•typ′ic** (-tĭp′ĭk) *adj.*

Mon•o•type (mŏn′ə-tīp′). A trademark used for a typesetting machine operated from a keyboard that activates a unit that casts and sets individual characters.

mon•o•va•lent (mŏn′ə-vā′lənt) *adj.* **1.** *Chemistry.* Having a valence of 1; univalent. **2.** *Immunology.* **a.** Containing antigens from a single strain of a microorganism: *a monovalent vaccine.* **b.** Having only one site of attachment. Used of an antibody or antigen. **—mon′o•va′lence, mon′o•va′len•cy** *n.*

mon•ox•ide (mə-nŏk′sīd′) *n.* An oxide with each molecule containing one oxygen atom.

mon•o•zy•got•ic (mŏn′ō-zī-gŏt′ĭk) *adj.* Derived from a single fertilized ovum or embryonic cell mass. Used especially of identical twins.

Mon•roe (mən-rō′). **1.** A city of northeast-central Louisiana east of Shreveport. Founded in 1785, it is an industrial center. Population, 57,597. **2.** A city of southeast Michigan on Lake Erie southwest of Detroit. It was settled c. 1778 and today is a manufacturing and shipping center. Population, 23,531.

Monroe, Harriet. 1860–1936. American poet who founded and edited (1912–1936) *Poetry.*

Monroe, James. 1758–1831. The fifth President of the United States (1817–1825), whose administration was marked by the acquisition of Florida (1819), the Missouri Compromise (1820), in which Missouri was declared a slave state, and the profession of the Monroe Doctrine (1823), which declared U.S. opposition to European interference in the Americas.

Monroe, Marilyn. Originally Norma Jean Baker. 1926–1962. American actress noted for her great sex appeal. She appeared in several motion pictures, including *Some Like It Hot* (1959).

Mon•roe•ville (mən-rō′vĭl′). A borough of southwest Pennsylvania, a residential suburb of Pittsburgh. Population, 30,977.

Mon•ro•vi•a (mən-rō′vē-ə). **1.** The capital and largest city of Liberia, in the northwest part of the country on the Atlantic Ocean. It was founded in 1822 as a haven for freed slaves and named after James Monroe. Population, 243,243. **2.** A city of southern California, a suburb of Los Angeles in the foothills of the San Gabriel Mountains. Population, 30,531.

mons (mŏnz) *n., pl.* **mon•tes** (mŏn′tēz). A protuberance of the human body, especially that formed by the pubic bones. [Latin *mōns,* mountain. See **men-**[2] in Appendix.]

Mons (mōɴs). A city of southwest Belgium near the French border southwest of Brussels. It was an important cloth market in the 14th century. Population, 91,868.

Mon•sei•gneur (môɴ-sĕ-nyœr′) *n., pl.* **Mes•sei•gneurs** (mā-sĕ-nyœr′). *Abbr.* **Msgr., Mgr.** Used as an honorific in French-speaking areas, especially as accorded to princes and prelates. [French, from Old French : *mon,* my; see MONSIEUR + *seigneur,* lord, sir; see SEIGNIOR.]

Mon•sieur (mə-syœ′) *n., pl.* **Mes•sieurs** (mā-syœ′, mĕs′ərz). **1.** *Abbr.* **M.** Used as a courtesy title before the surname, full name, or professional title of a man in a French-speaking area: *Monsieur Cartier; Monsieur Jacques Cartier.* **2. monsieur.** Used as a form of polite address for a man in a French-speaking area. [French, from Old French : *mon,* my (from Latin *meum,* accusative of *meus;* see **me-**[1] in Appendix) + *sieur,* lord, sir; see SEIGNIOR.]

Mon•si•gnor also **mon•si•gnor** (mŏn-sēn′yər) *n. Abbr.* **Msgr., Mgr.** *Roman Catholic Church.* **1.** A title and an office conferred on a male cleric by a pope. **2.** Used as a form of address prefixed to the name of such a cleric. [Italian, from French *Monseigneur.* See MONSEIGNEUR.] **—Mon′si•gnor′i•al** (mŏn′sēn-yôr′ē-əl, -yōr′-) *adj.*

mon•soon (mŏn-so͞on′) *n.* **1.** A wind system that influences large climatic regions and reverses direction seasonally. **2. a.** A wind from the southwest or south that brings heavy rainfall to southern Asia in the summer. **b.** The rain that accompanies this wind. [Obsolete Dutch *monssoen,* from Portuguese *monção,* from Arabic *mawsim,* season.] **—mon•soon′al** *adj.*

mons pubis *n., pl.* **montes pubis.** A rounded fleshy protuberance situated over the pubic bones that becomes covered with hair during puberty. [New Latin *mōns pūbis* : Latin *mōns,* mount + Latin *pūbis,* genitive of *pūbēs,* pubis.]

mon•ster (mŏn′stər) *n.* **1. a.** An imaginary or legendary creature, such as a centaur or Harpy, that combines parts from various animal or human forms. **b.** A creature having a strange or frightening appearance. **2.** An animal, a plant, or other organism having structural defects or deformities. **3.** *Pathology.* A fetus or an infant that is grotesquely abnormal and usually not viable. **4.** A very large animal, plant, or object. **5.** One who inspires horror or disgust: *a monster of selfishness.* [Middle English *monstre,* from Old French, from Latin *mōnstrum,* portent, monster, from *monēre,* to warn. See **men-**[1] in Appendix.]

mon•strance (mŏn′strəns) *n. Roman Catholic Church.* A receptacle in which the host is held. Also called *ostensorium.* [Middle English, from Old French, from Medieval Latin *mōnstrantia,* from Latin *mōnstrāns, mōnstrant-,* present participle of *mōnstrāre,* to show, from *mōnstrum,* portent, monster. See MONSTER.]

mon•stros•i•ty (mŏn-strŏs′ĭ-tē) *n., pl.* **-ties. 1.** One that is monstrous. **2.** The quality or character of being monstrous. [Middle English *monstruosite,* from Old French, from Late Latin *mōnstrōsitās,* from Latin *mōnstruōsus,* monstrous. See MONSTROUS.]

mon•strous (mŏn′strəs) *adj.* **1.** Shockingly hideous or frightful. See Synonyms at **outrageous. 2.** Exceptionally large; enormous: *a monstrous wave.* **3.** Deviating greatly from the norm in appearance or structure; abnormal. **4.** Of or resembling a fabulous monster. [Middle English, from Old French *monstruos,* from Latin *mōnstruōsus,* from *mōnstrum,* portent, monster. See MONSTER.] **—mon′strous•ly** *adv.* **—mon′strous•ness** *n.*

mons ve•ne•ris (vĕn′ər-ĭs) *n., pl.* **montes veneris.** The female mons pubis. [New Latin *mōns veneris* : Latin *mōns,* mount + Latin *Veneris,* genitive of *Venus,* Venus.]

Mont. *abbr.* Montana.

mon•tage (mŏn-täzh′, môɴ-) *n.* **1. a.** A single pictorial composition made by juxtaposing or superimposing many pictures or designs. **b.** The art or process of making such a composition. **2. a.** A rapid succession of different images or shots in a movie. **b.** The use of such successive images as a cinematic technique. **3.** A composite of closely juxtaposed elements: *a montage of voices on an audiotape.* **—montage** *tr.v.* **-taged, -tag•ing, -tag•es.** To use or incorporate in a montage. [French, from *monter,* to mount, from Old French. See MOUNT[1].]

Mon•tag•nais (mŏn′tən-yā′) *n., pl.* **Montagnais. 1. a.** A Native American people inhabiting an extensive area in Quebec and Labrador. **b.** A member of this people. **2.** The Algonquian language of the Montagnais and Naskapi. [Canadian French, from French *montagne,* mountain. See MONTAGNARD.]

Mon•ta•gnard also **mon•ta•gnard** (mŏn′tən-yärd′) *—n.* A member of a people inhabiting the mountains and highlands of southern Vietnam near the border of Cambodia. *—adj.* Of or relating to the Montagnards or their culture. [French, mountaineer, from *montagne,* mountain, from Old French *montaigne.* See MOUNTAIN.]

Mon•ta•gu (mŏn′tə-gyo͞o′), **Ashley.** Born 1905. British-born American anthropologist whose books, such as *The Natural Superiority of Women* (1953), helped popularize anthropology.

Montagu, Lady **Mary Wortley.** 1689–1762. English writer noted for her erudite and amusing letters, first published in *Turkish Letters* (1763).

Mon·taigne (mŏn-tān′, môn-tĕn′yə), **Michel Eyquem de.** 1533–1592. French essayist whose lively personal essays are considered the highest expression of 16th-century French prose.

Mon·ta·le (mōn-tä′lā, -lĕ), **Eugenio.** 1896–1981. Italian poet whose works greatly influenced 20th-century Italian literature. He won the 1975 Nobel Prize for literature.

Mon·tan·a (mŏn-tăn′ə). *Abbr.* **MT, Mont.** A state of the northwest United States bordering on Canada. It was admitted as the 41st state in 1889. Most of the area passed to the United States through the Louisiana Purchase of 1803 and was explored by Lewis and Clark in 1805 and 1806. Split for many years among other western territories, the region was organized as the Montana Territory in 1864. Helena is the capital and Billings the largest city. Population, 786,690. **—Mon·tan′an** *adj. & n.*

mon·tane (mŏn-tān′, mŏn′tān′) *adj.* Of, growing in, or inhabiting mountain areas. [Latin *montānus,* from *mōns, mont-,* mountain. See **men-²** in Appendix.]

mon·tan wax (mŏn′tən, -tăn′) *n.* A hard, white wax obtained from lignite and used in the manufacture of polishes, paints, and phonograph records. [From Latin *montānus,* montane. See MONTANE.]

Mon·tauk (mŏn′tôk′) *n., pl.* **Montauk** or **-tauks. 1.a.** A Native American people formerly inhabiting the eastern end of Long Island in New York. **b.** A member of this people. **2.** The Algonquian language of the Montauk, dialectally related to Mohegan and Pequot. **3.** A member of any of various Algonquian peoples of eastern and central Long Island connected with the Montauk. [From a place name of Montauk origin.]

Montauk Point. The eastern extremity of Long Island, in southeast New York. It is a popular resort area.

Mont Blanc (mônt blăngk, môN bläN′). See Mont **Blanc.**

Mont·calm de Saint-Ve·ran (mŏnt-käm′ də săN′vā-räN′, môN-kälm′), Marquis **Louis Joseph de.** 1712–1759. French commander in Canada during the French and Indian War.

Mont·clair (mŏnt-klâr′). **1.** A city of southern California northeast of Pomona. It is a residential community in a citrus-growing area. Population, 22,628. **2.** A town of northeast New Jersey, a residential suburb of New York City. Population, 38,321.

mon·te (mŏn′tē) *n. Games.* A card game in which two cards are chosen from four laid out faceup and a player bets that one of the two will be matched in suit by the dealer before the other one. [Spanish, mountain, pile, monte, from Italian, from Latin *mōns, mont-,* mountain. See **men-²** in Appendix.]

Mon·te Al·bán (môn′tĕ äl-bän′). A ruined Zapotec city of southern Mexico near Oaxaca. Excavations (begun in 1931) have revealed that an advanced culture flourished here c. 200 B.C.

Mon·te·bel·lo (mŏn′tə-bĕl′ō). A city of southern California, a suburb of Los Angeles. Population, 52,929.

Mon·te Car·lo¹ (mŏn′tē kär′lō). A town of Monaco on the Mediterranean Sea and the French Riviera. It is a noted resort famed for its casino and luxurious hotels. Population, 11,599.

Mon·te Car·lo² (mŏn′tē kär′lō) *adj.* Of or relating to a problem-solving technique that uses random samples and other statistical methods for finding solutions to mathematical or physical problems. [After MONTE CARLO¹.]

Mon·te·go Bay (mŏn-tē′gō). A town of northwest Jamaica on the Caribbean Sea. Visited by Columbus in 1494, it is today a port and popular resort area. Population, 70,285.

mon·teith (mŏn-tēth′) *n.* A large punch bowl having a notched rim on which cups can be hung. [Possibly after *Monteith* (Monteigh), an eccentric 17th-century Scotsman who wore a cloak scalloped at the hem.]

Mon·te·ne·gro (mŏn′tə-nē′grō, -nĕg′rō). A region of southwest Yugoslavia bordering on the Adriatic Sea. An ancient Balkan state, it long resisted the Turks and from 1910 to 1918 was an independent kingdom. Montenegro then joined the newly formed Kingdom of the Serbs, Croats, and Slovenes, which became Yugoslavia after 1929.

Mon·te·rey (mŏn′tə-rā′). A city of western California south of San Francisco on **Monterey Bay,** an inlet of the Pacific Ocean. First settled in 1770 around a Franciscan mission, Monterey was a Spanish colonial capital for much of the time from 1774 to 1846, when it was taken by U.S. naval forces. Population, 27,558.

Monterey Park. A city of southern California, a residential suburb of Los Angeles. Population, 54,338.

mon·te·ro (mŏn-târ′ō) *n., pl.* **-ros.** A hunter's cap with side flaps. [Spanish, hunter, from *monte,* mountain, from Latin *mōns, mont-.* See MOUNTAIN.]

Mon·ter·rey (mŏn′tə-rā′, môn′tĕ-). A city of northeast Mexico east of Matamoros. Founded in 1579, the city was captured (September 1846) by Zachary Taylor's forces during the Mexican War. Population, 1,090,099.

mon·tes (mŏn′tēz) *n.* Plural of **mons.**

Mon·tes·quieu (mŏn′tə-skyōō′, môN-tĕ-skyœ′) Baron de la Brede et de Montesquieu. Title of Charles de Secondat. 1689–1755. French philosopher and jurist. An outstanding figure of the early French Enlightenment, he wrote *The Spirit of the Laws* (1748), a discourse on government.

Mon·tes·so·ri (mŏn′tĭ-sôr′ē, -sōr′ē), **Maria.** 1870–1952. Italian physician and pioneer educator.

Mon·tes·so·ri·an (mŏn′tĭ-sôr′ē-ən, -sōr′-) *adj.* Of or relating to the Montessori method.

Montessori method *n.* A method of educating young children that stresses development of a child's own initiative and natural abilities, especially through practical play. [After Maria MONTESSORI.]

Mon·teux (mŏn-tōō′, môN-tœ′), **Pierre.** 1875–1964. French-born American conductor of many major orchestras. He was noted as an interpreter of 20th-century music.

Mon·te·ver·di (mŏn′tə-vâr′dē, môn′tĕ-), **Claudio.** 1567–1643. Italian composer considered a founder of opera. His works include sacred music, many madrigals, and the opera *Orfeo* (1607).

Mon·te·vi·de·o (mŏn′tə-vĭ-dā′ō, -vĭd′ē-ō′, môn′tĕ-vē-*thĕ*′ô). The capital and largest city of Uruguay, in the southern part of the country on the Río de la Plata estuary. Founded by the Spanish c. 1726 on the site of a captured Portuguese fort, it became the capital after Uruguay achieved independence in 1828. Population, 1,237,227.

Mon·te·zu·ma II (mŏn′tĭ-zōō′mə). 1466?–1520. Last Aztec emperor in Mexico (1502–1520). He was overthrown by the Spanish conquistador Hernando Cortés.

Mont·fer·rat (mŏnt-fə-rät′). A historical region of northwest Italy south of the Po River. Claimed by a noble family of Mantua and the house of Savoy after 1612, it was finally awarded to Savoy by the Peace of Utrecht (1713).

Mont·fort (mŏnt′fərt, môN-fôr′), **Simon de.** Earl of Leicester. 1208?–1265. French-born English nobleman who led the baronial opposition to Henry III. After his military victory over the king at Lewes in southeast England (1264), Montfort was the effective ruler of England. In 1265 he called a representative legislature regarded as England's first full parliament.

Mont·gol·fier (mŏnt-gŏl′fē-ər, môN-gôl-fyā′), **Joseph Michel.** 1740–1810. French aeronautic inventor who with his brother **Jacques Étienne** (1745–1799) built and ascended in the first practical hot-air balloon (1783).

Mont·gom·er·y (mŏnt-gŭm′ə-rē, -gŭm′rē). The capital of Alabama, in the central part of the state south-southeast of Birmingham. From February to May 1861 it served as the capital of the Confederate States of America. Population, 177,857.

Montgomery, Sir **Bernard Law.** First Viscount Montgomery of Alamein. 1887–1976. British army officer who during World War II commanded the British victories over German forces in North Africa (1942).

Montgomery Village. A community of central Maryland, a suburb of Washington, D.C. Population, 16,600.

month (mŭnth) *n. Abbr.* **m., mo. 1.** A unit of time corresponding approximately to one cycle of the moon's phases, or about 30 days or 4 weeks. **2.** One of the 12 divisions of a year as determined by a calendar, especially the Gregorian calendar. Also called *calendar month.* **3.** A period extending from a date in one calendar month to the corresponding date in the following month. **4.** A sidereal month. **5.** A lunar month. **6.** A solar month. **—*idiom.* month of Sundays.** *Informal.* An indefinitely long period of time: *It will take you a month of Sundays to chop all that wood.* [Middle English *moneth,* from Old English *mōnath.* See **mē-²** in Appendix.]

USAGE NOTE: The singular *month,* preceded by a numeral (or number) and a hyphen, is used as a compound attributive: *a three-month vacation.* The plural possessive form without a hyphen is also possible: *a three months' vacation.*

month·ly (mŭnth′lē) *adj.* **1.** Occurring, appearing, or coming due every month: *a monthly meeting; monthly rent payments.* **2.** Continuing or lasting for a month. **—monthly** *adv.* Once a month; every month. **—monthly** *n., pl.* **-lies. 1.** A periodical publication appearing once each month. **2. monthlies.** *Informal.* The menses.

Mon·ti·cel·lo (mŏn′tĭ-chĕl′ō, -sĕl′ō). An estate of central Virginia southeast of Charlottesville. Designed by Thomas Jefferson, it was begun in 1770 and was his home for 56 years.

mon·ti·cule (mŏn′tĭ-kyōōl′) *n.* A minor cone of a volcano. [French, from Late Latin *monticulus,* diminutive of Latin *mōns, mont-,* mountain. See **men-²** in Appendix.]

Mont·mar·tre (môN-mär′trə). A hill and district of northern Paris, France, on the Right Bank. It is noted for its nightlife and for its associations with artists such as Van Gogh, Toulouse-Lautrec, and Utrillo.

Mont·par·nasse (môN-pär-näs′). A district of south-central Paris, France, on the Left Bank. Its cafés have long been famous as gathering places for artists, writers, and intellectuals.

Mont·pel·ier (mŏnt-pēl′yər). The capital of Vermont, in the north-central part of the state. Founded in 1780, it became the state capital in 1805. Population, 8,241.

Mont·pel·lier (môN-pĕl-yā′). A city of southern France near the Mediterranean Sea west-northwest of Marseilles. Founded in the eighth century, it was purchased by Philip VI of France in 1349. Population, 197,231.

Mon·tre·al (mŏn′trē-ôl′) or **Mont·ré·al** (môN′rā-äl′). A city of southern Quebec, Canada, on **Montreal Island** in the St. Lawrence River. Named after Mount Royal, a hill at its center, it was founded by the French as Ville Marie de Montréal in 1642 and

monteith
Late 18th-century English

Montezuma II

ă pat	oi boy
ā pay	ou out
âr care	ŏŏ took
ä father	ōō boot
ĕ pet	ŭ cut
ē be	ûr urge
ĭ pit	th thin
ī pie	*th* this
îr pier	hw which
ŏ pot	zh vision
ō toe	ə about, item
ô paw	♦ regionalism

Stress marks: ′ (primary); ′ (secondary), as in **dictionary** (dĭk′shə-nĕr′ē)

monument
Washington Monument, Washington, D.C., designed by Robert Mills

grew rapidly as a fur-trading center. The English captured the city in 1760. Population, 980,354.

Montreal North or **Mont·ré·al-Nord** (môɴ′rā-äl-nôr′). A town of southern Quebec, Canada, a suburb of Montreal on Montreal Island. Population, 94,914.

Mon·treuil (môɴ-trœ′yə). A town of north-central France, an industrial suburb of Paris. Population, 93,368.

Mon·trose (mŏn-trōz′), First Marquis of. Title of James Graham. 1612–1650. Scottish Covenanter who changed allegiance (1643) and led a force of Highlanders in a series of military victories on behalf of Charles I during the English Civil War.

Mont Roy·al (môɴ rwä-yäl′) or **Mount Roy·al** (roi′əl). A town of southern Quebec, Canada, a suburb of Montreal on Montreal Island. Population, 19,247.

Mont-Saint-Mi·chel (môɴ-săɴ-mē-shĕl′). A small island off the coast of northwest France in an arm of the English Channel.

Mont·ser·rat (mŏnt′sə-răt′). An island in the Leeward Islands of the British West Indies northwest of Guadaloupe. It was colonized by the English after 1632 but held by the French at various periods before being awarded to Great Britain in 1783.

Mont·ville (mŏnt′vĭl′). A town of southeast Connecticut on the Thames River north-northwest of New London. It was settled in 1670. Population, 16,455.

mon·u·ment (mŏn′yə-mənt) *n.* **1.** A structure, such as a building or sculpture, erected as a memorial. **2.** An inscribed marker placed at a grave; a tombstone. **3.** Something venerated for its enduring historic significance or association with a notable past person or thing: *traditions that are monuments to an earlier era.* **4.a.** An outstanding, enduring achievement: *a translation that is a monument of scholarship.* **b.** An exceptional example: *"Thousands of them wrote texts, some of them monuments of dullness"* (Robert L. Heilbroner). **5.** An object, such as a post or stone, fixed in the ground so as to mark a boundary or position. **6.** A written document, especially a legal one. [Middle English, from Latin *monumentum,* memorial, from *monēre,* to remind. See **men-**[1] in Appendix.]

mon·u·men·tal (mŏn′yə-mĕn′tl) *adj.* **1.** Of, resembling, or serving as a monument. **2.** Impressively large, sturdy, and enduring. **3.** Of outstanding significance: *Einstein's monumental contributions to physics.* **4.** Astounding: *monumental cowardice; monumental talent.* **—mon′u·men·tal′i·ty** (-mĕn-tăl′ĭ-tē) *n.* **—mon′u·men′tal·ly** *adv.*

mon·u·men·tal·ize (mŏn′yə-mĕn′tl-īz′) *tr.v.* **-ized, -iz·ing, -iz·es.** To memorialize with a monument.

mon·u·ron (mŏn′yə-rŏn′) *n.* A crystalline compound, $C_9H_{11}ClN_2O$, used as a herbicide for grasses and broadleaf weeds. [MON(O)– + UR(EA) + –ON[3].]

Mon·za (mōn′zə, môn′tsä). A city of northern Italy north-northeast of Milan. An ancient capital of Lombardy, it is now a major industrial center. Population, 122,103.

mon·zo·nite (mŏn-zō′nīt′, mŏn′zə-nīt′) *n.* An igneous rock composed chiefly of plagioclase and orthoclase, with small amounts of other minerals. [French, after Mount *Monzoni* in northeast Italy.] **—mon′zo·nit′ic** (mŏn′zə-nĭt′ĭk) *adj.*

moo (mo͞o) *intr.v.* **mooed, moo·ing, moos.** To emit the deep, bellowing sound made by a cow; low. **—moo** *n., pl.* **moos.** The lowing of a cow or a similar sound. [Imitative.]

mooch (mo͞och) *v.* **mooched, mooch·ing, mooch·es.** *Slang.* *—tr.* **1.** To obtain or try to obtain by begging; cadge. See Synonyms at **cadge. 2.** To steal; filch. *—intr.* **1.** To get or try to get something free of charge; sponge: *lived by mooching off friends.* **2.** To wander about aimlessly. **3.** To skulk around; sneak. [Middle English *mowchen,* probably from Old French *muchier,* to hide, skulk.] **—mooch′er** *n.*

mood[1] (mo͞od) *n.* **1.** A state of mind or emotion. **2.** A pervading impression of an observer: *the somber mood of the painting.* **3.** An incidence of sulking or angry behavior. **4.** Inclination; disposition. [Middle English *mod,* from Old English *mōd,* disposition. See **mē-**[1] in Appendix.]

SYNONYMS: *mood, humor, temper.* These nouns refer to a temporary state of mind or feeling. *Mood* is the most inclusive term: *a contentious mood; a cheerful mood. "I was in no mood to laugh and talk with strangers"* (Mary Wollstonecraft Shelley). *Humor* often implies a state of mind resulting from one's characteristic disposition or temperament; it sometimes suggests fitfulness or variability: *The humor of the Cabinet shifted after the scandal was exposed. "All which had been done . . . was the effect not of humor, but of system"* (Edmund Burke). *Temper* most often refers to a state of mind marked by irritability or intense anger: *"The nation was in such a temper that the smallest spark might raise a flame"* (Macaulay).

mood[2] (mo͞od) *n.* **1.** *Grammar.* A set of verb forms or inflections used to indicate the speaker's attitude toward the factuality or likelihood of the action or condition expressed. In English the indicative mood is used to make factual statements, the subjunctive mood to indicate doubt or unlikelihood, and the imperative mood to express a command. **2.** *Logic.* The arrangement or form of a syllogism. [Alteration of MODE.]

mood·y (mo͞o′dē) *adj.* **-i·er, -i·est. 1.** Given to frequent changes of mood; temperamental. **2.** Subject to periods of depression; sulky. **3.** Expressive of a mood, especially a sullen or gloomy mood. **—mood′i·ly** *adv.* **—mood′i·ness** *n.*

moon
Top: 4th day of new moon
Center: Full moon
Bottom: 24th day of new moon

moonscape
Astronaut Harrison H. Schmitt on the moon, December 1972

Moo·dy (mo͞o′dē), **Dwight Lyman.** 1837–1899. American evangelist who toured major American and British cities and founded several educational institutions.

Moody, Helen Wills. See Helen Newington **Wills.**

Moody, William Henry. 1853–1917. American jurist who served as an associate justice of the U.S. Supreme Court (1906–1910).

moo goo gai pan (mo͞o′ go͞o′ gī′ păn′) *n.* A Cantonese dish of chicken, mushrooms, vegetables, and spices sautéed together. [Cantonese, corresponding to Mandarin *mú gū jī piān* : *mú gū,* mushroom + *jī,* chicken + *piān,* slice.]

moo·la or **moo·lah** (mo͞o′lə) *n. Slang.* Money. [Origin unknown.]

moon (mo͞on) *n.* **1.** The natural satellite of Earth, visible by reflection of sunlight and having a slightly elliptical orbit, approximately 356,000 kilometers (221,600 miles) distant at perigee and 406,997 kilometers (252,950 miles) at apogee. Its mean diameter is 3,475 kilometers (2,160 miles), its mass approximately one eightieth that of Earth, and its average period of revolution around Earth 29 days 12 hours 44 minutes calculated with respect to the sun. **2.** A natural satellite revolving around a planet. **3.** The moon as it appears at a particular time in its cycle of phases: *the full moon; a half moon.* **4.** A month, especially a lunar month. **5.** A disk, globe, or crescent resembling the natural satellite of Earth. **6.** Moonlight. **7.** *Slang.* The bared buttocks. **—moon** *v.* **mooned, moon·ing, moons.** *—intr.* **1.** To wander about or pass time languidly and aimlessly. **2.** To yearn or pine as if infatuated. **3.** *Slang.* To expose one's buttocks in public as a prank or disrespectful gesture. *—tr. Slang.* To expose one's buttocks to (others) as a prank or disrespectful gesture: *"threatened to moon a passing . . . camera crew"* (Vanity Fair). [Middle English *moone,* from Old English *mōna.* See **mē-**[2] in Appendix.]

moon·beam (mo͞on′bēm′) *n.* A ray of moonlight.

moon·blind (mo͞on′blīnd′) *adj.* Affected with moon blindness.

moon blindness *n.* Recurrent inflammation of a horse's eyes, often resulting in eventual blindness. Also called *mooneye.*

moon·calf (mo͞on′kăf′, -käf′) *n.* **1.** A fool. **2.** A freak.

moon·child (mo͞on′chīld′) *n.* One who is born under the sign of Cancer. [From the astrological association of Cancer and the moon.]

moon dog *n.* A paraselene.

moon·eye (mo͞on′ī′) *n.* **1.** A silvery freshwater fish of the family Hiodontidae, especially *Hiodon tergisus* of eastern North America. **2.** See **moon blindness.**

moon·eyed (mo͞o′īd′) *adj.* Moonblind.

moon-faced (mo͞on′fāst′) *adj.* Having a round face.

moon·fish (mo͞on′fĭsh′) *n., pl.* **moonfish** or **-fish·es. 1.** Any of several marine fishes of the family Carangidae, found in warm coastal waters of North and South America and having short, compressed bodies and a silver to yellowish color. Also called *dollarfish.* **2.** See **opah.**

moon·flow·er (mo͞on′flou′ər) *n.* Any of several night-blooming vines related to the morning glories.

moon·light (mo͞on′līt′) *n.* The light reflected from the surface of the moon. **—moonlight** *intr.v.* **-light·ed, -light·ing, -lights.** *Informal.* To work at another job, often at night, in addition to one's full-time job. **—moon′light′er** *n.*

moon·lit (mo͞on′lĭt′) *adj.* Lighted by moonlight.

moon·quake (mo͞on′kwāk′) *n.* A quake or series of vibrations on the moon similar to an earthquake but usually of very low magnitude.

moon·rise (mo͞on′rīz′) *n.* The event or time of the appearance of the moon above the eastern horizon.

moon·scape (mo͞on′skāp′) *n.* **1.** A view or picture of the surface of the moon. **2.** A desolate landscape.

moon·seed (mo͞on′sēd′) *n.* Any of several dioecious vines of the closely related genera *Cocculus* and *Menispermum,* having inconspicuous flowers and red or blackish fruit.

moon·set (mo͞on′sĕt′) *n.* The event or time of the disappearance of the moon below the western horizon.

moon shell *n.* Any of various marine gastropod mollusks of the family Naticidae, having a smooth, rounded shell.

♦**moon·shine** (mo͞on′shīn′) *n.* **1.** Moonlight. **2.** *Informal.* Foolish talk or thought; nonsense. **3.** Illegally distilled whiskey. In this sense, also called ♦*white lightning.* **—moonshine** *intr.v.* **-shined, -shin·ing, -shines.** To distill and sell liquor illegally. **—moon′shin′er** *n.*

moon·stone (mo͞on′stōn′) *n.* A variety of feldspar valued as a gem for its pearly translucence.

moon·struck (mo͞on′strŭk′) also **moon·strick·en** (-strĭk′ən) *adj.* **1.** Dazed or distracted with romantic sentiment. **2.** Affected by insanity; crazed. [From the belief that the moon caused insanity.]

moon·walk (mo͞on′wôk′) *n.* A walk on the surface of the moon by an astronaut. **—moonwalk** *intr.v.* **-walked, -walk·ing, -walks.** To walk on the surface of the moon. **—moon′walk′er** *n.*

moon·ward (mo͞on′wərd) *adv. & adj.* Toward the moon.

moon·wort (mo͞on′wûrt′, -wôrt′) *n.* See **grape fern.**

moon·y (mo͞o′nē) *adj.* **-i·er, -i·est. 1.** Of or suggestive of the moon or moonlight. **2.** Moonlit. **3.** Dreamy in mood or nature; absent-minded.

moor[1] (mo͝or) *v.* **moored, moor·ing, moors.** —*tr.* **1.** To make fast (a vessel, for example) by means of cables, anchors, or lines: *moor a ship to a dock; a dirigible moored to a tower.* **2.** To fix in place; secure. See Synonyms at **fasten.** —*intr.* **1.** To secure a vessel or an aircraft with lines or anchors. **2.** To be secured with lines or anchors: *The freighter moored alongside the wharf.* [Middle English *moren.*]

moor[2] (mo͝or) *n.* A broad area of open land, often high but poorly drained, with patches of heath and peat bogs. [Middle English *mor,* from Old English *mōr.*]

Moor (mo͝or) *n.* **1.** A member of a Moslem people of mixed Berber and Arab descent, now living chiefly in northwest Africa. **2.** One of the Moslems who invaded Spain in the 8th century and established a civilization in Andalusia that lasted until the late 15th century. [Middle English *More,* from Old French, from Medieval Latin *Mōrus,* from Latin *Maurus,* Mauritanian, from Greek *Mauros.*]

moor·age (mo͝or′ĭj) *n.* **1.** The act or an instance of mooring. **2.** A place where a ship or an aircraft may be moored. **3.** A charge for mooring.

moor cock *n.* The male red grouse.

Moore (mo͝or, môr). A city of central Oklahoma, an industrial suburb of Oklahoma City. Population, 35,063.

Moore, Alfred. 1755–1810. American jurist who served as an associate justice of the U.S. Supreme Court (1799–1804).

Moore, Clement Clarke. 1779–1863. American scholar who wrote the Christmas poem "A Visit from St. Nicholas" (1823).

Moore, George. 1852–1933. Irish writer whose works include poetry, drama, criticism, and novels, such as *Esther Waters* (1894).

Moore, George Edward. 1873–1958. British philosopher whose theories influenced 20th-century epistemology and linguistic analysis.

Moore, Henry. 1898–1986. British sculptor whose works, mostly semiabstract human figures, are characterized by smooth, organic forms.

Moore, Marianne Craig. 1887–1972. American poet whose descriptive works are characterized by wit and irony.

Moore, Thomas. 1779–1852. Irish romantic poet. Many of his nostalgic and patriotic lyrics, such as "The Minstrel Boy," were set to traditional Irish tunes.

moor·fowl (mo͝or′foul′) *n.* See **red grouse.**

Moor·head (mo͝or′hĕd′, môr′-). A city of western Minnesota on the Red River opposite Fargo, North Dakota. Founded in 1871, it is a trade center in an agricultural region. Population, 29,998.

moor·hen (mo͝or′hĕn′) *n. Chiefly British.* **1.** A common, widely distributed species of gallinule, *Gallinula chloropus.* **2.** The female red grouse.

moor·ing (mo͝or′ĭng) *n.* **1.** A place or structure to which a vessel or aircraft can be moored. **2.** Equipment, such as anchors or chains, for holding fast a vessel or an aircraft. **3.** Often **moorings.** Elements providing stability or security: *lost their emotional moorings during the war.*

Moor·ish (mo͝or′ĭsh) *adj.* **1.** Of or relating to the Moors or their culture. **2.** Of, relating to, or being a style of Spanish architecture of the 8th to the 16th century, characterized by the horseshoe arch and ornate decoration.

moor·land (mo͝or′lănd′) *n.* Land consisting of moors.

moose (mo͞os) *n., pl.* **moose.** A hoofed mammal *(Alces alces)* found in forests of northern North America and in Eurasia and having a broad, pendulous muzzle and large, palmate antlers in the male. [Eastern Abenaki *mos.*]

moose·bird (mo͞os′bûrd′) *n.* See **gray jay.**

Moose·head Lake (mo͞os′hĕd′). A lake of west-central Maine north of Augusta. It is the center of a popular resort area.

Moose Jaw (mo͞os jô). A city of south-central Saskatchewan, Canada, west of Regina. Founded in 1882, it is a processing center for an agricultural and oil-producing area. Population, 33,941.

Moose River. A river, about 547 km (340 mi) long, of northeast Ontario, Canada, flowing northeast to James Bay.

moose·wood (mo͞os′wo͝od′) *n.* **1.** See **striped maple. 2.** See **leatherwood** (sense 1).

moot (mo͞ot) *n.* **1.** *Law.* A hypothetical case argued by law students as an exercise. **2.** An ancient English meeting, especially a representative meeting of the freemen of a shire. —**moot** *tr.v.* **moot·ed, moot·ing, moots. 1.a.** To bring up as a subject for discussion or debate. **b.** To discuss or debate. See Synonyms at **broach[1]. 2.** *Law.* To plead or argue (a case) in a moot court. —**moot** *adj.* **1.** Subject to debate; arguable: *a moot question.* **2.a.** *Law.* Without legal significance, through having been previously decided or settled. **b.** Of no practical importance; irrelevant. [Middle English, meeting, from Old English *mōt, gemōt.*] —**moot′ness** *n.*

USAGE NOTE: As an adjective *moot* has come to be widely used to mean "no longer important, irrelevant," as in *It's a purely moot question which corporation you make your rent check out to; Brown will get the money in either case.* This usage may be originally the result of a misinterpretation of its legal sense in phrases such as *a moot question.* A number of critics have objected to this use, but it was accepted by 59 percent of the Usage Panel in the sentence *The nominee himself chastised the White House for failing to do more to support him, but his concerns became moot when a number of Republicans announced that they, too, would oppose the nomination.*

moot court *n. Law.* A mock court where hypothetical cases are tried for the training of law students.

mop (mŏp) *n.* **1.** A household implement made of absorbent material attached to a typically long handle and used for washing, dusting, or drying floors. **2.** A loosely tangled bunch or mass: *a mop of unruly hair.* —**mop** *v.* **mopped, mop·ping, mops.** —*tr.* To wash or wipe with or as if with a mop: *mopped the hallway; mopping the spilled water; mopped her forehead with a towel.* —*intr.* To use a mop to wash or dry surfaces: *mopped along the baseboards.* —***phrasal verb.* mop up. 1.** To clear (an area) of remaining enemy troops after a victory. **2.** *Informal.* To perform the minor tasks that conclude a project or an activity. [Middle English *mappe,* perhaps from Old French dialectal, napkin, from Latin *mappa,* towel, cloth. See MAP.] —**mop′per** *n.*

mop·board (mŏp′bôrd′, -bōrd′) *n.* See **baseboard.**

mope (mōp) *intr.v.* **moped, mop·ing, mopes. 1.a.** To be gloomy or dejected. **b.** To brood or sulk. See Synonyms at **brood. 2.** To move in a leisurely or aimless manner; dawdle. —**mope** *n.* **1.** A person given to gloomy or dejected moods. **2. mopes.** Low spirits; the blues. Often used with *the.* [Origin unknown.] —**mop′er** *n.* —**mop′ish, mop′ey** *adj.* —**mop′ish·ly** *adv.*

mo·ped (mō′pĕd′) *n.* A lightweight motorized bicycle that can be pedaled as well as driven by a low-powered gasoline engine. [From MO(TOR) + PED(AL).]

mop·pet (mŏp′ĭt) *n.* A young child. [From obsolete *mop,* fool, child, from Middle English *moppe.*]

mop-up (mŏp′ŭp′) *n.* The act or an instance of mopping up; a concluding operation.

mo·quette (mō-kĕt′) *n.* **1.** A heavy fabric with a thick nap, used for upholstery. **2.** A carpet with a deep, tufted pile. [French, alteration of obsolete *moucade.*]

MOR *abbr.* Middle-of-the-road.

mor. *abbr.* Morocco (leather).

Mor. *abbr.* **1.** Morocco. **2.** Moroccan.

mo·ra (môr′ə, mōr′ə) *n., pl.* **mo·rae** (môr′ē, mōr′ē) or **mo·ras.** The minimal unit of metrical time in quantitative verse, equal to the short syllable. [Latin, pause.]

Mo·rad·a·bad (mə-rä′də-bäd′, môr′ə-də-băd′). A city of north-central India east-northeast of Delhi. Founded in 1625, it is an important manufacturing center. Population, 330,051.

mo·raine (mə-rān′) *n.* An accumulation of boulders, stones, or other debris carried and deposited by a glacier. [French, from French dialectal *morena,* mound of earth, from Provençal *morre,* muzzle, from Vulgar Latin **murrum.*] —**mo·rain′al, mo·rain′ic** *adj.*

mor·al (môr′əl, mŏr′-) *adj.* **1.** Of or concerned with the judgment of the goodness or badness of human action and character: *moral scrutiny; a moral quandary.* **2.** Teaching or exhibiting goodness or correctness of character and behavior: *a moral lesson.* **3.** Conforming to standards of what is right or just in behavior; virtuous: *a moral life.* **4.** Arising from conscience or the sense of right and wrong: *a moral obligation.* **5.** Having psychological rather than physical or tangible effects: *a moral victory; moral support.* **6.** Based on strong likelihood or firm conviction, rather than on the actual evidence: *a moral certainty.* —**moral** *n.* **1.** The lesson or principle contained in or taught by a fable, a story, or an event. **2.** A concisely expressed precept or general truth; a maxim. **3. morals.** Rules or habits of conduct, especially of sexual conduct, with reference to standards of right and wrong: *a person of loose morals; a decline in the public morals.* [Middle English, from Old French, from Latin *mōrālis,* from *mōs, mōr-,* custom. See **mē-[1]** in Appendix.] —**mor′al·ly** *adv.*

SYNONYMS: *moral, ethical, virtuous, righteous.* These adjectives mean in accord with principles or rules of right or good conduct. *Moral* applies to personal character and behavior, especially sexual conduct, measured against prevailing standards of rectitude: *"The fact that man knows right from wrong proves his* intellectual *superiority to the other creatures; but the fact that he can* do *wrong proves his* moral *inferiority to any creature that* cannot*"* (Mark Twain). *Ethical* stresses conformity with idealistic standards of right and wrong, as those applicable to the practices of lawyers and doctors: *"The world has achieved brilliance without conscience. Ours is a world of nuclear giants and ethical infants"* (Omar N. Bradley). *Virtuous* implies moral excellence and loftiness of character; in a narrower sense it refers to sexual chastity: *"The life of the nation is secure only while the nation is honest, truthful, and virtuous"* (Frederick Douglass). *Righteous* emphasizes moral uprightness and especially the absence of guilt or sin; when it is applied to actions, reactions, or impulses, it often implies justifiable outrage: *"The effectual fervent prayer of a righteous man availeth much"* (James 5:16). *"He was . . . stirred by righteous wrath"* (John Galsworthy).

mo·rale (mə-răl′) *n.* The state of the spirits of a person or group as exhibited by confidence, cheerfulness, discipline, and willingness to perform assigned tasks. [French, morality, good

Moorish

moose
Bull moose
Alces alces

moped

ă pat	oi boy
ā pay	ou out
âr care	o͝o took
ä father	o͞o boot
ĕ pet	ŭ cut
ē be	ûr urge
ĭ pit	th thin
ī pie	*th* this
îr pier	hw which
ŏ pot	zh vision
ō toe	ə about, item
ô paw	♦ regionalism

Stress marks: **′** (primary); ′ (secondary), as in **dictionary** (dĭk′shə-nĕr′ē)

moray

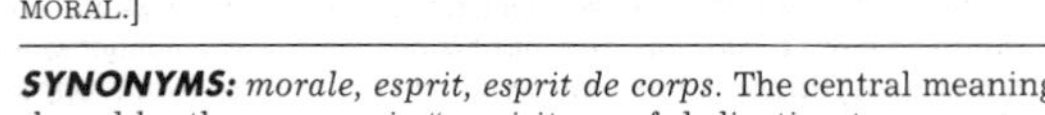

conduct, from feminine of *moral,* moral, from Old French. See MORAL.]

SYNONYMS: *morale, esprit, esprit de corps.* The central meaning shared by these nouns is "a spirit, as of dedication to a common goal, that unites a group": *the high morale of the troops; the esprit of an orchestra; the esprit de corps of a football team.*

moral hazard *n.* A risk to an insurance company resulting from uncertainty about the honesty of the insured.

mor·al·ism (môr′ə-lĭz′əm, mŏr′-) *n.* **1.** A conventional moral maxim or attitude. **2.** The act or practice of moralizing. **3.** Often undue concern for morality.

mor·al·ist (môr′ə-lĭst, mŏr′-) *n.* **1.** A teacher or student of morals and moral problems. **2.** One who follows a system of moral principles. **3.** One who is unduly concerned with the morals of others.

mor·al·is·tic (môr′ə-lĭs′tĭk, mŏr′-) *adj.* **1.** Characterized by or displaying a concern with morality. **2.** Marked by a narrow-minded morality. **—mor′al·is′ti·cal·ly** *adv.*

mo·ral·i·ty (mə-răl′ĭ-tē, mô-) *n., pl.* **-ties. 1.** The quality of being in accord with standards of right or good conduct. **2.** A system of ideas of right and wrong conduct: *religious morality; Christian morality.* **3.** Virtuous conduct. **4.** A rule or lesson in moral conduct.

morality play *n.* A drama in the 15th and 16th centuries using allegorical characters to portray the soul's struggle to achieve salvation.

mor·al·ize (môr′ə-līz′, mŏr′-) *v.* **-ized, -iz·ing, -iz·es.** *—intr.* To think about or express moral judgments or reflections. *—tr.* **1.** To interpret or explain the moral meaning of. **2.** To improve the morals of; reform. **—mor′al·i·za′tion** (-ə-lĭ-zā′shən) *n.* **—mor′al·iz′er** *n.*

moral philosophy *n.* Ethics.

mo·rass (mə-răs′, mô-) *n.* **1.** An area of low-lying, soggy ground. **2.** Something that hinders, engulfs, or overwhelms: *a morass of detail.* [Dutch *moeras,* from Middle Dutch *maras,* from Old French *mareis,* probably of Germanic origin. See **mori-** in Appendix.]

Sir Thomas More
1527 portrait by Hans Holbein the Younger

mor·a·to·ri·um (môr′ə-tôr′ē-əm, -tōr′-, mŏr′-) *n., pl.* **-to·ri·ums** or **-to·ri·a** (-tôr′ē-ə, -tōr′-). **1.** *Law.* **a.** An authorization to a debtor, such as a bank or nation, permitting temporary suspension of payments. **b.** An authorized period of delay in the performance of an obligation. **2.** A suspension of an ongoing or planned activity. [From Late Latin, neuter of *morātōrius,* delaying. See MORATORY.]

mor·a·to·ry (môr′ə-tôr′ē, -tōr′ē, mŏr′-) *adj.* Authorizing delay in payment. [French *moratoire,* from Late Latin *morātōrius,* delaying, from Latin *morātus,* past participle of *morārī,* to delay, from *mora,* delay.]

Mo·ra·va (môr′ə-və, mô′rä-vä). **1.** A river of central Czechoslovakia flowing about 386 km (240 mi) generally southward to the Danube River near Bratislava. **2.** A river of eastern Yugoslavia rising in two forks and flowing about 209 km (130 mi) north-northwest to the Danube River east of Belgrade.

Mo·ra·vi·a (mə-rā′vē-ə, mô-). A region of central Czechoslovakia. Settled by a Slavic people at the end of the sixth century A.D., it became an independent kingdom in 870 but fell to the Magyars in 906 and later to the Bohemians. It was incorporated into Czechoslovakia in 1918.

Mo·ra·vi·a (mō-rä′vē-ə, mô-rä′vyä), **Alberto.** Pen name of Alberto Pincherle. 1907–1990. Italian writer best known for his novels, such as *Time of Desecration* (1978).

morel
Common morel
Morchella esculenta

Mo·ra·vi·an (mə-rā′vē-ən) *n.* **1.** A native or inhabitant of Moravia. **2.** A group of Czech dialects spoken in Moravia. **3.** A member of a Protestant denomination founded in Saxony in 1722 by Hussite emigrants from Moravia. **—Moravian** *adj.* **1.** Of or relating to Moravia or its people, dialects, or culture. **2.** Of or relating to the Moravian denomination.

Moravian Gate or **Moravian Gap.** A mountain pass of central Europe between the Sudetes and the western Carpathian Mountains. It was long a strategic trade route.

mo·ray (môr′ā, mə-rā′) *n.* Any of numerous chiefly tropical, brightly colored marine eels of the family Muraenidae that are ferocious fighters and commonly inhabit coral reefs. [Portuguese *moréia,* from Latin *mūrēna,* from Greek *muraina.*]

Mor·ay Firth (mûr′ē). An inlet of the North Sea on the northeast coast of Scotland. It is the northern outlet of the Caledonian Canal system.

mor·bid (môr′bĭd) *adj.* **1.a.** Of, relating to, or caused by disease; pathological or diseased. **b.** Psychologically unhealthy or unwholesome. *"He suffered much from a morbid acuteness of the senses"* (Edgar Allan Poe). **2.** Characterized by preoccupation with unwholesome thoughts or feelings: *read the account of the murder with a morbid interest.* **3.** Gruesome; grisly. [Latin *morbidus,* diseased, from *morbus,* disease. See **mer-** in Appendix.] **—mor′bid·ly** *adv.* **—mor′bid·ness** *n.*

Morgan

mor·bid·i·ty (môr-bĭd′ĭ-tē) *n., pl.* **-ties. 1.** The quality of being morbid; morbidness. **2.** The rate of incidence of a disease.

mor·da·cious (môr-dā′shəs) *adj.* **1.** Given to biting; biting. **2.** Caustic; sarcastic. [Latin *mordāx, mordāc-* (from *mordēre,* to bite; see **mer-** in Appendix) + -IOUS.] **—mor·da′cious·ly** *adv.* **—mor·dac′i·ty** (-dăs′ĭ-tē) *n.*

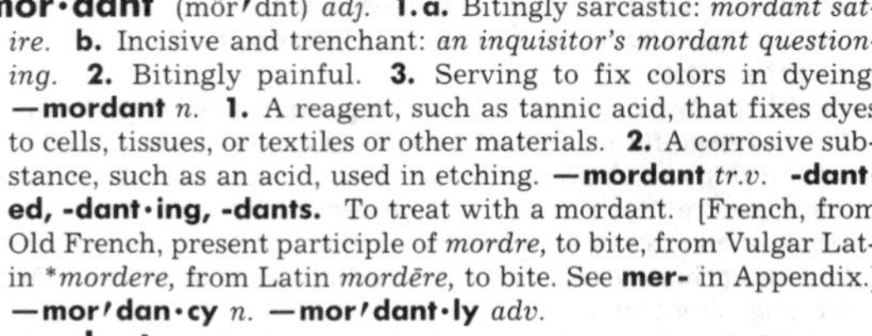

mor·dant (môr′dnt) *adj.* **1.a.** Bitingly sarcastic: *mordant satire.* **b.** Incisive and trenchant: *an inquisitor's mordant questioning.* **2.** Bitingly painful. **3.** Serving to fix colors in dyeing. **—mordant** *n.* **1.** A reagent, such as tannic acid, that fixes dyes to cells, tissues, or textiles or other materials. **2.** A corrosive substance, such as an acid, used in etching. **—mordant** *tr.v.* **-dant·ed, -dant·ing, -dants.** To treat with a mordant. [French, from Old French, present participle of *mordre,* to bite, from Vulgar Latin **mordere,* from Latin *mordēre,* to bite. See **mer-** in Appendix.] **—mor′dan·cy** *n.* **—mor′dant·ly** *adv.*

mor·dent (môr′dnt, môr-dĕnt′) *n.* *Music.* A melodic ornament in which a principal tone is rapidly alternated with the tone a half or full step below. [German, from Italian *mordente,* from *mordere,* to bite, from Vulgar Latin **mordere,* from Latin *mordēre.* See **mer-** in Appendix.]

Mord·vin·i·a (môrd-vĭn′ē-ə) also **Mor·do·vi·a** (môr-dō′vē-ə). A region of southwest Russia. Settled by a Finno-Ugric people first mentioned in the sixth century A.D., it was annexed by Russia in 1552.

more (môr, mōr) *adj.* Comparative of **many, much. 1.a.** Greater in number: *a hall with more seats.* **b.** Greater in size, amount, extent, or degree: *more land; more support.* **2.** Additional; extra: *She needs some more time.* **—more** *n.* A greater or additional quantity, number, degree, or amount: *The more I see of you the more I like you.* **—more** *pron.* *(used with a pl. verb).* A greater or additional number of persons or things: *I opened only two bottles but more were in the refrigerator.* **—more** *adv.* Comparative of **much. 1.a.** To or in a greater extent or degree: *loved him even more.* **b.** Used to form the comparative of many adjectives and adverbs: *more difficult; more softly.* See Usage Note at **perfect. 2.** In addition: *phoned twice more.* **3.** Moreover; furthermore. **—*idioms.* more and more.** To a steadily increasing extent or degree: *getting more and more worried.* **more or less. 1.** About; approximately: *holds two tons, more or less.* **2.** To an undetermined degree: *were more or less in agreement.* [Middle English, from Old English *māra* and *māre.* See **mē-**[3] in Appendix.]

More (môr, mōr), **Hannah.** 1745–1833. British writer whose works include tragedies, such as *Percy* (1777), the novel *Coelebs in Search of a Wife* (1809), and religious tracts.

More, Sir **Thomas.** 1478–1535. English politician, humanist scholar, and writer who refused to comply with the Act of Supremacy, by which English subjects were enjoined to recognize Henry VIII's authority over the pope, and was imprisoned in the Tower of London and beheaded for treason. His political essay *Utopia* (1516), speculates about life under an ideal government.

Mo·reau River (môr′ō, mōr′ō). A river of northwest South Dakota flowing about 402 km (250 mi) to the Missouri River.

mo·reen (mə-rēn′, mô-) *n.* A sturdy ribbed fabric of wool, cotton, or wool and cotton, often with an embossed finish, used for clothing and upholstery. [Possibly from MOIRÉ.]

mo·rel (mə-rĕl′, mô-) *n.* Any of various edible mushrooms of the genus *Morchella* and related genera, characterized by a brownish spongelike cap. [French *morille,* from Old French, perhaps from Vulgar Latin **maurīcula,* feminine diminutive of Latin *Maurus,* Mauritanian, Moor. See MOOR.]

Mo·re·lia (mə-rāl′yə, mô-rĕ′lyä). A city of southwest Mexico west-northwest of Mexico City. Founded in 1541 as Valladolid, it was renamed in 1828 after the revolutionary hero José María Morelos y Pavón (1765–1815). Population, 297,544.

mo·rel·lo (mə-rĕl′ō) *n., pl.* **-los.** A variety of the sour cherry *(Prunus cerasus* var. *austera)* having double flowers and fruit with dark red skin. [Perhaps from Italian *amarello,* from Medieval Latin *amārellum,* diminutive of Latin *amārus,* bitter.]

more·o·ver (môr-ō′vər, mōr-, môr′ō′vər, mōr′-) *adv.* Beyond what has been stated; besides. See Synonyms at **also.**

mo·res (môr′āz′, -ēz, mōr′-) *pl.n.* **1.** The accepted traditional customs and usages of a particular social group. **2.** Moral attitudes. **3.** Manners; ways. [Latin *mōrēs,* pl. of *mōs,* custom. See **mē-**[1] in Appendix.]

Mo·resque (mô-rĕsk′, mə-) *adj.* Characteristic of Moorish art or architecture. **—Moresque** *n.* An ornament or a decoration in Moorish style. [French, from Old French, from Spanish *Morisco,* Morisco. See MORISCO.]

Mor·gan (môr′gən) *n.* Any of a breed of American saddle and trotting horses noted for strength, speed, and endurance. [After Justin *Morgan* (1747–1798), American schoolteacher.]

Morgan, Daniel. 1736–1802. American Revolutionary soldier who commanded the defeat of the British at the Battle of Cowpens, South Carolina (1781).

Morgan, Sir **Henry.** 1635?–1688. Welsh buccaneer who raided Spanish ships and settlements in the Caribbean and was acting governor of Jamaica (1680–1682).

Morgan, John Hunt. 1825–1864. American Confederate soldier who led cavalry raids behind Union lines in Tennessee, Kentucky, Indiana, and Ohio.

Morgan, John Pierpont. 1837–1913. American financier and philanthropist noted for his reorganization and control of major railroads, his consolidation of the U.S. Steel Corporation (1901), and his collection of art and the establishment of the Morgan Library in New York City, which was donated to the public (1924) by his son **John Pierpont, Jr.** (1867–1943).

Mor·gan, Lewis Henry. 1818–1881. American anthropologist who studied Native Americans, particularly the Seneca.

Mor·gan, Thomas Hunt. 1866–1945. American biologist. He won a 1933 Nobel Prize for discoveries concerning the hereditary function of chromosomes.

mor·ga·nat·ic (môr′gə-năt′ĭk) *adj.* Of or being a legal marriage between a person of royal or noble birth and a partner of lower rank, in which it is agreed that no titles or estates of the royal or noble partner are to be shared by the partner of inferior rank nor by any of the offspring of the marriage. [New Latin *morganāticus,* from Medieval Latin *(mātrimōnium ad) morganāticam,* (marriage for the) morning-gift, of Germanic origin.] **—mor′ga·nat′i·cal·ly** *adv.*

Morgan City. A city of southern Louisiana south of Baton Rouge. Settled in 1850, it is a trade center. Population, 16,114.

Morgan Hill. A city of western California southeast of San Jose. It is a processing center. Population, 17,060.

mor·gan·ite (môr′gə-nīt′) *n.* A rosy-pink variety of beryl, valued as a semiprecious gem. [After John Pierpont MORGAN.]

Morgan le Fay (lə fā′) *n.* In Arthurian legend, the sorceress sister and enemy of King Arthur.

Mor·gan·town (môr′gən-toun′). A city of northern West Virginia on the Monongahela River near the Pennsylvania border. It is a shipping and industrial center. Population, 27,605.

mor·gen (môr′gən) *n., pl.* **morgen** or **-gens.** A Dutch and South African unit of land area equal to 2.1 acres. [Dutch, morning (referring to the amount of land that can be plowed in a morning), from Middle Dutch *morghen.*]

morgue (môrg) *n.* **1.** A place in which the bodies of persons found dead are kept until identified and claimed or until arrangements for burial have been made. **2.** A reference file in a newspaper or magazine office. [French, from *la Morgue,* building in Paris used as a morgue, probably from *morgue,* haughty manner, from Old French *morguer,* to look at solemnly, from Vulgar Latin **murricāre,* to make a face, from **murrum,* muzzle.]

mor·i·bund (môr′ə-bŭnd′, mŏr′-) *adj.* **1.** Approaching death; about to die. **2.** On the verge of becoming obsolete: *moribund customs; a moribund way of life.* [Latin *moribundus,* from *morī,* to die. See **mer-** in Appendix.] **—mor′i·bun′di·ty** (-bŭn′dĭ-tē) *n.* **—mor′i·bund′ly** *adv.*

mo·ri·on (môr′ē-ŏn′, mŏr′-) *n.* A crested metal helmet with a curved peak in front and back, worn by soldiers in the 16th and 17th centuries. [French, from Spanish *morrión,* from *morro,* round object, probably from Vulgar Latin **murrum,* muzzle.]

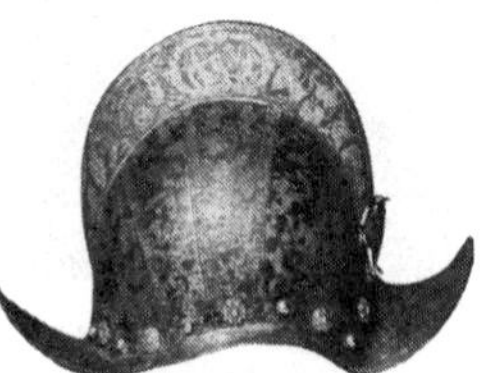

morion

Mo·ris·co (mə-rĭs′kō) *n., pl.* **-cos** or **-coes.** A Moor, especially a Spanish Moor. [Spanish, from *Moro,* Moor, from Latin *Maurus.* See MOOR.] **—Mo·ris′co** *adj.*

Mor·i·son (môr′ĭ-sən, mŏr′-), **Samuel Eliot.** 1887–1976. American historian noted for his works on maritime history.

Mo·ri·sot (mô-rē-zō′), **Berthe.** 1841–1895. French impressionist painter most admired for her graceful canvases featuring women and children.

Mor·ley (môr′lē), **Christopher Darlington.** 1890–1957. American writer who was a founder and editor (1924–1941) of *Saturday Review.*

Morley, Edward Williams. 1838–1923. American chemist and physicist who with Albert Michelson disproved the existence of ether, the hypothetical medium of electromagnetic waves.

Mor·mon (môr′mən) *Mormon Church. n.* **1.** An ancient prophet who appeared to Joseph Smith and imparted to him a sacred history of the Americas, which Smith translated and published as the Book of Mormon in 1830. **2.** A member of the Mormon Church. In this sense, also called *Latter-day Saint.* **—Mormon** *adj.* Of or relating to the Mormons, their religion, or the Mormon Church. **—Mor′mon·ism** *n.*

Mormon Church *n.* A church founded by Joseph Smith at Palmyra in western New York in 1830 and having its headquarters since 1847 in Salt Lake City, Utah. Its doctrines are based chiefly on the Bible, the Book of Mormon, and other revelations made to church leaders. Also called *Church of Jesus Christ of Latter-day Saints.*

Mormon cricket *n.* A large, wingless, long-horned grasshopper *(Anabrus simplex)* of the western United States that is often destructive to crops.

morn (môrn) *n.* **1.** The morning. **2.** The dawn. [Middle English, from Old English *morgen.*]

Mor·nay (môr-nā′) *adj.* Being or served with a white sauce flavored with grated cheese and seasonings: *eggs Mornay.* [Perhaps after Philippe de MORNAY.]

Mornay, Philippe de. Known as Duplessis-Mornay. Called "Pope of the Huguenots." 1549–1623. French Huguenot leader during the reigns of Henry III and Henry IV.

morn·ing (môr′nĭng) *n. Abbr.* **m. 1.** The first or early part of the day, lasting from midnight to noon or from sunrise to noon. **2.** The dawn. **3.** The first or early part; the beginning: *the morning of a new nation.* [Middle English, from *morn,* morn. See MORN.]

morn·ing-af·ter pill (môr′nĭng-ăf′tər) *n.* A pill containing a drug, especially an estrogen or estrogen substitute such as diethylstilbestrol, that prevents implantation of a fertilized ovum and is therefore effective as a contraceptive after sexual intercourse.

morning glory *n.* Any of numerous, usually twining vines of the related genera *Argyreia, Calystegia, Convolvulus, Merremia,* and *Ipomoea,* having funnel-shaped, variously colored flowers that close late in the day.

Morn·ing Prayer (môr′nĭng prâr) *n.* The liturgical service used for morning worship in the Anglican Church. Also called *matins.*

morning sickness *n.* Nausea and vomiting upon rising in the morning, especially during early pregnancy.

morning star *n.* A planet, especially Venus, visible in the east just before or at sunrise.

Mo·ro (môr′ō, mōr′ō) *n., pl.* **Moro** or **-ros. 1.** A member of any of the predominantly Moslem Malay tribes of the southern Philippines. **2.** Any of the Austronesian languages of the Moro. [Spanish, Moor, Moro, from Latin *Maurus,* Moor. See MOOR.]

mo·roc·co (mə-rŏk′ō) *n., pl.* **-cos.** *Abbr.* **mor.** A soft, fine leather of goatskin tanned with sumac, used for book bindings and shoes. [After MOROCCO.]

Mo·roc·co (mə-rŏk′ō). *Abbr.* **Mor.** A country of northwest Africa on the Mediterranean Sea and the Atlantic Ocean. Inhabited from ancient times by Berbers, the region became a Roman province in the 1st century B.C. and was overrun by Arabs in the 7th century A.D. European powers first penetrated the area in the 15th century. Morocco achieved independence in 1956. Rabat is the capital and Casablanca the largest city. Population, 20,419,555. **—Mo·roc′can** *adj. & n.*

Moro Gulf. An inlet of the Celebes Sea southwest of Mindanao, Philippines.

mo·ron (môr′ŏn′, mōr′-) *n.* **1.** A person regarded as very stupid. **2.** *Psychology.* A person of mild mental retardation having a mental age of from 7 to 12 years and generally having communication and social skills enabling some degree of academic or vocational education. The term belongs to a classification system no longer in use and is now considered offensive. [From Greek *mōron,* neuter of *mōros,* stupid, foolish.] **—mo·ron′ic** (mə-rŏn′ĭk, mô-) *adj.* **—mo·ron′i·cal·ly** *adv.* **—mo′ron′ism, mo·ron′i·ty** (mə-rŏn′ĭ-tē, mô-) *n.*

Mo·ro·ni (mə-rō′nē, mô-). The capital of the Comoros, on Great Comoro Island at the northern end of the Mozambique Channel. Population, 20,112.

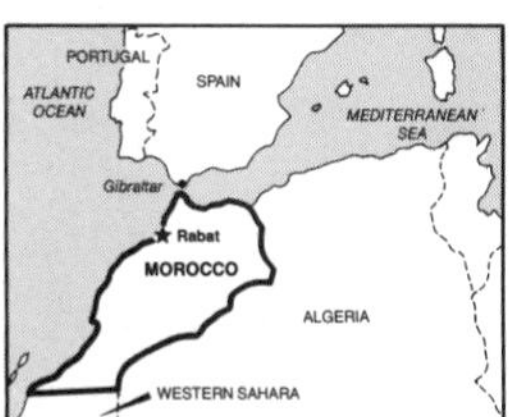

Morocco

mo·rose (mə-rōs′, mô-) *adj.* Sullenly melancholy; gloomy. See Synonyms at **glum.** [Latin *mōrōsus,* peevish, from *mōs, mōr-,* self-will, caprice, manner. See **mē-**[1] in Appendix.] **—mo·rose′ly** *adv.* **—mo·rose′ness** *n.*

morph (môrf) *n.* **1.** *Linguistics.* **a.** An allomorph. **b.** A phoneme or sequence of phonemes that is assumed to be an allomorph though its assignment to a particular morpheme has not been established. **2.** *Biology.* One of various distinct forms of an organism or a species.

morph. *abbr.* **1.** Morphological. **2.** Morphology.

morph– *pref.* Variant of **morpho–.**

–morph *suff.* **1.** Form; shape; structure: *endomorph.* **2.** Morpheme: *allomorph.* [Greek *-morphos,* from *morphē,* shape.]

mor·phal·lax·is (môr′fə-lăk′sĭs) *n., pl.* **-lax·es** (-lăk′sēz). The regeneration of a body part by means of structural or cellular reorganization with only limited production of new cells, observed primarily in invertebrate organisms, such as certain lobsters. [New Latin : MORPH(O)– + Greek *allaxis,* exchange (from *allassein,* to exchange, from *allos,* other; see **al-**[1] in Appendix).]

mor·pheme (môr′fēm′) *n. Linguistics.* A meaningful linguistic unit consisting of a word, such as *man,* or a word element, such as *-ed* in *walked,* that cannot be divided into smaller meaningful parts. [French *morphème,* blend of Greek *morphē,* form and French *phonème,* phoneme; see PHONEME.] **—mor·phem′ic** *adj.* **—mor·phem′i·cal·ly** *adv.*

mor·phem·ics (môr-fē′mĭks) *n. (used with a sing. verb). Linguistics.* **1.** The study, description, and classification of morphemes. **2.** The morphemic structure of a language.

Mor·phe·us (môr′fē-əs, -fyo͞os′) *n.* The god of dreams in Ovid's *Metamorphoses.* **—Mor′phe·an** (-fē-ən) *adj.*

mor·phi·a (môr′fē-ə) *n.* See **morphine.** [New Latin, from Latin *Morpheus,* Morpheus.]

–morphic *suff.* Having a specified shape or form: *geomorphic.*

mor·phine (môr′fēn′) *n.* A bitter, crystalline alkaloid, $C_{17}H_{19}NO_3 \cdot H_2O$, extracted from opium, the soluble salts of which are used in medicine as an analgesic, a light anesthetic, or a sedative. Also called *morphia.* [French, from *Morphée,* Morpheus, from Latin *Morpheus.*]

mor·phin·ism (môr′fē-nĭz′əm, môr′fə-) *n.* **1.** Addiction to morphine. **2.** A diseased condition caused by habitual or addictive use of morphine. **—mor′phin·ist** *n.*

–morphism *suff.* The condition or quality of having a specified form: *homomorphism.*

mor·pho (môr′fō) *n., pl.* **mor·phos.** Any of various large, brightly colored butterflies of the genus *Morpho,* found in tropical parts of Central and South America and including especially *M. menelaus* and *M. rhetenor.* These butterflies are noted for the brilliant iridescent blue color of their wings. [New Latin *Morphō,* genus name, from Greek, epithet of Aphrodite, perhaps from *morphē,* shape, form.]

morpho– or **morph–** *pref.* **1.** Form; shape; structure: *morphogenesis.* **2.** Morpheme: *morphophonemics.* [From Greek *morphē,* shape.]

mor·pho·gen·e·sis (môr′fō-jĕn′ĭ-sĭs) *n.* Formation of the structure of an organism or part; differentiation and growth of

ă pat	oi boy
ā pay	ou out
âr care	o͝o took
ä father	o͞o boot
ĕ pet	ŭ cut
ē be	ûr urge
ĭ pit	th thin
ī pie	*th* this
îr pier	hw which
ŏ pot	zh vision
ō toe	ə about, item
ô paw	♦ regionalism

Stress marks: ′ (primary); ′ (secondary), as in **dictionary** (dĭk′shə-nĕr′ē)

Samuel F.B. Morse
1866 photograph attributed to Mathew Brady

tissues and organs during development. **—mor′pho·ge·net′ic** (-jə-nĕt′ĭk), **mor′pho·gen′ic** *adj.* **—mor′pho·ge·net′i·cal·ly** *adv.*

mor·phol·o·gy (môr-fŏl′ə-jē) *n., pl.* **-gies.** *Abbr.* **morph., morphol. 1. a.** The branch of biology that deals with the form and structure of organisms without consideration of function. **b.** The form and structure of an organism or one of its parts: *the morphology of a cell; the morphology of vertebrates.* **2.** *Linguistics.* The study of the structure and form of words in language or a language, including inflection, derivation, and the formation of compounds. **—mor′pho·log′i·cal** (-fə-lŏj′ĭ-kəl), **mor′pho·log′ic** *adj.* **—mor′pho·log′i·cal·ly** *adv.* **—mor·phol′o·gist** *n.*

mor·pho·pho·ne·mics (môr′fō-fə-nē′mĭks) *n. Linguistics.* **1.** *(used with a pl. verb).* The changes in pronunciation undergone by allomorphs of morphemes as they are modified by neighboring sounds, as the plural allomorphs in *cat-s, dog-s, box-es,* or as they are modified for grammatical reasons in the course of inflection or derivation, as *house* versus *to house* and *housing.* **2.** *(used with a sing. verb).* The study of the morphophonemics of a language. **—mor′pho·pho·ne′mic** *adj.*

mor·pho·sis (môr-fō′sĭs) *n., pl.* **-ses** (-sēz). The manner in which an organism or any of its parts changes form or undergoes development. [Greek *morphōsis,* process of forming, from *morphoun,* to form, from *morphē,* form.]

-morphous *suff.* Having a specified shape or form: *polymorphous.* [Greek *-morphos,* from *morphē,* shape.]

mor·ris (môr′ĭs, mŏr′-) *n.* An English folk dance in which a story is enacted by costumed dancers. [Middle English *moreys (daunce),* morris (dance), from *moreys,* Moorish, from Old French *morois,* from *More,* Moor. See MOOR.] **—mor′ris** *adj.*

Mor·ris (môr′ĭs, mŏr′-), **Esther Hobart McQuigg Slack.** 1814–1902. American suffragist who was instrumental in the passage of women's suffrage in Wyoming Territory (1869).

Morris, Gouverneur. 1752–1816. American political leader and diplomat who led the committee that produced the final draft of the U.S. Constitution (1787).

Morris, Robert. 1734–1806. American Revolutionary politician and financier. A signer of the Declaration of Independence, he raised money for the Continental Army and was financially ruined by land speculation.

Morris, William. 1834–1896. British poet, painter, craftsman, and social reformer best remembered for his poetry, including the epic *Sigurd the Volsung* (1876).

Morris chair *n.* A large easy chair with arms, an adjustable back, and removable cushions. [After William MORRIS.]

Morris Jes·up (jĕs′əp), **Cape.** A cape of northern Greenland on the Arctic Ocean. It is the northernmost point in the world.

Mor·ris·on (môr′ĭ-sən, mŏr′-), **Toni.** Born 1931. American writer whose novels include *Sula* (1973) and *Beloved* (1987).

Mor·ris·town (môr′ĭs-toun′, mŏr′-). **1.** A town of northern New Jersey west-northwest of Newark. The Continental Army encamped here during the winters of 1776–1777 and 1779–1780. Population, 16,614. **2.** A city of northeast Tennessee east-northeast of Knoxville. Population, 19,683.

Mor·ro Castle (môr′ō, mŏr′ō). A fort at the entrance to the harbor of Havana, Cuba. Built by the Spanish (1589–1597) to protect the city from buccaneers, it was captured by the British in 1762 and bombarded by American forces during the Spanish-American War (1898).

mor·row (môr′ō, mŏr′ō) *n.* **1.** The following day: *resolved to set out on the morrow.* **2.** The time immediately subsequent to a particular event. **3.** *Archaic.* The morning. [Middle English *morwe, morow,* variant of *morwen,* from Old English *morgen,* morning.]

Mörs (mœrs). See **Moers.**

Morse (môrs), **Samuel Finley Breese.** 1791–1872. American painter and inventor. A portraitist whose subjects included Lafayette, he refined (1838) and patented (1854) the telegraph and developed the telegraphic code that bears his name.

Morse code *n.* Either of two codes used for transmitting messages in which letters of the alphabet and numbers are represented by various sequences of dots and dashes or short and long signals. [After Samuel Finley Breese MORSE.]

A	B	C	D
•—	—•••	•• •	—••
E	F	G	H
•	•—•	——•	••••
I	J	K	L
••	—•—•	—•—	—
M	N	O	P
——	—•	• •	•••••
Q	R	S	T
••—•	• ••	•••	—
U	V	W	X
••—	•••—	•——	•—••
	Y	Z	
	•• ••	••• •	

Morse code

mor·sel (môr′səl) *n.* **1.** A small piece of food. **2.** A tasty delicacy; a tidbit. **3.** A small amount; a piece: *a morsel of gossip.* **4.** One that is delightful and extremely pleasing. [Middle English, from Old French, diminutive of *mors,* bite, from Latin *morsum,* from neuter past participle of *mordēre,* to bite. See **mer-** in Appendix.]

mort¹ (môrt) *n.* The note sounded on a hunting horn to announce the death of a deer. [Middle English, death, from Old French, from Latin *mors, mort-.* See **mer-** in Appendix.]

mort² (môrt) *n.* A great number or quantity. [Perhaps from MORTAL.]

mor·ta·del·la (môr′tə-dĕl′ə) *n.* An Italian sausage made of pork, beef, and cubes of pork fat, flavored with wine and spices and smoked, steamed, or baked. [Italian, feminine diminutive of *murtato,* seasoned with myrtle berries, from Latin *myrtātus, murtātus,* from *myrtus, myrta,* myrtle. See MYRTLE.]

mortar

mor·tal (môr′tl) *adj.* **1.** Liable or subject to death. **2.** Of or relating to humankind; human: *the mortal limits of understanding.* **3.** Of, relating to, or accompanying death: *mortal throes.* **4.** Causing death; fatal: *a mortal wound.* See Synonyms at **fatal. 5.** Fighting or fought to the death; unrelenting: *a mortal enemy; a mortal attack.* **6.** Of great intensity or severity; dire: *mortal terror.* **7.** Conceivable: *no mortal reason for us to go.* **8.** Used as an intensive: *a mortal fool.* **—mortal** *n.* A human being. [Middle English, from Old French, from Latin *mortālis,* from *mors, mort-,* death. See **mer-** in Appendix.] **—mor′tal·ly** *adv.*

mor·tal·i·ty (môr-tăl′ĭ-tē) *n., pl.* **-ties. 1.** The quality or condition of being mortal. **2.** Death, especially of large numbers; heavy loss of life: *the mortality wrought by an epidemic.* **3.** Death rate. **4.** The rate of failure or loss: *the high mortality among family-run farms.*

mortal sin *n. Theology.* A sin, such as first-degree murder or perjury, that is so heinous it deprives the soul of sanctifying grace and causes damnation.

mor·tar (môr′tər) *n.* **1.** A vessel in which substances are crushed or ground with a pestle. **2.** A machine in which materials are ground and blended or crushed. **3. a.** A portable, muzzle-loading cannon used to fire shells at low velocities, short ranges, and high trajectories. Also called *trench mortar.* **b.** Any of several similar devices, such as one that shoots life lines across a stretch of water. **4.** Any of various bonding materials used in masonry, surfacing, and plastering, especially a plastic mixture of cement or lime, sand, and water that hardens in place and is used to bind together bricks or stones. **—mortar** *tr.v.* **-tared, -tar·ing, -tars. 1.** To bombard with mortar shells. **2.** To plaster or join with mortar. [Middle English *morter,* from Old English *mortere* and from Old French *mortier,* both from Latin *mortārium.* See **mer-** in Appendix.]

mor·tar·board (môr′tər-bôrd′, -bōrd′) *n.* **1.** A square board with a handle used for holding and carrying masonry mortar. **2.** An academic cap topped by a flat square.

mortarboard

mort·gage (môr′gĭj) *n. Abbr.* **mtg., mtge. 1.** A temporary, conditional pledge of property to a creditor as security for performance of an obligation or repayment of a debt. **2.** A contract or deed specifying the terms of a mortgage. **3.** The claim of a mortgagee upon mortgaged property. **—mortgage** *tr.v.* **-gaged, -gag·ing, -gag·es. 1.** To pledge or convey (property) by means of a mortgage. **2.** To make subject to a claim or risk; pledge against a doubtful outcome: *mortgaged their political careers by taking an unpopular stand.* [Middle English *morgage,* from Old French : *mort,* dead (from Vulgar Latin **mortus,* from Latin *mortuus,* past participle of *morī,* to die; see **mer-** in Appendix) + *gage,* pledge (of Germanic origin).]

WORD HISTORY: The great jurist Sir Edward Coke, who lived from 1552 to 1634, has explained why the term *mortgage* comes from the Old French words *mort,* "dead," and *gage,* "pledge." It seemed to him that it had to do with the doubtfulness of whether or not the mortgagor will pay the debt. If the mortgagor does not, then the land pledged to the mortgagee as security for the debt "is taken from him for ever, and so dead to him upon condition, &c. And if he doth pay the money, then the pledge is dead as to the [mortgagee]." This etymology, as understood by 17th-century attorneys, of the Old French term *morgage,* which we adopted, may well be correct. The term has been in English much longer than the 17th century, being first recorded in Middle English with the form *morgage* and the figurative sense "pledge" in a work written before 1393.

mort·ga·gee (môr′gĭ-jē′) *n.* One that holds a mortgage.

mort·ga·gor (môr′gĭ-jôr′, môr′gĭ-jər) also **mort·gag·er** (môr′gĭ-jər) *n.* One that mortgages property.

mor·tice (môr′tĭs) *n. & v.* Variant of **mortise.**

mor·ti·cian (môr-tĭsh′ən) *n.* See **funeral director.** [Latin *mors, mort-,* death; see MORTAL + -ICIAN.]

mor·ti·fi·ca·tion (môr′tə-fĭ-kā′shən) *n.* **1.** A feeling of shame, humiliation, or wounded pride. **2.** Discipline of the body and the appetites by self-denial or self-inflicted privation. **3.** *Pathology.* Death or decay of one part of a living body; gangrene or necrosis.

mor·ti·fy (môr′tə-fī′) *v.* **-fied, -fy·ing, -fies.** *—tr.* **1.** To cause to experience shame, humiliation, or wounded pride; humiliate. **2.** To discipline (one's body and physical appetites) by self-denial or self-inflicted privation. *—intr.* **1.** To practice ascetic discipline or self-denial of the body and its appetites. **2.** *Pathology.* To undergo mortification; become gangrenous or necrosed. [Middle English *mortifien,* to deaden, subdue, from Old French *mortifier,* from Latin *mortificāre,* to kill : *mors, mort-,* death; see **mer-** in Appendix + *-ficāre,* -fy.]

Mor·ti·mer (môr′tə-mər), **Roger de.** 1287–1330. Welsh rebel and lover of Edward II's wife, Isabella (1292–1358), with whom he raised an army to invade England from France (1326). They deposed Edward (1327) and ruled until 1330, when Edward III seized power and Mortimer was condemned to death.

mor·tise also **mor·tice** (môr′tĭs) *—n.* **1.** A usually rectangular cavity in a piece of wood, stone, or other material, prepared to receive a tenon and thus form a joint. **2.** *Printing.* A hole cut in a plate for insertion of type. *—tr.v.* **-tised, -tis·ing, -tis·es** also **-ticed, -tic·ing, -tic·es. 1.** To join or fasten securely, as with a mortise and tenon. **2.** To make a mortise in. **3.** *Printing.* **a.** To cut a hole in (a plate) for the insertion of type. **b.** To cut such a hole and insert (type). [Middle English *mortaise,* from Old French, perhaps from Arabic *murtazz,* fastened, from *irtazza,* to be fixed (in place).]

mort·main (môrt′măn′) *n.* **1.** *Law.* Perpetual ownership of real estate by institutions such as churches that cannot transfer or sell it. **2.** The often oppressive influence of the past on the present. [Middle English *mortemayne,* from Old French *mortemain* : *morte,* feminine of *mort,* dead; see MORTGAGE + *main,* hand (from Latin *manus;* see **man-**[2] in Appendix).]

Mor·ton (môr′tn), **Ferdinand Joseph La Menthe.** Known as "Jelly Roll." 1885–1941. American musician and composer who recorded seminal jazz works during the 1920's.

Morton, Levi Parsons. 1824–1920. Vice President of the United States (1889–1893) under Benjamin Harrison.

Morton, Thomas. Died c. 1647. English-born American colonist who was twice deported to England (1628 and 1630) by Puritans who disapproved of his business practices and frolicsome ways.

Morton, William Thomas Green. 1819–1868. American dentist who demonstrated the use of ether as an anesthetic (1846).

Morton Grove. A village of northeast Illinois, a suburb of Chicago. Population, 23,747.

mor·tu·ar·y (môr′cho͞o-ĕr′ē) *n., pl.* **-ies.** A place, especially a funeral home, where dead bodies are kept before burial or cremation. [Middle English *mortuarie,* gift to a parish priest from the estate of the deceased, funeral service, from Anglo-Norman, from Latin *mortuārium,* receptacle for dead things, neuter of *mortuārius,* of the dead, from *mortuus,* dead, past participle of *morī,* to die. See **mer-** in Appendix.]

mor·u·la (môr′yə-lə, môr′ə-) *n., pl.* **-lae** (-lē′). The spherical embryonic mass of blastomeres formed before the blastula and resulting from cleavage of the fertilized ovum. [New Latin, feminine diminutive of Latin *mōrum,* mulberry.] **—mor′u·lar** *adj.* **—mor′u·la′tion** *n.*

MOS *abbr.* **1.** Metal-oxide semiconductor. **2.** Military occupational specialty.

mos. *abbr.* Months.

mo·sa·ic (mō-zā′ĭk) *n.* **1.a.** A picture or decorative design made by setting small colored pieces, as of stone or tile, into a surface. **b.** The process or art of making such pictures or designs. **2.** A composite picture made of overlapping, usually aerial, photographs. **3.** Something that resembles a mosaic: *a mosaic of testimony from various witnesses.* **4.** *Botany.* A virus disease of plants, resulting in light and dark areas in the leaves, which often become shriveled and dwarfed. **5.** A photosensitive surface, as in the iconoscope of a television camera. **6.** *Biology.* An individual exhibiting mosaicism. **—mosaic** *tr.v.* **-icked, -ick·ing, -ics. 1.** To make by mosaic: *mosaic a design on a rosewood box.* **2.** To adorn with or as if with mosaic: *mosaic a sidewalk.* [Middle English *musycke,* from Old French *mosaique,* from Old Italian *mosaico,* from Medieval Latin *mūsāicum,* neuter of *mūsāicus,* of the Muses, from Latin *Mūsa,* Muse, from Greek *Mousa.* See **men-**[1] in Appendix.] **—mo·sa′i·cist** (mō-zā′ĭ-sĭst) *n.*

Mo·sa·ic (mō-zā′ĭk) *adj.* Of or relating to Moses or the laws and writings attributed to him.

mosaic gold *n.* Ormolu. [From its use in making mosaics.]

mo·sa·i·cism (mō-zā′ĭ-sĭz′əm) *n.* A condition in which tissues of genetically different types occur in the same organism.

Mosaic Law *n.* The ancient law of the Hebrews, attributed to Moses and contained in the Pentateuch. Also called *Law of Moses.*

mo·sa·saur (mō′sə-sôr′) *n.* Any of various very large extinct aquatic lizards of the genus *Mosasaurus,* having modified limbs that served as paddles for swimming. These lizards, thought to have been viviparous and carnivorous, may be early ancestors of the modern monitor lizard. [New Latin *Mosasaurus,* genus name : Latin *Mosa,* the Meuse River (where fossils of the genus were first discovered) + Greek *sauros,* lizard.]

Mos·by (mōz′bē), **John Singleton.** 1833–1916. American Confederate soldier who led a small cavalry unit, Mosby's Rangers, on raids against advanced Union positions.

mos·cha·tel (mŏs′kə-tĕl′, mŏs′kə-tĕl′) *n.* A perennial herb *(Adoxa moschatellina)* native to northern regions of Eurasia and North America, having greenish-white, musk-scented flowers. Also called *muskroot.* [French *moscatelle,* from Italian *moscatella,* feminine diminutive of *moscato,* musk, from Late Latin *muscus.* See MUSK.]

Mos·cow (mŏs′kou, -kō). **1.** The capital and largest city of Russia, in the west-central part of the country on the **Moscow River,** flowing about 499 km (310 mi) eastward to the Oka River. Inhabited since Neolithic times and first mentioned in Russian chronicles in 1147, Moscow became the capital of the principality of Muscovy and by the 15th century was the capital of the Russian state. The capital was transferred to St. Petersburg in 1712 but returned to Moscow by the Soviets in 1918. Population, 8,408,000. **2.** A city of northwest Idaho on the Washington border north of Lewiston. It is the seat of the University of Idaho (chartered 1889). Population, 16,513.

Mo·sel (mō′zəl). See **Moselle**[1].

Mo·selle[1] (mō-zĕl′) also **Mo·sel** (mō′zəl). A river rising in the Vosges Mountains of northeast France and flowing about 547 km (340 mi) to the Rhine River in western Germany.

Mo·selle[2] (mō-zĕl′) *n.* A light, dry white wine produced in the valley of the Moselle River.

Mos·es (mō′zĭz, -zĭs). In the Old Testament, the Hebrew prophet and lawgiver who led the Israelites out of Egypt.

Moses, Anna Mary Robertson. Known as "Grandma Moses." 1860–1961. American painter noted for her primitive and colorful paintings of rural scenes.

mo·sey (mō′zē) *intr.v.* **-seyed, -sey·ing, -seys.** *Informal.* **1.** To move in a leisurely, relaxed way; saunter: *moseyed over to the club after lunch.* **2.** To get going; move along. [Origin unknown.]

mo·shav (mō-shäv′) *n., pl.* **mo·sha·vim** (mō′shä-vēm′). An Israeli cooperative settlement consisting of small separate farms. [Modern Hebrew *môšāb,* from Hebrew, dwelling.]

Mos·lem (mŏz′ləm, mŏs′-) or **Mus·lim** (mŭz′ləm, mo͝oz′-, mŭs′-, mo͝os′-) *n.* A believer in or adherent of Islam. [Arabic *muslim.* See MUSLIM.] **—Mos′lem** *adj.*

USAGE NOTE: *Moslem* is the form predominantly preferred in journalism and popular usage. *Muslim* is preferred by scholars and by English-speaking adherents of Islam.

Moslem calendar *n.* The lunar calendar used by Moslems, reckoned from the year of the Hegira in A.D. 622. See table at **calendar.**

Mos·ley (mōz′lē), Sir **Oswald Ernald.** 1896–1980. British politician and the founder and leader of the British fascist party.

mosque (mŏsk) *n.* A Moslem house of worship. [French *mosquée,* from Old French *mousquaie,* from Old Italian *moschea,* from *moscheta,* from Old Spanish *mezquita,* from Arabic *masjid,* from *sajada,* to worship.]

♦ **mos·qui·to** (mə-skē′tō) *n., pl.* **-toes** or **-tos.** Any of various two-winged insects of the family Culicidae, in which the female of most species is distinguished by a long proboscis for sucking blood. Some species are vectors of diseases such as malaria and yellow fever. Also called ♦ *skeeter.* See Regional Note at **possum.** [Spanish and Portuguese, from diminutive of *mosca,* fly, from Latin *musca.*]

WORD HISTORY: Flies will never be popular creatures, in spite or because of their omnipresence. Two examples of the fly's influence on our lives can be found in the etymologies of the words *mosquito* and *musket,* both of which can be traced back to *musca,* the Latin word for fly. This Latin word became *mosca* in Spanish and Portuguese, Romance languages that developed from Vulgar Latin. *Mosquito,* the diminutive of *mosca,* was borrowed into English (first recorded around 1583) with the same sense "mosquito" that it had in Spanish and Portuguese. The Romance language French was the source of our word *musket* (first recorded around 1587), which came from French *mousquet,* but this word entered French from yet another Romance language, Italian. From the descendant of Latin *musca,* Italian *mosca,* was formed the diminutive *moschetta* with the senses "bolt for a catapult" and "small artillery piece." From *moschetta* came *moschetto,* "musket," the source of French *mousquet.* The use of *moschetta,* literally "little fly," to mean "bolt from a crossbow" can be ascribed to the fact that both bolt and insect fly, buzz, and sting.

Mos·qui·to (mə-skē′tō) *n., pl.* **Mosquito** or **-tos.** See **Miskito.**

mosquito boat *n. Chiefly British.* A PT boat.

Mosquito Coast. A region of eastern Nicaragua and northeast Honduras. A British protectorate from 1655 to 1860, it then became an autonomous state known as the Mosquito Kingdom. In 1894 Nicaragua appropriated the territory, and in 1960 the northern part was awarded to Honduras.

mosquito fern *n.* Any of several free-floating ferns of the genus *Azolla* of warm regions, having two-lobed minute leaves arranged in two rows.

mosquito fish *n.* Any of various fishes that feed on the larvae of mosquitoes, especially a small gambusia *(Gambusia affinis)* native to the southeast United States but introduced into many parts of the world for use in controlling mosquito populations.

♦ **mosquito hawk** *n.* **1.** See **nighthawk** (sense 1a). **2.** *Lower Southern U.S.* See **dragonfly.** See Regional Note at **dragonfly.**

mosquito net *n.* A fine net or screen used to keep out mosquitoes.

moss (môs, mŏs) *n.* **1.a.** Any of various green, usually small, nonvascular plants of the class Musci of the division Bryophyta. **b.** A patch or covering of such plants. **2.** Any of various other unrelated plants having a similar appearance or manner of growth, such as the club moss, Irish moss, and Spanish moss. **—moss** *tr.v.* **mossed, moss·ing, moss·es.** To cover with moss. [Middle English, from Old English *mos,* bog and from Medieval Latin *mossa,* moss (of Germanic origin).]

moss animal *n.* See **bryozoan.**

moss·back (môs′băk′, mŏs′-) *n.* **1.** An old shellfish or turtle with a growth of algae on its back. **2.** An old, large, or sluggish fish. **3.** An extremely conservative or old-fashioned person. **—moss′backed′** *adj.*

Möss·bau·er (mœs′bou′ər, môs′-, mŏs′-), **Rudolf Ludwig.** Born 1929. German physicist. He shared a 1961 Nobel Prize for his method of producing and measuring recoil-free gamma rays.

Mössbauer effect *n.* The recoilless emission of gamma rays by radioactive nuclei of crystalline solids, and the subsequent absorption of the emitted rays by other nuclei. [After Rudolf Ludwig MÖSSBAUER.]

moss·bunk·er (môs′bŭng′kər, mŏs′-) *n.* See **menhaden.** [Dutch *marsbanker.*]

mosaic
Detail of c. 500 A.D. mosaic of a Syrian queen

Grandma Moses

mosque
Selimiye Mosque in Edirne, Turkey, designed by Sinan (1489–1588)

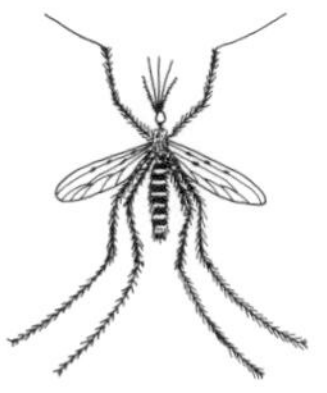

mosquito
Common malaria mosquito *Anopheles quadrimaculatus*

ă pat	oi boy
ā pay	ou out
âr care	o͝o took
ä father	o͞o boot
ĕ pet	ŭ cut
ē be	ûr urge
ĭ pit	th thin
ī pie	*th* this
îr pier	hw which
ŏ pot	zh vision
ō toe	ə about, item
ô paw	♦ regionalism

Stress marks: ′ (primary); ′ (secondary), as in **dictionary** (dĭk′shə-nĕr′ē)

moss campion *n.* A low-growing plant *(Silene acaulis)* of cool regions, having purplish-red flowers and forming dense, cushionlike mats.

moss green *n. Color.* A moderate yellow green to grayish or moderate olive or dark yellowish green. **—moss′-green′** (môs′grēn′, mŏs′-) *adj.*

moss·grown (môs′grōn′, mŏs′-) *adj.* **1.** Overgrown with moss. **2.** Old-fashioned: *mossgrown ideas about family life.*

mos·so (môs′sō) *adv. Music.* With motion or animation. Used chiefly as a direction. [Italian, past participle of *muovere,* to move, from Latin *movēre.* See **meuə-** in Appendix.]

moss pink *n.* A low-growing eastern North American plant *(Phlox subulata)* forming dense, mosslike mats and widely cultivated for its profuse pink or white flowers.

Moss Point (môs, mŏs). A city of extreme southeast Mississippi east of Biloxi. Population, 18,998.

moss rose *n.* A variety of rose *(Rosa centifolia)* native to the Caucasus, having a mossy flower stalk and calyx and fragrant pink flowers, used as a source of attar.

moss-troop·er (môs′trōō′pər, mŏs′-) *n.* **1.** One of a band of raiders operating in the bogs on the borders of England and Scotland during the 17th century. **2.** A plunderer; a marauder.

moss·y (mô′sē, mŏs′ē) *adj.* **-i·er, -i·est. 1.** Covered with moss or something like moss: *mossy banks.* **2.** Resembling moss. **3.** Old-fashioned; antiquated. **—moss′i·ness** *n.*

most (mōst) *adj.* Superlative of **many, much. 1.a.** Greatest in number: *won the most votes.* **b.** Greatest in amount, extent, or degree: *has the most compassion.* **2.** In the greatest number of instances: *Most fish have fins.* **—most** *n.* **1.** The greatest amount or degree: *She has the most to gain.* **2.** *Slang.* The greatest, best, or most exciting. Used with *the*: *That party was the most!* **—most** *pron. (used with a sing. or pl. verb).* The greatest part or number: *Most of the town was destroyed. Most of the books were missing.* **—most** *adv.* Superlative of **more, much. 1.** In or to the highest degree or extent. Used with many adjectives and adverbs to form the superlative degree: *most honest; most impatiently.* **2.** Very: *a most impressive piece of writing.* **3.** *Informal.* Almost: *Most everyone agrees.* **—*idiom.* at (the) most.** At the maximum: *We saw him for ten minutes at the most. She ran two miles at most.* [Middle English, from Old English *mǣst, māst.* See **mē-**[3] in Appendix. Adv., sense 3, probably short for ALMOST.]

-most *suff.* **1.** Most: *innermost.* **2.** Nearest to: *aftmost.* [Middle English, alteration (influenced by *most,* most; see MOST) of *-mest,* from Old English : *-mo, -ma,* superlative suff. + *-est,* superlative suff.]

mos·tac·cio·li (mô-stä′chə-lē′, -stät′chô-) *n.* Short, tubular pasta with slanted ends. [Italian, pl. of *mostacciolo,* cake, bun, from Latin *mustāceum,* cake made with must, from *mustum,* must. See MUST[3].]

most-fav·ored-na·tion (mōst′fā′vərd-nā′shən) *adj.* Of or relating to the status or terms embodied in a commercial treaty by which each signatory agrees to accord the other the same treatment that is or will be accorded to any other nation.

most·ly (mōst′lē) *adv.* **1.** For the greatest part; mainly. **2.** Generally; usually.

Mó·sto·les (mô′stô-lĕs′). A city of central Spain, an industrial suburb of Madrid. Population, 164,304.

Mo·sul (mō-sōōl′, mō′səl). A city of northern Iraq on the Tigris River north-northwest of Baghdad. An important center on the historical caravan route across northern Mesopotamia, it became part of the Ottoman Empire in the 16th century. Population, 570,926.

mot (mō) *n.* A witty or incisive remark. [French, from Old French, word, saying, probably from Vulgar Latin **mŏttum,* from Late Latin *muttum,* grunt, mutter, of imitative origin.]

mote[1] (mōt) *n.* A very small particle; a speck: *"Dust motes hung in a slant of sunlight"* (Anne Tyler). [Middle English *mot,* from Old English.]

mote[2] (mōt) *aux.v. Archaic.* May; might. [Middle English *moten,* from Old English *mōtan.* See **med-** in Appendix.]

mo·tel (mō-tĕl′) *n.* An establishment that provides lodging for motorists in rooms usually having direct access to an open parking area. Also called *motor court, motor lodge.* [Blend of MOTOR and HOTEL.]

mo·tet (mō-tĕt′) *n. Music.* A polyphonic composition based on a text of a sacred nature and usually sung without accompaniment. [Middle English, from Old French, diminutive of *mot,* word. See MOT.]

moth (môth, mŏth) *n., pl.* **moths** (môthz, mŏthz, môths, mŏths). **1.** Any of numerous insects of the order Lepidoptera, generally distinguished from butterflies by their nocturnal activity, hairlike or feathery antennae, stout bodies, and the frenulum that holds the front and back wings together. **2.** A clothes moth. [Middle English *motthe,* from Old English *moththe.*]

moth·ball (môth′bôl′, mŏth′-) *n.* **1.** A marble-sized ball, originally of camphor but now of naphthalene, stored with clothes to repel moths. **2. mothballs. a.** A condition of long storage for possible future use: *put the battleship into mothballs.* **b.** A condition of being set aside or discarded: *decided to put the plan into mothballs.* **—mothball** *tr.v.* **-balled, -ball·ing, -balls. 1.** To remove (a ship, for example) from active service or use and put into protective storage. **2.** To defer indefinitely; shelve: *mothball a project.*

moth-eat·en (môth′ēt′n, mŏth′-) *adj.* **1.** Eaten away by moth larvae. **2.** Old and timeworn; stale: *a moth-eaten phrase.* **3.** Shabby; decrepit.

moth·er[1] (mŭth′ər) *n.* **1.** A woman who conceives, gives birth to, or raises and nurtures a child. **2.** A female parent of an animal. **3.** A female ancestor. **4.** A woman who holds a position of authority or responsibility similar to that of a mother: *a den mother.* **5.** *Roman Catholic Church.* **a.** A mother superior. **b.** Used as a form of address for such a woman. **6.** A woman who creates, originates, or founds something: *"the discovery of radium, which made Marie Curie mother to the Atomic Age"* (Alden Whitman). **7.** A creative source; an origin: *Philosophy is the mother of the sciences.* **8.** Used as a title for a woman respected for her wisdom and age. **9.** Maternal love and tenderness: *brought out the mother in her.* **10.** *Vulgar Slang.* Something considered extraordinary, as in disagreeableness, size, or intensity. **—mother** *adj.* **1.** Relating to or being mother. **2.** Characteristic of a mother: *mother love.* **3.** Being the source or origin: *the mother church.* **4.** Derived from or as if from one's mother; native: *one's mother language.* **—mother** *tr.v.* **-ered, -er·ing, -ers. 1.** To give birth to; create and produce. **2.** To watch over, nourish, and protect maternally. See Usage Note at **father.** [Middle English *moder, mother,* from Old English *mōdor.* See **māter-** in Appendix.]

moth·er[2] (mŭth′ər) *n.* A stringy slime composed of yeast cells and bacteria that forms on the surface of fermenting liquids and is added to wine or cider to start the production of vinegar. [Probably alteration (influenced by MOTHER[1]) of obsolete Dutch *moeder,* from Middle Dutch, probably from *moeder,* mother of children. See **māter-** in Appendix.]

moth·er·board (mŭth′ər-bôrd′, -bōrd′) *n. Computer Science.* The main board of a computer, usually containing the circuitry for the central processing unit, keyboard, and monitor and often having slots for accepting additional circuitry.

Moth·er Car·ey's chicken (mŭth′ər kâr′ēz) *n.* A petrel, especially a storm petrel. [Possibly translation and alteration of Medieval Latin *mater cāra,* Virgin Mary : Latin *mater,* mother + Latin *cāra,* dear.]

mother cell *n.* A cell that divides to produce two or more daughter cells.

mother country *n.* **1.** The country of one's birth or one's ancestors. **2.** The country from which the settlers of a territory originally came.

mother figure *n.* An older woman, often one in a position of power or influence, who elicits the emotions usually reserved for a mother.

moth·er·fuck·er (mŭth′ər-fŭk′ər) *n. Obscene.* **1.** A person regarded as thoroughly despicable. **2.** Something regarded as thoroughly unpleasant, frustrating, or despicable.

Mother Goose *n.* The imaginary author of *Mother Goose's Tales,* a collection of nursery rhymes first published in London in the 18th century.

mother hen *n.* A person who fusses over others in an overly protective manner.

moth·er·hood (mŭth′ər-hōōd′) *n.* **1.** The state of being a mother. **2.** The qualities of a mother. **3.** Mothers considered as a group.

moth·er·house (mŭth′ər-hous′) *n.* **1.** The convent in which the mother superior of a religious community lives. **2.** The original convent of a religious community.

Mother Hub·bard (hŭb′ərd) *n.* A woman's loose, unbelted dress. [Probably from illustrations of *Mother Hubbard,* character in a nursery rhyme by Sarah Catherine Martin (1768–1826), British writer.]

moth·er·ing (mŭth′ər-ĭng) *n.* The nurturing and raising of a child or children by a mother: *"Because they are involved in careers and mothering, many women lead exhausting lives"* (David E. Bloom).

moth·er-in-law (mŭth′ər-ĭn-lô′) *n., pl.* **moth·ers-in-law** (mŭth′ərz-). **1.** The mother of one's wife or husband. **2.** *Archaic.* A stepmother.

moth·er·land (mŭth′ər-lănd′) *n.* **1.** One's native land. **2.** The land of one's ancestors. **3.** A country considered as the origin of something.

moth·er·less (mŭth′ər-ləs′) *adj.* **1.** Having no living mother. **2.** Having no known mother. **—moth′er·less·ness** *n.*

mother lode *n.* **1.** The main vein of ore in a region. **2.** An abundant or rich source: *"the kind . . . who makes Boston the mother lode of advance men"* (David Nyhan).

moth·er·ly (mŭth′ər-lē) *adj.* **1.** Of, like, or appropriate to a mother: *motherly love.* **2.** Showing the affection of a mother. **—motherly** *adv.* In a manner befitting a mother. **—moth′er·li·ness** *n.*

moth·er-of-pearl (mŭth′ər-əv-pûrl′) *n.* The pearly internal layer of certain mollusk shells, used to make decorative objects. Also called *nacre.* **—moth′er-of-pearl′** *adj.*

Moth·er's Day (mŭth′ərz) *n.* The second Sunday in May, observed in the United States in honor of mothers.

moth·ers-in-law (mŭth′ərz-ĭn-lô′) *n.* Plural of **mother-in-law.**

mother superior *n., pl.* **mothers superior** or **mother superiors.** A woman in charge of a religious community of women.

mother tongue *n.* **1.** One's native language. **2.** A parent language.

Moth·er·well (mŭth′ər-wĕl′), **Robert.** 1915–1991. American artist whose abstract expressionist paintings are characterized by brilliantly colored amorphous figures.

Moth·er·well and Wish·aw (mŭth′ər-wĕl′, -wəl; wĭsh′ô). A burgh of south-central Scotland on the Clyde River southeast of Glasgow. Population, 149,900.

mother wit *n.* Innate intelligence or common sense.

moth·er·wort (mŭth′ər-wûrt′, -wôrt′) *n.* Any of several Eurasian plants of the genus *Leonurus*, especially *L. cardiaca*, a weed having clusters of small purple or pink flowers and spine-tipped calyx lobes. [Middle English *moderwort* : *moder,* womb (from its use in treating diseases of the uterus); see MOTHER[1] + *wort,* wort; see WORT[1].]

moth·proof (môth′pro͞of′, mŏth′-) *adj.* Resistant to damage by moths. **—mothproof** *tr.v.* **-proofed, -proof·ing, -proofs.** To make resistant to damage by moths. **—moth′proof′er** *n.*

moth·y (mô′thē, mŏth′ē) *adj.* **-i·er, -i·est. 1.** Infested by moths. **2.** Moth-eaten.

mo·tif (mō-tēf′) *n.* **1.a.** A recurrent thematic element in an artistic or literary work. **b.** A dominant theme or central idea. **2.** *Music.* A short significant phrase in a composition. **3.** A repeated figure or design in architecture or decoration. See Synonyms at **figure.** [French, from Old French, motive. See MOTIVE.]

mo·tile (mōt′l, mō′tīl′) *adj.* **1.** *Biology.* Moving or having the power to move spontaneously: *motile spores.* **2.** *Psychology.* Of or relating to mental imagery that arises primarily from sensations of bodily movement and position rather than from visual or auditory sensations. [Latin *mōtus,* motion, from past participle of *movēre,* to move; see MOTION + –ILE[1].] **—mo·til′i·ty** (mō-tĭl′ĭ-tē) *n.*

mo·tion (mō′shən) *n.* **1.** The act or process of changing position or place. **2.** A meaningful or expressive change in the position of the body or a part of the body; a gesture. **3.** Active operation: *set the plan in motion.* **4.** The ability or power to move: *lost motion in his arm.* **5.** The manner in which the body moves, as in walking. **6.** A prompting from within; an impulse or inclination: *resigned of her own motion.* **7.** *Music.* Melodic ascent and descent of pitch. **8.** *Law.* An application made to a court for an order or a ruling. **9.** A formal proposal put to the vote under parliamentary procedures. **10.a.** A mechanical device or piece of machinery that moves or causes motion; a mechanism. **b.** The movement or action of such a device. **—motion** *v.* **-tioned, -tion·ing, -tions.** —*tr.* To direct by making a gesture: *motioned us to our seats.* —*intr.* To signal by making a gesture: *motioned to her to enter.* **—*idiom.* go through the motions.** To do something in a mechanical manner indicative of a lack of interest or involvement. [Middle English *mocioun,* from Old French *motion,* from Latin *mōtiō, mōtiōn-,* from *mōtus,* past participle of *movēre,* to move. See **meuə-** in Appendix.]

mo·tion·less (mō′shən-lĭs) *adj.* Having or making no motion. **—mo′tion·less·ly** *adv.* **—mo′tion·less·ness** *n.*

motion picture *n.* **1.** A movie. **2. motion pictures.** The movie industry. **—mo′tion-pic′ture** (mō′shən-pĭk′chər) *adj.*

motion sickness *n.* Nausea and dizziness induced by motion, as in travel by aircraft, car, or ship.

motion study *n.* See **time and motion study.**

mo·ti·vate (mō′tə-vāt′) *tr.v.* **-vat·ed, -vat·ing, -vates.** To provide with an incentive; move to action; impel. **—mo′ti·va′tor** *n.*

mo·ti·va·tion (mō′tə-vā′shən) *n.* **1.a.** The act or process of motivating. **b.** The state of being motivated. **2.** Something that motivates; an inducement or incentive. **—mo′ti·va′tion·al** *adj.* **—mo′ti·va′tion·al·ly** *adv.*

motivational research *n.* Systematic analysis of the motives behind consumer decisions, used especially by advertisers and marketers to assess attitudes toward products and services. Also called *motivation research.*

mo·tive (mō′tĭv) *n.* **1.** An emotion, desire, physiological need, or similar impulse that acts as an incitement to action. **2.** (mō′tĭv, mō-tēv′). A motif in art, literature, or music. **—motive** *adj.* **1.** Causing or able to cause motion: *motive power.* **2.** Impelling to action: *motive pleas.* **3.** Of or constituting an incitement to action. **—motive** *tr.v.* **-tived, -tiv·ing, -tives.** To motivate. [Middle English *motif, motive,* from Old French *motif,* from Late Latin *mōtīvus,* of motion, from Latin *mōtus,* past participle of *movēre,* to move. See **meuə-** in Appendix.]

mo·tiv·ic (mō-tĭv′ĭk′) *adj.* *Music.* Of or relating to a motif: *sparse motivic improvisations.*

mo·ti·vi·ty (mōtĭv′ĭ-tē) *n., pl.* **-ties.** The power of moving or causing motion.

mot juste (mō zhüst′) *n., pl.* **mots justes** (mō zhüst′). Exactly the right word or expression. [French : *mot,* word + *juste,* right.]

mot·ley (mŏt′lē) *adj.* **1.** Having elements of great variety or incongruity; heterogenous: *"Most Ivy League freshman classes are chosen from a motley collection of constituencies . . . and a bare majority of entering students can honestly be called scholars"* (New York Times). See Synonyms at **miscellaneous. 2.** Having many colors; variegated; parti-colored: *a motley tunic.* **—motley** *n., pl.* **-leys. 1.** The parti-colored attire of a court jester. **2.** A heterogeneous, often incongruous mixture of elements. [Middle English *motlei,* variegated cloth, variegated, probably Anglo-Norman, probably from Middle English *mot,* speck. See MOTE[1].]

Mot·ley (mŏt′lē), **John Lothrop.** 1814–1877. American historian and diplomat whose written works include *The Rise of the Dutch Republic* (1856).

mot·mot (mŏt′mŏt′) *n.* Any of several tropical American birds of the family Momotidae, usually having green and blue plumage with long tail feathers that spread out at the tip. [New Latin *motmot,* probably of imitative origin.]

mo·to·cross (mō′tō-krôs′, -krŏs′) *n. Abbr.* **MX** *Sports.* A cross-country motorcycle race over a closed course of rough terrain with steep hills and sharp curves. [French *moto-cross* : *moto,* motorcycle (short for *motocyclette,* from *moto-,* motor, from *moteur,* from Latin *mōtor,* mover; see MOTOR) + CROSS-COUNTRY.]

mo·to·neu·ron (mō′tə-no͝or′ŏn′, -nyo͝or′-) *n.* A motor neuron. [MOTO(R) + NEURON.]

mo·tor (mō′tər) *n.* **1.** Something, such as a machine or an engine, that produces or imparts motion. **2.** A device that converts any form of energy into mechanical energy, especially an internal-combustion engine or an arrangement of coils and magnets that converts electric current into mechanical power. **3.** A motor vehicle, especially an automobile. **—motor** *adj.* **1.** Causing or producing motion: *motor power.* **2.** Driven by or having a motor. **3.** Of or for motors or motor vehicles: *motor oil.* **4.** Of, relating to, or designating nerves that carry impulses from the nerve centers to the muscles. **5.** Involving or relating to movements of the muscles: *motor coordination; a motor reflex.* **—motor** *v.* **-tored, -tor·ing, -tors.** —*intr.* To drive or travel in a motor vehicle. —*tr.* To carry by motor vehicle. [Middle English *motour,* prime mover, from Latin *mōtor,* from *mōtus,* past participle of *movēre,* to move. See **meuə-** in Appendix.]

mo·tor·bike (mō′tər-bīk′) *n.* **1.** A lightweight motorcycle. **2.** A pedal bicycle that has an attached motor.

mo·tor·boat (mō′tər-bōt′) *n.* *Nautical.* A boat propelled by an internal-combustion engine or other motor. Also called *powerboat.*

mo·tor·bus (mō′tər-bŭs′) *n., pl.* **-bus·es** or **-bus·ses.** A passenger bus that is powered by a motor. Also called *motor coach.*

mo·tor·cade (mō′tər-kād′) *n.* A procession of motor vehicles, as in a parade. **—mo′tor·cade′** *v.*

mo·tor·car (mō′tər-kär′) *n.* See **automobile.**

motor coach *n.* See **motorbus.**

motor cortex *n.* The area of the cerebral cortex where impulses from the nerve centers to the muscles originate.

motor court *n.* See **motel.**

mo·tor·cy·cle (mō′tər-sī′kəl) *n.* A two-wheeled motor vehicle resembling a heavy bicycle, sometimes having two saddles and a sidecar with a third wheel. **—mo′tor·cy′cle** *v.* **—mo′tor·cy′clist** *n.*

motor drive *n.* A system consisting of an electric motor and accessory parts, used to power machinery. **—mo′tor-driv′en** (mō′tər-drĭv′ən) *adj.*

motor home *n.* A motor vehicle built on a truck or bus chassis and designed to serve as self-contained living quarters for recreational travel.

motor inn *n.* An urban motel usually having several stories. Also called *motor hotel.*

mo·tor·ist (mō′tər-ĭst) *n.* One who drives or travels in an automotive vehicle.

mo·tor·ize (mō′tə-rīz′) *tr.v.* **-ized, -iz·ing, -iz·es. 1.** To equip with a motor. **2.** To supply with motor-driven vehicles. **3.** To provide with automobiles. **—mo′tor·i·za′tion** (-tər-ĭ-zā′shən) *n.*

motor lodge *n.* See **motel.**

mo·tor·man (mō′tər-mən) *n.* One who drives an electrically powered streetcar, locomotive, or subway train.

motor mouth *n.* *Slang.* An incessant talker.

motor neuron *n.* A neuron that conveys impulses from the central nervous system to a muscle, gland, or other effector tissue.

motor pool *n.* A centrally managed group of motor vehicles intended for the use of personnel, as of a governmental agency or military installation.

motor scooter *n.* A two-wheeled vehicle with small wheels and a low-powered gasoline engine geared to the rear wheel.

motor vehicle *n.* A self-propelled wheeled conveyance, such as a car or truck, that does not run on rails.

mo·tor·way (mō′tər-wā′) *n.* *Chiefly British.* A superhighway.

Mott (mŏt), **John Raleigh.** 1865–1955. American religious leader. He shared the 1946 Nobel Peace Prize for his leadership of the YMCA.

Mott, Lucretia Coffin. 1793–1880. American feminist and social reformer who was active in the antislavery movement and with Elizabeth Cady Stanton called the first convention for women's rights, held at Seneca Falls, New York (1848).

♦ **motte[1]** also **mott** (mŏt) *n.* *Western U.S.* A copse or small stand of trees on a prairie. [American Spanish *mata,* from Spanish, shrub, probably from Late Latin *matta,* mat. See MAT[1].]

♦ **motte[2]** also **mott** (mŏt) *n.* *Upper Southern U.S.* A tuft of human or animal hair standing up on the head or body. [From French, from Old French *mote,* mound. See MOAT.]

mot·tle (mŏt′l) *tr.v.* **-tled, -tling, -tles.** To mark with spots or blotches of different shades or colors. **—mottle** *n.* **1.** A spot or

motorboat

motorcycle

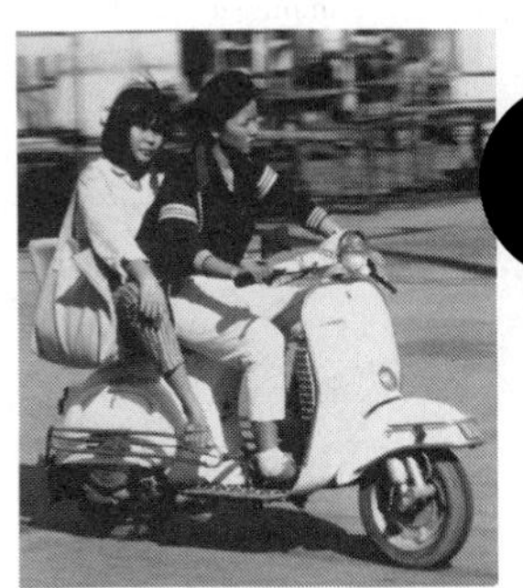

motor scooter

ă pat	oi boy
ā pay	ou out
âr care	o͝o took
ä father	o͞o boot
ĕ pet	ŭ cut
ē be	ûr urge
ĭ pit	th thin
ī pie	*th* this
îr pier	hw which
ŏ pot	zh vision
ō toe	ə about, item
ô paw	♦ regionalism

Stress marks: ′ (primary); ′ (secondary), as in **dictionary** (dĭk′shə-nĕr′ē)

mountain ash
American mountain ash
Sorbus americana

mountaineer
Climbing a wall of ice

mountain laurel
Kalmia latifolia

Louis Mountbatten

blotch of color. **2.** A variegated pattern, as on marble. [Probably back-formation from MOTLEY.] **—mot′tler** *n.*

mot·tled (mŏt′ld) *adj.* Spotted or blotched with different shades or colors.

mottled enamel *n.* Discolored and spotted tooth enamel caused by excessive amounts of fluorides in drinking water.

mot·to (mŏt′ō) *n., pl.* **-toes** or **-tos. 1.** A brief statement used to express a principle, a goal, or an ideal. See Synonyms at **saying. 2.** A sentence, phrase, or word of appropriate character inscribed on or attached to an object. **3.** A maxim adopted as a guide to one's conduct. [Italian, word, motto, probably from Vulgar Latin *mŏttum, word. See MOT.]

mouch (mo͞och) *v. Chiefly British.* Variant of **mooch.**

moue (mo͞o) *n.* A small grimace; a pout. [French, from Old French *moe,* of Germanic origin.]

mou·flon also **mouf·flon** (mo͞of′lŏn′) *n., pl.* **mouflon** or **-flons** also **moufflon** or **-flons.** A small, wild European sheep *(Ovis musimon),* native to Sardinia and Corsica and having large curving horns in the male. [French, alteration of Italian dialectal *muvrone,* from Late Latin *mufrō, mufrōn-.*]

mouil·lé (mo͞o-yā′) *adj. Linguistics.* Pronounced as a palatal sound, as the *ll* in French *fille.* [French, past participle of *mouiller,* to moisten, palatalize, from Old French *moillier,* to soften by soaking. See MOIL.]

mou·jik (mo͞o-zhēk′, -zhĭk′) *n.* Variant of **muzhik.**

mou·lage (mo͞o-läzh′) *n.* **1.** A mold, as of a footprint, made for use in a criminal investigation. **2.** The making of such a mold or cast, as with plaster of Paris. [French, from Old French, fee for inspection of wood by use of a standard frame, from *mouler,* to mold, measure with a standard frame, from *moule,* mold. See MOLD[1].]

mould[1] (mōld) *n. & v. Chiefly British.* Variant of **mold[1].**

mould[2] (mōld) *n. & v. Chiefly British.* Variant of **mold[2].**

mould[3] (mōld) *n. Chiefly British.* Variant of **mold[3].**

moul·der (mōl′dər) *v. Chiefly British.* Variant of **molder.**

mould·ing (mōl′dĭng) *n. Chiefly British.* Variant of **molding.**

mould·y (mōl′dē) *adj. Chiefly British.* Variant of **moldy.**

mou·lin (mo͞o-lăɴ′) *n.* A nearly vertical shaft or cavity worn in a glacier by surface or rock debris falling through a crack in the ice. [French, mill, moulin, from Old French *molin,* mill, from Late Latin *molīnum.* See MILL[1].]

Moul·mein (mo͞ol-mān′, mōl-). A city of southern Burma on the Gulf of Martaban east of Rangoon. Population, 219,991.

moult (mōlt) *v. & n. Chiefly British.* Variant of **molt.**

mound (mound) *n.* **1.** A pile of earth, gravel, sand, rocks, or debris heaped for protection or concealment. **2.** A natural elevation, such as a small hill. **3.** A raised mass, as of hay; a heap. See Synonyms at **heap. 4.** *Archaeology.* A large pile of earth or stones marking a burial site. **5.** *Baseball.* The slightly elevated pitcher's area in the center of the diamond. **6.** *Archaic.* A hedge or fence. **—mound** *tr.v.* **mound·ed, mound·ing, mounds. 1.** To fortify or conceal with a mound. **2.** To heap into a raised mass. [Origin unknown.]

mound·bird (mound′bûrd′) *n.* See **megapode.**

mound builder *n.* See **megapode.**

Mound Builder (mound) *n.* A member of any of various Native American peoples flourishing from around the 5th century B.C. to the 16th century A.D. especially in the Ohio and Mississippi valleys, practicing settled agriculture and known for their often large burial and effigy mounds.

mount[1] (mount) *v.* **mount·ed, mount·ing, mounts.** *—tr.* **1.** To climb or ascend: *mount stairs.* **2.** To place oneself upon; get up on: *mount a horse; mount a platform.* **3.** To climb onto (a female) for copulation. Used of male animals. **4. a.** To furnish with a horse for riding. **b.** To set on a horse: *mount the saddle.* **5.** To set in a raised position: *mount a bed on blocks.* **6. a.** To fix securely to a support: *mount an engine in a car.* **b.** To place or fix on or in the appropriate support or setting for display or study: *mount stamps in an album; mount a specimen on a slide.* **7.** To provide with scenery, costumes, and other equipment necessary for production: *mount a play.* **8.** To organize and equip: *mount an army.* **9.** To prepare and set in motion: *mount an attack.* **10. a.** To set in position for use: *mount guns.* **b.** To carry as equipment: *The warship mounted ten guns.* **11.** To post (a guard). *—intr.* **1.** To go upward; rise. **2.** To get up on something, as a horse or bicycle. **3.** To increase in amount, extent, or intensity: *Expenses are mounting up. Costs quickly mounted.* See Synonyms at **rise. —mount** *n.* **1.** The act or manner of mounting. **2.** A means of conveyance, such as a horse, on which to ride. **3.** An opportunity to ride a horse in a race. **4.** An object to which another is affixed or on which another is placed for accessibility, display, or use, especially: **a.** A glass slide for use with a microscope. **b.** A hinge used to fasten stamps in an album. **c.** A setting for a jewel. **d.** An undercarriage or stand on which a device rests while in service. [Middle English *mounten,* from Old French *monter,* from Vulgar Latin **montāre,* from Latin *mōns, mont-,* mountain. See **men-[2]** in Appendix.] **—mount′a·ble** *adj.* **—mount′er** *n.*

mount[2] (mount) *n.* **1.** *Abbr.* **mt., Mt.** A mountain or hill. Used especially as part of a proper name. **2.** Any of the seven fleshy cushions around the edges of the palm of the hand in palmistry. [Middle English *mont,* from Old English *munt* and from Old French *mont, munt,* both from Latin *mōns, mont-.* See **men-[2]** in Appendix.]

moun·tain (moun′tən) *n.* **1.** *Abbr.* **mt., Mt., mtn., Mtn.** A natural elevation of the earth's surface having considerable mass, generally steep sides, and a height greater than that of a hill. **2. a.** A large heap: *a mountain of laundry.* **b.** A huge quantity: *a mountain of trouble.* [Middle English *mountaine,* from Old French *montaigne, muntaigne,* from Vulgar Latin **montānea,* from feminine of **montāneus,* of a mountain, from Latin *montānus,* from *mōns, mont-,* mountain. See **men-[2]** in Appendix.] **—moun′tain·y** *adj.*

mountain ash *n.* Any of various deciduous trees of the genus *Sorbus,* such as the rowan, having clusters of small white flowers and bright orange-red berries arranged in clusters.

mountain avens *n.* A creeping evergreen plant *(Dryas octopetala)* in the rose family, widely distributed in northern portions of Eurasia and North America and having flowers with white petals and feathery styles.

mountain beaver *n.* See **sewellel.**

mountain bluebird *n.* A bluebird *(Sialia currucoides)* of the western United States, having a light blue breast.

Moun·tain Brook (moun′tən). A city of north-central Alabama, a suburb of Birmingham. Population, 19,718.

mountain cat *n.* See **mountain lion.**

mountain climbing *n. Sports.* The climbing of mountains, especially the scaling of rock faces by means of special equipment and technique.

mountain cranberry *n.* See **cowberry.**

mountain dew *n.* Illegally distilled corn liquor.

moun·tain·eer (moun′tə-nîr′) *n.* **1.** A native or inhabitant of a mountainous area. **2.** *Sports.* One who climbs mountains for sport. **—mountaineer** *intr.v.* **-eered, -eer·ing, -eers.** *Sports.* To climb mountains for sport.

moun·tain·eer·ing (moun′tn-ēr′ĭng) *n. Sports.* The climbing of mountains for sport.

mountain goat *n.* A goat antelope *(Oreamnos americanus)* of the northwest North American mountains, having short, curved black horns and shaggy, yellowish-white hair and beard. Also called *Rocky Mountain goat.*

mountain laurel *n.* An evergreen shrub *(Kalmia latifolia)* of eastern North America, having leathery, poisonous leaves and clusters of pink or white flowers. Also called *calico bush.*

♦ **mountain lion** *n.* A large, powerful, wild cat *(Felis concolor)* of mountainous regions of the Western Hemisphere, having an unmarked tawny body. Also called *catamount, cougar, mountain cat,* ♦*painter,* ♦*panther,* ♦*puma.*

moun·tain·ous (moun′tə-nəs) *adj.* **1.** Having many mountains. **2.** Resembling a mountain in size: *mountainous waves.*

mountain range *n.* A series of mountain ridges alike in form, direction, and origin.

mountain sheep *n.* **1.** See **bighorn. 2.** A wild sheep inhabiting a mountainous area.

mountain sickness *n.* Altitude sickness brought on by the diminished oxygen pressure at mountain elevations.

moun·tain·side (moun′tən-sīd′) *n.* The side of a mountain.

Mountain Standard Time *n. Abbr.* **MST, M.S.T.** Standard time in the seventh time zone west of Greenwich, England, reckoned at 105° west and used in the Rocky Mountain states of the United States. Also called *Mountain Time.*

moun·tain·top (moun′tən-tŏp′) *n.* The summit of a mountain.

Mountain View. A city of western California on San Francisco Bay northwest of San Jose. Population, 58,655.

mountain whitefish *n.* A whitefish *(Prospium williamsoni)* with a slender body and short head, found in mountain streams of western North America.

Mount Ath·os (mount ăth′ŏs, ā′thŏs, ä′thôs). See **Athos.**

Mount·bat·ten (mount-băt′n), **Louis.** First Earl Mountbatten of Burma. 1900–1979. British naval officer and colonial administrator who was supreme Allied commander in southeast Asia (1943–1946) and the last viceroy and governor-general of India (1947). He was assassinated by the Irish Republican Army.

Mount Clem·ens (klĕm′ənz). A city of southeast Michigan north-northeast of Detroit. Population, 18,806.

Mount Des·ert Island (dĕz′ərt). An island in the Atlantic Ocean off the southern coast of Maine. Named by 17th-century French explorers for its *Monts Deserts,* or "wilderness peaks," it is a popular summer resort.

moun·te·bank (moun′tə-băngk′) *n.* **1.** A hawker of quack medicines who attracts customers with stories, jokes, or tricks. **2.** A flamboyant charlatan. See Synonyms at **impostor. —mountebank** *v.* **-banked, -bank·ing, -banks.** *—intr.* To act as a mountebank. *—tr. Archaic.* To ensnare or prevail over with trickery. [Italian *montambanco,* from the phrase *monta im banco,* one gets up onto the bench : *monta,* one gets up, third person sing. present tense of *montare,* to get up (from Vulgar Latin **montāre;* see MOUNT[1]) + *im,* onto (variant of *in,* on, onto, from Latin; see IN–[2]) + *banco,* bench (variant of *banca,* from Old Italian, bench, table, from Old High German *bank*).]

Mount·ie also **Mount·y** (moun′tē) *n., pl.* **-ies.** *Informal.* A member of the Royal Canadian Mounted Police.

mount•ing (moun′tĭng) *n.* Something that serves as a support, setting, or backing: *a mounting for a gem.*

Mount•lake Terrace (mount′lāk′). A city of northwest Washington south of Everett. Population, 16,534.

Mount Leb•a•non (lĕb′ə-nən, -nŏn′). A community of southwest Pennsylvania, a suburb of Pittsburgh. Population, 34,414.

Mount Pleas•ant (plĕz′ənt). A city of central Michigan west-northwest of Saginaw. Oil was discovered nearby in 1928. Population, 23,746.

Mount Pros•pect (prŏs′pĕkt′). A village of northeast Illinois, an industrial suburb of Chicago. Population, 52,634.

Mount Roy•al (roi′əl). See **Mont Royal.**

Mount Ver•non[1] (vûr′nən). An estate of northeast Virginia on the Potomac River near Washington, D.C. It was the home of George Washington from 1752 until his death in 1799.

Mount Ver•non[2] (vûr′nən). **1.** A city of south-central Illinois east-southeast of East St. Louis. It is a trade and industrial center in a farming region. Population, 16,995. **2.** A city of southeast New York adjacent to the Bronx. Primarily residential, it was laid out as a planned community in the 1850's. Population, 66,713.

Mount•y (moun′tē) *n.* Variant of **Mountie.**

mourn (môrn, mōrn) *v.* **mourned, mourn•ing, mourns.** —*intr.* **1.** To feel or express grief or sorrow. See Synonyms at **grieve. 2.** To show grief for a death by conventional signs, as by wearing black clothes. **3.** To make a low, indistinct, mournful sound. Used especially of a dove. —*tr.* **1.** To feel or express deep regret for: *mourned the wasted years.* **2.** To grieve over (someone who has died). **3.** To utter sorrowfully. [Middle English *mournen,* from Old English *murnan.* See **(s)mer-**[1] in Appendix.] **—mourn′er** *n.* **—mourn′ing•ly** *adv.*

mourn•ful (môrn′fəl, mōrn′-) *adj.* **1.** Feeling or expressing sorrow or grief; sorrowful. **2.** Causing or suggesting sadness or melancholy: *the mournful sound of a train whistle.* **—mourn′ful•ly** *adv.* **—mourn′ful•ness** *n.*

mourn•ing (môr′nĭng, mōr′-) *n.* **1.** The actions or expressions of one who has suffered a bereavement. **2.** Conventional outward signs of grief for the dead, such as a black armband or black clothes. **3.** The period during which a death is mourned.

mourning cloak *n.* A large butterfly *(Nymphalis antiopa)* of Europe and North America, having purplish-brown wings with a broad yellow border.

mourning dove *n.* A grayish-brown, swift-flying wild dove *(Zenaidura macroura)* of North America, noted for its mournful call. Also called *turtledove.*

mourning warbler *n.* A yellow and olive warbler *(Oporornis philadelphia)* of eastern North America, having a bluish gray hood set off by a black band on its breast.

Mous•cron (mo͞o-skrôɴ′) also **Moes•kroen** (mo͞os′kro͞on′). A city of western Belgium near the French border west-southwest of Brussels. It was founded as a frontier station. Population, 54,402.

mouse (mous) *n., pl.* **mice** (mīs). **1.a.** Any of numerous small rodents of the families Muridae and Cricetidae, such as the common house mouse *(Mus musculus),* characteristically having a pointed snout, small, rounded ears, and a long, naked or almost hairless tail. **b.** Any of various similar or related animals, such as the jumping mouse, the vole, or the jerboa. **2.** A cowardly or timid person. **3.** *Informal.* A discolored swelling under the eye caused by a blow; a black eye. **4.** *pl.* **mice** or **mous•es** (mous′ĭz). *Computer Science.* A hand-held, button-activated input device that when rolled along a flat surface directs an indicator to move correspondingly about a computer screen, allowing the operator to move the indicator freely, as to select operations or manipulate text or graphics. **—mouse** (mouz) *intr.v.* **moused, mous•ing, mous•es. 1.** To hunt mice. **2.** To search furtively for something; prowl. [Middle English *mous,* from Old English *mūs.* See **mūs-** in Appendix.]

mouse deer *n.* See **chevrotain.** [Probably alteration (influenced by MOOSE and MOUSE) of MUSK DEER.]

mouse-ear chickweed (mous′îr′) *n.* Any of numerous herbs of the genus *Cerastium,* having opposite leaves and cylindrical capsules with ten toothlike projections.

mous•er (mou′zər) *n.* An animal, especially a cat, that catches mice.

mouse-tail (mous′tāl′) *n.* A plant of the genus *Myosurus,* especially *M. minimus,* having a taillike flower spike.

mouse•trap (mous′trăp′) *n.* A trap for catching mice. **—mousetrap** *tr.v.* **-trapped, -trap•ping, -traps.** To trap or ensnare, as by a stratagem.

mous•ey (mou′sē, -zē) *adj.* Variant of **mousy.**

mous•ing (mou′zĭng) *n. Nautical.* A binding or metal shackle around the point and shank of a hook to prevent it from slipping from an eye. [From MOUSE, a large mouselike knot on a rope.]

mous•sa•ka (mo͞o-sä′kə, mo͞o′sä-kä′) *n.* A Greek dish consisting of layers of ground lamb or beef and sliced eggplant topped with a cheese sauce and baked. [Serbo-Croatian, from Turkish *mussakka,* from Arabic *musakka.*]

mousse (mo͞os) *n.* **1.** Any of various chilled desserts made with flavored whipped cream, gelatin, and eggs. *chocolate mousse.* **2.** A molded dish containing meat, fish, or shellfish combined with whipped cream and gelatin. **3.** An aerosol foam used to control and style the hair. **—mousse** *tr.v.* **moussed, mouss•ing, mouss•es.** To apply a styling foam to (the hair). [French, foam, mousse, from Old French, moss, foam, partly of Germanic origin and partly from Latin *mulsa,* hydromel, from feminine of *mulsus,* honey-sweet; see **melit-** in Appendix.]

mousse•line (mo͞os-lēn′) *n.* **1.** A fine sheer fabric resembling muslin, originally made in Mosul, Iraq. **2.** A hollandaise sauce to which whipped cream has been added. **3.** An aspic containing whipped cream. [French. See MUSLIN.]

mousseline de soie (də swä′) *n., pl.* **mousselines de soie.** A fine, crisp fabric made of silk or rayon. [French : *mousseline,* muslin + *de,* of + *soie,* silk.]

mous•tache (mŭs′tăsh′, mə-stăsh′) *n.* Variant of **mustache.**

mous•ta•chioed (mə-stăch′ōd, -stăsh′ē-ōd′, -stä′shōd, -shē-ōd′) *adj.* Variant of **mustachioed.**

Mous•te•ri•an (mo͞o-stîr′ē-ən) *adj. Archaeology.* Designating or belonging to a Middle Paleolithic culture following the Acheulian and associated with Neanderthal man, characterized by the use of flaked tools. [French *moustérien,* after *Le Moustier,* a cave in southwest France.]

mous•y also **mous•ey** (mou′sē, -zē) *adj.* **-i•er, -i•est. 1.** Resembling a mouse, especially: **a.** Having a drab, pale brown color: *mousy hair.* **b.** Having small, sharp features: *a mousy face.* **c.** Quiet; timid; shy. **2.** Infested with mice.

mouth (mouth) *n., pl.* **mouths** (mouthz). **1.a.** The body opening through which an animal takes in food. **b.** The cavity lying at the upper end of the alimentary canal, bounded on the outside by the lips and inside by the oropharynx and containing in higher vertebrates the tongue, gums, and teeth. **c.** This cavity regarded as the source of sounds and speech. **d.** The opening to any cavity or canal in an organ or a bodily part. **2.** The part of the lips visible on the human face. **3.** A person viewed as a consumer of food: *has three mouths to feed at home.* **4.** A pout, grimace, or similar expression. **5.a.** Utterance; voice: *gave mouth to her doubts.* **b.** A tendency to talk excessively or unwisely. **c.** Impudent or vulgar talk: *Watch your mouth.* **6.** A spokesperson; a mouthpiece. **7.** A natural opening, as the part of a stream or river that empties into a larger body of water or the entrance to a harbor, canyon, valley, or cave. **8.** The opening through which a container is filled or emptied. **9.** The opening between the jaws of a vise or other holding or gripping tool. **10.** *Music.* **a.** An opening in the pipe of an organ. **b.** The opening in the mouthpiece of a flute across which the player blows. **—mouth** (mouth) *v.* **mouthed, mouth•ing, mouths.** —*tr.* **1.** To speak or pronounce, especially: **a.** To declare in a pompous manner; declaim: *mouthing his opinions of the candidates.* **b.** To utter without conviction or understanding: *mouthing empty compliments.* **c.** To form soundlessly: *I mouthed the words as the others sang.* **d.** To utter indistinctly; mumble. **2.** To take or move around in the mouth. —*intr.* **1.** To orate affectedly; declaim. **2.** To grimace. **—*phrasal verb.* mouth off.** *Slang.* **a.** To express one's opinions or complaints in a loud, indiscreet manner. **b.** To speak impudently; talk back. [Middle English, from Old English *mūth.* See **men-**[2] in Appendix.]

mouth•breed•er (mouth′brē′dər) *n.* Any of various fishes, especially of the genera *Haplochromis* and *Tilapia,* that carry their eggs and young in the mouth.

mouth•ful (mouth′fo͝ol′) *n.* **1.** The amount of food or other material that can be placed or held in the mouth at one time. **2.** A small amount to be tasted or eaten. **3.** A long word, name, or phrase that is difficult to pronounce. **4.** An important or perceptive remark: *You said a mouthful!*

mouth•ing (mou′thĭng) *n.* A bombastic or empty phrase or speech. Often used in the plural: *mouthings about morality.*

mouth organ *n. Music.* **1.** See **harmonica** (sense 1). **2.** See **panpipe.**

mouth•part (mouth′pärt′) *n.* Any of the parts of the mouth of an insect or other arthropod, especially a part or an organ adapted to a specific way of feeding.

mouth•piece (mouth′pēs′) *n.* **1.** A part, as of a musical instrument or a telephone, that functions in or near the mouth. **2.** *Sports.* A protective rubber device worn over the teeth, as by boxers. **3.** *Informal.* One, such as a spokesperson, through which views are expressed. **4.** *Slang.* A defense lawyer.

mouth-to-mouth resuscitation (mouth′tə-mouth′) *n.* A technique used to resuscitate a person who has stopped breathing, in which the rescuer presses his or her mouth against the mouth of the victim and, allowing for passive exhalation, forces air into the lungs at intervals of several seconds.

mouth•wash (mouth′wŏsh′, -wôsh′) *n.* A flavored, usually antiseptic solution used for cleaning the mouth and freshening the breath.

mouth•wa•ter•ing or **mouth-wa•ter•ing** (mouth′wô′tər-ĭng) *adj.* Appealing to the sense of taste; appetizing: *the mouth-watering aroma of a baking pie.*

mouth•y (mou′thē, -thē) *adj.* **-i•er, -i•est. 1.** Annoyingly talkative. **2.** Given to ranting or bombast. **—mouth′i•ness** *n.*

mou•ton (mo͞o′tŏn′) *n.* Sheepskin that has been sheared and processed to resemble beaver or seal. —*attributive.* Often used to modify another noun: *mouton jackets; a mouton hat.* [French, sheep, from Old French. See MUTTON.]

mou•ton•née (mo͞o′tə-nā′) also **mou•ton•néed** (-nād′) *adj. Geology.* Rounded by glacial action into a shape likened to a sheep's back. Used of a rock formation. [Short for French *roche moutonnée* : *roche,* rock + *moutonnée,* fleecy, past participle of *moutonner,* to make fleecy (from *mouton,* sheep; see MOUTON).]

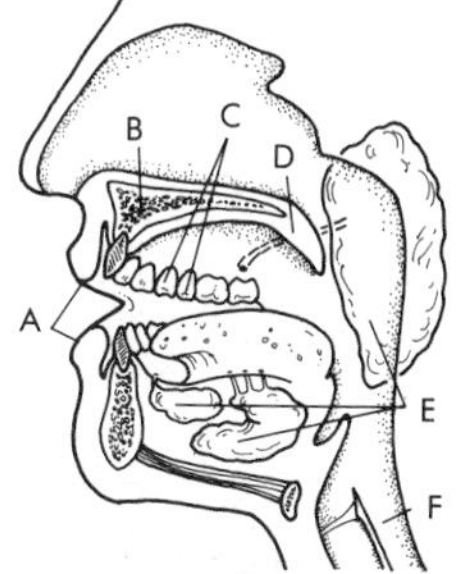

mouth
A. Lips
B. Hard palate
C. Teeth
D. Soft palate
E. Salivary glands
F. Esophagus

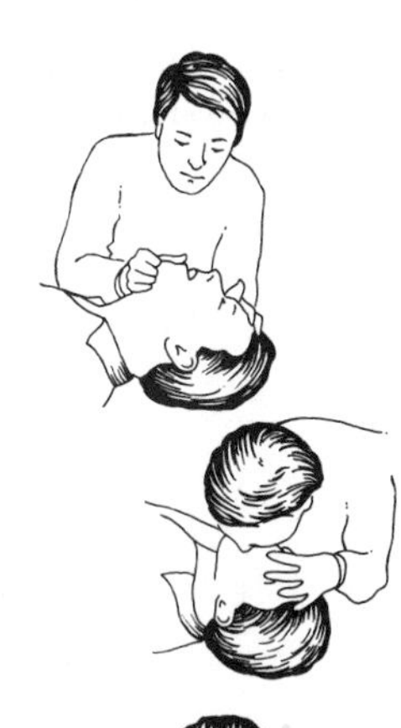

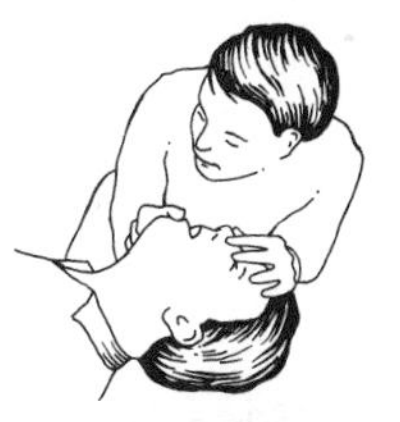

mouth-to-mouth resuscitation
Top: Tilt head of victim back to open air passage
Center: Pinch victim's nose closed and breathe into victim's mouth
Bottom: Listen for sounds of victim breathing on own; if necessary, repeat procedure 15 breaths per minute

ă pat	oi boy
ā pay	ou out
âr care	o͝o took
ä father	o͞o boot
ĕ pet	ŭ cut
ē be	ûr urge
ĭ pit	th thin
ī pie	*th* this
îr pier	hw which
ŏ pot	zh vision
ō toe	ə about, item
ô paw	♦ regionalism

Stress marks: **′** (primary); ′ (secondary), as in **dictionary** (dĭk′shə-nĕr′ē)

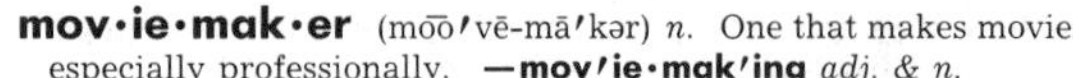

mov·a·ble also **move·a·ble** (mo͞o′və-bəl) —*adj.* **1.** Possible to move: *a movable stove; a movable rock.* **2.** Varying in date from year to year: *a movable holiday.* **3.** *Law.* Of or relating to personal property that can be moved. —*n.* **1.** Something, especially a piece of furniture, that can be moved. **2.** Often **movables.** *Law.* Personal property. **—mov′a·bil′i·ty, mov′a·ble·ness** *n.* **—mov′a·bly** *adv.*

movable feast *n.* A religious holiday, such as Easter, that changes in date from year to year.

movable type *n. Printing.* Type in which each character is cast on a separate piece of metal.

move (mo͞ov) *v.* **moved, mov·ing, moves.** —*intr.* **1.** To change in position from one point to another: *moved away from the window.* **2.** To progress in sequence; go forward: *a novel that moves slowly.* **3.** To follow a specified course: *Earth moves around the sun.* **4.** To progress toward a particular state or condition: *moving up in the company; moved into the lead.* **5.** To go from one residence or location to another; relocate. **6.** To start off; depart. **7.** To be disposed of by sale: *Woolens move slowly in the summer.* **8.** To change posture or position; stir: *was afraid to move.* **9.** *Games.* To change the position of a piece in a board game. **10.** To be put in motion or to turn according to a prescribed motion. Used of machinery. **11.** To exhibit great activity or energy. **12.** To initiate an action; act. **13.** To be active in a particular environment: *moves in diplomatic circles.* **14.** To stir the emotions: *words that have the power to move.* **15.** To make a formal motion in parliamentary procedure: *move for an adjournment.* **16.** To evacuate. Used of the bowels. —*tr.* **1.** To change the place or position of: *moved her office; could not move his arm.* **2.** To cause to go from one place to another: *moved the crowd away.* **3.** *Games.* To change (a piece) from one position to another in a board game: *moved a pawn.* **4.** To change the course of: *moved the discussion to other matters.* **5.** To dislodge from a fixed point of view, as by persuasion: *"Speak to him, ladies, see if you can move him"* (Shakespeare). **6.** To prompt to an action; rouse: *Anger moved her to speak out.* **7. a.** To set or keep in motion. **b.** To cause to function. **c.** To cause to progress or advance. **8. a.** To arouse the emotions of; affect. **b.** To excite or provoke to the expression of an emotion: *The film moved me to tears.* See Synonyms at **affect**[1]. **9. a.** To propose or request in formal parliamentary procedure: *moved that a vote be taken.* **b.** To make formal application to (a court, for example). **10.** To dispose of by sale: *moved the new merchandise quickly.* **11.** To cause (the bowels) to evacuate. **—move** *n.* **1. a.** The act or an instance of moving. **b.** A particular manner of moving: *made some intricate moves on the dance floor.* **2.** A change of residence or location. **3.** *Games.* **a.** An act of transferring a piece from one position to another in board games. **b.** The prescribed manner in which a piece may be played. **c.** A participant's turn to make a play. **4.** An action taken to achieve an objective; a maneuver: *a move to halt the arms race.* ***—phrasal verb.*** **move in.** To begin to occupy a residence or place of business. ***—idioms.*** **get a move on.** *Informal.* To get started; get going. **move in on. 1.** To make intrusive advances toward; intrude on. **2.** To attempt to seize control of: *moving in on their territory.* **on the move. 1.** Busily moving about; active: *A nurse is on the move all day.* **2.** Going from one place to another: *troops on the move.* **3.** Making progress; advancing: *a technology that is clearly on the move.* [Middle English *moven,* from Old French *movoir,* from Latin *movēre.* See **meue-** in Appendix.]

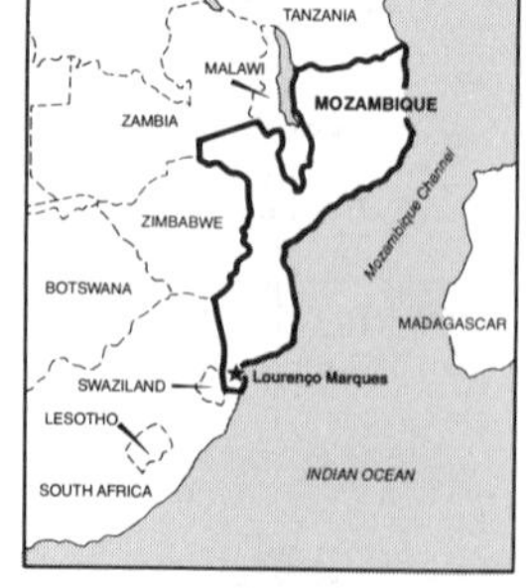

Mozambique

move·a·ble (mo͞o′və-bəl) *adj. & n.* Variant of **movable.**

move·ment (mo͞ov′mənt) *n.* **1. a.** The act or an instance of moving; a change in place or position. **b.** A particular manner of moving. **2.** A change in the location of troops, ships, or aircraft for tactical or strategic purposes. **3. a.** A series of actions and events taking place over a period of time and working to foster a principle or policy: *a movement toward world peace.* **b.** An organized effort by supporters of a common goal: *an early leader of the labor movement.* **4.** A tendency or trend: *a movement toward larger kitchens.* **5.** A change in the market price of a security or commodity. **6. a.** An evacuation of the bowels. **b.** The matter so evacuated. **7.** The suggestion or illusion of motion in a painting, sculpture, or design. **8.** The progression of events in the development of a literary plot. **9.** The rhythmical or metrical structure of a poetic composition. **10.** *Music.* A self-contained section of a composition. **11.** A mechanism, such as the works of a watch, that produces or transmits motion.

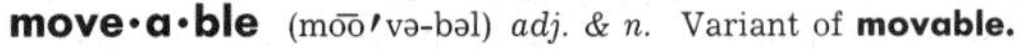

Wolfgang Amadeus Mozart

mov·er (mo͞o′vər) *n.* **1.** One that moves: *a fast mover in corporate circles.* **2.** One that transports household or office goods from one location to another as an occupation.

mover and shaker *n., pl.* **movers and shakers.** One who wields power and influence in a sphere of activity: *"the importance of hanging out with the movers and shakers of the art world"* (Richard Colvin).

mov·ie (mo͞o′vē) *n.* **1. a.** A sequence of photographs projected onto a screen with sufficient rapidity as to create the illusion of motion and continuity. **b.** A connected cinematic narrative represented in this form. **2.** A theater that shows movies. **3. movies. a.** A showing of a movie. Often used with *the.* **b.** The movie industry. —*attributive.* Often used to modify another noun: *a movie producer; movie stars.* [Shortening and alteration of MOVING PICTURE.]

mov·ie·dom (mo͞o′vē-dəm) *n.* See **filmdom.**

mov·ie·go·er (mo͞o′vē-gō′ər) *n.* One who goes to see movies. **—mov′ie·go′ing** *adj. & n.*

mov·ie·mak·er (mo͞o′vē-mā′kər) *n.* One that makes movies, especially professionally. **—mov′ie·mak′ing** *adj. & n.*

mov·ing (mo͞o′vĭng) *adj.* **1.** Changing or capable of changing position: *a moving target.* **2.** Relating to or involved in a transfer of furnishings from one location to another: *moving expenses; moving van.* **3.** Causing or producing motion. **4.** Involving a motor vehicle in motion: *a moving violation.* **5.** Arousing or capable of arousing deep emotion: *a moving account of the tragedy.* **—mov′ing·ly** *adv.*

SYNONYMS: *moving, stirring, poignant, touching, pathetic, affecting.* These adjectives mean arousing or capable or arousing deep, usually somber emotion. *Moving* is the least specific: *"A . . . widow . . . has laid her case of destitution before him in a very moving letter"* (Nathaniel Hawthorne). Something *stirring* excites strong, turbulent, but not unpleasant feelings, as of inspiration: *An advocate for the homeless gave a stirring speech about their plight. Poignant* suggests the evocation of keen, painful emotion: *"Poignant grief cannot endure forever"* (W.H. Hudson). *Touching* emphasizes sympathy or tenderness: *Her expression of gratitude was simple and touching. Pathetic* stresses pity and compassion: *"The old, rather shabby room struck her as extraordinarily pathetic"* (John Galsworthy). *Affecting* applies especially to what is heart-rending or bittersweet: *The homecoming of the released hostages and their reunion with their families was an affecting scene.*

moving picture *n.* A movie.

moving sidewalk *n.* A conveyor for transporting pedestrians along a flat expanse.

mow[1] (mou) *n.* **1.** The place in a barn where hay, grain, or other feed is stored. **2.** A stack of hay or other feed stored in a barn. [Middle English, stack of hay, from Old English *mūga.*]

mow[2] (mō) *v.* **mowed, mowed** or **mown** (mōn), **mow·ing, mows.** —*tr.* **1.** To cut down (grass or grain) with a scythe or a mechanical device. **2.** To cut (grass or grain) from: *mow the lawn.* —*intr.* To cut down grass or other growth. ***—phrasal verb.*** **mow down. 1.** To destroy in great numbers as if cutting down, as in battle. **2.** To overwhelm: *mowed down the opposition with strong arguments.* [Middle English *mowen,* from Old English *māwan.* See **mē-**[4] in Appendix.] **—mow′er** (mō′ər) *n.*

mox·ie (mŏk′sē) *n. Slang.* **1.** The ability to face difficulty with spirit and courage. **2.** Aggressive energy; initiative: *"His prose has moxie, though it rushes and stumbles from a pent-up surge"* (Patricia Hampl). **3.** Skill; know-how. [From *Moxie,* trademark for a soft drink.]

moy·en âge (mwä-yĕn äzh′) *n.* The Middle Ages. [French : *moyen,* middle + *âge,* age.]

Mo·zam·bique (mō′zəm-bēk′, -zăm-). *Abbr.* **Moz.** A country of southeast Africa. The Portuguese colonized the area beginning in 1505 and governed it as part of their Indian holdings until 1752, when a separate administrative unit was formed. As Portuguese East Africa it became an overseas province in 1951, but increasing nationalist feeling and guerrilla activity forced Portugal to grant Mozambique its independence in 1975. Maputo is the capital and the largest city. Population, 12,130,000. **—Mo′zam·bi′can** (-bē′kən) *adj. & n.*

Mozambique Channel. An arm of the Indian Ocean between Madagascar and the mainland of southeast Africa.

Moz·ar·ab (mō-zăr′əb) *n.* One of a group of Spanish Christians who adopted certain aspects of Arab culture under Moslem rule but practiced a modified form of Christian worship. [Spanish *Mozárabe,* from Arabic *musta'rib,* would-be Arab, from *'arab,* Arab.] **—Moz·ar′a·bic** *adj.*

Mo·zart (mōt′särt), **Wolfgang Amadeus.** 1756–1791. Austrian composer considered among the greatest and most prolific composers in history. Of his more than 600 compositions, the finest works, including three symphonies (1788) and the operas *Don Giovanni* (1787) and *The Magic Flute* (1791), were written in the last five years of his short life.

mo·zet·ta (mō-zĕt′ə, mōt-sĕt′tä) *n.* Variant of **mozzetta.**

♦ **mo·zo** (mō′zō) *n., pl.* **-zos.** *Southwestern U.S.* **1.** A man who helps with a pack train or serves as a porter. **2.** An assistant. [Spanish, boy, servant, mozo, from Old Spanish *moço.*]

♦ ***REGIONAL NOTE:*** In the world of pack trains and cattle roundups, a *mozo* provides a useful pair of extra hands. Back home on the ranch, the mozo helps with odd jobs, especially heavy work around the house. In the southwest United States *mozo* has taken on a general sense of "assistant," even in areas not related to ranching: *"An enterprising deputy of the opposition Partido de Acción Nacional (PAN) called a quorum count, only to find that . . . many of the reclining figures occasionally raising their hands were mozos (attendants)"* (Latin America). In fact, to call an assistant a *mozo* is essentially to call him a "boy," for *mozo* is Spanish for "young man." Even though a mozo may not be a boy in years, the word is not used disparagingly. In other languages porters or guides are commonly referred to as "boys"—for example, *gillie,* from Scottish Gaelic *gille,* means "boy."

moz·za·rel·la (mŏt′sə-rĕl′ə, mōt′-) *n.* A mild, white Italian cheese that has a rubbery texture and is often eaten melted, as on pizza. [Italian, diminutive of *mozza,* a cut, mozzarella, from *moz-*

zare, to cut off, from *mozzo,* mutilated, from Vulgar Latin **mutius,* from Latin *mutilis.*]

moz·zet·ta or **mo·zet·ta** (mō-zĕt′ə, mōt-sĕt′tä) *n. Roman Catholic Church.* A short, hooded cape worn over the rochet by the pope and by bishops and other dignitaries. [Italian, from Medieval Latin *almutia.*]

mp or **m.p.** *abbr.* **1.** Melting point. **2.** *Music.* Mezzo piano.

MP or **M.P.** *abbr.* **1.** Member of Parliament. **2.** Military police. **3.** Military police officer. **4.** Mounted police.

M.P.A. *abbr.* **1.** Master of Public Administration. **2.** Master of Public Accounting.

M.P.E. *abbr.* Master of Public Education.

mpg or **m.p.g.** *abbr.* Miles per gallon.

mph or **m.p.h.** *abbr.* Miles per hour.

M.P.H. *abbr.* Master of Public Health.

Mr. (mĭs′tər) *n., pl.* **Messrs.** (mĕs′ərz). Used as a courtesy title before the surname or full name of a man. See Usage Note at **Ms.** [Middle English, abbreviation of *maister,* master. See MASTER.]

Mr. Char·lie or **Mister Char·lie** (chär′lē) *n. Offensive Slang.* A white person or white people considered as a group. [From the name *Charlie,* nickname for *Charles.*]

Mr. Clean *n. Slang.* A man who adheres to the highest standards of personal and professional conduct, especially a public figure of unquestioned integrity. [From *Mr. Clean,* trademark used for a cleaning product.]

M.R.E. *abbr.* Meals Ready to Eat.

MRI *abbr.* Magnetic resonance imaging.

mRNA *abbr.* Messenger RNA.

Mr. Right *n. Slang.* The man who would make an ideal mate: *"self-help guides for women in search of Mr. Right"* (Los Angeles Times).

Mrs. (mĭs′ĭz) *n., pl.* **Mmes.** (mā-däm′, -dăm′). **1.** Used as a courtesy title for a married or widowed woman before the surname or full name of her husband: *Mrs. Doe; Mrs. John Doe.* **2.** Used as a courtesy title for a married, widowed, or divorced woman before her own surname or full name: *Mrs. Doe; Mrs. Jane Doe.* See Usage Note at **Ms.** [Abbreviation of MISTRESS.]

Mrs. Grun·dy (grŭn′dē) *n.* An extremely conventional or priggish person. [After *Mrs. Grundy,* character alluded to in the play *Speed the Plough* by Thomas Morton (1764–1838), British playwright.]

ms *abbr.* Millisecond.

MS *abbr.* **1.** Mississippi. **2.** Multiple sclerosis.

Ms. also **Ms** (mĭz) *n., pl.* **Mses.** also **Mses** also **Mss.** or **Mss** (mĭz′ĭz). Used as a courtesy title before the surname or full name of a woman or girl: *Ms. Doe; Ms. Jane Doe.* [Blend of MISS and MRS.]

USAGE NOTE: *Ms.* has come to be widely used in both professional and social contexts. Many women prefer it to *Miss* or *Mrs.* because they feel that information about their marital status properly belongs to the realm of private life and is often inappropriate to many of the contexts in which such titles are used. Many people also find *Ms.* convenient, since information about an addressee's marital status is not always available. But there are also many women who continue to prefer *Miss* or *Mrs.,* and practices vary widely according to the region and social setting. • The use of *Ms.* is equivalent to that of *Mr.*: *Mr. Green, Mr. Paul Green; Ms. Smith, Ms. Judith Smith.* If a woman keeps her own name after marriage, *Ms.* is the appropriate courtesy title: if Judith Smith marries Paul Green and does not change her name to Green, *Ms. Smith* is the appropriate title and *Mrs. Smith* is incorrect. If a woman takes her husband's name, either *Ms.* or *Mrs.* may be used, although *Ms.* should not be used if the woman is addressed by her husband's given name and surname: *Ms. Green, Ms. Judith Green,* but not *Ms. Paul Green.* Some women who keep their own names for professional purposes use the title *Miss* in that context, while others use *Ms.*

MS. or **MS** also **ms.** or **ms** *abbr.* Manuscript.

M.S. *abbr. Latin.* Magister Scientiae (Master of Science).

M.Sc. *abbr. Latin.* Magister Scientiae (Master of Science).

MS-DOS (ĕm′ĕs-dôs′, -dŏs′). A trademark for a microcomputer operating system.

msec *abbr.* Millisecond.

Mses. (mĭz′ĭz) also **Mses** *n.* Plurals of **Ms.**

MSG *abbr.* Monosodium glutamate.

msg. *abbr.* Message.

Msgr. *abbr.* **1.** Monseigneur. **2.** Monsignor.

M.Sgt. or **MSGT** *abbr.* Master sergeant.

MSH *abbr.* Melanocyte-stimulating hormone.

M.S. in L.S. *abbr.* Master of Science in Library Science.

m.s.l. or **M.S.L.** *abbr.* Mean sea level.

M.S.N. *abbr.* Master of Science in Nursing.

Mss. (mĭz′ĭz) or **Mss** *n.* Plurals of **Ms.**

MSS. or **MSS** also **mss.** or **mss** *abbr.* Manuscripts.

MST or **M.S.T.** *abbr.* Mountain Standard Time.

M.S.T.S. *abbr.* Military Sea Transportation Service.

M.S.W. *abbr.* **1.** Master of Social Welfare. **2.** Master of Social Work.

Mt *abbr. Bible.* Matthew.

MT *abbr.* **1.** Machine translation. **2.** Megaton. **3.** Montana. **4.** Or **M.T.** Mountain Time.

mt. or **Mt.** *abbr.* Mount; mountain.

m.t. or **M.T.** *abbr.* Metric ton.

mtg. *abbr.* **1.** Meeting. **2.** Mortgage.

mtge. *abbr.* Mortgage.

mtn. or **Mtn.** *abbr.* Mountain.

mts. or **Mts.** *abbr.* Mountains.

mu (myo͞o, mo͞o) *n.* The 12th letter of the Greek alphabet. See table at **alphabet.** [Greek, of Phoenician origin; akin to Hebrew *mēm.*]

Mu·bar·ak (mo͞o-bär′ək), **Hosni.** Born 1929. Egyptian politician who was appointed president after the assassination of Anwar el-Sadat (1981).

muc– *pref.* Variant of **muco–.**

much (mŭch) *adj.* **more** (môr, mōr), **most** (mōst). Great in quantity, degree, or extent: *not much rain; much affection.* **—much** *n.* **1.** A large quantity or amount: *Much has been written.* **2.** Something great or remarkable: *I've never been much to look at.* **—much** *adv.* **more, most. 1.** To a great degree or extent: *much smarter.* **2.** Just about; almost: *much the same.* **3.** Frequently; often: *doesn't get out much.* **—*idiom.* much less.** And certainly not: *"Happiness is an emotion not often spoken of at the magazine, much less experienced"* (Brendan Gill). [Middle English *muche,* short for *muchel,* from Old English *mycel.* See **meg-** in Appendix.]

much as *conj.* However much: *Much as she needed the job, she had to refuse.*

much·ness (mŭch′nĭs) *n.* Greatness of quantity, degree, or extent.

muci– *pref.* Variant of **muco–.**

mu·cic acid (myo͞o′sĭk) *n.* An organic acid, $HOOC\text{-}(CHOH)_4COOH$, often derived from milk sugar.

mu·cif·er·ous (myo͞o-sĭf′ər-əs) *adj.* Secreting, producing, or containing mucus.

mu·ci·lage (myo͞o′sə-lĭj) *n.* **1.** A sticky substance used as an adhesive. **2.** A gummy substance obtained from certain plants. [Middle English *muscilage,* gelatinous plant substance, from Old French *mucilage,* from Late Latin *mūcilāgō, mūcilāgin-,* from Latin *mūcēre,* to be musty, from *mūcus,* mucus.]

mu·ci·lag·i·nous (myo͞o′sə-lăj′ə-nəs) *adj.* **1.** Resembling mucilage; moist and sticky. **2.** Relating to or secreting mucilage.

mu·cin (myo͞o′sĭn) *n.* Any of a group of glycoproteins found especially in the secretions of mucous membranes. **—mu′cin·ous** *adj.*

muck (mŭk) *n.* **1.** A moist, sticky mixture, especially of mud and filth. **2.** Moist farmyard dung; manure. **3.** Dark, fertile soil containing decaying vegetable matter. **4.** Something filthy or disgusting. **5.** Earth, rocks, or clay excavated in mining. **—muck** *tr.v.* **mucked, muck·ing, mucks. 1.** To fertilize with manure or compost. **2.** To make dirty with or as if with muck. **3.** To remove muck or dirt from (a mine, for example). **—*phrasal verbs.* muck about.** *Chiefly British.* To spend time idly; putter. **muck up.** *Informal.* To bungle, damage, or ruin. [Middle English *muk,* of Scandinavian origin; akin to Old Norse *myki,* dung.] **—muck′i·ly** *adv.* **—muck′y** *adj.*

muck·a·muck (mŭk′ə-mŭk′) *n. Slang.* A high muckamuck. [Short for HIGH MUCKAMUCK.]

muck·rake (mŭk′rāk′) *intr.v.* **-raked, -rak·ing, -rakes.** To search for and expose misconduct in public life. [From the man with the muckrake, who cannot look up to heaven because he is so obsessed with the muck of worldly profit, in *Pilgrim's Progress* by John Bunyan.] **—muck′rak′er** *n.*

muck·worm (mŭk′wûrm′) *n.* Any wormlike insect larva, as of certain beetles, that lives and grows in manure.

muco– or **muci–** or **muc–** *pref.* **1.** Mucus: *mucoprotein.* **2.** Mucosa: *mucin.* [From Latin *mūcus,* mucus.]

mu·co·cu·ta·ne·ous (myo͞o′kō-kyo͞o-tā′nē-əs) *adj.* Of or relating to the skin and a mucous membrane.

mu·coid (myo͞o′koid′) *n.* Any of various glycoproteins, especially a mucoprotein, similar to the mucins. **—mucoid** *adj.* Of, relating to, or resembling mucus.

mu·co·lyt·ic (myo͞o′kə-lĭt′ĭk) *adj.* Breaking down or hydrolyzing mucus or mucopolysaccharides.

mu·co·pep·tide (myo͞o′kō-pĕp′tīd) *n.* See **peptidoglycan.**

mu·co·pol·y·sac·cha·ride (myo͞o′kō-pŏl′ē-săk′ə-rīd′) *n.* See **glycosaminoglycan.**

mu·co·pro·tein (myo͞o′kō-prō′tēn′, -prō′tē-ĭn) *n.* Any of a group of organic compounds, such as the mucins, that consist of a complex of proteins and glycosaminoglycons and are found in body tissues and fluids.

mu·co·pu·ru·lent (myo͞o′kō-pyo͝or′ə-lənt, -yə-lənt) *adj.* Containing mucus and pus.

mu·co·sa (myo͞o-kō′sə) *n., pl.* **-sae** (-sē) or **-sas.** See **mucous membrane.** [From Latin, feminine of *mūcōsus,* mucous. See MUCOUS.] **—mu·co′sal** *adj.*

mu·cous (myo͞o′kəs) *adj.* **1.** Containing, producing, or secreting mucus: *a mucous tissue.* **2.** Relating to, consisting of, or resembling mucus: *a mucous substance.* [Latin *mūcōsus,* from *mūcus,* mucus.]

mucous membrane *n.* A membrane lining all body passages

ă pat	oi boy
ā pay	ou out
âr care	o͝o took
ä father	o͞o boot
ĕ pet	ŭ cut
ē be	ûr urge
ĭ pit	th thin
ī pie	*th* this
îr pier	hw which
ŏ pot	zh vision
ō toe	ə about, item
ô paw	♦ regionalism

Stress marks: **′** (primary); ′ (secondary), as in **dictionary** (dĭk′shə-nĕr′ē)

that communicate with the air, such as the respiratory and alimentary tracts, and having cells and associated glands that secrete mucus. Also called *mucosa.*

mu·co·vis·ci·do·sis (myo͞o′kō-vĭs′ĭ-dō′sĭs) *n.* See **cystic fibrosis.**

mu·cro (myo͞o′krō) *n., pl.* **mu·cro·nes** (myo͞o-krō′nēz). A sharp, pointed part or organ, especially a sharp terminal point, as of a leaf or shell. [Latin *mūcrō, mūcrōn-,* sharp point.]

mu·cro·nate (myo͞o′krə-nāt′) *adj.* Of or having a mucro; ending abruptly in a sharp point: *mucronate feathers; a mucronate leaf.* **—mu′cro·na′tion** *n.*

mu·cro·nes (myo͞o-krō′nēz) *n.* Plural of **mucro.**

mu·cus (myo͞o′kəs) *n.* The viscous, slippery substance that consists chiefly of mucin, water, cells, and inorganic salts and is secreted as a protective lubricant coating by cells and glands of the mucous membranes. [Latin *mūcus.*]

mud (mŭd) *n.* **1.** Wet, sticky, soft earth, as on the banks of a river. **2.** *Slang.* Wet plaster, mortar, or cement. **3.** Slanderous or defamatory charges or comments: *slinging mud at his opponent.* **—mud** *tr.v.* **mud·ded, mud·ding, muds.** To cover or spatter with or as if with mud. [Middle English *mudde,* probably from Middle Low German and Middle Dutch *modde.*]

mud·bug (mŭd′bŭg′) *n.* See **crayfish** (sense 1).

♦**mud cat** *n. Chiefly Southern U.S.* See **catfish.**

♦**mud dauber** *n. Midland U.S.* See **mud wasp** (sense 1).

mud·der (mŭd′ər) *n.* A racehorse that runs well on a wet or muddy track.

muff²

mud·dle (mŭd′l) *v.* **-dled, -dling, -dles.** *—tr.* **1.** To make turbid or muddy. **2.** To mix confusedly; jumble. **3.** To confuse or befuddle (the mind), as with alcohol. See Synonyms at **confuse.** **4.** To mismanage or bungle. **5.** To stir or mix (a drink) gently. *—intr.* To think, act, or proceed in a confused or aimless manner: *muddled along through my high-school years.* **—muddle** *n.* **1.** A disordered condition; a mess. **2.** Mental confusion. ***—phrasal verb.* muddle through.** To push on to a favorable outcome in a disorganized way. [Possibly from obsolete Dutch *moddelen,* to make water muddy, from Middle Dutch, frequentative of **modden,* to make muddy, from *modde,* mud.] **—mud′dler** *n.*

mud·dle-head·ed (mŭd′l-hĕd′ĭd) *adj.* **1.** Mentally confused. **2.** Inept; blundering. **—mud′dle-head′ed·ness** *n.*

mud·dy (mŭd′ē) *adj.* **-di·er, -di·est. 1.** Full of or covered with mud. **2.a.** Not bright or pure: *a muddy color.* **b.** Not clear; cloudy, as with sediment: *muddy coffee.* **3.** Lacking luster; dull: *a muddy complexion.* **4.** Confused or vague: *muddy thinking.* **—muddy** *tr.v.* **-died, -dy·ing, -dies. 1.** To make dirty or muddy. **2.** To make dull or cloudy. **3.** To make obscure or confused. **—mud′di·ly** *adv.* **—mud′di·ness** *n.*

mud eel *n.* A small amphibian *(Siren lacertina),* found in swamps and shallow waters of the southeast United States, that is eellike in appearance and has only front legs, which are partially concealed by external gills.

Mu·dé·jar (mo͞o-thĕ′här) *n., pl.* **Mu·déja·res** (-hä-rĕs′). A Moslem who remained in Spain after it had been reconquered by the Christians in the Middle Ages. **—Mudéjar** *adj.* Of or relating to a style of Spanish architecture of the 13th to 16th centuries, combining Moorish and Gothic forms: *"Geometric designs . . . interlaced friezes, and coffered ceilings mark the Mudejar style"* (Teague Jackson). [Spanish, possibly from Arabic *dajana,* to remain, stay.]

mud·fish (mŭd′fĭsh′) *n., pl.* **mudfish** or **-fish·es.** See **bowfin.**

mud flat *n.* Low-lying muddy land that is covered at high tide and exposed at low tide.

mud·flow (mŭd′flō′) *n.* A downhill movement of soft wet earth and debris, made fluid by rain or melted snow and often building up great speed.

mud·guard (mŭd′gärd′) *n.* A shield over or behind a vehicle's wheel to prevent mud or water from splashing onto that vehicle or a following vehicle. Also called *splashguard.*

mud hen *n.* Any of various birds, such as the coot or rail, inhabiting marshy or coastal regions.

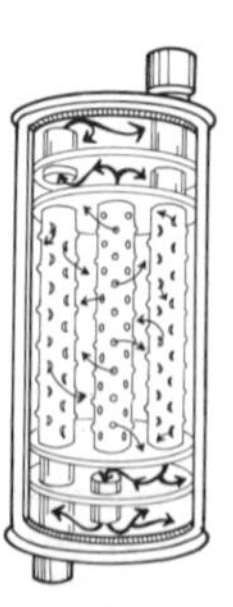

muffler
Reverse-flow muffler

mud minnow *n.* Any of various very small fishes of the family Umbridae, especially of the genus *Umbra,* living in the muddy areas of North American lakes and ponds and often used as bait.

♦**mud puppy** also **mud·pup·py** (mŭd′pŭp′ē) *n., pl.* **mud pup·pies** also **mud·pup·pies. 1.** Any of several large North American salamanders of the genus *Necturus,* especially *N. maculosus,* that live in lakes and streams and have conspicuous clusters of dark red external gills. Also called *water dog.* **2.** *Northern U.S.* See **catfish.**

mu·dra (mə-drä′) *n.* A series of symbolic body postures and hand movements used in East Indian classical dancing. [Sanskrit *mudrā,* seal, mystery, mudra.]

mud·room (mŭd′ro͞om′, -ro͝om′) *n.* A small room or entryway in a house where wet or muddy footwear and clothing can be removed.

mud·sill (mŭd′sĭl′) *n.* The lowest sill, block, or timber supporting a building, located at or below ground level.

mud·skip·per (mŭd′skĭp′ər) *n.* Any of several fishes of the family Gobiidae, especially of the genus *Periophthalmus,* that are found along the western coast of tropical Africa and in the Indo-Pacific region and are able to survive out of water and maneuver on land.

mud·slide (mŭd′slīd′) *n.* A mudflow, especially a slow-moving one.

mud·sling·er (mŭd′slĭng′ər) *n.* One who makes malicious charges and otherwise attempts to discredit an opponent, as in a political campaign. **—mud′sling′ing** *n.*

mud snake *n.* A burrowing snake *(Farancia abacura)* of swamps and lowlands of the southeast United States, having black scales with reddish markings.

mud·stone (mŭd′stōn′) *n.* A fine-grained, dark gray sedimentary rock, formed from silt and clay and similar to shale but without laminations.

mud turtle *n.* Any of various small turtles of the genus *Kinosternon,* having hinged lobes on the ventral part of the shell and found in slow-moving fresh waters throughout the Western Hemisphere.

♦**mud wasp** *n.* **1.** *Northeastern U.S.* Any of various wasps that build nests of mud with cellular compartments for eggs and paralyzed prey. Also called ♦*mud dauber.* **2.** See **potter wasp.**

Muen·ster or **Mun·ster** (mŭn′stər, mo͝on′-) *n.* A semisoft, creamy cheese of mild flavor. [After *Munster,* a town of northeast France.]

mues·li (myo͞oz′lē) *n.* A mixture of usually untoasted rolled oats and dried fruit, often used as a breakfast cereal. [German dialectal, diminutive of German *Mus,* mush, from Middle High German *muos,* a meal, mushlike food, from Old High German.]

mu·ez·zin (myo͞o-ĕz′ĭn, mo͞o-) *n. Islam.* The crier who calls the faithful to prayer five times a day. [Ottoman Turkish *müezzin* or Persian *muazzin,* from Arabic *mu'aḏḏin,* active participle of *'aḏḏana,* to cause to listen, from *'udn,* ear.]

muff¹ (mŭf) *v.* **muffed, muff·ing, muffs.** *—tr.* **1.** To perform or handle clumsily; bungle. See Synonyms at **botch. 2.** *Sports.* To fail to make (a catch). *—intr.* To perform an act clumsily. **—muff** *n.* **1.** A clumsy or bungled action. **2.** *Sports.* A failure to make a catch. [Origin unknown.]

muff² (mŭf) *n.* **1.** A small cylindrical fur or cloth cover, open at both ends, in which the hands are placed for warmth. **2.** A cluster of feathers on the side of the face of certain breeds of fowl. [Dutch *mof,* from Middle Dutch *moffel,* from Old French *moufle,* mitten, from Medieval Latin *muffula,* perhaps of Germanic origin.]

muf·fin (mŭf′ĭn) *n.* **1.** A small, cup-shaped quick bread, often sweetened and usually served warm. **2.** An English muffin. [Possibly from Low German *Muffen,* pl. of *Muffe,* small cake, from Middle Low German.]

muffin pan *n.* A baking pan in the form of connected cup-shaped molds, used in making muffins and cupcakes.

muf·fle¹ (mŭf′əl) *tr.v.* **-fled, -fling, -fles. 1.** To wrap up, as in a blanket or shawl, for warmth, protection, or secrecy. **a.** To wrap or pad in order to deaden the sound: *muffled the drums.* **b.** To deaden (a sound): *The sand muffled the hoofbeats.* **2.** To make vague or obscure: *"His message was so muffled by learning and 'artiness'"* (Walter Blair). **3.** To repress; stifle. **—muffle** *n.* **1.** Something that muffles. **2.** A kiln or part of a kiln in which pottery can be fired without being exposed to direct flame. [Middle English *muflen,* possibly from Old French *mofler,* to stuff, from *mofle,* glove. See MUFF².]

muf·fle² (mŭf′əl) *n.* The fleshy, hairless snout of certain mammals, such as ruminants. [French *mufle,* perhaps blend of *moufle,* chubby face (from Old French; see MUFF²) and *museau,* muzzle (from Old French *musel;* see MUZZLE).]

muf·fler (mŭf′lər) *n.* **1.** A heavy scarf worn around the neck for warmth. **2.** A device that absorbs noise, especially one used with an internal-combustion engine.

♦**muf·fu·let·ta** (mo͞o′fə-lĕt′ə) *n. New Orleans.* A sandwich made with a large round roll of Italian bread split in half and filled with layers of hard salami, ham, provolone, and olive salad. [Italian dialectal, bread with a filling, from Italian *muffa,* mold, probably of Germanic origin.]

♦ ***REGIONAL NOTE:*** The New Orleans *muffeletta* is one of the few large American sandwiches not made with a long crusty roll. Instead, it is made by filling a round loaf of Italian bread with layers of hard salami, ham, provolone, and olive salad. The shape of the bread and the presence of the olive salad distinguishes the muffuletta from the *submarine sandwich.* Marian Burros of the *New York Times* traces the creation of the muffuletta to Salvatore Lupa's Central Grocery in New Orleans in 1910. The sandwich was a favorite lunch for farmers on their trips into town.

---

muf·ti¹ (mŭf′tē, mo͝of′-) *n., pl.* **-tis.** A Moslem scholar who interprets the shari'a. [Arabic *muftī,* from *'aftā,* to decide by legal opinion.]

muf·ti² (mŭf′tē) *n., pl.* **-tis.** Civilian dress, especially when worn by one who normally wears a uniform. [Probably from MUFTI¹.]

mug¹ (mŭg) *n.* **1.** A heavy cylindrical drinking cup usually having a handle. **2.** The amount that such a cup can hold. [Perhaps of Scandinavian origin.]

mug² (mŭg) *n.* **1.** *Informal.* **a.** The human face. See Synonyms at **face. b.** The area of the human mouth, chin, and jaw. **c.** A grimace. **d.** A mug shot. **2.** A thug; a hoodlum. **3.** *Chiefly Brit-*

ish. A victim or dupe. **—mug** *v.* **mugged, mug·ging, mugs.** *—tr.* **1.** *Informal.* To photograph (a person's face) for police files. **2.** To threaten or assault (a person) with the intent to rob. *—intr.* To make exaggerated facial expressions, especially for humorous effect. [Probably from MUG[1] (possibly in allusion to mugs decorated with grotesque faces).]

WORD HISTORY: Various senses of the term *mug* illustrate uses and abuses of the human face. One use to which the face was put in the 18th century was as a form of decoration for cups or mugs. It is probably from these grotesque and striking faces that *mug* came to mean "face," the word in this sense being first recorded in 1708. The next recorded development of *mug* is its use as a verb in 1818 in the sense "to strike in the face." This verb has developed the sense "to attack and rob," all too familiar to urban dwellers. The face's role in conveying emotion explains the development of the verb sense "to make faces, grimace," recorded first in 1855. Another sense of the noun, "photograph or portrait of the face," found earliest in 1887, is an obvious development, although it is ironic that those who mug criminally end up in a mug book. The use of the face to express affection explains the sense "to kiss, fondle," recorded first in Australia in 1890.

Mu·ga·be (mo͝o-gä′bē), **Robert Gabriel.** Born 1924. Zimbabwean politician who led the Black nationalist struggle against the white minority government of Rhodesia. After Zimbabwe's independence (1980), he was elected prime minister.

mug·ger[1] (mŭg′ər) *n.* **1.** One who commits a mugging. **2.** One who makes exaggerated faces, as in performing.

mug·ger[2] (mŭg′ər) *n.* A large crocodile *(Crocodilus palustris)* of southwest Asia, having a very broad wrinkled snout. [Hindi *magar,* from Sanskrit *makaraḥ,* crocodile, of Dravidian origin.]

mug·ging (mŭg′ĭng) *n.* An assault upon a person especially with the intent to rob.

mug·gy (mŭg′ē) *adj.* **-gi·er, -gi·est.** Warm and extremely humid. [Probably from Middle English *mugen,* to drizzle; akin to Old Norse *mugga,* a drizzle.] **—mug′gi·ness** *n.*

mu·gho pine or **mu·go pine** (myo͞o′gō, mo͞o′-) *n.* A shrubby, prostrate European pine *(Pinus mugo)* widely cultivated as an ornamental. [French, from Italian *mugo.*]

mug shot *n. Informal.* A photograph of a person's face, especially one made for police files.

mug·wump (mŭg′wŭmp′) *n.* **1.** A person who acts independently or remains neutral, as in politics. **2.** Often **Mugwump.** A Republican who bolted the party in 1884, refusing to support presidential candidate James G. Blaine. [Massachusett *mugguomp, mummugguomp,* war leader.] **—mug′wump′er·y** *n.*

Mu·ham·mad (mo͝o-hăm′ĭd, -hä′mĭd). See **Mohammed.**

Muhammad, Elijah. 1897–1975. American activist and leader of the Black Muslims (1934–1975) who favored political, social, and economic independence for Black Americans.

Mu·ham·mad·an or **Mu·ham·med·an** (mo͝o-hăm′ĭ-dən) *adj. & n.* Variants of **Mohammedan.**

Mu·ham·mad·an·ism (mo͝o-hăm′ĭ-də-nĭz′əm) *n.* Variant of **Mohammedanism.**

Mu·har·ram (mo͞o-hăr′əm) also **Mo·har·ram** (mō-) or **Mu·har·rum** (mo͞o-) *n.* **1.** The first month of the Moslem calendar. See table at **calendar. 2.** A Shiite festival held during the first ten days of this month. [Arabic *Muḥarram,* from past participle of *ḥarrama,* to forbid.]

Muir (myo͝or), **John.** 1838–1914. British-born American naturalist who promoted the creation of national parks.

mu·ja·hi·deen also **mu·ja·he·deen** or **mu·ja·hi·din** (mo͞o-jä′hĕ-dēn′) *pl.n.* Moslem guerrilla warriors engaged in a jihad: *"As a fighting force, the mujahideen still retain a grim determination to pursue their jihad (holy war) against the invaders from the north"* (Edward Girardet). [Arabic or Persian *mujāhidīn,* pl. of *mujāhid,* one who fights in a jihad, from *jihād,* jihad.]

mu·jik (mo͞o-zhēk′, -zhĭk′) *n.* Variant of **muzhik.**

Muk·den (mo͝ok′dən, -dĕn′, mo͝ok′-). See **Shenyang.**

muk·luk (mŭk′lŭk′) *n.* **1.** A soft boot made of reindeer skin or sealskin and worn by Eskimos. **2.** A slipper with a soft sole resembling this boot. [Yupik Eskimo *maklak,* bearded seal.]

mu·lat·to (mo͝o-lăt′ō, -lä′tō, myo͞o-) *n., pl.* **-tos** or **-toes. 1.** A person having one white and one Black parent. **2.** A person of mixed white and Black ancestry. [Spanish, from Arabic *muwallad,* person of mixed race, from *walada,* to engender, give birth.]

mul·ber·ry (mŭl′bĕr′ē, -bə-rē) *n.* **1. a.** Any of several deciduous trees of the genus *Morus,* having unisexual flowers in drooping catkins and edible multiple fruit. **b.** The sweet fruit of any of these trees. **2.** Any of several similar or related trees. **3.** *Color.* A grayish to dark purple. In this sense, also called *murrey.* [Middle English *mulberrie,* from Old English *mōrberie* and Middle Low German *mūlberi, mūrberi* : both from Latin *mōrum* + Old English *berie,* berry or Old High German *beri,* berry; see **bhā-[1]** in Appendix.] **—mul′ber′ry** *adj.*

mulch (mŭlch) *n.* A protective covering, usually of organic matter such as leaves, straw, or peat, placed around plants to prevent the evaporation of moisture, the freezing of roots, and the growth of weeds. **—mulch** *tr.v.* **mulched, mulch·ing, mulch·es.** To cover or surround with mulch. [Probably from Middle English *melsche, molsh,* soft, from Old English *melsc,* mellow, mild. See **mel-[1]** in Appendix.]

mulct (mŭlkt) *n.* A penalty such as a fine. **—mulct** *tr.v.* **mulct·ed, mulct·ing, mulcts. 1.** To penalize by fining or demanding forfeiture. **2.** To acquire by trickery or deception. **3.** To defraud or swindle. [From Middle English *multen,* to fine, from Latin *multāre, mulctāre,* from *mulcta,* fine.]

mule[1] (myo͞ol) *n.* **1.** The sterile hybrid offspring of a male donkey and a female horse, characterized by long ears and a short mane. **2.** A sterile hybrid, as between a canary and other birds or between certain plants. **3.** *Informal.* A stubborn person. **4.** A spinning machine that makes thread or yarn from fibers. **5.** A small, usually electric tractor or locomotive used for hauling over short distances. **6.** *Slang.* A person who serves as a courier of illegal drugs. [Middle English, from Old French *mul* and from Old English *mūl,* both from Latin *mūlus.*]

mule[1]

mule[2] (myo͞ol) *n.* A slipper that has no counter or strap to fit around the heel. [Probably French, slipper, possibly from Middle Dutch *muil,* ultimately from Latin *mulleus (calceus),* reddish-purple (ceremonial shoe).]

mule deer *n.* A brownish-gray deer *(Odocoileus hemionus)* of western North America, having long mulelike ears, large branching antlers in the male, and a black-tipped tail. Also called *black-tailed deer.*

mule·skin·ner (myo͞ol′skĭn′ər) *n. Informal.* A driver of mules.

mu·le·ta (mo͞o-lā′tə, -lĕt′ə) *n.* A short red cape suspended from a hollow staff, used by a matador to maneuver a bull during the final passes before a kill. [Spanish, small mule, crutch, muleta, diminutive of *mula,* she-mule, from Latin *mūla,* feminine of *mūlus,* mule.]

mu·le·teer (myo͞o′lə-tîr′) *n.* A driver of mules. [French *muletier,* from Old French, from *mulet,* diminutive of *mul,* mule. See MULE[1].]

mu·ley (myo͞o′lē, mo͞ol′ē, mo͞o′lē) *adj.* Having no horns: *muley cattle.* **—muley** *n., pl.* **-leys.** An animal without horns, especially a cow. [From Irish Gaelic *maol* (from Old Irish *mael*) or from Welsh *moel,* bald, hornless.]

Mul·ha·cén (mo͞o′lä-sän′, -thĕn′). A mountain, 3,480.4 m (11,411 ft) high, of southern Spain in the Sierra Nevada east of Granada. It is the highest point in the country.

Mül·heim (mo͞ol′hīm, myo͞ol′-, mül′-). A city of west-central Germany on the Ruhr River east of Duisburg. First mentioned in 1093, it passed to Prussia in 1815. Population, 173,190.

Mul·house (mə-lo͞oz′, mü-). A city of northeast France south of Colmar. Dating from at least 803, it became a free imperial city in 1308, allied itself with the Swiss from the 15th to the 18th century, and in 1798 voted to join France. Population, 112,157.

mu·li·eb·ri·ty (myo͞o′lē-ĕb′rĭ-tē) *n.* **1.** The state of being a woman. **2.** Femininity. [Latin *muliēbritās,* state of womanhood (as against maidenhood), from *muliēbris,* womanly, from *mulier,* woman.]

mul·ish (myo͞o′lĭsh) *adj.* Stubborn and intractable; recalcitrant. See Synonyms at **obstinate. —mul′ish·ly** *adv.* **—mul′ish·ness** *n.*

mull[1] (mŭl) *tr.v.* **mulled, mull·ing, mulls.** To heat and spice (wine, for example). [Origin unknown.]

mull[2] (mŭl) *v.* **mulled, -ing, mulls.** *—tr.* To go over extensively in the mind; ponder. *—intr.* To ruminate; ponder: *mull over a plan.* See Synonyms at **ponder.** [Probably Middle English *mullen,* to moisten, crumble. See MOIL.]

mull[3] (mŭl) *n.* A soft, thin muslin used in dresses and for trimmings. [Short for *mulmull,* from Hindi *malmal.*]

Mull (mŭl). An island of western Scotland in the Inner Hebrides. It is the largest island of the group and is separated from the mainland on the northeast by the **Sound of Mull.**

mul·lah also **mul·la** (mŭl′ə, mo͝ol′ə) *n. Islam.* **1.** A male religious teacher or leader. **2.** Used as a form of address for such a man. [Urdu *mullā,* from Persian, from Arabic *mawlā,* master.] **—mul′lah·ism** *n.*

mul·lein (mŭl′ən) *n.* Any of various Eurasian plants of the genus *Verbascum,* especially *V. thapsus,* a tall plant having closely clustered yellow flowers and leaves covered with dense, woolly down. Also called *flannel leaf, velvet plant.* [Middle English *moleine,* from Anglo-Norman, probably from *mol,* soft, from Latin *mollis.* See MOUILLÉ.]

mullein pink *n.* See **rose campion.**

mul·ler (mŭl′ər) *n.* An implement of stone or other hard substance used as a pestle to grind paints or drugs. [Middle English *molour,* probably from *mullen,* to grind. See MULL[2].]

Mul·ler (mŭl′ər), **Hermann Joseph.** 1890–1967. American geneticist. He won a 1946 Nobel Prize for the study of the hereditary effect of x-rays on genes.

Mül·ler (mŭl′ər, myo͞o′lər, mü′-), **(Friedrich) Max.** 1823–1900. German-born British philologist and Orientalist noted for his studies of Sanskrit language and literature.

Müller, Johann. Known as **Re·gi·o·mon·ta·nus** (rē′jē-ō-mŏn-tā′nəs, -tä′-, rĕj′ē-). 1436–1476. German mathematician and astronomer who established the study of algebra and trigonometry in Germany and contributed to the revival of astronomy during the Renaissance.

Müller, Karl Alex. Born 1927. Swiss physicist. He shared a 1987 Nobel Prize for pioneering research in superconductivity.

Mül·le·ri·an mimicry (myo͞o-lîr′ē-ən, mə-, mĭ-) *n.* A form of protective mimicry in which two or more distasteful or harmful

ă pat	oi boy
ā pay	ou out
âr care	o͝o took
ä father	o͞o boot
ĕ pet	ŭ cut
ē be	ûr urge
ĭ pit	th thin
ī pie	*th* this
îr pier	hw which
ŏ pot	zh vision
ō toe	ə about, item
ô paw	♦ regionalism

Stress marks: ′ (primary); ′ (secondary), as in **dictionary** (dĭk′shə-nĕr′ē)

species, especially of insects, closely resemble each other and are therefore avoided equally by all their natural predators. [After Fritz (Johann Friedrich Theodor) *Müller* (1821–1897), German-born Brazilian zoologist.]

mul·let (mŭl′ĭt) *n., pl.* **mullet** or **-lets. 1.** Any of various stout-bodied, edible fishes of the family Mugilidae, found worldwide in tropical and temperate coastal waters and some freshwater streams. Also called *gray mullet.* **2.** The red mullet. [Middle English *molet,* from Medieval Latin *mulettus,* probably from Old French *mulet,* from *mul,* from Latin *mullus,* from Greek *mullos.*]

mul·li·gan (mŭl′ĭ-gən) *n. Sports.* A golf shot not tallied against the score, granted in informal play after a poor shot especially from the tee. [Probably from the name *Mulligan.*]

mulligan stew *n.* A stew made of bits of various meats and vegetables. [Probably from the name *Mulligan.*]

mul·li·ga·taw·ny (mŭl′ĭ-gə-tô′nē) *n., pl.* **-nies.** An East Indian soup having a meat or chicken base and curry seasoning. [Tamil *miḷagutaṇṇī* : *miḷagu,* pepper + *taṇṇīr,* cool water (*taṇ,* cool + *nīr,* water).]

Mul·li·kan (mŭl′ĭ-kən), **Robert Sanderson.** 1896–1986. American chemist and physicist. He won a 1966 Nobel Prize for research on the bond between atoms in a molecule.

mul·lion (mŭl′yən) *n.* A vertical strip dividing the panes of a window. [Alteration of Middle English *moniel,* from Anglo-Norman *moynel,* perhaps from *moienel,* middle, from *moien,* from Latin *mediānus,* from *medius.* See **medhyo-** in Appendix.] **—mul′lioned** *adj.*

Mul·ro·ney (mŭl-rō′nē, -ro͞o′-), **(Martin) Brian.** Born 1939. Canadian politician who was elected prime minister in 1984.

Mul·tan (mo͞ol-tän′). A city of east-central Pakistan southwest of Lahore. Conquered c. 326 B.C. by Alexander the Great, it was captured by Tamerlane in 1398 and was under British jurisdiction from 1849 until 1947. Population, 694,000.

multi– *pref.* **1.** Many; much; multiple: *multicolor.* **2.a.** More than one: *multiparous.* **b.** More than two: *multilateral.* [Middle English, from Old French, from Latin, from *multus,* much, many. See **mel-**[2] in Appendix.]

mul·ti·ad·dress (mŭl′tē-ăd′rĕs′, -tī-) *adj. Computer Science.* Of, relating to, or designating a storage system of data-processing computers in which it is possible to store instructions or quantities in more than one position.

mul·ti·cel·lu·lar (mŭl′tē-sĕl′yə-lər, -tī-) *adj.* Having or consisting of many cells: *multicellular organisms.* **—mul′ti·cel′lu·lar′i·ty** (-lăr′ĭ-tē) *n.*

mul·ti·col·or (mŭl′tĭ-kŭl′ər) also **mul·ti·col·ored** (-kŭl′-ərd) *adj.* **1.** Having many colors. **2.** *Printing.* Capable of printing in two or more colors simultaneously.

mul·ti·cul·tur·al (mŭl′tē-kŭl′chər-əl, -tī-) *adj.* Of, relating to, or including several cultures.

mul·ti·den·tate (mŭl′tĭ-dĕn′tāt) *adj.* Having many teeth or toothlike processes.

mul·ti·di·men·sion·al (mŭl′tĭ-dĭ-mĕn′shə-nəl) *adj.* Of, relating to, or having several dimensions. **—mul′ti·di·men′sion·al′i·ty** (-shə-năl′ĭ-tē) *n.*

mul·ti·di·rec·tion·al (mŭl′tē-dĭ-rĕk′shə-nəl, -dī-, -tī-) *adj.* **1.** Reaching out in several directions: *a multidirectional campaign.* **2.** Operating or functioning in more than one direction: *a multidirectional television antenna; multidirectional stereo speakers.*

mul·ti·dis·ci·pli·nar·y (mŭl′tē-dĭs′ə-plə-nĕr′ē, -tī-) *adj.* Of, relating to, or making use of several disciplines at once: *a multidisciplinary approach to teaching.*

mul·ti·eth·nic (mŭl′tē-ĕth′nĭk, -tī-) *adj.* Of, relating to, or including several ethnic groups.

mul·ti·fac·et·ed (mŭl′tē-făs′ĭ-tĭd, -tī-) *adj.* Having many facets or aspects. See Synonyms at **versatile.**

mul·ti·fac·to·ri·al (mŭl′tĭ-făk-tôr′ē-əl, -tōr′-) *adj.* Involving, dependent on, or controlled by several factors. **—mul′ti·fac·tor′i·al·ly** *adv.*

mul·ti·fam·i·ly (mŭl′tē-făm′ə-lē, -tī-) *adj.* Of, relating to, or intended for use by several families: *a multifamily house.*

mul·ti·far·i·ous (mŭl′tə-fâr′ē-əs) *adj.* Having great variety; diverse. See Synonyms at **versatile.** [From Latin *multifāriam,* in many places : *multi-,* multi- + *-fāriam,* adv. suff.; see **dhē-** in Appendix.] **—mul′ti·far′i·ous·ly** *adv.* **—mul′ti·far′i·ous·ness** *n.*

mul·ti·fid (mŭl′tə-fĭd′) *adj. Biology.* Having many clefts forming lobes: *multifid leaves.*

mul·ti·flo·ra rose (mŭl′tə-flôr′ə, -flōr′ə) *n.* A climbing or sprawling shrub *(Rosa multiflora)* of eastern Asia, having clusters of small fragrant flowers. It is the origin of many horticultural varieties. [Partial translation of New Latin *Rosa multiflōra,* species name : Latin *rosa,* rose + Late Latin *multiflōra,* feminine of *multiflōrus,* multiflorous (Latin *multi-,* multi- + Latin *flōs, flōr-,* flower; see FLORA).]

mul·ti·flo·rous (mŭl′tə-flôr′əs, -flōr′-) *adj. Botany.* Bearing many flowers.

mul·ti·foil (mŭl′tə-foil′) *n. Architecture.* A flat object or opening with scalloped edges or ornaments.

mul·ti·fold (mŭl′tə-fōld′) *adj.* Numerous and varied; manifold.

mul·ti·form (mŭl′tə-fôrm′) *adj.* Occurring in or having many forms or shapes. **—mul′ti·for′mi·ty** (-fôr′mĭ-tē) *n.*

mul·ti·gen·er·a·tion·al (mŭl′tĭ-jĕn′ə-rā′shə-nəl) *adj.* Of or relating to several generations: *multigenerational traditions.*

mul·ti·grav·i·da (mŭl′tĭ-grăv′ĭ-də) *n.* A woman who has had two or more previous pregnancies. [MULTI– + *primigravida* (Latin *prīmus,* first; see PRIME + Latin *gravida,* feminine of *gravidus,* pregnant; see GRAVID).]

mul·ti·lane (mŭl′tē-lān′, -tī-) *adj.* Having several lanes: *a multilane highway.*

mul·ti·lat·er·al (mŭl′tĭ-lăt′ər-əl) *adj.* **1.** Having many sides. **2.** Involving more than two nations or parties: *multilateral trade agreements.* **—mul′ti·lat′er·al·ly** *adv.*

mul·ti·lay·ered (mŭl′tē-lā′ərd, -tī-) *adj.* Consisting of or involving several individual layers or levels.

mul·ti·lev·el (mŭl′tə-lĕv′əl) *adj.* Having several levels: *a multilevel parking garage.*

mul·ti·lin·gual (mŭl′tē-lĭng′gwəl, -tī-) *adj.* **1.** Of, including, or expressed in several languages: *a multilingual dictionary.* **2.** Using or having the ability to use several languages: *a multilingual translator.* **—mul′ti·lin′gual·ism** *n.*

mul·ti·loc·u·lar (mŭl′tĭ-lŏk′yə-lər) *adj.* Having or consisting of many small compartments or cavities.

mul·ti·me·di·a (mŭl′tē-mē′dē-ə, -tī-) *pl.n. (used with a sing. verb).* **1.** The combined use of several media, such as movies, slides, music, and lighting, especially for the purpose of education or entertainment. **2.** The use of several mass media, such as television, radio, and print, especially for the purpose of advertising or publicity. Also called *mixed media.* —*attributive.* Often used to modify another noun: *a multimedia presentation; a multimedia advertising campaign.*

mul·ti·mil·lion·aire (mŭl′tē-mĭl′yə-nâr′, -tī-) *n.* One whose financial assets are worth several million dollars.

mul·ti·na·tion·al (mŭl′tē-năsh′ə-nəl, -năsh′nəl, -tī-) *adj.* **1.** Having operations, subsidiaries, or investments in more than two countries: *a multinational corporation.* **2.** Of or involving more than two countries: *a multinational research project.* **—multinational** *n.* A company or corporation operating in more than two countries. **—mul′ti·na′tion·al·ism** *n.*

mul·ti·no·mi·al (mŭl′tĭ-nō′mē-əl) *n. Mathematics.* See **polynomial** (sense 2a). [MULTI– + (BI)NOMIAL.] **—mul′ti·no′mi·al** *adj.*

multinomial theorem *n. Mathematics.* The theorem that establishes the rule for forming the terms of a polynomial expansion.

mul·ti·nu·cle·ar (mŭl′tē-no͞o′klē-ər, -nyo͞o′-, -tī-) *adj.* Multinucleate.

mul·ti·nu·cle·ate (mŭl′tē-no͞o′klē-ət, -nyo͞o′-, -tī-) also **mul·ti·nu·cle·at·ed** (-ā′tĭd) *adj.* Having two or more nuclei: *the multinucleate cells of striated muscle.*

mul·ti·pack (mŭl′tĭ-păk′) *n.* A packaged product containing more than two items.

mul·tip·a·ra (mŭl-tĭp′ər-ə) *n., pl.* **-ras -rae** (-rē). A woman who has given birth two or more times.

mul·tip·a·rous (mŭl-tĭp′ər-əs) *adj.* **1.** Having given birth two or more times. **2.** Giving birth to more than one offspring at a time. **—mul′ti·par′i·ty** (mŭl′tĭ-păr′ĭ-tē) *n.*

mul·ti·par·tite (mŭl′tĭ-pär′tīt′) *adj.* **1.** Divided into many parts. **2.** Involving more than two nations or parties; multilateral.

mul·ti·par·ty (mŭl′tə-pär′tē) *adj.* Of, relating to, or involving more than two political parties.

mul·ti·ped (mŭl′tə-pĕd′) also **mul·ti·pede** (-pēd′) —*adj.* Having many feet. —*n.* An animal with many feet.

mul·ti·ple (mŭl′tə-pəl) *adj.* Having, relating to, or consisting of more than one individual, element, part, or other component; manifold. **—multiple** *n. Mathematics.* A number that may be divided by another number with no remainder: *4, 6, and 12 are multiples of 2.* [French, from Old French, from Late Latin *multiplum,* a multiple : Latin *multi-,* multi- + Latin *-plus,* -fold; see **pel-**[2] in Appendix.]

multiple allele *n.* Any of a set of three or more alleles, or alternative states of a gene, only two of which can be present in a diploid organism.

mul·ti·ple-choice (mŭl′tə-pəl-chois′) *adj.* **1.** Offering several answers from which the correct one is to be chosen: *a multiple-choice question.* **2.** Consisting of questions of this type: *a multiple-choice test.*

multiple factor *n.* See **polygene.**

multiple fruit *n.* A fruit, such as a fig, mulberry, or pineapple, derived from several flowers that are combined into a single structure.

multiple myeloma *n.* A malignant proliferation of plasma cells in bone marrow causing numerous tumors and characterized by the presence of abnormal proteins in the blood.

multiple neuritis *n.* Inflammation of several nerves at one time, as in leprosy. Also called *polyneuritis.*

multiple personality *n.* A psychological disorder, sometimes occurring as a symptom of schizophrenia, in which a person exhibits two or more disassociated personalities, each functioning as a distinct entity. Also called *split personality.*

multiple sclerosis *n. Abbr.* **MS** A chronic degenerative disease of the central nervous system in which gradual destruction of myelin occurs in patches throughout the brain or spinal cord or both, interfering with the nerve pathways and causing muscular weakness, loss of coordination, and speech and visual disturbances. It occurs chiefly in young adults and is thought to be caused by a defect in the immune system that may be of genetic or viral origin.

multiple star *n.* A group of three or more stars, usually with a common gravitational center, that appear as one to the unaided eye.

multiple store *n. Chiefly British.* A chain store.

mul·ti·plet (mŭl′tə-plĕt′, -plĭt) *n. Physics.* **1.** A spectral line having more than one component, representing slight variations in the energy states characteristic of an atom. **2.** Any of several classes or groupings of subatomic particles, such as the nucleon, that are similar in most properties but different in electric charge. [MULTIPL(E) + (DOUBL)ET.]

mul·ti·plex (mŭl′tə-plĕks′) *adj.* **1.** Relating to, having, or consisting of multiple elements or parts: *"the whole complex and multiplex detail of the noble science of dinner"* (Thomas Love Peacock). **2.** Relating to being a system of simultaneous communication of two or more messages on the same wire or radio channel. **—multiplex** *n.* A building, especially a movie theater or dwelling, with multiple separate units. **—multiplex** *v.* **-plexed, -plex·ing, -plex·es.** *—intr.* To send messages or signals simultaneously using a multiplex system. *—tr.* To send simultaneously using a multiplex system. [Middle English, a multiple, from Latin, various, complicated : *multi-,* multi- + *-plex,* -fold; see **plek-** in Appendix.]

mul·ti·pli·a·ble (mŭl′tə-plī′ə-bəl) also **mul·ti·plic·a·ble** (-plĭk′ə-bəl) *adj.* That can be multiplied: *multipliable fractions.*

mul·ti·pli·cand (mŭl′tə-plĭ-kănd′) *n. Mathematics.* The number that is or is to be multiplied by another. In 8 × 32, the multiplicand is 32. [Latin *multiplicandum,* neuter gerundive of *multiplicāre,* to multiply. See MULTIPLY[1].]

mul·tip·li·cate (mŭl-tĭp′lĭ-kĭt) *adj.* **1.** Having more than one layer or fold, as some shells or leaves. **2.** Multiple. [Middle English, from Latin *multiplicātus,* past participle of *multiplicāre,* to multiply. See MULTIPLY[1].]

mul·ti·pli·ca·tion (mŭl′tə-plĭ-kā′shən) *n.* **1.** The act or process of multiplying or the condition of being multiplied. **2.** Propagation of plants and animals; procreation. **3.** *Mathematics.* **a.** The operation that, for integers, consists of adding a number (the multiplicand) to itself a certain number of times. The operation is extended to other real numbers according to the rules governing the multiplication of integers. **b.** Any of certain analogous operations involving expressions other than real numbers. **—mul′ti·pli·ca′tion·al** *adj.*

multiplication sign *n. Mathematics.* The sign used to indicate multiplication, a times sign (×) or a raised dot (•).

multiplication table *n. Mathematics.* A table, used as an aid in memorization, that lists the products of certain numbers multiplied together, typically the numbers 1 to 12.

mul·ti·pli·ca·tive (mŭl′tə-plĭk′ə-tĭv, mŭl′tə-plĭ-kā′tĭv) *adj.* **1.** Tending to multiply or capable of multiplying or increasing. **2.** Having to do with multiplication. **—mul′ti·pli′ca·tive·ly** *adv.*

multiplicative inverse *n. Mathematics.* See **inverse** (sense 2a).

mul·ti·plic·i·ty (mŭl′tə-plĭs′ĭ-tē) *n., pl.* **-ties. 1.** The state of being various or manifold: *the multiplicity of architectural styles on that street.* **2.** A large number: *a multiplicity of ideas.* [Middle English, from Old French *multiplicite,* from Late Latin *multiplicitās,* from *multiplex,* various. See MULTIPLEX.]

mul·ti·pli·er (mŭl′tə-plī′ər) *n.* **1.** One that multiplies: *This old house is becoming a multiplier of expenses.* **2.** *Mathematics.* The number by which another number is multiplied. In 8 × 32, the multiplier is 8. **3.** *Physics.* A device, such as a phototube, used to enhance or increase an effect.

mul·ti·ply[1] (mŭl′tə-plī′) *v.* **-plied, -ply·ing, -plies.** *—tr.* **1.** To increase the amount, number, or degree of. **2.** *Mathematics.* To perform multiplication on. *—intr.* **1.** To grow in amount, number, or degree. See Synonyms at **increase. 2.** To breed or propagate. **3.** *Mathematics.* To perform multiplication. [Middle English *multiplien,* from Old French *multiplier,* from Latin *multiplicāre,* from *multiplex,* multiplex. See MULTIPLEX.]

mul·ti·ply[2] (mŭl′tə-plē′) *adv.* In many or multiple ways.

mul·ti·po·lar (mŭl′tĭ-pō′lər) *adj.* Having or conceiving multiple centers of power or influence: *a multipolar world; a multipolar approach to foreign policy.*

mul·ti·port (mŭl′tĭ-pôrt′, -pōrt′) *adj.* Having, relating to, or being a system of multiple ports for injecting fuel separately into each cylinder of an engine.

mul·ti·pronged (mŭl′tĭ-prôngd′, -prŏngd′) *adj.* **1.** Having many prongs. **2.** Involving several different directions, aspects, or elements: *a multipronged attack; a multipronged tax bill.*

mul·ti·pur·pose (mŭl′tē-pûr′pəs, -tī-) *adj.* Designed or used for several purposes: *a multipurpose room; multipurpose software.*

mul·ti·ra·cial (mŭl′tē-rā′shəl, -tī-) *adj.* Made up of, involving, or acting on behalf of various races: *a multiracial society.*

mul·ti·ra·cial·ism (mŭl′tē-rā′shə-lĭz′əm, -tī-) *n.* Equality of political representation and social acceptance in a society made up of various races.

mul·ti·re·lig·ious (mŭl′tē-rĭ-lĭj′əs, -tī-) *adj.* Made up of, involving, or acting on behalf of various religions or religious groups.

mul·ti·screen (mŭl′tĭ-skrēn′) *adj.* Having or using several movie, slide, or video screens.

mul·ti·sense (mŭl′tĭ-sĕns′) *adj.* Having multiple meanings: *a multisense word.*

mul·ti·sen·so·ry (mŭl′tĭ-sĕn′sə-rē) *adj.* Relating to or involving several bodily senses: *multisensory methods of reading instruction.*

mul·ti·serv·ice (mŭl′tĭ-sûr′vĭs) *adj.* **1.** Offering or involving a variety of services: *a multiservice agency for the elderly.* **2.** Involving, relating to, or composed of members of various branches of the armed forces.

mul·ti·sport (mŭl′tĭ-spôrt′, -spōrt′) also **mul·ti·sports** (-spôrts′, -spōrts′) *adj. Sports.* **1.** Composed of, involving, or accommodating several sports: *a multisport competition; a multisport stadium.* **2.** Skilled in several sports: *a multisport athlete.*

mul·ti·stage (mŭl′tĭ-stāj′) *adj.* **1.** Functioning in more than one stage: *a multistage design project.* **2.** Relating to or composed of two or more propulsion units.

multistage rocket *n.* A rocket composed of two or more propulsion units that fire in succession. Also called *step rocket.*

mul·ti·state (mŭl′tĭ-stāt′) *adj.* Of, relating to, or involving several states: *a multistate environmental campaign.*

mul·ti·sto·ry (mŭl′tĭ-stôr′ē, -stōr′ē) also **mul·ti·sto·ried** (-stôr′ēd, -stōr′-) *adj.* Having several stories: *a multistory hotel.*

mul·ti·track (mŭl′tĭ-trăk′) *adj.* **1.** Having, using, or produced with multiple recording tracks: *a multitrack tape recorder.* **2.** Having several different aspects, elements, or functions: *multitrack negotiations; a multitrack business executive.* **3.** Having or using several schedules: *students in a multitrack program with staggered vacations.*

mul·ti·tude (mŭl′tĭ-to͞od′, -tyo͞od′) *n.* **1.** The condition or quality of being numerous. **2.** A very great number. **3.** The masses; the populace: *the concerns of the multitude.* [Middle English, from Old French, from Latin *multitūdō,* from *multus,* many. See **mel-[2]** in Appendix.]

SYNONYMS: *multitude, host, legion, army.* These nouns all denote a very great number of people or things. *Multitude* is the most general term: *a multitude of friends; a multitude of reasons. Host* and *legion* both stress impressively, sometimes countlessly large numbers: *a host of ideas; a legion of complaints. Army* emphasizes order and often purposeful association: *an army of mosquitoes; an army of firefighters.*

mul·ti·tu·di·nous (mŭl′tĭ-to͞od′n-əs, -tyo͞od′-) *adj.* **1.** Very numerous; existing in great numbers. **2.** Consisting of many parts. **3.** Populous; crowded. [From Latin *multitūdō, multitūdin-,* multitude. See MULTITUDE.] **—mul′ti·tu′di·nous·ly** *adv.* **—mul′ti·tud′in·ous·ness** *n.*

mul·ti·va·lent (mŭl′tĭ-vā′lənt, mŭl-tĭv′ə-lənt) *adj.* **1.** *Chemistry.* Polyvalent. **2.** *Genetics.* Of or relating to the association of three or more homologous chromosomes during the first division of meiosis. **3.** *Immunology.* Having several sites of attachment for an antibody or antigen. **4.** Having various meanings or values: *subtle, multivalent allegory.* **—mul′ti·va′lence** *n.*

mul·ti·ver·si·ty (mŭl′tĭ-vûr′sĭ-tē) *n., pl.* **-ties.** A university that has numerous constituent and affiliated institutions, such as separate colleges, campuses, and research centers. [MULTI– + (UNI)VERSITY.]

mul·ti·vi·ta·min (mŭl′tə-vī′tə-mĭn) *adj.* Containing many vitamins. **—multivitamin** *n.* A preparation containing many vitamins.

mul·ti·vol·tine (mŭl′tĭ-vōl′tēn) *adj.* Producing several broods in a single season: *multivoltine moths.* [MULTI– + French *-voltine,* having a given number of broods in one season (from Italian *volta,* time, turn, from Old Italian; see VOLT[2]).]

mum[1] (mŭm) *adj.* Not verbalizing; silent. **—mum** *interj.* Used as a command to stop speaking. ***—idiom.* mum's the word.** Say nothing of the secret you know: *Mum's the word on the surprise party.* [Middle English.]

mum[2] (mŭm) *intr.v.* **mummed, mum·ming, mums. 1.** To act or play in a pantomime. **2.** To go merrymaking in a mask or disguise especially during a festival. [Middle English *mummen,* from Old French *momer,* to wear a mask.]

mum[3] (mŭm) *n. Chiefly British.* Mother. [Short for MUMMY[2].]

mum[4] (mŭm) *n.* A chrysanthemum.

mum[5] (mŭm) *n.* A strong beer originally brewed in Brunswick, Germany. [German *Mumme.*]

mum·ble (mŭm′bəl) *v.* **-bled, -bling, -bles.** *—tr.* **1.** To utter indistinctly by lowering the voice or partially closing the mouth: *mumbled an insincere apology.* **2.** To chew slowly or ineffectively without or as if without teeth. *—intr.* **1.** To speak words indistinctly, as by lowering the voice or partially closing the mouth. **2.** To chew food slowly or ineffectively, as if with the gums. **—mumble** *n.* A low, indistinct sound or utterance. [Middle English *momelen,* from Middle Dutch *mommelen.*] **—mum′bler** *n.* **—mum′bly** *adj.*

mum·ble·ty-peg (mŭm′bəl-tē-pĕg′, mŭm′blē-pĕg′) also **mum·ble-the-peg** (mŭm′bəl-*th*ə-pĕg′) *n. Games.* A game in which players toss a jackknife in various prescribed ways, with

ă pat	oi boy
ā pay	ou out
âr care	o͝o took
ä father	o͞o boot
ĕ pet	ŭ cut
ē be	ûr urge
ĭ pit	th thin
ī pie	*th* this
îr pier	hw which
ŏ pot	zh vision
ō toe	ə about, item
ô paw	♦ regionalism

Stress marks: **′** (primary); ′ (secondary), as in **dictionary** (dĭk′shə-nĕr′ē)

mummer
Parading in Philadelphia

the object being to make the blade stick firmly into the ground. [From the phrase *mumble the peg,* from the fact that originally the loser had to pull up with his teeth a peg driven into the ground.]

mum·bo jum·bo or **mum·bo-jum·bo** (mŭm′bō-jŭm′bō) *n., pl.* **mum·bo jum·bos** or **mum·bo-jum·bos. 1.** Unintelligible or incomprehensible language; gibberish. **2.** Language or ritualistic activity intended to confuse. **3.** A complicated or obscure ritual. **4.** An object believed to have supernatural powers; a fetish. [Perhaps of Mandingo origin.]

mu meson *n. Physics.* See **muon.**

Mum·ford (mŭm′fərd), **Lewis.** 1895–1990. American social critic and writer whose works decry dehumanizing technology and call for a return to humanitarian and moral values.

mum·mer (mŭm′ər) *n.* **1.** A masked or costumed merrymaker, especially at a festival. **2.a.** One who acts or plays in a pantomime. **b.** An actor. [Middle English, from Old French *momeur,* from *momer,* to wear a mask, pantomime.]

mum·mer·y (mŭm′ə-rē) *n., pl.* **-ies. 1.** A performance by mummers. **2.** A pretentious or hypocritical show or ceremony. [French *mommerie,* from Old French *momer,* to wear a mask, pantomime.]

mum·mi·chog (mŭm′ĭ-chŏg′) *n.* A stout-bodied killifish *(Fundulus heteroclitus)* of the Atlantic coast south of the Gulf of St. Lawrence, valued especially as bait. [Narragansett *moamitteaūg.*]

mum·mi·fy (mŭm′ə-fī′) *v.* **-fied, -fy·ing, -fies.** —*tr.* **1.** To make into a mummy by embalming and drying. **2.** To cause to shrivel and dry up. —*intr.* To shrivel or dry up like a mummy. **—mum′mi·fi·ca′tion** (-fĭ-kā′shən) *n.*

mum·my[1] (mŭm′ē) *n., pl.* **-mies. 1.** The dead body of a human being or an animal that has been embalmed and prepared for burial, as according to the practices of the ancient Egyptians. **2.** A withered, shrunken, or well-preserved body that resembles an embalmed body. [Middle English *mummie,* medicinal material from embalmed corpses, from Old French *momie,* from Medieval Latin *mumia,* from Arabic *mūmiyā′,* from *mūm,* wax.]

mum·my[2] (mŭm′ē) *n., pl.* **-mies.** *Informal.* Mother. [Alteration of MAMMY.]

mumps (mŭmps) *pl.n. (used with a sing. or pl. verb).* An acute, inflammatory, contagious disease caused by a paramyxovirus and characterized by swelling of the salivary glands, especially the parotids, and sometimes of the pancreas, ovaries, or testes. This disease, mainly affecting children, can be prevented by vaccination. [From pl. of dialectal *mump,* grimace.]

munch (mŭnch) *v.* **munched, munch·ing, munch·es.** —*intr.* **1.** To chew food audibly or with a steady working of the jaws. **2.** To eat with pleasure. —*tr.* To chew or eat (food) audibly or with pleasure. [Middle English *monchen.*] **—munch′er** *n.*

Munch (mo͝ongk), **Edvard.** 1863–1944. Norwegian artist whose works include *The Scream* (1893) and *Frieze of Life* (1897).

Münch·hau·sen also **Mun·chau·sen** (mŭn′chou′zən, mŭnch′hou′-, mün**KH**′hou′-), Baron **Karl Friedrich Hieronymus von.** 1720–1797. German soldier and raconteur known for his fantastic stories about his adventures.

munch·ies (mŭn′chēz) *pl.n. Slang.* **1.** Food for snacking. **2.** A craving for snack foods. Often used with *the: an attack of the munchies.*

munch·kin (mŭnch′kĭn) *n.* **1.** A very small person, especially one with an elflike appearance. **2.** *Informal.* A child. **3.** *Informal.* A minor official. [After the *Munchkins,* characters in *The Wonderful Wizard of Oz* by L. Frank Baum.]

Edvard Munch
1895 self-portrait

Mun·cie (mŭn′sē). A city of east-central Indiana northeast of Indianapolis. Established on the site of an earlier Delaware settlement, it was the setting for Robert and Helen Lynd's pioneering sociological study *Middletown* (1929). Population, 77,216.

mun·dane (mŭn-dān′, mŭn′dān′) *adj.* **1.** Of, relating to, or typical of this world; secular. **2.** Relating to, characteristic of, or concerned with commonplaces. [Middle English *mondeine,* from Old French *mondain,* from Latin *mundānus,* from *mundus,* world.] **—mun·dane′ly** *adv.* **—mun·dane′ness** *n.*

Mun·de·lein (mŭn′dl-īn′). A village of northeast Illinois southwest of Waukegan. Population, 17,053.

mung bean (mŭng) *n.* **1.** An Asian plant *(Vigna radiata)* in the pea family, widely cultivated for its edible seeds and pods. It is the chief source of bean sprouts. **2.** The seeds or pods of this plant. [Hindi *mūg,* from Sanskrit *mudgaḥ.*]

mu·ni (myo͞o′nē) *Informal. adj.* Municipal. **—muni** *n., pl.* **-nis.** A municipal bond.

Mu·nich (myo͞o′nĭk). A city of southeast Germany near the Bavarian Alps southeast of Augsburg. Founded in 1158, it has long been the center of Bavaria. Adolf Hitler organized the Nazi Party here after World War I and signed the Munich Pact, widely regarded as a symbol of appeasement, with Great Britain, France, and Italy in 1938. The city was largely rebuilt after extensive Allied bombing in World War II. Population, 1,267,451.

mural

mu·nic·i·pal (myo͞o-nĭs′ə-pəl) *adj.* **1.a.** Of, relating to, or typical of a municipality. **b.** Having local self-government. **c.** Issued on the authority of a local or state government. **2.** Of or relating to the internal affairs of a nation. **—municipal** *n.* A municipal bond: *invested in tax-free municipals.* [Latin *mūnicipālis,* from *mūnicipium,* town, from *mūniceps,* citizen : *mūnus,* public office, duty; see **mei-**[1] in Appendix + *capere,* to take; see **kap-** in Appendix.] **—mu·nic′i·pal·ly** *adv.*

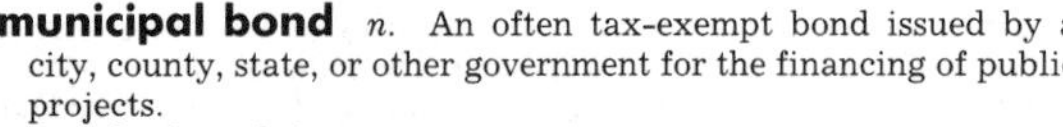

municipal bond *n.* An often tax-exempt bond issued by a city, county, state, or other government for the financing of public projects.

mu·nic·i·pal·i·ty (myo͞o-nĭs′ə-păl′ĭ-tē) *n., pl.* **-ties. 1.** A political unit, such as a city or town, incorporated for local self-government. **2.** A body of officials appointed to manage the affairs of a local political unit.

mu·nic·i·pal·ize (myo͞o-nĭs′ə-pə-līz′) *tr.v.* **-ized, -iz·ing, -iz·es. 1.** To place under municipal ownership. **2.** To make into a municipality. **—mu·nic′i·pal·i·za′tion** (-pə-lĭ-zā′shən) *n.*

mu·nif·i·cent (myo͞o-nĭf′ĭ-sənt) *adj.* **1.** Very liberal in giving; generous. **2.** Showing great generosity: *a munificent gift.* See Synonyms at **liberal.** [Latin *mūnificēns, mūnificent-,* from *mūnificus* : *mūnus,* gift; see **mei-**[1] in Appendix + *facere,* to make; see FACT.] **—mu·nif′i·cence** *n.* **—mu·nif′i·cent·ly** *adv.*

mu·ni·ment (myo͞o′nə-mənt) *n.* **1. muniments.** *Law.* Documentary evidence by which one can defend a title to property or a claim to rights. **2.** *Archaic.* A means of defense or protection. [Middle English, from Old French, from Medieval Latin *mūnīmentum,* from Latin, defense, protection, from *mūnīre,* to fortify.]

mu·ni·tion (myo͞o-nĭsh′ən) *n.* War materiel, especially weapons and ammunition. Often used in the plural. **—munition** *tr.v.* **-tioned, -tion·ing, -tions.** To supply with munitions. [Middle English *municion,* privilege supported by a document, from Old French, fortification, from Latin *mūnītiō, mūnītiōn-,* from *mūnītus,* past participle of *mūnīre,* to defend.]

Mu·ñoz Ma·rín (mo͞o-nyōs′ mä-rēn′), **Luis.** 1898–1980. Puerto Rican journalist and politician who served as the first elected governor of Puerto Rico (1948–1964).

Mun·ro (mən-rō′), **Alice.** Born 1931. Canadian writer noted for vivid novels and short stories of life in rural Ontario.

Munro, Hector Hugh. Pen name Saki. 1870–1916. British writer known for his witty and sometimes bitter short stories, published in collections such as *The Chronicles of Clovis* (1911).

Mun·see (mŭn′sē) *n.* **1.** One of the two Algonquian languages of the Delaware peoples, spoken in northern New Jersey, downstate New York, and western Long Island. **2.** A speaker of this language.

Mun·ster[1] (mŭn′stər). **1.** A historical region and province of southwest Ireland. It was one of the kingdoms of ancient Ireland. **2.** A town of northwest Indiana, a suburb of Gary on the Illinois border. Population, 20,671.

Mun·ster[2] (mŭn′stər, mo͝on′-) *n.* Variant of **Muenster.**

Mün·ster (mo͝on′stər, mŭn′-, mün′-). A city of west-central Germany north-northeast of Cologne. Founded c. 800 as a Carolingian episcopal see, it was a prominent member of the Hanseatic League after the 14th century. Population, 272,626.

mun·tin (mŭn′tən) *n.* A strip of wood or metal separating and holding panes of glass in a window. [Middle English *mountaunt,* upright post or stud, from Old French *montant,* from present participle of *monter,* to mount. See MOUNT[1].]

munt·jac also **munt·jak** (mŭnt′jăk′) *n.* Any of several small deer of the genus *Muntiacus* of southeast Asia and the East Indies. [Malay *mênjangan,* deer.]

mu·on (myo͞o′ŏn′) *n. Physics.* An elementary particle in the lepton family (not a meson), having a mass 209 times that of the electron, a negative electric charge, and a mean lifetime of 2.2 × 10^{-6} second. Also called *mu meson.* See table at **subatomic particle.** [Short for MU MESON.]

muon neutrino *n. Physics.* A stable elementary particle in the lepton family having a mass less than 0.49 times that of the electron and no charge. See table at **subatomic particle.**

mup·pie (mŭp′ē) *n. Informal.* A middle-aged or mature professional person, especially one considered to be affluent, ambitious, and trendy. [M(IDDLE-AGED) + (Y)UPPIE.]

Mur (mo͝or) also **Mu·ra** (mo͝or′ə). A river, about 483 km (300 mi) long, of south-central Austria and northern Yugoslavia flowing east, northeast, south, and southeast to the Drava River.

mu·ral (myo͝or′əl) *n.* A very large image, such as a painting or an enlarged photograph, applied directly to a wall or ceiling. **—mural** *adj.* **1.** Of, relating to, or resembling a wall. **2.** Painted on or applied to a wall. [Middle English, of a wall, from Old French, from Latin *mūrālis,* from *mūrus,* wall.] **—mu′ral·ist** *n.*

mu·raled also **mu·ralled** (myo͝or′əld) *adj.* Decorated with murals or a mural: *muraled halls.*

mu·ram·ic acid (myo͞o-răm′ĭk) *n.* An amino sugar, $C_9H_{17}NO_7$, found in the peptidoglycan layer of the cell walls of many bacteria. [Latin *mūrus,* wall + AM(IDE) + –IC.]

Mu·ra·sa·ki Shi·ki·bu (mo͞o′rä-sä′kē shē′kē-bo͞o′), Baroness. 978?–1031? Japanese writer whose masterpiece *The Tale of Genji* is considered to be the first full novel.

Mu·rat (myo͞o-rä′, mü-), **Joachim.** 1767?–1815. French marshal who aided Napoleon's coup d'état (1799) and was appointed king of Naples (1808).

Mur·chi·son River (mûr′chĭ-sən). An intermittent river of western Australia flowing about 708 km (440 mi) generally southwest to the Indian Ocean.

Mur·cia (mûr′shə, -shē-ə, mo͝or′thyä). **1.** A region and former kingdom of southeast Spain on the Mediterranean Sea. Settled by Carthaginians, it was conquered by the Moors in the 8th century and became an independent Moorish kingdom in the 11th century. **2.** A city of southeast Spain north-northwest of Cartagena. Originally a Roman settlement, it was the capital of the ancient kingdom of Murcia. Population, 200,300.

mur·der (mûr′dər) *n.* **1.** The unlawful killing of one human being by another, especially with premeditated malice. **2.** *Slang.* Something that is very uncomfortable, difficult, or hazardous: *The rush hour traffic is murder.* **—murder** *v.* **-dered, -der·ing, -ders.** *—tr.* **1.** To kill (another human being) unlawfully. **2.** To kill brutally or inhumanly. **3.** To put an end to; destroy: *murdered their chances.* **4.** To spoil by ineptness; mutilate: *a speech that murdered the English language.* **5.** *Slang.* To defeat decisively; trounce. *—intr.* To commit murder. ***—idioms.*** **get away with murder.** *Informal.* To escape punishment for or detection of an egregiously blameworthy act. **murder will out.** Secrets or misdeeds will eventually be disclosed. [Middle English *murther,* from Old English *morthor.* See **mer-** in Appendix.] **—mur′der·er** *n.* **—mur′der·ess** *n.*

mur·der·ous (mûr′dər-əs) *adj.* **1.** Capable of, guilty of, or intending murder: *a group of murderous thugs.* **2.** Characteristic of or giving rise to murder or bloodshed: *murderous mistrust.* **3.** *Informal.* Capable of devastating or overwhelming: *a murderous exam.* **—mur′der·ous·ly** *adv.* **—mur′der·ous·ness** *n.*

Mur·doch (mûr′dŏk′), **(Jean) Iris.** Born 1919. Irish-born writer whose novels include *The Sea, the Sea* (1978).

mu·re·in (myo͝or′ē-ĭn, myo͝or′ēn′) *n.* See **peptidoglycan.** [MUR(AMIC ACID) + –EIN.]

Mu·re·şul (mo͞or′ə-so͞ol′, mo͞o′rĕ-sho͞ol′) or **Mu·reş** (mo͞o′rĕsh). A river rising in the Carpathian Mountains of north-central Romania and flowing about 756 km (470 mi) generally westward into southern Hungary.

mu·rex (myo͝or′ĕks) *n., pl.* **mu·ri·ces** (myo͝or′ĭ-sēz′) or **mu·rex·es.** Any of various marine gastropods of the genus *Murex* common in tropical seas and having rough, spiny shells, especially *M. trunculus,* the source of Tyrian purple. [New Latin *Mūrex,* genus name, from Latin *mūrex,* purple-fish.]

Mur·frees·bor·o (mûr′frēz-bûr′ō, -bŭr′ō). A city of central Tennessee southeast of Nashville. The state capital from 1819 to 1825, it was the site of a hard-fought Union victory in the Battle of Murfreesboro (December 31, 1862–January 2, 1863). Population, 32,845.

Mur·gab also **Mur·ghab** (mo͝or-gäb′). A river rising in northeast Afghanistan and flowing about 853 km (530 mi) generally west and northwest to the Kara Kum Desert.

mu·ri·at·ic acid (myo͝or′ē-ăt′ĭk) *n.* Hydrochloric acid. [Latin *muriāticus,* pickled, from *muria,* brine.]

mu·ri·cate (myo͝or′ĭ-kāt′) also **mu·ri·cat·ed** (-kā′tĭd) *adj.* Covered with many short spines. [Latin *mūricātus,* shaped like a murex, pointed, from *mūrex,* murex.]

mu·ri·ces (myo͝or′ĭ-sēz′) *n.* A plural of **murex.**

Mu·ril·lo (myo͞o-rĭl′ō, mo͞o-rē′lyô), **Bartolomé Esteban.** 1617–1682. Spanish painter of genre scenes, portraits, and religious subjects, such as *Immaculate Conception* (1668).

mu·rine (myo͝or′īn′) *adj.* **1.** Of or relating to a member of the rodent family Muridae, including rats and mice. **2.** Caused, transmitted, or affected by rodents of the family Muridae: *a murine plague.* **—murine** *n.* A murine rodent. [Latin *mūrīnus,* of mice, from *mūs, mūr-,* mouse. See **mūs-** in Appendix.]

murine typhus *n.* A comparatively mild, acute, endemic form of typhus caused by the microorganism *Rickettsia typhi,* transmitted from rats to human beings by fleas and characterized by fever, headache, and muscular pain.

murk also **mirk** (mûrk) *—n.* Partial or total darkness; gloom. *—adj. Archaic.* Partially or totally dark; gloomy. [Middle English *mirke,* from Old Norse *myrkr* or Old English *mirce.*]

murk·y also **mirk·y** (mûr′kē) *adj.* **-i·er, -i·est. 1.** Dark, dim, or gloomy: *a murky dungeon.* See Synonyms at **dark. 2.a.** Heavy and thick with smoke, mist, or fog; hazy. **b.** Darkened or clouded with sediment: *murky waters.* **3.** Lacking clarity or distinctness; obscure. **—murk′i·ly** *adv.* **—murk′i·ness** *n.*

Mur·mansk (mo͝or-mänsk′, mo͝or′mənsk). A city of northwest Russia on the northern Kola Peninsula on an inlet of the Barents Sea. A major ice-free port, it was the terminus of an important supply line to the U.S.S.R. in World Wars I and II. Population, 419,000.

mur·mur (mûr′mər) *n.* **1.** A low, indistinct, continuous sound: *spoke in a murmur; the murmur of the waves.* **2.** An indistinct, whispered, or confidential complaint; a mutter. **3.** *Medicine.* An abnormal sound, usually emanating from the heart, that sometimes indicates a diseased condition. **—murmur** *v.* **-mured, -mur·ing, -murs.** *—intr.* **1.** To make a low, continuous, indistinct sound or succession of sounds. **2.** To complain in low mumbling tones; grumble. *—tr.* To say in a low indistinct voice; utter indistinctly: *murmured his approval.* [Middle English *murmure,* from Old French, from Latin *murmur,* a humming, roaring.] **—mur′mur·er** *n.* **—mur′mur·ing·ly** *adv.* **—mur′mur·ous** *adj.* **—mur′mur·ous·ly** *adv.*

Mu·rom (mo͝or′əm). A city of west-central Russia on the Oka River southwest of Gorky. One of the oldest cities in Russia, it was first mentioned in a chronicle of 862. Population, 121,000.

Mur·phy (mûr′fē) *n., pl.* **-phies.** *Slang.* **1.** Also **murphy.** A Murphy game. **2. murphy.** A potato. [From *Murphy,* a common Irish name.]

Murphy, William Francis. Known as "Frank." 1890–1949. American jurist who served as an associate justice of the U.S. Supreme Court (1940–1949).

Murphy bed *n.* A bed that folds or swings into a closet for concealment. [After William Lawrence *Murphy* (1876–1959), American inventor.]

Murphy game also **murphy game** *n. Slang.* Any of various confidence games often having the services of a prostitute as a lure and brought off by switching an envelope containing the victim's cash with one containing scrap paper.

Mur·phy's Law (mûr′fēz) *n.* Any of certain humorous axioms stating that anything that can possibly go wrong, will go wrong. [From the name *Murphy.*]

mur·rain (mûr′ĭn) *n.* **1.** Any of various highly infectious diseases of cattle, as anthrax. **2.** *Obsolete.* A pestilence or dire disease. [Middle English *moreine,* from Old French *morine,* from Medieval Latin *morina,* from Latin *morī,* to die. See **mer-** in Appendix.]

Mur·ray (mûr′ē). A city of northern Utah, an industrial suburb of Salt Lake City. Population, 25,750.

Murray, (George) Gilbert (Aimé). 1866–1957. Australian-born British classical scholar and pacifist noted for his verse translations of Greek dramas and for his advocacy of the League of Nations and the United Nations.

Murray, Sir **James Augustus Henry.** 1837–1915. British philologist and the original lexicographer (1879–1915) of the *Oxford English Dictionary.*

Murray, Lindley. 1745–1826. American grammarian who wrote several widely used schoolbooks, including *Grammar of the English Language* (1795).

Murray River. A river of southeast Australia rising in the Australian Alps and flowing about 2,589 km (1,609 mi) northwest then south to an arm of the Indian Ocean south of Adelaide.

murre (mûr) *n., pl.* **murre** or **murres.** Any of several large auks of the genus *Uria,* having black plumage and white markings. [Origin unknown.]

mur·rey (mûr′ē) *n. Color.* See **mulberry** (sense 3). [Middle English *murrei,* from Old French *more,* from Latin *mōrum,* mulberry, blackberry.] **—mur′rey** *adj.*

Mur·row (mûr′ō, mŭr′ō), **Edward R(oscoe).** 1908–1965. American broadcast journalist noted for his dramatic factual reports from London during World War II.

Mur·rum·bidg·ee (mûr′əm-bĭj′ē). A river of southeast Australia rising in the Australian Alps and flowing about 1,689 km (1,050 mi) westward to the Murray River.

Mur·rys·ville (mûr′ēz-vĭl′, mŭr′-). A borough of southwest Pennsylvania, a suburb of Pittsburgh. Population, 16,036.

mur·ther (mûr′*th*ər) *n. & v. Obsolete.* Variant of **murder.**

mus. *abbr.* **1.** Museum. **2.** Music; musical; musician.

Mus.B. *abbr. Latin.* Musicae Baccalaureus (Bachelor of Music).

Mus·ca (mŭs′kə) *n.* A constellation in the polar region of the Southern Hemisphere near Apus and Carina. [Latin *musca,* fly.]

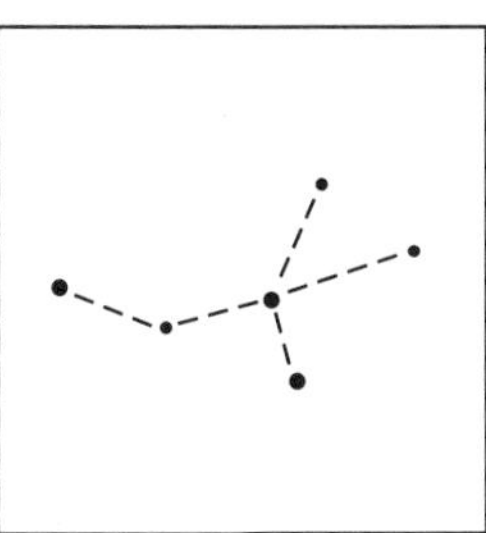

Musca

Mus·ca·det (mŭs′kə-dā′) *n.* A dry white wine made from grapes originating in the Loire River valley. [French, from Old French, from *musc,* musky odor. See MUSK.]

mus·ca·dine (mŭs′kə-dīn′, -dĭn) *n.* A woody vine *(Vitis rotundifolia)* of the southeast United States, bearing a musky grape used to make wine. Also called *scuppernong.* [Alteration of MUSCATEL.]

mus·ca·rine (mŭs′kə-rēn′) *n.* A highly toxic alkaloid, $C_9H_{20}NO_2$, related to the cholines, derived from the red form of the mushroom *Amanita muscaria* and found in decaying animal tissue. [New Latin *muscaria,* Amanita species (from Latin *muscārius,* of flies, from *musca,* fly) + –INE[2].] **—mus′ca·rin′ic** (-rĭn′ĭk) *adj.*

mus·cat (mŭs′kăt′, -kət) *n.* **1.** Any of various sweet white grapes used for making wine or raisins. **2.** Muscatel wine. [French, from Old French, from Old Provençal *muscat, from *musc,* musk, from Late Latin *muscus.* See MUSK.]

Mus·cat (mŭs′kăt′, -kət, mŭs-kăt′). The capital of Oman, in the northern part of the country on the Gulf of Oman. Held by Portugal from 1508 to 1648, it became the capital of Oman in 1741. Population, 30,000.

Muscat and O·man (ō-män′). See **Oman.**

mus·ca·tel (mŭs′kə-tĕl′) *n.* **1.** A rich, sweet wine made from muscat grapes. **2.** A muscat grape or raisin. [Middle English *muscadelle,* partly from Medieval Latin *muscātellum* (from *muscātus,* nutmeg, musky, from Late Latin *muscus,* musk; see MUSK) and partly from Old French *muscadel* (from Old Provençal, diminutive of *muscat, muscat. See MUSCAT).]

Mus·ca·tine (mŭs′kə-tēn′). A city of southeast Iowa on the Mississippi River west-southwest of Davenport. Founded in 1833, it grew as a river port and lumber center. Population, 23,467.

mus·cid (mŭs′ĭd) *n.* A fly of the family Muscidae, which includes the common housefly. **—muscid** *adj.* Of or belonging to the family Muscidae. [From New Latin *Muscidae,* family name, from *Musca,* type genus, from Latin *musca,* fly.]

mus·cle (mŭs′əl) *n.* **1.** A tissue composed of fibers capable of contracting to effect bodily movement. **2.** A contractile organ consisting of a special bundle of muscle tissue, which moves a particular bone, part, or substance of the body: *the heart muscle; the muscles of the arm.* **3.** Muscular strength: *enough muscle to be a high jumper.* **4.** *Informal.* Power or authority: *put some mus-*

ă pat	oi boy
ā pay	ou out
âr care	o͝o took
ä father	o͞o boot
ĕ pet	ŭ cut
ē be	ûr urge
ĭ pit	th thin
ī pie	*th* this
îr pier	hw which
ŏ pot	zh vision
ō toe	ə about, item
ô paw	♦ regionalism

Stress marks: ′ (primary); ′ (secondary), as in **dictionary** (dĭk′shə-nĕr′ē)

cle into law enforcement. —*intr.* **-cled, -cling, -cles.** *Informal.* To make one's way by or as if by force. [Middle English, from Old French, from Latin *mūsculus,* diminutive of *mūs,* mouse. See **mūs-** in Appendix.] —**mus′cly** *adj.*

mus·cle·bound also **mus·cle-bound** (mŭs′əl-bound′) *adj.* **1.** Having inelastic, overdeveloped muscles, usually as the result of excessive exercise. **2. a.** Hindered by or as if by overdeveloped muscles. **b.** Characterized by inflexibility; rigid.

muscle car *n.* A high-performance automobile, often with flashy, sporty styling.

muscle fiber *n.* A cylindrical, multinucleate cell composed of numerous myofibrils that contracts when stimulated.

mus·cle·man also **mus·cle man** (mŭs′əl-măn′) *n. Informal.* **1.** A man who is physically powerful, especially one with well-developed muscles. **2.** A strong man hired as a bodyguard or thug.

muscle spindle *n.* A stretch receptor in vertebrate muscle.

mus·co·vite (mŭs′kə-vīt′) *n.* A potassium aluminum silicate mineral, $KAl_2(AlSi_3O_{10})(OH)_2$, the most common form of mica, which ranges from colorless or pale yellow to gray and brown, has a pearly luster, and is used as an insulator. Also called *white mica.* [*Muscovy glass,* its former name + –ITE[1].]

Mus·co·vite (mŭs′kə-vīt′) *n.* A native or resident of Moscow or Muscovy. —**Muscovite** *adj.* Of or relating to Moscow, Muscovy, or the Muscovites.

Mus·co·vy (mŭs′kə-vē). A historical region and former principality in west-central Russia. Centered on Moscow, it was founded c. 1280 and existed as a separate entity until the 16th century, when it was united with another principality to form the nucleus of the early Russian empire. The name was then used for the expanded territory.

Muscovy duck *n.* A greenish-black, gooselike duck *(Cairina moschata),* having heavy red wattles and found wild from Mexico to northern Argentina but widely domesticated around the world for its succulent flesh. Also called *musk duck.* [Alteration (influenced by MUSCOVY) of *musk duck.*]

mus·cu·lar (mŭs′kyə-lər) *adj.* **1.** Of, relating to, or consisting of muscle: *muscular contraction.* **2.** Having well-developed muscles: *a muscular build.* **3.** Having or suggesting great power; forceful or vigorous. **4.** Having or suggesting an emphasis on hard physical activity, as at the expense of subtlety: *muscular religion; muscular reasoning that does not take the details into account.* [From Latin *mūsculus,* muscle. See MUSCLE.] —**mus′cu·lar′i·ty** (-lăr′ĭ-tē) *n.* —**mus′cu·lar·ly** *adv.*

SYNONYMS: *muscular, athletic, brawny, burly, sinewy.* The central meaning shared by these adjectives is "strong and powerfully built": *a muscular boxer; a robust and athletic young woman; brawny arms; a burly stevedore; a lean and sinewy frame.*

muscular dystrophy *n. Abbr.* **MD 1.** Any of a group of progressive muscle disorders caused by a defect in one or more genes that control muscle function and characterized by gradual irreversible wasting of skeletal muscle. **2.** Duchenne's muscular dystrophy.

mus·cu·la·ture (mŭs′kyə-lə-chŏŏr′) *n.* The system or arrangement of muscles in a body or a body part. [French, from Latin *mūsculus,* muscle. See MUSCLE.]

mus·cu·lo·skel·e·tal (mŭs′kyə-lō-skĕl′ĭ-tl) *adj.* Relating to or involving the muscles and the skeleton. [Latin *mūsculus,* muscle; see MUSCLE + SKELETAL.]

Mus.D. *abbr. Latin.* Musicae Doctor (Doctor of Music).

Mus.Dr. *abbr. Latin.* Musicae Doctor (Doctor of Music).

muse (myo͞oz) *v.* **mused, mus·ing, mus·es.** —*intr.* To be absorbed in one's thoughts; engage in meditation. See Synonyms at **ponder.** —*tr.* To consider or say thoughtfully: *mused that it might take longer to drive than walk.* —**muse** *n.* A state of meditation. [Middle English *musen,* from Old French *muser* (possibly from *mus,* snout, from Medieval Latin *mūsum*) or of Germanic origin.] —**mus′ing·ly** *adv.*

Muse (myo͞oz) *n.* **1.** *Greek Mythology.* Any of the nine daughters of Mnemosyne and Zeus, each of whom presided over a different art or science. **2. muse. a.** A guiding spirit. **b.** A source of inspiration. **3. muse.** A poet. [Middle English, from Old French, from Latin *Mūsa,* from Greek *Mousa.* See **men-**[1] in Appendix.]

mu·se·ol·o·gy (myo͞o′zē-ŏl′ə-jē) *n.* The discipline of museum design, organization, and management. —**mu′se·o·log′i·cal** (-ə-lŏj′ĭ-kəl) *adj.* —**mu′se·o·log′i·cal·ly** *adv.* —**mu′se·ol′o·gist** *n.*

mu·sette (myo͞o-zĕt′) *n.* **1.** *Music.* **a.** A small French bagpipe operated with a bellows and having a soft sound. **b.** A soft pastoral air that imitates bagpipe music. **2.** A musette bag. [Middle English, from Old French, diminutive of *muse,* from *muser,* to play the musette, muse. See MUSE.]

musette bag *n.* A small canvas or leather bag with a shoulder strap, as one used by soldiers or travelers.

mu·se·um (myo͞o-zē′əm) *n. Abbr.* **mus.** A building, place, or institution devoted to the acquisition, conservation, study, exhibition, and educational interpretation of objects having scientific, historical, or artistic value. —*attributive.* Often used to modify another noun: *museum exhibits; museum tours.* [Latin *Mūsēum,* from Greek *Mouseion,* shrine of the Muses, from *Mouseios,* of the Muses, from *Mousa,* Muse. See **men-**[1] in Appendix.]

mu·se·um·go·er (myo͞o-zē′əm-gō′ər) *n.* **1.** A visitor to a museum. **2.** One who visits museums frequently.

mush[1] (mŭsh) *n.* **1.** A thick porridge or pudding of cornmeal boiled in water or milk. **2.** Something thick, soft, and pulpy. **3.** *Informal.* Mawkish sentimentality, affection, or amorousness. —**mush** *tr.v.* **mushed, mush·ing, mush·es.** To reduce to mush; mash or crush. [Probably alteration of MASH.]

mush[2] (mŭsh) *v.* **mushed, mush·ing, mush·es.** —*intr.* To travel, especially over snow with a dogsled. —*tr.* To drive (a dogsled or team of dogs). —**mush** *n.* A journey, especially by dogsled. —**mush** *interj.* Used to command a team of dogs to begin pulling or move faster. [Possibly alteration of French *marchons,* first person pl. imperative of *marchier,* to walk, go, from Old French. See MARCH[1].] —**mush′er** *n.*

♦ **mush bread** *n. Midland & Lower Southern U.S.* See **johnnycake.** See Regional Note at **johnnycake.**

Mu·shin (mo͞o′shĭn′). A city of southwest Nigeria, an industrial and residential suburb of Lagos. Population, 234,500.

mush·room (mŭsh′ro͞om′, -ro͝om′) *n.* **1.** Any of various fleshy fungi of the class Basidiomycota, characteristically having an umbrella-shaped cap borne on a stalk, especially any of the edible kinds, as those of the genus *Agaricus.* **2.** Something shaped like one of these fungi. —**mushroom** *intr.v.* **-roomed, -room·ing, -rooms. 1.** To multiply, grow, or expand rapidly: *The population mushroomed in the postwar decades.* **2.** To swell or spread out into a shape similar to a mushroom. —**mushroom** *adj.* **1.** Relating to, consisting of, or containing mushrooms: *mushroom sauce.* **2.** Resembling a mushroom in shape: *a mushroom cloud.* **3.** Resembling mushrooms in rapidity of growth or evanescence: *mushroom towns.* [Middle English *musheron,* from Anglo-Norman *moscheron, musherum,* from Old French *mousseron,* from Medieval Latin *musariō, musariōn-.*]

mush·y (mŭsh′ē, mo͝osh′ē) *adj.* **-i·er, -i·est. 1.** Resembling mush in consistency; soft. **2.** *Informal.* **a.** Excessively sentimental. See Synonyms at **sentimental. b.** Given to or displaying mawkish affection or amorousness. —**mush′i·ly** *adv.* —**mush′i·ness** *n.*

Mu·si·al (myo͞o′zē-əl), **Stanley Frank.** Known as "Stan the Man." Born 1920. American baseball player who as an outfielder and first baseman accrued a lifetime batting average of .331 and hit 475 home runs and 3,630 base hits.

mu·sic (myo͞o′zĭk) *n. Abbr.* **mus. 1.** The art of arranging sounds in time so as to produce a continuous, unified, and evocative composition, as through melody, harmony, rhythm, and timbre. **2.** Vocal or instrumental sounds possessing a degree of melody, harmony, or rhythm. **3. a.** A musical composition. **b.** The written or printed score for such a composition. **c.** Such scores considered as a group: *We keep our music in a stack near the piano.* **4.** A musical accompaniment. **5.** A particular category or kind of music. **6.** An aesthetically pleasing or harmonious sound or combination of sounds: *the music of the wind.* [Middle English, from Old French *musique,* from Latin *mūsica,* from Greek *(hē) mousikē (tekhnē),* (art) of the Muses, feminine of *mousikos,* of the Muses, from *Mousa,* Muse. See **men-**[1] in Appendix.]

mu·si·cal (myo͞o′zĭ-kəl) *adj. Abbr.* **mus. 1.** Of, relating to, or capable of producing music: *a musical instrument.* **2.** Characteristic of or resembling music; melodious: *a musical speaking voice.* **3.** Set to or accompanied by music: *a musical revue.* **4.** Devoted to or skilled in music. —**musical** *n. Abbr.* **mus. 1.** A play or movie in which an often simple plot, developed by dialogue, is interspersed with songs and sometimes dances. **2.** *Archaic.* A musicale. —**mu′si·cal·ly** *adv.*

musical chairs *pl.n. (used with a sing. verb).* **1.** *Games.* A game in which players walk to music around a group of chairs containing one chair fewer than the number of players and rush to sit down when the music stops. The player left standing in each round is eliminated. **2.** *Informal.* A rearrangement, as of the elements of a problem, having little practical significance.

musical comedy *n.* A play or movie in which dialogue is interspersed with songs; a musical.

mu·si·cale (myo͞o′zĭ-kăl′) *n.* A program of music performed at a party or social gathering. [French, from *(soirée) musicale,* musical (evening), from *musique,* music. See MUSIC.]

mu·si·cal·i·ty (myo͞o′zĭ-kăl′ĭ-tē) *n.* **1.** The quality or condition of being musical. **2.** Musical sensitivity or talent.

mu·si·cal·ize (myo͞o′zĭ-kə-līz′) *tr.v.* **-ized, -iz·ing, -iz·es.** To adapt for performance with singing and musical accompaniment; set to music: *musicalize a play by Shakespeare.* —**mu′si·cal·i·za′tion** (-kə-lĭ-zā′shən) *n.*

musical saw *n. Music.* A handsaw on which varying musical tones are produced by flexing the blade and stroking it with a violin bow or striking it with a hammer.

music box *n. Music.* A music-making device consisting of a housing or box enclosing a sounding mechanism, especially one in which a row of tuned steel teeth are plucked by pins set in a revolving cylinder to produce a melody.

music drama *n. Music.* An opera in which the continuity is not interrupted by arias, recitatives, or ensembles, and in which the music reflects or embodies the action of the drama.

music hall *n.* **1.** An auditorium for musical performances. **2.** *Chiefly British.* **a.** A vaudeville theater. **b.** Vaudeville.

mu·si·cian (myo͞o-zĭsh′ən) *n. Abbr.* **mus.** One who composes, conducts, or performs music, especially instrumental music.

[Middle English *musicien,* from Old French, from Latin *mūsica,* music. See MUSIC.] **—mu·si′cian·ly** *adj.* **—mu·si′cian·ship′** *n.*

music of the spheres *n.* A perfectly harmonious music, inaudible on Earth, thought by Pythagoras and later classical and medieval philosophers to be produced by the movement of celestial bodies.

mu·si·col·o·gy (myo͞o′zĭ-kŏl′ə-jē) *n.* The historical and scientific study of music. **—mu′si·co·log′i·cal** (-kə-lŏj′ĭ-kəl) *adj.* **—mu′si·co·log′i·cal·ly** *adv.* **—mu′si·col′o·gist** *n.*

music video *n.* A filmed or videotaped rendition of a recorded song, often portraying musicians performing the song or including visual images interpreting the lyrics.

mu·sique con·crète (mo͞o-zēk′ kŏn-krĕt′, mü-zēk kôɴ-krĕt′) *n. Music.* Electronic music composed of instrumental and natural sounds often altered or distorted in the recording process. [French : *musique,* music + *concrète,* concrete.]

musk (mŭsk) *n.* **1.a.** A greasy secretion with a powerful odor, produced in a glandular sac beneath the skin of the abdomen of the male musk deer and used in the manufacture of perfumes. **b.** A similar secretion produced by certain other animals, such as the otter or civet. **c.** A synthetic chemical resembling natural musk in odor or use. **2.a.** The odor of musk. **b.** An odor similar to musk. **3.** A musk deer. [Middle English, from Old French *musc,* from Late Latin *muscus,* from Greek *moskhos,* from Persian *mušk,* probably from Sanskrit *muṣkaḥ,* testicle.]

musk deer *n.* A small, antlerless deer *(Moschus moschiferus)* of the mountainous regions of central and northeast Asia, the male of which secretes musk.

musk duck *n.* **1.** See **Muscovy duck. 2.** A waterfowl *(Biziura lobata)* of Australia, the male of which has a leathery chin lobe and emits a musky odor during the breeding season.

mus·keg (mŭs′kĕg′) also **mas·keg** (măs′-) *n.* A swamp or bog formed by an accumulation of sphagnum moss, leaves, and decayed matter resembling peat. [Cree *maskek.*]

Mus·ke·gon (mŭ-skē′gən). A city of southwest Michigan west-northwest of Grand Rapids at the mouth of the **Muskegon River,** which flows about 365 km (227 mi) from west-central Michigan southwest to Lake Michigan. The city was founded on the site of a fur-trading post. Population, 40,823.

mus·kel·lunge or **mus·ke·lunge** (mŭs′kə-lŭnj′) also **mas·ki·nonge** (măs′kə-nŏng′, -nŏnj′) *n., pl.* **muskellunge** or **-lung·es** or **muskelunge** or **-lung·es** also **maskinonge** or **-nong·es.** A large food and game fish *(Esox masquinongy),* the largest member of the pike family, found in lakes and rivers of the northern United States and southern Canada. [Canadian French *maskinongé,* from Ojibwa *maashkinoozhe.*]

mus·ket (mŭs′kĭt) *n.* A smoothbore shoulder gun used from the late 16th through the 18th century. [French *mousquet,* from Italian *moschetto,* a type of crossbow, musket, diminutive of *mosca,* fly, from Latin *musca.*]

mus·ket·eer (mŭs′kĭ-tîr′) *n.* **1.** A soldier armed with a musket. **2.** A member of the French royal household bodyguard in the 17th and 18th centuries. [French *mousquetaire,* from *mousquet,* musket. See MUSKET.]

mus·ket·ry (mŭs′kĭ-trē) *n.* **1.** The technique of using small arms. **2.** Muskets considered as a group. **3.** Musketeers considered as a group.

Mus·kho·ge·an (mŭs-kō′gē-ən) *n.* Variant of **Muskogean.**

mus·kie or **mus·ky** (mŭs′kē) *n., pl.* **-kies.** The muskellunge.

Mus·kie (mŭs′kē), **Edmund Sixtus.** Born 1914. American politician. A Democratic U.S. senator from Maine (1958–1980), he also served as U.S. secretary of state (1980–1981).

musk mallow *n.* **1.** See **abelmosk. 2.** A European and North African herb *(Malva moschata)* naturalized in eastern North America.

musk·mel·on (mŭsk′mĕl′ən) *n.* **1.** Any of several varieties of the melon *Cucumis melo,* such as the cantaloupe, having fruit characterized by a netted rind and edible flesh with a musky aroma. **2.** The fruit of any of these plants.

Mus·ko·ge·an also **Mus·kho·ge·an** (mŭs-kō′gē-ən) *n.* A family of Native American languages of the southeast United States that includes Choctaw, Chickasaw, Creek, and Alabama.

Mus·ko·gee[1] (mŭs-kō′gē) *n.* See **Creek.** [Creek *maask-óoki.*]

Mus·ko·gee[2] (mə-skō′gē). A city of eastern Oklahoma on the Arkansas River southeast of Tulsa. Founded in 1872, it is a trade and industrial center. Population, 40,011.

musk ox or **musk·ox** (mŭsk′ŏks′) *n., pl.* **musk oxen** or **-ox·en** (-ŏk′sən). A large, stocky ox *(Ovibos moschatus)* native to the coastal regions of northern Canada and Greenland, having broad flat horns with curved tips and a long, shaggy, brown or black coat and emitting a musky odor.

musk·rat (mŭs′krăt′) *n., pl.* **muskrat** or **-rats. 1.** A large aquatic rodent *(Ondatra zibethica)* of North America, related to the lemming and the vole and having a dense brown coat and musk glands under a broad, flat tail. Also called *musquash, water rat.* **2.** The fur of this rodent.

musk·root (mŭsk′ro͞ot′, -ro͝ot′) *n.* See **moschatel.**

musk rose *n.* A prickly Mediterranean shrub *(Rosa moschata)* cultivated for its clustered, musk-scented white flowers.

musk turtle *n.* Any of several small freshwater turtles of the genus *Sternotherus* of the eastern United States and Canada, which emit a musky odor when disturbed.

musk·y[1] (mŭs′kē) *adj.* **-i·er, -i·est.** Of, relating to, or having the odor of musk. **—musk′i·ness** *n.*

mus·ky[2] (mŭs′kē) *n.* Variant of **muskie.**

Mus·lim (mŭz′ləm, mo͝oz′-, mŭs′-, mo͝os′-) *n.* **1.** Variant of **Moslem. 2.** A Black Muslim. [Arabic *muslim,* one who surrenders, active participle of *'aslama,* to surrender, from Syriac *'ašlem.*] **—Mus′lim** *adj.*

mus·lin (mŭz′lĭn) *n.* Any of various sturdy cotton fabrics of plain weave, used especially for sheets. [French *mousseline,* from Italian *mussolina,* from *Mussolo,* Mosul, Iraq, from Arabic *Al-Mawṣil.*]

Mus.M. *abbr. Latin.* Musicae Magister (Master of Music).

mus·quash (mŭs′kwŏsh′, -kwôsh′) *n.* See **muskrat** (sense 1). [Perhaps of Massachusett origin; akin to Western Abenaki *mòsk-was.*]

muss (mŭs) *tr.v.* **mussed, muss·ing, muss·es.** To make messy or untidy; rumple. **—muss** *n.* A state of disorder; a mess. [Probably alteration of MESS.] **—muss′i·ly** *adv.* **—muss′i·ness** *n.* **—muss′y** *adj.*

mus·sel (mŭs′əl) *n.* **1.** Any of several marine bivalve mollusks, especially the edible members of the family Mytilidae and in particular *Mytilus edulis,* a blue-black species raised commercially in Europe. Mussels are often found attached to rocky surfaces or the sides of ships. **2.** Any of several freshwater bivalve mollusks of the genera *Anodonta* and *Unio,* found in the central United States, that burrow in the sand or mud of lakes and streams. [Alteration (possibly influenced by Dutch *mossel,* from Middle Dutch *mosscele*) of Middle English *muscle,* from Old English *muscelle,* from Medieval Latin *mūscula,* from Latin *mūsculus,* sea mussel. See MUSCLE.]

Mus·sel·shell (mŭs′əl-shĕl′). A river of central Montana flowing about 483 km (300 mi) to the Missouri River.

Mus·set (mo͞o-sā′, mü-), **(Louis Charles) Alfred de.** 1810–1857. French writer. A leading poet of the French romantic movement, he also wrote comedies of manners.

Mus·so·li·ni (mo͞o′sə-lē′nē, mo͝os′ə-, mo͝os′sô-), **Benito.** Known as "Il Duce." 1883–1945. Italian Fascist dictator and prime minister (1922–1943) who conducted an expansionist foreign policy, formalized an alliance with Germany (1939), and brought Italy into World War II (1940). Dismissed by Victor Emmanuel III (1943), he led a puppet Nazi government in northern Italy until 1945, when he was assassinated.

Mus·sorg·sky (mə-zôrg′skē, -sôrg′-, mo͞o′sərg-), **Modest Petrovich.** 1839–1881. Russian composer whose works include the opera *Boris Godunov* and the piano suite *Pictures at an Exhibition* (both 1874).

Mus·sul·man (mŭs′əl-mən) *n., pl.* **-men** or **-mans.** *Archaic.* A Moslem. [Turkish *musulmān,* probably alteration of Arabic *muslim,* Muslim. See MUSLIM.]

must[1] (mŭst) *v. —aux.* **1.** To be obliged or required by morality, law, or custom: *Citizens must register in order to vote.* **2.** To be compelled, as by a physical necessity or requirement: *Plants must have oxygen in order to live.* **3.** Used to express a command or an admonition: *You must not go there alone. You simply must be careful.* **4.** To be determined to; have as a fixed resolve: *If you must leave, do it quietly.* **5.a.** Used to indicate inevitability or certainty: *We all must die.* **b.** Used to indicate logical probability or presumptive certainty: *If the lights were on, they must have been at home.* —*intr. Archaic.* To be required or obliged to go: *"I must from hence"* (Shakespeare). **—must** *n.* Something that is absolutely required or indispensable: *Promptness on the job is a must. Comfortable shoes are a must when taking a walking tour of Wales.* —*attributive.* Often used to modify another noun: *a new book that is must reading; a list of must legislation for the session.* [Middle English *moste,* from Old English *mōste,* past tense of *mōtan,* to be allowed. See **med-** in Appendix.]

must[2] (mŭst) *n.* The quality or condition of being stale or musty. [Probably back-formation from MUSTY.]

must[3] (mŭst) *n.* The unfermented or fermenting juice expressed from fruit, especially grapes. [Middle English, from Old English, from Latin *mustum,* neuter of *mustus,* new, fresh.]

must[4] (mŭst) *n.* Variant of **musth.**

must[5] (mŭst) *n.* Musk. [Scottish, from Old French, variant of *musc.* See MUSK.]

mus·tache also **mous·tache** (mŭs′tăsh′, mə-stăsh′) *n.* **1.** The hair growing on the human upper lip, especially when cultivated and groomed. **2.** Something similar to the cultivated, groomed hair on the human upper lip, as: **a.** A group of bristles or hairs about the mouth of an animal. **b.** Distinctive coloring or feathers near the beak of a bird. **c.** Food or drink sticking conspicuously to the upper lip, as after a deep draft: *a milk mustache.* [French *moustache,* from Italian dialectal *mustaccio,* from Medieval Greek *moustakion,* from Greek *mustax,* mustache, upper lip.]

mus·tached (mŭs′tăsht) *adj.* Variant of **mustachioed.**

mus·ta·chio (mə-stăsh′ō, -stăsh′ē-ō′, -stä′shō, -shē-ō′) *n., pl.* **-chios.** A mustache, especially a luxuriant one. [Ultimately from Italian dialectal *mustaccio,* mustache. See MUSTACHE.]

mus·ta·chioed also **mous·ta·chioed** (mə-stăsh′ōd, -stăsh′ē-ōd′, -stä′shōd, -shē-ōd′) or **mus·tached** (mŭs′tăsht) *adj.* Having or wearing a mustache.

musk ox
Musk ox bull
Ovibos moschatus

Benito Mussolini

ă **pat**	oi **boy**
ā **pay**	ou **out**
âr **care**	o͝o **took**
ä **father**	o͞o **boot**
ĕ **pet**	ŭ **cut**
ē **be**	ûr **urge**
ĭ **pit**	th **thin**
ī **pie**	*th* **this**
îr **pier**	hw **which**
ŏ **pot**	zh **vision**
ō **toe**	ə **about, item**
ô **paw**	♦ **regionalism**

Stress marks: ′ (primary); ′ (secondary), as in **dictionary** (dĭk′shə-nĕr′ē)

mus·tang (mŭs′tăng′) *n.* A small, hardy wild horse of the North American plains, descended from Arabian horses and brought to the New World by Spanish explorers. [American Spanish *mesteño, mestengo,* stray animal, from Old Spanish, from *mesta,* association of livestock owners, from Medieval Latin *(animalia) mixta,* assorted (animals), from Latin, neuter pl. past participle of *miscēre,* to mix. See **meik-** in Appendix.]

mus·tard (mŭs′tərd) *n.* **1.a.** Any of various Eurasian plants of the genus *Brassica,* especially *B. nigra* and *B. juncea,* which are cultivated for their pungent seeds. **b.** A condiment made from the powdered seeds of some of these plants. **2.** A member of the mustard family. **3.** *Color.* A dark yellow to light olive brown. ***—idiom.*** **cut the mustard.** To perform up to expectations or to a required standard. [Middle English, from Old French *mustarde,* from Latin *mustum,* must, unfermented wine. See MUST[3].] **—mus′tard·y** *adj.*

mustard family *n.* A large family of herbs, the Cruciferae (Brassicaceae), characterized by pungent juice and four-petaled flowers arranged in a cross and including important vegetables such as broccoli, Brussels sprouts, cabbage, cauliflower, kale, radishes, and watercress.

mustard gas *n.* An oily, volatile liquid, $(ClCH_2CH_2)_2S$, that is corrosive to the skin and mucous membranes and causes severe, sometimes fatal respiratory damage. It was introduced in World War I as a chemical warfare agent. [From its smell.]

mustard oil *n.* An oil obtained from mustard seeds, used in making soap.

mustard plaster *n.* A medicinal plaster made with a pastelike mixture of powdered black mustard, flour, and water, used especially as a counterirritant. Also called *sinapism.*

mus·te·line (mŭs′tə-līn′, -lĭn) *adj.* Of, relating to, or belonging to Mustelidae, the family of fur-bearing mammals that includes the badger, mink, otter, and weasel. [Latin *mūstēlīnus,* of a weasel, from *mūstēla,* weasel, probably from *mūs,* mouse. See **mūs-** in Appendix.]

mute
On a trumpet

mus·ter (mŭs′tər) *v.* **-tered, -ter·ing, -ters.** *—tr.* **1.** To call (troops) together, as for inspection. **2.** To cause to come together; gather: *Bring all the volunteers you can muster.* **3.** To call forth; summon up: *mustering up her strength for the ordeal.* See Synonyms at **call.** *—intr.* To assemble or gather: *mustering for inspection.* **—muster** *n.* **1.a.** A gathering, especially of troops, for service, inspection, review, or roll call. **b.** The persons assembled for such a gathering. **2.** A muster roll. **3.** A gathering or collection: *a muster of business leaders at a luncheon.* **4.** A flock of peacocks. See Synonyms at **flock[1].** ***—phrasal verbs.*** **muster in.** To enlist in military service: *She mustered in at the age of 18.* **muster out.** To leave or be discharged from military service: *He mustered out when the war ended.* [Middle English *mustren,* from Old French *moustrer,* from Latin *mōnstrāre,* to show, from *mōnstrum,* sign, portent, from *monēre,* to warn. See **men-[1]** in Appendix.]

muster roll *n.* **1.** The official roll of persons in a military or naval unit. **2.** An inventory; a roster.

musth also **must** (mŭst) *n.* An annual period of heightened aggressiveness and sexual activity in male elephants, during which violent frenzies occur. [Urdu *mast,* from Persian, drunk.]

must·n't (mŭs′ənt). Must not.

must-read (mŭst′rēd′) *n. Slang.* A piece of writing, such as a book, an article, or a salient part of one of these, that should or must be read: *Not many must-reads were published this summer.* **—must′-read′** *adj.*

must-see (mŭst′sē′) *n. Slang.* Something that should or must be seen: *a brief sightseeing tour hitting the must-sees; a movie that's a must-see.* **—must′-see′** *adj.*

must·y (mŭs′tē) *adj.* **-i·er, -i·est. 1.** Stale or moldy in odor or taste. **2.a.** Hackneyed or trite; dull. **b.** Out of date; antiquated. **c.** Out of use or practice; rusty. [Alteration of obsolete *moisty,* from MOIST.] **—must′i·ly** *adv.* **—must′i·ness** *n.*

mu·ta·ble (myo͞o′tə-bəl) *adj.* **1.a.** Capable of or subject to change or alteration. **b.** Prone to frequent change; inconstant: *mutable weather patterns.* **2.** Tending to undergo genetic mutation: *a mutable organism; a mutable gene.* [Middle English, from Latin *mūtābilis,* from *mūtāre,* to change. See MUTATE.] **—mu′ta·bil′i·ty, mu′ta·ble·ness** *n.* **—mu′ta·bly** *adv.*

mu·ta·gen (myo͞o′tə-jən, -jĕn′) *n.* An agent, such as ultraviolet light or a radioactive element, that can induce or increase the frequency of mutation in an organism. [MUTA(TION) + -GEN.] **—mu′ta·gen′ic** *adj.* **—mu′ta·gen′i·cal·ly** *adv.* **—mu′ta·ge·nic′i·ty** (-jə-nĭs′ĭ-tē) *n.*

mu·ta·gen·e·sis (myo͞o′tə-jĕn′ĭ-sĭs) *n., pl.* **-ses** (-sēz′). Formation or development of a mutation. [MUTA(TION) + -GENESIS.]

mu·ta·gen·ize (myo͞o′tə-jĕn′īz) *tr.v.* **-ized, -iz·ing, -iz·es.** To cause or induce mutation in (a cell or an organism).

mu·tant (myo͞ot′nt) *n.* **1.** An individual, an organism, or a new genetic character arising or resulting from mutation. **2.** *Slang.* One that is suggestive of a genetic mutant, as in bizarre appearance, inaptitude, or genesis in an unhealthy environment: *"These . . . remakes are neither dreams nor recognizable reality. They're mutants."* (Vincent Canby). **—mutant** *adj.* **1.** Resulting from or undergoing mutation: *a mutant strain of bacteria.* **2.** *Slang.* Suggestive of a genetic mutant, as in appearance, inaptitude, or genesis in an unhealthy environment: *gangs of disaffected mutant teenagers.* [Latin *mūtāns, mūtant-,* present participle of *mūtāre,* to change. See MUTATE.]

mu·tase (myo͞o′tās, -tāz) *n.* Any enzyme that catalyzes the rearrangement of atoms within a molecule, especially one that causes the transfer of a phosphate group from one carbon atom to another. [Latin *mūtāre,* to change, move; see MUTATE + -ASE.]

mu·tate (myo͞o′tāt, myo͞o-tāt′) *intr. & tr.v.* **-tat·ed, -tat·ing, -tates.** To undergo or cause to undergo mutation. [Latin *mūtāre, mūtāt-,* to change. See **mei-[1]** in Appendix.] **—mu′ta′tive** (-tā′tĭv, -tə-tĭv) *adj.*

mu·ta·tion (myo͞o-tā′shən) *n.* **1.** The act or process of being altered or changed. **2.** An alteration or change, as in nature, form, or quality. **3.** *Genetics.* **a.** A sudden structural change within a gene or chromosome of an organism resulting in the creation of a new character or trait not found in the parental type. **b.** The process by which such a sudden structural change occurs, either through an alteration in the nucleotide sequence of the DNA coding for a gene or through a change in the physical arrangement of a chromosome. **c.** A mutant. **4.** *Linguistics.* The change, especially an umlaut, that is caused in a sound by its assimilation to another sound. [Middle English *mutacioun,* from Old French *mutacion,* from Latin *mūtātiō, mūtātiōn-,* from past participle of *mūtāre,* to change. See MUTATE.] **—mu·ta′tion·al** *adj.* **—mu·ta′tion·al·ly** *adv.*

mu·ta·tis mu·tan·dis (mo͞o-tä′tĭs mo͞o-tän′dĭs) *adv. Abbr.* **m.m.** The necessary changes having been made; having substituted new terms. [Latin *mūtātīs mūtandīs* : *mūtātīs,* ablative pl. past participle of *mūtāre,* to change + *mūtandīs,* ablative pl. gerundive of *mūtāre.*]

mutch·kin (mŭch′kĭn) *n. Scots.* A unit of liquid measure equal to 0.9 U.S. pint (0.42 liter). [Middle English *muchekyn,* from Middle Dutch *mudseken,* diminutive of *mutse,* a kind of measure, from Latin *modius,* grain measure. See **med-** in Appendix.]

mute (myo͞ot) *adj.* **mut·er, mut·est. 1.** Refraining from producing speech or vocal sound. **2.a.** Unable to speak. **b.** Unable to vocalize, as certain animals. See Synonyms at **dumb. 3.** Expressed without speech; unspoken: *a mute appeal.* **4.** *Law.* Refusing to plead when under arraignment. **5.** *Linguistics.* **a.** Not pronounced; silent, as the *e* in the word *house.* **b.** Pronounced with a temporary stoppage of breath, as the sounds (p) and (b); plosive; stopped. **—mute** *n.* **1.** *Offensive.* One who is incapable of speech. **2.** *Law.* A defendant who refuses to plead when under arraignment. **3.** *Music.* Any of various devices used to muffle or soften the tone of an instrument. **4.** *Linguistics.* **a.** A silent letter. **b.** A plosive; a stop. **—mute** *tr.v.* **mut·ed, mut·ing, mutes. 1.** To soften or muffle the sound of. **2.** To soften the tone, color, shade, or hue of. [Middle English *muet,* from Old French, from diminutive of *mu,* from Latin *mūtus.*] **—mute′ly** *adv.* **—mute′ness** *n.*

mut·ed (myo͞o′tĭd) *adj.* **1.a.** Muffled; indistinct: *a muted voice.* **b.** Mute or subdued; softened: *muted colors.* **2.** *Music.* Produced by or provided with a mute. **—mut′ed·ly** *adv.*

mute swan *n.* A white swan *(Cygnus olor)* native to Europe and Asia and widely introduced elsewhere, having an orange bill with a black knob at the base and being much less vocal than most swans.

mu·ti·late (myo͞ot′l-āt′) *tr.v.* **-lat·ed, -lat·ing, -lates. 1.** To deprive of a limb or an essential part; cripple. **2.** To disfigure by damaging irreparably: *mutilate a statue.* See Synonyms at **batter[1]. 3.** To make imperfect by excising or altering parts. [Latin *mutilāre, mutilāt-,* from *mutilus,* maimed.] **—mu′ti·la′tion** *n.* **—mu′ti·la′tive** *adj.* **—mu′ti·la′tor** *n.*

mu·ti·neer (myo͞ot′n-îr′) *n.* One who takes part in a mutiny. [Obsolete French *mutinier,* from Old French *mutin,* rebellious. See MUTINY.]

mu·ti·nous (myo͞ot′n-əs) *adj.* **1.** Of, relating to, engaged in, disposed to, or constituting mutiny. See Synonyms at **insubordinate. 2.** Unruly; disaffected: *a mutinous child.* **3.** Turbulent and uncontrollable: *"mutinous passions, and conflicting fears"* (Percy Bysshe Shelley). [From obsolete *mutine,* mutiny. See MUTINY.] **—mu′ti·nous·ly** *adv.* **—mu′ti·nous·ness** *n.*

mu·ti·ny (myo͞ot′n-ē) *n., pl.* **-nies.** Open rebellion against constituted authority, especially rebellion of sailors against superior officers. See Synonyms at **rebellion. —mutiny** *intr.v.* **-nied, -ny·ing, -nies.** To engage in mutiny. [Obsolete *mutine,* from Old French *mutin,* rebellious, from *muete,* revolt, from Vulgar Latin **movita,* from Latin *movēre,* to move. See MOVE.]

mut·ism (myo͞o′tĭz′əm) *n.* The condition of being unable to speak as a result of a physical or psychological disorder.

mu·ton (myo͞o′tŏn′) *n.* The smallest unit of DNA at which a mutation can occur; a nucleotide. [MUT(ATION) + -ON[1].]

Mu·tsu·hi·to (mo͞o′tso͞o-hē′tō). Imperial name **Mei·ji** (mā′jē′). 1852–1912. Emperor of Japan (1867–1912) who presided over the transformation of feudal Japan into a modern constitutional state.

mutt (mŭt) *n. Informal.* **1.** A mongrel dog. **2.** A person regarded as stupid. [Short for MUTTONHEAD.]

WORD HISTORY: Clipping not of sheep but of a word having to do with sheep has given us our term *mutt* for a mongrel dog. Clipping or abbreviating words, a standard process of word formation, sheared *mutt* from *muttonhead,* a pejorative term meaning "a stupid person," based on the notion that sheep are stupid. *Mutt* in its first recorded use in 1901 is used in the same senses as *muttonhead,* but it is soon recorded (1904) as a term of contempt for a horse and then (1906) for a dog. We can be reasonably certain that the *New Yorker* critic writing in 1970 that "The cast includes a Sheepdog . . . a Mutt Bitch," had no awareness that a sheepdog would make the ideal mutt.

mut·ter (mŭt′ər) *v.* **-tered, -ter·ing, -ters.** —*intr.* **1.** To speak indistinctly in low tones. **2.** To complain or grumble morosely. —*tr.* To utter or say in low, indistinct tones. **—mutter** *n.* A low grumble or indistinct utterance. [Middle English *muttren,* possibly from Latin *muttīre.*] **—mut′ter·er** *n.*

mut·ton (mŭt′n) *n.* The flesh of fully grown sheep. [Middle English, from Old French *mouton, moton,* from Medieval Latin *multō, multōn-,* of Celtic origin. See **mel-**[1] in Appendix.]

mut·ton-bird (mŭt′n-bûrd′) *n.* See **sooty shearwater.**

mut·ton·chops (mŭt′n-chŏps′) *pl.n.* Side whiskers that are narrow at the temple, broad along the lower cheek or jawline, and separated by a shaven chin.

mut·ton·fish (mŭt′n-fĭsh′) *n., pl.* **muttonfish** or **-fish·es.** **1.** An eelpout *(Macrozoarces americanus)* of the coastal waters of northeast North America. **2.** Mutton snapper.

mut·ton·head (mŭt′n-hĕd′) *n. Informal.* A person regarded as stupid; a fool. [From the proverbial stupidity of sheep.] **—mut′ton·head′ed** *adj.*

mutton snapper *n.* An olive-green snapper *(Lutjanus analis)* of warm western Atlantic waters, valued as a source of food and as a game fish.

Mut·tra (mŭt′rə). See **Mathura.**

mu·tu·al (myōō′chōō-əl) *adj.* **1.** Having the same relationship each to the other: *mutual predators.* **2.** Directed and received in equal amount; reciprocal: *mutual respect.* **3.** Possessed in common: *mutual interests.* **4.** Of, relating to, or in the form of mutual insurance. **—mutual** *n.* A mutual fund. [French *mutuel,* from Old French, from Latin *mūtuus,* borrowed. See **mei-**[1] in Appendix.] **—mu′tu·al′i·ty** (-ăl′ĭ-tē) *n.* **—mu′tu·al·ly** *adv.*

USAGE NOTE: *Mutual* is uncontroversially used to describe a reciprocal relationship between two or more things, in which use it can be paraphrased by expressions involving *between* or *each other.* Thus *their mutual animosity* means "their animosity for each other" or "the animosity between them," and *a mutual defense treaty* is one in which each party agrees to come to the defense of the other. But *mutual* is also widely used where one might expect "common," as in *The bill serves the mutual interests of management and labor* and particularly in the expression *our mutual friend,* which was widespread even before Charles Dickens used it as the title of a novel. Critics have often objected to this use, but it is well established in reputable writing. However, *mutual* in this latter sense is reserved to describe relations that hold between two or more specific parties and a third person or thing. It cannot be used as a substitute for *common* in the sense "general": *English is the common* (not *mutual*) *language of the island. It is commonly* (not *mutually*) *believed that Spanish is an easier language than French.*

mutual assured destruction *n. Abbr.* **MAD** Severe, unavoidable reciprocal damage that superpowers are likely to inflict on each other or their allies in a nuclear war, conceived as the heart of a doctrine of nuclear deterrence.

mutual fund *n.* An investment company that continually offers new shares and buys existing shares back on demand and uses its capital to invest in diversified securities of other companies. **—mu′tu·al-fund′** (myōō′chōō-əl-fŭnd′) *adj.*

mutual inductance *n. Abbr.* **M** The ratio of the electromotive force in a circuit to the corresponding change of current in a neighboring circuit.

mutual induction *n.* The production of an electromotive force in a circuit resulting from a change of current in a neighboring cirucuit.

mutual insurance *n.* An insurance system in which the insured persons become company members, each paying specified amounts into a common fund from which members are entitled to indemnification in case of loss.

mu·tu·al·ism (myōō′chōō-ə-lĭz′əm) *n.* An association between organisms of two different species in which each member benefits. **—mu′tu·al·is′tic** *adj.*

mu·tu·al·ize (myōō′chōō-ə-līz′) *v.* —*tr.* **-ized, -iz·ing, -iz·es.** **1.** To make mutual. **2.** To set up or reorganize (a corporation) so that the majority of common stock is owned by customers or employees. —*intr.* To become mutual. **—mu′tu·al·i·za′tion** (-ə-lĭ-zā′shən) *n.*

muu·muu (mōō′mōō′) *n.* A long, loose dress that hangs free from the shoulders. [Hawaiian *mu'umu'u,* cut off, muumuu.]

Muy·bridge (mī′brĭj′), **Eadweard.** Originally Edward James Muggeridge. 1830–1904. British-born American motion-picture pioneer noted for his photographs of horses in motion, taken by a series of still cameras.

Mu·zak (myōō′zăk′). A trademark used for recorded background music transmitted by wire or radio, as to places of business, on a subscription basis.

mu·zhik also **mou·jik** or **mu·jik** or **mu·zjik** (mōō-zhēk′, -zhĭk′) *n.* A peasant in czarist Russia. [Russian, from *muzh,* man. See **man-**[1] in Appendix.]

Muz·tag or **Muz·tagh** (mōōs-tä′, -täg′). A mountain, 7,286.8 m (23,891 ft) high, in the Kunlun Range of western China near the Indian border.

Muz·tag·a·ta also **Muz·tagh A·ta** (mōōs-tä′ə-tä′, mōōs-täg′-). A mountain, 7,550.9 m (24,757 ft) high, of the **Muztagata Range** in western China near the Tadzikhistan border.

Muz·tagh (mōōs-tä′, -täg′). See **Muztag.**

muz·zle (mŭz′əl) *n.* **1.** The forward, projecting part of the head of certain animals, such as dogs, including the mouth, nose, and jaws; the snout. **2.** A leather or wire restraining appliance that, when fitted over an animal's snout, prevents biting and eating. **3.** The forward, discharging end of the barrel of a firearm. **4.** A restraint on free movement or expression: *had a muzzle put on their high spirits.* **—muzzle** *tr.v.* **-zled, -zling, -zles.** **1.** To put a muzzle on (an animal). **2.** To restrain from expression: *tried to muzzle the opposition.* [Middle English *mosel,* from Old French *musel,* from Medieval Latin *mūsellum,* diminutive of *mūsus,* snout, from Latin *mūsum.*] **—muz′zler** *n.*

muz·zle·load·er (mŭz′əl-lō′dər) *n.* A firearm that is loaded at the muzzle. **—muz′zle·load′ing** *adj.*

muz·zy (mŭz′ē) *adj.* **-zi·er, -zi·est.** **1.** Mentally confused; muddled. **2.** Blurred; indistinct. [Origin unknown.] **—muz′zi·ly** *adv.* **—muz′zi·ness** *n.*

mV *abbr.* Millivolt.

MV *abbr.* **1.** Mean variation. **2.** Megavolt.

MVP *abbr. Sports.* Most valuable player.

mW *abbr.* Milliwatt.

MW *abbr.* Megawatt.

Mwe·ru (mwā′rōō), **Lake.** A lake of central Africa on the Zaire-Zambia border west of Lake Tanganyika.

Mx *abbr.* Maxwell (measurement).

MX *abbr. Sports.* Motocross.

mxd. *abbr.* Mixed.

my (mī) *adj.* The possessive form of **I.** **1.** Used as a modifier before a noun: *my boots; my accomplishments.* **2.** Used preceding various forms of polite, affectionate, or familiar address: *My friend, you are so right.* **3.** Used in various interjectional phrases: *My word! My goodness!* **—my** *interj.* Used as an exclamation of surprise, pleasure, or dismay: *Oh, my! What a tiring day!* [Middle English *mi,* from Old English *mīn.* See **me-**[1] in Appendix.]

m.y. *abbr.* Million years.

my– *pref.* Variant of **myo–.**

my·al·gi·a (mī-ăl′jē-ə, -jə) *n.* Muscular pain or tenderness, especially when diffuse and nonspecific. **—my·al′gic** (-jĭk) *adj.*

Myan·mar (myän-mä′). See **Burma.**

my·as·the·ni·a (mī′əs-thē′nē-ə) *n.* **1.** Abnormal muscular weakness or fatigue. **2.** Myasthenia gravis. **—my′as·then′ic** (-thĕn′ĭk) *adj.*

myasthenia gra·vis (grăv′ĭs) *n.* A disease characterized by progressive fatigue and generalized weakness of the skeletal muscles, especially those of the face, neck, arms, and legs, caused by impaired transmission of nerve impulses following an autoimmune attack on acetylcholine receptors. [New Latin : MYASTHENIA + Latin *gravis,* heavy, severe.]

myc (mĭk) *n.* Any of a group of vertebrate oncogenes whose product, a DNA binding protein, is thought to promote the growth of tumor cells. [Possibly from *my(elo)c(ytomatosis virus).*]

myc. *abbr.* **1.** Mycological. **2.** Mycology.

myc– *pref.* Variant of **myco–.**

Myc·a·le (mĭk′ə-lē). A promontory of western Asia Minor. In 479 B.C. it was the site of a major Greek victory over the Persian fleet.

my·ce·li·um (mī-sē′lē-əm) *n., pl.* **-li·a** (-lē-ə). **1.** The vegetative part of a fungus, consisting of a mass of branching, threadlike hyphae. **2.** A similar mass of fibers formed by certain bacteria. [New Latin : MYC(O)– + Greek *hēlos,* wart.] **—my·ce′li·al** (-lē-əl) *adj.*

My·ce·nae (mī-sē′nē). An ancient Greek city in the northeast Peloponnesus that flourished during the Bronze Age as the center of an early civilization.

My·ce·nae·an (mī′sə-nē′ən) *adj.* **1.** Of or relating to Mycenae or its inhabitants. **2.** Of, relating to, or being the Aegean civilization that spread its influence from Mycenae to many parts of the Mediterranean region from about 1580 to 1120 B.C. **3.** Of, relating to, or being the archaic dialect of Greek written in the Linear B script. **—Mycenaean** *n.* **1.** A native or inhabitant of Mycenae. **2.** Mycenaean Greek.

–mycete *suff.* Fungus: *basidiomycete.* [New Latin *-mycētēs,* from Greek *mukēs, mukēt-,* fungus.]

my·ce·to·ma (mī′sĭ-tō′mə) *n., pl.* **-mas** or **-ma·ta** (-mə-tə). A chronic, slowly progressing bacterial or fungal infection usually of the foot or leg, characterized by nodules that discharge an oily pus. [Greek *mukēs, mukēt-,* fungus + –OMA.] **—my′ce·to′ma·tous** (-tō′mə-təs, -tŏm′ə-) *adj.*

–mycin *suff.* A substance derived from a bacterium in the order Actinomycetales: *neomycin.* [MYC(O)– (so called because the bacteria from which the substances were first derived were originally mistaken for fungi) + –IN.]

myco– or **myc–** *pref.* Fungus: *mycology.* [From Greek *mukēs,* fungus.]

ă pat	oi boy
ā pay	ou out
âr care	ŏŏ took
ä father	ōō boot
ĕ pet	ŭ cut
ē be	ûr urge
ĭ pit	th thin
ī pie	*th* this
îr pier	hw which
ŏ pot	zh vision
ō toe	ə about, item
ô paw	♦ regionalism

Stress marks: ′ (primary); ′ (secondary), as in **dictionary** (dĭk′shə-nĕr′ē)

my·co·bac·te·ri·um (mī′kō-băk-tîr′ē-əm) *n., pl.* **-te·ri·a** (-tîr′ē-ə). Any of various slender, rod-shaped, aerobic bacteria of the genus *Mycobacterium,* which includes the bacteria that cause tuberculosis and leprosy. **—my′co·bac·ter′i·al** *adj.*

mycol. *abbr.* **1.** Mycological. **2.** Mycology.

my·col·o·gy (mī-kŏl′ə-jē) *n., pl.* **-gies.** *Abbr.* **myc., mycol. 1.** The branch of botany that deals with fungi. **2.** The fungi native to a region. **3.** The composition or characteristics of a particular fungus: *the mycology of rusts and mildews.* **—my′co·log′i·cal** (-kə-lŏj′ĭ-kəl), **my′co·log′ic** *adj.* **—my′col·og′i·cal·ly** *adv.* **—my·col′o·gist** *n.*

my·coph·a·gous (mī-kŏf′ə-gəs) *adj.* Fungivorous. **—my·coph′a·gy** (-ə-jē) *n.*

my·co·plas·ma (mī′kō-plăz′mə) *n.* Any of numerous parasitic, pathogenic microorganisms of the genus *Mycoplasma* that lack a true cell wall, are gram-negative, and need sterols such as cholesterol for growth. In human beings, one species is a primary cause of nonbacterial pneumonia. Also called *pleuropneumonia-like organism.* **—my′co·plas′mal** *adj.*

my·cor·rhi·za or **my·co·rhi·za** (mī′kə-rī′zə) *n., pl.* **-zae** (-zē) or **-zas.** *Botany.* The symbiotic association of the mycelium of a fungus with the roots of certain plants, such as conifers, beeches, or orchids. [MYCO– + Greek *rhiza,* root; see **wrād-** in Appendix.] **—my′cor·rhi′zal** *adj.*

my·co·sis (mī-kō′sĭs) *n., pl.* **-ses** (-sēz). **1.** A fungal infection in or on a part of the body. **2.** A disease caused by a fungus.

my·co·tox·i·co·sis (mī′kō-tŏk′sĭ-kō′sĭs) *n.* Poisoning caused by ingestion of a mycotoxin.

my·co·tox·in (mī′kō-tŏk′sĭn) *n.* A toxin produced by a fungus.

my·dri·a·sis (mĭ-drī′ə-sĭs) *n.* Prolonged, abnormal dilatation of the pupil of the eye caused by disease or a drug. [Latin, from Greek *mudriasis.*]

myd·ri·at·ic (mĭd′rē-ăt′ĭk) *adj.* Causing dilatation of the pupils. **—mydriatic** *n.* A mydriatic drug. [From MYDRIASIS.]

myel– *pref.* Variant of **myelo–.**

my·e·len·ceph·a·lon (mī′ə-lĕn-sĕf′ə-lŏn′) *n.* The posterior portion of the embryonic hindbrain, from which the medulla oblongata develops. **—my′e·len·ce·phal′ic** (-sə-făl′ĭk) *adj.*

my·e·lin (mī′ə-lĭn) also **my·e·line** (-lĭn, -lēn′) *n.* A white fatty material, composed chiefly of lipids and lipoproteins, that encloses certain axons and nerve fibers. Also called *medulla.* **—my′e·lin′ic** *adj.*

my·e·li·nat·ed (mī′ə-lə-nā′tĭd) *adj.* Having a myelin sheath: *myelinated nerve fibers.*

my·e·li·na·tion (mī′ə-lə-nā′shən) *n.* Variant of **myelinization.**

my·e·line (mī′ə-lĭn, -lēn′) *n.* Variant of **myelin.**

my·e·li·ni·za·tion (mī′ə-lə-nĭ-zā′shən) also **my·e·li·na·tion** (-nā′shən) *n.* The process of forming a myelin sheath.

myelin sheath *n.* The insulating envelope of myelin that surrounds the core of a nerve fiber or axon and facilitates the transmission of nerve impulses. In the peripheral nervous system, the sheath is formed from the cell membrane of the Schwann cell and, in the central nervous system, from oligodendrocytes. Also called *medullary sheath.*

my·e·li·tis (mī′ə-lī′tĭs) *n.* **1.** Inflammation of the spinal column. **2.** Osteomyelitis.

myelo– or **myel–** *pref.* **1.** Spinal cord: *myelitis.* **2.** Bone marrow: *myeloma.* [New Latin, from Greek *muelos,* marrow, probably from *mus,* muscle. See **mūs-** in Appendix.]

my·e·lo·blast (mī′ə-lə-blăst′) *n.* An immature cell of the bone marrow that is the precursor of a myelocyte. **—my′e·lo·blas′tic** *adj.*

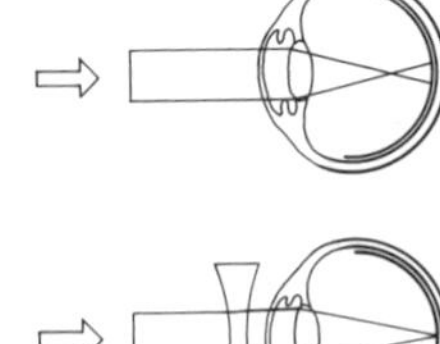
myopia
Top: Before correction
Bottom: After correction

my·e·lo·cyte (mī′ə-lə-sīt′) *n.* A large cell of the bone marrow that is a precursor of the mature granulocyte of the blood. **—my′e·lo·cyt′ic** (-sĭt′ĭk) *adj.*

my·e·lo·fi·bro·sis (mī′ə-lō-fī-brō′sĭs) *n.* Proliferation of fibroblastic cells in bone marrow, causing anemia and sometimes enlargement of the spleen and liver.

my·e·log·e·nous (mī′ə-lŏj′ə-nəs) also **my·e·lo·gen·ic** (-lə-jĕn′ĭk) *adj.* Originating in or produced by the bone marrow.

my·e·lo·gram (mī′ə-lə-grăm′) *n.* An x-ray of the spinal cord after injection of air or a radiopaque substance into the subarachnoid space. **—my′e·log′ra·phy** (-lŏg′rə-fē) *n.*

my·e·loid (mī′ə-loid′) *adj.* **1.** Of, relating to, or derived from the bone marrow. **2.** Of or relating to the spinal cord.

my·e·lo·ma (mī′ə-lō′mə) *n., pl.* **-mas** or **-ma·ta** (-mə-tə). A malignant tumor formed by the cells of the bone marrow. **—my′e·lo′ma·toid′** (-toid′) *adj.*

my·e·lo·pro·lif·er·a·tive (mī′ə-lō-prə-lĭf′ə-rā′tĭv, -ər-ə-tĭv) *adj.* Relating to or characterized by the proliferation of cells of the bone marrow: *myeloproliferative syndromes.*

my·ia·sis (mī′ə-sĭs, mī-ī′ə-sĭs) *n., pl.* **my·ia·ses** (mī′ə-sēz′). **1.** Infestation of tissue by fly larvae. **2.** A disease resulting from infestation of tissue by fly larvae. [Greek *muia, mua,* fly + –IASIS.]

Myk·o·nos (mĭk′ə-nŏs′, -nōs′, mē′kô-nôs′) also **Mí·ko·nos** (mē′kô-nôs′). An island of southeast Greece in the Cyclades Islands of the Aegean Sea. It is a popular resort.

My Lai (mē′ lī′). A village of southern Vietnam where more than 300 unarmed civilians, including women and children, were massacred by U.S. troops (March 1968) during the Vietnam War.

My·lar (mī′lär′). A trademark used for a thin strong polyester film. This trademark often occurs in print as an attributive: *"Mylar star balloons dangle from the ceiling, the pianist strokes her ivories, and waiters . . . waltz through the crowd"* (San Francisco Chronicle). It also occurs in lowercase: *"The* [printers] *use standard fabric ribbon cartridges or high-carbon mylar cartridges"* (Byte).

my·lo·nite (mī′lə-nīt′) *n.* A fine-grained laminated rock formed by the shifting of rock layers along faults. [Greek *mulōn,* mill (from *mulē,* handmill; see **melə-** in Appendix) + –ITE[1].]

my·na or **my·nah** also **mi·na** (mī′nə) *n.* Any of various starlings of southeast Asia, having bluish-black or dark brown coloration and yellow bills. Certain species, especially the hill myna *(Gracula religiosa),* are known for mimicry of human speech. [Hindi *mainā,* perhaps from Sanskrit *madanaḥ,* from *madana-,* delightful, joyful, from *madati,* it bubbles.]

myn·heer also **men·eer** (mə-nîr′) *n.* **1.** Often **Mynheer** also **Meneer. a.** Used as a courtesy title before the name of a man in a Dutch-speaking area. **b.** Used as a form of polite address for a man in a Dutch-speaking area. **2.** *Informal.* A Dutchman. [Dutch *mijnheer* : *mijn,* my (from Middle Dutch; see **me-**[1] in Appendix) + *heer,* lord (from Middle Dutch *here*).]

myo– or **my–** *pref.* Muscle: *myograph.* [New Latin, from Greek *mus,* muscle. See **mūs-** in Appendix.]

myocardial infarction *n. Abbr.* **MI** Necrosis of a region of the myocardium caused by an interruption in the supply of blood to the heart.

my·o·car·di·tis (mī′ō-kär-dī′tĭs) *n.* Inflammation of the myocardium.

my·o·car·di·um (mī′ō-kär′dē-əm) *n., pl.* **-di·a** (-dē-ə). The muscular tissue of the heart. [New Latin : MYO– + Greek *kardia,* heart; see **kerd-** in Appendix.] **—my′o·car′di·al** *adj.*

my·oc·lo·nus (mī-ŏk′lə-nəs) *n.* A sudden twitching of muscles or parts of muscles, without any rhythm or pattern, occurring in various brain disorders. **—my′o·clon′ic** (mī′ə-klŏn′ĭk) *adj.*

my·o·e·lec·tric (mī′ō-ĭ-lĕk′trĭk) *adj.* Of or relating to the electrical properties of muscle tissue from which impulses may be amplified, used especially in the control or operation of prosthetic devices.

my·o·fib·ril (mī′ə-fī′brəl, -fĭb′rəl) *n.* Any of the threadlike fibrils that make up the contractile part of a striated muscle fiber. Also called *sarcostyle.*

my·o·fil·a·ment (mī′ə-fĭl′ə-mənt) *n.* Any of the ultramicroscopic filaments, made up of actin and myosin, that are the structural units of a myofibril.

my·o·gen·ic (mī′ə-jĕn′ĭk) also **my·o·ge·net·ic** (mī′ō-jə-nĕt′ĭk) *adj.* **1.** Giving rise to or forming muscular tissue. **2.** Of muscular origin; arising from the muscles.

my·o·glo·bin (mī′ə-glō′bĭn) *n.* The form of hemoglobin found in muscle fibers, having a higher affinity for oxygen than hemoglobin of the blood.

my·o·graph (mī′ə-grăf′) *n.* An instrument for recording muscular contractions.

my·ol·o·gy (mī-ŏl′ə-jē) *n.* The scientific study of muscles. **—my′o·log′ic** (mī′ə-lŏj′ĭk) *adj.* **—my·ol′o·gist** *n.*

my·o·ma (mī-ō′mə) *n., pl.* **-mas** or **-ma·ta** (-mə-tə). A tumor composed of muscle tissue. **—my·o′ma·tous** (-ō′mə-təs, -ŏm′ə-) *adj.*

my·o·neu·ral (mī′ə-nŏŏr′əl, -nyŏŏr′-) *adj.* Of or relating to both muscles and nerves, especially to nerve endings in muscle tissue.

my·op·a·thy (mī-ŏp′ə-thē) *n., pl.* **-thies.** A disease of muscle or muscle tissue. **—my′o·path′ic** (mī′ə-păth′ĭk) *adj.*

my·ope (mī′ōp′) *n.* One affected by myopia. [French, from Late Latin *myops,* near-sighted, from Greek *muōps.* See MYOPIA.]

my·o·pi·a (mī-ō′pē-ə) *n.* **1.** A visual defect in which distant objects appear blurred because their images are focused in front of the retina rather than on it; nearsightedness. Also called *short sight.* **2.** Lack of discernment or long-range perspective in thinking or planning: *"For Lorca, New York is a symbol of spiritual myopia"* (Edwin Honig). [Greek *muōpia,* from *muōps,* near-sighted : *muein,* to close the eyes + *ōps,* eye; see **okʷ-** in Appendix.] **—my·op′ic** (-ŏp′ĭk, -ō′pĭk) *adj.* **—my·op′i·cal·ly** *adv.*

my·o·sin (mī′ə-sĭn) *n.* The commonest protein in muscle cells, responsible for the elastic and contractile properties of muscle. It combines with actin to form actomyosin. [Greek *muos,* genitive of *mus,* muscle; see MYO– + *–in.*]

my·o·sis (mī-ō′sĭs) *n.* Variant of **miosis.**

my·o·si·tis (mī′ə-sī′tĭs) *n.* Inflammation of a muscle, especially a voluntary muscle, characterized by pain, tenderness, and sometimes spasm in the affected area.

my·o·so·tis (mī′ə-sō′tĭs) *n.* Any of various plants of the genus *Myosotis,* such as the forget-me-not. [New Latin *Myosōtis,* genus name, from Latin *myosōtis,* mouse-ear, a kind of plant, from Greek *muosōtis* : *muos,* genitive of *mus,* mouse; see **mūs-** in Appendix + *ous, ōt-,* ear; see **ous-** in Appendix.]

my·o·tome (mī′ə-tōm′) *n.* **1.** The segment of a somite in a vertebrate embryo that differentiates into skeletal muscle. **2.** A muscle or group of muscles derived from one somite and innervated by a single segment of a spinal nerve.

my·o·to·ni·a (mī′ə-tō′nē-ə) *n.* Tonic spasm or temporary rigidity of one or more muscles, often characteristic of various muscular disorders. **—my'o·ton'ic** (-tŏn'ĭk) *adj.*

My·ra (mī'rə). An ancient Lycian city of southern Asia Minor. A major seaport, it was one of the chief cities of the region.

Myr·dal (mür'däl', mîr'-), **Alva.** 1902–1986. Swedish sociologist and diplomat. She shared the 1982 Nobel Peace Prize for her role in the United Nations nuclear disarmament negotiations.

Myrdal, (Karl) Gunnar. 1898–1987. Swedish economist. He shared a 1974 Nobel Prize for work on the theory of optimum allocation of resources.

myr·i·ad (mĭr'ē-əd) *adj.* **1.** Constituting a very large, indefinite number; innumerable: *the myriad fish in the ocean.* **2.** Composed of numerous diverse elements or facets: *the myriad life of the metropolis.* **—myriad** *n.* **1.** A vast number: *the myriads of bees in the hive.* **2.** *Archaic.* Ten thousand. [Greek *murias, muriad-,* ten thousand, from *murios,* countless.]

USAGE NOTE: Throughout most of its history in English *myriad* was used as a noun, as in *a myriad of men.* In the 19th century it began to be used as an adjective, as in *myriad men;* this usage became so well entrenched that many people came to consider it as the only correct possibility. In fact, both uses have not only ample precedent in English but also etymological justification from Greek, inasmuch as the Greek word *murias* from which *myriad* derives could be used as either a noun or an adjective. Both uses may be considered equally acceptable, as in Samuel Taylor Coleridge's *"Myriad myriads of lives."*

myr·i·a·pod also **myr·i·o·pod** (mĭr'ē-ə-pŏd') *n.* Any of several arthropods, such as the centipede or millipede, having segmented bodies, one pair of antennae, and at least nine pairs of legs. [From New Latin *Myriapoda,* class name : Greek *murias,* ten thousand; see MYRIAD + New Latin *-poda,* -pod.] **—myr'i·ap'o·dous** (-ăp'ə-dəs) *adj.*

my·ris·tic acid (mə-rĭs'tĭk, mī-) *n.* A fatty acid, $CH_3(CH_2)_{12}COOH$, occurring in animal and vegetable fats and used in the manufacture of cosmetics, soaps, perfumes, and flavorings. [Greek *muristikos,* fragrant, from *muron,* perfume.]

myrmeco– *pref.* Ant: *myrmecology.* [Greek *murmēko-,* from *murmēx,* ant.]

myr·me·col·o·gy (mûr'mĭ-kŏl'ə-jē) *n.* The branch of entomology that deals with ants. **—myr'me·co·log'i·cal** (-kə-lŏj'ĭ-kəl) *adj.* **—myr'me·col'o·gist** *n.*

myr·me·co·phile (mûr'mĭ-kə-fīl') *n.* An organism, such as a beetle, that habitually shares the nest of an ant colony. **—myr'me·coph'i·lous** (-kŏf'ə-ləs) *adj.* **—myr'me·coph'i·ly** (-kŏf'ə-lē) *n.*

Myr·mi·don (mûr'mə-dŏn', -dn) *n.* **1.** *Greek Mythology.* A member of a warlike Thessalian people who were ruled by Achilles and followed him on the expedition against Troy. **2. myrmidon.** A faithful follower who carries out orders without question. [From Middle English *Mirmidones,* Myrmidons, from Latin *Myrmidones,* from Greek *Murmidones.*]

my·rob·a·lan (mī-rŏb'ə-lən, mə-) *n.* **1.** See **cherry plum. 2.** See **Indian almond. 3.** The fruit of any of these plants. [Obsolete French *mirobolan,* from Latin *myrobalanum,* fragrant oil of the ben-nut, from Greek *murobalanos* : *muron,* perfume + *balanos,* acorn.]

myrobalan plum *n.* See **cherry plum.**

My·ron (mī'rən). Fifth century B.C. Greek sculptor of the *Discus Thrower.*

myrrh (mûr) *n.* **1.** An aromatic gum resin obtained from several trees and shrubs of the genus *Commiphora* of India, Arabia, and eastern Africa, used in perfume and incense. Also called *balm of Gilead.* **2.** See **sweet cicely** (sense 2). [Middle English *mirre,* from Old English *myrrha,* from Latin, from Greek *murrha,* probably of Semitic origin.]

myr·tle (mûr'tl) *n.* **1.** Any of several evergreen shrubs or trees of the genus *Myrtus,* especially *M. communis,* an aromatic shrub native to the Mediterranean region and western Asia, having pink or white flowers and blue-black berries and widely cultivated as a hedge plant. **2.** See **periwinkle**[2] (sense 1). [Middle English *mirtille,* from Old French, from Medieval Latin *myrtillus,* diminutive of Latin *myrtus,* from Greek *murtos.*]

Myr·tle Beach (mûr'tl). A city of eastern South Carolina on the Atlantic Ocean east of Columbia. Population, 18,758.

my·self (mī-sĕlf') *pron.* **1.** That one identical with me. **a.** Used reflexively as the direct or indirect object of a verb or as the object of a preposition: *I bought myself a new car.* **b.** Used for emphasis: *I myself was certain of the facts.* **c.** Used in an absolute construction: *In office myself, I helped her get a job.* **2.** My normal or healthy condition or state: *I'm feeling myself again.* [Middle English *mi-self,* from Old English *mē selfum, mē selfne* : *mē,* me; see **me-**[1] in Appendix + *selfum, selfne,* dative and accusative of *self;* see SELF.]

USAGE NOTE: The reflexive pronouns, such as *myself, ourselves, yourself, yourselves, himself,* and *herself,* are often used as emphatic forms: *Like yourself, I have no apologies to make.* The practice is particularly common in compound phrases: *Mrs. Evans or yourself will have to pick them up at the airport.* These usages have been common in the writing of reputable authors for several centuries: *"To myself, mountains are the beginning and end of all natural scenery"* (John Ruskin). The strongest criticism that can be made of these uses of reflexives is that like other emphatic devices they may easily be overused, and when the pronoun refers to the writer or speaker, the result of the emphasis may be an implication of pomposity or self-importance.

My·si·a (mĭsh'ē-ə). An ancient region of northwest Asia Minor. It passed successively to Lydia, Persia, Macedon, Syria, Pergamum, and Rome. **—My'si·an** *adj. & n.*

my·sid (mī'sĭd) *n.* Any of various small, shrimplike, chiefly marine crustaceans of the order Mysidacea, the females of which carry their eggs in a pouch beneath the thorax. Also called *opossum shrimp.* [From New Latin *Mysis, Mysid-,* type genus, from Greek *musis,* a closing, from *muein,* to close the lips or eyes.]

my·so·pho·bi·a (mī'sō-fō'bē-ə) *n.* An abnormal fear of dirt or contamination. [Greek *musos,* uncleanness + –PHOBIA.]

My·sore (mī-sôr', -sōr'). A city of southern India southwest of Bangalore. Inhabited before the 3rd century B.C., it was the center of a Moslem state after the late 16th century and was occupied by the British in 1831. Population, 441,754.

mys·ta·gogue (mĭs'tə-gŏg', -gôg') *n.* **1.** One who prepares candidates for initiation into a mystery cult. **2.** One who holds or spreads mystical doctrines. [From Latin *mystagōgus,* from Greek *mustagōgos* : *mustēs,* an initiate; see MYSTERY[1] + *agōgos,* guide, leader (from *agein,* to lead; see **ag-** in Appendix).] **—mys'ta·gog'ic** (-gŏj'ĭk) *adj.* **—mys'ta·go'gy** (-gō'jē) *n.*

mys·te·ri·ous (mĭ-stîr'ē-əs) *adj.* **1.** Of, relating to, or being a mystery: *mysterious and infinite truths.* **2.** Simultaneously arousing wonder and inquisitiveness, and eluding explanation or comprehension: *a mysterious visitor.* [French *mystérieux,* from *mystère,* secret, from Latin *mystērium.* See MYSTERY[1].] **—mys·te'ri·ous·ly** *adv.* **—mys·te'ri·ous·ness** *n.*

SYNONYMS: *mysterious, esoteric, arcane, occult, inscrutable.* These adjectives mean beyond human power to explain or understand. Something *mysterious* arouses wonder and inquisitiveness and at the same time eludes explanation or comprehension: *a mysterious noise; mysterious symbols. "The sea lies all about us. . . . In its mysterious past it encompasses all the dim origins of life"* (Rachel Carson). What is *esoteric* is mysterious because it is known and understood by only a small, select group, as by a circle of initiates or the members of a profession: *a compilation of esoteric philosophical theories. Arcane* applies to what is hidden from the knowledge of all but those having the key to a secret: *the arcane science of dowsing. Occult* suggests knowledge reputedly gained only by secret, magical, or supernatural means: *occult powers; the occult sciences.* Something that is *inscrutable* cannot be fathomed by means of investigation or scrutiny: *an inscrutable smile. "It is not for me to attempt to fathom the inscrutable workings of Providence"* (Earl of Birkenhead).

mys·ter·y[1] (mĭs'tə-rē) *n., pl.* **-ies. 1.** Something that is not fully understood or that baffles or eludes the understanding; an enigma: *How he got in is a mystery. Even after all the testimonies, the murder remained a mystery.* **2.** A mysterious character or quality: *a landscape with mystery and charm.* **3.** A work of fiction, drama, or film dealing with a puzzling crime. **4.** Often **mysteries.** The skills, lore, or practices that are peculiar to a particular activity or group and are regarded as the special province of initiates: *the mysteries of Freemasonry; the mysteries of cooking game.* **5.** *Theology.* A religious truth that is incomprehensible to the reason and knowable only through divine revelation. **6. a.** An incident from the life of Jesus, especially the Incarnation, Passion, Crucifixion, or Resurrection, of particular importance for redemption. **b.** *Roman Catholic Church.* One of the 15 incidents from the lives of Jesus or the Blessed Virgin Mary, such as the Annunciation or the Ascension, serving as the subject of meditation during recitation of the rosary. **7. a.** One of the Christian sacraments, especially the Eucharist. **b. mysteries.** The consecrated elements of the Eucharist. **8. a.** A religious cult practicing secret rites to which only initiates are admitted. **b.** A secret rite of such a cult. [Middle English *misterie,* from Latin *mystērium,* from Greek *mustērion,* secret rite, from *mustēs,* an initiate, from *muein,* to close the eyes, initiate.]

mys·ter·y[2] (mĭs'tə-rē) *n., pl.* **-ies. 1.** *Archaic.* A trade or an occupation. **2.** *Archaic.* A guild, as of merchants or artisans. **3.** A mystery play. [Middle English *misterie,* service, craft, from Medieval Latin *misterium,* craft-guild, from Late Latin, alteration of Latin *ministerium,* occupation, from *minister,* assistant, servant. See **mei-**[2] in Appendix.]

mystery play *n.* A medieval drama based on scriptural events especially in the life of Jesus. [From MYSTERY[1] or MYSTERY[2].]

mys·tic (mĭs'tĭk) *adj.* **1.** Of or relating to religious mysteries or occult rites and practices. **2.** Of or relating to mysticism or mystics. **3.** Inspiring a sense of mystery and wonder. **4. a.** Mysterious; strange. **b.** Enigmatic; obscure. **5.** Mystical. **—mystic** *n.* One who practices or believes in mysticism or a given form of mysticism: *Protestant mystics.* [Middle English *mystik,* from Latin *mysticus,* from Greek *mustikos,* from *mustērion,* secret rite. See MYSTERY[1].]

mys·ti·cal (mĭs'tĭ-kəl) *adj.* **1.** Of or having a spiritual reality or import not apparent to the intelligence or senses. **2.** Of, relating to, or stemming from direct communion with ultimate reality or God: *a mystical religion.* **3.** Of or founded on subjective experience: *mystical theories about the securities market.* **4.** Of

ă pat	oi boy
ā pay	ou out
âr care	ŏŏ took
ä father	ōō boot
ĕ pet	ŭ cut
ē be	ûr urge
ĭ pit	th thin
ī pie	*th* this
îr pier	hw which
ŏ pot	zh vision
ō toe	ə about, item
ô paw	♦ regionalism

Stress marks: **'** (primary); ' (secondary), as in **dictionary** (dĭk'shə-nĕr'ē)

or relating to mystic rites or practices. **5.** Unintelligible; cryptic. **—mys′ti·cal·ly** *adv.* **—mys′ti·cal·ness** *n.*

mys·ti·cete (mĭs′tĭ-sēt′) *n.* See **baleen whale.** [New Latin *mysticētus,* from Greek *mustikētos,* alteration of *(ho) mus to kētos,* (the) whale (called) the mouse : *mus,* mouse; see **mūs-** in Appendix + *kētos,* whale.] **—mys′ti·ce′tous** (-sē′təs) *adj.*

mys·ti·cism (mĭs′tĭ-sĭz′əm) *n.* **1.a.** Immediate consciousness of the transcendent or ultimate reality or God. **b.** The experience of such communion as described by mystics. **2.** A belief in the existence of realities beyond perceptual or intellectual apprehension that are central to being and directly accessible by subjective experience. **3.** Vague, groundless speculation.

mys·ti·fi·ca·tion (mĭs′tə-fĭ-kā′shən) *n.* **1.** The act or an instance of mystifying. **2.** The fact or condition of being mystified. **3.** Something intended to mystify.

mys·ti·fy (mĭs′tə-fī′) *tr.v.* **-fied, -fy·ing, -fies. 1.** To confuse or puzzle mentally; bewilder. See Synonyms at **puzzle. 2.** To make obscure or mysterious. [French *mystifier* : *mystère,* mystery (from Latin *mystērium;* see MYSTERY[1]) + *-fier,* -fy.] **—mys′ti·fi′er** *n.* **—mys′ti·fy′ing·ly** *adv.*

mys·tique (mĭ-stēk′) *n.* An aura of heightened value, interest, or meaning surrounding something, arising from attitudes and beliefs that impute special power or mystery to it: *the cowboy mystique; the mystique of existentialism.* [French, mystical, mystique, from Latin *mysticus.* See MYSTIC.]

myth (mĭth) *n.* **1.a.** A traditional, typically ancient story dealing with supernatural beings, ancestors, or heroes that serves as a fundamental type in the world view of a people, as by explaining aspects of the natural world or delineating the psychology, customs, or ideals of society: *the myth of Eros and Psyche; a creation myth.* **b.** Such stories considered as a group: *the realm of myth.* **2.** A story, a theme, an object, or a character regarded as embodying an aspect of a culture: *a star whose fame turned her into a myth; the pioneer myth of suburbia.* **3.** A fiction or half-truth, especially one that forms part of an ideology. **4.** A fictitious story, person, or thing: *"German artillery superiority on the Western Front was a myth"* (Leon Wolff). [New Latin *mȳthus,* from Late Latin *mȳthos,* from Greek *muthos.*]

myth. *abbr.* Mythological; mythology.

myth·i·cal (mĭth′ĭ-kəl) also **myth·ic** (-ĭk) *adj.* **1.** Of or existing in myth: *the mythical unicorn.* **2.** Imaginary; fictitious. **3.** Often **mythic.** Of, relating to, or having the nature of a myth: *a novel of almost mythic consequence.* **—myth′i·cal·ly** *adv.*

myth·i·cize (mĭth′ĭ-sīz′) *tr.v.* **-cized, -ciz·ing, -ciz·es. 1.** To turn (a person or an event) into myth: *mythicizing the American trucker.* **2.** To interpret as a myth or in terms of mythology.

myth·mak·er (mĭth′mā′kər) *n.* One that creates myths or mythical situations. **—myth′mak·ing** *n.*

my·thog·ra·pher (mĭ-thŏg′rə-fər) *n.* One who records, narrates, or comments on myths. [From Greek *muthographos,* writer of legends : *muthos,* word, story + *-graphos,* -grapher.]

my·thog·ra·phy (mĭ-thŏg′rə-fē) *n., pl.* **-phies. 1.** The artistic representation of mythical subjects. **2.** A collection of myths, often with critical commentary.

my·thoi (mī′thoi, mĭth′oi) *n.* Plural of **mythos.**

mythol. *abbr.* Mythological; mythology.

myth·o·log·i·cal (mĭth′ə-lŏj′ĭ-kəl) also **myth·o·log·ic** (-ĭk) *adj. Abbr.* **myth., mythol. 1.** Of, relating to, or recorded in myths or mythology. **2.** Fabulous; imaginary. **—myth′o·log′i·cal·ly** *adv.*

my·thol·o·gist (mĭ-thŏl′ə-jĭst) *n.* A student or scholar of mythology.

my·thol·o·gize (mĭ-thŏl′ə-jīz′) *v.* **-gized, -giz·ing, -giz·es.** *—tr.* To convert into myth; mythicize. *—intr.* **1.** To construct or relate a myth. **2.** To interpret or write about myths or mythology. **—my·thol′o·giz′er** *n.*

my·thol·o·gy (mĭ-thŏl′ə-jē) *n., pl.* **-gies.** *Abbr.* **myth., mythol. 1.a.** A body or collection of myths belonging to a people and addressing their origin, history, deities, ancestors, and heroes. **b.** A body of myths concerning an individual, event, or institution: *"A new mythology, essential to the . . . American funeral rite, has grown up"* (Jessica Mitford). **2.** The field of scholarship dealing with the systematic collection and study of myths. [French *mythologie,* from Late Latin *mȳthologia,* from Greek *muthologia,* story-telling : *muthos,* story + *-logia,* -logy.]

myth·o·ma·ni·a (mĭth′ə-mā′nē-ə, -mān′yə) *n.* A compulsion to embroider the truth, engage in exaggeration, or tell lies. **—myth′o·ma′ni·ac′** (-ăk′) *n.*

myth·o·poe·ic or **myth·o·pe·ic** (mĭth′ə-pē′ĭk) also **myth·o·po·et·ic** (-pō-ĕt′ĭk) *adj.* **1.** Of or relating to the making of myths. **2.** Serving to create or engender myths; productive in mythmaking. [From Greek *muthopoios,* composer of fiction, from *muthopoiein,* to relate a story : *muthos,* story + *poiein,* to make; see **kʷei-**[2] in Appendix.] **—myth′o·poe′ia** (-pē′ə), **myth′o·po·e′sis** (-pō-ē′sĭs) *n.*

my·thos (mī′thŏs, mĭth′ŏs) *n., pl.* **my·thoi** (mī′thoi, mĭth′oi). **1.** Myth. **2.** Mythology. **3.** The pattern of basic values and attitudes of a people, characteristically transmitted through myths and the arts. [Greek *muthos.*]

myx– *pref.* Variant of **myxo–.**

myx·a·moe·ba also **myx·a·me·ba** (mĭk′sə-mē′bə) *n., pl.* **-bas** also **-bae** (-bē). A slime mold at a stage when it is an amoebalike free-swimming cell and before it fuses to form a plasmodium.

myx·e·de·ma or **myx·oe·de·ma** (mĭk′sĭ-dē′mə) *n.* A disease caused by decreased activity of the thyroid gland in adults and characterized by dry skin, swellings around the lips and nose, mental deterioration, and a subnormal basal metabolic rate. **—myx′e·dem′a·tous** (-dĕm′ə-təs, -dē′mə-), **myx′e·dem′ic** (-dĕm′ĭk) *adj.*

myxo– or **myx–** *pref.* Mucus: *myxoma.* [New Latin, from Greek *muxa,* mucus, slime.]

myx·o·bac·te·ri·um (mĭk′sō-băk-tîr′ē-əm) *n., pl.* **-te·ri·a** (-tîr′ē-ə). Any of numerous gram-negative, rod-shaped saprophytic bacteria of the phylum Myxobacteria, typically found embedded in slime in which they form complex colonies and noted for their ability to move by gliding along surfaces without any known organ of locomotion.

myx·oe·de·ma (mĭk′sĭ-dē′mə) *n.* Variant of **myxedema.**

myx·oid (mĭk′soid′) *adj.* Containing mucus; mucoid.

myx·o·ma (mĭk-sō′mə) *n., pl.* **-mas** or **-ma·ta** (-mə-tə). A benign tumor, most often found in the heart, that is composed of connective tissue embedded in mucus. **—myx·o′ma·tous** (-sō′mə-təs, -sŏm′ə-) *adj.*

myx·o·ma·to·sis (mĭk-sō′mə-tō′sĭs) *n., pl.* **-ses** (-sēz). **1.** A highly infectious, usually fatal disease of rabbits that is caused by a pox virus and is characterized by many skin tumors similar to myxomas. **2.** A condition characterized by the growth of many myxomas.

myx·o·my·cete (mĭk′sō-mī′sēt) *n.* See **slime mold** (sense 2). [MYXO– + –MYCETE.]

myx·o·vi·rus (mĭk′sə-vī′rəs) *n., pl.* **-rus·es.** Any of a group of RNA-containing viruses, including those that cause influenza, typically having an affinity for certain mucins and causing agglutination of red blood cells.

ă pat	oi boy
ā pay	ou out
âr care	ŏŏ took
ä father	ōō boot
ĕ pet	ŭ cut
ē be	ûr urge
ĭ pit	th thin
ī pie	*th* this
îr pier	hw which
ŏ pot	zh vision
ō toe	ə about, item
ô paw	♦ regionalism

Stress marks: ′ (primary); ′ (secondary), as in **dictionary** (dĭk′shə-nĕr′ē)

n¹ or **N** (ĕn) *n., pl.* **n's** or **N's.** **1.** The 14th letter of the modern English alphabet. **2.** Any of the speech sounds represented by the letter *n.* **3.** The 14th in a series. **4.** Something shaped like the letter N.

n² *abbr.* **1.** Or **N.** *Printing.* En. **2.** *Mathematics.* Indefinite number. **3.** Neutron. **4.** Also **N** or **n.** *Chemistry.* Normal.

N¹ The symbol for the element **nitrogen.**

N² *abbr.* **1.** Avogadro's number. **2.** *Games.* Knight. **3.** Newton. **4.** Also **N.** or **n** or **n.** North; northern.

n. *abbr.* **1.** *Latin.* Natus (born). **2.** *Business.* Net. **3.** Or **N.** Noon. **4.** Note. **5.** *Grammar.* Noun. **6.** Number.

N. *abbr.* Norse.

'n' or **'n** *conj. Informal.* And: *scratch 'n sniff.*

Na The symbol for the element **sodium.** [From New Latin *natrium,* from French *natron,* natron. See NATRON.]

Na. *abbr. Bible.* Nahum.

N.A. *abbr.* **1.** Narcotics Anonymous. **2.** National Academy. **3.** North America. **4.** Or **n/a.** Not applicable.

NAACP or **N.A.A.C.P.** *abbr.* National Association for the Advancement of Colored People.

nab (năb) *tr.v.* **nabbed, nab·bing, nabs.** *Informal.* **1.** To seize (a fugitive or wrongdoer); arrest. **2.** To grab; snatch. [Perhaps variant of dialectal *nap,* to seize, probably of Scandinavian origin.] **—nab'ber** *n.*

NAB *abbr.* New American Bible.

Nab·a·tae·a (năb'ə-tē'ə). An ancient kingdom of Arabia in present-day Jordan. It flourished from the fourth century B.C. to A.D. 106, when it was conquered by Rome. The "rose-red city" of Petra was its capital.

Nab·a·tae·an also **Nab·a·te·an** (năb'ə-tē'ən) *n.* **1.** A subject of the kingdom of Nabataea. **2.** The Aramaic dialect of the Nabataeans. **—Nab'a·tae'an** *adj.*

Na·blus (năb'ləs, nä'bləs) also **Nab·u·lus** (năb'ə-lo͞os'). A city in the West Bank north of Jerusalem. An ancient Canaanite town, it was the biblical home of Jacob and the chief city of Samaria. Population, 64,000.

na·bob (nā'bŏb') *n.* **1.** A governor in India under the Mogul Empire. Also called *nawab.* **2.** A person of wealth and prominence. [Hindi *nawāb, nabāb,* from Arabic *nuwwāb,* pl. of *nā'ib,* deputy.]

Na·bo·kov (nə-bô'kəf, nä'bə-kôf', năb'ə-), **Vladimir Vladimirovich.** 1899–1977. Russian-born American writer of poetry, short stories, and novels, most notably the satirical *Lolita* (1955).

Nab·u·lus (năb'ə-lo͞os'). See **Nablus.**

na·celle (nə-sĕl') *n.* A separate streamlined enclosure on an aircraft for sheltering the crew or cargo or housing an engine. [French, dinghy, gondola, from Old French *nacele,* small boat, from Late Latin *nāvicella,* diminutive of Latin *nāvis,* ship. See **nāu-** in Appendix.]

na·cho (nä'chō') *n., pl.* **-chos.** A small, often triangular piece of tortilla topped with cheese or chili-pepper sauce and broiled. [American Spanish, possibly diminutive of the name *Ignacio* or alteration of *ñato,* pug-nosed, ugly, poor (alteration of Spanish *chato,* flat, snub-nosed, from Vulgar Latin **plattus,* flat; see PLATE).]

Nac·og·do·ches (năk'ə-dō'chĭz). A city of eastern Texas east of Waco. Settled in 1779 on the site of a Spanish mission founded in 1716, it is today a processing and manufacturing center. Population, 27,149.

na·cre (nā'kər) *n.* See **mother-of-pearl.** [French, from Old French *nacle,* from Old Italian *naccaro,* drum, nacre, from Arabic *naqqārah,* small drum.] **—na'cred** (-kərd), **na'cre·ous** (-krē-əs) *adj.*

nacreous cloud *n.* A cloud resembling a cirrus, showing iridescent coloration when the sun is several degrees below the horizon. [From NACRE (from the iridescent coloring of mother-of-pearl).]

NACU *abbr.* National Association of Colleges and Universities.

NAD (ĕn'ā-dē') *n.* A coenzyme, $C_{21}H_{27}N_7O_{14}P_2$, occurring in most living cells and utilized alternately as an oxidizing or reducing agent in various metabolic processes. [From *n(icotinamide) a(denine) d(inucleotide),* one of its chemical names.]

Na-Den·e also **Na·Dé·né** (nä-dĕn'ē) *n.* A proposed phylum of North American Indian languages including Athabaskan, Tlingit, and possibly Haida. [Haida *náa-,* house, to live, and Tlingit *naa,* tribe + Proto-Athapaskan **dənæ,* person.] **—Na-Den'e** *adj.*

Na·der (nā'dər), **Ralph.** Born 1934. American lawyer and pioneer in the field of consumer protectionism.

NADH (ĕn'ā-dē-āch') *n.* The reduced form of NAD. [NAD + H[1].]

na·dir (nā'dər, -dîr') *n.* **1.** *Astronomy.* A point on the celestial sphere directly below the observer, diametrically opposite the zenith. **2.** The lowest point: *the nadir of their fortunes.* [Middle English, from Medieval Latin, from Arabic *naẓīr (as-samt),* opposite (the zenith).]

NADP (ĕn-ā'dē-pē') *n.* A coenzyme, $C_{21}H_{28}N_7O_{17}P_3$, occurring in most living cells and utilized similarly to NAD but interacting with different metabolites. [From *n(icotinamide) a(denine) d(inucleotide) p(hosphate),* one of its chemical names.]

NADPH (ĕn'ā-dē'pē-āch') *n.* The reduced form of NADP. [NADP + H[1].]

nae (nā) *adv. Scots.* **1.** No. **2.** Not.

naff¹ (năf) *adj. Chiefly British.* Unstylish, clichéd, or outmoded. [Possibly of dialectal origin.]

naff² (năf) *intr.v.* **naff·ed, naff·ing, naffs.** *Chiefly British.* To fool around or go about: *"naffing about in a tutu"* (Suzanne Lowry). ***—phrasal verb.*** **naff off.** Used in the imperative as a signal of angry dismissal. [Origin unknown.]

WORD HISTORY: In the dual tradition of looking to one's betters for models of how to use language and American obeisance to British usage, let us look at two British words spelled *naff.* One is an adjective, meaning "clichéd, unstylish" (first recorded in 1969), that may be derived from dialectal words such as *naffhead,* "simpleton," or *niffy-naffy,* "stupid." The other *naff* is a verb, usually used in the imperative in combination with *off* (first recorded in 1959). This is the delicate injunction that members of the royal family such as Princess Anne have used in requesting members of the press to beat it. The origin of *naff* is unknown, but it has been suggested that *naff* may be related to an older English slang term *naf,* meaning "the female sexual organ." *Naf* has been derived from a backward spelling of *fan,* from *fanny.*

Na·fud (nă-fo͞od'). See **Nefud.**

nag¹ (năg) *v.* **nagged, nag·ging, nags.** *—tr.* **1.** To annoy by constant scolding, complaining, or urging. **2.** To torment persistently, as with anxiety or pain. *—intr.* **1.** To scold, complain, or find fault constantly: *nagging at the children.* **2.** To be a constant source of anxiety or annoyance: *The half-remembered quotation nagged at my mind.* **—nag** *n.* One who nags. [Probably of Scandinavian origin; akin to Old Norse *gnaga,* to bite, gnaw.] **—nag'ger** *n.* **—nag'ging·ly** *adv.*

nag² (năg) *n.* **1.** A horse, especially: **a.** An old or worn-out horse. **b.** *Slang.* A racehorse. **2.** *Archaic.* A small saddle horse or pony. [Middle English *nagge,* possibly of Low German origin.]

Na·ga Hills (nä'gə) also **Na·ga·land** (-lănd'). A region on the India-Burma border. Its people were subdued by the British from 1865 to 1880.

na·ga·na also **n'ga·na** (nə-gä'nə) *n.* An often fatal disease of African ungulates caused by various species of trypanosomes and transmitted by the bite of the tsetse fly. Also called *tsetse disease.* [Nguni (Zulu) *u-nakane.*]

Na·ga·no (nä-gä'nō). A city of central Honshu, Japan, northwest of Tokyo. It is a religious center with diverse industries in a silk-producing region. Population, 336,967.

Na·ga·sa·ki (nä'gə-sä'kē, năg'ə-săk'ē). A city of western Kyushu, Japan, on **Nagasaki Bay,** an inlet of the East China Sea. The first Japanese port to be opened to foreign trade in the 16th century, Nagasaki was devastated by the second atomic bomb

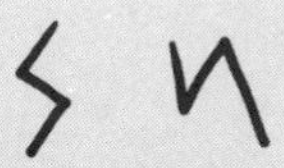

Phoenician
The Phoenician alphabet used this sign to stand for the *n* in *nūn,* "fish."

Early Greek
The Greeks adopted the letter without change and called it *nu.*

Roman
Only a bit of straightening under the Roman stylus and chisel remained to produce the modern shape of capital N.

used in World War II (August 9, 1945). Population, 449,382.

Na·go·ya (nə-goi′ə, nä′gô-yä′). A city of central Honshu, Japan, at the head of Ise Bay east of Kyoto. A fortress town in the 16th century, it was rebuilt after heavy bombing in World War II. Population, 2,116,350.

Nag·pur (näg′po͝or′). A city of central India northeast of Bombay. Founded in the 18th century, it passed to the British in 1853 and is today an important commercial and industrial center. Population, 1,219,461.

Nah. *abbr. Bible.* Nahum.

Na·ha (nä′hä). A city of southwest Okinawa, Japan, in the Ryukyu Islands on the East China Sea. It is a port and the commercial center of the islands. Population, 303,680.

Na·hua·tl (nä′wät′l) *n., pl.* **Nahuatl** or **-tls. 1.** A member of any of various Indian peoples of central Mexico, including the Aztecs. **2.** The Uto-Aztecan language of the Nahuatl. [Spanish *náhuatl,* from Nahuatl, that which pleases the ear.]

Na·hum (nā′həm, nā′əm) *n. Bible.* **1.** A Hebrew prophet of the seventh century B.C. who predicted the fall of Nineveh. **2.** *Abbr.* **Na., Nah.** See table at **Bible.**

NAIA *abbr.* National Association of Intercollegiate Athletes.

nai·ad (nā′əd, -ăd′, nī′-) *n., pl.* **-a·des** (-ə-dēz′) or **-ads. 1.** *Greek Mythology.* One of the nymphs who lived in and presided over brooks, springs, and fountains. **2.** The aquatic nymph of certain insects, such as the mayfly, damselfly, or dragonfly. **3.** An aquatic plant of the genus *Naias.* [Middle English, from Latin *nāias, nāiad-,* from Greek *naias,* probably from *naein,* to flow. See **(s)nāu-** in Appendix.]

Nai·du (nī′do͞o), **Sarojini.** 1879–1949. Indian poet and reformer noted for her famine-relief efforts and her delicate, sentimental poetry, written in English.

na·if or **na·ïf** (nä-ēf′) *adj. & n.* Variants of **naive.**

nail (nāl) *n.* **1.** A slim, pointed piece of metal hammered into material as a fastener. **2. a.** A fingernail or toenail. **b.** A claw or talon. **3.** Something resembling a nail in shape, sharpness, or use. **4.** A measure of length formerly used for cloth, equal to 1/16 yard (5.7 cm). —*tr.* **nailed, nail·ing, nails. 1.** To fasten, join, or attach with or as if with a nail. **2.** To cover, enclose, or shut by fastening with nails: *nail up a window.* **3.** To keep fixed, motionless, or intent: *Fear nailed me to my seat.* **4.** *Slang.* **a.** To stop and seize; catch: *Police nailed the suspect.* **b.** To detect and expose: *nailed the senator in a lie; nail corruption before it gets out of control.* **5.** *Slang.* **a.** To strike or bring down, especially with something shot or hurled: *nail a bird in flight.* **b.** To gain thorough understanding of; master: *a brilliant student who nailed all her courses in thermodynamics.* **6.** *Baseball.* To put out (a base runner). —***phrasal verb.* nail down. 1.** To discover or establish conclusively: *nailed down the story by checking all the facts.* **2.** To win: *nailed down another victory in the golf tournament.* [Middle English, from Old English *nægl,* fingernail, toenail. See **nogh-** in Appendix.] —**nail′er** *n.*

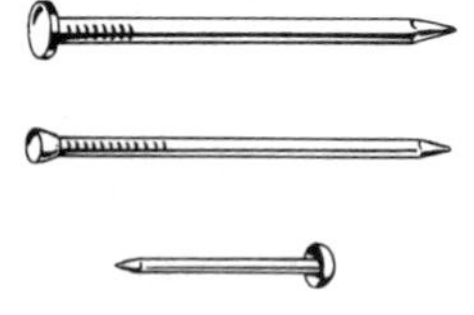

nail
Top: Box nail
Center: Finishing nail
Bottom: Upholstery nail

nail bed *n.* The formative layer of cells at the base of the fingernail or toenail; the matrix.

nail·brush (nāl′brŭsh′) *n.* A small brush with firm bristles used for scrubbing the hands and cleaning the fingernails.

nail file *n.* A small flat file used for shaping and smoothing the fingernails.

nail fold *n.* A fold of hard skin overlapping the base and sides of a fingernail or toenail.

nail polish *n.* A clear or colored cosmetic lacquer applied to the fingernails or toenails.

nail punch *n.* See **nail set.**

nail scissors *pl.n. (used with a sing. or pl. verb).* Small scissors with short, curved blades for trimming and shaping fingernails or toenails.

nail set *n.* A tool used for driving a nail so that its head is below or flush with a surface. Also called *nail punch.*

nain·sook (nān′so͝ok′) *n.* A soft, light cotton material, often with a woven stripe. [Hindi *nainsukh,* pleasant : *nain,* eye (from Sanskrit *nayanam,* from *nayati,* he leads) + *sukh,* pleasure (from Sanskrit *sukha-,* pleasant).]

Nai·paul (nī′pôl), **V(idiadhar) S(urajprasad).** Born 1932. West Indian-born British writer whose short stories, travel essays, and novels, such as *A Bend in the River* (1979), present an increasingly pessimistic view of the Third World.

nai·ra (nī′rə) *n.* See table at **currency.** [Alteration of NIGERIA.]

Nai·ro·bi (nī-rō′bē). The capital and largest city of Kenya, in the south-central part of the country. Founded in 1899, it became the seat of government for British East Africa in 1905 and capital of independent Kenya in 1963. Population, 827,775.

Nai·smith (nā′smĭth′), **James.** 1861–1939. Canadian-born American educator who originated the game of basketball (1891).

na·ive or **na·ïve** (nä-ēv′) also **na·if** or **na·ïf** (nä-ēf′) —*adj.* **1. a.** Lacking worldliness and sophistication; artless. **b.** Simple and credulous as a child; ingenuous. **2.** Lacking critical ability or analytical insight; not subtle or learned: *"this extravagance of metaphors, with its naive bombast"* (H.L. Mencken). **3. a.** Not previously subjected to experiments: *testing naive mice.* **b.** Not having previously taken or received a particular drug: *persons naive to marijuana.* —*n.* One who is artless, credulous, or uncritical. [French *naïve,* feminine of *naïf,* from Old French, natural, native, from Latin *nātīvus,* native, rustic, from *nātus,* past participle of *nāscī,* to be born. See **gene-** in Appendix.] —**na·ive′ly** *adv.* —**na·ive′ness** *n.*

SYNONYMS: *naive, simple, ingenuous, unsophisticated, natural, unaffected, guileless, artless.* These adjectives mean free from guile, cunning, or sham. *Naive* suggests the simplicity of nature; it sometimes connotes a credulity that impedes effective functioning in a practical world: *"this naive simple creature, with his straightforward and friendly eyes so eager to believe appearances"* (Arnold Bennett). *Simple* stresses absence of complexity, artifice, pretentiousness, or dissimulation; it may imply a favorable quality, such as openness of character, or an unfavorable one, such as lack of good sense: *"Those of highest worth and breeding are most simple in manner and attire"* (Francis Parkman). *"He was one of those simple men that love and sympathize with children"* (W.H. Hudson). *"Among simple people she had the reputation of being a prodigy of information"* (Harriet Beecher Stowe). *Ingenuous* denotes childlike directness, simplicity, and innocence; it connotes an inability to mask one's feelings: *an ingenuous admission of responsibility. Unsophisticated* indicates absence of worldly wisdom: *The sights of Paris bowled over the unsophisticated tourists. Natural* stresses spontaneity that is the result of freedom from self-consciousness or inhibitions: *"When Kavanagh was present, Alice was happy, but embarrassed; Cecelia, joyous and natural"* (Henry Wadsworth Longfellow). *Unaffected* implies sincerity and lack of affectation: *"With men he can be rational and unaffected, but when he has ladies to please, every feature works"* (Jane Austen). *Guileless* signifies absence of insidious or treacherous cunning: *a harmless, honest, guileless creature; a guileless, disarming look. Artless* stresses absence of plan or purpose, as to mislead, and suggests a lack of concern for or awareness of the reaction produced in others: *a woman of artless grace and simple goodness.*

na·ive·té or **na·ïve·té** (nä′ēv-tā′, nä-ē′vĭ-tā′) *n.* **1.** The state or quality of being artless, credulous, or uncritical. **2.** An artless, credulous, or uncritical statement or act. [French *naïveté,* from Old French *naivete,* native disposition, from *naif,* artless. See NAIVE.]

na·ive·ty or **na·ïve·ty** (nä-ēv′tē, -ē′vĭ-tē) *n.* Artlessness or credulity; naiveté.

Najd (nǎjd). See **Nejd.**

na·ked (nā′kĭd) *adj.* **1.** Having no clothing on the body; nude. **2.** Having no covering, especially the usual one: *a naked sword.* **3.** Devoid of vegetation, trees, or foliage: *the naked ground; naked tree limbs.* **4.** Being without addition, concealment, disguise, or embellishment: *the naked facts; naked ambition.* **5.** Devoid of a specified quality, characteristic, or element: *a look that was naked of all pretense.* **6.** Exposed to harm; vulnerable: *"naked to mine enemies"* (Shakespeare). **7.** *Botany.* **a.** Not encased in ovaries: *naked seeds.* **b.** Unprotected by scales: *naked buds.* **c.** Lacking a perianth: *naked flowers.* **d.** Without leaves or pubescence: *naked stalks.* **8.** *Zoology.* Lacking outer covering such as scales, fur, feathers, or a shell. [Middle English, from Old English *nacod.* See **nogʷ-** in Appendix.] —**na′ked·ly** *adv.* —**na′ked·ness** *n.*

naked eye *n.* The eye unassisted by an optical instrument.

naked option *n.* An opening transaction in an option when the underlying asset is not owned by the investor writing the option. If a stock on which such an investor has written a call option is then called by the option holder, the investor must purchase shares in the market for delivery and is therefore caught naked. Also called *uncovered option.*

Nal·chik (näl′chĭk). A city of southwest Russia southeast of Rostov. Founded as a fortress town c. 1818, it is now an industrial center and a health resort. Population, 227,000.

na·led (nā′lĕd′) *n.* A nonpersistent chemical, $C_4H_7O_4PBr_2Cl_2$, used for mosquito control and as an insecticide against crop pests. [Origin unknown.]

na·li·dix·ic acid (nā′lĭ-dĭk′sĭk) *n.* A compound, $C_{12}H_{12}N_2O_3$, used to treat infections of the genital and urinary tracts caused by gram-negative bacteria. [Shortening and alteration of *naphthyridin* and *carboxylic acid,* elements of one of its chemical names.]

nal·or·phine (năl′ər-fēn′, năl-ôr′fēn) *n.* A drug, $C_{19}H_{21}NO_3$, derived from morphine, used to treat respiratory depression and other effects of an overdose of narcotics. [Short for *N-allylnormorphine,* its chemical name.]

nal·ox·one (năl′ək-sōn′, nə-lŏk′sōn) *n.* A drug, $C_{19}H_{21}NO_4$, used as an antagonist to narcotic drugs, such as morphine. [Short for *N-allyldihydrohydroxynormorphinone,* its chemical name.]

nal·trex·one (năl-trĕk′sōn) *n.* A drug, $C_{20}H_{23}NO_4$, used as an antagonist to narcotic drugs. [*N-allyl* (N[1] + AL(LYL)) + *trex-* (of unknown origin) + -ONE.]

Nam (näm, năm). Vietnam.

NAM or **N.A.M.** *abbr.* National Association of Manufacturers.

Na·ma (nä′mä, -mə) *n., pl.* **Nama** or **-mas. 1.** A member of a Khoikhoin people of southwest Africa. **2.** The Khoikhoin language of the Nama.

Na·ma·land (nä′mə-lănd′). See **Namaqualand.**

Na·man·gan (nä′mən-gän′, nə-mən-). A city of eastern Uzbekistan east of Tashkent. It has textile and food-processing industries. Population, 275,000.

Na·ma·qua·land (nə-mä′kwə-lănd′) or **Na·ma·land** (nä′mə-). A mostly arid region of southwest Africa divided by the

Orange River into **Great Namaqualand** in Namibia and **Little Namaqualand** in South Africa.

nam·ay·cush (năm′ī-kŭsh′, năm′ā-) *n.* See **lake trout.** [Cree *namekos.*]

nam·by-pam·by (năm′bē-păm′bē) *adj.* **1.** Insipid and sentimental. **2.** Lacking vigor or decisiveness; spineless. **—namby-pamby** *n., pl.* **-bies.** One that is insipid, sentimental, or weak. [After *Namby-Pamby,* a satire on the poetry of Ambrose Philips (1674–1749) by Henry Carey (1687?–1743).]

WORD HISTORY: We are being very literary when we call someone a *namby-pamby.* This word is derived from the name of Ambrose Philips, a little-known poet who wrote verse that incurred the sharp ridicule of two other 18th-century poets, Alexander Pope and his friend Henry Carey. Their ridicule, inspired by political differences and literary rivalry, actually had little to do with the quality of Philips's poetry. In poking fun at some children's verse written by Philips, Carey used the nickname *Namby Pamby:* "So the Nurses get by Heart Namby Pamby's Little Rhimes." Pope then used the name in the 1733 edition of his satirical epic *The Dunciad.* The first part of Carey's coinage came from *Amby,* or *Ambrose. Pamby* repeated the sound and form but added the initial of Philips's name. Such a process of repetition is called reduplication. After being popularized by Pope, *namby-pamby* went on to be used generally for people or things that are insipid, sentimental, or weak.

name (nām) *n.* **1.** A word or words by which an entity is designated and distinguished from others. *some of the most famous names of the 20th century.* **2.** A word or group of words used to describe or evaluate, often disparagingly. **3.** Representation or repute, as opposed to reality: *a democracy in name, a police state in fact.* **4.a.** General reputation: *a bad name.* **b.** A distinguished reputation; renown. **5.** An illustrious or outstanding person: *some of the most famous names of the 20th century.* **—name** *tr.v.* **named, nam·ing, names. 1.** To give a name to: *named the child after both grandparents.* **2.** To mention, specify, or cite by name: *named the primary colors.* **3.** To call by an epithet: *named them all cowards.* **4.** To nominate for or appoint to a duty, an office, or an honor. **5.** To specify or fix: *We need to name the time for our meeting.* **—name** *adj. Informal.* Well-known by a name: *a name performer.* ***—idioms.*** **in the name of.** By the authority of: *Open up in the name of the law!* **to (one's) name.** Belonging to one: *I don't have a hat to my name.* [Middle English, from Old English *nama.* See **nō-men-** in Appendix.] **—nam′a·ble, name′a·ble** *adj.* **—nam′er** *n.*

SYNONYMS: *name, designation, denomination, title, appellation, cognomen.* These nouns all denote the word or words by which someone or something is called and identified. *Name* is the general term: *I can't recall the child's name. "What is friendship but a name?"* (Oliver Goldsmith). A *designation* is a name given principally to classify according to distinguishing characteristics: *During the Depression a shantytown was known by the designation "Hooverville." Denomination,* also a categorizing term, is applied especially to classes of persons or things: *pickpockets, formerly known by the denomination "cutpurse." Title,* applied to people, indicates rank or position and generally connotes distinction and respect (*a prince who renounced his title when he became an American citizen*); applied to entities such as literary or musical forms, it is a distinguishing name (*looking for a colorful and evocative title for the book*). An *appellation* is a name other than a proper name that describes or characterizes and that gains currency primarily through use: *hasn't yet earned the appellation of expert. Cognomen* is frequently used as the equivalent of a first name or a surname or often a nickname: *Rufus, an unusual cognomen; a king renowned under the cognomen "the Just."* See also Synonyms at **appoint, celebrity.**

name brand *n.* **1.** A trademark or distinctive name identifying a product or manufacturer. **2.** The product or its manufacturer. **—name′-brand′** (nām′brănd′) *adj.*

name-call·ing (nām′kô′lĭng) *n.* Verbal abuse; insulting language: *"name-calling, mud-slinging, suits and countersuits"* (Wall Street Journal).

name day *n.* **1.** The feast day of the saint after whom one is named. **2.** The day on which one is baptized.

name-drop (nām′drŏp′) *intr.v.* **-dropped, -drop·ping, -drops.** To mention casually the names of illustrious or famous people in order to imply that one is on familiar terms with them, intended as a means of self-promotion. **—name′-drop′per** *n.* **—name′-drop′ping** *n.*

name·less (nām′lĭs) *adj.* **1.** Having or bearing no name: *nameless stars.* **2.** Unknown by name; obscure: *the nameless dead.* **3.** Not designated by name; anonymous: *a nameless benefactor.* **4.** Defying description; inexpressible: *nameless horror.* **—name′less·ly** *adv.* **—name′less·ness** *n.*

name·ly (nām′lē) *adv.* That is to say; specifically.

name of the game *n. Slang.* The essential or indispensable part or quality necessary for success of an activity or enterprise or the fulfillment of a goal: *"The name of the game was to get the story"* (David Fitzpatrick).

name·plate (nām′plāt′) *n.* **1.** A plate or plaque, as on an office door, inscribed with a name. **2.** See **masthead** (sense 3).

name·sake (nām′sāk′) *n.* One that is named after another. [From the phrase *for the name's sake.*]

name·tag (nām′tăg′) *n.* A badge of personal identification worn to permit access to areas, such as government installations or industrial plants, or gatherings, such as conventions or sales meetings.

name·tape (nām′tāp′) *n.* A small strip of cloth showing the owner's name, sewn or glued to a garment.

Na·mib Desert (nä′mĭb). A dry region of southwest Africa extending along the coast of Namibia between the Atlantic Ocean and the interior plateau.

Na·mib·i·a (nə-mĭb′ē-ə). Formerly **South-West Af·ri·ca** (south′wĕst′ ăf′rĭ-kə). A country of southwest Africa on the Atlantic Ocean. A German protectorate after 1884, it was occupied in 1915 by South Africa, which governed it under a League of Nations mandate from 1920 to 1946 but refused to accept the United Nations trusteeship that replaced the mandate. Namibia achieved full independence in March 1990. Windhoek is the capital. Population, 1,099,000. **—Na·mib′i·an** *adj. & n.*

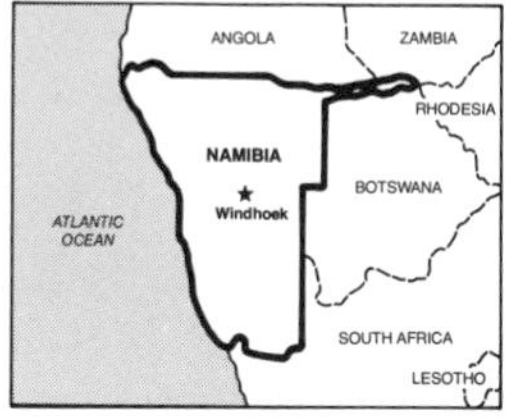

Namibia

Nam·oi (năm′oi′). A river, about 846 km (526 mi) long, of southeast Australia flowing generally northwest to a tributary of the Darling River.

Nam·pa (năm′pə). A city of southwest Idaho west-southwest of Boise. It is a processing and shipping center for an irrigated farming region. Population, 25,112.

Na·mur (nă-mo͝or′, nä-mür′). A city of south-central Belgium on the Meuse River southeast of Brussels. Strategically located, it has been the scene of numerous sieges and battles, notably in the 17th century and in World Wars I and II. Population, 101,860.

Nan (nän). A river of western Thailand flowing about 563 km (350 mi) generally southward to join the Ping River and form the Chao Phraya.

nan·a (năn′ə, nä′nə) *n.* **1.** A grandmother. **2.** A nurse or nursemaid. [Of baby-talk origin.]

Na·nai·mo (nə-nī′mō). A city of southwest British Columbia, Canada, on Vancouver Island and the Strait of Georgia west of Vancouver. Population, 47,069.

Na·nak (nä′nək). 1469–1538? Indian religious leader who broke from orthodox Hinduism to found Sikhism.

nance (năns) *n. Offensive Slang.* Used as a disparaging term for an effeminate man, especially a gay or homosexual man. [Short for the name *Nancy.*]

Nan·chang (nän′chäng′). A city of southeast China on the Gan Jiang southeast of Wuhan. Dating from the 12th century, it is the capital of Jiangxi province. Population, 1,088,800.

Nan·cy (năn′sē, näɴ-sē′). A city of northeast France east of Paris. The capital of the duchy and region of Lorraine, the city passed to France in 1766. Population, 96,317.

NAND gate (nănd) *n. Computer Science.* A logic circuit that produces an output inverse to that of an AND gate. [N(OT) + AND.]

Nan·da De·vi (nŭn′də dā′vē). A peak, 7,821.7 m (25,645 ft) high, of the Himalaya Mountains in northern India.

na·nism (nā′nĭz′əm, năn′ĭz′-) *n.* **1.** *Ecology.* The condition of being stunted or dwarfed, as in certain climates. **2.** See **dwarfism.** [French *nanisme,* from Latin *nānus,* dwarf, from Greek *nanos.* See NANO–.]

Nan·ga Par·bat (nŭng′gə pûr′bət). A peak, 8,131.3 m (26,660 ft), of the Himalaya Mountains in northwest Kashmir.

Nan·jing (nän′jĭng′) also **Nan·king** (năn′kĭng′, nän′-). A city of east-central China on the Yangtze River (Chang Jiang) northwest of Shanghai. The capital of China from the third to the sixth century A.D. and again from 1368 to 1421, it was opened to foreign trade by the Treaty of Nanking in 1842. It was Sun Yat-sen's capital from 1912 to 1927 and Chiang Kai-shek's capital from 1928 to 1937, when it was captured by the Japanese. Reclaimed by Chinese forces in 1946, it is now the capital of Jiangsu province. Population, 2,250,000.

nan·keen (năn-kēn′) also **nan·kin** (-kēn′, -kĭn′) *n.* **1.a.** A sturdy yellow or buff cotton cloth. **b. nankeens.** Trousers made of this cloth. **2. Nankeen.** A Chinese porcelain with a blue-and-white pattern. [After NANJING.]

Nan·king (năn′kĭng′, nän′-). See **Nanjing.**

Nan Ling (nän′ lĭng′). A mountain range of southeast China running roughly east to west along the northern border of Guangdong province.

Nan·ning (nän′nĭng′). A city of extreme southern China west of Guangzhou. The capital of Guangxi Zhuangzu, it is highly industrialized. Population, 564,900.

nanno– *pref.* Variant of **nano–** (sense 1).

nan·no·fos·sil also **nan·o·fos·sil** (năn′ə-fŏs′əl) *n.* A very small fossil organism, especially one of the nannoplankton.

nan·no·plank·ton also **nan·o·plank·ton** (năn′ə-plăngk′tən) *n.* Aquatic organisms constituting very small or the smallest forms of plankton.

nan·ny also **nan·nie** (năn′ē) *n., pl.* **-nies.** A children's nurse. [Alteration of NANA.] **—nan′ny·ish** *adj.*

nan·ny·ber·ry (năn′ē-bĕr′ē) *n.* See **sheepberry.** [From nanny goats' taste for them.]

nanny goat *n.* A female goat. [From *Nanny,* nickname for Anne.]

nano– *pref.* **1.** Often **nanno–.** Extremely small: *nannoplank-*

ă pat	oi boy
ā pay	ou out
âr care	o͝o took
ä father	o͞o boot
ĕ pet	ŭ cut
ē be	ûr urge
ĭ pit	th thin
ī pie	*th* this
îr pier	hw which
ŏ pot	zh vision
ō toe	ə about, item
ô paw	♦ regionalism

Stress marks: ′ (primary); ′ (secondary), as in **dictionary** (dĭk′shə-nĕr′ē)

ton. **2.** One-billionth (10^{-9}): *nanosecond.* [Greek *nanos, nannos,* little old man, dwarf, from *nannas,* uncle, from *nanna,* aunt.]

nan·o·fos·sil (năn′ə-fŏs′əl) *n.* Variant of **nannofossil.**

nan·o·gram (năn′ə-grăm′) *n. Abbr.* **ng** One billionth (10^{-9}) of a gram.

nan·o·me·ter (năn′ə-mē′tər) *n. Abbr.* **nm** One billionth (10^{-9}) of a meter.

nan·o·plank·ton (năn′ə-plăngk′tən) *n.* Variant of **nannoplankton.**

nan·o·sec·ond (năn′ə-sĕk′ənd) *n. Abbr.* **ns, nsec** One billionth (10^{-9}) of a second.

Nan·sen (năn′sən, nän′-), **Fridtjof.** 1861–1930. Norwegian explorer, zoologist, and politician who led an Arctic expedition (1893–1896) and directed the League of Nations relief programs for refugees of World War I. He won the 1922 Nobel Peace Prize.

Nansen bottle *n.* An ocean-water sampling bottle with spring-loaded valves at both ends that are closed at an appropriate depth by a messenger device sent down the wire connecting the bottle to the surface. [After Fridtjof NANSEN.]

Nan Shan (nän′ shän′). See **Qilian Shan.**

Nan·terre (näN-tĕr′). A city of north-central France, an industrial suburb of Paris on the Seine River. Population, 88,578.

Nantes (nănts, näNt). A city of western France on the Loire River west of Tours. Dating to pre-Roman times, it was captured by Norse raiders in the ninth century and later fell to the dukes of Brittany. The Edict of Nantes, granting limited religious and civil liberties to the Huguenots, was issued in 1598 by Henry IV of France and revoked in 1685 by Louis XIV. Population, 240,539.

Nan·ti·coke[1] (năn′tĭ-kōk′) *n., pl.* **Nanticoke** or **-cokes. 1.a.** A Native American people formerly inhabiting Delaware and eastern Maryland between the Chesapeake Bay and the Atlantic coast. **b.** A member of this people. **2.** The Algonquian language of the Nanticoke.

Nan·ti·coke[2] (năn′tĭ-kōk′). A city of southeast Ontario, Canada, on Lake Erie south-southeast of Hamilton. It is in a resort region. Population, 19,816.

Nan·tong also **Nan·tung** (nän′to͝ong′). A city of east-central China on the northern bank of the Yangtze River (Chang Jiang) estuary east of Nanjing. Population, 300,000.

Nan·tuck·et (năn-tŭk′ĭt). An island of southeast Massachusetts south of Cape Cod, from which it is separated by **Nantucket Sound,** an arm of the Atlantic Ocean. Settled in 1659, the island was part of New York from 1660 to 1692, when it was ceded to Massachusetts. It was a whaling center until the mid-1850's and is now a popular resort. **—Nan·tuck′et·er** *n.*

Nan·tung (nän′to͝ong′). See **Nantong.**

Naoi·se (nē′sē, nā′-) *n.* The husband of Deidre in Irish legend.

Na·o·mi (nā-ō′mē). In the Old Testament, the mother-in-law of Ruth.

nap[1] (năp) *n.* A brief sleep, often during the day. **—nap** *intr.v.* **napped, nap·ping, naps. 1.** To sleep for a brief period, often during the day; doze. **2.** To be unaware of imminent danger or trouble. [Middle English, from *nappen,* to doze, from Old English *hnappian.*]

WORD HISTORY: The famous verse 4 in Psalm 121, rendered in the King James Version as "Behold, he that keepeth Israel shall neither slumber nor sleep," is rendered in a Middle English translation as "Loo, ha shal not nappen ne slepen that kepeth ireal." The word *nappen* is indeed the Middle English ancestor of our word *nap.* Lest it be thought undignified to say that God could nap, it must be realized that our word *nap* was at one time not associated only with the younger and older members of society nor simply with short periods of rest. The ancestors of our word, Old English *hnappian* and its descendant, Middle English *nappen,* could both refer to prolonged periods of sleep as well as short ones and also, as in the quotation from Psalm 121, to sleepiness. But these senses have been lost. Since the word has become less dignified, we would not find *nap* used in a translation of Psalm 121 any longer.

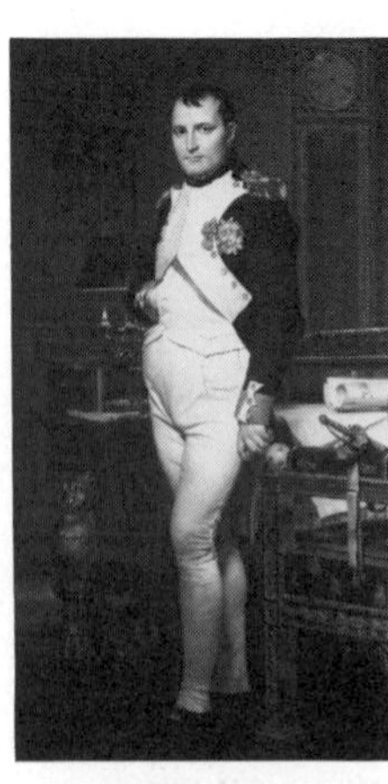

Napoleon I
Detail from *Napoleon in his Study,* 1812, by Jacques Louis David

nap[2] (năp) *n.* A soft or fuzzy surface on fabric or leather. **—nap** *tr.v.* **napped, nap·ping, naps.** To form or raise a soft or fuzzy surface on (fabric or leather). [Alteration (perhaps influenced by obsolete French *nape,* tablecloth) of Middle English *noppe,* from Middle Dutch.]

nap[3] (năp) *tr.v.* **napped, nap·ping, naps.** To pour or put a sauce or gravy over (a cooked dish): *"a stuffed veal chop napped with an elegant Port sauce"* (Jay Jacobs). [French *napper,* from *nappe,* cover. See NAPPE.]

nap[4] (năp) *n.* **1.** *Games.* **a.** A card game that resembles whist. **b.** The highest bid in this game, announcing the intention to win five tricks, the maximum number in a hand. Also called *napoleon.* **2.** See **napoleon** (sense 2). [Short for NAPOLEON.]

na·pa or **nap·pa** (năp′ə, nä′pə) *n.* See **Chinese cabbage.** [Probably Japanese *nappa,* greens.]

Nap·a (năp′ə). A city of western California north of Oakland. It is a center of the **Napa Valley,** a mountainous region that is famous for its vineyards. Population, 50,879.

NAPA *abbr.* National Association of Performing Artists.

na·palm (nā′päm′) *n.* **1.a.** An aluminum soap of various fatty acids that when mixed with gasoline makes a firm jelly used in some bombs and in flamethrowers. **b.** This jelly. **2.** An incendiary mixture of polystyrene, benzene, and gasoline. [*naphthenate,* salt of naphthenic acid (from NAPHTHENE) + PALM(ITATE).] **—na′palm′** *v.*

Nap·a·ta (năp′ə-tə). An ancient city of Nubia near the Fourth Cataract of the Nile River in modern-day Sudan. It flourished during the eighth century B.C.

nape (nāp, năp) *n.* The back of the neck. [Middle English.]

Na·per·ville (nā′pər-vĭl′). A city of northeast Illinois, a manufacturing suburb of Chicago. Population, 42,330.

na·per·y (nā′pə-rē) *n., pl.* **-ies.** Household linen, especially table linen. [Middle English *naperie,* from Old French, from *nape, nappe,* tablecloth. See NAPPE.]

Naph·ta·li (năf′tə-lī′). In the Old Testament, a son of Jacob and the forebear of one of the tribes of Israel.

naph·tha (năf′thə, năp′-) *n.* **1.** Any of several highly volatile, flammable liquid mixtures of hydrocarbons distilled from petroleum, coal tar, and natural gas and used as fuel, as solvents, and in making various chemicals. **2.** *Obsolete.* Petroleum. [Latin, from Greek, liquid bitumen, of Persian origin.] **—naph′thous** *adj.*

naph·tha·lene also **naph·tha·line** (năf′thə-lēn′, năp′-) or **naph·tha·lin** (-lĭn) *n.* A white crystalline compound, $C_{10}H_8$, derived from coal tar or petroleum and used in manufacturing dyes, moth repellents, and explosives and as a solvent. Also called *tar camphor.* [NAPHTH(A) + AL(COHOL) + -ENE.] **—naph′tha·len′ic** (-lĕn′ĭk) *adj.*

naph·thene (năf′thēn′, năp′-) *n.* Any of several cycloalkane hydrocarbons having the general formula C_nH_{2n} and found in various petroleums. [NAPHTH(A) + -ENE.] **—naph·then′ic** (-thĕn′ĭk) *adj.*

naph·thol (năf′thôl′, -thōl′, -thŏl′, năp′-) also **naph·tol** (-tôl, -tōl, -tŏl) *n.* An organic compound, $C_{10}H_7OH$, occurring in two isomeric forms, alpha-naphthol and beta-naphthol. [NAPHTH(ALENE) + -OL[2].]

Na·pi·er (nā′pē-ər, nə-pîr′), Sir **Charles James.** 1782–1853. British general who conquered (1843) and governed (1843–1847) Sind in present-day Pakistan.

Napier, John. Laird of Merchiston. 1550–1617. Scottish mathematician who invented logarithms and introduced the use of the decimal point in writing numbers.

Na·pier·i·an logarithm (nə-pîr′ē-ən, nā-) *n. Abbr.* **ln** *Mathematics.* See **natural logarithm.** [After John NAPIER.]

Na·pi·er's bones (nā′pē-ərz, nə-pîrz′) *pl.n.* *(used with a sing. verb). Mathematics.* A set of graduated rods used to perform multiplication quickly. [After John NAPIER.]

na·pi·form (nā′pə-fôrm′) *adj.* Shaped like a turnip: *napiform roots.* [Latin *nāpus,* turnip + -FORM.]

nap·kin (năp′kĭn) *n.* **1.** A piece of cloth or absorbent paper used at table to protect the clothes or wipe the lips and fingers. **2.** A cloth or towel. **3.** A sanitary napkin. **4.** *Chiefly British.* A diaper. [Middle English : Old French *nape, nappe,* tablecloth; see NAPPE + *-kin,* -kin.]

Na·ples (nā′pəlz). **1.** Also **Na·po·li** (nä′pô-lē). A city of south-central Italy on the **Bay of Naples,** an arm of the Tyrrhenian Sea. Founded by Greeks c. 600 B.C., Naples was conquered by the Romans in the fourth century B.C. and eventually became an independent duchy (eighth century A.D.) and capital of the kingdom of Naples (1282–1860). Population, 1,210,503. **2.** A city of southwest Florida on the Gulf of Mexico south of Fort Myers. It has a shrimp-fishing industry. Population, 17,581.

Na·po (nä′pō). A river of northeast Ecuador and northern Peru flowing about 1,126 km (700 mi) east and southeast to the Amazon River.

na·po·le·on (nə-pō′lē-ən, -pōl′yən) *n.* **1.** A rectangular piece of pastry made with crisp, flaky layers filled with custard cream. **2.** A 20-franc gold coin formerly used in France. Also called *nap.* **3.** *Games.* See **nap**[4] (sense 1). [After NAPOLEON I.]

Na·po·le·on I (nə-pō′lē-ən, -pōl′yən). Originally Napoleon Bonaparte. Called "the Little Corporal." 1769–1821. Emperor of the French (1804–1814). A brilliant military strategist, he deposed the French Directory (1799) and proclaimed himself first counsel and, later, emperor (1804). His military and political might gripped Continental Europe but failed to encompass Great Britain. After a disastrous winter campaign in Russia (1812), he was forced to abdicate by a coalition of French marshals (1814). Having been exiled to the island of Elba, he escaped, briefly regained power, and was ultimately defeated at Waterloo (1815) and exiled for life to the island of St. Helena. His codification of laws, the Napoleonic Code, still forms the basis of French civil law. **—Na·po′le·on′ic** (-ŏn′ĭk) *adj.*

Napoleon II. Originally François Charles Joseph Bonaparte. Called "the Eaglet." 1811–1832. Titular king of Rome who succeeded his father, Napoleon I, as emperor of the French (1814) but remained a politically powerless figure.

Napoleon III. Originally Charles Louis Napoleon Bonaparte. Known as Louis Napoleon. 1808–1873. Emperor of the French (1852–1871). A nephew of Napoleon I, he led the Bonapartist opposition to Louis Philippe and became president of the Second Republic (1848). After proclaiming himself emperor (1852), he instituted reforms and rebuilt Paris. His successful imperialist ventures were overshadowed by a failed campaign in Mexico (1861–1867) and the Franco-Prussian War (1870–1871), which resulted in his deposition.

Na·po·li (nä′pô-lē). See **Naples** (sense 1).
nap·pa (năp′ə, nä′pə) *n.* Variant of **napa.**
nappe (năp) *n.* **1.** A sheet of water flowing over a dam or similar structure. **2.** *Geology.* A large sheetlike body of rock that has been moved far from its original position. **3.** *Mathematics.* Either of the two parts into which a cone is divided by the vertex. [French, tablecloth, nappe, from Old French, tablecloth, from Latin *mappa,* napkin. See MAP.]
nap·py[1] (năp′ē) *adj.* **-pi·er, -pi·est. 1.** Having a nap; fuzzy. **2.** Kinky; frizzy.
nap·py[2] (năp′ē) *n., pl.* **-pies.** A round, shallow cooking or serving dish with a flat bottom and sloping sides. [Probably from dialectal *nap,* bowl, from Middle English, from Old English *hnæp.*]
nap·py[3] (năp′ē) *n., pl.* **-pies.** *Chiefly British.* A diaper. [Alteration of NAPKIN.]
na·prap·a·thy (nə-prăp′ə-thē) *n., pl.* **-thies.** Treatment of disease by manipulation of joints, muscles, and ligaments, based on the belief that many diseases are caused by displacement of connective tissues. [Czech *naprava,* correction (from Slavic *pravŭ,* right; see **per[1]** in Appendix) + -PATHY.] **—nap′ra·path′** (năp′rə-păth′) *n.*
na·prox·en (nə-prŏk′sən) *n.* A drug, $C_{14}H_{14}O_3$, used to reduce inflammation and pain, especially in the treatment of arthritis. [Shortening and alteration of *methoxynaphthylpropionic acid,* one of its chemical names.]
nap·time (năp′tīm′) *n.* The usual time for taking a nap.
Na·ra (när′ə). A city of south-central Honshu, Japan, east of Osaka. An ancient cultural and religious center, it was the first permanent capital of Japan (710–784). Population, 327,702.
Nar·ba·da (nər-bŭd′ə). See **Narmada.**
Nar·bonne (när-bŏn′, -bôn′). A city of southern France near the Mediterranean coast southwest of Montpellier. Thought to have been the first Roman colony established in Transalpine Gaul (118 B.C.), it was an important seaport until its harbor silted up in the 14th century. Population, 41,565.
narc or **nark** (närk) *n. Slang.* A law enforcement officer who deals with narcotics violations. [Short for *narcotics agent.*]
nar·ce·ine (när′sē-ēn′, -ĭn′) *n.* A bitter crystalline alkaloid, $C_{23}H_{27}NO_8$, obtained from opium and formerly used in medicine as a substitute for morphine. [French *narcéine* : Greek *narkē,* numbness + *-ine,* alkaloid; see -INE[2].]
nar·cism (när′sĭz′əm) *n.* Variant of **narcissism.**
nar·cis·si (när-sĭs′ī′, -sĭs′ē) *n.* A plural of **narcissus.**
nar·cis·sism (när′sĭ-sĭz′əm) also **nar·cism** (-sĭz′əm) *n.* **1.** Excessive love or admiration of oneself. See Synonyms at **conceit. 2.** Erotic pleasure derived from contemplation or admiration of one's own body or self, especially as a fixation on or a regression to an infantile stage of development. [After NARCISSUS.] **—nar′cis·sist** *n.* **—nar′cis·sis′tic** *adj.* **—nar′cis·sis′ti·cal·ly** *adv.*
nar·cis·sus (när-sĭs′əs) *n., pl.* **-cis·sus·es** or **-cis·si** (-sĭs′ī′, -sĭs′ē). Any of several widely cultivated bulbous plants of the genus *Narcissus,* having long narrow leaves and usually white or yellow flowers characterized by a cup-shaped or trumpet-shaped central crown. [Latin, from Greek *narkissos* (influenced by *narkē,* numbness, from its narcotic properties).]
Nar·cis·sus (när-sĭs′əs) *n. Greek Mythology.* A youth who pined away in love for his own image in a pool of water and was transformed into the flower that bears his name.
narco– *pref.* **1.** Numbness; stupor; lethargy: *narcolepsy.* **2.** Narcotic drug: *narcoanalysis.* [Greek *narko-,* from *narkoun,* to numb, from *narkē,* numbness.]
nar·co·a·nal·y·sis (när′kō-ə-năl′ĭ-sĭs) *n., pl.* **-ses** (-sēz′). Psychotherapy conducted while the patient is in a sleeplike state induced by barbiturates or other drugs, especially as a means of releasing repressed feelings or thoughts. **—nar′co·an′a·lyt′ic** (-ăn′ə-lĭt′ĭk) *adj.*
nar·co·dol·lar (när′kō-dŏl′ər) *n.* A U.S. dollar acquired from illegal drug traffic. Often used in the plural.
nar·co·klep·toc·ra·cy (när′kō-klĕp-tŏk′rə-sē) *n., pl.* **-cies. 1.** A group of people within a country engaged with drug dealers in large-scale narcotics traffic, theft, corruption, and violence. **2.** A country or government in which such activities are widespread. [NARCO(TIC) + KLEPTO(MANIA) + -CRACY.]
nar·co·lep·sy (när′kə-lĕp′sē) *n., pl.* **-sies.** A disorder characterized by sudden and uncontrollable, though often brief, attacks of deep sleep, sometimes accompanied by paralysis and hallucinations. **—nar′co·lep′tic** (-lĕp′tĭk) *adj.*
nar·co·ma (när-kō′mə) *n., pl.* **-mas** also **-ma·ta** (-mə-tə). Stupor induced by a narcotic. [New Latin *narcōma,* from Greek *narkoun,* to benumb. See NARCOSIS.]
nar·co·sis (när-kō′sĭs) *n., pl.* **-ses** (-sēz). A condition of deep stupor or unconsciousness produced by a drug or other chemical substance. [New Latin *narcōsis,* from Greek *narkōsis,* a numbing, from *narkoun,* to benumb, from *narkē,* numbness.]
nar·co·syn·the·sis (när′kō-sĭn′thĭ-sĭs) *n., pl.* **-ses** (-sēz′). Narcoanalysis directed toward making the patient recall repressed memories and emotional traumas.
nar·cot·ic (när-kŏt′ĭk) *n.* **1.** An addictive drug, such as opium, that reduces pain, alters mood and behavior, and usually induces sleep or stupor. Natural and synthetic narcotics are used in medicine to control pain. **2.** A soothing, numbing agent or thing: *"There was the blessed narcotic of bridge, at the Colony or at the home of friends"* (Louis Auchincloss). **—narcotic** *adj.* **1.** Inducing sleep or stupor; causing narcosis. **2.** Of or relating to narcotics, their effects, or their use. **3.** Of, relating to, or intended for one addicted to a narcotic. [Middle English *narcotik,* from Old French *narcotique,* from Medieval Latin *narcōticum,* from Greek *narkōtikon,* neuter of *narkōtikos,* numbing, from *narkōsis,* a numbing. See NARCOSIS.] **—nar·cot′i·cal·ly** *adv.*
nar·co·tism (när′kə-tĭz′əm) *n.* **1.** Addiction to narcotics such as opium, heroin, or morphine. **2.** Narcosis. [French *narcotisme,* from *narcotique,* narcotic. See NARCOTIC.]
nar·co·tize (när′kə-tīz′) *tr.v.* **-tized, -tiz·ing, -tiz·es. 1.** To place under the influence of a narcotic. **2.** To put to sleep; lull. **3.** To dull; deaden. **—nar′co·ti·za′tion** (-tĭ-zā′shən) *n.*
nard (närd) *n.* See **spikenard** (sense 1). [Middle English *narde,* from Old French, from Latin *nardus,* from Greek *nardos,* probably ultimately from Sanskrit *naladam,* Indian spikenard.]
nar·es (nâr′ēz) *n.* Plural of **naris.**
Na·rew also **Na·rev** (nä′rəf). A river rising in western Belorussia and flowing about 442 km (275 mi) to northeast Poland and then generally west and southwest to the Western Bug River near its confluence with the Vistula River.
nar·ghi·le also **nar·gi·leh** (när′gə-lē′) *n.* See **hookah.** [French *narghilé,* obsolete variant of *narguilé,* from Persian *nārgīleh,* from *nārgīl,* coconut, of Indic origin.]
nar·is (nâr′ĭs) *n., pl.* **-es** (-ēz). An external opening in the nasal cavity of a vertebrate; a nostril. [Latin *nāris.* See **nas-** in Appendix.] **—nar′i·al** (-ē-əl) *adj.*
nark[1] (närk) *n. Slang.* Variant of **narc.**
nark[2] (närk) *Chiefly British. n.* An informer, especially a police informer. **—nark** *intr.v.* **narked, nark·ing, narks.** To be an informer. [Perhaps from Romany *nāk,* nose. See **nas-** in Appendix.]
Nar·ma·da (nər-mŭd′ə) also **Nar·ba·da** (-bŭd′ə). A river of central India flowing about 1,247 km (775 mi) westward to the Gulf of Cambay. Sacred to Hindus, it is said to have sprung from the body of the god Shiva.
Nar·ra·gan·sett also **Nar·ra·gan·set** (năr′ə-găn′sĭt) *n., pl.* **Narragansett** or **-setts** also **Narraganset** or **-sets. 1.a.** A Native American people formerly inhabiting Rhode Island west of Narragansett Bay, with present-day descendants in the same area. The Narragansett were nearly exterminated during King Philip's War in 1675–1676. **b.** A member of this people. **c.** The Algonquian language of the Narragansett. **2.** Any of a breed of small sturdy saddle horse developed in Rhode Island. [From a Narragansett place name.] **—Nar′ra·gan′sett** *adj.*
Narragansett Bay. A deep inlet of the Atlantic Ocean in eastern Rhode Island.
nar·rate (năr′āt′, nă-rāt′) *v.* **-rat·ed, -rat·ing, -rates.** *—tr.* **a.** To tell (a story, for example) in speech or writing. **b.** To give an account of (events, for example). See Synonyms at **describe.** *—intr.* **1.** To give an account or a description. **2.** To supply a running commentary for a movie or performance. [Latin *narrāre, narrāt-,* from *gnārus,* knowing. See **gnō-** in Appendix.] **—nar′rat·a·bil′i·ty** *n.* **—nar′rat·a·ble** *adj.* **—nar′ra′tor, nar′rat′er** *n.*
nar·ra·tion (nă-rā′shən) *n.* **1.** The act, process, or an instance of narrating. **2.** Narrated material. **—nar·ra′tion·al** *adj.*
nar·ra·tive (năr′ə-tĭv) *n.* **1.** A narrated account; a story. **2.** The art, technique, or process of narrating. **3.** *Computer Science.* A comment. **—narrative** *adj.* **1.** Consisting of or characterized by the telling of a story: *narrative poetry.* **2.** Of or relating to narration: *narrative skill.* **—nar′ra·tive·ly** *adv.*
nar·row (năr′ō) *adj.* **-row·er, -row·est. 1.** Of small or limited width, especially in comparison with length. **2.** Limited in area or scope; cramped. **3.** Lacking flexibility; rigid: *narrow opinions.* **4.** Barely sufficient; close: *a narrow margin of victory.* **5.** Painstakingly thorough or attentive; meticulous: *narrow scrutiny.* **6.** *Linguistics.* Tense. **—narrow** *v.* **-rowed, -row·ing, -rows.** *—tr.* **1.** To reduce in width or extent; make narrower. **2.** To limit or restrict: *narrowed the possibilities down to three.* *—intr.* To become narrower; contract. **—narrow** *n.* **1.** A part of little width, as a pass through mountains. **2. narrows.** *(used with a sing. or pl. verb).* **a.** A body of water with little width that connects two larger bodies of water. **b.** A part of a river or an ocean current that is not wide. [Middle English *narwe,* from Old English *nearu.*] **—nar′row·ish** *adj.* **—nar′row·ly** *adv.* **—nar′row·ness** *n.*
nar·row-bod·ied (năr′ō-bŏd′ēd) *adj.* Being or designating a jet aircraft having a narrow fuselage with seats for passengers on either side of a single aisle running the length of the fuselage.
nar·row·cast (năr′ō-kăst′) *intr.v.* **-cast, -cast·ing, -casts.** To transmit, as by cable, programs confined to the interests of a specific group of viewers, subscribers, or listeners, such as physicians, businesspeople, or teenagers. [NARROW + (BROAD)CAST.] **—nar′row·cast′er** *n.*
narrow gauge *n.* **1.** A distance between the rails of a railroad track that is less than the standard width of 56½ inches (143.5 centimeters). **2.** A locomotive, car, or railway line of this gauge. **—nar′row-gauge′** (năr′ō-gāj′), **nar′row-gauged′** (-gājd′) *adj.*
nar·row-mind·ed (năr′ō-mīn′dĭd) *adj.* Lacking tolerance,

ă pat	oi boy
ā pay	ou out
âr care	ŏŏ took
ä father	ōō boot
ĕ pet	ŭ cut
ē be	ûr urge
ĭ pit	th thin
ī pie	*th* this
îr pier	hw which
ŏ pot	zh vision
ō toe	ə about, item
ô paw	♦ regionalism

Stress marks: ′ (primary); ′ (secondary), as in **dictionary** (dĭk′shə-nĕr′ē)

breadth of view, or sympathy; petty. **—nar′row-mind′ed·ly** *adv.* **—nar′row-mind′ed·ness** *n.*

Nar·rows (năr′ōz). A strait of southeast New York between Brooklyn and Staten Island in New York City and connecting Upper and Lower New York Bay.

nar·thex (när′thĕks′) *n. Architecture.* **1.** A portico or lobby of an early Christian or Byzantine church or basilica, originally separated from the nave by a railing or screen. **2.** An entrance hall leading to the nave of a church. [Late Greek *narthē*, from Greek, box, giant fennel, of Indic origin.]

Nar·vá·ez (när-vä′ăs′, -ĕth), **Pánfilo de.** 1470?–1528. Spanish conquistador who was sent to capture and replace the disloyal Hernando Cortés in Mexico but was himself captured and imprisoned by Cortés (1520–1522).

nar·whal also **nar·wal** (när′wəl) or **nar·whale** (-hwāl′, -wāl′) *n.* An Arctic whale *(Monodon monoceros)* that has a spotted pelt and is characterized in the male by a long spirally twisted ivory tusk projecting from the left side of its head. [Alteration of Norwegian or Danish *narhval*, from Old Norse *nāhvalr* : *nār*, corpse (from its whitish color) + *hvalr*, whale.]

nar·y (nâr′ē) *adj.* Not one: *"Frequently, measures of major import . . . glide through these chambers with nary a whisper of debate"* (George B. Merry). [Alteration of *ne'er a.*]

NASA (năs′ə) *abbr.* National Aeronautics and Space Administration.

na·sal (nā′zəl) *adj.* **1.** Of, in, or relating to the nose. **2.** *Linguistics.* Articulated by lowering the soft palate so that air resonates in the nasal cavities and passes out the nose, as in the pronunciation of the nasal consonants (m), (n), and (ng) or the nasalized vowel of French *bon.* **3.** Characterized by or resembling a resonant sound produced through the nose: *a nasal whine.* **—nasal** *n.* **1.** *Linguistics.* A nasal consonant. **2.** A nasal part or bone, forming part of the bridge of the nose. **3.** The nosepiece of a helmet. [Possibly from Middle English *nasale*, from Medieval Latin *nāsālis*, from Latin *nāsus*, nose. See **nas-** in Appendix.] **—na·sal′i·ty** (nā-zăl′ĭ-tē) *n.* **—na′sal·ly** *adv.*

narwhal
Male and female narwhals
Monodon monoceros

nasal index *n.* The ratio of the width to the height of the nose, multiplied by 100, used in anthropological measurements.

na·sal·ize (nā′zə-līz′) *tr. & intr.v.* **-ized, -iz·ing, -iz·es.** *Linguistics.* To make nasal or produce nasal sounds. **—na′sal·i·za′tion** (nā′zə-lĭ-zā′shən) *n.*

Nas·by (năz′bē), **Petroleum V.** See David Ross **Locke.**

NASCAR *abbr.* National Association of Stock Car Auto Racing.

nas·cence (năs′əns, nā′səns) *n.* A coming into being; birth. See Synonyms at **beginning.**

nas·cent (năs′ənt, nā′sənt) *adj.* Coming into existence; emerging: *"the moral shock of our nascent imperialism"* (Richard Hofstadter). [Latin *nāscēns, nāscent-*, present participle of *nāscī*, to be born. See **gene-** in Appendix.] **—nas′cen·cy** *n.*

NASD *abbr.* National Association of Securities Dealers.

NASDAQ *abbr.* National Association of Securities Dealers Automated Quotation System.

Gamal Abdel Nasser

nase·ber·ry (nāz′bĕr′ē) *n.* See **sapodilla.** [Alteration of Spanish *néspera*, from Latin *mespila*, medlar. See MEDLAR.]

Nase·by (nāz′bē). A village of central England near Northampton. Nearby on June 14, 1645, Oliver Cromwell's Parliamentarian forces decisively defeated Royalist troops led by Charles I and Prince Rupert.

Nash (năsh), **Ogden.** 1902–1971. American writer known for his droll epigrammatic verse, much of which appeared in the *New Yorker.*

Nash or **Nashe** (năsh), **Thomas.** 1567–1601. English writer noted for his witty, often invective literary criticism and for *The Unfortunate Traveller* (1594), possibly the best Elizabethan narrative work.

Nash·u·a (năsh′o͞o-ə). A city of southern New Hampshire on the Merrimack River south of Manchester. Settled c. 1655, it developed as a textile center in the early 19th century. Population, 67,865.

Nash·ville¹ (năsh′vĭl′). The capital of Tennessee, in the north-central part of the state northeast of Memphis. Founded in 1779 as Fort Nashborough, it was renamed in 1784 and became the permanent capital in 1843. Nashville is known especially for its music industry. Population, 455,651.

Nash·ville² (năsh′vĭl′) *n. Music.* **1.** Country music. **2.** The country music industry. [After NASHVILLE¹.]

Na·sik (nä′sĭk). A town of west-central India northeast of Bombay. It is a Hindu pilgrimage center noted for its brass and copper ware. Population, 262,428.

na·si·on (nā′zī-ŏn′) *n.* The point in the skull where the nasal and frontal bones unite. [New Latin *nāsion* : NAS(O)– + Greek *-ion*, diminutive suff.]

Nas·ka·pi (năs′kə-pē) *n.*, *pl.* **Naskapi** or **-pis. 1.a.** A Native American people inhabiting northern Quebec and Labrador. **b.** A member of this people. **2.** The variety of Montagnais spoken by the Naskapi. [French, of Montagnais origin.]

nasturtium

naso– *pref.* Nose: *nasopharynx.* [New Latin, from Latin *nāsus*, nose. See **nas-** in Appendix.]

na·so·fron·tal (nā′zō-frŭn′təl) *adj.* Of or relating to the nasal and frontal bones.

na·so·phar·ynx (nā′zō-făr′ĭngks) *n.*, *pl.* **-pha·ryn·ges** (-fə-rĭn′jēz) or **-phar·ynx·es.** The part of the pharynx above the soft palate that is continuous with the nasal passages. **—na′so·pha·ryn′ge·al** (-fə-rĭn′jē-əl, -jəl, -făr′ən-jē′əl) *adj.*

Nas·sau (năs′ô′). **1.** (*also* nä′sou′). A region and former duchy of central Germany north and east of the Main and Rhine rivers. The region became a duchy in 1806 and was absorbed by Prussia in 1866. Members of the original dynasty subsequently ruled Luxembourg and the Netherlands (as the house of Orange). **2.** The capital and largest city of the Bahamas, on the northeast coast of New Providence Island in the Atlantic Ocean east of Miami, Florida. Settled in the 17th century, it was a haven for pirates in the 18th century. Population, 135,000.

Nas·ser (năs′ər, nä′sər), **Gamal Abdel.** 1918–1970. Egyptian army officer and politician who served as prime minister (1954–1956) and president (1956–1958) of Egypt and as president of the United Arab Republic (1958–1970).

Nasser, Lake. A lake of southeast Egypt and northern Sudan. It was formed in the 1960's by the construction of the Aswan High Dam on the Nile river. The rising waters of the lake submerged many historic sites.

Nass River (năs). A river of western British Columbia, Canada, flowing about 380 km (236 mi) southwest through the Coast Mountains to the Pacific Ocean north of Prince Rupert.

Nast (năst), **Thomas.** 1840–1902. German-born American editorial cartoonist whose caricatures in *Harper's Weekly* contributed to the downfall of the Tweed Ring in New York City. He also established the donkey and the elephant as symbols of the Democratic and Republican parties.

nas·tic (năs′tĭk) *adj.* Of, relating to, or characterized by the tendency in plant parts to move in a direction determined by an internal stimulus, as an increased rate of cellular growth on one surface or side of the plant part. [Greek *nastos*, pressed close (from *nassein*, to press) + –IC.]

nas·tur·tium (nə-stûr′shəm, nă-) *n.* **1.** Any of various New World plants of the genus *Tropaeolum*, having pungent juice and long-spurred, usually yellow, orange, or red irregular flowers. **2.** *Color.* A brilliant orange yellow. [Middle English *nasturcium*, a kind of cress, from Latin *nasturtium* : perhaps *nāsus*, nose; see **nas-** in Appendix + **tortāre*, frequentative of *torquēre*, to twist (from its pungent smell); see **terkʷ-** in Appendix.]

nas·ty (năs′tē) *adj.* **-ti·er, -ti·est. 1.a.** Disgustingly dirty. **b.** Physically repellent. **2.** Morally offensive; indecent. See Synonyms at **offensive. 3.** Malicious; spiteful: *"Will he say nasty things at my funeral?"* (Ezra Pound). **4.** Very unpleasant or annoying: *nasty weather; a nasty trick.* See Synonyms at **dirty. 5.** Painful or dangerous; grave: *a nasty accident.* **6.** Exasperatingly difficult to solve or handle: *a nasty puzzle; a nasty problem.* **—nasty** *n.*, *pl.* **-ties.** One that is nasty: *"It is the business of museums to present us with nasties as well as with fine things"* (Country Life). [Middle English *nasti*, possibly alteration of Old French *nastre*, bad, short for *villenastre* : *vilein*, bad; see VILLAIN + *-astre*, pejorative suff. (from Latin *-aster*).] **—nas′ti·ly** *adv.* **—nas′ti·ness** *n.*

–nasty *suff.* Nastic response or change: *epinasty.* [Greek *nastos*, pressed down; see NASTIC + –Y².]

nat. *abbr.* **1.** National. **2.** Native. **3.** Natural.

na·tal (nāt′l) *adj.* **1.** Of, relating to, or accompanying birth: *natal injuries.* **2.** Of or relating to the time or place of one's birth. [Middle English, from Latin *nātālis*, from *nātus*, past participle of *nāscī*, to be born. See **gene-** in Appendix.]

Na·tal (nə-tăl′, -täl′, -tôl′). **1.** A region of southeast Africa on the Indian Ocean. First sighted by Vasco da Gama on Christmas Day 1497 and named *Terra Natalis*, it was acquired by the British in the 1820's and 1830's and settled by the Boers after 1836. Natal became a British colony in 1843 and was later a separate colony (after 1856) and then a founding province of the country of South Africa (1910). **2.** A city of northeast Brazil on the Atlantic Ocean north of Recife. Founded in the late 1590's, it was occupied by the Dutch from 1633 to 1654. Population, 376,446.

Na·tal brown (nə-tăl′, -täl′) *n. Color.* A grayish brown.

na·tal·i·ty (nā-tăl′ĭ-tē, nə-) *n.*, *pl.* **-ties.** See **birthrate.** [NATAL + (MORTAL)ITY.]

Na·tal plum (nə-tăl′, -täl′) *n.* A South African evergreen shrub *(Carissa grandiflora)* often cultivated as a hedge plant, having forked spines, white flowers, and an edible scarlet berry.

na·tant (nāt′nt) *adj.* Floating or swimming in water. [Latin *natāns, natant-*, present participle of *natāre*, to swim. See **snā-** in Appendix.]

Na·tash·quan or **Na·tash·kwan** (nə-tăsh′kwən). A river of eastern Canada rising in southern Labrador and flowing about 388 km (241 mi) across Quebec to the Gulf of St. Lawrence.

na·ta·tion (nā-tā′shən, nă-) *n.* The act or skill of swimming. [Latin *natātiō, natātiōn-*, from *natātus*, past participle of *natāre*, to swim. See **snā-** in Appendix.]

na·ta·to·ri·al (nā′tə-tôr′ē-əl, -tōr′-, năt′ə-) also **na·ta·to·ry** (nā′tə-tôr′ē, -tōr′ē, năt′ə-) *adj.* Of, relating to, adapted for, or characterized by swimming: *a natatorial appendage; natatorial birds.* [From Late Latin *natātōrius*, from Latin *natātor*, swimmer, from *natātus*, past participle of *natāre*, to swim. See **snā-** in Appendix.]

natch (năch) *adv. Slang.* Of course; naturally. [Shortening and alteration of NATURALLY.]

Natch·ez¹ (năch′ĭz) *n.*, *pl.* **Natchez. 1.a.** A Native American people formerly located on the lower Mississippi River near present-day Natchez. The Natchez ceased to exist as a people after war with the French in the early 18th century. **b.** A member of this people. **2.** The language of the Natchez. [French, from Natchez.] **—Natch′ez** *adj.*

Natch·ez² (năch′ĭz). A city of southwest Mississippi on the Mississippi River south-southwest of Vicksburg. Founded as a fortified settlement in 1716, it was held successively by France, Great Britain, Spain, and the United States. Natchez prospered especially as the southern terminus of the **Natchez Trace,** an old road connecting the city with Nashville, Tennessee, that was commercially and strategically important in the late 18th and early 19th centuries. Population, 22,015.

Natch·i·toches (năk′ĭ-tŏsh′). A city of northwest-central Louisiana southeast of Shreveport. It was founded c. 1714 as a French military and trading post. Population, 16,664.

NATE *abbr.* National Association of Teachers of English.

na·tes (nā′tēz) *pl.n.* The buttocks. [Latin *natēs,* pl. of *natis,* buttock.]

Na·than (nā′thən). In the Old Testament, a prophet during the reigns of David and Solomon.

Nathan, George Jean. 1882–1958. American writer, editor, and critic who founded and edited (1924–1930) the *American Mercury* with H.L. Mencken.

Nathan, Maud. 1862–1946. American reformer who was a founder and director (1898–1917) of the National Consumer's League, which pressured industry by the threat of consumer boycotts to institute better working conditions.

Na·than·ael (nə-thăn′yəl). See Saint **Bartholomew.**

nathe·less (nāth′lĭs) also **nath·less** (năth′-) *adv. Archaic.* Nevertheless; notwithstanding. [Middle English, from Old English *nā thē lǣs,* not less by that : *nā,* no; see NO¹ + *thē, thȳ,* instrumental case of *se,* this, that; see **to-** in Appendix + *lǣs,* less; see LESS.]

Na·tick¹ (nā′tĭk) *n.* The variety of Massachusett presumed to have been spoken in the mission town of Natick, Massachusetts, and used in the Massachusett Bible.

Na·tick² (nā′tĭk). A town of northeast Massachusetts, a residential and industrial suburb of Boston. Population, 29,461.

na·tion (nā′shən) *n.* **1.** A relatively large group of people organized under a single, usually independent government; a country. **2.** The government of a sovereign state. **3.** A people who share common customs, origins, history, and frequently language; a nationality: *"Historically the Ukrainians are an ancient nation which has persisted and survived through terrible calamity"* (Robert Conquest). **4.a.** A federation or tribe, especially one composed of Native Americans. **b.** The territory occupied by such a federation or tribe. [Middle English *nacioun,* from Old French *nation,* from Latin *nātiō, nātiōn-,* from *nātus,* past participle of *nāscī,* to be born. See **genə-** in Appendix.] **—na′tion·hood′** *n.* **—na′tion·less** *adj.*

Na·tion (nā′shən), **Carry Amelia Moore.** 1846–1911. American temperance crusader who conducted a series of raids on saloons, in which she would break bottles of liquor and destroy barroom furniture with a hatchet.

na·tion·al (năsh′ə-nəl, năsh′nəl) *adj. Abbr.* **nat., natl. 1.** Of, relating to, or belonging to a nation as an organized whole: *a national anthem.* **2.** Of or relating to nationality: *their national origin.* **3.** Characteristic of or peculiar to the people of a nation: *a national trait.* **4.** Of or maintained by the government of a nation: *a national landmark.* **5.** Being in the interest of one's own nation: *Isolationism is a strictly national policy.* **6.** Devoted to one's own nation or its interests; patriotic. **—national** *n.* **1.** A citizen of a particular nation. See Synonyms at **citizen. 2.** Often **nationals.** *Sports & Games.* A contest or tournament involving participants from all parts of a nation. **—na′tion·al·ly** *adv.*

national bank *n.* **1.** A bank in a system of federally chartered privately owned banks in the United States, each required by law to be an investing member of its district Federal Reserve Bank and insured by the Federal Deposit Insurance Corporation. **2.** A bank associated with national finances and usually owned or controlled by a government.

Na·tion·al City (năsh′ə-nəl, năsh′nəl). A city of southern California, a residential and industrial suburb of San Diego on San Diego Bay. Population, 48,772.

national debt *n.* The total financial obligations of a national government.

national forest *n.* A large expanse of forest that is protected by a government and may be harvested or hunted in only under controlled conditions.

National Guard *n. Abbr.* **NG, N.G.** The military reserve units controlled by each state of the United States, equipped by the federal government, and subject to the call of either the federal or the state government.

National Guardmember *n.* A member of a National Guard unit.

national income *n.* The total net value of all goods and services produced within a nation over a specified period of time, representing the sum of wages, profits, rents, interest, and pension payments to residents of the nation.

na·tion·al·ism (năsh′ə-nə-lĭz′əm, năsh′nə-) *n.* **1.** Devotion to the interests or culture of a particular nation. **2.** The belief that nations will benefit from acting independently rather than collectively, emphasizing national rather than international goals. **3.** Aspirations for national independence in a country under foreign domination. **—na′tion·al·ist** *n.* **—na′tion·al·is′tic** *adj.* **—na′tion·al·is′ti·cal·ly** *adv.*

na·tion·al·i·ty (năsh′ə-năl′ĭ-tē, năsh-năl′-) *n., pl.* **-ties. 1.** The status of belonging to a particular nation by origin, birth, or naturalization. **2.** A people having common origins or traditions and often constituting a nation. **3.** Existence as a politically autonomous entity; national independence. **4.** National character. **5.** Nationalism.

na·tion·al·ize (năsh′ə-nə-līz′, năsh′nə-) *tr.v.* **-ized, -iz·ing, -iz·es. 1.** To convert from private to governmental ownership and control: *nationalize the steel industry.* **2.a.** To make national in character, scope, or notoriety: *"His high profile on such issues as abortion . . . has already begun to nationalize his image"* (Kenneth L. Woodward). **b.** To render distinctively national: *characteristics and issues that have tended to nationalize American political life.* **—na′tion·al·i·za′tion** (-shə-nə-lĭ-zā′shən) *n.* **—na′tion·al·iz′er** *n.*

national monument *n.* A natural landmark or a structure or site of historic interest set aside by a national government and maintained for public enjoyment or study.

national park *n.* A tract of land declared public property by a national government with a view to its preservation and development for purposes of recreation and culture.

national seashore *n.* A seacoast recreational area that is protected and maintained by the federal government for public use.

National Socialism *n.* Nazism.

na·tion-state (nā′shən-stāt′) *n.* A political unit consisting of an autonomous state inhabited especially by a predominantly homogeneous people.

na·tion·wide (nā′shən-wīd′) *adv. & adj.* Throughout a whole nation: *a speech that was broadcast nationwide; nationwide opposition to the tax hike.*

na·tive (nā′tĭv) *adj. Abbr.* **nat. 1.** Existing in or belonging to one by nature; innate: *native ability.* **2.** Being such by birth or origin: *a native Scot.* **3.** Being one's own because of the place or circumstances of one's birth: *our native land.* **4.** Originating, growing, or produced in a certain place or region; indigenous: *a plant native to Asia.* **5.** Of, belonging to, or characteristic of the original inhabitants of a particular place. **6.** Occurring in nature pure or uncombined with other substances: *native copper.* **7.** Natural; unaffected: *native beauty.* **8.** *Archaic.* Closely related, as by birth or race. **—native** *n. Abbr.* **nat. 1.a.** One born in or connected with a place by birth: *a native of Scotland now living in the United States.* **b.** One of the original inhabitants or lifelong residents of a place. **2.** An animal or a plant that originated in a particular place or region. [Middle English, from Old French *natif,* from Latin *nātīvus,* from *nātus,* past participle of *nāscī,* to be born. See **genə-** in Appendix.] **—na′tive·ly** *adv.* **—na′tive·ness** *n.*

SYNONYMS: *native, indigenous, endemic, autochthonous, aboriginal.* These adjectives mean of, belonging to, or connected with a specific place or country by virtue of birth or origin. *Native* implies birth or origin in the specified place: *a native Frenchman; the native North American sugar maple. Indigenous* specifies that something or someone is native rather than coming or being brought in from elsewhere: *The tomato is indigenous to South America. The Ainu are indigenous to the northernmost islands of Japan.* Something *endemic* is prevalent in or peculiar to a particular locality or people: *Food shortages and starvation are endemic in certain parts of the world. Autochthonous* applies to what arises in the locality where it is found and has not been exposed to or has resisted change from outside sources: *Bartók collected autochthonous folk melodies and used them in his compositions. Aboriginal* describes what has existed from the beginning; it is often applied to the earliest known inhabitants of a place: *aboriginal chiefs; the aboriginal population; aboriginal nature.* See also Synonyms at **crude.**

Na·tive American (nā′tĭv) *n.* A member of any of the aboriginal peoples of the Western Hemisphere. The ancestors of the Native Americans are generally considered to have entered the Americas from Asia by way of the Bering Strait sometime during the late glacial epoch. Also called *American Indian, Amerindian, Indian.* **—Native American** *adj.*

USAGE NOTE: The term *Indian* has always been a misnomer for the earliest inhabitants of the Americas. Many people now prefer *Native American* both as a corrective to Columbus's mistaken appellation and as a means of avoiding the romantic and generally offensive stereotypes associated with phrases such as *wild Indian* or *cowboys and Indians.* Certainly there is great merit in a term that distinguishes the peoples indigenous to the Americas from the inhabitants of India, and wherever such confusion might exist *Native American* is an obvious choice. It is also preferred by many contemporary writers when emphasizing ethnic pride, as in *"Only the Native American can lay claim to equality in suffering with the Afro-American in this nation"* (S. Allen Counter). However, it should not be assumed that *Indian* is necessarily offensive or out of date. On the contrary, *Indian* is firmly rooted in English in neutral terms such as *Plains Indian, Paleo-Indian,* and *Indian summer,* as well as in numerous plant and place names, and in locutions of this kind there is no possibility of substitution. Furthermore, many Native Americans and others sympathetic to Native American issues continue to use *Indian* as a term of pride and respect, as in *"It was about this time that* [my mother] *began to see herself as an Indian. That dim native heritage became a fascination and a cause for her"* (N. Scott Momaday) and *"The desperate struggles of the Indian people for survival in this century are too widespread and various to be treated in a single volume"* (Peter Matthiessen). • The compound terms *American Indian* and the less frequent *Amerindian* offer an unambiguous and unproblematic alternative where *Native American* might seem out of place, as in certain historical contexts or in references to groups outside the boundaries of the United States. *Indian* is also a useful adjunct to the name of a people when it cannot be assumed that the reader is familiar with their cultural identity; thus one might say *the Wampanoag Indians* or *the Quiché Indians of Guatemala* rather than adding a gloss such as *the Quiché, a Native American people of Guatemala.* • *Native American* and *Indian* are not exact equivalents when referring to the aboriginal peoples of Canada and Alaska. *Native American,* the broader term, is properly used of all such peoples, whereas *Indian* is customarily used of the northern Athabaskan and Algonquian peoples in contrast to the Eskimo and the Aleut.

nativity
The Nativity
by Lorenzo Lotto
(1480?–1556)

na·tive-born (nā′tĭv-bôrn′) *adj.* Belonging to a place by birth.

na·tiv·ism (nā′tĭ-vĭz′əm) *n.* **1.** A sociopolitical policy, especially in the United States in the 19th century, favoring the interests of indigenous inhabitants over those of immigrants. **2.** The reestablishment or perpetuation of native cultural traits, especially in opposition to acculturation. **3.** *Philosophy.* The doctrine that the mind produces ideas that are not derived from external sources. **—na′tiv·ist** *n.* **—na′tiv·is′tic** *adj.*

na·tiv·i·ty (nə-tĭv′ĭ-tē, nā-) *n., pl.* **-ties. 1.** Birth, especially the place, conditions, or circumstances of being born. **2. Nativity. a.** The birth of Jesus. **b.** A representation, such as a painting, of Jesus's birth. **c.** Christmas. **3.** A horoscope for the time of one's birth. [Middle English *nativite,* from Old French, from Latin *nātīvitās,* from *nātīvus,* born. See NATIVE.]

natl. *abbr.* National.

NATO *abbr.* North Atlantic Treaty Organization.

na·tri·u·re·sis (nā′trə-yo͞o-rē′sĭs) *n.* Excretion of excessive amounts of sodium in the urine. [New Latin *natriūrēsis* : *natrium,* sodium (from French *natron,* natron; see NATRON) + *ūrēsis,* urination (from Greek *ourēsis,* from *ourein,* to urinate; see URETIC).] **—na′tri·u·ret′ic** (-rĕt′ĭk) *adj.*

na·tro·lite (nā′trə-līt′) *n.* A mineral in the zeolite family with composition $Na_2(Al_2Si_3O_{10})\cdot 2H_2O$. [NATRO(N) + –LITE.]

na·tron (nā′trŏn′, -trən) *n.* A mineral of hydrous sodium carbonate, $Na_2CO_3\cdot 10H_2O$, often found crystallized with other salts. [French, from Spanish *natrón,* from Arabic *naṭrūn,* niter, from Greek *nitron.* See NITER.]

Nat·ta (nä′tä), **Giulio.** 1903–1979. Italian chemist. He shared a 1963 Nobel Prize for research on polymers.

nat·ter (năt′ər) *intr.v.* **-tered, -ter·ing, -ters.** To talk idly; chatter. [Variant of *gnatter.*]

nat·ty (năt′ē) *adj.* **-ti·er, -ti·est.** Neat, trim, and smart; dapper. [Perhaps variant of obsolete *netty,* from *net,* elegant, from Middle English, from Old French. See NEAT[1].] **—nat′ti·ly** *adv.* **—nat′ti·ness** *n.*

nat·u·ral (năch′ər-əl, năch′rəl) *adj. Abbr.* **nat. 1.** Present in or produced by nature: *a natural pearl.* **2.** Of, relating to, or concerning nature: *a natural environment.* **3.** Conforming to the usual or ordinary course of nature: *a natural death.* **4. a.** Not acquired; inherent: *Love of power is natural to some people.* **b.** Having a particular character by nature: *a natural leader.* See Synonyms at **normal. c.** *Biology.* Not produced or changed artificially; not conditioned: *natural immunity; a natural reflex.* **5.** Characterized by spontaneity and freedom from artificiality, affectation, or inhibitions. See Synonyms at **naive. 6.** Not altered, treated, or disguised: *natural coloring; natural produce.* **7.** Faithfully representing nature or life. **8.** Expected and accepted: *"In Willie's mind marriage remained the natural and logical sequence to love"* (Duff Cooper). **9.** Established by moral certainty or conviction: *natural rights.* **10.** Being in a state regarded as primitive, uncivilized, or unregenerate. **11. a.** Related by blood: *the natural parents of the child.* **b.** Born of unwed parents; illegitimate: *a natural child.* **12.** *Mathematics.* Of or relating to positive integers. **13.** *Music.* **a.** Not sharped or flatted. **b.** Having no sharps or flats. **—natural** *n.* **1. a.** One having all the qualifications necessary for success: *You are a natural for this job.* **b.** One suited by nature for a certain purpose or function: *She is a natural at mathematics.* **2.** *Music.* **a.** The sign (♮) placed before a note to cancel a preceding sharp or flat. **b.** A note so affected. **3.** *Color.* A yellowish gray to pale orange yellow. **4.** *Games.* A combination in certain card and dice games that wins immediately. **5.** An Afro hairstyle. [Middle English, from Old French, from Latin *nātūrālis,* from *nātūra,* nature. See NATURE.] **—nat′u·ral·ness** *n.*

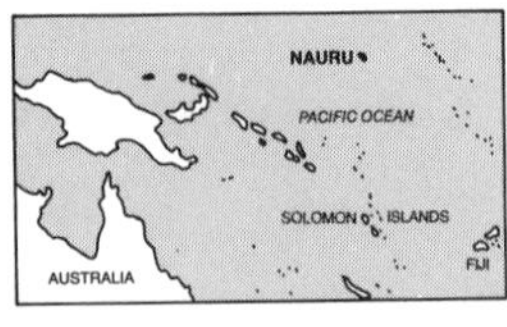

Nauru

natural childbirth *n.* Childbirth in which medical intervention is minimized and the mother often practices relaxation and breathing techniques to control pain and ease delivery.

natural food *n.* Food that does not contain any additives, such as preservatives or artificial coloring.

natural gas *n. Abbr.* **NG, N.G.** A mixture of hydrocarbon gases that occurs with petroleum deposits, principally methane together with varying quantities of ethane, propane, butane, and other gases, and is used as a fuel and in the manufacture of organic compounds.

natural history *n.* **1.** The study and description of organisms and natural objects, especially their origins, evolution, and interrelationships. **2.** A collection of facts about the development of a natural process or object: *the natural history of an insect.*

nat·u·ral·ism (năch′ər-ə-lĭz′əm, năch′rə-) *n.* **1.** Factual or realistic representation, especially: **a.** The practice of describing precisely the actual circumstances of human life in literature. **b.** The practice of reproducing subjects as precisely as possible in the visual arts. **2. a.** A movement or school advocating such precise representation. **b.** The principles and methods of such a movement or of its adherents. **3.** *Philosophy.* The system of thought holding that all phenomena can be explained in terms of natural causes and laws without attributing moral, spiritual, or supernatural significance to them. **4.** *Theology.* The doctrine that all religious truths are derived from nature and natural causes and not from revelation. **5.** Conduct or thought prompted by natural desires or instincts.

nat·u·ral·ist (năch′ər-ə-lĭst, năch′rə-) *n.* **1.** One versed in natural history, especially in zoology or botany. **2.** One who believes in and follows the tenets of naturalism.

nat·u·ral·is·tic (năch′ər-ə-lĭs′tĭk, năch′rə-) *adj.* **1.** Imitating or producing the effect or appearance of nature. **2.** Of, relating to, or being in accordance with the doctrines of naturalism. **—nat′u·ral·is′ti·cal·ly** *adv.*

nat·u·ral·ize (năch′ər-ə-līz′, năch′rə-) *v.* **-ized, -iz·ing, -iz·es.** *—tr.* **1.** To grant full citizenship to (one of foreign birth). **2.** To adopt (something foreign) into general use. **3.** To adapt or acclimate (a plant or an animal) to a new environment; introduce and establish as if native. **4.** To cause to conform to nature. *—intr.* To become naturalized or acclimated; undergo adaptation. **—nat′u·ral·iz′a·ble** *adj.* **—nat′u·ral·i·za′tion** (-lĭ-zā′shən) *n.*

natural killer cell *n.* A killer cell that is activated by double-stranded RNA and fights off viral infections and tumors.

natural language *n.* A human written or spoken language as opposed to a computer language.

natural law *n.* A law or body of laws that derives from nature and is believed to be binding upon human actions apart from or in conjunction with laws established by human authority.

natural logarithm *n. Symbol* **ln** *Mathematics.* A logarithm in which the base is the irrational number e (= 2.71828 . . .). For example, $\ln 10 = \log_e 10 = 2.30258$. Also called *Napierian logarithm.*

nat·u·ral·ly (năch′ər-ə-lē, năch′rə-) *adv.* **1.** In a natural manner. **2.** By nature; inherently. **3.** Without a doubt; surely.

natural number *n. Mathematics.* One of the set of positive whole numbers; a positive integer.

natural philosophy *n.* The study of nature and the physical universe. **—natural philosopher** *n.*

natural resource *n.* A material source of wealth, such as timber, fresh water, or a mineral deposit, that occurs in a natural state and has economic value.

natural science *n.* A science, such as biology, chemistry, or physics, that deals with the objects, phenomena, or laws of nature and the physical world. **—natural scientist** *n.*

natural selection *n.* The process in nature by which, according to Darwin's theory of evolution, only the organisms best adapted to their environment tend to survive and transmit their genetic characters in increasing numbers to succeeding generations while those less adapted tend to be eliminated.

natural theology *n.* A theology holding that knowledge of God may be acquired by human reason alone without the aid of revealed knowledge.

natural virtue *n.* Cardinal virtue.

na·ture (nā′chər) *n.* **1.** The material world and its phenomena. **2.** The forces and processes that produce and control all the phenomena of the material world: *the laws of nature.* **3.** The world of living things and the outdoors: *the beauties of nature.* **4.** A primitive state of existence, untouched and uninfluenced by civilization or artificiality: *couldn't tolerate city life anymore and went back to nature.* **5.** *Theology.* Humankind's natural state as distinguished from the state of grace. **6.** A kind or sort: *confidences of a personal nature.* See Synonyms at **type. 7.** The essential characteristics and qualities of a person or thing: *"She was only strong and sweet and in her nature when she was really deep in trouble"* (Gertrude Stein). **8.** The fundamental character or disposition of a person; temperament: *"Strange natures made a brotherhood of ill"* (Percy Bysshe Shelley). **9.** The natural or real aspect of a person, place, or thing. See Synonyms at **disposition. 10.** The processes and functions of the body. [Middle English, essential properties of a thing, from Old French, from Latin *nātūra,* from *nātus,* past participle of *nāscī,* to be born. See **gene-** in Appendix.]

na·tured (nā′chərd) *adj.* Having a nature or temperament of a specified kind. Often used in combination: *mean-natured; sweet-natured.*

nature study *n.* The study of natural objects and phenomena, especially animal and plant life, often as an introductory subject in school.

nature trail *n.* A trail, as through woods or by a seashore, usually with natural features labeled especially for study.

na•tur•ism (nā′chə-rĭz′əm) *n.* Nudism. —**na′tur•ist** *n.*

na•tur•op•a•thy (nā′chə-rŏp′ə-thē) *n., pl.* **-thies.** A system of therapy that relies on natural remedies, such as sunlight supplemented with diet and massage, to treat illness. [NATUR(E) + –PATHY.] —**na′tur•o•path′** (nā′chər-ə-păth′, nə-cho͝or′-) *n.* —**na•tur′o•path′ic** (nə-cho͝or′ə-păth′ĭk) *adj.*

Nau•cra•tis (nô′krə-tĭs). An ancient city of Egypt in the Nile River delta southeast of Alexandria. Greek colonists probably settled here in the seventh century B.C.

Nau•ga•hyde (nô′gə-hīd′). A trademark used for an artificial leather made of vinyl-coated fabric. This trademark, which often occurs in print as an attributive, sometimes occurs in figurative contexts as well: *"We sat down on a Naugahyde couch and beanbag chair"* (New York Times). *"A good sun block lotion is recommended because most race fans get so engrossed they hardly notice their faces turning to Naugahyde"* (AutoWeek).

Nau•ga•tuck (nô′gə-tŭk′). A town of west-central Connecticut south of Waterbury on the **Naugatuck River,** about 105 km (65 mi) long. Population, 26,456.

naught also **nought** (nôt) —*n.* **1.** Nonexistence; nothingness. **2.** The figure 0; a cipher; a zero. —*pron.* Nothing: *All their work was for naught.* —*adj.* **1.** Nonexistent. **2.** Insignificant. [Middle English, from Old English *nāwiht* : *nā,* no; see **ne** in Appendix + *wiht,* thing; see **wekti-** in Appendix.]

naugh•ty (nô′tē) *adj.* **-ti•er, -ti•est. 1.** Behaving disobediently or mischievously: *a naughty child.* **2.** Indecent; improper: *a naughty wink.* **3.** *Archaic.* Wicked; immoral. —**naughty** *n., pl.* **-ties.** One that is naughty. [Middle English *noughti,* wicked, from *nought,* nothing, evil, from Old English *nāwiht,* nothing. See NAUGHT.] —**naugh′ti•ly** *adv.* —**naugh′ti•ness** *n.*

WORD HISTORY: Words have changes in their fortunes over time just as people and institutions do. The word *naughty* at one time might have been high on one's list as an all-purpose word similar to *bad* or *nice.* During the 16th century one could use *naughty* to mean "unhealthy, unpleasant, bad (with respect to weather), vicious (of an animal), inferior, or bad in quality" (one could say "very naughtie figes" or "naughty corrupt water"). All of these senses have disappeared, however, and *naughty* is now used mainly in contexts involving mischief or indecency. This recalls its early days in Middle English (with the form *noughti*), when the word was restricted to the senses "evil, hostile, ineffectual, and needy." Middle English *noughti,* first recorded in works written in the last quarter of the 14th century, was derived from *nought,* which as a noun had senses such as "evil," as a pronoun meant "nothing," and as an adjective could mean such things as "immoral, weak, useless." *Nought* was descended from Old English *nāwiht,* with similar senses, a compound made up of *nā,* "no," and *wiht,* "thing, being." Thus *naughty,* in a sense, has risen from nothing, but its fortunes have been better than they are at present.

nau•pli•us (nô′plē-əs) *n., pl.* **-pli•i** (-plē-ī′). The free-swimming first stage of the larva of certain crustaceans, having an unsegmented body with three pairs of appendages and a single median eye. [Latin, a kind of shellfish, from Greek *nauplios.*] —**nau′pli•al** (-əl) *adj.*

Na•u•ru (nä-o͞o′ro͞o). Formerly **Pleas•ant Island** (plĕz′ənt). An island country of the central Pacific Ocean just south of the equator and west of Kiribati. Discovered by the British in 1798, the coral atoll was annexed by Germany in 1888 and administered by Australia from 1919 until it became independent in 1968. Yaren is the capital. Population, 8,000. —**Na•u′ru•an** *adj. & n.*

nau•se•a (nô′zē-ə, -zhə, -sē-ə, -shə) *n.* **1.** A feeling of sickness in the stomach characterized by an urge to vomit. See Usage Note at **nauseous. 2.** Strong aversion; disgust. [Middle English, from Latin, from Greek *nautia, nausiē,* seasickness, from *nautēs,* sailor, from *naus,* ship. See **nāu-** in Appendix.]

nau•se•ant (nô′zē-ənt, -zhē-, -sē-, -shē-) *adj.* Inducing nausea or vomiting. —**nau′se•ant** *n.*

nau•se•ate (nô′zē-āt′, -zhē-, -sē-, -shē-) *intr. & tr.v.* **-at•ed, -at•ing, -ates. 1.** To feel or cause to feel nausea. **2.** To feel or cause to feel loathing or disgust. See Synonyms at **disgust.** See Usage Note at **nauseous.** [Latin *nauseāre, nauseāt-,* from *nausea,* nausea. See NAUSEA.] —**nau′se•at′ing•ly** *adv.* —**nau′se•a′tion** *n.*

nau•seous (nô′shəs, -zē-əs) *adj.* **1.** Causing nausea; sickening: *"the most nauseous offal fit for the gods"* (John Fowles). **2.** *Usage Problem.* Affected with nausea. —**nau′seous•ly** *adv.*

USAGE NOTE: Traditional critics have insisted that *nauseous* is appropriately used only to mean "causing nausea" and that it is incorrect to use it to mean "affected with nausea," as in *Roller coasters make me nauseous.* In this example, *nauseated* is preferred by 72 percent of the Usage Panel. What is curious, however, is that 88 percent of the Panelists indicated that they would prefer *nauseating* in the sentence *The children looked a little green from too many candy apples and nauseous rides.* Thus it appears that like a handful of other words such as *transpire, nauseous* is actively used mainly in the sense in which it is considered incorrect. • While the use of *nauseous* to mean "affected with nausea" may incur critical displeasure, it should be pointed out in its defense not only that it is quite common among educated speakers but that it is subtly distinct from *nauseated* in this sense. *Nauseated* is a passive participle, and hence suggests a condition induced by a specific external cause. By contrast, *nauseous* is an adjective that refers to an occurrent state whose cause may be nonspecific or unknown. The person who reports that *I woke up this morning feeling nauseous* might not be willing to accept that he or she had been *nauseated* by any external agent.

Nau•sic•a•a (nô-sĭk′ē-ə, -ā-ə, nou-) *n. Greek Mythology.* In the *Odyssey,* a maiden who befriended the stranded Odysseus.

naut. *abbr.* Nautical.

nau•ti•cal (nô′tĭ-kəl) *adj. Abbr.* **naut.** Of, relating to, or characteristic of ships, shipping, sailors, or navigation on a body of water. [From Latin *nauticus,* from Greek *nautikos,* from *nautēs,* sailor, from *naus,* ship. See **nāu-** in Appendix.] —**nau′ti•cal•ly** *adv.*

SYNONYMS: *nautical, marine, maritime, naval.* The central meaning shared by these adjectives is "of or relating to the sea, ships, shipping, sailors, or navigation": *nautical charts; marine insurance; maritime law; a naval officer.*

nautilus
Chambered nautilus
Nautilus pompilius

nautical mile *n. Abbr.* **nm, n.m., NM** A unit of length used in sea and air navigation, based on the length of one minute of arc of a great circle, especially an international and U.S. unit equal to 1,852 meters (about 6,076 feet). Also called *sea mile.*

nau•ti•li (nôt′l-ī′) *n.* A plural of **nautilus.**

nau•ti•loid (nôt′l-oid′) *n.* A mollusk of the subclass Nautiloidea, which includes the nautiluses and numerous extinct species known only from fossils. [From New Latin *Nautiloidea,* subclass name : Latin *nautilus,* nautilus; see NAUTILUS + Greek *-oidēs,* -oid.] —**nau′ti•loid** *adj.*

nau•ti•lus (nôt′l-əs) *n., pl.* **nau•ti•lus•es** or **nau•ti•li** (nôt′l-ī′). **1.** A cephalopod mollusk of the genus *Nautilus,* especially *N. pompilius,* found in the Indian and Pacific oceans and having a spiral, pearly-lined shell with a series of air-filled chambers. Also called *chambered nautilus, pearly nautilus.* **2.** The paper nautilus. [Latin, from Greek *nautilos,* sailor, nautilus, from *nautēs,* mariner, from *naus,* ship. See **nāu-** in Appendix.]

nav. *abbr.* **1.** Naval. **2.** Navigable. **3.** Navigation.

Nav•a•jo also **Nav•a•ho** (năv′ə-hō′, nä′və-) *n., pl.* **Navajo** or **-jos** also **Navaho** or **-hos. 1.a.** A Native American people inhabiting extensive reservation lands in Arizona, New Mexico, and southeast Utah. The most populous of contemporary Native American groups in the United States, the Navajo are noted as skilled weavers, potters, and silversmiths. **b.** A member of this people. **2.** The Apachean language of the Navajo. [American Spanish *Navajó,* originally a place-name, from Tewa *navahū,* large arroyo with cultivated fields.] —**Nav′a•jo′** *adj.*

na•val (nā′vəl) *adj. Abbr.* **nav. 1.** Of or relating to ships or shipping. See Synonyms at **nautical. 2.** Of or relating to a navy. **3.** Having a navy: *a great naval power.* [Middle English, from Old French, from Latin *nāvālis,* from *nāvis,* ship. See **nāu-** in Appendix.]

naval architect *n.* One who designs ships.

naval stores *pl.n. Nautical.* Products, such as turpentine or pitch, originally used to caulk the seams of wooden ships.

Na•varre (nə-vär′, nä-). A historical region and former kingdom of southwest Europe in the Pyrenees of northern Spain and southwest France. Inhabited from early times by ancestors of the Basques, it was ruled by a Basque dynasty from the 9th to the 13th century. The southern part was annexed to Spain (1512–1515), while the northern part remained an independent kingdom until it was incorporated into the French crown lands in 1589.

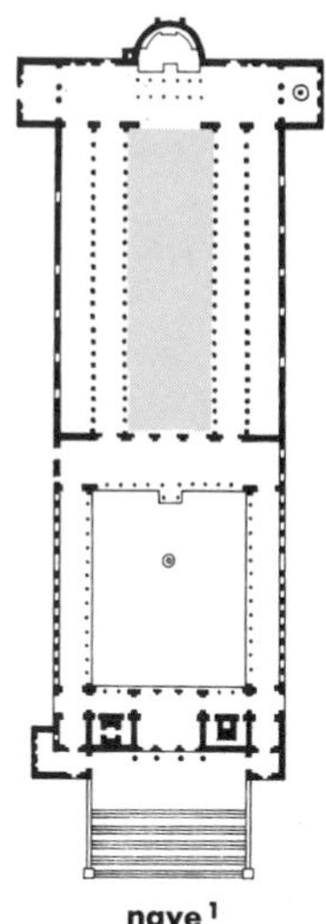

nave¹

nave¹ (nāv) *n.* The central part of a church, extending from the narthex to the chancel and flanked by aisles. [Medieval Latin *nāvis,* from Latin, ship (probably from its shape). See **nāu-** in Appendix.]

nave² (nāv) *n.* The hub of a wheel. [Middle English, from Old English *nafu.* See **nobh-** in Appendix.]

na•vel (nā′vəl) *n.* **1.** The mark on the surface of the abdomen of mammals where the umbilical cord was attached during gestation. Also called *umbilicus.* **2.** A central point; a middle. [Middle English, from Old English *nafela.* See **nobh-** in Appendix.]

na•vel-gaz•ing (nā′vəl-gā′zĭng) *n. Slang.* Excessive introspection, self-absorption, or a concentration on a single issue to the detriment of a broad view and a full grasp of problems or circumstances: *"The optimistic trend masks a looming problem, which has sent the travel industry into a renewed bout of navel-gazing"* (Financial Times).

navel orange *n.* A sweet, usually seedless orange having at its apex a navellike formation enclosing an underdeveloped fruit.

na•vel•wort (nā′vəl-wûrt′, -wôrt′) *n.* **1.** See **pennywort** (sense a). **2.** Any of various Eurasian plants of the genus *Omphalodes,* having one-sided cymes of usually blue flowers. **3.** See **water pennywort.** [From the navellike depression on its leaves.]

na•vic•u•lar (nə-vĭk′yə-lər) *n. Anatomy.* **1.** A comma-shaped bone of the human wrist, located in the first row of carpals. **2.** A concave bone of the human foot, located between the talus and the metatarsals. Also called *scaphoid.* —**navicular** *adj.* Shaped like a boat; scaphoid. [From Latin *nāvicula,* boat, diminutive of *nāvis,* ship. See **nāu-** in Appendix.]

nav•i•ga•ble (năv′ĭ-gə-bəl) *adj. Abbr.* **nav. 1.** Sufficiently deep or wide to provide passage for vessels: *navigable waters; a navigable river.* **2.** That can be steered. Used of boats, ships, or aircraft. **—nav′i·ga·bil′i·ty, nav′i·ga·ble·ness** *n.* **—nav′i·ga·bly** *adv.*

nav·i·gate (năv′ĭ-gāt′) *v.* **-gat·ed, -gat·ing, -gates.** *—tr.* **1.** To plan, record, and control the course and position of (a ship or an aircraft). **2.** To follow a planned course on, across, or through: *navigate a stream.* *—intr.* **1.** To control the course of a ship or an aircraft. **2.** To voyage over water in a boat or ship; sail. **3.a.** To make one's way: *navigated with difficulty through the crowd.* **b.** *Informal.* To walk: *He was too unsteady on his legs to navigate.* [Latin *nāvigāre, nāvigāt-* : *nāvis,* ship; see **nāu-** in Appendix + *agere,* to drive, lead; see **ag-** in Appendix.]

nav·i·ga·tion (năv′ĭ-gā′shən) *n. Abbr.* **nav. 1.** The theory and practice of navigating, especially the charting of a course for a ship or an aircraft. **2.** Travel or traffic by vessels, especially commercial shipping. **—nav′i·ga′tion·al** *adj.*

nav·i·ga·tor (năv′ĭ-gā′tər) *n.* **1.** One who navigates. **2.** A device that directs the course of an aircraft or a missile.

Nav·ra·ti·lo·va (năv′rə-tĭ-lō′və, nä′vrə-), **Martina.** Born 1956. Czechoslovakian-born American tennis player who won nine Wimbledon women's singles championships (1978, 1979, 1982–1987, and 1990), more singles titles than any other player.

nav·vy (năv′ē) *n., pl.* **-vies.** *Chiefly British.* A laborer, especially one employed in construction or excavation projects. [Short for NAVIGATOR, canal laborer (obsolete).]

na·vy (nā′vē) *n., pl.* **-vies. 1.** All of a nation's warships. **2.** Often **Navy.** A nation's entire military organization for sea warfare and defense, including vessels, personnel, and shore establishments. **3.** A group of ships; a fleet. **4.** *Color.* Navy blue. [Middle English, from Old French *navie,* from Latin *nāvigia,* pl. of *nāvigium,* ship, from *nāvigāre,* to sail. See NAVIGATE.]

navy bean *n.* Any of several varieties of the kidney bean, cultivated for their edible white seeds. [From its former use as a standard provision of the U.S. Navy.]

navy blue *n. Color.* A dark grayish blue. [From the color of the British naval uniform.]

Navy Cross *n.* A decoration awarded by the U.S. Navy for exceptional heroism in action.

navy gray *n. Color.* A dark gray.

navy junior *n.* The child of a member of the U.S. Navy, typically a career officer.

navy yard *n.* A dockyard for the construction, repair, equipping, or docking of naval vessels.

na·wab (nə-wŏb′) *n.* See **nabob** (sense 1).

Nax·os or **Náx·os** (năk′sŏs, -sōs, -səs, näk′sôs). An island of southeast Greece in the Aegean Sea. The largest of the Cyclades, it was famous in ancient times as a center of Dionysian worship.

nay (nā) *adv.* **1.** No: *All but four Democrats voted nay.* **2.** And moreover: *He was ill-favored, nay, hideous.* **—nay** *n.* **1.** A denial or refusal. **2.** A negative vote or voter. [Middle English, from Old Norse *nei* : *ne,* not; see **ne** in Appendix + *ei,* ever; see **aiw-** in Appendix.]

nay·say (nā′sā′) *tr.v.* **-said** (-sĕd′), **-say·ing, -says** (-sĕz′). To say no to; deny or oppose: *They will naysay any policy that includes the use of nuclear weapons.*

nay·say·er (nā′sā′ər) *n.* **1.** One who is assertively negative in attitude. **2.** One who critically disagrees.

Naz·a·rene (năz′ə-rēn′, năz′ə-rēn′) *n.* **1.a.** A native or inhabitant of Nazareth. **b.** Jesus. **2.** A member of a sect of early Christians of Jewish origin who retained many of the prescribed Jewish observances. **3.** A member of an American Protestant denomination, the Church of the Nazarene, that follows many of the doctrines of early Methodism. **—Nazarene** *adj.* Of or relating to Nazareth or its inhabitants. [Middle English, from Late Latin *Nazarēnus,* from Greek *Nazarēnos,* from *Nazaret,* Nazareth.]

Naz·a·reth (năz′ər-əth). A town of northern Israel southeast of Haifa. Settled in prehistoric times, it is first mentioned in the New Testament as the boyhood home of Jesus. The modern town is a trade center and pilgrimage site. Population, 46,300.

Na·zi (nät′sē, năt′-) *n., pl.* **-zis. 1.** A member of the National Socialist German Workers' Party, founded in Germany in 1919 and brought to power in 1933 under Adolf Hitler. **2.** Often **nazi.** An adherent or advocate of policies characteristic of Nazism; a fascist. **—Nazi** *adj.* Of, relating to, controlled by, or typical of the National Socialist German Workers' Party. [German, short for *Nationalsozialistische deutsche Arbeiter-Partei,* National Socialist German Workers' Party.] **—Na′zi·fi·ca′tion** (-sə-fĭ-kā′shən) *n.* **—Na′zi·fy′** (-sə-fī′) *v.*

Na·zi·mo·va (nə-zĭm′ə-və, -zyĕ′mə-), **Alla.** 1879–1945. Russian-born American actress noted as an interpreter of the works of Ibsen, Chekhov, and O'Neill.

Na·zism (nät′sĭz′əm, năt′-) also **Na·zi·ism** (-sē-ĭz′əm) *n.* The ideology and practice of the Nazis, especially the policy of racist nationalism, national expansion, and state control of the economy.

nebula
Lagoon nebula in Sagittarius

Nb The symbol for the element **niobium.**

NB also **N.B.** *abbr.* New Brunswick.

Nb. *abbr. Bible.* Numbers.

n.b. or **N.B.** *abbr.* Nota bene.

NBA also **N.B.A.** *abbr.* **1.** National Basketball Association. **2.** National Boxing Association.

NbE *abbr.* North by east.

NbW *abbr.* North by west.

NC *abbr.* **1.** No charge. **2.** No credit. **3.** *Business.* Noncallable. **4.** Or **N.C.** North Carolina.

NC-17 (ĕn′sē-sĕv′ən-tēn′) *n.* A movie rating that allows admission to no one under the age of 17. *—attributive.* Often used to modify another noun: *an NC-17 movie.* [*N(o) c(hildren under) 17 (admitted).*]

NCAA or **N.C.A.A.** *abbr.* National Collegiate Athletic Association.

NCC *abbr.* National Council of Churches.

NCO or **N.C.O.** *abbr.* Noncommissioned officer.

NCTE *abbr.* National Council of Teachers of English.

NCTM *abbr.* National Council of Teachers of Mathematics.

Nd The symbol for the element **neodymium.**

ND or **N.D.** *abbr.* North Dakota.

n.d. or **N.D.** *abbr.* No date.

N.Dak. *abbr.* North Dakota.

NDEA *abbr.* National Defense Education Act.

Nde·be·le (ən′də-bĕl′ā) *n., pl.* **Ndebele** or **-les. 1.** A member of a Zulu people of southwest Zimbabwe. **2.** The Nguni language of the Ndebele. Also called *Matabele.*

Ndja·me·na or **N'dja·me·na** or **N'Dja·me·na** (ən-jä′mə-nə). Formerly **Fort-La·my** (fôr-lä-mē′). The capital and largest city of Chad, in the southwest part of the country on the Shari River. Founded by the French in 1900, it was renamed in 1973. Population, 303,000.

Ndo·la (ən-dō′lə). A city of north-central Zambia north of Lusaka on the border with Zaire. It is a commercial and manufacturing center in a copper-mining region. Population, 250,490.

Ndong·o (ən-dông′gō) *n., pl.* **Ndongo** or **-os.** See **Mbundu** (sense 3).

Ne The symbol for the element **neon** (sense 1).

NE *abbr.* **1.** Nebraska. **2.** Or **N.E.** New England. **3.a.** Northeast. **b.** Northeastern. **4.** Not equal to.

Ne. *abbr. Bible.* Nehemiah.

NEA *abbr.* National Education Association.

Ne·an·der·thal (nē-ăn′dər-thôl′, -tôl′, nā-än′dər-täl′) *n.* **1.** Neanderthal man. **2.** *Slang.* A crude or boorish person. **—Neanderthal** *adj.* **1.** Of, having to do with, or resembling Neanderthal man. **2.** *Slang.* Crude or boorish. **—Ne·an′der·thal′oid′** (-thô′loid′, -tô′-, -tä′-) *adj.*

Neanderthal man *n.* An extinct species or race of human beings, *Homo neanderthalensis,* living during the late Pleistocene Age in the Old World and associated with Middle Paleolithic tools. [After *Neanderthal,* a valley of Germany west of Düsseldorf.]

ne·an·throp·ic (nē′ən-thrŏp′ĭk) *adj.* Of or relating to members of the extant species *Homo sapiens* as compared with other, now extinct species of *Homo.* [NE(O)– + ANTHROP(O)– + –IC.]

Ne·a·pol·i·tan (nē′ə-pŏl′ĭ-tən) *adj.* Of, belonging to, or characteristic of Naples, Italy. **—Neapolitan** *n.* A native or resident of Naples, Italy. [Middle English, from Latin *Neapolitānus,* from Greek *neapolitēs,* from *Neapolis,* Naples, Italy.]

Neapolitan ice cream *n.* Ice cream in brick form, with layers of different colors and flavors.

neap tide (nēp) *n.* A tide that occurs when the difference between high and low tide is least; the lowest level of high tide. Neap tide comes twice a month, in the first and third quarters of the moon. [Middle English *neep,* from Old English *nēp(flōd),* neap (tide).]

near (nîr) *adv.* **near·er, near·est.** *Abbr.* **nr 1.** To, at, or within a short distance or interval in space or time. **2.** Just about; almost; nearly: *was near exhausted from the labor; near dead after the assault.* **3.** With or in a close relationship. **—near** *adj.* **nearer, nearest.** *Abbr.* **nr 1.** Close in time, space, position, or degree: *near equals.* **2.** Closely related by kinship or association; intimate: *a near relative; a near and dear friend.* See Synonyms at **close. 3.a.** Nearly occurring but not actually happening: *a near victory; a near disaster.* **b.** Just barely avoided: *a near hit by the incendiary bomb.* **4.a.** Closely corresponding to or resembling an original: *a near likeness.* **b.** Closely resembling the genuine article: *a dress of near satin; near silver beads.* **5.a.** Closer of two or more: *Take the near street and then turn right.* **b.** Being on the left side of an animal or a vehicle. **c.** Being the animal or vehicle on the left. **6.** Short and direct: *the nearest route to town.* **7.** Stingy; parsimonious. **—near** *prep.* Close to: *an inn near London.* **—near** *v.* **neared, near·ing, nears.** *—tr.* To come close or closer to. *—intr.* To draw near or nearer; approach. [Middle English *ner,* from Old English *nēar,* from comparative of *nēah,* close, near. See **nēhw-iz** in Appendix.] **—near′ness** *n.*

near beer *n.* A malt liquor that does not contain enough alcohol to be considered an alcoholic beverage.

near·by (nîr′bī′) *adj.* Located a short distance away; close at hand. See Synonyms at **close. —nearby** *adv.* Not far away.

Ne·arc·tic (nē-ärk′tĭk, -är′tĭk) *adj.* Of or designating the biogeographic region that includes the Arctic and Temperate areas of North America and Greenland. [NE(O)– + ARCTIC.]

Near East (nîr). A region of southwest Asia generally thought to include Turkey, Lebanon, Israel, Iraq, Jordan, Saudi Arabia, and the other countries of the Arabian Peninsula. Egypt and Sudan in northeast Africa are sometimes considered part of the region. **—Near East′ern** *adj.*

near gale *n. Meteorology.* See **moderate gale.**

Near Islands. A group of islands of southwest Alaska. The westernmost of the Aleutian Islands, they were occupied by Japan from June 1942 until May–June 1943.

near·ly (nîr′lē) *adv.* **1.** Almost but not quite: *The coat nearly fits.* **2.** In a close manner; intimately: *a matter nearly affecting our interests.*

near miss *n.* **1.** A narrowly avoided collision involving two or more aircraft, ships, boats, or motor vehicles. **2.** A missile strike that is extremely close to but not directly on target.

near point *n.* The nearest point at which an object can be seen distinctly by the eye.

near rhyme *n.* See **off rhyme.**

near·sight·ed (nîr′sī′tĭd) *adj.* Unable to see distant objects clearly; myopic. **—near′sight′ed·ly** *adv.* **—near′sight′ed·ness** *n.*

near-term (nîr′tûrm′) *adj.* Of, for, or involving a short period of time in the near future.

neat¹ (nēt) *adj.* **neat·er, neat·est. 1.** Orderly and clean; tidy. **2.** Orderly and precise in procedure; systematic. **3.** Marked by ingenuity and skill; adroit: *a neat turn of phrase.* **4.** Not diluted or mixed with other substances: *neat whiskey.* **5.** Left after all deductions; net: *neat profit.* **6.** *Slang.* Wonderful; terrific: *That was a neat party.* [Anglo-Norman *neit,* clear, pure, variant of Old French *net,* from Latin *nitidus,* elegant, gleaming, from *nitēre,* to shine.] **—neat′ly** *adv.* **—neat′ness** *n.*

SYNONYMS: *neat, tidy, trim, shipshape, spick-and-span, spruce, trig.* These adjectives mean marked by good order and cleanliness. *Neat* implies a pleasingly clean and orderly condition: *a neat room; neat hair. Tidy* emphasizes precise arrangement and order: *"When she saw me come in tidy and well dressed, she even smiled"* (Charlotte Brontë). *Trim* stresses especially smart appearance resulting from neatness, tidiness, and pleasing proportions: *"A trim little sailboat was dancing out at her moorings"* (Herman Melville). *Shipshape* evokes the meticulous order and neatness that might be found aboard a ship: *"We'll try to make this barn a little more shipshape"* (Rudyard Kipling). *Spick-and-span* suggests the immaculate freshness and cleanliness of something new: *"young men in spick-and-span uniforms"* (Edith Wharton). *Spruce* implies neatness and smartness, as of dress or appearance: *"a good-looking man; spruce and dapper, and very tidy"* (Anthony Trollope). *Trig* suggests sprightly smartness: *"the trig corporal, with the little visorless cap worn so jauntily"* (William Dean Howells).

neat² (nēt) *n., pl.* **neat.** *Archaic.* A cow or other domestic bovine animal. [Middle English *net,* from Old English *nēat.*]

neat·en (nēt′n) *tr.v.* **-ened, -en·ing, -ens.** To put into order; make neat.

neath or **'neath** (nēth) *prep.* Beneath.

neat·herd (nēt′hûrd′) *n. Archaic.* A cowherd.

neat's-foot oil (nēts′fo͝ot′) *n.* A light yellow oil obtained from the feet and shinbones of cattle, used chiefly to dress leather.

neb (nĕb) *n.* **1. a.** A beak of a bird. **b.** A nose; a snout. **2.** A projecting part, especially a nib. [Middle English, from Old English.]

NEB *abbr.* New English Bible.

neb·bish (nĕb′ĭsh) *n.* A person regarded as weak-willed or timid. [Yiddish *nebekh,* poor, unfortunate, of Slavic origin. See **bhag-** in Appendix.] **—neb′bish·y** *adj.*

NEbE *abbr.* Northeast by east.

NEbN *abbr.* Northeast by north.

Ne·bras·ka (nə-brăs′kə). *Abbr.* **NE, Nebr.** A state of the central United States in the Great Plains. It was admitted as the 37th state in 1867. The region became part of the United States through the Louisiana Purchase of 1803 and was made a separate territory by the Kansas-Nebraska Act of 1854. Its present boundaries were established in 1861. Lincoln is the capital and Omaha the largest city. Population, 1,569,825.

Ne·bras·kan (nə-brăs′kən) *adj.* **1.** Of or relating to Nebraska. **2.** *Geology.* Of or relating to the first glacial stage of the Pleistocene in North America. **—Nebraskan** *n.* A native or resident of Nebraska.

Neb·u·chad·nez·zar II (nĕb′ə-kəd-nĕz′ər, nĕb′yə-). 630?–562 B.C. King of Babylonia (605–562) who captured (597) and destroyed (586) Jerusalem and carried the Israelites into captivity in Babylonia.

neb·u·la (nĕb′yə-lə) *n., pl.* **-lae** (-lē′) or **-las. 1.** *Astronomy.* **a.** A diffuse mass of interstellar dust or gas or both, visible as luminous patches or areas of darkness depending on the way the mass absorbs or reflects incident radiation. **b.** See **galaxy** (sense 1a). **2.** *Pathology.* **a.** A cloudy spot on the cornea. **b.** Cloudiness in the urine. **3.** A liquid medication applied by spraying. [Middle English *nebule,* cloud, mist, from Latin *nebula.* See **nebh-** in Appendix.] **—neb′u·lar** *adj.*

nebular hypothesis *n.* A theory of the origin of the solar system according to which a rotating nebula cooled and contracted, throwing off rings of matter that contracted into the planets and their moons, while the great mass of the condensing nebula became the sun.

neb·u·lize (nĕb′yə-līz′) *tr.v.* **-lized, -liz·ing, -liz·es. 1.** To convert (a liquid) to a fine spray; atomize. **2.** To treat with a medicated spray. **—neb′u·li·za′tion** (-lĭ-zā′shən) *n.* **—neb′u·liz′er** *n.*

neb·u·los·i·ty (nĕb′yə-lŏs′ĭ-tē) *n., pl.* **-ties. 1.** The quality or condition of being nebulous. **2.** *Astronomy.* **a.** A nebula. **b.** A mass of material constituting a nebula.

neb·u·lous (nĕb′yə-ləs) *adj.* **1.** Cloudy, misty, or hazy. **2.** Lacking definite form or limits; vague: *nebulous assurances of future cooperation.* **3.** Of, relating to, or characteristic of a nebula. [Middle English, from Latin *nebulōsus,* from *nebula,* cloud. See **nebh-** in Appendix.] **—neb′u·lous·ly** *adv.* **—neb′u·lous·ness** *n.*

nec·es·sar·i·ly (nĕs′ĭ-sâr′ə-lē, -sĕr′-) *adv.* Of necessity; inevitably.

nec·es·sar·y (nĕs′ĭ-sĕr′ē) *adj.* **1.** Absolutely essential. See Synonyms at **indispensable. 2.** Needed to achieve a certain result or effect; requisite: *the necessary tools.* **3. a.** Unavoidably determined by prior conditions or circumstances; inevitable: *the necessary results of overindulgence.* **b.** Logically inevitable. **4.** Required by obligation, compulsion, or convention: *made the necessary apologies.* **—necessary** *n., pl.* **-ies.** Something indispensable. [Middle English *necessarie,* from Old French *necessaire,* from Latin *necessārius,* from *necesse.* See **ked-** in Appendix.]

ne·ces·si·tar·i·an·ism (nə-sĕs′ĭ-târ′ē-ə-nĭz′əm) *n. Philosophy.* The doctrine holding that events are inevitably determined by preceding causes. **—ne·ces′si·tar′i·an** *adj. & n.*

ne·ces·si·tate (nə-sĕs′ĭ-tāt′) *tr.v.* **-tat·ed, -tat·ing, -tates. 1.** To make necessary or unavoidable. **2.** To require or compel. [Medieval Latin *necessitāre, necessitāt-,* from Latin *necessitās,* necessity. See NECESSITY.] **—ne·ces′si·ta′tion** *n.* **—ne·ces′si·ta′tive** *adj.*

ne·ces·si·tous (nə-sĕs′ĭ-təs) *adj.* **1.** Needy; indigent. **2.** Compelling; urgent. [French *nécessiteux,* from Old French, necessary, from *necessite,* necessity. See NECESSITY.] **—ne·ces′si·tous·ly** *adv.*

ne·ces·si·ty (nə-sĕs′ĭ-tē) *n., pl.* **-ties. 1. a.** The condition or quality of being necessary. **b.** Something necessary: *The necessities of life include food, clothing, and shelter.* **2. a.** Something dictated by invariable physical laws. **b.** The force exerted by circumstance. **3.** The state or fact of being in need. **4.** Pressing or urgent need, especially that arising from poverty. See Synonyms at **need.** ***—idiom.* of necessity.** As an inevitable consequence; necessarily. [Middle English *necessite,* from Old French, from Latin *necessitās,* from *necesse,* necessary. See NECESSARY.]

Ne·chak·o (nə-chăk′ō). A river, about 462 km (287 mi) long, of central British Columbia, Canada, flowing northeast then east to the Fraser River at Prince George.

Nech·es (nĕch′ĭz). A river of eastern Texas flowing about 669 km (416 mi) south and southeast to Sabine Lake.

neck (nĕk) *n.* **1.** The part of the body joining the head to the shoulders or trunk. **2.** The part of a garment around or near the neck. **3.** *Anatomy.* **a.** A narrow or constricted part of a structure, as of a bone or an organ, that joins its parts; a cervix. **b.** The part of a tooth between the crown and the root. **4.** A relatively narrow elongation, projection, or connecting part: *a neck of land; the neck of a flask.* **5.** *Music.* The narrow part along which the strings of an instrument extend to the pegs. **6.** *Geology.* Solidified lava filling the vent of an extinct volcano. **7.** The siphon of a bivalve mollusk, such as a clam. **8.** A narrow margin: *won by a neck.* **—neck** *v.* **necked, neck·ing, necks.** *—intr. Informal.* To kiss and caress amorously. *—tr.* To strangle or decapitate (a fowl). [Middle English *nekke,* from Old English *hnecca.*] **—neck′less** *adj.*

neck
Devils Tower, Wyoming

neck and neck *adv. & adj.* Nip and tuck, as in a race.

Neck·ar (nĕk′ər, -är). A river of southwest Germany rising in the Black Forest and flowing about 337 km (228 mi) generally north and west to the Rhine River at Mannheim.

neck·band (nĕk′bănd′) *n.* The band around the collar of a garment.

necked (nĕkt) *adj.* Having a neck or neckline of a specified kind. Often used in combination: *a long-necked bird; a low-necked dress.*

Neck·er (nĕk′ər, nĕ-kĕr′), **Jacques.** 1732–1804. French financier and politician who advocated the formation of the States-General to effect financial reform. His brief dismissal by Louis XVI (1789) precipitated the storming of the Bastille.

neck·er·chief (nĕk′ər-chĭf, -chēf′) *n.* A kerchief worn around the neck.

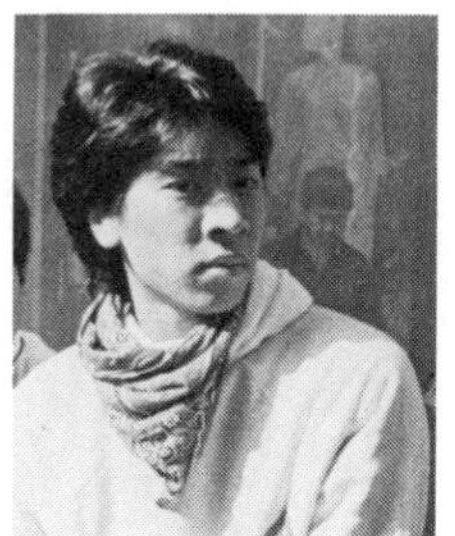
neckerchief

neck·ing (nĕk′ĭng) *n.* **1.** *Architecture.* A molding between the upper part of a column and the projecting part of the capital. **2.** *Informal.* The act or practice of amorously kissing and caressing.

neck·lace (nĕk′lĭs) *n.* **1.** An ornament worn around the neck. **2.** Something felt to resemble this neck ornament, as in shape: *a necklace of hundreds of tiny islands.*

neck·line (nĕk′līn′) *n.* The line formed by the edge of a garment at or near the neck.

neck of the woods *n., pl.* **necks of the woods.** *Informal.* A region; a neighborhood.

neck·piece (nĕk′pēs′) *n.* A scarf, often of fur.

neck·tie (nĕk′tī′) *n.* A narrow fabric band of varying length worn around the neck and tied in a knot or bow close to the throat.

neck·wear (nĕk′wâr′) *n.* Articles, such as neckties worn around the neck.

ă pat	oi boy
ā pay	ou out
âr care	o͝o took
ä father	o͞o boot
ĕ pet	ŭ cut
ē be	ûr urge
ĭ pit	th thin
ī pie	*th* this
îr pier	hw which
ŏ pot	zh vision
ō toe	ə about, item
ô paw	♦ regionalism

Stress marks: ′ (primary); ′ (secondary), as in **dictionary** (dĭk′shə-nĕr′ē)

necro– or **necr–** *pref.* **1.** Dead body; corpse: *necrophilia.* **2.** Death: *necrobiosis.* [Greek *nekro-,* from *nekros.* See **nek-**[1] in Appendix.]

nec·ro·bi·o·sis (nĕk′rō-bī-ō′sĭs) *n.* The natural death of cells or tissues through aging, as distinguished from necrosis or pathological death. **—nec′ro·bi·ot′ic** (-ŏt′ĭk) *adj.*

ne·crol·o·gy (nə-krŏl′ə-jē, nĕ-) *n., pl.* **-gies. 1.** A list of people who have died, especially in the recent past or during a specific period. **2.** An obituary. **—nec′ro·log′ic** (nĕk′rə-lŏj′ĭk), **nec′ro·log′i·cal** *adj.* **—ne·crol′o·gist** *n.*

nec·ro·man·cy (nĕk′rə-măn′sē) *n.* **1.** The practice of supposedly communicating with the spirits of the dead in order to predict the future. **2.** Black magic; sorcery. **3.** Magic qualities. [Alteration of Middle English *nigromancie,* from Old French *nigremancie,* from Medieval Latin *nigromantia,* alteration (influenced by Latin *niger,* black) of Late Latin *necromantia,* from Greek *nekromanteia* : *nekros,* corpse; see **nek-**[1] in Appendix + *manteia,* divination; see –MANCY.] **—nec′ro·man′cer** *n.* **—nec′ro·man′tic** (-măn′tĭk) *adj.*

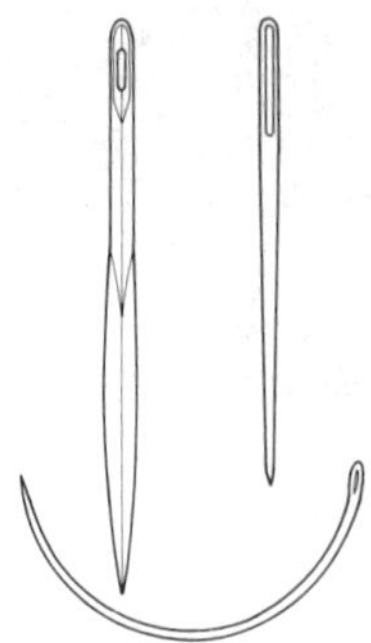

needle
Sailmaking needle (*top left*), tapestry needle (*top right*), and curved embroidery needle (*bottom*)

nec·ro·pha·gia (nĕk′rə-fā′jə) *n.* The act or practice of feeding on dead bodies or carrion.

ne·croph·a·gous (nə-krŏf′ə-gəs, nĕ-) *adj.* Feeding on carrion or corpses: *necrophagous organisms.*

nec·ro·phil·i·a (nĕk′rə-fĭl′ē-ə) also **nec·roph·i·lism** (nĭ-krŏf′ə-lĭz′əm, nĕ-) *n.* **1.** Obsessive fascination with death and corpses. **2.** Erotic attraction to or sexual contact with corpses. **—nec′ro·phil′i·ac′** (-ē-ăk′) *adj. & n.* **—nec′ro·phile′** (-fīl′) *n.* **—nec′ro·phil′ic** (-fĭl′ĭk) *adj.*

nec·ro·pho·bi·a (nĕk′rə-fō′bē-ə) *n.* An abnormal fear of death or corpses. **—nec′ro·pho′bic** *adj.*

ne·crop·o·lis (nə-krŏp′ə-lĭs, nĕ-) *n., pl.* **-lis·es** or **-leis** (-lās′). A cemetery, especially a large and elaborate one belonging to an ancient city. [Greek *nekropolis* : *nekro-,* necro- + *polis,* city; see **pelə-**[3] in Appendix.]

nec·rop·sy (nĕk′rŏp′sē) *n., pl.* **-sies.** See **autopsy** (sense 1). **—nec′rop′sy** *v.*

ne·crose (nĕ-krōs′, -krōz′, nĕk′rōs′, -rōz′) *intr. & tr.v.* **-crosed, -cros·ing, -cros·es.** To undergo or cause to undergo necrosis. [Back-formation from NECROSIS.]

ne·cro·sis (nə-krō′sĭs, nĕ-) *n., pl.* **-ses** (-sēz′). Death of cells or tissues through injury or disease, especially in a localized area of the body. [Late Latin *necrōsis,* a causing to die, killing, from Greek *nekrōsis,* death, from *nekroun,* to make dead, from *nekros,* corpse. See **nek-**[1] in Appendix.] **—ne·crot′ic** (-krŏt′ĭk) *adj.*

nec·ro·tize (nĕk′rə-tīz′) *intr. & tr.v.* **-tized, -tiz·ing, -tiz·es.** To undergo necrosis or cause to necrose.

ne·crot·o·my (nĭ-krŏt′ə-mē, nĕ-) *n., pl.* **-mies. 1.** Surgical excision of dead tissue. **2.** Dissection of a dead body.

nec·tar (nĕk′tər) *n.* **1.** A sweet liquid secreted by flowers of various plants, consumed by pollinators, such as hummingbirds and insects, and gathered by bees for making honey. **2.** *Greek & Roman Mythology.* The drink of the gods. **3.** A delicious or invigorating drink. [Latin, from Greek *nektar.* See **nek-**[1] in Appendix.] **—nec′tar·ous** *adj.*

nec·tar·ine (nĕk′tə-rēn′) *n.* A variety of aromatic peach of ancient origin, having a smooth, waxy skin. [From obsolete *nectarine,* sweet as nectar, from NECTAR.]

nec·ta·ry (nĕk′tə-rē) *n., pl.* **-ries.** A glandlike organ, located outside or within a flower, that secretes nectar. [New Latin *nectārium,* from NECTAR.] **—nec·tar′i·al** (-târ′ē-əl) *adj.*

Ne·der·land (nē′dər-lănd′). A city of southeast Texas between Beaumont and Port Arthur. Population, 16,855.

née also **nee** (nā) *adj.* **1.** Born. Used to indicate the maiden name of a married woman. **2.** *Usage Problem.* Formerly known as. [French, feminine past participle of *naître,* to be born, from Old French *naistre,* from Latin *nāscī.* See **genə-** in Appendix.]

USAGE NOTE: The traditional conventions of address dictate that *née* or *nee* be followed only by a family name (which is, to be sure, the only name one has at birth): *Mrs. Mary Parks, née Case,* not *née Mary Case.* • *Née* is a feminine form in French, and both its spelling and its pronunciation indicate that it has not been fully nativized. Its use to describe men who have changed their names is likely to raise eyebrows among people who recognize the etymology of the word, unless the intention is clearly jocular. A phrase like *John Smith, née Schmidt,* would be more accurately—and less affectedly—paraphrased with an unexceptionally English word such as *born* or *formerly known as.*

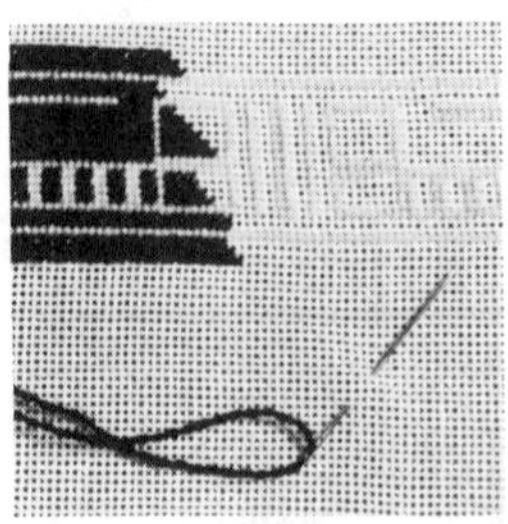

needlepoint

need (nēd) *n.* **1.** A lack of something required or desirable: *crops in need of water; a need for affection.* **2.** Something required or wanted; a requisite: *Our needs are modest.* **3.** Necessity; obligation: *There is no need for you to go.* **4.** A condition of poverty or misfortune: *The family is in dire need.* **—need** *v.* **need·ed, need·ing, needs. —need** *aux.* To be under the necessity of or the obligation to: *They need not come.* *—tr.* To have need of; require: *The family needs money.* *—intr.* **1.** To be in need or want. **2.** To be necessary. [Middle English *nede,* from Old English *nēod, nēd,* distress, necessity.]

SYNONYMS: *need, necessity, exigency, requisite.* These nouns denote a condition in which something essential is required or wanted; they also refer to that which is required or wanted. *Need* is the most general: *There's no need to be concerned. She is serene and contented; her emotional and spiritual needs are being met. Necessity* more strongly than *need* suggests urgency, inevitability, or unavoidable obligation: *"I think the necessity of being ready increases.—Look to it"* (Abraham Lincoln). *"The rehabilitation of the cabin became a necessity"* (Bret Harte). *Exigency* implies acute urgency, especially that arising from conditions or circumstances such as those of an emergency: *"No . . . more pernicious* [doctrine] *was ever invented . . . than that any of* [the Constitution's] *provisions can be suspended during any of the great exigencies of government"* (David Davis) *Requisite* applies to something indispensable: *"a place where the three grand requisites of water, fuel and fodder were to be obtained"* (James Fenimore Cooper). See also Synonyms at **lack.**

USAGE NOTE: Depending on the sense, the verb *need* behaves sometimes like an auxiliary verb (such as *can* or *may*) and sometimes like a main verb (such as *want* or *try*). When used as a main verb, *need* agrees with its subject, takes *to* before the verb following it, and combines with *do* in questions, negations, and certain other constructions: *He needs to go. Does he need to go so soon? He doesn't need to go.* When used as an auxiliary verb, *need* does not agree with its subject, does not take *to* before the verb following it, and does not combine with *do*: *He needn't go. Need he go so soon?* The auxiliary forms of *need* are used primarily in present-tense questions, negations, and conditional clauses. They differ subtly in meaning from the main verb forms in that they always refer to an externally imposed obligation. Hence one might say *You needn't* (or less formally, *don't need to*) *fill out both forms,* but where the sense of necessity is internal to the subject, only the main verb can be used: *I don't need to* (not *needn't*) *be told how to manage my own affairs.* Note also that the use of *need* as an auxiliary is often accompanied by a presupposition that the activity in question has in fact been performed. *The boys needn't have spoken frankly* implies that they did in fact speak frankly, whereas the sentence *The boys did not need to speak frankly* does not; only the latter could be followed by a clause like *they conveyed their meanings by indirection.*

need·ful (nēd′fəl) *adj.* Necessary; required. See Synonyms at **indispensable. —need′ful·ly** *adv.* **—need′ful·ness** *n.*

Need·ham (nē′dəm). A town of eastern Massachusetts, a mainly residential suburb of Boston. Population, 27,901.

nee·dle (nēd′l) *n.* **1.a.** A small, slender implement used for sewing or surgical suturing, made usually of polished steel and having an eye at one end through which a length of thread is passed and held. **b.** Any one of various other implements, such as one used in knitting or crocheting. **2.** A small, pointed stylus used to transmit vibrations from the grooves of a phonograph record. **3.a.** A slender pointer or indicator on a dial, scale, or similar part of a mechanical device. **b.** A magnetic needle. **4.a.** A hypodermic needle. **b.** *Informal.* A hypodermic injection; a shot. **5.** A narrow stiff leaf, as those of conifers. **6.** A fine, sharp projection, as a spine of a sea urchin or a crystal. **7.** A sharp-pointed instrument used in engraving. **8.** *Informal.* A goading, provoking, or teasing remark or act. **—needle** *v.* **-dled, -dling, -dles.** *—tr.* **1.** To prick, pierce, or stitch with a small, slender, sharp-pointed implement. **2.** *Informal.* To goad, provoke, or tease. **3.** *Slang.* To increase the alcoholic content of (a beverage). *—intr.* To sew or do similar work with a small, slender, sharp-pointed implement. [Middle English *nedle,* from Old English *nǣdl.* See **(s)nē-** in Appendix.] **—nee′dler** *n.*

nee·dle·craft (nēd′l-krăft′) *n.* The art or process of needlework.

nee·dle·fish (nēd′l-fĭsh′) *n., pl.* **needlefish** or **-fish·es. 1.** Any of several marine fishes of the family Belonidae, having slender bodies, needlelike teeth, and narrow jaws. **2.** Any of various other fishes, such as the pipefish, having projecting jaws.

needle grass *n.* See **feather grass.**

nee·dle·point (nēd′l-point′) *n.* **1.** Decorative needlework on canvas, usually in a diagonal stitch covering the entire surface of the material. **2.** A type of lace worked on paper patterns with a needle. In this sense, also called *point lace.* **—nee′dle·point′** *v.*

need·less (nēd′lĭs) *adj.* Not needed or wished for; unnecessary. **—need′less·ly** *adv.* **—need′less·ness** *n.*

needle valve *n.* A valve having a slender point fitting into a conical seat, used to regulate accurately the flow of a liquid or gas.

nee·dle·work (nēd′l-wûrk′) *n.* Work, such as sewing or embroidery, that is done with a needle.

need·n't (nēd′nt). Need not.

needs (nēdz) *adv.* Of necessity; necessarily: *We must needs go.* [Middle English *nedes,* from *nede,* from Old English *nēde,* genitive of *nēd,* necessity. See NEED.]

need·y (nē′dē) *adj.* **-i·er, -i·est.** Being in need; impoverished. See Synonyms at **poor. —need′i·ness** *n.*

Né·el (nā-ĕl′), **Louis Eugène Félix.** Born 1904. French physicist. He shared a 1970 Nobel Prize for his research on magnetism.

neem (nēm) *n.* A tall, usually evergreen East Indian tree *(Azadirachta indica)* widely cultivated in tropical Asia for its timber, resin, bitter bark, and aromatic seed oil. [Hindi *nīm,* from Sanskrit *nimbah.*]

Nee·nah (nē′nə). A city of eastern Wisconsin on Lake Winnebago north-northeast of Oshkosh. Population, 23,272.

ne'er (nâr) *adv.* Never.

ne'er-do-well (nâr′do͞o-wĕl′) *n.* An idle, irresponsible person. **—ne'er′-do-well′** *adj.*

ne·far·i·ous (nə-fârʹē-əs) *adj.* Infamous by way of being extremely wicked. [Latin *nefārius,* from *nefās,* crime, transgression : *ne-,* not; see **ne** in Appendix + *fās,* divine law; see **dhē-** in Appendix.] —**ne·farʹi·ous·ly** *adv.* —**ne·farʹi·ous·ness** *n.*

Nef·er·ti·ti (nĕfʹər-tēʹtē). 14th century B.C. Queen of Egypt as the wife of Akhenaton.

Ne·fud (nĕ-fo͞odʹ) also **Na·fud** (nă-). A desert region of northern Saudi Arabia. It is noted for its sudden violent winds.

neg. *abbr.* Negative.

ne·gate (nĭ-gātʹ) *tr.v.* **-gat·ed, -gat·ing, -gates. 1.** To make ineffective or invalid; nullify. See Synonyms at **neutralize. 2.** To rule out; deny. See Synonyms at **deny. 3.** *Computer Science.* To perform the operation NOT gate. [Latin *negāre, negāt-,* to deny. See **ne** in Appendix.] —**ne·gaʹtor, ne·gatʹer** *n.*

ne·ga·tion (nĭ-gāʹshən) *n.* **1.** The act or process of negating. **2.** A denial, contradiction, or negative statement. **3.** The opposite or absence of something regarded as actual, positive, or affirmative. —**ne·gaʹtion·al** *adj.*

neg·a·tive (nĕgʹə-tĭv) *adj. Abbr.* **neg. 1.a.** Expressing, containing, or consisting of a negation, refusal, or denial: *gave a negative answer to our request for funding.* **b.** Indicating opposition or resistance: *a negative reaction to the new advertising campaign.* **2.** Having no positive features: *negative ideas; a negative outlook on life.* **3.** Marked by or exhibiting features, such as hostility, that cannot be deemed positive or constructive: *conducted a negative campaign against his opponent.* **4.** *Medicine.* Not indicating the presence of microorganisms, disease, or a specific condition. **5.** *Logic.* Designating a proposition that denies agreement between a subject and its predicate. **6.** *Mathematics.* **a.** Relating to or designating a quantity less than zero. **b.** Relating to or designating the sign (−). **c.** Relating to or designating a quantity to be subtracted from another. **d.** Relating to or designating a quantity, a number, an angle, a velocity, or a direction in a sense opposite to another of the same magnitude indicated or understood to be positive. **7.** *Physics.* **a.** Relating to or designating an electric charge of the same sign as that of an electron, indicated by the symbol (−). **b.** Relating to or designating a body having an excess of electrons. **8.** *Chemistry.* Of or designating an ion, the anion, that is attracted to a positive electrode. **9.** *Biology.* Moving or turning away from a stimulus, such as light: *a negative tropism.* —**negative** *n.* **1.** A statement or an act indicating or expressing a contradiction, denial, or refusal. See Usage Note at **affirmative. 2.a.** A statement or an act that is highly critical of another or of others: *campaign advertising that was based solely on negatives.* **b.** Something that lacks all positive, affirmative, or encouraging features; an element that is the counterpoint of the positive: *"Life is full of overwhelming odds. You can't really eliminate the negatives but you can diminish them"* (Art Linkletter). **c.** A feature or characteristic that is not deemed positive, affirmative, or desirable: *"As voters get to know his liberal views, his negatives will rise"* (Richard M. Nixon). *"I'm known for being very forthright and honest in my opinions. If that's a negative, it's a negative"* (Kitty Dukakis). **3.** *Grammar.* A word or part of a word, such as *no, not,* or *non-,* that indicates negation. See Usage Note at **double negative. 4.** The side in a debate that contradicts or opposes the question being debated. **5.a.** An image in which the light areas of the object rendered appear dark and the dark areas appear light. **b.** A film, plate, or other photographic material containing such an image. **6.** *Mathematics.* A negative quantity. —**negative** *tr.v.* **-tived, -tiv·ing, -tives. 1.** To refuse to approve; veto. **2.** To deny; contradict. See Synonyms at **deny. 3.** To demonstrate to be false; disprove. **4.** To counteract or neutralize. [Middle English, from Old French *negatif,* from Latin *negātīvus,* from *negātus,* past participle of *negāre,* to deny. See NEGATE.] —**negʹa·tive·ly** *adv.* —**negʹa·tive·ness, negʹa·tivʹi·ty** (-tĭvʹĭ-tē) *n.*

negative feedback *n.* Feedback that reduces the output of a system, as the action of heat on a thermostat to limit the output of a furnace.

negative prescription *n. Law.* See **prescription** (sense 5).

negative transfer *n.* The interference of previous learning in the process of learning something new, such as switching from an old manual typewriter to a computer keyboard.

neg·a·tiv·ism (nĕgʹə-tĭ-vĭzʹəm) *n.* **1.** A habitual attitude of skepticism or resistance to the suggestions, orders, or instructions of others. **2.** Behavior characterized by persistent refusal, without apparent or logical reasons, to act on or carry out suggestions, orders, or instructions of others. —**negʹa·tiv·ist** *n.* —**negʹa·tiv·isʹtic** *adj.*

neg·a·tron (nĕgʹə-trŏnʹ) *n.* An electron with a negative charge, as contrasted with a positron. [NEGA(TIVE) + (ELEC)TRON.]

Ne·gev (nĕgʹĕv) also **Ne·geb** (-ĕb). A hilly desert region of southern Israel. Assigned to Israel after the partition of Palestine in 1948, it has various mineral resources.

ne·glect (nĭ-glĕktʹ) *tr.v.* **-glect·ed, -glect·ing, -glects. 1.** To pay little or no attention to; fail to heed; disregard: *neglected their warnings.* **2.** To fail to care for or attend to properly: *neglects her appearance.* **3.** To fail to do or carry out, as through carelessness or oversight: *neglected to return the call.* —**neglect** *n.* **1.** The act or an instance of neglecting something. **2.** The state of being neglected. **3.** Habitual lack of care. [Latin *neglegere, neglēct-* : *neg-,* not; see **ne** in Appendix + *legere,* to choose, pick up; see **leg-** in Appendix.] —**ne·glectʹer** *n.*

ne·glect·ful (nĭ-glĕktʹfəl) *adj.* Characterized by neglect; heedless: *neglectful of their responsibilities.* See Synonyms at **negligent.** —**ne·glectʹful·ly** *adv.* —**ne·glectʹful·ness** *n.*

neg·li·gee also **neg·li·gée** or **neg·li·gé** (nĕgʹlĭ-zhāʹ, nĕgʹlĭ-zhāʹ) *n.* **1.** A woman's loose dressing gown, often of soft, delicate fabric. **2.** Informal or incomplete attire. [French *négligée,* from feminine past participle of *négliger,* to neglect, from Latin *neglegere.* See NEGLECT.]

neg·li·gence (nĕgʹlĭ-jəns) *n.* **1.** The state or quality of being negligent. **2.** A negligent act or a failure to act. **3.** *Law.* Failure to exercise the degree of care considered reasonable under the circumstances, resulting in an unintended injury to another party.

neg·li·gent (nĕgʹlĭ-jənt) *adj.* **1.** Characterized by or inclined to neglect, especially habitually. **2.** Characterized by careless ease or informality; casual. **3.** *Law.* Guilty of negligence. [Middle English, from Old French, from Latin *neglegēns, neglegent-,* present participle of *neglegere,* to neglect. See NEGLECT.] —**negʹli·gent·ly** *adv.*

SYNONYMS: *negligent, derelict, lax, neglectful, remiss, slack.* The central meaning shared by these adjectives is "guilty of a lack of due care or concern": *an accident caused by a negligent driver; was derelict in his civic responsibilities; lax in attending classes; neglectful of her own financial security; remiss of you not to pay your bill; slack in maintaining discipline.*

neg·li·gi·ble (nĕgʹlĭ-jə-bəl) *adj.* Not significant or important enough to be worth considering. [NEGLIG(ENT) + –IBLE.] —**negʹli·gi·bilʹi·ty, negʹli·gi·ble·ness** *n.* —**negʹli·gi·bly** *adv.*

ne·go·tia·ble (nĭ-gōʹshə-bəl, -shē-ə-) *adj.* **1.** Easy or possible to negotiate or be negotiated: *negotiable demands; a negotiable road.* **2.** Transferable from one person to another by delivery or by delivery and endorsement: *negotiable securities.* —**ne·goʹtia·bilʹi·ty** *n.* —**ne·goʹtia·bly** *adv.*

ne·go·ti·ant (nĭ-gōʹshē-ənt, -shənt) *n.* One that negotiates.

ne·go·ti·ate (nĭ-gōʹshē-ātʹ) *v.* **-at·ed, -at·ing, -ates.** —*intr.* To confer with another or others in order to come to terms or reach an agreement: *"It is difficult to negotiate where neither will trust"* (Samuel Johnson). —*tr.* **1.** To arrange or settle by discussion and mutual agreement: *negotiate a contract.* **2.a.** To transfer title to or ownership of (a promissory note, for example) to another party by delivery or by delivery and endorsement in return for value received. **b.** To sell or discount (assets or securities, for example). **3.a.** To succeed in going over or coping with: *negotiate a sharp curve.* **b.** To succeed in accomplishing or managing: *negotiate a difficult musical passage.* [Latin *negōtiārī, negōtiāt-,* to transact business, from *negōtium,* business : *neg-,* not; see **ne** in Appendix + *ōtium,* leisure.] —**ne·goʹti·aʹtor** *n.* —**ne·goʹtia·toʹry** (-shə-tôrʹē, -tōrʹē, -shē-ə-) *adj.*

ne·go·ti·a·tion (nĭ-gōʹshē-āʹshən) *n.* The act or process of negotiating: *successful negotiation of a contract; entered into labor negotiations.*

Ne·gress (nēʹgrĭs) *n. Offensive.* A Black woman or girl.

USAGE NOTE: Like the feminine forms of other ethnic terms, such as *Jewess,* the word *Negress* is now widely regarded as offensive, since it seems to imply that Black women constitute a distinct racial category. Where reference to gender is relevant, the phrase *Black* (or *African-American* or *Afro-American*) *woman* should be used: *The program will particularly benefit Black women, for whom higher education opportunities have been severely limited.* See Usage Note at **Jewess.**

Ne·gri·to (nĭ-grēʹtō) *n., pl.* **-tos** or **-toes.** A member of any of various peoples of short stature inhabiting parts of Malaysia, the Philippines, and southeast Asia. [Spanish, diminutive of *negro,* Black person. See NEGRO.]

ne·gri·tude or **Ne·gri·tude** (nēʹgrĭ-to͞odʹ, -tyo͞odʹ, nĕgʹrĭ-) *n.* An aesthetic and ideological concept affirming the independent nature, quality, and validity of Black culture. [French *négritude,* from *nègre,* Black person, from Spanish *negro.* See NEGRO.]

Ne·gro (nēʹgrō) *n., pl.* **-groes. 1.** A member of a major human racial division traditionally distinguished by physical characteristics such as brown to black pigmentation and often tightly curled hair, especially one of various peoples of sub-Saharan Africa. **2.** A person of Negro descent: *"Discrimination is a hellhound that gnaws at Negroes in every waking moment of their lives to remind them that the lie of their inferiority is accepted as truth in the society dominating them"* (Martin Luther King, Jr.). See Usage Note at **black.** [Spanish and Portuguese *negro,* black, Black person, from Latin *niger, nigr-,* black.] —**Neʹgro** *adj.*

Ne·gro (nāʹgrō, nĕʹgrô, -gro͞o), **Rio. 1.** A river rising in central Argentina and flowing about 644 km (400 mi) eastward to the Atlantic Ocean. **2.** A river rising in southern Brazil and flowing about 805 km (500 mi) generally southwest to the Uruguay River in central Uruguay. **3.** A river of northwest South America flowing about 2,253 km (1,400 mi) from eastern Colombia to the Amazon River near Manaus, Brazil.

Ne·groid (nēʹgroidʹ) *Anthropology. adj.* Of, relating to, or being a major human racial classification traditionally distinguished by physical characteristics such as brown to black pigmentation and often tightly curled hair and including peoples indigenous to sub-Saharan Africa. No longer in scientific use. —**Negroid** *n.* A

Nefertiti
XVIII Dynasty
limestone bust

ă pat	oi boy
ā pay	ou out
âr care	o͝o took
ä father	o͞o boot
ĕ pet	ŭ cut
ē be	ûr urge
ĭ pit	th thin
ī pie	*th* this
îr pier	hw which
ŏ pot	zh vision
ō toe	ə about, item
ô paw	♦ regionalism

Stress marks: ʹ (primary); ʹ (secondary), as in **dictionary** (dĭkʹshə-nĕrʹē)

member of this racial division. No longer in scientific use. [NE-GR(O) + –OID.]

Ne·gro·phile (nē′grə-fīl′) *n.* One who admires and supports Black people and their culture. **—Ne′gro·phil′ism** (nē′grə-fĭ′lĭz′əm, nĭ-grŏf′ə-) *n.*

Ne·gro·phobe (nē′grə-fōb′) *n.* One who fears or dislikes Black people and their culture. **—Ne′gro·pho′bi·a** (-fō′bē-ə) *n.*

Ne·gros (nā′grōs, nĕ′grôs). An island of the central Philippines in the Visayan Islands between Panay and Cebu.

ne·gus (nē′gəs) *n.* A beverage made of wine, hot water, lemon juice, sugar, and nutmeg. [After Francis *Negus* (died 1732), English army officer.]

Ne·gus (nē′gəs, nĭ-go͞os′) *n.* Used formerly as a title for emperors of Ethiopia. [Amharic *negūs,* from Ethiopic *nĕgūsă,* king of kings.]

Neh. *abbr. Bible.* Nehemiah.

Ne·he·mi·ah (nē′hə-mī′ə, nē′ə-) *n. Bible.* **1.** A Jewish leader and governor of Judea in the fifth century B.C. **2.** *Abbr.* **Neh.** See table at **Bible.**

Neh·ru (nā′ro͞o), Pandit **Motilal.** 1861–1931. Indian nationalist politician who was an associate of Mahatma Gandhi and an influential leader in the years leading to India's independence. His son **Jawaharlal Nehru** (1889–1964), also greatly involved in the movement for self-governance, was the political heir to Gandhi and the first prime minister of independent India (1947–1964).

neigh (nā) *n.* The long, high-pitched sound made by a horse. **—neigh** *intr.v.* **neighed, neigh·ing, neighs.** To utter the characteristic sound of a horse; whinny. [From Middle English *neighen,* to neigh, from Old English *hnǣgan,* probably of imitative origin.]

neigh·bor (nā′bər) *n.* **1.** One who lives near or next to another. **2.** A person, place, or thing adjacent to or located near another. **3.** A fellow human being. **4.** Used as a form of familiar address. **—neighbor** *v.* **-bored, -bor·ing, -bors.** *—tr.* To lie close to or border directly on. *—intr.* To live or be situated close by. **—neighbor** *adj.* Situated or living near another: *a neighbor state.* [Middle English *neighebor,* from Old English *nēahgebūr* : *nēah,* near; see **nēhw-iz** in Appendix + *gebūr,* dweller; see **bheuə-** in Appendix.]

WORD HISTORY: Loving one's neighbor as oneself would be much easier, or perhaps much more difficult, if the word *neighbor* had kept to its etymological meaning. The source of our word, the assumed West Germanic form **nāhgabūr,* was a compound of the words **nēhwiz,* "near," and **būram,* "dweller, especially a farmer." A neighbor, then, was a near dweller. *Nēahgebūr,* the Old English descendant of this West Germanic word, and its descendant in Middle English, *neighebor,* and our Modern English *neighbor* have all retained the literal notion, even though one can now have many neighbors whom one does not know, a situation that would have been highly unlikely in earlier times. The extension of this word to mean "fellow" is probably attributable to the Christian concern with the treatment of one's fellow human beings, as in the passage in Matthew 19:19 that urges love of one's neighbor.

neigh·bor·hood (nā′bər-ho͝od′) *n.* **1.** A district or an area with distinctive characteristics: *a neighborhood of fine homes; an ethnic neighborhood.* **2.** The people who live near one another or in a particular district or area: *The noise upset the entire neighborhood.* **3.** The surrounding area; vicinity: *happened to be in the neighborhood.* **4.** *Informal.* Approximate amount or range: *in the neighborhood of five million dollars.* **5.** Friendliness appropriate to a neighbor: *a feeling of neighborhood.* **6.** *Mathematics.* The set of points surrounding a specified point, each of which is within a certain, usually small distance from the specified point. *—attributive.* Often used to modify another noun: *neighborhood schools; neighborhood housing.*

neigh·bor·ly (nā′bər-lē) *adj.* Having or exhibiting the qualities of a friendly neighbor. **—neigh′bor·li·ness** *n.*

neigh·bour (nā′bər) *n., v., & adj. Chiefly British.* Variant of **neighbor.**

Neil·son (nēl′sən), **William Allan.** 1869–1946. British-born American scholar and lexicographer noted for his editions of Shakespeare (1906 and 1942).

Nei Mong·gol (nā′ mŏn′gōl′, mŏng′-) also **In·ner Mon·go·li·a** (ĭn′ər mŏng-gō′lē-ə, -gōl′yə, mŏn-). An autonomous region of northeast China. Originally the southern section of Mongolia, it was annexed by the Manchus in 1635 and became an integral part of China in 1911. Hohhot is the capital. Population, 20,070,000.

Neis·se (nī′sə). A river, about 225 km (140 mi) long, rising in northwest Czechoslovakia and flowing generally north along the border of Germany and Poland to the Oder River.

nei·ther (nē′thər, nī′-) *adj.* Not one or the other; not either: *Neither shoe feels comfortable.* **—neither** *pron.* Not either one; not the one or the other: *Neither of the twins is here. Neither will do. Neither of them is incorrect.* **—neither** *conj.* **1.** Not either; not in either case. Used with the correlative conjunction *nor*: *Neither we nor they want it. She neither called nor wrote. I got neither the gift nor the card.* **2.** Also not: *If he won't go, neither will she.* **—neither** *adv.* Similarly not; also not: *Just as you would not, so neither would they.* [Middle English, from Old English *nāwther, nāhwæther* (influenced by *æghwæther, ægther,* either; see EITHER) : *nā,* not; see **ne** in Appendix + *hwæther,* which of two; see **kʷo-** in Appendix.]

USAGE NOTE: According to the traditional rule, *neither* is used only to mean "not one or the other of two." To refer to "none of several," *none* is preferred: *None* (not *neither*) *of the three opposition candidates would make a better president than the incumbent.* • The traditional rule also holds that *neither* is grammatically singular: *Neither candidate is having an easy time with the press.* However, it is often used with a plural verb, especially when followed by *of* and a plural: *Neither of the candidates are really expressing their own views.* • As a conjunction *neither* is properly followed by *nor,* not *or,* in formal style: *Neither prayers nor curses* (not *or curses*) *did any good.* See Usage Note at **either, every, he¹, none, nor¹, or¹.**

Nei·va (nā′və, -vä). A city of south-central Colombia on the Magdalena River south-southwest of Bogotá. It is a processing center in a coffee-growing region. Population, 179,609.

Nejd (nĕjd) also **Najd** (năjd). A vast plateau region of the central Arabian Peninsula. Formerly a separate kingdom, it was the nucleus for the modern state of Saudi Arabia.

nek·ton (nĕk′tən, -tŏn′) *n.* The collection of marine and freshwater organisms that can swim freely and are generally independent of currents, ranging in size from microscopic organisms to whales. [Greek *nēkton,* neuter of *nēktos,* swimming, from *nēkhein,* to swim. See **snā-** in Appendix.] **—nek·ton′ic** (-tŏn′ĭk) *adj.*

nel·ly or **nel·lie** (nĕl′ē) *n., pl.* **-lies.** *Offensive Slang.* Used as a disparaging term for an effeminate gay or homosexual man. [Probably from the name *Nelly,* nickname for *Helen.*]

nel·son (nĕl′sən) *n. Sports.* Any of several wrestling holds in which the user places an arm under the opponent's upper arm or armpit and presses the wrist or the palm of the hand against the back of the opponent's neck. [Perhaps from the name *Nelson.*]

Nel·son (nĕl′sən), **Horatio.** Viscount Nelson. 1758–1805. British admiral who defeated the French fleet in the Battle of the Nile (1798), thus ending Napoleon's attempt to conquer Egypt, and destroyed French and Spanish naval forces at Trafalgar (1805), where he was mortally wounded.

Nelson, Samuel. 1792–1873. American jurist who served as an associate justice of the U.S. Supreme Court (1845–1872).

Nelson River. A river of Manitoba, Canada, flowing about 644 km (400 mi) generally north and northeast from Lake Winnipeg to Hudson Bay.

Nem·an (nĕm′ən, nyĕ′mən) also **Nie·men** (nē′mən, nyĕ′-). A river of western Belorussia flowing about 933 km (580 mi) west and north through Lithuania to the Baltic Sea.

nemat– *pref.* Variant of **nemato–.**

nem·a·ti·cide (nĕm′ə-tĭ-sīd′, nə-măt′ĭ-) *n.* Variant of **nematocide.**

nemato– or **nemat–** *pref.* Thread; threadlike: *nematocyst.* [New Latin *nēmato-,* from Greek *nēma, nēmat-,* thread. See **(s)nē-** in Appendix.]

nem·a·to·cide also **nem·a·ti·cide** (nĕm′ə-tĭ-sīd′, nə-măt′ĭ-) *n.* A substance or preparation used to kill nematodes. **—nem′a·to·cid·al** (-sīd′l) *adj.*

nem·a·to·cyst (nĕm′ə-tə-sĭst′, nĭ-măt′ə-) *n.* A capsule within specialized cells of certain coelenterates, such as jellyfish, containing a barbed, threadlike tube that delivers a paralyzing sting when propelled into attackers and prey. Also called *stinging cell.* **—nem′a·to·cys′tic** *adj.*

nem·a·tode (nĕm′ə-tōd′) *n.* Any of several worms of the phylum Nematoda, having unsegmented, cylindrical bodies, often narrowing at each end, and including parasitic forms such as the hookworm and pinworm. Also called *roundworm.* [From New Latin *Nēmatoda,* phylum name : NEMATO– + New Latin *-ōda* (alteration of Greek *-oeidēs,* -oid).] **—nem′a·tode′** *adj.*

nem·a·tol·o·gy (nĕm′ə-tŏl′ə-jē) *n.* The branch of zoology that deals with nematodes. **—nem′a·to·log′i·cal** (nĕm′ə-tl-ŏj′ĭkəl) *adj.* **—nem′a·tol′o·gist** *n.*

Nem·bu·tal (nĕm′byə-tôl′). A trademark used for the sedative pentobarbital sodium.

Ne·me·a (nē′mē-ə). A valley of northern Argolis in ancient Greece. Its temple of Zeus was the site of the Nemean games after 573 B.C. **—Ne′me·an** *adj. & n.*

ne·mer·te·an (nĭ-mûr′tē-ən) also **nem·er·tine** (nĕm′ər-tīn′) *—n.* Any of several velvety, usually brightly colored worms of the phylum Nemertina (or Nemertea) that have a flat, unsegmented body with an extensible proboscis and live in the sea or in the mud of the intertidal zone. Also called *ribbon worm.* *—adj.* Of or belonging to the phylum Nemertina (or Nemertea). [From New Latin *Nēmertēs,* type genus, from Greek, name of a Nereid.]

nem·e·sis (nĕm′ĭ-sĭs) *n., pl.* **-ses** (-sēz′). **1.** A source of harm or ruin: *Uncritical trust is my nemesis.* **2.** Retributive justice in its execution or outcome: *To follow the proposed course of action is to invite nemesis.* **3.** An opponent that cannot be beaten or overcome. **4.** One that inflicts retribution or vengeance. **5. Nemesis.** *Greek Mythology.* The goddess of retributive justice or vengeance. [Greek, retribution, the goddess Nemesis, from *nemein,* to allot. See **nem-** in Appendix.]

Nen Chiang (nŭn′ chyăng′). See **Nen Jiang.**

ne·ne (nā′nā) *n.* A rare wild goose *(Branta sandvicensis)* of the

nene
Branta sandvicensis

Hawaiian Islands, having a grayish-brown body with a black face. [Hawaiian *nēnē*.]

Nen·ets (nĕn′ĕts) *n., pl.* **Nenets. 1.** A member of a reindeer-herding people of the northeast European and northwest Siberian U.S.S.R. **2.** The Uralic language of this people. Also called *Samoyed.* [Nenets, human being, Nenets.]

Nen Jiang (nŭn′ jyäng′) also **Nen Chiang** (chyäng′). A river, about 1,191 km (740 mi) long, of northeast China flowing generally southward to the Songhua Jiang.

neo– *pref.* **1.** New; recent: *Neolithic.* **2.a.** New and different: *neoimpressionism.* **b.** New and abnormal: *neoplasm.* **3.** New World: *Neotropical.* [Greek, from *neos,* new. See **newo-** in Appendix.]

ne·o·ars·phen·a·mine (nē′ō-ärs-fĕn′ə-mēn′) *n.* A yellow powder, $C_{13}H_{13}As_2N_2NaO_4S$, containing arsenic, formerly used in the treatment of syphilis and yaws.

ne·o·clas·si·cism also **Ne·o·clas·si·cism** (nē′ō-klăs′ĭ-sĭz′əm) *n.* A revival of classical aesthetics and forms, especially: **a.** A revival in literature in the late 17th and 18th centuries, characterized by a regard for the classical ideals of reason, form, and restraint. **b.** A revival in the 18th and 19th centuries in architecture and art, especially in the decorative arts, characterized by order, symmetry, and simplicity of style. **c.** A movement in music in the late 19th and early 20th centuries that sought to return to the style of the pre-Romantic composers. **—ne′o·clas′sic, ne′o·clas′si·cal** *adj.*

ne·o·co·lo·ni·al·ism (nē′ō-kə-lō′nē-ə-lĭz′əm) *n.* A policy whereby a major power uses economic and political means to perpetuate or extend its influence over underdeveloped nations or areas: *"Strong elements of neocolonialism persist in the economic relations of the rich and poor countries"* (Scientific American). **—ne′o·co·lo′ni·al** *adj.* **—ne′o·co·lo′ni·al·ist** *n.*

ne·o·con (nē′ō-kŏn′) *n. Informal.* A neoconservative: *"The neocons and hard-liners have long felt that no Soviet leader could be trusted"* (New York Times).

ne·o·con·ser·va·tism also **ne·o-con·ser·va·tism** (nē′ō-kən-sûr′və-tĭz′əm) *n.* An intellectual and political movement in favor of political, economic, and social conservatism that arose in opposition to the perceived liberalism of the 1960's: *"The neoconservatism of the 1980s is a replay of the New Conservatism of the 1950s, which was itself a replay of the New Era philosophy of the 1920s"* (Arthur M. Schlesinger, Jr.).

ne·o·con·ser·va·tive (nē′ō-kən-sûr′və-tĭv) *n.* One who follows or supports neoconservatism: *"Neoconservatives are heavily represented at the White House and exert maximum pressure on presidential policy"* (Joseph C. Harsch). **—ne′o·con·ser′va·tive** *adj.*

ne·o·cor·tex (nē′ō-kôr′tĕks′) *n., pl.* **-ti·ces** (-tĭ-sēz′) or **-tex·es.** The dorsal region of the cerebral cortex, especially large in higher mammals and the most recently evolved part of the brain. Also called *neopallium.* **—ne′o·cor′ti·cal** (-tĭ-kəl) *adj.*

Ne·o-Dar·win·ism (nē′ō-där′wə-nĭz′əm) *n.* Darwinism as modified by the findings of modern genetics. **—Ne′o-Dar·win′i·an** (-där-wĭn′ē-ən) *adj.* **—Ne′o-Dar′win·ist** *n.*

ne·o·dym·i·um (nē′ō-dĭm′ē-əm) *n. Symbol* **Nd** A bright, silvery rare-earth metal element, found in monazite and bastnaesite and used for coloring glass and for doping some glass lasers. Atomic number 60; atomic weight 144.24; melting point 1,024°C; boiling point 3,027°C; specific gravity 6.80 or 7.004 (depending on allotropic form); valence 3. See table at **element.** [NEO– + (DI-) DYMIUM.]

ne·o-ex·pres·sion·ism (nē′ō-ĭk-sprĕsh′ə-nĭz′əm) *n.* An art movement based on expressionism that developed in the early 1980's in Germany, Italy, and the United States and is characterized by crudely drawn, garishly colored canvases depicting violent or erotic subject matter. **—ne′o-ex·pres′sion·ist** *adj. & n.*

ne·o·fas·cism (nē′ō-făsh′ĭz′əm) *n.* A fringe movement inspired by the tenets and methods of fascism or Nazism. **—ne′o·fas′cist** *adj. & n.*

Ne·o-Freud·i·an (nē′ō-froi′dē-ən) *adj.* Of, relating to, or characterizing any psychoanalytic system based on but modifying Freudian doctrine by emphasizing social factors, interpersonal relations, or other cultural influences in personality development or in causation of the neuroses. **—Ne′o-Freud′i·an** *n.*

Ne·o·gae·a also **Ne·o·ge·a** (nē′ə-jē′ə) *n.* A region that is coextensive with the Neotropical region and is considered one of the primary biogeographic realms. [New Latin : NEO– + Greek *gaia,* earth.] **—Ne′o·gae′an** *adj.*

ne·o·gen·e·sis (nē′ō-jĕn′ĭ-sĭs) *n.* **1.** *Biology.* Regeneration of tissue. **2.** *Mineralogy.* The formation of new minerals. **—ne′o·ge·net′ic** (-jə-nĕt′ĭk) *adj.*

ne·o·im·pres·sion·ism or **ne·o-im·pres·sion·ism** (nē′ō-ĭm-prĕsh′ə-nĭz′əm) *n.* A movement in late 19th-century painting led by Georges Seurat that was stricter and more formal than impressionism in composition and employed pointillism as a technique. **—ne′o·im·pres′sion·ist** *adj. & n.*

Ne·o-La·marck·ism (nē′ō-lə-mär′kĭz′əm) *n.* The theory, based on Lamarckism, that response to environmental influence can be inherited and transmitted through the action of natural selection. **—Ne′o-La·marck′i·an** (-mär′kē-ən) *adj. & n.*

ne·o·lib·er·al (nē′ō-lĭb′ər-əl, -lĭb′rəl) *n.* One who follows or supports neoliberalism: *"Old liberals esteem big institutions (except big business); neoliberals disdain bureaucracy and champion the entrepreneur"* (Jonathan Alter). **—neoliberal** *adj.*

ne·o·lib·er·al·ism (nē′ō-lĭb′ər-ə-lĭz′əm, -lĭb′rə-) *n.* A political movement beginning in the 1960's that blends traditional liberal concerns for social justice with an emphasis on economic growth.

ne·o·lith (nē′ə-lĭth′) *n.* A stone implement of the Neolithic Period. [Back-formation from NEOLITHIC.]

Ne·o·lith·ic (nē′ə-lĭth′ĭk) *adj. Archaeology.* Of or relating to the cultural period beginning around 10,000 B.C. in the Middle East and later elsewhere, characterized by the development of agriculture and the making of polished stone implements.

ne·ol·o·gism (nē-ŏl′ə-jĭz′əm) *n.* **1.** A new word, expression, or usage. **2.** The creation or use of new words or senses. **3.** *Psychiatry.* A meaningless word used by a psychotic. **4.** *Theology.* A new doctrine or a new interpretation of scripture. **—ne·ol′o·gist** *n.* **—ne·ol′o·gis′tic, ne·ol′o·gis′ti·cal** *adj.*

ne·ol·o·gize (nē-ŏl′ə-jīz′) *intr.v.* **-gized, -giz·ing, -giz·es.** To coin or use neologisms.

ne·ol·o·gy (nē-ŏl′ə-jē) *n., pl.* **-gies.** Neologism. **—ne′o·log′i·cal** (nē′ə-lŏj′ĭ-kəl) *adj.* **—ne′o·log′i·cal·ly** *adv.*

Ne·o-Mal·thu·sian·ism (nē′ō-măl-thōō′zhə-nĭz′əm, -môl-) *n.* A doctrine advocating control of population growth. **—Ne′o-Mal·thu′sian** *adj. & n.*

ne·o·my·cin (nē′ə-mī′sĭn) *n.* A broad-spectrum antibiotic produced from strains of the actinomycete *Streptomyces fradiae* and used especially in the form of its sulfate as an intestinal antiseptic in surgery.

ne·on (nē′ŏn′) *n.* **1.** *Symbol* **Ne** A rare, inert gaseous element occurring in the atmosphere to the extent of 18 parts per million and obtained by fractional distillation of liquid air. It is colorless but glows reddish orange in an electric discharge and is used in display and television tubes. Atomic number 10; atomic weight 20.183; melting point −248.67°C; boiling point −245.95°C. See table at **element. 2.** Neon tetra. [Greek, neuter of *neos,* new. See **newo-** in Appendix.]

ne·o·na·tal (nē′ō-nāt′l) *adj.* Of or relating to newborn infants or an infant: *neonatal care; neonatal disorders.* **—ne′o·na′tal·ly** *adv.*

ne·o·nate (nē′ə-nāt′) *n.* A newborn infant, especially one less than four weeks old. [NEO– + Latin *nātus,* past participle of *nāscī,* to be born; see **genə-** in Appendix.]

ne·o·na·tol·o·gy (nē′ō-nā-tŏl′ə-jē) *n.* The branch of pediatrics that deals with the diseases and care of newborn infants. **—ne′o·na·tol′o·gist** *n.*

ne·o-Na·zi (nē′ō-nät′sē, -năt′-) *n.* A member of a fringe group inspired by Adolf Hitler's Nazis. **—ne′o-Na′zism** *n.*

neon tetra *n.* A small tropical American freshwater fish *(Hyphessobrycon innesi)* of the upper Amazon River, having blue and red markings and often kept in aquariums.

ne·o-or·tho·dox·y (nē′ō-ôr′thə-dŏk′sē) *n.* A Protestant movement that arose during World War I and is closely associated with Karl Barth. It opposes liberalism and aims to revive adherence to certain theological, especially Calvinist doctrines of the Reformation. **—ne′o-or′tho·dox′** *adj.*

ne·o·pal·li·um (nē′ō-păl′ē-əm) *n.* See **neocortex.**

ne·o·phyte (nē′ə-fīt′) *n.* **1.** A recent convert to a belief; a proselyte. **2.** A beginner or novice: *a neophyte at politics.* **3.a.** *Roman Catholic Church.* A newly ordained priest. **b.** A novice of a religious order or congregation. [Middle English, from Late Latin *neophytus,* from Greek *neophutos* : *neo-,* neo- + *-phutos,* planted (from *phuein,* to bring forth; see **bheuə-** in Appendix).]

ne·o·pla·sia (nē′ō-plā′zhə, -zhē-ə) *n.* **1.** Formation of new tissue. **2.** Formation of a neoplasm or neoplasms.

ne·o·plasm (nē′ə-plăz′əm) *n.* An abnormal new growth of tissue in animals or plants; a tumor. **—ne′o·plas′tic** (-plăs′tĭk) *adj.*

Ne·o-Pla·to·nism also **Ne·o·pla·to·nism** (nē′ō-plāt′n-ĭz′əm) *n.* **1.** A philosophical system developed at Alexandria in the third century A.D. by Plotinus and his successors. It is based on Platonism with elements of mysticism and some Judaic and Christian concepts and posits a single source from which all existence emanates and with which an individual soul can be mystically united. **2.** A revival of Neo-Platonism or a system derived from it, as in the Middle Ages. **—Ne′o-Pla·ton′ic** (-plə-tŏn′ĭk) *adj.* **—Ne′o-Pla′to·nist** *n.*

ne·o·prene (nē′ə-prēn′) *n.* A synthetic rubber produced by polymerization of chloroprene and used in weather-resistant products, adhesives, shoe soles, paints, and rocket fuels. [NEO– + (CHLORO)PRENE.]

Ne·op·tol·e·mus (nē′ŏp-tŏl′ə-məs) *n. Greek Mythology.* A son of Achilles who killed Priam during the taking of Troy.

Ne·o-Scho·las·ti·cism (nē′ō-skə-lăs′tĭ-sĭz′əm) *n.* A chiefly Roman Catholic intellectual movement that arose in the late 19th century and seeks to revive medieval Scholasticism by infusing it with modern concepts. **—Ne′o-Scho·las′tic** (-lăs′tĭk) *adj.*

Ne·o·sho (nē-ō′shō, -shə). A river rising in east-central Kansas and flowing about 740 km (460 mi) southeast and south to the Arkansas River in eastern Oklahoma.

ne·o·stig·mine (nē′ō-stĭg′mēn, -mĭn) *n.* Either of two related white crystalline compounds, $C_{12}H_{19}BrN_2O_2$ or $C_{13}H_{22}N_2O_6S$, that opposes the action of acetylcholinesterase and is used in the treatment of glaucoma, myasthenia gravis, and var-

neoclassicism
West Building of the National Gallery of Art in Washington, D.C., designed by John Russell Pope (1874–1937)

ă pat	oi boy
ā pay	ou out
âr care	ŏŏ took
ä father	ōō boot
ĕ pet	ŭ cut
ē be	ûr urge
ĭ pit	th thin
ī pie	*th* this
îr pier	hw which
ŏ pot	zh vision
ō toe	ə about, item
ô paw	♦ regionalism

Stress marks: ′ (primary); ′ (secondary), as in **dictionary** (dĭk′shə-nĕr′ē)

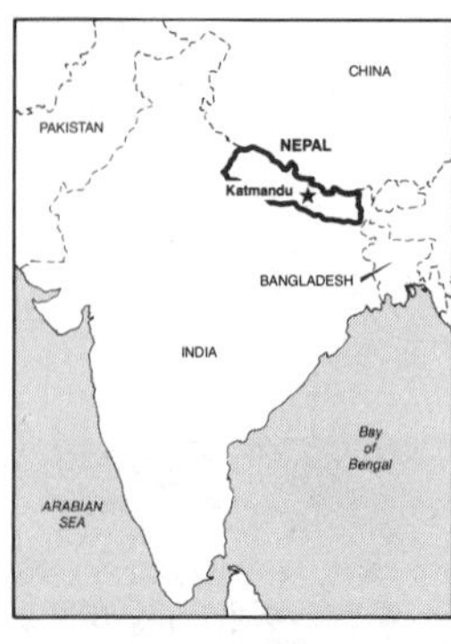

Nepal

ious postoperative conditions. [NEO– + (PHYSO)STIGMINE.]

Ne·o-Sur·re·al·ism or **ne·o·sur·real·ism** also **ne·o·sur·real·ism** (nē′ō-sə-rē′ə-lĭz′əm) *n.* A revival of surrealism mixed with pop art in the late 1970's and the 1980's, marked by an attempt to illustrate the bizarre imagery of dreams or the subconscious mind in painting and photography. **—Ne′o-Sur·re′al·ist** *n.* **—Ne′o-Sur·re·al·is′tic** *adj.*

ne·ot·e·ny (nē-ŏt′n-ē) *n.* **1.** Retention of juvenile characteristics in the adults of a species, as among certain amphibians. **2.** The attainment of sexual maturity by an organism still in its larval stage. [New Latin *neotenia* : NEO– + Greek *teinein, ten-,* to extend; see TENESMUS.] **—ne′o·ten′ic** (nē′ə-tĕn′ĭk, -tē′nĭk), **ne·ot′e·nous** (-ŏt′n-əs) *adj.*

ne·o·ter·ic (nē′ə-tĕr′ĭk) *adj.* Of recent origin; modern. **—neoteric** *n.* A modern writer or philosopher. [Late Latin *neōtericus,* from Greek *neōterikos,* from *neōteros,* younger, comparative of *neos,* new. See **newo-** in Appendix.]

Ne·o·trop·i·cal (nē′ō-trŏp′ĭ-kəl) *adj.* Of or designating the biogeographic region stretching southward from the Tropic of Cancer and including southern Mexico, Central and South America, and the West Indies: *Neotropical flora and fauna.*

ne·o·type (nē′ə-tīp′) *n.* A new specimen selected to replace a holotype that has been lost or destroyed.

NEP or **N.E.P.** *abbr.* **1.** New Economic Policy. **2. N.E.P.** Non-English proficient.

Ne·pal (nə-pôl′, -päl′, -păl′, nā-). *Abbr.* **Nep.** A country of central Asia in the Himalaya Mountains between India and southeast China. Inhabited since ancient times, the region was ruled in the medieval era by a Rajput dynasty. Great Britain recognized Nepal's full sovereignty in 1923, and since 1951 it has been a constitutional monarchy. Katmandu is the capital and the largest city. Population, 15,022,839.

Nep·al·ese (nĕp′ə-lēz′, -lēs′) *n., pl.* **Nepalese. 1.** A native or inhabitant of Nepal. **2.** The Nepali language. **—Nepalese** *adj.* Of or relating to Nepal or its people, language, or culture.

Ne·pal·i (nə-pô′lē, -pä′-, -păl′ē) *n., pl.* **-is. 1.** A native or inhabitant of Nepal. **2.** The Indic language of Nepal, closely related to Hindi. **—Nepali** *adj.* Of or relating to Nepal or its people, language, or culture.

Ne·pe·an (nə-pē′ən). A city of southeast Ontario, Canada, a suburb of Ottawa. Population, 84,361.

ne·pen·the (nĭ-pĕn′thē) *n.* **1.** A drug mentioned in the *Odyssey* as a remedy for grief. **2.** Something that induces forgetfulness of sorrow or eases pain. [Alteration of Latin *nēpenthes,* from Greek *nēpenthes (pharmakon),* grief-banishing (drug), nepenthe : *nē-,* not; see **ne** in Appendix + *penthos,* grief; see **kʷent(h)-** in Appendix.] **—ne·pen′the·an** (-thē-ən) *adj.*

neph·e·line (nĕf′ə-lēn′, -lĭn) also **neph·e·lite** (-līt′) *n.* A mineral of sodium-aluminum or potassium-aluminum silicate, occurring worldwide in igneous rocks and used in the manufacture of ceramics and enamels. [From Greek *nephelē,* cloud (because its fragments become cloudy when placed in nitric acid). See **nebh-** in Appendix.] **—neph′e·lin′ic** (-lĭn′ĭk) *adj.*

neph·e·lin·ite (nĕf′ə-lĭ-nīt′) *n.* An igneous rock consisting chiefly of pyroxene and nepheline.

neph·e·lite (nĕf′ə-līt′) *n.* Variant of **nepheline.**

neph·e·lom·e·ter (nĕf′ə-lŏm′ĭ-tər) *n.* An apparatus used to measure the size and concentration of particles in a liquid by analysis of light scattered by the liquid. [Greek *nephelē,* cloud; see **nebh-** in Appendix + –METER.] **—neph′e·lo·met′ric** (-lō-mĕt′rĭk) *adj.* **—neph′e·lom′e·try** *n.*

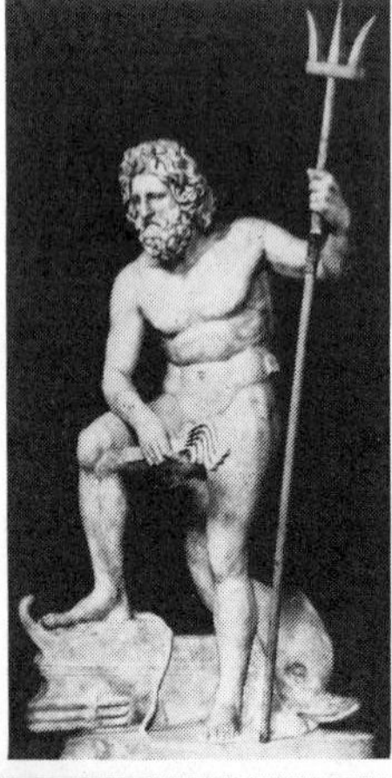

Neptune[1]
Top: Roman god
Bottom: Neptune's Great Dark Spot, photographed by Voyager 2 in August 1989

neph·ew (nĕf′yōō) *n.* **1.** A son of one's brother or sister or the brother or sister of one's spouse. **2.** The illegitimate son of an ecclesiastic who has taken a vow of celibacy. [Middle English *neveu, nepheu,* from Old French *nevo, neveu,* from Latin *nepōs.* See **nepōt-** in Appendix.]

ne·phol·o·gy (nĕ-fŏl′ə-jē) *n.* The branch of meteorology that deals with clouds. [Greek *nephos,* cloud; see **nebh-** in Appendix + –LOGY.] **—neph′o·log′i·cal** (nĕf′ə-lŏj′ĭ-kəl) *adj.*

nephr– *pref.* Variant of **nephro–.**

ne·phrec·to·my (nə-frĕk′tə-mē) *n., pl.* **-mies.** Surgical removal of a kidney.

neph·ric (nĕf′rĭk) *adj.* Relating to or connected with a kidney.

ne·phrid·i·um (nə-frĭd′ē-əm) *n., pl.* **-i·a** (-ē-ə). **1.** A tubular excretory organ in many invertebrates, such as mollusks and earthworms. **2.** The excretory organ of a vertebrate embryo from which the kidney develops. [NEPHR(O)– + New Latin *-idium,* having a small form (from Greek *-idion*).] **—ne·phrid′i·al** *adj.*

neph·rite (nĕf′rīt′) *n.* A white to dark green variety of jade, chiefly a metasilicate of iron, calcium, and magnesium. [Greek *nephros,* kidney (from the belief that it cured kidney diseases) + –ITE[1].]

ne·phrit·ic (nə-frĭt′ĭk) *adj.* **1.** Of or relating to the kidneys; renal. **2.** Of, relating to, or affected with nephritis.

ne·phri·tis (nə-frī′tĭs) *n., pl.* **-phrit·i·des** (-frĭt′ĭ-dēz′) or **-phri·tis·es.** Any of various acute or chronic inflammations of the kidneys, such as Bright's disease.

nerd
From *If I Ran the Zoo* by Dr. Seuss

nephro– or **nephr–** *pref.* Kidney; kidneylike structure: *nephrotomy.* [From Greek *nephros,* kidney.]

ne·phrog·e·nous (nə-frŏj′ə-nəs) or **neph·ro·gen·ic** (nĕf′rə-jĕn′ĭk) *adj.* **1.** Originating in the kidney. **2.** Able to develop into kidney tissue.

ne·phrol·o·gy (nə-frŏl′ə-jē) *n.* The science that deals with the kidneys, especially their functions or diseases. **—ne·phrol′o·gist** *n.*

neph·ron (nĕf′rŏn) *n.* Any of the numerous filtering units of the vertebrate kidney that remove waste matter from the blood. [German, from Greek *nephros,* kidney.]

ne·phrop·a·thy (nə-frŏp′ə-thē) *n., pl.* **-thies.** A disease or an abnormality of the kidney. **—neph′ro·path′ic** (nĕf′rə-păth′ĭk) *adj.*

ne·phro·sis (nə-frō′sĭs) *n., pl.* **-ses** (-sēz). A disease of the kidneys marked by degenerative lesions, especially of the winding uriniferous tubules. **—ne·phrot′ic** (-frŏt′ĭk) *adj.*

neph·ro·stome (nĕf′rə-stōm′) *n.* The ciliated funnel-shaped inner opening of a nephridium into the coelom in some invertebrates and lower vertebrates. [NEPHRO– + Greek *stoma,* mouth.]

ne·phrot·o·my (nə-frŏt′ə-mē) *n., pl.* **-mies.** Surgical incision into the kidney.

ne plus ul·tra (nē′ plŭs ŭl′trə, nā′ plōōs ōōl′trä) *n.* **1.** The highest point, as of excellence or achievement; the ultimate. **2.** The most profound degree, as of a condition or quality. [Latin *nē plūs ultrā,* (go) no more beyond (this point) : *nē,* no + *plūs,* more + *ultrā,* beyond.]

nep·o·tism (nĕp′ə-tĭz′əm) *n.* Favoritism shown or patronage granted to relatives, as in business. [French *népotisme,* from Italian *nepotismo,* from *nepote,* nephew, from Latin *nepōs, nepōt-.* See **nepōt-** in Appendix.] **—nep′o·tist** *n.* **—nep′o·tis′tic, nep′o·tis′ti·cal** *adj.*

Nep·tune[1] (nĕp′tōōn′, -tyōōn′) *n.* **1.a.** *Roman Mythology.* The god of the sea. **b.** The sea. **2.** The eighth planet from the sun, having a sidereal period of revolution around the sun of 164.8 years at a mean distance of 4.5 billion kilometers (2.8 billion miles), a mean radius of 24,000 kilometers (15,000 miles), and a mass 17.2 times that of Earth. [Latin *Neptūnus.*] **—Nep·tu′ni·an** (-tōō′nē-ən, -tyōō′-) *adj.*

Nep·tune[2] (nĕp′tōōn′, -tyōōn′). A community of east-central New Jersey south of Asbury Park. It is an industrial center in a coastal resort area. Population, 28,366.

nep·tu·ni·um (nĕp-tōō′nē-əm, -tyōō′-) *n. Symbol* **Np** A silvery, metallic, naturally radioactive element, atomic number 93, the first of the transuranium elements. Its longest-lived isotope is Np-237 with a half-life of 2.1 million years. Found in trace quantities in uranium ores, it is produced synthetically by nuclear reactions. See table at **element.** [After the planet NEPTUNE[1] (from the fact that it follows uranium in the periodic table).]

ne·ral (nîr′ăl) *n. Chemistry.* A structural isomer of citral that is obtained from the oxidation of nerol and is used to make perfumes and flavorings. [NER(OL) + –AL[3].]

nerd also **nurd** (nûrd) *n. Slang.* **1.** A person regarded as stupid, inept, or unattractive. **2.** A person who is single-minded or accomplished in scientific pursuits but is felt to be socially inept. [Perhaps after *Nerd,* a character in *If I Ran the Zoo,* by Theodor Seuss Geisel.] **—nerd′y** *adj.*

WORD HISTORY: The word *nerd* and *a* nerd, undefined but illustrated, first appeared in 1950 in Dr. Seuss's *If I Ran the Zoo*: "And then, just to show them, I'll sail to Ka-Troo And Bring Back an It-Kutch a Preep and a Proo a Nerkle a Nerd and a Seersucker, too!" (The nerd itself is a small humanoid creature looking comically angry, like a thin, cross Chester A. Arthur.) *Nerd* next appears, with a gloss, in the February 10, 1957, issue of the Glasgow, Scotland, *Sunday Mail* in a regular column entitled "ABC for SQUARES": "Nerd—a square, any explanation needed?" Many of the terms defined in this "ABC" are unmistakable Americanisms, such as *hep, ick,* and *jazzy,* as is the gloss "square," the current meaning of *nerd.* The third appearance of *nerd* in print is back in the United States in 1970 in *Current Slang*: "*Nurd* [sic], someone with objectionable habits or traits. . . . An uninteresting person, a 'dud.'" Authorities disagree on whether the two nerds—Dr. Seuss's small creature and the teenage slang term in the *Glasgow Sunday Mail*—are the same word. Some experts claim there is no semantic connection and the identity of the words is fortuitous. Others maintain that Dr. Seuss is the true originator of *nerd* and that the word *nerd* ("comically unpleasant creature") was picked up by the five- and six-year-olds of 1950 and passed on to their older siblings, who by 1957, as teenagers, had restricted and specified the meaning to the most comically obnoxious creature of their own class, a "square."

Ne·re·id (nîr′ē-ĭd) *n.* **1.** *Greek Mythology.* Any of the sea nymphs, the 50 daughters of Nereus. **2.** The satellite of Neptune that is third in distance from the planet. [Latin *Nērēis, Nērēid-,* from Greek, from *Nēreus,* Nereus.]

ne·re·is (nîr′ē-ĭs) *n., pl.* **ne·re·i·des** (nə-rē′ĭ-dēz′). See **clamworm.** [Latin *Nērēis,* Nereid. See NEREID.]

Ne·re·us (nîr′ē-əs, nîr′yōōs′) *n. Greek Mythology.* A sea god, son of Oceanus and Gaea and father of the Nereids.

Ne·ri (nā′rē), Saint **Philip.** Italian name Filippo Neri. 1515–1595. Italian ecclesiastic who founded (1564) a religious order, the Fathers of the Oratory, and advised the Holy See to absolve Henry IV of France.

ne·rit·ic (nə-rĭt′ĭk) *adj.* Of, relating to, or inhabiting the ocean waters between the low tide mark and a depth of about a hundred fathoms (200 meters): *neritic plankton.* [German *neritisch,* perhaps ultimately from *Nēreus,* Nereus.]

Nernst (nĕrnst), **Walther Hermann.** 1864–1941. German physicist and chemist. He won a 1920 Nobel Prize for his work in thermochemistry.

Ne•ro (nîr′ō, nē′rō). A.D. 37–68. Emperor of Rome (54–68) whose early reign was dominated by his mother, Agrippina the Younger. He had his mother and wife murdered, and he may have set the Great Fire of Rome (64). His cruelty and irresponsibility provoked widespread revolts, which led to his suicide. **—Ne•ro′ni•an** (nĭ-rō′nē-ən) *adj.*

ne•rol (nîr′ôl, -ōl, -ŏl, nĕr′-) *n. Chemistry.* A colorless liquid, $C_9H_{17}COH$, derived from orange blossoms and used in perfumery. [NER(OLI OIL) + -OL¹.]

ner•o•li oil (nĕr′ə-lē) *n.* An essential oil distilled from orange flowers and used in perfumery. [French *néroli,* from Italian *neroli,* after Anna Maria de la Trémoille, 17th-century princess of *Nerola.*]

nerts (nûrts) *interj. Slang.* Used to express disgust, contempt, or refusal. [Alteration of NUTS.]

Ne•ru•da (nĕ-ro͞o′də, *-thä*), **Pablo.** 1904–1973. Chilean poet and diplomat whose literary tone of despair, evident in his early works, evolved into one reflecting the socialist commitment of the government of Salvador Allende. He won the 1971 Nobel Prize for literature.

ner•vate (nûr′vāt′) *adj. Botany.* Having veins. Used of leaves.

ner•va•tion (nûr-vā′shən) *n.* A pattern of veins or nerves; venation.

nerve (nûrv) *n.* **1.** Any of the cordlike bundles of fibers made up of neurons through which sensory stimuli and motor impulses pass between the brain or other parts of the central nervous system and the eyes, glands, muscles, and other parts of the body. Nerves form a network of pathways for conducting information throughout the body. **2.** The sensitive tissue in the pulp of a tooth. **3.** A sore point or sensitive subject: *The criticism touched a nerve.* **4.a.** Courage and control under pressure: *lost his nerve at the last minute.* **b.** Fortitude; stamina. **c.** Forceful quality; boldness. **d.** Brazen boldness; effrontery: *had the nerve to deny it.* See Synonyms at **temerity. 5. nerves.** Nervous agitation caused by fear, anxiety, or stress: *an attack of nerves.* **6.** A vein or rib in the wing of an insect. **7.** The midrib and larger veins in a leaf. **—nerve** *tr.v.* **nerved, nerv•ing, nerves.** To give strength or courage to. **—*idioms.* get on (someone's) nerves.** To irritate or exasperate. **strain every nerve.** To make every effort. [Middle English, sinew, nerve, from Old French *nerf,* from Medieval Latin *nervus,* from Latin. See **(s)neəu-** in Appendix.]

nerve block *n.* A blocking of the passage of impulses along a nerve, especially by administration of a local anesthetic.

nerve cell *n.* **1.** See **neuron. 2.** The body of a neuron without its axon and dendrites.

nerve center *n.* **1.** A group of closely connected nerve cells that perform a specific function. **2.** A source of power or control: *Our Boston office is the nerve center of the corporation.*

nerve fiber *n.* A threadlike process of a neuron, especially the prolonged axon that conducts nerve impulses.

nerve gas *n.* Any of various poisonous gases that interfere with the functioning of nerves by inhibiting cholinesterase.

nerve growth factor *n. Abbr.* **NGF** A protein that stimulates the growth of sympathetic and sensory nerve cells.

nerve impulse *n.* A wave of physical and chemical excitation along a nerve fiber in response to a stimulus, accompanied by a transient change in electric potential in the membrane of the fiber.

nerve•less (nûrv′lĭs) *adj.* **1.** Lacking strength or energy; spiritless; weak. **2.** Lacking courage; spineless or cowardly. **3.** Calm and controlled in trying circumstances; cool. **—nerve′less•ly** *adv.* **—nerve′less•ness** *n.*

nerve net *n.* A diffuse network of cells that conducts impulses in all directions from the area stimulated, forming a primitive nervous system in ctenophores, coelenterates, and certain other organisms.

nerve-rack•ing or **nerve-wrack•ing** (nûrv′răk′ĭng) *adj.* Intensely distressing or irritating to the nerves.

nerve trunk *n.* The main stem of a nerve, consisting of a bundle of nerve fibers bound together by a tough sheet of connective tissue.

Ner•vi (nĕr′vē), **Pier Luigi.** 1891–1979. Italian architect and pioneer in the decorative use of reinforced concrete.

ner•vos•i•ty (nûr-vŏs′ĭ-tē) *n.* The quality or state of being nervous. [Latin *nervōsitās,* sinewy strength, from *nervōsus,* sinewy. See NERVOUS.]

nerv•ous (nûr′vəs) *adj.* **1.a.** Of or relating to the nerves or nervous system: *nervous tissue.* **b.** Stemming from or affecting the nerves or nervous system: *a nervous disorder.* **2.** Easily agitated or distressed; high-strung or jumpy. **3.** Marked by or having a feeling of unease or apprehension: *nervous moments before takeoff.* **4.** Vigorous in style or feeling; spirited: *"the nervous thrust of a modern creation"* (Henry A. Kissinger). **5.** *Archaic.* Strong; sinewy. [Middle English, sinewy, containing nerves, from Latin *nervōsus,* sinewy, from *nervus,* sinew. See NERVE.] **—nerv′ous•ly** *adv.* **—nerv′ous•ness** *n.*

nervous breakdown *n.* A severe or incapacitating emotional disorder, especially when occurring suddenly and marked by depression.

nervous Nel•lie or **nervous Nel•ly** (nĕl′ē) *n., pl.* **-lies.** *Informal.* An unduly timid or anxious person.

nervous system *n. Anatomy.* The system that regulates the body's responses to internal and external stimuli. In vertebrates it consists of the brain, spinal cord, nerves, ganglia, and parts of the receptor and effector organs.

ner•vure (nûr′vyər) *n.* **1.** *Botany.* See **vein** (sense 2). **2.** *Zoology.* See **vein** (sense 3). [French, from Old French *nerveure,* strap, from *nerf,* sinew, from Latin *nervus.* See NERVE.]

nerv•y (nûr′vē) *adj.* **-i•er, -i•est. 1.** Arrogantly impudent; brazen. **2.** Showing or requiring courage and fortitude; bold. **3.** *Chiefly British.* Jumpy; nervous. **4.** *Archaic.* Full of muscular force; sinewy. **—nerv′i•ness** *n.*

n.e.s. or **N.E.S.** *abbr.* Not elsewhere specified.

nes•cience (nĕsh′əns, nĕsh′ē-əns, nĕsh′-, nĕs′ē-əns, nē′sē-) *n.* **1.** Absence of knowledge or awareness; ignorance. **2.** Agnosticism. [Late Latin *nescientia,* from Latin *nesciēns, nescient-,* present participle of *nescīre,* to be ignorant : *ne-,* not; see **ne** in Appendix + *scīre,* to know; see **skei-** in Appendix.] **—nes′cient** *adj. & n.*

ness (nĕs) *n.* A cape or headland. [Middle English *ness,* from Old English *næss.* See **nas-** in Appendix.]

Ness (nĕs), **Loch.** A lake of north-central Scotland. It drains through the **Ness River** into the Moray Firth and is part of the Caledonian Canal system. The Loch Ness Monster is reputed to inhabit its deep waters.

-ness *suff.* State; quality; condition; degree: *brightness.* [Middle English *-nes,* from Old English.]

Nes•sel•rode (nĕs′əl-rōd′) *n.* A mixture of chopped and boiled chestnuts, maraschino cherries, candied fruits, and liqueur or rum, used as a sauce or in puddings, ice cream, or pies. [After Count Karl Robert von *Nesselrode* (1780–1862), Russian politician.]

nest (nĕst) *n.* **1.a.** A container or shelter made by a bird out of twigs, grass, or other material to hold its eggs and young. **b.** A similar structure in which fish, insects, or other animals deposit eggs or keep their young. **c.** A place in which young are reared; a lair. **d.** A number of insects, birds, or other animals occupying such a place: *a nest of hornets.* **2.** A place affording snug refuge or lodging; a home. **3.a.** A place or an environment that fosters rapid growth or development, especially of something undesirable; a hotbed: *a nest of criminal activity.* **b.** Those who occupy or frequent such a place or environment. **4.a.** A set of objects of graduated size that can be stacked together, each fitting within the one immediately larger: *a nest of tables.* **b.** A cluster of similar things. **5.** *Computer Science.* A subroutine or set of data contained sequentially within another. **6.** A group of weapons in a prepared position: *a machine-gun nest.* **—nest** *v.* **nest•ed, nest•ing, nests. —nest** *intr.v.* **1.** To build or occupy a nest. **2.** To create and settle into a warm and secure refuge. **3.** To hunt for birds' nests, especially in order to collect the eggs. **4.** To fit together in a stack. **—nest** *tr.v.* **1.** To place in or as if in a nest. **2.** To put snugly together or inside one another: *to nest boxes.* [Middle English, from Old English.]

nest egg *n.* **1.** An artificial or natural egg placed in a nest to induce a bird to continue to lay eggs in that place. **2.** A sum of money put by as a reserve.

♦**nest•er** (nĕs′tər) *n.* **1.** One, such as a bird, that nests. **2.** *Western U.S.* A squatter, homesteader, or farmer who settles in cattle-grazing territory.

nes•tle (nĕs′əl) *v.* **-tled, -tling, -tles.** *—intr.* **1.** To settle snugly and comfortably: *The cat nestled among the pillows.* **2.** To lie in a sheltered position: *a cottage that nestles in the wood.* **3.** To draw or press close, as in affection; snuggle: *The child nestled up to her mother.* **4.** *Archaic.* To nest. *—tr.* **1.** To snuggle or press contentedly: *The baby nestled its head on my shoulder.* **2.** To place or settle as if in a nest: *I nestled the puppy in my arms.* [Middle English *nestlen,* to make a nest, from Old English *nestlian,* from *nest,* nest.] **—nes′tler** *n.*

nest•ling (nĕst′lĭng, nĕs′-) *n.* **1.** A bird too young to leave its nest. **2.** A young child.

Nes•tor (nĕs′tər, -tôr′) *n. Greek Mythology.* **1.** A hero celebrated as an elderly and wise counselor to the Greeks at Troy. **2.** Often **nestor.** A venerable and wise old man. [Greek *Nestōr.*]

Nes•to•ri•an (nĕ-stôr′ē-ən, -stōr′-) *adj. Theology.* **1.** Of or relating to the doctrine of Nestorius, declared heretical in 431, that two distinct persons, divine and human, existed within Jesus. **2.** Of, relating to, or being an Eastern church that adheres to this doctrine. **—Nestorian** *n.* A member of the Nestorian church. **—Nes•to′ri•an•ism** *n.*

Nes•to•ri•us (nĕ-stôr′ē-əs, -stōr′-). Died A.D. 451. Syrian-born patriarch of Constantinople whose belief that Jesus had two distinct natures, human and divine, and that Mary was the mother of only his human nature was declared heretical (431).

net¹ (nĕt) *n.* **1.** An openwork fabric made of threads or cords that are woven or knotted together at regular intervals. **2.** Something made of openwork fabric, especially: **a.** A device for capturing birds, fish, or insects. **b.** A barrier against flying insects: *a mosquito net.* **c.** A mesh for holding the hair in place. **d.** Something that entraps; a snare. **e.** A fine mesh fabric used as curtain or dress material or as the foundation for various laces. **3.** *Sports.* **a.** A barrier of meshwork cord or rope strung between two posts to divide a court in half, as in tennis and badminton. **b.**

Nero
First-century A.D.
Roman bust

nest
Top: Sora nest
Center: Osprey nest
Bottom: c. 1810 English nest of tables, possibly by Thomas Sheraton; once owned by Napoleon Bonaparte

ă pat	oi boy
ā pay	ou out
âr care	o͝o took
ä father	o͞o boot
ĕ pet	ŭ cut
ē be	ûr urge
ĭ pit	th thin
ī pie	*th* this
îr pier	hw which
ŏ pot	zh vision
ō toe	ə about, item
ô paw	♦ regionalism

Stress marks: ′ (primary); ′ (secondary), as in **dictionary** (dĭk′shə-nĕr′ē)

A ball that is hit into this meshwork barrier. **c.** The goal in soccer, hockey, and lacrosse. **4.** A meshed network of lines, figures, or fibers. **5.** A radio, television, or telephone network. **6.** *Computer Science.* See **network** (sense 4b). **—net** *tr.v.* **net·ted, net·ting, nets. 1.** To catch or ensnare in or as if in a net. **2.** To cover, protect, or surround with or as if with a net. **3.** *Sports.* To hit (a ball) into the net. **4.** To make into a net. [Middle English, from Old English. See **ned-** in Appendix.] **—net′ter** *n.*

net² (nĕt) *adj.* **1.** *Abbr.* **n.** *Business.* **a.** Remaining after all deductions have been made, as for expenses: *net profit.* **b.** Remaining after tare is deducted: *net weight.* **2.** Ultimate; final: *the net result.* **—net** *n.* **1.** *Abbr.* **n.** *Business.* A net amount, as of profit or weight. **2.** The main point; the essence: *the net of our discussion.* **—net** *tr.v.* **net·ted, net·ting, nets. 1.** To bring in or yield as profit. **2.** To clear as profit. [Middle English, elegant, remaining after deductions, from Old French, elegant, and from Old Italian *netto,* remaining after deductions, both from Latin *nitidus,* clean, elegant. See NEAT¹.]

Netherlands

NET *abbr.* National Educational Television.

net asset value *n.* The market value of all securities owned by a mutual fund, minus its total liabilities, divided by the number of shares issued.

net·back (nĕt′băk′) *n.* Linkage of the price of crude oil to the market price of products refined from it. *—attributive.* Often used to modify another noun: *netback deals; netback agreements.*

Neth. *abbr.* Netherlands.

neth·er (nĕth′ər) *adj.* Located beneath or below; lower or under: *the nether regions of the earth.* [Middle English, from Old English *neothera,* from *neother,* down.]

Neth·er·lands (nĕth′ər-ləndz). Often called **Hol·land** (hŏl′ənd). *Abbr.* **Neth.** A country of northwest Europe on the North Sea. Inhabited by Germanic tribes during Roman times, the region passed to the Franks (4th–8th century), the Holy Roman Empire (10th century), the dukes of Burgundy (14th–15th century), and then to the house of Hapsburg. The northern part of the region formed the Union of Utrecht in 1579 and achieved its independence as the United Provinces in 1648 after the Thirty Years' War. In the 17th century the country enjoyed great commercial prosperity and expanded its territories in the East and West Indies and elsewhere, although it lost this supremacy to Great Britain and France in the 18th century. The kingdom of the Netherlands, proclaimed at the Congress of Vienna (1814–1815), included Belgium until 1830. Amsterdam is the constitutional capital and the largest city; The Hague is the seat of government. Population, 14,394,600. **—Neth′er·land′ish** (-lăn′dĭsh) *adj.*

Netherlands An·til·les (ăn-tĭl′ēz). Formerly **Dutch West In·dies** (dŭch; ĭn′dēz). An autonomous territory of the Netherlands consisting of several islands in the Caribbean Sea, including Curaçao and Bonaire off the coast of Venezuela and Saba, St. Eustatius, and the southern portion of St. Martin in the northern Windward Islands. Willemstad, on Curaçao, is the capital. Population, 192,056.

neth·er·most (nĕth′ər-mōst′) *adj.* Farthest down; lowest.

neth·er·world also **neth·er world** (nĕth′ər-wûrld′) *n.* **1.** The world of the dead; Hades. **2.** The underworld; hell. **3.** The lower depths of society: *"In this black-white nether world, nobody judged the customers"* (Malcolm X). **—neth′er·world′ly** *adj.*

net·keep·er (nĕt′kē′pər) *n.* *Sports.* See **goalkeeper.**

net knot *n.* See **karyosome.**

net·su·ke (nĕt′sə-kē′) *n.* A small toggle, often in the form of an elaborately carved ivory or wood figure, used to secure a purse or small container suspended on a silk cord from the sash of a kimono. [Japanese.]

netsuke
Mid 19th-century Japanese inro suspended from a netsuke

net·ting (nĕt′ĭng) *n.* **1.** An openwork fabric; a net. **2.** The act or process of making a net. **3.** The act or process of fishing with a net.

net·tle (nĕt′l) *n.* **1.** Any of numerous plants of the genus *Urtica,* having toothed leaves, unisexual apetalous flowers, and stinging hairs that cause skin irritation on contact. **2.** Any of various hairy, stinging, or prickly plants. **—nettle** *tr.v.* **-tled, -tling, -tles. 1.** To sting with or as if with a nettle. **2.** To irritate; vex. [Middle English, from Old English *netele.* See **ned-** in Appendix.]

nettle rash *n.* See **hives.**

net·tle·some (nĕt′l-səm) *adj.* Causing irritation or distress; vexatious.

net ton *n.* See **ton** (sense 1).

net·work (nĕt′wûrk′) *n.* **1.** An openwork fabric or structure in which cords, threads, or wires cross at regular intervals. **2.** Something resembling an openwork fabric or structure in form or concept, especially: **a.** A system of lines or channels that cross or interconnect: *a network of railroads.* **b.** A complex, interconnected group or system: *an espionage network.* **c.** An extended group of people with similar interests or concerns who interact and remain in informal contact for mutual assistance or support. **3. a.** A chain of radio or television broadcasting stations linked by wire or microwave relay. **b.** A company that produces the programs for these stations. **4. a.** A group or system of electric components and connecting circuitry designed to function in a specific manner. **b.** *Computer Science.* A system of computers interconnected by telephone wires or other means in order to share information. Also called *net.* **—network** *v.* **-worked, -work·ing, -works.** *—tr.* **1.** To cover with or as if with an openwork fabric or structure. **2.** To broadcast over a radio or television network. **3.** *Computer Science.* To connect (computers) into a network. *—intr.* To interact or engage in informal communication with others for mutual assistance or support. **—net′work′er** *n.*

net·work·ing (nĕt′wûr′kĭng) *n.* An informal system whereby persons having common interests or concerns assist each other, as in the exchange of information or the development of professional contacts.

Ne·tza·hual·có·yotl (nĕ-tsä′wäl-kō′yōt′l). A city of south-central Mexico, a suburb of Mexico City. Population, 1,341,230.

Neu·bran·den·burg (noi-brän′dən-bûrg′, -bŏŏrk′). A city of northeast Germany north of Berlin. Founded in 1248, it is an industrial center. Population, 82,451.

Neu·châ·tel (nōō′shə-tĕl′, nyōō′-, nœ-shä-), **Lake of.** A narrow lake of northwest Switzerland near the French border. It is in a picturesque region with notable vineyards.

Neuf·châ·tel (nōō′shə-tĕl′, nœ′shä-) *n.* A soft, white cheese made from skimmed or whole milk. [After *Neufchâtel,* a town of northeast France.]

Neuil·ly (nœ-yē′) or **Neuil·ly-sur-Seine** (-yē-sŏŏr-sĕn′, -sür-). A city of north-central France, a residential and industrial suburb of Paris. Population, 64,170.

neume or **neum** (nōōm, nyōōm) *n.* *Music.* A sign used in the notation of plainsong during the Middle Ages, surviving today in transcriptions of Gregorian chants. [Middle English, series of notes sung on one syllable, from Medieval Latin *pneuma,* from Greek, breath. See PNEUMA.] **—neu·mat′ic** (noō-măt′ĭk, nyoō-) *adj.*

Neu·mün·ster (noi-mün′stər). A city of north-central Germany south-southwest of Kiel. Founded in the 12th century, it is a transportation and industrial center. Population, 78,743.

neur. *abbr.* **1.** Neurological. **2.** Neurology.

neur– *pref.* Variant of **neuro–.**

neu·ral (nŏŏr′əl, nyŏŏr′-) *adj.* **1.** Of or relating to a nerve or the nervous system. **2.** Of, relating to, or located on the same side of the body as the spinal cord; dorsal. **—neu′ral·ly** *adv.*

neural arch *n.* A bony or cartilaginous arch that arises from the dorsal side of a vertebra to enclose the spinal cord.

neural crest *n.* The part of the ectoderm in a vertebrate embryo that lies on either side of the neural tube and develops into the cranial, spinal, and autonomic ganglia.

neu·ral·gia (nōō-răl′jə, nyōō-) *n.* Sharp, severe paroxysmal pain extending along a nerve or group of nerves. **—neu·ral′gic** *adj.*

neural plate *n.* The thickened dorsal plate of ectoderm that differentiates into the neural tube and neural crest.

neural tube *n.* A dorsal tubular structure in the vertebrate embryo formed by longitudinal folding of the neural plate and differentiating into the brain and spinal cord.

neural tube defect *n.* Any of various congenital defects of the brain and spinal cord, such as spina bifida, resulting from incomplete closing of the neural tube in an embryo.

neu·ra·min·i·dase (nŏŏr′ə-mĭn′ĭ-dās′, -dāz′, nyŏŏr′-) *n.* A hydrolytic enzyme that breaks down mucoproteins and is found chiefly in microorganisms of the respiratory and intestinal tracts. [*neuraminic acid* (NEUR(O)– + *amin(e)* + –IC) + –ID(E) + –ASE.]

neu·ras·the·ni·a (nŏŏr′əs-thē′nē-ə, nyŏŏr′-) *n.* A neurotic disorder characterized by chronic fatigue and weakness, loss of memory, and generalized aches and pains. It was formerly thought to result from exhaustion of the nervous system. **—neu′ras·then′ic** (-thĕn′ĭk) *adj. & n.* **—neu′ras·then′i·cal·ly** *adv.*

neu·rec·to·my (nōō-rĕk′tə-mē, nyōō-) *n., pl.* **-mies.** Surgical removal of a nerve or part of a nerve.

neu·ri·lem·ma (nŏŏr′ə-lĕm′ə, nyŏŏr′-) *n.* The delicate membranous covering of a nerve fiber. [Alteration (influenced by Greek *lemma,* husk; see LEMMA²) of French *névrilème* : *névr-,* nerve (from Greek *neuro-,* neuro-) + Greek *eilēma,* veil (from *eilein,* to wind, turn; see **wel-²** in Appendix).] **—neu′ri·lem′mal** *adj.*

neu·ris·tor (nōō-rĭs′tər, nyōō-) *n.* An electronic device that is capable of relaying a signal without attenuation in velocity. [NEUR(ON) + (TRANS)ISTOR.]

neu·ri·tis (nōō-rī′tĭs, nyōō-) *n.* Inflammation of a nerve or group of nerves, characterized by pain, loss of reflexes, and atrophy of the affected muscles. **—neu·rit′ic** (-rĭt′ĭk) *adj.*

neuro– or **neur–** *pref.* **1.** Nerve: *neuroblast.* **2.** Neural: *neuropathology.* [Greek, sinew, string, from *neuron.* See **(s)neəu-** in Appendix.]

neu·ro·a·nat·o·my (nŏŏr′ō-ə-năt′ə-mē, nyŏŏr′-) *n., pl.* **-mies. 1.** The branch of anatomy that deals with the nervous system. **2.** The neural structure of an organ or a part: *the neuroanatomy of the eye.* **—neu′ro·an′a·tom′i·cal** (-ăn′ə-tŏm′ĭ-kəl) *adj.* **—neu′ro·a·nat′o·mist** *n.*

neu·ro·bi·ol·o·gy (nŏŏr′-ō-bī-ŏl′ə-jē, nyŏŏr′-) *n.* The biological study of the nervous system. **—neu′ro·bi′o·log′i·cal** (-bī′ə-lŏj′ĭ-kəl) *adj.* **—neu′ro·bi·ol′o·gist** *n.*

neu·ro·blast (nŏŏr′ə-blăst′, nyŏŏr′-) *n.* An embryonic cell from which a nerve cell develops.

neu·ro·blas·to·ma (nŏŏr′ō-blă-stō′mə, nyŏŏr′-) *n., pl.* **-mas** or **-ma·ta** (-mə-tə). A malignant tumor composed of neuroblasts, originating in the autonomic nervous system or the adrenal medulla and occurring chiefly in infants and young children.

neu·ro·chem·is·try (no͝or′ō-kĕm′ĭ-strē, nyo͝or′-) *n.* The study of the chemical composition and processes of the nervous system and the effects of chemicals on it. **—neu′ro·chem′i·cal** (-kəl) *adj.* **—neu′ro·chem′ist** *n.*

neu·ro·en·do·crine (no͝or′ō-ĕn′də-krĭn, -krēn′, -krīn′, nyo͝or′-) *adj.* Of, relating to, or involving the interaction between the nervous system and the hormones of the endocrine glands: *the neuroendocrine apparatus in birds.*

neu·ro·en·do·cri·nol·o·gy (no͝or′ō-ĕn′də-krə-nŏl′ə-jē, nyo͝or′-) *n.* The study of the interaction between the nervous system and the endocrine glands and their secretions. **—neu′ro·en′do·cri·no·log′i·cal** (-krĭn′ə-lŏj′ĭ-kəl) *adj.* **—neu′ro·en′do·cri·nol′o·gist** *n.*

neu·ro·fi·bril (no͝or′ə-fī′brəl, -fĭb′rəl, nyo͝or′-) *n.* Any of the long, thin, microscopic fibrils that run through the body of a neuron and extend into the axon and dendrites. **—neu′ro·fi′bril·lar′y** (-brə-lĕr′ē) *adj.*

neu·ro·fi·bro·ma (no͝or′ō-fī-brō′mə, nyo͝or′-) *n., pl.* **-mas** or **-ma·ta** (-mə-tə). A usually benign tumor originating in peripheral nerve fibers and composed chiefly of Schwann cells.

neu·ro·fi·bro·ma·to·sis (no͝or′ō-fī′brō-mə-tō′sĭs, nyo͝or′-) *n. Abbr.* **NF** A genetic disease characterized by the formation of neurofibromas, sometimes accompanied by physical deformation and a predisposition to brain tumors and various forms of cancer.

neu·ro·fil·a·ment (no͝or′ə-fĭl′ə-mənt, nyo͝or′-) *n.* Any of the long, fine threads that make up a neurofibril. **—neu′ro·fil′a·men′tous** (-mĕn′təs) *adj.*

neu·ro·gen·e·sis (no͝or′ə-jĕn′ĭ-sĭs, nyo͝or′-) *n., pl.* **-ses** (-sēz′). Formation of nervous tissue.

neu·ro·ge·net·ics (no͝or′ō-jə-nĕt′ĭks, nyo͝or′-) *n. (used with a sing. verb).* The study of the genetic factors that contribute to the development of neurological disorders.

neu·ro·gen·ic (no͝or′ə-jĕn′ĭk, nyo͝or′-) *adj.* **1.** Originating in the nerves or nervous tissue: *a neurogenic tumor.* **2.** Caused or affected by the nerves or nervous system: *neurogenic disorders.* **—neu′ro·gen′i·cal·ly** *adv.*

neu·rog·li·a (no͞o-rŏg′lē-ə, nyo͞o-, no͝or′ə-glē′ə, -glī′-, nyo͝or′-) *n.* The delicate network of branched cells and fibers that supports the tissue of the central nervous system. Also called *glia.* [NEURO– + Medieval Greek *glia,* glue; see ZOOGLEA.] **—neu·rog′li·al** *adj.*

neu·ro·hor·mone (no͝or′ō-hôr′mōn, nyo͝or′-) *n.* A hormone secreted by or acting on a part of the nervous system. **—neu′ro·hor·mo′nal** *adj.*

neu·ro·hy·poph·y·sis (no͝or′ō-hī-pŏf′ĭ-sĭs, -hĭ-, nyo͝or′-) *n., pl.* **-ses** (-sēz′). The posterior portion of the pituitary gland, having a rich supply of nerve fibers and releasing oxytocin and vasopressin. **—neu′ro·hy′po·phys′e·al, neu′ro·hy′po·phys′i·al** (-hī′pə-fĭz′ē-əl, -hĭp′ə-, -hĭ-pŏf′ə-sē′əl) *adj.*

neurol. *abbr.* Neurology.

neu·ro·lep·tic (no͝or′ə-lĕp′tĭk, nyo͝or′-) *n.* A tranquilizing drug, especially one used in treating mental disorders. **—neuroleptic** *adj.* Having a tranquilizing effect. [French *neuroleptique* : *neuro-,* nerve (from Greek; see NEURO–) + *-leptique,* affecting (from Greek *lēptikos,* seizing, from *lēptos,* seized, from *lambanein, lēp-,* to seize, take).]

neu·rol·o·gy (no͞o-rŏl′ə-jē, nyo͞o-) *n. Abbr.* **neur., neurol.** The medical science that deals with the nervous system and disorders affecting it. **—neu′ro·log′ic** (no͝or′ə-lŏj′ĭk, nyo͝or′-), **neu′ro·log′i·cal** (-ĭ-kəl) *adj.* **—neu′ro·log′i·cal·ly** *adv.* **—neu·rol′o·gist** *n.*

neu·ro·ma (no͞o-rō′mə, nyo͞o-) *n., pl.* **-mas** or **-ma·ta** (-mə-tə). A tumor composed of nerve tissue.

neu·ro·mus·cu·lar (no͝or′ō-mŭs′kyə-lər, nyo͝or′-) *adj.* **1.** Of, relating to, or affecting both nerves and muscles. **2.** Having the characteristics of both nervous and muscular tissue.

neu·ron (no͝or′ŏn′, nyo͝or′-) also **neu·rone** (-ōn′) *n.* Any of the impulse-conducting cells that constitute the brain, spinal column, and nerves, consisting of a nucleated cell body with one or more dendrites and a single axon. Also called *nerve cell.* [Greek, sinew, string, nerve. See **(s)neəu-** in Appendix.] **—neu′ron·al** (no͞o-rōn′l, nyo͞o-, no͝or′ə-nəl, nyo͝or′-), **neu·ron′ic** *adj.* **—neu·ron′i·cal·ly** *adv.*

neu·ro·pa·thol·o·gy (no͝or′ō-pə-thŏl′ə-jē, nyo͝or′-) *n.* The scientific study of diseases of the nervous system. **—neu′ro·path′o·log′ic** (-păth′ə-lŏj′ĭk), **neu′ro·path′o·log′i·cal** (-ĭ-kəl) *adj.* **—neu′ro·pa·thol′o·gist** *n.*

neu·rop·a·thy (no͞o-rŏp′ə-thē, nyo͞o-) *n., pl.* **-thies.** A disease or an abnormality of the nervous system.

neu·ro·phar·ma·col·o·gy (no͝or′ō-fär′mə-kŏl′ə-jē, nyo͝or′-) *n.* The study of the action of drugs on the nervous system. **—neu′ro·phar′ma·co·log′i·cal** (-kə-lŏj′ĭ-kəl) *adj.* **—neu′ro·phar′ma·col′o·gist** *n.*

neu·ro·phys·i·ol·o·gy (no͝or′ō-fĭz′ē-ŏl′ə-jē, nyo͝or′-) *n.* The branch of physiology that deals with the functions of the nervous system. **—neu′ro·phys′i·o·log′ic** (-ə-lŏj′ĭk), **neu′ro·phys′i·o·log′i·cal** *adj.* **—neu′ro·phys′i·ol′o·gist** *n.*

neu·ro·psy·chi·a·try (no͝or′ō-sĭ-kī′ə-trē, -sī-, nyo͝or′-) *n. Abbr.* **NP** The combined medical study of neurological and psychiatric disorders. **—neu′ro·psy′chi·at′ric** (-sī′kē-ăt′rĭk) *adj.* **—neu′ro·psy·chi′a·trist** *n.*

neu·ro·psy·chol·o·gy (no͝or′ō-sī-kŏl′ə-jē, nyo͝or′-) *n.* The branch of psychology that deals with the relationship between the nervous system, especially the brain, and cerebral or mental functions such as language, memory, and perception. **—neu′ro·psy′cho·log′i·cal** (-sī′kə-lŏj′ĭ-kəl) *adj.* **—neu′ro·psy·chol′o·gist** *n.*

neu·rop·ter·an (no͞o-rŏp′tər-ən, nyo͞o-) *n.* A carnivorous insect of the order Neuroptera, such as the ant lion or dobsonfly, having four net-veined wings and mouthparts adapted for chewing. **—neuropteran** *adj.* Of or belonging to the Neuroptera. [From New Latin *Neuroptera,* order name : Greek *neuron,* vein, tendon; see NEURON + Greek *ptera,* pl. of *pteron,* wing; see –PTER.] **—neu·rop′ter·ous** *adj.*

neu·ro·ra·di·ol·o·gy (no͝or′ō-rā′dē-ŏl′ə-jē, nyo͝or′-) *n.* **1.** The branch of radiology that deals with the nervous system. **2.** The use of x-rays in diagnosis and treatment of disorders of the nervous system. **—neu′ro·ra′di·o·log′i·cal** (-ə-lŏj′ĭ-kəl) *adj.* **—neu′ro·ra′di·ol′o·gist** *n.*

neu·ro·sci·ence (no͝or′ō-sī′əns, nyo͝or′-) *n.* Any of the sciences, such as neuroanatomy and neurobiology, that deal with the nervous system. **—neu′ro·sci′en·tif′ic** (-sī′ən-tĭf′ĭk) *adj.* **—neu′ro·sci′en·tist** (-sī′ən-tĭst) *n.*

neu·ro·se·cre·tion (no͝or′ō-sĭ-krē′shən, nyo͝or′-) *n.* **1.** The secretion of substances, such as hormones, by nerve cells. **2.** A substance secreted by this process. **—neu′ro·se·cre′to·ry** (-krē′tə-rē) *adj.*

neu·ro·sen·so·ry (no͝or′ō-sĕn′sə-rē, nyo͝or′-) *adj.* Of or relating to the sensory activity or functions of the nervous system: *neurosensory cells.*

neu·ro·sis (no͞o-rō′sĭs, nyo͞o-) *n., pl.* **-ses** (-sēz). Any of various mental or emotional disorders, such as hypochondria or neurasthenia, arising from no apparent organic lesion or change and involving symptoms such as insecurity, anxiety, depression, and irrational fears.

neu·ro·sur·ger·y (no͝or′ō-sûr′jə-rē, nyo͝or′-) *n., pl.* **-ies.** Surgery on any part of the nervous system. **—neu′ro·sur′geon** (-jən) *n.* **—neu′ro·sur′gi·cal** (-jĭ-kəl) *adj.*

neu·rot·ic (no͞o-rŏt′ĭk, nyo͞o-) *adj.* **1.** Of, relating to, derived from, or affected with a neurosis: *a neurotic disorder; neurotic symptoms.* **2.** *Informal.* Overly anxious: *neurotic about punctuality.* **—neurotic** *n.* **1.** A person suffering from a neurosis. **2.** *Informal.* A person prone to excessive anxiety and emotional upset. **—neu·rot′i·cal·ly** *adv.*

neu·rot·o·my (no͞o-rŏt′ə-mē, nyo͞o-) *n., pl.* **-mies.** The surgical cutting or stretching of a nerve, usually to relieve pain.

neu·ro·tox·in (no͝or′ō-tŏk′sĭn, nyo͝or′-) *n.* A toxin that damages or destroys nerve tissue. **—neu′ro·tox′ic** (-tŏk′sĭk) *adj.* **—neu′ro·tox·ic′i·ty** (-tŏk-sĭs′ĭ-tē) *n.*

neu·ro·trans·mit·ter (no͝or′ō-trăns′mĭt-ər, -trănz′-, nyo͝or′-) *n.* A chemical substance, such as acetylcholine or dopamine, that transmits nerve impulses across a synapse.

neu·ro·trop·ic (no͝or′ə-trŏp′ĭk, -trō′pĭk, nyo͝or′-) *adj.* Tending to affect or attack nervous tissue: *a neurotropic venom.* **—neu·rot′ro·pism** (no͞o-rŏt′rə-pĭz′əm, nyo͞o-) *n.*

neus·ton (no͞o′stŏn, nyo͞o′-) *n.* The collection of minute or microscopic organisms that inhabit the surface layer of a body of water. [Greek *neuston,* neuter of *neustos,* swimming, from *nein,* to swim. See **(s)nāu-** in Appendix.]

Neuse (no͞os, nyo͞os). A river of east-central North Carolina flowing about 442 km (275 mi) southeast to Pamlico Sound.

Neuss (nois). A city of west-central Germany across the Rhine River from Düsseldorf. Built on the site of a Roman camp, it was chartered in the 12th century and held by France from 1794 to 1815, when it passed to Prussia. Population, 143,762.

Neus·tri·a (no͞o′strē-ə, nyo͞o′-). The western part of the kingdom of the Merovingian Franks from the sixth to the eighth century, in present-day northwest France. After 912 the name was applied to Normandy. **—Neu′stri·an** *adj. & n.*

neut. *abbr.* **1.** Neuter. **2.** Neutral.

neu·ter (no͞o′tər, nyo͞o′-) *adj. Abbr.* **neut. 1.** *Grammar.* **a.** Neither masculine nor feminine in gender. **b.** Neither active nor passive; intransitive. Used of verbs. **2. a.** *Biology.* Having undeveloped or imperfectly developed sexual organs: *the neuter caste in social insects.* **b.** *Botany.* Having no pistils or stamens; asexual. **c.** *Zoology.* Sexually undeveloped. **3.** Taking no side; neutral. **—neuter** *n.* **1.** *Grammar.* **a.** The neuter gender. **b.** A neuter word. **c.** A neuter noun. **2.** A castrated animal. **3.** A sexually undeveloped or imperfectly developed insect, such as a worker bee. **4.** A plant without stamens or pistils. **5.** One that is neutral. **—neuter** *tr.v.* **-tered, -ter·ing, -ters.** To castrate or spay. [Middle English *neutre,* from Old French, from Latin *neuter,* neither, neuter : *ne-,* not; see **ne** in Appendix + *uter,* either; see **kʷo-** in Appendix.]

neu·tral (no͞o′trəl, nyo͞o′-) *adj. Abbr.* **neut. 1.** Not aligned with, supporting, or favoring either side in a war, dispute, or contest. **2.** Belonging to neither side in a controversy: *on neutral ground.* **3.** Belonging to neither kind; not one thing or the other; indifferent. **4.** Sexless; neuter. **5.** *Chemistry.* **a.** Of or relating to a solution or compound that is neither acidic nor alkaline. **b.** Of or relating to a compound that does not ionize in solution. **6.** *Physics.* **a.** Of or relating to a particle, an object, or a system that has neither positive nor negative electric charge. **b.** Of or relating to a particle, an object, or a system that has a net electric charge of zero. **7.** *Color.* Of or indicating a color, such as gray, black, or

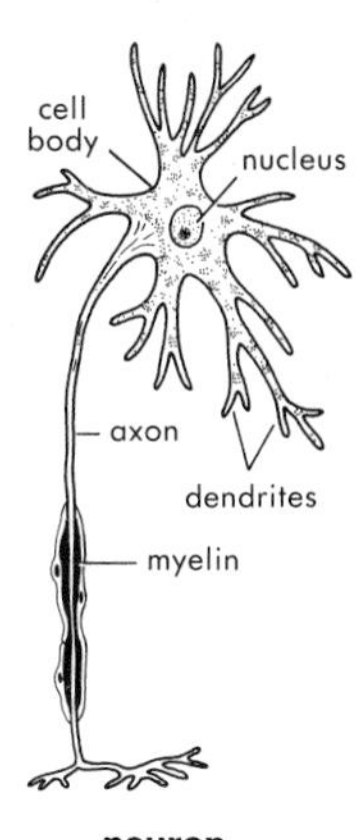

neuron

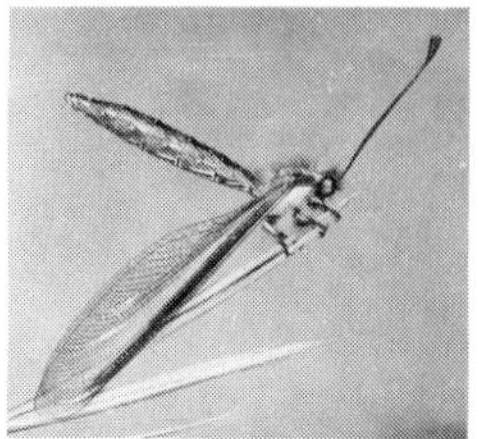

neuropteran
Adult ant lion

ă **pat**	oi **boy**
ā **pay**	ou **out**
âr **care**	o͝o **took**
ä **father**	o͞o **boot**
ĕ **pet**	ŭ **cut**
ē **be**	ûr **urge**
ĭ **pit**	th **thin**
ī **pie**	*th* **this**
îr **pier**	hw **which**
ŏ **pot**	zh **vision**
ō **toe**	ə **about, item**
ô **paw**	♦ **regionalism**

Stress marks: ′ (primary); ′ (secondary), as in **dictionary** (dĭk′shə-nĕr′ē)

white, that lacks hue; achromatic. **8.** *Linguistics.* Pronounced with the tongue in a middle position, neither high nor low, as the *a* in *around.* **—neutral** *n.* **1.a.** A nation nonaligned with either side in a war. **b.** A citizen of such a nation. **2.** One who takes no side in a controversy: *"I am by disposition one of life's neutrals, a human Switzerland"* (John Gregory Dunne). **3.** *Color.* A neutral hue. **4.** A position in which a set of gears is disengaged so that power cannot be transmitted. [Middle English *neuteral,* from Old French *neutral,* from Latin *neutrālis,* grammatically neuter, from *neuter, neutr-.* See NEUTER.] **—neu′tral·ly** *adv.*

Neu·tral (no͞o′trəl, nyo͞o′-) *n., pl.* **Neutral** or **-trals.** **1.** A confederacy of Iroquoian-speaking Native American peoples formerly inhabiting the northern shore of Lake Erie. The Neutral were destroyed by the Iroquois in the mid-17th century. **2.** A member of this people.

♦ **neutral ground** *n. Louisiana & Southern Mississippi.* See **median strip.**

♦ ***REGIONAL NOTE:*** The strip of grass dividing the opposing lanes of an avenue or a highway is known by a variety of terms in the United States. The most common term is *median strip* or *median.* In upstate New York it is called a *mall,* and in Pennsylvania, a *medial strip.* In the Upper Midwest the strip is known as a *meridian,* a *boulevard,* or a *boulevard strip.* In Louisiana and southern Mississippi the term used is *neutral ground*—"as if the highway were a battle zone," observes Craig M. Carver in *American Regional Dialects.*

neu·tral·ism (no͞o′trə-lĭz′əm, nyo͞o′-) *n.* **1.** The state of being neutral; neutrality. **2.** A political policy or advocacy of nonalignment or noninvolvement in conflicting alliances and of attempting to mediate or conciliate in conflicts between states: *"Neutralism differs from neutrality in that it is an attitude of mind in time of peace rather than a legal status in time of war"* (London Times). **—neu′tral·ist** *adj. & n.* **—neu′tral·is′tic** *adj.*

neu·tral·i·ty (no͞o-trăl′ĭ-tē, nyo͞o-) *n.* The state or policy of being neutral, especially nonparticipation in war.

neu·tral·i·za·tion (no͞o′trə-lĭ-zā′shən, nyo͞o′-) *n.* **1.a.** The act or process of neutralizing. **b.** The state or quality of being neutralized. **2.** *Chemistry.* A reaction between an acid and a base that yields a salt and water.

neu·tral·ize (no͞o′trə-līz′, nyo͞o′-) *tr.v.* **-ized, -iz·ing, -iz·es.** **1.** To make neutral. **2.** To counterbalance or counteract the effect of; render ineffective. **3.** To declare neutral and therefore inviolable during a war. **4.** *Chemistry.* **a.** To make (a solution) neutral. **b.** To cause (an acid or a base) to undergo neutralization. **5.** *Medicine.* To counteract the effect of (a drug or toxin). **6.** *Slang.* To remove as a threat, especially by killing. **—neu′tral·iz′er** *n.*

SYNONYMS: *neutralize, negate, nullify, counteract.* These verbs mean to make something ineffective by or as if by applying an opposite or counterbalancing force. *Neutralize* implies a state of ineffectiveness, inaction, or inoperativeness: *"American life is a powerful solvent. It seems to neutralize every intellectual element . . . and to fuse it in the native good will, complacency, thoughtlessness, and optimism"* (George Santayana). *Negate* and *nullify* suggest cancellation of validity, force, usefulness, value, consequence, or significance: *Terror momentarily negated the effects of his injury. "The* [15th] *Amendment nullifies sophisticated as well as simple-minded modes of discrimination"* (Felix Frankfurter). *Counteract* frequently implies the opposition of forces thought of as being desirable and undesirable; it may suggest action taken as a corrective measure: *The prime minister addressed the nation in an effort to counteract the damage the scandal had done to his credibility.*

neutral spirits *pl.n. (used with a sing. or pl. verb).* Ethyl alcohol distilled at or above 190 proof and used frequently in blended alcoholic beverages.

neu·tri·no (no͞o-trē′nō, nyo͞o-) *n., pl.* **-nos.** Any of three electrically neutral subatomic particles in the lepton family. See table at **subatomic particle.** [Italian, from *neutro,* neuter, from Latin *neuter, neutr-.* See NEUTER.]

neu·tron (no͞o′trŏn′, nyo͞o′-) *n. Abbr.* **n** An electrically neutral subatomic particle in the baryon family, having a mass 1,839 times that of the electron, stable when bound in an atomic nucleus, and having a mean lifetime of approximately 1.0×10^3 seconds as a free particle. It and the proton form nearly the entire mass of atomic nuclei. See table at **subatomic particle.** [NEUTR(AL) + -ON[1].]

neutron bomb *n.* A nuclear bomb that would produce great numbers of neutrons but little blast and thus destroy life but spare property.

neutron star *n.* A celestial body hypothesized to occur in a terminal stage of stellar evolution, essentially consisting of a superdense mass of neutrons and having a powerful gravitational attraction from which only neutrinos and high-energy photons can escape, thus rendering the body invisible except to x-ray detection.

neu·tro·phil (no͞o′trə-fĭl′, nyo͞o′-) *adj.* Not stained strongly or definitely by either acid or basic dyes but stained readily by neutral dyes. Used especially of white blood cells. **—neutrophil** *n.* A neutrophil cell, especially an abundant type of granular white blood cell that is highly destructive of microorganisms. [NEUTR(AL) + -PHIL(E).] **—neu′tro·phile′** (-fīl′), **neu′tro·phil′ic** (-fĭl′ĭk) *adj.*

Nev. *abbr.* Nevada.

Ne·va (nē′və, nyĭ-vä′). A river of northwest Russia flowing about 74 km (46 mi) from Lake Ladoga to the Gulf of Finland, an arm of the Baltic Sea.

Ne·vad·a (nə-văd′ə, -vä′də). *Abbr.* **NV, Nev.** A state of the western United States. It was admitted as the 36th state in 1864. Part of the area ceded by Mexico to the United States in 1848, it was made into a separate territory in 1861 after an influx of settlers who were drawn by the discovery (1859) of the Comstock Lode. Carson City is the capital and Las Vegas the largest city. Population, 800,493. **—Ne·vad′an, Ne·vad′i·an** *adj. & n.*

né·vé (nā-vā′) *n.* **1.** The upper part of a glacier where the snow turns into ice. **2.a.** A snow field at the head of a glacier. **b.** The granular snow typically found in such a field. [French, from French dialectal *névi,* from Vulgar Latin **nivātum,* from neuter of Latin *nivātus,* cooled by snow, from *nix, niv-,* snow.]

Nev·el·son (nĕv′əl-sən), **Louise.** 1899–1988. Russian-born American sculptor whose massive works, often of wood, cast metal, and found objects, are characterized by complex and rhythmic abstract shapes.

nev·er (nĕv′ər) *adv.* **1.** Not ever; on no occasion; at no time: *He had never been there before. You never can be sure.* **2.** Not at all; in no way; absolutely not: *Never fear. That will never do.* [Middle English, from Old English *nǣfre* : *ne,* not; see **ne** in Appendix + *ǣfre,* ever; see **aiw-** in Appendix.]

nev·er-end·ing (nĕv′ər-ĕn′dĭng) *adj.* Having no foreseeable end: *the never-ending search for happiness.*

nev·er·more (nĕv′ər-môr′, -mōr′) *adv.* Never again.

nev·er-nev·er land (nĕv′ər-nĕv′ər) *n.* An imaginary and wonderful place; a fantasy land. [After *Never-Never Land,* fictional setting used in the play *Peter Pan* by J.M. Barrie.]

nev·er·the·less (nĕv′ər-thə-lĕs′) *adv.* In spite of that; nonetheless; however: *a small, nevertheless fatal error.*

Ne·vis (nē′vĭs, nĕv′ĭs). One of the Leeward Islands of the eastern West Indies in the Caribbean Sea. It was colonized by the English after 1628 and is now part of St. Christopher-Nevis.

ne·vus (nē′vəs) *n., pl.* **-vi** (-vī′). A congenital growth or mark on the skin, such as a mole or birthmark. [Latin *naevus.*] **—ne′void′** (-void′) *adj.*

new (no͞o, nyo͞o) *adj.* **new·er, new·est.** **1.** Having been made or come into being only a short time ago; recent: *a new law.* **2.a.** Still fresh: *a new coat of paint.* **b.** Never used or worn before now: *a new car; a new hat.* **3.** Just found, discovered, or learned: *new information.* **4.** Not previously experienced or encountered; novel or unfamiliar: *ideas new to her; visiting new places.* **5.** Different from the former or the old: *the new morality.* **6.** Recently obtained or acquired: *new political power; new money.* **7.** Additional; further: *new sources of energy.* **8.** Recently arrived or established in a place, position, or relationship: *new neighbors; a new president.* **9.** Changed for the better; rejuvenated: *The nap has made a new person of me.* **10.** Being the later or latest in a sequence: *a new edition.* **11.** Currently fashionable: *a new dance.* **12. New.** In the most recent form, period, or development. **13.** Inexperienced or unaccustomed: *new at the job; new to the trials of parenthood.* **—new** *adv.* Freshly; recently. Often used in combination: *new-mown.* [Middle English *newe,* from Old English *nīwe, nēowe.* See **newo-** in Appendix.] **—new′ness** *n.*

SYNONYMS: *new, fresh, novel, newfangled, original.* These adjectives describe what has existed for only a short time, has only lately come into use, or has only recently arrived at a state or position, as of prominence. *New* is the most general: *a new movie; new clothes; a new friend; a new popular hero. "It is time for a new generation of leadership, to cope with new problems and new opportunities. For there is a new world to be won"* (John F. Kennedy). Something *fresh* has or has retained qualities of newness such as briskness, brightness, or purity: *The police found fresh fingerprints on the light switch. Identifying the virus gave scientists fresh hope of discovering a vaccine. Novel* applies to what is both new and strikingly unusual: *"The Spaniards were astonished at these novel maneuvers* [by musketeers on skates] *upon the ice"* (John Lothrop Motley). *Newfangled* suggests that something is needlessly novel; the term is often derogatory: *"the newfangled doctrine of utility"* (John Galt). Something that is *original* is novel and the first of its kind: *"The science of pure mathematics, in its modern development, may claim to be the most original creation of the human spirit"* (Alfred North Whitehead).

New Age *adj.* Of or relating to a complex of spiritual and consciousness-raising movements of the 1980's covering a range of themes from a belief in spiritualism and reincarnation to advocacy of holistic approaches to health and ecology. **—New Age** *n. Music.* Modern music characterized by quiet improvisation on instruments such as the acoustic piano, the guitar, or a synthesizer and marked by a dreamy texture and touches of ethnic instrumentation. **—New Ager** *n.*

New Al·ba·ny (ôl′bə-nē). A city of southern Indiana on the Ohio River opposite Louisville, Kentucky. It was a shipbuilding center in the 19th century. Population, 37,103.

New Am·ster·dam (ăm′stər-dăm′). A settlement established in 1624 by the Dutch at the mouth of the Hudson River on the southern end of Manhattan Island. It was the capital of New

Netherland from 1626 to 1664, when it was captured by the British and renamed New York.

New·ark (no͞o′ərk, nyo͞o′-). **1.** A city of western California south-southeast of Oakland. On the eastern coast of San Francisco Bay, it is largely residential. Population, 32,126. **2.** (*also* -ärk′). A city of northwest Delaware west-southwest of Wilmington. Settled c. 1694, it is the seat of the University of Delaware (established 1743). Population, 25,247. **3.** A city of northeast New Jersey on **Newark Bay,** an inlet of the Atlantic Ocean, opposite Jersey City and west of New York City. It was settled by Puritans in 1666 and is today a heavily industrialized port of entry. Population, 329,248. **4.** A city of central Ohio east of Columbus. It is an industrial and processing center in an area marked by notable earthworks erected by the Mound Builders. Population, 41,200.

New Bed·ford (bĕd′fərd). A city of southeast Massachusetts on Buzzards Bay east-southeast of Fall River. Settled in the mid-1600's, it was a major whaling port in the first half of the 19th century. Population, 98,478.

New Ber·lin (bûr-lĭn′). A city of southeast Wisconsin, a suburb of Milwaukee. Population, 30,529.

new blood *n.* New people considered as a revitalizing force, as in an organization.

New·bolt (no͞o′bōlt′, nyo͞o′-), Sir **Henry John.** 1862–1938. British writer and editor known for his naval histories.

new·born (no͞o′bôrn′, nyo͞o′-) *adj.* **1.** Very recently born: *a newborn baby.* **2.** Born anew: *newborn courage.* —**newborn** *n.* A neonate.

New Braun·fels (broun′fəlz). A city of south-central Texas northeast of San Antonio. Founded by German immigrants, it has a textile industry. Population, 22,402.

New Brigh·ton (brīt′n). A city of southeast Minnesota, a suburb of Minneapolis–St. Paul. Population, 23,269.

New Brit·ain[1] (brĭt′n). A volcanic island of Papua New Guinea, in the southwest Pacific Ocean. The largest island in the Bismarck Archipelago, it was first visited and named by William Dampier in 1700 and was controlled by Germany after 1884 and by Australia from 1920 until 1975, when Papua New Guinea achieved independence.

New Brit·ain[2] (brĭt′n). A city of central Connecticut south-southwest of Hartford. Tin and brass industries were established here in the 18th century. Population, 73,840.

New Bruns·wick (brŭnz′wĭk). **1.** *Abbr.* **NB, N.B.** A province of eastern Canada on the Gulf of St. Lawrence. Part of French Acadia and then the province of Nova Scotia, it became a separate province in 1784 after an influx of Loyalists from the newly independent United States. New Brunswick joined Nova Scotia, Quebec, and Ontario to form the confederated Dominion of Canada in 1867. Fredericton is the capital and St. John the largest city. Population, 696,405. **2.** A city of central New Jersey on the Raritan River southwest of Newark. Settled in 1681, it served as headquarters for both the British and Continental armies during the American Revolution. Population, 41,442.

New·burg also **New·burgh** (no͞o′bûrg′, nyo͞o′-) *adj.* Served in a rich sauce made of cream, egg yolks, butter, and sherry: *lobster Newburg; seafood Newburg.* [Origin unknown.]

Newburgh. A city of southeast New York on the Hudson River south-southwest of Poughkeepsie. Founded c. 1709, it was George Washington's headquarters from April 1782 until August 1783. Population, 23,438.

New Cal·e·do·ni·a (kăl′ĭ-dō′nē-ə, -dōn′yə). A French overseas territory in the southwest Pacific Ocean consisting of the island of **New Caledonia** and several smaller islands. The island of New Caledonia was named by Capt. James Cook in 1774 and annexed by France in 1853. It was a penal colony from 1864 to 1894. Nouméa is the territorial capital. Population, 145,368.

New Ca·naan (kā′nən). A town of southwest Connecticut north-northeast of Stamford. Population, 17,931.

New Cas·tile (kăs-tēl′). A historical region of central Spain that combined with Old Castile to the north to form the kingdom of Castile. It was united with Aragon after the marriage of Ferdinand and Isabella (1479).

New·cas·tle (no͞o′kăs′əl, nyo͞o′-). **1.** A town of southern Ontario, Canada, on Lake Ontario east of Toronto. It was established in a dairy and farm region. Population, 32,229. **2.** Or **New·cas·tle-un·der-Lyme** (-ŭn′dər-līm′). A municipal borough of west-central England south-southwest of Stoke. It has brick, tile, and clothing industries. Population, 74,200. **3.** Or **Newcastle upon Tyne** (tīn). A borough of northeast England on the Tyne River north of Leeds. Built on the site of a Roman military station, it became a coal-shipping port in the 13th century and was the principal center for coal exports after the 16th century. Its prominence in the trade gave rise to the expression *to carry coals to Newcastle,* meaning "to do something superfluous or unnecessary." Population, 285,300.

New Cas·tle (kăs′əl). **1.** A city of east-central Indiana south of Muncie. It is a trade center in an agricultural region. There are prehistoric mounds in the area. Population, 20,056. **2.** A city of western Pennsylvania north-northwest of Pittsburgh. Various mineral deposits and manufactures are important to its economy. Population, 33,621.

New·cas·tle-un·der-Lyme (no͞o′kăs′əl-ŭn′dər-līm′, nyo͞o′-). See **Newcastle** (sense 2).

Newcastle upon Tyne (tīn). See **Newcastle** (sense 3).

new-col·lar (no͞o′kŏl′ər, nyo͞o′-) *adj.* Of or relating to a class of workers between blue-collar and white-collar who hold primarily service and clerical jobs.

New·comb (no͞o′kəm, nyo͞o′-), **Simon.** 1835–1909. American astronomer who updated the tables indicating the position of the moon, the planets, and important stars.

new·com·er (no͞o′kŭm′ər, nyo͞o′-) *n.* One who has only recently arrived.

New Criticism *n.* A method of literary evaluation and interpretation practiced chiefly in the mid-20th century that emphasizes close examination of a text with minimum regard for the biographical or historical circumstances in which it was produced. —**New Critic** *n.*

New Deal *n.* **1.** The programs and policies to promote economic recovery and social reform introduced during the 1930's by President Franklin D. Roosevelt. **2.** The period during which these programs and policies were developed. —**New Dealer** *n.*

New Del·hi (dĕl′ē). The capital of India, in the north-central part of the country south of Delhi. It was constructed between 1912 and 1929 to replace Calcutta as the capital of British India and officially inaugurated in 1931. New Delhi is also a trade center and transportation hub. Population, 273,036.

new·el (no͞o′əl, nyo͞o′-) *n.* **1.** A vertical support at the center of a circular staircase. **2.** A post that supports a handrail at the bottom or at the landing of a staircase. [Middle English *nouel, niewel,* from Old French *noiel,* from Vulgar Latin **nōdellus,* little knot, diminutive of Latin *nōdulus,* diminutive of *nōdus,* knot. See NODE.]

New Eng·land (ĭng′glənd). *Abbr.* **NE, N.E.** A region of the northeast United States comprising the modern-day states of Maine, New Hampshire, Vermont, Massachusetts, Connnecticut, and Rhode Island. —**New Eng′land·er** *n.*

New England boiled dinner *n.* A dish consisting of meat simmered with carrots, potatoes, and cabbage.

New England clam chowder *n.* A thick soup made with clams, onions, salt pork, potatoes, and milk.

New England Range. A mountain range and plateau of southeast Australia in the northern part of the Great Dividing Range.

New English *n.* See **Modern English.**

New English Bible *n.* A modern translation of the Bible prepared by a British interdenominational team and published in 1970.

Newf. *abbr.* Newfoundland.

new·fan·gled (no͞o′făng′gəld, nyo͞o′-) *adj.* **1.** New and often needlessly novel. See Synonyms at **new.** **2.** Fond of novelty. [Middle English *newfanglyd,* fond of novelty, alteration of *neufangel* : *new,* new; see NEW + *-*fangel,* taken; see **pag-** in Appendix.] —**new′fan′gled·ness** *n.*

new-fash·ioned (no͞o′făsh′ənd, nyo͞o′-) *adj.* **1.** Up-to-date; current. **2.** Created in a new form or fashion.

New For·est (fôr′ĭst, fŏr′-). A region of southern England. Set aside as a hunting ground by William the Conqueror in 1079, it is mostly administrated as public parkland.

new·found (no͞o′found′, nyo͞o′-) *adj.* Recently discovered: *a newfound pastime.*

New·found·land[1] (no͞o′fən-lənd, -lănd′, -fənd-, nyo͞o′-). *Abbr.* **NF, Newf., Nfld.** A province of eastern Canada including the island of **Newfoundland** and nearby islands and the mainland area of Labrador with its adjacent islands. Newfoundland joined the confederation in 1949. Vikings probably visited the region c. 1000, but the area was not known to European fishermen and explorers until John Cabot's voyages in the late 15th century. England claimed Newfoundland in 1583, although the claims were disputed by France until the Treaty of Paris (1763). The province of Quebec continued to claim Labrador until 1927. St. John's is the capital and the largest city. Population 567,681. —**New′found·land·er** *n.*

New·found·land[2] (no͞o′fən-lənd, nyo͞o′-) *n.* Any of a breed of large, strong dog developed in Newfoundland and having a thick, usually black coat.

New France (frăns). The possessions of France in North America from the 16th century until the Treaty of Paris (1763), when the French holdings were awarded to Great Britain and Spain. At its greatest extent it included much of southeast Canada, the Great Lakes region, and the Mississippi Valley. British and French rivalry for control of the territory led to the four conflicts known collectively in the New World as the French and Indian Wars (1689–1763).

New Geor·gia Island (jôr′jə). An island of the Solomon islands in the southwest Pacific Ocean. It was occupied by the Japanese in 1942 and recaptured by the Allies in August 1943.

New Gra·na·da (grə-nä′də). A former Spanish colony of northern South America including present-day Colombia, Ecuador, Panama, and Venezuela. It was under Spanish rule from the 1530's to 1819.

New Greek *n.* See **Modern Greek.**

New Guin·ea (gĭn′ē). An island in the southwest Pacific Ocean north of Australia. The western half is part of Indonesia, and the eastern half forms the major portion of Papua New Guinea. It was probably first sighted by the Portuguese in 1511 and

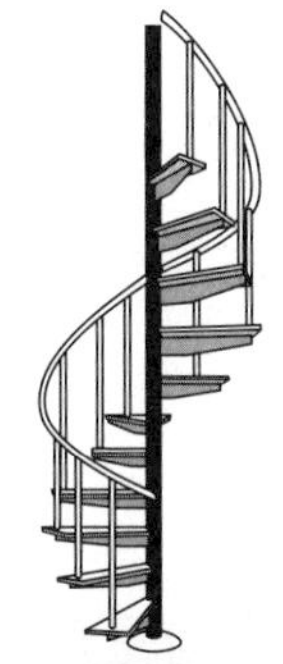

newel
Top: Of a circular staircase
Bottom: At the landing of a staircase

Newfoundland[2]

ă pat	oi boy
ā pay	ou out
âr care	o͝o took
ä father	o͞o boot
ĕ pet	ŭ cut
ē be	ûr urge
ĭ pit	th thin
ī pie	*th* this
îr pier	hw which
ŏ pot	zh vision
ō toe	ə about, item
ô paw	♦ regionalism

Stress marks: ′ (primary); ′ (secondary), as in **dictionary** (dĭk′shə-nĕr′ē)

named for the Guinea coast of western Africa. **—New Guin′e·an** *adj. & n.*

New Guinea, Trust Territory of. A former trust territory of Australia consisting of northeast New Guinea, the Bismarck Archipelago, and Bougainville in the Solomon Islands. It was placed under Australian jurisdiction after World War II and was gradually broken up between 1963 and 1973.

New Hamp·shire (hămp′shər, -shîr′, hăm′-). *Abbr.* **NH, N.H.** A state of the northeast United States between Vermont and Maine. It was admitted as one of the original Thirteen Colonies in 1788. First explored in 1603, it was settled by colonists from Massachusetts during the 1620's and 1630's and became a separate colony in 1741. New Hampshire was the first colony to declare its independence from Great Britain and the first to establish its own government (January 1776). Concord is the capital and Manchester the largest city. Population, 920,610. **—New Hamp′shir·ite′** *n.*

New Har·mo·ny (här′mə-nē). A village of southwest Indiana on the Wabash River west-northwest of Evansville. It was founded in 1814 by the Harmony Society led by George Rapp and was the site (1825–1828) of a utopian community established by Robert Owen. Population, 945.

New Ha·ven (hā′vən). A city of southern Connecticut on Long Island Sound northeast of Bridgeport. Settled 1637–1638 by Puritans, it was the center of a theocratic colony that was joined with Connecticut in 1664. From 1701 to 1875 it was joint capital with Hartford. Population, 126,109.

New Hebrew *n.* The Hebrew language as used from the mid-18th century until 1948. Also called *Modern Hebrew.*

New Heb·ri·des (hĕb′rĭ-dēz′). See **Vanuatu.**

New Hope (hōp). A city of southeast Minnesota, a residential suburb of Minneapolis. Population, 23,087.

New·house (no͞o′hous′, nyo͞o′-), **S(amuel) I(rving).** 1895–1979. American publisher who built and controlled a vast media conglomerate, based on 31 newspapers nationwide.

New I·be·ri·a (ī-bîr′ē-ə). A city of southern Louisiana southwest of Baton Rouge. Settled by Acadians after c. 1765, it is a processing and shipping center. Population, 32,766.

New·ing·ton (no͞o′ĭng-tən, nyo͞o′-). A town of north-central Connecticut southwest of Hartford. Population, 28,841.

New Ire·land (īr′lənd). A volcanic island of the southwest Pacific Ocean in the Bismarck Archipelago. First sighted in 1616, it was thought to be part of the island of New Britain until 1797. New Ireland was a German protectorate from 1884 to 1914 and now belongs to Papua New Guinea.

new·ish (no͞o′ĭsh, nyo͞o′-) *adj.* Fairly new.

New Jer·sey (jûr′zē). *Abbr.* **NJ, N.J.** A state of the east-central United States on the Atlantic Ocean. It was admitted as one of the original Thirteen Colonies in 1787. The region was settled by Dutch and Swedish colonists in the 1620's and 1630's, was ceded to the English as part of New Netherland in 1664, and became a royal province in 1702. The colony was strategically important in the American Revolution and was the site of a number of major battles. Trenton is the capital and Newark the largest city. Population, 7,365,011. **—New Jer′sey·ite′** *n.*

New Je·ru·sa·lem (jə-ro͞o′sə-ləm, -zə-) *n.* **1.** *Theology.* The final resting place of souls redeemed by Jesus. **2.** An ideal community on earth.

New Journalism *n.* Journalism that is characterized by the reporter's subjective interpretations and often features fictional dramatized elements to emphasize personal involvement. **—New Journalist** *n.*

New Ken·sing·ton (kĕn′zĭng-tən). A city of southwest Pennsylvania on the Allegheny River east-northeast of Pittsburgh. Population, 17,660.

New Kingdom. Ancient Egypt during the XVIII–XX Dynasties, from c. 1580 to 1090 B.C. The New Kingdom was noted for its territorial expansion and richness of art and architecture under rulers such as Amenhotep III and Rameses II.

New Latin *n.* Latin as used since about 1500.

New Left *n.* A political movement originating in the United States in the 1960's, especially among college students, marked by active advocacy of radical changes in government, politics, and society. **—New Leftist** *n.*

New Lon·don (lŭn′dən). A city of southeast Connecticut at the mouth of the Thames River near Long Island Sound. Laid out by John Winthrop in 1646, it was an important whaling center during the 19th century. Population, 28,842.

new·ly (no͞o′lē, nyo͞o′-) *adv.* **1.** Not long ago; recently: *newly baked bread.* **2.** Once more; anew: *a newly painted room.* **3.** In a new or different way; freshly: *an old idea newly phrased.*

new·ly·wed (no͞o′lē-wĕd′, nyo͞o′-) *n.* A person recently married.

New·man (no͞o′mən, nyo͞o′-), **John Henry.** 1801–1890. British prelate and theologian. A founder of the Oxford movement, he converted to Roman Catholicism (1845) and was made a cardinal (1879).

New·mar·ket (no͞o′mär′kĭt, nyo͞o′-). **1.** A town of southeast Ontario, Canada, north of Toronto. It is an industrial community. Population, 29,753. **2.** An urban district of eastern England east of Cambridge. It has been a center for horse racing since the early 17th century. Population, 16,235.

new math *n.* Mathematics taught in elementary and secondary schools that constructs mathematical relationships from set theory. Also called *new mathematics.*

New Mex·i·co (mĕk′sĭ-kō′). *Abbr.* **NM, N.M., N.Mex.** A state of the southwest United States on the Mexican border. It was admitted as the 47th state in 1912. Site of prehistoric cultures that long preceded the Pueblo civilization encountered by the Spanish in the 16th century, the region was governed as a province of Mexico after 1821 and ceded to the United States by the Treaty of Guadalupe Hidalgo in 1848. Sante Fe is the capital and Albuquerque the largest city. Population, 1,303,445. **—New Mex′i·can** *adj. & n.*

New Mil·ford (mĭl′fərd). **1.** A town of western Connecticut on the Housatonic River north-northeast of Danbury. Founded in the early 1700's, it is a manufacturing center in a summer resort region. Population, 19,420. **2.** A borough of northeast New Jersey east-northeast of Paterson. Settled in 1695 by French Huguenots, it is primarily residential. Population, 16,876.

new moon *n.* **1.** The phase of the moon occurring when it passes between the earth and the sun and is invisible or visible only as a narrow crescent at sunset. **2.** The crescent moon.

New Neth·er·land (nĕth′ər-lənd). A Dutch colony in North America along the Hudson and lower Delaware rivers. The first settlement was made at Fort Orange (now Albany, New York) in 1624, although the colony centered on New Amsterdam at the tip of Manhattan Island after 1625–1626. New Netherland was annexed by the English and renamed New York in 1664.

New Norwegian *n.* A Norwegian national standard language based on the spoken, especially rural dialects, devised in 1853 and recognized as a second national language in 1885. Also called *Landsmål, Nynorsk.*

New Or·leans (ôr′lē-ənz, ôr′lənz, ôr-lēnz′). A city of southeast Louisiana between the Mississippi River and Lake Pontchartrain. Founded in 1718, it became the capital of a French colony in 1722 and passed to the United States as part of the Louisiana Purchase of 1803. French influence continued to dominate the city, however, especially in the Vieux Carré and in the celebration of Mardi Gras. Population, 557,482. **—New Or·lea′ni·an** (ôr-lē′nē-ən, -lēn′yən) *n.*

new penny *n.* See **penny** (sense 3a).

New Phil·a·del·phi·a (fĭl′ə-dĕl′fē-ə). A city of northeast central Ohio south of Canton. Population, 16,883.

New·port (no͞o′pôrt′, -pōrt′, nyo͞o′-). **1.** A municipal borough of southern England. It is the administrative and commercial center of the Isle of Wight in the English Channel. Population, 23,570. **2.** A city of northern Kentucky on the Ohio River opposite Cincinnati, Ohio. Laid out in 1791, it is an industrial center. Population, 21,587. **3.** A city of southeast Rhode Island at the mouth of Narragansett Bay south-southeast of Providence. Settled in 1639, it was an important economic center in pre-Revolutionary times and in the 19th century became a fashionable summer resort where the wealthy built palatial "cottages" such as the Breakers and Marble House. Population 29,259. **4.** A borough of southeast Wales on an inlet of the Severn estuary northeast of Cardiff. It is an industrial center. Population 134,200.

Newport Beach. A city of southern California on the Pacific Ocean south of Santa Ana. It is a popular seaside and yachting resort. Population, 64,556.

Newport News. An independent city of southeast Virginia at the mouth of the James River off Hampton Roads north-northwest of Norfolk. Settled c. 1620, it gained economic importance with the beginning of its shipbuilding industry in the 1880's. Population, 144,903.

New Prov·i·dence (prŏv′ĭ-dəns). An island of the Bahamas in the West Indies.

New River. A river of the southeast United States flowing about 515 km (320 mi) from the Blue Ridge in northwest North Carolina northeast across southwest Virginia then northwest to the Allegheny Plateau in south-central West Virginia.

New Ro·chelle (rə-shĕl′, rō-). A city of southeast New York on Long Island Sound east of Mount Vernon. Settled by Huguenots in 1688, it is mainly residential with some light industry. Population, 70,794.

news (no͞oz, nyo͞oz) *pl.n. (used with a sing. verb).* **1.a.** Information about recent events or happenings, especially as reported by newspapers, periodicals, radio, or television. **b.** A presentation of such information, as in a newspaper or on a newscast. **2.** New information of any kind: *The requirement was news to him.* **3.** Newsworthy material: *"a public figure on a scale unimaginable in America; whatever he did was news"* (James Atlas). [Middle English *newes,* new things, tidings, pl. of *newe,* new thing, new. See NEW.] **—news′less** *adj.*

SYNONYMS: *news, advice, intelligence, tidings, word.* The central meaning shared by these nouns is "information about hitherto unknown events and happenings": *just heard the good news; sent advice that the mortgage would be foreclosed; a source of intelligence about the negotiations; tidings of victory; received word of the senator's death.*

WORD HISTORY: If you take the first letters of the directions North, East, West, and South, it is true that you have the letters of the word *news,* but it is not true that you have the etymology of *news,* contrary to what has often been thought. The history of the word is much less clever than this and not at all unexpected. *News* is simply the plural of the noun *new,* which we use, for example, in the adage "Out with the old, in with the new." The first recorded user of this plural to mean "tidings" may have been James I of Scotland; a work possibly written by him around 1437 contains the words "Awak . . . I bring The [thee] newis [news] glad." It is pleasant to see that the first news was good. However, his descendant James I of England is the first person recorded (1616) to have said "No newis is better than evill newis," or as we would put it, "No news is good news."

---

news agency *n.* An organization that provides news coverage to subscribers, as to newspapers or periodicals. Also called *press agency, press association.*

news•boy (no͞oz′boi′, nyo͞oz′-) *n.* A boy who sells or delivers newspapers.

news•break (no͞oz′brāk′, nyo͞oz′-) *n.* **1.** An urgent or immediate item of news. **2.** The act or an instance of interrupting previously scheduled radio or television programming in order to report a newsworthy event or story. Also called *news flash.*

news•cast (no͞oz′kăst′, nyo͞oz′-) *n.* A radio or television broadcast of the news. [NEWS + (BROAD)CAST.] —**news′cast′er** *n.*

news conference *n.* See **press conference.**

news flash *n.* See **newsbreak.**

news•gath•er•ing (no͞oz′găth′ər-ĭng, nyo͞oz′-) *adj.* Of, relating to, or involving the research and reportage of news: *a worldwide newsgathering operation.* —**news′gath′er•ing** *n.*

news•girl (no͞oz′gûrl′, nyo͞oz′-) *n.* A girl who sells or delivers newspapers.

New Si•be•ri•an Islands (sī-bîr′ē-ən). An archipelago of northeast Russia in the Arctic Ocean between the Laptev and East Siberian seas.

news•let•ter (no͞oz′lĕt′ər, nyo͞oz′-) *n.* A printed report giving news or information of interest to a special group.

news•mag•a•zine (no͞oz′măg′ə-zēn′, nyo͞oz′-) *n.* A magazine, usually published weekly, that contains reports and analyses of current events.

news•mak•er (no͞oz′mā′kər, nyo͞oz′-) *n.* One that is newsworthy.

news•man (no͞oz′măn′, -mən, nyo͞oz′-) *n.* A man who gathers, reports, or edits news.

news•mon•ger (no͞oz′mŭng′gər, -mŏng′-, nyo͞oz′-) *n.* One who spreads news, especially a gossip.

New Spain (spān). **1.** A former Spanish viceroyalty (1521–1821) in North America, including the southwest United States, Mexico, Central America north of Panama, and some West Indian islands. It also included the islands of the Philippines and was administered from Mexico City. **2.** The former Spanish possessions in the New World. At its greatest extent, New Spain comprised South America (except Brazil), Central America, Mexico, the West Indies, Florida, and much of the land west of the Mississippi River.

news•pa•per (no͞oz′pā′pər, nyo͞oz′-) *n.* **1.** A publication, usually issued daily or weekly, containing current news, editorials, feature articles, and usually advertising. **2.** See **newsprint.** —*attributive.* Often used to modify another noun: *a newspaper reporter; newspaper sales.*

news•pa•per•ing (no͞oz′pā′pər-ĭng, nyo͞oz′-) *n.* Journalism.

news•pa•per•man (no͞oz′pā′pər-măn′, nyo͞oz′-) *n.* **1.** A man who owns or publishes a newspaper. **2.** A man who is a newspaper reporter, writer, or editor.

news•pa•per•wom•an (no͞oz′pā′pər-wo͝om′ən, nyo͞oz′-) *n.* **1.** A woman who owns or publishes a newspaper. **2.** A woman who is a newspaper reporter, writer, or editor.

new•speak (no͞o′spēk′, nyo͞o′-) *n.* Deliberately ambiguous and contradictory language used to mislead and manipulate the public. [From *Newspeak,* a language invented by George Orwell in the novel *1984.*]

news•peo•ple (no͞oz′pē′pəl, nyo͞oz′-) *pl.n.* Newspersons considered as a group.

news•per•son (no͞oz′pûr′sən, nyo͞oz′-) *n.* A newsman or a newswoman.

news•print (no͞oz′prĭnt′, nyo͞oz′-) *n.* Inexpensive paper made from wood pulp and used chiefly for printing newspapers. Also called *newspaper.*

news•reel (no͞oz′rēl′, nyo͞oz′-) *n.* A short film dealing with recent or current events.

news release *n.* A prepared publicity or news announcement; a handout.

news•room (no͞oz′ro͞om′, -ro͝om′, nyo͞oz′-) *n.* A room, as in a newspaper office or radio or television station, where news stories are written and edited.

news•stand (no͞oz′stănd′, nyo͞oz′-) *n.* An open booth or stand at which newspapers and periodicals are sold.

New Style *n. Abbr.* **N.S.** The current method of reckoning the months and days of the year according to the Gregorian calendar.

New Swe•den (swēd′n). A Swedish colony in North America on the Delaware River. Founded in 1638, it included parts of present-day Pennsylvania, New Jersey, and Delaware. The Dutch under Peter Stuyvesant took the colony in 1655.

news•week•ly (no͞oz′wēk′lē, nyo͞oz′-) *n., pl.* **-lies.** A weekly newsmagazine or newspaper that reports current events.

news•wom•an (no͞oz′wo͝om′ən, nyo͞oz′-) *n.* A woman who gathers, reports, or edits news.

news•wor•thy (no͞oz′wûr′thē, nyo͞oz′-) *adj.* **-thi•er, -thi•est.** Of sufficient interest or importance to the public to warrant reporting in the media. —**news′wor′thi•ness** *n.*

news•y (no͞o′zē, nyo͞o′-) *adj.* **-i•er, -i•est.** *Informal.* Full of news; informative. —**news′i•ness** *n.*

newt (no͞ot, nyo͞ot) *n.* Any of several small, slender, often brightly colored salamanders of the genus *Triturus* and related genera, living chiefly on land but becoming aquatic during the breeding season. [Middle English *neute,* from the phrase *an eute,* variant of *evete,* from Old English *efete.*]

New Testament *n. Bible.* **1.** *Abbr.* **New Test., NT, N.T.** The Gospels, Acts, Pauline and other Epistles, and the Book of Revelation, together viewed by Christians as forming the record of the new dispensation belonging to the Church. **2.** See table at **Bible.**

New Thought *n.* A modern religious movement that emphasizes spiritual healing and the creative power of positive thought.

new•ton (no͞ot′n, nyo͞ot′n) *n. Abbr.* **N** In the meter-kilogram-second system, the unit of force required to accelerate a mass of one kilogram one meter per second per second, equal to 100,000 dynes. See table at **measurement.** [After Sir Isaac NEWTON.]

New•ton (no͞ot′n, nyo͞ot′n). **1.** A city of south-central Kansas north of Wichita. Russian Mennonites settled here in the early 1870's. Population, 16,332. **2.** A city of eastern Massachusetts, a mainly residential suburb of Boston. The city comprises a number of villages, including **Newton Corner, Newton Center, Newton Upper Falls,** and **Newton Lower Falls.** Population 83,622.

Newton, Sir **Isaac.** 1642–1727. English mathematician and scientist who invented differential calculus and formulated the theories of universal gravitation, terrestrial mechanics, and color. His treatise on gravitation, presented in *Principia Mathematica* (1687), was supposedly inspired by the sight of a falling apple. —**New•to′ni•an** *adj.*

new town *n.* A planned urban community designed for self-sufficiency and providing housing, educational, commercial, and recreational facilities for its residents.

New•town (no͞o′toun′, nyo͞o′-). A town of southwest Connecticut on the Housatonic River east-northeast of Danbury. It is a manufacturing center. Population, 19,107.

new wave *n.* **1.** Often **New Wave.** A movement in French cinema in the 1960's, led by directors such as Jean Luc Godard and François Truffaut, that abandoned traditional narrative techniques in favor of greater use of symbolism and abstraction and dealt with themes of social alienation, psychopathology, and sexual love. Also called *nouvelle vague.* **2.** An avant-garde or experimental movement, as in the arts. **3.** *Music.* An emotionally detached style of rock music marked by the use of synthesized sound and a repetitive beat. [Translation of French *nouvelle vague* : *nouvelle,* new + *vague,* wave.]

New West•min•ster (wĕst-mĭn′stər). A city of southwest British Columbia, Canada, a suburb of Vancouver on the Fraser River. It was the capital of the province from 1860 to 1866. Population, 38,550.

New World (wûrld). The Western Hemisphere. The term was first used by the Italian historian Peter Martyr (1457–1526), whose *De Rebus Oceanicis et Novo Orbe* (1516) chronicled the discovery of America.

New Year *n.* The first day or days of the calendar year.

New Year's Day (yîrz) *n.* January 1, the first day of the year, celebrated as a holiday in many countries.

New Year's Eve (yîrz) *n.* The eve of New Year's Day.

New York (yôrk). *Abbr.* **NY, N.Y. 1.** A state of the northeast United States. It was admitted as one of the original Thirteen Colonies in 1788. First explored by Samuel de Champlain and Henry Hudson, the region was claimed by the Dutch in 1624 but fell to the English in 1664–1667. The building of the Erie Canal and railroad lines in the 1820's and 1830's led to development of the western part of the state and great economic prosperity, establishing New York City as the financial center of the nation. Albany is the capital and New York City the largest metropolis. Population, 17,558,072. **2.** Or **New York City.** A city of southern New York on New York Bay at the mouth of the Hudson River. Founded by the Dutch as New Amsterdam, it was renamed by the English in honor of the Duke of York. It is the largest city in the country and a financial, cultural, trade, shipping, and communications center. Originally consisting only of Manhattan Island, it was rechartered in 1898 to include the five present-day boroughs of Manhattan, the Bronx, Brooklyn, Queens, and Staten Island. Population, 7,071,030. —**New York′er** *n.*

New York aster *n.* A wild aster *(Aster novi-belgi)* of eastern North America, with pointed leaves and bluish-violet flowers.

New York Bay. An arm of the Atlantic Ocean at the mouth of the Hudson River between western Long Island and northeast New Jersey. It is divided into **Upper New York Bay** and **Lower New York Bay** by the Narrows.

New York City. *Abbr.* **NYC, N.Y.C.** See **New York** (sense 2).

New York minute *n. Slang.* An extremely short period of time: *"If we could find* [a merger in another city] *that would work as well, we'd do it in a New York minute"* (Jonathan Golden).

New York State Barge Canal. A system of inland waterways, about 845 km (525 mi) long, traversing New York State and

newsstand

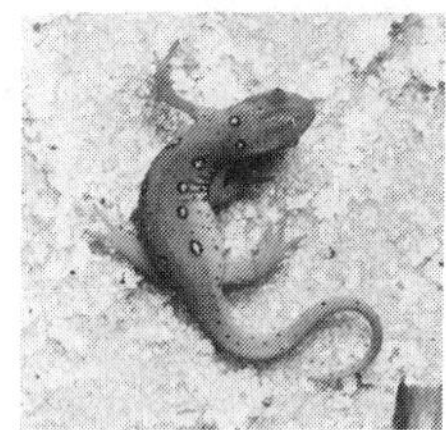

newt

Isaac Newton
c. 1726 painting
by an unknown artist

ă pat	oi boy
ā pay	ou out
âr care	o͝o took
ä father	o͞o boot
ĕ pet	ŭ cut
ē be	ûr urge
ĭ pit	th thin
ī pie	*th* this
îr pier	hw which
ŏ pot	zh vision
ō toe	ə about, item
ô paw	♦ regionalism

Stress marks: ′ (primary); ′ (secondary), as in **dictionary** (dĭk′shə-nĕr′ē)

connecting the Great Lakes with the Hudson River and Lake Champlain.

New Zea·land (zē′lənd). *Abbr.* **N.Z.** An island country in the southern Pacific Ocean southeast of Australia. Discovered by Abel Tasman in 1642, the islands were visited and explored by Capt. James Cook four times between 1769 and 1777. The first settlements were made in 1840 by the British, who claimed the region as a crown colony. New Zealand was set off from Australia in 1841, received dominion status in 1907, and became fully independent in 1931. Wellington is the capital and Auckland the largest city. Population, 3,265,300. **—New Zea′land·er** *n.*

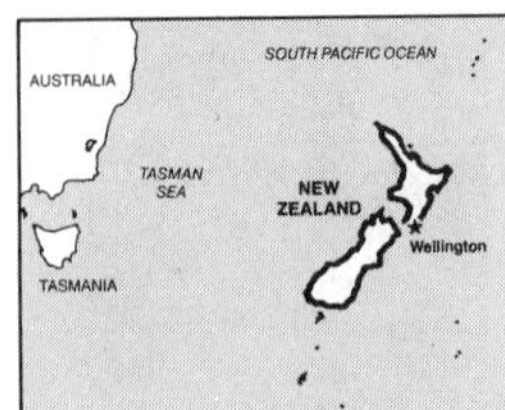

New Zealand

NEX *abbr.* Navy exchange.

next (nĕkst) *adj.* **1.** Nearest in space or position; adjacent: *the next room.* **2.** Immediately following, as in time, order, or sequence: *next week; the next item on the list.* **—next** *adv.* **1.** In the time, order, or place nearest or immediately following: *reading this book next; our next oldest child.* **2.** On the first subsequent occasion: *when next I write.* **—next** *n.* The next person or thing: *The next will be better.* **—*idiom.* next to. 1.** Adjacent to: *the car next to hers.* **2.** Following in order or degree: *Next to skiing, she likes hiking.* **3.** Almost; practically: *next to impossible.* [Middle English *nexte,* from Old English *nīehsta, nēhst,* superlative of *nēah,* near. See **nēhw-iz** in Appendix.]

next door *adv.* To or in the adjacent house, building, apartment, or room. **—next′-door′** (nĕkst′dôr′, -dōr′) *adj.*

next friend *n. Law.* A person appointed by or admitted to a court to act in behalf of a minor or other party under legal disability.

next of kin *n., pl.* **next of kin. 1.** The person or persons most closely related by blood to another person. **2.** *Law.* **a.** The closest relative of a deceased person. **b.** *(used with a pl. verb).* The relative or relatives entitled to share in the personal property of one who dies intestate.

Niagara Falls[1]
American Falls

nex·us (nĕk′səs) *n., pl.* **nexus** or **-us·es. 1.** A means of connection; a link or tie: *"this nexus between New York's . . . real-estate investors and its . . . politicians"* (Wall Street Journal). **2.** A connected series or group. **3.** The core or center: *"The real nexus of the money culture* [was] *Wall Street"* (Bill Barol). [Latin, past participle of *nectere,* to bind. See **ned-** in Appendix.]

Ney (nā), **Michel.** Duc d'Elchingen and Prince de la Moskowa. 1769–1815. French marshal who brilliantly commanded the rear guard in Napoleon I's retreat from Moscow (1812) and later deserted Louis XVIII to aid Napoleon at Waterloo (1815).

Nez Perce (nĕz′ pûrs′, nĕs′) also **Nez Per·cé** (pər-sā′) *n., pl.* **Nez Perce** or **Nez Per·ces** (pûr′sĭz) also **Nez Percé** or **Nez Per·cés** (-sāz′). **1.a.** A Native American people formerly inhabiting the lower Snake River and its tributaries in western Idaho, northeast Oregon, and southeast Washington, with present-day populations in western Idaho and northeast Washington. **b.** A member of this people. **2.** The Sahaptian language of the Nez Perce. [French *Nez-Percé* : *nez,* nose + *percé,* past participle of *percer,* to pierce.]

NF *abbr.* **1. N.F.** National Formulary. **2.** Neurofibromatosis. **3.** Newfoundland.

n/f *abbr.* No funds.

NFC *abbr. Sports.* National Football Conference.

NFL *abbr. Sports.* National Football League.

Nfld. *abbr.* Newfoundland.

ng *abbr.* Nanogram.

NG or **N.G.** *abbr.* **1.** National Guard. **2.** No good. **3.** Natural gas.

Nga·mi (əng-gä′mē), **Lake.** A lake of northern Botswana north of the Kalahari Desert. The marshy lake covered an extensive area during the Pleistocene epoch but was greatly reduced in size during the 1880's, when papyrus growth blocked the mouth of its main tributary.

n'ga·na (nə-gä′nə) *n.* Variant of **nagana.**

NGF *abbr.* Nerve growth factor.

NGU *abbr.* Nongonococcal urethritis.

ngul·trum (əng-gŭl′trəm) *n.* See table at **currency.** [Bhutanese.]

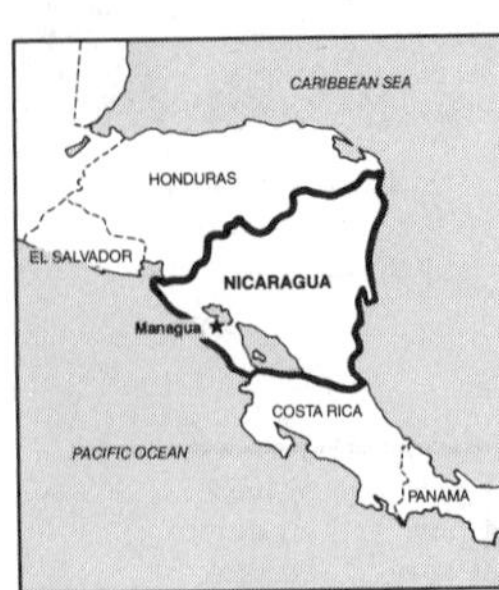

Nicaragua

Ngu·ni (əng-go͞o′nē) *n., pl.* **Nguni** or **-nis. 1.** A member of a group of peoples of southern and southeast Africa, including the Swazi, Ndebele, Xhosa, and Zulu. **2.** Any of the Bantu languages of the Nguni.

ngwee (əng-gwē′) *n., pl.* **ngwee.** See table at **currency.** [Nyanja, bright, ngwee.]

NH or **N.H.** *abbr.* New Hampshire.

NHI *abbr.* National Health Insurance.

NHL *abbr. Sports.* National Hockey League.

NHS *abbr.* National Health Service.

Ni The symbol for the element **nickel** (sense 1).

ni·a·cin (nī′ə-sĭn) *n.* A white crystalline acid, C_5H_4NCOOH, that is a component of the vitamin B complex found in meat, wheat germ, dairy products, and yeast and is used to treat and prevent pellagra. Also called *nicotinic acid.* [NI(COTINIC) AC(ID) + -IN.]

Ni·ag·a·ra (nī-ăg′rə, -ər-ə) *n.* A torrent or flood: *"engulfed by the Niagara of Americanisms that flowed over them"* (Wall Street Journal). [After NIAGARA (FALLS)[1].]

Niagara Falls[1]. Falls in the Niagara River between the cities of Niagara Falls, New York, and Niagara Falls, Ontario, Canada. The falls are divided by Goat Island into the American Falls, 50.9 m (167 ft) high, and the Canadian Falls, 48.2 m (158 ft) high.

Niagara Falls[2]. 1. A city of southeast Ontario, Canada, on the Niagara River opposite Niagara Falls, New York. It is a port of entry and an important industrial center. Population, 70,960. **2.** A city of western New York on the Niagara River north-northwest of Buffalo. Occupied by the French in the 1680's, captured by the British in 1759, and settled by Americans in 1805, it was held by the British during the War of 1812. Population, 71,384.

Niagara River. A river flowing about 55 km (34 mi) from Lake Erie to Lake Ontario. It forms part of the boundary between western New York and Ontario, Canada.

Nia·mey (nē-ä′mā, nyä-mā′). The capital and largest city of Niger, in the southwest part of the country on the Niger River. It is an important commercial center. Population, 399,100.

nib (nĭb) *n.* **1.a.** The sharpened point of a quill pen. **b.** A tapered point of a pen, designed to be inserted into a penholder or fountain pen. **2.** A sharp point or tip. **3.** A bird's beak or bill. [Alteration of NEB.]

nib·ble (nĭb′əl) *v.* **-bled, -bling, -bles.** *—tr.* **1.** To bite at gently and repeatedly. **2.** To eat with small, quick bites or in small morsels: *nibble a cracker.* **3.** To wear away or diminish bit by bit: *"If you start compromising too early . . . they nibble you to death"* (People). *—intr.* To take small or hesitant bites: *fish nibbling at the bait.* **—nibble** *n.* **1.** A very small quantity, especially of food; a morsel. **2.** The act or an instance of nibbling. [Middle English *nebyllen;* akin to Low German *nibbelen.*]

Ni·be·lung (nē′bə-lo͝ong′) *n. Mythology.* **1.** Any of a race of subterranean dwarfs whose hoard of riches and magic ring were taken from them by Siegfried. **2.** A follower of Siegfried. **3.** One of the Burgundian kings in the *Nibelungenlied.* [German, from Middle High German *Nibelunc,* from Old High German *Nibulunc, Nibilung.*]

Ni·be·lung·en·lied (nē′bə-lo͝ong′ən-lēd′) *n. Mythology.* A Middle High German epic poem written in the early 13th century and based on the legends of Siegfried and of the Burgundian kings.

nib·lick (nĭb′lĭk) *n. Sports.* An iron-headed golf club with the face slanted at a greater angle than any other iron except a wedge; a nine iron. [Origin unknown.]

nibs (nĭbz) *n. Informal.* A person in authority, especially one who is self-important. Used with *his* or *her*: *His nibs says we must do it.* [Perhaps alteration of NOB[2].]

Nic. *abbr.* Nicaragua.

Ni·cae·a (nī-sē′ə). An ancient city of Bithynia in northwest Asia Minor. Dating from the fourth century B.C., it flourished during Roman times. The Nicene Creed was adopted at an ecumenical council convened here in A.D. 325. **—Ni·cae′an** *adj.*

Nic·a·ra·gua (nĭk′ə-rä′gwə). *Abbr.* **Nic.** A country of Central America on the Caribbean Sea and the Pacific Ocean. Its Caribbean coastline was discovered by Columbus in 1502, and the first settlements were made by the Spanish in 1524. Nicaragua was ruled as part of Guatemala until it declared its independence from Spain in 1821. Managua is the capital and the largest city. Population, 2,823,979. **—Ni′ca·ra′guan** *adj. & n.*

Nicaragua, Lake. The largest lake of Central America, in southwest Nicaragua. The freshwater lake contains fish, such as tuna and sharks, usually found only in salt water because it was part of the Caribbean Sea until land masses rose around it in prehistoric times.

nic·co·lite (nĭk′ə-līt′) *n.* A nickel ore, essentially nickel arsenide, NiAs, found in America and Europe. [New Latin *niccolum,* nickel (perhaps from Swedish *nickel;* see NICKEL) + -ITE[1].]

nice (nīs) *adj.* **nic·er, nic·est. 1.** Pleasing and agreeable in nature: *had a nice time.* **2.** Having a pleasant or attractive appearance: *a nice dress; a nice face.* **3.** Exhibiting courtesy and politeness: *a nice gesture.* **4.** Of good character and reputation; respectable. **5.** Overly delicate or fastidious; fussy. **6.** Showing or requiring great precision or sensitive discernment; subtle: *a nice distinction; a nice sense of style.* **7.** Done with delicacy and skill: *a nice bit of craft.* **8.** Used as an intensive with *and*: *nice and warm.* **9.** *Obsolete.* **a.** Wanton; profligate: *"For when mine hours/Were nice and lucky, men did ransom lives/Of me for jests"* (Shakespeare). **b.** Affectedly modest; coy: *"Ere . . . /The nice Morn on th'* Indian *steep,/From her cabin'd loop-hole peep"* (John Milton). [Middle English, foolish, from Old French, from Latin *nescius,* ignorant, from *nescīre,* to be ignorant. See NESCIENCE.] **—nice′ly** *adv.* **—nice′ness** *n.*

Nice (nēs). A city of southeast France on the Mediterranean Sea northeast of Cannes. Controlled by various royal houses after the 13th century, the city was finally ceded to France in 1860. Population, 337,085.

Ni·cene Creed (nī′sēn′, nī-sēn′) *n. Theology.* A formal statement of doctrine of the Christian faith adopted at the Council of Nicaea in A.D. 325 to defend orthodoxy from Arianism and expanded in later councils.

nice-nel·ly (nīs′nĕl′ē) *adj.* **1.** Priggish. **2.** Marked by the use of euphemism: *nice-nelly language.* [From the name *Nelly,* nickname for *Helen.*] **—nice′-nel′ly·ism** *n.*

ni·ce·ty (nī′sĭ-tē) *n., pl.* **-ties. 1.** The quality of showing or requiring careful, precise treatment: *the nicety of a diplomatic exchange.* **2.** Delicacy of character or feeling; fastidiousness;

scrupulousness. **3.** A fine point, small detail, or subtle distinction: *the niceties of etiquette.* **4.** An elegant or refined feature; an amenity: *the niceties of civilized life.* [Middle English *nicete,* silliness, exactitude, from Old French, silliness, from *nice,* silly. See NICE.]

niche (nĭch, nēsh) *n.* **1.** A recess in a wall, as for holding a statue or an urn. **2.** A cranny, hollow, or crevice, as in rock. **3.a.** A situation or an activity specially suited to a person's interests, abilities, or nature: *found her niche in life.* **b.** A special area of demand for a product or service: *"One niche that is approaching mass-market proportions is held by regional magazines"* (Brad Edmondson). **4.** *Ecology.* **a.** The function or position of an organism or a population within an ecological community. **b.** The particular area within a habitat occupied by an organism. **—niche** *tr.v.* **niched, nich•ing, nich•es.** To place in a niche. [French, from Old French, from *nichier,* to nest (from Vulgar Latin **nīdicāre,* from Latin *nīdus,* nest) or from Old Italian *nicchio,* seashell (perhaps from Latin *mītulus,* mussel).]

Nich•o•las (nĭk′ə-ləs), Saint. Fourth century A.D. Bishop of Myra in Asia Minor who is often associated with Santa Claus and the custom of gift-giving at Christmas.

Nicholas I. 1796–1855. Czar of Russia (1825–1855) who suppressed the Decembrist movement and led Russia into the Crimean War (1853–1856).

Nicholas II. 1868–1918. The last czar of Russia (1894–1917), whose reign was marked by defeat in the Russo-Japanese War (1904–1905), the 1905 Revolution, the court influence of the unpopular Rasputin, involvement in World War I, and governmental incompetence, all of which helped precipitate the Revolution of 1917. Forced to abdicate, he and his family were executed by the Bolsheviks.

Nicholas of Cu•sa (kyōō′zə, -sə). 1401–1464. German prelate, scientist, and philosopher who emphasized the incompleteness of the human knowledge of God and nature.

Ni•ci•as (nĭsh′ē-əs, nĭs′-). Died 413 B.C. Athenian general and politician who arranged (421) a briefly observed truce with Sparta during the Peloponnesian War and was captured and killed during his command of the siege of Syracuse.

nick (nĭk) *n.* **1.** A shallow notch, cut, or indentation on an edge or a surface: *nicks in the table; razor nicks on his chin.* **2.** *Chiefly British.* A prison or police station. **3.** *Printing.* A groove down the side of a piece of type used to ensure that it is correctly placed. **—nick** *tr.v.* **nicked, nick•ing, nicks. 1.a.** To cut a nick or notch in. **b.** To cut into and wound slightly: *A sliver of glass nicked my hand.* **2.** To cut short; check: *nicked an impulse to flee.* **3.** *Slang.* To cheat, especially by overcharging. **4.** *Chiefly British.* **a.** To steal. **b.** To arrest. ***—idiom.* in the nick of time.** Just at the critical moment; just in time. [Middle English *nik,* possibly alteration (influenced by *nokke,* notch; see NOCK) of *niche.* See NICHE.]

nick•el (nĭk′əl) *n.* **1.** *Symbol* **Ni** A silvery, hard, ductile, ferromagnetic metallic element used in alloys, in corrosion-resistant surfaces and batteries, and for electroplating. Atomic number 28; atomic weight 58.71; melting point 1,453°C; boiling point 2,732°C; specific gravity 8.902; valence 0, 1, 2, 3. See table at **element. 2.** A U.S. coin worth five cents, made of a nickel and copper alloy. **3.** *Slang.* A nickel bag. **—nickel** *tr.v.* **-eled, -el•ing, -els** or **-elled, -el•ling, -els.** To coat with nickel. [Swedish, short for *kopparnickel,* niccolite, partial translation of German *Kupfernickel : Kupfer,* copper + *Nickel,* demon, rascal, from the deceptive copper color of the ore (from the name *Nikolaus,* Nicholas).]

nick•el-and-dime (nĭk′əl-ən-dīm′) *Informal. adj.* **1.** Involving or paying only a small amount of money: *a nickel-and-dime job.* **2.** Minor; small-time: *"a nickel-and-dime operation run out of a single borrowed room"* (New York). **—nickel-and-dime** *v.* **nick•el-and-dimed, nick•el-and-dim•ing, nick•el-and-dimes** or **nick•eled-and-dimed, nick•el•ing-and-dim•ing, nick•els-and-dimes.** *—intr.* To spend very little money. *—tr.* **1.** To drain or destroy bit by bit, especially financially: *nickel-and-dimed the project to death.* **2.** To accumulate in small amounts: *"nickel-and-diming a substantial bankroll together"* (Newsweek).

nickel bag *n. Slang.* A specified amount of an unlawful drug, packaged and sold for a fixed price, usually about five dollars. [NICKEL, five dollars (slang).]

nick•el•ic (nĭ-kĕl′ĭk) *adj.* **1.** Of or containing nickel. **2.** Of or containing trivalent nickel, $Ni_3{}^+$.

nick•el•if•er•ous (nĭk′ə-lĭf′ər-əs) *adj.* Bearing or containing nickel. Used of ores.

nick•el•o•de•on (nĭk′ə-lō′dē-ən) *n.* **1.** An early movie theater charging an admission price of five cents. **2.** A player piano. **3.** A jukebox. [NICKEL + *(Mel)odeon,* music hall; see MELODEON.]

nick•el•ous (nĭk′ə-ləs) *adj.* **1.** Of or containing nickel. **2.** Of or containing bivalent nickel, $Ni_2{}^+$.

nickel silver *n.* A silvery, hard, corrosion-resistant, ductile, malleable alloy of copper, zinc, and nickel, used in tableware and as a structural material for hospital and restaurant equipment. Also called *German silver.*

nick•er (nĭk′ər) *intr.v.* **-ered, -er•ing, -ers.** To neigh softly. [Perhaps alteration of *neigher, nicher,* frequentative of NEIGH.] **—nick′er** *n.*

Nick•laus (nĭk′ləs), **Jack William.** Born 1940. American golfer who won 17 major international tournaments, including 6 Masters' championships.

nick•nack (nĭk′năk′) *n.* Variant of **knickknack.**

nick•name (nĭk′nām′) *n.* **1.** A descriptive name added to or replacing the actual name of a person, place, or thing. **2.** A familiar or shortened form of a proper name. **—nickname** *tr.v.* **-named, -nam•ing, -names. 1.** To give a nickname to. **2.** *Archaic.* To call by an incorrect name; misname. [Middle English *neke name,* from the phrase *an eke name : eke,* addition (from Old English *ēaca;* see **aug-** in Appendix) + *name,* name; see NAME.] **—nick′nam′er** *n.*

Nic•o•bar Islands (nĭk′ə-bär′). An island group in the Bay of Bengal northwest of Sumatra. They are part of the Andaman and Nicobar Islands belonging to India.

Nic•o•let (nĭk′ə-lā′, nē-kô-lĕ′), **Jean.** 1598–1642. French explorer who was the first European to reach the Great Lakes region (1634).

Nic•ol•son (nĭk′əl-sən), Sir **Harold George.** 1886–1968. British diplomat and writer noted for his literary criticism and his biographies of Tennyson, Swinburne, and George V.

Nic•o•me•di•a (nĭk′ə-mē′dē-ə). An ancient city of northwest Asia Minor near the Bosporus in present-day Turkey. It flourished from 264 B.C. until it was sacked by Goths in A.D. 258. Diocletian chose it for the capital of his Eastern Roman Empire, but it was soon superseded by Byzantium.

Nic•o•si•a (nĭk′ə-sē′ə). The capital and largest city of Cyprus, in the north-central part of the island. Founded probably before the seventh century B.C., it fell to the Venetians in 1489 and the Turks in 1571. It became the capital when Cyprus gained independence in 1960. Population, 48,221.

niche

ni•co•ti•an•a (nĭ-kō′shē-ăn′ə, -ä′nə, -ā′nə) *n.* Any of various flowering annual or perennial herbs of the genus *Nicotiana,* native to the Americas and including the tobacco plant and ornamental species with fragrant flowers. [New Latin *(herba) nicotiāna,* (herb of) Nicot, nicotiana, after Jean *Nicot* (1530?–1600), French diplomat.]

nicotin– *pref.* **1.** Nicotine: *nicotinic.* **2.** Nicotinic acid: *nicotinamide.* [From NICOTINE.]

nic•o•tin•a•mide adenine dinucleotide (nĭk′ə-tĭn′ə-mīd′, -tē′nə-) *n.* NAD.

nic•o•tine (nĭk′ə-tēn′) *n.* A colorless, poisonous alkaloid, $C_{10}H_{14}N_2$, derived from the tobacco plant and used as an insecticide. It is the substance in tobacco to which smokers can become addicted. [French, from New Latin *nicotiāna.* See NICOTIANA.]

nic•o•tin•ic (nĭk′ə-tĭn′ĭk, -tē′nĭk) *adj.* **1.** Of or relating to nicotine. **2.** Of or relating to niacin.

nicotinic acid *n.* See **niacin.** [So called because it is often obtained by oxidizing nicotine.]

nic•o•tin•ism (nĭk′ə-tē-nĭz′əm) *n.* Nicotine poisoning, caused by excessive use of tobacco and marked by depression of the central and autonomic nervous systems.

Ni•co•ya (nĭ-kō′yə, nē-kô′yä), **Gulf of.** An inlet of the Pacific Ocean between **Nicoya Peninsula** and the northwest mainland of Costa Rica.

nic•tate (nĭk′tāt′) *v.* Variant of **nictitate.**

nic•tat•ing membrane (nĭk′tā′tĭng) *n.* Variant of **nictitating membrane.**

nic•ti•tate (nĭk′tĭ-tāt′) also **nic•tate** (nĭk′tāt′) *intr.v.* **-tat•ed, -tat•ing, -tates.** To wink. See Synonyms at **blink.** [Medieval Latin *nictitāre, nictitāt-,* frequentative of Latin *nictāre.*] **—nic′ti•ta′tion** *n.*

nic•ti•tat•ing membrane (nĭk′tĭ-tā′tĭng) also **nic•tat•ing membrane** (nĭk′tā′tĭng) *n.* A transparent inner eyelid in birds, reptiles, and some mammals that closes to protect and moisten the eye. Also called *third eyelid.*

ni•date (nī′dāt) *tr.v.* **-dat•ed, -dat•ing, -dates.** To become implanted in the uterus. Used of a fertilized cell. [NID(US) + -ATE[1].] **—ni•da′tion** *n.*

nid•der•ing (nĭd′ər-ĭng) *n. Archaic.* A cowardly person; a wretch. [Misreading of Middle English *nithing,* from Old English *nīthing,* from Old Norse *nīdhingr,* from *nīdh,* scorn.]

nide (nīd) *n.* A nest or brood of pheasants. See Synonyms at **flock[1].** [Latin *nīdus,* nest.]

ni•di (nī′dī) *n.* A plural of **nidus.**

ni•dic•o•lous (nī-dĭk′ə-ləs) *adj.* Remaining in the nest after hatching until able to fly. Used of a bird. [Latin *nīdus,* nest + -COLOUS.]

ni•dif•u•gous (nī-dĭf′yə-gəs) *adj.* Leaving the nest a short time after hatching. Used of a bird. [Latin *nīdus,* nest + Latin *-fugus,* fleeing (from *fugere,* to flee; see FUGITIVE).]

nid•i•fy (nĭd′ə-fī′) *intr.v.* **-fied, -fy•ing, -fies.** To build a nest. [Latin *nīdificāre : nīdus,* nest + *-ficāre,* -fy.] **—nid′i•fi•ca′tion** (-fĭ-kā′shən) *n.*

ni•dus (nī′dəs) *n., pl.* **-dus•es** or **-di** (-dī). **1.** A nest, especially one for the eggs of insects, spiders, or small animals. **2.** A cavity where spores develop. **3.** *Pathology.* A central point or focus of bacterial growth in a living organism. **4.** A point or place at which something originates, accumulates, or develops, as the center around which salts of calcium, uric acid, or bile acid form calculi. [Latin *nīdus.*]

Nie•buhr (nē′bo͝or′, -bər), **Barthold George.** 1776–1831. German historian whose influential history of Rome (published 1811–1832) established the modern scientific study of history.

Niebuhr, Reinhold. 1892–1971. American theologian who

Nicholas II

ă pat	oi boy
ā pay	ou out
âr care	o͝o took
ä father	o͞o boot
ĕ pet	ŭ cut
ē be	ûr urge
ĭ pit	th thin
ī pie	*th* this
îr pier	hw which
ŏ pot	zh vision
ō toe	ə about, item
ô paw	♦ regionalism

Stress marks: ′ (primary); ′ (secondary), as in **dictionary** (dĭk′shə-nĕr′ē)

Friedrich Nietzsche

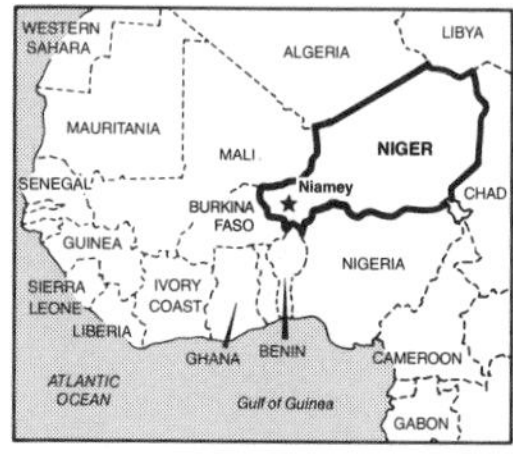

Niger

Nigeria

Florence Nightingale
Photographed c. 1857

wrote primarily about morality and Christianity's refusal to confront social problems.

niece (nēs) *n.* **1.** The daughter of one's brother or sister or of the brother or sister of one's spouse. **2.** The illegitimate daughter of an ecclesiastic who has taken a vow of celibacy. [Middle English *nece,* from Old French, from Vulgar Latin **neptia,* from Latin *neptis.* See **nepōt-** in Appendix.]

ni·el·lo (nē-ĕl′ō) *n., pl.* **-el·li** (-ĕl′ē) or **-el·los. 1.** Any of several black metallic alloys of sulfur with copper, silver, or lead, used to fill an incised design on the surface of another metal. **2.** A surface or an object decorated with one of these alloys. **3.** The art or process of ornamenting metal surfaces with one of these alloys. **—niello** *tr.v.* **-loed, -lo·ing, -los.** To decorate or inlay with niello. [Italian, from Medieval Latin *nigellum,* from neuter of Latin *nigellus,* diminutive of *niger,* black.] **—ni·el′list** *n.*

niels·bohr·i·um (nēlz-bôr′ē-əm, -bōr′-) *n.* Element 105. [After Niels Henrik David BOHR.]

Niel·sen (nēl′sən), **Carl August.** 1865–1931. Danish composer whose polytonal and contrapuntal works include several symphonies, the opera *Saul and David* (1903), and chamber works.

Nie·men (nē′mən, nyĕ′-). See **Neman.**

Nie·mey·er Soa·res Fil·ho (nē′mī′ər swä′rĕsh fēl′yo͞o), **Oscar.** Born 1907. Brazilian architect. Influenced by Le Corbusier, he directed the creation of Brasília (1950–1960).

Nie·tzsche (nē′chə, -chē), **Friedrich Wilhelm.** 1844–1900. German philosopher who reasoned that Christianity's emphasis on the afterlife makes its believers less able to cope with earthly life. He argued that the ideal human being, the *Ubermensch,* would be able to channel passions creatively instead of suppressing them. His written works include *Thus Spake Zarathustra* (1883–1892). **—Nie′tzsche·an** *adj. & n.*

Nif·l·heim (nĭv′əl-hām′) *n. Mythology.* The realm of the dead in Norse myth. [Old Norse *niflheimr* : *nifl-,* mist, dark; see **nebh-** in Appendix + *heimr,* home; see **tkei-** in Appendix.]

nif·ty (nĭf′tē) *Slang. adj.* **-ti·er, -ti·est.** First-rate; great: *a nifty idea.* **—nifty** *n., pl.* **-ties.** A nifty person or thing, especially a clever joke. [Origin unknown.] **—nif′ti·ly** *adv.* **—nif′ti·ness** *n.*

Nig. *abbr.* Nigeria.

ni·gel·la (nī-jĕl′ə) *n.* See **wild fennel.** [Middle English, from Late Latin, black cumin, fennel, from feminine of Latin *nigellus,* blackish, diminutive of *niger,* black.]

Ni·ger (nī′jər). A country of west-central Africa. Niger came under the French sphere of influence after the Conference of Berlin (1884–1885) and was made a separate colony within French West Africa in 1922. It achieved independence in 1960. Niamey is the capital and the largest city. Population, 5,772,000.

Ni·ger-Con·go (nī′jər-kŏng′gō) *n.* A large and widely dispersed language family of sub-Saharan Africa that includes the Mande, West Atlantic, and Central Niger-Congo branches.

Ni·ge·ri·a (nī-jîr′ē-ə). *Abbr.* **Nig.** A country of western Africa on the Gulf of Guinea. Exploited by Portuguese, British, French, and Dutch traders in the 17th and 18th centuries, Nigeria was eventually claimed by the British, who consolidated the northern and southern sections into one colony in 1914. The country attained its independence in 1960. Lagos is the present capital and the largest city. Abuja is being developed as a new capital district. Population, 89,117,500. **—Ni·ge′ri·an** *adj. & n.*

Ni·ger-Kor·do·fan·i·an (nī′jər-kôr′də-făn′ē-ən, -făn′yən) *n.* The largest language family of sub-Saharan Africa, consisting of the Niger-Congo and Kordofanian branches.

Niger River. A river of western Africa rising in Guinea and flowing about 4,183 km (2,600 mi) in a wide arc through Mali, Niger, and Nigeria to the Gulf of Guinea.

nig·gard (nĭg′ərd) *n.* A stingy, grasping person; a miser. **—niggard** *adj.* Stingy; miserly. [Middle English *nigard,* perhaps from *nig,* stingy person, of Scandinavian origin.]

nig·gard·ly (nĭg′ərd-lē) *adj.* **1.** Grudging and petty in giving or spending. See Synonyms at **stingy. 2.** Meanly small; scanty or meager: *left the waiter a niggardly tip.* **—nig′gard·li·ness** *n.* **—nig′gard·ly** *adv.*

nig·ger (nĭg′ər) *n. Offensive Slang.* **1.a.** Used as a disparaging term for a Black person: *"You can only be destroyed by believing that you really are what the white world calls a nigger"* (James Baldwin). **b.** Used as a disparaging term for a member of any dark-skinned people. **2.** Used as a disparaging term for a member of any socially, economically, or politically deprived group of people: *"Gun owners are the new niggers . . . of society"* (John Aquilino). [Alteration of dialectal *neger,* black person, from French *nègre,* from Spanish *negro.* See NEGRO.]

nig·gle (nĭg′əl) *intr.v.* **-gled, -gling, -gles. 1.** To be preoccupied with trifles or petty details. **2.** To find fault constantly and trivially; carp. See Synonyms at **quibble.** [Perhaps of Scandinavian origin.] **—nig′gler** *n.*

nig·gling (nĭg′lĭng) *adj.* **1.** Petty, especially in a nagging or annoying way; trifling: *a pointless dispute over niggling details.* **2.** Overly concerned with details; exacting and fussy. **—nig′gling** *n.* **—nig′gling·ly** *adv.*

nigh (nī) *adv.* **nigh·er, nigh·est. 1.** Near in time, place, or relationship: *Evening draws nigh.* **2.** Nearly; almost: *talked for nigh onto two hours.* **—nigh** *adj.* **nigher, nighest. 1.** Being near in time, place, or relationship; close. See Synonyms at **close. 2.a.** Being on the left side of an animal or a vehicle: *pulling hard on the nigh rein.* **b.** Being the animal or vehicle on the left: *the nigh horse.* **—nigh** *prep.* Not far from; near. **—nigh** *tr. & intr.v.* **nighed, nigh·ing, nighs.** To come near to or draw near. [Middle English *neigh,* from Old English *nēah, nēh.* See **nēhw-iz** in Appendix.]

night (nīt) *n.* **1.a.** The period between sunset and sunrise, especially the hours of darkness. **b.** This period considered as a unit of time: *for two nights running.* **c.** This period considered from its conditions: *a rainy night.* **2.** The period between dusk and midnight of a given day: *either late Thursday night or early Friday morning.* **3.a.** The period between evening and bedtime. **b.** This period considered from its activities: *a night at the opera.* **c.** This period set aside for a specific purpose: *Parents' Night at school.* **4.a.** The period between bedtime and morning: *spent the night at a motel.* **b.** One's sleep during this period: *had a restless night.* **5.** Nightfall: *worked from morning to night.* **6.** Darkness: *vanished into the night.* **7.a.** A time or condition of gloom, obscurity, ignorance, or despair: *"In a real dark night of the soul it is always three o'clock in the morning"* (F. Scott Fitzgerald). **b.** A time or condition marked by absence of moral or ethical values: *"He never would have let us go untroubled into the night of private greed"* (Anthony Lewis). **—night** *adj.* **1.** Of or relating to the night: *the night air.* **2.** Intended for use at night: *a night light.* **3.** Working during the night: *the night nurse.* **4.** Active chiefly at night: *night prowlers.* **5.** Occurring after dark: *night baseball.* [Middle English, from Old English *niht.* See **nek^w-t-** in Appendix.]

night-blind (nīt′blīnd′) *adj.* Affected with night blindness.

night blindness *n.* A condition of the eyes in which vision is normal in daylight or other strong light but is abnormally weak or completely lost at night or in dim light. The condition may result from vitamin A deficiency, disease, or hereditary factors. Also called *nyctalopia.*

night-bloom·ing cereus (nīt′blo͞o′mĭng) *n.* Any of various night-blooming cacti of the genera *Hylocereus, Nyctocereus, Peniocereus,* and *Selenicereus,* having large fragrant flowers.

night·cap (nīt′kăp′) *n.* **1.** A usually alcoholic drink taken just before bedtime. **2.** *Sports & Games.* The last event in a day's competition, especially the final game in a baseball doubleheader. **3.** A cloth cap worn especially in bed.

night·clothes (nīt′klōz′, -klōthz′) *pl.n.* Clothes, such as pajamas or a nightgown, worn in bed. Also called *nightdress, nightwear.*

night·club (nīt′klŭb′) *n.* An establishment that stays open late at night and provides food, drink, entertainment, and music for dancing. Also called *nightspot.* **—night′club′ber** *n.* **—night′club′by** *adj.*

night court *n. Law.* A criminal court holding sessions at night for routine disposition of charges and granting of bail.

night crawler *n.* Any of various large earthworms that crawl out from the ground at night and are often used as fish bait. Also called *nightwalker.*

night·dress (nīt′drĕs′) *n.* **1.** See **nightgown. 2.** See **nightclothes.**

night·fall (nīt′fôl′) *n.* The approach of darkness; dusk.

night·glow (nīt′glō′) *n.* Airglow occurring at night.

night·gown (nīt′goun′) *n.* A loose garment worn in bed by women and girls. Also called *nightdress.*

night·hawk (nīt′hôk′) *n.* **1.a.** Any of several chiefly nocturnal birds of the genus *Chordeiles,* especially *C. minor,* having mottled grayish-brown feathers with a white spot on the wings. Also called *bullbat, mosquito hawk.* **b.** The European nightjar. **2.** *Informal.* A night owl.

night heron *n.* Any of several nocturnal or crepuscular herons of the genus *Nycticorax,* especially the black-crowned heron, *N. nycticorax.*

night·ie or **night·y** (nī′tē) *n., pl.* **-ies.** *Informal.* A nightgown.

night·in·gale (nīt′n-gāl′, nī′tĭng-) *n.* **1.** A European songbird *(Luscinia megarhynchos)* with reddish-brown plumage, noted for the melodious song of the male at night during the breeding season. **2.** Any of various other nocturnal songbirds of the genus *Luscinia.* [Middle English, from Old English *nihtegale* : *niht,* night; see NIGHT + *galan,* to sing; see **ghel-[1]** in Appendix.]

Night·in·gale (nīt′n-gāl′, nī′tĭng-), **Florence.** Known as "the Lady with the Lamp." 1820–1910. British nurse who organized (1854) and directed a unit of field nurses during the Crimean War and is considered the founder of modern nursing.

night·jar (nīt′jär′) *n.* A goatsucker, especially *Caprimulgus europaeus* of Europe, having gray and brown mottled plumage with long, slender white wings and a short bill. [NIGHT + JAR[2] (from its harsh call).]

night jasmine *n.* **1.** An Asian shrub or small tree *(Nyctanthes arbortristis)* having opposite leaves and small, fragrant flowers with an orange corolla tube and white corolla lobes. **2.** A West Indian shrub *(Cestrum nocturnum)* having small greenish-white flowers that are very fragrant at night.

night latch *n.* A spring lock that can be opened from the inside by turning a knob but from the outside only with a key.

night letter *n. Abbr.* **NLT** A telegram sent at night at a reduced rate for delivery the next morning.

night·life (nīt′līf′) *n.* Social activities or entertainment available or pursued in the evening.

night-light (nītʹlītʹ) *n.* A small, dim light left on all night.

night·long (nītʹlôngʹ, -lŏngʹ) *adj.* Lasting through the night. **—nightlong** *adv.* Through the night; all night.

night·ly (nītʹlē) *adj.* **1.** Of or occurring during the night; nocturnal: *the cat's nightly prowl.* **2.** Happening or done every night: *the physician's nightly rounds.* **—nightʹly** *adv.*

night·mare (nītʹmârʹ) *n.* **1.** A dream arousing feelings of intense fear, horror, and distress. **2.** An event or experience that is intensely distressing. **3.** A demon or spirit once thought to plague sleeping people. [Middle English, a female demon that afflicts sleeping people : *night,* night; see NIGHT + *mare,* goblin (from Old English; see **mer-** in Appendix).] **—nightʹmarʹish** *adj.* **—nightʹmarʹish·ly** *adv.* **—nightʹmarʹish·ness** *n.*

night owl *n. Informal.* A person who habitually stays up and is active late into the night.

night·rid·er (nītʹrīʹdər) *n.* One of a secret band of mounted, usually masked white men who engaged in nocturnal terrorism for revenge or intimidation in the southern United States especially during Reconstruction.

night·scape (nītʹskāpʹ) *n.* **1.** A view or representation of a night scene. **2.** A night scene considered together with all the elements and features constituting it: *"a nightscape of black shiny streets and glistening light"* (David Denby). **3.** A situation likened to a scene late at night: *"His trip . . . is an eerie nightscape full of rubble and reflexive violence"* (Time).

night school *n.* A school that holds classes in the evening.

night·shade (nītʹshādʹ) *n.* **1.** Any of several plants of the genus *Solanum,* such as the bittersweet nightshade, most of which have a poisonous juice. **2.** Any of various similar or related plants, such as belladonna. [Middle English, from Old English *nihtscada* : *niht,* night; see NIGHT + *sceadu,* shade.]

night shift or **night·shift** (nītʹshĭftʹ) *n.* **1.** A group of employees working during the night in a factory or business. **2.** The period of time for such work.

night·shirt (nītʹshûrtʹ) *n.* A long, loose shirt worn in bed, especially by men.

night soil *n.* Human excrement collected for use as fertilizer.

night·spot (nītʹspŏtʹ) *n.* See **nightclub.**

night·stand (nītʹstăndʹ) *n.* See **night table.**

night·stick (nītʹstĭkʹ) *n.* A club carried by a police officer.

night table *n.* A small table or stand placed at a bedside. Also called *nightstand.*

night terror *n.* A state of intense fear and agitation sometimes experienced, especially by children, on awakening from a stage of sleep not associated with dreaming but characterized by extremely vivid hallucinations.

night·time (nītʹtīmʹ) *n.* The time between sunset and sunrise. **—nighttime** *adj.* Occurring in or appropriate for use during the night: *nighttime activities; nighttime attire.*

night·walk·er (nītʹwôʹkər) *n.* **1.** One, especially a robber or prostitute, who walks the streets at night. **2.** See **night crawler.**

night watch *n.* **1.** A watch or guard kept during the night. **2.** The person or persons on such a watch.

night watchman *n.* A man who serves as a guard during the night.

night·wear (nītʹwârʹ) *n.* See **nightclothes.**

night·y (nīʹtē) *n.* Variant of **nightie.**

ni·gres·cence (nī-grĕsʹəns) *n.* **1.** The process of becoming black or dark. **2.** Blackness or darkness, as of complexion. [From *nigrescent,* blackish, from Latin *nigrēscēns, nigrēscent-,* present participle of *nigrēscere,* to become black, from *niger, nigr-,* black.] **—ni·gresʹcent** *adj.*

ni·gro·sine (nīʹgrə-sēnʹ, -sĭn) *n.* Any of a class of dyes, varying from blue to black, used in the manufacture of inks and for dyeing wood and textiles. [Latin *niger, nigr-,* black + -OS(E)[2] + -INE[2].]

NIH *abbr.* National Institutes of Health.

ni·hil·ism (nīʹə-lĭzʹəm, nēʹ-) *n.* **1.** *Philosophy.* **a.** An extreme form of skepticism that denies all existence. **b.** A doctrine holding that all values are baseless and that nothing can be known or communicated. **2.** Rejection of all distinctions in moral or religious value and a willingness to repudiate all previous theories of morality or religious belief. **3.** The belief that destruction of existing political or social institutions is necessary for future improvement. **4.** Also **Nihilism.** A diffuse, revolutionary movement of mid 19th-century Russia that scorned authority and tradition and believed in reason, materialism, and radical change in society and government through terrorism and assassination. **5.** *Psychiatry.* A delusion, experienced in some mental disorders, that the world or one's mind, body, or self does not exist. [Latin *nihil,* nothing; see **ne** in Appendix + -ISM.] **—niʹhil·ist** *n.* **—niʹhil·isʹtic** *adj.* **—niʹhil·isʹti·cal·ly** *adv.*

ni·hil·i·ty (nī-hĭlʹĭ-tē, nē-) *n.* Nonexistence; nothingness. [French *nihilité,* from Old French, from Medieval Latin *nihilitās,* from Latin *nihil,* nothing. See NIHILISM.]

ni·hil ob·stat (nīʹhĭl ŏbʹstätʹ, -stătʹ, nēʹ-) *n.* **1.** *Roman Catholic Church.* An attestation by a church censor that a book contains nothing damaging to faith or morals. **2.** Official approval, especially of an artistic work. [Latin, nothing hinders : *nihil,* nothing + *obstat,* third person sing. present tense of *obstāre,* to hinder.]

Ni·i·ga·ta (nēʹē-gäʹtə, -tä). A city of northwest Honshu, Japan, on the Sea of Japan north-northwest of Tokyo. It is a leading port with a major chemical industry. Population 475,633.

Ni·i·ha·u (nēʹē-houʹ, nēʹhouʹ). An island of northwest Hawaii west of Kauai Island. It is used mainly for cattle grazing.

Ni·jin·sky (nĭ-zhĭnʹskē, -jĭnʹ-), **Vaslav** or **Waslaw.** 1890–1950. Russian-born dancer and choreographer noted for his leading roles with Diaghilev's Ballets Russes in Paris and for his choreography of *The Rites of Spring* (1913) and other ballets.

Nij·me·gen (nīʹmā'gən, -KHən). A city of eastern Netherlands on the Waal River near the German border. Founded in Roman times, it later became a free imperial city and a member of the Hanseatic League. Population, 147,102.

-nik *suff.* One associated with or characterized by: *beatnik; peacenik.* [Yiddish and Russian (Yiddish, from Russian), of Slavic origin.]

Ni·ke (nīʹkē) *n. Greek Mytholology.* The goddess of victory.

Nik·ko (nĭkʹō, nēʹkō). A town of central Honshu, Japan, north of Tokyo. It is a pilgrimage center famed for its ornate temples and shrines. Population, 21,705.

Ni·ko·la·yev (nĭkʹə-läʹyəf, nyĭ-kə-). A city of southern Ukraine at the mouth of the Western Bug River northeast of Odessa. Founded c. 1784 as a fortress, it became a shipbuilding center in the 1780's. Population, 486,000.

nil (nĭl) *n.* Nothing; zero. [Latin *nīl,* contraction of *nihil.* See **ne** in Appendix.] **—nil** *adj.*

Nile (nīl). The longest river in the world, flowing about 6,677 km (4,150 mi) through eastern Africa from its most remote sources in Burundi to a delta on the Mediterranean Sea in northeast Egypt. The main headstreams, the **Blue Nile** and the **White Nile,** join at Khartoum in Sudan to form the Nile proper. The river has been used for irrigation in Egypt since at least 4000 B.C., a function now regulated largely by the Aswan High Dam.

Nile blue *n. Color.* A light greenish blue.

Nile crocodile *n.* A large crocodile *(Crocodylus niloticus)* common in all parts of Africa except the Sahara and the northern coast and known to attack domestic animals and human beings.

Nile green *n. Color.* A moderate yellow green to vivid light green.

Niles (nīlz). **1.** A village of northeast Illinois, an industrial suburb of Chicago on the Chicago River. Population, 30,363. **2.** A city of northeast Ohio north-northwest of Youngstown. It is an iron and steel center. Population, 23,088.

nil·gai (nĭlʹgīʹ) *n., pl.* **-gais** or **nilgai.** A large, long-legged antelope *(Boselaphus tragocamelus)* of India, the male of which has short, sturdy horns and a tuft of long hair under the chin. [Hindi *nīlgāī,* feminine of *nīlgāw* : Sanskrit *nīla-,* dark blue + Sanskrit *gauḥ,* ox, cow; see GAYAL.]

nill (nĭl) *v.* **nilled, nill·ing, nills.** *Obsolete.* —*tr.* Not to will; not to wish. —*intr.* To be unwilling; will not. [Middle English *nilen,* from Old English *nyllan* : *ne,* not; see **ne** in Appendix + *willan,* to desire; see **wel-**[1] in Appendix.]

Ni·lo-Sa·har·an (nīʹlō-sə-hărʹən, -häʹrən) *n.* A language family of sub-Saharan Africa spoken in the interior from Nigeria to Kenya and including Kanuri, Nubian, and the Nilotic languages.

Ni·lot·ic (nī-lŏtʹĭk) *adj.* **1.** Of or relating to the Nile or the Nile Valley. **2.** Of or relating to the peoples who speak Nilotic languages. **—Nilotic** *n.* A large group of Nilo-Saharan languages, spoken in southern Sudan, Uganda, Kenya, and northern Tanzania and including Masai. [Latin *Nīlōticus,* from *Nīlōtis,* from Greek *Neilōtis,* from *Neilos,* Nile.]

nil·po·tent (nĭl-pōtʹnt, nĭlʹpōtʹnt) *n. Mathematics.* An algebraic quantity that when raised to a certain power equals zero. [NIL + Latin *potēns, potent-,* having power; see POTENT.] **—nil·poʹten·cy** *n.*

Nils·son (nĭlʹsən), **Birgit.** Born 1918. Swedish operatic soprano noted for her Wagnerian roles.

nim[1] (nĭm) *tr. & intr.v.* **nimmed, nim·ming, nims.** *Archaic.* To steal; pilfer. [Middle English *nimen,* to take, from Old English *niman.* See **nem-** in Appendix.]

nim[2] (nĭm) *n. Games.* A game in which players in turn remove small objects from a collection, such as matchsticks arranged in rows, and attempt to take, or avoid taking, the last one. [Perhaps from German *nimm,* third person sing. imperative of *nehmen,* to take, from Middle High German *nemen,* from Old High German *neman.* See **nem-** in Appendix.]

nim·bi (nĭmʹbīʹ) *n.* A plural of **nimbus.**

nim·ble (nĭmʹbəl) *adj.* **-bler, -blest. 1.** Quick, light, or agile in movement or action; deft: *nimble fingers.* **2.** Quick, clever, and acute in devising or understanding: *nimble wits.* [Middle English *nemel,* from Old English *nǣmel,* quick to seize, and *numol,* quick at learning; see **nem-** in Appendix.] **—nimʹble·ness** *n.* **—nimʹbly** *adv.*

SYNONYMS: *nimble, agile, quick, brisk, facile, spry.* These adjectives mean moving, performing, or done quickly, lightly, and adroitly. *Nimble* suggests rapidity, ease, and deftness: *as nimble as a deer; nimble feet. "For nimble thought can jump both sea and land"* (Shakespeare). *Agile* implies dexterity, as in the use of the hands: *as sleek and agile as a gymnast; an agile intellect. Quick* connotes readiness, liveliness, energy, and speed: *a quick mind; "quick of foot"* (Charles Dickens). *Brisk* suggests sprightliness and a spirited quality: *played the concerto at a brisk tempo. "Tom*

Vaslav Nijinsky
In character as a slave for *Scheherazade,* 1910

Nike
Detail from a fifth-century B.C. Greek bell krater

ă **pat**	oi **boy**
ā **pay**	ou **out**
âr **care**	o͝o **took**
ä **father**	o͞o **boot**
ĕ **pet**	ŭ **cut**
ē **be**	ûr **urge**
ĭ **pit**	th **thin**
ī **pie**	*th* **this**
îr **pier**	hw **which**
ŏ **pot**	zh **vision**
ō **toe**	ə **about, item**
ô **paw**	♦ **regionalism**

Stress marks: ʹ (primary); ʹ (secondary), as in **dictionary** (dĭkʹshə-nĕrʹē)

Birch is as brisk as a bee in conversation" (Samuel Johnson). *Facile* implies ease and fluency of performance; sometimes it has the disparaging implications of superficiality, cursoriness, or glibness: *a facile hand; the gift of facile expression; "can dazzle anyone anywhere with his facile tongue"* (Suzanne Perney). *Spry* usually suggests unexpected speed and energy of motion: *The old dog was so spry that it was in the door and halfway up the stairs before we could stop it.* See also Synonyms at **dexterous.**

nimbostratus
Nimbostratus clouds releasing rain

nim·bo·stra·tus (nĭm′bō-strā′təs, -străt′əs) *n., pl.* **-stra·ti** (-strā′tī, -străt′ī). A low, gray, often dark cloud that precipitates rain, snow, or sleet. [NIMB(US) + STRATUS.]

nim·bus (nĭm′bəs) *n., pl.* **-bi** (-bī′) or **-bus·es. 1.** A cloudy radiance said to surround a classical deity when on earth. **2.** A radiant light that appears usually in the form of a circle or halo about or over the head in the representation of a god, demigod, saint, or sacred person such as a king or an emperor. **3.** A splendid atmosphere or aura, as of glamour, that surrounds a person or thing. **4.** A rain cloud, especially a low dark layer of clouds such as a nimbostratus. [Latin, cloud. See **nebh-** in Appendix.]

NIM·BY also **nim·by** (nĭm′bē) *n., pl.* **NIM·BYs** also **nim·bys.** *Slang.* One who objects to the establishment in one's neighborhood of projects, such as incinerators, prisons, or shelters for the homeless, that are believed to be dangerous, unsightly, or otherwise undesirable. [*N(ot) i(n) m(y) b(ack) y(ard).*] **—nim′by·ness** *n.*

Nîmes (nēm). A city of southern France northeast of Montpellier. Thought to have been founded by Greek colonists, it was one of the leading cities of Roman Gaul. Population, 124,220.

ni·mi·e·ty (nĭ-mī′ĭ-tē) *n.* Superfluity; excess. [Late Latin *nimietās,* from Latin *nimius,* excessive, from *nimis,* excessively. See **ne** in Appendix.]

nim·i·ny-pim·i·ny (nĭm′ə-nē-pĭm′ə-nē) *adj.* Affectedly delicate or refined; mincing. [Perhaps alteration of NAMBY-PAMBY.] **—nim′i·ny-pim′i·ny** *n.*

Nim·itz (nĭm′ĭts), **Chester Williams.** 1885–1966. American admiral of the Pacific fleet during World War II who halted Japanese expansion and ultimately destroyed the Japanese fleet with a strategy based largely on the use of aircraft carriers.

nim·rod also **Nim·rod** (nĭm′rŏd′) *n.* A hunter.

Nimrod. In the Old Testament, a mighty hunter and king of Shinar who was a grandson of Ham and a great-grandson of Noah.

Nim·rud (nĭm-rōōd′). An ancient city of Assyria south of present-day Mosul, Iraq.

Nin (nēn, nĭn), **Anaïs.** 1903–1977. French-born American writer known for *The Diary of Anaïs Nin 1931–1966* (published 1966–1980).

nin·com·poop (nĭn′kəm-pōōp′, nĭng′-) *n.* A person regarded as silly, foolish, or stupid. [Origin unknown.] **—nin′com·poop′er·y** *n.*

nine (nīn) *n.* **1.** The cardinal number equal to 8 + 1. **2.** The ninth in a set or sequence. **3.** Something having nine parts, units, or members. **4.** *Games.* A playing card marked with nine pips. **5.** A set of nine persons or things, especially: **a.** *Baseball.* The nine players on a side, or the whole team. **b. Nine.** *Greek Mythology.* The nine Muses. **6.** A size, as in clothing or shoes, designated as nine. **7.** *Sports.* The first or second 9 holes of an 18-hole golf course. ***—idiom.* to the nines.** *Informal.* To the highest degree: *dressed to the nines.* [Middle English, from Old English *nigon.* See **newn̥** in Appendix.] **—nine** *adj. & pron.*

nine-band·ed armadillo (nīn′băn′dĭd) *n.* The most common species of armadillo, *Dasypus novemcinctus,* usually having nine jointed bands of bony plates. The females give birth to quadruplets from one egg.

nine·bark (nīn′bärk′) *n.* Any of several shrubs of the genus *Physocarpus,* especially *P. opulifolius* of eastern North America, having peeling or shredding bark and clusters of small white flowers. [From the many layers in its bark.]

nine days' wonder (dāz) *n.* A thing or an event that creates a brief sensation.

nine-banded armadillo
Dasypus novemcinctus

nine·pin (nīn′pĭn′) *n. Sports.* **1. ninepins.** *(used with a sing. or pl. verb).* A bowling game in which nine wooden pins are the target. **2.** A wooden pin used in the game of ninepins.

nine·teen (nīn-tēn′) *n.* **1.** The cardinal number equal to 18 + 1. **2.** The 19th in a set or sequence. [Middle English *nintene,* from Old English *nigontēne.* See **newn̥** in Appendix.] **—nine·teen′** *adj. & pron.*

nine·teenth (nīn-tēnth′) *n.* **1.** The ordinal number matching the number 19 in a series. **2.** One of 19 equal parts. **—nine·teenth′** *adv. & adj.*

nine·ti·eth (nīn′tē-ĭth) *n.* **1.** The ordinal number matching the number 90 in a series. **2.** One of 90 equal parts. **—nine′ti·eth** *adv. & adj.*

nine-to-fiv·er (nīn′tə-fī′vər) *n.* One who works regular daytime hours, as in an office.

nine·ty (nīn′tē) *n., pl.* **-ties. 1.** The cardinal number equal to 9 × 10. **2. nineties. a.** Often **Nineties.** The decade from 90 to 99 in a century. **b.** A decade or the numbers from 90 to 99: *My grandparents are in their nineties. The temperature stayed in the nineties.* [Middle English *ninti,* from Old English *nigontig.* See **newn̥** in Appendix.] **—nine′ty** *adj. & pron.*

Nin·e·veh (nĭn′ə-və). An ancient city of Assyria on the Tigris River opposite the site of present-day Mosul, Iraq. As capital of the Assyrian Empire, it enjoyed great influence and prosperity, especially under Sennacherib and Ashurbanipal (seventh century B.C.). The city was captured and destroyed by Babylonia and its allies in 612 B.C.

Ning·bo (nĭng′bō′) also **Ning·po** (-pō′). A city of eastern China east-southeast of Hangzhou on Hangzhou Bay. Built on a site occupied since the eighth century, it was used as a trading post by the Portuguese from 1520 to 1545 and became a treaty port in 1842. Population, 350,000.

Ning·xia Hui·zu (nĭng′shyä′ hwē′dzōō′) also **Ning·sia Hui** (hwē′). An autonomous region of northern China. Formerly a province, it was incorporated into Gansu in 1954 but reconstituted as a region in 1958. Yinchuan is the capital. Population, 4,150,000.

nin·ja (nĭn′jə) *n., pl.* **ninja** or **-jas.** A member of a class of 14th-century Japanese mercenary agents who were trained in the martial arts and hired for covert operations such as assassination and sabotage. *—attributive.* Often used to modify another noun: *ninja weapons.* [Japanese : *nin,* to endure + *ja,* person.]

nin·ny (nĭn′ē) *n., pl.* **-nies.** A fool; a simpleton. [Perhaps alteration of INNOCENT.]

Ni·ño (nēn′yō) *n.* El Niño.

ni·non (nē′nŏn′) *n.* A sheer fabric of silk, rayon, or nylon made in a variety of tight smooth weaves or open lacy patterns. [Probably from French *Ninon,* nickname for *Anne.*]

ninth (nīnth) *n.* **1.** The ordinal number matching the number nine in a series. **2.** One of nine equal parts. **3.** *Music.* **a.** A harmonic or melodic interval of an octave and a second. **b.** The tone at the upper limit of such an interval. **c.** A chord consisting of a root with its third, seventh, and ninth. [Middle English *ninthe,* from Old English *nigonthe,* from *nigon,* nine. See **newn̥** in Appendix.] **—ninth** *adv. & adj.*

Ni·o·be (nī′ə-bē) *n. Greek Mythology.* The daughter of Tantalus who turned to stone while bewailing the loss of her children.

ni·o·bite (nī′ə-bīt′) *n.* Columbite. [NIOB(IUM) + –ITE [1].]

ni·o·bi·um (nī-ō′bē-əm) *n. Symbol* **Nb** A silvery, soft, ductile metallic element that occurs chiefly in columbite-tantalite and is used in steel alloys, arc welding, and superconductivity research. Atomic number 41; atomic weight 92.906; melting point 2,468°C; boiling point 4,927°C; specific gravity 8.57; valence 2, 3, 5. See table at **element.** [After NIOBE (so called because it is extracted from tantalite).]

Ni·o·brar·a (nī′ə-brâr′ə). A river, about 692 km (430 mi) long, rising in eastern Wyoming and flowing generally eastward to the Missouri River in northeast Nebraska.

Niort (nyôr). A city of western France southeast of Nantes. Originally a Gallo-Roman town, it was a stronghold of the Huguenots in the 16th and 17th centuries. Population, 58,203.

nip¹ (nĭp) *v.* **nipped, nip·ing, nips.** *—tr.* **1.** To seize and pinch or bite: *The fish nipped the wader's toe.* **2.** To remove or sever by pinching or snipping: *nipped off the plant leaf.* **3.** To bite or sting with the cold; chill. **4.** To check or cut off the growth or development of: *a conspiracy that was nipped in the bud by the police.* See Synonyms at **blast. 5.** *Slang.* **a.** To snatch up hastily. **b.** To take (the property of another) unlawfully; steal. *—intr. Chiefly British.* To move quickly; dart. **—nip** *n.* **1.** The act or an instance of seizing or pinching. **2. a.** A pinch or snip that cuts off or removes a small part: *He gave a small nip to each corner of the cloth.* **b.** The small bit or portion so removed: *There were nips of construction paper all over the child's table.* **3. a.** A sharp, stinging quality, as of frosty air. **b.** Severely sharp cold or frost. **4.** A cutting remark. **5.** A sharp, biting flavor; a tang: *the nip of Mexican salsa.* [Middle English *nippen,* perhaps from Middle Dutch *nipen.*]

nip² (nĭp) *Informal. n.* A small amount of liquor. **—nip** *v.* **nipped, nip·ping, nips.** *—tr.* To sip (alcoholic liquor) in small amounts: *had been nipping brandy. —intr.* To take a sip or sips of alcoholic liquor: *nips all day long.* [Probably short for *nipperkin,* of Dutch or Low German origin.]

ni·pa (nē′pə) *n.* **1.** A large palm *(Nipa frutescens)* of the Philippines and Australia, having long leaves often used for thatching. **2.** An alcoholic beverage made from the sap of this plant. [New Latin, from Malay *nipah.*]

nip and tuck *adv. & adj.* So close that the advantage or lead shifts from one to another and is virtually indeterminable; neck and neck.

Nip·i·gon (nĭp′ĭ-gŏn′), **Lake.** A lake of southwest-central Ontario, Canada, north of Lake Superior.

Nip·is·sing (nĭp′ĭ-sĭng′), **Lake.** A lake of southeast Ontario, Canada, between the Ottawa River and Georgian Bay.

nip·per (nĭp′ər) *n.* **1.** A tool, such as pliers or pincers, used for squeezing or nipping. Often used in the plural. **2.** A pincerlike part, such as the large claw of a crustacean. **3.** *Chiefly British.* A small boy.

nip·ping (nĭp′ĭng) *adj.* **1.** Sharp and biting, as the cold. **2.** Bitingly sarcastic. **—nip′ping·ly** *adv.*

nip·ple (nĭp′əl) *n.* **1.** The small projection near the center of the mammary gland containing the outlets of the milk ducts through which young mammals obtain milk from the adult female; a teat. **2. a.** The rubber cap on a bottle from which a baby nurses. **b.** A pacifier for an infant. **3.** Any of various devices functioning like or resembling a nipple, especially: **a.** A regulated opening for discharging a liquid, as in a small stopcock. **b.**

A pipe coupling threaded on both ends. **c.** A short extension of pipe to which a nozzle can be attached. **d.** A small projection through which grease in a grease gun can be forced into a bearing. **4.** A natural or geographic projection resembling a nipple, as a mountain crest. [From obsolete *neble,* diminutive of NEB.]

nip·ple·wort (nĭp′əl-wûrt′, -wôrt′) *n.* A European annual plant *(Lapsana communis)* naturalized in eastern North America, having a milky juice and small yellow flower heads. [From its former use in folk medicine to treat breast tumors.]

Nip·pon (nĭ-pŏn′, nĭp′ŏn, nē-pôn′). Japan. The name was derived from the Chinese characters for "the place where the sun comes from," or the Land of the Rising Sun.

Nip·pon·ese (nĭp′ə-nēz′, -nēs′) *adj. & n.* Japanese.

Nip·pur (nĭ-po͝or′). An ancient city of Babylonia on the Euphrates River southeast of Babylon. It was an important religious center in Sumerian times.

nip·py (nĭp′ē) *adj.* **-pi·er, -pi·est. 1.** Tending to nip: *an exuberant, nippy puppy.* **2.** Sharp or biting: *nippy cheese.* **3.** Bitingly cold: *a nippy fall day.* **—nip′pi·ly** *adv.* **—nip′pi·ness** *n.*

nip-up (nĭp′ŭp′) *n. Sports.* An acrobatic spring from a supine to an upright position.

N.Ire. *abbr.* Northern Ireland.

nir·va·na (nîr-vä′nə, nər-) *n.* **1.** Often **Nirvana. a.** *Buddhism.* The ineffable ultimate in which one has attained disinterested wisdom and compassion. **b.** *Hinduism.* Emancipation from ignorance and the extinction of all attachment. **2.** An ideal condition of rest, harmony, stability, or joy. [Sanskrit *nirvāṇam,* a blowing out, extinction, nirvana : *nis-, nir-,* out, away + *vāti,* it blows; see **wē-** in Appendix.]

Niš also **Nish** (nĭsh). A city of eastern Yugoslavia near the Bulgarian border. The birthplace of Constantine the Great, it was held at various times by Bulgarians, Hungarians, Turks, and Serbians. Population, 151,600.

Ni·san (nĭs′ən, nē-sän′) *n.* The seventh month of the year in the Jewish calendar. See table at **calendar.** [Hebrew *nisān,* from Akkadian *nissanu,* the first month of the year, from Sumerian *nisag,* first fruits.]

Ni·sei (nē-sā′, nē′sā′) *n., pl.* **Nisei** or **-seis.** A person born in America of parents who emigrated from Japan. [Japanese : *ni,* second + *sei,* generation.]

Nish (nĭsh). See **Niš.**

Ni·shi·no·mi·ya (nĭsh′ə-nō′mē-ä, nē′shē-nô′mē-yä′). A city of southern Honshu, Japan, on Osaka Bay east of Kobe. It is a resort and an industrial center. Population, 421,267.

ni·si (nī′sī′) *adj. Law.* Taking effect at a specified date unless cause is shown for modification or nullification: *a decree nisi.* [Latin *nisī,* unless. See **ne** in Appendix.]

Nis·sen hut (nĭs′ən) *n.* A prefabricated building of corrugated steel in the shape of a half cylinder, used especially by military personnel as a shelter. [After Peter Norman *Nissen* (1871–1930), British army officer and mining engineer.]

ni·sus (nī′səs) *n., pl.* **nisus.** An effort or endeavor to realize an aim. [Latin *nīsus,* from past participle of *nītī,* to strive.]

nit¹ (nĭt) *n.* The egg or young of a parasitic insect, such as a louse. [Middle English, from Old English *hnitu.*] **—nit′ty** *adj.*

nit² (nĭt) *n.* A unit of illuminative brightness equal to one candle per square meter, measured perpendicular to the rays of the source. [From Latin *nitor,* brightness, from *nitēre,* to shine.]

NIT *abbr.* **1.** National Intelligence Test. **2.** *Sports.* National Invitational Tournament.

ni·ter (nī′tər) *n.* A white, gray, or colorless mineral of potassium nitrate, KNO_3, used in making gunpowder. Also called *saltpeter.* [Middle English *nitre,* sodium carbonate, natron, from Old French, from Latin *nitrum,* from Greek *nitron,* from Egyptian *ntr.*]

Ni·te·rói (nē′tə-roi′). A city of southeast Brazil on Guanabara Bay opposite Rio de Janeiro. Founded in 1671, it is a residential and industrial center. Population, 382,736.

nit·pick (nĭt′pĭk′) *intr.v.* **-picked, -pick·ing, -picks.** To be concerned with or find fault with insignificant details. See Synonyms at **quibble. —nit′pick′er** *n.*

nit·pick·ing (nĭt′pĭk′ĭng) *n.* Minute, trivial, unnecessary, and unjustified criticism or faultfinding.

nitr– *pref.* Variant of **nitro–.**

Ni·tra (nē′trə). A city of south-central Czechoslovakia on the **Nitra River,** a tributary of the Danube. Dating from Roman times, Nitra was a religious center after the ninth century and became a free city in 1248. Population, 83,338.

ni·trate (nī′trāt′, -trĭt) *n.* **1.** The univalent radical NO_3 or a compound containing it, as a salt or an ester of nitric acid. **2.** Fertilizer consisting of sodium nitrate or potassium nitrate. **—nitrate** *tr.v.* **-trat·ed, -trat·ing, -trates.** To treat with nitric acid or a nitrate, usually to change (an organic compound) into a nitrate. **—ni·tra′tion** *n.* **—ni′tra′tor** *n.*

nitrate bacterium *n.* Any of several nitrobacteria that convert nitrites to nitrates by oxidation. Also called *nitric bacterium.*

ni·tre (nī′tər) *n. Chiefly British.* Variant of **niter.**

ni·tric (nī′trĭk) *adj.* Of, derived from, or containing nitrogen, especially in a valence state higher than that in a comparable nitrous compound.

nitric acid *n.* A transparent, colorless to yellowish, fuming corrosive liquid, HNO_3, a highly reactive oxidizing agent used in the production of fertilizers, explosives, and rocket fuels and in a wide variety of industrial metallurgical processes. Also called *aqua fortis.*

nitric bacterium *n.* See **nitrate bacterium.**

nitric oxide *n.* A colorless, poisonous gas, NO, produced as an intermediate during the manufacture of nitric acid from ammonia or atmospheric nitrogen.

ni·tride (nī′trīd′) *n.* A compound containing nitrogen with another more electropositive element, such as phosphorus or a metal.

ni·tri·fy (nī′trə-fī′) *tr.v.* **-fied, -fy·ing, -fies. 1.** To oxidize (an ammonia compound) into nitric acid, nitrous acid, or any nitrate or nitrite, especially by the action of nitrobacteria. **2.** To treat or combine with nitrogen or compounds containing nitrogen. **—ni′tri·fi·ca′tion** (-fĭ-kā′shən) *n.* **—ni′tri·fi′er** *n.*

ni·trile also **ni·tril** (nī′trəl) *n.* An organic cyanide containing a CN group. [NITR(O)– + *-ile,* chemical suff. (probably variant of –YL).]

ni·trite (nī′trīt′) *n.* The univalent radical NO_2 or a compound containing it, such as a salt or an ester of nitrous acid.

nitrite bacterium *n.* Any of several nitrobacteria that convert ammonia to nitrites by oxidation. Also called *nitrous bacterium.*

nitro– or **nitr–** *pref.* **1.** Nitrate; niter: *nitrobacterium.* **2. a.** Nitrogen: *nitrile.* **b.** Containing the univalent group NO_2: *nitromethane.* [New Latin, from Latin *nitrum,* natron. See NITER.]

ni·tro·bac·te·ri·um (nī′trō-băk-tîr′ē-əm) *n., pl.* **-te·ri·a** (-tîr′ē-ə). Any of various soil bacteria that take part in the nitrogen cycle, oxidizing ammonium compounds into nitrites or nitrites into nitrates.

ni·tro·ben·zene (nī′trō-bĕn′zēn′, -bĕn-zēn′) *n.* A poisonous organic compound, $C_6H_5NO_2$, either bright yellow crystals or an oily liquid, having the odor of almonds and used in the manufacture of aniline, insulating compounds, and polishes.

ni·tro·cel·lu·lose (nī′trō-sĕl′yə-lōs′, -lōz′) *n.* A pulpy or cottonlike polymer derived from cellulose treated with sulfuric and nitric acids and used in the manufacture of explosives, collodion, plastics, and solid monopropellants. Also called *guncotton, cellulose nitrate.* **—ni′tro·cel′lu·los′ic** (-lō′sĭk, -zĭk) *adj.*

ni·tro·chlo·ro·form (nī′trō-klôr′ə-fôrm′, -klōr′-) *n.* See **chloropicrin.**

ni·tro·fu·ran (nī′trō-fyo͝or′ăn′, -fyo͝o-răn′) *n.* Any of several drugs derived from furan that are used to inhibit bacterial growth.

ni·tro·fur·an·to·in (nī′trō-fyo͝o-răn′tō-ĭn) *n.* A derivative of nitrofuran, $C_8H_6N_4O_5$, used in the treatment of bacterial infections of the urinary tract. [NITROFURAN + *(hydan)toin,* a chemical compound; see DIPHENYLHYDANTOIN.]

ni·tro·gen (nī′trə-jən) *n. Symbol* **N** A nonmetallic element that constitutes nearly four fifths of the air by volume, occurring as a colorless, odorless, almost inert diatomic gas, N_2, in various minerals and in all proteins and used in a wide variety of important manufactures, including ammonia, nitric acid, TNT, and fertilizers. Atomic number 7; atomic weight 14.0067; melting point −209.86°C; boiling point −195.8°C; valence 3, 5. See table at **element.** [French *nitrogène* : *nitro-,* nitric acid (from New Latin; see NITRO–) + *-gène,* -gen.] **—ni·trog′e·nous** (nī-trŏj′ə-nəs) *adj.*

ni·trog·e·nase (nī-trŏj′ə-nās′, -nāz′, nī′trə-jə-) *n.* An enzyme of nitrogen-fixing bacteria that activates the conversion of nitrogen to ammonia.

nitrogen balance *n.* The difference between the amount of nitrogen taken into the body or the soil and the amount excreted or lost.

nitrogen cycle *n.* **1.** *Ecology.* The circulation of nitrogen in nature, consisting of a cycle of chemical reactions in which atmospheric nitrogen is compounded, dissolved in rain, and deposited in the soil, where it is assimilated and metabolized by bacteria and plants, eventually returning to the atmosphere by bacterial decomposition of organic matter. **2.** *Physics.* See **carbon-nitrogen cycle.**

nitrogen dioxide *n.* A poisonous brown gas, NO_2, often found in smog and automobile exhaust fumes and synthesized for use as a nitrating agent, a catalyst, and an oxidizing agent.

nitrogen fixation *n.* **1.** The conversion of atmospheric nitrogen into compounds, such as ammonia, by natural agencies or various industrial processes. **2.** The conversion by certain soil microorganisms, such as rhizobia, of atmospheric nitrogen into compounds that plants and other organisms can assimilate. **—ni′tro·gen-fix′er** (nī′trə-jən-fĭk′sər) *n.* **—ni′tro·gen-fix′ing** *adj.*

ni·trog·en·ize (nī-trŏj′ə-nīz′, nī′trə-jə-) *tr.v.* **-ized, -iz·ing, -iz·es.** To combine or treat with nitrogen or a nitrogen compound.

nitrogen narcosis *n.* A condition of confusion or stupor resulting from increased levels of dissolved nitrogen in the blood, as that occurring in deep-sea divers breathing air under high pressure.

ni·tro·glyc·er·in also **ni·tro·glyc·er·ine** (nī′trō-glĭs′ər-ĭn, -trə-) *n.* A thick, pale yellow liquid, $CH_2NO_3CHNO_3CH_2NO_3$, that is explosive on concussion or exposure to sudden heat. It is used in the production of dynamite and blasting gelatin and as a vasodilator in medicine.

ni·tro·hy·dro·chlo·ric acid (nī′trō-hī′drə-klôr′ĭk, -klōr′-) *n.* See **aqua regia.**

ă pat	oi boy
ā pay	ou out
âr care	o͝o took
ä father	o͞o boot
ĕ pet	ŭ cut
ē be	ûr urge
ĭ pit	th thin
ī pie	*th* this
îr pier	hw which
ŏ pot	zh vision
ō toe	ə about, item
ô paw	♦ regionalism

Stress marks: ′ (primary); ′ (secondary), as in **dictionary** (dĭk′shə-nĕr′ē)

Pat Nixon

Richard M. Nixon
Photographed in 1969

No[1]

ni·tro·meth·ane (nī'trō-mĕth'ān') *n.* A colorless, oily liquid, CH_3NO_2, used in making dyes and resins, in organic synthesis, and as a rocket propellant.

ni·tro·par·af·fin (nī'trō-păr'ə-fĭn) *n.* Any of a group of organic compounds formed by replacing one or more of the hydrogen atoms of a paraffin hydrocarbon with the univalent group, NO_2, as in nitromethane, CH_3NO_2.

ni·tros·a·mine (nī-trō'sə-mēn', nī'trōs-ăm'ēn) *n.* Any of a class of organic compounds with the general formula R_2NNO or RNHNO, present in various foods and other products and found to be carcinogenic in laboratory animals. [Latin *nitrōsus,* full of natron (from *nitrum,* natron; see NITER) + AMINE.]

ni·tro·starch (nī'trə-stärch') *n.* A highly explosive orange powder, $C_{12}H_{12}(NO_2)_8O_{10}$, derived from starch and used for demolition.

ni·trous (nī'trəs) *adj.* Of, derived from, or containing nitrogen, especially in a valence state lower than that in a comparable nitric compound.

nitrous acid *n.* A weak inorganic acid, HNO_2, existing only in solution or in the form of its salts.

nitrous bacterium *n.* See **nitrite bacterium.**

nitrous oxide *n.* A colorless, sweet-tasting gas, N_2O, used as a mild anesthetic in dentistry and surgery.

nits-and-lice (nĭts'ən-līs') *n. (used with a sing. or pl. verb).* A plant *(Hypericum drummondii)* of the central United States having narrow leaves and yellow flowers.

Nit·ti (nĭt'ē, nēt'tē), **Francesco Saverio.** 1868–1953. Italian economist and politician who served as prime minister (1919–1920) and was exiled in 1924 by Mussolini.

nit·ty-grit·ty (nĭt'ē-grĭt'ē) *n. Informal.* The specific or practical details; the heart of a matter. [Origin unknown.]

nit·wit (nĭt'wĭt') *n.* A person regarded as stupid or silly. [Probably obsolete *nit,* nothing (from German dialectal, from Middle High German *niht, nit;* see NIX[2]) + WIT[1].]

Ni·u·e (nē-o͞o'ā). An island dependency of New Zealand in the south-central Pacific Ocean east of Tonga. Discovered by Capt. James Cook in 1774, it became internally self-governing in 1974. Alofi is the capital. Population, 3,578.

ni·val (nī'vəl) *adj.* Of, relating to, or growing in or under snow: *nival species of plants.* [Latin *nivālis,* from *nix, niv-,* snow.]

niv·e·ous (nĭv'ē-əs) *adj.* Resembling snow; snowy. [From Latin *niveus,* from *nix, niv-,* snow.]

Ni·ver·nais (nĭv'ər-nā', nē-vĕr-nĕ'). A historical region and former province of central France. A countship after the ninth century, it passed to various noble families before being incorporated into the royal domain by Louis XIV in 1669.

nix[1] (nĭks) *n. Mythology.* A water sprite of German mythology, usually in human form or half-human and half-fish. [German, from Middle High German *nickes,* from Old High German *nihhus.*]

nix[2] (nĭks) *Slang. n.* Nothing. **—nix** *adv.* Not so; no. **—nix** *tr.v.* **nixed, nix·ing, nix·es.** To forbid, refuse, or veto: *Congress nixed the tax hike.* [German dialectal, from Middle High German *nihtes,* genitive of *niht,* from Old High German *niwiht* : *ni,* not, no; see **ne** in Appendix + *wiht,* thing; see **wekti-** in Appendix.]

nix·ie also **nix·y** (nĭk'sē) *n., pl.* **-ies.** *Slang.* A misaddressed or illegibly addressed piece of mail, therefore undeliverable. [From NIX[2].]

Nix·on (nĭk'sən), **Richard Milhous.** Born 1913. The 37th President of the United States (1969–1974). Vice President (1953–1961) under Dwight D. Eisenhower, he lost the 1960 presidential election to John F. Kennedy. Elected President in 1968, he visited China (1972) and established détente with the U.S.S.R. Although he increased U.S. military involvement in Southeast Asia, he was also responsible for the eventual withdrawal of U.S. troops. When Congress recommended three articles of impeachment for Nixon's involvement in the Watergate scandal, he resigned from office (August 9, 1974).

Nixon, Thelma Catherine Ryan. Known as "Pat." Born 1912. First Lady of the United States (1969–1974) as the wife of President Richard M. Nixon. She worked to make the White House more accessible for disabled and sightless people.

Ni·zam (nĭ-zăm', -zăm', nī-) *n.* **1.** Used formerly as a title for rulers of Hyderabad, India. **2. nizam** *pl.* **nizam.** A Turkish soldier, especially in the 19th century. [Urdu *nizām(-almulk),* governor (of the empire), from Arabic *niẓām,* order, arrangement, from *naẓama,* to arrange.]

Nizh·ne·var·tovsk (nĭzh'nə-vär-tôfsk', nyĭzh-). A city of central Russia on the Ob River. A huge oil field was discovered nearby in 1965. Population, 190,000.

Nizh·niy Ta·gil (nĭzh'nē tə-gēl', nyē'zhnē tə-gyēl'). A city of central Russia in the east-central Ural Mountains. Founded in 1725, it is a metallurgical center. Population, 419,000.

Nizh·ny Nov·go·rod (nĭzh'nē nŏv'gə-rŏd', nyē'zhnē nôv'gə-rət). See **Gorky.**

NJ or **N.J.** *abbr.* New Jersey.

Nkru·mah (ən-kro͞o'mə, əng-), **Kwame.** 1909–1972. Ghanaian politician. Instrumental in achieving Ghana's independence from Great Britain (1957), he became president (1960) but was deposed in a coup d'état (1966).

NKVD or **N.K.V.D.** *abbr.* Narodny Kommissariat Vnutrennikh Del (Peoples' Commissariat of Internal Affairs).

NL or **N.L.** *abbr.* **1.** *Baseball.* National League. **2.** Also **n.l.** New line. **3.** New Latin. **4.** *Latin.* Non licet (not permitted). **5.** *Latin.* Non liquet (not clear).

NLF *abbr.* National Liberation Front.

NLRB or **N.L.R.B.** *abbr.* National Labor Relations Board.

NLT *abbr.* Night letter.

nm *abbr.* **1.** Nanometer. **2.** Nuclear magneton. **3.** Also **n.m.** or **NM.** Nautical mile.

NM or **N.M.** *abbr.* New Mexico.

N.Mex. *abbr.* New Mexico.

NMI *abbr.* No middle initial.

NMR *abbr.* Nuclear magnetic resonance.

NNE *abbr.* North-northeast.

NNW *abbr.* North-northwest.

no[1] (nō) *adv.* **1.** Used to express refusal, denial, disbelief, emphasis, or disagreement: *No, I'm not going. No, you're wrong.* **2.** Not at all; not by any degree. Often used with the comparative: *no better; no more.* **3.** Not: *whether or no.* **—no** *n., pl.* **noes** (nōz). **1.** A negative response; a denial or refusal: *The proposal produced only noes.* **2.** A negative vote or voter. [Middle English, from Old English *nā* : *ne,* not; see **ne** in Appendix + *ā,* ever; see **aiw-** in Appendix.]

no[2] (nō) *adj.* **1.** Not any; not one; not a: *No cookies are left.* **2.** Not at all; not close to being: *He is no child.* **3.** Hardly any: *got there in no time flat.* See Usage Note at **nor[1].** [Middle English, variant of *non,* from Old English *nān,* none : *ne,* not; see **ne** in Appendix + *ān,* one; see ONE.]

No[1] also **Noh** (nō) *n., pl.* **No** also **Noh.** The classical drama of Japan, with music and dance performed in a highly stylized manner by elaborately dressed performers on an almost bare stage. [Japanese *nō,* talent, ability, No, from Chinese *néng.*]

No[2] The symbol for the element **nobelium.**

No (nō), **Lake.** A lake of south-central Sudan. Formed by the flood waters of the White Nile, it varies in size seasonally.

no. or **No.** *abbr.* **1.** North; northern. **2.** Number.

NOAA *abbr.* National Oceanic and Aeronautic Administration.

no-ac·count (nō'ə-kount') *adj. Informal.* Worthless; good-for-nothing: *my no-account brother-in-law.*

No·a·chi·an (nō-ā'kē-ən) also **No·ach·ic** (-ăk'ĭk) or **No·ach·i·cal** (-ĭ-kəl) *adj.* **1.** *Bible.* Of or relating to Noah or his time. **2.** Antiquated; ancient; long obsolete.

No·ah (nō'ə). In the Old Testament, the patriarch who was chosen by God to build an ark, in which he, his family, and a pair of every animal were saved from the Flood.

No·a·tak (nō-ā'tək, -täk). A river of northwest Alaska rising in the Brooks Range and flowing about 644 km (400 mi) westward to Kotzebue Sound.

nob[1] (nŏb) *n.* **1.** *Slang.* The human head. **2.** *Games.* The jack of the suit turned up by the dealer in cribbage, scoring one point for the holder: *one for his nob.* [Perhaps variant of KNOB.]

nob[2] (nŏb) *n. Chiefly British.* A person of wealth or social standing: *"The nobs were forever snubbing the snobs"* (Conor Cruise O'Brien). [Possibly from NOB[1] or KNOB.]

nob·ble (nŏb'əl) *tr.v.* **-bled, -bling, -bles.** *Chiefly British.* **1.** To disable (a racehorse), especially by drugging. **2.** To win (a person) over. **3.** To outdo or get the better of by devious means. **4.** To filch or steal. **5.** To kidnap. [Origin unknown.] **—nob'bler** *n.*

nob·by (nŏb'ē) *adj.* **-bi·er, -bi·est.** Fashionable; stylish. [From NOB[2].]

No·bel (nō-bĕl'), **Alfred Bernhard.** 1833–1896. Swedish chemist and engineer who invented dynamite (1866) and bequeathed his fortune to institute the Nobel Prizes.

No·bel·ist (nō-bĕl'ĭst) *n.* A recipient of a Nobel prize.

no·bel·i·um (nō-bĕl'ē-əm) *n. Symbol* **No** A radioactive transuranic element in the actinide series, artificially produced in trace amounts. Its longest-lived isotope is No 255 with a half-life of 3 minutes. Atomic number 102. See table at **element.** [After Alfred Bernhard NOBEL.]

Nobel Prize *n.* Any of the six international prizes awarded annually by the Nobel Foundation for outstanding achievements in the fields of physics, chemistry, physiology or medicine, literature, and economics and for the promotion of world peace. [After Alfred Bernhard NOBEL.]

no·bil·i·ar·y (nō-bĭl'ē-ĕr'ē, -bĭl'yə-rē) *adj.* Of or relating to the nobility. [French *nobiliaire,* from Latin *nōbilis,* noble. See NOBLE.]

nobiliary particle *n.* A preposition used as a mark of noble rank before a title or surname, as German *van* in *Ludwig van Beethoven* and French *de* in *Simone de Beauvoir.*

no·bil·i·ty (nō-bĭl'ĭ-tē) *n., pl.* **-ties.** **1.** A class of persons distinguished by high birth or rank and in Great Britain including dukes and duchesses, marquises and marchionesses, earls and countesses, viscounts and viscountesses, and barons and baronesses: *"The old English nobility of office made way for the Norman nobility of faith and landed wealth"* (Winston S. Churchill). **2.** Noble rank or status: *Congress may not grant titles of nobility.* **3.** The state or quality of being exalted in character. [Middle English *nobilite,* the quality of being noble, from Old French, from Latin *nōbilitās,* from *nōbilis,* noble. See NOBLE.]

no·ble (nō'bəl) *adj.* **-bler, -blest.** **1.** Possessing hereditary rank in a political system or social class derived from a feudalistic stage of a country's development. **2.a.** Having or showing qualities of high moral character, such as courage, generosity, or honor: *a noble spirit.* **b.** Proceeding from or indicative of such a character; showing magnanimity: *"What poor an instrument/May do a noble deed!"* (Shakespeare). **3.** Grand and stately in appearance; majestic: *"a mighty Spanish chestnut, bare now of leaves, but in summer a noble tree"* (Richard Jeffries). **4.** *Chemistry.* Inactive or inert. **—noble** *n.* **1.** A member of the nobility. **2.** A gold coin formerly used in England, worth half of a mark. [Middle English, from Old French, from Latin *nōbilis.* See **gnō-** in Appendix.] **—no′ble·ness** *n.* **—no′bly** *adv.*

noble gas *n.* Any of the elements in Group O of the periodic table, including helium, neon, argon, krypton, xenon, and radon, which are monatomic and with limited exceptions chemically inert. Also called *inert gas.*

no·ble·man (nō′bəl-mən) *n.* A man of noble rank.

noble metal *n.* A metal or an alloy, such as gold, that is highly resistant to oxidation and corrosion.

noble rot *n.* A parasitic fungus *(Botrytis cinerea)* that attacks ripe grapes and causes an increase in their sugar content. Certain wines, such as the French Sauternes and the Hungarian Tokay, are produced from such grapes.

no·blesse (nō-blĕs′) *n.* **1.** Noble birth or condition. **2.** The members of the nobility, especially the French nobility. [Middle English, from Old French, from *noble,* noble, from Latin *nōbilis.* See NOBLE.]

noblesse o·blige (ō-blēzh′) *n.* Benevolent, honorable behavior considered to be the responsibility of persons of high birth or rank. [French, nobility obligates : *noblesse,* nobility + *oblige,* third person sing. present tense of *obliger,* to obligate.]

no·ble·wom·an (nō′bəl-wo͝om′ən) *n.* A woman of noble rank.

no·bod·y (nō′bŏd′ē, -bŭd′ē, -bə-dē) *pron.* No person; not anyone: *Nobody told you to go.* **—nobody** *n., pl.* **-ies.** A person of no importance or influence.

no·cent (nō′sənt) *adj.* Causing injury; harmful. [Middle English *nocent,* guilty, from Latin *nocēns, nocent-,* present participle of *nocēre,* to harm. See **nek-**[1] in Appendix.]

no·ci·cep·tive (nō′sĭ-sĕp′tĭv) *adj.* **1.** Causing pain. Used of a stimulus. **2.** Caused by or responding to a painful stimulus: *a nociceptive spinal reflex.* [From NOCICEPTOR.]

no·ci·cep·tor (nō′sĭ-sĕp′tər) *n.* A sensory receptor that responds to pain. [Latin *nocēre,* to hurt; see NOCENT + (RE)CEPTOR.]

nock (nŏk) *n.* **1.** The groove at either end of a bow for holding the bowstring. **2.** The notch in the end of an arrow that fits on the bowstring. **—nock** *tr.v.* **nocked, nock·ing, nocks. 1.** To put a nock in (a bow or an arrow). **2.** To fit (an arrow) to a bowstring. [Middle English *nokke.*]

noct– *pref.* Variant of **nocti–.**

noc·tam·bu·lism (nŏk-tăm′byə-lĭz′əm) also **noc·tam·bu·la·tion** (-tăm′byə-lā′shən) *n.* See **sleepwalking.** [NOCT(I)– + Latin *ambulāre,* to walk + –ISM.] **—noc·tam′bu·list** *n.*

nocti– or **noct–** *pref.* Night: *noctilucent.* [New Latin, from Latin *nox, noct-,* night. See **nekʷ-t-** in Appendix.]

noc·ti·lu·ca (nŏk′tə-lo͞o′kə) *n.* Any of various bioluminescent dinoflagellates of the genus *Noctiluca* that when grouped in large numbers make the sea phosphorescent. [New Latin *Noctilūca,* genus name, from Latin *noctilūca,* lantern, moon : *nocti-,* nocti- + *lūcēre,* to shine; see **leuk-** in Appendix.]

noc·ti·lu·cent (nŏk′tə-lo͞o′sənt) *adj.* Luminous at night. Used especially of certain high clouds.

noc·tu·id (nŏk′cho͞o-ĭd) *n.* Any of numerous, usually dull-colored night-flying moths of the family Noctuidae, having a well-developed proboscis for sucking nectar and larvae such as the cutworms and armyworms that are destructive to young trees and other crops. Also called *owlet moth.* **—noctuid** *adj.* Of, relating to, or belonging to the family Noctuidae. [From New Latin *Noctuidae,* family name, from *Noctua,* type genus, from Latin *noctua,* night owl. See **nekʷ-t-** in Appendix.]

noc·tule (nŏk′cho͞ol′) *n.* A large, reddish-brown insectivorous bat of the genus *Nyctalus,* found in Eurasia, Indonesia, and the Philippines and typically dwelling in the hollows of trees. [French, from Italian *nottola,* bat, owl, from Late Latin *noctula,* from Latin, diminutive of *noctua,* night owl. See **nekʷ-t-** in Appendix.]

noc·turn (nŏk′tûrn′) *n.* Any of the three canonical divisions of the office of matins. [Middle English *nocturne,* from Medieval Latin *nocturna,* from Latin, feminine of *nocturnus,* of the night. See NOCTURNAL.]

noc·tur·nal (nŏk-tûr′nəl) *adj.* **1.** Of, relating to, or occurring in the night: *nocturnal stillness.* **2.** *Botany.* Having flowers that open during the night. **3.** *Zoology.* Most active at night: *nocturnal animals.* [Middle English, from Old French, from Late Latin *nocturnālis,* from Latin *nocturnus,* from *nox, noct-,* night. See **nekʷ-t-** in Appendix.] **—noc·tur′nal·ly** *adv.*

noc·turne (nŏk′tûrn′) *n.* **1.** A painting of a night scene. **2.** *Music.* An instrumental composition of a pensive, dreamy mood, especially one for the piano. [French, from Old French, nocturnal, from Latin *nocturnus.* See NOCTURNAL.]

noc·u·ous (nŏk′yo͞o-əs) *adj.* Harmful; noxious. [From Latin *nocuus,* from *nocēre,* to harm. See **nek-**[1] in Appendix.] **—noc′u·ous·ly** *adv.*

nod (nŏd) *v.* **nod·ded, nod·ding, nods.** *—intr.* **1.** To lower and raise the head quickly, as in agreement or acknowledgment. **2.** To let the head fall forward when sleepy; doze momentarily: *nodded off on the train.* **3.** To be careless or momentarily inattentive as if sleepy; lapse: *Even Homer nods.* **4.** To sway, move up and down, or droop, as flowers in the wind. *—tr.* **1.** To lower and raise (the head) quickly in agreement or acknowledgment. **2.** To express by lowering and raising the head: *He nodded his agreement.* **3.** To summon, guide, or send by nodding the head: *The chairperson nodded us into the room.* **—nod** *n.* **1.** A forward or up-and-down movement of the head, usually expressive of drowsiness or agreement: *gave a nod of affirmation.* **2.** An indication of approval or assent: *The contestant got the nod from the judges.* [Middle English *nodden;* perhaps akin to Middle High German *notten.*] **—nod′der** *n.*

nod·al (nōd′l) *adj.* Of, relating to, resembling, being, or situated near or at a node. **—nod′al·ly** *adv.*

nod·ding pogonia (nŏd′ĭng) *n.* A North American orchid *(Triphora trianthophora)* having nodding flower buds and ascending, pink or white flowers.

nod·dle (nŏd′l) *n.* The head. [Middle English *noddel,* back of the head, perhaps from Latin *nōdulus,* lump, knob. See NODULE.]

nod·dy (nŏd′ē) *n., pl.* **-dies. 1.** A dunce or fool; a simpleton. **2.** Any of several terns of the genera *Anous* and *Micranous,* found in tropical waters and having a dark brown or black color with a white or gray head. [Perhaps from obsolete *noddy,* foolish, possibly from NOD.]

node (nōd) *n.* **1.** A knob, knot, protuberance, or swelling. **2.a.** *Botany.* The point on a stem where a leaf is attached or has been attached; a joint. **b.** See **knot**[1] (sense 7). **3.** *Physics.* A point or region of virtually zero amplitude in a periodic system. **4.** *Mathematics.* The point at which a continuous curve crosses itself. **5.** *Computer Science.* A terminal in a computer network. **6.** *Astronomy.* **a.** Either of two diametrically opposite points at which the orbit of a planet intersects the ecliptic. **b.** Either of two points at which the orbit of a satellite intersects the orbital plane of a planet. [Middle English, lump in the flesh, from Latin *nōdus,* knot. See **ned-** in Appendix.]

node of Ran·vier (rän′vyā, rän-vyā′, räɴ-) *n., pl.* **nodes of Ranvier.** A constriction in the myelin sheath, occurring at varying intervals along the length of a nerve fiber. [After Louis Antoine *Ranvier* (1835–1922), French histologist.]

no·di (nō′dī) *n.* Plural of **nodus.**

no·dose (nō′dōs′) *adj.* Characterized by or having many nodes or protuberances, jointed or knobby at intervals. **—no·dos′i·ty** (-dŏs′ĭ-tē) *n.*

nod·ule (nŏj′o͞ol) *n.* **1.** A small knotlike protuberance. **2.** *Anatomy.* A small mass of tissue or aggregation of cells. **3.** *Botany.* A small knoblike outgrowth, as those found on the roots of many leguminous plants. **4.** *Mineralogy.* A small rounded lump of a mineral or mixture of minerals, usually harder than the surrounding rock or sediment. [Middle English, from Latin *nōdulus,* diminutive of *nōdus,* knot. See **ned-** in Appendix.] **—nod′u·lar** (nŏj′ə-lər), **nod′u·lose′** (-lōs′) , **nod′u·lous** (-ləs) *adj.*

no·dus (nō′dəs) *n., pl.* **-di** (-dī). A difficult situation or problem; a complication. [Latin *nōdus,* knot. See **ned-** in Appendix.]

NOED also **N.O.E.D.** *abbr.* New Oxford English Dictionary.

No·ël also **No·el** (nō-ĕl′) *n.* **1.** Christmas. **2. noël** also **noel.** A Christmas carol. [Middle English *noel,* from Old French, variant of *nael,* from Latin *nātālis (diēs),* (day) of birth, from *nātus,* past participle of *nāscī,* to be born. See **gene-** in Appendix.]

No·el-Ba·ker (nō′əl-bā′kər), **Philip John.** 1889–1982. British politician who helped draft the Covenant of the League of Nations (1919) and the United Nations Charter (1945). He won the 1959 Nobel Peace Prize.

noes (nōz) *n.* Plural of **no**[1]**.**

no·e·sis (nō-ē′sĭs) *n.* *Psychology.* The cognitive process; cognition. [Greek *noēsis,* understanding, from *noein,* to perceive, from *nous,* mind.]

no·et·ic (nō-ĕt′ĭk) *adj.* Of, relating to, originating in, or apprehended by the intellect. [Greek *noētikos,* from *noēsis,* understanding. See NOESIS.]

no-fault (nō′fôlt′) *adj.* **1.** Of, indicating, or being a system of motor vehicle insurance in which accident victims are compensated by their insurance companies without assignment of blame. **2.** *Law.* Of, indicating, or being a type of divorce in which blame is assigned to neither party.

no-frills (nō′frĭlz′) *adj.* *Informal.* Marked by the absence of extra or special features; basic: *no-frills housing; no-frills airline service.*

nog[1] (nŏg) *n.* **1.** A wooden block built into a masonry wall to hold nails that support joinery structures. **2.** A wooden peg or pin. [Origin unknown.]

nog[2] (nŏg) *n.* Eggnog.

No·gal·es (nō-găl′ĭs, -gä′lĭs). A city of southern Arizona south of Tucson on the Mexican border adjacent to **Nogales,** Mexico. Both cities are ports of entry and tourist centers. Nogales, Arizona, has a population of 15,683; Nogales, Mexico, has 14,254 inhabitants.

nog·gin (nŏg′ĭn) *n.* **1.** A small mug or cup. **2.** A unit of liquid measure equal to one quarter of a pint. **3.** *Slang.* The human head. [Origin unknown.]

no-go (nō′gō′) *adj.* Not in a suitable condition for proceeding

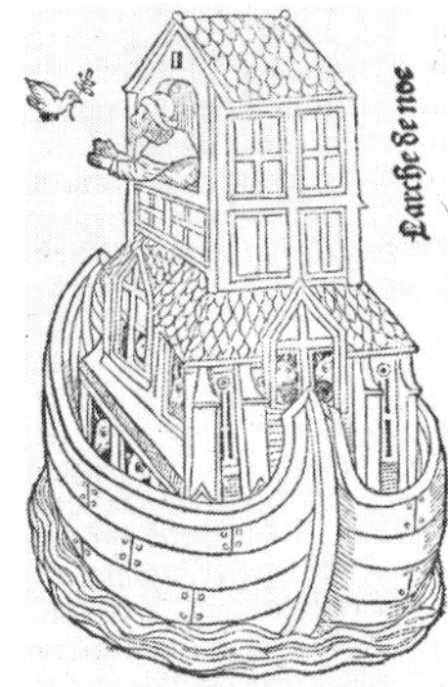

Noah
15th-century French rendering of Noah in his ark, from *La Mer des Histoires*

Alfred Nobel

ă pat	oi boy
ā pay	ou out
âr care	o͝o took
ä father	o͞o boot
ĕ pet	ŭ cut
ē be	ûr urge
ĭ pit	th thin
ī pie	*th* this
îr pier	hw which
ŏ pot	zh vision
ō toe	ə about, item
ô paw	♦ regionalism

Stress marks: ′ (primary); ′ (secondary), as in **dictionary** (dĭk′shə-nĕr′ē)

or functioning properly: *The space launch was no-go.* **—no-go** *n., pl.* **no-goes.** A situation in which planned operations cannot be effectuated, as in the case of the launch of spacecraft: *The flight is a no-go because of technical problems.*

no-good (nō′go͝od′) *adj.* Having no value, use, merit, or virtue. **—no-good** *n.* One that is worthless.

No·gu·chi (nō-go͞o′chē), **Hideyo.** 1876–1928. Japanese-born American bacteriologist who discovered the cause and worked toward a treatment of syphilis and yellow fever.

Noguchi, Isamu. Born 1904. American sculptor noted for his abstract works of bronze, stone, and terra cotta.

Noh (nō) *n.* Variant of **No**[1].

no-hit (nō′hĭt′) *adj. Baseball.* Of, relating to, or being a no-hitter.

no-hit·ter (nō′hĭt′ər) *n. Baseball.* A game in which one pitcher allows the opposing team no hits.

no-holds-barred (nō′hōldz′bärd′) *adj. Informal.* Open and unrestrained: *"These paintings and charcoal drawings . . . are slightly tame compared with the no-holds-barred forcefulness of his self-generated vision"* (Christopher Andreae).

no·how (nō′hou′) *adv. Non-Standard.* In no way; not at all.

noil (noil) *n.* A short fiber combed from long fibers during the preparation of textile yarns. [Perhaps from Middle English **noil,* from Old French *noel,* from Medieval Latin *nōdellus,* from Latin, diminutive of *nōdus,* knot. See NODE.]

noise (noiz) *n.* **1.a.** Sound or a sound that is loud, unpleasant, unexpected, or undesired. **b.** Sound or a sound of any kind: *The only noise was the wind in the pines.* **2.** A loud outcry or commotion: *"Whatever the fate of Eureka, it should have some positive effects, even if modest in comparison to its political noise, for the technological cooperation of European firms"* (Foreign Affairs). **3.** *Physics.* A disturbance, especially a random and persistent disturbance, that obscures or reduces the clarity of a signal. **4.** *Computer Science.* Irrelevant or meaningless data generated by a computer along with desired data. **5.** *Informal.* **a.** A complaint or protest. **b.** Rumor; talk. **c. noises.** Remarks or actions intended to convey a specific impression or to attract attention: *"The U.S. is making appropriately friendly noises to the new Socialist Government"* (Flora Lewis). **—noise** *v.* **noised, nois·ing, nois·es.** *—tr.* To spread the rumor or report of. *—intr.* **1.** To talk much or volubly. **2.** To be noisy; make noise. [Middle English, from Old French, perhaps from Vulgar Latin **nausea,* discomfort, from Latin *nausea,* seasickness. See NAUSEA.]

SYNONYMS: *noise, din, racket, uproar, pandemonium, hullabaloo, hubbub, clamor, babel.* These nouns refer to loud, confused, or disagreeable sound or sounds. *Noise* is the least specific: *deafened by the noise in the subway; the noise of cannon fire.* A *din* is a jumble of loud, usually discordant sounds: *The din in the factory ends abruptly when the noon whistle sounds. Racket* is loud, distressing noise: *Can you imagine the racket made by a line of empty trailer trucks rolling along cobblestone streets? Uproar, pandemonium,* and *hullabaloo* imply disorderly tumult together with loud, bewildering sound: *"The evening uproar of the howling monkeys burst out"* (W.H. Hudson). *"When night came, it brought with it a pandemonium of dancing and whooping, drumming and feasting"* (Francis Parkman). *The first performance of the iconoclastic composition caused a tremendous hullabaloo in the audience. Hubbub* emphasizes turbulent activity, as of those engaged in commerce, and concomitant din: *We couldn't hear the starting announcement above the hubbub of bettors, speculators, tipsters, and touts. Clamor* is loud, usually sustained noise, as of a public outcry of dissatisfaction: *"not in the clamor of the crowded street"* (Henry Wadsworth Longfellow). *The debate was interrupted by a clamor of opposition. Babel* stresses confusion of vocal sounds arising from simultaneous utterance and random mixture of languages: *My outstanding memory of the diplomatic reception is of elegantly dressed guests chattering in a babel of tongues.*

WORD HISTORY: For those who find that too much noise makes them ill, it will come as no surprise that the word *noise* possibly can be traced back to the Latin word *nausea,* "seasickness, feeling of sickness." Our words *nausea* and *noise* are doublets, that is, words borrowed in different forms from the same word. *Nausea,* first recorded probably before 1425, was borrowed directly from Latin. *Noise,* on the other hand, first recorded around the beginning of the 13th century, came to us through Old French, probably ultimately from Latin, which explains its change in form. The unrecorded change in sense probably took place in Vulgar Latin. Old French *nois,* descended from Latin *nausea,* meant "sound, din, uproar, quarrel," all senses that came into Middle English with the word. *Noise,* however, is an example of how words can change for the better, for a noise can be pleasant as well as unpleasant, as in the sentence "The only noise was the wind in the pines."

noise·less (noiz′lĭs) *adj.* Making or marked by no noise. See Synonyms at **still**[1]. **—noise′less·ly** *adv.* **—noise′less·ness** *n.*

noise·mak·er (noiz′mā′kər) *n.* One that makes noise, especially a device such as a horn or rattle used to make noise at a party. **—noise′mak′ing** *n.*

noise pollution *n.* Environmental noise that is annoying, distracting, or physically harmful. Also called *sound pollution.*

noi·sette (nwä-zĕt′) *n.* A small round piece of meat, especially loin or fillet of lamb, veal, or pork. **—noisette** *adj.* Made or flavored with hazelnuts. [French, from Old French, diminutive of *nois,* nut, from Latin *nux.*]

noi·some (noi′səm) *adj.* **1.** Offensive to the point of arousing disgust; foul: *a noisome odor.* **2.** Harmful or dangerous: *noisome fumes.* [Middle English *noiesom* : *noie,* harm (short for *anoi,* annoyance, from Old French, from *anoier,* to annoy; see ANNOY) + *-som,* adj. suff.; see –SOME[1].] **—noi′some·ly** *adv.* **—noi′some·ness** *n.*

nois·y (noi′zē) *adj.* **-i·er, -i·est. 1.** Making noise: *a small, noisy dog.* **2.** Full of, characterized by, or accompanied by noise: *a noisy cafeteria.* **—nois′i·ly** *adv.* **—nois′i·ness** *n.*

no·lens vo·lens (nō′lĕnz vō′lĕnz, nō′lĕns wō′lĕns) *adv.* Whether willing or unwilling. [Latin *nōlēns volēns* : *nōlēns,* present participle of *nolle,* to be unwilling + *volēns,* present participle of *velle,* to wish, be willing.]

no·li-me-tan·ge·re (nō′lē-mē-tăn′jə-rē, nō′lī-) *n.* **1.** A warning or prohibition against meddling, touching, or interfering. **2.** A representation of Jesus appearing to Mary Magdalen after his resurrection. [Late Latin *nōlī mē tangere,* do not touch me (Jesus's words to Mary Magdalene, John 20:17) : Latin *nōlī,* do not, imperative of *nolle,* to be unwilling + Latin *mē,* me + Latin *tangere,* to touch.]

nol·le pros·e·qui (nŏl′ē prŏs′ĭ-kwī′, -kwē′) *n. Abbr.* **nol. pros.** *Law.* A declaration that the plaintiff in a civil case or the prosecutor in a criminal case will drop prosecution of all or part of a suit or an indictment. [Latin *nolle prōsequī,* to be unwilling to pursue : *nolle,* to be unwilling + *prōsequī,* to pursue.]

no·lo (nō′lō) *n., pl.* **-los.** *Law.* Nolo contendere.

no-load (nō′lōd′) *adj. Business.* Sold directly to customers at net asset value without a sales commission: *a no-load mutual fund.*

no·lo con·ten·de·re (nō′lō kən-tĕn′də-rē) *n. Law.* A plea made by the defendant in a criminal action that is substantially but not technically an admission of guilt and subjects the defendant to punishment but permits denial of the alleged facts in other proceedings. [Latin *nōlō contendere,* I do not wish to contend : *nōlō,* first person sing. present tense of *nolle,* to be unwilling + *contendere,* to contend.]

no-lose (nō′lo͞oz′) *adj. Slang.* Certain to end happily or successfully: *"It is a no-lose situation: The hungry get the food, the donors get a tax deduction"* (Los Angeles Times).

nol-pros (nŏl′prŏs′) *tr.v.* **-prossed, -pros·sing, -pros·ses.** *Law.* To drop prosecution of by entering a nolle prosequi in court records.

nol. pros. *abbr. Law.* Nolle prosequi.

nom. *abbr.* Nominative.

no·ma (nō′mə) *n.* A severe, often gangrenous inflammation of the mouth or genitals, occurring usually after an infectious disease and found most often in children in poor hygienic or malnourished condition. [Latin *nomē,* ulcer, from Greek. See **nem-** in Appendix.]

no·mad (nō′măd′) *n.* **1.** A member of a group of people who have no fixed home and move according to the seasons from place to place in search of food, water, and grazing land. **2.** A person with no fixed residence who roams about; a wanderer. [French *nomade,* from Latin *nomas, nomad-,* from Greek *nomas,* wandering in search of pasture. See **nem-** in Appendix.] **—no·mad′ic** *adj.* **—no·mad′i·cal·ly** *adv.* **—no′mad′ism** *n.*

no man's land (mănz) *n.* **1.** Land under dispute by two opposing parties, especially the field of battle between the lines of two opposing entrenched armies. **2.** An area of uncertainty or ambiguity. **3.** An unclaimed or unowned piece of land.

nom·ar·chy (nŏm′är′kē) *n., pl.* **-chies.** Any of the administrative provinces of the modern Greek state. [Modern Greek *nomarkhia,* from Greek, district : *nomos,* district; see NOME + *-arkhia,* -archy.]

nom·bril (nŏm′brəl) *n. Heraldry.* The point on an escutcheon between the fess point and the base point; the midpoint in the lower half of the escutcheon. [French, from Old French, from *(un) ombril,* (a) navel, from Vulgar Latin **umbilīculus,* from Latin, diminutive of *umbilīcus.* See **nobh-** in Appendix.]

nom de guerre (nŏm′ də gâr′) *n., pl.* **noms de guerre** (nŏm′). A fictitious name; a pseudonym. [French : *nom,* name + *de,* of + *guerre,* war.]

nom de plume (nŏm′ də plo͞om′) *n., pl.* **noms de plume** (nŏm′). See **pen name.** [French : *nom,* name + *de,* of + *plume,* pen.]

nome (nōm) *n.* **1.** A province of Pharaonic, Hellenistic, and Roman Egypt. **2.** A nomarchy. [Greek *nomos,* district, custom. See **nem-** in Appendix.]

Nome (nōm). A city of western Alaska on Norton Sound and the southern coast of Seward Peninsula. It was founded as a gold-mining camp in 1896 and was an important center of the Alaskan gold rush from 1899 to 1903. Population, 2,301.

no·men·cla·tor (nō′mən-klā′tər) *n.* One who assigns names, as in scientific classification. [Latin *nōmenclātor,* a slave who accompanied his master to tell him the names of people he met, variant of *nōmenculātor* : *nōmen,* name; see **nō-men-** in Appendix + *calātor,* servant, crier (from *calāre,* to call; see **kelə-**[2] in Appendix).]

no·men·cla·to·ri·al (nō′mən-klə-tôr′ē-əl, -tōr′-) *adj.* Of or relating to nomenclature.

no·men·cla·ture (nō′mən-klā′chər, nō-mĕn′klə-) *n.* **1.** A system of names used in an art or a science: *the nomenclature of mineralogy.* **2.** The procedure of assigning names to the kinds and groups of organisms listed in a taxonomic classification: *the rules of nomenclature in botany.* [Latin *nōmenclātūra,* from *nōmenclātor,* nomenclator. See NOMENCLATOR.]

no·men·kla·tu·ra (nō′mən-klä-to͝or′ə, nô′myĕn-klä-to͝or′ä) *n.* **1.** The system of patronage to senior positions in the bureaucracy of the Soviet Union and some other Communist states, controlled by committees at various levels of the Communist Party. **2.** *(used with a pl. verb).* The lists of appointees matching the lists of patronage positions in such a system. **3.** *(used with a pl. verb).* The appointees to these positions: *"The . . . nomenklatura are perceived as draft-immune"* (Anthony Arnold). **4.** The stratified, privileged class composed of these appointees. [Russian, from Latin *nōmenclātūra,* list of names. See NOMENCLATURE.]

nom·i·nal (nŏm′ə-nəl) *adj.* **1.a.** Of, resembling, relating to, or consisting of a name or names. **b.** Assigned to or bearing a person's name: *nominal shares.* **2.** Existing in name only. **3.** *Philosophy.* Of or relating to nominalism. **4.** Insignificantly small; trifling: *a nominal sum.* **5.** *Business.* **a.** Of, relating to, or being the amount or face value of a sum of money or a stock certificate, for example, and not the purchasing power or market value. **b.** Of, relating to, or being the rate of interest or return without adjustment for compounding or inflation. **6.** *Grammar.* Of or relating to a noun or word group that functions as a noun. **7.** *Aerospace & Engineering.* According to plan or design: *a nominal flight check.* **—nominal** *n.* *Grammar.* A word or group of words functioning as a noun. [Middle English *nominalle,* of nouns, from Latin *nōminālis,* of names, from *nōmen, nōmin-,* name. See **nŏmen-** in Appendix.] **—nom′i·nal·ly** *adv.*

nom·i·nal·ism (nŏm′ə-nə-lĭz′əm) *n.* *Philosophy.* The doctrine holding that abstract concepts, general terms, or universals have no objective reference but exist only as names. **—nom′i·nal·ist** *n.* **—nom′i·nal·is′tic** *adj.*

nominal quote *n.* The approximate price of a security when there is no firm bid or asking price. Also called *subject quote.*

nominal value *n.* See **par value.**

nominal wages *pl.n.* Wages measured in terms of money paid, not in terms of purchasing power.

nom·i·nate (nŏm′ə-nāt′) *tr.v.* **-nat·ed, -nat·ing, -nates. 1.** To propose by name as a candidate, especially for election. **2.** To designate or appoint to an office, a responsibility, or an honor. See Synonyms at **appoint.** [Latin *nōmināre, nōmināt-,* to name, from *nōmen, nōmin-,* name. See **nŏ-men-** in Appendix.] **—nom′i·na′tor** *n.*

nom·i·na·tion (nŏm′ə-nā′shən) *n.* **1.** The act or an instance of appointing a person to office. **2.** The act or an instance of submitting a name for candidacy or appointment. **3.** The state of being nominated.

nom·i·na·tive (nŏm′ə-nā′tĭv) *adj.* *Abbr.* **nom. 1.a.** Appointed to office. **b.** Nominated as a candidate for office. **2.** Having or bearing a person's name: *nominative shares.* **3.** (-nə-tĭv). *Grammar.* Of, relating to, or belonging to a case of the subject of a finite verb (as *I* in *I wrote the letter*) and of words identified with the subject of a copula, such as a predicate nominative (as *children* in *These are his children*). **—nominative** (-nə-tĭv) *n.* *Grammar.* The nominative case.

nom·i·nee (nŏm′ə-nē′) *n.* **1.** One who has been nominated to an office or for a candidacy. **2.** A person or an organization in whose name a security is registered though true ownership is held by another party. [NOMIN(ATE) + -EE[1].]

nom·o·graph (nŏm′ə-grăf′, nō′mə-) or **nom·o·gram** (-grăm′) *n.* **1.** A graph consisting of three coplanar curves, each graduated for a different variable so that a straight line cutting all three curves intersects the related values of each variable. **2.** A chart representing numerical relationships. [Greek *nomos,* law; see **nem-** in Appendix + -GRAPH.] **—nom′o·graph′ic** *adj.* **—no·mog′ra·phy** (nō-mŏg′rə-fē) *n.*

no·mol·o·gy (nō-mŏl′ə-jē) *n.* The study and discovery of general physical and logical laws. [Greek *nomos,* law; see **nem-** in Appendix + -LOGY.] **—nom′o·log′ic** (nŏm′ə-lŏj′ĭk, nō′mə-), **nom′o·log′i·cal** (-ĭ-kəl) *adj.* **—nom′o·log′i·cal·ly** *adv.* **—no·mol′o·gist** *n.*

nom·o·thet·ic (nŏm′ə-thĕt′ĭk) or **nom·o·thet·ic·al** (-ĭk-əl) *adj.* **1.** Of or relating to lawmaking; legislative. **2.** Based on system of law. **3.** Of or relating to the philosophy of law. **4.** Of or relating to the study or discovery of general scientific laws. [Greek *nomothetikos* : *nomos,* law; see **nem-** in Appendix + *thetikos,* thetic; see THETIC.] **—nom·o·thet′i·cal·ly** *adv.*

-nomy *suff.* A system of laws governing or a body of knowledge about a specified field: *aeronomy.* [Greek *-nomia,* from *nomos,* law. See **nem-** in Appendix.]

non- *pref.* Not: *noncombatant.* [Middle English, from Old French, from Latin *nōn,* not. See **ne** in Appendix.]

nona- *pref.* Ninth; nine: *nonagon.* [From Latin *nōnus,* ninth. See **newn̥** in Appendix.]

non·age (nŏn′ĭj, nō′nĭj) *n.* **1.** The period during which one is legally underage. **2.** A period of immaturity: *"The bravest achievements were always accomplished in the nonage of a nation"* (Thomas Paine). [Middle English *nounage,* from Anglo-Norman, variant of Old French *nonaage* : *non-,* non- + *aage,* age; see AGE.]

non·a·ge·nar·i·an (nŏn′ə-jə-nâr′ē-ən, nō′nə-) *n.* A person 90 years old or between 90 and 100 years old. [From Latin *nōnāgēnārius,* from *nōnāgēnī,* ninety each, from *nōnāgintā,* ninety : *nōnus,* ninth; see NONA- + *-gintā,* ten times; see **dekm̥** in Appendix.] **—non′a·ge·nar′i·an** *adj.*

non·ag·gres·sion (nŏn′ə-grĕsh′ən) *n.* Lack of intention to show aggression against a foreign government or nation. *—attributive.* Often used to modify another noun: *a nonaggression policy; nonaggression treaties.*

non·a·gon (nŏn′ə-gŏn′, nō′nə-) *n.* A polygon with nine sides.

non·al·co·hol·ic (nŏn′ăl-kə-hô′lĭk, -hŏl′ĭk) *n.* A beverage usually containing less than 0.5 percent alcohol by volume. **—nonalcoholic** *adj.* **1.** Of, relating to, or being a beverage whose alcohol content is very low or negligible. **2.** Containing no alcohol: *nonalcoholic medication.* **3.** Dealcoholized.

non·a·ligned (nŏn′ə-līnd′) *adj.* Not allied with any other nation or bloc; neutral: *A group of 20 nonaligned nations urged a treaty to ban space weapons.* **—non′a·lign′ment** *n.*

non·a·no·ic acid (nŏn′ə-nō′ĭk) *n.* See **pelargonic acid.** [*nonane,* a paraffin (NONA- + -ANE, so called because it is ninth in the methane series) + -OIC.]

non·ap·pear·ance (nŏn′ə-pîr′əns) *n.* *Law.* **1.** Failure of a defendant to appear in an action. **2.** Failure of a witness or party to appear in response to a subpoena or notice.

non·as·sess·a·ble (nŏn′ə-sĕs′ə-bəl) *adj.* **1.** Impossible to estimate, set, or determine: *nonassessable damages.* **2.** Of or relating to capital stock for which owners cannot be assessed additional funds to cover any liabilities of the firm and therefore cannot lose any more than their original investments.

non·bank (nŏn′băngk′) *adj.* Of, relating to, or done by a business or an institution that is not a bank but performs similar services.

non·be·liev·er (nŏn′bĕ-lē′vər) *n.* One who does not believe or have faith, as in God or a philosophy.

non·black or **non-Black** or **non-black** (nŏn-blăk′) *n.* A person who is not Black. **—non·black′** *adj.*

non·book (nŏn′bo͝ok′) *n.* A book having little or no literary merit or substance, often published to exploit a fad. **—nonbook** *adj.* Of, relating to, or being something other than a book, such as microfilm or microfiche in a library.

non·busi·ness (nŏn′bĭz′nĭs) *adj.* **1.** Unrelated to business or industry. **2.** Unrelated to one's own business or employment.

non·call·a·ble (nŏn-kô′lə-bəl) *adj.* *Abbr.* **NC** *Business.* Of or relating to a provision of some bond and preferred stock issues that prohibits the issuer from redeeming the security before a certain date or until maturity.

non·ca·lor·ic (nŏn′kə-lôr′ĭk, -lŏr′-) *adj.* Having few or no calories: *a noncaloric soft drink.*

non·can·di·date (nŏn-kăn′dĭ-dāt′, -dĭt) *n.* *Informal.* A person who has announced that he or she is not a candidate, especially for political office.

nonce (nŏns) *n.* The present or particular occasion: *"Her tendency to discover a touch of sadness had for the nonce disappeared"* (Theodore Dreiser). [From Middle English *for the nones,* for the occasion, alteration of *for then anes* : *for,* for; see FOR + *then,* neuter dative sing. of *the;* see THE[1] + *ones, anes,* once; see ONCE.]

nonce word *n.* A word occurring, invented, or used just for a particular occasion; for example, the word *mileconsuming* in *"the wagon beginning to fall into its slow and mileconsuming clatter"* (William Faulkner).

non·cha·lance (nŏn′shə-läns′) *n.* Casual lack of concern: *"The contemptuous nonchalance of her trailed hand irritated him"* (Elizabeth Bowen).

non·cha·lant (nŏn′shə-länt′) *adj.* Seeming to be coolly unconcerned or indifferent. See Synonyms at **cool.** [French, from Old French, present participle of *nonchaloir,* to be unconcerned : *non-,* non- + *chaloir,* to cause concern to (from Latin *calēre,* to be warm, heat up; see **kelə-**[1] in Appendix).] **—non′cha·lant′ly** *adv.*

WORD HISTORY: A nonchalant person is not likely to become warm or heated about anything, a fact that is underscored by the etymology of the word *nonchalant. Non-,* the first part of the word, is easy to spot as a familiar negative prefix; since this word was formed in Old French, we have *non-,* the Old French descendant of Latin *nōn-.* The second element, *chalant,* is the Old French present participle of the verb *chaloir,* meaning "to be concerned." This in turn came from the Latin word *calēre,* which from its concrete sense "to be hot or warm" developed the figurative sense "to be roused or fired with hope, zeal, or anger." The word *nonchalant* is first recorded in English before 1734, although French *nonchalance,* a derivative of French *nonchalant,* seems to have entered English first. English *nonchalance* is first recorded in 1678.

non·chro·mo·som·al (nŏn′krō-mə-sō′məl) *adj.* Not situated on or involving a chromosome: *nonchromosomal DNA.*

non·cit·i·zen (nŏn-sĭt′ĭ-zən) *n.* See **alien** (sense 1).

non·clear·ing member (nŏn-klîr′ĭng) *n.* A member of a securities exchange that does not belong to the exchange's clearing facility but pays another firm to provide the service.

non·com (nŏn′kŏm′) *n.* *Informal.* A noncommissioned officer.

ă **pat**	oi **boy**
ā **pay**	ou **out**
âr **care**	o͝o **took**
ä **father**	o͞o **boot**
ĕ **pet**	ŭ **cut**
ē **be**	ûr **urge**
ĭ **pit**	th **thin**
ī **pie**	*th* **this**
îr **pier**	hw **which**
ŏ **pot**	zh **vision**
ō **toe**	ə **about, item**
ô **paw**	♦ **regionalism**

Stress marks: ′ (primary); ′ (secondary), as in **dictionary** (dĭk′shə-nĕr′ē)

non·com·bat·ant (nŏn′kəm-băt′nt, -kŏm′bə-tnt) *n.* **1.** A member of the armed forces, such as a chaplain or surgeon, whose duties lie outside combat. **2.** A civilian in wartime, especially one in a war zone.

non·com·mis·sioned officer (nŏn′kə-mĭsh′ənd) *n. Abbr.* **NCO, N.C.O.** An enlisted member of the armed forces, such as a corporal, sergeant, or petty officer, appointed to a rank conferring leadership over other enlisted personnel.

non·com·mit·tal (nŏn′kə-mĭt′l) *adj.* Refusing commitment to a particular opinion or course of action; not revealing what one feels or thinks: *"His face was the color of a freshly baked pork pie and as noncommittal"* (Thomas Pynchon). **—non′com·mit′tal·ly** *adv.*

non·com·pet·i·tive bid (nŏn′kəm-pĕt′ĭ-tĭv) *n.* A method of purchasing U.S. Treasury bills at the weekly public auction by agreeing to purchase a given amount of securities at the average price set at the auction.

non·com·pli·ance (nŏn′kəm-plī′əns) *n.* Failure or refusal to comply. **—non′com·pli′ant** *adj. & n.*

non com·pos men·tis (nŏn kŏm′pəs mĕn′tĭs) *adj. Law.* Not of sound mind and hence not legally responsible; mentally incompetent. [Latin *nōn compos mentis* : *nōn,* not + *compos,* in control + *mentis,* genitive sing. of *mēns,* mind.]

non·con·duc·tor (nŏn′kən-dŭk′tər) *n.* A material that conducts little or no electricity, heat, or sound.

non·con·form·ist (nŏn′kən-fôr′mĭst) *n.* **1.** One who does not conform to, or refuses to be bound by, accepted beliefs, customs, or practices. **2.** Often **Nonconformist.** A member of a Protestant church not observing the doctrines, usage, or polity of a national or established church, especially the Church of England. **—non′con·form′ist** *adj.* **—non′con·form′ism** *n.*

non·con·form·i·ty (nŏn′kən-fôr′mĭ-tē) *n.* **1.** Refusal or failure to conform to accepted customs, beliefs, or practices. **2.** Often **Nonconformity.** Refusal to accept or conform to the doctrines, usage, or polity of the Church of England.

non·con·trib·u·to·ry (nŏn′kən-trĭb′yə-tôr′ē, -tōr′ē) *adj.* Of or relating to a pension plan in which participating members or employees are not required to support the plan with their own contributions.

non·co·op·er·a·tion (nŏn′kō-ŏp′ə-rā′shən) *n.* Failure or refusal to cooperate, especially nonviolent civil disobedience against a government or an occupying power. **—non′co·op′er·a′tion·ist** *n.* **—non′co·op′er·a·tive** (-ŏp′ər-ə-tĭv, -ŏp′ə-rā′-) *adj.* **—non′co·op′er·a′tor** *n.*

non·count·a·ble noun (nŏn-koun′tə-bəl) *n. Linguistics.* A mass noun.

non·cred·it (nŏn-krĕd′ĭt) *adj.* Of, relating to, or constituting an educational course that does not offer credit toward an academic degree.

non·cus·to·di·al (nŏn′kŭ-stō′dē-əl) *adj.* **1.** Not having custody of one's children after a divorce or separation: *a noncustodial parent.* **2.** Of or relating to a lack of child custody: *noncustodial households.*

non·dair·y (nŏn-dâr′ē) *adj.* Containing no milk or dairy products: *nondairy coffee creamer.*

non·de·duct·i·ble (nŏn′dĭ-dŭk′tə-bəl) *adj.* Not deductible, especially for income-tax purposes.

non·de·nom·i·na·tion·al (nŏn′dĭ-nŏm′ə-nā′shə-nəl) *adj.* Not restricted to or associated with a religious denomination.

non·de·script (nŏn′dĭ-skrĭpt′) *adj.* Lacking distinctive qualities; having no individual character or form: *"This expression gave temporary meaning to a set of features otherwise nondescript"* (Katherine Anne Porter). [NON– + Latin *dēscrīptus,* past participle of *dēscrībere,* to describe; see DESCRIBE.] **—non′de·script′** *n.*

non·de·struc·tive (nŏn′dĭ-strŭk′tĭv) *adj.* Of, relating to, or being a process that does not result in damage to the material under investigation or testing. **—non′de·struc′tive·ly** *adv.*

non·di·rec·tive (nŏn′dĭ-rĕk′tĭv, -dī-) *adj.* Of, relating to, or being a psychotherapeutic or counseling technique in which the therapist takes an unobtrusive role in order to encourage free expression by the client or patient.

non·dis·crim·i·na·tion (nŏn′dĭ-skrĭm′ə-nā′shən) *n.* **1.** Absence of discrimination. **2.** The practice or policy of refraining from discrimination. **—non′dis·crim′i·na·to′ry** (-nə-tôr′ē, -tōr′ē) *adj.*

non·dis·junc·tion (nŏn′dĭs-jŭngk′shən) *n. Biology.* The failure of paired chromosomes or sister chromatids to separate and go to different cells during meiosis. **—non′dis·junc′tion·al** *adj.*

non·dis·tinc·tive (nŏn′dĭ-stĭngk′tĭv) *adj. Linguistics.* Not phonemically distinctive; not serving to distinguish meaning.

non·drink·er (nŏn-drĭng′kər) *n.* One who does not drink alcoholic beverages.

non·dur·a·ble (nŏn-dŏŏr′ə-bəl, -dyŏŏr′-) *adj.* Not enduring; being in a state of constant consumption: *nondurable items such as paper products.* **—nondurable** *n.* A consumable item: *nondurables such as food.*

none (nŭn) *pron.* **1.** No one; not one; nobody: *None dared to do it.* **2.** Not any: *None of my classmates survived the war.* **3.** No part; not any: *none of your business.* **—none** *adv.* **1.** Not at all: *He is none too ill.* **2.** In no way: *The jeans looked none the better for having been washed.* [Middle English, from Old English *nān* : *ne,* no, not; see **ne** in Appendix + *ān,* one; see **oi-no-** in Appendix.]

USAGE NOTE: It is widely asserted that *none* is equivalent to *no one,* and hence requires a singular verb and singular pronoun: *None of the prisoners* was *given his soup.* It is true that *none* is etymologically derived from the Old English word *ān,* "one," but the word has been used as both a singular and a plural noun from Old English onward. The plural use can be found in reputable sources such as the King James Bible, Dryden, and Burke; and H.W. Fowler described the traditional rule as "a mistake." Either a singular or a plural verb is acceptably used in a sentence such as *None of the conspirators has* (or *have*) *been brought to trial.* When *none* is modified by *almost,* however, it is difficult to avoid treating the word as a plural: *Almost none of the officials were* (not *was*) *interviewed by the committee. None* can only be plural in its use in sentences such as *None but his most loyal supporters believe* (not *believes*) *his story.* See Usage Notes at **every, neither.**

non·e·go (nŏn-ē′gō, -ĕg′ō) *n.* All that is not part of the ego or the conscious self. [Translation of German *Nichtich* : *nicht,* not + *Ich,* I, ego.]

non·e·las·tic (nŏn′ĭ-lăs′tĭk) *adj.* Having or exhibiting no elasticity.

non·e·lect·ed (nŏn′ĭ-lĕk′tĭd) *adj.* Having reached an office or an official position without going through the elective process: *powerful nonelected bureaucrats.*

non·en·ti·ty (nŏn-ĕn′tĭ-tē) *n., pl.* **-ties. 1.** A person regarded as being of no importance or significance. **2.** Nonexistence. **3.** Something that does not exist or that exists only in the imagination.

nones (nōnz) *pl.n.* **1.** The ninth day before the ides of a month; in the ancient Roman calendar, the seventh day of March, May, July, or October and the fifth day of the other months. **2.** *Ecclesiastical.* **a.** The fifth of the seven canonical hours. No longer in liturgical use. **b.** The time of day appointed for this service, usually the ninth hour after sunrise. [Middle English, from Old French, from Latin *nōnae,* feminine pl. of *nōnus,* ninth. See **newn̥** in Appendix.]

non·es·sen·tial (nŏn′ĭ-sĕn′shəl) *adj.* **1.** Having little or no importance; not essential. **2.** *Biochemistry.* Being a substance that is required for normal functioning but does not need to be included in the diet because of the body's ability to synthesize it from other nutrients.

none·such also **non·such** (nŭn′sŭch′) *n.* **1.** A person or thing without equal. See Synonyms at **paragon. 2.** See **black medic. —none′such′** *adj.*

no·net (nō-nĕt′) *n. Music.* **1.** A combination of nine instruments or voices. **2.** A composition written for such a combination. [Italian *nonetto,* from diminutive of *nono,* ninth, from Latin *nōnus.* See NONES.]

none·the·less (nŭn′thə-lĕs′) *adv.* Nevertheless; however.

non-Eu·clid·e·an (nŏn′yōō-klĭd′ē-ən) *adj. Mathematics.* Of, relating to, or being any of several modern geometries that are not based on the postulates of Euclid.

non·e·vent (nŏn′ĭ-vĕnt′) *n. Informal.* An anticipated or highly publicized event that does not occur or proves anticlimactic or boring.

non·ex·ist·ence (nŏn′ĭg-zĭs′təns) *n.* **1.** The condition of not existing. **2.** Something that does not exist. **—non′ex·ist′ent** *adj.*

non·ex·plo·sive (nŏn′ĭk-splō′sĭv) *adj.* That will not explode: *a nonexplosive fuel; nonexplosive gases.* **—non′ex·plo′sive** *n.*

non·fat (nŏn′făt′) *adj.* Lacking fat solids or having the fat content removed: *nonfat milk.*

non·fea·sance (nŏn-fē′zəns) *n. Law.* Failure to perform an act that is either an official duty or a legal requirement. [NON– + (MIS)FEASANCE.]

non·fer·rous (nŏn-fĕr′əs) *adj.* **1.** Not composed of or containing iron. **2.** Of or relating to metals other than iron.

non·fic·tion (nŏn-fĭk′shən) *n.* **1.** Prose works other than fiction: *I've read her novels but not her nonfiction.* **2.** The category of literature consisting of works of this kind. **—non·fic′tion·al** *adj.*

nonfiction novel *n.* A factual or historical narrative written in the form of a novel: *Truman Capote's* In Cold Blood *is a nonfiction novel.*

non·flam·ma·ble (nŏn-flăm′ə-bəl) *adj.* Not flammable, especially not readily ignited and not rapidly burned.

non·food (nŏn′fōōd′) *adj.* Of, relating to, or being something that is not food but is sold in a supermarket, as housewares, stationery, and school supplies. *—attributive.* Often used to modify another noun: *nonfood items; nonfood sales.*

non·gon·o·coc·cal urethritis (nŏn′gŏn-ə-kŏk′əl) *n. Abbr.* **NGU** An inflammation of the urethra similar to that of gonorrhea but caused by the rickettsia *Chlamydia trachomatis* and occurring mostly among males as an early symptom of chlamydia.

non·grad·ed (nŏn-grā′dĭd) *adj.* **1.** Being without grade levels: *a nongraded elementary school.* **2.** Consisting of particles of essentially the same size, as soil.

non gra·ta (nŏn grä′tə, grăt′ə, nōn) *adj.* Not welcome; not approved: *The aide, having been declared non grata, was expelled from the country.* [From PERSONA NON GRATA.]

non·he·ro (nŏn-hîr′ō) *n., pl.* **-roes.** An antihero.

non·i·den·ti·cal (nŏn′ī-dĕn′tĭ-kəl) *adj.* **1.** Not being the same; different. **2.** Fraternal: *nonidentical twins.*

no·nil·lion (nō-nĭl′yən) *n.* **1.** The cardinal number equal to 10^{30}. **2.** *Chiefly British.* The cardinal number equal to 10^{54}. [French : Latin *nōnus,* ninth; see NONA– + French *million,* million (from Old French *milion;* see MILLION).] **—no·nil′lion** *adj.*

no·nil·lionth (nō-nĭl′yənth) *n.* **1.** The ordinal number nonillion in a series. **2.** One of nonillion equal parts. **—no·nil′lionth** *adv. & adj.*

non·im·mi·grant (nŏn-ĭm′ĭ-grənt) *n.* **1.** An alien, such as a tourist or a member of a ship's crew, who enters a country for a temporary stay. **2.** An alien who returns to his or her own country after a stay abroad. *—attributive.* Often used to modify another noun: *nonimmigrant status.*

non·in·duc·tive (nŏn′ĭn-dŭk′tĭv) *adj. Electricity.* Having low or zero inductance.

non-in·su·lin-de·pen·dent diabetes (nŏn-ĭn′sə-lĭn-dĭ-pĕn′dənt) *n.* See **diabetes mellitus** (sense 2).

non·in·ter·ven·tion (nŏn′ĭn-tər-vĕn′shən) *n.* Failure or refusal to intervene, especially in the affairs of another nation. **—non′in·ter·ven′tion·ist** *n.*

non·in·tro·spec·tive (nŏn′ĭn-trə-spĕk′tĭv) *adj.* Unable or unwilling to examine one's conscience or soul.

non·in·va·sive (nŏn′ĭn-vā′sĭv) *adj.* **1.** Not penetrating the body, as by incision or injection: *noninvasive surgery; a noninvasive diagnostic method.* **2.** Not invading healthy tissue: *noninvasive cancer of the bladder.*

non·in·volve·ment (nŏn′ĭn-vŏlv′mənt) *n.* **1.** Lack of emotional involvement. **2.** Failure or refusal to become involved, especially in the affairs of another nation; nonintervention.

non·is·sue (nŏn′ĭsh′o͞o) *n.* A matter of so little import that it ought not become a focus of controversy and comment: *She felt that the matter of her attire should have been a nonissue.*

non·join·der (nŏn-join′dər) *n. Law.* Omission of a party, plaintiff, defendant, or cause of action that should have been included as a part of an action or a suit.

non·judg·men·tal (nŏn′jŭj-mĕn′tl) *adj.* Refraining from judgment, especially one based on personal ethical standards.

non·ju·ror (nŏn-jo͝or′ər, -ôr′) *n.* **1.** One who refuses to take an oath, as of allegiance. **2. Nonjuror.** A beneficed Anglican clergyman who refused to take the Oaths of Allegiance and Supremacy to William and Mary and their successors after the Glorious Revolution of 1688. [NON– + JUROR, one who takes an oath (obsolete).] **—non·jur′ing** *adj.*

non·lead·ed (nŏn-lĕd′ĭd) *adj.* Containing no lead; lead-free.

non·lin·e·ar (nŏn-lĭn′ē-ər) *adj.* **1.** Not in a straight line. **2.** *Mathematics.* **a.** Occurring as a result of a nonadditive operation. **b.** Containing a variable with an exponent other than one. Used of an equation.

non·lit·er·ate (nŏn-lĭt′ər-ĭt) *adj.* Having no written language; preliterate. **—non·lit′er·ate** *n.*

non·mar·ket·a·ble (nŏn-mär′kĭ-tə-bəl) *adj.* **1.** Of or relating to a security that may not be sold by one investor to another but is generally redeemable by the issuer within limitations; nonnegotiable. **2.** Difficult or impossible to market: *a nonmarketable product.*

non·mem·ber firm (nŏn-mĕm′bər) *n.* A firm that is not a member of a securities exchange and must work through member firms to have its orders executed on the exchange floor.

non·met·al (nŏn-mĕt′l) *n.* Any of a number of elements, such as oxygen or sulfur, that lack the physical and chemical properties of metals.

non·me·tal·lic (nŏn′mə-tăl′ĭk) *adj.* **1.** Not metallic. **2.** *Chemistry.* Of, relating to, or being a nonmetal.

non·mor·al (nŏn-môr′əl, -mŏr′-) *adj.* **1.** Unrelated to moral or ethical considerations. **2.** Having no moral or ethical standards; lacking a moral sense.

non·neg·a·tive (nŏn-nĕg′ə-tĭv) *adj. Mathematics.* Of, relating to, or being a quantity that is either positive or zero.

non·ne·go·tia·ble (nŏn′nĭ-gō′shə-bəl, -shē-ə-) *adj.* **1.** Difficult or impossible to settle by arbitration, mediation, or mutual concession: *a nonnegotiable demand.* **2.** Nonmarketable.

non·nu·cle·ar (nŏn-no͞o′klē-ər, -nyo͞o′-) *adj.* **1.** Not causing, involving, or operated by nuclear energy. **2.** Not possessing nuclear weapons.

no-no (nō′nō′) *n., pl.* **-noes.** *Informal.* **1.** Something unacceptable or impermissible: *"Even though his company wasn't the one involved in the case, what he did is considered a definite no-no"* (Mike Royko). **2.** A social blunder; a faux pas.

non·ob·jec·tive (nŏn′əb-jĕk′tĭv) *adj.* Of, relating to, or being a style of art in which natural objects are not represented realistically; abstract.

non·ob·serv·ance (nŏn′əb-zûr′vəns) *n.* Failure or refusal to observe, as a religious custom or holiday. **—non′ob·serv′ant** *adj.* **—non′ob·serv′ant·ly** *adv.*

non ob·stan·te (nŏn′ əb-stăn′tē, -stän′-, nōn′) *prep. Abbr.* **non obs., non obst.** Notwithstanding. [Middle English, from Medieval Latin *nōn obstante (aliquō statūtō in contrārium),* notwithstanding (any statute to the contrary) : Latin *nōn,* not + Latin *obstante,* ablative present participle of *obstāre,* to withstand.]

no-non·sense (nō-nŏn′sĕns′, -səns) *adj.* Not tolerating irrelevancies; direct, efficient, and practical: *the no-nonsense tones of a stern parent; plain, no-nonsense meals at a diner.*

non·ox·y·nol-9 (nŏn-ŏk′sə-nôl′nīn′, -nŏl′-, -nōl′-) *n.* A spermicide widely used in contraceptive creams, foams, and lubricants. [By shortening and rearrangement of *nonylphenylhydroxynonaoxyethylene.*]

non·pa·reil (nŏn′pə-rĕl′) *adj.* Having no equal; peerless: *the Yankees' nonpareil center fielder.* **—nonpareil** *n.* **1.** A person or thing that has no equal; a paragon. See Synonyms at **paragon. 2.** See **painted bunting. 3.** A small, flat chocolate drop covered with white pellets of sugar. [Middle English *nounparalle,* from Old French *nonpareil* : *non-,* non- + *pareil,* equal (from Vulgar Latin **pariculus,* diminutive of Latin *pār,* equal; see **perə-**[2] in Appendix).]

non·par·ti·san (nŏn-pär′tĭ-zən, -sən) *adj.* Based on, influenced by, affiliated with, or supporting the interests or policies of no single political party: *a nonpartisan commission; nonpartisan opinions.* **—non·par′ti·san** *n.* **—non·par′ti·san·ship′** *n.*

non·per·sis·tent (nŏn′pər-sĭs′tənt) *adj.* Having a short life or existence under natural conditions: *a nonpersistent pesticide; a nonpersistent infection.*

non·per·son (nŏn-pûr′sən) *n.* A person whose existence is systematically ignored or concealed, especially one whose removal from the attention and memory of the public is sought for reasons of ideological or political deviation.

non·plus (nŏn-plŭs′) *tr.v.* **-plused, -plus·ing, -plus·es** also **-plussed, -plus·sing, -plus·ses.** To put at a loss as to what to think, say, or do; bewilder. **—nonplus** *n.* A state of perplexity, confusion, or bewilderment. [From Latin *nōn plūs,* no more : *nōn,* not; see NON– + *plūs,* more; see **pelə-**[1] in Appendix.]

non·pre·scrip·tion (nŏn′prĭ-skrĭp′shən) *adj.* Sold legally without a physician's prescription; over-the-counter: *nonprescription drugs.*

non·pro·duc·tive (nŏn′prə-dŭk′tĭv) *adj.* **1.** Not yielding or producing: *nonproductive land.* **2.** Not engaged in the direct production of goods: *nonproductive personnel.* **—nonproductive** *n.* A person who produces no useful work. **—non′pro·duc′tive·ly** *adv.*

non·pro·fes·sion·al (nŏn′prə-fĕsh′ə-nəl) *n.* One who is not a professional. **—non′pro·fes′sion·al** *adj.* **—non′pro·fes′sion·al·ly** *adv.*

non·prof·it (nŏn-prŏf′ĭt) *adj.* Not seeking or producing a profit or profits: *a nonprofit organization.*

non·pro·lif·er·a·tion (nŏn′prə-lĭf′ə-rā′shən) *adj.* Of, relating to, or calling for an end to the acquisition of nuclear weapons by additional nations: *a nonproliferation treaty.*

non·pros (nŏn′prŏs′) *tr.v.* **-prossed, -pros·sing, -pros·ses.** *Law.* To enter a judgment of non prosequitur against (a plaintiff). [Short for NON PROSEQUITUR.]

non pro·se·qui·tur (nŏn′ prə-sĕk′wĭ-tər, nōn′) *n. Law.* The judgment entered against a plaintiff who fails to appear in court to prosecute a suit. [Late Latin *nōn prosequitur,* he does not prosecute : Latin *nōn,* not + *prōsequitur,* third person sing. present tense of *prōsequī,* to prosecute.]

non·read·er (nŏn-rē′dər) *n.* A person who cannot or does not read, especially a child who takes a long time learning to read.

non·re·com·bi·nant (nŏn′rē-kŏm′bə-nənt) *adj.* Not resulting from or involved in genetic recombination: *nonrecombinant microbial cells.*

non·re·cov·er·a·ble (nŏn′rĭ-kŭv′ər-ə-bəl) *adj.* That cannot be recovered, especially from waste materials or ore.

non·rep·re·sen·ta·tion·al (nŏn-rĕp′rĭ-zĕn-tā′shə-nəl) *adj.* Of, relating to, or being a style of art in which natural objects are not represented realistically; nonobjective.

♦ **non·res·i·dent** (nŏn-rĕz′ĭ-dənt, -dĕnt′) *adj.* **1.** Not living in a particular place: *nonresident students who commute to classes.* **2.** *Chiefly New England.* Of, relating to, or being real estate owned by persons who are resident only in the summer. See Regional Note at **summercater. —non·res′i·dence, non·res′i·den·cy** *n.* **—non·res′i·dent** *n.*

non·re·sis·tance (nŏn′rĭ-zĭs′təns) *n.* **1.** The practice or principle of complete obedience to authority even if unjust or arbitrary. **2.** The practice or principle of refusing to resort to force even in defense against violence.

non·re·sis·tant (nŏn′rĭ-zĭs′tənt) *adj.* **1.** Not resistant, especially to a disease or an environmental factor, such as heat or moisture. **2.** Submissively obedient. **—non′re·sis′tant** *n.*

non·re·stric·tive (nŏn′rĭ-strĭk′tĭv) *adj.* **1.** Not restrictive: *nonrestrictive zoning.* **2.** *Grammar.* Of, relating to, or being a subordinate clause or phrase that describes but does not identify or restrict the meaning of the noun, phrase, or clause it modifies, as the clause *who live in a small condo* in the sentence *The Smiths, who live in a small condo, have 11 cats.*

non·re·turn·a·ble (nŏn′rĭ-tûr′nə-bəl) *adj.* **1.** That cannot be returned: *Merchandise on sale is generally nonreturnable.* **2.** Not exchangeable for a deposit: *nonreturnable bottles.*

non·rig·id (nŏn-rĭj′ĭd) *adj.* **1.** Not rigid: *a nonrigid frame.* **2.** Of, relating to, or being a lighter-than-air aircraft that holds its shape by gas pressure.

non·sched·uled (nŏn-skĕj′o͞old) *adj.* Operating without a

ă pat	oi boy
ā pay	ou out
âr care	o͝o took
ä father	o͞o boot
ĕ pet	ŭ cut
ē be	ûr urge
ĭ pit	th thin
ī pie	*th* this
îr pier	hw which
ŏ pot	zh vision
ō toe	ə about, item
ô paw	♦ regionalism

Stress marks: ′ (primary); ′ (secondary), as in **dictionary** (dĭk′shə-nĕr′ē)

Norfolk Island pine
Araucaria heterophylla

regular schedule of passenger or cargo flights: *a nonscheduled airline.*

non·sec·tar·i·an (nŏn′sĕk-târ′ē-ən) *adj.* Not limited to or associated with a particular religious denomination. **—non′sec·tar′i·an·ism** *n.*

non·self (nŏn-sĕlf′) *n.* That which the immune system identifies as foreign to the body.

non·sense (nŏn′sĕns′, -səns) *n.* **1.** Words or signs having no intelligible meaning: *a message that was nonsense until decoded.* **2.** Subject matter, behavior, or language that is foolish or absurd. **3.** Extravagant foolishness or frivolity: *a clown's exuberant nonsense.* **4.** Matter of little or no importance or usefulness: *a chatty letter full of gossip and nonsense.* **5.** Insolent talk or behavior; impudence: *wouldn't take any nonsense from the children.* **6.** *Genetics.* A section within a strand of messenger RNA containing a nucleotide triplet that codes for no amino acid. Nonsense cannot be read during protein synthesis and so terminates the polypeptide chain.

nonsense verse *n.* Verse characterized by humor or whimsy and often featuring nonce words.

non·sen·si·cal (nŏn-sĕn′sĭ-kəl) *adj.* **1.** Lacking intelligible meaning: *a nonsensical jumble of words.* **2.** Foolish; absurd: *nonsensical ideas.* **—non·sen′si·cal′i·ty** (-kăl′ĭ-tē), **non·sen′si·cal·ness** (-kəl-nĭs) *n.* **—non·sen′si·cal·ly** *adv.*

non se·qui·tur (nŏn sĕk′wĭ-tər, -to͝or′) *n.* **1.** An inference or conclusion that does not follow from the premises or evidence. **2.** A statement that does not follow logically from what preceded it. [Latin *nōn sequitur,* it does not follow : *nōn,* not + *sequitur,* third person sing. present tense of *sequī,* to follow.]

non·sex·ist (nŏn-sĕk′sĭst) *adj.* **1.** Not discriminating on the basis of gender: *nonsexist hiring policies.* **2.** Not promoting sexual stereotypes: *nonsexist terminology such as* firefighter *and* flight attendant.

non·sig·nif·i·cant (nŏn′sĭg-nĭf′ĭ-kənt) *adj.* **1.** Not significant. **2.** Having, producing, or being a value obtained from a statistical test that lies within the limits for being of random occurrence. **—non′sig·nif′i·cance** *n.* **—non′sig·nif′i·cant·ly** *adv.*

non·sked (nŏn′skĕd′) *n.* *Informal.* A nonscheduled airline or cargo plane. [Shortening and alteration of NONSCHEDULED.]

non·skid (nŏn′skĭd′) *adj.* Designed to prevent or inhibit skidding: *nonskid tires.*

non·smok·er (nŏn′smō′kər) *n.* One who does not smoke tobacco.

non·smok·ing (nŏn′smō′kĭng) *adj.* **1.** Not engaging in the smoking of tobacco: *nonsmoking passengers.* **2.** Designated or reserved for nonsmokers: *the nonsmoking section of a restaurant.* **3.** Of or relating to abstinence from smoking tobacco: *corporate nonsmoking policies.*

non·stan·dard also **non-stan·dard** (nŏn-stăn′dərd) *adj.* **1.** Varying from or not adhering to the standard: *nonstandard lengths of board.* **2.** *Linguistics.* Associated with a language variety used by uneducated speakers or socially disfavored groups.

USAGE NOTE: The term *nonstandard* was introduced by linguists and lexicographers to describe usages and language varieties that had previously been labeled with terms such as *vulgar* and *illiterate. Nonstandard* is not simply a euphemism but reflects the empirical discovery that the varieties used by low-prestige groups have rich and systematic grammatical structures and that their stigmatization more often reflects a judgment about their speakers rather than any inherent deficiencies in logic or expressive power. Note, however, that the use of nonstandard forms is not necessarily restricted to the communities with which they are associated in the public mind. Many educated speakers freely use forms such as *can't hardly* or *ain't I* to set a popular or informal tone. • Some dictionaries use the term *substandard* to describe forms, such as *ain't,* associated with uneducated speech, while reserving *nonstandard* for forms such as *irregardless,* which are common in writing but are still regarded by many as uneducated. But *substandard* is itself susceptible of disparaging interpretation, and most linguists and lexicographers now use only *nonstandard,* the practice followed in this Dictionary.

non·start·er (nŏn-stär′tər) *n.* **1.** One that fails to start. **2.** An idea, a proposal, or a candidate with no chance of being accepted or successful: *"Many lawmakers are pronouncing the budget a nonstarter"* (Christian Science Monitor).

non·ste·roi·dal (nŏn′stĭ-roid′l, -stĕ-) also **non·ster·oid** (nŏn-stîr′oid, -stĕr′-) *—adj.* Not being or containing a steroid: *a nonsteroidal anti-inflammatory drug.* *—n.* A drug or other substance not containing a steroid.

non·stick (nŏn′stĭk′) *adj.* Permitting easy removal of adherent food particles: *a frying pan with a nonstick surface.*

non·stop (nŏn′stŏp′) *adj.* **1.** Made or done without stops: *a nonstop flight.* **2.** Unceasing; unremitting: *nonstop criticism.* **—non′stop′** *adv.*

non·such (nŭn′sŭch′) *n.* Variant of **nonesuch.**

non·suit (nŏn-so͞ot′) *Law. n.* A judgment against a plaintiff for failure to prosecute the case or to introduce sufficient evidence. **—nonsuit** *tr.v.* **-suit·ed, -suit·ing, -suits.** To render a judgment of nonsuit against (a plaintiff). [Middle English, failure of a plaintiff to prosecute, from Anglo-Norman *nounsuite* : *noun-,* no (from Latin *nōn;* see NON–) + *suite,* suit; see SUIT.]

non·sup·port (nŏn′sə-pôrt′, -pōrt′) *n.* *Law.* Failure to provide for the maintenance of one's legal dependents.

non·tar·get (nŏn-tär′gĭt) *adj.* Not being the target, as of an agent or a weapon: *effects of radiotherapy on nontarget cells.*

non·ten·ured (nŏn-tĕn′yərd, -yo͝ord′) *adj.* Not having or leading to tenure: *a nontenured academic post.*

non·triv·i·al (nŏn-trĭv′ē-əl) *adj.* **1.** Not trivial; of some importance. **2.** *Mathematics.* Of, relating to, or being an expression in which at least one variable is not equal to zero.

non trop·po (nŏn trô′pō, nōn) *adv. & adj.* *Music.* In moderation. Used to modify a direction: *adagio non troppo.* [Italian : *non,* not + *troppo,* too much.]

non-U (nŏn-yo͞o′) *adj.* *Chiefly British.* Not characteristic of the upper class, especially in language usage. [NON– + U[2].]

non·un·ion (nŏn-yo͞on′yən) *adj.* **1.** Not belonging to a labor union: *nonunion plumbers.* **2.** Not recognizing or dealing with a labor union or employing union members: *a nonunion shop.*

non·u·ple (nŏn′yə-pəl) *adj.* **1.** Consisting of nine members, parts, or elements. **2.** Multiplied by nine. **—nonuple** *n.* A number or total that is nine times as great as another. [French *nonuple* (on the model of *quadruple,* quadruple; see QUADRUPLE) from Latin *nōnus,* nine. See NONA–.]

non·us·er (nŏn-yo͞o′zər) *n.* One who refrains from the use of something, as of narcotic drugs or alcohol.

non·ver·bal (nŏn-vûr′bəl) *adj.* **1.** Being other than verbal: *nonverbal communication.* **2.** Involving little use of language: *a nonverbal intelligence test.* **3.** Measuring low on a scale of verbal ability.

non·vi·a·ble (nŏn-vī′ə-bəl) *adj.* **1.** Not capable of living or developing: *a nonviable fetus.* **2.** Not workable or practicable: *a nonviable idea.*

non·vi·o·lence (nŏn-vī′ə-ləns) *n.* **1.** Lack of violence. **2.** The doctrine, policy, or practice of rejecting violence in favor of peaceful tactics as a means of gaining political objectives. **—non·vi′o·lent** *adj.* **—non·vi′o·lent·ly** *adv.*

non·vot·er (nŏn-vō′tər) *n.* A person who does not vote or has no right to vote.

non·white (nŏn-hwīt′, -wīt′) *n.* A person who is not white. **—non′white′** *adj.*

non·wo·ven (nŏn-wō′vən) *adj.* Made by a process not involving weaving. Used of textiles. **—nonwoven** *n.* Material or a fabric made by a process not involving weaving.

non·ze·ro (nŏn-zîr′ō, -zē′rō) *adj.* *Mathematics.* Not equal to zero.

noo·dle[1] (no͞od′l) *n.* A narrow, ribbonlike strip of dried dough, usually made of flour, eggs, and water. [German *Nudel.*]

noo·dle[2] (no͞od′l) *n.* *Slang.* **1.** The human head. **2.** A person regarded as weak, foolish, or stupid. [Probably alteration of NODDLE.]

noo·dle[3] (no͞od′l) *intr.v.* **-dled, -dling, -dles.** *Music.* To improvise music on an instrument in an idle, haphazard fashion. [Imitative.]

nook (no͝ok) *n.* **1.** A small corner, alcove, or recess, especially one in a large room. **2.** A hidden or secluded spot. [Middle English *nok,* probably of Scandinavian origin; akin to Norwegian dialectal *nōk,* hook.]

noon (no͞on) *n.* *Abbr.* **n., N. 1.a.** Twelve o'clock in the daytime; midday. **b.** The time or point in the sun's path at which the sun is on the local meridian. Also called *noontide, noontime.* **2.** The highest point; the zenith. **3.** *Archaic.* Midnight. *—attributive.* Often used to modify another noun: *noon meals; noon meetings.* [Middle English *non,* from Old English *nōn,* canonical hour of nones (3 P.M. in early Middle Ages), from Late Latin *nōna (hōra),* ninth (hour after sunrise), nones, feminine sing. of Latin *nōnus,* ninth. See **newn̥** in Appendix.]

noon·day (no͞on′dā′) *n.* Midday; noon.

no one *pron.* No person; nobody.

noon·tide (no͞on′tīd′) *n.* See **noon** (sense 1).

noon·time (no͞on′tīm′) *n.* See **noon** (sense 1).

noose (no͞os) *n.* **1.** A loop formed in a rope by means of a slipknot so that it binds tighter as the rope is pulled. Also called *running noose.* **2.** A snare or trap. **—noose** *tr.v.* **noosed, noos·ing, noos·es. 1.** To capture or hold by or as if by a noose. **2.** To make a noose of or in. [Middle English *nose,* probably from Old French *nos, nous,* knot, from Latin *nōdus.* See NODE.]

Noot·ka (no͞ot′kə, no͝ot′-) *n., pl.* **Nootka** or **-kas. 1.a.** A Native American people inhabiting Vancouver Island in British Columbia and Cape Flattery in northwest Washington. **b.** A member of this people. **2.** The Wakashan language of the Nootka. [After NOOTKA (SOUND).] **—Noot′ka** *adj.*

Nootka cypress *n.* See **Alaska cedar** (sense 1). [After NOOTKA (SOUND).]

Nootka Sound. An inlet of the Pacific Ocean on the western coast of Vancouver Island in southwest British Columbia, Canada.

n.o.p. *abbr.* Not otherwise provided for.

no·pal (nō′pəl, nō-päl′, -păl′) *n.* Any of several cacti of the genus *Nopalea,* especially *N. cochenillifera,* found chiefly in Mexico and having reddish flowers with an erect perianth and long, exserted stamens. [American Spanish, from Nahuatl *nopalli.*]

no-par (nō′pär′) *adj.* Being without face value; having no par value: *a no-par stock certificate.*

nope (nōp) *adv.* *Informal.* No. [Alteration of NO[1].]

nor¹ (nôr; nər *when unstressed*) *conj.* And not; or not; not either: *has neither phoned nor written us; life forms that are neither plants nor animals.* [Middle English, blend of *ne,* no; see NO¹, and *or,* or; see OR¹.]

USAGE NOTE: The traditional rule requires that *nor* be used following *neither* in expressions in which the negation is carried over to the second element: *He is neither able nor* (not *or*) *willing to go. Nor* is likewise required when a negation is carried over into the second of two independent clauses, in which case it also triggers inversion of the subject and the auxiliary verb in the second clause: *He cannot find anyone now, nor does he expect to find anyone in the future; Jane will never compromise with Bill, nor will Bill compromise with Jane.* When the first negative is expressed by *not* or *never,* however, and when the second conjoined element is a verb phrase, the use of *nor* is often optional: *He will not permit the change, or* (or *nor*) *even consider it.* When a noun phrase of the type *no this or that* is introduced by *no, or* is more common than *nor: He has no experience or interest* (less frequently *nor interest*) *in chemistry. Or* is also more common than *nor* when such a noun phrase, adjective phrase, or adverb phrase is introduced by *not*: *He is not a philosopher or a statesman. We were not rich or happy.* See Usage Notes at **neither, or¹.**

♦ **nor²** (nôr, nər *when unstressed*) *conj. Regional.* Than. [Middle English, perhaps ultimately from *nor,* nor. See NOR¹.]

Nor. *abbr.* **1.** Norman. **2.** North. **3.** Norway; Norwegian.

nor– *pref.* An unaltered parent compound: *norepinephrine.* [Short for NORMAL.]

NORAD *abbr.* North American Air Defense Command.

nor·a·dren·a·lin (nôr′ə-drĕn′ə-lĭn) *n.* See **norepinephrine.**

nor·ad·ren·er·gic (nôr′ăd-rə-nûr′jĭk) *adj.* Stimulated by or releasing norepinephrine: *noradrenergic neurons.* **—nor′ad·ren·er′gi·cal·ly** *adv.*

Noraid or **NORAID** *abbr.* Irish Northern Aid Committee.

Nor·co (nôr′kō, nōr′-). A city of southern California west-southwest of Riverside. It is an industrial center in an agricultural region. Population, 21,126.

Nor·dau (nôr′dou′), **Max Simon.** 1849–1923. Hungarian-born German writer and Zionist leader in Europe (1895–1923) whose written works concern social and moral questions.

Nor·den·skjöld (nôr′dn-shōld′, -shəld, no͝or′dən-shœld′), Baron **Nils Adolf Erik.** 1832–1901. Finnish-born Swedish explorer and geologist who was the first to navigate the Northeast Passage (1878–1880).

Nor·dic (nôr′dĭk) *adj.* **1.** Of, relating to, or characteristic of Scandinavia or its peoples, languages, or cultures. **2.** Of or relating to a human physical type exemplified by the tall, narrow-headed, light-skinned, blond-haired peoples of Scandinavia. **3.** *Sports.* Of or relating to ski competition featuring ski jumping and cross-country racing. **—Nordic** *n.* A person of the Nordic physical type. [French *nordique,* from *nord,* north, from Old French *nort,* from Old English *north.* See **ner-¹** in Appendix.]

Nord·kyn (nôr′kən, -kün), **Cape.** The northernmost point of the European mainland, in northern Norway east of North Cape.

Nord·mann fir (nôrd′mən) *n.* A widely planted evergreen tree *(Abies nordmanniana)* native to Greece, Turkey, and the Caucasus, having erect, reddish-brown cones. [After Alexander von *Nordmann* (1803–1866), Finnish naturalist.]

Nord-Ost·see Ka·nal (nört-ôst′zā kä-näl′). See **Kiel Canal.**

nor′east·er (nôr-ē′stər) *n.* A northeaster.

nor·ep·i·neph·rine (nôr′ĕp-ə-nĕf′rĭn) *n.* A substance, $C_8H_{11}NO_3$, both a hormone and neurotransmitter, secreted by the adrenal medulla and the nerve endings of the sympathetic nervous system to cause vasoconstriction and increases in heart rate, blood pressure, and the sugar level of the blood. Also called *noradrenalin.*

nor·eth·in·drone (nôr-ĕth′ĭn-drōn′) *n.* A progestational hormone, $C_{20}H_{26}O_2$, similar in effect to progesterone, used especially in oral contraceptives. [Alteration and rearrangement of chemical name, such as *norethynylandrostenolone.*]

Nor·folk (nôr′fək, -fôk). **1.** A historical region of eastern England bordering on the North Sea. Settled in prehistoric times, it was part of the Anglo-Saxon kingdom of East Anglia. Its name means the "northern people," as opposed to the "southern people" of Suffolk. **2.** A city of northeast Nebraska northwest of Omaha. It is a processing and trade center in an agricultural region. Population, 19,449. **3.** An independent city of southeast Virginia on Hampton Roads southeast of Richmond. Founded in 1682 and today the largest city of Virginia, it has been a major naval base since the American Revolution. Population, 266,979.

Norfolk Island. An island territory of Australia in the southern Pacific Ocean northeast of Sydney.

Norfolk Island pine *n.* An evergreen tree *(Araucaria heterophylla)* with incurved, decurrent needles, native to Norfolk Island in the South Pacific and widely grown as an indoor plant.

Norfolk jacket *n.* A belted jacket with two box pleats in front and back. [After NORFOLK, England.]

Norfolk terrier *n.* Any of an English breed of small, sturdy, short-legged terriers identical with the Norwich terrier except for ears that bend forward. [After NORFOLK, England.]

NOR gate (nôr) *n. Computer Science.* A logic circuit that produces an output inverse to that of an OR gate. [N(OT) + OR GATE.]

Nor·gay (nôr′gā), **Tenzing.** 1914–1986. Sherpa guide who with Sir Edmund Hillary made the first ascent of Mount Everest (1953).

no·ri (nôr′ē) *n., pl.* **-ris.** An edible, dried preparation of red algae of the genus *Porphyra.* [Japanese.]

no·ri·a (nôr′ē-ə, nōr′-) *n.* A water wheel with buckets attached to its rim, used to raise water from a stream, especially for transfer to an irrigation channel. [Spanish, from Arabic *nā'ūrah.*]

noria

Nor·i·cum (nôr′ĭ-kəm, nŏr′-). An ancient country and province of the Roman Empire south of the Danube River in present-day Austria west of Vienna. It was incorporated into the Roman Empire in the first century B.C. and prospered as a frontier colony until it was overrun by Germanic peoples in the fifth century A.D.

No·rilsk (nə-rēlsk′). A city of north-central Russia. Founded in 1935, it is the center of an important mining region. Population, 180,000.

nor·ite (nôr′īt) *n.* See **gabbro.** [Norwegian *Norge,* Norway + –ITE¹.] **—nor·it′ic** (nô-rĭt′ĭk) *adj.*

norm (nôrm) *n.* **1.** A standard, model, or pattern regarded as typical: *the current middle-class norm of two children per family.* **2.** *Mathematics.* **a.** A mode. **b.** An average. **c.** The length of a vector. [French *norme,* from Old French, from Latin *norma,* carpenter's square, norm. See **gnō-** in Appendix.]

norm. *abbr.* Normal.

Norm. *abbr.* Norman.

Nor·ma (nôr′mə) *n.* A constellation in the Southern Hemisphere within the Milky Way near Lupus and Ara. [Latin *norma,* carpenter's square. See **gnō-** in Appendix.]

nor·mal (nôr′məl) *adj.* **1.** *Abbr.* **norm.** Conforming with, adhering to, or constituting a norm, standard, pattern, level, or type; typical: *normal room temperature; one's normal weight; normal diplomatic relations.* **2.** *Abbr.* **norm.** *Biology.* Functioning or occurring in a natural way; lacking observable abnormalities or deficiencies. **3.** *Abbr.* **n, N, n.** *Chemistry.* **a.** Designating a solution having one gram equivalent weight of solute per liter of solution. **b.** Designating an aliphatic hydrocarbon having a straight and unbranched chain of carbon atoms. **4.** *Abbr.* **norm.** *Mathematics.* Being at right angles; perpendicular. **5.** *Abbr.* **norm. a.** Relating to or characterized by average intelligence or development. **b.** Free from emotional disorder. **—normal** *n. Abbr.* **norm. 1.** Something normal; the standard: *scored close to the normal.* **2.** The usual or expected state, form, amount, or degree. **3. a.** Correspondence to a norm. **b.** An average. **4.** *Mathematics.* A perpendicular, especially a perpendicular to a line tangent to a plane curve or to a plane tangent to a space curve. [Middle English, from Late Latin *normālis,* from Latin, made according to the square, from *norma,* carpenter's square. See **gnō-** in Appendix.] **—nor′mal·ly** *adv.*

SYNONYMS: *normal, regular, natural, typical.* These adjectives mean not deviating from what is common, usual, or to be expected. *Normal* stresses adherence to an established standard, model, or pattern: *normal body temperature; normal curiosity. Regular* indicates unvarying conformity with a fixed rule or principle or a uniform procedure: *her regular bedtime; regular attendance at school.* What is *natural* is proper to, consonant with, or in accord with one's inherent nature or character: *a natural fear of nuclear war; a grandparent's natural affection for a grandchild. Typical* stresses adherence to those qualities, traits, or characteristics that identify a kind, group, or category: *a typical American; a painting typical of the Impressionist school.*

Nor·mal (nôr′məl). A town of central Illinois north-northeast of Bloomington. It is the seat of Illinois State University (founded 1857). Population, 35,672.

nor·mal·cy (nôr′məl-sē) *n.* Normality.

normal distribution *n.* A theoretical frequency distribution for a set of variable data, usually represented by a bell-shaped curve symmetrical about the mean. Also called *Gaussian distribution.*

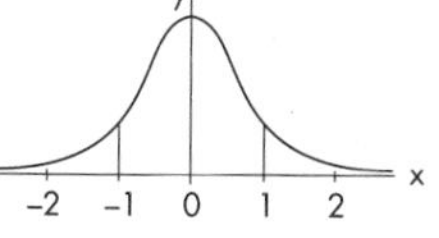

normal distribution

nor·mal·i·ty (nôr-măl′ĭ-tē) *n.* **1.** The state or fact of being normal; normalcy. **2.** The concentration of a solution, expressed in gram equivalent weights of solute per liter of solution.

nor·mal·ize (nôr′mə-līz′) *tr.v.* **-ized, -iz·ing, -iz·es. 1.** To make normal, especially to cause to conform to a standard or norm: *normalize a patient's temperature; normalizing relations with a former enemy nation.* **2.** To make (a text or language) regular and consistent, especially with respect to spelling or style. **3.** To remove strains and reduce coarse crystalline structures in (metal), especially by heating and cooling. **—nor′mal·i·za′tion** (-mə-lĭ-zā′shən) *n.* **—nor′mal·iz′er** *n.*

normal school *n.* A school that trains teachers, chiefly for the elementary grades. [Translation of French *école normale* (so called because the first school so named was intended as a model) : *école,* school + *normal,* normal.]

Nor·man¹ (nôr′mən) *n. Abbr.* **Norm., Nor. 1. a.** A member of a Scandinavian people who settled in northern France in the tenth century. **b.** A descendant of this people, especially one ruling or inhabiting England from the time of the Norman Conquest. **2.** A native or inhabitant of Normandy. **—Norman** *adj. Abbr.* **Norm., Nor. 1.** Of or relating to Normandy, the Normans, their

ă pat	oi boy
ā pay	ou out
âr care	o͝o took
ä father	o͞o boot
ĕ pet	ŭ cut
ē be	ûr urge
ĭ pit	th thin
ī pie	*th* this
îr pier	hw which
ŏ pot	zh vision
ō toe	ə about, item
ô paw	♦ regionalism

Stress marks: ′ (primary); ′ (secondary), as in **dictionary** (dĭk′shə-nĕr′ē)

culture, or their language. **2.** Of or being a style of Romanesque architecture that was introduced from Normandy into England before 1066 and that flourished until about 1200. [Middle English, from Old French *Normant,* from Old Norse *Nordhmadhr* (*nordhr,* north + *madhr,* man) and from Old English *Norman* (variant of *Northman* : *north,* north; see **ner-¹** in Appendix + *man,* man; see **man-¹** in Appendix).]

Nor·man² (nôr′mən). A city of central Oklahoma south of Oklahoma City. The University of Oklahoma opened here in 1892. Population, 68,020.

Norman Conquest *n.* The conquest of England by the Normans under William the Conqueror beginning in 1066.

Nor·man·dy (nôr′mən-dē). A historical region and former province of northwest France on the English Channel. Part of ancient Gaul, the region was successively conquered by the Romans, Franks, and Norse; passed to England after the Norman Conquest (1066) and during the Hundred Years' War (1337–1453); and was restored to France in 1450. Its beaches were the focal point of Allied landings on D-day (June 6, 1944) in World War II.

Norman French *n.* The dialect of Old French used in medieval Normandy.

nor·ma·tive (nôr′mə-tĭv) *adj.* Of, relating to, or prescribing a norm or standard: *normative grammar.* **—nor′ma·tive·ly** *adv.* **—nor′ma·tive·ness** *n.*

nor·mo·cyte (nôr′mə-sīt′) *n.* A red blood cell having normal size, shape, or color. [Latin *norma,* norm; see NORM + –CYTE.]

nor·mo·ten·sive (nôr′mō-tĕn′sĭv) *adj.* Having normal blood pressure; not hypertensive or hypotensive. [Latin *norma,* norm; see NORM + (HYPER)TENSIVE.] **—nor′mo·ten′sive** *n.*

nor·mo·ther·mi·a (nôr′mō-thûr′mē-ə) *n.* A condition of normal body temperature. [Latin *norma,* norm; see NORM + THERM(O)– + –IA¹.] **—nor′mo·ther′mic** *adj.*

Norn (nôrn) *n. Mythology.* Any of the three goddesses of fate in Norse myth.

nor·nic·o·tine (nôr-nĭk′ə-tēn′) *n.* A colorless liquid alkaloid, $C_9H_{12}N_2$, extracted from tobacco and used as a plant insecticide.

Nor·ridge (nôr′ĭj, nŏr′-). A village of northeast Illinois, a suburb of Chicago. Population, 16,483.

Nor·ris (nôr′ĭs, nŏr′-), **Benjamin Franklin Jr.** Known as "Frank." 1870–1902. American writer noted for his naturalistic novels about American life, including *McTeague* (1899). His brother **Charles Gilman Norris** (1881–1945) and sister-in-law **Kathleen Thompson Norris** (1880–1966) were also writers.

Norris, George William. 1861–1944. American politician. A U.S. representative (1903–1913) and senator (1913–1943) from Nebraska, he was instrumental in the founding of the Tennessee Valley Authority (1933) and drafted the 20th Amendment to the U.S. Constitution, which limits the President to two full terms.

Nor·rish (nôr′ĭsh, nŏr′-), **Ronald George Wreyford.** 1897–1978. British chemist. He shared a 1967 Nobel Prize for research on high-speed chemical reactions.

Nor·ris·town (nôr′ĭs-toun′, nŏr′-). A borough of southeast Pennsylvania on the Schuylkill River northwest of Philadelphia. Population, 34,684.

Norr·kö·ping (nôr′chœ′pĭng). A city of southeast Sweden on **Norrköping Bay,** an inlet of the Baltic Sea southwest of Stockholm. The city was chartered in 1384 and is today a major manufacturing center. Population, 118,451.

Norse (nôrs) *adj. Abbr.* **N. 1.** Of or relating to medieval Scandinavia or its peoples, languages, or cultures. **2.** Of or relating to Norway or its people, language, or culture. **3.** Of, relating to, or being the branch of the North Germanic languages that includes Norwegian, Icelandic, and Faeroese. **—Norse** *n. Abbr.* **N. 1. a.** The people of Scandinavia; the Scandinavians. **b.** The people of Norway; the Norwegians. **c.** Speakers of Norwegian, Icelandic, and Faeroese. **2. a.** See **North Germanic. b.** Any of the West Scandinavian languages, especially Norwegian. [Probably Dutch *Noorsch,* Scandinavian, from Middle Dutch *Noortsch,* from *nort,* north. See **ner-¹** in Appendix.]

Norse·man (nôrs′mən) *n.* A member of any of the peoples of medieval Scandinavia.

north (nôrth) *n. Abbr.* **N, N., n, n., No., no., Nor. 1. a.** The direction along a meridian 90° counterclockwise from east; the direction to the left of sunrise. **b.** The cardinal point on the mariner's compass located at 0°. **2.** An area or a region lying in the north. **3.** Often **North. a.** The northern part of the earth. **b.** The northern part of a region or country. **4. North.** The northern part of the United States, especially the states that fought for the Union in the Civil War. **—north** *adj. Abbr.* **N, N., n, n., No., no., Nor. 1.** To, toward, of, facing, or in the north. **2.** Originating in or coming from the north: *a cold north wind.* **—north** *adv. Abbr.* **N, N., n, n., No., no., Nor.** In, from, or toward the north. [Middle English, from Old English *north.* See **ner-¹** in Appendix.]

North, Frederick. Second Earl of Guilford. Known as "Lord North." 1732–1792. British politician who served as prime minister (1770–1782) under George III and instituted policies that led to the rebellion of the American colonies.

North Ad·ams (ăd′əmz). A city of northwest Massachusetts north-northeast of Pittsfield. It was settled c. 1737. Population, 18,063.

North Af·ri·ca (ăf′rĭ-kə). A region of northern Africa generally considered to include the modern-day countries of Morocco, Algeria, Tunisia, and Libya. **—North Af′ri·can** *adj. & n.*

North A·mer·i·ca (ə-mĕr′ĭ-kə). *Abbr.* **N.A.** The northern continent of the Western Hemisphere, extending northward from the Colombia-Panama border and including Central America, Mexico, the islands of the Caribbean Sea, the United States, Canada, the Arctic Archipelago, and Greenland. **—North A·mer′i·can** *adj. & n.*

North·amp·ton (nôr-thămp′tən, nôrth-hămp′-). **1.** A borough of central England north-northwest of London. Its Norman castle was the meeting place for parliaments from the 12th to the 14th century. Population, 158,900. **2.** A city of west-central Massachusetts on the Connecticut River north of Springfield. It is the seat of Smith College (founded 1875). Population, 29,286.

North An·do·ver (ăn′dō′vər). A town of northeast Massachusetts on the Merrimack River east-northeast of Lowell. It was a textile center in the 19th century. Population, 20,129.

North Ar·ling·ton (är′lĭng-tən). A borough of northeast New Jersey, a residential and industrial suburb of Newark on the Passaic River. Population, 16,587.

North At·lan·ta (ăt-lăn′tə). A community of northwest Georgia, a suburb of Atlanta. Population, 22,800.

North At·lan·tic Ocean (ăt-lăn′tĭk). The northern part of the Atlantic Ocean, extending northward from the equator to the Arctic Ocean.

North At·tle·bor·o (ăt′l-bûr′ō, -bŭr′ō). A town of southeast Massachusetts north-northeast of Providence, Rhode Island. It was settled in 1669. Population, 21,095.

North Bay. A city of southeast Ontario, Canada, on Lake Nipissing east-southeast of Sudbury. It is a trade center in a lumber and mining region. Population, 51,268.

North Ber·gen (bûr′gən). A community of northeast New Jersey north of Jersey City and across the Hudson River from Manhattan Island. Population, 47,019.

north·bound (nôrth′bound′) *adj.* Going toward the north.

North·brook (nôrth′brŏŏk′). A village of northeast Illinois, a residential and industrial suburb of Chicago. Population, 30,735.

North Bruns·wick (brŭnz′wĭk). A community of central New Jersey southwest of New Brunswick. Population, 22,220.

north by east *n. Abbr.* **NbE** The direction or point on the mariner's compass halfway between due north and north-northeast, or 11°15′ east of due north. **—north by east** *adv. & adj. Abbr.* **NbE** Toward or from north by east.

north by west *n. Abbr.* **NbW** The direction or point on the mariner's compass halfway between due north and north-northwest, or 11°15′ west of due north. **—north by west** *adv. & adj. Abbr.* **NbW** Toward or from north by west.

North Ca·na·di·an River (kə-nā′dē-ən). A river rising in northeast New Mexico and flowing about 1,223 km (760 mi) generally southeast to the Canadian River in eastern Oklahoma.

North Cape. 1. The northernmost point of North Island, New Zealand, projecting into the southern Pacific Ocean. **2.** A promontory on an island of northern Norway west of Cape Nordkyn. It is considered the northernmost important extremity of the continent of Europe.

North Car·o·li·na (kăr′ə-lī′nə). *Abbr.* **NC, N.C.** A state of the southeast United States bordering on the Atlantic Ocean. It was admitted as one of the original Thirteen Colonies in 1789. First settled c. 1653, it was part of the province of Carolina until 1691 and became a separate colony in 1711 and a royal colony in 1729. North Carolina seceded in May 1861 and was readmitted to the Union in 1868. Raleigh is the capital and Charlotte the largest city. Population, 5,881,385. **—North Car·o·lin′i·an** (-lĭn′ē-ən) *adj. & n.*

North Channel. A strait between Scotland and Northern Ireland. It connects the Atlantic Ocean with the Irish Sea.

North Charles·ton (chärl′stən). A city of southeast South Carolina, a suburb of Charleston. Population, 65,630.

North Chi·ca·go (shĭ-kä′gō, -kô′-). A city of northeast Illinois, an industrial suburb of Waukegan on Lake Michigan. Population, 38,774.

North·cliffe (nôrth′klĭf′), Viscount. See Alfred Charles William **Harmsworth.**

North Country. 1. The northern section of England north of the Humber estuary. **2.** A geographic and economic region comprising Alaska and the Yukon Territory of Canada.

North Da·ko·ta (də-kō′tə). *Abbr.* **ND, N.D., N.Dak.** A state of the north-central United States bordering on Canada. It was admitted as the 39th state in 1889. Acquired through the Louisiana Purchase (1803) and a border treaty with Great Britain (1818), the region became part of the Dakota Territory in 1861. It was set off from South Dakota when statehood was achieved. Bismarck is the capital and Fargo the largest city. Population, 652,717. **—North Da·ko′tan** *adj. & n.*

North Downs (dounz). See **Downs.**

north·east (nôrth-ēst′, nôr-ēst′) *n. Abbr.* **NE 1.** The direction or point on the mariner's compass halfway between due north and due east, or 45° east of due north. **2.** An area or a region lying in the northeast. **3. Northeast.** A region of the northeast United States, generally including the New England states, New York, and sometimes Pennsylvania and New Jersey. **—northeast** *adj. Abbr.* **NE 1.** To, toward, of, facing, or in the northeast. **2.** Originating in or coming from the northeast: *a northeast wind.*

—**northeast** *adv.* *Abbr.* **NE** In, from, or toward the northeast. —**north·east′ern** *adj.*

northeast by east *n.* *Abbr.* **NEbE** The direction or point on the mariner's compass halfway between northeast and east-northeast, or 56°15′ east of due north. —**northeast by east** *adv. & adj.* *Abbr.* **NEbE** Toward or from northeast by east.

northeast by north *n.* *Abbr.* **NEbN** The direction or point on the mariner's compass halfway between northeast and north-northeast, or 33°45′ east of due north. —**northeast by north** *adv. & adj.* *Abbr.* **NEbN** Toward or from northeast by north.

north·east·er (nôrth-ē′stər, nôr-ē′-) *n.* A storm or gale blowing from the northeast.

north·east·er·ly (nôrth-ē′stər-lē, nôr-ē′-) *adj.* **1.** Situated toward the northeast. **2.** Coming or being from the northeast. —**north·east′er·ly** *adv.*

Northeast Pas·sage (păs′ĭj). A water route along the northern coast of Europe and Asia between the Atlantic and Pacific oceans. A goal of navigators since the 15th century, it was first traversed by Nils A.E. Nordenskjöld in 1878 to 1880.

north·east·ward (nôrth-ēst′wərd, nôr-ēst′-) *adv. & adj.* Toward, to, or in the northeast. —**northeastward** *n.* A northeastward direction, point, or region. —**north·east′ward·ly** *adv. & adj.* —**north·east′wards** *adv.*

north·er (nôr′*th*ər) *n.* A sudden cold gale coming from the north.

north·er·ly (nôr′*th*ər-lē) *adj.* **1.** Situated toward the north. **2.** Coming or being from the north: *northerly winds.* —**northerly** *n., pl.* **-lies.** A storm or wind coming from the north. —**north′er·ly** *adv.*

north·ern (nôr′*th*ərn) *adj.* *Abbr.* **N, N., n, n., No., no. 1.** Situated in, toward, or facing the north. **2.** Coming from the north: *northern breezes.* **3.** Native to or growing in the north. **4.** Often **Northern.** Of, relating to, or characteristic of northern regions or the North. **5.** Being north of the equator. [Middle English *northerne,* from Old English. See **ner-**[1] in Appendix.] —**north′ern·ness′** *n.*

Northern Cross *n.* See **Cygnus.**

Northern Crown *n.* See **Corona Borealis.**

Northern Dvi·na (dvē-nä′). See **Dvina** (sense 1).

north·ern·er also **North·ern·er** (nôr′*th*ər-nər) *n.* A native or inhabitant of the north, especially the northern United States.

northern harrier *n.* A slim-bodied hawk *(Circus cyaneus)* found in marshy areas of northern North America and Eurasia, having an owllike face and a white patch on the tail. Also called *hen harrier, marsh hawk.*

Northern Hemisphere *n.* **1.** The half of the earth north of the equator. **2.** *Astronomy.* The half of the celestial sphere north of the celestial equator.

Northern Ire·land (īr′lənd). *Abbr.* **N.Ire.** A division of the United Kingdom in the northeast section of the island of Ireland. The province occupies much of the ancient Irish kingdom of Ulster and is often known by that name. It was colonized by the British in the 17th century and became a part of the United Kingdom in 1920. Civil strife between the Protestant majority of Northern Ireland and the largely Catholic population of the Republic of Ireland has erupted frequently since the late 1960's. Belfast is the capital and the largest city. Population, 1,488,077.

Northern Kingdom. See **Israel**[2].

northern lights *pl.n.* See **aurora borealis.**

Northern Mar·i·an·a Islands (măr′ē-ăn′ə, mâr′-, mä′-rē-ä′nä). See **Mariana Islands.**

north·ern·most (nôr′*th*ərn-mōst′) *adj.* Farthest north.

northern oriole *n.* A species of American songbird *(Icterus galbula)* composed of two subspecies, the Baltimore and Bullock's orioles.

Northern Paiute *n.* **1.** See **Paiute** (sense 1a). **2.** The Uto-Aztecan language of the Northern Paiute.

northern pike *n.* See **pike**[2] (sense 1).

Northern prickly ash *n.* See **toothache tree.**

Northern Shoshone *n.* See **Shoshone** (sense 1a).

Northern Spor·a·des (spôr′ə-dēz′, spô-rä′*th*ĕs). See **Sporades.**

Northern Spy *n.* A large, yellowish-red, late-ripening apple. [Origin unknown.]

North Fort My·ers (mī′ərz). A community of southwest Florida on the Caloosahatchee River opposite Fort Myers. Population, 17,200.

North Frig·id Zone (frĭj′ĭd). See **Frigid Zone.**

North Fri·sian Islands (frĭzh′ən, frē′zhən). See **Frisian Islands.**

North Germanic *n.* A subdivision of the Germanic languages that includes Norwegian, Icelandic, Swedish, Danish, and Faeroese. Also called *Norse, Scandinavian.*

North·glenn (nôrth-glĕn′). A city of north-central Colorado, a residential suburb of Denver. Population, 29,847.

North Ha·ven (hā′vən). A town of southern Connecticut north-northeast of New Haven. Settled c.1650, it is mainly residential. Population, 22,080.

north·ing (nôr′thĭng, -*th*ĭng) *n.* **1.** The difference in latitude between two positions as a result of a movement to the north. **2.** Progress toward the north.

North Island. An island of New Zealand separated from South Island by Cook Strait. It is the smaller but more populous of the country's two principal islands.

North Kar·roo (kə-ro͞o′). See **Karroo.** [Origin unknown.]

North Kings·town (kĭngz′stən). A town of south-central Rhode Island on Narragansett Bay south-southwest of Providence. The site was settled by Roger Williams in 1641. Population, 21,938.

North Ko·re·a (kə-rē′ə, kô-, kō-). A country of northeast Asia on the Korean Peninsula. Inhabited since ancient times, the region was occupied by Japan from 1910 to 1945. The Soviet-controlled northern territory attained its present-day boundaries after the cease-fire ending the Korean War (1950–1953). Pyongyang is the capital and the largest city. Population, 18,317,000. —**North Ko·re′an** *adj. & n.*

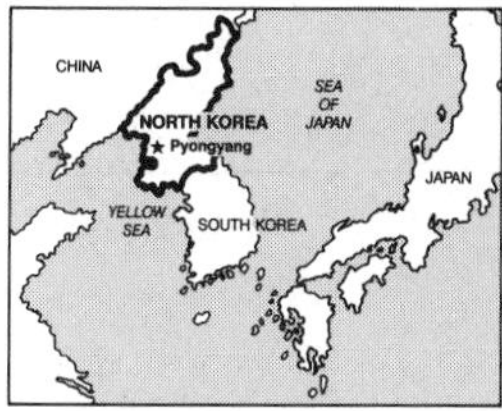

North Korea

north·land also **North·land** (nôrth′lănd′, -lənd) *n.* A region in the north of a country or an area. —**north′land′er** *n.*

North Las Ve·gas (läs vā′gəs). A city of southeast Nevada, a residential suburb of Las Vegas. Population, 42,739.

North Lau·der·dale (lô′dər-dāl′). A city of southeast Florida near the Everglades northwest of Fort Lauderdale. Population, 18,479.

North Lit·tle Rock (lĭt′l rŏk′). A city of central Arkansas on the Arkansas River opposite Little Rock. Originally named Silver City after a small vein of ore discovered in the area, it is now a trade and manufacturing center. Population, 64,391.

North Loup (lo͞op). A river, about 341 km (212 mi) long, of north-central Nebraska flowing southeast to unite with the Middle Loup and South Loup rivers and form the Loup River.

North·man (nôrth′mən) *n.* A Norseman.

North Mas·sa·pe·qua (măs′ə-pē′kwə). A community of southeast New York on Long Island near Massapequa. It is mainly residential. Population, 23,100.

North Mi·am·i (mī-ăm′ē, -ăm′ə). A city of southeast Florida, a suburb of Miami on Biscayne Bay. Population, 42,566.

North Miami Beach. A city of southeast Florida, a resort community on the Atlantic Ocean north of Miami Beach. Population, 36,481.

North Minch (mĭnch). See **Minch.**

north-north·east (nôrth′nôrth-ēst′, nôr′nôr-ēst′) *n.* *Abbr.* **NNE** The direction or point on the mariner's compass halfway between due north and northeast, or 22°30′ east of due north. —**north-northeast** *adj.* *Abbr.* **NNE** To, toward, of, facing, or in the north-northeast. —**north-northeast** *adv.* *Abbr.* **NNE** In, from, or toward the north-northeast.

north-north·west (nôrth′nôrth-wĕst′, nôr′nôr-wĕst′) *n.* *Abbr.* **NNW** The direction or point on the mariner's compass halfway between due north and northwest, or 22°30′ west of due north. —**north-northwest** *adj.* *Abbr.* **NNW** To, toward, of, facing, or in the north-northwest. —**north-northwest** *adv.* *Abbr.* **NNW** In, from, or toward the north-northwest.

North Olm·sted (ŭm′stĕd′). A city of northeast Ohio, a residential and industrial suburb of Cleveland. Population, 36,486.

North Pa·ci·fic Ocean (pə-sĭf′ĭk). The northern part of the Pacific Ocean, extending northward from the equator to the Arctic Ocean.

North Plain·field (plān′fēld′). A borough of northeast-central New Jersey west-southwest of Elizabeth. It is mainly residential. Population, 19,108.

North Platte (plăt). A city of west-central Nebraska at the confluence of the North Platte and South Platte rivers west of Grand Island. It is a processing and shipping center. Population, 24,479.

North Platte River. A river rising in the Park Range of northern Colorado and flowing about 1,094 km (680 mi) north into southeast Wyoming then east and southeast through west-central Nebraska, where it joins the South Platte River to form the Platte River.

North Po·lar Region (pō′lər). See **Polar Regions.**

North Pole *n.* **1.a.** The northern end of Earth's axis of rotation, a point in the Arctic Ocean. **b.** The celestial zenith of this terrestrial point. **c. north pole.** The northern end of the axis of rotation of a planet or other celestial body. **2. north pole.** The north-seeking magnetic pole of a straight magnet.

North Prov·i·dence (prŏv′ĭ-dəns). A town of northeast Rhode Island, a mainly residential suburb of Providence. Population, 29,188.

North Rich·land Hills (rĭch′lənd, -lən). A city of northeast Texas, a residential suburb of Fort Worth. Population, 30,592.

North Ridge·ville (rĭj′vĭl′). A city of northeast Ohio west-southwest of Cleveland. It is mainly residential. Population, 21,522.

North River. An estuary of the Hudson River between New Jersey and New York City flowing into Upper New York Bay. It was so named by the Dutch to distinguish it from the "South River," known today as the Delaware River.

Nor·throp (nôr′thrəp), **John Howard.** 1891–1987. American biochemist. He shared a 1946 Nobel Prize for discovering methods of producing pure enzymes and virus proteins.

North Roy·al·ton (roi′əl-tən). A city of northeast Ohio, a residential suburb of Cleveland. Population, 17,671.

North Sas·katch·e·wan (să-skăch′ə-wän′, -wən). A river of south-central Canada flowing about 1,223 km (760 mi) gener-

ă pat	oi boy
ā pay	ou out
âr care	o͝o took
ä father	o͞o boot
ĕ pet	ŭ cut
ē be	ûr urge
ĭ pit	th thin
ī pie	*th* this
îr pier	hw which
ŏ pot	zh vision
ō toe	ə about, item
ô paw	♦ regionalism

Stress marks: ′ (primary); ′ (secondary), as in **dictionary** (dĭk′shə-nĕr′ē)

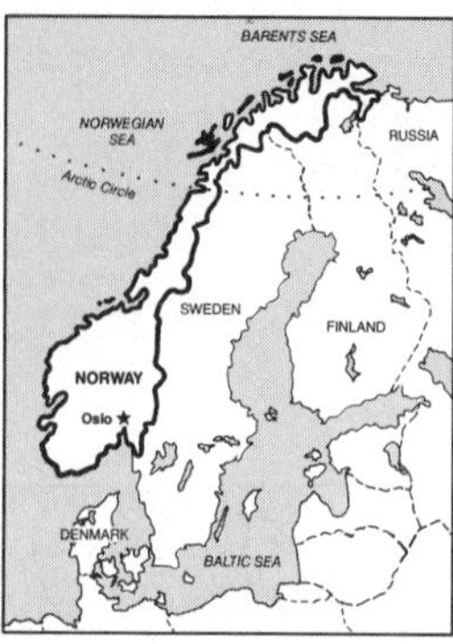

Norway

Norway maple
Acer platanoides

Norway spruce
Picea abies

ally eastward from the Rocky Mountains in western Alberta to central Saskatchewan where it joins the South Saskatchewan to form the Saskatchewan River.

North Sea. An arm of the Atlantic Ocean between Great Britain and northwest Europe. It is connected with the English Channel by the Strait of Dover. Major reserves of oil and natural gas were discovered beneath its waters in the late 1960's.

North Slope. A region of northern Alaska between the Brooks Range and the Arctic Ocean. There are oil and natural gas reserves in the area around Prudhoe Bay.

North Star *n.* See **Polaris.**

North Tem·per·ate Zone (tĕm′pər-ĭt, tĕm′prĭt). See **Temperate Zone.**

North Ton·a·wan·da (tŏn′ə-wŏn′də). A city of western New York on the Niagara River north of Buffalo. It is a port of entry and manufacturing center. Population, 35,760.

North Tru·chas Peak (tro͞o′chəs). See **Truchas Peaks.**

North·um·ber·land Strait (nôr-thŭm′bər-lənd). An arm of the Gulf of St. Lawrence separating Prince Edward Island from New Brunswick and Nova Scotia in southeastern Canada.

North·um·bri·a (nôr-thŭm′brē-ə). An Anglo-Saxon kingdom of northern England formed in the seventh century by the union of Bernicia and Deira, Angle kingdoms originally established c. A.D. 500. Much of Northumbria fell to invading Danes in the ninth century and was annexed to Wessex in 954.

North·um·bri·an (nôr-thŭm′brē-ən) *adj.* **1.** Of or relating to Northumbria or its Old English dialect. **2.** Of or relating to the former or present-day county of Northumberland in northeast England. —**Northumbrian** *n.* **1.** A native or inhabitant of Northumbria. **2.** A native or inhabitant of Northumberland. **3.** The Old English dialect of Northumbria.

North Van·cou·ver (văn-ko͞o′vər). A city of southwest British Columbia, Canada, on an inlet of the Strait of Georgia opposite Vancouver. Population, 33,952.

North Vi·et·nam (vē-ĕt′näm′, -năm′, vē′ĭt-, vyĕt′-). A former country of southeast Asia. It existed from 1954, after the fall of the French at Dien Bien Phu, to 1975, when the South Vietnamese government collapsed at the end of the Vietnam War. It is now part of the country of Vietnam. —**North Vi·et′nam·ese′** (-nə-mēz′, -mēs′) *adj. & n.*

north·ward (nôrth′wərd) *adv. & adj.* Toward, to, or in the north. —**northward** *n.* A northern direction, point, or region. —**north′ward·ly** *adv. & adj.* —**north′wards** *adv.*

North Wa·zir·i·stan (wə-zîr′ĭ-stăn′, -stän′). See **Waziristan.**

north·west (nôrth-wĕst′, nôr-wĕst′) *n. Abbr.* **NW 1.** The direction or point on the mariner's compass halfway between due north and due west, or 45° west of due north. **2.** An area or a region lying in the northwest. **3. Northwest. a.** A historical region of the north-central United States west of the Mississippi River and north of the Missouri River. **b.** A region of the northwest United States, generally including Washington, Oregon, and Idaho. —**northwest** *adj. Abbr.* **NW 1.** To, toward, of, facing, or in the northwest. **2.** Originating in or coming from the northwest: *a northwest wind.* —**northwest** *adv. Abbr.* **NW** In, from, or toward the northwest. —**north·west′ern** *adj.*

northwest by north *n. Abbr.* **NWbN** The direction or point on the mariner's compass halfway between northwest and north-northwest, or 33°45′ west of due north. —**northwest by north** *adv. & adj. Abbr.* **NWbN** Toward or from northwest by north.

northwest by west *n. Abbr.* **NWbW** The direction or point on the mariner's compass halfway between northwest and west-northwest, or 56°15′ west of due north. —**northwest by west** *adv. & adj. Abbr.* **NWbW** Toward or from northwest by west.

north·west·er (nôrth-wĕs′tər, nôr-wĕs′-) *n.* A storm or gale blowing from the northwest.

north·west·er·ly (nôrth-wĕs′tər-lē, nôr-wĕs′-) *adj.* **1.** Situated toward the northwest. **2.** Coming or being from the northwest. —**north·west′er·ly** *adv.*

North-West Fron·tier Province (nôrth-wĕst′ frŭn-tîr′). A historical region of northwest Pakistan on the Afghanistan border. Long a strategic area because of its proximity to the Khyber Pass, it is the traditional home of the Pathans, an Indo-Iranian people. The region was annexed by the British in 1849 and became part of Pakistan after independence was achieved in 1947.

Northwest Pas·sage (păs′ĭj). A water route from the Atlantic to the Pacific through the Arctic Archipelago of northern Canada and along the northern coast of Alaska. Sought by navigators since the 16th century, the existence of such a route was proved in the early 19th century, but the passage was not traversed until the Norwegian explorer Roald Amundsen led an expedition across it in 1903 to 1906. The ice-breaking tanker *Manhattan* was the first commercial ship to cross the passage (1969), after the discovery of oil in northern Alaska.

Northwest Territories. *Abbr.* **NT, NWT, N.W.T.** A territory of northern Canada including the Arctic Archipelago, islands in the northern Hudson Bay, and the mainland north of latitude 60° north. It joined the confederation in 1870. Sir Martin Frobisher was the first European to reach the area, but major exploration of the region was spearheaded by Henry Hudson in the 17th century, Alexander Mackenzie in the 18th century, and Sir John Franklin in the 19th century. The Hudson's Bay Company transferred its holdings to Canada in 1869–1870, leading to the formation of the territory and the creation of the provinces of Manitoba (1870) and Alberta and Saskatchewan (1905). Yellowknife is the capital and the largest city. Population, 45,741.

Northwest Territory. Formerly **Old Northwest.** A historical region of the north-central United States extending from the Ohio and Mississippi rivers to the Great Lakes. The area was ceded to the United States by the Treaty of Paris in 1783. It was officially designated a territory in 1787 and later split up into the territories and present-day states of Ohio, Indiana, Illinois, Michigan, Wisconsin, and part of Minnesota. Control over the territory was a major issue in the War of 1812.

north·west·ward (nôrth-wĕst′wərd) *adv. & adj.* Toward, to, or in the northwest. —**northwestward** *n.* A northwestward direction, point, or region. —**north·west′ward·ly** *adv. & adj.* —**north·west′wards** *adv.*

North Yem·en (yĕm′ən, yä′mən). The former country of Yemen (1962–1990).

Nor·ton (nôr′tn), **Charles Eliot.** 1827–1908. American educator, writer, and editor who founded the *Nation* (1865) and edited the *North American Review* (1864–1868).

Norton Shores. A city of western Michigan on Lake Michigan south of Muskegon. Population, 22,025.

Norton Sound. An inlet of the Bering Sea in western Alaska south of Seward Peninsula.

nor·trip·ty·line (nôr-trĭp′tə-lēn′) *n.* A tricyclic compound, $C_{19}H_{21}N$, used as a tranquilizer and an antidepressant. [NOR– + (AMI)TRIPTYLINE.]

Norw. *abbr.* Norway; Norwegian.

Nor·walk (nôr′wôk′). **1.** A city of southern California north-northeast of Long Beach. It was settled in the 1850's. Population, 85,232. **2.** A city of southwest Connecticut on Long Island Sound northeast of Stamford. Founded in the mid-1600's, it was burned by the British in the American Revolution. Population 77,767.

Nor·way (nôr′wā′). *Abbr.* **Nor., Norw.** A country of northern Europe in the western part of the Scandinavian Peninsula. Beginning in the 9th century, Norway was ruled by numerous petty kingdoms, and raiding parties reached Normandy, Iceland, Greenland, islands off Scotland and Ireland, and the coast of the New World. Norway was finally unified in the 12th century and reached the height of its medieval prosperity in the 13th century. After 1397 it was controlled at various times by Denmark and Sweden. Independence was achieved in 1905. Oslo is the capital and the largest city. Population, 4,122,707.

Norway maple *n.* A tall Eurasian tree *(Acer platanoides)* having greenish-yellow flowers and drooping fruits with horizontally spreading wings, widely cultivated in North America as a shade tree.

Norway pine *n.* See **red pine.** [After *Norway*, a town of southwest Maine.]

Norway rat *n.* The common domestic rat *(Rattus norvegicus)*, which is highly destructive and found worldwide, especially in populated areas. Also called *brown rat.*

Norway spruce *n.* A tall evergreen tree *(Picea abies)* with long, dark green needles, native to Europe and widely cultivated in North America.

Nor·we·gian (nôr-wē′jən) *adj. Abbr.* **Norw., Nor.** Of or relating to Norway or its people, language, or culture. —**Norwegian** *n. Abbr.* **Norw., Nor. 1.** A native or inhabitant of Norway. **2. a.** Dano-Norwegian. **b.** New Norwegian. [From Medieval Latin *Norvegia*, Norway (influenced by NORWAY), from Old Norse *Norvegr* : *nordhr*, north; see **ner-**[1] in Appendix + *vegr*, region; see **wegh-** in Appendix.]

Norwegian elkhound *n.* Any of a Scandinavian breed of hunting dog, having a compact body, heavy grayish coat, and a tail that curls over the back.

Norwegian Sea. A section of the Atlantic Ocean off the coast of Norway north of the North Sea.

Nor·wich. 1. (nŏr′ĭch). A borough of eastern England northeast of London. The city was sacked by Danes in the 11th century and devastated by the Black Death in 1348. Population, 125,900. **2.** (nôr′wĭch′, nŏr′-). A city of southeast Connecticut north of New London. It is an industrial center and the birthplace of Benedict Arnold. Population, 38,074.

Norwich terrier *n.* Any of an English breed of small, sturdy, short-legged terriers, identical with the Norfolk terrier except for ears that stand straight up. [After NORWICH, England.]

Nor·wood (nôr′wo͝od′). **1.** A town of eastern Massachusetts, a chiefly residential suburb of Boston. Population, 29,711. **2.** A city of southwest Ohio surrounded by Cincinnati, of which it is a residential suburb with various light industries. Population, 26,342.

nos. or **Nos.** *abbr.* Numbers.

n.o.s. *abbr.* Not otherwise specified.

nose (nōz) *n.* **1.** The part of the human face or the forward part of the head of other vertebrates that contains the nostrils and organs of smell and forms the beginning of the respiratory tract. **2.** The sense of smell: *a dog with a good nose.* **3.** The ability to detect, sense, or discover as if by smell: *has a nose for gossip.* **4.** The characteristic smell of a wine or liqueur; bouquet. **5.** *Informal.* The nose considered as a symbol of prying: *Keep your nose out of my business.* **6.** Something, such as the forward end of an aircraft, a rocket, or a submarine, that resembles a nose in shape or position. —**nose** *v.* **nosed, nos·ing, nos·es.** —*tr.* **1.** To find out by or as if by smell: *nosed out the thieves' hiding place.* **2.** To touch with the nose; nuzzle. **3.** To move, push, or make with or as if with the nose. **4.** To advance the forward part of cautiously: *nosed the car into the flow of traffic.* —*intr.* **1.** To smell or sniff. **2.** *Informal.* To search or inquire meddlesomely; snoop or pry: *nosing around looking for opportunities.* **3.** To advance with caution: *The ship nosed into its berth.* —***phrasal verb.*** **nose out.** To defeat by a narrow margin. —***idioms.*** **down (one's) nose.** *Informal.* With disapproval, contempt, or arrogance: *Year-round residents here look down their noses at the summer people.* **on the nose.** Exactly; precisely: *predicted the final score on the nose.* **under (someone's) nose.** In plain view: *The keys are right under your nose.* [Middle English, from Old English *nosu.* See **nas-** in Appendix.]

nose·bag (nōz′băg′) *n.* See **feedbag.**

nose·band (nōz′bănd′) *n.* The part of a bridle or halter that passes over an animal's nose. Also called *nosepiece.*

nose·bleed (nōz′blēd′) *n.* A nasal hemorrhage; bleeding from the nose.

nose cone *n.* The forwardmost, usually separable section of a rocket or guided missile that is shaped to offer minimum aerodynamic resistance and often bears protective cladding against heat.

nose·dive (nōz′dīv′) *n.* **1.** A very steep dive of an aircraft. **2.** A sudden, swift drop or plunge: *Stock prices took a nosedive.*

nose-dive (nōz′dīv′) *intr.v.* **-dived** or **-dove** (-dōv′), **-div·ing, -dives.** To perform a nosedive. —**nose′-div′er** *n.*

no-see-um (nō-sē′əm) *n.* See **punkie.** [Alteration of *you can't see 'em.*]

nose·gay (nōz′gā′) *n.* A small bunch of flowers. See Synonyms at **bouquet.** [Middle English : *nose,* nose; see NOSE + *gai,* joyous, ornament; see GAY.]

nose job *n.* *Informal.* Plastic surgery on the nose, especially to improve its appearance; rhinoplasty.

nose·piece (nōz′pēs′) *n.* **1.** A piece of armor that forms part of a helmet and protects the nose. **2.** The part of a pair of eyeglasses that fits across the nose. **3.** See **noseband. 4.** The part of a microscope, often rotatable, to which one or more objective lenses are attached.

nos·ey (nō′zē) *adj.* Variant of **nosy.**

nosh (nŏsh) *Informal. n.* A snack or light meal. —**nosh** *intr.v.* **noshed, nosh·ing, nosh·es.** To eat a snack or light meal: *noshed on a bagel between classes.* [Yiddish *nash,* from *nashn,* to eat sweets, nibble on, from Middle High German *naschen,* to nibble, from Old High German *hnascōn.*] —**nosh′er** *n.*

no-show (nō′shō′) *Informal. n.* One that is expected but does not appear, especially: **a.** A person who reserves a place, as on an airplane, but neither uses nor cancels the reservation. **b.** A person who buys a ticket for an event but does not attend. **c.** A person who unexplainedly fails to keep an appointment. —**no-show** *adj.* Requiring little or no actual attendance or work: *a no-show political patronage job.*

nos·ing (nō′zĭng) *n.* **1.a.** The horizontally projecting edge of a stair tread. **b.** A shield covering this edge. **2.** A projecting edge of a molding.

noso– *pref.* Disease: *nosography.* [Greek, from *nosos,* a disease.]

no·sog·ra·phy (nō-sŏg′rə-fē, -zŏg′-) *n.* The systematic description of diseases. —**no·sog′ra·pher** *n.* —**no′so·graph′ic** (nō′sə-grăf′ĭk), **no′so·graph′i·cal** (-ĭ-kəl) *adj.*

no·sol·o·gy (nō-sŏl′ə-jē, -zŏl′-) *n., pl.* **-gies. 1.** The branch of medicine that deals with the classification of diseases. **2.** A classification of diseases. —**no′so·log′i·cal** (-sə-lŏj′ĭ-kəl), **no′so·log′ic** (-ĭk) *adj.* —**no′so·log′i·cal·ly** *adv.* —**no·sol′o·gist** *n.*

nos·tal·gi·a (nŏ-stăl′jə, nə-) *n.* **1.** A bittersweet longing for things, persons, or situations of the past. **2.** The condition of being homesick; homesickness. [Greek *nostos,* a return home; see **nes-**[1] in Appendix + –ALGIA.] —**nos·tal′gic** (-jĭk) *adj.* —**nos·tal′gi·cal·ly** *adv.*

nos·toc (nŏs′tŏk′) *n.* A freshwater blue-green alga of the genus *Nostoc,* forming spherical colonies of filaments embedded in a gelatinous substance. [New Latin, coined by Paracelsus.]

Nos·tra·da·mus (nŏs′trə-dā′məs, -dä′-, nō′strə-). Originally Michel de Notredame. 1503–1566. French physician and astrologer who wrote *Centuries* (1555), a book of prophecies.

nos·tril (nŏs′trəl) *n.* Either of the external openings of the nose; a naris. [Middle English *nostrille,* from Old English *nosthyrl* : *nosu,* nose; see **nas-** in Appendix + *thyrl,* hole; see **terə-**[2] in Appendix.]

nos·trum (nŏs′trəm) *n.* **1.** A medicine whose effectiveness is unproved and whose ingredients are usually secret; a quack remedy. **2.** A favorite but untested remedy for problems or evils. [From Latin *nostrum (remedium),* our (remedy), neuter of *noster.* See **nes-**[2] in Appendix.]

nos·y or **nos·ey** (nō′zē) *adj.* **-i·er, -i·est.** *Informal.* **1.** Given to prying into the affairs of others; snoopy. See Synonyms at **curious. 2.** Prying; inquisitive. —**nos′i·ly** *adv.* —**nos′i·ness** *n.*

not (nŏt) *adv.* In no way; to no degree. Used to express negation, denial, refusal, or prohibition: *I will not go. You may not have any.* [Middle English, alteration of *naught, nought.* See NAUGHT.]

USAGE NOTE: Care should be taken with the placement of *not* and other negatives in a sentence in order to avoid ambiguity. *All elephants are not friendly* could be taken to mean either "All elephants are unfriendly" or "Not all elephants are friendly." Similarly, the sentence *Kim didn't sleep until noon* could mean either "Kim went to sleep at noon" or "Kim got up before noon." • In formal writing the *not only . . . but also* construction should be used in such a way that each of its elements is followed by a construction of the same type. Instead of *She not only bought a new car but a new lawnmower,* write *She bought not only a new car but a new lawnmower;* in the second version, both *not only* and *but also* are followed by noun phrases. • In the *not only* construction *also* is often omitted when the second part of the sentence merely intensifies the first: *She is not only smart but brilliant. He not only wanted the diamond but wanted it desperately.* See Usage Note at **only.**

no·ta (nō′tə) *n.* Plural of **notum.**

no·ta be·ne (nō′tə bĕn′ē, bē′nē). *Abbr.* **n.b., N.B.** Used to direct attention to something particularly important. [Latin *notā bene,* note well : *notā,* sing. imperative of *notāre,* to note + *bene,* well.]

no·ta·bil·i·ty (nō′tə-bĭl′ĭ-tē) *n., pl.* **-ties. 1.** The state or quality of being eminent or worthy of notice. **2.** A prominent or notable person.

no·ta·ble (nō′tə-bəl) *adj.* **1.** Worthy of note or notice; remarkable: *notable beauty; sled dogs that are notable for their stamina.* **2.** Characterized by excellence or distinction; eminent: *formed a commission of notable citizens.* See Synonyms at **noted.** —**notable** *n.* **1.** A person of distinction or great reputation. See Synonyms at **celebrity. 2.** Often **Notable.** One of a council of prominent persons in pre-Revolutionary France called into assembly to deliberate at times of emergency. [Middle English, from Old French, from Latin *notābilis,* from *notāre,* to note, from *nota,* note. See NOTE.] —**no′ta·ble·ness** *n.* —**no′ta·bly** *adv.*

no·tar·i·al (nō-târ′ē-əl) *adj.* **1.** Of or relating to a notary public. **2.** Executed or drawn up by a notary public. —**no·tar′i·al·ly** *adv.*

no·ta·rize (nō′tə-rīz′) *tr.v.* **-rized, -riz·ing, -riz·es.** To certify (the validity of a signature on a document, for example) as a notary public. —**no′ta·ri·za′tion** (-rĭ-zā′shən) *n.*

no·ta·ry (nō′tə-rē) *n., pl.* **-ries.** A notary public. [Middle English *notarie,* from Old French *notaire, notarie,* from Latin *notārius,* relating to shorthand, shorthand writer, from *nota,* mark. See NOTE.]

notary public *n., pl.* **notaries public.** *Abbr.* **N.P.** A person legally empowered to witness and certify the validity of documents and to take affidavits and depositions.

no·tate (nō′tāt) *tr.v.* **-tat·ed, -tat·ing, -tates.** To put into notation. [Back-formation from NOTATION.]

no·ta·tion (nō-tā′shən) *n.* **1.a.** A system of figures or symbols used in a specialized field to represent numbers, quantities, tones, or values: *musical notation.* **b.** The act or process of using such a system. **2.** A brief note; an annotation: *marginal notations.* [Latin *notātiō, notātiōn-,* from *notātus,* past participle of *notāre,* to note, from *nota,* note. See NOTE.] —**no·ta′tion·al** *adj.*

notch (nŏch) *n.* **1.a.** A V-shaped cut. **b.** Such a cut used for keeping a record. **2.** A narrow pass between mountains. **3.** *Informal.* A level or degree: *a notch or two higher in quality.* —**notch** *tr.v.* **notched, notch·ing, notch·es. 1.** To cut a notch in. **2.** To record by or as if by making notches: *notched the score on a stick.* **3.** *Informal.* To achieve; score: *notched 30 wins in a single season.* [Probably from the phrase **an otch,* from French *oche,* from Old French, from *ochier,* to notch.]

notch·back (nŏch′băk′) *n.* An automobile having a roof that drops off sharply to the top of the rear compartment.

note (nōt) *n.* *Abbr.* **n. 1.** A brief record, especially one written down to aid the memory: *took notes during the lecture.* **2.** A brief informal letter. See Synonyms at **letter. 3.** A formal written diplomatic or official communication. **4.** A comment or an explanation, as on a passage in a text. **5.a.** A piece of paper currency. **b.** A certificate issued by a government or a bank and sometimes negotiable as money. **c.** A promissory note. **6.** *Music.* **a.** A tone of definite pitch. **b.** A symbol for such a tone, indicating pitch by its position on the staff and duration by its shape. **c.** A key of an instrument, such as a piano. **7.** The characteristic vocal sound made by a songbird or other animal: *the clear note of a cardinal.* **8.** The sign of a particular quality or emotion: *ended his plea on a note of despair; a note of gaiety in her manner.* See Synonyms at **sign. 9.** Importance; consequence: *Nothing of note happened.* **10.** Notice; observation: *quietly took note of the scene.* **11.** *Obsolete.* A song, melody, or tune. —**note** *tr.v.* **not·ed, not·ing, notes. 1.** To observe carefully; notice. See Synonyms at **see**[1]. **2.** To make a note of; write down: *noted the time of each arrival.* **3.** To show; indicate: *a reporter who is careful to note sources of information.* **4.** To make mention of; remark: *noted the lateness of their arrival.* [Middle English, from Old French, from Latin *nota,* annotation. See **gnō-** in Appendix.] —**not′er** *n.*

note·book (nōt′bo͝ok′) *n.* A book of blank pages for notes.

No·teć (nô′tĕch′). A river of northwest Poland flowing about 434 km (270 mi) generally westward. It is connected by canal with the Vistula River.

not·ed (nō′tĭd) *adj.* Distinguished by reputation; famous: *a noted physician.* —**not′ed·ly** *adv.* —**not′ed·ness** *n.*

Norwegian elkhound

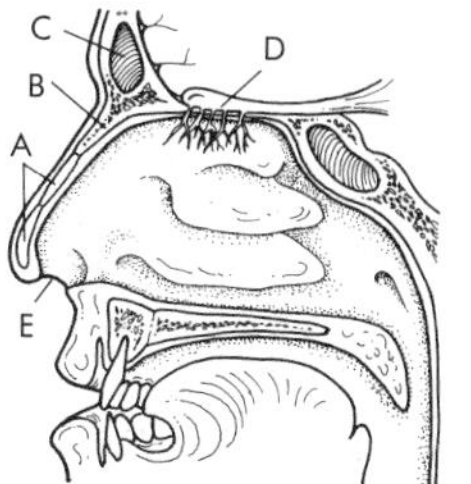

nose
A. Cartilage
B. Bone
C. Frontal sinus
D. Olfactory bulb
E. Nostril

Nostradamus
1562 portrait

ă pat	oi boy
ā pay	ou out
âr care	o͝o took
ä father	o͞o boot
ĕ pet	ŭ cut
ē be	ûr urge
ĭ pit	th thin
ī pie	*th* this
îr pier	hw which
ŏ pot	zh vision
ō toe	ə about, item
ô paw	♦ regionalism

Stress marks: **′** (primary); ′ (secondary), as in **dictionary** (dĭk′shə-nĕr′ē)

SYNONYMS: *noted, celebrated, eminent, famed, famous, illustrious, notable, preeminent, renowned.* The central meaning shared by these adjectives is "widely known and esteemed": *a noted author; a celebrated musician; an eminent scholar; a famed scientist; a famous actor; an illustrious judge; a notable historian; a preeminent archaeologist; a renowned painter.*
ANTONYM: *obscure.*

note of hand *n., pl.* **notes of hand.** See **promissory note.**

note·wor·thy (nōt′wûr′*thē*) *adj.* **-thi·er, -thi·est.** Deserving notice or attention; notable: *a noteworthy advance in cancer research.* **—note′wor′thi·ly** *adv.* **—note′wor′thi·ness** *n.*

NOT gate (nŏt) *n. Computer Science.* A logic circuit that produces an output inverse to the input. [From NOT.]

noth·ing (nŭth′ĭng) *pron.* **1.** No thing; not anything: *The box contained nothing. I've heard nothing about it.* **2.** No part; no portion: *Nothing remains of the old house but the cellar hole.* **3.** One of no consequence, significance, or interest: *The new non-smoking policy is nothing to me.* **—nothing** *n.* **1.** Something that has no existence. **2.** Something that has no quantitative value; zero: *a score of two to nothing.* **3.** One that has no substance or importance; a nonentity: *"A nothing is a dreadful thing to hold onto"* (Edna O'Brien). **—nothing** *adj.* Insignificant or worthless: *"the utterly nothing role of a wealthy suitor"* (Bosley Crowther). **—nothing** *adv.* In no way or degree; not at all: *She looks nothing like her sister.* ***—idiom.*** **nothing doing.** *Informal.* Certainly not. [Middle English, from Old English *nāthing* : *nā*, no; see NO[2] + *thing*, thing; see THING.]

USAGE NOTE: According to the traditional rule, *nothing* is invariably treated as a singular, even when followed by an exception phrase containing a plural noun: *Nothing except your fears stands* (not *stand*) *in your way. Nothing but roses meets* (not *meet*) *the eye.*

noth·ing·ness (nŭth′ĭng-nĭs) *n.* **1.** The condition or quality of being nothing; nonexistence. **2.** Empty space; a void. **3.** Lack of consequence; insignificance. **4.** Something inconsequential or insignificant.

no·tice (nō′tĭs) *n.* **1.** The act of noting or observing; perception or attention: *That detail escaped my notice.* **2.** Respectful attention or consideration: *grateful for the teacher's notice.* **3.** A written or printed announcement: *a notice of sale.* **4.a.** A formal announcement, notification, or warning, especially an announcement of one's intention to withdraw from an agreement or leave a job: *give one's employer two weeks' notice; raised the price without notice.* **b.** The condition of being formally warned or notified: *put us on notice for chronic lateness.* **5.** A printed critical review, as of a play or book. **—notice** *tr.v.* **-ticed, -tic·ing, -tic·es. 1.** To take notice of; observe: *noticed a figure in the doorway.* See Synonyms at **see**[1]. **2.** To perceive with the mind; detect: *noticed several discrepancies.* **3.** To comment on; mention. **4.** To treat with courteous attention. **5.** To give or file a notice of: *noticed the court case for next Tuesday.* [Middle English, knowledge, from Old French, from Latin *nōtitia*, from *nōtus*, known, past participle of *nōscere*, to get to know. See **gnō-** in Appendix.]

no·tice·a·ble (nō′tĭ-sə-bəl) *adj.* **1.** Evident; observable: *noticeable changes in temperature; a noticeable lack of friendliness.* **2.** Worthy of notice; significant. **—no′tice·a·bil′i·ty** *n.* **—no′tice·a·bly** *adv.*

SYNONYMS: *noticeable, observable, marked, conspicuous, prominent, outstanding, salient, remarkable, signal, arresting, striking.* These adjectives mean attracting notice. *Noticeable* and *observable* both refer to something that can be readily noticed or observed: *"His long, feminine eyelashes were very noticeable"* (Joseph Conrad). *The movements of the prowler were observable from the window.* What is *marked* is emphatically evident: *He walks with a marked limp. The play is a marked success. Conspicuous* applies to what is immediately apparent and noteworthy: *Her outlandish attire made her conspicuous in the crowd. "Conspicuous consumption of valuable goods is a means of reputability to the gentleman of leisure"* (Thorstein Veblen). *Prominent* and *outstanding* connote a standing out among others, especially others of its kind: *A new theory of the origin of language is the most prominent feature of the book. Einstein and Churchill were among the outstanding figures of the 20th century.* What is *salient* is so prominent and consequential that it seems to leap out and claim the attention: *"Defenders of the pit bull always seem to miss the salient point that it is the ferocity of the bite, not the number of bites, that has made the dog so feared today"* (Sports Illustrated). *Remarkable* describes what elicits comment because it is unusual or extraordinary: *"This story of Mongolian conquests is surely the most remarkable in all history"* (H.G. Wells). *Signal* suggests that something is notably remarkable: *"I had an Opportunity of doing his Majesty . . . a most signal Service"* (Jonathan Swift). *Arresting* applies to what attracts and holds the attention: The Miraculous Mandarin *is one of Bartók's most arresting compositions. Striking* describes something that seizes the attention and produces a vivid impression on the sight or the mind: *The child bears a striking resemblance to the parents.* See also Synonyms at **perceptible.**

no·ti·fi·ca·tion (nō′tə-fĭ-kā′shən) *n.* **1.** The act or an instance of notifying. **2.** Something, such as a letter, by which notice is given.

no·ti·fy (nō′tə-fī′) *tr.v.* **-fied, -fy·ing, -fies. 1.** To give notice to; inform: *notified the citizens of the curfew by posting signs.* **2.** *Chiefly British.* To give notice of; make known. [Middle English *notifien*, from Old French *notifier*, from Latin *nōtificāre* : *notus*, known, past participle of *nōscere*, to get to know; see **gnō-** in Appendix + *-ficāre*, -fy.] **—no′ti·fi′er** *n.*

no·tion (nō′shən) *n.* **1.** A belief or opinion. **2.** A mental image or representation; an idea or conception. **3.** A fanciful impulse; a whim. See Synonyms at **idea. 4. notions.** Small lightweight items for household use, such as needles, buttons, and thread. [Middle English *nocioun*, concept, from Latin *nōtiō*, *nōtiōn-*, from *nōtus*, known, past participle of *nōscere*, to get to know. See **gnō-** in Appendix.]

no·tion·al (nō′shə-nəl) *adj.* **1.** Of, containing, or being a notion; mental or imaginary. **2.** Speculative or theoretical. **3.** *Linguistics.* Conveying an idea of a thing or an action; having full lexical meaning as distinguished from relational meaning. The word *did* is notional in *We did the work* and relational in *We did not agree.* **—no′tion·al·ly** *adv.*

no·to·chord (nō′tə-kôrd′) *n.* **1.** A flexible rodlike structure that forms the main support of the body in the lowest chordates, such as the lancelet; a primitive backbone. **2.** A similar structure in embryos of higher vertebrates, from which the spinal column develops. [Greek *nōton*, back + CHORD[2].] **—no′to·chord′al** *adj.*

No·to·gae·a or **No·to·ge·a** (nō′tə-jē′ə). A zoogeographic region including Australia, New Zealand, and the islands of the southwest Pacific Ocean.

no·to·ri·e·ty (nō′tə-rī′ĭ-tē) *n.* The quality or condition of being notorious; ill fame.

no·to·ri·ous (nō-tôr′ē-əs, -tōr′-) *adj.* Known widely and usually unfavorably; infamous: *a notorious gangster; a district notorious for vice.* [From Medieval Latin *nōtōrius*, well-known, from Latin *nōtus*, known, past participle of *nōscere*, to get to know. See **gnō-** in Appendix.] **—no·to′ri·ous·ly** *adv.* **—no·to′ri·ous·ness** *n.*

no·tor·nis (nō-tôr′nĭs) *n., pl.* **notornis.** Any of several flightless New Zealand birds, now rare, of the genus *Notornis*, especially the takahe. [New Latin *Notornis*, genus name : Greek *notos*, south + Greek *ornis*, bird; see **or-** in Appendix.]

No·tre Dame Mountains (nō′trə dām′, däm′, nō′tər). A section of the Appalachian Mountains extending about 805 km (500 mi) from the Green Mountains of Vermont into the Gaspé Peninsula of southeast Quebec, Canada.

no-trump (nō′trŭmp′) *n. Games.* **1.** A declaration to play a hand without a trump suit in bridge and other card games. **2.** A hand played without a trump suit. **—no′-trump′** *adj.*

Not·ta·way (nŏt′ə-wā′). A river, about 644 km (400 mi) long, of southwest Quebec, Canada, flowing northwest into James Bay.

Not·ting·ham (nŏt′ĭng-əm). A borough of central England north of Leicester. Charles I raised his standard here in 1642, marking the beginning of the English Civil War. The city has long been a center for the manufacture of textiles, lace, and hosiery. According to tradition, it is the birthplace of Robin Hood. Population, 277,500.

no·tum (nō′təm) *n., pl.* **-ta** (-tə). The dorsal part of the thoracic segment of an insect. [New Latin *nōtum*, from Greek *nōton*, back.]

not·with·stand·ing (nŏt′wĭth-stăn′dĭng, -wĭth-) *prep.* In spite of: *The teams played on, notwithstanding the rain.* **—notwithstanding** *adv.* All the same; nevertheless: *We proceeded, notwithstanding.* **—notwithstanding** *conj.* In spite of the fact that; although. [Middle English *notwithstandinge* (translation of Medieval Latin *nōn obstante*; see NON OBSTANTE) : *not*, not; see NOT + *withstanding*, present participle of *withstanden*, to resist; see WITHSTAND.]

Nouak·chott (nwäk-shŏt′). The capital and largest city of Mauritania, in the western part of the country on the Atlantic Ocean. It was chosen as capital in 1957. Population, 150,000.

nou·gat (no͞o′gət) *n.* A confection made from a sugar or honey paste into which nuts are mixed. [French, from Provençal, from *nougo*, nut, from Old Provençal *noga*, from Vulgar Latin **nuca*, from Latin *nux*, *nuc-*, nut.]

nought (nôt) *n., pron., & adj.* Variant of **naught.**

Nou·mé·a (no͞o-mā′ə). The capital of New Caledonia, on the southwest coast of the island of New Caledonia in the southwest Pacific Ocean. It was an Allied air base in World War II. Population, 60,112.

nou·me·non (no͞o′mə-nŏn′) *n., pl.* **-na** (-nə). *Philosophy.* **1.** An object that can be intuited only by the intellect and not perceived by the senses. **2.** An object independent of intellectual intuition of it or of sensuous perception of it. Also called *thing-in-itself.* **3.** In the philosophy of Kant, an object, such as the soul, that cannot be known through perception, although its existence can be demonstrated. [German, from Greek *noumenon*, from neuter present middle participle of *noein*, to perceive by thought, from *nous*, mind.] **—nou′men·al** (-mə-nəl) *adj.*

noun (noun) *n. Abbr.* **n.** *Grammar.* A word that is used to name a person, place, thing, quality, or action and can function as the subject or object of a verb, the object of a preposition, or an appositive. [Middle English, name, noun, from Anglo-Norman, from Latin *nōmen, nōmin-*. See **nō-men-** in Appendix.]

nour·ish (nûr′ĭsh, nŭr′-) *tr.v.* **-ished, -ish·ing, -ish·es. 1.** To provide with food or other substances necessary for life and growth; feed. **2.** To foster the development of; promote: *"Athens was an imperial city, nourished by the tribute of subjects"* (V. Gordon Childe). **3.** To keep alive; maintain: *nourish a hope.* [Middle English *norishen,* from Old French *norrir, norriss-,* from Vulgar Latin **nutrīre,* from Latin *nūtrīre.* See **(s)nāu-** in Appendix.] **—nour′ish·er** *n.*

nour·ish·ment (nûr′ĭsh-mənt, nŭr′-) *n.* **1.a.** The act of nourishing. **b.** The state of being nourished. **2.** Something that nourishes; food.

nous (no͞os, nous) *n.* **1.** *Philosophy.* **a.** Reason and knowledge as opposed to sense perception. **b.** The rational part of the individual human soul. **c.** The principle of the cosmic mind or soul responsible for the rational order of the cosmos. **d.** In Stoicism, the equivalent of Logos. **e.** In Neo-Platonism, the image of the absolute good, containing the cosmos of intelligible beings. **2.** *Chiefly British.* Good sense; shrewdness: *"Hillela had the nous to take up with the General when he was on the up-and-up again"* (Nadine Gordimer). [Greek.]

nou·veau riche (no͞o′vō rēsh′) *n., pl.* **nou·veaux riches** (no͞o′vō rēsh′). One who has recently become rich, especially one who flaunts newly acquired wealth. [French : *nouveau,* new + *riche,* rich.]

nou·velle cuisine (no͞o-vĕl′) *n.* A contemporary school of French cooking that seeks to bring out the natural flavors of foods and substitutes light, low-calorie sauces and stocks for the traditional heavy butter-based and cream-based preparations. [French : *nouvelle,* new + *cuisine,* cuisine.]

nouvelle vague (väg′) *n.* See **new wave** (sense 1). [French : *nouvelle,* new + *vague,* wave.]

Nov. or **Nov** *abbr.* November.

no·va (nō′və) *n., pl.* **-vae** (-vē) or **-vas.** A star that suddenly becomes much brighter and then gradually returns to its original brightness over a period of weeks to years. [New Latin *(stēlla) nova,* new (star), nova, feminine of Latin *novus,* new. See **newo-** in Appendix.]

no·vac·u·lite (nō-văk′yə-līt′) *n.* A very hard, dense, even-textured, silica-bearing sedimentary rock used in whetstones. [Latin *novācula,* razor + -ITE[1].]

no·vae (nō′vē) *n.* A plural of **nova.**

No·va I·gua·çu (nô′vä ē′gwä-so͞o′). A city of southeast Brazil, an industrial suburb of Rio de Janeiro. Population, 491,766.

No·va·ra (nō-vär′ə, -vä′rä). A city of northwest Italy west of Milan. The Austrians defeated the Piedmontese here in 1849. Population, 101,635.

No·va Sco·tia (nō′və skō′shə). *Abbr.* **NS, N.S.** A province of eastern Canada comprising a mainland peninsula and the adjacent Cape Breton Island. It joined the confederation in 1867. The first successful settlement was made by the French at Port Royal (now Annapolis Royal) in 1610. France and Great Britain bitterly contested the area, part of Acadia, until 1763, when the Treaty of Paris awarded the French possessions in North America to the British. During the 18th century many Scots immigrated to the region, leading to its name, a Latinized version of "New Scotland." Halifax is the capital and the largest city. Population, 847,442. **—No′va Sco′tian** *adj. & n.*

no·va·tion (nō-vā′shən) *n. Law.* Substitution of a new obligation for an old one. [Late Latin *novātiō, novātiōn-,* from Latin, a renewing, from *novātus,* past participle of *novāre,* to make new, from *novus,* new. See **newo-** in Appendix.]

No·va·to (nə-vä′tō). A city of western California north of San Rafael. It is mainly residential. Population, 43,916.

No·va·ya Zem·lya (nō′və-yə zĕm′lē-ä′, zĭm-lyä′). An archipelago of north-central Russia in the Arctic Ocean between the Barents and Kara seas. Consisting of two main islands and many smaller ones, the archipelago has mineral deposits and an economy based on fishing, sealing, and trapping.

nov·el[1] (nŏv′əl) *n.* **1.** A fictional prose narrative of considerable length, typically having a plot that is unfolded by the actions, speech, and thoughts of the characters. **2.** The literary genre represented by novels. [Ultimately from Italian *novella,* from Old Italian, piece of news, chit-chat, tale, from Vulgar Latin **novella,* from neuter pl. of Latin *novellus,* diminutive of *novus,* new. See **newo-** in Appendix.]

nov·el[2] (nŏv′əl) *adj.* Strikingly new, unusual, or different. See Synonyms at **new.** [Middle English, from Old French, from Latin *novellus,* diminutive of *novus.* See **newo-** in Appendix.] **—nov′el·ly** *adv.*

nov·el·ette (nŏv′ə-lĕt′) *n.* A short novel.

nov·el·ist (nŏv′ə-lĭst) *n.* A writer of novels.

nov·el·is·tic (nŏv′ə-lĭs′tĭk) *adj.* Of, relating to, or characteristic of novels. **—nov′el·is′ti·cal·ly** *adv.*

nov·el·ize (nŏv′ə-līz′) *tr.v.* **-ized, -iz·ing, -iz·es. 1.** To write a novel based on: *novelize a popular movie.* **2.** To turn into fiction; fictionalize: *novelize one's personal experiences.* **—nov′el·i·za′tion** (-ə-lĭ-zā′shən) *n.* **—nov′el·iz′er** *n.*

no·vel·la (nō-vĕl′ə) *n., pl.* **-vel·las** or **-vel·le** (-vĕl′ē, -vĕl′ā). **1.** A short prose tale often characterized by moral teaching or satire. **2.** A short novel. [Italian. See NOVEL[1].]

nov·el·ty (nŏv′əl-tē) *n., pl.* **-ties. 1.** The quality of being novel; newness. **2.** Something new and unusual; an innovation. **3.** A small mass-produced article, such as a toy or trinket.

No·vem·ber (nō-vĕm′bər) *n. Abbr.* **Nov., Nov** The 11th month of the year in the Gregorian calendar. See table at **calendar.** [Middle English *Novembre,* from Old French, from Latin *November,* ninth month, from *novem,* nine. See **newn̥** in Appendix.]

no·ve·na (nō-vē′nə) *n., pl.* **-nas** or **-nae** (-nē). *Roman Catholic Church.* A recitation of prayers and devotions for a special purpose during nine consecutive days. [Medieval Latin *novēna,* from feminine of Latin *novēnus,* nine each, from *novem,* nine. See **newn̥** in Appendix.]

no·ver·cal (nō-vûr′kəl) *adj.* Of, relating to, or characteristic of a stepmother. [Latin *novercālis,* from *noverca,* stepmother. See **newo-** in Appendix.]

Nov·go·rod (nŏv′gə-rŏd′, nôv′gə-rət). A city of northwest Russia south-southeast of St. Petersburg. One of the oldest cities in Russia, it was strategically and economically important in the Middle Ages because of its location on the chief trade routes of eastern Europe. The city was overrun by Moscow in 1478 and lost its commercial dominance to St. Petersburg after 1703. Population, 220,000.

No·vi (nō′vī′). A village of southeast Michigan northwest of Detroit. Metal products are among its manufactures. Population, 22,525.

nov·ice (nŏv′ĭs) *n.* **1.** A person new to a field or activity; a beginner. **2.** A person who has entered a religious order but has not yet taken final vows. In this sense, also called *novitiate.* [Middle English, from Old French, from Medieval Latin *novīcius,* from Latin, recently entered into a condition, from Latin *novus,* new. See **newo-** in Appendix.]

No·vi Sad (nō′vē säd′). A city of northeast Yugoslavia on the Danube River northwest of Belgrade. It became a free city of Austria-Hungary in 1748 and was the center of a Serbian literary revival in the 18th and early 19th centuries. Population, 170,800.

no·vi·ti·ate also **no·vi·ci·ate** (nō-vĭsh′ē-ĭt, -āt′) *n.* **1.** The period of being a novice. **2.** A place where novices live. **3.** See **novice** (sense 2). [Medieval Latin *novīciātus,* from *novīcius,* novice. See NOVICE.]

no·vo·bi·o·cin (nō′və-bī′ə-sĭn) *n.* An antibiotic, $C_{31}H_{36}N_2O_{11}$, produced by the actinomycete *Streptomyces nivens* and used to treat infections by gram-positive bacteria. [Probably Latin *novus,* new; see NOVICE + (ANTI)BIO(TIC) + -IN.]

No·vo·cain (nō′və-kān′). A trademark used for an anesthetic preparation of procaine.

No·vo·cher·kassk (nō′və-chər-käsk′, nə-və-chĭr-). A city of southwest Russia northeast of Rostov. Founded in 1805, it is a commercial center. Population, 186,000.

No·vo Ham·bur·go (nô′vo͝o äNm-bo͞or′go͞o). A city of southern Brazil north of Pôrto Alegre. It was founded by German immigrants in the 19th century. Population, 133,221.

No·vo·kuz·netsk (nō′və-ko͝oz-nĕtsk′, nə-və-ko͝oz-nyĕtsk′). A city of south-central Russia southeast of Novosibirsk. Founded by Cossacks in 1617, it was developed as an iron and steel center in the 1930's. Population, 577,000.

No·vo·ros·siysk (nō′və-rə-sēsk′, nə-və-). A city of southwest Russia on the Black Sea south-southwest of Rostov. It is a shipbuilding center. Population, 175,000.

No·vo·si·birsk (nō′və-sə-bîrsk′, nə-və-sĭ-). A city of south-central Russia on the Ob River east of Omsk. An important transportation hub on the Trans-Siberian Railroad, it prospered after the development of the Kuznetsk Basin. Population, 1,393,000.

now (nou) *adv.* **1.** At the present time: *goods now on sale; the now aging dictator.* **2.** At once; immediately: *Stop now.* **3.** In the immediate past; very recently: *left the room just now.* **4.** At this point in the series of events; then: *The ship was now listing to port.* **5.** Nowadays. **6.** In these circumstances; as things are: *Now we won't be able to stay.* **7.a.** Used to introduce a command, reproof, or request: *Now pay attention.* **b.** Used to indicate a change of subject or to preface a remark: *Now, let's get down to work.* **—now** *conj.* Seeing that; since: *Now that spring is here, we can expect milder weather.* **—now** *n.* The present time or moment: *wouldn't work up to now.* **—now** *adj.* **1.** Of the present time; current: *our now governor.* **2.** *Slang.* Currently fashionable; trendy: *the now sound of this new rock band.* **—*idiom.* now and again** (or **then).** Occasionally. [Middle English, from Old English *nū.* See **nu-** in Appendix.] **—now′ness** *n.*

NOW *abbr.* National Organization for Women.

NOW account (nou) *n.* An interest-bearing savings account against which drafts may be written. [*n(egotiable) o(rder of) w(ithdrawal).*]

now·a·days (nou′ə-dāz′) *adv.* During the present time; now. [Middle English *nouadaies* : *nou,* now; see NOW + *a* (variant of *on,* on; see ON) + *daies,* genitive of *dai,* day; see DAY.]

no·way (nō′wā′) also **no·ways** (-wāz′) *adv. Informal.* In no way or degree; nowise. **—noway** also **no way** *interj.* Used to express emphatic negation.

no·where (nō′hwâr′, -wâr′) *adv.* **1.** Not anywhere. **2.** To no place or result: *protested the ruling but got nowhere.* **—nowhere** *n.* A remote or unknown place: *a cabin in the middle of nowhere.*

ă pat	oi boy
ā pay	ou out
âr care	o͝o took
ä father	o͞o boot
ĕ pet	ŭ cut
ē be	ûr urge
ĭ pit	th thin
ī pie	*th* this
îr pier	hw which
ŏ pot	zh vision
ō toe	ə about, item
ô paw	♦ regionalism

Stress marks: **′** (primary); ′ (secondary), as in **dictionary** (dĭk′shə-nĕr′ē)

no·wheres (nō′hwârz′, -wârz′) *adv. Non-Standard.* Nowhere.

no·whith·er (nō′hwĭth′ər, -wĭth′-) *adv.* In no definite direction.

no-win (nō′wĭn′) *adj. Informal.* Certain to end in failure or disappointment: *trapped in a no-win situation.*

no·wise (nō′wīz′) *adv.* In no way, manner, or degree; not at all.

nox·ious (nŏk′shəs) *adj.* **1.** Harmful to living things; injurious to health: *noxious chemical wastes.* **2.** Harmful to the mind or morals; corrupting: *noxious ideas.* [Middle English *noxius,* from Latin, from *noxa,* damage. See **nek-¹** in Appendix.] **—nox·ious·ly** *adv.* **—nox′ious·ness** *n.*

Noyes (noiz), **Alfred.** 1880–1958. British poet whose works, traditional in style, concern nature and science, English history, and his conversion to Catholicism.

Noyes, John Humphrey. 1811–1886. American religious leader who founded (1848) an experimental community at Oneida, New York, based on his belief in perfectionism and communal living.

noz·zle (nŏz′əl) *n.* **1.** A projecting part with an opening, as at the end of a hose, for regulating and directing a flow of fluid. **2.** *Slang.* The human nose. [Middle English *noselle,* socket on a candlestick, diminutive of *nose.* See NOSE.]

Np The symbol for the element **neptunium.**

NP *abbr.* **1.** Neuropsychiatry. **2.** *Grammar.* Noun phrase. **3.** Nurse practitioner.

N.P. *abbr.* Notary public.

NPN *abbr.* Nonprotein nitrogen.

NPR *abbr.* National Public Radio.

nr *abbr.* Near.

NRA *abbr.* **1.** National Recovery Administration. **2.** National Rifle Association. **3.** Naval Reserve Association.

NRC *abbr.* **1.** National Research Council. **2.** Nuclear Regulatory Commission.

ns *abbr.* Nanosecond.

NS *abbr.* **1.** Also **N.S.** Nova Scotia. **2.** Nuclear ship.

n.s. *abbr.* **1.** New series. **2.** Not specified.

N.S. *abbr.* New Style.

n/s *abbr.* Not sufficient.

NSA *abbr.* National Security Agency.

NSC *abbr.* National Security Council.

NSE *abbr.* National Stock Exchange.

nsec *abbr.* Nanosecond.

NSF *abbr.* National Science Foundation.

n.s.f. or **N.S.F.** *abbr.* Not sufficient funds.

N.S.P.C.A. *abbr.* National Society for the Prevention of Cruelty to Animals.

NT *abbr.* **1.** Also **N.T.** *Bible.* New Testament. **2.** Northwest Territories.

–n't. Not.

nth (ĕnth) *adj.* **1.** Relating to an indefinitely large ordinal number: *ten to the nth power.* **2.** Highest; utmost: *delighted to the nth degree.* [N², indefinite number + –TH³.]

nth root *n. Mathematics.* See **root¹** (sense 9a).

n.t.p. or **N.T.P.** *abbr.* Normal temperature and pressure.

NTSB *abbr.* National Transportation Safety Board.

nt.wt. *abbr.* Net weight.

nu (no͞o, nyo͞o) *n.* The 13th letter of the Greek alphabet. See table at **alphabet.** [Greek, of Semitic origin; akin to Hebrew *nûn,* nun.]

nu·ance (no͞o′äns′, nyo͞o′-, no͞o-äns′, nyo͞o-) *n.* **1.** A subtle or slight degree of difference, as in meaning, feeling, or tone; a gradation. **2.** Expression or appreciation of subtle shades of meaning, feeling, or tone: *a rich artistic performance, full of nuance.* [French, from Old French, from *nuer,* to shade, cloud, from *nue,* cloud, from Vulgar Latin **nūba,* from Latin *nūbēs.*] **—nu·anced′** *adj.*

SYNONYMS: *nuance, gradation, shade.* The central meaning shared by these nouns is "a slight variation or differentiation between nearly identical entities": *sensitive to delicate nuances of style; gradations of feeling from infatuation to deep affection; subtle shades of meaning.*

nub (nŭb) *n.* **1.** A protuberance or knob. **2.** A small lump. **3.** The essence; the core: *the nub of a story.* [Variant of *knub,* probably from Low German *knubbe,* from Middle Low German, variant of *knobbe.*] **—nub′by** *adj.*

Nu·ba (no͞o′bə, nyo͞o′-) *n., pl.* **Nuba. 1.** A member of any of several peoples inhabiting the hills of south-central Sudan. **2.** See **Nubian** (sense 2).

Nu·bi·a (no͞o′bē-ə, nyo͞o′-). A desert region and ancient kingdom in the Nile River valley of southern Egypt and northern Sudan. After the 20th century B.C. it was controlled by the rulers of Egypt, although in the 8th and 7th centuries an independent kingdom arose that conquered Eygpt and ruled as the XXV Dynasty (712–663). Converted to Christianity in the 6th century A.D., Nubia united with Ethiopia but fell to the Moslems in the 14th century. Much of the region was flooded by the completion of the Aswan High Dam in the 1960's.

Nu·bi·an (no͞o′bē-ən, nyo͞o′-) *adj.* Of or relating to Nubia or its peoples, languages, or cultures. **—Nubian** *n.* **1.** A native or inhabitant of Nubia. **2.** Any of a group of closely related Nilo-Saharan languages spoken in the Sudan. In this sense, also called *Nuba.*

Nubian Desert. A desert region of northeast Sudan extending east of the Nile River to the Red Sea.

nu·bile (no͞o′bĭl, -bīl′, nyo͞o′-) *adj.* **1.** Ready for marriage; of a marriageable age or condition. Used of young women. **2.** Sexually mature and attractive. Used of young women. [Latin *nūbilis,* from *nūbere,* to take a husband.] **—nu·bil′i·ty** (no͞o-bĭl′ĭ-tē, nyo͞o-) *n.*

nu·cel·lus (no͞o-sĕl′əs, nyo͞o-) *n., pl.* **-cel·li** (-sĕl′ī). *Botany.* The central portion of an ovule in which the embryo sac develops; the megasporangium. [New Latin, from *nux, nuc-,* nut.] **—nu·cel′lar** *adj.*

nu·cha (no͞o′kə, nyo͞o′-) *n.* The nape of the neck. [Middle English, spinal cord, from Medieval Latin, from Arabic *nuḫḫ,* marrow.] **—nu′chal** *adj.*

nucle– *pref.* Variant of **nucleo–.**

nu·cle·ar (no͞o′klē-ər, nyo͞o′-) *adj.* **1.** *Biology.* Of, relating to, or forming a nucleus: *a nuclear membrane.* **2.** *Physics.* Of or relating to atomic nuclei. **3.** Using or derived from the energy of atomic nuclei; atomic. **4.** Of, using, or possessing atomic or hydrogen bombs: *nuclear war; nuclear nations.* [From NUCLEUS.]

nuclear age *n.* The atomic age.

nuclear emulsion *n. Physics.* Any of several photographic emulsions used to detect and visually display the paths of charged subatomic particles, especially of charged cosmic ray particles.

nuclear energy *n.* **1.** The energy released by a nuclear reaction, especially by fission or fusion. **2.** Nuclear energy regarded as a source of power. Also called *atomic energy.*

nuclear envelope *n.* See **nuclear membrane.**

nuclear family *n.* A family unit consisting of a mother and father and their children.

nuclear force *n. Physics.* Strong interaction.

nu·cle·ar-free zone (no͞o′klē-ər-frē′, nyo͞o′-) *n.* An area in which the siting of nuclear weapons or reactors is banned.

nu·cle·ar·ize (no͞o′klē-ə-rīz′, nyo͞o′-) *tr.v.* **-ized, -iz·ing, -iz·es.** To equip with nuclear weapons. **—nu′cle·ar·i·za′tion** (-ər-ĭ-zā′shən) *n.*

nuclear magnetic resonance *n. Abbr.* **NMR** The absorption of electromagnetic radiation of a specific frequency by an atomic nucleus that is placed in a strong magnetic field, used especially in spectroscopic studies of molecular structure and in medicine to measure rates of metabolism.

nuclear magneton *n. Physics.* A unit of the magnetic moment of a nucleon.

nuclear medicine *n.* The branch of medicine that deals with the use of radionuclides in diagnosis and treatment of disease.

nuclear membrane *n.* The double-layered membrane enclosing the nucleus of a cell. Also called *nuclear envelope.*

nuclear physics *n. (used with a sing. verb).* The scientific study of the forces, reactions, and internal structures of atomic nuclei.

nuclear power *n.* Power, especially electricity, the source of which is nuclear fission or fusion.

nuclear reaction *n.* A reaction, as in fission, fusion, or radioactive decay, that alters the energy, composition, or structure of an atomic nucleus.

nuclear reactor *n.* Any of several devices in which a chain reaction is initiated and controlled, with the resulting heat typically used for power generation and the neutrons and fission products used for military, experimental, and medical purposes.

nuclear weapon *n.* A device, such as a bomb or warhead, whose great explosive power derives from the release of nuclear energy.

nuclear winter *n.* A worldwide darkening and cooling of the atmosphere with consequent devastation of surviving life forms, believed by some scientists to be a probable outcome of large-scale nuclear war.

nu·cle·ase (no͞o′klē-ās′, -āz′, nyo͞o′-) *n.* Any of several enzymes, such as endonucleases and exonucleases, that hydrolyze nucleic acids.

nu·cle·ate (no͞o′klē-ĭt, nyo͞o′-) *adj.* Nucleated. **—nucleate** (-āt′) *v.* **-at·ed, -at·ing, -ates.** *—tr.* **1.** To bring together into a nucleus. **2.** To act as a nucleus for. **3.** To provide a nucleus for. *—intr.* To form a nucleus. **—nu′cle·a′tion** *n.* **—nu′cle·a′tor** *n.*

nu·cle·at·ed (no͞o′klē-ā′tĭd, nyo͞o′-) *adj.* Having a nucleus or nuclei: *the nucleated cell of a spermatozoon.*

nu·cle·i (no͞o′klē-ī′, nyo͞o′-) *n.* A plural of **nucleus.**

nu·cle·ic acid (no͞o-klē′ĭk, -klā′-, nyo͞o-) *n.* Any of a group of complex compounds found in all living cells and viruses, composed of purines, pyrimidines, carbohydrates, and phosphoric acid. Nucleic acids in the form of DNA and RNA control cellular function and heredity.

nu·cle·in (no͞o′klē-ĭn, nyo͞o′-) *n.* Any of the substances present in the nucleus of a cell, consisting chiefly of proteins, phosphoric acids, and nucleic acids. **—nu′cle·in′ic** *adj.*

nucleo– or **nucle–** *pref.* **1.** Nucleus: *nucleon; nucleoplasm.* **2.** Nucleic acid: *nucleoprotein.* [From NUCLEUS.]

nu·cle·o·cap·sid (no͞o′klē-ō-kăp′sĭd, nyo͞o′-) *n.* The basic structure of a virus, consisting of a core of nucleic acid enclosed in a protein coat.

nu·cle·o·his·tone (no͞o′klē-ō-hĭs′tōn′, nyo͞o′-) *n.* A nucleoprotein whose protein component is a histone.

nu·cle·oid (no͞o′klē-oid′, nyo͞o′-) *n.* The part of a bacterium or virus that contains nucleic acid and is analogous in function to the nucleus of a eucaryotic cell.

nu·cle·o·late (no͞o′klē-ə-lāt′, nyo͞o′-) also **nu·cle·o·lat·ed** (-lā′tĭd) *adj.* Having a nucleolus or nucleoli. [NUCLEOL(US) + -ATE[1].]

nu·cle·o·lus (no͞o-klē′ə-ləs, nyo͞o-) *n., pl.* **-li** (-lī′). *Biology.* A small, typically round, granular body composed of protein and RNA in the nucleus of a cell, usually associated with a specific chromosomal site and involved in ribosomal RNA synthesis and the formation of ribosomes. [Latin, diminutive of *nucleus,* kernel. See NUCLEUS.] **—nu·cle′o·lar** (-lər) *adj.*

nu·cle·on (no͞o′klē-ŏn′, nyo͞o′-) *n.* A proton or a neutron, especially as part of an atomic nucleus. See table at **subatomic particle.** **—nu′cle·on′ic** *adj.*

nu·cle·on·ics (no͞o′klē-ŏn′ĭks, nyo͞o′-) *n. (used with a sing. verb).* **1.** The study of the behavior and characteristics of nucleons or atomic nuclei. **2.** Development of instruments for use in nuclear research. [From NUCLEON.]

nucleon number *n.* See **mass number.**

nu·cle·o·phile (no͞o′klē-ə-fīl′, nyo͞o′-) *n.* A chemical compound or group that is attracted to nuclei and tends to donate or share electrons.

nu·cle·o·plasm (no͞o′klē-ə-plăz′əm, nyo͞o′-) *n.* The protoplasm of a cell nucleus. Also called *karyoplasm.* **—nu′cle·o·plas′mic, nu′cle·o·plas·mat′ic** (-ō-plăz-măt′ĭk) *adj.*

nu·cle·o·pro·tein (no͞o′klē-ō-prō′tēn′, -prō′tē-ĭn, nyo͞o′-) *n.* Any of a group of substances found in the nuclei of all living cells and in viruses, composed of a protein and a nucleic acid.

nu·cle·o·side (no͞o′klē-ə-sīd′, nyo͞o′-) *n.* Any of various compounds consisting of a sugar, usually ribose or deoxyribose, and a purine or pyrimidine base, especially a compound obtained by hydrolysis of a nucleic acid, such as adenosine or guanine.

nu·cle·o·some (no͞o′klē-ə-sōm′, nyo͞o′-) *n.* Any of the repeating subunits of chromatin, consisting of a DNA chain coiled around a core of histones. **—nu′cle·o·som′al** (-sō′məl) *adj.*

nu·cle·o·syn·the·sis (no͞o′klē-ō-sĭn′thĭ-sĭs, nyo͞o′-) *n.* The process by which heavier chemical elements are synthesized from hydrogen nuclei in the interiors of stars. **—nu′cle·o·syn·thet′ic** (-sĭn-thĕt′ĭk) *adj.*

nu·cle·o·tid·ase (no͞o′klē-ə-tī′dās, -dāz, nyo͞o′-) *n.* An enzyme that catalyzes the hydrolysis of a nucleotide to a nucleoside and phosphoric acid.

nu·cle·o·tide (no͞o′klē-ə-tīd′, nyo͞o′-) *n.* Any of various compounds consisting of a nucleoside combined with a phosphate group and forming the basic constituent of DNA and RNA. [Alteration of NUCLEOSIDE.]

nu·cle·us (no͞o′klē-əs, nyo͞o′-) *n., pl.* **-cle·i** (-klē-ī′) or **-cle·us·es. 1.** A central or essential part around which other parts are gathered or grouped; a core: *the nucleus of a city.* **2.** Something regarded as a basis for future development and growth; a kernel: *a few paintings that formed the nucleus of a great art collection.* **3.** *Biology.* A large, membrane-bound, usually spherical protoplasmic structure within a living cell, containing the cell's hereditary material and controlling its metabolism, growth, and reproduction. **4.** *Botany.* **a.** The central kernel of a nut or seed. **b.** The center of a starch granule. **5.** *Anatomy.* A group of specialized nerve cells or a localized mass of gray matter in the brain or spinal cord. **6.** *Physics.* The positively charged central region of an atom, composed of protons and neutrons and containing almost all of the mass of the atom. **7.** *Chemistry.* A group of atoms bound in a structure, such as a benzene ring, that is resistant to alteration in chemical reactions. **8.** *Astronomy.* **a.** The central portion of the head of a comet. **b.** The central or brightest part of a nebula or galaxy. **9.** *Meteorology.* A particle on which water vapor molecules accumulate in free air to form a droplet or ice crystal. [Latin *nuculeus, nucleus,* kernel, from *nucula,* little nut, diminutive of *nux, nuc-,* nut.]

nu·clide (no͞o′klīd′, nyo͞o′-) *n.* A type of atom specified by its atomic number, atomic mass, and energy state, such as carbon 14. **—nu·clid′ic** (no͞o-klĭd′ĭk, nyo͞o-) *adj.*

nude (no͞od, nyo͞od) *adj.* **nud·er, nud·est. 1.** Being without clothing; naked. **2.** *Law.* Lacking any of various legal requisites, such as evidence. **—nude** *n.* **1.** An unclothed human figure, especially an artistic representation. **2.** The condition of being unclothed. [Latin *nūdus.* See **nogʷ-** in Appendix.] **—nude′ly** *adv.* **—nu′di·ty** (no͞o′dĭ-tē, nyo͞o′-), **nude′ness** *n.*

nudge[1] (nŭj) *tr.v.* **nudged, nudg·ing, nudg·es. 1.** To push against gently, especially in order to gain attention or give a signal. **2.** To come close to; near: *"The temperature was nudging 105 degrees in the shade"* (Scouting). **—nudge** *n.* A gentle push. [Probably of Scandinavian origin.] **—nudg′er** *n.*

nudge[2] or **nudzh** (no͝oj) *Slang.* —*n.* One who persistently pesters, annoys, or complains. —*v.* **nudged, nudg·ing, nudg·es** or **nudzhed, nudzh·ing, nudzh·es.** —*tr.* To annoy persistently; pester. —*intr.* To complain or carp persistently. [From Yiddish *nudyen,* to pester, bore, from Polish *nudzić.*]

nudi– *pref.* Naked; bare: *nudibranch.* [Latin *nūdi-,* from *nūdus,* naked. See **nogʷ-** in Appendix.]

nu·di·branch (no͞o′də-brăngk′, nyo͞o′-) *n.* See **sea slug.** [From New Latin *Nudibranchia,* order name : NUDI– + BRANCHIA.] **—nu′di·bran′chi·ate** (-brăng′kē-ĭt), **nu′di·bran′chi·an** (-kē-ən) *adj. & n.*

nud·ism (no͞o′dĭz′əm, nyo͞o′-) *n.* The belief in or practice of going nude, especially in secluded, sexually mixed groups for reasons of health. **—nud′ist** *adj. & n.*

nud·nik also **nud·nick** (no͝od′nĭk) *n. Slang.* An obtuse, boring, or bothersome person; a pest. [Yiddish, *nudne,* boring (from *nudyen,* to bore; see NUDGE[2]) + *-nik,* -nik.]

nudzh (no͝oj) *n. & v. Slang.* Variant of **nudge[2].**

Nu·e·ces (no͞o-ā′sĭs, nyo͞o-). A river of southern Texas flowing about 507 km (315 mi) to **Nueces Bay,** an inlet of the Gulf of Mexico near Corpus Christi.

Nue·vo La·re·do (no͞o-ā′vō lə-rā′dō, nwĕ′vô lä-rĕ′thô). A city of northeast Mexico across the Rio Grande from Laredo, Texas. Founded in 1755, it was part of Laredo until the end of the Mexican War in 1848. Population, 201,731.

nu·ga·to·ry (no͞o′gə-tôr′ē, -tōr′ē, nyo͞o′-) *adj.* **1.** Of little or no importance; trifling. **2.** Having no force; invalid. See Synonyms at **vain.** [Latin *nūgātōrius,* from *nūgātor,* trifler, from *nūgārī,* to trifle, from *nūgae,* jokes.]

nug·get (nŭg′ĭt) *n.* **1.** A small, solid lump, especially of gold. **2.** A small compact portion or unit: *nuggets of information.* [Perhaps diminutive of English dialectal *nug,* lump.]

nui·sance (no͞o′səns, nyo͞o′-) *n.* **1.** One that is inconvenient, annoying, or vexatious; a bother: *Having to stand in line was a nuisance. The disruptive child was a nuisance to the class.* **2.** *Law.* A use of property or course of conduct that interferes with the legal rights of others by causing damage, annoyance, or inconvenience. [Middle English, from Old French, from *nuire, nuis-,* to harm, from Vulgar Latin **nocere,* from Latin *nocēre.* See **nek-[1]** in Appendix.]

nuisance tax *n.* A small excise tax levied on separate purchases and collected directly from the purchaser.

nuke (no͞ok, nyo͞ok) *Slang. n.* **1.** A nuclear device or weapon. **2.** A nuclear-powered electric generating plant. **—nuke** *tr.v.* **nuked, nuk·ing, nukes. 1.** To attack with nuclear weapons. **2.** To heat in a microwave oven: *"I obtained this soup by nuking one cup of water and mixing that with . . . bouillon"* (Judy Markey). [Shortening and alteration of NUCLEAR.]

Nu·ku·a·lo·fa (no͞o′ko͞o-ə-lô′fə). The capital of Tonga in the southwest Pacific Ocean. Population, 21,745.

null (nŭl) *adj.* **1.** Having no legal force; invalid: *render a contract null and void.* **2.** Of no consequence, effect, or value; insignificant. **3.** Amounting to nothing; absent or nonexistent: *a null result.* **4.** *Mathematics.* Of or relating to a set having no members or to zero magnitude. **—null** *tr.v.* **nulled, null·ing, nulls.** To make null. **—null** *n.* **1.** Zero; nothing. **2.** An instrument reading of zero. [French *nul,* from Old French, from Latin *nūllus.* See **ne** in Appendix.]

nul·lah (nŭl′ə) *n.* A ravine or gully, especially in southern Asia. [Hindi *nālā,* rivulet, probably of Dravidian origin.]

Null·ar·bor Plain (nŭl′ə-bôr′, nŭl-är′bər). A region of south-central Australia south of the Great Victoria Desert and north of the Great Australian Bight.

null character *n. Computer Science.* A data control character that fills computer time by adding nonsignificant zeros to a data sequence.

nul·li·fi·ca·tion (nŭl′ə-fĭ-kā′shən) *n.* **1.a.** The act of nullifying. **b.** The state of being nullified. **2.** Refusal or failure of a U.S. state to recognize or enforce a federal law within its boundaries. **—nul′li·fi·ca′tion·ist** *n.*

nul·li·fi·er (nŭl′ə-fī′ər) *n.* **1.** One that nullifies. **2.** One who believes in nullification as a means by which U.S. states may resist federal laws.

nul·li·fy (nŭl′ə-fī′) *tr.v.* **-fied, -fy·ing, -fies. 1.** To make null; invalidate. **2.** To counteract the force or effectiveness of. See Synonyms at **neutralize.** [Latin *nūllificāre,* to despise : *nūllus,* none; see **ne** in Appendix + *-ficāre,* -fy.]

nul·lip·a·ra (nə-lĭp′ər-ə) *n.* A woman who has never given birth. [Latin *nūllus,* none; see **ne** in Appendix + –PARA.] **—nul·lip′a·rous** *adj.*

nul·li·ty (nŭl′ĭ-tē) *n., pl.* **-ties. 1.** The state or quality of being null. **2.** Something that is null, especially an act having no legal validity.

num. *abbr.* **1.** Number. **2.** Numeral.

Num. *abbr. Bible.* Numbers.

numb (nŭm) *adj.* **numb·er, numb·est. 1.** Deprived of the power to feel or move normally; benumbed: *toes numb with cold; too numb with fear to cry out.* **2.** Emotionally unresponsive; indifferent: *numb to yet another appeal.* **—numb** *tr. & intr.v.* **numbed, numb·ing, numbs.** To make or become numb. [Middle English *nome,* variant of *nomin,* past participle of *nimen,* to seize, from Old English *niman.* See **nem-** in Appendix.] **—numb′ly** *adv.* **—numb′ness** *n.*

WORD HISTORY: One of the more frequently used words in English, *take,* is evidence of the importance of the Scandinavian influence on English. Chiefly Danes and Norwegians, the invaders and settlers of the 8th through the 11th century contributed more

ă **pat**	oi **boy**
ā **pay**	ou **out**
âr **care**	o͝o **took**
ä **father**	o͞o **boot**
ĕ **pet**	ŭ **cut**
ē **be**	ûr **urge**
ĭ **pit**	th **thin**
ī **pie**	*th* **this**
îr **pier**	hw **which**
ŏ **pot**	zh **vision**
ō **toe**	ə **about, item**
ô **paw**	♦ **regionalism**

Stress marks: **′** (primary); ′ (secondary), as in **dictionary** (dĭk′shə-nĕr′ē)

than 900 words to the English language, but perhaps few so important as *take.* The Old Norse word *taka* was adopted as Old English *tacan,* the ancestor of our *take.* But Old English already had a word that paralleled *tacan* in sense, and that was *niman.* In Middle English *nimen,* from *niman,* still thrived, but by the 16th century the word had all but disappeared, surviving today only as *nim* in the archaic sense "to steal." However, all was not lost, for the past participle of *nimen, nomin,* was used as an adjective, meaning "deprived of the power of movement, unable to move, paralyzed." We know this word in the form *numb,* from which the new verb *numb* has been derived.

num•ber (nŭm′bər) *n.* **1.** *Mathematics.* **a.** A member of the set of positive integers; one of a series of symbols of unique meaning in a fixed order that can be derived by counting. **b.** A member of any of the further sets of mathematical objects, such as negative integers and real numbers, that can be derived from the positive integers by induction. **2. numbers.** Arithmetic. **3.** *Abbr.* **no., n., num., No. a.** A symbol or word used to represent a number. **b.** A numeral or a series of numerals used for reference or identification: *his telephone number; the apartment number.* **4. a.** A position in an ordered sequence that corresponds to one of the positive integers: *the house that is number three from the corner; ranked number six in her class.* **b.** One item in a group or series considered to be in numerical order: *an old number of a magazine.* **5.** A total; a sum: *the number of feet in a mile.* **6.** An indefinite quantity of units or individuals: *The crowd was small in number. A number of people complained about the poor lighting in the museum.* **7. numbers. a.** A large quantity; a multitude: *Numbers of people visited the fair.* **b.** Numerical superiority: *The South had leaders, the North numbers.* **8.** *Grammar.* The indication, as by inflection, of the singularity or plurality of a linguistic form. **9. numbers. a.** Metrical feet or lines; verses: *"These numbers will I tear, and write in prose"* (Shakespeare). **b.** *Obsolete.* Poetic meter. **10. numbers.** *Archaic.* Musical periods or measures. **11. numbers.** *(used with a sing. or pl. verb). Games.* A numbers game. **12. Numbers.** *(used with a sing. verb). Abbr.* **Nb., Num.** *Bible.* See table at **Bible. 13.** One of the separate offerings in a program of music or other entertainment: *The band's second number was a ballad.* **14.** *Slang.* A frequently repeated, characteristic speech, argument, or performance: *The suspects will do their usual number—protesting innocence—and then confess.* **15.** *Slang.* A person or thing singled out for a particular characteristic: *a suspect who was a crafty number.* **—number** *v.* **-bered, -ber•ing, -bers.** *—tr.* **1.** To assign a number to. **2.** To determine the number or amount of; count. **3.** To total in number or amount; add up to. **4.** To include in a group or category: *He was numbered among the lost.* **5.** To mention one by one; enumerate. **6.** To limit or restrict in number: *Our days are numbered.* *—intr.* **1.** To call off numbers; count: *numbering to ten.* **2.** To constitute a group or number: *The applicants numbered in the thousands.* ***—idioms.*** **by the numbers. 1.** In unison as numbers are called out by a leader: *performing calisthenics by the numbers.* **2.** In a strict, step-by-step or mechanical way. **do a number on.** *Slang.* To defeat, abuse, or humiliate in a calculated and thorough way. **get** (or **have**) **(someone's) number.** To determine or know someone's real character or motives. **without** (or **beyond**) **number.** Too many to be counted; countless: *Mosquitoes without number filled the yard.* [Middle English *nombre,* from Old French, from Latin *numerus.* See **nem-** in Appendix.] **—num′ber•er** *n.*

Rudolf Nureyev

USAGE NOTE: As a collective noun *number* may take either a singular or a plural verb. It takes a singular verb when it is preceded by the definite article *the: The number of skilled workers is small.* It takes a plural verb when preceded by the indefinite article *a: A number of the workers are unskilled.*

number cruncher *n.* *Slang.* **1.** One that is able to perform complex, lengthy calculations. **—number crunching** *n.*

num•ber•less (nŭm′bər-lĭs) *adj.* Innumerable; countless: *numberless lies and other prevarications.*

number line *n.* *Mathematics.* A line that graphically expresses the real numbers as a series of points distributed about a point arbitrarily designated as zero and in which the magnitude of each number is represented by the distance of the corresponding point from zero.

number one *n.* **1.** One that is first in rank, order, or importance. **2.** *Slang.* One's own interests; oneself: *watching out for number one.* **—number one** *adj.* **1.** First in rank, order, or importance: *the number one team in the nation; our number one problem.* **2.** Foremost in quality; first-rate: *bought some number one farmland.*

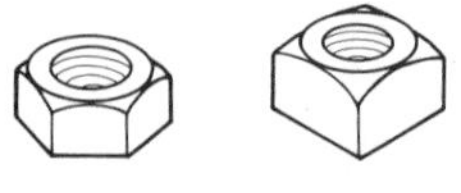

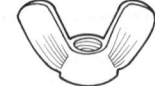

nut
Hexagonal (*top left*), square (*top right*), and wing (*bottom*)

num•bers game (nŭm′bərz) *n.* *Games.* A lottery in which bets are made on an unpredictable number, such as a daily stock quotation.

number system *n.* *Mathematics.* Any system of naming or representing numbers, as the decimal system or the binary system. Also called *numeral system.*

numb•fish (nŭm′fĭsh′) *n., pl.* **numbfish** or **-fish•es.** See **electric ray.**

numb•skull (nŭm′skŭl′) *n.* Variant of **numskull.**

nu•men (no͞o′mən, nyo͞o′-) *n., pl.* **-mi•na** (-mə-nə). **1.** A presiding divinity or spirit of a place. **2.** A spirit believed by animists to inhabit certain natural phenomena or objects. **3.** Creative energy; genius. [Latin *nūmen,* nod of the head, divine power, numen.]

nu•mer•a•ble (no͞o′mər-ə-bəl, nyo͞o′-) *adj.* That can be counted; countable: *numerable assets.* [Latin *numerābilis,* from *numerāre,* to count, from *numerus,* number. See NUMBER.]

nu•mer•al (no͞o′mər-əl, nyo͞o′-) *n.* *Abbr.* **num. 1.** A symbol or mark used to represent a number. **2. numerals.** The numbers, usually the last two digits, indicating by year a graduating class in a school or college. **—numeral** *adj.* Of, relating to, or representing numbers. [From Middle English, of number, from Late Latin *numerālis,* from Latin *numerus,* number. See NUMBER.] **—nu′mer•al•ly** *adv.*

numeral system *n.* *Mathematics.* See **number system.**

nu•mer•ar•y (no͞o′mə-rĕr′ē, nyo͞o′-) *adj.* Of or relating to a number or numbers. [Medieval Latin *numerārius,* from Late Latin, an accountant, from Latin *numerus,* number. See NUMBER.]

nu•mer•ate (no͞o′mə-rāt′, nyo͞o′-) *tr.v.* **-at•ed, -at•ing, -ates.** To enumerate; count. **—numerate** (-mər-ĭt) *adj.* Able to think and express oneself effectively in quantitative terms. [Latin *numerāre, numerāt-,* from *numerus,* number. See NUMBER.] **—nu′mer•a•cy** (-mər-ə-sē) *n.*

nu•mer•a•tion (no͞o′mə-rā′shən, nyo͞o′-) *n.* **1.** The act or process of counting or numbering; enumeration. **2.** A system of numbering.

nu•mer•a•tor (no͞o′mə-rā′tər, nyo͞o′-) *n.* **1.** *Mathematics.* **a.** The expression written above the line in a common fraction to indicate the number of parts of the whole. **b.** An expression to be divided by another; a dividend. **2.** One that numbers; an enumerator.

nu•mer•ic (no͞o-mĕr′ĭk, nyo͞o-) *n.* A number or numeral. **—numeric** *adj.* Variant of **numerical.** [Probably back-formation from NUMERICAL.]

nu•mer•i•cal (no͞o-mĕr′ĭ-kəl, nyo͞o-) also **nu•mer•ic** (-mĕr′ĭk) *adj.* **1.** Of or relating to a number or series of numbers: *numerical order.* **2.** Designating number or a number: *a numerical symbol.* **3.** Expressed in or counted by numbers: *numerical strength.* [From Latin *numerus,* number. See NUMBER.] **—nu•mer′i•cal•ly** *adv.*

numerical analysis *n.* The study of approximation techniques for solving mathematical problems, taking into account the extent of possible errors.

numerical control *n.* Control of a process or machine by encoded commands that are commonly prepared by a computer.

numerical taxonomy *n.* The branch of taxonomy that uses mathematical methods to evaluate observable differences and similarities between taxonomic groups. Also called *taximetrics.*

numerical value *n.* See **absolute value** (sense 1).

numeric keypad *n.* *Computer Science.* A keypad.

nu•mer•ol•o•gy (no͞o′mə-rŏl′ə-jē, nyo͞o′-) *n.* The study of the occult meanings of numbers and their supposed influence on human life. [Latin *numerus,* number; see NUMBER + -LOGY.] **—nu′mer•o•log′i•cal** (-mər-ə-lŏj′ĭ-kəl) *adj.* **—nu′mer•ol′o•gist** *n.*

nu•mer•ous (no͞o′mər-əs, nyo͞o′-) *adj.* Amounting to a large number; many. [Middle English, from Latin *numerōsus,* from *numerus,* number. See NUMBER.] **—nu′mer•ous•ly** *adv.* **—nu′mer•ous•ness** *n.*

Nu•mid•i•a (no͞o-mĭd′ē-ə, nyo͞o-). An ancient country of northwest Africa corresponding roughly to present-day Algeria. It was part of the Carthaginian empire before the Punic Wars and became a separate kingdom after 201 B.C. Conquered by Rome in 46 B.C. and invaded by the Vandals in the fifth century A.D., Numidia was overrun by the Arabs in the eighth century. **—Nu•mid′i•an** *adj. & n.*

nu•mi•na (no͞o′mə-nə, nyo͞o′-) *n.* Plural of **numen.**

nu•mi•nous (no͞o′mə-nəs, nyo͞o′-) *adj.* **1.** Of or relating to a numen; supernatural. **2.** Filled with or characterized by a sense of a supernatural presence: *a numinous place.* **3.** Spiritually elevated; sublime. [From Latin *nūmen, nūmin-,* numen.]

numis. *abbr.* Numismatic; numismatics.

nu•mis•mat•ic (no͞o′mĭz-măt′ĭk, -mĭs-, nyo͞o′-) *adj.* *Abbr.* **numis. 1.** Of or relating to coins or currency. **2.** Of or relating to numismatics. [French *numismatique,* from Late Latin *numisma, numismat-,* coin, variant of Latin *nomisma,* from Greek, custom, current coin, from *nomizein,* to have in use, from *nomos,* custom. See **nem-** in Appendix.] **—nu′mis•mat′i•cal•ly** *adv.*

nu•mis•mat•ics (no͞o′mĭz-măt′ĭks, -mĭs-, nyo͞o′-) *n.* *(used with a sing. verb). Abbr.* **numis.** The study or collection of money, coins, and often medals. **—nu•mis′ma•tist** (no͞o-mĭz′mə-tĭst, -mĭs′-, nyo͞o-) *n.*

num•mu•lar (nŭm′yə-lər) *adj.* Shaped like a coin; oval or circular. [From Latin *nummulus,* diminutive of *nummus,* coin, probably from Greek *nomimos,* customary, legal. See **nem-** in Appendix.]

num•mu•lite (nŭm′yə-līt′) *n.* A large, coin-shaped, fossil foraminifer of the genus *Nummulites,* widely distributed in limestone formations from the Eocene Epoch to the Miocene Epoch of the Cenozoic. [From New Latin *Nummulītēs,* type genus, from Latin *nummulus,* diminutive of *nummus,* coin, probably from Greek *nomimos,* customary, legal. See **nem-** in Appendix.] **—num′mu•lit′ic** (-lĭt′ĭk) *adj.*

num•skull also **numb•skull** (nŭm′skŭl′) *n.* A person regarded as stupid.

nun¹ (nŭn) *n.* A woman who belongs to a religious order or congregation devoted to active service or meditation, living under vows of poverty, chastity, and obedience. [Middle English, from Old English *nunne* and from Old French *nonne,* both from Late Latin *nonna,* feminine of *nonnus,* tutor, monk.]

nun² (no͝on) *n.* The 14th letter of the Hebrew alphabet. See table at **alphabet.** [Hebrew *nûn.*]

Nunc Di·mit·tis (nŭngk′ dĭ-mĭt′ĭs, no͝ongk′) *n.* A Christian canticle or hymn using the words of Simeon in Luke 2:29–32, beginning *"Nunc dimittis servum tuum"* ("Now lettest thou thy servant depart"). [Late Latin : Latin *nunc,* now + Latin *dīmittis,* second person sing. present tense of *dīmittere,* to send away.]

nun·cha·ku (nŭn-chä′ko͞o) *n.* A pair of hardwood sticks joined by a chain or cord and used as a weapon. [Origin unknown.]

nun·ci·a·ture (nŭn′sē-ə-cho͝or′, -chər, no͞on′-) *n.* The office or term of office of a nuncio. [Italian *nunciatura,* from *nuncio,* nuncio. See NUNCIO.]

nun·ci·o (nŭn′sē-ō′, no͞on′-) *n., pl.* **-os.** A papal ambassador or representative. [Italian, from Latin *nūntius,* messenger. See **neu-** in Appendix.]

nun·cle (nŭng′kəl) *n. Chiefly British.* An uncle: *"Can you make no use of nothing, nuncle?"* (Shakespeare). [From the phrase *an uncle.*]

nun·cu·pa·tive (nŭn′kyə-pā′tĭv, nŭng′-, nŭn-kyo͞o′pə-tĭv) *adj. Law.* Delivered orally to witnesses rather than written: *a nuncupative will.* [Medieval Latin *nūncupātīvus,* from Late Latin, so-called, from Latin *nūncupātus,* past participle of *nūncupāre,* to name : *nōmen,* name; see **nō-men-** in Appendix + *capere,* to take; see **kap-** in Appendix.]

Nun·ea·ton (nŭ-nēt′n). A municipal borough of central England north of Coventry. It is a textile center in a coal-mining region. Population, 113,200.

Nu·ni·vak (no͞o′nə-văk′). An island off western Alaska in the Bering Sea. It was first sighted by Russian explorers in 1821.

nun·ner·y (nŭn′ə-rē) *n., pl.* **-ies.** A convent of nuns.

nup·tial (nŭp′shəl, -chəl) *adj.* **1.** Of or relating to marriage or the wedding ceremony. **2.** Of, relating to, or occurring during the mating season: *the nuptial plumage of male birds.* **—nuptial** *n.* Often **nuptials.** A wedding ceremony. [Middle English *nupcialle,* from Old French *nuptial,* from Latin *nuptiālis,* from *nuptiae,* wedding, from *nupta,* feminine past participle of *nūbere,* to take a husband.] **—nup′tial·ly** *adv.*

nurd (nûrd) *n. Slang.* Variant of **nerd.**

Nu·rem·berg (no͝or′əm-bûrg′, nyo͝or′-) also **Nürn·berg** (no͝orn′bĕrk′, nürn′-). A city of southeast Germany north-northwest of Munich. First mentioned in 1050, it became a free imperial city in the 13th century and was a center of the German cultural renaissance in the 15th and 16th centuries. From 1933 to 1938 it was the site of annual Nazi party congresses. Largely destroyed in World War II, the city served as the venue for the Allied trials of war criminals (1945–1946). Population, 468,352.

Nu·re·yev (no͝or′ĭ-yĕf, no͞o-rā′-), **Rudolf.** Born 1938. Russian-born ballet dancer and choreographer. Noted for his athletic grace, stage presence, and partnership with Margot Fonteyn, he was the most celebrated male dancer of his day.

Nu·ri·stan (no͝or′ĭ-stăn′, -stän′). A region of northeast Afghanistan on the southern slopes of the Hindu Kush.

Nu·ri·sta·ni (no͝or′ĭ-stä′nē) *n., pl.* **Nuristani** or **-nis.** A member of a Dardic-speaking people inhabiting parts of the Hindu Kush in northeast Afghanistan. Also called *Kafir.*

Nürn·berg (no͝orn′bĕrk′, nürn′-). See **Nuremberg.**

nurse (nûrs) *n.* **1.** A person educated and trained to care for the sick or disabled. **2.a.** A woman employed to suckle children other than her own; a wet nurse. **b.** A woman employed to take care of a child; a nursemaid. **3.** One that serves as a nurturing or fostering influence or means: *"Town life is the nurse of civilization"* (C.L.R. James). **4.** *Zoology.* A worker ant or bee that feeds and cares for the colony's young. **—nurse** *v.* **nursed, nurs·ing, nurs·es.** *—tr.* **1.** To serve as a nurse for: *nursed the patient back to health.* **2.** To feed at the breast; suckle. **3.** To try to cure by special care or treatment: *nurse a cough with various remedies.* **4.** To treat carefully, especially in order to prevent pain: *He nursed his injured knee by shifting his weight to the other leg.* **5.** To manage or guide carefully; look after with care; foster: *nursed her business through the depression.* See Synonyms at **nurture.** **6.** To bear privately in the mind: *nursing a grudge.* **7.** To consume slowly, especially in order to conserve: *nursed one drink for the whole evening.* *—intr.* **1.** To serve as a nurse. **2.** To take nourishment from the breast; suckle. [Middle English *norice, nurse,* wet nurse, from Old French *norrice,* from Vulgar Latin **nutrīcia,* from Late Latin *nūtrīcia,* from feminine of Latin *nūtrīcius,* that suckles, from *nūtrīx, nūtrīc-,* wet nurse. See **(s)nāu-** in Appendix.] **—nurs′er** *n.*

nurse·maid (nûrs′mād′) *n.* A woman employed to take care of children.

nurse practitioner *n. Abbr.* **NP** A registered nurse with special training for providing primary health care, including many tasks customarily performed by a physician.

nurs·er·y (nûr′sə-rē, nûrs′rē) *n., pl.* **-ies. 1.** A room or area in a household set apart for the use of children. **2.a.** A place for the temporary care of children in the absence of their parents. **b.** A nursery school. **3.** A place where plants are grown for sale, transplanting, or experimentation. **4.** A place in which something is produced, fostered, or developed. [Middle English *noricerie,* probably from Old French *norricerie,* from *norrice,* nursemaid. See NURSE.]

nursery rhyme *n.* A short, rhymed poem or tale for children.

nursery school *n.* A school for children, usually between the ages of three and five, who are not old enough to attend kindergarten. **—nursery schooler** *n.*

nurse's aide (nûr′sĭz) *n., pl.* **nurses' aides.** A person who assists nurses at a hospital or other medical facility in tasks requiring little or no formal training or education.

nurs·ing (nûr′sĭng) *n.* **1.** The profession of a nurse. **2.** The tasks or care of a nurse.

nursing home *n.* A private establishment that provides living quarters and care for the elderly or the chronically ill.

nurs·ling (nûrs′lĭng) *n.* **1.** A nursing infant or young animal. **2.** A carefully nurtured person or thing.

nur·tur·ance (nûr′chər-əns) *n.* The providing of loving care and attention. **—nur′tur·ant** *adj.*

nur·ture (nûr′chər) *n.* **1.** Something that nourishes; sustenance. **2.** The act of bringing up. **3.** *Biology.* The sum of environmental influences and conditions acting on an organism. **—nurture** *tr.v.* **-tured, -tur·ing, -tures. 1.** To nourish; feed. **2.** To educate; train. **3.** To help grow or develop; cultivate: *nurture a student's talent.* [Middle English, from Old French, from Late Latin *nūtrītūra,* act of suckling, from Latin *nūtrītus,* past participle of *nūtrīre,* to suckle. See **(s)nāu-** in Appendix.] **—nur′tur·er** *n.*

SYNONYMS: *nurture, cultivate, foster, nurse.* The central meaning shared by these verbs is "to promote and sustain the growth and development of": *nurturing hopes; cultivating tolerance; foster friendly relations; nursed the fledgling business through an economic downturn.*

nut (nŭt) *n.* **1.a.** An indehiscent, hard-shelled, one-loculated, one-seeded fruit, such as an acorn or a hazelnut. **b.** A seed borne within a fruit having a hard shell, as in the peanut, almond, or walnut. **c.** The kernel of any of these. **2.** *Slang.* **a.** A crazy or eccentric person. **b.** An enthusiast; a buff: *a movie nut.* **3.** *Informal.* A difficult endeavor or problem: *Painting the closet was a tough nut to crack.* **4.** *Slang.* The human head. **5.** *Music.* **a.** A ridge of wood at the top of the fingerboard or neck of a stringed instrument, over which the strings pass. **b.** A device at the lower end of the bow for a stringed instrument, used for tightening the hairs. **6.** A small block of metal or wood with a central, threaded hole that is designed to fit around and secure a bolt or screw. **7.** *Slang.* **a.** The cost of launching a business venture. **b.** The operating expenses of a theater, theatrical production, or similar enterprise: *"The* [theater] *has simply failed to attract enough paying customers per week to meet its nut"* (Variety). **8. nuts.** *Vulgar Slang.* The testicles. **—nut** *intr.v.* **nut·ted, nut·ting, nuts.** To gather or hunt for nuts. [Middle English *nute,* from Old English *hnutu.*] **—nut′ter** *n.*

nu·ta·tion (no͞o-tā′shən, nyo͞o-) *n.* **1.** The act or an instance of nodding the head. **2.** A wobble in a spinning gyroscope or other rotating body. **3.** *Astronomy.* A small periodic motion of the celestial pole of Earth with respect to the pole of the ecliptic. **4.** *Botany.* A slight curving or circular movement in a stem, as of a twining plant, caused by irregular growth rates of different parts. [Latin *nūtātiō, nūtātiōn-,* from *nūtātus,* past participle of *nūtāre,* frequentative of *-nuere,* to nod.] **—nu·ta′tion·al** *adj.*

nut case *n. Slang.* A person regarded as eccentric or crazy.

nut·crack·er (nŭt′krăk′ər) *n.* **1.** An implement used to crack nuts, typically consisting of two hinged metal levers between which the nut is squeezed. **2.a.** Any of various birds of the genus *Nucifraga,* especially *N. caryocatactes* of northern Eurasia and *N. columbiana* of western North America, that are related to the crow and feed chiefly on the seeds of pine cones. **b.** See **nuthatch.**

nut·gall (nŭt′gôl′) *n.* A nutlike swelling produced on an oak or other tree by certain parasitic wasps. Also called *gallnut.*

nut·hatch (nŭt′hăch′) *n.* Any of several small, short-tailed birds of the family Sittidae, having a long sharp bill and known for climbing down trees headfirst. Also called *nutcracker.* [Middle English *notehache* : *note,* nut; see NUT + *hache,* hatchet, from Old French, perhaps of Germanic origin (from its habit of wedging nuts in bark and hacking them open).]

nut house *n. Slang.* A mental health facility.

nut·let (nŭt′lĭt) *n.* **1.** A small nut. **2.** The stone or pit of certain fruits such as the peach or cherry.

Nut·ley (nŭt′lē). A town of northeast New Jersey, a residential suburb of Newark. Population, 28,998.

nut·meat (nŭt′mēt′) *n.* The edible kernel of a nut.

nut·meg (nŭt′mĕg′) *n.* **1.** An evergreen tree *(Myristica fragrans)* native to the East Indies and cultivated for its spicy seeds. **2.** The hard, aromatic seed of this tree, used as a spice when grated or ground. **3.** *Color.* A grayish to moderate brown. [Middle English *notemuge,* probably ultimately from Old French *nois mugede,* alteration of *nois muscade,* nut smelling like musk, from Old Provençal *notz muscada* : *notz,* nut (from Latin *nux, nuc-,* nut) + *muscada,* smelling like musk (from *musc,* musk, from Late Latin *muscus;* see MUSK).]

nutcracker

nuthatch
White-breasted nuthatch
Sitta carolinensis

nutmeg
Myristica fragrans

ă pat	oi boy
ā pay	ou out
âr care	o͝o took
ä father	o͞o boot
ĕ pet	ŭ cut
ē be	ûr urge
ĭ pit	th thin
ī pie	*th* this
îr pier	hw which
ŏ pot	zh vision
ō toe	ə about, item
ô paw	♦ regionalism

Stress marks: ′ (primary); ′ (secondary), as in **dictionary** (dĭk′shə-nĕr′ē)

nut pick also **nut·pick** (nŭt′pĭk′) *n.* A small, sharp-pointed tool used for digging the meat from nuts.

nut pine *n.* See **piñon.**

nu·tri·a (no͞o′trē-ə, nyo͞o′-) *n.* **1.** See **coypu. 2.** The light-brown fur of the coypu. [Spanish, from Vulgar Latin *nutria, variant of Latin *lutra.* See **wed-**[1] in Appendix.]

nu·tri·ent (no͞o′trē-ənt, nyo͞o′-) *n.* A source of nourishment, especially a nourishing ingredient in a food. **—nutrient** *adj.* Providing nourishment. [Latin *nūtriēns, nutrient-,* present participle of *nūtrīre,* to suckle. See **(s)nāu-** in Appendix.]

nu·tri·ment (no͞o′trə-mənt, nyo͞o′-) *n.* **1.** A source of nourishment; food. **2.** An agent that promotes growth or development. [Middle English, from Latin *nūtrīmentum,* from *nūtrīre,* to suckle. See **(s)nāu-** in Appendix.] **—nu′tri·men′tal** (-mĕn′tl) *adj.*

nu·tri·tion (no͞o-trĭsh′ən, nyo͞o-) *n.* **1.** The process of nourishing or being nourished, especially the process by which a living organism assimilates food and uses it for growth and for replacement of tissues. **2.** The science or study that deals with food and nourishment, especially in human beings. **3.** A source of nourishment; food. [Middle English *nutricion,* from Old French *nutrition,* from Late Latin *nūtrītiō, nūtrītiōn-,* from Latin *nūtrītus,* past participle of *nūtrīre,* to suckle. See **(s)nāu-** in Appendix.] **—nu·tri′tion·al** *adj.* **—nu·tri′tion·al·ly** *adv.*

nu·tri·tion·ist (no͞o-trĭsh′ə-nĭst, nyo͞o-) *n.* One who is trained or an expert in the field of nutrition.

nu·tri·tion·ist's calorie (no͞o-trĭsh′ə-nĭsts, nyo͞o-) *n.* See **calorie** (sense 3b).

nu·tri·tious (no͞o-trĭsh′əs, nyo͞o-) *adj.* Providing nourishment; nourishing. [From Latin *nūtrītius,* from *nūtrīx, nūtrīc-,* nurse. See **(s)nāu-** in Appendix.] **—nu·tri′tious·ly** *adv.* **—nu·tri′tious·ness** *n.*

nu·tri·tive (no͞o′trĭ-tĭv, nyo͞o′-) *adj.* **1.** Nutritious; nourishing. **2.** Of or relating to nutrition. [Middle English *nutritif,* from Old French, from Late Latin *nūtrītīvus,* from Latin *nūtrītus,* past participle of *nūtrīre,* to suckle. See **(s)nāu-** in Appendix.] **—nu′tri·tive·ly** *adv.*

nuts (nŭts) *Slang. adj.* **1.** Crazy; insane. **2.** Extremely enthusiastic: *I'm nuts about opera.* **—nuts** *interj.* Used to express contempt, disappointment, or refusal. [From NUT.]

nuts and bolts *pl.n. Slang.* The basic working components or practical aspects: "[proposing] *lofty goals without specifying the nuts and bolts of how they are to be achieved"* (Village Voice). **—nuts′-and-bolts′** (nŭts′ən-bōlts′) *adj.*

nut sedge *n.* Either of two Old World sedges *(Cyperus esculentus* or *C. rotundus)* having aromatic tubers. [From the shape of the tubers.]

nut·shell (nŭt′shĕl′) *n.* The shell enclosing the meat of a nut. ***—idiom.*** **in a nutshell.** In a few words; concisely: *Just give me the facts in a nutshell.*

nut·ty (nŭt′ē) *adj.* **-ti·er, -ti·est. 1.** Containing or producing nuts: *nutty trees.* **2.** Having a flavor like that of nuts: *The wild turkey often has a nutty taste when cooked.* **3.** *Slang.* Crazy; idiotic: *a nutty idea.* **—nut′ti·ly** *adv.* **—nut′ti·ness** *n.*

nux vom·i·ca (nŭks vŏm′ĭ-kə) *n.* A tree *(Strychnos nux-vomica)* native to southeast Asia, having poisonous seeds that are the source of the medicinal alkaloids strychnine and brucine. [Medieval Latin : Latin *nux,* nut + Medieval Latin *vomica,* feminine of *vomicus,* emetic (from Latin *vomere,* to vomit; see **weme-** in Appendix).]

nuz·zle (nŭz′əl) *v.* **-zled, -zling, -zles.** *—tr.* **1.** To rub or push against gently with or as if with the nose or snout: *stroked and nuzzled the kitten.* **2.** To root or move with the snout. *—intr.* **1.** To make rubbing or pressing motions with or as if with the nose or snout. **2.** To nestle together. [Middle English *noselen,* to bend down, perhaps back-formation from *noselyng,* on the face, prostrate, from *nose,* nose. See NOSE.] **—nuz′zler** *n.*

NV *abbr.* **1.** Nevada. **2.** Not voting.

NW *abbr.* **1.** Northwest. **2.** Northwestern.

NWbN *abbr.* Northwest by north.

NWbW *abbr.* Northwest by west.

NWT or **N.W.T.** *abbr. Abbr.* **Northwest Territories.**

n.wt. *abbr.* Net weight.

NY or **N.Y.** *abbr.* New York.

nya·la (nyä′lə) *n., pl.* **nyala** or **-las.** Any of several African antelopes of the genus *Tragelaphus,* having vertical stripes on the sides of the body, including especially *T. angasi* of southeast Africa, the male of which has spiral horns and long black hair along the neck and the underside. [Probably of Bantu origin.]

Nyan·ja (nyăn′jə) *n.* A Bantu language closely related to Chewa and spoken in Malawi.

Ny·as·a (nī-ăs′ə, nyä′sä), **Lake.** Also **Lake Ma·la·wi** (mə-lä′wē). A lake of southeast-central Africa between Tanzania, Mozambique, and Malawi.

Ny·as·a·land (nī-ăs′ə-lănd′, nyä′sä-). See **Malawi.**

NYC or **N.Y.C.** *abbr.* New York City.

nyc·ta·lo·pi·a (nĭk′tə-lō′pē-ə) *n.* See **night blindness.** [Late Latin *nyctalōpia,* from Greek *nuktalōps,* night-blind : *nux, nukt-,* night; see **nekʷ-t-** in Appendix + *alaos,* blind + *ōps, ōp-,* eye; see **okʷ-** in Appendix.] **—nyc′ta·lo′pic** (-lō′pĭk, -lŏp′ĭk) *adj.*

nyc·tit·ro·pism (nĭk-tĭt′rə-pĭz′əm) *n. Botany.* The tendency of the leaves of some plants to change their position at nightfall. [Greek *nux, nukt-,* night; see **nekʷ-t-** in Appendix + –TROPISM.] **—nyc′ti·tro′pic** (-tĭ-trō′pĭk, -trŏp′ĭk) *adj.*

nyc·to·pho·bi·a (nĭk′tə-fō′bē-ə) *n.* An abnormal fear of the night or darkness. [Greek *nux, nukt-,* night; see NYCTALOPIA + –PHOBIA.]

Nye (nī), **Edgar Wilson.** Known as "Bill." 1850–1896. American humorist. Many of his anecdotes of American life were first published in the Laramie, Wyoming, *Boomerang.*

Nyí·regy·há·za (nē′rĕj-hä′zô, nyē′rĕd-yə-). A city of northeast Hungary north of Debrecen. Inhabited since the 13th century, it was destroyed by the Turks in the 16th century and rebuilt in the 18th century. Population, 90,200.

ny·lon (nī′lŏn′) *n.* **1.a.** Any of a family of high-strength, resilient synthetic polymers, the molecules of which contain the recurring amide group CONH. **b.** Cloth or yarn made from one of these synthetic materials. **2. nylons.** Stockings made of one of these synthetic materials. *—attributive.* Often used to modify another noun: *nylon stockings; a nylon curtain.* [Coined by its inventors, E.I. Du Pont de Nemours and Co., Inc.]

nymph (nĭmf) *n.* **1.** *Greek & Roman Mythology.* Any of numerous minor deities represented as beautiful maidens inhabiting and sometimes personifying features of nature such as trees, waters, and mountains. **2.** A girl, especially a beautiful one. **3.** The larval form of certain insects, such as silverfish and grasshoppers, usually resembling the adult form but smaller and lacking fully developed wings. In this sense, also called *nympha.* [Middle English *nimphe,* from Old French, from Latin *nympha,* from Greek *numphē.*] **—nymph′al** (nĭm′fəl) *adj.*

nym·pha (nĭm′fə) *n., pl.* **-phae** (-fē). **1.** See **nymph** (sense 3). **2. nymphae.** The labia minora. [Latin, from Greek *numphē.*]

nym·pha·lid (nĭm′fə-lĭd) *n.* Any of various medium to large butterflies of the family Nymphalidae, found worldwide and characterized by vestigial forelegs and often brilliant coloring. [From New Latin *Nymphălidae,* family name, from *Nymphălis,* type genus, ultimately from Latin *nympha,* nymph, from Greek *numphē.*]

nym·phet (nĭm-fĕt′, nĭm′fĭt) *n.* A pubescent girl regarded as sexually desirable.

nym·pho·lep·sy (nĭm′fə-lĕp′sē) *n., pl.* **-sies. 1.** A frenzy supposed by ancient peoples to have been induced by nymphs. **2.** An emotional frenzy. [From NYMPHOLEPT.] **—nym′pho·lep′tic** (-lĕp′tĭk) *adj.*

nym·pho·lept (nĭm′fə-lĕpt′) *n.* One who is in a state of nympholepsy. [Greek *numpholēptos,* caught by nymphs, frenzied : *numphē,* nymph + *lēptos,* seized (from *lambanein, lēp-,* to seize).]

nym·pho·ma·ni·a (nĭm′fə-mā′nē-ə, -mān′yə) *n.* Excessive sexual desire in a female. [New Latin : Greek *numphē,* nymph + –MANIA.] **—nym′pho·ma′ni·ac′** (-nē-ăk′) *adj. & n.* **—nym′pho·ma·ni′a·cal** (-mə-nī′ə-kəl) *adj.*

Ny·norsk (no͞o-nôrsk′, nü′nôshk′) *n.* See **New Norwegian.** [Norwegian : *ny,* new (from Old Norse *nȳr;* see SPAN-NEW) + *norsk,* Norwegian (from *noregsk, from Old Norse *Nōregr,* Norway).]

NYP *abbr.* Not yet published.

NYSE *abbr.* New York Stock Exchange.

nys·tag·mus (nĭ-stăg′məs) *n.* A rapid, involuntary, oscillatory motion of the eyeball. [New Latin, from Greek *nustagmos,* drowsiness.] **—nys·tag′mic** (-mĭk) *adj.*

nys·ta·tin (nĭs′tə-tĭn) *n.* An antibiotic, $C_{46}H_{77}NO_{19}$, produced by the actinomycete *Streptomyces noursei* and used especially in the treatment of fungal infections. [*N(ew) Y(ork) Stat(e)* + –IN.]

N.Z. *abbr.* New Zealand.

ă pat	oi **boy**
ā pay	ou **out**
âr **care**	o͝o **took**
ä **father**	o͞o **boot**
ĕ pet	ŭ cut
ē be	ûr **urge**
ĭ pit	th **thin**
ī pie	*th* **this**
îr **pier**	hw **which**
ŏ pot	zh vision
ō **toe**	ə about, item
ô **paw**	♦ regionalism

Stress marks: ′ (primary); ′ (secondary), as in **dictionary** (dĭk′shə-nĕr′ē)

o¹ or **O** (ō) *n., pl.* **o's** or **O's.** **1.** The 15th letter of the modern English alphabet. **2.** Any of the speech sounds represented by the letter *o.* **3.** The 15th in a series. **4.** Something shaped like the letter O. **5.** A zero. **6. O.** A human blood type of the ABO system.

o² *abbr.* **1. O** or **O.** *Printing.* Octavo. **2.** Ohm.

O¹ (ō) *interj.* **1.** Used before the name of or a pronoun referring to a person or thing being formally addressed: *"How can I put it to you, O you who prepare to travel with important matters on your mind?"* (Jo Durden-Smith). **2.** Used to express surprise or strong emotion: *"O how I laugh when I think of my vague indefinite riches"* (Henry David Thoreau).

O² The symbol for the element **oxygen.**

O³ *abbr.* **1.** Or **O.** Ocean. **2.** Also **o.** Old. **3.** Also **O.** or **o.** Order. **4.** *Baseball.* Out.

o. *abbr. Latin.* Octarius (pint).

O. *abbr.* Ohio.

-o *suff.* Used to form an informal, abbreviated, or slang word or variant: *ammo.* [Perhaps from OH.]

-o- Used as a connective to join word elements: *acidophilic.* [Middle English, from Old French, from Latin, from Greek, thematic vowel of nouns and adjectives used in combination.]

o/a *abbr.* On or about.

oaf (ōf) *n.* A person regarded as stupid or clumsy. [Old Norse *alfr,* elf, silly person. See **albho-** in Appendix.] **—oaf′ish** *adj.* **—oaf′ish·ly** *adv.* **—oaf′ish·ness** *n.*

O·a·hu (ō-ä′ho͞o). An island of central Hawaii between Molokai and Kauai. It is the chief island of the state, with major tourist areas, including Waikiki Beach and Diamond Head, and a U.S. naval base at Pearl Harbor.

oak (ōk) *n.* **1. a.** Any of numerous monoecious deciduous or evergreen trees or shrubs of the genus *Quercus,* bearing acorns as fruit. **b.** The durable wood of any of these trees or shrubs. **c.** Something made of this wood. **2.** Any of various similar trees or shrubs, such as the poison oak. **3.** *Color.* Any of various brown shades resembling the wood of an oak in color. [Middle English *ok,* from Old English *āc.*] **—oak′en** (ō′kən) *adj.*

oak apple *n.* An insect gall on oak trees, caused by certain wasp larvae.

Oak Creek (ōk). A city of southeast Wisconsin, an industrial suburb of Milwaukee on Lake Michigan. Population, 16,932.

Oak Forest. A city of northeast Illinois, a residential suburb of Chicago. Population, 26,096.

Oak·land (ōk′lənd). A city of western California on San Francisco Bay opposite San Francisco. Founded on a site settled by Spanish colonists in 1820, it is a port and rail terminus connected with other communities in the Bay Area by bridge, tunnel, and rapid transit. Population, 339,288.

Oakland Park. A city of southeast Florida on the Atlantic Ocean north of Fort Lauderdale. Population, 23,035.

Oak Lawn. A village of northeast Illinois, a residential suburb of Chicago with some light industry. Population, 60,690.

oak leaf cluster *n.* A decoration of bronze or silver oak leaves and acorns given to holders of various U.S. military medals in recognition of acts entitling them to another award of the same medal.

Oak·ley (ōk′lē), **Annie.** 1860–1926. American sharpshooter. She was the star attraction of Buffalo Bill's Wild West Show.

Oak Park. **1.** A village of northeast Illinois, a residential suburb of Chicago. Ernest Hemingway was born here. Population, 54,887. **2.** A city of southeast Michigan, a mainly residential suburb of Detroit. Population, 31,537.

Oak Ridge. A city of eastern Tennessee west of Knoxville. It was founded in 1942 as a research facility to produce materials needed for the first atomic bomb. Population, 27,662.

oa·kum (ō′kəm) *n.* Loose hemp or jute fiber, sometimes treated with tar, creosote, or asphalt, used chiefly for caulking seams in wooden ships and packing pipe joints. [Middle English *okom,* from Old English *ācumba.* See **gembh-** in Appendix.]

Oak·ville (ōk′vĭl′). A town of southeast Ontario, Canada, on Lake Ontario southwest of Toronto. It is a summer resort and manufacturing center. Population, 75,773.

oak wilt *n.* A disease of oak trees caused by the fungus *Chalara quercina* and often resulting in wilting and dropping of leaves.

oar (ôr, ōr) *n. Nautical.* **1.** A long, thin, usually wooden pole with a blade at one end, used to row or steer a boat. **2.** A person who rows a boat. **—oar** *v.* **oared, oar·ing, oars.** *—tr.* **1.** To propel with or as if with oars or an oar. **2.** To traverse with or as if with oars or an oar: *an hour to oar the strait.* *—intr.* To move forward by or as if by rowing: *oared strongly across the finish line.* [Middle English *or,* from Old English *ār.*] **—oared** *adj.* **—oar′less** *adj.*

oar·fish (ôr′fĭsh′, ōr′-) *n., pl.* **oarfish** or **-fish·es.** A widely distributed marine fish *(Regalecus glesne)* having a slender, silvery body up to 11 meters (36 feet) in length, a bright red dorsal fin along its entire length, and an undulating motion in swimming resembling that of a snake.

oar·lock (ôr′lŏk′, ōr′-) *n. Nautical.* A device, usually a U-shaped metal hoop on a swivel in the gunwale, used to hold an oar in place and as a fulcrum in rowing.

oars·man (ôrz′mən, ōrz′-) *n. Nautical.* A man who rows, especially an expert in rowing; a rower.

oars·wom·an (ôrz′wo͝om′ən) *n. Nautical.* A woman who rows, especially an expert in rowing; a rower.

OAS *abbr.* Organization of American States.

o·a·sis (ō-ā′sĭs) *n., pl.* **-ses** (-sēz). **1.** A fertile or green spot in a desert or wasteland, made so by the presence of water. **2.** A situation or place preserved from surrounding unpleasantness; a refuge: *an oasis of serenity amid chaos.* [Late Latin, from Greek, probably of Egyptian origin.]

oast (ōst) *n.* A kiln for drying hops or malt or drying and curing tobacco. [Middle English *ost,* from Old English *āst.*]

oat (ōt) *n.* **1.** Often **oats.** *(used with a sing. or pl. verb).* **a.** Any of various grasses of the genus *Avena,* especially *A. sativa,* widely cultivated for their edible grains. **b.** The grain of any of these plants, used as food and fodder. **2.** *Archaic.* A musical pipe made of an oat straw. [Middle English *ote,* from Old English *āte.*]

oat·cake (ōt′kāk′) *n.* A flattened cake of baked oatmeal.

oat·en (ōt′n) *adj.* Of, made of, or containing oats, oatmeal, or oat straw: *oaten fodder.*

oat·er (ō′tər) *n. Slang.* A movie about frontier or cowboy life; a western. [From the prominence of horses, known for their taste for oats, in such films.]

Oates (ōts), **Joyce Carol.** Born 1938. American writer whose works often concern love and violence in American society. Among her novels is *A Garden of Earthly Delights* (1967).

Oates, Titus. 1649–1705. English conspirator. His story of a Jesuit plot to assassinate Charles II (1678) resulted in the execution of many innocent Catholics.

oat grass *n.* **1.** Any of various grasses of the genera *Arrhenatherum* and *Danthonia.* **2.** Any of several oatlike grasses.

oath (ōth) *n., pl.* **oaths** (ōthz, ōths). **1. a.** A solemn, formal declaration or promise to fulfill a pledge, often calling on God or a sacred object as witness. **b.** The words or formula of such a declaration or promise. **c.** Something declared or promised. **2.** An irreverent or blasphemous use of the name of God or something held sacred. **3.** An imprecation; a curse. [Middle English *oth,* from Old English *āth.*]

oat·meal (ōt′mēl′) *n.* **1.** Meal made from oats; rolled or ground oats. **2.** A porridge made from rolled or ground oats.

Oa·xa·ca (wə-hä′kə). A city of southeast Mexico south of Orizaba. It was probably founded in 1486 as an Aztec garrison post and was conquered by the Spanish in 1521. Population, 154,223.

Ob (ŏb, ôb, ôp). A river, about 3,700 km (2,300 mi) long, of western and central Russia flowing generally northward to the **Gulf of Ob,** an arm of the Arctic Ocean.

OB or **Ob.** also **ob.** *abbr.* Obstetric; obstetrician; obstetrics.

ob. *abbr.* **1.** *Latin.* Obiit (he or she died). **2.** *Latin.* Obiter (incidentally). **3.** *Music.* Oboe.

Ob. *abbr. Bible.* Obadiah.

Phoenician
Originally a picture of a round eye (with a dot in the middle to represent the pupil), the 15th letter of the Phoenician alphabet stood for the Semitic sound at the beginning of *'ayin,* "eye."

Early Greek
Because this sound did not occur in Greek, the Greeks were able to assign this letter to the vowel *o.*

Roman
The simple, eloquent shape of this remarkable cultural artifact has not been changed by daily use for well over three thousand years.

oasis

ob– *pref.* Inverse; inversely: *obcordate.* [New Latin, short for *obversē,* obversely, from Latin *obversus,* past participle of *obvertere,* to turn toward : *ob-,* toward, against (from *ob,* toward, against, before; see **epi** in Appendix) + *vertere,* to turn; see VERSUS.]

o·ba (ō′bə) *n.* A hereditary chief or king among various peoples of Benin and Nigeria. [Of African origin.]

O·ba·di·ah (ō′bə-dī′ə) *n. Bible.* **1.** Also **Ab·di·as** (ăb-dī′əs). A Hebrew prophet of the sixth century B.C. **2.** *Abbr.* **Ob., Obad.** See table at **Bible.**

ob·bli·ga·to also **ob·li·ga·to** (ŏb′lĭ-gä′tō) *Music.* —*adj.* Not to be left out; indispensable. Used of an accompaniment that is an integral part of a piece. —*n., pl.* **-tos** or **-ti** (-tē). An obbligato accompaniment. [Italian, past participle of *obbligare,* to obligate, from Latin *obligāre,* to oblige. See OBLIGE.]

ob·com·pressed (ŏb′kəm-prĕst′) *adj.* Flattened from back to front rather than from side to side, as in the fruits of pennycress or peppergrass.

ob·cor·date (ŏb-kôr′dāt′) *adj. Botany.* Heart-shaped, with the point of attachment at the narrow end: *an obcordate leaf.*

ob·du·ra·cy (ŏb′dŏŏr-ə-sē, -dyŏŏr-) *n.* The state or quality of being intractable or hardened.

ob·du·rate (ŏb′dŏŏ-rĭt, -dyŏŏ-) *adj.* **1.a.** Hardened in wrongdoing or wickedness; stubbornly impenitent: *"obdurate conscience of the old sinner"* (Sir Walter Scott). **b.** Hardened against feeling; hardhearted: *an obdurate miser.* **2.** Not giving in to persuasion; intractable. See Synonyms at **inflexible.** [Middle English *obdurat,* from Late Latin *obdūrātus,* past participle of *obdūrāre,* to harden, from Latin, to be hard, endure : *ob-,* intensive pref.; see OB– + *dūrus,* hard; see **deru-** in Appendix.] **—ob′du·rate·ly** *adv.* **—ob′du·rate·ness** *n.*

obelisk

O.B.E. *abbr.* Order of the British Empire.

o·be·ah (ō′bē-ə) also **o·bi** (ō′bē) *n.* **1.** A form of religious belief of African origin, practiced in some parts of the West Indies, Jamaica, and nearby tropical America, involving sorcery. **2.** An object, a charm, or a fetish used in the practice of this religion. [Black and West Indian English, of West African origin; akin to Efik *ubio,* anything noxious, something put in the ground to cause sickness or death, bad omen.]

o·be·di·ence (ō-bē′dē-əns) *n.* **1.a.** The quality or condition of being obedient. **b.** The act of obeying. **2.a.** A sphere of ecclesiastical authority. **b.** A group of people under such authority.

o·be·di·ent (ō-bē′dē-ənt) *adj.* Dutifully complying with the commands, orders, or instructions of one in authority. [Middle English, from Old French, from Latin *oboediēns, oboedient-,* present participle of *oboedīre,* to obey. See OBEY.] **—o·be′di·ent·ly** *adv.*

SYNONYMS: *obedient, biddable, compliant, acquiescent, submissive, docile, amenable, tractable.* These adjectives mean carrying or willing to carry out the orders, requests, or wishes of another. *Obedient* implies acceptance of and submission to authority: *an obedient pupil; an obedient soldier. "The obedient colonies in this scheme are heavily taxed; the refractory remain unburdened"* (Edmund Burke). One who is *biddable* follows directions or obeys commands: *"A more gentle and biddable invalid . . . can hardly be conceived"* (Henry Kingsley). *Compliant* and *acquiescent* suggest a disposition to yield to authority meekly and without protest: *children compliant with the parental will; too acquiescent to challenge the propriety of offering a bribe. Submissive* implies an inclination or a willingness to submit without resistance and sometimes with deference to the control of another: *"replacing the troublemakers with more submissive people from the masses of unemployed"* (Suzanne Muchnic). One who is *docile* is receptive to being taught and willing to be led, supervised, or directed by another: *"A State which dwarfs its men, in order that they may be more docile instruments in its hands even for beneficial purposes—will find that with small men no great thing can really be accomplished"* (John Stuart Mill). *Amenable* suggests an agreeable responsiveness to authority, advice, or suggestion: *a high-spirited and rebellious girl not at all amenable to persuasion. Tractable* applies to those who can be handled, dealt with, or managed, especially with ease: *"the natives . . . being . . . of an intelligent tractable disposition"* (Samuel Butler).

o·bei·sance (ō-bā′səns, ō-bē′-) *n.* **1.** A gesture or movement of the body, such as a curtsy, that expresses deference or homage. **2.** An attitude of deference or homage. [Middle English *obeisaunce,* from Old French *obeissance,* from *obeissant,* present participle of *obeir,* to obey. See OBEY.] **—o·bei′sant** *adj.*

ob·e·li (ŏb′ə-lī′) *n.* Plural of **obelus.**

o·be·lia (ō-bēl′yə) *n.* Any of various colonial marine hydroids of the genus *Obelia,* having various specialized feeding and reproductive polyps and growing in a branchlike form. Colonies of obelia are found as a delicate furlike growth on the wooden piles of piers and wharves. [New Latin *Obelia,* genus name, probably from Greek *obelias,* a loaf baked on a spit, from *obelos,* a spit.]

ob·e·lisk (ŏb′ə-lĭsk) *n.* **1.** A tall, four-sided shaft of stone, usually tapered and monolithic, that rises to a point. **2.** *Printing.* The dagger sign (†), used especially as a reference mark. In this sense, also called *dagger, obelus.* [Latin *obeliscus,* from Greek *obeliskos,* diminutive of *obelos,* a spit, obelisk.] **—ob′e·lis′cal** (-lĭs′kəl) *adj.* **—ob′e·lis′koid′** (-koid′) *adj.*

ob·e·lize (ŏb′ə-līz′) *tr.v.* **-lized, -liz·ing, -liz·es.** To mark or annotate with an obelus. [Greek *obelizein,* from *obelos,* obelus.]

ob·e·lus (ŏb′ə-ləs) *n., pl.* **-li** (-lī′). **1.** A mark (— or ÷) used in ancient manuscripts to indicate a doubtful or spurious passage. **2.** *Printing.* See **obelisk** (sense 2). [Middle English, from Late Latin *obelus,* from Greek *obelos,* a spit, obelus.]

o·ben·to (ō-bĕn′tō) or **ben·to** (bĕn′-) *n., pl.* **-tos.** A Japanese meal that is packed in a partitioned lacquered box. [Japanese *obento* : *o,* pref. + *bento,* box lunch.]

O·ber·am·mer·gau (ō′bər-äm′ər-gou′). A town of southern Germany in the Bavarian Alps south-southwest of Munich. It is famed for its Passion plays, held every ten years since 1634 in thanksgiving for deliverance from the Black Death in 1633.

O·ber·hau·sen (ō′bər-hou′zən). A city of west-central Germany in the Ruhr Valley west-northwest of Essen. It is a port, rail junction, and industrial center. Population, 223,265.

O·ber·on (ō′bə-rŏn′, -rən) *n.* **1.** The king of the fairies and husband of Titania in medieval folklore. **2.** The satellite of Uranus that is fifth in distance from the planet. [French, from Old French *Auberon,* of Germanic origin. See **albho-** in Appendix.]

o·bese (ō-bēs′) *adj.* Extremely fat; grossly overweight. See Synonyms at **fat.** [Latin *obēsus,* from past participle of **obedere,* to eat away : *ob-,* away; see OB– + *edere,* to eat; see **ed-** in Appendix.] **—o·bese′ly** *adv.* **—o·bese′ness** *n.*

o·be·si·ty (ō-bē′sĭ-tē) *n.* The condition of being obese; increased body weight caused by excessive accumulation of fat.

o·bey (ō-bā′) *v.* **o·beyed, o·bey·ing, o·beys.** —*tr.* **1.** To carry out or fulfill the command, order, or instruction of. **2.** To carry out or comply with (a command, for example). —*intr.* To behave obediently. [Middle English *obeien,* from Old French *obeir,* from Latin *oboedīre,* to listen to : *ob-,* to; see OB– + *audīre,* to hear; see **au-** in Appendix.] **—o·bey′er** *n.*

ob·fus·cate (ŏb′fə-skāt′, ŏb-fŭs′kāt′) *tr.v.* **-cat·ed, -cat·ing, -cates. 1.** To make so confused or opaque as to be difficult to perceive or understand: *"A great effort was made . . . to obscure or obfuscate the truth"* (Robert Conquest). **2.** To render indistinct or dim; darken: *The fog obfuscated the shore.* [Latin *obfuscāre, obfuscāt-,* to darken : *ob-,* over; see OB– + *fuscāre,* to darken (from *fuscus,* dark).] **—ob′fus·ca′tion** *n.* **—ob·fus′ca·to′ry** (ŏb-fŭs′kə-tôr′ē, -tōr′ē, əb-) *adj.*

ob-gyn (ō′bē-jē′wī-ĕn′) *n. Informal.* **1.** The combined practice or field of obstetrics and gynecology. **2.** A specialist in this field; an obstetrician-gynecologist.

o·bi¹ (ō′bē) *n.* A wide sash fastened in the back with a large flat bow, worn by women in Japan as a part of the traditional dress. [Japanese.]

o·bi² (ō′bē) *n.* Variant of **obeah.**

O·bie (ō′bē) *n.* An award that is given annually for exceptional achievement in off-Broadway theater. [From *O.B.,* abbr. for OFF-BROADWAY.]

o·bit (ō′bĭt, ō-bĭt′) *n. Informal.* An obituary. [Middle English, death, record of date of death, from Old French, death, from Latin *obitus.* See OBITUARY.]

o·bi·ter dic·tum (ō′bĭ-tər dĭk′təm) *n., pl.* **obiter dic·ta** (dĭk′tə). **1.** *Law.* An opinion voiced by a judge that has only incidental bearing on the case in question and is therefore not binding. Also called *dictum.* **2.** An incidental remark or observation; a passing comment. [Latin, something said in passing : *obiter,* in passing + *dictum,* from neuter past participle of *dīcere,* to say.]

o·bit·u·ar·y (ō-bĭch′ōō-ĕr′ē) *n., pl.* **-ies.** A published notice of a death, sometimes with a brief biography of the deceased. [Medieval Latin *obituārius,* (report) of death, from Latin *obitus,* death, from past participle of *obīre,* to meet, meet one's death : *ob-,* toward; see OB– + *īre,* to go; see **ei-** in Appendix.] **—o·bit′u·ar′y** *adj.*

obj. *abbr.* **1.** *Grammar.* Object; objective. **2.** Objection.

ob·ject (ŏb′jĭkt, -jĕkt′) *n.* **1.** Something perceptible by one or more of the senses, especially by vision or touch; a material thing. **2.** A focus of attention, feeling, thought, or action: *an object of contempt.* **3.** The purpose, aim, or goal of a specific action or effort: *the object of the game.* **4.** *Abbr.* **obj.** *Grammar.* **a.** A noun or substantive that receives or is affected by the action of a verb within a sentence. **b.** A noun or substantive following and governed by a preposition. **5.** *Philosophy.* Something intelligible or perceptible by the mind. **—object** (əb-jĕkt′) *v.* **-ject·ed, -ject·ing, -jects.** —*intr.* **1.** To present a dissenting or opposing argument; raise an objection: *objected to the testimony of the witness.* **2.** To be averse to or express disapproval of something: *objects to modern materialism.* —*tr.* To put forward in or as a reason for opposition; offer as criticism: *They objected that discipline was lacking.* [Middle English, from Old French, from Medieval Latin *obiectum,* thing put before the mind, from neuter past participle of Latin *obicere,* to put before : *ob-,* before, toward; see OB– + *iacere,* to throw; see **yē-** in Appendix. V., from Middle English *obiecten,* from Old French *objecter,* from Latin *obiectāre,* frequentative of *obicere,* to hinder, oppose.] **—ob·jec′tor** *n.*

SYNONYMS: *object, protest, kick, demur, remonstrate, expostulate.* These verbs mean to express opposition to something, most often by presenting arguments against it. *Object* implies the expression of disapproval or distaste: *The general public objects to the use of drugs. "Freedom of the press in Britain is freedom to print such of the proprietor's prejudices as the advertisers don't object to"* (Hannen Swaffer). *Protest* suggests strong opposition, usually forthrightly expressed: *The patient protested to the recep-*

tionist when he was kept waiting. "We should, therefore, protest openly everything . . . that smacks of discrimination or slander" (Mary McLeod Bethune). *Kick* implies the expression of strong negative feelings, often of anger or rebellion: *"a rampant heresy, such as . . . Would make all women kick against their Lords"* (Tennyson). *I won't kick if you insist on paying the bill.* To *demur* is to raise an objection that may delay decision or action: *We proposed that dinner be served before the last guest arrived, but the hostess demurred. Remonstrate* implies the presentation of objections, complaints, or reproof in the form of argument or pleading: *"The people of Connecticut . . . remonstrated against the bill"* (George Bancroft). To *expostulate* is to express objection in the form of earnest reasoning: *Her parents expostulated with her on the foolhardiness of her behavior.* See also Synonyms at **intention.**

object ball *n. Games.* The ball in billiards or pool that a player hits or intends to hit first with the cue ball.

object glass *n.* See **objective** (sense 4).

ob·jec·ti·fy (əb-jĕk′tə-fī′) *tr.v.* **-fied, -fy·ing, -fies. 1.** To present (something or someone) as an object; depersonalize: *"Because we have objectified animals, we are able to treat them impersonally"* (Barry Lopez). **2.** To make objective. To impart reality to; make objective; externalize. **—ob·jec′ti·fi·ca′tion** (-fĭ-kā′shən) *n.* **—ob·jec′ti·fi′er** *n.*

ob·jec·tion (əb-jĕk′shən) *n. Abbr.* **obj. 1.** The act of objecting. **2.** A statement presented in opposition. **3.** A ground, reason, or cause for expressing opposition.

ob·jec·tion·a·ble (əb-jĕk′shə-nə-bəl) *adj.* Arousing disapproval; offensive: *objectionable behavior.* **—ob·jec′tion·a·bil′i·ty, ob·jec′tion·a·ble·ness** *n.* **—ob·jec′tion·a·bly** *adv.*

ob·jec·tive (əb-jĕk′tĭv) *adj.* **1.** Of or having to do with a material object. **2.** Having actual existence or reality. **3.a.** Uninfluenced by emotions or personal prejudices: *an objective critic.* See Synonyms at **fair**[1]. **b.** Based on observable phenomena; presented factually: *an objective appraisal.* **4.** *Medicine.* Indicating a symptom or condition perceived as a sign of disease by someone other than the person affected. **5.** *Abbr.* **obj.** *Grammar.* **a.** Of, relating to, or being the case of a noun or pronoun that serves as the object of a verb. **b.** Of or relating to a noun or pronoun used in this case. **—objective** *n.* **1.** Something that actually exists. **2.** Something worked toward or striven for; a goal. See Synonyms at **intention. 3.** *Abbr.* **obj.** *Grammar.* **a.** The objective case. **b.** A noun or pronoun in the objective case. **4.** The lens or lens system in a microscope or other optical instrument that first receives light rays from the object and forms the image. In this sense, also called *object glass, objective lens, object lens.* **—ob·jec′tive·ly** *adv.* **—ob·jec′tive·ness** *n.*

objective complement *n. Grammar.* A noun, an adjective, or a pronoun serving as a complement to a verb and qualifying its direct object, as *governor* in *They elected him governor.*

objective correlative *n.* A situation or a sequence of events or objects that evokes a particular emotion in a reader or an audience.

objective lens *n.* See **objective** (sense 4).

ob·jec·tiv·ism (ŏb-jĕk′tə-vĭz′əm) *n.* **1.** *Philosophy.* One of several doctrines holding that all reality is objective and external to the mind and that knowledge is reliably based on observed objects and events. **2.** An emphasis on objects rather than feelings or thoughts in literature or art. **—ob·jec′tiv·ist** *n.* **—ob·jec′tiv·is′tic** *adj.*

ob·jec·tiv·i·ty (ŏb′jĕk-tĭv′ĭ-tē) *n.* **1.** The state or quality of being objective. **2.** External or material reality.

ob·jec·ti·vize (əb-jĕk′tə-vīz′) *tr.v.* **-vized, -viz·ing, -viz·es.** To make objective or impersonal; objectify. **—ob·jec′ti·vi·za′tion** (-vĭ-zā′shən) *n.*

object language *n.* See **target language.**

object lens *n.* See **objective** (sense 4).

object lesson *n.* **1.** A concrete illustration of a moral or principle. **2.** A lesson taught by using a material object.

ob·jet d'art (ôb′zhĕ där′) *n., pl.* **ob·jets d'art** (ôb′zhĕ där′). An object of artistic merit. [French : *objet,* object + *de,* of + *art,* art.]

ob·jet trou·vé (ôb-zhā′ tro͞o-vā′) *n., pl.* **ob·jets trou·vés** (ôb-zhā′ tro͞o-vā′). See **found object.** [French : *objet,* object + *trouvé,* past participle of *trouver,* to find.]

ob·jur·gate (ŏb′jər-gāt′, ŏb-jûr′gāt′) *tr.v.* **-gat·ed, -gat·ing, -gates.** To scold or rebuke sharply; berate. [Latin *obiūrgāre, obiūrgāt-* : *ob-,* against; see OB– + *iūrgāre,* to scold, sue at law (probably *iūs, iūr-,* law; see **yewes-** in Appendix + *agere,* to do, proceed; see **ag-** in Appendix).] **—ob′jur·ga′tion** *n.* **—ob·jur′ga·to′ri·ly** (ŏb-jûr′gə-tôr′ə-lē, -tōr′-) *adv.* **—ob·jur′ga·to′ry** (-tôr′ē, -tōr′ē) *adj.*

obl. *abbr.* **1.** Oblique. **2.** Oblong.

ob·lan·ce·o·late (ŏb-lăn′sē-ə-lāt′) *adj. Botany.* Lance-shaped but broadest above the middle and tapering toward the base: *an oblanceolate leaf.*

o·blast (ô′bləst, ô′bläst′) *n.* An administrative territorial division within a constituent republic of the Soviet Union. [Russian *oblast',* from Old Church Slavonic : *ob,* on; see **epi** in Appendix + *vlastĭ,* power; see **wal-** in Appendix.]

ob·late[1] (ŏb′lāt′, ŏ-blāt′) *adj.* **1.** Having the shape of a spheroid generated by rotating an ellipse about its shorter axis. **2.** Having an equatorial diameter greater than the distance between poles; compressed along or flattened at the poles: *Planet Earth is an oblate solid.* [Probably New Latin *oblātus* : Latin *ob-,* toward; see OB– + Latin *lātus,* past participle of *ferre,* to carry (as in Latin *prōlātus,* prolate; see PROLATE); see **tele-** in Appendix.] **—ob′late′ly** *adv.* **—ob′late′ness** *n.*

ob·late[2] (ŏb′lāt′) *n.* **1.** A layperson dedicated to religious life. **2. Oblate.** *Roman Catholic Church.* A member of one of various religious communities for men or women. [Medieval Latin *oblātus,* from Latin, past participle of *offerre,* to offer. See OFFER.]

ob·la·tion (ə-blā′shən, ō-blā′-) *n.* **1.** The act of offering something, such as worship or thanks, to a deity. **2. Oblation. a.** The act of offering the bread and wine of the Eucharist. **b.** Something offered, especially the bread and wine of the Eucharist. **3.** A charitable offering or gift. [Middle English *oblacioun,* from Old French *oblacion,* from Late Latin *oblātiō, oblātiōn-,* from Latin *oblātus,* past participle of *offerre,* to offer. See OFFER.] **—ob·la′tion·al, ob′la·to′ry** (ŏb′lə-tôr′ē, -tōr′ē) *adj.*

ob·li·gate (ŏb′lĭ-gāt′) *tr.v.* **-gat·ed, -gat·ing, -gates. 1.** To bind, compel, or constrain by a social, legal, or moral tie. See Synonyms at **force. 2.** To cause to be grateful or indebted; oblige. **3.** To commit (money, for example) in order to fulfill an obligation. **—obligate** (-gĭt, -gāt′) *adj.* **1.** *Biology.* Able to exist or survive only in a particular environment or by assuming a particular role: *an obligate parasite; an obligate anaerobe.* **2.** Absolutely indispensable; essential. [Latin *obligāre, obligāt-.* See OBLIGE.] **—ob′li·ga·ble** (-gə-bəl) *adj.* **—ob′li·gate·ly** *adv.* **—ob′li·ga′tor** *n.*

ob·li·ga·tion (ŏb′lĭ-gā′shən) *n.* **1.** The act of binding oneself by a social, legal, or moral tie. **2.a.** A social, legal, or moral requirement, such as a duty, contract, or promise that compels one to follow or avoid a particular course of action. **b.** A course of action imposed by society, law, or conscience by which one is bound or restricted. **3.** The constraining power of a promise, contract, law, or sense of duty. **4.** *Law.* **a.** A legal agreement stipulating a specified payment or action, especially if the agreement also specifies a penalty for failure to comply. **b.** The document containing the terms of such an agreement. **5.a.** Something owed as payment or in return for a special service or favor. **b.** The service or favor for which one is indebted to another. **6.** The state, fact, or feeling of being indebted to another for a special service or favor received. **—ob′li·ga′tion·al** *adj.*

SYNONYMS: *obligation, responsibility, duty.* These nouns refer to a course of action that is demanded of a person, as by law or conscience. *Obligation* usually applies to a specific constraint arising from a particular cause: *"Then in the marriage union, the independence of the husband and wife will be equal, their dependence mutual, and their obligations reciprocal"* (Lucretia Mott). *Responsibility* stresses accountability for the fulfillment of an obligation: *"I believe that every right implies a responsibility; every opportunity, an obligation; every possession, a duty"* (John D. Rockefeller, Jr.). *Duty* applies especially to constraint deriving from moral or ethical considerations: *"I therefore believe it is my duty to my country to love it, to support its Constitution, to obey its laws, to respect its flag, and to defend it against all enemies"* (William Tyler Page).

ob·li·ga·to (ŏb′lĭ-gä′tō) *adj. & n. Music.* Variant of **obbligato.**

o·blig·a·to·ry (ə-blĭg′ə-tôr′ē, -tōr′ē, ŏb′lĭ-gə-) *adj.* **1.** Morally or legally constraining; binding. **2.** Imposing or recording an obligation: *a bill obligatory.* **3.** Of the nature of an obligation; compulsory: *Attendance is obligatory. Mathematics is an obligatory course.* **4.** *Biology.* Obligate. **—o·blig′a·to′ri·ly** *adv.*

o·blige (ə-blīj′) *v.* **o·bliged, o·blig·ing, o·blig·es.** *—tr.* **1.** To constrain by physical, legal, social, or moral means. **2.** To make indebted or grateful: *I am obliged to you for your gracious hospitality.* **3.** To do a service or favor for: *They obliged us by arriving early.* *—intr.* To do a service or favor: *The soloist obliged with yet another encore.* [Middle English *obligen,* from Old French *obligier,* from Latin *obligāre* : *ob-,* to; see OB– + *ligāre,* to bind; see **leig-** in Appendix.] **—o·blig′er** *n.*

SYNONYMS: *oblige, accommodate, favor.* The central meaning shared by these verbs is "to perform a service or a courteous act for": *obliged me by keeping the matter quiet; accommodating her by lending her money; favor an audience with an encore.* See also Synonyms at **force.**
ANTONYM: *disoblige.*

ob·li·gee (ŏb′lə-jē′) *n. Law.* One to whom another is bound by contract or legal agreement.

o·blig·ing (ə-blī′jĭng) *adj.* Ready to do favors for others; accommodating. See Synonyms at **amiable. —o·blig′ing·ly** *adv.* **—o·blig′ing·ness** *n.*

ob·li·gor (ŏb′lĭ-gôr′, -jôr′) *n. Law.* One who binds oneself to another by contract or legal agreement.

o·blique (ō-blēk′, ə-blēk′) *adj. Abbr.* **obl. 1.a.** Having a slanting or sloping direction, course, or position; inclined. **b.** *Mathematics.* Designating geometric lines or planes that are neither parallel nor perpendicular. **2.** *Botany.* Having sides of unequal length or form: *an oblique leaf.* **3.** *Anatomy.* Situated in a slanting position; not transverse or longitudinal: *oblique muscles or ligaments.* **4.a.** Indirect or evasive: *oblique political maneu-*

ă pat	oi boy
ā pay	ou out
âr care	o͝o took
ä father	o͞o boot
ĕ pet	ŭ cut
ē be	ûr urge
ĭ pit	th thin
ī pie	*th* this
îr pier	hw which
ŏ pot	zh vision
ō toe	ə about, item
ô paw	♦ regionalism

Stress marks: **′** (primary); ′ (secondary), as in **dictionary** (dĭk′shə-nĕr′ē)

vers. **b.** Devious, misleading, or dishonest: *gave oblique answers to the questions.* **5.** Not direct in descent; collateral. **6.** *Grammar.* Designating any noun case except the nominative or the vocative. **—oblique** *n.* **1.** An oblique thing, such as a line, direction, or muscle. **2.** *Nautical.* The act of changing course by less than 90°. **—oblique** (ō-blēk′, ə-blēk′) *adv.* At an angle of 45°. [Middle English, from Old French, from Latin *oblīquus.*] **—o·blique′ly** *adv.* **—o·blique′ness** *n.*

oblique angle *n. Mathematics.* An angle, such as an acute or obtuse angle, that is not a right angle or a multiple of a right angle.

oblique rhyme *n.* See **off rhyme.**

oblique triangle *n. Mathematics.* A triangle having no right angle.

o·bliq·ui·ty (ō-blĭk′wĭ-tē, ə-blĭk′-) *n., pl.* **-ties. 1.** The quality or condition of being oblique. **2. a.** A deviation from a vertical or horizontal line, plane, position, or direction. **b.** The angle or extent of such a deviation. **3. a.** A mental deviation or aberration. **b.** Immoral conduct. **4. a.** Obscurity in conduct or verbal expression: *"It may be that the candor of contemporary literature creates a nostalgia for indirection, obliquity and deferral"* (Anatole Broyard). **b.** An obscure statement. **—o·bliq′ui·tous** *adj.*

oboe

o·blit·er·ate (ə-blĭt′ə-rāt′, ō-blĭt′-) *tr.v.* **-at·ed, -at·ing, -ates. 1.** To do away with completely so as to leave no trace. See Synonyms at **abolish. 2.** To wipe out, rub off, or erase (writing or other markings). **3.** *Medicine.* To remove completely (a body organ or part), as by surgery, disease, or radiation. [Latin *oblitterāre, oblitterāt-*, to erase, from *ob litterās*, in *ob litterās scrībere*, to write over letters (*ob*, over; see OB– + *litterās*, accusative pl. of *littera*, letter) and from *oblītus*, past participle of *oblīvīscī*, to forget; see OBLIVION.] **—o·blit′er·a′tion** *n.* **—o·blit′er·a′tive** (-ə-rā′tĭv, -ər-ə-tĭv) *adj.* **—o·blit′er·a′tor** *n.*

o·bliv·i·on (ə-blĭv′ē-ən) *n.* **1.** The condition or quality of being completely forgotten: *"He knows that everything he writes is consigned to posterity (oblivion's other, seemingly more benign, face)"* (Joyce Carol Oates). **2.** The act or an instance of forgetting; total forgetfulness: *sought the great oblivion of sleep.* **3.** Official overlooking of offenses; amnesty. [Middle English, from Old French, from Latin *oblīviō, oblīviōn-*, from *oblīvīscī*, to forget. See **lei-** in Appendix.]

o·bliv·i·ous (ə-blĭv′ē-əs) *adj.* **1.** Lacking all memory; forgetful. **2.** Lacking conscious awareness; unmindful. See Synonyms at **forgetful. —o·bliv′i·ous·ly** *adv.* **—o·bliv′i·ous·ness** *n.*

USAGE NOTE: In an earlier survey a majority of the Usage Panel accepted the use of both *of* and *to* with *oblivious: The party appeared oblivious to* (or *of*) *the mounting pressures for political reform.*

ob·long (ŏb′lông′, -lŏng′) *adj. Abbr.* **obl. 1.** Deviating from a square, circular, or spherical form by being elongated in one direction. **2.** Having the shape of or resembling a rectangle or an ellipse. **3.** *Botany.* Having a somewhat elongated form with approximately parallel sides: *an oblong leaf.* **—oblong** *n.* An object or a figure, such as a rectangle, with an elongated shape. [Middle English, from Latin *oblongus* : *ob-*, intensive pref. (sense uncertain); see OB– + *longus*, long; see **del-**[1] in Appendix.]

ob·lo·quy (ŏb′lə-kwē) *n., pl.* **-quies. 1.** Abusively detractive language or utterance; calumny: *"I have had enough obloquy for one lifetime"* (Anthony Eden). **2.** The condition of disgrace suffered as a result of abuse or vilification; ill repute. See Synonyms at **disgrace.** [Middle English *obloqui*, from Late Latin *obloquium*, abusive contradiction, from Latin *obloquī*, to interrupt : *ob-*, against; see OB– + *loquī*, to speak; see **tolkʷ-** in Appendix.]

ob·nox·ious (ŏb-nŏk′shəs, əb-) *adj.* **1.** Very objectionable; odious. See Synonyms at **hateful. 2.** Exposed to harm, injury, or evil: *"The town . . . now lies obnoxious to its foes"* (John Bunyan). **3.** *Archaic.* Deserving of or liable to censure. [Latin *obnoxiōsus*, subordinate, from *obnoxius*, subject, liable : *ob-*, to; see OB– + *noxa*, injury; see **nek-**[1] in Appendix.] **—ob·nox′ious·ly** *adv.* **—ob·nox′ious·ness** *n.*

observatory
U.S. Naval Observatory in Washington, D.C.

o·boe (ō′bō) *n. Abbr.* **ob.** *Music.* **1.** A slender woodwind instrument with a conical bore and a double reed mouthpiece, having a range of three octaves and a penetrating, poignant sound. **2.** A reed stop in an organ that produces a sound similar to that of the oboe. [Italian, from French *hautbois.* See HAUTBOY.] **—o′bo·ist** *n.*

ob·ol (ŏb′əl) also **ob·o·lus** (ŏb′ə-ləs) *n., pl.* **-ols** also **-o·li** (-ə-lī′). A silver coin or unit of weight equal to one sixth of a drachma, formerly used in ancient Greece. [Latin *obolus*, from Greek *obolos*, variant of *obelos*, spit, obol.]

ob·o·vate (ŏb-ō′vāt′) *adj. Botany.* Egg-shaped and flat, with the narrow end attached to the stalk: *an obovate leaf.*

ob·o·void (ŏb-ō′void′) *adj. Botany.* Egg-shaped and solid, with the narrow end attached to the stem: *an obovoid fruit.*

O·bre·gón (ō-brā-gôn′, ô-vrĕ-), **Álvaro.** 1880–1928. Mexican soldier and politician who overthrew Venustiano Carranza in 1920. As president (1920–1924 and 1928) he initiated numerous social reforms before he was assassinated.

O'Bri·en (ō-brī′ən), **Edna.** Born 1932. Irish writer whose works, including *Johnny I Hardly Knew You* (1977), explore the lives of women in modern-day Ireland.

obs. *abbr.* **1.** Obscure. **2.** Observation. **3.** Or **Obs.** Observatory. **4.** Obsolete. **5.** Obstetric; obstetrician; obstetrics.

ob·scene (ŏb-sēn′, əb-) *adj.* **1.** Offensive to accepted standards of decency or modesty. See Synonyms at **coarse. 2.** Inciting lustful feelings; lewd. **3.** Offensive or repulsive to the senses; loathsome: *"The way he writes about the disease that killed her is simply obscene"* (Michael Korda). [Latin *obscēnus.*] **—ob·scene′ly** *adv.*

ob·scen·i·ty (ŏb-sĕn′ĭ-tē, əb-) *n., pl.* **-ties. 1.** The state or quality of being obscene. **2.** Indecency, lewdness, or offensiveness in behavior, expression, or appearance. **3.** Something, such as a word, an act, or an expression, that is indecent or lewd. **4.** Something that is offensive or repulsive to the senses: *"What had once been a gentle hill covered with lush grass turned into a brown obscenity of bare earth and smoke"* (Tom Clancy).

ob·scur·ant (ŏb-skyo͝or′ənt, əb-) *n.* One who opposes intellectual advancement and political reform. **—obscurant** *adj.* **1.** Characterized by opposition to intellectual advancement and political reform. **2.** Tending to make obscure: *an obscurant bank of clouds.*

ob·scur·ant·ism (ŏb-skyo͝or′ən-tĭz′əm, əb-, ŏb′skyo͝o-răn′-) *n.* **1.** The principles or practice of obscurants. **2.** A policy of withholding information from the public. **3. a.** A style in art and literature characterized by deliberate vagueness or obliqueness. **b.** An example or instance of this style. **—ob·scur′ant·ist** *n.*

ob·scure (ŏb-skyo͝or′, əb-) *adj.* **-scur·er, -scur·est.** *Abbr.* **obs. 1.** Deficient in light; dark. **2. a.** So faintly perceptible as to lack clear delineation; indistinct. See Synonyms at **dark. b.** Indistinctly heard; faint. **c.** *Linguistics.* Having the reduced, neutral sound represented by schwa (ə). **3. a.** Far from centers of human population: *an obscure village.* **b.** Out of sight; hidden: *an obscure retreat.* **4.** Not readily noticed or seen; inconspicuous: *an obscure flaw.* **5.** Of undistinguished or humble station or reputation: *an obscure poet; an obscure family.* **6.** Not clearly understood or expressed; ambiguous or vague: *"an impulse to go off and fight certain obscure battles of his own spirit"* (Anatole Broyard). See Synonyms at **ambiguous. —obscure** *tr.v.* **-scured, -scur·ing, -scures. 1.** To make dim or indistinct: *Smog obscured our view.* See Synonyms at **block. 2.** To conceal in obscurity; hide: *"Unlike the origins of most nations, America's origins are not obscured in the mists of time"* (National Review). **3.** *Linguistics.* To reduce (a vowel) to the neutral sound represented by schwa (ə). **—obscure** *n.* Something obscure or unknown. [Middle English, from Old French *obscur*, from Latin *obscūrus.* See **(s)keu-** in Appendix.] **—ob·scure′ly** *adv.* **—ob·scure′ness** *n.*

ob·scu·ri·ty (ŏb-skyo͝or′ĭ-tē, əb-) *n., pl.* **-ties. 1.** Deficiency or absence of light; darkness. **2. a.** The quality or condition of being unknown: *"Even utter obscurity need not be an obstacle to* [political] *success"* (New Republic). **b.** One that is unknown. **3. a.** The quality or condition of being imperfectly known or difficult to understand: *"writings meant to be understood . . . by all, composed without deliberate obscurity or hidden motives"* (National Review). **b.** An instance of being imperfectly known or difficult to understand.

ob·se·qui·ous (ŏb-sē′kwē-əs, əb-) *adj.* Full of or exhibiting servile compliance; fawning. [Middle English, from Latin *obsequiōsus*, from *obsequium*, compliance, from *obsequī*, to comply : *ob-*, to; see OB– + *sequī*, to follow; see **sekʷ-**[1] in Appendix.] **—ob·se′qui·ous·ly** *adv.* **—ob·se′qui·ous·ness** *n.*

ob·se·quy (ŏb′sĭ-kwē) *n., pl.* **-quies.** A funeral rite or ceremony. Often used in the plural. [Middle English *obsequi*, from Old French *obseque*, from Medieval Latin *obsequiae*, alteration (influenced by Latin *exsequiae*, funeral rites) of Latin *obsequia*, pl. of *obsequium*, compliance, dutiful service. See OBSEQUIOUS.]

ob·serv·a·ble (əb-zûr′və-bəl) *adj.* **1.** Possible to observe: *observable phenomena; an observable change in demeanor.* See Synonyms at **noticeable. 2.** Deserving or worthy of note; noteworthy: *an observable anniversary.* **—observable** *n. Physics.* A physical property, such as weight or temperature, that can be observed or measured directly, as distinguished from a quantity, such as work or entropy, that must be derived from observed quantities. **—ob·serv′a·bly** *adv.*

ob·ser·vance (əb-zûr′vəns) *n.* **1.** The act or practice of observing or complying with a law, custom, command, or rule. **2.** The act or custom of keeping or celebrating a holiday or other ritual occasion. **3.** A customary rite or ceremony. **4.** The act of watching; observation: *"Consider how much intellect was needed in the architect, and how much observance of nature"* (John Ruskin). **5.** *Roman Catholic Church.* The rule governing a religious order.

ob·ser·vant (əb-zûr′vənt) *adj.* **1.** Quick to perceive or apprehend; alert: *an observant traveler.* See Synonyms at **careful. 2.** Diligent in observing a law, custom, duty, or principle: *observant of the speed limit.* **—ob·ser′vant·ly** *adv.*

ob·ser·va·tion (ŏb′zər-vā′shən) *n. Abbr.* **obs. 1. a.** The act or faculty of observing. **b.** The fact of being observed. **2. a.** The act of noting and recording something, such as a phenomenon, with instruments. **b.** The result or record of such notation: *a meteorological observation.* **3.** A comment or remark. See Synonyms at **comment. 4.** An inference or a judgment that is acquired from or based on observing. **—ob′ser·va′tion·al** *adj.* **—ob′ser·va′tion·al·ly** *adv.*

ob·ser·va·to·ry (əb-zûr′və-tôr′ē, -tōr′ē) *n., pl.* **-ries.** *Abbr.* **obs., Obs. 1.** A building, a place, or an institution designed and equipped for making observations of astronomical, meteorological, or other natural phenomena. **2.** A structure overlooking an extensive view. [French *observatoire* (influenced by CONSERVATORY), from *observer,* to observe, from Old French. See OBSERVE.]

ob·serve (əb-zûrv′) *v.* **-served, -serv·ing, -serves.** —*tr.* **1.** To be or become aware of, especially through careful and directed attention; notice. **2.** To watch attentively: *observe a child's behavior.* **3.** To make a systematic or scientific observation of: *observe the orbit of the moon.* **4.** To say casually; remark. **5.** To adhere to or abide by: *observe the terms of a contract.* **6.** To keep or celebrate (a holiday, for example): *observe an anniversary.* —*intr.* **1.** To take notice. **2.** To say something; make a comment or remark. **3.** To watch or be present without participating actively: *We were invited to the conference solely to observe.* [Middle English *observen,* to conform to, from Old French *observer,* from Latin *observāre,* to abide by, watch : *ob-,* over; see OB– + *servāre,* to keep, watch; see **ser-**[1] in Appendix.] **—ob·serv′ing·ly** *adv.*

SYNONYMS: *observe, keep, celebrate, commemorate, solemnize.* These verbs are compared as they mean to give proper heed to or show proper reverence for something, such as a rule, custom, or holiday. *Observe* stresses respectful adherence, as to law or tradition, often in the form of compliance with prescribed rites: *observe the speed limit; observe the Sabbath. Keep* contrasts with *break* and *violate;* it implies actions such as the discharge of a duty or the fulfillment of a promise: *He said he would help, and he kept his word. Celebrate* in this comparison emphasizes observance in the form of rejoicing or festivity: *We are planning a surprise party to celebrate her birthday.* To *commemorate* is to honor the memory of a past event; *solemnize* implies dignity and gravity in the celebration of an occasion: *"It* [July 2, 1776] *ought to be commemorated as the day of deliverance . . . It ought to be solemnized with pomp and parade . . . from one end of this continent to the other, from this time forward forevermore"* (John Adams). See also Synonyms at **see**[1].

ob·serv·er (əb-zûr′vər) *n.* **1.** One that observes: *an observer of local customs; observers of religious holidays.* **2.** A delegate sent to observe and report on the proceedings of an assembly or a meeting but not vote or otherwise participate. **3.a.** A crew member on a military aircraft who makes observations. **b.** A member of an armed force who watches and reports from an observation post.

ob·sess (əb-sĕs′, ŏb-) *v.* **-sessed, -sess·ing, -sess·es.** —*tr.* To preoccupy the mind of excessively. —*intr.* To have the mind excessively preoccupied with a single emotion or topic: *"She's dead. And you're still obsessing"* (Scott Turow). [Latin *obsidēre, obsess-,* to beset, occupy : *ob-,* on; see OB– + *sedēre,* to sit; see **sed-** in Appendix.] **—ob·ses′sor** *n.*

ob·ses·sion (əb-sĕsh′ən, ŏb-) *n.* **1.** Compulsive preoccupation with a fixed idea or an unwanted feeling or emotion, often accompanied by symptoms of anxiety. **2.** A compulsive, often unreasonable idea or emotion. **—ob·ses′sion·al** *adj.* **—ob·ses′sion·al·ly** *adv.*

ob·ses·sive (əb-sĕs′ĭv, ŏb-) *adj.* **1.** Of, relating to, characteristic of, or causing an obsession: *obsessive gambling.* **2.** Excessive in degree or nature: *an obsessive need to win.* **—ob·ses′sive** *n.* **—ob·ses′sive·ly** *adv.* **—ob·ses′sive·ness** *n.*

ob·ses·sive-com·pul·sive (əb-sĕs′ĭv-kəm-pŭl′sĭv, ŏb-) *adj.* Relating to or characterized by a tendency to dwell on unwanted thoughts or ideas or perform certain repetitious rituals, especially as a defense against anxiety from unconscious conflicts: *obsessive-compulsive behavior.* **—obsessive-compulsive** *n.* An obsessive-compulsive person.

ob·sid·i·an (ŏb-sĭd′ē-ən) *n.* A usually black or banded, hard volcanic glass that displays shiny, curved surfaces when fractured and is formed by rapid cooling of lava. [Latin *obsidiānus,* misreading of *obsiānus (lapis),* Obsian (stone), obsidian, after *Obsius,* a Roman who supposedly discovered it or a similar mineral.]

ob·so·lesce (ŏb′sə-lĕs′) *intr.v.* **-lesced, -lesc·ing, -lesc·es.** To undergo the process of becoming obsolete. [Latin *obsolēscere.* See OBSOLESCENT.]

ob·so·les·cent (ŏb′sə-lĕs′ənt) *adj.* **1.** Being in the process of passing out of use or usefulness; becoming obsolete. **2.** *Biology.* Gradually disappearing; imperfectly or only slightly developed. Used of an organ or other part of an animal or a plant. [Latin *obsolēscēns, obsolēscent-,* present participle of *obsolēscere,* to fall into disuse : *ob-,* away; see OB– + *solēre,* to be accustomed to.] **—ob′so·les′cence** *n.* **—ob′so·les′cent·ly** *adv.*

ob·so·lete (ŏb′sə-lēt′, ŏb′sə-lēt′) *adj.* **1.** *Abbr.* **obs.** No longer in use: *an obsolete word.* See Synonyms at **old. 2.** Outmoded in design, style, or construction: *an obsolete locomotive.* **3.** *Biology.* Vestigial or imperfectly developed, especially in comparison with other individuals or related species; not clearly marked or seen; indistinct. Used of an organ or other part of an animal or a plant. **—obsolete** *tr.v.* **-let·ed, -let·ing, -letes.** To cause to become obsolete. [Latin *obsolētus,* past participle of *obsolēscere,* to fall into disuse. See OBSOLESCENT.] **—ob′so·lete′ly** *adv.* **—ob′so·lete′ness** *n.* **—ob′so·let′ism** *n.*

ob·sta·cle (ŏb′stə-kəl) *n.* One that opposes, stands in the way of, or holds up progress. [Middle English, from Old French, from Latin *obstāculum,* from *obstāre,* to hinder : *ob-,* against; see OB– + *stāre,* to stand; see **stā-** in Appendix.]

SYNONYMS: *obstacle, obstruction, bar, barrier, block, hindrance, impediment, snag.* All of these nouns refer to something that prevents action or slows progress. *Obstacle* applies to something that stands in the way and must be removed, circumvented, or surmounted: *"We combat obstacles in order to get repose"* (Henry Adams). An *obstruction* makes passage or progress difficult: *a sandbar that is an obstruction to navigation. Bar* and *barrier* suggest an obstruction that confines or prevents exit or entry: *"Tyranny may always enter—there is no charm, no bar against it—the only bar against it is a large resolute breed of men"* (Walt Whitman). *"Literature is my Utopia . . . No barrier of the senses shuts me out from the sweet, gracious discourse of my book friends"* (Helen Keller). *Block* suggests obstruction that effectively prevents all passage: *The student failed the examination because of a mental block. Hindrance* and *impediment* are applied to something that interferes with or delays passage or progress: *"an attachment that would be a hindrance to him in any honorable career"* (Thomas Hardy). *Overcrowded prisons are an impediment to the rehabilitation of criminals.* A *snag* is an unforeseen or hidden, often transitory obstacle: *The tourist ran up against a snag in the form of a lost passport.*

obstacle course *n.* **1.** A training course filled with obstacles, such as ditches and walls, that must be negotiated speedily by troops undergoing training or participants in an obstacle race. **2.** A situation full of obstacles that must be overcome.

obstacle race *n. Sports.* A race in which the participants are required to go through, under, or over a number of obstacles.

obstet. *abbr.* Obstetric; obstetrics.

ob·stet·ric (ŏb-stĕt′rĭk, əb-) also **ob·stet·ri·cal** (-rĭ-kəl) *adj. Abbr.* **OB, ob., Ob., obs., obstet.** Of or relating to the profession of obstetrics or the care of women during and after pregnancy. [Latin *obstetrīcius,* pertaining to a midwife, from *obstetrīx, obstetrīc-,* midwife, from *obstāre,* to stand opposite to : *ob-,* opposite to; see OB– + *stāre,* to stand; see **stā-** in Appendix.] **—ob·stet′ri·cal·ly** *adv.*

ob·ste·tri·cian (ŏb′stĭ-trĭsh′ən) *n. Abbr.* **OB, ob., Ob., obs.** A physician who specializes in obstetrics.

ob·stet·rics (ŏb-stĕt′rĭks, əb-) *n. (used with a sing. or pl. verb). Abbr.* **OB, ob., Ob., obs., obstet.** The branch of medicine that deals with the care of women during pregnancy, childbirth, and the recuperative period following delivery.

ob·sti·na·cy (ŏb′stə-nə-sē) *n., pl.* **-cies. 1.** The state or quality of being stubborn or refractory. **2.** The act or an instance of being stubborn or refractory.

ob·sti·nate (ŏb′stə-nĭt) *adj.* **1.** Stubbornly adhering to an attitude, an opinion, or a course of action; obdurate. **2.** Difficult to manage, control, or subdue; refractory. **3.** Difficult to alleviate or cure: *an obstinate headache.* [Middle English *obstinat,* from Latin *obstinātus,* past participle of *obstināre,* to persist. See **stā-** in Appendix.] **—ob′sti·nate·ly** *adv.* **—ob′sti·nate·ness** *n.*

SYNONYMS: *obstinate, stubborn, headstrong, stiff-necked, bullheaded, pigheaded, mulish, dogged, pertinacious.* These adjectives are compared as they mean tenaciously unwilling or marked by tenacious unwillingness to yield. *Obstinate* implies unreasonable rigidity, as in the face of argument, persuasion, entreaty, or attack: *"Mr. Quincy labored hard with the governor to obtain his assent, but he was obstinate"* (Benjamin Franklin). *Stubborn* pertains to innate, often perverse resoluteness or unyieldingness: *"She was very stubborn when her mind was made up"* (Samuel Butler). One who is *headstrong* is stubbornly, often recklessly willful: *The headstrong young couple entered into a marriage doomed to failure. Stiff-necked* implies stubbornness combined with arrogance or aloofness: *The stiff-necked old Brahmin returned to Boston. Bullheaded* suggests foolish or irrational obstinacy, and *pigheaded,* stupid obstinacy: *Don't be bullheaded; see a doctor. "It's a pity pious folks are so apt to be pigheaded"* (Harriet Beecher Stowe). *Mulish* implies the obstinacy and intractability associated with a mule: *"Obstinate is no word for it, for she is mulish"* (Ouida). *Dogged* emphasizes stubborn perseverance: *dogged persistence; "two warring ideals in one dark body, whose dogged strength alone keeps it from being torn asunder"* (W.E.B. Du Bois). *Pertinacious* stresses a tenacity of purpose, opinion, or course of action that is sometimes viewed as vexatious: *She is the most vocal and pertinacious of all the critics of the policy.*

ob·strep·er·ous (ŏb-strĕp′ər-əs, əb-) *adj.* **1.** Noisily and stubbornly defiant. **2.** Aggressively boisterous. [From Latin *obstreperus,* noisy, from *obstrepere,* to make a noise against : *ob-,* against; see OB– + *strepere,* to make a noise (of imitative origin).] **—ob·strep′er·ous·ly** *adv.* **—ob·strep′er·ous·ness** *n.*

ob·struct (əb-strŭkt′, ŏb-) *tr.v.* **-struct·ed, -struct·ing, -structs. 1.** To block or fill (a passage) with obstacles or an obstacle. See Synonyms at **block. 2.** To impede, retard, or interfere with; hinder: *obstructed my progress.* See Synonyms at **hinder**[1]. **3.** To get in the way of so as to hide from sight. [Latin *obstruere, obstrūct-* : *ob-,* against; see OB– + *struere,* to pile up; see **ster-**[2] in Appendix.] **—ob·struct′er, ob·struc′tor** *n.* **—ob·struc′tive** *adj.* **—ob·struc′tive·ly** *adv.* **—ob·struc′tive·ness** *n.*

ob·struc·tion (əb-strŭk′shən, ŏb-) *n.* **1.** One that obstructs; an obstacle. See Synonyms at **obstacle. 2.a.** The act or an instance of obstructing. **b.** The condition of being obstructed. **3.** The act of causing a delay or an attempt to cause a delay in the

ă pat	oi boy
ā pay	ou out
âr care	ŏŏ took
ä father	ōō boot
ĕ pet	ŭ cut
ē be	ûr urge
ĭ pit	th thin
ī pie	*th* this
îr pier	hw which
ŏ pot	zh vision
ō toe	ə about, item
ô paw	♦ regionalism

Stress marks: **′** (primary); ′ (secondary), as in **dictionary** (dĭk′shə-nĕr′ē)

conduct of business, especially in a legislative body. **4.** *Sports.* The act of impeding another player in a match or race.

ob·struc·tion·ist (əb-strŭk′shə-nĭst, ŏb-) *n.* One who systematically blocks or interrupts a process, especially one who attempts to impede passage of legislation by the use of delaying tactics, such as a filibuster. **—ob·struc′tion·ism** *n.* **—ob·struc′tion·is′tic** *adj.*

obstruction of justice *n. Law.* The criminal offense, under common law and according to the statutes of many jurisdictions, of obstructing the administration and due process of law: *"the violations of the Constitution, the abuse of power, the obstruction of justice, the subversion of government, the lies to Congress and the American people"* (Arthur M. Schlesinger, Jr.).

ob·stru·ent (ŏb′stro͞o-ənt) *adj.* Obstructing or closing natural openings or passages of the body. **—obstruent** *n.* **1.** An obstruent medicine or agent. **2.** *Linguistics.* A sound, such as a stop, a fricative, or an affricate, that is produced with complete blockage or at least partial constriction of the airflow through the nose or mouth. [Latin *obstruēns, obstruent-,* present participle of *obstruere,* to obstruct. See OBSTRUCT.]

ob·tain (əb-tān′, ŏb-) *v.* **-tained, -tain·ing, -tains.** *—tr.* To succeed in gaining possession of as the result of planning or endeavor; acquire. *—intr.* **1.** To be established, accepted, or customary: *"standards, proprieties that no longer obtain"* (Meg Greenfield). **2.** *Archaic.* To succeed. [Middle English *obteinen,* from Old French *obtenir,* from Latin *obtinēre* : *ob-,* intensive pref.; see OB– + *tenēre,* to hold; see **ten-** in Appendix.] **—ob·tain′a·ble** *adj.* **—ob·tain′er** *n.*

ob·tect (ŏb-tĕkt′) also **ob·tect·ed** (-tĕk′tĭd) *adj.* Having the wings and appendages enclosed or covered by a secretion that forms a hard shell or horny case, as the pupae of most butterflies and moths. [Latin *obtēctus,* past participle of *obtegere,* to cover over : *ob-,* over; see OB– + *tegere,* to cover; see **(s)teg-** in Appendix.]

ob·test (ŏb-tĕst′) *tr.v.* **-test·ed, -test·ing, -tests.** To supplicate; entreat. [Latin *obtestārī* : *ob-,* to; see OB– + *testārī,* to call as a witness (from *testis,* witness; see **trei-** in Appendix).] **—ob′tes·ta′tion** *n.*

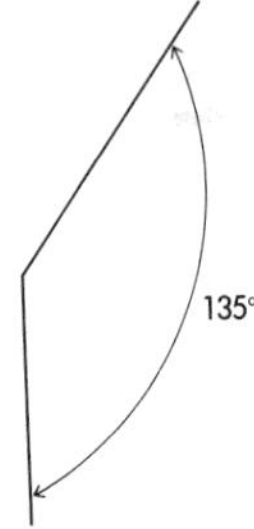

obtuse angle

ob·trude (ŏb-tro͞od′, əb-) *v.* **-trud·ed, -trud·ing, -trudes.** *—tr.* **1.** To impose (oneself or one's ideas) on others with undue insistence or without invitation. See Synonyms at **intrude. 2.** To thrust out; push forward. *—intr.* To impose oneself on others. [Latin *obtrūdere* : *ob-,* against; see OB– + *trūdere,* to thrust; see **treud-** in Appendix.] **—ob·trud′er** *n.* **—ob·tru′sion** (-tro͞o′zhən) *n.*

ob·tru·sive (ŏb-tro͞o′sĭv, -zĭv, əb-) *adj.* **1.** Thrusting out; protruding: *an obtrusive rock formation.* **2.** Tending to push self-assertively forward; brash: *the obtrusive behavior of a spoiled child.* **3.** Undesirably noticeable: *an obtrusive scar.* [From Latin *obtrūsus,* past participle of *obtrūdere,* to obtrude. See OBTRUDE.] **—ob·tru′sive·ly** *adv.* **—ob·tru′sive·ness** *n.*

ob·tund (ŏb-tŭnd′) *tr.v.* **-tund·ed, -tund·ing, -tunds.** To make less intense; dull or deaden. [Middle English *obtunden,* from Latin *obtundere* : *ob-,* against; see OB– + *tundere,* to beat.] **—ob·tund′ent** *adj.* **—ob·tun′di·ty** *n.*

ob·tu·rate (ŏb′tə-rāt′, -tyə-) *tr.v.* **-rat·ed, -rat·ing, -rates.** To close or obstruct. [Latin *obtūrāre, obtūrāt-* : *ob-,* ob- + *-tūrāre,* to stop up; see **teue-** in Appendix.] **—ob′tu·ra′tion** *n.*

ob·tu·ra·tor (ŏb′tə-rā′tər, -tyə-) *n.* **1.** An organic structure, such as the soft palate, that closes an opening in the body. **2.** A prosthetic device serving to close an opening in the body.

ob·tuse (ŏb-to͞os′, -tyo͞os′, əb-) *adj.* **-tus·er, -tus·est. 1.** Lacking quickness of perception or intellect. See Synonyms at **stupid. 2.a.** Not sharp, pointed, or acute in form; blunt. **b.** *Botany.* Having a blunt or rounded tip: *an obtuse leaf.* [Middle English, from Old French, from Latin *obtūsus,* past participle of *obtundere,* to blunt. See OBTUND.] **—ob·tuse′ly** *adv.* **—ob·tuse′ness** *n.*

obtuse angle *n. Mathematics.* An angle greater than 90° and less than 180°.

ob·verse (ŏb-vûrs′, əb-, ŏb′vûrs′) *adj. Abbr.* **obv. 1.** Facing or turned toward the observer: *the obverse side of a statue.* **2.** Serving as a counterpart or complement. **—obverse** (ŏb′vûrs′, ŏb-vûrs′, əb-) *n.* **1.** The side of a coin, medal, or badge that bears the principal stamp or design. **2.** The more conspicuous of two possible alternatives, cases, or sides: *the obverse of this issue.* **3.** *Logic.* The counterpart of a proposition obtained by exchanging the affirmative for the negative quality of the whole proposition and then negating the predicate: *The obverse of "Every act is predictable" is "No act is unpredictable."* [Latin *obversus,* past participle of *obvertere,* to turn toward. See OBVERT.] **—ob·verse′ly** *adv.*

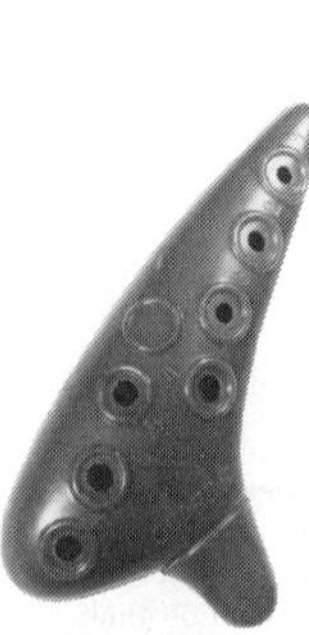

ocarina

ob·ver·sion (ŏb-vûr′zhən, -shən, əb-) *n.* **1.** The process of obverting or the condition so resulting. **2.** *Logic.* Inference of the obverse of a proposition.

ob·vert (ŏb-vûrt′, əb-) *tr.v.* **-vert·ed, -vert·ing, -verts. 1.** To turn (something) so as to present another side or aspect to view. **2.** To alter the appearance of. **3.** *Logic.* To subject (a proposition) to obversion. [Latin *obvertere,* to turn toward : *ob-,* toward; see OB– + *vertere,* to turn; see **wer-**[2] in Appendix.]

ob·vi·ate (ŏb′vē-āt′) *tr.v.* **-at·ed, -at·ing, -ates.** To anticipate and dispose of effectively; render unnecessary. See Synonyms at **prevent.** [Latin *obviāre, obviāt-,* to hinder, from *obvius,* in the way. See OBVIOUS.] **—ob′vi·a′tion** *n.* **—ob′vi·a′tor** *n.*

ob·vi·ous (ŏb′vē-əs) *adj.* **1.** Easily perceived or understood; quite apparent. See Synonyms at **apparent. 2.** Easily seen through because of a lack of subtlety; transparent: *an obvious political ploy.* **3.** *Archaic.* Standing in the way or in front. [From Latin *obvius,* from *obviam,* in the way, within reach : *ob-,* against; see OB– + *viam,* accusative sing. of *via,* way; see **wegh-** in Appendix.] **—ob′vi·ous·ly** *adv.* **—ob′vi·ous·ness** *n.*

oc. or **Oc.** *abbr.* Ocean.

o.c. *abbr. Latin.* Opere citato (in the work cited).

O.C. *abbr.* **1.** Officer Commanding. **2.** Old Catholic.

o/c *abbr.* Overcharge.

o·ca (ō′kə) *n.* **1.** A perennial plant *(Oxalis tuberosa)* of the high Andes, grown for its edible tubers. **2.** The tubers of this plant. [Spanish, possibly from Quechua *oqa.*]

O·cal·a (ō-kăl′ə). A city of north-central Florida south-southeast of Gainesville. Population, 37,170.

oc·a·ri·na (ŏk′ə-rē′nə) *n. Music.* A small terra-cotta or plastic wind instrument with finger holes, a mouthpiece, and an elongated ovoid shape. [Italian, from dialectal *ucarenna,* diminutive of Italian *oca,* goose (from the fact that its mouthpiece is shaped like a goose's beak), from Vulgar Latin **auca,* from **avica,* from Latin *avis,* bird. See **awi-** in Appendix.]

OCAS *abbr.* Organization of Central American States.

O'Ca·sey (ō-kā′sē), **Sean.** 1880–1964. Irish playwright. His dramas include *Juno and the Paycock* (1924) and *The Plough and the Stars* (1926).

occ. *abbr.* **1.** Occident; occidental. **2.** Occupation.

Oc·cam (ŏk′əm), **William of.** See William of **Ockham.**

Oc·cam's razor (ŏk′əmz) *n.* Variant of **Ockham's razor.**

occas. *abbr.* Occasional; occasionally.

oc·ca·sion (ə-kā′zhən) *n.* **1.a.** An event or a happening; an incident. **b.** The time at which an event occurs. **2.** A significant event. **3.** A favorable or appropriate time or juncture; an opportunity. See Synonyms at **opportunity. 4.** Something that brings on or precipitates an action, a condition, or an event, especially the immediate cause. See Synonyms at **cause. 5.** Something that provides a reason or justification; a ground. **6.** A need created by a particular circumstance: *"He must buy what he has little occasion for"* (Laurence Sterne). **7.** A large or important social gathering. **8. occasions.** *Archaic.* Personal requirements or necessities. **—occasion** *tr.v.* **-sioned, -sion·ing, -sions.** To provide occasion for; cause: *"The year's annual reports occasion an especially revealing glimpse of how corporations lend . . . embellishment to the stark numbers of the comptroller's office"* (Mark Muro). **—*idiom.* on occasion.** From time to time; now and then. [Middle English, from Old French, from Latin *occāsiō, occāsiōn-,* from *occāsus,* past participle of *occidere,* to fall : *ob-,* down; see OB– + *cadere,* to fall; see **kad-** in Appendix.]

oc·ca·sion·al (ə-kā′zhə-nəl) *adj. Abbr.* **occas. 1.a.** Occurring from time to time. See Synonyms at **periodic. b.** Not habitual; infrequent: *took an occasional glass of wine.* **2.** Created for a special occasion: *occasional verse.* **3.** Intended for use as the occasion requires: *an occasional chair.* **4.** Acting as a cause. **5.** Acting in a specified capacity from time to time: *an occasional hunter.*

oc·ca·sion·al·ly (ə-kā′zhə-nə-lē) *adv. Abbr.* **occas.** Now and then; from time to time.

oc·ci·dent (ŏk′sĭ-dənt, -dĕnt′) *n. Abbr.* **occ. 1.** Western lands or regions; the west. **2. Occident.** The countries of Europe and the Western Hemisphere. [Middle English, from Old French, from Latin *occidēns, occident-,* from present participle of *occidere,* to set (used of the sun). See OCCASION.]

oc·ci·den·tal or **Oc·ci·den·tal** (ŏk′sĭ-dĕn′tl) *—adj. Abbr.* **occ.** Of or relating to the countries of the Occident or their peoples or cultures; western. *—n.* A native or inhabitant of an Occidental country; a westerner.

Oc·ci·den·tal·ism (ŏk′sĭ-dĕn′tl-ĭz′əm) *n.* The characteristic traits or customs of Occidental peoples.

oc·ci·den·tal·ize or **Oc·ci·den·tal·ize** (ŏk′sĭ-dĕn′tl-īz′) *tr.v.* **-ized, -iz·ing, -iz·es.** To make Occidental in character or way of life. **—oc′ci·den′tal·i·za′tion** (-ĭ-zā′shən) *n.*

oc·cip·i·ta (ŏk-sĭp′ĭ-tə) *n.* A plural of **occiput.**

oc·cip·i·tal (ŏk-sĭp′ĭ-tl) *adj.* Of or relating to the occiput or to the occipital bone: *an occipital fracture.* **—occipital** *n.* The occipital bone. **—oc·cip′i·tal·ly** *adv.*

occipital bone *n.* A curved, trapezoid compound bone that forms the lower posterior part of the skull; the occipital.

occipital lobe *n.* The posterior lobe of each cerebral hemisphere, having the shape of a three-sided pyramid and containing the visual center of the brain.

oc·ci·put (ŏk′sə-pŭt′, -pət) *n., pl.* **oc·cip·i·ta** (ŏk-sĭp′ĭ-tə) or **oc·ci·puts.** The back part of the head or skull. [Middle English, from Latin *occiput, occipit-* : *ob-,* against; see OB– + *caput,* head; see **kaput-** in Appendix.]

Oc·cleve (ŏk′lēv′), **Thomas.** See Thomas **Hoccleve.**

oc·clude (ə-klo͞od′) *v.* **-clud·ed, -clud·ing, -cludes.** *—tr.* **1.** To cause to become closed; obstruct: *occlude an artery.* **2.** To prevent the passage of: *occlude light; occlude the flow of blood.* **3.** *Chemistry.* To absorb or adsorb and retain (a substance). **4.** *Meteorology.* To force (air) upward from Earth's surface, as when a cold front overtakes and undercuts a warm front. **5.** *Dentistry.* To bring together (the upper and lower teeth) in proper alignment for chewing. —*intr. Dentistry.* To close so that the cusps fit together. Used of the teeth of the upper and lower jaws. [Latin *occlūdere* : *ob-*, intensive pref.; see OB– + *claudere,* to close.] **—oc·clud′ent** *adj.*

oc·clud·ed front (ə-klo͞o′dĭd) *n. Meteorology.* The front formed when a cold front occludes a warm front.

oc·clu·sal (ə-klo͞o′zəl, -səl) *adj.* Of or relating to occlusions of the teeth, especially the chewing or biting surfaces: *occlusal wear.*

oc·clu·sion (ə-klo͞o′zhən) *n.* **1.a.** The process of occluding. **b.** Something that occludes. **2.** *Medicine.* An obstruction or a closure of a passageway or vessel. **3.** *Dentistry.* The alignment of the teeth of the upper and lower jaws when brought together. **4.** *Meteorology.* **a.** The process of occluding air masses. **b.** An occluded front. **5.** *Linguistics.* Closure at some point in the vocal tract that blocks the flow of air in the production of an oral or a nasal stop. [From Latin *occlūsus,* past participle of *occlūdere,* to occlude. See OCCLUDE.]

oc·clu·sive (ə-klo͞o′sĭv, -zĭv) *adj.* Occluding or tending to occlude. **—occlusive** *n. Linguistics.* An oral or a nasal stop.

oc·cult (ə-kŭlt′, ŏk′ŭlt′) *adj.* **1.** Of, relating to, or dealing with supernatural influences, agencies, or phenomena. **2.** Beyond the realm of human comprehension; inscrutable. **3.** Available only to the initiate; secret: *occult lore.* See Synonyms at **mysterious. 4.** Hidden from view; concealed. **5.a.** *Medicine.* Detectable only by microscopic examination or chemical analysis, as a minute blood sample. **b.** Not accompanied by readily detectable signs or symptoms: *occult carcinoma.* **—occult** *n.* Occult practices or techniques: *a student of the occult.* **—occult** (ə-kŭlt′) *v.* **-cult·ed, -cult·ing, -cults.** —*tr.* **1.** To conceal or cause to disappear from view. **2.** *Astronomy.* To conceal by occultation: *The moon occulted Mars.* —*intr.* To become concealed or extinguished at regular intervals: *a lighthouse beacon that occults every 45 seconds.* [Latin *occultus,* secret, past participle of *occulere,* to cover over. See **kel-**[1] in Appendix.] **—oc·cult′ly** *adv.* **—oc·cult′ness** *n.*

oc·cul·ta·tion (ŏk′ŭl-tā′shən) *n.* **1.** The act of occulting or the state of being occulted. **2.** *Astronomy.* **a.** The passage of a celestial body across a line between an observer and another celestial object, as when the moon moves between the earth and the sun in a solar eclipse. **b.** The progressive blocking of light, radio waves, or other radiation from a celestial source during such a passage. **c.** An observational technique for determining the position or radiant structure of a celestial source so occulted: *a lunar occultation of a quasar.* [Middle English *occultacion,* from Latin *occultātiō, occultātiōn-,* from *occultātus,* past participle of *occultāre,* frequentative of *occulere,* to conceal. See OCCULT.]

oc·cult·ism (ə-kŭl′tĭz′əm, ŏk′ŭl-) *n.* **1.** The study of the supernatural. **2.** A belief in occult powers and the possibility of bringing them under human control. **—oc·cult′ist** *n.*

oc·cu·pan·cy (ŏk′yə-pən-sē) *n., pl.* **-cies. 1.a.** The act of occupying or the condition of being occupied. **b.** The state of being an occupant or a tenant. **2.a.** The period during which one owns, rents, or uses certain premises or land. **b.** The use to which something occupied is put: *a building for commercial occupancy.* **3.** *Law.* The act of taking possession of previously unowned property with the intent of obtaining the right to own it.

oc·cu·pant (ŏk′yə-pənt) *n.* **1.** One that occupies a position or place: *the occupant of the honorary professorial chair; the occupants of a beehive.* **2.** One who has certain legal rights to or control over the premises occupied; a tenant or an owner. **3.** *Law.* One that is the first to take possession of something previously unowned.

oc·cu·pa·tion (ŏk′yə-pā′shən) *n. Abbr.* **occ. 1.a.** An activity that serves as one's regular source of livelihood; a vocation. **b.** An activity engaged in especially as a means of passing time; an avocation. **2.a.** The act or process of holding or possessing a place. **b.** The state of being held or possessed. **3.a.** Invasion, conquest, and control of a nation or territory by foreign armed forces. **b.** The military government exercising control over an occupied nation or territory. [Middle English *occupacioun,* from Old French *occupacion,* from Latin *occupātiō, occupātiōn-,* from *occupātus,* past participle of *occupāre,* to occupy. See OCCUPY.]

oc·cu·pa·tion·al (ŏk′yə-pā′shə-nəl) *adj.* Of, relating to, or caused by engagement in a particular occupation: *occupational hazards.* **—oc′cu·pa′tion·al·ly** *adv.*

occupational disease *n.* A disease, such as byssinosis or black lung, resulting from the conditions of a person's work, trade, or occupation.

occupational medicine *n.* The branch of medicine that deals with the prevention and treatment of diseases and injuries occurring at work or in specific occupations.

occupational therapy *n. Abbr.* **OT** The use of productive or creative activity in the treatment or rehabilitation of physically or emotionally disabled people. **—occupational therapist** *n.*

oc·cu·py (ŏk′yə-pī′) *tr.v.* **-pied, -py·ing, -pies. 1.** To fill up (time or space): *a lecture that occupied three hours.* **2.** To dwell or reside in. **3.** To hold or fill (an office or a position). **4.** To seize possession of and maintain control over by or as if by conquest. **5.** To engage, employ, or busy (oneself). [Middle English *occupien,* alteration of Old French *occuper,* from Latin *occupāre,* to seize : *ob-,* intensive pref.; see OB– + *capere,* to take; see **kap-** in Appendix.] **—oc′cu·pi′er** *n.*

oc·cur (ə-kûr′) *intr.v.* **-curred, -cur·ring, -curs. 1.** To take place; come about. See Synonyms at **happen. 2.** To be found to exist or appear: *Heavy rains occur during a summer monsoon.* **3.** To come to mind: *The idea never occurred to me.* [Latin *occurrere* : *ob-,* toward; see OB– + *currere,* to run; see **kers-** in Appendix.]

oc·cur·rence (ə-kûr′əns) *n.* **1.** The act or an instance of occurring. **2.** Something that takes place. **—oc·cur′rent** *adj.*

SYNONYMS: *occurrence, happening, event, incident, episode, circumstance.* These nouns all refer to something that takes place or comes to pass. *Occurrence* and *happening* are the most general: *an everyday occurrence; a happening of no great importance. Event* usually signifies a notable occurrence: *The events of the day are reported on the evening news. "Great events make me quiet and calm; it is only trifles that irritate my nerves"* (Victoria). *Incident* may apply to a minor occurrence: *Errors are inescapable incidents in the course of scientific research.* The term may also refer to a distinct event of sharp identity and significance: *His debut at Carnegie Hall was the first of a succession of exciting incidents in his life.* An *episode* is an incident in the course of a progression or within a larger sequence: *"Happiness was but the occasional episode in a general drama of pain"* (Thomas Hardy). *Circumstance* in this comparison denotes a particular incident or occurrence: *"What schoolboy of fourteen is ignorant of this remarkable circumstance?"* (Macaulay).

o·cean (ō′shən) *n.* **1.** *Abbr.* **oc.** The entire body of salt water that covers more than 70 percent of the earth's surface. **2.** Often **Ocean.** *Abbr.* **O, O., Oc.** Any of the principal divisions of the ocean, including the Atlantic, Pacific, and Indian oceans, their southern extensions in Antarctica, and the Arctic Ocean. **3.** A great expanse or amount: *"that ocean of land which is Russia"* (Henry A. Kissinger). [Middle English *occean,* from Old French, from Latin *ōceanus,* from Greek *Ōkeanos,* the god Oceanus, a great river encircling the earth.]

o·cean·ar·i·um (ō′shə-nâr′ē-əm) *n., pl.* **-i·ums** or **-i·a** (-ē-ə). A large aquarium for the study or display of marine life.

o·cea·naut (ō′shə-nôt′, -nŏt′) *n.* See **aquanaut.**

o·cean·front (ō′shən-frŭnt′) *n.* Land bordering an ocean: *Condominiums crowd the oceanfront.* —*attributive.* Often used to modify another noun: *oceanfront cottages; oceanfront promenades.*

o·cean·go·ing (ō′shən-gō′ĭng) *adj.* Made or used for ocean voyages.

O·ce·an·i·a (ō′shē-ăn′ē-ə, -ā′nē-ə, -ä′nē-ə). The islands of the southern, western, and central Pacific Ocean, including Melanesia, Micronesia, and Polynesia. The term is sometimes extended to encompass Australia, New Zealand, and the Malay Archipelago. **—O′ce·an′i·an** *adj. & n.*

o·ce·an·ic (ō′shē-ăn′ĭk) *adj.* **1.** Of or relating to the ocean: *"Like many oceanic islands, Bermuda was originally free of all mammals except the bat"* (Dwight Holing). **2.** Produced by or living in an ocean, especially in the open sea rather than in shallow coastal waters. **3.** Resembling an ocean in expanse; vast: *oceanic steppes.*

O·ce·a·nid (ō-sē′ə-nĭd) *n., pl.* **O·ce·an·i·des** (ō′sē-ăn′ĭ-dēz′). *Greek Mythology.* Any of the ocean nymphs believed to be the daughters of Oceanus and Tethys. [Greek *ōkeanis, ōkeanid-,* from *Ōkeanos,* Oceanus.]

o·cean·og·ra·phy (ō′shə-nŏg′rə-fē) *n. Abbr.* **oceanog.** The exploration and scientific study of the ocean and its phenomena. Also called *oceanology.* **—o′cean·og′ra·pher** *n.* **—o′cean·o·graph′ic** (ō′shə-nə-grăf′ĭk), **o′cean·o·graph′i·cal** *adj.* **—o′cean·o·graph′i·cal·ly** *adv.*

o·cean·ol·o·gy (ō′shə-nŏl′ə-jē) *n.* See **oceanography. —o′cean·o·log′ic** (ō′shə-nə-lŏj′ĭk), **o′cean·o·log′i·cal** (-ĭ-kəl) *adj.* **—o′cean·o·log′i·cal·ly** *adv.* **—o′cean·ol′o·gist** *n.*

ocean perch *n.* See **rosefish.**

O·cean·side (ō′shən-sīd′). A city of southern California north-northwest of San Diego. It is a seaside resort and trade center.

ocean sunfish *n.* A marine fish *(Mola mola)* with a large globular body, found in warm and temperate seas. Also called *mola.*

O·ce·a·nus (ō-sē′ə-nəs) *n. Greek Mythology.* A Titan god of the outer sea encircling the earth and the father of the Oceanides and the river gods.

oc·el·lat·ed (ŏs′ə-lā′tĭd, ō′sə-, ō-sĕl′ā′-) also **oc·el·late** (-lāt′) *adj.* **1.** Having an ocellus or ocelli. **2.** Resembling an ocellus. **3.** Having spots. [Latin *ocellātus,* having little eyes, from *ocellus,* diminutive of *oculus,* eye. See OCELLUS.] **—oc′el·la′tion** *n.*

o·cel·lus (ō-sĕl′əs) *n., pl.* **o·cel·li** (ō-sĕl′ī′). **1.** A small simple eye, found in many invertebrates, usually consisting of a few sensory cells and a single lens. **2.** A marking that resembles an eye, as on the tail feathers of a male peacock; an eyespot. [Latin, diminutive of *oculus,* eye. See **okʷ-** in Appendix.] **—o·cel′lar** (ō-sĕl′ər) *adj.*

oc·e·lot (ŏs′ə-lŏt′, ō′sə-) *n.* A nocturnal wildcat *(Felis pardalis* or *Leopardus pardalis)* of the brush and forests of the southwest United States and Central and South America, having a grayish or yellow coat with black spots. [French, from Nahuatl *ocelotl.*]

o·cher or **o·chre** (ō′kər) *n.* **1.** Any of several earthy mineral oxides of iron occurring in yellow, brown, or red and used as pigments. **2.** *Color.* A moderate orange yellow, from moderate or deep orange to moderate or strong yellow. [Middle English *oker,*

ocelot
Felis pardalis

ă pat	oi boy
ā pay	ou out
âr care	o͝o took
ä father	o͞o boot
ĕ pet	ŭ cut
ē be	ûr urge
ĭ pit	th thin
ī pie	*th* this
îr pier	hw which
ŏ pot	zh vision
ō toe	ə about, item
ô paw	♦ regionalism

Stress marks: ′ (primary); ′ (secondary), as in **dictionary** (dĭk′shə-nĕr′ē)

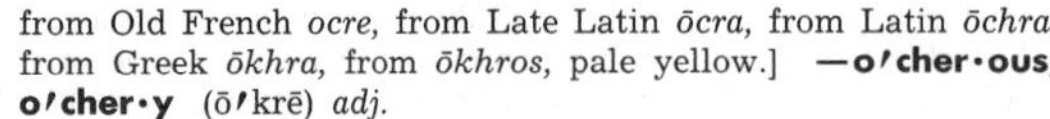
from Old French *ocre,* from Late Latin *ōcra,* from Latin *ōchra,* from Greek *ōkhra,* from *ōkhros,* pale yellow.] **—o′cher·ous, o′cher·y** (ō′krē) *adj.*

och·loc·ra·cy (ŏk-lŏk′rə-sē) *n., pl.* **-cies.** Government by the masses; mob rule. [French *ochlocratie,* from Greek *okhlokratia* : *okhlos,* mob; see **wegh-** in Appendix + *-kratia,* -cracy.] **—och′lo·crat′** (ŏk′lə-krăt′) *n.* **—och′lo·crat′ic, och′lo·crat′i·cal** *adj.* **—och′lo·crat′i·cal·ly** *adv.*

och·lo·pho·bi·a (ŏk′lə-fō′bē-ə) *n.* An abnormal fear of crowds. [Greek *okhlos,* crowd; see **wegh-** in Appendix + -PHOBIA.] **—och′lo·pho′bic** *adj. & n.*

O·cho·a (ō-chō′ə), **Severo.** Born 1905. Spanish-born American biochemist. He shared a 1959 Nobel Prize for work on the biological synthesis of nucleic acids.

o·chre (ō′kər) *n.* Variant of **ocher.**

Ochs (ŏks), **Adolph Simon.** 1858–1935. American newspaper publisher who published the *New York Times* (1896–1935) and directed the Associated Press (1900–1935).

Ock·ham also **Oc·cam** (ŏk′əm), **William of.** 1285?–1349? English scholastic philosopher who rejected the reality of universal concepts.

Ock·ham's razor also **Oc·cam's razor** (ŏk′əmz) *n.* A rule in science and philosophy stating that entities should not be multiplied needlessly. This rule is interpreted to mean that the simplest of two or more competing theories is preferable and that an explanation for unknown phenomena should first be attempted in terms of what is already known. Also called *law of parsimony.* [After William of OCKHAM.]

o'clock (ə-klŏk′) *adv.* **1.** Of or according to the clock: *three o'clock.* **2.** According to an imaginary clock dial with the observer at the center and 12 o'clock considered as straight ahead in horizontal position or straight up in vertical position. Used to indicate relative position: *enemy planes at 10 o'clock.* [Short for *of the clock.*]

Oc·mul·gee (ōk-mŭl′gē). A river, about 410 km (255 mi) long, of Georgia rising near Atlanta and flowing southeast to join the Oconee River and form the Altahama River.

O·co·nee (ə-kō′nē). A river rising in the Blue Ridge of northern Georgia and flowing about 454 km (282 mi) generally south to join the Ocmulgee River and form the Altahama River.

O'Con·nor (ō-kŏn′ər), **Flannery.** 1925–1964. American writer whose novels include *Wise Blood* (1952) and *The Violent Bear It Away* (1960).

Sandra Day O'Connor
Photographed in 1990

O'Connor, Sandra Day. Born 1930. American jurist. In 1981 she was appointed the first woman associate justice of the U.S. Supreme Court.

O'Connor, Thomas Power. Known as "Tay Pay." 1848–1929. Irish journalist and politician who entered Parliament in 1880 and served for 49 years, leading to his nickname "the Father of the House of Commons."

ocotillo
Fouquieria splendens in bloom

o·co·til·lo (ō′kə-tē′yō) *n., pl.* **-los.** A cactuslike tree *(Fouquieria splendens)* of Mexico and the southwest United States, having clusters of scarlet tubular flowers. [American Spanish, diminutive of *ocote,* a Mexican pine, from Nahuatl *ocotl,* pitch pine.]

OCR *abbr. Computer Science.* **1.** Optical character reader. **2.** Optical character recognition.

oc·re·a (ŏk′rē-ə) *n., pl.* **-re·ae** (-rē-ē′). *Botany.* A sheath formed at the node of a stem by the fusion of two stipules, as in the rhubarb plant. [Latin, greave.]

OCS *abbr.* Officer Candidate School.

oct. *abbr. Printing.* Octavo.

Oct. or **Oct** *abbr.* October.

oct– or **octa–** *pref.* Variants of **octo–.**

oc·tad (ŏk′tăd′) *n.* A group or sequence of eight. [Greek *oktas, oktad-,* from *oktō,* eight. See **oktō(u)** in Appendix.] **—oc·tad′ic** *adj.*

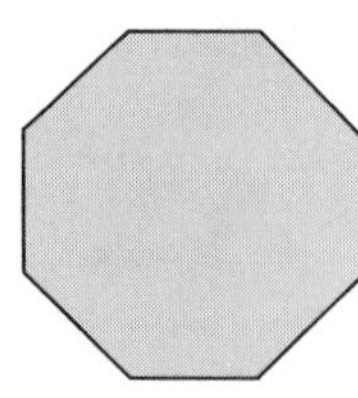
octagon

oc·ta·gon (ŏk′tə-gŏn′) *n.* A polygon with eight sides and eight angles.

oc·tag·o·nal (ŏk-tăg′ə-nəl) *adj.* Having eight sides and eight angles. **—oc·tag′o·nal·ly** *adv.*

oc·ta·he·dra (ŏk′tə-hē′drə) *n.* A plural of **octahedron.**

oc·ta·he·dral (ŏk′tə-hē′drəl) *adj.* Having eight plane surfaces. **—oc′ta·he′dral·ly** *adv.*

oc·ta·he·dron (ŏk′tə-hē′drən) *n., pl.* **-drons** or **-dra** (-drə). A polyhedron with eight plane surfaces.

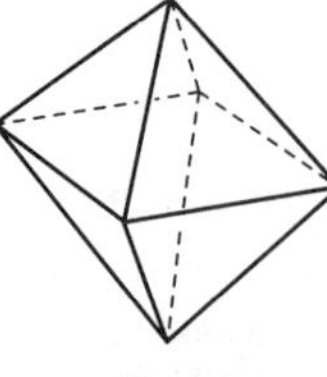
octahedron

oc·tal (ŏk′təl) *adj.* Of, relating to, or based on the number eight: *an octal number system.*

oc·tam·e·ter (ŏk-tăm′ĭ-tər) also **oc·tom·e·ter** (-tŏm′-) *n.* A line of verse consisting of eight metrical feet.

oc·tan·dri·ous (ŏk-tăn′drē-əs) *adj. Botany.* Having eight stamens.

oc·tane (ŏk′tān′) *n.* **1.** Any of various isomeric paraffin hydrocarbons with the formula C_8H_{18}, found in petroleum and used as a fuel and solvent. **2.** An octane number.

octane number *n.* A numerical representation of the antiknock properties of motor fuel, compared with a standard reference fuel, such as isooctane, which has an octane number of 100. Also called *octane rating.*

Oc·tans (ŏk′tănz′) *n.* The constellation that includes the southern celestial pole. [Latin, half quadrant, from *octō,* eight. See **oktō(u)** in Appendix.]

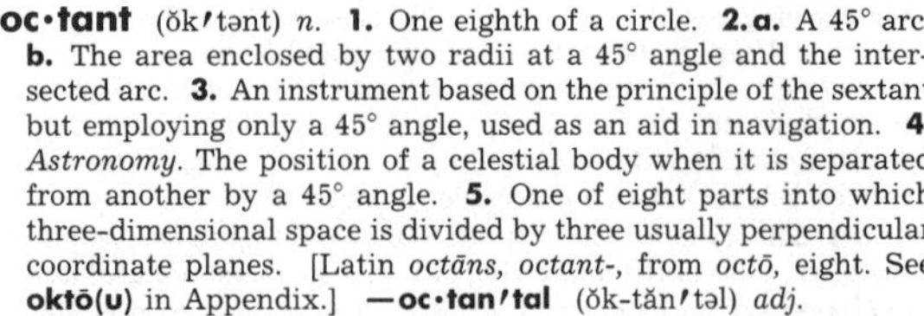
oc·tant (ŏk′tənt) *n.* **1.** One eighth of a circle. **2.a.** A 45° arc. **b.** The area enclosed by two radii at a 45° angle and the intersected arc. **3.** An instrument based on the principle of the sextant but employing only a 45° angle, used as an aid in navigation. **4.** *Astronomy.* The position of a celestial body when it is separated from another by a 45° angle. **5.** One of eight parts into which three-dimensional space is divided by three usually perpendicular coordinate planes. [Latin *octāns, octant-,* from *octō,* eight. See **oktō(u)** in Appendix.] **—oc·tan′tal** (ŏk-tăn′təl) *adj.*

oc·ta·pep·tide (ŏk′tə-pĕp′tīd) *n.* A polypeptide, such as angiotensin, that is composed of eight amino acids.

oc·tave (ŏk′tĭv, -tāv′) *n.* **1.** *Music.* **a.** The interval of eight diatonic degrees between two tones, one of which has twice as many vibrations per second as the other. **b.** A tone that is eight full tones above or below another given tone. **c.** Two tones eight diatonic degrees apart that are sounded together. **d.** The consonance that results when two tones eight diatonic degrees apart are sounded. **e.** A series of tones included within this interval or the keys of an instrument that produce such a series. **f.** An organ stop that produces tones an octave above those usually produced by the keys played. **g.** The interval between any two frequencies having a ratio of 2 to 1. **2.** *Ecclesiastical.* **a.** The eighth day after a feast day, counting the feast day as one. **b.** The entire period between a feast day and the eighth day following it. **3.** A group or series of eight. **4.a.** A group of eight lines of poetry, especially the first eight lines of a Petrarchan sonnet. Also called *octet.* **b.** A poem or stanza containing eight lines. **5.** *Sports.* A rotating parry in fencing. [Middle English, eighth day after a feast day, from Old French, from Medieval Latin *octāva (diēs),* from Latin, feminine of *octāvus,* eighth, from *octō,* eight. See **oktō(u)** in Appendix.] **—oc·ta′val** (ŏk-tā′vəl, ŏk′tə-vəl) *adj.*

Oc·ta·vi·an (ŏk-tā′vē-ən). See **Augustus.**

oc·ta·vo (ŏk-tā′vō, -tä′-) *n., pl.* **-vos.** *Abbr.* **o, O, O., oct.** *Printing.* **1.** The page size, from 5 by 8 inches to 6 by 9½ inches, of a book composed of printer's sheets folded into eight leaves. **2.** A book composed of octavo pages. Also called *eightvo.* [Medieval Latin *(in) octāvō,* (in) an eighth, from Latin, ablative sing. of *octāvus,* eighth, from *octō,* eight. See **oktō(u)** in Appendix.]

oc·tet (ŏk-tĕt′) *n.* **1.** *Music.* **a.** A composition written for eight voices or eight instruments. **b.** A group of eight singers or eight instrumentalists. **2.** A group of eight: *"A train of heavy wagons rumbled north on the Winnipeg Trail, drawn by octets of oxen, the drovers walking alongside"* (Garrison Keillor). **3.** See **octave** (sense 4a). **4.** A set of eight valence electrons in an atom or ion, forming a stable configuration. [Alteration (influenced by OCTO–, and DUET) of Italian *ottetto,* from *otto,* eight, from Latin *octō.* See **oktō(u)** in Appendix.]

oc·til·lion (ŏk-tĭl′yən) *n.* **1.** The cardinal number equal to 10^{27}. **2.** *Chiefly British.* The cardinal number equal to 10^{48} [OCT(O)– + (M)ILLION.] **—oc·til′lion** *adj.*

oc·til·lionth (ŏk-tĭl′yənth) *n.* **1.** The ordinal number that matches the number octillion in a series. **2.** One of octillion equal parts. **—oc·til′lionth** *adv. & adj.*

octo– or **octa–** or **oct–** *pref.* Eight: *octane.* [Greek *okta-, oktō-* (from *oktō*) and Latin *octō-* (from *octō*); see **oktō(u)** in Appendix.]

Oc·to·ber (ŏk-tō′bər) *n.* **1.** *Abbr.* **Oct., Oct** The tenth month of the year in the Gregorian calendar. See table at **calendar. 2.** *Chiefly British.* Ale brewed in October. [Middle English *Octobre,* from Old French and from Old English *October,* both from Latin *Octōber,* eighth month, from *octō,* eight. See **oktō(u)** in Appendix.]

oc·to·dec·i·mo (ŏk′tə-dĕs′ə-mō′) *n., pl.* **-mos.** *Printing.* **1.** The page size, 4 by 6½ inches, of a book composed of printer's sheets folded into 18 leaves or 36 pages. **2.** A book composed of octodecimo pages. Also called *eighteenmo.* [Late Latin *(in) octōdecimō,* (in) an eighteenth, ablative sing. of *octōdecimus,* eighteenth, from Latin *octōdecim,* eighteen : *octō,* eight; see **oktō(u)** in Appendix + *decem,* ten; see **dekm̥** in Appendix.]

oc·to·ge·nar·i·an (ŏk′tə-jə-nâr′ē-ən) *adj.* Being between 80 and 90 years of age. **—octogenarian** *n.* A person between 80 and 90 years of age. [From French *octogénaire,* from Latin *octōgēnārius,* containing eighty, from *octōgēnī,* eighty each, from *octōgintā,* eighty : *octō,* eight; see **oktō(u)** in Appendix + *-gintā,* ten times; see **dekm̥** in Appendix.]

oc·to·nar·y (ŏk′tə-nĕr′ē) *adj.* **1.** Of or relating to the number eight. **2.** Consisting of eight members or of groups containing eight. **—octonary** *n., pl.* **-ies.** A group or set of eight. [Latin *octōnārius,* containing eight, from *octōnī,* eight each, from *octō,* eight. See **oktō(u)** in Appendix.]

oc·to·pi (ŏk′tə-pī′) *n.* A plural of **octopus.**

oc·to·ploid (ŏk′tə-ploid′) *adj.* Having eight haploid sets of chromosomes in a body cell. **—octoploid** *n.* An octoploid organism.

oc·to·pod (ŏk′tə-pŏd′) *n.* Any of various cephalopod mollusks of the order Octopoda, such as an octopus, having eight tentacles. [From New Latin *Octōpoda,* order name, from Greek *oktōpoda,* neuter pl. of *oktōpous,* octopus. See OCTOPUS.] **—oc′to·pod′, oc′to·pod′ous** *adj.*

oc·to·pus (ŏk′tə-pəs) *n., pl.* **-pus·es** or **-pi** (-pī′). **1.** Any of numerous carnivorous marine mollusks of the genus *Octopus* or related genera, found worldwide. The octopus has a rounded soft body, eight tentacles with each bearing two rows of suckers, a large distinct head, and a strong beaklike mouth. Also called *dev-*

ilfish. **2.** Something, such as a multinational corporation, that has many powerful, centrally controlled branches. [New Latin *Octōpus,* genus name, from Greek *oktōpous,* eight-footed : *oktō,* eight; see **oktō(u)** in Appendix + *pous,* foot; see **ped-** in Appendix.]

oc·to·roon (ŏk′tə-ro͞on′) *n.* A person whose ancestry is one-eighth Black. [OCTO– + (QUAD)ROON.]

oc·to·syl·la·ble (ŏk′tə-sĭl′ə-bəl) *n.* **1.** Also **oc·to·syl·lab·ic** (ŏk′tō-sĭ-lăb′ĭk). **a.** A line of verse containing eight syllables. **b.** A poem having eight syllables in each line. **2.** A word of eight syllables. **—oc′to·syl·lab′ic** *adj.*

oc·tu·ple (ŏk′tə-pəl, -to͞o′pəl, -tyo͞o′-) *adj.* **1.** Having eight parts, members, or copies. **2.** Multiplied by eight; eightfold. **—octuple** *n.* A quantity eight times as great as another. **—octuple** *tr.v.* **-pled, -pling, -ples.** To multiply by eight. [Latin *octuplus* : *octō-,* octo- + *-plus,* fold; see **pel-**[2] in Appendix.]

oc·u·lar (ŏk′yə-lər) *adj.* **1.a.** Of or relating to the eye: *ocular exercises; ocular muscles.* **b.** Resembling the eye in form or function: *ocular spots; an ocular organ.* **2.** Of or relating to the sense of sight: *an ocular aberration.* **3.** Seen by the eye; visual: *ocular proof.* **—ocular** *n.* The eyepiece of an optical instrument. [Late Latin *oculāris,* from Latin *oculus,* eye. See **ok^w-** in Appendix.]

oc·u·list (ŏk′yə-lĭst) *n.* **1.** A physician who treats diseases of the eyes; an ophthalmologist. **2.** An optometrist. [From Latin *oculus,* eye. See **ok^w-** in Appendix.]

oc·u·lo·gy·ric (ŏk′yə-lō-jī′rĭk) *adj.* Of or relating to the turning of the eyeballs in the sockets. [Latin *oculus,* eye; see OCULIST + GYR(O)– + –IC.]

oculogyric crisis *n.* A spasmodic movement of the eyeballs into a fixed position, usually upward, that persists for several minutes or hours.

oc·u·lo·mo·tor (ŏk′yə-lō-mō′tər) *adj.* **1.** Of or relating to movements of the eyeball: *an oculomotor muscle.* **2.** Of or relating to the oculomotor nerve. [Latin *oculus,* eye; see **ok^w-** in Appendix + MOTOR.]

oculomotor nerve *n.* Either of the third pair of cranial nerves, which originate in the mesencephalon and control most of the muscles that move the eyeballs.

Od or **Odd** (ŏd) *interj. Archaic.* Used as a mild oath. [Alteration of GOD.]

OD (ō′dē′) *Slang. n.* **1.a.** An overdose of a drug. **b.** An overdose of a substance or thing. **2.** One who has taken an overdose. **—OD** *intr.v.* **OD′d, OD′ing, OD′s.** To overdose: *OD'd on chocolate cake.* [O(VER)D(OSE).]

o.d. *abbr.* **1.** *Latin.* Oculus dexter (right eye). **2.** Olive drab. **3.** On demand. **4.** Outside diameter.

O.D. *abbr.* **1.** Doctor of Optometry. **2.** Officer of the day. **3.** Also **o/d.** Overdraft. **4.** Overdrawn.

o·da·lisque also **o·da·lisk** (ō′də-lĭsk′) *n.* A concubine or woman slave in a harem. [French, from Turkish *ōdalik,* chambermaid : *ōdah,* room + *-lik,* suff. expressing function.]

odd (ŏd) *adj.* **odd·er, odd·est.** **1.** Deviating from what is ordinary, usual, or expected; strange or peculiar: *an odd name; odd behavior.* See Synonyms at **strange.** **2.** Being in excess of the indicated or approximate number, extent, or degree. Often used in combination: *invited 30-odd guests.* **3.a.** Constituting a remainder: *had some odd dollars left over.* **b.** Small in amount: *jingled the odd change in his pockets.* **4.a.** Being one of an incomplete pair or set: *an odd shoe.* **b.** Remaining after others have been paired or grouped. **5.** *Mathematics.* Designating an integer not divisible by two, such as 1, 3, and 5. **6.** Not expected, regular, or planned: *called at odd intervals.* **7.** Remote; out-of-the-way: *found the antique shop in an odd corner of town.* **—odd** *n.* **1.** Something odd. **2.** *Sports.* **a.** In the United States, a golf score one stroke higher than the score of one's opponent. **b.** In Great Britain, a golfing handicap of one stroke given to a superior player or an advantage of one stroke taken away from an inferior player's score in order to equalize the chances of winning. [Middle English *odde,* from Old Norse *oddi,* point of land, triangle, odd number.] **—odd′ly** *adv.* **—odd′ness** *n.*

Odd (ŏd) *interj.* Variant of **Od.**

odd·ball (ŏd′bôl′) *n. Informal.* A person regarded as eccentric.

Odd Fellow *n.* A member of the Independent Order of Odd Fellows, a fraternal and benevolent secret society.

odd·ish (ŏd′ĭsh) *adj.* Somewhat odd.

odd·i·ty (ŏd′ĭ-tē) *n., pl.* **-ties.** **1.** One that is odd. **2.** The state or quality of being odd; strangeness.

odd job *n.* Any of various nonspecialized, unrelated jobs, usually domestic, unskilled, or menial.

odd·job·ber also **odd-job·ber** (ŏd′jŏb′ər) *n.* One who performs casual and occasional work, especially unskilled or domestic jobs, for a living.

odd lot *n.* A quantity that differs from a standard trading unit, especially an amount of stock of fewer than 100 shares. **—odd′-lot′** (ŏd′lŏt′) *adj.*

odd man out *n., pl.* **odd men out.** One who, because of strangeness of behavior or belief, stands alone in or out from a group.

odd·ment (ŏd′mənt) *n.* **1.a.** Something left over. **b. oddments.** Odds and ends. **2.** An oddity.

odd-pin·nate (ŏd′pĭn′āt′) *adj. Botany.* Pinnately compound with a single terminal leaflet, as in the leaves of the rose plant. **—odd′-pin′nate′ly** *adv.*

odds (ŏdz) *pl.n.* **1.** A certain number of points given beforehand to a weaker side in a contest to equalize the chances of all participants. See Synonyms at **advantage.** **2.a.** The ratio of the probability of an event's occurring to the probability of its not occurring. **b.** The likelihood of the occurrence of one thing rather than the occurrence of another thing, as in a contest: *The odds are that she will get the nomination on the first ballot.* **3.** *Games.* A ratio expressing the amount by which the stake of one bettor differs from that of an opposing bettor. **4.** An amount or a degree by which one thing exceeds or falls short of another: *won the contest by considerable odds.* **—*idioms.* at odds.** In disagreement; in conflict: *"The artist and the self-critic . . . are, with a few felicitous exceptions, forever at odds"* (Joyce Carol Oates). **by all odds.** In every possible way; unquestionably: *By all odds it is the best film of the year.* [Pl. of ODD.]

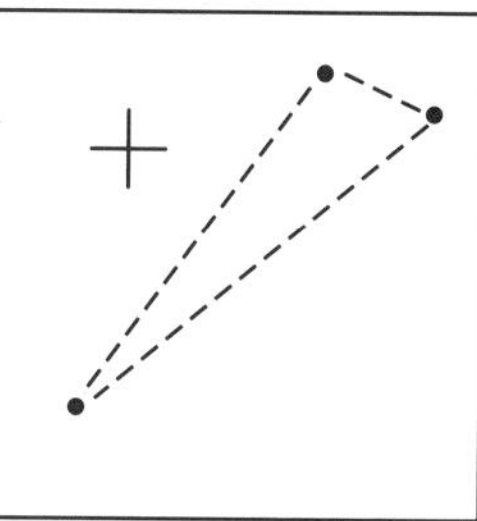

Octans

odds and ends *pl.n.* Miscellaneous items or remnants.

odds·mak·er (ŏdz′mā′kər) *n. Games.* One who calculates and sets betting odds based on the prediction of the result of a contest such as a horserace or an election.

odds-on (ŏdz′ŏn′, -ôn′) *adj. Informal.* More likely than others to win; having a good chance of success: *"I was the odds-on favorite to become the next president of the Ford Motor Company"* (Lee Iacocca).

ode (ōd) *n.* **1.** A lyric poem of some length, usually of a serious or meditative nature and having an elevated style and formal stanzaic structure. **2.a.** A choric song of classical Greece, often accompanied by a dance and performed at a public festival or as part of a drama. **b.** A classical Greek poem modeled on the choric ode and usually having a three-part structure consisting of a strophe, an antistrophe, and an epode. [French, choric song, from Old French, from Late Latin *ōdē, ōda,* from Greek *aoidē, ōidē,* song. See **wed-**[2] in Appendix.] **—od′ic** (ō′dĭk) *adj.*

octopus

–ode *suff.* **1.** Way; path: *electrode.* **2.** Electrode: *dynode.* [Greek *-odos,* from *hodos.*]

o·de·a (ō-dē′ə, ō′dē-ə) *n.* Plural of **odeum.**

O·den·se (ōd′n-sə, o͞od′-). A city of southern Denmark on Fyn Island near the **Odense Fjord,** an arm of the Kattegat. Founded in the tenth century, Odense is the birthplace of Hans Christian Andersen. Population, 170,961.

O·der (ō′dər). A river of central Europe flowing about 904 km (562 mi) from north-central Czechoslovakia through Poland and Germany to the Baltic Sea.

O·des·sa (ō-dĕs′ə). **1.** (*also* ə-dyĕ′sə). A city of south-central Ukraine on **Odessa Bay,** an arm of the Black Sea. Said to occupy the site of an ancient Greek colony that disappeared between the 3rd and 4th centuries A.D., Odessa was established as a Tartar fortress in the 14th century. Population, 1,126,000. **2.** A city of western Texas south-southwest of Lubbock. It was a small ranching town until the discovery of oil reserves in the area. Population, 90,027.

O·dets (ō-dĕts′), **Clifford.** 1906–1963. American playwright known for his powerful works of the Depression era, including *Waiting for Lefty* (1935) and *Golden Boy* (1937).

o·de·um (ō-dē′əm, ō′dē-) *n., pl.* **o·de·a** (ō-dē′ə, ō′dē-ə). **1.** A small building of ancient Greece and Rome used for public performances of music and poetry. **2.** A contemporary theater or concert hall. [Latin *ōdēum,* from Greek *ōideion,* from *aoidē, ōidē,* song. See ODE.]

O·din (ō′dĭn) *n. Mythology.* The Norse god of wisdom, war, art, culture, and the dead and the supreme deity and creator of the cosmos and human beings. [Old Norse *Ōdhinn.* See **wet-**[1] in Appendix.]

o·di·ous (ō′dē-əs) *adj.* Arousing or meriting strong dislike, aversion, or intense displeasure. See Synonyms at **hateful.** [Middle English, from Old French *odieus,* from Latin *odiōsus,* from *odium,* hatred. See ODIUM.] **—o′di·ous·ly** *adv.* **—o′di·ous·ness** *n.*

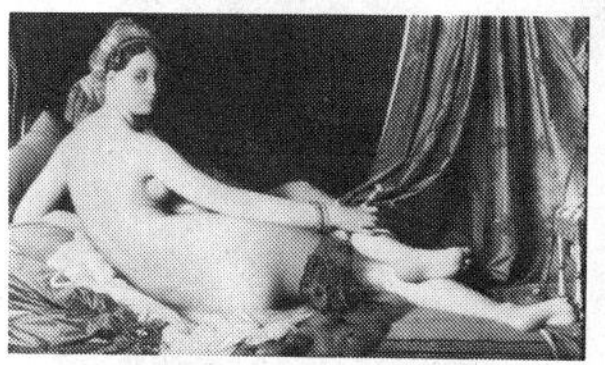

odalisque
La Grande Odalisque,
1814, by Jean Auguste
Dominique Ingres

o·di·um (ō′dē-əm) *n.* **1.** The state or quality of being odious. **2.** Strong dislike, contempt, or aversion. **3.** A state of disgrace resulting from hateful or detestable conduct. See Synonyms at **disgrace.** [Latin, hatred. See **od-** in Appendix.]

O·do·a·cer (ō′dō-ā′sər) also **O·do·va·car** or **O·do·va·kar** (-vā′kər). A.D. 434?–493. Germanic tribal leader who in 476 deposed Romulus Augustulus (reigned 475–476), bringing the Western Roman Empire to an end.

o·do·graph (ō′də-grăf′) *n.* An instrument for recording the distance and course traveled by a vehicle. [Greek *hodos,* journey + –GRAPH.]

o·dom·e·ter (ō-dŏm′ĭ-tər) *n.* An instrument that indicates distance traveled by a vehicle. [French *odomètre,* from Greek *hodometron* : Greek *hodos,* journey + Greek *metron,* measure; see –METER.] **—o·dom′e·try** *n.*

–odon *suff.* An animal having a specified kind of teeth: *sphenodon.* [New Latin, from Greek *odōn,* tooth. See **dent-** in Appendix.]

o·do·nate (ōd′n-āt′, ō-dŏn′-) *n.* Any of the large predacious winged insects of the order Odonata, which includes the dragonflies and damselflies, characterized by long brightly colored bodies, two pairs of membranous wings, and large compound eyes. **—odonate** *adj.* Of or belonging to the order Odonata. [From

ă **pat**	oi **boy**
ā **pay**	ou **out**
âr **care**	o͝o **took**
ä **father**	o͞o **boot**
ĕ **pet**	ŭ **cut**
ē **be**	ûr **urge**
ĭ **pit**	th **thin**
ī **pie**	*th* **this**
îr **pier**	hw **which**
ŏ **pot**	zh **vision**
ō **toe**	ə **a**bout, it**e**m
ô **paw**	♦ regionalism

Stress marks: **′** (primary); ′ (secondary), as in **dictionary** (dĭk′shə-nĕr′ē)

New Latin *Odōnata,* order name, from Greek *odōn,* tooth. See –ODON.]

odont– *pref.* Variant of **odonto–.**

–odont *suff.* Having teeth of a specified kind: *pleurodont.* [From Greek *odous, odont-,* tooth. See **dent-** in Appendix.]

o·don·tal·gia (ō′dŏn-tăl′jə, -jē-ə) *n.* A toothache. **—o′don·tal′gic** *adj.*

–odontia *suff.* The form of, condition of, or manner of treating the teeth: *orthodontia.*

odonto– or **odont–** *pref.* Tooth: *odontophore.* [Greek, from *odous, odont-,* tooth. See **dent-** in Appendix.]

o·don·to·blast (ō-dŏn′tə-blăst′) *n.* One of the cells forming the outer surface of dental pulp that produces the dentin of a tooth. **—o·don′to·blas′tic** *adj.*

o·don·toid (ō-dŏn′toid′) *adj.* **1.** Resembling a tooth. **2.** Of or relating to the odontoid process: *the odontoid ligaments.*

odontoid process *n.* A small, toothlike, upward projection from the second vertebra of the neck around which the first vertebra rotates.

o·don·tol·o·gy (ō′dŏn-tŏl′ə-jē) *n.* The study of the structure, development, and abnormalities of the teeth. **—o·don′to·log′i·cal** (-tə-lŏj′ĭ-kəl) *adj.* **—o·don′to·log′i·cal·ly** *adv.* **—o′don·tol′o·gist** *n.*

o·don·to·phore (ō-dŏn′tə-fôr′, -fōr′) *n.* A structure at the base of the mouth of most mollusks over which the radula is drawn back and forth in breaking up food. **—o′don·toph′o·ral** (ō′dŏn-tŏf′ər-əl), **o′don·toph′o·rine′** (-ə-rīn′, -rĭn), **o′don·toph′o·rous** (-ər-əs) *adj.*

o·dor (ō′dər) *n.* **1.** The property or quality of a thing that affects, stimulates, or is perceived by the sense of smell. See Synonyms at **smell. 2.** A sensation, stimulation, or perception of the sense of smell. **3.** A strong, pervasive quality: *An odor of sadness permeated the gathering.* **4.** Esteem; repute: *a doctrine that is not currently in good odor.* [Middle English *odour,* from Old French, from Latin *odor.*]

o·dor·if·er·ous (ō′də-rĭf′ər-əs) *adj.* Having or giving off an odor. **—o′dor·if′er·ous·ly** *adv.* **—o′dor·if′er·ous·ness** *n.*

o·dor·less (ō′dər-lĭs) *adj.* Having no odor. **—o′dor·less·ly** *adv.* **—o′dor·less·ness** *n.*

o·dor·ous (ō′dər-əs) *adj.* Having a distinctive odor: *odorous jasmine flowers; odorous garbage.* **—o′dor·ous·ly** *adv.* **—o′dor·ous·ness** *n.*

o·dour (ō′dər) *n. Chiefly British.* Variant of **odor.**

O·do·va·car or **O·do·va·kar** (ō′dō-vā′kər). See **Odoacer.**

O·dys·seus (ō-dĭs′yo͞os′, ō-dĭs′ē-əs) *n. Greek Mythology.* The king of Ithaca, a leader of the Greeks in the Trojan War, who reached home after ten years of wandering.

od·ys·sey (ŏd′ĭ-sē) *n., pl.* **-seys. 1.** An extended adventurous voyage or trip. **2.** An intellectual or spiritual quest: *an odyssey of discovery.* [After the *Odyssey,* a Homeric epic recounting the wanderings of Odysseus after the fall of Troy, from Greek *Odusseia,* from *Odusseus,* Odysseus.]

Oe *abbr.* Oersted.

OE also **O.E.** *abbr.* Old English.

OECD *abbr.* Organization for Economic Cooperation and Development.

oe·de·ma (ĭ-dē′mə) *n. Pathology & Botany.* Variant of **edema.**

oed·i·pal also **Oed·i·pal** (ĕd′ə-pəl, ē′də-) *adj.* Of, relating to, or characteristic of the Oedipus complex: *oedipal conflicts.* **—oed′i·pal·ly** *adv.*

Oedipus
With the sphinx

Oed·i·pus (ĕd′ə-pəs, ē′də-) *n. Greek Mythology.* A son of Laius and Jocasta, who was abandoned at birth and unwittingly killed his father and then married his mother. [Latin, from Greek *Oidipous* : *oidein,* to swell + *pous,* foot; see OCTOPUS.]

Oedipus complex *n.* In psychoanalysis, a subconscious sexual desire in a child, especially a male child, for the parent of the opposite sex, usually accompanied by hostility to the parent of the same sex. If unresolved naturally, this complex may result in neurosis and an inability to form normal sexual relationships in adulthood.

OEM *abbr.* Original equipment manufacturer.

oe·nol·o·gy (ē-nŏl′ə-jē) *n.* Variant of **enology.** [Greek *oinos,* wine + –LOGY.] **—oe′no·log′i·cal** (ē′nə-lŏj′ĭ-kəl) *adj.* **—oe·nol′o·gist** *n.*

oe·no·mel (ē′nə-mĕl′) *n.* An ancient Greek beverage consisting of wine and honey. [Late Latin *oenomeli,* from Greek *oinomeli* : *oinos,* wine + *meli,* honey; see **melit-** in Appendix.]

OEO *abbr.* Office of Economic Opportunity.

o'er (ôr, ōr) *prep. & adv.* Over.

oer·sted (ûr′stĕd′) *n. Abbr.* **Oe** The centimeter-gram-second electromagnetic unit of magnetic intensity, equal to the magnetic intensity one centimeter from a unit magnetic pole. [After Hans Christian *Oersted* (1777–1851), Danish physicist.]

oe·soph·a·gus (ĭ-sŏf′ə-gəs) *n.* Variant of **esophagus.**

oes·tro·gen (ĕs′trə-jən) *n.* Variant of **estrogen.**

oes·trus (ĕs′trəs) *n.* Variant of **estrus.**

oeu·vre (œ′vrə) *n., pl.* **oeu·vres** (œ′vrə). **1.** A work of art. **2.** The sum of the lifework of an artist, a writer, or a composer. [French, from Old French *uevre,* work, from Latin *opera,* from pl. of *opus,* work. See OPUS.]

of (ŭv, ŏv; əv *when unstressed*) *prep.* **1.** Derived or coming from; originating at or from: *men of the north.* **2.** Caused by; resulting from: *a death of tuberculosis.* **3.** Away from; at a distance from: *a mile east of here.* **4.** So as to be separated or relieved from: *robbed of one's dignity; cured of distemper.* **5.** From the total or group comprising: *give of one's time; two of her friends; most of the cases.* **6.** Composed or made from: *a dress of silk.* **7.** Associated with or adhering to: *a man of your religion.* **8.** Belonging or connected to: *the rungs of a ladder.* **9. a.** Possessing; having: *a person of honor.* **b.** On one's part: *very nice of you.* **10.** Containing or carrying: *a basket of groceries.* **11.** Specified as; named or called: *a depth of ten feet; the Garden of Eden.* **12.** Centering on; directed toward: *a love of horses.* **13.** Produced by; issuing from: *products of the vine.* **14.** Characterized or identified by: *a year of famine.* **15. a.** With reference to; about: *think highly of her proposals; will speak of it later.* **b.** In respect to: *slow of speech.* **16.** Set aside for; taken up by: *a day of rest.* **17.** Before; until: *five minutes of two.* **18.** During or on a specified time: *of recent years.* **19.** By: *beloved of the family.* **20.** Used to indicate an appositive: *that idiot of a driver.* **21.** *Archaic.* On: *"A plague of all cowards, I say"* (Shakespeare). [Middle English, from Old English. See **apo-** in Appendix.]

USAGE NOTE: Grammarians have sometimes condemned categorically the so-called double genitive construction, as in *a friend of my father's; a book of mine.* The construction is well supported by literary precedent, however, and serves a useful purpose. Thus there is no substitute for the double genitive in a sentence such as *That's the only friend of yours that I've ever met,* since sentences such as *That's your only friend that I've ever met* and *That's your only friend, whom I've ever met* are obviously impossible.

OF *abbr. Baseball.* Outfield; outfielder.

O'Fao·lain (ō-făl′ən, ō-fā′lən), **Sean.** 1900–1991. Irish writer. His short stories are contained in volumes such as *Midsummer Night Madness* (1932) and *The Heat of the Sun* (1966).

o·fay (ō′fā′) *n. Offensive Slang.* Used as a disparaging term for a white person. [Possibly of West African origin.]

WORD HISTORY: The commonly seen etymology of *ofay*—Pig Latin for *foe*—is perhaps of less interest than the more likely story of this word's origins. The word, which is first recorded in the first quarter of the 20th century, must have been in use much longer if it is, as some scholars think, borrowed from an African source. Although this source has not been pinned down, the suggested possibilities are in themselves interesting. One would trace it to the Ibibio word *afia,* "white or light-colored." Another would have it come from Yoruba *ofe,* a word that was said in order to protect oneself from danger. The term was then transferred to white people, regarded as a danger to Black people throughout the wretched days of slavery and beyond.

off (ôf, ŏf) *adv.* **1.** From a place or position: *drove off.* **2. a.** At a certain distance in space or time: *a mile off; a week off.* **b.** From a given course or route; aside: *swerved off into a ditch.* **c.** Into a state of unconsciousness: *I must have dozed off.* **3. a.** So as to be no longer on, attached, or connected: *shaved off his mustache.* **b.** So as to be divided: *marked off the playing field by yards.* **4.** So as to be no longer continuing, operating, or functioning: *switched off the radio.* **5.** So as to be completely removed, finished, or eliminated: *kill off the mice.* **6.** So as to be smaller, fewer, or less: *Sales dropped off.* **7.** So as to be away from work or duty: *They took a day off.* **8.** Offstage. **—off** *adj.* **1. a.** Distant or removed; farther: *the off side of the barn.* **b.** Remote; slim: *stopped by on the off chance that they're home.* **2.** Not on, attached, or connected: *with his shoes off.* **3.** Not operating or operational: *The oven is off.* **4.** No longer taking place; canceled: *The wedding is off.* **5.** Slack: *Production was off this year.* **6. a.** Not up to standard; below a normal or satisfactory level: *Your pitching is off today.* **b.** Not accurate; incorrect: *Your statistical results are off.* **c.** Somewhat crazy; eccentric: *I think that person is a little off.* **7.** Started on the way; going: *I'm off to see the president.* **8. a.** Absent or away from work or duty: *He's off every Tuesday.* **b.** Spent away from work or duty: *My off day is Saturday.* **9. a.** Being on the right side of an animal or a vehicle. **b.** Being the animal or vehicle on the right. **10.** *Nautical.* Farthest from the shore; seaward. **11.** *Sports.* Toward or designating the side of the field facing the batsman in cricket. **12.** Off-color. **—off** *prep.* **1.** So as to be removed or distant from: *The bird hopped off the branch.* **2.** Away or relieved from: *off duty.* **3. a.** By consuming: *living off locusts and honey.* **b.** With the means provided by: *living off my pension.* **c.** *Informal.* From: *"What else do you want off me?"* (Jimmy Breslin). **4.** Extending or branching out from: *an artery off the heart.* **5.** Not up to the usual standard of: *off his game.* **6.** So as to abstain from: *went off narcotics.* **7.** *Nautical.* To seaward of: *a mile off Sandy Hook.* **—off** *v.* **offed, off·ing, offs.** —*intr.* To go away; leave: *Off with you or I'll call the police.* —*tr. Slang.* To murder. [Variant of Middle English *of,* from Old English. See **apo-** in Appendix.]

USAGE NOTE: In Modern English the compound preposition *off of* is generally regarded as informal and is best avoided in formal speech and writing: *He stepped off* (not *off of*) *the platform. Off* is informal as well in its use to indicate a source: formal style requires *I borrowed it from* (not *off*) *my brother.*

off. *abbr.* Office; officer; official.

Of·fa (ô′fə). Died 796. King of Mercia (757–796). With Charlemagne he signed the first recorded English commercial treaty (796).

off-air (ôf′âr′, ŏf′-) *adj.* Spoken, occurring, or used not during broadcasting or not while being recorded for broadcasting: *an off-air argument; off-air discussion.*

of·fal (ô′fəl, ŏf′əl) *n.* **1.** Waste parts, especially of a butchered animal. **2.** Refuse; rubbish. [Middle English : *of-*, off (from Old English, from *of;* see **apo-** in Appendix) + *fal*, fall.]

off and on *adv.* In an intermittent manner: *slept off and on last night.*

off·beat (ôf′bēt′, ŏf′-) *n. Music.* An unaccented beat in a measure. **—offbeat** (ôf′bēt′, ŏf′-) *adj. Slang.* Not conforming to an ordinary type or pattern; unconventional: *offbeat humor.*

off-Broad·way (ôf′brôd′wā′, ŏf′-) *n.* Theatrical work, often experimental and inexpensive, presented outside the Broadway entertainment district of New York City. **—off-Broadway** *adj.* **1.** Of, relating to, or being theatrical activity that is chiefly experimental and inexpensive, carried on outside the New York City entertainment district. **2.** Located outside the Broadway entertainment district. **—off′-Broad′way′** *adv.*

off-col·or (ôf′kŭl′ər, ŏf′-) *adj.* **1.** Exhibiting bad taste: *an off-color joke.* **2.** Varying from the usual, expected, or required color. **3.** Not in good health or spirits.

Of·fen·bach (ôf′ən-bäk′, -bäкн′). A city of central Germany north-northeast of Mannheim on the Main River. First mentioned in the tenth century, it is an industrial center noted for its leather goods. Population, 107,378.

Of·fen·bach (ô′fən-bäk′, ŏf′ən-, ô-fĕn-bäk′), **Jacques.** 1819–1880. French composer noted for his operettas and the opera *Tales of Hoffman* (performed 1881).

of·fence (ə-fĕns′) *n. Chiefly British.* Variant of **offense.**

of·fend (ə-fĕnd′) *v.* **-fend·ed, -fend·ing, -fends.** —*tr.* **1.** To cause displeasure, anger, resentment, or wounded feelings in. **2.** To be displeasing or disagreeable to: *Onions offend my sense of smell.* **3.a.** To transgress; violate: *offend all laws of humanity.* **b.** To cause to sin. —*intr.* **1.** To result in displeasure: *Bad manners may offend.* **2.a.** To violate a moral or divine law; sin. **b.** To violate a rule or law: *offended against the curfew.* [Middle English *offenden*, from Old French *offendre*, from Latin *offendere.* See **gʷhen-** in Appendix.]

SYNONYMS: *offend, insult, affront, outrage.* These verbs mean to cause resentment, humiliation, or hurt. To *offend* is to cause displeasure, wounded feelings, or repugnance in another: *"He often offended men who might have been useful friends"* (John Lothrop Motley). *Insult* implies gross insensitivity, insolence, or contemptuous rudeness resulting in shame or embarrassment: *"His letters . . . boil with sarcastic gibes and insulting remarks on the subject of universal suffrage"* (Mario Vargas Llosa). To *affront* is to insult openly, usually intentionally: *Affronted at his impertinence, she stared at him coldly and wordlessly. Outrage* implies the flagrant violation of a person's integrity, pride, or sense of right and decency: *"Agnes . . . was outraged by what seemed to her Rose's callousness"* (Mrs. Humphry Ward).

of·fend·er (ə-fĕn′dər) *n.* One that offends, especially one that breaks a public law: *youthful offenders.*

of·fense (ə-fĕns′) *n.* **1.a.** The act of causing anger, resentment, displeasure, or affront. **b.** The state of being offended. **2.a.** A violation or an infraction of a moral or social code; a transgression or a sin. **b.** A transgression of law; a crime. **3.** Something that outrages moral sensibilities: *Genocide is an offense to all civilized human beings.* **4.** (ŏf′ĕns′). The act of attacking or assaulting. **5.** (ŏf′ĕns′). *Sports.* **a.** A team in possession of the ball or puck. **b.** Scoring ability or potential. **c.** The means or tactics used in an attempt to score points. [Middle English, from Old French *ofense*, from Latin *offēnsa*, from feminine past participle of *offendere*, to offend. See OFFEND.]

SYNONYMS: *offense, crime, sin, error.* These nouns are related in denoting a violation or an infraction of a moral, social, or legal code. *Offense* applies most broadly: *The phrase* between you and I *is often considered an offense against proper usage. Juveniles convicted of criminal offenses are sent to reformatories. Crime* refers both to an act committed or omitted in violation of—and punishable by—law and to a serious or grave offense: *"treason, bribery, or other high crimes and misdemeanors"* (U.S. Constitution, Article II) *"Is it . . . a crime to love too well?"* (Alexander Pope). A *sin* is a transgression of religious or moral law; more loosely it applies to something regarded as being utterly wrong: *"The sins of the fathers are to be laid upon the children"* (Shakespeare). *"The only deadly sin I know is cynicism"* (Henry L. Stimson). *Error* is departure from what is morally right; the term often suggests bad judgment or lack of awareness rather than willful violation: *"All men are liable to error; and most men are . . . under temptation to it"* (John Locke).

of·fen·sive (ə-fĕn′sĭv) *adj.* **1.** Disagreeable to the senses: *an offensive odor.* **2.** Causing anger, displeasure, resentment, or affront: *an offensive gesture.* **3.a.** Making an attack: *The offensive troops gained ground quickly.* **b.** Of, relating to, or designed for attack: *offensive weapons.* **4.** (ŏf′ĕn-). *Sports.* Of or relating to a team having possession of a ball or puck: *the offensive line.* **—offensive** *n.* **1.** An attitude or a position of attack: *a peace offensive.* **2.** An attack or assault: *led a massive military offensive.* **—of·fen′sive·ly** *adv.* **—of·fen′sive·ness** *n.*

SYNONYMS: *offensive, disgusting, loathsome, nasty, repellent, repulsive, revolting, vile.* The central meaning shared by these adjectives is "extremely unpleasant to the senses or feelings": *an offensive remark; disgusting language; a loathsome disease; a nasty smell; a repellent demand; repulsive behavior; revolting food; vile thoughts.* See also Synonyms at **hateful.**

of·fer (ô′fər, ŏf′ər) *v.* **-fered, -fer·ing, -fers.** —*tr.* **1.** To present for acceptance or rejection; proffer: *offered me a drink.* **2.a.** To put forward for consideration; propose: *offer an opinion.* **b.** To present in order to meet a need or satisfy a requirement: *offered new statistics in order to facilitate the decision-making process.* **3.a.** To present for sale. **b.** To provide; furnish: *a hotel that offers conference facilities.* **4.** To propose as payment; bid. **5.** To present as an act of worship: *offer up prayers.* **6.** To exhibit readiness or desire to do; volunteer: *offered to carry the packages.* **7.** To put up; mount: *partisans who offered strong resistance to the invaders.* **8.** To threaten: *offered to leave without them if they didn't hurry.* **9.** To produce or introduce on the stage: *The repertory group is offering two new plays this season.* —*intr.* **1.** To present an offering in worship or devotion. **2.** To make an offer or a proposal, especially of marriage. **3.** To present itself: *"This plan was dropped, because of its risk, and because a better offered"* (T.E. Lawrence). **—offer** *n.* **1.** The act of offering: *an offer of assistance.* **2.** Something, such as a suggestion, proposal, bid, or recommendation, that is offered. **3.** *Law.* A proposal that if accepted constitutes a legally binding contract. **4.** The condition of being offered, especially for sale: *thousands of bushels of wheat on offer.* **5.a.** An attempt; a try. **b.** A show of intention. [Middle English *offren*, from Old English *offrian*, to present in worship and from Old French *offrir*, to propose, present, both from Latin *offerre*, to present, offer : *ob-*, to; see OB– + *ferre*, to bring; see **bher-¹** in Appendix.] **—of′fer·er, of′fer·or** *n.*

SYNONYMS: *offer, proffer, tender, present.* These verbs are compared as they mean to put before another for acceptance or rejection. *Offer* is the basic general term in this group: *the hostess offered us a cup of coffee. Many department stores offer television sets. I offered him some money for his help. "She offered no response"* (Arnold Bennett). *Proffer* implies voluntary action motivated especially by courtesy or generosity: *"Mr. van der Luyden . . . proffered to Newland low-voiced congratulations"* (Edith Wharton). To *tender* is to offer formally; it may connote polite observance of amenities: *She tendered her respects. The chief of staff is expected to tender his resignation this week. Present* suggests formality and often a measure of ceremony: *The impresario will present an expanded series of concerts next season. The ambassador presented her credentials to the monarch. "A footman entered, and presented . . . some mail on a silver tray"* (Winston Churchill).

of·fer·ing (ô′fər-ĭng, ŏf′ər-) *n.* **1.** The act of making an offer. **2.** Something, such as stock, that is offered. **3.** A presentation made to a deity as an act of religious worship or sacrifice; an oblation. **4.** A contribution or gift, especially one made at a religious service.

of·fer·to·ry (ô′fər-tôr′ē, -tōr′ē, ŏf′ər-) *n., pl.* **-ries. 1.** Often **Offertory. a.** One of the principal parts of the Eucharistic liturgy at which bread and wine are offered to God by the celebrant. **b.** A musical setting for this part of the liturgy. **2.** A collection of offerings at a religious service. [Middle English *offertori*, from Late Latin *offertōrium*, from Latin *offerre*, to offer. See OFFER.]

off·hand (ôf′hănd′, ŏf′-) *adv.* Without preparation or forethought; extemporaneously. **—offhand** also **off·hand·ed** (-hăn′dĭd) *adj.* Performed or expressed without preparation or forethought. See Synonyms at **extemporaneous. —off′-hand′ed·ly** *adv.* **—off′hand′ed·ness** *n.*

off-hour (ôf′our′, ŏf′-) *n.* A period of time during which motor vehicular and pedestrian traffic is light.

of·fice (ô′fĭs, ŏf′ĭs) *n. Abbr.* **off. 1.a.** A place in which business, clerical, or professional activities are conducted. **b.** The administrative personnel, executives, or staff working in such a place. **2.** A duty or function assigned to or assumed by someone. See Synonyms at **function. 3.** A position of authority, duty, or trust given to a person, as in a government or corporation: *the office of vice president.* **4.a.** A subdivision of a governmental department: *the U.S. Patent Office.* **4.b.** A major executive division of a government: *the British Home Office.* **5.** A public position: *seek office.* **6. offices.** *Chiefly British.* The parts of a house, such as the laundry and kitchen, in which servants carry out household work. **7.** Often **offices.** A usually beneficial act performed for another. **8.** *Ecclesiastical.* A ceremony, rite, or service, usually prescribed by liturgy, especially: **a.** The canonical hours. **b.** A prayer service in the Anglican Church, such as Morning or Evening Prayer. **c.** A ceremony, rite, or service for a special purpose, especially a rite for the dead. —*attributive.* Often used

ă pat	oi boy
ā pay	ou out
âr care	ŏŏ took
ä father	ōō boot
ĕ pet	ŭ cut
ē be	ûr urge
ĭ pit	th thin
ī pie	*th* this
îr pier	hw which
ŏ pot	zh vision
ō toe	ə about, item
ô paw	♦ regionalism

Stress marks: ′ (primary); ′ (secondary), as in **dictionary** (dĭk′shə-nĕr′ē)

to modify another noun: *office furniture; office buildings.* [Middle English, from Old French, duty, from Latin *officium.* See **dhē-** in Appendix.]

office boy *n.* A boy or young man employed in a business office to do odd jobs.

office girl *n.* A girl or young woman employed in a business office to do odd jobs.

of·fice·hold·er (ô′fĭs-hōl′dər, ŏf′ĭs-) *n.* One who holds public office.

office park *n.* An area in a suburb or a town in which a number of office buildings are constructed together with ancillary structures such as those housing health clubs, day-care centers, and restaurants.

of·fi·cer (ô′fĭ-sər, ŏf′ĭ-) *n. Abbr.* **off. 1.** One who holds an office of authority or trust in an organization, such as a corporation or government. **2.** One who holds a commission in the armed forces. **3.** A person licensed in the merchant marine as master, mate, chief engineer, or assistant engineer. **4.** A police officer. [Middle English, from Old French *officier,* from Medieval Latin *officārius,* from Latin *officium,* service, duty. See OFFICE.]

officer of the day *n., pl.* **officers of the day.** *Abbr.* **O.D.** A military officer who, for a given day, assumes responsibility for security, order, and supervision of the guard.

officer of the deck *n., pl.* **officers of the deck.** A naval officer assigned to represent the commanding officer of a vessel or an installation for a specified period during which he or she is superior to all officers below the executive officer.

of·fi·cial (ə-fĭsh′əl) *adj. Abbr.* **off. 1.** Of or relating to an office or a post of authority: *official duties.* **2.** Authorized by a proper authority; authoritative: *official permission.* **3.** Holding office or serving in a public capacity: *an official representative.* **4.** Characteristic of or befitting a person of authority; formal: *an official banquet.* **5.** Authorized by or contained in the U.S. Pharmacopoeia or National Formulary. Used of drugs. **—official** *n. Abbr.* **off. 1.** One who holds an office or a position, especially one who acts in a subordinate capacity for an institution such as a corporation or governmental agency. **2.** *Sports.* A referee or an umpire. [From Middle English, ecclesiastical officer, from Old French, from Latin *officiālis,* an attendant of an office, from *officium,* duty, service. See OFFICE.] **—of·fi′cial·dom** *n.* **—of·fi′cial·ly** *adv.*

of·fi·cial·ese (ə-fĭsh′ə-lēz′, -lēs′) *n.* Language characteristic of official documents or statements, especially when obscure, pretentiously wordy, or excessively formal.

of·fi·cial·ism (ə-fĭsh′ə-lĭz′əm) *n.* Rigid adherence to official regulations, forms, and procedures.

of·fi·ci·ant (ə-fĭsh′ē-ənt) *n.* One who performs a religious rite or presides over a religious service or ceremony.

of·fi·ci·ar·y (ə-fĭsh′ē-ĕr′ē) *n., pl.* **-ies. 1.** A body of officials or officers. **2.** An official or officer. **—officiary** *adj.* **1.** Attached to or resulting from an office held. Used of a title. **2.** Having a title resulting from the holding of an office. Used of a dignitary.

of·fi·ci·ate (ə-fĭsh′ē-āt′) *intr.v.* **-at·ed, -at·ing, -ates. 1.** To perform the duties and functions of an office or a position of authority. **2.** To serve as an officiant. **3.** *Sports.* To serve as a referee or an umpire. [Medieval Latin *officiāre, officiāt-,* to conduct, from Latin *officium,* service, duty. See OFFICE.] **—of·fi′ci·a′tion** *n.* **—of·fi′ci·a′tor** *n.*

of·fic·i·nal (ə-fĭs′ə-nəl, ô′fĭ-sī′nəl, ŏf′ĭ-) *adj.* **1.** Readily available in pharmacies; not requiring special preparation. **2.** Recognized by a pharmacopoeia: *an officinal herb.* **—officinal** *n.* An officinal drug. [French, from Medieval Latin *officīnālis,* of a storeroom or workshop, from Latin *officīna,* workshop, alteration of *opificīna,* from *opifex, opific-,* workman : *opus,* work; see **op-** in Appendix + *facere,* to do; see **dhē-** in Appendix.] **—of·fic′i·nal·ly** *adv.*

of·fi·cious (ə-fĭsh′əs) *adj.* **1.** Marked by excessive eagerness in offering unwanted services or advice to others: *an officious host; officious attention.* **2.** Informal; unofficial. **3.** *Archaic.* Eager to render services or help others. [Latin *officiōsus,* obliging, dutiful, from *officium,* duty. See OFFICE.] **—of·fi′cious·ly** *adv.* **—of·fi′cious·ness** *n.*

off·ing (ô′fĭng, ŏf′ĭng) *n. Nautical.* The part of the sea visible from shore that is very distant or beyond anchoring ground. **—*idiom.* in the offing. 1.** In the near or immediate future; soon to come: *with exams finished and graduation in the offing.* **2.** Nearby; at hand.

off·ish (ô′fĭsh, ŏf′ĭsh) *adj.* Inclined to be distant and reserved; aloof. **—off′ish·ly** *adv.* **—off′ish·ness** *n.*

off-key (ôf′-kē′, ŏf′-) *adj.* **1.** *Music.* Pitched higher or lower than the correct notes of a melody. **2.** Being out of accord with what is considered normal or appropriate: *a high-flown, off-key speech by a newcomer.* **—off′key′** *adv.*

off-lim·its (ôf-lĭm′ĭts, ŏf-) *adj.* Not to be entered or frequented by a designated group: *a bar that is off-limits to troops.*

off-line (ôf′līn′, ŏf′-) *adj. Computer Science.* **1.** Not under the control of a central computer, as in a manufacturing process or an experiment. **2.** Not connected to a computer or computer network.

off·load or **off-load** (ôf′lōd′, ŏf′-) *v.* **-load·ed, -load·ing, -loads.** —*tr.* **1.** To unload (a vehicle or container). **2.** *Computer Science.* To transfer (data) to a peripheral device. **3.** *Slang.* To get rid of and pass on to (another): *"He does come close to offloading some of the blame for the launch on . . . the dear old media"* (Meg Greenfield). —*intr.* To unload a vehicle or container.

off of *prep. Informal.* Off. See Usage Note at **off.**

off-off-Broad·way also **Off-Off-Broad·way** (ôf′ôf-brôd′wā′, ŏf′ŏf-) *n.* The avant-garde or experimental theatrical productions of New York City, typically performed in small or multipurpose venues. **—off′-off-Broad′way** *adv. & adj.*

off-peak (ôf′pēk′, ŏf′-) *adj.* Not in the period of most frequent or heaviest use: *lower rates for telephone calls made during off-peak hours; travelers who take advantage of off-peak fares.*

off-piste (ôf′pēst′, ŏf′-) *adj. Sports.* Existing or taking place on snow that has not been compacted into tracks: *off-piste skiing.*

off-price (ôf′prīs′, ŏf′-) *adj.* **1.** Of, relating to, or being a retail store that sells merchandise at prices lower than usual. **2.** For sale at prices lower than usual: *off-price assortments of women's clothing.*

off·print (ôf′prĭnt′, ŏf′-) *Printing. n.* A reproduction of or an excerpt from an article that was originally contained in a larger publication. **—offprint** *tr.v.* **-print·ed, -print·ing, -prints.** To reproduce or reprint (an article or excerpt).

off-put·ting (ôf′po͝ot′ĭng, ŏf′-) *adj.* Tending to disconcert or repel: *"The trappings of upper-class life are off-putting and sterile"* (Elizabeth Hess).

off rhyme *n.* A partial or imperfect rhyme, often using assonance or consonance only, as in *dry* and *died* or *grown* and *moon.* Also called *half rhyme, near rhyme, oblique rhyme, slant rhyme.*

off-road (ôf′rōd′, ŏf′-) *adj.* Existing, taking place, or designed for use off paved or public roads or in rugged terrain: *off-road sports such as snowmobiling.* **—off′-road′** *adv.*

off-road vehicle *n. Abbr.* **ORV** A vehicle, such as a dune buggy, designed for use off paved or public roads or in rough terrain.

off·scour·ing (ôf′skour′ĭng, ŏf′-) *n.* **1.** Something that is scoured off or disposed of; refuse. Often used in the plural. **2.** A person regarded as fallen from society; an outcast. Often used in the plural.

off-screen or **off·screen** (ôf′-skrēn′, ŏf′-) *adj.* **1.** Existing or occurring outside the frame of a movie or television screen: *sounds of off-screen mayhem.* **2.** Existing or occurring out of public view or knowledge; private. **—off′-screen′** *adv.*

off-sea·son (ôf′-sē′zən, ŏf′-) *n.* A part of the year marked by a cessation or lessening of normal activity, as of a business. **—off′-sea′son** *adv. & adj.*

off·set (ôf′sĕt′, ŏf′-) *n.* **1.** An agent, an element, or a thing that balances, counteracts, or compensates for something else. **2.** One thing set off or developed from something else. **3.** The start or initial stage; the outset. **4.** *Architecture.* A ledge or recess in a wall formed by a reduction in thickness above; a setoff. **5.** *Botany.* A shoot that develops laterally at the base of a plant, often rooting to form a new plant. **6.** *Geology.* A spur of a mountain range or hills. **7.** A bend in a pipe, bar, or other straight continuous piece made to allow it to pass around an obstruction. **8.** A short distance measured perpendicularly from the main line in surveying, used to help in calculating the area of an irregular plot. **9.** A descendant of a race or family; an offshoot. **10.** *Printing.* **a.** An unintentional or faulty transfer of wet ink from a printed sheet to another surface in contact with it. Also called *setoff.* **b.** Offset printing. **—offset** (ôf′sĕt′, ŏf′-, ôf-sĕt′, ŏf-) *v.* **-set, -set·ting, -sets.** —*tr.* **1.** To counterbalance, counteract, or compensate for: *fringe benefits designed to offset low salaries.* **2.** *Printing.* **a.** To cause (printed matter) to transfer or smear on another surface. **b.** To produce by offset printing. **3.** To make or form an offset in (a wall, bar, or pipe). —*intr.* **1.** To develop, project, or be situated as an offset. **2.** *Printing.* To become marked by or cause an unintentional transfer of ink. **—off′set′** *adv. & adj.*

offset printing *n.* The process of printing by indirect image transfer, especially by using a metal or paper plate to ink a smooth rubber cylinder that transfers the ink to the paper.

off·shoot (ôf′sho͞ot′, ŏf′-) *n.* **1.** Something that branches out or derives its existence or origin from a particular source. See Synonyms at **branch. 2.** A branch, descendant, or member of a family or social group. **3.** *Botany.* A lateral shoot from the main stem of a plant.

off·shore (ôf′shôr′, -shōr′, ŏf′-) *adj.* **1.** Moving or directed away from the shore: *an offshore wind.* **2. a.** Located at a distance from the shore: *an offshore mooring; offshore oil-drilling platforms.* **b.** Located or based in a foreign country and not subject to tax laws: *offshore bank accounts; offshore investments.* **—offshore** *adv.* **1.** Away from the shore: *The storm moved offshore.* **2.** At a distance from the shore: *a boat moored offshore.*

off·side (ôf′sīd′, ŏf′-) also **off·sides** (-sīdz′) *Sports.* —*adv. & adj.* Illegally ahead of the ball or puck. —*n.* An offside motion or play.

off-site (ôf′sīt′, ŏf′-) *adj.* Taking place or located away from the site, as of a particular activity: *an off-site waste treatment operation.* **—off′-site′** *adv.*

off-speed (ôf′spēd′, ŏf′-) *adj. Sports.* Slower than expected: *an off-speed pitch; an off-speed backhand.*

off·spring (ôf′sprĭng′, ŏf′-) *n., pl.* **offspring. 1.** The progeny or descendants of a person, an animal, or a plant considered as a group. **2.** A child of particular parentage. **3.** A result; a product.

[Middle English *ofspring,* from Old English : *of,* off; see OFF + *springan,* to rise.]

off-stage or **off•stage** (ôf′stāj′, ŏf′-) —*adj.* **1.** Situated or taking place in the area of a stage that is invisible to the audience. **2.** Of, relating to, or taking place in private life: *an off-stage persona.* —*adv.* **1.** Away from the area of a stage visible to the audience. **2.a.** In private life: *an actor known off-stage by another name.* **b.** Behind the scenes; not visible to the public: *The meetings between the leaders took place off-stage.*

off-the-cuff (ôf′thə-kŭf′, ŏf′-) *adv. & adj.* Without preparation; impromptu: *answered off-the-cuff; an off-the-cuff toast.*

off-the-rack (ôf′thə-răk′, ŏf′-) *adj.* Of, relating to, or being merchandise, especially clothing, made in standard sizes; ready-made.

off-the-rec•ord (ôf′thə-rĕk′ərd, ŏf′-) *adv. & adj.* Not for publication or attribution: *spoke off-the-record to the press; off-the-record comments by the senator.*

off-the-shelf (ôf′thə-shĕlf′, ŏf′-) *adj.* Of, relating to, or being merchandise carried in stock that is usable without modification. —**off′-the-shelf′** *adv.*

off-the-wall (ôf′thə-wôl′, ŏf′-) *adj. Informal.* **1.** Very unconventional or unusual: *manic, off-the-wall creativity; off-the-wall humor.* **2.** Exhibiting bizarre behavior; crazy: *their off-the-wall friends.*

off-track (ôf′trăk′, ŏf′-) *adj. Sports & Games.* Of or relating to gambling on races that is conducted away from a racetrack.

off-track bet•ting (bĕt′ĭng) *n. Abbr.* **OTB** *Sports & Games.* A system of placing bets away from a racetrack.

off-white (ôf′hwīt′, -wīt′, ŏf′-) *n. Color.* A grayish or yellowish white. —**off′-white′** *adj.*

off year *n.* **1.** A year in which no major political elections occur. **2.** A year of reduced activity or production: *an off year for soybean crops.*

O'Fla•her•ty (ō-flă′hər-tē), **Liam.** 1896–1984. Irish writer known especially for his short stories, collected in *Two Lovely Beasts* (1948) and *The Pedlar's Revenge* (1976).

O.F.M. *abbr.* Order of Friars Minor.

oft (ôft, ŏft) *adv.* Often. Often used in combination: *his oft-expressed philosophy; oft-repeated tales.* [Middle English, from Old English. See **upo** in Appendix.]

of•ten (ô′fən, ŏf′ən, ôf′tən, ŏf′-) *adv.* **-er, -est.** Many times; frequently. [Middle English, alteration (probably influenced by *selden,* seldom) of *oft,* from Old English. See **upo** in Appendix.]

of•ten•times (ô′fən-tīmz′, ôf′tən-, ŏf′ən-, ŏf′tən-) also **oft•times** (ôf′tīmz′, ŏf′-) *adv.* Frequently; repeatedly.

OG or **O.G.** *abbr.* Officer of the guard.

og•am (ŏg′əm, ō′əm) *n.* Variant of **ogham.**

Og•bo•mo•sho (ŏg′bə-mō′shō). A city of southwest Nigeria north-northeast of Ibadan. Population, 514,400.

Og•den (ŏg′dən, ŏg′-). A city of northern Utah north of Salt Lake City. Settled by Mormons in the 1840's, it is a railroad junction with varied industries. Population, 64,407.

Ogden, Charles Kay. 1889–1957. British psychologist and educator who designed Basic English, a simplified form of English made up of 850 words.

o•gee (ō′jē′) *n. Architecture.* **1.** A double curve with the shape of an elongated S. **2.** A molding having the profile of an S-shaped curve. **3.** An arch formed by two S-shaped curves meeting at a point. [Middle English *oggifs, ogeus,* pl. of *ogif,* ogive. See OGIVE.]

O•gee•chee (ō-gē′chē). A river, about 402 km (250 mi) long, of eastern Georgia flowing generally southeast to the Atlantic Ocean.

og•ham or **og•am** (ŏg′əm, ō′əm) *n.* **1.a.** An alphabetic system of inscribed notches for vowels and lines for consonants used to write Old Irish, chiefly on the edges of memorial stones, from the fifth to the early seventh century. **b.** A character used in this alphabet. **2.a.** An inscription in the ogham alphabet. **b.** A stone inscribed in the ogham alphabet. [Irish Gaelic, from Old Irish *ogom,* after *Ogma,* name of a Celtic god.]

o•give (ō′jīv′) *n.* **1.** *Statistics.* **a.** A distribution curve in which the frequencies are cumulative. **b.** A frequency distribution. **2.** *Architecture.* **a.** A diagonal rib of a Gothic vault. **b.** A pointed arch. [Middle English *ogif* and French *ogive,* diagonal rib of a vault, both from Old French *augive,* probably from Vulgar Latin **obviātīva,* from Late Latin *obviāta,* feminine past participle of *obviāre,* to resist. See OBVIATE.] —**o•gi′val** *adj.*

O•gla•la (ō-glä′lə) *n., pl.* **Oglala** or **-las. 1.** A Native American people constituting a subdivision of the Teton Sioux, formerly inhabiting the Black Hills region of western South Dakota, with a present-day population mainly in southwest South Dakota. **2.** A member of this people.

o•gle (ō′gəl, ô′gəl) *v.* **o•gled, o•gling, o•gles.** —*tr.* **1.** To stare at. **2.** To stare at impertinently, flirtatiously, or amorously. —*intr.* To stare in an impertinent, flirtatious, or amorous manner. See Synonyms at **gaze.** —**ogle** *n.* An impertinent, flirtatious, or amorous stare. [Perhaps from Low German *oghelen, oegeln,* frequentative of *oegen,* to eye, from *oghe, oge,* eye. See **okʷ-** in Appendix.] —**o′gler** *n.*

O•gle•thorpe (ō′gəl-thôrp′), **James Edward.** 1696–1785. English soldier, philanthropist, and colonizer. He secured a charter for the colony of Georgia (1732) as a refuge for unemployed debtors newly released from prison.

o•gre (ō′gər) *n.* **1.** A giant or monster in legends and fairy tales that eats human beings. **2.** A person who is felt to be particularly cruel, brutish, or hideous. [French, probably ultimately from Latin *Orcus,* god of the underworld.] —**o′gre•ish** (ō′gər-ĭsh, ō′grĭsh) *adj.*

o•gress (ō′grĭs) *n.* **1.** A female giant or monster in legends and fairy tales that eats human beings. **2.** A woman who is felt to be particularly cruel, brutish, or hideous.

oh (ō) *interj.* **1.** Used to express strong emotion, such as surprise, fear, anger, or pain. **2.** Used in direct address: *Oh, sir! You forgot your keys.* **3.** Used to indicate understanding or acknowledgment of a statement.

OH *abbr.* Ohio.

O'Hair (ō-hâr′), **Madalyn Murray.** Born 1919. American reformer who won the 1963 U.S. Supreme Court case *Murray* v. *Curlett,* in which prayer exercises in public schools were declared unconstitutional.

O'Ha•ra (ō-hâr′ə, ō-hăr′ə), **John Henry.** 1905–1970. American writer who contributed short stories to the *New Yorker* and wrote novels such as *Ten North Frederick* (1955).

O. Hen•ry (ō hĕn′rē). See William Sydney **Porter.**

O'Hig•gins (ō-hĭg′ĭnz), **Bernardo.** 1778–1842. Chilean general and politician who ruled Chile (1817–1823) after its revolt against the Spanish.

O•hi•o (ō-hī′ō). *Abbr.* **OH, O.** A state of the north-central United States in the Great Lakes region. It was admitted as the 17th state in 1863. In prehistoric times Mound Builders inhabited the region, which was first explored by La Salle in 1669. The French-British rivalry for control of the area led to the last of the French and Indian Wars (1754–1763), in which the French were defeated. Ohio was part of the vast area ceded to the United States by the Treaty of Paris in 1783 and became part of the Old Northwest by the Ordinance of 1787. It became a separate territory in 1799. Columbus is the capital and Cleveland the largest city. Population, 10,797,624. —**O•hi′o•an** *adj. n.*

Ohio buckeye *n.* A large shrub or tree *(Aesculus glabra)* of the central United States, having compound leaves and yellowish-green flowers.

Ohio River. A river formed by the confluence of the Allegheny and Monongahela rivers in western Pennsylvania and flowing about 1,578 km (981 mi) to the Mississippi River at Cairo in southern Illinois.

ohm (ōm) *n. Abbr.* **o** A unit of electrical resistance equal to that of a conductor in which a current of one ampere is produced by a potential of one volt across its terminals. See table at **measurement.** [After Georg Simon OHM.] —**ohm′ic** *adj.* —**ohm′i•cal•ly** *adv.*

Ohm (ōm), **Georg Simon.** 1789–1854. German physicist noted for his contributions to mathematics, acoustics, and the measurement of electrical resistance.

ohm•me•ter (ōm′mē′tər) *n.* An instrument for direct measurement in ohms of the resistance of a conductor in ohms.

OHMS or **O.H.M.S.** *abbr.* **1.** On Her Majesty's Service. **2.** On His Majesty's Service.

o•ho (ō-hō′) *interj.* Used to express surprise or mock astonishment.

-oic *suff.* Containing a carboxyl group or one of its derivatives: *decanoic acid.* [–O– + –IC.]

-oid *suff.* **1.** Resembling; having the appearance of; related to: *acanthoid.* **2.** One that resembles something specified or has a specified quality: *humanoid.* [Greek *-oeidēs,* from *eidos,* shape, form. See **weid-** in Appendix.]

o•id•i•um (ō-ĭd′ē-əm) *n., pl.* **-i•a** (-ē-ə). A thin-walled spore produced by fragmentation in certain filamentous fungi. [New Latin *Oidium,* fungus genus, from Greek *ōion,* egg. See OO–.]

oil (oil) *n.* **1.** Any of numerous mineral, vegetable, and synthetic substances and animal and vegetable fats that are generally slippery, combustible, viscous, liquid or liquefiable at room temperatures, soluble in various organic solvents such as ether but not in water, and used in a great variety of products, especially lubricants and fuels. **2.a.** Petroleum. **b.** A petroleum derivative, such as a machine oil or lubricant. **3.** A substance with an oily consistency. **4.** Oil paint. **5.** A painting done in oil paint. **6.** Insincere flattery. —**oil** *tr.v.* **oiled, oil•ing, oils.** To lubricate, supply, cover, or polish with oil. —***idiom.*** **oil (someone's) hand** (or **palm).** *Informal.* **1.** To bribe: *an attorney who tried to oil the judge's hand in order to obtain a directed verdict favorable to his client.* **2.** To give a tip to: *oiled the headwaiter's palm.* [Middle English, from Old French *oile,* from Latin *oleum,* olive oil, from Greek *elaion,* **elaiwon,* from *elaia, elaiwā,* olive.]

oil beetle *n.* Any of various blister beetles of the genus *Meloe* that exude an oily yellow substance from the joints of the legs when disturbed.

oil•bird (oil′bûrd′) *n.* See **guacharo.**

oil cake *n.* The solid residue that is left after certain oily seeds, such as cottonseed and linseed, have been pressed free of their oil. It is ground and used as cattle feed or fertilizer.

oil•can (oil′kăn′) *n.* A can for oil, especially a can with a spout constructed to release oil drop by drop, as for lubricating machinery. Also called *oiler.*

oil•cloth (oil′klôth′, -klŏth′) *n.* Fabric treated with clay, oil, and pigments to make it waterproof.

oil color *n.* See **oil paint.**

ogee

ă pat	oi boy
ā pay	ou out
âr care	ŏŏ took
ä father	ōō boot
ĕ pet	ŭ cut
ē be	ûr urge
ĭ pit	th thin
ī pie	*th* this
îr pier	hw which
ŏ pot	zh vision
ō toe	ə about, item
ô paw	♦ regionalism

Stress marks: ′ (primary); ′ (secondary), as in **dictionary** (dĭk′shə-nĕr′ē)

oil well
In front of the State Capitol, Oklahoma City, Oklahoma

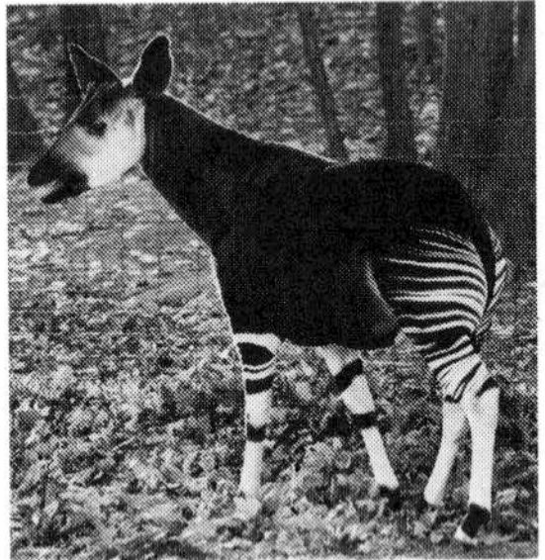

okapi
Okapia johnstoni

Georgia O'Keeffe

Oil·dale (oil′dāl′). A community of south-central California, an oil-producing suburb of Bakersfield. Population, 23,382.

oiled (oild) *adj.* **1.** Treated with oil. **2.** *Slang.* Intoxicated; drunk.

oil·er (oi′lər) *n.* **1.** One that oils engines or machinery. **2.** *Nautical.* **a.** An oil tanker. **b.** A ship that burns oil as fuel. **3.** See **oilcan. 4.** See **oil well. 5.** *Informal.* An oilskin garment.

oil field *n.* An area with reserves of recoverable petroleum, especially one with several oil-producing wells.

oil gland *n.* **1.** A gland, such as a sebaceous gland, that secretes an oily substance. **2.** See **uropygial gland.**

oil of turpentine *n.* See **turpentine** (sense 1).

oil of vitriol *n.* See **sulfuric acid.**

oil paint *n.* A paint in which the vehicle is a drying oil. Also called *oil color.*

oil painting *n.* **1.** A painting done in oil paints. **2.** The art or practice of painting with oils.

oil palm *n.* **1.** A tall palm tree *(Elaeis guineensis)* native to tropical Africa, having nutlike fruits that yield a commercially valuable oil. Also called *African oil palm.* **2.** Any of several palms that yield oil.

oil pan *n.* The bottom of the crankcase in an internal-combustion engine, serving as an oil reservoir.

oil·pa·per (oil′pā′pər) *n.* Paper that is soaked in oil to make it transparent and water-resistant.

oil patch *n. Informal.* The oil-producing region of the United States that includes Texas, Oklahoma, and Louisiana.

Oil Rivers (oil). A large delta region of the Niger River in southern Nigeria. The **Oil Rivers Protectorate** was administered by the British Royal Niger Company from 1885 to 1893.

oil sand *n.* A stratum of sand or sandstone containing petroleum.

oil-seed rape (oil′sēd′) *n.* See **rape²**.

oil shale *n.* A black or dark brown shale containing hydrocarbons that yield petroleum by distillation.

oil·skin (oil′skĭn′) *n.* **1.** Cloth treated with oil to make it waterproof. **2.** A garment made of oilskin.

oil slick *n.* A layer of oil floating on the surface of water.

oil·stone (oil′stōn′) *n.* A fine-grained whetstone lubricated with oil, used for fine sharpening.

oil well *n.* A hole drilled or dug in the earth from which petroleum flows or is pumped. Also called *oiler.*

oil·y (oi′lē) *adj.* **-i·er, -i·est. 1.** Of or relating to oil. **2.** Impregnated, smeared with, or containing oil; greasy. **3.** Excessively suave in action or behavior; unctuous. See Synonyms at **unctuous.** **—oil′i·ly** *adv.* **—oil′i·ness** *n.*

oink (oingk) *n.* The characteristic grunting noise of a hog. [Imitative.] **—oink** *v.*

oint·ment (oint′mənt) *n.* A highly viscous or semisolid substance used on the skin as a cosmetic, an emollient, or a medicament; a salve. [Middle English *oinement,* from Old French *oignement,* from Vulgar Latin **unguimentum,* from Latin *unguentum.* See UNGUENT.]

Oise (wäz). A river rising in the Ardennes Mountains of southern Belgium and flowing about 299 km (186 mi) generally southwest to the Seine River in northern France.

O·i·ta (ō′ĭ-tä′, ō-ē′tä). A city of northeast Kyushu, Japan, east-northeast of Nagasaki. It was a castle town in the 16th century and traded extensively with the Portuguese. Population, 390,105.

OJ *abbr.* Orange juice.

O·jib·wa (ō-jĭb′wā′, -wə) also **O·jib·way** (-wā′) *n., pl.* **Ojibwa** or **-was** also **Ojibway** or **-ways. 1.a.** A Native American people originally located north of Lake Huron before moving westward in the 17th and 18th centuries into Michigan, Wisconsin, Minnesota, western Ontario, and Manitoba, with later migrations onto the northern Great Plains in North Dakota, Montana, and Saskatchewan. **b.** A member of this people. **2.** The Algonquian language of the Ojibwa. Also called *Chippewa.* [Ojibwa *ojibwe.*]

O·jos Del Sa·la·do (ō′hōz dĕl′ sə-lä′dō, ō′hôs dĕl sä-lä′thô). A peak, 6,874.3 m (22,539 ft) high, in the Andes on the border between Argentina and Chile.

OK¹ or **O.K.** or **o·kay** (ō-kā′) *Informal.—n., pl.* **OK's** or **O.K.'s** or **o·kays.** Approval; agreement: *got her supervisor's OK before taking a day off.* *—tr.v.* **OK'd, OK'ing, OK's** or **O.K.'d, O.K.'ing, O.K.'s** or **o·kayed, o·kay·ing, o·kays.** To approve of or agree to; authorize. *—interj.* Used to express approval or agreement. [Abbreviation of *oll korrect,* slang respelling of *all correct.*] **—OK** *adv. & adj.*

WORD HISTORY: Although we use this word hundreds of times a week whether things are OK or not, we have probably rarely wondered about its history. That history is in fact a brief one, the word being first recorded in 1839, though it was no doubt in circulation before then. Much scholarship has been expended on the origins of *OK,* but Allen Walker Read has conclusively proved that *OK* is based on a sort of joke. Someone pronounced the phrase *all correct* as *oll* (or *orl*) *correct,* and the same person or someone else spelled it *oll korrect,* which abbreviated gives us *OK.* This term gained wide currency by being used as a political slogan by the 1840 Democratic candidate Martin Van Buren, who was nicknamed *Old Kinderhook* because he was born in Kinderhook, New York. An editorial of the same year, referring to the receipt of a pin with the slogan *O.K.,* had this comment: "frightful letters . . . significant of the birth-place of Martin Van Buren, old Kinderhook, as also the rallying word of the Democracy of the late election, 'all correct' . . . Those who wear them should bear in mind that it will require their most strenuous exertions . . . to make all things O.K."

OK² *abbr.* Oklahoma.

O·ka (ō-kä′). **1.** A river, about 1,488 km (925 mi) long, of western Russia flowing north, east, and northeast to join the Volga River near Gorky. **2.** A river rising in the Sayan Mountains of south-central Russia and flowing about 965 km (600 mi) generally north to the Angara River.

O·ka·nog·an (ō′kə-nŏg′ən). Also in Canada **O·ka·na·gan** (ō′kə-nŏg′ən). A river, about 483 km (300 mi) long, flowing southward from **Lake Okanagan** in southern British Columbia, Canada, to the Columbia River in north-central Washington.

o·ka·pi (ō-kä′pē) *n., pl.* **okapi** or **-pis.** A ruminant forest mammal *(Okapia johnstoni)* of the Congo River basin in Africa, related to the giraffe but smaller and having a short neck, reddish-brown body, creamy white cheeks, and whitish stripes and bands on the legs. [Perhaps of Mbuba origin.]

O·ka·van·go (ō′kə-văng′gō). A river of southwest-central Africa flowing about 1,609 km (1,000 mi) from central Angola to the **Okavango Basin** or **Okavango Swamp,** a marshy region of northern Botswana.

o·kay (ō-kā′) *n., v., & interj.* Variant of **OK¹**.

O·ka·ya·ma (ō′kä-yä′mä). A city of western Honshu, Japan, on an inlet of the Inland Sea west of Kobe. It is an industrial center and a railroad hub. Population, 572,423.

O·ka·za·ki (ō-kä′zä-kē, ō′kə-zä′kē). A city of southern Honshu, Japan, southeast of Nagoya. Population, 284,996.

O·kee·cho·bee (ō′kĭ-chō′bē), **Lake.** A lake of southeast Florida north of the Everglades. It is a link in the **Okeechobee Waterway,** or **Cross-Florida Waterway,** a water route from the Atlantic Ocean to the Gulf of Mexico.

O'Keeffe (ō-kēf′), **Georgia.** 1887–1986. American painter known especially for her sensuous close-up paintings of flowers.

O·ke·fe·no·kee Swamp (ō′kə-fə-nō′kē). A large swampy area of southeast Georgia and northeast Florida.

O'Kel·ly (ō-kĕl′ē), **Seán Thomas.** 1883–1966. Irish political leader. A founder of Sinn Fein, he later served as president of Ireland (1945–1959).

O·khotsk (ō-kŏtsk′, ə-KHôtsk′), **Sea of.** An arm of the northwest Pacific Ocean west of the Kamchatka Peninsula and Kuril Islands. It is connected with the Sea of Japan by narrow straits.

O·kie (ō′kē) *n. Offensive Slang.* Used as a disparaging term for a migrant farm worker, especially one from Oklahoma during the 1930's. [OK(LAHOMA) + -IE.]

O·ki·na·wa (ō′kĭ-nä′wə, -nou′-). An island group of the central Ryukyu Islands in the western Pacific Ocean southwest of Japan. In World War II **Okinawa,** the largest island in the group, was the scene of fierce combat between the Japanese and U.S. Army and Marine forces (April 1–June 21, 1945). The islands were returned to the Japanese in 1972.

O·kla·ho·ma (ō′klə-hō′mə). *Abbr.* **OK, Okla.** A state of the south-central United States. It was admitted as the 46th state in 1907. First explored by the Spanish, it was opened to settlement in 1889. The western part was organized in 1890 as the Oklahoma Territory, which was merged with the adjoining Indian Territory to form the present state boundaries. The Dust Bowl of the 1930's forced many farmers to move west as migrant laborers. Oklahoma City is the capital and the largest city. Population, 3,025,495. **—O′kla·ho′man** *adj. & n.*

Oklahoma City. The capital and largest city of Oklahoma, in the central part of the state. It was settled during the land rush of April 1889 and became the capital in 1910. Population, 403,213.

Ok·mul·gee (ōk-mŭl′gē). A city of east-central Oklahoma south of Tulsa. Population, 16,263.

O·ko·lo·na (ō′kə-lō′nə). A community of northwest Kentucky, a suburb of Louisville. Population, 20,039.

♦**o·kra** (ō′krə) *n.* **1.** A tall tropical Asian annual plant *(Abelmoschus esculentus)* widely cultivated in warm regions for its edible, mucilaginous green pods. Also called *gumbo.* **2.** The edible pods of this plant, used in soups and as a vegetable. Also called ♦*gumbo.* **3.** See **gumbo** (sense 2). [Of West African origin; akin to Akan (Twi) *nkruma.*]

Ok·to·ber·fest (ŏk-tō′bər-fĕst′) *n.* An autumn festival that usually emphasizes merrymaking and the consumption of beer. [German : *Oktober,* October (from Latin *Octōber;* see OCTOBER) + *Fest,* festival (from Middle High German *vëst,* from Latin *fēstum,* from neuter of *fēstus,* festive; see **dhēs-** in Appendix).]

-ol¹ *suff.* An alcohol or a phenol: *glycerol.* [From (ALCOH)OL.]

-ol² *suff.* Variant of **-ole.**

O·laf II (ō′läf, ō′ləf, ōō′läf) or **O·lav II** (ō′läv). Known as Saint Olaf. 995?–1030. Patron saint and king of Norway (1016–1028). He was converted to Christianity in 1013.

Ö·land (œ′lănd′). A narrow island of southeast Sweden in the Baltic Sea. It is a summer resort with an important fishing fleet. There are numerous Stone Age monuments on the island.

O·la·the (ō-lā′thə). A city of eastern Kansas southwest of Kansas City. It has varied manufacturing industries. Population, 37,258.

O·lav II (ō′läv). See **Olaf II.**

old (ōld) *adj.* **old·er, old·est. 1.a.** Having lived or existed for a relatively long time; far advanced in years or life. **b.** Relatively advanced in age: *Pamela is our oldest child.* **2.** Made long ago; in existence for many years: *an old book.* **3.** Of or relating to a long life or to people who have had long lives: *a ripe old age.* **4.** Having or exhibiting the physical characteristics of age: *a prematurely old face.* **5.** Having or exhibiting the wisdom of age; mature: *a child who is old for his years.* **6.** Having lived or existed for a specified length of time: *She was 12 years old.* **7.a.** Belonging to a remote or former period in history; ancient: *old fossils.* **b.** Belonging to or being of an earlier time: *her old classmates.* **8.** Often **Old.** *Abbr.* **O, o.** Being the earlier or earliest of two or more related objects, stages, versions, or periods. **9.** *Geology.* **a.** Having become slower in flow and less vigorous in action. Used of a river. **b.** Having become simpler in form and of lower relief. Used of a landform. **10.** Exhibiting the effects of time or long use; worn: *an old coat.* **11.** Known through long acquaintance; long familiar: *an old friend.* **12.** Skilled or able through long experience; practiced. **13.** Often **ol′** (ōl). **a.** Used as an intensive: *Come back any old time. Don't give me any ol' excuse.* **b.** Used to express affection or familiarity: *Good ol' Sam.* **—old** *n.* **1.** An individual of a specified age: *a five-year-old.* See Usage Note at **elder[1]**. **2.** Old people considered as a group. Used with *the*: *caring for the old.* **3.** Former times; yore: *in days of old.* [Middle English, from Old English *eald.* See **al-[2]** in Appendix.] **—old′ness** *n.*

SYNONYMS: *old, ancient, archaic, antediluvian, obsolete, antique, antiquated.* These adjectives describe what belongs to or dates from an earlier time or period. *Old* is the most general term: *old lace; an old saying; old colleagues; an old Dutch painting. Ancient* pertains to the distant past: *"the hills,/Rock-ribbed, and ancient as the sun"* (William Cullen Bryant). *Archaic* implies a very remote, often primitive period: *an archaic Greek bronze of the seventh century* B.C. *He was convicted under an archaic statute that had never been repealed. Antediluvian* applies to what is so old and outdated that it seems to belong to the period preceding the biblical Flood: *lived in a ramshackle, antediluvian tenement; "a branch of one of your antediluvian families"* (William Congreve). *Obsolete* indicates the fact of having fallen into disuse: *an obsolete custom; obsolete methods of research. "Either man is obsolete or war is"* (R. Buckminster Fuller). *Antique* is applied both to what is very old and to what is especially appreciated or valued because of its age: *"in hat of antique shape"* (Matthew Arnold). *She collects antique French furniture and porcelains. Antiquated* describes what is out of date, no longer fashionable, or discredited: *"No idea is so antiquated that it was not once modern. No idea is so modern that it will not someday be antiquated"* (Ellen Glasgow). See also Synonyms at **elderly.**

old boy *n. Chiefly British.* A graduate of a public school for boys.

old-boy network (ōld′boi′) *n.* An informal, exclusive system of mutual assistance and friendship through which men belonging to a particular group, such as the alumni of a school, exchange favors and connections, as in politics or business: *"Working-class kids . . . had no old-boy network to turn to in times of trouble"* (Bill Barich).

Old Bulgarian *n.* See **Old Church Slavonic.**

Old Cas·tile (kăs-tēl′). A historical region of north-central Spain that combined with New Castile to the south to form the kingdom of Castile. It was united with Aragon after the marriage of Ferdinand and Isabella (1479).

Old·cas·tle (ōld′kăs′əl, -kä′səl), Sir **John.** Lord Cobham. 1377?–1417. English Lollard conspirator who was burned alive for heresy.

Old Catholic *n.* A member of an independent religious organization formed by a group of German Roman Catholics who refused to accept the doctrine of papal infallibility proclaimed by the Vatican Council in 1870.

Old Church Slavonic *n.* The language used by Cyril and Methodius in their translation of the Bible and still used as a liturgical language by several churches of Eastern Orthodoxy in Slavic countries and elsewhere. This language was used in early literary manuscripts. Also called *Church Slavonic, Old Bulgarian.*

old country *n.* The native country of an immigrant.

Old Danish *n.* The Danish language from the beginning of the 12th to the end of the 14th century.

Old Dutch *n.* The Dutch language from the beginning of the 12th to the middle of the 13th century.

old·en (ōl′dən) *adj.* Of, relating to, or belonging to time long past; old or ancient: *olden days.* [Middle English : *old,* old; see OLD + *-en,* adj. suff.; see –EN[2].]

Ol·den·burg (ōl′dən-bûrg′, -bo͝ork′). A city of northwest Germany west of Bremen. First mentioned in 1108, it was chartered in 1345. Population, 138,469.

Oldenburg, Claes Thure. Born 1929. Swedish-born American sculptor best known for his "soft sculptures" of household objects made from stuffed vinyl and canvas.

Old English *n. Abbr.* **OE, O.E. 1.** The English language from the middle of the 5th to the beginning of the 12th century. Also called *Anglo-Saxon.* **2.** *Printing.* See **black letter.**

Old English sheepdog *n.* Any of an English breed of sturdy dog, having a docked tail and a thick, shaggy, bluish-gray and white coat with fur that hangs over the eyes.

Old Faith·ful (fāth′fəl). A geyser in Yellowstone National Park in northwest Wyoming. Its eruptions, which last about 4 minutes, occur on the average of once every 65 minutes (the intervals can vary from 33 to 90 minutes). The geyser sends up a column of hot water and steam ranging from 35.4 to 53.4 m (116 to 175 ft) high.

old-fash·ioned (ōld′făsh′ənd) *adj.* **1.** Of a style or method formerly in vogue; outdated. **2.** Attached to or favoring methods, ideas, or customs of an earlier time: *old-fashioned parents.* **—old-fashioned** *n.* A cocktail made of whiskey, bitters, sugar, and fruit.

♦**old-field** (ōld′fēld′) *n. Virginia.* An overcultivated field allowed to lie fallow.

Old·field (ōld′fēld′), **Berna Eli.** Known as "Barney." 1878–1946. American automobile racer who was the first driver to break the mile-a-minute speed barrier (1903).

♦**old-field colt** *n. Virginia.* An illegitimate child. Also called ♦*catch colt,* ♦*woods colt.* [From the unsupervised breeding of horses in unfrequented fields.]

♦ ***REGIONAL NOTE:*** *Old-field colt* is one of several old-fashioned regional euphemisms for an illegitimate child. The term is native to the Virginia Piedmont, where *old-field* refers to an overcultivated field allowed to lie fallow. Being isolated and usually undisturbed, these fields provided a place for unplanned breeding of horses and, figuratively, of children. A related Southern expression is *woods colt.* The Western U.S. equivalent is *catch colt.*

Old French *n.* The French language from the 9th to the early 16th century.

Old Frisian *n.* The Frisian language until about 1575.

old girl *n. Chiefly British.* A graduate of a public school for girls.

old-girl network (ōld′-gûrl′) *n.* An informal, exclusive system of mutual assistance and friendship through which women belonging to a particular group, such as the alumnae of a school, exchange favors and connections, as in politics or business: *"Companies rely on an old-girl network whereby representatives use friends as contacts"* (New York Times).

Old Glory *n.* The flag of the United States.

old gold *n. Color.* A dark yellow, from light olive or olive brown to deep or strong yellow. **—old′-gold′** (ōld′gōld′) *adj.*

old growth *n.* Forest or woodland having a mature ecosystem characterized by the presence of old woody plants and the wildlife and smaller plants associated with them. **—old′-growth′** (ōld′grōth′) *adj.*

old guard also **Old Guard** *n.* A conservative, often reactionary element of a class, society, or political group. [Translation of French *Vieille Garde,* the imperial guard of Napoleon I.]

Old·ham (ōl′dəm). A borough of northwest England northeast of Manchester. Population, 221,800.

old hand *n.* One who is experienced; a veteran: *an old hand at international politics.*

old hat *adj.* **1.** Behind the times; old-fashioned: *Last year's styles will be old hat soon.* **2.** Overused; trite: *That prank is old hat.*

Old High German *n.* High German from the middle of the 9th to the end of the 11th century.

Old Icelandic *n.* Icelandic from the middle of the 12th to the middle of the 16th century.

old·ie (ōl′dē) *n.* Something old, especially a song that was once popular.

Old Iranian *n.* Any of the Iranian languages in use before the beginning of the Christian era.

Old Irish *n.* The Irish language from 725 to about 950.

Old Italian *n.* The Italian language until the middle of the 16th century.

Old Kingdom. Ancient Egypt during the III–VI Dynasties, from c. 2980 to 2475 B.C. The Old Kingdom was noted as "the Age of the Pyramids," with magnificent monuments built by rulers such as Cheops.

old lady *n. Slang.* **1.** One's mother. **2.a.** One's wife. **b.** One's girlfriend, especially a lover with whom one lives.

Old Latin *n.* The earliest recorded Latin, found in inscriptions from the beginning of the sixth century B.C. and in literature from the middle of the third century B.C. until the middle of the first century B.C.

old-line (ōld′līn′) *adj.* **1.** Adhering to conservative or reactionary principles: *an old-line senator.* **2.** Long established: *an old-line New England family.*

♦**old maid** *n.* **1.** *Offensive.* Used as a disparaging term for a woman, especially an older woman, who is not married. **2.** *Informal.* A person regarded as being primly fastidious. **3.** *Games.* **a.** A card game in which the player who holds a designated card at the end is the loser. **b.** The loser of this game. **4.** *Chiefly Southern U.S.* See **zinnia. —old′-maid′ish** (ōld′mā′dĭsh) *adj.*

♦**old maid flower** *n. Chiefly Southern U.S.* See **zinnia.**

old man *n.* **1.** *Slang.* One's father. **2.** *Slang.* **a.** One's husband. **b.** One's boyfriend, especially a lover with whom one lives. **3.** *Informal.* **a.** A man in authority; a boss. **b.** Often **Old Man.**

okra
Abelmoschus esculentus

Old English sheepdog

ă pat	oi boy
ā pay	ou out
âr care	o͝o took
ä father	o͞o boot
ĕ pet	ŭ cut
ē be	ûr urge
ĭ pit	th thin
ī pie	*th* this
îr pier	hw which
ŏ pot	zh vision
ō toe	ə about, item
ô paw	♦ regionalism

Stress marks: ′ (primary); ′ (secondary), as in **dictionary** (dĭk′shə-nĕr′ē)

The commanding officer, especially of a U.S. naval vessel. **4.** See **southernwood.**

old-man-and-wom·an (ōld′măn′ənd-wo͝om′ən) *n., pl.* **old-man-and-wom·ans** (-wo͝om′ənz). See **houseleek.**

old-man cactus (ōld′măn′) *n.* A treelike central Mexican cactus *(Cephalocereus senilis)* having rose-colored flowers and tufts of long, white hair on the tips of its branches.

old-man's-beard (ōld′mănz-bîrd′) *n.* **1.** Any of various plants having parts suggestive of a beard, as Spanish moss. **2.** See **fringe tree. 3.** See **virgin's bower.**

old master *n.* **1.** A distinguished European artist of the period from about 1500 to the early 1700's, especially one of the great painters of this period. **2.** A work created by one of these artists.

old money *n.* **1.** The inherited wealth of established upper-class families. **2.** A person, family, or lineage possessing inherited wealth: *married old money.*

old moon *n.* The waning moon.

♦ **Old Nick** (nĭk) *n.* The Devil; Satan. See Regional Note at **Old Scratch.**

Old Norse *n. Abbr.* **ON, O.N. 1.** The North Germanic languages until the middle of the 14th century. **2.a.** Old Icelandic. **b.** Old Norwegian.

olecranon

Old North French *n.* The dialects of Old French spoken in northern France, especially in Normandy and Picardy.

Old Northwest. See **Northwest Territory.**

Old Norwegian *n.* The Norwegian language from the middle of the 12th century to the end of the 14th century.

Old Persian *n.* An Old Iranian language attested in cuneiform inscriptions dating from the sixth to the fifth century B.C.

Old Portuguese *n.* The Portuguese language until the middle of the 16th century.

Old Provençal *n.* The Provençal language before the middle of the 16th century.

Old Prussian *n.* The Baltic language of eastern Prussia that became extinct in the 18th century.

old rose *n. Color.* A dark pink to grayish or moderate red.

Old Russian *n.* The Russian language as used in documents from the middle of the 11th to the end of the 16th century.

Old Saxon *n.* The Low German language of the continental Saxons until the 12th century.

old school *n.* A group committed to traditional ideas or practices: *a diplomat of the old school.*

old-school tie (ōld′sko͞ol′) *n.* **1.** A necktie that has the colors of a British public school. **2.** The upper-middle-class solidarity and system of mutual assistance attributed to alumni of British public schools. **3.** The narrow, clannish attitudes characteristic of the members of a clique.

♦ **Old Scratch** *n. Chiefly Southern U.S.* The Devil; Satan. [Probably alteration of *scrat,* from Middle English, hermaphrodite goblin, from Old Norse *skratte,* wizard, goblin.]

♦ ***REGIONAL NOTE:*** *Old Scratch,* like *Old Nick,* is a nickname for the devil. In the last century it was widely used in the eastern United States, especially in New England, as is evident from the Devil's name for himself in the well-known Stephen Vincent Benét short story, "The Devil and Daniel Webster." Now the term has been regionalized to the South. *Old Scratch* is attested in the *Oxford English Dictionary* from the 18th century onward in Great Britain: *"He'd have pitched me to Old Scratch"* (Anthony Trollope). The source of the name is probably the Old Norse word *skratte,* meaning "a wizard, goblin, monster, or devil."

old snow *n.* See **firn.**

Old Spanish *n.* Spanish before the middle of the 16th century.

old·squaw (ōld′skwô′) *n.* A marine duck *(Clangula hyemalis)* that is black with a white breast and is found in Arctic and North Temperate regions. Also called *long-tailed duck, oldwife.*

old·ster (ōld′stər) *n. Informal.* An elderly person.

Old Stone Age *n.* The Paleolithic Age.

old style *n.* **1.** *Printing.* A style of type originating in the 18th century and characterized by slight contrast between light and heavy strokes and slanting serifs. **2. Old Style.** *Abbr.* **O.S.** The method of reckoning dates according to the Julian calendar.

Old Swedish *n.* Swedish from the early 13th to the late 14th century.

Old Testament *n. Abbr.* **OT, O.T. 1.** *Bible.* The first of the two main divisions of the Christian Bible, corresponding to the Hebrew Scriptures. See table at **Bible. 2.** The covenant of God with Israel as distinguished in Christianity from the dispensation of Jesus constituting the New Testament.

old-time (ōld′tīm′) *adj.* Of, relating to, or characteristic of a time in the past.

old-tim·er (ōld′tī′mər) *n. Informal.* **1.a.** An elderly person. **b.** A person with considerable tenure or experience in a given place or activity; a veteran. **2.** Something very old or antiquated.

Old Turkic *n.* The language of the oldest texts of the Turkic dialects, written in a variety of scripts from the 7th to the 12th century.

Ol·du·vai Gorge (ōl′də-vī′, ôl′do͞o-). A ravine in northern Tanzania west of Mount Kilimanjaro. It contains archaeological sites rich in fossils and Paleolithic implements.

Old Welsh *n.* The Welsh language before the 12th century.

ă pat	oi boy
ā pay	ou out
âr care	o͝o took
ä father	o͞o boot
ĕ pet	ŭ cut
ē be	ûr urge
ĭ pit	th thin
ī pie	*th* this
îr pier	hw which
ŏ pot	zh vision
ō toe	ə about, item
ô paw	♦ regionalism

Stress marks: ′ (primary); ′ (secondary), as in **dictionary** (dĭk′shə-nĕr′ē)

old·wife (ōld′wīf′) *n., pl.* **-wives** (-wīvz′). **1.** See **oldsquaw. 2.** Any of various fishes such as the alewife and the menhaden.

old wives' tale (wīvz) *n.* A superstitious belief or story belonging to traditional folklore.

Old World (wûrld). The Eastern Hemisphere. The term is often used to refer specifically to Europe.

ole– *pref.* Variant of **oleo–.**

–ole or **–ol** *suff.* **1.** A usually heterocyclic chemical compound containing a five-membered ring: *pyrrole.* **2.** A chemical compound, especially an ether, that does not contain hydroxyl: *eucalyptol.* [French, from Latin *oleum,* oil. See OIL–.]

o·lé (ō-lā′) *interj.* Used to express excited approval. **—olé** *n.* A cry of "olé." [Spanish, perhaps from Arabic *wallah,* by God!, used as an expression of admiration.]

o·le·a (ō′lē-ə) *n.* A plural of **oleum.**

o·le·ag·i·nous (ō′lē-ăj′ə-nəs) *adj.* **1.** Of or relating to oil. **2.** Falsely or smugly earnest; unctuous: *oleaginous flattery.* See Synonyms at **unctuous.** [From Middle English *oliaginose* and from French *oléagineux* (from Old French), both from Latin *oleāginus,* of the olive tree, from *olea,* olive tree, alteration (influenced by *oleum,* olive oil) of *olīva.* See OLIVE.] **—o′le·ag′i·nous·ly** *adv.* **—o′le·ag′i·nous·ness** *n.*

O·le·an (ō′lē-ăn′, ō′lē-ăn′). A city of western New York on the Allegheny River near the Pennsylvania border. It produces varied manufactures. Population, 18,207.

o·le·an·der (ō′lē-ăn′dər, ō′lē-ăn′dər) *n.* A poisonous Eurasian evergreen shrub *(Nerium oleander)* having fragrant white, rose, or purple flowers, whorled leaves, and long follicles containing numerous comose seeds. Also called *rosebay.* [Medieval Latin, probably alteration of Late Latin *lorandrum,* alteration (influenced by *laurea,* laurel) of Latin *rhododendron.* See RHODODENDRON.]

o·le·as·ter (ō′lē-ăs′tər) *n.* **1.** A small Eurasian tree *(Elaeagnus angustifolia)* having oblong silvery leaves, fragrant greenish flowers, and olivelike fruit. **2.** The fruit of this tree. Also called *Russian olive, silverberry.* [Middle English, from Latin, from *olea,* olive tree. See OLEAGINOUS.]

o·le·ate (ō′lē-āt′) *n.* An ester or a salt of oleic acid.

o·lec·ra·non (ō-lĕk′rə-nŏn′) *n.* The large process on the upper end of the ulna that projects behind the elbow joint and forms the point of the elbow. [Greek *ōlekranon* : *ōlenē,* elbow; see **el-** in Appendix + *kranion,* skull, head; see **ker-**[1] in Appendix.] **—o·lec′ra·nal** (-nəl), **o′le·cra′ni·al** (ō′lĭ-krā′nē-əl), **o′le·cra′ni·an** (-nē-ən) *adj.*

o·le·fin (ō′lə-fĭn) *n.* Any of a class of unsaturated open-chain hydrocarbons such as ethylene, having the general formula C_nH_{2n}; an alkene with only one carbon-carbon double bond. [French *(gaz) oléfiant,* oil-forming (gas), ethylene : Latin *oleum,* oil; see OIL + *-fiant,* present participle of *-fier,* -fy.] **—o′le·fin′ic** *adj.*

o·le·ic (ō-lē′ĭk) *adj. Chemistry.* **1.** Of, relating to, or derived from oil. **2.** Of or relating to oleic acid.

oleic acid *n.* An oily liquid, $C_{17}H_{33}COOH$, occurring in animal and vegetable oils and used in making soap.

o·le·in (ō′lē-ĭn) also **o·le·ine** (-ĭn, -ēn′) *n.* An oily yellow liquid, $(C_{17}H_{33}COO)_3C_3H_5$, occurring naturally in most fats and oils and used as a textile lubricant.

O·lek·ma (ŏ-lĕk′mə). A river, about 1,319 km (820 mi) long, of eastern Russia flowing north to the Lena River.

O·le·nek (ŏl′ən-yôk′, ə-lə-nyôk′). A river of northeast Russia flowing about 2,172 km (1,350 mi) to the Laptev Sea.

o·le·o (ō′lē-ō′) *n., pl.* **-os.** Margarine. [Short for OLEOMARGARINE.]

oleo– or **ole–** *pref.* Oil: *oleoresin.* [French *oléo-,* from *oléine,* olein, from Latin *oleum,* oil. See OIL.]

o·le·o·graph (ō′lē-ə-grăf′) *n.* A chromolithograph printed with oil paint on canvas in imitation of an oil painting. **—o′le·og′ra·pher** (-ŏg′rə-fər) *n.* **—o′le·o·graph′ic** *adj.* **—o′le·og′ra·phy** *n.*

o·le·o·mar·ga·rine (ō′lē-ō-mär′jə-rĭn, -rēn′) *n.* Margarine.

o·le·o·res·in (ō′lē-ō-rĕz′ĭn) *n.* A naturally occurring mixture of an oil and a resin extracted from various plants, such as pine or balsam fir. **—o′le·o·res′in·ous** *adj.*

o·le·um (ō′lē-əm) *n., pl.* **o·le·a** (ō′lē-ə) or **o·le·ums.** A corrosive solution of sulfur trioxide in sulfuric acid. [Latin, olive oil. See OIL.]

O level *n. Chiefly British.* **1.** The earlier of two standardized tests in a secondary school subject. **2.** The educational background and skills required to pass this test. [O(RDINARY) LEVEL.]

ol·fac·tion (ŏl-făk′shən, ōl-) *n.* **1.** The sense of smell. **2.** The act or process of smelling. [Latin *olfactus,* past participle of *olfacere,* to smell; see OLFACTORY + –ION.]

ol·fac·tom·e·ter (ŏl′făk-tŏm′ĭ-tər, ōl′-) *n.* An apparatus for measuring the acuity of the sense of smell. [OLFACT(ION) + –METER.] **—ol·fac′to·met′ric** (-tə-mĕt′rĭk) *adj.* **—ol′fac·tom′e·try** *n.*

ol·fac·to·ry (ŏl-făk′tə-rē, -trē, ōl-) *adj.* Of, relating to, or contributing to the sense of smell. [Latin *olfactōrius,* used to sniff at, from *olfactus,* past participle of *olfacere,* to smell : *olēre,* to smell + *facere,* to do; see FACT.]

olfactory bulb *n.* The bulblike distal end of the olfactory lobe, where the olfactory nerves begin.

olfactory lobe *n.* A projection of the lower anterior portion of each cerebral hemisphere, functioning in the sense of smell.

olfactory nerve *n.* Either of the first pair of cranial nerves that conduct impulses from the mucous membranes of the nose to the olfactory bulb.

♦**ol·i·cook** (ō′lĭ-ko͝ok′, ŏl′ĭ-) *n. Hudson Valley.* See **doughnut** (sense 1). [Dutch *oliekoek* : *olie,* oil (from Middle Dutch, from Latin *oleum, olium;* see OIL) + *koeke,* cake.]

♦ ***REGIONAL NOTE:*** Originally brought to the Hudson Valley of New York by settlers from the Netherlands, a few items of Dutch vocabulary have survived there from colonial times until the present. The word *olicook,* meaning "doughnut," comes from Dutch *oliekoek*—literally, "oil cake." And the Dutch word *kill* for a small running stream is used throughout New York State. *Stoop,* "a small porch," comes from Dutch *stoep;* this word is now in general use in the Northeast and beyond.

olig– *pref.* Variant of **oligo–.**

ol·i·garch (ŏl′ĭ-gärk′, ō′lĭ-) *n.* A member of a small governing faction. [Greek *oligarkhēs* : *oligos,* few + *-arkhēs,* -arch.]

ol·i·gar·chy (ŏl′ĭ-gär′kē, ō′lĭ-) *n., pl.* **-chies. 1.a.** Government by a few, especially by a small faction of persons or families. **b.** Those making up such a government. **2.** A state governed by a few persons. **—ol′i·gar′chic, ol′i·gar′chi·cal** *adj.*

oligo– or **olig–** *pref.* Few: *oligosaccharide.* [Greek, from *oligos,* little, few.]

Ol·i·go·cene (ŏl′ĭ-gō-sēn′, ō′lĭ-) *Geology. adj.* Of, relating to, or being the geologic time and deposits of the epoch in the Tertiary Period of the Cenozoic Era that extended from the Eocene Epoch to the Miocene Epoch. See table at **geologic time.** **—Oligocene** *n.* **1.** The Oligocene Epoch. **2.** The deposits of the Oligocene Epoch.

ol·i·go·chaete or **ol·i·go·chete** (ŏl′ĭ-gō-kēt′, ō′lĭ-) *n.* Any of various annelid worms of the class Oligochaeta, including the earthworms and a few small freshwater forms. [From New Latin *Oligochaeta,* class name : OLIGO– + CHAETA.] **—ol′i·go·chae′tous** (-kē′təs) *adj.*

ol·i·go·clase (ŏl′ĭ-gō-klās′, -klāz′, ō′lĭ-) *n. Geology.* See **plagioclase.** [OLIGO– + Greek *klasis,* cleavage; see PLAGIOCLASE.]

ol·i·go·den·dro·cyte (ŏl′ĭ-gō-dĕn′drə-sīt′, ō′lĭ-) *n.* One of the cells comprising the oligodendroglia.

ol·i·go·den·drog·li·a (ŏl′ĭ-gō-dĕn-drŏg′lē-ə, ō′lĭ-) *n.* Neuroglia consisting of cells similar to but smaller than astrocytes, found in the central nervous system and associated with the formation of myelin. [OLIGO– + DENDRO– + (NEURO)GLIA.]

o·lig·o·mer (ə-lĭg′ə-mər) *n.* A polymer that consists of two, three, or four monomers. **—o·lig′o·mer′ic** (-mĕr′ĭk) *adj.* **—o·lig′o·mer′i·za′tion** *n.*

ol·i·go·nu·cle·o·tide (ŏl′ĭ-gō-no͞o′klē-ə-tīd, -nyo͞o′-, ō′lĭ-) *n.* A short polymeric chain of two to ten nucleotides.

ol·i·goph·a·gous (ŏl′ĭ-gŏf′ə-gəs, ō′lĭ-) *adj.* Feeding on a restricted range of food substances, especially a limited number of plants. Used chiefly of insects. **—ol′i·goph′a·gy** (-jē) *n.*

ol·i·gop·o·ly (ŏl′ĭ-gŏp′ə-lē, ō′lĭ-) *n., pl.* **-lies.** A market condition in which sellers are so few that the actions of any one of them will materially affect price and have a measurable impact on competitors. [OLIGO– + (MONO)POLY.] **—ol′i·gop′o·lis′tic** (-lĭs′tĭk) *adj.*

ol·i·gop·so·ny (ŏl′ĭ-gŏp′sə-nē, ō′lĭ-) *n., pl.* **-nies.** A market condition in which purchasers are so few that the actions of any one of them can materially affect price and the costs that competitors must pay. [OLIG(O)– + (MON)OPSONY.] **—ol′i·gop′so·nis′tic** (-nĭs′tĭk) *adj.*

ol·i·go·sac·cha·ride (ŏl′ĭ-gō-săk′ə-rīd′, ō′lĭ-) *n.* A carbohydrate that consists of a relatively small number of monosaccharides.

ol·i·go·tro·phic (ŏl′ĭ-gō-trō′fĭk, -trŏf′ĭk, ō′lĭ-) *adj.* Lacking in plant nutrients and having a large amount of dissolved oxygen throughout. Used of a pond or lake. **—ol′i·got′ro·phy** (-gŏt′rə-fē) *n.*

O·lin·da (ō-lĭn′də, o͞o-lēN′dä). A city of northeastern Brazil, a suburb of Recife on the Atlantic Ocean. It was founded in 1537 and held by the Dutch from 1630 to 1654. Population, 266,751.

o·lin·go (ō-lĭng′gō) *n., pl.* **-gos.** A small, nocturnal, chiefly arboreal mammal of the genus *Bassaricyon* native to Central and South America, resembling the kinkajou but having a nonprehensile tail. [American Spanish, howler monkey.]

o·li·o (ō′lē-ō′) *n., pl.* **-os. 1.** A heavily spiced stew of meat, vegetables, and chickpeas. **2.a.** A mixture or medley; a hodgepodge. **b.** A collection of various artistic or literary works or musical pieces; a miscellany. **3.** Vaudeville or musical entertainment presented between the acts of a burlesque or minstrel show. [Alteration of Spanish *olla,* pot. See OLLA.]

ol·i·va·ceous (ŏl′ə-vā′shəs) *adj. Color.* Olive-green.

ol·ive (ŏl′ĭv) *n.* **1.** A Mediterranean evergreen tree *(Olea europaea)* having fragrant white flowers, usually lance-shaped leathery leaves, and edible drupes. **2.** The small, ovoid fruit of this tree, an important food and source of oil. **3.** *Color.* A yellow green of low to medium lightness and low to moderate saturation. [Middle English, from Latin *olīva,* from Greek *elaia, elaiwā.*] **—ol′ive** *adj.*

ol·ive-backed thrush (ŏl′ĭv-băkt′) *n.* A North American thrush *(Hylocichla ustulata)* having a dark olive-brown back and common in spruce and fir forests. Also called *Swainson's thrush.*

olive branch *n.* **1.** A branch of an olive tree regarded as an emblem of peace. **2.** An offer of peace: *bore an olive branch to the new round of negotiations.*

olive drab *n. Abbr.* **o.d. 1.** *Color.* A grayish olive to dark olive brown or olive gray. **2.a.** Cloth of this color, often used in military uniforms. **b.** Also **olive drabs.** A uniform made from cloth of this color. **—ol′ive-drab′** (ŏl′ĭv-drăb′) *adj.*

olive green *n. Color.* A green-yellow hue of low to medium lightness and low to moderate saturation. **—ol′ive-green′** (ŏl′ĭv-grēn′) *adj.*

o·liv·e·nite (ō-lĭv′ə-nīt′) *n.* A mineral, $Cu_2(AsO_4)(OH)$, a basic arsenate of copper, that is brown, olive green, or gray in color and found in copper deposits. [German *Olivenit* : *Olive,* olive (from Latin *olīva;* see OLIVE) + *-it,* n. suff. (from Latin *-īta;* see –ITE[1]).]

olive oil *n.* Oil pressed from olives, used in salad dressings, for cooking, as an ingredient in soaps, and as an emollient.

Ol·i·ver (ŏl′ə-vər), **Joseph.** Known as "King Oliver." 1885?–1938. American jazz musician and composer who had a great influence on the style of Louis Armstrong.

Ol·ives (ŏl′ivz), **Mount of.** Also **Ol·i·vet** (ŏl′ə-vĕt′). A ridge of hills in the West Bank east of Jerusalem. At its western foot is the biblical site of the Garden of Gethsemane.

ol·ive·wood (ŏl′ĭv-wo͝od′) *n.* An evergreen tree *(Cassine laneana)* native to Bermuda, having oblanceolate leaves, unisexual flowers, and creamy-white fruit.

O·liv·i·er (ō-lĭv′ē-ā′), Sir **Laurence Kerr.** Baron Olivier of Brighton. 1907–1989. British actor and director best known for his interpretations of Shakespeare's Othello and Richard III.

ol·i·vine (ŏl′ə-vēn′) *n.* A mineral silicate of iron and magnesium, principally $(Mg, Fe)_2SiO_4$, found in igneous and metamorphic rocks and used as a structural material in refractories and in cements. Also called *chrysolite.* [OLIVE (from its color) + –INE[1].] **—ol′i·vin′ic** (-vĭn′ĭk), **ol′i·vi·nit′ic** (-və-nĭt′ĭk) *adj.*

♦**ol·la** (ŏl′ə, ô′yä) *n.* **1.** *South Texas.* An earthenware crock. **2.** An olla podrida. [Spanish, from Old Spanish, from Latin, variant of *aula, aulla,* pot, jar.]

♦ ***REGIONAL NOTE:*** The unglazed earthenware *olla,* a large crock or jar, was used for generations in parts of the United States where Spanish language and culture predominate, particularly in South Texas and California. The olla was usually used to store water on a patio and was wrapped in burlap to keep the water cool.

olla po·dri·da (pə-drē′də, pô-*thrē*′thä) *n., pl.* **ol·la po·dri·das** also **ol·las po·dri·das. 1.** A stew of highly seasoned meat and vegetables. **2.** An assorted mixture; a miscellany: *"All the conversations were in English . . . the whole olla podrida spiced with the latest gossip"* (William Pearson). [Spanish : *olla,* olla; see OLLA + *podrida,* feminine of *podrido,* rotten (from Latin *putridus;* see PUTRID).]

Ol·mec (ŏl′mĕk, ōl′-) *n., pl.* **Olmec** or **-mecs. 1.** An early Mesoamerican Indian civilization centered in the Veracruz region of southeast Mexico that flourished before the Maya and whose cultural influence was widespread throughout southern Mexico and Central America. **2.** A member of any of various peoples who contributed to the Olmec civilization.

Olm·sted (ōm′stĕd′, -stĭd), **Frederick Law.** 1822–1903. American landscape architect who was the chief designer of Central Park in New York City (1858–1861).

ol·o·gy (ŏl′ə-jē) *n., pl.* **-gies.** *Informal.* A branch of learning: *"amphibology, parisology, and other ologies"* (Evan Esar). [From *-ology* (as in *biology, geology,* etc.).]

O·lo·mouc (ô′lô-mōts′). A city of north-central Czechoslovakia on the Morava River northeast of Brno. Possibly founded as a Roman fortress, it was ceded to Hungary in 1478 and was the capital of Moravia until c. 1640. Population, 105,516.

Olsz·tyn (ôl′shtĭn). A city of northern Poland southeast of Gdańsk. Founded by the Teutonic Knights in 1348, it was ceded to Poland in 1466 and to Prussia in 1772. It reverted to Poland in 1945. Population, 147,100.

O·lym·pi·a[1] (ō-lĭm′pē-ə, ə-lĭm′-). A plain of southern Greece in the northwest Peleponnesus. It was a religious center devoted to the worship of Zeus and the site of the ancient Olympic games. The statue of the Olympian Zeus by Phidias was one of the Seven Wonders of the World.

O·lym·pi·a[2] (ō-lĭm′pē-ə, ə-lĭm′-). The capital of Washington, in the western part of the state on the southern end of Puget Sound. Settled in 1845, it became the territorial capital in 1853. Population, 27,447.

O·lym·pi·ad (ō-lĭm′pē-ăd′) *n.* **1.** An interval of four years between celebrations of the Olympic games, by which the ancient Greeks reckoned dates. **2.** *Sports.* A celebration of the modern Olympic games. [Back-formation from Middle English *Olympiades,* Olympiads, from Latin *Olympias, Olympiad-,* from Greek *Olumpias,* from *Olumpia,* Olympia, Greece, site of the Olympic games.]

Olympia Heights. A community of southeast Florida, a suburb of Miami. Population, 33,112.

olive
Olea europaea

Laurence Olivier
Photographed in 1958

olla
c. 1885

O·lym·pi·an (ō-lĭm′pē-ən) *adj.* **1.** *Greek Mythology.* Of or relating to the greater gods and goddesses of the ancient Greek pantheon, whose abode was Mount Olympus. **2.a.** Majestic in manner. **b.** Superior to mundane affairs. **c.** Surpassing all others in scope and effect: *Olympian efforts were mounted to keep the city from going bankrupt.* **3.** *Sports.* Of or relating to the Olympic games. **4.** Of or relating to the region of Olympia in Greece or its inhabitants. **—Olympian** *n.* **1.** *Greek Mythology.* One of the 12 major gods and goddesses inhabiting Mount Olympus. **2.** One who is superior to all others: *an intellectual Olympian.* **3.** A contestant in either the ancient or the modern Olympic games. **4.** A native or inhabitant of the region of Olympia in Greece.

Olympian games *pl.n.* See **Olympic games** (sense 2).

Olympia oyster *n.* A small oyster *(Ostrea lurida)* native to the Pacific coast of North America. [After OLYMPIA^2.]

O·lym·pic (ō-lĭm′pĭk) *adj.* *Sports.* Of or relating to the Olympic games.

Olympic games *pl.n.* **1.** *Sports.* A group of modern international athletic contests held every four years in a different city. Also called *Olympics.* **2.** A Pan-Hellenic festival in ancient Greece consisting of athletic games and contests of choral poetry and dance, first celebrated in 776 B.C. and held periodically until A.D. 393 on the plain of Olympia in honor of the Olympian Zeus. Also called *Olympian games.*

Olympic lift·ing (lĭf′tĭng) *n.* *Sports.* A weightlifting competition in which participants compete in the snatch and the clean and jerk.

Olympic Mountains. A range of the Coast Ranges on the **Olympic Peninsula** of northwest Washington. The rugged peninsula is bounded by the Pacific Ocean, the Strait of Juan de Fuca, and Puget Sound. On the western slope of the mountains is a rain forest with an annual precipitation of more than 330 cm (130 in).

O·lym·pics (ō-lĭm′pĭks) *pl.n.* *Sports.* See **Olympic games** (sense 1).

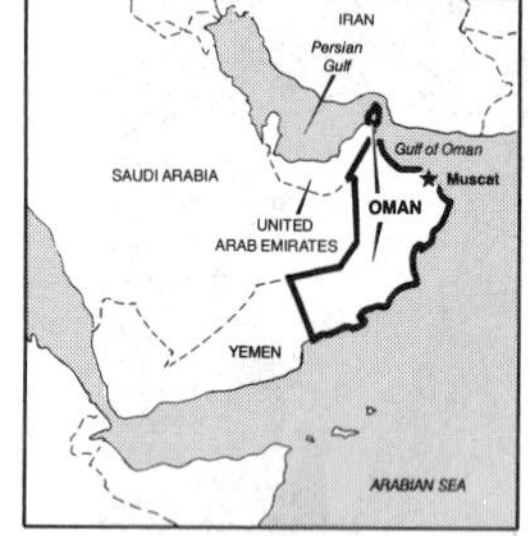

Oman

O·lym·pus (ə-lĭm′pəs, ō-lĭm′-). A mountain range of northern Greece near the Aegean coast. It rises to 2,918.9 m (9,570 ft) at **Mount Olympus,** the highest point in Greece and home of the mythical Greek gods.

O·lyn·thus (ō-lĭn′thəs). An ancient city of northeast Greece on the coast of Macedonia. As head of the Chalcidian League after the late fifth century B.C., it opposed the threats of Athens and Sparta but was captured briefly by Athens and subjugated by Sparta in 379. Philip of Macedon destroyed the city in 348.

Om^1 (ôm). A river, 724 km (450 mi) long, of south-central Russia flowing westward to the Irtysh River at Omsk.

Om^2 also **Aum** (ōm) *n.* *Hinduism & Buddhism.* The supreme and most sacred syllable, consisting in Sanskrit of the three sounds (a), (u), and (m), representing various fundamental triads and believed to be the spoken essence of the universe. It is uttered as a mantra and in affirmations and blessings. [Sanskrit *om.*]

OM. *abbr.* Ostmark.

O.M. *abbr.* Order of Merit.

–oma *suff.* Tumor: *lipoma.* [New Latin *-ōma,* from Greek *-ōma, -ōmat-,* n. suff.]

O·ma·ha^1 (ō′mə-hô′, -hä′) *n., pl.* **Omaha** or **-has. 1.a.** A Native American people inhabiting northeast Nebraska since the late 17th century. The Omaha are closely related to the Ponca in language and history. **b.** A member of this people. **2.** The Siouan language of the Omaha. [Omaha *umóNhoN.*] **—O′ma·ha** *adj.*

O·ma·ha^2 (ō′mə-hô′, -hä′). A city of eastern Nebraska on the Missouri River and the Iowa border. Founded in 1854 with the opening of the Nebraska Territory, it grew as a supply point for westward migration and was territorial capital from 1855 to 1867. Population, 313,911.

O·man (ō-män′). Formerly **Mus·cat and Oman** (mŭs′kăt′, -kət, mŭs-kăt′). A sultanate of the southeast Arabian Peninsula on the **Gulf of Oman,** an arm of the Arabian Sea. Much of the area was controlled by the Portuguese from 1508 to 1659 and the Turks until 1741. Muscat is the capital. Population, 891,000. **—O·man′i** (ō-mä′nē) *adj. & n.*

O·mar Khay·yám (ō′mär kī-yäm′, -ăm′). 1050?–1123. Persian poet, mathematician, and astronomer remembered for his collection of quatrains *The Rubáiyat of Omar Khayyám,* translated by Edward FitzGerald (1859).

o·ma·sum (ō-mā′səm) *n., pl.* **-sa** (-sə). The third division of the stomach of a ruminant animal, located between the abomasum and the reticulum. Also called *manyplies.* [Latin *omāsum,* bullock's tripe, probably of Celtic origin.]

O·may·yad (ō-mī′ăd). See **Umayyad.**

OMB *abbr.* Office of Management and Budget.

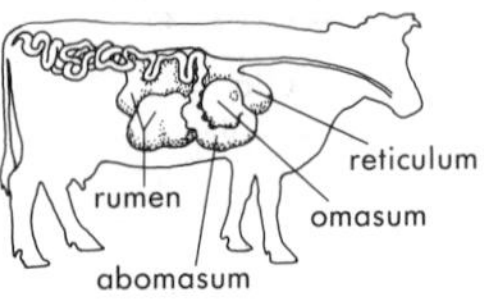

omasum

om·bre also **om·ber** (ŏm′bər) or **hom·bre** (hŏm′bər, ŏm′-) *n.* *Games.* A card game, played by three players with 40 cards, that was popular in Europe during the 17th and 18th centuries. [Spanish *hombre,* man, ombre, from Latin *homō.* See **dhghem-** in Appendix.]

om·buds·man (ŏm′bŭdz′mən, -bədz-, -bo͝odz′-) *n.* **1.** A man who investigates complaints, reports findings, and mediates fair settlements, especially between aggrieved parties such as consumers or students and an institution, an organization, or a company. **2.** A government official, especially in Scandinavian countries, who investigates citizens' complaints against the government or its functionaries. [Swedish, from Old Norse *um-*

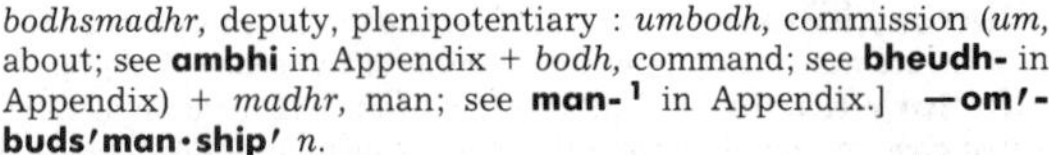
bodhsmadhr, deputy, plenipotentiary : *umbodh,* commission (*um,* about; see **ambhi** in Appendix + *bodh,* command; see **bheudh-** in Appendix) + *madhr,* man; see **man-**^{1} in Appendix.] **—om′-buds′man·ship′** *n.*

WORD HISTORY: The word *ombudsman* looks as if its constituents would be familiar, judging from the element *man,* but it is difficult to think of what *ombuds* could mean. *Ombudsman* is from Swedish, a Germanic language in the same family as English, and *man* in Swedish corresponds to our word *man. Ombud* means "commissioner, agent," coming from Old Norse *umbodh,* "charge, commission, administration by a delegacy," *umbodh* being made up of *um,* "regarding," and *bodh,* "command." In Old Norse an *umbodhsmadhr* was a "trusty manager, commissary." In Swedish an *ombudsman* was a deputy who looked after the interests and legal affairs of a group such as a trade union or business. In 1809 the office of *riksdagens justitieombudsman* was created to act as an agent of justice, that is, to see after the interests of justice in affairs between the government and its citizens. This office of ombudsman and the word *ombudsman* have been adopted elsewhere, as in individual states in the United States. The term has also been expanded in sense to include people who perform the same function for business corporations or newspapers.

om·buds·per·son (ŏm′bŭdz-pûr′sən, -bədz-, -bo͝odz-) *n.* An ombudsman or ombudswoman. [OMBUDS(MAN) + PERSON.] **—om′buds·per′son·ship′** *n.*

om·buds·wom·an (ŏm′bŭdz-wo͝om′ən, -bədz-, -bo͝odz-) *n.* A woman who investigates complaints, reports findings, and mediates fair settlements between aggrieved persons such as consumers or students and an institution, an organization, or a company. [OMBUDS(MAN) + WOMAN.] **—om′buds·wom′an·ship′** *n.*

Om·dur·man (ŏm′do͝or-män′). A city of northeast-central Sudan on the White Nile opposite Khartoum. Anglo-Egyptian troops defeated Mahdi forces near here on September 2, 1898. Population, 526,287.

–ome *suff.* Mass: *biome.* [New Latin *-ōma, -ōmat-,* from Greek, n. suff.]

o·me·ga (ō-mĕg′ə, ō-mē′gə, ō-mā′-) *n.* **1.** The 24th letter of the Greek alphabet. See table at **alphabet. 2.** The end. **3.** See **omega hyperon. 4.** See **omega meson.** [Greek *ō mega* : *ō,* the letter o + *mega,* neuter of *megas,* large, great; see **meg-** in Appendix.]

omega hyperon *n.* A subatomic particle in the baryon family having a rest mass of 3,272 times that of the electron, a unit negative electron charge, and an average lifetime of 8×10^{-11} second. Also called *omega.* See table at **subatomic particle.**

omega meson *n.* A neutral meson having a rest mass 1,532 times that of the electron and an average lifetime of 606×10^{-23} second. Also called *omega.* See table at **subatomic particle.**

om·e·let also **om·e·lette** (ŏm′ə-lĭt, ŏm′lĭt) *n.* A dish consisting of beaten eggs cooked until set and folded over, often around a filling. [French *omelette,* from Old French *amlette,* alteration of *alumette,* variant of *alumelle,* probably from *(la) lemelle,* (the) knife blade, from Latin *lāmella,* diminutive of *lāmina,* thin plate.]

o·men (ō′mən) *n.* **1.** A phenomenon supposed to portend good or evil; a prophetic sign. **2.** Prognostication; portent: *birds of ill omen.* **—omen** *tr.v.* **o·mened, o·men·ing, o·mens.** To be a prophetic sign of; portend. [Latin *ōmen.*]

o·men·tum (ō-mĕn′təm) *n., pl.* **-ta** (-tə) or **-tums.** *Anatomy.* One of the folds of the peritoneum that connect the stomach with other abdominal organs, especially: **a.** The greater omentum. **b.** The lesser omentum. [Latin *ōmentum.*] **—o·men′tal** (-təl) *adj.*

o·mer (ō′mər, ō′mĕr) *n.* *Judaism.* **1.** An ancient Hebrew unit of dry measure equal to $\frac{1}{10}$ ephah, about 3.5 liters (3.7 quarts). **2.a.** An offering of a sheaf or an omer of the first harvest of barley to a priest in the Temple on the second day of Passover. **b. Omer.** A 49-day liturgical season, originally a harvest festival, from the second day of Passover to the first day of Shavuot, during which marriages are prohibited and signs of mourning are observed, except during Passover and on Lag b'Omer. [Hebrew *'ōmer,* a measure.]

om·i·cron (ŏm′ĭ-krŏn′, ō′mĭ-) *n.* The 15th letter of the Greek alphabet. See table at **alphabet.** [Greek *o mikron* : *o,* the letter o + *mikron,* neuter of *mikros,* small.]

om·i·nous (ŏm′ə-nəs) *adj.* **1.** Menacing; threatening: *ominous black clouds; ominous rumblings of discontent.* **2.** Of or being an omen, especially an evil one. [Latin *ōminōsus,* from *ōmen, ōmin-,* omen.] **—om′i·nous·ly** *adv.* **—om′i·nous·ness** *n.*

o·mis·si·ble (ō-mĭs′ə-bəl) *adj.* Possible to omit: *an omissible passage in the text.* [From Latin *omissus,* past participle of *omittere,* to disregard. See OMIT.]

o·mis·sion (ō-mĭsh′ən) *n.* **1.** The act or an instance of omitting. **2.** The state of having been omitted. **3.** Something omitted or neglected. [Middle English, from Old French, from Late Latin *omissiō, omissiōn-,* from Latin *omissus,* past participle of *omittere,* to disregard. See OMIT.]

o·mis·sive (ō-mĭs′ĭv) *adj.* Characterized by omission or omitting: *omissive crimes; was omissive of responsibility.*

o·mit (ō-mĭt′) *tr.v.* **o·mit·ted, o·mit·ting, o·mits. 1.** To fail to include or mention; leave out: *omit a word.* **2.a.** To pass over; neglect. **b.** To desist or fail in doing; forbear. [Middle English *omitten,* from Latin *omittere* : *ob-,* against, away; see OB– + *mittere,* to send.]

O·mi·ya (ō-mē′ə, ô′mē-yä′). A city of east-central Honshu, Japan, a commercial suburb of Tokyo. Population, 373,015.

om·ma·tid·i·um (ŏm′ə-tĭd′ē-əm) *n., pl.* **-i·a** (-ē-ə). One of the structural elements, resembling a single simplified eye, that make up the compound eye of insects and other arthropods. [New Latin, diminutive of Greek *omma, ommat-,* eye. See **okʷ-** in Appendix.] **—om′ma·tid′i·al** (-ē-əl) *adj.*

om·mat·o·phore (ō-măt′ə-fôr′, -fōr′) *n.* A movable stalk ending with an eye, as found in certain snails. [Greek *omma, ommat-,* eye; see **okʷ-** in Appendix + –PHORE.] **—om′ma·toph′o·rous** (ŏm′ə-tŏf′ər-əs) *adj.*

Om·mi·ad (ō-mī′ăd). See **Umayyad.**

omni– *pref.* All: *omnidirectional.* [Latin, from *omnis,* all. See **op-** in Appendix.]

om·ni·bus (ŏm′nĭ-bŭs′, -bəs) *n.* **1.** A long motor vehicle for passengers; a bus. **2.** A printed anthology of the works of one author or of writings on related subjects. **—omnibus** *adj.* Including or covering many things or classes: *an omnibus trade bill.* [French, from Latin, for all, dative pl. of *omnis,* all. See **op-** in Appendix.]

om·ni·di·rec·tion·al (ŏm′nē-dĭ-rĕk′shə-nəl, -dī-) *adj.* Capable of transmitting or receiving signals in all directions, as an antenna.

omnidirectional radio range *n.* See **omnirange.**

om·ni·far·i·ous (ŏm′nĭ-fâr′ē-əs) *adj.* Of all kinds: *omnifarious knowledge.* [From Latin *omnifāriam,* on every side : *omni-,* omni- + *-fāriam,* adv. suff.; see **dhē-** in Appendix.] **—om′ni·far′i·ous·ly** *adv.* **—om′ni·far′i·ous·ness** *n.*

om·nip·o·tent (ŏm-nĭp′ə-tənt) *adj.* Having unlimited or universal power, authority, or force; all-powerful. See Usage Note at **infinite. —omnipotent** *n.* **1.** One having unlimited power or authority: *the bureaucratic omnipotents.* **2. Omnipotent.** God. Used with *the.* [Middle English, from Old French, from Latin *omnipotēns, omnipotent-* : *omni-,* omni- + *potēns,* present participle of *posse,* to be able; see **poti-** in Appendix.] **—om·nip′o·tence, om·nip′o·ten·cy** *n.* **—om·nip′o·tent·ly** *adv.*

om·ni·pres·ent (ŏm′nĭ-prĕz′ənt) *adj.* Present everywhere simultaneously. [Medieval Latin *omnipresēns, omnipresent-* : Latin *omni-,* omni- + Latin *praesēns,* present participle of *praeesse,* to be present; see PRESENT[1].] **—om′ni·pres′ence** *n.*

om·ni·range (ŏm′nĭ-rānj′, -nē-) *n.* A radio network that provides aircraft with complete information on bearings. Also called *omnidirectional radio range.*

om·nis·cient (ŏm-nĭsh′ənt) *adj.* Having total knowledge; knowing everything: *an omniscient deity; the omniscient narrator.* **—omniscient** *n.* **1.** One having total knowledge. **2. Omniscient.** God. Used with *the.* [Medieval Latin *omnisciēns, omniscient-* : Latin *omni-,* omni- + Latin *sciēns* (present participle of *scīre,* to know; see **skei-** in Appendix).] **—om·nis′cience, om·nis′cien·cy** *n.* **—om·nis′cient·ly** *adv.*

om·ni·um-gath·er·um (ŏm′nē-əm-găth′ər-əm) *n.* A miscellaneous collection; a hodgepodge. [Latin *omnium,* genitive pl. of *omnis,* all; see **op-** in Appendix + *gatherum* (alteration of GATHER).]

om·ni·vore (ŏm′nə-vôr′, -vōr′) *n.* **1.** An omnivorous person or animal. **2.** One that takes in everything available, as with the mind. [From New Latin *Omnivora,* omnivores, from neuter pl. of Latin *omnivorus,* omnivorous. See OMNIVOROUS.]

om·niv·o·rous (ŏm-nĭv′ər-əs) *adj.* **1.** Eating both animal and vegetable foods. **2.** Taking in everything available: *an inquiring, omnivorous mind.* [From Latin *omnivorus* : *omni-,* omni- + *-vorus,* -vorous.] **—om·niv′o·rous·ly** *adv.* **—om·niv′o·rous·ness** *n.*

Om·o·lon (ŏm′ə-lôn′). A river, about 965 km (600 mi) long, of northeast Russia flowing to the Kolyma River.

om·pha·los (ŏm′fə-lŏs′, -ləs) *n., pl.* **-li** (-lē). **1.** The navel. **2.** A central part; a focal point. [Greek. See **nobh-** in Appendix.]

Omsk (ômsk). A city of south-central Russia at the confluence of the Irtysh and Om rivers. It was founded in 1716. Population, 1,108,000.

on (ŏn, ôn) *prep.* **1.a.** Used to indicate position above and supported by or in contact with: *The vase is on the table. We rested on our hands and knees.* **b.** Used to indicate contact with or extent over (a surface) regardless of position: *a picture on the wall; a rash on my back.* **c.** Used to indicate location at or along: *the pasture on the south side of the river; a house on the highway.* **d.** Used to indicate proximity: *a town on the border.* **e.** Used to indicate attachment to or suspension from: *beads on a string.* **f.** Used to indicate figurative or abstract position: *on the young side, but experienced; on her third beer; stopped on chapter two.* **2.a.** Used to indicate actual motion toward, against, or onto: *jumped on the table; the march on Washington.* **b.** Used to indicate figurative or abstract motion toward, against, or onto: *going on six o'clock; came on the answer by accident.* **3.a.** Used to indicate occurrence at a given time: *on July third; every hour on the hour.* **b.** Used to indicate the particular occasion or circumstance: *On entering the room, she saw him.* **4.a.** Used to indicate the object affected by actual, perceptible action: *The spotlight fell on the actress. He knocked on the door.* **b.** Used to indicate the object affected by a figurative action: *Have pity on them.* **c.** Used to indicate the object of an action directed, tending, or moving against it: *an attack on the fortress.* **d.** Used to indicate the object of perception or thought: *gazed on the vista; meditated on his actions.* **5.** Used to indicate the agent or agency of a specified action: *cut his foot on the broken glass; talked on the telephone.* **6.a.** Used to indicate a medicine or other corrective taken or undertaken routinely: *went on a strict diet.* **b.** Used to indicate a substance that is the cause of an addiction, a habit, or an altered state of consciousness: *high on dope.* **7.** Used to indicate a source or basis: *"We will reach our judgments not on intentions or on promises but on deeds and on results"* (Margaret Thatcher). **8.a.** Used to indicate the state or process of: *on leave; on fire; on the way.* **b.** Used to indicate the purpose of: *travel on business.* **c.** Used to indicate a means of conveyance: *ride on a train.* **d.** Used to indicate availability by means of: *beer on tap; a physician on call.* **9.** Used to indicate belonging to: *a nurse on the hospital staff.* **10.** Used to indicate addiction or repetition: *heaped error on error.* **11.a.** Concerning; about: *a book on astronomy.* **b.** Concerning and to the disadvantage of: *We have some evidence on him.* **12.** *Informal.* In one's possession; with: *I haven't a cent on me.* **13.** At the expense of; compliments of: *drinks on the house.* **—on** *adv.* **1.** In or into a position or condition of being supported by or in contact with something: *Put the coffee on.* **2.** In or into a position of being attached to or covering something: *Put your clothes on.* **3.** In the direction of something: *He looked on while the ship docked.* **4.a.** Toward or at a point lying ahead in space or time; forward: *The play moved on to the next city.* **b.** At or to a more distant point in time or space: *I'll do it later on.* **5.** In a continuous course: *He worked on quietly.* **6.a.** In or into performance or operation: *Turn on the radio.* **b.** In progress or action; in a state of activity: *The show must go on.* **7.** In or at the present position or condition: *stay on; hang on.* **8.** In a condition of being scheduled for or decided upon: *There is a party on tonight.* **—on** *adj.* **1.** Being in operation: *The television is on.* **2.a.** Engaged in a given function or activity, such as a vocal or dramatic role: *You're on in five minutes!* **b.** Under or behaving as if under observation: *A minister is always on.* **3.** *Slang.* Functioning or performing at a high degree of competence or energy: *The goalie is really on.* **4.a.** Planned; intended: *Our calendar is open; we have nothing on for this weekend.* **b.** Happening; taking place: *The parade is on.* **—*idioms.* be on to.** *Slang.* To be aware of or have information about: *You'll never deceive us again; we're on to you.* **on and off.** Intermittently. **on and on.** Without stopping; continuously. [Middle English, from Old English *an, on.* See **an-** in Appendix.]

USAGE NOTE: To indicate motion toward a position, both *on* and *onto* can be used: *The cat jumped on the table. The cat jumped onto the table. Onto* is more specific, however, in indicating that the motion was initiated from an outside point. *He wandered onto the battlefield* means that he began his wandering at some point off the battlefield. *He wandered on the battlefield* may mean that his wandering began on the battlefield. • In constructions where *on* is an adverb attached to a verb, it should not be joined with *to* to form the single word *onto: move on to* (not *onto*) *new subjects; hold on to* (not *onto*) *our gains.* • In their uses to indicate spatial relations, *on* and *upon* are often interchangeable: *It was resting on* (or *upon*) *two supports. She took it on* (or *upon*) *herself to finish the project. We saw a finch light on* (or *upon*) *a bough.* To indicate a relation between two things, however, instead of between an action and an end point, *upon* cannot always be used: *Hand me the book on* (not *upon*) *the table. It was the only town on* (not *upon*) *the main line.* Similarly, *upon* cannot always be used in place of *on* when the relation is not spatial: *He wrote a book on* (not *upon*) *alchemy. She will be here on* (not *upon*) *Tuesday.*

ON *abbr.* **1.** Also **O.N.** Old Norse. **2.** Ontario.

–on[1] *suff.* **1.a.** Subatomic particle: *baryon.* **b.** Unit; quantum: *photon.* **2.** Basic hereditary unit: *codon.* [From ION.]

–on[2] *suff.* Inert gas: *radon.* [New Latin, from (ARG)ON.]

–on[3] *suff.* A chemical compound that is not a ketone or a compound that contains oxygen in a carbonyl group: *parathion.* [Alteration of –ONE.]

on-a·gain, off-a·gain (ŏn′ə-gĕn′ ôf′ə-gĕn′, ŏf-, ôn′-) *adj.* *Informal.* Existing or continuing sporadically; intermittent or occasional: *an on-again, off-again correspondence.*

on·a·ger (ŏn′ə-jər) *n.* **1.** A fast-running wild ass *(Equus hemionus* subsp. *onager)* of central Asia, having an erect mane and a broad black stripe along its back. **2.** An ancient and medieval stone-propelling siege engine. [Middle English, from Late Latin, from Latin, wild ass, from Greek *onagros* : *onos,* ass + *agrios,* wild; see **agro-** in Appendix.]

on-air (ŏn′âr′, ôn′-) *adj.* Spoken, occurring, or used during broadcasting or while being recorded for broadcasting: *an on-air argument; changed his on-air name.*

o·nan·ism (ō′nə-nĭz′əm) *n.* **1.** Masturbation. **2.** Coitus interruptus. [After *Onan,* son of Judah (Genesis 38:9).] **—o′nan·ist** *n.* **—o′nan·is′tic** *adj.*

O·nas·sis (ō-năs′ĭs, ō-nä′sĭs), **Aristotle.** 1906?–1975. Turkish-born Greek financier and shipping magnate.

Onassis, Jacqueline Lee Bouvier Kennedy. See Jacqueline Lee Bouvier **Kennedy.**

on·board or **on-board** (ŏn-bôrd′, -bōrd′, ôn-) *adj.* Carried aboard a vehicle or vessel. **—on·board′** *adv.*

once (wŭns) *adv.* **1.** One time only: *once a day.* **2.** At one time in the past; formerly. **3.** At any time; ever: *Once known, his face*

ă pat	oi boy
ā pay	ou out
âr care	ŏŏ took
ä father	ōō boot
ĕ pet	ŭ cut
ē be	ûr urge
ĭ pit	th thin
ī pie	*th* this
îr pier	hw which
ŏ pot	zh vision
ō toe	ə about, item
ô paw	♦ regionalism

Stress marks: **′** (primary); ′ (secondary), as in **dictionary** (dĭk′shə-nĕr′ē)

is never forgotten. **4.** By one degree of relationship: *my first cousin once removed.* **—once** *n.* A single occurrence; one time: *Once will have to do. You can go just this once.* **—once** *conj.* As soon as; if ever; when: *Once he goes, we can clean up.* **—once** *adj.* Having been formerly; former: *the once capital of the nation.* **—*idiom.* at once. 1.** All at one time; simultaneously: *Everything happened at once. The view of the skyline is at once awesome, grand, and disappointing.* **2.** Immediately; instantly: *Leave the room at once.* [Middle English *ones,* from *on,* one, from Old English *ān.* See **oi-no-** in Appendix.]

once-o•ver (wŭns′ō′vər) *n. Informal.* A quick but comprehensive survey or performance: *Let's give this memorandum the once-over.*

on•cho•cer•ci•a•sis (ŏng′kō-sər-kī′ə-sĭs) *n.* A disease caused by infestation with filarial worms of the genus *Onchocerca,* especially a disease of human beings caused by *O. volvulus* and characterized by nodular swellings on the skin and lesions of the eyes. Transmitted by black flies, the disease occurs in tropical regions of Africa and Central America. Also called *river blindness.* [New Latin : *Onchocerca,* genus name (Greek *onkos,* barb + Greek *kerkos,* tail) + –IASIS.]

Eugene O'Neill

on•co•gene (ŏn′kə-jēn, ŏng′-) *n.* A gene that causes the transformation of normal cells into cancerous tumor cells, especially a viral gene that transforms a host cell into a tumor cell. [Greek *onkos,* mass, tumor; see ONCOLOGY + GENE.]

on•co•gen•e•sis (ŏn′kō-jĕn′ĭ-sĭs, ŏng′-) *n.* The formation and development of tumors. [Greek *onkos,* mass, tumor; see **nek-**[2] in Appendix + –GENESIS.]

on•co•gen•ic (ŏn′kō-jĕn′ĭk, ŏng′-) *adj.* Tending to cause or give rise to tumors: *an oncogenic virus.* [Greek *onkos,* mass, tumor; see ONCOLOGY + –GENIC.] **—on′co•ge•nic′i•ty** (-jə-nĭs′ĭ-tē) *n.*

on•col•o•gy (ŏn-kŏl′ə-jē, ŏng-) *n.* The branch of medicine that deals with tumors, including study of their development, diagnosis, treatment, and prevention. [Greek *onkos,* mass, tumor; see **nek-**[2] in Appendix + –LOGY.] **—on′co•log′i•cal** (-kə-lŏj′ĭ-kəl), **on′co•log′ic** (-lŏj′ĭk) *adj.* **—on•col′o•gist** *n.*

on•com•ing (ŏn′kŭm′ĭng, ôn′-) *adj.* Coming nearer; approaching: *an oncoming storm.* **—oncoming** *n.* An approach; an advance.

on•cor•na•vi•rus (ŏn-kôr′nə-vī′rəs, ŏng-) *n.* Any of a group of viruses that contain single-stranded RNA and produce tumors in birds and mammals. [Greek *onkos,* mass, tumor; see ONCOLOGY + RNA + VIRUS.]

one (wŭn) *adj.* **1.** Being a single entity, unit, object, or living being; not two or more. **2.** Characterized by unity; undivided: *They spoke with one voice.* **3.a.** Of the same kind or quality: *two animals of one species.* **b.** Forming a single entity of two or more components: *three chemicals combining into one solution.* **4.** Being a single member or element of a group, category, or kind: *I'm just one player on the team.* **5.** Being a single thing in contrast with or relation to another or others of its kind: *One day is just like the next.* **6.** Occurring or existing as something indefinite, as in time or position: *He will come one day.* **7.** Occurring or existing as something particular but unspecified, as in time past: *late one evening.* **8.** *Informal.* Used as an intensive: *That is one fine dog.* **9.** Being the only individual of a specified or implied kind: *the one person I could marry; the one horse that can win this race.* **—one** *n.* **1.** The cardinal number, represented by the symbol 1, designating the first such unit in a series. **2.** A single person or thing; a unit: *This is the one I like best.* **—one** *pron.* **1.** An indefinitely specified individual: *She visited one of her cousins.* **2.** An unspecified individual; anyone: *"The older one grows the more one likes indecency"* (Virginia Woolf). **—*idioms.* at one.** In accord or unity. **one and all.** Everyone. **one by one.** Individually in succession. [Middle English *on,* from Old English *ān.* See **oi-no-** in Appendix.]

USAGE NOTE: When constructions headed by *one* appear as the subject of a sentence or relative clause, there may be a question as to whether the verb should be singular or plural. Such a construction is exemplified in the sentence *One of every ten rotors was found defective.* Although the plural *were* is sometimes used in such sentences, an earlier survey found that the singular was preferred by a large majority of the Usage Panel. • Another problem is raised by constructions such as *one of those people who* or its variants. In the sentence *The defeat turned out to be one of the most costly blows that were ever inflicted on our forces,* most grammarians would hold that the plural *were* is correct, inasmuch as the subject of the verb is the plural noun *blows.* However, constructions of this sort are often used with a singular verb even by the best writers. Note also that when the phrase containing *one* is introduced by the definite article, the verb in the relative clause must be singular: *He is the only one of the students who has* (not *have*) *already taken Latin.* See Usage Note at **he**[1].

-one *suff.* **1.** A ketone: *acetone.* **2.** A chemical compound containing oxygen, especially in a carbonyl group: *lactone.* [Perhaps from Greek *-ōnē,* feminine patronymic suff.]

one-act•er (wŭn′ăk′tər) *n.* A play consisting of only one act.

one another *pron.* Used to indicate a reciprocal relationship or reciprocal actions among the members of the set referred to by the antecedent, often with the implication that the actions are temporally ordered: *The students help one another. The waiters followed one another into the room.* See Usage Note at **each other.**

one-armed bandit (wŭn′ärmd′) *n. Games.* A slot machine for gambling operated by pulling a lever on the side.

one-base hit (wŭn′bās′) *n. Baseball.* A base hit by which a batter can reach first base safely.

one-di•men•sion•al (wŭn′dĭ-mĕn′shə-nəl, -dī-) *adj.* **1.** Having or existing in one dimension only. **2.** Lacking depth; superficial.

O•ne•ga (ō-nē′gə, ə-nyĕ′-), **Lake.** A lake of northwest Russia between Lake Ladoga and the White Sea.

Onega Bay. An arm of the White Sea in northwest Russia. It receives the **Onega River,** about 418 km (260 mi) long.

one-hand•ed (wŭn′hăn′dĭd) *adj.* **1.** Having or making use of only one hand. **2.** Calling for or brought about by the use of only one hand. **—one′-hand′ed** *adv.*

one-horse (wŭn′hôrs′) *adj.* **1.** Drawn by or using only one horse: *a one-horse carriage.* **2.** Very small or insignificant: *a one-horse town.*

O•nei•da[1] (ō-nī′də) *n., pl.* **Oneida** or **-das. 1.a.** A Native American people formerly inhabiting central New York south of Oneida Lake, with present-day populations in Wisconsin, New York, and Ontario. The Oneida are one of the original members of the Iroquois confederacy. **b.** A member of this people. **2.** The Iroquoian language of the Oneida. [Oneida *one·nyóte',* erected stone, a village name.]

O•nei•da[2] (ō-nī′də). A city of central New York east-northeast of Syracuse. The Oneida Community, a Utopian society established in 1848 by John Humphrey Noyes, was nearby. It prospered through its manufacture of silverware and was reorganized in 1881 as a joint stock company. Population, 10,810.

Oneida Lake. A lake of central New York northeast of Syracuse. It is part of the New York State Barge Canal system.

O'Neill (ō-nēl′), **Eugene Gladstone.** 1888–1953. American playwright. Among his works are *Mourning Becomes Electra* (1931) and *Long Day's Journey into Night* (produced 1956). He won the 1936 Nobel Prize for literature.

o•nei•ric (ō-nī′rĭk) *adj.* Of, relating to, or suggestive of dreams. [Greek *oneiros,* dream + –IC.]

o•nei•ro•man•cy (ō-nī′rə-măn′sē) *n.* The practice of predicting the future through interpretation of dreams. [Greek *oneiros,* dream + –MANCY.] **—o•nei′ro•man′cer** *n.*

one-lin•er (wŭn′lī′nər) *n.* A short joke or witticism, usually expressed in a single sentence.

one-man (wŭn′măn′) *adj.* **1.** Consisting of a single man: *a one-man bobsled team; built a one-man business empire.* **2.** Designed for or restricted to one person: *a one-man tent.*

one-man show *n.* **1.** An exhibition or a performance featuring the artistic work of one man. **2.** An effort or operation controlled by one person: *"The magazine has been a one-man show, with no editorial conferences and with every ultimate decision coming from our . . . secretive leader"* (Brendan Gill).

one•ness (wŭn′nĭs) *n.* **1.** The quality or state of being one; singleness: *the infinite oneness of God.* **2.** Singularity; uniqueness. **3.** The condition of being undivided; wholeness. **4.** Sameness of character: *the disagreeable oneness of roadside landscapes.* **5.** Unison; agreement: *oneness of mind and purpose.*

one-night stand (wŭn′nīt′) *n.* **1.a.** A performance by a traveling musical or dramatic performer or group in one place on one night only. **b.** The place at which such a performance is given. **2.** *Slang.* A sexual encounter that is limited to only one occasion.

one-off (wŭn′ôf′, -ŏf′) *adj. Chiefly British.* Happening, done, or made only once. **—one-off** *n.* Something that is not repeated or reproduced.

one-on-one (wŭn′ŏn-wŭn′, -ôn-) *adj.* **1.** Consisting of or being direct communication or exchange between two people: *one-on-one instruction.* **2.** *Sports.* Man-to-man. **—one′-on-one′** *adv.*

one-per•son (wŭn′pûr′sən) *adj.* **1.** Consisting of a single person. **2.** Designed for or restricted to one person.

one-piece (wŭn′pēs′) *adj.* Consisting of or fashioned in a single whole piece: *a one-piece swimsuit.*

on•er•ous (ŏn′ər-əs, ō′nər-) *adj.* **1.** Troublesome or oppressive; burdensome. See Synonyms at **burdensome. 2.** *Law.* Entailing obligations that exceed advantages. [Middle English, from Old French *onereus,* from Latin *onerōsus,* from *onus, oner-,* burden.] **—on′er•ous•ly** *adv.* **—on′er•ous•ness** *n.*

one•self (wŭn-sĕlf′) also **one's self** (wŭn sĕlf′, wŭnz sĕlf′) *pron.* **1.** One's own self: **a.** Used reflexively as the direct or indirect object of a verb or the object of a preposition: *One can congratulate oneself on one's victories.* **b.** Used in an absolute construction: *When in charge oneself, one may rearrange the committees as one pleases.* **2.** One's normal or healthy condition or state.

one-shot (wŭn′shŏt′) *adj. Informal.* **1.** Becoming effective after only one attempt: *looked for a one-shot solution to the problem.* **2.** Being the only one and unlikely to be repeated: *The funding was a one-shot deal.*

one-sid•ed (wŭn′-sī′dĭd) *adj.* **1.** Favoring one side or group; partial or biased: *a one-sided view.* **2.** Larger or more developed on one side: *a one-sided pattern.* **3.** Existing or occurring on one side only. **—one′-sid′ed•ly** *adv.* **—one′-sid′ed•ness** *n.*

one-size-fits-all (wŭn′sīz-fĭts-ôl′) *adj.* **1.** Relating to or being a garment or covering designed to accommodate a wide range of sizes. **2.** *Informal.* Appealing or answering to a wide range of tastes or needs: *a one-size-fits-all candidate.*

one-step (wŭn′stĕp′) *n.* **1.** A ballroom dance consisting of a series of unbroken rapid steps in 2/4 time. **2.** A piece of music for this dance. **—one-step** *intr.v.* **-stepped, -step·ping, -steps.** To perform this dance.

one·time (wŭn′tīm′) *adj.* Former: *a onetime boxing champion.*

one-time (wŭn′tīm′) *adj.* Only once: *a one-time winner in 1970.*

one-to-one (wŭn′tə-wŭn′) *adj.* **1.** Allowing the pairing of each member of a class uniquely with a member of another class. **2.** *Mathematics.* Relating to or being a correspondence that assigns to each member of one set a unique member of another set.

one-track (wŭn′trăk′) *adj.* Obsessively limited to a single idea or purpose: *a one-track mind.*

one-two (wŭn′to͞o′) *n.* A one-two punch.

one-two punch *n.* **1.** *Sports.* A combination of two blows delivered in rapid succession in boxing, especially a left lead followed by a right cross. **2.** *Informal.* An especially forceful or effective combination or sequence of two things.

one-up (wŭn′ŭp′) *tr.v.* **-upped, -up·ping, -ups.** *Informal.* To keep one step ahead of (a competitor or an opponent).

one-up·man·ship (wŭn-ŭp′mən-shĭp′) *n.* *Informal.* The art of outdoing or showing up a rival or competitor, as in exploits, privileges, or honors.

one-way (wŭn′wā′) *adj.* *Abbr.* **OW** **1.** Moving or permitting movement in one direction only: *a one-way street.* **2.** Providing for travel in one direction only: *a one-way ticket.*

one-wom·an (wŭn′wo͝om′ən) *adj.* Consisting of a single woman: *a one-woman bobsled team; built a one-woman business empire.*

one-woman show *n.* An exhibition or a performance featuring the artistic work of one woman.

on·go·ing (ŏn′gō′ĭng, ôn′-) *adj.* **1.** Currently taking place: *an ongoing festival.* **2.** In progress or evolving.

ONI *abbr.* Office of Naval Intelligence.

on·ion (ŭn′yən) *n.* **1.** A bulbous plant *(Allium cepa)* cultivated worldwide as a vegetable. **2.** The rounded, edible bulb of this plant, composed of fleshy, tight, concentric leaf bases having a pungent odor and taste. [Middle English *oinyon,* from Old French *oignon,* from Latin *uniō, uniōn-.*]

On·ions (ŭn′yənz), **Charles Talbut.** 1873–1965. British philologist and lexicographer who was coeditor of the *Oxford English Dictionary* from 1914 to 1933.

on·ion·skin (ŭn′yən-skĭn′) *n.* A thin, strong, translucent paper.

on·lay (ŏn′lā′, ôn′-) *n.* **1.** Something laid or applied over something else, as to add relief to a surface. **2.** *Medicine.* A graft applied to the surface of the recipient organ or structure. **3.** *Dentistry.* A cast, usually made of gold, attached to the occlusal surface of a tooth.

on-line (ŏn′līn′, ôn′-) *adj.* **1.** *Computer Science.* **a.** Under the control of a central computer, as in a manufacturing process or an experiment. **b.** Connected to a computer network. **c.** Accessible via a computer or computer network: *an on-line database.* **2.** In progress; ongoing: *on-line editorial projects.*

on·load (ŏn′lōd′, ôn′-) *v.* **-load·ed, -load·ing, -loads.** *—tr.* To load (a vehicle or container). *—intr.* To load a vehicle or container.

on·look·er (ŏn′lo͝ok′ər, ôn′-) *n.* One that looks on; a spectator.

on·ly (ōn′lē) *adj.* **1.** Alone in kind or class; sole. **2.** Standing alone by reason of superiority or excellence. **—only** *adv.* **1.** Without anyone or anything else; alone: *room for only one passenger.* **2.a.** At the very least: *If you would only come home. The story was only too true.* **b.** And nothing else or more: *I only work here.* **3.** Exclusively; solely: *facts known only to us.* **4.a.** In the last analysis or final outcome: *actions that will only make things worse.* **b.** With the final result; nevertheless: *received a raise only to be laid off.* **5.a.** As recently as: *called me only last month.* **b.** In the immediate past: *only just saw her.* **—only** *conj.* **1.** Were it not that; except. **2.a.** With the restriction that; but: *You may go, only be careful.* **b.** However; and yet: *The merchandise is well made, only we can't use it.* [Middle English, from Old English *ānlīc* : *ān,* one; see ONE + *-līc,* having the form of; see -LY[1].]

USAGE NOTE: When used as an adverb, *only* should be placed with care to avoid ambiguity. Generally this means having *only* adjoin the word or words that it limits. Variation in the placement of *only* can change the meaning of the sentence, as the following examples show: *Dictators respect only force; they are not moved by words. Dictators only respect force; they do not worship it. She picked up the receiver only when he entered, not before. She only picked up the receiver when he entered; she didn't dial the number.* Though strict grammarians insist that the rule for placement of *only* should always be followed, there are occasions when placement of *only* earlier in the sentence seems much more natural. In the following example *only* is placed according to the rule: *The committee can make its decision by Friday of next week only if it receives a copy of the latest report.* Placement of *only* earlier in the sentence, immediately after *can,* would serve the rhetorical function of warning the reader that a condition on the statement follows. See Usage Note at **not.**

on·o·mas·tic (ŏn′ə-măs′tĭk) *adj.* **1.** Of, relating to, or explaining a name or names. **2.** Of or relating to onomastics. [French *onomastique,* from Greek *onomastikos,* from *onomazein,* to name, from *onoma,* name. See **nō-men-** in Appendix.]

on·o·mas·tics (ŏn′ə-măs′tĭks) *n.* *(used with a sing. or pl. verb).* **1.a.** The study of the origins and forms of proper names. **b.** The study of the origins and forms of terms used in specialized fields. **2.** The system that underlies the formation and use of proper names or terms used in specialized fields.

on·o·mat·o·poe·ia (ŏn′ə-măt′ə-pē′ə, -mä′tə-) *n.* The formation or use of words such as *buzz* or *murmur* that imitate the sounds associated with the objects or actions they refer to. [Late Latin, from Greek *onomatopoiia,* from *onomatopoios,* coiner of names : *onoma, onomat-,* name; see **nō-men-** in Appendix + *poiein,* to make; see **k^{w}ei-[2]** in Appendix.] **—on′o·mat′o·poe′ic, on′o·mat′o·po·et′ic** (-pō-ĕt′ĭk) *adj.* **—on′o·mat′o·poe′i·cal·ly, on′o·mat′o·po·et′i·cal·ly** *adv.*

On·on·da·ga (ŏn′ən-dô′gə, -dä′-, -dā′-) *n., pl.* **Onondaga** or **-gas.** **1.a.** A Native American people formerly inhabiting the eastern Finger Lakes region of west-central New York, with present-day populations in this same area and in southeast Ontario. The Onondaga are one of the original members of the Iroquois confederacy. **b.** A member of this people. **2.** The Iroquoian language of the Onondaga. [Onondaga *onó·ntà'ke,* on the hill, a village name.] **—On′on·da′gan** *adj.*

on·rush (ŏn′rŭsh′, ôn′-) *n.* **1.** A forward rush or flow. **2.** A violent physical or verbal attack; an assault. **—on′rush′ing** *adj.*

On·sa·ger (ôn′sä′gər), **Lars.** 1903–1976. Norwegian-born American chemist. He won a 1968 Nobel Prize for the development of a system of equations in thermodynamics.

on-screen or **on·screen** (ŏn′skrēn′, ôn′-) *adj. & adv.* **1.** Within sight of the viewer of a movie or television screen. **2.** Within public view; in public.

on·set (ŏn′sĕt′, ôn′-) *n.* **1.** An onslaught; an assault. **2.** A beginning; a start: *the onset of a cold.*

on·shore (ŏn′shôr′, -shōr′, ôn′-) *adj.* **1.** Moving or directed toward the shore: *an onshore wind.* **2.** Located on the shore: *an onshore beacon; an onshore patrol.* **—onshore** *adv.* Toward the shore: *The wind shifted onshore.*

on·side (ŏn′sīd′, ôn′-) *adv. & adj.* *Sports.* In such a position as to be able to play or receive a ball or puck legally.

on-site (ŏn′sīt′, ôn′-) *adj.* Done or located at the site, as of a particular activity: *an on-site filming.* **—on′-site′** *adv.*

on·slaught (ŏn′slôt′, ôn′-) *n.* **1.** A violent attack. **2.** An overwhelming outpouring: *an onslaught of third-class mail.* [Alteration (influenced by obsolete *slaughte,* slaughter) of Dutch *aanslag,* a striking at, from Middle Dutch *aenslach* : *aen,* on; see **an-** in Appendix + *slach,* a striking.]

on-stage or **on·stage** (ŏn-stāj′, ôn-) *—adj.* Situated or taking place in the area of a stage that is visible to the audience. *—adv.* In or into the area of a stage that is visible to the audience.

on-stream (ŏn′strēm′, ôn′-) *adv. & adj.* In or into operation or production.

Ont. *abbr.* Ontario.

ont– *pref.* Variant of **onto–.**

–ont *suff.* Cell; organism: *-biont.* [From Greek *ōn, ont-,* present participle of *einai,* to be. See **es-** in Appendix.]

On·tar·i·o (ŏn-târ′ē-ō′). **1.** *Abbr.* **ON, Ont.** A province of east-central Canada. It joined the confederation in 1867. First visited by French explorers in the early 1600's, it passed to the British in 1763 and became part of the province of Quebec in 1774. It was called Upper Canada after its division from Quebec (then Lower Canada) in 1791. Reunited with Lower Canada in 1841, it became a separate province with the formation of the confederation. Toronto is the capital and the largest city. Population, 8,625,107. **2.** A city of southern California east of Los Angeles. It is a residential and industrial center. Population, 88,280.

Ontario, Lake. The smallest of the Great Lakes, between southeast Ontario, Canada, and northwest New York. The St. Lawrence Seaway and Welland Ship Canal connect with the lake to afford passage by oceangoing vessels to the other Great Lakes.

on-the-job (ŏn′thə-jŏb′, ôn′-) *adj.* Acquired or learned while working at a job: *on-the-job training.*

on-the-rec·ord (ôn′thə-rĕk′ərd, ŏn′-) *adj.* Intended for publication or attribution: *on-the-record comments by the senator.* **—on′-the-rec′ord** *adv.*

on-the-scene (ŏn′thə-sēn′, ôn′-) *adj.* Being at the site of an action or event: *an on-the-scene reporter.*

on·tic (ŏn′tĭk) *adj.* *Philosophy.* Relating to or possessing real existence.

on·to (ŏn′to͞o′, -tə, ôn′-) *prep.* **1.** On top of; to a position on; upon: *The dog jumped onto the chair.* See Usage Note at **on.** **2.** *Informal.* Fully aware of; informed about: *The police are onto the robbers' plans.* **—onto** *adj.* *Mathematics.* Of, relating to, or being a mapping such that every element of the set referred to is the image of an element in another.

onto– or **ont–** *pref.* **1.** Existence; being: *ontology.* **2.** Organism: *ontogeny.* [Late Greek, from Greek *ōn, ont-,* present participle of *einai,* to be. See **es-** in Appendix.]

onion
Allium cepa

ă pat	oi boy
ā pay	ou out
âr care	o͝o took
ä father	o͞o boot
ĕ pet	ŭ cut
ē be	ûr urge
ĭ pit	th thin
ī pie	*th* this
îr pier	hw which
ŏ pot	zh vision
ō toe	ə about, item
ô paw	♦ regionalism

Stress marks: **′** (primary); ′ (secondary), as in **dictionary** (dĭk′shə-nĕr′ē)

on·to·gen·e·sis (ŏn′tō-jĕn′ĭ-sĭs) *n., pl.* **-ses** (-sēz′). See **ontogeny.**

on·tog·e·ny (ŏn-tŏj′ə-nē) *n., pl.* **-nies.** The origin and development of an individual organism from embryo to adult. Also called *ontogenesis.* **—on′to·ge·net′ic** (ŏn′tō-jə-nĕt′ĭk) *adj.* **—on′to·ge·net′i·cal·ly** *adv.*

on·tol·o·gy (ŏn-tŏl′ə-jē) *n.* The branch of metaphysics that deals with the nature of being. **—on′to·log′i·cal** (ŏn′tə-lŏj′ĭ-kəl) *adj.* **—on′to·log′i·cal·ly** *adv.* **—on·tol′o·gist** *n.*

o·nus (ō′nəs) *n.* **1.** A difficult or disagreeable responsibility or necessity; a burden or an obligation. **2.a.** A stigma. **b.** Blame. **3.** The burden of proof: *The onus was on the defense attorney.* [Latin.]

on·ward (ŏn′wərd, ôn′-) *adj.* Moving or tending forward. **—onward** also **on·wards** (-wərdz) *adv.* In a direction or toward a position that is ahead in space or time; forward.

on·y·chol·y·sis (ŏn′ĭ-kŏl′ĭ-sĭs) *n.* The separation or loosening of a fingernail or toenail from its nail bed. [New Latin : Greek *onux, onukh-,* nail, claw; see ONYX + –LYSIS.]

on·y·choph·o·ran (ŏn′ĭ-kŏf′ər-ən) *n.* Any of numerous wormlike carnivorous animals of the phylum Onychophora, common in tropical and temperate forest regions and having characteristics of both arthropods and annelid worms. Also called *peripatus, velvet worm.* [From New Latin *Onychophora,* phylum name : Greek *onux, onukh-,* nail, claw; see ONYX + Greek *-phora,* neuter pl. of *-phoros,* -phore.] **—on′y·choph′o·ran** *adj.*

–onym *suff.* Word; name: *acronym.* [Greek *-ōnumon,* neuter of *-ōnumos,* having a specified kind of name, from *onuma,* name. See **nō-men-** in Appendix.]

–onymy *suff.* A set of names; the study of a kind of names: *toponymy.* [Greek *-ōnumia,* from *-ōnumos,* having a specified kind of name, from *onuma,* name. See **nō-men-** in Appendix.]

on·yx (ŏn′ĭks) *n.* A chalcedony that occurs in bands of different colors and is used as a gemstone, especially in cameos and intaglios. [Middle English *onix,* from Old French, from Latin *onyx,* from Greek *onux,* nail, onyx. See **nogh-** in Appendix.]

oo– *pref.* Egg; ovum: *oogenesis.* [Greek *ōio-,* from *ōion,* egg. See **awi-** in Appendix.]

o·o·cyst (ō′ə-sĭst′) *n.* A thick-walled structure in which sporozoan zygotes develop and that serves to transfer them to new hosts.

o·o·cyte (ō′ə-sīt′) *n.* A cell from which an egg or ovum develops by meiosis; a female gametocyte.

O.O.D. *abbr.* Officer of the deck.

O′o·dham (ō′ə-däm) *n., pl.* **O′odham** or **-dhams.** See **Papago.**

oo·dles (o͞od′lz) *pl.n. Informal.* A great amount or number: *oodles of fun.* [Origin unknown.]

o·o·ga·mete (ō′ə-găm′ēt′, -gə-mēt′) *n.* A female gamete, especially the larger of two gametes produced by an oogamous species.

o·og·a·mous (ō-ŏg′ə-məs) *adj.* Characterized by or having small motile male gametes and large nonmotile female gametes. **—o·og′a·my** *n.*

o·o·gen·e·sis (ō′ə-jĕn′ĭ-sĭs) *n.* The formation, development, and maturation of an ovum. **—o′o·ge·net′ic** (-jə-nĕt′ĭk) *adj.*

o·o·go·ni·um (ō′ə-gō′nē-əm) *n., pl.* **-ni·a** (-nē-ə) or **-ni·ums. 1.** A cell that arises from a primordial germ cell and differentiates into an oocyte in the ovary. **2.** A female reproductive structure in certain thallophytes, usually a rounded cell or sac containing one or more oospheres. [OO– + New Latin *gonium,* cell (from Greek *gonos,* seed; see GONO–).] **—o′o·go′ni·al** (-nē-əl) *adj.*

ooh (o͞o) *interj.* Used to express pleasure, satisfaction, surprise, or great joy. **—ooh** *intr.v.* **oohed, ooh·ing, oohs.** To exclaim in pleasure, satisfaction, surprise, or great joy: *The crowd was oohing and aahing at the panda's enclosure.* **—ooh** *n.*

o·o·lem·ma (ō′ə-lĕm′ə) *n.* See **zona pellucida.** [OO– + Greek *lemma,* husk; see LEMMA[2].]

o·o·lite (ō′ə-līt′) also **o·o·lith** (-lĭth′) *n.* **1.** A small round calcareous grain found, for example, in limestones. **2.** Rock, usually limestone, composed of oolites. **—o′o·lit′ic** (-lĭt′ĭk) *adj.*

o·ol·o·gy (ō-ŏl′ə-jē) *n.* The branch of zoology that deals with the study of eggs, especially birds' eggs. **—o′o·log′ic** (ō′ə-lŏj′ĭk), **o′o·log′i·cal** (-ĭ-kəl) *adj.* **—o′o·log′i·cal·ly** *adv.* **—o·ol′o·gist** *n.*

oo·long (o͞o′lông′, -lŏng′) *n.* A dark Chinese tea that has been partially fermented before drying. [Chinese (Mandarin) *wū lóng* : *wū,* dark, black + *lóng,* dragon.]

oo·mi·ak (o͞o′mē-ăk′) *n.* Variant of **umiak.**

oom·pah (o͞om′pä, o͞om′-) also **oom·pah-pah** (o͞om′pä-pä′) *n. Music.* A rhythmic sound made by a tuba or other brass instrument. [Imitative.]

oomph (o͞omf) *n. Slang.* **1.** Spirited vigor: *"There is not much oomph in the economy, but there is nothing seriously pushing it down"* (Murray L. Weidenbaum). **2.** Physical or sexual attractiveness. [Expressive of exertion.]

o·o·pho·rec·to·my (ō′ə-fə-rĕk′tə-mē) *n., pl.* **-mies.** See **ovariectomy.**

o·o·pho·ri·tis (ō′ə-fə-rī′tĭs) *n.* Inflammation of an ovary. Also called *ovaritis.*

Oort cloud (ôrt, ōrt) *n.* A swarm of comets orbiting the sun at a distance of one to two light-years, proposed as a source of comets that pass near the sun. [After Jan Hendrix *Oort* (born 1900), Dutch astronomer.]

o·o·sphere (ō′ə-sfîr′) *n.* A large nonmotile female gamete or egg cell, formed in an oogonium and ready for fertilization.

o·o·spore (ō′ə-spôr′, -spōr′) *n.* A fertilized female cell or zygote, especially one with thick chitinous walls, developed from a fertilized oosphere. **—o′o·spor′ic** (-spôr′ĭk, -spŏr′-), **o·os′-po·rous** (ō-ŏs′pər-əs, ō′ə-spôr′əs, -spōr′-) *adj.*

Oost·en·de (ō-stĕn′də). See **Ostend.**

o·o·the·ca (ō′ə-thē′kə) *n., pl.* **-cae** (-sē). The egg case of certain insects and mollusks. **—o′o·the′cal** *adj.*

o·o·tid (ō′ə-tĭd′) *n.* A haploid cell that results from the meiotic division of an oocyte and becomes a female gamete or an ovum. [OO– + (SPERMA)TID.]

ooze[1] (o͞oz) *v.* **oozed, ooz·ing, ooz·es.** *—intr.* **1.** To flow or leak out slowly, as through small openings. **2.** To disappear or ebb slowly: *His courage oozed away.* **3.** To progress slowly but steadily: *"Over grass bleached colorless by strong outback sun, the herd oozes forward"* (Geraldine Brooks). **4.** To exude moisture. **5.** To emit a particular essence or quality: *The house oozed with charm.* *—tr.* **1.** To give off; exude. **2.** To emit or radiate in abundance: *She oozes confidence.* **—ooze** *n.* **1.** The act of oozing. **2.** Something that oozes. **3.** An infusion of vegetable matter, as from oak bark, used in tanning. [Middle English *wosen,* from *wose,* juice, from Old English *wōs.*]

ooze[2] (o͞oz) *n.* **1.** Soft mud or slime. **2.** A layer of mudlike sediment on the floor of oceans and lakes, composed chiefly of remains of microscopic sea animals. **3.** Muddy ground. [Middle English *wose,* from Old English *wāse.*]

ooz·y[1] (o͞o′zē) *adj.* **-i·er, -i·est.** Exuding moisture. **—ooz′i·ly** *adv.* **—ooz′i·ness** *n.*

ooz·y[2] (o͞o′zē) *adj.* **-i·er, -i·est.** Of, resembling, or containing ooze: *soft, oozy ground.* **—ooz′i·ly** *adv.* **—ooz′i·ness** *n.*

OP *abbr.* **1.** Observation post. **2.** Out of print.

op. or **Op.** *abbr.* **1.** Operation. **2.** Opus.

O.P. *abbr. Roman Catholic Church.* Order of Preachers (Dominican).

o·pac·i·fi·er (ō-păs′ə-fī′ər) *n.* A chemical agent added to a material, such as rocket propellant, to make it opaque.

o·pac·i·ty (ō-păs′ĭ-tē) *n., pl.* **-ties. 1.** The quality or state of being opaque. **2.** Something opaque. **3.a.** Obscurity; impenetrability. **b.** Dullness of mind. [French *opacité,* from Old French, from Latin *opācitās,* from *opācus,* dark.]

o·pah (ō′pə) *n.* A large, oval-shaped, vividly colored marine fish *(Lampris regius)* that has edible red flesh. Also called *moonfish.* [Of West African origin; akin to Ibo *uba.*]

o·pal (ō′pəl) *n.* A translucent mineral of hydrated silica, often used as a gem. [Middle English *opalus,* from Latin, alteration of Greek *opallios,* probably from Sanskrit *upalaḥ,* from *upara-,* lower, from *upa,* below. See **upo** in Appendix.] **—o′pal·ine′** (ō′pə-līn′, -lēn′) *adj.*

o·pal·esce (ō′pə-lĕs′) *intr.v.* **-esced, -esc·ing, -lesc·es.** To exhibit an iridescent shimmer of colors. [Back-formation from OPALESCENCE.]

o·pal·es·cent (ō′pə-lĕs′ənt) *adj.* Exhibiting a milky iridescence like that of an opal. **—o′pal·es′cence** *n.*

o·paque (ō-pāk′) *adj.* **1.a.** Impenetrable by light; neither transparent nor translucent. **b.** Not reflecting light; having no luster: *an opaque finish.* **2.** Impenetrable by a form of radiant energy other than visible light: *a chemical solution opaque to x-rays.* **3.a.** So obscure as to be unintelligible: *"opaque, elusive, minimal meanings"* (John Simon). **b.** Obtuse of mind; dense. See Synonyms at **dark.** **—opaque** *n.* Something that is opaque, especially an opaque pigment used to darken parts of a photographic print or negative. [Middle English *opake,* shady, and French *opaque,* opaque (from Old French, shady), both from Latin *opācus.*] **—o·paque′ly** *adv.* **—o·paque′ness** *n.*

op art also **Op Art** (ŏp) *n.* A school of abstract art characterized by the use of geometric shapes and brilliant colors to create optical illusions, as of motion, and free the art of all but visual associations. [OP(TICAL) ART.]

op. cit. *abbr. Latin.* Opere citato (in the work cited).

OPEC (ō′pĕk′) *n.* Organization of Petroleum Exporting Countries.

op-ed page or **Op-Ed page** (ŏp′-ĕd′) *n.* A newspaper page, usually opposite the editorial page, that features articles expressing personal viewpoints. [OP(POSITE) + ED(ITORIAL).]

O·pe·li·ka (ō′pə-lī′kə). A city of eastern Alabama east-northeast of Montgomery. Population, 22,087.

Op·e·lou·sas (ŏp′ə-lo͞o′səs). A city of south-central Louisiana west-northwest of Baton Rouge. It was founded by French traders c. 1756 and served briefly as the state capital in 1862. Population, 18,903.

♦ **o·pen** (ō′pən) *adj.* **1.a.** Affording unobstructed entrance and exit; not shut or closed. **b.** Affording unobstructed passage or view: *open waters; the open countryside.* **2.a.** Having no protecting or concealing cover: *an open wound; an open sports car.* **b.** Completely obvious; blatant: *open disregard of the law.* **c.** Carried on in full view: *open warfare; open family strife.* **3.a.** Not sealed or tied: *an open package.* **b.** Spread out; unfolded: *an open book.* **4.** Having interspersed gaps, spaces, or intervals: *open ranks; an open weave.* **5.a.** Accessible to all; unrestricted as to participants: *an open competition.* **b.** Free from limitations, boundaries, or restrictions: *open registration.* **c.** Enterable by registered voters regardless of political affiliation: *an open primary.* **6.a.** Lacking effective regulation: *an open town in which gambling predominated.* **b.** Not legally repressed: *open drug trafficking.* **7.a.** Susceptible; vulnerable: *open to interpretation; an issue that is open to question.* **b.** Willing to consider or deal with: *open to suggestions.* **8.a.** Available; obtainable: *The job is still open.* **b.** Available for use: *an open account; the only course open to us.* **9.** Ready to transact business: *The store is open.* **10.** Not engaged or filled: *has an open hour for emergency cases.* **11.** Not yet decided; subject to further thought: *an open question.* **12.a.** Characterized by lack of pretense or reserve; candid: *Please be open with me.* See Synonyms at **frank**[1]. **b.** Free of prejudice; receptive to new ideas and arguments: *She listened to the proposal with an open mind.* **c.** Generous: *He is very open with his time.* **13.** *Printing.* **a.** Widely spaced or leaded. Used of typeset or other printed matter. **b.** Having constituent elements separated by a space in writing or printing: *The word* sea gull *is an open compound.* **14.** *Music.* **a.** Not stopped by a finger. Used of a string or hole of an instrument. **b.** Produced by an unstopped string or hole or without the use of slides, valves, or keys: *an open note on a trumpet.* **c.** Played without a mute: *an open wind instrument.* **15.a.** Articulated with the tongue in a low position, as the vowel in *far.* **b.** Ending in a vowel or diphthong: *an open syllable.* **16.** Designating a method of punctuation in which commas and other marks are used sparingly. **17.** Being in operation; live: *an open microphone.* **18.** *New England.* Clear. Used of weather. See Regional Note at **fair**[1]. **19.** *Electricity.* Containing a gap across which electricity cannot pass. **20.** *Mathematics.* **a.** Of or relating to an interval containing neither of its endpoints. **b.** Of, relating to, or being a set such that at least one neighborhood of every point in the set is within the set. **c.** Of, relating to, or being a set that is the complement of a closed set. **—open** *v.* **o·pened, o·pen·ing, o·pens.** —*tr.* **1.** To release from a closed or fastened position. **2.** To remove obstructions from; clear. **3.** To make or force an opening in: *open an old wound.* **4.** To form spaces or gaps between: *soldiers opening ranks.* **5.a.** To remove the cover, cork, or lid from. **b.** To remove the wrapping from; undo. **6.** To unfold so that the inner parts are displayed; spread out: *open a newspaper.* **7.a.** To get (something) going; initiate: *open a campaign.* **b.** To commence the operation of: *open a new business.* **8.** *Games.* To begin (the action in a game of cards) by making the first bid, placing the first bet, or playing the first lead. **9.** To make available for use: *opened the area to commercial development.* **10.** To make more responsive or understanding. **11.** To reveal the secrets of; bare. **12.** *Law.* To recall (an order or a judgment) for a reexamination of its merits. —*intr.* **1.** To become open: *The door opened slowly.* **2.** To draw apart; separate: *The wound opened under pressure.* **3.** To spread apart; unfold. **4.** To come into view; become revealed: *The plain opened before us.* **5.** To become receptive or understanding. **6.a.** To begin; commence: *The meeting opened with a call to order.* **b.** To begin business or operation. **7.** To give the first public performance: *The play opens next week.* **8.** *Games.* To make a bid, bet, or lead in starting a game of cards. **9.** To give access: *The room opens onto a terrace.* **—open** *n.* **1.** An unobstructed area of land or water. **2.** The outdoors: *camping in the open.* **3.** An undisguised or unconcealed state: *brought the problem out into the open.* **4.** *Sports & Games.* A tournament or contest in which both professional and amateur players may participate. ***—phrasal verb.*** **open up. 1.** To spread out; unfold: *A green valley opened up before us.* **2.a.** To begin operation: *The new store opens up next month.* **b.** To begin firing: *The artillery opened up at dawn.* **3.** *Informal.* To speak freely and candidly: *At last the frightened witness opened up and told the truth.* **4.** To make an opening in by cutting: *The surgeon opened up the patient's chest.* **5.** To make available or accessible: *open up new markets.* **6.** *Informal.* To accelerate. Used of a motor vehicle. ***—idioms.*** **open fire.** To begin firing on. **open (one's) eyes.** To become aware of the truth of a situation. [Middle English, from Old English. See **upo** in Appendix.] **—o′pen·ly** *adv.* **—o′pen·ness** *n.*

open admissions *pl.n. (used with a sing. or pl. verb).* A policy that permits enrollment of a student in a college or university without regard to academic qualifications. Also called *open enrollment.*

open adoption *n.* An arrangement in which contact between the adoptive and biological parents is allowed or maintained.

o·pen-air (ō′pən-âr′) *adj.* Outdoor: *an open-air concert.*

o·pen-and-shut (ō′pən-ən-shŭt′) *adj.* So obvious as to present no difficulties; easily determined: *an open-and-shut case.*

open chain *n.* An arrangement of atoms that does not form a ring, as in silicon compounds and various carbon compounds, such as aliphatic hydrocarbons.

open city *n.* A city that is declared demilitarized during a war, thus gaining immunity from attack under international law.

open classroom *n.* **1.** A system of elementary education in which instruction and activities are informally structured, flexible, and individualized. **2.** A school or classroom in which this system is practiced.

open door *n.* **1.** Unhindered opportunity; free access. **2.** Admission to all on equal terms. **3.** A policy whereby a nation trades with all other nations on equal terms. **—o′pen-door′** (ō′pən-dôr′, -dōr′) *adj.*

o·pen-end (ō′pən-ĕnd′) *adj.* **1.** Having no definite limit of duration or amount: *an open-end contract.* **2.** Permitting the borrowing of additional funds under existing terms: *an open-end mortgage.*

o·pen-end·ed (ō′pən-ĕn′dĭd) *adj.* **1.** Not restrained by definite limits, restrictions, or structure. **2.** Allowing for or adaptable to change. **3.** Inconclusive or indefinite: *"faintly bemused and uneasily open-ended about the whole horrible business"* (Charles Michener). **4.** Allowing for a spontaneous, unstructured response: *an open-ended question.*

open-end investment company *n.* A mutual fund.

open enrollment *n.* See **open admissions.**

o·pen·er (ō′pə-nər) *n.* **1.** One that opens, especially a device used to cut open cans or pry up bottle caps. **2.** *Games.* **a.** The player who starts the betting in cards. **b. openers.** Cards of sufficient value to enable the holder to open the betting. **3.** The first act in a theatrical variety show. **4.** *Sports.* The first game in a series. ***—idiom.*** **for openers.** *Informal.* To begin with: *"Out of 54 potential jurors, they knocked 20 off . . . just for openers"* (Joseph DiMona).

o·pen-eyed (ō′pən-īd′) *adj.* **1.** Having the eyes wide open, as in surprise. **2.** Watchful and alert.

o·pen-faced (ō′pən-fāst′) *adj.* **1.** Having a face that seems to exhibit honesty and sincerity. **2.** Having a side uncovered: *an open-faced sandwich.*

o·pen·hand·ed (ō′pən-hăn′dĭd) *adj.* Giving freely; generous. See Synonyms at **liberal.** **—o′pen·hand′ed·ly** *adv.* **—o′pen·hand′ed·ness** *n.*

o·pen·heart·ed (ō′pən-här′tĭd) *adj.* **1.** Frank. **2.** Kindly. **—o′pen·heart′ed·ly** *adv.* **—o′pen·heart′ed·ness** *n.*

o·pen-hearth (ō′pən-härth′) *adj.* **1.** Designating or being a reverberatory furnace used in the production of high-quality steel. **2.** Of or relating to the steel produced in such a furnace.

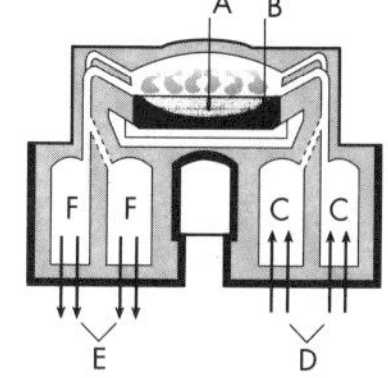

open-hearth
Open-hearth furnace
A. Molten pig iron
B. Hearth
C. Heating chamber (hot)
D. Preheated gas and air entry
E. Gas and air escape
F. Heating chamber (cold)

o·pen-heart surgery (ō′pən-härt′) *adj.* Surgery in which the thoracic cavity is opened to expose the heart and the blood is recirculated and oxygenated by a heart-lung machine.

open house *n.* **1.** A social event in which hospitality is extended to all. **2.** An occasion when a school or an institution is open for visiting and observation by the public. **3.a.** A period of time during which a house or an apartment for sale is held open for public viewing. **b.** A house or an apartment open for such viewing.

o·pen·ing (ō′pə-nĭng) *n.* **1.** The act or an instance of becoming open or being made to open. **2.** An open space serving as a passage or gap. **3.** A breach or an aperture. **4.** A clearing in the woods. **5.** The first part or stage, as of a book. **6.** The first performance: *the opening of a play.* **7.** A formal commencement of operation: *attended the opening of the new museum.* **8.** *Games.* A specific pattern or series of beginning moves in certain games, especially chess. **9.** An opportunity affording a chance of success. See Synonyms at **opportunity.** **10.** An unfilled job or position; a vacancy.

opening transaction *n.* **1.** The first transaction for a security during a trading day. **2.** An option order that establishes a new investment position or increases the size of an existing investment position.

open interval *n.* *Mathematics.* See **interval** (sense 5).

open letter *n.* A published letter on a subject of general interest, addressed to a person but intended for general readership.

open loop *n.* *Computer Science.* A control system that is not self-correcting.

open market *n.* A freely competitive market operating without restrictions.

open marriage *n.* A marriage in which the partners agree that each is free to engage in extramarital relationships.

o·pen-mind·ed (ō′pən-mīn′dĭd) *adj.* Having or showing receptiveness to new and different ideas or the opinions of others. See Synonyms at **broad-minded.** **—o′pen-mind′ed·ly** *adv.* **—o′pen-mind′ed·ness** *n.*

o·pen-mouthed (ō′pən-mouthd′, -moutht′) *adj.* **1.** Having the mouth open. **2.** Gaping in astonishment or wonder. **3.** Loudly insistent. **—o′pen-mouth′ed·ly** *adv.* **—o′pen-mouth′ed·ness** *n.*

open season *n.* **1.** The period during which it is legal to hunt or catch game or fish. **2.** *Informal.* A time of unrestrained harassment, criticism, or attack: *"By 1950 it was open season on Communists and their fellow travelers"* (Boston).

open secret *n.* Something supposedly secret but in fact generally known.

open sentence *n.* *Mathematics.* An expression that contains at least one unknown quantity and becomes true or false when a test value is substituted for the unknown.

open sesame *n.* A means of attaining a goal that has been repeatedly successful. [From the magical formula *Open Sesame* used by Ali Baba in the *Arabian Nights* to open the door of the robbers' cave.]

open shop *n.* A business or factory in which workers are employed without regard to union membership.

open stock *n.* Merchandise kept in stock so as to enable customers to replace or supplement articles, such as dishes, purchased in sets.

o·pen·work (ō′pən-wûrk′) *n.* Ornamental or structural

ă **pat**	oi **boy**
ā **pay**	ou **out**
âr **care**	o͝o **took**
ä **father**	o͞o **boot**
ĕ **pet**	ŭ **cut**
ē **be**	ûr **urge**
ĭ **pit**	th **thin**
ī **pie**	*th* **this**
îr **pier**	hw **which**
ŏ **pot**	zh **vision**
ō **toe**	ə **about, item**
ô **paw**	♦ **regionalism**

Stress marks: **′** (primary); ′ (secondary), as in **dictionary** (dĭk′shə-nĕr′ē)

work, as of embroidery or metal, containing numerous openings, usually in set patterns.

op·er·a¹ (ŏp′ər-ə, ŏp′rə) *n. Music.* **1.** A theatrical presentation in which a dramatic performance is set to music. **2.** The score of such a work. **3.** A theater designed primarily for operas. —*attributive.* Often used to modify another noun: *opera stars; an opera libretto.* [Italian, work, opera, from Latin, work, service. See **op-** in Appendix.]

o·pe·ra² (ō′pər-ə, ŏp′ər-ə) *n.* A plural of **opus.**

op·er·a·ble (ŏp′ər-ə-bəl, ŏp′rə-) *adj.* **1.** Being such that use or operation is possible: *an operable machine.* **2.** Possible to put into practice; practicable: *an operable plan.* **3.** Treatable by surgical operation with a reasonable degree of safety and chance of success: *an operable cancer.* —**op′er·a·bil′i·ty** *n.* —**op′er·a·bly** *adv.*

o·pé·ra bouffe (ŏp′ər-ə bo͞of′, ŏp′rə, ô-pā-rä bo͞o′) *n. Music.* A comic, often farcical opera. [French, from Italian *opera buffa.* See OPERA BUFFA.]

o·pe·ra buf·fa (ŏp′ər-ə bo͞o′fə, ŏp′rə, ô′pĕ-rä bo͞of′fä) *n. Music.* A comic opera of the 18th century. [Italian : *opera,* opera + *buffa,* feminine of *buffo,* comic.]

o·pé·ra co·mique (ŏp′ər-ə kŏ-mēk′, ŏp′rə, ô-pā-rä kô-mēk′) *n. Music.* See **comic opera.** [French : *opéra,* opera + *comique,* comic.]

opera glass (ŏp′ər-ə, ŏp′rə) *n.* A pair of small, low-powered binoculars for use especially at a theatrical performance. Often used in the plural.

op·er·a·go·er (ŏp′ər-ə-gō′ər, ŏp′rə-) *n.* One who frequently attends operas.

opera house *n.* A theater designed chiefly for the performance of operas.

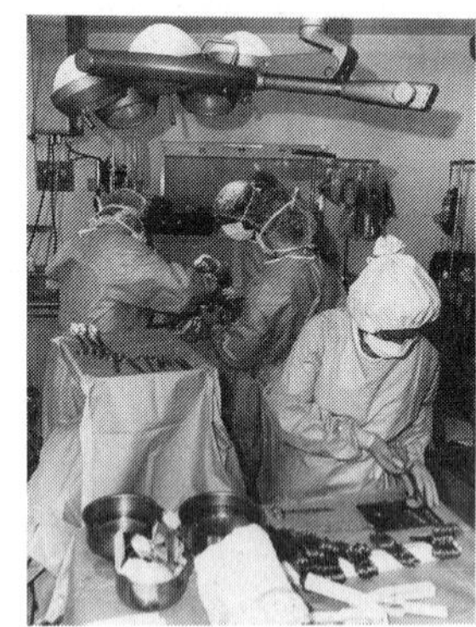

operating room

op·er·and (ŏp′ər-ənd) *n. Mathematics.* A quantity on which an operation is performed. [From Latin *operandum,* neuter gerundive of *operārī,* to operate. See OPERATE.]

op·er·ant (ŏp′ər-ənt) *adj.* **1.** Operating to produce effects; effective. **2.** *Psychology.* Of, relating to, or being a response that occurs spontaneously and is identified by its reinforcing or inhibiting effects. —**operant** *n.* **1.** One that operates. **2.** *Psychology.* An element of operant behavior. [Latin *operāns, operant-,* present participle of *operārī,* to work. See OPERATE.] —**op′er·ant·ly** *adv.*

operant conditioning *n. Psychology.* A process of behavior modification in which a subject is encouraged to behave in a desired manner through positive or negative reinforcement each time a specific behavior is exhibited, so that the subject comes to associate the pleasure or displeasure of the reinforcement with the behavior.

op·er·ate (ŏp′ə-rāt′) *v.* **-at·ed, -at·ing, -ates.** —*intr.* **1.** To perform a function; work: *The motor operates smoothly.* **2.** To perform surgery. **3. a.** To exert an influence: *forces operating on the economy.* **b.** To produce a desired or proper effect: *a drug that operates quickly.* **4.** To carry on a military or naval action or campaign. **5.** *Informal.* To conduct business in an irregular or devious manner: *drug dealers operating in residential and urban areas.* —*tr.* **1.** To control the functioning of; run: *operate a sewing machine.* **2.** To conduct the affairs of; manage: *operate a business.* [Latin *operārī, operāt-,* from *opera,* work. See **op-** in Appendix.]

op·er·at·ic (ŏp′ə-răt′ĭk) *adj. Music.* Of, related to, or typical of the opera: *an operatic aria.* [From OPERA¹.] —**op′er·at′i·cal·ly** *adv.*

op·er·at·ics (ŏp′ə-răt′ĭks) *n.* (*used with a sing. or pl. verb*). Exaggerated behavior of a type associated with grand opera; histrionics.

op·er·at·ing room (ŏp′ə-rā′tĭng) *n. Abbr.* **O.R., OR** A room equipped for performing surgical operations.

operating system *n. Computer Science.* Software designed to control the hardware of a specific data-processing system in order to allow users and application programs to employ it easily.

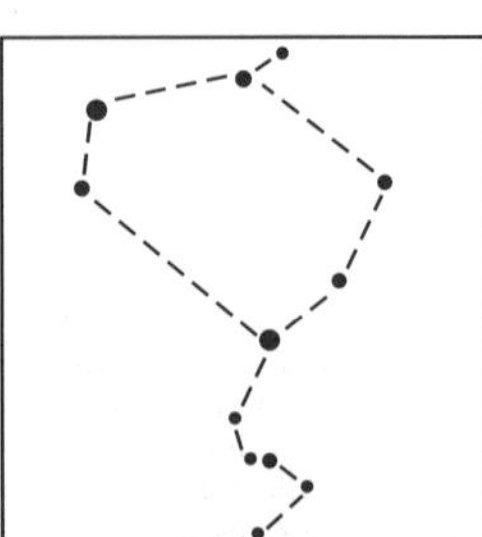

Ophiuchus

op·er·a·tion (ŏp′ə-rā′shən) *n. Abbr.* **op., Op. 1.** The act or process of operating or functioning. **2.** The state of being operative or functional: *a factory in operation.* **3.** A process or series of acts involved in a particular form of work: *the operation of building a house.* **4.** An instance or a method of efficient, productive activity: *That restaurant is quite an operation.* **5.** An unethical or illegal business: *a fencing operation for stolen goods.* **6.** *Medicine.* A surgical procedure for remedying an injury, an ailment, a defect, or a dysfunction. **7.** *Mathematics.* A process or an action, such as addition, substitution, transposition, or differentiation, performed in a specified sequence and in accordance with specific rules. **8.** *Computer Science.* An action resulting from a single instruction. **9. a.** A military or naval action, campaign, or mission. **b. operations.** The headquarters or center from which a military action, flights into and out of an airfield, or other activities are controlled. **10. operations.** The division of an organization that carries out the major planning and operating functions.

op·er·a·tion·al (ŏp′ə-rā′shə-nəl) *adj.* **1.** Of or relating to an operation or a series of operations. **2.** Of, intended for, or involved in military operations. **3.** Fit for proper functioning; ready for use: *an operational aircraft.* **4.** Being in effect or operation: *"de facto apartheid still operational even in the 'new' African nations"* (Leslie Marmon Silko). —**op′er·a′tion·al·ly** *adv.*

op·er·a·tion·al·ism (ŏp′ə-rā′shə-nə-lĭz′əm) *n. Philosophy.* The view that all theoretical terms in science must be defined only by their procedures or operations. —**op′er·a′tion·al·ist** *n.*

operation code *n. Computer Science.* **1.** The portion of a set of operation descriptions that specifies the operation to be performed. **2.** The set of operations in a computer. Also called *order code.*

op·er·a·tions research (ŏp′ə-rā′shənz) *n. Abbr.* **OR** Mathematical or scientific analysis of a process or an operation, used in making decisions.

op·er·a·tive (ŏp′ər-ə-tĭv, -ə-rā′tĭv, ŏp′rə-) *adj.* **1.** Being in effect; having force; operating: *"Two major tendencies are operative in the American political system"* (Heinz Eulau). **2.** Functioning effectively; efficient. **3.** Engaged in or concerned with physical or mechanical activity. **4.** Of, relating to, or resulting from a surgical operation. —**operative** *n.* **1.** A skilled worker, especially in industry. **2. a.** A secret agent; a spy. **b.** A private detective. —**op′er·a·tive·ly** *adv.*

op·er·a·tor (ŏp′ə-rā′tər) *n.* **1.** One who operates a machine or device: *a switchboard operator.* **2.** The owner or manager of a business or an industrial enterprise. **3.** One who deals aggressively in stocks or commodities. **4.** *Informal.* A person who is adept at accomplishing goals through shrewd or unscrupulous maneuvers. **5.** *Mathematics.* A symbol, such as a plus sign, that represents an operation. **6.** A chromosomal segment of DNA that regulates the activity of the structural genes of an operon by interacting with a specific repressor.

o·per·cu·la (ō-pûr′kyə-lə) *n. Biology.* A plural of **operculum.**

o·per·cu·late (ō-pûr′kyə-lĭt) also **o·per·cu·lat·ed** (-lā′tĭd) *adj. Biology.* Having an operculum.

o·per·cu·lum (ō-pûr′kyə-ləm) *n., pl.* **-la** (-lə) or **-lums.** *Biology.* A lid or flap covering an aperture, such as the gill cover in some fishes or the horny shell cover in snails or other mollusks. [Latin, lid, from *operīre,* to cover. See **wer-⁴** in Appendix.] —**o·per′cu·lar** (-lər) *adj.* —**o·per′cu·lar·ly** *adv.*

op·e·ret·ta (ŏp′ə-rĕt′ə) *n. Music.* A theatrical production that has many of the musical elements of opera but is lighter and more popular in subject and style and contains spoken dialogue. Also called *light opera.* [Italian, diminutive of *opera,* opera. See OPERA¹.]

op·er·on (ŏp′ə-rŏn′) *n.* A unit of gene activity consisting of a sequence of genetic material that functions in a coordinated manner by means of an operator, a promoter, and one or more structural genes. [OPER(ATOR) + –ON¹.]

op·er·ose (ŏp′ə-rōs′) *adj.* **1.** Involving great labor; laborious. **2.** Industrious. [Latin *operōsus,* from *opus, oper-,* work. See **op-** in Appendix.] —**op′er·ose′ly** *adv.* —**op′er·ose′ness** *n.*

o·phid·i·an (ō-fĭd′ē-ən) *adj.* Of, relating to, or resembling snakes. —**ophidian** *n.* A member of the suborder Ophidia or Serpentes; a snake. [From New Latin *Ophidia,* suborder name, from Greek *ophis,* snake.]

oph·i·o·lite (ŏf′ē-ə-līt′, ō′fē-) *n.* Any of a group of igneous and metamorphic rocks, rich in iron and magnesium, whose origin is associated with an early phase of the development of a geosyncline. [Greek *ophis,* snake + –LITE.]

oph·i·ol·o·gy (ŏf′ē-ŏl′ə-jē, ō′fē-) *n.* The branch of herpetology that deals with snakes. [Greek *ophis,* snake + –LOGY.] —**oph′i·o·log′i·cal** (-ə-lŏj′ĭ-kəl) *adj.* —**oph′i·ol′o·gist** *n.*

oph·i·oph·a·gous (ŏf′ē-ŏf′ə-gəs, ō′fē-) *adj.* Feeding on snakes. [From Greek *ophiophagos* : *ophis,* snake + *-phagos,* -phagous.]

oph·ite (ŏf′īt′, ō′fīt′) *n.* **1.** A mottled green rock composed of diabase. **2.** Any of various green rocks, such as serpentine. [Middle English *ophites,* from Latin *ophītēs,* from Greek *ophitēs (lithos),* serpentlike (stone), from *ophis,* serpent.]

o·phit·ic (ō-fĭt′ĭk, ō-fĭt′-) *adj.* **1.** Of or relating to ophite. **2.** Having a texture composed of lath-shaped plagioclase crystals in a matrix of pyroxene crystals.

Oph·i·u·chus (ŏf′ē-yo͞o′kəs, ō′fē-) *n.* A constellation in the equatorial region near Hercules and Scorpius. [Latin *Ophiūchus,* from Greek *ophioukhos* : *ophis,* serpent + *okhos,* holder, from *ekhein,* to hold, see **segh-** in Appendix.]

oph·i·ur·oid (ŏf′ē-yo͝or′oid, ō′fē-) *n.* See **brittle star.** [From New Latin *Ophiūroidea,* class name : *Ophiūra,* type genus (Greek *ophis,* snake + Greek *-oura,* neuter pl. of *-ouros,* tailed, from *oura,* tail; see OXYURIASIS) + Greek *-oeidēs,* -oid.]

ophthalm– *pref.* Variant of **ophthalmo–.**

oph·thal·mi·a (ŏf-thăl′mē-ə, ŏp-) *n.* Inflammation of the eye, especially of the conjunctiva. [Middle English *obtalmia,* from Old French *obtalmie* and Medieval Latin *obtalmia,* both from Late Latin *ophthalmia,* from Greek, from *ophthalmos,* eye. See OPHTHALMO–.]

oph·thal·mic (ŏf-thăl′mĭk, ŏp-) *adj.* Of or relating to the eye; ocular.

oph·thal·mi·tis (ŏf′thəl-mī′tĭs, -thăl-, ŏp′-) *n.* Inflammation of the eye.

ophthalmo– or **ophthalm–** *pref.* Eye; eyeball: *ophthalmoscope.* [Greek, from *ophthalmos,* eye. See **okʷ-** in Appendix.]

oph·thal·mol·o·gist (ŏf′thəl-mŏl′ə-jĭst, -thăl-, ŏp′-) *n.* A physician who specializes in ophthalmology.

oph·thal·mol·o·gy (ŏf′thəl-mŏl′ə-jē, -thăl-, ŏp′-) *n.* The branch of medicine that deals with the anatomy, functions, pathology, and treatment of the eye. **—oph·thal′mo·log′ic** (-thăl′mə-lŏj′ĭk), **oph·thal′mo·log′i·cal** (-ĭ-kəl) *adj.* **—oph·thal′mo·log′i·cal·ly** *adv.*

oph·thal·mo·scope (ŏf-thăl′mə-skōp′, ŏp-) *n.* An instrument for examining the interior structures of the eye, especially the retina, consisting of a mirror that reflects light into the eye and a central hole through which the eye is examined. **—oph·thal′mo·scop′ic** (-skŏp′ĭk), **oph·thal′mo·scop′i·cal** (-ĭ-kəl) *adj.* **—oph′thal·mos′co·py** (ŏf′thăl-mŏs′kə-pē, ŏp′-) *n.*

-opia *suff.* A visual condition or defect of a specified kind: *anisometropia.* [Greek *-ōpia,* from *ōps, ōp-,* eye. See PELOPS.]

o·pi·ate (ō′pē-ĭt, -āt′) *n.* **1.** Any of various sedative narcotics containing opium or one or more of its natural or synthetic derivatives. **2.** A drug, hormone, or other chemical substance having sedative or narcotic effects similar to those containing opium or its derivatives: *a natural brain opiate.* Also called *opioid.* **3.** Something that dulls the senses and induces relaxation or torpor. **—opiate** *adj.* **1.a.** Containing opium or any of its derivatives. **b.** Resembling opium or its derivatives in activity. **2.** Inducing sleep or sedation; soporific. **3.** Causing dullness or apathy; deadening. **—opiate** (-āt′) *tr.v.* **-at·ed, -at·ing, -ates. 1.** To subject to the action of an opiate. **2.** To dull or deaden as if with a narcotic drug. [Middle English, from Medieval Latin *opiātum,* from Latin *opium,* opium. See OPIUM.]

o·pine (ō-pīn′) *tr.v.* **o·pined, o·pin·ing, o·pines.** To hold or state as an opinion. [Middle English *opinen,* from Old French *opiner,* from Latin *opīnārī,* to suppose.]

o·pin·ion (ə-pĭn′yən) *n.* **1.** A belief or conclusion held with confidence but not substantiated by positive knowledge or proof: *"The world is not run by thought, nor by imagination, but by opinion"* (Elizabeth Drew). **2.** A judgment based on special knowledge and given by an expert: *a medical opinion.* **3.** A judgment or an estimation of the merit of a person or thing: *has a low opinion of braggarts.* **4.** The prevailing view: *public opinion.* **5.** *Law.* A formal statement by a court or other adjudicative body of the legal reasons and principles for the conclusions of the court. [Middle English, from Old French, from Latin *opīniō, opīniōn-.*]

SYNONYMS: *opinion, view, sentiment, feeling, belief, conviction, persuasion.* These nouns signify something a person believes or accepts as being sound or true. *Opinion* is applicable to a judgment, especially a personal judgment, based on grounds insufficient to rule out the possibility of dispute: *It is wise to seek a second medical opinion before submitting to surgery. "A little group of willful men, representing no opinion but their own, have rendered the great Government of the United States helpless and contemptible"* (Woodrow Wilson). *View* stresses individuality of outlook: *"My view is . . . that freedom of speech means that you shall not do something to people either for the views they have or the views they express"* (Hugo L. Black). *Sentiment* and especially *feeling* stress the role of emotion as a determinant: *"If men are to be precluded from offering their sentiments on a matter which may involve the most serious and alarming consequences . . . reason is of no use to us"* (George Washington). *The economist gave us her feelings on the causes of inflation.* A *belief* is a conclusion, not necessarily derived firsthand, to which one subscribes strongly: *"Our belief in any particular natural law cannot have a safer basis than our unsuccessful critical attempts to refute it"* (Karl Popper). *Conviction* is a belief that excludes doubt: *"Responsible journalism is journalism responsible in the last analysis to the editor's own conviction of what, whether interesting or only important, is in the public interest"* (Walter Lippmann). *Persuasion* applies to a confidently held opinion not necessarily based on intellectual considerations: *"He had a strong persuasion that Likeman was wrong"* (H.G. Wells).

o·pin·ion·at·ed (ə-pĭn′yə-nā′tĭd) *adj.* Holding stubbornly and often unreasonably to one's own opinions. [Probably from obsolete *opinionate* : OPINION + -ATE[1].] **—o·pin′ion·at′ed·ly** *adv.* **—o·pin′ion·at′ed·ness** *n.*

o·pin·ion·a·tive (ə-pĭn′yə-nā′tĭv) *adj.* **1.** Of, based on, or of the nature of an opinion. **2.** Opinionated. **—o·pin′ion·a′tive·ly** *adv.*

o·pi·oid (ō′pē-oid′) *n.* See **opiate** (sense 2). **—opioid** *adj.* Opiate. [OPI(UM) + -OID.]

o·pis·tho·branch (ə-pĭs′thə-brăngk′) *n., pl.* **-branchs.** Any of various marine gastropod mollusks of the subclass or order Opisthobranchia, characterized by gills, a shell that is reduced or absent, and two pairs of tentacles. [From New Latin *Opisthobranchia,* order name : Greek *opistho-* (from *opisthen,* behind; see **epi** in Appendix) + Greek *brankhia,* pl. of *brankhion,* gill.]

op·is·thog·na·thous (ŏp′ĭs-thŏg′nə-thəs) *adj.* Having receding jaws. [Greek *opistho-* (from *opisthen,* behind; see **epi** in Appendix) + -GNATHOUS.] **—op′is·thog′na·thism** *n.*

o·pi·um (ō′pē-əm) *n.* **1.** A bitter, yellowish-brown, strongly addictive narcotic drug prepared from the dried juice of unripe pods of the opium poppy and containing alkaloids such as morphine, codeine, and papaverine. **2.** Something that numbs or stupefies. [Middle English, from Latin, from Greek *opion,* diminutive of *opos,* vegetable juice.]

opium poppy *n.* An annual plant *(Papaver somniferum)* native to Turkey and adjacent areas, having grayish-green leaves and variously colored flowers.

O·po·le (ô-pô′lə). A city of southern Poland on the Oder River southeast of Wroclaw. Originally a Slavic settlement, it passed to Prussia in 1742 and was assigned to Poland by the Potsdam Conference of 1945. Population, 124,000.

O·por·to (ō-pôr′tō, ō-pōr′-) also **Por·to** or **Pôr·to** (pôr′to͞o). A city of northwest Portugal near the mouth of the Douro River north of Lisbon. Probably of pre-Roman origin, it was captured by the Moors in 716. Population, 327,368.

♦**o·pos·sum** (ə-pŏs′əm, pŏs′əm) *n., pl.* **opossum** or **-sums. 1.** Any of various nocturnal, usually arboreal marsupials of the family Didelphidae, especially *Didelphis marsupialis* of the Western Hemisphere, having a thick coat of hair, a long snout, and a long prehensile tail. See Regional Note at **possum. 2.** Any of several similar marsupials of Australia belonging to the family Phalangeridae. [Virginia Algonquian.]

WORD HISTORY: The word *opossum* takes us back to the earliest days of the United States. The settlement of Jamestown, Virginia, was founded in 1607 by the London Company, chartered for the planting of colonies. Even though the first years were difficult, promotional literature was glowing. In one such piece, *A True Declaration of the Estate of the Colonie in Virginia,* published in 1610, we find this passage: "There are . . . Apossouns, in shape like to pigges." This is the first recorded use of *opossum,* although in a spelling that differs from the one later settled on to reproduce the sound of the Virginia Algonquian word from which our word came. The word *opossum* and its shortened form *possum,* first recorded in 1613 in more promotional literature, remind us of a time when the New World was still very new, settlers were few, and the inhabitants for whom the New World was not new were plentiful.

opossum shrimp *n.* See **mysid.**

opp. *abbr.* Opposite.

Op·pen·hei·mer (ŏp′ən-hī′mər), **J(ulius) Robert.** 1902–1967. American physicist who directed the Los Alamos, New Mexico, laboratory during the development of the first atomic bomb (1942–1945).

op·po·nent (ə-pō′nənt) *n.* One that opposes another or others in a battle, contest, controversy, or debate. **—opponent** *adj.* **1.** Acting against an antagonist or opposing force: *opponent armies.* **2.** Located in front. [Latin *oppōnēns, oppōnent-,* present participle of *oppōnere,* oppose. See OPPOSE.] **—op·po′nen·cy** *n.*

SYNONYMS: *opponent, adversary, antagonist.* These nouns all mean one who offers opposition. An *opponent* opposes, resists, or combats: *"two men, one . . . a zealous supporter and the other a zealous opponent of the system pursued"* (Macaulay). *Adversary* suggests a more formidable opponent and can imply animosity: *"the Adversary of God and Man,/Satan"* (John Milton). *"And do as adversaries do in law,/Strive mightily, but eat and drink as friends"* (Shakespeare). An *antagonist* is an actively hostile opponent: *"He that wrestles with us strengthens our nerves, and sharpens our skill. Our antagonist is our helper"* (Edmund Burke). See also Synonyms at **enemy.**

op·por·tune (ŏp′ər-to͞on′, -tyo͞on′) *adj.* **1.** Suited or right for a particular purpose: *an opportune place to make camp.* **2.** Occurring at a fitting or advantageous time: *an opportune arrival.* [Middle English, from Old French *opportun,* from Latin *opportūnus,* from *ob portum (veniēns),* (coming) toward port : *ob,* to; see OB- + *portum,* accusative of *portus,* harbor; see **per-**[2] in Appendix.] **—op′por·tune′ly** *adv.* **—op′por·tune′ness** *n.*

SYNONYMS: *opportune, seasonable, timely, well-timed.* The central meaning shared by these adjectives is "occurring, coming, or done at the right, fitting, or favorable time": *waited for the opportune moment; seasonable summer storms; a timely warning; a well-timed attack.*
ANTONYM: *inopportune.*

op·por·tun·ist (ŏp′ər-to͞o′nĭst, -tyo͞o′-) *n.* One who takes advantage of any opportunity to achieve an end, often with no regard for principles or consequences. **—op′por·tun′ism** *n.*

op·por·tun·is·tic (ŏp′ər-to͞o-nĭs′tĭk, -tyo͞o-) *adj.* Taking immediate advantage, often unethically, of any circumstance of possible benefit.

opportunistic infection *n.* An infection by a microorganism that normally does not cause disease but becomes pathogenic when the body's immune system is impaired and unable to fight off infection, as in AIDS and certain other diseases.

op·por·tu·ni·ty (ŏp′ər-to͞o′nĭ-tē, -tyo͞o′-) *n., pl.* **-ties. 1.a.** A favorable or advantageous circumstance or combination of circumstances. **b.** A favorable or suitable occasion or time. **2.** A chance for progress or advancement.

SYNONYMS: *opportunity, occasion, opening, chance, break.* All these nouns refer to a favorable or advantageous circumstance or combination of circumstances. *Opportunity* is an auspicious state of affairs or a suitable time: *"He would . . . trust to time and opportunity for the gratification of his revenge"* (Frederick Marryat). *"If you prepare yourself . . . you will be able to grasp op-*

ophthalmoscope

opium poppy
Papaver somniferum

opossum

ă pat	oi boy
ā pay	ou out
âr care	o͝o took
ä father	o͞o boot
ĕ pet	ŭ cut
ē be	ûr urge
ĭ pit	th thin
ī pie	*th* this
îr pier	hw which
ŏ pot	zh vision
ō toe	ə about, item
ô paw	♦ regionalism

Stress marks: **′** (primary); ′ (secondary), as in **dictionary** (dĭk′shə-nĕr′ē)

portunity for broader experience when it appears" (Eleanor Roosevelt). *Occasion* suggests the proper time for action: *"Who would do ill ne'er wants* [lacks] *occasion"* (George Herbert). *I seized the occasion to set the record straight.* An *opening* is an opportunity affording a good possibility of success: *The lawyer waited patiently for her opening, then exposed the inconsistency in the testimony.* *Chance* often implies an opportunity that arises through luck or accident: *This is a chance for the two of you to get acquainted. Don't throw this chance away; it won't come around again.* A *break* is an often sudden piece of luck, especially good luck: *When the star was taken ill, the understudy finally got her first big break. "The best you get is an even break"* (Franklin P. Adams).

op·pos·a·ble (ə-pō′zə-bəl) *adj.* **1.** Possible to oppose or resist. **2.** That can be placed opposite something else: *The thumb is an opposable digit.* **—op·pos′a·bil′i·ty** *n.*

op·pose (ə-pōz′) *v.* **-posed, -pos·ing, -pos·es.** —*tr.* **1.** To be in contention or conflict with: *oppose the enemy force.* **2.** To be resistant to: *opposes new ideas.* **3.** To place opposite in contrast or counterbalance. **4.** To place so as to be opposite something else. —*intr.* To act or be in opposition. [Middle English *opposen,* to question, interrogate, from Old French *opposer,* alteration (influenced by *poser,* to place; see POSE[1]) of Latin *oppōnere,* to oppose (*ob-,* against; see OB– + *pōnere,* to put; see **apo-** in Appendix).] **—op·pos′er** *n.*

SYNONYMS: *oppose, fight, combat, resist, withstand, contest.* These verbs are compared as they mean to set someone or something in opposition to another, as in an effort to overcome or defeat. *Oppose* has the fewest connotations: *oppose a legislative bill; was opposed to nuclear reactors. "The idea is inconsistent with our constitutional theory and has been stubbornly opposed . . . since the early days of the Republic"* (E.B. White). *Fight* and *combat* suggest vigor and aggressiveness: *fight corruption; combating disease. "All my life I have fought against prejudice and intolerance"* (Harry S. Truman). *"We are not afraid . . . to tolerate any error so long as reason is left free to combat it"* (Thomas Jefferson). To *resist* is to strive to fend off or offset the actions, effects, or force of: *"Pardon was freely extended to all who had resisted the invasion"* (John R. Green). *"My servants . . . resisted the adoption of this plan"* (A.W. Kinglake). *Withstand* often implies successful resistance: *"Neither the southern provinces, nor Sicily, could have withstood his power"* (Henry Hallam). To *contest* is to call something into question and take an active stand against it: *I don't contest your right to dispose of your property as you see fit, but I doubt the propriety of this bequest.*

op·po·site (ŏp′ə-zĭt) *adj. Abbr.* **opp. 1.** Placed or located directly across from something else or from each other: *opposite sides of a building.* **2.** Facing the other way; moving or tending away from each other: *opposite directions.* **3.** Altogether different, as in nature, quality, or significance: *The effect of the medication was opposite to that intended.* **4.** *Botany.* Growing in pairs on either side of a stem: *opposite leaves.* **—opposite** *n.* **1.** One that is opposite or contrary to another. **2.** An opponent or antagonist. **3.** An antonym. **—opposite** *adv.* In an opposite position: *They sat opposite at the table.* **—opposite** *prep.* **1.** Across from or facing: *parked the car opposite the bank.* **2.** In a complementary dramatic role to: *He played opposite her.* [Middle English, from Old French, from Latin *oppositus,* past participle of *oppōnere,* oppose. See OPPOSE.] **—op′po·site·ly** *adv.* **—op′po·site·ness** *n.*

SYNONYMS: *opposite, contrary, antithetical, contradictory.* These adjectives mean marked by a natural or innate and irreconcilable opposition. Two things that are altogether different are *opposite*: *Antonyms are words of opposite meaning. "It is said that opposite characters make a union happiest"* (Charles Reade). *Contrary* stresses extreme divergence: *Democrats and Republicans often hold contrary opinions.* *Antithetical* emphasizes diametrical opposition: *She engaged in practices entirely antithetical to her professed beliefs.* *Contradictory* implies denial or inconsistency: *"contradictory attributes of unjust justice and loving vindictiveness"* (John Morley).

opposite number *n.* A person who holds a position in an organization or a system that corresponds to that of a person in another organization or system; a counterpart: *"had a face-to-face . . . conference with his opposite number at the American Embassy"* (Frederick Forsyth).

op·po·si·tion (ŏp′ə-zĭsh′ən) *n.* **1.a.** The act of opposing or resisting. **b.** The condition of being in conflict; antagonism: *"The history of men's opposition to women's emancipation is more interesting perhaps than the story of that emancipation itself"* (Virginia Woolf). **2.** Placement opposite to or in contrast with another. **3.** Something that serves as an obstacle. **4.** Often **Opposition.** A political party or an organized group opposed to the group, party, or government in power. **5.** *Astronomy.* **a.** The position of two celestial bodies when their longitude differs by 180°, especially a configuration in which the earth lies on a straight line between the sun and a superior planet or the moon. **b.** The position of the superior planet or the moon in this configuration. **6.** *Logic.* The relation existing between two propositions having an identical subject and predicate but differing in quantity, quality, or both. **7.** *Linguistics.* Contrast in a language between two phonemes or other linguistically important elements. **—op′po·si′tion·al** *adj.*

op·po·si·tion·ist (ŏp′ə-zĭsh′ə-nĭst) *n.* A member of an opposition. **—op′po·si′tion·ist** *adj.*

op·press (ə-prĕs′) *tr.v.* **-pressed, -press·ing, -press·es. 1.** To keep down by severe and unjust use of force or authority: *a people who were oppressed by tyranny.* **2.** To weigh heavily on: *Poverty oppresses the spirit.* **3.** *Obsolete.* To overwhelm or crush. [Middle English *oppressen,* from Old French *opresser,* back-formation from *oppression,* oppression, from Latin *oppressiō, oppressiōn-,* from *oppressus,* past participle of *opprimere* : *ob-,* against; see OB– + *premere,* to press; see **per-[4]** in Appendix.] **—op·pres′sor** *n.*

op·pres·sion (ə-prĕsh′ən) *n.* **1.a.** The act of oppressing; arbitrary and cruel exercise of power: *"There can be no really pervasive system of oppression . . . without the consent of the oppressed"* (Florynce R. Kennedy). **b.** The state of being oppressed. **2.** Something that oppresses. **3.** A feeling of being heavily weighed down in mind or body.

op·pres·sive (ə-prĕs′ĭv) *adj.* **1.** Difficult to bear; burdensome: *oppressive laws.* **2.** Exercising power arbitrarily and often unjustly; tyrannical. **3.** Weighing heavily on the senses or spirit: *oppressive weather.* See Synonyms at **burdensome. —op·pres′sive·ly** *adv.* **—op·pres′sive·ness** *n.*

op·pro·bri·ous (ə-prō′brē-əs) *adj.* **1.** Expressing contemptuous reproach; scornful or abusive: *opprobrious epithets.* **2.** Bringing disgrace; shameful or infamous: *opprobrious conduct.* **—op·pro′bri·ous·ly** *adv.*

op·pro·bri·um (ə-prō′brē-əm) *n.* **1.** Disgrace arising from exceedingly shameful conduct; ignominy. See Synonyms at **disgrace. 2.** Scornful reproach or contempt: *a term of opprobrium.* **3.** A cause of shame or disgrace. [Latin, from *opprobrāre,* to reproach : *ob-,* against; see OB– + *probum,* reproach; see **bher-[1]** in Appendix.]

op·pugn (ə-pyo͞on′) *tr.v.* **-pugned, -pugn·ing, -pugns.** To oppose, contradict, or call into question. [Middle English *oppugnen,* from Latin *oppugnāre,* to attack : *ob-,* against; see OB– + *pugnāre,* to fight with the fist; see **peuk-** in Appendix.] **—op·pugn′er** *n.*

op·sin (ŏp′sĭn) *n.* A protein of the retina, especially the protein constituent of rhodopsin, that makes up one of the visual pigments. [Probably back-formation from RHODOPSIN.]

–opsis *suff.* Something resembling a specified thing: *caryopsis.* [Greek, sight, seeing, like, from *opsis,* sight, appearance. See **okʷ-** in Appendix.]

op·son·ic (ŏp-sŏn′ĭk) *adj.* Of, relating to, or produced by opsonins. [OPSON(IN) + –IC.]

op·so·nin (ŏp′sə-nĭn) *n.* An antibody in blood serum that causes bacteria or other foreign cells to become more susceptible to the action of phagocytes. [Latin *opsōnāre,* to buy provisions (from Greek *opsōnein,* from *opson,* condiment, delicacy) + –IN.]

op·so·nize (ŏp′sə-nīz′) *tr.v.* **-nized, -niz·ing, -niz·es.** To make (bacteria or other cells) more susceptible to the action of phagocytes. [From OPSONIN.] **—op′so·ni·za′tion** (-nĭ-zā′shən) *n.*

–opsy *suff.* Examination: *biopsy.* [Greek *-opsia,* sight, seeing, from *opsis.* See **okʷ-** in Appendix.]

opt (ŏpt) *intr.v.* **opt·ed, opt·ing, opts.** To make a choice or decision: *opted for early retirement; opted not to go.* **—*phrasal verb.* opt out.** *Slang.* To choose not to participate in something: *"give individual schools the right to opt out of the local educational authority"* (Newsweek). [French *opter,* from Old French, from Latin *optāre.*]

opt. *abbr.* **1.** *Grammar.* Optative. **2.** Optical; optician; optics. **3.** Optimum. **4.** Optional.

op·ta·tive (ŏp′tə-tĭv) *adj.* **1.** Expressing a wish or choice. **2.** *Abbr.* **opt.** *Grammar.* **a.** Of, relating to, or being a mood of verbs in some languages, such as Greek, used to express a wish. **b.** Designating a statement using a verb in the subjunctive mood to indicate a wish or desire, as in *Had I the means, I would do it.* **—optative** *n. Abbr.* **opt.** *Grammar.* **1.** The optative mood. **2.** A verb or an expression in the optative mood. [Middle English *optatif,* from Old French, from Late Latin *optātīvus,* from Latin *optātus,* past participle of *optāre,* to wish.] **—op′ta·tive·ly** *adv.*

op·tic (ŏp′tĭk) *adj.* **1.** Of or relating to the eye or vision. **2.** Of or relating to the science of optics or optical equipment. **—optic** *n.* **1.** An eye. **2.** Any of the lenses, prisms, or mirrors of an optical instrument. [Middle English *optik,* from Old French *optique,* from Medieval Latin *opticus,* from Greek *optikos,* from *optos,* visible. See **okʷ-** in Appendix.]

op·ti·cal (ŏp′tĭ-kəl) *adj. Abbr.* **opt. 1.** Of or relating to sight; visual: *an optical defect.* **2.** Designed to assist sight: *optical instruments.* **3.** Of or relating to optics. **4.** Relating to or using visible light: *optical astronomy.* **5.** Using light-sensitive devices. **—op′ti·cal·ly** *adv.*

optical activity *n. Chemistry.* A property caused by asymmetrical molecular structure that enables a substance to rotate the plane of incident polarized light.

optical art *n.* Op art.

optical character reader *n. Abbr.* **OCR** *Computer Science.* A device used for optical character recognition.

optical character recognition *n. Abbr.* **OCR** *Computer*

Science. The use of light-sensitive devices to identify and encode printed or handwritten characters.

optical computer *n. Computer Science.* A computer that uses holograms for compact data storage and laser beams for connections. Most optical computers use electronic components for computation.

optical disk or **optical disc** *n. Computer Science.* A plastic-coated disk that stores digital data, such as music or text, as tiny pits etched into the surface and is read with a laser scanning the surface. Also called *laser disk.*

optical fiber *n.* A flexible optically transparent fiber, usually made of glass or plastic, through which light can be transmitted by successive internal reflections.

optical illusion *n.* A visually perceived image that is deceptive or misleading.

optical maser *n.* A laser, especially one that produces visible radiation.

optic axis *n.* An optical path through a crystal along which a ray of light can pass without undergoing double refraction.

optic chiasma *n.* A structure in the brain forming the partial intersection or crossing of the optic nerve fibers on the underside of the hypothalamus. Also called *optic chiasm.*

optic cup *n. Embryology.* A two-walled cuplike depression, formed by invagination of the optic vesicle, that develops into the pigmented and sensory layers of the retina. Also called *eyecup.*

optic disk *n. Anatomy.* See **blind spot** (sense 1).

op·ti·cian (ŏp-tĭsh′ən) *n. Abbr.* **opt. 1.** One that makes lenses and eyeglasses. **2.** One that sells lenses, eyeglasses, and other optical instruments.

optic lobe *n.* Either of two lobes of the dorsal part of the mesencephalon, containing primary visual centers.

optic nerve *n.* Either of the second pair of cranial nerves that arise from the retina and carry visual information to the thalamus and other parts of the brain.

op·tics (ŏp′tĭks) *n. (used with a sing. verb). Abbr.* **opt.** The branch of physics that deals with light and vision, chiefly the generation, propagation, and detection of electromagnetic radiation having wavelengths greater than x-rays and shorter than microwaves.

optic vesicle *n. Embryology.* An evagination on either side of the embryonic forebrain from which the optic nerve and retina develop.

op·ti·ma (ŏp′tə-mə) *n.* A plural of **optimum.**

op·ti·mal (ŏp′tə-məl) *adj.* Most favorable or desirable; optimum. **—op′ti·mal·ly** *adv.*

op·ti·mism (ŏp′tə-mĭz′əm) *n.* **1.** A tendency to expect the best possible outcome or dwell on the most hopeful aspects of a situation: *"There is a touch of optimism in every worry about one's own moral cleanliness"* (Victoria Ocampo). **2.** *Philosophy.* **a.** The doctrine, asserted by Leibnitz, that this world is the best of all possible worlds. **b.** The belief that the universe is improving and that good will ultimately triumph over evil. [French *optimisme,* from New Latin *optimum,* the greatest good. See OPTIMUM.]

op·ti·mist (ŏp′tə-mĭst) *n.* **1.** One who usually expects a favorable outcome. **2.** A believer in philosophical optimism. **—op′ti·mis′tic** *adj.* **—op′ti·mis′ti·cal·ly** *adv.*

op·ti·mi·za·tion (ŏp′tə-mĭ-zā′shən) *n.* The procedure or procedures used to make a system or design as effective or functional as possible, especially the mathematical techniques involved.

op·ti·mize (ŏp′tə-mīz′) *tr.v.* **-mized, -miz·ing, -miz·es. 1.** To make as perfect or effective as possible. **2.** To make the most of.

op·ti·mum (ŏp′tə-məm) *n., pl.* **-ma** (-mə) or **-mums.** *Abbr.* **opt. 1.** The point at which the condition, degree, or amount of something is the most favorable. **2.** *Biology.* The most favorable condition for growth and reproduction. **—optimum** *adj.* Most favorable or advantageous; best. [Latin, neuter sing. of *optimus,* best. See **op-** in Appendix.]

op·tion (ŏp′shən) *n.* **1.** The act of choosing; choice. See Synonyms at **choice. 2.** The power or freedom to choose. **3. a.** The exclusive right, usually obtained for a fee, to buy or sell something within a specified time at a set price. **b.** The privilege of demanding fulfillment of a contract at a specified time. **c.** A right to buy or sell specific securities or commodities at a stated price within a specified time. **d.** The right of the holder of an insurance policy to specify the manner in which payments are to be made or credited to the policyholder. **4.** Something chosen or available as a choice. **5.** An item or a feature that may be chosen to replace or enhance standard equipment, as in a car. **—option** *tr.v.* **-tioned, -tion·ing, -tions. 1.** To acquire or grant an option on: *"had optioned for a film several short stories about two policemen"* (Barbara Goldsmith). **2.** *Baseball.* To transfer (a player) to a minor-league club with the option of recalling him within a specified period of time. [Latin *optiō, optiōn-.*]

op·tion·al (ŏp′shə-nəl) *adj. Abbr.* **opt.** Left to choice; not compulsory or automatic. **—op′tion·al·ly** *adv.*

option play *n. Football.* An offensive play in which a back has the choice of running with the ball or throwing a forward pass.

op·tom·e·trist (ŏp-tŏm′ĭ-trĭst) *n.* A person who is professionally trained and licensed to examine the eyes for visual defects, diagnose problems or impairments, and prescribe corrective lenses or provide other types of treatment.

op·tom·e·try (ŏp-tŏm′ĭ-trē) *n.* The practice or profession of an optometrist. [Greek *optos,* visible; see **ok^w-** in Appendix + -METRY.] **—op′to·met′ric** (ŏp′tə-mĕt′rĭk), **op′to·met′ri·cal** (-rĭ-kəl) *adj.*

op·u·lence (ŏp′yə-ləns) also **op·u·len·cy** (-lən-sē) *n.* **1.** Wealth; affluence. **2.** Great abundance; profusion.

op·u·lent (ŏp′yə-lənt) *adj.* **1.** Possessing or exhibiting great wealth; affluent. **2.** Characterized by rich abundance; luxuriant. [Latin *opulentus.* See **op-** in Appendix.] **—op′u·lent·ly** *adv.*

o·pun·ti·a (ō-pŭn′shē-ə, -shə) *n.* Any of various cacti of the genus *Opuntia,* especially the prickly pear. [Latin *(herba) Opūntia,* Opuntian (herb), after *Opūs, Opūnt-,* an ancient town of east-central Greece.]

o·pus (ō′pəs) *n., pl.* **o·pe·ra** (ō′pər-ə, ŏp′ər-ə) or **o·pus·es.** *Abbr.* **op., Op.** A creative work, especially a musical composition numbered to designate the order of a composer's works. [Latin. See **op-** in Appendix.]

o·pus·cule (ō-pŭs′kyo͞ol) *n.* A small, minor work. [Latin *opusculum,* diminutive of *opus,* work. See OPUS.]

o·quas·sa (ō-kwăs′ə, ō-kwä′sə) *n., pl.* **oquassa** or **-sas.** A freshwater trout *(Salvelinus oquassa)* found in the Rangeley Lakes in western Maine. [After Lake *Oquassa,* a lake of western Maine.]

or[1] (ôr; ər *when unstressed*) *conj.* **1. a.** Used to indicate an alternative, usually only before the last term of a series: *hot or cold; this, that, or the other.* **b.** Used to indicate the second of two alternatives, the first being preceded by *either* or *whether*: *Your answer is either ingenious or wrong. She didn't know whether to laugh or cry.* **c.** *Archaic.* Used to indicate the first of two alternatives, with the force of *either* or *whether.* **2.** Used to indicate a synonymous or equivalent expression: *acrophobia, or fear of great heights.* **3.** Used to indicate uncertainty or indefiniteness: *two or three.* [Middle English, from *other,* or (from Old English *other,* from *oththe*) and from *outher* (from Old English *āhwæther, āther;* see EITHER).]

USAGE NOTE: When all the elements in a series connected by *or* are singular, the verb they govern is singular: *Tom or Jack is coming. Beer, ale, or wine is included in the charge.* When all the elements are plural, the verb is plural. When the elements do not agree in number, some grammarians have suggested that the verb be governed by the element to which it is nearer: *Tom or his sisters are coming. The girls or their brother is coming. Cold symptoms or headache is the usual first sign.* Other grammarians, however, have argued that such constructions must be avoided and that substitutes be found in which the problem of agreement does not arise: *Either Tom is coming or his sisters are. The usual first sign may be either cold symptoms or a headache.* See Usage Notes at **and/or, either, neither, nor**[1]**.**

or[2] (ôr) *Archaic. conj.* Before. Followed by *ever* or *ere*: *"I doubt he will be dead or ere I come"* (Shakespeare). **—or** *prep.* Before. [Middle English, variant of *er,* from Old English *ǣr,* soon, early, and from Old Norse *ār;* see **ayer-** in Appendix.]

or[3] (ôr) *n. Heraldry.* Gold, represented in heraldic engraving by a white field sprinkled with small dots. [Middle English, from Old French, from Latin *aurum.*]

OR *abbr.* **1.** Or **O.R.** Operating room. **2.** Operations research. **3.** Oregon. **4.** Owner's risk.

-or[1] *suff.* One that performs a specified action: *accelerator.* [Middle English *-or, -our,* from Old French *-eor, -eur* and Anglo-Norman *-our, -ur,* all from Latin *-or, -ōr-.*]

-or[2] *suff.* State; quality; activity: *valor.* [Middle English *-our,* from Old French *-eur,* from Latin *-or, -ōr-.*]

o·ra (ôr′ə, ōr′ə) *n.* Plural of **os**[1]**.**

or·ach also **or·ache** (ôr′ĭch, ŏr′-) *n.* Any of various plants of the genus *Atriplex,* especially *A. hortensis,* having edible, spinachlike leaves. [Middle English *orage,* arage, from Old French *arrache,* from Vulgar Latin **ātripica,* from Latin *ātriplex, ātriplic-,* from Greek *atraphaxus.*]

or·a·cle (ôr′ə-kəl, ŏr′-) *n.* **1. a.** A shrine consecrated to the worship and consultation of a prophetic deity, as that of Apollo at Delphi. **b.** A person, such as a priestess, through whom a deity is held to respond when consulted. **c.** The response given through such a medium, often in the form of an enigmatic statement or allegory. **2. a.** A person considered to be a source of wise counsel or prophetic opinions. **b.** An authoritative or wise statement or prediction. **3.** *Theology.* A command or revelation from God. **4.** In the Old Testament, the sanctuary of the Temple. [Middle English, from Old French, from Latin *ōrāculum,* from *ōrāre,* to speak.]

o·rac·u·lar (ô-răk′yə-lər, ō-răk′-) *adj.* **1.** Of, relating to, or being an oracle. **2.** Resembling or characteristic of an oracle: **a.** Solemnly prophetic. **b.** Enigmatic; obscure. [From Latin *ōrāculum,* oracle, from *ōrāre,* to speak.] **—o·rac′u·lar′i·ty** (-lăr′ĭ-tē) *n.* **—o·rac′u·lar·ly** *adv.*

O·ra·dea (ô-räd′yä). A city of northwest Romania near the Hungarian border. Hungary ceded it to Romania in 1919 and again after World War II. Population, 206,206.

o·ral (ôr′əl, ōr′-) *adj.* **1.** Spoken rather than written. See Usage Note at **verbal. 2.** Of or relating to the mouth: *oral surgery.* **3.** Used in or taken through the mouth: *an oral thermometer; an oral vaccine.* **4.** Consisting of or using speech: *oral instruction.* **5.** *Linguistics.* Articulated through the mouth only, with the nasal

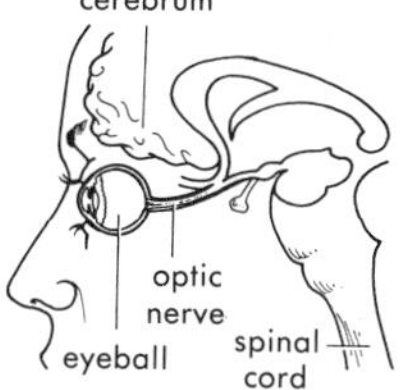

optic nerve

orach
Atriplex patula

ă pat	oi boy
ā pay	ou out
âr care	o͝o took
ä father	o͞o boot
ĕ pet	ŭ cut
ē be	ûr urge
ĭ pit	th thin
ī pie	*th* this
îr pier	hw which
ŏ pot	zh vision
ō toe	ə about, item
ô paw	♦ regionalism

Stress marks: ′ (primary); ′ (secondary), as in **dictionary** (dĭk′shə-nĕr′ē)

passages closed. **6.** *Psychology.* Of or relating to the first stage of psychosexual development in psychoanalytic theory, during which the mouth is the chief focus of exploration and pleasure. **—oral** *n.* An academic examination in which questions and answers are spoken rather than written. Often used in the plural. [Late Latin *ōrālis,* from Latin *ōs, ōr-,* mouth. See **ōs-** in Appendix.] **—o′ral·ly** *adv.*

oral contraceptive *n.* A pill, typically containing estrogen or progesterone, that inhibits ovulation and thereby prevents conception. Also called *birth control pill.*

o·ral-for·mu·la·ic (ôr′əl-fôr′myə-lā′ĭk, ōr′-) *adj.* Of or relating to poetry in which traditional material is improvised at each performance by using verbal formulas as an aid to memory.

oral history *n.* **1.** Historical information, usually tape-recorded, obtained in interviews with persons having firsthand knowledge. **2.** An audiotape or a written account of such an interview or interviews.

oral hygiene *n.* See **dental hygiene.**

oral sex *n.* Sexual activity involving oral stimulation of one's partner's sex organs.

oral tradition *n.* The spoken relation and preservation, from one generation to the next, of a people's cultural history and ancestry, often by a storyteller in narrative form.

O·ran (ō-rän′, ô-räɴ′). A city of northwest Algeria on the **Gulf of Oran,** an inlet of the Mediterranean Sea west-southwest of Algiers. Built on a site occupied since prehistoric times, Oran was captured by the Spanish in 1509 and by the Turks in 1708. It was occupied by the French in 1831 and held by Vichy France during World War II. Population, 409,788.

o·rang (ō-răng′, ô′răng) *n. Informal.* An orangutan.

orangutan
Pongo pygmaeus

or·ange (ôr′ĭnj, ŏr′-) *n.* **1.a.** Any of several southeast Asian evergreen trees of the genus *Citrus,* widely cultivated in warm regions and having fragrant white flowers and round fruit with a yellowish or reddish rind and a sectioned, pulpy interior, especially *C. sinensis,* the sweet orange, and *C. aurantium,* the Seville or sour orange. **b.** The fruit of any of these trees, having a sweetish, acidic juice. **2.** Any of several similar plants, such as the Osage orange. **3.** *Color.* The hue of that portion of the visible spectrum lying between red and yellow, evoked in the human observer by radiant energy with wavelengths of approximately 590 to 630 nanometers; any of a group of colors between red and yellow in hue, of medium lightness and moderate saturation. [Middle English, from Old French *pume orenge,* translation and alteration (influenced by *Orenge,* Orange, a town in France) of Old Italian *melarancio : mela,* fruit + *arancio,* orange tree (alteration of Arabic *nāranj,* from Persian *nārang,* from Sanskrit *nāraṅgaḥ,* possibly of Dravidian origin).] **—or′ange** *adj.*

WORD HISTORY: Oranges imported to China from the United States reflect a journey come full circle, for the orange had worked its way westward for centuries, originating in China, then being introduced to India, and traveling on to the Middle East, into Europe, and finally to the New World. The history of the word *orange* keeps step with this journey only part of the way. The word is possibly ultimately of Dravidian origin, that is, it comes from a language or languages in a large non-Indo-European family of languages, including Tamil and Telegu, that are spoken in southern India and northern Sri Lanka. The Dravidian word or words were adopted into the Indo-European language Sanskrit with the form *nāraṅgaḥ.* As the fruit passed westward, so did the word, as evidenced by Persian *nārang* and Arabic *nāranj.* Arabs brought the first oranges to Spain, and the fruit rapidly spread throughout Europe. The important word for the development of our term is Old Italian *melarancio,* derived from *mela,* "fruit," and *arancio,* "orange tree," from Arabic *nāranj.* Old Italian *melarancio* was translated into Old French as *pume orenge,* the *o* replacing the *a* because of the influence of the name of the town of Orange, from which oranges reached the northern part of France. The final stage of the odyssey of the word was its borrowing into English from the Old French form *orenge.* Our word is first recorded in Middle English in a text probably composed around 1380, a time preceding the arrival of the orange in the New World.

orb

Or·ange¹ (ôr′ĭnj, ŏ′-). Princely family of Europe ruling continously in the Netherlands since 1815. The name was first used for a former principality of southeast France that passed to the house of Nassau in 1530.

Or·ange² (ôr′ĭnj, ŏr′-). **1.** A city of southern California north-northeast of Santa Ana. It is a manufacturing center in a citrus-growing area. Population, 91,788. **2.** A city of northeast New Jersey, a chiefly residential suburb of Newark and New York City. Population, 31,136. **3.** A city of southeast Texas east of Beaumont. It is a port and processing center. Population, 23,628.

or·ange·ade (ôr′ĭn-jād′, ŏr′-) *n.* A beverage of orange juice, sugar, and water.

Orange Free State. A province and historical region of east-central South Africa. European settlement of the area began early in the 1800's and accelerated with an influx of Boer farmers after 1835. Great Britain annexed the region as the **Orange River Sovereignty** in 1848 and granted it independence as the Orange Free State in 1854. In 1900, during the Boer War, Great Britain once again annexed the territory, this time as the **Orange River Colony.** The renamed Orange Free State formed an independent government in 1907 and became a founding province of South Africa in 1910.

orange hawkweed *n.* A European perennial weed *(Hieracium aurantiacum)* common on the Pacific coast and the eastern regions of North America, having hairy leaves and clusters of orange-red flower heads. Also called *devil's paintbrush.*

Or·ange·man (ôr′ĭnj-mən, ŏr′-) *n.* **1.** A member of a secret society founded in Northern Ireland in 1795 to maintain the political and religious ascendancy of Protestantism. **2.** A Protestant Irishman. [After William, Prince of ORANGE¹, later King William III of England, Scotland, and Ireland.]

orange milkweed *n.* See **butterfly weed.**

orange pekoe *n.* A grade of black tea consisting of the end buds of the shoot or their surrounding two full leaves. [From the orange color of its infusion.]

Orange River. A river, about 2,092 km (1,300 mi) long, of Lesotho, South Africa, and Namibia flowing southwest, northwest, and west to the Atlantic Ocean.

or·ange·root (ôr′ənj-ro͞ot′, -ro͝ot′, ŏr′-) *n.* See **goldenseal.**

or·ange·ry (ôr′ĭnj-rē, ŏr′-) *n., pl.* **-ries.** A sheltered place, especially a greenhouse, used for the cultivation of orange trees in cool climates.

orange stick *n.* A stick of orangewood with tapered ends, used in manicuring.

Or·ange·vale (ôr′ĭnj-vāl′, ŏr′-). A community of north-central California, a suburb of Sacramento. Population, 20,585.

or·ange·wood (ôr′ĭnj-wo͝od′, ŏr′-) *n.* The fine-grained wood of the orange tree, used in fine woodwork.

o·rang·u·tan (ô-răng′ə-tăn′, ō-răng′-, ə-răng′-) also **o·rang·ou·tang** (-ə-tăng′) *n.* An arboreal anthropoid ape *(Pongo pygmaeus)* of Borneo and Sumatra, having a shaggy reddish-brown coat, very long arms, and no tail. [Malay *ōrang hūtan : ōrang,* man + *hūtan,* wilderness, jungle.]

o·rate (ô-rāt′, ō-rāt′, ôr′āt′, ōr′-) *intr.v.* **o·rat·ed, o·rat·ing, o·rates.** To speak in a formal, pompous manner. [Latin *ōrāre, ōrāt-,* to pray, speak publicly.]

o·ra·tion (ô-rā′shən, ō-rā′-) *n.* **1.** A formal speech, especially one given on a ceremonial occasion. **2.** A speech delivered in a high-flown or pompous manner. [Middle English *oracion,* prayer, from Late Latin *ōrātiō, ōrātiōn-,* from Latin, discourse, from *ōrātus,* past participle of *ōrāre,* to speak.]

or·a·tor (ôr′ə-tər, ŏr′-) *n.* **1.** One who delivers an oration. **2.** An eloquent and skilled public speaker. **—or′a·tor·ship′** *n.*

Or·a·to·ri·an (ôr′ə-tôr′ē-ən, -tōr′-) *n. Roman Catholic Church.* A member of an Oratory.

or·a·tor·i·cal (ôr′ə-tôr′ĭ-kəl, ŏr′ə-tŏr′-) *adj.* Of or characteristic of an orator or oratory. **—or′a·tor′i·cal·ly** *adv.*

or·a·to·ri·o (ôr′ə-tôr′ē-ō′, -tōr′-, ŏr′-) *n., pl.* **-os.** *Music.* A composition for voices and orchestra, telling a sacred story without costumes, scenery, or dramatic action. [Italian, after *Oratorio,* the Oratory of Saint Philip Neri at Rome, where famous musical services were held in the 16th century.]

or·a·to·ry¹ (ôr′ə-tôr′ē, -tōr′ē, ŏr′-) *n.* **1.** The art of public speaking. **2.** Eloquence or skill in making speeches to the public. **3.** Public speaking marked by the use of overblown rhetoric. [Latin *(ars) ōrātōria,* (art) of speaking, feminine sing. of *ōrātōrius,* oratorical, from *ōrātor,* speaker, from *ōrāre,* to speak.]

or·a·to·ry² (ôr′ə-tôr′ē, -tōr′ē, ŏr′-) *n., pl.* **-ries.** **1.** A place for prayer, such as a small private chapel. **2.** Also **Oratory. a.** A Roman Catholic religious society founded in 1575 by Saint Philip Neri and consisting of secular priests. **b.** A branch or church of this society. [Middle English *oratorie,* from Old French, from Late Latin *ōrātōrium,* place of prayer, from Latin, neuter of *ōrātōrius,* for praying, from *ōrāre,* to pray.]

orb (ôrb) *n.* **1.** A sphere or spherical object. **2.a.** A celestial body, such as the sun or moon. **b.** *Archaic.* The planet Earth. **3.** One of a series of concentric transparent spheres thought by ancient and medieval astronomers to revolve about Earth and carry the celestial bodies. **4.** A globe surmounted by a cross, used as a symbol of monarchial power and justice. **5.** An eye or eyeball. **6.** *Archaic.* Something of circular form; a circle or an orbit. **7.** *Archaic.* A range of endeavor or activity; a province. **—orb** *v.* **orbed, orb·ing, orbs.** *—tr.* **1.** To shape into a circle or sphere. **2.** *Archaic.* To encircle; enclose. *—intr. Archaic.* To move in an orbit. [Middle English *orbe,* orbit, from Old French, from Latin *orbis,* circle, disk, orbit.]

or·bic·u·lar (ôr-bĭk′yə-lər) *adj.* **1.** Circular or spherical. **2.** *Botany.* Circular and flat. Used especially of leaves. [Middle English *orbiculer,* from Old French *orbiculaire,* from Late Latin *orbiculāris,* from Latin *orbiculus,* diminutive of *orbis,* circle, disk.] **—or·bic′u·lar′i·ty** (-lăr′ĭ-tē) *n.* **—or·bic′u·lar·ly** *adv.*

or·bic·u·late (ôr-bĭk′yə-lĭt, -lāt′) also **or·bic·u·lat·ed** (-lā′tĭd) *adj.* Orbicular. [Latin *orbiculātus,* from *orbiculus,* diminutive of *orbis,* circle, disk.] **—or·bic′u·late·ly** *adv.*

Or·bi·son (ôr′bĭ-sən), **Roy.** 1936–1988. American singer and songwriter noted for his smooth tenor voice. Many of his ballads were made popular by later musicians.

or·bit (ôr′bĭt) *n.* **1.a.** The path of a celestial body or an artificial satellite as it revolves around another body. **b.** One complete revolution of such a body. **2.** The path of a body in a field of force surrounding another body; for example, the movement of an atomic electron in relation to a nucleus. **3.a.** A range of activity, experience, or knowledge. **b.** A range of control or influence: *"What magnetism drew these quaking ruined creatures into his orbit?"* (Malcolm Lowry). See Synonyms at **range.** **4.** Either of two bony cavities in the skull containing an eye and its external structures; an eye socket. **—orbit** *v.* **-bit·ed, -bit·ing, -bits.** *—tr.* **1.** To put into an orbit: *orbit a satellite.* **2.** To revolve around (a center of attraction): *The moon orbits Earth. —intr.* To move in an orbit. [Middle English *orbite,* eye socket, from Old French, from Latin *orbita,* orbit, probably from *orbis.*]

or·bit·al (ôr′bĭ-tl) *adj.* Of or relating to an orbit. **—orbital** *n.* The wave function of an electron in an atom or molecule, indicating the electron's probable location.

orbital velocity *n.* **1.** The velocity at which a body revolves about another body. **2.** The minimum velocity required to place or maintain a satellite in orbit.

or·bi·teer (ôr′bĭ-tîr′) *v.* **-teered, -teer·ing, -teers.** *Sports. —tr.* To make one's way up (tall mountains) by walking around instead of scaling. *—intr.* To engage in the sport of walking around tall mountains. **—or′bi·teer′ing** *n.*

or·bit·er (ôr′bĭ-tər) *n.* Something that orbits, especially a spacecraft that orbits a planet or moon without landing on it.

or·ca (ôr′kə) *n.* See **killer whale.** [Latin *ōrca,* whale, probably alteration (probably influenced by *orca,* vessel) of Greek *orux, orug-,* pickax, a kind of large fish or whale, perhaps from *orussein,* to dig.]

orch. *abbr. Music.* Orchestra.

or·chard (ôr′chərd) *n.* **1.** An area of land devoted to the cultivation of fruit or nut trees. **2.** The trees cultivated in such an area. [Middle English, from Old English *orceard,* alteration of *ortgeard* : perhaps *wyrt, wort,* plant; see WORT[1] + *geard,* yard; see **gher-**[1] in Appendix.]

orchard grass *n.* A Eurasian grass *(Dactylis glomerata)* widely planted in pastures.

or·char·dist (ôr′chər-dĭst) *n.* One who owns or cultivates an orchard.

or·ches·tra (ôr′kĭ-strə, -kĕs′trə) *n. Abbr.* **orch. 1.** *Music.* **a.** A large group of musicians who play together on various instruments, usually including strings, woodwinds, brass instruments, and percussion instruments. **b.** The instruments played by such a group. **2.** The area in a theater or concert hall where the musicians sit, immediately in front of and below the stage. **3. a.** The front section of seats nearest the stage in a theater. **b.** The entire main floor of a theater. **4.** A semicircular space in front of the stage used by the chorus in ancient Greek theaters. [Latin *orchēstra,* the space in front of the stage in Greek theaters where the chorus performed, from Greek *orkhēstra,* from *orkheisthai,* to dance.] **—or·ches′tral** (ôr-kĕs′trəl) *adj.* **—or·ches′tral·ly** *adv.*

or·ches·trate (ôr′kĭ-strāt′) *tr.v.* **-trat·ed, -trat·ing, -trates. 1.** *Music.* To compose or arrange (music) for performance by an orchestra. **2.** To arrange or control the elements of, as to achieve a desired overall effect: *orchestrated a successful political campaign.* **—or′ches·tra′tor** *n.*

or·ches·tra·tion (ôr′kĭ-strā′shən) *n.* **1.** *Music.* **a.** A composition that has been orchestrated. **b.** Arrangement of music for performance by an orchestra. **2.** Arrangement or control: *orchestration of events.*

or·ches·tri·on (ôr-kĕs′trē-ən) also **or·ches·tri·na** (ôr′kĭ-strē′nə) *n. Music.* A large mechanical instrument resembling a barrel organ that produces sound in imitation of an orchestra. [ORCHESTR(A) + (MELOD)EON.]

or·chid (ôr′kĭd) *n.* **1. a.** A member of the orchid family. **b.** The flower of any of these plants, especially one cultivated for ornament. **2.** *Color.* A pale to light purple, from grayish to purplish pink to strong reddish purple. [From New Latin *Orchideae,* family name, from Latin *orchis,* from Greek *orkhis,* testicle, orchid (from the slope of its root).] **—or′chid** *adj.*

or·chi·da·ceous (ôr′kĭ-dā′shəs) *adj.* **1.** Of, relating to, or characteristic of the orchid family. **2.** Suggesting ostentatious luxury; showy. [From New Latin *Orchidaceae,* family name, from Latin *orchis,* orchid. See ORCHID.]

or·chi·dec·to·my (ôr′kĭ-dĕk′tə-mē) *n., pl.* **-mies.** Variant of **orchiectomy.**

orchid family *n.* A large family of epiphytic or terrestial perennial herbs, the Orchidaceae, found chiefly in the tropics and subtropics and characterized by bilaterally symmetrical, showy flowers with an inferior ovary and dustlike seeds.

orchid tree *n.* **1.** A small southeast Asian tree *(Bauhinia variegata)* in the pea family, having showy, irregular lavender or purple flowers and deeply emarginate leaves. **2.** A tree *(Amherstia nobilis)* of Burma, having compound leaves and a great profusion of large, irregular, yellow-spotted, scarlet flowers.

or·chi·ec·to·my (ôr′kē-ĕk′tə-mē) or **or·chi·dec·to·my** (-kĭ-dĕk′-) *n., pl.* **-mies.** Surgical removal of one or both testes. [Greek *orkhis, orkhi-,* testicle + -ECTOMY.]

or·chil (ôr′kĭl, -chĭl) also **ar·chil** (är′-) *n.* **1.** Any of several lichens, chiefly of the genera *Roccella* and *Lecanora,* from which a dye is obtained. **2.** The reddish dyestuff obtained from any of these organisms. [Middle English *orchell,* ultimately from Old Catalan *orxella,* from Mozarabic *'urğāla.*]

or·chis (ôr′kĭs) *n.* Any of numerous orchids of the genus *Orchis,* having magenta, white, or magenta-spotted flowers. [Latin, orchid. See ORCHID.]

Or·cus (ôr′kəs) *n. Roman Mythology.* **1.** The world of the dead; Hades. **2.** Pluto, the god of the underworld.

ord. *abbr.* **1.** Order. **2.** Ordinal. **3.** Ordinance. **4.** Ordnance.

or·dain (ôr-dān′) *tr.v.* **-dained, -dain·ing, -dains. 1. a.** To invest with ministerial or priestly authority; confer holy orders on. **b.** To authorize as a rabbi. **2.** To order by virtue of superior authority; decree or enact. **3.** To prearrange unalterably; predestine: *by fate ordained.* See Synonyms at **dictate.** [Middle English *ordeinen,* from Old French *ordener, ordein-,* from Latin *ōrdināre,* to organize, appoint to office, from *ōrdō, ōrdin-,* order. See **ar-** in Appendix.] **—or·dain′er** *n.* **—or·dain′ment** *n.*

or·deal (ôr-dēl′) *n.* **1.** A difficult or painful experience, especially one that severely tests character or endurance. See Synonyms at **trial. 2.** A method of trial in which the accused was subjected to physically painful or dangerous tests, the result being regarded as a divine judgment of guilt or innocence. [Alteration (influenced by DEAL[1]) of Middle English *ordal,* trial by ordeal, from Old English *ordāl.* See **dail-** in Appendix.]

ordeal bean *n.* See **Calabar bean.** [So called from its alleged use as a test for witchcraft.]

or·der (ôr′dər) *n. Abbr.* **ord., O, O., o. 1.** A condition of logical or comprehensible arrangement among the separate elements of a group. **2. a.** A condition of methodical or prescribed arrangement among component parts such that proper functioning or appearance is achieved: *"Order, cleanliness, seemliness make a structure that is half support, half ritual"* (Florida Scott-Maxwell). **b.** Condition or state in general: *in good order.* **3. a.** The established system of social organization: *"Every revolution exaggerates the evils of the old order"* (C. Wright Mills). **b.** A condition in which freedom from disorder or disruption is maintained through respect for established authority: *finally restored order in the rebellious provinces.* **4.** A sequence or an arrangement of successive things. **5.** The prescribed form or customary procedure: *the order of worship.* **6.** An authoritative indication to be obeyed; a command or direction. **7. a.** A command given by a superior military officer requiring obedience, as in the execution of a task. **b. orders.** Formal written instructions to report for military duty at a specified time and place. **8. a.** A commission or an instruction to buy, sell, or supply something. **b.** That which is supplied, bought, or sold. **9. a.** A request made by a customer at a restaurant for a portion of food. **b.** The food requested. **10.** *Law.* A direction or command delivered by a court or other adjudicative body and entered into the record but not necessarily included in the final judgment or verdict. **11.** *Ecclesiastical.* **a.** Any of several grades of the Christian ministry: *the order of priesthood.* **b.** Often **orders.** The rank of an ordained Christian minister or priest. **c.** Often **orders.** The sacrament or rite of ordination. **12.** Any of the nine grades or choirs of angels. **13.** A group of persons living under a religious rule: *Order of Saint Benedict.* **14.** An organization of people united by a common fraternal bond or social aim. **15. a.** A group of people upon whom a government or sovereign has formally conferred honor for unusual service or merit, entitling them to wear a special insignia: *the Order of the Garter.* **b.** The insignia worn by such people. **16.** Often **orders.** A social class: *the lower orders.* **17.** A class defined by the common attributes of its members; a kind. **18.** Degree of quality or importance; rank: *poetry of a high order.* **19.** *Architecture.* **a.** Any of several styles of classical architecture characterized by the type of column employed: *the Corinthian order.* **b.** A style of building: *a cathedral of the Gothic order.* **20.** *Biology.* A taxonomic category of organisms ranking above a family and below a class. See table at **taxonomy. 21.** *Mathematics.* **a.** The sum of the exponents to which the variables in a term are raised; degree. **b.** An indicated number of successive differentiations to be performed. **c.** The number of elements in a finite group. **d.** The number of rows or columns in a determinant or matrix. **—order** *v.* **-dered, -der·ing, -ders.** *—tr.* **1.** To issue a command or an instruction to. **2.** To give a command or an instruction for: *The judge ordered a recount of the ballots.* **3.** To direct to proceed as specified: *ordered them off the property.* **4.** To give an order for; request to be supplied with. **5.** To put into a methodical, systematic arrangement. See Synonyms at **arrange. 6.** To predestine; ordain. *—intr.* To give an order or orders; request that something be done or supplied. ***—idioms.*** **in order that.** So that. **in order to.** For the purpose of. **in short order.** With no delay; quickly. **on order.** Requested but not yet delivered. **on the order of. 1.** Of a kind or fashion similar to; like: *a house on the order of a mountain lodge.* **2.** Approximately; about: *equipment costing on the order of a million dollars.* **to order.** According to the buyer's specifications. [Middle English *ordre,* from Old French, variant of *ordene,* from Latin *ōrdō, ōrdin-.* See **ar-** in Appendix.] **—or′der·er** *n.*

order arms *n.* **1.** A position in the military manual of arms in which the rifle is held vertically next to the right leg with its butt resting on the ground. **2.** A command to assume order arms.

order code *n. Computer Science.* See **operation code.**

or·der·ly (ôr′dər-lē) *adj.* **1. a.** Free from disorder; neat: *an orderly desk.* **b.** Having a systematic arrangement: *an orderly universe.* **2.** Marked by or adhering to method or system: *orderly in the upkeep of his rooms.* **3.** Devoid of violence or disruption; peaceful: *an orderly transition of governments.* **—orderly** *n., pl.* **-lies. 1.** An attendant who does routine, nonmedical work in a hospital. **2.** A soldier assigned to attend a superior officer and perform various tasks. **—orderly** *adv.* Systematically; regularly. **—or′der·li·ness** *n.*

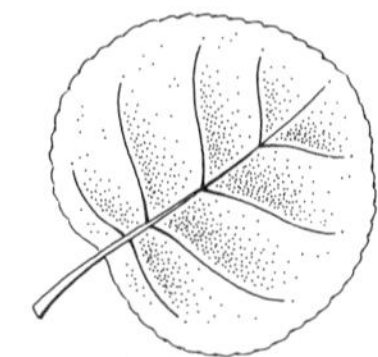

orbicular

ă pat	oi boy
ā pay	ou out
âr care	o͝o took
ä father	o͞o boot
ĕ pet	ŭ cut
ē be	ûr urge
ĭ pit	th thin
ī pie	*th* this
îr pier	hw which
ŏ pot	zh vision
ō toe	ə about, item
ô paw	♦ regionalism

Stress marks: **′** (primary); ′ (secondary), as in **dictionary** (dĭk′shə-nĕr′ē)

SYNONYMS: *orderly, methodical, systematic.* These adjectives mean proceeding in or observant of a prescribed pattern or arrangement. *Orderly* especially implies correct or customary procedure or proper or harmonious arrangement: *Firefighters supervised the orderly evacuation of the building. Workers set up chairs on the stage in orderly and symmetrical rows. Methodical* stresses adherence to a logically and carefully planned succession of steps: *The pattern supplies methodical instructions for cutting and assembling the parts of the garment. The methodical housekeeper performs tasks according to a schedule. Systematic* emphasizes observance of a coordinated and orderly set of procedures constituting part of a complex but unitary whole: *Scientists are conducting systematic research into antigens to combat immune disorders.*

order of battle *n., pl.* **orders of battle.** The identification, command structure, strength, and disposition of personnel, equipment, and units of an armed force.

order of business *n., pl.* **orders of business.** A matter, such as a task, that must be addressed.

order of magnitude *n., pl.* **orders of magnitude. 1.** An estimate of size or magnitude expressed as a power of ten: *Earth's mass is of the order of magnitude of* 10^{22} *tons; that of the sun is* 10^{27} *tons.* **2.** A range of values between a designated lower value and an upper value ten times as large: *The masses of Earth and the sun differ by five orders of magnitude.*

order of the day *n., pl.* **orders of the day. 1.** The business to be considered or done by a legislature or other body on a particular day. Often used in the plural. **2.** The characteristic or most significant aspect or activity: *Volatility is the order of the day in the stock market.*

or·di·nal (ôr′dn-əl) *adj. Abbr.* **ord. 1.** Being of a specified position in a numbered series: *an ordinal rank of seventh.* **2.** Of or relating to a taxonomic order. **—ordinal** *n. Abbr.* **ord. 1.** An ordinal number. **2.** *Ecclesiastical.* **a.** A book of instructions for daily services. **b.** A book of forms for ordination. [Middle English *ordinel,* orderly, regular, from Late Latin *ōrdinālis,* ordinal, from Latin *ōrdō, ōrdin-,* order. See **ar-** in Appendix. N., sense 2, from Middle English, from Medieval Latin *ōrdināle,* from Late Latin, neuter sing. of *ōrdinālis,* ordinal.]

ordinal number *n.* A number indicating position in a series or order. The ordinal numbers are first (1st), second (2nd), third (3rd), and so on.

or·di·nance (ôr′dn-əns) *n. Abbr.* **ord. 1.** An authoritative command or order. **2.** A custom or practice established by long usage. **3.** A Christian rite, especially the Eucharist. **4.** A statute or regulation, especially one enacted by a city government. [Middle English *ordinaunce,* from Old French *ordenance,* from Medieval Latin *ōrdinantia,* from Latin *ōrdināns, ōrdinant-,* present participle of *ōrdināre,* to ordain, from *ōrdō, ōrdin-,* order. See **ar-** in Appendix.]

or·di·nar·i·ly (ôr′dn-âr′ə-lē, ôr′dn-ĕr′-) *adv.* **1.** As a general rule; usually: *ordinarily home by six.* **2.** In the commonplace or usual manner: *ordinarily dressed pedestrians on the street.* **3.** To the usual extent or degree: *an ordinarily small profit.*

or·di·nar·y (ôr′dn-ĕr′ē) *adj.* **1.** Commonly encountered; usual. **2. a.** Of no exceptional ability, degree, or quality; average. **b.** Of inferior quality; second-rate. **3.** Having immediate rather than delegated jurisdiction, as a judge. **4.** *Mathematics.* Designating a differential equation containing no more than two variables and derivatives of one with respect to the other. **—ordinary** *n., pl.* **-ies. 1.** The usual or normal condition or course of events: *Nothing out of the ordinary occurred.* **2.** *Law.* **a.** A judge or other official with immediate rather than delegated jurisdiction. **b.** The judge of a probate court in some states of the United States. **3.** Often **Ordinary.** *Ecclesiastical.* **a.** The part of the Mass that remains unchanged from day to day. **b.** A division of the Roman Breviary containing the unchangeable parts of the office other than the Psalms. **c.** A cleric, such as the residential bishop of a diocese, with ordinary jurisdiction over a specified territory. **4.** *Heraldry.* One of the simplest and commonest charges, such as the bend and the cross. **5.** *Chiefly British.* **a.** A complete meal provided at a fixed price. **b.** A tavern or an inn providing such a meal. [Middle English *ordinarie,* from Old French, from Latin *ōrdinārius,* from *ōrdō, ōrdin-,* order. See **ar-** in Appendix.] **—or′di·nar′i·ness** *n.*

Ordinary level *n. Chiefly British.* O level.

ordinary seaman *n. Abbr.* **O.S.** A seaman of the lowest grade in the merchant marine.

or·di·nate (ôr′dn-ĭt, -āt′) *adj.* Arranged in regular rows, as the spots on the wings of an insect. **—ordinate** *n. Symbol* **y** *Mathematics.* The plane Cartesian coordinate representing the distance from a specified point to the x-axis, measured parallel to the y-axis. [Middle English, properly ordered, from Latin *ōrdinātus,* past participle of *ōrdināre,* to set in order, from *ōrdō, ōrdin-,* order. See **ar-** in Appendix.]

or·di·na·tion (ôr′dn-ā′shən) *n.* **1.** The act of ordaining or the state of being ordained. **2.** *Ecclesiastical.* The ceremony of consecration to the ministry. **3.** An arrangement or ordering.

or·di·nes (ôr′də-nēz′) *n. Roman Catholic Church.* A plural of **ordo.**

ordn. *abbr.* Ordnance.

ă pat	oi boy
ā pay	ou out
âr care	o͝o took
ä father	o͞o boot
ĕ pet	ŭ cut
ē be	ûr urge
ĭ pit	th thin
ī pie	*th* this
îr pier	hw which
ŏ pot	zh vision
ō toe	ə about, item
ô paw	♦ regionalism

Stress marks: ′ (primary); ′ (secondary), as in **dictionary** (dĭk′shə-nĕr′ē)

ord·nance (ôrd′nəns) *n. Abbr.* **ord., ordn. 1.** Military materiel, such as weapons, ammunition, combat vehicles, and equipment. **2.** The branch of an armed force that procures, maintains, and issues weapons, ammunition, and combat vehicles. **3.** Cannon; artillery. [Middle English *ordnaunce,* variant of *ordinaunce,* order, military provision. See ORDINANCE.]

or·do (ôr′dō) *n., pl.* **-di·nes** (-də-nēz′) or **-dos.** *Roman Catholic Church.* An annual calendar containing instructions for the Mass and office to be celebrated on each day of the year. [Medieval Latin *ōrdō,* from Latin, order. See **ar-** in Appendix.]

or·don·nance (ôr′dn-əns, ôr′dô-näns′) *n.* The arrangement of elements in a literary or artistic composition or an architectural plan. [French, variant of Old French *ordenance,* an arranging. See ORDINANCE.]

Or·dos (ôr′dŏs). A sandy desert plateau region of Nei Monggol (Inner Mongolia) in northern China bounded on the south and east by the Great Wall.

Or·do·vi·cian (ôr′də-vĭsh′ən) *adj.* Of, relating to, or designating the geologic time, system of rocks, and sedimentary deposits of the second period of the Paleozoic Era, characterized by the appearance of primitive fishes. See table at **geologic time. —Ordovician** *n.* The Ordovician Period. [From Latin *Ordovicēs,* an ancient Celtic tribe of Wales, from Celtic *Ordovices.* See **weik-³** in Appendix.]

or·dure (ôr′jər) *n.* **1.** Excrement; dung. **2.** Something morally offensive; filth. [Middle English, from Old French, from *ord,* filthy, from Latin *horridus,* frightful, from *horrēre,* to shudder.]

Or·dzho·ni·kid·ze (ôr′jŏn-ĭ-kĭd′zə, ər-jə-nyĭ-kyē′dzĭ). A city of southwest Russia at the foot of the Caucasus Mountains southwest of Grozny. Founded in 1784 as a fortress, it is a metallurgical center. Population, 303,000.

ore (ôr, ōr) *n.* A mineral or an aggregate of minerals from which a valuable constituent, especially a metal, can be profitably mined or extracted. [Middle English, from Old English *ōra* and from Old English *ār,* brass, copper, bronze.]

Ore. *abbr.* Oregon.

ö·re (œ′rə) *n., pl.* **öre.** See table at **currency.** [Danish and Norwegian *ore* and Swedish *öre,* all from Latin *aureus,* gold coin, from *aurum,* gold.]

o·re·ad (ôr′ē-ăd′, ōr′-) *n. Greek Mythology.* Any of a group of mountain nymphs. [Latin *Orēas, Orēad-,* from Greek *Oreias,* from *oreios,* of a mountain, from *oros,* mountain.]

Ör·e·bro (œ′rə-bro͞o′). A city of south-central Sweden west of Stockholm. Known since the 11th century, it has often been the site of national assemblies. Population, 117,569.

o·reg·a·no (ə-rĕg′ə-nō′, ô-rĕg′-) *n.* A perennial Eurasian herb *(Origanum vulgare)* of the mint family, having aromatic leaves that are used as a seasoning. [Spanish *orégano,* wild marjoram, from Latin *orīganum,* from Greek *origanon,* probably of North African origin.]

Or·e·gon (ôr′ĭ-gən, -gŏn′, ŏr′-). **1.** *Abbr.* **OR, Ore.** A state of the northwest United States in the Pacific Northwest. It was admitted as the 33rd state in 1859. Claimed by the United States after Capt. Robert Gray explored the mouth of the Columbia River in 1792, the area was further explored by Lewis and Clark in 1805 and was soon the site of fur-trading posts. The **Oregon Country,** a region encompassing all the land from the California border to Alaska and the Pacific Ocean to the Rocky Mountains, was held jointly by Great Britain and the United States from 1818 until 1846, when the international boundary was fixed at the 49th parallel. In 1848 the **Oregon Territory** was created, including all of present-day Washington and Idaho. The state's current boundaries were established in 1853. Salem is the capital and Portland the largest city. Population, 2,633,149. **2.** A city of northwest Ohio, an industrial suburb of Toledo on Lake Erie. Population, 18,675. **—Or′e·go′ni·an** (-gō′nē-ən) *adj. n.*

Oregon grape *n.* Any of various evergreen shrubs of the genus *Mahonia,* especially *M. aquifolium* of northwest North America, having compound leaves with spiny-toothed leaflets and black berries with blue bloom.

Oregon myrtle *n.* See **California laurel.**

Oregon pine *n.* The wood of the Douglas fir.

Oregon Trail. A historical overland route to the western United States extending from various cities on the Missouri River to the Oregon Country and later Oregon Territory. The trail was opened in 1842, and by 1845 more than 3,000 migrants had made the arduous journey. After the coming of the railroad, the trail fell into disuse and was finally abandoned in the 1870's.

o·re·ide (ôr′ē-īd′, ōr′-) *n.* Variant of **oroide.**

O·rel (ô-rĕl′, ō-rĕl′, ôr-yôl′). A city of western Russia on the Oka River south of Moscow. Founded in 1564 as a fortified settlement, it is an industrial center and a railroad junction. Population, 328,000.

O·rem (ôr′əm, ōr′-). A city of north-central Utah north-northwest of Provo. It is a manufacturing center in an irrigated farming area. Population, 52,399.

O·ren·burg (ôr′ən-bûrg′, ōr′-, ə-rĭn-bo͝ork′). Formerly (1938–1957) **Chka·lov** (chə-kä′ləf, chkä′-). A city of western Russia on the Ural River. Founded as a fortress in 1735, it is a processing center. Population, 519,000.

O·ren·se (ô-rĕn′sĕ). A city of northwest Spain east of Vigo. Its hot sulfur springs have been known since Roman times. Population, 85,500.

O·res·tes (ô-rĕs′tēz) *n. Greek Mythology.* The son of Agamemnon and Clytemnestra, who with his sister Electra avenged the murder of his father by murdering his mother and her lover Aegisthus.

O·re·sund or **Ø·re·sund** (œ′rə-sŭn′, -so͝ond′). A narrow strait between southern Sweden and eastern Denmark connecting the Baltic Sea with the Kattegat.

Orff (ôrf), **Carl.** 1895–1982. German composer and educator who developed a well-known system of music instruction for children, using percussion instruments and motion.

or·fray (ôr′frā′) *n.* Variant of **orphrey.**

org. *abbr.* **1.** Organic. **2.a.** Organization. **b.** Organized.

or·gan (ôr′gən) *n.* **1.** *Music.* **a.** An instrument consisting of a number of pipes that sound tones when supplied with air and a keyboard that operates a mechanism controlling the flow of air to the pipes. Also called *pipe organ.* **b.** Any one of various other instruments, such as the electronic organ, that resemble a pipe organ either in mechanism or sound. **2.** *Biology.* A differentiated part of an organism, such as an eye, a wing, or a leaf, that performs a specific function. **3.** An instrument or agency dedicated to the performance of specified functions: *The FBI is an organ of the Justice Department.* **4.** An instrument or a means of communication, especially a periodical issued by a political party, business firm, or other group. [Middle English, from Old French *organe* and from Old English *organe,* both from Latin *organum,* tool, instrument, from Greek *organon.* See **werg-** in Appendix.]

organ– *pref.* Variant of **organo–.**

or·ga·na[1] (ôr′gə-nə) *n.* A plural of **organon.**

or·ga·na[2] (ôr′gə-nə) *n.* A plural of **organum**[1].

or·gan·dy also **or·gan·die** (ôr′gən-dē) *n., pl.* **-dies.** A stiff transparent fabric of cotton or silk, used for trim, curtains, and light apparel. [French *organdi,* perhaps after Old French *Organzi* (Urgench), a city of western Uzbekistan.]

or·gan·elle (ôr′gə-nĕl′) *n.* A differentiated structure within a cell, such as a mitochondrion, vacuole, or chloroplast, that performs a specific function. [New Latin *organella,* diminutive of Medieval Latin *organum,* organ of the body, from Latin, implement, tool. See ORGAN.]

organ grinder *n.* A musician who plays a hurdy-gurdy and usually performs on the street.

or·gan·ic (ôr-găn′ĭk) *adj. Abbr.* **org. 1.** Of, relating to, or affecting organs or an organ of the body: *an organic disease.* **2.** Of, relating to, or derived from living organisms: *organic matter.* **3.a.** Using or produced with fertilizers of animal or vegetable matter, using no synthetic fertilizers or pesticides: *organic gardening; organic vegetables.* **b.** Free from chemical injections or additives, such as antibiotics or hormones: *organic chicken.* **c.** Simple, healthful, and close to nature: *an organic lifestyle.* **4.a.** Having properties associated with living organisms. **b.** Resembling a living organism in organization or development; interconnected: *society as an organic whole.* **5.** Constituting an integral part of a whole; fundamental. **6.** *Law.* Denoting or relating to the fundamental or constitutional laws and precepts of a government or an organization. **7.** *Chemistry.* Of or designating carbon compounds. **—or·gan′i·cal·ly** *adv.* **—or′gan·ic′i·ty** (ôr′gə-nĭs′ĭ-tē) *n.*

organic chemistry *n.* The chemistry of carbon compounds.

or·gan·i·cism (ôr-găn′ĭ-sĭz′əm) *n.* **1.** The theory that all disease is associated with structural alterations of organs. **2.** The theory that the total organization of an organism, rather than the functioning of individual organs, is the principal or exclusive determinant of every life process. **3.** The concept that society is analogous to a biological organism. **—or·gan′i·cist** *n.*

or·gan·ism (ôr′gə-nĭz′əm) *n.* **1.** An individual form of life, such as a plant, an animal, a bacterium, a protist, or a fungus; a body made up of organs, organelles, or other parts that work together to carry on the various processes of life. **2.** A system regarded as analogous in its structure or functions to a living body: *the social organism.* **—or′gan·is′mal** (-nĭz′məl), **or′gan·is′mic** (-mĭk) *adj.* **—or′gan·is′mi·cal·ly** *adv.*

or·gan·ist (ôr′gə-nĭst) *n. Music.* One who plays the organ.

or·gan·i·za·tion (ôr′gə-nĭ-zā′shən) *n. Abbr.* **org. 1.a.** The act or process of organizing. **b.** The state or manner of being organized: *a high degree of organization.* **2.** Something that has been organized or made into an ordered whole. **3.** Something made up of elements with varied functions that contribute to the whole and to collective functions; an organism. **4.** A group of persons organized for a particular purpose; an association: *a benevolent organization.* **5.a.** A structure through which individuals cooperate systematically to conduct business. **b.** The administrative personnel of such a structure. **—or′gan·i·za′tion·al** *adj.* **—or′gan·i·za′tion·al·ly** *adv.*

or·gan·ize (ôr′gə-nīz′) *v.* **-ized, -iz·ing, -iz·es.** *—tr.* **1.** To put together into an orderly, functional, structured whole. **2.a.** To arrange in a coherent form; systematize: *organized her thoughts before speaking.* **b.** To arrange in a desired pattern or structure: *"The painting is organized about a young reaper enjoying his noonday rest"* (William Carlos Williams). **3.** To arrange systematically for harmonious or united action: *organize a strike.* See Synonyms at **arrange. 4.a.** To establish as an organization: *organize a club.* See Synonyms at **found**[1]. **b.** To induce (employees) to form or join a labor union. **c.** To induce the employees of (a business or an industry) to form or join a union: *organize a factory. —intr.* **1.** To develop into or assume an organic structure. **2.** To form or join an activist group, especially a labor union. [Middle English *organisen,* from Old French *organiser,* from Medieval Latin *organizāre,* from Latin *organum,* tool, instrument. See ORGAN.] **—or′gan·iz′er** *n.*

or·gan·ized (ôr′gə-nīzd′) *adj. Abbr.* **org. 1.** Functioning within a formal structure, as in the coordination and direction of activities. **2.** Affiliated in an organization, especially a union. **3.** Efficient and methodical.

organized crime *n.* **1.** Widespread criminal activities, such as prostitution, interstate theft, or illegal gambling, that occur within a centrally controlled formal structure. **2.** The people and the groups involved in such criminal activities.

organo– or **organ–** *pref.* **1.** Organ: *organotherapy.* **2.** Organic: *organomercurial.* [Greek, from *organon.* See ORGAN.]

or·gan·o·chlo·rine (ôr-găn′ə-klôr′ēn′, -ĭn, -klōr′-) *n.* Any of various hydrocarbon pesticides, such as DDT, that contain chlorine. **—or·gan·o·chlo′rine** *adj.*

organ of Cor·ti (kôr′tē) *n.* A specialized structure located on the inner surface of the basilar membrane of the cochlea containing hair cells that transmit sound vibrations to the nerve fibers. [After Alfonso *Corti* (1822–1888), Italian anatomist.]

or·gan·o·gen·e·sis (ôr′gə-nō-jĕn′ĭ-sĭs, ôr-găn′ə-) *n., pl.* **-ses** (-sēz′). The formation and development of the organs of living things. **—or′gan·o·ge·net′ic** (-jə-nĕt′ĭk) *adj.* **—or′gan·o·ge·net′i·cal·ly** *adv.*

or·gan·og·ra·phy (ôr′gə-nŏg′rə-fē) *n., pl.* **-phies.** Scientific description of the organs of living things. **—or′gan·o·graph′ic** (-nə-grăf′ĭk) *adj.* **—or′gan·o·graph′i·cal·ly** *adv.*

or·gan·o·lep·tic (ôr′gə-nō-lĕp′tĭk, ôr-găn′ə-) *adj.* **1.** Relating to perception by a sensory organ. **2.** Involving the use of sense organs: *organoleptic tests.* [French *organoleptique* : Greek *organo-,* organo- + Greek *lēptikos,* receptive (from *lēptos,* taken, seized, from *lambanein,* to take).] **—or′gan·o·lep′ti·cal·ly** *adv.*

organ
Pipes and console

or·gan·ol·o·gy (ôr′gə-nŏl′ə-jē) *n.* The branch of biology that deals with the structure and function of organs. **—or′gan·o·log′ic** (ôr′gə-nə-lŏj′ĭk, ôr-găn′ə-), **or′gan·o·log′i·cal** (-ĭ-kəl) *adj.*

or·gan·o·mer·cu·ri·al (ôr-găn′ō-mər-kyo͝or′ē-əl) *n.* An organic compound that contains mercury. **—or·gan·o·mer·cu′ri·al** *adj.*

or·gan·o·me·tal·lic (ôr′gə-nō-mə-tăl′ĭk, ôr-găn′ō-) *adj.* Of, relating to, or constituting an organic compound containing a metal, especially a compound in which a metal atom is bonded directly to a carbon atom.

or·ga·non (ôr′gə-nŏn′) also **or·ga·num** (-nəm) *n., pl.* **-na** (-nə) or **-nons** also **-na** or **-nums.** A set of principles for use in scientific or philosophical investigation. [Greek, tool, organ of the body, instrument. See **werg-** in Appendix.]

or·gan·o·phos·phate (ôr′gə-nō-fŏs′fāt, ôr-găn′ə-) *n.* Any of several organic compounds containing phosphorus, some of which are used as fertilizers and pesticides. **—or′gan·o·phos′phate** *adj.*

or·gan·o·phos·pho·rus (ôr′gə-nō-fŏs′fər-əs, -fŏs-fôr′əs, -fōr′-, ôr-găn′ə-) *n.* An organophosphate. **—or′gan·o·phos′pho·rus, or′gan·o·phos′pho·rous** (ôr′gə-nō-fŏs′fər-əs, -fŏs-fôr′əs, -fōr′-, ôr-găn′ə-) *adj.*

or·gan·o·ther·a·py (ôr′gə-nō-thĕr′ə-pē, ôr-găn′ō-) *n., pl.* **-pies.** Treatment of disease with animal endocrine organs or extracts such as insulin and thyroxin. **—or′gan·o·ther′a·peu′tic** (-thĕr′ə-pyo͞o′tĭk) *adj.*

or·gan·ot·ro·pism (ôr′gə-nŏt′rə-pĭz′əm) also **or·gan·ot·ro·py** (-pē) *n.* The attraction of certain chemical compounds or microorganisms to specific tissues or organs of the body. **—or′gan·o·trop′ic** (ôr′gə-nō-trŏp′ĭk, -trō′pĭk, ôr-găn′ō-) *adj.* **—or′gan·o·trop′i·cal·ly** *adv.*

or·gan-pipe cactus (ôr′gən-pīp′) *n.* A tall, treelike cactus *(Lemaireocereus marginatus)* native to central Mexico and the southwest United States.

organ point *n. Music.* See **pedal point.**

or·ga·num[1] (ôr′gə-nəm) *n., pl.* **-na** (-nə) or **-nums.** *Music.* Any of several types of vocal polyphonic music, in two, three, or four parts, of the 9th to the early 13th century. [Medieval Latin, from Late Latin, church organ. See ORGAN.]

or·ga·num[2] (ôr′gə-nəm) *n., pl.* **-nums.** Variant of **organon.**

organ-pipe cactus

or·gan·za (ôr-găn′zə) *n.* A sheer, stiff fabric of silk or synthetic material used for trimming, neckwear, or evening dresses. [Probably after *Organzi* (Urgench), a city of southwest Central Asian U.S.S.R.]

or·gan·zine (ôr′gən-zēn′) *n.* A raw-silk thread, usually used as a warp thread. [French *organsin,* from Italian *organzino,* probably after *Organzi* (Urgench), a city of southwest Central Asian U.S.S.R.]

or·gasm (ôr′găz′əm) *n.* **1.** The highest point of sexual excitement, characterized by strong feelings of pleasure and marked normally by ejaculation of semen by the male and by vaginal contractions in the female. Also called *climax.* **2.** A similar point of intensity of emotional excitement. [French *orgasme* or New Latin *orgasmus,* both from Greek *orgasmos,* swelling, excitement, from *organ,* to swell up, be excited.] **—or·gas′mic** (ôr-găz′mĭk), **or·gas′tic** (-tĭk) *adj.* **—or·gas′mi·cal·ly, or·gas′ti·cal·ly** *adv.*

OR gate (ôr) *n. Computer Science.* A logic circuit that emits a signal if either or both of its input wires receive a signal. [From OR[1].]

or·geat (ôr′zhä′) *n.* A sweet flavoring of orange and almond used in cocktails and food. [French, from Old French, from Old Provençal *orjat,* from *ordj, orge,* barley, from Latin *hordeum.*]

or·gi·as·tic (ôr′jē-ăs′tĭk) *adj.* Of, relating to, or characteristic of an orgy. [Greek *orgiastikos,* from *orgiastēs,* celebrant of orgies, from *orgiazein,* to celebrate orgies, from *orgia,* orgies. See ORGY.] **—or′gi·ast′** *n.* **—or′gi·as′ti·cal·ly** *adv.*

or·gone (ôr′gōn) *n.* A theoretical universal life force emanating from all organic material that purportedly can be captured with a boothlike device and used to restore psychological well-being. [Probably : ORG(ANISM) + —ONE.]

or·gy (ôr′jē) *n., pl.* **-gies. 1.** A revel involving unrestrained indulgence, especially sexual activity. **2.** Uncontrolled or immoderate indulgence in an activity: *an orgy of spending.* See Synonyms at **binge. 3.** A secret rite in the cults of ancient Greek or Roman deities, typically involving frenzied singing, dancing, drinking, and sexual activity. [From *orgies,* secret rites, from Old French, from Latin *orgia,* from Greek. See **werg-** in Appendix.]

WORD HISTORY: The word *orgy* has become connected in the minds of many of us with unrestrained sexual activity, but its origins are much less licentious. We can trace the word as far back as the Indo-European root *werg–,* meaning "to do" and the source of our word *work.* Greek *orgia,* "secret rites, worship," also comes from the root *werg–,* by way of the form **worg–.* The Greek word was used with reference to the worship and the rites practiced in the worship of various deities, such as Orpheus and Dionysus. The word in Greek did not denote sexual activity, although this was a part of some of the various rites. The rites of Dionysus, for example, included only music, dancing, drinking, and the eating of animal sacrifices. Having passed through Latin and Old French into English the word *orgy* is first recorded in English with reference to the secret rites of the Greek and Roman religions in 1589. It is interesting to note that the word is first recorded with its modern sense in 18th-century English and perhaps in 17th-century French. Whether this speaks to a greater licentiousness in society or not must be left to the historian, but certainly the religious nature of the word has gone into eclipse.

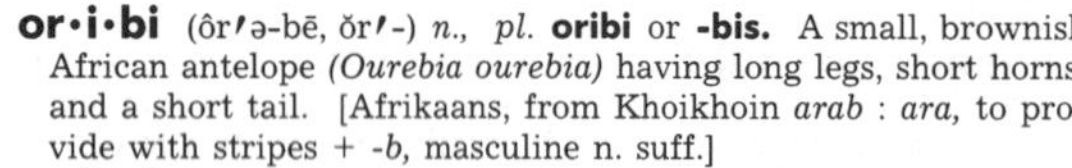

oriel

or·i·bi (ôr′ə-bē, ŏr′-) *n., pl.* **oribi** or **-bis.** A small, brownish African antelope *(Ourebia ourebia)* having long legs, short horns, and a short tail. [Afrikaans, from Khoikhoin *arab* : *ara,* to provide with stripes + *-b,* masculine n. suff.]

o·ri·el (ôr′ē-əl, ōr′-) *n.* A projecting bay window, supported from below with a corbel or bracket. [Middle English, from Old French *oriol,* porch, from Medieval Latin *oriolum.*]

o·ri·ent (ôr′ē-ənt, -ĕnt′, ōr′-) *n.* **1. Orient.** The countries of Asia, especially of eastern Asia. **2. a.** The luster characteristic of a pearl of high quality. **b.** A pearl having exceptional luster. **3.** *Archaic.* The place on the horizon where the sun rises; the east. **—orient** *adj.* **1.** Having exceptional luster: *orient gemstones.* **2.** *Archaic.* Eastern; oriental. **3.** *Archaic.* Rising in the sky; ascending. **—orient** (ôr′ē-ĕnt′, ōr′-) *v.* **-ent·ed, -ent·ing, -ents.** *—tr.* **1.** To locate or place in a particular relation to the points of the compass: *orient the swimming pool north and south.* **2.** To locate or place (something) so as to face the east, especially to build (a church) with the nave laid out west to east and the main altar at the eastern end. **3.** To align or position with respect to a point or system of reference: *oriented the telescope toward the moon; oriented her interests toward health care.* **4.** To determine the bearings of. **5.** To make familiar with or adjusted to facts, principles, or a situation. **6.** To focus (the content of a story or film, for example) toward the concerns and interests of a specific group. *—intr.* **1.** To turn toward the east. **2.** To become adjusted or aligned. [Middle English, from Old French, from Latin *oriēns, orient-,* rising sun, east, from present participle of *orīrī,* to arise, be born. See **er-[1]** in Appendix.]

o·ri·en·tal (ôr′ē-ĕn′tl, ōr′-) *adj.* **1.** Often **Oriental.** Of or relating to the countries of the Orient or their peoples or cultures; eastern: *"Oriental immigration"* (S.I. Hayakawa). **2. Oriental.** Of or designating the biogeographic region that includes Asia south of the Himalaya Mountains and the islands of the Malay Archipelago. **3.** Lustrous and valuable: *oriental pearls.* **4. a.** Of or relating to a genuine or superior gem: *an oriental ruby.* **b.** Relating to or designating corundum that resembles another stone in color. **—oriental** *n.* Often **Oriental.** *Offensive.* Used as a disparaging term for an Asian person. See Usage Note at **Asian. —o′ri·en′tal·ly** *adv.*

Oriental black mushroom *n.* See **shiitake.**

Oriental garlic *n.* See **Chinese chive.**

o·ri·en·ta·li·a or **O·ri·en·ta·li·a** (ôr′ē-ĕn-tā′lē-ə, -tāl′yə, ōr′-) *pl.n.* Things, especially decorative objects, produced in or associated with eastern Asia.

O·ri·en·tal·ism also **o·ri·en·tal·ism** (ôr′ē-ĕn′tl-ĭz′əm, ōr′-) *n.* **1.** A quality, mannerism, or custom specific to or characteristic of the Orient. **2.** Scholarly knowledge of eastern cultures, languages, and peoples. **—O′ri·en′tal·ist** *n.*

o·ri·en·tal·ize also **O·ri·en·tal·ize** (ôr′ē-ĕn′tl-īz′, ōr′-) *v.* **-ized, -iz·ing, -iz·es.** *—tr.* To give an oriental character or appearance to. *—intr.* To become oriental in character.

Oriental poppy *n.* A southwest Asian plant *(Papaver orientale)* widely cultivated for its brilliant scarlet and black flowers.

Oriental radish *n.* See **daikon.**

Oriental rug *n.* Any of numerous kinds of rugs made by hand in the Orient.

or·i·en·tate (ôr′ē-ĕn-tāt′, -ən-, ōr′-) *v.* **-tat·ed, -tat·ing, -tates.** *—tr.* To orient: *"He . . . stood for a moment, orientating himself exactly in the light of his knowledge"* (John le Carré). *—intr.* To face or turn to the east.

o·ri·en·ta·tion (ôr′ē-ĕn-tā′shən, -ən-, ōr′-) *n.* **1.** The act of orienting or the state of being oriented. **2.** Location or position relative to the points of the compass. **3.** The construction of a church so that its longitudinal axis is from west to east and its main altar is at the eastern end. **4.** The direction followed in the course of a trend, movement, or development. **5. a.** A tendency of thought; a general inclination: *a Marxist orientation.* **b.** Sexual orientation. **6. a.** An adjustment or adaptation to a new environment, situation, custom, or set of ideas. **b.** Introductory instruction concerning a new situation: *orientation for incoming students.* **7.** *Psychology.* Awareness of the objective world in relation to one's self.

or·i·en·teer·ing (ôr′ē-ĕn-tîr′ĭng, -ən-, ōr′-) *n. Sports.* A cross-country race in which competitors use a map and compass to find their way through unfamiliar territory. [Alteration of Swedish *orientering,* from *orientera,* to orient, from French *orienter,* from *orient,* east. See ORIENT.] **—or′i·en·teer′** *n.*

or·i·fice (ôr′ə-fĭs, ŏr′-) *n.* An opening, especially to a cavity or passage of the body; a mouth or vent. [Middle English, from Old French, from Late Latin *ōrificium* : Latin *ōs, ōr-,* mouth; see **ōs-** in Appendix + Latin *-ficium,* a making, doing (from *facere,* to make; see **dhē-** in Appendix).] **—or′i·fi′cial** (-fĭsh′əl) *adj.*

or·i·flamme (ôr′ə-flăm′, ŏr′-) *n.* **1.** An inspiring standard or symbol. **2.** The red or orange-red flag of the Abbey of Saint Denis in France, used as a standard by the early kings of France. [Middle English *oriflamble,* banner of St. Denis, from Old French, variant of *oriflambe,* possibly from Medieval Latin *aurea flamma, auriflamma* (Latin *aurea,* feminine of *aureus,* golden, from *aurum,* gold + Latin *flamma,* flame; see FLAME) or alteration of Old French **lorie flambe,* from Late Latin *laurea flammula,* laureled standard (Latin *laureus,* of laurel; see LAUREATE + Latin *flammula,* banner, diminutive of *flamma,* flame).]

orig. *abbr.* Origin; original; originally.

o·ri·ga·mi (ôr′ĭ-gä′mē) *n., pl.* **-mis. 1.** The art or process, originating in Japan, of folding paper into shapes representing flowers and birds, for example. **2.** A decorative object made by folding paper. [Japanese : *ori,* to fold + *kami,* paper.]

Or·i·gen (ôr′ĭ-jĕn′, -jən, ŏr′-). A.D.185?–254? Greek Christian philosopher known for his interpretations of the Old Testament, contained in *Hexapla.*

or·i·gin (ôr′ə-jĭn, ŏr′-) *n. Abbr.* **orig. 1.** The point at which something comes into existence or from which it derives or is derived. **2.** Ancestry: *"We cannot escape our origins, however hard we try"* (James Baldwin). **3.** The fact of originating; rise or derivation: *The rumor had its origin in an impulsive remark.* **4.** *Anatomy.* The point of attachment of a muscle that remains relatively fixed during contraction. **5.** *Mathematics.* The point of intersection of coordinate axes, as in the Cartesian coordinate system. [Middle English *origine,* ancestry, from Latin *orīgō, orīgin-,* from *orīrī,* to arise, be born. See **er-[1]** in Appendix.]

SYNONYMS: *origin, inception, source, root.* These nouns signify the point at which something originates. *Origin* is the point at which something comes into existence: *The origins of some words are unknown. "Man with all his noble qualities . . . still bears in his bodily frame the indelible stamp of his lowly origin"* (Charles Darwin). When *origin* refers to people, it means parentage or ancestry: *"He came . . . of mixed French and Scottish origin"* (Charlotte Brontë). *Inception* is the beginning, as of an action or process: *Between the inception of the litigation and its final disposition the plaintiff's first attorney retired. Source* can refer to the point of origin of a stream or a river: *"the Alpine sources of the Rhine"* (John Foster Kirk). In another sense the term signifies the point at which something springs into being or from which it derives or is obtained: *"one great original source of revenue . . . the wages of labor"* (Adam Smith). *"The mysterious . . . is the source of all true art and science"* (Albert Einstein). *Root* often denotes what is considered the fundamental cause of or basic reason for something: *"Lack of money is the root of all evil"* (George Bernard Shaw). *"Most of the problems a President has to face have their roots in the past"* (Harry S. Truman).

o·rig·i·nal (ə-rĭj′ə-nəl) *adj. Abbr.* **orig. 1.** Preceding all others in time; first. **2. a.** Not derived from something else; fresh and unusual: *an original play, not an adaptation.* **b.** Showing a marked departure from previous practice; new: *a truly original approach.* See Synonyms at **new. 3.** Productive of new things or new ideas; inventive: *an original mind.* **4.** Being the source from which a copy, reproduction, or translation is made. **—original** *n.* **1.** A first form from which other forms are made or developed: *Later models of the car retained many features of the original.* **2. a.** An authentic work of art: *bought an original, not a print.* **b.** Work that has been composed firsthand: *kept the original but sent a photocopy to his publisher.* **3.** A person who is appealingly odd or curious; a character. **4.** *Archaic.* The source from which something arises; an originator. [Middle English, from Old French, from Latin *orīginālis,* from *orīgō, orīgin-,* source. See ORIGIN.]

o·rig·i·nal·ism (ə-rĭj′ə-nə-lĭz′əm) *n.* The belief that the U.S. Constitution should be interpreted according to the intent of those who composed and adopted it. **—o·rig′i·nal·ist** *adj. & n.*

o·rig·i·nal·i·ty (ə-rĭj′ə-năl′ĭ-tē) *n., pl.* **-ties. 1.** The quality of being original. **2.** The capacity to act or think independently. **3.** Something original.

o·rig·i·nal·ly (ə-rĭj′ə-nə-lē) *adv. Abbr.* **orig. 1.** With reference to origin: *originally named Johnston.* **2.** At first: *not what I had originally expected.* **3.** In a highly distinctive manner: *interpreted the flute solo most originally.*

original sin *n.* According to Christian theology, the condition of sin that marks all human beings as a result of Adam's first act of disobedience.

o·rig·i·nate (ə-rĭj′ə-nāt′) *v.* **-nat·ed, -nat·ing, -nates.** *—tr.* To bring into being; create: *originated the practice of monthly reports.* *—intr.* To come into being; start. See Synonyms at **stem**[1]. **—o·rig′i·na′tion** *n.* **—o·rig′i·na′tive** *adj.* **—o·rig′i·na′tive·ly** *adv.* **—o·rig′i·na′tor** *n.*

origination fee *n.* A fee, often a percentage of the total principal of a loan, charged by a lender to a borrower on initiation of the loan.

O·ril·lia (ô-rĭl′yə, ō-rĭl′-). A city of southeast Ontario, Canada, north of Toronto. Population, 23,955.

o·ri·na·sal (ôr′ə-nā′zəl, ŏr′-) *Linguistics. adj.* Pronounced with both nasal and oral passages open. **—orinasal** *n.* An orinasal speech sound, such as a French nasal vowel. [Latin *ōs, ōr-,* mouth; see **ōs-** in Appendix + NASAL.]

O·rin·da (ə-rĭn′də, ô-rĭn′-, ō-rĭn′-). A community of western California, a residential suburb of the Oakland-Berkeley metropolitan area. Population, 16,825.

O-ring (ō′rĭng′) *n.* A flat ring made of rubber or plastic, used as a gasket.

O·ri·no·co (ôr′ə-nō′kō, ōr′-). A river of Venezuela flowing more than 2,414 km (1,500 mi), partly along the Colombia-Venezuela border, to the Atlantic Ocean.

o·ri·ole (ôr′ē-ōl′, ōr′-) *n.* **1.** Any of various Old World passerine birds of the family Oriolidae, of which the males are characteristically black and bright yellow or orange. **2.** Any of various similar New World birds of the family Icteridae. [Obsolete French *oriol,* from Old French, from Latin *aureolus,* diminutive of *aureus,* golden, from *aurum,* gold.]

O·ri·on (ō-rī′ən, ə-rī′-) *n.* **1.** *Greek Mythology.* A giant hunter, pursuer of the Pleiades and lover of Eos, killed by Artemis. **2.** A constellation in the celestial equator near Gemini and Taurus, containing the stars Betelgeuse and Rigel. [Middle English *Orioun,* from Latin *Ōrīōn,* from Greek.]

or·i·son (ôr′ĭ-sən, -zən, ŏr′-) *n.* A prayer. [Middle English *orisoun,* from Old French *orison,* from Late Latin *ōrātiō, ōrātiōn-.* See ORATION.]

O·ri·ya (ô-rē′yə) *n.* The Indic language of Orissa, a state in eastern India.

O·ri·za·ba (ôr′ĭ-zä′bə, ōr′-, ô′rē-sä′vä). A city of east-central Mexico west of Veracruz. It is a manufacturing center and popular resort. Population, 114,848.

Orizaba, Mount. See **Citlaltépetl.**

Ork·ney Islands (ôrk′nē). An archipelago comprising about 70 islands in the Atlantic Ocean and the North Sea off the northeast coast of Scotland. Settled by Picts, the islands were a Norse dependency after 875 and became part of Scotland in 1472.

Or·lan·do (ôr-lăn′dō). A city of central Florida east-northeast of Tampa. It is a trade and processing center with aerospace and electronics industries. Population, 128,394.

Or·lan·do (ôr-lăn′dō, -län′-), **Vittorio Emanuele.** 1860–1952. Italian politician who served as prime minister of Italy (1917–1919) and was the Italian delegate at the Paris Peace Conference (1919–1920).

Or·land Park (ôr′lənd). A village of northeast Illinois, a residential and manufacturing suburb of Chicago. Population, 23,035.

Or·lé·a·nais (ôr′lē-ə-nā′, ôr-lā-ä-nĕ′). A historical region and former province of north-central France. Most of the area has been part of the royal domain since the tenth century.

Or·le·an·ist (ôr′lē-ə-nĭst) *n.* A supporter of the Orléans branch of the French royal family, descended from a younger brother of Louis XIV.

Or·lé·ans (ôr-lā-äɴ′). A city of north-central France on the Loire River south-southwest of Paris. Founded by Celts and conquered by Julius Caesar in 52 B.C., the city was taken by Clovis I in A.D. 498 and became the center of the Frankish kingdom of **Orléans** in 511. It became a principal residence of the Capetian kings in the tenth century. The siege of Orléans by the English (1428–1429) was lifted by troops led by Joan of Arc, the Maid of Orléans. Population, 102,117.

Or·lon (ôr′lŏn′). A trademark used for an acrylic fiber or yarns made from this fiber.

or·lop (ôr′lŏp′) *n. Nautical.* The lowest deck of a ship, especially a warship, having at least four decks. [Middle English *overlop,* floor covering a ship's hold, from Middle Low German *overlōp* : *over,* over; see **uper** in Appendix + *lōp,* a running.]

Or·ly (ôr′lē, ôr-lē′). A city of north-central France, a suburb of Paris. Orly Field is a major international airport serving the Paris region. Population, 23,766.

Or·man·dy (ôr′mən-dē), **Eugene.** 1899–1985. Hungarian-born American conductor who directed the Philadelphia Orchestra from 1938 to 1980.

Or·mazd also **Or·muzd** (ôr′məzd) *n.* The chief deity of Zoroastrianism, the creator of the world, the source of light, and the embodiment of good. [Persian *Ormazd,* from Old Persian *Auramazda,* from Avestan *ahurō mazdå.* See AHURA MAZDA.]

or·mer (ôr′mər) *n. Chiefly British.* An abalone, especially of the species *Haliotis tuberculata,* found chiefly in the Channel Islands. [French dialectal, from French *ormier,* short for *oreille-de-mer,* translation of Latin *auris maris,* sea-ear : *auris,* ear; see **ous-** in Appendix + *maris,* genitive of *mare,* sea; see **mori-** in Appendix.]

or·mo·lu (ôr′mə-lo͞o′) *n.* **1.** Any of several copper and zinc or tin alloys resembling gold in appearance and used to ornament furniture, moldings, architectural details, and jewelry. **2.** An imitation of gold. [French *or moulu* : *or,* gold (from Old French; see OR[3]) + obsolete French *molu,* past participle of *moudre,* to grind up (from Old French, from Latin *molere;* see **melə-** in Appendix).]

Or·mond Beach (ôr′mənd). A city of northeast Florida on the Atlantic Ocean north of Daytona Beach. Population, 21,378.

Or·muz (ôr′mŭz′, ôr-mo͞oz′), **Strait of.** See Strait of **Hormuz.**

Or·muzd (ôr′məzd) *n.* Variant of **Ormazd.**

or·na·ment (ôr′nə-mənt) *n.* **1.** Something that decorates or adorns; an embellishment. **2.** A person considered as a source of pride, honor, or credit: *a ballerina who is an ornament to the world of dance.* **3.** *Music.* A note or group of notes that embellishes a melody. **—ornament** (-mĕnt′) *tr.v.* **-ment·ed, -ment·ing, -ments. 1.** To furnish with ornaments: *ornamented the windows with hanging plants.* **2.** To be an ornament to: *"The babies ornament her ankles, dangle from her pant legs"* (Carolyn Chute). [Middle English *ournement,* from Old French *ornement,* from Latin *ōrnāmentum,* from *ōrnāre,* to adorn. See **ar-** in Appendix.] **—or′na·ment′er** *n.*

or·na·men·tal (ôr′nə-mĕn′tl) *adj.* Of, relating to, or serving as an ornament or a decoration. **—ornamental** *n.* Something that serves as ornamentation, especially a plant grown for its beauty. **—or′na·men′tal·ly** *adv.*

or·na·men·ta·tion (ôr′nə-mĕn-tā′shən) *n.* **1.a.** The act or process of decorating, adorning, or embellishing. **b.** The state of being decorated, adorned, or embellished. **2.** Something that decorates or adorns; an embellishment.

or·nate (ôr-nāt′) *adj.* **1.** Elaborately, heavily, and often excessively ornamented. **2.** Flashy, showy, or florid in style or manner; flowery. [Middle English, from Latin *ōrnātus,* past participle of *ōrnāre,* to embellish. See **ar-** in Appendix.] **—or·nate′ly** *adv.* **—or·nate′ness** *n.*

SYNONYMS: *ornate, florid, flamboyant, baroque, rococo.* These adjectives mean elaborately, often excessively ornamented. *Ornate* implies lavishness and heaviness: *a building with an ornate façade; "ornate rhetoric taught out of the rule of Plato"* (John Milton). Something *florid* is both ornate and flowery: *The senator gave a florid speech. Flamboyant* relates to a French Gothic architectural style marked by wavy flamelike forms; in a less technical sense the term suggests excessively vivid color, overwrought design, or striking audacity or verve: *flamboyant red hair; flamboyant handwriting; "that flamboyant but egotistical figure, Alexander the Great"* (H.G. Wells). *Baroque* applies to a European artistic style marked by ornate scrolls and curves. It often connotes rich, sometimes bizarre or incongruous ornamentation: *"the building . . . coldly classical or frantically baroque"* (William Dean Howells). *Rococo* describes the 18th-century European style that grew out of the baroque and is characterized by profuse ornamentation, such as graceful and delicate shells and foliage. It can also connote immoderate, perhaps even ridiculous complexity: *an exquisite gilded rococo mirror; rococo notions of an imperial presidency; "a rococo combination of warm slivers of buttery Scotch salmon encircling dollops of crème fraîche, each speckled with a different caviar"* (Bryan Miller).

or·ner·y (ôr′nə-rē) *adj.* **-i·er, -i·est.** Mean-spirited, disagreeable, and contrary in disposition; cantankerous. See Synonyms at **contrary.** [Alteration of ORDINARY.] **—or′ner·i·ness′** *n.*

ornith. *abbr.* **1.** Ornithologic; ornithological. **2.** Ornithology.

ornith– *pref.* Variant of **ornitho–.**

or·nith·ic (ôr-nĭth′ĭk) *adj.* Of, relating to, or characteristic of birds.

or·ni·thine (ôr′nə-thēn′) *n.* An amino acid, $C_5H_{12}N_2O_2$, formed by hydrolyzing arginine and important in the formation of urea. [*ornithuric acid,* an acid found in birds' urine (ORNITH(O)– + URIC ACID) + –INE[2].]

or·nith·is·chi·an (ôr′nə-thĭs′kē-ən) *n.* A dinosaur of the order Ornithischia, having a pelvic structure similar to that of birds. **—ornithischian** *adj.* Of, belonging to, or characteristic of the order Ornithischia. [From New Latin *Ornithischia,* order name : ORNITH(O)– + Greek *iskhion,* hip joint.]

ornitho– or **ornith–** *pref.* Bird: *ornithosis.* [New Latin, from Greek, from *ornis, ornith-,* bird. See **or-** in Appendix.]

or·ni·thol·o·gy (ôr′nə-thŏl′ə-jē) *n. Abbr.* **ornith.** The branch of zoology that deals with the study of birds. **—or′ni·tho·log′ic** (-thə-lŏj′ĭk), **or′ni·tho·log′i·cal** (-ĭ-kəl) *adj.* **—or′ni·tho·log′i·cal·ly** *adv.* **—or′ni·thol′o·gist** *n.*

Orion

ă pat	oi boy
ā pay	ou out
âr care	o͝o took
ä father	o͞o boot
ĕ pet	ŭ cut
ē be	ûr urge
ĭ pit	th thin
ī pie	*th* this
îr pier	hw which
ŏ pot	zh vision
ō toe	ə about, item
ô paw	♦ regionalism

Stress marks: ′ (primary); ′ (secondary), as in **dictionary** (dĭk′shə-nĕr′ē)

José Orozco

or·ni·thop·ter (ôr′nə-thŏp′tər) *n.* A machine shaped like an aircraft that is held aloft and propelled by wing movements.

or·ni·tho·sis (ôr′nə-thō′sĭs) *n.* Psittacosis, especially as contracted by human beings from birds.

oro– *pref.* Mountain: *orogeny.* [Greek, from *oros,* mountain.]

o·rog·e·ny (ô-rŏj′ə-nē) also **or·o·gen·e·sis** (ôr′ə-jĕn′ĭ-sĭs, ŏr′-) *n.* The process of mountain formation, especially by a folding and faulting of the earth's crust. **—or′o·gen′ic** (ôr′ə-jĕn′ĭk, ŏr′-) *adj.* **—or′o·gen′i·cal·ly** *adv.*

o·rog·ra·phy (ô-rŏg′rə-fē) *n.* The study of the physical geography of mountains and mountain ranges. **—or′o·graph′ic** (ôr′ə-grăf′ĭk, ŏr′-), **or′o·graph′i·cal** (-ĭ-kəl) *adj.* **—or′o·graph′i·cal·ly** *adv.*

o·ro·ide (ôr′ō-īd′, ŏr′-) also **o·re·ide** (-ē-īd′) *n.* An alloy of copper, zinc, and tin, used in imitation gold jewelry. [Alteration of French *oréide* : *or,* gold; see OR[3] + *-éide,* resembling (from Greek *-oeidēs,* -oid).]

o·rol·o·gy (ô-rŏl′ə-jē) *n.* The study of mountains. **—o′ro·log′i·cal** (ôr′ə-lŏj′ĭ-kəl, ŏr′-) *adj.* **—o′ro·log′i·cal·ly** *adv.* **—o·rol′o·gist** *n.*

O·ro·mo (ô-rō′mō) *n., pl.* **Oromo** or **-mos. 1.** A member of a widely acculturated people of southern and central Ethiopia and northern Kenya. **2.** The Cushitic language of the Oromo. Also called *Galla.*

O·ron·tes (ô-rŏn′tēz). A river, about 402 km (250 mi) long, flowing through Lebanon, Syria, and southern Turkey to the Mediterranean Sea. It is used extensively for irrigation.

o·ro·phar·ynx (ôr′ō-făr′ĭngks, ŏr′-) *n., pl.* **-pha·ryn·ges** (-fə-rĭn′jēz) or **-phar·ynx·es.** The part of the pharynx between the soft palate and the epiglottis. [Latin *ōs, ōr-,* mouth; see OS[1] + PHARYNX.] **—o′ro·pha·ryn′ge·al** (-fə-rĭn′jē-əl, -făr′ən-jē′əl) *adj.*

o·ro·tund (ôr′ə-tŭnd′, ŏr′-) *adj.* **1.** Pompous and bombastic: *orotund talk.* **2.** Full in sound; sonorous: *orotund tones.* [From alteration of Latin *ōre rotundō,* with a round mouth : *ōre,* ablative of *ōs,* mouth; see **ōs-** in Appendix + *rotundō,* ablative of *rotundus,* round; see ROTUND.] **—o′ro·tun′di·ty** (ôr′ə-tŭn′dĭ-tē, ŏr′-) *n.*

O·roz·co (ō-rôs′kō), **José Clemente.** 1883–1949. Mexican painter noted for his frescoes.

or·phan (ôr′fən) *n.* **1.a.** A child whose parents are dead. **b.** A child who has been deprived of parental care and has not been adopted. **2.** A young animal without a mother. **3.** One that lacks support, supervision, or care: *A lack of corporate interest has made the subsidiary an orphan.* **—orphan** *adj.* **1.** Deprived of parents. **2.** Intended for orphans: *an orphan home.* **3.** Lacking support or supervision; abandoned: *"an aggregation of every orphan technology at the Pentagon, stuff that's been around for years that nobody would buy"* (Harper's). **—orphan** *tr.v.* **-phaned, -phan·ing, -phans.** To deprive (a child) of one parent or both parents. [Middle English, from Late Latin *orphanus,* from Greek *orphanos,* orphaned. See **orbh-** in Appendix.] **—or′phan·hood′** *n.*

or·phan·age (ôr′fə-nĭj) *n.* **1.** A public institution for the care and protection of children without parents. **2.** The condition of being a child without parents.

orrery
c. 1800 miniature orrery
by Edward Troughton

Or·phe·us (ôr′fē-əs, -fyo͞os′) *n. Greek Mythology.* A legendary Thracian poet and musician whose music had the power to move even inanimate objects and who almost succeeded in rescuing his wife Eurydice from Hades. [Greek.] **—Or·phe′an** (ôr-fē′ən, ôr′fē-ən) *adj.*

Or·phic (ôr′fĭk) *adj.* **1.** *Greek Mythology.* Of or ascribed to Orpheus: *the Orphic poems; Orphic mysteries.* **2.** Of, relating to, or characteristic of the dogmas, mysteries, and philosophical principles set forth in the poems ascribed to Orpheus. **3.** Capable of casting a charm or spell; entrancing. **4.** Often **orphic.** Mystic or occult. [Greek *Orphikos,* from *Orpheus,* Orpheus.] **—Or′phi·cal·ly** *adv.*

Or·phism (ôr′fĭz′əm) *n.* **1.** An ancient Greek mystery religion arising in the sixth century B.C. from a synthesis of pre-Hellenic beliefs with the Thracian cult of Zagreus and soon becoming mingled with the Eleusinian mysteries and the doctrines of Pythagoras. **2.** Often **orphism.** A short-lived movement in early 20th-century painting, derived from cubism but marked by a lyrical style and the use of bold color. [French *orphisme,* from *Orphée,* Orpheus, from Greek *Orpheus.*] **—Or′phist** *n.*

José Ortega y Gasset

or·phrey (ôr′frē) also **or·fray** (-frā′) *n., pl.* **-phreys** also **-frays. 1.** A band of elaborate embroidery decorating the front of certain ecclesiastical vestments. **2.** Elaborate embroidery, especially when made of gold. [Middle English *orfrey,* alteration of *orfreis,* from Old French, from Medieval Latin *aurifrigium* : Latin *aurum,* gold + Latin *Phrygius,* Phrygian.]

or·pi·ment (ôr′pə-mənt) *n.* Arsenic trisulfide, As_2S_3, a yellow mineral used as a pigment. [Middle English, from Old French, from Latin *auripigmentum* : *aurum,* gold + *pigmentum,* pigment; see PIGMENT.]

or·pine (ôr′pĭn) *n.* Any of several succulent plants of the genus *Sedum,* especially the Eurasian species *S. telephium,* having clusters of reddish-purple flowers. Also called *live-forever.* [Middle English *orpin,* from Old French, from *orpiment,* orpiment. See ORPIMENT.]

Or·ping·ton (ôr′pĭng-tən) *n.* Any of a breed of large, white-skinned domestic fowls having a single comb and unfeathered legs, originally bred in England for both meat and eggs. [After *Orpington,* a district of southeast England.]

Orr (ôr), **Robert.** Called "Bobby." Born 1948. Canadian-born hockey player. He led the National Hockey League in scoring in 1970 and 1975 and was the first defenseman to score more than 100 points in a season.

or·re·ry (ôr′ə-rē, ŏr′-) *n., pl.* **-ries.** A mechanical model of the solar system. [After Charles Boyle, Fourth Earl of *Orrery* (1676–1731), for whom one was made.]

or·ris (ôr′ĭs, ŏr′-) *n.* **1.** Any of several species of iris having a fragrant rootstock, especially a variety of the hybrid *Iris germanica.* **2.** The fragrant rootstock of the orris, used in perfumes and cosmetics. In this sense, also called *orrisroot.* [Probably alteration of Middle English *yreos,* from Medieval Latin, alteration of Latin *īris.* See IRIS.]

or·ris·root (ôr′ĭs-ro͞ot′, -ro͝ot′, ŏr′-) *n.* See **orris** (sense 2).

Orsk (ôrsk). A city of western Russia on the Ural River east-southeast of Orenburg. It is an industrial center in an area with rich mineral deposits. Population, 266,000.

ort (ôrt) *n.* **1.** A small scrap or leaving of food after a meal is completed. Often used in the plural. **2.** A scrap; a bit. [Middle English *orte,* food left by animals, probably from Middle Dutch : *oor,* out; see **ud-** in Appendix + *eten,* to eat; see **ed-** in Appendix.]

Or·te·ga (ôr-tā′gə, -tĕ′gä), **Daniel.** Born 1945. Nicaraguan revolutionary leader and politician. He helped establish the Government of National Reconstruction after the overthrow of the Somoza regime (1979) and later served as president (1984–1990).

Or·te·ga y Gas·set (ôr-tā′gə ē gä-sĕt′), **José.** 1883–1955. Spanish philosopher. His most famous work, *The Revolt of the Masses* (1929), argues that human beings are essentially unequal and that an intellectual elite is necessary.

orth. *abbr.* **1.** Orthopedic. **2.** Orthopedics.

orth– *pref.* Variant of **ortho–.**

or·thi·con (ôr′thĭ-kŏn′) *n.* A television camera pickup tube, more sensitive than the iconoscope, that uses a low-velocity electron beam to scan a photoactive mosaic. Also called *image orthicon.* [ORTH(O)– + ICON(OSCOPE).]

or·tho (ôr′thō) *adj.* Orthochromatic. [From ORTHO–.]

ortho– or **orth–** *pref.* **1.** Straight; upright; vertical: *orthotropous.* **2.** Perpendicular: *orthorhombic.* **3.** Correct; correction: *orthopsychiatry.* **4.** The most fully hydrated form of an acid or of its salts: *orthoboric acid.* **5.** Diatomic molecules in which the nuclei have the same spin direction: *orthohydrogen.* **6.** Of or relating to one of three possible isomers of a benzene ring with two attached chemical groups in which the carbon atoms with attached groups are adjacent: ortho-*dibromobenzene.* [Middle English, from Old French, from Latin, from Greek, from *orthos,* straight, correct, right.]

or·tho·cen·ter (ôr′thō-sĕn′tər) *n.* The point of intersection of the three altitudes of a triangle.

or·tho·chro·mat·ic (ôr′thō-krō-măt′ĭk) *adj.* **1.** Of, having, or accurately reproducing the colors of nature. **2.** Of or relating to a film, plate, or emulsion that is sensitive to all colors except red and renders red as dark gray and blue and green as light gray. **—or′tho·chro′ma·tism** (-krō′mə-tĭz′əm) *n.*

or·tho·clase (ôr′thə-klās′, -klāz′) *n.* A variety of feldspar, essentially potassium aluminum silicate, $KAlSi_3O_8$, characterized by a monoclinic crystalline structure and found in igneous or granitic rock. Also called *potash feldspar.* [Greek *ortho-,* ortho- + Greek *klasis,* a breaking (from *klan,* to break).]

or·tho·clas·tic (ôr′thə-klăs′tĭk) *adj. Geology.* Having right-angled cleavage.

or·tho·don·tia (ôr′thə-dŏn′shə) or **or·tho·don·ture** (-dŏn′chər) *n.* Orthodontics.

or·tho·don·tics (ôr′thə-dŏn′tĭks) *n. (used with a sing. verb).* The dental specialty and practice of preventing and correcting irregularities of the teeth, as by the use of braces. **—or′tho·don′tic** *adj.* **—or′tho·don′ti·cal·ly** *adv.* **—or′tho·don′tist** *n.*

or·tho·don·ture (ôr′thə-dŏn′chər) *n.* Variant of **orthodontia.**

or·tho·dox (ôr′thə-dŏks′) *adj.* **1.** Adhering to the accepted or traditional and established faith, especially in religion. **2.** Adhering to the Christian faith as expressed in the early Christian ecumenical creeds. **3. Orthodox. a.** Of or relating to any of the churches or rites of the Eastern Orthodox Church. **b.** Of or relating to Orthodox Judaism. **4.** Adhering to what is commonly accepted, customary, or traditional: *an orthodox view of world affairs.* **—orthodox** *n.* **1.** One that is orthodox. **2. Orthodox.** A member of an Eastern Orthodox church. [Middle English *orthodoxe,* from Old French, from Late Latin *orthodoxus,* from Late Greek *orthodoxos* : Greek *ortho-,* ortho- + Greek *doxa,* opinion (from *dokein,* to think; see **dek-** in Appendix).] **—or′tho·dox′ly** *adv.*

Orthodox Church *n.* The Eastern Orthodox Church.

Orthodox Judaism *n.* The branch of Judaism that is governed by adherence to the Torah as interpreted in the Talmud.

orthodox sleep *n.* Sleep characterized by a slow alpha rhythm and the absence of REM.

or·tho·dox·y (ôr′thə-dŏk′sē) *n., pl.* **-ies. 1.** The quality or state of being orthodox. **2.** Orthodox practice, custom, or belief. **3. Orthodoxy. a.** The beliefs and practices of the Eastern Orthodox Church. **b.** Orthodox Judaism.

or·tho·e·py (ôr-thō′ə-pē, ôr′thō-ĕp′ē) *n. Linguistics.* **1.**

The study of the pronunciation of words. **2.** The customary pronunciation of words. [Greek *orthoepeia,* correctness of diction : *ortho-,* ortho- + *epos, epe-,* word; see **wekʷ-** in Appendix.] **—or′tho·ep′ic** (-ĕp′ĭk), **or′tho·ep′i·cal** (-ĕp′ĭ-kəl) *adj.* **—or·tho′e·pist** *n.*

or·tho·gen·e·sis (ôr′thō-jĕn′ĭ-sĭs) *n.* **1.** *Biology.* The theory that the evolution of a species is influenced most strongly by internal factors and is not subject to the external forces of natural selection. **2.** The theory that all cultures pass through sequential periods in the same order. **—or′tho·ge·net′ic** (-jə-nĕt′ĭk) *adj.* **—or′tho·ge·net′i·cal·ly** *adv.*

or·thog·o·nal (ôr-thŏg′ə-nəl) *adj. Mathematics.* Relating to or composed of right angles. [From Greek *orthogōnios* : *ortho-,* ortho- + *gōnia,* angle; see **genu-¹** in Appendix.] **—or·thog′o·nal·ly** *adv.*

orthogonal projection *n.* The two-dimensional graphic representation of an object formed by the perpendicular intersections of lines drawn from points on the object to a plane of projection. Also called *orthographic projection.*

or·tho·graph·ic (ôr′thə-grăf′ĭk) also **or·tho·graph·i·cal** (-ĭ-kəl) *adj.* **1.** Of or relating to orthography. **2.** Spelled correctly. **3.** *Mathematics.* Having perpendicular lines. **—or′tho·graph′i·cal·ly** *adv.*

orthographic projection *n.* See **orthogonal projection.**

or·thog·ra·phy (ôr-thŏg′rə-fē) *n., pl.* **-phies. 1.** The art or study of correct spelling according to established usage. **2.** The aspect of language study concerned with letters and their sequences in words. **3.** A method of representing the sounds of language or a language by letters and diacritics; spelling. **—or·thog′ra·pher, or·thog′ra·phist** *n.*

or·tho·mo·lec·u·lar (ôr′thō-mə-lĕk′yə-lər) *adj.* Of, relating to, or being a theory holding that mental diseases or abnormalities result from various chemical imbalances or deficiencies and can be cured by restoring proper levels of chemical substances, such as vitamins and minerals, in the body.

or·tho·pe·dics also **or·tho·pae·dics** (ôr′thə-pē′dĭks) *n. (used with a sing. verb). Abbr.* **orth.** The branch of medicine that deals with the prevention or correction of injuries or disorders of the skeletal system and associated muscles, joints, and ligaments. [From *orthopedic,* from French *orthopédique,* from *orthopédie,* orthopedic surgery : Greek *ortho-,* ortho- + Greek *paideia,* child-rearing (from *pais, paid-,* child; see **pau-** in Appendix).] **—or′tho·pe′dic** *adj.* **—or′tho·pe′di·cal·ly** *adv.* **—or′tho·pe′dist** *n.*

or·tho·psy·chi·a·try (ôr′thō-sī-kī′ə-trē, -sĭ-) *n.* The psychiatric study, treatment, and prevention of emotional and behavioral problems, especially of those that arise during early development. **—or′tho·psy′chi·at′ric** (-sī′kē-ăt′rĭk), **or′tho·psy′chi·at′ri·cal** (-rĭ-kəl) *adj.* **—or′tho·psy·chi′a·trist** *n.*

or·thop·ter·an (ôr-thŏp′tər-ən) also **or·thop·ter·on** (-tə-rŏn′, -tər-ən) *n.* An insect of the order Orthoptera, characterized by folded membranous hind wings covered by narrow, leathery forewings and mouthparts that are adapted for chewing. Insects of this order include the locusts, cockroaches, crickets, and grasshoppers. [From New Latin *Orthoptera,* order name : Greek *ortho-,* ortho- + Greek *ptera,* neuter pl. of *pteron,* wing; see **pet-** in Appendix.] **—or·thop′ter·an, or·thop′ter·ous, or·thop′ter·al** *adj.*

or·tho·rhom·bic (ôr′thō-rŏm′bĭk) *adj.* Of or relating to a crystalline structure of three mutually perpendicular axes of different length.

or·tho·scop·ic (ôr′thə-skŏp′ĭk) *adj.* **1.** Having normal vision; free from visual distortion. **2.** Giving an undistorted image. Used of an optical instrument.

or·tho·stat·ic (ôr′thə-stăt′ĭk) *adj.* Relating to or caused by standing upright: *orthostatic hypotension.* [ORTHO— + Greek *statos,* standing; see STATIC + —IC.]

or·thot·ics (ôr-thŏt′ĭks) *n. (used with a sing. verb).* The science that deals with the use of specialized mechanical devices to support or supplement weakened or abnormal joints or limbs. [From New Latin *orthōsis, orthōt-,* artificial support, brace, from Greek, a straightening, from *orthoun,* to straighten, from *orthos,* straight.] **—or·thot′ic** *adj. & n.* **—or·thot′ist** (ôr-thŏt′ĭst, ôr′-thə-tĭst) *n.*

or·tho·trop·ic (ôr′thə-trŏp′ĭk, -trō′pĭk) *adj.* **1.** Tending to grow or form along a vertical axis. **2.** Of or relating to a bridge deck consisting of steel plates supported by ribs underneath. **—or′tho·trop′i·cal·ly** *adv.* **—or·thot′ro·pism** (ôr-thŏt′rə-pĭz′əm) *n.*

or·thot·ro·pous (ôr-thŏt′rə-pəs) *adj. Botany.* Growing straight, so that the micropyle is at the end opposite the stalk. Used of an ovule.

Ort·les (ôrt′lās) also **Ort·ler** (-lər). A range of the Alps in northern Italy rising to 3,901.6 m (12,792 ft) at **Ortles** peak.

or·to·lan (ôr′tl-ən) *n.* **1.** A small, brownish Old World bunting *(Emberiza hortulana),* eaten as a delicacy. **2.** Any of several New World birds, such as the bobolink and the sora. [French, from Provençal, gardener, ortolan, from Latin *hortulānus,* from *hortulus,* diminutive of *hortus,* garden. See **gher-¹** in Appendix.]

Or·ton (ôr′tn), **Joe.** Full name John Kingsley Orton. 1933–1967. British playwright noted for his black comedies, including *Entertaining Mr. Sloane* (1964) and *What the Butler Saw* (1969).

O·ru·ro (ô-ro͞o′rô). A city of western Bolivia southeast of La Paz. At an altitude of 3,708.5 m (12,159 ft), it depends on mineral deposits found in the area for its economy. Population, 178,393.

ORV *abbr.* Off-road vehicle.

Or·well (ôr′wĕl′, -wəl), **George.** Pen name of Eric Arthur Blair. 1903–1950. British writer whose imaginative fiction attacks totalitarianism and reflects his concern with social justice. His works include *Animal Farm* (1945) and *1984* (1949).

Or·well·i·an (ôr-wĕl′ē-ən) *adj.* Of, relating to, or evocative of the works of George Orwell, especially the satirical novel *1984,* which depicts a futuristic totalitarian state.

-ory *suff.* **1.** Of, relating to, or characterized by: *advisory.* **2.** A place or thing used for or connected with: *crematory.* [Middle English *-orie,* from Old North French and Anglo-Norman, from Latin *-ōrius,* adj. suff., and *-ōrium,* n. suff.]

o·ryx (ôr′ĭks, ōr′-, ŏr′-) *n., pl.* **oryx** or **o·ryx·es.** Any of several African antelopes of the genus *Oryx,* including the gemsbok, having long, straight or slightly curved horns and a hump above the shoulders. [Latin, from Greek *orux,* pickax, gazelle (from its sharp horns), perhaps from *orussein,* to dig.]

or·zo (ôr′zō) *n.* A kind of pasta shaped like pearls of barley, frequently prepared with lamb in Greek cuisine. [Italian, barley, orzo, from Latin *hordeum.*]

os¹ (ŏs) *n., pl.* **o·ra** (ôr′ə, ōr′ə). A mouth or an opening. [Latin *ōs,* mouth. See **ōs-** in Appendix.]

os² (ŏs) *n., pl.* **os·sa** (ŏs′ə). A bone. [Latin, bone. See **ost-** in Appendix.]

os³ (ōs) *n., pl.* **os·ar** (ō′sär′). See **esker.** [Swedish *ås,* ridge, from Old Norse *āss.*]

Os The symbol for the element **osmium.**

o.s. *abbr.* **1.** *Latin.* Oculus sinister (left eye). **2.** Old series. **3.** Or **o/s.** Out of stock.

O.S. *abbr.* **1.** Or **O/S.** Old Style. **2.** Ordinary seaman.

OSA or **O.S.A.** *abbr.* Order of Saint Augustine.

O·sage (ō′sāj′, ō-sāj′) *n., pl.* **Osage** or **O·sag·es. 1.a.** A Native American people formerly inhabiting western Missouri and later southeast Kansas, with a present-day population in north-central Oklahoma. Substantial oil reserves were discovered on Osage lands in the early 20th century. **b.** A member of this people. **2.** The Siouan language of the Osage. [French, from Osage *wazházhe,* tribal name.] **—O′sage′** *adj.*

Osage orange *n.* A dioecious spiny tree *(Maclura pomifera),* native to Arkansas and Texas and having pulpy, inedible, orange-like multiple fruit.

Osage River. A river, about 579 km (360 mi) long, of central Missouri rising as the confluence of two smaller streams on the Kansas border and flowing east and northeast through the Lake of the Ozarks and on to the Missouri River near Jefferson City.

O·sa·ka (ō-sä′kə, ô′sä-kä′). A city of southern Honshu, Japan, on **Osaka Bay,** an inlet of the Pacific Ocean. Osaka was the leading commercial center of Japan during the feudal period and today is highly industrialized. Population, 2,636,260.

os·ar (ō′sär′) *n.* Plural of **os³.**

O·sas·co (o͞o-säs′ko͞o). A city of southeast Brazil, an industrial suburb of São Paulo. Population, 474,543.

OSB or **O.S.B.** *abbr.* Order of Saint Benedict.

Os·born (ŏz′bərn, -bôrn′), **Henry Fairfield.** 1857–1935. American paleontologist who was president (1908–1935) of the American Museum of Natural History in New York City.

Os·borne (ŏz′bərn, -bôrn′, -bōrn′), **John James.** Born 1929. British playwright and member of the Angry Young Men who is best known for his first play, *Look Back in Anger* (1956).

Osborne, Thomas Mott. 1859–1926. American prison reformer. As warden of Sing Sing state prison (1914–1916) he introduced a number of self-help programs for prisoners.

Os·can (ŏs′kən) *n.* **1.** A member of an ancient people of Campania. **2.** The Italic language of the Oscans. **—Os′can** *adj.*

Os·car (ŏs′kər) *n.* Any of the golden statuettes awarded annually by the Academy of Motion Picture Arts and Sciences for achievement in movies.

Oscar II also **Os·kar II** (ôs′kär). 1829–1907. King of Sweden from 1872 to 1907 and of Norway from 1872 to 1905, when he gave up the throne to Haakon VII.

Os·ce·o·la (ŏs′ē-ō′lə, ō′sē-). 1804?–1838. Seminole leader who resisted the removal of his people from Florida in the 1830's. He died under suspicious circumstances after being tricked into surrendering (1837).

os·cil·late (ŏs′ə-lāt′) *intr.v.* **-lat·ed, -lat·ing, -lates. 1.** To swing back and forth with a steady, uninterrupted rhythm. **2.** To waver, as between conflicting opinions or courses of action; vacillate: *"The court has oscillated over the decades from more liberal to less, more conservative to less, depending upon who was president at the time of vacancies"* (Gordon J. Humphrey). See Synonyms at **swing. 3.** *Physics.* To vary between alternate extremes, usually within a definable period of time. [Latin *ōscillāre, ōscillāt-,* from *ōscillum,* swing, probably from *ōscillum,* small mask of Bacchus, diminutive of *ōs,* mouth. See **ōs-** in Appendix.] **—os′cil·la′tor** *n.* **—os′cil·la·to′ry** (-lə-tôr′ē, -tōr′ē) *adj.*

WORD HISTORY: The rather dry word *oscillate* may become a bit less dry as we learn its story. It is possible that it goes back to the Latin word *ōscillum,* a diminutive of *ōs,* "mouth," meaning "small

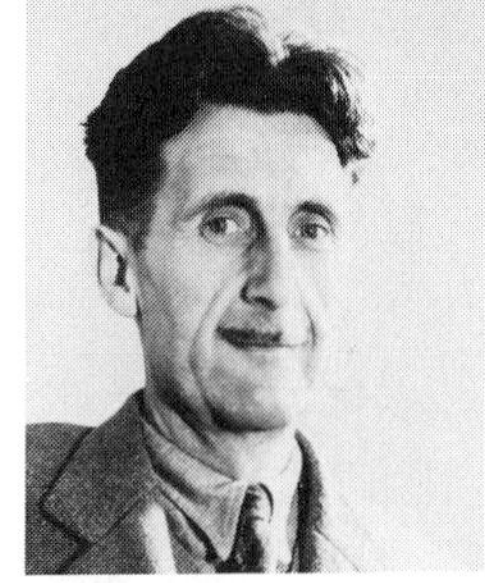

George Orwell

ă pat	oi boy
ā pay	ou out
âr care	o͝o took
ä father	o͞o boot
ĕ pet	ŭ cut
ē be	ûr urge
ĭ pit	th thin
ī pie	*th* this
îr pier	hw which
ŏ pot	zh vision
ō toe	ə about, item
ô paw	♦ regionalism

Stress marks: **′** (primary); ′ (secondary), as in **dictionary** (dĭk′shə-nĕr′ē)

mouth." In a passage in the *Georgics,* Virgil applies the word to a small mask of Bacchus hung from trees to move back and forth in the breeze. From this word *ōscillum* may have come another word *ōscillum,* meaning "something, such as a swing, that moves up and down or back and forth." And this *ōscillum* was the source of the verb *ōscillāre,* "to ride in a swing," and the noun (from the verb) *ōscillātio,* "the action of swinging or oscillating." The words have given us, respectively, our verb *oscillate,* first recorded in 1726, and our noun *oscillation,* first recorded in 1658. The next time one sees something oscillating, one might think of that small mask of Bacchus swinging from a pine tree in the Roman countryside.

os·cil·la·tion (ŏs′ə-lā′shən) *n.* **1.a.** The act of oscillating. **b.** The state of being oscillated. **2.** A single oscillatory cycle. **—os′cil·la′tion·al** *adj.*

os·cil·lo·gram (ə-sĭl′ə-grăm′) *n.* **1.** The graph traced by an oscillograph. **2.** An instantaneous oscilloscope trace or photograph. [OSCILLO(GRAPH) + –GRAM.]

os·cil·lo·graph (ə-sĭl′ə-grăf′) *n.* A device that records oscillations, as of an electric current and voltage. [OSCILL(ATION) + –GRAPH.] **—os·cil′lo·graph′ic** *adj.* **—os·cil′lo·graph′i·cal·ly** *adv.* **—os′cil·log′ra·phy** (ŏs′ə-lŏg′rə-fē) *n.*

os·cil·lo·scope (ə-sĭl′ə-skōp′) *n.* An electronic instrument that produces an instantaneous trace on the screen of a cathode-ray tube corresponding to oscillations of voltage and current. [OSCILL(ATION) + –SCOPE.] **—os·cil′lo·scop′ic** (-skŏp′ĭk) *adj.*

os·cine (ŏs′īn′) *adj.* Of, relating to, or belonging to the Oscines, a large suborder of passerine birds that includes most songbirds. **—oscine** *n.* A bird of the suborder Oscines. [From New Latin *Oscinēs,* suborder name, from Latin *oscinēs,* pl. of *oscen,* bird used in augury. See **kan-** in Appendix.]

os·ci·tance (ŏs′ĭ-təns) *n.* Oscitancy.

os·ci·tan·cy (ŏs′ĭ-tən-sē) *n., pl.* **-cies. 1.** The act of yawning. **2.** The state of being drowsy or inattentive; dullness. [From *oscitant,* yawning, from Latin *ōscitāns, ōscitant-,* present participle of *ōscitāre,* to yawn : *ōs,* mouth; see **ōs-** in Appendix + *citāre,* to move; see **kei-**[2] in Appendix.] **—os′ci·tant** *adj.*

Osiris

Os·co-Um·bri·an (ŏs′kō-ŭm′brē-ən) *n.* A subdivision of the Italic languages that consists of Oscan and Umbrian.

os·cu·la (ŏs′kyə-lə) *n.* Plural of **osculum.**

os·cu·lant (ŏs′kyə-lənt) *adj.* **1.** *Biology.* Intermediate in characteristics between two similar or related taxonomic groups. **2.** Closely adhering or joined; embracing. [Latin *ōsculāns, ōsculant-,* present participle of *ōsculārī,* to kiss. See OSCULATE.]

os·cu·late (ŏs′kyə-lāt′) *v.* **-lat·ed, -lat·ing, -lates.** —*tr.* **1.** To kiss. **2.** *Mathematics.* To have three or more points coincident with. —*intr.* To come together; contact. [Latin *ōsculārī, ōsculāt-,* from *ōsculum,* kiss, diminutive of *ōs,* mouth. See **ōs-** in Appendix.]

os·cu·la·tion (ŏs′kyə-lā′shən) *n.* **1.a.** The act of kissing. **b.** A kiss. **2.** *Mathematics.* A contact, as between two curves or surfaces, at three or more common points. **—os′cu·la·to′ry** (ŏs′-kyə-lə-tôr′ē, -tōr′ē) *adj.*

os·cu·lum (ŏs′kyə-ləm) also **os·cule** (-kyo͞ol′) *n., pl.* **-cu·la** (-kyə-lə) also **-cules.** The mouthlike opening in a sponge, used to expel water. [Latin, diminutive of *ōs,* mouth. See **ōs-** in Appendix.] **—os′cu·lar** *adj.*

-ose[1] *suff.* Possessing; having the characteristics of; full of: *cymose.* [Middle English, variant of *-ous,* from Latin *-ōsus.*]

-ose[2] *suff.* **1.** Carbohydrate: *fructose.* **2.** Product of protein hydrolysis: *proteose.* [French, from *glucose,* glucose. See GLUCOSE.]

OSF or **O.S.F.** *abbr.* Order of Saint Francis.

OSHA (ō′shə) *n.* Occupational Safety and Health Administration.

Osh·a·wa (ŏsh′ə-wä′, -wə). A city of southeast Ontario, Canada, on Lake Ontario east-northeast of Toronto. Founded on the site of a French trading post, it is a manufacturing center. Population, 117,519.

Osh·kosh (ŏsh′kŏsh). A city of eastern Wisconsin on Lake Winnebago north-northwest of Fond du Lac. It grew as a lumber town in the latter half of the 19th century. Population, 50,016.

osprey
Pandion haliaetus

O·shog·bo (ō-shŏg′bō). A city of southwest Nigeria northeast of Ibadan. It is primarily a farm trade and commercial center. Population, 336,000.

o·sier (ō′zhər) *n.* **1.a.** Any of several willows having long rodlike twigs used in basketry, especially the Eurasian *Salix viminalis* and *S. purpurea.* **b.** A twig of one of these trees. **2.** Any of various similar or related trees. [Middle English, from Old English *oser* and Old French *osier,* both from Medieval Latin *osera, osiera.*]

O·si·jek (ô′sē-ĕk, -yĕk′). A city of northern Yugoslavia on the Drava River east-southeast of Zagreb. The city was under Turkish rule from 1526 to 1687. Population, 103,600.

O·si·ris (ō-sī′rĭs) *n.* *Mythology.* The ancient Egyptian god whose annual death and resurrection personified the self-renewing vitality and fertility of nature.

-osis *suff.* **1.** Condition; process; action: *osmosis.* **2.** Diseased or abnormal condition: *neurosis.* **3.** Increase; formation: *leukocytosis.* [Latin *-ōsis,* from Greek, n. suff.]

Os·kar II (ôs′kär). See **Oscar II.**

Os·lo (ŏz′lō, ŏs′-). Formerly (1624–1925) **Chris·ti·a·ni·a** (krĭs′tē-ăn′ē-ə, -än′-, krĭs′chē-). The capital and largest city of Norway, in the southeast part of the country at the head of the **Oslo Fjord,** a deep inlet of the Skagerrak. Founded c. 1050, Oslo was rebuilt and renamed in 1624 by Christian IV (1577–1648; reigned 1588–1648). It has been the capital of the country since 1299. Population, 448,747.

Os·man I (ŏz′mən, ôs′-, ŏs-män′) also **Oth·man I** (ŏth′mən, o͞oth-män′). 1258–1326? Founder of the Ottoman dynasty that ruled Turkey after the 13th century.

Os·man·li (ŏz-măn′lē, ŏs-) *n., pl.* **-lis. 1.** An Ottoman Turk. **2.** Ottoman Turkish. **—Osmanli** *adj.* Ottoman. [Turkish *osmānli* : OSMAN (I) + *-li,* adj. suff.]

os·mat·ic (ŏz-măt′ĭk) *adj.* Having or characterized by a well-developed sense of smell. [From Greek *osmē,* smell.]

os·me·te·ri·um (ŏz′mĭ-tîr′ē-əm) *n., pl.* **-te·ri·a** (-tîr′ē-ə). An eversible glandular sac on the first thoracic segment of many caterpillars that secretes an unpleasant-smelling substance to ward off predators. [New Latin *osmētērium,* from Greek *osmē,* smell.]

os·mic[1] (ŏz′mĭk) *adj.* Of, relating to, or containing osmium, especially in a compound with a valence of 4 or a valence higher than that in a comparable osmous compound. [OSM(IUM) + –IC.]

os·mic[2] (ŏz′mĭk) *adj.* Of or relating to odors or the sense of smell. [Greek *osmē,* smell + –IC.] **—os′mi·cal·ly** *adv.*

osmic acid *n.* See **osmium tetroxide.**

os·mics (ŏz′mĭks) *n.* *(used with a sing. verb).* The science that deals with smells and the olfactory sense.

os·mi·ous (ŏz′mē-əs) *adj.* Variant of **osmous.**

os·mi·rid·i·um (ŏz′mə-rĭd′ē-əm) *n.* A mineral that is a natural alloy of osmium and iridium with small inclusions of platinum, rhodium, and other metals, used in needles and wearing points. Also called *iridosmine.* [OSM(IUM) + IRIDIUM.]

os·mi·um (ŏz′mē-əm) *n.* *Symbol* **Os** A bluish-white, hard metallic element, found in small amounts in osmiridium, nickel, and platinum ores. It is used as a platinum hardener and in making pen points, phonograph needles, and instrument pivots. Atomic number 76; atomic weight 190.2; melting point 3,000°C; boiling point 5,000°C; specific gravity 22.57; valence 2, 3, 4, 8. See table at **element.** [From Greek *osmē,* smell (from the strong odor of osmium tetroxide).]

osmium tetroxide *n.* A poisonous compound, OsO_4, with a pungent smell, used in solution to stain and fix biological material, especially lipids. Also called *osmic acid.*

os·mom·e·ter (ŏz-mŏm′ĭ-tər, ŏs-) *n.* A device for measuring osmotic pressure. [OSMO(SIS) + –METER.] **—os′mo·met′ric** (ŏz′mə-mĕt′rĭk, ŏs′-) *adj.* **—os·mom′e·try** *n.*

os·mo·reg·u·la·tion (ŏz′mə-rĕg′yə-lā′shən, ŏs′-) *n.* *Physiology.* Maintenance of an optimal, constant osmotic pressure in the body of a living organism. [OSMO(SIS) + REGULATION.] **—os′mo·reg′u·la·to′ry** (-lə-tôr′ē, -tōr′ē) *adj.*

os·mose (ŏz′mōs′, ŏs′-) *intr. & tr.v.* **-mosed, -mos·ing, -mos·es.** To diffuse or cause to diffuse by osmosis. [Back-formation from OSMOSIS.]

os·mo·sis (ŏz-mō′sĭs, ŏs-) *n., pl.* **-ses** (-sēz). **1.a.** Diffusion of fluid through a semipermeable membrane until there is an equal concentration of fluid on both sides of the membrane. **b.** The tendency of fluids to diffuse in such a manner. **2.** A gradual, often unconscious process of assimilation or absorption: *learned French by osmosis while residing in Paris for 15 years.* [From obsolete *osmose,* from earlier *endosmose,* from French : Greek *endo-,* endo- + Greek *ōsmos,* thrust, push (from *ōthein,* to push).] **—os·mot′ic** (-mŏt′ĭk) *adj.* **—os·mot′i·cal·ly** *adv.*

osmotic pressure *n.* The pressure exerted by the flow of water through a semipermeable membrane separating two solutions with different concentrations of solute.

osmotic shock *n.* The rupture of bacterial or other cells in a solution following a sudden reduction in osmotic pressure. Osmotic shock is sometimes induced to release cellular components for biochemical analysis.

os·mous (ŏz′məs) also **os·mi·ous** (-mē-əs) *adj.* Of, relating to, or containing osmium in a compound with a valence lower than that in a comparable osmic compound. [OSM(IUM) + –OUS.]

os·mun·da (ŏz-mŭn′də) also **os·mund** (ŏz′mənd) *n.* Any of several ferns of the genus *Osmunda,* having erect, bipinnately compound fronds and deeply contracted fertile pinnules. The fibrous roots are sometimes used as a potting medium for cultivated plants, and the young crosiers are used as food. [New Latin *Osmunda,* genus name, from Middle English *osmunde,* a kind of fern, from Old French *osmonde.*]

Os·na·brück (ŏz′nə-bro͝ok′, ôs′nä-brük′). A city of northwest Germany northeast of Münster. It was a member of the Hanseatic League and an important center of the linen trade in the Middle Ages. Population, 153,587.

os·na·burg (ŏz′nə-bûrg′) *n.* A heavy, coarse cotton fabric, used for grain sacks, upholstery, and draperies. [After *Osnaburg* (Osnabrück).]

os·prey (ŏs′prē, -prā) *n., pl.* **-preys. 1.** A fish-eating hawk *(Pandion haliaetus)* having plumage that is dark on the back and white below. Also called *fish hawk.* **2.** A plume formerly used to trim women's hats. [Middle English *osprai,* from Anglo-Norman *ospreit,* from Medieval Latin *avis prede,* bird of prey : Latin *avis,* bird; see **awi-** in Appendix + Latin *praedae,* genitive of *praeda,* booty, prey; see **ghend-** in Appendix.]

OSS *abbr.* Office of Strategic Services.

os·sa (ŏs′ə) *n.* Plural of **os**[2].

Os·sa (ŏs′ə), **Mount.** A peak, 1,979.1 m (6,489 ft) high, of the Olympus Mountains in northern Greece.

os·sa·ture (ŏs′ə-chŏŏr′, -chər) *n.* A framework or skeleton, as for a building or statue. [French, from Latin *os, oss-,* bone. See OS[2].]

os·se·in (ŏs′ē-ĭn) *n.* The collagen component of bone. [OSSE(OUS) + –IN.]

os·se·ous (ŏs′ē-əs) *adj.* Composed of, containing, or resembling bone; bony. [From Latin *osseus,* from *os, oss-,* bone. See **ost-** in Appendix.] **—os′se·ous·ly** *adv.*

Os·set (ŏs′ĭt, ŏ-sĕt′, ŏ-sēt′) also **Os·sete** (ŏs′ēt′, ŏ-sēt′) *n.* A member of a people of mixed Iranian and Caucasian origin inhabiting Ossetia.

Os·se·tia (ŏ-sē′shə, ə-syĕ′tĭ-yə). A region of the central Caucasus in Georgia and southwest Russia. The area was annexed by Russia between 1801 and 1806. **—Os·se′tian** *adj. & n.*

Os·set·ic (ŏ-sĕt′ĭk) *adj.* Of or relating to Ossetia, the Ossets, or their language or culture. **—Ossetic** *n.* The Iranian language of the Ossets.

os·si·a (ō-sē′ə) *conj. Music.* Or else. Used to designate an alternate section or passage. [Italian, from *o sia,* or let it be : *o,* or (from Latin *aut*) + *sia,* third person sing. present subjunctive of *essere,* to be (from Latin *esse;* see **es-** in Appendix).]

Os·sian (ŏsh′ən, ŏs′ē-ən) *n.* A legendary Gaelic hero and bard of the third century A.D.

os·si·cle (ŏs′ĭ-kəl) *n.* A small bone, especially one of the three bones of the middle ear. [Latin *ossiculum,* diminutive of *os,* bone. See **ost-** in Appendix.] **—os·sic′u·lar** (ŏ-sĭk′yə-lər), **os·sic′u·late** (-lĭt) *adj.*

Os·si·etz·ky (ŏs′ē-ĕt′skē ô′sē-), **Carl von.** 1889–1938. German journalist and pacifist who was imprisoned (1931–1932 and 1933–1936) for exposing Germany's military buildup. He won the 1935 Nobel Peace Prize.

os·si·fi·ca·tion (ŏs′ə-fĭ-kā′shən) *n.* **1.** The natural process of bone formation. **2.a.** The hardening or calcification of soft tissue into a bonelike material. **b.** A mass or deposit of such material. **3.a.** The process of becoming set in a rigidly conventional pattern, as of behavior, habits, or beliefs. **b.** Rigid, unimaginative convention.

os·si·frage (ŏs′ə-frĭj, -frāj′) *n.* **1.** See **lammergeier. 2.** *Archaic.* An osprey. [Latin *ossifraga,* from *ossifragus,* bone-breaking : *os, oss-,* bone; see **ost-** in Appendix + *frangere,* to break; see **bhreg-** in Appendix.]

os·si·fy (ŏs′ə-fī′) *v.* **-fied, -fy·ing, -fies.** *—intr.* **1.** To change into bone; become bony. **2.** To become set in a rigidly conventional pattern: *"The central ideas of liberalism have ossified"* (Jeffrey Hart). *—tr.* **1.** To convert (a membrane or cartilage, for example) into bone. **2.** To mold into a rigidly conventional pattern. [Latin *os, oss-,* bone; see **ost-** in Appendix + –FY.] **—os·sif′ic** (ŏ-sĭf′ĭk) *adj.*

Os·si·ning (ŏs′ə-nĭng′). A village of southeast New York on the Hudson River north of White Plains. Incorporated in 1813 as Sing Sing, it was renamed in 1901. Sing Sing state prison, established in 1824, is here. Population, 20,196.

os·so bu·co (ō′sō bo͞o′kō, ŏs′sō) *n., pl.* **osso bu·cos.** An Italian dish consisting of braised veal shanks in white wine. [Italian *ossobuco,* marrowbone : *osso,* bone + *buco,* hole.]

os·su·ar·y (ŏsh′o͞o-ĕr′ē, ŏs′yo͞o-) *n., pl.* **-ies.** A container or receptacle, such as an urn or a vault, for holding the bones of the dead. [Late Latin *ossuārium,* from neuter of Latin *ossuārius,* of bones, from *os, oss-,* bone. See **ost-** in Appendix.]

oste– *pref.* Variant of **osteo–.**

os·te·al (ŏs′tē-əl) *adj.* **1.** Bony; osseous. **2.** Relating to bone or to the skeleton.

os·te·i·tis (ŏs′tē-ī′tĭs) *n.* Inflammation of bone or bony tissue.

Ost·end (ŏs-tĕnd′, ŏs′tĕnd′) also **Oost·en·de** (ō-stĕn′də). A city of northwest Belgium on the North Sea west-southwest of Bruges. It was a German submarine base during World War I and was severely damaged by Allied bombing during World War II. Population, 69,129.

os·ten·si·ble (ŏ-stĕn′sə-bəl) *adj.* Represented or appearing as such; ostensive: *His ostensible purpose was charity, but his real goal was popularity.* [French, from Medieval Latin *ostēnsibilis,* from Latin *ostēnsus,* past participle of *ostendere,* to show : *ob-,* ob- + *tendere,* to stretch; see **ten-** in Appendix.] **—os·ten′si·bly** *adv.*

os·ten·sive (ŏ-stĕn′sĭv) *adj.* Seeming or professed; ostensible. [Late Latin *ostēnsīvus,* from Latin *ostēnsus,* past participle of *ostendere,* to show. See OSTENSIBLE.] **—os·ten′sive·ly** *adv.*

os·ten·so·ri·um (ŏs′tən-sôr′ē-əm, -sōr′-) also **os·ten·so·ry** (ŏ-stĕn′sə-rē) *n., pl.* **-so·ri·a** (-sôr′ē-ə, -sōr′-) also **-so·ries.** *Roman Catholic Church.* See **monstrance.** [Medieval Latin *ostēnsōrium,* from Latin *ostēnsus,* past participle of *ostendere,* to show. See OSTENSIBLE.]

os·ten·ta·tion (ŏs′tĕn-tā′shən, -tən-) *n.* **1.** Pretentious display meant to impress others; boastful showiness. **2.** *Archaic.* The act or an instance of showing; an exhibition. [Middle English *ostentacioun,* from Old French *ostentacion,* from Latin *ostentātiō, ostentātiōn-,* from *ostentāre,* frequentative of *ostendere,* to show. See OSTENSIBLE.]

os·ten·ta·tious (ŏs′tĕn-tā′shəs, -tən-) *adj.* Characterized by or given to ostentation; pretentious. See Synonyms at **showy. —os′ten·ta′tious·ly** *adv.*

osteo– or **oste–** *pref.* Bone: *osteoarthritis.* [Greek, from *osteon,* bone. See **ost-** in Appendix.]

os·te·o·ar·thri·tis (ŏs′tē-ō-är-thrī′tĭs) *n.* A form of arthritis, occurring mainly in older persons, that is characterized by chronic degeneration of the cartilage of the joints. Also called *degenerative joint disease.* **—os′te·o·ar·thrit′ic** (-thrĭt′ĭk) *adj.*

os·te·o·blast (ŏs′tē-ə-blăst′) *n.* A cell from which bone develops; a bone-forming cell. **—os′te·o·blas′tic** *adj.*

os·te·oc·la·sis (ŏs′tē-ŏk′lə-sĭs) *n., pl.* **-ses** (-sēz′). **1.** The process of dissolution and resorption of bony tissue. **2.** Surgical fracture of a bone, performed to correct a deformity. [OSTEO– + Greek *klasis,* breakage (from *klan,* to break).]

os·te·o·clast (ŏs′tē-ə-klăst′) *n.* **1.** A large multinucleate cell found in growing bone that resorbs bony tissue, as in the formation of canals and cavities. **2.** An instrument used in surgical osteoclasis. [OSTEO– + Medieval Latin *-clastēs,* breaker (from Late Greek *-klastēs,* from Greek *klastos,* broken, from *klan,* to break).] **—os′te·o·clas′tic** *adj.*

os·te·o·cyte (ŏs′tē-ə-sīt′) *n.* A branched cell embedded in the matrix of bone tissue.

os·te·o·gen·e·sis (ŏs′tē-ə-jĕn′ĭ-sĭs) *n., pl.* **-ses** (-sēz′). The formation and development of bony tissue. **—os′te·o·ge·net′ic** (-ō-jə-nĕt′ĭk) *adj.* **—os′te·og′e·nous** (-ŏj′ə-nəs) *adj.*

osteogenesis im·per·fec·ta (ĭm′pər-fĕk′tə) *n.* A hereditary disease characterized by abnormally brittle, easily fractured bones. [New Latin : OSTEOGENESIS + Latin *imperfecta,* feminine of *imperfectus,* incomplete.]

os·te·o·gen·ic (ŏs′tē-ə-jĕn′ĭk) *adj.* **1.** Derived from or composed of bone-forming tissue. **2.** Of or relating to osteogenesis.

osteogenic sarcoma *n.* See **osteosarcoma.**

os·te·oid (ŏs′tē-oid′) *adj.* Resembling bone. **—osteoid** *n.* The bone matrix, especially before calcification.

os·te·ol·o·gy (ŏs′tē-ŏl′ə-jē) *n., pl.* **-gies. 1.** The branch of anatomy that deals with the structure and function of bones. **2.** The bone structure or system of an animal. **—os′te·o·log′i·cal** (-ə-lŏj′ĭ-kəl) *adj.* **—os′te·o·log′i·cal·ly** *adv.* **—os′te·ol′o·gist** *n.*

os·te·ol·y·sis (ŏs′tē-ŏl′ĭ-sĭs) *n.* Dissolution or degeneration of bone tissue through disease. **—os′te·o·lyt′ic** (-ə-lĭt′ĭk) *adj.*

os·te·o·ma (ŏs′tē-ō′mə) *n., pl.* **-mas** or **-ma·ta** (-mə-tə). A benign tumor composed of bony tissue, often developing on the skull.

os·te·o·ma·la·cia (ŏs′tē-ō-mə-lā′shə, -shē-ə) *n.* A disease occurring mostly in adult women that results from a deficiency in vitamin D or calcium and is characterized by a softening of the bones with accompanying pain and weakness. [New Latin : OSTEO– + Greek *malakia,* softness (from *malakos,* soft; see **mel-**[1] in Appendix).]

os·te·o·ma·ta (ŏs′tē-ō′mə-tə) *n.* A plural of **osteoma.**

os·te·o·my·e·li·tis (ŏs′tē-ō-mī′ə-lī′tĭs) *n.* Inflammation of bone and bone marrow.

os·te·o·path (ŏs′tē-ə-păth′) also **os·te·op·a·thist** (ŏs′tē-ŏp′ə-thĭst) *n.* A physician who practices osteopathy.

os·te·op·a·thy (ŏs′tē-ŏp′ə-thē) *n.* A system of medicine based on the theory that disturbances in the musculoskeletal system affect other bodily parts, causing many disorders that can be corrected by various manipulative techniques in conjunction with conventional medical, surgical, pharmacological, and other therapeutic procedures. **—os′te·o·path′ic** (-ə-păth′ĭk) *adj.* **—os′te·o·path′i·cal·ly** *adv.*

os·te·o·phyte (ŏs′tē-ə-fīt′) *n.* A small, abnormal bony outgrowth. **—os′te·o·phyt′ic** (-fĭt′ĭk) *adj.*

os·te·o·plas·tic (ŏs′tē-ə-plăs′tĭk) *adj.* **1.** Of or relating to osteoplasty. **2.** Relating to or functioning in bone formation.

os·te·o·plas·ty (ŏs′tē-ə-plăs′tē) *n., pl.* **-ties.** Surgical repair or alteration of bone.

os·te·o·po·ro·sis (ŏs′tē-ō-pə-rō′sĭs) *n., pl.* **-ses** (-sēz). A disease in which the bones become extremely porous, are subject to fracture, and heal slowly, occurring especially in women following menopause and often leading to curvature of the spine from vertebral collapse. [New Latin : OSTEO– + Greek *poros,* passage, pore; see PORE[2] + –OSIS.] **—os′te·o·po·rot′ic** (-rŏt′ĭk) *adj.*

os·te·o·sar·co·ma (ŏs′tē-ō-sär-kō′mə) *n., pl.* **-ma·ta** (-mə-tə) or **-mas.** A malignant bone tumor. Also called *osteogenic sarcoma.*

os·te·o·sis (ŏs′tē-ō′sĭs) also **os·to·sis** (-tō′sĭs) *n.* The formation of bony tissue, especially over connective or other tissue.

os·te·ot·o·my (ŏs′tē-ŏt′ə-mē) *n., pl.* **-mies.** Surgical division or sectioning of bone. **—os′te·ot′o·mist** *n.*

os·ti·a (ŏs′tē-ə) *n.* Plural of **ostium.**

Os·ti·a (ŏs′tē-ə, ô′styä). An ancient city of west-central Italy at the mouth of the Tiber River. According to legend, it was founded in the seventh century B.C. Ostia developed as a port after the first century B.C. and declined after the third century A.D.

Os·ti·ak (ŏs′tē-ăk′) *n.* Variant of **Ostyak.**

os·ti·ar·y (ŏs′tē-ĕr′ē) *n., pl.* **-ies. 1.** *Roman Catholic Church.* One who is ordained in the lowest of the former minor orders. **2.** A church doorkeeper. [Middle English *hostiary,* from

ă pat	oi boy
ā pay	ou out
âr care	o͝o took
ä father	o͞o boot
ĕ pet	ŭ cut
ē be	ûr urge
ĭ pit	th thin
ī pie	*th* this
îr pier	hw which
ŏ pot	zh vision
ō toe	ə about, item
ô paw	♦ regionalism

Stress marks: ′ (primary); ′ (secondary), as in **dictionary** (dĭk′shə-nĕr′ē)

Latin *ōstiārius,* doorkeeper, from *ōstium,* door, from *ōs,* mouth. See **ōs-** in Appendix.]

os·ti·na·to (ŏs′tĭ-nä′tō) *n., pl.* **-tos.** *Music.* A short melody or phrase that is constantly repeated, usually the same part at the same pitch. [Italian, from Latin *obstinātus,* stubborn, past participle of *obstināre,* to persist. See OBSTINATE.]

os·ti·ole (ŏs′tē-ōl′) *n.* A small opening or pore, as of a fruiting body. [Latin *ōstiolum,* diminutive of *ōstium,* opening. See OSTIUM.] **—os′ti·o′lar** (ŏs′tē-ō′lər, ŏ-stī′ə-) *adj.*

os·ti·um (ŏs′tē-əm) *n., pl.* **-ti·a** (-tē-ə). **1.** A small opening or orifice, as in a body organ or passage. **2.** Any of the small openings or pores in a sponge. [Latin *ōstium,* door, opening, from *ōs,* mouth. See **ōs-** in Appendix.]

os·tler (ŏs′lər) *n.* Variant of **hostler.**

ost·mark (ôst′märk′, ŏst′-) *n. Abbr.* **OM.** A former monetary unit of East Germany worth 100 pfennigs. [German : *Ost,* east (from Middle High German *ōst, ōsten,* from Old High German *ōstan;* see **aus-** in Appendix) + *Mark,* mark (from Middle High German *marke, marc;* see MARK[2]).]

os·to·mate (ŏs′tə-māt′) *n.* One who has had an ostomy.

os·to·my (ŏs′tə-mē) *n., pl.* **-mies.** Surgical construction of an artificial excretory opening, as a colostomy or ileostomy. [From (COL)OSTOMY.]

os·to·sis (ŏs-tō′sĭs) *n.* Variant of **osteosis.**

os·tra·cism (ŏs′trə-sĭz′əm) *n.* **1.a.** The act of banishing or excluding. **b.** Banishment or exclusion from a group; disgrace. **2.** In Athens and other cities of ancient Greece, the temporary banishment by popular vote of a citizen considered dangerous to the state. [French *ostracisme,* from Greek *ostrakismos,* from *ostrakizein,* to ostracize. See OSTRACIZE.]

os·tra·cize (ŏs′trə-sīz′) *tr.v.* **-cized, -ciz·ing, -ciz·es. 1.** To exclude from a group. See Synonyms at **blackball. 2.** To banish by ostracism, as in ancient Greece. [Greek *ostrakizein,* from *ostrakon,* shell, potsherd (from the potsherds used as ballots in voting for ostracism). See **ost-** in Appendix.]

os·tra·cod (ŏs′trə-kŏd′) *n.* Any of various minute, chiefly freshwater crustaceans of the subclass Ostracoda, having a bivalve carapace. [New Latin *Ostracōda,* subclass name, from Greek *ostrakōdēs,* testaceous, from *ostrakon,* shell. See **ost-** in Appendix.]

Os·tra·va (ô′strä-vä). A city of north-central Czechoslovakia near the Oder River. Population, 325,431.

ostrich
Male Masai ostrich
Struthio camelus massaicus

os·trich (ŏs′trĭch, ôs′-) *n., pl.* **ostrich** or **-trich·es. 1.a.** A large, swift-running flightless bird *(Struthio camelus)* of Africa, characterized by a long bare neck, small head, and two-toed feet. It is the largest living bird. **b.** A rhea. **2.** One who tries to avoid disagreeable situations by refusing to face them. [Middle English, from Old French *ostrusce, ostrice* and Medieval Latin *ostrica,* both from Vulgar Latin **avis strūthiō* : Latin *avis,* bird; see **awi-** in Appendix + Late Latin *strūthiō,* ostrich; see STRUTHIOUS.]

ostrich fern *n.* A fern *(Matteuccia struthiopteris)* of northern temperate regions, having long plumelike fronds that form a crown.

Os·tro·goth (ŏs′trə-gŏth′) *n.* One of a tribe of eastern Goths that conquered and ruled Italy from A.D. 493 to 555. [From Middle English *Ostrogotes,* Ostrogoths, from Late Latin *Ostrogothī* : *ostro-,* eastern (of Germanic origin; see **aus-** in Appendix) + *Gothī,* Goths (of Germanic origin).] **—Os′tro·goth′ic** *adj.*

Ost·wald (ôst′wôld′, ôst′vält), **Wilhelm.** 1853–1932. German chemist. He won a 1909 Nobel Prize for work on catalysis and chemical equilibrium.

Os·ty·ak also **Os·ti·ak** (ŏs′tē-ăk′) *n.* **1.** A member of a Finno-Ugric people inhabiting western Siberia. **2.** The Ugric language of this people. [Russian, from Ostyak *āsyakh,* pl. of *āskho,* person from the Ob River, from *Ās,* the Ob River.]

OSU or **O.S.U.** *abbr.* Order of Saint Ursula.

Os·wald (ŏz′wôld′), **Lee Harvey.** 1939–1963. American alleged assassin of President John F. Kennedy (November 22, 1963). He was shot while under arrest (November 24).

Os·we·go (ŏs-wē′gō). A city of north-central New York at the mouth of the **Oswego River,** about 37 km (23 mi) long, on Lake Ontario northwest of Syracuse. A British trading post was founded in Oswego c. 1722. Population, 19,793.

Oś·wię·cim (ôsh-vyĕn′chĕm, -tsĕm). Formerly **Ausch·witz** (oush′vĭts′). A city of southern Poland west of Cracow. During World War II it was the site of the largest Nazi concentration camp. Population, 45,700.

OT[1] also **O.T.** *abbr. Bible.* Old Testament.

OT[2] *abbr.* **1.** Occupational therapy. **2.** Also **o.t.** or **O.T.** Overtime.

ot– *pref.* Variant of **oto–.**

ostrich fern
Matteuccia struthiopteris

O·ta·hei·te apple (ō′tə-hē′tē, -hā′-) *n.* See **ambarella.** [After *Otaheite* (Tahiti).]

Otaheite orange *n.* A widely cultivated house plant, believed to be a hybrid between *Citrus limon* and *C. reticulata,* resembling a miniature orange tree and having lemon-shaped, insipid fruit. [After *Otaheite* (Tahiti).]

o·tal·gi·a (ō-tăl′jē-ə, -jə) *n.* Pain in the ear; earache. **—o·tal′gic** *adj.*

OTB *abbr. Sports & Games.* Off-track betting.

OTC also **O.T.C.** *abbr.* **1.** Officers' Training Corps. **2.** Over-the-counter.

oth·er (ŭth′ər) *adj.* **1.a.** Being the remaining one of two or more: *the other ear.* **b.** Being the remaining ones of several: *His other books are still in storage.* **2.** Different from that or those implied or specified: *Any other person would tell the truth.* **3.** Of a different character or quality: *"a strange, other dimension . . . where his powers seemed to fail"* (Lance Morrow). **4.** Of a different time or era either future or past: *other centuries; other generations.* **5.** Additional; extra: *I have no other shoes.* **6.** Opposite or contrary; reverse: *the other side.* **7.** Alternate; second: *every other day.* **8.** Of the recent past: *just the other day.* **—other** *n.* **1.a.** The remaining one of two or more: *One took a taxi, and the other walked home.* **b. others.** The remaining ones of several: *After her departure the others resumed the discussion.* **2.a.** A different person or thing: *one hurricane after the other.* **b.** An additional person or thing: *How many others will come later?* **—other** *pron.* **1.** A different or an additional person or thing: *We'll get someone or other to replace him.* **2. others.** People aside from oneself: *"the eyes of others our prisons; their thoughts our cages"* (Virginia Woolf). **—other** *adv.* In another way; otherwise; differently: *She performed other than perfectly.* [Middle English, from Old English *ōther.* See **al-[1]** in Appendix.]

oth·er-di·rect·ed (ŭth′ər-dĭ-rĕk′tĭd, -dī-) *adj.* Directed or guided chiefly by external standards as opposed to one's own standards or values. **—oth′er-di·rect′ed·ness** *n.*

oth·er·ness (ŭth′ər-nĭs) *n.* The quality or condition of being other or different, especially if exotic or strange: *"We're going to see in Europe . . . religion, royalty, picturesqueness, otherness"* (Anatole Broyard).

oth·er·wise (ŭth′ər-wīz′) *adv.* **1.** In another way; differently: *She thought otherwise.* **2.** Under other circumstances: *Otherwise I might have helped.* **3.** In other respects: *an otherwise logical mind.* **—otherwise** *adj.* Other than supposed; different: *The evidence is otherwise.* [Middle English, from Old English *(on) ōthere wīsan,* (in) another manner : *ōthre,* dative of *ōther,* other + *wīsan,* dative of *wīse,* manner; see WISE[2].]

oth·er·world (ŭth′ər-wûrld′) *n.* A world or existence beyond earthly reality.

oth·er·world·ly (ŭth′ər-wûrld′lē) *adj.* **1.** Of, relating to, or characteristic of another world, especially a mystical or transcendental world: *"The effect was dreamy, otherworldy"* (Gioia Diliberto). **2.** Devoted to the world of the mind; concerned with intellectual or imaginative things. **3.** Concerned with an afterlife, especially when inattentive to the present. **—oth′er·world′li·ness** *n.*

Oth·man (ŏth′mən) *n., pl.* **-mans.** *Archaic.* An Ottoman Turk; a Turk. [After *Othman,* variant of OSMAN (I).] **—Oth′man** *adj.*

Oth·man I (ŏth′mən, ŏŏth-män′). See **Osman I.**

O·tho I (ō′thō, ō′tō). See **Otto I.**

o·tic (ō′tĭk, ŏt′ĭk) *adj.* Of, relating to, or located near the ear; auricular. [Greek *ōtikos,* from *ous, ōt-,* ear. See **ous-** in Appendix.]

–otic *suff.* **1.** Of, relating to, or characterized by a specified condition or process: *anabiotic.* **2.** Having a specified disease or abnormal condition: *epizootic.* **3.** Characterized by an increase or formation of a specified kind: *leukocytotic.* [French *-otique,* from Latin *-ōticus,* from Greek *-ōtikos,* adj. suff.]

o·ti·ose (ō′shē-ōs′, ō′tē-) *adj.* **1.** Lazy; indolent. **2.** Of no use. **3.** Ineffective; futile. See Synonyms at **vain.** [Latin *ōtiōsus,* idle, from *ōtium,* leisure.] **—o′ti·ose′ly** *adv.* **—o′ti·os′i·ty** (-ŏs′ĭ-tē) *n.*

O·tis (ō′tĭs), **Elisha Graves.** 1811–1861. American inventor of the first passenger elevator (installed 1857).

Otis, James. 1725–1783. American Revolutionary politician and publicist whose speeches and pamphlets influenced American sentiment against the British.

o·ti·tis (ō-tī′tĭs) *n.* Inflammation of the ear. **—o·tit′ic** (ō-tĭt′ĭk) *adj.*

otitis media *n.* Inflammation of the middle ear, occurring commonly in children as a result of infection and often causing pain and temporary hearing loss. [New Latin : OTITIS + Latin *media,* feminine of *medius,* middle.]

O·to (ō′tō) *n., pl.* **Oto** or **O·tos. 1.a.** A Native American people formerly inhabiting eastern Nebraska along the Platte River, with present-day descendants living with the Missouri in north-central Oklahoma. **b.** A member of this people. **2.** The Siouan language of the Oto, dialectically related to Iowa.

oto– or **ot–** *pref.* Ear: *otology.* [New Latin, from Greek *ous, ōt-,* ear. See **ous-** in Appendix.]

o·to·cyst (ō′tə-sĭst′) *n.* **1.** The structure formed by invagination of the embryonic ectodermal tissue that develops into the inner ear. **2.** See **statocyst. —o′to·cys′tic** *adj.*

otol. *abbr.* Otology.

o·to·lar·yn·gol·o·gy (ō′tō-lăr′ĭng-gŏl′ə-jē) *n.* The branch of medicine that deals with diagnosis and treatment of diseases of the ear, nose, and throat. Also called *otorhinolaryngology.* **—o′to·lar·yn′go·log′i·cal** (-lə-rĭng′gə-lŏj′ĭ-kəl) *adj.* **—o′to·lar′yn·gol′o·gist** *n.*

o·to·lith (ō′tə-lĭth′) *n.* One of many minute calcareous particles found in the inner ear of certain lower vertebrates and in the statocysts of many invertebrates. **—o′to·lith′ic** *adj.*

o·tol·o·gy (ō-tŏl′ə-jē) *n. Abbr.* **otol.** The branch of medicine that deals with the structure, function, and pathology of the ear.

—o′to·log′i·cal (ō′tə-lŏj′ĭ-kəl) *adj.* **—o·tol′o·gist** *n.*

o·to·rhi·no·lar·yn·gol·o·gy (ō′tō-rī′nō-lăr′ĭng-gŏl′ə-jē) *n.* See **otolaryngology. —o′to·rhi′no·la·ryn′go·log′i·cal** (-lə-rĭng′gə-lŏj′ĭ-kəl) *adj.* **—o′to·rhi′no·lar′yn·gol′o·gist** *n.*

WORD HISTORY: Otorhinolaryngology is the type of medical specialty that drives the layperson to despair, both of pronouncing the word properly (ō′tō-rī′nō-lăr′ĭng-gŏl′ə-jē) and of having any notion of what it means. The words *ear, nose,* and *throat* are quite clear, however, and that is what is meant by *oto–, rhino–,* and *laryngo–,* which are the forms of Greek *ous,* "ear," *rhis,* "nose," and *larunx,* "larynx or upper part of the windpipe," respectively, when used in combination with other word forms.

o·to·scle·ro·sis (ō′tō-sklə-rō′sĭs) *n.* A disease of the ear in which the movement of the stapes within the oval window becomes impeded by abnormal deposits of spongy bone, leading to a progressive loss of hearing. **—o′to·scle·rot′ic** (-rŏt′ĭk) *adj.*

o·to·scope (ō′tə-skōp′) *n.* An instrument for examining the interior of the ear, especially the eardrum, consisting essentially of a magnifying lens and a light.

o·to·tox·ic (ō′tə-tŏk′sĭk) *adj.* Having a toxic effect on the structures of the ear, especially on its nerve supply. **—o′to·tox·ic′i·ty** (-tŏk-sĭs′ĭ-tē) *n.*

O·tran·to (ō-trăn′tō), **Strait of.** A passage between southeast Italy and western Albania connecting the Adriatic Sea with the Ionian Sea.

OTS also **O.T.S.** *abbr.* Officers' Training School.

ot·tar (ŏt′ər) *n.* Variant of **attar.**

ot·ta·va (ō-tä′və) *adv. & adj. Music.* At an octave higher or lower than the notes written. Used chiefly as a direction, positioned above or below a staff. [Italian *(all')ottava,* (at the) octave, from Medieval Latin *octāva,* from Latin, feminine of *octāvus,* eighth. See OCTAVE.]

ottava ri·ma (rē′mə) *n.* A stanza of verse consisting of eight lines in iambic pentameter rhyming *abababcc.* [Italian : *ottava,* feminine of *ottavo,* eighth + *rima,* rhyme.]

Ot·ta·wa¹ (ŏt′ə-wə, -wä′, -wô′) *n., pl.* **Ottawa** or **-was. 1.a.** A Native American people formerly inhabiting the northern shore of Lake Huron, with later settlements throughout the upper Great Lakes region. Present-day Ottawa populations are located mainly in southern Ontario, northern Michigan, and Oklahoma. **b.** A member of this people. **2.** The dialect of Ojibwa spoken by the Ottawa. [Ojibwa *odaawaa.*]

Ot·ta·wa² (ŏt′ə-wə). **1.** The capital of Canada, in southeast Ontario at the confluence of the Ottawa River and the Rideau Canal. It was founded as Bytown during the construction of the Rideau Canal and renamed Ottawa in 1854. Victoria chose it as the capital of the United Provinces of Canada in 1858. In 1867 it became the capital of the newly formed confederation. Population, 295,163. **2.** A city of north-central Illinois southwest of Chicago. It was the site of the first Lincoln-Douglas debate (1858). Population, 18,166.

Ottawa River. A river, about 1,126 km (700 mi) long, rising in the Laurentian Plateau of southwest Quebec, Canada, and flowing west and southeast in a V-shaped course to the St. Lawrence River near Montreal. It was an important waterway for early fur traders and missionaries.

ot·ter (ŏt′ər) *n., pl.* **otter** or **-ters. 1.** Any of various aquatic, carnivorous mammals of the genus *Lutra* and allied genera, related to the minks and weasels and having webbed feet and dense, dark brown fur. **2.** The fur of this mammal. [Middle English *oter,* from Old English *otor.* See **wed-¹** in Appendix.]

Ot·ter·bein (ŏt′ər-bīn′), **Philip William.** 1726–1813. German-born American religious leader who was a founder (1789) of the United Brethren in Christ.

otter hound *n.* Any of a breed of hardy dog developed in England for hunting otters, having slightly webbed feet and a thick, coarse coat with an oily undercoat.

ot·to (ŏt′ō) *n.* Variant of **attar.**

Ot·to I (ŏt′ō, ôt′ō) also **O·tho I** (ō′thō, ō′tō). Known as "Otto the Great." 912–973. King of Germany (936–973) and first Holy Roman emperor (962–973). He united Italy and Burgundy under German control.

ot·to·man (ŏt′ə-mən) *n., pl.* **-mans. 1.a.** An upholstered sofa or divan without arms or a back. **b.** An upholstered low seat or cushioned footstool. **2.** A heavy silk or rayon fabric with a corded texture, usually used for coats and trimmings. [French *ottomane,* feminine of *ottoman,* Ottoman. See OTTOMAN.]

Ot·to·man (ŏt′ə-mən) *n., pl.* **-mans.** A Turk, especially a member of the family or tribe of Osman I. **—Ottoman** *adj.* **1.** Of or relating to the Ottoman Empire or its people, language, or culture. **2.** Turkish. [French, from Italian *ottomano,* from Arabic *'uṯmānī,* of Uthman, from *'Uṯman,* Osman I.]

Ottoman Empire. Also called **Turk·ish Empire** (tûr′kĭsh). A vast Turkish sultanate of southwest Asia, northeast Africa, and southeast Europe. It was founded in the 13th century by Osman I and ruled by his descendents until its dissolution after World War I. Originally a small state controlled by Ottoman or Osmanli Turks, it spread rapidly, superseding the Byzantine Empire in the east.

Ottoman Turkish *n.* The Turkic language spoken in Turkey, the Balkan Peninsula, Cyprus, the Soviet Union, West Germany, and elsewhere.

Ot·tum·wa (ə-tŭm′wə, ō-tŭm′-). A city of southeast Iowa southeast of Des Moines. It is a commercial center in a farming and coal-mining area. Population, 27,381.

oua·ba·in (wä-bā′ĭn) *n.* A white poisonous glycoside, $C_{29}H_{44}O_{12}{\cdot}8H_2O$, extracted from the seeds of the African trees *Strophanthus gratus* and *Acokanthera ouabaio,* that is used as a heart stimulant and by some African peoples as a dart poison. [From French *ouabaïo,* from Somali *wabayo.*]

Ouach·i·ta Mountains (wŏsh′ĭ-tô′). A low mountain range between the Arkansas and Red rivers extending about 322 km (200 mi) from central Arkansas to southeast Oklahoma and rising to 839.7 m (2,753 ft).

Ouachita River. A river, about 965 km (600 mi) long, rising in the Ouachita Mountains of western Arkansas and flowing east, southeast, and south into eastern Louisiana.

Oua·ga·dou·gou (wä′gə-do͞o′go͞o). The capital and largest city of Burkina Faso, in the central part of the country. It was founded in the late 11th century and is today a trade and distribution center. Population, 345,150.

ou·bli·ette (o͞o′blē-ĕt′) *n.* A dungeon with a trap door in the ceiling as its only means of entrance or exit. [French, from *oublier,* to forget, from Old French *oblider,* from Vulgar Latin **oblītāre,* from Latin *oblītus,* past participle of *oblīvīscī.* See **lei-** in Appendix.]

ouch¹ (ouch) *interj.* Used to express sudden pain or displeasure.

ouch² (ouch) *n.* **1.** A setting for a precious stone. **2.** A brooch or buckle set with jewels. **3.** *Obsolete.* A clasp; a brooch. [Middle English *ouche,* from Anglo-Norman, alteration of *(une) nouch,* (a) brooch, of Germanic origin. See **ned-** in Appendix.]

oud (o͞od) *n. Music.* An instrument of northern Africa and southwest Asia resembling a lute. [Arabic *'ūd.*]

Oudh (oud). A historical region of north-central India. Dating from at least the 4th century A.D., it was ruled by the Moguls after the 16th century and annexed by Great Britain in 1856. The annexation was a major cause of the Indian Mutiny (1857–1858).

ought¹ (ôt) *aux.v.* **1.** Used to indicate obligation or duty: *You ought to work harder than that.* **2.** Used to indicate advisability or prudence: *You ought to wear a raincoat.* **3.** Used to indicate desirability: *You ought to have been there; it was great fun.* **4.** Used to indicate probability or likelihood: *She ought to finish by next week.* [Middle English *oughten,* to be obliged to, from *oughte,* owned, from Old English *āhte,* past tense of *āgan,* to possess. See **ĕik-** in Appendix.]

USAGE NOTE: *Ought to* is sometimes used without a following verb if the meaning is clear: *Should we begin soon? Yes, we ought to.* In questions and negative sentences, especially those with contractions, *to* is also sometimes omitted: *Oughtn't we be going soon?* Although the omission of *to* was formerly possible in English, it is now considered nonstandard. • Usages such as *He hadn't ought to come* and *She shouldn't ought to say that* are common in many varieties of American English. They should be avoided in written English, however, in favor of the more standard variant *ought not to.*

ought² (ôt) *pron. & adv.* Variant of **aught¹.**

ought³ (ôt) *n.* Variant of **aught².**

ought⁴ (ôt) *v. Obsolete.* A past participle of **owe.**

ou·gui·ya (o͞o-gē′yə) *n.* See table at **currency.** [Native word in Mauritania.]

Oui·da (wē′də). See Marie Louise de la **Ramée.**

Oui·ja (wē′jə, -jē). A trademark used for a board with the alphabet and other symbols on it, and a planchette that is thought, when touched with the fingers, to move in such a way as to spell out spiritualistic and telepathic messages on the board.

Ouj·da (o͞oj-dä′). A city of northeast Morocco near the Algerian border. Founded in 944, it was occupied by the French in 1844, 1859, and 1907. Population, 260,082.

Ou·lu (ō′lo͞o, ou′-). A city of west-central Finland on the Gulf of Bothnia at the mouth of the **Oulu River,** about 105 km (65 mi) long. Oulu was chartered in 1610. Population, 96,525.

ounce¹ (ouns) *n. Abbr.* **oz, oz. 1.a.** A unit of weight in the U.S. Customary System, an avoirdupois unit equal to 437.5 grains (28.35 grams). **b.** A unit of apothecary weight, equal to 480 grains (31.10 grams). See table at **measurement. 2.** A fluid ounce. See table at **measurement. 3.** A tiny bit: *not an ounce of sympathy.* [Middle English *unce,* from Old French, from Latin *uncia.* See **oi-no-** in Appendix.]

ounce² (ouns) *n.* See **snow leopard.** [Middle English *unce,* from Old French *once,* alteration of *lonce,* from Vulgar Latin **luncea,* from Latin *lynx, lync-,* lynx, from Greek *lunx.* See **leuk-** in Appendix.]

our (our) *adj.* The possessive form of **we.** Used as a modifier before a noun: *our accomplishments; our hometown.* [Middle English, from Old English *ūre.* See **nes-²** in Appendix.]

Our Father (our) *n.* See **Lord's Prayer.**

Our Lady *n.* The Virgin Mary.

ours (ourz) *pron. (used with a sing. or pl. verb).* Used to indicate the one or ones belonging to us: *The original of the painting is ours. If your car doesn't start, take ours.* [Middle English *oures,* from *oure,* our, from Old English *ūre.* See **nes-²** in Appendix.]

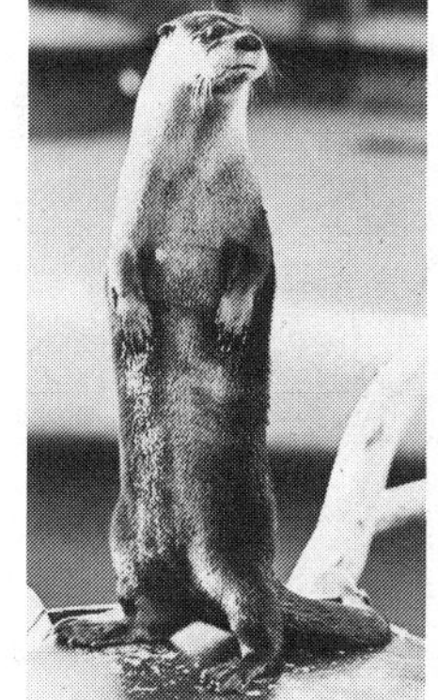

otter
North American river otter
Lutra canadensis

ottoman
c. 1882 American ottoman
by the Herter brothers
(fl. 1865–1908)

ă pat	oi boy
ā pay	ou out
âr care	o͝o took
ä father	o͞o boot
ĕ pet	ŭ cut
ē be	ûr urge
ĭ pit	th thin
ī pie	*th* this
îr pier	hw which
ŏ pot	zh vision
ō toe	ə about, item
ô paw	♦ regionalism

Stress marks: **′** (primary); ′ (secondary), as in **dictionary** (dĭk′shə-nĕr′ē)

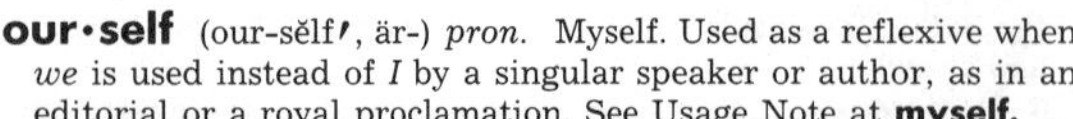

our·self (our-sĕlf′, är-) *pron.* Myself. Used as a reflexive when *we* is used instead of *I* by a singular speaker or author, as in an editorial or a royal proclamation. See Usage Note at **myself.**

our·selves (our-sĕlvz′, är-) *pron.* **1.** Those ones identical with us. **a.** Used reflexively as the direct or indirect object of a verb or the object of a preposition: *We bought ourselves an espresso machine.* **b.** Used for emphasis: *We ourselves were certain of the facts.* **c.** Used in an absolute construction: *Feeling chilly ourselves, we moved the party indoors.* **2.** Our normal or healthy condition or state: *We're feeling ourselves again after our bout with the flu.* See Usage Note at **myself.**

outboard motor

–ous *suff.* **1.** Possessing; full of; characterized by: *joyous.* **2.** Having a valence lower than that of a specified element in compounds or ions named with adjectives ending in *-ic*: *ferrous.* [Middle English, from Old French *-ous, -eus, -eux,* from Latin *-ōsus* and *-us,* adj. suff.]

ou·sel (o͞o′zəl) *n.* Variant of **ouzel.**

Ouse River (o͞oz). **1.** Also **Great Ouse River.** A river, about 249 km (155 mi) long, rising in south-central England and meandering east and northeast to the Wash, an inlet of the North Sea. **2.** A river, about 97 km (60 mi) long, of northeast England flowing southeast to join the Trent River and form the Humber River.

oust (oust) *tr.v.* **oust·ed, oust·ing, ousts. 1.** To eject from a position or place; force out: *"the American Revolution, which ousted the English"* (Virginia S. Eifert). **2.** To take the place of, especially by force; supplant. See Synonyms at **eject.** [Middle English *ousten,* from Anglo-Norman *ouster,* from Latin *obstāre,* to hinder. See OBSTACLE.]

oust·er (ous′tər) *n.* **1.a.** The act of ejecting, forcing out, or supplanting. **b.** The state of being ejected, forced out, or supplanted. **2.** One that ejects, forces out, or supplants another. **3.** *Law.* The act of forcing one out of possession or occupancy of material property to which one is entitled; illegal or wrongful dispossession. [Anglo-Norman, to oust, ouster. See OUST.]

out (out) *adv.* **1.** In a direction away from the inside: *go out of the office.* **2.** Away from the center or middle: *The troops fanned out.* **3.a.** Away from a usual place: *stepped out for a drink of water; went out for the evening.* **b.** Out of normal position: *threw his back out.* **4.a.** From inside a building or shelter into the open air; outside: *The boy went out to play.* **b.** In the open air; outside: *Is it snowing out?* **5.a.** From within a container or source: *drained the water out.* **b.** From among others: *picked out the thief in the crowd.* **6.a.** To exhaustion or depletion: *The supplies have run out.* **b.** Into extinction or imperceptibility: *The fire has gone out.* **c.** To a finish or conclusion: *Play the game out.* **d.** To the fullest extent or degree: *all decked out for the dance.* **e.** In or into competition or directed effort: *went out for the basketball team; was out to win.* **7.a.** Into being or evident existence: *The new car models have come out.* **b.** Into public circulation: *The paper came out early today.* **8.** Into view: *The moon came out.* **9.** Without inhibition; boldly: *Speak out.* **10.** Into possession of another or others; into distribution: *giving out free passes.* **11.a.** Into disuse or an unfashionable status: *Narrow ties have gone out.* **b.** Into a state of deprivation or loss: *voted the incompetent governor out.* **c.** Out of consideration: *A taxi is out, because we haven't the money.* **12.** In the time following; afterward: *"to gauge economic conditions six months out"* (Christian Science Monitor). **13.** *Baseball.* So as to be retired, or counted as an out: *He grounded out to the shortstop.* **14.** Used in two-way radio to indicate that a transmission is complete and no reply is expected. **—out** *adj.* **1.** Exterior; external: *the out surface of a ship's hull.* **2.** Directed away from a place or center; outgoing: *the out doorway.* **3.** No longer fashionable. **4.** *Baseball.* Not allowed to continue to bat or run; retired. **—out** *prep.* **1.** Forth from; through: *He fell out the window.* **2.** Beyond or outside of: *Out this door is the garage.* **—out** *n.* **1.** One that is out, especially one who is out of power. **2.** *Informal.* A means of escape: *The window was my only out.* **3.** *Abbr.* **O** *Baseball.* **a.** A play in which a batter or base runner is retired. **b.** The player retired in such a play. **4.** *Sports.* A serve or return that falls out of bounds in a court game. **5.** *Printing.* A word or other part of a manuscript omitted from the printed copy. **—out** *v.* **out·ed, out·ing, outs.** *—intr.* To be disclosed or revealed; come out: *Truth will out.* *—tr.* **1.** *Sports.* To send (a tennis ball, for example) outside the court or playing area. **2.** *Chiefly British.* To knock unconscious. **—*idiom.* on the outs.** *Informal.* Not on friendly terms; disagreeing. [Middle English, from Old English *ūt.* See **ud-** in Appendix.]

out– *pref.* In a way that surpasses, exceeds, or goes beyond: *outdistance.* [From OUT.]

out·age (ou′tĭj) *n.* **1.** A quantity or portion of something lacking after delivery or storage. **2.** A temporary suspension of operation, especially of electric power.

outcrop

out and away *adv.* By far: *She's out and away the best swimmer on the team.*

out-and-out (out′n-out′) *adj.* Complete; thoroughgoing: *An out-and-out capitalist.*

out-and-out·er (out′ən-ou′tər) *n.* One who goes to extremes.

out·back (out′băk′) *adv.* Out to or in remote, rural country, especially in Australia or New Zealand. **—outback** (out′băk′) *n.* The remote, rural part of a country, especially of Australia or New Zealand. *—attributive.* Often used to modify another noun: *outback life; outback ranches.* **—out′back′er** *n.*

out·bal·ance (out-băl′əns) *tr.v.* **-anced, -anc·ing, -anc·es.** To exceed in influence or significance; outweigh.

out·bid (out-bĭd′) *tr.v.* **-bid, -bid·den** (-bĭd′n) or **-bid, -bid·ding, -bids.** To bid higher than: *We outbid our rivals at the auction.*

out·board (out′bôrd′, -bōrd′) *adj.* **1.** *Nautical.* **a.** Situated or positioned outside the hull of a vessel. **b.** Being in a position that is away from the center line of the hull of a ship. **2.** Situated or positioned toward or nearer the end of a wing of an aircraft. **—outboard** *n.* **1.** An outboard motor. **2.** A boat with an outboard motor. **—out′board′** *adv.*

outboard motor *n. Nautical.* A detachable engine mounted on outboard brackets or on the stern of a boat.

out·bound (out′bound′) *adj.* Outward bound; headed away: *outbound trains.*

out·break (out′brāk′) *n.* **1.** A sudden increase: *an outbreak of influenza.* **2.** A sudden eruption; an outburst: *"an outbreak of strikes, violent agitation, and arrests"* (Samuel Chew).

out·breed (out′brēd′) *tr.v.* **-bred** (-brĕd′), **-breed·ing, -breeds.** To subject to outbreeding.

out·breed·ing (out′brē′dĭng) *n.* **1.** The breeding of distantly related or unrelated individuals, often producing a hybrid of superior quality. **2.** *Anthropology.* The mating of persons from different groups, often as a consequence of taboos against marriage within the group.

out·build·ing (out′bĭl′dĭng) *n.* A building separate from but associated with a main building.

out·burst (out′bûrst′) *n.* A sudden, violent display, as of activity or emotion: *an outburst of indignation.*

out·call (out′kôl′) *n.* A visit by a professional person to a client or patient's home; a house call.

out·cast (out′kăst′) *n.* One that has been excluded from a society or system. **—out′cast′** *adj.*

out·caste (out′kăst′) *n.* In India, one who has been expelled from or has abandoned one's caste.

out·class (out-klăs′) *tr.v.* **-classed, -class·ing, -class·es.** To surpass decisively, so as to appear of a higher class.

out·come (out′kŭm′) *n.* A natural result; a consequence. See Synonyms at **effect.**

out·crop (out′krŏp′) *n.* A portion of bedrock or other stratum protruding through the soil level. **—outcrop** (out-krŏp′) *intr.v.* **-cropped, -crop·ping, -crops.** To protrude above the soil, as rock formations.

out·cross (out′krôs′, -krŏs′) *tr.v.* **-crossed, -cross·ing, -cross·es.** To cross (animals or plants) by breeding individuals of different strains but usually of the same breed. **—outcross** *n.* **1.** The process of outcrossing. **2.** Offspring produced by outcrossing.

out·cry (out′krī′) *n., pl.* **-cries. 1.** A loud cry or clamor. **2.** A strong protest or objection: *public outcry over the rise in prices.*

out·curve (out′kûrv′) *n. Baseball.* A pitched ball that curves away from the batter.

out·date (out-dāt′) *tr.v.* **-dat·ed, -dat·ing, -dates.** To replace or make obsolete or old-fashioned.

out·dat·ed (out-dā′tĭd) *adj.* Out-of-date; old-fashioned.

out·did (out-dĭd′) *v.* Past tense of **outdo.**

out·dis·tance (out-dĭs′təns) *tr.v.* **-tanced, -tanc·ing, -tanc·es. 1.** To outrun, especially in a long-distance race. **2.** To surpass by a wide margin, especially through superior skill or endurance: *a sales force that outdistanced its competitors in volume sold.*

out·do (out-do͞o′) *tr.v.* **-did** (-dĭd′), **-done** (-dŭn′), **-do·ing, -does** (-dŭz′). To do more or better than in performance or action. See Synonyms at **excel.**

out·door (out′dôr′, -dōr′) also **out-of-door** (out′əv-dôr′, -dōr′) *adj.* Located in, done in, or suited to the open air: *badminton and other outdoor games.*

out·doors (out-dôrz′, -dōrz′) also **out-of-doors** (out′əv-dôrz′, -dōrz′) *—adv.* In or into the open; outside: *walking outdoors for fresh air.* *—n.* **1.** The open air. **2.** An area away from human settlements.

out·doors·man (out-dôrz′mən, -dōrz′-) *n.* A man who spends considerable time in outdoor pursuits, such as hunting or fishing.

out·doors·wo·man (out-dôrz′wo͝om′ən, -dōrz′-) *n.* A woman who spends considerable time in outdoor pursuits, such as hunting and fishing.

out·door·sy (out-dôr′zē, -dōr′-) *adj. Informal.* **1.** Associated with the outdoors: *outdoorsy hobbies such as fishing.* **2.** Showing a liking for the outdoors: *"backpackers, mountain climbers, cross-country skiers, and other no-nonsense outdoorsy types"* (New Yorker).

out·er (ou′tər) *adj.* **1.** Located on the outside; external. **2.** Farther than another from the center or middle. **3.** Relating to the body or its appearance rather than the mind or spirit.

outer ear *n.* See **external ear.**

Out·er Heb·ri·des (out′ər hĕb′rĭ-dēz′). See **Hebrides.**

Outer Mon·go·li·a (mŏng-gō′lē-ə, -gōl′yə, mŏn-). See **Mongolia** (sense 2).

out·er·most (ou′tər-mōst′) *adj.* Most distant from the center or inside; outmost.

outer planet *n.* Any of the five planets, Jupiter, Saturn, Uranus, Neptune, and Pluto, with orbits outside that of Mars.

outer space *n.* Any region of space beyond limits determined with reference to the boundaries of a celestial body or system, especially: **a.** The region of space immediately beyond Earth's atmosphere. **b.** Interplanetary or interstellar space.

out·er·wear (ou′tər-wâr′) *n.* Clothing, such as hats, coats, and gloves, for use outdoors.

out·face (out-fās′) *tr.v.* **-faced, -fac·ing, -fac·es. 1.** To overcome with a bold or self-assured look; stare down. **2.** To defy or resist.

out·fall (out′fôl′) *n.* The place where a sewer, drain, or stream discharges.

out·field (out′fēld′) *n. Abbr.* **OF** *Baseball.* **1.** The playing area extending outward from the diamond, divided into left, center, and right field. **2.** The position played by an outfielder. **3.** The members of a team playing in the outfield.

out·field·er (out′fēl′dər) *n. Abbr.* **OF** *Baseball.* A player who defends left, center, or right field.

out·fit (out′fĭt′) *n.* **1.** A set of tools or equipment for a specialized purpose: *a welder's outfit.* See Synonyms at **equipment. 2.** A set of clothing, often with accessories. **3.** *Informal.* An association of persons, especially a military unit or a business organization. **4.** The act of equipping. **—outfit** *tr.v.* **-fit·ted, -fit·ting, -fits.** To provide with necessary equipment: *This store outfits skiers.* See Synonyms at **furnish. —out′fit′ter** *n.*

out·flank (out-flăngk′) *tr.v.* **-flanked, -flank·ing, -flanks. 1.** To maneuver around and behind the flank of (an opposing force). **2.** To gain a tactical advantage over (a competitor, for example).

out·flow (out′flō′) *n.* **1.** The act or the process of flowing out: *watched the heavy outflow of the tide.* **2. a.** Something that flows out: *an outflow of water from a power plant.* **b.** The amount flowing out: *a heavy outflow of cash from the country.* **—outflow** *intr.v.* **-flowed, -flow·ing, -flows.** To issue or stream out, in or as if in a flow: *Too much money is outflowing from our household.*

out·fox (out-fŏks′) *tr.v.* **-foxed, -fox·ing, -fox·es.** To surpass (another) in cleverness or cunning; outsmart.

out-front (out′frŭnt′) *adj. Informal.* Straightforward, frank, and candid: *out-front news reporting.*

out·gas (out′găs′) *v.* **-gassed, -gas·sing, -gas·ses.** —*tr.* To remove embedded gas from (a solid), as by heating or reducing the pressure. —*intr.* To lose gas, as from a solid.

out·gen·er·al (out-jĕn′ər-əl) *tr.v.* **-aled, -al·ing, -als.** To surpass (another, especially an opponent) in leadership.

out·giv·ing (out′gĭv′ĭng) *adj.* Friendly and responsive; outgoing.

out·go (out-gō′) *tr.v.* **-went** (-wĕnt′), **-gone** (-gôn′, -gŏn′), **-go·ing, -goes** (-gōz′). To go beyond; exceed or surpass. **—outgo** (out′gō′) *n., pl.* **-goes. 1.** Something that goes out, especially an expenditure. **2.** The act or process of going out.

out·go·ing (out′gō′ĭng) *adj.* **1. a.** Going out or away; departing: *an outgoing passenger train.* **b.** Retiring from or relinquishing a place, a position, or an office: *the outgoing chairperson.* **c.** Addressed for sending: *outgoing mail.* **2.** Sociable and responsive to others; friendly: *a warm, outgoing personality.* **3.** Intended to be taken out, as from a restaurant: *outgoing orders of Chinese food.* **—out·go′ing·ness** *n.*

out·gone (out-gôn′, -gŏn′) *v.* Past participle of **outgo.**

out·grew (out-gro͞o′) *v.* Past tense of **outgrow.**

out-group (out′gro͞op′) *n.* A group of people excluded from or not belonging to one's own group, especially when viewed as subordinate or contemptibly different.

out·grow (out-grō′) *tr.v.* **-grew** (-gro͞o′), **-grown** (-grōn′), **-grow·ing, -grows. 1.** To grow too large for: *The child outgrew all his clothes.* **2.** To lose or discard in the course of maturation: *She outgrew her youthful idealism.* **3.** To surpass in growth: *Spring lambs were outgrowing the piglets.*

out·growth (out′grōth′) *n.* **1.** The act or process of growing out. **2.** A product of growing out; an offshoot: *an outgrowth of new shoots on a branch.* **3.** A result or consequence: *Inflation is an outgrowth of war.*

out·guess (out-gĕs′) *tr.v.* **-guessed, -guess·ing, -guess·es. 1.** To anticipate correctly the actions of. **2.** To gain the advantage over (another) by cleverness or forethought; outwit.

out·gun (out′gŭn′) *tr.v.* **-gunned, -gun·ning, -guns. 1.** To surpass in military force. **2.** To overwhelm or defeat.

out·haul (out′hôl′) *n. Nautical.* A rope used to extend a sail along a spar or boom.

out·house (out′hous′) *n.* **1.** A small, enclosed structure having one or two holes in a seat built over a pit and serving as an outdoor toilet. **2.** An outbuilding, as on a farm.

out·ing (ou′tĭng) *n.* **1.** An excursion, typically a pleasure trip. **2.** A walk outdoors.

outing flannel *n.* A soft, lightweight cotton fabric, usually with a short nap on both sides.

out·laid (out-lād′) *v.* Past tense and past participle of **outlay.**

out·land (out′lănd′, -lənd) *n.* **1.** A foreign land. **2. outlands.** The outlying areas of a country; the provinces. **—out′land′** *adj.*

out·land·er (out′lăn′dər) *n.* **1.** A person from a foreign country; a foreigner. **2.** A stranger.

out·land·ish (out-lăn′dĭsh) *adj.* **1.** Conspicuously unconventional; bizarre. See Synonyms at **strange. 2.** Strikingly unfamiliar. **3.** Located far from civilized areas. **4.** *Archaic.* Of foreign origin; not native. **—out·land′ish·ly** *adv.* **—out·land′ish·ness** *n.*

out·last (out-lăst′) *tr.v.* **-last·ed, -last·ing, -lasts.** To last longer than. See Synonyms at **outlive.**

out·law (out′lô′) *n.* **1. a.** A fugitive from the law. **b.** A habitual criminal. **c.** A rebel; a nonconformist: *a social outlaw.* **2.** A person excluded from normal legal protection and rights. **3.** A wild or vicious horse or other animal. **—outlaw** *tr.v.* **-lawed, -law·ing, -laws. 1.** To declare illegal: *outlawed the sale of firearms.* **2.** To place under a ban; prohibit: *outlawed smoking in the house.* **3.** To deprive (one declared to be a criminal fugitive) of the protection of the law. [Middle English *outlaue,* from Old English *ūtlaga,* from Old Norse *ūtlagi,* from *ūtlagr,* outlawed, banished : *ūt,* out; see **ud-** in Appendix + *lög,* law; see **legh-** in Appendix.] **—out′law′** *adj.*

WORD HISTORY: The word *outlaw* brings to mind cattle rustlers and gunslingers of the Wild West, but it comes to us from a much earlier time, when guns were not yet invented but cattle stealing was. *Outlaw* can be traced back to the Old Norse word *ūtlagr,* "outlawed, banished," made up of *ūt,* "out," and *lög,* "law." An *ūtlagi* (derived from *ūtlagr*) was someone outside the protection of the law. The Scandinavians, who invaded and settled in England during the 8th through the 11th century, gave us the Old English word *ūtlaga,* which designated someone who because of criminal acts must give up his property to the crown and could be killed without recrimination. The legal status of the outlaw became less severe over the course of the Middle Ages. However, the looser use of the word to designate criminals in general, which arose in Middle English, lives on in tales of the Wild West.

out·law·ry (out′lô′rē) *n., pl.* **-ries. 1.** The act or process of outlawing or the state of having been outlawed. **2.** Defiance of the law. [Middle English *outlauerie,* from Anglo-Norman *utlagerie* and from Medieval Latin *ūtlagāria,* both from Old English *ūtlaga,* outlaw. See OUTLAW.]

out·lay (out′lā′) *n.* **1.** The spending or disbursement of money: *the weekly outlay on groceries.* **2.** An amount spent; an expenditure: *"huge new outlays for the military"* (New York Times). **—outlay** (out-lā′) *tr.v.* **-laid** (-lād′), **-lay·ing, -lays.** To spend or disburse (money).

out·let (out′lĕt′, -lĭt) *n.* **1. a.** A passage for escape or exit; a vent. **b.** A means of release or gratification, as for energies, drives, or desires: *exercised as an outlet for frustration.* **2. a.** A stream that flows out of a lake or pond. **b.** The mouth of a river where it flows into a larger body of water. **c.** The point of intersection of a driveway and a road, especially in a rural area. **3. a.** A commercial market for goods or services. **b.** A store that sells the goods of a particular manufacturer or wholesaler. **4.** A receptacle, especially one mounted in a wall, that is connected to a power supply and equipped with a socket for a plug.

outhouse

out·li·er (out′lī′ər) *n.* **1.** One whose domicile lies at an appreciable distance from one's place of business. **2.** A portion of stratified rock separated from a main formation by erosion.

out·line (out′līn′) *n.* **1. a.** A line marking the outer contours or boundaries of an object or a figure. **b.** The shape of an object or a figure. **2. a.** A style of drawing in which objects are delineated in contours without shading. **b.** A sketch done in this style. **3. a.** A general description covering the main points of a subject: *an outline of American literature.* **b.** A statement summarizing the important points of a text. **c.** A summary of a written work or speech, usually analyzed in headings and subheadings. **4.** A preliminary draft or plan, as of a project or proposal. **—outline** *tr.v.* **-lined, -lin·ing, -lines. 1.** To draw an outline of. **2.** To display or accentuate the outline of. **3.** To give the main features or various aspects of; summarize: *outlined the major provisions of the tax bill.*

SYNONYMS: *outline, contour, profile, silhouette.* The central meaning shared by these nouns is "a line defining the boundary and shape of an object, a mass, or a figure": *the outline of the mountains against the sunset; saw the contour of the island from the airplane; the profile of a king on a coin; saw the dark silhouette of the family waving farewell.*

out·live (out-lĭv′) *tr.v.* **-lived, -liv·ing, -lives. 1.** To live longer than: *She outlived her son.* **2.** To continue in use or existence long enough to survive (something else): *a regulation that has outlived its usefulness.*

SYNONYMS: *outlive, outlast, survive.* These verbs all mean to live or exist longer than another person or thing. *Outlive* frequently implies the capacity for enduring after the death of another or after a particular time: *outlived her friends. Outlast,* often interchangeable with *outlive,* more commonly stresses longer duration in time: *anxiety that outlasted its cause. Survive* may also be used with reference merely to living longer than another: *He is survived by his wife and children.* Frequently, however, to *survive* is to remain alive following something potentially destructive to life: *She survived the plane crash.*

out·look (out′lo͝ok′) *n.* **1.** A point of view; an attitude: *a positive outlook.* **2.** Expectation for the future: *the long-term out-*

ă pat	oi boy
ā pay	ou out
âr care	o͝o took
ä father	o͞o boot
ĕ pet	ŭ cut
ē be	ûr urge
ĭ pit	th thin
ī pie	*th* this
îr pier	hw which
ŏ pot	zh vision
ō toe	ə about, item
ô paw	♦ regionalism

Stress marks: ′ (primary); ′ (secondary), as in **dictionary** (dĭk′shə-nĕr′ē)

look for economic growth. **3.a.** A place where something can be viewed. **b.** The view seen from such a place. **4.** The act of looking out.

out loud *adv.* Loud enough to be audible; aloud: *read the poem out loud.*

out·ly·ing (out′lī′ĭng) *adj.* Relatively distant or remote from a center or middle: *outlying regions.*

out·man (out-măn′) *tr.v.* **-manned, -man·ning, -mans. 1.** To exceed in manpower; outnumber: *The country's army was outmanned and outgunned.* **2.** To get the better of; overwhelm or defeat: *Our team was outmanned six to one.*

out·ma·neu·ver (out′mə-no͞o′vər, -nyo͞o′-) *tr.v.* **-vered, -ver·ing, -vers. 1.** To overcome (an opponent) by artful, clever maneuvering. **2.** To excel in maneuverability: *The car outmaneuvers all others of its class.*

out·match (out-măch′) *tr.v.* **-matched, -match·ing, -match·es.** To prove greater or better than; surpass.

out-mi·grant (out′mī′grənt) *n.* One that out-migrates.

out-mi·grate (out′mī′grāt) *intr.v.* **-grat·ed, -grat·ing, -grates.** To move out of one community, region, or country in order to reside in another. **—out′-mi·gra′tion** *n.*

out·mode (out-mōd′) *tr.v.* **-mod·ed, -mod·ing, -modes.** To cause to become unfashionable or obsolete.

out·mod·ed (out-mō′dĭd) *adj.* **1.** Not in fashion; unfashionable: *outmoded attire; outmoded ideas.* **2.** No longer usable or practical; obsolete: *outmoded machinery.*

out·most (out′mōst′) *adj.* Farthest out; outermost.

out·mus·cle (out-mŭs′əl) *tr.v.* **-cled, -cling, -cles.** *Informal.* To dominate or defeat by means of superior strength or power.

out·num·ber (out-nŭm′bər) *tr.v.* **-bered, -ber·ing, -bers.** To exceed the number of; be more numerous than.

out of *prep.* **1.a.** From within to the outside of: *got out of the car.* **b.** From a given condition: *came out of her trance.* **c.** From an origin, a source, or a cause: *made out of wood.* **d.** In, especially intermittently in: *works out of the main office.* **2.a.** In a position or situation beyond the range, boundaries, limits, or sphere of: *The plane flew out of sight.* **b.** In a state or position away from the expected or usual: *out of practice; out of touch with reality.* **3.** From among: *five out of six votes.* **4.** In or into a condition of no longer having: *We're out of coffee; We were tricked out of our savings.* ***—idiom.* out of it.** *Slang.* Not aware of or participating in a particular group, pursuit, or trend.

out-of-bod·y (out′əv-bŏd′ē) *adj.* Of, relating to, or marked by the psychological sensation of perceiving oneself from an external perspective, as though the mind or soul has left the physical body and is acting of its own volition: *convinced she had an out-of-body experience while undergoing surgery.*

out-of-bounds (out′əv-boundz′) *adv.* Beyond the designated boundaries or limits.

out-of-court (out′əv-kôrt′, -kōrt) *adj.* *Law.* Managed or agreed upon between disputing parties without a judicial decision: *reached an out-of-court settlement.*

out-of-date (out′əv-dāt′) *adj.* Out of style or use; outmoded.

out-of-door (out′əv-dôr′, -dōr′) *adj.* Variant of **outdoor.**

out-of-doors (out′əv-dôrz′, -dōrz′) *adv. & n.* Variant of **outdoors.**

out of pocket *adv.* **1.** Without funds or assets: *a traveler who was caught out of pocket.* **2.** In a state of having experienced a loss, especially a financial one.

out-of-pock·et (out′əv-pŏk′ĭt) *adj.* **1.** Calling for the spending of cash: *out-of-pocket expenses.* **2.** Lacking funds: *hungry, cold, and out-of-pocket travelers.*

out-of-state (out′əv-stāt′) *adj.* Of, relating to, or being from another state.

out-of-stat·er (out′əv-stā′tər) *n.* **1.** A visitor, such as a tourist, from another state. **2.** A legal resident of one state who lives for a period of time in another state in order to attend school, for example.

out-of-the-way (out′əv-*th*ə-wā′) *adj.* **1.** Being in a remote or secluded location: *a quiet, out-of-the-way resort.* **2.** Being out of the ordinary; unusual: *out-of-the-way memorabilia.* **3.** Improper; offensive: *out-of-the-way remarks.*

out-of-town (out′əv-toun′) *adj.* **1.** Of, relating to, or being from another town or city. **2.** Happening in another town or city: *the out-of-town début of a new musical.*

out-of-town·er (out′əv-tou′nər) *n.* A visitor from another town or city.

out·pace (out-pās′) *tr.v.* **-paced, -pac·ing, -pac·es.** To surpass or outdo (another), as in speed, growth, or performance.

out·pa·tient (out′pā′shənt) *n.* A patient who is admitted to a hospital or clinic for treatment that does not require an overnight stay. *—attributive.* Often used to modify another noun: *outpatient wards; outpatient facilities.*

out·per·form (out′pər-fôrm′) *tr.v.* **-formed, -form·ing, -forms.** To surpass (another) in performance.

out·place (out′plās′) *tr.v.* **-placed, -plac·ing, -plac·es.** To terminate the employment of. **—out′placed′** *adj.*

out·place·ment (out′plās′mənt) *n.* The process of facilitating a terminated employee's search for a new job by provision of professional services, such as counseling, paid for by the employing company.

out·plac·er (out′plā′sər) *n.* A specialist in outplacement services.

out·play (out-plā′) *tr.v.* **-played, -play·ing, -plays.** *Sports & Games.* To surpass (an opponent) in skill or technique or in scoring points.

out·point (out-point′) *tr.v.* **-point·ed, -point·ing, -points. 1.** *Nautical.* To sail closer to the wind than (another vessel). **2.** *Sports.* To surpass (an opponent) in the number of points won.

out·poll (out-pōl′) *tr.v.* **-polled, -poll·ing, -polls.** To win more votes than: *She outpolled her rival by a wide margin.*

out·post (out′pōst′) *n.* **1.a.** A detachment of troops stationed at a distance from a main force to guard against surprise attacks. **b.** The station occupied by such troops. **c.** A usually small military base established in another country. **2.** An outlying settlement.

out·pour (out-pôr′, -pōr′) *tr.v.* **-poured, -pour·ing, -pours.** To flow out rapidly; pour out. **—outpour** (out′pôr′, -pōr′) *n.* A rapid outflow; an outpouring: *an outpour of sympathy.* **—out·pour′er** *n.*

out·pour·ing (out′pôr′ĭng, -pōr′-) *n.* **1.** The act of pouring out. **2.** Something that pours out or is poured out; an outflow: *an outpouring of lava; an outpouring of charges and countercharges.*

out-proc·ess (out-prŏs′ĕs, -prō′sĕs) *tr.v.* **-essed, -ess·ing, -ess·es.** To generate the required paperwork in order to process (military personnel) out of one tour of duty into another or out of the armed forces: "[He] *was now out-processed from Vietnam duty via Okinawa*" (W.E.B. Griffin).

out·put (out′po͝ot′) *n.* **1.** The act or process of producing; production. **2.a.** An amount produced or manufactured during a certain time. **b.** Intellectual or creative production: *literary output; artistic output.* **3.a.** The energy, power, or work produced by a system. **b.** *Computer Science.* The information produced by a computer from a specific input. **—output** *tr.v.* **-put·ted** or **-put, -put·ting, -puts.** To produce or manufacture (something) during a certain time.

out·race (out-rās′) *tr.v.* **-raced, -rac·ing, -rac·es.** To surpass in speed or performance.

out·rage (out′rāj′) *n.* **1.** An act of extreme violence or viciousness. **2.** An act grossly offensive to decency, morality, or good taste. **3.** A deplorable insult. **4.** Resentful anger aroused by a violent or offensive act. **—outrage** *tr.v.* **-raged, -rag·ing, -rag·es. 1.** To offend grossly against (standards of decency or morality); commit an outrage on. **2.** To produce anger or resentment in: *Incompetence outraged him.* See Synonyms at **offend.** [Middle English, from Old French, from *outre,* beyond. See OUTRÉ.]

out·ra·geous (out-rā′jəs) *adj.* **1.a.** Grossly offensive to decency or morality. **b.** Being well beyond the bounds of good taste: *outrageous epithets.* **2.** Having no regard for morality. **3.** Violent or unrestrained in temperament or behavior. **4.a.** Extremely unusual or unconventional; extraordinary: *loved to dress in outrageous clothing; found some outrageous bargains.* **b.** Being beyond all reason; extravagant or immoderate: *spends an outrageous amount on entertainment.* **—out·ra′geous·ly** *adv.* **—out·ra′geous·ness** *n.*

SYNONYMS: *outrageous, flagrant, atrocious, monstrous.* These adjectives mean grievously or conspicuously bad or appalling; the terms are often used interchangeably. Something *outrageous* is grossly offensive to decency, morality, or good taste: *an outrageous lie; was subjected to outrageous cruelty.* What is *flagrant* is glaringly or scandalously reprehensible: *"The adherence of the United States to the Monroe Doctrine may force the United States . . . in flagrant cases of such wrongdoing . . . to the exercise of an international police power"* (Theodore Roosevelt). *Atrocious* means extremely wicked or cruel: *Murder is an atrocious crime. Monstrous* describes what is shockingly hideous or frightful: *"There was no excess too monstrous for them to commit"* (Nicholas P.S. Wiseman).

out·ran (out-răn′) *v.* Past tense of **outrun.**

out·range (out-rānj′) *tr.v.* **-ranged, -rang·ing, -rang·es.** To exceed (another) in range: *a ballistic missile that outranged all others in its class.*

out·rank (out-răngk′) *tr.v.* **-ranked, -rank·ing, -ranks.** To rank higher than.

ou·tré (o͞o-trā′) *adj.* Highly unconventional; eccentric or bizarre: *"outré and affected stage antics"* (Michael Heaton). [French, from Old French, defeated, past participle of *outrer,* to pass someone, from *outre,* beyond, from Latin *ultrā.* See **al-**[1] in Appendix.]

out·reach (out-rēch′) *tr.v.* **-reached, -reach·ing, -reach·es. 1.** To surpass (another) in reach: *She had to outreach her opponent to win the fencing match.* **2.** To be more or greater than; exceed: *Demand has outreached supply.* **—outreach** (out′rēch′) *n.* **1.** The act or process of reaching out: *could not allay the outreach of human intellect.* **2.** Extent or length of reach: *the vast outreach of technology; the outreach of a forest fire from mountains to suburbs.* **3.** A systematic attempt to provide services beyond conventional limits, as to particular segments of a community: *an educational outreach to illiterate adults.*

Ou·tre·mont (o͞o′trə-mŏnt′, o͞o-trə-môɴ′). A city of southern Quebec, Canada, a residential section of Greater Montreal on Montreal Island. Population, 24,338.

out·ride (out-rīd′) *tr.v.* **-rode** (-rōd′), **-rid·den** (-rĭd′n), **-rid·ing, -rides. 1.** To ride faster, farther, or better than; outstrip. **2.** To withstand successfully; ride out: *outride a storm at sea.* **—outride** *n.* An unstressed syllable or cluster of syllables within a given metrical unit that is omitted from the scansion pattern in sprung rhythm. [N., coined by Gerard Manley HOPKINS.]

out·rid·er (out′rī′dər) *n.* **1.** A guide; an escort. **2.** One that goes in advance; a forerunner. **3.** A mounted attendant who rides in front of or beside a carriage.

out·rig·ger (out′rĭg′ər) *n.* **1.** *Nautical.* **a.** A projecting beam or spar run out from the side of a vessel to help in securing the masts or from a mast to be used in extending a rope or sail. **b.** A long, thin float attached parallel to a seagoing canoe by projecting spars as a means of preventing it from capsizing. **c.** A vessel fitted with such a float or beam. **d.** A support for an oarlock projecting from the side of a racing shell. **e.** A racing shell fitted with such a support. **2.** A projecting frame extending laterally beyond the main structure of a vehicle, an aircraft, or a machine to stabilize the structure or support an extending part.

out·right (out′rīt′, -rīt′) *adv.* **1.** Without reservation or qualification; openly: *finally responded outright to the question.* **2.** Completely and entirely; wholly: *denied the charges outright.* **3.** At once; straightway: *were killed outright in the crash.* **4.** Without additional payments owing, constraints, or stipulations: *owns the property outright.* **—outright** (out′rīt′) *adj.* **1.** Presented without reservation; unqualified: *an outright gift.* **2.a.** Complete; total: *outright victory.* **b.** Thoroughgoing; out-and-out: *outright viciousness; an outright coward.* **3.** Made without constraints, stipulations, or additional payments owed: *outright sale of the property.* **4.** *Archaic.* Moving straight onward. **—out′right′ly** *adv.* **—out′right′ness** *n.*

out·rode (out-rōd′) *v.* Past tense of **outride.**

out·run (out-rŭn′) *tr.v.* **-ran** (-răn′), **-run, -run·ning, -runs. 1.a.** To run faster than. **b.** To escape from: *outrun one's creditors.* **2.** To go beyond; exceed: *"Man's ingenuity has outrun his intelligence"* (Joseph Wood Krutch).

out·sell (out-sĕl′) *tr.v.* **-sold** (-sōld′), **-sell·ing, -sells. 1.** To surpass (another) in an amount sold: *a book that outsold all others of its kind.* **2.** To outdo (another) in selling: *a salesperson who outsold her colleagues.*

out·set (out′sĕt′) *n.* **1.** The beginning; the start: *Problems arose at the very outset.* **2.** An initial stage, as of an activity: *The outset of any major project can be difficult.*

out·shine (out-shīn′) *v.* **-shone** (-shōn′), **-shin·ing, -shines.** —*tr.* **1.a.** To shine brighter than. **b.** To be more beautiful, splendid, or flamboyant than. **2.** To surpass in obvious excellence; outdo. —*intr.* To shine forth.

out·shoot (out-sho͞ot′) *tr.v.* **-shot** (-shŏt′), **-shoot·ing, -shoots.** To shoot better than (another): *a pistol that easily outshoots others in its class; a basketball player who outshot all others on the team.* **—outshoot** (out′sho͞ot′) *n.* A protuberance, a projection, or an outgrowth: *outshoots of brush on the high mountain slopes.*

out·side (out-sīd′, out′sīd′) *n.* **1.** The part or parts that face out; the outer surface. **2.a.** The part or side of an object that is presented to the viewer; the external aspect. **b.** Outward aspect or appearance: *"You'll never persuade me that I can't tell what men are by their outsides"* (George Eliot). **3.** The space beyond a boundary or limit. **4.** *Sports.* A position at a distance from the inside or center, as of a playing field or racetrack. **5.** The utmost limit; the maximum: *We'll be leaving in ten days at the outside.* **—outside** *adj.* **1.a.** Of, relating to, or being on or near the outer side; outer: *the outside margin.* **b.** Of, restricted to, or situated on the outer side of an enclosure or a boundary; external: *an outside door lock; an outside antenna.* **2.** Located away from the inside or center: *the outside traffic lane.* **3.a.** Acting, occurring, originating, or being at a place beyond certain limits: *knew little of the outside world.* **b.** Gaining or providing access to the external side: *an outside telephone line.* **4.a.** Not belonging to or originating in a certain group or association: *requested outside assistance; deplored outside interference.* **b.** Being beyond the limits of one's usual work or responsibilities: *My outside interests are skiing and sailing.* **5.** Extreme, uttermost: *The costs have exceeded even our outside estimates.* **6.** Very unlikely; remote: *only an outside possibility of winning the tournament.* **7.** *Baseball.* Passing on the side of home plate away from the batter. Used of a pitch. **—outside** *adv.* **1.** On or to the outer or external side. **2.** Outdoors. **—outside** *prep.* **1.** On or to the outer or external side of: *saw someone outside the window.* **2.** Beyond the limits of: *a little place outside the city.* **3.** With the exception of; except: *We have no other information outside the figures already given.*

outside of *prep.* Outside.

out·sid·er (out-sī′dər) *n.* **1.a.** One who is excluded from a party, an association, or a set. **b.** One who is isolated or detached from the activities or concerns of one's own community. **2.** A contestant given little chance of winning; a long shot. **—out·si′der·ness** *n.*

out·sight (out′sīt′) *n.* The faculty or act of clearly perceiving and understanding external things.

out·size (out′sīz′) *n.* **1.** An unusual size, especially a very large size. **2.** A garment of unusual size. **—outsize** also **out·sized** (-sīzd′) *adj.* Unusually large, weighty, or extensive.

out·skirt (out′skûrt′) *n.* The part or region remote from a central district, as of a city or town. Often used in the plural: *on the outskirts of Paris.*

out·smart (out-smärt′) *tr.v.* **-smart·ed, -smart·ing, -smarts.** To gain the advantage over by cunning; outwit.

out·soar (out-sôr′, -sōr′) *tr.v.* **-soared, -soar·ing, -soars.** To soar beyond or to a higher place than.

out·sold (out-sōld′) *v.* Past tense and past participle of **outsell.**

out·sole (out′sōl′) *n.* The outer sole of a shoe or boot.

out·source (out′sôrs′, -sōrs′) *tr.v.* **-sourced, -sourc·ing, -sourc·es.** To farm out (work, for example) to an outside provider or manufacturer in order to cut costs.

out·sourc·ing (out′sôr′sĭng, -sōr′-) *n.* The procuring of services or products, such as the parts used in manufacturing a motor vehicle, from an outside supplier or manufacturer in order to cut costs.

out·speak (out-spēk′) *v.* **-spoke** (-spōk′), **-spo·ken** (-spō′kən), **-speak·ing, -speaks.** —*tr. Archaic.* To speak better or more cogently than (another). —*intr.* To speak out.

out·spend (out-spĕnd′) *tr.v.* **-spent** (-spĕnt), **-spend·ing, -spends. 1.** To spend beyond the limits of: *outspends his earnings.* **2.** To outdo in spending: *outspends all her relatives at Christmas.*

out·spent (out-spĕnt′) *adj.* Completely exhausted.

out·spoke (out-spōk′) *v.* Past tense of **outspeak.**

out·spo·ken (out-spō′kən) *v.* Past participle of **outspeak.** **—outspoken** *adj.* **1.** Spoken without reserve; candid. **2.** Frank and unreserved in speech. See Synonyms at **frank**[1]. **—out·spo′ken·ly** *adv.* **—out·spo′ken·ness** *n.*

out·spread (out-sprĕd′) *tr. & intr.v.* **-spread, -spread·ing, -spreads.** To stretch or extend or to be stretched or extended. **—outspread** (out′sprĕd′) *n.* **1.** The act of spreading out. **2.** Something spread out; an expanse. **—outspread** *adj.* Spread out; extended.

out·stand (out-stănd′) *intr.v.* **-stood** (-sto͝od′), **-stand·ing, -stands.** To stand out plainly.

out·stand·ing (out-stăn′dĭng, out′stăn′-) *adj.* **1.** Standing out among others of its kind; prominent. See Synonyms at **noticeable. 2.** Superior to others of its kind; distinguished. **3.** Projecting upward or outward; standing out. **4.** Still in existence; not settled or resolved: *outstanding debts; a long outstanding problem.* **5.** Publicly issued and sold: *outstanding stocks and bonds.* **—out·stand′ing·ly** *adv.*

out·stare (out-stâr′) *tr.v.* **-stared, -star·ing, -stares.** To overcome by or as if by staring; stare down.

out·sta·tion (out′stā′shən) *n.* A remote station or post.

out·stay (out-stā′) *tr.v.* **-stayed, -stay·ing, -stays. 1.** To stay longer than (another or others); overstay: *guests who outstayed their welcome.* **2.** To show greater endurance than: *She outstayed her opponents and won the race.*

out·stood (out-sto͝od′) *v.* Past tense and past participle of **outstand.**

out·stretch (out-strĕch′) *tr.v.* **-stretched, -stretch·ing, -stretch·es.** To stretch out; extend.

out·strip (out-strĭp′) *tr.v.* **-stripped, -strip·ping, -strips. 1.** To leave behind; outrun. **2.** To exceed or surpass: *"Material development outstripped human development"* (Edith Hamilton). See Synonyms at **excel.**

out·stroke (out′strōk′) *n.* An outward stroke, especially the stroke of an engine piston moving toward the crankshaft.

out·take (out′tāk′) *n.* **1.a.** A section or scene, as of a movie, that is filmed but not used in the final version. **b.** A complete version, as of a recording, that is dropped in favor of another version. **2.** An opening for outward discharge; a vent.

out·talk (out-tôk′) *tr.v.* **-talked, -talk·ing, -talks. 1.** To outdo (another) in talking. **2.** To outwit by talking.

out·think (out-thĭngk′) *tr.v.* **-thought** (-thôt), **-think·ing, -thinks. 1.** To outdo (another) in thinking. **2.** To outwit by thinking.

out·thrust (out-thrŭst′) *intr. & tr.v.* **-thrust·ed, -thrust·ing, -thrusts.** To extend or cause to extend outward. **—outthrust** (out′thrŭst′) *n.* Something, such as an outcropping of rocks, that extends outward.

out·turn (out′tûrn′) *n.* A total amount produced during a given period; output.

out·vote (out-vōt′) *tr.v.* **-vot·ed, -vot·ing, -votes. 1.** To outdo in voting: *The county seat outvoted the smaller towns.* **2.** To defeat (an opponent or a proposal, for example) in voting.

out·wait (out-wāt′) *tr.v.* **-wait·ed, -wait·ing, -waits. 1.** To delay until the end of; wait out: *had to outwait the traffic jam.* **2.** To get the better of or overcome by refraining from action: *sat back and decided to outwait my opponent.*

out·ward (out′wərd) *adj.* **1.** Of, located on, or moving toward the outside or exterior; outer. **2.** Relating to the physical self: *a concern with outward beauty rather than with inward reflections.* **3.** Purely external; superficial: *outward composure.* **—outward** *adv.* **1.** Also **out·wards** (-wərdz). Toward the outside; away from a central point. **2.** *Archaic.* On the outside; externally. **—outward** *n.* The material or external world: *"There is nothing here,/Which, from the outward to the inward brought,/Molded thy baby thought"* (Tennyson). [Middle English, from Old English *ūtweard* : *ūt,* out; see OUT + *-weard,* -ward.] **—out′ward·ness** *n.*

outrigger

ă pat	oi boy
ā pay	ou out
âr care	o͝o took
ä father	o͞o boot
ĕ pet	ŭ cut
ē be	ûr urge
ĭ pit	th thin
ī pie	*th* this
îr pier	hw which
ŏ pot	zh vision
ō toe	ə about, item
ô paw	♦ regionalism

Stress marks: ′ (primary); **′** (secondary), as in **dictionary** (dĭk′shə-nĕr′ē)

out•ward-bound (out′wərd-bound′) *adj.* Headed out, as toward the open sea: *an outward-bound tanker.*

out•ward•ly (out′wərd-lē) *adv.* **1.** On the outside or exterior; externally. **2.** Toward the outside. **3.** In regard to outward condition, conduct, or manifestation: *outwardly a perfect gentleman.*

out•wash (out′wŏsh′, -wôsh′) *n.* Sediment deposited by streams flowing away from a melting glacier.

out•wear (out-wâr′) *tr.v.* **-wore** (-wôr′, -wōr′), **-worn** (-wôrn′, -wōrn′), **-wear•ing, -wears. 1.** To last longer than; outlast: *durable clothing that outwears other brands.* **2.** To get over (something) by the passage of time; outgrow: *"He . . . may outwear those unattractive qualities of character"* (Westminster Gazette).

out•weigh (out-wā′) *tr.v.* **-weighed, -weigh•ing, -weighs. 1.** To weigh more than. **2.** To be more significant than; exceed in value or importance: *The benefits outweigh the risks.*

out•went (out-wĕnt′) *v.* Past tense of **outgo.**

out•wit (out-wĭt′) *tr.v.* **-wit•ted, -wit•ting, -wits. 1.** To surpass in cleverness or cunning; outsmart. **2.** *Archaic.* To surpass in intelligence.

out•wore (out-wôr′, -wōr′) *v.* Past tense of **outwear.**

out•work (out-wûrk′) *tr.v.* **-worked** or **-wrought** (-rôt′), **-work•ing, -works. 1.** To work better or faster than. **2.** To complete (something); work (something) out. **—outwork** (out′-wûrk′) *n.* A minor fortification constructed beyond a main defensive position or fortification.

out•worn (out-wôrn′, -wōrn′) *v.* Past participle of **outwear. —outworn** *adj.* No longer acceptable, usable, or practical: *an outworn penal code; outworn clothes.*

out•wrought (out-rôt′) *v.* A past tense and a past participle of **outwork.**

ovenbird
Seiurus aurocapillus

ou•zel also **ou•sel** (o͞o′zəl) *n.* A water ouzel. [Middle English *osel,* from Old English *ōsle.*]

ou•zo (o͞o′zō) *n., pl.* **-zos.** A colorless, unsweetened Greek liqueur flavored with anise. [Modern Greek.]

ov– *pref.* Variant of **ovi–.**

o•va (ō′və) *n.* Plural of **ovum.**

o•val (ō′vəl) *adj.* **1.** Resembling an egg in shape. **2.** Resembling an ellipse in shape; elliptical. **—oval** *n.* **1.** An egg-shaped or elliptical form or figure. **2.** An elliptical track, as for racing or athletic events. [Medieval Latin *ōvālis,* from Latin *ōvum,* egg. See **awi-** in Appendix.] **—o′val•ly** *adv.* **—o′val•ness** *n.*

ov•al•bu•min (ŏv′əl-byo͞o′mĭn, ō′vəl-) *n.* The albumin of egg white. [Alteration of Late Latin *ōvī albūmen* : Latin *ōvī,* genitive sing. of *ōvum,* egg; see OVUM + *albūmen,* white of an egg; see ALBUMEN.]

O•val Office (ō′vəl) *n.* **1.** The office of the President of the United States, situated in the White House. **2.** The office, authority, or executive power of the President of the United States; the presidency.

oval window *n.* The oval opening in the middle ear to which the base of the stapes is connected and through which the ossicles of the ear transmit sound vibrations to the cochlea.

o•var•i•ec•to•my (ō-vâr′ē-ĕk′tə-mē) *n., pl.* **-mies.** Surgical removal of one ovary or both. Also called *oophorectomy.*

o•var•i•ot•o•my (ō-vâr′ē-ŏt′ə-mē) *n., pl.* **-mies. 1.** An ovariectomy. **2.** Surgical incision into an ovary, as to perform a biopsy or remove a tumor.

o•va•ri•tis (ō′və-rī′tĭs) *n.* See **oophoritis.**

o•va•ry (ō′və-rē) *n., pl.* **-ries. 1.** The usually paired female or hermaphroditic reproductive organ that produces ova and, in vertebrates, estrogen and progesterone. **2.** *Botany.* The ovule-bearing lower part of a pistil that ripens into a fruit. [New Latin *ōvārium,* from Latin *ōvum,* egg. See **awi-** in Appendix.] **—o•var′i•an** (ō-vâr′ē-ən), **o•var′i•al** (-ē-əl) *adj.*

o•vate (ō′vāt′) *adj.* **1.** Shaped like an egg; oval. **2.** *Botany.* Broad and rounded at the base and tapering toward the end: *an ovate leaf.* [Latin *ōvātus,* from *ōvum,* egg. See **awi-** in Appendix.] **—o′vate′ly** *adv.*

o•va•tion (ō-vā′shən) *n.* **1.** Enthusiastic, prolonged applause. **2.** A show of public homage or welcome. **3.** An ancient Roman victory ceremony of somewhat less importance than a triumph. [Latin *ovātiō, ovātiōn-,* a Roman victory ceremony, from *ovātus,* past participle of *ovāre,* to rejoice.] **—o•va′tion•al** *adj.*

ov•en (ŭv′ən) *n.* A chamber or enclosed compartment for heating, baking, or roasting food, as in a stove, or for firing, baking, hardening, or drying objects, as in a kiln. [Middle English, from Old English *ofen.*]

overalls

ov•en•a•ble (ŭv′ə-nə-bəl) *adj.* Of, relating to, or being heat-resistant paper packaging, as for use in a kitchen oven, especially a microwave oven: *ovenable paperboard trays.*

ov•en•bird (ŭv′ən-bûrd′) *n.* **1.** A thrushlike North American warbler *(Seiurus aurocapillus)* having a shrill call and characteristically building a domed, oven-shaped nest on the ground. Also called *teacher bird.* **2.** Any of various South American birds of the family Furnariidae, especially of the genus *Furnarius.* [From its oven-shaped nest.]

ov•en•proof (ŭv′ən-pro͞of′) *adj.* Capable of resisting the heat produced in a kitchen oven: *an ovenproof casserole dish.*

ov•en•ware (ŭv′ən-wâr′) *n.* Baking dishes, as of glass or pottery, that are heat-resistant and can be used for baking and serving food.

o•ver (ō′vər) *prep.* **1.** In or at a position above or higher than: *a sign over the door; a hawk gliding over the hills.* **2. a.** Above and across from one end or side to the other: *a jump over the fence.* **b.** To the other side of; across: *strolled over the bridge.* **c.** Across the edge of and down: *fell over the cliff.* **3.** On the other side of: *a village over the border.* **4. a.** Upon the surface of: *put a coat of varnish over the woodwork.* **b.** On top of or down upon: *clubbed him over the head; tripped over the toys.* **5. a.** Through the extent of; all through: *walked over the grounds; looked over the report.* **b.** Through the medium of; via: *addressed us over the loudspeaker; can't tell you over the phone.* **6.** So as to cover: *put rocks over a cave entrance; threw a shawl over her shoulders.* **7.** Up to or higher than the level or height of: *The water was over my shoulders.* **8. a.** Through the period or duration of: *records maintained over two years.* **b.** Until or beyond the end of: *stayed over the holidays.* **9.** More than in degree, quantity, or extent: *over ten miles; over a thousand dollars.* **10. a.** In superiority to: *won a narrow victory over her rival; a distinct advantage over our competitors.* **b.** In preference to: *selected him over all the others.* **11.** In a position to rule or control: *The director presides over the meeting. There is no one over him in the department.* **12.** So as to have an effect or influence on: *the change that came over you.* **13.** While occupied with or engaged in: *a chat over coffee.* **14.** With reference to; concerning: *an argument over methods.* **—over** *adv.* **1.** Above the top or surface: *climbed the ladder and peered over.* **2. a.** Across to another or opposite side: *stopped at the curb, then crossed over.* **b.** Across the edge, brink, or brim: *The coffee spilled over.* **c.** Across an intervening space: *Throw the ball over.* **3. a.** Across a distance in a particular direction or at a location: *lives over in England.* **b.** To another often specified place or position: *Move your chair over toward the fire.* **c.** To one's place of residence or business: *invited us over for cocktails.* **4.** Throughout an entire area or region: *wandered all over.* **5. a.** To a different opinion or allegiance: *win someone over.* **b.** So as to be comprehensible, acceptable, or effective; across: *eventually got my point over.* **6.** To a different person, condition, or title: *sign the property over.* **7.** So as to be completely enclosed or covered: *The river froze over. Engineers sealed the tunnel entrance over.* **8.** Completely through; from beginning to end: *Think the problem over. Let's read the memo over.* **9. a.** From an upright position: *kicked the bookstand over.* **b.** From an upward position to an inverted or reversed position: *turn the paper over.* **10.** Another time; again: *counted his cards over; had to do it over.* **11.** In repetition: *made me write it ten times over.* **12.** In addition or excess; in surplus: *lots of food left over.* **13.** Beyond or until a specified time: *stay a day over.* **14. a.** At an end: *Summer is over.* **b.** Used in two-way radio to indicate that a transmission is complete and a reply is awaited. **—over** *adj.* **1.** External; outer. **2.** Excessive; extreme. **3. a.** Not yet used up; remaining. **b.** Extra; surplus. **—over** *n. Sports.* A series of six balls bowled from one end of a cricket pitch. **—over** *tr.v.* **o•vered, o•ver•ing, o•vers.** To jump over: *Horse and rider overed the stile with ease.* ***—idioms.* over against.** As opposed to; contrasted with. **over with.** Completely finished; done: *Let's get the shopping over with. Are we over with all this shopping?* [Middle English, from Old English *ofer.* See **uper** in Appendix.]

o•ver•a•bun•dance (ō′vər-ə-bŭn′dəns) *n.* A going or being beyond what is needed, desired, or appropriate; an excess: *teenagers with an overabundance of energy.* **—o′ver•a•bun′dant** *adj.* **—o′ver•a•bun′dant•ly** *adv.*

o•ver•a•chieve (ō′vər-ə-chēv′) *intr.v.* **-chieved, -chiev•ing, -chieves.** To perform better or achieve more success than expected. **—o′ver•a•chieve′ment** *n.* **—o′ver•a•chiev′er** *n.*

o•ver•act (ō′vər-ăkt′) *v.* **-act•ed, -act•ing, -acts.** *—tr.* To act (a dramatic role) with unnecessary exaggeration. *—intr.* **1.** To exaggerate a role; overplay. **2.** To act over and above what is required; overdo in acting. **—o′ver•ac′tion** *n.*

o•ver•ac•tive (ō′vər-ăk′tĭv) *adj.* Active to an excessive or abnormal degree: *an overactive child.* **—o′ver•ac•tiv′i•ty** *n.*

o•ver•age¹ (ō′vər-ĭj) *n.* **1.** An amount, as of money or goods, that is actually on hand and exceeds the listed amount in records or books. **2.** A surplus; an excess.

o•ver•age² (ō′vər-āj′) *adj.* **1.** Beyond the proper or required age. **2.** Older than usual for a particular position or activity. **3.** Too old to be of use or service: *an overage vehicle.*

o•ver•ag•gres•sive (ō′vər-ə-grĕs′ĭv) *adj.* Aggressive to an excessive degree. **—o′ver•ag•gres′sive•ly** *adv.* **—o′ver•ag•gres′sive•ness** *n.*

o•ver•all (ō′vər-ôl′) *adj.* **1.** From one end to the other: *the overall length of the house.* **2.** Including everything; comprehensive: *the overall costs of medical care.* **3.** Regarded as a whole; general: *My overall impression was favorable.* **—overall** *adv.* (ō′vər-ôl′). On the whole; generally: *enjoyed the performance overall.* **—overall** *n. Chiefly British.* **1.** A loose-fitting protective outer garment; a smock. **2. overalls.** Loose-fitting trousers, usually of strong fabric, with a bib front and shoulder straps, often worn over regular clothing as protection from dirt.

o•ver•am•bi•tious (ō′vər-ăm-bĭsh′əs) *adj.* Ambitious to an excessive degree. **—o′ver•am•bi′tion** *n.* **—o′ver•am•bi′tious•ly** *adv.* **—o′ver•am•bi′tious•ness** *n.*

over and above *prep.* In addition to: *travel expenses over and above entertainment costs.*

over and over *adv.* Again and again; repeatedly.

o•ver•anx•ious (ō′vər-ăngk′shəs, -ăng′shəs) *adj.* Anxious to an excessive degree. **—o′ver·anx·i′e·ty** (-ăng-zī′ĭ-tē), **o′ver·anx′ious·ness** (-ăngk′shəs-nĭs, -ăng′-) *n.* **—o′ver·anx′ious·ly** *adv.*

o·ver·arch (ō′vər-ärch′) *tr.v.* **-arched, -arch·ing, -arch·es.** To form an arch over: *Grape vines overarched the garden path.*

o·ver·arch·ing (ō′vər-är′chĭng) *adj.* **1.** Forming an arch overhead or above: *overarching branches.* **2.** Extending over or throughout: *"I am not sure whether the missing ingredient . . . is surprise or an overarching radiance"* (John Simon). **—o′ver·arch′ing·ly** *adv.*

o·ver·arm[1] (ō′vər-ärm′) *adj. Sports.* **1.** Executed with the arm raised above the shoulder; overhand: *an overarm throw.* **2.** Of, relating to, or being a stroke in swimming that is begun with the arm lifted and stretched forward over the shoulder.

o·ver·arm[2] (ō′vər-ärm′) *tr.v.* **-armed, -arm·ing, -arms.** To supply (a nation, for example) with an excess of weaponry, especially nuclear missiles.

o·ver·armed (ō′vər-ärmd′) *adj.* Supplied with excessive weaponry: *"parallels between the overarmed Britain and Germany of 1914 and the overarmed United States and Soviet Union of today"* (Tony Gibbs).

o·ver·as·sess (ō′vər-ə-sĕs′) *tr.v.* **-sessed, -sess·ing, -sess·es.** To assess (property or a property owner) at too high a tax figure; overtax. **—o′ver·as·sess′ment** *n.*

o·ver·ate (ō′vər-āt′) *v.* Past tense of **overeat.**

o·ver·awe (ō′vər-ô′) *tr.v.* **-awed, -aw·ing, -awes.** To control or subdue by inspiring awe.

o·ver·bal·ance (ō′vər-băl′əns) *v.* **-anced, -anc·ing, -anc·es.** *—tr.* **1.** To have greater weight or importance than. **2.** To throw off balance. *—intr.* To lose one's balance. **—overbalance** (ō′vər-băl′əns) *n.* **1.** An excess in weight or quantity. **2.** Something that overbalances or more than equals something else.

o·ver·bear (ō′vər-bâr′) *v.* **-bore** (-bôr′, -bōr′), **-borne** (-bôrn′), **-bear·ing, -bears.** *—tr.* **1.** To crush or press down on with physical force. **2.** To prevail over, as if by superior weight or force; dominate. **3.** To be more important than; outweigh. *—intr.* To bear an overabundance of fruit or offspring.

o·ver·bear·ing (ō′vər-bâr′ĭng) *adj.* **1.** Domineering in manner; arrogant: *an overbearing person.* See Synonyms at **dictatorial.** **2.** Overwhelming in power or significance; predominant. **—o′ver·bear′ing·ly** *adv.* **—o′ver·bear′ing·ness** *n.*

o·ver·bid (ō′vər-bĭd′) *v.* **-bid, -bid·den** (-bĭd′n) or **-bid, -bid·ding, -bids.** *—tr.* **1.** To outbid (a person) for something, as at an auction. **2.** *Games.* To bid more than the value of (one's hand in bridge, for example). *—intr.* To bid higher than the actual value of something. **—overbid** (ō′vər-bĭd′) *n.* A bid higher than another bid. **—o′ver·bid′der** *n.*

o·ver·bite (ō′vər-bīt′) *n.* A malocclusion of the teeth in which the front upper incisor and canine teeth project over the lower.

o·ver·blew (ō′vər-blo͞o′) *v.* Past tense of **overblow.**

o·ver·blouse (ō′vər-blous′, -blouz′) *n.* A blouse fashioned for wearing outside the waistband of a skirt or slacks.

o·ver·blow (ō′vər-blō′) *tr.v.* **-blew** (-blo͞o′), **-blown** (-blōn′), **-blow·ing, -blows.** To blow (a wind instrument) so as to produce an overtone instead of a fundamental tone.

o·ver·blown (ō′vər-blōn′) *v.* Past participle of **overblow.** **—overblown** *adj.* **1.a.** Done to excess; overdone: *overblown decorations.* **b.** Full of empty or pretentious language; bombastic: *overblown oratory.* **2.** Past the stage of full bloom: *overblown roses.* **3.** Very fat; obese. **4.** Having been blown down or over: *a pile of overblown saplings.*

o·ver·board (ō′vər-bôrd′, -bōrd′) *adv.* Over or as if over the side of a boat or ship. **—*idiom.* go overboard.** To go to extremes, especially as a result of enthusiasm.

o·ver·book (ō′vər-bo͝ok′) *v.* **-booked, -book·ing, -books.** *—tr.* To take reservations for (an airline flight, for example) beyond the capacity for accommodation. *—intr.* To take reservations beyond the capacity for accommodation: *a restaurant that regularly overbooks for dinner.* **—o′ver·book′ing** *n.*

o·ver·bore (ō′vər-bôr′, -bōr′) *v.* Past tense of **overbear.**

o·ver·borne (ō′vər-bôrn′) *v.* Past participle of **overbear.** **—overborne** *adj.* Overpowered or overcome: *hikers overborne by fatigue.*

o·ver·bought (ō′vər-bôt′) *v.* Past tense and past participle of **overbuy.** **—overbought** *adj.* Characterized by excessively high prices owing to prior heavy buying and a concomitant rise in prices: *an overbought stock market.*

o·ver·build (ō′vər-bĭld′) *v.* **-built** (-bĭlt′), **-build·ing, -builds.** *—tr.* **1.** To build over or on top of. **2.** To construct more buildings in (an area) than necessary. **3.** To build with excessive size or elaboration. *—intr.* To construct more homes, office buildings, or commercial complexes than necessary in an area.

o·ver·bur·den (ō′vər-bûr′dn) *tr.v.* **-dened, -den·ing, -dens.** **1.** To burden with too much weight; overload. **2.** To subject to an excessive burden or strain; overtax. **—overburden** (ō′vər-bûr′dn) *n.* **1.** An excessive burden; an overload. **2.** *Geology.* **a.** Material overlying a useful mineral deposit. **b.** Sedimentary rock covering older crystalline layers. **3.** *Archaeology.* A sterile stratum overlying a stratum bearing traces of the culture being studied.

o·ver·buy (ō′vər-bī′) *v.* **-bought** (-bôt′), **-buy·ng, -buys.** *—tr.* **1.** To buy in excessive amounts. **2.** To buy (stock) on margin in excess of one's ability to provide further security if prices drop. *—intr.* To buy goods beyond one's means or needs.

o·ver·call (ō′vər-kôl′) *v.* **-called, -call·ing, o·ver·calls.** *Games.* *—tr.* To bid beyond or in excess of (a previous bid or player) in a game of cards. *—intr.* To bid higher than one's opponent when one's partner has not bid in bridge. **—overcall** (ō′vər-kôl′) *n.* **1.** *Games.* **a.** An overbid. **b.** An instance of overcalling in bridge. **2.** The amount of additional money, often 10 to 20 percent of the original amount invested, that can be requested from the financial backers of a theatrical production.

o·ver·came (ō′vər-kām′) *v.* Past tense of **overcome.**

o·ver·ca·pac·i·ty (ō′vər-kə-păs′ĭ-tē) *n.* Too great a capacity for production of commodities or delivery of services in relation to actual need: *the problem of overcapacity in many large industries.*

o·ver·cap·i·tal·ize (ō′vər-kăp′ĭ-tl-īz′) *tr.v.* **-ized, -iz·ing, -iz·es.** **1.** To provide an excess amount of capital for (a business enterprise). **2.** To estimate the value of (property) too highly. **3.** To place an unlawfully or unreasonably high value on the nominal capital of (a corporation). **—o′ver·cap′i·tal·i·za′tion** (-ĭ-zā′shən) *n.*

o·ver·cast (ō′vər-kăst′, ō′vər-kăst′) *adj.* **1.a.** Covered or obscured, as with clouds or mist. **b.** Clouded over. **2.** Gloomy; melancholy. **3.** Sewn with long, overlying stitches in order to prevent raveling, as the raw edges of fabric. **—overcast** (ō′vər-kăst′) *n.* **1.** A covering, as of mist or clouds. **2.** An arch or a support for a passage over another passage in a mine. **3.** A cast made in fishing that falls beyond the point intended. **4.** An overcast stitch or seam. **—overcast** (ō′vər-kăst′, ō′vər-kăst′) *v.* **-cast, -cast·ing, -casts.** *—tr.* **1.** To make cloudy or gloomy. **2.** To cast beyond (the intended point) with a fishing rod. **3.** To sew with long, overlying stitches. *—intr.* To become cloudy or gloomy.

o·ver·cast·ing (ō′vər-kăs′tĭng) *n.* **1.a.** The act of sewing raw edges of material with long, overlying stitches to prevent raveling. **b.** The stitching so done. **2.** The stitch used to overcast.

o·ver·cau·tious (ō′vər-kô′shəs) *adj.* Excessively cautious; unduly careful. **—o′ver·cau′tious·ly** *adv.* **—o′ver·cau′tious·ness** *n.*

o·ver·charge (ō′vər-chärj′) *v.* **-charged, -charg·ing, -charg·es.** *—tr.* **1.** To charge (a party) an excessive price for something. **2.** To fill too full; overload. **3.** To overstate or exaggerate. *—intr.* To charge too much. **—overcharge** (ō′vər-chärj′) *n.* **1.** *Abbr.* **o/c.** An excessive charge or price. **2.** A load or burden that is too full or heavy.

o·ver·cloud (ō′vər-kloud′) *v.* **-cloud·ed, -cloud·ing, -clouds.** *—tr.* **1.** To cover with clouds. **2.** To make dark and gloomy. *—intr.* To become cloudy.

o·ver·coat (ō′vər-kōt′) *n.* **1.** A heavy coat worn over ordinary clothing in cold weather. **2.** An additional, protective coating, as of paint.

o·ver·coat·ing (ō′vər-kō′tĭng) *n.* An overcoat, as of varnish or paint.

o·ver·come (ō′vər-kŭm′) *v.* **-came** (-kām′), **-come, -com·ing, -comes.** *—tr.* **1.** To defeat (another) in competition or conflict; conquer. See Synonyms at **defeat.** **2.** To prevail over; surmount: *tried to overcome the obstacles of poverty.* **3.** To overpower, as with emotion; affect deeply. *—intr.* To surmount opposition; be victorious.

o·ver·com·mit (ō′vər-kə-mĭt′) *v.* **-mit·ted, -mit·ting, -mits.** *—tr.* **1.** To bind or obligate (oneself, for example) beyond the capacity for realization. **2.** To allocate or apportion (money, goods, or resources) in amounts incapable of replacement. *—intr.* To be or become overcommitted. **—o′ver·com·mit′ment** *n.*

o·ver·com·pen·sate (ō′vər-kŏm′pən-sāt′) *v.* **-sat·ed, -sat·ing, -sates.** *—intr.* To engage in overcompensation. *—tr.* To pay (someone) too much; compensate excessively. **—o′ver·com·pen′sa·to′ry** (-kəm-pĕn′sə-tôr′ē, -tōr′ē) *adj.*

o·ver·com·pen·sa·tion (ō′vər-kŏm′pən-sā′shən) *n.* Excessive compensation, especially the exertion of effort in excess of that needed to compensate for a physical or psychological characteristic or defect.

o·ver·con·fi·dent (ō′vər-kŏn′fĭ-dənt) *adj.* Excessively confident; presumptuous. **—o′ver·con′fi·dence** *n.* **—o′ver·con′fi·dent·ly** *adv.*

o·ver·cor·rect (ō′vər-kə-rĕkt′) *v.* **-rect·ed, -rect·ing, -rects.** *—tr.* To correct beyond what is needed, appropriate, or usual, especially when resulting in a mistake. *—intr.* To correct something to an excessive or unusual degree. **—o′ver·cor·rec′tion** *n.*

o·ver·crit·i·cal (ō′vər-krĭt′ĭ-kəl) *adj.* Inclined to judge too severely; hypercritical. **—o′ver·crit′i·cal·ly** *adv.* **—o′ver·crit′i·cal·ness** *n.*

o·ver·crop (ō′vər-krŏp′) *tr.v.* **-cropped, -crop·ping, -crops.** To exhaust the fertility of (land) by continuous cultivation of crops.

o·ver·crowd (ō′vər-kroud′) *v.* **-crowd·ed, -crowd·ing, -crowds.** *—tr.* To cause to be excessively crowded: *a system of consolidation that only overcrowded the classrooms.* *—intr.* To crowd together excessively.

o·ver·de·vel·op (ō′vər-dĭ-vĕl′əp) *tr.v.* **-oped, -op·ing, -ops.** **1.** To develop to excess: *muscles that were overdeveloped by weightlifting.* **2.** To process (a photographic plate or film) too

ă pat	oi boy
ā pay	ou out
âr care	o͝o took
ä father	o͞o boot
ĕ pet	ŭ cut
ē be	ûr urge
ĭ pit	th thin
ī pie	*th* this
îr pier	hw which
ŏ pot	zh vision
ō toe	ə about, item
ô paw	♦ regionalism

Stress marks: ′ (primary); ′ (secondary), as in **dictionary** (dĭk′shə-nĕr′ē)

long or in too concentrated a solution. **—o′ver·de·vel′op·ment** *n.*

o·ver·do (ō′vər-do͞o′) *v.* **-did** (-dĭd′), **-done** (-dŭn′), **-do·ing, -does** (-dŭz′). —*tr.* **1.a.** To do, use, or stress to excess; carry (something) too far: *overdid the diet and became malnourished.* **b.** To exaggerate: *overdid the compliments.* **2.** To wear out the strength of; overtax. **3.** To cook (food) too long. —*intr.* To do too much; go to extremes: *We always overdo at Christmas.* **—o′ver·do′er** *n.*

o·ver·dog (ō′vər-dôg′, -dŏg′) *n. Informal.* One that has a significant advantage: *"a champion of the overdog who provides tax breaks for the rich while cutting social services for the poor"* (Leon Daniel). [OVER + (UNDER)DOG.]

o·ver·dom·i·nance (ō′vər-dŏm′ə-nəns) *n.* The condition of a heterozygote having a phenotype that is more pronounced or better adapted than that of either homozygote. **—o′ver·dom′i·nant** *adj.*

o·ver·done (ō′vər-dŭn′) *v.* Past participle of **overdo.**

o·ver·dose (ō′vər-dōs′) *n.* An excessive dose, especially of a narcotic. **—overdose** (ō′vər-dōs′) *v.* **-dosed, -dos·ing, -dos·es.** —*intr.* To take an overdose. —*tr.* To administer too large a dose or too many doses to.

o·ver·draft (ō′vər-drăft′) *n.* **1.a.** The act of overdrawing a bank account. **b.** *Abbr.* **O.D., o/d.** The amount overdrawn. **c.** The maximum amount of credit extended to a customer. **2.** Also **o·ver·draught** (-drăft′). **a.** A current of air made to pass over the ignited fuel in a furnace. **b.** A series of flues in a brick kiln designed to force air down from the top. **c.** The air so forced.

o·ver·draw (ō′vər-drô′) *v.* **-drew** (-dro͞o′), **-drawn** (-drôn′), **-draw·ing, -draws.** —*tr.* **1.** To draw against (a bank account) in excess of credit. **2.** To pull back too far: *overdraw a bow.* **3.** To spoil the effect of by exaggeration in telling or describing. —*intr.* To make an overdraft.

o·ver·dress (ō′vər-drĕs′) *v.* **-dressed, -dress·ing, -dress·es.** —*intr.* To dress oneself more formally or elaborately than appropriate or desirable. —*tr.* To dress (oneself) more formally or elaborately than appropriate or desirable. **—overdress** (ō′vər-drĕs′) *n.* A skirted garment, such as a pinafore, worn over other outer clothing.

o·ver·drew (ō′vər-dro͞o′) *v.* Past tense of **overdraw.**

o·ver·drive (ō′vər-drīv′) *n.* **1.** A gearing mechanism of a motor vehicle engine that reduces the power output required to maintain driving speed in a specific range by lowering the gear ratio. **2.** *Informal.* A state of heightened activity or concentration: *shifted into overdrive toward the end of the semester.* **—overdrive** (ō′vər-drīv′) *tr.v.* **-drove** (-drōv′), **-driv·en** (-drĭv′ən), **-driv·ing, -drives. 1.** To drive (a vehicle) too far or too long. **2.** To push (oneself) too far, as in the performance of tasks.

o·ver·dub (ō′vər-dŭb′) *tr.v.* **-dubbed, -dub·bing, -dubs.** To add (supplementary recorded sound) to a previously taped musical recording especially in order to heighten the total effect. **—overdub** *n.* Additional recorded sound that is blended into a musical recording: *instrumental overdubs.*

o·ver·due (ō′vər-do͞o′, -dyo͞o′) *adj.* **1.** Being unpaid when due: *an overdue bill.* **2.** Coming or arriving after the scheduled or expected time: *an overdue train.* **3.a.** Expected or required but not yet having come about. **b.** Being something that should have occurred earlier. See Synonyms at **tardy.**

o·ver·ea·ger (ō′vər-ē′gər) *adj.* Excessively eager; too ardent. **—o′ver·ea′ger·ly** *adv.* **—o′ver·ea′ger·ness** *n.*

o·ver·eat (ō′vər-ēt′) *intr.v.* **-ate** (-āt′), **-eat·en** (-ēt′n), **-eat·ing, -eats.** To eat to excess, especially when habitual. **—o′ver·eat′er** *n.*

o·ver·em·pha·size (ō′vər-ĕm′fə-sīz′) *tr. & intr.v.* **-sized, -siz·ing, -siz·es.** To place too much emphasis on or employ too much emphasis. **—o′ver·em′pha·sis** (-sĭs) *n.*

o·ver·es·ti·mate (ō′vər-ĕs′tə-māt′) *tr.v.* **-mat·ed, -mat·ing, -mates. 1.** To estimate too highly. **2.** To esteem too greatly. **—o′ver·es′ti·mate** (-mĭt) *n.* **—o′ver·es′ti·ma′tion** *n.*

o·ver·ex·ert (ō′vər-ĭg-zûrt′) *tr.v.* **-ert·ed, -ert·ing, -erts.** To exert (oneself) too much; overtax. **—o′ver·ex·er′tion** *n.*

o·ver·ex·pose (ō′vər-ĭk-spōz′) *tr.v.* **-posed, -pos·ing, -pos·es. 1.** To expose too long or too much: *Don't overexpose the children to television.* **2.** To expose (a photographic film or plate) too long or with too much light. **—o′ver·ex·po′sure** (-ĭk-spō′zhər) *n.*

o·ver·ex·tend (ō′vər-ĭk-stĕnd′) *tr.v.* **-tend·ed, -tend·ing, -tends. 1.** To expand or disperse beyond a safe or reasonable limit: *overextended their defenses.* **2.** To obligate (oneself) beyond a limit, especially a financial one. **—o′ver·ex·ten′sion** *n.*

o·ver·fa·mil·iar (ō′vər-fə-mĭl′yər) *adj.* Too familiar, as: **a.** Exceedingly common or ordinary: *overfamiliar sayings.* **b.** Unduly forward or brash; offensively presumptuous: *She displayed an overfamiliar attitude toward her superiors.* **—o′ver·fa·mil′iar′i·ty** (-mĭl′yăr′ĭ-tē, -mĭl′ē-ăr′-) *n.*

o·ver·fa·tigue (ō′vər-fə-tēg′) *n.* Excessive fatigue.

o·ver·feed (ō′vər-fēd′) *tr. & intr.v.* **-fed** (-fĕd′), **-feed·ing, -feeds.** To feed or eat too often or too much.

o·ver·fill (ō′vər-fĭl′) *v.* **-filled, -fill·ing, -fills.** —*tr.* To fill (something) to overflowing. —*intr.* To become too full.

o·ver·fish (ō′vər-fĭsh′) *v.* **-fished, -fish·ing, -fish·es.** —*tr.* To fish (a body of water) to such a degree as to upset the ecological balance or cause depletion of living creatures. —*intr.* To fish a body of water so extensively as to exhaust the supply of fish or shellfish.

o·ver·flew (ō′vər-flo͞o′) *v.* Past tense of **overfly.**

o·ver·flight (ō′vər-flīt′) *n.* An aircraft flight over a particular area, especially over foreign territory.

o·ver·flow (ō′vər-flō′) *v.* **-flowed, -flow·ing, -flows.** —*intr.* **1.** To flow or run over the top, brim, or banks. **2.** To be filled beyond capacity, as a container or waterway. **3.** To have a boundless supply; be superabundant. See Synonyms at **teem**[1]. —*tr.* **1.** To flow over the top, brim, or banks of. **2.** To spread or cover over; flood. **3.** To cause to fill beyond capacity. **—overflow** (ō′vər-flō′) *n.* **1.** The act of overflowing. **2.** Something that flows over; an excess. **3.** An outlet or a vent through which excess liquid may escape. **4.** *Computer Science.* A condition in which a calculation produces a unit of data too large to be stored in the location allotted to it.

o·ver·fly (ō′vər-flī′) *tr.v.* **-flew** (-flo͞o′), **-flown** (-flōn′), **-fly·ing, -flies. 1.** To fly over (a particular area or territory) in an aircraft or a spacecraft. **2.** To fly beyond or past; overshoot: *The plane overflew the runway and crashed.*

o·ver·gar·ment (ō′vər-gär′mənt) *n.* An outer garment.

o·ver·glaze (ō′vər-glāz′) *n.* **1.** An outer coat of glaze on a piece of pottery. **2.** A painted or printed decoration applied over a glaze. **—overglaze** (ō′vər-glāz′, ō′vər-glāz′) *tr.v.* **-glazed, -glaz·ing, -glaz·es.** To apply an overglaze to. **—overglaze** *adj.* Applied or designed for applying over a ceramic glaze.

o·ver·graze (ō′vər-grāz′) *tr.v.* **-grazed, -graz·ing, -graz·es.** To permit animals to graze (vegetational cover) excessively, to the detriment of the vegetation.

o·ver·grow (ō′vər-grō′, ō′vər-grō′) *v.* **-grew** (-gro͞o′), **-grown** (-grōn′), **-grow·ing, -grows.** —*tr.* **1.** To grow over with herbage or foliage. **2.** To grow beyond or too large for. —*intr.* **1.** To grow beyond normal or usual size. **2.** To become grown over, as with unwanted vegetation or weeds.

o·ver·growth (ō′vər-grōth′) *n.* A usually abundant, luxurious growth over or on something else: *an overgrowth of ivy on the old house.*

o·ver·hand (ō′vər-hănd′) also **o·ver·hand·ed** (ō′vər-hăn′dĭd) —*adj.* **1.** Executed with the hand brought forward and down from above the level of the shoulder: *an overhand pitch; an overhand stroke.* **2.** Sewn with close, vertical stitches drawing two edges together, with each stitch passing over the seam formed by the edges. —*adv.* In an overhand manner. —*n.* **1.** An overhand throw, stroke, or delivery. **2.** An overhand stitch or seam. —*tr.v.* **-hand·ed, -hand·ing, -hands.** To sew with overhand stitches.

overhand knot *n.* A knot formed by making a loop in a piece of cord and pulling the end through it. Also called *single knot.*

o·ver·hang (ō′vər-hăng′) *v.* **-hung** (-hŭng′), **-hang·ing, -hangs.** —*tr.* **1.** To project or extend beyond. **2.** To loom over: *The threat of nuclear war overhangs modern society.* **3.** To ornament with hangings. —*intr.* To project over something that lies beneath. See Synonyms at **bulge. —overhang** (ō′vər-hăng′) *n.* **1.** A projecting part, such as an architectural structure or a rock formation. **2.** An amount of projection: *an overhang of six inches.* **3.** *Nautical.* The part of a bow or stern that projects over the water.

o·ver·haul (ō′vər-hôl′, ō′vər-hôl′) *tr.v.* **-hauled, -haul·ing, -hauls. 1.a.** To examine or go over carefully for needed repairs. **b.** To dismantle in order to make repairs. **c.** *Nautical.* To slacken (a line) or to release and separate the blocks of (a tackle). **2.** To make extensive renovations or revisions on; renovate: *proposals to overhaul the health care system.* **3.** To catch up with; overtake. **—overhaul** (ō′vər-hôl′) *n.* **1.** An act of overhauling. **2.** A repair job. **—o′ver·haul′er** *n.*

o·ver·head (ō′vər-hĕd′) *adj.* **1.** Located, functioning, or originating from above. **2.** Of or relating to the operating expenses of a business. **—overhead** *n.* **1.** The operating expenses of a business, including the costs of rent, utilities, interior decoration, and taxes, exclusive of labor and materials. **2.** *Nautical.* The top surface in an enclosed space of a ship. **3.** Something, such as a light fixture, that is located above head height. **4.** *Sports.* A stroke in a game, such as tennis or badminton, that is made with a hard downward motion from above the head. **5.** An overhead projector. **—overhead** (ō′vər-hĕd′) *adv.* Over or above the level of the head; high or higher up: *look overhead.*

overhead projector *n.* A projector capable of projecting enlarged images of written or pictorial material onto a screen or wall from a transparency placed horizontally below the projector and lighted from underneath.

o·ver·hear (ō′vər-hîr′) *v.* **-heard** (-hûrd′), **-hear·ing, -hears.** —*tr.* To hear (speech or someone speaking) without the speaker's awareness or intent. —*intr.* To hear something without the speaker's awareness or intent. **—o′ver·hear′er** *n.*

o·ver·heat (ō′vər-hēt′) *v.* **-heat·ed, -heat·ing, -heats.** —*tr.* **1.** To heat too much. **2.** To cause to become excited, agitated, or overstimulated. —*intr.* To become hot or excited.

o·ver·hit (ō′vər-hĭt′) *v.* **-hit, -hit·ting, -hits.** *Sports.* —*tr.* **1.** To hit (a tennis ball, for example) too hard or too far. **2.** To hit beyond, as in golf: *overhit his approach.* —*intr.* To overhit a ball.

o·ver·hung (ō′vər-hŭng′) *v.* Past tense and past participle of

overhang. —**overhung** (ō′vər-hŭng′) *adj.* Suspended from above: *an overhung door.*

o·ver·hy·drate (ō′vər-hī′drāt) *tr.v.* **-drat·ed, -drat·ing, -drates.** To cause to take excessive fluids into the body, as through intravenous injection. —**o′ver·hy·dra′tion** *n.*

o·ver·hype (ō′vər-hīp′) *tr.v.* **-hyped, -hyp·ing, -hypes.** *Slang.* To promote or publicize to excess: *Promoters grossly overhyped the movie.*

o·ver·in·dulge (ō′vər-ĭn-dŭlj′) *v.* **-dulged, -dulg·ing, -dulg·es.** —*tr.* **1.** To indulge (a desire, craving, or habit) to excess: *overindulging a fondness for chocolate.* **2.** To indulge (a person) excessively: *overindulges his children.* —*intr.* To indulge in something to excess. —**o′ver·in·dul′gence** *n.* —**o′ver·in·dul′gent** *adj.* —**o′ver·in·dul′gent·ly** *adv.*

o·ver·joy (ō′vər-joi′) *tr.v.* **-joyed, -joy·ing, -joys.** To fill with joy; delight. —**o′ver·joyed′** (-joid′) *adj.*

o·ver·kill (ō′vər-kĭl′) *n.* **1.** Destructive nuclear capacity exceeding the amount needed to destroy an enemy. **2.** Excessive killing. **3.** An excess of what is necessary or appropriate for a particular end: *"government overkill in dealing with dissent"* (Jesse Unruh). —**overkill** (ō′vər-kĭl′) *tr.v.* **-killed, -kill·ing, -kills.** To destroy (an enemy or enemy target) with more nuclear force than necessary.

o·ver·lad·en (ō′vər-lād′n) *adj.* Loaded or burdened too heavily.

o·ver·laid (ō′vər-lād′) *v.* Past tense and past participle of **overlay**[1].

o·ver·lain (ō′vər-lān′) *v.* Past participle of **overlie.**

o·ver·land (ō′vər-lănd′, -lənd) *adj.* Accomplished, traversing, or passing over the land instead of the ocean: *an overland journey; an overland route.* —**overland** *adv.* By way of land: *traveled overland to the ranch.*

O·ver·land (ō′vər-lənd). A city of eastern Missouri, a suburb of St. Louis. Population, 19,620.

Overland Park. A city of northeast Kansas, a residential suburb of Kansas City. Population, 81,784.

Overland Trail. Any of several trails, such as the Oregon Trail or the Santa Fe Trail, of westward migration in the United States. The term is sometimes used to refer collectively to all the overland migration routes from the Missouri River to the Pacific Ocean.

o·ver·lap (ō′vər-lăp′) *v.* **-lapped, -lap·ping, -laps.** —*tr.* **1.** To lie or extend over and cover part of. **2.** To have an area or a range in common with. —*intr.* **1.** To lie over and partly cover something. **2.** To correspond in character or function: *Their duties overlap.* **3.** *Mathematics.* To have one or more elements in common. Used of sets. —**overlap** (ō′vər-lăp′) *n.* **1.** A part or portion that overlaps or is overlapped. **2.** An instance of overlapping.

o·ver·lay[1] (ō′vər-lā′) *tr.v.* **-laid** (-lād′), **-lay·ing, -lays.** **1.** To lay or spread over or on. **2.a.** To cover the surface of with a decorative layer or design: *overlay wood with silver.* **b.** To embellish superficially: *a simple tune that was overlaid with ornate harmonies.* **3.** *Printing.* To put an overlay on. —**overlay** (ō′vər-lā′) *n.* **1.** Something that is laid over or covers something else. **2.** A layer of decoration, such as gold leaf or wood veneer, applied to a surface. **3.** *Printing.* A piece of paper used on a press tympan to vary the pressure that produces light and dark tones. **4.** A transparent sheet containing graphic matter, such as labels or colored areas, placed on illustrative matter to be incorporated into it.

o·ver·lay[2] (ō′vər-lā′) *v.* Past tense of **overlie.**

o·ver·leaf (ō′vər-lēf′) *adv.* On the other side of the page or leaf.

o·ver·leap (ō′vər-lēp′) *tr.v.* **-leaped** or **-leapt** (-lĕpt′), **-leap·ing, -leaps.** **1.** To leap across or over. **2.** To defeat (oneself or one's purpose) by going too far.

o·ver·learn (ō′vər-lûrn′) *tr.v.* **-learned** also **-learnt** (-lûrnt′), **-learn·ing, -learns.** To continue working at (a skill, for example) after becoming proficient.

o·ver·lie (ō′vər-lī′) *tr.v.* **-lay** (-lā′), **-lain** (-lān′), **-ly·ing, -lies.** **1.** To lie over or on. **2.** To smother (a newborn infant or an animal) by lying upon.

o·ver·load (ō′vər-lōd′) *tr.v.* **-load·ed, -load·ing, -loads.** To load too heavily. —**overload** (ō′vər-lōd′) *n.* An excessive load.

o·ver·long (ō′vər-lông′, -lŏng′) *adj.* Excessively long: *an overlong play.* —**overlong** *adv.* For too long: *talked overlong.*

o·ver·look (ō′vər-lo͝ok′) *tr.v.* **-looked, -look·ing, -looks.** **1.a.** To look over or at from a higher place. **b.** To rise above, especially so as to afford a view over: *The tower overlooks the sea.* **2.a.** To fail to notice or consider; miss. **b.** To ignore deliberately or indulgently; disregard. **3.** To look over; examine. **4.** To watch over; oversee. See Synonyms at **supervise.** —**overlook** (ō′vər-lo͝ok′) *n.* An elevated place that affords an extensive view: *a scenic overlook.*

o·ver·lord (ō′vər-lôrd′) *n.* **1.** A lord having power or supremacy over other lords. **2.** One in a position of supremacy or domination over others. —**o′ver·lord′ship** *n.*

o·ver·ly (ō′vər-lē) *adv.* To an excessive degree.

o·ver·man (ō′vər-mən) *n.* **1.** A person having authority over others, especially an overseer or a shift supervisor. **2.** (ō′vər-măn′). See **superman** (sense 2). —**overman** (ō′vər-măn′) *tr.v.* **-manned, -man·ning, -mans.** To provide with more personnel than necessary. [Sense 2, translation of German *Übermensch* : *über,* higher + *Mensch,* man.]

o·ver·man·tel (ō′vər-măn′tl) *n.* A decorative structure or an ornamental panel situated above a mantelpiece. —**o′ver·man′tel** *adj.*

o·ver·mas·ter (ō′vər-măs′tər) *tr.v.* **-tered, -ter·ing, -ters.** To overpower by superior force; overcome.

o·ver·match (ō′vər-măch′) *tr.v.* **-matched, -match·ing, -match·es.** **1.** To be more than a match for; exceed or defeat. **2.** To match with a superior opponent. —**overmatch** (ō′vər-măch′) *n.* A contest in which one opponent is distinctly superior.

o·ver·med·i·cate (ō′vər-mĕd′ĭ-kāt′) *tr.v.* **-cat·ed, -cat·ing, -cates.** To medicate (a patient) excessively. —**o′ver·med′i·ca′tion** *n.*

o·ver·much (ō′vər-mŭch′) *adj.* Too much; excessive. —**overmuch** *adv.* In excess. —**overmuch** (ō′vər-mŭch′, ō′vər-mŭch′) *n.* An excessive amount.

o·ver·night (ō′vər-nīt′) *adj.* **1.** Lasting for, extending over, or remaining during a night: *an overnight trip; an overnight guest.* **2.** For use over a single night or for a short journey: *overnight supplies.* **3.** Mailed for guaranteed delivery on the next day: *an overnight package.* **4.** Happening as if in a single night; sudden: *an overnight success.* —**overnight** (ō′vər-nīt′) *adv.* **1.** During or for the length of the night: *Let the meat marinate overnight.* **2.** In or as if in the course of one night; suddenly: *became a sensation overnight.* —**overnight** *n.* An overnight stay or trip. —**overnight** (ō′vər-nīt′) *intr.v.* **-night·ed, -night·ing, -nights.** To spend the night: *overnighting at a country inn.*

overnight bag *n.* A small piece of luggage used to carry items needed for an overnight stay. Also called *overnight case.*

o·ver·night·er (ō′vər-nī′tər) *n.* **1.** An overnight. **2.** One making an overnight stay or trip. **3.** Something relating to or used for overnight travel.

o·ver·op·ti·mis·tic (ō′vər-ŏp′tə-mĭs′tĭk) *adj.* Excessively optimistic. —**o′ver·op′ti·mism** *n.* —**o′ver·op′ti·mis′ti·cal·ly** *adv.*

o·ver·paid (ō′vər-pād′) *v.* Past tense and past participle of **overpay.**

o·ver·pass (ō′vər-păs′) *n.* A passage, roadway, or bridge that crosses above another roadway or thoroughfare. —**overpass** (ō′vər-păs′) *tr.v.* **-passed** or **-past** (-păst′), **-pass·ing, -pass·es.** **1.** To pass over or across; traverse. **2.** To go beyond; surpass. **3.** To go over (a limit or boundary); transgress. **4.** To overlook or disregard.

overpass
On the Pennsylvania Turnpike

o·ver·pay (ō′vər-pā′) *v.* **-paid** (-pād′), **-pay·ing, -pays.** —*tr.* **1.** To pay (a party) too much. **2.** To pay an amount in excess of (a sum due). —*intr.* To pay too much. —**o′ver·pay′ment** *n.*

o·ver·per·suade (ō′vər-pər-swād′) *tr.v.* **-suad·ed, -suad·ing, -suades.** To persuade (someone) to act contrary to inclination or choice. —**o′ver·per·sua′sion** *n.*

o·ver·play (ō′vər-plā′) *v.* **-played, -play·ing, -plays.** —*tr.* **1.a.** To present (a dramatic role, for example) in an exaggerated manner. **b.** To emphasize or stress unduly. **2.** To overestimate the strength of (one's holding or position) with resulting defeat: *overplayed his hand and lost the game.* **3.** *Sports.* To hit (a golf ball) beyond the green. —*intr.* To overdo a role or an effect.

o·ver·plus (ō′vər-plŭs′) *n.* An amount in excess of need; a surplus.

o·ver·pop·u·late (ō′vər-pŏp′yə-lāt′) *v.* **-lat·ed, -lat·ing, -lates.** —*tr.* To fill (an area, for example) with excessive population to the detriment of the inhabitants, resources, or environment. —*intr.* To breed to excess: *wild animals that overpopulated and then starved.*

o·ver·pop·u·la·tion (ō′vər-pŏp′yə-lā′shən) *n.* Excessive population of an area to the point of overcrowding, depletion of natural resources, or environmental deterioration.

o·ver·pow·er (ō′vər-pou′ər) *tr.v.* **-ered, -er·ing, -ers.** **1.** To overcome or vanquish by superior force; subdue. **2.** To affect so strongly as to make helpless or ineffective; overwhelm. **3.** To supply with excessive mechanical power.

o·ver·pow·er·ing (ō′vər-pou′ər-ĭng) *adj.* So strong as to be overwhelming: *an overpowering need for solitude.* —**o′ver·pow′er·ing·ly** *adv.*

o·ver·praise (ō′vər-prāz′) *tr.v.* **-praised, -prais·ing, -prais·es.** To praise excessively.

o·ver·pre·scribe (ō′vər-prĭ-skrīb′) *v.* **-scribed, -scrib·ing, -scribes.** —*intr.* To prescribe an excessive amount of a medication. —*tr.* To prescribe (a medication) in excess of the amount needed. —**o′ver·pre·scrip′tion** (-skrĭp′shən) *n.*

o·ver·pres·sure (ō′vər-prĕsh′ər) *n.* A transient air pressure, such as the shock wave from an explosion, that is greater than the surrounding atmospheric pressure. —**overpressure** *tr.v.* **-sured, -sur·ing, -sures.** To cause or subject to overpressure. —**o′ver·pres′sur·i·za′tion** (-ĭ-zā′shən) *n.*

o·ver·price (ō′vər-prīs′) *tr.v.* **-priced, -pric·ing, -pric·es.** To put too high a price or value on.

o·ver·print (ō′vər-prĭnt′) *tr.v.* **-print·ed, -print·ing, -prints.** To imprint over with something more, especially to print over with another color. —**overprint** (ō′vər-prĭnt′) *n.* **1.** A mark or an impression made by overprinting. **2.a.** A mark or words printed over a postage stamp to note a change in use or a special occasion. **b.** A stamp so marked.

ă pat	oi boy
ā pay	ou out
âr care	o͝o took
ä father	o͞o boot
ĕ pet	ŭ cut
ē be	ûr urge
ĭ pit	th thin
ī pie	*th* this
îr pier	hw which
ŏ pot	zh vision
ō toe	ə about, item
ô paw	♦ regionalism

Stress marks: ′ (primary); ′ (secondary), as in **dictionary** (dĭk′shə-nĕr′ē)

o·ver·priv·i·leged (ō′vər-prĭv′ə-lĭjd) *adj.* Having an excess of opportunities or advantages. **—o′ver·priv′i·leged** *n.*

o·ver·prize (ō′vər-prīz′) *tr.v.* **-prized, -priz·ing, -priz·es.** To value too highly.

o·ver·pro·duce (ō′vər-prə-do͞os′, -dyo͞os′) *tr.v.* **-duced, -duc·ing, -duc·es.** To produce in excess of need or demand. **—o′ver·pro·duc′er** *n.* **—o′ver·pro·duc′tion** (-dŭk′shən) *n.*

o·ver·proof (ō′vər-pro͞of′) *adj.* Containing a greater proportion of alcohol than proof spirit, especially containing more than 50 percent alcohol by volume.

o·ver·pro·por·tion (ō′vər-prə-pôr′shən, -pōr′-) *tr.v.* **-tioned, -tion·ing, -tions.** To make larger and out of proportion to what is normal, desired, or appropriate. **—o′ver·pro·por′tion** *n.* **—o′ver·pro·por′tion·ate** (-shə-nĭt) *adj.* **—o′ver·pro·por′tion·ate·ly** *adv.*

o·ver·pro·tect (ō′vər-prə-tĕkt′) *tr.v.* **-tect·ed, -tect·ing, -tects.** To protect too much; coddle: *overprotected their children.* **—o′ver·pro·tec′tion** *n.* **—o′ver·pro·tec′tive** *adj.* **—o′ver·pro·tec′tive·ness** *n.*

o·ver·qual·i·fied (ō′vər-kwŏl′ə-fīd′) *adj.* Educated or skilled beyond what is necessary or desired for a particular job.

o·ver·ran (ō′vər-răn′) *v.* Past tense of **overrun.**

o·ver·rate (ō′vər-rāt′) *tr.v.* **-rat·ed, -rat·ing, -rates.** To overestimate the merits of; rate too highly.

o·ver·reach (ō′vər-rēch′) *v.* **-reached, -reach·ing, -reach·es.** —*tr.* **1.** To reach or extend over or beyond. **2.** To miss by reaching too far or attempting too much: *overreach a goal.* **3.** To defeat (oneself) by going too far or by doing or trying to gain too much. **4.** To get the better of, especially by deceitful cleverness; outwit. —*intr.* **1.** To reach or go too far. **2.** To overreach oneself. **3.** To outwit or cheat others. **4.** To strike the front part of a hind foot against the rear or side part of a forefoot or foreleg on the same side of the body. Used of a horse. **—o′ver·reach′** *n.* **—o′ver·reach′er** *n.*

o·ver·re·act (ō′vər-rē-ăkt′) *intr.v.* **-act·ed, -act·ing, -acts.** To react with unnecessary or inappropriate force, emotional display, or violence. **—o′ver·re·ac′tion** *n.* **—o′ver·re·ac′tive** *adj.*

o·ver·re·fine (ō′vər-rĭ-fīn′) *tr.v.* **-fined, -fin·ing, -fines.** To refine beyond a desired or appropriate point. **—o′ver·re·fined′** *adj.* **—o′ver·re·fine′ment** *n.*

o·ver·reg·u·late (ō′vər-rĕg′yə-lāt′) *tr.v.* **-lat·ed, -lat·ing, -lates.** To burden excessively with rules and regulations: *did not want to overregulate the airlines.* **—o′ver·reg′u·la′tion** *n.*

o·ver·rep·re·sent·ed (ō′vər-rĕp′rĭ-zĕn′tĭd) *adj.* Represented in excessive or disproportionately large numbers: *"Some groups, and most notably some races, may be overrepresented and others may be underrepresented"* (Scientific American). **—o′ver·rep′re·sen·ta′tion** (-zĕn-tā′shən, -zən-) *n.*

o·ver·ride (ō′vər-rīd′) *tr.v.* **-rode** (-rōd′), **-rid·den** (-rĭd′n), **-rid·ing, -rides. 1.a.** To ride across. **b.** To ride beyond. **2.** To trample on. **3.** To ride (a horse) too hard. **4.a.** To prevail over; conquer: *Budgetary concerns overrode all other considerations.* **b.** To declare null and void; set aside: *override the President's veto.* **c.** To counteract the normal operation of (an automatic control). **5.** To extend over; overlap. **—override** (ō′vər-rīd′) *n.* **1.** A sales commission collected by an executive in addition to the commission received by a subordinate salesperson. **2.** See **royalty** (sense 9). **3.** A mechanism or system used to counteract an automatic control. **4.** The act or an instance of nullifying.

o·ver·rid·ing (ō′vər-rī′dĭng) *adj.* First in priority; more important than all others: *Our overriding concern is the eradication of illiteracy.* **—o′ver·rid′ing·ly** *adv.*

o·ver·ripe (ō′vər-rīp′) *adj.* **1.** Too ripe. **2.** Marked by decay or decline. **—o′ver·ripe′ly** *adv.* **—o′ver·ripe′ness** *n.*

o·ver·rode (ō′vər-rōd′) *v.* Past tense of **override.**

o·ver·ruff (ō′vər-rŭf′) *intr. & tr.v.* **-ruffed, -ruff·ing, -ruffs.** *Games.* To overtrump. **—o′ver·ruff′** *n.*

o·ver·rule (ō′vər-ro͞ol′) *tr.v.* **-ruled, -rul·ing, -rules. 1.a.** To disallow the action or arguments of, especially by virtue of higher authority: *The defense attorney's objection was overruled by the judge.* **b.** To decide or rule against: *overrule a policy decision.* **c.** To declare null and void; reverse. **2.** To rule over: *a powerful empire that overruled the continent.* **3.** To dominate by strong influence; prevail over.

o·ver·run (ō′vər-rŭn′) *v.* **-ran** (-răn′), **-run, -run·ning, -runs.** —*tr.* **1.a.** To seize the positions of and defeat conclusively: *The position of the forward infantry was overrun by large numbers of enemy troops at dawn.* **b.** To spread or swarm over destructively: *Locusts overran the prairie.* **2.** To spread swiftly throughout: *The new fashion overran the country.* **3.** To overflow: *The river overran its banks.* **4.a.** To run beyond or past; overshoot: *The plane overran the end of the runway.* **b.** To run or extend beyond a limit set by; exceed: *Your speech has overrun the time limit.* **5.** *Printing.* **a.** To rearrange or move (set type or pictures) from one column, line, or page to another. **b.** To set too much type for. **c.** To print (a job order) in a quantity larger than that ordered. —*intr.* **1.** To run over; overflow. **2.** To go beyond the normal or desired limit. **—overrun** (ō′vər-rŭn′) *n.* **1.** An act of overrunning. **2.** The amount by which something overruns. **3.a.** The exceeding of estimated costs for product development and manufacture covered by contract. **b.** The amount by which actual costs exceed estimates. **4.** *Printing.* A run over and above the quantity ordered by a customer.

o·ver·saw (ō′vər-sô′) *v.* Past tense of **oversee.**

o·ver·scale (ō′vər-skāl′) or **o·ver·scaled** (-skāld′) *adj.* Being of a size or scope that is greater than usual; unusually large or extensive: *overscale furniture; an overscaled jacket.*

o·ver·score (ō′vər-skôr′, -skōr′) *tr.v.* **-scored, -scor·ing, -scores.** To cross out by drawing a line or lines over or through.

o·ver·sea (ō′vər-sē′, ō′vər-sē′) *adv. & adj.* Overseas.

o·ver·seas (ō′vər-sēz′, ō′vər-sēz′) *adv.* Beyond the sea; abroad. **—overseas** *adj.* Of, relating to, originating in, or situated in countries across the sea.

overseas cap *n.* See **garrison cap.**

o·ver·see (ō′vər-sē′) *tr.v.* **-saw** (-sô′), **-seen** (-sēn′), **-see·ing, -sees. 1.** To watch over and direct; supervise. See Synonyms at **supervise. 2.** To subject to scrutiny; examine or inspect.

o·ver·se·er (ō′vər-sē′ər) *n.* **1.** One who keeps watch over and directs the work of others, especially laborers. **2.** A supervisor or superintendent.

o·ver·sell (ō′vər-sĕl′) *tr.v.* **-sold** (-sōld′), **-sell·ing, -sells. 1.** To contract to sell more of (a stock or commodity) than can be delivered. **2.** To be too eager or insistent in attempting to sell something to. **3.** To present with excessive or unwarranted enthusiasm; overpraise. **—o′ver·sell′** *n.*

o·ver·sen·si·tive (ō′vər-sĕn′sĭ-tĭv) *adj.* Extremely or excessively sensitive. **—o′ver·sen′si·tive·ness, o′ver·sen′si·tiv′i·ty** *n.*

o·ver·set (ō′vər-sĕt′) *v.* **-set, -set·ting, -sets.** —*tr.* **1.** To throw into a confused or disturbed state; upset: *"The news is sure to overset him"* (Charles Dickens). **2.** *Printing.* **a.** To set (type or copy) in excess of what is needed. **b.** To set too much type for (a given space). —*intr. Printing.* To set too much material for a given space. **—overset** (ō′vər-sĕt′) *n. Printing.* Too much typeset matter.

o·ver·sew (ō′vər-sō′, ō′vər-sō′) *tr.v.* **-sewed, -sewn** (-sōn′) or **-sewed -sew·ing, -sews.** To sew with overhand stitches.

o·ver·sexed (ō′vər-sĕkst′) *adj.* Having or showing an excessive sexual appetite or interest in sexual matters.

o·ver·shad·ow (ō′vər-shăd′ō) *tr.v.* **-owed, -ow·ing, -ows. 1.** To cast a shadow over; darken or obscure. **2.** To make insignificant by comparison; dominate.

o·ver·shirt (ō′vər-shûrt′) *n.* A shirt worn over another shirt or over other clothing without being tucked into the waistband.

o·ver·shoe (ō′vər-sho͞o′) *n.* An article of footwear worn over a shoe as protection from water, snow, or cold.

o·ver·shoot (ō′vər-sho͞ot′) *v.* **-shot** (-shŏt′), **-shoot·ing, -shoots.** —*tr.* **1.** To shoot or pass over or beyond. **2.** To miss by or as if by shooting, hitting, or propelling something too far. **3.** To fly beyond or past; overrun: *The plane overshot the runway.* **4.** To go beyond; exceed. —*intr.* To shoot or go too far. **—o′ver·shoot′** *n.*

o·ver·shot (ō′vər-shŏt′) *v.* Past tense and past participle of **overshoot. —overshot** (ō′vər-shŏt′) *adj.* Having an upper part projecting beyond the lower: *an overshot jaw.* **—overshot** (ō′vər-shŏt′) *n.* A pattern in weaving made when filling threads are passed over two or more warp threads at a time.

o·ver·sight (ō′vər-sīt′) *n.* **1.** An unintentional omission or mistake. See Synonyms at **error. 2.** Watchful care or management; supervision.

o·ver·sim·ple (ō′vər-sĭm′pəl) *adj.* Too simple; not thoroughgoing: *an oversimple explanation of a complex phenomenon.* **—o′ver·sim′ply** *adv.*

o·ver·sim·pli·fy (ō′vər-sĭm′plə-fī′) *v.* **-fied, -fy·ing, -fies.** —*tr.* To simplify to the point of causing misrepresentation, misconception, or error. —*intr.* To cause distortion or error by extreme simplification of a subject. **—o′ver·sim′pli·fi·ca′tion** (-fĭ-kā′shən) *n.* **—o′ver·sim′pli·fi′er** *n.*

o·ver·size (ō′vər-sīz′) *n.* **1.** A size that is larger than usual. **2.** An oversize article or object. **—oversize** (ō′vər-sīz′) also **o·ver·sized** (-sīzd′) *adj.* Larger in size than usual or necessary.

o·ver·skirt (ō′vər-skûrt′) *n.* An outer skirt, especially a shorter one worn draped over another skirt.

o·ver·sleep (ō′vər-slēp′) *v.* **-slept** (-slĕpt′), **-sleep·ing, -sleeps.** —*intr.* To sleep beyond one's usual or intended time for waking. —*tr.* To sleep beyond the time for: *I overslept my appointment.*

o·ver·sold (ō′vər-sōld′) *v.* Past tense and past participle of **oversell. —oversold** *adj.* Characterized by prices regarded as excessively low because of prior heavy selling and a concomitant decline in prices: *an oversold stock market.*

o·ver·soul (ō′vər-sōl′) *n.* In New England transcendentalism, a spiritual essence or vital force in the universe in which all souls participate and that therefore transcends individual consciousness.

o·ver·spe·cial·ize (ō′vər-spĕsh′ə-līz′) *intr.v.* **-ized, -iz·ing, -iz·es.** To specialize to an extreme degree. **—o′ver·spe′cial·i·za′tion** (-spĕsh′ə-lĭ-zā′shən) *n.* **—o′ver·spe′cial·ized′** *adj.*

o·ver·spend (ō′vər-spĕnd′) *v.* **-spent** (-spĕnt′), **-spend·ing, -spends.** —*intr.* To spend more than is prudent or necessary. —*tr.* **1.** To spend in excess of: *overspend one's income.* **2.** To exhaust: *was overspent with toil.* —**o′ver·spend′er** *n.*

o·ver·spill (ō′vər-spĭl′) *intr.v.* **-spilled** or **-spilt** (-spĭlt), **-spill·ing, -spills.** To spill over. —**overspill** (ō′vər-spĭl′) *n.* **1.** The act of spilling over. **2.** Something that spills over: *an overspill of milk.* **3.** *Chiefly British.* Movement of people from overcrowded cities to less populated areas.

o·ver·spread (ō′vər-sprĕd′) *tr.v.* **-spread, -spread·ing, -spreads.** To spread or extend over the surface of: *Dark clouds are overspreading the sky.* —**o′ver·spread′** *n.*

o·ver·staff (ō′vər-stăf′) *tr.v.* **-staffed, -staff·ing, -staffs.** To supply with too many employees: *Management was careful not to overstaff the agency.*

o·ver·state (ō′vər-stāt′) *tr.v.* **-stat·ed, -stat·ing, -states.** To state in exaggerated terms. See Synonyms at **exaggerate.** —**o′ver·state′ment** *n.*

o·ver·stay (ō′vər-stā′) *tr.v.* **-stayed, -stay·ing, -stays.** To stay beyond the set limits or expected duration of; outstay: *The guests overstayed their welcome.*

o·ver·step (ō′vər-stĕp′) *tr.v.* **-stepped, -step·ping, -steps.** To go beyond (a limit); exceed: *overstepped the bounds of taste.*

o·ver·stock (ō′vər-stŏk′) *tr.v.* **-stocked, -stock·ing, -stocks.** To stock more of (something) than necessary or desirable. —**overstock** (ō′vər-stŏk′) *n.* An excessive supply.

o·ver·sto·ry (ō′vər-stôr′ē, -stōr′ē) *n.* The uppermost layer of foliage that forms a forest canopy.

o·ver·strain (ō′vər-strān′) *v.* **-strained, -strain·ing, -strains.** —*tr.* To subject to excessive strain, especially to force beyond a natural or proper limit: *overstraining the environment.* —*intr.* To put forth too much physical effort.

o·ver·stress (ō′vər-strĕs′) *tr.v.* **-stressed, -stress·ing, -stress·es.** **1.** To place too much emphasis on. **2.** To subject to excessive physical or emotional stress. **3.** To subject to mechanical force or pressure to the point of deformation. —**o′ver·stress′** *n.*

o·ver·stretch (ō′vər-strĕch′) *v.* **-stretched, -stretch·ing, -stretch·es.** —*tr.* **1.** To stretch excessively; overstrain. **2.** To stretch or extend over. —*intr.* To stretch one's body or muscles to the point of strain or injury.

o·ver·stride (ō′vər-strīd′) *tr.v.* **-strode** (-strōd′), **-strid·den** (-strĭd′n), **-strid·ing, -strides.** **1.** To stride over, across, or farther than. **2.** To sit or stand astride. **3.** To stride faster than or beyond, as in a competition. **4.** To go beyond; surpass.

o·ver·strung (ō′vər-strŭng′) *adj.* **1.** Too sensitive, nervous, or tense. **2.** Too tightly strung: *an overstrung archery bow.*

o·ver·stuff (ō′vər-stŭf′) *tr.v.* **-stuffed, -stuff·ing, -stuffs.** **1.** To stuff too much into: *overstuff a suitcase.* **2.** To upholster (an armchair, for example) deeply and thickly.

o·ver·sub·scribe (ō′vər-səb-skrīb′) *tr.v.* **-scribed, -scrib·ing, -scribes.** To subscribe for (something) in excess of available supply: *The opera season was oversubscribed.* —**o′ver·sub·scrip′tion** (-skrĭp′shən) *n.*

o·ver·sup·ply (ō′vər-sə-plī′) *n., pl.* **-plies.** A supply in excess of what is appropriate or required. —**oversupply** (ō′vər-sə-plī′) *tr.v.* **-plied, -ply·ing, -plies.** To supply in excess of what is appropriate or required: *oversupplied the troops with blankets; oversupplied blankets to the troops.*

o·vert (ō-vûrt′, ō′vûrt′) *adj.* **1.** Open and observable; not hidden, concealed, or secret: *overt hostility; overt intelligence gathering.* **2.** Of, relating to, or being military or intelligence operations sanctioned or mandated by Congress: *overt aid to the rebels.* [Middle English, from Old French, past participle of *ovrir,* to open, from Vulgar Latin **ōperīre,* alteration (influenced by Latin *cōperīre,* to cover) of Latin *aperīre.* See **wer-**[4] in Appendix.] —**o·vert′ly** *adv.* —**o·vert′ness** *n.*

o·ver·take (ō′vər-tāk′) *tr.v.* **-took** (-to͝ok′), **-tak·en** (-tā′kən), **-tak·ing, -takes.** **1.a.** To catch up with; draw even or level with. **b.** To pass after catching up with. **2.** To come upon unexpectedly; take by surprise: *geopolitical strategists who were overtaken by events in the Middle East.*

o·ver·tax (ō′vər-tăks′) *tr.v.* **-taxed, -tax·ing, -tax·es.** **1.** To subject to an excessive burden or strain. **2.** To tax in excess of what is appropriate or just. —**o′ver·tax·a′tion** *n.*

o·ver-the-air (ō′vər-*th*ē-âr′) *adj.* Of, relating to, or being a medium of broadcast transmission, such as radio or television: *over-the-air programming.*

o·ver-the-count·er (ō′vər-*th*ə-koun′tər) *adj. Abbr.* **OTC, O.T.C.** **1.** Not listed or available on an officially recognized stock exchange but traded in direct negotiation between buyers and sellers: *over-the-counter stocks.* **2.** That can be sold legally without a doctor's prescription: *over-the-counter drugs.*

o·ver-the-hill (ō′vər-*th*ə-hĭl′) *adj. Informal.* **1.** Past the peak of one's youthful vigor. **2.** Far along in life; old.

o·ver·throw (ō′vər-thrō′) *tr.v.* **-threw** (-thro͞o′), **-thrown** (-thrōn′), **-throw·ing, -throws.** **1.** To throw over; overturn. **2.** To bring about the downfall or destruction of, especially by force or concerted action: *a plot to overthrow the government.* **3.** *Sports.* To throw an object over and beyond (an intended mark): *The infielder overthrew first base.* —**overthrow** (ō′vər-thrō′) *n.* **1.** An instance of overthrowing, especially one that results in downfall or destruction. **2.** *Sports.* The throwing of a ball over and beyond a target, especially in baseball.

SYNONYMS: *overthrow, overturn, subvert, topple, upset.* The central meaning shared by these verbs is "to cause the downfall, destruction, abolition, or undoing of": *overthrow an empire; overturn existing institutions; subverting civil order; toppled the government; unable to upset the will.*

o·ver·thrust fault (ō′vər-thrŭst′) *n. Geology.* A fault in which one section of crust has ridden up over another.

o·ver·time (ō′vər-tīm′) *n. Abbr.* **OT, o.t., O.T.** **1.** Time beyond an established limit, as: **a.** Working hours in addition to those of a regular schedule. **b.** *Sports.* A period of playing time added after the expiration of the set time limit. **2.** Payment for additional work done outside of regular working hours. —**overtime** *adv.* Beyond the established time limit, especially that of the normal working day: *The newspaper staff worked overtime.* —**overtime** (ō′vər-tīm′) *tr.v.* **-timed, -tim·ing, -times.** To exceed the desired timing for: *overtime a photo exposure.*

o·ver·tone (ō′vər-tōn′) *n.* **1.** Often **overtones.** An ulterior, usually implicit meaning or quality; an implication or a hint: *an overtone of anger barely masked; praise with overtones of envy.* **2.** See **harmonic** (sense 1).

o·ver·took (ō′vər-to͝ok′) *v.* Past tense of **overtake.**

o·ver·top (ō′vər-tŏp′) *tr.v.* **-topped, -top·ping, -tops.** **1.** To extend or rise over or beyond the top of; tower above. **2.** To take precedence over; override: *"Religion overtopped the common affairs of life"* (Albert C. Baugh). **3.** To be greater or better than; surpass.

o·ver·trade (ō′vər-trād′) *v.* **-trad·ed, -trad·ing, -trades.** —*intr.* To engage in trading to a degree that is in excess of one's finances or the demands of the market. —*tr.* To trade (stock, for example) in this manner.

o·ver·train (ō′vər-trān′) *v.* **-trained, -train·ing, -trains.** *Sports.* —*tr.* To train too much: *a coach who overtrained the athletes before the championship.* —*intr.* To engage in excessive training: *a boxer who overtrained.*

o·ver·trick (ō′vər-trĭk′) *n. Games.* A card trick won in excess of contract or game, as in bridge.

o·ver·trump (ō′vər-trŭmp′, ō′vər-trŭmp′) *v.* **-trumped, -trump·ing, -trumps.** *Games.* —*intr.* To play a trump higher than one previously played on a trick. —*tr.* To trump with a higher trump card than any played on the same trick.

o·ver·ture (ō′vər-cho͝or′) *n.* **1.** *Music.* **a.** An instrumental composition intended especially as an introduction to an extended work, such as an opera or oratorio. **b.** A similar orchestral work, such as one written as a concert piece or an introduction to a play. **2.** An introductory section or part, as of a poem; a prelude. **3.** An act, an offer, or a proposal that indicates readiness to undertake a course of action or open a relationship. —**overture** *tr.v.* **-tured, -tur·ing, -tures.** **1.** To present as an introduction or a proposal. **2.** To present or make an offer or a proposal to. [Middle English, opening, from Old French, from Vulgar Latin **ōpertūra,* alteration (influenced by Latin *cōperīre,* to cover) of Latin *apertūra,* from *apertus,* past participle of *aperīre,* to open. See **wer-**[4] in Appendix.]

o·ver·turn (ō′vər-tûrn′) *v.* **-turned, -turn·ing, -turns.** —*tr.* **1.** To cause to turn over or capsize; upset. **2.a.** To cause the ruin or destruction of; overthrow. See Synonyms at **overthrow. b.** *Law.* To invalidate or reverse (a decision) by legal means: *"his continuing legal battles to overturn a draft-evasion conviction"* (Robert Lipsyte). —*intr.* To turn over or capsize. —**overturn** (ō′vər-tûrn′) *n.* **1.** The act or process of overturning. **2.** The state of having been overturned.

o·ver·use (ō′vər-yo͞oz′) *tr.v.* **-used, -us·ing, -us·es.** To use to excess. —**overuse** (ō′vər-yo͞os′) *n.* Excessive use.

o·ver·val·ue (ō′vər-văl′yo͞o) *tr.v.* **-ued, -u·ing, -ues.** To assign too high a value to: *overvalued the painting.* —**o′ver·val′u·a′tion** *n.*

o·ver·view (ō′vər-vyo͞o′) *n.* **1.** A broad, comprehensive view; a survey. **2.** A summary or review.

o·ver·wear (ō′vər-wâr′) *tr.v.* **-wore** (-wôr′, -wōr′), **-worn** (-wôrn′, -wōrn′), **-wear·ing, -wears.** To wear out; exhaust.

o·ver·wea·ry (ō′vər-wîr′ē) *adj.* So weary as to be totally exhausted. —**overweary** *tr.v.* **-ried, -ry·ing, -ries.** To tire out utterly; exhaust.

o·ver·ween·ing (ō′vər-wē′nĭng) *adj.* **1.** Presumptuously arrogant; overbearing: *had a witty but overweening manner about him.* **2.** Excessive; immoderate: *overweening ambition.* —**o′ver·ween′ing·ly** *adv.*

o·ver·weigh (ō′vər-wā′) *tr.v.* **-weighed, -weigh·ing, -weighs.** **1.** To have more weight than. **2.** To weigh down excessively; overburden or oppress.

o·ver·weight (ō′vər-wāt′) *adj.* Weighing more than is normal, necessary, or allowed, especially having more body weight than is considered normal or healthy for one's age or build. —**overweight** (ō′vər-wāt′) *n.* **1.** More weight than is normal, necessary, or allowed. **2.** Greater weight or importance; preponderance. —**overweight** (ō′vər-wāt′) *tr.v.* **-weight·ed, -weight·ing, -weights.** **1.** To weigh down too heavily; overload. **2.** To give too much emphasis, importance, or consideration to.

o·ver·whelm (ō′vər-hwĕlm′, -wĕlm′) *tr.v.* **-whelmed, -whelm·ing, -whelms.** **1.** To surge over and submerge; engulf: *waves overwhelming the rocky shoreline.* **2.a.** To defeat com-

ă pat	oi boy
ā pay	ou out
âr care	o͝o took
ä father	o͞o boot
ĕ pet	ŭ cut
ē be	ûr urge
ĭ pit	th thin
ī pie	*th* this
îr pier	hw which
ŏ pot	zh vision
ō toe	ə about, item
ô paw	♦ regionalism

Stress marks: ′ (primary); ′ (secondary), as in **dictionary** (dĭk′shə-nĕr′ē)

pletely and decisively: *Our team overwhelmed the visitors by 40 points.* **b.** To affect deeply in mind or emotion: *Despair overwhelmed me.* **3.** To present with an excessive amount: *They overwhelmed us with expensive gifts.* **4.** To turn over; upset: *The small craft was overwhelmed by the enormous waves.*

o·ver·whelm·ing (ō′vər-hwĕl′mĭng, -wĕl′-) *adj.* Overpowering in effect or strength: *overwhelming joy; an overwhelming majority.* **—o′ver·whelm′ing·ly** *adv.*

o·ver·wind (ō′vər-wīnd′) *tr.v.* **-wound** (-wound′), **-wind·ing, -winds.** To wind too tightly: *overwound the watch and broke the spring.*

o·ver·win·ter (ō′vər-wĭn′tər) *intr.v.* **-tered, -ter·ing, -ters. 1.** To remain alive through the winter: *sheep that overwintered on the steppe.* **2.** To pass or spend the winter: *We usually overwinter in the Bahamas.* **—overwinter** (ō′vər-wĭn′tər) *adj.* Occurring during the period of winter.

o·ver·with·hold (ō′vər-wĭth-hōld′, -wĭ*th*-) *v.* **-held** (-hĕld′), **-hold·ing, -holds.** *—tr.* **1.** To deduct (an amount in withholding tax) beyond the tax owed. **2.** To subject to overwithholding. *—intr.* To deduct too much withholding tax.

o·ver·wore (ō′vər-wôr′, -wōr′) *v.* Past tense of **overwear.**

o·ver·work (ō′vər-wûrk′) *v.* **-worked, -work·ing, -works.** *—tr.* **1.** To force to work too hard or too long. **2. a.** To rework to excess: *overwork a speech.* **b.** To use too often: *"'Vulnerable' and 'volatile' were the most overworked adjectives of the '70s"* (David Ansen). **3.** To decorate the entire surface of. *—intr.* To work too long or too hard. **—overwork** (ō′vər-wûrk′) *n.* Excessive work.

o·ver·worn (ō′vər-wôrn′, -wōrn′) *v.* Past participle of **overwear.**

o·ver·wound (ō′vər-wound′) *v.* Past tense and past participle of **overwind.**

o·ver·write (ō′vər-rīt′) *v.* **-wrote** (-rōt′), **-writ·ten** (-rĭt′n), **-writ·ing, -writes.** *—tr.* **1.** To cover (something) with writing. **2.** To write about in an artificial or an excessively elaborate, wordy style. *—intr.* To write artificial, excessively elaborate, or wordy prose.

Jesse Owens
Photographed at the 1936 Summer Olympics in Berlin, Germany

o·ver·wrought (ō′vər-rôt′) *adj.* **1.** Excessively nervous or excited; agitated. **2.** Extremely elaborate or ornate; overdone: *overwrought prose style.*

o·ver·zeal·ous (ō′vər-zĕl′əs) *adj.* Excessively enthusiastic: *overzealous movie fans; an overzealous manager.* **—o′ver·zeal′ous·ly** *adv.* **—o′ver·zeal′ous·ness** *n.*

ovi– or **ovo–** or **ov–** *pref.* Egg; ovum: *oviferous.* [Latin *ōvi-*, from *ōvum,* egg. See **awi-** in Appendix.]

o·vi·cide (ō′vĭ-sīd′) *n.* A chemical agent that kills eggs, especially the eggs of insects. **—o′vi·cid′al** (-sīd′l) *adj.*

Ov·id (ŏv′ĭd). 43 B.C.–A.D. 17. Roman poet known for his explorations of love, especially the *Art of Love* (c. 1 B.C.) and *Metamorphoses* (c. A.D. 8). **—O·vid′i·an** (ŏ-vĭd′ē-ən) *adj.*

o·vi·duct (ō′vĭ-dŭkt′) *n.* A tube through which the ova pass from the ovary to the uterus or to the outside. **—o′vi·duc′tal** *adj.*

O·vie·do (ō-vyā′dō, ô-vyĕ′*th*ô). A city of northwest Spain near the Cantabrian Mountains. Founded c. 760, it flourished as the capital of Asturian kings until 910. Population, 189,376.

o·vif·er·ous (ō-vĭf′ər-əs) *adj.* Bearing or producing ova.

o·vi·form (ō′və-fôrm′) *adj.* Shaped like an egg; ovoid.

O·vim·bun·du (ō′vĭm-bōōn′dōō) *n., pl.* **Ovimbundu** or **-dus.** See **Mbundu** (sense 1).

o·vine (ō′vīn′) *adj.* Of, relating to, or characteristic of sheep; sheeplike. **—ovine** *n.* An ovine animal. [Late Latin *ovīnus,* from Latin *ovis,* sheep. See **owi-** in Appendix.]

o·vip·a·ra (ō-vĭp′ər-ə) *pl.n.* Oviparous animals considered as a group. [Latin *ōvipara,* neuter pl. of *ōviparus,* egg-laying : *ōvi-,* ovi- + *-parus,* -parous.]

o·vip·a·rous (ō-vĭp′ər-əs) *adj.* Producing eggs that hatch outside the body. **—o′vi·par′i·ty** (ō′və-păr′ĭ-tē) *n.* **—o·vip′a·rous·ly** *adv.*

owl
Snowy owl
Nyctea scandiaca

o·vi·pos·it (ō′və-pŏz′ĭt) *intr.v.* **-it·ed, -it·ing, -its.** To lay eggs, especially by means of an ovipositor. **—o′vi·po·si′tion** (-pə-zĭsh′ən) *n.* **—o′vi·po·si′tion·al** *adj.*

o·vi·pos·i·tor (ō′və-pŏz′ĭ-tər) *n.* **1.** A tubular structure, usually concealed but sometimes extending outside the abdomen, with which many female insects deposit eggs. **2.** A similar organ of certain fishes.

o·vi·sac (ō′vĭ-săk′) *n.* An egg-containing capsule, such as an ootheca or a Graafian follicle.

ovo– *pref.* Variant of **ovi–.**

o·void (ō′void′) also **o·voi·dal** (ō-void′l) *—adj.* Shaped like an egg; ovate. *—n.* Something that is shaped like an egg.

o·vo·lac·to·veg·e·tar·i·an (ō′vō-lăk′tō-vĕj′ĭ-târ′ē-ən) *n.* A vegetarian whose diet includes milk or milk products and eggs.

o·vo·lo (ō′və-lō′) *n., pl.* **-li** (-lī′). *Architecture.* A rounded convex molding, often a quarter section of a circle or an ellipse. [Obsolete Italian, diminutive of *uovo, ovo,* egg, from Latin *ōvum.* See **awi-** in Appendix.]

o·von·ic (ō-vŏn′ĭk) *adj.* Of or relating to a device whose operation is based on the Ovshinsky effect. [OV(SHINSKY EFFECT) + (ELECTR)ONIC.]

o·vo·tes·tis (ō′vō-tĕs′tĭs) *n., pl.* **-tes** (-tēz′). A hermaphroditic reproductive organ that produces both sperm and eggs, found in certain gastropods.

o·vo·vi·vip·a·rous (ō′vō-vī-vĭp′ər-əs) *adj.* Producing eggs that hatch within the female's body without obtaining nourishment from it. Used of certain fishes and reptiles and many invertebrates. **—o′vo·vi′vi·par′i·ty** (-vī′və-păr′ĭ-tē), **o′vo·vi·vip′a·rous·ness** (-vĭp′ər-əs-nĭs) *n.* **—o′vo·vi·vip′a·rous·ly** *adv.*

Ov·shin·sky effect (ŏv-shĭn′skē, ôv-) *n.* The effect by which a specific glassy thin film switches from a nonconductor to a semiconductor upon application of a minimum voltage. [After Stanford R. *Ovshinsky* (born 1922), American inventor.]

o·vu·late (ō′vyə-lāt′, ŏv′yə-) *intr.v.* **-lat·ed, -lat·ing, -lates.** To produce ova; discharge eggs from the ovary. [From OVULE.] **—o′vu·la′tion** *n.* **—o′vu·la·to′ry** (-lə-tôr′ē, -tōr′ē) *adj.*

o·vule (ō′vyōōl, ŏv′yōōl) *n.* **1.** *Botany.* A minute structure in seed plants, containing the embryo sac and surrounded by the nucellus, that develops into a seed after fertilization. **2.** *Zoology.* A small or immature ovum. [New Latin *ōvulum,* diminutive of Latin *ōvum,* egg. See **awi-** in Appendix.] **—o′vu·lar** (ō′vyə-lər, ŏv′yə-), **o′vu·lar′y** (-lĕr′ē) *adj.*

o·vum (ō′vəm) *n., pl.* **o·va** (ō′və). The female reproductive cell or gamete of animals; egg. [Latin *ōvum,* egg. See **awi-** in Appendix.]

ow (ou) *interj.* Used especially in response to sudden pain.

OW *abbr.* One-way.

O·wa·ton·na (ō′wə-tŏn′ə). A city of southeast Minnesota south of Minneapolis. Population, 18,632.

owe (ō) *v.* **owed, ow·ing, owes.** *—tr.* **1.** To be indebted to the amount of: *He owes me five dollars.* **2.** To have a moral obligation to render or offer: *I owe them an apology.* **3.** To be in debt to: *We owe the plumber for services rendered.* **4.** To be indebted or obliged for: *owed their riches to oil; owes her good health to diet and exercise.* **5.** To bear (a certain feeling) toward a person or persons: *You seem to owe your neighbors a grudge.* **6.** *Archaic.* To have as a possession; own. *—intr.* To be in debt: *She still owes for the car.* [Middle English *owen,* from Old English *āgan,* to possess. See **ēik-** in Appendix.]

Ow·en (ō′ĭn), Sir **Richard.** 1804–1892. British anatomist and paleontologist who was an early opponent of Darwin's theories of evolution.

Owen, Robert. 1771–1858. Welsh-born British manufacturer and social reformer who attempted to establish a cooperative community at New Harmony in Indiana (1825–1828).

Owen, Wilfred. 1893–1918. British poet whose work reflects his experiences in World War I. He was killed in battle.

Ow·ens (ō′ĭnz), **Jesse.** 1913–1980. American track star. He won four gold medals at the 1936 Olympics, upsetting Adolf Hitler's plans to use the games as evidence of Aryan superiority.

O·wens·bor·o (ō′ĭnz-bûr′ō, -bŭ′ō). A city of northwest Kentucky on the Ohio River west-southwest of Louisville. Settled c. 1800, it is a tobacco market. Population, 54,450.

Owen Sound. A city of southeast Ontario, Canada, on **Owen Sound,** an inlet of Georgian Bay. It is a port and railroad terminal with varied industries. Population, 19,883.

Owens River. A river, about 193 km (120 mi) long, of eastern California rising in the Sierra Nevada and flowing generally southward, formerly to **Owens Lake,** now a dry lake bed near Mount Whitney, and currently via aqueduct to the reservoirs of Los Angeles.

Owen Stan·ley Range (stăn′lē). A mountain range extending about 483 km (300 mi) southeast to northwest on New Guinea Island in Papua New Guinea. It rises to 4,075.7 m (13,363 ft).

ow·ing (ō′ĭng) *adj.* Still to be paid; due.

owing to *prep.* Because of; on account of: *I couldn't attend, owing to illness.*

owl (oul) *n.* **1.** Any of various often nocturnal birds of prey of the order Strigiformes, having hooked and feathered talons, large heads with short hooked beaks, large eyes set forward, and fluffy plumage that allows for almost noiseless flight. **2.** Any of a breed of domestic pigeons resembling owls. [Middle English *owle,* from Old English *ūle,* of imitative origin.]

owl·et (ou′lĭt) *n.* A small or young owl.

owlet moth *n.* See **noctuid.**

owl·ish (ou′lĭsh) *adj.* Resembling or characteristic of an owl. **—owl′ish·ly** *adv.* **—owl′ish·ness** *n.*

owl's claws (oulz) *pl.n. (used with a sing. or pl. verb).* A perennial plant *(Helenium hoopesii)* of western North America, having large, rayed, yellow flower heads clustered in loose corymbs.

owl's clover *n.* Any of various New World plants of the genus *Orthocarpus,* having bracteate spikes, variously colored flowers, and tubular bilabiate corolla. [From the resemblance of the flowers of some species to owls' faces.]

own (ōn) *adj.* Of or belonging to oneself or itself: *She makes her own clothes.* **—own** *n.* That which belongs to one: *It is my own.* **—own** *v.* **owned, own·ing, owns.** *—tr.* **1. a.** To have or possess as property: *owns a chain of restaurants.* **b.** To have control over: *For a time, enemy planes owned the skies.* **2.** To admit as being in accordance with fact, truth, or a claim; acknowledge. *—intr.* To make a full confession or acknowledgment: *When confronted with the evidence the thief owned up.* See Synonyms at **acknowledge.** **—*idioms.* of (one's) own.** Belonging completely to oneself: *a room of one's own.* **on (one's) own. 1.** By one's own efforts: *She got the job on her own.* **2.** Responsible for oneself; independent of outside help or control: *He is now out of college and on his own.* [Middle English *owen,* from Old English *āgen.* See **ēik-** in Appendix.] **—own′er** *n.*

own·er·ship (ō′nər-shĭp′) *n.* **1.** The state or fact of being an owner. **2.** Legal right to the possession of a thing.

O·wos·so (ō-wŏs′ō). A city of central Michigan west of Flint. It is a trade center in a farming region. Population, 16,455.

O·wy·hee (ō-wī′ē, -hē). A river, about 483 km (300 mi) long, of southwest Idaho, northern Nevada, and southeast Oregon. It empties into the Snake River.

ox (ŏks) *n., pl.* **ox·en** (ŏk′sən). **1.** An adult castrated bull of the genus *Bos,* especially *B. taurus,* used chiefly as a draft animal. **2.** A bovine mammal. [Middle English, from Old English *oxa.*]

ox– *pref.* Variant of **oxo–.**

ox·a·cil·lin (ŏk′sə-sĭl′ĭn) *n.* A semisynthetic penicillin effective against penicillin-resistant infections, especially those of staphylococci. [OX(O)– + A(ZOLE) + (PENI)CILLIN.]

ox·al·ac·e·tate (ŏk′səl-ăs′ĭ-tāt′) *n.* Variant of **oxaloacetate.**

ox·al·a·cet·ic acid (ŏk-săl′ə-sē′tĭk, ŏk′sə-lə-) *n.* Variant of **oxaloacetic acid.**

ox·a·late (ŏk′sə-lāt′) *n.* A salt or an ester of oxalic acid. **—oxalate** *tr.v.* **-lat·ed, -lat·ing, -lates.** To treat (a specimen) with an oxalate or oxalic acid. [OXAL(IC ACID) + –ATE[2].]

ox·al·ic acid (ŏk-săl′ĭk) *n.* A poisonous, colorless crystalline organic acid, HOOCCOOH·$2H_2O$, found in many plants, such as spinach, and used as a bleach and rust remover. [Latin *oxalis,* wood sorrel; see OXALIS + –IC.]

ox·a·lis (ŏk′sə-lĭs, ŏk-săl′ĭs) *n.* Any of numerous plants of the genus *Oxalis,* having often cloverlike compound leaves with three leaflets and variously colored flowers that are usually clustered in umbels. Also called *wood sorrel.* [Latin *oxalis,* wood sorrel, from Greek, from *oxus,* sour. See **ak-** in Appendix.]

ox·a·lo·ac·e·tate (ŏk′sə-lō-ăs′ĭ-tāt′) or **ox·al·ac·e·tate** (-ăs′ĭ-tāt′) *n.* A salt or an ester of oxaloacetic acid. [OXAL(IC ACID) + ACET(IC ACID) + –ATE[2].]

ox·a·lo·a·ce·tic acid (ŏk′sə-lō-ə-sē′tĭk, ŏk-săl′ō-) or **ox·al·a·ce·tic acid** (ŏk-sĕl′ə-sē′tĭk, ŏk′sə-lə-) *n.* A colorless crystalline dicarboxylic acid, $C_4H_4O_5$, that is formed by oxidation of malic acid in the Krebs cycle and by transamination from aspartic acid. It is important as an intermediate in the metabolism of carbohydrates and a precursor in the synthesis of amino acids. [OXAL(IC ACID) + ACETIC ACID.]

ox·az·e·pam (ŏk-săz′ə-păm′) *n.* A tranquilizing drug, $C_{15}H_{11}ClN_2O_2$, related to benzodiazepine and used especially in the treatment of insomnia and alcohol withdrawal. [(HYDR)OX(Y) + (BENZODI)AZEP(INE) + AM(INE).]

ox·blood red (ŏks′blŭd′) *n. Color.* A dark or deep red to medium reddish brown.

ox·bow (ŏks′bō′) *n.* **1.** A U-shaped piece of wood that fits under and around the neck of an ox, with its upper ends attached to the bar of the yoke. **2.a.** A U-shaped bend in a river. **b.** The land within such a bend of a river. **—ox′bow′** *adj.*

oxbow lake *n.* A crescent-shaped lake formed when a meander of a river or stream is cut off from the main channel.

Ox·bridge (ŏks′brĭj′) *n. Chiefly British.* Oxford and Cambridge universities, especially when regarded as the seat of traditional academic and social excellence, privilege, and exclusiveness. **—Oxbridge** *adj.* Of, relating to, or characteristic of Oxbridge: *spoke with an Oxbridge accent.*

ox·en (ŏk′sən) *n.* Plural of **ox.**

Ox·en·stier·na also **Ox·en·stjer·na** (o͝ok′sən-shĕr′nə, ŏk′-), Count **Axel Gustafsson.** 1583–1654. Swedish politician who virtually ruled Sweden as leader of the council of regency during the minority of Christina (1632–1644).

ox·eye (ŏks′ī′) *n.* **1.** Either of two Eurasian plants of the genus *Buphthalum,* having daisylike flowers with yellow rays and dark centers. **2.** Any of various New World plants of the genus *Heliopsis,* having similar flowers. **3.** A round or oval dormer window.

oxeye daisy *n.* See **daisy** (sense 1).

ox·ford (ŏks′fərd) *n.* **1.** A sturdy, low shoe that laces over the instep. **2.** A cotton cloth of a tight basket weave, used primarily for shirts. [After OXFORD, England.]

Ox·ford (ŏks′fərd). **1.** A borough of south-central England on the Thames River west-northwest of London. First mentioned in 912, it was chartered in 1605. Oxford University, with its famed "dreaming spires," was founded in the 12th century and still dominates the center of the city. Population, 114,400. **2.** A city of northern Mississippi south-southeast of Memphis, Tennessee. It is the seat of the University of Mississippi ("Old Miss"), established in 1844, and was William Faulkner's home town. Population, 9,882. **3.** A village of southwest Ohio northwest of Hamilton near the Indiana border. Mainly residential, it is the seat of Miami University (founded 1809). Population, 17,655.

oxford gray *n. Color.* A dark gray. [After OXFORD, England.]

Oxford movement *n.* A movement within the Church of England, originating at Oxford University in 1833, that sought to link the Anglican Church more closely to the Roman Catholic Church.

ox·heart (ŏks′härt′) *n.* A variety of cultivated cherry having sweet, juicy fruit. [From its shape.]

ox·i·dant (ŏk′sĭ-dənt) *n.* See **oxidizer.** [French *oxidant,* present participle of *oxider,* to oxidize, from *oxide,* oxide. See OXIDE.]

ox·i·dase (ŏk′sĭ-dās′, -dāz′) *n.* Any of a group of enzymes that catalyze oxidation, especially an enzyme that reacts with molecular oxygen to catalyze the oxidation of a substrate. [OXID(ATION) + –ASE.] **—ox′i·da′sic** *adj.*

ox·i·da·tion (ŏk′sĭ-dā′shən) *n.* **1.** The combination of a substance with oxygen. **2.** A reaction in which the atoms in an element lose electrons and the valence of the element is correspondingly increased. [French, from *oxider,* to oxidize, from *oxide,* oxide. See OXIDE.] **—ox′i·da′tive** *adj.* **—ox′i·da′tive·ly** *adv.*

ox·i·da·tion-re·duc·tion (ŏk′sĭ-dā′shən-rĭ-dŭk′shən) *n.* A chemical reaction in which an atom or ion loses electrons to another atom or ion. *—attributive.* Often used to modify another noun: *an oxidation-reduction reaction; oxidation-reduction equilibrium.*

oxidative phosphorylation *n.* The process in cell metabolism by which respiratory enzymes in the mitochondria synthesize ATP from ADP during the oxidation of reduced NAD by molecular oxygen.

ox·ide (ŏk′sīd′) *n.* A binary compound of an element or a radical with oxygen. [French : *ox(ygène),* oxygen; see OXYGEN + *(ac)ide,* acid (from Latin *acidus,* tart, acid; see ACID).] **—ox·id′ic** (ŏk-sĭd′ĭk) *adj.*

ox·i·dize (ŏk′sĭ-dīz′) *v.* **-dized, -diz·ing, -diz·es.** *Chemistry.* *—tr.* **1.** To combine with oxygen; make into an oxide. **2.** To increase the positive charge or valence of (an element) by removing electrons. **3.** To coat with oxide. *—intr.* To become oxidized. **—ox′i·diz′a·ble** *adj.* **—ox′i·di·za′tion** (-dĭ-zā′shən) *n.*

ox·i·diz·er (ŏk′sĭ-dī′zər) *n.* A substance that oxidizes another substance; an oxidizing agent. Also called *oxidant.*

ox·i·do·re·duc·tase (ŏk′sĭ-dō-rĭ-dŭk′tās′, -tāz′) *n.* An enzyme that catalyzes an oxidation-reduction reaction. [OXID(ATION) + REDUCT(ION) + –ASE.]

ox·ime (ŏk′sēm) *n.* Any of a group of compounds containing a CNOH group, formed by treating aldehydes or ketones with hydroxylamine. [OX(O)– + IM(ID)E.]

ox·im·e·ter (ŏk-sĭm′ĭ-tər) *n.* A device for measuring the oxygen saturation of arterial blood. **—ox′i·met′ric** (-mĕt′rĭk) *adj.* **—ox′i·met′ri·cal·ly** *adv.* **—ox·im′e·try** *n.*

ox·lip (ŏks′lĭp′) *n.* A Eurasian primrose *(Primula elatior)* having yellow flowers clustered in a one-sided umbel. [Middle English *oxeslippe,* from Old English *oxanslyppe* : *oxan,* genitive sing. of *oxa,* ox + *slyppe,* slimy substance; see **sleubh-** in Appendix.]

Ox·nard (ŏks′närd′). A city of southern California west-northwest of Los Angeles on the Pacific coast. It is a commercial and industrial center. Population, 108,195.

oxo– or **ox–** *pref.* Oxygen: *oxime.* [From OXYGEN.]

Ox·on Hill (ŏk′sŏn, -sən). A community of central Maryland, a suburb of Washington, D.C. Population, 36,267.

Ox·o·ni·an (ŏk-sō′nē-ən) *adj.* Of, relating to, or characteristic of Oxford or Oxford University. **—Oxonian** *n.* **1.** A native or inhabitant of Oxford. **2.** A person who studies or has studied at Oxford University. [From Medieval Latin *Oxōnia,* Oxford, from Old English *Oxnaford* : *oxena,* genitive pl. of *oxa,* ox; see OX + *ford,* ford; see FORD.]

ox·peck·er (ŏks′pĕk′ər) *n.* Either of two African starlings *(Buphagus africanus* or *B. erythrorhyncus)* that feed on the ticks found on the hides of large wild or domestic animals. Also called *tickbird.*

ox·tail (ŏks′tāl′) *n.* The tail of an ox, especially when used for food. **—ox′tail′** *adj.*

Ox·us (ŏk′səs). See **Amu Darya.**

oxy– *pref.* Oxygen, especially additional oxygen: *oxyacetylene.* [From OXYGEN.]

ox·y·a·cet·y·lene (ŏk′sē-ə-sĕt′l-ĭn, -ēn′) *adj.* Of or using a mixture of acetylene and oxygen: *an oxyacetylene torch.*

ox·y·ac·id (ŏk′sē-ăs′ĭd) *n.* An oxygen-containing acid.

ox·y·ceph·a·ly (ŏk′sē-sĕf′ə-lē) *n., pl.* **-lies.** A congenital abnormality of the skull in which the top of the head assumes a conical or pointed shape. Also called *acrocephaly.* [From Greek *oxukephalos,* sharp-headed : *oxus,* sharp; see OXYGEN + *–kephalos,* -cephalous.] **—ox′y·ce·phal′ic** (-sə-făl′ĭk), **ox′y·ceph′a·lous** *adj.*

ox·y·co·done (ŏk′sĭ-kō′dōn′) *n.* A narcotic alkaloid, $C_{18}H_{21}NO_4$, related to codeine, used as an analgesic and a sedative chiefly in the form of its hydrochloride salt. [From chemical name *(dihydrohydr)oxycod(ein)one.*]

ox·y·gen (ŏk′sĭ-jən) *n. Symbol* **O** A nonmetallic element constituting 21 percent of the atmosphere by volume that occurs as a diatomic gas, O_2, and in many compounds such as water and iron ore. It combines with most elements, is essential for plant and animal respiration, and is required for nearly all combustion. Atomic number 8; atomic weight 15.9994; melting point −218.4°C; boiling point −183.0°C; gas density at 0°C 1.429 grams per liter; valence 2. See table at **element.** [French *oxygène* : Greek *oxus,* sharp, acid; see **ak-** in Appendix + French *-gène,* -gen.] **—ox′y·gen′ic** (-jĕn′ĭk) *adj.* **—ox′y·gen′i·cal·ly** *adv.* **—ox·yg′e·nous** (ŏk-sĭj′ə-nəs) *adj.*

ox·y·gen·ase (ŏk′sĭ-jə-nās′, -nāz′) *n.* An oxidoreductase

ox
Bos grunniens

ă pat	oi boy
ā pay	ou out
âr care	o͝o took
ä father	o͞o boot
ĕ pet	ŭ cut
ē be	ûr urge
ĭ pit	th thin
ī pie	*th* this
îr pier	hw which
ŏ pot	zh vision
ō toe	ə about, item
ô paw	♦ regionalism

Stress marks: **′** (primary); ′ (secondary), as in **dictionary** (dĭk′shə-nĕr′ē)

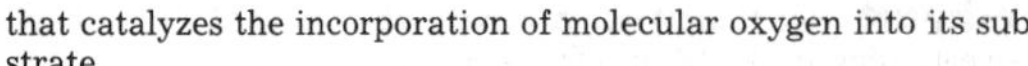

that catalyzes the incorporation of molecular oxygen into its substrate.

ox·y·gen·ate (ŏk′sĭ-jə-nāt′) also **ox·y·gen·ize** (-jə-nīz′) *tr.v.* **-at·ed, -at·ing, -ates** also **-ized, -iz·ing, -iz·es.** To treat, combine, or infuse with oxygen. **—ox′y·gen·a′tion** *n.* **—ox′y·gen·a′tor** *n.*

oxygen debt *n.* The amount of extra oxygen required by muscle tissue during recovery from vigorous exercise.

oxygen demand *n.* Biochemical oxygen demand.

oxygen mask *n.* A masklike device placed over the mouth and nose and through which oxygen is supplied from an attached storage tank.

oxygen tent *n.* A canopy placed over the head and shoulders or over the entire body of a patient to provide oxygen at a higher level than normal.

ox·y·he·mo·glo·bin (ŏk′sē-hē′mə-glō′bĭn) *n.* A bright-red chemical complex of hemoglobin and oxygen that transports oxygen to the tissues.

ox·y·hy·dro·gen (ŏk′sē-hī′drə-jən) *adj.* Of or using a mixture of hydrogen and oxygen: *an oxyhydrogen torch.*

ox·y·me·taz·o·line (ŏk′sē-mĭ-tăz′ə-lēn′, -mĕt′ə-zō-) *n.* A vasoconstricting drug, $C_{16}H_{24}N_2O$, that is used topically in the form of its hydrochloride salt to reduce nasal congestion. [Alteration of chemical name *(tertbutyldi)met(hylhydr)oxy(benzylimid)azoline.*]

ox·y·mo·ron (ŏk′sē-môr′ŏn′, -mōr′-) *n., pl.* **-mo·ra** (-môr′ə, -mōr′ə) or **-rons.** A rhetorical figure in which incongruous or contradictory terms are combined, as in *a deafening silence* and *a mournful optimist.* [Greek *oxumōron,* from neuter of *oxumōros,* pointedly foolish : *oxus,* sharp; see OXYGEN + *mōros,* foolish, dull.] **—ox′y·mo·ron′ic** (-mə-rŏn′ĭk) *adj.* **—ox′y·mo·ron′i·cal·ly** *adv.*

ox·y·sul·fide (ŏk′sē-sŭl′fīd′) *n.* A sulfide compound in which part of the sulfur has been replaced by oxygen.

ox·y·tet·ra·cy·cline (ŏk′sē-tĕt′rə-sī′klĭn, -klēn′) *n.* A broad-spectrum antibiotic, $C_{22}H_{24}N_2O_9$, derived from the actinomycete *Streptomyces rimosus* and used to treat a variety of bacterial infections.

ox·y·to·ci·a (ŏk′sĭ-tō′shē-ə, -shə) *n.* An unusually rapid childbirth.

ox·y·to·cic (ŏk′sĭ-tō′sĭk) *adj.* Hastening or facilitating childbirth, especially by stimulating contractions of the uterus. Used of a drug. **—oxytocic** *n.* An oxytocic drug. [From alteration (influenced by Late Greek *oxutokia, sudden delivery) of Greek *ōkutokios,* oxytocic : Greek *ōkus,* swift; see **ōku-** in Appendix + *tokos,* birth; see **tek-** in Appendix.]

ox·y·to·cin (ŏk′sĭ-tō′sĭn) *n.* A short polypeptide hormone, $C_{43}H_{66}N_{12}O_{12}S_2$, released from the posterior lobe of the pituitary gland, that stimulates the contraction of smooth muscle of the uterus during labor and facilitates ejection of milk from the breast during nursing.

ox·y·tone (ŏk′sĭ-tōn′) *adj.* **1.** Relating to or being a Greek word that has an acute accent on its last syllable. **2.** Relating to or being a word that has a heavy stress accent on its last syllable. **—oxytone** *n.* A word having the stress or the acute accent on the last syllable. [Greek *oxutonos* : *oxus,* sharp; see OXYURIASIS + *tonos,* tone; see TONE.]

ox·y·u·ri·a·sis (ŏk′sē-yŏŏ-rī′ə-sĭs) *n.* Infestation with pinworms. [New Latin *Oxyuris,* type genus (Greek *oxus,* sharp; see **ak-** in Appendix + Greek *oura,* tail; see **ors-** in Appendix) + -IASIS.]

oy·er and ter·mi·ner (oi′ər; tûr′mə-nər) *n. Law.* **1.** A hearing or trial. **2.** A court of general criminal jurisdiction in some states of the United States. **3.a.** A commission empowering a judge in Great Britain to hear and rule on a criminal case at the assizes. **b.** The court in Great Britain where such a hearing is held. [Middle English, partial translation of Anglo-Norman *oyer et terminer,* to hear and determine : *oyer,* to hear + *terminer,* to determine.]

o·yez (ō′yĕs′, ō′yĕz′, ō′yā′) also **o·yes** (ō′yĕs′) *—interj.* Used three times in succession to introduce the opening of a court of law. *—n., pl.* **o·yes·ses** (ō′yĕs′ĭz). This cry, used to open a court. [Middle English, from Anglo-Norman, hear ye, imperative pl. of *oyer,* to hear, from Latin *audīre.* See **au-** in Appendix.]

WORD HISTORY: Hearing the cry "Oyez, oyez, oyez," in a courtroom may have puzzled more than one auditor, especially if pronounced "O yes." (Many people have thought that in fact it is like *O yes.*) This cry serves to remind us that up until the 18th century, speaking English in a British court of law was not required and one could instead use Law French, a form of French that evolved after the Norman Conquest, when Anglo-Norman became the language of the official class in England. *Oyez* descends from the Anglo-Norman *oyez,* the plural imperative form of *oyer,* "to hear"; thus *oyez* means "hear ye" and was used as a call for silence and attention. Although it would have been much heard in Medieval England, it is first recorded as an English word fairly late in the Middle English period, in a work composed around 1425.

oys·ter (oi′stər) *n.* **1.a.** Any of several edible bivalve mollusks of the family Ostreidae, especially of the genera *Crassostrea* and *Ostrea,* that live chiefly in shallow marine waters and have a rough, irregularly shaped shell. **b.** Any of various similar or related bivalve mollusks, such as the pearl oyster. **2.** An edible bit of muscle found in the hollow of the pelvic bone of a fowl. **3.a.** A special delicacy. **b.** Something from which benefits may be extracted. **4.** *Slang.* A close-mouthed person. **—oyster** *intr.v.* **-tered, -ter·ing, -ters.** To gather, dredge for, or raise oysters. [Middle English *oistre,* from Old French, from Latin *ostreum, ostrea,* from Greek *ostreon.* See **ost-** in Appendix.]

Oys·ter Bay (oi′stər). A village of southeast New York on northeast Long Island on an inlet of Long Island Sound. Nearby is Sagamore Hill, Theodore Roosevelt's estate, which is now a national historic site. Population, 7,200.

oyster bed *n.* A place where oysters breed or are raised.

oys·ter·catch·er (oi′stər-kăch′ər) *n.* Any of several wading birds of the genus *Haematopus,* having black and white plumage and a long orange bill and feeding on oysters, clams, and limpets.

oystercatcher

oyster crab *n.* A small crab *(Pinnotheres ostreum)* that lives commensally inside the shell of a bivalve mollusk such as an oyster or a clam.

oyster cracker *n.* A small, dry, usually round soda cracker.

oys·ter·man (oi′stər-mən) *n.* **1.** One who gathers, cultivates, or sells oysters. **2.** *Nautical.* An oyster-dredging vessel.

oyster mushroom *n.* Any of several edible mushrooms of the genus *Pleurotus,* having a soft, flavorful, grayish cap.

♦ **oyster plant** *n. Chiefly Southern U.S.* See **salsify.**

oys·ters Rockefeller (oi′stərz) *pl.n.* Oysters cooked with spinach and a seasoned cream sauce. [Perhaps after John Davison ROCKEFELLER.]

oyster white *n. Color.* A pale yellowish green to light gray.

oz also **oz.** *abbr.* Ounce.

Oz (ŏz) *n.* An unreal, magical, often bizarre place: *regarded New York City as the Oz of the Northeast.* Also called *Land of Oz.* [After the fantasy land *Oz* created by L. Frank Baum in *The Wonderful World of Oz* and other novels.]

oz ap *abbr.* Apothecaries' ounce.

O·zark Plateau or **O·zark Mountains** (ō′zärk′). An upland region of the south-central United States extending from southwest Missouri across Arkansas into eastern Oklahoma.

O·zarks (ō′zärks′), **Lake of the.** A lake of central Missouri formed by Bagnell Dam (completed 1931) on the Osage River.

oz av *abbr.* Avoirdupois ounce.

O·za·wa (ō-zä′wə), **Seiji.** Born 1935. Japanese-born conductor. He directed the San Francisco Symphony (1970–1976) and was named director of the Boston Symphony Orchestra in 1973.

Seiji Ozawa
Photographed in 1972

o·zo·ce·rite (ō′zō-sîr′īt′) also **o·zo·ke·rite** (-kîr′-) *n.* A yellow-brown to black or green hydrocarbon wax, found in irregular veins in sandstones and used in making electrical insulation and polishes. [Greek *ozein,* to smell + Greek *kēros,* wax + -ITE[1].]

o·zone (ō′zōn′) *n.* **1.** A blue gaseous allotrope of oxygen, O_3, formed naturally from diatomic oxygen by electric discharge or exposure to ultraviolet radiation. It is an unstable, powerfully bleaching, poisonous oxidizing agent with a pungent, irritating odor, used to deodorize air, purify water, treat industrial wastes and as a bleach. **2.** *Informal.* Fresh, pure air. [German *Ozon,* from Greek *ozon,* neuter present participle of *ozein,* to smell.] **—o·zo′nic** (ō-zō′nĭk, ō-zŏn′ĭk), **o′zon′ous** (ō′zō′nəs) *adj.*

ozone layer *n.* A region of the upper atmosphere, between about 15 and 30 kilometers (10 and 20 miles) in altitude, containing a relatively high concentration of ozone that absorbs solar ultraviolet radiation in a wavelength range not screened by other atmospheric components. Also called *ozonosphere.*

o·zo·nide (ō′zō-nīd′, -zə-) *n.* Any of various, often explosive chemicals formed by attachment of ozone to the double bond of an unsaturated compound and used in analytical chemistry to locate such bonds.

o·zo·nize (ō′zō-nīz′, -zə-) *tr.v.* **-nized, -niz·ing, -niz·es. 1.** To treat or impregnate with ozone. **2.** To convert (oxygen) to ozone. **—o′zon·iz′er** *n.*

o·zo·no·sphere (ō-zō′nə-sfîr′) *n.* See **ozone layer. —o·zo′no·spher′ic** (-sfîr′ĭk, -sfĕr′-), **o·zo′no·spher′i·cal** (-ĭ-kəl) *adj.*

o·zo·sto·mi·a (ō′zə-stō′mē-ə) *n.* Foul-smelling breath; halitosis. [From Greek *ozostomos,* having bad breath : *ozein,* to smell + *-stomos,* mouthed (from *stoma,* mouth).]

oz t *abbr.* Troy ounce.

ă pat	oi boy
ā pay	ou out
âr care	ŏŏ took
ä father	ōō boot
ĕ pet	ŭ cut
ē be	ûr urge
ĭ pit	th thin
ī pie	*th* this
îr pier	hw which
ŏ pot	zh vision
ō toe	ə about, item
ô paw	♦ regionalism

Stress marks: **′** (primary); ′ (secondary), as in **dictionary** (dĭk′shə-nĕr′ē)

Pp

p¹ or **P** (pē) *n., pl.* **p's** or **P's.** **1.** The 16th letter of the modern English alphabet. **2.** Any of the speech sounds represented by the letter *p.* **3.** The 16th in a series. **4.** Something shaped like the letter P.

p² *Physics.* The symbol for **momentum** (sense 1).

p³ *abbr.* **1.** Or **p.** *Music.* Piano (a direction). **2.** *Physics.* Proton.

P¹ The symbol for the element **phosphorus.**

P² *abbr.* **1.** *Genetics.* Parental generation. **2.** *Physics.* Parity. **3.** *Games.* Pawn. **4.** *Bible.* Peter. **5.** Petite. **6.** *Physics.* Pressure.

P³ *abbr.* First class (airline transportation).

p. *abbr.* **1.** Page. **2.** Part. **3.** *Grammar.* Participle. **4.** *Grammar.* Past. **5.** Penny. **6.** Per. **7.** Peseta. **8.** Peso. **9.** Pint. **10.** Pipe. **11.** Pole. **12.** Population. **13.** Or **P.** President. **14.** Or **P.** Prince. **15.** Pro. **16.** Purl.

P. *abbr.* Priest.

pa (pä) *n. Informal.* Father; papa. [Short for PAPA.]

Pa¹ The symbol for the element **protactinium.**

Pa² *abbr.* Pascal.

PA *abbr.* **1.** Or **Pa.** Pennsylvania. **2.** Public-address system.

p.a. *abbr.* Per annum.

P.A. *abbr.* **1.** Physician's assistant. **2.** Or **P/A.** *Law.* Power of attorney. **3.** Or **PA.** Press agent. **4.** Or **PA.** *Law.* Prosecuting attorney.

pa'an·ga (päng′gə, pä-äng′-) *n.* See table at **currency.** [Tongan.]

PABA (pä′bə) *n.* A crystalline para form of aminobenzoic acid that is part of the vitamin B complex and is widely used in sunscreens to absorb ultraviolet light. [P(ARA)-A(MINO)B(ENZOIC) A(CID).]

pab·lum (păb′ləm) *n.* Trite, insipid, or simplistic writing, speech, or conceptualization: *"We have to settle for the pablum that passes for the inside dope"* (Julie Salamon). [From PABLUM.]

Pab·lum (păb′ləm). A trademark used for a bland, soft cereal for infants.

pab·u·lum (păb′yə-ləm) *n.* **1.** A substance that gives nourishment; food. **2.** Insipid intellectual nourishment: *"TV . . . gobbled up comedy material and spat it out as pabulum"* (Ralph Corliss). [Latin *pābulum.* See **pā-** in Appendix. Sense 2, by confusion with PABLUM.]

pac also **pack** (păk) *n.* **1.** A moccasin or soft shoe designed to be worn inside a boot. **2.** A shoepac. [Short for *shoepac,* alteration (influenced by SHOE) of pidgin Delaware *seppock,* shoe, from Unami Delaware *chípahko,* shoes.]

PAC (păk) *n., pl.* **PAC's** or **PACs.** A political action committee.

Pac. *abbr.* Pacific.

pa·ca (pä′kə, păk′ə) *n.* A large nocturnal burrowing rodent of the genus *Cuniculus,* found in South and Central America and similar to the agouti, especially the spotted species *C. paca* that lives on plants and fruit and is hunted for its edible flesh. [Portuguese and American Spanish, both from Tupi *páca.*]

pace¹ (pās) *n.* **1.** A step made in walking; a stride. **2.** A unit of length equal to 30 inches (0.76 meter). **3.** The distance spanned by a step or stride, especially: **a.** The modern version of the Roman pace, measuring five English feet. Also called *geometric pace.* **b.** Thirty inches at quick marching time or 36 at double time. **c.** Five Roman feet or 58.1 English inches, measured from the point at which the heel of one foot is raised to the point at which it is set down again after an intervening step by the other foot. **4.a.** The rate of speed at which a person, an animal, or a group walks or runs. **b.** The rate of speed at which an activity or a movement proceeds. **5.** A manner of walking or running: *a jaunty pace.* **6.** A gait of a horse in which both feet on one side leave and return to the ground together. **—pace** *v.* **paced, pac·ing, pac·es.** *—tr.* **1.** To walk or stride back and forth across: *paced the floor nervously.* **2.** To measure by counting the number of steps needed to cover a distance. **3.** To set or regulate the rate of speed for. **4.** To train (a horse) in a particular gait, especially the pace. *—intr.* **1.** To walk with long, deliberate steps. **2.** To go at the pace. Used of a horse or rider. [Middle English, from Old French *pas,* from Latin *passus,* from past participle of *pandere,* to stretch, spread out. See **pete-** in Appendix.]

pa·ce² (pā′sē, pä′chā, -kā) *prep.* With the permission of; with deference to. Used to express polite or ironically polite disagreement: *I have not, pace my detractors, entered into any secret negotiations.* [Latin *pāce,* ablative of *pāx,* peace. See **pag-** in Appendix.] **—pa′ce** *adv.*

pace car (pās) *n. Sports.* A usually high-performance automobile that leads a group of competing cars through the pace lap of a race but does not participate in the race.

pace lap (pās) *n. Sports.* The initial lap of a motor vehicle race in which the racers warm up their engines and prepare for a fast start.

pace·mak·er (pās′mā′kər) *n.* **1.** *Sports.* One who sets the pace in a race. Also called *pacer, pacesetter.* **2.** A leader in a field: *the fashion house that is the pacemaker.* Also called *pacesetter.* **3.a.** *Biology.* A part of the body, such as the mass of muscle fibers of the sinoatrial node, that sets the pace or rhythm of physiological activity. **b.** *Medicine.* Any of several usually miniaturized and surgically implanted electronic devices used to stimulate or regulate contractions of the heart muscle. **4.** *Biochemistry.* A substance that regulates a series of related reactions. **—pace′mak′ing** *adj. & n.*

pac·er (pā′sər) *n.* **1.** A horse trained to pace. **2.** *Sports.* See **pacemaker** (sense 1).

pace·set·ter (pās′sĕt′ər) *n.* **1.** *Sports.* See **pacemaker** (sense 1). **2.** See **pacemaker** (sense 2). **—pace′set′ting** *adj. & n.*

pa·cha (pä′shə, păsh′ə, pə-shä′) *n.* Variant of **pasha.**

pa·chin·ko (pə-chĭng′kō) *n. Games.* A Japanese gambling game played on a vertical pinball machine. [Japanese.]

pa·chi·si (pə-chē′zē) *n.* An ancient game of India similar to backgammon that uses cowrie shells instead of dice. [Hindi *pacīsī,* from *pacīs,* twenty-five : Sanskrit *pañca,* five; see **penkʷe** in Appendix + Sanskrit *viṁśatiḥ,* twenty; see **wīkm̥tī** in Appendix.]

pach·ou·li (pə-cho͞o′lē, păch′o͞o-lē) *n.* Variant of **patchouli.**

Pa·chu·ca (pə-cho͞o′kə, pä-cho͞o′kä) also **Pachuca de So·to** (dĭ sō′tō, dĕ). A city of central Mexico north-northeast of Mexico City. It was founded in 1534 as a silver-mining center on the site of an ancient Toltec city. Population, 110,351.

pa·chu·co (pə-cho͞o′kō) *n., pl.* **-cos.** A Mexican-American youth or teenager, especially one who dresses in flamboyant clothes and belongs to a neighborhood gang. [American Spanish, possibly alteration of *payuco,* yokel, from *payo,* rustic.]

pach·y·derm (păk′ĭ-dûrm′) *n.* Any of various large, thick-skinned, hoofed mammals such as the elephant, rhinoceros, or hippopotamus. [French *pachyderme,* from New Latin **Pachyderma,* sing. of *Pachydermata,* obsolete order name, from Greek *pakhudermos,* thick-skinned : *pakhus,* thick + *derma,* skin; see DERMA¹.] **—pach′y·der′mal, pach′y·der′mic, pach′y·der′mous** *adj.*

pach·y·der·ma·tous (păk′ĭ-dûr′mə-təs) *adj.* **1.** Of, relating to, or characteristic of a pachyderm. **2.** Thick-skinned; insensitive. [New Latin *Pachydermata,* obsolete order name; see PACHYDERM + -OUS.]

pach·y·san·dra (păk′ĭ-săn′drə) *n.* Any of several plants of the genus *Pachysandra,* especially the evergreen *P. terminalis* native to Japan, having toothed leaves and inconspicuous white unisexual flowers. Also called *Japanese spurge.* [New Latin *Pachysandra,* genus name : Greek *pakhus,* thick + New Latin *-andrus,* -androus (after its thick stamens).]

pach·y·tene (păk′ĭ-tēn′) *n.* The third stage of the prophase of meiosis during which the homologous chromosomes become short and thick and divide into four distinct chromatids. [French *pachytène* : Greek *pakhus,* thick + *-tène,* ribbon (from Latin *taenia;* see TAENIA).]

pa·cif·a·rin (pə-sĭf′ər-ĭn) *n.* Any of various bacterial products that, introduced in small amounts, protect an organism from an infection or a disease without killing the infectious agent. [Origin unknown.]

Pacif. *abbr.* Pacific.

pa·cif·ic (pə-sĭf′ĭk) also **pa·cif·i·cal** (-ĭ-kəl) *adj.* **1.** Tending

Phoenician
To represent the sound of *p,* the Phoenicians made use of a sign they called *pē.*

Early Greek
In adapting the Phoenician alphabet the Greeks retained the letter's value and called it *pi.*

Roman
In the course of time it made its way to Rome, where it was slightly altered to take on the shape we know today.

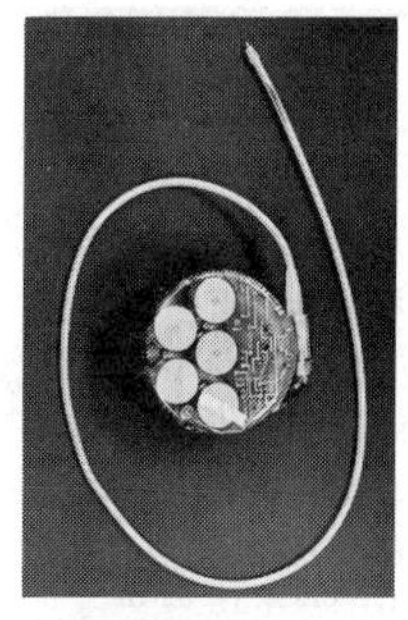

pacemaker

pad¹
Lacrosse goalie

to diminish or put an end to conflict; appeasing. **2.** Of a peaceful nature; tranquil. [French *pacifique,* from Old French *pacifice,* from Latin *pācificus* : *pāx, pāc-,* peace; see **pag-** in Appendix + *-ficus,* -fic.] **—pa·cif'i·cal·ly** *adv.*

Pa·cif·i·ca (pə-sĭf'ĭ-kə). A city of western California on the Pacific coast south of San Francisco. It is mainly residential. Population, 36,866.

pac·i·fi·ca·tion (păs'ə-fĭ-kā'shən) *n.* **1.** The act of pacifying or the condition of being pacified; appeasement. **2.a.** Reduction, as of a rebellious district, to peaceful submission: *"Real pacification is hard to get in the Vietnamese countryside"* (McGeorge Bundy). **b.** Practical measures or policy aiming to effect this type of submission. **3.** Often **Pacification.** A peace treaty: *the Pacification of Ghent.* **—pa·cif'i·ca'tor** (pə-sĭf'ĭ-kā'tər) *n.* **—pa·cif'i·ca·to'ry** (-kə-tôr'ē, -tōr'ē) *adj.*

Pa·cif·ic Islands (pə-sĭf'ĭk), **Trust Territory of the.** A group of more than 2,000 islands and islets of the northwest Pacific Ocean administered by the United States as a United Nations trust territory from 1947 to 1978. It originally included the Caroline, Marianas (excluding Guam), and Marshall islands. Parts of the territory are now self-governing. **—Pacific Islander** *n.*

pa·cif·i·cism (pə-sĭf'ĭ-sĭz'əm) *n.* Pacifism. **—pa·cif'i·cist** *n.*

Pacific Northwest. A region of the northwest United States usually including the states of Washington and Oregon. The term is also used to refer to the southwest part of British Columbia, Canada.

Pacific Ocean. The largest of the world's oceans, divided into the **North Pacific** and the **South Pacific.** It extends from the western Americas to eastern Asia and Australia.

Pacific Rim. The countries and landmasses surrounding the Pacific Ocean, often considered as a socioeconomic region.

Pacific Standard Time *n. Abbr.* **PST, P.S.T.** Standard time in the eighth time zone west of Greenwich, England, reckoned at 120° west and used, for example, in the Pacific coastal states of the United States. Also called *Pacific Time.*

pac·i·fi·er (păs'ə-fī'ər) *n.* A rubber or plastic nipple or teething ring for a baby to suck or chew on.

pac·i·fism (păs'ə-fĭz'əm) *n.* **1.** The belief that disputes between nations should and can be settled peacefully. **2.a.** Opposition to war or violence as a means of resolving disputes. **b.** Such opposition demonstrated by refusal to participate in military action. [French *pacifisme,* from *pacifique,* pacific. See PACIFIC.] **—pac'i·fist** *n.* **—pac'i·fis'tic** *adj.* **—pac'i·fis'ti·cal·ly** *adv.*

pac·i·fy (păs'ə-fī') *tr.v.* **-fied, -fy·ing, -fies. 1.** To ease the anger or agitation of. **2.** To end war, fighting, or violence in; establish peace in. [Middle English *pacifien,* from Old French *pacifier,* from Latin *pācificāre* : *pāx, pāc-,* peace; see **pag-** in Appendix + *-ficāre,* -fy.] **—pac'i·fi'a·ble** *adj.*

SYNONYMS: *pacify, mollify, conciliate, appease, placate.* These verbs all refer to allaying another's anger, belligerence, discontent, or agitation. To *pacify* is to restore calm to or establish peace in: *"The explanation . . . was merely an invention framed to pacify his guests"* (Charlotte Brontë). *An army was required in order to pacify the islands. Mollify* stresses the soothing of hostile feelings: *"In that case go ahead with the project," she said, mollified by his agreeable manner. Conciliate* usually implies winning over, often by reasoning and with mutual concessions: *"A wise government knows how to enforce with temper or to conciliate with dignity"* (George Grenville). *Appease* and *placate* suggest the satisfaction of claims or demands or the tempering of antagonism, often through the granting of concessions: *The child is adept at appeasing her parents' anger with a joke or compliment. Even a written apology failed to placate the indignant hostess.*

Pa·cin·i·an corpuscle (pə-sĭn'ē-ən) *n.* An encapsulated receptor found in deep layers of the skin that senses vibratory pressure and touch. [After Filippo *Pacini* (1812–1883), Italian anatomist.]

pack¹ (păk) *n. Abbr.* **pk. 1.a.** A collection of items tied up or wrapped; a bundle. **b.** A container made to be carried on the back of a person or an animal. **2.** The amount, as of food, that is processed and packaged at one time or in one season. **3.** A small package containing a standard number of identical or similar items: *a pack of matches.* **4.a.** A complete set of related items: *a pack of cards.* **b.** *Informal.* A large amount; a heap: *earned a pack of money.* **5.a.** A group of animals, such as dogs or wolves, that run and hunt together. See Synonyms at **flock¹. b.** A gang of people: *a pack of hoodlums.* **c.** An organized troop having common interests: *a Cub Scout pack.* **6.** A mass of large pieces of floating ice driven together. **7.** *Medicine.* **a.** The swathing of a patient or a body part in hot, cold, wet, or dry materials, such as cloth towels, sheets, or blankets. **b.** The materials so used. **c.** A material, such as gauze, that is therapeutically inserted into a body cavity or wound; packing. **8.** An ice pack; an ice bag. **9.** A cosmetic paste that is applied to the skin, allowed to dry, and then rinsed off. **—pack** *v.* **packed, pack·ing, packs.** —*tr.* **1.** To fold, roll, or combine into a bundle; wrap up. **2.a.** To put into a receptacle for transporting or storing: *pack one's belongings.* **b.** To fill up with items: *pack one's trunk.* **3.** To process and put into containers in order to preserve, transport, or sell: *packed the fruit in jars.* **4.a.** To bring together (persons or things) closely; crowd together: *managed to pack 300 students into the lecture hall.* **b.** To fill up tight; cram. **5.** *Medicine.* **a.** To wrap (a patient) in a pack. **b.** To insert a pack into a body cavity or wound. **6.** To wrap tightly for protection or to prevent leakage: *pack a valve stem.* **7.** To press together; compact firmly: *packed the clay and straw into bricks.* **8.** *Informal.* To carry, deliver, or have available for action: *a thug who packed a pistol; a fighter who packs a hard punch; a storm that packed winds in excess of 75 miles an hour.* **9.** To send unceremoniously: *The parents packed both children off to bed.* **10.** To constitute (a voting panel) by appointment, selection, or arrangement in such a way that it is favorable to one's purposes or point of view; rig: *"In 1937 Roosevelt threatened to pack the court"* (New Republic). —*intr.* **1.** To place one's belongings in boxes or luggage for transporting or storing. **2.** To be susceptible of compact storage: *Dishes pack more easily than glasses.* **3.** To form lumps or masses; become compacted. ***—idiom.* pack it in.** *Informal.* To cease work or activity: *Let's pack it in for the day.* [Middle English *pak,* possibly of Low German origin.] **—pack'a·bil'i·ty** *n.* **—pack'a·ble** *adj.*

pack² (păk) *n.* Variant of **pac.**

pack·age (păk'ĭj) *n. Abbr.* **pkg. 1.** A wrapped or boxed object; a parcel. **2.** A container in which something is packed for storage or transportion. **3.a.** A preassembled unit. **b.** A commodity, such as food, uniformly processed and containerized. **4.** A proposition or an offer composed of several items, each of which must be accepted. **—package** *tr.v.* **-aged, -ag·ing, -ag·es.** To place into a package or make a package of. **—pack'ag·er** *n.*

package store *n.* A store that sells sealed bottles of alcoholic beverages for consumption off the premises.

pack·ag·ing (păk'ə-jĭng) *n.* **1.** The act, process, industry, art, or style of packing. **2.** Material used for making packages. **3.** The manner in which something, such as a proposal or product, or someone, such as a candidate or an author, is presented to the public.

pack animal *n.* An animal, such as a mule, used to carry loads.

packed (păkt) *adj.* **1.** Crowded to capacity: *a packed theater.* **2.** Compressed: *ground covered with wet, heavily packed leaves.* **3.** *Informal.* Filled with. Often used in combination: *a thrill-packed television series.*

pack·er (păk'ər) *n.* **1.** One that packs: *a packer of boxes in a warehouse.* **2.** One whose occupation is the processing and packing of wholesale goods, usually meat products: *meat packers.*

pack·et (păk'ĭt) *n. Abbr.* **pkt. 1.** A small package or bundle. **2.** *Informal.* A sizable sum of money. **3.** *Nautical.* A boat, usually a coastal or river steamer, that plies a regular route and carries passengers, freight, and mail. **4.** *Computer Science.* A short block of data transmitted in a packet switching network. [Middle English *pekette,* probably diminutive of *pak,* pack. See PACK¹.]

packet switch·ing (swĭch'ĭng) *n.* *Computer Science.* A method of data transmission in which small blocks of data are transmitted rapidly over a channel dedicated to the connection only for the duration of the packet's transmission.

pack·horse (păk'hôrs') *n.* A horse used as a pack animal.

pack ice *n.* Floating ice that has been driven together into a single mass.

pack·ing (păk'ĭng) *n.* **1.** The act or process of one that packs. **2.** The processing and packaging of manufactured products, especially food products. **3.** A material used to prevent leakage or seepage, as around a pipe joint. **4.a.** The insertion of gauze or other material into a body cavity or wound for therapeutic purposes. **b.** The material so used; a pack.

packing fraction *n.* *Physics.* The quotient of the algebraic difference between the isotopic mass and the mass number of a nuclide, divided by its mass number, often interpreted as a measure of stability.

pack·ing·house (păk'ĭng-hous') *n.* **1.** A firm that slaughters, processes, and packs livestock into meat and meat products. **2.** A firm that processes and packs food products other than meat.

pack·man (păk'măn', -mən) *n.* A peddler.

♦ **pack rat** *n.* **1.** Any of various small North American rodents of the genus *Neotoma* that collect in or around their nests a great variety of small objects. Also called *trade rat, wood rat.* **2.** *Western U.S.* A petty thief. **3.** *Slang.* A collector of miscellaneous objects.

pack·sack (păk'săk') *n.* A canvas or leather traveling bag designed to be carried while strapped to the shoulders.

pack·sad·dle (păk'săd'l) *n.* A saddle on which loads can be secured.

pack·thread (păk'thrĕd') *n.* A strong two-ply or three-ply twine for sewing or tying packages or bundles.

pack train *n.* A line of animals, such as horses or mules, loaded with supplies for an expedition.

pact (păkt) *n.* **1.** A formal agreement, such as one between nations; a treaty. **2.** A compact; a bargain. [Middle English, from Old French, from Latin *pactum,* from neuter sing. past participle of *pacīscī,* to agree. See **pag-** in Appendix.]

pad¹ (păd) *n.* **1.** A thin, cushionlike mass of soft material used to fill, to give shape, or to protect against jarring, scraping, or other injury. **2.** A flexible saddle without a frame. **3.** An ink-soaked cushion used to ink a rubber stamp. **4.** A number of sheets of paper of the same size stacked one on top of the other and glued together at one end; a tablet. **5.** The broad, floating leaf of an aquatic plant such as the water lily. **6.a.** The cush-

ă pat	oi boy
ā pay	ou out
âr care	ŏŏ took
ä father	ōō boot
ĕ pet	ŭ cut
ē be	ûr urge
ĭ pit	th thin
ī pie	*th* this
îr pier	hw which
ŏ pot	zh vision
ō toe	ə about, item
ô paw	♦ regionalism

Stress marks: **'** (primary); ' (secondary), as in **dictionary** (dĭk'shə-nĕr'ē)

ionlike flesh on the underpart of the toes and feet of many animals. **b.** The foot of such an animal. **7.** The fleshy underside of the end of a finger or toe. **8. a.** A launch pad. **b.** A helipad. **9.** A keypad. **10.** *Slang.* One's apartment or room. **—pad** *tr.v.* **pad·ded, pad·ding, pads. 1.** To line or stuff with soft material. **2.** To lengthen (something written or spoken) with extraneous material: *pad a résumé; pad an expense account.* **—*idiom.* on the pad.** *Slang.* Taking bribes. [Origin unknown.] **—pad′less** *adj.*

pad² (păd) *v.* **pad·ded, pad·ding, pads.** *—intr.* **1.** To go about on foot. **2.** To move or walk about almost inaudibly. *—tr.* To go along (a route) on foot: *padding the long road into town.* **—pad** *n.* **1.** A muffled sound resembling that of soft footsteps. **2.** A horse with a plodding gait. [Probably of Low German origin; akin to *path.*] **—pad′der** *n.*

Pa·dang (pä′däng′, pä-däng′). A city of western Indonesia on the Indian Ocean and the west-central coast of Sumatra Island. It is a major port, trading in tea, coffee, and spices. Population, 296,680.

pa·dauk (pə-dôk′) also **pa·douk** (-do͝ok′) *n.* **1.** A tropical tree *(Pterocarpus indicus)* native to southeast Asia, having reddish wood with a mottled or striped black grain. **2.** The wood of this tree, used mainly for decorative cabinetwork. Also called *amboyna.* [Burmese.]

pad·ding (păd′ĭng) *n.* **1.** The act of stuffing, filling, or lining. **2.** A soft material used to make pads or a pad. **3.** Extraneous material added to written work to make it longer.

pad·dle¹ (păd′l) *n.* **1.** *Nautical.* A wooden implement having a blade at one end or sometimes at both ends, used without an oarlock to propel a canoe or small boat. **2.** Any of various implements resembling the paddle of a boat or canoe, as: **a.** An iron tool for stirring molten ore in a furnace. **b.** A tool with a shovellike blade used to mix materials in glassmaking. **c.** A potter's pallet. **d.** A narrow board used to beat clothes in laundering by hand. **e.** A flattened board used to administer physical punishment. **f.** *Sports.* A light wooden racket used in playing table tennis. **3.** A board on a paddle wheel. **4.** A flipper or flattened appendage of certain animals. **5.** The act of paddling. **—paddle** *v.* **-dled, -dling, -dles.** *—intr.* **1.** *Nautical.* **a.** To propel a watercraft with paddles or a paddle. **b.** To row slowly and gently. **2.** To move through water by means of repeated short strokes of the limbs. *—tr.* **1.** *Nautical.* **a.** To propel (a watercraft) with paddles or a paddle. **b.** To convey in a watercraft propelled by paddles. **2.** To spank with a paddle, especially as a punishment. **3.** To stir or shape (material) with a paddle. [Middle English *padell,* implement used for cleaning a plowshare, perhaps from Medieval Latin *padela.*] **—pad′dler** *n.*

pad·dle² (păd′l) *intr.v.* **-dled, -dling, -dles. 1.** To dabble about in shallow water; splash gently with the hands or feet. **2.** To move with a waddling motion; toddle. [Perhaps of Low German origin.]

pad·dle·ball (păd′l-bôl′) *n.* *Sports.* **1.** A game for two to four participants played with a wooden or plastic perforated paddle and a ball similar to a tennis ball on a court having one, three, or four walls. **2.** The ball used in this game.

pad·dle·board (păd′l-bôrd′, -bōrd′) *n.* *Sports.* A long, narrow, floatable board used especially in surfing.

pad·dle·boat (păd′l-bōt′) *n.* *Nautical.* A boat, especially a steamship, propelled through the water by paddle wheels on each side or by one paddle wheel astern. Also called *paddle wheeler.*

pad·dle·fish (păd′l-fĭsh′) *n., pl.* **paddlefish** or **-fish·es.** A fish of the family Polyodontidae, having a long paddle-shaped snout, especially *Polyodon spathula* of the Mississippi River basin. Also called *spoonbill.*

paddle wheel *n.* *Nautical.* A wheel with boards or paddles affixed around its circumference, usually driven by steam to propel a ship. **—pad′dle-wheel′** (păd′l-hwēl′, -wēl′) *adj.*

paddle wheeler *n.* *Nautical.* See **paddleboat.**

pad·dling (păd′lĭng, păd′l-ĭng) *n.* **1.** *Nautical.* The act of moving a boat by means of a paddle. **2.** A whipping or spanking with a paddle.

pad·dock (păd′ək) *n.* **1.** A fenced area, usually near a stable, used chiefly for grazing horses. **2.** *Sports.* **a.** An enclosure at a racetrack where the horses are assembled, saddled, and paraded before each race. **b.** An area of an automobile racetrack where cars are prepared before a race. **3.** *Australian.* A piece of fenced-in land. **—paddock** *tr.v.* **-docked, -dock·ing, -docks.** To confine in a paddock. [Alteration of Middle English *parrok,* from Old English *pearroc.*]

pad·dy (păd′ē) *n., pl.* **-dies. 1.** Rice, especially in the husk, whether gathered or still in the field. **2.** A specially irrigated or flooded field where rice is grown. [Malay *padi.*]

Pad·dy (păd′ē) *n.* *Offensive Slang.* Used as a disparaging term for an Irishman. [Nickname for Irish Gaelic *Pádraig,* Patrick.]

paddy field *n.* A rice paddy.

paddy wagon *n.* *Slang.* A van used by police for taking suspects into custody. [Origin unknown.]

Pa·der·born (pä′dər-bôrn′). A city of west-central Germany northwest of Kassel. It joined the Hanseatic League in the 13th century and passed to Prussia in 1802. Population, 109,514.

Pa·de·rew·ski (păd′ə-rĕf′skē, -rĕv′-, pä′də-), **Ignace Jan.** 1860–1941. Polish pianist and politician who served as prime minister (1919–1920) and led (1940–1941) the exiled Polish government.

Pa·di·shah (pä′dĭ-shä′) *n.* **1.** Used formerly as a title for the monarch of Iran. **2.** Used formerly as a title for the sultan of Turkey. [Persian *pādshāh* : Old Persian *pati-,* master; see **poti-** in Appendix + Persian *shāh,* king.]

pad·lock (păd′lŏk′) *n.* A detachable lock with a U-shaped bar hinged at one end, designed to be passed through the staple of a hasp or a link in a chain and then snapped shut. **—padlock** *tr.v.* **-locked, -lock·ing, -locks.** To lock up with or as if with a padlock. [Middle English *padlok* : *pad-,* of unknown meaning + *lok,* lock; see LOCK¹.]

pa·douk (pə-do͝ok′) *n.* Variant of **padauk.**

pa·dre (pä′drā, -drē) *n.* **1.** Father. Used as a form of address for a priest in Italy, Spain, Portugal, and Latin America. **2.** *Informal.* A military chaplain. **3.** *Chiefly British.* A parson. [Spanish, Italian, or Portuguese, all from Latin *pater, patr-,* father. See **peter-** in Appendix.]

pa·dro·ne (pə-drō′nē, -nā) *n., pl.* **-nes** (-nēz, -nāz) or **-ni** (-nē). **1.** An owner or a manager, especially of an inn; a proprietor. **2.** A man who exploitatively employs or finds work for Italian immigrants in America. [Italian, from Latin *patrōnus,* patron. See PATRON.] **—pa·dro′nism** *n.*

Pad·u·a (păj′o͞o-ə, păd′yo͞o-ə). A city of northeast Italy west of Venice. An important cultural center during the Middle Ages, it was known for its artistic and architectural works by Giotto, Mantegna, and Donatello. Galileo taught at its university from 1592 to 1610. Population, 231,337.

pad·u·a·soy (păj′o͞o-ə-soi′) *n.* **1.** A rich, heavy silk fabric with a corded effect. **2.** A hanging or garment made of this fabric. [Alteration (influenced by PADUA) of French *pou-de-soie,* from Old French *pout-de-soie* : *pout,* of uncertain meaning + *de,* of (from Latin *dē,* of; see DE–) + *soie,* silk (from Vulgar Latin *sēta, from Late Latin *saeta,* raw silk, from Latin, bristle).]

Pa·du·cah (pə-do͞o′kə, -dyo͞o′-). A city of western Kentucky on the Ohio River and the Illinois border. It is a tobacco market and manufacturing center. Population, 29,315.

pae·an also **pe·an** (pē′ən) *n.* **1.** *Music.* A song of joyful praise or exultation. **2.** A fervent expression of joy or praise: *"The art . . . was a paean to paganism"* (Will Durant). **3.** An ancient Greek hymn of thanksgiving or invocation, especially to Apollo. [Latin *paeān,* hymn of thanksgiving, often addressed to Apollo, from Greek *paian,* from *Paian,* a title of Apollo.] **—pae′an·is′tic** (-ĭs′tĭk) *adj.*

paed– or **paedo–** *pref.* Variants of **pedo–².**

pae·do·gen·e·sis also **pe·do·gen·e·sis** (pē′dō-jĕn′ĭ-sĭs) *n.* Reproduction of young during the larval or preadult stage, occurring chiefly in insects. **—pae′do·ge·net′ic** (-jə-nĕt′ĭk) *adj.*

paed·o·morph also **ped·o·morph** (pĕd′ə-môrf′, pē′də-) *n.* An organism that retains juvenile characteristics in the adult form.

paed·o·mor·phism also **ped·o·mor·phism** (pĕd′ə-môr′fĭz′əm, pē′də-) *n.* Retention of juvenile characteristics in the adult, occurring in mammals. **—paed′o·mor′phic** (-fĭk) *adj.*

paed·o·mor·pho·sis also **ped·o·mor·pho·sis** (pĕd′ə-môr′fə-sĭs, pē′də-) *n., pl.* **-ses** (-sēz′). Phylogenetic change in which juvenile characteristics are retained in the adult form of an organism.

pa·el·la (pä-ĕl′ə, pä-ā′lyä, -ā′yä) *n.* A saffron-flavored Spanish dish made with varying combinations of rice, vegetables, meat, chicken, and seafood. [Catalan, frying pan, paella, from Old French *paelle,* frying pan, pot, from Latin *patella,* diminutive of *patina,* pan. See PATEN.]

pae·on (pē′ən, -ŏn′) *n.* In quantitative verse, a foot of one long syllable and three short syllables occurring in any order. [Latin *paeōn,* from Greek *paiōn,* from *paian, paiōn,* paean. See PAEAN.]

Paes·tum (pĕs′təm, pē′stəm). An ancient city of southern Italy on the Gulf of Salerno. Founded as a Greek colony before 600 B.C., it flourished as part of Magna Graecia and was taken by Rome in 273 B.C.

pa·gan (pā′gən) *n.* **1.** One who is not a Christian, Moslem, or Jew; a heathen. **2.** One who has no religion. **3.** A non-Christian. **4.** A hedonist. **—pagan** *adj.* **1.** Not Christian, Moslem, or Jewish. **2.** Professing no religion; heathen. [Middle English, from Late Latin *pāgānus,* from Latin, country-dweller, civilian, from *pāgus,* country, rural district. See **pag-** in Appendix.] **—pa′gan·dom** (-dəm) *n.* **—pa′gan·ish** *adj.* **—pa′gan·ism** *n.*

Pa·ga·ni·ni (păg′ə-nē′nē, pä′gä-), **Nicolo.** 1782–1840. Italian violinist and composer whose works include six violin concertos and many other virtuoso violin pieces.

pa·gan·ize (pā′gə-nīz′) *tr. & intr.v.* **-ized, -iz·ing, -iz·es.** To make or become pagan. **—pa′gan·i·za′tion** (-gə-nĭ-zā′shən) *n.*

page¹ (pāj) *n.* **1.** *Abbr.* **p., pg. a.** One side of a leaf, as of a book, letter, newspaper, or manuscript, especially the entire leaf: *tore a page from the book.* **b.** The writing or printing on one side of a leaf. **c.** The type set for printing one side of a leaf. **2.** A noteworthy or memorable event: *a new page in history.* **3.** *Computer Science.* **a.** A quantity of memory storage equal to between 512 and 4,096 bytes. **b.** A quantity of source program coding equal to between 8 and 64 lines. **4. pages.** A source or record of knowledge: *in the pages of science.* **—page** *tr.v.* **paged, pag·**

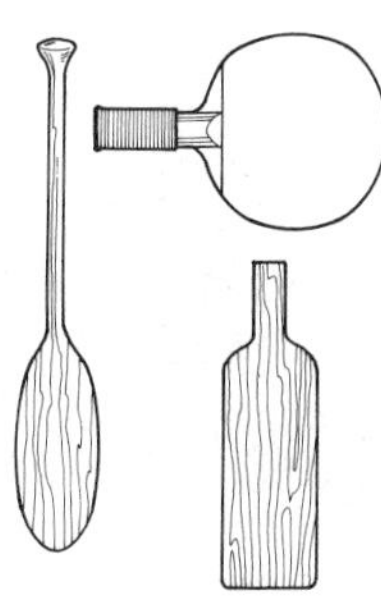

paddle¹
Canoe (*left*), table tennis (*top right*), and pottery (*bottom right*)

paddle wheel
On the *Mississippi Queen*

paddy
Rice paddies in Java

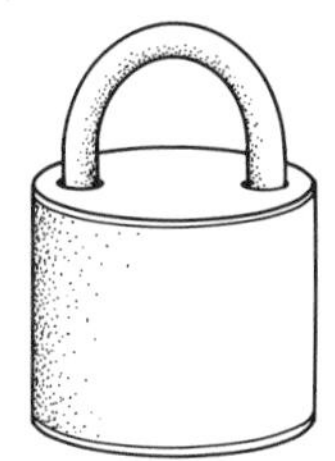

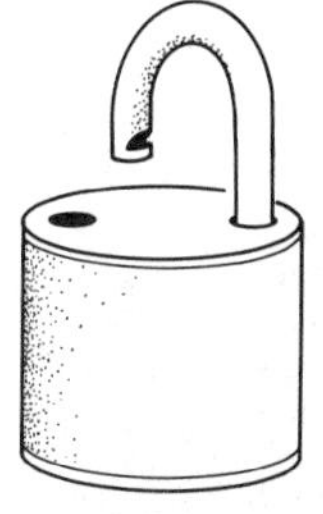

padlock
Top: Locked
Bottom: Unlocked

pagoda

ing, pag•es. 1. To number the pages of; paginate. **2.** To turn the pages of: *page through a magazine.* [French, alteration of Old French *pagine,* from Latin *pāgina.* See **pag-** in Appendix.] **—page′ful′** *n.*

page[2] (pāj) *n.* **1.** A boy who acted as a knight's attendant as the first stage of training for chivalric knighthood. **2.** A youth in ceremonial employment or attendance at court. **3.a.** One who is employed to run errands, carry messages, or act as a guide in a hotel, theater, or club. **b.** One who is similarly employed in the U.S. Congress or another legislature. **4.** A boy who holds the bride's train at a wedding. **—page** *tr.v.* **paged, pag•ing, pag•es. 1.** To summon or call (a person) by name. **2.** To summon or call (a person) by means of a beeper. **3.** To attend as a page. [Middle English, from Old French, possibly from Italian *paggio,* perhaps ultimately from Greek *paidion,* diminutive of *pais, paid-,* child. See **pau-** in Appendix.]

Page (pāj), **Thomas Nelson.** 1853–1922. American writer and diplomat remembered for his nostalgic works about the Old South, such as *Two Little Confederates* (1888) and *Red Rock* (1898).

Page, Walter Hines. 1855–1918. American journalist and diplomat. As U.S. ambassador to Great Britain (1913–1918) he encouraged American participation in World War I.

pag•eant (păj′ənt) *n.* **1.** An elaborate public dramatic presentation that usually depicts a historical or traditional event. **2.** A spectacular procession or celebration. **3.** Colorful, showy display; pageantry or pomp. [Middle English *pagin, pagent,* moveable stage for a mystery play, mystery play, alteration of Medieval Latin *pāgina,* probably from Latin, page. See **pag-** in Appendix.]

Mohammed Reza Pahlavi

pag•eant•ry (păj′ən-trē) *n., pl.* **-ries. 1.** Pageants and their presentation. **2.a.** Grand display; pomp. **b.** Empty pomp or show; flashy display.

page•boy (pāj′boi′) *n.* **1.** One, usually a boy, who acts or serves as a page. **2.** A hairstyle, usually shoulder-length, with the ends of the hair curled under smoothly in a loose roll.

pag•er (pā′jər) *n.* See **beeper** (sense 2).

Pag•et (păj′ĭt), Sir **James.** 1814–1899. British surgeon and pathologist who discovered (1834) the cause of trichinosis.

Pag•et's disease (păj′ĭts) *n.* **1.** A disease, occurring chiefly in old age, in which the bones become enlarged and weakened, often resulting in fracture or deformation. **2.** A form of breast cancer affecting the areola and nipple. [After Sir James PAGET.]

page-turn•er (pāj′tûr′nər) *n. Informal.* A very interesting, exciting, or suspenseful book, usually a novel: *"The book is a page-turner"* (Frank Conroy).

pag•i•nal (păj′ə-nəl) *adj.* **1.** Of, relating to, or consisting of pages. **2.** Page for page: *a paginal facsimile.* [Late Latin *pāginālis,* from Latin *pāgina,* page. See PAGE[1].]

pag•i•nate (păj′ə-nāt′) *tr.v.* **-nat•ed, -nat•ing, -nates.** To number the pages of; page. [From Latin *pāgina,* page. See PAGE[1].]

pag•i•na•tion (păj′ə-nā′shən) *n.* **1.** The system by which pages are numbered. **2.** The arrangement and number of pages in a book, as noted in a catalog or bibliography.

pag•ing (pā′jĭng) *n. Computer Science.* The transfer of pages of data between a computer's main memory and an auxiliary memory.

pa•go•da (pə-gō′də) *n.* **1.** A religious building of the Far East, especially a many-storied Buddhist tower, erected as a memorial or shrine. **2.** A structure, such as a garden pavilion, built in imitation of a many-storied Buddhist tower. [Portuguese *pagode,* perhaps from Tamil *pagavadi,* from Sanskrit *bhagavatī,* goddess, from *bhagavant-,* blessed, from *bhagaḥ,* good fortune. See **bhag-** in Appendix.]

painted lady
Vanessa cardui

Pa•go Pa•go (päng′ō-päng′ō, păng′gō-păng′gō, päng′gō-päng′gō, pä′gō-pä′gō, pă′gō-pă′gō) also **Pan•go Pan•go** (päng′ō päng′ō, păng′gō păng′gō, päng′gō päng′gō). The capital of American Samoa, on the southern coast of Tutuila Island. It is a port and naval station. Population, 3,075.

pah (pä) *interj.* Used to express disgust or irritation.

pah•la•vi (pä′lə-vē′) *n., pl.* **-vis.** A gold coin formerly used in Iran. [Persian *pahlawī,* after Reza Shah *Pahlavi* (1878–1944), Shah of Iran.]

Pah•la•vi (pä′lə-vē′) also **Peh•le•vi** (pā′-) *n.* An Iranian language used in Persia during the reign of the Sassanids. [Persian *pahlawī,* from *Pahlav,* Parthia, from Old Persian *Parthava-.*]

Pahlavi, Mohammed Reza. 1919–1980. Shah of Iran from 1941 to 1979, when he was deposed by Islamic fundamentalists.

paid[1] (pād) *v.* Past tense and past participle of **pay**[1].

paid[2] (pād) *v. Nautical.* A past tense and a past participle of **pay**[2].

Paige (pāj), **Leroy Robert.** Known as "Satchel." 1906–1982. American baseball player who became the first Black pitcher in the American League (1948).

painter[1]
House painter

pail (pāl) *n.* **1.** A watertight cylindrical vessel, open at the top and fitted with a handle; a bucket. **2.** The amount that a pail can hold. [Middle English *paile,* probably from Old French *paele,* warming pan, perhaps from Latin *patella,* small pan. See PAELLA.] **—pail′ful′** *n.*

pail•lard (pī-yär′) *n.* A slice of veal, chicken, or beef that is pounded until very thin and quickly grilled, broiled, or sautéed with high heat. [Origin unknown.]

pail•lasse also **pal•liasse** (păl-yăs′, păl′yăs′) *n.* A thin mattress filled with straw or sawdust. [French, from Old French, from *paille,* straw, from Late Latin *palea,* from Latin, chaff.]

pail•lette (pä-yĕt′, pā-, pă-lĕt′) *n.* **1.** A small piece of metal or foil used in painting with enamel. **2.** A spangle used to ornament a dress or costume. [French, from Old French, diminutive of *paille,* straw. See PAILLASSE.] **—pail•let′ted** *adj.*

pain (pān) *n.* **1.** An unpleasant sensation occurring in varying degrees of severity as a consequence of injury, disease, or emotional disorder. **2.** Suffering or distress. **3. pains.** The pangs of childbirth. **4. pains.** Great care or effort: *take pains with one's work.* **5.** *Informal.* A source of annoyance; a nuisance. **—pain** *v.* **pained, pain•ing, pains.** *—tr.* To cause pain to; hurt or injure. *—intr.* To be the cause of pain. ***—idiom.* on** (or **under**) **pain of.** Subject to the penalty of a specified punishment, such as death. [Middle English, from Old French *peine,* from Latin *poena,* penalty, pain, from Greek *poinē,* penalty. See **kʷei-**[1] in Appendix.]

SYNONYMS: *pain, ache, pang, smart, stitch, throe, twinge.* The central meaning shared by these nouns is "a sensation of severe physical discomfort": *abdominal pain; aches and cramps in a leg; the pangs of childbirth; aspirin that alleviated the smart; a stitch in the side; the throes of dying; a twinge of arthritis.* See also Synonyms at **effort.**

Paine (pān), **Robert Treat.** 1731–1814. American Revolutionary leader and jurist. A signer of the Declaration of Independence, he later served as a justice of the Massachusetts supreme court (1790–1804).

Paine, Thomas. 1737–1809. British-born American writer and Revolutionary leader who wrote the pamphlet *Common Sense* (1776) arguing for American independence from Britain. In England he published *The Rights of Man* (1791–1792), a defense of the French Revolution.

Paines•ville (pānz′vĭl′). A city of northeast Ohio northeast of Cleveland. Population, 16,391.

pain•ful (pān′fəl) *adj.* **1.** Causing pain. **2.** Full of pain. **3.** Requiring care and labor; irksome: *a painful task.* **4.** *Archaic.* Diligent; careful. **—pain′ful•ly** *adv.* **—pain′ful•ness** *n.*

pain in the neck *n., pl.* **pains in the neck.** *Informal.* One that is a source of annoyance; a nuisance.

pain•kill•er (pān′kĭl′ər) *n.* An agent, such as an analgesic drug, that relieves pain. **—pain′kill′ing** *adj.*

pain•less (pān′lĭs) *adj.* Free from complication or pain: *a painless operation.* **—pain′less•ly** *adv.* **—pain′less•ness** *n.*

pains•tak•ing (pānz′tā′kĭng) *adj.* Marked by or requiring great pains; very careful and diligent. See Synonyms at **meticulous. —painstaking** *n.* Extremely careful and diligent work or effort. **—pains′tak′ing•ly** *adv.*

paint (pānt) *n.* **1.a.** A liquid mixture, usually of a solid pigment in a liquid vehicle, used as a decorative or protective coating. **b.** The thin, dry film formed by such a mixture when applied to a surface. **c.** The solid pigment before it is mixed with a vehicle. **2.** A cosmetic, such as rouge, that is used to give color to the face; makeup. **3.** See **pinto. —paint** *v.* **paint•ed, paint•ing, paints.** *—tr.* **1.** To make (a picture) with paints. **2.a.** To represent in a picture with paints. **b.** To depict vividly in words. **3.** To coat or decorate with paint: *paint a house.* **4.** To apply cosmetics to. **5.** To apply medicine to; swab: *paint a wound.* **6.** *Computer Science.* To display (graphic data) on a video terminal. *—intr.* **1.** To practice the art of painting pictures. **2.** To cover something with paint. **3.** To apply cosmetics to oneself: *"Let her paint an inch thick, to this favor she must come"* (Shakespeare). **4.** To serve as a surface to be coated with paint: *These nonporous surfaces paint badly with a brush.* ***—idiom.* paint the town red.** *Slang.* To go on a spree. [From Middle English *painten,* to paint, from Old French *peintier,* from *peint,* past participle of *peindre,* from Latin *pingere.* See **peig-** in Appendix.] **—paint′a•bil′i•ty** *n.* **—paint′a•ble** *adj.*

paint•brush (pānt′brŭsh′) *n.* **1.** A brush for applying paint. **2.** The Indian paintbrush.

paint•ed (pān′tĭd) *adj.* **1.** Represented in paint. **2.a.** Covered or decorated with paint. **b.** Brightly colored; gaudy. **3.** Excessively or improperly made up with cosmetics.

painted bunting *n.* A small finch *(Passerina ciris)* of the southern United States and Mexico, the male of which has brilliant multicolored plumage. Also called *nonpareil.*

painted cup *n.* See **Indian paintbrush.**

Paint•ed Desert (pān′tĭd). A plateau region of north-central Arizona east of the Colorado and Little Colorado rivers. Irregularly eroded layers of red and yellow sediment and clay have left striking bands of color.

painted lady *n.* A widely distributed butterfly *(Vanessa cardui)* having brown, black, and orange markings. Also called *cosmopolite, thistle butterfly.*

paint•er[1] (pān′tər) *n.* One who paints, either as an artist or a worker.

pain•ter[2] (pān′tər) *n. Nautical.* A rope attached to the bow of a boat, used for tying up, as when docking or towing. [Middle English *peintour,* probably from Old French *pentoir,* strong rope, from *pendre,* to hang, from Vulgar Latin **pendere,* from Latin *pendēre.* See **(s)pen-** in Appendix.]

♦**pain·ter³** (pān′tər) *n. Chiefly Upper Southern U.S.* See **mountain lion.** [Alteration of PANTHER.]

paint·er·ly (pān′tər-lē) *adj.* **1.** Of, relating to, or characteristic of a painter; artistic. **2. a.** Having qualities unique to the art of painting. **b.** Of, relating to, or being a style of painting marked by openness of form, with shapes distinguished by variations of color rather than by outline or contour. **—paint′er·li·ness** *n.*

paint·er's colic (pān′tərz) *n.* Chronic intestinal pains and constipation caused by lead poisoning. Also called *lead colic.* [So called because the disease is often caused by exposure to lead-base paint.]

paint·ing (pān′tĭng) *n.* **1.** The process, art, or occupation of coating surfaces with paint for a utilitarian or an artistic effect. **2.** A picture or design in paint.

pair (pâr) *n., pl.* **pair** or **pairs.** *Abbr.* **pr. 1.** Two corresponding persons or items, similar in form or function and matched or associated: *a pair of shoes.* **2.** One object composed of two joined, similar parts that are dependent upon each other: *a pair of pliers.* **3. a.** Two persons who are joined in marriage or engagement. **b.** Two persons who have something in common and are considered together: *a pair of hunters.* **c.** Two mated animals. **d.** Two animals joined together in work. See Synonyms at **couple. 4.** *Games.* Two playing cards of the same denomination. **5.** Two members of a deliberative body with opposing opinions on a given issue who agree to abstain from voting on the issue, thereby offsetting each other. **6.** *Chemistry.* An electron pair. **—pair** *v.* **paired, pair·ing, pairs.** *—tr.* **1.** To arrange in sets of two; couple. **2.** To join in a pair; mate. **3.** To provide a partner for. *—intr.* **1.** To form pairs or a pair. **2.** To join in marriage; mate. [Middle English, from Old French *paire,* from Latin *paria,* equals, pl. of *pār,* a pair, from *pār,* equal. See **pere-²** in Appendix.]

USAGE NOTE: *Pair* as a noun can be followed by a singular or plural verb. The singular is always used when *pair* denotes the set taken as a single entity: *This pair of shoes is on sale.* A plural verb is used when the members are considered as individuals: *The pair are working more harmoniously now.* After a number other than one *pair* itself can be either singular or plural, but the plural is now more common: *She bought six pairs* (or *pair*) *of stockings.*

pair bond *n.* The temporary or permanent association formed between a female and male animal during courtship and mating. **—pair bonding** *n.*

pair of compasses *n.* See **compass** (sense 2).

pair of virginals *n. Music.* See **virginal².**

pair production *n.* The simultaneous creation of a subatomic particle and its antiparticle from another form of energy, especially the production of a positron and an electron from a gamma ray photon in a strong electric field, such as that surrounding a nucleus.

pai·sa (pī-sä′) *n., pl.* **-se** (-sā′) or **-sas** (-säs′). See table at **currency.** [Hindi *paisā,* perhaps from *pā′ī,* unit of currency. See PIE³.]

pai·sa·no (pī-zä′nō) also **pai·san** (-zän′) *n., pl.* **-sa·nos** also **-sans. 1.** A countryman; a compatriot. **2.** *Slang.* A friend; a pal. [Spanish, from French *paysan,* from Old French *paisant,* peasant. See PEASANT.]

pai·se (pī-sā′) *n.* A plural of **paisa.**

pais·ley (pāz′lē) *adj.* **1.** Made of a soft wool fabric with a colorful, woven or printed and swirled pattern of abstract, curved shapes. **2.** Marked with this pattern. **—paisley** *n., pl.* **-leys.** An article of clothing made of paisley fabric. [After PAISLEY.]

Pais·ley (pāz′lē). A burgh of southwest Scotland west of Glasgow. It has been a textile center since the early 18th century and became famous in the 19th century for its colorful patterned shawls. Population, 86,100.

Pai·ute also **Pi·ute** (pī′yo͞ot′) *n., pl.* **Paiute** or **-utes** also **Piute** or **-utes. 1.** Either of two distinct Native American peoples inhabiting parts of the Great Basin, specifically: **a.** A group occupying eastern Oregon, western Nevada, and adjacent areas of northeast California. Also called *Northern Paiute.* **b.** A group occupying southern Utah and Nevada, northern Arizona, and adjacent areas of southeast California. Also called *Southern Paiute.* **2.** A member of either of these peoples. **—Pai′ute′** *adj.*

pa·ja·ma (pə-jä′mə, -jăm′ə) *n.* **1.** A loose-fitting garment consisting of trousers and a jacket, worn for sleeping or lounging. Often used in the plural. **2.** Loose-fitting trousers worn in the Far East by men and women. Often used in the plural. *—attributive.* Often used to modify another noun: *a pajama top; a pajama party.* [Hindi *pāijāma,* loose-fitting trousers : Persian *pāī,* leg (from Middle Persian; see **ped-** in Appendix) + Persian *jāmah,* garment.]

Pak. *abbr.* Pakistan.

pak choi (bŏk′ choi′) *n.* Variant of **bok choy.**

Pak·i·stan (păk′ĭ-stăn′, pä′kĭ-stän′). *Abbr.* **Pak.** A country of southern Asia. Occupying land crisscrossed by ancient invasion paths, Pakistan was the home of the prehistoric Indus Valley civilization, which flourished until overrun by Aryans c. 1500 B.C. After being conquered by numerous rulers and powers, it passed to the British as part of India and became a separate Moslem state in 1947. The country originally included what is now Bangladesh, which declared its independence in 1971. Islamabad is the capital and Karachi the largest city. Population, 83,782,000. **—Pak′i·stan′i** (-stăn′ē, -stä′nē) *adj. & n.*

pal (păl) *Informal. n.* A friend; a chum. **—pal** *intr.v.* **palled, pal·ling, pals.** To associate as friends or chums. Often used with *around.* [Romany *phral, phal;* akin to Sanskrit *bhrātā,* brother. See **bhrāter-** in Appendix.]

WORD HISTORY: *Pal,* like *buddy* and *chum,* has an informal, thoroughly "American" ring to it. One might think that *pal* had been a fixture in the English language forever. In fact, *pal* is a fairly recent acquisition from a rather exotic source—the language of the Gypsies. First recorded in English in the 17th century, *pal* was borrowed from Romany, the Indic language of the Gypsies, specifically from a word meaning "brother, comrade," which occurs as *phal* in the Romany spoken in England and *phral* in the Romany spoken in Europe. Gypsies speak an Indic language because they originally migrated to Europe from the border region between Iran and India. In other Indic languages we find related words meaning "brother," such as Hindustani *bhāi,* Prakrit *bhāda* or *bhāyā,* and Sanskrit *bhrātā.* All these terms trace their ancestry to the same Indo-European word that our word *brother* does.

Pal. *abbr.* Palestine.

pal·ace (păl′ĭs) *n.* **1.** The official residence of a royal personage. **2.** *Chiefly British.* The official residence of a high dignitary, such as a bishop or an archbishop. **3. a.** A large or splendid residence. **b.** A large, often gaudily ornate building used for entertainment or exhibitions. [Middle English, from Old French *palais,* from *Palātium,* Palatine Hill, Rome (from its being the site where emperors built their homes), imperial residence.]

pal·a·din (păl′ə-dĭn) *n.* **1.** A paragon of chivalry; a heroic champion. **2.** A strong supporter or defender of a cause: *"the paladin of plain speaking"* (Arthur M. Schlesinger, Jr.). **3.** Any of the 12 peers of Charlemagne's court. [French, from Italian *paladino,* from Late Latin *palātīnus,* palatine. See PALATINE¹.]

palae– or **palaeo–** *pref.* Variants of **paleo–.**

pa·laes·tra (pə-lĕs′trə) *n.* Variant of **palestra.**

pal·an·quin also **pal·an·keen** (păl′ən-kēn′) *n.* A covered litter carried on poles on the shoulders of two or four men, formerly used in eastern Asia. [Portuguese *palanquim,* from Javanese *pēlangki,* from Pali *pallaṅko,* from Sanskrit *paryaṅkaḥ, palyaṅkaḥ,* couch, bed.]

pa·la·pa (pə-lä′pə) *n.* **1.** An open-sided dwelling with a thatched roof made of dried palm leaves. **2.** A structure, such as a bar or restaurant in a tropical resort, that is open-sided and thatched with palm leaves. [Perhaps from American Spanish, a kind of palm tree.]

pal·at·a·ble (păl′ə-tə-bəl) *adj.* **1.** Acceptable to the taste; sufficiently agreeable in flavor to be eaten. **2.** Acceptable or agreeable to the mind or sensibilities: *a palatable solution to the problem.* **—pal′at·a·bil′i·ty, pal′at·a·ble·ness** *n.* **—pal′at·a·bly** *adv.*

pal·a·tal (păl′ə-təl) *adj.* **1.** Of or relating to the palate. **2.** *Linguistics.* **a.** Produced with the front of the tongue near or against the hard palate, as the (y) in English *young.* **b.** Produced with the blade of the tongue near the hard palate, as the (ch) in English *chin.* **c.** Produced with the front of the tongue in a forward position. Used of a vowel. **—palatal** *n. Linguistics.* A palatal sound. **—pal′a·tal·ly** *adv.*

pal·a·tal·ize (păl′ə-tə-līz′) *tr.v.* **-ized, -iz·ing, -iz·es.** *Linguistics.* To pronounce as or alter to a palatal sound. **—pal′a·tal·i·za′tion** (-tə-lĭ-zā′shən) *n.*

pal·ate (păl′ĭt) *n.* **1.** The roof of the mouth in vertebrates having a complete or partial separation of the oral and nasal cavities and consisting of the hard palate and the soft palate. **2.** *Botany.* The projecting part on the lower lip of a bilabiate corolla that closes the throat, as in a snapdragon. **3.** The sense of taste: *delicacies pleasing to the most refined palate.* [Middle English, from Old French *palat,* from Latin *palātum,* perhaps of Etruscan origin.]

pa·la·tial (pə-lā′shəl) *adj.* **1.** Of or suitable for a palace: *palatial furnishings.* **2.** Of the nature of a palace, as in spaciousness or ornateness: *a palatial yacht.* [From Latin *Palātium,* imperial residence. See PALACE.] **—pa·la′tial·ly** *adv.*

pa·lat·i·nate (pə-lăt′n-āt′, -ĭt) *n.* The office, powers, or territory of a palatine.

Pa·lat·i·nate (pə-lăt′n-ĭt). Either of two historical districts and former states of southern Germany. The **Lower Palatinate** is in southwest Germany between Luxembourg and the Rhine River; the **Upper Palatinate** is to the east in eastern Bavaria. They were once under the jurisdiction of the counts palatine, who became electors of the Holy Roman Empire in 1356 and were then known as electors palatine.

pal·a·tine¹ (păl′ə-tīn′) *n.* **1. a.** A soldier of the palace guard of the Roman emperors, formed in the time of Diocletian. **b.** A soldier of a major division of the Roman army formed in the time of Constantine I. **2.** Used as a title for various administrative officials of the late Roman and Byzantine empires. **3.** A feudal lord exercising sovereign power over his lands. In this sense, also called *palsgrave.* **—palatine** *adj.* **1.** Belonging to or fit for a palace. **2.** Of or relating to a palatine or palatinate. [From Middle English, ruled by an independent lord, from Old French *palatin,* from Late Latin *palātīnus,* palace official, from Latin *palātīnus,* from *Palātium,* imperial residence. See PALACE.]

pal·a·tine² (păl′ə-tīn′) *adj.* **1.** Of or relating to the palate: *the palatine tonsils.* **2.** Of or relating to either of two bones that

paisley

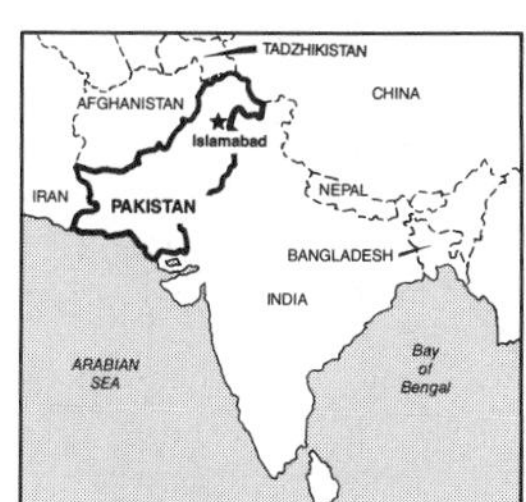

Pakistan

palapa
Meetinghouse, Saleaula Village, Savaii Island

ă pat	oi boy
ā pay	ou out
âr care	o͝o took
ä father	o͞o boot
ĕ pet	ŭ cut
ē be	ûr urge
ĭ pit	th thin
ī pie	*th* this
îr pier	hw which
ŏ pot	zh vision
ō toe	ə about, item
ô paw	♦ regionalism

Stress marks: ′ (primary); ′ (secondary), as in **dictionary** (dĭk′shə-nĕr′ē)

pale[1]

make up the hard palate. **—palatine** *n.* Either of the two bones that make up the hard palate.

Pal·a·tine[1] (păl′ə-tīn′). The most important of the seven hills of ancient Rome. Traditionally the location of the earliest Roman settlement, it was the site of many imperial palaces, including ones built by Tiberius, Nero, and Domitian. **—Pal′a·tine** *adj.*

Pal·a·tine[2] (păl′ə-tīn′). A village of northeast Illinois, a residential suburb of Chicago. Population, 32,166.

Pa·lau (pä-lou′, pə-). See **Belau.**

pa·lav·er (pə-lăv′ər, -lä′vər) *n.* **1. a.** Idle chatter. **b.** Talk intended to charm or beguile. **2.** *Obsolete.* A parley between European explorers and representatives of local populations, especially in Africa. **—palaver** *v.* **-ered, -er·ing, -ers.** —*tr.* To flatter or cajole. —*intr.* To chatter idly. [Portuguese *palavra,* speech, alteration of Late Latin *parabola,* speech, parable. See PARABLE.]

Pa·la·wan (pə-lä′wən, pä-lä′wän). A long, narrow island of the southwest Philippines north of Borneo. It lies between the Sulu Sea and the **Palawan Passage** of the South China Sea.

pa·laz·zo (pə-lät′sō) *n., pl.* **-zi** (-sē) or **-zos.** A large, splendid residence or public building, such as a palace or museum. [Italian, from Latin *Palātium,* imperial residence. See PALACE.]

pale[1] (pāl) *n.* **1.** A stake or pointed stick; a picket. **2.** A fence enclosing an area. **3.** The area enclosed by a fence or boundary. **4.** *Heraldry.* A wide vertical band in the center of an escutcheon. **5. Pale.** The medieval dominions of the English in Ireland. Used with *the.* **—pale** *tr.v.* **paled, pal·ing, pales.** To enclose with pales; fence in. **—*idiom.* beyond the pale.** Irrevocably unacceptable or unreasonable: *behavior that was quite beyond the pale.* [Middle English, from Old French *pal,* from Latin *pālus.* See **pag-** in Appendix.]

pale[2] (pāl) *adj.* **pal·er, pal·est. 1.** Whitish in complexion; pallid. **2.** *Color.* **a.** Of a low intensity of color; light. **b.** Having high lightness and low saturation. **3.** Of a low intensity of light; dim or faint: *"a late afternoon sun coming through the el tracks and falling in pale oblongs on the cracked, empty sidewalks"* (Jimmy Breslin). **4.** Feeble; weak: *a pale rendition of the aria.* **—pale** *v.* **paled, pal·ing, pales.** —*tr.* To cause to turn pale. —*intr.* **1.** To become pale; blanch: *paled with fright.* **2.** To decrease in relative importance. [Middle English, from Old French, from Latin *pallidus,* from *pallēre,* to be pale. See **pel-**[1] in Appendix.] **—pale′ly** *adv.* **—pale′ness** *n.*

pale– *pref.* Variant of **paleo–.**

pa·le·a (pā′lē-ə) *n., pl.* **-le·ae** (-lē-ē′). **1.** A small chafflike bract enclosing the flower of a grass. **2.** The chaffy scales on the receptacle of a flower head in a plant of the composite family, as the sunflower. [Latin, chaff.]

Pa·le·arc·tic (pā′lē-ärk′tĭk, -är′tĭk) *adj.* Of or relating to the biogeographic region that includes Europe, the northwest coast of Africa, and Asia north of the Himalaya Mountains, especially with respect to distribution of animals.

pale-dry (pāl′drī′) *adj.* Light in color and dry in flavor: *pale-dry ginger ale.*

pa·le·eth·nol·o·gy (pā′lē-ĕth-nŏl′ə-jē) *n., pl.* **-gies.** The ethnology of early human beings. **—pa′le·eth′no·log′ic** (-ĕth′nə-lŏj′ĭk), **pa′le·eth′no·log′i·cal** (-ĭ-kəl) *adj.*

pale·face (pā′fās′) *n. Slang.* A white person.

Pa·lem·bang (pä′ləm-băng′, -lĕm-). A city of Indonesia on southeast Sumatra Island. Center of a powerful Hindu kingdom in the seventh and eighth centuries, it became a Dutch trading post in 1617 and was later occupied intermittently by the British. Population, 787,187.

palette

Pa·len·que (pä-lĕng′kĕ). An ancient Mayan city of southern Mexico southeast of Villahermosa. The Temple of Inscriptions is noted for its hieroglyphic tablets.

paleo– or **pale–** or **palaeo–** or **palae–** *pref.* **1.** Ancient; prehistoric; old: *paleobotany.* **2.** Early; primitive: *paleoanthropology.* [Greek *palaio-,* from *palaios,* ancient, from *palai,* long ago. See **k**^{w}**el-**[2] in Appendix.]

pa·le·o·an·throp·ic (pā′lē-ō-ăn-thrŏp′ĭk) *adj.* Of or relating to extinct members of the genus *Homo* that preceded *H. sapiens.*

pa·le·o·an·thro·pol·o·gy (pā′lē-ō-ăn′thrə-pŏl′ə-jē) *n.* The study of humanlike creatures more primitive than *Homo sapiens.* **—pa′le·o·an′thro·po·log′ic** (-pə-lŏj′ĭk), **pa′le·o·an′thro·po·log′i·cal** (-ĭ-kəl) *adj.* **—pa′le·o·an′thro·pol′o·gist** *n.*

pa·le·o·bi·o·chem·is·try (pā′lē-ō-bī′ō-kĕm′ĭ-strē) *n., pl.* **-tries. 1.** The biochemical constituents of fossil organisms. **2.** The study of the development and evolution of biochemicals and biochemical processes. **—pa′le·o·bi′o·chem′i·cal** (-ĭ-kəl) *adj.*

pa·le·o·bi·o·ge·og·ra·phy (pā′lē-ō-bī′ō-jē-ŏg′rə-fē) *n.* The study of the geographic distribution of fossil organisms. **—pa′le·o·bi′o·ge′o·graph′ic** (-jē′ə-grăf′ĭk), **pa′le·o·bi′o·ge′o·graph′i·cal** (-ĭ-kəl) *adj.*

pa·le·o·bot·a·ny (pā′lē-ō-bŏt′n-ē) *n.* The branch of paleontology that deals with plant fossils and ancient vegetation. **—pa′le·o·bo·tan′ic** (-bə-tăn′ĭk), **pa′le·o·bo·tan′i·cal** (-ĭ-kəl) *adj.* **—pa′le·o·bo·tan′i·cal·ly** *adv.* **—pa′le·o·bot′a·nist** *n.*

Pa·le·o·cene (pā′lē-ə-sēn′) *adj.* Of, belonging to, or designating the geologic time, rock series, and sedimentary deposits of the first epoch of the Tertiary Period, preceding the Eocene Epoch and characterized by the appearance of placental mammals. See table at **geologic time. —Paleocene** *n.* **1.** The Paleocene Epoch. **2.** The deposits of the Paleocene Epoch.

pa·le·o·e·col·o·gy (pā′lē-ō-ĭ-kŏl′ə-jē) *n.* The branch of ecology that deals with the interaction between ancient or prehistoric organisms and their environment. **—pa′le·o·ec′o·log′i·cal** (-ĕk′ə-lŏj′ĭ-kəl, -ē′kə-), **pa′le·o·ec′o·log′ic** (-lŏj′ĭk) *adj.* **—pa′le·o·e·col′o·gist** *n.*

pa·le·og·ra·phy (pā′lē-ŏg′rə-fē) *n.* **1.** The study and scholarly interpretation of ancient written documents. **2.** The documents so studied. **—pa′le·og′ra·pher** *n.* **—pa′le·o·graph′ic** (-ə-grăf′ĭk), **pa′le·o·graph′i·cal** (-ĭ-kəl) *adj.*

Pa·le·o-In·di·an (pā′lē-ō-ĭn′dē-ən) *adj.* Of or relating to prehistoric human culture in the Western Hemisphere from the earliest habitation to around 5,000 B.C. Paleo-Indian cultures are distinguished especially by the various projectile points they produced. **—Pa′le·o-In′di·an** *n.*

pa·le·o·lith (pā′lē-ə-lĭth′) *n.* A stone implement of the Paleolithic Age. [Back-formation from PALEOLITHIC.]

Pa·le·o·lith·ic (pā′lē-ə-lĭth′ĭk) *adj.* Of, belonging to, or designating the cultural period beginning with the earliest chipped stone tools, about 750,000 years ago, until the beginning of the Mesolithic Age, about 15,000 years ago. **—Paleolithic** *n.* The Paleolithic Age.

pa·le·on·tol·o·gy (pā′lē-ŏn-tŏl′ə-jē) *n.* The study of the forms of life existing in prehistoric or geologic times, as represented by the fossils of plants, animals, and other organisms. **—pa′le·on′to·log′ic** (-ŏn′tə-lŏj′ĭk), **pa′le·on′to·log′i·cal** (-ĭ-kəl) *adj.* **—pa′le·on·tol′o·gist** *n.*

Pa·le·o·zo·ic (pā′lē-ə-zō′ĭk) *adj.* Of, belonging to, or designating the era of geologic time that includes the Cambrian, Ordovician, Silurian, Devonian, Mississippian, Pennsylvanian, and Permian periods and is characterized by the appearance of marine invertebrates, primitive fishes, land plants, and primitive reptiles. See table at **geologic time. —Paleozoic** *n.* The Paleozoic Era.

pa·le·o·zo·ol·o·gy (pā′lē-ō-zō-ŏl′ə-jē) *n.* The branch of paleontology that deals with animal fossils and ancient animal life. **—pa′le·o·zo′o·log′i·cal** (-zō′ə-lŏj′ĭ-kəl) *adj.* **—pa′le·o·zo·ol′o·gist** *n.*

Pa·ler·mo (pə-lûr′mō, -lâr′-, pä-lĕr′mô). A city of northwest Sicily, Italy, on the Tyrrhenian Sea. Founded by Phoenicians c. eighth century B.C., it later became a Carthaginian military base and was conquered by Rome in 254–253. The Arabs held the city from A.D. 831 until 1072, when it became capital of the independent kingdom of Sicily (until 1194). Population, 699,691.

Pal·es·tine (păl′ĭ-stīn′). Often called "the Holy Land." *Abbr.* **Pal.** A historical region of southwest Asia between the eastern Mediterranean shore and the Jordan River roughly coextensive with modern Israel and the West Bank. Occupied since prehistoric times, it has been ruled by Hebrews, Egyptians, Romans, Byzantines, Arabs, and Turks. A British League of Nations mandate oversaw the affairs of the area from 1920 until 1948, when Israel declared itself a separate state and the West Bank territory was awarded to Jordan. Israel occupied the Jordanian area west of the Jordan River in 1967. In November 1988 the Palestine Liberation Organization under Yasir Arafat declared its intention of forming an Arab state of Palestine, probably including the West Bank, the Gaza Strip, and the Arab sector of Jerusalem. **—Pal′es·tin′i·an** (-stĭn′ē-ən) *adj. & n.*

pa·les·tra also **pa·laes·tra** (pə-lĕs′trə) *n., pl.* **-trae** (-trē) or **-tras.** A public place in ancient Greece for training and practice in wrestling and other athletics. [Middle English *palestre,* from Old French, from Latin *palaestra,* from Greek *palaistra,* from *palaiein,* to wrestle.] **—pa·les′tral, pa·les′tri·an** *adj.*

Pa·le·stri·na (păl′ĭ-strē′nə, pä′lĕ-strē′nä), **Giovanni Pierluigi da.** 1526?–1594. Italian composer known especially for his Masses. His other works include motets and madrigals.

pal·ette (păl′ĭt) *n.* **1.** A board, typically with a hole for the thumb, which an artist can hold while painting and on which the artist mixes colors. **2. a.** The range of colors used in a particular painting or by a particular artist: *a limited palette.* **b.** The range of qualities inherent in nongraphic art forms such as music and literature. [French, from Old French, small potter's shovel, diminutive of *pale,* shovel, spade, from Latin *pāla.* See **pag-** in Appendix.]

palette knife *n.* A knife with a thin flexible blade, used by artists for mixing, scraping, or applying paint.

Pa·ley (pā′lē), **William.** 1743–1805. British theologian and utilitarian philosopher. Among his works are *The Principles of Moral and Political Philosophy* (1785).

Paley, William S. 1901–1990. American broadcasting executive who founded the Columbia Broadcasting System (1929).

pal·frey (pôl′frē) *n., pl.* **-freys.** *Archaic.* A saddle horse, especially one for a woman to ride. [Middle English, from Old French *palefrei,* from Medieval Latin *palafrēdus,* alteration of Late Latin *paraverēdus,* post horse for secondary routes, extra horse : Greek *para,* extra, beyond; see **per**[1] in Appendix + Latin *verēdus,* post horse, of Celtic origin. See **reidh-** in Appendix.]

Pal·grave (păl′grāv′, pôl′-), **Francis Turner.** 1824–1897. British poet and anthologist known for his *Golden Treasury of the Best Songs and Lyrical Poems in the English Language* (1861).

Pa·li (pä′lē) *n.* A Prakit language that is a scriptural and liturgical language of Hinayana Buddhism. [Short for Sanskrit *pālibhāṣā,* language of the row, series of Buddhist sacred texts, from *pāliḥ,* row, perhaps of Dravidian origin.]

pal·i·mo·ny (păl′ə-mō′nē) *n. Informal.* An allowance for support made under court order and given usually by one person to his or her former lover or live-in companion after they have separated. [Blend of PAL and ALIMONY.]

pal·imp·sest (păl′ĭmp-sĕst′) *n.* **1.** A manuscript, typically of papyrus or parchment, that has been written on more than once, with the earlier writing incompletely erased and often legible. **2.** An object, a place, or an area that reflects its history: *"Spaniards in the sixteenth century . . . saw an ocean moving south . . . through a palimpsest of bayous and distributary streams in forested paludal basins"* (John McPhee). [Latin *palimpsēstum,* from Greek *palimpsēston,* neuter of *palimpsēstos,* scraped again : *palin,* again; see **kʷel-**[1] in Appendix + *psēn,* to scrape.]

pal·in·drome (păl′ĭn-drōm′) *n.* **1.** A word, phrase, verse, or sentence that reads the same backward or forward. For example: *A man, a plan, a canal, Panama!* **2.** A segment of double-stranded DNA in which the nucleotide sequence of one strand reads in reverse order to that of the complementary strand. [From Greek *palindromos,* running back again, recurring : *palin,* again; see **kʷel-**[1] in Appendix + *dromos,* a running.] **—pal′in·dro′mic** (-drō′mĭk, -drŏm′ĭk) *adj.*

pal·ing (pā′lĭng) *n.* **1.** One of a row of upright, pointed sticks forming a fence; a pale. **2.** Pointed sticks used in making fences; pales. **3.** A fence made of pales or pickets.

pal·in·gen·e·sis (păl′ĭn-jĕn′ĭ-sĭs) *n., pl.* **-ses** (-sēz′). **1.** The doctrine of transmigration of souls; metempsychosis. **2.** *Biology.* The repetition by a single organism of various stages in the evolution of its species during embryonic development. [Greek *palin,* again; see **kʷel-**[1] in Appendix + -GENESIS.] **—pal′in·ge·net′ic** (-jə-nĕt′ĭk) *adj.* **—pal′in·ge·net′i·cal·ly** *adv.*

pal·i·node (păl′ə-nōd′) *n.* **1.** A poem in which the author retracts something said in a previous poem. **2.** A formal statement of retraction. [From Late Latin *palinōdia,* from Greek *palinōidia* : *palin,* again; see **kʷel-**[1] in Appendix + *ōidē,* song; see PARODY.]

pal·i·sade (păl′ĭ-sād′) *n.* **1.a.** A fence of pales forming a defense barrier or fortification. **b.** One of the pales of such a fence. **2. palisades.** A line of lofty, steep cliffs, usually along a river. **—palisade** *tr.v.* **-sad·ed, -sad·ing, -sades.** To equip or fortify with palisades or a palisade. [French *palissade,* from Old French, from Old Provençal *palissada,* from *palissa,* stake, from Vulgar Latin **pālīcea,* from Latin *pālus.* See **pag-** in Appendix.]

palisade cell *n. Botany.* One of the columnar cells of palisade parenchyma.

palisade parenchyma *n. Botany.* A leaf tissue composed of columnar cells containing numerous chloroplasts in which the long axis of each cell is perpendicular to the leaf surface.

Pal·i·sades (păl′ĭ-sādz′). A row of cliffs in northeast New Jersey along the western bank of the Hudson River.

pal·ish (pā′lĭsh) *adj.* Slightly pale.

Palk Strait (pôk, pôlk). A waterway between southeast India and northern Sri Lanka.

pall[1] (pôl) *n.* **1.** A cover for a coffin, bier, or tomb, often made of black, purple, or white velvet. **2.** A coffin, especially one being carried to a grave or tomb. **3.a.** A covering that darkens or obscures: *a pall of smoke over the city.* **b.** A gloomy effect or atmosphere: *"A pall of depressed indifference hung over Petrograd during February and March 1916"* (W. Bruce Lincoln). **4.** *Ecclesiastical.* **a.** A linen cloth or a square of cardboard faced with cloth used to cover the chalice. **b.** See **pallium** (sense 2). **—pall** *tr.v.* **palled, pall·ing, palls.** To cover with or as if with a pall. [Middle English *pal,* from Old English *pæll,* cloak, covering, from Latin *pallium.*]

pall[2] (pôl) *v.* **palled, pall·ing, palls.** *—intr.* **1.** To become insipid, boring, or wearisome. **2.** To have a dulling, wearisome, or boring effect. **3.** To become cloyed or satiated. *—tr.* **1.** To cloy; satiate. **2.** To make vapid or wearisome. [Middle English *pallen,* to grow feeble, probably short for *appallen.* See APPALL.]

pal·la·di·a (pə-lā′dē-ə) *n.* A plural of **palladium**[2].

Pal·la·di·an[1] (pə-lā′dē-ən) *adj.* **1.** *Greek Mythology.* Of, relating to, or characteristic of Athena. **2.** Of, relating to, or characterized by wisdom or study. [From Latin *Palladius,* from Greek *Palladios,* from *Pallas, Pallad-,* Pallas Athena.]

Pal·la·di·an[2] (pə-lā′dē-ən) *adj.* **1.** Of or characteristic of the Renaissance architectural style of Palladio. **2.** Of or characteristic of an architectural style of the mid 18th century derived from that of Palladio, especially in Britain.

pal·la·dic (pə-lā′dĭk, -lăd′ĭk) *adj.* Of or designating compounds that contain palladium, especially with valence 4.

Pal·la·dio (pə-lā′dē-ō, pä-lä′dyô), **Andrea.** 1508–1580. Italian architect who developed a style based on the classicism of ancient Rome, breaking with the ornate conventions of the Italian Renaissance. His works include the Villa Rotonda and the Palazzo Chiericati in Venice.

pal·la·di·um[1] (pə-lā′dē-əm) *n. Symbol* **Pd** A soft, ductile, steel-white, tarnish-resistant, metallic element occurring naturally with platinum, especially in gold, nickel, and copper ores. Because it can absorb large amounts of hydrogen, it is used as a purification filter for hydrogen and a catalyst in hydrogenation. It is alloyed for use in electric contacts, jewelry, nonmagnetic watch parts, and surgical instruments. Atomic number 46; atomic weight 106.4; melting point 1,552°C; boiling point 3,140°C; specific gravity 12.02 (20°C); valence 2, 3, 4. See table at **element.** [From PALLAS (discovered at the same time as the element).]

pal·la·di·um[2] (pə-lā′dē-əm) *n., pl.* **-di·a** (-dē-ə) or **-di·ums. 1.** A safeguard, especially one viewed as a guarantee of the integrity of social institutions: *the Bill of Rights, palladium of American civil liberties.* **2.** A sacred object that was believed to have the power to preserve a city or state possessing it. [Middle English *Palladion,* a statue of Pallas Athena believed to protect Troy, from Old French *palladion,* from Latin *Palladium,* from Greek *Palladion,* from *Pallas, Pallad-,* Pallas Athena.]

pal·la·dous (pə-lā′dəs, păl′ə-dəs) *adj.* Of or designating compounds that contain palladium, especially with valence 2.

Pal·las (păl′əs) *n.* **1.** One of the largest asteroids, the second to be discovered. **2.** *Greek Mythology.* Athena. [After PALLAS (ATHENA).]

Pallas A·the·na (ə-thē′nə) also **Pallas A·the·ne** (-nē) *n. Greek Mythology.* Athena.

pall·bear·er (pôl′bâr′ər) *n.* One of the persons carrying or attending a coffin at a funeral.

pal·let[1] (păl′ĭt) *n.* **1.** A projection on a machine part, such as a pawl for controlling the motion of a ratchet wheel in a watch escapement, that engages the teeth of a ratchet wheel to convert reciprocating motion to rotary motion or vice versa. **2.** A wooden, shovellike potter's tool used for mixing and shaping clay. **3.** A tool used for printing or gilding letters on book bindings or taking up and applying gold leaf. **4.** A portable platform used for storing or moving cargo or freight. **5.** A painter's palette. [Middle English *palet,* tongue depressor, from Old French *palete,* small potter's shovel. See PALETTE.]

♦ **pal·let**[2] (păl′ĭt) *n.* **1.** A narrow, hard bed or straw-filled mattress. **2.** *Chiefly Southern U.S.* A temporary bed made from bedding arranged on the floor, especially for a child. [Middle English *paillet,* from Anglo-Norman, bundle of straw, from *paille,* straw, from Late Latin *palea.* See PAILLASSE.]

pal·li·a (păl′ē-ə) *n.* A plural of **pallium.**

pal·li·al (păl′ē-əl) *adj.* **1.** Of or relating to the cerebral cortex. **2.** Of or relating to the mantle of a mollusk, brachiopod, or bird. [PALLIUM + -AL[1].]

pal·liasse (păl-yăs′, păl′yăs′) *n.* Variant of **paillasse.**

pal·li·ate (păl′ē-āt′) *tr.v.* **-at·ed, -at·ing, -ates. 1.** To make (an offense or crime) seem less serious; extenuate. **2.** To make less severe or intense; mitigate: *tried unsuccessfully to palliate the widespread discontent.* **3.** To relieve the symptoms of a disease or disorder. [Middle English *palliaten,* from Late Latin *palliāre, palliāt-,* to cloak, palliate, from Latin *pallium,* cloak.] **—pal′li·a′tion** *n.* **—pal′li·a′tor** *n.*

SYNONYMS: *palliate, extenuate, gloss, gloze, whitewash.* The central meaning shared by these verbs is "to cause a fault or offense to seem less grave or less reprehensible": *palliate a crime; couldn't extenuate the malfeasance; glossing over an unethical transaction; glozing sins and iniquities; whitewashed official complicity in political extortion.* See also Synonyms at **relieve.**

pal·li·a·tive (păl′ē-ā′tĭv, -ē-ə-tĭv) *adj.* **1.** Tending or serving to palliate. **2.** Relieving or soothing the symptoms of a disease or disorder without effecting a cure. **—palliative** *n.* One that palliates, especially a palliative drug or medicine. **—pal′li·a′tive·ly** *adv.*

pal·lid (păl′ĭd) *adj.* **1.** Having an abnormally pale or wan complexion: *the pallid face of the invalid.* **2.** Lacking intensity of color or luminousness. **3.** Lacking in radiance or vitality; dull: *pallid prose.* [Latin *pallidus,* from *pallēre,* to be pale. See **pel-**[1] in Appendix.] **—pal′lid·ly** *adv.* **—pal′lid·ness** *n.*

pal·li·um (păl′ē-əm) *n., pl.* **pal·li·ums** or **pal·li·a** (păl′ē-ə). **1.** A cloak or mantle worn by the ancient Greeks and Romans. **2.** *Ecclesiastical.* A vestment worn by the pope and conferred by him on archbishops and sometimes on bishops. Also called *pall.* **3.a.** The mantle of gray matter forming the cerebral cortex. **b.** The mantle of a mollusk, brachiopod, or bird. [Latin.]

pall-mall (pĕl′mĕl′, păl′măl′, pôl′môl′) *n. Games.* **1.** A 17th-century game in which a boxwood ball was struck with a mallet to drive it through an iron ring suspended at the end of an alley. **2.** The alley in which this game was played. [Obsolete French *pallemaille,* from Italian *pallamaglio* : *palla,* ball (of Germanic origin; see **bhel-**[2] in Appendix) + *maglio,* mallet (from Latin *malleus;* see **melə-** in Appendix).]

Pall Mall (păl′ măl′, pĕl′ mĕl′). A fashionable street in London, England, noted as the site of St. James's Palace and many private clubs. It derives its name from the game pall-mall, which was played on the grounds of the palace in the 17th century.

pal·lor (păl′ər) *n.* Extreme or unnatural paleness. [Middle English *pallour,* from Old French *palor,* from Latin *pallor,* from *pallēre,* to be pale. See **pel-**[1] in Appendix.]

pal·ly (păl′ē) *adj.* **-li·er, -li·est.** *Informal.* Having the relationship of friends or chums.

palm[1] (päm) *n.* **1.a.** The inner surface of the hand that extends from the wrist to the base of the fingers. **b.** The similar part of the forefoot of a quadruped. **2.** A unit of length equal to either the width or the length of the hand. **3.** The part of a glove or mitten that covers the palm of the hand. **4.** *Nautical.* A metal shield worn by sailmakers over the palm of the hand and used to

Palladian[2]
The Basilica, Venice, Italy

pallbearer
Burial at Arlington National Cemetery, Virginia

pallet[1]
Unloading cargo stacked on a pallet; unused pallets appear in the background

ă pat	oi boy
ā pay	ou out
âr care	o͝o took
ä father	o͞o boot
ĕ pet	ŭ cut
ē be	ûr urge
ĭ pit	th thin
ī pie	*th* this
îr pier	hw which
ŏ pot	zh vision
ō toe	ə about, item
ô paw	♦ regionalism

Stress marks: **′** (primary); ′ (secondary), as in **dictionary** (dĭk′shə-nĕr′ē)

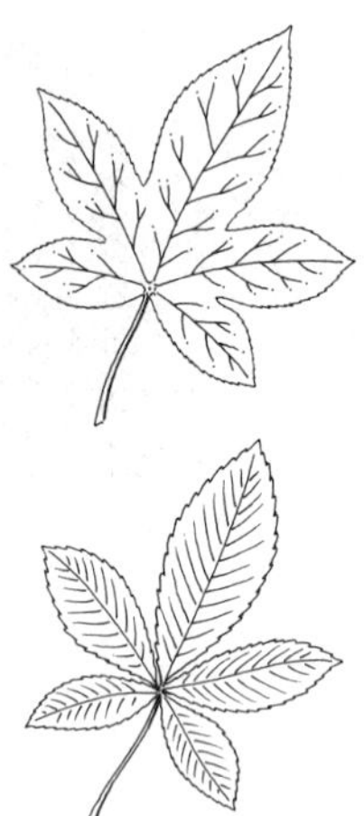

palmate
Top: Compound palmate leaf
Bottom: Digitately compound palmate leaf

force a needle through heavy canvas. **5.** *Nautical.* The blade of an oar or paddle. **6.** The flattened part of the antlers of certain animals, such as the moose. **—palm** *tr.v.* **palmed, palm·ing, palms. 1.** To conceal (something) in the palm of the hand, as in cheating at dice or cards or in a sleight-of-hand trick. **2.** To pick up furtively. **3.** *Basketball.* To commit a violation by letting (the ball) rest momentarily in the palm of the hand while dribbling. **—*phrasal verb.* palm off.** To dispose of or pass off by deception. [Middle English *paume,* from Old French, from Latin *palma,* palm tree, palm of the hand. See **pele-**[2] in Appendix.] **—palm′ful′** *n.*

palm[2] (päm) *n.* **1.** Any of various chiefly tropical evergreen trees, shrubs, or woody vines of the family Palmae (or Arecaceae), characteristically having unbranched trunks with a crown of large pinnate or palmate leaves having conspicuous parallel venation. **2.** A leaf of a palm tree, carried as an emblem of victory, success, or joy. **3.** Triumph; victory. **4.** A small metallic representation of a palm leaf added to a military decoration that has been awarded more than one time. [Middle English, from Old English and from Old French *palme,* both from Latin *palma,* palm of the hand, palm tree (from the shape of the tree's leaves). See **pele-**[2] in Appendix.]

Pal·ma (päl′mä) also **Palma de Mal·lor·ca** (də mä-yôr′kä, *thĕ* mä-lyôr′kä). A city of western Majorca Island, Spain, on the **Bay of Palma,** an inlet of the Mediterranean Sea. Population, 311,197.

pal·mar (păl′mər, päl′-, pä′mər) *adj.* Of, relating to, or corresponding to the palm of the hand or an animal's paw: *palmar folds.*

pal·ma·ry (păl′mə-rē, päl′-, pä′mə-) *adj.* Outstanding; great.

pal·mate (păl′māt′, päl′-, pä′māt′) also **pal·mat·ed** (-mā′tĭd) *adj.* **1.** Having a shape similar to that of a hand with the fingers extended: *palmate antlers; palmate coral.* **2.** *Botany.* Having three or more veins, leaflets, or lobes radiating from one point; digitate: *a palmate leaf.* **3.** *Zoology.* Having webbed toes, as the feet of many water birds. **—pal′mate′ly** *adv.*

pal·ma·ti·fid (păl-mā′tə-fĭd, pä-mā′-) *adj. Botany.* Divided palmately about halfway to the base: *a palmatifid leaf.*

Olaf Palme
Photographed in 1980

pal·ma·tion (păl-mā′shən, päl-, pä-mā′-) *n.* **1.** The state of being palmate. **2. a.** A palmate structure or form. **b.** A division or part of a palmate structure.

pal·ma·ti·sect (păl-mā′tĭ-sĕkt′, päl-, pä-mā′-) *adj.* Divided deeply in a palmate fashion, almost to the base: *the palmatisect leaves of the Japanese maple.*

Palm Bay (päm). A city of eastern Florida on the Indian River lagoon southeast of Orlando. It is a resort. Population, 18,560.

Palm Beach. A city of southeast Florida on a barrier beach of the Atlantic Ocean north of Fort Lauderdale. It was developed as a fashionable resort by Henry Flagler in the 1890's. Population, 9,729.

palm civet *n.* Any of various large nocturnal, arboreal civets of the subfamily Paradoxurinae of southern Asia and tropical Africa, especially the common Asian species *Paradoxurus hermaphroditus,* having spotted fur and a long tail.

palm crab *n.* A large crab *(Birgus latro)* of the islands of the South Pacific that lives in burrows and feeds mainly on coconuts.

Pal·me (päl′mə), **Olaf.** 1927–1986. Swedish politician. As premier (1969–1976 and 1982–1986) he was widely respected for his efforts toward peace and disarmament. Palme was assassinated in 1986.

palm·er (pä′mər) *n.* A medieval European pilgrim who carried a palm branch as a token of having visited the Holy Land.

Pal·mer (pä′mər, päl′-), **Alice Elvira Freeman.** 1855–1902. American educator who was president of Wellesley College (1882–1888) and dean of women at the University of Chicago (1892–1895).

Palmer, Arnold. Born 1929. American golfer who was the first to win four Masters championships (1958, 1960, 1962, and 1964).

Palmer, Daniel David. 1845–1913. Canadian-born American founder of chiropractic. In 1898 he established the Palmer School of Chiropractic in Iowa.

Palmer, George Herbert. 1842–1933. American scholar and educator. Among his works are *The Field of Ethics* (1901) and *The Autobiography of a Philosopher* (1930).

Palmer Archipelago. Formerly **Ant·arc·tic Archipelago** (ănt-ärk′tĭk, -är′tĭk). An island group between the southern tip of South America and the northwest coast of the Antarctic Peninsula. The islands are claimed by Great Britain.

Palmer Peninsula. See **Antarctic Peninsula.**

Pal·mer·ston (pä′mər-stən, päl′-), Third Viscount. Title of Henry John Temple. 1784–1865. British politician remembered for his efforts to maintain the balance of power in Europe. He served as prime minister (1855–1858 and 1859–1865).

palmette
Detail from the frieze of the Erechtheum in Athens, Greece, showing two palmettes and one anthemion

palm·er·worm (pä′mər-wûrm′) *n.* Any of several caterpillars that injure fruit trees by feeding on their leaves, especially the small green caterpillar of the North American moth *Dichomeris ligulella.* [From the way they suddenly appear in large numbers like a throng of pilgrims.]

pal·mette (păl-mĕt′) *n.* A stylized palm leaf used as a decorative element, notably in Persian rugs and in classical moldings, reliefs, frescoes, and vase paintings. [French, diminutive of *palme,* palm, from Old French, from Latin *palma.* See PALM[2].]

pal·met·to (păl-mĕt′ō) *n., pl.* **-tos** or **-toes. 1.** Any of several small, mostly tropical palms having fan-shaped leaves, especially one of the genus *Sabal,* such as *S. palmetto* of the southeast United States. Also called *sabal.* **2.** Leaf strips of any of these plants, used in weaving. [Spanish *palmito,* diminutive of *palma,* palm tree, from Latin. See PALM[2].]

Pal·mi·ra (päl-mîr′ə, -mē′rä). A city of western Colombia southwest of Bogotá on the Pan-American Highway. Coffee and tobacco are grown in the area. Population, 174,425.

palm·ist (pä′mĭst) also **palm·is·ter** (-mĭ-stər) *n.* One who practices palmistry. [Probably back-formation from PALMISTRY.]

palm·is·try (pä′mĭ-strē) *n.* The practice or art of telling fortunes from the lines, marks, and patterns on the palms of the hands. [Middle English *palmestrie,* from *palme, paume,* palm. See PALM[1].]

pal·mi·tate (păl′mĭ-tāt′, päl′-, pä′mĭ-) *n.* An ester or salt of palmitic acid. [PALMIT(IC) ACID + -ATE[2].]

pal·mit·ic acid (păl-mĭt′ĭk, päl-, pä-mĭt′-) *n.* A fatty acid, $C_{15}H_{31}COOH$, occurring in many natural oils and fats and used in making soaps. [French *palmitique,* from *palmite,* pith of the palm tree. See PALMITIN.]

pal·mi·tin (păl′mĭ-tĭn, päl′-, pä′mĭ-) *n.* The glyceryl ester, $C_3H_5(OOC_{16}H_{31})_3$, of palmitic acid, found in palm oil and animal fats and used to manufacture soap. Also called *tripalmitin.* [French *palmitine,* perhaps from *palmite,* pith of the palm tree, from Portuguese *palmito,* diminutive of *palma,* palm, from Latin *palma.* See PALM[2].]

palm oil *n.* A yellowish fatty oil obtained especially from the crushed nuts of an African palm *(Elaeis guineensis)* and used in the manufacture of soaps, chocolates, cosmetics, and candles.

Palm Springs. A city of southeast California east-southeast of Riverside. It is a desert oasis and popular resort with hot springs known to the Spanish as early as 1774. Population, 32,271.

palm sugar *n.* Sugar made from the sap of various palm trees.

Palm Sunday *n.* The Sunday before Easter, observed by Christians in commemoration of Jesus's entry into Jerusalem, when palm fronds were strewn before him.

palm·y (pä′mē) *adj.* **-i·er, -i·est. 1.** Of or relating to palm trees. **2.** Covered with palm trees. **3.** Prosperous; flourishing: *palmy times for stockbrokers.*

pal·my·ra (păl-mī′rə) *n.* A tall, dioecious palm *(Borassus flabellifer)* of tropical Africa and Asia that has large fanlike leaves. Also called *palmyra palm.* [Alteration (influenced by PALMYRA) of Portuguese *palmeira,* from *palma,* palm tree, from Latin. See PALM[2].]

Pal·my·ra (păl-mī′rə). An ancient city of central Syria northeast of Damascus. Said to have been built by Solomon, it prospered under the Romans because of its location on the trade route from Egypt to the Persian Gulf. The city was partially destroyed by the emperor Aurelian after a people's revolt in A.D. 273.

Pal·o Al·to (păl′ō ăl′tō). A city of western California northwest of San Jose. It is a residential community with an electronics industry. Population, 55,225.

Pal·o·mar (păl′ə-mär′), **Mount.** A peak, 1,868.4 m (6,126 ft) high, of southern California northeast of San Diego. It is the site of an observatory with one of the world's largest reflecting telescopes.

pal·o·mi·no (păl′ə-mē′nō) *n., pl.* **-nos.** A horse with a golden or tan coat and a white or cream-colored mane and tail, thought to have been developed from Arabian stock. [American Spanish, from Spanish, young dove, perhaps from Italian *palombino,* dove-colored, from Latin *palumbīnus,* pertaining to ring-doves, from *palumbēs,* ringdove. See **pel-**[1] in Appendix.]

pa·loo·ka (pə-lo͞o′kə) *n.* **1.** *Sports.* An incompetent or easily defeated athlete, especially a prizefighter. **2.** *Slang.* A stupid or clumsy person. [Origin unknown.]

Pa·los Hills (pā′ləs). A city of northeast Illinois, a suburb of Chicago. Population, 16,654.

Pa·louse (pə-lo͞os′) *n., pl.* **Palouse** or **Pa·louses. 1.** A Sahaptin-speaking Native American people formerly inhabiting an area of southeast Washington and northwest Idaho, with present-day descendants in northeast Washington. **2.** A member of this people.

Palouse River. A river, about 225 km (140 mi) long, rising in northwest Idaho and flowing west and south to the Snake River in southeast Washington.

pa·lo ver·de (păl′ō vûr′dē, vûrd′) *n.* **1.** A spiny, nearly leafless, bushy tree *(Cercidium floridum)* of the southwest United States, having showy yellow flowers and blue-green bark. **2.** Any of several similar or related shrubs. [American Spanish : Spanish *palo,* tree (from Latin *pālus,* stake; see PALE[1]) + Spanish *verde,* green (from Latin *viridis*).]

palp (pălp) *n. Zoology.* An elongated, often segmented appendage usually found near the mouth in invertebrate organisms such as mollusks, crustaceans, and insects, the functions of which may include sensation, locomotion, and feeding. Also called *palpus.* [French *palpe,* from New Latin *palpus,* from Latin, a touching. See **pōl-** in Appendix.]

pal·pa·ble (păl′pə-bəl) *adj.* **1.** Capable of being handled, touched, or felt; tangible: *"Anger rushed out in a palpable wave through his arms and legs"* (Herman Wouk). **2.** Easily perceived; obvious: *"There was a palpable sense of expectation in the court"* (Nelson DeMille). See Synonyms at **perceptible. 3.** *Medicine.* That can be felt by palpating: *a palpable tumor.* [Middle English, from Old French, from Late Latin *palpābilis,* from Latin *palpāre,* to touch gently. See **pōl-** in Appendix.] **—pal′pa·bil′i·ty** *n.* **—pal′pa·bly** *adv.*

pal·pal (păl′pəl) *adj.* Of, relating to, or characteristic of a palp.

pal·pate[1] (păl′pāt′) *tr.v.* **-pat·ed, -pat·ing, -pates.** To examine or explore by touching (an organ or area of the body), usually as a diagnostic aid. See Synonyms at **touch.** [Latin *palpāre, palpāt-,* to touch gently. See **pōl-** in Appendix.] **—pal·pa′tion** *n.* **—pal′pa′tor** *n.* **—pal′pa·tor′y** (-pə-tôr′ē, -tōr′ē) *adj.*

pal·pate[2] (păl′pāt′) *adj.* Having a palp or palps.

pal·pe·bra (păl′pə-brə, păl-pē′-) *n., pl.* **-pe·brae** (-pə-brē′, -pē′brē) also **-pe·bras.** *Anatomy.* An eyelid. [Latin. See **pōl-** in Appendix.] **—pal′pe·bral** (păl′pə-brəl, păl-pē′brəl, -pĕb′rəl) *adj.*

pal·pi (păl′pī′) *n. Zoology.* Plural of **palpus.**

pal·pi·tant (păl′pĭ-tənt) *adj.* **1.** Shaking; trembling. **2.** Undergoing pulsation; pulsating. [Latin *palpitāns, palpitant-,* present participle of *palpitāre,* to palpitate. See PALPITATE.]

pal·pi·tate (păl′pĭ-tāt′) *intr.v.* **-tat·ed, -tat·ing, -tates. 1.** To move with a slight tremulous motion; tremble, shake, or quiver. **2.** To beat with excessive rapidity; throb. See Synonyms at **pulsate.** [Latin *palpitāre, palpitāt-,* frequentative of *palpāre,* to touch gently. See **pōl-** in Appendix.] **—pal′pi·tat′ing·ly** *adv.*

pal·pi·ta·tion (păl′pĭ-tā′shən) *n.* **1.** A trembling or shaking. **2.** Irregular, rapid beating or pulsation of the heart.

pal·pus (păl′pəs) *n., pl.* **-pi** (-pī). *Zoology.* See **palp.** [Latin, a toweling, the soft palm of the hand. See PALP.]

pals·grave (pôlz′grāv′) *n.* See **palatine[1]** (sense 3). [Obsolete Dutch *paltsgrave,* from Middle Dutch *palsgrēve, palsgrave* : *pals,* palatine (from Vulgar Latin *palantia, palace, from Latin *palātia,* pl. of *Palātium,* imperial palace; see PALACE) + Middle Dutch *grēve, grave,* count.]

pal·sied (pôl′zēd) *adj.* **1.** Affected with palsy. **2.** Trembling or shaking.

pal·sy (pôl′zē) *n., pl.* **-sies. 1.** Complete or partial muscle paralysis, often accompanied by loss of sensation and uncontrollable body movements or tremors. **2.a.** A weakening or debilitating influence. **b.** An enfeebled condition or debilitated state thought to result from such an influence. **3.** A fit of strong emotion marked by the inability to act: *"Flaherty dithered in a little palsy of indignation"* (Anthony Burgess). **—palsy** *tr.v.* **-sied, -sy·ing, -sies. 1.a.** To paralyze. **b.** To deprive of strength. **2.** To make helpless, as with fear. [Middle English *palsie,* alteration of Old French *paralisie,* alteration of Latin *paralysis.* See PARALYSIS.]

pal·sy-wal·sy (păl′zē-wăl′zē) *adj. Slang.* Having or appearing to have the close relationship of chums. [Reduplication of *palsy,* alteration of PALLY.]

pal·ter (pôl′tər) *intr.v.* **-tered, -ter·ing, -ters. 1.** To talk or act insincerely or misleadingly; equivocate. See Synonyms at **lie[2]. 2.** To be capricious; trifle. **3.** To quibble, especially in bargaining. [Origin unknown.] **—pal′ter·er** *n.*

pal·try (pôl′trē) *adj.* **-tri·er, -tri·est. 1.** Lacking in importance or worth; trivial. See Synonyms at **trivial. 2.** Wretched or contemptible. [Probably from obsolete and dialectal *paltry,* trash, perhaps from Low German *paltrig,* ragged, from *palte,* rag.] **—pal′tri·ly** *adv.* **—pal′tri·ness** *n.*

pa·lu·dal (pə-lo͞od′l, păl′yə-dəl) *adj.* Of or relating to a swamp; marshy. [Latin *palūs, palūd-,* marsh. See **pele-[1]** in Appendix.]

pal·u·dism (păl′yə-dĭz′əm) *n.* See **malaria** (sense 1). [From Latin *palūs, palūd-,* marsh. See **pele-[1]** in Appendix.]

pal·y[1] (pā′lē) *adj.* **-i·er, -i·est.** *Archaic.* Pale.

pal·y[2] (pā′lē) *adj. Heraldry.* Divided into several equal parts by perpendicular lines. Used of a field. [Middle English, from Old French *pale,* from *pal,* stake. See PALE[1].]

pal·y·nol·o·gy (păl′ə-nŏl′ə-jē) *n.* The scientific study of spores and pollen. [Greek *palunein,* to sprinkle + –LOGY.] **—pal′y·no·log′i·cal** (-nə-lŏj′ĭ-kəl), **pal′y·no·log′ic** *adj.* **—pal′y·no·log′i·cal·ly** *adv.* **—pal′y·nol′o·gist** *n.*

pam (păm) *n. Games.* The jack of clubs and highest trump in certain variations of loo. [Probably ultimately from the Greek name *Pamphilos.*]

pam. *abbr.* Pamphlet.

Pa·mir (pə-mîr′, pä-). A mountainous region of south-central Asia mostly in Tadzhikistan with extensions in northern Afghanistan, northern Kashmir, and western China. The Pamirs rise to 7,500 m (24,590 ft).

Pam·li·co Sound (păm′lĭ-kō′). An inlet of the Atlantic Ocean between the eastern coast of North Carolina and a row of low, sandy barrier islands. Fish, oysters, and wildlife abound.

pam·pa (păm′pə) *n., pl.* **-pas** (-pəz, -pəs). In South America, a treeless, grassland area. [American Spanish, from Quechua, flat field.]

Pam·pa (păm′pə). A city of northwest Texas in the Panhandle east-northeast of Amarillo. It is an industrial and shipping center in a cattle and oil area. Population, 21,396.

Pam·pas (păm′pəz, -pəs). A vast plain of south-central South America. The Pampas extend for about 1,610 km (1,000 mi) from the lower Paraná River to south-central Argentina.

pam·pas grass (păm′pəs) *n.* A grass *(Cortaderia selloana)* of southern South America, having silvery plumes and growing in large clumps more than three meters (ten feet) tall.

pam·pe·an also **Pam·pe·an** (păm′pē-ən, păm-pē′ən) *adj.* Of or relating to a pampa or the Pampas or their inhabitants.

pam·per (păm′pər) *tr.v.* **-pered, -per·ing, -pers. 1.** To treat with excessive indulgence: *pampered their child.* **2.** To give in to; gratify: *He pampered his ambition for wealth and fame.* **3.** *Archaic.* To indulge with rich food; glut. [Middle English *pamperen,* probably of Low German origin.] **—pam′per·er** *n.*

SYNONYMS: *pamper, indulge, humor, spoil, coddle, mollycoddle, baby.* These verbs all mean to cater excessively to someone or to his or her desires or feelings. To *pamper* is to gratify appetites, tastes, or desires, as for rich food or luxurious comforts: *Cosseted and pampered from earliest childhood, he believed the world had been invented for his entertainment. "He was pampering the poor girls's lust for singularity and self-glorification"* (Charles Kingsley). *Indulge* suggests a kindly or excessive lenience in yielding to wishes, inclinations, or impulses, especially those better left unfulfilled: *"The truth is, I do indulge myself a little the more in pleasure"* (Samuel Pepys). *"Pelham . . . felt that an ally so little used to control . . . might well be indulged in an occasional fit of waywardness"* (Macaulay). *Humor* implies compliance with or accommodation to another's mood or idiosyncrasies: *"Human life is . . . but like a froward child, that must be played with and humored a little to keep it quiet till it falls asleep"* (William Temple). *Spoil* implies oversolicitude or excessive indulgence that adversely affects the character, nature, or attitude: *"He seems to be in no danger of being spoilt by good fortune"* (George Gissing). *Coddle* and *mollycoddle* point to tender, overprotective care that often leads to weakening of character: *"I would not coddle the child"* (Samuel Johnson). *Stop mollycoddling me; I'm a grown person. Baby* suggests bestowing on someone the indulgence and attention one might give to an infant: *"I should like to be made much of, and tended—yes, babied"* (Adeline D.T. Whitney).

pam·pe·ro (păm-pâr′ō, päm-) *n., pl.* **-ros.** A strong, cold southwest wind that blows across the Pampas. [American Spanish, from *pampa,* pampa. See PAMPA.]

pam·phlet (păm′flĭt) *n. Abbr.* **pam., pph. 1.** An unbound printed work, usually with a paper cover. **2.** A short essay or treatise, usually on a current topic, published without a binding. [Middle English *pamflet,* from Medieval Latin *pamfletus,* from *Pamphiletus,* diminutive of *Pamphilus,* a short amatory Latin poem of the 12th century, from Greek *pamphilos,* beloved by all : *pan-,* pan- + *philos,* beloved.] **—pam′phlet·ar′y** (păm′flĭ-tĕr′ē) *adj.*

pam·phlet·eer (păm′flĭ-tîr′) *n.* A writer of pamphlets or other short works taking a partisan stand on an issue. **—pamphleteer** *intr.v.* **-eered, -eer·ing, -eers.** To write and publish pamphlets.

Pam·plo·na (păm-plō′nə, päm-plô′nä). A city of northern Spain east-southeast of Bilbao. An ancient Basque city, it was captured by the Visigoths, Franks, and Moors and became the capital of the kingdom of Navarre (824–1512). The annual running of the bulls during the feast of San Fermin was celebrated in Ernest Hemingway's *The Sun Also Rises* (1926). Population, 181,688.

pam·pro·dac·ty·lous (păm′prō-dăk′tə-ləs) *adj.* Having all toes pointing forwards. Used of certain birds. [PAN– + PRO–[2] + DACTYL(O)– + –OUS.]

pan[1] (păn) *n.* **1.** A shallow, wide, open container, usually of metal and without a lid, used for holding liquids, cooking, and other domestic purposes. **2.** A vessel similar in form to a pan, especially: **a.** An open, metal dish used to separate gold or other metal from gravel or waste by washing. **b.** Either of the receptacles on a balance or pair of scales. **c.** A vessel used for boiling and evaporating liquids. **3.a.** A basin or depression in the earth, often containing mud or water. **b.** A natural or artificial basin used to obtain salt by evaporating brine. **c.** Hardpan. **4.** A freely floating piece of ice that has broken off a larger floe. **5.** The small cavity in the lock of a flintlock used to hold powder. **6.** *Slang.* The face. See Synonyms at **face. 7.** *Informal.* Severe criticism, especially a negative review: *gave the film a pan.* **—pan** *v.* **panned, pan·ning, pans.** *—tr.* **1.** To wash (gravel, for example) in a pan for gold or other precious metal. **2.** To cook (food) in a pan: *panned the fish right after catching it.* **3.** *Informal.* To criticize or review harshly. *—intr.* **1.** To wash gravel, sand, or other sediment in a pan. **2.** To yield gold as a result of washing in a pan. **—*phrasal verb.* pan out.** To turn out well; be successful: *"If I don't pan out as an actor I can still go back to school"* (Saul Bellow). [Middle English, from Old English *panne,* from West Germanic *panna, probably from Vulgar Latin *patna, from Latin *patina,* shallow pan, platter, from Greek *patanē.* See **pete-** in Appendix.]

WORD HISTORY: "But Dr. Brett cautioned that what sounds exciting from the Moon does not always pan out in the laboratory" (*London Daily Telegraph,* December 14, 1972). If Dr. Brett had been talking about hunting for gold on the moon, there would be a solid connection between his use of the expression *pan out* and its original use in gold mining. *Pan out,* like the verb *pan* itself, comes from the noun *pan* in the sense "a shallow circular metal vessel used in washing gold from gravel." The expression *pan out* was used in a variety of senses, including "to wash gold-bearing earth in a pan"; "to obtain gold by washing ore in a miner's pan"; and with reference to a mine or mineral-bearing soil, "to produce

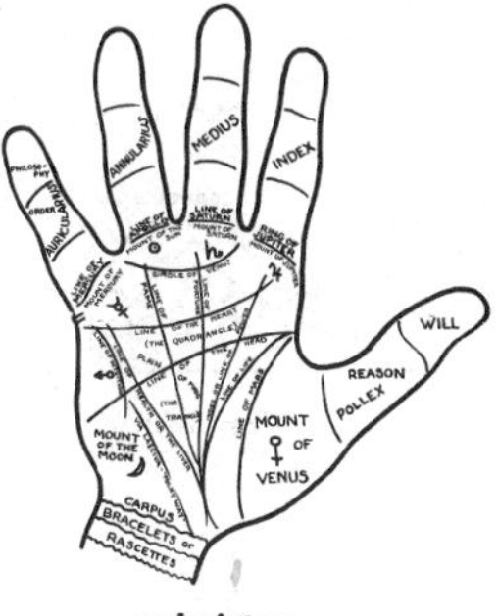

palmistry

ă pat	oi boy
ā pay	ou out
âr care	o͝o took
ä father	o͞o boot
ĕ pet	ŭ cut
ē be	ûr urge
ĭ pit	th thin
ī pie	*th* this
îr pier	hw which
ŏ pot	zh vision
ō toe	ə about, item
ô paw	♦ regionalism

Stress marks: ′ (primary); ′ (secondary), as in **dictionary** (dĭk′shə-nĕr′ē)

Pan

gold or minerals." From such literal usages *pan out* was transferred to other situations. In Frederick Whymper's *Travel and Adventure in the Territory of Alaska,* published in 1868, we are told that " 'It panned out well' means that 'it gave good returns.' " All these uses occurred first in American English, making the expression a true Americanism.

pan² (păn) *n.* **1.** A leaf of the betel vine. **2.** A chewing preparation of this leaf with betel nuts, spices, and lime, used in the Far East. [Hindi *pān,* from Sanskrit *parṇam,* feather, betel leaf. See **per-²** in Appendix.]

pan³ (păn) *v.* **panned, pan·ning, pans.** —*intr.* To move a movie or television camera to follow an object or create a panoramic effect. —*tr.* To move (a camera) so as to follow a moving object or create a panoramic effect. [Short for PANORAMA or PANORAMIC.]

Pan (păn) *n. Greek Mythology.* The god of woods, fields, and flocks, having a human torso and head with a goat's legs, horns, and ears. [Middle English, from Latin *Pān,* from Greek *Pan.*]

Pan. *abbr.* Panama.

pan– *pref.* **1.** All: *panorama.* **2. Pan–.** Involving all of or the union of a specified group: *Pan-Hellenic.* **3.** General; whole: *panleukopenia.* [Greek, from *pan,* neuter of *pas, pant-,* all. See **pant-** in Appendix.]

pan·a·ce·a (păn′ə-sē′ə) *n.* A remedy for all diseases, evils, or difficulties; a cure-all. [Latin *panacēa,* from Greek *panakeia,* from *panakēs,* all-healing : *pan-,* pan- + *akos,* cure.] **—pan′a·ce′an** *adj.*

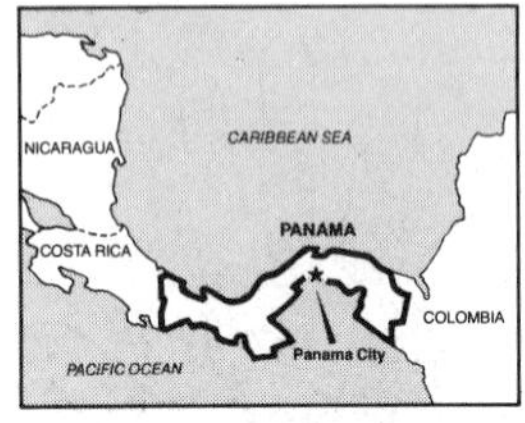

Panama

pa·nache (pə-năsh′, -näsh′) *n.* **1.** Dash; verve. **2.** A bunch of feathers or a plume, especially on a helmet. [French, plume, verve, from Italian *pinnacchio,* plume, from Late Latin *pinnāculum,* diminutive of Latin *pinna,* feather, wing. See **pet-** in Appendix.]

pa·na·da (pə-nä′də) *n.* A paste or gruel of bread crumbs, toast, or flour combined with milk, stock, or water and used for making soups, binding forcemeats, or thickening sauces. [Spanish, from *pan,* bread, from Latin *pānis.* See **pā-** in Appendix.]

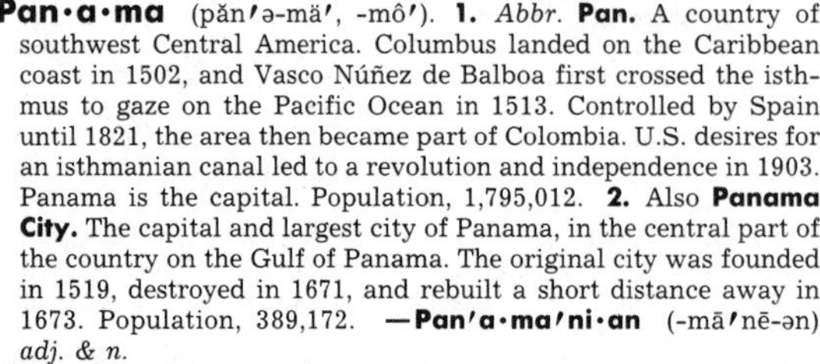

Pan·a·ma (păn′ə-mä′, -mô′). **1.** *Abbr.* **Pan.** A country of southwest Central America. Columbus landed on the Caribbean coast in 1502, and Vasco Núñez de Balboa first crossed the isthmus to gaze on the Pacific Ocean in 1513. Controlled by Spain until 1821, the area then became part of Colombia. U.S. desires for an isthmanian canal led to a revolution and independence in 1903. Panama is the capital. Population, 1,795,012. **2.** Also **Panama City.** The capital and largest city of Panama, in the central part of the country on the Gulf of Panama. The original city was founded in 1519, destroyed in 1671, and rebuilt a short distance away in 1673. Population, 389,172. **—Pan′a·ma′ni·an** (-mā′nē-ən) *adj. & n.*

Panama hat

Panama, Gulf of. A wide inlet of the Pacific Ocean on the southern coast of Panama.

Panama, Isthmus of. Formerly **Isthmus of Da·ri·én** (dâr′ē-ĕn′, dār-yĕn′). An isthmus of Central America connecting North and South America and separating the Pacific Ocean from the Caribbean Sea.

Panama Canal. A ship canal, about 82 km (51 mi) long, crossing the Isthmus of Panama in the Canal Zone and connecting the Caribbean Sea with the Pacific Ocean. It was begun by the French in 1881, but the project was abandoned in 1889. The United States gained construction rights after Panama declared its independence in 1903, and the canal was opened to traffic on August 15, 1914. A 1977 treaty stipulated that the Panamanians gain full rights of sovereignty over the canal on December 31, 1999.

Panama Canal Zone. See **Canal Zone.**

Panama City. **1.** A city of northwest Florida on the Gulf of Mexico east-southeast of Pensacola. It is a resort and fishing center and a port of entry. Population, 33,346. **2.** See **Panama** (sense 2).

Panama hat *n.* A natural-colored, hand-plaited hat made from leaves of the jipijapa plant of South and Central America.

Panama Red *n.* Marijuana of Panamanian origin that is slightly red and very potent.

Pan-A·mer·i·can (păn′ə-mĕr′ĭ-kən) *adj.* Of or relating to North, South, and Central America.

Pan-American Highway. A system of roadways, about 25,744 km (16,000 mi) long, extending from Alaska to Chile and linking the nations of the Western Hemisphere.

Pan·a·mint Range (păn′ə-mĭnt′). A rugged range of mountains in eastern California between Death Valley and the **Panamint Valley.**

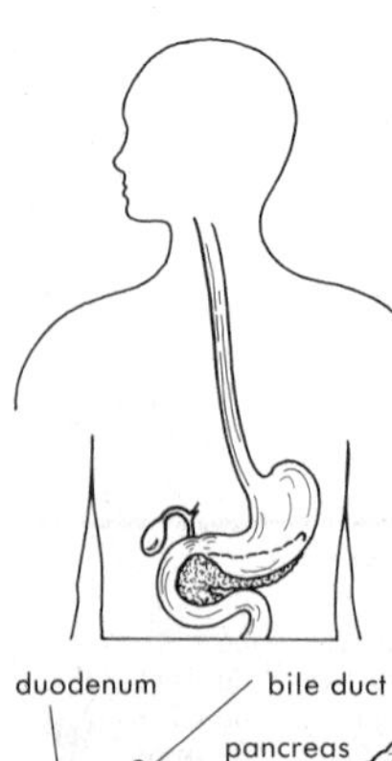

pancreas

pan·a·tel·a (păn′ə-tĕl′ə) also **pan·e·tel·a** or **pan·e·tel·la** (păn′ĭ-) *n.* A long, slender cigar. [Spanish, biscuit, cigar, from American Spanish, long thin biscuit, from Italian *panatella,* diminutive of *panata,* panada, from *pane,* bread, from Latin *pānis.* See **pā-** in Appendix.]

Pa·nay (pə-nī′, pä-). An island of the central Philippines in the Visayan Islands northwest of Negros. Corn and rice are among its crops.

pan-broil (păn′broil′) *tr.v.* **-broiled, -broil·ing, -broils.** To cook (steak, for example) over direct heat in an uncovered, usually ungreased skillet.

♦**pan·cake** (păn′kāk′) *n.* A thin cake made of batter that is poured onto a hot, greased surface and cooked on both sides until brown. Also called ♦*battercake,* ♦*flannel cake,* ♦*flapjack,* ♦*griddlecake,* ♦*hotcake.* **—pancake** *v.* **-caked, -cak·ing, -cakes.** —*intr.* To make a pancake landing in an aircraft. —*tr.* To cause (an aircraft) to make a pancake landing.

Pan-Cake (păn′kāk′). A trademark used for a semisolid cosmetic or theatrical makeup pressed into a flat cake and usually applied with a damp sponge.

pancake landing *n.* An irregular or emergency landing in which an aircraft drops flat to the ground from a low altitude.

pan·cet·ta (păn-chĕt′ə) *n.* Italian bacon that has been cured in salt and spices and then air-dried. [Italian, diminutive of *pancia,* belly, from Latin *pantex, pantic-.*]

pan·chax (păn′chăks′) *n.* Any of various small, brightly colored Old World tropical fishes of the genus *Aplocheilus* and related genera, often kept in home aquariums. [New Latin, former genus name.]

Pan·chen La·ma (pän′chən lä′mə) *n.* One of Tibet's two grand lamas, the other being the Dalai Lama. [Tibetan : *paṇchen,* great scholar (Sanskrit *paṇḍitaḥ,* scholar; see PUNDIT + Tibetan *chen-po,* great) + Tibetan *bla-ma,* monk.]

pan·chro·mat·ic (păn′krō-măt′ĭk) *adj.* Sensitive to all colors: *panchromatic film.* **—pan·chro′ma·tism** (-krō′mə-tĭz′əm) *n.*

pan·cra·ti·um (păn-krā′shē-əm) *n.* An athletic contest in ancient Greece that involved boxing and wrestling. [Latin, from Greek *pankration* : *pan-,* all (from neuter of *pas, pant-;* see **pant-** in Appendix) + *kratos,* strength; see –CRACY.]

pan·cre·as (păng′krē-əs, păn′-) *n.* A long, irregularly shaped gland in vertebrates, lying behind the stomach, that secretes pancreatic juice into the duodenum and insulin, glucagon, and somatostatin into the bloodstream. [Greek *pankreas* : *pan-,* all (from neuter of *pas, pant-;* see **pant-** in Appendix) + *kreas,* flesh; see **kreuə-** in Appendix.] **—pan′cre·at′ic** (păng′krē-ăt′ĭk, păn′-) *adj.*

pancreat– *pref.* Variant of **pancreato–.**

pan·cre·a·tec·to·my (păng′krē-ə-tĕk′tə-mē, păn′-) *n., pl.* **-mies.** Surgical removal of all or part of the pancreas.

pancreatic juice *n.* A clear, alkaline secretion of the pancreas containing enzymes that aid in the digestion of proteins, carbohydrates, and fats.

pan·cre·a·tin (păng′krē-ə-tĭn, păn′-, păn-krē′ə-tĭn) *n.* A mixture of the enzymes of pancreatic juice, such as amylase, lipase, and trypsin, extracted from animals such as cattle or hogs and used as a digestive aid.

pan·cre·a·ti·tis (păng′krē-ə-tī′tĭs, păn′-) *n.* Inflammation of the pancreas.

pancreato– or **pancreat–** *pref.* Pancreas: *pancreatin.* [From Greek *pankreas, pankreat-,* pancreas. See PANCREAS.]

pan·cre·o·zy·min (păng′krē-ō-zī′mĭn, păn′-) *n.* See **cholecystokinin.** [PANCRE(AS) + ZYM(O)– + –IN.]

pan·cy·to·pe·ni·a (păn′sī-tə-pē′nē-ə) *n.* See **aplastic anemia.**

pan·da (păn′də) *n.* **1.** A rare, bearlike mammal *(Ailuropoda melanoleuca)* of the mountains of China and Tibet (Xizang), having woolly fur with distinctive black and white markings. Also called *giant panda, panda bear.* **2.** A small, raccoonlike mammal *(Ailurus fulgens)* of northeast Asia, having reddish fur, white face markings, and a long ringed tail. Also called *lesser panda, red panda.* [French, perhaps of Nepalese origin.]

panda car *n. Chiefly British.* A police cruiser. [From a similarity of color tone distribution.]

pan·dae·mo·ni·um (păn′də-mō′nē-əm) *n.* Variant of **pandemonium.**

pan·da·nus (păn-dā′nəs, -dăn′əs) *n.* Any of numerous palmlike dioecious trees and shrubs of the genus *Pandanus* of the Old World tropics, having large prop roots and a crown of narrow, spiny leaves that yield a fiber used in weaving mats and similar articles. Also called *screw pine.* [New Latin *Pandanus,* genus name, from Malay *pandan,* screw pine.] **—pan′da·na′ceous** (păn′də-nā′shəs) *adj.*

panda plant *n.* A succulent perennial herb *(Kalanchoe tomentosa)* native to Madagascar, having usually oblong obovate leaves covered with a dense silvery felt and surrounded by a rusty brown crenate margin. [From the color pattern of the leaves.]

Pan·da·rus (păn′dər-əs) also **Pan·dar** (-dər) *n.* **1.** The leader of the Lycians, slain by Diomedes in the *Iliad.* **2.** The procurer of Cressida for Troilus in medieval romance.

Pan·de·an pipe (păn-dē′ən) *n. Music.* See **panpipe.** [From PAN.]

pan·dect (păn′dĕkt′) *n.* **1.** A comprehensive digest or complete treatise. **2. pandects.** A complete body of laws; a legal code. **3. Pandects.** A digest of Roman civil law, compiled for the emperor Justinian in the sixth century A.D. and part of the Corpus Juris Civilis. In this sense, also called *Digest.* [Latin *pandectēs,* encyclopedia, from Greek *pandektēs,* all-receiving : *pan-,* pan- + *dektēs,* receiver (from *dekhesthai,* to receive, accept; see **dek-** in Appendix).]

pan·dem·ic (păn-dĕm′ĭk) *adj.* **1.** Widespread; general. **2.** *Medicine.* Epidemic over a wide geographic area: *pandemic influenza.* **—pandemic** *n.* A pandemic disease. [From Late Latin *pandēmus,* from Greek *pandēmos,* of all the people : *pan-,* pan- + *dēmos,* people; see **dā-** in Appendix.]

pan·de·mo·ni·um also **pan·dae·mo·ni·um** (păn′də-mō′nē-əm) *n.* **1.** A very noisy place: *"The whole lobby was a perfect pandemonium, and the din was terrific"* (Jerome K. Jerome). **2.** Wild uproar or noise. See Synonyms at **noise.** [From *Pandæmonium,* capital of Hell in *Paradise Lost,* an epic poem by John Milton : Greek *pan-,* pan- + Late Latin *daemonium,* demon (from Greek *daimonion,* from *daimōn,* lesser god, demon; see DEMON).] **—pan′de·mo′ni·ac** (-nē-ăk′) *adj.*

pan·der (păn′dər) *intr.v.* **-dered, -der·ing, -ders. 1.** To act as a go-between or liaison in sexual intrigues; function as a procurer. **2.** To cater to the lower tastes and desires of others or exploit their weaknesses: *"He refused to pander to nostalgia and escapism"* (New York Times). [Middle English *Pandare,* Pandarus, from Old Italian *Pandaro,* from Latin *Pandarus,* from Greek *Pandaros.*] **—pan′der** *n.*

pan·der·er (păn′dər-ər) *n.* **1.** A sexual procurer. **2.** One who caters to or exploits the lower tastes and desires of others.

P and H or **p. and h.** *abbr.* Postage and handling.

pan·dit (păn′dĭt) or **pun·dit** (pŭn′-) *n.* **1.** A Brahman scholar or learned man. **2.** Used as a title of respect for a learned man in India. [Hindi *paṇḍit,* from Sanskrit *paṇḍitaḥ.* See PUNDIT.]

P and L or **p. and l.** *abbr. Accounting.* Profit and loss.

Pan·do·ra (păn-dôr′ə, -dōr′ə) *n. Greek Mythology.* The first woman, bestowed upon humankind as a punishment for Prometheus's theft of fire. Entrusted with a box containing all the ills that could plague people, she opened it out of curiosity and thereby released all the evils of human life.

Pan·do·ra's box (păn-dôr′əz, -dōr′-) *n.* A source of many unforeseen troubles: *"Reform is a Pandora's box; opening up the system can lead to a loss of economic and political control"* (Russell Watson).

pan·dore (păn′dôr′, -dōr′) *n. Music.* See **bandore.** [Ultimately Greek *pandoura.*]

pan·dow·dy (păn-dou′dē) *n., pl.* **-dies.** Sliced fruit baked with sugar and spices in a deep dish, with a thick top crust. [Perhaps from obsolete dialectal *pandoulde,* custard : PAN[1] + dialectal *dowl,* to mix dough in a hurry (probably variant of DOUGH).]

pan·du·rate (păn-do͝or′ĭt, -dyo͝or′-) also **pan·du·ri·form** (-ə-fôrm′) *adj. Botany.* Having rounded ends and a contracted center; fiddle-shaped: *pandurate leaves.* [From Late Latin *pandūra,* three-string lute, from Greek *pandoura.*]

pane (pān) *n.* **1. a.** One of the glass-filled divisions of a window or door. **b.** The glass used in such a division. **2.** A panel, as of a door or wall. **3.** One of the flat surfaces or facets of an object, such as a bolt, having many sides. [Middle English, section, pane of glass, from Old French *pan,* piece of cloth, panel, from Latin *pannus,* cloth. See **pan-** in Appendix.]

paned (pānd) *adj.* Having a specified kind or number of panes. Often used in combination: *clear-paned windows; double-paned French doors.*

pan·e·gyr·ic (păn′ə-jĭr′ĭk, -jī′rĭk) *n.* **1.** A formal eulogistic composition intended as a public compliment. **2.** Elaborate praise or laudation; an encomium. [Latin *panēgyricus,* from Greek *panēgurikos (logos),* (speech) at a public assembly, panegyric, from *panēguris,* public assembly : *pan-,* pan- + *aguris,* assembly, marketplace; see **ger-** in Appendix.] **—pan′e·gyr′i·cal** *adj.* **—pan′e·gyr′i·cal·ly** *adv.*

pan·e·gyr·ist (păn′ə-jĭr′ĭst, -jī′rĭst) *n.* One who writes or delivers panegyrics; a eulogist.

pan·e·gy·rize (păn′ə-jə-rīz′) *v.* **-rized, -riz·ing, -riz·es.** *—tr.* To eulogize. *—intr.* To compose, deliver, or indulge in panegyrics.

pan·el (păn′əl) *n.* **1.** A flat, usually rectangular piece forming a raised, recessed, or framed part of the surface in which it is set. **2.** The space or section in a fence or railing between two posts. **3.** A vertical section of fabric; a gore. **4. a.** A thin wooden board, used as a surface for an oil painting. **b.** A painting on such a board. **5. a.** A board having switches or buttons to control an electric device. **b.** An instrument panel. **6.** A section of a telephone switchboard. **7.** *Law.* **a.** The complete list of persons summoned for jury duty. **b.** Those persons selected from this list to compose a jury. **c.** A jury. **8. a.** A group of people gathered to plan or discuss an issue, judge a contest, or act as a team on a radio or television quiz program. **b.** A discussion by such a group. **—panel** *tr.v.* **-eled, -el·ing, -els** or **-elled, -el·ling, -els. 1.** To cover or furnish with panels. **2.** To decorate with panels. **3.** To separate into panels. **4.** *Law.* To select or impanel (a jury). [Middle English, piece of cloth, from Old French, probably from Vulgar Latin **pannellus,* diminutive of Latin *pannus,* cloth. See **pan-** in Appendix.]

panel discussion *n.* A discussion of a subject of public interest by a group of persons forming a panel, often before an audience.

pan·el·ing (păn′ə-lĭng) *n.* A section of panels or paneled wall.

pan·el·ist (păn′ə-lĭst) *n.* A member of a panel.

pan·el·ized (păn′ə-līzd′) *adj.* Consisting of or characterized by prefabricated wall, floor, and roof sections that are shipped to and assembled at the building site: *panelized housing.* **—pan′el·i·za′tion** (-ə-lĭ-zā′shən) *n.*

panel truck *n.* A small delivery truck with a fully enclosed body.

pan·en·ceph·a·li·tis (păn′ĕn-sĕf′ə-lī′tĭs) *n.* **1.** Encephalitis that affects both the gray and white matter of the brain, resulting in progressive loss of mental and motor functions. **2.** Subacute sclerosing panencephalitis.

pan·e·tel·a or **pan·e·tel·la** (păn′ĭ-tĕl′ə) *n.* Variants of **panatela.**

pan·et·to·ne (păn′ĭ-tō′nē) *n., pl.* **-nes** or **-ni** (-nē). A festive Italian yeast cake flavored with candied fruit peels and raisins. [Italian, augmentative of *panetto,* a small loaf, diminutive of *pane,* bread, from Latin *pānis.* See PANADA.]

pan fish *n.* A fish small enough to be fried whole in a pan.

pan-fry also **pan·fry** (păn′frī′) *tr.v.* **-fried, -fry·ing, -fries.** To fry in a frying pan or skillet with a small amount of fat.

pan·ful (păn′fo͝ol′) *n.* The amount that a pan can hold.

pang (păng) *n.* **1.** A sudden sharp spasm of pain. See Synonyms at **pain. 2.** A sudden, sharp feeling of emotional distress. **—pang** *tr.v.* **panged, pang·ing, pangs.** To cause to feel pangs; distress acutely. [Origin unknown.]

Pan·gae·a also **Pan·ge·a** (păn-jē′ə) *n.* A hypothetical supercontinent that included all the landmasses of the earth before the Triassic Period. When continental drift began, Pangaea broke up into Laurasia and Gondwanaland. [PAN– + Greek *gaia,* earth.]

pan·gen·e·sis (păn-jĕn′ĭ-sĭs) *n.* A theory of heredity proposed by Charles Darwin in which gemmules containing hereditary information from every part of the body coalesce in the gonads and are incorporated into the reproductive cells. **—pan′ge·net′ic** (-jə-nĕt′ĭk) *adj.* **—pan′ge·net′i·cal·ly** *adv.*

Pan·gloss·i·an (păn-glŏs′ē-ən, -glôs′-, păng-) *adj.* Blindly or naively optimistic. [After *Pangloss,* an optimist in *Candide,* a satire by Voltaire.]

pan·go·lin (păng′gə-lĭn, păn′-) *n.* Any of several long-tailed, scale-covered mammals of the order Pholidota of tropical Africa and Asia, having a long snout and a sticky tongue for catching and eating ants and termites. Also called *scaly anteater.* [Malay *pêngguling* : *pêng-,* instrumental pref. + *guling,* to roll over (from its habit of rolling up into a ball when frightened).]

Pan·go Pan·go (päng′ō päng′ō, păng′gō păng′gō, päng′gō päng′gō). See **Pago Pago.**

pan·gram (păn′grăm′, -grəm, păng′-) *n.* A sentence that uses all the letters of the alphabet. **—pan′gram·mat′ic** (-grə-măt′ĭk) *adj.*

pan·han·dle[1] (păn′hăn′dl) *v.* **-dled, -dling, -dles.** *Informal.* *—intr.* To approach strangers and beg for money or food. *—tr.* **1.** To approach and beg from (a stranger). **2.** To obtain by approaching and begging from a stranger: *panhandled money.* See Synonyms at **cadge.** [Back-formation from *panhandler,* beggar : perhaps PAN[1] + HANDLER.] **—pan′han′dler** *n.*

pan·han·dle[2] (păn′hăn′dl) *n.* **1.** The handle of a pan. **2.** Often **Panhandle.** A narrow strip of territory projecting from a larger, broader area, as in Alaska, Idaho, Oklahoma, Texas, and West Virginia.

Pan-Hel·len·ic also **Pan·hel·len·ic** (păn′hə-lĕn′ĭk) *adj.* **1.** Of or relating to all Greek peoples or a movement to unify them. **2.** Of or relating to all Greek-letter fraternities and sororities.

pan·hu·man (păn-hyo͞o′mən) *adj.* Of or relating to all humanity.

pan·ic (păn′ĭk) *n.* **1.** A sudden, overpowering terror, often affecting many people at once. See Synonyms at **fear. 2.** A sudden widespread alarm concerning finances, often resulting in a rush to sell property: *a stock-market panic.* **3.** *Slang.* One that is uproariously funny. **—panic** *adj.* **1.** Of, relating to, or resulting from sudden, overwhelming terror: *panic flight.* **2.** Of or resulting from a financial panic: *panic selling of securities.* **3.** Often **Panic.** *Mythology.* Of or relating to Pan. **—panic** *tr. & intr.v.* **-icked, -ick·ing, -ics.** To affect or be affected with panic. See Synonyms at **frighten.** [From French *panique,* terrified, from Greek *Panikos,* of Pan (a source of terror, as in flocks or herds), groundless (used of fear), from *Pan,* Pan. See PAN.] **—pan′ick·y** *adj.*

panic button *n. Slang.* A signal for a hasty, emotional response to an emergency: *Stay calm; there's no need to hit the panic button.*

panic disorder *n.* A psychological disorder characterized by the occurrence of intense attacks of anxiety in specific circumstances and situations, usually resulting in the development of one or more phobias.

panic grass *n.* Any of numerous grasses of the genus *Panicum,* many of which are grown for grain and fodder. [Middle English *panik,* from Old French, from Latin *pānicum.*]

pan·i·cle (păn′ĭ-kəl) *n. Botany.* A branched cluster of flowers in which the branches are racemes. [Latin *pānicula,* feminine diminutive of *pānus,* a swelling, main stalk of a panicle.] **—pan′i·cled** *adj.*

pan·ic-strick·en (păn′ĭk-strĭk′ən) also **pan·ic-struck** (-strŭk′) *adj.* Overcome by panic; terrified.

pa·nic·u·late (pə-nĭk′yə-lĭt, -lāt′) also **pa·nic·u·lat·ed** (-lā′tĭd) *adj. Botany.* Growing or arranged in a panicle. [New Latin *pāniculātus,* from Latin *pānicula,* panicle. See PANICLE.] **—pa·nic′u·late·ly** *adv.*

Pa·ni·ni (pä-nē′nē). fl. 400 B.C. Indian grammarian. His *Ashtadhyayi,* one of the first works of descriptive linguistics, presents grammatical rules for Sanskrit.

Pan·ja·bi (pŭn-jä′bē, -jăb′ē) *n. & adj.* Variant of **Punjabi.**

pan·jan·drum (păn-jăn′drəm) *n.* An important or self-

panda
Giant panda
Ailuropoda melanoleuca

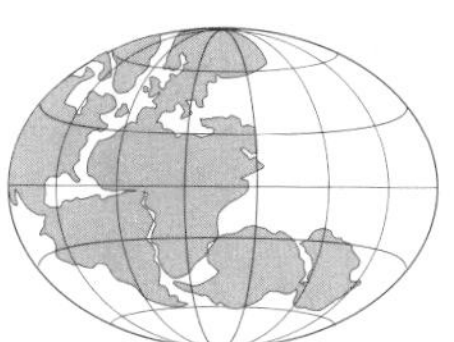

Pangaea

ă pat	oi boy
ā pay	ou out
âr care	o͝o took
ä father	o͞o boot
ĕ pet	ŭ cut
ē be	ûr urge
ĭ pit	th thin
ī pie	*th* this
îr pier	hw which
ŏ pot	zh vision
ō toe	ə about, item
ô paw	♦ regionalism

Stress marks: **′** (primary); ′ (secondary), as in **dictionary** (dĭk′shə-nĕr′ē)

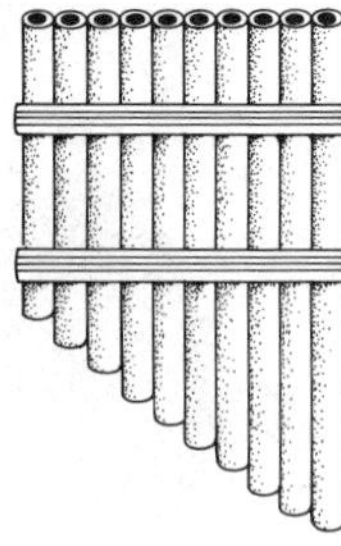

panpipe

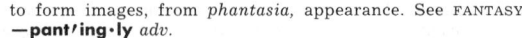

important person: *"a panjandrum of the publishing business"* (Nat Hentoff). [After the Grand *Panjandrum,* a character in a nonsense farrago written by Samuel Foote (1720–1777).]

Pank·hurst (păngk′hûrst′), **Emmeline Goulden.** 1858–1928. British suffrage leader who advocated militancy and violence in order to gain public recognition. With her daughters **Christabel Pankhurst** (1880–1958) and **Sylvia Pankhurst** (1882–1960) she founded (1903) the Women's Social and Political Union, a women-only, nonpartisan group whose motto was "Deeds, not Words."

pan·leu·ko·pe·ni·a also **pan·leu·co·pe·ni·a** (păn′lo͞o-kə-pē′nē-ə) *n.* See **distemper**[1] (sense 1b).

pan·mic·tic (păn-mĭk′tĭk) *adj.* Of or relating to panmixia. [PAN– + Greek *miktos,* mixed (from *mignunai,* to mix; see **meik-** in Appendix) + –IC.]

pan·mix·i·a (păn-mĭk′sē-ə) also **pan·mix·is** (-mĭk′sĭs) *n.* Random mating within a breeding population. [From PAN– + Greek *mixis,* act of mingling (from *mignunai,* to mix; see **meik-** in Appendix).]

Pan·mun·jom (păn′mo͞on′jŭm′). A village of northwest South Korea just south of the 38th parallel. Truce negotiations for the Korean War were held here from October 1951 to July 27, 1953, when the truce was officially signed.

panne (păn) *n.* A special finish for velvet and satin that produces a high luster. [French, a soft cloth, from Old French *penne, pane,* fur lining, from Latin *pinna, penna,* feather. See PENNA.]

pan·nier (păn′yər, păn′ē-ər) *n.* **1.** A large wicker basket, especially: **a.** One of a pair of baskets carried on the shoulders of a person or on either side of a pack animal. **b.** A basket carried on a person's back. **2.** A basket or pack, usually one of a pair, that fastens to the rack of a bicycle and hangs over the side of one of the wheels. **3.a.** A framework of wire, bone, or other material formerly used to expand a woman's skirt at the hips. **b.** A skirt or an overskirt puffed out at the hips. [Middle English *panier,* from Old French, from Latin *pānārium,* breadbasket, from *pānis,* bread. See **pā-** in Appendix.] **—pan′niered** *adj.*

Pan·no·ni·a (pə-nō′nē-ə). An ancient Roman province of central Europe including present-day western Hungary and northern Yugoslavia. Its people were finally subjugated by Rome in A.D. 9. **—Pan·no′ni·an** *adj. & n.*

pa·no·cha (pə-nō′chə) also **pa·no·che** (-chē) *n.* **1.** A coarse grade of Mexican sugar. **2.** Variants of **penuche.** [American Spanish, probably from Spanish *panoja, panocha,* ear of grain, panicle, from Latin *pānicula.* See PANICLE.]

pan·o·ply (păn′ə-plē) *n., pl.* **-plies. 1.** A splendid or striking array: *a panoply of colorful flags.* See Synonyms at **display. 2.** Ceremonial attire with all accessories: *a portrait of the general in full panoply.* **3.** Something that covers and protects: *a porcupine's panoply of quills.* **4.** The complete arms and armor of a warrior. [Greek *panoplia* : *pan-,* pan- + *hopla,* arms, armor, pl. of *hoplon,* weapon.]

pan·op·tic (păn-ŏp′tĭk) also **pan·op·ti·cal** (-tĭ-kəl) *adj.* Including everything visible in one view. [From Greek *panoptos,* seen of all : *pan-,* pan- + *optos,* visible; see **ok**[w]**-** in Appendix.]

pan·o·ram·a (păn′ə-răm′ə, -rä′mə) *n.* **1.** An unbroken view of an entire surrounding area. **2.** A comprehensive presentation; a survey: *a panorama of American literature.* **3.** A picture or series of pictures representing a continuous scene, often exhibited a part at a time by being unrolled and passed before the spectator. **4.** A mental vision of a series of events. [PAN– + Greek *horama,* sight (from *horan,* to see; see **wer-**[3] in Appendix).] **—pan′o·ram′ic** (-răm′ĭk) *adj.* **—pan′o·ram′i·cal·ly** *adv.*

pan·pipe (păn′pīp′) *n. Music.* A primitive wind instrument consisting of a series of pipes or reeds of graduated length bound together, played by blowing across the top open ends. Often used in the plural. Also called *mouth organ, Pandean pipe, syrinx.* [PAN + PIPE.]

Pantheon
Rome, Italy

pan·sex·u·al (păn-sĕk′sho͞o-əl) *adj.* Exhibiting or suggesting a sexuality that has many different forms, objects, and outlets. **—pan′sex·u·al′i·ty** (-ăl′ĭ-tē) *n.*

pan·sper·mi·a (păn-spûr′mē-ə) *n.* The theory that microorganisms or biochemical compounds from outer space are responsible for originating life on Earth and possibly in other parts of the universe where suitable atmospheric conditions exist. [Greek, mixture of all seeds : *pan-,* pan- + *sperma,* seed; see SPERM[1].]

pan·sy (păn′zē) *n., pl.* **-sies. 1.** Any of various plants of the genera *Achimenes* or *Viola,* especially *V. tricolor* or its hybrids, having flowers with velvety petals of various colors. **2.** *Color.* A deep to strong violet. **3.** *Offensive Slang.* **a.** Used as a disparaging term for a man or boy who is considered effeminate. **b.** Used as a disparaging term for a gay or homosexual man. [Middle English *pancy,* from Old French *pensee,* thought, remembrance, pansy, from feminine past participle of *penser,* to think. See PENSIVE.]

pant[1] (pănt) *v.* **pant·ed, pant·ing, pants.** *—intr.* **1.** To breathe rapidly in short gasps, as after exertion. **2.** To beat loudly or heavily; throb or pulsate. **3.** To give off loud puffs, especially while moving. **4.** To long demonstratively; yearn: *was panting for a chance to play.* *—tr.* To utter hurriedly or breathlessly: *I panted my congratulations to the winner of the race.* **—pant** *n.* **1.** A short, labored breath; a gasp. **2.** A throb; a pulsation. **3.** A short, loud puff, as of steam from an engine. [Middle English *panten,* perhaps alteration of Old French *pantaisier,* from Vulgar Latin **pantasiāre,* from Greek *phantasioun,* to form images, from *phantasia,* appearance. See FANTASY.] **—pant′ing·ly** *adv.*

pant[2] (pănt) *n.* **1.** Trousers. Often used in the plural. **2.** Underpants. Often used in the plural. **—*idiom.* with (one's) pants down.** *Slang.* In an embarrassing position. [Short for *pantaloon.*]

WORD HISTORY: It would seem unlikely that the name of a 4th-century Roman Catholic saint should be the ultimate source of a word for a modern article of clothing commonly worn by both men and women. *Pants,* however, can be traced back to Pantaleon, the patron saint of Venice. He became so closely associated with the inhabitants of that city that the Venetians became popularly known as *Pantaloni.* Consequently, among the commedia dell'arte's stock characters the representative Venetian (a stereotypically wealthy but miserly merchant) was called *Pantalone.* His name in French, *Pantalon,* was borrowed into English (first recorded around 1590). During the middle of the 17th century the French came to identify him with one particular style of trousers, and this same style became known as *pantaloons* in English. *Pantaloons* was later applied to another style of trousers that came into fashion toward the end of the 18th century, tight-fitting garments that had begun to replace knee breeches. After that *pantaloons* was used to refer to trousers in general. The last step in the development of the word *pants* met with some resistance. This abbreviation of *pantaloon* was considered vulgar and, as Oliver Wendell Holmes put it, "a word not made for gentlemen, but 'gents.' " First found in the writings of Edgar Allan Poe in 1840, *pants* has replaced the "gentleman's word" in English and has lost all obvious connection to Saint Pantaleon.

pan·ta·let also **pan·ta·lette** (păn′tə-lĕt′) *n.* **1.** Long underpants trimmed with ruffles extending below the skirt, worn by women in the mid-19th century. Often used in the plural. **2.** A frill attached to the leg of underpants. Often used in the plural. [From PANTALOON.]

Pan·ta·lo·ne (păn′tə-lō′nā, pän′tä-lô′nĕ) *n.* Variant of **Pantaloon** (sense 1).

pan·ta·loon (păn′tə-lo͞on′) *n.* **1.a.** Men's wide breeches extending from waist to ankle, worn especially in England in the late 17th century. Often used in the plural. **b.** Tight trousers extending from waist to ankle with straps passing under the instep, worn especially in the 19th century. Often used in the plural. **2.** Trousers; pants. Often used in the plural. [French *pantalon,* a kind of trouser, from *Pantalon,* Pantaloon. See PANTALOON.]

Pan·ta·loon (păn′tə-lo͞on′) *n.* **1.** Often **Pan·ta·lo·ne** (păn′tə-lō′nā, pän′tä-lô′nĕ). A character in the commedia dell'arte, portrayed as a foolish old man in tight trousers and slippers. **2.** A stock character in modern pantomime, the butt of a clown's jokes. [French *Pantalon,* from Italian *Pantalone,* after San *Pantalone,* or Saint Pantaleon (died A.D. 303), Roman physician and martyr.]

pan·the·ism (păn′thē-ĭz′əm) *n.* **1.** A doctrine identifying the Deity with the universe and its phenomena. **2.** Belief in and worship of all gods. **—pan′the·ist** *n.* **—pan′the·is′tic, pan′the·is′ti·cal** *adj.* **—pan′the·is′ti·cal·ly** *adv.*

pan·the·on (păn′thē-ŏn′, -ən) *n.* **1. Pantheon.** A circular temple in Rome, completed in 27 B.C. and dedicated to all the gods. **2.** A temple dedicated to all gods. **3.** All the gods of a people. **4.** A public building commemorating and dedicated to the heroes and heroines of a nation. **5.** A group of persons most highly regarded for contributions to a field or an endeavor: *the pantheon of modern physics.* [Middle English *Panteon,* Pantheon, from Latin *Pantheon,* from Greek *Pantheion,* shrine of all the gods, from neuter sing. of *pantheios,* of all the gods : *pan-,* pan- + *theos,* god; see **dhēs-** in Appendix.]

pan·ther (păn′thər) *n.* **1.** The leopard, especially in its black, unspotted form. **2.** See **mountain lion.** [Middle English *pantere,* from Old French and from Old English *panthera,* both from Latin *panthēra,* from Greek *panthēr.*]

pant·ie or **pant·y** (păn′tē) *n., pl.* **pant·ies.** Short underpants for women or children. Often used in the plural. [Diminutive of PANT[2].]

pan·tile (păn′tīl′) *n.* A roofing tile with an S-shaped profile, laid so that the down curve of one tile overlaps the up curve of the next one. [PAN[1] + TILE.] **—pan′tiled′** *adj.*

pan·tof·fle also **pan·to·fle** (păn-tŏf′əl, -tō′fəl, -to͞o′fəl, păn′tə-fəl) *n.* A slipper. [Middle English *pantufle,* from Old French *pantoufle.*]

pan·to·graph (păn′tə-grăf′) *n.* **1.** An instrument for copying a plane figure to a desired scale, consisting of styluses for tracing and copying mounted on four jointed rods in the form of a parallelogram with extended sides. **2.** A similarly jointed framework, such as a power-collecting trolley on an electric locomotive or an extensible telephone arm. [Greek *panto-,* all (from *pas, pant-;* see PAN–) + –GRAPH.] **—pan′to·graph′ic** *adj.*

pan·to·mime (păn′tə-mīm′) *n.* **1.** Communication by means of gesture and facial expression: *Some tourists make themselves understood abroad by pantomime.* **2.a.** The telling of a story without words, by means of bodily movements, gestures, and facial expressions. **b.** A play, dance, or other theatrical performance characterized by such wordless storytelling. **c.** An ancient Roman theatrical performance in which one actor played all the parts by means of gesture and movement, accompanied by a narrative chorus. **d.** A player in such a performance. **3.** A traditional British Christmas entertainment for children, usually based on nursery tales and featuring stock characters in costume who sing, dance, and perform skits. **—pantomime** *v.* **-mimed, -mim·ing, -mimes.** *—tr.* To represent or express by pantomime: *pantomine a story on the stage; pantomimed "baby" by cradling an imaginary infant.* *—intr.* To express oneself in pantomime. [Latin *pantomīmus,* a pantomimic actor, from Greek *pantomimos* : *panto-,* all (from *pas, pant-;* see PAN—) + *mimos,* mime.] **—pan′to·mim′ic** (-mĭm′ĭk) *adj.* **—pan′to·mim′ist** (-mī′mĭst) *n.*

pan·to·then·ate (păn′tə-thĕn′āt′, păn-tŏth′ə-nāt′) *n.* A salt or an ester of pantothenic acid. [PANTOTHEN(IC ACID) + —ATE[2].]

pan·to·then·ic acid (păn′tə-thĕn′ĭk) *n.* A yellow, oily acid, $C_9H_{17}NO_5$, belonging to and found widely in plant and animal tissues. [From Greek *pantothen,* from all sides : *panto-,* all (from *pas, pant-;* see PAN—) + *-othen,* adverbial suff. (for motion from).]

pan·toum (păn-to͞om′) *n.* A verse form composed of quatrains in which the second and fourth lines are repeated as the first and third lines of the following quatrain. [French, from Malay *pantun,* verse composed using metonymy.]

pan·trop·ic (păn-trŏp′ĭk, -trō′pĭk) *adj.* Having an affinity for or indiscriminately affecting many kinds of tissue: *pantropic viruses.*

pan·try (păn′trē) *n., pl.* **-tries. 1.** A small room or closet, usually off a kitchen, where food, tableware, linens, and similar items are stored. **2.** A small room used for the preparation of cold foods. [Middle English *pantrie,* from Old French *paneterie,* bread-closet, from *panetier,* pantry servant, from *pan,* bread, from Latin *pānis.* See **pā-** in Appendix.]

pant·suit also **pants suit** (pănt′so͞ot′) *n.* A woman's suit having trousers instead of a skirt. **—pant′suit′ed** *adj.*

pant·y (păn′tē) *n.* Variant of **pantie.**

pant·y·hose or **pant·y hose** (păn′tē-hōz′) *pl.n.* A woman's one-piece undergarment consisting of underpants and stretchable stockings.

panty raid *n.* A raid on a girls' dormitory by college boys to obtain undergarments as trophies.

pant·y·waist (păn′tē-wāst′) *n.* **1.** A child's undergarment consisting of a shirt and pants buttoned together at the waist. **2.** *Slang.* A boy or man who is considered weak or effeminate. **—pant′y·waist′** *adj.*

pan·zer (păn′zər, pänt′sər) *n.* A German armored vehicle, such as a tank, especially of the type used during World War II. **—panzer** *adj.* **1.** Of or equipped with armored vehicles: *a panzer division.* **2.** Of or relating to an armored division. [German, short for *Panzerdivision,* armored unit, from *Panzer,* tank, armor, from Middle High German *panzier,* armor, from Old French *pancier,* armor for the belly, from *pance,* belly. See PAUNCH.]

Pa·o·li (pou′lē, pä′ō-), **Pasquale di.** 1725–1807. Corsican patriot who led the struggle for independence from Genoa.

Pao·ting (bou′dĭng′). See **Baoding.**

Pao·tow (bou′tō′). See **Baotou.**

♦**pap**[1] (păp) *n.* **1.** *Midland U.S.* A teat or nipple. **2.** Something resembling a nipple. [Middle English *pappe,* probably from Latin *papilla.* See PAPILLA.]

pap[2] (păp) *n.* **1.** Soft or semiliquid food, as for infants. **2.** Material lacking real value or substance: *TV shows that offer nothing but pap.* **3.** *Slang.* Money and favors obtained as political patronage: *"self-seeking politicians primarily interested in patronage, privilege, and pap"* (Fiorello H. La Guardia). [Middle English, from Old French *papa,* from Latin, children's word for food.]

pa·pa (pä′pə, pə-pä′) also **pop·pa** (pä′pə) *n. Informal.* Father. [French. See **papa** in Appendix.]

pa·pa·cy (pā′pə-sē) *n., pl.* **-cies. 1.** The office and jurisdiction of a pope. **2.** The period of time during which a pope is in office. **3.** A succession or line of popes: *the Medici papacy.* **4. Papacy.** *Roman Catholic Church.* The system of church government headed by the pope. [Middle English *papacie,* from Medieval Latin *pāpātia,* from Late Latin *pāpa,* pope. See POPE.]

Pa·pa·do·pou·los (păp′ə-dŏp′ə-ləs, pä′pä-dô′po͞o-lôs), **George.** Born 1919. Greek military officer and politician who became premier after a 1967 coup. He was overthrown in 1973.

Pa·pa·go (păp′ə-gō′, pä′pə-) *n., pl.* **Papago** or **-gos. 1.a.** A Native American people inhabiting desert regions of southern Arizona and northern Sonora, a state of northwest Mexico. **b.** A member of this people. **2.** The Uto-Aztecan language of this people, dialectically related to Pima. Also called *O'odham, Tohono O'odham.*

pa·pa·in (pə-pā′ĭn, -pī′ĭn) *n.* An enzyme capable of digesting protein, obtained from the unripe fruit of the papaya and used as a meat tenderizer and in medicine as a digestive aid. [PAPA(YA) + —IN.]

pa·pal (pā′pəl) *adj.* **1.** Of, relating to, or issued by a pope: *the papal succession; a papal bull.* **2.** Of or relating to the Roman Catholic Church. [Middle English, from Old French, from Medieval Latin *pāpālis,* from Late Latin *pāpa,* pope. See POPE.] **—pa′pal·ly** *adv.*

Pa·pal States (pā′pəl). A group of territories in central Italy ruled by the popes from 754 until 1870. They were originally given to the papacy by Pepin the Short and reached their greatest extent in 1859. The last papal state—the Vatican City—was formally established as a separate state by the Lateran Treaty of 1929.

Pap·an·dre·ou (păp′ən-drā′o͞o, pä′pän-drĕ′-), **Andreas George.** Born 1919. Greek politician who served as premier (1981–1989).

Pa·pa·ni·co·laou test (pä′pə-nē′kə-lou′, păp′ə-nĭk′ə-lou′) *n.* The Pap smear.

pa·pa·raz·zo (pä′pə-rät′sō) *n., pl.* **-zi** (-sē). A freelance photographer who doggedly pursues celebrities to take candid pictures for sale to magazines and newspapers. [After Signor *Paparazzo,* a character in *La Dolce Vita,* a movie by Federico Fellini.]

pa·pav·er·ine (pə-păv′ə-rēn′, -ər-ĭn) *n.* A nonaddictive opium derivative, $C_{20}H_{21}NO_4$, used medicinally to relieve spasms of smooth muscle. [Latin *papāver,* poppy + —INE[2].]

pa·paw also **paw·paw** (pô′pô′) *n.* **1.** A deciduous tree *(Asimina triloba)* of the eastern and southeast United States, having flowers with three sepals, three petals, and numerous stamens and fleshy, edible fruit. **2.** The fruit of this tree. **3.** See **papaya.** [Ultimately from Spanish and obsolete Portuguese *papaya,* papaya; see PAPAYA.]

pa·pa·ya (pə-pä′yə) *n.* **1.** An evergreen, usually dioecious, tropical American tree *(Carica papaya)* having a crown of palmately divided leaves with pinnate lobes and large, yellow, edible fruit. **2.** The fruit of this tree. Also called *papaw.* [Spanish and Portuguese, both of Cariban origin.]

Pa·pe·e·te (pä′pē-ā′tā, pə-pē′tē). The capital of the overseas territory of French Polynesia, a port on the northwest coast of Tahiti in the Society Islands of the southern Pacific Ocean. It is a commercial and tourist center. Population, 23,496.

Pa·pen (pä′pən), **Franz von.** 1879–1969. German politician and diplomat who served as vice chancellor (1933–1934) and ambassador to Austria (1934–1938) and Turkey (1939–1944).

pa·per (pā′pər) *n.* **1.** A material made of cellulose pulp, derived mainly from wood, rags, and certain grasses, processed into flexible sheets or rolls by deposit from an aqueous suspension, and used chiefly for writing, printing, drawing, wrapping, and covering walls. **2.** A single sheet of this material. **3.** One or more sheets of paper bearing writing or printing, especially: **a.** A formal written composition intended to be published, presented, or read aloud; a scholarly essay or treatise. **b.** A piece of written work for school; a report or theme. **c.** *Often* **papers.** An official document, especially one establishing the identity of the bearer. **4. papers.** A collection of letters, diaries, and other writings, especially by one person: *the Madison papers.* **5.** Commercial documents that represent value and can be transferred from owner to owner; negotiable instruments considered as a group: *"billions more invested in American stocks, bonds, certificates of deposit, and other paper"* (Christian Science Monitor). **6.** A newspaper. **7.** Wallpaper. **8.** A wrapper made of paper, often with its contents: *a paper of pins.* **9.** *Slang.* **a.** A free pass to a theater. **b.** The audience admitted with free passes. **—paper** *tr.v.* **-pered, -per·ing, -pers. 1.** To cover, wrap, or line with paper. **2.** To cover with wallpaper. **3.** To supply with paper. **4.** *Slang.* To issue free passes for (a theater, for example). **5.** To construct (something) in haste and with little forethought: *papered together a new coalition of political convenience.* **—paper** *adj.* **1.** Made of paper. **2.** Resembling paper, as in thinness or flimsiness. **3.** Of or relating to clerical work: *paper duties.* **4. a.** Existing only in printed or written form: *paper profits; a paper corporation.* **b.** Planned but not realized; theoretical. ***—phrasal verb.*** **paper over. 1.** To put or keep out of sight; conceal: *paper over a deficit with accounting gimmicks.* **2.** To downplay or gloss over (differences, for example), especially in order to maintain a nominal, apparent, or temporary unity. ***—idiom.*** **on paper. 1.** In writing or print. **2.** In theory, as opposed to actual performance or fact: *a good team on paper but not in the field.* [Middle English, from Old French *papier,* from Latin *papȳrus,* papyrus plant, papyrus paper, from Greek *papuros.*] **—pa′per·er** *n.*

pa·per·back (pā′pər-băk′) *n.* A book having a flexible paper binding. **—pa′per·back′, pa′per·backed′** *adj.*

paper birch *n.* A North American birch tree *(Betula papyrifera)* having paperlike white bark used to make baskets, toy canoes, and other articles. Also called *canoe birch.*

pa·per·board (pā′pər-bôrd′, -bōrd′) *n.* Cardboard; pasteboard.

pa·per·bound (pā′pər-bound′) *adj.* Bound in paper; paperback.

pa·per·boy (pā′pər-boi′) *n.* A boy who sells or delivers newspapers.

paper clip also **pa·per·clip** (pā′pər-klĭp′) *n.* A wire or plastic clip for holding sheets of paper together. Also called ♦*gem clip.*

paper cutter *n.* A device for trimming paper to desired dimensions, typically a ruled board with a long pivoted cutting knife attached to one side.

pa·per·girl (pā′pər-gûrl′) *n.* A girl who sells or delivers newspapers.

pa·per·hang·er (pā′pər-hăng′ər) *n.* **1.** One whose occupation is covering or decorating walls with wallpaper; a paperer. **2.** *Slang.* One who passes bad checks. **—pa′per·hang′ing** *n.*

pa·per·knife (pā′pər-nīf′) *n.* A thin, dull knife used for opening sealed envelopes, slitting uncut pages of books, and creasing paper.

pa·per·mak·ing (pā′pər-mā′kĭng) *n.* The process or craft of making paper. **—pa′per·mak′er** *n.*

pantry

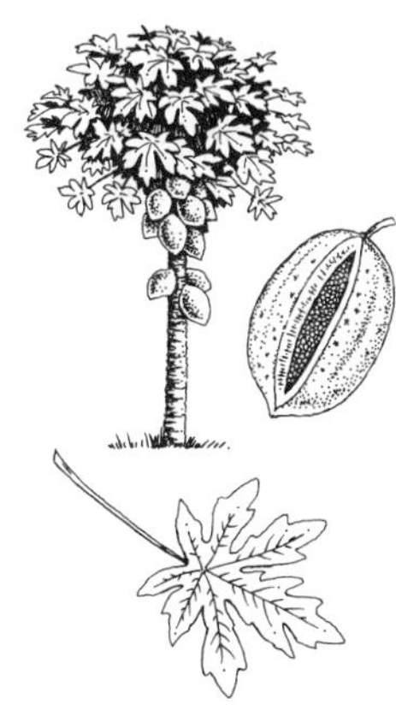

papaya
Carica papaya

ă pat	oi boy
ā pay	ou out
âr care	o͝o took
ä father	o͞o boot
ĕ pet	ŭ cut
ē be	ûr urge
ĭ pit	th thin
ī pie	*th* this
îr pier	hw which
ŏ pot	zh vision
ō toe	ə about, item
ô paw	♦ regionalism

Stress marks: ′ (primary); ′ (secondary), as in **dictionary** (dĭk′shə-nĕr′ē)

pa·per money *n.* Currency in the form of government notes and bank notes.

paper mulberry *n.* An eastern Asian ornamental deciduous tree *(Broussonetia papyrifera)* having bark that can be processed into a paperlike fabric.

paper nautilus *n.* A cephalopod mollusk *(Argonauta argo)* with eight tentacles, the female of which inhabits a paper-thin shell that later acts as an egg case. Also called *argonaut.*

paper plant *n.* See **papyrus** (sense 1).

pa·per-thin (pā′pər-thĭn′) *adj.* Very thin or shallow: *a paper-thin membrane.*

paper tiger *n.* One that is seemingly dangerous and powerful but is in fact timid and weak: *"They are paper tigers, weak and indecisive"* (Frederick Forsyth).

paper trail *n. Informal.* Documentary evidence of one's actions: *"Judges leave a paper trail, a track record of opinions that tell, literally, where they are coming from"* (Ellen Goodman).

pa·per-train (pā′pər-trān′) *tr.v.* **-trained, -train·ing, -trains.** To train (a dog, for example) to urinate and defecate indoors on paper.

paper wasp *n.* Any of various social wasps, such as the hornet, that builds papery nests from chewed wood pulp.

pa·per·weight (pā′pər-wāt′) *n.* A small, heavy, often decorative object that is placed on loose papers to hold them down.

pa·per·work also **pa·per work** (pā′pər-wûrk′) *n.* Work involving the handling of reports, letters, and forms.

pa·per·y (pā′pə-rē) *adj.* Resembling paper, as in thickness or texture. **—pa′per·i·ness** *n.*

pap·e·terie (păp′ĭ-trē, păp-trē′) *n.* A box used to hold stationery and other writing materials. [French, from Old French *papetier,* papermaking, from *papier,* paper. See PAPER.]

papillote

Pa·pia·men·tu (pä′pyə-mĕn′to͞o) also **Pa·pia·men·to** (-tō) *n.* A creole based on Portuguese and pidginized Spanish and spoken in the Netherlands Antilles. [From Papiamentu *papia,* talk, probably from Portuguese *papaguear, papear,* to chatter, from *papagaio,* parrot.]

pa·pier-mâ·ché (pā′pər-mə-shā′, pă-pyā′-) *n.* A material, made from paper pulp or shreds of paper mixed with glue or paste, that can be molded into various shapes when wet and becomes hard and suitable for painting and varnishing when dry. [French : *papier,* paper; see PAPER + *mâché,* past participle of *mâcher,* to chew (from Old French *maschier,* from Latin *masticāre;* see MASTICATE).] **—pa′pier-mâ·ché** *adj.*

pa·pil·i·o·na·ceous (pə-pĭl′ē-ə-nā′shəs) *adj.* Having a bilaterally symmetrical corolla somewhat resembling a butterfly, characteristic of most plants of the pea family. [Latin *pāpiliō, pāpiliōn-,* butterfly; see PAVILION + –ACEOUS.]

pa·pil·la (pə-pĭl′ə) *n., pl.* **-pil·lae** (-pĭl′ē). **1.** A small nipplelike projection, such as a protuberance on the skin, at the root of a hair or feather, or at the base of a developing tooth. **2.** One of the small, round or cone-shaped protuberances on the top of the tongue that contain taste buds. **3.** A pimple or pustule. **4.** *Botany.* A minute projection on the surface of a stigma, petal, or leaf. [Latin, nipple, diminutive of *papula,* swelling, pimple.] **—pap′il·lar′y** (păp′ə-lĕr′ē, pə-pĭl′ə-rē) *adj.* **—pap′il·late′** (păp′ə-lāt′, pə-pĭl′ĭt) *adj.* **—pap·il·lose** (păp′ə-lōs′, pə-pĭl′ōs′) *adj.*

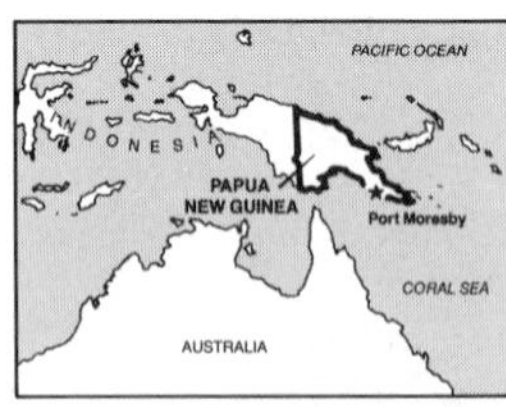

Papua New Guinea

pap·il·lo·ma (păp′ə-lō′mə) *n., pl.* **-mas** or **-ma·ta** (-mə-tə). A small benign epithelial tumor, such as a wart, consisting of an overgrowth of cells on a core of smooth connective tissue. **—pap′il·lo′ma·tous** *adj.*

pap·il·lon (păp′ə-lŏn′, pä′pē-yôN) *n.* Any of a breed of small dog related to the spaniel, having a long silky coat, a bushy tail that curves over its back, and large ears shaped like the wings of a butterfly. [French, from Old French, butterfly, from Latin *pāpiliō, pāpiliōn-.* See PAVILION.]

pap·il·lote (pä′pē-yōt′, păp′ē-) *n.* **1.** A frilled paper cover used to decorate the bone end of a cooked chop or cutlet. **2.** An oiled paper or foil wrapper in which certain foods are baked. [French, from Old French, ornament for the hair, from feminine of *papillot,* diminutive of *papillon,* butterfly, from Latin *pāpiliō, pāpiliōn-.* See PAVILION.]

pa·pist (pā′pĭst) *n. Offensive.* A Roman Catholic. [New Latin *pāpista,* from Late Latin *pāpa.* See POPE.] **—pa′pist, pa·pis′tic** (pə-pĭs′tĭk) *adj.* **—pa′pist·ry** *n.*

pa·poose (pă-po͞os′, pə-) *n.* A Native American infant or very young child. [Narragansett *papoòs,* child.]

pa·po·va·vi·rus (pə-pō′və-vī′rəs) *n., pl.* **-rus·es.** Any of a group of DNA-containing viruses that are associated with or cause papillomas or polyomas in animals. [PA(PILLOMA) + PO(LYOMA) + VA(CUOLATION) + VIRUS.]

Papp (păp), **Joseph.** 1921–1991. American stage producer and director known for his productions of *Hair* (1967) and *A Chorus Line* (1975).

pap·pa·ta·ci fever (pä′pə-tä′chē) *n.* See **sandfly fever.** [Italian *pappataci,* sandfly : *pappare,* to eat (from Latin *pappāre,* from *pappa,* food) + *-taci,* silently (from *tacito,* past participle of *tacere,* to be silent, from Latin *tacēre*).]

pap·pus (păp′əs) *n., pl.* **pap·pi** (păp′ī). A modified calyx, composed of scales, bristles, or featherlike hairs, in plants of the composite family, such as the dandelion and the thistle. [Latin, old man, down on certain seeds, from Greek *pappos.* See **papa** in Appendix.] **—pap′pose** (-ōs), **pap′pous** (-əs) *adj.*

pap·py[1] (păp′ē) *adj.* **-pi·er, -pi·est.** Of or resembling pap; mushy.

pap·py[2] (păp′ē) *n., pl.* **-pies.** *Informal.* Father. [Diminutive of PAPA.]

pa·pri·ka (pă-prē′kə, pə-, păp′rĭ-kə) *n.* **1.** A mild, powdered seasoning made from sweet red peppers. **2.** *Color.* A dark to deep or vivid reddish orange. [Hungarian, from Serbian, from *papar,* ground pepper, from Slavic **pipru,* from Latin *piper.* See PEPPER.]

Pap smear (păp) *n.* A test for cancer, especially of the female genital tract, in which a smear of exfoliated cells is specially stained and examined under a microscope for pathological changes. Also called *Pap test, smear test.* [After George *Papanicolaou* (1883–1962), American anatomist.]

Pap·u·a (păp′yo͞o-ə, pä′po͞o-ä′), **Gulf of.** A large inlet of the Coral Sea on the southeast coast of New Guinea.

Pap·u·an (păp′yo͞o-ən) *adj.* **1.** Of or relating to the peoples, languages, or cultures of Papua New Guinea or New Guinea. **2.** Of or relating to the Papuan language. **—Papuan** *n.* **1.** A native or inhabitant of Papua New Guinea or New Guinea. **2.** A member of any of the indigenous peoples of New Guinea and neighboring islands. **3.** Any of the indigenous languages of New Guinea, New Britain, and the Solomon Islands.

Papua New Guin·ea (gĭn′ē). An island country of the southwest Pacific Ocean comprising the eastern half of New Guinea, the Bismarck Archipelago, the western Solomons, and adjacent islands. Formerly an Australian territory, the country became self-governing in 1973 and fully independent in 1975. Port Moresby, on New Guinea, is the capital and the largest city. Population, 3,010,727. **—Pap′u·a New Guin′e·an** *adj. & n.*

pap·ule (păp′yo͞ol) also **pap·u·la** (-yə-lə) *n., pl.* **-ules** also **-u·lae** (-yə-lē′). A small, solid, usually inflammatory elevation of the skin that does not contain pus. [Latin *papula.*] **—pap′u·lar** (-yə-lər) *adj.*

pa·py·ri (pə-pī′rī′) *n.* A plural of **papyrus.**

pap·y·rol·o·gy (păp′ə-rŏl′ə-jē) *n.* The study of papyrus manuscripts. **—pap′y·ro·log′ic** (păp′ər-ə-lŏj′ĭk, pə-pī′rə-), **pap′y·ro·log′i·cal** (-ĭ-kəl) *adj.*

pa·py·rus (pə-pī′rəs) *n., pl.* **-rus·es** or **-ri** (-rī′). **1.** A tall, aquatic, Mediterranean sedge *(Cyperus papyrus)* having numerous drooping rays grouped in umbels. Also called *Egyptian paper rush, paper plant.* **2.a.** A material on which to write made from the pith or the stems of this sedge, used especially by the ancient Egyptians, Greeks, and Romans. **b.** A document written on this material. [Middle English *papirus,* from Latin *papȳrus,* from Greek *papuros.*]

par (pär) *n.* **1.** An amount or a level considered to be average; a standard: *performing up to par; did not yet feel up to par.* **2.** An equality of status, level, or value; equal footing: *a local product on a par with the best foreign makes.* **3.** The established value of a monetary unit expressed in terms of a monetary unit of another country using the same metal standard. **4.** The face value of a stock, bond, or other negotiable instrument: *sold the bond at par.* **5.** *Sports.* The number of golf strokes considered necessary to complete a hole or course in expert play. **—par** *tr.v.* **parred, par·ring, pars.** *Sports.* To score par on (a hole or course) in golf. **—par** *adj.* **1.** Equal to the standard; normal: *a solid, par performance.* **2.** Of or relating to monetary face value. [From Latin *pār,* equal, that which is equal. See **pere-**[2] in Appendix.]

par. *abbr.* **1.** Paragraph. **2.** Parallel. **3.** Parenthesis. **4.** Parish.

Par. *abbr.* Paraguay.

par– *pref.* Variant of **para–**[1].

pa·ra (pä-rä′, pä′rä) *n.* See table at **currency.** [Serbo-Croatian, from Turkish, from Persian *parāh,* piece, para.]

para–[1] or **par–** *pref.* **1.** Beside; near; alongside: *parathyroid.* **2.** Beyond: *paranormal.* **3.** Incorrect; abnormal: *paresthesia.* **4.** Similar to; resembling: *paratyphoid fever.* **5.** Subsidiary; assistant: *paraprofessional.* **6.** Isomeric; polymeric: *paraldehyde.* **7.** A diatomic molecule in which the nuclei have opposite spin directions: *parahydrogen.* **8.** Of or relating to one of three possible isomers of a benzene ring with two attached chemical groups in which the carbon atoms with attached groups are separated by two unsubstituted carbon atoms: para-*bromoiodobenzene.* [Greek, from *para,* beside. See **per**[1] in Appendix.]

para–[2] *pref.* Parachute; parachutist: *paratroops.* [From PARACHUTE.]

–para *suff.* A woman who has given birth to a specified number of children: *multipara.* [Latin, from *parere,* to give birth. See **pere-**[1] in Appendix.]

Pa·rá (pə-rä′). See **Belém.**

par·a-a·mi·no·ben·zo·ic acid (păr′ə-ə-mē′nō-bĕn-zō′ĭk, -ăm′ə-) *n.* PABA.

par·a·bi·o·sis (păr′ə-bī-ō′sĭs) *n., pl.* **-ses** (-sēz). **1.** The natural or surgical union of anatomical parts of two organisms, usually involving exchange of blood, as in the development of Siamese twins or in certain transplant operations. **2.** A temporary suspension of conductivity or excitability in a nerve. **—par′a·bi·ot′ic** (-ŏt′ĭk) *adj.* **—par′a·bi·ot′i·cal·ly** *adv.*

par·a·blast (păr′ə-blăst′) *n.* The nutritive yolk of a meroblastic egg. **—par′a·blas′tic** *adj.*

par·a·ble (păr′ə-bəl) *n.* A simple story illustrating a moral or religious lesson. [Middle English, from Old French, from Late Latin *parabola,* from Greek *parabolē,* from *paraballein,* to com-

ă pat	oi boy
ā pay	ou out
âr care	o͝o took
ä father	o͞o boot
ĕ pet	ŭ cut
ē be	ûr urge
ĭ pit	th thin
ī pie	*th* this
îr pier	hw which
ŏ pot	zh vision
ō toe	ə about, item
ô paw	♦ regionalism

Stress marks: ′ (primary); ′ (secondary), as in **dictionary** (dĭk′shə-nĕr′ē)

pare : *para-*, beside; see PARA–[1] + *ballein*, to throw; see **g^w^ele-** in Appendix.]

pa·rab·o·la (pə-răb′ə-lə) *n.* **1.** A plane curve formed by the intersection of a right circular cone and a plane parallel to an element of the cone. **2.** A plane curve formed by the locus of points equidistant from a fixed line and a fixed point not on the line. [New Latin, from Greek *parabolē*, comparison, application, parabola (from the relationship between the line joining the vertices of a conic and the line through its focus and parallel to its directrix), from *paraballein*, to compare. See PARABLE.]

par·a·bol·ic (păr′ə-bŏl′ĭk) also **par·a·bol·i·cal** (-ĭ-kəl) *adj.* **1.** Of or similar to a parable. **2.** Of or having the form of a parabola or paraboloid. [Ultimately from Greek *parabolē*, comparison; see PARABLE. Sense 2, from PARABOLA.] **—par′a·bol′i·cal·ly** *adv.*

pa·rab·o·loid (pə-răb′ə-loid′) *n.* A surface having parabolic sections parallel to a single coordinate axis and elliptic sections perpendicular to that axis. **—pa·rab′o·loi′dal** (-loid′l) *adj.*

Par·a·cel·sus (păr′ə-sĕl′səs), **Philippus Aureolus.** 1493–1541. German-Swiss alchemist and physician who introduced the concept of disease to medicine. He held that illness was the result of external agents attacking the body rather than imbalances within the body and advocated the use of chemicals against disease-causing agents.

par·a·chute (păr′ə-sho͞ot′) *n.* **1.** An apparatus used to retard free fall from an aircraft, consisting of a light, usually hemispherical canopy attached by cords to a harness and worn or stored folded until deployed in descent. **2.** Any of various similar unpowered devices that are used for retarding free-speeding or free-falling motion. **3.** See **patagium** (sense 1). **—parachute** *v.* **-chut·ed, -chut·ing, -chutes.** *—tr.* To drop (supplies or troops, for example) by means of a parachute. *—intr.* To descend by means of a parachute. [French : *para(sol)*, parasol; see PARASOL + *chute*, fall; see CHUTE.] **—par′a·chut′ic** *adj.* **—par′a·chut′ist, par′a·chut′er** *n.*

parachute spinnaker *n. Nautical.* An oversize spinnaker used on racing yachts.

Par·a·clete (păr′ə-klēt′) *n.* The Holy Spirit. [Middle English *Paraclit*, from Old French *Paraclet*, from Latin *Paraclētus*, from Greek *Paraklētos*, from *parakalein*, to invoke : *para-*, to the side of; see PARA–[1] + *kalein*, *klē-*, to call; see **kele-**[2] in Appendix.]

pa·rade (pə-rād′) *n.* **1.a.** An organized public procession on a festive or ceremonial occasion. **b.** The participants in such a procession. **2.a.** A regular place of assembly for reviews of troops. Also called *parade ground.* **b.** A ceremonial review of troops. **c.** The troops taking part in such a review. **3.** A line or extended group of moving persons or things: *a parade of strollers on the mall.* **4.** An extended, usually showy succession: *a parade of fads and styles.* **5.** An ostentatious show; an exhibition: *make a parade of one's talents.* See Synonyms at **display. 6.** A public square or promenade. **—parade** *v.* **-rad·ed, -rad·ing, -rades.** *—intr.* **1.** To take part in a parade; march in a public procession: *The circus performers and animals paraded down Main Street.* **2.** To assemble for a ceremonial military review. **3.** To stroll in public, especially so as to be seen; promenade. **4.** To behave so as to attract attention; show off. *—tr.* **1.** To cause to take part in a parade: *paraded the floats past city hall.* **2.** To assemble (troops) for a ceremonial review. **3.** To march or walk through or around: *parade the campus.* **4.** To exhibit ostentatiously; flaunt: *paraded their wealth.* See Synonyms at **show.** [Probably French, from Old French, exhibition, from *parer*, to embellish, from Latin *parāre*, to prepare. See **pere-**[1] in Appendix.] **—pa·rad′er** *n.*

par·a·di·chlo·ro·ben·zene (păr′ə-dī-klôr′ə-bĕn′zēn′, -bĕn-zēn′, -klōr′-) *n.* A white crystalline compound, $C_6H_4Cl_2$, used as a germicide and an insecticide.

par·a·did·dle (păr′ə-dĭd′l) *n. Music.* A pattern of drumbeats characterized by four basic beats and alternating left-handed and right-handed strokes on the successive primary beats. [Probably imitative.]

par·a·digm (păr′ə-dīm′, -dĭm′) *n.* **1.** An example that serves as pattern or model. **2.** A list of all the inflectional forms of a word taken as an illustrative example of the conjugation or declension to which it belongs. [Middle English, example, from Late Latin *paradīgma*, from Greek *paradeigma*, from *paradeiknunai*, to compare : *para-*, alongside; see PARA–[1] + *deiknunai*, to show; see **deik-** in Appendix.] **—par′a·dig·mat′ic** (-dĭg-măt′ĭk) *adj.*

par·a·dise (păr′ə-dīs′, -dīz′) *n.* **1.** Often **Paradise.** The Garden of Eden. **2.** *Theology.* **a.** The abode of righteous souls after death; heaven. **b.** An intermediate resting place for righteous souls awaiting the Resurrection. **3.** A place of ideal beauty or loveliness. **4.** A state of delight. [Middle English *paradis*, from Old French, from Late Latin *paradīsus*, from Greek *paradeisos*, garden, enclosed park, paradise, from Avestan *pairi-daēza-*, enclosure, park : *pairi-*, around; see **per**[1] in Appendix + *daēza-*, wall; see **dheigh-** in Appendix.] **—par′a·di·si′a·cal** (-dĭ-sī′ə-kəl, -zī′-), **par′a·di·si′ac** (-ăk) , **par′a·di·sa′i·cal** (-dĭ-sā′ĭ-kəl, -zā′-) , **par′a·di·sa′ic** (-ĭk) , **par′a·dis′al** (-dī′səl, -zəl) *adj.* **—par′a·di·si′a·cal·ly, par′a·di·sa′i·cal·ly, par′a·dis′al·ly** *adv.*

WORD HISTORY: Perhaps the supreme example of the semantic process known as melioration is the word *paradise.* In tracing this word from its origins to its present status, we see an elevation, or melioration, of meaning that raises the word to new heights. The history begins with the Avestan (the eastern dialect of Old Iranian) word *pairi-daēza–*, "enclosure," made up of *pairi*, "around," and *daēza–*, "wall." The Greek military leader and historian Xenophon, who served with Greek mercenaries in Persia, first used the Greek word *paradeisos* adopted from the Avestan word to refer to the Persian kings' and nobles' parks or pleasure grounds. This Greek word extended to mean "garden" or "orchard" was an obvious choice for translators of the Bible into Greek to use both for the Garden of Eden and the Abode of the Blessed, or heaven. The Greek word was adopted into Late Latin and was used much as we might expect in its biblical senses in ecclesiastical Latin (Late Latin *paradīsus*). The Old English word *paradis* taken from Latin is found, but our word probably really established itself in Middle English (first recorded before 1200), derived both from Latin and from Old French, which had adopted the word from Latin.

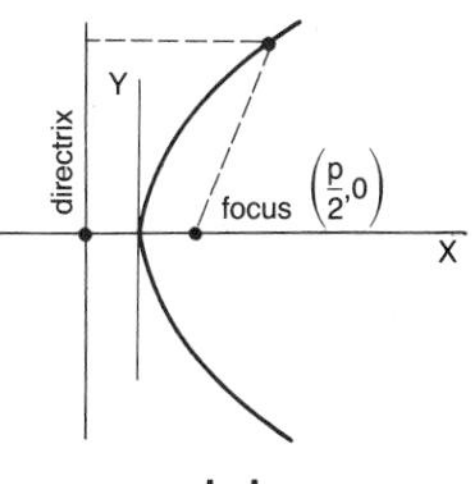

parabola
$y^2 = 2px$

par·a·dor (păr′ə-dôr′, pä′rä-*th*ôr′) *n., pl.* **-dors** or **-dor·es** (-*th*ô′rĕs). A government-run country hotel in Spain or Latin America. [Spanish, from *parar*, to stop, from Latin *parāre*, to prepare. See PARADE.]

par·a·dox (păr′ə-dŏks′) *n.* **1.** A seemingly contradictory statement that may nonetheless be true: *the paradox that standing is more tiring than walking.* **2.** One exhibiting inexplicable or contradictory aspects: *"You have the paradox of a Celt being the smooth Oxonian"* (Anthony Burgess). **3.** An assertion that is essentially self-contradictory, though based on a valid deduction from acceptable premises. **4.** A statement contrary to received opinion. [Latin *paradoxum*, from Greek *paradoxon*, from neuter sing. of *paradoxos*, conflicting with expectation : *para-*, beyond; see PARA–[1] + *doxa*, opinion (from *dokein*, to think; see **dek-** in Appendix).] **—par′a·dox′i·cal** *adj.* **—par′a·dox′i·cal·ly** *adv.* **—par′a·dox′i·cal·ness** *n.*

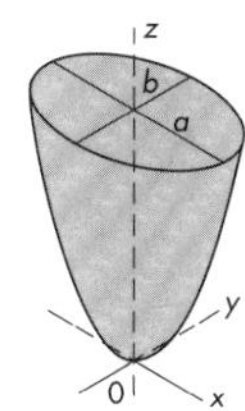

paraboloid

paradoxical sleep *n.* See **REM sleep.**

par·a·drop (păr′ə-drŏp′) *n.* Delivery of supplies to a place by parachute. **—paradrop** *tr.v.* **-dropped, -drop·ping, -drops.** To deliver by parachute.

par·aes·the·sia (păr′ĭs-thē′zhə) *n.* Variant of **paresthesia.**

par·af·fin (păr′ə-fĭn) *n.* **1.** A waxy, white or colorless, solid hydrocarbon mixture used to make candles, wax paper, lubricants, and sealing materials. Also called *paraffin wax.* **2.** *Chemistry.* A member of the alkane series. **3.** *Chiefly British.* Kerosene. **—paraffin** *tr.v.* **-fined, -fin·ing, -fins.** To saturate, impregnate, or coat with paraffin. [German *Paraffin* : Latin *parum*, little, not very; see **pau-** in Appendix + Latin *affīnis*, associated with (from its lack of affinity with other material); see AFFINED.] **—par′af·fin′ic** *adj.*

paraffin series *n. Chemistry.* See **alkane series.**

paraffin wax *n.* See **paraffin** (sense 1).

par·a·for·mal·de·hyde (păr′ə-fôr-măl′də-hīd′) *n.* A white solid polymer of formaldehyde, $(HCHO)_n$, where *n* is at least 6, used as a disinfectant, fumigant, and fungicide.

par·a·gen·e·sis (păr′ə-jĕn′ĭ-sĭs) also **par·a·ge·ne·sia** (-jə-nē′zhə, -zhē-ə) *n.* The order in which a formation of associated minerals is generated. **—par′a·ge·net′ic** (-jə-nĕt′ĭk) *adj.*

parachute

par·a·gon (păr′ə-gŏn′, -gən) *n.* **1.** A model of excellence or perfection of a kind; a peerless example: *a paragon of virtue.* **2.a.** An unflawed diamond weighing at least 100 carats. **b.** A very large spherical pearl. **3.** *Printing.* A type size of 20 points. **—paragon** *tr.v.* **-goned, -gon·ing, -gons. 1.** To compare; parallel. **2.** To equal; match. [Obsolete French, from Old French, from Old Italian *paragone*, from *paragonare*, to test on a touchstone, perhaps from Greek *parakonan*, to sharpen : *para-*, alongside; see PARA–[1] + *akonē*, whetstone; see **ak-** in Appendix.]

SYNONYMS: *paragon, nonesuch, nonpareil.* The central meaning shared by these nouns is "a person or thing so excellent as to have no equal": *Paris, the paragon of cities; a suspension bridge that is the nonesuch of beauty and utility; thought her grandchildren were nonpareils.*

par·a·graph (păr′ə-grăf′) *n. Abbr.* **par. 1.** A distinct division of written or printed matter that begins on a new, usually indented line, consists of one or more sentences, and typically deals with a single thought or topic or quotes one speaker's continuous words. **2.** A mark (¶) used to indicate where a new paragraph should begin or to serve as a reference mark. **3.** A brief article, notice, or announcement, as in a newspaper. **—paragraph** *tr.v.* **-graphed, -graph·ing, -graphs.** To divide or arrange into paragraphs. [Middle English *paragraf*, from Old French *paragrafe*, from Medieval Latin *paragraphus*, from Greek *paragraphos*, line showing a break in sense or a change of speakers in a dialogue, from *paragraphein*, to write beside : *para-*, beside; see PARA–[1] + *graphein*, to write; see **gerbh-** in Appendix.] **—par′a·graph′ic, par′a·graph′i·cal** *adj.*

Par·a·guay (păr′ə-gwī′, -gwā′). *Abbr.* **Par.** A country of south-central South America. Entirely landlocked, the region was first explored in 1516 and grew around the colony of Asunción (founded in the 1530's). Full independence from Spain was achieved in 1811. Asunción is the capital and the largest city. Population, 3,026,165. **—Par′a·guay′an** *adj. & n.*

Paraguay

Paraguay River. A river rising in southwest Brazil and flow-

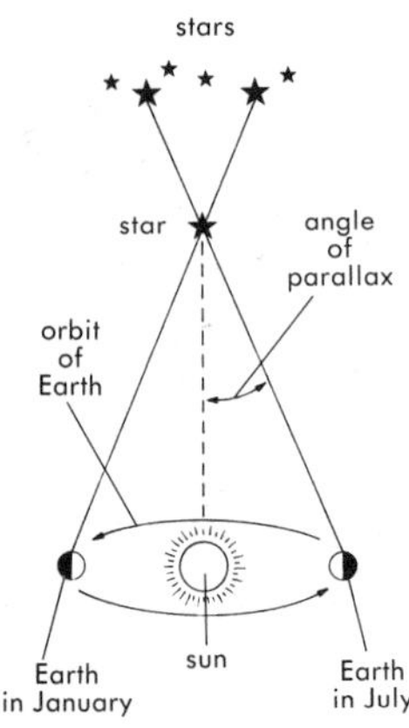

parallax

ing about 2,574 km (1,600 mi) southward to the Paraná River in southwest Paraguay.

Paraguay tea *n.* See **maté** (sense 2).

Pa·ra·í·ba (păr′ə-ē′bə, pä′rä-ē′bä) also **Paraíba do Sul** (do͞o so͞ol′). A river, about 1,046 km (650 mi) long, of southeast Brazil emptying into the Atlantic Ocean near Campos.

par·a·in·flu·en·za (păr′ə-ĭn′flo͞o-ĕn′zə) *adj.* Of, relating to, or designating any of a group of paramyxoviruses that are similar to the viruses that cause influenza and are associated with various respiratory infections, especially in children.

par·a·jour·nal·ism (păr′ə-jûr′nə-lĭz′əm) *n.* Subjective journalism that uses some of the techniques or license of fiction. **—par′a·jour′nal·ist** *n.* **—par′a·jour′nal·is′tic** *adj.*

par·a·keet (păr′ə-kēt′) *n.* Any of various small slender parrots, usually having long tapering tails and often kept as pets. [Spanish *periquito,* probably diminutive of *Perico,* diminutive of *Pedro,* Peter.]

par·al·de·hyde (pə-răl′də-hīd′) *n.* A colorless liquid polymer, $C_6H_{12}O_3$, of acetaldehyde, used as a solvent and a sedative.

par·a·le·gal (păr′ə-lē′gəl) *adj. Law.* Of, relating to, or being a person with specialized training who assists an attorney. **—par′a·le′gal** *n.*

par·al·lax (păr′ə-lăks′) *n.* An apparent change in the direction of an object, caused by a change in observational position that provides a new line of sight. [French *parallaxe,* from Greek *parallaxis,* from *parallassein,* to change : *para-,* among; see PARA–[1] + *allassein,* to exchange (from *allos,* other; see **al-**[1] in Appendix).] **—par′al·lac′tic** (-lăk′tĭk) *adj.*

par·al·lel (păr′ə-lĕl′) *adj. Abbr.* **par. 1.** Being an equal distance apart everywhere: *dancers in two parallel rows.* **2.** *Mathematics.* **a.** Of, relating to, or designating two or more straight coplanar lines that do not intersect. **b.** Of, relating to, or designating two or more planes that do not intersect. **c.** Of, relating to, or designating a line and a plane that do not intersect. **d.** Of, relating to, or designating curves or surfaces everywhere equidistant. **3. a.** Having comparable parts, analogous aspects, or readily recognized similarities: *the parallel lives of two contemporaries.* **b.** Having the same tendency or direction: *parallel motives and aims.* **4.** *Grammar.* Having identical or equivalent syntactic constructions in corresponding clauses or phrases. **5.** *Music.* Moving consistently by the same intervals: *harmony with parallel voices.* **6.** *Electronics.* Denoting a circuit or part of a circuit connected in parallel. **7.** *Computer Science.* **a.** Of or relating to the simultaneous transmission of all the bits of a byte over separate wires: *a parallel part; a parallel printer.* **b.** Of or relating to the simultaneous performance of multiple operations: *parallel processing.* **—parallel** *adv.* In a parallel relationship or manner: *a road and a railway that run parallel.* **—parallel** *n. Abbr.* **par. 1.** *Mathematics.* One of a set of parallel geometric figures, such as lines or planes. **2. a.** One that closely resembles or is analogous to another: *a unique event, without parallel in history.* **b.** A comparison indicating likeness; an analogy. **3.** The condition of being parallel; near similarity or exact agreement in particulars; parallelism. **4.** Any of the imaginary lines representing degrees of latitude that encircle the earth parallel to the plane of the equator. **5.** *Printing.* A sign indicating material referred to in a note or reference. **6.** *Electronics.* An arrangement of components in a circuit that splits the current into two or more paths. Used chiefly in the phrase *in parallel.* **—parallel** *tr.v.* **-leled, -lel·ing, -lels** also **-lelled, -lel·ling, -lels. 1.** To make or place parallel to something else: *paralleled the ditch to the highway.* **2.** To be or extend parallel to: *a trail that parallels the crater rim.* **3.** To be similar or analogous to: *claimed that fetal development parallels the evolution of the species.* **4.** To be or provide an equal for; match. **5.** To show to be analogous; compare or liken: *critics who have paralleled the novel's plot to an ancient myth.* [Latin *parallēlus,* from Greek *parallēlos* : *para,* beside; see PARA–[1] + *allēlōn,* of one another (from *allos,* other; see **al-**[1] in Appendix).]

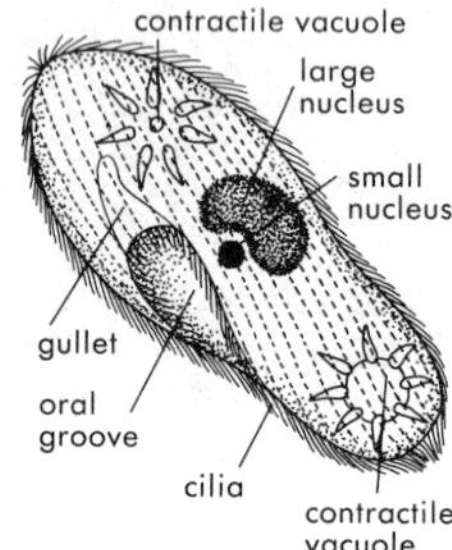

paramecium

USAGE NOTE: In its mathematical usage *parallel* is an absolute term—two lines either do or do not intersect—and as such does not admit of qualification as to degree. Some grammarians have argued that this restriction should apply as well to nontechnical uses of the word. According to this logic, one may not say *The two roads have been made more parallel,* except perhaps as a loose way of saying what is rendered more precisely by expressions such as *more nearly parallel.* Like the analogous objection that has been made to the comparison of *equal,* the point betrays a misconception about the relation between mathematical concepts and their ordinary-language equivalents. Applied to objects in the world, *parallel* can only denote a rough approximation to a geometric ideal. A pair of rails or parked cars cannot be truly parallel in the mathematician's sense of the term but only more or less so, just as a road or shelf cannot be truly straight in the geometric sense but nonetheless may be described as very straight or relatively straight. The grammarians' compunctions make even less sense when applied to metaphorical uses of *parallel,* as in *The difficulties faced by the Republicans are quite parallel to those that confronted the Democrats four years ago,* in which the intended meaning has nothing to do with the possibility of intersection but instead suggests the structural correspondence of two distinct situations. In this sense, parallelism is clearly a matter of degree and the word *parallel* can be modified accordingly. See Usage Notes at **equal, perfect, unique.**

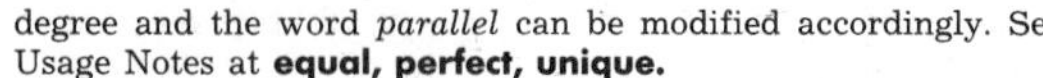

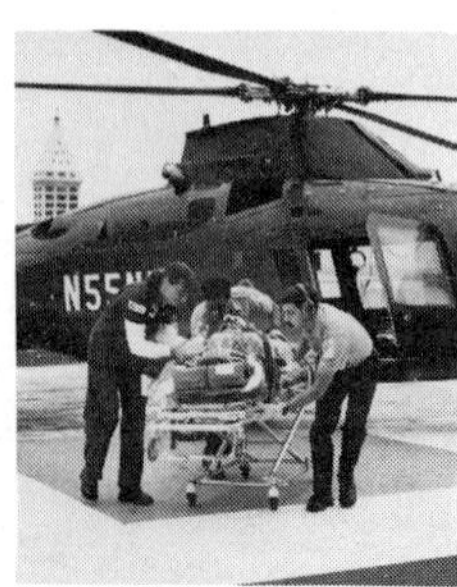
paramedic
Traveling by medevac helicopter

parallel bars *pl.n. Sports.* An apparatus for gymnastic exercises consisting of two horizontal bars set parallel to each other in adjustable upright supports.

parallel cousin *n.* A cousin who is the child of one's mother's sister or one's father's brother.

par·al·lel·e·pi·ped (păr′ə-lĕl′ə-pī′pĭd, -pĭp′ĭd) *n.* A solid with six faces, each a parallelogram and each being parallel to the opposite face. [Greek *parallēlepipedon* : *parallēlos,* parallel; see PARALLEL + *epipedon,* plane surface, from neuter sing. of *epipedos,* level (*epi-,* epi- + *pedon,* ground; see **ped-** in Appendix).]

par·al·lel·ism (păr′ə-lĕ-lĭz′əm) *n.* **1.** The quality or condition of being parallel; a parallel relationship. **2.** Likeness, correspondence, or similarity in aspect, course, or tendency. **3.** *Grammar.* The use of identical or equivalent syntactic constructions in corresponding clauses. **4.** *Philosophy.* The doctrine that to every mental change there corresponds a concomitant but causally unconnected physical alteration.

par·al·lel·o·gram (păr′ə-lĕl′ə-grăm′) *n.* A four-sided plane figure with opposite sides parallel. [Late Latin *parallēlogrammum,* from Greek *parallēlogrammon,* from neuter sing. of *parallēlogrammos,* bounded by parallel lines : *parallēlos,* parallel; see PARALLEL + *grammē,* line; see **gerbh-** in Appendix.]

pa·ral·o·gism (pə-răl′ə-jĭz′əm) *n.* A fallacious or illogical argument or conclusion. [Late Latin *paralogismus,* from Greek *paralogismos,* from *paralogos,* unreasonable : *para-,* beyond; see PARA–[1] + *logos,* reason; see **leg-** in Appendix.] **—pa·ral′o·gist** *n.* **—pa·ral′o·gis′tic** *adj.*

Par·a·lym·pic Games (păr′ə-lĭm′pĭk) *pl.n. Sports.* An international competition for physically impaired athletes. [PARA–[1] + (O)LYMPIC.] **—par′a·lym′pi·an** *adj. & n.*

par·a·lyse (păr′ə-līz′) *v. Chiefly British.* Variant of **paralyze.**

pa·ral·y·sis (pə-răl′ĭ-sĭs) *n., pl.* **-ses** (-sēz′). **1. a.** Loss or impairment of the ability to move a body part, usually as a result of damage to its nerve supply. **b.** Loss of sensation over a region of the body. **2.** Inability to move or function; total stoppage or severe impairment of activity: *fear that led to national paralysis.* [Latin, from Greek *paralusis,* from *paraluein,* to disable, loosen : *para-,* on one side; see PARA–[1] + *luein,* to release; see **leu-** in Appendix.]

paralysis ag·i·tans (ăj′ĭ-tănz′) *n.* See **Parkinson's disease.** [New Latin *paralysis agitāns* : Latin *paralysis,* palsy + Latin *agitāns,* present participle of *agitāre,* to shake.]

par·a·lyt·ic (par′ə-lĭt′ĭk) *adj.* **1.** Of or relating to paralysis. **2.** Characteristic of or resembling paralysis. **3.** Affected with paralysis; paralyzed. **—paralytic** *n.* A person affected with paralysis. **—par′a·lyt′i·cal·ly** *adv.*

par·a·lyze (păr′ə-līz′) *tr.v.* **-lyzed, -lyz·ing, -lyz·es. 1.** To affect with paralysis; cause to be paralytic. **2.** To make unable to move or act: *paralyzed by fear.* **3.** To impair the progress or functioning of; make inoperative or powerless: *strict regulations that paralyze economic activity.* [French *paralyser,* from *paralysie,* paralysis, from Old French, from Latin *paralysis.* See PARALYSIS.] **—par′a·ly·za′tion** (-lĭ-zā′shən) *n.* **—par′a·lyz′er** *n.* **—par′a·lyz′ing·ly** *adv.*

par·a·mag·net (păr′ə-măg′nĭt) *n.* A paramagnetic substance. [Back-formation from PARAMAGNETIC.]

par·a·mag·net·ic (păr′ə-măg-nĕt′ĭk) *adj.* Relating to or being a substance in which an induced magnetic field is parallel and proportional to the intensity of the magnetizing field but is much weaker than in ferromagnetic materials. **—par′a·mag·net′i·cal·ly** *adv.* **—par′a·mag′net·ism** (-măg′nĭ-tĭz′əm) *n.*

Par·a·mar·i·bo (păr′ə-măr′ə-bō′). The capital and largest city of Suriname, on the Suriname River near its mouth on the Atlantic Ocean. Settled by the British from Barbados in the 1630's, it came under Dutch rule in 1815. Population, 67,905.

par·a·mat·ta or **par·ra·mat·ta** (păr′ə-măt′ə) *n.* A fine, lightweight, silk and wool or cotton and wool dress fabric. [After PARRAMATTA.]

par·a·me·ci·um (păr′ə-mē′shē-əm, -sē-əm) *n., pl.* **-ci·a** (-shē-ə, -sē-ə) or **-ci·ums.** Any of various freshwater ciliate protozoans of the genus *Paramecium,* usually oval and having an oral groove for feeding. [New Latin *Paramēcium,* genus name, from Greek *paramēkēs,* oblong in shape : *para-,* alongside; see PARA–[1] + *mēkos,* length; see **māk-** in Appendix.]

par·a·med·ic (păr′ə-mĕd′ĭk) *n.* A person who is trained to give emergency medical treatment or assist medical professionals.

par·a·med·i·cal (păr′ə-mĕd′ĭ-kəl) *adj.* Of, relating to, or being a person trained to give emergency medical treatment or assist medical professionals.

par·a·ment (păr′ə-mənt) *n., pl.* **-ments** or **-men·ta** (-mĕn′tə). An ecclesiastical vestment or hanging. [From Middle English *paramentes,* ornamentation, adornments, from Old French *parement,* ornament, from Medieval Latin *parāmentum,* from *parāre,* to decorate, from Latin, to prepare. See PARE.]

pa·ram·e·ter (pə-răm′ĭ-tər) *n.* **1.** *Mathematics.* **a.** A constant in an equation that varies in other equations of the same general form, especially such a constant in the equation of a curve or surface that can be varied to represent a family of curves or surfaces. **b.** One of a set of independent variables that express the coordinates of a point. **2.a.** One of a set of measurable factors, such as temperature and pressure, that define a system and determine its behavior and are varied in an experiment. **b.** *Usage Problem.* A factor that restricts what is possible or what results: *"all the parameters of shelter—where people will live, what mode of housing they will choose, and how they will pay for it"* (New York). **c.** A factor that determines a range of variations; a boundary: *an experimental school that keeps expanding the parameters of its curriculum.* **3.** *Statistics.* A quantity, such as a mean, that is calculated from data and describes a population. **4.** *Usage Problem.* A distinguishing characteristic or feature. [New Latin *parametrum,* a line through the focus and parallel to the directrix of a conic : Greek *para-,* beside; see PARA–[1] + Greek *metron,* measure; see –METER.] **—par′a·met′ric** (păr′ə-mĕt′rĭk), **par′a·met′ri·cal** *adj.* **—par′a·met′ri·cal·ly** *adv.*

USAGE NOTE: In recent years *parameter* has become the archetype for the borrowing of scientific terms into general usage and as such has occasioned a good deal of skeptical comment. Some of its new uses can be justified as useful extensions of the technical senses of the word. For example, the provisions of a zoning ordinance that limit the height or density of new construction can be reasonably likened to mathematical parameters that establish the limits of other variables. Therefore one can properly say *The zoning commission announced new planning parameters for the historic Lamping district of the city.* But other uses suggest that the writer has not understood the technical sense and has chosen it primarily as a way of injecting an aura of scientific precision into what would otherwise be a pedestrian communication. Thus there is no semantic justification for using *parameter* as a general substitute for *characteristic,* as in *The Judeo-Christian ethic is one of the important parameters of Western culture,* an example found unacceptable by 80 percent of the Usage Panel. • Some of the difficulties with nontechnical use of *parameter* appear to arise from its resemblance to the word *perimeter,* with which it shares the sense "limit," though the two words differ in their precise meaning. This confusion doubtless explains the use of *parameter* in a sentence such as *U.S. forces report that the parameters of the mine area in the Gulf are fairly well established,* where the word *perimeter* would have expressed the intended sense more exactly. This example of a use of *parameter* was unacceptable to 61 percent of the Usage Panel.

par·a·mil·i·tar·y (păr′ə-mĭl′ĭ-tĕr′ē) *adj.* Of, relating to, or being a group of civilians organized in a military fashion, especially to operate in place of or assist regular army troops. **—paramilitary** *n., pl.* **-ies.** A member of a paramilitary force.

par·am·ne·sia (păr′ăm-nē′zhə) *n.* **1.** A distortion of memory in which fantasy and objective experience are confused. **2.** An inability to recall the meanings of common words.

pá·ra·mo (pä′rə-mō′, păr′ə-) *n., pl.* **-mos.** A treeless alpine plateau of the Andes and tropical South America. [American Spanish *páramo,* from Spanish, wasteland.]

par·a·morph (păr′ə-môrf′) *n.* A mineral crystal formed or affected by paramorphism. Also called *allomorph.*

par·a·mor·phine (păr′ə-môr′fēn′) *n.* See **thebaine.**

par·a·mor·phism (păr′ə-môr′fĭz′əm) *n.* Structural alteration of a mineral without change of chemical composition. **—par′a·mor′phic** (-fĭk), **par′a·mor′phous** (-fəs) *adj.*

par·a·mount (păr′ə-mount′) *adj.* **1.** Of chief concern or importance: *tending first to one's paramount needs.* **2.** Supreme in rank, power, or authority. See Synonyms at **dominant.** **—paramount** *n.* One that has the highest rank, power, or authority. [Anglo-Norman *paramont,* above : *par,* by (from Latin *per;* see **per**[1] in Appendix) + *amont,* above, upward; see AMOUNT.] **—par′a·mount′cy** *n.* **—par′a·mount′ly** *adv.*

Par·a·mount (păr′ə-mount′). A city of southern California southeast of Los Angeles. Originally a dairy center, it became industrialized after the 1950's. Population, 36,407.

par·a·mour (păr′ə-mo͝or′) *n.* A lover, especially one in an adulterous relationship. [Middle English, from *par amour,* by way of love, passionately, from Anglo-Norman : *par,* by (from Latin *per;* see **per**[1] in Appendix) + *amour,* love (from Latin *amor,* from *amāre,* to love).]

Pa·ram·us (pə-răm′əs). A borough of northeast New Jersey northeast of Paterson. It is mainly residential. Population, 26,474.

par·am·y·lum (pă-răm′ə-ləm) also **par·am·y·lon** (-lən) *n.* A carbohydrate resembling starch that is composed of glucose and forms the reserve foodstuff of certain algae.

par·a·myx·o·vi·rus (păr′ə-mĭk′sə-vī′rəs) *n., pl.* **-rus·es.** Any of a group of viruses that contain RNA and are similar to but larger and more variable in size than the related myxovirus. The paramyxoviruses include the Sendai virus, the parainfluenza viruses, and the viruses that cause measles and mumps.

Pa·ra·ná (păr′ə-nä′, pä′rä-). A city of northeast Argentina on the Paraná River north of Rosario. It is a river port accessible for oceangoing vessels. Population, 161,638.

Pa·ra·na·í·ba (păr′ə-nə-ē′bə, pä′rä-nä-ē′bä). A river, about 805 km (500 mi) long, of south-central Brazil. It is one of the headstreams of the Paraná River.

Paraná River. A river of central South America rising in east-central Brazil at the confluence of the Rio Grande and the Paranáiba and flowing about 2,896 km (1,800 mi) generally southwest to its junction with the Paraguay River then south and east to join the Uruguay River and form the Río de la Plata estuary in eastern Argentina.

pa·rang (pä′răng′) *n.* A short, heavy, straight-edged knife used in Malaysia and Indonesia as a tool and weapon. [Malay.]

par·a·noi·a (păr′ə-noi′ə) *n.* **1.** A psychotic disorder characterized by delusions of persecution or grandeur, often strenuously defended with apparent logic and reason. **2.** Extreme, irrational distrust of others. [Greek, madness, from *paranoos,* demented : *para-,* beyond; see PARA–[1] + *nous, noos,* mind.]

par·a·noi·ac (păr′ə-noi′ăk′, -noi′ĭk) *n.* A paranoid. **—paranoiac** *adj.* Of, relating to, or resembling paranoia.

par·a·noid (păr′ə-noid′) *adj.* **1.** Relating to, characteristic of, or affected with paranoia. **2.** Exhibiting or characterized by extreme fear or distrust of others: *a paranoid suspicion that the phone might be bugged.* **—paranoid** *n.* One affected with paranoia.

par·a·nor·mal (păr′ə-nôr′məl) *adj.* Beyond the range of normal experience or scientific explanation: *such paranormal phenomena as telepathy; a medium's paranormal powers.* **—par′a·nor·mal′i·ty** (-nôr-măl′ĭ-tē) *n.* **—par′a·nor′mal·ly** *adv.*

par·a·pa·re·sis (păr′ə-pə-rē′sĭs, -păr′ĭ-sĭs) *n., pl.* **-ses** (-sēz). Partial paralysis of the lower extremities.

par·a·pet (păr′ə-pĭt, -pĕt′) *n.* **1.** A low protective wall or railing along the edge of a raised structure such as a roof or balcony. **2.** An earthen or stone embankment protecting soldiers from enemy fire. See Synonyms at **bulwark.** [French, from Italian *parapetto* : *parare,* to shield; see PARASOL + *petto,* chest (from Latin *pectus*).]

parapet

par·aph (păr′əf, pə-răf′) *n.* A flourish made after or below a signature, originally to prevent forgery. [French *paraphe,* from Old French *paraffe,* abbreviated signature, from Medieval Latin *paraphus,* paragraph sign, short for *paragraphus.* See PARAGRAPH.]

par·a·pher·na·lia (păr′ə-fər-nāl′yə, -fə-nāl′yə) *pl.n.* *(used with a sing. or pl. verb).* **1.** Personal belongings. **2.** The articles used in a particular activity; equipment: *a photographer's paraphernalia.* See Synonyms at **equipment.** **3.** *Law.* A married woman's personal property exclusive of her dowry, according to common law. [Medieval Latin *paraphernālia,* neuter pl. of *paraphernālis,* pertaining to a married woman's property exclusive of her dowry, from Late Latin *parapherna,* a married woman's property exclusive of her dowry, from Greek : *para-,* beyond; see PARA–[1] + *phernē,* dowry; see **bher-**[1] in Appendix.]

par·a·phrase (păr′ə-frāz′) *n.* **1.** A restatement of a text or passage in another form or other words, often to clarify meaning. **2.** The restatement of texts in other words as a studying or teaching device. **—paraphrase** *v.* **-phrased, -phras·ing, -phras·es.** *—tr.* To restate in a paraphrase. *—intr.* To compose a paraphrase. [French, from Latin *paraphrasis,* from Greek, from *paraphrazein,* to paraphrase : *para-,* alongside; see PARA–[1] + *phrazein,* to show, explain; see **gʷhren-** in Appendix.] **—par′a·phras′a·ble** *adj.* **—par′a·phras′er** *n.*

par·a·phras·tic (păr′ə-frăs′tĭk) or **par·a·phras·ti·cal** (-tĭ-kəl) *adj.* Of, relating to, or having the nature of paraphrase. [Medieval Latin *paraphrasticus,* from Greek *paraphrastikos,* from *paraphrazein,* to paraphrase. See PARAPHRASE.] **—par′a·phras′ti·cal·ly** *adv.*

pa·raph·y·sis (pə-răf′ĭ-sĭs) *n., pl.* **-ses** (-sēz′). One of the erect, sterile filaments often occurring among the reproductive organs of certain fungi, algae, and mosses. [New Latin : PARA–[1] + Greek *phusis,* nature, growth; see PHYSIC.]

par·a·ple·gi·a (păr′ə-plē′jē-ə, -jə) *n.* Complete paralysis of the lower half of the body including both legs, usually caused by damage to the spinal cord. [Greek *paraplēgiē,* hemiplegia, from *paraplēssesthai,* to be paralyzed, from *paraplēssein,* to strike on one side : *para-,* beside; see PARA–[1] + *plēssein,* to strike; see **plāk-**[2] in Appendix.] **—par′a·ple′gic** (-plē′jĭk) *adj. & n.*

par·a·po·di·um (păr′ə-pō′dē-əm) *n., pl.* **-di·a** (-dē-ə). One of the fleshy paired appendages of polychete annelids that function in locomotion and breathing.

par·a·prax·is (păr′ə-prăk′sĭs) *n., pl.* **-prax·es** (-prăk′sēz). *Psychology.* A minor error, such as a slip of the tongue, thought to reveal a subconscious motive. [PARA–[1] + Greek *praxis,* act, action; see PRAXIS.]

par·a·pro·fes·sion·al (păr′ə-prə-fĕsh′ə-nəl) *n.* A trained worker who is not a member of a given profession but assists a professional. **—paraprofessional** *adj.* Of, relating to, or performing the work of a paraprofessional.

par·a·psy·chol·o·gy (păr′ə-sī-kŏl′ə-jē) *n.* The study of the evidence for psychological phenomena, such as telepathy, clairvoyance, and psychokinesis, that are inexplicable by science. **—par′a·psy′cho·log′i·cal** (-sī′kə-lŏj′ĭ-kəl) *adj.* **—par′a·psy·chol′o·gist** *n.*

par·a·quat (păr′ə-kwŏt′) *n.* A colorless compound, $C_{12}H_{14}Cl_2N_2$, or a related yellow compound, $C_{12}H_{14}N_2(CH_3SO_4)_2$, used as a herbicide. [PARA–[1] + QUAT(ERNARY).]

Pa·rá rubber (pə-rä′, păr′ə) *n.* Rubber obtained from various tropical South American trees of the genus *Hevea,* especially *H. brasiliensis.* [After *Pará,* a state of northern Brazil.]

par·a·sail (păr′ə-sāl′) *n.* A special parachute with winglike extensions that lifts a rider in its harness up and through the air when towed by an automobile or motorboat. **—parasail** *intr.v.*

ă pat	oi boy
ā pay	ou out
âr care	o͝o took
ä father	o͞o boot
ĕ pet	ŭ cut
ē be	ûr urge
ĭ pit	th thin
ī pie	*th* this
îr pier	hw which
ŏ pot	zh vision
ō toe	ə about, item
ô paw	♦ regionalism

Stress marks: **′** (primary); ′ (secondary), as in **dictionary** (dĭk′shə-nĕr′ē)

-sailed, -sail·ing, -sails. To be pulled into the air while harnessed to such a parachute. **—par′a·sail′er** *n.*

par·a·sang (păr′ə-săng′) *n.* An ancient Persian unit of distance, usually estimated at 3.5 miles (5.6 kilometers). [Latin *parasanga,* from Greek *parasangēs,* of Iranian origin.]

par·a·se·le·ne (păr′ə-sĭ-lē′nē) *n., pl.* **-nae** (-nē). A luminous spot on a lunar halo. [PARA–[1] + Greek *selēnē,* moon.] **—par′a·se·le′nic** (-lē′nĭk, -lĕn′ĭk) *adj.*

par·a·sen·so·ry (păr′ə-sĕn′sə-rē) *adj.* Extrasensory. **—par′a·sen·so′ri·ly** (-sôr′ə-lē, -sōr′-) *adv.*

par·a·sex·u·al (păr′ə-sĕk′sho͞o-əl) *adj.* Of, relating to, or involving a form of reproduction in which recombination of genes from different individuals occurs without meiosis and fertilization. **—par′a·sex′u·al′i·ty** (-ăl′ĭ-tē) *n.*

par·a·site (păr′ə-sīt′) *n.* **1.** *Biology.* An organism that grows, feeds, and is sheltered on or in a different organism while contributing nothing to the survival of its host. **2. a.** One who habitually takes advantage of the generosity of others without making any useful return. **b.** One who lives off and flatters the rich; a sycophant. **3.** A professional dinner guest, especially in ancient Greece. [Latin *parasītus,* a person who lives by amusing the rich, from Greek *parasitos,* person who eats at someone else's table, parasite : *para-,* beside; see PARA–[1] + *sitos,* grain, food.]

par·a·sit·ic (păr′ə-sĭt′ĭk) also **par·a·sit·i·cal** (-ĭ-kəl) *adj.* **1.** Of, relating to, or characteristic of a parasite. **2.** Caused by a parasite: *parasitic diseases.* **—par′a·sit′i·cal·ly** *adv.*

par·a·sit·i·cide (păr′ə-sĭt′ĭ-sīd′) *n.* An agent or a preparation used to destroy parasites. **—parasiticide** *adj.* Destructive to parasites. **—par′a·sit′i·ci′dal** (-sīd′l) *adj.*

par·a·sit·ism (păr′ə-sĭ-tĭz′əm, -sī-) *n.* **1.** The characteristic behavior or mode of existence of a parasite or parasitic population. **2.** Parasitosis.

par·a·sit·ize (păr′ə-sĭ-tīz′, -sī-) *tr.v.* **-ized, -iz·ing, -iz·es.** To live on or in (a host) as a parasite.

par·a·sit·oid (păr′ə-sĭ-toid′, -sī′toid) *n.* Any of various insects, such as the ichneumon fly, whose larvae are parasites that eventually kill their hosts. **—parasitoid** *adj.* Of or relating to a parasitic insect of this kind.

par·a·si·tol·o·gy (păr′ə-sĭ-tŏl′ə-jē, -sī-) *n.* The scientific study of parasitism. **—par′a·si′to·log′ic** (-sī′tə-lŏj′ĭk), **par′a·si′to·log′i·cal** (-ĭ-kəl) *adj.* **—par′a·si·tol′o·gist** *n.*

par·a·si·to·sis (păr′ə-sĭ-tō′sĭs, -sī-) *n., pl.* **-ses** (-sēz). A disease resulting from parasitic infestation.

parasol

par·a·sol (păr′ə-sôl′, -sŏl′) *n.* A light, usually small umbrella carried as protection from the sun. [French, from Italian *parasole* : *parare,* to shield (from Latin *parāre,* to prepare; see **perə-**[1] in Appendix) + *sole,* sun (from Latin *sōl;* see **sāwel-** in Appendix).] **—par′a·soled′** *adj.*

par·a·som·ni·a (păr′ə-sŏm′nē-ə) *n.* Any of several disorders that frequently interfere with sleep, occurring especially among children and including sleepwalking, night terrors, and bed-wetting. [Probably PARA–[1] + (IN)SOMNIA.]

par·a·stat·al (păr′ə-stāt′l) *adj.* Owned or controlled wholly or partly by the government: *a parastatal mining corporation.* **—parastatal** *n.* A company or an agency owned or controlled wholly or partly by the government.

par·a·sym·pa·thet·ic (păr′ə-sĭm′pə-thĕt′ĭk) *adj.* Of, relating to, or affecting the parasympathetic nervous system: *parasympathetic agents.* **—parasympathetic** *n.* **1.** The parasympathetic nervous system. **2.** Any of the nerves of this system. **—par′a·sym′pa·thet′i·cal·ly** *adv.*

parasympathetic nervous system *n.* The part of the autonomic nervous system originating in the brain stem and the lower part of the spinal cord that, in general, inhibits or opposes the physiological effects of the sympathetic nervous system, as in tending to stimulate digestive secretions, slow the heart, constrict the pupils, and dilate blood vessels.

par·a·sym·pa·tho·mi·met·ic (păr′əsĭm′pə-thō-mĭ-mĕt′ik, -mī-) *adj.* Producing effects similar to those produced when a parasympathetic nerve is stimulated. **—parasympathomimetic** *n.* A drug or an agent that produces such effects.

par·a·syn·the·sis (păr′ə-sĭn′thĭ-sĭs) *n., pl.* **-ses** (-sēz′). The formation of words by a combination of compounding and adding an affix, as in *downhearted,* formed from *down* plus *heart* plus *-ed,* not *down* plus *hearted.* **—par′a·syn·thet′ic** (-thĕt′ĭk) *adj.*

par·a·tax·is (păr′ə-tăk′sĭs) *n.* The juxtaposition of clauses or phrases without the use of coordinating or subordinating conjunctions, as *It was cold; the snows came.* [Greek, a placing side by side, from *paratassein,* to arrange side by side : *para-,* beside; see PARA–[1] + *tassein,* to arrange.] **—par′a·tac′tic** (-tăk′tĭk), **par′a·tac′ti·cal** (-tĭ-kəl) *adj.* **—par′a·tac′ti·cal·ly** *adv.*

parbuckle

par·a·thi·on (păr′ə-thī′ŏn) *n.* A highly poisonous yellowish liquid agricultural insecticide, $(C_2H_5O)_2P(S)OC_6H_4NO_2$. [PARA–[1] + *thio(phosphate),* phosphoric acid salt (THIO– + PHOSPHATE) + –ON[3].]

par·a·thy·roid (păr′ə-thī′roid) *adj.* Of, relating to, or obtained from the parathyroid glands: *a parathyroid extract.* **—parathyroid** *n.* **1.** The parathyroid gland. **2.** A parathyroid hormone.

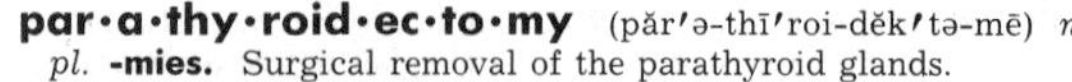

par·a·thy·roid·ec·to·my (păr′ə-thī′roi-dĕk′tə-mē) *n., pl.* **-mies.** Surgical removal of the parathyroid glands.

parathyroid gland *n.* Any of usually four small kidney-shaped glands that lie in pairs near or within the posterior surface of the thyroid gland and secrete a hormone necessary for the metabolism of calcium and phosphorus.

parathyroid hormone *n. Abbr.* **PTH** A hormone produced by the parathyroid glands that regulates the amount of calcium in the body.

par·a·troop·er (păr′ə-tro͞o′pər) *n.* A member of the paratroops.

par·a·troops (păr′ə-tro͞ops′) *pl.n.* Infantry trained and equipped to parachute. **—par′a·troop′** *adj.*

par·a·ty·phoid fever (păr′ə-tī′foid′) *n.* An acute intestinal disease, similar to typhoid fever but less severe, caused by food contaminated with certain bacteria of the genus *Salmonella.*

par·a·vane (păr′ə-vān′) *n.* A device equipped with sharp teeth and towed alongside a ship to cut the mooring cables of submerged mines.

par·boil (pär′boil′) *tr.v.* **-boiled, -boil·ing, -boils. 1.** To cook partially by boiling for a brief period: *parboiled and then sautéed the new potatoes.* **2.** To subject to intense, often uncomfortable heat. [Middle English *parboilen,* to boil partly, to boil thoroughly (influenced by *part,* part), from Old French *parboillir,* to boil thoroughly, from Late Latin *perbullīre* : Latin *per-,* thoroughly; see PER– + Latin *bullīre,* to boil.]

par·buck·le (pär′bŭk′əl) *n.* **1.** A rope sling for rolling cylindrical objects up or down an inclined plane. **2.** A sling for raising or lowering an object vertically. **—parbuckle** *tr.v.* **-led, -ling, -les.** To raise or lower with such a sling. [Alteration (influenced by BUCKLE) of *parbunkel.*]

Par·cae (pär′sē) *pl.n. Roman Mythology.* The Fates. [Latin. See **perə-**[1] in Appendix.]

par·cel (pär′səl) *n.* **1.** Something wrapped up or packaged; a package. **2.** A plot of land, usually a division of a larger area. **3.** A quantity of merchandise offered for sale. **4.** A group or company; a pack: *"this youthful parcel of noble bachelors"* (Shakespeare). **—parcel** *tr.v.* **-celed, -cel·ing, -cels** also **-celled, -cel·ling, -cels. 1.** To divide into parts and distribute: *parceled out the land to their three children.* **2.** To make into a parcel; package. **3.** *Nautical.* To wind protective strips of canvas around (rope). [Middle English, from Old French, portion, from Vulgar Latin **particella,* diminutive of Latin *particula,* diminutive of *pars, part-,* part. See **perə-**[2] in Appendix.]

parcel post *n. Abbr.* **p.p., P.P.** A postal service or department that handles and delivers packages.

par·ce·nar·y (pär′sə-nĕr′ē) *n., pl.* **-ies.** *Law.* See **coparcenary** (sense 1). [Anglo-Norman *parcenarie,* from *parcen,* portion, division. See PARCENER.]

par·ce·ner (pär′sə-nər) *n. Law.* See **coparcener.** [Middle English, from Anglo-Norman, from *parcen,* portion, division, from Vulgar Latin **partiō, partiōn-,* from Latin *partitiō, partitiōn-.* See PARTITION.]

parch (pärch) *v.* **parched, parch·ing, parch·es.** *—tr.* **1.** To make extremely dry, especially by exposure to heat: *The midsummer sun parched the earth.* See Synonyms at **burn**[1]. **2.** To make thirsty. **3.** To dry or roast (corn, for example) by exposing to heat. *—intr.* **1.** To become very dry. See Synonyms at **dry. 2.** To become thirsty. [Middle English *parchen.*]

Par·chee·si (pär-chē′zē). A trademark used for a board game based on the ancient game of pachisi.

parch·ment (pärch′mənt) *n.* **1.** The skin of a sheep or goat prepared as a material on which to write or paint. **2.** A written text or drawing on a sheet of this material. **3.** Paper made in imitation of this material. [Middle English *parchemin, parchement* (influenced by Medieval Latin *pergamentum,* from Late Latin *pergamīna*), from Old French *parchemin,* from Late Latin *pergamīna,* variant of Latin *pergamēna,* parchment, from feminine of *Pergamēnus,* of Pergamum, from Greek *Pergamēnos,* after *Pergamon* (Pergamum), an ancient Greek city and kingdom of Asia Minor.]

pard (pärd) *n.* A leopard or other large cat. [Middle English *parde,* from Old French, from Latin *pardus,* from Greek *pardos,* probably of Iranian origin.]

◆**pard·ner** (pärd′nər) *n. Regional.* A partner, companion, or friend. [Variant of PARTNER.]

par·don (pär′dn) *tr.v.* **-doned, -don·ing, -dons. 1.** To release (a person) from punishment; exempt from penalty: *a convicted criminal who was pardoned by the governor.* **2.** To let (an offense) pass without punishment. **3.** To make courteous allowance for; excuse: *Pardon me, I'm in a hurry.* See Synonyms at **forgive. —pardon** *n.* **1.** The act of pardoning. **2.** *Law.* **a.** Exemption of a convicted person from the penalties of an offense or a crime by the power of the executor of the laws. **b.** An official document or warrant declaring such an exemption. **3.** Allowance or forgiveness for an offense or a discourtesy: *begged the host's pardon for leaving early.* **4.** *Roman Catholic Church.* An indulgence. [Middle English *pardonen,* from Old French *pardoner,* from Vulgar Latin **perdōnāre,* to give wholeheartedly : Latin *per-,* intensive pref.; see PER– + Latin *dōnāre,* to present, forgive (from *dōnum,* gift; see **dō-** in Appendix).] **—par′don·a·ble** *adj.* **—par′don·a·ble·ness** *n.* **—par′don·a·bly** *adv.*

par·don·er (pär′dn-ər) *n.* **1.** One that pardons: *a pardoner of* *the sins of others.* **2.** A medieval ecclesiastic authorized to raise money for religious works by granting papal indulgences to contributors.

Par·du·bi·ce (pär′do͞o-bĭ′tsə). A city of northwest-central Czechoslovakia on the Elbe River east of Prague. It is an industrial center. Population, 93,822.

pare (pâr) *tr.v.* **pared, par·ing, pares. 1.** To remove the outer covering or skin of with a knife or similar instrument: *pare apples.* **2.** To remove by or as if by cutting, clipping, or shaving: *pared off the excess dough.* **3.** To reduce as if by cutting off outer parts; trim: *pare expenses.* [Middle English *paren,* from Old French *parer,* to prepare, trim, from Latin *parāre,* to prepare. See **perə-**[1] in Appendix.] **—par′er** *n.*

par·e·gor·ic (păr′ə-gôr′ĭk, -gŏr′-) *n.* A camphorated tincture of opium, taken internally for the relief of diarrhea and intestinal pain. [Late Latin *parēgoricus,* soothing, from Greek *parēgorikos,* from *parēgorein,* to talk over, soothe, from *parēgoros,* consoling : *para-,* beside; see PARA–[1] + *agora,* agora; see AGORA[1].]

paren. *abbr.* Parenthesis.

pa·ren·chy·ma (pə-rĕng′kə-mə) *n.* **1.** *Anatomy.* The tissue characteristic of an organ, as distinguished from associated connective or supporting tissues. **2.** *Botany.* The primary tissue of higher plants, composed of thin-walled cells and forming the greater part of leaves, roots, the pulp of fruit, and the pith of stems. [New Latin, from Greek *parenkhuma,* visceral flesh, from *parenkhein,* to pour in beside : *para-,* beside; see PARA–[1] + *en-,* in; see **en** in Appendix + *khein,* to pour; see **gheu-** in Appendix.] **—pa·ren′chy·mal, par′en·chym′a·tous** (păr′ĕn-kĭm′ə-təs) *adj.* **—par′en·chym′a·tous·ly** *adv.*

par·ent (pâr′ənt, păr′-) *n.* **1.** One who begets, gives birth to, or nurtures and raises a child; a father or a mother. **2.** An ancestor; a progenitor. **3.** An organism that produces or generates offspring. **4.** A guardian; a protector. **5.** A source or cause; an origin: *Despair is the parent of rebellion.* **—parent** *v.* **-ent·ed, -ent·ing, -ents.** *—tr.* **1.** *Usage Problem.* To act as a parent to; raise and nurture: *"A genitor who does not parent the child is not its parent"* (Ashley Montagu). **2.** To cause to come into existence; originate. *—intr. Usage Problem.* To act as a parent. [Middle English, from Old French, from Latin *parēns, parent-,* from past active participle of *parere,* to give birth. See **perə-**[1] in Appendix.] **—par′ent·hood′** *n.*

USAGE NOTE: The Usage Panel is better disposed to accept the verb *parent* than in previous surveys, though a majority continues to find it unacceptable. In 1968 it was acceptable to only 19 percent of the Panel; in the most recent survey 45 percent accepted it in the sentence *In looking for foster homes, we give preference first to relatives and second to families with prior experience in parenting.* • The use of the verb *parent* to mean "act as a parent to" is not entirely new: it occurs as early as 1884 in a metaphorical context. But its use in a literal sense with respect to children is a recent development and reflects a modern reconceptualization of family life. The word is not completely synonymous with the traditional expression *raise a child,* though the precise nature of the differences may depend on the context. For some speakers, use of the word suggests a self-conscious shift from child to parent as the focus of the parental relationship, and it may be this implication that feeds critical reservations about the verb. But the usage also reflects a widespread practical realization that the activities required of a parent extend well beyond the direct interaction with the child emphasized in *child raising.* Thus the *parenting* classes for young parents offered by schools and state agencies encompass not only the activities traditionally associated with raising a child but also topics such as personal self-sufficiency, household financial management, and methods of dealing with schools and health care agencies. See Usage Note at **father.**

par·ent·age (pâr′ən-tĭj, păr′-) *n.* **1.** Descent from parents; lineage: *of humble parentage.* **2.** The state or relationship of being a parent. **3.** Derivation from a source; origin.

pa·ren·tal (pə-rĕn′tl) *adj.* **1.** Of, relating to, or characteristic of a parent. **2.** *Genetics.* Of or designating the generation of organisms from which hybrid offspring are produced. **—pa·ren′tal·ly** *adv.*

par·en·ter·al (pă-rĕn′tər-əl) *adj.* **1.** *Physiology.* Located outside the alimentary canal. **2.** *Medicine.* Taken into the body or administered in a manner other than through the digestive tract, as by intravenous or intramuscular injection. **—par·en′ter·al·ly** *adv.*

pa·ren·the·sis (pə-rĕn′thĭ-sĭs) *n., pl.* **-ses** (-sēz′). *Abbr.* **par., paren. 1.** Either or both of the upright curved lines, (or), used to mark off explanatory or qualifying remarks in writing or printing or enclose a sum, product, or other expression considered or treated as a collective entity in a mathematical operation. **2. a.** A qualifying or amplifying word, phrase, or sentence inserted within written matter in such a way as to be independent of the surrounding grammatical structure. **b.** A comment departing from the theme of discourse; a digression. **3.** An interruption of continuity; an interval: *"This is one of the things I wasn't prepared for—the amount of unfilled time, the long parentheses of nothing"* (Margaret Atwood). [Late Latin, insertion of a letter or syllable in a word, from Greek, from *parentithenai,* to insert : *para-,* beside; see PARA–[1] + *en-,* in; see **en** in Appendix + *tithenai,* to put; see **dhē-** in Appendix.]

par·en·thet·i·cal (păr′ən-thĕt′ĭ-kəl) also **par·en·thet·ic** (-ĭk) *adj.* **1.** Set off within or as if within parentheses; qualifying or explanatory: *a parenthetical remark.* **2.** Using or containing parentheses. **—par′en·thet′i·cal·ly** *adv.*

par·ent·ing (pâr′ən-tĭng, păr′-) *n. Usage Problem.* The rearing of a child or children, especially the care, love, and guidance given by a parent. See Usage Note at **parent.**

parent language *n.* A language from which a later language is derived: *Latin is the parent language of Italian and French.*

pa·ren·ty (pə-rĕn′tē) *n.* Variant of **perentie.**

pa·re·sis (pə-rē′sĭs, păr′ĭ-sĭs) *n.* **1.** Slight or partial paralysis. **2.** General paresis. [Greek, act of letting go, paralysis, from *parienai,* to let fall : *para-,* beside; see PARA–[1] + *hienai,* to throw; see **yē-** in Appendix.] **—pa·ret′ic** (pə-rĕt′ĭk) *adj. & n.* **—pa·ret′i·cal·ly** *adv.*

par·es·the·sia also **par·aes·the·sia** (păr′ĭs-thē′zhə) *n.* A skin sensation, such as burning, prickling, itching, or tingling, with no apparent physical cause. [New Latin : PARA–[1] + Greek *aisthēsis,* feeling; see ANESTHESIA + –IA[1].] **—par′es·thet′ic** (-thĕt′ĭk) *adj.*

Pa·re·to (pə-rā′tō, pä-rĕ′tô), **Vilfredo.** 1848–1923. Italian economist and sociologist whose theories influenced the development of Italian fascism.

pa·re·u (pä′rā-o͞o′) *n.* A rectangular piece of cloth worn especially in Polynesia as a wraparound skirt or loincloth. [Tahitian.]

pa·re·ve (pä′rə-və) also **par·ve** (pär′və) *adj. Judaism.* Prepared without meat, milk, or their derivatives and therefore permissible to be eaten with both meat and dairy dishes according to dietary laws: *pareve margarine.* [Yiddish *pareve.*]

par ex·cel·lence (pär ĕk-sə-läNs′) *adj.* Being the best or truest of a kind; quintessential: *a diplomat par excellence.* [French : *par,* by + *excellence,* preeminence.]

par·fait (pär-fā′) *n.* **1.** A dessert made of cream, eggs, sugar, and flavoring frozen together and served in a tall glass. **2.** A dessert made of several layers of different flavors of ice cream or ices, variously garnished and served in a tall glass. [French, from Old French, perfect, from Latin *perfectus.* See PERFECT.]

parfait glass *n.* A tall, slender glass with a short stem, used in serving a parfait.

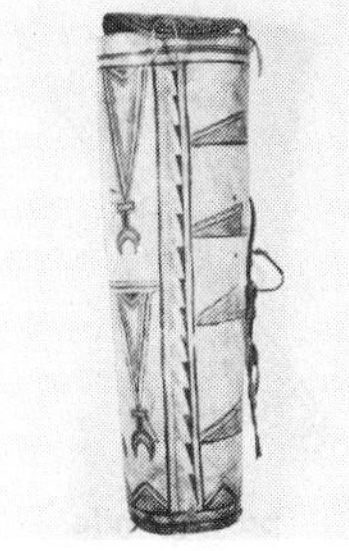

parfleche
Painted Comanche bonnet case

par·fleche (pär′flĕsh′) *n.* **1.** An untanned animal hide soaked in lye and water to remove the hair and then dried on a stretcher. **2.** An article, such as a shield, made of this hide. [Canadian French *parflèche* : French *parer,* to parry, defend; see PARRY + French *flèche,* arrow; see FLÈCHE.]

par·get (pär′jĭt) *n.* **1.** A mixture, such as plaster or roughcast, used to coat walls and line chimneys. **2.** Ornamental work in plaster. **3.** A cement mixture used to waterproof outer walls. **—parget** *tr.v.* **-get·ed, -get·ing, -gets** also **-get·ted, -get·ting, -gets.** To cover or adorn with parget. [Middle English, probably from *pargetten,* to parget, from Old French *pargeter, parjeter,* to throw about (*par-,* intensive pref., from Latin *per;* see **per**[1] in Appendix + *jeter,* to throw, from Latin *iactāre,* frequentative of *iacere;* see **yē-** in Appendix) and from Old French *porgeter,* to roughcast a wall (*por-,* forward, ultimately from Latin *porrō;* see **per**[1] in Appendix + *iactāre,* to throw).] **—par′get·ing** *n.*

parget
Framing a painting

par·he·li·a (pär-hē′lē-ə, -hēl′yə) *n.* Plural of **parhelion.**

par·he·lic circle (pär-hē′lĭk) *n.* A luminous halo visible at the height of the sun and parallel to the horizon, caused by the sun's rays reflecting off atmospheric ice crystals. Also called *parhelic ring.*

par·he·li·on (pär-hē′lē-ən, -hēl′yən) *n., pl.* **-he·li·a** (-hē′lē-ə, -hēl′yə). A bright spot sometimes appearing on either side of the sun, often on a luminous ring or halo. [Latin *parēlion,* from Greek : *para-,* beside; see PARA–[1] + *hēlios,* sun; see **sāwel-** in Appendix.] **—par·he′lic** (-hē′lĭk) *adj.*

pa·ri·ah (pə-rī′ə) *n.* **1.** A social outcast: *"Shortly Tom came upon the juvenile pariah of the village, Huckleberry Finn, son of the town drunkard"* (Mark Twain). **2.** A member of a low caste of agricultural and domestic workers in southern India and Burma. [Tamil *paṟaiyar,* pl. of *paṟaiyan,* pariah caste, from *paṟai,* festival drum.]

WORD HISTORY: In the word *pariah,* which can be used for anyone who is a social outcast, independent of social position, we have a reminder of a much more rigid social system, where only certain people could be pariahs. The caste system of India placed members of the pariah caste very low in society; until 1949 they were also known as *untouchables.* The word *pariah,* however, which we have extended in meaning, came into English from Tamil *paṟaiyar,* the plural of *paṟaiyan,* the caste name, which literally means "(hereditary) drummer" and comes from the word *paṟai,* the name of a drum used at certain festivals. The word is first recorded in English in 1613. Its use in English and its extension in use probably owe much to the close relationship that developed between Great Britain and India. Indeed, many of the British servants in India were from the pariah caste.

Par·i·an (pâr′ē-ən, păr′-) *adj.* **1.** Of or relating to the island of Páros or its inhabitants. **2.** Of or being a type of white, semitranslucent marble quarried at Páros and highly valued in ancient times for making sculptures. **3.** Of or being a fine white porcelain. **—Parian** *n.* **1.** A native or inhabitant of Páros. **2.** Parian marble. **3.** Parian porcelain.

ă pat	oi boy
ā pay	ou out
âr care	o͝o took
ä father	o͞o boot
ĕ pet	ŭ cut
ē be	ûr urge
ĭ pit	th thin
ī pie	*th* this
îr pier	hw which
ŏ pot	zh vision
ō toe	ə about, item
ô paw	♦ regionalism

Stress marks: **′** (primary); ′ (secondary), as in **dictionary** (dĭk′shə-nĕr′ē)

Pa·ri·cu·tin (pä-rē′ko͞o-tēn′). A volcano, 2,272.3 m (7,450 ft) high, of west-central Mexico west of Mexico City. It erupted from a cornfield in February 1943 and grew more than 458 m (1,500 ft) in that year alone.

pa·ri·es (pâr′ē-ēz′) *n., pl.* **pa·ri·e·tes** (pə-rī′ĭ-tēz′). A wall of a body part, organ, or cavity. Often used in the plural. [Latin *pariēs,* wall.]

pa·ri·e·tal (pə-rī′ĭ-təl) *adj.* **1.** Relating to or forming the wall of a body part, organ, or cavity. **2.** Of or relating to either of the parietal bones. **3.** *Botany.* Borne on the inside of the ovary wall. Used of the ovules or placentas in flowering plants. **4.** Dwelling within or having authority within the walls or buildings of a college. **—parietal** *n.* **1.** A parietal part, such as a wall or bone. **2. parietals.** The rules governing the visiting privileges of members of the opposite sex in college or university dormitories. [Middle English, from Late Latin *parietālis,* of a wall, from Latin *pariēs, pariet-,* wall.]

parietal bone *n.* Either of two large, irregularly quadrilateral bones between the frontal and occipital bones that together form the sides and top of the skull.

parietal cell *n.* One of the large peripheral cells of the mucous membrane of the stomach that secrete hydrochloric acid.

parietal lobe *n.* The division of each hemisphere of the brain that lies beneath each parietal bone.

pa·ri·e·tes (pə-rī′ĭ-tēz′) *n.* Plural of **paries.**

par·i-mu·tu·el (păr′ĭ-myo͞o′cho͞o-əl) *n. Sports & Games.* **1.** A system of betting on races whereby the winners divide the total amount bet, after deducting management expenses, in proportion to the sums they have wagered individually. **2.** A machine that records such bets and computes the payoffs. [French *pari-mutuel* : *pari,* wager (from *parier,* to wager, from Latin *pariāre,* to settle a debt, from *pār, par-,* equal; see **perə-²** in Appendix) + *mutuel,* mutual (from Old French; see MUTUAL).]

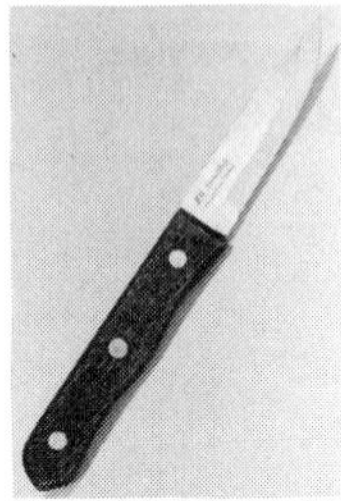

paring knife

par·ing (pâr′ĭng) *n.* Something, such as a skin or peel, that has been pared off.

paring knife *n.* A small knife with a short blade and a firm handle, used in paring fruit and vegetables.

pa·ri pas·su (păr′ē păs′o͞o, păr′ī, pär′ē) *adv.* At an equal pace; side by side: *inflation and interest rates increasing pari passu.* [Latin *parī passū* : *parī,* ablative of *pār,* equal + *passū,* ablative of *passus,* step.]

par·i·pin·nate (păr′ĭ-pĭn′āt, -ĭt) *adj. Botany.* Pinnately compound with two terminal leaflets: *paripinnate leaves.* [Latin *pār, par-,* equal, a pair + PINNATE.]

Par·is¹ (păr′ĭs) *n. Greek Mythology.* The prince of Troy whose abduction of Helen provoked the Trojan War.

Par·is² (păr′ĭs). **1.** The capital and largest city of France, in the north-central part of the country on the Seine River. Founded as a fishing village on the Île de la Cité, Paris (then called Lutetia) was captured and fortified by the Romans in 52 B.C. Clovis I made it the capital of his kingdom after A.D. 486, and Hugh Capet established it as the capital of France after his accession to the throne in 987. Through the succeeding centuries, Paris grew rapidly as a commercial, cultural, and industrial center. The city was occupied by the Germans in World War II from June 14, 1940, to August 25, 1944. Population, 2,149,900. **2.** A city of northeast Texas northeast of Dallas. It is a trade and processing center in the Red River valley. Population, 25,498.

parka

Paris, Matthew. 1200?–1259. English monk and chronicler. His *Chronica Majora* traced the history of the world from the creation to 1259.

Paris daisy *n.* See **marguerite** (sense 1).

Paris green *n.* A poisonous emerald-green powder, $(CuO)_3As_2O_3{\cdot}Cu(C_2H_3O_2)_2$, used as a pigment, an insecticide, and a wood preservative.

par·ish (păr′ĭsh) *n. Abbr.* **par. 1.a.** An administrative part of a diocese that has its own church in the Anglican, Roman Catholic, and some other churches. **b.** The members of such a parish; a religious community attending one church. **2.** A political subdivision of a British county, usually corresponding in boundaries to an original ecclesiastical parish. **3.** An administrative subdivision in Louisiana that corresponds to a county in other U.S. states. [Middle English, from Old French *parroche,* from Late Latin *parochia,* diocese, alteration of *paroecia,* from Late Greek *paroikia,* from Greek, a sojourning, from *paroikos,* neighboring, neighbor, sojourner : *para-,* near; see PARA–¹ + *oikos,* house; see **weik-¹** in Appendix.]

pa·rish·ion·er (pə-rĭsh′ə-nər) *n.* A member of a parish. [Middle English, from *parishon,* parishioner, from Old French *parochien,* from *parroche,* parish. See PARISH.]

par·i·ty¹ (păr′ĭ-tē) *n., pl.* **-ties. 1.** Equality, as in amount, status, or value. **2.** Functional equivalence, as in the weaponry or military strength of adversaries: *"A problem that has troubled the U.S.-Soviet relationship from the beginning has been the issue of parity"* (Charles William Maynes). **3.** The equivalent in value of a sum of money expressed in terms of a different currency at a fixed, official rate of exchange. **4.** Equality of prices of goods or securities in two different markets. **5.** A level for farm-product prices maintained by governmental support and intended to give farmers the same purchasing power they had during a chosen base period. **6.** *Mathematics.* The even or odd quality of an integer. If two integers are both odd or both even, they are said to have the same parity; if one is odd and one even, they have different parity. **7.** *Abbr.* **P** *Physics.* **a.** An intrinsic symmetry property of subatomic particles that is characterized by the behavior of the wave function of such particles under reflection through the origin of spatial coordinates. **b.** A quantum number, either +1 (even) or −1 (odd), that mathematically describes this property. **8.** *Computer Science.* **a.** The even or odd quality of the number of 1's or 0's in a binary code, often used to determine the integrity of data especially after transmission. **b.** A parity bit. [French *parité,* from Old French *parite,* from Late Latin *paritās,* from *pār, par-,* equal. See PAIR.]

par·i·ty² (păr′ĭ-tē) *n. Medicine.* **1.** The condition of having given birth. **2.** The number of children borne by one woman. [Latin *parere,* to give birth, bring forth; see **perə-¹** in Appendix + –ITY.]

parity bit *n. Computer Science.* A bit added to a binary code that indicates parity and is used to check the integrity of data.

park (pärk) *n. Abbr.* **pk. 1.** An area of land set aside for public use, as: **a.** A piece of land with few or no buildings within or adjoining a town, maintained for recreational and ornamental purposes. **b.** A landscaped city square. **c.** A large tract of rural land kept in its natural state and usually reserved for the enjoyment and recreation of visitors. **2.** A broad, fairly level valley between mountain ranges: *the high parks of the Rocky Mountains.* **3.** A tract of land attached to a country house, especially when including extensive gardens, woods, pastures, or a game preserve. **4.** *Sports.* A stadium or an enclosed playing field: *a baseball park.* **5.a.** An area where military vehicles or artillery are stored and serviced. **b.** The materiel kept in such an area. **6.** An area in or near a town designed and usually zoned for a certain purpose: *a commercial park.* **7.** See **parking lot** (sense 1). **—park** *v.* **parked, park·ing, parks.** *—tr.* **1.** To put or leave (a vehicle) for a time in a certain location. **2.** *Aerospace.* To place (a spacecraft or satellite) in a usually temporary orbit. **3.** *Informal.* To place or leave temporarily: *parked the baby with neighbors; parking cash in a local bank account.* **4.** To assemble (artillery or other equipment) in a military park. *—intr.* **1.** To park a motor vehicle: *pulled over and parked next to the curb.* **2.** *Slang.* To engage in kissing and caressing in a vehicle stopped in a secluded spot. [Middle English, game preserve, enclosed tract of land, from Old French *parc,* of Germanic origin.] **—park′er** *n.*

Park (pärk), **Mungo.** 1771–1806. Scottish explorer in Africa known for his expeditions on the Niger River (1795–1796 and 1805).

par·ka (pär′kə) *n.* **1.** A hooded fur pullover outer garment worn in the Arctic. **2.** A coat or jacket with a hood and usually a warm lining for cold-weather wear. [Alaskan Russian, pelt, ultimately of Nenets origin.]

Park Avenue. A wide thoroughfare extending north to south on the East Side of Manhattan Island. Traditionally associated with luxurious apartment houses, it is now the location of many high-rise commercial buildings.

Park Chung Hee (pärk′ chŭng′ hē′). 1917–1979. South Korean politician who became president of South Korea after a military coup (1961) and assumed dictatorial powers in 1972. He was assassinated in 1979.

Par·ker (pär′kər), **Charlie.** Known as "Bird." 1920–1955. American musician and composer. A leader of the bop movement in jazz, Parker is best remembered for his smooth, moody improvisations.

Parker, Dorothy Rothschild. 1893–1967. American writer noted for her satirical wit. She was drama critic for *Vanity Fair* (1916–1917) and book critic for the *New Yorker* (1927–1933).

Parker, Sir **(Horatio) Gilbert (George).** 1862–1932. Canadian writer whose works include *The Seats of the Mighty* (1896) and *The Power and the Glory (1925).*

Parker, Matthew. 1504–1575. English prelate who served as archbishop of Canterbury from 1559 until his death and was instrumental in establishing ecclesiastical forms for the Anglican Church.

Parker, Theodore. 1810–1860. American cleric and social reformer known for his abolitionist activities.

Parker House roll *n.* A yeast-leavened roll, shaped by folding a flat round of dough in half. [After the *Parker House,* a hotel in Boston, Massachusetts.]

Par·kers·burg (pär′kərz-bûrg′). A city of northwest West Virginia at the confluence of the Little Kanawha and Ohio rivers north of Charleston. It is an industrial and commercial center in a coal region. Population, 39,967.

Park Forest. A village of northeast Illinois, a residential suburb of Chicago. Population, 26,222.

♦**park·ing** (pär′kĭng) *n.* **1.** The act or practice of temporarily leaving a vehicle or maneuvering a vehicle into a certain location. **2.** Space in which to park vehicles or a vehicle: *ample parking behind the building.* **3.** *Upper Midwest.* The grass strip, often planted with shade trees, between a sidewalk and a street. **4.** *Slang.* Kissing or caressing in a vehicle stopped in a secluded spot.

♦ ***REGIONAL NOTE:*** *Parking* is an Upper Midwestern term for the grass strip, often planted with shade trees, between a sidewalk and a street. The presence of this word also in Western states attests to the close linguistic connection, owing to settlement patterns, between the Upper Midwest and the West.

parking lot *n.* **1.** An area for parking motor vehicles. Also called *park.* **2.** *Slang.* A traffic jam.

parking meter *n.* A coin-operated device that registers the amount of time purchased for the parking of a motor vehicle, at the expiration of which the driver is liable for a fine.

parking orbit *n. Aerospace.* A temporary orbit for a spacecraft.

Par·kin·son (pär′kĭn-sən), **C(yril) Northcote.** Born 1909. British historian noted for his humorous works that ridicule the inefficiency of bureaucracies.

Par·kin·son·ism (pär′kĭn-sə-nĭz′əm) *n.* **1.** Any of a group of nervous disorders similar to Parkinson's disease, marked by muscular rigidity, tremor, and impaired motor control and often having a specific cause, such as the use of certain drugs or frequent exposure to toxic chemicals. Also called *Parkinson's syndrome.* **2.** Parkinson's disease. [From PARKINSON'S DISEASE.]

Par·kin·son's disease (pär′kĭn-sənz) *n.* A progressive nervous disease occuring most often after the age of 50, associated with the destruction of brain cells that produce dopamine and characterized by muscular tremor, slowing of movement, partial facial paralysis, peculiarity of gait and posture, and weakness. Also called *paralysis agitans, shaking palsy.* [After James *Parkinson* (1755–1824), British physician.]

Parkinson's Law *n.* Any of several satirical observations propounded as economic laws, especially "Work expands to fill the time available for its completion." [After C(yril) Northcote PARKINSON.]

Parkinson's syndrome *n.* See **Parkinsonism** (sense 1).

park·land (pärk′lănd′) *n.* **1.** Land within or suitable for public parks: *Alaska's vast federal parkland.* **2.** Grassland with scattered clusters of trees or shrubs.

Park·land (pärk′lənd). A community of west-central Washington, a residential suburb of Tacoma. Population, 22,300.

Park·man (pärk′mən), **Francis.** 1823–1893. American historian whose works include *The California and Oregon Trail* (1849) and *Pioneers of France in the New World* (1865).

Park Range. A range of the Rocky Mountains in north-central Colorado and southern Wyoming rising to 4,357.2 m (14,286 ft) at Mount Lincoln in Colorado.

Park Ridge. A city of northeast Illinois, a chiefly residential suburb of Chicago. Population, 38,704.

Park·rose (pärk′rōz′). A community of northwest Oregon, a suburb of Portland. Population, 21,103.

Parks (pärks), **Rosa.** Born 1913. American civil rights leader. Her refusal to give up her seat on a bus to a white man in Montgomery, Alabama, resulted in a city-wide boycott of the bus company and stirred the civil rights movement across the nation.

park·way (pärk′wā′) *n. Abbr.* **pkwy, pky** A broad landscaped highway, often divided by a planted median strip.

parl. *abbr.* **1.** Also **Parl.** Parliament. **2.** Parliamentary.

par·lance (pär′ləns) *n.* **1.** A particular manner of speaking; idiom: *legal parlance.* **2.** Speech, especially a conversation or parley. [Old French, from *parler,* to speak. See PARLEY.]

par·lan·do (pär-län′dō) also **par·lan·te** (-tā) *adv. & adj. Music.* To be sung in a style suggestive of speech. Used chiefly as a direction. [Italian, present participle of *parlare,* to speak, from Vulgar Latin *paraulāre. See PARLEY.]

par·lay (pär′lā′, -lē) *tr.v.* **-layed, -lay·ing, -lays. 1.** *Games.* To bet (an original wager and its winnings) on a subsequent event. **2.** To maneuver (an asset) to great advantage: *parlayed some small investments into a large fortune.* **—parlay** *n. Games.* A bet comprising the sum of a prior wager plus its winnings or a series of bets made in such a manner. [Alteration of *paroli,* staking of double the sum staked before in faro, from French, from obsolete Italian, probably from Italian *parare,* to place a bet, from Latin *parāre,* to prepare. See PARE.]

par·ley (pär′lē) *n., pl.* **-leys.** A discussion or conference, especially one between enemies over terms of truce or other matters. **—parley** *intr.v.* **-leyed, -ley·ing, -leys.** To have a discussion, especially with an enemy. See Synonyms at **confer.** [Middle English, from Old French *parlee,* from feminine past participle of *parler,* to talk, from Vulgar Latin *paraulāre, from Late Latin *parabolāre,* from Late Latin *parabola,* discourse. See PARABLE.]

par·lia·ment (pär′lə-mənt) *n. Abbr.* **parl., Parl. 1.** A national representative body having supreme legislative powers within the state. **2. Parliament.** The national legislature of various countries, especially that of the United Kingdom, made up of the House of Lords and the House of Commons. [Middle English, a meeting about national concerns, from Old French *parlement,* from *parler,* to talk. See PARLEY.]

par·lia·men·tar·i·an (pär′lə-mĕn-târ′ē-ən) *n.* **1.** One who is expert in parliamentary procedures, rules, or debate. **2.** A member of a parliament. **3. Parliamentarian.** A supporter of the Long Parliament during the English Civil War and the Commonwealth; a Roundhead.

par·lia·men·ta·ry (pär′lə-mĕn′tə-rē, -mĕn′trē) *adj. Abbr.* **parl. 1.** Of, relating to, or resembling a parliament. **2.** Enacted or decreed by a parliament. **3.** Being in accord with the rules and customs of a parliament. **4. a.** Having a parliament. **b.** Characterized by an executive consisting of cabinet ministers selected from and responsible to the parliament: *parliamentary government.*

parliamentary law *n.* A body of rules governing procedure in legislative and deliberative assemblies.

par·lor (pär′lər) *n.* **1.** A room in a private home set apart for the entertainment of visitors. **2.** A small lounge or sitting room affording limited privacy, as at an inn or a tavern. **3.** A room equipped and furnished for a special function or business: *a tanning parlor.* [Middle English *parlur,* from Old French, from *parler,* to talk. See PARLEY.]

parlor car *n.* A railroad car for day travel fitted with individual reserved seats. Also called *chair car.*

parlor game *n. Games.* A game that can be played indoors.

parlor grand *n. Music.* A grand piano shorter in length than a concert grand yet longer than a baby grand.

par·lour (pär′lər) *n. Chiefly British.* Variant of **parlor.**

par·lous (pär′ləs) *adj.* **1.** Perilous; dangerous: *a parlous journey on stormy seas.* **2.** *Obsolete.* Dangerously cunning. [Middle English, variant of *perilous,* perilous, from *peril,* peril. See PERIL.] **—par′lous·ly** *adv.*

Par·ma (pär′mə). **1.** A city of north-central Italy southeast of Milan. Founded by Romans in 183 B.C., it became a free city in the 12th century and was the center of the duchy of Parma and Piacenza after 1545. It became part of the kingdom of Sardinia in 1860 and of Italy in 1861. Population, 176,750. **2.** A city of northeast Ohio, a suburb of Cleveland. Population, 92,547.

Parma Heights. A city of northeast Ohio, a residential suburb of Cleveland. Population, 23,112.

Par·men·i·des (pär-mĕn′ĭ-dēz′). Born 515? B.C. Greek philosopher and a founder of the Eleatic school.

Par·me·san (pär′mə-zän′, -zăn′, -zən) *n.* A hard, sharp, dry Italian cheese made from skim milk and usually served grated as a garnish. [French, from Old French *permigean,* of Parma, from Old Italian *parmigiano.* See PARMIGIANA.]

par·mi·gia·na (pär′mĭ-zhä′nə, -jä′-) *adj.* Made or covered with Parmesan cheese: *eggplant parmigiana.* [Italian, feminine of *parmigiano,* of Parma, after PARMA, Italy.]

Par·mi·gia·ni·no (pär′mĭ-jä-nē′nō, -mē-) or **Par·mi·gia·no** (-jä′nō), **Il.** 1503–1540. Italian Mannerist painter and etcher whose work is characterized by elongation of form and includes *Vision of Saint Jerome* (1527).

Par·na·í·ba (pär′nə-ē′bə, -nä-ē′bä). A river, about 1,287 km (800 mi) long, of northeast Brazil flowing generally northward to the Atlantic Ocean.

Par·nas·si·an (pär-năs′ē-ən) *adj.* Of or relating to poetry. **—Parnassian** *n.* A member of a school of late 19th-century French poets whose work is characterized by detachment and emphasis on metrical form. [From Latin *Parnassius,* of Parnassus, from Greek *parnasios,* after *Parnasos* (Parnassus), a mountain in Greece sacred to Apollo and the Muses. N., from French *parnassien,* after *Le Parnasse contemporain,* the group's first anthology of poetry (1866), from *Parnasse,* Parnassus, from Latin *Parnassus,* from Greek *Parnasos.*]

Par·nas·sus (pär-năs′əs) also **Par·nas·sós** (-nä-sôs′). A mountain, about 2,458 m (8,060 ft) high, of central Greece north of the Gulf of Corinth. In ancient times it was sacred to Apollo, Dionysus, and the Muses. Delphi was at the foot of the mountain.

Par·nell (pär-nĕl′, pär′nəl), **Charles Stewart.** 1846–1891. Irish nationalist leader who served as a member of the British parliament (1875–1891) and led Ireland's Home Rule Movement.

pa·ro·chi·al (pə-rō′kē-əl) *adj.* **1.** Of, relating to, supported by, or located in a parish. **2.** Narrowly restricted in scope or outlook; provincial: *parochial attitudes.* [Middle English, from Old French, from Late Latin *parochiālis,* from *parochia,* diocese. See PARISH.] **—pa·ro′chi·al·ism** *n.* **—pa·ro′chi·al·ist** *n.* **—pa·ro′chi·al·ly** *adv.*

parochial school *n.* A school supported by a church parish.

par·o·dy (păr′ə-dē) *n.* **-dies. 1. a.** A literary or artistic work that imitates the characteristic style of an author or a work for comic effect or ridicule. See Synonyms at **caricature. b.** The genre of literature comprising such works. **2.** Something so bad as to be equivalent to intentional mockery; a travesty: *The trial was a parody of justice.* **3.** *Music.* The practice, popular in the 15th and 16th centuries, of significantly reworking an already established composition, especially the incorporation into the Mass of material borrowed from other works, such as motets or madrigals. **—parody** *tr.v.* **-died, -dy·ing, -dies.** To make a parody of. See Synonyms at **imitate.** [Latin *parōdia,* from Greek *parōidia* : *para-,* subsidiary to; see PARA–[1] + *ōidē,* song; see **wed-**[2] in Appendix.] **—pa·rod′ic** (pə-rŏd′ĭk), **pa·rod′i·cal** (-ĭ-kəl) *adj.* **—par′o·dist** *n.* **—par′o·dis′tic** *adj.*

pa·rol (pə-rōl′, păr′əl) *Law. n.* An oral statement or utterance: *by parol.* **—parol** *adj.* Expressed or evidenced by word of mouth; not written. [Middle English *parole,* from Anglo-Norman, from Vulgar Latin *paraula. See PAROLE.]

pa·role (pə-rōl′) *n.* **1.** *Law.* **a.** The release of a prisoner whose term has not expired on condition of sustained lawful behavior that is subject to regular monitoring by an officer of the law for a set period of time. **b.** The duration of such conditional release. **2.** A password used by an officer of the day, an officer on guard, or the personnel commanded by such an officer. **3.** Word of honor, especially that of a prisoner of war who is granted freedom only after promising to lay down arms. **4.** *Linguistics.* The act of speaking; a particular utterance or word. *—attributive.* Often used to modify another noun: *a parole board; parole viola-*

Rosa Parks

ă pat	oi boy
ā pay	ou out
âr care	ŏŏ took
ä father	ōō boot
ĕ pet	ŭ cut
ē be	ûr urge
ĭ pit	th thin
ī pie	*th* this
îr pier	hw which
ŏ pot	zh vision
ō toe	ə about, item
ô paw	♦ regionalism

Stress marks: ′ (primary); ′ (secondary), as in **dictionary** (dĭk′shə-nĕr′ē)

parquetry
Parquet floor

tions. **—parole** *tr.v.* **-roled, -rol·ing, -roles.** To release (a prisoner) on parole. [French, promise, word, from Vulgar Latin **paraula,* from Latin *parabola,* discourse. See PARABLE.]

pa·rol·ee (pə-rō′lē′) *n.* One who is released on parole.

par·o·no·ma·sia (păr′ə-nō-mā′zhə, -zhē-ə) *n.* **1.** Word play; punning. **2.** A pun. [Latin, from Greek, from *paronomazein,* to call by a different name : *para-,* beside; see PARA–[1] + *onomazein,* to name; see ONOMASTIC.] **—par′o·no·mas′tic** (-măs′tĭk), **par′o·no·ma′sial** (-mā′zhəl, -zhē-əl) *adj.* **—par′o·no·mas′ti·cal·ly** *adv.*

par·o·nych·i·a (păr′ə-nĭk′ē-ə) *n. Medicine.* Inflammation of the tissue surrounding a nail. [Latin *parōnychia,* from Greek *parōnukhia* : *para-,* around; see PARA–[1] + *onux, onukh-,* nail; see **nogh-** in Appendix.] **—par′o·nych′i·al** *adj.*

par·o·nym (păr′ə-nĭm′) *n.* A paronymous word. [Greek *parōnumon,* from neuter sing. of *parōnumos,* derivative. See PARONYMOUS.] **—par′o·nym′ic** *adj.*

pa·ron·y·mous (pə-rŏn′ə-məs) *adj.* Allied by derivation from the same root; having the same stem; for example, *beautiful* and *beauteous.* [Greek *parōnumos,* derivative : *para-,* beside; see PARA–[1] + *onuma,* name; see **nō-men-** in Appendix.]

Pá·ros also **Par·os** (pâr′ŏs, pä′rôs). An island of southeast Greece in the Aegean Sea. One of the Cyclades, it was settled by Ionians and later founded colonies of its own in the seventh century B.C. The island was held by the Ottoman Turks from 1537 to 1832, when it became part of Greece. A fine white, semitranslucent marble quarried on the island was used by sculptors as early as the sixth century B.C.

Catherine Parr
c. 1545 portrait by an unknown artist

pa·ros·mi·a (pə-rŏz′mē-ə) *n.* A distortion of the sense of smell, as in smelling odors that are not present. [PAR(A)–[1] + Greek *osmē,* smell + –IA[1].]

pa·rot·id (pə-rŏt′ĭd) *n.* A parotid gland. **—parotid** *adj.* **1.** Situated near the ear: *the parotid region of the face.* **2.** Of or relating to a parotid gland.

pa·rot·i·dec·to·my (pə-rŏt′ĭ-dĕk′tə-mē) *n., pl.* **-mies.** Surgical removal of the parotid gland.

parotid gland *n.* Either of the pair of salivary glands situated below and in front of each ear. [New Latin *parōtis, parōtid-,* from Latin, tumor near the ear, from Greek : *para-,* beside; see PARA–[1] + *ous, ōt-,* ear; see **ous-** in Appendix.]

par·o·ti·tis (păr′ə-tī′tĭs) also **pa·rot·i·di·tis** (pə-rŏt′ĭ-dī′tĭs) *n.* Inflammation of the parotid glands, as in mumps. **—par′o·tit′ic** (-tĭt′ĭk) *adj.*

par·ous (păr′əs, pâr′-) *adj.* Having given birth one or more times. [From –PAROUS.]

–parous *suff.* Giving birth to; producing: *multiparous.* [From Latin *-parus,* from *parere,* to give birth. See **perə-[1]** in Appendix.]

Par·ou·si·a (pär′o͞o-sē′ə, pə-ro͞o′zē-ə) *n.* The Second Coming. [Greek, presence, Parousia, from feminine present participle of *pareinai,* to be present : *para-,* beside; see PARA–[1] + *einai,* to be; see **es-** in Appendix.]

par·ox·ysm (păr′ək-sĭz′əm) *n.* **1.** A sudden outburst of emotion or action: *a paroxysm of laughter.* **2.** *Medicine.* **a.** A sudden attack, recurrence, or intensification of a disease. **b.** A spasm or fit; a convulsion. [Middle English *paroxism,* periodic attack of a disease, from Medieval Latin *paroxysmus,* from Greek *paroxusmos,* from *paroxunein,* to stimulate, irritate : *para-,* intensive pref.; see PARA–[1] + *oxunein,* to goad, sharpen (from *oxus,* sharp; see **ak-** in Appendix).] **—par′ox·ys′mal** (-ək-sĭz′məl) *adj.* **—par′ox·ys′mal·ly** *adv.*

Maxfield Parrish

par·ox·y·tone (pă-rŏk′sĭ-tōn′) *adj.* Having an acute accent on the next to last syllable. Used of some words in Greek and certain Romance languages, such as French and Portuguese. **—paroxytone** *n.* A paroxytone word. [Greek *paroxutonos* : *para-,* beside; see PARA–[1] + *oxutonos,* oxytone; see OXYTONE.]

par·quet (pär-kā′) *n.* **1.** A floor made of parquetry. **2.** The art or process of making parquetry. **3. a.** The part of the main floor of a theater between the orchestra pit and the parquet circle. **b.** The entire main floor of a theater. **—parquet** *tr.v.* **-queted** (-kād′), **-quet·ing** (-kā′ĭng), **-quets** (-kāz′). **1.** To furnish with a floor of parquetry. **2.** To make (a floor, for example) of parquetry. [French, parquetry, from Old French, diminutive of *parc,* enclosure. See PARK.]

parquet circle *n.* The part of the main floor of a theater that lies under the balcony section. Also called *parterre.*

par·quet·ry (pär′kĭ-trē) *n., pl.* **-ries.** Inlay of wood, often of different colors, that is worked into a geometric pattern or mosaic and is used especially for floors. [French *parqueterie,* from *parquet.* See PARQUET.]

parr (pär) *n., pl.* **parr** or **parrs. 1.** A young salmon during its first two years of life, when it lives in fresh water. **2.** The young of various other fishes. [Origin unknown.]

Parr (pär), **Catherine.** 1512–1548. Queen of England as the sixth and last wife of Henry VIII.

par·ral (păr′əl) *n. Nautical.* Variant of **parrel.**

par·ra·mat·ta (păr′ə-măt′ə) *n.* Variant of **paramatta.**

Par·ra·mat·ta (păr′ə-măt′ə). A city of southeast Australia, a manufacturing suburb of Sydney. It was founded in 1788. Population, 131,800.

parrot

par·rel also **par·ral** (păr′əl) *n. Nautical.* A sliding loop of rope or chain by which a running yard or gaff is connected to, while still being able to move vertically along, the mast. [Middle English *perel, parrail,* short for *appareil,* apparel, rigging. See APPAREL.]

par·ri·cide (păr′ĭ-sīd′) *n.* **1.** The murdering of one's father, mother, or other near relative. **2.** One who commits such a murder. [Latin *parricīda* and *parricīdium* : *pāri-, parri-,* kin + *-cīda, -cīdium,* -cide.] **—par′ri·cid′al** (-sīd′l) *adj.* **—par′ri·cid′al·ly** *adv.*

Par·ring·ton (păr′ĭng-tən), **Vernon Louis.** 1871–1929. American literary historian and philosopher known especially for his *Main Currents in American Thought* (1927–1930).

Par·rish (păr′ĭsh), **Anne.** 1760–1800. American philanthropist who founded (1795) the Philadelphia House of Industry, the first charitable institution for women in the United States.

Parrish, Maxfield Frederick. 1870–1966. American artist known for his colorful murals, magazine covers, and book illustrations.

Par·ris Island (păr′ĭs). An island of the Sea Islands off southern South Carolina. It has been a U.S. Marine Corps training installation since 1915.

par·rot (păr′ət) *n.* **1.** Any of numerous tropical and semitropical birds of the order Psittaciformes, characterized by a short hooked bill, brightly colored plumage, and, in some species, the ability to mimic human speech or other sounds. **2.** One who imitates the words or actions of another, especially without understanding them. **—parrot** *tr.v.* **-rot·ed, -rot·ing, -rots.** To repeat or imitate, especially without understanding. [Probably from French dialectal *Perrot,* diminutive of *Pierre,* Peter.] **—par′rot·er** *n.*

parrot fever *n.* See **psittacosis.**

par·rot·fish (păr′ət-fĭsh′) *n., pl.* **parrotfish** or **-fish·es.** Any of various brightly colored tropical marine fishes, especially of the family Scaridae, having fused teeth resembling a parrot's beak.

par·ry (păr′ē) *v.* **-ried, -ry·ing, -ries.** *—tr.* **1.** To deflect or ward off (a fencing thrust, for example). **2.** To deflect, evade, or avoid: *He skillfully parried the question with a clever reply.* *—intr.* To deflect or ward off a thrust or blow. **—parry** *n., pl.* **-ries. 1.** The deflecting or warding off of a thrust or blow, as in fencing. **2.** An evasive answer or action. [Probably from French *parez,* imperative of *parer,* to defend, from Italian *parare,* from Latin *parāre,* to prepare. See **perə-[1]** in Appendix.]

Par·ry (păr′ē), Sir **William Edward.** 1790–1855. British navigator who commanded three expeditions in search of the Northwest Passage (1819–1820, 1821–1823, and 1824–1825).

Parry Channel. A water route through the central Arctic Archipelago of Northwest Territories, Canada, linking Baffin Bay on the east with the Beaufort Sea on the west.

Parry Islands. A group of islands of northern Northwest Territories, Canada, in the Arctic Ocean north of Victoria Island.

parse (pärs) *v.* **parsed, pars·ing, pars·es.** *—tr.* **1.** To break (a sentence) down into its component parts of speech with an explanation of the form, function, and syntactical relationship of each part. **2.** To describe (a word) by stating its part of speech, form, and syntactical relationships in a sentence. **3.** To examine closely or subject to detailed analysis, especially by breaking up into components: *"What are we missing by parsing the behavior of chimpanzees into the conventional categories recognized largely from our own behavior?"* (Stephen Jay Gould). **4.** *Computer Science.* To analyze or separate (input, for example) into more easily processed components. Used of software. *—intr.* To admit of being parsed: *sentences that do not parse easily.* [Probably from Middle English *pars,* part of speech, from Latin *pars (ōrātiōnis),* part (of speech). See **perə-[2]** in Appendix.] **—pars′er** *n.*

par·sec (pär′sĕk′) *n.* A unit of astronomical length based on the distance from Earth at which stellar parallax is one second of arc and equal to 3.258 light-years, 3.086×10^{13} kilometers, or 1.918×10^{13} miles. [PAR(ALLAX) + SEC(OND)[1].]

Par·see also **Par·si** (pär′sē, pär-sē′) *n., pl.* **-sees** also **-sis. 1.** A member of a Zoroastrian religious sect in India, descended from Persians. **2.** The Iranian dialect used in the religious literature of the Parsees. [Persian *Pārsī,* from *Pārs,* Persia, from Old Persian *Pārsā.*] **—Par′see′ism** *n.*

par·si·mo·ni·ous (pär′sə-mō′nē-əs) *adj.* Excessively sparing or frugal. See Synonyms at **stingy.** **—par′si·mo′ni·ous·ly** *adv.* **—par′si·mo′ni·ous·ness** *n.*

par·si·mo·ny (pär′sə-mō′nē) *n.* **1.** Unusual or excessive frugality; extreme economy or stinginess. **2.** Adoption of the simplest assumption in the formulation of a theory or in the interpretation of data, especially in accordance with the rule of Ockham's razor. [Middle English *parcimony,* from Latin *parsimōnia,* from *parsus,* past participle of *parcere,* to spare.]

pars·ley (pär′slē) *n., pl.* **-leys. 1.** A member of the parsley family. **2.** A cultivated Eurasian herb *(Petroselinum crispum)* having flat or curled, ternately compound leaves that are used for seasoning or as a garnish. [Middle English *persely,* from Old English *petersilie* and Old French *persil,* both ultimately from Late Latin *petrosillum,* alteration of Latin *petroselīnum,* from Greek *petroselinon* : *petra,* rock + *selinon,* celery.]

pars·leyed (pär′slēd) *adj.* Prepared or garnished with parsley: *parsleyed potatoes; a parsleyed rack of lamb.*

parsley family *n.* A large family of aromatic herbs, the Umbelliferae (Apiaceae), characterized by compound leaves and small flowers grouped in umbels and including vegetables such as carrots, celery, dill, parsley, and parsnips and spices such as anise, coriander, and cumin.

pars·nip (pär′snĭp) *n.* **1.** A strong-scented plant *(Pastinaca sativa)* cultivated for its long, white, edible, fleshy root. **2.** The root of this plant. [Middle English *pasnepe,* alteration (influenced by *nep,* turnip) of Old French *pasnaie,* from Latin *pastināca,* from *pastinum,* a kind of two-pronged dibble.]

par·son (pär′sən) *n.* **1.** An Anglican cleric with full legal control of a parish under ecclesiastical law; a rector. **2.** A member of the clergy, especially a Protestant minister. [Middle English, parish priest, from Old French *persone,* from Medieval Latin *persōna,* from Latin, character. See PERSON.]

par·son·age (pär′sə-nĭj) *n.* The official residence usually provided by a church for its parson; a rectory.

parson bird *n.* See **tui.**

Par·sons (pär′sənz), **Betty.** Born 1900. American artist and arts patron whose New York gallery was a center of the abstract expressionist movement in the late 1940's.

Parsons, Talcott. 1902–1979. American sociologist noted for developing the structural-functional approach to studying social systems. **—Par·son′i·an** (pär-sō′nē-ən) *adj.*

Parsons, William. Third Earl of Rosse. 1800–1867. British astronomer known for his improvements to telescope construction.

par·son's nose (pär′sənz) *n. Informal.* See **pope's nose.**

Parsons table *n.* A sturdy, usually rectangular table with flush surfaces and straight, block legs that are equal in thickness to the top of the table and form its four corners. [After the *Parsons* School of Design in New York City.]

part (pärt) *n. Abbr.* **p., pt. 1.** A portion, division, piece, or segment of a whole. **2.** Any of several equal portions or fractions that can constitute a whole or into which a whole can be divided: *a mixture of two parts flour to one part sugar.* **3.** A division of a literary work: *a novel in three parts.* **4.a.** An organ, a member, or another division of an organism. **b. parts.** The external genitalia. **5.** A component that can be separated from or attached to a system; a detachable piece: *spare parts for cars.* **6.** A role: *She has the main part in the play.* **7.** One's responsibility, duty, or obligation; share: *We each do our part to keep the house clean.* **8.** Often **parts.** Individual endowment or ability; talent. **9.** Often **parts.** A region, area, land, or territory: *"Minding your own business is second nature in these parts"* (Boston). **10.** The line where the hair on the head is parted. **11.** *Music.* **a.** The music or score for a particular instrument, as in an orchestra. **b.** One of the melodic divisions or voices of a contrapuntal composition. **—part** *v.* **part·ed, part·ing, parts.** *—tr.* **1.** To divide or break into separate parts. **2.** To break up (a relationship) by separating the elements involved: *parted company.* **3.** To put or keep apart: *No one could part the two friends.* **4.** To comb (hair, for example) away from a dividing line, as on the scalp. **5.** *Archaic.* To divide into shares or portions. *—intr.* **1.** To become divided or separated: *The curtain parted in the middle.* **2.** To go apart from one another; separate: *They parted as friends. They were forced to part from one another.* **3.** To separate or divide into ways going in different directions: *The road parts about halfway into the forest.* **4.** To go away; depart. See Synonyms at **separate. 5.** To disagree by factions: *The committee parted over the issue of pay raises for employees.* **6.** *Archaic.* To die. **—part** *adv.* Partially; in part: *part yellow, part green.* **—part** *adj.* Not full or complete; partial: *a part owner of the business.* ***—phrasal verb.*** **part with.** To give up or let go of; relinquish. ***—idioms.*** **for (one's) part.** So far as one is concerned. **for the most part.** To the greater extent; generally or mostly. **in good part.** Good-naturedly or with good grace; without taking offense: *take a joke in good part.* **in part.** To some extent; partly. **on the part of.** Regarding or with respect to the one specified: *Brilliant strategy on the part of Confederate forces ensured their victory at Chancellorsville.* **part and parcel.** A basic or essential part: *Working overtime is part and parcel of his job.* **take part.** To join in; participate: *He took part in the celebration.* **take (someone's) part.** To side with in a disagreement; support. [Middle English, from Old French, from Latin *pars, part-.* See **perə-**[2] in Appendix.]

part. *abbr.* **1.** Particle. **2.** Particular.

par·take (pär-tāk′) *v.* **-took** (-to͝ok′), **-tak·en** (-tā′kən), **-tak·ing, -takes.** *—intr.* **1.** To take or have a part or share; participate. **2.** To take or be given part or portion: *The guests partook of a delicious dinner.* **3.** To have part of the quality, nature, or character of something. See Synonyms at **share**[1]. *—tr.* To take or have a part in; share in. [Back-formation from *partaker,* one who partakes, from Middle English *part-taker* (translation of Latin *particeps,* participant).] **—par·tak′er** *n.*

part·ed (pär′tĭd) *adj.* **1.** Separated or divided into parts. **2.** Being or kept apart; separated. **3.** *Botany.* Cleft almost to the base, so as to have distinct divisions or lobes. **4.** *Archaic.* Deceased.

par·terre (pär-târ′) *n.* **1.** An ornamental flower garden having the beds and paths arranged to form a pattern. **2.** See **parquet circle.** [French, from Old French, ornamental garden, from *par terre,* on the ground : *par,* over, on; see PARAMOUNT + *terre,* ground (from Old French, from Latin *terra,* earth; see **ters-** in Appendix).]

par·the·no·car·py (pär′thə-nō-kär′pē) *n.* The production of fruit without fertilization. [Greek *parthenos,* virgin + Greek *karpos,* fruit; see –CARP + –Y[2].] **—par′the·no·car′pic** *adj.* **—par′the·no·car′pi·cal·ly** *adv.*

par·the·no·gen·e·sis (pär′thə-nō-jĕn′ĭ-sĭs) *n.* A form of reproduction in which an unfertilized egg develops into a new individual, occurring commonly among insects and certain other arthropods. [New Latin : Greek *parthenos,* virgin + GENESIS.] **—par′the·no·ge·net′ic** (-jə-nĕt′ĭk) *adj.* **—par′the·no·ge·net′i·cal·ly** *adv.*

par·the·nog·e·none (pär′thə-nŏj′ə-nōn′) *n.* An organism produced by parthenogenesis. [PARTHENOGEN(ESIS) + *-one,* basic unit (variant of –ON[1]).]

Par·the·non (pär′thə-nŏn′, -nən) *n.* The chief temple of the goddess Athena built on the acropolis at Athens between 447 and 432 B.C. and considered a supreme example of Doric architecture. [Latin *Parthenōn,* from Greek, from *parthenos,* virgin.]

Par·thi·a (pär′thē-ə). An ancient country of southwest Asia corresponding to modern northeast Iran. It was included in the Assyrian and Persian empires, the Macedonian empire of Alexander the Great, and the Syrian empire. A Parthian kingdom lasted from c. 250 B.C. to A.D. 226, reaching the height of its influence and land holdings at the beginning of the first century B.C. Its people, of Scythian stock, were noted as horsemen and archers.

Par·thi·an (pär′thē-ən) *adj.* **1.** Of or relating to Parthia or its people, language, or culture. **2.** Delivered in or as if in retreat: *"a Parthian volley of expletives from Uncle Billy"* (Bret Harte). **—Parthian** *n.* **1.** A native or inhabitant of Parthia. **2.** The Iranian language of the Parthians.

par·tial (pär′shəl) *adj.* **1.** Of, relating to, being, or affecting only a part; not total; incomplete: *The plan calls for partial deployment of missiles. The police have only a partial description of the suspect.* **2.** Favoring one person or side over another or others; biased or prejudiced: *a decision that was partial to the plaintiff.* **3.** Having a particular liking or fondness for something or someone: *partial to detective novels.* **4.** *Mathematics.* Of, relating to, or being operations or sequences of operations, such as differentiation and integration, when applied to only one of several variables at a time. **—partial** *n.* **1.** *Music.* See **harmonic** (sense 1). **2.** *Mathematics.* A partial derivative. [Middle English *parcial,* from Old French, from Late Latin *partiālis,* from Latin *pars, part-,* part. See PART.] **—par′tial·ness** *n.*

partial derivative *n. Mathematics.* The derivative with respect to a single variable of a function of two or more variables, regarding other variables as constants.

partial differential equation *n. Mathematics.* A differential equation containing at least one partial derivative.

partial differentiation *n. Mathematics.* Differentiation with respect to a single variable in a function of several variables, regarding other variables as constants.

partial fraction *n.* One of a set of fractions having an algebraic sum equal to a specified fraction.

par·ti·al·i·ty (pär′shē-ăl′ĭ-tē, pär-shăl′-) *n., pl.* **-ties. 1.** The state of being partial. **2.** Favorable prejudice or bias. **3.** A special fondness; a predilection: *a child with a grown-up partiality for rare and expensive foods.* See Synonyms at **predilection.**

par·tial·ly (pär′shə-lē) *adv.* To a degree; not totally.

partial pressure *n.* The pressure that one component of a mixture of gases would exert if it were alone in a container.

partial tone *n. Music.* See **harmonic** (sense 1).

par·ti·ble (pär′tə-bəl) *adj.* That can be parted, divided, or separated; divisible: *a partible estate.*

par·tic·i·pant (pär-tĭs′ə-pənt) *n.* One that participates, shares, or takes part in something. **—participant** *adj.* Sharing in or taking part; participating. **—par·tic′i·pance** *n.*

par·tic·i·pate (pär-tĭs′ə-pāt′) *v.* **-pat·ed, -pat·ing, -pates.** *—intr.* **1.** To take part in something: *participated in the festivities.* **2.** To share in something: *If only I could participate in your good fortune.* See Synonyms at **share**[1]. *—tr. Archaic.* To partake of. [Latin *participāre, participāt-,* from *particeps, particip-,* partaker : *pars, part-,* part; see PART + *capere,* to take; see **kap-** in Appendix.] **—par·tic′i·pa′tive** *adj.* **—par·tic′i·pa′tor** *n.*

par·tic·i·pa·tion (pär-tĭs′ə-pā′shən) *n.* The act of taking part or sharing in something: *Teachers often encourage class participation.* **—par·tic′i·pa′tion·al** *adj.*

par·tic·i·pa·to·ry (pär-tĭs′ə-pə-tôr′ē, -tōr′ē) *adj.* Marked by, requiring, or involving participation, especially affording the opportunity for individual participation: *a participatory democracy.*

par·ti·cip·i·al (pär′tĭ-sĭp′ē-əl) *Grammar. adj.* Of, relating to, consisting of, or formed with a participle. **—participial** *n.* A participle. [Latin *participiālis,* from *participium,* participle. See PARTICIPLE.] **—par′ti·cip′i·al·ly** *adv.*

par·ti·ci·ple (pär′tĭ-sĭp′əl) *n. Abbr.* **p.** *Grammar.* A form of a verb that in some languages, such as English, can function independently as an adjective, such as the past participle *baked* in *We had some baked beans,* and is used with an auxiliary verb to indicate tense, aspect, or voice, as the past participle *baked* in the passive sentence *The beans were baked too long.* [Middle English, from Old French, variant of *participe,* from Latin *participium,* from *particeps, particip-,* partaker. See PARTICIPATE.]

USAGE NOTE: The "dangling participle" is quite common in speech, where it often passes unremarked; but its use in writing can lead to unintentional absurdities, as in *He went to watch his horse take a turn around the track carrying a copy of the breeders' guide under his arm.* Even when the construction occasions no

parsnip
Pastinaca sativa

parterre
Garden at the Governor's Palace in Colonial Williamsburg, Virginia

Parthenon
On the Acropolis, Athens, Greece

ă pat	oi boy
ā pay	ou out
âr care	o͝o took
ä father	o͞o boot
ĕ pet	ŭ cut
ē be	ûr urge
ĭ pit	th thin
ī pie	*th* this
îr pier	hw which
ŏ pot	zh vision
ō toe	ə about, item
ô paw	♦ regionalism

Stress marks: ′ (primary); ′ (secondary), as in **dictionary** (dĭk′shə-nĕr′ē)

ambiguity, it is likely to distract the reader, who will ordinarily be operating on the assumption that a participle or other modifying phrase will be associated with the noun phrase that is immediately adjacent to it. Thus the sentence *Turning the corner, the view was quite different* would be better rewritten as *The view was quite different when we turned the corner* or *Turning the corner, we saw a different view.* • A number of expressions originally derived from active participles are now well established as prepositions of a kind, and these may be used freely to introduce phrases that are not associated with the immediately adjacent noun phrase. Such expressions include *concerning, considering, failing, granting, judging by,* and *speaking of.* Thus one may write *Speaking of politics, the elections have been postponed* or *Considering the hour, it is surprising that he arrived at all.*

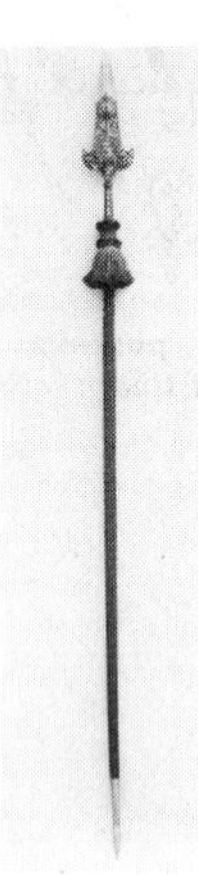

partisan²

par·ti·cle (pär′tĭ-kəl) *n. Abbr.* **part. 1.** A very small piece or part; a tiny portion or speck. **2.** A very small or the smallest possible amount, trace, or degree: *not a particle of doubt.* **3.** *Physics.* **a.** A body whose spatial extent and internal motion and structure, if any, are irrelevant in a specific problem. **b.** An elementary particle. **c.** A subatomic particle. See table at **subatomic particle. 4.** *Grammar & Linguistics.* **a.** An uninflected item that has grammatical function but does not clearly belong to one of the major parts of speech, such as *up* in *look up* or *to* in English infinitives. **b.** In some systems of grammatical analysis, any short function word, including articles, prepositions, and conjunctions. **5.** *Roman Catholic Church.* **a.** A small piece of a consecrated host. **b.** One of the smaller, individual hosts. **6.** *Archaic.* A small division or section of something written, such as a clause of a document. [Middle English, from Latin *particula,* diminutive of *pars, part-,* part. See PART.]

particle beam *n.* A beam of atoms or subatomic particles that have been accelerated by a particle accelerating device, aimed by magnets, and focused by a lens.

par·ti·cle·board (pär′tĭ-kəl-bôrd′, -bōrd′) *n.* A structural material made of wood fragments, such as chips or shavings, that are mechanically pressed into sheet form and bonded together with resin.

particle physics *n.* The branch of physics that deals with subatomic particles.

par·ti-col·ored (pär′tē-kŭl′ərd) *adj.* Having parts, sections, or areas colored differently from each other; pied: *Shapes seem to emerge from the painting's parti-colored ground.* [From Obsolete *party,* variegated, from Middle English *parti,* from Old French, divided, striped, past participle of *partir,* to divide. See PARTY.]

par·tic·u·lar (pər-tĭk′yə-lər, pə-tĭk′-) *adj. Abbr.* **part. 1.** Of, belonging to, or associated with a specific person, group, thing, or category; not general or universal: *She has a particular preference for Chinese art.* **2.** Separate and distinct from others of the same group, category, or nature: *We will make an exception in this particular case.* **3.** Worthy of note; exceptional: *a piano performance of particular depth and fluidity.* **4. a.** Of, relating to, or providing details: *gave a particular description of the room.* **b.** Attentive to or concerned with details or niceties, often excessively so; meticulous or fussy. See Synonyms at **detailed. 5.** *Logic.* Encompassing some but not all of the members of a class or group. Used of a proposition. **—particular** *n.* **1.** An individual item, fact, or detail: *correct in every particular.* See Synonyms at **item. 2.** Often **particulars.** An item or a detail of information or news: *The police refused to divulge the particulars of the case.* **3.** Often **particulars.** A separate case or an individual thing or instance, especially one that can be distinguished from a larger category or class: *"What particulars were ambushed behind these generalizations?"* (Aldous Huxley). **4.** *Logic.* A particular proposition. **—*idiom.* in particular.** Particularly; especially. [Middle English *particuler,* from Old French, from Late Latin *particulāris,* from Latin *particula,* diminutive of *pars, part-,* part. See PART.]

par·tic·u·lar·ism (pər-tĭk′yə-lə-rĭz′əm, pə-tĭk-) *n.* **1.** Exclusive adherence to, dedication to, or interest in one's own group, party, sect, or nation. **2.** A principle of allowing each state in a nation or federation to act independently of the central authority, especially in promoting its own economic interests. **3.** *Theology.* The belief that a person can gain salvation only by God's free choice. **—par·tic′u·lar·ist** *n.* **—par·tic′u·lar·is′tic** *adj.*

par·tic·u·lar·i·ty (pər-tĭk′yə-lăr′ĭ-tē, pə-tĭk′-) *n., pl.* **-ties. 1.** The quality or state of being particular rather than general. **2.** Exactitude of detail, especially in description: *a travel account written with almost excruciating particularity.* **3.** Attention to or concern with detail; fastidiousness: *a scholar known for her particularity.* **4.** A specific point or detail; a particular. **5.** An individual characteristic; a peculiarity: *each small town with its special particularities and ancient customs.*

par·tic·u·lar·ize (pər-tĭk′yə-lə-rīz′, pə-tĭk-) *v.* **-ized, -iz·ing, -iz·es.** *—tr.* **1.** To mention, describe, or treat individually; itemize or specify. **2.** To make particular as opposed to general or universal. *—intr.* To go into or give details or particulars. **—par·tic′u·lar·i·za′tion** (-lər-ĭ-zā′shən) *n.* **—par·tic′u·lar·iz′er** *n.*

par·tic·u·lar·ly (pər-tĭk′yə-lər-lē, pə-tĭk′-) *adv.* **1.** To a great degree; especially: *I particularly like the brown shoes.* **2.** With particular reference or emphasis; individually or specifically: *"Everyone has a moment in history which belongs particularly to him"* (John Knowles). **3.** With regard to particulars; in detail.

par·tic·u·late (pər-tĭk′yə-lĭt, -lāt′, pär-) *adj.* Of, relating to, or formed of separate particles. **—particulate** *n.* A particulate substance. [From Latin *particula,* a small part. See PARTICLE.]

part·ing (pär′tĭng) *n.* **1. a.** The act or process of separating or dividing. **b.** The state of being separated or divided. **2.** A departure or leave-taking. **—parting** *adj.* Given, received, or done on departing or separating: *a parting gift.* **—*idiom.* parting of the ways.** A point of divergence, especially one of great moment.

parting shot *n.* An act of aggression or retaliation, such as a retort or threat, that is made upon one's departure or at the end of a heated discussion. [Perhaps alteration of PARTHIAN.]

par·ti pris (pär′tē prē′) *n., pl.* **par·tis pris** (pär′tē). An inclination for or against something or someone that affects judgment; prejudice or bias. [French : *parti,* decision, side + *pris,* taken.]

par·ti·san¹ (pär′tĭ-zən) *n.* **1.** A fervent, sometimes militant supporter or proponent of a party, cause, faction, person, or idea. **2.** A member of an organized body of fighters who attack or harass an enemy, especially within occupied territory; a guerrilla. **—partisan** *adj.* **1.** Of, relating to, or characteristic of a partisan or partisans. **2.** Devoted to or biased in support of a party, group, or cause: *partisan politics.* [French, from Old French, from Old Italian dialectal *partisano,* variant of Old Italian *partigiano,* from *parte,* part, from Latin *pars, part-.* See PART.] **—par′ti·san·ship′** *n.*

par·ti·san² also **par·ti·zan** (pär′tĭ-zən) *n.* A weapon having a blade with lateral projections mounted on the end of a long shaft, used chiefly in the 16th and 17th centuries. [French *partizane,* from Italian dialectal **(arma) partisana,* partisan (weapon), feminine sing. of *partisano,* supporter. See PARTISAN¹.]

par·ti·ta (pär-tē′tə) *n. Music.* **1.** An instrumental piece composed of a series of variations, as a suite. **2.** One of the variations contained in such a piece. [Italian, from feminine past participle of *partire,* divide, from Latin *partīre.* See PARTITE.

par·tite (pär′tīt′) *adj.* Divided into parts. [Latin *partītus,* past participle of *partīre,* to divide, from *pars, part-,* part. See PART.]

par·ti·tion (pär-tĭsh′ən) *n.* **1. a.** The act or process of dividing something into parts. **b.** The state of being so divided. **2. a.** Something that divides or separates, as a wall dividing one room or cubicle from another. **b.** A wall, septum, or other separating membrane in an organism. **3.** A part or section into which something has been divided. **4.** Division of a country into separate, autonomous nations. **5.** *Mathematics.* **a.** An expression of a positive integer as a sum of positive integers. **b.** The decomposition of a set into a family of mutually exclusive sets. **6.** *Computer Science.* A location in memory assigned to a program. **7.** *Law.* Division of property, especially real estate. **—partition** *tr.v.* **-tioned, -tion·ing, -tions. 1.** To divide into parts, pieces, or sections. **2.** To divide or separate by means of a partition: *We partitioned off the alcove to make another bedroom.* **3.** To divide (a country) into separate, autonomous nations. [Middle English *particioun,* from Old French *partition,* from Latin *partītiō, partītiōn-,* from *partītus,* past participle of *partīre,* to divide, from *pars, part-,* part. See PART.] **—par·ti′tion·ment** *n.*

par·ti·tion·ist (pär-tĭsh′ə-nĭst) *n.* One who advocates partition of a country.

par·ti·tive (pär′tĭ-tĭv) *adj.* **1.** Dividing or serving to divide something into parts; marked by division. **2.** *Grammar.* Indicating a part as distinct from a whole, as *some of the coffee* in the sentence *She drank some of the coffee.* **—partitive** *n. Grammar.* **1.** A partitive word, such as *many* or *less.* **2.** A partitive construction or case. [Middle English, from Old French *partitif,* from Medieval Latin *partītīvus,* from Latin *partītus,* past participle of *partīre,* to divide. See PARTITE.] **—par′ti·tive·ly** *adv.*

par·ti·zan (pär′tĭ-zən) *n.* Variant of **partisan².**

part·let (pärt′lĭt) *n.* A collared, usually ruffled covering for the neck and shoulders, popular in 16th-century Europe and worn especially by women. [Alteration of Middle English *patelet,* from Old French *patelete,* band of cloth, diminutive of *pate,* paw. See PATOIS.]

part·ly (pärt′lē) *adv.* In part or in some degree; not completely.

part·ner (pärt′nər) *n.* **1.** One that is united or associated with another or others in an activity or a sphere of common interest, especially: **a.** A member of a business partnership. **b.** A spouse. **c.** Either of two persons dancing together. **d.** *Sports & Games.* One of a pair or team in a sport or game, such as tennis or bridge. **2.** Often **partners.** *Nautical.* A wooden framework used to strengthen a ship's deck at the point where a mast or other structure passes through it. **—partner** *v.* **-nered, -ner·ing, -ners.** *—tr.* **1.** To make a partner of. **2.** To bring together as partners. **3.** To be the partner of. *—intr.* To work or perform as a partner. [Middle English *partener,* alteration (influenced by *part,* part) of *parcener,* parcener. See PARCENER.]

SYNONYMS: *partner, colleague, ally, confederate.* These nouns all denote one who is united or associated with another, as in a venture or relationship. A *partner* participates in a relationship in which each member has equal status: *a partner in a law firm; husbands and wives who are ideal partners.* A *colleague* is an associate in an occupation, such as a profession: *a colleague and fellow professor.* An *ally* is one who associates with another, at least temporarily in a common cause: *The United States and the Soviet Union were allies in World War II.* A *confederate* is a member of a confederacy, a league, or an alliance; sometimes the term signifies a collaborator in a suspicious venture: *The confederates,* *undefeated, pushed onward. The burglar was caught, but his confederate got away.*

part·ner·ship (pärtʹnər-shĭpʹ) *n.* **1.** The state of being a partner. **2.a.** A legal contract entered into by two or more persons in which each agrees to furnish a part of the capital and labor for a business enterprise, and by which each shares a fixed proportion of profits and losses. **b.** The persons bound by such a contract. **3.** A relationship between individuals or groups that is characterized by mutual cooperation and responsibility, as for the achievement of a specified goal: *Neighborhood groups formed a partnership to fight crime.*

part of speech *n., pl.* **parts of speech. 1.** One of a group of traditional classifications of words according to their functions in context, including the noun, pronoun, verb, adjective, adverb, preposition, conjunction, and interjection, and sometimes the article. **2.** A word considered as a part of speech.

par·ton (pärʹtŏnʹ) *n.* A hypothetical elementary particle believed to be a constituent of hadrons. [PART(ICLE) + –ON[1].]

par·took (pär-to͝okʹ) *v.* Past tense of **partake.**

par·tridge (pärʹtrĭj) *n., pl.* **partridge** or **-tridg·es. 1.** Any of several plump-bodied Old World game birds, especially of the genera *Perdix* and *Alectoris,* related to the pheasants and grouse. **2.** Any of several birds, such as the ruffed grouse or the bobwhite, similar or related to the partridge. [Middle English *partrich,* from Old French *perdriz,* alteration of *perdis,* from Latin *perdīx,* from Greek *perdix.* See **perd-** in Appendix.]

par·tridge·ber·ry (pärʹtrĭj-bĕrʹē) *n.* A creeping, evergreen, perennial plant *(Mitchella repens)* of eastern North America, having small white flowers and scarlet berries. Also called *twinberry.*

partridge pea *n.* An annual plant *(Cassia fasciculata)* of eastern and central North America in the pea family, having yellow flowers and sensitive leaves with numerous leaflets.

part song *n. Music.* **1.** A homophonic choral composition, especially of the 19th century. **2.** A polyphonic song of the premadrigal period.

part-time (pärtʹtīmʹ) *adj.* For or during less than the customary or standard time: *a part-time job.* **—partʹ-timeʹ** *adv.* **—partʹ-timʹer** *n.*

par·tu·ri·ent (pär-to͝orʹē-ənt, -tyo͝orʹ-) *adj.* **1.** About to bring forth young; being in labor. **2.** Of or relating to giving birth. **3.** About to produce or come forth with something, such as an idea or a discovery. [Latin *parturiēns, parturient-,* present participle of *parturīre,* to be in labor, from *partus,* past participle of *parere,* to give birth. See **perə-[1]** in Appendix.] **—par·tuʹri·en·cy** *n.*

par·tu·ri·fa·cient (pär-to͝orʹə-fāʹshənt, -tyo͝orʹ-) *adj.* Inducing or facilitating childbirth. **—parturifacient** *n.* A drug facilitating childbirth. [Latin *parturīre,* to be in labor; see PARTURIENT + –FACIENT.]

par·tu·ri·tion (pärʹtyo͞o-rĭshʹən, -to͞o-, pärʹchə-) *n.* The act or process of giving birth; childbirth. [Late Latin *parturītiō, parturītiōn-,* from Latin *parturītus,* past participle of *parturīre,* to be in labor. See PARTURIENT.]

part·way (pärtʹwāʹ) *adv. Informal.* To a certain degree or distance; in part: *partway to town; not even partway reasonable.*

par·ty (pärʹtē) *n., pl.* **-ties. 1.a.** A social gathering especially for pleasure or amusement: *a cocktail party.* **b.** A group of people who have gathered to participate in an activity. See Synonyms at **band[2]. 2.** An established political group organized to promote and support its principles and candidates for public office. **3.a.** A person or group involved in an enterprise; a participant or an accessory: *I refuse to be a party to your silly scheme.* **b.** *Law.* A person or group involved in a legal proceeding as a litigant. **4.a.** A subscriber to a telephone party line. **b.** A person using a telephone. **5.** A person: *"And though Grainger was a spry old party, such steps couldn't be his"* (Anthony Hyde). **6.** A selected group of soldiers: *a raiding party.* **7.** *Slang.* **a.** An act of sexual intercourse. **b.** An orgy. **—party** *adj.* **1.** Of, relating to, or participating in an established political organization: *party members; party politics.* **2.** Suitable for use at a social gathering: *party dresses; a party hat.* **3.** Characteristic of a pleasurable social gathering: *a party atmosphere.* **—party** *intr.v.* **-tied, -ty·ing, -ties.** *Informal.* To celebrate or carouse at or as if at a party: *That night we partied until dawn.* [Middle English *partie,* part, side, group, from Old French, from feminine past participle of *partir,* to divide, from Latin *partīre,* from *pars, part-,* part. See PART.]

USAGE NOTE: *Party* is unexceptionable when used to refer to a participant in a social arrangement, as in *She was not named as a party in the conspiracy.* It is this sense that underlies the legal use of the term, as when one speaks of the *parties to a contract.* The legal use has in turn led to the presence of the word in many fixed expressions, such as *injured party* and *third party.* But *party* is also widely used as a general substitute for *person,* as in *Would all parties who left packages at the desk please reclaim their property.* This usage has been established for many centuries, but in the Victorian era it came to be associated with the language of the semieducated (the *Oxford English Dictionary* describes it as "shoppy"), and it has been the subject of many later criticisms. This use of *party* may have been reinforced by its modern adoption by telephone operators. In other contexts, when used in earnest, it may be perceived as a superfluous variant for *person.* But the jocular use of the term is well established, particular in references such as *a wise old party.*

par·ty·go·er (pärʹtē-gōʹər) *n.* One who attends parties or a party: *The lobby was filled with partygoers.*

party line *n.* **1.** A telephone circuit connecting two or more subscribers with the same exchange. **2.** One or more of the policies or principles of a political party to which loyal members are expected to adhere. **—party liner, parʹty-linʹer** (pärʹtē-līʹnər) *n.*

par·ty poop·er also **par·ty-poop·er** (pärʹtē-po͞oʹpər) *n. Slang.* One who declines to participate with enthusiasm, especially in the recreational activities of a group.

party wall *n. Law.* A wall built on the boundary line of adjoining properties and shared by both owners. [Obsolete *party,* shared, divided, from Old French *parti.* See PARTI-COLORED.]

pa·rure (pə-ro͝orʹ) *n.* A set of matched jewelry or other ornaments. [French, from Old French, adornment, from *parer,* to adorn. See PARE.]

par value *n.* The value imprinted on a security, such as a stock certificate or bond, used to calculate a payment, such as a dividend or interest; face value. Also called *nominal value.*

par·ve (pärʹvə) *adj. Judaism.* Variant of **pareve.**

par·ve·nu (pärʹvə-no͞oʹ, -nyo͞oʹ) *n.* A person who has suddenly risen to a higher social and economic class and has not yet gained social acceptance by others in that class. [French, from past participle of *parvenir,* to arrive, from Latin *pervenīre* : *per,* through; see **per[1]** in Appendix + *venīre,* to come; see **gʷā-** in Appendix.] **—parʹve·nuʹ** *adj.*

par·vis (pärʹvĭs) *n.* **1.** An enclosed courtyard or space at the entrance to a building, especially a cathedral, that is sometimes surrounded by porticoes or colonnades. **2.** One of the porticoes or colonnades surrounding such a space. [Middle English, from Old French, alteration of *pareis,* paradise, from Late Latin *paradīsus,* garden, paradise. See PARADISE.]

par·vo (pärʹvō) *n., pl.* **-vos.** A parvovirus.

par·vo·vi·rus (pärʹvō-vīʹrəs) *n., pl.* **-rus·es.** Any of a group of small viruses that contain DNA in an icosahedral protein shell and cause disease in many vertebrates, especially mammals such as dogs and cattle. [Latin *parvus,* small; see **pau-** in Appendix + VIRUS.]

pas (pä) *n., pl.* **pas** (pä). **1.** A step or dance. **2.** The right to go before; precedence. [French, from Old French, from Latin *passus,* step. See PACE[1].]

Pas·a·de·na (păsʹə-dēʹnə). **1.** A city of southern California northeast of Los Angeles. It is famous for its Rose Bowl and annual Tournament of Roses parade. Population, 119,374. **2.** A city of southeast Texas, an industrial suburb of Houston. The Lyndon B. Johnson Manned Space Center is nearby. Population, 112,560.

Pa·sar·ga·dae (pə-särʹgə-dēʹ). A ruined city of ancient Persia northeast of Persepolis. It was Cyrus the Great's capital and is said to have been founded by him in 550 B.C.

Pa·say (päʹsī). A city of southwest Luzon, Philippines, a suburb of Manila on the eastern shore of Manila Bay. Population, 287,770.

Pas·ca·gou·la (păsʹkə-go͞oʹlə). A city of extreme southeast Mississippi east of Biloxi on Mississippi Sound. It is a port of entry, fishing center, and coastal resort. Population, 29,318.

pas·cal (pă-skălʹ, pä-skälʹ) *n.* **1.** *Abbr.* **Pa** A unit of pressure equal to one newton per square meter. See table at **measurement. 2. Pascal** or **PASCAL.** A high-level computer programming language designed to support structured programming and used in teaching, applications, and systems programming. [After Blaise PASCAL.]

Pas·cal (pă-skălʹ, pä-skälʹ), **Blaise.** 1623–1662. French philosopher and mathematician. Among his achievements are the invention of an adding machine and the development of the modern theory of probability.

Blaise Pascal
Detail of a portrait by Philippe de Champaigne (1602–1674)

pas·cal celery also **Pas·chal celery** (păsʹkəl) *n.* Any of several types of commercially grown celery having unblanched green stalks. [Origin unknown.]

Pasch (păsk) *n.* **1.** Passover. **2.** Easter. [Middle English, from Old French *pasche,* from Late Latin *pascha,* Passover, Easter, from Late Greek *paskha,* from Aramaic *pasḥā,* passover; akin to Hebrew *pesaḥ,* Pesach. See PESACH.] **—Pasʹchal, pasʹchal** *adj.*

Paschal celery *n.* Variant of **pascal celery.**

paschal lamb *n.* **1.** The lamb sacrificed at the first Passover. **2. Paschal Lamb.** Jesus. **3. Paschal Lamb.** See **Agnus Dei** (sense 1).

Pas·co (păsʹkō). A city of southeast Washington on the Columbia River near its confluence with the Snake and Yakima rivers. It grew during World War II as a supply center for the nearby Hanford Atomic Works. Population, 17,944.

pas de bour·rée (pä də bo͞o-rāʹ, bo͞o-) *n., pl.* **pas de bourrée.** A short running or walking step in ballet, usually executed on pointe. [French : *pas,* step + *de,* of + *bourrée,* bourrée.]

Pas de Ca·lais (pä də kă-lāʹ, kălʹā, kä-lĕʹ). The Strait of Dover.

pas de chat (shä) *n., pl.* **pas de chat.** A ballet jump in which the feet are lifted, one after the other, to the level of the opposite knee. [French : *pas,* step + *de,* of + *chat,* cat.]

pas de deux (dœ) *n., pl.* **pas de deux. 1.** A dance for two, especially in ballet. **2.** A close relationship between two people

ă pat	oi boy
ā pay	ou out
âr care	o͝o took
ä father	o͞o boot
ĕ pet	ŭ cut
ē be	ûr urge
ĭ pit	th thin
ī pie	*th* this
îr pier	hw which
ŏ pot	zh vision
ō toe	ə about, item
ô paw	♦ regionalism

Stress marks: **ʹ** (primary); ʹ (secondary), as in **dictionary** (dĭkʹshə-nĕrʹē)

or things, as during an activity. [French : *pas,* step + *de,* of, for + *deux,* two.]

pas de quat·re (kăt′rə) *n., pl.* **pas de quatre.** A dance for four. [French : *pas,* step + *de,* of, for + *quatre,* four.]

pas de trois (trwä) *n., pl.* **pas de trois.** A dance for three. [French : *pas,* step + *de,* of, for + *trois,* three.]

pa·se (pä′sā) *n.* One of several usually one-handed maneuvers in bullfighting in which the matador presents and moves the cape to attract a close, passing charge of the bull. [Spanish, from *pasar,* to pass, from Vulgar Latin **passāre.* See PASS.]

pa·se·o (pä-sā′ō) *n., pl.* **-os. 1.** A slow, easy stroll or walk outdoors. **2.** The street, series of streets, or walkway along which such a walk is taken. **3.** In bullfighting, the formal procession into the ring of the players, including the matadors, banderilleros, and horses, that occurs just before the first bull is fought. [Spanish, from *pasear,* to take a stroll, frequentative of *pasar,* to go, pass. See PASE.]

pash (păsh) *n. Slang.* **a.** A romantic infatuation: *"She develops a sudden pash for Richard . . . a widower with a . . . son"* (Los Angeles Times). **b.** The object of such an infatuation. [Short for PASSION.]

pa·sha also **pa·cha** (pä′shə, păsh′ə, pə-shä′) *n.* Used formerly as a title for military and civil officers, especially in Turkey and northern Africa. [Turkish *paşa.*]

Pash·to (pŭsh′tō) also **Push·tu** (pŭsh′to͞o) *n.* An Iranian language that is the principal vernacular language of Afghanistan and parts of western Pakistan. Also called *Afghan.* [Persian *pashtu,* from Pashto.]

Pa·siph·a·ë (pə-sĭf′ə-ē′) *n. Greek Mythology.* **1.** The wife of Minos and mother, by a white bull, of the Minotaur. **2. Pasiphae.** The satellite of Jupiter that is 16th in distance from the planet.

pa·so do·ble also **pa·so·do·ble** (pä′sō-dō′blā, -dô′vlĕ) *n., pl.* **paso do·bles** also **pa·so·do·bles** (-blāz, -vlĕs). **1.** A lively Spanish dance. **2.** Music for or in the rhythm of this dance, set in march time and often played at bullfights. [Spanish : *paso,* step + *doble,* double.]

pasque·flow·er (păsk′flou′ər) *n.* Any of several plants of the genus *Anemone,* especially *A. patens,* having large blue, purple, or white flowers, each producing many conspicuously plumed achenes. [Alteration (influenced by *pasque,* Easter, from their flowering in April) of obsolete *passeflower,* from French *passefleur : passer,* to pass; see PASS + *fleur,* flower; see FLOWER.]

pas·qui·nade (păs′kwə-nād′) *n.* A satire or lampoon, especially one that ridicules a specific person, traditionally written and posted in a public place. **—pasquinade** *tr.v.* **-nad·ed, -nad·ing, -nades.** To ridicule with a pasquinade; satirize or lampoon. [French, from Italian *pasquinata,* after *Pasquino,* nickname given to a statue in Rome, Italy, on which lampoons were posted.] **—pas′qui·nad′er** *n.*

pass (păs) *v.* **passed, pass·ing, pass·es.** *—intr.* **1.** To move on or ahead; proceed. **2.** To extend; run: *The river passes through our land.* **3.a.** To move by: *The band passed and the crowd cheered.* **b.** To move past another vehicle: *The sports car passed on the right.* **4.** To gain passage despite obstacles: *pass through difficult years.* **5.** To move past in time; elapse: *The days passed quickly.* **6.a.** To be transferred from one to another; circulate: *The wine passed around the table.* **b.** *Sports.* To transfer a ball or puck to a teammate. **7.** To be communicated or exchanged between persons: *Loud words passed in the corridor.* **8.** To be transferred or conveyed to another by will or deed: *The title passed to the older heir.* **9.** To undergo transition from one condition, form, quality, or characteristic to another: *Daylight passed into darkness.* **10.** To come to an end: *My anger suddenly passed. The headache finally passed.* **11.** To cease to exist; die: *The patient passed on during the night.* **12.** To happen; take place: *What passed during the day?* **13.a.** To be allowed to happen without notice or challenge: *Let their rude remarks pass.* **b.** *Games.* To decline one's turn to play or bid. **14.** To undergo an examination or a trial with favorable results. **15.a.** To serve as a barely acceptable substitute: *The spare tire was nearly bald but would pass until we bought a new one.* **b.** To be accepted as a member of a group by denying one's own ancestry or background. **16.** To be approved or adopted: *The motion to adjourn passed.* **17.** *Law.* **a.** To pronounce an opinion, a judgment, or a sentence. **b.** To sit in adjudication. **18.** To be voided: *Luckily the kidney stone passed before she had to be hospitalized.* **19.** *Sports.* To thrust or lunge in fencing. *—tr.* **1.** To go by without stopping; leave behind. **2.a.** To go by without paying attention to; disregard or ignore: *If you pass the new photographs in the collection, you'll miss some outstanding ones.* **b.** To fail to pay (a dividend). **3.** To go beyond; surpass: *The inheritance passed my wildest dreams.* **4.** To go across; go through: *We passed the border into Mexico.* **5.a.** To undergo (a trial or an examination) with favorable results: *She passed every test.* **b.** To cause or allow to go through a trial, a test, or an examination successfully: *The instructor passed all the candidates.* **6.a.** To cause to move: *We passed our hands over the fabric.* **b.** To cause to move into a certain position: *pass a ribbon around a package.* **c.** To cause to move as part of a process: *pass liquid through a filter.* **d.** To cause to go by: *The officers passed their troops in review before the general.* **e.** *Baseball.* To walk (a batter). **7.** To allow to go by or elapse; spend: *He passed his winter in Vermont.* **8.a.** To cause to be transferred from one to another; circulate: *They passed the news quickly.* **b.** To hand over to someone else: *Please pass the bread.* **c.** *Sports.* To transfer (a ball, for example) to a teammate, as by throwing. **d.** To cause to be accepted; circulate fraudulently: *pass counterfeit money.* **e.** *Law.* To transfer title or ownership of. **9.** To discharge (body waste, for example); void. **10.a.** To approve; adopt: *The legislature passed the bill.* **b.** To be sanctioned, ratified, or approved by: *The bill passed the House of Representatives.* **11.** To pronounce; utter: *pass judgment; pass sentence on an offender.* **—pass** *n.* **1.** The act of passing; passage. **2.** A way, such as a narrow gap between mountains, that affords passage around, over, or through a barrier. See Synonyms at **way. 3.a.** A permit, a ticket, or an authorization to come and go at will. **b.** A free ticket entitling one to transportation or admisssion. **c.** Written leave of absence from military duty. **4.a.** A sweep or run by an aircraft over an area or a target. **b.** A single complete cycle of operations, as by a machine or computer program. **5.** A condition or situation, often critical in nature; a predicament. See Synonyms at **crisis. 6.** A sexual invitation or overture. **7.** A motion of the hand or the waving of a wand. **8.a.** *Sports.* A transfer of a ball or puck between teammates. **b.** *Sports.* A lunge or thrust in fencing. **c.** *Baseball.* A base on balls. **9.** *Games.* **a.** A refusal to bid, draw, bet, or play. **b.** A winning throw of the dice in craps. **10.** A pase. ***—phrasal verbs.* pass away. 1.** To pass out of existence; end. **2.** To die. **pass for.** To be accepted as or believed to be: *You could pass for a teenager. The fake painting passed for an original.* **pass off.** To offer, sell, or put into circulation (an imitation) as genuine: *pass off glass as a gemstone.* **pass out.** To lose consciousness. **pass over.** To leave out; disregard. **pass up.** *Informal.* To let go by; reject: *pass up a chance for promotion; an opportunity too good to pass up.* ***—idioms.* bring to pass.** To cause to happen. **come to pass.** To occur. **pass muster.** To pass an examination or inspection; measure up to a given standard. **pass (one's) lips. 1.** To be eaten or drunk. **2.** To issue or be spoken: *Rumors never passed her lips.* **pass the buck.** *Slang.* To shift responsibility or blame to another. **pass the time of day.** To exchange greetings or engage in pleasantries. **pass the torch.** To relinquish (responsibilities, for example) to another or others. [Middle English *passen,* from Old French *passer,* from Vulgar Latin *passāre,* from Latin *passus,* step. See PACE¹.] **—pass′er** *n.*

USAGE NOTE: The past tense and past participle of *pass* is *passed: They passed* (or *have passed*) *our home. Time had passed slowly. Past* is the corresponding adjective (*in centuries past*), adverb (*drove past*), preposition (*past midnight; past the crisis*), and noun (*lived in the past*).

pass. *abbr.* **1.** Passage; passenger. **2.** *Grammar.* Passive.

pass·a·ble (păs′ə-bəl) *adj.* **1.** That can be passed, traversed, or crossed; navigable: *a passable road.* **2.** Acceptable for general circulation: *passable currency.* **3.** Satisfactory but not outstanding; adequate: *The actors gave passable performances but the singers seemed unrehearsed.* **4.** That can be legislated: *a passable bill.* **—pass′a·ble·ness** *n.* **—pass′a·bly** *adv.*

pas·sa·ca·glia (pä′sə-käl′yə, păs′ə-kăl′yə) *n.* **1.** *Music.* A musical form of the 17th and 18th centuries consisting of continuous variations on a ground bass in 3/4 time and similar to the chaconne. **2.** A courtly dance of the period that was performed to such music. [Italian, From Spanish *pasacalle : pasar,* to pass, step; see PASE + *calle,* street (from Latin *callis, call-,* path).]

pas·sade (pə-säd′) *n.* **1.** A dressage technique in which the horse is made to course repeatedly over the same spot. **2.** A passing flirtation or romance: *"How can it be that the sympathy between two people like ourselves . . . should end from one day to another like a mere passade?"* (Edith Wharton). [French, passado, passade, from Italian *passata,* from *passare,* to pass. See PASSAGE².]

pas·sa·do (pə-sä′dō) *n., pl.* **-dos** or **-does.** A fencing maneuver in which the foil is thrust forward and one foot advanced at the same time. [Alteration of French *passade.* See PASSADE.]

pas·sage¹ (păs′ĭj) *n. Abbr.* **pass. 1.** The act or process of passing, especially: **a.** A movement from one place to another, as by going by, through, over, or across; transit or migration. **b.** The process of elapsing: *the passage of time.* **c.** The process of passing from one condition or stage to another; transition: *the passage from childhood to adulthood.* **d.** Enactment into law of a legislative measure. **2.** A journey, especially one by air or water: *a rough passage on the stormy sea.* **3.** The right to travel as a passenger, especially on a ship: *book passage; pay for one's passage.* **4.** The right, permission, or power to come and go freely: *Only medical supply trucks were granted safe passage through enemy territory.* **5.a.** A path, channel, or duct through, over, or along which something may pass: *the nasal passages.* **b.** A corridor. See Synonyms at **way. 6.a.** An occurrence or event: *"Another encouraging passage took place . . . when heads of state . . . took note of the extraneous factors affecting their economies that are beyond their control"* (Helen Kitchen). **b.** Something, such as an exchange of words or blows, that occurs between two persons: *a passage at arms.* **7.a.** A segment of a written work or speech: *a celebrated passage from Shakespeare.* **b.** *Music.* A segment of a composition, especially one that demonstrates the virtuousity of the composer or performer: *a passage of exquisite beauty, played to perfection.* **c.** A section of a painting or other piece of artwork; a detail. **8.** *Physiology.* An act of emptying, as of the bowels. **9.** *Biology.* The process of passing or maintaining a group of microorganisms or cells through a series of hosts or cultures. **10.** *Ob-*

solete. Death. [Middle English, from Old French, from *passer,* to pass. See PASS.]

pas·sage² (păs′ĭj, pə-säzh′) *n.* A slow, cadenced trot in which the horse alternately raises and returns to the ground first one diagonal pair of feet, then the other. **—passage** *v.* **-saged, -sag·ing, -sag·es.** *—intr.* To execute such a trot in dressage. *—tr.* To cause (a horse) to execute such a trot in dressage. [French, from *passager,* to execute a passage, alteration (influenced by *passer,* to pass) of *passéger,* from Italian *passeggiare,* from *passare,* to pass, from Vulgar Latin **passāre,* from Latin *passus,* step. See PACE¹.]

pas·sage·way (păs′ĭj-wā′) *n.* A way allowing passage, especially a corridor.

pas·sage·work (păs′ĭj-wûrk′) *n. Music.* **1.** A portion of a composition of little thematic or structural importance that permits a performer to make a display of technique, especially in the rapid execution of scales and arpeggios: *the intricate passagework of a Beethoven pastorale.* **2.** A musician's performance of this portion of a composition: *her virtuosic passagework.*

Pas·sa·ic (pə-sā′ĭk). A city of northeast New Jersey south of Paterson on the **Passaic River,** about 129 km (80 mi) long. Settled by Dutch traders in 1678, the city is highly industrialized. Population, 52,463.

pass-a·long also **pass·a·long** (păs′ə-lông′, -lŏng′) *n.* The policy, practice, or act of paying for an increased cost by raising the price charged to one's customers or clients: *"Landlords . . . went to court . . . to allow a fel cost pass-along to tenants in rent-controlled apartments"* (New York Post). Also called *pass-through.*

Pas·sa·ma·quod·dy (păs′ə-mə-kwŏd′ē) *n., pl.* **Passamaquoddy** or **-dies. 1.a.** A Native American people formerly inhabiting parts of coastal Maine and New Brunswick along the Bay of Fundy, with present-day descendants in eastern Maine. The Passamaquoddy helped form the Abenaki confederacy in the mid-18th century. **b.** A member of this people. **2.** The Algonquian language of the Passamaquoddy, dialectally related to Malecite. [Of Micmac origin.]

Passamaquoddy Bay. An arm of the Bay of Fundy between southern New Brunswick, Canada, and eastern Maine.

pas·sant (păs′ənt) *adj. Heraldry.* Being a beast facing and walking toward the viewer's left with one front leg raised. [Middle English, from Old French, present participle of *passer,* to pass. See PASS.]

pass·book (păs′bo͝ok′) *n. Abbr.* **P.B. 1.** See **bankbook. 2.** A book in which a merchant records credit sales. **3.** An obligatory document in South Africa that identifies a Black person by tribe and enumerates official restrictions placed on the person regarding the right to work, travel, or establish residence. In this sense, also called *reference book.*

pas·sé (pă-sā′) *adj.* **1.** No longer current or in fashion; out-of-date. **2.** Past the prime; faded or aged. [French, past participle of *passer,* to pass, from Old French. See PASS.]

passed ball (păst) *n. Baseball.* A pitch that should have been fielded by the catcher but was missed, allowing a runner to advance a base.

pas·sel (păs′əl) *n. Informal.* A large quantity or group: *"The President faces a passel of domestic issues"* (Christian Science Monitor). [Alteration of PARCEL.]

passe·men·terie (păs-mĕn′trē) *n.* Ornamental trimming for a garment, as braid, lace, or metallic beads. [French, from *passement,* ornamental braid, cloth, from Old French, a passing, from *passer,* to pass. See PASS.]

pas·sen·ger (păs′ən-jər) *n. Abbr.* **pass. 1.** A person who travels in a conveyance, such as a car or train, without participating in its operation. **2.** *Informal.* One that participates only passively in an activity. **3.** A wayfarer or traveler. [Middle English *passinger,* alteration of *passager,* from Old French *passageor,* from *passager,* passing, from *passage,* passage. See PASSAGE¹.]

passenger pigeon *n.* An extinct migratory bird *(Ectopistes migratorius)* abundant in eastern North America until the latter part of the 19th century.

passe-par·tout (păs pär-to͞o′) *n.* **1.** Something, such as a master key, that permits one to pass or go at will. **2.a.** A border, such as a mat, that is used to frame or mount a picture. **b.** An adhesive tape or a gummed paper used for a similar purpose. [French : *passer,* to pass + *partout,* everywhere.]

passe·pied (päs-pyā′) *n.* **1.** A spirited court dance, popular in France and England in the 17th and 18th centuries, resembling a minuet but faster. **2.** Music for or in the rhythm of this dance. [French : *passer,* to pass; see PASS + *pied,* foot (from Old French, from Latin *pēs, ped-;* see PEDAL).]

pas·ser·by also **pas·ser-by** (păs′ər-bī′, -bī′) *n., pl.* **pas·sers·by** also **pas·sers-by** (păs′ərz-). A person who passes by, especially casually or by chance.

pas·ser·ine (păs′ə-rīn′) *adj.* Of or relating to birds of the order Passeriformes, which includes perching birds and songbirds such as the jays, blackbirds, finches, warblers, and sparrows. **—passerine** *n.* A bird of the order Passeriformes. [Latin *passerīnus,* of sparrows, from *passer,* sparrow.]

pas·sers·by also **pas·sers-by** (păs′ərz-bī′, -bī′) *n.* Plurals of **passerby.**

pas seul (pä sœl′) *n., pl.* **pas seuls** (pä sœl′). A dance for one person. [French : *pas,* step + *seul,* solo.]

pass-fail (păs′fāl′) *adj.* Of, relating to, or being a system of grading in which a student simply passes or fails instead of receiving a traditional letter grade: *a pass-fail course.* **—pass-fail** *n.* This kind of a grading system.

pas·si·ble (păs′ə-bəl) *adj.* Capable of feeling or suffering; sensitive: *a passible type of personality.* [Middle English, from Old French, from Latin *passibilis,* from Latin *passus,* past participle of *patī,* to suffer. See **pē(i)-** in Appendix.] **—pas′si·bil′i·ty** *n.*

pas·sim (păs′ĭm) *adv.* Throughout or frequently; here and there. Used in textual annotation to indicate that something, such as a word or passage, occurs frequently in the work cited. [Latin, from *passus,* past participle of *pandere,* to scatter, spread out. See **pete-** in Appendix.]

pass·ing (păs′ĭng) *adj.* **1.** Moving by; going past: *A small child waved to the passing cars.* **2.** Of brief duration; transitory: *a passing fancy.* **3.** Cursory or superficial; casual: *a passing glance.* **4.** Allowing one to pass a test, a course of study, an inspection, or an examination; satisfactory: *a passing grade.* **5.** *Archaic.* Very or great; surpassing: *"'Tis a passing shame"* (Shakespeare). **—passing** *adv.* Very; surpassingly: *"I will mention only one particular aspect of the current mess because . . . this one is surely something new and passing strange"* (Walker Percy). **—passing** *n.* **1.** The act of one that passes or the fact of having passed: *the passing of another summer.* **2.** A place where or a means by which one can pass. **3.** Death. ***—idiom.* in passing.** While going by; incidentally. **—pass′ing·ly** *adv.*

passing note *n. Music.* A note that is not part of a particular chord but is placed between two chords to provide a smooth melodic transition from one to the other. Also called *passing tone.*

passing shot *n. Sports.* A forceful shot, as in tennis or handball, that travels to one side out of the reach of one's opponent.

passing tone *n. Music.* See **passing note.**

pas·sion (păsh′ən) *n.* **1.** A powerful emotion, such as love, joy, hatred, or anger. **2.a.** Ardent love. **b.** Strong sexual desire; lust. **c.** The object of such love or desire. **3.a.** Boundless enthusiasm: *His skills as a player don't quite match his passion for the game.* **b.** The object of such enthusiasm: *soccer is her passion.* **4.** An abandoned display of emotion, especially of anger: *He's been known to fly into a passion without warning.* **5. Passion. a.** The sufferings of Jesus in the period following the Last Supper and including the Crucifixion. **b.** A narrative, musical setting, or pictorial representation of Jesus's sufferings. **6.** *Archaic.* Martyrdom. **7.** *Archaic.* Passivity. [Middle English, from Old French, from Medieval Latin *passiō, passiōn-,* sufferings of Jesus or a martyr, from Late Latin, physical suffering, martyrdom, sinful desire, from Latin, an undergoing, from *passus,* past participle of *patī,* to suffer. See **pē(i)-** in Appendix.]

SYNONYMS: *passion, fervor, fire, zeal, ardor.* These nouns all denote powerful, intense emotion. *Passion* is a deep, overwhelming emotion: *"an ardent, generous, perhaps an immoderate passion for fame"* (Edmund Burke). *"There is not a passion so strongly rooted in the human heart as envy"* (Richard Brinsley Sheridan). The term may signify sexual desire but can also refer to anger: *"He flew into a violent passion and abused me mercilessly"* (H.G. Wells). *Fervor* is great warmth and intensity of feeling: *"The union of the mathematician with the poet, fervor with measure, passion with correctness, this surely is the ideal"* (William James). *Fire* is burning passion: *"In our youth our hearts were touched with fire"* (Oliver Wendell Holmes, Jr.). *Zeal* is strong, enthusiastic devotion to a cause, an ideal, or a goal and tireless diligence in its furtherance: *"his fervent zeal for the interests of the state"* (Macaulay). *"We are sometimes stirred by emotion and take it for zeal"* (Thomas à Kempis). *Ardor* is fiery intensity of feeling: *"the furious ardor of my zeal repressed"* (Charles Churchill). See also Synonyms at **feeling.**

pas·sion·al (păsh′ə-nəl) *adj.* Of, relating to, or filled with passion. **—passional** *n.* A book of the sufferings of saints and martyrs.

pas·sion·ate (păsh′ə-nĭt) *adj.* **1.** Capable of, having, or dominated by powerful emotions: *a family of passionate personalities.* **2.** Wrathful by temperament; choleric. **3.** Marked by strong sexual desire; amorous or lustful. **4.** Showing or expressing strong emotion; ardent: *a passionate speech against injustice.* **5.** Arising from or marked by passion: *a teacher who is passionate about her subject.* **—pas′sion·ate·ly** *adv.* **—pas′sion·ate·ness** *n.*

pas·sion·flow·er (păsh′ən-flou′ər) *n.* Any of various climbing, tendril-bearing, chiefly tropical American vines of the genus *Passiflora,* having large, showy flowers with a fringelike crown and a conspicuous stalk that bears the stamens and pistil. [From the resemblance of its parts to the instruments of the Passion.]

passion fruit *n.* The edible fruit of the passionflower.

Pas·sion·ist (păsh′ə-nĭst) *n.* A member of a Roman Catholic religious order founded in Italy in 1720 by Saint Paul of the Cross (1694–1775) and dedicated to promoting devotion to the Passion of Christ chiefly by missionary work.

pas·sion·less (păsh′ən-lĭs) *adj.* **1.** Lacking strong emotion or feeling: *a rather passionless plea for clemency.* **2.** Unbiased or impartial; detached: *a newspaper's passionless account of a sensational trial.*

Passion play *n.* A dramatic performance, of medieval origin,

passant

passionflower

ă pat	oi boy
ā pay	ou out
âr care	o͝o took
ä father	o͞o boot
ĕ pet	ŭ cut
ē be	ûr urge
ĭ pit	th thin
ī pie	*th* this
îr pier	hw which
ŏ pot	zh vision
ō toe	ə about, item
ô paw	♦ regionalism

Stress marks: **′** (primary); ′ (secondary), as in **dictionary** (dĭk′shə-nĕr′ē)

that represents the events associated with the Passion of Jesus.

Passion Sunday *n.* The second Sunday before Easter.

Pas·sion·tide (păsh′ən-tīd′) *n.* The two weeks between Passion Sunday and Easter.

Passion Week *n.* The week between Passion Sunday and Palm Sunday.

pas·si·vate (păs′ə-vāt′) *v.* **-vat·ed, -vat·ing, -vates.** —*tr.* **1.** To treat or coat (a metal) in order to reduce the chemical reactivity of its surface. **2.** To coat (a semiconductor, for example) with an oxide layer to protect against contamination and increase electrical stability. **—pas′si·va′tion** *n.* **—pas′si·va·tor** *n.*

pas·sive (păs′ĭv) *adj.* **1.** Receiving or subjected to an action without responding or initiating an action in return. **2.** Accepting or submitting without objection or resistance; compliant. **3.** Not participating, acting, or operating; inert. See Synonyms at **inactive. 4.** Of, relating to, or being certain bonds or shares that do not bear financial interest. **5.** Of, relating to, or being a solar heating or cooling system that uses no external mechanical power. **6.** *Abbr.* **pass.** *Grammar.* Of, relating to, or being a verb form or voice used to indicate that the grammatical subject is the object of the action or the effect of the verb. For example, in the sentence *They were impressed by his manner, were impressed* is in the passive voice. **7.** *Chemistry.* Unreactive except under special or extreme conditions; inert. **8.** *Electronics.* Exhibiting no gain or contributing no energy: *a passive circuit element.* **9.** *Psychology.* Relating to or characteristic of an inactive or submissive role in a relationship, especially a sexual relationship. **—passive** *n.* **1.** *Abbr.* **pass.** *Grammar.* **a.** The passive voice. **b.** A verb or construction in the passive voice. **2.** One that is submissive or inactive. Often used in the plural: *"And the rest of us, we passives of the world, proceeded . . . as if nothing untoward had happened"* (Martin Gottfried). [Middle English, from Old French *passif,* from Latin *passīvus,* capable of suffering, from *passus,* past participle of *patī,* to suffer. See **pē(i)-** in Appendix.] **—pas′sive·ly** *adv.* **—pas′sive·ness** *n.*

passive immunity *n.* Immunity acquired by the transfer of antibodies from another individual, as through injection or placental transfer to a fetus. **—passive immunization** *n.*

passive resistance *n.* Resistance by nonviolent methods, such as fasting or demonstrating in protests, to a government, an occupying power, or specific laws. **—passive resister** *n.*

passive restraint *n.* An automatic safety device, such as an air bag, in a motor vehicle that protects a person during a crash.

passive smoking *n.* The involuntary inhalation of tobacco smoke by a person, especially a nonsmoker, who occupies an area with smokers or a smoker.

passive transfer *n.* The transfer of skin-sensitizing antibodies from the blood of an allergic individual to that of a nonallergic individual in order to test the sensitized area for an allergic reaction to specific allergens.

passive transport *n.* The movement of a chemical substance across a cell membrane without expenditure of energy by the cell, as in diffusion.

pas·siv·ism (păs′ə-vĭz′əm) *n.* Passive character, attitude, quality, or behavior. **—pas′siv·ist** *n.*

pas·siv·i·ty (pă-sĭv′ĭ-tē) *n.* The condition or quality of being passive; inactivity, quiescence, or submissiveness.

pass·key (păs′kē′) *n.* **1.** See **master key. 2.** See **skeleton key.**

Pass·o·ver (păs′ō′vər) *n. Judaism.* A holiday beginning on the 14th of Nisan and traditionally continuing for eight days, commemorating the exodus of the Jews from Egypt. [Translation of Hebrew *pesaḥ,* Pesach. See PESACH.]

pass·port (păs′pôrt′, -pōrt′) *n.* **1.** An official government document that certifies one's identity and citizenship and permits a citizen to travel abroad. **2.** An official permit issued by a foreign country allowing one to transport goods or to travel through that country. **3.** An official document issued by an allied foreign government to a ship, especially a neutral merchant ship in time of war, authorizing it to enter and travel through certain waters freely. **4.** Something that gives one the right or privilege of passage, entry, or acceptance: *Hard work was her passport to success.* [French *passeport,* from Old French : *passer,* to pass; see PASS + *port,* port; see PORT[1].]

pass-through (păs′thro͞o′) *n.* **1.** An opening between two rooms, especially a shelved space between a kitchen and dining room that is used for passing food. **2.** A route through which something is permitted to pass. **3.** A security that passes through payments made by debtors, thus providing investors with regular returns. Also called *pass-through security.* **4.** See **pass-along. —pass-through** *adj.*

pass·word (păs′wûrd′) *n.* **1.** A secret word or phrase that one uses to gain admittance or access to information. **2.** *Computer Science.* A sequence of characters required to gain access to a computer system.

Pas·sy (pă-sē′, pä-), **Frédéric.** 1822–1912. French economist and pacifist who founded the International League for Permanent Peace (1867). In 1901 he shared the first Nobel Peace Prize.

Passy, Paul Édouard. 1859–1940. French philologist who founded the International Phonetic Association (1894).

Louis Pasteur

past (păst) *adj.* **1.** No longer current; gone by; over: *His youth is past.* **2.** Having existed or occurred in an earlier time; bygone: *past events; in years past.* **3.a.** Earlier than the present time; ago: *40 years past.* **b.** Just gone by or elapsed: *in the past few days.* **4.** Having served formerly in a given capacity, especially an official one: *a past president; a past inmate of a cell.* **5.** *Abbr.* **p.** *Grammar.* Of, relating to, or being a verb tense or form used to express an action or a condition prior to the time it is expressed. **—past** *n.* **1.** The time before the present. **2.a.** Previous background, career, experiences, and activities: *an elderly person with a distinguished past.* **b.** A former period of someone's life kept secret or thought to be shameful: *a family with a checkered past.* **3.** *Abbr.* **p.** *Grammar.* **a.** The past tense. **b.** A verb form in the past tense. **—past** *adv.* So as to pass by or go beyond: *He waved as he walked past.* **—past** *prep.* **1.** Beyond in time; later than or after: *past midnight; a quarter past two.* **2.** Beyond in position; farther than: *The house is about a mile past the first stoplight. They walked past the memorial in silence.* **3.a.** Beyond the power, scope, extent, or influence of: *The problem is past the point of resolution.* **b.** Beyond in development or appropriateness: *The child is past drinking from a bottle. You're past sucking your thumb, so don't do it.* **4.** Beyond the number or amount of: *The child couldn't count past 20.* See Usage Note at **pass.** [Middle English, from past participle of *passen,* to pass. See PASS.]

pas·ta (päs′tə) *n.* **1.** Paste or dough made of wheat flour, eggs, and water, often formed into shapes and dried and used in a variety of recipes after being boiled. **2.** A prepared dish containing pasta as its main ingredient. [Italian, from Late Latin, paste, pastry cake. See PASTE[1].]

paste[1] (pāst) *n.* **1.** A smooth viscous mixture, as of flour and water or of starch and water, that is used as an adhesive for joining light materials, such as paper and cloth. **2.** A soft, smooth, thick mixture, as: **a.** A smooth dough of water, flour, and butter or other shortening, used in making pastry. **b.** A food that has been pounded until it is reduced to a smooth, creamy mass: *anchovy paste.* **c.** A sweet, doughy candy or confection: *rolled apricot paste.* **3.** The moist clay or clay mixture used in making porcelain or pottery. Also called *pâte.* **4.a.** A hard, brilliant, lead-containing glass used in making artificial gems. **b.** A gem made of this glass. In this sense, also called *strass.* **—paste** *tr.v.* **past·ed, past·ing, pastes. 1.** To cause to adhere by or as if by applying paste. **2.** To cover with something by or as if by pasting: *He pasted the wall with burlap. The wall is pasted with splotches.* [Middle English, from Old French, from Late Latin *pasta,* from Greek, barley-porridge, from neuter pl. of *pastos,* sprinkled, salted, from *passein,* to sprinkle. See **kwēt-** in Appendix.]

paste[2] (pāst) *tr.v.* **past·ed, past·ing, pastes.** *Slang.* To punch or strike. **—paste** *n.* A hard blow. [Probably alteration of BASTE[3].]

paste·board (pāst′bôrd′, -bōrd′) *n.* **1.** A thin, firm board made of sheets of paper pasted together or pressed paper pulp. **2.** A card, especially: **a.** A ticket. **b.** *Games.* A playing card. **c.** A visiting card. **—pasteboard** *adj.* **1.** Made of pasteboard. **2.** Of inferior quality; flimsy or unsubstantial.

paste·down (pāst′doun′) *n.* The portion of the endpaper that is pasted to the cover of a book.

pas·tel (pă-stĕl′) *n.* **1.a.** A drawing medium of dried paste made of ground pigments and a water-based binder that is manufactured in crayon form. **b.** A crayon of this material. **2.a.** A picture or sketch drawn with this type of crayon. **b.** The art or process of drawing with pastels. **3.** A soft, delicate hue; a pale color: *a room done all in pastels.* **4.** A sketchy or brief prose work. **—pastel** *adj.* **1.** Of, relating to, or made of pastel. **2.** Pale and soft in color. [French, from Italian *pastello,* material made into a paste, from Late Latin *pastellus,* woad dye, diminutive of *pasta,* paste. See PASTE[1].] **—pas·tel′ist, pas·tel′list** *n.*

past·er (pā′stər) *n.* **1.** One that applies or covers with paste. **2.** A paper sticker.

pas·tern (păs′tərn) *n.* **1.** The part of a horse's foot between the fetlock and hoof. **2.** An analogous part of the leg of a dog or other quadruped. [Alteration of Middle English *pastron,* hobble, pastern, from Old French *pasturon,* diminutive of *pasture,* pasture, tether, alteration of **pastoire,* from Latin *pāstōria,* feminine sing. of *pāstōrius,* of herdsmen, from *pāstor,* shepherd. See PASTOR.]

Pas·ter·nak (păs′tər-năk′, pə-styĭr-näk′), **Boris Leonidovich.** 1890–1960. Russian writer whose *Doctor Zhivago* (1957), a novel of disillusionment with the Russian Revolution, was banned by Soviet authorities. He was forced to refuse the 1958 Nobel Prize for literature.

paste-up (pāst′ŭp′) *n.* **1.** A composition of light, flat objects pasted onto a sheet of paper, board, or other backing, as: **a.** A layout of an image to be printed, such as a book cover. **b.** A collage. **2.** The art or process of making such a composition.

Pas·teur (păs-tûr′, pä-stœr′), **Louis.** 1822–1895. French chemist who founded modern microbiology, invented the process of pasteurization, and developed vaccines for anthrax, rabies, and chicken cholera. **—Pas·teur′i·an** *adj.*

Pasteur effect *n.* The inhibiting effect of oxygen on the process of fermentation. [After Louis PASTEUR.]

pas·teur·i·za·tion (păs′chər-ĭ-zā′shən, păs′tər-) *n.* **1.** The act or process of heating a beverage or other food, such as milk or beer, to a specific temperature for a specific period of time in order to kill microorganisms that could cause disease, spoilage, or undesired fermentation. **2.** The act or process of destroying most microorganisms in certain foods, such as fish or clam meat, by irradiating them with gamma rays or other radiation to prevent spoilage. [After Louis PASTEUR.]

pas·teur·ize (păs′chə-rīz′, păs′tə-) *tr.v.* **-ized, -iz·ing, -iz·es.** To subject (a beverage or other food) to pasteurization. **—pas′teur·iz′er** *n.*

Pasteur treatment *n.* A treatment for infection by the rabies virus in which a series of increasingly strong inoculations with attenuated virus is given to stimulate antibody production during the incubation period of the disease. [After Louis PASTEUR.]

pas·tic·cio (pă-stē′chō, -chē-ō, pä-) *n., pl.* **-ci** (-chē). A work or style produced by borrowing fragments, ingredients, or motifs from various sources; a potpourri. [Italian, from Vulgar Latin **pastīcium,* pasty. See PATISSERIE.]

pas·tiche (pă-stēsh′, pä-) *n.* **1.** A dramatic, literary, or musical piece openly imitating the previous works of other artists, often with satirical intent. **2.** A pasticcio of incongruous parts; a hodgepodge: *"In . . . a city of splendid Victorian architecture . . . there is a rather pointless pastiche of Dickensian London down on the waterfront"* (Economist). [French, from Italian *pasticcio.* See PASTICCIO.]

past·ies (pā′stēz′) *pl.n.* A pair of adhesive patches used to conceal a woman's nipples and worn principally by exotic dancers or striptease performers.

pas·tille (pă-stēl′) also **pas·til** (păs′tĭl) *n.* **1.** A small medicated or flavored tablet; a troche. **2.** A tablet containing aromatic substances that is burned to fumigate or deodorize the air. **3.** A pastel paste or crayon. [French, from Spanish *pastilla,* perfume pellet, and Italian *pastillo,* pastille, both from Latin *pastillus,* little loaf, medicine tablet, diminutive of *pānis,* bread. See **pā-** in Appendix.]

pas·time (păs′tīm′) *n.* An activity that occupies one's spare time pleasantly: *Sailing is her favorite pastime.* [Middle English *passe tyme,* translation of French *passe temps* : *passer,* to pass + *temps,* time.]

pas·ti·na (pă-stē′nə) *n.* Tiny pieces of pasta, often cooked in soups or used as baby food. [Italian, diminutive of *pasta,* pasta. See PASTA.]

pas·tis (pă-stēs′) *n.* A French licorice-flavored liqueur, usually drunk as an apéritif. [French, muddle, pastis, from Old Provençal *pastitz,* paste, pasty, from Vulgar Latin **pastīcium.* See PATISSERIE.]

past master *n. Abbr.* **PM, P.M. 1.** One who has formerly held the position of master in an organization, especially a social one such as a lodge or club. **2.** One who is thoroughly experienced and skilled in a particular craft or activity.

past·ness (păst′nĭs) *n.* **1.** The quality or condition of being past. **2.** The emotion or feeling evoked by memory: *"the one wave of recaptured pastness with which many a gifted writer makes his debut"* (John Simon).

Pas·to (päs′tō). A city of southwest Colombia near the Ecuadorian border. Founded in 1539, it was the site of an 1832 treaty by which Colombia and Ecuador became separate states. Population, 196,800.

pas·tor (păs′tər) *n.* **1.** A Christian minister or priest having spiritual charge over a congregation or other group. **2.** A layperson having spiritual charge over a person or group. **3.** A shepherd. **—pastor** *tr.v.* **-tored, -tor·ing, -tors.** To serve or act as pastor of. [Middle English, from Old French, from Latin *pāstor,* shepherd. See **pā-** in Appendix.] **—pas′tor·ship′** *n.*

pas·tor·al (păs′tər-əl) *adj.* **1.a.** Of or relating to shepherds or herders. **b.** Of, relating to, or used for animal husbandry. **2.a.** Of or relating to the country or country life; rural. **b.** Charmingly simple and serene; idyllic. See Synonyms at **rural. 3.** Of, relating to, or being a literary or other artistic work that portrays or evokes rural life, usually in an idealized manner. **4.** Of or relating to a pastor or the duties of a pastor: *pastoral duties; a pastoral letter.* **—pastoral** *n.* **1.** A literary or other artistic work that portrays or evokes rural life, usually in an idealized manner. **2.** *Music.* A pastorale. [Middle English, from Old French, from Latin *pāstōrālis,* from *pāstor,* shepherd. See PASTOR.] **—pas′tor·al·ly** *adv.*

pas·to·rale (păs′tə-räl′, -răl′, -rä′lē, pä′stə-) *n., pl.* **-ra·li** (-rä′lē) or **-rales. 1.** *Music.* An instrumental or vocal composition with a tender melody in a moderately slow rhythm, suggestive of traditional shepherds' music and idyllic rural life. **2.** A dramatic performance or opera, popular in the 16th and 17th centuries, that was based on a rural theme or subject. [Italian, of herdsmen, pastorale, from Latin *pāstōrālis.* See PASTORAL.]

Pas·tor·al Epistles (păs′tər-əl) *n. Bible.* The three New Testament Epistles, two addressed to Timothy and one to Titus, that are attributed to Saint Paul and concerned with the duties of ministers and certain issues of Church doctrine.

pas·to·ra·li (păs′tə-rä′lē, pä′stə-) *n.* A plural of **pastorale.**

pas·tor·al·ism (păs′tər-ə-lĭz′əm, pä′stər-) *n.* **1.** The quality or state of being pastoral. Used especially of a literary work. **2.** A social and economic system based on the raising and herding of livestock. **—pas′tor·al·ist** *n.*

pas·tor·al·ize (păs′tər-ə-līz′) *tr.v.* **-ized, -iz·ing, -iz·es. 1.** To make pastoral, especially to convert (an industrial society or economy) to an agricultural society or economy. **2.** To set in or render into a pastoral form. **—pas′tor·al·i·za′tion** (-ə-lĭ-zā′shən) *n.*

pas·tor·ate (păs′tər-ĭt) *n.* **1.** The office, rank, or jurisdiction of a pastor. **2.** A pastor's term of office with one congregation. **3.** A body of pastors.

♦**pas·to·ri·um** (pă-stôr′ē-əm, -stōr′-) *n., pl.* **-ums.** *Chiefly Southern U.S.* The residence of a pastor; a parsonage. [PAST(OR) + Latin *-orium,* n. suff.; see -ORY.]

past participle *n. Abbr.* **pp., p.p., P.P.** *Grammar.* A verb form indicating past or completed action or time that is used as a verbal adjective in phrases such as *baked beans* and *finished work* and with auxiliaries to form the passive voice or perfect and pluperfect tenses in constructions such as *She had baked the beans* and *The work was finished.* Also called *perfect participle.*

past perfect *n. Grammar.* See **pluperfect** (sense 1).

pas·tra·mi (pə-strä′mē) *n., pl.* **-mis.** A highly seasoned smoked cut of beef, usually taken from the shoulder. [Yiddish *pastrame,* from Rumanian *pastrámă.*]

pas·try (pā′strē) *n., pl.* **-tries. 1.** Dough or paste consisting primarily of flour, water, and shortening that is baked and often used as a crust for foods such as pies. **2.a.** Baked sweet foods made with pastry: *Viennese pastry.* **b.** One of these baked foods. [Middle English *pastree,* from *paste,* paste, dough. See PASTE[1].]

past tense *n. Grammar.* A verb tense used to express an action or a condition that occurred in or during the past. For example, in *While she was sewing, he read aloud, was sewing* and *read* are in the past tense.

pas·tur·age (păs′chər-ĭj) *n.* **1.** The grass or other vegetation eaten by grazing animals. **2.** Land covered with grass or vegetation suitable for grazing animals. **3.** The business of grazing cattle.

pas·ture (păs′chər) *n.* **1.a.** Grass or other vegetation eaten as food by grazing animals. **b.** Ground on which such vegetation grows, especially that which is set aside for use by domestic grazing animals. **2.** The feeding or grazing of animals. **—pasture** *v.* **-tured, -tur·ing, -tures.** *—tr.* **1.** To herd (animals) into a pasture to graze. **2.** To provide (animals) with pasturage. Used of land. **3.a.** To graze on (land or vegetation). **b.** To use (land) as pasture. *—intr.* To graze in a pasture. ***—idiom.* put out to pasture. 1.** To herd (grazing animals) into pasturable land. **2.** *Informal.* To retire or compel to retire from work or a full workload. [Middle English, from Old French, from Late Latin *pāstūra,* from Latin *pāstus,* past participle of *pāscere,* to feed. See **pā-** in Appendix.] **—pas′tur·a·ble** *adj.* **—pas′tur·er** *n.*

pasture

pas·ture·land (păs′chər-lănd′) *n.* Land suitable for grazing.

past·y[1] (pā′stē) *adj.* **-i·er, -i·est. 1.** Resembling paste in consistency. **2.** Having a pale, lifeless appearance; pallid: *an unhealthy, pasty complexion.* **—past′i·ness** *n.*

pas·ty[2] (păs′tē) *n., pl.* **-ties.** *Chiefly British.* A pie or turnover, especially one filled with seasoned meat or fish. [Middle English *pastey,* from Old French *paste,* from Vulgar Latin **pastāta,* from Late Latin *pasta,* paste. See PASTE[1].]

PA system (pē′ā′) *n.* A public-address system.

pat[1] (păt) *v.* **pat·ted, pat·ting, pats.** *—tr.* **1.a.** To tap gently with the open hand or with something flat. **b.** To stroke lightly as a gesture of affection. **2.** To mold by tapping gently with the hands or a flat implement. *—intr.* **1.** To run or walk with a tapping sound. **2.** To hit something or against something gently or lightly. **—pat** *n.* **1.** A light, gentle stroke or tap. **2.** The sound made by a light stroke or tap or by light footsteps. **3.** A small mass shaped by or as if by patting: *a pat of butter.* ***—idiom.* pat on the back.** A word or gesture of praise or approval: *received a pat on the back for doing a good job.* [From Middle English, a blow, perhaps of imitative origin.]

pat[2] (păt) *adj.* **1.** Trite or glib; superficially complete or satisfactory: *A pat answer is not going to satisfy an inquisitive audience.* **2.a.** Timely or opportune. **b.** Suitable; fitting. **3.** *Games.* Being a poker hand that is strong enough to make drawing cards unlikely to improve it. **—pat** *adv. Informal.* Completely, exactly, or perfectly: *They've got the system down pat. He has the lesson pat.* [From PAT[1].] **—pat′ly** *adv.* **—pat′ness** *n.*

pat. *abbr.* Patent.

pa·ta·ca (pə-tä′kə) *n.* See table at **currency.** [Portuguese, from Arabic *'abū ṭāqah.*]

pa·ta·gi·um (pə-tā′jē-əm) *n., pl.* **-gi·a** (-jē-ə). **1.** A thin membrane extending between the body and a limb to form a wing or winglike extension, as in bats and flying squirrels. Also called *parachute.* **2.** An expandable, membranous fold of skin between the wing and body of a bird. [Latin *patagium,* gold edging on a woman's tunic, perhaps from Greek **patageion,* from *patagos,* clatter, of imitative origin.] **—pa·ta′gi·al** (-jē-əl) *adj.*

Pat·a·go·ni·a (păt′ə-gō′nē-ə, -gōn′yə). A tableland region of South America in southern Argentina and Chile extending from the Río Colorado to the Straits of Magellan and from the Andes to the Atlantic Ocean. The study of its original inhabitants, the Tehuelche ("the Patagonian giants"), and its unusual wildlife have attracted many scientific expeditions, including that of Charles Darwin (1831–1836). **—Pat′a·go′ni·an** *adj. & n.*

Patagonian hare *n.* See **mara.**

pa·ta·phys·ics (pä′tə-fĭz′ĭks) *n. (used with a sing. verb).* The French absurdist concept of a philosophy or science dedicated to studying what lies beyond the realm of metaphysics, intended as a parody of the methods and theories of modern science and often expressed in nonsensical language. [French *pataphysique,* alteration of Greek *ta epi ta metaphusika,* things after the metaphysics : *epi,* after; see EPI– + *metaphusika,* metaphysics; see METAPHYSICS.]

ă pat	oi boy
ā pay	ou out
âr care	ŏŏ took
ä father	ōō boot
ĕ pet	ŭ cut
ē be	ûr urge
ĭ pit	th thin
ī pie	*th* this
îr pier	hw which
ŏ pot	zh vision
ō toe	ə about, item
ô paw	♦ regionalism

Stress marks: ′ (primary); ′ (secondary), as in **dictionary** (dĭk′shə-nĕr′ē)

pa·tas (pä′təs) *n., pl.* **patas.** Any of several long-tailed terrestrial monkeys of the genus *Erythrocebus* of western Africa that are closely related to the guenons, especially *E. patas,* which has reddish fur and a black nose. [French, from Wolof *pata.*]

patch[1] (păch) *n.* **1.a.** A small piece of material affixed to another, larger piece to conceal, reinforce, or repair a worn area, hole, or tear. **b.** A small piece of cloth used for patchwork. **2.** A small cloth badge affixed to a garment as a decoration or an insignia, as of a military unit. **3.a.** A dressing or covering applied to protect a wound or sore. **b.** A pad or shield of cloth worn over an eye socket or an injured eye. **c.** A transdermal patch. **4.** A beauty spot applied to a woman's face or shoulder to conceal an imperfection or to enhance the fairness of her skin. **5.a.** A small piece, part, or section, especially that which differs from or contrasts with the whole: *a patch of thin ice; patches of sunlight.* **b.** A small plot or piece of land, especially one that produces or is used for growing specific vegetation: *a briar patch; a bean patch.* **6.** A temporary, removable electronic connection, as one between two components in a communications system. **—patch** *v.* **patched, patch·ing, patch·es.** *—tr.* **1.** To put a patch or patches on. **2.** To make by sewing scraps of material together: *patch a quilt.* **3.** To mend, repair, or put together, especially hastily, clumsily, or poorly: *They patched together the broken statues with glue and plaster. The delegates will be forced to patch up their differences.* **4.** To connect temporarily (electronic components), as with a patch cord. *—intr. Electronics.* To be connected temporarily. [Middle English *pacche,* perhaps alteration of *pece, pieche,* piece. See PIECE.] **—patch′a·ble** *adj.* **—patch′er** *n.*

patch[2] (păch) *n.* A fool or clown; a dolt. [Perhaps from Italian dialectal *paccio,* from Old Italian.]

patch cord *n.* A conductor with a plug at each end that is used to temporarily connect components of an electronic system.

patch·ou·li also **patch·ou·ly** or **pach·ou·li** (pə-cho͞o′lē, păch′o͞o-lē) *n., pl.* **-lis** also **-lies** or **-lis. 1.** A small southeast Asian shrub *(Pogostemon cablin)* in the mint family, having leaves that yield a fragrant oil used in the manufacture of perfumes. **2.** A perfume made from the oil of this plant. [Tamil *paccuḷi.*]

patch pocket *n.* An unfitted flat pocket on the outside of a garment.

patch test *n.* A test for allergic sensitivity in which a suspected allergen is applied to the skin on a small surgical pad.

patchwork
Detail of
a patchwork quilt

patch·work (păch′wûrk′) *n.* **1.** Needlework consisting of varicolored patches of material sewn together, as in a quilt. **2.** A collection of miscellaneous or incongruous parts; a jumble.

patch·y (păch′ē) *adj.* **-i·er, -i·est. 1.** Made up of or marked by patches: *patchy trousers.* **2.** Uneven in quality or performance: *Their work is patchy at best.* **—patch′i·ly** *adv.* **—patch′i·ness** *n.*

patd. *abbr.* Patented.

pate (pāt) *n.* **1.** The human head, especially the top of the head: *a bald pate.* **2.** The intellect; one's brains. [Middle English.] **—pat′ed** *adj.*

pâte (pät) *n.* See **paste**[1] (sense 3). [French, from Old French *paste,* paste. See PASTE[1].]

pâ·té (pä-tā′) *n.* **1.** A meat paste, such as pâté de foie gras. **2.** A small pastry filled with meat or fish. [French, from Old French *paste,* paste, pâté. See PASTE[1].]

pâ·té de foie gras (pä-tā′ də fwä grä′) *n., pl.* **pâtés de foie gras** (pä-tā′). A paste made from goose liver, pork fat, onions, mushrooms, and often truffles. [French : *pâté,* pâté + *de,* of + *foie,* liver + *gras,* fat.]

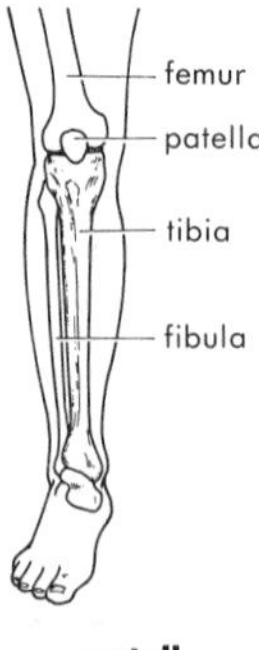

patella

pa·tel·la (pə-tĕl′ə) *n., pl.* **-tel·lae** (-tĕl′ē). **1.a.** A flat triangular bone located at the front of the knee joint. Also called *kneecap.* **b.** A dish-shaped anatomical formation. **2.** A pan or dish in ancient Rome. [Latin, diminutive of *patina,* plate, pan. See PATEN.] **—pa·tel′lar, pa·tel′late** (-tĕl′ĭt, -āt′) *adj.*

pa·tel·li·form (pə-tĕl′ə-fôrm′) *adj.* Shaped like a pan, dish, or cup: *the patelliform shell of the limpet.* [Latin *patella,* small plate, pan; see PATELLA + -FORM.]

pat·en also **pat·in** (păt′n) *n.* **1.** A plate, usually of gold or silver, that is used to hold the host during the celebration of the Eucharist. Also called *patina.* **2.** A plate or shallow dish, especially an artifact from an ancient civilization. **3.** A thin disk of or resembling metal. [Middle English, from Old French *patene,* from Medieval Latin *patina,* from Latin, pan, from Greek *patanē,* platter. See **pete-** in Appendix.]

pa·ten·cy (pāt′n-sē) *n.* **1.** The state or quality of being obvious. **2.** *Biology.* The state or quality of being open, expanded, or unblocked.

pat·ent (păt′nt) *n. Abbr.* **pat. 1.a.** A grant made by a government that confers upon the creator of an invention the sole right to make, use, and sell that invention for a set period of time. **b.** Letters patent. **c.** An invention protected by such a grant. **2.a.** A grant made by a government that confers on an individual fee-simple title to public lands. **b.** The official document of such a grant. **c.** The land so granted. **3.** An exclusive right or title. **—patent** *adj.* **1.** *Abbr.* **pat. a.** Protected or conferred by a patent or letters patent: *a patent right.* **b.** Of, relating to, or dealing in patents: *patent law.* **2.** (*also* pāt′nt). Obvious; plain. See Synonyms at **apparent. 3.** (pāt′nt). *Biology.* **a.** Not blocked; open. **b.** Spreading open; expanded. **4.** Of, relating to, or being a nonprescription drug or other medical preparation that is often protected by a trademark. **5.** Of high quality. Used of flour. **6.** (*also* păt′nt). *Archaic.* Open to general inspection. Used especially of documents. **—patent** *tr.v.* **-ent·ed, -ent·ing, -ents. 1.** To obtain a patent on or for (an invention, for example). **2.** To invent, originate, or be the proprietor of (an idea, for example). **3.** To grant a patent to or for. [Middle English, document granting a right, short for *(lettre) patent,* open (letter), from Old French *(lettre) patente,* from Latin *patēns, patent-,* open, present participle of *patēre,* to be open. See **pete-** in Appendix.] **—pat′ent·a·bil′i·ty** *n.* **—pat′ent·a·ble** *adj.*

pat·ent·ed (păt′n-tĭd) *adj.* **1.** Characteristic of, unique to, or originated by a particular person or group: *Throughout the campaign, the candidate refuted his rival's criticisms with a series of patented responses.* **2.** Protected or conferred by a patent or letters patent: *a patented process.*

pat·ent·ee (păt′n-tē′) *n.* The party that possesses or has been granted a patent.

patent leather *n.* Black leather finished to a hard, glossy surface and used especially for shoes and clothing accessories. [So called because it is made by a once-patented process.]

patent log *n. Nautical.* A torpedo-shaped instrument with rotary fins that is dragged from the stern of a vessel to measure the speed or distance traveled. Also called *screw log, taffrail log.*

pat·ent·ly (păt′nt-lē, păt′-) *adv.* In a patent manner; openly, plainly, or clearly: *a patently false statement.*

patent office *n.* A government bureau that studies claims for, grants, and maintains records of patents.

pat·en·tor (păt′n-tər, păt′n-tôr′) *n.* One that grants a patent.

pa·ter (pā′tər) *n. Chiefly British.* Father. [Latin. See **peter-** in Appendix.]

Pa·ter (pā′tər), **Walter Horatio.** 1839–1894. British writer remembered for his volumes of criticism, including *Studies in the History of the Renaissance* (1873) and *Appreciations* (1889).

pa·ter·fa·mil·i·as (pā′tər-fə-mĭl′ē-əs, pä′-, păt′ər-) *n., pl.* **pa·tres·fa·mil·i·as** (pā′trēz-fə-mĭl′ē-əs, pä′-, păt′rēz-). A man who is the head of a household or the father of a family. [Latin *paterfamiliās* : *pater,* father; see PATER + *familiās,* archaic genitive of *familia,* family; see FAMILY.]

pa·ter·nal (pə-tûr′nəl) *adj.* **1.** Relating to or characteristic of a father or fatherhood; fatherly. **2.** Received or inherited from a father: *a paternal trait.* **3.** Related through one's father: *my paternal aunt.* [Middle English, from Old French, from Late Latin *paternālis,* from Latin *paternus,* from *pater,* father. See **peter-** in Appendix.] **—pa·ter′nal·ly** *adv.*

pa·ter·nal·ism (pə-tûr′nə-lĭz′əm) *n.* A policy or practice of treating or governing people in a fatherly manner, especially by providing for their needs without giving them rights or responsibilities. **—pa·ter′nal·ist** *adj. & n.* **—pa·ter′nal·is′tic** *adj.* **—pa·ter′nal·is′ti·cal·ly** *adv.*

pa·ter·ni·ty (pə-tûr′nĭ-tē) *n., pl.* **-ties. 1.** The state of being a father; fatherhood. **2.** Descent on a father's side; paternal descent. **3.** Authorship; origin. **—paternity** *adj.* Of or relating to a lawsuit brought by a woman attempting to establish that a particular man is the father of her child and so must provide the child with financial support: *paternity case; paternity suit.* [Middle English *paternite,* from Old French, from Late Latin *paternitās,* from Latin *paternus,* paternal. See PATERNAL.]

paternity leave *n.* A leave of absence from work granted to a father to care for an infant.

paternity test *n.* A test using blood group identification of a mother, child, and putative father to establish the probability of paternity. **—paternity testing** *n.*

pa·ter·nos·ter (pā′tər-nŏs′tər, pä′-, păt′ər-) *n.* **1.** Often **Paternoster.** The Lord's Prayer. **2.** One of the large beads on a rosary on which the Lord's Prayer is said. **3.** A sequence of words spoken as a prayer or a magic formula. **4.** A weighted fishing line having several jointed attachments for hooks connected by bead-like swivels. **5.** An elevator constructed of a series of doorless compartments hung on chains that move slowly and continuously, allowing passengers to step on and off at will. [Middle English, from Old English, from Late Latin : Latin *pater,* father; see PATER + Latin *noster,* our; see **nes-**[2] in Appendix.]

Pat·er·son (păt′ər-sən). A city of northeast New Jersey at the falls of the Passaic River north of Newark. It was founded in 1791 as an industrial settlement of the Society for Establishing Useful Manufactures, chartered by Alexander Hamilton and others to promote independent American enterprise. Population, 137,970.

Paterson, William. 1745–1806. Irish-born American Revolutionary leader and jurist. A member of the Constitutional Convention (1787), he later served as an associate justice of the U.S. Supreme Court (1793–1806).

path (păth, päth) *n., pl.* **paths** (păthz, päthz, păths, päths). **1.** A trodden track or way. **2.** A road, way, or track made for a particular purpose: *a bicycle path.* **3.** The route or course along which something travels or moves: *the path of a hurricane.* **4.** A course of action or conduct: *the path of righteousness.* [Middle English, from Old English *pæth.* See **pent-** in Appendix.]

path. or **pathol.** *abbr.* **1.** Pathological. **2.** Pathology.

path– *pref.* Variant of **patho–.**

–path *suff.* **1.** A practitioner of a specified kind of medical treatment: *naturopath.* **2.** One affected by a specified kind of disorder: *sociopath.* [Back-formation from -PATHY.]

Pa·than (pə-tän′) *n.* A member of a Pashto-speaking people of eastern Afghanistan and northwest Pakistan, constituting the majority population of Afghanistan. [Hindi *Paṭhān,* from Pashto *Pĕṣtana,* pl. of *Pĕṣtūn,* an Afghan, from *paṣtu,* Pashto.]

pa·thet·ic (pə-thĕt′ĭk) also **pa·thet·i·cal** (-ĭ-kəl) *adj.* **1.** Arousing or capable of arousing sympathetic sadness and compassion. **2.** Arousing or capable of arousing scornful pity. [French *pathétique,* from Late Latin *patheticus,* from Greek *pathētikos,* sensitive, from *pathētos,* liable to suffer, from *pathos,* suffering. See **k^{w}ent(h)-** in Appendix.] **—pa·thet′i·cal·ly** *adv.*

SYNONYMS: *pathetic, pitiful, pitiable, piteous, lamentable.* These adjectives describe one that inspires or deserves pity. Something *pathetic* elicits sympathetic sadness and compassion: *"Everything human is pathetic"* (Mark Twain). Often the word refers to what is so poor that it arouses scornful pity: *The academic standards in the school were pathetic.* Both *pitiful* and *pitiable* apply to what is touchingly sad: *"She told a most pitiful story"* (Samuel Butler). *"The emperor had been in a state of pitiable vacillation"* (William Hickling Prescott). Sometimes the terms connote contemptuous pity, as for what is hopelessly inept or inadequate: *"If when the chips are down, the world's most powerful nation . . . acts like a pitiful, helpless giant, the forces of totalitarianism and anarchy will threaten free nations and free institutions throughout the world"* (Richard M. Nixon). *"That cold accretion called the world, which, so terrible in the mass, is so unformidable, even pitiable, in its units"* (Thomas Hardy). *Piteous* applies to what cries out for pity: *"They . . . made piteous lamentation to us to save them"* (Daniel Defoe). *Lamentable* suggests the evocation of pity mixed with sorrow: *"Tell thou the lamentable tale of me,/And send the hearers weeping to their beds"* (Shakespeare). See also Synonyms at **moving.**

pathetic fallacy *n.* The attribution of human emotions or characteristics to inanimate objects or to nature; for example, *angry clouds; a cruel wind.*

path·find·er (păth′fīn′dər, päth′-) *n.* One that discovers a new course or way, especially through or into unexplored regions. **—path′find′ing** *adj.*

patho– or **path–** *pref.* Disease; suffering: *pathogen.* [New Latin, from Greek, from *pathos,* suffering. See **k^{w}ent(h)-** in Appendix.]

path·o·bi·ol·o·gy (păth′ō-bī-ŏl′ə-jē) *n.* See **pathology** (sense 1).

path·o·gen (păth′ə-jən) *n.* An agent that causes disease, especially a living microorganism such as a bacterium or fungus.

path·o·gen·e·sis (păth′ə-jĕn′ĭ-sĭs) also **pa·thog·e·ny** (pă-thŏj′ə-nē) *n.* The development of a diseased or morbid condition.

path·o·gen·ic (păth′ə-jĕn′ĭk) also **path·o·ge·net·ic** (-jə-nĕt′ĭk) *adj.* **1.** Capable of causing disease. **2.** Originating or producing disease. **3.** Of or relating to pathogenesis. **—path′o·gen′i·cal·ly** *adv.* **—path′o·ge·nic′i·ty** (-jə-nĭs′ĭ-tē) *n.*

pa·thog·e·ny (pă-thŏj′ə-nē) *n.* Variant of **pathogenesis.**

pa·thog·no·mon·ic (pə-thŏg′nə-mŏn′ĭk, păth′əg-nō-) *adj.* Characteristic or symptomatic of a particular disease or condition. [Greek *pathognōmonikos* : *patho-,* patho- + *gnōmonikos,* able to judge (from *gnōmōn,* interpreter; see **gnō-** in Appendix).]

pa·thog·ra·phy (pă-thŏg′rə-fē) *n.* **1.** The retrospective study, often by a physician, of the possible influence and effects of disease on the life and work of a historical personage or group. **2.** A style of biography that overemphasizes the negative aspects of a person's life and work, such as failure, unhappiness, illness, and tragedy: "[It] *falls into pathography's technique of emphasizing the sensational underside of its subject's life"* (Joyce Carol Oates).

path·o·log·i·cal (păth′ə-lŏj′ĭ-kəl) also **path·o·log·ic** (-ĭk) *adj. Abbr.* **path., pathol. 1.** Of or relating to pathology. **2.** Relating to or caused by disease. **3.** Of, relating to, or manifesting behavior that is habitual and compulsive: *a pathological liar.* **—path′o·log′i·cal·ly** *adv.*

pa·thol·o·gy (pă-thŏl′ə-jē) *n., pl.* **-gies.** *Abbr.* **path., pathol. 1.** The scientific study of the nature of disease and its causes, processes, development, and consequences. Also called *pathobiology.* **2.** The anatomic or functional manifestations of a disease: *the pathology of cancer.* **3.** A departure or deviation from a normal condition: *"Neighborhoods plagued by a self-perpetuating pathology of joblessness, welfare dependency, crime"* (Time). **—pa·thol′o·gist** *n.*

path·o·phys·i·ol·o·gy (păth′ō-fĭz′ē-ŏl′ə-jē) *n.* **1.** The functional changes associated with or resulting from disease or injury. **2.** The scientific study of such changes. Also called *physiopathology.* **—path′o·phys′i·o·log′ic** (-ə-lŏj′ĭk), **path′o·phys′i·o·log′i·cal** (-ĭ-kəl) *adj.* **—path′o·phys′i·ol′o·gist** *n.*

pa·thos (pā′thŏs′, -thôs′) *n.* **1.** A quality, as of an experience or a work of art, that arouses feelings of pity, sympathy, tenderness, or sorrow. **2.** The feeling, as of sympathy or pity, so aroused. [Greek, suffering. See **k^{w}ent(h)-** in Appendix.]

path·way (păth′wā′, päth′-) *n.* **1.** A path. **2.** *Physiology.* **a.** A course usually followed by a body part or process. **b.** A chain of nerve fibers along which impulses normally travel. **c.** A sequence of enzymatic or other reactions by which one biological material is converted to another.

–pathy *suff.* **1.** Feeling; suffering; perception: *telepathy.* **2.a.** Disease: *neuropathy.* **b.** A system of treating disease: *homeopathy.* [Greek *-patheia,* from *pathos.* See **k^{w}ent(h)-** in Appendix.]

pa·tience (pā′shəns) *n.* **1.** The capacity, quality, or fact of being patient. **2.** *Chiefly British.* The game solitaire.

SYNONYMS: *patience, long-suffering, resignation, forbearance.* These nouns all denote the capacity to endure hardship, difficulty, or inconvenience without complaint. *Patience* emphasizes calmness, self-control, and the willingness or ability to tolerate delay: *"Our patience will achieve more than our force"* (Edmund Burke). *"No fear can stand up to hunger, no patience can wear it out"* (Joseph Conrad). *Long-suffering* is long and patient endurance, as of wrong or provocation: *The general, a man by no means notable for docility and long-suffering, flew into a rage. Resignation* implies an unresisting acceptance of or submission to something trying, as out of despair or necessity: *Too timorous to protest the disrespect with which she was being treated, the young woman could only accept it with resignation. Forbearance* denotes restraint, as in retaliating, demanding what is due, or voicing disapproval or condemnation: *"It is the mutual duty of all to practice Christian forbearance, love, and charity towards each other"* (Patrick Henry). *The parents showed remarkable forbearance toward their defiant and unruly son.*

pa·tient (pā′shənt) *adj.* **1.** Bearing or enduring pain, difficulty, provocation, or annoyance with calmness. **2.** Marked by or exhibiting calm endurance of pain, difficulty, provocation, or annoyance. **3.** Tolerant; understanding: *an unfailingly patient leader and guide.* **4.** Persevering; constant: *With patient industry, she revived the failing business and made it thrive.* **5.** Capable of calmly awaiting an outcome or a result; not hasty or impulsive. **6.** Capable of bearing or enduring pain, difficulty, provocation, or annoyance: *"My uncle Toby was a man patient of injuries"* (Laurence Sterne). **—patient** *n.* **1.** One who receives medical attention, care, or treatment. **2.** *Archaic.* One who suffers. [Middle English *pacient,* from Old French, from Latin *patiēns, patient-,* present participle of *patī,* to endure. See **pē(i)-** in Appendix.] **—pa′tient·ly** *adv.*

pat·in (păt′n) *n.* Variant of **paten.**

pat·i·na[1] (păt′n-ə) *n., pl.* **pat·i·nae** (păt′n-ē). See **paten** (sense 1). [Medieval Latin, from Latin, plate. See PATEN.]

pat·i·na[2] (păt′n-ə, pə-tē′nə) also **pa·tine** (pă-tēn′) *n.* **1.** A thin greenish layer, usually basic copper sulfate, that forms on copper or copper alloys, such as bronze, as a result of corrosion. **2.** The sheen on any surface, produced by age and use. **3.** A change in appearance produced by long-standing behavior, practice, or use: *a face etched with a patina of fine lines and tiny wrinkles.* [Italian, from Latin, plate (from the incrustation on ancient metal plates and dishes). See PATEN.]

pat·i·naed (păt′n-ĭd, pə-tē′nĭd) *adj.* Having a coating, covering, or sheen; patinated. Used especially to describe the corrosive green layer that forms on copper and its alloys.

pat·i·nate (păt′n-āt′) *v.* **-nat·ed, -nat·ing, -nates.** —*tr.* To furnish with a patina. —*intr.* To acquire or become covered with a patina.

pa·tine (pă-tēn′) *tr.v.* **-tined, -tin·ing, -tines.** To coat with a patina. **—patine** *n.* Variant of **patina**[2]. [French *patiner,* from *patine,* patina, from Italian *patina.* See PATINA[2].]

pat·i·o (păt′ē-ō′, pä′tē-ō′) *n., pl.* **-os. 1.** An outdoor space for dining or recreation that adjoins a residence and is often paved. **2.** A roofless inner courtyard, typically found in Spanish and Spanish-style dwellings. [Spanish, from Old Spanish, possibly from Old Provençal *patu, pati,* pasture, perhaps from Latin *pactum,* agreement. See PACT.]

pa·tis·se·rie (pə-tĭs′ə-rē, pä-tēs-rē′) *n.* A bakery specializing in French pastry. [French *pâtisserie,* from Old French *pastiserie,* from *pasticier,* to make pastry, from **pastitz,* pastry, from Vulgar Latin **pastīcium,* from Late Latin *pasta,* dough. See PASTE[1].]

Pát·mos also **Pat·mos** (păt′mŏs, -məs, pät′môs). An island of southeast Greece in the Dodecanese Islands of the Aegean Sea. Saint John was exiled to the island c. A.D. 95 and according to tradition wrote the Book of Revelation here.

Pat·na (pŭt′nə). A city of northeast India on the Ganges River northwest of Calcutta. It served as Asoka's capital in the 3rd century B.C. and as a Mogul viceregal capital in the 16th century. Population, 776,371.

pat·ois (păt′wä′, pă-twä′) *n., pl.* **pat·ois** (păt′wäz′, pă-twä′). **1.** A regional dialect, especially one without a literary tradition. **2.a.** A creole. **b.** Nonstandard speech. **3.** The special jargon of a group; cant. See Synonyms at **dialect.** [French, from Old French, possibly from *pate,* paw, from Vulgar Latin **patta,* perhaps of imitative origin.]

Pa·ton (pāt′n), **Alan Stewart.** 1903–1988. South African writer noted for his novels *Cry, the Beloved Country* (1948) and *Too Late the Phalarope* (1953). He was a founder and leader (1953–1968) of the Liberal Party of South Africa.

Pa·tos (păt′əs, pä′to͞os), **Lagoa dos.** A shallow tidal lagoon of southeast Brazil. Separated from the Atlantic Ocean by a wide sandbar, it is an important fishing ground.

patr– *pref.* Variant of **patri–.**

Pá·trai (pä′trĕ) **Pa·tras** (pə-trăs′, păt′rəs). A city of southern Greece in the northwest Peloponnesus on the **Gulf of Pátrai,** or **Gulf of Patras,** an inlet of the Ionian Sea. The city was an important trade center by the fifth century B.C. but declined before the Roman conquest of Greece (146 B.C.). Its commercial impor-

ă pat	oi **boy**
ā pay	ou **out**
âr care	o͝o **took**
ä father	o͞o **boot**
ĕ pet	ŭ **cut**
ē be	ûr **urge**
ĭ pit	th **thin**
ī pie	*th* **this**
îr pier	hw **which**
ŏ pot	zh **vision**
ō toe	ə **about, item**
ô paw	♦ **regionalism**

Stress marks: **′** (primary); ′ (secondary), as in **dictionary** (dĭk′shə-nĕr′ē)

tance revived during the Middle Ages. Population, 142,163.

pa·tres·fa·mil·i·as (pā′trēz-fə-mĭl′ē-əs, pä′-, păt′rēz-) *n.* Plural of **paterfamilias.**

patri– or **patr–** *pref.* Father, paternal: *patrilineal.* [Latin (from *pater, patr-,* father) and Greek (from *patēr, patr-,* father; see **pəter-** in Appendix).]

pa·tri·arch (pā′trē-ärk′) *n.* **1.** A man who rules a family, clan, or tribe. **2.** In the Old Testament: **a.** One of the antediluvian progenitors of the human race, from Adam to Noah. **b.** Abraham, Isaac, Jacob, or any of Jacob's 12 sons, the eponymous progenitors of the 12 tribes of Israel. **3.** Used formerly as a title for the bishops of Rome, Constantinople, Jerusalem, Antioch, and Alexandria. **4.** *Roman Catholic Church.* A bishop who holds the highest episcopal rank after the pope. **5.** *Eastern Orthodox Church.* Any one of the bishops of the sees of Constantinople, Antioch, Alexandria, Moscow, and Jerusalem who has authority over other bishops. **6.** *Judaism.* The head of the Sanhedrin in Syrian Palestine from about 180 B.C. to A.D. 429. **7.** *Mormon Church.* A high dignitary of the priesthood empowered to invoke blessings. **8.** One who is regarded as the founder or original head of an enterprise, an organization, or a tradition. **9.** A very old, venerable man; an elder. **10.** The oldest member of a group: *the patriarch of the herd.* [Middle English *patriarche,* from Old French, from Late Latin *patriarcha,* from Greek *patriarkhēs* : *patria,* lineage (from *patēr, patr-,* father; see **pəter-** in Appendix) + *-arkhēs,* -arch.]

pa·tri·ar·chal (pā′trē-är′kəl) also **pa·tri·ar·chic** (-är′kĭk) *adj.* **1.** Of, relating to, or characteristic of a patriarch. **2.** Of or relating to a patriarchy: *a patriarchal social system.* **3.** Ruled by a patriarch: *a patriarchal see.* **—pa′tri·ar′chal·ism** *n.* **—pa′tri·ar′chal·ly** *adv.*

patriarchal cross

patriarchal cross *n.* A Latin cross having two horizontal bars, of which the upper is the shorter.

pa·tri·ar·chate (pā′trē-är′kĭt, -kāt′) *n.* **1.** The territory, rule, or rank of a patriarch. **2.** See **patriarchy.**

pa·tri·ar·chic (pā′trē-är′kĭk) *adj.* Variant of **patriarchal.**

pa·tri·ar·chy (pā′trē-är′kē) *n., pl.* **-chies. 1.** A social system in which the father is the head of the family and descent is traced through the father's side of the family. **2.** A family, community, or society based on this system or governed by men. Also called *patriarchate.*

pa·tri·cian (pə-trĭsh′ən) *n.* **1.** A person of refined upbringing, manners, and tastes. **2.** A member of an aristocracy; an aristocrat. **3.** A member of one of the noble families of the ancient Roman Republic, which before the third century B.C. had exclusive rights to the Senate and the magistracies. **4.** Used as a title for members of a class of honorary nobility appointed by the Byzantine emperors. **5.** A member of the hereditary ruling class in the medieval free cities of Italy and Germany. [Middle English *patricion,* from Old French *patricien,* from Latin *patricius,* from *patrēs (cōnscrīptī),* enrolled fathers, senators, pl. of *pater, patr-,* father. (See **pəter-** in Appendix).] **—pa·tri′cian** *adj.* **—pa·tri′cian·ly** *adv.*

pa·tri·ci·ate (pə-trĭsh′ē-ĭt, -āt′) *n.* **1.** Nobility or aristocracy. **2.** The rank, position, or term of office of a patrician. [Latin *patriciātus,* from *patricius,* patrician. See PATRICIAN.]

pat·ri·cide (păt′rĭ-sīd′) *n.* **1.** The act of murdering one's father. **2.** One who murders one's father. [Late Latin *patricīdium* and *patricīda* : Latin *patri-,* patri- + *-cīdium, -cīda,* -cide.] **—pat′ri·cid′al** (păt′rĭ-sīd′l) *adj.*

Pat·rick (păt′rĭk), Saint. A.D. 389?–461? Christian missionary and patron saint of Ireland.

pat·ri·cli·nous (păt′rĭ-klī′nəs) *adj.* Variant of **patroclinous.**

pat·ri·lin·e·age (păt′rə-lĭn′ē-ĭj) *n.* The line of descent as traced through the paternal side of a family.

pat·ri·lin·e·al (păt′rə-lĭn′ē-əl) *adj.* Relating to, based on, or tracing ancestral descent through the paternal line.

pat·ri·lo·cal (păt′rə-lō′kəl) *adj.* *Anthropology.* Of or relating to the residence of a husband's kin group or clan. **—pat′ri·lo′cal·ly** *adv.*

pat·ri·mo·ny (păt′rə-mō′nē) *n., pl.* **-nies. 1.a.** An inheritance from a father or other ancestor. **b.** An inheritance or a legacy; heritage. **2.** An endowment or estate belonging to an institution, especially a church. [Middle English, from Old French *patrimoine,* from Latin *patrimōnium,* from *pater, patr-,* father. See **pəter-** in Appendix.] **—pat′ri·mo′ni·al** *adj.* **—pat′ri·mo′ni·al·ly** *adv.*

pa·tri·ot (pā′trē-ət, -ŏt′) *n.* One who loves, supports, and defends one's country. [French *patriote,* from Old French, compatriot, from Late Latin *patriōta,* from Greek *patriōtēs,* from *patrios,* of one's fathers, from *patēr, patr-,* father. See **pəter-** in Appendix.]

pa·tri·ot·ic (pā′trē-ŏt′ĭk) *adj.* Feeling, expressing, or inspired by love for one's country. **—pa′tri·ot′i·cal·ly** *adv.*

pa·tri·ot·ism (pā′trē-ə-tĭz′əm) *n.* Love of and devotion to one's country.

Pa·tri·ots' Day (pā′trē-əts, -ŏts′) *n.* The third Monday in April, a holiday in Maine and Massachusetts commemorating the battles of Lexington and Concord in 1775, which began the American Revolution.

pa·tris·tic (pə-trĭs′tĭk) also **pa·tris·ti·cal** (-tĭ-kəl) *adj.* Of or relating to the fathers of the early Christian church or their writings. **—pa·tris′ti·cal·ly** *adv.*

pa·tris·tics (pə-trĭs′tĭks) *n. (used with a sing. verb).* **1.** The study of the lives, writings, and doctrines of the Church fathers. **2.** The writings of the Church fathers.

pat·ro·cli·nous (păt′rə-klī′nəs) also **pat·ri·cli·nous** (-rĭ-) *adj.* Having inherited characteristics that more closely resemble the father's side than the mother's side. [PATR(I)– + Greek *klinein,* to lean; see **klei-** in Appendix + –OUS.]

Pa·tro·clus (pə-trō′kləs) *n.* *Greek Mythology.* A Greek warrior, attendant, and friend to Achilles, who was killed by Hector in the Trojan War.

pa·trol (pə-trōl′) *n.* **1.** The act of moving about an area especially by an authorized and trained person or group, for purposes of observation, inspection, or security. **2.** A person or group of persons who perform such an act. **3.a.** A military unit sent out on a reconnaissance or combat mission. **b.** One or more military vehicles, boats, ships, or aircraft assigned to guard or reconnoiter a given area. **4.** A division of a Boy Scout troop consisting of between six and eight boys. **—patrol** *v.* **-trolled, -trol·ling, -trols.** —*tr.* To engage in a patrol of. —*intr.* To engage in a patrol. [French *patrouille,* from *patrouiller,* to patrol, alteration of Old French *patouiller,* to paddle about in mud, patrol, probably from *pate,* paw. See PATOIS.] **—pa·trol′ler** *n.*

patrol car *n.* See **squad car.**

pa·trol·man (pə-trōl′mən) *n.* **1.** A policeman who patrols or polices an assigned area. **2.** One who patrols an assigned area.

patrol torpedo boat *n.* A PT boat.

patrol wagon *n.* An enclosed police truck used to convey prisoners.

pa·trol·wom·an (pə-trōl′wo͝om′ən) *n.* A policewoman who patrols or polices an assigned area.

pa·tron (pā′trən) *n.* **1.** One that supports, protects, or champions someone or something, such as an institutuion, an event, or a cause; a sponsor or benefactor: *a patron of the arts.* **2.** A customer, especially a regular customer. **3.** (*also* pä-trōn′). The owner or manager of an establishment, especially a restaurant or an inn of France or Spain. **4.a.** A noble or wealthy person in ancient Rome who granted favor and protection to someone in exchange for certain services. **b.** A slave owner in ancient Rome who freed a slave without relinquishing all legal claim to him. **5.** One who possesses the right to grant an ecclesiastical benefice to a member of the clergy. **6.** A patron saint. **7.** *Nautical.* The captain or master of a ship, especially a barge. [Middle English, from Old French, from Medieval Latin *patrōnus,* from Latin, from *pater, patr-,* father. See **pəter-** in Appendix.] **—pa′tron·al** (pā′trə-nəl) *adj.*

pa·tron·age (pā′trə-nĭj, păt′rə-) *n.* **1.** Support, encouragement, or championship, as of a person, an institution, an event, or a cause, from a patron. **2.** Support or encouragement proffered in a condescending manner: *It seems our little establishment has finally been deemed worthy of the bank's patronage.* **3.** The trade given to a commercial establishment by its customers: *Shopkeepers thanked Christmas shoppers for their patronage.* **4.** Customers or patrons considered as a group; clientele: *The grand old hotel has a loyal but demanding patronage.* **5.a.** The power to distribute or appoint people to governmental or political positions. **b.** The act of distributing or appointing people to such positions. **c.** The positions so distributed or filled. **6.** The right to grant an ecclesiastical benefice to a member of the clergy.

pa·tron·ess (pā′trə-nĭs) *n.* **1.** A woman who supports, protects, or champions someone or something, such as an institution, an event, or a cause; a sponsor or benefactor. **2.** A woman who possesses the right to grant an ecclesiastical benefice to a member of the clergy. **3.** A patron saint.

pa·tron·ize (pā′trə-nīz′, păt′rə-) *tr.v.* **-ized, -iz·ing, -iz·es. 1.** To act as a patron to; support or sponsor. **2.** To go to as a customer, especially on a regular basis. **3.** To treat in a condescending manner. **—pa′tron·i·za′tion** (-trə-nĭ-zā′shən) *n.* **—pa′tron·iz′ing·ly** *adv.*

patron saint *n.* A saint who is regarded as the intercessor and advocate in heaven of a nation, place, craft, activity, or person.

pat·ro·nym·ic (păt′rə-nĭm′ĭk) *adj.* Of, relating to, or derived from the name of one's father or a paternal ancestor. **—patronymic** *n.* A name so derived. [Late Latin *patrōnymicus,* from Greek *patrōnumikos,* from *patrōnumos,* named after one's father : *patēr, patr-,* father + *onuma,* name; see **nō-men-** in Appendix.] **—pat′ro·nym′i·cal·ly** *adv.*

pa·troon (pə-tro͞on′) *n.* A landholder in New Netherland who, under Dutch colonial rule, was granted proprietary and manorial rights to a large tract of land in exchange for bringing 50 new settlers to the colony. [Dutch, from French *patron,* patron, master, from Old French. See PATRON.]

pat·sy (păt′sē) *n., pl.* **-sies.** *Slang.* A person easily taken advantage of, cheated, blamed, or ridiculed. [Perhaps from Italian *pazzo,* fool, from Old Italian *paccio.*]

pat·ten (păt′n) *n.* Any one of various types of wooden-soled footwear, such as a sandal, shoe, or clog, worn to increase one's height or to keep one's feet out of the mud. [Middle English *patin,* from Old French, perhaps from *pate,* paw, hoof. See PATOIS.]

Pat·ten (păt′n), **Gilbert.** Pen name Burt L. Standish. 1866–1945. American writer who created the hero Frank Merriwell and wrote numerous children's adventure stories.

pat·ter¹ (păt′ər) *v.* **-tered, -ter·ing, -ters.** —*intr.* **1.** To make a quick succession of light, soft tapping sounds: *Rain pat-*

tered steadily against the glass. **2.** To move with quick, light, softly audible steps. —*tr.* To cause to patter. —**patter** *n.* A quick succession of light, soft tapping sounds: *the patter of rain on the rooftops.* [Frequentative of PAT[1].]

pat·ter[2] (păt′ər) *v.* **-tered, -ter·ing, -ters.** —*intr.* **1.** To speak or chatter glibly and rapidly. **2.** To mumble prayers in a mechanical manner. —*tr.* To utter in a glib, rapid, or mechanical manner. —**patter** *n.* **1.** The jargon of a particular group; cant. **2.** Glib, rapid speech, as of an auctioneer, a salesperson, or a comedian. **3.** Meaningless talk; chatter. [Middle English *patren,* from *paternoster,* paternoster (from the mechanical and rapid recitation of the prayer). See PATERNOSTER.] —**pat′ter·er** *n.*

pat·tern (păt′ərn) *n.* **1.a.** A model or an original used as an archetype. **b.** A person or thing considered worthy of imitation. **2.** A plan, diagram, or model to be followed in making things: *a dress pattern.* **3.** A representative sample; a specimen. See Synonyms at **ideal. 4.a.** An artistic or decorative design: *a paisley pattern.* See Synonyms at **figure. b.** A design of natural or accidental origin: *patterns of bird formations.* **5.** A consistent, characteristic form, style, or method, as: **a.** A composite of traits or features characteristic of an individual or a group: *one's pattern of behavior.* **b.** Form and style in an artistic work or body of artistic works. **6.a.** The configuration of gunshots upon a target that is used as an indication of skill in shooting. **b.** The distribution and spread, around a targeted region, of spent shrapnel, bomb fragments, or shot from a shotgun. **7.** Enough material to make a complete garment. **8.** A test pattern. **9.** The flight path of an aircraft about to land: *a flight pattern.* —**pattern** *v.* **-terned, -tern·ing, -terns.** —*tr.* **1.** To make, mold, or design by following a pattern: *We patterned this plan on the previous one. My daughter patterned her military career after her father's.* **2.** To cover or ornament with a design or pattern. —*intr.* To make a pattern. [Middle English *patron,* from Old French. See PATRON.]

pat·tern·ing (păt′ər-nĭng) *n.* **1.** Design, structure, or configuration of a form, style, or method. **2.** A method of physical therapy in which a rigid pattern of exercises is imposed to stimulate weak or paralyzed nerves and muscles to act on their own.

pat·tern·mak·er also **pattern maker** (păt′ərn-mā′kər) *n.* One who makes patterns, as for sewing, carpentry, or industrial machinery. —**pat′tern·mak′ing** *n.*

Pat·ter·son (păt′ər-sən). American family of journalists, including **Robert Wilson Patterson** (1850–1910), editor in chief of the *Chicago Tribune* (1899–1910). His son **Joseph Medill Patterson** (1879–1946) founded (1919) the *New York Daily News,* and his daughter **Eleanor Medill Patterson** (1884–1948) founded (1939) the *Washington Times-Herald.*

Patterson, Floyd. Born 1935. American prizefighter who held the world heavyweight title from 1956 to 1959 and 1960 to 1962.

Pat·ti (păt′ē, pä′tē), **Adelina.** 1843–1919. Spanish-born Italian operatic soprano. She was the most celebrated coloratura soprano of the 19th century.

Pat·ton (păt′n), **George Smith, Jr.** 1885–1945. American general. In World War II he led the Third Army's sweep across France and into Germany (1944–1945).

pat·ty (păt′ē) *n., pl.* **-ties. 1.** A small rounded, flattened cake of food, especially one made from ingredients that have been previously ground, chopped, or minced: *a hamburger patty; a peppermint patty.* **2.** A patty shell. **3.** A small pie; a pasty. [French *pâté,* pâté, from Old French *paste,* paste. See PASTY[2].]

pat·ty·pan squash (păt′ē-păn′) *n.* A variety of squash *(Cucurbita Pepo)* having a wheel-shaped fruit about three inches high and nine inches in diameter, ribbed white skin, and creamy white flesh.

patty shell *n.* A decorative, edible shell of baked puff pastry that is made to be filled with other food, such as creamed meat, seafood, vegetables, or fruit.

pat·u·lous (păch′ə-ləs) also **pat·u·lent** (-lənt) *adj. Botany.* Spreading or expanded: *patulous branches.* [From Latin *patulus,* from *patēre,* to be open. See **pete-** in Appendix.] —**pat′u·lous·ly** *adv.* —**pat′u·lous·ness** *n.*

pat·zer (pät′sər, păt′-) *n. Slang.* A poor or amateurish chess player. [Probably from German, bungler, from *patzen,* to bungle.]

Pau (pō). A city of southwest France in the foothills of the Pyrenees south of Bordeaux. It is a year-round tourist center noted for its scenery and winter sports. Population, 83,790.

PAU also **P.A.U.** *abbr.* Pan American Union.

pau·ci·ty (pô′sĭ-tē) *n.* **1.** Smallness of number; fewness. **2.** Scarcity; dearth: *a paucity of natural resources.* [Middle English *paucite,* from Old French, from Latin *paucitās,* from *paucus,* few. See **pau-** in Appendix.]

Paul (pôl), Saint. A.D. 5?–67? Apostle to the Gentiles whose life and teachings are set forth in his epistles and the Acts of the Apostles. —**Paul′ine** (-īn, -ēn) *adj.*

Paul I[1]. 1754–1801. Russian czar (1796–1801) who led the first Russian military campaigns against Napoleonic France (1798–1800). His tyrannical reign was ended the following year in a coup d'état.

Paul I[2]. 1901–1964. King of Greece (1947–1964). After taking refuge in South Africa during World War II he returned to Greece in 1946 and succeeded to the throne the following year.

Paul III. Originally Alessandro Farnese. 1468–1549. Pope (1534–1549) who initiated the Catholic Reformation and accepted (1545) the Jesuit order into the Church.

Paul VI. Originally Giovanni Battista Montini. 1897–1978. Pope (1963–1978) noted for easing regulations on fasting and interfaith marriages.

Paul, Alice. 1885–1977. American feminist who founded (1916) the separatist National Woman's Party and wrote (1923) the first equal rights amendment to be considered by the U.S. Congress.

Paul Bun·yan (pôl′ bŭn′yən) *n.* A giant lumberjack who performs superhuman acts in American folklore.

Pau·li (pou′lē), **Wolfgang.** 1900–1958. Austrian-born American physicist. He won a 1945 Nobel Prize for work on atomic fissions.

Pau·li exclusion principle (pô′lē, pou′-) *n.* See **exclusion principle.** [After Wolfgang PAULI.]

Pau·ling (pô′lĭng), **Linus Carl.** Born 1901. American chemist. He won a 1954 Nobel Prize for work on the nature of chemical bonding and the 1962 Nobel Peace Prize for his efforts toward disarmament.

Linus Pauling
Photographed in 1962

Paul·ist (pô′lĭst) *n.* A member of the Roman Catholic Missionary Society of Saint Paul the Apostle, founded in New York in 1858.

pau·low·ni·a (pô-lō′nē-ə) *n.* Any of several Chinese deciduous trees of the genus *Paulownia,* having large, heart-shaped, opposite leaves and pyramidal panicles of purplish or white flowers with a spotted interior. Also called *princess tree.* [New Latin, genus name, after Princess Anna *Paulovna* (1795–1865), Russian princess and queen of William II of the Netherlands.]

paunch (pônch, pänch) *n.* **1.** The belly, especially a protuding one; a potbelly. **2.** See **rumen.** [Middle English *paunche,* from Old French *panche,* from Latin *pantex.*]

paunch·y (pôn′chē, pän′-) *adj.* **-i·er, -i·est.** Having a potbelly. —**paunch′i·ness** *n.*

pau·per (pô′pər) *n.* **1.** One who is extremely poor. **2.** One living on or eligible for public charity. [From Latin, poor. See **pau-** in Appendix.]

pau·per·ism (pô′pə-rĭz′əm) *n.* The quality or state of being a pauper.

pau·per·ize (pô′pə-rīz′) *tr.v.* **-ized, -iz·ing, -iz·es.** To make a pauper of; impoverish. —**pau′per·i·za′tion** (-pər-ĭ-zā′shən) *n.*

pau·piette (pō-pyĕt′) *n.* A thin slice of meat or fish wrapped around a forcemeat or vegetable filling. [French, probably from obsolete *poulpe,* fleshy part, from Old French *polpe,* from Latin *pulpa.*]

Pau·sa·ni·as (pô-sā′nē-əs). fl. second century A.D. Greek geographer and historian who wrote *Periegesis of Greece,* a valuable source on the topography and history of ancient Greece.

pause (pôz) *intr.v.* **paused, paus·ing, paus·es. 1.** To cease or suspend an action temporarily. **2.** To linger; tarry: *paused for a while under the huge oak tree.* **3.** To hesitate: *He paused before replying.* —**pause** *n.* **1.** A temporary cessation. **2.** A delay or suspended reaction, as from uncertainty; a hesitation: *After a pause the audience broke into cheers.* **3.** A break, stop, or rest, often for a calculated purpose or effect: *After a dramatic pause, the lawyer finished her summation.* **4.a.** *Music.* A sign indicating that a note or rest is to be held. **b.** A break or rest in a line of poetry; a caesura. **5.** Reason for hesitation: *The immensity of the task gives one pause.* [From Middle English, pause, from Old French, from Latin *pausa,* from Greek *pausis,* from *pauein,* to stop.]

SYNONYMS: *pause, intermission, recess, respite, suspension.* The central meaning shared by these nouns is "a temporary stop, as in activity": *a short pause in the conversation; a concert with the usual 15-minute intermission; the legislature's summer recess; toiling without respite; a suspension of work.*

Luciano Pavarotti

pa·vane also **pa·van** (pə-vän′, -văn′) *n.* **1.** A slow, stately court dance of the 16th and 17th centuries. **2.** A piece of music for this dance. [French *pavane,* from Italian *pavana,* from feminine of *pavano,* of Padua, from dialectal *pavàn,* from *Pava,* dialectal variant of *Padova,* Padua.]

Pav·a·rot·ti (păv′ə-rŏt′ē, pä′vä-rôt′tē), **Luciano.** Born 1935. Italian-born tenor whose notable operatic roles include the Duke of Mantua in *Rigoletto* and Radames in *Aïda.*

pave (pāv) *tr.v.* **paved, pav·ing, paves. 1.** To cover with a pavement. **2.** To cover uniformly, as if with pavement. **3.** To be or compose the pavement of. —***idiom.* pave the way.** To make progress or development easier: *experiments that paved the way for future research.* [Middle English *paven,* from Old French *paver,* from Latin *pavīre,* to beat, tread down. See **peu-** in Appendix.] —**pav′er** *n.*

pa·vé (pă-vā′, păv′ā) *n.* A setting of precious stones placed together so closely that no metal shows: *diamonds in pavé.* [French, from past participle of *paver,* to pave, from Old French. See PAVE.] —**pa·vé** *adj.*

pave·ment (pāv′mənt) *n.* **1.a.** A hard, smooth surface, especially of a public area or thoroughfare, that will bear travel. **b.** The material with which such a surface is made. **2.** *Chiefly British.* A sidewalk.

Pa·vi·a (pə-vē′ə, pä-vē′ä). A city of northwest Italy south of Milan. Originally a Roman stronghold known as Ticinum, it served as capital of the Lombard kings before 1359 and later became a leading Italian city-state. Population, 85,056.

ă pat	oi boy
ā pay	ou out
âr care	ŏŏ took
ä father	ōō boot
ĕ pet	ŭ cut
ē be	ûr urge
ĭ pit	th thin
ī pie	*th* this
îr pier	hw which
ŏ pot	zh vision
ō toe	ə about, item
ô paw	♦ regionalism

Stress marks: ′ (primary); ′ (secondary), as in **dictionary** (dĭk′shə-nĕr′ē)

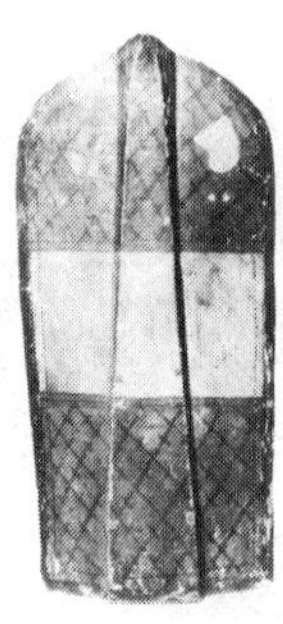

pavis
15th-century German

Anna Pavlova
In character for
The Dying Swan

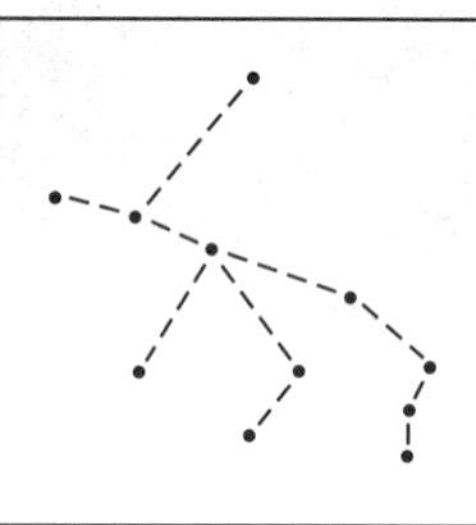

Pavo

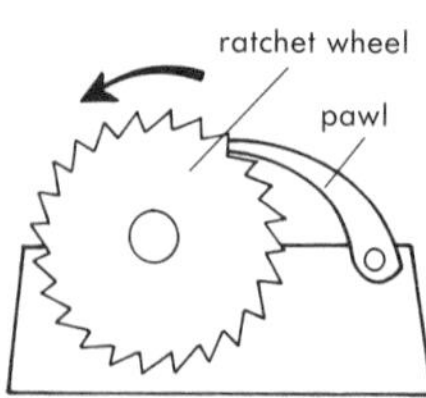

pawl

pawn²
Chess piece

pav·id (păv′ĭd) *adj.* Exhibiting or experiencing fear; timid. [Latin *pavidus*, from *pavēre*, to fear. See **peu-** in Appendix.]

pa·vil·ion (pə-vĭl′yən) *n.* **1.** An ornate tent. **2.a.** A light, sometimes ornamental roofed structure, used for amusement or shelter, as at parks or fairs: *a picnic pavilion.* **b.** A usually temporary structure erected at a fair or show for use by an exhibitor: *the French pavilion at the World's Fair.* **c.** A large structure housing sports or entertainment facilities; an arena. **3.** A structure or another building connected to a larger building; an annex. **4.** One of a group of related buildings forming a complex, as of a hospital. **5.** The lower surface of a brilliant-cut gem, slanting outward from the culet to the girdle. **—pavilion** *tr.v.* **-ioned, -ion·ing, -ions. 1.** To cover or furnish with or as if with a pavilion. **2.** To put in or as if in a pavilion. [Middle English *pavilon*, from Old French *pavillon*, from Latin *pāpiliō, pāpiliōn-*, butterfly, tent.]

pav·ing (pā′vĭng) *n.* **1.** The act or technique of laying pavement. **2.** A pavement. **3.** Material used for pavement.

pav·is also **pav·isse** (păv′ĭs) *n.* A medieval shield large enough to protect the whole body. [Middle English, from Old French *pavais*, from Old Italian *pavese*, from PAVIA.]

Pav·lo·dar (păv′lə-där′, pə-vlə-). A town of northeast Kazakhstan on the Irtysh River southeast of Omsk. It is a processing and shipping center in a rich agricultural region. Population, 315,000.

Pav·lov (păv′lôf′, -lôv′, păv′ləf), **Ivan Petrovich.** 1849–1936. Russian physiologist who is best known for discovering the conditioned response. He won a 1904 Nobel Prize for research on the nature of digestion. **—Pav·lo′vi·an** (păv-lō′vē-ən, -lô′-) *adj.*

Pav·lo·va (păv-lō′və, päv-, păv′lə-, päv′-), **Anna.** 1882–1931. Russian ballerina famous for her roles in *Swan Lake* and *Les Sylphides.*

Pavlovian conditioning *n.* Classical conditioning. [After Ivan Petrovich PAVLOV.]

Pa·vo (pā′vō) *n.* A constellation in the Southern Hemisphere near Apus and Indus. [Latin *pāvō*, peacock.]

pav·o·nine (păv′ə-nīn′) *adj.* **1.** Of or resembling a peacock. **2.** Resembling a peacock's tail in color, design, or iridescence. [Latin *pāvōnīnus*, from *pāvō*, peacock.]

paw (pô) *n.* **1.** The nailed or clawed foot of an animal, especially of a quadruped. **2.** *Informal.* A human hand, especially a large, clumsy one: *"Lennie dabbled his big paw in the water"* (John Steinbeck). **—paw** *v.* **pawed, paw·ing, paws.** *—tr.* **1.** To strike with the paw or paws. **2.** To strike or scrape with a beating motion: *The bull pawed the ground before charging.* **3.** To handle clumsily, rudely, or with too much familiarity. See Synonyms at **touch.** *—intr.* **1.** To scrape the ground with the forefeet: *The horse pawed restlessly.* **2.** To handle someone or something clumsily, rudely, or with too much familiarity: *Don't paw at everything you see.* [Middle English *pawe*, from Old French *powe.*] **—paw′er** *n.*

pawk·y (pô′ke) *adj.* **-i·er, -i·est.** *Chiefly British.* Shrewd and cunning, often in a humorous manner. [From English dialectal *pawk*, a trick.]

pawl (pôl) *n.* A hinged or pivoted device adapted to fit into a notch of a ratchet wheel to impart forward motion or prevent backward motion. [Probably from Dutch *pal*, from Latin *pālus*, stake. See **pag-** in Appendix.]

pawn¹ (pôn) *n.* **1.** Something given as security for a loan; a pledge or guaranty. **2.** The condition of being held as a pledge against the payment of a loan: *jewels in pawn.* **3.** A person serving as security; a hostage. **4.** The act of pawning. **—pawn** *tr.v.* **pawned, pawn·ing, pawns. 1.** To give or deposit (personal property) as security for the payment of money borrowed. **2.** To risk; hazard: *pawn one's honor.* [Middle English *paun*, from Old French *pan*, of Germanic origin.] **—pawn′a·ble** *adj.* **—pawn′age** *n.* **—pawn′er** (pô′nər), **paw′nor′** (-nôr′) *n.*

pawn² (pôn) *n.* **1.** *Abbr.* **P** *Games.* A chess piece of lowest value that may move forward one square at a time or two squares in the first move, capture other pieces only on a one-square diagonal forward move, and be promoted to any piece other than a king upon reaching the eighth rank. **2.** A person or an entity used to further the purposes of another: *an underdeveloped nation that was a pawn in international politics.* [Middle English, from Old French *pedon, paon*, from Medieval Latin *pedō, pedōn-*, foot soldier, from Late Latin, one who has wide feet, from Latin *pēs, ped-*, foot. See **ped-** in Appendix.]

pawn·bro·ker (pôn′brō′kər) *n.* One that lends money at interest in exchange for personal property deposited as security. **—pawn′bro′king** *n.*

Paw·nee (pô-nē′) *n., pl.* **Pawnee** or **-nees. 1.a.** A Native American people formerly inhabiting the Platte River valley in south-central Nebraska and northern Kansas, with a present-day population in north-central Oklahoma. The Pawnee comprised a confederation of four relatively independent tribes living in permanent villages. **b.** A member of this people. **2.** The Caddoan language of the Pawnee. [North American French *Pani*, of Illinois origin, ultimately of Siouan origin.]

pawn·shop (pôn′shŏp′) *n.* The shop of a pawnbroker.

pawn ticket *n.* A receipt for goods pawned.

paw·paw (pô′pô) *n.* Variant of **papaw.**

Paw·tuck·et (pô-tŭk′ĭt, pə-). A city of northeast Rhode Island, an industrial suburb of Providence. The first successful water-powered cotton mill in the United States was built here (1790–1793) by Samuel Slater. Population, 71,204.

pay¹ (pā) *v.* **paid** (pād), **pay·ing, pays.** *—tr.* **1.** To give money to in return for goods or services rendered: *pay the cashier.* **2.** To give (money) in exchange for goods or services: *paid three dollars for a hamburger; paid an hourly wage.* **3.** To discharge or settle (a debt or an obligation): *paying taxes; paid the bill.* **4.a.** To give recompense for; requite: *a kindness that cannot be paid back.* **b.** To give recompense to; reward or punish: *I'll pay him back for his insults.* **5.** To bear (a cost or penalty, for example) in recompense: *She paid the price for her unpopular opinions.* **6.** To yield as a return: *a savings plan that paid 12 percent interest.* **7.** To afford an advantage to; profit: *It paid us to be generous.* **8.** To give or bestow: *paying compliments; paying attention.* **9.** To make (a visit or call). **10.** *Past tense and past participle* **paid** or **payed** (pād) To let out (a line or cable) by slackening. *—intr.* **1.** To give money in exchange for goods or services. **2.** To discharge a debt or an obligation. **3.** To bear a cost or penalty in recompense: *You'll pay for this mischief!* **4.** To be profitable or worthwhile: *It doesn't pay to get angry.* **—pay** *adj.* **1.** Of, relating to, giving, or receiving payments. **2.** Requiring payment to use or operate: *a pay telephone.* **3.** Yielding valuable metal in mining: *a pay streak.* **—pay** *n.* **1.** The act of paying or state of being paid. **2.** Money given in return for work done; salary; wages. **3.a.** Recompense or reward: *Your thanks are pay enough.* **b.** Retribution or punishment. **4.** Paid employment: *the workers in our pay.* **5.** A person considered with regard to his or her credit or reliability in discharging debts. **—*phrasal verbs.* pay off. 1.** To pay the full amount on (a debt). **2.** To effect profit: *a bet that paid off poorly.* **3.** To get revenge for or on; requite. **4.** To pay the wages due to (an employee) upon discharge. **5.** *Informal.* To bribe. **6.** *Nautical.* To turn or cause to turn (a vessel) to leeward. **pay out. 1.** To give (money) out; spend. **2.** To let out (a line or rope) by slackening. **pay up.** To give over the full monetary amount demanded. **—*idioms.* pay (one's) dues.** To earn a given right or position through hard work, long-term experience, or suffering: *She paid her dues in small-town theaters before getting a part in a Broadway play.* **pay (one's) way.** To contribute one's own share; pay for oneself. **pay the piper.** To bear the consequences of something. **pay through the nose.** *Informal.* To pay excessively. [Middle English *paien*, from Old French *paiier*, from Late Latin, to appease, from Latin *pācāre*, to pacify, from *pāx, pāc-*, peace. See **pag-** in Appendix.]

WORD HISTORY: Given the unpeaceful feelings one often has in paying bills or income taxes, it is difficult to believe that the word *pay* ultimately derives from the Latin word *pāx*, "peace." However, it is not the peace of the one who pays that is involved in this development of meaning. From *pāx*, meaning "peace" and also "a settlement of hostilities," was derived the word *pācāre*, "to impose a settlement on peoples or territories." In Late Latin *pācāre* was extended in sense to mean "to appease." The Old French word *paiier* that developed from Latin *pācāre* came to have the specific application "to pacify or satisfy a creditor," a sense that came into Middle English along with the word *paien* (first recorded around the beginning of the 13th century), the ancestor of our word *pay*.

pay² (pā) *tr.v.* **payed** or **paid** (pād), **pay·ing, pays.** *Nautical.* To coat or cover (seams of a ship, for example) with waterproof material such as tar or asphalt. [Obsolete French *peier*, from Old French, from Latin *picāre*, from *pix, pic-*, pitch.]

pay·a·ble (pā′ə-bəl) *adj.* **1.** Requiring payment on a certain date; due. **2.** Requiring payment to a particular person or entity. **3.** Capable of producing profit: *a payable business venture.* **—payable** *n.* Money owed to a creditor. Often used in the plural: *tried to balance inventory, payables, and receivables.*

pay-as-you-go also **pay as you go** (pā′əz-yo͞o-gō′) *n.* The system or practice of paying debts as they are incurred. **—pay′-as-you-go′** *adj.*

pay·back (pā′băk′) *n.* **1.a.** The return gained from or paid on an investment: *"One problem with space ventures is that the up-front costs are enormous and the paybacks uncertain and far off at best"* (Eric Gelman). **b.** The return on an investment equal to the amount invested: *expect a payback within six years.* **2.** A benefit gained as the result of a previous action. **3.** The act or process of paying back.

pay cable *n.* Pay-TV that is received over a cable.

pay·check (pā′chĕk′) *n.* **1.** A check issued to an employee in payment of salary or wages. **2.** Salary or wages: *The new appropriations bill could mean a larger paycheck for state employees.*

pay·day (pā′dā′) *n.* The day on which employees' salaries or wages are paid.

pay dirt *n.* **1.** Earth, ore, or gravel that is profitable to mine. **2.** *Informal.* A useful or profitable discovery or venture.

PAYE or **P.A.Y.E.** *abbr.* **1.** Pay as you earn. **2.** Pay as you enter.

payed¹ (pād) *v.* A past tense and a past participle of **pay¹** (sense 10).

payed² (pād) *v.* *Nautical.* A past tense and a past participle of **pay².**

pay·ee (pā-ē′) *n.* One to whom money is paid.

pay equity *n.* Comparable worth.

pay·er (pā′ər) *n.* **1.** One that pays: *a prompt payer of bills.* **2.** One named responsible for paying a bill or note.

pay·load (pā′lōd′) *n.* **1.** The revenue-producing part of a cargo. **2. a.** The total weight of passengers and cargo that an aircraft carries or can carry. **b.** The total weight of the instruments, crew, and life-support systems that a spacecraft carries or can carry. **c.** The passengers, crew, instruments, or equipment carried by an aircraft, a spacecraft, or a rocket. **3.** The explosive charge carried in the warhead of a missile.

Pay·load·er (pā′lō′dər). A trademark used for an excavating machine with a large scoop in front for moving and lifting earth, rocks, and rubble.

pay·mas·ter (pā′măs′tər) *n.* A person in charge of paying wages and salaries.

pay·ment (pā′mənt) *n. Abbr.* **pmt., pt., payt. 1.** The act of paying or the state of being paid. **2.** An amount paid: *received a large payment.* **3.** One's due, reward, or punishment; requital.

pay·nim (pā′nĭm) *n. Archaic.* **1.** A non-Christian, especially a Moslem. **2.** A pagan or heathen. [Middle English *painim,* from Old French *paienime,* heathendom, from Late Latin *pāgānismus,* from *pāgānus,* pagan. See PAGAN.]

pay·off (pā′ôf′, -ŏf′) *n.* **1. a.** Full payment of a salary or wages. **b.** The time of such payment. **2.** *Informal.* **a.** A final settlement or reckoning. **b.** The climax of a narrative or sequence of events. **3.** Final retribution or revenge. **4.** *Informal.* A bribe.

pay·o·la (pā-ō′lə) *n.* **1.** Bribery, especially the bribing of disc jockeys to promote records. **2.** A bribe, especially one given to a disc jockey. [Probably PAY(OFF) + *(Victr)ola,* a phonograph.]

pay·out (pā′out′) *n.* **1.** The act or an instance of paying out. **2.** A percentage of corporate earnings that is paid as dividends to shareholders.

pay·roll also **pay roll** (pā′rōl′) *n. Abbr.* **PR 1.** A list of employees receiving wages or salaries, with the amounts due to each. **2.** The total sum of money to be paid out to employees at a given time.

pay station *n.* A coin-operated telephone for public use.

payt. *abbr.* Payment.

pay-TV (pā′tē-vē′) *n.* A system for receiving television broadcasts by making subscription payments, as by renting a device that unscrambles the broadcaster's scrambled signal. Also called *pay television.*

Paz (päz, päs), **Octavio.** Born 1914. Mexican writer whose essays, including *The Labyrinth of Solitude* (1950), and volumes of poetry, such as *Sun Stone* (1957), often explore the Mexican identity. He won the 1990 Nobel Prize for literature.

Pb The symbol for the element **lead**[2] (sense 1). [Latin *plumbum,* lead.]

P.B. *abbr.* **1.** Passbook. **2.** Prayer book.

PBS *abbr.* Public Broadcasting Service.

PBX also **P.B.X.** *abbr.* Private branch exchange.

PC *abbr. Computer Science.* Personal computer.

p.c. *abbr.* **1.** Percent. **2.** Post card. **3.** *Latin.* Post cibum (after meals).

P.C. *abbr.* **1.** Past Commander. **2.** Police constable. **3.** Post commander. **4.** Privy Council.

p/c or **P/C** *abbr.* **1.** Also **p.c.** Petty cash. **2.** Prices current.

PCB (pē′sē-bē′) *n.* Any of a family of industrial compounds produced by chlorination of biphenyl, noted primarily as an environmental pollutant that accumulates in animal tissue with resultant pathogenic and teratogenic effects. [P(OLY)C(HLORINATED) B(IPHENYL).]

PCP[1] (pē′sē-pē′) *n.* Phencyclidine. [From the chemical name *p(henyl)c(yclohexyl)p(iperidine).*]

PCP[2] *abbr.* **1.** Pneumocystis pneumonia. **2.** Progressive-Conservative Party.

pct. *abbr.* Percent.

Pd The symbol for the element **palladium**[1].

pd. *abbr.* Paid.

p.d. or **P.D.** *abbr.* Per diem.

P.D. *abbr.* **1.** Police Department. **2.** Postal district. **3.** Potential difference.

Pd.B. *abbr. Latin.* Pedagogiae Baccalaureus (Bachelor of Pedagogy).

Pd.D. *abbr. Latin.* Pedagogiae Doctor (Doctor of Pedagogy).

Pd.M. *abbr. Latin.* Pedagogiae Magister (Master of Pedagogy).

PDT or **P.D.T.** *abbr.* Pacific Daylight Time.

pe[1] (pā) *n.* The 17th letter of the Hebrew alphabet. See table at **alphabet.** [Hebrew *pē,* mouth, pe.]

pe[2] also **p.e.** *abbr.* Printer's error.

PE *abbr.* Prince Edward Island.

P.E. *abbr.* **1.** Physical Education. **2.** *Statistics.* Probable error. **3.** Professional Engineer.

pea (pē) *n.* **1.** A member of the pea family. **2.** A Eurasian climbing annual vine *(Pisum sativum)* cultivated in all temperate zones, having compound leaves with terminal leaflets modified into tendrils and globose, edible seeds enclosed in a green, elongated pod. **3.** The seed of this plant, used as a vegetable. **4.** Also **peas.** The unopened pods of this plant. **5.** Any of several plants of the genus *Lathyrus,* such as the sweet pea or the beach pea. [Back-formation from Middle English *pease* (mistaken for pl.), from Old English *pise, piose,* from Late Latin *pīsa,* variant of Latin *pīsum,* from Greek *pison.*]

pea bean *n.* The navy bean.

Pea·bod·y (pē′bŏd′ē, -bə-dē). A city of northeast Massachusetts west of Salem. Settled c. 1633 and later called South Danvers, it was renamed after George Peabody in 1868. Population, 45,976.

Peabody, Elizabeth Palmer. 1804–1894. American educator and writer who founded the first kindergarten in the United States (1860).

Peabody, George. 1795–1869. American merchant and philanthropist. He established numerous museums and libraries, including the Peabody Institute of Baltimore and the Peabody Museum at Harvard University.

pea·bod·y bird (pē′bŏd′ē, -bə-dē) *n.* The white-throated sparrow. [Probably imitative of its song.]

peace (pēs) *n.* **1.** The absence of war or other hostilities. **2.** An agreement or a treaty to end hostilities. **3.** Freedom from quarrels and disagreement; harmonious relations: *roommates living in peace with each other.* **4.** Public security and order: *was arrested for disturbing the peace.* **5.** Inner contentment; serenity: *peace of mind.* **—peace** *interj.* Used as a greeting or farewell, and as a request for silence. ***—idioms.* at peace. 1.** In a state of tranquillity; serene: *She is at peace with herself and her friends.* **2.** Free from strife: *Everyone wants to live in a world at peace.* **keep** (or **hold**) **one's peace.** To be silent. **keep the peace.** To maintain or observe law and order: *officers who were sworn to keep the peace.* [Middle English *pes,* from Old French *pais, pes,* from Latin *pāx, pāc-.* See **pag-** in Appendix.]

peace·a·ble (pē′sə-bəl) *adj.* **1.** Inclined or disposed to peace; promoting calm: *They met in a peaceable spirit.* **2.** Peaceful; undisturbed. **—peace′a·ble·ness** *n.* **—peace′a·bly** *adv.*

Peace Corps (pēs) *n.* A federal government organization, set up in 1961, that trains and sends American volunteers abroad to work with people of developing countries on projects for technological, agricultural, and educational improvement.

peace·ful (pēs′fəl) *adj.* **1.** Undisturbed by strife, turmoil, or disagreement; tranquil. See Synonyms at **calm. 2.** Inclined or disposed to peace; peaceable. **3.** Of or characteristic of a condition of peace. **—peace′ful·ly** *adv.* **—peace′ful·ness** *n.*

peace·keep·er (pēs′kē′pər) *n.* **1.** One that preserves or promotes peace: *the peacekeeper in the family.* **2.** A member of a military force engaging in peacekeeping activities, often under international sanction.

peace·keep·ing (pēs′kē′pĭng) *adj.* Of or relating to the preservation of peace, especially the supervision by international forces of a truce between hostile nations. **—peace′keep′ing** *n.*

peace·mak·er (pēs′mā′kər) *n.* One that makes peace, especially by settling disputes. **—peace′mak′ing** *adj. & n.*

peace·nik (pēs′nĭk) *n. Informal.* A political activist who publicly opposes war, a particular war, or the proliferation of weapons; a pacifist.

peace offering *n.* An offering made to an adversary in the interests of peace or reconciliation.

peace officer *n.* A law enforcement officer, such as a sheriff, who is responsible for maintaining civil peace.

peace pipe *n.* A calumet.

Peace River. A river, about 1,521 km (945 mi) long, rising in central British Columbia, Canada, and flowing east to Alberta then northeast to the Slave River near Lake Athabasca. It was long an important waterway for fur traders.

peace sign *n.* A hand sign made with the palm forward and the middle and index fingers forming a V, used to express a desire for peace.

peace·time (pēs′tīm′) *n.* A time free from war. **—peace′time′** *adj.*

peach[1] (pēch) *n.* **1. a.** A small Chinese tree *(Prunus persica)* widely cultivated throughout temperate regions, having pink flowers and edible fruit. **b.** The soft, juicy fruit of this tree, having yellow flesh, downy, red-tinted yellow skin, and a deeply sculptured stone containing a single seed. **2.** *Color.* A light moderate to strong yellowish pink to light orange. **3.** *Informal.* A particularly admirable or pleasing person or thing. [Middle English *peche,* from Old French, a peach, from Latin *persica,* peach tree, ultimately from *persicus,* Persian, from PERSIA.]

peach[2] (pēch) *v.* **peached, peach·ing, peach·es.** *—intr.* To inform on someone; turn informer: *"Middle-level bureaucrats cravenly peach on their bosses* [when] *one of them does something the tiniest bit illegal"* (National Observer). *—tr.* To inform against: *"He has peached me and all the others, to save his life"* (Daniel Defoe). [Middle English *pechen,* from *apechen,* to accuse (probably from Anglo-Norman **anpecher,* from Late Latin *impedicāre,* to entangle; see IMPEACH) and from *empechen,* to accuse; see IMPEACH.]

peach palm *n.* A densely spiny Amazonian palm *(Bactris gasipaes)* widely cultivated in the New World tropics as an ornamental and a food plant, having an edible heart and a highly nutritious, mealy fruit wall.

peach·y (pē′chē) *adj.* **-i·er, -i·est. 1.** Resembling a peach, especially in color or texture. **2.** *Informal.* Splendid; fine. **—peach′i·ness** *n.*

pea coat *n.* See **pea jacket.**

pea·cock (pē′kŏk′) *n.* **1. a.** A male peafowl, distinguished by its crested head, brilliant blue or green plumage, and long modified back feathers that are marked with iridescent eyelike spots and that can be spread in a fanlike form. **b.** A peafowl, either

pea
Pisum sativum

peach[1]
Prunus persica

peacock
Blue peacock
Pavo cristatus

ă pat	oi boy
ā pay	ou out
âr care	o͝o took
ä father	o͞o boot
ĕ pet	ŭ cut
ē be	ûr urge
ĭ pit	th thin
ī pie	*th* this
îr pier	hw which
ŏ pot	zh vision
ō toe	ə about, item
ô paw	♦ regionalism

Stress marks: ′ (primary); ′ (secondary), as in **dictionary** (dĭk′shə-nĕr′ē)

male or female. **2.** A vain person; a dandy. **—peacock** *intr.v.* **-cocked, -cock·ing, -cocks.** To strut about like a peacock; exhibit oneself vainly. [Middle English *pocock, pecok : po,* peacock (from Old English *pawa, pēa,* peafowl, from Latin *pāvō,* peacock) + Middle English *cok;* see COCK[1].] **—pea′cock′ish, pea′cock′y** *adj.*

Pea·cock (pē′kŏk′), **Thomas Love.** 1785–1866. British writer noted for his satirical novels, including *Headlong Hall* (1816) and *Nightmare Abbey* (1818).

peacock blue *n. Color.* A moderate to dark or strong greenish blue. **—pea′cock-blue′** (pē′kŏk-blo͞o′) *adj.*

peacock orchid *n.* See **acidanthera.**

pea family *n.* A large and widespread family of plants, the Leguminosae (Fabaceae), characterized by stipulate, usually compound leaves, often bilaterally symmetrical flowers, and legume fruits and including important food plants such as beans, peas, and soybeans.

pea·fowl (pē′foul′) *n., pl.* **peafowl** or **-fowls.** Either of two large pheasants, *Pavo cristatus* of India and Sri Lanka or *P. muticus* of southeast Asia. [PEA(COCK) + FOWL.]

peag also **peage** (pēg) *n.* See **wampum** (sense 1). [Short for WAMPUMPEAG.]

pea green *n. Color.* A moderate, strong, or brilliant yellow green. **—pea′-green′** (pē′grēn′) *adj.*

pea·hen (pē′hĕn′) *n.* A female peafowl. [Middle English *pohen, pehenne : po,* peacock; see PEACOCK + *hen,* female bird; see HEN.]

pea jacket *n.* A short, warm, double-breasted coat of heavy wool, worn especially by sailors. Also called *pea coat.* [Probably translation of Dutch *pijjekker, pij* : a kind of coarse cloth (from Middle Dutch *pīe*) + *jekker,* jacket.]

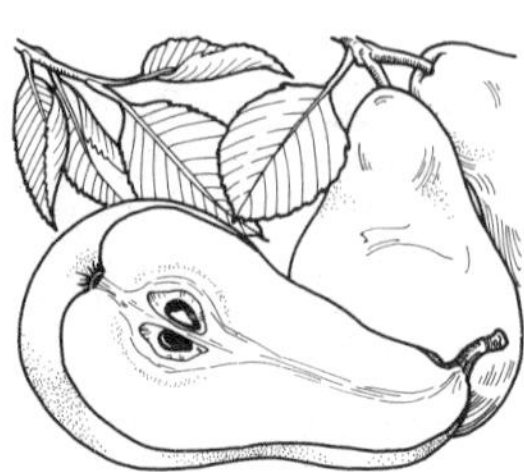
pear
Pyrus communis

peak[1] (pēk) *n. Abbr.* **pk. 1.** A tapering, projecting point; a pointed extremity: *the peak of a cap; the peak of a roof.* **2. a.** The pointed summit of a mountain. **b.** The mountain itself. **3. a.** The point of a beard. **b.** A widow's peak. **4.** The point of greatest development, value, or intensity: *a novel written at the peak of the writer's career.* See Synonyms at **summit. 5.** *Physics.* The highest value attained by a varying quantity: *a peak in current.* **6.** *Nautical.* **a.** The narrow portion of a ship's hull at the bow or stern. **b.** The upper after corner of a fore-and-aft sail. **c.** The outermost end of a gaff. **—peak** *v.* **peaked, peak·ing, peaks.** *—tr.* **1.** *Nautical.* To raise (a gaff) above the horizontal. **2.** To bring to a maximum of development, value, or intensity. *—intr.* **1.** To be formed into a peak or peaks: *Beat the egg whites until they peak.* **2.** To achieve a maximum of development, value, or intensity: *Sales tend to peak just before the holidays.* **—peak** *adj.* Approaching or constituting the maximum: *working at peak efficiency.* [Probably Middle English *pike, peke.* See PIKE[5].]

pearl[1]
Double strand of pearls

peak[2] (pēk) *intr.v.* **peaked, peak·ing, peaks.** To become sickly, emaciated, or pale. [Origin unknown.]

peaked[1] (pēkt, pē′kĭd) *adj.* Ending in a peak; pointed: *a peaked cap.*

peak·ed[2] (pē′kĭd) *adj.* Having a sickly appearance: *You're looking a little peaked today.*

peak flow meter *n.* A portable instrument that detects minute decreases in air flow, used by people with asthma to monitor small changes in breathing capacity.

peal (pēl) *n.* **1.** A ringing of a set of bells, especially a change or set of changes rung on bells. **2.** A set of bells tuned to each other; a chime. **3.** A loud burst of noise: *peals of laughter.* **—peal** *v.* **pealed, peal·ing, peals.** *—intr.* To sound in a peal; ring. *—tr.* To sound loudly and sonorously. [Middle English *pele,* a bell peal, especially as a summons to church, short for *apel,* appeal. See APPEAL.]

Peale (pēl). American family of painters, including **Charles Willson Peale** (1741–1827) and his brother **James Peale** (1749–1831). Four of Charles's children became painters: **Raphael Peale** (1774–1825), **Rembrandt Peale** (1778–1860), **Rubens Peale** (1784–1865), and **Titian Peale** (1799–1885). James's two daughters, **Anna Claypoole Peale** (1791–1878) and **Sarah Miriam Peale** (1800–1885), were also artists.

Peale, Norman Vincent. Born 1898. American cleric known for his popular self-help book *The Power of Positive Thinking* (1952).

pe·an (pē′ən) *n.* Variant of **paean.**

Robert E. Peary
c. 1896 photograph by George N. Rockwood (1833–1911)

♦**pea·nut** (pē′nŭt′) *n.* **1.** A prostrate southern Brazilian plant *(Arachis hypogaea)* widely cultivated in tropical and warm temperate regions, having yellow flowers on stalks that bend over so that the seed pods ripen underground. **2.** The edible, nutlike, oily seed of this plant, used for food and as a source of oil. Also called ♦*goober,* ♦*goober pea.* **3.** *Slang.* **a.** A person small in stature. **b.** A person who is regarded as being insignificant. **4. peanuts.** *Informal.* A very small amount of money; a trifling sum. **—peanut** *adj. Slang.* Having little or no importance; insignificant: *peanut politicians.*

peanut brittle *n.* A hard toffee containing peanuts.

peanut butter *n.* A paste made from ground roasted peanuts.

peanut oil *n.* The oil pressed from peanuts, used for cooking, in soaps, and as a solvent for pharmaceutical preparations.

pear (pâr) *n.* **1.** A widely cultivated tree *(Pyrus communis)* in the rose family, having glossy leaves, white flowers grouped in a corymb, and edible fruit. **2.** The fruit of this tree, spherical at the base and tapering toward the stalk. [Middle English *pere,* from Old English *peru,* a pear, ultimately from Vulgar Latin **pira,* from Latin, pl. of *pirum.*]

pearl[1] (pûrl) *n.* **1.** A smooth, lustrous, variously colored deposit, chiefly calcium carbonate, formed around a grain of sand or other foreign matter in the shells of certain mollusks and valued as a gem. **2.** Mother-of-pearl; nacre. **3.** One that is highly regarded for one's beauty or value. **4.** *Printing.* A type size measuring approximately five points. **5.** *Color.* A yellowish white. **—pearl** *v.* **pearled, pearl·ing, pearls.** *—tr.* **1.** To decorate or cover with or as if with pearls. **2.** To make into the shape or color of pearls. *—intr.* **1.** To dive or fish for pearls or pearl-bearing mollusks. **2.** To form beads resembling pearls. [Middle English *perle,* from Old French, from Latin **pernula,* diminutive of *perna,* ham, seashell (from the shape of the shell).]

pearl[2] (pûrl) *v. & n.* Variant of **purl[2].**

Pearl (pûrl). A city of central Mississippi, a suburb of Jackson. Population, 20,778.

pearl ash *n.* An impure form of potassium carbonate.

Pearl City. A village of Hawaii on Pearl Harbor in southern Oahu. It was severely damaged during the attack on Pearl Harbor (December 7, 1941). Population 33,000.

pearl danio *n.* A slender freshwater tropical fish *(Brachydanio albolineatus),* having silvery scales and popular as an aquarium fish.

pearl diver *n.* A person who dives in search of mollusks containing pearls.

pearl·er (pûr′lər) *n.* **1.** A pearl diver. **2.** A boat engaged in seeking or trading pearls.

pearl·es·cent (pûr-lĕs′ənt) *adj.* Having a luster resembling that of pearls.

pearl gray *n. Color.* A light gray, from yellowish to light bluish gray. **—pearl′-gray′** (pûrl′grā′) *adj.*

Pearl Harbor[1]. An inlet of the Pacific Ocean on the southern coast of Oahu, Hawaii, west of Honolulu. It became the site of a naval base after the United States annexed Hawaii in 1900. On Sunday, December 7, 1941, Japanese planes attacked the base without warning, destroying or severely damaging 19 naval vessels and some 200 aircraft. The United States entered World War II the following day.

Pearl Harbor[2] *n.* A swift surprise attack that usually causes great destruction: *"The Teheran takeover was the Pearl Harbor of the Foreign Service"* (Moorhead Kennedy). [After PEARL HARBOR[1].]

pearl·ite (pûr′līt′) *n.* **1.** A mixture of ferrite and cementite forming distinct layers or bands in slowly cooled carbon steels. **2.** Variant of **perlite.**

pearl millet *n.* A tropical Old World grass *(Pennisetum americanum)* having long, dense flowering panicles and whitish grains that are used as food. Also called *African millet.*

pearl oyster *n.* Any of several bivalve marine mollusks of the genus *Pinctada* and related genera of tropical waters, especially *P. margaritifera,* a major commercial source of pearls.

Pearl River. A river, about 780 km (485 mi) long, of central and southern Mississippi flowing southwest then south to the Gulf of Mexico. Its lower course forms part of the Mississippi-Louisiana border.

pearl·y (pûr′lē) *adj.* **-i·er, -i·est. 1.** Resembling pearls. **2.** Covered or decorated with pearls or mother-of-pearl.

pearly everlasting *n.* A rhizomatous plant *(Anaphalis margaritacea)* having woolly, gray-green foliage and long-lasting, whitish flower heads.

pearly nautilus *n.* See **nautilus** (sense 1).

pear psylla *n.* A small plant louse *(Psylla pyricola)* that is a destructive pest of pear trees, especially in the northeast United States.

Pear·son (pîr′sən), **Andrew Russell.** Known as "Drew." 1897–1969. American journalist famous for exposing political corruption in Washington, D.C. He was the coauthor of *Washington Merry-Go-Round* (1931).

Pearson, Lester Bowles. 1897–1972. Canadian politician who served as prime minister (1963–1968). He won the 1957 Nobel Peace Prize for his role in the negotiation of a solution to the Suez crisis (1956).

pear thrips *n.* A minute leaf-eating insect *(Taeniothrips inconsequens),* originally native to Europe, that is a common pest of pear, maple, almond, and other trees in the eastern United States.

Pea·ry (pîr′ē), **Robert Edwin.** 1856–1920. American naval officer and Arctic explorer who led the expedition credited with first reaching the North Pole (1909).

Peary Land. A peninsula of northern Greenland extending into the Arctic Ocean. Robert E. Peary first explored it on his 1891–1892 expedition.

peas·ant (pĕz′ənt) *n.* **1.** A member of the class constituted by small farmers and tenants, sharecroppers, and laborers on the land where they form the main labor force in agriculture. **2.** A country person; a rustic. **3.** An uncouth, crude, or ill-bred person; a boor. [Middle English *paissaunt,* from Old French *paisant,* from *pais,* country, from Late Latin *pāgēnsis,* inhabitant of a district, from Latin *pāgus,* district. See **pag-** in Appendix.]

peas·ant·ry (pĕz′ən-trē) *n.* **1.** The social class constituted by peasants. **2.** The condition, rank, or conduct of a peasant.

peas·cod (pēz′kŏd′) *n.* Variant of **peasecod.**

pease (pēz) *n., pl.* **pease** or **peas·en** (pē′zən). *Archaic.* A pea. [Middle English. See PEA.]

pease·cod also **peas·cod** (pēz′kŏd′) *n.* The pod of the pea.

peas·en (pē′zən) *n. Archaic.* A plural of **pease.**

pea·shoot·er (pē′sho͞o′tər) *n.* A toy consisting of a small tube through which dried peas or other pellets are blown.

pea soup *n.* **1.** A purée or soup made of cooked dried peas. **2.** *Slang.* Dense fog.

peat (pēt) *n.* Partially carbonized vegetable matter, usually mosses, found in bogs and used as fertilizer and fuel. [Middle English *pete,* perhaps from Medieval Latin *peta.*] **—peat′y** *adj.*

peat bog *n.* See **bog** (sense 1).

peat moss *n.* **1.** Any of various mosses of the genus *Sphagnum,* growing in very wet places. **2.** The partly carbonized remains of these plants, used as a mulch and plant food.

peau de soie (pō′ də-swä′) *n.* A soft silk fabric of satin weave having a dull finish. [French : *peau,* skin + *de,* of + *soie,* silk.]

pea·vey also **pea·vy** (pē′vē) *n., pl.* **-veys** also **-vies.** An implement consisting of a wooden shaft with a metal point and a hinged hook near the end, used to handle logs. [After Joseph *Peavey* (fl. 1875), American inventor.]

peb·ble (pĕb′əl) *n.* **1.** A small stone, especially one worn smooth by erosion. **2.a.** Clear, colorless quartz; rock crystal. **b.** A lens made of such quartz. **3.** *Geology.* A rock fragment between 4 and 64 millimeters (0.16 and 2.51 inches) in diameter, especially one that has been naturally rounded. **4.** An irregularly rough, grainy surface, as on leather or paper. **—pebble** *tr.v.* **-bled, -bling, -bles. 1.** To pave with pebbles. **2.** To impart an irregularly rough, grainy surface to (leather or paper). **3.** To pelt with pebbles. [Middle English *pobble, pibel, pebul,* from Old English *papol-,* as in *papolstān,* pebblestone.] **—peb′bly** *adj.*

pebble plant *n.* See **fig marigold.**

pec (pĕk) *n. Slang.* A pectoral muscle. Often used in the plural: *"Beneath those pecs there beats a heart"* (Leon Wieseltier).

pe·can (pĭ-kän′, -kăn′, pē′kăn) *n.* **1.** A deciduous tree *(Carya illinoinensis)* of the central and southern United States, having deeply furrowed bark, pinnately compound leaves, and edible nuts. **2.** The smooth, thin-shelled oval nut of this tree. [North American French *pacane,* from Illinois *pakani.*]

pec·ca·ble (pĕk′ə-bəl) *adj.* Liable to sin. [Medieval Latin *peccābilis,* from Latin *peccāre,* to sin. See **ped-** in Appendix.] **—pec′ca·bil′i·ty** *n.*

pec·ca·dil·lo (pĕk′ə-dĭl′ō) *n., pl.* **-loes** or **-los.** A small sin or fault. [Spanish *pecadillo,* diminutive of *pecado,* sin, and Italian *peccadiglio,* diminutive of *peccato,* sin, both from Latin *peccātum,* from neuter of *peccātus,* past participle of *peccāre,* to sin. See **ped-** in Appendix.]

pec·cant (pĕk′ənt) *adj.* **1.** Sinful; guilty. **2.** Violating a rule or an accepted practice; erring. [Latin *peccāns, peccant-,* present participle of *peccāre,* to sin. See **ped-** in Appendix.] **—pec′can·cy** *n.* **—pec′cant·ly** *adv.*

pec·ca·ry (pĕk′ə-rē) *n., pl.* **-ries.** Any of several piglike hoofed mammals of the family Tayassuidae, found in North, Central, and South America and having long, dark, dense bristles. [Ultimately from Carib *pakira.*]

pec·ca·vi (pĕ-kä′wē, -vē, -kā′vī′) *n., pl.* **-vis.** A confession of sin. [Latin *peccāvī,* I have sinned, first person sing. perfect tense of *peccāre,* to sin. See PECCABLE.]

Pe·cho·ra (pə-chôr′ə, -chōr′ə, pyĭ-). A river of northwest Russia flowing about 1,802 km (1,120 mi) northward into **Pechora Bay,** an arm of the Barents Sea.

peck[1] (pĕk) *v.* **pecked, peck·ing, pecks.** *—tr.* **1.** To strike with the beak or a pointed instrument. **2.** To make (a hole, for example) by striking repeatedly with the beak or a pointed instrument. **3.** To grasp and pick up with the beak: *The bird pecked insects from the log.* **4.** *Informal.* To kiss briefly and casually. *—intr.* **1.** To make strokes with the beak or a pointed instrument. **2.** To eat in small, sparing bits; nibble: *He pecked at his dinner.* **3.** To criticize repeatedly; carp. **—peck** *n.* **1.a.** A stroke or light blow with the beak or a pointed instrument. **b.** A mark or hole made by such a stroke. **2.** *Informal.* A light, quick kiss. [Middle English *pecken,* probably variant of *piken,* to peck (perhaps influenced by Middle Low German *pekken*). See PICK[1].]

peck[2] (pĕk) *n. Abbr.* **pk. 1.a.** A unit of dry volume or capacity in the U.S. Customary System equal to 8 quarts or approximately 537.6 cubic inches. **b.** A unit of dry volume or capacity in the British Imperial System equal to 8 quarts or approximately 554.8 cubic inches. See table at **measurement. 2.** A container holding or measuring a peck. **3.** *Informal.* A large quantity; a lot: *a peck of troubles.* [Middle English.]

Peck (pĕk), **Annie Smith.** 1850–1935. American explorer and mountain climber. Her most notable ascents include the volcano Popocatépetl in Mexico (1897) and Huascarán in the Peruvian Andes (1908).

Peck, Gregory. Born 1916. American actor who is best known for his portrayals of strong and courageous characters. Among his films are *Spellbound* (1950) and *To Kill a Mockingbird* (1962).

peck·er (pĕk′ər) *n.* **1.** One that pecks, as a bird's bill. **2.** *Chiefly British Slang.* Courage. **3.** *Vulgar Slang.* The penis.

♦**peck·er·wood** (pĕk′ər-wo͝od′) *n. Chiefly Southern U.S.* See **woodpecker.** See Regional Note at **everwhere.**

Peck·ham (pĕk′əm), **Rufus Wheeler.** 1838–1909. American jurist who served as an associate justice of the U.S. Supreme Court (1896–1909).

peck·ing order (pĕk′ĭng) *n.* **1.** A hierarchy among a group, as of people, classes, or nations: *"The astronauts had developed a pecking order that was military in its rigidity"* (Tom Wolfe). **2.** The social hierarchy in a flock of domestic fowl in which each bird pecks subordinate birds and submits to being pecked by dominant birds.

peck·ish (pĕk′ĭsh) *adj.* **1.** Ill-tempered; irritable. **2.** *Chiefly British.* Somewhat hungry. [From PECK[1], to eat.]

Peck's bad boy (pĕks) *n.* A person whose bad behavior embarrasses and annoys others. [After *Peck's Bad Boy and His Pa,* by George Wilbur Peck (1840–1916), American writer.]

Peck·sniff·i·an (pĕk-snĭf′ē-ən) *adj.* Hypocritically benevolent; sanctimonious. [After Seth *Pecksniff,* a character in *Martin Chuzzlewit,* a novel by Charles Dickens.]

pe·co·ri·no (pĕk′ə-rē′nō) *n., pl.* **-nos.** An Italian cheese, especially Romano, made from ewe's milk. [Italian, of ewes, pecorino, from *pecora,* ewe, sheep, from Latin, cattle, pl. of *pecus, pecor-.* See **peku-** in Appendix.]

Pe·cos (pā′kəs). A river of eastern New Mexico and western Texas flowing about 1,490 km (926 mi) south and southeast to the Rio Grande.

Pécs (pāch). A city of southwest Hungary near the Yugoslavian border south-southwest of Budapest. It was a Celtic settlement and later the capital of a Roman province. Population, 175,477.

pec·tase (pĕk′tās′, -tāz′) *n.* See **pectinesterase.** [PECT(IN) + -ASE.]

pec·tate (pĕk′tāt′) *n.* A salt or an ester of pectic acid. [PECT(IC ACID) + -ATE[2].]

pec·ten (pĕk′tən) *n., pl.* **-tens** or **-ti·nes** (-tə-nēz′). **1.** A body structure or an organ resembling a comb, as the ridged part of the eyelid of reptiles and birds. **2.** A scallop of the genus *Pecten.* [Latin *pecten, pectin-,* comb.]

pec·tic acid (pĕk′tĭk) *n.* A transparent gelatinous acid, $C_{17}H_{24}O_{16}$, insoluble in water, formed by the hydrolysis of certain esters of pectin. [French *pectique,* related to pectin, from Greek *pēktikos,* coagulating, from *pēktos,* coagulated. See PECTIN.]

pec·tin (pĕk′tĭn) *n.* Any of a group of water-soluble colloidal carbohydrates of high molecular weight found in ripe fruits, such as apples, plums, and grapefruit, and used to jell various foods, drugs, and cosmetics. [French *pectine,* from Greek *pēktos,* coagulated, from *pēgnunai,* to coagulate. See **pag-** in Appendix.] **—pec′tic, pec′tin·ous** *adj.*

pec·ti·nate (pĕk′tə-nāt′) also **pec·ti·nat·ed** (-nā′tĭd) *adj.* Having projections resembling the teeth of a comb; comblike. **—pec′ti·na′tion** *n.*

pec·ti·nes (pĕk′tə-nēz′) *n.* A plural of **pecten.**

pec·tin·es·ter·ase (pĕk′tə-nĕs′tə-rās′, -rāz′) *n.* An enzyme found in certain plants, bacteria, and fungi that catalyzes the hydrolysis of pectin to pectic acid and methanol. Also called *pectase.*

pec·to·ral (pĕk′tər-əl) *adj.* **1.** Relating to or situated in the breast or chest: *a pectoral muscle; the pectoral cavity.* **2.** Useful in relieving disorders of the chest or respiratory tract. **3.** Worn on the chest or breast: *a pectoral cross.* **—pectoral** *n.* **1.** A muscle or an organ of the chest. **2.** A pectoral fin. **3.** A medicine for relieving disorders of the chest or respiratory tract. **4.** An ornament or a decoration worn on the chest. [Probably Latin *pectorālis,* from *pectus, pector-,* breast. N., sense 4, Middle English, from Old French, from Latin *pectorāle,* breastplate, from neuter of *pectorālis,* pectoral.]

pectoral arch *n.* See **pectoral girdle.**

pectoral fin *n.* Either of the anterior pair of fins attached to the pectoral girdle of fishes, corresponding to the forelimbs of higher vertebrates.

pectoral girdle *n.* A bony or cartilaginous structure in vertebrates, attached to and supporting the forelimbs or anterior fins. Also called *pectoral arch.*

pectoral sandpiper *n.* A New World sandpiper *(Calidris melanotos)* with brownish streaks on the upper part of the breast. The male inflates its breast during courtship.

pec·u·late (pĕk′yə-lāt′) *tr. & intr.v.* **-lat·ed, -lat·ing, -lates.** To embezzle (funds) or engage in embezzlement. [Latin *peculārī, peculāt-,* from *pecūlium,* private property. See **peku-** in Appendix.] **—pec′u·la′tion** *n.* **—pec′u·la′tor** *n.*

pe·cu·liar (pĭ-kyo͞ol′yər) *adj.* **1.** Unusual or eccentric; odd. **2.** Distinct from all others. See Synonyms at **strange. 3.** Belonging distinctively or primarily to one person, group, or kind; special or unique: *rights peculiar to the rich; a species peculiar to this area.* **—peculiar** *n.* **1.** A privilege or property that is exclusively one's own. **2.** *Chiefly British.* A church or parish under the jurisdiction of a diocese different from that in which it lies. [Middle English *peculier,* personal, from Latin *pecūliāris,* from *pecūlium,* private property. See **peku-** in Appendix.] **—pe·cu′liar·ly** *adv.*

pe·cu·li·ar·i·ty (pĭ-kyo͞o′lē-ăr′ĭ-tē, -kyo͞ol-yăr′-) *n., pl.* **-ties. 1.** The quality or state of being peculiar. **2.** A notable or distinctive feature or characteristic. **3.** An eccentricity; an idiosyncrasy.

pe·cu·ni·ar·y (pĭ-kyo͞o′nē-ĕr′ē) *adj.* **1.** Of or relating to money: *a pecuniary loss; pecuniary motives.* See Synonyms at **financial. 2.** Requiring payment of money: *a pecuniary offense.*

peavey

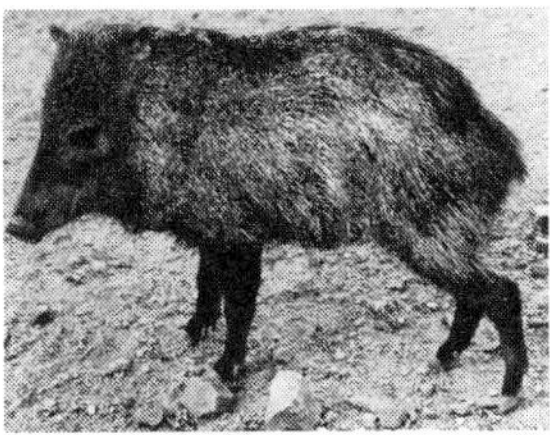

peccary
Collared peccary
Tayassu tajacu

pectoral

ă pat	oi boy
ā pay	ou out
âr care	o͝o took
ä father	o͞o boot
ĕ pet	ŭ cut
ē be	ûr urge
ĭ pit	th thin
ī pie	*th* this
îr pier	hw which
ŏ pot	zh vision
ō toe	ə about, item
ô paw	♦ regionalism

Stress marks: ′ (primary); ′ (secondary), as in **dictionary** (dĭk′shə-nĕr′ē)

[Latin *pecūniārius*, from *pecūnia*, property, wealth. See **peku-** in Appendix.]

ped–¹ *pref.* Variant of **pedo–¹**.

ped–² *pref.* Variant of **pedo–²**.

–ped or **–pede** *suff.* Foot: *maxilliped.* [From Latin *pēs, ped-*, foot. See **ped-** in Appendix.]

ped·a·gog·ic (pĕd′ə-gŏj′ĭk, -gō′jĭk) also **ped·a·gog·i·cal** (-gŏj′ĭ-kəl, -gō′jĭ-) *adj.* **1.** Of, relating to, or characteristic of pedagogy. **2.** Characterized by pedantic formality: *a haughty, pedagogic manner.* **—ped′a·gog′i·cal·ly** *adv.*

ped·a·gog·ics (pĕd′ə-gŏj′ĭks, -gō′jĭks) *n.* *(used with a sing. verb).* The art of teaching; pedagogy.

ped·a·gogue (pĕd′ə-gŏg′, -gôg′) *n.* **1.** A schoolteacher; an educator. **2.** One who instructs in a pedantic or dogmatic manner. [Middle English *pedagoge*, from Old French, from Latin *paedagōgus*, slave who supervised children, including taking them to and from school, from Greek *paidagōgos* : *paido-*, boy; see PEDO–¹ + *agōgos*, leader (from *agein*, to lead; see **ag-** in Appendix).] **—ped′a·gogu′ish** *adj.*

ped·a·go·gy (pĕd′ə-gō′jē, -gŏj′ē) *n.* **1.** The art or profession of teaching. **2.** Preparatory training or instruction. [French *pédagogie*, from Old French, from Greek *paidagōgia*, from *paidagōgos*, slave who took children to and from school. See PEDAGOGUE.]

ped·al (pĕd′l) *n.* **1.a.** A foot-operated lever used for actuating or controlling a mechanism, as in a loom, a sewing machine, a piano, or an organ. **b.** A similar foot-operated part attached to a crank and used for powering various devices, such as a bicycle. **2.** *Music.* **a.** A pedal point. **b.** A pedal keyboard. **—pedal** *adj.* **1.** Of or relating to a pedal. **2.** (*also* pēd′l). Of or relating to a foot or footlike part: *the pedal extremities.* **—pedal** *v.* **-aled, -al·ing, -als** or **-alled, -al·ling, -als.** —*intr.* **1.** To use or operate a pedal or pedals. **2.** To ride a bicycle. —*tr.* To operate the pedals of. [French *pédale*, from Italian *pedale*, from Latin *pedālis*, one foot long, from *pēs, ped-*, foot. See **ped-** in Appendix.]

ped·al·er also **ped·al·ler** (pĕd′l-ər) *n.* One who rides a pedal-driven vehicle, such as a bicycle.

pe·dal·fer (pĭ-dăl′fər) *n.* Soil rich in alumina and iron and deficient in carbonates, found in and characteristic of humid regions. [PED(O)–¹ + AL(UMINUM) + Latin *ferrum*, iron.]

pedal keyboard *n.* *Music.* A keyboard of pedals in an instrument such as a pipe organ.

ped·al·ler (pĕd′l-ər) *n.* Variant of **pedaler.**

pedal piano *n.* *Music.* A piano with a pedal keyboard.

pedal point *n.* *Music.* A note, usually in the bass and on the tonic or the dominant, sustained through harmonic changes in the other parts. Also called *organ point.* [POINT, musical note.]

pedal pushers *pl.n.* Calf-length slacks worn by women and girls. [From their originally being worn by bicyclists.]

pedal steel *n.* *Music.* An electronically amplified guitar mounted on legs, with up to ten strings whose pitch can be altered by sliding a steel bar across them or by depressing pedals attached to them. Also called *pedal steel guitar.*

ped·ant (pĕd′nt) *n.* **1.** One who pays undue attention to book learning and formal rules. **2.** One who exhibits one's learning or scholarship ostentatiously. **3.** *Obsolete.* A schoolmaster. [French *pédant* or Italian *pedante* (French, from Italian), possibly from Vulgar Latin **paedēns, *paedent-*, present participle of **paedere*, to instruct, probably from Greek *paiduein*, from *pais, paid-*, child. See PEDO–².]

pe·dan·tic (pə-dăn′tĭk) *adj.* Characterized by a narrow, often ostentatious concern for book learning and formal rules: *a pedantic attention to details.* **—pe·dan′ti·cal·ly** *adv.*

SYNONYMS: *pedantic, academic, bookish, donnish, scholastic.* The central meaning shared by these adjectives is "marked by a narrow, often tiresome focus on or display of learning and especially its trivial aspects": *a pedantic style of writing; an academic insistence on precision; a bookish vocabulary; donnish refinement of speech; scholastic and excessively subtle reasoning.*

pedicab

ped·ant·ry (pĕd′n-trē) *n.*, *pl.* **-ries.** **1.** Pedantic attention to detail or rules. **2.** An instance of pedantic behavior. **3.** The habit of mind or manner characteristic of a pedant.

ped·ate (pĕd′āt′) *adj.* **1.** Resembling or functioning as a foot: *pedate appendages.* **2.** *Zoology.* Having feet: *pedate larvae.* **3.** *Botany.* Having palmately divided lobes with the lateral lobes cleft or divided: *a pedate leaf.* [Latin *pedātus*, past participle of *pedāre*, to furnish with feet, from *pēs, ped-*, foot. See **ped-** in Appendix.]

ped·dle (pĕd′l) *v.* **-dled, -dling, -dles.** —*tr.* **1.a.** To travel about selling (wares): *peddling goods from door to door.* **b.** To engage in the illicit sale of (narcotics). **2.** *Informal.* To seek to disseminate; give out: *peddling lies.* —*intr.* **1.** To travel about selling wares. **2.** To occupy oneself with trifles. [Back-formation from PEDDLER. V., intr., sense 2, probably inluenced by PIDDLE.]

ped·dler (pĕd′lər) *n.* One who travels about selling wares for a living; a hawker. [Middle English *pedlere*, probably alteration of *peddere*, from Medieval Latin *pedārius*, crozier bearer, from Latin *pēs, ped-*, foot. See PEDI–.]

–pede *suff.* Variant of **–ped.**

ped·er·ast (pĕd′ə-răst′) *n.* A man who has a sexual relationship with a boy. [Greek *paiderastēs* : *pais, paid-*, child; see PEDO–² + *erastēs*, lover (from *erasthai*, to love).] **—ped′er·as′ty** *n.*

pe·des (pĕd′ās′) *n.* Plural of **pes.**

ped·es·tal (pĕd′ĭ-stəl) *n.* **1.** An architectural support or base, as for a column or statue. **2.** A support or foundation. **3.** A position of high regard or adoration. **—pedestal** *tr.v.* **-taled, -tal·ing, -tals** or **-talled, -tal·ling, -tals.** To place on or provide with a pedestal. [Obsolete French *pedestal*, from Italian *piedestallo* : *piede*, foot (from Latin *pēs*; see PEDI–) + *di*, of (from Latin *dē*; see DE–) + *stallo*, stall (of Germanic origin; see **stel-** in Appendix).]

pe·des·tri·an (pə-dĕs′trē-ən) *n.* A person traveling on foot; a walker. **—pedestrian** *adj.* **1.** Of, relating to, or made for pedestrians: *a pedestrian bridge.* **2.** Going or performed on foot: *a pedestrian journey.* **3.** Undistinguished; ordinary: *pedestrian prose.* See Synonyms at **dull.** [From Latin *pedester, pedestr-*, going on foot, from *pedes*, a pedestrian, from *pēs, ped-*, foot. See **ped-** in Appendix.] **—pe·des′tri·an·ism** *n.*

pe·des·tri·an·ize (pĭ-dĕs′trē-ə-nīz′) *tr.v.* **-ized, -iz·ing, -iz·es.** To convert (a street) into a mall or pedestrian walkway. **—pe·des′tri·an·i·za′tion** (-ə-nĭ-zā′shən) *n.*

pedi– *pref.* Foot: *pediform.* [Latin, from *pēs, ped-*, foot. See **ped-** in Appendix.]

pe·di·a·tri·cian (pē′dē-ə-trĭsh′ən) also **pe·di·at·rist** (-ăt′rĭst) *n.* A physician who specializes in pediatrics.

pe·di·at·rics (pē′dē-ăt′rĭks) *n.* *(used with a sing. verb).* The branch of medicine that deals with the care of infants and children and the treatment of their diseases. **—pe′di·at′ric** *adj.*

pe·di·at·rist (pē′dē-ăt′rĭst) *n.* Variant of **pediatrician.**

ped·i·cab (pĕd′ĭ-kăb′) *n.* A small three-wheeled vehicle having a seat, pedals, and handlebars in front for the operator and a usually hooded cab in back for passengers.

ped·i·cel (pĕd′ĭ-səl, -sĕl′) *n.* **1.** *Biology.* A small stalk, part, or organ, especially one serving as a support. **2.** *Botany.* **a.** A stalk bearing a single flower in an inflorescence. **b.** A support for a fern sporangium or moss capsule. Also called *pedicle.* [New Latin *pedicellus*, diminutive of Latin *pediculus*, diminutive of *pēs, ped-*, foot. See **ped-** in Appendix.] **—ped′i·cel′lar** (-sĕl′ər) *adj.*

ped·i·cel·late (pĕd′ĭ-sĕl′ĭt, -āt′) *adj.* *Biology.* Having or supported by a pedicel.

ped·i·cle (pĕd′ĭ-kəl) *n.* **1.** See **pedicel.** **2.** A slender, footlike or stemlike part, as at the base of a tumor. [Latin *pediculus*, diminutive of *pēs, ped-*, foot. See PEDICEL.]

pe·dic·u·lar (pə-dĭk′yə-lər) *adj.* Of, relating to, or caused by lice. [Latin *pēdiculāris*, from *pēdiculus*, diminutive of *pēdis*, louse. See **pezd-** in Appendix.]

pe·dic·u·late (pə-dĭk′yə-lĭt, -lāt′) *adj.* Of, relating to, or being the marine teleost fishes of the order Pediculati, characterized by pectoral fins extending from an armlike process and a dorsal fin ray that serves as a lure for prey. **—pediculate** *n.* A pediculate fish. [From New Latin *Pediculātī*, order name, from Latin *pediculus*, diminutive of *pēs, ped-*, foot. See PEDI–.]

pe·dic·u·lo·sis (pə-dĭk′yə-lō′sĭs) *n.* Infestation with lice. [Latin *pēdiculus*, diminutive of *pēdis*, louse; see PEDICULAR + –OSIS.] **—pe·dic′u·lous** (-ləs) *adj.*

ped·i·cure (pĕd′ĭ-kyo͝or′) *n.* **1.a.** Cosmetic care of the feet and toenails. **b.** A cosmetic treatment of the feet and toenails. **2.** A podiatrist. [French *pédicure* : Latin *pēs, ped-*, foot; see PEDI– + Latin *cūra*, care; see CURE.] **—ped′i·cure′** *v.* **—ped′i·cur′ist** *n.*

ped·i·form (pĕd′ə-fôrm′) *adj.* Shaped like a foot.

ped·i·gree (pĕd′ĭ-grē′) *n.* **1.a.** A line of ancestors; a lineage. **b.** A list of ancestors; a family tree. **2.** A chart of an individual's ancestors used in human genetics to analyze Mendelian inheritance of certain traits, especially of familial diseases. **3.** A list of the ancestors of a purebred animal. [Middle English *pedegru*, from Anglo-Norman *pe de grue* : *pe*, foot (from Latin *pēs*; see PEDI–) + *de*, of (from Latin *dē*; see DE–) + *grue*, crane (from the resemblance of a crane's foot to the lines of succession on a genealogical chart) (from Vulgar Latin **grūa*, from Latin *grūs, gru-*; see **gera-²** in Appendix).] **—ped′i·greed′** *adj.*

ped·i·ment (pĕd′ə-mənt) *n.* **1.a.** A wide, low-pitched gable surmounting the façade of a building in the Grecian style. **b.** A triangular element, similar to or derivative of a Grecian pediment, used widely in architecture and decoration. **2.** *Geology.* A broad, gently sloping rock surface at the base of a steeper slope, often covered with alluvium, formed primarily by erosion. [Alteration (influenced by Latin *pēs, ped-*, foot see PEDI–) of earlier *perement*, probably alteration of PYRAMID.] **—ped′i·men′tal** (-mĕn′tl) *adj.* **—ped′i·ment′ed** *adj.*

ped·i·palp (pĕd′ə-pălp′) *n.* One of the second pair of appendages near the mouth of a spider or other arachnid that are modified for various reproductive, predatory, or sensory functions.

ped·lar (pĕd′lər) *n.* *Chiefly British.* Variant of **peddler.**

pedo–¹ or **ped–** *pref.* Soil: *pedocal.* [From Greek *pedon*, soil, earth. See **ped-** in Appendix.]

pedo–² or **ped–** or **paed–** or **paedo–** *pref.* Child; children: *pedodontics.* [Greek *paido-*, from *pais, paid-*, child. See **pau-** in Appendix.]

ped·o·cal (pĕd′ə-kăl′) *n.* A soil of semiarid and arid regions that is rich in calcium carbonate and lime. [PEDO–¹ + CAL(CIUM).] **—ped′o·cal′ic** *adj.*

pe·do·don·tia (pē′də-dŏn′shə) *n.* Pedodontics.

pe·do·don·tics (pē′də-dŏn′tĭks) *n.* *(used with a sing. verb).* The branch of dentistry that deals with the care and treatment of children's teeth. —**pe′do·don′tist** (-dŏn′tĭst) *n.*

ped·o·gen·e·sis[1] (pĕd′ə-jĕn′ĭ-sĭs) *n.* The process of soil formation.

pe·do·gen·e·sis[2] (pē′dō-jĕn′ĭ-sĭs) *n.* Variant of **paedogenesis.**

pe·dol·o·gy[1] (pē-dŏl′ə-jē) *n.* The study of the physical and mental development and characteristics of children. —**pe′do·log′ic** (-də-lŏj′ĭk), **pe′do·log′i·cal** (-ĭ-kəl) *adj.* —**pe′do·log′i·cal·ly** *adv.* —**pe·dol′o·gist** *n.*

pe·dol·o·gy[2] (pĭ-dŏl′ə-jē, pĕ-) *n.* The scientific study of soils, including their origins, characteristics, and uses. —**ped′o·log′ic** (pĕd′l-ŏj′ĭk), **ped′o·log′i·cal** (-ĭ-kəl) *adj.* —**ped′o·log′i·cal·ly** *adv.* —**pe·dol′o·gist** *n.*

pe·dom·e·ter (pĭ-dŏm′ĭ-tər) *n.* An instrument that gauges the approximate distance traveled on foot by registering the number of steps taken.

ped·o·morph (pĕd′ə-môrf′, pē′də-) *n.* Variant of **paedomorph.**

pe·do·mor·phism (pĕd′ə-môr′fĭz′əm, pē′də-) *n.* Variant of **paedomorphism.**

ped·o·mor·pho·sis (pĕd′ə-môr′fə-sĭs, pē′də-) *n.* Variant of **paedomorphosis.**

ped·o·phile (pĕd′ə-fīl′, pē′də-) *n.* An adult who is sexually attracted to a child or children. —**ped′o·phil′ic** (-fĭl′ĭk) *adj.*

ped·o·phil·i·a (pĕd′ə-fĭl′ē-ə, pē′də-) *n.* Sexual attraction felt by an adult toward a child or children. —**ped′o·phil′i·ac** (-ăk) *adj. & n.*

Pe·dro I (pā′drō, pĕ′dro͞o). 1798–1834. Brazilian political leader who declared Brazil's independence from Portugal in 1822 and served as the country's first emperor from 1822 until 1831, when he abdicated and fled to Europe.

Pedro II. 1825–1891. Brazilian emperor (1831–1889) who assumed the throne after the abdication of his father, Pedro I. His later reign was marked by the abolition of slavery.

pe·dun·cle (pĭ-dŭng′kəl, pē′dŭng′kəl) *n.* **1.** *Botany.* The stalk of an inflorescence or a stalk bearing a solitary flower in a one-flowered inflorescence. **2.** *Zoology.* A stalklike structure in invertebrate animals, usually serving as an attachment for a larger part or structure. **3.** *Anatomy.* A stalklike bundle of nerve fibers connecting different parts of the brain. **4.** *Medicine.* The stalklike base to which a polyp or tumor is attached. [New Latin *pedunculus,* diminutive of Latin *pēs, ped-,* foot. See **ped-** in Appendix.] —**pe·dun′cu·lar** (pĭ-dŭng′kyə-lər) *adj.*

pe·dun·cu·late (pĭ-dŭng′kyə-lĭt, -lāt′) also **pe·dun·cu·lat·ed** (-lā′tĭd) *adj.* Having or supported on a peduncle.

pee[1] (pē) *n.* The letter *p.*

pee[2] (pē) *Slang. intr.v.* **peed, pee·ing, pees.** To urinate. —**pee** *n.* **1.** Urine. **2.** An act of urination. [From the first letter of PISS.]

Pee Dee (pē′ dē′) also **Great Pee Dee** (grāt). A river, about 375 km (233 mi) long, of south-central North Carolina and northeast South Carolina.

peek (pēk) *intr.v.* **peeked, peek·ing, peeks. 1.** To glance quickly. **2.** To look or peer furtively, as from a place of concealment. **3.** To be only partially visible, as if peering or emerging from hiding: *Tiny crocuses peeked through the snow in March.* —**peek** *n.* A brief or furtive look. [Middle English *piken,* perhaps alteration of Middle Dutch *kieken,* variant of *kīken.*]

peek·a·boo (pēk′ə-bo͞o′) *n.* A game for amusing a small child, in which one covers one's face or hides and then returns to view saying "Peekaboo!" —**peekaboo** *adj.* **1.** Decorated with embroidered holes or eyelets. **2.** Made of a sheer or transparent fabric. [PEEK + BOO[1].]

Peeks·kill (pēk′skĭl′). A city of southeast New York on the Hudson River north of White Plains. Strategically important in the American Revolution, it was burned by the British in 1777. Population, 18,236.

peel[1] (pēl) *n.* The skin or rind of certain fruits and vegetables. —**peel** *v.* **peeled, peel·ing, peels.** —*tr.* **1.** To strip or cut away the skin, rind, or bark from; pare. **2.** To strip away; pull off: *peeled the label from the jar.* —*intr.* **1.** To lose or shed skin, bark, or other covering. **2.** To come off in thin strips or pieces, as bark, skin, or paint: *Her sunburned skin began to peel.* **3.** *Slang.* To remove one's clothes; undress. —***phrasal verb.*** **peel off. 1.** To leave flight formation in order to land or make a dive. Used of an aircraft. **2.** To leave or depart. [From Middle English *pilen, pelen,* to peel, from Old French *peler,* and Old English *pilian* (both from Latin *pilāre,* to deprive of hair, from *pilus,* hair) and from Old French *pillier,* to tug, pull, plunder (from Latin *pilleum,* felt cap).]

peel[2] (pēl) *n.* **1.** A long-handled, shovellike tool used by bakers to move bread or pastries into and out of an oven. **2.** *Printing.* A T-shaped pole used for hanging up freshly printed sheets of paper to dry. [Middle English, from Old French *pele,* from Latin *pāla,* spade, peel. See **pag-** in Appendix.]

peel[3] (pēl) *n.* A fortified house or tower of a kind constructed in the borderland of Scotland and England in the 16th century. [Middle English *pel,* stake, small castle, from Anglo-Norman, stockade, variant of Old French, stake, from Latin *pālus.* See **pag-** in Appendix.]

Peel (pēl), Sir **Robert.** 1788–1850. British politician. As home secretary (1822–1827 and 1828–1830) he established the London police force (1829) and helped pass the Catholic Emancipation Act (1829). He later served as prime minister (1834–1835 and 1841–1846).

peel·a·ble (pēl′ə-bəl) *adj.* **1.** Having a peel or rind that can be peeled off: *peelable fruits and vegetables.* **2.** That can be removed and used again: *peelable address labels.*

peel·er[1] (pē′lər) *n.* **1.** One that peels, especially a kitchen implement for peeling the rinds or skins from fruits or vegetables. **2.** *Slang.* A stripteaser.

peel·er[2] (pē′lər) *n.* *Chiefly British.* A police officer. [After Sir Robert PEEL.]

peel·ing (pē′lĭng) *n.* A piece or strip, as of skin or vegetable rind, that has been peeled off.

Peel River. A river, about 644 km (400 mi) long, of northern Yukon Territory and western Northwest Territories, Canada, flowing east and north to the Mackenzie River.

peen (pēn) *n.* The end of a hammerhead opposite the flat striking surface, often wedge-shaped or ball-shaped and used for chipping, indenting, and metalworking. —**peen** *tr.v.* **peened, peen·ing, peens.** To hammer, bend, or shape with a peen. [Probably of Scandinavian origin.]

Pee·ne·mün·de (pā′nə-mo͝on′də, -mün′-). A village of northeast Germany on an offshore island in the Baltic Sea. It was a center for the development of guided missiles, especially the V-1 and V-2, prior to and during World War II (1937–1945).

peep[1] (pēp) *intr.v.* **peeped, peep·ing, peeps. 1.** To utter short, soft, high-pitched sounds, like those of a baby bird; cheep. **2.** To speak in a hesitant, thin, high-pitched voice. —**peep** *n.* **1.** A short, soft, high-pitched sound or utterance, like that of a baby bird. **2.** A slight sound or utterance: *I don't want to hear a peep out of you.* **3.** Any of various small North American sandpipers. [Middle English **pepen,* probably alteration of *pipen,* from Old English *pīpian,* to pipe, from Old English *pīpe,* tube, musical instrument, and from Latin *pīpāre,* to peep; see PIPE.]

peep[2] (pēp) *v.* **peeped, peep·ing, peeps.** —*intr.* **1.** To peek furtively; steal a quick glance. **2.** To peer through a small aperture or from behind something. **3.** To appear as though emerging from a hiding place: *the moon peeping through the clouds.* —*tr.* To cause to emerge or become partly visible: *He peeped his head through the door.* —**peep** *n.* **1.** A quick or furtive look or glance. **2.** A first glimpse or appearance: *the peep of dawn.* [Middle English *pepen,* perhaps alteration of *piken,* to peek. See PEEK.]

peep·er[1] (pē′pər) *n.* A creature that makes short, high-pitched sounds, especially a frog.

peep·er[2] (pē′pər) *n.* **1.** One who peeks furtively. **2.** *Slang.* An eye.

peep·hole (pēp′hōl′) *n.* A small hole or crevice through which one may peep. Also called *eyehole.*

peep·ing Tom (pē′pĭng tŏm) *n.* A person who gets pleasure, especially sexual pleasure, from secretly watching others; a voyeur. [After the legendary *Peeping Tom* of Coventry, England, who was the only person to see the naked Lady Godiva.]

WORD HISTORY: In an age when we can speak of *peeping Tom cameras* or *electronic peeping Toms* we have indeed come far from the time of the legendary peeping Tom. Godgifu (fl. 1040–1080), Lady Godiva to us, pledged her legendary ride as a means of persuading her husband, Leofric, Earl of Mercia, to lower taxes. In the original version of the story she was observed by all the townspeople as she disrobed, but in a much later version of the story a tailor or butcher named Tom was the only person to observe her as she rode by, everyone else having shuttered their windows as they had been asked. *Peeping Tom,* first recorded around 1796, has become a term for a voyeur, not at all a pleasant fate for this legendary fellow. As W.H. Auden has said, "Peeping Toms Are never praised, like novelists or bird watchers,/For their keenness of observation."

peep·show also **peep show** (pēp′shō′) *n.* **1.** An exhibition of pictures or objects viewed through a small hole or magnifying glass. Also called *raree show.* **2.** A short pornographic film presentation seen usually in a small coin-operated projection booth.

peep sight *n.* A rear sight of a firearm consisting of an adjustable eyepiece with a small opening through which the front sight and the target are aligned.

pee·pul also **pi·pal** (pē′pəl) *n.* A fig tree *(Ficus religiosa)* native to India, having broadly ovate leaves with a long terminal projection. It is regarded as sacred by Buddhists. Also called *bo tree.* [Hindi *pīpal,* from Sanskrit *pippalam.*]

peer[1] (pîr) *intr.v.* **peered, peer·ing, peers. 1.** To look intently, searchingly, or with difficulty. See Synonyms at **gaze. 2.** To be partially visible; show: *The moon peered from behind dark clouds.* [Middle English *piren* (probably from Frisian *piren*) and *peren* (short for *aperen,* to appear; see APPEAR).]

peer[2] (pîr) *n.* **1.** A person who has equal standing with another or others, as in rank, class, or age: *children who are easily influenced by their peers.* **2.a.** A nobleman. **b.** A man who holds a peerage by descent or appointment. **3.** *Archaic.* A companion; a fellow: *"To stray away into these forests drear,/Alone, without a peer"* (John Keats). [Middle English, from Old French *per,* equal, peer, from Latin *pār.* See **perə-**[2] in Appendix.]

peer·age (pîr′ĭj) *n.* **1.** The rank, title, or jurisdiction of a peer or peeress; a duchy, marquisate, county, viscountcy, or barony. **2.**

ă pat	oi boy
ā pay	ou out
âr care	o͝o took
ä father	o͞o boot
ĕ pet	ŭ cut
ē be	ûr urge
ĭ pit	th thin
ī pie	*th* this
îr pier	hw which
ŏ pot	zh vision
ō toe	ə about, item
ô paw	♦ regionalism

Stress marks: ′ (primary); ′ (secondary), as in **dictionary** (dĭk′shə-nĕr′ē)

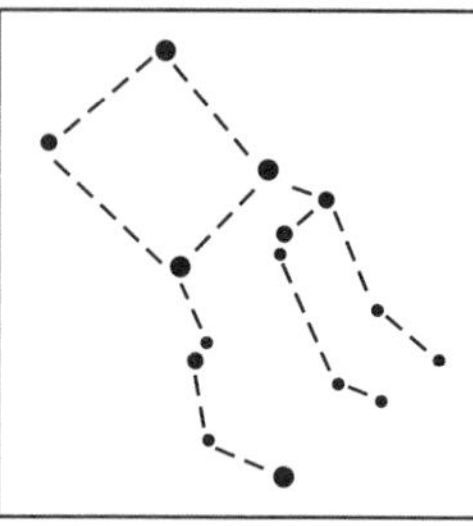

Pegasus
Top: Fourth-century B.C. Greek coin
Bottom: Constellation

I.M. Pei

Pelé
Photographed in 1984 at an exhibition match

pelican
Brown pelican
Pelecanus occidentalis

Peers and peeresses considered as a group. **3.** A book listing peers, peeresses, and their families.

peer·ess (pîr′ĭs) *n.* **1.a.** A noblewoman. **b.** A woman who holds a peerage by descent or appointment. **2.** A woman who holds a title by association, as the wife or widow of a peer.

peer·less (pîr′lĭs) *adj.* Being such as to have no match; incomparable. **—peer′less·ly** *adv.* **—peer′less·ness** *n.*

peet·weet (pēt′wēt′) *n.* See **spotted sandpiper.** [Imitative of its call.]

peeve (pēv) *tr.v.* **peeved, peev·ing, peeves.** To cause to be annoyed or resentful. See Synonyms at **annoy. —peeve** *n.* **1.** A vexation; a grievance. **2.** A resentful mood: *in a peeve about the delays.* [Back-formation from PEEVISH.]

pee·vish (pē′vĭsh) *adj.* **1.a.** Querulous or discontented. **b.** Ill-tempered. **2.** Contrary; fractious. [Middle English *pevish,* possibly from Latin *perversus,* past participle of *perversus.* See PERVERSE.] **—pee′vish·ly** *adv.* **—pee′vish·ness** *n.*

pee·wee[1] (pē′wē) *n. Informal.* One, such as a child, that is relatively or unusually small. [Probably reduplication of WEE.] **—pee′wee** *adj.*

pee·wee[2] (pē′wē) *n.* Variant of **pewee.**

pee·wit (pē′wĭt′, pyo͞o′ĭt) *n.* Variant of **pewit.**

peg (pĕg) *n.* **1.a.** A small cylindrical or tapered pin, as of wood, used to fasten things or plug a hole. **b.** A similar pin forming a projection that may be used as a support or boundary marker. **2.** *Music.* One of the pins of a stringed instrument that are turned to tighten or slacken the strings so as to regulate their pitch. **3.** A degree or notch, as in estimation: *Our opinion of him went up a few pegs after he did the dishes.* **4.** *Chiefly British.* A drink of liquor. **5.** *Baseball.* A low and fast throw made to put a base runner out. **6.** *Informal.* A leg, especially a wooden one. **—peg** *v.* **pegged, peg·ging, pegs.** *—tr.* **1.** To fasten or plug with a peg or pegs. **2.** To designate or mark by means of a peg or pegs. **3.** To fix (a price) at a certain level or within a certain range. **4.** *Informal.* To classify; categorize: *I pegged her as an opportunist. Why do you have me pegged as the rowdy one?* **5.** *Informal.* To throw. *—intr.* To work steadily; persist: *pegged away until our luck turned.* ***—idiom.* take (someone) down a peg.** To reduce the pride of; humble. [Middle English *pegge,* from Middle Dutch.]

Peg·a·sus (pĕg′ə-səs) *n.* **1.** *Greek Mythology.* A winged horse that with a stroke of his hoof caused the fountain Hippocrene to spring forth from Mount Helicon. **2.** A constellation in the Northern Hemisphere near Aquarius and Andromeda. [Middle English, from Latin *Pēgasus,* from Greek *Pēgasos.*]

peg·board (pĕg′bôrd′, -bōrd′) *n.* **1.** *Games.* **a.** A board perforated with a pattern of holes into which pegs can be fitted for playing certain games. **b.** A game played by fitting pegs into holes in a board. **2.** A board fitted with pegs for hanging clothing.

Peg-Board (pĕg′bôrd′, -bō′rd). A trademark used for a type of hardboard with rows of regularly spaced holes into which hooks may be inserted for storing or displaying objects.

peg leg *n. Informal.* An artificial leg.

peg·ma·tite (pĕg′mə-tīt′) *n.* A coarse-grained granite, sometimes rich in rare elements such as uranium, tungsten, and tantalum. [Greek *pēgma, pēgmat-,* something fastened together (from *pēgnunai,* to fasten; see **pag-** in Appendix) + —ITE[1].] **—peg′ma·tit′ic** (-tĭt′ĭk) *adj.*

Peh·le·vi (pā′lə-vē′) *n.* Variant of **Pahlavi.**

Pei (pā), **I(eoh) M(ing).** Born 1917. Chinese-born American architect who designed Government Center in Boston and Place Ville Marie in Montreal.

P.E.I. *abbr.* Prince Edward Island.

pei·gnoir (pān-wär′, pĕn-) *n.* A woman's loose-fitting dressing gown. [French, from Old French *peignouer,* linen covering used while combing oneself, from *peigner,* to comb the hair, from Latin *pectināre,* from *pecten, pectin-,* comb.]

Pei·ping (pā′pĭng′). See **Beijing.**

Pei·pus (pī′pəs), **Lake.** A lake between eastern Estonia and western Russia. Alexander Nevski defeated the Teutonic Knights on the frozen lake in 1242.

Peirce (pîrs, pûrs), **Benjamin.** 1809–1880. American mathematician and astronomer known for his studies of Uranus, Neptune, and Saturn's rings.

Peirce, Charles Sanders. 1839–1914. American philosopher, mathematician, and scientist who cofounded pragmatism and made numerous contributions to logic.

Pei·sis·tra·tus (pī-sĭs′trə-təs, pī-). See **Pisistratus.**

pej·o·ra·tion (pĕj′ə-rā′shən, pē′jə-) *n.* **1.** The process or condition of worsening or degenerating. **2.** *Linguistics.* The process by which the meaning of a word becomes negative or less elevated over a period of time, as *silly,* which formerly meant "deserving sympathy, helpless or simple," has come to mean "showing a lack of good sense, frivolous." [Medieval Latin *pēiōrātiō, pēiōrātiōn-,* from Late Latin *pēiōrātus,* past participle of *pēiōrāre,* to make worse, from Latin *pēior,* worse. See **ped-** in Appendix.]

pe·jor·a·tive (pĭ-jôr′ə-tĭv, -jŏr′-, pĕj′ə-rā′tĭv, pē′jə-) *adj.* **1.** Tending to make or become worse. **2.** Disparaging; belittling. **—pejorative** *n.* A disparaging or belittling word or expression. **—pe·jor′a·tive·ly** *adv.*

pek·an (pĕk′ən) *n.* See **fisher** (sense 2a). [Canadian French *pékan,* from Eastern Abenaki *pékané.*]

pe·kin (pē′kĭn′) *n.* **1.** A striped or figured silk fabric. **2.** Also **Pekin.** A large white duck of a Chinese breed, widely raised in the United States for food. [French *pékin,* after *Pékin* (Beijing), China.]

Pe·kin (pē′kĭn). A city of central Illinois, an industrial suburb of Peoria on the Illinois River. Population, 33,967.

Pe·king (pē′kĭng′, pā′-). See **Beijing.**

Peking duck *n.* A Chinese dish of roast duck with crispy skin. [After *Peking* (Beijing), China.]

Pe·king·ese (pē′kĭng-ēz′, -ēs′) also **Pe·kin·ese** (pē′kə-nēz′, -nēs′) *n., pl.* **Pekingese** also **Pekinese. 1.** A native or resident of Peking (Beijing). **2.** The Chinese dialect of Peking. **3.** (pē′kə-nēz′, -nēs′). Any of a breed of small dog developed in China, having a flat nose, a long-haired coat, short bowed forelegs, and a tail that curls over its back. **—Pe′king·ese′** *adj.*

Peking man *n.* An early member of an extinct species of human beings, considered a subspecies of *Homo erectus* and known from fossil remains of the Pleistocene Epoch. Also called *sinanthropus.* [After *Peking* (Beijing), China.]

pe·koe (pē′kō) *n.* A grade of black tea consisting of the leaves around the buds. [Chinese (Amoy) *pek ho* : *pek,* white + *ho,* down, fine feathers.]

pel·age (pĕl′ĭj) *n.* **1.** The coat of a mammal, consisting of hair, fur, wool, or other soft covering, as distinct from bare skin. **2.** Something felt to resemble the coat of a mammal: *"The hardwoods were a soft pale green in the dark pelage of the conifers"* (Peter Matthiessen). [French, from Old French, from *peil, pel,* hair, from Latin *pilus.*]

Pe·la·gi·an·ism (pə-lā′jē-ə-nĭz′əm) *n.* The theological doctrine propounded by Pelagius, a British monk, and condemned as heresy by the Roman Catholic Church in A.D. 416. It denied original sin and affirmed the ability of human beings to be righteous by the exercise of free will. **—Pe·la′gi·an** *adj. & n.*

pe·lag·ic (pə-lăj′ĭk) *adj.* Of, relating to, or living in open oceans or seas rather than waters adjacent to land or inland waters: *pelagic birds.* [Latin *pelagicus,* from Greek *pelagikos,* from *pelagos,* sea. See **plāk-[1]** in Appendix.]

pel·ar·gon·ic acid (pĕl′är-gŏn′ĭk, -gō′nĭk) *n.* A colorless or yellow oil, $CH_3(CH_2)_7COOH$, used in the manufacture of lacquers, plastics, and pharmaceuticals. Also called *nonanoic acid.* [PELARGON(IUM) + —IC.]

pel·ar·go·ni·um (pĕl′är-gō′nē-əm) *n.* Any of various herbs and shrubs of the genus *Pelargonium,* which includes the geraniums. [New Latin *Pelargonium,* genus name, from Greek *pelargos,* stork (from the resemblance of a stork's bill to its capsules). See **pel-[1]** in Appendix.]

Pe·las·gi·an (pə-lăz′jē-ən) *n.* A member of a people living in the region of the Aegean Sea before the coming of the Greeks. [Middle English, from Latin *Pelasgus,* from Greek *Pelasgos.*] **—Pe·las′gi·an, Pe·las′gic** (-jĭk) *adj.*

Pe·lé (pā′lā). Real name Edson Arantes do Nascimento. Born 1940. Brazilian soccer player who led his national team to three World Cup championships (1958, 1962, and 1970). He later played for the New York Cosmos (1975–1977).

pe·lec·y·pod (pə-lĕs′ə-pŏd′) *n.* See **lamellibranch.** [From New Latin *Pelecypoda,* class name : Greek *pelekus,* ax + New Latin *-poda,* -pod.]

Pe·lée (pə-lā′), **Mount.** A volcano, about 1,373 m (4,500 ft) high, on northern Martinique in the French West Indies. Its eruption on May 8, 1902, killed some 40,000 people.

pel·er·ine (pĕl′ə-rēn′, pĕl′ər-ĭn) *n.* A woman's cape, usually short, with points in front. [French *pèlerine,* from feminine of *pèlerin,* pilgrim, from Late Latin *pelegrīnus.* See PILGRIM.]

Pe·le·us (pē′lē-əs, pēl′yo͞os′) *n. Greek Mythology.* A son of Aeacus and the father of Achilles.

Pe·lew (pə-lo͞o′, pē-). See **Belau.**

pelf (pĕlf) *n.* Wealth or riches, especially when dishonestly acquired. [Middle English, from Medieval Latin *pelfra, pelfa,* probably from Old French *pelfre.*]

pel·i·can (pĕl′ĭ-kən) *n.* Any of various large, web-footed birds of the genus *Pelecanus* of tropical and warm regions, having a long straight bill from which hangs a distensible pouch of skin for catching and holding fish. [Middle English, from Old English *pellican* and from Old French *pelican,* both from Late Latin *pelicānus,* from Greek *pelekan.*]

Pe·li·on (pē′lē-ən, -ôn′), **Mount.** A peak, 1,601.9 m (5,252 ft) high, of northeast Greece in eastern Thessaly. According to Greek legend, it was the home of the centaurs, especially Chiron.

pe·lisse (pə-lēs′) *n.* **1.** A long cloak or outer robe, usually of fur or with a fur lining. **2.** A woman's loose, light cloak, often with openings for the arms. [French, from Old French *pelice,* from Late Latin *pellīcia,* from Latin, feminine of *pellīcius,* made of skin, from *pellis,* skin. See **pel-[3]** in Appendix.]

pe·lite (pē′līt′) *n.* Sedimentary rock composed of fine fragments, as of clay or mud. [Greek *pēlos,* clay + —ITE[1].] **—pe·lit′ic** (pĭ-lĭt′ĭk) *adj.*

Pel·la (pĕl′ə). An ancient city of Greek Macedonia. It was the capital of Macedonia from the fourth century to 168 B.C., when the territory was conquered by the Romans.

pel·lag·ra (pə-lăg′rə, -lā′-, -lä′grə) *n.* A disease caused by a deficiency of niacin and protein in the diet and characterized by skin eruptions, digestive and nervous system disturbances, and eventual mental deterioration. [Italian : *pelle,* skin (from Latin *pellis;* see **pel-³** in Appendix) + *-agra,* a seizure (from Latin, from Greek, from *agra,* a seizing; see **ag-** in Appendix).] **—pel·lag′rous** *adj.*

pel·lag·rin (pə-lăg′rĭn, -lā′-, -lä′grĭn) *n.* A person affected with pellagra. [From PELLAGRA.]

pel·let (pĕl′ĭt) *n.* **1.** A small, solid or densely packed ball or mass, as of food, wax, or medicine. **2. a.** A bullet or piece of small shot. **b.** A stone ball, used as a catapult missile or a primitive cannonball. **—pellet** *tr.v.* **-let·ed, -let·ing, -lets. 1.** To make or form into pellets. **2.** To strike with pellets. [Middle English *pelet,* from Old French *pelote,* from Vulgar Latin *pilotta, diminutive of Latin *pila,* ball.]

pel·li·cle (pĕl′ĭ-kəl) *n.* A thin skin or film, such as an organic membrane or a liquid film. [French, from Latin *pellicula,* husk, diminutive of *pellis,* skin. See **pel-³** in Appendix.] **—pel·lic′u·lar** (pə-lĭk′yə-lər) *adj.*

pel·li·to·ry (pĕl′ĭ-tôr′ē, -tōr′ē) *n., pl.* **-ries. 1.** A small Mediterranean plant *(Anacyclus pyrethrum)* containing a volatile oil once used for the relief of toothache and facial neuralgia. **2.** Any of various monoecious plants of the genus *Parietaria,* having long, narrow leaves with hairy tufts at the base and apetalous flowers. [Middle English *peletre, peletori,* from Old French *piretre, peletre,* from Latin *pyrethrum.* See PYRETHRUM.]

pell-mell also **pell·mell** (pĕl′mĕl′) *adv.* **1.** In a jumbled, confused manner; helter-skelter. **2.** In frantic, disorderly haste; headlong: *"I went to work pell-mell, blotted several sheets of paper with choice floating thoughts"* (Washington Irving). [French *pêle-mêle,* from Old French *pesle mesle,* probably reduplication of *mesle,* imperative of *mesler,* to mix. See MEDDLE.] **—pell′-mell′** *adj. & n.*

pel·lu·cid (pə-lo͞o′sĭd) *adj.* **1.** Admitting the passage of light; transparent or translucent. See Synonyms at **clear. 2.** Transparently clear in style or meaning: *pellucid prose.* [Latin *pellūcidus,* from *pellūcēre,* to shine through : *per-,* through; see PER– + *lūcēre,* to shine; see **leuk-** in Appendix.] **—pel·lu·cid′i·ty, pel·lu′cid·ness** *n.* **—pel·lu′cid·ly** *adv.*

Pel·ly (pĕl′ē). A river, about 531 km (330 mi) long, of central Yukon Territory, Canada, flowing generally northwest to the Yukon River.

Pe·lop·i·das (pə-lŏp′ĭ-dəs). Died 364 B.C. Theban general who helped liberate Thebes from the Spartans in 379. He was killed in battle at Cynoscephalae.

Pel·o·pon·ne·sus or **Pel·o·pon·ne·sos** (pĕl′ə-pə-nē′səs) also **Pel·o·pon·nese** (pĕl′ə-pə-nēz′, -nēs′). A peninsula forming the southern part of Greece south of the Gulf of Corinth. It was dominated by Sparta until the fourth century B.C. **—Pel′o·pon·ne′sian** (-nē′zhən, -shən) *adj. & n.*

Pe·lops (pē′lŏps′) *n. Greek Mythology.* The son of Tantalus and father of Atreus. [Latin, from Greek : *pelios,* dark; see **pel-¹** in Appendix + *ōps,* face, eye; see **okʷ-** in Appendix.]

pe·lo·ri·a (pə-lôr′ē-ə, -lōr′-) *n.* Unusual regularity in the form of a flower that is normally irregular. [New Latin, from Greek *pelōros,* monstrous, from *pelōr,* monster. See **kʷer-** in Appendix.] **—pe·lor′ic** (-lôr′ĭk, -lŏr′-) *adj.*

pe·lo·rus (pə-lôr′əs, -lōr′-) *n., pl.* **-rus·es.** *Nautical.* A fixed compass card on which bearings relative to a ship's heading are taken. [Origin unknown.]

pe·lo·ta (pə-lō′tə) *n. Sports.* **1.** Jai alai. **2.** The ball used in jai alai. [Spanish, from Old French *pelote,* pellet. See PELLET.]

Pe·lo·tas (pə-lō′təs, pĭ-lô′täs). A city of southeast Brazil on a lagoon south-southwest of Pôrto Alegre. It is a major producer of dried beef. Population, 196,919.

pelt¹ (pĕlt) *n.* **1.** The skin of an animal with the fur or hair still on it. **2.** A stripped animal skin ready for tanning. [Middle English, probably from Old French *pelete,* diminutive of *pel,* skin, from Latin *pellis.* See PELTRY.]

pelt² (pĕlt) *v.* **pelt·ed, pelt·ing, pelts.** *—tr.* **1.** To strike or assail repeatedly with or as if with blows or missiles; bombard: *pelted each other with snowballs.* **2.** To cast, hurl, or throw (missiles): *children who pelted stones at the neighbors' windows.* **3.** To strike repeatedly: *Hailstones pelted the tent.* *—intr.* **1.** To beat or strike heavily and repeatedly. **2.** To move at a vigorous gait. **—pelt** *n.* **1.** A sharp blow; a whack. **2.** A rapid pace: *galloped away at a pelt.* [Middle English *pelten,* variant of *pilten,* perhaps ultimately from Latin *pultāre,* to beat, variant of *pulsāre,* frequentative of *pellere,* to strike. See **pel-⁵** in Appendix.] **—pelt′er** *n.*

pel·tate (pĕl′tāt′) *adj.* Having a flat circular structure attached to a stalk near the center, rather than at or near the margin; shield-shaped: *the peltate leaf of the nasturtium.* [Latin *peltātus,* armed with a small shield, from Latin *pelta,* small shield, from Greek *peltē.* See **pel-³** in Appendix.] **—pel′tate′ly** *adv.*

pelt·ing (pĕl′tĭng) *adj. Archaic.* Paltry; petty: *"This land . . . /Is now leas'd out . . . /Like to a tenement or pelting farm"* (Shakespeare). [Perhaps from dialectal *pelt,* trash.]

pel·try (pĕl′trē) *n.* Undressed pelts considered as a group. [Middle English, from Old French *peleterie,* from *peletier,* furrier, from *pel,* skin, from Latin *pellis.* See **pel-³** in Appendix.]

pel·ves (pĕl′vēz) *n.* A plural of **pelvis.**

pel·vic (pĕl′vĭk) *adj.* Of, in, near, or relating to the pelvis: *a pelvic artery.*

pelvic arch *n.* See **pelvic girdle.**

pelvic fin *n.* Either of a pair of lateral hind fins of fishes, attached to the pelvic girdle and corresponding to the hind limbs of higher vertebrates.

pelvic girdle *n.* A bony or cartilaginous structure in vertebrates, attached to and supporting the hind limbs or fins. Also called *pelvic arch.*

pelvic inflammatory disease *n. Abbr.* **PID** Inflammation of the female genital tract, especially of the fallopian tubes, caused by any of several microorganisms, chiefly chlamydia and gonococci, and characterized by severe abdominal pain, high fever, vaginal discharge, and in some cases destruction of tissue that can result in sterility.

pel·vim·e·try (pĕl-vĭm′ĭ-trē) *n.* Measurement of the dimensions and capacity of the pelvis, especially of the adult female pelvis. **—pel·vim′e·ter** *n.*

pel·vis (pĕl′vĭs) *n., pl.* **-vis·es** or **-ves** (-vēz). **1. a.** A basin-shaped structure of the vertebrate skeleton, composed of the innominate bones on the sides, the pubis in front, and the sacrum and coccyx behind, that rests on the lower limbs and supports the spinal column. **b.** The cavity formed by this structure. **2.** The hollow funnel in the outlet of the kidney, into which urine is discharged before entering the ureter. In this sense, also called *renal pelvis.* [Latin *pēlvis,* basin.]

Pem·ba (pĕm′bə). An island of Tanzania in the Indian Ocean north of Zanzibar. In the 16th and 17th centuries the Portuguese occupied the island, which passed under British control in 1890.

Pem·broke Pines (pĕm′bro͝ok′, -brōk′). A city of southeast Florida, a residential suburb of Fort Lauderdale. Population, 35,776.

pem·mi·can also **pem·i·can** (pĕm′ĭ-kən) *n.* **1.** A food prepared by Native Americans from lean, dried strips of meat pounded into paste, mixed with fat and berries, and pressed into small cakes. **2.** A food made chiefly from beef, dried fruit, and suet, used as emergency rations. [Cree *pimihkaam,* pemmican.]

pem·o·line (pĕm′ə-lēn′) *n.* A white, crystalline synthetic compound, $C_9H_8N_2O_2$, used as a mild stimulant of the central nervous system, usually in combination with magnesium hydroxide, especially in treating depression. [From chemical name *p(h)e(nyli)m(inooxooxaz)ol(id)ine.*]

pem·phi·gus (pĕm′fĭ-gəs, pĕm-fī′gəs) *n.* Any of several acute or chronic skin diseases characterized by groups of itching blisters. [New Latin, from Greek *pemphix, pemphig-,* pustule.] **—pem′phi·gous** *adj.*

pen¹ (pĕn) *n.* **1.** An instrument for writing or drawing with ink or similar fluid, especially: **a.** A ballpoint pen. **b.** A fountain pen. **c.** A pen point. **d.** A penholder and its pen point. **e.** A quill. **2.** An instrument for writing regarded as a means of expression: *"Tyranny has no enemy so formidable as the pen"* (William Cobbett). **3.** A writer or an author: *a hired pen.* **4.** A style of writing: *wrote plays with a witty pen.* **5. pens.** Pinions. **6.** The chitinous internal shell of a squid. **—pen** *tr.v.* **penned, pen·ning, pens.** To write or compose with or as if with a pen. [Middle English *penne,* from Old French, from Late Latin *penna,* from Latin, feather. See **pet-** in Appendix.] **—pen′ner** *n.*

pen² (pĕn) *n.* **1. a.** A fenced enclosure for animals. **b.** The animals kept in such an enclosure. **c.** Any of various enclosures, such as a bullpen or playpen, used for a variety of purposes. **2.** A repair dock for submarines. **—pen** *tr.v.* **penned** or **pent** (pĕnt), **pen·ning, pens.** To confine in or as if in a pen. See Synonyms at **enclose.** [Middle English, from Old English *penn.*]

pen³ (pĕn) *n.* A female swan. [Origin unknown.]

pen⁴ (pĕn) *n. Informal.* A penitentiary; a prison. [Short for PENITENTIARY.]

pe·nal (pē′nəl) *adj.* **1.** Of, relating to, or prescribing punishment, as for breaking the law. **2.** Subject to punishment; legally punishable: *a penal offense.* **3.** Serving as or constituting a means or place of punishment: *penal servitude; a penal colony.* [Middle English, from Old French *peinal* and from Medieval Latin *pēnālis,* both from Latin *poenālis,* from *poena,* penalty, from Greek *poinē.* See **kʷei-¹** in Appendix.] **—pe′nal·ly** *adv.*

penal code *n. Law.* A body of laws relating to crimes and offenses and the penalties for their commission.

pe·nal·ize (pē′nə-līz′, pĕn′ə-) *tr.v.* **-ized, -iz·ing, -iz·es. 1.** To subject to a penalty, especially for infringement of a law or an official regulation. See Synonyms at **punish. 2.** To impose a handicap on; place at a disadvantage. **—pe′nal·i·za′tion** (-nə-lĭ-zā′shən) *n.*

pen·al·ty (pĕn′əl-tē) *n., pl.* **-ties. 1.** A punishment established by law or authority for a crime or an offense. **2.** Something, especially a sum of money, required as a forfeit for an offense. **3.** The disadvantage or painful consequences resulting from an action or a condition: *neglected his health and paid the penalty.* **4.** *Sports.* A punishment, handicap, or loss of advantage imposed on a team or competitor for infraction of a rule. **5.** Often **penalties.** *Games.* Points scored in contract bridge by the opponents when the declarer fails to make a bid. *—attributive.* Often used to modify another noun: *a penalty kick; a penalty stroke.* [Middle English *penalte,* from Old French *penalite,* from Medieval Latin *poenālitās,* from Latin *poenālis,* penal. See PENAL.]

penalty box *n.* An area to the side of an ice-hockey rink in which penalized players wait out the time of their penalties.

pen·ance (pĕn′əns) *n.* **1.** An act of self-mortification or devotion performed voluntarily to show sorrow for a sin or other wrongdoing. **2.** A sacrament in some Christian churches that in-

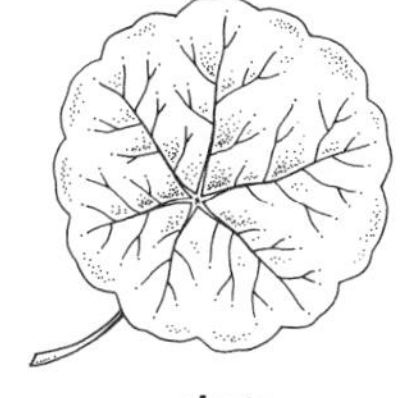

peltate

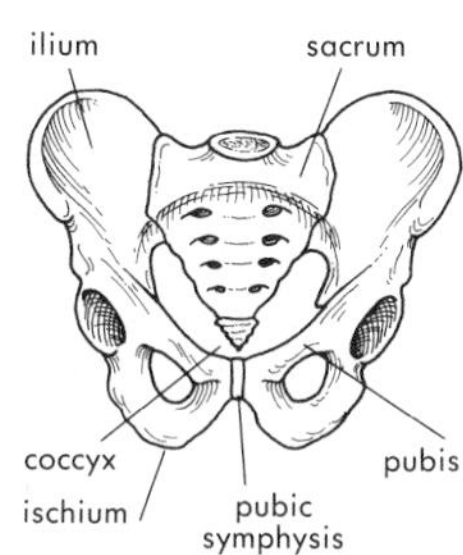

pelvis

ă pat	oi boy
ā pay	ou out
âr care	o͝o took
ä father	o͞o boot
ĕ pet	ŭ cut
ē be	ûr urge
ĭ pit	th thin
ī pie	*th* this
îr pier	hw which
ŏ pot	zh vision
ō toe	ə about, item
ô paw	♦ regionalism

Stress marks: **′** (primary); ′ (secondary), as in **dictionary** (dĭk′shə-nĕr′ē)

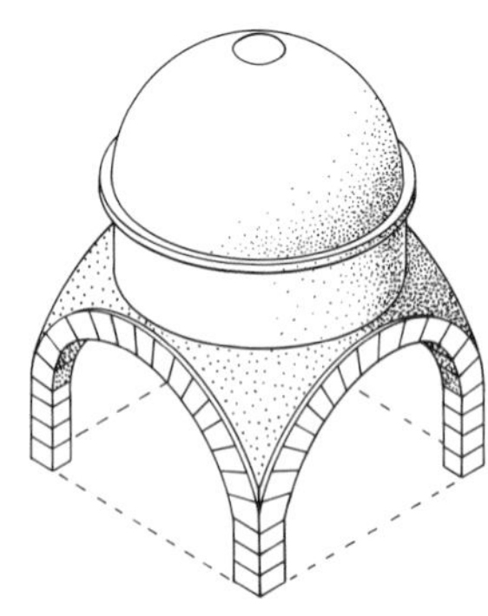

pendentive

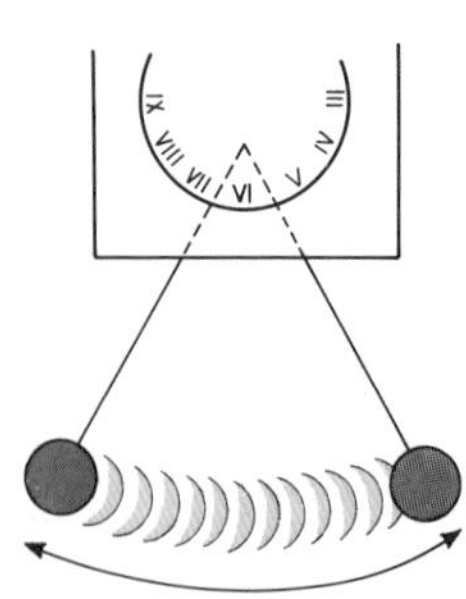

pendulum

cludes contrition, confession to a priest, acceptance of punishment, and absolution. In this sense, also called *reconciliation.* **—penance** *tr.v.* **-anced, -anc·ing, -anc·es.** To impose penance upon. [Middle English, from Old French, from Latin *paenitentia,* penitence, from *paenitēns, paenitent-,* penitent. See PENITENT.]

Pe·nang (pə-năng′, pē′näng′). See **George Town** (sense 1).

Pe·na·tes (pə-nā′tēz, -nä′-) *pl.n. Roman Mythology.* The Roman gods of the household, tutelary deities of the home and of the state, whose cult was closely connected and often identified with that of the Lares. [Latin *Penātēs,* from *penus,* foodstuff, interior of a house.]

pence (pĕns) *n. Chiefly British.* A plural of **penny** (sense 3).

pen·cel also **pen·sil** (pĕn′səl) *n.* A narrow flag, streamer, or pennon, especially one carried at the top of a lance or spear. [Middle English, from Old French *penoncel,* diminutive of *penon,* pennon. See PENNON.]

pen·chant (pĕn′chənt) *n.* A definite liking; a strong inclination. See Synonyms at **predilection.** [French, from present participle of *pencher,* to incline, from Old French, from Vulgar Latin **pendicāre,* from Latin *pendēre,* to hang. See **(s)pen-** in Appendix.]

pen·cil (pĕn′səl) *n.* **1.** A narrow, generally cylindrical implement for writing, drawing, or marking, consisting of a thin rod of graphite, colored wax, or similar substance encased in wood or held in a mechanical holder. **2.** Something shaped or used like a pencil, especially a narrow medicated or cosmetic stick: *an eyebrow pencil.* **3. a.** A style or technique in drawing or delineating. **b.** Descriptive skill: *"His characters are drawn with a strong pencil"* (Henry Hallam). **c.** An artist's brush, especially a fine one. **4.** *Physics.* A beam of radiant energy in the form of a narrow cone or cylinder. **5.** *Mathematics.* A family of geometric objects, such as lines, that have a common property, such as passage through a given line in a given plane. **—pencil** *tr.v.* **-ciled, -cil·ing, -cils** also **-cilled, -cil·ling, -cils.** **1.** To write or produce by using a pencil. **2.** To mark or color with or as if with a pencil. [Middle English *pencel,* artist's brush, from Old French *pincel, peincel,* from Vulgar Latin **pēnicellus,* alteration of Latin *pēnicillus,* diminutive of *pēniculus,* diminutive of *pēnis,* tail, brush. See **pes-** in Appendix.] **—pen′cil·er, pen′cil·ler** *n.*

pencil pusher *n. Informal.* One whose job involves writing and other paperwork.

pen·dant¹ also **pen·dent** (pĕn′dənt) *n.* **1.** Something suspended from something else, especially an ornament or a piece of jewelry attached to a necklace or bracelet. **2.** A hanging lamp or chandelier. **3.** A sculptured ornament suspended from a vaulted Gothic roof or ceiling. **4.** One of a matched pair; a companion piece. [Middle English *pendaunt,* from Old French *pendant,* from present participle of *pendre,* to hang, from Vulgar Latin **pendere,* from Latin *pendēre.* See **(s)pen-** in Appendix.]

pen·dant² (pĕn′dənt) *adj.* Variant of **pendent¹.**

Pen·del·i·kón (pĕn-dĕl′ĭ-kŏn′, pĕn′dĕ-lē-kôn′). A mountain, about 1,119 m (3,670 ft) high, of east-central Greece northeast of Athens. White marble quarried here was used for many of the buildings of ancient Athens.

pen·dent¹ also **pen·dant** (pĕn′dənt) *adj.* **1.** Hanging down; dangling; suspended. **2.** Projecting; overhanging. **3.** Awaiting settlement; pending. [Middle English *pendant* (influenced by Latin *pendēns, pendent-,* present participle of *pendēre,* to hang), from Old French. See PENDANT¹.] **—pen′dent·ly** *adv.*

pen·dent² (pĕn′dənt) *n.* Variant of **pendant¹.**

pen·den·tive (pĕn-dĕn′tĭv) *n. Architecture.* A triangular section of vaulting between the rim of a dome and each adjacent pair of the arches that support it. [French *pendentif,* from Latin *pendēns, pendent-,* hanging, present participle of *pendēre,* to hang. See **(s)pen-** in Appendix.]

pend·ing (pĕn′dĭng) *adj.* **1.** Not yet decided or settled; awaiting conclusion or confirmation. **2.** Impending; imminent. **—pending** *prep.* **1.** While in the process of; during. **2.** While awaiting; until. [French *pendant,* pendant, pending (from Old French; see PENDENT¹) + –ING¹.]

Pend O·reille (pŏn′də-rā′). A river, about 161 km (100 mi) long, rising in **Pend Oreille Lake** in northern Idaho and flowing generally northwest through northeast Washington to the Columbia River just north of the British Columbia, Canada, border.

pen·du·lar (pĕn′jə-lər, pĕn′dyə-, -də-) *adj.* Of or resembling the motion of a pendulum; swinging back and forth.

pen·du·lous (pĕn′jə-ləs, pĕn′dyə-, -də-) *adj.* **1.** Hanging loosely; suspended so as to swing or sway. **2.** Wavering; undecided. [From Latin *pendulus,* from *pendēre,* to hang. See **(s)pen-** in Appendix.] **—pen′du·lous·ly** *adv.* **—pen′du·lous·ness** *n.*

pen·du·lum (pĕn′jə-ləm, pĕn′dyə-, pĕn′də-) *n.* **1.** A body suspended from a fixed support so that it swings freely back and forth under the influence of gravity, commonly used to regulate various devices, especially clocks. Also called *simple pendulum.* **2.** Something that swings back and forth from one course, opinion, or condition to another: *the pendulum of public opinion.* [New Latin, probably from Italian *pendolo,* pendulous, pendulum, from Latin *pendulus,* hanging. See PENDULOUS.]

Pe·nel·o·pe (pə-nĕl′ə-pē) *n. Greek Mythology.* The wife of Odysseus and mother of Telemachus. Penelope was made immortal by Circe.

pe·ne·plain also **pe·ne·plane** (pē′nə-plān′) *n. Geology.* A nearly flat land surface representing an advanced stage of erosion. [Latin *paene, pēne,* almost + PLAIN.]

pe·nes (pē′nēz) *n. Anatomy.* A plural of **penis.**

pen·e·tra·ble (pĕn′ĭ-trə-bəl) *adj.* Capable of being penetrated: *penetrable defenses; a penetrable wall.* **—pen′e·tra·bil′i·ty** *n.* **—pen′e·tra·bly** *adv.*

pen·e·tra·li·a (pĕn′ĭ-trā′lē-ə) *pl.n.* **1.** The innermost parts of a building, especially the sanctuary of a temple. **2.** The most private or secret parts; recesses: *the penetralia of the soul.* [Latin *penetrālia,* from neuter pl. of *penetrālis,* inner, from *penetrāre,* to penetrate. See PENETRATE.]

pen·e·tram·e·ter (pĕn′ĭ-trăm′ĭ-tər) *n.* Variant of **penetrometer.**

pen·e·trance (pĕn′ĭ-trəns) *n.* The frequency, under given environmental conditions, with which a specific genotype is expressed by those individuals that possess it.

pen·e·trant (pĕn′ĭ-trənt) *adj.* Penetrating; piercing: *a penetrant wind from the north.* **—penetrant** *n.* Something that penetrates or is capable of penetrating.

pen·e·trate (pĕn′ĭ-trāt′) *v.* **-trat·ed, -trat·ing, -trates.** *—tr.* **1.** To enter or force a way into; pierce. **2. a.** To enter into and permeate: *The insistent rhythm of piano practice penetrated each room of the house.* **b.** To cause to be permeated or diffused; steep. **3.** To insert the penis into the vagina or anus of. **4.** To enter (an organization, for example), usually surreptitiously, so as to gain influence or information; infiltrate. **5.** To enter and gain a share of (a market): *penetrated the home-computer market with an affordable new model.* **6.** To grasp the inner significance of; understand. **7.** To see through: *keen eyes that penetrate the darkness.* **8.** To affect deeply, as by piercing the consciousness or emotions. *—intr.* **1.** To pierce or enter into something; make a way in or through something. **2.** To gain admittance or access. **3.** To gain insight. [Latin *penetrāre, penetrāt-,* from *penitus,* deeply.] **—pen′e·tra′tor** *n.*

pen·e·trat·ing (pĕn′ĭ-trā′tĭng) *adj.* **1.** Able or seeming to penetrate: *The penetrating odor of garlic soon filled the entire apartment.* **2.** Keenly perceptive or understanding; acute: *The lecture provided penetrating insight into foreign affairs.* **—pen′e·trat′ing·ly** *adv.*

pen·e·tra·tion (pĕn′ĭ-trā′shən) *n.* **1.** The act or process of piercing or penetrating something, especially: **a.** The act of entering a country or an organization so as to establish influence or gain information: *"If the policy is accepted that the Soviet Union has a right to penetrate her immediate neighbors for security, penetration of the next immediate neighbors becomes . . . equally logical"* (W. Averell Harriman). **b.** An attack that penetrates enemy territory or a military front. **c.** Insertion of the penis into the vagina or anus. **2.** The power or ability to penetrate. **3.** The depth reached by a projectile after hitting its target. **4. a.** The degree to which a commodity, for example, is sold or recognized in a particular market. **b.** The extent of influence that one culture or nation has on another. **5.** The capacity or action of understanding; insight.

pen·e·tra·tive (pĕn′ĭ-trā′tĭv) *adj.* **1.** Tending to penetrate; penetrant. **2.** Displaying keen insight; acute.

pen·e·trom·e·ter (pĕn′ĭ-trŏm′ĭ-tər) also **pen·e·tram·e·ter** (-trăm′ĭ-tər) *n.* **1.** A device for measuring the penetrating power of radiation, especially x-rays. **2.** A device for measuring the penetrability of semisolids.

Peng·hu (pŭng′ho͞o′). See **Pescadores.**

Peng·pu (pŭng′po͞o′). See **Bengbu.**

pen·guin (pĕng′gwĭn, pĕn′-) *n.* **1.** Any of various stout, flightless marine birds of the family Spheniscidae, of cool regions of the Southern Hemisphere, having flipperlike wings and webbed feet adapted for swimming and diving, and short scalelike feathers that are white in front and black on the back. **2.** *Obsolete.* The great auk. [Possibly from Welsh *pen gwyn,* White Head (name of an island in Newfoundland), great auk : *pen,* chief, head + *gwynn,* white; see **weid-** in Appendix.]

pen·hold·er (pĕn′hōl′dər) *n.* **1.** A holder for a pen point. **2.** A rack or cup for holding a pen or pens.

–penia *suff.* Lack; deficiency: *leukopenia.* [New Latin, from Greek *penia,* poverty, lack. See **(s)pen-** in Appendix.]

pen·i·cil·la·mine (pĕn′ĭ-sĭl′ə-mēn′) *n.* A degradation product of penicillin, $C_5H_{11}NO_2S$, that is used as a chelating agent and in the treatment of rheumatoid arthritis and copper poisoning. [PENICILL(IN) + –AMINE.]

pen·i·cil·late (pĕn′ĭ-sĭl′ĭt, -āt′) *adj.* Having or resembling a tuft or brush of fine hairs, as those on caterpillars and certain grasses. [Latin *pēnicillus,* brush; see PENCIL + –ATE².] **—pen′i·cil′late·ly** *adv.* **—pen′i·cil·la′tion** *n.*

pen·i·cil·li·a (pĕn′ĭ-sĭl′ē-ə) *n.* A plural of **penicillium.**

pen·i·cil·lin (pĕn′ĭ-sĭl′ĭn) *n.* Any of a group of broad-spectrum antibiotic drugs obtained from penicillium molds or produced synthetically, most active against gram-positive bacteria and used in the treatment of various infections and diseases. [PENICILL(IUM) + –IN.]

pen·i·cil·lin·ase (pĕn′ĭ-sĭl′ĭ-nās′) *n.* Any of various enzymes, produced by certain bacteria, that hydrolyze penicillin and are used in medicine to treat allergic reactions to penicillin.

pen·i·cil·li·um (pĕn′ĭ-sĭl′ē-əm) *n., pl.* **-cil·li·ums** or **-cil·li·a** (-sĭl′ē-ə). Any of various characteristically bluish-green fungi of the genus *Penicillium* that grow as molds on decaying fruits and ripening cheese and are used in the production of penicillin and in making cheese. [New Latin *Pēnicillium*, genus name, from Latin *pēnicillus*, brush. See PENCIL.]

pe·nile (pē′nīl′, -nəl) *adj.* Of or relating to the penis.

pen·in·su·la (pə-nĭn′syə-lə, -sə-lə) *n.* A piece of land that projects into a body of water and is connected with the mainland by an isthmus. [Latin *paenīnsula* : *paene*, almost + *īnsula*, island.] **—pen·in′su·lar** *adj.*

pe·nis (pē′nĭs) *n., pl.* **-nis·es** or **-nes** (-nēz). *Anatomy.* **1.** The male organ of copulation in higher vertebrates, homologous with the clitoris. In mammals, it also serves as the male organ of urinary excretion. **2.** Any of various copulatory organs in males of lower animals. [Latin *pēnis*. See **pes-** in Appendix.]

penis envy *n. Psychology.* The wish of a girl or woman to have a penis, postulated by Sigmund Freud as a cause of feelings of inferiority and neurotic behavior.

pen·i·tence (pĕn′ĭ-təns) *n.* The condition or quality of being penitent; regret for wrongdoing.

SYNONYMS: *penitence, compunction, contrition, remorse, repentance.* The central meaning shared by these nouns is "a feeling of regret for one's sins or misdeeds": *showed no penitence; ended the relationship without compunction; pangs of contrition; tears of remorse; sincere repentance.*

pen·i·tent (pĕn′ĭ-tənt) *adj.* Feeling or expressing remorse for one's misdeeds or sins. **—penitent** *n.* **1.** One who is penitent. **2.** A person performing penance under the direction of a confessor. [Middle English, from Old French, from Medieval Latin *pēnitēns, pēnitent-*, from Latin *paenitēns*, present participle of *paenitēre*, to repent.] **—pen′i·tent·ly** *adv.*

Pen·i·ten·te (pĕn′ĭ-tĕn′tā, -tē) *n.* A member of a Roman Catholic brotherhood in parts of the Southwest, of Native American and Hispanic origin, that celebrates the Passion with rites involving fasting and self-flagellation. [Spanish, from Latin *paenitēns, paenitent-*, penitent. See PENITENT.]

pen·i·ten·tial (pĕn′ĭ-tĕn′shəl) *adj.* **1.** Of, relating to, or expressing penitence. **2.** Of or relating to penance. **—penitential** *n.* **1.** A book or set of church rules concerning the sacrament of penance. **2.** A penitent. **—pen′i·ten′tial·ly** *adv.*

pen·i·ten·tia·ry (pĕn′ĭ-tĕn′shə-rē) *n., pl.* **-ries. 1.** A prison for those convicted of major crimes. **2.** *Roman Catholic Church.* **a.** A tribunal of the Roman Curia having jurisdiction in matters relating to penance, dispensations, and papal absolutions. **b.** A priest whose special function is the administration of the sacrament of penance in a particular church or diocese. **—penitentiary** *adj.* **1.** Of or for the purpose of penance; penitential. **2.** Relating to or used for punishment or reform of criminals or wrongdoers. **3.** Resulting in or punishable by imprisonment in a penitentiary: *a penitentiary offense.* [Middle English *penitenciarie*, penance officer, episcopal prison, from Medieval Latin *pēnitentiāria*, feminine of *pēnitentiārius*, from Latin *paenitentia*, penitence, from *paenitēns*, penitent. See PENITENT.]

Pen·ki (bŭn′jē′). See **Benxi.**

pen·knife (pĕn′nīf′) *n.* A small pocketknife. [So called because it was originally used for cutting quill pens.]

pen·light (pĕn′līt′) *n.* A small flashlight having the size and shape of a fountain pen.

pen·man (pĕn′mən) *n.* **1.** A copyist; a scribe. **2.** An expert in penmanship. **3.** An author; a writer.

pen·man·ship (pĕn′mən-shĭp′) *n.* The art, skill, style, or manner of handwriting; calligraphy.

Penn (pĕn), **William.** 1644–1718. English Quaker colonizer in America. He founded the colony of Pennsylvania in 1681.

Penn, Sir **William.** 1621–1670. English admiral who led the English fleet during the Dutch War (1665–1667).

Penn. *abbr.* Pennsylvania.

pen·na (pĕn′ə) *n., pl.* **pen·nae** (pĕn′ē). A contour feather of a bird, as distinguished from a down feather or a plume. [Latin, feather. See **pet-** in Appendix.] **—pen·na′ceous** (pĕ-nā′shəs) *adj.*

Penna. *abbr.* Pennsylvania.

pen·nae (pĕn′ē) *n.* Plural of **penna.**

pen name also **pen·name** (pĕn′nām′) *n.* A pseudonym used by a writer. Also called *nom de plume.*

pen·nant (pĕn′ənt) *n.* **1.** *Nautical.* A long, tapering, usually triangular flag, used on ships for signaling or identification. **2.** A flag or an emblem similar in shape to a ship's pennant. **3.** *Sports.* **a.** A flag that symbolizes the championship of a league, especially a professional baseball league. **b.** The championship symbolized by such a flag. [Blend of PENDANT[1] and PENNON.]

pen·nate (pĕn′āt′) also **pen·nat·ed** (pĕn′ā′tĭd) *adj.* **1.** Having feathers or wings. **2.** *Botany.* Pinnate. **3.** Of or relating to diatoms of the class Pennales, distinguished by bilaterally symmetrical form. [Latin *pennātus*, from *penna*, feather. See **pet-** in Appendix.]

pen·ne (pĕn′ā) *n., pl.* **penne.** Short, tubular pasta with diagonally cut ends. [Italian, pl. of *penna*, feather, quill pen, from Latin. See PENNA.]

Pen·ney (pĕn′ē), **James Cash.** 1875–1971. American business executive who built the J.C. Penney chain and pioneered the practice of employee profit-sharing.

Penn Hills. A community of southwest Pennsylvania, a residential suburb of Philadelphia. Population, 57,632.

pen·ni (pĕn′ē) *n., pl.* **pen·nis** or **pen·ni·a** (pĕn′ē-ə). See table at **currency.** [Finnish, possibly from Swedish *penning*.]

pen·ni·less (pĕn′ē-lĭs, pĕn′ə-) *adj.* **1.** Entirely without money. **2.** Very poor. See Synonyms at **poor. —pen′ni·less·ly** *adv.* **—pen′ni·less·ness** *n.*

Pen·nine Alps (pĕn′īn′). A range of the Alps extending southwest to northeast along the Swiss-Italian border from Great St. Bernard Pass to Simplon Pass. It rises to 4,636.9 m (15,203 ft) at Monte Rosa.

Pen·nines (pĕn′īnz′) also **Pennine Chain.** A range of hills extending about 257 km (160 mi) southward from the Cheviot Hills on the Scottish border to central England. Sometimes called "the backbone of England," it rises to 893.7 m (2,930 ft).

pen·non (pĕn′ən) *n.* **1.** A long, narrow banner or streamer borne upon a lance. **2.** A pennant, banner, or flag. **3.** A pinion; a wing. [Middle English, from Old French *penon*, streamer, feather of an arrow, augmentative of *penne*, feather, from Latin *penna*. See **pet-** in Appendix.] **—pen′noned** *adj.*

William Penn
c. 1700 chalk portrait
by Francis Place
(1647–1728)

pen·non·cel also **pen·non·celle** (pĕn′ən-sĕl′) *n.* A small pennon, flag, or streamer borne on a lance. [Middle English *penoncel*, from Old French, diminutive of *penon*, pennon. See PENNON.]

Penn·sau·ken (pĕn-sô′kĭn). A community of southwest New Jersey, an industrial and residential suburb of Camden and Philadelphia, Pennsylvania. Population, 33,775.

Penn·syl·va·nia (pĕn′səl-vān′yə, -vā′nē-ə). *Abbr.* **PA, Pa., Penn., Penna.** A state of the eastern United States. It was admitted as one of the original Thirteen Colonies in 1787. First explored in the early 1600's, the region was settled by Swedes in 1634 and granted by royal charter to William Penn in 1681. The Mason-Dixon Line (surveyed in 1763–1767) established the colony's southern boundary and was extended westward in 1784. Pennsylvania played a crucial role in the American Revolution and in the formation of the new republic. Harrisburg is the capital and Philadelphia the largest city. Population, 11,864,751.

Pennsylvania Dutch *n.* **1.** The descendants of German and Swiss immigrants who settled in Pennsylvania in the 17th and 18th centuries. **2.** The dialect of High German spoken by the Pennsylvania Dutch. Also called *Dutch, Pennsylvania German.* **3.** The style of folk art and decorative arts developed by the Pennsylvania Dutch. [Alteration of German *Deutsch*, German. See PLATTDEUTSCH.]

Penn·syl·va·nian (pĕn′səl-vān′yən, -vā′nē-ən) *adj.* **1.** Of or relating to Pennsylvania. **2.** *Geology.* Of, belonging to, or being the geologic time, system of rocks, and sedimentary deposits of the sixth period of the Paleozoic Era, characterized by the development of coal-bearing rock formations. See table at **geologic time. —Pennsylvanian** *n.* **1.** A native or resident of Pennsylvania. **2.** *Geology.* The Pennsylvanian Period. [After PENNSYLVANIA.]

pen·ny (pĕn′ē) *n., pl.* **-nies. 1.** See table at **currency. 2.** *Abbr.* **p.** In the United States and Canada, the coin that is worth one cent. **3.** *pl.* **pence** (pĕns). **a.** *Abbr.* **p.** A coin used in Great Britain since 1971, worth 1/100 of a pound. Also called *new penny.* **b.** *Abbr.* **d.** A coin formerly used in Great Britain, worth 1/12 of a shilling or 1/240 of a pound. **4.** Any of various coins of small denomination. **5.** A sum of money. *—attributive.* Often used to modify another noun: *a penny arcade; penny candy.* ***—idiom.*** **pretty penny.** A considerable sum of money: *I paid a pretty penny for that ring.* [Middle English, an English coin, from Old English *penig*.]

pennywhistle

penny ante *n.* **1.** *Games.* A poker game in which the highest bet is limited to a penny or another small sum. **2.** *Informal.* A business proposal or transaction on a trivial scale. **—pen′ny-an′te** (pĕn′ē-ăn′tē) *adj.*

pen·ny·cress (pĕn′ē-krĕs′) *n.* Any of several plants of the genus *Thlaspi*, having small, flattened seed pods with winglike margins, especially the Eurasian species *T. arvense*, a weed naturalized throughout North America.

penny pincher *n. Informal.* A very stingy person.

pen·ny-pinch·ing (pĕn′ē-pĭn′chĭng) *adj.* Giving or spending money grudgingly; niggardly. See Synonyms at **stingy. —pen′ny-pinch′ing** *n.*

pen·ny·roy·al (pĕn′ē-roi′əl) *n.* **1.** A Eurasian mint *(Mentha pulegium)* having small lilac-blue flowers and ovate or nearly orbicular leaves that yield a useful, aromatic oil. **2.** An aromatic plant *(Hedeoma pulegioides)* of eastern North America, having purple-blue flowers and glabrous leaves that yield an oil used as an insect repellent. [Probably by folk etymology from Middle English *puliol real*, from Anglo-Norman : *puliol*, thyme (from Latin *pūlegium*) + *real*, royal (from Latin *rēgālis*; see REGAL).]

pen·ny·weight (pĕn′ē-wāt′) *n. Abbr.* **dwt., pwt.** A unit of troy weight equal to 24 grains, 1/20 of a troy ounce or approximately 1.555 grams.

pen·ny·whis·tle also **pen·ny whis·tle** (pĕn′ē-hwĭs′əl, -wĭs′-) *n. Music.* An inexpensive fipple flute, usually having a plastic mouthpiece and a tin body.

pen·ny-wise or **pen·ny·wise** (pĕn′ē-wīz′) *adj.* Careful in dealing with small sums of money or small matters.

pen·ny·wort (pĕn′ē-wûrt′, -wôrt′) *n.* Any of several plants having rounded leaves suggestive of pennies, as: **a.** A Eurasian

ă pat	oi boy
ā pay	ou out
âr care	o͝o took
ä father	o͞o boot
ĕ pet	ŭ cut
ē be	ûr urge
ĭ pit	th thin
ī pie	*th* this
îr pier	hw which
ŏ pot	zh vision
ō toe	ə about, item
ô paw	♦ regionalism

Stress marks: ′ (primary); ′ (secondary), as in **dictionary** (dĭk′shə-nĕr′ē)

plant *(Umbilicus rupestris)* having thick, peltate leaves and yellowish-green flowers. Also called *navelwort.* **b.** A North American plant *(Obolaria virginica)* having fleshy leaves and small white or purplish flowers.

pen•ny•worth (pĕn′ē-wûrth′) *n.* **1.** As much as a penny will buy. **2.** A small amount; a modicum. **3.** A bargain: *got my pennyworth at that price.*

Pe•nob•scot (pə-nŏb′skət, -skŏt′) *n., pl.* **Penobscot** or **-scots. 1.a.** A Native American people inhabiting Penobscot Bay and the Penobscot River valley in Maine. The Penobscot, who joined the Abenaki confederacy in the mid-18th century, are represented in the Maine legislature by a nonvoting delegate. **b.** A member of this people. **2.** The Algonquian language of the Penobscot, a dialect of Eastern Abenaki. [From a Penobscot place name.] **—Pe•nob′scot** *adj.*

Penobscot River. A river rising in several lakes and tributaries in western and central Maine and flowing about 563 km (350 mi) to **Penobscot Bay,** an inlet of the Atlantic Ocean. The river is an important source of power for pulpwood and paper mills. The bay was first explored by English navigators in 1603.

pe•nol•o•gy also **poe•nol•o•gy** (pē-nŏl′ə-jē) *n.* The study, theory, and practice of prison management and criminal rehabilitation. [Latin *poena,* penalty (from Greek *poinē;* see **kʷei-**[1] in Appendix) + –LOGY.] **—pe′no•log′i•cal** (pē′nə-lŏj′ĭ-kəl) *adj.* **—pe′no•log′i•cal•ly** *adv.* **—pe•nol′o•gist** *n.*

pen•on•cel (pĕn′ən-sĕl′) *n.* Variant of **pennoncel.**

pen pal *n.* A person with whom one becomes acquainted through a friendly, regular correspondence.

pen point *n.* **1.** A tapering metal device with a split point that fits into a holder and is used for writing; a nib. **2.** The point or tip of a pen.

Pen•sa•co•la (pĕn′sə-kō′lə). A city of extreme northwest Florida on **Pensacola Bay,** an inlet of the Gulf of Mexico. Originally settled by the Spanish in 1559, the city passed back and forth between the Spanish, French, and British until it was captured by Andrew Jackson in 1814 during the War of 1812. It formally became part of the United States in 1821. Population, 57,619.

pen•sil (pĕn′səl) *n.* Variant of **pencel.**

pen•sile (pĕn′sīl′) *adj.* **1.** Hanging loosely; suspended: *the pensile nest of the Baltimore oriole.* **2.** Having or building a hanging nest. Used of birds. [Latin *pēnsilis,* from *pēnsus,* past participle of *pendēre,* to hang. See **(s)pen-** in Appendix.]

pen•sion[1] (pĕn′shən) *n.* A sum of money paid regularly as a retirement benefit or by way of patronage. **—pension** *tr.v.* **-sioned, -sion•ing, -sions. 1.** To grant a pension to. **2.** To retire or dismiss with a pension: *"Some French farmers suggest that the Government pension off the older and less efficient farmers"* (E.J. Dionne, Jr.). [Middle English *pensioun,* payment, from Old French *pension,* from Latin *pēnsiō, pēnsiōn-,* from *pēnsus,* past participle of *pendere,* to weigh, pay. See **(s)pen-** in Appendix.] **—pen′sion•a•ble** *adj.*

pen•sion[2] (päɴ-syôɴ′) *n.* **1.** A boarding house or small hotel in Europe: *"A pension had somewhat less to offer than a hotel; it was always smaller, and never elegant; it sometimes offered breakfast, and sometimes not"* (John Irving). **2.** Accommodations or the payment for accommodations, especially at a boarding house or small hotel in Europe. **3.** Room and board. [French, from Old French, payment. See PENSION[1].]

pen•sion•ar•y (pĕn′shə-nĕr′ē) *adj.* **1.** Constituting a pension. **2.** Mercenary; venal. **—pensionary** *n., pl.* **-ies. 1.** A pensioner. **2.** A hireling.

pen•sion•er (pĕn′shə-nər) *n.* **1.** One who receives a pension. **2.** One who is dependent on the bounty of another. **3.** *Obsolete.* **a.** A gentleman-at-arms. **b.** An attendant; a retainer.

pen•sive (pĕn′sĭv) *adj.* **1.** Deeply, often wistfully or dreamily thoughtful. **2.** Suggestive or expressive of melancholy thoughtfulness. [Middle English *pensif,* from Old French, from *penser,* to think, from Latin *pēnsāre,* frequentative of *pendere,* to weigh. See **(s)pen-** in Appendix.] **—pen′sive•ly** *adv.* **—pen′sive•ness** *n.*

SYNONYMS: *pensive, contemplative, reflective, meditative, thoughtful.* These adjectives mean characterized by or disposed to thought, especially serious or deep thought. *Pensive* often connotes thought of a wistful, dreamy, or sad quality: *"while pensive poets painful vigils keep"* (Alexander Pope). *Seeing the depth of her despair, he grew pensive. Contemplative* implies slow, directed consideration, often with conscious intent of achieving better understanding or spiritual or aesthetic enrichment: *"The Contemplative Atheist is rare . . . And yet they seem to be more than they are"* (Francis Bacon). *Reflective* suggests careful, analytical deliberation, as in reappraising past experience: *"Cromwell was of the active, not the reflective temper"* (John Morley). *Meditative* implies earnest, sustained thought: *The scholar was reticent, aloof, and meditative. Thoughtful* can refer to absorption in thought or to the habit of reflection and circumspection: *The judge looked thoughtful, then granted the motion. Thoughtful voters viewed the proposed legislation with alarm.*

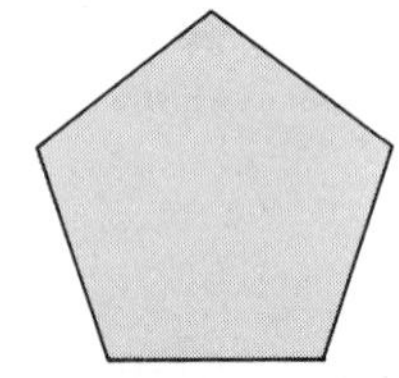

pentagon
Top: Polygonal figure
Bottom: The Pentagon, Arlington, Virginia

pen•ste•mon (pĕn-stē′mən, pĕn′stə-mən) *n.* Any of numerous plants of the genus *Penstemon,* native to North America and eastern Asia, having opposite leaves, flowers with a usually two-lipped, variously colored corolla, and capsules containing many seeds. Also called *beardtongue.* [New Latin *Pēnstēmōn,* genus name : Greek *pente,* five; see **penkʷe** in Appendix + Greek *stēmōn,* thread; see **stā-** in Appendix.]

pen•stock (pĕn′stŏk′) *n.* **1.** A sluice or gate used to control a flow of water. **2.** A pipe or conduit used to carry water to a water wheel or turbine.

pent (pĕnt) *v.* A past tense and a past participle of **pen**[2]**. —pent** *adj.* Penned or shut up; closely confined.

penta– or **pent–** *pref.* Five: *pentamerous.* [Greek, from *pente,* five. See **penkʷe** in Appendix.]

pen•ta•chlo•ro•phe•nol (pĕn′tə-klôr′ə-fē′nōl′, -nôl′, -nŏl′, -klōr′-) *n.* A toxic white crystalline compound, C_6Cl_5OH, used in solution as a fungicide and wood preservative.

pen•ta•cle (pĕn′tə-kəl) *n.* A five-pointed star formed by five straight lines connecting the vertices of a pentagon and enclosing another pentagon in the completed figure. Also called *pentagram.* [Medieval Latin **pentaculum* : Greek *penta-,* penta- + Latin *-culum,* diminutive suff.]

pen•tad (pĕn′tăd′) *n.* A group of five. [Greek *pentas, pentad-,* group of five, from *pente,* five. See **penkʷe** in Appendix.]

pen•ta•dac•tyl (pĕn′tə-dăk′təl) also **pen•ta•dac•ty•late** (-tə-lĭt, -lāt′) *adj.* Having five fingers or toes on each hand or foot. [Latin *pentadactylus,* from Greek *pentadaktulos* : *penta-,* penta- + *daktulos,* finger.] **—pen′ta•dac′tyl•ism** *n.*

pen•ta•gon (pĕn′tə-gŏn′) *n.* **1.** A polygon having five sides and five interior angles. **2. Pentagon.** The United States military establishment. Used with *the.* [Late Latin *pentagōnum,* from Greek *pentagōnon* : *penta-,* penta- + *-gōnon,* -gon.] **—pen•tag′o•nal** (pĕn-tăg′ə-nəl) *adj.* **—pen•tag′o•nal•ly** *adv.*

Pen•ta•gon•ese (pĕn′tə-gŏn-ēz′, -ēs′) *n.* United States military jargon: *"Being open and egalitarian, Americans characteristically speak in a straight-forward, declarative manner—discounting Pentagonese and other jargon"* (Jack Pitman).

pen•ta•gram (pĕn′tə-grăm′) *n.* See **pentacle.**

pen•ta•he•dron (pĕn′tə-hē′drən) *n., pl.* **-drons** or **-dra** (-drə). A solid having five plane faces. **—pen′ta•he′dral** (-drəl) *adj.*

pen•tam•er•ous (pĕn-tăm′ər-əs) *adj.* **1.** Having five similar parts. **2.** Having flower parts, such as petals, sepals, and stamens, in sets of five, as in the geranium. **—pen•tam′er•ism** *n.*

pen•tam•e•ter (pĕn-tăm′ĭ-tər) *n.* **1.** A line of verse consisting of five metrical feet. **2.** English verse composed in iambic pentameter. [Latin, from Greek *pentametros* : *penta-,* penta- + *metron,* measure; see METER[1].]

pen•tane (pĕn′tān′) *n.* Any of three colorless, flammable isomeric hydrocarbons, C_5H_{12}, derived from petroleum and used as solvents.

pen•tan•gu•lar (pĕn-tăng′gyə-lər) *adj.* Having five angles.

pen•ta•pep•tide (pĕn′tə-pĕp′tīd) *n.* A polypeptide composed of five amino acids.

pen•ta•ploid (pĕn′tə-ploid′) *adj.* Having five haploid sets of chromosomes. **—pentaploid** *n.* A pentaploid individual.

pen•ta•quine (pĕn′tə-kwēn′, -kwĭn) also **pen•ta•quin** (-kwĭn) *n.* A synthetic drug, $C_{18}H_{27}N_3O$, used with quinine in the prevention or treatment of malaria. [PENTA– + QUIN(OLIN)E.]

pen•tar•chy (pĕn′tär′kē) *n., pl.* **-chies. 1.** Government by five rulers. **2.** A body of five joint rulers. **3.** An association or federation of five governments, each ruled by a different leader. [Greek *pentarkhia* : *penta-,* penta- + *-arkhia,* -archy.] **—pen•tar′chi•cal** (pĕn-tär′kĭ-kəl) *adj.*

pen•ta•stich (pĕn′tə-stĭk′) *n.* A poem or stanza having five lines. [From Late Greek *pentastikhos,* of five lines : *penta-,* penta- + *stikhos,* line; see **steigh-** in Appendix.]

pen•ta•stome (pĕn′tə-stōm′) *n.* See **tongue worm.** [From New Latin *Pentastomum,* genus name : PENTA– + *-stomum,* neuter of *-stomus,* mouthed (from STOMA).]

Pen•ta•teuch (pĕn′tə-to͞ok′, -tyo͞ok′) *n.* The first five books of the Hebrew Scriptures. [Middle English *Pentateuke,* from Late Latin *Pentateuchus,* from Greek *Pentateukhos* : *penta-,* penta- + *teukhos,* implement, vessel, scroll case; see **dheugh-** in Appendix.] **—Pen′ta•teuch′al** *adj.*

pen•tath•lete (pĕn-tăth′lēt) *n.* *Sports.* An athlete who participates in a pentathlon.

pen•tath•lon (pĕn-tăth′lən, -lŏn′) *n.* *Sports.* **1.** An athletic contest in which each participant competes in five track and field events, usually sprinting, hurdling, long jumping, and discus and javelin throwing. **2.** The modern pentathlon. [Greek : *penta-,* penta- + *athlon,* contest.]

pen•ta•ton•ic (pĕn′tə-tŏn′ĭk) *adj.* *Music.* Of or using only five tones, especially the first, second, third, fifth, and sixth tones of a diatonic scale.

pen•ta•va•lent (pĕn′tə-vā′lənt) *adj.* Having a valence of 5.

pen•taz•o•cine (pĕn-tăz′ə-sēn′) *n.* A synthetic narcotic drug, $C_{19}H_{27}NO$, used as a nonaddictive analgesic, often in place of morphine. [PENT(A)– + AZO– + –INE[2].]

Pen•te•cost (pĕn′tĭ-kôst′, -kŏst′) *n.* **1.** The seventh Sunday after Easter, commemorating the descent of the Holy Spirit upon the disciples. Also called *Whitsunday.* **2.** *Judaism.* See **Shavuot.** [Middle English *pentecoste,* from Old English *Pentecosten,* from Late Latin *Pentēcostē,* from Greek *pentēkostē (hēmera),* fiftieth (day), feminine of *pentēkostos,* fiftieth, from *pentēkonta,* fifty. See **penkʷe** in Appendix.]

Pen•te•cos•tal (pĕn′tĭ-kŏs′təl, -kô′stəl) *adj.* **1.** Of, relating to, or occurring at Pentecost. **2.** Of, relating to, or being any of various Christian religious congregations whose members seek to be filled with the Holy Spirit, in emulation of the Apostles at Pentecost. **—Pentecostal** *n.* A member of a Pentecostal congregation: *"Pentecostals rejected the belief of many fundamentalists that . . . God had ceased to reveal himself to man"* (John B. Judis). **—Pen'te·cos'tal·ism** *n.* **—Pen'te·cos'tal·ist** *adj. & n.*

pent·house (pĕnt'hous') *n.* **1.a.** An apartment or dwelling situated on the roof of a building. **b.** A residence, often with a terrace, on the top floor or floors of a building. **c.** A structure housing machinery on the roof of a building. **2.** A shed or sloping roof attached to the side of a building or wall. **3.** *Sports.* The sloping roof that rises from the inner wall to the outer wall surrounding three sides of the court in court tennis, off which the ball is served. [Alteration of Middle English *pentis, pentace,* a shed attached to a wall of a building, from Anglo-Norman *pentiz,* penthouses, from Old French *apentiz,* penthouse, from *apent,* past participle of *apendre,* to belong, depend, from Medieval Latin *appendere,* from Latin, to hang, suspend. See APPEND.]

WORD HISTORY: The word *penthouse* and the structure it denotes have both come a long way. The word goes back to Latin *appendere,* "to cause to be suspended." In Medieval Latin *appendere* developed the sense "to belong, depend," a sense that passed into *apendre,* the Old French development of *appendere.* From *apent,* the past participle of *apendre,* came the derivative *apentiz,* "low building behind or beside a house," and the Anglo-Norman plural form *pentiz.* The form without the *a–* was then borrowed into Middle English, giving us *pentis* (first recorded about 1300), which was applied to sheds or lean-tos added on to buildings. Because these structures often had sloping roofs, the word was connected with the French word *pente,* "slope," and the second part of the word changed to *house,* which could mean simply "a building for human use." The use of the term with reference to fancy penthouse apartments developed from the application of the word to a structure built on the roof to cover such things as a stairway or an elevator shaft. *Penthouse* then came to mean an apartment built on a rooftop and finally the top floor of an apartment building.

Pen·tic·ton (pĕn-tĭk'tən). A city of southern British Columbia, Canada, east of Vancouver at the southern shore of Okanagan Lake. It is a trade center in a resort area. Population, 23,181.

pen·ti·men·to (pĕn'tə-mĕn'tō) *n., pl.* **-ti** (-tē). An underlying image in a painting, as an earlier painting, a part of a painting, or an original draft, that shows through, usually when the top layer of paint has become transparent with age. [Italian, correction, pentimento, from *pentire,* to repent, from Latin *paenitēre.*]

Pent·land Firth (pĕnt'lənd). A narrow channel between northeast Scotland and the Orkney Islands.

pent·land·ite (pĕnt'lən-dīt') *n.* A yellowish-brown nickel iron sulfide that is the principal ore of nickel. [French, after Joseph B. *Pentland* (1797–1873), Irish scientist.]

pen·to·bar·bi·tal sodium (pĕn'tə-bär'bĭ-tôl', -tăl') *n.* A white crystalline or powdery barbiturate, $C_{11}H_{17}N_2O_3Na$, used as a hypnotic, a sedative, and an anticonvulsive drug. Also called *pentobarbitone.*

pen·to·bar·bi·tone (pĕn'tə-bär'bĭ-tōn') *n.* See **pentobarbital sodium.** [PENT(A)– + BARBIT(URIC ACID) + –ONE.]

pen·to·san (pĕn'tə-săn') *n.* Any of a group of polysaccharides found with cellulose in many woody plants and yielding pentoses on hydrolysis.

pen·tose (pĕn'tōs', -tōz') *n.* Any of a class of monosaccharides having five carbon atoms per molecule and including ribose and several other sugars.

Pen·to·thal (pĕn'tə-thôl'). A trademark used for thiopental sodium.

pent·ox·ide (pĕnt-ŏk'sīd') *n.* A compound having five atoms of oxygen combined with another element or radical.

pent-up (pĕnt'ŭp') *adj.* Not given expression; repressed: *pent-up emotions.*

pen·tyl (pĕn'təl) *n.* See **amyl.**

pen·tyl·ene·tet·ra·zol (pĕn'tə-lēn'tĕt'rə-zôl', -zōl', -zŏl') *n.* A drug, $C_6H_{10}N_4$, that is a stimulant of the central nervous system and is used chiefly as an analeptic. [PENT(A)– + (METH)YLENE + TETR(A)– + AZ(O)– + –OL(E).]

pe·nu·che also **pe·nu·chi** (pə-no͞o'chē) or **pa·no·cha** (-nō'chə), **pa·no·che** (-chē) *n.* A fudgelike confection of brown sugar, cream or milk, and chopped nuts. [Variant of PANOCHA.]

pe·nuch·le or **pe·nuck·le** (pē'nŭk'əl) *n. Games.* Variants of **pinochle.**

pe·nult (pē'nŭlt', pĭ-nŭlt') also **pe·nul·ti·ma** (pĭ-nŭl'tə-mə) *n.* **1.** The next to the last item in a series. **2.** *Linguistics.* The next to the last syllable in a word. [Short for *penultima,* from Latin *paenultima,* feminine of *paenultimus,* next to last : *paene,* almost + *ultimus,* last; see ULTIMATE.]

pe·nul·ti·mate (pĭ-nŭl'tə-mĭt) *adj.* **1.** Next to last. **2.** *Linguistics.* Of or relating to the penult of a word: *penultimate stress.* **—penultimate** *n.* The next to the last. [From Latin *paenultimus.* See PENULT.] **—pe·nul'ti·mate·ly** *adj.*

pe·num·bra (pĭ-nŭm'brə) *n., pl.* **-brae** (-brē) or **-bras. 1.** A partial shadow, as in an eclipse, between regions of complete shadow and complete illumination. See Synonyms at **shade. 2.** The grayish outer part of a sunspot. **3.** An area in which something exists to a lesser or an uncertain degree: *"The First Amendment has a penumbra where privacy is protected from governmental intrusion"* (Joseph A. Califano, Jr.). **4.** An outlying, surrounding region; a periphery: *"Downtown Chicago and its penumbra also stand rejuvenated"* (John McCormick). [New Latin : Latin *paene,* almost + Latin *umbra,* shadow.] **—pe·num'bral, pe·num'brous** *adj.*

pe·nu·ri·ous (pə-no͝or'ē-əs, -nyo͝or'-) *adj.* **1.** Ungenerously or pettily unwilling to spend money. See Synonyms at **stingy. 2.** Yielding little; barren: *a penurious land.* **3.** Poverty-stricken; destitute. [From Medieval Latin *pēnūriōsus,* from Latin *pēnūria,* want.] **—pe·nu'ri·ous·ly** *adv.* **—pe·nu'ri·ous·ness** *n.*

pen·u·ry (pĕn'yə-rē) *n.* **1.** Extreme want or poverty; destitution. **2.** Extreme dearth; barrenness or insufficiency. [Middle English *penurie,* from Latin *pēnūria,* want.]

Pe·nu·ti·an (pə-no͞o'tē-ən, -shən) *n.* A proposed stock of North American Indian languages spoken in Pacific coastal areas from California into British Columbia. [From the reconstructed words for "two" in two of its subgroups.]

Pen·za (pĕn'zə, pyĕn'-). A city of west-central Russia south-southwest of Kazan. Founded as a fortress in 1666 and chartered in 1682, it is a railroad junction and major industrial center. Population, 527,000.

Pen·zance (pĕn-zăns'). A municipal borough of southwest England west-southwest of Plymouth. It is a port and summer resort and was frequently raided by pirates until the 18th century. Population, 19,521.

Pen·zi·as (pĕnt'sē-əs), **Arno Allan.** Born 1933. German-born American physicist. He shared a 1978 Nobel Prize for work on cosmic microwave radiation.

pe·on (pē'ŏn', pē'ən) *n.* **1.a.** An unskilled laborer or farm worker of Latin America or the southwest United States. **b.** Such a worker bound in servitude to a landlord creditor. **2.** A menial worker; a drudge. **3.** (*also* pyo͞on). An Indian or Ceylonese messenger, servant, or foot soldier. [Spanish, day laborer, from Medieval Latin *pedō, pedōn-,* foot soldier. See PIONEER. Sense 3, possibly from Portuguese *peão,* from Medieval Latin *pedō.*]

pe·on·age (pē'ə-nĭj) *n.* **1.** The condition of being a peon. **2.** A system by which debtors are bound in servitude to their creditors until their debts are paid.

pe·o·ny (pē'ə-nē) *n., pl.* **-nies.** Any of various garden plants of the genus *Paeonia,* having large, variously colored flowers with numerous stamens and several pistils. [Middle English *pione,* from Old English *pēonie* and Anglo-Norman *peonie,* both from Medieval Latin *peōnia,* from Latin *paeōnia,* from Greek *paiōnia,* perhaps from *Paiōn,* Apollo, physician of the gods.]

peo·ple (pē'pəl) *n., pl.* **people. 1.** Human beings considered as a group or in indefinite numbers: *People were dancing in the street. I met all sorts of people.* **2.** A body of persons living in the same country under one national government; a nationality. **3.** *pl.* **peo·ples.** A body of persons sharing a common religion, culture, language, or inherited condition of life. **4.** Persons with regard to their residence, class, profession, or group: *city people.* **5.** The mass of ordinary persons; the populace. Used with *the*: *"those who fear and distrust the people, and wish to draw all powers from them into the hands of the higher classes"* (Thomas Jefferson). **6.** The citizens of a political unit, such as a nation or a state; the electorate. Used with *the.* **7.** Persons subordinate to or loyal to a ruler, a superior, or an employer: *The queen showed great compassion for her people.* **8.** Family, relatives, or ancestors. **9.** *Informal.* Animals or other beings distinct from human beings: *Rabbits and squirrels are the furry, little people of the woods.* **—people** *tr.v.* **-pled, -pling, -ples.** To furnish with or as if with people; populate. [Middle English *peple,* from Old French *pueple,* from Latin *populus,* of Etruscan origin.] **—peo'pler** *n.*

USAGE NOTE: Used as a plural *people* is a form with no exactly corresponding singular. (English is not odd in this respect: the equivalent word is anomalous in Spanish, Italian, Russian, and many other languages.) In the past, grammarians have sometimes insisted that *people* is a collective noun that should not be used as a substitute for *persons* when referring to a specific number of individuals, as in *Six people were arrested.* But *people* has always been used in such contexts, and the distinction is now so widely ignored in general writing that it seems pedantic to insist on it. *Persons* is still preferred in quasilegal contexts, however, as in *Vehicles containing fewer than three persons may not use the left lane during rush hours.* Only the singular *person* is used in compounds involving a specific numeral: *a six-person car; a two-person show.* But *people* is used in other compounds: *people mover; people power.* These examples are exceptions to the general rule that plural nouns cannot be used in such compounds; note that we do not say *teethpaste* or *books-burning.* See Usage Note at **man.**

peo·ple·hood (pē'pəl-ho͝od') *n.* The state or condition of being a people or one of a people: *"As symbols go, few are as national and sectarian as the menorah. It is the symbol of Jewish peoplehood"* (Charles Krauthammer).

people mover *n.* A means of mass transit, such as a moving sidewalk or a monorail, used to transport people, usually along a fixed route.

Peo·ple's Party (pē'pəlz) *n.* See **Populist Party.**

ă pat	oi boy
ā pay	ou out
âr care	o͝o took
ä father	o͞o boot
ĕ pet	ŭ cut
ē be	ûr urge
ĭ pit	th thin
ī pie	*th* this
îr pier	hw which
ŏ pot	zh vision
ō toe	ə about, item
ô paw	♦ regionalism

Stress marks: ' (primary); ' (secondary), as in **dictionary** (dĭk'shə-nĕr'ē)

People's Republic *n.* A political organization founded and controlled by a national Communist party.

Pe·or·i·a[1] (pē-ôr′ē-ə, -ōr′-) *n., pl.* **Peoria** or **-as. 1.** A Native American people forming part of the Illinois confederacy. **2.** A member of this people.

Pe·or·i·a[2] (pē-ôr′ē-ə, -ōr′-). A city of northwest-central Illinois on the Illinois River north of Springfield. Founded on the site of a French fort established by La Salle in 1680, it is a transportation and industrial center. Population, 124,160.

pep (pĕp) *Informal. n.* Energy and high spirits; vim: *"The duchess is full of pep, that particularly American word that expresses precisely her energy and gaiety"* (Suzy Menkes). **—pep** *tr.v.* **pepped, pep·ping, peps.** To bring energy or liveliness to; invigorate: *The good news pepped him up.* [Short for PEPPER.]

pep·er·o·mi·a (pĕp′ə-rō′mē-ə) *n.* Any of numerous succulent tropical herbs of the genus *Peperomia,* having simple, entire, palmately veined leaves and numerous minute, unisexual flowers densely grouped in cylindrical spikes. [New Latin *Peperomia,* genus name : from Greek *peperi,* pepper; see PEPPER + Greek *homos,* same; see HOMO–.]

pe·pi·no (pə-pē′nō) *n., pl.* **-nos. 1.** A spiny Andean shrub *(Solanum muricatum)* having bright blue flowers and ovoid, violet-purple fruits with edible, yellow, aromatic, acid flesh. **2.** The fruit of this plant. [American Spanish, from Spanish, cucumber, from Latin *pepō,* melon. See PEPO.]

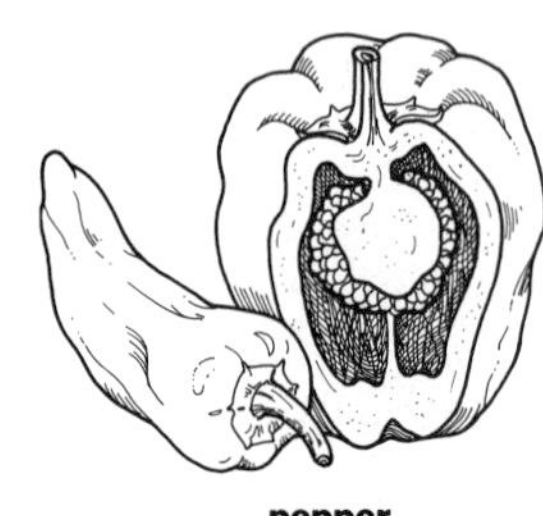
pepper

Pep·in the Short (pĕp′ĭn). Also known as **Pepin III.** 714?–768. King of the Franks (751–768). He defended papal interests and established the core territory of the Papal States.

pep·los (pĕp′ləs, -lŏs′) also **pep·lus** (-ləs) *n., pl.* **-los·es** also **-lus·es.** A loose outer robe worn by women in ancient Greece. Also called *peplum.* [Greek.]

pep·lum (pĕp′ləm) *n., pl.* **-lums. 1.** A short overskirt or ruffle attached at the waistline of a jacket, blouse, or dress. **2.** See **peplos.** [Latin, robe of state, from Greek *peplon,* neuter of *peplos,* peplos.] **—pep′lumed** *adj.*

pep·lus (pĕp′ləs) *n.* Variant of **peplos.**

pe·po (pē′pō) *n., pl.* **-pos.** The fruit of any of various related plants, such as the cantaloupe, watermelon, cucumber, squash, pumpkin, and melon, having a hard or leathery rind, fleshy pulp, and numerous flattened seeds. [Latin, a kind of melon, from Greek *pepōn,* ripe. See **pekʷ-** in Appendix.]

pep·per (pĕp′ər) *n.* **1.** Black pepper. **2.** Any of several plants of the genus *Piper,* as cubeb, betel, and kava. **3. a.** Any of several tropical American, cultivated forms of *Capsicum frutescens* or *C. annuum,* having podlike, many-seeded, variously colored berries. **b.** The podlike fruit of any of these plants, varying in size, shape, and degree of pungency, with the milder types including the bell pepper and pimiento, and the more pungent types including the cherry pepper. **4.** Any of various condiments made from the more pungent varieties of *Capsicum frutescens,* such as cayenne pepper, tabasco pepper, and chili. Also called *hot pepper.* **5.** *Baseball.* A warm-up exercise in which players standing a short distance from a batter field the ball and toss it to the batter, who hits each toss back to the fielders. Also called *pepper game.* **—pepper** *tr.v.* **-pered, -per·ing, -pers. 1.** To season or sprinkle with pepper. **2.** To sprinkle liberally; dot. **3.** To shower with or as if with small missiles. See Synonyms at **barrage**[2]. **4.** To make (a speech, for example) lively and vivid with wit or invective. [Middle English *peper,* from Old English *pipor,* from Latin *piper,* from Greek *peperi,* from Sanskrit *pippalī,* from *pippalam,* pepper tree.]

pepper mill

pep·per-and-salt (pĕp′ər-ən-sôlt′) *adj.* Having a close mixture of black and white: *a pepper-and-salt beard.*

pep·per·box (pĕp′ər-bŏks′) *n.* See **peppershaker.**

pep·per·bush (pĕp′ər-bo͝osh′) *n. Botany.* Sweet pepperbush.

pep·per·corn (pĕp′ər-kôrn′) *n.* **1.** A dried berry of the pepper vine *Piper nigrum.* **2.** A small or insignificant thing.

pep·per·cress (pĕp′ər-krĕs′) *n.* See **peppergrass.**

pepper game *n. Baseball.* See **pepper** (sense 5).

pep·per·grass (pĕp′ər-grăs′) *n.* Any of several plants of the genus *Lepidium,* especially the North American species *L. virginicum,* having small white flowers and pungent foliage and seeds. Also called *peppercress, pepperwort.*

pep·per·idge (pĕp′ər-ĭj) *n.* See **sour gum.** [Origin unknown.]

pepper mill *n.* A utensil for grinding peppercorns.

pep·per·mint (pĕp′ər-mĭnt′) *n.* **1.** A plant, *Mentha piperita,* having small purple or white flowers and downy leaves that yield a pungent oil. **2.** The oil from this plant or a preparation made from it, used as a flavoring. **3.** A candy or lozenge flavored with this oil.

pep·per·o·ni (pĕp′ə-rō′nē) *n., pl.* **-nis. 1.** A highly spiced pork and beef sausage. **2.** A slice of this type of sausage. [Italian *peperoni,* pl. of *peperone,* pimento, red pepper, augmentative of *pepe,* pepper, from Latin *piper.* See PEPPER.]

pepper pot *n.* **1.** A soup made with vegetables and tripe or other meat, seasoned with pepper, and often containing dumplings. Also called *Philadelphia pepper pot.* **2.** A thick West Indian stew of meat or fish, vegetables, and regional condiments. **3.** See **peppershaker.**

peppermint
Mentha piperita

Pep·per·rell (pĕp′ər-əl), Sir **William.** 1696–1759. American merchant and colonial official. After his defeat of French forces at Louisbourg on Cape Breton Island (1745) he was the first American to be made a baronet by the British Crown (1746).

pep·per·shak·er (pĕp′ər-shā′kər) *n.* A container with small holes in the top for sprinkling ground pepper. Also called *pepperbox, pepper pot.*

pepper tree also **pep·per·tree** (pĕp′ər-trē′) *n.* Any of several evergreen trees of the genus *Schinus,* especially *S. molle,* native to South America, having compound leaves, yellowish-white flowers clustered in branching panicles, and small rose-colored drupes. Also called *California pepper tree.*

pep·per·wood (pĕp′ər-wo͝od′) *n.* See **Hercules' club** (sense 2).

pep·per·wort (pĕp′ər-wûrt′, -wôrt′) *n.* **1.** Any of various aquatic or marsh ferns of the genus *Marsilea,* having floating, four-parted palmate leaves rising from long runners. Also called *water clover.* **2.** See **peppergrass.**

pep·per·y (pĕp′ə-rē) *adj.* **1.** Of, containing, or resembling pepper; sharp or pungent in flavor. **2.** Vigorously sharp-tempered: *a peppery sales clerk.* **3.** Sharp and stinging in style or content; vivid or fiery: *peppery criticism.* **—pep′per·i·ness** *n.*

pep pill *n. Slang.* A tablet or capsule containing a stimulant drug, especially an amphetamine.

pep·py (pĕp′ē) *adj.* **-i·er, -i·est.** *Informal.* Full of or characterized by energy and high spirits; lively. **—pep′pi·ly** *adv.* **—pep′pi·ness** *n.*

pep·sin also **pep·sine** (pĕp′sĭn) *n.* **1.** A digestive enzyme found in gastric juice that catalyzes the breakdown of protein to peptides. **2.** A substance containing pepsin, obtained from the stomachs of hogs and calves and used as a digestive aid. [Greek *pepsis,* digestion (from *peptein,* to digest; see **pekʷ-** in Appendix) + –IN.]

pep·sin·o·gen (pĕp-sĭn′ə-jən) *n.* The inactive precursor to pepsin, formed in the cells of the mucous membrane of the stomach and converted to pepsin by hydrochloric acid during digestion.

pep talk *n. Informal.* A speech of exhortation, as to a team or staff, meant to instill enthusiasm or bolster morale.

pep·tic (pĕp′tĭk) *adj.* **1. a.** Of, relating to, or assisting digestion: *peptic secretion.* **b.** Induced by or associated with the action of digestive secretions: *a peptic ulcer.* **2.** Of, relating to, or involving pepsin. **3.** Capable of digesting. **—peptic** *n.* A digestive agent. [Latin *pepticus,* from Greek *peptikos,* digested, from *peptos,* from *peptein,* to digest. See **pekʷ-** in Appendix.]

pep·ti·dase (pĕp′tĭ-dās′, -dāz′) *n.* An enzyme that hydrolyzes peptides into amino acids.

pep·tide (pĕp′tīd′) *n.* Any of various natural or synthetic compounds containing two or more amino acids linked by the carboxyl group of one amino acid and the amino group of another. [PEPT(ONE) + –IDE.] **—pep·tid′ic** (-tĭd′ĭk) *adj.* **—pep·tid′i·cal·ly** *adv.*

peptide bond *n.* The chemical bond formed between the carboxyl groups and amino groups of neighboring amino acids, constituting the primary linkage of all protein structures.

pep·ti·do·gly·can (pĕp′tĭ-dō-glī′kən, -kăn′) *n.* A polymer found in the cell walls of prokaryotes that consists of polysaccharide and peptide chains in a strong molecular network. Also called *mucopeptide, murein.* [PEPTIDE + *glycan,* a polysaccharide.]

pep·tize (pĕp′tīz′) *tr.v.* **-tized, -tiz·ing, -tiz·es.** To disperse (a precipitate) to form a colloid. [Greek *peptein,* to digest; see **pekʷ-** in Appendix + –IZE.] **—pep′ti·za′tion** (-tĭ-zā′shən) *n.* **—pep′tiz′er** *n.*

pep·tone (pĕp′tōn′) *n.* Any of various compounds obtained by acid or enzyme hydrolysis of natural protein and used as nutrients in culture media. [German *Pepton,* from Greek *peptos,* digested, from *peptein,* to digest. See **pekʷ-** in Appendix.] **—pep·ton′ic** (-tŏn′ĭk) *adj.*

pep·to·nize (pĕp′tə-nīz′) *tr.v.* **-nized, -niz·ing, -niz·es. 1.** To convert (protein) into a peptone. **2.** To dissolve (food) by means of a proteolytic enzyme. **3.** To combine with peptone. **—pep′to·ni·za′tion** (-nĭ-zā′shən) *n.*

Pepys (pēps, pĕp′ĭs), **Samuel.** 1633–1703. English civil servant whose diary includes detailed descriptions of the Great Fire of London (1665) and the Great Plague (1666). **—Pepys′i·an** *adj.*

Pe·quot (pē′kwŏt′) *n., pl.* **Pequot** or **-quots. 1. a.** A Native American people formerly inhabiting eastern Connecticut, with present-day descendants in the same area. The Pequot and the Mohegan were the same people until the Mohegan broke away under Uncas in the early 17th century. **b.** A member of this people. **2.** The Algonquian language of the Pequot, dialectally related to Mohegan and Montauk. **—Pe′quot** *adj.*

per (pûr) *prep. Abbr.* **p. 1.** To, for, or by each; for every: *Gasoline once cost 40 cents per gallon.* **2.** *Usage Problem.* According to; by: *Changes were made to the manuscript per the author's instructions.* **3.** By means of; through. **—per** *adv. Informal.* **1.** For each one; apiece: *sold the cookies for one dollar per.* **2.** Per hour: *was driving at 60 miles per.* [Latin. See **per**[1] in Appendix.]

USAGE NOTE: *Per* is appropriately used in the description of ratios (*five miles per day; 20 dollars per person*). In its more general use to mean "according to" (as in *per the terms of the contract*), it is best reserved for business and legal communications, unless the writer seeks a tone of jocular formality.

per. *abbr.* **1.** Period. **2.** Person.

per– *pref.* **1.** Thoroughly; completely; intensely: *perfervid.* **2.** Containing an element in its highest oxidation state: *perchloric acid.* **3.** Containing a large or the largest possible proportion of an element: *peroxide.* **4.** Containing the peroxy group: *peracid.* [Latin, from *per,* through. See **per**[1] in Appendix.]

per·ac·id (pûr′ăs′ĭd) *n.* **1.** Any of various acids containing the peroxy group. **2.** An acid, such as perchloric acid, containing the largest proportion of oxygen in a series of related acids.

per·ad·ven·ture (pûr′əd-vĕn′chər, pĕr′-) *adv. Archaic.* Perhaps; perchance. **—peradventure** *n.* Chance or uncertainty; doubt. [Middle English *per aventure,* from Old French, by chance : *per,* through (from Latin; see PER) + *aventure,* chance; see ADVENTURE.]

per·am·bu·late (pə-răm′byə-lāt′) *v.* **-lat·ed, -lat·ing, -lates.** *—tr.* **1.** To walk through. **2.** To inspect (an area) on foot. *—intr.* To walk about; roam or stroll. [Latin *perambulāre, perambulāt-* : *per-,* per- + *ambulāre,* to walk.] **—per·am′bu·la′tion** *n.* **—per·am′bu·la·to′ry** (-lə-tôr′ē, -tōr′ē) *adj.*

per·am·bu·la·tor (pə-răm′byə-lā′tər) *n. Chiefly British.* A baby carriage.

per an·num (pər ăn′əm) *adv. Abbr.* **p.a.** By the year; annually: *A subscription costs 12 dollars per annum.* [Latin : *per,* per + *annum,* accusative of *annus,* year.]

per·bo·rate (pər-bôr′āt′, -bōr′-) *n.* A salt containing the radical BO_3, formed from a borate and hydrogen peroxide.

per·cale (pər-kāl′) *n.* A closely woven cotton fabric used for sheets and clothing. [French, from Persian *pargālah,* rag.]

per·ca·line (pûr′kə-lēn′) *n.* A fine cotton fabric, usually glazed, used especially for linings and in the bindings of books. [French, diminutive of *percale,* percale. See PERCALE.]

per cap·i·ta (pər kăp′ĭ-tə) *adv. & adj.* **1.** Per unit of population; per person: *In that year, Americans earned $15,304 per capita. Among the states, Connecticut has a high per capita income.* **2.** Equally to each individual. [Medieval Latin, by heads : Latin *per,* per + Latin *capita,* accusative pl. of *caput,* head.]

per·ceive (pər-sēv′) *tr.v.* **-ceived, -ceiv·ing, -ceives. 1.** To become aware of directly through any of the senses, especially sight or hearing. **2.** To achieve understanding of; apprehend. See Synonyms at **see**[1]. [Middle English *perceiven,* from Old French *perceivre,* from Latin *percipere* : *per-,* per- + *capere,* to seize; see **kap-** in Appendix.] **—per·ceiv′a·ble** *adj.* **—per·ceiv′a·bly** *adv.* **—per·ceiv′er** *n.*

per·cent also **per cent** (pər-sĕnt′) *—adv. Abbr.* **p.c., pct.** Out of each hundred; per hundred. *—n.* **1.** *pl.* **percent** also **per cent** One part in a hundred: *The report states that 42 percent of the alumni contributed to the endowment.* Also called *per centum.* **2.** *pl.* **percents.** A percentage or portion: *She has invested a large percent of her salary.* **3. percents.** *Chiefly British.* Public securities yielding interest at a specified percentage. *—adj.* Paying or demanding interest at a specified percentage: *a 5½ percent checking account.* [From *per cent.,* abbreviation of *per centum,* by the hundred : *per,* per; see PER + *centum,* hundred; see **dekm̥** in Appendix.]

USAGE NOTE: Statistically speaking, a quantity can be increased by any percentage but cannot be decreased by more than 100 percent. Once pollution has been reduced by 100 percent, for example, it ceases to exist, and no further reduction is possible. In defiance of this logic, however, advertisers sometimes refer to *a 150 percent decrease in lost luggage* or *a new dental rinse that reduces plaque on teeth by over 300 percent.* On reflection, it is possible to infer the intended meaning in these examples—presumably the rinse is three times as effective as some other tooth-cleaning procedure—but the ostensible claim is logically nonsensical, and the phrasing serves mostly to obscure the fact that the standard of comparison has not been made explicit. The latter phrase was unacceptable to 66 percent of the Usage Panel.

per·cent·age (pər-sĕn′tĭj) *n.* **1.a.** A fraction or ratio with 100 understood as the denominator; for example, 0.98 equals a percentage of 98. **b.** The result obtained by multiplying a quantity by a percent. **2.** A proportion or share in relation to a whole; a part: *The hecklers constituted only a small percentage of the audience.* **3.** An amount, such as an allowance, a duty, or a commission, that varies in proportion to a larger sum, such as total sales: *work for a percentage.* **4.** *Informal.* Advantage; gain: *There is no percentage in work without pay.*

USAGE NOTE: *Percentage,* when preceded by *the,* takes a singular verb: *The percentage of unskilled workers is small.* When preceded by *a,* it takes either a singular or plural verb, depending on the number of the noun in the prepositional phrase that follows: *A small percentage of the workers are unskilled. A large percentage of the crop has spoiled.*

per·cen·tile (pər-sĕn′tīl′) *n.* One of a set of points on a scale arrived at by dividing a group into parts in order of magnitude. For example, a score higher than 97 percent of those attained on an examination is said to be in the 97th percentile.

per cen·tum (pər sĕn′təm) *n.* See **percent** (sense 1). [Latin.] See PERCENT.]

per·cept (pûr′sĕpt′) *n.* **1.** The object of perception. **2.** A mental impression of something perceived by the senses, viewed as the basic component in the formation of concepts; a sense datum. [From Latin *perceptum,* neuter past participle of *percipere,* to perceive. See PERCEIVE.]

per·cep·ti·ble (pər-sĕp′tə-bəl) *adj.* Capable of being perceived by the senses or the mind: *perceptible sounds in the night.* [Late Latin *perceptibilis,* from Latin *perceptus,* past participle of *percipere,* to perceive. See PERCEIVE.] **—per·cep′ti·bil′i·ty** *n.* **—per·cep′ti·bly** *adv.*

SYNONYMS: *perceptible, palpable, appreciable, noticeable, discernible.* These adjectives apply to what is capable of being apprehended with the mind or through the senses as being real. *Perceptible* is the least specific: *After quite a perceptible pause, during which he consulted his notes, the lecturer continued. Palpable* applies both to what is perceptible by means of the sense of touch and to what is readily perceived by the mind: *"I felt as if my soul were grappling with a palpable enemy"* (Mary Wollstonecraft Shelley). *"The advantages Mr. Falkland possessed . . . are palpable"* (William Godwin). What is *appreciable* is capable of being estimated or measured: *Appreciable amounts of noxious waste are still being dumped into the harbor. Noticeable* means easily observed: *noticeable shadows under her eyes; a noticeable tremor in his voice. Discernible* means distinguishable, especially by the faculty of vision or the intellect: *The skyline is easily discernible even at a distance of several miles. The newspaper reports no discernible progress in the negotiations.*

per·cep·tion (pər-sĕp′shən) *n.* **1.** The process, act, or faculty of perceiving. **2.** The effect or product of perceiving. **3.** *Psychology.* **a.** Recognition and interpretation of sensory stimuli based chiefly on memory. **b.** The neurological processes by which such recognition and interpretation are effected. **4.a.** Insight, intuition, or knowledge gained by perceiving. **b.** The capacity for such insight. [Middle English *percepcioun,* from Old French *percepcion,* from Latin *perceptiō, perceptiōn-,* from *perceptus,* past participle of *percipere,* to perceive. See PERCEIVE.] **—per·cep′tion·al** *adj.*

per·cep·tive (pər-sĕp′tĭv) *adj.* **1.** Of or relating to perception: *perceptive faculties.* **2.a.** Having the ability to perceive; keen in discernment. **b.** Marked by discernment and understanding; sensitive. **—per·cep′tive·ly** *adv.* **—per′cep·tiv′i·ty** (pûr′sĕp-tĭv′ĭ-tē), **per·cep′tive·ness** (pər-sĕp′tĭv-nĭs) *n.*

per·cep·tu·al (pər-sĕp′cho͞o-əl) *adj.* Of, based on, or involving perception. **—per·cep′tu·al·ly** *adv.*

perch[1] (pûrch) *n.* **1.** A rod or branch serving as a roost for a bird. **2.a.** An elevated place for resting or sitting. **b.** A position that is secure, advantageous, or prominent. **3.** A pole, stick, or rod. **4.** *Chiefly British.* **a.** A linear measure equal to 5.50 yards or 16.5 feet (5.03 meters); a rod. **b.** One square rod of land. **5.** A unit of cubic measure used in stonework, usually 16.5 feet by 1.0 foot by 1.5 feet, or 24.75 cubic feet (0.70 cubic meter). **6.** A frame on which cloth is laid for examination of quality. **—perch** *v.* **perched, perch·ing, perch·es.** *—intr.* **1.** To alight or rest on a perch; roost: *A raven perched high in the pine.* **2.** To stand, sit, or rest on an elevated place or position. *—tr.* **1.** To place on or as if on a perch: *The child perched the glass on the edge of the counter.* **2.** To lay (cloth) on a perch in order to examine it. [Middle English *perche,* from Old French, from Latin *pertica,* stick, pole.]

perch[2] (pûrch) *n., pl.* **perch** or **perch·es. 1.** Any of various spiny-finned freshwater fishes of the genus *Perca,* especially either of two edible species, *P. flavescens,* of North America, and *P. fluviatilis,* of Europe. **2.** Any of various similar or related fishes, such as the pike perch or the grouper. [Middle English *perche,* from Old French, from Latin *perca,* from Greek *perkē.*]

per·chance (pər-chăns′) *adv.* Perhaps; possibly. [Middle English, from Anglo-Norman *par chance* : *par,* by (from Latin *per;* see PER) + *chance,* chance (from Old French; see CHANCE).]

perch·er (pûr′chər) *n.* **1.** One that perches. **2.** A bird whose feet are adapted for perching.

Per·che·ron (pûr′chə-rŏn′, -shə-) *n.* Any of a breed of gray or black draft horse originally used in France for drawing artillery and heavy coaches but now bred in other countries for general purposes. [French, from *Perche,* a historical region of northwest France.]

per·chlo·rate (pər-klôr′āt′, -klōr′-) *n.* An ester or a salt of perchloric acid.

per·chlo·ric acid (pər-klôr′ĭk, -klōr′-) *n.* A clear, colorless liquid, $HClO_4$, explosively unstable under some conditions, that is a powerful oxidant used as a catalyst and in explosives.

per·chlo·ride (pər-klôr′īd′, -klōr′-) also **per·chlo·rid** (-klôr′ĭd, -klōr′-) *n.* A chloride having more chlorine than other chlorides of the same element.

per·chlor·o·eth·yl·ene (pər-klôr′ō-ĕth′ə-lēn′, -klōr′-) *n.* A colorless, nonflammable organic solvent, $Cl_2C{:}CCl_2$, used in dry-cleaning solutions and as an industrial solvent.

per·cia·tel·li (pûr′chə-tĕl′ē, pĕr′chä-tĕl′lē) *n.* Long tubular pasta thicker than spaghetti. [Italian dialectal, diminutive pl. of *perciato,* past participle of *perciare,* to pierce, from Old French *percer,* pierce. See PIERCE.]

per·cip·i·ent (pər-sĭp′ē-ənt) *adj.* Having the power of perceiving, especially perceiving keenly and readily. **—percipient** *n.* One that perceives. [Latin *percipiēns, percipient-,* present parti-

ă pat	oi boy
ā pay	ou out
âr care	o͝o took
ä father	o͞o boot
ĕ pet	ŭ cut
ē be	ûr urge
ĭ pit	th thin
ī pie	*th* this
îr pier	hw which
ŏ pot	zh vision
ō toe	ə about, item
ô paw	♦ regionalism

Stress marks: ′ (primary); ′ (secondary), as in **dictionary** (dĭk′shə-nĕr′ē)

Père David's deer
Elaphurus davidianus

peregrine falcon
Continental peregrine falcon
Falco peregrinus

ciple of *percipere,* to perceive. See PERCEIVE.] **—per·cip′i·ence, per·cip′i·en·cy** *n.*

per·coid (pûr′koid′) also **per·coi·de·an** (pər-koi′dē-ən) *—adj.* Of or relating to the Percoidea, a large suborder of spiny-finned fishes that includes the perches, sunfishes, groupers, and grunts. *—n.* A fish belonging to the suborder Percoidea. [From New Latin *Percoidea,* suborder name : Latin *perca,* perch; see PERCH² + New Latin *-oidea,* pl. of *-oidēs,* resembling (from Greek *-oeidēs;* see —OID).]

per·co·late (pûr′kə-lāt′) *v.* **-lat·ed, -lat·ing, -lates.** *—tr.* **1.** To cause (liquid, for example) to pass through a porous substance or small holes; filter. **2.** To pass or ooze through: *Water percolated the sand.* **3.** To make (coffee) in a percolator. *—intr.* **1.** To drain or seep through a porous material or filter. **2.** *Informal.* To become lively or active. **—percolate** (-lĭt, -lāt′) *n.* A liquid that has been percolated. [Latin *percōlāre, percōlāt-* : *per-,* per- + *cōlāre,* to filter (from *cōlum,* sieve).] **—per′co·la′tion** *n.*

per·co·la·tor (pûr′kə-lā′tər) *n.* A coffeepot in which boiling water is forced repeatedly up through a central tube to filter back down through a basket of ground coffee beans.

per con·tra (pər kŏn′trə) *adv.* **1.** On the contrary. **2.** By way of contrast. [Latin : *per,* per + *contrā,* against.]

per·cur·rent (pər-kûr′ənt) *adj.* Of or relating to a midrib that extends throughout the entire length of a leaf. [Latin *percurrēns, percurrent-,* present participle of *percurrere,* to run through : *per-,* per- + *currere,* to run; see **kers-** in Appendix.]

per·cuss (pər-kŭs′) *tr.v.* **-cussed, -cuss·ing, -cuss·es.** To strike or tap firmly, as in medical percussion: *The doctor percussed the patient's chest.* [Latin *percutere, percuss-,* to strike hard : *per-,* per- + *quatere,* to strike; see **kwēt-** in Appendix.]

per·cus·sion (pər-kŭsh′ən) *n.* **1.** The striking together of two bodies, especially when noise is produced. **2.** The sound, vibration, or shock caused by the striking together of two bodies. **3.** The act of detonating a percussion cap in a firearm. **4.** A method of medical diagnosis in which various areas of the body, especially the chest, back, and abdomen, are tapped to determine by resonance the condition of internal organs. **5.** *Music.* **a.** The section of a band or an orchestra composed of percussion instruments. **b.** Percussion instruments or their players considered as a group. [Latin *percussiō, percussiōn-,* from *percussus,* past participle of *percutere,* to percuss. See PERCUSS.]

percussion cap *n.* A thin metal cap containing gunpowder or another detonator that explodes on being struck.

percussion instrument *n. Music.* An instrument, such as a drum, xylophone, piano, or maraca, in which sound is produced by one object striking another.

per·cus·sion·ist (pər-kŭsh′ə-nĭst) *n. Music.* One who plays percussion instruments.

per·cus·sive (pər-kŭs′ĭv) *adj.* Of, relating to, or characterized by percussion. **—per·cus′sive·ly** *adv.* **—per·cus′sive·ness** *n.*

per·cu·ta·ne·ous (pûr′kyo͞o-tā′nē-əs) *adj. Medicine.* Passed, done, or effected through the skin. **—per′cu·ta′ne·ous·ly** *adv.*

Per·cy (pûr′sē), Sir **Henry.** Known as "Hotspur." 1364–1403. English soldier who was killed while leading an uprising against Henry IV (1403).

Percy, Thomas. 1729–1811. English prelate, antiquary, and poet who edited *Reliques of Ancient English Poetry* (1765).

per di·em (pər dē′əm, dī′əm) *adv. Abbr.* **p.d., P.D.** By the day; per day. **—per diem** *adj.* **1.** Reckoned on a daily basis; daily. **2.** Paid by the day. **—per diem** *n., pl.* **per diems.** An allowance for daily expenses. [Latin : *per,* per + *diem,* accusative of *diēs,* day.]

per·di·tion (pər-dĭsh′ən) *n.* **1. a.** Loss of the soul; eternal damnation. **b.** Hell: *"Him the Almighty Power/Hurl'd headlong . . . /To bottomless perdition, there to dwell"* (John Milton). **2.** *Archaic.* Utter ruin. [Middle English *perdicion,* from Old French *perdicion,* from Late Latin *perditiō, perditiōn-,* from Latin *perditus,* past participle of *perdere,* to lose : *per-,* per- + *dare,* to give; see **dō-** in Appendix.]

per·du or **per·due** (pər-do͞o′, -dyo͞o′) *n. Obsolete.* A soldier sent on an especially dangerous mission. [From French *sentinelle perdue,* forward sentry : *sentinelle,* sentinel + *perdu,* past participle of *perdre,* to lose (from Latin *perdere;* see PERDITION).]

per·du·ra·ble (pər-do͝or′ə-bəl, -dyo͝or′-) *adj.* Extremely durable; permanent. [Middle English, from Old French, from Late Latin *perdūrābilis,* from Latin *perdūrāre,* to endure : *per-,* per- + *dūrāre,* to last; see **deuə-** in Appendix.] **—per·du′ra·bil′i·ty** *n.* **—per·du′ra·bly** *adv.*

per·dure (pər-do͝or′, -dyo͝or′) *intr.v.* **-dured, -dur·ing, -dures.** To last permanently; endure. [Middle English *perduren,* from Old French *pardurer,* from Latin *perdūrāre.* See PERDURABLE.]

père (pĕr) *n.* **1.** Used after a man's surname to distinguish between father and son: *Dumas père primarily wrote novels, while dramas occupied Dumas fils.* **2. Père.** *Roman Catholic Church.* Used as a title for certain priests. [French, from Old French *pedre,* from Latin *pater.* See **pəter-** in Appendix.]

Père Da·vid's deer (pâr′ dä-vēdz′, dā′vĭdz) *n.* A large reddish-brown Chinese deer *(Elaphurus davidianus)* surviving only in domesticated herds and having antlers whose tips point backward, a long donkeylike tail, and hoofs that make a cracking sound in walking. [After *Père* Armand *David* (1826–1900), French missionary and naturalist.]

per·e·gri·nate (pĕr′ĭ-grə-nāt′) *v.* **-nat·ed, -nat·ing, -nates.** *—intr.* To journey or travel from place to place, especially on foot. *—tr.* To travel through or over; traverse. [Latin *peregrīnārī, peregrīnāt-,* from *peregrīnus,* foreigner. See PEREGRINE.] **—per′e·gri·na′tion** *n.* **—per′e·gri·na′tor** *n.*

per·e·grine (pĕr′ə-grĭn, -grēn′) *adj.* **1.** Foreign; alien. **2.** Roving or wandering; migratory. **—peregrine** *n.* A peregrine falcon. [Middle English, from Old French, from Medieval Latin *peregrīnus,* wandering, pilgrim, from Latin, foreigner, from *pereger,* being abroad : *per,* through; see PER + *ager,* land; see **agro-** in Appendix.]

peregrine falcon *n.* A widely distributed, swift-flying bird of prey *(Falco peregrinus),* having gray and white plumage, much used in falconry. Also called *duck hawk.* [Middle English, translation of Medieval Latin *falcō peregrīnus* (so called because they were caught in passage rather than taken from the nest as were eyas falcons).]

Pe·rei·ra (pə-rĕr′ə, pĕ-rā′rä). A city of west-central Colombia west of Bogotá. It is a distribution center for a coffee, livestock, and mineral region. Population, 232,311.

Per·el·man (pĕr′əl-mən), **S(idney) J(oseph).** 1904–1979. American writer known especially for his satirical pieces in the *New Yorker.*

per·emp·to·ry (pə-rĕmp′tə-rē) *adj.* **1.** Putting an end to all debate or action: *a peremptory decree.* **2.** Not allowing contradiction or refusal; imperative: *The officer issued peremptory commands.* **3.** Having the nature of or expressing a command; urgent: *The teacher spoke in a peremptory tone.* **4.** Offensively self-assured; dictatorial: *a swaggering, peremptory manner.* [Latin *peremptōrius,* from *peremptus,* past participle of *perimere,* to take away : *per-,* per- + *emere,* to obtain; see **em-** in Appendix.] **—per·emp′to·ri·ly** *adv.* **—per·emp′to·ri·ness** *n.*

per·en·nate (pĕr′ə-nāt′, pə-rĕn′āt) *intr.v.* **-nat·ed, -nat·ing, -nates.** To survive from one growing season to the next, often with a period of reduced or arrested growth between seasons. Used of plants or plant parts. [Latin *perennāre, perennāt-,* to last many years, from *perennis,* lasting for years. See PERENNIAL.] **—per′en·na′tion** *n.*

per·en·ni·al (pə-rĕn′ē-əl) *adj.* **1.** Lasting or active through the year or through many years. **2. a.** Lasting an indefinitely long time; enduring: *perennial happiness.* **b.** Appearing again and again; recurrent. See Synonyms at **continual. 3.** *Botany.* Living three or more years. **—perennial** *n.* **1.** *Botany.* A perennial plant. **2.** Something that recurs or seems to recur on a yearly or continual basis: *"that hardy perennial, the budget deficit"* (David S. Broder). [Latin *perennis (per-,* throughout; see PER + *annus,* year; see **at-** in Appendix) + —AL¹.] **—per·en′ni·al·ly** *adv.*

pe·ren·tie also **pa·ren·ty** (pə-rĕn′tē) *n., pl.* **-ties.** A monitor *(Varanus giganteus)* of Australia that burrows in desert areas and often grows to a length of 2.5 meters (8 feet) or more. It is the largest Australian lizard. [Probably from Diyari (Aboriginal language of south-central Australia) *pirindi.*]

per·e·stroi·ka (pĕr′ĭ-stroi′kə, pyĕ-ryĭ-stroi′kä) *n.* **1.** The organizational restructuring of the Soviet economy and bureaucracy that was begun in the mid 1980's. **2.** An economic and bureaucratic restructuring: *"For several years now . . . the U.S. has been going through its own perestroika at the cost of unemployment and all kinds of painful but ultimately beneficial change"* (Peter Fuhrman). [Russian *perestroĭka* : *pere-,* around, again (from Old Russian; see **per¹** in Appendix) + *stroĭka,* construction (from *stroit',* to build, from Old Russian *stroiti,* from *strojĭ,* order; see **ster-²** in Appendix).]

Pe·rez Es·qui·vel (pĕr′əs ĕs′kē-vĕl′, pĕr′ĕs), **Adolfo.** Born 1932. Argentine civil rights leader. He won the 1980 Nobel Peace Prize for his efforts to promote human rights in Latin America.

Pérez Gal·dós (gäl-dōs′), **Benito.** 1843–1920. Spanish writer known especially for his *Episodios Nacionales* (1873–1912), a series of 46 historical novels.

per·fect (pûr′fĭkt) *adj. Abbr.* **perf. 1.** Lacking nothing essential to the whole; complete of its nature or kind. **2.** Being without defect or blemish: *a perfect specimen.* **3.** Thoroughly skilled or talented in a certain field or area; proficient. **4.** Completely suited for a particular purpose or situation: *She was the perfect actress for the part.* **5. a.** Completely corresponding to a description, standard, or type: *a perfect circle; a perfect gentleman.* **b.** Accurately reproducing an original: *a perfect copy of the painting.* **6.** Complete; thorough; utter: *a perfect fool.* **7.** Pure; undiluted; unmixed: *perfect red.* **8.** Excellent and delightful in all respects: *a perfect day.* **9.** *Botany.* Having both stamens and pistils in the same flower; monoclinous. **10.** *Grammar.* Of, relating to, or constituting a verb form expressing action completed prior to a fixed point of reference in time. **11.** *Music.* **a.** Designating the three basic intervals of the octave, fourth, and fifth. **b.** Designating a cadence or chord progression from the dominant to the tonic at the end of a phrase or piece of music. **—perfect** *n. Abbr.* **perf. 1.** *Grammar.* The perfect tense. **2.** A verb or verb form in the perfect tense. **—perfect** (pər-fĕkt′) *tr.v.* **-fect·ed, -fect·ing, -fects.** To bring to perfection or completion. [Middle English *perfit,* from Old French *parfit,* from Latin *perfectus,* past participle of *perficere,* to finish : *per-,* per- + *facere,* to do; see **dhē-** in Appendix.] **—per·fect′er** *n.* **—per′fect·ness** *n.*

SYNONYMS: *perfect, consummate, faultless, flawless, impeccable.* The central meaning shared by these adjectives is "being wholly without flaw": *a perfect diamond; a consummate performer; faultless logic; a flawless instrumental technique; speaks impeccable French.*
ANTONYM: *imperfect.*
USAGE NOTE: *Perfect* has often been described as an absolute term like *chief* and *prime,* hence not allowing modification by *more, quite, relatively,* and other qualifiers of degree. But the qualification of *perfect* has numerous reputable precedents (most notably in the preamble to the U.S. Constitution in the phrase *"in order to form a more perfect Union"*). What is more, the stricture is philosophically dubious. There can be no mathematically perfect forms in nature; therefore to say that any actual circle is "perfect" can mean only that it approximates the geometric ideal of circularity, a quality that it can obviously have to a greater or lesser degree. By the same token, *perfect* freely allows comparison in examples such as *There could be no more perfect spot for the picnic,* where it is used to mean "ideal for the purposes." See Usage Notes at **complete, equal, parallel, unique.**

per·fec·ta (pər-fĕk′tə) *n. Sports & Games.* See **exacta.** [From American Spanish *(quiniela) perfecta,* perfect (quinella), feminine of *perfecto,* perfect, from Latin *perfectus.* See PERFECT.]

perfect game *n.* **1.** *Baseball.* A complete game in which no opposing batter reaches first base. **2.** *Sports.* A game in bowling in which a player bowls 12 successive strikes.

per·fect·i·ble (pər-fĕk′tə-bəl) *adj.* Capable of becoming perfect or being made perfect: *perfectible prose.* **—per·fect′i·bil′i·ty** *n.*

per·fec·tion (pər-fĕk′shən) *n.* **1.** The quality or condition of being perfect. **2.** The act or process of perfecting: *Perfection of the invention took years.* **3.** A person or thing considered to be perfect. **4.** An instance of excellence.

per·fec·tion·ism (pər-fĕk′shə-nĭz′əm) *n.* **1.** A propensity for being displeased with anything that is not perfect or does not meet extremely high standards. **2.** A belief that moral or spiritual perfection can be achieved by people in this life. **—per·fec′tion·ist** *adj. & n.* **—per·fec′tion·ist′ic** *adj.*

per·fec·tive (pər-fĕk′tĭv) *adj.* **1.** Tending toward perfection. **2.** *Grammar.* Of or being a verb in the perfective aspect. **—perfective** *n. Grammar.* **1.** The perfective aspect. **2.** A verb in the perfective aspect. **—per·fec′tive·ly** *adv.* **—per·fec′tive·ness, per′fec·tiv′i·ty** (pûr′fĕk-tĭv′ĭ-tē) *n.*

perfective aspect *n. Grammar.* An aspect of verbs that expresses a completed action as distinct from a continuing or not necessarily completed action.

per·fect·ly (pûr′fĭkt-lē) *adv.* **1.** In a perfect manner or to a perfect degree. **2.** To a complete or full degree or extent; wholly: *The diners were perfectly satisfied with the meal.* See Usage Note at **perfect.**

perfect number *n. Mathematics.* A positive integer that is equal to the sum of its integral factors, including 1 but excluding itself.

per·fec·to (pər-fĕk′tō) *n., pl.* **-tos.** A cigar of standard length, thick in the center and tapered at each end. [From Spanish, perfect, from Latin *perfectus.* See PERFECT.]

perfect participle *n. Grammar.* See **past participle.**

perfect pitch *n. Music.* See **absolute pitch** (sense 2).

perfect rhyme *n.* **1.** Rhyme in which the final accented vowel and all succeeding consonants or syllables are identical, while the preceding consonants are different, for example, *great, late; rider, beside her; dutiful, unbeautiful.* Also called *full rhyme, true rhyme.* **2.** Rime riche.

perfect square *n. Mathematics.* An integer that is the square of an integer.

perfect year *n.* In the Jewish calendar, an ordinary year of 355 days or a leap year of 385 days.

per·fer·vid (pər-fûr′vĭd) *adj.* Extremely or extravagantly eager; impassioned or zealous. **—per·fer′vid·ly** *adv.* **—per·fer′vid·ness** *n.*

per·fid·i·ous (pər-fĭd′ē-əs) *adj.* Of, relating to, or marked by perfidy; treacherous. See Synonyms at **faithless.** **—per·fid′i·ous·ly** *adv.*

per·fi·dy (pûr′fĭ-dē) *n., pl.* **-dies.** **1.** Deliberate breach of faith; calculated violation of trust; treachery. **2.** The act or an instance of treachery. [Latin *perfidia,* from *perfidus,* treacherous : *per,* through; see PER + *fidēs,* faith; see **bheidh-** in Appendix.]

per·fo·li·ate (pər-fō′lē-ĭt) *adj.* Of or relating to a sessile leaf or bract that completely clasps the stem and is apparently pierced by it. [New Latin *perfoliātus* : Latin *per,* through; see PER + Latin *foliātus,* bearing leaves (from *folium,* leaf; see **bhel-**[3] in Appendix).] **—per·fo′li·a′tion** *n.*

per·fo·rate (pûr′fə-rāt′) *v.* **-rat·ed, -rat·ing, -rates.** *—tr.* **1.** To pierce, punch, or bore a hole or holes in; penetrate. **2.** To pierce or stamp with rows of holes, as those between postage stamps, to allow easy separation. *—intr.* To pass into or through something. **—perforate** (pûr′fər-ĭt, -fə-rāt′) *adj.* Having been perforated. [Latin *perforāre, perforāt-* : *per-,* per- + *forāre,* to bore.] **—per′fo·ra·ble** (-fər-ə-bəl) *adj.* **—per′fo·ra′tive** *adj.* **—per′fo·ra′tor** *n.*

per·fo·rat·ed (pûr′fə-rā′tĭd) *adj.* Having a hole or holes, especially a row of small holes.

per·fo·ra·tion (pûr′fə-rā′shən) *n.* **1.** A hole or series of holes punched or bored through something, especially a hole in a series, separating sections in a sheet or roll. **2. a.** The act of perforating. **b.** The state of being perforated.

per·force (pər-fôrs′, -fōrs′) *adv.* By necessity; by force of circumstance. [Middle English *par force,* from Old French : *par,* by (from Latin *per;* see PER) + *force,* force; see FORCE.]

per·form (pər-fôrm′) *v.* **-formed, -form·ing, -forms.** *—tr.* **1.** To begin and carry through to completion; do: *The surgeon performed the operation.* **2.** To take action in accordance with the requirements of; fulfill: *perform one's contractual obligations.* **3. a.** To enact (a feat or role) before an audience. **b.** To give a public presentation of; present: *The theater group performed a three-act play.* *—intr.* **1.** To carry on; function: *a car that performs well on curves.* **2.** To fulfill an obligation or requirement; accomplish something as promised or expected. **3.** To portray a role or demonstrate a skill before an audience: *The juggler performed atop a unicycle.* **4.** To present a dramatic or musical work or other entertainment before an audience. [Middle English *performen,* from Anglo-Norman *performer,* from Old French *parfornir* : *par-,* intensive pref. (from Latin *per-,* per-) + *fournir,* to furnish; see FURNISH.] **—per·form′a·ble** *adj.* **—per·form′er** *n.*

SYNONYMS: *perform, execute, accomplish, achieve, effect, fulfill, discharge.* These verbs signify to carry through to completion. To *perform* is to carry out an action, an undertaking, or a procedure; the word often connotes observance of due form or the exercise of skill or care: *The ship's captain performed the wedding ceremony. The orchestra and chorus performed an Easter oratorio. Sophisticated laser experiments are performed regularly in the laboratory. Execute* implies performing a task or putting something into effect in accordance with a plan or design: *"To execute laws is a royal office; to execute orders is not to be a king"* (Edmund Burke). *The violinist had the technical skill to execute the cadenza, with its double stops and harmonics, with brilliance. Accomplish* connotes the successful completion of something, often of something that requires tenacity or talent: *"Make one brave push and see what can be accomplished in a week"* (Robert Louis Stevenson). *He accomplished his purpose, the rapid acquisition of enormous profits, only by making risky investments.* To *achieve* is to accomplish something especially by dint of effort or despite difficulty; the term often implies a significant result: *"Some are born great . . . Some achieve greatness . . . And some have greatness thrust upon them"* (Shakespeare). *Greater benefits can be achieved through diplomatic channels than by acts of aggression. Effect* suggests the power of an agent to bring about a desired result: *Even the antibiotics the doctor prescribed didn't effect a complete cure.* To *fulfill* is to live up to expectations or satisfy demands, wishes, or requirements: *It is unrealistic to hope that all one's desires can be fulfilled. She fulfilled her obligations to her parents.* To *discharge* an obligation or duty is to perform all the steps necessary for its fulfillment: *"I have found it impossible to carry the heavy burden of responsibility and to discharge my duties as King as I would wish to do"* (Edward VIII).

per·form·ance (pər-fôr′məns) *n.* **1.** The act of performing or the state of being performed. **2.** The act or style of performing a work or role before an audience. **3.** The way in which someone or something functions: *The pilot rated the airplane's performance in high winds.* **4.** A presentation, especially a theatrical one, before an audience. **5.** Something performed; an accomplishment.

performance art *n.* A form of theatrical art in which thematically related works in a variety of media are presented simultaneously or successively to an audience. **—performance artist** *n.*

per·form·ing arts (pər-fôr′mĭng) *pl.n.* Arts, such as dance, drama, and music, that are performed before an audience.

per·fume (pûr′fyo͞om′, pər-fyo͞om′) *n.* **1.** A substance that emits and diffuses a fragrant odor, especially a volatile liquid distilled from flowers or prepared synthetically. **2.** A pleasing, agreeable scent or odor. See Synonyms at **fragrance.** **—perfume** (pər-fyo͞om′) *tr.v.* **-fumed, -fum·ing, -fumes.** To impregnate with fragrance; impart a pleasant odor to. [French *parfum,* from Old Italian *parfumo,* from *parfumare,* to fill with smoke : *par-,* intensive pref. (from Latin *per-,* per-) + *fumare,* to smoke (from Latin *fūmāre,* from *fūmus,* smoke).]

per·fum·er (pər-fyo͞o′mər) *n.* One that makes or sells perfumes.

per·fum·er·y (pər-fyo͞o′mə-rē) *n., pl.* **-ies.** **1.** Perfumes. **2.** An establishment that makes or sells perfume. **3.** The art of making perfume.

per·func·to·ry (pər-fŭngk′tə-rē) *adj.* **1.** Done routinely and with little interest or care: *The operator answered the phone with a perfunctory greeting.* **2.** Acting with indifference; showing little interest or care. [Late Latin *perfūnctōrius,* from Latin *perfūnctus,* past participle of *perfungī,* to get through with : *per-,* per- + *fungī,* to perform.] **—per·func′to·ri·ly** *adv.* **—per·func′to·ri·ness** *n.*

per·fuse (pər-fyo͞oz′) *tr.v.* **-fused, -fus·ing, -fus·es.** **1.** To coat or permeate with liquid, color, or light; suffuse. **2.** To pour or diffuse (a liquid, for example) over or through something. [Latin *perfundere, perfūs-,* to pour over : *per-,* per- + *fundere,* to

ă pat	oi boy
ā pay	ou out
âr care	o͝o took
ä father	o͞o boot
ĕ pet	ŭ cut
ē be	ûr urge
ĭ pit	th thin
ī pie	*th* this
îr pier	hw which
ŏ pot	zh vision
ō toe	ə about, item
ô paw	♦ regionalism

Stress marks: **′** (primary); ′ (secondary), as in **dictionary** (dĭk′shə-nĕr′ē)

pour; see **gheu-** in Appendix.] **—per·fu′sive** (pər-fyo͞o′sĭv, -zĭv) *adj.*

per·fu·sion (pər-fyo͞o′zhən) *n.* **1.** The act of perfusing. **2.** The injection of fluid into a blood vessel in order to reach an organ or tissues, usually to supply nutrients and oxygen.

Per·ga·mum (pûr′gə-məm). An ancient Greek city and kingdom of western Asia Minor in modern-day western Turkey. It passed to Rome in the second century B.C. and was noted for its sculpture and its library, which Mark Antony gave to Cleopatra.

per·go·la (pûr′gə-lə) *n.* An arbor or a passageway of columns supporting a roof of trelliswork on which climbing plants are trained to grow. [Italian, from Latin *pergula.*]

pergola

Per·go·le·si (pĕr′gə-lā′zē, -gô-lĕ′-), **Giovanni Battista.** 1710–1736. Italian composer who wrote the comic opera *The Maid as Mistress* (1733).

per·haps (pər-hăps′) *adv.* Maybe; possibly. [From Middle English *perhap* : *per,* by (from Latin; see PER) + *hap,* chance; see HAP.]

peri– *pref.* **1.** Around; about; enclosing: *perimysium.* **2.** Near: *perinatal.* [Greek, from *peri.* See **per**[1] in Appendix.]

per·i·anth (pĕr′ē-ănth′) *n.* The outer envelope of a flower, consisting of either the calyx or the corolla, or both. [French *périanthe,* from New Latin *perianthum* : Greek *peri-,* peri- + Greek *anthos,* flower.]

per·i·apt (pĕr′ē-ăpt′) *n.* A charm worn as protection against mischief and disease; an amulet. [French *périapte,* from Greek *periapton,* from *periaptos,* hung around : *peri-,* peri- + *haptos,* fastened (from *haptein,* to fasten).]

per·i·aq·ue·duc·tal (pĕr′ē-ăk′wĭ-dŭk′təl) *adj.* Situated around the aqueduct of the brain: *the periaqueductal gray matter.*

Per·i·bon·ca (pĕr′ə-bŏng′kə). A river, about 451 km (280 mi) long, of central Quebec, Canada, flowing southward through **Peribonca Lake** to Lake St. John.

per·i·car·di·a (pĕr′ĭ-kär′-dē-ə) *n.* Plural of **pericardium.**

per·i·car·di·tis (pĕr′ĭ-kär-dī′tĭs) *n.* Inflammation of the pericardium.

per·i·car·di·um (pĕr′ĭ-kär′dē-əm) *n., pl.* **-di·a** (-dē-ə). The membranous sac filled with serous fluid that encloses the heart and the roots of the aorta and other large blood vessels. [New Latin, from Greek *perikardion,* from *perikardios,* around the heart : *peri-,* peri- + *kardia,* heart; see **kerd-** in Appendix.] **—per′i·car′di·al** (-dē-əl), **per′i·car′di·ac′** (-dē-ăk′) *adj.*

per·i·carp (pĕr′ĭ-kärp′) *n.* **1.** *Botany.* The wall of a ripened ovary; fruit wall. **2.** A membranous structure surrounding the cystocarp of red algae. **—per′i·car′pi·al** *adj.*

per·i·chon·dri·um (pĕr′ĭ-kŏn′drē-əm) *n., pl.* **-dri·a** (-drē-ə). The fibrous membrane of connective tissue covering the surface of cartilage except at the endings of joints. [New Latin : PERI– + Greek *khondrion,* diminutive of *khondros,* cartilage; see CHONDRO–.] **—per′i·chon′dri·al** (-drē-əl) *adj.*

per·i·clase (pĕr′ĭ-klās′, -klāz′) *n.* A mineral form of magnesium oxide, MgO, usually occurring in cubic crystals or grains. [German *Periklas* : Greek *peri-,* intensive pref.; see PERI– + Greek *klasis,* breaking (from its perfect cleavage).]

Per·i·cles (pĕr′ĭ-klēz′). Died 429 B.C. Athenian leader noted for advancing democracy in Athens and for ordering the construction of the Parthenon. **—Per′i·cle′an** (-klē′ən) *adj.*

Pericles
Copy of a mid fifth-century B.C. herma attributed to Cresilas (fl. 450–430 B.C.)

per·i·cline (pĕr′ĭ-klīn′) *n.* A variety of albite occurring as elongated white crystals. [From Greek *periklinēs,* sloping on all sides : *peri-,* peri- + *klinein,* to slope; see **klei-** in Appendix.]

per·i·cra·ni·um (pĕr′ĭ-krā′nē-əm) *n., pl.* **-ni·a** (-nē-ə). The external periosteum that covers the outer surface of the skull. [New Latin, from Greek *perikranion,* from *perikranios,* around the skull : *peri-,* peri- + *kranion,* cranium; see CRANIUM.] **—per′i·cra′ni·al** *adj.*

per·i·cy·cle (pĕr′ĭ-sī′kəl) *n.* A plant tissue characteristic of the roots, located between the endodermis and phloem. [French *péricycle,* from Greek *perikuklos,* spherical : *peri-,* peri- + *kuklos,* circle; see CYCLE.] **—per′i·cy′clic** (-sī′klĭk, -sĭk′lĭk) *adj.*

per·i·derm (pĕr′ĭ-dûrm′) *n.* The outer layers of tissue of woody roots and stems, consisting of the cork cambium and the tissues produced by it, such as cork. **—per′i·der′mal, per′i·der′mic** *adj.*

pe·rid·i·um (pə-rĭd′ē-əm) *n., pl.* **-i·a** (-ē-ə). The covering of the spore-bearing organ in many fungi. [New Latin *pēridium,* from Greek *pēridion,* diminutive of *pēra,* leather pouch.] **—pe·rid′i·al** (-ē-əl) *adj.*

per·i·dot (pĕr′ĭ-dŏt′, -dō′) *n.* A yellowish-green variety of olivine used as a gem. [Middle English, from Old French.] **—per′i·dot′ic** (-dŏt′ĭk, -dō′tĭk) *adj.*

per·i·do·tite (pĕr′ĭ-dō-tīt′, pə-rĭd′ə-) *n.* Any of a group of igneous rocks composed mainly of olivine and various pyroxenes and having a granitelike texture.

per·i·gee (pĕr′ə-jē) *n.* **1.** The point nearest the earth's center in the orbit of the moon or a satellite. **2.** The point in any orbit nearest to the body being orbited. [French *périgée,* from Medieval Latin *perigēum,* from Late Greek *perigeion* : Greek *peri-,* peri- + Greek *gē,* earth.] **—per′i·ge′al** (-jē′əl), **per′i·ge′an** (-jē′ən) *adj.*

pe·rig·y·nous (pə-rĭj′ə-nəs) *adj. Botany.* **1.** Having sepals, petals, and stamens around the edge of a cuplike receptacle containing the ovary, as in flowers of the rose or cherry. **2.** Of or being perigynous flower parts: *perigynous stamens.* **—pe·rig′y·ny** (-ə-nē) *n.*

per·i·he·li·on (pĕr′ə-hē′lē-ən, -hēl′yən) *n., pl.* **-he·li·a** (-hē′lē-ə, -hēl′yə). The point nearest the sun in the orbit of a planet or other celestial body. [Alteration of New Latin *perihēlium* : PERI– + Greek *hēlios,* sun; see **sāwel-** in Appendix.] **—per′i·he′li·al** (-hē′lē-əl, -hēl′yəl) *adj.*

per·i·kar·y·on (pĕr′ĭ-kăr′ē-ŏn′, -ən) *n., pl.* **-kar·y·a** (-kăr′ē-ə). The cell body of a neuron, containing the nucleus and organelles. [PERI– + Greek *karuon,* nut; see KARYO–.] **—per′i·kar′y·al** (-ē-əl) *adj.*

per·il (pĕr′əl) *n.* **1.a.** Imminent danger. **b.** Exposure to the risk of harm or loss. **2.** Something that endangers or involves risk. **—peril** *tr.v.* **-iled, -il·ing, -ils** also **-illed, -il·ling, -ils.** To expose to danger or the chance of injury; imperil. [Middle English, from Old French, from Latin *perīculum.* See **per-**[3] in Appendix.]

pe·ril·la (pə-rĭl′ə) *n.* **1.** An annual Asian plant *(Perilla frutescens)* having opposite leaves, a bell-shaped calyx, and flowers with a short, white, tubular corolla. It is widely cultivated as an ornamental and for its oily seeds. **2.** The oil from the seeds of this plant, widely used in the manufacture of paint, varnish, and artificial leather and as a substitute for linseed oil. [New Latin, genus name.]

per·il·ous (pĕr′ə-ləs) *adj.* Full of or involving peril; dangerous. **—per′il·ous·ly** *adv.* **—per′il·ous·ness** *n.*

per·i·lymph (pĕr′ə-lĭmf′) *n.* The fluid in the space between the membranous and bony labyrinths of the inner ear. **—per′i·lym·phat′ic** (-lĭm-făt′ĭk) *adj.*

pe·rim·e·ter (pə-rĭm′ĭ-tər) *n.* **1.** *Mathematics.* **a.** A closed curve bounding a plane area. **b.** The length of such a boundary. **2.** The outer limits of an area. See Synonyms at **circumference. 3.** A fortified strip or boundary usually protecting a military position. [Middle English *perimetre,* from Latin *perimetros,* from Greek : *peri-,* peri- + *metron,* measure; see METER[2].] **—per′i·met′ric** (pĕr′ə-mĕt′rĭk), **per′i·met′ri·cal** (-rĭ-kəl) *adj.* **—per′i·met′ri·cal·ly** *adv.*

per·i·morph (pĕr′ə-môrf′) *n.* A mineral that encloses a different mineral. **—per′i·mor′phic, per′i·mor′phous** *adj.* **—per′i·mor′phism** *n.*

per·i·my·si·um (pĕr′ə-mĭzh′ē-əm, -mĭz′ē-əm) *n., pl.* **-my·si·a** (-mĭzh′ē-ə, -mĭz′ē-ə). The sheath of connective tissue enveloping bundles of muscle fibers. [New Latin : PERI– + Greek *mus,* muscle; see **mūs-** in Appendix.]

per·i·na·tal (pĕr′ə-nāt′l) *adj.* Of, relating to, or being the period around childbirth, especially the five months before and one month after birth: *perinatal mortality; perinatal care.* **—per′i·na′tal·ly** *adv.*

per·i·na·tol·o·gy (pĕr′ə-nā-tŏl′ə-jē) *n.* The medical study of fetuses and infants during the perinatal period.

per·i·ne·a (pĕr′ə-nē′ə) *n.* Plural of **perineum.**

per·i·neph·ri·um (pĕr′ə-nĕf′rē-əm) *n., pl.* **-ri·a** (-rē-ə). The connective and fatty tissue surrounding a kidney. [New Latin, from Greek *perinephros,* fat around the kidneys : *peri-,* peri- + *nephros,* kidney.] **—per′i·neph′ral** (-nĕf′rəl), **per′i·neph′ri·al** (-rē-əl) , **per′i·neph′ric** (-rĭk) *adj.*

per·i·ne·um (pĕr′ə-nē′əm) *n., pl.* **-ne·a** (-nē′ə). **1.** The portion of the body in the pelvis occupied by urogenital passages and the rectum, bounded in front by the pubic arch, in the back by the coccyx, and laterally by part of the hipbone. **2.** The region between the scrotum and the anus in males, and between the posterior vulva junction and the anus in females. [Middle English, from Medieval Latin *perinaeon,* from Greek *perinaion* : *peri-,* peri- + *inan,* to excrete.] **—per′i·ne′al** (-nē′əl) *adj.*

per·i·neu·ri·um (pĕr′ə-no͝or′ē-əm, -nyo͝or′-) *n., pl.* **-neu·ri·a** (-no͝or′ē-ə, -nyo͝or′-). The sheath of connective tissue enclosing a bundle of nerve fibers. [New Latin : PERI– + Greek *neuron,* nerve; see NEURON.] **—per′i·neu′ri·al** *adj.*

pe·ri·od (pîr′ē-əd) *n. Abbr.* **per. 1.** An interval of time characterized by the occurrence of a certain condition, event, or phenomenon: *a period of economic prosperity.* **2.** An interval of time characterized by the prevalence of a specified culture, ideology, or technology: *artifacts of the pre-Columbian period.* **3.** An interval regarded as a distinct evolutionary or developmental phase: *Picasso's early career is divided into his blue period and rose period.* **4.** *Geology.* A unit of time, longer than an epoch and shorter than an era. **5.** Any of various arbitrary units of time, especially: **a.** Any of the divisions of the academic day. **b.** *Sports & Games.* A division of the playing time of a game. **6.** *Physics & Astronomy.* The time interval between two successive occurrences of a recurrent event or phases of an event; a cycle. **7.** An instance or occurrence of menstruation. **8.** A point or portion of time at which something is ended; a completion or conclusion. **9.** The full pause at the end of a spoken sentence. **10.** A punctuation mark (.) indicating a full stop, placed at the end of declarative sentences and other statements thought to be complete, and after many abbreviations. **11.** A sentence of several carefully balanced clauses in formal writing. **12.a.** A metrical unit of quantitative verse consisting of two or more cola. **b.** An analogous unit or division of classical Greek or Latin prose. **13.** *Music.* A group of two or more phrases within a composition, made up of 8 or 16 measures and terminating with a cadence. **14.** *Mathematics.* **a.** The least interval in the range of the independent variable of a periodic function of a real variable in which all possible values of the dependent variable are assumed. **b.** A group of digits separated by commas in a written number. **c.** The number of digits that repeat in a repeating decimal. For example, $\frac{1}{7}$ = 0.142857142857 . . . has a six-digit period. **15.** *Chemistry.* A sequence of elements arranged in order of increasing atomic number and forming one of the horizontal rows in the periodic table. **—period** *adj.* Of, belonging to, or representing a certain historical age or time: *a period piece; period furniture.* [Middle English *periode,* from Old French, from Medieval Latin *periodus,* from Latin *perihodos,* rhetorical period, from Greek *periodos,* circuit : *peri-,* peri- + *hodos,* way.]

SYNONYMS: *period, epoch, era, age, term.* These nouns refer to a portion or length of time. *Period* is the most general: *a short waiting period; one of the most difficult periods of her life; worked for a period of ten years; the Romantic period in music. Epoch* refers to a period regarded as being remarkable or memorable: *"We enter on an epoch of constitutional retrogression"* (John R. Green). An *era* is a period of time notable because of new or different aspects or events: *"How many a man has dated a new era in his life from the reading of a book"* (Henry David Thoreau). An *age* is usually a period marked by a particular distinctive characteristic: *the age of Newton; the Iron Age. "These principles form the bright constellation which has . . . guided our steps through an age of revolution and reformation"* (Thomas Jefferson). A *term* is a period of time to which limits have been set: *Senators are elected for a term of six years.*

WORD HISTORY: Perhaps more than once one may have wondered why the word *period* has the sense "punctuation mark (.)" as well as some of its other senses having to do with time. The answer to this question lies in the senses of the Greek word *periodos* from which our word is descended. *Periodos,* made up of *peri–,* "around," and *hodos,* "way," meant such things as "going round, way round, going round in a circle, circuit," and with regard to time "cycle or period of time." The word also meant "the period of menstruation." In rhetoric it referred to "a group of words organically related in grammar and sense." The Greek word was adopted into Latin as *perihodos* with only its rhetorical sense and one other sense, but in Medieval Latin it reacquired senses it had in Greek, such as "cycle," and acquired a new sense, "a punctuation mark used at the end of a rhetorical period." Although this sense is recorded in Medieval Latin, it is not recorded in English until 1609. But the word *period* had entered Middle English from Medieval Latin and Old French, first being recorded in a work written around 1425 in the sense "a cycle of recurrence of a disease."

pe·ri·od·ic (pĭr′ē-ŏd′ĭk) *adj.* **1.** Having or marked by repeated cycles. **2.** Happening or appearing at regular intervals. **3.** Recurring or reappearing from time to time; intermittent. **4.** Characterized by periodic sentences. **—pe′ri·od′i·cal·ly** *adv.*

SYNONYMS: *periodic, sporadic, intermittent, occasional, fitful.* These adjectives all mean recurring or reappearing now and then. Something *periodic* occurs at regular or at least generally predictable intervals: *periodic feelings of anxiety. Sporadic* implies appearance or occurrence in scattered, irregular, unpredictable, or isolated instances: *a city subjected to sporadic bombing raids. Intermittent* describes something that stops and starts at intervals: *intermittent rain showers.* What is *occasional* happens at random and irregularly: *occasional outbursts of temper.* Something *fitful* occurs in spells and often abruptly: *fitful bursts of energy.*

USAGE NOTE: *Periodic* has long been used loosely to mean "occasional, intermittent," but this usage may be confusing for readers who are accustomed to using the word only in its narrower sense of "at regular or predictable intervals." Thus the writer who said *Parker's losses at the track were not covered by his periodic winners* invited the (most likely unintended) inference that Parker had a system that enabled him to pick winners at regular intervals. Substitution of *occasional* in this context would have resolved the ambiguity.

per·i·od·ic acid (pûr′ī-ŏd′ĭk) *n.* A white, crystalline inorganic acid, $HIO_4 \cdot 2H_2O$, used as an oxidizer.

pe·ri·od·i·cal (pĭr′ē-ŏd′ĭ-kəl) *adj.* **1.** Periodic. **2.a.** Published at regular intervals of more than one day. **b.** Of or relating to a publication issued at such intervals. **—periodical** *n.* A publication issued at regular intervals of more than one day.

periodical cicada *n.* A cicada of the genus *Magicicada* of the eastern United States whose 17-year or 13-year life cycle consists almost entirely of a nymphal stage spent underground. Upon emerging from this stage, the periodical cicada transforms into a winged adult, mates, lays eggs, and dies shortly thereafter. Also called *seventeen-year locust.*

pe·ri·o·dic·i·ty (pĭr′ē-ə-dĭs′ĭ-tē) *n., pl.* **-ties. 1.** The quality or state of being periodic; recurrence at regular intervals. **2.** The tendency of chemical elements with similar positions in the periodic table to have similar properties. **3.** The position of an element in the periodic table.

pe·ri·od·ic law (pĭr′ē-ŏd′ĭk) *n. Chemistry.* The principle that the properties of the elements recur periodically as their atomic numbers increase.

pe·ri·od·ic sentence (pĭr′ē-ŏd′ĭk) *n.* A sentence in which the main clause or its predicate is withheld until the end, as in *Despite heavy winds, the plane landed safely.*

pe·ri·od·ic table (pĭr′ē-ŏd′ĭk) *n. Chemistry.* A tabular arrangement of the elements according to their atomic numbers so that elements with similar properties are in the same column.

per·i·o·don·tal (pĕr′ē-ə-dŏn′tl) *adj.* **1.** Surrounding or encasing a tooth: *a periodontal ligament.* **2.** Relating to or affecting tissue and structures surrounding and supporting the teeth. **—per′i·o·don′tal·ly** *adv.*

per·i·o·don·tia (pĕr′ē-ə-dŏn′shə) *n.* Periodontics.

per·i·o·don·tics (pĕr′ē-ə-dŏn′tĭks) *n. (used with a sing. verb).* The branch of dentistry that deals with the study and treatment of periodontal disease. **—per′i·o·don′tic, per′i·o·don′ti·cal** *adj.* **—per′i·o·don′tist** *n.*

per·i·o·nych·i·um (pĕr′ē-ō-nĭk′ē-əm) *n., pl.* **-i·a** (-ē-ə). The border of epidermal tissue surrounding a fingernail or toenail. [New Latin : PERI– + Greek *onux,* nail; see **nogh-** in Appendix.]

per·i·os·te·um (pĕr′ē-ŏs′tē-əm) *n., pl.* **-te·a** (-tē-ə). The dense fibrous membrane covering the surface of bones except at the joints and serving as an attachment for muscles and tendons. [New Latin, from Late Latin *periosteon,* from Greek, from *periosteos,* around the bone : *peri-,* peri- + *osteon,* bone; see **ost-** in Appendix.] **—per′i·os′te·al** (-tē-əl), **per′i·os′te·ous** (-tē-əs) *adj.*

per·i·os·ti·tis (pĕr′ē-ŏs-tī′tĭs) *n.* Inflammation of the periosteum. **—per′i·os·tit′ic** (-tĭt′ĭk) *adj.*

per·i·os·tra·cum (pĕr′ē-ŏs′trə-kəm) *n., pl.* **-ca** (-kə). The hard chitinous outer covering of the shell of many mollusks, especially freshwater ones, that protects the shell from the erosive action of water. [New Latin : PERI– + Greek *ostrakon,* shell; see OSTRACOD.]

per·i·o·tic (pĕr′ē-ō′tĭk) *adj.* **1.** Situated around the ear. **2.** Of or relating to the bones immediately around the inner ear.

per·i·pa·tet·ic (pĕr′ə-pə-tĕt′ĭk) *adj.* **1.** Walking about or from place to place; traveling on foot. **2. Peripatetic.** Of or relating to the philosophy or teaching methods of Aristotle, who conducted discussions while walking about in the Lyceum of ancient Athens. **—peripatetic** *n.* **1.** One who walks from place to place; an itinerant. **2. Peripatetic.** A follower of the philosophy of Aristotle; an Aristotelian. [Middle English *peripatetik,* from Latin *peripatēticus,* from Greek *peripatētikos,* from *peripatein,* to walk about : *peri-,* peri- + *patein,* to walk; see **pent-** in Appendix.]

pe·rip·a·tus (pə-rĭp′ə-təs) *n.* See **onychophoran.** [New Latin *Peripatus,* genus name, from Greek *peripatos,* walking about, from *peripatein,* to walk about. See PERIPATETIC.]

per·i·pe·te·ia also **per·i·pe·ti·a** (pĕr′ə-pə-tē′ə, -tī′ə) *n.* A sudden change of events or reversal of circumstances, especially in a literary work. [Greek, from *peripiptein,* to change suddenly : *peri-,* peri- + *piptein,* to fall; see **pet-** in Appendix.]

pe·rip·e·ty (pə-rĭp′ĭ-tē) *n.* Peripeteia. [French *péripétie,* from Greek *peripeteia.* See PERIPETEIA.]

pe·riph·er·al (pə-rĭf′ər-əl) *adj.* **1.** Related to, located in, or constituting an outer boundary or periphery. **2.** Perceived or perceiving near the outer edges of the retina: *peripheral vision.* **3.** *Anatomy.* **a.** Of the surface or outer part of a body or organ; external. **b.** Of, relating to, or being part of the peripheral nervous system. **4.** Of minor relevance or importance. **5.** Auxiliary. **—peripheral** *n. Computer Science.* An auxiliary device, such as a printer, modem, or storage system, that works in conjunction with a computer. **—pe·riph′er·al·ly** *adv.*

peripheral nervous system *n.* The part of the vertebrate nervous system constituting the nerves outside the central nervous system and including the cranial nerves, the spinal nerves, and the sympathetic and parasympathetic nervous systems.

pe·riph·er·y (pə-rĭf′ə-rē) *n., pl.* **-ies. 1.** A line that forms the boundary of an area; a perimeter. See Synonyms at **circumference. 2.** The surface of a solid. **3.a.** The outermost part or region within a precise boundary. **b.** A zone constituting an imprecise boundary. [Middle English *periferie,* from Medieval Latin *periferia,* from Late Latin *peripheria,* from Greek *periphereia,* from *peripherēs,* carrying around : *peri-,* peri- + *pherein,* to carry; see **bher-**[1] in Appendix.]

pe·riph·ra·sis (pə-rĭf′rə-sĭs) *n., pl.* **-ses** (-sēz′). **1.** The use of circumlocution. **2.** A circumlocution. [Latin, from Greek, from *periphrazein,* to express periphrastically : *peri-,* peri- + *phrazein,* to say; see **gʷhren-** in Appendix.]

per·i·phras·tic (pĕr′ə-frăs′tĭk) *adj.* **1.** Having the nature of or characterized by periphrasis. **2.** *Grammar.* Constructed by using an auxiliary word rather than an inflected form; for example, *of father* is the periphrastic possessive case of *father* but *father's* is the inflected possessive case, and *did say* is the periphrastic past tense of *say* but *said* is the inflected past tense. **—per′i·phras′ti·cal·ly** *adv.*

pe·riph·y·ton (pə-rĭf′ĭ-tŏn′) *n.* Sessile organisms, such as algae and small crustaceans, that live attached to surfaces projecting from the bottom of a freshwater aquatic environment. [New Latin, from Greek *periphuton,* from neuter sing. of *periphutos,* planted all over, from *periphuein,* to grow around, cling to : *peri-,* peri- + *phuein,* to grow; see **bheuə-** in Appendix.]

per·i·plasm (pĕr′ə-plăz′əm) *n.* The region near or immediately within a bacterial or other cell wall, outside the plasma membrane. **—per′i·plas′mic** *adj.*

per·i·plast (pĕr′ə-plăst′) *n.* **1.** An outer layer surrounding the

periodical cicada

ă pat	oi boy
ā pay	ou out
âr care	o͝o took
ä father	o͞o boot
ĕ pet	ŭ cut
ē be	ûr urge
ĭ pit	th thin
ī pie	*th* this
îr pier	hw which
ŏ pot	zh vision
ō toe	ə about, item
ô paw	♦ regionalism

Stress marks: **′** (primary); ′ (secondary), as in **dictionary** (dĭk′shə-nĕr′ē)

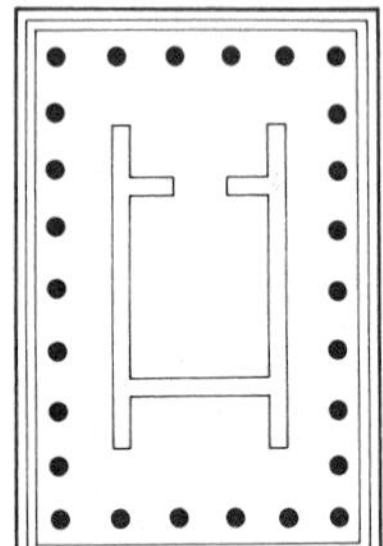
peristyle
Plan of a Greek temple

periwinkle[2]
Common periwinkle
Vinca minor

Frances Perkins

cell membrane of certain microorganisms, such as a spirochete. **2.** A cell membrane or cell wall.

per·i·proct (pĕr′ə-prŏkt′) *n.* The area around the anus in certain invertebrates, such as echinoderms. [PERI– + Greek *prōktos,* anus.]

pe·rip·ter·al (pə-rĭp′tər-əl) *adj. Architecture.* Having a single row of columns on all sides. [From Latin *peripteros,* from Greek : *peri-,* peri- + *pteron,* wing; see **pet-** in Appendix.]

pe·rique (pə-rēk′) *n.* A strongly flavored black tobacco grown in Louisiana and used in various blends. [Louisiana French, perhaps from *Périque,* nickname of *Pierre Chenet,* a Louisiana tobacco grower.]

per·i·sarc (pĕr′ĭ-särk′) *n.* A horny external covering that encloses the polyp colonies of certain hydrozoans. [PERI– + Greek *sarx, sark-,* flesh.] **—per′i·sar′cal, per′i·sar′cous** *adj.*

per·i·scope (pĕr′ĭ-skōp′) *n.* Any of various tubular optical instruments that contain reflecting elements, such as mirrors and prisms, to permit observation from a position displaced from a direct line of sight. **—per′i·scop′ic** (-skŏp′ĭk), **per′i·scop′i·cal** (-ĭ-kəl) *adj.*

per·ish (pĕr′ĭsh) *v.* **-ished, -ish·ing, -ish·es.** *—intr.* **1.** To die or be destroyed, especially in a violent or untimely manner: *"Must then a Christ perish in torment in every age to save those who have no imagination?"* (George Bernard Shaw). **2.** To pass from existence; disappear gradually: *"Man will go down into the pit, and all his thoughts will perish"* (A.J. Balfour). **3.** *Chiefly British.* To spoil or deteriorate. *—tr.* To bring to destruction; destroy: *"Many foul blights/Perish'd his hard won gains"* (Thomas Hood). **—*idiom.* perish the thought.** Used to express the wish that one not even think about something. [Middle English *perishen,* from Old French *perir, periss-,* to perish, from Latin *perīre* : *per-,* per- + *īre,* to go; see **ei-** in Appendix.]

per·ish·a·ble (pĕr′ĭ-shə-bəl) *adj.* Subject to decay, spoilage, or destruction. **—perishable** *n.* Something, especially foodstuff, subject to decay or spoilage. Often used in the plural. **—per′ish·a·bil′i·ty, per′ish·a·ble·ness** *n.* **—per′ish·a·bly** *adv.*

per·i·sperm (pĕr′ĭ-spûrm′) *n. Botany.* The nutritive tissue that is derived from the nucleus and surrounds the embryo of the seed.

pe·ris·so·dac·tyl (pə-rĭs′ō-dăk′təl) *Zoology. adj.* **1.** Having an uneven number of toes. **2.** Of or relating to certain hoofed mammals, such as horses and rhinoceroses, of the order Perissodactyla, that have an uneven number of toes. **—perissodactyl** *n.* A hoofed mammal of the order Perissodactyla. [New Latin *perissodactylus,* from Greek *perissodaktulos* : *perissos,* irregular, uneven (from *peri,* beyond); see **per**[1] in Appendix + *daktulos,* finger.] **—pe·ris′so·dac′ty·lous** (-dăk′tə-ləs) *adj.*

per·i·stal·sis (pĕr′ĭ-stôl′sĭs, -stăl′-) *n., pl.* **-ses** (-sēz). The wavelike muscular contractions of the alimentary canal or other tubular structures by which contents are forced onward toward the opening. [New Latin, from Greek *peristaltikos,* peristaltic, from *peristellein,* to wrap around : *peri-,* peri- + *stellein,* to place; see **stel-** in Appendix.] **—per′i·stal′tic** (-stôl′tĭk, -stăl′-) *adj.* **—per′i·stal′ti·cal·ly** *adv.*

per·i·stome (pĕr′ĭ-stōm′) *n.* **1.** *Botany.* A fringe of toothlike appendages surrounding the mouth of a moss capsule. **2.** *Zoology.* The area or parts around the mouth in certain invertebrates. **—per′i·sto′mal** (-stō′məl), **per′i·sto′mi·al** (-stō′mē-əl) *adj.*

per·i·style (pĕr′ĭ-stīl′) *n. Architecture.* **1.** A series of columns surrounding a building or enclosing a court. **2.** A court enclosed by columns. [French *péristyle,* from Latin *peristȳlum,* from Greek *peristulon,* from neuter of *peristulos,* surrounded by columns : *peri-,* peri- + *stulos,* pillar; see **stā-** in Appendix.] **—per′i·sty′lar** (-stī′lər) *adj.*

per·i·the·ci·um (pĕr′ə-thē′shē-əm, -sē-əm) *n., pl.* **-ci·a** (-shē-ə, -sē-ə). A small flask-shaped fruiting body in ascomycetous fungi that contains the ascospores. [New Latin : PERI– + Greek *thēkion,* diminutive of *thēkē,* case; see **dhē-** in Appendix.] **—per′i·the′ci·al** (-shē-əl, -sē-əl) *adj.*

per·i·to·ne·um also **per·i·to·nae·um** (pĕr′ĭ-tn-ē′əm) *n., pl.* **-to·ne·a** also **-to·nae·a** (-tn-ē′ə). The serous membrane that lines the walls of the abdominal cavity and folds inward to enclose the viscera. [Middle English, from Late Latin *peritonaeum,* from Greek *peritonaion,* from *peritonaios,* stretched across, from *peritonos,* stretched around : *peri-,* peri- + *teinein,* to stretch; see **ten-** in Appendix.] **—per′i·to·ne′al** *adj.* **—per′i·to·ne′al·ly** *adv.*

per·i·to·ni·tis (pĕr′ĭ-tn-ī′tĭs) *n.* Inflammation of the peritoneum.

per·i·trich (pĕr′ĭ-trĭk′) *n., pl.* **pe·rit·richs** also **pe·rit·ri·cha** (pə-rĭt′rĭ-kə). Any of various protozoans, such as the vorticella, having a wide oral opening surrounded by cilia. [From New Latin *Peritrichida,* former order name : PERI– + Greek *thrix, trikh-,* hair.]

pe·rit·ri·chous (pə-rĭt′rĭ-kəs) *adj.* **1.** Having flagella uniformly distributed over the body surface, as certain bacteria. **2.** Having a band of cilia around the mouth, as certain protozoans. **3.** Of or relating to peritrichs. **—pe·rit′ri·chous·ly** *adv.*

per·i·vis·cer·al (pĕr′ə-vĭs′ər-əl) *adj.* Surrounding the viscera: *a perivisceral sinus.*

per·i·wig (pĕr′ĭ-wĭg′) *n.* A wig, especially a peruke. [Alteration of Old French *perruque.* See PERUKE.]

per·i·win·kle[1] (pĕr′ĭ-wĭng′kəl) *n.* **1.** Any of several small, often edible marine snails, especially of the genus *Littorina,* having thick, cone-shaped, whorled shells. **2.** The shell of any of the periwinkles. [Middle English **periwinkle,* probably alteration (influenced by *pervinkle,* periwinkle (plant); see PERIWINKLE[2]) of Old English *pīnewincle* : Latin *pīna,* mussel (from Greek *pinē*) + Old English *-wincel,* snail shell.]

per·i·win·kle[2] (pĕr′ĭ-wĭng′kəl) *n.* **1.** Any of several shrubby, trailing, evergreen plants of the genus *Vinca,* especially *V. minor,* having glossy, dark green, opposite leaves and flowers with a blue, funnel-shaped corolla. Also called *myrtle.* **2.** Any of several erect herbs of the genus *Catharanthus,* especially *C. roseus,* having flowers with a rose-pink or white salverform corolla and a closed throat. [Middle English *pervinkle,* diminutive of *pervinke,* from Old English *pervince,* from Latin *(vinca) pervinca,* from *pervincīre,* to wind about.]

per·jure (pûr′jər) *tr.v.* **-jured, -jur·ing, -jures.** *Law.* To render (oneself) guilty of perjury by deliberately testifying falsely under oath. [Middle English *perjuren,* from Old French *perjurer,* from Latin *periūrāre* : *per-,* per- + *iūrāre,* to swear; see **yewes-** in Appendix.] **—per′jur·er** *n.*

per·ju·ry (pûr′jə-rē) *n., pl.* **-ries. 1.** *Law.* The deliberate, willful giving of false, misleading, or incomplete testimony under oath. **2.** The breach of an oath or a promise. [Middle English *periurie,* from Anglo-Norman, from Latin *periūrium,* from *periūrāre,* to perjure. See PERJURE.] **—per·ju′ri·ous** (pər-jo͝or′ē-əs) *adj.* **—per·ju′ri·ous·ly** *adv.*

perk[1] (pûrk) *v.* **perked, perk·ing, perks.** *—intr.* **1.** To stick up or jut out: *dogs' ears that perk.* **2.** To carry oneself in a lively and jaunty manner. *—tr.* To cause to stick up quickly: *The dog perked its ears at the noise.* **—perk** *adj.* Perky. **—*phrasal verb.* perk up. 1.** To regain or cause to regain one's good spirits or liveliness. **2.** To refresh the appearance of: *New furniture and paint perked up the room.* [Possibly Middle English *perken,* to perch, from *perk,* rod, perch, probably from Medieval Latin *perca* and from Old French *perche, perce,* both from Latin *pertica,* rod. See PERCH[1].]

perk[2] (pûrk) *n. Informal.* A perquisite: *"Temper tantrums over perks are more common than the American taxpayer might like to believe"* (Maureen Dowd).

perk[3] (pûrk) *intr.v.* **perked, perk·ing, perks.** *Informal.* To percolate: *The coffee was perking on the stove.*

Per·kins (pûr′kĭnz), **Frances.** 1882–1965. American social reformer and public official. As U.S. secretary of labor (1933–1945) she was the first woman to hold a cabinet position.

Perkins, Maxwell Evarts. 1884–1946. American editor who helped develop the talents of a number of great writers, including F. Scott Fitzgerald, Ernest Hemingway, and Thomas Wolfe.

perk·y (pûr′kē) *adj.* **-i·er, -i·est. 1.** Having a buoyant or self-confident air; briskly cheerful. **2.** Jaunty; sprightly. **—perk′i·ly** *adv.* **—perk′i·ness** *n.*

per·lite also **pearl·ite** (pûr′līt′) *n.* A natural volcanic glass similar to obsidian but having distinctive concentric cracks and a relatively high water content. In a fluffy heat-expanded form perlite is used as a lightweight aggregate, in fire-resistant insulation, and in soil for potted plants. [French (from *perle,* pearl, from Old French; see PEARL[1]) or German *Perlite* (from *Perle,* pearl, ultimately from Vulgar Latin **pernula*).] **—per·lit′ic** (pər-lĭt′ĭk) *adj.*

Perl·man (pûrl′mən), **Itzhak.** Born 1945. Israeli-born American violinist noted for his technical brilliance.

perm (pûrm) *Informal. n.* A permanent. **—perm** *tr.v.* **permed, perm·ing, perms.** To give (hair) a permanent.

Perm (pĕrm, pyĕrm). A city of west-central Russia on the Kama River in the foothills of the Ural Mountains. Settled since early times, it grew rapidly as an industrial center in the 19th century. Population, 1,056,000.

perm. *abbr.* Permanent.

per·ma·cul·ture (pûr′mə-kŭl′chər) *n.* A system of perennial agriculture emphasizing the use of renewable natural resources and the enrichment of local ecosystems. [PERMA(NENT) + (AGRI)CULTURE.]

per·ma·frost (pûr′mə-frôst′, -frŏst′) *n.* Permanently frozen subsoil, occurring throughout the Polar Regions and locally in perennially frigid areas. [PERMA(NENT) + FROST.]

Perm·al·loy (pûr′mə-loi′, pûrm-ăl′oi′). A trademark used for any of several alloys of nickel and iron having high magnetic permeability. This trademark often occurs in lowercase in print: *"Structures of permalloy . . . form input/output tracks and storage loops"* (Aviation Week & Space Technology). *"The record and playback heads . . . are made of hardened permalloy"* (Stereo Review). *"They are hard, strong . . . permalloys"* (High Technology).

per·ma·nence (pûr′mə-nəns) *n.* The quality or condition of being permanent; permanency.

per·ma·nen·cy (pûr′mə-nən-sē) *n.* Permanence: *the permanency of the Roman Forum.*

per·ma·nent (pûr′mə-nənt) *adj. Abbr.* **perm. 1.** Lasting or remaining without essential change: *"the universal human yearning for something permanent, enduring, without shadow of change"* (Willa Cather). **2.** Not expected to change in status, condition, or place: *a permanent address; permanent secretary to the president.* **—permanent** *n.* A long-lasting hair wave produced by applying a chemical lotion to the hair while wet, winding the hair on rollers, and drying it with heat. Also called *permanent* *wave.* [Middle English, from Old French, from Latin *permanēns, permanent-*, present participle of *permanēre*, to endure : *per-*, throughout; see PER– + *manēre,* to remain; see **men-**[3] in Appendix.] **—per′ma·nent·ly** *adv.* **—per′ma·nent·ness** *n.*

WORD HISTORY: In this world of impermanence it seems that we have tried to hold on to a few things at least by using the word *permanent.* Coming ultimately from the present participle *permanēns* of Latin *permanēre,* "to endure," Middle English *permanent* (first recorded around 1425) also had to do with the enduring and the stable. When we consider some of the applications of this adjective, as in *permanent press, permanent tooth,* we are struck by the relative evanescence of the so-called permanent. But perhaps never more so than in the case of the permanent wave. When asked what this phenomenon was, one journalist wrote in 1932, "(so far as my experience goes): a wave that is anything but permanent."

permanent magnet *n.* A piece of magnetic material that retains its magnetism after it is removed from a magnetic field.

permanent press *n.* **1.** A chemical process in which fabrics are permanently shaped and treated for wrinkle resistance. **2.** A fabric treated by permanent press. Also called *durable press.* **—per′ma·nent-press′** (pûr′mə-nənt-prĕs′) *adj.*

permanent tooth *n.* One of the second set of teeth in mammals that grow as the milk teeth are shed. Human beings have 32 permanent teeth.

permanent wave *n.* See **permanent.**

per·man·ga·nate (pər-măng′gə-nāt′) *n.* Any of the salts of permanganic acid, all of which are strong oxidizing agents. [PERMANGAN(IC ACID) + –ATE[2].]

per·man·gan·ic acid (pûr′măn-găn′ĭk, -măng-) *n.* An unstable inorganic acid, $HMnO_4$, existing only in dilute solution. Its purple aqueous solution is used as an oxidizing agent.

per·me·a·bil·i·ty (pûr′mē-ə-bĭl′ĭ-tē) *n., pl.* **-ties. 1.** The property or condition of being permeable. **2.** The rate of flow of a liquid or gas through a porous material.

per·me·a·ble (pûr′mē-ə-bəl) *adj.* That can be permeated or penetrated, especially by liquids or gases: *permeable membranes; rock that is permeable by water.* **—per′me·a·bly** *adv.*

per·me·ance (pûr′mē-əns) *n.* A measure of the ability of a magnetic circuit to conduct magnetic flux; the reciprocal of reluctance. [From Latin *permeāre,* to penetrate. See PERMEATE.]

per·me·ase (pûr′mē-ās′) *n.* An enzyme that promotes the passage of a substance across a cell membrane. [PERME(ATE) + –ASE.]

per·me·ate (pûr′mē-āt′) *v.* **-at·ed, -at·ing, -ates.** *—tr.* **1.** To spread or flow throughout; pervade: *"Our thinking is permeated by our historical myths"* (Freeman J. Dyson). See Synonyms at **charge. 2.** To pass through the openings or interstices of: *liquid permeating a membrane.* *—intr.* To spread through or penetrate something. [Latin *permeāre, permeāt-,* to penetrate : *per-,* through; see PER– + *meāre,* to pass; see **mei-**[1] in Appendix.] **—per′me·ant** (-ənt), **per′me·a′tive** (-ā′tĭv) *adj.* **—per′me·a′tion** *n.*

Per·mi·an (pûr′mē-ən, pĕr′-) *Geology. adj.* Of, belonging to, or designating the geologic time, system of rocks, and sedimentary deposits of the seventh and last period of the Paleozoic Era. See table at **geologic time. —Permian** *n.* The Permian Period. [After *Perm,* a historical region of eastern European U.S.S.R.]

per·mis·si·ble (pər-mĭs′ə-bəl) *adj.* Permitted; allowable: *permissible tax deductions; permissible behavior in school.* **—per·mis′si·bil′i·ty, per·mis′si·ble·ness** *n.* **—per·mis′si·bly** *adv.*

per·mis·sion (pər-mĭsh′ən) *n.* **1.** The act of permitting. **2.** Consent, especially formal consent; authorization. [Middle English, from Old French, from Latin *permissiō, permissiōn-,* from *permissus,* past participle of *permittere,* to permit. See PERMIT.]

SYNONYMS: *permission, authorization, consent, leave, license, sanction.* The central meaning shared by these nouns is "approval for a course of action that is granted by one in authority": *was refused permission to smoke; seeking authorization to begin construction; gave their consent to the marriage; will ask leave to respond to the speaker; was given license to depart; gave sanction to the project.*
ANTONYM: *prohibition.*

per·mis·sive (pər-mĭs′ĭv) *adj.* **1.** Granting or inclined to grant permission; tolerant or lenient. **2.** Permitting discretion; optional. **3.** *Archaic.* Not forbidden; permitted. **—per·mis′sive·ly** *adv.* **—per·mis′sive·ness** *n.*

per·mit (pər-mĭt′) *v.* **-mit·ted, -mit·ting, -mits.** *—tr.* **1.** To allow the doing of (something); consent to: *permit the sale of alcoholic beverages.* **2.** To grant consent or leave to (someone); authorize: *permitted him to explain.* **3.** To afford opportunity or possibility for: *weather that permits sailing.* *—intr.* To afford opportunity; allow: *if circumstances permit.* **—permit** (pûr′mĭt, pər-mĭt′) *n.* **1.** Permission, especially in written form. **2.** A document or certificate giving permission to do something; a license or warrant: *a building permit.* [Middle English *permitten,* from Latin *permittere* : *per-,* through; see PER– + *mittere,* to let go.] **—per′mit·tee′** (pûr′mĭ-tē′) *n.* **—per·mit′ter** *n.*

USAGE NOTE: In the sense "to allow for, be consistent with," *permit* is often accompanied by *of* when its subject is inanimate: *The wording of the note permits of several interpretations.* But *permit of* should not be used in the sense "to give permission": *The law permits* (not *permits of) camping on the beach.*

per·mit·tiv·i·ty (pûr′mĭ-tĭv′ĭ-tē) *n., pl.* **-ties.** *Physics.* A measure of the ability of a material to resist the formation of an electric field within it. Also called *dielectric constant, relative permittivity.*

per·mu·ta·tion (pûr′myo͝o-tā′shən) *n.* **1.** A complete change; a transformation. **2.** The act of altering a given set of objects in a group. **3.** *Mathematics.* An ordered arrangement of the elements of a set. **—per′mu·ta′tion·al** *adj.*

per·mute (pər-myo͞ot′) *tr.v.* **-mut·ed, -mut·ing, -mutes. 1.** To change the order of. **2.** *Mathematics.* To subject to permutation. [Middle English *permuten,* from Old French *permuter,* from Latin *permūtāre* : *per-,* per- + *mūtāre,* to change; see **mei-**[1] in Appendix.] **—per·mut′a·bil′i·ty** *n.* **—per·mut′a·ble** *adj.* **—per·mut′a·bly** *adv.*

per·ni·cious (pər-nĭsh′əs) *adj.* **1.a.** Tending to cause death or serious injury; deadly: *a pernicious virus.* **b.** Causing great harm; destructive: *pernicious rumors.* **2.** *Archaic.* Evil; wicked. [Middle English, from Old French *pernicios,* from Latin *perniciōsus,* from *perniciēs,* destruction : *per-,* per- + *nex, nec-,* violent death; see **nek-**[1] in Appendix.] **—per·ni′cious·ly** *adv.* **—per·ni′cious·ness** *n.*

pernicious anemia *n.* A severe anemia most often affecting older adults, caused by failure of the stomach to absorb vitamin B_{12} and characterized by abnormally large red blood cells, gastrointestinal disturbances, and lesions of the spinal cord.

per·nick·e·ty (pər-nĭk′ĭ-tē) *adj.* Persnickety. [Origin unknown.]

Pe·rón (pə-rōn′, pĕ-rôn′), **Juan Domingo.** 1895–1974. Argentine soldier and president (1946–1955 and 1973–1974). His second wife, **(Maria) Eva Duarte de Perón** (1919–1952), known as "Evita," was popular for her charitable works. Perón was succeeded in office by his third wife, **Maria Estela Martínez de Perón** (born 1931), known as "Isabelita," who was ousted by the military in 1976.

per·o·ne·al (pĕr′ə-nē′əl) *adj.* Of or relating to the fibula or to the outer portion of the leg. [From Greek *peronē,* pin of a brooch, fibula. See **per-**[2] in Appendix.]

per·o·ral (pər-ôr′əl, -ōr′-) *adj.* Through or by way of the mouth: *a peroral infection; peroral administration of fluids.* **—per·o′ral·ly** *adv.*

per·o·rate (pĕr′ə-rāt′) *intr.v.* **-rat·ed, -rat·ing, -rates. 1.** To conclude a speech with a formal recapitulation. **2.** To speak at great length, often in a grandiloquent manner; declaim. [Latin *perōrāre, perōrāt-* : *per-,* per- + *ōrāre,* to speak.] **—per′o·ra′tion** *n.* **—per′o·ra′tion·al** *adj.*

per·ox·i·dase (pə-rŏk′sĭ-dās′, -dāz′) *n.* Any of a group of enzymes that occur especially in plant cells and catalyze the oxidation of a substance by a peroxide.

per·ox·ide (pə-rŏk′sīd′) *n.* **1.** A compound, such as sodium peroxide, Na_2O_2, that contains a peroxyl group and yields hydrogen peroxide when treated with an acid. **2.** Hydrogen peroxide. **—peroxide** *tr.v.* **-id·ed, -id·ing, -ides. 1.** To treat with peroxide. **2.** To bleach (hair) with hydrogen peroxide. **—per·ox′ide′** *adj.* **—per′ox·id′ic** (pûr′ŏk-sĭd′ĭk) *adj.*

per·ox·i·some (pə-rŏk′sĭ-sōm′) *n.* A cell organelle containing enzymes, such as catalase and oxidase, that catalyze the production and breakdown of hydrogen peroxide. [PEROXI(DE) + –SOME[3].] **—per·ox′i·som′al** (-sō′məl) *adj.*

peroxy– *pref.* Containing the bivalent group O_2: *peroxybenzoic acid.* [PER– + OXY–.]

perp (pûrp) *n. Slang.* One who perpetrates a crime.

perp. *abbr.* Perpendicular.

per·pend (pər-pĕnd′) *v.* **-pend·ed, -pend·ing, -pends.** *—tr.* To consider carefully; ponder. *—intr.* To be attentive; reflect. [Latin *perpendere* : *per-,* per- + *pendere,* to weigh; see **(s)pen-** in Appendix.]

per·pen·dic·u·lar (pûr′pən-dĭk′yə-lər) *adj. Abbr.* **perp. 1.** *Mathematics.* Intersecting at or forming right angles. **2.** Being at right angles to the horizontal; vertical. See Synonyms at **vertical. 3.** Often **Perpendicular.** Of or relating to a style of English Gothic architecture of the 14th and 15th centuries, characterized by emphasis of the vertical element. **—perpendicular** *n.* **1.** *Mathematics.* A line or plane perpendicular to a given line or plane. **2.** A perpendicular position. **3.** A device, such as a plumb line, used in marking the vertical from a given point. **4.** A vertical or nearly vertical line or plane. [Middle English *perpendiculer,* from Old French, from Latin *perpendiculāris,* from *perpendiculum,* plumb line, from *perpendere,* to weigh carefully : *per-,* per- + *pendere,* to weigh; see **(s)pen-** in Appendix.] **—per′pen·dic′u·lar′i·ty** (-lăr′ĭ-tē) *n.* **—per′pen·dic′u·lar·ly** *adv.*

per·pe·trate (pûr′pĭ-trāt′) *tr.v.* **-trat·ed, -trat·ing, -trates.** To be responsible for; commit: *perpetrate a crime; perpetrate a practical joke.* [Latin *perpetrāre, perpetrāt-,* to accomplish : *per-,* per- + *patrāre,* to bring about (from *pater,* father; see **pəter-** in Appendix).] **—per′pe·tra′tion** *n.* **—per′pe·tra′tor** *n.*

per·pet·u·al (pər-pĕch′o͞o-əl) *adj.* **1.** Lasting for eternity. **2.**

ă pat	oi boy
ā pay	ou out
âr care	o͝o took
ä father	o͞o boot
ĕ pet	ŭ cut
ē be	ûr urge
ĭ pit	th thin
ī pie	*th* this
îr pier	hw which
ŏ pot	zh vision
ō toe	ə about, item
ô paw	♦ regionalism

Stress marks: **′** (primary); ′ (secondary), as in **dictionary** (dĭk′shə-nĕr′ē)

Continuing or lasting for an indefinitely long time. **3.** Instituted to be in effect or have tenure for an unlimited duration: *a treaty of perpetual friendship.* **4.** Continuing without interruption. See Synonyms at **continual. 5.** Flowering throughout the growing season. [Middle English *perpetuel,* from Old French, from Latin *perpetuālis,* from *perpetuus,* continuous : *per-,* per- + *petere,* to go toward; see **pet-** in Appendix.] **—per·pet′u·al·ly** *adv.*

perpetual calendar *n.* A chart or mechanical device that indicates the day of the week corresponding to any given date over a period of many years.

perpetual motion *n.* The hypothetical continuous operation of an isolated mechanical device or other closed system without a sustaining energy source.

per·pet·u·ate (pər-pĕch′o͞o-āt′) *tr.v.* **-at·ed, -at·ing, -ates. 1.** To cause to continue indefinitely; make perpetual. **2.** To prolong the existence of; cause to be remembered: *The new library will perpetuate its founder's great love of learning.* [Latin *perpetuāre, perpetuāt-,* from *perpetuus,* continuous. See PERPETUAL.] **—per·pet′u·ance, per·pet′u·a′tion** *n.* **—per·pet′u·a′tor** *n.*

per·pe·tu·i·ty (pûr′pĭ-to͞o′ĭ-tē, -tyo͞o′-) *n., pl.* **-ties. 1.** The quality or condition of being perpetual: *"The perpetuity of the Church was an article of faith"* (Morris L. West). **2.** Time without end; eternity. **3.** *Law.* **a.** The condition of an estate that is limited so as to be inalienable either perpetually or longer than the period determined by law. **b.** An estate so limited. **4.** An annuity payable indefinitely. ***—idiom.* in perpetuity.** For an indefinite period of time; forever.

per·phen·a·zine (pər-fĕn′ə-zēn′) *n.* A crystalline compound, $C_{21}H_{26}ClN_3OS$, used as a tranquilizer especially in the treatment of psychosis and to prevent or alleviate nausea and vomiting. [Shortening and rearrangement of chemical name *(chloro)phen(othiazinpropylpi)perazine(ethanol).*]

Per·pi·gnan (pĕr-pē-nyäɴ′). A city of southern France near the Spanish border and the Mediterranean Sea. Probably founded in the 10th century, it was capital of the Spanish kingdom of Roussillon after the 12th century and became part of France in 1659. Population, 111,669.

per·plex (pər-plĕks′) *tr.v.* **-plexed, -plex·ing, -plex·es. 1.** To confuse or trouble with uncertainty or doubt. See Synonyms at **puzzle. 2.** To make confusedly intricate; complicate. [Back-formation from Middle English *perplexed,* puzzled. See PERPLEXED.] **—per·plex′ing·ly** *adv.*

per·plexed (pər-plĕkst′) *adj.* **1.** Filled with confusion or bewilderment; puzzled. **2.** Full of complications or difficulty; involved. [Middle English, from *perplex,* confused, from Old French *perplexe,* from Latin *perplexus* : *per-,* per- + *plexus,* past participle of *plectere,* to entwine; see **plek-** in Appendix.] **—per·plex′ed·ly** (-plĕk′sĭd-lē) *adv.*

per·plex·i·ty (pər-plĕk′sĭ-tē) *n., pl.* **-ties. 1.** The state of being perplexed or puzzled. **2.** The state of being intricate or complicated: *"the perplexity of life in twentieth-century America"* (Daniel J. Boorstin). **3.** Something that perplexes.

per·qui·site (pûr′kwĭ-zĭt) *n.* **1.** A payment or profit received in addition to a regular wage or salary, especially a benefit expected as one's due. See Synonyms at **right. 2.** A tip; a gratuity. **3.** Something claimed as an exclusive right: *"Politics was the perquisite of the upper class"* (Richard B. Sewall). [From Middle English *perquisites,* property acquired otherwise than by inheritance, from Medieval Latin *perquīsītum,* acquisition, from Latin, neuter past participle of *perquīrere,* to search diligently for : *per-,* per- + *quaerere,* to seek.]

Per·rault (pə-rō′, pĕ-), **Charles.** 1628–1703. French writer. His *Contes de ma Mère l'Oye* (c. 1697) includes "Tom Thumb" and "Sleeping Beauty."

Per·rin (pĕ-răɴ′), **Jean Baptiste.** 1870–1942. French physicist and chemist. He won a 1926 Nobel Prize for work on the discontinuous structure of matter and his discovery of the equilibrium of sedimentation.

Per·rot (pə-rō′, pĕ-), **Nicolas.** 1644–1717. French explorer and trader. In 1689 he claimed the upper Mississippi River region for France.

per·ry (pĕr′ē) *n., pl.* **-ries.** A fermented, often effervescent beverage made from pears. [Middle English *pere,* from Old French *pere,* from Vulgar Latin **pirātum,* from Latin *pirum,* pear.]

Per·ry (pĕr′ē), **Antoinette.** 1888–1946. American actress and director. The Antoinette Perry Awards, or Tony Awards, are named for her.

Perry, Matthew Calbraith. 1794–1858. American naval officer who opened diplomatic and trade relations between the United States and Japan (1854).

Perry, Oliver Hazard. 1785–1819. American naval officer who led the fleet that defeated the British in the Battle of Lake Erie (1813) during the War of 1812.

Perry, Ralph Barton. 1876–1957. American philosopher and educator. Among his works are *The New Realism* (1912) and *Thought and Character of William James* (1935).

pers. *abbr.* **1.** Person. **2.** Personal.

Pers. *abbr.* Persia; Persian.

perse (pûrs) *adj. Color.* Dark grayish blue or purple. [Middle English *pers,* from Old French, from Medieval Latin *persus,* back-formation from Latin *Persicus,* Persian, from *Persa,* a Persian.]

Persian cat

per se (pər sā′, sē′) *adv.* Of, in, or by itself or oneself; intrinsically. [Latin *per sē* : *per,* per + *sē,* itself.]

Perse (pĕrs, pûrs), **Saint-John.** See Alexis Saint-Léger **Léger.**

per·se·cute (pûr′sĭ-kyo͞ot′) *tr.v.* **-cut·ed, -cut·ing, -cutes. 1.** To oppress or harass with ill-treatment, especially because of race, religion, sexual orientation, or beliefs. **2.** To annoy persistently; bother. [Middle English, from Old French *persecuter,* back-formation from *persecuteur,* persecutor, from Late Latin *persecūtor,* from *persecūtus,* past participle of *persequī,* to persecute, from Latin, to pursue : *per-,* per- + *sequī,* to follow; see **sekʷ-¹** in Appendix.] **—per′se·cu·tee′** (-kyo͞o-tē′) *n.* **—per′se·cu′tive, per′se·cu·to′ry** (-kyo͞o-tôr′ē, -tōr′ē, -kyo͞o′tə-rē) *adj.* **—per′se·cu′tor** *n.*

per·se·cu·tion (pûr′sĭ-kyo͞o′shən) *n.* **1.** The act or practice of persecuting on the basis of race, religion, sexual orientation, or beliefs that differ from those of the persecutor. **2.** The condition of being persecuted. **—per′se·cu′tion·al** *adj.*

Per·se·id (pûr′sē-ĭd) *n., pl.* **Per·se·ids** or **Per·se·i·des** (pər-sē′ĭ-dēz′). One of a shower of meteors that appears to originate in the vicinity of the constellation Perseus during the second week of August. [From Latin *Perseus,* the constellation Perseus; see PERSEUS, or from Greek *Persēides,* pl. of *Persēis,* offspring of Perseus (from *Perseus,* Perseus).]

Per·seph·o·ne (pər-sĕf′ə-nē) *n. Greek Mythology.* The daughter of Demeter and Zeus who was abducted by Hades but rescued by her mother and thereafter spent six months of the year on earth and six months in the underworld.

Per·sep·o·lis (pər-sĕp′ə-lĭs). An ancient city of Persia northeast of modern Shiraz in southwest Iran. It was the ceremonial capital of Darius I and his successors. Its ruins include the palaces of Darius and Xerxes and a citadel that contained the treasury looted by Alexander the Great.

Per·se·us (pûr′sē-əs, -syo͞os′) *n.* **1.** *Greek Mythology.* The son of Danaë and Zeus and husband of Andromeda who killed the Gorgon Medusa. **2.** A constellation in the Northern Hemisphere near Andromeda and Auriga. [Latin, from Greek.]

per·se·ver·ance (pûr′sə-vîr′əns) *n.* **1.** Steady persistence in adhering to a course of action, a belief, or a purpose; steadfastness. **2.** *Theology.* The Calvinistic doctrine that those who have been chosen by God will continue in a state of grace to the end and will finally be saved.

SYNONYMS: *perseverance, persistence, tenacity, pertinacity.* Each of these nouns means steadfast singleness of purpose, as in the pursuit of a goal, despite difficulties or obstacles. *Perseverance* suggests praiseworthy and enduring patience: *" 'Tis known by the name of perseverance in a good cause,—and of obstinacy in a bad one"* (Laurence Sterne). *"Great works are performed, not by strength, but perseverance"* (Samuel Johnson). *Persistence* always implies firm resolve but may connote an obstinate, annoying quality: *"Persistence and courage are the most womanly no less than the most manly qualities"* (Margaret Fuller). *Tenacity* and especially *pertinacity* suggest stubborn, often perverse persistence: *"The Scots fought with desperate tenacity"* (John Morley). *"Again and again . . . with the inexorable pertinacity of a child intent upon some object important to itself, did he renew his efforts"* (Nathaniel Hawthorne).

per·sev·er·ate (pər-sĕv′ə-rāt′) *intr.v.* **-at·ed, -at·ing, -ates.** *Psychology.* To manifest or experience perseveration. [Back-formation from PERSEVERATION.] **—per·sev′er·a′tive** *adj.*

per·sev·er·a·tion (pər-sĕv′ə-rā′shən) *n.* **1.** *Psychology.* **a.** Uncontrollable repetition of a particular response, such as a word, phrase, or gesture, despite the absence or cessation of a stimulus, usually caused by brain injury or other organic disorder. **b.** The tendency to continue or repeat an act or activity after the cessation of the original stimulus. **2.** The act or an instance of persevering; perseverance.

per·se·vere (pûr′sə-vîr′) *intr.v.* **-vered, -ver·ing, -veres.** To persist in or remain constant to a purpose, an idea, or a task in the face of obstacles or discouragement. [Middle English *perseveren,* from Old French *perseverer,* from Latin *persevērāre,* from *persevērus,* very serious : *per-,* per- + *sevērus,* severe; see **wēro-** in Appendix.] **—per′se·ver′ing·ly** *adv.*

Per·shing (pûr′shĭng, -zhĭng), **John Joseph.** Known as "Black Jack." 1860–1948. American general who commanded the American Expeditionary Force in Europe during World War I and served as army chief of staff (1921–1924).

Per·sia (pûr′zhə, -shə). *Abbr.* **Pers. 1.** Also **Per·sian Empire** (-zhən, -shən). A vast empire of southwest Asia founded by Cyrus II after 546 B.C. and brought to the height of its power and glory by Darius I and his son Xerxes. Alexander the Great conquered the empire in 334 B.C. A later empire was established by the Sassanids (A.D. 226–637). **2.** See **Iran.**

Per·sian (pûr′zhən, -shən) *adj. Abbr.* **Pers.** Of or relating to Persia or Iran, or to their peoples, languages, or cultures. **—Persian** *n.* **1.** A native or inhabitant of Persia or Iran. **2.** Any of the western Iranian dialects or languages of ancient or medieval Persia and modern Iran.

Persian cat *n.* A stocky domestic cat having long silky fur, short legs, and a broad, round head with small ears.

Persian Empire. See **Persia** (sense 1).

Persian Gulf also **A·ra·bi·an Gulf** (ə-rā′bē-ən). An arm of the Arabian Sea between the Arabia Peninsula and southwest Iran. It has been an important trade route since ancient times and gained added strategic significance after the discovery of oil in the Gulf States in the 1930's.

Persian lamb *n.* **1.** The lamb of the karakul sheep of Asia. **2.** The pelt of a Persian lamb, having glossy, tightly curled fur.

Persian melon *n.* A variety of melon *(Cucumis melo)* having a strongly netted, unridged rind and musky, orange-colored flesh.

per·si·flage (pûr′sə-fläzh′) *n.* **1.** Light good-natured talk; banter. **2.** Light or frivolous manner of discussing a subject. [French, from *persifler,* to banter : *per-,* intensive pref. (from Latin; see PER–) + *siffler,* to whistle (from Old French, from Late Latin *sīfilāre,* alteration of Latin *sībilāre*).]

per·sim·mon (pər-sĭm′ən) *n.* **1.** Any of various chiefly tropical trees of the genus *Diospyros,* having hard wood and orange-red fruit that is edible only when completely ripe. **2.** The fruit of any of these trees. [Of Virginia Algonquian origin.]

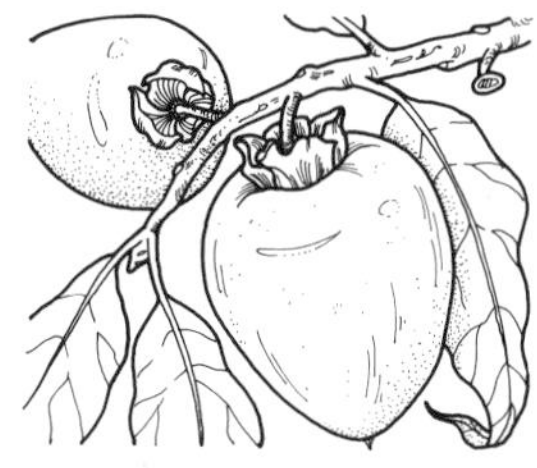
persimmon

per·sist (pər-sĭst′, -zĭst′) *intr.v.* **-sist·ed, -sist·ing, -sists. 1.** To be obstinately repetitious, insistent, or tenacious. **2.** To hold firmly and steadfastly to a purpose, a state, or an undertaking despite obstacles, warnings, or setbacks. **3.** To continue in existence; last: *hostilities that have persisted for years.* [Latin *persistere* : *per-,* per- + *sistere,* to stand; see **stā-** in Appendix.] **—per·sis′ter** *n.*

per·sist·ence (pər-sĭs′təns, -zĭs′-) *n.* **1.** The act of persisting. **2.** The state or quality of being persistent; persistency. See Synonyms at **perseverance. 3.** Continuance of an effect after the cause is removed: *persistence of vision.*

per·sist·en·cy (pər-sĭs′tən-sē) *n.* Persistence.

per·sist·ent (pər-sĭs′tənt, -zĭs′-) *adj.* **1.** Refusing to give up or let go; persevering obstinately. **2.** Insistently repetitive or continuous: *a persistent ringing of the telephone.* **3.** Existing or remaining in the same state for an indefinitely long time; enduring: *persistent rumors; a persistent infection.* **4.** *Botany.* Lasting past maturity without falling off, as the calyx on an eggplant or the scales of a pine cone. **5.** *Zoology.* Retained permanently, rather than disappearing in an early stage of development: *the persistent gills of fishes.* **—per·sist′ent·ly** *adv.*

per·snick·e·ty (pər-snĭk′ĭ-tē) *adj.* **1.a.** Overly particular about trivial details; fastidious. **b.** Snobbish; pretentious. **2.** Requiring strict attention to detail; demanding: *a persnickety job.* [Alteration of *pernickety.* See PERNICKETY.] **—per·snick′e·ti·ness** *n.*

per·son (pûr′sən) *n. Abbr.* **per., pers. 1.** A living human being. Often used in combination: *chairperson; spokesperson; salesperson.* **2.** An individual of specified character: *a person of importance.* See Usage Note at **man. 3.** The composite of characteristics that make up an individual personality; the self. **4.** The living body of a human being: *searched the prisoner's person.* **5.** Physique and general appearance. **6.** *Law.* A human being or an organization with legal rights and duties. **7.** *Theology.* The separate individualities of the Father, Son, and Holy Spirit, as distinguished from the essence of the Godhead that unites them. **8.** *Grammar.* **a.** Any of three groups of pronoun forms with corresponding verb inflections that distinguish the speaker (first person), the individual addressed (second person), and the individual or thing spoken of (third person). **b.** Any of the different forms or inflections expressing these distinctions. **9.** A character or role, as in a play; a guise: *"Well, in her person, I say I will not have you"* (Shakespeare). **—*idiom.* in person.** In one's physical presence; personally: *applied for the job in person.* [Middle English, from Old French *persone,* from Latin *persōna,* mask, role, person, probably from Etruscan *phersu,* mask.]

per·so·na (pər-sō′nə) *n.* **1.** *pl.* **-nas** or **-nae** (-nē) A voice or character representing the speaker in a literary work. **2. personae.** The characters in a dramatic or literary work. **3.** *pl.* **personas.** The role that one assumes or displays in public or society; one's public image or personality, as distinguished from the inner self. [Latin. See PERSON.]

per·son·a·ble (pûr′sə-nə-bəl) *adj.* Pleasing in personality or appearance; attractive. **—per′son·a·ble·ness** *n.* **—per′son·a·bly** *adv.*

per·son·age (pûr′sə-nĭj) *n.* **1.** A character in a literary work. **2.a.** A person. **b.** A person of distinction. See Synonyms at **celebrity.** [Middle English, person, from Old French, from *persone,* person. See PERSON.]

persona gra·ta (grä′tə, grăt′ə) *adj.* Fully acceptable or welcome, especially to a foreign government: *The diplomat was persona grata.* [Latin *persōna,* person + *grata,* acceptable.]

per·son·al (pûr′sə-nəl) *adj. Abbr.* **pers. 1.** Of or relating to a particular person; private: *"Like their personal lives, women's history is fragmented, interrupted"* (Elizabeth Janeway). **2.a.** Done, made, or performed in person: *a personal appearance.* **b.** Done to or for or directed toward a particular person: *a personal favor.* **3.** Concerning a particular person and his or her private business, interests, or activities; intimate: *I have something personal to tell you.* **4.a.** Aimed pointedly at the most intimate aspects of a person, especially in a critical or hostile manner: *an uncalled-for, highly personal remark.* **b.** Tending to make remarks, or be unduly questioning, about another's affairs: *She always becomes personal in an argument.* **5.** Of or relating to the body or physical being: *personal cleanliness.* **6.** Relating to or having the nature of a person or self-conscious being: *belief in a personal God.* **7.** *Law.* Relating to a person's movable property: *personal possessions.* **8.** *Grammar.* Indicating grammatical person. **—personal** *n. Abbr.* **pers. 1.** A personal item or notice in a newspaper. **2. personals.** A column in a newspaper or magazine featuring personal notices.

personal care *n.* The occupation of attending to the physical needs of people who are disabled or otherwise unable to take care of themselves, including tasks such as bathing, management of bodily functions, and cooking.

personal computer *n. Abbr.* **PC.** *Computer Science.* A microcomputer for use by an individual, as in an office or at home or school.

personal effects *pl.n.* Privately owned items, such as keys, an identification card, or a wallet or watch, that are regularly worn or carried on one's person.

personal equation *n. Psychology.* **1.** Those characteristics of a person that cause variation in observation, judgment, and reasoning. **2.** An allowance or adjustment made for such variation.

personal foul *n. Sports.* A foul in a game, such as basketball or football, that usually involves body contact with or willful roughing of an opponent.

per·son·a·li·a (pûr′sə-nā′lē-ə, -nāl′yə) *pl.n.* **1.** Personal allusions or references. **2.** Personal belongings or affairs. [Latin *persōnālia,* neuter pl. of *persōnālis,* relating to a person. See PERSONALITY.]

per·son·al·ism (pûr′sə-nə-lĭz′əm) *n.* **1.** The quality of being characterized by purely personal modes of expression or behavior; idiosyncrasy. **2.** *Philosophy.* Any of various theories of subjective idealism regarding personality as the key to the interpretation of reality. **—per′son·al·ist** *adj. & n.* **—per′son·al·is′tic** *adj.*

per·son·al·i·ty (pûr′sə-năl′ĭ-tē) *n., pl.* **-ties. 1.** The quality or condition of being a person. **2.** The totality of qualities and traits, as of character or behavior, that are peculiar to a specific person. **3.** The pattern of collective character, behavioral, temperamental, emotional, and mental traits of a person: *Though their personalities differed, they got along as friends.* **4.** Distinctive qualities of a person, especially those distinguishing personal characteristics that make one socially appealing: *won the election more on personality than on capability.* See Synonyms at **disposition. 5.a.** A person as the embodiment of distinctive traits of mind and behavior. **b.** *Usage Problem.* A person of prominence or notoriety: *television personalities.* **6.** Often **personalities.** An offensively personal remark: *Let's not engage in personalities.* **7.** The distinctive characteristics of a place or situation: *furnishings that give a room personality.* —*attributive.* Often used to modify another noun: *personality disorders; a personality problem.* [Middle English *personalite,* from Old French, from Late Latin *persōnālitās,* from Latin *persōnālis,* personal, from *persōna,* person. See PERSON.]

USAGE NOTE: *Personality* is often used to mean "celebrity," particularly in popular journalism, as in *The show features interviews with entertainment personalities.* A case can be made for the usage, since many of the persons so described are best known simply for who they are rather than what they have done. Thus *personality* may be an appropriate description of someone who is best known by virtue of his or her frequent appearances as a television host or an advertising spokesperson, but it is slighting when used of people whose renown is based on substantive achievements. Perhaps for this reason, the word was unacceptable to 57 percent of the Usage Panel in an earlier survey.

personality inventory *n.* A questionnaire that is scored to yield a profile of the particular traits or characteristics that make up the respondent's personality.

personality test *n.* A test, usually involving a standardized series of questions or tasks, used to describe or evaluate a subject's personality characteristics.

per·son·al·ize (pûr′sə-nə-līz) *tr.v.* **-ized, -iz·ing, -iz·es. 1.** To take (a general remark or characterization) in a personal manner. **2.** To attribute human or personal qualities to; personify. **3.** To have printed, engraved, or monogrammed with one's name or initials: *personalized the stationery; personalized the bath towels.* **—per′son·al·i·za′tion** (-sə-nə-lĭ-zā′shən) *n.*

per·son·al·ly (pûr′sə-nə-lē) *adv.* **1.** Without the intervention of another; in person: *I thanked them personally.* **2.** As far as oneself is concerned: *Personally, I don't mind.* **3.** As a person: *I admire his skill but dislike him personally.* **4.** In a personal manner: *Don't take the disparaging remarks personally.*

personal pronoun *n. Grammar.* A pronoun designating the person speaking (*I, me, we, us*), the person spoken to (*you*), or the person or thing spoken about (*he, she, it, they, him, her, them*).

personal property *n.* Temporary or movable property.

per·son·al·ty (pûr′sə-nəl-tē) *n., pl.* **-ties.** *Law.* Personal property; chattels. [Anglo-Norman *personalte,* from Late Latin *persōnālitās,* personality. See PERSONALITY.]

persona non gra·ta (nŏn grä′tə, grăt′ə) *adj.* Fully unacceptable or unwelcome, especially to a foreign government: *The diplomat was persona non grata.* [Latin *persōna,* person + *nōn,* not + *grata,* acceptable.]

per·son·ate[1] (pûr′sə-nāt′) *tr.v.* **-at·ed, -at·ing, -ates. 1.** To play the role or portray the part of (a character); impersonate. **2.** To endow with personal qualities; personify. **3.** *Law.* To assume the identity of, with intent to deceive. [Late Latin *per-*

ă pat	oi boy
ā pay	ou out
âr care	ŏŏ took
ä father	ōō boot
ĕ pet	ŭ cut
ē be	ûr urge
ĭ pit	th thin
ī pie	*th* this
îr pier	hw which
ŏ pot	zh vision
ō toe	ə about, item
ô paw	♦ regionalism

Stress marks: ′ (primary); ′ (secondary), as in **dictionary** (dĭk′shə-nĕr′ē)

sōnāre, persōnāt-, to bear the character of, represent, from Latin *persōna,* person. See PERSON.] **—per′son·a′tion** *n.* **—per′son·a′tive** *adj.* **—per′son·a′tor** *n.*

per·son·ate² (pûr′sə-nĭt) *adj. Botany.* Having two lips, with the throat closed by a prominent palate. Used of a corolla, such as that of the snapdragon. [Latin *persōnātus,* masked, from *persōna,* mask. See PERSON.]

per·son·hood (pûr′sən-ho͝od′) *n.* The state or condition of being a person, especially having those qualities that confer distinct individuality: *"finding her own personhood as a campus activist"* (Walter Shapiro).

per·son·i·fi·ca·tion (pər-sŏn′ə-fĭ-kā′shən) *n.* **1.** The act of personifying. **2.** A person or thing typifying a certain quality or idea; an embodiment or exemplification: *"He's invisible, a walking personification of the Negative"* (Ralph Ellison). **3.** A figure of speech in which inanimate objects or abstractions are endowed with human qualities or are represented as possessing human form, as in *Hunger sat shivering on the road* or *Flowers danced about the lawn.* Also called *prosopopeia.* **4.** Artistic representation of an abstract quality or idea as a person.

per·son·i·fy (pər-sŏn′ə-fī′) *tr.v.* **-fied, -fy·ing, -fies. 1.** To think of or represent (an inanimate object or abstraction) as having personality or the qualities, thoughts, or movements of a living being: *"To make history or psychology alive I personify it"* (Anaïs Nin). **2.** To represent (an object or abstraction) by a human figure. **3.** To represent (an abstract quality or idea): *This character personifies evil.* **4.** To be the embodiment or perfect example of: *"Stalin now personified bolshevism in the eyes of the world"* (A.J.P. Taylor). [French *personnifier,* from *personne,* person, from Old French *persone.* See PERSON.] **—per·son′i·fi′er** *n.*

per·son·nel (pûr′sə-nĕl′) *n.* **1.a.** The body of persons employed by or active in an organization, business, or service. **b.** *(used with a pl. verb).* Persons. **2.** An administrative division of an organization concerned with the body of persons employed by or active in it and often acting as a liaison between different departments. *—attributive.* Often used to modify another noun: *personnel problems; personnel matters.* [French, from Old French, personal, from Latin *persōnālis.* See PERSONALITY.]

per·son-to-per·son (pûr′sən-tə-pûr′sən) *adj.* **1.** Of or relating to a long-distance telephone call chargeable only when the caller speaks to an indicated person at the number reached. **2.** Involving direct communication or contact between persons: *a person-to-person interview.* **—per′son-to-per′son** *adv.*

per·spec·tive (pər-spĕk′tĭv) *n.* **1.** The technique of representing three-dimensional objects and depth relationships on a two-dimensional surface. **2.a.** A view or vista. **b.** A mental view or outlook: *"It is useful occasionally to look at the past to gain a perspective on the present"* (Fabian Linden). **3.** The appearance of objects in depth as perceived by normal binocular vision. **4.a.** The relationship of aspects of a subject to each other and to a whole: *a perspective of history; a need to view the problem in the proper perspective.* **b.** Subjective evaluation of relative significance; a point of view: *the perspective of the displaced homemaker.* **c.** The ability to perceive things in their actual interrelations or comparative importance: *tried to keep my perspective throughout the crisis.* **—perspective** *adj.* Of, relating to, seen, or represented in perspective. [Middle English, science of optics (influenced by French *perspective,* perspective, alteration of Italian *prospettiva,* from *prospetto,* new, from Latin *prōspectus;* see PROSPECT), from Medieval Latin *perspectīva (ars),* feminine of *perspectīvus,* optical, from *perspectus,* past participle of *perspicere,* to inspect : *per-,* per- + *specere,* to look; see **spek-** in Appendix.] **—per·spec′tiv·al** *adj.* **—per·spec′tive·ly** *adv.*

per·spi·ca·cious (pûr′spĭ-kā′shəs) *adj.* Having or showing penetrating mental discernment; clear-sighted. See Synonyms at **shrewd.** [From Latin *perspicāx, perspicāc-,* from *perspicere,* to look through. See PERSPECTIVE.] **—per′spi·ca′cious·ly** *adv.* **—per′spi·ca′cious·ness** *n.*

per·spi·cac·i·ty (pûr′spĭ-kăs′ĭ-tē) *n.* Acuteness of perception, discernment, or understanding.

per·spi·cu·i·ty (pûr′spĭ-kyo͞o′ĭ-tē) *n.* **1.** The quality of being perspicuous; clearness and lucidity: *"He was at pains to insist on the perspicuity of what he wrote"* (Lionel Trilling). **2.** Perspicacity.

per·spic·u·ous (pər-spĭk′yo͞o-əs) *adj.* Clearly expressed or presented; easy to understand. [From Latin *perspicuus,* from *perspicere,* to see through. See PERSPICACIOUS.] **—per·spic′u·ous·ly** *adv.* **—per·spic′u·ous·ness** *n.*

per·spi·ra·tion (pûr′spə-rā′shən) *n.* **1.** The fluid, consisting of water with small amounts of urea and salts, that is excreted through the pores of the skin by the sweat glands; sweat. **2.** The act or process of perspiring. **—per·spir′a·to′ry** (pər-spīr′ə-tôr′ē, -tōr′ē, pûr′spər-ə-) *adj.*

per·spire (pər-spīr′) *v.* **-spired, -spir·ing, -spires.** *—intr.* To excrete perspiration through the pores of the skin. *—tr.* To expel through external pores; exude. [Latin *perspīrāre,* to blow steadily : *per-,* through; see PER– + *spīrāre,* to breathe.]

per·suade (pər-swād′) *tr.v.* **-suad·ed, -suad·ing, -suades.** To induce to undertake a course of action or embrace a point of view by means of argument, reasoning, or entreaty: *"to make children fit to live in a society by persuading them to learn and accept its codes"* (Alan W. Watts). See Usage Note at **convince.** [Latin *persuādēre* : *per-,* per- + *suādēre,* to urge; see **swād-** in Appendix.] **—per·suad′a·ble** *adj.* **—per·suad′er** *n.*

SYNONYMS: *persuade, induce, prevail, convince.* These verbs are compared as they mean to succeed in causing a person to do or consent to something. *Persuade* means to win someone over, as by reasons, advice, urging, or personal forcefulness: *Nothing can persuade her to change her mind once it is made up.* To *induce* is to lead, as to a course of action, by means of influence or persuasion: *"Pray what could induce him to commit so rash an action?"* (Oliver Goldsmith). One *prevails* on somebody who resists: *"He had prevailed upon the king to spare them"* (Daniel Defoe). To *convince* is to persuade by the use of argument or evidence: *"In science the credit goes to the man who convinces the world, not to the man to whom the idea first occurs"* (Francis Darwin).

per·sua·si·ble (pər-swā′zə-bəl, -sə-bəl) *adj.* Capable of being persuaded; persuadable. **—per·sua′si·bil′i·ty, per·sua′si·ble·ness** *n.*

per·sua·sion (pər-swā′zhən) *n.* **1.** The act of persuading or the state of being persuaded: *"The persuasion of a democracy to big changes is at best a slow process"* (Harold J. Laski). **2.** The ability or power to persuade: *"Three foremost aids to persuasion which occur to me are humility, concentration, and gusto"* (Marianne Moore). **3.** A strongly held opinion; a conviction. See Synonyms at **opinion. 4.a.** A body of religious beliefs; a religion: *worshipers of various persuasions.* **b.** A party, faction, or group holding to a particular set of ideas or beliefs. **5.** *Informal.* Kind; sort. [Middle English, from Old French, from Latin *persuāsiō, persuāsiōn-,* from *persuāsus,* past participle of *persuādēre,* to persuade. See PERSUADE.]

per·sua·sive (pər-swā′sĭv, -zĭv) *adj.* Tending or having the power to persuade: *a persuasive argument.* **—per·sua′sive·ly** *adv.* **—per·sua′sive·ness** *n.*

pert (pûrt) *adj.* **pert·er, pert·est. 1.** Trim and stylish in appearance; jaunty: *a pert hat.* **2.** High-spirited; vivacious. **3.** Impudently bold; saucy. [Middle English, unconcealed, bold, short for *apert,* obvious, frank (probably influenced by Old French *aspert, espert,* clever, from Latin *expertus,* expert; see EXPERT), from Old French, from Latin *apertus,* open, past participle of *aperīre,* to open. See **wer-⁴** in Appendix.] **—pert′ly** *adv.* **—pert′ness** *n.*

pert. *abbr.* Pertaining.

per·tain (pər-tān′) *intr.v.* **-tained, -tain·ing, -tains. 1.** To have reference; relate: *evidence that pertains to the accident.* **2.** To belong as an adjunct, part, holding, or quality. **3.** To be fitting or suitable. [Middle English *pertenen, pertainen,* from Old French *partenir,* from Latin *pertinēre* : *per-,* per- + *tenēre,* to hold; see **ten-** in Appendix.]

Perth (pûrth). **1.** A city of southwest Australia near the Indian Ocean. Founded in 1829, it grew rapidly after the discovery of gold in the region in the 1890's. Population, 82,600. **2.** A burgh of central Scotland on the Tay River north-northwest of Edinburgh. The capital of Scotland from the 11th to the mid-15th century, it was the site of John Knox's sermon against idolatry in 1559. Population, 42,000.

Perth Am·boy (ăm′boi′). A city of east-central New Jersey on Raritan Bay opposite Staten Island. It was settled in the late 17th century and is today an industrial center and port of entry. Population, 38,951.

per·ti·na·cious (pûr′tn-ā′shəs) *adj.* **1.** Holding tenaciously to a purpose, belief, opinion, or course of action. **2.** Stubbornly or perversely persistent. See Synonyms at **obstinate.** [From Latin *pertināx, pertināc-* : *per-,* per- + *tenāx,* tenacious (from *tenēre,* to hold; see **ten-** in Appendix).] **—per′ti·na′cious·ly** *adv.* **—per′ti·na′cious·ness** *n.*

per·ti·nac·i·ty (pûr′tn-ăs′ĭ-tē) *n.* The quality or state of being pertinacious. See Synonyms at **perseverance.**

per·ti·nent (pûr′tn-ənt) *adj.* Having logical, precise relevance to the matter at hand. See Synonyms at **relevant.** [Middle English, from Old French *partenant, pertinent,* from Latin *pertinēns, pertinent-,* present participle of *pertinēre,* to pertain. See PERTAIN.] **—per′ti·nence, per′ti·nen·cy** *n.* **—per′ti·nent·ly** *adv.*

per·turb (pər-tûrb′) *tr.v.* **-turbed, -turb·ing, -turbs. 1.** To disturb greatly; make uneasy or anxious. **2.** To throw into great confusion. **3.** *Physics & Astronomy.* To cause perturbation, as of a celestial orbit. [Middle English *perturben,* from Old French *perturber,* from Latin *perturbāre* : *per-,* per- + *turbāre,* to throw into disorder (from *turba,* confusion, perhaps from Greek *turbē*).] **—per·turb′a·ble** *adj.*

per·tur·ba·tion (pûr′tər-bā′shən) *n.* **1.a.** The act of perturbing. **b.** The state of being perturbed; agitation. **2.a.** A small change in a physical system. **b.** *Physics & Astronomy.* Variation in a designated orbit, as of a planet, resulting from the influence of one or more external bodies. **—per′tur·ba′tion·al** *adj.*

per·tus·sis (pər-tŭs′ĭs) *n.* See **whooping cough. —per·tus′sal** *adj.*

Pe·ru (pə-ro͞o′). A country of western South America on the Pacific Ocean. Inhabited since at least the 9th millennium B.C., it was the center of an Incan empire established after the 12th century A.D. The Spanish under Pizarro conquered the empire in 1533 and set up in 1542 the viceroyalty of Peru, which at one time included Panama and all of Spanish South America. Peru achieved full independence from Spain in 1824. Lima is the capital and the largest city. Population, 17,031,221. **—Pe·ru′vi·an** (-vē-ən) *adj. & n.*

Peru Current *n.* See **Humboldt Current.**

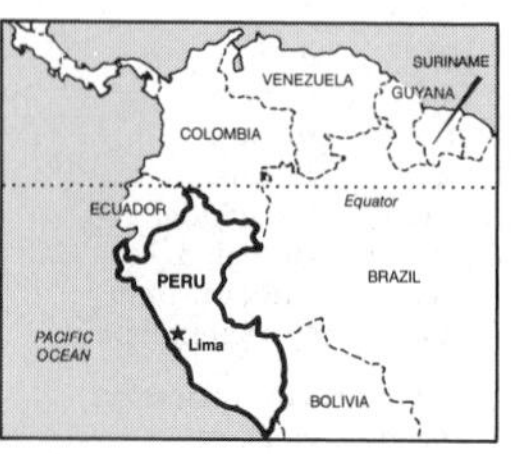

Peru

Pe·ru·gia (pə-ro͞o′jə, -jē-ə, pĕ-ro͞o′jä). A city of central Italy on a hill overlooking the Tiber River north of Rome. An important Etruscan settlement, it fell to the Romans c. 310 B.C. and became a Lombard duchy in A.D. 592 and a free city in the 12th century. Population, 142,522. **—Pe·ru′gian** *adj. & n.*

Pe·ru·gi·no (pĕr′ə-jē′nō, pĕ′ro͞o-), **Il.** 1445–1523? Italian painter whose best-known work is a fresco in the Sistine Chapel, *Christ Giving the Keys to Saint Peter* (1481–1482).

pe·ruke (pə-ro͞ok′) *n.* A wig, especially one worn by men in the 17th and 18th centuries; a periwig. [French *perruque,* from Old French, head of hair, from Old Italian *perrucca.*]

pe·ruse (pə-ro͞oz′) *tr.v.* **-rused, -rus·ing, -rus·es.** To read or examine, typically with great care. [Middle English *perusen,* to use up : Latin *per-,* per- + Middle English *usen,* to use; see USE.] **—pe·rus′a·ble** *adj.* **—pe·rus′al** *n.* **—pe·rus′er** *n.*

USAGE NOTE: *Peruse* has long meant "to read thoroughly" and is often used loosely when one could use the word *read* instead. The worst that can be said about the latter use is that it is excessively literary or precious. However, common misuse of the word in the sense "to glance over, skim," as in *I only had a moment to peruse the manual quickly,* was unacceptable to 66 percent of the Usage Panel.

Per·utz (pə-ro͞otz′, pĕr′əts), **Max Ferdinand.** Born 1914. Austrian-born English biochemist. He shared a 1962 Nobel Prize for determining the molecular structure of blood components.

Peruvian balsam *n.* Balsam of Peru.

Peruvian bark *n.* See **cinchona** (sense 2).

Pe·ruz·zi (pə-ro͞ot′sē, pĕ-), **Baldassare.** 1481–1536. Italian architect and painter. In 1520 he was appointed architect for Saint Peter's in Rome.

per·vade (pər-vād′) *tr.v.* **-vad·ed, -vad·ing, -vades.** To be present throughout; permeate. See Synonyms at **charge.** [Latin *pervādere* : *per-,* through; see PER– + *vādere,* to go.] **—per·vad′er** *n.* **—per·va′sion** (-vā′zhən) *n.*

per·va·sive (pər-vā′sĭv, -zĭv) *adj.* Having the quality or tendency to pervade or permeate: *the pervasive odor of garlic.* [From Latin *pervāsus,* past participle of *pervādere,* to pervade. See PERVADE.] **—per·va′sive·ly** *adv.* **—per·va′sive·ness** *n.*

per·verse (pər-vûrs′, pûr′vûrs′) *adj.* **1.** Directed away from what is right or good; perverted. **2.** Obstinately persisting in an error or a fault; wrongly self-willed or stubborn. **3.a.** Marked by a disposition to oppose and contradict. **b.** Arising from such a disposition. See Synonyms at **contrary. 4.** Cranky; peevish. [Middle English *pervers,* from Old French, from Latin *perversus,* past participle of *pervertere,* to pervert. See PERVERT.] **—per·verse′ly** *adv.* **—per·verse′ness** *n.*

per·ver·sion (pər-vûr′zhən, -shən) *n.* **1.a.** The act of perverting. **b.** The state of being perverted. **2.** A sexual practice or act considered abnormal or deviant. **—per·ver′sive** (-sĭv, -zĭv) *adj.*

per·ver·si·ty (pər-vûr′sĭ-tē) *n., pl.* **-ties. 1.** The quality or state of being perverse. **2.** An instance of being perverse.

per·vert (pər-vûrt′) *tr.v.* **-vert·ed, -vert·ing, -verts. 1.** To cause to turn away from what is right, proper, or good; corrupt. **2.** To bring to a bad or worse condition; debase. **3.** To put to a wrong or improper use; misuse. See Synonyms at **corrupt. 4.** To interpret incorrectly; misconstrue or distort: *an analysis that perverts the meaning of the poem.* **—pervert** (pûr′vûrt′) *n.* One who practices sexual perversion. [Middle English *perverten,* from Old French *pervertir,* from Latin *pervertere* : *per-,* per- + *vertere,* to turn; see **wer-[2]** in Appendix.] **—per·vert′er** *n.* **—per·vert′i·ble** *adj.*

per·vert·ed (pər-vûr′tĭd) *adj.* **1.** Deviating from what is considered right and correct: *a perverted idea of justice.* **2.** Of, relating to, or practicing sexual perversion. **3.** Marked by misinterpretation or distortion: *a perverted translation of an epic poem.* **—per·vert′ed·ly** *adv.* **—per·vert′ed·ness** *n.*

per·vi·ous (pûr′vē-əs) *adj.* **1.** Open to passage or entrance; permeable. **2.** Open to arguments, ideas, or change; approachable. [From Latin *pervius* : *per-,* through; see PER– + *via,* way; see **wegh-** in Appendix.] **—per′vi·ous·ly** *adv.* **—per′vi·ous·ness** *n.*

pes (pās) *n., pl.* **pe·des** (pĕd′ās′). A foot or footlike part, especially the foot of a four-footed vertebrate. [Latin *pēs.* See **ped-** in Appendix.]

Pe·sach (pā′säKH′, pĕ′-) *n. Judaism.* Passover. [Hebrew *pesaḥ,* from *pāsaḥ,* to pass over.]

pe·sade (pə-säd′, -zäd′) *n.* The act or position of a horse when rearing on its hind legs with its forelegs in the air. [French, alteration (influenced by *peser,* to weigh, from Old French *poiser, peser*; see POISE[1]) of obsolete *posade,* from Old Italian *posata,* a pause, from *posare,* to pause, from Late Latin *pausāre.* See POSE[1].]

Pe·sa·ro (pā′zə-rō′, pĕ′zä-rô). A city of north-central Italy on the Adriatic Sea west of Florence. On the site of a Roman colony, it became part of the Papal States in 1631. Population, 90,147.

Pes·ca·do·res (pĕs′kə-dôr′ēz, -ĭs, -dōr′-). In Pinyin **Peng·hu** (pŭng′ho͞o′). An island group of Taiwan in Taiwan Strait between the western coast of Taiwan and southwest China. The name, meaning "fishermen's islands," was given to the group by the Portuguese in the 16th century. Ceded to Japan in 1895 and returned to China after World War II, the islands have been administered by Taiwan since 1949.

Pes·ca·ra (pə-skär′ə, pĕ-skä′rä). A city of central Italy on the Adriatic Sea east-northeast of Rome. It is an industrial and commercial center. Population, 131,345.

pe·se·ta (pə-sā′tə) *n. Abbr.* **p., pta.** See table at **currency.** [Spanish, diminutive of *peso,* peso. See PESO.]

pe·se·wa (pā-sā′wä) *n., pl.* **pesewa** or **-was.** See table at **currency.** [From Akan *pésewabo,* dark blue seed of a plant, formerly used as the smallest gold weight.]

Pe·sha·war (pə-shä′wər). A city of northwest Pakistan northwest of Lahore. It has long been strategically important for its proximity to the Khyber Pass. Population, 500,000.

pes·ky (pĕs′kē) *adj.* **-ki·er, -ki·est.** *Informal.* Troublesome; annoying: *a pesky mosquito.* [Probably alteration of PEST.] **—pes′ki·ly** *adv.* **—pes′ki·ness** *n.*

pe·so (pā′sō) *n., pl.* **-sos.** *Abbr.* **p.** See table at **currency.** [Spanish, from Latin *pēnsum,* something weighed, from neuter past participle of *pendere,* to weigh. See **(s)pen-** in Appendix.]

pes·sa·ry (pĕs′ə-rē) *n., pl.* **-ries. 1.** Any of various devices worn in the vagina to support or correct the position of the uterus or rectum. **2.** A contraceptive diaphragm. **3.** A medicated vaginal suppository. [Middle English *pessarie,* from Late Latin *pessārium,* from *pessus, pessum,* from Greek *pessos,* oval-shaped stone, pessary.]

pes·si·mism (pĕs′ə-mĭz′əm) *n.* **1.** A tendency to stress the negative or unfavorable or to take the gloomiest possible view: *"We have seen too much defeatism, too much pessimism, too much of a negative approach"* (Margo Jones). **2.** The doctrine or belief that this is the worst of all possible worlds and that all things ultimately tend toward evil. **3.** The doctrine or belief that the evil in the world outweighs the good. [French *pessimisme* (on the model of French *optimisme,* optimism), from Latin *pessimus,* worst. See **ped-** in Appendix.] **—pes′si·mist** *n.* **—pes′si·mis′tic** *adj.* **—pes′si·mis′ti·cal·ly** *adv.*

pest (pĕst) *n.* **1.** An annoying person or thing; a nuisance. **2.** An injurious plant or animal, especially one harmful to human beings. **3.** A deadly epidemic disease; a pestilence. [French *peste,* pestilence, from Old French, from Latin *pestis.*]

Pest (pĕst, pĕsht). A former town of north-central Hungary on the left bank of the Danube River. Since 1873 it has been part of Budapest.

Pes·ta·loz·zi (pĕs′tə-lŏt′sē, -tä-lôt′-), **Johann Heinrich.** 1746–1827. Swiss educational reformer whose teaching theories, based on respect and attention to the individual, laid the foundation for the reform of education in the 19th century.

pes·ter (pĕs′tər) *tr.v.* **-tered, -ter·ing, -ters.** To harass with petty annoyances; bother. See Synonyms at **harass.** [Probably short for French *empestrer,* to constrain, embarrass (probably also influenced by PEST), from Old French, from Vulgar Latin **impāstōriāre* : Latin *in-,* in; see IN–[2] + Vulgar Latin **pastōria,* a hobble, from Latin, feminine of *pāstōrius,* of a herdsman, from Latin *pāstor,* herdsman. See **pā-** in Appendix.] **—pes′ter·er** *n.*

pest·hole (pĕst′hōl′) *n.* A place that is considered a breeding ground for epidemic disease.

pest house *n.* A hospital for patients affected with plague or other infectious disease.

pes·ti·cide (pĕs′tĭ-sīd′) *n.* A chemical used to kill pests, especially insects. **—pes′ti·cid′al** (-sīd′l) *adj.*

pes·tif·er·ous (pĕ-stĭf′ər-əs) *adj.* **1.a.** Producing or breeding infectious disease. **b.** Infected with or contaminated by an epidemic disease. **2.** Morally evil or deadly; pernicious. **3.** Bothersome; annoying. [Middle English, from Latin *pestiferus,* variant of *pestifer* : *pestis,* pestilence; see PEST + *-fer,* -fer.] **—pes·tif′er·ous·ly** *adv.* **—pes·tif′er·ous·ness** *n.*

pes·ti·lence (pĕs′tə-ləns) *n.* **1.a.** A usually fatal epidemic disease, especially bubonic plague. **b.** An epidemic of such a disease. **2.** A pernicious, evil influence or agent.

pes·ti·lent (pĕs′tə-lənt) *adj.* **1.** Tending to cause death; deadly. **2.** Likely to cause an epidemic disease. **3.** Infected with or contaminated with a contagious disease. **4.** Morally, socially, or politically harmful; pernicious. See Synonyms at **poisonous. 5.** Causing annoyance or disapproval. [Middle English, from Old French, from Latin *pestilēns, pestilent-,* from *pestis,* pestilence. See PEST.]

pes·ti·len·tial (pĕs′tə-lĕn′shəl) *adj.* Pestilent. See Synonyms at **poisonous. —pes′ti·len′tial·ly** *adv.*

pes·tle (pĕs′əl, pĕs′təl) *n.* **1.** A club-shaped, hand-held tool for grinding or mashing substances in a mortar. **2.** A large bar moved vertically to stamp or pound, as in a press or mill. **—pestle** *v.* **-tled, -tling, -tles.** —*tr.* To pound, grind, or mash with or as if with a pestle. —*intr.* To use a pestle. [Middle English *pestel,* from Old French, from Latin *pistillum.*]

pes·to (pĕs′tō) *n.* A sauce consisting of usually fresh basil, garlic, pine nuts, olive oil, and grated cheese. [Italian, from past participle of *pistare, pestare,* to pound. See PISTON.]

pet[1] (pĕt) *n.* **1.** An animal kept for amusement or companionship. **2.** An object of the affections. **3.** A person especially loved or indulged; a favorite: *the teacher's pet.* **—pet** *adj.* **1.** Kept as a pet: *a pet cat.* **2.a.** Particularly cherished or indulged: *a pet grandchild.* **b.** Expressing or showing affection: *a pet name.* **3.** Being a favorite: *a pet topic.* **—pet** *v.* **pet·ted, pet·ting, pets.** —*tr.* To stroke or caress gently; pat. See Synonyms at **caress.**

peruke
Portrait of a Man by Jeremiah Theus (1716–1774)

pestle
In a mortar

ă pat	oi boy
ā pay	ou out
âr care	o͝o took
ä father	o͞o boot
ĕ pet	ŭ cut
ē be	ûr urge
ĭ pit	th thin
ī pie	*th* this
îr pier	hw which
ŏ pot	zh vision
ō toe	ə about, item
ô paw	♦ regionalism

Stress marks: ′ (primary); ′ (secondary), as in **dictionary** (dĭk′shə-nĕr′ē)

—*intr. Informal.* To make love by fondling and caressing. [Scottish Gaelic *peata,* tame animal, pet, from Old Irish.] —**pet′ter** *n.*

pet² (pĕt) *n.* A fit of bad temper or pique. —**pet** *intr.v.* **pet·ted, pet·ting, pets.** To be sulky and peevish. [Origin unknown.]

PET *abbr.* Positron emission tomography.

pet. *abbr.* Petroleum.

Pet. *abbr. Bible.* Peter.

Pe·tah Tiq·wa (pĕt′ə tĭk′və, -vä, pĕ′täкн). A city of central Israel east of Tel Aviv–Jaffa. Founded in 1878, it is an industrial center in an agricultural region. Population, 128,300.

Pé·tain (pā-tăɴ′), **Henri Philippe.** 1856–1951. French soldier and politician who led the pro-German government of unoccupied Vichy France (1940–1944).

pet·al (pĕt′l) *n.* A unit of a corolla, usually showy and colored. [New Latin *petalum,* from Greek *petalon,* leaf. See **pete-** in Appendix.] —**pet′aled, pet′alled** *adj.*

-petal *suff.* Moving toward: *basipetal.* [From New Latin *-petus,* from Latin *petere,* to seek. See **pet-** in Appendix.]

pet·al·if·er·ous (pĕt′l-ĭf′ər-əs) *adj.* Bearing petals.

pet·al·ine (pĕt′l-ĭn, -īn′) *adj.* Of or resembling a petal.

pet·al·oid (pĕt′l-oid′) *adj.* Resembling a petal.

pet·al·ous (pĕt′l-əs) *adj.* Having petals.

Pet·a·lu·ma (pĕt′l-o͞o′mə). A city of western California north-northwest of San Rafael. Founded in 1833, it is a trade and processing center. Population, 33,834.

pe·tard (pĭ-tärd′) *n.* **1.** A small bell-shaped bomb used to breach a gate or wall. **2.** A loud firecracker. [French *pétard,* from Old French, from *peter,* to break wind, from *pet,* a breaking of wind, from Latin *pēditum,* from neuter past participle of *pēdere,* to break wind. See **pezd-** in Appendix.]

Peter the Great

pet·a·sos or **pet·a·sus** (pĕt′ə-səs) *n.* **1.** A wide-brimmed hat worn by ancient Greeks and Romans. **2.** *Greek Mythology.* The winged hat of Hermes. [Greek. See **pete-** in Appendix.]

pet·cock (pĕt′kŏk′) *n.* A small valve or faucet used to drain or reduce pressure, as from a boiler. [Perhaps PET¹ + COCK¹.]

pe·te·chi·a (pə-tē′kē-ə) *n., pl.* **-chi·ae** (-kē-ī′). A small purplish spot on a body surface, such as the skin or a mucous membrane, caused by a minute hemorrhage and often seen in typhus. [New Latin, from Italian *petecchie,* pl. of *petecchia,* spot on skin, perhaps from Vulgar Latin **petīcula,* short for **impetīcula,* diminutive of Latin *impetīx, impetīc-,* variant of *impetīgo.* See IMPETIGO.] —**pe·te′chi·al** *adj.* —**pe·te′chi·ate** (-ĭt) *adj.*

pe·ter¹ (pē′tər) *intr.v.* **-tered, -ter·ing, -ters. 1.** To diminish slowly and come to an end; dwindle. Often used with *out: Their enthusiasm soon petered out.* **2.** To become exhausted. Used with *out.* [Origin unknown.]

pe·ter² (pē′tər) *n. Vulgar Slang.* The penis. [From the name *Peter.*]

Pe·ter (pē′tər) *n. Abbr.* **P., Pet.** *Bible.* See table at **Bible.**

Peter, Saint. Died c. A.D. 67. The chief of the 12 Apostles. He is traditionally regarded as the first bishop of Rome.

Peter I. Known as "Peter the Great." 1672–1725. Russian czar (1682–1725) who extended his territory around the Baltic and Caspian shores and reformed the administration of the state.

Peter II. 1923–1970. Yugoslavian king (1934–1945). After spending World War II in exile, he was forced to abdicate by the Communist government.

Roger Tory Peterson

Pe·ter·bor·ough (pē′tər-bûr′ə, -bər-ə, -bŭr′ō). **1.** A city of southeast Ontario, Canada, northeast of Toronto. Settled in the 1820's as a lumbering town, it is now an industrial center and a railroad junction. Population, 60,620. **2.** A municipal borough of east-central England east of Leicester. Catherine of Aragon is buried in the cathedral here. Population, 126,200.

Peter Pan collar *n.* A small, close-fitting, usually flat collar with rounded ends meeting in front. [After *Peter Pan,* the boy protagonist of *Peter Pan, or The Boy Who Wouldn't Grow Up,* a play by J.M. Barrie.]

Peter Principle *n.* The theory that an employee within an organization will advance to his or her level of incompetence and remain there. [After Laurence Johnston *Peter* (1919–1990).]

Pe·ters·burg (pē′tərz-bûrg′). An independent city of southeast Virginia on the Appomattox River south of Richmond. A prolonged siege (June 15, 1864–April 3, 1865) during the Civil War led to the fall of Richmond and the subsequent surrender of the Confederate general Robert E. Lee. Population, 41,055.

Pe·ter·son (pē′tər-sən), **Roger Tory.** Born 1908. American ornithologist and artist noted for his bird paintings and guidebooks.

Petrarch

Pe·ter's pence (pētərz) *n. Roman Catholic Church.* **1.** A tax of one penny per household paid in medieval England to the Papal See. **2.** *Roman Catholic Church.* An annual voluntary contribution made by Roman Catholics toward the expenses of the Holy See. In this sense, also called *hearth money.* [Middle English *Peteres pens,* pl. of *Peteres peni* : *Peteres,* genitive of *Peter,* Saint Peter + *peni,* penny (from the tradition that Saint Peter founded the papacy); see PENNY.]

Peter the Hermit. Also called "Peter of Amiens." 1050?–1115? French monk and preacher of the First Crusade (1095).

pet·i·o·lar (pĕt′ē-ō′lər) *adj.* Of, relating to, or growing on a petiole: *a petiolar sheath.*

pet·i·o·late (pĕt′ē-ə-lāt′, pĕt′ē-ō′lĭt) *adj.* Having a petiole.

pet·i·ole (pĕt′ē-ōl′) *n.* **1.** *Botany.* The stalk by which a leaf is attached to a stem. Also called *leafstalk.* **2.** *Zoology.* A slender, stalklike part, as that connecting the thorax and abdomen in certain insects. [Latin *petiolus,* variant of *peciolus,* little foot, fruit stalk, probably from **pediciolus,* diminutive of *pediculus.* See PEDICEL.] —**pet′i·oled′** *adj.*

pet·i·o·lule (pĕt′ē-ō-lo͞ol′, pĕt′ē-ŏl′yo͞ol) *n.* The stalk of a leaflet in a compound leaf.

pet·it also **pet·ty** (pĕt′ē) *adj. Law.* Lesser; minor. [Middle English, from Old French.]

pet·it bourgeois (pĕt′ē; pə-tē′) *n.* A member of the petite bourgeoisie. [French *petit-bourgeois* : *petit,* small + *bourgeois,* bourgeois.] —**pet·it′-bour·geois′** *adj.*

pe·tite (pə-tēt′) *adj.* Small, slender, and trim. Used of a girl or woman. See Synonyms at **small.** —**petite** *n. Abbr.* **P** A clothing size for short, slender women. [French, feminine of *petit.* See PETIT.] —**pe·tite′ness** *n.*

petite bourgeoisie *n.* The lower middle class, including small businesspeople, tradespeople, and craftworkers. [French *petite-bourgeoisie* : *petite,* small + *bourgeoisie,* bourgeoisie.]

petite mar·mite (mär-mēt′) *n.* **1.** Broth made and served in a small, covered earthenware casserole. **2.** The casserole used for cooking and serving this broth. [French : *petite,* little + *marmite,* kettle.]

pet·it four (pĕt′ē fôr′, fōr′) *n., pl.* **pe·tits fours** or **pet·it fours** (pĕt′ē fôrz′, fōrz′). A small, square-cut, frosted and decorated piece of pound cake or sponge cake. [French : *petit,* little + *four,* oven.]

pe·ti·tion (pə-tĭsh′ən) *n.* **1.** A solemn supplication or request to a superior authority; an entreaty. **2.** A formal written document requesting a right or benefit from a person or group in authority. **3.** *Law.* **a.** A formal written application requesting a court for a specific judicial action: *a petition for appeal.* **b.** The judicial action asked for in any such request. **4.** Something requested or entreated. —**petition** *v.* **-tioned, -tion·ing, -tions.** —*tr.* **1.** To address a petition to. **2.** To ask for by petition; request formally. —*intr.* To make a request, especially formally: *petitioned for retrial.* [Middle English *peticion,* from Old French *petition,* from Latin *petītiō, petītiōn-,* from *petītus,* past participle of *petere,* to request. See **pet-** in Appendix.] —**pe·ti′tion·ar′y** (pə-tĭsh′ə-nĕr′ē) *adj.* —**pe·ti′tion·er** *n.*

pe·ti·ti·o prin·ci·pi·i (pə-tĭsh′ē-ō′ prĭn-sĭp′ē-ē′, -ē-ī′) *n. Logic.* The fallacy of assuming in the premise of an argument that which one wishes to prove in the conclusion; a begging of the question. [Medieval Latin *petītiō prīncipiī* : Latin *petītiō,* request + Latin *prīncipiī,* genitive of *prīncipium,* beginning.]

pet·it juror also **pet·ty juror** (pĕt′ē) *n. Law.* A member of a petit jury.

pet·it jury also **pet·ty jury** (pĕt′ē) *n. Law.* A jury that sits at civil and criminal trials. Also called *trial jury.*

pet·it larceny also **pet·ty larceny** (pĕt′ē) *n. Law.* The theft of objects whose value is below a certain arbitrary standard.

pet·it mal (pĕt′ē mäl′, măl′) *n.* A form of epilepsy, occurring most often in adolescents and children, characterized by frequent but transient lapses of consciousness and only rare spasms or falling. [French : *petit,* small + *mal,* illness.]

pet·it point (pĕt′ē point′) *n.* **1.** A small stitch used in needlepoint. **2.** Needlepoint done with a small stitch. [French : *petit,* small + *point,* stitch.]

pet·its pois (pĕt′ē pwä′, pə-tē′) *pl.n.* Very small green peas. [French : *petits,* pl. of *petit,* little + *pois,* pl. of *pois,* pea.]

pet·nap·ping (pĕt′năp′ĭng) *n.* The stealing of a pet, such as a dog or cat, usually for sale to experimental laboratories or for ransom. [PET¹ + (KID)NAP.] —**pet′nap′per** *n.*

Pe·tö·fi (pĕt′ə-fē, pĕ′tœ-), **Sándor.** 1823–1849. Hungarian lyric poet and revolutionary hero best known for his patriotic songs and the epic poem *Janos the Hero* (1845).

pet peeve *n. Informal.* Something about which one frequently complains; a particular personal vexation.

petr. *abbr.* Petrology.

petr- *pref.* Variant of **petro-.**

Pe·tra (pē′trə, pĕt′rə). An ancient ruined city of Edom in present-day southwest Jordan. It flourished as a trade center from the 4th century B.C. until its capture by the Romans in A.D. 106. The city was taken by Moslems in the 7th century and by Crusaders in the 12th century. The ruins of the "rose-red city" were discovered in 1812.

Pe·trarch (pē′trärk′, pĕt′rärk′) or **Pe·trar·ca** (pĕ-trär′kä), **Francesco.** 1304–1374. Italian poet, scholar, and humanist who is famous for *Canzoniere,* a collection of love lyrics. —**Pe·trarch′an** (pĭ-trär′kən) *adj.*

Petrarchan sonnet *n.* A sonnet containing an octave with the rhyme pattern *abbaabba* and a sestet of various rhyme patterns such as *cdecde* or *cdcdcd.* Also called *Italian sonnet.* [After Francesco PETRARCH.]

pet·rel (pĕt′rəl) *n.* Any of numerous black, gray, or white sea birds of the order Procellariiformes, especially the storm petrel. [Perhaps alteration (perhaps influenced by *Saint Peter* walking on the water, from the fact that the bird flies so close to the water as to appear to be walking on the water) of earlier *pitteral.*]

petri– *pref.* Variant of **petro–.**

pe·tri dish (pē′trē) *n.* A shallow circular dish with a loose-fitting cover, used to culture bacteria or other microorganisms. [After Julius R. *Petri* (1852–1921), German bacteriologist.]

Pe·trie (pē′trē), Sir **(William Matthew) Flinders.** 1853–1942. British Egyptologist known especially for his excavations at Memphis and Thebes.

pet·ri·fac·tion (pĕt′rə-făk′shən) also **pet·ri·fi·ca·tion** (-fĭ-kā′shən) *n.* **1.** A process of fossilization in which dissolved minerals replace organic matter. **2.** The state of being stunned or paralyzed with fear.

Pet·ri·fied Forest (pĕt′rə-fīd′). A section of the Painted Desert in eastern Arizona reserved for its stonelike trees dating from the Triassic Period.

pet·ri·fy (pĕt′rə-fī′) *v.* **-fied, -fy·ing, -fies.** —*tr.* **1.** To convert (wood or other organic matter) into a stony replica by petrifaction. **2.** To cause to become stiff or stonelike; deaden. **3.** To stun or paralyze with terror; daze. —*intr.* To become stony, especially by petrifaction. [Middle English *petrifien,* to harden, from Old French *petrifier* : Latin *petra,* rock (from Greek) + Old French *-fier,* -fy.]

Pe·trine (pē′trīn′) *adj.* Of or relating to Saint Peter. [Late Latin *Petrus,* Saint Peter + –INE[1].]

petro– or **petri–** or **petr–** *pref.* **1.** Rock; stone: *petroglyph.* **2.** Petroleum: *petrochemistry.* [Greek, from *petros,* stone.]

pet·ro·chem·i·cal (pĕt′rō-kĕm′ĭ-kəl) *n.* A chemical derived from petroleum or natural gas. —**pet′ro·chem′i·cal** *adj.*

pet·ro·chem·is·try (pĕt′rō-kĕm′ĭ-strē) *n.* **1.** The chemistry of petroleum and its derivatives. **2.** The branch of geochemistry that deals with the chemical composition of rocks.

pet·ro·dol·lars (pĕt′rō-dŏl′ərz) *pl.n.* Money in any number of currencies that is paid to oil-producing countries, which then deposit it into Western banks.

petrog. *abbr.* Petrography.

pet·ro·gen·e·sis (pĕt′rō-jĕn′ĭ-sĭs) *n.* The branch of petrology that deals with the origin of rocks, especially igneous rocks. —**pet′ro·ge·net′ic** (-jə-nĕt′ĭk) *adj.*

pet·ro·glyph (pĕt′rə-glĭf′) *n. Archaeology.* A carving or line drawing on rock, especially one made by prehistoric people. —**pet′ro·glyph′ic** *adj.*

Pet·ro·grad (pĕt′rə-grăd′, pyĭ-trə-grät′). See **Leningrad.**

pe·trog·ra·phy (pə-trŏg′rə-fē) *n. Abbr.* **petrog.** The description and classification of rocks. —**pe·trog′ra·pher** *n.* —**pet′ro·graph′ic** (pĕt′rə-grăf′ĭk), **pet′ro·graph′i·cal** (-ĭ-kəl) *adj.* —**pet′ro·graph′i·cal·ly** *adv.*

pet·rol (pĕt′rəl) *n. Chiefly British.* Gasoline. [French *(essence de) pétrole,* (essence of) petroleum, gasoline, from Old French *petrole,* petroleum, from Medieval Latin *petrōleum.* See PETROLEUM.]

petrol. *abbr.* Petrology.

pet·ro·la·tum (pĕt′rə-lā′təm, -lä′təm) *n.* See **petroleum jelly.** [From PETROL.]

pe·tro·le·um (pə-trō′lē-əm) *n. Abbr.* **pet.** A thick, flammable, yellow-to-black mixture of gaseous, liquid, and solid hydrocarbons that occurs naturally beneath the earth's surface, can be separated into fractions including natural gas, gasoline, naphtha, kerosene, fuel and lubricating oils, paraffin wax, and asphalt and is used as raw material for a wide variety of derivative products. [Middle English, from Medieval Latin *petrōleum* : Latin *petra,* rock (from Greek) + Latin *ōleum,* oil; see OIL.]

petroleum jelly *n.* A colorless-to-amber semisolid mixture of hydrocarbons obtained from petroleum and used in lubricants and medicinal ointments. Also called *petrolatum.*

pe·trol·ic (pə-trŏl′ĭk) *adj.* Of, relating to, or derived from petroleum.

pe·trol·o·gy (pə-trŏl′ə-jē) *n. Abbr.* **petr., petrol.** The branch of geology that deals with the origin, composition, structure, and alteration of rocks. —**pet′ro·log′ic** (pĕt′rə-lŏj′ĭk), **pet′ro·log′i·cal** (-ĭ-kəl) *adj.* —**pet′ro·log′i·cal·ly** *adv.* —**pe·trol′o·gist** *n.*

Pe·tro·ni·us (pĭ-trō′nē-əs), **Gaius.** Known as "Petronius Arbiter." Died A.D. 66. Roman writer and courtier who is credited with writing the *Satyricon.*

Pet·ro·pav·lovsk (pĕt′rə-păv′lôfsk′, pyĭ-trə-päv′ləfsk). **1.** A city of north-central Kazakhstan west of Novosibirsk. It was founded as a fort in 1752. Population, 226,000. **2.** Or **Pet·ro·pav·lovsk-Kam·chat·ski** (-kăm-chăt′skē, -kə-chyät′-). A city of eastern Russia on the Pacific coast of the Kamchatka Peninsula. Ice-free seven months a year, it is a major port and naval base. Population, 245,000.

Pe·tróp·o·lis (pə-trŏp′ə-lĭs, pĭ-trô′pŏŏ-). A city of southeast Brazil north of Rio de Janeiro. Mainly residential with some light industry, it was formerly the summer residence of Emperor Dom Pedro II. Population, 150,249.

pet·ro·pol·i·tics (pĕt′rō-pŏl′ĭ-tĭks) *n. (used with a sing. or pl. verb).* The strategic practice of controlling petroleum sales so as to achieve international political and economic ends.

pe·tro·sal (pə-trō′səl) *adj.* Relating to or located near the petrous portion of the temporal bone. [From Latin *petrōsus,* rocky. See PETROUS.]

pet·rous (pĕt′rəs) *adj.* **1.** Of, relating to, or resembling rock, especially in hardness; stony. **2.** Of or relating to the very dense, hard portion of the temporal bone that forms a protective case for the inner ear. [Middle English, from Old French *petros,* from Latin *petrōsus,* rocky, from *petra,* rock, from Greek.]

Pet·ro·za·vodsk (pĕt′rə-zə-vŏtsk′, pyĭ-trə-zə-vôtsk′). A city of northwest Russia on Lake Onega northeast of St. Petersburg. Peter the Great built an ironworks here in 1703. Population, 255,000.

pe-tsai (bā′tsī′) *n.* See **Chinese cabbage.** [Alteration of Chinese (Mandarin) *bái cài.* See BOK CHOY.]

PET scan (pĕt) *n.* A cross-sectional image produced by a PET scanner.

PET scanner *n.* A device that produces cross-sectional x-rays of metabolic processes by means of positron emission tomography. [P(OSITRON) E(MISSION) T(OMOGRAPHY).]

PET scanning *n.* The act or process of using a PET scanner.

pet·ti (pĕt′ē) *n., pl.* **-tis. 1.** A woman's petticoat. **2.** A petti-slip.

pet·ti·coat (pĕt′ē-kōt′) *n.* **1.** A woman's slip or underskirt that is often full and trimmed with ruffles or lace. Also called *pettiskirt.* **2.** Something, such as a decorative valance or flounce, that resembles a woman's underskirt. **3.** *Offensive Slang.* A woman or girl. —**petticoat** *adj. Slang.* **1.** Female; feminine. **2.** Of, relating to, or carried out by women. [Middle English *peticote* : *peti,* small; see PETTY + *cote,* coat; see COAT.] —**pet′ti·coat′ed** *adj.*

petticoat narcissus *n.* A small southwest European daffodil *(Narcissus bulbocodium)* having yellow flowers with narrow perianth segments and a longer corona.

pet·ti·fog (pĕt′ē-fŏg′, -fôg′) *intr.v.* **-fogged, -fog·ging, -fogs.** To act like a pettifogger. See Synonyms at **quibble.** [Back-formation from PETTIFOGGER.]

pet·ti·fog·ger (pĕt′ē-fŏg′ər, -fô′gər) *n.* **1.** A petty, quibbling, unscrupulous lawyer. **2.** One who quibbles over trivia. [Probably PETTY + obsolete *fogger,* pettifogger.] —**pet′ti·fog′ger·y** *n.*

pet·ting (pĕt′ĭng) *n. Informal.* The act or practice of amorously embracing, kissing, and caressing one's partner.

petting zoo *n.* A collection of farm animals, such as goats, ducks, and sheep, and sometimes docile wild animals such as turtles or deer, for children to feed and pet.

pet·tish (pĕt′ĭsh) *adj.* Ill-tempered; peevish. [Probably from PET[2].] —**pet′tish·ly** *adv.* —**pet′tish·ness** *n.*

pet·ti·skirt (pĕt′ē-skûrt′) *n.* See **petticoat** (sense 1).

pet·ti·slip (pĕt′ē-slĭp′) *n.* A half-slip usually trimmed with a decorative edging.

pet·ti·toes (pĕt′ē-tōz′) *pl.n.* **1.** The feet of a pig used as food. **2.** Human feet or toes, especially those of a child. [Possibly from earlier *pettytoe,* offal (influenced by PETTY and TOE), possibly from Old French *petite oye,* giblets of a goose : *petite,* small + *oye,* goose (from Late Latin *auca;* see OCARINA).]

pet·ty (pĕt′ē) *adj.* **-ti·er, -ti·est. 1.** Of small importance; trivial: *a petty grievance.* **2.** Marked by narrowness of mind, ideas, or views. **3.** Marked by meanness or lack of generosity, especially in trifling matters. **4.** Secondary in importance or rank; subordinate. See Synonyms at **trivial. 5.** *Law.* Variant of **petit.** [Middle English *peti,* from Old French, variant of *petit.* See PETIT.] —**pet′ti·ly** *adv.* —**pet′ti·ness** *n.*

petty apartheid *n.* A system of racial segregation that focuses principally on public places, such as restaurants, hotels, and public transportation.

petty cash *n. Abbr.* **p/c, P/C, p.c.** A small fund of money for incidental expenses, as in an office.

petty juror *n. Law.* Variant of **petit juror.**

petty jury *n. Law.* Variant of **petit jury.**

petty larceny *n. Law.* Variant of **petit larceny.**

petty officer *n. Abbr.* **PO, P.O.** A noncommissioned naval officer intermediate in rank between enlisted personnel and commissioned officers.

pet·u·lant (pĕch′ə-lənt) *adj.* **1.** Unreasonably irritable or ill-tempered; peevish. **2.** Contemptuous in speech or behavior. [Latin *petulāns, petulant-,* insolent, from *petere,* to assail. See **pet-** in Appendix.] —**pet′u·lance, pet′u·lan·cy** *n.* —**pet′u·lant·ly** *adv.*

pe·tu·nia (pĭ-tōōn′yə, -tyōōn′-) *n.* **1.** Any of various widely cultivated South American plants of the genus *Petunia,* having alternate, entire leaves and funnel-shaped flowers in colors from white to purple. **2.** *Color.* A moderate to dark purple. [New Latin *Petunia,* genus name, from obsolete French *pétun,* tobacco, from Portuguese *petum,* of Tupi-Guarani origin.]

WORD HISTORY: "Tobacco is a dirty weed," as the song goes (it also perversely admits "I like it, I like it"), but tobacco has some nice relatives in the nightshade family, such as the tomato, red pepper, and eggplant. One of its more beautiful relatives, the petunia, is actually named for tobacco. This curious story begins when the Portuguese in South America picked up their word *petum,* meaning "tobacco," from a Tupi-Guarani word, such as Tupi *petyn.* From Portuguese the word made its way into French (*pétun*), from which English borrowed the word (*petun* remains an archaic word for tobacco). The name of the genus *petunia* was formed in New Latin (1789) from French *pétun* because of the

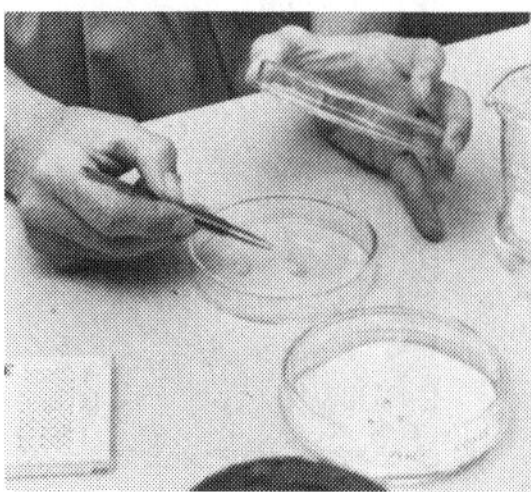

petri dish

petroglyph
Newspaper Rock at Indian Creek, Utah

petunia

ă pat	oi boy
ā pay	ou out
âr care	ŏŏ took
ä father	ōō boot
ĕ pet	ŭ cut
ē be	ûr urge
ĭ pit	th thin
ī pie	*th* this
îr pier	hw which
ŏ pot	zh vision
ō toe	ə about, item
ô paw	♦ regionalism

Stress marks: ′ (primary); ′ (secondary), as in **dictionary** (dĭk′shə-nĕr′ē)

close relationship of the petunia genus to tobacco. English *petunia,* taken from Modern Latin, is first recorded around 1825.

pew

pe•tun•tze or **pe•tun•tse** (pə-to͞on′tsē) *n.* A variety of feldspar sometimes mixed with kaolin and used in Chinese porcelain. [Chinese (Mandarin) *bāi dūnzi* : *bāi,* white + *dūnzi,* block of stone.]

Pevs•ner (pĕvz′nər, pyĕf′snĭr), **Antoine.** 1886–1962. Russian artist. With his brother Naum Gabo he set forth the principles of constructivism in the *Realist Manifesto* (1920).

pew (pyo͞o) *n.* **1.** One of the long, fixed benches with backs that are arranged in rows for the seating of a congregation in church. **2.** An enclosed compartment in a church that provides seating for a number of people, such as a family. [Middle English *pewe,* probably from Old French *puie,* balcony, from Latin *podia,* pl. of *podium,* balcony. See PODIUM.]

pe•wee also **pee•wee** (pē′wē) *n.* Any of various small, olive-gray North American flycatchers of the genus *Contopus,* especially a wood pewee. [Imitative of its call.]

pe•wit also **pee•wit** (pē′wĭt′, pyo͞o′ĭt) *n.* See **lapwing.** [Imitative of its call.]

pew•ter (pyo͞o′tər) *n.* **1.** Any of numerous silver-gray alloys of tin with various amounts of antimony, copper, and sometimes lead, used widely for fine kitchen utensils and tableware. **2.** Pewter articles considered as a group. [Middle English *pewtre,* from Old French *peutre,* from Vulgar Latin **peltrum.*] —**pew′ter** *adj.*

pe•yo•te (pā-ō′tē) also **pe•yo•tl** (-ōt′l) *n.* **1.** A spineless, dome-shaped cactus *(Lophophora williamsii)* native to Mexico and the southwest United States, having buttonlike tubercles that are chewed fresh or dry as a narcotic drug by certain Native American peoples. Also called *mescal.* **2.** See **mescal button. 3.** See **mescaline.** [American Spanish, from Nahuatl *peyotl.*]

pf. *abbr.* **1.** Preferred. **2.** Pfennig.

PFC also **Pfc** *abbr.* Private first class.

pfd. *abbr.* Preferred.

pfen•nig (fĕn′ĭg) *n., pl.* **pfen•nigs** or **pfen•ni•ge** (fĕn′ĭ-gə). *Abbr.* **pf., pfg.** See table at **currency.** [German, from Middle High German *pfennic,* from Old High German *pfenning.*]

pfft (ft, pft) *interj.* Used to express or indicate a usually sudden disappearance or ending.

pfg. *abbr.* Pfennig.

Pforz•heim (fôrts′hīm, fōrts′-, pfôrts′-). A city of southwest Germany west-northwest of Stuttgart. Chartered c. 1195, it has a noted jewelry and watchmaking industry. Population, 104,023.

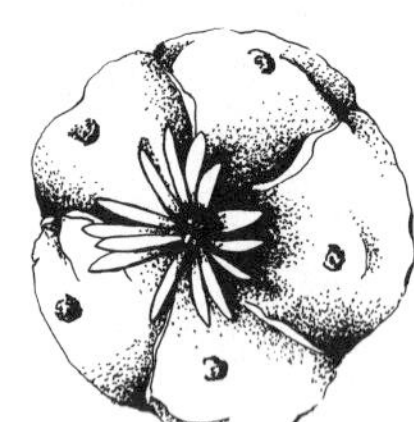
peyote
Lophophora williamsii

PG (pē′jē′) *n.* A movie rating that allows admission of persons of all ages but suggests parental guidance in the case of children. —*attributive.* Often used to modify another noun: *a PG movie.* [P(ARENTAL) + G(UIDANCE).]

pg. *abbr.* Page.

Pg. *abbr.* Portuguese.

PG-13 (pē′jē′thûr-tēn′) *n.* A movie rating that allows admission of persons of all ages but suggests parental guidance in the case of children under the age of 13. —*attributive.* Often used to modify another noun: *a PG-13 movie.*

P.G. *abbr.* **1.** Paying guest. **2.** Postgraduate.

PGA *abbr.* Professional Golfers' Association.

pH (pē′āch′) *n. Chemistry.* A measure of the acidity or alkalinity of a solution, numerically equal to 7 for neutral solutions, increasing with increasing alkalinity and decreasing with increasing acidity. The pH scale commonly in use ranges from 0 to 14. [*p(otential of) h(ydrogen).*]

Ph *abbr. Bible.* Philippians.

PH also **P.H.** *abbr.* **1.** Public Health. **2.** Purple Heart.

ph. *abbr.* Phase.

PHA *abbr.* Public Housing Administration.

phac•o•e•mul•si•fi•ca•tion (făk′ō-ĭ-mŭl′sə-fĭ-kā′shən) *n.* Removal of a cataract by emulsifying the lens ultrasonically. [Greek *phakos,* lentil, lentil-shaped object; see **bha-bhā-** in Appendix + EMULSIFICATION.]

Phae•dra (fē′drə, fĕd′rə) *n. Greek Mythology.* The daughter of Pasiphaë and wife of Theseus who killed herself after accusing her stepson Hippolytus of rape.

Phae•drus (fē′drəs, fĕd′rəs). fl. first century A.D. Roman fabulist who wrote a collection of fables based on those attributed to Aesop.

Pha•ë•thon (fā′ə-thŏn′, -thən) *n. Greek Mythology.* A son of the sun god Helios who was killed by Zeus while trying to drive his father's chariot across the sky. [Latin *Phaetōn, Phaethōn,* from Greek *Phaethōn.*]

phaeton

pha•e•ton (fā′ĭ-tn) *n.* **1.** A light, four-wheeled open carriage, usually drawn by a pair of horses. **2.** A touring car. [French *phaéton,* from *Phaeton,* Phaethon, from Old French, from Latin *Phaethōn.* See PHAËTHON.]

phage (fāj) *n.* A bacteriophage.

–phage *suff.* One that eats: *macrophage.* [From Greek *-phagos,* eating, from *phagein,* to eat. See **bhag-** in Appendix.]

–phagia or **–phagy** *suff.* The eating of a specified substance or eating in a specified manner: *dysphagia.* [Greek, from *phagein,* to eat. See **bhag-** in Appendix.]

phago– *pref.* Eating; consuming: *phagocyte.* [Greek, from *phagein,* to eat. See **bhag-** in Appendix.]

phag•o•cyte (făg′ə-sīt′) *n.* A cell, such as a white blood cell, that engulfs and absorbs waste material, harmful microorganisms, or other foreign bodies in the bloodstream and tissues. —**phag′o•cyt′ic** (-sĭt′ĭk) *adj.*

phagocytic index *n.* The average number of bacteria ingested by each phagocyte in an individual's blood after a mixture of the blood serum, bacteria, and phagocytes has been incubated.

phag•o•cy•tize (făg′ə-sĭ-tīz′, -sī′-) *tr.v.* **-tized, -tiz•ing, -tiz•es.** To ingest by phagocytosis; phagocytose.

phag•o•cy•tose (făg′ə-sĭ-tōs′, -tōz′, -sī′tōs, -tōz) *tr.v.* **-tosed, -tos•ing, -tos•es.** To phagocytize. [Back-formation from PHAGOCYTOSIS.]

phag•o•cy•to•sis (făg′ə-sī-tō′sĭs) *n.* The engulfing and ingestion of bacteria or other foreign bodies by phagocytes. —**phag′o•cy•tot′ic** (-tŏt′ĭk) *adj.*

phag•o•some (făg′ə-sōm′) *n.* A membrane-bound vesicle found in a cell by an inward folding of the cell membrane to hold foreign matter taken into the cell by phagocytosis.

–phagous *suff.* Eating; feeding on: *ichthyophagous.* [From Latin *-phagus,* from Greek *-phagos,* from *phagein,* to eat. See **bhag-** in Appendix.]

–phagy *suff.* Variant of **–phagia.**

pha•lan•gal (fə-lăng′gəl, fā-) *adj. Anatomy.* Variant of **phalangeal.**

pha•lange (fā′lănj′, fə-lănj′) *n.* See **phalanx** (sense 3). [French, from Old French, body of infantrymen, from Latin, from Greek *phalanx, phalang-,* log, battle array, bone between the finger and toe joints. See PHALANX.]

pha•lan•ge•al (fə-lăn′jē-əl, fā-) also **pha•lan•gal** (fə-lăng′gəl, fā-) or **pha•lan•ge•an** (fə-lăn′jē-ən, fā-) *adj. Anatomy.* Of or relating to a phalanx or phalanges.

pha•lan•ger (fə-lăn′jər) *n.* Any of various small arboreal marsupials of the family Phalangeridae, of Australia and adjacent islands, having a long tail and dense woolly fur and including the cuscus and the flying phalanger. [New Latin, from Greek *phalanx, phalang-,* toe bone (from its fused hind toes). See PHALANX.]

pha•lan•ges (fə-lăn′jēz, fā-) *n.* A plural of **phalanx.**

phal•an•ster•y (făl′ən-stĕr′ē) *n.* **-ies. 1.a.** A self-sustaining cooperative community of the followers of Fourierism. Also called *phalanx.* **b.** The buildings in such a community. **2.** An association resembling a Fourierist phalanstery. [French *phalanstère* : *phalange,* phalanx (from Latin *phalanx, phalang-;* see PHALANX) + *monastère,* monastery (from Late Latin *monastērium;* see MONASTERY).] —**phal′an•ste′ri•an** (-stîr′ē-ən) *adj. & n.* —**phal′an•ste′ri•an•ism** *n.*

pha•lanx (fā′lăngks′, făl′ăngks′) *n., pl.* **pha•lanx•es** or **pha•lan•ges** (fə-lăn′jēz, fā-). **1.** A compact or close-knit body of people: *"formed a solid phalanx in defense of the Constitution and Protestant religion"* (G.M. Trevelyan). **2.** A formation of infantry carrying overlapping shields and long spears, developed by Philip II of Macedon and used by Alexander the Great. **3.** *pl.* **phalanges.** *Anatomy.* A bone of a finger or toe. Also called *phalange.* **4.** See **phalanstery** (sense 1a). [Latin *phalanx, phalang-,* from Greek.]

phal•a•rope (făl′ə-rōp′) *n.* Any of several small wading birds of the family Phalaropodidae, resembling sandpipers but having lobed toes that enable them to swim. [French, from New Latin *phalaropus* : Greek *phalaris,* coot (from *phalaros,* having a white spot; see **bhel-**[1] in Appendix) + Greek *pous,* foot; see **ped-** in Appendix.]

phal•li (făl′ī′) *n.* A plural of **phallus.**

phal•lic (făl′ĭk) *adj.* **1.** Of, relating to, or resembling a phallus. **2.** Of or relating to the cult of the phallus as an embodiment of generative power: *phallic worship.* **3.** Of or relating to the third stage of psychosexual development in psychoanalytic theory during which the genital organs first become the focus of sexual feeling. [Greek *phallikos,* from *phallos,* phallus. See PHALLUS.] —**phal′li•cal•ly** *adv.*

phal•lus (făl′əs) *n., pl.* **phal•li** (făl′ī′) or **phal•lus•es. 1.** *Anatomy.* **a.** The penis. **b.** The sexually undifferentiated tissue in an embryo that becomes the penis or clitoris. **2.** A representation of the penis and testes as an embodiment of generative power. **3.** The immature penis considered in psychoanalysis as the libidinal object of infantile sexuality in the male. [Late Latin, from Greek *phallos.* See **bhel-**[2] in Appendix.]

–phane or **–phan** *suff.* A substance resembling something specified: *tryptophan.* [From Greek *-phanēs,* appearing, from *phainesthai,* to appear. See **bhā-**[1] in Appendix.]

phan•er•o•gam (făn′ər-ə-găm′, fə-nâr′ə-) *n.* A plant that produces seeds. [New Latin *phanerogamus* : Greek *phaneros,* visible (from *phainein,* to cause to appear; see **bhā-**[1] in Appendix) + Greek *gamos,* marriage; see –GAMOUS.] —**phan′er•o•gam′ic, phan′er•og′a•mous** (făn′ə-rŏg′ə-məs) *adj.*

phan•tasm (făn′tăz′əm) *n.* **1.** Something apparently seen but having no physical reality; a phantom or an apparition. Also called *phantasma.* **2.** An illusory mental image. Also called *phantasma.* **3.** In Platonic philosophy, objective reality as perceived and distorted by the five senses. [Middle English *fantasme,* from Old French, from Latin *phantasma,* from Greek, from *phantazein,* to make visible, from *phantos,* visible, from *phainein,* to show. See **bhā-**[1] in Appendix.] —**phan•tas′mal** (făn-tăz′məl), **phan•tas′mic** (-tăz′mĭk) *adj.*

phan•tas•ma (făn-tăz′mə) *n., pl.* **-ma•ta** (-mə-tə). See

phantasm (senses 1, 2). [Ultimately from Greek. See PHANTASM.]

phan·tas·ma·go·ri·a (făn-tăz′mə-gôr′ē-ə, -gōr′-) also **phan·tas·ma·go·ry** (făn-tăz′mə-gôr′ē, -gōr′ē) *n.* **1.a.** A fantastic sequence of haphazardly associative imagery, as seen in dreams or fever. **b.** A constantly changing scene composed of numerous elements. **2.** Fantastic imagery as represented in art. [Alteration of obsolete French *phantasmagorie,* art of creating supernatural illusions : perhaps *fantasme,* illusion (from Old French; see PHANTASM) + *allégorie,* allegory, allegorical visual representation (from Old French, allegory, from Latin *allēgoria;* see ALLEGORY).] **—phan·tas′ma·gor′ic** (-gôr′ĭk, -gŏr′-) *adj.* **—phan·tas′ma·gor′i·cal·ly** *adv.*

phan·tom also **fan·tom** (făn′təm) *—n.* **1.a.** Something apparently seen, heard, or sensed, but having no physical reality; a ghost or an apparition. **b.** Something elusive or delusive. **2.** An image that appears only in the mind; an illusion. **3.** Something dreaded or despised. *—adj.* **1.** Resembling, characteristic of, or being a phantom; illusive. **2.** Fictitious; nonexistent: *phantom employees on the payroll.* [Middle English *fantom,* from Old French *fantosme,* probably from Vulgar Latin **phantauma,* from Greek dialectal **phantagma,* from Greek *phantasma.* See PHANTASM.]

phantom limb pain *n.* Pain or discomfort felt by an amputee in the area of the missing limb.

phar. or **Phar.** *abbr.* **1.** Pharmaceutical. **2.** Pharmacist. **3.** Pharmacopoeia. **4.** Pharmacy.

Phar·aoh also **phar·aoh** (fâr′ō, fā′rō) *n.* **1.** A king of ancient Egypt. **2.** A tyrant. [Middle English *Pharao,* from Late Latin *Pharaō,* from Greek *Pharaō,* from Hebrew *Par'ōh,* from Egyptian *pr-'o : pr,* house + *'o,* great.] **—Phar′a·on′ic** (fâr′ā-ŏn′ĭk) *adj.*

pharaoh ant *n.* A tiny, yellowish-red ant *(Monomorium pharaonis)* that infests human dwellings throughout the world.

Pharaoh hound *n.* Any of a breed of sleek, swift-running hunting dog originating in Egypt and having a short, glossy, tan coat and large, pointed ears.

Phar.B. *abbr. Latin.* Pharmaciae Baccalaureus (Bachelor of Pharmacy).

Phar.D. *abbr. Latin.* Pharmaciae Doctor (Doctor of Pharmacy).

phar·i·sa·ic (făr′ĭ-sā′ĭk) also **phar·i·sa·i·cal** (-sā′ĭ-kəl) *adj.* **1. Pharisaic, Pharisaical.** Of, relating to, or characteristic of the Pharisees. **2.** Hypocritically self-righteous and condemnatory. **—phar′i·sa′i·cal·ly** *adv.* **—phar′i·sa′i·cal·ness** *n.*

phar·i·sa·ism (făr′ĭ-sā-ĭz′əm) also **phar·i·see·ism** (-sē-ĭz′əm) *n.* **1. Pharisaism, Phariseeism.** The doctrines and practices of the Pharisees. **2.** Hypocritical observance of the letter of religious or moral law without regard for the spirit; sanctimoniousness.

phar·i·see (făr′ĭ-sē) *n.* **1. Pharisee.** A member of an ancient Jewish sect that emphasized strict interpretation and observance of the Mosaic law in both its oral and written form. **2.** A hypocritically self-righteous person. [Middle English *pharise,* from Old English *fariseus* and from Old French *pharise,* both from Late Latin *pharīsaeus,* from Greek *pharisaios,* from Aramaic *pĕrīšayyā.*]

phar·i·see·ism (făr′ĭ-sē-ĭz′əm) *n.* Variant of **pharisaism.**

pharm. or **Pharm.** *abbr.* **1.** Pharmaceutical. **2.** Pharmacist. **3.** Pharmacopoeia. **4.** Pharmacy.

Phar.M. *abbr. Latin.* Pharmaciae Magister (Master of Pharmacy).

phar·ma·ceu·ti·cal (fär′mə-sōō′tĭ-kəl) also **phar·ma·ceu·tic** (-tĭk) *—adj. Abbr.* **phar., Phar., pharm., Pharm.** Of or relating to pharmacy or pharmacists. *—n. Abbr.* **phar., Phar., pharm., Pharm.** A pharmaceutical product or preparation. [From Late Latin *pharmaceuticus,* from Greek *pharmakeutikos,* from *pharmakeutēs,* preparer of drugs, variant of *pharmakeus,* from *pharmakon,* drug.] **—phar′ma·ceu′ti·cal·ly** *adv.*

phar·ma·ceu·tics (fär′mə-sōō′tĭks) *n.* **1.** *(used with a sing. verb).* The science of preparing and dispensing drugs. **2.** *(used with a pl. verb).* Pharmaceutical preparations; medicinal drugs.

phar·ma·cist (fär′mə-sĭst) *n. Abbr.* **phar., Phar., pharm., Pharm.** A person trained in pharmacy; a druggist.

pharmaco– *pref.* Drug; medicine: *pharmacognosy.* [Greek, from *pharmakon,* poison, drug.]

phar·ma·co·dy·nam·ics (fär′mə-kō-dī-năm′ĭks) *n. (used with a sing. verb).* The study of the action or effects of drugs on living organisms. **—phar′ma·co′dy·nam′ic** *adj.* **—phar′ma·co′dy·nam′i·cal·ly** *adv.*

phar·ma·co·ge·net·ics (fär′mə-kō-jə-nĕt′ĭks) *n. (used with a sing. verb).* The study of genetic factors that influence an organism's reaction to a drug. **—phar′ma·co·ge·net′ic** *adj.*

phar·ma·cog·no·sy (fär′mə-kŏg′nə-sē) *n.* The branch of pharmacology that deals with drugs in their crude or natural state. [PHARMACO– + Greek *gnōsis,* knowledge; see GNOSIS.] **—phar′ma·cog′no·sist** *n.* **—phar′ma·cog·nos′tic** (-kŏg-nŏs′tĭk) *adj.*

phar·ma·co·ki·net·ics (fär′mə-kō-kĭ-nĕt′ĭks, -kī-) *n. (used with a sing. verb).* **1.** The process by which a drug is absorbed, distributed, metabolized and eliminated by the body. **2.** The study of this process. **—phar′ma·co·ki·net′ic** *adj.*

phar·ma·col·o·gy (fär′mə-kŏl′ə-jē) *n.* **1.** The science of drugs, including their composition, uses, and effects. **2.** The characteristics or properties of a drug, especially those that make it medically effective. **—phar′ma·co·log′ic** (-kə-lŏj′ĭk), **phar′ma·co·log′i·cal** (-ĭ-kəl) *adj.* **—phar′ma·co·log′i·cal·ly** *adv.* **—phar′ma·col′o·gist** *n.*

phar·ma·co·poe·ia also **phar·ma·co·pe·ia** (fär′mə-kə-pē′ə) *n. Abbr.* **phar., Phar., pharm., Pharm. 1.** A book containing an official list of medicinal drugs together with articles on their preparation and use. **2.** A collection or stock of drugs. [New Latin, from Greek *pharmakopoiia,* preparation of drugs, from *pharmakopoios,* preparing drugs : *pharmako-,* pharmaco- + *-poios,* preparing (from *poiein,* to make; see **kʷei-²** in Appendix).] **—phar′ma·co·poe′ial** (-pē′əl) *adj.* **—phar′ma·co·poe′ist** (-pē′ĭst) *n.*

phar·ma·co·ther·a·py (fär′mə-kō-thĕr′ə-pē) *n., pl.* **-pies.** Treatment of disease through the use of drugs.

phar·ma·cy (fär′mə-sē) *n., pl.* **-cies.** *Abbr.* **phar., Phar., pharm., Pharm. 1.** The art of preparing and dispensing drugs. **2.** A place where drugs are sold; a drugstore. In this sense, also called *apothecary.* [Middle English *farmacie,* a purgative, from Old French, from Medieval Latin *pharmacīa,* a medicine, from Greek *pharmakeia,* use of drugs, from *pharmakon,* drug. See PHARMACO–.]

pha·ros (fâr′ŏs′) *n.* A lighthouse. [Latin, from Greek, after *Pharos,* a peninsula, formerly an island, in the Mediterranean Sea at Alexandria, Egypt, and the site of an ancient lighthouse, one of the Seven Wonders of the World.]

Pharr (fär). A city of extreme southern Texas west-northwest of Brownsville. It is a processing center. Population, 21,381.

Phar·sa·lus (fär-sā′ləs) or **Phar·sa·la** (fär′sä-lä). An ancient city of Thessaly in northeast Greece. Julius Caesar decisively defeated Pompey nearby in 48 B.C.

pharyng– *pref.* Variant of **pharyngo–.**

pha·ryn·ge·al (fə-rĭn′jē-əl, -jəl, făr′ĭn-jē′əl) also **pha·ryn·gal** (fə-rĭng′gəl) *—adj.* Of, relating to, located in, or coming from the pharynx. *—n. Linguistics.* A speech sound produced in the pharynx. [From New Latin *pharyngeus,* from *pharynx, pharyng-,* pharynx. See PHARYNX.]

phar·yn·gec·to·my (făr′ən-jĕk′tə-mē) *n., pl.* **-mies.** Surgical removal of part or all of the pharynx.

pha·ryn·ges (fə-rĭn′jēz) *n.* A plural of **pharynx.**

phar·yn·gi·tis (făr′ĭn-jī′tĭs) *n.* Inflammation of the pharynx.

pharyngo– or **pharyng–** *pref.* Pharynx: *pharyngoscope.* [New Latin, from Greek *pharungo-,* from *pharunx, pharung-.* See PHARYNX.]

pha·ryn·go·cele (fə-rĭng′gə-sēl′) *n.* Protrusion of mucous membrane through the wall of the pharynx; hernia of the pharynx.

phar·yn·gol·o·gy (făr′ĭn-gŏl′ə-jē, făr′ĭng-) *n.* The medical study of the pharynx and its diseases.

pha·ryn·go·scope (fə-rĭng′gə-skōp′) *n.* An instrument used in examining the pharynx. **—phar′yn·gos′co·py** (făr′ĭn-gŏs′kə-pē, făr′ĭng-) *n.*

phar·ynx (făr′ĭngks) *n., pl.* **pha·ryn·ges** (fə-rĭn′jēz) or **phar·ynx·es.** The section of the alimentary canal that extends from the mouth and nasal cavities to the larynx, where it becomes continuous with the esophagus. [New Latin *pharynx, pharyng-,* from Greek *pharunx.*]

phase (fāz) *n. Abbr.* **ph. 1.** A distinct stage of development: *"The American occupation of Japan fell into three successive phases"* (Edwin O. Reischauer). **2.** A temporary manner, attitude, or pattern of behavior: *just a passing phase.* **3.** An aspect; a part: *every phase of the operation.* **4.** *Astronomy.* One of the cyclically recurring apparent forms of the moon or a planet. **5.** *Physics.* **a.** A particular stage in a periodic process or phenomenon. **b.** The fraction of a complete cycle elapsed as measured from a specified reference point and often expressed as an angle. **6.** *Chemistry.* **a.** Any of the forms or states, solid, liquid, gas, or plasma, in which matter can exist, depending on temperature and pressure. **b.** A discrete homogeneous part of a material system that is mechanically separable from the rest, as is ice from water. **7.** *Biology.* A characteristic form, appearance, or stage of development that occurs in a cycle or that distinguishes some individuals of a group: *the white color phase of a weasel; the swarming phase of locusts.* **—phase** *tr.v.* **phased, phas·ing, phas·es. 1.** To plan or carry out systematically by phases. **2.** To set or regulate so as to be synchronized. ***—phrasal verbs.*** **phase in.** To introduce, one stage at a time. **phase out.** To bring or come to an end, one stage at a time. ***—idioms.*** **in phase.** In a correlated or synchronized way. **out of phase.** In an unsynchronized or uncorrelated way. [Back-formation from New Latin *phasēs,* phases of the moon, from Greek, pl. of *phasis,* appearance, from *phainein,* to show. See **bhā-¹** in Appendix.] **—pha′sic** (fā′zĭk) *adj.*

SYNONYMS: *phase, aspect, facet, angle, side.* These nouns refer to a particular or possible way of viewing something, such as an object, a situation, or a process. *Phase* may denote a change in an object itself rather than in the viewpoint of an observer (*an ermine in its winter color phase*), but the term also refers to a stage or period of change or development: *"A phase of my life was closing tonight, a new one opening tomorrow"* (Charlotte Brontë). *Aspect* is the way something appears to an observer at a specific vantage point: *"In our description of nature the purpose is . . . to track down . . . relations between the manifold aspects of our experience"* (Niels Bohr). A *facet* is one of numerous aspects, as of a

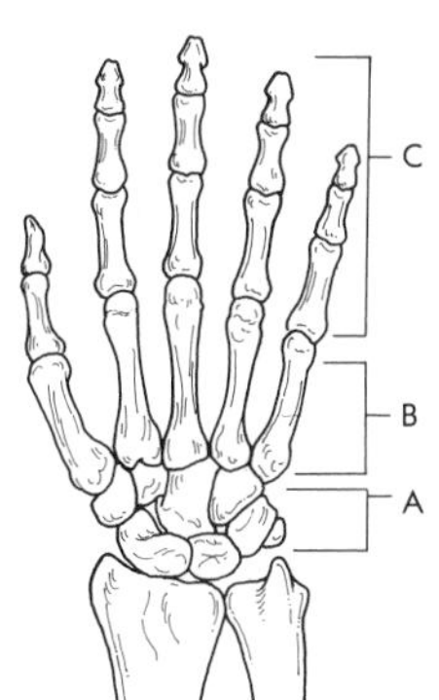

phalanx
A. Phalanges
B. Metacarpus
C. Carpus

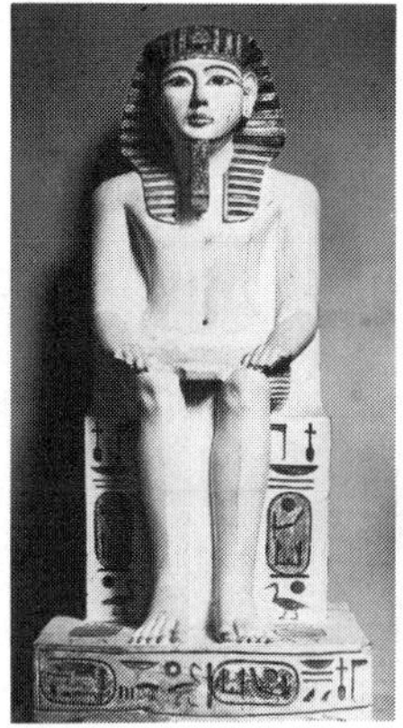

Pharaoh
Of the XII Dynasty

ă pat	oi boy
ā pay	ou out
âr care	ŏŏ took
ä father	ōō boot
ĕ pet	ŭ cut
ē be	ûr urge
ĭ pit	th thin
ī pie	*th* this
îr pier	hw which
ŏ pot	zh vision
ō toe	ə about, item
ô paw	♦ regionalism

Stress marks: **′** (primary); ′ (secondary), as in **dictionary** (dĭk′shə-nĕr′ē)

problem: *studying the many facets of life in manufacturing towns after the Industrial Revolution. Angle* suggests a limitation of perspective, frequently with emphasis on the observer's own point of view: *an account of the causes of World War II from the angle of the Allies. Side* refers to something having two or more parts or aspects: *"Much might be said on both sides"* (Joseph Addison).

---

phase contrast microscope *n.* A microscope that uses the differences in the phase of light transmitted or reflected by a specimen to form distinct, contrasting images of different parts of the specimen.

phased array (fāzd) *n.* An arrangement of dipoles on a radar antenna, in which the phase of each dipole is controlled by a computer so that the beam can scan very rapidly.

phase•down (fāz′doun′) *n.* A gradual reduction.

phase-in (fāz′ĭn′) *n.* A gradual introduction: *a phase-in of new personal policies.*

phase microscope *n.* A phase contrast microscope.

phase modulation *n. Abbr.* **pm, p-m** A type of electronic modulation in which the phase of a carrier wave is varied in order to transmit the information contained in the signal.

phase•out (fāz′out′) *n.* A gradual discontinuation.

phase rule *n. Physics.* A rule stating that the number of degrees of freedom in a material system at equilibrium is equal to the number of components minus the number of phases plus the constant 2. For example, the system of water vapor, liquid water, and solid ice has zero degrees of freedom because the three phases of vapor, liquid, and solid coexist in the one component, water.

–phasia *suff.* A speech disorder of a specified kind: *dysphasia.* [Greek, speech, from *phasis,* utterance, from *phanai,* to say, speak. See **bhā-**[2] in Appendix.]

phas•mid (făz′mĭd) *n.* Any of various insects of the order Phasmida, including the leaf insects and walking sticks, especially common in tropical areas and resembling foliage in color and form. [From New Latin *Phasmida,* order name, from *Phasma,* type genus, from Greek *phasma,* apparition, from *phainein,* to show. See PHASE.]

phat•ic (făt′ĭk) *adj.* Of, relating to, or being speech used to share feelings or to establish a mood of sociability rather than to communicate information or ideas. [From Greek *phatos,* spoken, from *phanai,* to speak. See –PHASIA.] **—phat′i•cal•ly** *adv.*

pheasant
Phasianus colchicus

Ph.B. *abbr. Latin.* Philosophiae Baccalaureus (Bachelor of Philosophy).

Ph.C. *abbr.* Pharmaceutical Chemist.

Ph.D. *abbr. Latin.* Philosophiae Doctor (Doctor of Philosophy).

pheas•ant (fĕz′ənt) *n., pl.* **pheas•ants** or **pheasant. 1.** Any of various Old World birds of the family Phasianidae, especially the ring-necked pheasant introduced in North America, characteristically having long tails and, in the males of many species, brilliantly colored plumage. **2.** Any of several other birds that resemble the pheasant, such as the partridge. [Middle English *fesaunt,* from Old French *fesan,* from Latin *phāsiānus,* from Greek *phasianos (ornis),* (bird) of the Phasis River, pheasant, from *Phasis,* the Phasis River of western Georgia.]

phel•lem (fĕl′əm, -ĕm′) *n. Botany.* See **cork** (sense 4). [German : Greek *phellos,* cork; see **bhel-**[2] in Appendix + *-em* (as in *Phloëm,* phloem; see PHLOEM).]

phel•lo•derm (fĕl′ə-dûrm′) *n.* A tissue produced inwardly by the cork cambium. [Greek *phellos,* cork; see **bhel-**[2] in Appendix + –DERM.] **—phel′lo•der′mal** *adj.*

phel•lo•gen (fĕl′ə-jən) *n.* See **cork cambium.** [Greek *phellos,* cork; see **bhel-**[2] in Appendix + –GEN.] **—phel′lo•ge•net′ic** (-jə-nĕt′ĭk), **phel′lo•gen′ic** (-jĕn′ĭk) *adj.*

phen– *pref.* Variant of **pheno–.**

phe•na•caine (fē′nə-kān′, fĕn′ə-) *n.* A white crystalline compound, $C_{18}H_{22}N_2O_2$, used in the form of its hydrochloride as a local anesthetic in ophthalmology. [PHEN(O)– + A(CETO–) + –CAINE.]

phe•nac•e•tin (fə-năs′ĭ-tĭn) *n.* See **acetophenetidin.** [Rearrangement of chemical name ACETOPHENETIDIN.]

phen•a•cite (fĕn′ə-sīt′) or **phen•a•kite** (-kīt′) *n.* A natural beryllium silicate, Be_2SiO_4, occurring as vitreous crystals sometimes used as gems. [Greek *phenax, phenak-,* impostor + –ITE[1].]

phe•nan•threne (fə-năn′thrēn′) *n.* A colorless crystalline hydrocarbon, $C_{14}H_{10}$, obtained by fractional distillation of coal-tar oils and used in dyes, drugs, and explosives. [PHEN(O)– + ANTHR(AC)ENE.]

phen•ar•sa•zine chloride (fə-när′sə-zēn′) *n.* A highly poisonous yellow crystalline compound, $C_{12}H_9AsClN$, used as a poison gas and sometimes with tear gas. Also called *diphenylaminechloroarsine.* [PHEN(O)– + ARS(ENIC) + AZINE.]

phen•a•zine (fĕn′ə-zēn′) also **phen•a•zin** (-zĭn) *n.* A yellow crystalline compound, $C_6H_4N_2C_6H_4$, used in the manufacture of dyes.

phen•cy•cli•dine (fĕn-sī′klĭ-dēn′, -dĭn, -sĭk′lĭ-) *n.* A drug, $C_{17}H_{25}N$, used in veterinary medicine as an anesthetic and illegally as a hallucinogen; PCP. [PHEN(O)– + CYCL(O)– + –ID(E) + –INE[2].]

phen•el•zine (fĕn′əl-zēn′) *n.* A monoamine oxidase inhibitor, $C_8H_{12}N_2$, used especially in the form of its sulfate as an antidepressant. [PHEN(O)– + E(THY)L + (HYDRA)ZINE.]

phe•net•ic (fĭ-nĕt′ĭk) *adj.* Of, relating to, or designating a system of classification of organisms based on overall or observable similarities rather than on phylogenetic or evolutionary relationships. [PHEN(OTYPE) + –ETIC.] **—phe•net′i•cal•ly** *adv.*

phe•net•ics (fĭ-nĕt′ĭks) *n. (used with a sing. verb).* The phenetic system of taxonomic classification. **—phe•net′i•cist** (-ĭ-sĭst) *n.*

phe•nix (fē′nĭks) *n.* Variant of **phoenix.**

Phe•nix City (fē′nĭks). A city of eastern Alabama on the Chattahoochee River across from Columbus, Georgia. It is a processing center in a cotton-growing area. Population, 27,012.

pheno– or **phen–** *pref.* **1.** Showing; displaying: *phenotype.* **2.a.** Related to or derived from benzene: *phenol.* **b.** Containing phenyl: *phenothiazine.* [Greek *phaino-,* from *phainein,* to show. See **bhā-**[1] in Appendix.]

phe•no•bar•bi•tal (fē′nō-bär′bĭ-tôl′, -tăl′) *n.* A crystalline barbiturate, $C_{12}H_{12}N_2O_3$, used medicinally as a sedative, a hypnotic, and an anticonvulsant.

phe•no•bar•bi•tone (fē′nō-bär′bĭ-tōn′) *n. Chiefly British.* Phenobarbital.

phe•no•cop•y (fē′nə-kŏp′ē) *n., pl.* **-ies.** An environmentally induced, nonhereditary variation in an organism, closely resembling a genetically determined trait. [PHENO(TYPE) + COPY.]

phe•no•cryst (fē′nə-krĭst′) *n.* A conspicuous, usually large, crystal embedded in porphyritic igneous rock. [PHENO– + CRYST(AL).] **—phe′no•crys′tic** *adj.*

phe•nol (fē′nôl′, -nōl′, -nŏl′) *n.* **1.** A caustic, poisonous, white crystalline compound, C_6H_5OH, derived from benzene and used in resins, plastics, and pharmaceuticals and in dilute form as a disinfectant and antiseptic. Also called *carbolic acid.* **2.** Any of a class of aromatic organic compounds having at least one hydroxyl group attached directly to the benzene ring.

phe•no•late (fē′nə-lāt′) *n.* A salt of phenol. Also called *phenoxide.*

phe•no•lic (fĭ-nō′lĭk, -nŏl′ĭk) *adj.* Of, relating to, containing, or derived from phenol. **—phenolic** *n.* Any of various synthetic thermosetting resins, obtained by the reaction of phenols with simple aldehydes and used to make molded products and as coatings and adhesives. Also called *phenolic resin.*

phe•nol•o•gy (fĭ-nŏl′ə-jē) *n.* **1.** The scientific study of periodic biological phenomena, such as flowering, breeding, and migration, in relation to climatic conditions. **2.** The relationship between a periodic biological phenomenon and climatic conditions. [PHENO(MENON) + –LOGY.] **—phe′no•log′i•cal** (fē′nə-lŏj′ĭ-kəl) *adj.* **—phe′no•log′i•cal•ly** *adv.* **—phe•nol′o•gist** *n.*

phe•nol•phthal•ein (fē′nōl-thăl′ēn′, -thăl′ē-ĭn, -thā′lēn′, -thā′lē-ĭn) *n.* A white or pale yellow crystalline powder, $C_{20}H_{14}O_4$, used as an acid-base indicator, in making dyes, and in medicine as a laxative.

phenol red *n.* A red, water-soluble dye, $C_{19}H_{14}O_5S$, used as an acid-base indicator and in medicine to test kidney function and renal blood flow.

phe•nom (fĭ-nŏm′) *n. Slang.* A phenomenon, especially a remarkable or outstanding person.

phe•nom•e•na (fĭ-nŏm′ə-nə) *n.* Plural of **phenomenon.**

phe•nom•e•nal (fĭ-nŏm′ə-nəl) *adj.* **1.** Of, relating to, or constituting phenomena or a phenomenon. **2.** Extraordinary; outstanding: *a phenomenal feat of memory.* **3.** *Philosophy.* Known or derived through the senses rather than through the mind. **—phe•nom′e•nal•ly** *adv.*

phe•nom•e•nal•ism (fĭ-nŏm′ə-nə-lĭz′əm) *n. Philosophy.* The doctrine, set forth by David Hume and his successors, that percepts and concepts actually present in the mind constitute the sole object of knowledge, with the objects of perception themselves, their origin outside the mind, or the nature of the mind itself remaining forever beyond inquiry. **—phe•nom′e•nal•ist** *n.* **—phe•nom′e•nal•is′tic** *adj.* **—phe•nom′e•nal•is′ti•cal•ly** *adv.*

phe•nom•e•nol•o•gy (fĭ-nŏm′ə-nŏl′ə-jē) *n. Philosophy.* **1.** The study of all possible appearances in human experience, during which considerations of objective reality and of purely subjective response are left out of account. **2.** A movement based on this study, originated about 1905 by Edmund Husserl. **—phe•nom′e•no•log′i•cal** (-nə-lŏj′ĭ-kəl) *adj.* **—phe•nom′e•no•log′i•cal•ly** *adv.* **—phe•nom′e•nol′o•gist** *n.*

phe•nom•e•non (fĭ-nŏm′ə-nŏn′, -nən) *n., pl.* **-na** (-nə). **1.** An occurrence, a circumstance, or a fact that is perceptible by the senses. **2.** *pl.* **-nons. a.** An unusual, significant, or unaccountable fact or occurrence; a marvel. **b.** A remarkable or outstanding person; a paragon. See Synonyms at **wonder. 3.** *Philosophy.* **a.** That which appears real to the mind, regardless of whether its underlying existence is proved or its nature understood. **b.** In Kantian philosophy, the appearance of an object to the mind as opposed to its existence in and of itself, independent of the mind. **4.** *Physics.* An observable event. [Late Latin *phaenomenon,* from Greek *phainomenon,* from neuter present participle of *phainesthai,* to appear. See **bhā-**[1] in Appendix.]

USAGE NOTE: *Phenomenon* is the only singular form of this noun; *phenomena* is the usual plural. *Phenomenons* may also be used as the plural in nonscientific writing when the meaning is "extraordinary things, occurrences, or persons": *They were phenomenons in the history of music.*

phe·no·thi·a·zine (fē′nō-thī′ə-zēn′, -nə-) *n.* **1.** A yellow organic compound, $C_{12}H_9NS$, used in insecticides, livestock anthelmintics, and dyes. **2.** Any of a group of drugs derived from this compound and used as major tranquilizers in the treatment of psychiatric disorders, such as schizophrenia.

phe·no·type (fē′nə-tīp′) *n.* **1.a.** The observable physical or biochemical characteristics of an organism, as determined by both genetic makeup and environmental influences. **b.** The expression of a specific trait, such as stature or blood type, based on genetic and environmental influences. **2.** An individual or group of organisms exhibiting a particular phenotype. **—phe′no·typ′ic** (-tĭp′ĭk), **phe′no·typ′i·cal** (-ĭ-kəl) *adj.* **—phe′no·typ′i·cal·ly** *adv.*

phe·nox·ide (fĭ-nŏk′sīd′) *n.* See **phenolate.**

phe·nox·y·ben·za·mine (fē-nŏk′sē-bĕn′zə-mēn′) *n.* A long-acting alpha-adrenergic blocking agent, $C_{18}H_{22}ClNO{\cdot}HCl$, used to treat high blood pressure, excessive sweating, and tachycardia caused by pheochromocytoma.

phen·tol·a·mine (fĕn-tŏl′ə-mēn′) *n.* An adrenergic blocking agent, $C_{17}H_{19}N_3O$, used especially in the diagnosis and treatment of pheochromocytoma. [PHEN(O)– + TOL(UIDINE) + AMINE.]

phen·yl (fĕn′əl, fē′nəl) *n.* The univalent organic radical C_6H_5, derived from benzene by removal of one hydrogen atom. **—phe·nyl′ic** (fĭ-nĭl′ĭk) *adj.*

phen·yl·al·a·nine (fĕn′əl-ăl′ə-nēn′, fē′nəl-) *n.* An essential amino acid, $C_6H_5CH_2CH(NH_2)COOH$, that occurs as a constituent of many proteins and is normally converted to tyrosine in the human body. It is necessary for growth in infants and for nitrogen equilibrium in adults.

phen·yl·bu·ta·zone (fĕn′əl-byo͞o′tə-zōn′) *n.* A white or light yellow compound, $C_{19}H_{20}N_2O_2$, used as an anti-inflammatory and analgesic drug in the treatment of arthritis, bursitis, and gout. [PHENYL + BUT– + AZO– + –ONE.]

phen·yl·ene (fĕn′ə-lēn′, fē′nə-) *n.* A bivalent organic radical, C_6H_4, derived from benzene by removal of two hydrogen atoms.

phen·yl·eph·rine (fĕn′əl-ĕf′rēn, fē′nəl-) *n.* An adrenergic drug, $C_9H_{13}NO_2$, that is a powerful vasoconstrictor and is used to relieve nasal congestion, dilate the pupils, and maintain blood pressure during anesthesia. [PHENYL + (EPIN)EPHRINE.]

phen·yl·ke·to·nur·i·a (fĕn′əl-kēt′n-o͝or′ē-ə, -yo͝or′-, fē′nəl-) *n.* *Abbr.* **PKU** A genetic disorder in which the body lacks the enzyme necessary to metabolize phenylalanine to tyrosine. Left untreated, the disorder can cause brain damage and progressive mental retardation as a result of the accumulation of phenylalanine and its breakdown products. **—phen′yl·ke′to·nur′ic** *adj. & n.*

phen·yl·pro·pa·nol·a·mine (fĕn′əl-prō′pə-nŏl′ə-mēn′, fē′nəl-) *n.* *Abbr.* **PPA** An adrenergic drug, $C_9H_{13}NO$, that acts as a vasoconstrictor and is used as a nasal decongestant, a bronchodilator, an appetite suppressant, and a mild stimulant.

phen·yl·thi·o·car·ba·mide (fĕn′əl-thī′ō-kär′bə-mīd′, -kär-băm′īd, fē′nəl-) *n.* *Abbr.* **PTC** A crystalline compound, $C_6H_5NHCSNH_2$, that tastes intensely bitter to people with a specific dominant gene and is used to test for the presence of the gene. Also called *phenylthiourea.*

phen·yl·thi·o·u·rea (fĕn′əl-thī′ō-yo͞o-rē′ə, fē′nəl-) *n.* See **phenylthiocarbamide.**

phen·y·to·in (fĕn′ĭ-tō′ĭn, fə-nĭt′ō-) *n.* An anticonvulsant drug, $C_{15}H_{12}N_2O_2$, chemically related to the barbiturates and used most commonly in the treatment of epilepsy. Also called *diphenylhydantoin.* [(DI)PHENY(LHYDAN)TOIN.]

phe·o·chro·mo·cy·to·ma (fē′ō-krō′mō-sī-tō′mə) *n., pl.* **-mas** or **-ma·ta** (-mə-tə). A usually benign tumor of the adrenal medulla or the sympathetic nervous system in which the affected cells secrete increased amounts of epinephrine or norepinephrine. [*pheochromocyte,* chromaffin cell (Greek *phaios,* dusky + CHROMO– + –CYTE) + –OMA.]

phe·re·sis (fə-rē′sĭs, fĕr′ə-) *n.* *Informal.* Apheresis.

pher·o·mone (fĕr′ə-mōn′) *n.* A chemical secreted by an animal, especially an insect, that influences the behavior or development of others of the same species. [Greek *pherein,* to carry; see **bher-**[1] in Appendix + (HOR)MONE.] **—pher′o·mon′al** *adj.*

phew (fyo͞o) *interj.* Used to express relief, fatigue, surprise, or disgust.

Ph.G. *abbr.* Graduate in Pharmacy.

phi (fī) *n.* The 21st letter of the Greek alphabet. See table at **alphabet.** [Late Greek, from Greek *phei.*]

phi·al (fī′əl) *n.* A vial. [Middle English *fiole,* from Old French, from Late Latin *fiola,* shallow vessel, alteration of Latin *phiala,* from Greek *phialē.*]

Phi Be·ta Kap·pa (fī′ bā′tə kăp′ə, bē′tə) *n.* **1.** An honorary society, founded in 1776, of college students and graduates whose members are chosen on the basis of high academic standing. **2.** A member of this society. [From the initials of the society's motto in Greek *philosophia biou kubernētēs,* philosophy the guide of life : *philosophia,* philosophy + *biou,* genitive of *bios* + *kubernētēs,* guide.]

Phid·i·as (fĭd′ē-əs). fl. fifth century B.C. Athenian sculptor who supervised work on the Parthenon. His statue of Zeus at Olympia was one of the Seven Wonders of the World.

phil. *abbr.* Philosopher; philosophical; philosophy.

Phil. *abbr.* **1.** *Bible.* Philippians. **2.** Philippines.

phil– *pref.* Variant of **philo–.**

–phil *suff.* Variant of **–phile.**

Phil·a·del·phi·a (fĭl′ə-dĕl′fē-ə). **1.** An ancient city of Asia Minor northeast of the Dead Sea in modern-day Jordan. The chief city of the Ammonites, it was enlarged and embellished by Ptolemy II Philadelphus (285–246 B.C.) and named in honor of him. Amman, the capital of Jordan, is now on the site. **2.** The largest city of Pennsylvania, in the southeast part of the state on the Delaware River. It was founded as a Quaker colony by William Penn in 1681 on the site of an earlier Swedish settlement. The First and Second Continental Congresses (1774 and 1775–1776) and the Constitutional Convention (1787) met in the city, which served as the capital of the United States from 1790 to 1800. Population, 1,688,210. **—Phil′a·del′phi·an** *adj. & n.*

Philadelphia lawyer *n.* A shrewd attorney adept at the discovery and manipulation of legal technicalities. [After PHILADELPHIA, Pennsylvania.]

Philadelphia pepper pot *n.* See **pepper pot** (sense 1).

Phi·lae (fī′lē). A former island in the Nile River of southeast Egypt. Site of many ancient temples and monuments, it was particularly noted for its temple dedicated to Isis. The island is now covered by the waters of Lake Nasser.

phi·lan·der (fĭ-lăn′dər) *intr.v.* **-dered, -der·ing, -ders. 1.** To carry on a sexual affair, especially an extramarital affair, with a woman one cannot or does not intend to marry. **2.** To engage in many love affairs, especially with a frivolous or casual attitude. [From *philander,* lover, from *Philander,* former literary name for a lover, from Greek *philandros,* loving or fond of men : *phil-, philo-,* philo- + *anēr, andr-,* man; see **ner-**[2] in Appendix.] **—phi·lan′der·er** *n.*

phil·an·throp·ic (fĭl′ən-thrŏp′ĭk) also **phil·an·throp·i·cal** (-ĭ-kəl) *adj.* **1.** Of, relating to, or marked by philanthropy; humanitarian. **2.** Organized to provide humanitarian or charitable assistance: *a philanthropic society.* See Synonyms at **benevolent. —phil′an·throp′i·cal·ly** *adv.*

phi·lan·thro·py (fĭ-lăn′thrə-pē) *n., pl.* **-pies. 1.** The effort or inclination to increase the well-being of humankind, as by charitable aid or donations. **2.** Love of humankind in general. **3.** Something, such as an activity or institution, intended to promote human welfare. [Late Latin *philanthrōpia,* from Greek, from *philanthrōpos,* humane, benevolent : *phil-, philo-,* philo- + *anthrōpos,* man, mankind.] **—phi·lan′thro·pist** *n.*

phi·lat·e·ly (fĭ-lăt′l-ē) *n.* The collection and study of postage stamps, postmarks, and related materials; stamp collecting. [French *philatélie* : Greek *phil-, philo-,* philo- + Greek *ateleia,* exemption from payment (because a postage stamp indicates prepayment of postage) (*a-,* without; see A–[1] + *telos,* tax, charge; see **tele-** in Appendix).] **—phil′a·tel′ic** (fĭl′ə-tĕl′ĭk), **phil′a·tel′i·cal** (-ĭ-kəl) *adj.* **—phil′a·tel′i·cal·ly** *adv.* **—phi·lat′e·list** *n.*

–phile or **–phil** *suff.* **1.** One that loves or has a strong affinity or preference for: *audiophile.* **2.** Loving; having a strong affinity or preference for: *Francophile.* [New Latin *-philus,* from Greek *-philos,* beloved, dear, from *philos,* beloved, loving.]

Phi·le·mon (fĭ-lē′mən, fī-) *n.* **1.** *Abbr.* **Philem., Phm** *Bible.* See table at **Bible. 2.** *Greek Mythology.* A poor elderly man who, with his wife Baucis, treated the disguised Zeus so hospitably that as a reward their humble cottage was transformed into a magnificent temple.

phil·har·mon·ic (fĭl′här-mŏn′ĭk, fĭl′ər-) *Music. adj.* **1.** Devoted to or appreciative of music. **2.** Relating to a symphony orchestra. **—philharmonic** also **Philharmonic** *n.* A symphony orchestra or the group that supports it. [French *philharmonique,* from Italian *filarmonico* : Greek *phil-, philo-,* philo- + Greek *harmonika,* theory of music, from neuter pl. of *harmonikos,* musical; see HARMONIC.]

phil·hel·lene (fĭl-hĕl′ēn′) also **phil·hel·len·ist** (-hĕl′ə-nĭst) *n.* One who admires Greece or the Greeks. [Greek *philellēn* : *phil-,* philo- + *Hellēn,* Greek.] **—phil′hel·len′ic** (fĭl′hĕ-lĕn′ĭk) *adj.* **—phil·hel′len·ism** *n.*

Phil. I. *abbr.* Philippine Islands.

–philia *suff.* **1.** Tendency toward: *hemophilia.* **2.** Abnormal attraction to: *necrophilia.* [New Latin, from Greek *philia,* friendship, from *philos,* loving.]

–philiac *suff.* **1.** One that has a tendency toward: *hemophiliac.* **2.** One that has an abnormal attraction to: *coprophiliac.* [–PHILIA + –AC.]

–philic *suff.* Variant of **–philous.**

Phil·ip (fĭl′ĭp). Died 1676. Wampanoag leader who waged King Philip's War (1675–1676) against New England colonists who had encroached on Native American territory.

Philip, Prince. Duke of Edinburgh. Born 1921. Husband of Elizabeth II of Great Britain. The great-great-grandson of Victoria, he was given the title Prince in 1957.

Philip, Saint. fl. first century A.D. One of the 12 Apostles. In the New Testament he is present at the feeding of the 5,000.

Philip II[1]**.** 382–336 B.C. King of Macedon (359–336) who built the army that defeated a Greek coalition at Chaeronea (338) and achieved a peace settlement in which all the states except Sparta participated.

Prince Philip
Photographed in 1985

ă pat	oi boy
ā pay	ou out
âr care	o͝o took
ä father	o͞o boot
ĕ pet	ŭ cut
ē be	ûr urge
ĭ pit	th thin
ī pie	*th* this
îr pier	hw which
ŏ pot	zh vision
ō toe	ə about, item
ô paw	♦ regionalism

Stress marks: **′** (primary); ′ (secondary), as in **dictionary** (dĭk′shə-nĕr′ē)

Philip II² or **Philip Au·gus·tus** (ô-gŭs′təs). 1165–1223. King of France (1180–1223). His reign was marked by greater control over feudal lords and an expansion of royal territories.

Philip II³. 1527–1598. King of Spain (1556–1598), of Naples and Sicily (1554–1598), and of Portugal (1580–1598) as Philip I. In 1588 he launched the Spanish Armada in an unsuccessful attempt to invade England.

Philip IV. Known as "Philip the Fair." 1268–1314. King of France (1285–1314) and of Navarre (1284–1305) as the husband of Joan I of Navarre (1273–1305). His reign was marked by controversy with the papacy and expansion of royal prerogative.

Philip V. 238–179 B.C. King of Macedon (221–179) who won the First Macedonian War with Rome (205) but was defeated in the Second Macedonian War (197).

Philip VI. 1293–1350. King of France (1328–1350). The first Valois king, his reign was dominated by the Hundred Years' War.

Philip Au·gus·tus (ô-gŭs′təs). See **Philip II²**.

Phi·lip·pi (fĭ-lĭp′ī). An ancient town of north-central Macedonia, Greece, near the Aegean Sea. It was the site of Antony and Octavian's decisive defeat of Brutus and Cassius in 42 B.C. **—Phi·lip′pi·an** (-lĭp′ē-ən) *adj. & n.*

Phi·lip·pi·ans (fĭ-lĭp′ē-ənz) *pl.n.* *(used with a sing. verb).* *Abbr.* **Ph, Phil.** *Bible.* See table at **Bible.**

Phi·lip·pic (fĭ-lĭp′ĭk) *n.* **1.** Any of the orations of Demosthenes against Philip of Macedon in the fourth century B.C. **2.** Any of the orations of Cicero against Antony in 44 B.C. **3. philippic.** A verbal denunciation characterized by harsh, often insulting language; a tirade.

Philippine mahogany *n.* **1.** Any of various southeast Asian hardwood trees of the genus *Shorea* and related genera. **2.** The wood of any of these trees.

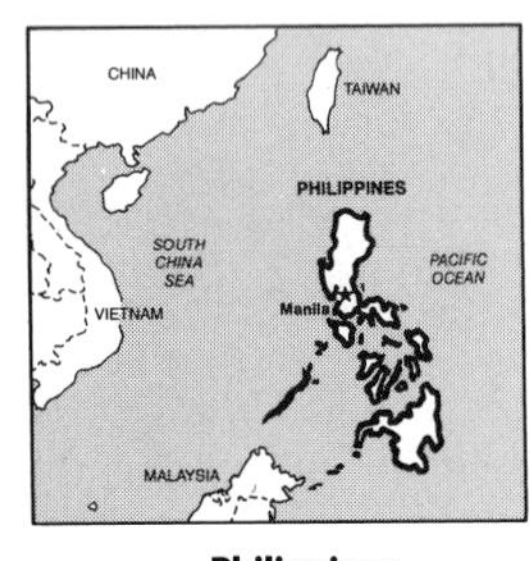

Philippines

Phil·ip·pines (fĭl′ə-pēnz′, fĭl′ə-pēnz′). *Abbr.* **Phil.** A country of eastern Asia consisting of the **Philippine Islands,** an archipelago in the western Pacific Ocean southeast of China. First sighted by Magellan's expedition in 1521, the islands were colonized by the Spanish after 1565 and came under U.S. control in 1898 after the Spanish-American War. A commonwealth was created in 1935 and full independence achieved in 1946. The islands were occupied by Japan during much of World War II. Political turmoil led to the dictatorship of Ferdinand Marcos after 1965 and his exile in 1986 following the election of Corazon Aquino. Manila is the capital and the largest city. Population, 48,098,460. **—Phil′ip·pine** *adj.*

Philippine Sea. A section of the western Pacific Ocean east of the Philippines and west of the Marianas.

Phil·ips (fĭl′ĭps), **Ambrose.** Called "Namby Pamby." 1674–1749. British poet known especially for his collection *Pastorals* (1709).

Phil. Is. *abbr.* Philippine Islands.

Phi·lis·ti·a (fĭ-lĭs′tē-ə). An ancient region of southwest Palestine. Strategically located on a trade route from Egypt to Syria, the cities of the region formed a loose confederacy important in biblical times.

Phil·is·tine (fĭl′ĭ-stēn′, fĭ-lĭs′tĭn, -tēn′) *n.* **1.** A member of an Aegean people who settled ancient Philistia around the 12th century B.C. **2.a.** A smug, ignorant, especially middle-class person who is regarded as being indifferent or antagonistic to artistic and cultural values. **b.** One who lacks knowledge in a specific area. **—Philistine** *adj.* **1.** Of or relating to ancient Philistia. **2.** Often **philistine.** Boorish; barbarous: *"our plastic, violent culture, with its philistine tastes and hunger for novelty"* (Lloyd Rose). [From Middle English *Philistines,* Philistines, from Late Latin *Philistīnī,* from Greek *Philistinoi,* from Hebrew *Pĕlištîm,* from *Pĕlešet,* Philistia.]

WORD HISTORY: It has never been good to be a Philistine. Samson, Saul, and David in the Bible helped bring the Philistines into prominence because they were such prominent opponents. Even though the Philistines have long since disappeared, their name has lived on in the Old Testament. The English name for them, *Philistines,* which goes back through Late Latin and Greek to Hebrew, is first found in Middle English, where *Philistiens,* the ancestor of our word, is recorded in a work composed before 1325. Beginning in the 17th century *philistine* was used as a common noun usually in the plural to refer to various groups considered the enemy, such as literary critics. In Germany in the same century it is said that in a memorial at Jena for a student who had been killed in a town-gown quarrel, the minister preached a sermon from the text "Philister über dir Simson! [The Philistines be upon thee, Samson!]," the words of Delilah to Samson after she attempted to render him powerless before his Philistine enemies. From this usage it is said that German students came to use *Philister,* the German equivalent of *Philistine,* to denote nonstudents and hence uncultured or materialistic people. Both usages were picked up in English in the early 19th century.

Phil·is·tin·ism also **phi·lis·tin·ism** (fĭl′ĭ-stē-nĭz′əm, fĭ-lĭs′tə-nĭz′əm, -tē-nĭz′əm) *n.* An attitude of smug ignorance and conventionalism, especially toward artistic and cultural values.

Phil·lips (fĭl′ĭps). A trademark used for a screw with a head having two intersecting perpendicular slots and for a screwdriver with a tip shaped to fit into these slots.

Phillips, Wendell. 1811–1884. American abolitionist who served as president of the American Antislavery Society from 1865 to 1870.

Phil·lips·burg (fĭl′ĭps-bûrg′). A town of northwest New Jersey on the Delaware River northwest of Trenton. Settled in the early 1700's, it is an industrial center. Population, 16,647.

phil·lu·men·ist (fə-lo͞o′mə-nĭst) *n.* One who collects matchbooks or matchboxes. [PHIL(O)– + Latin *lūmen,* light; see **leuk-** in Appendix + –IST.]

philo– or **phil–** *pref.* Having a strong affinity or preference for; loving: *philoprogenitive.* [Greek, from *philos,* beloved, loving.]

phil·o·den·dron (fĭl′ə-dĕn′drən) *n., pl.* **-drons** or **-dra** (-drə). Any of various climbing tropical American plants of the genus *Philodendron,* many of which are cultivated as houseplants. [From Greek, neuter of *philodendros,* fond of trees (from the fact that in its tropical American habitat it twines around trees) : *philo-,* philo- + *dendron,* tree; see **deru-** in Appendix.]

Phi·lo Ju·dae·us (fī′lō jo͞o-dē′əs, -dā′-). Also Philo of Alexandria. 30? B.C.–A.D. 45? Alexandrian Jewish philosopher known for his attempts to reconcile religious faith and philosophical reason.

phi·lol·o·gy (fĭ-lŏl′ə-jē) *n.* *Abbr.* **philol. 1.** Literary study or classical scholarship. **2.** See **historical linguistics.** [Middle English *philologie,* from Latin *philologia,* love of learning, from Greek, from *philologos,* fond of learning or of words : *philo-,* philo- + *logos,* reason, speech; see –LOGY.] **—phi·lol′o·ger, phi·lol′o·gist** *n.* **—phil′o·log′ic** (fĭl′ə-lŏj′ĭk), **phil′o·log′i·cal** (-ĭ-kəl) *adj.* **—phil′o·log′i·cal·ly** *adv.*

phil·o·mel (fĭl′ə-mĕl′) *n.* A nightingale. [Alteration (influenced by French *philomèle,* from Latin *Philomēla,* Philomela) of Middle English *phylomene,* from Medieval Latin *philomēna,* from Latin *Philomēla,* Philomela. See PHILOMELA.]

Phil·o·me·la (fĭl′ə-mē′lə) *n.* *Greek Mythology.* A princess of Athens who, after being raped by her brother-in-law, Tereus, was avenged by her sister, Procne, and was later turned into a swallow or nightingale while fleeing Tereus. [Latin *Philomēla,* from Greek *Philomēlē.*]

phil·o·pro·gen·i·tive (fĭl′ō-prō-jĕn′ĭ-tĭv) *adj.* **1.** Producing many offspring; prolific. **2.** Loving one's own offspring or children in general. **3.** Of or relating to love of children. **—phil′o·pro·gen′i·tive·ly** *adv.* **—phil′o·pro·gen′i·tive·ness** *n.*

philos. *abbr.* Philosopher; philosophical; philosophy.

phi·lo·sophe (fĭl′ə-sŏf′, fē′lô-zôf′) *n.* Any of the leading philosophical, political, and social writers of the 18th-century French Enlightenment. [French, from Old French, philosopher. See PHILOSOPHER.]

phi·los·o·pher (fĭ-lŏs′ə-fər) *n.* *Abbr.* **phil., philos. 1.** A student of or specialist in philosophy. **2.** A person who lives and thinks according to a particular philosophy. **3.** A person who is calm and rational under any circumstances. [Middle English *philosophre,* from Old French *philosophe,* from Latin *philosophus,* from Greek *philosophos,* lover of wisdom, philosopher : *philo-,* philo- + *sophia,* knowledge, learning.]

phi·los·o·phers' stone also **phi·los·o·pher's stone** (fĭ-lŏs′ə-fərz) *n.* A substance that was believed to have the power of transmuting base metal into gold. Also called *elixir.*

phil·o·soph·i·cal (fĭl′ə-sŏf′ĭ-kəl) also **phil·o·soph·ic** (-ĭk) *adj.* *Abbr.* **phil., philos. 1.** Of, relating to, or based on a system of philosophy. **2.** Characteristic of a philosopher, as in equanimity, enlightenment, and wisdom. **—phil′o·soph′i·cal·ly** *adv.*

phi·los·o·phize (fĭ-lŏs′ə-fīz′) *v.* **-phized, -phiz·ing, -phiz·es.** *—intr.* **1.** To speculate in a philosophical manner. **2.** To set forth or express a moralistic, often superficial philosophy. *—tr.* To consider (a matter) from a philosophical standpoint. **—phi·los′o·phiz′er** *n.*

phi·los·o·phy (fĭ-lŏs′ə-fē) *n., pl.* **-phies.** *Abbr.* **phil., philos. 1.a.** Love and pursuit of wisdom by intellectual means and moral self-discipline. **b.** The investigation of causes and laws underlying reality. **c.** A system of philosophical inquiry or demonstration. **2.** Inquiry into the nature of things based on logical reasoning rather than empirical methods. **3.** The critique and analysis of fundamental beliefs as they come to be conceptualized and formulated. **4.** The synthesis of all learning. **5.** All learning except technical precepts and practical arts. **6.** All the disciplines presented in university curriculums of science and the liberal arts, except medicine, law, and theology. **7.** The science comprising logic, ethics, aesthetics, metaphysics, and epistemology. **8.** A system of motivating concepts or principles: *the philosophy of a culture.* **9.** A basic theory; a viewpoint: *an original philosophy of advertising.* **10.** The system of values by which one lives: *has an unusual philosophy of life.* [Middle English *philosophie,* from Old French, from Latin *philosophia,* from Greek, from *philosophos,* lover of wisdom, philosopher. See PHILOSOPHER.]

–philous or **–philic** *suff.* Having a strong affinity or preference for; loving: *anemophilous.* [From New Latin *-philus,* from Greek *philos,* beloved, loving.]

phil·ter also **phil·tre** (fĭl′tər) *—n.* **1.** A love potion. **2.** A magic potion or charm. *—tr.v.* **-tered, -ter·ing, -ters** also **-tred, -tring, -tres.** To enchant with or as if with a philter. [French *philtre,* from Old French, from Latin *philtrum,* from Greek *philtron* : *philein,* to love (from *philos,* beloved, loving) + *-tron,* instrumental suff.]

phi·mo·sis (fī-mō′sĭs, fĭ-) *n., pl.* **-ses** (-sēz). An abnormal constriction of the foreskin that prevents it from being drawn back to uncover the glans penis. [New Latin *phimōsis,* from Greek, a muzzling, phimosis, from *phimoun,* to muzzle, from *phimos,* muzzle.]

phleb– *pref.* Variant of **phlebo–.**

phle·bi·tis (flĭ-bī′tĭs) *n.* Inflammation of a vein. —**phle·bit′ic** (-bĭt′ĭk) *adj.*

phlebo– or **phleb–** *pref.* Vein: *phlebology.* [Greek, from *phleps, phleb-,* blood vessel, vein.]

phle·bog·ra·phy (flĭ-bŏg′rə-fē) *n.* See **venography.** —**phle′bo·gram** (flē′bə-grăm′) *n.* —**phle′bo·graph′ic** (-grăf′ĭk) *adj.*

phle·bol·o·gy (flĭ-bŏl′ə-jē) *n.* The branch of medicine that deals with veins and their diseases.

phleb·o·scle·ro·sis (flĕb′ō-sklə-rō′sĭs) *n.* The thickening or hardening of the walls of veins.

phle·bot·o·mist (flə-bŏt′ə-mĭst) *n.* **1.** One who practices phlebotomy. **2.** One who draws blood for analysis or transfusion.

phle·bot·o·mize (flĭ-bŏt′ə-mīz′) *tr.v.* **-mized, -miz·ing, -miz·es.** To perform a phlebotomy on; bleed.

phle·bot·o·mus fever (flə-bŏt′ə-məs) *n.* See **sandfly fever.** [New Latin *Phlebotomus,* sandfly genus (from Late Latin *phlebotomus,* lancet, from Greek *phlebotomos,* opening a vein. See PHLEBOTOMY).]

phle·bot·o·my (flĭ-bŏt′ə-mē) *n., pl.* **-mies.** The act or practice of opening a vein by incision or puncture to remove blood as a therapeutic treatment. Also called *venesection.* [Middle English *flebotomie,* from Old French *flebothomie,* from Late Latin *phlebotomia,* from Greek, from *phlebotomos,* opening a vein : *phlebo-,* phlebo- + *-tomos,* cutting; see –TOME.] —**phleb′o·tom′ic** (flĕb′ə-tŏm′ĭk), **phleb′o·tom′i·cal** (-ĭ-kəl) *adj.*

Phleg·e·thon (flĕg′ə-thŏn′) *n. Greek Mythology.* A river of fire, one of the five rivers of Hades. [Middle English *Flegeton,* from Latin *Phlegethōn,* from Greek, from the present participle of *phlegethein,* to blaze, variant of *phlegein,* to burn. See **bhel-**[1] in Appendix.]

phlegm (flĕm) *n.* **1.** Thick, sticky, stringy mucus secreted by the mucous membrane of the respiratory tract, as during a cold or other respiratory infection. **2.** One of the four humors of ancient physiology, described as cold and moist and thought to cause sluggishness, apathy, and evenness of temper. **3.** Sluggishness of temperament. **4.** Calm self-possession; equanimity. [Middle English *fleume,* mucous discharge, the humor phlegm, from Old French, from Medieval Latin *phlegma, flegma,* from Late Latin *phlegma,* the humor phlegm, from Greek, heat, the humor phlegm, from *phlegein,* to burn. See **bhel-**[1] in Appendix.] —**phlegm′y** *adj.*

phleg·mat·ic (flĕg-măt′ĭk) also **phleg·mat·i·cal** (-ĭ-kəl) *adj.* **1.** Of or relating to phlegm; phlegmy. **2.** Having or suggesting a calm, sluggish temperament; unemotional. [Middle English *fleumatik,* from Old French *fleumatique,* from Late Latin *phlegmaticus,* full of phlegm, from Greek *phlegmatikos,* from *phlegma, phlegmat-,* heat, the humor phlegm, from *phlegein,* to burn. See **bhel-**[1] in Appendix.] —**phleg·mat′i·cal·ly** *adv.*

phlo·em (flō′ĕm′) *n.* The food-conducting tissue of vascular plants, consisting of sieve tubes, fibers, parenchyma, and sclereids. [German, from Greek *phloios,* bark. See **bhleu-** in Appendix.]

phlo·gis·tic (flō-jĭs′tĭk) *adj.* **1.** Of or relating to phlogiston. **2.** *Medicine.* Of, relating to, or inducing inflammation or fever; inflammatory.

phlo·gis·ton (flō-jĭs′tŏn′, -tən) *n.* A hypothetical substance formerly thought to be a volatile constituent of all combustible substances released as flame in combustion. [From Greek, neuter of *phlogistos,* inflammable, from *phlogizein,* to set on fire, from *phlox, phlog-,* flame. See **bhel-**[1] in Appendix.]

phlog·o·pite (flŏg′ə-pīt′) *n.* A yellow to dark brown mica, $K(Mg,Fe)_3AlSi_3O_{10}(OH)_2$, used in insulation. [Greek *phlogōpos,* fiery-looking (*phlox, phlog-,* flame; see **bhel-**[1] in Appendix + *ōps,* eye, face; see **okʷ-** in Appendix) + –ITE[1].]

phlox (flŏks) *n., pl.* **phlox** or **phlox·es.** Any of various North American plants of the genus *Phlox,* having opposite leaves and flowers with a variously colored salverform corolla. [Latin *phlox,* a kind of flame-colored flower, from Greek, flame, wallflower. See **bhel-**[1] in Appendix.]

phlyc·te·na also **phlyc·tae·na** (flĭk-tē′nə) *n., pl.* **-nae** (-nē). A small blister or vesicle, especially one of multiple blisters caused by a mild burn. [New Latin, from Greek *phluktaina,* blister, from *phluzein,* to boil over. See **bhleu-** in Appendix.] —**phlyc′ten′ar** (flĭk′tĕn′ər) *adj.*

Phm *abbr. Bible.* Philemon.

Ph.M. *abbr. Latin.* Philosophiae Magister (Master of Philosophy).

Phnom Penh (pə-nôm′ pĕn′, nŏm′). The capital and largest city of Cambodia, in the southwest part of the country on the Mekong River. It was founded in the 14th century and became the capital of the Khmer after c. 1432 and the capital of Cambodia in 1867. The city suffered greatly during civil strife in the country beginning in 1970. Population, 400,000.

–phobe *suff.* One that fears or is averse to a specified thing: *ailurophobe.* [French, from Latin *-phobus,* from Greek *-phobos,* fearing, from *phobos,* fear. See **bhegʷ-** in Appendix.]

pho·bi·a (fō′bē-ə) *n.* **1.** A persistent, abnormal, or irrational fear of a specific thing or situation that compels one to avoid the feared stimulus. **2.** A strong fear, dislike, or aversion. [From Late Latin *-phobia,* -phobia.]

–phobia *suff.* An intense, abnormal, or illogical fear of a specified thing: *xenophobia.* [Late Latin, from Greek, from *phobos,* fear. See **bhegʷ-** in Appendix.]

pho·bic (fō′bĭk) *adj.* Of, relating to, arising from, or having a phobia. —**phobic** *n.* One who has a phobia.

–phobic or **–phobous** *suff.* **1.** Having a fear of or an aversion for: *xenophobic.* **2.** Lacking an affinity for: *lyophobic.* [Late Latin *-phobicus,* from Greek *-phobikos,* from *-phobia,* -phobia.]

Pho·bos (fō′bəs) *n.* The larger and inner of the two planetary satellites of Mars. [Greek, fear, deity who personifies fear, from *phobos,* fear. See –PHOBE.]

–phobous *suff.* See **–phobic.**

Pho·cae·a (fō-sē′ə). An ancient Ionian Greek city of western Asia Minor on the Aegean Sea in present-day Turkey. It was an important maritime state c. 1000 to 600 B.C. but declined after a Persian siege in 540.

pho·cine (fō′sīn) *adj. Zoology.* Of, relating to, or resembling seals. [From Latin *phōca,* seal, from Greek *phōkē.*]

Pho·cis (fō′sĭs). A historical region of central Greece north of the Gulf of Corinth. In early times (before 590 B.C.) it controlled the oracle at Delphi. The region was ultimately conquered by Philip II of Macedon.

pho·co·me·li·a (fō′kō-mē′lē-ə, -mēl′yə) *n.* A birth defect in which the upper portion of a limb is absent or poorly developed, so that the hand or foot attaches to the body by a short, flipperlike stump. [New Latin *phōcomelia* : Greek *phōkē,* seal + Greek *melos,* limb.]

phoe·be (fē′bē) *n.* Any of several medium-sized birds of the genus *Sayornis,* of North America, noted for the flicking motion of the tail. [Imitative of its song (influenced by the name *Phoebe*).]

Phoe·be (fē′bē) *n.* **1.** *Greek Mythology.* The goddess Artemis. **2.** The moon. **3.** The satellite of Saturn that is 17th in distance from the planet. [Middle English *phebe,* from Latin *Phoebē,* from Greek *Phoibē,* from feminine of *phoibos,* shining.]

Phoe·bus (fē′bəs) *n.* **1.** *Greek Mythology.* Apollo, the god of the sun. **2.** The sun. [Middle English *phebus,* from Latin *Phoebus,* from Greek *phoibos,* shining, Apollo.]

Phoe·ni·cia (fĭ-nĭsh′ə, -nē′shə). An ancient maritime country of southwest Asia consisting of city-states along the eastern Mediterranean Sea in present-day Syria and Lebanon. Its people became the foremost navigators and traders of the Mediterranean by 1250 B.C. and established numerous colonies, including Carthage in northern Africa. The Phoenicians traveled to the edges of the known world at the time and introduced their alphabet, based on symbols for sounds rather than cuneiform or hieroglyphic representations, to the Greeks and other early peoples.

Phoe·ni·cian (fĭ-nĭsh′ən, -nē′shən) *adj.* Of or relating to ancient Phoenicia or its people, language, or culture. —**Phoenician** *n.* **1.** A native or inhabitant of ancient Phoenicia. **2.** The Semitic language of ancient Phoenicia. [Middle English *Phenicien,* from Latin *Phoenīcia,* feminine of *Phoenīcius,* from *Phoenīcē,* Phoenicia.]

phoe·nix also **phe·nix** (fē′nĭks) *n.* **1.** *Mythology.* A bird in Egyptian mythology that lived in the desert for 500 years and then consumed itself by fire, later to rise renewed from its ashes. **2.** A person or thing of unsurpassed excellence or beauty; a paragon. **3. Phoenix.** A constellation in the Southern Hemisphere near Tucana and Sculptor. [Middle English *fenix,* from Old English and Old French, both from Medieval Latin *fēnix,* from Latin *phoenix,* from Greek *phoinix.*]

Phoenix. The capital and largest city of Arizona, in the south-central part of the state northwest of Tucson. Settled c. 1868, it became territorial capital in 1889 and state capital in 1912. The city is noted as a winter and health resort. Population, 789,704.

Phoenix Islands. A group of eight small islands in the central Pacific Ocean north of Samoa. Discovered between 1823 and 1840 by British and American explorers, they were administered at various times by one or both of the countries and are now part of Kiribati.

phon (fŏn) *n.* A unit of apparent loudness, equal in number to the intensity in decibels of a 1,000-hertz tone judged to be as loud as the sound being measured. [German, from Greek *phōnē,* sound. See PHONE[1].]

phon. *abbr.* **1.** Phonetic; phonetics. **2.** Phonology.

phon– *pref.* Variant of **phono–.**

pho·nate (fō′nāt′) *intr.v.* **-nat·ed, -nat·ing, -nates.** To utter speech sounds; vocalize. —**pho·na′tion** *n.*

phone[1] (fōn) *Informal. n.* **1.** A telephone. **2.** An earphone. —**phone** *v.* **phoned, phon·ing, phones.** —*intr.* To telephone. —*tr.* **1.** To get in touch with by telephone. **2.** To impart (information or news, for example) by telephone. [Short for TELEPHONE.]

phone[2] (fōn) *n. Linguistics.* A speech sound considered without reference to its status as a phoneme or an allophone in a language. [Greek *phōnē,* sound, voice. See **bhā-**[2] in Appendix.]

–phone *suff.* **1.** Sound: *homophone.* **2.** Device that receives or emits sound: *geophone.* **3.** Speaker of a language: *Anglophone.* [From Greek *phōnē,* sound, voice. See **bhā-**[2] in Appendix.]

phlox
Blue phlox
Phlox divaricata

phoebe

phoenix
On its funeral pyre

ă pat	oi boy
ā pay	ou out
âr care	ŏŏ took
ä father	ōō boot
ĕ pet	ŭ cut
ē be	ûr urge
ĭ pit	th thin
ī pie	*th* this
îr pier	hw which
ŏ pot	zh vision
ō toe	ə about, item
ô paw	♦ regionalism

Stress marks: **′** (primary); ′ (secondary), as in **dictionary** (dĭk′shə-nĕr′ē)

phone book *n. Informal.* A telephone book.

phone booth *n. Informal.* A telephone booth.

pho·ne·mat·ic (fō′nĭ-măt′ĭk) *adj. Linguistics.* Phonemic.

pho·neme (fō′nēm′) *n. Linguistics.* The smallest phonetic unit in a language that is capable of conveying a distinction in meaning, as the *m* of *mat* and the *b* of *bat* in English. [French *phonème,* from Greek *phōnēma, phōnēmat-,* utterance, sound produced, from *phōnein,* to produce a sound, from *phōnē,* sound, voice. See **bhā-**[2] in Appendix.]

pho·ne·mic (fə-nē′mĭk, fō-) *adj. Linguistics.* **1.** Of or relating to phonemes. **2.** Of or relating to phonemics. **3.** Serving to distinguish phonemes or distinctive features. **—pho·ne′mi·cal·ly** *adv.*

pho·ne·mics (fə-nē′mĭks, fō-) *n. (used with a sing. verb). Linguistics.* The study and establishment of the phonemes of a language. **—pho·ne′mi·cist** (-mĭ-sĭst) *n.*

pho·net·ic (fə-nĕt′ĭk) *adj. Abbr.* **phon.** *Linguistics.* **1.** Of or relating to phonetics. **2.** Representing the sounds of speech with a set of distinct symbols, each designating a single sound: *phonetic spelling.* **3.** Of, relating to, or being features of pronunciation that are not phonemically distinctive in a language, as aspiration of consonants or vowel length in English. [New Latin *phōnēticus,* representing speech sounds, from Greek *phōnētikos,* vocal, from *phōnētos,* to be spoken, from *phōnein,* to produce a sound, from *phōnē,* sound, voice. See **bhā-**[2] in Appendix.] **—pho·net′i·cal** *adj.* **—pho·net′i·cal·ly** *adv.*

phonetic alphabet *n.* **1.** *Linguistics.* A standardized set of symbols used in phonetic transcription. **2.** Any of various systems of code words for identifying letters in voice communication.

pho·ne·ti·cian (fō′nĭ-tĭsh′ən) also **pho·net·i·cist** (fə-nĕt′ĭ-sĭst) *n. Linguistics.* An expert in phonetics.

pho·net·ics (fə-nĕt′ĭks) *n. (used with a sing. verb). Abbr.* **phon.** *Linguistics.* **1.** The branch of linguistics that deals with the sounds of speech and their production, combination, description, and representation by written symbols. **2.** The system of sounds of a particular language.

pho·ney (fō′nē) *adj. & n.* Variant of **phony.**

phon·ic (fŏn′ĭk) *adj. Linguistics.* Of, relating to, or having the nature of sound, especially speech sounds. **—phon′i·cal·ly** *adv.*

phon·ics (fŏn′ĭks) *n. (used with a sing. verb).* **1.** A method of teaching elementary reading and spelling based on the phonetic interpretation of ordinary spelling. **2.** Phonetics.

pho·no (fō′nō) *n., pl.* **-nos.** *Informal.* A phonograph.

phono– or **phon–** *pref.* Sound; voice; speech: *phonology.* [Greek *phōno-,* from *phōnē,* sound, voice. See **bhā-**[2] in Appendix.]

phonograph

pho·no·car·di·o·gram (fō′nə-kär′dē-ə-grăm′) *n.* A graphic record of heart sounds and murmurs that is produced by a phonocardiograph.

pho·no·car·di·o·graph (fō′nə-kär′dē-ə-grăf′) *n.* An instrument consisting of microphones and recording equipment used to monitor and record heart sounds and murmurs. **—pho′no·car′di·o·graph′ic** *adj.* **—pho′no·car′di·og′ra·phy** (-ŏg′rə-fē) *n.*

pho·no·gram (fō′nə-grăm′) *n. Linguistics.* A character or symbol, as in a phonetic alphabet, representing a word or phoneme in speech. **—pho′no·gram′ic, pho′no·gram′mic** *adj.* **—pho′no·gram′i·cal·ly, pho′no·gram′mi·cal·ly** *adv.*

pho·no·graph (fō′nə-grăf′) *n.* A machine that reproduces sound by means of a stylus in contact with a grooved rotating disk. **—pho′no·graph′ic** *adj.* **—pho′no·graph′i·cal·ly** *adv.*

WORD HISTORY: In considering the makeup of the word *phonograph* or the related word *gramophone,* one has no difficulty understanding why they contain *phono–* or *–phone,* both going back to Greek *phōnē,* "sound, voice." Why, however, do these words contain *–graph* and *gram–,* which have to do with writing, going back to Greek *graphein,* "to write," and Greek *gramma,* "something written, letter of the alphabet," respectively? *Gramophone* is in fact simply an inversion of the earlier *phonogram,* the more important word to explain therefore. Both *phonogram* and *phonograph* were first used to denote characters that represented speech sounds, *phonograph* being found in such a use earlier (1835–1840) than *phonogram* (1860). But in the second half of the 19th century sounds were reproduced in ways other than writing. The earliest device to be called a *phonograph* was a machine that picked up sound vibrations by means of a membrane and recorded them with a point that traced them on a cylinder. Thomas Edison's famous device was also known as the *phonograph* (first reference found in 1877, the year of its invention); it too used the principle of tracing sound on a cylinder. After this the word *phonogram,* probably under the influence of the word *telegram,* was used to refer to a sound recording made by a phonograph (first such use found in 1879), and in 1884 the *gramophone,* whose name was formed by inverting the term *phonogram,* was patented by Emile Berliner.

pho·nog·ra·phy (fə-nŏg′rə-fē, fō-) *n.* **1.** *Linguistics.* The science or practice of transcribing speech by means of symbols representing elements of sound; phonetic transcription. **2.** A system of shorthand based on phonetic transcription. **—pho·nog′ra·pher, pho·nog′ra·phist** *n.*

pho·no·lite (fō′nə-līt′) *n.* A light-colored volcanic rock composed largely of feldspars. **—pho′no·lit′ic** (-lĭt′ĭk) *adj.*

pho·nol·o·gy (fə-nŏl′ə-jē, fō-) *n., pl.* **-gies.** *Abbr.* **phon.** *Linguistics.* **1.** The study of speech sounds in language or a language with reference to their distribution and patterning and to tacit rules governing pronunciation. **2.** The sound system of a language: *the phonology of English.* **—pho·no·log′ic** (fō′nə-lŏj′ĭk), **pho′no·log′i·cal** (-ĭ-kəl) *adj.* **—pho′no·log′i·cal·ly** *adv.* **—pho·nol′o·gist** *n.*

pho·non (fō′nŏn′) *n. Physics.* The quantum of acoustic or vibrational energy, considered a discrete particle and used especially in mathematical models to calculate thermal and vibrational properties of solids.

pho·no·re·cep·tion (fō′nō-rĭ-sĕp′shən) *n.* Perception of or response to sound waves. **—pho′no·re·cep′tor** (-tər) *n.*

pho·no·scope (fō′nə-skōp′) *n.* A device that produces a visible display of the mechanical properties of a sounding body, especially of musical instruments.

pho·no·type (fō′nə-tīp′) *n.* **1.** A phonetic symbol used in printing. **2.** Text printed in phonetic symbols. **—pho′no·typ′ic** (fō′nə-tĭp′ĭk), **pho′no·typ′i·cal** (-ĭ-kəl) *adj.* **—pho′no·typ′i·cal·ly** *adv.*

pho·no·typ·y (fō′nə-tī′pē) *n. Linguistics.* The practice of transcribing speech sounds by means of phonetic symbols. **—pho′no·typ′ist** *n.*

pho·ny also **pho·ney** (fō′nē) *—adj.* **-ni·er, -ni·est. 1.a.** Not genuine or real; counterfeit: *a phony credit card.* **b.** False; spurious: *a phony name.* **2.** Not truthful; deceptive: *a phony excuse.* **3.a.** Insincere or hypocritical. **b.** Giving a false impression of truth or authenticity. *—n., pl.* **-nies** also **-neys. 1.** Something not genuine; a fake. **2.a.** One who is insincere or pretentious. **b.** An impostor; a hypocrite. [Alteration of *fawney,* gilt brass ring used by swindlers, from Irish Gaelic *fáinne,* ring, from Old Irish.] **—pho′ni·ly** *adv.* **—pho′ni·ness** *n.*

–phony *suff.* Sound: *telephony.* [Greek *-phōnia,* from *phōnē,* sound, voice. See **bhā-**[2] in Appendix.]

phoo·ey (fo͞o′ē) *interj.* Used to express disgust, disbelief, or contempt.

pho·rate (fôr′āt′, fōr′-) *n.* A toxic liquid, $C_7H_{17}O_2PS_3$, used as an insecticide especially in soil treatment. [From chemical name *(phos)phor(odithio)ate* : PHOSPHORUS + *dithioate* (DI–[1] + THIO– + –ATE[2]).]

–phore *suff.* Bearer; carrier: *chromatophore.* [From Greek *-phoros,* bearing, from *pherein,* to carry. See **bher-**[1] in Appendix.]

–phoresis *suff.* Transmission: *electrophoresis.* [From Greek *phorēsis,* a carrying, from *phorein,* frequentative of *pherein,* to bear. See **bher-**[1] in Appendix.]

phor·e·sy (fôr′ĭ-sē) *n.* A symbiotic relationship, especially among arthropods and some fishes, in which one organism transports another organism of a different species. [New Latin *phorēsia,* from Greek *phorēsis,* a carrying. See –PHORESIS.]

pho·ro·nid (fə-rō′nĭd) *n.* Any of the small, wormlike marine animals of the phylum Phoronida, inhabiting a chitinous tube and having a U-shaped digestive tract. **—phoronid** *adj.* Of or belonging to the phylum Phoronida. [From New Latin *Phoronida,* phylum name, from *Phorōnis,* type genus, probably from Latin, Phoronean, Argive (name of Io, priestess of Argos), from *Phorōneus,* son of Inachus, king of Argos, from Greek.]

–phorous *suff.* Bearing: *gonophorous.* [From Greek *-phoros,* from *pherein,* to carry. See **bher-**[1] in Appendix.]

phos– *pref.* Light: *phosgene.* [From Greek *phōs,* light. See **bhā-**[1] in Appendix.]

phos·gene (fŏs′jēn′, fŏz′-) *n.* A colorless volatile liquid or gas, $COCl_2$, used as a poison gas and in making glass, dyes, resins, and plastics.

phosph– *pref.* Variant of **phospho–.**

phos·pham·i·don (fŏs-făm′ĭ-dŏn′) *n.* A colorless insecticide, $C_{10}H_{19}ClNO_5P$, used to control mites, beetles, aphids, and other plant pests. [PHOSPH(ATE) + AMID(E) + –ON[3].]

phos·pha·tase (fŏs′fə-tās′, -tāz′) *n.* Any of numerous enzymes that catalyze the hydrolysis of esters of phosphoric acid and are important in the absorption and metabolism of carbohydrates, nucleotides, and phospholipids and in the calcification of bone. [PHOSPHAT(E) + –ASE.]

♦ **phos·phate** (fŏs′fāt′) *n.* **1.** A salt or an ester of phosphoric acid. **2.** A fertilizer containing phosphorus compounds. **3.** *Chicago.* A soda fountain drink made by blending carbonated water with flavored syrup. [PHOSPH(O)– + –ATE[2].] **—phos·phat′ic** (fŏs-făt′ĭk) *adj.*

phosphate rock *n.* Any of various rocks composed largely of phosphate minerals, especially apatite, used as fertilizer and as a source of phosphorous compounds.

phos·pha·tide (fŏs′fə-tīd′) *n.* See **phospholipid.** [PHOSPHAT(E) + –IDE.] **—phos′pha·tid′ic** (-tĭd′ĭk) *adj.*

phos·pha·tize (fŏs′fə-tīz′) *tr.v.* **-tized, -tiz·ing, -tiz·es. 1.** To change into phosphates or a phosphate. **2.** To treat with phosphate or phosphoric acid. **—phos′pha·ti·za′tion** (-tĭ-zā′shən) *n.*

phos·pha·tu·ri·a (fŏs′fə-to͝or′ē-ə, -tyo͝or′-) *n.* An excess of phosphates in the urine. [PHOSPHAT(E) + –URIA.] **—phos′pha·tu′ric** *adj.*

phos·phene (fŏs′fēn′) *n.* A sensation of light caused by excitation of the retina by mechanical or electrical means rather than by light, as when the eyeballs are pressed through closed lids.

[French *phosphène* : Greek *phōs,* light; see PHOS– + Greek *phainein,* to cause to appear, to show; see **bhā-**[1] in Appendix.]

phos·phide (fŏs′fīd′) also **phos·phid** (-fĭd) *n.* A compound of phosphorus and a more electropositive element or radical.

phos·phine (fŏs′fēn′) also **phos·phin** (-fĭn) *n.* **1.** A colorless, spontaneously flammable poisonous gas, PH_3, having a fishy odor and used as a doping agent for solid-state components. **2.** Any of several organic compounds having the structure of an amine but with phosphorus in place of nitrogen.

phos·phite (fŏs′fīt′) *n.* A salt or an ester of phosphorous acid.

phospho– or **phosph–** *pref.* **1.** Phosphorus: *phosphine.* **2.** Phosphate: *phospholipid.* [From PHOSPHORUS.]

phos·pho·cre·a·tine (fŏs′fō-krē′ə-tēn′) also **phos·pho·cre·a·tin** (-tĭn) *n.* An organic compound, $C_4H_{10}N_3O_5P$, found in muscle tissue and capable of storing and providing energy for muscular contraction. Also called *creatine phosphate.*

phos·pho·fruc·to·ki·nase (fŏs′fō-frŭk′tō-kī′nās, -frŏŏk′-) *n.* A glycolytic enzyme that catalyzes the phosphorylation of fructose phosphate. [PHOSPHO– + Latin *fructus,* fruit; see FRUIT + KINASE.]

phos·pho·lip·id (fŏs′fō-lĭp′ĭd) *n.* Any of various phosphorous-containing lipids, such as lecithin and cephalin, that are composed mainly of fatty acids, a phosphate group, and a simple organic molecule. Also called *phosphatide.*

phos·pho·ni·um (fŏs-fō′nē-əm) *n.* A univalent radical, PH_4, derived from phosphine. [PHOSPH(O)– + (AMM)ONIUM.]

phos·pho·pro·tein (fŏs′fō-prō′tēn′, -tē-ĭn) *n.* Any of a group of proteins, such as casein, containing chemically bound phosphoric acid.

phos·phor (fŏs′fər, -fôr′) *n.* **1.** A substance that exhibits phosphorescence. **2.** The phosphorescent coating on the inside of the screen of a cathode-ray tube. [Latin *Phōsphorus,* the morning star. See PHOSPHORUS.]

phosphor bronze *n.* A hard, strong, corrosion-resistant bronze containing tin and a small amount of phosphorus, used in machine parts, springs, and fine tubing.

phos·pho·resce (fŏs′fə-rĕs′) *intr.v.* **-resced, -resc·ing, -resc·es.** To persist in emitting light, unaccompanied by sensible heat or combustion, after exposure to and removal of a source of radiation. [Probably back-formation from PHOSPHORESCENT.]

phos·pho·res·cence (fŏs′fə-rĕs′əns) *n.* **1.** Persistent emission of light following exposure to and removal of incident radiation. **2.** Emission of light without burning or by very slow burning without appreciable heat, as from the slow oxidation of phosphorous: *"He saw the phosphorescence of the Gulf weed in the water"* (Ernest Hemingway). **—phos′pho·res′cent** *adj.* **—phos′pho·res′cent·ly** *adv.*

phos·phor·ic (fŏs-fôr′ĭk, -fŏr′-) *adj.* Of, relating to, or containing phosphorus, especially with a valence of 5 or a valence higher than that of a comparable phosphorous compound.

phosphoric acid *n.* A clear colorless liquid, H_3PO_4, used in fertilizers, detergents, food flavoring, and pharmaceuticals.

phos·pho·rism (fŏs′fə-rĭz′əm) *n.* Chronic phosphorus poisoning.

phos·pho·rite (fŏs′fə-rīt′) *n.* A sedimentary rock consisting predominantly of apatite and other phosphates. [PHOSPHOR(US) + –ITE[1].]

phos·pho·rous (fŏs′fər-əs, fŏs-fôr′əs, -fōr′-) *adj.* Of, relating to, or containing phosphorus, especially with a valence of 3 or a valence lower than that of a comparable phosphoric compound.

phosphorous acid *n.* A white or yellowish hygroscopic crystalline solid, H_3PO_3, used as a reducing agent and to produce phosphite salts.

phos·pho·rus (fŏs′fər-əs) *n.* **1.** *Symbol* **P** A highly reactive, poisonous, nonmetallic element occurring naturally in phosphates, especially apatite, and existing in three allotropic forms, white (or sometimes yellow), red, and black. An essential constituent of protoplasm, it is used in safety matches, pyrotechnics, incendiary shells, and fertilizers and to protect metal surfaces from corrosion. Atomic number 15; atomic weight 30.9738; melting point (white) 44.1°C; boiling point 280°C; specific gravity (white) 1.82; valence 3, 5. See table at **element.** **2.** A phosphorescent substance. [Latin *Phōsphorus,* morning star, from Greek, bringing light, morning star : *phōs,* light; see **bhā-**[1] in Appendix + *-phoros,* -phorous.]

phos·pho·ryl·ase (fŏs′fər-ə-lās′, -lāz′) *n.* An enzyme that catalyzes the production of glucose phosphate from glycogen and inorganic phosphate.

phos·pho·ryl·ate (fŏs′fər-ə-lāt′) *tr.v.* **-at·ed, -at·ing, -ates.** To add a phosphate group to (an organic molecule). **—phos′pho·ryl·a′tion** *n.* **—phos′pho·ryl·a′tive** *adj.*

phot (fōt) *n. Physics.* A unit of illumination equal to one lumen per square centimeter. [Greek *phōs, phōt-,* light. See **bhā-**[1] in Appendix.]

phot– *pref.* Variant of **photo–.**

pho·tic (fō′tĭk) *adj.* **1.** Of or relating to light. **2.** Penetrated by or receiving light. **3.** Designating or relating to the layer of a body of water that is penetrated by sufficient sunlight for photosynthesis: *the photic zone of the ocean.*

pho·to (fō′tō) *Informal. n., pl.* **-tos.** A photograph. **—photo** *tr. & intr.v.* **-toed, -to·ing, -tos.** To photograph or take photographs.

photo– or **phot–** *pref.* **1.** Light; radiant energy: *photosynthesis.* **2.** Photographic: *photomontage.* **3.** Photoelectric: *photoemission.* [Greek *phōto-,* from *phōs, phōt-.* See **bhā-**[1] in Appendix.]

pho·to·ac·tive (fō′tō-ăk′tĭv) *adj.* **1.** Capable of responding to light photoelectrically. **2.** Capable of responding to sunlight or ultraviolet radiation by chemical reaction. **—pho′to·ac·tiv′i·ty** *n.*

pho·to·au·to·troph (fō′tō-ô′tə-trŏf′, -trōf′) *n.* An organism capable of synthesizing its own food from inorganic substances using light as an energy source. Green plants and photosynthetic bacteria are photoautotrophs. **—pho′to·au′to·troph′ic** *adj.* **—pho′to·au′to·troph′i·cal·ly** *adv.*

pho·to·bi·ol·o·gy (fō′tō-bī-ŏl′ə-jē) *n.* The study of the effects of light on living organisms and biological processes. **—pho′to·bi′o·log′ic** (-bī′ə-lŏj′ĭk), **pho′to·bi′o·log′i·cal** (-ĭ-kəl) *adj.*

pho·to·bi·ot·ic (fō′tō-bī-ŏt′ĭk) *adj. Biology.* Depending on light for life and growth.

pho·to·cell (fō′tō-sĕl′) *n.* A photoelectric cell.

photochemical smog *n.* Air pollution produced by the action of sunlight on hydrocarbons, nitrogen oxides, and other pollutants.

pho·to·chem·is·try (fō′tō-kĕm′ĭ-strē) *n.* The chemistry of the effects of light on chemical systems. **—pho′to·chem′i·cal** (-ĭ-kəl) *adj.* **—pho′to·chem′i·cal·ly** *adv.*

pho·to·co·ag·u·la·tion (fō′tō-kō-ăg′yə-lā′shən) *n.* Surgical coagulation of tissue by means of intense light energy, such as a laser beam, performed to destroy abnormal tissues or to form adhesive scars, especially in ophthalmology. **—pho′to·co·ag′u·late** *v.*

pho·to·com·pose (fō′tō-kəm-pōz′) *tr.v.* **-posed, -pos·ing, -pos·es.** *Printing.* To prepare (written matter) for printing by photocomposition. **—pho′to·com·pos′er** *n.*

pho·to·com·po·si·tion (fō′tō-kŏm′pə-zĭsh′ən) *n. Printing.* The preparation of manuscript for printing by the projection of images of type characters on photographic film, which is then used to make printing plates. Also called *phototypesetting.*

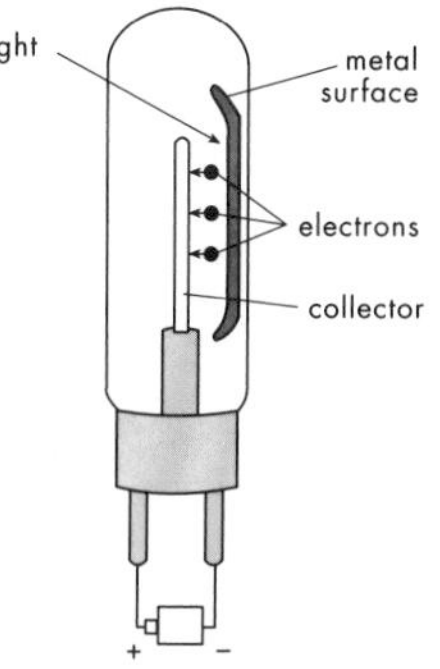

photoelectric cell

pho·to·con·duc·tiv·i·ty (fō′tō-kŏn′dŭk-tĭv′ĭ-tē) *n., pl.* **-ties.** Electrical conductivity affected by exposure to light. **—pho′to·con·duc′tion** *n.* **—pho′to·con·duc′tive** *adj.*

pho·to·cop·i·er (fō′tə-kŏp′ē-ər) *n.* A machine for photographically reproducing written, printed, or graphic material, especially by xerography.

pho·to·cop·y (fō′tə-kŏp′ē) *tr.v.* **-cop·ied, -cop·y·ing, -cop·ies.** To make a photographic reproduction of (printed or graphic material), especially by xerography. **—photocopy** *n., pl.* **-cop·ies.** A photographic or xerographic reproduction.

pho·to·cur·rent (fō′tō-kûr′ənt, -kŭr′-) *n.* An electric current produced by illumination of a photoelectric material.

pho·to·de·com·po·si·tion (fō′tō-dē-kŏm′pə-zĭsh′ən) *n.* Chemical breakdown caused by radiant energy.

pho·to·de·grad·a·ble (fō′tō-dĭ-grā′də-bəl) *adj.* Capable of being chemically broken down by light: *photodegradable plastic containers.*

pho·to·dis·in·te·gra·tion (fō′tō-dĭs-ĭn′tĭ-grā′shən) *n.* Nuclear disintegration or transformation caused by absorption of high-energy radiation, as of gamma rays.

pho·to·dra·ma (fō′tə-drä′mə, -drăm′ə) *n.* See **photoplay.**

pho·to·du·pli·cate (fō′tō-dōō′plĭ-kāt′, -dyōō′-) *tr.v.* **-cat·ed, -cat·ing, -cates.** To photocopy. **—photoduplicate** (-kĭt) *n.* A photocopy. **—pho′to·du′pli·ca′tion** *n.*

pho·to·dy·nam·ic (fō′tō-dī-năm′ĭk) *adj.* **1.** Of or relating to the energy of light. **2.** Enhancing the effects of or inducing a toxic reaction to light, especially to ultraviolet light. **—pho′to·dy·nam′i·cal·ly** *adv.*

pho·to·dy·nam·ics (fō′tō-dī-năm′ĭks) *n. (used with a sing. verb).* The science that deals with the activating effects of light on living organisms.

pho·to·e·lec·tric (fō′tō-ĭ-lĕk′trĭk) also **pho·to·e·lec·tri·cal** (-trĭ-kəl) *adj.* Of or relating to the electric effects, especially increased conductivity, caused by light. **—pho′to·e·lec′tri·cal·ly** *adv.*

photoelectric cell *n.* An electronic device having an electrical output that varies in response to incident radiation, especially to visible light. Also called *electric eye.*

photoelectric effect *n.* Ejection of electrons from a substance by incident electromagnetic radiation, especially by visible light.

pho·to·e·lec·tron (fō′tō-ĭ-lĕk′trŏn′) *n.* An electron released or ejected from a substance by photoelectric effect.

pho·to·e·mis·sion (fō′tō-ĭ-mĭsh′ən) *n.* Emission of photoelectrons, especially from metallic surfaces.

pho·to·en·grave (fō′tō-ĕn-grāv′) *tr.v.* **-graved, -grav·ing, -graves.** To reproduce by photoengraving; make a photoengraving of. **—pho′to·en·grav′er** *n.*

pho·to·en·grav·ing (fō′tō-ĕn-grā′vĭng) *n.* **1.** The process of reproducing graphic material by transferring the image photographically to a plate or another surface, which is then etched for printing. **2.** A plate prepared by this process. **3.** A reproduction made by this process.

pho·to-es·say also **pho·to es·say** (fō′tō-ĕs′ā′) *n.* A story

ă pat	oi boy
ā pay	ou out
âr care	ŏŏ took
ä father	ōō boot
ĕ pet	ŭ cut
ē be	ûr urge
ĭ pit	th thin
ī pie	*th* this
îr pier	hw which
ŏ pot	zh vision
ō toe	ə about, item
ô paw	♦ regionalism

Stress marks: **′** (primary); ′ (secondary), as in **dictionary** (dĭk′shə-nĕr′ē)

told chiefly through photographs usually supplemented by a written commentary. —**pho′to·es′say·ist** *n.*

photo finish *n.* **1.** *Sports.* A race in which the leading contestants cross the finish line so close together that the winner must be determined by a photograph taken at the moment of crossing. **2.** *Informal.* An extremely close competition.

pho·to·fin·ish·ing (fō′tō-fĭn′ĭ-shĭng) *n.* The act or business of developing camera films and printing photographs for customers. —**pho′to·fin′ish·er** *n.*

pho·to·flash (fō′tō-flăsh′) *n.* See **flashbulb.**

pho·to·flood (fō′tō-flŭd′) *n.* A reusable electric lamp that produces a bright continuous light for photographic illumination. Also called *photoflood lamp.*

pho·to·fluor·o·gram (fō′tə-flo͝or′ə-grăm′, -flôr′-, -flōr′-) *n.* A photograph made by photofluorography.

pho·to·fluor·og·ra·phy (fō′tō-flo͝o-rŏg′rə-fē, -flô-, -flō-) *n.* The photographic record of x-ray images produced by a flouroscope. Also called *fluorography.* —**pho′to·fluor·o·graph′ic** (-flo͝or′ə-grăf′ĭk, -flôr′-, -flōr′-) *adj.*

pho·tog (fə-tŏg′) *n. Informal.* A person who takes photographs, especially as a profession; a photographer.

photog. *abbr.* Photograph; photographic; photography.

pho·to·gel·a·tin process (fō′tō-jĕl′ə-tĭn) *n.* See **collotype** (sense 1).

pho·to·gene (fō′tə-jēn′) *n.* See **afterimage.**

pho·to·gen·ic (fō′tə-jĕn′ĭk) *adj.* **1.** Attractive as a subject for photography. **2.** *Biology.* Producing or emitting light; phosphorescent: *photogenic bacteria.* **3.** Caused or produced by light: *photogenic seizures.* —**pho′to·gen′i·cal·ly** *adv.*

pho·to·gram (fō′tə-grăm′) *n.* **1.** An image produced without a camera by placing an object in contact with film or photosensitive paper and exposing it to light. **2.** A photograph.

pho·to·gram·me·try (fō′tə-grăm′ĭ-trē) *n.* **1.** The process of making maps or scale drawings from photographs, especially aerial photographs. **2.** The process of making precise measurements by means of photography. —**pho′to·gram·met′ric** (-grə-mĕt′rĭk) *adj.* —**pho′to·gram′me·trist** *n.*

pho·to·graph (fō′tə-grăf′) *n. Abbr.* **photog.** An image, especially a positive print, recorded by a camera and reproduced on a photosensitive surface. —**photograph** *v.* **-graphed, -graph·ing, -graphs.** —*tr.* To take a photograph of. —*intr.* **1.** To practice photography. **2.** To be the subject for photographs: *She photographs well.* —**pho′to·graph′a·ble** *adj.* —**pho·tog′ra·pher** (fə-tŏg′rə-fər) *n.*

pho·to·graph·ic (fō′tə-grăf′ĭk) also **pho·to·graph·i·cal** (-ĭ-kəl) *adj. Abbr.* **photog. 1.** Of, relating to, or consisting of photography or a photograph. **2.** Used in photography: *a photographic lens.* **3.** Resembling a photograph, especially representing or simulating something with great accuracy and fidelity of detail. **4.** Capable of forming accurate and lasting impressions: *a photographic memory.* —**pho′to·graph′i·cal·ly** *adv.*

pho·tog·ra·phy (fə-tŏg′rə-fē) *n. Abbr.* **photog. 1.** The art or process of producing images of objects on photosensitive surfaces. **2.** The art, practice, or occupation of taking and printing photographs. **3.** A body of photographs.

pho·to·gra·vure (fō′tə-grə-vyo͝or′) *n.* The process of printing from an intaglio plate, etched according to a photographic image.

pho·to·he·li·o·graph (fō′tō-hē′lē-ə-grăf′) *n.* A telescope equipped to photograph the sun.

pho·to·jour·nal·ism (fō′tō-jûr′nə-lĭz′əm) *n.* Journalism in which a news story is presented primarily through photographs with supplementary written copy. —**pho′to·jour′nal·ist** *n.* —**pho′to·jour′nal·is′tic** *adj.*

pho·to·ki·ne·sis (fō′tō-kĭ-nē′sĭs, -kī-) *n.* Movement as a response to light. —**pho′to·ki·net′ic** (-nĕt′ĭk) *adj.*

pho·to·lith·o·graph (fō′tō-lĭth′ə-grăf′) *n.* A picture made by photolithography. —**photolithograph** *tr.v.* **-graphed, -graph·ing, -graphs.** To reproduce by means of photolithography; make a photolithograph of. —**pho′to·li·thog′ra·pher** (-lĭ-thŏg′rə-fər) *n.*

pho·to·li·thog·ra·phy (fō′tō-lĭ-thŏg′rə-fē) *n.* A planographic printing process using plates made according to a photographic image. —**pho′to·lith′o·graph′ic** (-lĭth′ə-grăf′ĭk) *adj.* —**pho′to·lith′o·graph′i·cal·ly** *adv.*

pho·tol·y·sis (fō-tŏl′ĭ-sĭs) *n.* Chemical decomposition induced by light or other radiant energy. —**pho′to·lyt′ic** (fō′-tə-lĭt′ĭk) *adj.* —**pho′to·lyt′i·cal·ly** *adv.*

photom. *abbr. Physics.* Photometry.

pho·to·map (fō′tə-măp′) *n.* A map made by superimposing orienting data and markings on an aerial photograph. —**photomap** *v.* **-mapped, -map·ping, -maps.** —*tr.* To make a photomap of. —*intr.* To make a photomap.

pho·to·me·chan·i·cal (fō′tō-mĭ-kăn′ĭ-kəl) *adj.* Of, relating to, or involving any of various methods by which plates are prepared for printing by means of photography. —**pho′to·me·chan′i·cal·ly** *adv.*

pho·tom·e·ter (fō-tŏm′ĭ-tər) *n.* An instrument for measuring a property of light, especially luminous intensity or flux.

pho·tom·e·try (fō-tŏm′ĭ-trē) *n. Abbr.* **photom.** *Physics.* Measurement of the properties of light, especially luminous intensity. —**pho′to·met′ric** (fō′tə-mĕt′rĭk), **pho′to·met′ri·cal** (-rĭ-kəl) *adj.* —**pho′to·met′ri·cal·ly** *adv.* —**pho·tom′e·trist** *n.*

pho·to·mi·cro·graph (fō′tō-mī′krə-grăf′) *n.* A photograph made through a microscope. Also called *microphotograph.* —**photomicrograph** *tr.v.* **-graphed, -graph·ing, -graphs.** To photograph (an object) through a microscope. —**pho′to·mi·crog′ra·pher** (-mī-krŏg′rə-fər) *n.* —**pho′to·mi′cro·graph′ic** *adj.* —**pho′to·mi·crog′ra·phy** *n.*

pho·to·mi·cro·scope (fō′tō-mī′krə-skōp′) *n.* An instrument consisting of a microscope, camera apparatus, and light source used for making photomicrographs. —**pho′to·mi′cro·scop′ic** (-skŏp′ĭk) *adj.*

pho·to·mon·tage (fō′tō-mŏn-täzh′, -môn-) *n.* **1.** The technique of making a picture by assembling pieces of photographs, often in combination with other types of graphic material. **2.** The composite picture produced by this technique.

pho·to·mu·ral (fō′tō-myo͝or′əl) *n.* A greatly enlarged photograph or series of photographs placed on a wall especially as decoration. —**pho′to·mu′ral·ist** *n.*

pho·ton (fō′tŏn′) *n.* **1.** The quantum of electromagnetic energy, generally regarded as a discrete particle having zero mass, no electric charge, and an indefinitely long lifetime. See table at **subatomic particle. 2.** A unit of retinal illumination, equal to the amount of light that reaches the retina through 1 square millimeter of pupil area from a surface having a brightness of 1 candela per square meter. —**pho·ton′ic** *adj.*

pho·to·neg·a·tive (fō′tō-nĕg′ə-tĭv) *adj. Biology.* Repelled by light, exhibiting a negative phototactic or phototropic response.

pho·to·nu·cle·ar (fō′tō-no͞o′klē-ər, -nyo͞o′-) *adj.* Of or relating to a nuclear reaction induced by photons.

pho·to-off·set (fō′tō-ôf′sĕt′, -ŏf′-) *n.* A method of offset printing using photomechanical plates.

photo opportunity *n.* A brief period reserved for the press to photograph the participants in a newsworthy event.

pho·to·pe·ri·od (fō′tō-pîr′ē-əd) *n.* The duration of an organism's daily exposure to light, considered especially with regard to the effect of the exposure on growth and development. —**pho′to·pe′ri·od′ic** (-ŏd′ĭk), **pho′to·pe′ri·od′i·cal** (-ĭ-kəl) *adj.*

pho·to·pe·ri·od·ism (fō′tō-pîr′ē-ə-dĭz′əm) also **pho·to·pe·ri·o·dic·i·ty** (-dĭs′ĭ-tē) *n., pl.* **-isms** also **-i·ties.** The response of an organism to changes in its photoperiod, especially as indicated by vital processes.

pho·to·phil·ic (fō′tə-fĭl′ĭk) also **pho·toph·i·lous** (fō-tŏf′-ə-ləs) *adj. Biology.* Growing or functioning best in strong light.

pho·to·pho·bi·a (fō′tə-fō′bē-ə) *n.* **1.** An abnormal sensitivity to or intolerance of light, especially by the eyes, as may be caused by eye inflammation, lack of pigmentation in the iris, or various diseases. **2.** An abnormal or irrational fear of light.

pho·to·pho·bic (fō′tə-fō′bĭk) *adj.* **1.** Exhibiting photophobia. **2.** Avoiding light. **3.** Growing best in the absence of light; photonegative.

pho·to·phore (fō′tə-fôr′, -fōr′) *n.* A light-producing organ found especially in marine fishes that emits light from specialized structures or derives light from symbiotic luminescent bacteria.

pho·to·phos·phor·y·la·tion (fō′tō-fŏs′fôr-ə-lā′shən, -fər-) *n.* Phosphorylation induced by radiant energy in photosynthesis.

pho·to·pi·a (fō-tō′pē-ə) *n.* Vision in bright light, mediated by cone cells of the retina; daylight vision. —**pho·to′pic** (-tō′pĭk, -tŏp′ĭk) *adj.*

pho·to·play (fō′tə-plā′) *n.* A play filmed or arranged for filming as a movie. Also called *photodrama.*

pho·to·pos·i·tive (fō′tō-pŏz′ĭ-tĭv) *adj. Biology.* Drawn to light; exhibiting a positive phototactic or phototropic response.

pho·to·prod·uct (fō′tō-prŏd′əkt) *n.* The product of a photochemical reaction.

pho·to·re·ac·tion (fō′tō-rē-ăk′shən) *n.* A photochemical reaction.

pho·to-re·al·ism (fō′tō-rē′ə-lĭz′əm) *n.* A style of painting that resembles photography in its meticulous attention to realistic detail. —**pho′to-re′al·ist** *adj.* & *n.* —**pho′to-re′al·is′tic** *adj.*

pho·to·re·cep·tion (fō′tō-rĭ-sĕp′shən) *n.* The detection, absorption, and use of light, as for vision in animals or phototropism and photosynthesis in plants. —**pho′to·re·cep′tive** *adj.*

pho·to·re·cep·tor (fō′tō-rĭ-sĕp′tər) *n.* A nerve ending, cell, or group of cells specialized to sense or receive light.

pho·to·re·con·nais·sance (fō′tō-rĭ-kŏn′ə-səns, -zəns) *n.* Photographic aerial reconnaissance especially of military targets.

pho·to·res·pi·ra·tion (fō′tō-rĕs′pə-rā′shən) *n.* Oxidation of carbohydrates in plants with the release of carbon dioxide during photosynthesis.

pho·to·sen·si·tive (fō′tō-sĕn′sĭ-tĭv) *adj.* **1.** Sensitive or responsive to light or other radiant energy. **2.** *Medicine* Abnormally sensitive or reactive to light.

pho·to·sen·si·tiv·i·ty (fō′tō-sĕn′sĭ-tĭv′ĭ-tē) *n., pl.* **-ties. 1.** Sensitivity or responsiveness to light. **2.** *Medicine.* An abnormally heightened response, especially of the skin, to sunlight or ultraviolet radiation, caused by certain disorders or chemicals and characterized by a toxic or allergic reaction.

pho·to·sen·si·ti·za·tion (fō′tō-sĕn′sĭ-tĭ-zā′shən) *n.* The act or process of inducing photosensitivity.

pho·to·sen·si·tize (fō′tō-sĕn′sĭ-tīz′) *tr.v.* **-tized, -tiz·ing, -tiz·es.** To make (an organism, a cell, or a substance) photosensitive.

pho·to·set (fō′tō-sĕt′) *tr.v.* **-set, -set·ting, -sets.** *Printing.* To photocompose. **—pho′to·set′ter** *n.*

pho·to·sphere (fō′tə-sfîr′) *n.* The visible outer layer of a star, especially of the sun. **—pho′to·spher′ic** (-sfîr′ĭk, -sfĕr′ĭk) *adj.*

Pho·to·stat (fō′tə-stăt′). A trademark used for a photographic device for making positive or negative copies of graphic matter. This trademark often occurs in lowercase in print: *"denying into evidence photostats produced of insurance claims filed for stolen property"* (United States Law Week). *"a framed photostat of the 1901 school-system payroll"* (U.S. News & World Report). *"displayed a photostat copy of a certified letter"* (Los Angeles Times).

pho·to·syn·thate (fō′tō-sĭn′thāt) *n.* A chemical product of photosynthesis.

pho·to·syn·the·sis (fō′tō-sĭn′thĭ-sĭs) *n.* The process in green plants and certain other organisms by which carbohydrates are synthesized from carbon dioxide and water using light as an energy source. Most forms of photosynthesis release oxygen as a byproduct. **—pho′to·syn·thet′ic** (-sĭn-thĕt′ĭk) *adj.* **—pho′to·syn·thet′i·cal·ly** *adv.*

pho·to·syn·the·size (fō′tō-sĭn′thĭ-sīz′) *v.* **-sized, -siz·ing, -siz·es.** *—tr.* To synthesize by the process of photosynthesis. *—intr.* To perform the process of photosynthesis.

pho·to·tax·is (fō′tō-tăk′sĭs) *n.* *Biology.* The movement of an organism or a cell toward or away from a source of light. **—pho′to·tac′tic** (-tăk′tĭk) *adj.* **—pho′to·tac′ti·cal·ly** *adv.*

pho·to·ther·a·py (fō′tō-thĕr′ə-pē) *n., pl.* **-pies.** The treatment of a disorder, especially of the skin, by exposure to light, including ultraviolet and infrared radiation. **—pho′to·ther′a·peu′tic** (-thĕr′ə-pyo͞o′tĭk) *adj.*

pho·tot·o·nus (fō-tŏt′n-əs) *n.* *Biology.* The state of being sensitive to or irritated by light. **—pho′to·ton′ic** (fō′tə-tŏn′ĭk) *adj.*

pho·to·tox·ic (fō′tō-tŏk′sĭk) *adj.* Rendering the skin susceptible to damage by light. Used of certain medications and cosmetics. **—pho′to·tox·ic′i·ty** (-tŏk-sĭs′ĭ-tē) *n.*

pho·to·tran·sis·tor (fō′tō-trăn-zĭs′tər) *n.* A transistor having highly photosensitive electrical characteristics.

pho·to·troph (fō′tə-trŏf′, -trōf′) *n.* A photoautotroph. [PHOTO– + Greek *trophē*, nourishment.] **—pho′to·troph′ic** *adj.* **—pho′to·troph′i·cal·ly** *adv.*

pho·tot·ro·pism (fō-tŏt′rə-pĭz′əm) *n.* Growth or movement of a sessile organism toward or away from a source of light. **—pho′to·tro′pic** (fō′tə-trō′pĭk, -trŏp′ĭk) *adj.* **—pho′to·tro′pi·cal·ly** *adv.*

pho·to·tube (fō′tō-to͞ob′, -tyo͞ob′) *n.* An electron tube with a photosensitive cathode.

pho·to·type·set·ter (fō′tō-tīp′sĕt′ər) *n.* *Printing.* **1.** Any of various machines used in photocomposition. **2.** The operator of one of these machines.

pho·to·type·set·ting (fō′tō-tīp′sĕt′ĭng) *n.* *Printing.* See **photocomposition.**

pho·to·ty·pog·ra·phy (fō′tō-tī-pŏg′rə-fē) *n.* *Printing.* Photomechanical printing that resembles metal typography. **—pho′to·ty′po·graph′ic** (-tī′pə-grăf′ĭk), **pho′to·ty′po·graph′i·cal** (-ĭ-kəl) *adj.* **—pho′to·ty′po·graph′i·cal·ly** *adv.*

pho·to·vol·ta·ic (fō′tō-vŏl-tā′ĭk, -vōl-) *adj.* Capable of producing a voltage when exposed to radiant energy, especially light. **—pho′to·vol·ta′ic** *n.*

photovoltaic cell *n.* See **solar cell.**

phr. *abbr.* Phrase.

phrag·mi·tes (frăg-mī′tēz) *n.* Any of several perennial reeds of the genus *Phragmites* in the grass family, found worldwide in marshes and wetlands and having stems up to nearly 6 meters (20 feet) long. [Latin *phragmitēs*, kind of reed growing in hedges, from Greek *phragmitēs*, fencing in, from *phragma*, fence, from *phrassein*, to fence in.]

phrasal verb *n.* An English verb complex consisting of a verb and one or more following particles and acting as a complete syntactic and semantic unit, as *look up* in *She looked up the word in the dictionary* or *She looked the word up in the dictionary.*

phrase (frāz) *n.* *Abbr.* **phr. 1.** A sequence of words intended to have meaning. **2. a.** A characteristic way or mode of expression. **b.** A brief, apt, and cogent expression. **3.** A word or group of words read or spoken as a unit and separated by pauses or other junctures. **4.** *Grammar.* Two or more words in sequence that form a syntactic unit that is less than a complete sentence. **5.** *Music.* A segment of a composition, usually consisting of four or eight measures. **6.** A series of dance movements forming a unit in a choreographic pattern. **—phrase** *v.* **phrased, phras·ing, phras·es.** *—tr.* **1.** To express orally or in writing: *The speaker phrased several opinions.* **2.** To pace or mark off (something read aloud or spoken) by pauses. **3.** *Music.* **a.** To divide (a passage) into phrases. **b.** To combine (notes) in a phrase. *—intr.* **1.** To make or render phrases, as in reading aloud. **2.** *Music.* To perform a passage with the correct phrasing. [Latin *phrasis*, diction, from Greek, speech, diction, phrase, from *phrazein*, to point out, show. See **gʷhren-** in Appendix.] **—phras′al** *adj.* **—phras′al·ly** *adv.*

phrase book *n.* A book of idiomatic foreign language expressions and their translations.

phrase·mak·er (frāz′mā′kər) *n.* **1.** One, such as a speechwriter, who composes memorable or effective phrases. **2.** One who makes attractive but often meaningless phrases. In this sense, also called *phrasemonger.* **—phrase′mak′ing** *n.*

phrase marker *n.* *Grammar.* In generative grammar, a representation in the form of a tree diagram or labeled brackets of the constituent structure of a sentence.

phrase·mon·ger (frāz′mŭng′gər, -mŏng′-) *n.* See **phrasemaker** (sense 2). **—phrase′mon′ger·ing** *n.*

phra·se·o·gram (frā′zē-ə-grăm′) *n.* A symbol, such as one used in shorthand, that designates a particular phrase.

phra·se·o·graph (frā′zē-ə-grăf′) *n.* A phrase represented by a phraseogram. **—phra′se·o·graph′ic** *adj.*

phra·se·ol·o·gy (frā′zē-ŏl′ə-jē) *n., pl.* **-gies. 1.** The way in which words and phrases are used in speech or writing; style. **2.** A set of expressions used by a particular person or group: *nautical phraseology.* See Synonyms at **diction.** **—phra′se·o·log′i·cal** (-ə-lŏj′ĭ-kəl) *adj.* **—phra′se·ol′o·gist** *n.*

phras·ing (frā′zĭng) *n.* **1.** The act of making phrases. **2.** The manner in which an expression is phrased. See Synonyms at **diction. 3.** *Music.* The manner in which a phrase is rendered or interpreted.

phra·try (frā′trē) *n., pl.* **-tries. 1.** A kinship group constituting an intermediate division in the primitive structure of the Hellenic tribe or phyle, consisting of several patrilinear clans, and surviving in classical times as a territorial subdivision in the political and military organization of the Athenian state. **2.** *Anthropology.* An exogamous subdivision of the tribe, constituting two or more related clans. [Greek *phratria*, from *phratēr, phratr-*, fellow member of a clan. See **bhrāter-** in Appendix.] **—phra′tric** *adj.*

phre·at·ic (frē-ăt′ĭk) *adj.* Of or relating to ground water. [From Greek *phrear, phreat-*, well, spring. See **bhreu-** in Appendix.]

phre·at·o·phyte (frē-ăt′ə-fīt′) *n.* A deep-rooted plant that obtains water from a permanent ground supply or from the water table. **—phre·at′o·phyt′ic** (-fĭt′ĭk) *adj.*

phren. *abbr.* Phrenology.

phren– *pref.* Variant of **phreno–.**

phre·net·ic (frə-nĕt′ĭk) or **phre·net·i·cal** (-ĭ-kəl) *adj.* Variants of **frenetic.**

–phrenia *suff.* Mental disorder: *schizophrenia.* [From Greek *phrēn*, mind. See **gʷhren-** in Appendix.]

phren·ic (frĕn′ĭk, frē′nĭk) *adj.* **1.** Of or relating to the mind. **2.** *Anatomy.* Of or relating to the diaphragm: *the phrenic nerve.*

phre·ni·tis (frĭ-nī′tĭs) *n.* **1.** Inflammation of the diaphragm. **2.** Encephalitis. No longer in scientific use. **—phre·nit′ic** (-nĭt′ĭk) *adj.*

phreno– or **phren–** *pref.* **1.** Mind: *phrenology.* **2.** Diaphragm: *phrenic.* [Greek, from *phrēn, phren-*, diaphragm, midriff, heart, mind. See **gʷhren-** in Appendix.]

phre·nol·o·gy (frĭ-nŏl′ə-jē) *n.* *Abbr.* **phren.** The study of the shape and protuberances of the skull, based on the now discredited belief that they reveal character and mental capacity. **—phren′o·log′ic** (frĕn′ə-lŏj′ĭk, frē′nə-), **phren′o·log′i·cal** (-ĭ-kəl) *adj.* **—phre·nol′o·gist** *n.*

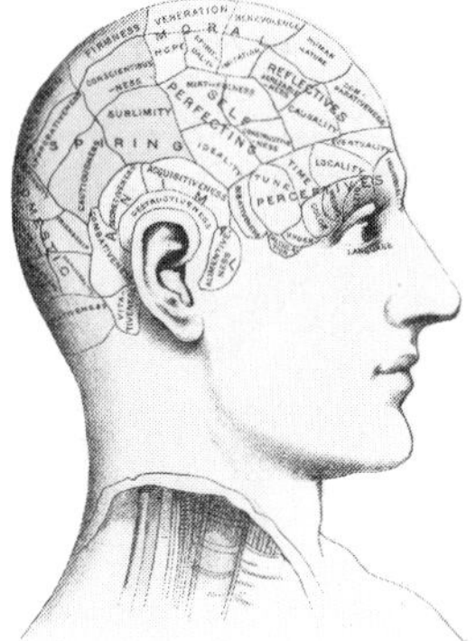

phrenology
Diagram showing the parts of the brain believed to control various personality traits

phren·sy (frĕn′zē) *n. & v.* *Archaic.* Variant of **frenzy.**

Phryg·i·a (frĭj′ē-ə). An ancient region of central Asia Minor in modern-day central Turkey. It was settled c. 1200 B.C. and flourished from the eighth to the sixth century, after which it came under the influence of Lydia, Persia, Greece, Rome, and Byzantium.

Phryg·i·an (frĭj′ē-ən) *adj.* Of or relating to Phrygia or its people, language, or culture. **—Phrygian** *n.* **1.** A native or inhabitant of Phrygia. **2.** The Indo-European language of the Phrygians.

Phrygian cap *n.* See **liberty cap.**

PHS *abbr.* Public Health Service.

phthal·ein also **phthal·eine** (thăl′ēn′, thăl′ē-ĭn, thā′lēn′, thā′lē-ĭn, -fthăl′-) *n.* Any of a group of chemical compounds formed by a reaction of phthalic anhydride with a phenol, from which certain synthetic dyes are derived. [PHTHAL(IC) + –EIN.]

phthal·ic (thăl′ĭk, fthăl′-) *adj.* **1.** Of, relating to, or derived from naphthalene. **2.** Relating to phthalic acid. [Short for *naphthalic acid* : NAPHTHAL(ENE) + –IC.]

phthalic acid *n.* A colorless crystalline organic acid, $C_6H_4(COOH)_2$, prepared from naphthalene and used in the synthesis of dyes, perfumes, and other organic compounds.

phthalic anhydride *n.* A white crystalline compound, $C_6H_4(CO)_2O$, prepared by oxidizing naphthalene and used in the manufacture of phthaleins and other dyes, resins, plasticizers, and insecticides.

phthal·in (thăl′ĭn, fthăl′-) *n.* Any of various colorless compounds derived from the reduction of phthaleins.

phthal·o·cy·a·nine (thăl′ō-sī′ə-nēn′, fthăl′-) *n.* Any of several stable, light-fast, blue or green organic pigments derived from the basic compound $(C_6H_4C_2N)_4N_4$ and used in enamels, printing inks, linoleum, and plastics. [PHTHAL(IC) + CYANINE.]

ă pat	oi boy
ā pay	ou out
âr care	o͝o took
ä father	o͞o boot
ĕ pet	ŭ cut
ē be	ûr urge
ĭ pit	th thin
ī pie	*th* this
îr pier	hw which
ŏ pot	zh vision
ō toe	ə about, item
ô paw	♦ regionalism

Stress marks: **′** (primary); ′ (secondary), as in **dictionary** (dĭk′shə-nĕr′ē)

phthi·ri·a·sis (thĭ-rī′ə-sĭs, thī-) *n.* Infestation with lice, especially crab lice; pediculosis. [Latin *phthīriāsis,* from Greek *phtheiriasis,* from *phtheirian,* to be lousy, from *phtheir,* louse.]

phthis·ic (tĭz′ĭk, thĭz′-) *n.* **1.** Variant of **phthisis. 2.** *Archaic.* Any illness of the lungs or throat, such as asthma or a cough. [Middle English *ptisike,* from Old French *ptisique,* from *phthisicus,* consumptive, from Greek *phthisikos,* from *phthisis,* wasting away, consumption. See PHTHISIS.] **—phthis′ic, phthis′i·cal** *adj.*

phthi·sis (thī′sĭs, tī′-) also **phthis·ic** (tĭz′ĭk, thĭz′-) *n.* **1.** A disease characterized by the wasting away or atrophy of the body or a part of the body. **2.** Tuberculosis of the lungs. No longer in scientific use. [Latin, from Greek, from *phthinein,* to waste away.]

phyco– *pref.* Seaweed; algae: *phycology.* [Greek *phuko-,* from *phukos,* seaweed.]

phy·co·bi·lin (fī′kō-bī′lĭn) *n.* Any of a group of water-soluble proteinaceous pigments that occur in red algae and cyanobacteria. [PHYCO– + Latin *bīlis,* bile + –IN.]

phy·co·cy·a·nin (fī′kō-sī′ə-nĭn) *n.* A blue phycobilin occurring especially in the cells of cyanobacteria.

phy·co·er·y·thrin (fī′kō-ĕr′ĭ-thrĭn) *n.* A red phycobilin occurring especially in the cells of red algae.

phy·col·o·gy (fī-kŏl′ə-jē) *n.* The branch of botany that deals with algae. Also called *algology.* **—phy′co·log′i·cal** (fī′kə-lŏj′ĭ-kəl) *adj.* **—phy·col′o·gist** *n.*

phy·co·my·cete (fī′kō-mī′sēt′, -mī-sēt′) *n.* Any of various fungi that resemble algae, including certain molds and mildews. [From New Latin *Phycomycetes,* class name : PHYCO– + –MYCETE.] **—phy′co·my·ce′tous** *adj.*

phylactery

Phyfe (fīf), **Duncan.** 1768?–1854. Scottish-born American cabinetmaker. His shop was one of the first to use factory methods of furniture construction.

phy·la (fī′lə) *n.* Plural of **phylum.**

phy·lac·ter·y (fĭ-lăk′tə-rē) *n., pl.* **-ies. 1.** *Judaism.* Either of two small leather boxes, each containing strips of parchment inscribed with quotations from the Hebrew Scriptures, one of which is strapped to the forehead and the other to the left arm by Orthodox and Conservative Jewish men during morning worship, except on the Sabbath and holidays. **2.a.** An amulet. **b.** A reminder. [Middle English *filaterie, philacterie,* from Old French *filatiere,* from Late Latin *phylactērium,* from Greek *phulaktērion,* guard's post, safeguard, phylactery, from *phulaktēr,* guard, from *phulax, phulak-*.]

phy·le (fī′lē) *n., pl.* **-lae** (-lē). A large citizens' organization based on kinship, constituting the largest political subdivision of an ancient Greek city-state. [Greek *phulē,* tribe, phyle. See **bheuə-** in Appendix.] **—phy′lic** *adj.*

phy·let·ic (fī-lĕt′ĭk) *adj.* Of or relating to the evolutionary descent and development of a species or group of organisms; phylogenetic. [From Greek *phuletikos,* of or for a tribesman, from *phuletēs,* tribesman, from *phulē,* tribe. See **bheuə-** in Appendix.] **—phy·let′i·cal·ly** *adv.*

phyll– *pref.* Variant of **phyllo–.**

–phyll *suff.* Leaf: *sporophyll.* [From Greek *phullon,* leaf. See PHYLLO–.]

phyl·lite (fĭl′īt′) *n.* A green, gray, or red metamorphic rock, similar to slate but often having a wavy surface and a distinctive micaceous luster. **—phyl·lit′ic** (fĭ-lĭt′ĭk) *adj.*

phyl·lo (fē′lō) *n.* Very thin sheets of pastry dough that make a flaky pastry used especially in Greek dishes. [Modern Greek *phullon,* from Greek, leaf. See PHYLLO–.]

phyllo– or **phyll–** *pref.* Leaf: *phylloid.* [Greek, from *phullon,* leaf. See **bhel-**[3] in Appendix.]

phyl·lo·clade (fĭl′ə-klād′) also **phyl·lo·clad** (-klăd′) *n.* A flattened branch or stem that performs the function of or resembles a leaf, as in the Christmas cactus. [New Latin *phyllocladium* : PHYLLO– + Greek *klados,* branch.]

phyl·lode (fĭl′ōd) also **phyl·lo·di·um** (fĭ-lō′dē-əm) *n., pl.* **-lodes** also **-lo·di·a** (-lō′dē-ə). A flattened leafstalk that functions as a leaf, as in an acacia. [New Latin *phyllōdium,* from Greek *phullōdēs,* leaflike : *phullon,* leaf; see PHYLLO– + *-ōdēs,* variant of *-oeidēs,* -oid (probably related to *ozein, od-,* to smell).] **—phyl·lo′di·al** *adj.*

phyl·loid (fĭl′oid′) *adj.* Resembling a leaf; leaflike.

phyl·lome (fĭl′ōm′) *n.* A leaf or a plant part that evolved from a leaf. **—phyl·lo′mic** (fĭ-lō′mĭk, -lŏm′ĭk) *adj.*

phyl·loph·a·gous (fĭ-lŏf′ə-gəs) *adj.* Feeding on leaves.

phyl·lo·pod (fĭl′ə-pŏd′) *n.* Any of various branchiopod crustaceans having swimming and respiratory appendages that resemble leaves. **—phyllopod** also **phyl·lop·o·dous** (fĭ-lŏp′ə-dəs) *adj.* Of or relating to the phyllopods. **—phyl·lop′o·dan** (fĭ-lŏp′ə-dən) *adj. & n.*

phyl·lo·tax·y (fĭl′ə-tăk′sē) also **phyl·lo·tax·is** (fĭl′ə-tăk′sĭs) *n., pl.* **-tax·ies** also **-tax·es. 1.** The arrangement of leaves on a stem. **2.** The principles governing leaf arrangement. **—phyl′lo·tac′tic** (-tăk′tĭk), **phyl′lo·tac′ti·cal** *adj.*

–phyllous *suff.* Having a specified kind or number of leaves: *gamophyllous.* [From New Latin *-phyllus,* from Greek *-phullos,* from *phullon,* leaf. See **bhel-**[3] in Appendix.]

phyl·lox·e·ra (fĭl′ŏk-sîr′ə, fĭ-lŏk′sər-ə) *n., pl.* **-rae** (-rē). Any of several small insects of the genus *Phylloxera* that are related to aphids, especially *P. vitifoliae,* a widely distributed species very destructive to grape crops. [New Latin *Phylloxera,* genus name : Greek *phullo-,* phyllo- + Greek *xēros,* dry.] **—phyl′lox·e′ran** *adj. & n.*

phy·lo·gen·e·sis (fī′lō-jĕn′ĭ-sĭs) *n.* See **phylogeny** (sense 1).

phy·lo·ge·net·ic (fī′lō-jə-nĕt′ĭk) *adj.* **1.** Of or relating to phylogeny or phylogenetics. **2.** Relating to or based on evolutionary development or history: *a phylogenetic classification of species.* **—phy′lo·ge·net′i·cal·ly** *adv.*

phy·lo·ge·net·ics (fī′lō-jə-nĕt′ĭks) *n. (used with a sing. verb).* The study of phylogeny.

phy·log·e·ny (fī-lŏj′ə-nē) *n., pl.* **-nies. 1.** The evolutionary development and history of a species or higher taxonomic grouping of organisms. Also called *phylogenesis.* **2.** The evolutionary development of an organ or other part of an organism: *the phylogeny of the amphibian intestinal tract.* **3.** The historical development of a tribe or racial group. [Greek *phulon,* race, class; see **bheuə-** in Appendix + –GENY.] **—phy′lo·gen′ic** (-jĕn′ĭk) *adj.*

phy·lum (fī′ləm) *n., pl.* **-la** (-lə). **1.** *Biology.* A primary division of a kingdom, as of the animal kingdom, ranking next above a class in size. See table at **taxonomy. 2.** *Linguistics.* A large division of possibly genetically related families of languages or linguistic stocks. [New Latin, from Greek *phulon,* class. See **bheuə-** in Appendix.]

phys. *abbr.* **1.** Physical. **2.** Physician. **3.** Physicist; physics. **4.** Physiological; physiology.

phys– *pref.* Variant of **physio–.**

phys. ed. or **phys ed** *abbr.* Physical education.

physi– *pref.* Variant of **physio–.**

phys·i·at·rics (fĭz′ē-ăt′rĭks) *n. (used with a sing. verb).* **1.** See **physical medicine. 2.** Physical therapy.

phys·i·at·rist (fĭz′ē-ăt′rĭst, fĭ-zī′ə-trĭst) *n.* **1.** A physician who specializes in physical medicine. **2.** A health care professional who administers physical therapy; a physical therapist.

phys·i·at·ry (fĭz′ē-ăt′rē, fĭ-zī′ə-trē) *n.* **1.** See **physical medicine. 2.** Physical therapy.

phys·ic (fĭz′ĭk) *n.* **1.** A medicine or drug, especially a cathartic. **2.** *Archaic.* The art or profession of medicine. **—physic** *tr.v.* **-icked, -ick·ing, -ics. 1.** To act on as a cathartic. **2.** To cure or heal. **3.** To treat with or as if with medicine. [Middle English *phisik,* from Old French *fisique,* medical science, natural science, from Latin, natural science, from Greek *phusikē,* feminine of *phusikos,* of nature, from *phusis,* nature. See **bheuə-** in Appendix.]

phys·i·cal (fĭz′ĭ-kəl) *adj. Abbr.* **phys. 1.a.** Of or relating to the body as distinguished from the mind or spirit. See Synonyms at **bodily. b.** Involving or characterized by vigorous bodily activity: *a physical dance performance.* **c.** *Slang.* Involving or characterized by violence: *"A real cop would get physical"* (TV Guide). **2.** Of or relating to material things: *our physical environment.* **3.** Of or relating to matter and energy or the sciences dealing with them, especially physics. **—physical** *n.* A physical examination. [Middle English *phisical,* medical, from Medieval Latin *physicālis,* from Latin *physica,* physics. See PHYSICS.] **—phys′i·cal′i·ty** (-kăl′ĭ-tē) *n.* **—phys′i·cal·ly** *adv.*

physical anthropology *n.* The branch of anthropology that deals with human evolutionary biology, racial variation, and classification. Also called *somatology.* **—physical anthropologist** *n.*

physical chemistry *n.* Scientific analysis of the properties and behavior of chemical systems primarily by physical theory and technique as, for example, the thermodynamic analysis of macroscopic chemical phenomena.

physical education *n. Abbr.* **P.E., phys. ed., phys ed** Education in the care and development of the human body, stressing athletics and including hygiene.

physical examination *n.* A medical examination to determine the condition of a person's health or physical fitness, especially for a specified activity or service.

physical geography *n.* The study of the natural features of the earth's surface, especially in its current aspects, including land formation, climate, currents, and distribution of flora and fauna. Also called *physiography.*

phys·i·cal·ism (fĭz′ĭ-kə-lĭz′əm) *n. Philosophy.* The doctrine that all phenomena can be described in spatiotemporal terms and consequently that any descriptive scientific statement can in principle be reduced to an empirically verifiable physical statement. **—phys′i·cal·ist** *n.* **—phys′i·cal·is′tic** *adj.*

phys·i·cal·ize (fĭz′ĭ-kə-līz′) *tr.v.* **-ized, -iz·ing, -iz·es. 1.** To express with the body: *physicalize one's emotions.* **2.** To describe or interpret in physical terms: *"a writer who physicalizes everything he feels"* (James Wolcott). **—phys′i·cal·i·za′tion** (-kə-lĭ-zā′shən) *n.*

physical medicine *n.* The branch of medicine that deals with the treatment, prevention, and diagnosis of disease by physical means, including manipulation, massage, and exercise, often with mechanical devices, and the application of heat, cold, electricity, radiation, and water. Also called *physiatrics, physiatry.*

physical science *n.* Any of the sciences, such as physics, chemistry, astronomy, and geology, that analyze the nature and properties of energy and nonliving matter.

physical therapy *n. Abbr.* **P.T.** The treatment of physical dysfunction or injury by the use of therapeutic exercise and the application of modalities, intended to restore or facilitate normal function or development. Also called *physiotherapy.* **—physical therapist** *n.*

phy·si·cian (fĭ-zĭsh′ən) *n.* **1.** *Abbr.* **phys.** A person licensed to practice medicine; a medical doctor. **2.** A person who practices general medicine as distinct from surgery. **3.** A person who heals or exerts a healing influence. [Middle English *fisicien,* from Old French, from *fisique,* medical science. See PHYSIC.]

phy·si·cian's assistant (fĭ-zĭsh′ənz) *n., pl.* **physicians' assistants.** *Abbr.* **P.A.** A person trained to provide basic medical services, usually under the supervision of a physician.

phys·i·cist (fĭz′ĭ-sĭst) *n. Abbr.* **phys.** A scientist who specializes in physics.

phys·i·co·chem·i·cal (fĭz′ĭ-kō-kĕm′ĭ-kəl) *adj.* **1.** Relating to both physical and chemical properties. **2.** Relating to physical chemistry.

phys·ics (fĭz′ĭks) *n.* **1.** *(used with a sing. verb). Abbr.* **phys.** The science of matter and energy and of interactions between the two, grouped in traditional fields such as acoustics, optics, mechanics, thermodynamics, and electromagnetism, as well as in modern extensions including atomic and nuclear physics, cryogenics, solid-state physics, particle physics, and plasma physics. **2.** *(used with a pl. verb).* Physical properties, interactions, processes, or laws: *the physics of supersonic flight.* **3.** *(used with a sing. verb). Archaic.* The study of the natural or material world and phenomena; natural philosophy. [From Latin *physica,* from Greek *(ta) phusika,* from neuter pl. of *phusikos,* of nature, from *phusis,* nature. See **bheuə-** in Appendix.]

physio– or **physi–** or **phys–** *pref.* **1.** Nature; natural: *physiography.* **2.** Physical: *physiotherapy.* [Greek *phusio-,* from *phusis,* nature. See **bheuə-** in Appendix.]

phys·i·og·no·my (fĭz′ē-ŏg′nə-mē, -ŏn′ə-mē) *n., pl.* **-mies. 1.a.** The art of judging human character from facial features. **b.** Divination based on facial features. **2.a.** Facial features, especially when regarded as revealing character. See Synonyms at **face. b.** Aspect and character of an inanimate or abstract entity: *the physiognomy of New England.* [Middle English *phisonomie,* from Old French *phisionomie,* from Late Latin *physiognōmia,* from Greek *phusiognōmia,* variant of *phusiognōmonia : phusio-,* physio- + *gnōmōn, gnōmon-,* interpreter; see **gnō-** in Appendix.] **—phys′i·og·nom′ic** (-ŏg-nŏm′ĭk, -ə-nŏm′ĭk), **phys′i·og·nom′i·cal** (-ĭ-kəl) *adj.* **—phys′i·og·nom′i·cal·ly** *adv.* **—phys′i·og′no·mist** *n.*

phys·i·og·ra·phy (fĭz′ē-ŏg′rə-fē) *n.* See **physical geography. —phys′i·og′ra·pher** *n.* **—phys′i·o·graph′ic** (-ə-grăf′ĭk), **phys′i·o·graph′i·cal** (-ĭ-kəl) *adj.* **—phys′i·o·graph′i·cal·ly** *adv.*

physiol. *abbr.* Physiological; physiology.

phys·i·o·log·i·cal (fĭz′ē-ə-lŏj′ĭ-kəl) also **phys·i·o·log·ic** (-ĭk) *adj. Abbr.* **phys., physiol. 1.** Of or relating to physiology. **2.** Being in accord with or characteristic of the normal functioning of a living organism. **3.** *Color.* Of or being an additive primary color. **—phys′i·o·log′i·cal·ly** *adv.*

physiological psychology *n.* See **psychophysiology. —physiological psychologist** *n.*

physiological saline *n.* A sterile solution of sodium chloride that is isotonic to body fluids, used to maintain living tissue temporarily and as a solvent for parenterally administered drugs.

phys·i·ol·o·gy (fĭz′ē-ŏl′ə-jē) *n. Abbr.* **phys., physiol. 1.** The biological study of the functions of living organisms and their parts. **2.** All the functions of a living organism or any of its parts. **—phys′i·ol′o·gist** *n.*

phys·i·o·pa·thol·o·gy (fĭz′ē-ō-pə-thŏl′ə-jē) *n.* See **pathophysiology. —phys′i·o·path′o·log′ic** (-păth′ə-lŏj′ĭk), **phys′i·o·path′o·log′i·cal** (-ĭ-kəl) *adj.* **—phys′i·o·pa·thol′o·gist** *n.*

phys·i·o·ther·a·py (fĭz′ē-ō-thĕr′ə-pē) *n.* See **physical therapy. —phys′i·o·ther′a·peu′tic** (-thĕr′ə-pyōō′tĭk) *adj.* **—phys′i·o·ther′a·pist** *n.*

phy·sique (fĭ-zēk′) *n.* The body considered with reference to its proportions, muscular development, and appearance: *"a short man with . . . the physique of a swimmer"* (John le Carré). [French, physical, physique, from Latin *physicus,* of nature, from Greek *phusikos,* from *phusis,* nature. See **bheuə-** in Appendix.] **—phy·siqued′** *adj.*

SYNONYMS: *physique, build, constitution.* The central meaning shared by these nouns is "bodily structure or development": *a child of delicate physique; a stocky build; a robust constitution.*

phy·so·stig·mine (fī′sō-stĭg′mēn′) also **phy·so·stig·min** (-mĭn) *n.* A crystalline alkaloid, $C_{15}H_{21}N_3O_2$, extracted from the Calabar bean, used in medicine as a miotic and cholinergic agent and to enhance memory in patients with Alzheimer's disease. Also called *eserine.* [New Latin *Physostigma,* genus name of the Calabar bean (Greek *phusa,* bellows + STIGMA) + –INE[2].]

phy·sos·to·mous (fī-sŏs′tə-məs) *adj.* Having a connecting tube between the air bladder and a part of the alimentary canal, as in certain fishes. [From Greek *phusa,* bladder + Greek *stoma,* mouth.]

phyt– *pref.* Variant of **phyto–.**

–phyte *suff.* **1.** A plant with a specified character or habitat: *halophyte.* **2.** A pathological growth: *osteophyte.* [From Greek *phuton,* plant, from *phuein,* to make grow. See **bheuə-** in Appendix.]

phyto– or **phyt–** *pref.* Plant: *phytogenesis.* [New Latin, from Greek *phuto-,* from *phuton,* plant, from *phuein,* to make grow. See **bheuə-** in Appendix.]

phy·to·chem·is·try (fī′tō-kĕm′ĭ-strē) *n.* The chemistry of plants. **—phy′to·chem′i·cal** (-ĭ-kəl) *adj.* **—phy′to·chem′i·cal·ly** *adv.* **—phy′to·chem′ist** *n.*

phy·to·chrome (fī′tə-krōm′) *n.* A cytoplasmic pigment of green plants that absorbs light and regulates dormancy, seed germination, and flowering.

phy·to·gen·e·sis (fī′tō-jĕn′ĭ-sĭs) also **phy·tog·e·ny** (fī-tŏj′ə-nē) *n.* The origin and evolutionary development of plants. **—phy′to·ge·net′ic** (-jə-nĕt′ĭk), **phy′to·ge·net′i·cal** (-ĭ-kəl) *adj.* **—phy′to·ge·net′i·cal·ly** *adv.*

phy·to·gen·ic (fī′tō-jĕn′ĭk) also **phy·tog·e·nous** (fī-tŏj′ə-nəs) *adj.* Having a plant origin, as coal.

phy·tog·e·ny (fī-tŏj′ə-nē) *n.* Variant of **phytogenesis.**

phy·to·ge·og·ra·phy (fī′tō-jē-ŏg′rə-fē) *n.* The study of the geographic distribution of plants. Also called *geobotany.* **—phy′to·ge·og′ra·pher** *n.* **—phy′to·ge′o·graph′i·cal** (-jē′ə-grăf′ĭ-kəl), **phy′to·ge′o·graph′ic** (-grăf′ĭk) *adj.*

phy·tog·ra·phy (fī-tŏg′rə-fē) *n.* The science of plant description; descriptive botany.

phy·to·he·mag·glu·ti·nin (fī′tō-hē′mə-glōōt′n-ĭn) *n.* A hemagglutinin extracted from a plant.

phy·to·hor·mone (fī′tō-hôr′mōn′) *n.* See **plant hormone.**

phy·tol (fī′tôl′, -tōl′) *n.* A liquid alcohol, $C_{20}H_{40}O$, used in the synthesis of vitamins E and K.

phy·tol·o·gy (fī-tŏl′ə-jē) *n.* The study of plants; botany. **—phy′to·log′ic** (fī′tə-lŏj′ĭk), **phy′to·log′i·cal** (-ĭ-kəl) *adj.*

phy·ton (fī′tŏn′) *n.* The smallest unit of plant structure. [New Latin, from Greek *phuton,* plant. See PHYTO–.] **—phy·ton′ic** *adj.*

phy·to·path·o·gen (fī′tō-păth′ə-jən) *n.* An organism that is pathogenic to a plant. **—phy′to·path′o·gen′ic** (-jĕn′ĭk) *adj.*

phy·to·pa·thol·o·gy (fī′tō-pə-thŏl′ə-jē) *n.* The science of plant diseases. **—phy′to·path′o·log′ic** (-păth′ə-lŏj′ĭk), **phy′to·path′o·log′i·cal** (-ĭ-kəl) *adj.* **—phy′to·pa·thol′o·gist** *n.*

phy·toph·a·gous (fī-tŏf′ə-gəs) *adj.* Feeding on plants, including shrubs and trees. Used especially of certain insects.

phy·to·plank·ton (fī′tō-plăngk′tən) *n.* Minute, free-floating aquatic plants. **—phy′to·plank·ton′ic** (-plăngk-tŏn′ĭk) *adj.*

phy·to·so·ci·ol·o·gy (fī′tō-sō′sē-ŏl′ə-jē, -shē-) *n.* The branch of ecology that deals with the characteristics, classification, relationships, and distribution of plant communities. **—phy′to·so′ci·o·log′i·cal** (-sō′sē-ə-lŏj′ĭ-kəl, -shē-) *adj.* **—phy′to·so′ci·ol′o·gist** *n.*

phy·to·tox·ic (fī′tō-tŏk′sĭk) *adj.* Poisonous to plants. **—phy′to·tox·ic′i·ty** (-tŏk-sĭs′ĭ-tē) *n.*

pi[1] (pī) *n., pl.* **pis. 1.** The 16th letter of the Greek alphabet. See table at **alphabet. 2.** *Mathematics.* A transcendental number, approximately 3.14159, represented by the symbol π, that expresses the ratio of the circumference to the diameter of a circle and appears as a constant in many mathematical expressions. [Medieval Greek, from Greek *pei,* of Phoenician origin; akin to Hebrew *pē.*]

pi[2] also **pie** (pī) *Printing.—n., pl.* **pis** also **pies.** An amount of type that has been jumbled or thrown together at random. *—v.* **pied, pi·ing, pies** also **pied, pie·ing, pies.** *—tr.* To jumble or mix up (type). *—intr.* To become jumbled. [Origin unknown.]

PI *abbr.* Private investigator.

pi·a (pī′ə, pē′ə) *n.* The pia mater. **—pi′al** *adj.*

Pia·cen·za (pyä-chĕn′zə, -tsä). A town of northern Italy on the Po River southeast of Milan. Founded by Romans as Placentia in 218 B.C., it became a free city and part of the Lombard League in the 12th century. Population, 108,177.

pi·ac·u·lar (pī-ăk′yə-lər) *adj.* **1.** Making expiation or atonement for a sacrilege: *piacular sacrifice.* **2.** Requiring expiation; wicked or blameworthy. [Latin *piāculāris,* from *piāculum,* propitiatory sacrifice, from *piāre,* to appease, from *pius,* dutiful.]

Pi·af (pē-äf′, pē′äf′), **Edith.** 1915–1963. French cabaret singer. Her best-remembered songs include *La Vie en Rose* and *Non, Je ne Regrette Rien.*

Edith Piaf

piaffe (pyăf) *intr.v.* **piaffed, piaf·fing, piaffes.** To perform the piaffer. [French *piaffer.*]

piaf·fer (pyăf′ər) *n.* A movement in which a horse trots in place with high action of the legs. [French, from *piaffer,* to strut, piaffe.]

Pia·get (pē′ə-zhā′, pyä-), **Jean.** 1896–1980. Swiss child psychologist noted for his studies of intellectual and cognitive development in children.

pia ma·ter (mā′tər, mä′tər) *n.* The fine vascular membrane that closely envelops the brain and spinal cord under the arachnoid and the dura mater. [Middle English, from Medieval Latin *pia māter* : Latin *pia,* tender + Latin *māter,* mother (translation of Arabic *'umm raqīqah*).]

pi·an·ism (pē-ăn′ĭz′əm, pē′ə-nĭz′əm) *n. Music.* The technique or execution of piano playing.

ă pat	oi boy
ā pay	ou out
âr care	ŏŏ took
ä father	ōō boot
ĕ pet	ŭ cut
ē be	ûr urge
ĭ pit	th thin
ī pie	*th* this
îr pier	hw which
ŏ pot	zh vision
ō toe	ə about, item
ô paw	♦ regionalism

Stress marks: ′ (primary); ′ (secondary), as in **dictionary** (dĭk′shə-nĕr′ē)

piano¹

Pablo Picasso
Photographed c. 1953

pi·a·nis·si·mo (pē′ə-nĭs′ə-mō′) *Music. adv. & adj. Abbr.* **pp, pp.** In a very soft or quiet tone. Used chiefly as a direction. **—pianissimo** *n., pl.* **-mos.** A part of a composition played very softly or quietly. [Italian, superlative of *piano,* soft. See PIANO².]

pi·an·ist (pē-ăn′ĭst, pē′ə-nĭst) *n. Music.* One who plays the piano.

pi·a·nis·tic (pē′ə-nĭs′tĭk) *adj. Music.* **1.** Of or relating to the piano. **2.** Well adapted to the piano. **—pi′a·nis′ti·cal·ly** *adv.*

pi·a·nis·tics (pē′ə-nĭs′tĭks) *n. (used with a sing. or pl. verb). Music.* **1.** The art or principles of piano playing. **2.** A show of virtuosity in playing the piano.

pi·an·o¹ (pē-ăn′ō, pyăn′ō) *n., pl.* **-os.** *Music.* An instrument with a manual keyboard actuating hammers that strike wire strings, producing sounds that may be softened or sustained by means of pedals. Also called *pianoforte.* [Italian, short for *pianoforte.* See PIANOFORTE.]

pi·a·no² (pē-ä′nō, pyä′-) *Music. adv. & adj. Abbr.* **p, p.** In a soft or quiet tone. Used chiefly as a direction. **—piano** *n., pl.* **-nos.** A passage to be played softly or quietly. [Italian, from Late Latin *plānus,* smooth, graceful, from Latin, flat. See **pelə-²** in Appendix.]

piano bar *n.* A cocktail lounge featuring entertainment by a pianist.

pi·an·o·for·te (pē-ăn′ō-fôr′tā, -fôr′tē, pē-ăn′ō-fôrt′) *n. Music.* See **piano¹.** [Italian, from *(clavicembalo con) piano (e) forte,* (harpsichord with) soft (and) loud : *piano,* soft; see PIANO² + *forte,* loud; see FORTE².]

piano hinge *n.* A long narrow hinge with a pin running the entire length of its joint.

pi·as·sa·va (pē′ə-sä′və) also **pi·as·sa·ba** (-sä′bə) *n.* **1.** Either of two South American palm trees, *Attalea funifera* or *Leopoldinia piassaba,* from which a strong, coarse fiber is obtained. **2.** The fiber of either of these plants, used for making ropes, brushes, and brooms. [Portuguese, from Tupi *plaçaba.*]

pi·as·ter also **pi·as·tre** (pē-ăs′tər, -ä′stər) *n.* **1.** See table at **currency. 2.** Piece of eight. [French *piastre,* from Italian *piastra,* thin metal plate, from Latin *emplastrum,* medical dressing. See PLASTER.]

pi·az·za (pē-ăz′ə, -ä′zə) *n., pl.* **-zas. 1.** *(also* pē-ät′sə, pyät′sä) *pl.* **pi·az·ze** (pē-ät′sə, pyät′sĕ). A public square in an Italian town. **2.** A roofed and arcaded passageway; a colonnade. **3.** A verandah. [Italian, from Latin *platēa,* street, from Greek *plateia (hodos),* broad (way), feminine of *platus,* broad. See **plat-** in Appendix.]

Piaz·zi (pyät′sē), **Giuseppi.** 1746–1826. Italian astronomer who discovered (1801) the first asteroid, Ceres.

pi·broch (pē′brŏKH′) *n. Music.* A series of variations on a traditional dirge or martial theme for the highland bagpipes. [Scottish Gaelic *piobaireachd,* pipe music, from *piobair,* piper, from *piob,* pipe, from Middle Irish *píp,* from Medieval Latin *pīpa,* from Vulgar Latin. See PIPE.]

pic (pĭk) *n., pl.* **pics** or **pix** (pĭks). *Slang.* **1.** A photograph. **2.** A movie. [Short for PICTURE.]

pi·ca¹ (pī′kə) *n. Printing.* **1.a.** A printer's unit of type size, equal to 12 points or about ⅙ of an inch. **b.** An equivalent unit of composition measurement used in determining the dimensions of lines, illustrations, or printed pages. **2.** A type size for typewriters, providing ten characters to the inch. [Probably from Medieval Latin *pīca,* list of church services (perhaps from the typeface used to print it).]

pi·ca² (pī′kə) *n.* An abnormal craving or appetite for nonfood substances, such as dirt, paint, or clay. [New Latin *pīca,* from Latin, magpie (from its omnivorous nature).]

pic·a·dor (pĭk′ə-dôr′, pē′kä-thôr′) *n., pl.* **pic·a·dors** or **pic·a·do·res** (pĭk′ə-dôr′ās, pē′kä-thô′rĕs). A horseman in a bullfight who lances the bull's neck muscles so that it will tend to keep its head low for the subsequent stages of the fight. [Spanish, from *picar,* to prick. See PICARO.]

pi·can·te (pĭ-kän′tā) *adj.* Prepared in such a way as to be spicy; having a sauce typically containing tomatoes, onions, peppers, vinegar, and other condiments. [Spanish, present participle of *picar,* to bite, prick. See PICARO.]

pi·ca·ra (pē′kä-rä′) *n., pl.* **-ras** (-räz′, -räs′). An adventuress. [Spanish *pícara,* feminine of *pícaro,* rogue. See PICARO.]

Pi·card (pē-kär′), **Jean.** 1620–1682. French cleric and astronomer who made an accurate measurement of a degree of meridian and subsequently calculated the circumference of the earth (1668–1670).

Pic·ar·dy (pĭk′ər-dē). A historical region of northern France bordering on the English Channel. The name was first used in the 13th century for a number of small feudal holdings. Picardy was contested by France and England during the Hundred Years' War and became part of the French crown lands in 1477.

pic·a·resque (pĭk′ə-rĕsk′, pē′kə-) *adj.* **1.** Of or involving clever rogues or adventurers. **2.** Of or relating to a genre of prose fiction that originated in Spain and depicts in realistic detail the adventures of a roguish hero, often with satiric or humorous effects. **—picaresque** *n.* One that is picaresque. [French, from Spanish *picaresco,* from *pícaro,* picaro. See PICARO.]

pi·ca·ro (pē′kä-rō) *n., pl.* **-ros** (-rōz′, -rōs′). A bohemian adventurer; a rogue. Also called *picaroon.* [Spanish *pícaro,* perhaps from *picar,* to prick, from Vulgar Latin **piccāre.* See PIQUE.]

pic·a·roon (pĭk′ə-ro͞on′) *n.* **1.a.** A pirate. **b.** A pirate ship. **2.** See **picaro. —picaroon** *intr.v.* **-rooned, -roon·ing, -roons.** To act as a pirate. [Spanish *picarón,* augmentative of *pícaro,* picaro. See PICARO.]

Pi·cas·so (pĭ-kä′sō, -kăs′ō), **Pablo.** 1881–1973. Spanish artist. One of the most prolific and influential artists of the 20th century, Picasso excelled in painting, sculpture, etching, stage design, and ceramics. With Georges Braque he launched cubism (1906–1925), and he introduced the technique of collage. Among Picasso's masterpieces are *Les Demoiselles d'Avignon* (1907) and *Guernica* (1937).

pic·a·yune (pĭk′ə-yo͞on′) *adj.* **1.** Of little value or importance; paltry. See Synonyms at **trivial. 2.** Petty; mean. **—picayune** *n.* **1.** A Spanish-American half-real piece formerly used in parts of the southern United States. **2.** A five-cent piece. **3.** Something of very little value; a trifle: *not worth a picayune.* [Louisiana French *picaillon,* small coin, from French, from Provençal *picaioun,* from *picaio,* money, perhaps from Old Provençal *piquar,* to jingle, clink, from Vulgar Latin **piccāre,* to pierce. See PIQUE.] **—pic′a·yun′ish** *adj.*

Pic·ca·dil·ly Circus (pĭk′ə-dĭl′ē). A traffic junction and popular meeting place in western London, England, noted for the statue known as *Eros.*

pic·ca·lil·li (pĭk′ə-lĭl′ē) *n., pl.* **-lis.** A pickled relish made of various chopped vegetables. [Probably alteration of PICKLE.]

Pic·card (pē-kärd′, -kär′), **Auguste.** 1884–1962. Swiss physicist and aeronaut known for his experiments at extreme altitudes and depths. He designed a balloon that in 1932 carried him to 16,946.7 meters (55,563 feet) and invented a bathyscaphe that in 1953 reached a depth of 3,151.3 meters (10,332 feet).

Piccard, Jean Felix. 1884–1963. Swiss-born American chemist and aeronautical engineer. In 1934 he reached a height of 17,557 meters (57,564 feet) in a balloon of his own design.

pic·ca·ta (pĭ-kä′tə) *adj.* Sliced, sautéed, and served in a sauce containing lemon, butter, and spices. Used of meat or fish. [Italian, feminine of *piccato,* larded, from French *piqué,* past participle of *piquer,* to prick, lard. See PIQUE.]

pic·co·lo¹ (pĭk′ə-lō′) *n., pl.* **-los.** *Music.* A small flute pitched an octave above a regular flute. [French, from Italian, short for *(flauto) piccolo,* small (flute).] **—pic′co·lo′ist** *n.*

pic·co·lo² (pĭk′ə-lō′) *adj. Music.* Of, relating to, or being an instrument considerably smaller than the usual size: *a piccolo trumpet; a piccolo concertina.* [Italian, small.]

pice (pīs) *n., pl.* **pice.** A monetary unit worth 1/64 of a rupee, formerly used in India. [Hindi *paisā.* See PAISA.]

pi·ce·ous (pī′sē-əs) *adj.* **1.** *Botany.* Of or relating to pitch. **2.** *Color.* Glossy black. [From Latin *piceus,* from *pix, pic-,* pitch.]

pich·i·ci·e·go (pĭch′ĭ-sē-ā′gō) also **pich·i·ci·a·go** (-ā′gō, -ä′gō) *n., pl.* **-gos. 1.** A small armadillo *(Chlamyphorus truncatus)* of Argentina, having pale pink armor and thick, silky white hair. **2.** A South American armadillo *(Burmeisteria retusa)* having yellow-brown armor and whitish hair. [American Spanish : Araucanian *pichi,* armadillo + Spanish *ciego,* blind (from Latin *caecus*).]

pick¹ (pĭk) *v.* **picked, pick·ing, picks.** *—tr.* **1.a.** To select from a group: *The best swimmer was picked.* See Synonyms at **choose. b.** To select or cull. **2.a.** To gather in; harvest: *They were picking cotton.* **b.** To gather the harvest from: *We picked the whole field in one day.* **3.a.** To remove the outer covering of; pluck: *pick a chicken clean of feathers.* **b.** To tear off bit by bit: *pick meat from the bones.* **4.** To remove extraneous matter from (the teeth). **5.** To poke and pull at (something) with the fingers. **6.** To break up, separate, or detach by means of a sharp, pointed instrument. **7.** To pierce or make (a hole) with a sharp, pointed instrument. **8.** To take up (food) with the beak; peck: *The parrot picked its seed.* **9.** To steal the contents of: *My pocket was picked.* **10.** To open (a lock) without the use of a key. **11.** To provoke: *pick a fight.* **12.** *Music.* **a.** To pluck (the strings) of an instrument: *picked the guitar while sitting alone on the deck.* **b.** To play (a tune) by plucking strings: *picked a melody out on the guitar.* *—intr.* **1.** To decide with care or forethought. **2.** To work with a pick. **3.** To find fault or make petty criticisms; carp: *He's always picking about something.* **4.** To be harvested or gathered: *The ripe apples picked easily.* **—pick** *n.* **1.** The act of picking, especially with a sharp, pointed instrument. **2.** The act of selecting or choosing; choice: *got first pick of the desserts.* **3.** Something selected as the most desirable; the best or choicest part: *the pick of the crop.* **4.** The amount or quantity of a crop that is picked by hand. ***—phrasal verbs.*** **pick apart.** To refute or find flaws in by close examination: *The lawyer picked the testimony apart.* **pick at. 1.** To pluck or pull at, especially with the fingers. **2.** To eat sparingly or without appetite: *The child just picked at her food.* **3.** *Informal.* To nag: *Don't pick at me day and night.* **pick off. 1.** To shoot after singling out: *The hunter picked the ducks off one by one.* **2.** *Baseball.* To catch (a base runner) off base and put out with a quick throw, as from the pitcher or catcher, often to a specified base. **3.** *Sports.* To intercept, as a football pass. **pick on.** To tease or bully. **pick out. 1.** To choose or select: *picked out the best piece of silk.* **2.** To discern from the surroundings; distinguish: *picked out their cousins from the crowd.* **pick over.** To sort out or examine item by item: *a shopper who picked over the grapes before purchasing them.* **pick up. 1.a.** To take up (something) by hand: *pick up a book.* **b.** To collect or gather: *picked up the broken pieces of glass.* **c.** To tidy up: *Let's pick up the living room.* **2.** To take on (passengers or freight, for example): *The bus picks up commuters at three stops.* **3.** *Informal.* **a.** To acquire casually or by accident: *picked up a mink coat on sale.* **b.** To acquire (knowledge) by learning or experience: *picked up French very quickly.* **c.** To claim: *picked up her shoes at the repair shop.* **d.** To buy: *picked up some beverages on the way home.* **e.** To accept (a bill or charge) in order to pay it: *Let me pick up the tab.* **f.** To come down with (a disease): *picked up a virus in the office.* **g.** To gain: *picked up five yards on that play.* **4.** *Informal.* To take into custody: *The coast guard picked up five smugglers.* **5.** *Slang.* To make casual acquaintance with, usually in anticipation of sexual relations. **6.a.** To come upon and follow: *The dog picked up the scent.* **b.** To come upon and observe: *We picked up two submarines on sonar.* **7.** To continue after a break: *Let's pick up the discussion after lunch.* **8.** *Informal.* To improve in condition or activity: *Sales picked up last fall.* **9.** *Slang.* To pack one's belongings: *She just picked up and left.* **—*idioms.*** **pick and choose.** To select with great care. **pick holes in.** To seek and discover flaws or a flaw in: *picked holes in the argument.* **pick (one's) way.** To find passage and make careful progress through it: *picked her way down the steep bank.* **pick (someone) to pieces.** To criticize sharply. **pick up on.** *Informal.* **1.** To take into the mind and understand, typically with speed: *picked up on the new approach and applied it to the project.* **2.** To notice: *learned to pick up on his superior's moods and act accordingly.* [Middle English *piken,* to prick, from Old English **pīcian,* to prick, and from Old French *piquer,* to pierce (from Vulgar Latin **piccāre;* see PIQUE).] **—pick′er** *n.*

pick² (pĭk) *n.* **1.** A tool for breaking hard surfaces, consisting of a curved bar sharpened at both ends and fitted to a long handle. **2.a.** Something, such as an ice pick, a toothpick, or a picklock, that is used for picking. **b.** A long-toothed comb, usually designed for use on curly hair. **c.** *Sports.* A pointed projection on the front of the blade of a figure skate. **3.** *Music.* A plectrum. [Middle English *pik,* variant of *pike,* sharp point. See PIKE⁵.]

pick³ (pĭk) *n.* **1.** A weft thread in weaving. **2.** A passage or throw of the shuttle in a loom. **—pick** *tr.v.* **picked, pick·ing, picks. 1.** To throw (a shuttle) across a loom. **2.** *Archaic.* To cast; pitch. [Dialectal, from *pick,* to pitch, thrust, variant of PITCH².]

pick·a·nin·ny (pĭk′ə-nĭn′ē) *n., pl.* **-nies.** *Offensive.* Used as a disparaging term for a young Black child. [Possibly from Spanish *pequeño,* small + *niño,* child, or Portuguese *pequenino,* diminutive of *pequeno,* small.]

pick·ax or **pick·axe** (pĭk′ăks′) *—n.* A pick, especially with one end of the head pointed and the other end with a chisel edge for cutting through roots. *—v.* **-axed, -ax·ing, -ax·es.** *—intr.* To use a pickax. *—tr.* To use a pickax on. [Middle English *picax,* alteration (influenced by *ax,* ax) of *picas,* from Old French *picois* (from *pic,* pick) and from Medieval Latin *pīcōsa,* both probably from Latin *pīcus,* woodpecker.]

picked¹ (pĭkt) *adj.* **1.** Chosen by careful selection: *a racing yacht sailed by a picked crew.* **2.** Gathered, harvested, or plucked: *baskets of picked cotton; a picked turkey.*

♦**picked²** (pĭkt) *adj. Regional.* Pointed: *a picked cap.* [From PICK².]

pick·er·el (pĭk′ər-əl, pĭk′rəl) *n., pl.* **pickerel** or **-els. 1.** Any of several small North American freshwater game and food fishes of the genus *Esox,* especially *E. reticulatus,* of the eastern and southern United States. **2.** Any of various fishes, such as the walleye, similar or related to the pickerel. **3.** *Chiefly British.* A young pike. [Middle English *pikerel,* diminutive of *pike,* pike. See PIKE².]

pick·er·el·weed (pĭk′ər-əl-wēd′, pĭk′rəl-) *n.* A freshwater plant *(Pontederia cordata)* of eastern North America, having heart-shaped leaves with long petioles and spikes of violet-blue flowers.

Pick·er·ing (pĭk′ər-ĭng). A town of southern Ontario, Canada, a suburb of Toronto on Lake Ontario. Population, 37,754.

Pickering, Edward Charles. 1846–1919. American astronomer noted for his work on stellar photometry. His brother **William Henry Pickering** (1858–1938) discovered Phoebe, the ninth moon of Saturn (1899), and predicted the existence of Pluto (1919).

pick·et (pĭk′ĭt) *n.* **1.** A pointed stake often driven into the ground to support a fence, secure a tent, tether animals, mark points in surveying, or, when pointed at the top, serve as a defense. **2.** A detachment of one or more troops, ships, or aircraft held in readiness or advanced to warn of an enemy's approach: *"The outlying sonar picket. . . . was to detect, localize, and engage any submarine trying to close the convoy"* (Tom Clancy). **3.a.** A person or group of persons stationed outside a place of employment, usually during a strike, to express grievance or protest and discourage entry by nonstriking employees or customers. **b.** A person or group of persons present outside a building to protest. **—picket** *v.* **-et·ed, -et·ing, -ets.** *—tr.* **1.** To enclose, secure, tether, mark out, or fortify with pickets. **2.a.** To post as a picket. **b.** To guard with a picket. **3.** To post a picket or pickets during a strike or demonstration. *—intr.* To act or serve as a picket. [French *piquet,* from Old French, from *piquer,* to prick. See PIQUE.] **—pick′et·er** *n.*

picket fence *n.* A fence of upright pointed pickets.

picket line *n.* A line or procession of people picketing a place of business or otherwise staging a public protest.

Pick·ett (pĭk′ĭt), **George Edward.** 1825–1875. American Confederate general known for leading the disastrous Pickett's Charge at Gettysburg (1863), in which three fourths of his troops were lost.

Pick·ford (pĭk′fərd), **Mary.** 1893–1979. Canadian-born American actress who received an Academy Award for her performance in *Coquette* (1929).

pick·ing (pĭk′ĭng) *n.* **1.** The act of one that picks. **2. pickings.** Something or a group of things that are or may be picked. **3.** Often **pickings. a.** Leftovers. **b.** A share of spoils.

pick·le (pĭk′əl) *n.* **1.** An edible product, such as a cucumber, that has been preserved and flavored in a solution of brine or vinegar. **2.** A solution of brine or vinegar, often spiced, for preserving and flavoring food. **3.** A chemical solution, such as an acid, that is used as a bath to remove scale and oxides from the surface of metals before plating or finishing. **4.** *Informal.* A disagreeable or troublesome situation; a plight. See Synonyms at **predicament. —pickle** *tr.v.* **-led, -ling, -les. 1.** To preserve or flavor (food) in a solution of brine or vinegar. **2.** To treat (metal) in a chemical bath. [Middle English *pikle,* highly seasoned sauce, probably from Middle Dutch *pekel,* pickle, brine.]

WORD HISTORY: Trade with the Low Countries across the North Sea was important to England in the later Middle Ages, and it is perhaps because of this trade that we have the word *pickle.* Middle English *pikel,* the ancestor of our word, is first recorded around 1400 with the meaning "a spicy sauce or gravy served with meat or fowl." This is a different sense from the one the word brings to mind now, but it is related somewhat in sense to its possible Middle Dutch source *pekel,* a solution, such as spiced brine, for preserving and flavoring food. After coming into English the word *pickle* expanded its sense range in several ways. It was applied, as it had been in Middle Dutch, to a pickling solution. Later *pickle* was used to refer to something so treated, such as a cucumber. The word also took on a figurative sense, "a troublesome situation," perhaps under the influence of a similar Dutch usage in the phrase *in de pekel zitten,* "sit in the pickle."

pick·led (pĭk′əld) *adj.* **1.** Preserved in or treated with pickle. **2.** *Slang.* Intoxicated; drunk.

pick·le·worm (pĭk′əl-wûrm′) *n.* The larva of a pyralid moth *(Diaphania nitidalis)* of the southern Atlantic and Gulf states of the United States, that feeds destructively on cucumbers, squash, pumpkins, and other gourds.

pick·lock (pĭk′lŏk′) *n.* **1.** A person who picks locks, especially a thief. **2.** An instrument for picking a lock.

pick-me-up (pĭk′mē-ŭp′) *n. Informal.* A drink, often an alcoholic beverage, taken as a stimulant or a cure for a hangover.

pick·off (pĭk′ôf′, -ŏf′) *n.* **1.** *Baseball.* A play in which a runner is caught off base and is put out by a quick throw, as from the pitcher or catcher. **2.** *Sports.* An interception, as in football.

pick·pock·et (pĭk′pŏk′ĭt) *n.* One who steals from pockets.

pick·proof (pĭk′pro͞of′) *adj.* Designed to prevent picking: *a pickproof lock.*

pick·up (pĭk′ŭp′) *n.* **1.a.** The act or process of picking up: *the pickup and delivery of farm produce.* **b.** *Sports.* The act of striking or fielding a ball after it has touched the ground: *a good pickup and throw from third base.* **c.** Capacity for acceleration: *a sports car with good pickup.* **d.** *Informal.* An improvement in condition or activity: *a pickup in sales.* **e.** *Slang.* An arrest by a law enforcement officer. **2.** One that is picked up, especially: **a.** Passengers or freight: *Taxi drivers expect good tips from airport pickups.* **b.** *Informal.* A hitchhiker. **c.** *Slang.* A stranger with whom casual acquaintance is made, usually in anticipation of sexual relations. **3.** *Accounting.* A balance brought forward. **4.** Previous journalistic copy to which succeeding copy is added. **5.** *Music.* The unstressed note or notes introductory to a phrase or composition. **6.** One that picks up, especially: **a.** A pickup truck. **b.** The rotary rake on a piece of machinery, such as a harvester, that picks up windrowed hay or straw. **7.** *Electronics.* **a.** A device that converts the oscillations of a phonograph needle into electrical impulses for subsequent conversion into sound. **b.** The tone arm of a record player. **8.a.** The reception of light or sound waves for conversion to electrical impulses. **b.** The apparatus used for such reception. **c.** A telecast originating outside a studio. **d.** The apparatus for transmitting a broadcast from an outside place to the broadcasting station. **—pickup** *adj.* Being, relating to, or involving a group of people assembled informally for a temporary purpose: *a pickup orchestra; a pickup baseball game.*

pickup truck *n.* A light truck with an open body and low sides.

pick·y (pĭk′ē) *adj.* **-i·er, -i·est.** *Informal.* Excessively meticulous; fussy.

pic·lo·ram (pĭk′lə-răm′, pī′klə-) *n.* A colorless compound, $C_6H_3Cl_3N_2O_2$, used as a herbicide. [PIC(OLINE) + (CH)LOR(O)– + AM(INE).]

pic·nic (pĭk′nĭk) *n.* **1.** A meal eaten outdoors, as on an excursion. **2.** *Slang.* An easy task or a pleasant experience. **3.** A shoulder of pork from which most of the butt has been removed. **—picnic** *intr.v.* **-nicked, -nick·ing, -nics.** To go on or participate in a picnic. [French *piquenique,* probably reduplication of *piquer,* to pick. See PIQUE.] **—pic′nick·er** *n.* **—pic′nick·y** *adj.*

pico– *pref.* **1.** One-trillionth (10^{-12}): *picosecond.* **2.** Very small: *picornavirus.* [Spanish *pico,* beak, small quantity, from Latin *beccus,* beak, of Celtic origin (influenced by Spanish *picar,* to prick; see PICARO).]

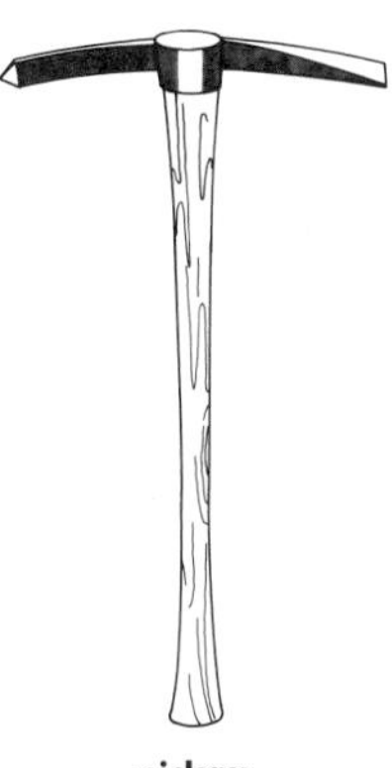

pickax

picket fence

Mary Pickford

pickup truck

ă pat	oi boy
ā pay	ou out
âr care	o͝o took
ä father	o͞o boot
ĕ pet	ŭ cut
ē be	ûr urge
ĭ pit	th thin
ī pie	*th* this
îr pier	hw which
ŏ pot	zh vision
ō toe	ə about, item
ô paw	♦ regionalism

Stress marks: **′** (primary); ′ (secondary), as in **dictionary** (dĭk′shə-nĕr′ē)

Pi·co del·la Mi·ran·do·la (pē′kō dĕl′ə mə-răn′də-lə, dĕl′lä mē-rän′dô-lä), Count **Giovanni.** 1463–1494. Italian Neo-Platonist philosopher famous for his 900 theses on a variety of scholarly subjects (1486).

pi·co·far·ad (pē′kə-făr′əd, -ăd, pī′-) *n.* One trillionth (10^{-12}) of a farad.

pi·co·gram (pē′kə-grăm′, pī′-) *n.* One trillionth (10^{-12}) of a gram.

pic·o·line (pĭk′ə-lēn′, pī′kə-) *n.* Any of three isomeric liquids, $C_5H_4N(CH_3)$, derived from coal tar, horse urine, and bone oil and used as an industrial solvent. [Latin *pix, pic-,* pitch + –OL[1] + –INE[2].]

pi·co·mole (pē′kə-mōl′, pī′-) *n.* One trillionth (10^{-12}) of a mole.

Pico Ri·ve·ra (rə-vîr′ə). A city of southern California, an industrial suburb of Los Angeles. Population, 53,459.

pi·cor·na·vi·rus (pē-kôr′nə-vī′rəs, pī-) *n., pl.* **-rus·es.** Any of a group of very small viruses, including the enteroviruses and the rhinoviruses, that infect animals and consist of RNA surrounded by an icosahedral protein shell. [PICO– + RNA + VIRUS.]

pi·co·sec·ond (pē′kə-sĕk′ənd, pī′-) *n. Abbr.* **psec.** One trillionth (10^{-12}) of a second.

pi·cot (pē′kō, pē-kō′) *n.* A small embroidered loop forming an ornamental edging on some ribbon and lace. —**picot** *tr.v.* **-coted** (-kōd), **-cot·ing** (-kō-ĭng), **-cots** (-kōz). To trim with small embroidered loops. [French, from Old French, from *pic,* point, from *piquer,* to prick. See PIQUE.]

pic·o·tee (pĭk′ə-tē′) *n.* A carnation having pale petals bordered by a darker color. [French *picoté,* marked with points, past participle of *picoter,* to mark with points, from *picot,* point, picot. See PICOT.]

pi·co·wave (pē′kə-wāv′, pī′-) *tr.v.* **-waved, -wav·ing, -waves.** To irradiate (food) with gamma rays in order to kill insects or worms. [PICO– + WAVE (from the extremely short wavelength of gamma radiation).]

pic·quet (pĭ-kā′) *n.* Variant of **piquet.**

picr– *pref.* Variant of **picro–.**

pic·rate (pĭk′rāt′) *n.* A salt or an ester of picric acid.

pic·ric acid (pĭk′rĭk) *n.* A poisonous, explosive yellow crystalline solid, $C_6H_2(NO_2)_3OH$, used in explosives, dyes, and antiseptics.

picro– or **picr–** *pref.* **1.** Bitter: *picrotoxin.* **2.** Picric acid: *picrate.* [Greek *pikro-,* from *pikros,* bitter. See **peig-** in Appendix.]

pic·ro·tox·in (pĭk′rə-tŏk′sĭn) *n.* A bitter crystalline compound, $C_{30}H_{34}O_{13}$, derived from the seed of an East Indian woody vine *(Animirta cocculus)* and used as a stimulant, especially in treating barbiturate poisoning. —**pic′ro·tox′ic** *adj.*

Pict (pĭkt) *n.* One of an ancient people of northern Britain. They remained undefeated by the Romans and in the ninth century joined with the Scots to form a kingdom later to become Scotland. [From Middle English *Pictes,* Picts, from Late Latin *Pictī,* from Latin *pictī,* pl. of *pictus,* painted. See PICTURE.]

Pict·ish (pĭk′tĭsh) *adj.* Of or relating to the Picts or their language or culture. —**Pictish** *n.* The language of the Picts, of uncertain affiliation, known chiefly from place names and extinct by the tenth century.

pic·to·gram (pĭk′tə-grăm′) *n.* See **pictograph.** [Latin *pictus,* past participle of *pingere,* to paint; see PICTOGRAPH + –GRAM.]

pic·to·graph (pĭk′tə-grăf′) *n.* **1.** A picture representing a word or idea; a hieroglyph. **2.** A record in hieroglyphic symbols. **3.** A pictorial representation of numerical data or relationships, especially a graph, but having each value represented by a proportional number of pictures. Also called *pictogram.* [Latin *pictus,* past participle of *pingere,* to paint; see **peig-** in Appendix + –GRAPH.] —**pic′to·graph′ic** *adj.* —**pic′to·graph′i·cal·ly** *adv.* —**pic·tog′ra·phy** (pĭk-tŏg′rə-fē) *n.*

Pic·tor (pĭk′tər) *n.* A constellation in the Southern Hemisphere near Columba and Dorado. [Latin *pictor,* painter, from *pingere,* to paint. See **peig-** in Appendix.]

pic·to·ri·al (pĭk-tôr′ē-əl, -tōr′-) *adj.* **1.** Relating to, characterized by, or composed of pictures. **2.** Represented as if in a picture: *pictorial prose.* **3.** Illustrated by pictures: *a pictorial history.* —**pictorial** *n.* An illustrated periodical. [From Latin *pictōrius,* from *pictor,* painter. See PICTOR.] —**pic·to′ri·al′i·ty** (-ăl′ĭ-tē), **pic·to′ri·al·ness** (-əl-nĭs) *n.* —**pic·to′ri·al·ly** *adv.*

pic·to·ri·al·ize (pĭk-tôr′ē-ə-līz′, -tōr′-) *tr.v.* **-ized, -iz·ing, -iz·es.** To show in pictures; illustrate: *pictorialized the changing seasons.* —**pic·to′ri·al·i·za′tion** (-ə-lĭ-zā′shən) *n.*

pic·ture (pĭk′chər) *n.* **1.** A visual representation or image painted, drawn, photographed, or otherwise rendered on a flat surface. **2.** A visible image, especially one on a flat surface: *the picture reflected in the lake.* **3.a.** A vivid or realistic verbal description: *a Shakespearean picture of guilt.* **b.** A vivid mental image. **4.** A person or an object bearing a marked resemblance to another: *She's the picture of her mother.* **5.** A person, an object, or a scene that typifies or embodies an emotion, a state of mind, or a mood: *Your face was the very picture of horror.* **6.** The chief circumstances of an event or time; a situation. **7.** A movie. **8.** A tableau vivant. —**picture** *tr.v.* **-tured, -tur·ing, -tures. 1.** To make a visible representation of. **2.** To form a mental image of; visualize. **3.** To describe vividly in words; make a verbal picture of: *He pictured her heroism in glowing language.* See Synonyms at **represent.** [Middle English, from Latin *pictūra,* from *pictus,* painted, past participle of *pingere,* to paint. See **peig-** in Appendix.]

ă pat	oi boy
ā pay	ou out
âr care	ŏŏ took
ä father	ōō boot
ĕ pet	ŭ cut
ē be	ûr urge
ĭ pit	th thin
ī pie	*th* this
îr pier	hw which
ŏ pot	zh vision
ō toe	ə about, item
ô paw	♦ regionalism

Stress marks: ′ (primary); ′ (secondary), as in **dictionary** (dĭk′shə-nĕr′ē)

picture card *n. Games.* See **face card.**

picture hat *n.* An elaborately decorated, broad-brimmed hat for women.

Pic·ture·phone (pĭk′chər-fōn′). A trademark used for a videophone.

picture puzzle *n. Games.* See **jigsaw puzzle.**

pic·tur·esque (pĭk′chə-rĕsk′) *adj.* **1.** Of, suggesting, or suitable for a picture: *picturesque rocky shores.* **2.** Striking or interesting in an unusual way; irregularly or quaintly attractive: *a picturesque French café.* **3.** Strikingly expressive or vivid: *picturesque language.* [Alteration of French *pittoresque,* from Italian *pittoresco,* from *pittore,* painter, from Latin *pictor,* from *pingere,* to paint. See **peig-** in Appendix.] —**pic′tur·esque′ly** *adv.* —**pic′tur·esque′ness** *n.*

picture tube *n.* A cathode-ray tube in a television receiver that translates received electrical signals into a visible picture on a luminescent screen. Also called *kinescope.*

picture window *n.* A large, usually single-paned window that provides a broad outside view.

pic·ul (pĭk′əl) *n.* Any of various units of weight used in southeast Asia and China and equal to 100 catties, especially a Chinese unit equal to 133⅓ pounds (about 60 kilograms). [Malay *pikul,* to carry the heaviest load a man can carry.]

PID *abbr.* Pelvic inflammatory disease.

pid·dle (pĭd′l) *v.* **-dled, -dling, -dles.** —*tr.* To use triflingly; squander: *piddle away one's time.* —*intr.* **1.** To spend time aimlessly; diddle. **2.** *Informal.* To urinate. [Origin unknown.]

pid·dling (pĭd′lĭng) *adj.* So trifling or trivial as to be beneath one's consideration.

pid·dock (pĭd′ək) *n.* A marine bivalve mollusk of the family Pholadidae, having a long shell with which it bores into wood, rock, and clay, often causing destruction of wharf pilings. [Origin unknown.]

pidg·in (pĭj′ən) *n.* A simplified form of speech that is usually a mixture of two or more languages, has a rudimentary grammar and vocabulary, is used for communication between groups speaking different languages, and is not spoken as a first or native language. [From PIDGIN ENGLISH.] —**pidg′in·i·za′tion** *n.* —**pidg′in·ize′** *v.*

Pid·gin English pid·gin English (pĭj′ən) *n.* Any of several pidgins based on English and now spoken mostly on the Pacific islands and in West Africa. [Alteration of *pigeon English,* from Pidgin English *pigeon,* business, perhaps from the Chinese pronunciation of English BUSINESS.]

pi-dog (pī′dôg′, -dŏg′) *n.* Variant of **pye-dog.**

pie[1] (pī) *n.* **1.** A baked food composed of a shell of pastry that is filled with fruit, meat, cheese, or other ingredients, and usually covered with a pastry crust. **2.** A layer cake having cream, custard, or jelly filling. **3.** A whole that can be shared: *"That would . . . enlarge the economic pie by making the most productive use of every investment dollar"* (New York Times). —*idiom.* **pie in the sky.** An empty wish or promise: *"To outlaw deficits . . . is pie in the sky"* (Howard H. Baker, Jr.). [Middle English.]

WORD HISTORY: The etymology of the word *pie* turns etymologists into Simple Simons, that is, we do not know what it is for certain. It may come from Medieval Latin *pica* or *pia,* "pie, pasty," but we do not know the origins of these words and the earliest use of the Middle English word *pie* is earlier (1199) than the first use of Medieval Latin *pica* (c. 1310) or *pia* (1230). It has been suggested that Medieval Latin *pica* may be from Latin *pīca,* "magpie." The connection could have been made because the miscellaneous nature of pie ingredients might have brought to mind either the magpie's piebald coloration or its habit of collecting miscellaneous items. In any case, the first pies contained fowl, fish, or meat; the first certain recorded mention of a fruit pie is in Robert Greene's *Arcadia,* published in 1590: "Thy breath is like the steame of apple-pyes."

pie[2] (pī) *n.* See **magpie** (sense 1). [Middle English, from Old French, from Latin *pīca.*]

pie[3] (pī) *n.* A monetary unit formerly in use in India and Pakistan. [Hindi *pā'ī,* from Sanskrit *pādikā,* quarter, from *pāt, pād-,* foot, leg. See **ped-** in Appendix.]

pie[4] (pī) *n.* An almanac of services used in the English church before the Reformation. [Medieval Latin *pīca.*]

pie[5] (pī) *n. & v. Printing.* Variant of **pi[2].**

pie·bald (pī′bôld′) *adj.* Spotted or patched, especially in black and white: *a piebald horse.* —**piebald** *n.* A piebald animal, especially a horse. [PIE[2] + BALD.]

piece (pēs) *n.* **1.** A thing considered as a unit or an element of a larger thing, quantity, or class; a portion: *a piece of string.* **2.** A portion or part that has been separated from a whole: *a piece of cake.* **3.** An object that is one member of a group or class: *a piece of furniture.* **4.** An artistic, musical, or literary work or composition: *"They are lively and well-plotted pieces, both in prose"* (Tucker Brooke). **5.** An instance; a specimen: *a piece of sheer folly.* **6.** A declaration of one's opinions or findings: *speak one's piece.* **7.** A coin: *a ten-cent piece.* **8.** *Games.* **a.** One of the counters or figures used in playing various board games. **b.** Any one of the chess figures other than a pawn. **9.** *Slang.* A firearm, especially a rifle. **10.** *Informal.* A given distance: *"There was farm country down the road on the right a piece"* (James Agee). **11.** *Vulgar Slang.* A sexually attractive person. **—piece** *tr.v.* **pieced, piec·ing, piec·es. 1.** To mend by adding pieces or a piece to. **2.** To join or unite the pieces of: *He pieced together the vase. She pieced together an account of what had gone on during the stormy meeting.* **—*idioms.* a piece of (one's) mind.** Frank and severe criticism; censure. **of a piece.** Belonging to the same class or kind. **piece by piece.** In stages: *took the clock apart piece by piece.* **piece of the action.** *Slang.* A share of an activity or of profits: *"a piece of the action in a Florida land deal"* (Shana Alexander). [Middle English *pece,* from Old French, from Vulgar Latin **pettia,* probably of Celtic origin.]

pièce de ré·sis·tance (pyĕs də rā-zē-stäns′) *n., pl.* **pièces de ré·sis·tance** (pyĕs). **1.** An outstanding accomplishment: *"The bison is an evolutionary pièce de résistance, the result of thousands of years of genetic development under the toughest weather and geographical conditions"* (B.J. Roche). **2.** The principal dish of a meal. [French : *pièce,* piece + *de,* of, with + *résistance,* staying power, lastingness.]

piece goods *pl.n.* Fabrics made and sold in standard lengths. Also called *yard goods.*

piece·meal (pēs′mēl′) *adv.* **1.** By a small amount at a time; in stages: *articles acquired piecemeal.* **2.** In pieces; apart. **—piecemeal** *adj.* Accomplished or made in stages. [Middle English *pecemeale* : *pece,* piece; see PIECE + *-mele,* by a fixed measure (from Old English *-mǣlum,* at a time, from dative pl. of *mǣl,* appointed time; see **mē-**[2] in Appendix).]

piece of cake *n. Informal.* Something very easy to do: *"Relearning to fly was a piece of cake"* (Burton Bernstein).

piece of eight *n., pl.* **pieces of eight.** An old Spanish silver coin. [From its original value of eight reals.]

piece of work *n.* A remarkable person, achievement, or product: *"He's a very tough piece of work"* (Ted Koppel).

piece·work (pēs′wûrk′) *n.* Work paid for according to the number of units turned out. **—piece′work′er** *n.*

pie chart *n.* A circular graph having radii dividing the circle into sectors proportional in angle and area to the relative size of the quantities represented. Also called *circle graph.*

pied[1] (pīd) *adj.* Patchy in color; splotched or piebald. [Middle English, from *pie,* magpie. See PIE[2].]

pied[2] (pīd) *v. Printing.* Past tense and past participle of **pi**[2].

pied-à-terre (pyā-dä-târ′) *n., pl.* **pieds-à-terre** (pyā-dä-târ′). A secondary or temporary place of lodging. [French : *pied,* foot + *à,* to, on + *terre,* ground.]

pied-billed grebe (pīd′bĭld′) *n.* A small, brown, North American diving bird *(Podilymbus podiceps)* having a short, heavy, whitish bill, found in freshwater ponds and marshes.

pied·mont (pēd′mŏnt′) *n.* An area of land formed or lying at the foot of a mountain or mountain range. **—piedmont** *adj.* Of, relating to, or constituting such an area of land. [After PIEDMONT.]

Pied·mont (pēd′mŏnt′). **1.** A historical region of northwest Italy bordering on France and Switzerland. Occupied by Rome in the 1st century B.C., it passed to Savoy in the 11th century and was the center of the Italian Risorgimento after 1814. **2.** A plateau region of the eastern United States extending from New York to Alabama between the Appalachian Mountains and the Atlantic coastal plain. **—Pied′mon·tese′** (-tēz′, -tēs′) *adj. & n.*

pied piper *n.* **1.** A person who offers others strong yet delusive enticements. **2.** One, such as a leader, who makes irresponsible promises. [After *The Pied Piper of Hamelin,* title and hero of a poem by Robert Browning.]

pie-eyed (pī′īd′) *adj. Slang.* Intoxicated; drunk.

Pie·gan (pē-găn′) *n., pl.* **Piegan** or **-gans. 1.** The southernmost tribe of the Blackfoot confederacy, inhabiting northwest Montana and southern Alberta. **2.** A member of this tribe.

pie plant *n.* See **rhubarb** (sense 1).

pier (pîr) *n.* **1.a.** A platform extending from a shore over water and supported by piles or pillars, used to secure, protect, and provide access to ships or boats. **b.** Such a structure used predominantly for entertainment. **2.** A supporting structure at the junction of connecting spans of a bridge. **3.** *Architecture.* Any of various vertical supporting structures, especially: **a.** A pillar, rectangular in cross section, supporting an arch or roof. **b.** The portion of a wall between windows. **c.** A reinforcing structure that projects from a wall; a buttress. [Middle English *per,* bridge support, partly from Norman French *pere, piere* (from Old French *puiere,* a support, from *puie,* support, from *puier,* to support, from Vulgar Latin **podiāre,* from Latin *podium,* platform; see PODIUM) and partly from Medieval Latin *pera* (from Old North French *pire, piere,* breakwater, possibly from Latin *petra,* rock, from Greek).]

pierce (pîrs) *v.* **pierced, pierc·ing, pierc·es.** *—tr.* **1.** To cut or pass through with or as if with a sharp instrument; stab or penetrate. **2.** To make a hole or opening in; perforate. **3.** To make a way through: *The path pierced the wilderness.* **4.** To sound sharply through: *His shout pierced the din.* **5.** To succeed in penetrating (something) with the eyes or the intellect: *Large glowing yellow eyes pierced the darkness.* *—intr.* To penetrate into or through something: *The rocket pierced through space.* [Middle English *percen,* from Old French *percer,* probably from Vulgar Latin **pertūsiāre,* from Latin *pertūsus,* past participle of *pertundere,* to bore through : *per-,* per- + *tundere,* to beat.] **—pierc′er** *n.* **—pierc′ing** *adj.* **—pierc′ing·ly** *adv.*

Pierce (pîrs), **Franklin.** 1804–1869. The 14th President of the United States (1853–1857). He was unable to reconcile the issue of slavery that divided the United States.

Pi·e·ri·a (pī-îr′ē-ə). A region of ancient Macedonia. It included Mount Olympus and Mount Pierus, seat of the worship of Orpheus and the Muses.

Pi·e·ri·an Spring (pī-îr′ē-ən) *n.* **1.** *Greek Mythology.* A spring in Macedonia, sacred to the Muses. **2.** A source of inspiration. [From Latin *Pīerius,* sacred to the Muses, from Greek *Pieria,* a region of Macedonia. See **peiə-** in Appendix.]

Pie·ro del·la Fran·ce·sca (pyâr′ō dĕl′ə frăn-chĕs′kə, frän-). 1420?–1492. Italian painter of the quattrocento whose works, including the fresco cycle *Legend of the True Cross* (1452–1459), show a mastery of geometric perspective.

Pierre (pîr). The capital of South Dakota, in the central part of the state on the Missouri River. Originally a small trading center, it thrived after the coming of the railroad and was chosen as state capital in 1889. Population, 11,973.

Pierre·fonds (pē-ĕr-fôn′, pyĕr-). A city of southern Quebec, Canada, on Montreal Island west of Montreal. Population, 38,390.

Pier·rot (pē′ə-rō′, pyĕ-rō′) *n.* A character in French pantomime, dressed in a floppy white outfit. [French, diminutive of the name *Pierre,* Peter, from Old French, from Latin *Petrus.*]

pie·tà also **Pie·tà** (pyā-tä′) *n.* A painting or sculpture of the Virgin Mary holding and mourning over the dead body of Jesus. [Italian, pity, a pietà, from Latin *pietās, pietās.* See PIETY.]

pi·e·tism (pī′ĭ-tĭz′əm) *n.* **1.** Stress on the emotional and personal aspects of religion. **2.** Affected or exaggerated piety. **3. Pietism.** A reform movement in the German Lutheran Church during the 17th and 18th centuries, which strove to renew the devotional ideal in the Protestant religion. [German *Pietismus,* from Latin *pietās, pietās,* piety. See PIETY.] **—pi′e·tist** *n.* **—pi′e·tis′tic, pi′e·tis′ti·cal** *adj.* **—pi′e·tis′ti·cal·ly** *adv.*

pi·e·ty (pī′ĭ-tē) *n., pl.* **-ties. 1.** The state or quality of being pious, especially: **a.** Religious devotion and reverence to God. **b.** Devotion and reverence to parents and family: *filial piety.* **2.** A devout act, thought, or statement. **3.a.** A position held conventionally or hypocritically. **b.** A statement of such a position: *"the liberated pieties of people who believe that social attitudes have kept pace with women's aspirations"* (Erica Abeel). [Middle English *piete,* mercy, pity, from Old French, from Latin *pietās, pietās,* dutiful conduct, from *pius, pīus,* dutiful.]

piezo– *pref.* Pressure: *piezoelectricity.* [From Greek *piezein,* to press tight, squeeze. See **sed-** in Appendix.]

pi·e·zo·e·lec·tric·i·ty (pī-ē′zō-ĭ-lĕk-trĭs′ĭ-tē, -ē′lĕk-, pē-ā′zō-) *n.* The generation of electricity or of electric polarity in dielectric crystals subjected to mechanical stress, or the generation of stress in such crystals subjected to an applied voltage. **—pi·e′zo·e·lec′tric, pi·e′zo·e·lec′tri·cal** *adj.* **—pi·e′zo·e·lec′tri·cal·ly** *adv.*

pi·e·zom·e·ter (pī′ĭ-zŏm′ĭ-tər, pē′ĭ-) *n.* An instrument for measuring pressure, especially high pressure. **—pi·e′zo·met′ric** (pī-ē′zə-mĕt′rĭk, pē-ā′zə-), **pi′e′zo·met′ri·cal** (-rĭ-kəl) *adj.* **—pi·e′zom′e·try** *n.*

pif·fle (pĭf′əl) *intr.v.* **-fled, -fling, -fles.** To talk or act in a feeble or futile way. **—piffle** *n.* Foolish or futile talk or ideas; nonsense. [Origin unknown.]

pig (pĭg) *n.* **1.a.** Any of several mammals of the family Suidae, having short legs, cloven hoofs, bristly hair, and a cartilaginous snout used for digging, especially the domesticated hog, *Sus scrofa,* when young or of comparatively small size. **b.** The edible parts of one of these mammals. **2.** *Informal.* A person regarded as being piglike, greedy, or gross. **3.a.** A crude block of metal, chiefly iron or lead, poured from a smelting furnace. **b.** A mold in which such metal is cast. **c.** Pig iron. **4.** *Offensive Slang.* Used as a disparaging term for a police officer. **5.** *Slang.* A member of the social or political establishment, especially one holding sexist or racist views. **—pig** *intr.v.* **pigged, pig·ging, pigs.** To give birth to pigs; farrow. **—*phrasal verb.* pig out.** *Slang.* To eat ravenously; gorge oneself: *"a parent who asks a child, 'Would you like to pig out on pizza?'"* (George F. Will). **—*idioms.* in a pig's eye.** *Slang.* Under no condition; never. **pig in a poke.** Something that is offered in a manner that conceals its true nature or value. **pig it.** *Slang.* To live in a piglike fashion. [Middle English *pigge,* young pig, probably from Old English **picga.*]

pig bed *n.* A bed of sand in which pigs of iron are cast.

pig·boat (pĭg′bōt′) *n. Slang.* A submarine.

pi·geon (pĭj′ən) *n.* **1.** Any of various birds of the widely distributed family Columbidae, characteristically having deep-chested bodies, small heads, and short legs, especially the rock dove or any of its domesticated varieties. **2.** *Slang.* One who is easily swindled; a dupe. [Middle English, from Old French *pijon,* probably from Vulgar Latin **pībiō, pībiōn-,* alteration of Late Latin *pīpiō,* young chirping bird, squab, from *pīpīre,* to chirp.]

pigeon breast *n.* A chest deformity marked by a projecting sternum, often occurring as a result of infantile rickets. Also called *chicken breast.* **—pi′geon-breast′ed** (pĭj′ən-brĕs′tĭd) *adj.*

pigeon hawk *n.* See **merlin.**

pi·geon·hole (pĭj′ən-hōl′) *n.* **1.** A small compartment or re-

pier
Top: Fishing pier
Bottom: Piers supporting a bridge

Franklin Pierce

pietà
Pietà by Michelangelo, Saint Peter's Cathedral, Rome

pigmy hippopotamus
Choeropsis liberiensis

pike²
Northern pike
Esox lucius

pilaster

ă pat | oi boy
ā pay | ou out
âr care | o͝o took
ä father | o͞o boot
ĕ pet | ŭ cut
ē be | ûr urge
ĭ pit | th thin
ī pie | *th* this
îr pier | hw which
ŏ pot | zh vision
ō toe | ə about, item
ô paw | ♦ regionalism

Stress marks: **ʹ** (primary); ʹ (secondary), as in **dictionary** (dĭkʹshə-nĕrʹē)

cess, as in a desk, for holding papers; a cubbyhole. **2.** A specific, often oversimplified category. **3.** The small hole or holes in a pigeon loft for nesting. **—pigeonhole** *tr.v.* **-holed, -hol·ing, -holes. 1.** To place or file in a small compartment or recess. **2.** To classify mentally; categorize. **3.** To put aside and ignore; shelve.

pigeon pea *n.* See **cajan pea.** [From the use of its seeds as pigeon feed.]

pi·geon-toed (pĭjʹən-tōdʹ) *adj.* Having the toes turned inward.

pig·fish (pĭgʹfĭshʹ) *n., pl.* **pigfish** or **-fish·es.** A North American grunt *(Orthopristis chrysoptera)* with a piglike mouth, found along the Atlantic and Gulf coasts of the United States and important as a food fish. Also called *hogfish.* [From the grunting sound it makes.]

pig·ger·y (pĭgʹə-rē) *n., pl.* **-ies. 1.** A place where pigs are raised or kept. **2.** Piggish conduct.

pig·gish (pĭgʹĭsh) *adj.* **1.** Greedy: *a piggish appetite.* **2.** Stubborn; pigheaded. **—pigʹgish·ly** *adv.* **—pigʹgish·ness** *n.*

pig·gy (pĭgʹē) *n., pl.* **-gies.** *Informal.* A little pig.

pig·gy·back (pĭgʹē-băkʹ) *adv. & adj.* **1.** On the shoulders or back: *ride piggyback; a piggyback ride.* **2.** By or relating to a method of transportation in which truck trailers are carried on trains, or cars on specially designed trucks. **3.** In connection with something larger or more important: *a tariff provision that came piggyback with the tax bill; a piggyback provision to a new piece of legislation.* **—piggyback** *n.* The act of transporting piggyback. **—piggyback** *v.* **-backed, -back·ing, -backs.** *—tr.* To cause to be aligned with (an issue, for example) that is larger or more important: *"a $21.5-million federal grant to piggyback city and state subsidies"* (New York). *—intr.* To function as if carried on the back of another: *"This reagent will piggyback onto an enzyme"* (Seth Rolbein). [Alteration of dialectal *pig back,* alteration of *pickaback, pickback, pick pack* : probably dialectal *pick,* to throw (variant of PITCH²) + BACK¹ or PACK¹.]

piggy bank *n.* A child's coin bank shaped like a pig.

pig·head·ed (pĭgʹhĕdʹĭd) *adj.* Stupidly obstinate. See Synonyms at **obstinate. —pigʹhead'ed·ly** *adv.* **—pigʹhead'ed·ness** *n.*

pig iron *n.* Crude iron cast in blocks.

pig Latin *n.* A jargon systematically formed by the transposition of the initial consonant to the end of the word and the suffixation of an additional syllable, as *igpay atinlay* for *pig Latin.*

pig lead (lĕd) *n.* Crude lead cast in blocks.

pig·let (pĭgʹlĭt) *n.* A young pig.

pig·ment (pĭgʹmənt) *n.* **1.** A substance used as coloring. **2.** Dry coloring matter, usually an insoluble powder to be mixed with water, oil, or another base to produce paint and similar products. **3.** A substance, such as chlorophyll or melanin, that produces a characteristic color in plant or animal tissue. **—pigment** *tr.v.* **-ment·ed, -ment·ing, -ments.** To color with pigment. [Middle English, spice, red dye, from Latin *pigmentum,* from *pingere,* to paint. See **peig-** in Appendix.] **—pigʹmen·tarʹy** (pĭgʹmən-tĕrʹē) *adj.*

pig·men·ta·tion (pĭgʹmən-tāʹshən) *n. Biology.* **1.** Coloration of tissues by pigment. **2.** Deposition of pigment by cells.

pigment cell *n. Biology.* See **chromatophore** (sense 1).

Pig·my (pĭgʹmē) *n. & adj.* Variant of **Pygmy.**

pigmy hippopotamus *n.* A small hippopotamus *(Choeropsis liberiensis)* of Liberia and the Ivory Coast, found in lowland forests and swamps.

pig·nut (pĭgʹnŭtʹ) *n.* **1.** Either of two deciduous trees *(Carya glabra* or *C. ovalis)* of the eastern United States, having pinnately compound leaves, male flowers grouped in catkins, and nuts with somewhat bitter kernels. **2.** The nut of either of these trees. **3.** The wood of either of these trees.

pig-out (pĭgʹoutʹ) *n. Slang.* The act or an instance of voracious eating by a person or group.

pig·pen (pĭgʹpĕnʹ) *n.* **1.** A pen for pigs. **2.** *Slang.* A dirty or very untidy place.

Pigs (pĭgz), **Bay of.** A small inlet of the Caribbean Sea on the southern coast of western Cuba. It was the site of an ill-fated invasion on April 17, 1961, when a force of 1,500 U.S.-trained guerrilla troops landed in an attempt to overthrow the government of Fidel Castro.

pig·skin (pĭgʹskĭnʹ) *n.* **1.** The skin of a pig. **2.** Leather made from the skin of a pig. **3.** *Sports.* A football. **4.** *Informal.* A saddle.

pigs·ney (pĭgzʹnē) *n., pl.* **-neys.** *Obsolete.* **1.** A darling. **2.** An eye. [Middle English *piggesnye* : *pigges,* genitive of *pigge,* pig; see PIG + *nye* (from *an eye,* an eye; see EYE).]

pig·sty (pĭgʹstīʹ) *n., pl.* **-sties. 1.** A shelter where pigs are kept. **2.** *Slang.* A dirty or very untidy place.

pig·tail (pĭgʹtālʹ) *n.* **1.** A plait of braided hair. **2.** A twisted roll of tobacco. **3.** See **flamingo flower. —pigʹtailedʹ** *adj.*

pig·weed (pĭgʹwēdʹ) *n.* **1.** A common weed *(Chenopodium album)* having lance-shaped leaves with a mealy surface and small green flowers. Also called *lamb's quarters.* **2.** A coarse cosmopolitan weed *(Amaranthus retroflexus)* having hairy leaves and stout, terminal panicles with dense, lateral spikes of green flowers. Also called *redroot.*

pi·ka (pēʹkə) *n.* Any of several small, tailless, furry mammals of the genus *Ochotona* of the mountains of North America and Eurasia, resembling guinea pigs but belonging to the order of lagomorphs that includes the hares and rabbits. Also called *coney, rock rabbit.* [Tungus *piika,* perhaps from Russian *pikat',* to squeak.]

pike¹ (pīk) *n.* A long spear formerly used by infantry. **—pike** *tr.v.* **piked, pik·ing, pikes.** To attack or pierce with a pike. [French *pique,* from Old French, from *piquer,* to prick. See PIQUE.] **—piked** *adj.*

pike² (pīk) *n., pl.* **pike** or **pikes. 1.** A freshwater game and food fish *(Esox lucius)* of the Northern Hemisphere that has a long snout and attains a length of over 1.2 meters (4 feet). Also called *northern pike.* **2.** Any of various similar or related fishes. [Middle English, perhaps from Old English *pīc,* sharp point (from its shape).]

pike³ (pīk) *n.* **1.** A turnpike. **2.a.** A tollgate on a turnpike. **b.** A toll paid. **—pike** *intr.v.* **piked, pik·ing, pikes.** To move quickly. ***—idiom.* come down the pike.** *Slang.* To come into prominence: *"a policy . . . allowing for little flexibility if an important new singer comes down the pike"* (Christian Science Monitor). [Short for TURNPIKE.]

pike⁴ (pīk) *n. Chiefly British.* A hill with a pointed summit. [Middle English, possibly of Scandinavian origin.]

pike⁵ (pīk) *n.* A spike or sharp point, as on the tip of a spear. [Middle English, from Old English *pīc.*]

Pike (pīk), **Zebulon Montgomery.** 1779–1813. American army officer and explorer noted for his expedition up the Arkansas River to the Rocky Mountains (1806–1807).

piked whale (pīkt) *n.* A small, dark gray whale *(Balaenoptera acutorostrata)* having a white underside and white bands on the flippers. Also called *minke whale.*

pike·perch (pīkʹpûrchʹ) *n., pl.* **pikeperch** or **-perch·es.** A fish, such as the walleye, that is related to the perch and resembles the pike.

pik·er (pīʹkər) *n. Slang.* **1.** A cautious gambler. **2.** A person regarded as petty or stingy. [Possibly from *Piker,* a poor migrant to California, after *Pike* County in eastern Missouri.]

Pikes Peak (pīks). A mountain, 4,303.6 m (14,110 ft) high, in the Front Range of the Rocky Mountains in central Colorado. It was discovered in 1806 by Zebulon M. Pike and is noted for the spectacular view from its summit.

pike·staff (pīkʹstăfʹ) *n.* **1.** The shaft of a pike. **2.** A walking stick tipped with a metal spike.

pi·laf or **pi·laff** (pĭ-läfʹ, pēʹläfʹ) also **pi·lau** (pĭ-läfʹ, -lôʹ, -louʹ, pēʹläfʹ, -lôʹ, -louʹ) *n.* A steamed rice dish often with meat, shellfish, or vegetables in a seasoned broth. [Persian *pilāw,* from Turkish *pilāv.*]

pi·lar (pīʹlər) *adj.* Of, relating to, or covered with hair. [New Latin *pilāris,* from Latin *pilus,* hair.]

pi·las·ter (pĭ-lăsʹtər) *n. Architecture.* A rectangular column with a capital and base, set into a wall as an ornamental motif. [French *pilastre,* from Old French, from Old Italian *pilastro,* from Medieval Latin *pīlaster* : Latin *pīla,* pillar + Latin *-aster,* n. suff., or blend of Latin *pīla,* pillar and Late Latin *parastatēs,* pilaster (from Greek, stay, supporter : *para-,* beside; see PARA–¹ + *-statēs,* -stat).]

Pi·late (pīʹlət), **Pontius.** fl. first century A.D. Roman governor of Judea who ordered Christ's crucifixion.

Pi·la·tus (pĭ-läʹtəs, pē-läʹto͞os). A peak, 2,121.3 m (6,955 ft) high, in the Alps of central Switzerland south-southwest of Lucerne. According to medieval folklore, the body of Pontius Pilate was thrown into a small lake on the mountain.

pi·lau (pĭ-läfʹ, -lôʹ, -louʹ, pēʹläfʹ, -lôʹ, -louʹ) *n.* Variant of **pilaf.**

pil·chard (pĭlʹchərd) *n.* Any of various small marine fishes related to the herrings, especially a commercially important edible species, *Sardina pilchardus,* of European waters. [Origin unknown.]

Pil·co·ma·yo (pĭlʹkō-mäʹyō, pēlʹ-). A river of central South America rising in central Bolivia and flowing about 1,609 km (1,000 mi) southeast along the Argentina-Paraguay border to the Paraguay River.

pile¹ (pīl) *n.* **1.** A quantity of objects stacked or thrown together in a heap. See Synonyms at **heap. 2.** *Informal.* A large accumulation or quantity: *a pile of trouble.* **3.** *Slang.* A large sum of money; a fortune: *made their pile in the commodities market.* **4.** A funeral pyre. **5.** A very large building or complex of buildings. See Synonyms at **building. 6.** A nuclear reactor. **7.** A voltaic pile. **—pile** *v.* **piled, pil·ing, piles.** *—tr.* **1.a.** To place or lay in or as if in a pile or heap: *piled books onto the table.* **b.** To load (something) with a heap or pile: *piled the table with books.* **2.** To heap (something) in abundance: *piled potato salad onto the plate.* *—intr.* **1.** To form a heap or pile. **2.** To move in, out, or forward in a disorderly mass or group: *pile into a bus; pile out of a car.* ***—phrasal verb.* pile up. 1.** To accumulate. **2.** *Informal.* To undergo a serious vehicular collision. [Middle English, from Old French, from Latin *pīla,* pillar.]

pile² (pīl) *n.* **1.** A heavy beam of timber, concrete, or steel, driven into the earth as a foundation or support for a structure. **2.** *Heraldry.* A wedge-shaped charge pointing downward. **3.** A Roman javelin. **—pile** *tr.v.* **piled, pil·ing, piles. 1.** To drive piles into. **2.** To support with piles. [Middle English, from Old English *pīl,* shaft, stake, from Latin *pīlum,* spear, pestle.]

pile³ (pīl) *n.* **1.a.** Cut or uncut loops of yarn forming the surface of certain fabrics, such as velvet, plush, and carpeting. **b.** The surface so formed. **2.** Soft, fine hair, fur, or wool. [From Middle English *piles,* hair, plumage, probably from Middle Dutch *pijl,* fine hair, and Middle Low German *pile,* downy plumage, both from Latin *pilus,* hair.] **—piled** *adj.*

pi·le·a (pī′lē-ə) *n.* Plural of **pileum.**

pi·le·at·ed (pī′lē-ā′tĭd) also **pi·le·ate** (-ĭt) *adj.* **1.** *Botany.* Having a pileus. **2.** Having a crest covering the pileum. Used of a bird. [From Latin *pīleātus,* wearing a pileus, from *pīleus,* felt cap.]

pileated woodpecker *n.* A large North American woodpecker *(Dryocopus pileatus)* having black and white plumage and a bright red crest.

pile driver *n.* **1.** A machine that drives a pile by raising a weight between guideposts and dropping it on the head of the pile. **2.** One who operates such a machine.

pi·le·i (pī′lē-ī′) *n.* Plural of **pileus.**

piles (pīlz) *pl.n.* See **hemorrhoid** (sense 2). [Middle English *piles,* from Medieval Latin *pilī,* from Latin *pila,* ball.]

pi·le·um (pī′lē-əm) *n., pl.* **-le·a** (-lē-ə). The top of a bird's head, extending from the base of the bill to the nape. [New Latin *pīleum,* from Latin *pīleus,* felt cap.]

pile·up or **pile-up** (pīl′ŭp′) *n.* **1.** *Informal.* A serious collision usually involving several motor vehicles. **2.** An accumulation: *"the pile-up of unsold autos"* (New York Times).

pi·le·us (pī′lē-əs) *n., pl.* **-le·i** (-lē-ī′). **1.** *Botany.* The umbrellalike fruiting structure forming the top of a stalked, fleshy fungus, such as a mushroom; the cap. **2.** A brimless, round skullcap worn by ancient Romans. **3.** See **caul** (sense 1). [New Latin *pīleus,* from Latin, cap.]

pile·wort (pīl′wûrt′, -wôrt′) *n.* Any of several plants, such as the lesser celandine and the fireweed, that are reputed to be effective in treating hemorrhoids. [From its use in treating piles.]

pil·fer (pĭl′fər) *v.* **-fered, -fer·ing, -fers.** *—tr.* To steal (a small amount or item). See Synonyms at **steal.** *—intr.* To steal or filch. [From Middle English *pilfre,* spoils, from Old French *pelfre.*] **—pil′fer·age** (-ĭj) *n.* **—pil′fer·er** *n.*

pil·grim (pĭl′grəm) *n.* **1.** A religious devotee who journeys to a shrine or sacred place. **2.** One who embarks on a quest for something conceived of as sacred. **3.** A traveler. **4. Pilgrim.** One of the English Separatists who founded the colony of Plymouth in New England in 1620. [Middle English, from Old French *peligrin,* from Late Latin *pelegrīnus,* alteration of Latin *peregrīnus,* foreigner. See PEREGRINE.]

pil·grim·age (pĭl′grə-mĭj) *n.* **1.** A journey to a sacred place or shrine. **2.** A long journey or search, especially one of exalted purpose or moral significance. **—pilgrimage** *intr.v.* **-aged, -ag·ing, -ag·es.** To go on a pilgrimage.

pilgrim bottle *n.* A costrel.

pi·li (pī′lī′) *n.* Plural of **pilus.**

pi·lif·er·ous (pī-lĭf′ər-əs) *adj.* Bearing or producing hair. [Latin *pilus,* hair + —FEROUS.]

pil·i·form (pĭl′ə-fôrm′) *adj.* Having the form of a hair. [Latin *pilus,* hair + —FORM.]

pil·ing (pī′lĭng) *n.* **1.** The act of driving piles. **2.** Piles considered as a group. **3.** A structure composed of piles.

Pil·i·pi·no (pĭl′ə-pē′nō) *n.* The Filipino language. [Tagalog, from *pilipino,* Filipino, from Spanish *filipino,* from *Filipinas,* the Philippines.]

pill¹ (pĭl) *n.* **1.** A small pellet or tablet of medicine, often coated, taken by swallowing whole or by chewing. **2.** *Informal.* An oral contraceptive. Used with *the.* **3.** *Slang.* Something, such as a baseball, that resembles a pellet of medicine. **4.** Something both distasteful and necessary. **5.** *Slang.* An insipid or ill-natured person. **—pill** *v.* **pilled, pil·ling, pills.** *—tr.* **1.** To dose with pills. **2.** To make into pills. **3.** *Slang.* To blackball. *—intr.* To form small balls resembling pills: *a sweater that pills.* [Middle English *pille,* from Middle Dutch or Middle Low German *pille* and Old French *pile,* all from Latin *pilula,* diminutive of *pila,* ball.]

pill² (pĭl) *v.* **pilled, pil·ling, pills.** *—intr. Chiefly British.* To come off, as in flakes or scales. *—tr. Archaic.* To subject to extortion. [Middle English *pillen,* to plunder, peel, from Old English *pilian;* see PEEL¹, and from Old French *piller,* to plunder; see PILLAGE.]

pil·lage (pĭl′ĭj) *v.* **-laged, -lag·ing, -lag·es.** *—tr.* **1.** To rob of goods by force, especially in time of war; plunder. **2.** To take as spoils. *—intr.* To take spoils by force. **—pillage** *n.* **1.** The act of pillaging. **2.** Something pillaged; spoils. [From Middle English, booty, from Old French, from *piller,* to plunder, from Vulgar Latin **pīliāre,* and from *peille,* rag (probably from Latin *pilleus, pīleus,* felt cap).] **—pil′lag·er** *n.*

pil·lar (pĭl′ər) *n.* **1.a.** A slender, freestanding, vertical support; a column. **b.** Such a structure or one similar to it used for decoration. **2.** One who occupies a central or responsible position: *a pillar of the state.* **—pillar** *tr.v.* **-lared, -lar·ing, -lars.** To support or decorate with pillars or a pillar. **—*idiom.* from pillar to post.** From one place to another; hither and thither. [Middle English, from Old French *pilier,* from Medieval Latin *pīlāre,* from Latin *pīla.*]

Pil·lars of Her·cu·les (pĭl′ərz; hûr′kyə-lēz′). The ancient name for two promontories at the eastern end of the Strait of Gibraltar and the entrance to the Mediterranean Sea. They are usually identified as Gibraltar in Europe and Jebel Musa in North Africa.

pill·box (pĭl′bŏks′) *n.* **1.** A small box for pills. **2.** A woman's small hat with upright sides and a flat crown. **3.** A low-roofed concrete emplacement for a machine gun or antitank gun.

pill bug *n.* A small terrestrial isopod crustacean of the genus *Armadillidium* closely related to the sow bug and having a convex, segmented, flexible body enabling it to curl into a ball when disturbed.

pil·lion (pĭl′yən) *n.* **1.** A pad or cushion for an extra rider behind the saddle on a horse or motorcycle. **2.** A bicycle or motorcycle saddle. [Probably from Scottish Gaelic *pillean,* diminutive of *peall,* rug, or Irish Gaelic *pillín,* diminutive of *pell,* rug, both from Old Irish *pell,* from Latin *pellis,* animal skin. See **pel-³** in Appendix.]

pil·lo·ry (pĭl′ə-rē) *n., pl.* **-ries.** A wooden framework on a post, with holes for the head and hands, in which offenders were formerly locked to be exposed to public scorn as punishment. **—pillory** *tr.v.* **-ried, -ry·ing, -ries.** **1.** To expose to ridicule and abuse. **2.** To put in a pillory as punishment. [Middle English, from Old French *pilori,* probably from Latin *pīla,* pillar.]

pil·low (pĭl′ō) *n.* **1.** A cloth case, stuffed with something soft, such as down, feathers, or foam rubber, used to cushion the head, especially during sleep. **2.** A decorative cushion. **3.** The pad on which bobbin lace is made. **—pillow** *v.* **-lowed, -low·ing, -lows.** *—tr.* **1.** To rest (one's head) on or as if on a pillow. **2.** To serve as a pillow for: *Grass pillowed my head.* *—intr.* **1.** To rest on or as if on a pillow. **2.** To assume the shape of a pillow. [Middle English, from Old English *pyle,* from West Germanic **pulwī,* from Latin *pulvīnus.*] **—pil′low·y** *adj.*

pillow block *n.* A block that encloses and supports a journal or shaft; a bearing.

pil·low·case (pĭl′ō-kās′) *n.* A removable covering for a pillow. Also called *pillowslip.*

pillow lace *n.* See **bobbin lace.**

pillow sham *n.* A decorative covering for a pillow on a bed.

pil·low·slip (pĭl′ō-slĭp′) *n.* See **pillowcase.**

pillow talk *n.* Intimate conversation between lovers, typically taking place in bed.

pi·lo·car·pine (pī′lō-kär′pēn′) *n.* A colorless or yellow poisonous compound, $C_{11}H_{16}N_2O_2$, obtained from the leaves of the jaborandi and used to induce sweating, promote salivation, and treat glaucoma. [New Latin *Pilocarpus,* jaborandi genus (Greek *pilos,* wool, felt + Greek *karpos,* fruit; see —CARP) + —INE².]

pi·lose (pī′lōs) also **pi·lous** (-ləs) *adj.* Covered with fine, soft hair. [Latin *pilōsus,* from *pilus,* hair.] **—pi·los′i·ty** (-lŏs′ĭ-tē) *n.*

pi·lot (pī′lət) *n.* **1.** One who operates or is licensed to operate an aircraft in flight. **2.** *Nautical.* **a.** One who, though not belonging to a ship's company, is licensed to conduct a ship into and out of port or through dangerous waters. **b.** The helmsman of a ship. **3.** One who guides or directs a course of action for others. **4.** The part of a tool, device, or machine that leads or guides the whole. **5.** A pilot light, as in a stove. **6.** A television program produced as a prototype of a series being considered for adoption by a network. **—pilot** *tr.v.* **-lot·ed, -lot·ing, -lots.** **1.** To serve as the pilot of. **2.** To steer or control the course of. See Synonyms at **guide.** **—pilot** *adj.* **1.** Serving as a tentative model for future experiment or development: *a pilot project.* **2.** Serving or leading as guide. [Obsolete French, helmsman, from Old French, from Old Italian *pilota,* alteration of *pedota,* probably from Medieval Greek **pēdōtēs,* from Greek *pēdon,* steering oar. See **ped-** in Appendix.]

WORD HISTORY: The pilot of an aircraft flying through the air has a foot on the ground not literally but etymologically. If we poke around in the etymological soil for the roots of the word *pilot,* we find that it goes back to the Indo-European root *ped-,* meaning "foot." From the lengthened-grade suffixed form *pēdo-* came the Greek word *pēdon,* "blade of an oar," and in the plural, "rudder." In Medieval Greek there is assumed to have existed the derivative *pēdōtēs,* "steersmen," which passed into Old Italian and acquired several forms, including *pedota,* and *pilota,* the form that was borrowed into Old French as *pilot.* English borrowed the word from French, and as *pilot* it has moved from the water to the air, first being recorded in 1848 with reference to an airborne pilot—a balloonist.

pi·lot·age (pī′lə-tĭj) *n.* **1.** *Nautical.* **a.** The technique or act of piloting. **b.** The fee paid to a pilot. **2.** Aerial navigation by visual identification of landmarks.

pilot balloon *n.* A small balloon used to determine wind velocity.

pilot bread *n.* Hardtack.

pilot burner *n.* **1.** A small service burner, as in a boiler system, kept lighted to ignite main fires. **2.** See **pilot light** (sense 1).

pilot cell *n.* A storage battery cell tested to determine the condition of the entire battery.

pilot engine *n.* A locomotive sent ahead of a train to check the track for safety and clearance.

pilot fish *n.* A small, slender marine fish *(Naucrates ductor)* that often swims in company with larger fishes, especially sharks and mantas.

pileated woodpecker
Dryocopus pileatus

Pilgrim
Detail of
Pilgrims Going to Church
by George Henry Boughton
(1833–1905)

pillory
At Colonial Williamsburg, Virginia

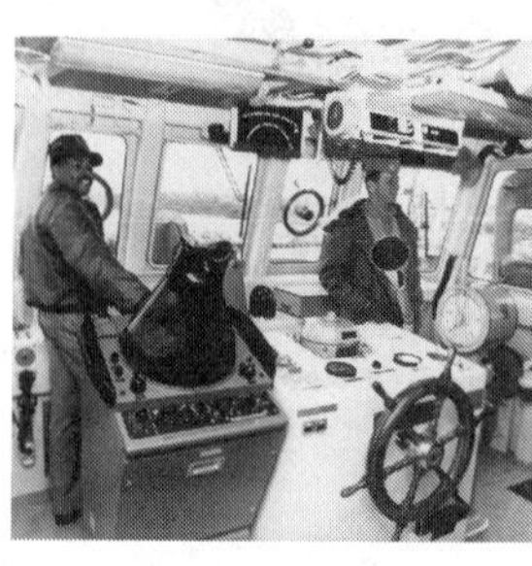

pilothouse

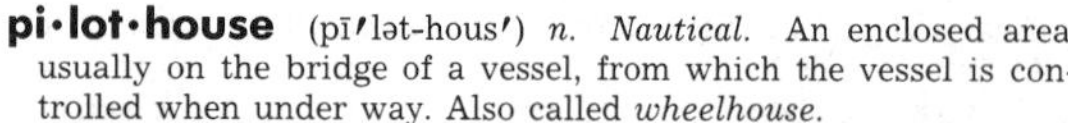

pi·lot·house (pī′lət-hous′) *n. Nautical.* An enclosed area, usually on the bridge of a vessel, from which the vessel is controlled when under way. Also called *wheelhouse.*

pi·lot·ing (pī′lə-tĭng) *n.* **1.** The occupation or service of a pilot. **2.** *Nautical.* Coastal navigation, as by reference to buoys and soundings.

pilot lamp *n.* A small electric lamp used to indicate that an electric circuit is energized. Also called *pilot light.*

pilot light *n.* **1.** A small jet of gas that is kept burning in order to ignite a gas burner, as in a stove. Also called *pilot burner.* **2.** See **pilot lamp.**

pilot whale *n.* Any of several large, usually black dolphins of the genus *Globicephala,* having an outward-curving globular forehead and noted for their occasional mass strandings. Also called *blackfish.*

pi·lous (pī′ləs) *adj.* **1.** Variant of **pilose. 2.** Of the nature of hair; consisting of hair; hairlike. [From Latin *pilōsus.* See PILOSE.]

Pil·sud·ski (pĭl-so͞ot′skē), **Jozef.** 1867–1935. Polish revolutionary leader and politician who was the first president (1918–1922) of independent Poland.

Pilt·down man (pĭlt′doun′) *n.* A supposed early species of human being postulated from a skull allegedly found in a gravel bed in about 1912 but determined in 1953 to be a fake constructed from a human cranium and the jawbone of an ape. [After *Piltdown* Common in southeast England.]

pil·ule (pĭl′yo͞ol) *n.* A small pill or pellet. [French, from Old French *pillule,* from Latin *pilula.* See PILL[1].] **—pil′u·lar** (pĭl′yə-lər) *adj.*

pi·lus (pī′ləs) *n., pl.* **-li** (-lī′). A hair or hairlike structure, especially on the surface of a cell or microorganism. [Latin.]

Pi·ma (pē′mə) *n., pl.* **Pima** or **-mas. 1.a.** A Native American people inhabiting south-central Arizona along the Gila and Salt rivers. **b.** A member of this people. **2.** The Uto-Aztecan language of the Pima, dialectally related to Papago. [From American Spanish *Pimahitos,* Pimas, from obsolete Pima *pimahaitu,* nothing.] **—Pi′man** *adj.*

pi·ma cotton (pē′mə) *n.* A very strong, high-grade cotton of medium staple developed from selected Egyptian cottons in the southwest United States. [After *Pima* County in southern Arizona.]

pi·men·to (pĭ-mĕn′tō) *n., pl.* **-tos. 1.** See **allspice. 2.** Variant of **pimiento.** [Spanish *pimiento,* red or green pepper, pepper plant, from *pimienta,* black pepper, pepper fruit, from Late Latin *pigmenta,* pl. of *pigmentum,* vegetable juice, condiment, pigment, from Latin, pigment, from *pingere,* to paint. See **peig-** in Appendix.]

pi meson *n. Physics.* See **pion.**

pi·mien·to (pĭ-mĕn′tō, -myĕn′tō) also **pi·men·to** (-mĕn′tō) *n., pl.* **-tos. 1.** A garden pepper *(Capsicum annuum)* having a mild, ripe, red fruit. **2.** The fruit of this plant, used in cookery, salad, and as stuffing for green olives. [Spanish. See PIMENTO.]

pimp (pĭmp) *n.* One who finds customers for a prostitute; a procurer. **—pimp** *intr.v.* **pimped, pimp·ing, pimps.** To serve as a procurer of prostitutes. [Origin unknown.]

pim·per·nel (pĭm′pər-nĕl′, -nəl) *n.* Any of various plants of the genus *Anagallis,* especially the scarlet pimpernel *(A. arvensis)* having opposite, entire leaves and small red, purple, or white flowers. [Middle English *pimpernelle,* from Old French, alteration of *piprenelle,* from Late Latin *pimpinella,* perhaps from Latin *piper,* pepper. See PEPPER.]

pim·ple (pĭm′pəl) *n.* A small red swelling of the skin, usually caused by acne; a papule or pustule. [Middle English.] **—pim′pled, pim′ply** *adj.*

pimp·mo·bile (pĭmp′mō-bēl′, -mə-) *n. Slang.* A flashy, oversize automobile used by or deemed suitable for use by a pimp.

pin (pĭn) *n.* **1.a.** A short, straight, stiff piece of wire with a blunt head and a sharp point, used especially for fastening. **b.** Something, such as a safety pin, that resembles such a piece of wire in shape or use. **c.** A whit; a jot: *didn't care a pin about the matter.* **2.** A slender, usually cylindrical piece of wood or metal for holding or fastening parts together, or serving as a support for suspending one thing from another, as: **a.** A thin rod for securing the ends of fractured bones. **b.** A peg for fixing the crown to the root of a tooth. **c.** A cotter pin. **d.** The part of a key stem entering a lock. **e.** *Music.* One of the pegs securing the strings and regulating their tension on a stringed instrument. **f.** *Nautical.* A belaying pin. **g.** *Nautical.* A thole pin. **3.** An ornament fastened to clothing by means of a clasp. **4.** A rolling pin. **5.** *Sports.* **a.** One of the wooden clubs at which the ball is aimed in bowling. **b.** A flagstick. **c.** See **fall** (sense 14a). **6. pins.** *Informal.* The legs: *spry for his age, and steady on his pins.* **7.** *Electronics.* A lead on a device that plugs into a socket to connect the device to a system. **8.** *Computer Science.* **a.** Any of the pegs on the platen of a printer, which engage holes at the edges of paper. **b.** Any of the styluses that form a dot matrix on a printer. **—pin** *tr.v.* **pinned, pin·ning, pins. 1.** To fasten or secure with or as if with a pin or pins. **2.** To transfix. **3.** To place in a position of trusting dependence: *He pinned his faith on an absurdity.* **4.a.** To hold fast; immobilize: *The passenger was pinned under the wreckage of the truck.* **b.** *Sports.* To win a fall from in wrestling. **5.** To give (a woman) a fraternity pin in token of attachment. **—pin** *adj.* Having a grain suggestive of the heads of pins. Used of leather.

piñata

pince-nez
Worn by Theodore Roosevelt

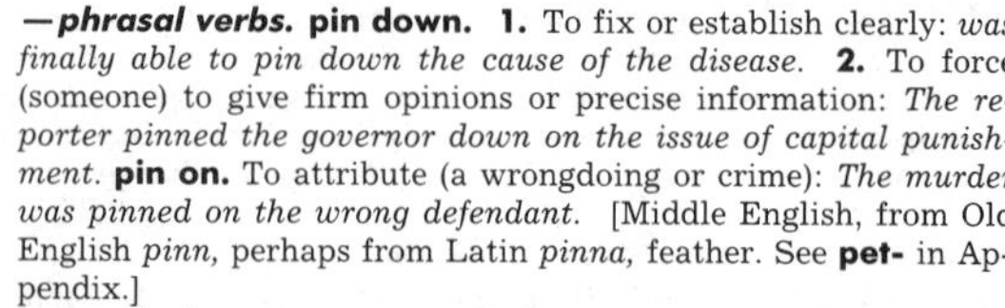

—*phrasal verbs.* pin down. 1. To fix or establish clearly: *was finally able to pin down the cause of the disease.* **2.** To force (someone) to give firm opinions or precise information: *The reporter pinned the governor down on the issue of capital punishment.* **pin on.** To attribute (a wrongdoing or crime): *The murder was pinned on the wrong defendant.* [Middle English, from Old English *pinn,* perhaps from Latin *pinna,* feather. See **pet-** in Appendix.]

pi·ña cloth (pēn′yə) *n.* A soft, sheer fabric made from the fibers of pineapple leaves. [Spanish *piña,* pine cone, pineapple, from Latin *pīnea,* pine cone, from *pīnus,* pine. See **peiə-** in Appendix.]

pi·ña co·la·da (pēn′yə kō-lä′də, kə-, pĭn′-) *n.* A mixed drink made of rum, coconut cream, and unsweetened pineapple juice. [Spanish, strained pineapple : *piña,* pineapple + *colada,* strained.]

pin·a·fore (pĭn′ə-fôr′, -fōr′) *n.* A sleeveless garment similar to an apron, worn especially by small girls as a dress or an overdress. [PIN + AFORE (so called because formerly pinned to the front of the dress).]

Pi·nang (pə-năng′, pē′näng′). See **George Town** (sense 1).

pi·nas·ter (pī-năs′tər) *n.* A Mediterranean pine tree *(Pinus pinaster)* having a characteristic pyramidal form and needles clustered in fascicles of two. [Latin, wild pine, from *pīnus,* pine. See PINE[1].]

pi·ña·ta (pēn-yä′tə) *n. Games.* A decorated container filled with candy and toys suspended from a height, intended to be broken by blindfolded children with sticks, and used as part of Christmas and birthday celebrations in certain Latin-American countries or at children's parties. [Spanish, from Italian *pignatta,* a kind of pot, probably from dialectal *pigna,* pine cone (from its shape), from Latin *pīnea.* See PINEAL.]

pin·ball (pĭn′bôl′) *n. Games.* A game played on a device in which the player operates a plunger to shoot a ball down or along a slanted surface having obstacles and targets.

pince-nez (păns′nā′, pĭns′-) *n., pl.* **pince-nez** (-nāz′, -nā′). Eyeglasses clipped to the bridge of the nose. [French : *pincer,* to pinch (from Old French *pincier;* see PINCH) + *nez,* nose (from Latin *nāsus;* see **nas-** in Appendix).]

pin·cer (pĭn′sər) *n.* **1.** An object resembling one of the grasping parts of a set of pincers. **2.** A maneuver in which an enemy force is attacked from two flanks and the front.

pin·cers (pĭn′sərz) also **pinch·ers** (pĭn′chərz) *pl.n. (used with a sing. or pl. verb).* **1.** A grasping tool having a pair of jaws and handles pivoted together to work in opposition. **2.** The articulated, prehensile claws of certain arthropods, such as the lobster. [Middle English *pinsours,* from Old French *pinceure,* from Old French *pincier,* to pinch. See PINCH.]

pinch (pĭnch) *v.* **pinched, pinch·ing, pinch·es.** *—tr.* **1.** To squeeze between the thumb and a finger, the jaws of a tool, or other edges. **2.** To squeeze or bind (a part of the body) in such a way as to cause discomfort or pain: *These shoes pinch my toes.* **3.** To nip, wither, or shrivel: *buds that were pinched by the frost; a face that was pinched with grief.* **4.** To straiten: *"A year and a half of the blockade has pinched Germany"* (William L. Shirer). **5.** *Slang.* To take (money or property) unlawfully; steal. See Synonyms at **steal. 6.** *Slang.* To take into custody; arrest. **7.** To move (something) by means of a pinch bar. **8.** *Nautical.* To head (a boat) very close into the wind. *—intr.* **1.** To press, squeeze, or bind painfully: *This collar pinches.* **2.** To be miserly. **3.** *Nautical.* To drag an oar at the end of a stroke. **—pinch** *n.* **1.** The act or an instance of pinching. **2.** An amount that can be held between thumb and forefinger: *a pinch of rosemary.* **3.** A painful, difficult, or straitened circumstance: *felt the pinch of the recession.* **4.** An emergency situation: *This coat will do in a pinch.* **5.** A narrowing of a mineral deposit, as in a mine. **6.** *Informal.* A theft. **7.** *Slang.* An arrest by a law enforcement officer. **—pinch** *adj. Baseball.* Relating to pinch-hitting or pinch runners: *a pinch single; a pinch steal of second base.* **—*idiom.* pinch pennies.** *Informal.* To be thrifty or miserly. [Middle English *pinchen,* from Old North French *pinchier, variant of Old French *pincier,* perhaps from Vulgar Latin *pīnctiāre.]

pinch bar *n.* A crowbar with a pointed projection at one end.

pinch·beck (pĭnch′bĕk′) *n.* **1.** An alloy of zinc and copper used as imitation gold. **2.** A cheap imitation. **—pinchbeck** *adj.* **1.** Made of pinchbeck. **2.** Imitation; spurious. [After Christopher *Pinchbeck* (1670?–1732), English watchmaker.]

pinch·cock (pĭnch′kŏk′) *n.* A clamp used to regulate or close a flexible tube, especially in laboratory apparatus.

pinch effect *n. Physics.* Radial constriction of flowing plasma or other matter carrying an electric current, caused by the magnetic field that is produced by the current.

pinch·ers (pĭn′chərz) *pl.n.* Variant of **pincers.**

pinch-hit (pĭnch′hĭt′) *intr.v.* **-hit, -hit·ting, -hits. 1.** *Baseball.* To bat in place of a player scheduled to bat, especially when a hit is badly needed. **2.** *Informal.* To substitute for another in a time of need. **—pinch hitter** *n.*

Pin·chot (pĭn′shō′), **Gifford.** 1865–1946. American conservationist and politician who served as chief of the U.S. Forest Service (1898–1910) and later helped found the Progressive Party (1912).

pinch·pen·ny (pĭnch′pĕn′ē) *adj.* **1.** Unwilling to give or spend money; penny-pinching. **2.** Characterized by scarcity of money: *a pinchpenny economy.* —**pinchpenny** *n., pl.* **-nies.** A penny pincher.

pinch runner *n. Baseball.* A substitute base runner.

Pinck•ney (pĭngk′nē), **Charles Cotesworth.** 1746–1825. American diplomat. As a minister to France (1797) he refused to offer a bribe to French negotiators, causing the conflict known as the XYZ Affair.

pin clover *n.* See **alfilaria.**

pin curl *n.* A usually damp, coiled strand of hair secured with a bobby pin or clip and combed into a wave or curl when dry.

pin•cush•ion (pĭn′ko͝osh′ən) *n.* A small, firm cushion into which pins are stuck when not in use.

Pin•dar (pĭn′dər). 522?–443? B.C. Greek lyric poet remembered especially for his *Odes.*

Pin•dar•ic (pĭn-dăr′ĭk) *adj.* **1.** Relating to or characteristic of the poetic style of Pindar. **2.** Of or characteristic of a Pindaric ode. —**Pindaric** *n.* A Pindaric ode.

Pindaric ode *n.* An ode in the form used by Pindar, consisting of a series of triads in which the strophe and antistrophe have the same stanza form and the epode has a different form.

Pin•dus Mountains (pĭn′dəs). A range of mountains extending about 161 km (100 mi) south from the southern border of Albania to northwest Greece and rising to 2,638.3 m (8,650 ft). They formed the border between ancient Thessaly and Epirus.

pine¹ (pīn) *n.* **1.** Any of various evergreen trees of the genus *Pinus,* having fascicles of needle-shaped leaves and producing woody, seed-bearing cones. These trees are widely cultivated for ornament and shade and for their timber and resinous sap, which yields turpentine and pine tar. **2.** Any of various other coniferous trees, such as the Norfolk Island pine. **3.** The wood of any of these trees. —*attributive.* Often used to modify another noun: *pine floors; pine walls.* [Middle English, from Old English *pīn-* (as in *pīntreow,* pine tree), from Latin *pīnus.* See **peiə-** in Appendix.]

pine² (pīn) *v.* **pined, pin•ing, pines.** —*intr.* **1.** To feel a lingering, often nostalgic desire. See Synonyms at **yearn. 2.** To wither or waste away from longing or grief: *pined away and died.* —*tr. Archaic.* To grieve or mourn for. —**pine** *n. Archaic.* Intense longing or grief. [Middle English *pinen,* from Old English *pīnian,* to cause to suffer, from **pīne,* pain, from Vulgar Latin **pēna,* penalty, variant of Latin *poena,* from Greek *poinē.* See **kʷei-¹** in Appendix.]

pin•e•al (pĭn′ē-əl, pī′nē-) *adj.* **1.** Having the form of a pine cone. **2.** Of or relating to the pineal body. [French *pinéal,* from Latin *pīnea,* pine cone, from feminine of *pīneus,* of pine, from *pīnus,* pine tree. See **peiə-** in Appendix.]

pineal body *n.* See **pineal gland.**

pineal eye *n.* See **third eye.**

pineal gland *n.* A small, cone-shaped organ in the brain of most vertebrates that secretes the hormone melatonin. Also called *epiphysis, pineal body, pineal organ.*

pine•ap•ple (pīn′ăp′əl) *n.* **1.a.** A tropical American plant *(Ananas comosus)* having large swordlike leaves and a large, fleshy, edible, multiple fruit with a terminal tuft of leaves. **b.** The fruit of this plant. **2.** *Slang.* A hand grenade. [Middle English *pinappel,* pine cone : *pine,* pine; see PINE¹ + *appel,* apple; see APPLE.]

pineapple weed *n.* A strongly aromatic, western North American plant *(Matricaria matricarioides)* having greenish-yellow discoid flower heads and an odor of pineapple when crushed.

Pine Bar•rens (pīn băr′ənz). A coastal plain region of southeast-central and southern New Jersey. Its extensive forests of pine, cedar, and oak were all but exhausted by the 1860's as the result of indiscriminate cutting for shipbuilding and charcoal making.

Pine Bluff (blŭf′). A city of southeast-central Arkansas south-southeast of Little Rock. Founded c. 1820 as Mount Marie, it was renamed in 1832. Population, 56,811.

pine•drops (pīn′drŏps′) *pl.n. (used with a sing. or pl. verb).* A purplish-brown, leafless, North American plant *(Pterospora andromedea)* living as a parasite on roots and having urn-shaped, reddish or white flowers arranged in a terminal raceme.

pine finch *n.* See **pine siskin.**

Pine Hills. A community of central Florida, a suburb of Orlando. Population, 26,000.

pine•land (pīn′lănd′, lənd) also **pine•lands** (-ləndz) *n.* A forested area in which pine trees predominate.

Pi•nel•las Park (pī-nĕl′əs). A city of west-central Florida, an industrial suburb of St. Petersburg. Population, 32,811.

pine mouse *n.* Any of various voles of the genus *Pitymys,* especially *P. pinetorum,* a tiny forest animal of eastern North America. Also called *pine vole.*

pi•nene (pī′nēn′) *n.* Either of two isomeric terpene liquids, $C_{10}H_{16}$, used as solvents and in making resins.

pine needle *n.* The needle-shaped leaf of a pine tree.

pine nut *n.* The edible seed of certain pines, such as the piñon.

Pi•ne•ro (pə-nîr′ō), Sir **Arthur Wing.** 1855–1934. British playwright noted for his farces, including *Dandy Dick* (1887).

pin•er•y (pī′nə-rē) *n., pl.* **-ies. 1.** A hothouse or plantation where pineapples are grown. **2.** A forest of pine trees.

Pines (pīnz), **Isle of.** An island in the Caribbean Sea off southwest Cuba. Discovered by Columbus in 1494, it was later a penal colony and a rendezvous for pirates. It was claimed by both the United States and Cuba until a 1925 treaty confirmed Cuba's sovereignty.

pine•sap (pīn′săp′) *n.* A fleshy white or reddish plant *(Monotropa hypopithys)* growing as a saprophyte or parasite on tree roots and having racemes with a few drooping flowers.

pine siskin *n.* A North American finch *(Carduelis pinus)* having streaked, brownish plumage. Also called *pine finch.*

pine snake *n.* Any of various bull snakes common in pine woods, especially *Pituophis melanoleucus,* of the eastern United States.

♦**pine straw** *n. Chiefly Southern U.S.* Dead, fallen pine needles.

pi•ne•ta (pī-nē′tə) *n.* Plural of **pinetum.**

pine tar *n.* A viscous or semisolid brown-to-black substance produced by the destructive distillation of pine wood and used in roofing compositions and as an expectorant and antiseptic.

pi•ne•tum (pī-nē′təm) *n., pl.* **-ta** (-tə). An area planted with pine trees or related conifers, especially for botanical study. [Latin *pīnētum,* pine grove, from *pīnus,* pine. See PINE¹.]

pine vole *n.* See **pine mouse.**

pine warbler *n.* A small, yellow-breasted songbird *(Dendroica pinus)* found in pine forests of the eastern United States.

pine•wood (pīn′wo͝od′) *n.* **1.** The wood of the pine tree. **2.** Often **pine•woods** (-wo͝odz′). A forest of pines.

pine•y (pī′nē) *adj.* Variant of **piny.**

pin•feath•er (pĭn′fĕth′ər) *n.* A growing feather still enclosed in its horny sheath, especially one just emerging through the skin.

pin•fish (pĭn′fĭsh′) *n., pl.* **pinfish** or **-fish•es.** A small, spiny-finned fish *(Lagodon rhomboides)* found along the southeast coast of the United States.

pin•fold (pĭn′fōld′) *n.* An enclosure where stray animals are confined. —**pinfold** *tr.v.* **-fold•ed, -fold•ing, -folds.** To confine in or as if in a pinfold. [Middle English *pynfold,* alteration of Old English *pundfald* : *pund-,* enclosure + *fald,* fold.]

ping (pĭng) *n.* **1.** A sharp, high-pitched sound, as that made by a bullet striking metal. **2.** See **knock** (sense 3). —**ping** *intr.v.* **pinged, ping•ing, pings.** To make a sharp, high-pitched, metallic sound. [Imitative.]

Ping (pĭng). A river, about 563 km (350 mi) long, of western Thailand. It is a major tributary of the Chao Phraya.

ping•er (pĭng′ər) *n.* A device used underwater to produce pulses of sound, as for an echo sounder.

pin•go (pĭng′gō) *n., pl.* **-gos** or **-goes.** An Arctic mound or conical hill, consisting of an outer layer of soil covering a core of solid ice. [Inupiaq or Inuit *pinguq.*]

Ping-Pong (pĭng′pông′, -pŏng′). A trademark used for table tennis and associated equipment. This trademark, variously styled, often occurs in figurative contexts and sometimes as a verb in print: *"Their dialogue is oblique and defensive, a Ping-Pong game of intellectual ploys, tiny digs and arch, veiled emotional prods"* (New York Times). *"The Q and A format gives the book a jerky, ping-pong rhythm"* (Nation). *"In fact,* [the movie] *ping-pongs interminably between two basic situations"* (Washington Times).

pin•guid (pĭn′gwĭd) *adj.* Fat; oily. [Latin *pinguis* + *-id* (as in LIQUID).]

pin•head (pĭn′hĕd′) *n.* **1.** The head of a pin. **2.** Something very small or insignificant. **3.** *Slang.* A person regarded as stupid. —**pin′head′ed** *adj.* —**pin′head′ed•ness** *n.*

pin•hole (pĭn′hōl′) *n.* A tiny puncture made by or as if by a pin.

pin•ion¹ (pĭn′yən) *n.* **1.** The wing of a bird. **2.** The outer rear edge of the wing of a bird, containing the primary feathers. **3.** A primary feather of a bird. —**pinion** *tr.v.* **-ioned, -ion•ing, -ions. 1.a.** To remove or bind the wing feathers of (a bird) to prevent flight. **b.** To cut or bind (the wings of a bird). **2.a.** To restrain or immobilize (a person) by binding the arms. **b.** To bind (a person's arms). **3.** To bind fast or hold down; shackle. [Middle English, from Old French *pignon,* from Vulgar Latin **pinniō, pinniōn-,* from Latin *penna, pinna,* feather. See PINNA.]

pin•ion² (pĭn′yən) *n.* A small cogwheel that engages or is engaged by a larger cogwheel or a rack. [French *pignon,* from Old French *peignon,* probably from *peigne,* comb, from Latin *pecten,* from *pectere,* to comb.]

pin•ite (pĭn′īt′, pē′nīt′) *n.* A gray, green, or brown mineral similar to mica, formed by chemical alteration of other minerals, such as cordierite. [After *Pini,* a mine in Saxony.]

pink¹ (pĭngk) *n.* **1.** *Color.* Any of a group of colors reddish in hue, of medium to high lightness, and of low to moderate saturation. **2.a.** Any of various plants of the genus *Dianthus,* such as the carnation and sweet William, often cultivated for their showy, fragrant flowers. **b.** Any of various other plants, such as the wild pink and the moss pink. **c.** A flower of any of these plants. **3.** The highest or best degree: *in the pink of health.* **4. pinks. a.** Light-colored trousers formerly worn as part of the winter semi-dress uniform by U.S. Army officers. **b.** The scarlet coat worn by fox hunters. **5.** *Slang.* A pinko. —**pink** *adj.* **pink•er, pink•est. 1.** *Color.* Of the color pink. **2.** *Slang.* Having moderately leftist political opinions. [Origin unknown.] —**pink′ness** *n.*

pink² (pĭngk) *tr.v.* **pinked, pink•ing, pinks. 1.** To stab lightly with a pointed weapon; prick. **2.** To decorate with a perforated pattern. **3.** To cut with pinking shears. [Middle English *pinken.*]

pine¹
Scotch pine
Pinus sylvestris

pineapple
Ananas comosus

ă pat	oi boy
ā pay	ou out
âr care	o͝o took
ä father	o͞o boot
ĕ pet	ŭ cut
ē be	ûr urge
ĭ pit	th thin
ī pie	*th* this
îr pier	hw which
ŏ pot	zh vision
ō toe	ə about, item
ô paw	♦ regionalism

Stress marks: ′ (primary); ′ (secondary), as in **dictionary** (dĭk′shə-nĕr′ē)

pinking shears

pinnace

pinnacle

pintail
Male pintail
Anas acuta

pink[3] (pĭngk) also **pink·ie** or **pink·y** (pĭng′kē) *n., pl.* **pinks** also **pink·ies.** *Nautical.* A sailing vessel with a narrow overhanging stern. [Middle English, from Middle Dutch *pinke.*]

pink bollworm *n.* The pinkish larva of a moth *(Pectinophora gossypiella)* that is destructive to the flowers and bolls of growing cotton.

pink-col·lar (pĭnk′kŏl′ər) *adj.* Of or relating to a class of jobs, such as typist or telephone operator, once traditionally filled by women.

Pin·ker·ton (pĭng′kər-tən), **Allan.** 1819–1884. Scottish-born American detective. His agency was notorious for breaking strikes and disrupting labor efforts to unionize.

pink·eye (pĭngk′ī′) *n.* An acute, very contagious form of conjunctivitis, caused by the hemophilic bacterium *Hemophilus aegyptius* and characterized by inflammation of the eyelids and eyeballs.

Pink·ham (pĭng′kəm), **Lydia Estes.** 1819–1883. American patent-medicine manufacturer. Her Vegetable Compound became the most widely advertised product of its time.

pink·ie[1] also **pink·y** (pĭng′kē) *n., pl.* **-ies.** *Informal.* The little finger. [Probably from Dutch *pinkje,* diminutive of *pink,* little finger.]

pink·ie[2] (pĭng′kē) *n. Nautical.* Variant of **pink[3].**

pink·ing shears (pĭng′kĭng) *pl.n.* Shears with notched blades, used to finish edges of cloth with a zigzag cut for decoration or to prevent raveling or fraying.

pink·ish (pĭng′kĭsh) *adj. Color.* Somewhat pink. **—pink′ish·ness** *n.*

pink lady *n.* A cocktail of gin, brandy, lemon or lime juice, egg white, and grenadine, shaken with cracked ice and strained.

pink·o (pĭng′kō) *n., pl.* **-os.** *Slang.* A person who holds moderately leftist political views; a pink.

pink·root (pĭngk′ro͞ot′, -ro͝ot′) *n.* A perennial plant *(Spigelia marilandica)* native to the southeast United States having flowers with a tubular corolla that is red outside and yellow inside. The rhizomes and roots were once used as a vermifuge. Also called *wormgrass.*

pink root *n.* A disease of onions and related bulbous plants caused by a fungus *(Pyrenochaeta terrestris)* and resulting in stunted growth and shriveled pink roots.

pink salmon *n.* A small salmon *(Oncorhynchus gorbuscha)* of Pacific waters, the male of which has a pink color and a conspicuous dorsal hump during the spawning season. Also called *humpback salmon.*

pink slip *n. Informal.* A notice of termination of employment. **—pink′-slip′** (pĭngk′slĭp′) *v.*

♦ **Pink·ster** also **Pinx·ter** (pĭngk′stər) *n. Regional.* Whitsunday or Whitsuntide. [Dutch, from Middle Dutch *pinxter,* ultimately from Gothic *paintekuste,* from Greek *pentēkostē,* fiftieth. See PENTECOST.]

pink·ster flower (pĭngk′stər) *n.* Variant of **pinxter flower.**

pink·y[1] (pĭng′kē) *n.* Variant of **pinkie[1].**

pink·y[2] (pĭng′kē) *n. Nautical.* Variant of **pink[3].**

pin money *n.* Money for incidental expenses.

pin·na (pĭn′ə) *n., pl.* **pin·nae** (pĭn′ē) or **pin·nas. 1.** *Botany.* A leaflet or primary division of a pinnately compound leaf. **2.** *Zoology.* A feather, wing, fin, or similar appendage. **3.** *Anatomy.* See **auricle** (sense 1a). [Latin, feather. See **pet-** in Appendix.] **—pin′nal** *adj.*

pin·nace (pĭn′ĭs) *n. Nautical.* **1.** A small sailing boat formerly used as a tender for merchant and war vessels. **2.** A small ship or ship's boat. [French *pinace,* from Old French, probably from Old Spanish *pinaza,* from *pino,* pine tree, boat, from Latin *pīnus.* See **peie-** in Appendix.]

pin·na·cle (pĭn′ə-kəl) *n.* **1.** *Architecture.* A small turret or spire on a roof or buttress. **2.** A tall, pointed formation, such as a mountain peak. **3.** The highest point; the culmination. See Synonyms at **summit.** **—pinnacle** *tr.v.* **-cled, -cling, -cles. 1.** To furnish with a pinnacle. **2.** To place on or as if on a pinnacle. [Middle English, from Old French, from Late Latin *pinnāculum,* diminutive of Latin *pinna,* feather. See **pet-** in Appendix.]

pin·nae (pĭn′ē) *n.* A plural of **pinna.**

pin·nate (pĭn′āt′) also **pin·nat·ed** (-ā′tĭd) *adj.* Resembling a feather; having parts or branches arranged on each side of a common axis: *a polyp with a pinnate form; pinnate leaves.* [Latin *pinnātus,* feathered, from *pinna,* feather. See **pet-** in Appendix.] **—pin′nate′ly** *adv.*

pinnati– *pref.* Resembling a feather: *pinnatifid.* [From Latin *pinnātus,* feathered. See PINNATE.]

pin·nat·i·fid (pĭ-năt′ə-fĭd) *adj.* Divided or cleft in a pinnate fashion. Used of certain leaves. **—pin·nat′i·fid·ly** *adv.*

pin·nat·i·ped (pĭ-năt′ə-pĕd′) *adj.* Having lobate toes. Used of birds.

pin·nat·i·sect (pĭ-năt′ĭ-sĕkt′) *adj.* Divided pinnately nearly to the midrib. Used of certain leaves.

pin·ni·grade (pĭn′ĭ-grād′) *adj.* Walking by means of finlike organs or flippers, as the seals and walruses. [PINN(A) + Latin *-gradus,* going (from *gradī,* to step; see **ghredh-** in Appendix).]

pin·ni·ped (pĭn′ə-pĕd′) *adj.* Of or belonging to the Pinnipedia, a suborder of carnivorous aquatic mammals that includes the seals, walruses, and similar animals having finlike flippers as organs of locomotion. **—pinniped** *n.* A mammal of the suborder Pinnipedia. [From New Latin *Pinnipedia,* order name : Latin *pinna,* feather; see PINNA + Latin *pēs, ped-,* foot; see –PED.]

pin·nule (pĭn′yo͞ol) also **pin·nu·la** (pĭn′yə-lə) *n., pl.* **pin·nules** also **pin·nu·lae** (pĭn′yə-lē′). **1.** *Botany.* Any of the ultimate leaflets of a bipinnately compound leaf. **2.** *Zoology.* A featherlike or plumelike organ or part, such as a small fin, or one of the appendages of a crinoid. [Latin *pinnula,* diminutive of *pinna,* feather. See **pet-** in Appendix.] **—pin′nu·lar** *adj.*

pin oak *n.* A deciduous tree *(Quercus palustris)* of eastern North America, having horizontal or drooping branches, sharply lobed leaves, and small acorns with a saucer-shaped cup.

pi·noch·le or **pi·noc·le** (pē′nŭk′əl, -nŏk′əl) **pe·nuch·le** or **pe·nuck·le** (pē′nŭk′əl) *n. Games.* **1.** A game of cards for two to four persons, played with a special deck of 48 cards, with points being scored by taking tricks and forming certain combinations. **2.** The combination of the queen of spades and jack of diamonds in this game. [Perhaps from German dialectal *Binokel,* beziquelike card game, from French dialectal *binocle,* spectacles, from New Latin *binoculus,* the two eyes : BI–[1] + Latin *oculus,* eye; see **okʷ-** in Appendix.]

pin·o·cy·to·sis (pĭn′ə-sī-tō′sĭs, -sī-, pī′nə-) *n.* Introduction of fluids into a cell by invagination of the cell membrane, followed by formation of vesicles within the cells. [Greek *pinein,* to drink; see **pō(i)-** in Appendix + CYT(O)– + –OSIS.] **—pin′o·cy·tot′ic** (-tŏt′ĭk) *adj.* **—pin′o·cy·tot′i·cal·ly** *adv.*

pi·no·le (pĭ-nō′lē) *n.* Meal made of ground corn or wheat and mesquite beans. [American Spanish, from Nahuatl *pinolli,* mixture of vanilla powder, spices, and ground toasted chocolate beans.]

pi·ñon also **pin·yon** (pĭn′yōn′, -yən) *n., pl.* **pi·ñons** or **pi·ño·nes** (pĭn-yō′nēz) also **pin·yons.** Any of several pine trees bearing edible, nutlike seeds, especially *Pinus edulis,* of the western United States and Mexico. Also called *nut pine.* [Spanish *piñón,* pine nut, pine cone, augmentative of *piña,* from Latin *pīnea,* from feminine of *pīneus,* of pine, from *pīnus,* pine tree. See **peie-** in Appendix.]

piñon jay also **pinyon jay** *n.* A small, dull blue, uncrested jay *(Gymnorhinus cyanocephala)* of western North America.

pi·not (pē′nō, pē-nō′) *n.* **1.** Any of several related white or red grapes chiefly grown in California and France and used for making wine. **2.** A white or red wine made from these grapes. [French, variant of *pineau,* diminutive of *pin,* pine tree (from the shape of the clusters of grapes), from Latin *pīnus.* See **peie-** in Appendix.]

pin·point (pĭn′point′) *n.* **1.** Something extremely small or trifling. **2.** A very small or sharp point: *a pinpoint of light.* **3.** A point on a map marking a precise location or target. **—pinpoint** *tr.v.* **-point·ed, -point·ing, -points. 1.** To locate or identify with precision. **2.** To take precise aim at: *pinpoint a target.* **3.** To direct attention to: *We pinpointed the flaws in his argument.* **—pinpoint** *adj.* **1.** Meticulously precise: *pinpoint accuracy.* **2.** Extremely small; minuscule: *pinpoint creatures.*

pin·prick (pĭn′prĭk′) *n.* **1.** A slight puncture made by or as if by a pin. **2.** An insignificant wound. **3.** A minor annoyance. **—pinprick** *tr.v.* **-pricked, -prick·ing, -pricks.** To puncture with or as if with a pin.

pins and nee·dles (pĭnz; nēd′lz) *pl.n.* A tingling sensation felt in a part of the body numbed from lack of circulation. ***—idiom.* on pins and needles.** In a state of tense anticipation.

pin·scher (pĭn′shər) *n.* A Doberman pinscher.

pin·set·ter (pĭn′sĕt′ər) *n.* An employee or a mechanical apparatus that sets up pins in a bowling alley.

Pinsk (pĭnsk, pyĕnsk). A city of southwest Belorussia south-southwest of Minsk. First mentioned in chronicles in 1097, it was the capital of the Pinsk duchy in the 13th century. Pinsk passed to Lithuania in 1320, to Poland in 1569, to Russia in 1793, back to Poland in 1921, and to the U.S.S.R. in 1945. Population, 109,000.

pin·stripe also **pin stripe** (pĭn′strīp′) *—n.* **1.** A very thin stripe, especially on a fabric. **2. a.** A fabric with very thin stripes, often used for suits. **b.** A suit made of such fabric. Often used in the plural. *—attributive.* Often used to modify another noun: *pinstripe suits; pinstripe fabric.* **—pin′striped′** *adj.*

pint (pīnt) *n. Abbr.* **p., pt. 1. a.** A unit of volume or capacity in the U.S. Customary System, used in liquid measure, equal to ⅛ gallon or 16 ounces (0.473 liter). **b.** A unit of volume or capacity in the U.S. Customary System, used in dry measure, equal to 1⁄16 peck or ½ quart (0.551 liter). **c.** A unit of volume or capacity in the British Imperial System, used in dry and liquid measure, equal to 0.568 liter. See table at **measurement. 2. a.** A container with a pint capacity. **b.** The amount of a substance that can be held in such a container. *—attributive.* Often used to modify another noun: *pint bottles; pint capacity.* [Middle English *pinte,* a unit of volume, from Old French, from Vulgar Latin **pīncta,* mark on a container, from feminine of **pīnctus,* past participle of Latin *pingere,* to paint. See **peig-** in Appendix.]

pin·ta (pĭn′tə, pēn′tä) *n.* A contagious skin disease prevalent in tropical America, caused by a spirochete *(Treponema carateum)* and characterized by extreme thickening and spotty discoloration of the skin. [Spanish, painted mark, colored spot, from Vulgar Latin **pīncta.* See PINT.]

pin·tail (pĭn′tāl′) *n., pl.* **pintail** or **-tails.** A duck *(Anas acuta)* of the Northern Hemisphere, having gray, brown, and white plumage and a sharply pointed tail. Also called *sprigtail.*

pin·ta·no (pĭn-tä′nō) *n., pl.* **pintano** or **-nos.** Any of various brilliantly colored damselfishes of the genus *Abudefduf,* especially the sergeant major. [American Spanish.]

Pin·ter (pĭn′tər), **Harold.** Born 1930. British playwright whose works, including *The Dumbwaiter* (1957) and *Birthday Party* (1958), create an atmosphere of menace. **—Pin′ter·esque′** (-ĕsk′) *adj.*

pin·tle (pĭn′tl) *n.* **1.** A pin or a bolt on which another part pivots. **2.** *Nautical.* The pin on which a rudder turns. **3.** The pin on which a gun carriage revolves. **4.** A hook or a bolt on the rear of a towing vehicle for attaching a gun or trailer. [Middle English *pintel,* from Old English, penis.]

pin·to (pĭn′tō) *n., pl.* **-tos** or **-toes.** A horse with patchy markings of white and another color. Also called *paint.* **—pinto** *adj.* Mottled; pied. [Spanish, piebald, spotted, from Vulgar Latin **pīnctus,* past participle of Latin *pingere,* to paint. See **peig-** in Appendix.]

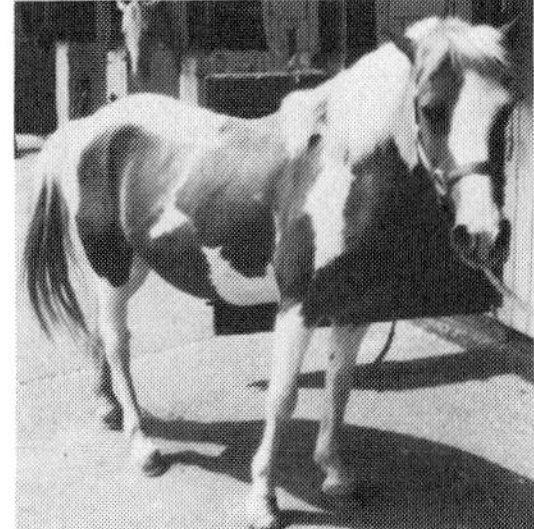

pinto

pinto bean *n.* A form of the common string bean that has mottled seeds and is grown chiefly in the southwest United States.

pint·size (pīnt′sīz′) also **pint·sized** (-sīzd′) *adj. Informal.* Of small dimensions; diminutive.

pin·up (pĭn′ŭp′) *n.* **1.a.** A picture, especially of a sexually attractive person, that is displayed on a wall. **b.** A person considered a suitable model for such a picture. **2.** Something intended to be affixed to a wall. **—pinup** *adj.* **1.** Suitable for a pinup. **2.** Designed to be attached to a wall.

pin·wale (pĭn′wāl′) *adj.* Made with narrow wales: *pinwale corduroy.*

pin·weed (pĭn′wēd′) *n.* Any of various North American perennial plants of the genus *Lechea,* having narrow leaves and numerous small flowers.

pin·wheel (pĭn′hwēl′, -wēl′) *n.* **1.** A toy consisting of vanes of colored paper or plastic pinned to a stick so that they revolve when blown on. **2.** A firework that forms a rotating wheel of colored flames. Also called *catherine wheel.* **3.** A wheel with a circle of pins at right angles to its face, used as a tripping device.

pin·work (pĭn′wûrk′) *n.* Fine stitches raised from the surface of the design in the embroidery of needlepoint lace.

pin·worm (pĭn′wûrm′) *n.* Any of various small nematode worms of the family Oxyuridae that are parasitic on horses, rabbits, and other mammals, especially *Enterobius vermicularis,* a species that infests the human intestines and rectum. Also called *threadworm.*

pin·wrench (pĭn′rĕnch′) *n.* A wrench having a projection designed to fit a hole in the object to be turned.

pinx. *abbr. Latin.* Pinxit (He or she painted it).

♦ **Pinx·ter** (pĭngk′stər) *n. Regional.* Variant of **Pinkster.**

pinx·ter flower also **pink·ster flower** (pĭngk′stər) *n.* A deciduous shrub *(Rhododendron periclymenoides)* of the southeast United States, having a funnel-shaped pink or purple corolla and flowers that bloom before the leaves appear.

pin·y also **pine·y** (pī′nē) *adj.* **-i·er, -i·est.** Relating to, suggestive of, or abounding in pines.

Pin·yin or **pin·yin** (pĭn′yĭn′, -yĭn) *n.* A system for transliterating Chinese ideograms into the Roman alphabet, officially adopted by the People's Republic of China in 1979. [Chinese (Mandarin) *pīn yīn,* to combine sounds into syllables : *pīn,* to combine + *yīn,* sound.]

pin·yon (pĭn′yōn′, -yən) *n.* Variant of **piñon.**

pinyon jay *n.* Variant of **piñon jay.**

Pin·za (pĭn′zə), **Ezio.** 1895–1957. Italian-born American operatic performer who was the leading basso at the Metropolitan Opera House in New York City (1926–1948).

Pin·zón (pĭn-zōn′, pēn-thôn′), **Martín Alonso.** 1440?–1493. Spanish navigator who commanded the *Pinta* on Christopher Columbus's first voyage to America (1492–1493). His brother **Vicente Yáñez Pinzón** (1460?–1524) was the first European explorer of the Amazon River (1500).

pi·o·let (pē′ə-lā′) *n.* An ice ax used in mountain climbing. [French, from French dialectal, diminutive of *piola,* small axe, from Old French **piola,* from Old Provençal, diminutive of *apcha, apia,* of Germanic origin; akin to Old High German *happa,* sickle.]

piolet

pi·on (pī′ŏn′) *n. Physics.* A semistable meson produced either in a neutral form with a mass 264 times that of an electron and a mean lifetime of 8.4×10^{-17} second or in a positively charged form with a mass 273 times that of an electron and a mean lifetime of 2.6×10^{-8} second. Also called *pi meson.* See table at **subatomic particle.** [Contraction of PI MESON.]

pi·o·neer (pī′ə-nîr′) *n.* **1.** One who ventures into unknown or unclaimed territory to settle. **2.** One who opens up new areas of thought, research, or development: *a pioneer in aviation.* **3.** A soldier who performs construction and demolition work in the field to facilitate troop movements. **4.** *Ecology.* An animal or plant species that establishes itself in a previously barren environment. **—pioneer** *adj.* **1.** Of, relating to, or characteristic of early settlers: *the pioneer spirit.* **2.** Leading the way; trailblazing: *a pioneer treatment for cancer.* **—pioneer** *v.* **-neered, -neer·ing, -neers.** *—tr.* **1.a.** To open up (an area) or prepare (a way): *rockets that pioneered outer space.* **b.** To settle (a region). **2.** To initiate or participate in the development of: *surgeons who pioneered organ transplants.* *—intr.* To act as a pioneer: *pioneered in development of the laser.* [French *pionnier,* from Old French *peonier,* foot soldier, from *peon,* from Medieval Latin *pedō, pedōn-,* from Late Latin, one who has broad feet, from Latin *pēs, ped-,* foot. See **ped-** in Appendix.]

pi·os·i·ty (pī-ŏs′ĭ-tē) *n., pl.* **-ties.** An exaggerated display of piety. [From PIOUS.]

pi·ous (pī′əs) *adj.* **1.** Having or exhibiting religious reverence; earnestly compliant in the observance of religion; devout. See Synonyms at **religious. 2.a.** Marked by conspicuous devoutness: *a pious and holy observation.* **b.** Marked by false devoutness; solemnly hypocritical: *a pious fraud.* **3.** Devotional: *pious readings.* **4.** Professing or exhibiting a strict, traditional sense of virtue and morality; high-minded. **5.** Commendable; worthy: *a pious effort.* [From Latin *pius,* dutiful.] **—pi′ous·ly** *adv.* **—pi′ous·ness** *n.*

Pioz·zi (pyôt′sē), **Hester Lynch.** Known as "Mrs. Thrale." 1741–1821. British writer whose books *Anecdotes of the Late Samuel Johnson* (1786) and *Letters to and from the Late Samuel Johnson* (1788) recount her friendship with the lexicographer.

pip¹ (pĭp) *n.* The small seed of a fruit, as that of an apple or orange. [Short for PIPPIN.]

pip² (pĭp) *tr.v.* **pipped, pip·ping, pips.** *Chiefly British.* **1.** To wound or kill with a bullet. **2.** To get the better of; defeat. **3.** To blackball. [Possibly from PIP³.]

pip³ (pĭp) *n.* **1.** *Games.* **a.** A dot indicating a unit of numerical value on dice or dominoes. **b.** A mark indicating the suit or numerical value of a playing card. **2.** A spot or a speck. **3.** A rootstock of certain flowering plants, especially the lily of the valley. **4.** Any of the small segments that make up the surface of a pineapple. **5.** *Informal.* A shoulder insignia indicating the rank of certain officers, as in the British Army. **6.** See **blip** (sense 1). [Origin unknown.]

pip⁴ (pĭp) *v.* **pipped, pip·ping, pips.** *—tr.* To break through (the shell) in hatching. Used of a chick. *—intr.* To peep or chirp, as a chick does. **—pip** *n.* A short, high-pitched radio signal. [Variant of PEEP¹ and PEEP².]

pip⁵ (pĭp) *n.* **1.a.** A disease of birds, characterized by a thick mucous discharge that forms a crust in the mouth and throat. **b.** The crust symptomatic of this disease. **2.** *Slang.* A minor, unspecified human ailment. [Middle English *pippe,* from Middle Dutch, phlegm, pip, from Medieval Latin **pippīta,* alteration of Latin *pītuīta.* See **peiə-** in Appendix.]

pi·pal (pē′pəl) *n.* Variant of **peepul.**

pipe (pīp) *n.* **1.a.** A hollow cylinder or tube used to conduct a liquid, gas, or finely divided solid. **b.** A section or piece of such a tube. **2.a.** A device for smoking, consisting of a tube of wood, clay, or other material with a small bowl at one end. **b.** An amount of smoking material, such as tobacco, needed to fill the bowl of a pipe; a pipeful. **3.** *Informal.* **a.** A tubular part or organ of the body. **b. pipes.** The passages of the human respiratory system. **4.** *Abbr.* **p. a.** A wine cask having a capacity of 126 gallons or 2 hogsheads (478 liters). **b.** This volume as a unit of liquid measure. **5.** *Abbr.* **p.** *Music.* **a.** A tubular wind instrument, such as a flute. **b.** Any of the tubes in an organ. **c. pipes.** A small wind instrument, consisting of tubes of different lengths bound together. **d. pipes.** A bagpipe. **6. pipes.** *Informal.* The vocal cords; the voice, especially as used in singing. **7.** A birdcall. **8.** *Nautical.* A whistle used for signaling crew members: *a boatswain's pipe.* **9.** *Geology.* **a.** A vertical, cylindrical vein of ore. **b.** One of the vertical veins of eruptive origin in which diamonds are found in South Africa. **10.** *Geology.* An eruptive passageway opening into the crater of a volcano. **11.** *Metallurgy.* A cone-shaped cavity in a steel ingot, formed during cooling by escaping gases. **—pipe** *v.* **piped, pip·ing, pipes.** *—tr.* **1.a.** To convey (liquid or gas) by means of pipes. **b.** To convey as if by pipes, especially to transmit by wire or cable: *piped music into the store.* **2.** To provide with pipes or connect with pipes. **3.a.** To play (a tune) on a pipe or pipes. **b.** To lead by playing on pipes. **4.** *Nautical.* **a.** To signal (crew members) with a boatswain's pipe. **b.** To receive aboard or mark the departure of by sounding a boatswain's pipe. **5.** To utter in a shrill, reedy tone. **6.** To furnish (a garment or fabric) with piping. **7.** To force through a pastry tube, as frosting onto a cake. **8.** *Slang.* To take a look at; notice. *—intr.* **1.** To play on a pipe. **2.** To speak shrilly; make a shrill sound. **3.** To chirp or whistle, as a bird does. **4.** *Nautical.* To signal the crew with a boatswain's pipe. **5.** *Metallurgy.* To develop conical cavities during solidification. ***—phrasal verbs.*** **pipe down.** *Slang.* To stop talking; be quiet. **pipe up.** To speak up. [Middle English, from Old English *pīpe,* from Vulgar Latin **pīpa,* from Latin *pīpāre,* to chirp.]

pipe bomb *n.* An explosive device contained in a metal pipe.

pipe clay *n.* A fine white clay used in making tobacco pipes and pottery and in whitening leather.

pipe cleaner *n.* A pliant, tufted, narrow rod used for cleaning the stem of a tobacco pipe.

pipe dream *n.* A fantastic notion or vain hope. [From the fantasies induced by smoking a pipe of opium.]

pipe·fish (pīp′fĭsh′) *n., pl.* **pipefish** or **-fish·es.** Any of various slim, elongated fishes of the family Syngnathidae, living in temperate and warm seas and characterized by a tubelike snout and an external covering of bony plates.

pipe fitter *n.* One that installs and repairs piping systems.

pipe·fit·ting (pīp′fĭt′ĭng) *n.* **1.** The act of connecting pipes. **2.** A trade that deals with the installation and repair of piping systems. **3.** A section of pipe, such as an elbow, used to connect two or more pipes.

ă pat	oi boy
ā pay	ou out
âr care	o͝o took
ä father	o͞o boot
ĕ pet	ŭ cut
ē be	ûr urge
ĭ pit	th thin
ī pie	*th* this
îr pier	hw which
ŏ pot	zh vision
ō toe	ə about, item
ô paw	♦ regionalism

Stress marks: **′** (primary); ′ (secondary), as in **dictionary** (dĭk′shə-nĕr′ē)

pipeline
Section of the Trans-Alaska Pipeline

pipkin

piranha

ă pat oi boy
ā pay ou out
âr care o͝o took
ä father o͞o boot
ĕ pet ŭ cut
ē be ûr urge
ĭ pit th thin
ī pie *th* this
îr pier hw which
ŏ pot zh vision
ō toe ə about, item
ô paw ♦ regionalism

Stress marks: **′** (primary); ′ (secondary), as in **dictionary** (dĭk**′**shə-nĕr′ē)

pipe·ful (pīp**′**fo͝ol′) *n.* The amount of smoking material that a pipe can hold.

pipe·line (pīp**′**līn′) *n.* **1.** A conduit of pipe, especially one used for the conveyance of water, gas, or petroleum products. **2.** A direct channel by which information is privately transmitted. **3.** A system through which something is conducted, especially as a means of supply: *"Farther down the pipeline are three other approaches to vaccine development"* (Boston Globe). **—pipeline** *tr.v.* **-lined, -lin·ing, -lines. 1.** To convey by or as if by a system of pipes. **2.** To lay a system of pipes through.

pipe organ *n. Music.* See **organ** (sense 1a).

pip·er (pī**′**pər) *n. Music.* **1.** One who plays on a pipe. **2.** One who plays the bagpipe.

pi·per·a·zine (pī-pĕr**′**ə-zēn′, pĭ-) *n.* A colorless crystalline compound, $C_4H_{10}N_2$, used as a hardener for epoxy resins, an antihistamine, and an anthelmintic. [PIPER(INE) + AZ(O)– + –INE[2].]

pi·per·i·dine (pĭ-pĕr**′**ĭ-dēn′, pī-) *n.* A strongly basic, colorless liquid, $C_5H_{10}NH$, used in the manufacture of rubber and as a curing agent in epoxy resins. [PIPER(INE) + –ID(E) + –INE[2].]

pip·er·ine (pĭp**′**ə-rēn′) *n.* A crystalline solid, $C_{17}H_{19}NO_3$, extracted from black pepper and used as flavoring and as an insecticide. [Latin *piper,* pepper; see PEPPER + –INE[2].]

pi·per·o·nal (pĭ-pĕr**′**ə-năl′, pī-) *n.* A white powder, $C_8H_6O_3$, having a floral odor, used as flavoring and in perfume. [PIPER(INE) + –ON(E) + –AL[3].]

pipe·stone (pīp**′**stōn′) *n.* A heat-hardened, compacted, red or pink clay stone used by Native American peoples for making tobacco pipes.

pi·pette also **pi·pet** (pī-pĕt**′**) *n.* A narrow, usually calibrated glass tube into which small amounts of liquid are suctioned for transfer or measurement. [French, from Old French, tube, diminutive of *pipe,* pipe, from Vulgar Latin **pīpa.* See PIPE.] **—pi·pette′** *v.*

pipe vine *n.* A deciduous woody vine *(Aristolochia durior)* of the eastern United States, having greenish, brown-mottled flowers shaped like a curved pipe. Also called *Dutchman's pipe.*

pipe wrench *n.* A wrench with two serrated jaws, one adjustable, for gripping and turning pipe.

pip·ing (pī**′**pĭng) *n.* **1.** A system of pipes, such as those used in plumbing. **2.** *Music.* **a.** The act of playing on a pipe. **b.** The music produced by a pipe when played. **3.** A shrill, high-pitched sound. **4.** A narrow tube of fabric, sometimes enclosing a cord, used for trimming seams and edges, as of slipcovers. **5.** A tubular ribbon of icing on a pastry. **—piping** *adj.* **1.** *Music.* Playing on a pipe. **2.** Having a high-pitched sound: *the piping voices of children.* **3.** Tranquil: *"in this weak piping time of peace"* (Shakespeare). **—*idiom.* piping hot.** Very hot: *piping hot biscuits.*

pip·i·strelle also **pip·i·strel** (pĭp**′**ĭ-strĕl′, pĭp′ĭ-strĕl**′**) *n.* Any of various very small insectivorous bats of the genus *Pipistrellus,* found throughout the world. [French, from Italian *pipistrello,* bat, alteration of Old Italian *vipistrello,* from Latin *vespertiliō.* See VESPERTILIONID.]

pip·it (pĭp**′**ĭt) *n.* Any of various widely distributed songbirds of the genus *Anthus,* characteristically having brownish upper plumage and a streaked breast. Also called *titlark.* [Imitative of its call.]

pip·kin (pĭp**′**kĭn) *n.* A small earthenware or metal cooking pot. [Possibly PIP(E), cask + –KIN.]

pip·pin (pĭp**′**ĭn) *n.* **1.** Any of several varieties of apple. **2.** The seed of a fleshy fruit; a pip. **3.** *Informal.* A person or a thing that is admired. [Middle English *pipin,* from Old French *pepin.*]

pip·sis·se·wa (pĭp-sĭs**′**ə-wô′, -wə) *n.* Any of several evergreen plants of the genus *Chimaphila,* especially the Eurasian species *C. umbellata,* having white or pinkish flowers grouped in a terminal corymb. Also called *prince's pine.* [Perhaps Eastern Abenaki *kpi-pskwáhsawe,* woods flower, pipsissewa.]

pip-squeak (pĭp**′**skwēk′) *n. Informal.* One that is small or insignificant.

Piq·ua (pĭk**′**wā′, -wə). A city of west-central Ohio north of Dayton. A supply base in the War of 1812, it is now an industrial center. Population, 20,480.

pi·quant (pē**′**kənt, -känt′, pē-känt**′**) *adj.* **1.** Pleasantly pungent or tart in taste; spicy. **2.a.** Appealingly provocative: *a piquant wit.* **b.** Charming, interesting, or attractive: *a piquant face.* **3.** *Archaic.* Causing hurt feelings; stinging. [French, from Old French, present participle of *piquer,* to prick. See PIQUE.] **—pi′quan·cy, pi′quant·ness** *n.* **—pi′quant·ly** *adv.*

pique (pēk) *n.* A state of vexation caused by a perceived slight or indignity; a feeling of wounded pride. **—pique** *tr.v.* **piqued, piqu·ing, piques. 1.** To cause to feel resentment or indignation. **2.** To provoke; arouse: *The portrait piqued her curiosity.* **3.** To pride (oneself): *He piqued himself on his stylish attire.* [French, a prick, irritation, from Old French, from *piquer,* to prick, from Vulgar Latin **piccāre,* ultimately of imitative origin.]

pi·qué (pĭ-kā**′**, pē-) *n.* A tightly woven fabric with various raised patterns, produced especially by a double warp. [French, past participle of *piquer,* to quilt, from Old French, to backstitch, prick. See PIQUE.]

pi·quet also **pic·quet** (pĭ-kā**′**) *n. Games.* A card game for two people, played with a deck from which all cards below the seven, aces being high, are omitted. [French.]

Pi·ra·ci·ca·ba (pîr′ə-sĭ-kä**′**bə, pē′rä-sĭ-kä**′**bä). A city of southeast Brazil northwest of São Paulo. It is a trade and shipping center with a noted agricultural institute. Population, 179,380.

pi·ra·cy (pī**′**rə-sē) *n., pl.* **-cies. 1.a.** Robbery committed at sea. **b.** A similar act of robbery, as the hijacking of an airplane. **2.** The unauthorized use or reproduction of copyrighted or patented material. **3.** The operation of an unlicensed, illegal radio or television station. [Medieval Latin *pīrātia,* from Late Greek *peirateia,* from Greek *peiratēs,* pirate. See PIRATE.]

Pi·rae·us (pī-rē**′**əs, pĭ-rā**′**-). A city of east-central Greece on the Saronic Gulf southwest of Athens. Its port was built in the 5th century B.C. and after extensive development in the mid-19th century became the principal seaport of the country. In ancient times it was connected with Athens by the Long Walls, two parallel walls some 183 m (600 ft) apart. Population, 196,389.

pi·ra·gua (pĭ-rä**′**gwə) *n. Nautical.* **1.** A canoe made by hollowing out a tree trunk; a dugout. **2.** A flat-bottomed sailing boat with two masts. [Spanish, from Carib.]

Pi·ran·del·lo (pîr′ən-dĕl**′**ō, pē′rän-dĕl**′**lô), **Luigi.** 1867–1936. Italian writer best known for his plays *Six Characters in Search of an Author* (1921) and *Tonight We Improvise* (1930). Pirandello won the 1934 Nobel Prize for literature.

Pi·ra·ne·si (pîr′ə-nā**′**zē, pē′rä-nĕ**′**-), **Giambattista.** 1720–1778. Italian architect and artist. His etchings of Rome and its ruins contributed to the revival of neoclassicism. **—Pi′ra·ne′si·an** *adj.*

pi·ra·nha also **pi·ra·ña** (pĭ-rän**′**yə, -răn**′**yə, -rä**′**nə, -răn**′**ə) *n.* Any of several tropical American freshwater fishes of the genus *Serrasalmus* that are voraciously carnivorous and often attack and destroy living animals. Also called *caribe.* [Portuguese, from Tupi : *pirá,* fish + *ánha,* to cut.]

pi·ra·ru·cu (pĭ-rär**′**ə-ko͞o**′**) *n.* See **arapaima.** [Portuguese *pirarucú,* from Tupi *pirá-rucú* : *pirá,* fish + *urucú,* red.]

pi·rate (pī**′**rĭt) *n.* **1.a.** One who robs at sea or plunders the land from the sea without commission from a sovereign nation. **b.** A ship used for this purpose. **2.** One who preys on others; a plunderer. **3.** One who makes use of or reproduces the work of another without authorization. **4.** One that operates an unlicensed, illegal television or radio station. **—pirate** *v.* **-rat·ed, -rat·ing, -rates.** —*tr.* **1.** To attack and rob (a ship at sea). **2.** To take (something) by piracy. **3.** To make use of or reproduce (another's work) without authorization. —*intr.* To act as a pirate; practice piracy. [Middle English, from Old French, from Latin *pīrāta,* from Greek *peiratēs,* from *peiran,* to attempt, from *peira,* trial. See **per-**[3] in Appendix.] **—pi·rat′ic** (pī-răt**′**ĭk), **pi·rat′i·cal** (-ĭ-kəl) *adj.* **—pi·rat′i·cal·ly** *adv.*

pirate perch *n.* A small North American freshwater fish *(Aphredoderus sayanus)* noted for having the anal opening near the throat.

Pire (pîr), **Dominique Georges.** 1910–1969. Belgian priest and humanitarian noted for his work with refugees after World War II. He won the 1958 Nobel Peace Prize.

pi·rog (pĭ-rōg**′**) *n., pl.* **-ro·ghi** or **-ro·gi** (-rō**′**gē). A large, flat, usually square or rectangular Russian pastry filled with finely chopped meat or cabbage often mixed with chopped hard-boiled eggs. [Russian, probably from *pir,* feast, from Old Church Slavonic *pirŭ.* See **pō(i)-** in Appendix.]

pi·rogue (pĭ-rōg**′**) *n. Nautical.* A canoe made from a hollowed tree trunk; a piragua. [French, from Spanish *piragua.* See PIRAGUA.]

pir·o·plasm (pĭr**′**ə-plăz′əm) *n.* See **babesia.** [New Latin *Piroplasma,* genus name : Latin *pirum,* pear + Greek *plasma,* image; see PLASMA.]

pir·o·plas·mo·sis (pĭr′ə-plăz-mō**′**sĭs) *n.* See **babesiosis.**

pi·rosh·ki (pĭ-rôsh**′**kē, -rŏsh**′**-) *pl.n.* Variant of **pirozhki.**

pir·ou·ette (pĭr′o͞o-ĕt**′**) *n.* A full turn of the body on the point of the toe or the ball of the foot in ballet. **—pirouette** *intr.v.* **-et·ted, -et·ting, -ettes.** To execute a pirouette. [French, from Old French *pirouet,* spinning top.]

pi·rozh·ki also **pi·rosh·ki** (pĭ-rôsh**′**kē, -rŏsh**′**-) *pl.n.* Small Russian pastries filled with finely chopped meat or cabbage, baked or fried. [Russian, pl. of *pirozhok,* diminutive of *pirog,* pirog. See PIROG.]

Pi·sa (pē**′**zə, -zä). A city of western Italy on the Arno River near the Tyrrhenian Sea. An important Etruscan town, it developed into a powerful maritime republic in the 9th to 11th centuries but was crushed by Genoa in 1284. Florence controlled the city from 1406 to 1509. The campanile of its cathedral, built 1174–c. 1350, is the famed Leaning Tower of Pisa. Population, 104,334. **—Pi′san** *adj. & n.*

pis al·ler (pē ză-lā**′**) *n.* The final recourse or expedient; the last resort. [French : *pis,* worse + *aller,* to go.]

Pi·sa·no (pē-zä**′**nō), **Andrea.** 1270?–1348. Italian sculptor. His best-known work is the depiction of the life of John the Baptist on the bronze doors of the Baptistery in Florence.

Pisano, Nicola or **Niccolò.** 1220–1284? Italian sculptor noted for combining classical and French Gothic styles. His works include the hexagonal pulpit of the Baptistry in Pisa. Nicola's son **Giovanni** (1245?–1314?), a sculptor and architect, designed the Church of the Franciscans in Naples (1268).

pis·ca·ry (pĭs**′**kə-rē) *n., pl.* **-ries. 1.** *Law.* The right to fish in waters owned by another. **2.** A fishery. [From Middle English *piscaries,* fishing rights, from Medieval Latin *piscāria,* from Latin, neuter pl. of *piscārius,* of fish, from *piscis,* fish. Sense 2, Medieval

Latin *piscārium* : Latin *piscis,* fish + Latin *-ārium,* -arium.]

Pis·cat·a·way (pĭs-kăt′ə-wā′). A community of north-central New Jersey north of New Brunswick. Founded before 1693, it is a manufacturing center. Population, 42,223.

pis·ca·to·ri·al (pĭs′kə-tôr′ē-əl, -tōr′-) or **pis·ca·to·ry** (pĭs′kə-tôr′ē, -tōr′ē) *adj.* **1.** Of or relating to fish or fishing. **2.** Involved in or dependent on fishing. [From Latin *piscātōrius,* from *piscātor,* fisherman, from *piscārī,* to fish, from *piscis,* fish.] **—pis′ca·to′ri·al·ly** *adv.*

Pi·sce·an (pī′sē-ən) *n.* One who is born under the sign of Pisces. **—Pi′sce·an** *adj.*

Pi·sces (pī′sēz) *pl.n. (used with a sing. verb).* **1.** A constellation in the equatorial region of the Northern Hemisphere near Aries and Pegasus. Also called *Fishes.* **2.a.** The 12th sign of the zodiac in astrology. Also called *Fishes.* **b.** One who is born under this sign. [Middle English, from Medieval Latin *Piscēs,* from Latin *piscēs,* pl. of *piscis,* fish.]

pisci– *pref.* Fish: *piscivorous.* [From Latin *piscis,* fish.]

pi·sci·cul·ture (pī′sĭ-kŭl′chər, pĭs′ĭ-) *n.* The breeding, hatching, and rearing of fish under controlled conditions. **—pi′sci·cul′tur·al** *adj.* **—pi′sci·cul′tur·ist** *n.*

pi·sci·form (pī′sĭ-fôrm′, pĭs′ĭ-) *adj.* Having the shape of a fish.

pi·sci·na (pĭ-sē′nə, -sī′nə, -shē′nə) *n., pl.* **-nae** (-nē). *Ecclesiastical.* A stone basin with a drain for carrying away the water used in ceremonial ablutions. [Middle English *piscine,* from Medieval Latin *piscīna,* from Latin, fish-pond, pool, from *piscis,* fish.] **—pis′ci·nal** (pĭs′ə-nəl) *adj.*

pi·scine (pī′sēn′, pĭs′īn′) *adj.* Of, relating to, or characteristic of a fish or fishes. [Medieval Latin *piscīnus,* from Latin *piscis,* fish.]

Pi·scis Aus·tri·nus (pī′sĭs ô-strī′nəs) *n.* A constellation in the Southern Hemisphere near Aquarius and Grus. [New Latin : Latin *piscis,* fish + Latin *austrinus,* southern.]

pi·sciv·o·rous (pĭ-sĭv′ər-əs, pī-) *adj.* Habitually feeding on fish; fish-eating.

pish (pĭsh) *interj.* Used to express disdain.

pi·shogue also **pi·shoge** (pĭ-shōg′) *n. Irish.* **1.** Black magic; sorcery. **2.** An evil spell; an incantation. [Irish Gaelic *piseog,* from Middle Irish *pisóc, piseóc.*]

pi·si·form (pī′sə-fôrm′) *adj.* Resembling a pea in size or shape. **—pisiform** *n. Anatomy.* A small bone at the junction of the ulna and the carpus. [Latin *pīsum,* pea; see PEA + –FORM.]

Pi·sis·tra·tus or **Pei·sis·tra·tus** (pī-sĭs′trə-təs, pĭ-). Died 527 B.C. Athenian tyrant (560–527) remembered for encouraging athletic contests and literary efforts.

pis·mire (pĭs′mīr′, pĭz′-) *n.* An ant. [Middle English *pissemyre* : *pisse,* urine (from the smell of the formic acid that ants secrete); see PISS + *mire,* ant (probably of Scandinavian origin; akin to Danish *myre*).]

pis·mo clam (pĭz′mō) *n.* A large, thick-shelled, edible marine clam *(Tivela stultorum)* of the southern Pacific coast of North America. [After *Pismo* Beach, a city of southwest California.]

pi·so·lite (pī′sə-līt′) *n. Geology.* **1.** Rock, usually limestone, composed of pisoliths. **2.** See **pisolith.** [Greek *pisos,* pea + –LITE.] **—pi′so·lit′ic** (-lĭt′ĭk) *adj.*

pi·so·lith (pī′sə-lĭth′, -zə-, pĭs′ə-, pĭz′ə-) *n. Geology.* A small rounded accretionary mass, usually of calcium carbonate, larger and less regular than an oolite. Also called *pisolite.* [Greek *pisos,* pea + –LITH.]

piss (pĭs) *Vulgar Slang. v.* **pissed, piss·ing, piss·es.** *—intr.* To urinate. *—tr.* **1.** To urinate on or in. **2.** To discharge (blood, for example) in the urine. **—piss** *n.* **1.** Urine. **2.** The act or an instance of urinating. ***—phrasal verb.* piss off.** To make or become angry. [Middle English *pissen,* from Old French *pissier,* from Vulgar Latin **pissiāre,* of imitative origin.]

piss·ant also **piss-ant** or **piss ant** (pĭs′ănt′) *Slang.—n.* A stickler for petty details. *—adj.* Exhibiting elaborate concern for petty details; niggling: *"Some pissant Texas court wants to make* [the company] *pay . . . more than $10 billion in reparations"* (New Republic).

Pis·sar·ro (pĭ-sär′ō, pē-), **Camille.** 1830–1903. French impressionist painter known for his rural scenes, including *Orchard in Blossom* (1877).

pissed (pĭst) *adj. Vulgar Slang.* **1.** Extremely irritated or angry. **2.** Intoxicated; drunk.

piss·er (pĭs′ər) *n. Vulgar Slang.* **1.** One that is extremely disagreeable. **2.** One that is extraordinary or remarkable.

pis·soir (pē-swär′) *n.* A public urinal located on the street in some European countries. [French, from Old French, from *pissier,* to urinate. See PISS.]

pis·ta·chi·o (pĭ-stăsh′ē-ō′, -stä′shē-ō′) *n., pl.* **-os. 1.a.** A deciduous tree *(Pistacia vera)* of central and western Asia, having pinnately compound leaves and dry, drupaceous, nutlike fruits. **b.** The nutlike fruit of this tree, having an edible, oily, green or yellow kernel. **2.** The flavor of these nuts. [Italian *pistacchio,* from Latin *pistacium,* pistachio nut, from Greek *pistakion,* from *pistakē,* pistachio tree, perhaps from Middle Persian **pistak.*]

pistachio green *n. Color.* A moderate to light yellowish or yellow green.

pis·ta·reen (pĭs′tə-rēn′) *n.* A small silver coin used in America and the West Indies during the 18th century. [Probably alteration of Spanish *peseta,* peseta. See PESETA.]

piste (pēst) *n. Sports.* A ski trail densely packed with snow. [French, from Italian *pista,* from obsolete *pistare,* to trample down, variant of *pestare.* See PISTON.]

pis·til (pĭs′təl) *n.* The female, ovule-bearing organ of a flower, including the stigma, style, and ovary. [French, from New Latin *pistillum,* from Latin, pestle (from its shape).]

pis·til·late (pĭs′tə-lāt′, -lĭt′) *adj.* **1.** Having one or more pistils. **2.** Having pistils but no stamens: *pistillate flowers.*

Pis·to·ia (pĭ-stoi′ə, pē -stō′yä). A city of north-central Italy northwest of Florence. Settled by Romans in the 6th century B.C., it was an important banking center in the 13th century A.D. and came under the influence of Florence in the 14th century. Population, 83,600.

pis·tol (pĭs′təl) *n.* A firearm designed to be held and fired with one hand. **—pistol** *tr.v.* **-toled, -tol·ing, -tols.** To shoot with such a handgun. [French *pistole,* from German, from Middle High German *pischulle,* from Czech *pišťala,* pipe, whistle, firearm, from *pištěti,* to whistle, of imitative origin.]

pis·tole (pĭ-stōl′) *n.* **1.** A gold coin equal to two escudos, formerly used in Spain. **2.** Any of several gold coins used in various European countries until the late 19th century. [French, back-formation from *pistolet,* diminutive of *pistole,* pistol. See PISTOL.]

pistol grip *n.* **1.a.** The grip of a pistol, shaped to fit the hand. **b.** A similar grip sometimes used on a rifle or other firearm. **2.** A grip used on certain tools, such as a saw, shaped to fit the hand.

pis·tol-whip (pĭs′təl-hwĭp′, -wĭp′) *tr.v.* **-whipped, -whip·ping, -whips.** To beat with a pistol.

pis·ton (pĭs′tən) *n.* **1.** A solid cylinder or disk that fits snugly into a larger cylinder and moves under fluid pressure, as in a reciprocating engine, or displaces or compresses fluids, as in pumps and compressors. **2.** *Music.* A valve mechanism in brass instruments for altering the pitch. [French, from Italian *pistone, pestone,* large pestle, from *pestare,* to pound, crush, from Late Latin *pistāre,* frequentative of Latin *pīnsere, pīnsāre.*]

piston ring *n.* An adjustable split metal ring that fits around a piston and seals the gap between the piston and the cylinder wall.

piston rod *n.* A connecting rod that transmits power to or is powered by a piston.

pis·tou (pē-stōō′) *n.* A sauce made of garlic, basil, tomato, Parmesan, and olive oil, used on pasta or in soups and stews. [French, from Provençal, from *pestar,* to crush, from Old Provençal, from Late Latin *pistāre.* See PISTON.]

pit¹ (pĭt) *n.* **1.** A natural or artificial hole or cavity in the ground. **2.a.** An excavation for the removal of mineral deposits; a mine. **b.** The shaft of a mine. **3.** A concealed hole in the ground used as a trap; a pitfall. **4.a.** Hell. **b.** A miserable or depressing place or situation. **c. pits.** *Slang.* The worst. Used with *the:* *"New York politics are the pits"* (Washington Star). **5.** A small indentation in a surface: *pits in a windshield.* **6.a.** A natural hollow or depression in the body or an organ. **b.** A small indented scar left in the skin by smallpox or other eruptive disease; a pockmark. **c.** *Informal.* An armpit. Often used in the plural. **7.** An enclosed, usually sunken area in which animals, such as dogs or gamecocks, are placed for fighting. **8.a.** The section directly in front of and below the stage of a theater, in which the musicians sit. **b.** *Chiefly British.* The ground floor of a theater behind the stalls. **9.a.** The section of an exchange where trading in a specific commodity is carried on. **b.** The gambling area of a casino. **10.a.** A sunken area in a garage floor from which mechanics may work on cars. **b.** Often **pits.** *Sports.* An area beside an auto racecourse where cars may be refueled or serviced during a race. Used with *the.* **11.** *Football.* The middle areas of the defensive and offensive lines. **12.** *Botany.* A cavity in the wall of a plant cell where there is no secondary wall, as in fibers, tracheids, and vessels. **—pit** *v.* **pit·ted, pit·ting, pits.** *—tr.* **1.** To mark with cavities, depressions, or scars: *a surface pitted with craters.* **2.** To set in direct opposition or competition: *a war that pitted brother against brother.* **3.** To place, bury, or store in a pit. *—intr.* **1.** To become marked with pits. **2.** To retain an impression after being indented. Used of the skin. **3.** To stop at a refueling area during an auto race. [Middle English, from Old English *pytt,* ultimately from Latin *puteus,* well. See **peu-** in Appendix.]

pit² (pĭt) *n.* The single, central kernel or stone of certain fruits, such as a peach or cherry. **—pit** *tr.v.* **pit·ted, pit·ting, pits.** To extract the pit from (a fruit). [Dutch, from Middle Dutch.]

pi·ta¹ (pē′tə) *n.* A round, flat bread of Middle Eastern origin that can be opened into a pocket for filling. Also called *pocket bread.* [Modern Greek *pētta, pita,* pie, cake, bread.]

pi·ta² (pē′tə) *n.* **1.** Any of several plants of the genus *Agave* that yield strong leaf fibers. Also called *istle.* **2.** The fiber of any of these plants, used in making cordage and paper. [Spanish, from Quechua, to complicate, discord, bother.]

pit·a·pat (pĭt′ə-păt′) *intr.v.* **-pat·ted, -pat·ting, -pats. 1.** To move with a series of quick, tapping steps. **2.** To make a repeated tapping sound. **—pitapat** *n.* A series of quick steps, taps, or beats. **—pitapat** *adv.* With a rapid tapping sound. [Imitative.]

pit boss *n.* An employee who supervises the gambling in a casino.

pit bull *n.* See **American Staffordshire terrier.**

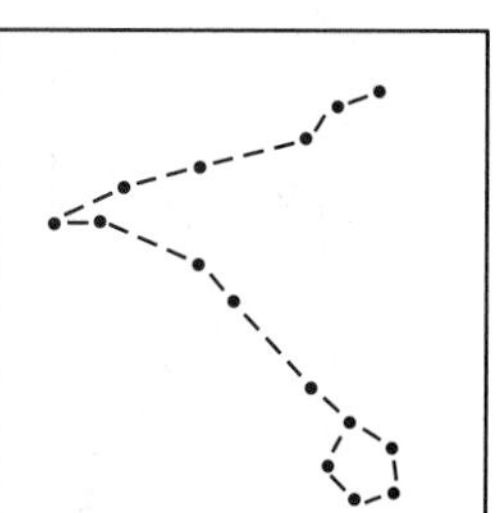
Pisces

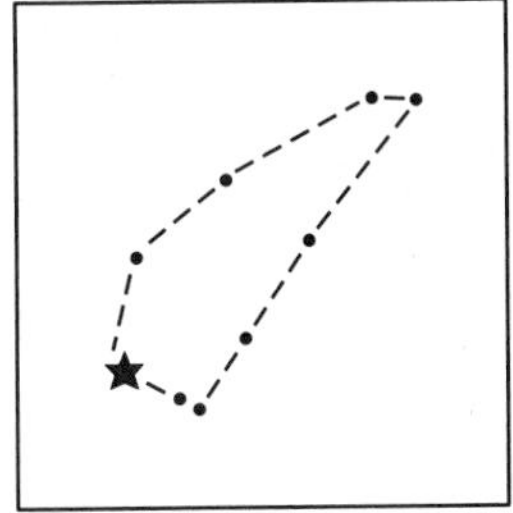
Piscis Austrinus

pistachio
Pistacia vera

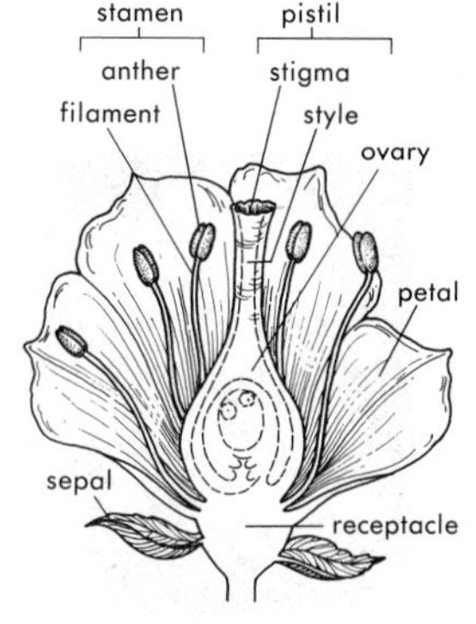

pistil

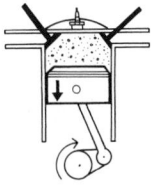

piston
Power stroke of an internal-combustion engine

pitcher²
1859 Tiffany sterling silver pitcher designed by Edward C. Moore (fl. 1848–1891)

pitcher plant
Sarracenia purpurea

pith helmet

pit-bull (pĭtʹbo͝olʹ) *adj. Slang.* Marked by or exhibiting great aggression, ruthlessness, and often bitterness: *"Pit-bull conservatives harbor the suspicion that their mission has been usurped by unbelievers"* (James Wolcott).

pit bull terrier *n.* See **American Staffordshire terrier.**

Pit·cairn Island (pĭtʹkârnʹ). A volcanic island of the southern Pacific Ocean east-southeast of Tahiti. Discovered by a British navigator in 1767, it was settled in 1790 by mutineers from H.M.S. *Bounty* and has been administered by the British since 1839.

pitch¹ (pĭch) *n.* **1.** Any of various thick, dark, sticky substances obtained from the distillation residue of coal tar, wood tar, or petroleum and used for waterproofing, roofing, caulking, and paving. **2.** Any of various natural bitumens, such as mineral pitch or asphalt. **3.** A resin derived from the sap of various coniferous trees, as the pines. **—pitch** *tr.v.* **pitched, pitch·ing, pitch·es.** To smear or cover with or as if with pitch. [Middle English *pich,* from Old English *pic* and from Anglo-Norman *piche,* both from Latin *pix, pic-.*]

pitch² (pĭch) *v.* **pitched, pitch·ing, pitch·es.** *—tr.* **1.a.** To throw, usually with careful aim. See Synonyms at **throw. b.** To discard by throwing: *pitched the can out the window.* **2.** *Baseball.* **a.** To throw (the ball) from the mound to the batter. **b.** To play (a game) as pitcher. **c.** To assign as pitcher. **3.** To erect or establish; set up: *pitched a tent; pitch camp.* **4.** To set firmly; implant; embed: *pitched stakes in the ground.* **5.** To set at a specified downward slant: *pitched the roof at a steep angle.* **6.a.** To set at a particular level, degree, or quality: *pitched her expectations too high.* **b.** *Music.* To set the pitch or key of. **c.** To adapt so as to be applicable; direct: *pitched his speech to the teenagers in the audience.* **7.** *Informal.* To attempt to promote or sell, often in a high-pressure manner: *"showed up on local TV to pitch their views"* (Business Week). **8.** *Sports.* To hit (a golf ball) in a high arc with backspin so that it does not roll very far after striking the ground. **9.** *Games.* To lead (a card), thus establishing the trump suit. *—intr.* **1.** To throw or toss something, such as a ball, horseshoe, or bale. **2.** *Baseball.* To play in the position of pitcher. **3.** To plunge headlong: *He pitched over the railing.* **4.a.** To stumble around; lurch. **b.** To buck, as a horse. **5.a.** *Nautical.* To dip bow and stern alternately. **b.** To oscillate about a lateral axis so that the nose lifts or descends in relation to the tail. Used of an aircraft. **c.** To oscillate about a lateral axis that is both perpendicular to the longitudinal axis and horizontal to the earth. Used of a missile or spacecraft. **6.** To slope downward: *The hill pitches steeply.* **7.** To set up living quarters; encamp; settle. **8.** *Sports.* To hit a golf ball in a high arc with backspin so that it does not roll very far after striking the ground. **—pitch** *n.* **1.** The act or an instance of pitching. **2.** *Baseball.* **a.** A throw of the ball by the pitcher to the batter. **b.** A ball so thrown. **3.** *Sports.* The rectangular area between the wickets in cricket, 22 yards (20.1 meters) by 10 feet (3.1 meters). Also called *wicket.* **4.a.** *Nautical.* The alternate dip and rise of the bow and stern of a ship. **b.** The alternate lift and descent of the nose and tail of an airplane. **5.a.** A steep downward slope. **b.** The degree of such a slope. **6.** *Architecture.* **a.** The angle of a roof. **b.** The highest point of a structure: *the pitch of an arch.* **7.** A level or degree, as of intensity: *worked at a feverish pitch.* **8.a.** *Acoustics.* The distinctive quality of a sound, dependent primarily on the frequency of the sound waves produced by its source. **b.** *Music.* The relative position of a tone within a range of musical sounds, as determined by this quality. **c.** *Music.* Any of various standards for this quality associating each tone with a particular frequency. **9.a.** The distance traveled by a machine screw in a single revolution. **b.** The distance between two corresponding points on adjacent screw threads or gear teeth. **c.** The distance between two corresponding points on a helix. **10.** The distance that a propeller would travel in an ideal medium during one complete revolution, measured parallel to the shaft of the propeller. **11.** *Informal.* **a.** A line of talk designed to persuade: "[his] *pious pitch for . . . austerity"* (Boston Globe). **b.** An advertisement. **12.** *Chiefly British.* The stand of a vender or hawker. **13.** *Games.* See **seven-up. 14.** *Printing.* The density of characters in a printed line, usually expressed as characters per inch. ***—phrasal verbs.*** **pitch in.** *Informal.* **1.** To set to work vigorously. **2.** To join forces with others; help or cooperate. **pitch into.** *Informal.* To attack verbally or physically; assault. **pitch on** (or **upon**). *Informal.* To succeed in choosing or achieving, usually quickly: *pitched on the ideal solution.* [Middle English *pichen,* probably from Old English **piccean,* causative of **pīcian,* to prick.]

pitch accent *n. Linguistics.* See **tonic accent.**

pitch-black (pĭchʹblăkʹ) *adj. Color.* Extremely dark; black as pitch.

pitch·blende (pĭchʹblĕndʹ) *n.* A massive variety of the mineral uraninite. [Partial translation of German *Pechblende* : *Pech,* pitch + *Blende,* blende; see BLENDE.]

pitch-dark (pĭchʹdärkʹ) *adj.* Extremely dark.

pitched battle (pĭcht) *n.* **1.** An intense battle fought in close contact by troops arranged in a predetermined formation. **2.** A fiercely waged battle or struggle between opposing forces.

pitch·er¹ (pĭchʹər) *n.* **1.** One that pitches. **2.** *Baseball.* The player who throws the ball from the mound to the batter. **3.** *Sports.* A seven iron used in golf.

pitch·er² (pĭchʹər) *n.* **1.** A container for liquids, usually having a handle and a lip or spout for pouring. **2.** *Botany.* A pitcherlike part, such as the leaf of a pitcher plant. [Middle English *picher,* from Old French *pichier,* alteration of *bichier,* from Medieval Latin *bicārium,* drinking cup, probably from Greek *bikos,* jar, possibly from Egyptian *bik,* oil vessel.]

Pitch·er (pĭchʹər), **Molly.** See Mary Ludwig Hays **McCauley.**

pitcher plant *n.* Any of various insectivorous plants of the genera *Sarracenia, Nepenthes,* or *Darlingtonia,* having pitcherlike leaves that attract and trap insects.

pitch·fork (pĭchʹfôrkʹ) *n.* A large, long-handled fork with sharp, widely spaced prongs for lifting and pitching hay. **—pitchfork** *tr.v.* **-forked, -fork·ing, -forks.** To lift or toss with or as if with a pitchfork. [Alteration (influenced by *pichen,* to throw) of Middle English *pikforke* : *pik,* pick; see PICK², or *pik,* spike; see PIKE⁵ + *forke,* fork; see FORK.]

pitch·ing niblick (pĭchʹĭng) *n. Sports.* An eight iron used in golf.

pitch·man (pĭchʹmən) *n.* **1.** A hawker of small wares, as on the streets or at a carnival. **2.** One who makes aggressive selling or promotional efforts. **3.** One who delivers commercials on radio or television.

pitch·out (pĭchʹoutʹ) *n.* **1.** *Baseball.* A pitch deliberately thrown high and away from the batter to make it easier for the catcher to throw out a base runner who is standing off a base or attempting to steal. **2.** *Football.* A lateral pass from the back receiving the snap from the center to another back behind the line of scrimmage.

pitch pine *n.* An eastern North American pine tree *(Pinus rigida)* that yields pitch or turpentine.

pitch pipe *n. Music.* A small pipe that, when sounded, gives the standard pitch for a piece of music or for tuning an instrument.

pitch·stone (pĭchʹstōnʹ) *n.* Any of various volcanic glasses distinguished by their dull pitchlike luster. [Translation of German *Pechstein.*]

pitch·y (pĭchʹē) *adj.* **-i·er, -i·est. 1.** Full of or covered with pitch. **2.** Resembling pitch in consistency. **3.** Extremely dark; black. **—pitchʹi·ness** *n.*

pit·e·ous (pĭtʹē-əs) *adj.* **1.** Demanding or arousing pity: *a piteous appeal for help.* See Synonyms at **pathetic. 2.** *Archaic.* Pitying; compassionate. [Middle English, from Old French *piteus,* from Late Latin *pietōsus, pĭetōsus,* merciful, from Latin *pietās, pĭetās,* compassion. See PIETY.] **—pitʹe·ous·ly** *adv.* **—pitʹe·ous·ness** *n.*

pit·fall (pĭtʹfôlʹ) *n.* **1.** An unapparent source of trouble or danger; a hidden hazard: *"potential pitfalls stemming from their optimistic inflation assumptions"* (New York Times). **2.** A concealed hole in the ground that serves as a trap.

pith (pĭth) *n.* **1.** *Botany.* The soft, spongelike, central cylinder of the stems of most flowering plants, composed mainly of parenchyma. **2.** *Zoology.* The soft inner substance of a feather or hair. **3.** The essential or central part; the heart or essence. See Synonyms at **substance. 4.** Strength; vigor; mettle. **5.** Significance; importance. **6.** *Archaic.* Spinal cord or bone marrow. **—pith** *tr.v.* **pithed, pith·ing, piths. 1.** To remove the pith from (a plant stem). **2.** To sever or destroy the spinal cord of, usually by means of a needle inserted into the vertebral canal. **3.** To kill (cattle) by cutting the spinal cord. [Middle English, from Old English *pitha.*]

pith·e·can·thro·pus (pĭthʹĭ-kănʹthrə-pəs, -kăn-thrōʹpəs) *n.* An extinct primate postulated from bones found in Java in 1891 and originally designated *Pithecanthropus erectus* because it was thought to represent a species evolutionarily between apes and human beings. Pithecanthropus is now classified as *Homo erectus.* [New Latin, genus name : Greek *pithēkos,* ape + Greek *anthrōpos,* man.] **—pithʹe·can·thropʹic** (-kən-thrŏpʹĭk) *adj.* **—pithʹe·canʹthro·pine** (-kănʹthrə-pīnʹ) *adj.*

pith·e·coid (pĭthʹĭ-koidʹ, pĭ-thēʹkoid) *adj.* **1.** Resembling or relating to the apes, especially the anthropoid apes. **2.** Of or belonging to a genus *(Pithecia)* of small, slender South American monkeys related to the titi. [Greek *pithēkos,* ape + –OID.]

pith helmet *n.* A lightweight hat made from dried pith and worn in tropical countries for protection from the sun.

pith ray *n.* The parenchymatous tissue that extends between the vascular bundles of a stem or root.

pith·y (pĭthʹē) *adj.* **-i·er, -i·est. 1.** Precisely meaningful; forceful and brief: *a pithy comment.* **2.** Consisting of or resembling pith. **—pithʹi·ly** *adv.* **—pithʹi·ness** *n.*

pit·i·a·ble (pĭtʹē-ə-bəl) *adj.* **1.** Arousing or deserving of pity or compassion; lamentable. **2.** Arousing disdainful pity. See Synonyms at **pathetic. —pitʹi·a·ble·ness** *n.* **—pitʹi·a·bly** *adv.*

pit·i·ful (pĭtʹĭ-fəl) *adj.* **1.** Inspiring or deserving pity. **2.** Arousing contemptuous pity, as through ineptitude or inadequacy. See Synonyms at **pathetic. 3.** *Archaic.* Filled with pity or compassion. **—pitʹi·ful·ly** *adv.* **—pitʹi·ful·ness** *n.*

pit·i·less (pĭtʹĭ-lĭs) *adj.* Having no pity; merciless. **—pitʹi·less·ly** *adv.* **—pitʹi·less·ness** *n.*

pit·man (pĭtʹmən) *n.* **1.** *pl.* **pit·men** (-mĕn). A worker employed inside a pit in various industrial operations, as in a coal mine. **2.** *pl.* **pit·mans** (-mənz). See **connecting rod.**

Pit·man (pĭtʹmən), Sir **Isaac.** 1813–1897. British educator and inventor (1837) of a system of shorthand.

Pit·ney (pĭtʹnē), **Mahlon.** 1858–1924. American jurist who served as an associate justice of the U.S. Supreme Court (1912–1922).

pi·ton (pēʹtŏnʹ) *n. Sports.* A metal spike fitted at one end with an eye for securing a rope and driven into rock or ice as a support in mountain climbing. [French, from Old French, nail.]

Pi·tot-stat·ic tube (pē′tō-stăt′ĭk, pē-tō′-) *n.* A device consisting of a Pitot tube and a static tube combined to measure simultaneously the total and static pressure in a fluid stream. It can be used in aircraft to determine relative wind speed.

Pi·tot tube (pē′tō, pē-tō′) *n.* A device, essentially a tube set parallel to the direction of fluid-stream movement and attached to a manometer, used to measure the total pressure of the fluid stream. [After Henri *Pitot* (1695–1771), French physicist.]

Pit River¹ (pĭt) *n.* See **Achomawi** (sense 1).

Pit River² (pĭt). A river, about 322 km (200 mi) long, of northern California flowing south and west to the Sacramento River.

pit·saw also **pit saw** (pĭt′sô′) *n.* A large saw for cutting logs, operated jointly by a person standing above the log and another in a pit underneath.

pit stop *n. Sports.* **1.** A stop at a pit for refueling or service during an automobile race. **2.** *Informal.* **a.** A brief stop for rest and refreshment, especially during an automobile trip. **b.** A place where such a stop is made.

Pitt¹ (pĭt), **William.** First Earl of Chatham. Known as "Pitt the Elder." 1708–1778. British political leader and orator who directed his country's military effort during the Seven Years' War (1756–1763).

Pitt² (pĭt), **William.** Second Earl of Chatham. Known as "Pitt the Younger." 1759–1806. British prime minister (1783–1801 and 1804–1806). He accomplished the Act of Union between Ireland and Britain (1800) but was unsuccessful in his efforts to achieve Catholic emancipation.

pit·ta (pĭt′ə) *n.* Any of several brightly colored perching birds of the family Pittidae that live in forests of Asia, Australia, and Africa and have a strong bill, short tail, and long legs. [Telugu *piṭṭa,* bird.]

pit·tance (pĭt′ns) *n.* **1.** A meager monetary allowance, wage, or remuneration. **2.** A very small amount: *not a pittance of remorse.* [Middle English *pitance,* from Old French, allowance of food to a monk or poor person, from Medieval Latin *pīetantia,* from **pīetāns, pīetant-,* present participle of **pīetāre,* to show compassion, from Latin *pietās, pietās,* piety. See PITY.]

pit·ted (pĭt′ĭd) *adj.* **1.** Marked by pits. **2.** Having the pit removed: *pitted dates.*

pit·ter-pat·ter (pĭt′ər-păt′ər) *n.* A rapid series of light, tapping sounds. —**pitter-patter** *intr.v.* **-tered, -ter·ing, -ters.** To make or move with a series of light, tapping sounds: *rain pitter-pattering on the roof.* [Imitative.]

pit·tos·po·rum (pĭ-tŏs′pər-əm, pĭt′ə-spôr′əm, -spōr′-) *n.* Any of various evergreen shrubs or plants of the genus *Pittosporum,* native to the warmer regions of the Old World and grown as ornamental or hedge plants in the southern United States and Pacific coastal states. [New Latin, genus name : Greek *pissa, pitta,* pitch + New Latin *spora,* spore; see SPORE.]

Pitts·burg (pĭts′bûrg′). **1.** A city of western California at the junction of the Sacramento and San Joaquin rivers northeast of Oakland. It is a manufacturing center in a fishing and farming region. Population, 33,034. **2.** A city of southeast Kansas near the Missouri border. Founded in 1876 as a mining town, it now has diversified industries. Population, 18,770.

Pitts·burgh (pĭts′bûrg′). A city of southwest Pennsylvania at the point where the confluence of the Allegheny and Monongahela rivers forms the Ohio River. Fort Duquesne was built on the site by the French c. 1750 and fell to the British in 1758, when it was renamed Fort Pitt. The village surrounding the fort grew rapidly after the opening of the Northwest Territory. The city today is highly industrialized. Population, 423,938.

Pitts·field (pĭts′fēld′). A city of western Massachusetts northwest of Springfield near the New York border. It is a center of the Berkshire Hills resort area. Population, 51,974.

pi·tu·i·cyte (pĭ-to͞o′ĭ-sīt′, -tyo͞o′-) *n.* A small branching cell of the posterior lobe of the pituitary gland. [PITUI(TARY) + -CYTE.]

pi·tu·i·tar·y (pĭ-to͞o′ĭ-tĕr′ē, -tyo͞o′-) *n., pl.* **-ies.** **1.** The pituitary gland. **2.** *Medicine.* An extract from the anterior or posterior lobes of the pituitary gland, prepared for therapeutic use. —**pituitary** *adj.* **1.** Of or relating to the pituitary gland. **2.** Of or secreting phlegm or mucus; mucous. [From Latin *pītuītārius,* of phlegm (from the early belief that it produced mucus), from *pītuīta,* phlegm. See **peie-** in Appendix.]

pituitary gland *n.* A small, oval endocrine gland attached to the base of the vertebrate brain and consisting of an anterior and a posterior lobe, the secretions of which control the other endocrine glands and influence growth, metabolism, and maturation. Also called *hypophysis, pituitary body.*

pit viper *n.* Any of various venomous snakes of the family Crotalidae, such as a copperhead, rattlesnake, or fer-de-lance, characterized by a small sensory pit below each eye.

pit·y (pĭt′ē) *n., pl.* **-ies.** **1.** Sympathy and sorrow aroused by the misfortune or suffering of another. **2.** A matter of regret: *It's a pity she can't attend the reception.* —**pity** *v.* **-ied, -y·ing, -ies.** —*tr.* To feel pity for. —*intr.* To feel pity. —***idiom.*** **have** (or **take**) **pity on.** To show compassion for. [Middle English *pite,* from Old French, from Latin *pietās,* piety, compassion, from *pius,* dutiful.] —**pit′y·ing·ly** *adv.*

SYNONYMS: *pity, compassion, commiseration, sympathy, condolence, empathy.* These nouns signify sympathetic, kindly concern aroused by the misfortune, affliction, or suffering of another. *Pity* often implies a feeling of sorrow that inclines one to help or to show mercy: *"Pity is the feeling which arrests the mind in the presence of whatsoever is grave and constant in human sufferings and unites it with the human sufferer"* (James Joyce). *Compassion* denotes deep awareness of the suffering of another and the wish to relieve it: *"Compassion is not weakness, and concern for the unfortunate is not socialism"* (Hubert H. Humphrey). *Commiseration* signifies the expression of pity or sorrow: *"They not unfrequently wonder why, from being born blind, they should be held to be objects of commiseration"* (Benjamin C. Brodie). *Sympathy* as it is compared here denotes the act of or capacity for sharing in the sorrows or troubles of another: *"They had little sympathy to spare for their unfortunate enemies"* (William Hickling Prescott). *Condolence* is a formal, conventional expression of pity, usually to relatives upon a death: *We extended our condolences to the bereaved family. Empathy* is a vicarious identification with and understanding of another's situation, feelings, and motives: *Empathy for the criminal's childhood misery does not imply exoneration of the crimes he committed as an adult.*

pit·y·ri·a·sis (pĭt′ĭ-rī′ə-sĭs) *n., pl.* **-ses** (-sēz′). Any of various skin diseases of humans and animals, characterized by epidermal shedding of flaky scales. [Greek *pituriasis,* from *pituron,* grain husk, dandruff.]

più (pyo͞o) *adv. Music.* More. Used to qualify an adjective or another adverb in directions. [Italian, from Latin *plūs.* See **pele-¹** in Appendix.]

Pi·us II (pī′əs). Originally Enea Silvio Piccolomini. 1405–1464. Pope (1458–1464) noted for his unsuccessful attempt to lead a crusade against the Turks.

Pius V, Saint. Originally Antonio Ghislieri. 1504–1572. Pope (1566–1572). A leading figure of the Catholic Reformation, he excommunicated Elizabeth I of England.

Pius VII. Originally Barnaba Gregorio Chiaramonti. 1742–1823. Pope (1800–1823) who was forced to crown Napoleon emperor in 1804.

Pius IX. Originally Giovanni Maria Mastai-Ferretti. 1792–1878. Pope (1846–1878) who summoned the First Vatican Council (1869–1870).

Pius X, Saint. Originally Giuseppe Melchiorre Sarto. 1835–1914. Pope (1903–1914) who was strongly opposed to religious modernism.

Pius XI. Originally Ambrogio Damiano Achille Ratti. 1857–1939. Pope (1922–1939) who signed a treaty with Benito Mussolini granting papal sovereignty over Vatican City.

Pius XII. Originally Eugenio Pacelli. 1876–1958. Pope (1939–1958) who maintained neutrality during World War II. He was later severely criticized for not taking forceful measures to aid European Jews.

Pi·ute (pī′yo͞ot′) *n.* Variant of **Paiute.**

piv·ot (pĭv′ət) *n.* **1.** A short rod or shaft on which a related part rotates or swings. **2.** A person or thing on which something depends or turns; the central or crucial factor. **3.** The act of turning on or as if on a pivot. —**pivot** *v.* **-ot·ed, -ot·ing, -ots.** —*tr.* **1.** To mount on, attach by, or provide with a pivot or pivots. **2.** To cause to rotate, revolve, or turn. —*intr.* To turn on or as if on a pivot: *"The plot . . . lacks direction, pivoting on Hamlet's incertitude"* (G. Wilson Knight). [French, from Old French.] —**piv′ot·a·ble** *adj.*

piv·ot·al (pĭv′ə-tl) *adj.* **1.** Of, relating to, or serving as a pivot. **2.** Being of vital or central importance; crucial: *"Its pivotal location has also exposed it to periodic invasions"* (Henry A. Kissinger). —**piv′ot·al·ly** *adv.*

pivot joint *n.* A joint in which a bone rotates around another; a joint permitting only rotating movement.

pix¹ (pĭks) *n.* A plural of **pic.**

pix² (pĭks) *n. Ecclesiastical.* Variant of **pyx.**

pix·el (pĭk′səl, -sĕl′) *n. Computer Science.* The smallest image-forming unit of a video display. [PIX¹ + EL(EMENT).]

pix·ie (pĭk′sē) *n.* Variant of **pixy.**

pix·i·lat·ed or **pix·il·lat·ed** (pĭk′sə-lā′tĭd) *adj.* **1.** Behaving as if mentally unbalanced; very eccentric. **2.** Whimsical; prankish. **3.** *Slang.* Intoxicated; drunk. [From PIXY.] —**pix′i·la′tion** *n.*

pix·y or **pix·ie** (pĭk′sē) —*n., pl.* **-ies.** A fairylike or elfin creature, especially one that is playful or mischievous. —*adj.* Playfully mischievous. [Origin unknown.] —**pix′y·ish** *adj.*

Pi·zar·ro (pĭ-zär′ō, pē-thär′ō, -sär′-), **Francisco.** 1475?–1541. Spanish explorer and conqueror of the Inca Empire of Peru (1531–1533). He founded the city of Lima in 1535.

pizz. *abbr. Music.* Pizzicato.

piz·za (pēt′sə) *n.* A baked pie of Italian origin consisting of a shallow breadlike crust covered with seasoned tomato sauce, cheese, and often other toppings, such as sausage or olives. [Italian, pie, tart, pizza.]

piz·zazz or **piz·zaz** (pĭ-zăz′) *n. Slang.* **1.** Dazzling style; flamboyance; flair. **2.** Vigorous spirit; energy or excitement. [Origin unknown.]

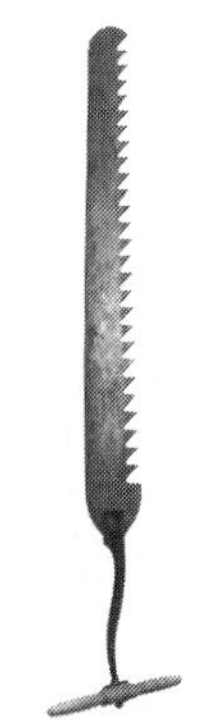

pitsaw

pit stop
During the Daytona 500

Francisco Pizarro
c. 1760 painting by an unknown artist

ă pat	oi boy
ā pay	ou out
âr care	o͝o took
ä father	o͞o boot
ĕ pet	ŭ cut
ē be	ûr urge
ĭ pit	th thin
ī pie	*th* this
îr pier	hw which
ŏ pot	zh vision
ō toe	ə about, item
ô paw	♦ regionalism

Stress marks: ′ (primary); ′ (secondary), as in **dictionary** (dĭk′shə-n

placard

piz·ze·ri·a (pēt′sə-rē′ə) *n.* A place where pizzas are made and sold. [Italian, from *pizza,* pizza, pie.]

piz·zi·ca·to (pĭt′sĭ-kä′tō) *Music. adj. Abbr.* **pizz.** Played by plucking rather than bowing the strings. **—pizzicato** *n., pl.* **-ti** (-tē). A pizzicato note or passage. [Italian, past participle of *pizzicare,* to pluck, from *pizzare,* to prick, from *pizzo,* point.] **—piz′zi·ca′to** *adv.*

piz·zle (pĭz′əl) *n.* **1.** The penis of an animal, especially a bull. **2.** A whip made from a bull's penis. [Possibly from Low German *pēsel,* diminutive of Middle Low German *pese,* penis, tendon.]

PK *abbr.* Psychokinesis.

pk. *abbr.* **1.** Pack. **2.** Park. **3.** Peak. **4.** Peck.

pkg. *abbr.* Package.

pkt. *abbr.* Packet.

PKU *abbr.* Phenylketonuria.

pkwy *abbr.* Parkway.

pky *abbr.* Parkway.

pl. *abbr.* **1.** Or **Pl.** Place. **2.** *Printing & Photography.* Plate. **3.** Plural.

PL/1 (pē′ĕl-wŭn′) *n. Computer Science.* A programming language designed for scientific and commercial uses at varying levels of complexity. [*p(rogramming) l(anguage) 1.*]

plac·a·ble (plăk′ə-bəl, plā′kə-) *adj.* Easily calmed or pacified; tolerant. [Middle English, agreeable, from Old French, from Latin *plācābilis,* from *plācāre,* to calm. See **plāk-**[1] in Appendix.] **—plac′a·bil′i·ty** *n.* **—plac′a·bly** *adv.*

plac·ard (plăk′ärd′, -ərd) *n.* **1.** A sign or notice for display in a public place. **2.** A small card or plaque, such as a name plate on a door. **—placard** *tr.v.* **-ard·ed, -ard·ing, -ards. 1.** To announce or advertise by means of placards. **2.** To post placards on or in. **3.** To display as a placard. [Middle English, official document, from Old French, from *plaquier,* to plaster, piece together, from Middle Dutch *placken,* to patch.] **—plac′ard′er** *n.*

pla·cate (plā′kāt′, plăk′āt′) *tr.v.* **-cat·ed, -cat·ing, -cates.** To allay the anger of, especially by making concessions; appease. See Synonyms at **pacify.** [Latin *plācāre, plācāt-,* to calm. See **plāk-**[1] in Appendix.] **—pla′cat′er** *n.* **—pla·ca′tion** (plā-kā′shən) *n.* **—pla′ca·to′ry** (-tôr′ē, -tōr′ē), **pla′ca′tive** (-kā′tĭv) *adj.*

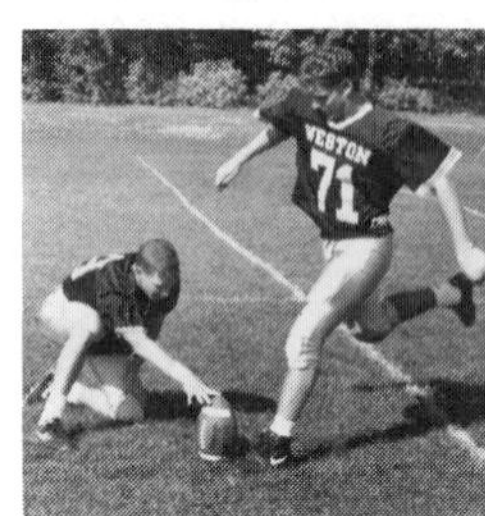

place kick

place (plās) *n.* **1.a.** An area with definite or indefinite boundaries; a portion of space. **b.** Room or space, especially adequate space: *There is place for everyone at the back of the room.* **2.a.** The particular portion of space occupied by or allocated to a person or thing. **b.** A building or an area set aside for a specified purpose: *a place of worship.* **3.a.** A dwelling; a house: *bought a place on the lake.* **b.** A business establishment or office. **c.** A locality, such as a town or a city: *visited many places.* **4.** Often **Place.** *Abbr.* **pl., Pl.** A public square or street with houses in a town. **5.a.** A space in which one person, such as a passenger or a spectator, can sit or stand. **b.** A setting for one person at a table. **6.** A position regarded as belonging to someone or something else; stead: *She was chosen in his place.* **7.** A particular point that one has reached, as in a book: *I have lost my place.* **8.** A particular spot, as on the body: *the place that hurts.* **9.a.** The proper or designated role or function: *the place of the media in a free society.* **b.** The proper or customary position or order: *These books are out of place.* **c.** A suitable setting or occasion: *not the place to argue.* **d.** The appropriate right or duty: *not her place to criticize.* **10.** Social station: *He overstepped his place.* **11.** A particular situation or circumstance: *Put yourself in my place.* **12.** High rank or status. **13.** A job, post, or position: *found a place in the company.* **14.** Relative position in a series; standing. **15.** *Games.* Second position for betting purposes, as in a horserace. **16.** The specified stage in a list of points to be made, as in an argument: *in the first place.* **17.** *Mathematics.* The position of a figure in a numeral or series. **—place** *v.* **placed, plac·ing, plac·es.** *—tr.* **1.** To put in or as if in a particular place or position; set. **2.** To put in a specified relation or order: *Place the words in alphabetical order.* **3.** To offer for consideration: *placed the matter before the board.* **4.** To find accommodation or employment for. **5.** To put into a particular condition: *placed him under arrest.* **6.** To arrange for the publication or display of: *place an advertisement in the newspaper.* **7.** To appoint to a post: *placed her in a key position.* **8.a.** To rank in an order or a sequence: *I'd place him second best.* **b.** To estimate: *placed the distance at 100 feet.* **9.** To identify or classify in a particular context: *could not place that person's face.* **10.a.** To give an order for: *place a bet.* **b.** To apply or arrange for: *place an order.* **11.** To adjust (one's voice) for the best possible effects. *—intr. Sports & Games.* To arrive among the first three finishers in a race, especially to finish second. ***—idioms.* in place. 1.** In the appropriate or usual position or order: *With everything in place, she started the slide show.* **2.** In the same spot; without moving forwards or backwards: *While marching in place, the band played a popular tune.* **in place of.** Instead of. **keep** (or **know**) **(one's) place.** To recognize one's social position and act according to traditional decorum. **put (someone) in (his** or **her) place.** To lower the dignity of (someone); humble. **place in the sun.** A dominant or favorable position or situation. [Middle English, from Old English *plæce* and Old French, open space (from Medieval Latin *placea,* from Vulgar Latin **plattea*), both from Latin *platēa,* broad street, from Greek *plateia (hodos),* broad (street), feminine of *platus.* See **plat-** in Appendix.] **—place′a·ble** *adj.* **—plac′er** *n.*

id

pla·ce·bo (plə-sē′bō) *n., pl.* **-bos** or **-boes. 1.a.** *Medicine.* A substance containing no medication and prescribed or given to reinforce a patient's expectation to get well. **b.** An inactive substance or preparation used as a control in an experiment or test to determine the effectiveness of a medicinal drug. **2.** Something of no intrinsic remedial value that is used to appease or reassure another. **3.** (plä-chā′bō). *Roman Catholic Church.* The service or office of vespers for the dead. [Middle English, from Late Latin *placēbō,* I shall please (the first word of the first antiphon of the service), first person sing. future tense of Latin *placēre,* to please. See **plāk-**[1] in Appendix.]

placebo effect *n.* A beneficial effect in a patient following a particular treatment that arises from the patient's expectations concerning the treatment rather than from the treatment itself.

place·hold·er (plās′hōl′dər) *n.* **1.** One who holds an office or a place, especially: **a.** One who acts as a deputy or a proxy. **b.** One who holds an appointed office in a government. **2.** In a mathematical or logical expression, a symbol that may be replaced by the name of any element of a set. **3.** In the decimal form of a number, a digit that is not significant.

place kick *n. Football.* A kick, as for a field goal, for which the ball is held or propped up in a fixed position on the ground. **—place′kick′** (plās′kĭk′) *v.* **—place′-kick′er** *n.*

place·man (plās′mən) *n. Chiefly British.* One who has a political appointment in the government.

place mat *n.* A protective table mat for a single setting of dishes and flatware.

place·ment (plās′mənt) *n.* **1.a.** The act of placing or arranging. **b.** The state of being placed or arranged. **2.a.** The finding of suitable accommodation or employment for applicants. **b.** Assignment of students to appropriate classes or programs. **3.** *Football.* **a.** The setting of the ball in position for a place kick. **b.** A place kick.

pla·cen·ta (plə-sĕn′tə) *n., pl.* **-tas** or **-tae** (-tē). **1.a.** A membranous vascular organ that develops in female mammals during pregnancy, lining the uterine wall and partially enveloping the fetus, to which it is attached by the umbilical cord. Following birth, the placenta is expelled. **b.** An organ with similar functions in some nonmammalian animals, such as certain sharks and reptiles. **2.** *Botany.* The part within the ovary of a flowering plant to which the ovules are attached. [New Latin, from Latin, flat cake, alteration of Greek *plakoenta,* from accusative of *plakoeis,* flat, from *plax, plak-,* flat land, surface. See **plāk-**[1] in Appendix.] **—pla·cen′tal** *adj.*

plac·en·ta·tion (plăs′ən-tā′shən) *n.* **1.a.** Formation of a placenta in the uterus. **b.** The type or structure of a placenta. **2.** *Botany.* Arrangement of placentas within the ovary.

Pla·cen·tia (plə-sĕn′chə, -shə). A city of southern California east-northeast of Long Beach. It is a residential community with light industries. Population, 35,041.

Placentia Bay. An inlet of the Atlantic Ocean in southeast Newfoundland, Canada. On August 14, 1941, Franklin D. Roosevelt and Winston Churchill signed the Atlantic Charter, setting forth the Allied aims for a postwar settlement, while aboard the British battleship *Prince of Wales* anchored in the bay.

plac·er (plăs′ər) *n.* **1.** A glacial or alluvial deposit of sand or gravel containing eroded particles of valuable minerals. **2.** A place where a placer deposit is washed to extract its mineral content. [Spanish, shoal, placer, from Catalan *placer,* shoal, from *plassa,* place, from Medieval Latin *placea.* See PLACE.]

placer mining *n.* The obtaining of minerals from placers by washing or dredging. **—placer miner** *n.*

Plac·er·ville (plăs′ər-vĭl′). A city of east-central California east-northeast of Sacramento. It grew with the discovery of gold nearby in 1848 and is still a mining center. Population, 6,739.

place setting *n.* A table service for one person.

plac·id (plăs′ĭd) *adj.* **1.** Undisturbed by tumult or disorder; calm or quiet. See Synonyms at **calm. 2.** Satisfied; complacent. [Latin *placidus,* from *placēre,* to please. See **plāk-**[1] in Appendix.] **—pla·cid′i·ty** (plə-sĭd′ĭ-tē), **plac′id·ness** (plăs′ĭd-nĭs) *n.* **—plac′id·ly** *adv.*

Plac·id (plăs′ĭd), **Lake.** A lake of northeast New York in the Adirondack Mountains. It is a noted winter sports center.

plack·et (plăk′ĭt) *n.* **1.** A slit in a dress, blouse, or skirt. **2.** A pocket, especially in a woman's skirt. [Origin unknown.]

plac·oid (plăk′oid) *adj.* Platelike, as the hard toothlike scales of sharks, skates, and rays. [Greek *plax, plak-,* flat land, surface; see **plāk-**[1] in Appendix + -OID.]

pla·fond (plə-fŏn′, plä-fôN′) *n.* A decorated ceiling. [French : *plat,* flat; see PLATE + *fond,* base, bottom; see FOND[2].]

pla·gal (plā′gəl) *adj. Music.* **1.** Of or being a medieval mode having a range from the fourth below to the fifth above its final tone. **2.** Of or being a cadence with the subdominant chord immediately preceding the tonic chord. [Medieval Latin *plagālis,* from *plaga,* plagal mode, from *plagius,* plagal, from Medieval Greek *plagios (ēkhos),* plagal (mode), from Greek, oblique, from *plagos,* side. See **plāk-**[1] in Appendix.]

plage (plăzh) *n.* **1.** A sandy beach at a seaside resort. **2.** A bright and intensely hot area in the sun's chromosphere, usually associated with a sunspot. [French, from Italian *piaggia,* ultimately from Greek *plagia,* neuter pl. of *plagios,* oblique, slanting. See PLAGAL.]

pla·gia·rism (plā′jə-rĭz′əm) *n.* **1.** The act of plagiarizing. **2.**

Something plagiarized. [From PLAGIARY.] **—pla′gia·rist** *n.* **—pla′gia·ris′tic** *adj.*

pla·gia·rize (plā′jə-rīz′) *v.* **-rized, -riz·ing, -riz·es.** *—tr.* **1.** To use and pass off as one's own (the ideas or writings of another). **2.** To appropriate for use as one's own passages or ideas from (another). *—intr.* To put forth as original to oneself the ideas or words of another. **—pla′gia·riz′er** *n.*

pla·gia·ry (plā′jə-rē) *n., pl.* **-ries. 1.** Plagiarism. **2.** *Archaic.* One who plagiarizes. [Latin *plagiārius,* kidnapper, plagiarist, from *plagium,* kidnapping, from *plaga,* net. See **plăk-**[1] in Appendix.]

plagio– *pref.* Slanting; inclining: *plagiotropism.* [Greek, oblique, from *plagios,* from *plagos,* side. See **plăk-**[1] in Appendix.]

pla·gi·o·clase (plā′jē-ə-klās′, -klāz′, plăj′ē-) *n.* Any of a common rock-forming series of triclinic feldspars, consisting of mixtures of sodium and calcium aluminum silicates. Also called *oligoclase.* [Greek *plagio-,* plagio- + Greek *klasis,* breaking (from *klan,* to break).]

pla·gi·ot·ro·pism (plā′jē-ŏt′rə-pĭz′əm) *n. Botany.* The tendency to grow at an oblique or horizontal angle. Used of roots, stems, or branches. **—pla′gi·o·tro′pic** (-ə-trō′pĭk, -trŏp′ĭk) *adj.* **—pla′gi·o·tro′pi·cal·ly** *adv.*

plague (plāg) *n.* **1.** A widespread affliction or calamity, especially one seen as divine retribution. **2.** A sudden destructive influx or injurious outbreak: *a plague of locusts; a plague of accidents.* **3.** A cause of annoyance; a nuisance: *"the plague of social jabbering"* (George Santayana). **4.** A highly infectious, usually fatal, epidemic disease, especially bubonic plague. **—plague** *tr.v.* **plagued, plagu·ing, plagues. 1.** To pester or annoy persistently or incessantly. See Synonyms at **harass. 2.** To afflict with or as if with a disease or calamity: *"Runaway inflation further plagued the wage- or salary-earner"* (Edwin O. Reischauer). [Middle English *plage,* blow, calamity, plague, from Late Latin *plāga,* from Latin, blow, wound. See **plăk-**[2] in Appendix. V., Middle English *plaghen,* from Middle Dutch, from *plaghe,* plague, from Late Latin *plāga.*] **—plagu′er** *n.*

pla·guy also **pla·guey** (plā′gē) *adj.* Vexatious; bothersome. **—pla′guy, pla′gui·ly** *adv.*

plaice (plās) *n., pl.* **plaice** or **plaic·es. 1.** A large edible marine flatfish *(Pleuronectes platessa)* of western European waters. **2.** Any of various flatfishes, such as *Hippoglossoides platessoides* of North American Atlantic waters, related to the plaice. [Middle English, from Old French *plais,* from Vulgar Latin **platīx,* alteration of Late Latin *platessa,* probably ultimately from Greek *platus,* broad. See **plat-** in Appendix.]

plaid (plăd) *n.* **1.** A rectangular woolen scarf of a tartan pattern worn over the left shoulder by Scottish Highlanders. **2.a.** Cloth with a tartan or checked pattern. **b.** A pattern of this kind. [Scottish Gaelic *plaide.*] **—plaid** *adj.*

plaid·ed (plăd′ĭd) *adj.* **1.** Made of plaid or having a plaid pattern. **2.** Wearing a plaid.

plain (plān) *adj.* **plain·er, plain·est.** *Abbr.* **pln. 1.** Free from obstructions; open; clear: *in plain view.* **2.** Obvious to the mind; evident: *make one's intention plain.* See Synonyms at **apparent. 3.** Not elaborate or complicated; simple: *plain food.* **4.** Straightforward; frank or candid: *plain talk.* **5.** Not mixed with other substances; pure: *plain water.* **6.** Common in rank or station; average; ordinary: *a plain man.* **7.** Not pretentious; unaffected. **8.** Marked by little or no ornamentation or decoration. **9.** Not dyed, twilled, or patterned: *a plain fabric.* **10.** Lacking beauty or distinction: *a plain face.* **11.** Sheer; utter; unqualified: *plain stupidity.* **12.** *Archaic.* Flat; level. **—plain** *n. Abbr.* **pln. 1.a.** An extensive, level, usually treeless area of land. **b.** A broad, level expanse, as a part of the sea floor or a lunar mare. **2.** Something free of ornamentation or extraneous matter. **—plain** *adv. Informal.* Clearly; simply: *plain stubborn.* [Middle English, from Old French, from Latin *plānus.* See **pele-**[2] in Appendix.] **—plain′ly** *adv.* **—plain′ness** *n.*

SYNONYMS: *plain, modest, simple, unostentatious, unpretentious.* The central meaning shared by these adjectives is "not ornate, ostentatious, or showy": *a plain hair style; a modest cottage; a simple dark suit; an unostentatious office; an unpretentious country church.*
ANTONYM: *ornate.*

plain·chant (plān′chănt′) *n. Roman Catholic Church.* See **plainsong** (sense 2). [French *plain-chant* (translation of Medieval Latin *cantus plānus*) : *plain,* plain; see PLAIN + *chant,* song; see CHANT.]

plain·clothes man or **plain·clothes·man** (plān′klōz′mən, -klōthz′-) *n.* A member of a police force, especially a detective, who wears civilian clothes on duty.

Plain·field (plān′fēld′). A city of northeast New Jersey southwest of Newark. Settled in 1684, it was formerly a residential town but has now become a trade and industrial center in a thickly populated area. Population, 45,555.

plain-Jane (plān′jān′) *adj.* Lacking adornment or pretension; basic or simple.

plain-laid (plān′lād′) *adj.* Made of three strands laid together with a right-hand twist. Used of a rope.

Plain People (plān) *pl.n.* Members of the Mennonites, Amish, or Dunkers, noted for their plain dress and simple style of life.

plain sailing *n. Informal.* Easy progress over a smooth and direct course: *After the editing of the book had been finished, it was plain sailing to the end of the project.* [Possibly variant of *plane sailing,* navigation as if on a plane surface, disregarding the curvature of the earth.]

Plains Indian (plānz) *n.* A member of any of the Native American peoples inhabiting the Great Plains of the United States and Canada. The Plains Indians spoke a variety of unrelated languages but shared certain cultural features such as nomadic buffalo hunting, the use of conical tepees, and a reliance on the horse in hunting and warfare.

plains·man (plānz′mən) *n.* An inhabitant or a settler of the plains, especially of the prairie regions of the United States.

plain·song (plān′sông′, -sŏng′) *n. Roman Catholic Church.* **1.a.** A Gregorian chant. **b.** A melody to which contrapuntal voices are added in Gregorian chant. **2.** Any medieval liturgical music without strict meter and traditionally sung without accompaniment. In this sense, also called *plainchant.* [Translation of Medieval Latin *cantus plānus.*]

plain·spo·ken (plān′spō′kən) *adj.* Frank; straightforward; blunt. **—plain′spo′ken·ness** *n.*

plaint (plānt) *n.* **1.** A complaint. **2.** An utterance of grief or sorrow; a lamentation. [Middle English, from Old French *plainte,* from Latin *plānctus,* lament, from past participle of *plangere,* to strike one's breast, lament. See **plăk-**[2] in Appendix.]

plain text or **plain·text** (plān′tĕkst′) *n.* The original form of a message as opposed to the encrypted form.

plain·tiff (plān′tĭf) *n. Abbr.* **plf.** *Law.* The party that institutes a suit in a court. [Middle English *plaintif,* from Anglo-Norman *pleintif,* from Old French *plaintif,* aggrieved. See PLAINTIVE.]

plain·tive (plān′tĭv) *adj.* Expressing sorrow; mournful or melancholy. [Middle English *plaintif,* from Old French, aggrieved, lamenting, from *plaint,* complaint. See PLAINT.] **—plain′tive·ly** *adv.* **—plain′tive·ness** *n.*

Plain·view (plān′vyo͞o′). A city of northwest Texas south of Amarillo. The city has large meat-packing and meat-processing industries. Population, 22,187.

Plain·ville (plān′vĭl′). A town of central Connecticut southwest of Hartford. It is a manufacturing center in a farming area. Population, 16,401.

plain weave *n.* A weave in which the filling threads and the warp threads interlace alternately, forming a checkerboard pattern. Also called *taffeta weave.*

plain-wo·ven (plān′wō′vən) *adj.* Made in plain weave.

plait (plāt, plăt) *n.* **1.** A braid, especially of hair. **2.** A pleat. **—plait** *tr.v.* **plait·ed, plait·ing, plaits. 1.** To braid. **2.** To pleat. **3.** To make by braiding. [Middle English *pleit,* fold, braid, possibly from *pleiten,* to fold, braid, alteration (influenced by Old French *pleit,* fold) of Old French *plier, pleiir,* from Latin *plicāre,* to fold. See **plek-** in Appendix.] **—plait′er** *n.*

plait

plan (plăn) *n.* **1.** A scheme, program, or method worked out beforehand for the accomplishment of an objective: *a plan of attack.* **2.** A proposed or tentative project or course of action: *had no plans for the evening.* **3.** A systematic arrangement of important parts; an outline or a sketch: *the plan of a story.* **4.** A drawing or diagram made to scale showing the structure or arrangement of something. **5.** In perspective rendering, one of several imaginary planes perpendicular to the line of vision between the viewer and the object being depicted. **—plan** *v.* **planned, plan·ning, plans.** *—tr.* **1.** To formulate a scheme or program for the accomplishment, enactment, or attainment of: *plan a campaign.* **2.** To have as a specific aim or purpose; intend: *They plan to buy a house.* **3.** To draw or make a graphic representation of. *—intr.* To make plans. [French, alteration (influenced by *plan,* flat surface; see PLAIN) of *plant,* ground plan, map (from *planter,* to plant, from Latin *plantāre,* from *planta,* sole of the foot. See **plat-** in Appendix).] **—plan′ner** *n.*

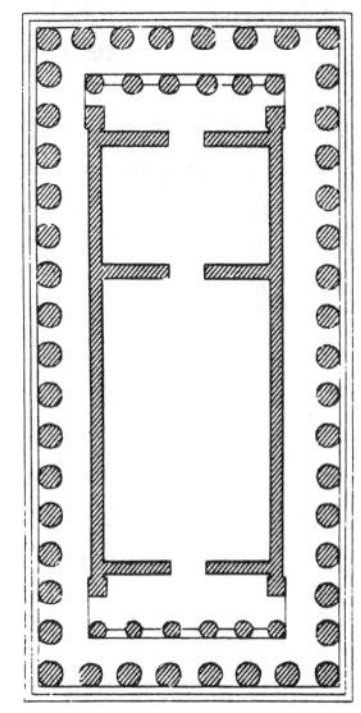

plan
Plan of the Parthenon, Athens, Greece

SYNONYMS: *plan, blueprint, design, project, scheme, strategy.* The central meaning shared by these nouns is "a method or program in accordance with which something is to be done or accomplished": *has no vacation plans; a blueprint for the reorganization of the company; social conventions that are a product of human design; an urban-renewal project; a new scheme for power conservation; a strategy for capturing a major market share.*

plan– *pref.* Variant of **plano–.**

pla·nar (plā′nər, -när′) *adj.* **1.** Of, relating to, or situated in a plane. **2.** Flat: *a planar surface.* **3.** Having a two-dimensional characteristic. [Late Latin *plānāris,* flat, from Latin *plānus.* See PLAIN.] **—pla·nar′i·ty** (plā-năr′ĭ-tē) *n.*

pla·nar·i·an (plə-nâr′ē-ən) *n.* Any of various small, chiefly freshwater turbellarian flatworms of the order Tricladida, having soft, broad, ciliated bodies, a three-branched digestive cavity, and the ability to regenerate body parts. [From New Latin *Plānāria,* genus name, from feminine of Late Latin *plānārius,* on level ground, from *plānus,* flat. See **pele-**[2] in Appendix.]

pla·na·tion (plā-nā′shən) *n.* The process of erosion and deposition in which a nearly level surface is produced, as by streams, wind, or ocean currents. [Latin *plānum,* flat surface; see PLANE[1] + –ATION.]

planch·et (plăn′chĭt) *n.* **1.** A flat disk of metal ready for stamping as a coin; a coin blank. **2.** A small shallow metal container in which a radioactive substance is deposited for measure-

ă pat	oi boy
ā pay	ou out
âr care	o͝o took
ä father	o͞o boot
ĕ pet	ŭ cut
ē be	ûr urge
ĭ pit	th thin
ī pie	*th* this
îr pier	hw which
ŏ pot	zh vision
ō toe	ə about, item
ô paw	♦ regionalism

Stress marks: **′** (primary); ′ (secondary), as in **dictionary** (dĭk′shə-nĕr′ē)

ment of its activity. [Diminutive of *planch,* flat plate, slab, from Middle English *plaunche,* plank, from Old French *planche,* from Late Latin *planca,* from feminine of Latin *plancus,* flat. See **plăk-**[1] in Appendix.]

plan•chette (plăn-shĕtʹ) *n.* A small triangular board supported by two casters and a vertical pencil which, when lightly touched by the fingertips, is said to spell out subconscious or supernatural messages. [French, from Old French, diminutive of *planche,* board. See PLANCHET.]

Planck (plängk), **Max Karl Ernst Ludwig.** 1858–1947. German physicist. He won a 1918 Nobel Prize for discoveries in connection with quantum theory.

Planck's constant (plängks) *n.* *Symbol* **h** The constant of proportionality relating the energy of a photon to the frequency of that photon, equal to approximately 6.626×10^{-34} joule-second. [After Max Karl Ernst Ludwig PLANCK.]

plane[1] (plān) *n.* **1.** *Mathematics.* A surface containing all the straight lines that connect any two points on it. **2.** A flat or level surface. **3.** A level of development, existence, or achievement: *scholarship on a high plane.* **4.** An airplane or a hydroplane. **5.** A supporting surface of an airplane; an airfoil or a wing. **—plane** *adj.* **1.** *Mathematics.* Of or being a figure lying in a plane: *a plane curve.* **2.** Flat; level. See Synonyms at **level.** [Latin *plānum,* flat surface, from neuter of *plānus,* flat. See **pelə-**[2] in Appendix. N., sense 4, short for AEROPLANE.] **—planeʹness** *n.*

WORD HISTORY: The plane in which we fly is properly named for a very important element of its structure—the wing that keeps it in the air. But the story behind this name is slightly complicated. To begin with, *plane* in the sense "winged vehicle," first recorded in April 1908, is a shortened form of *aeroplane.* In June of that year *plane* appeared in a quotation from the *London Times* that mentioned Mr. Wright. *Aeroplane,* first recorded in 1866, is made up of the prefix *aero–,* "air, aviation," and the word *plane,* referring to the structure designed to keep an air vehicle aloft. Originally the plane in such contexts was imagined as flat, hence the choice of the word *plane;* in practice this surface to curve slightly in order to work. The word *aeroplane* for the vehicle is first found in 1873. The first recorded appearance of the form *airplane* in our current sense, which uses *air–* instead of *aero–,* is found in 1907. An American flies in an *airplane* while a Briton still travels in an *aeroplane,* but both can catch a *plane.*

plane[2]
Bench plane

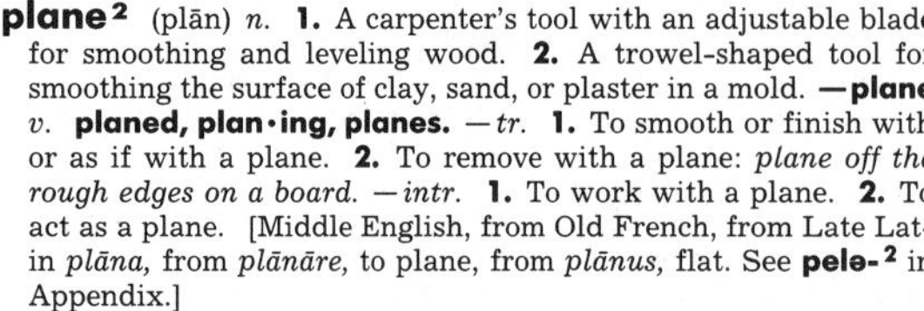

plane[2] (plān) *n.* **1.** A carpenter's tool with an adjustable blade for smoothing and leveling wood. **2.** A trowel-shaped tool for smoothing the surface of clay, sand, or plaster in a mold. **—plane** *v.* **planed, plan•ing, planes.** *—tr.* **1.** To smooth or finish with or as if with a plane. **2.** To remove with a plane: *plane off the rough edges on a board.* *—intr.* **1.** To work with a plane. **2.** To act as a plane. [Middle English, from Old French, from Late Latin *plāna,* from *plānāre,* to plane, from *plānus,* flat. See **pelə-**[2] in Appendix.]

plane[3] (plān) *intr.v.* **planed, plan•ing, planes. 1.** To rise partly out of the water, as a hydroplane does at high speeds. **2.** To soar or glide. **3.** To travel by airplane. [Middle English *planen,* to glide, soar, from Old French *planer,* from *plain,* flat, level, from Latin *plānus.* See **pelə-**[2] in Appendix.]

plane[4] (plān) *n.* The plane tree. [Middle English, from Old French, from Latin *platanus,* from Greek *platanos,* perhaps from *platus,* broad. See **plat-** in Appendix.]

plane angle *n.* *Mathematics.* An angle formed by two straight lines in the same plane.

plane geometry *n.* *Mathematics.* The geometry of planar figures.

plane•load (plānʹlōdʹ) *n.* The load that an airplane is capable of carrying.

plan•er (plāʹnər) *n.* **1.** One that planes, especially a machine tool that is used to smooth or finish the surfaces of wood or metal. **2.** *Printing.* A smooth block of wood used to level a form of type.

pla•ner tree (plāʹnər) *n.* A small, deciduous, elmlike swamp tree *(Planera aquatica)* of the southern United States, having small, ribbed, nutlike fruit. Also called *water elm.* [After Johann Jacob *Planer* (1743–1789), German botanist.]

plane•side (plānʹsīdʹ) *n.* The area adjacent to an airplane.

plan•et (plănʹĭt) *n.* **1.** A nonluminous celestial body larger than an asteroid or a comet, illuminated by light from a star, such as the sun, around which it revolves. In the solar system there are nine known planets: Mercury, Venus, Earth, Mars, Jupiter, Saturn, Uranus, Neptune, and Pluto. **2.** One of the seven celestial bodies, Mercury, Venus, the moon, the sun, Mars, Jupiter, and Saturn, visible to the naked eye and thought by ancient astronomers to revolve in the heavens about a fixed Earth and among fixed stars. **3.** One of the seven revolving astrological celestial bodies that in conjunction with the stars are believed to influence human affairs and personalities. [Middle English, from Old French *planete,* from Late Latin *planēta,* from Greek *planētēs,* variant of *planēs, planēt-,* from *planasthai,* to wander. See **pelə-**[2] in Appendix.]

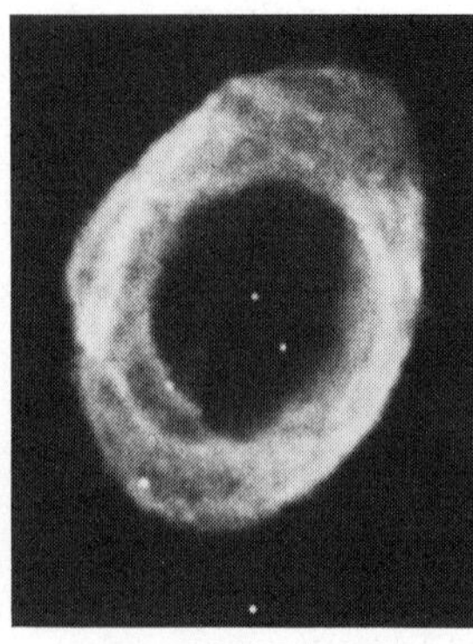

planetary nebula

plane table *n.* A portable surveying instrument consisting essentially of a drawing board and a ruler mounted on a tripod and used to sight and map topographical details.

plan•e•tar•i•um (plănʹĭ-târʹē-əm) *n., pl.* **-i•ums** or **-i•a** (-ē-ə). **1.** An apparatus or a model representing the solar system. **2. a.** An optical device for projecting images of celestial bodies and other astronomical phenomena onto the inner surface of a hemispherical dome. **b.** A building or room containing a planetarium, with seats for an audience.

plan•e•tar•y (plănʹĭ-tĕrʹē) *adj.* **1.** Of, relating to, or resembling the physical or orbital characteristics of a planet or the planets. **2. a.** Of or relating to the earth; terrestrial or earthly: *measured the planetary tilt in degrees.* **b.** Of or affecting the entire world; global: *a planetary consensus.* **3.** Wandering; erratic: *a planetary life.* **4.** Being or relating to a gear train consisting of a central gear with an internal ring gear and one or more pinions.

planetary nebula *n.* A nebula, such as the Ring Nebula, consisting of a hot, blue-white, central star surrounded by an envelope of expanding gas.

plan•e•tes•i•mal (plănʹĭ-tĕsʹə-məl) *n.* Any of innumerable small bodies thought to have orbited the sun during the formation of the planets. [PLANET + (INFINIT)ESIMAL.] **—planʹe•tesʹi•mal** *adj.*

planetesimal hypothesis *n.* The hypothesis that the planets and satellites of the solar system were formed by gravitational aggregation of planetesimals.

plan•e•toid (plănʹĭ-toidʹ) *n.* *Astronomy.* See **asteroid** (sense 1). **—planʹe•toiʹdal** (-toidʹl) *adj.*

plan•e•tol•o•gy (plănʹĭ-tŏlʹə-jē) *n.* The branch of astronomy that deals with the planets, satellites, and meteors of the solar system. **—planʹe•to•logʹi•cal** (plănʹĭ-tl-ŏjʹĭ-kəl) *adj.* **—planʹe•tolʹo•gist** *n.*

plane tree *n.* Any of several trees of the genus *Platanus,* having ball-shaped fruit clusters and, usually, outer bark that flakes off in patches.

planet wheel *n.* One of the small gear wheels in an epicyclic train.

plan•gent (plănʹjənt) *adj.* **1.** Loud and resounding: *plangent bells.* **2.** Expressing or suggesting sadness; plaintive: *"From a doorway came the plangent sounds of a guitar"* (Malcolm Lowry). [Latin *plangēns, plangent-,* present participle of *plangere,* to strike, lament. See **plăk-**[2] in Appendix.] **—planʹgen•cy** *n.* **—planʹgent•ly** *adv.*

plani– *pref.* Variant of **plano–.**

pla•nim•e•ter (plə-nĭmʹĭ-tər, plā-) *n.* An instrument that measures the area of a plane figure as a mechanically coupled pointer traverses the perimeter of the figure. **—plaʹni•metʹric** (plāʹnə-mĕtʹrĭk), **plaʹni•metʹri•cal** (-rĭ-kəl) *adj.* **—plaʹni•metʹri•cal•ly** *adv.* **—pla•nimʹe•try** *n.*

plan•ish (plănʹĭsh) *tr.v.* **-ished, -ish•ing, -ish•es.** To finish or smooth (metal) by rolling or hammering. [Middle English **planishen,* from Old French *planir, planiss-,* to make smooth, from *plan,* level, from Latin *plānus.* See **pelə-**[2] in Appendix.] **—planʹish•er** *n.*

pla•ni•sphere (plāʹnĭ-sfîrʹ) *n.* **1.** A representation of a sphere or part of a sphere on a plane surface. **2.** *Astronomy.* A polar projection of half or more of the celestial sphere on a chart equipped with an adjustable overlay to show the stars visible at a particular time and place. **—plaʹni•spherʹic** (-sfîrʹĭk, -sfĕrʹ-), **plaʹni•spherʹi•cal** (-ĭ-kəl) *adj.*

plank (plăngk) *n.* **1. a.** A piece of lumber cut thicker than a board. **b.** Such pieces of lumber considered as a group; planking. **2.** A foundation; a support. **3.** One of the articles of a political platform: *"Planks had been published by the subcommittees on farm policy, on education, on national defense"* (Theodore H. White). **—plank** *tr.v.* **planked, plank•ing, planks. 1.** To furnish or cover with planks: *plank a muddy pathway.* **2.** To bake or broil and serve (fish or meat) on a plank: *"Boards specially made for planking food have grooves . . . to hold juices"* (Springfield MA Daily News). **3.** To put or set down emphatically or with force. [Middle English, from Old North French *planke,* from Late Latin *planca,* from *plancus,* flat. See **plăk-**[1] in Appendix.]

plank•ing (plăngʹkĭng) *n.* **1.** Planks considered as a group. **2.** An object or a structure made of planks.

plank•ter (plăngkʹtər) *n.* One of the minute organisms that collectively constitute plankton. [Greek *planktēr,* wanderer, from *planktos,* wandering. See PLANKTON.]

plank•ton (plăngkʹtən) *n.* The collection of small or microscopic organisms, including algae and protozoans, that float or drift in great numbers in fresh or salt water, especially at or near the surface, and serve as food for fish and other larger organisms. [German, from Greek, neuter of *planktos,* wandering, from *plazein,* to turn aside. See **plăk-**[2] in Appendix.] **—plank•tonʹic** (-tŏnʹĭk) *adj.*

Planned Parenthood (plănd). A service mark used for an organization that provides family planning services.

Pla•no (plāʹnō). A city of northeast Texas, a manufacturing suburb of Dallas. Population, 72,331.

plano– or **plani–** or **plan–** *pref.* Flat: *planoconvex.* [From Latin *plānus,* flat. See **pelə-**[2] in Appendix.]

plan•o•blast (plănʹə-blăstʹ) *n.* The medusa of certain hydrozoans. [Greek *planos,* wandering (from *planasthai,* to wander; see PLANET) + *–blast.*]

pla•no•con•cave (plāʹnō-kŏn-kāvʹ, -kŏnʹkāvʹ) *adj.* Flat on one side and concave on the other: *a planoconcave lens.*

pla•no•con•vex (plāʹnō-kŏn-vĕksʹ, -kŏnʹvĕksʹ) *adj.* Flat on one side and convex on the other: *a planoconvex lens.*

plan•o•gam•ete (plănʹō-gămʹēt, -gə-mētʹ) *n.* A motile

gamete, especially one having undulipodia. [Greek *planos,* wandering; see PLANOBLAST + GAMETE.]

pla·nog·ra·phy (plə-nŏg′rə-fē, plā-) *n.* A process for printing from a smooth surface, as lithography or offset. **—pla′no·graph′ic** (plā′nə-grăf′ĭk) *adj.* **—pla′no·graph′i·cal·ly** *adv.*

pla·nom·e·ter (plə-nŏm′ĭ-tər, plā-) *n.* A flat metal plate for gauging the accuracy of a plane surface in precision metalworking. Also called *surface plate.* **—pla·nom′e·try** *n.*

plant (plănt) *n.* **1.** *Botany.* **a.** Any of various photosynthetic, eukaryotic, multicellular organisms of the kingdom Plantae characteristically producing embryos, containing chloroplasts, having cellulose cell walls, and lacking the power of locomotion. **b.** A plant having no permanent woody stem; an herb. **2.a.** A building or group of buildings for the manufacture of a product; a factory. **b.** The equipment, including machinery, tools, instruments, and fixtures and the buildings containing them, necessary for an industrial or manufacturing operation. **3.** The buildings, equipment, and fixtures of an institution: *the entire plant of a university.* **4.** A person or thing put into place in order to mislead or function secretly, especially: **a.** A person placed in a group of spectators to influence behavior. **b.** A person stationed in a given location as a spy or an observer. **c.** A misleading piece of evidence placed so as to be discovered. **d.** A remark or an action in a play or narrative that becomes important later. **5.** *Slang.* A scheming trick; a swindle. **—plant** *tr.v.* **plant·ed, plant·ing, plants. 1.a.** To place or set (seeds, for example) in the ground to grow. **b.** To place seeds or young plants in (land); sow: *plant a field in corn.* **2.a.** To place (spawn or young fish) in water or an underwater bed for cultivation: *plant oysters.* **b.** To stock with spawn or fish. **3.** To introduce (an animal) into an area. **4.** To set firmly in position; fix: *planted both feet on the ground.* **5.** To establish; found: *plant a colony.* **6.** To fix firmly in the mind; implant: *"The right of revolution is planted in the heart of man"* (Clarence Darrow). **7.a.** To station (a person) for the purpose of functioning in secret, as by observing, spying, or influencing behavior: *Detectives were planted all over the store.* **b.** To place so as to be discovered and to mislead: *planted a gun on the corpse to make the death look like suicide.* **8.** *Slang.* To conceal; hide. **9.** *Slang.* To deliver (a blow or punch). [Middle English *plante,* from Old English and Old French, both from Latin *planta,* shoot, sole of the foot. See **plat-** in Appendix.] **—plant′a·ble** *adj.*

Plan·tag·e·net (plăn-tăj′ə-nĭt). Family name of a line of English kings from Henry II to Richard III (1154–1485).

plan·tain[1] (plăn′tən) *n.* Any of various plants of the genus *Plantago* that produce dense spikes of small greenish flowers, especially either of two Eurasian weeds, *P. major* or *P. lanceolata.* Also called *ribwort.* [Middle English, from Old French, from Latin *plantāgō, plantāgin-,* from *planta,* sole of the foot (from its broad leaves). See **plat-** in Appendix.]

plan·tain[2] (plăn′tən) *n.* **1.** A large, tropical, treelike herb *(Musa paradisiaca)* of southeast Asia, resembling the banana and bearing similar fruit. **2.** The fruit of this plant, used as a staple food in tropical regions. [Spanish *plátano, plántano,* plane tree, plantain, from Latin *platanus.* See PLANE[4].]

plantain lily *n.* Any of several eastern Asian plants of the genus *Hosta,* widely cultivated for their large white, blue, or lilac flowers that are borne in a terminal, scapose, one-sided raceme. Also called *hosta.*

plan·tar (plăn′tər, -tär′) *adj.* Of, relating to, or occurring on the sole of the foot: *plantar warts.* [Latin *plantāris,* from *planta,* sole of the foot. See **plat-** in Appendix.]

plan·ta·tion (plăn-tā′shən) *n.* **1.** An area under cultivation. **2.** A group of cultivated trees or plants. **3.** A large estate or farm on which crops are raised, often by resident workers. **4.** A newly established settlement; a colony.

WORD HISTORY: It has probably seemed ironic to more than one reader that the same word *plantation* appears in the name *Plimoth Plantation,* a settlement of people seeking freedom of religion, albeit their particular form of religion, and also as the term for the estates of the pre-Civil War South with their beautiful mansions for the white elite and their hovels for the oppressed Black slaves. These two uses of the word *plantation* illustrate two sense developments of the word, which is first recorded in Middle English as *plantacioun* in a work probably written during the first quarter of the 15th century. Latin *plantātiō,* the source of our English word, originally meant "propagation of a plant, as from cuttings," but in Medieval Latin developed other related senses, such as "planting," "foundation, establishment," and "nursery, or collection of growing plants that have been planted." The two senses that were used in New England and in the South can thus be explained. The Plimoth sense is derived from the notion of a settlement or colony that has been established or planted in a new country. The Southern sense goes back to the notion of simply planting crops, in this case crops such as tobacco or cotton that are grown on estates or farms in subtropical or tropical climates and were at one time worked by slave labor.

Plan·ta·tion (plăn-tā′shən). A city of southeast Florida, a residential suburb of Fort Lauderdale. Population, 48,501.

plant bug *n.* An insect of the order Hemiptera whose mouthparts are adapted for piercing plants and sucking their juices.

Plant City (plănt). A city of west-central Florida east of Tampa. It is a processing center in a farming region. Population, 19,270.

plant·er (plăn′tər) *n.* **1.a.** One who plants: *a planter of beautiful gardens.* **b.** A machine or tool for planting seeds. **2.** The owner or manager of a plantation: *cotton and rice planters.* **3.** An early settler or colonist. **4.** A decorative container for a plant or small tree.

plant·er's punch (plăn′tərz) *n.* A drink of rum with lemon or lime juice, sugar syrup, water or soda, bitters, and grenadine.

plant hormone *n.* Any of various hormones produced by plants that control or regulate germination, growth, metabolism, or other physiological activities. Also called *phytohormone.*

plan·ti·grade (plăn′tĭ-grād′) *adj.* Walking with the entire sole of the foot on the ground, as human beings, bears, raccoons, and rabbits do. **—plantigrade** *n.* A plantigrade animal. [French : Latin *planta,* sole of the foot; see **plat-** in Appendix + Latin *-gradus,* going (from *gradī,* to walk, go; see **ghredh-** in Appendix).]

plant·let (plănt′lĭt) *n.* A young or small plant.

plant louse *n.* See **aphid.**

plan·u·la (plăn′yə-lə) *n., pl.* **-lae** (-lē′). The flat, free-swimming, ciliated larva of a coelenterate. [New Latin, from Latin, feminine diminutive of *plānus,* flat (from its shape). See **pelə-**[2] in Appendix.] **—plan′u·lar, plan′u·late′** (-lāt′) *adj.*

plaque (plăk) *n.* **1.** A flat plate, slab, or disk that is ornamented or engraved for mounting, as on a wall for decoration or on a monument for information. **2.** A small pin or brooch worn as an ornament or a badge of membership. **3.a.** *Pathology.* A small disk-shaped formation or growth; a patch. **b.** A deposit of fatty material on the inner lining of an arterial wall, characteristic of atherosclerosis. **c.** A scaly patch formed on the skin by psoriasis. **d.** A film of mucus and bacteria on a tooth surface. **e.** A clear, often round patch of lysed cells in an otherwise opaque layer of a bacteria or cell culture. [French, from Old French, metal plate, perhaps from Middle Dutch *placke,* disk, patch.]

plash (plăsh) *n.* **1.** A light splash. **2.** The sound of a light splash. **—plash** *v.* **plashed, plash·ing, plash·es.** *—tr.* To spatter (liquid) about; splash. *—intr.* To cause a light splash. [Possibly from Middle English *plashe,* pool of water, from Old English *plæsc.*]

-plasia or **-plasy** *suff.* Growth; development: *achondroplasia.* [New Latin, from Greek *plasis,* molding, from *plassein,* to mold. See **pelə-**[2] in Appendix.]

plasm (plăz′əm) *n.* **1.** See **germ plasm** (sense 3). **2.** Variant of **plasma.**

plasm– *pref.* Variant of **plasmo–.**

-plasm *suff.* Material forming cells or tissue: *cytoplasm.* [From PLASMA.]

plas·ma (plăz′mə) also **plasm** (plăz′əm) *n.* **1.a.** The clear, yellowish fluid portion of blood, lymph, or intramuscular fluid in which cells are suspended. **b.** Blood plasma. **2.** *Medicine.* Cell-free, sterilized blood plasma, used in transfusions. **3.** Protoplasm or cytoplasm. **4.** The fluid portion of milk from which the curd has been separated by coagulation; whey. **5.** *Physics.* An electrically neutral, highly ionized gas composed of ions, electrons, and neutral particles. It is a phase of matter distinct from solids, liquids, and normal gases. [New Latin, from Late Latin, image, figure, from Greek, from *plassein,* to mold. See **pelə-**[2] in Appendix.] **—plas·mat′ic** (plăz-măt′ĭk), **plas′mic** (-mĭk) *adj.*

plas·ma·blast (plăz′mə-blăst′) *n.* The precursor or stem cell of a plasma cell.

plasma cell *n.* An antibody-producing cell found in lymphoid tissue and derived from a B cell upon reaction with a specific antigen. Also called *plasmacyte.*

plas·ma·cyte (plăz′mə-sīt′) *n.* See **plasma cell.**

plas·ma·gel (plăz′mə-jĕl′) *n.* A jellylike state of cytoplasm, characteristically occurring in the pseudopod of the amoeba.

plas·ma·gene (plăz′mə-jēn′) *n.* A self-replicating hereditary structure thought to exist in cytoplasm and function in a manner analogous to, but independent of, chromosomal genes. **—plas′ma·gen′ic** (-jē′nĭk, -jĕn′ĭk) *adj.*

plas·ma·lem·ma (plăz′mə-lĕm′ə) *n.* See **cell membrane.** [PLASMA + Greek *lemma,* husk; see LEMMA[2].]

plasma membrane *n.* See **cell membrane.**

plas·ma·pher·e·sis (plăz′mə-fĕr′ĭ-sĭs, -fə-rē′-) *n.* A process in which plasma is taken from donated blood and the remaining components, mostly red blood cells, are returned to the donor. [PLASM(A) + Greek *aphairesis,* removal; see APHAERESIS.]

plas·ma·sol (plăz′mə-sôl′, -sŏl′, -sōl′) *n.* A state of cytoplasm that is more liquid than plasmagel.

plas·mid (plăz′mĭd) *n.* A circular, double-stranded unit of DNA that replicates within a cell independently of the chromosomal DNA. Plasmids are most often found in bacteria and are used in recombinant DNA research to transfer genes between cells.

plas·min (plăz′mĭn) *n.* A proteolytic enzyme in plasma that dissolves fibrin and other blood clotting factors. Also called *fibrinolysin.*

plas·min·o·gen (plăz-mĭn′ə-jən) *n.* The inactive precursor to plasmin that is found in body fluids and blood plasma.

plasmo– or **plasm–** *pref.* Plasma: *plasmin.* [From PLASMA.]

plas·mo·des·ma (plăz′mə-dĕz′mə) also **plas·mo·desm** (plăz′mə-dĕz′əm) *n., pl.* **-ma·ta** (-mə-tə) or **-mas** also **-desms.** *Botany.* A strand of cytoplasm that passes through

ă pat	oi boy
ā pay	ou out
âr care	ŏŏ took
ä father	ōō boot
ĕ pet	ŭ cut
ē be	ûr urge
ĭ pit	th thin
ī pie	*th* this
îr pier	hw which
ŏ pot	zh vision
ō toe	ə about, item
ô paw	♦ regionalism

Stress marks: ′ (primary); ′ (secondary), as in **dictionary** (dĭk′shə-nĕr′ē)

openings in cell walls and connects the protoplasts of adjacent living plant cells. [PLASMO– + Greek *desma,* bond (from *dein,* to bind).]

plasmodial slime mold *n.* See **slime mold** (sense 2).

plas·mo·di·um (plăz-mō′dē-əm) *n., pl.* **-di·a** (-dē-ə). **1.** A multinucleate mass of cytoplasm formed by the aggregation of a number of amoeboid cells, as that characteristic of the vegetative phase of the slime molds. **2.** A protozoan of the genus *Plasmodium,* which includes the parasites that cause malaria. [New Latin *Plasmodium,* genus name : PLASM(O)– + *-odium,* resembling (from Greek *-ōdēs,* variant of *-oeidēs,* -oid).] **—plas·mo′di·al** (-dē-əl) *adj.*

plastron
Fencer wearing a plastron

plas·mog·a·my (plăz-mŏg′ə-mē) *n., pl.* **-mies.** Fusion of two or more cells or protoplasts without fusion of the nuclei, as occurs in higher terrestrial fungi.

plas·mol·y·sis (plăz-mŏl′ĭ-sĭs) *n., pl.* **-ses** (-sēz′). Shrinkage or contraction of the protoplasm away from the wall of a living plant or bacterial cell, caused by loss of water through osmosis. **—plas′mo·lyt′ic** (plăz′mə-lĭt′ĭk) *adj.* **—plas′mo·lyt′i·cal·ly** *adv.*

plas·mo·lyze (plăz′mə-līz′) *v.* **-lyzed, -lyz·ing, -lyz·es.** *—tr.* To subject to plasmolysis. *—intr.* To undergo plasmolysis.

plas·mon (plăz′mŏn′) *n.* The aggregate of cytoplasmic or extranuclear genetic material in an organism. [German, from New Latin *plasma,* plasma. See PLASMA.]

–plast *suff.* A small body, structure, particle, or granule, especially of living matter; cell: *chloroplast.* [From Greek *plastos,* molded, from *plassein,* to mold. See **pelə-**[2] in Appendix.]

plas·ter (plăs′tər) *n.* **1.** A mixture of lime or gypsum, sand, and water, sometimes with fiber added, that hardens to a smooth solid and is used for coating walls and ceilings. **2.** Plaster of Paris. **3.** A pastelike mixture applied to a part of the body for healing or cosmetic purposes. Also called *sticking plaster.* **4.** *Chiefly British.* An adhesive bandage. *—attributive.* Often used to modify another noun: *plaster bandages; plaster walls.* **—plaster** *v.* **-tered, -ter·ing, -ters.** *—tr.* **1.** To cover, coat, or repair with plaster. **2.** To cover or hide with or as if with a coat of plaster: *plastered over our differences.* **3.** To apply a plaster to: *plaster an aching muscle.* **4. a.** To cover conspicuously, as with things pasted on; overspread: *plaster the walls with advertising.* **b.** To affix conspicuously, usually with a paste: *plaster notices on all the doors.* **5.** To make smooth by applying a sticky substance: *plaster one's hair with pomade.* **6.** To make adhere to another surface: *"His hair was plastered to his forehead"* (William Golding). **7.** *Informal.* **a.** To inflict heavy damage or injury on. **b.** To defeat decisively. *—intr.* To apply plaster. [Middle English, from Old English, medical dressing, and from Old French *plastre,* cementing material, both from Latin *emplastrum,* medical dressing, from Greek *emplastron,* from *emplassein,* to plaster on : *en-,* in, on; see EN–[2] + *plassein,* to mold; see **pelə-**[2] in Appendix.] **—plas′ter·er** *n.* **—plas′ter·y** *adj.*

plas·ter·board (plăs′tər-bôrd′, -bōrd′) *n.* A rigid board made of layers of fiberboard or paper bonded to a gypsum plaster core, used instead of plaster or wood panels in construction to form walls. Also called *gypsum board, wallboard.*

plaster cast *n.* **1.** A sculptured mold or cast in plaster of Paris. **2.** See **cast** (sense 11).

plas·tered (plăs′tərd) *adj. Slang.* Intoxicated; drunk.

plas·ter·ing (plăs′tər-ĭng) *n.* **1.** A layer or coating of plaster. **2.** *Informal.* A resounding defeat; a beating.

plaster of Par·is (păr′ĭs) *n.* Any of a group of gypsum cements, essentially hemihydrated calcium sulfate, $CaSO_4 \cdot \frac{1}{2}H_2O$, a white powder that forms a paste when mixed with water and hardens into a solid, used in making casts, molds, and sculpture. [Middle English, after PARIS[2], France.]

plas·ter·work (plăs′tər-wûrk′) *n.* Construction or ornamental work done with plaster.

plas·tic (plăs′tĭk) *adj.* **1.** Capable of being shaped or formed: *plastic material such as clay.* See Synonyms at **malleable. 2.** Relating to or dealing with shaping or modeling: *the plastic art of sculpture.* **3.** Having the qualities of sculpture; well-formed: *"the astonishing plastic beauty of the chorus girls"* (Frank Harris). **4.** Giving form or shape to a substance: *the plastic forces that create and wear down a mountain range.* **5.** Easily influenced; impressionable. **6.** Made of a plastic or plastics: *a plastic garden hose.* **7.** *Physics.* Capable of undergoing continuous deformation without rupture or relaxation. **8.** *Biology.* Capable of building tissue; formative. **9.** Marked by artificiality or superficiality; synthetic: *a TV host's plastic smile; a plastic world of fad, hype, and sensation.* **10.** *Informal.* Of or obtained by means of credit cards: *plastic money.* **—plastic** *n.* **1.** Any of various organic compounds produced by polymerization, capable of being molded, extruded, cast into various shapes and films, or drawn into filaments used as textile fibers. **2.** Objects made of plastic. **3.** *Informal.* A credit card or credit cards: *would accept cash or plastic in payment.* [Latin *plasticus,* from Greek *plastikos,* from *plastos,* molded, from *plassein,* to mold. See **pelə-**[2] in Appendix.] **—plas′ti·cal·ly** *adv.* **—plas·tic′i·ty** (plă-stĭs′ĭ-tē) *n.*

–plastic *suff.* Forming; growing; changing; developing: *metaplastic.* [Greek *plastikos,* fit for molding. See PLASTIC.]

plastic explosive *n.* A versatile explosive substance in the form of a moldable doughlike solid, used in bombs detonated by fuse or electrical impulse. Also called *plastique.*

plas·ti·cize (plăs′tĭ-sīz′) *tr. & intr. v.* **-cized, -ciz·ing, -ciz·es.** To make or become plastic. **—plas′ti·ci·za′tion** (-sĭ-zā′shən) *n.*

plas·ti·ciz·er (plăs′tĭ-sī′zər) *n.* Any of various substances added to plastics or other materials to make or keep them soft or pliable.

plastic surgery *n.* Surgery to remodel, repair, or restore body parts, especially by the transfer of tissue. **—plastic surgeon** *n.*

plas·tid (plăs′tĭd) *n.* Any of several pigmented cytoplasmic organelles found in plant cells and other organisms, having various physiological functions, such as the synthesis and storage of food. [From Greek *plastis, plastid-,* feminine of *plastēs,* molder, from *plastos,* molded. See PLASTIC.] **—plas·tid′i·al** (plăs-tĭd′ē-əl) *adj.*

plas·tique (plă-stēk′) *n.* See **plastic explosive.** [French, from Latin *plasticus,* plastic, of modeling. See PLASTIC.]

plas·tron (plăs′trən) *n.* **1.** A metal breastplate worn under a coat of mail. **2.** A quilted pad worn by fencers to protect the torso and side. **3.** A trimming on the front of a bodice. **4.** The front of a man's dress shirt. **5.** *Zoology.* The ventral part of the shell of a turtle or tortoise. [French, from Old French, from Old Italian *piastrone,* augmentative of *piastra,* thin metal plate. See PIASTER.] **—plas′tral** (-trəl) *adj.*

–plasty *suff.* Molding or forming surgically; plastic surgery: *dermatoplasty.* [Greek *-plastia,* from *plastos,* molded, from *plassein,* to mold. See **pelə-**[2] in Appendix.]

–plasy *suff.* Variant of **–plasia.**

plat[1] (plăt) *tr.v.* **plat·ted, plat·ting, plats.** To plait or braid. **—plat** *n.* A braid. [Middle English *platen,* alteration of *plaiten,* to fold, braid. See PLAIT.]

plat[2] (plăt) *n.* **1.** A piece of land; a plot. **2.** A map showing actual or planned features, such as streets and building lots. **—plat** *tr.v.* **plat·ted, plat·ting, plats.** To make a plat of: *plat a new town.* [Middle English, probably alteration (influenced by *plat,* something flat) of *plot.* See PLOT.]

plat. *abbr.* **1.** Plateau. **2.** Platform. **3.** Platoon.

Pla·ta (plä′tə, -tä), **Río de la.** A wide estuary of southeast South America between Argentina and Uruguay formed by the Paraná and Uruguay rivers and opening on the Atlantic Ocean.

Pla·tae·a (plə-tē′ə). An ancient city of central Greece southwest of Thebes. It was the site of a major Greek victory over the Persians in 479 B.C.

plat du jour (plä′ də zho͝or′) *n., pl.* **plats du jour** (plä′ də zho͝or′). A featured dish of the day at a restaurant. [French : *plat,* plate + *du,* of the + *jour,* day.]

plate (plāt) *n.* **1.** A smooth, flat, relatively thin, rigid body of uniform thickness. **2. a.** A sheet of hammered, rolled, or cast metal. **b.** A very thin applied or deposited coat of metal. **3. a.** A flat piece of metal forming part of a machine: *a boiler plate.* **b.** A flat piece of metal on which something is engraved. **4. a.** A thin piece of metal used for armor. **b.** Armor made of such pieces. **5.** *Abbr.* **pl.** *Printing.* **a.** A sheet of metal, plastic, rubber, paperboard, or other material prepared for use as a printing surface, such as an electrotype or a stereotype. **b.** A print of a woodcut, lithograph, or other engraved material, especially when reproduced in a book. **c.** A full-page book illustration, often in color and printed on paper different from that used on the text pages. **6.** *Abbr.* **pl.** *Photography.* A light-sensitive sheet of glass or metal on which a photographic image can be recorded. **7.** *Dentistry.* A thin metallic or plastic support fitted to the gums to anchor artificial teeth. **8.** *Architecture.* In wood-frame construction, a horizontal member, capping the exterior wall studs, upon which the roof rafters rest. **9.** *Baseball.* Home plate. **10. a.** A shallow dish in which food is served or from which it is eaten. **b.** The contents of such a dish: *ate a plate of spaghetti.* **c.** A whole course served on such a dish. **11.** Service and food for one person at a meal: *dinner at a set price per plate.* **12.** Household articles, such as hollowware, covered with a precious metal, such as silver or gold. **13.** A dish passed among the members of a group or congregation for the collection of offerings. **14.** *Sports.* **a.** A dish, cup, or other article of silver or gold offered as a prize. **b.** A contest, especially a horserace, offering such a prize. **15.** A thin cut of beef from the brisket. **16.** *Anatomy & Zoology.* **a.** A thin, flat layer or scale, as that of a fish. **b.** A platelike part, organ, or structure, such as that covering some reptiles. **17.** *Electricity.* **a.** An electrode, as in a storage battery or capacitor. **b.** The anode in an electron tube. **18.** *Geology.* In the theory of plate tectonics, one of the sections into which the earth's crust is divided and that is in constant motion relative to other plates, which are also in motion. **—plate** *tr.v.* **plat·ed, plat·ing, plates. 1.** To coat or cover with a thin layer of metal. **2.** To cover with armor plate: *plate a warship.* **3.** *Printing.* To make a stereotype or electrotype from. **4.** To give a glossy finish to (paper) by pressing between metal sheets or rollers. [Middle English, from Old French, from feminine of *plat,* flat, from Vulgar Latin **plattus,* from Greek *platus.* See **plat-** in Appendix.] **—plat′er** *n.*

pla·teau (plă-tō′) *n., pl.* **-teaus** or **-teaux** (-tōz′). **1.** *Abbr.* **plat.** An elevated, comparatively level expanse of land; a tableland. **2.** A relatively stable level, period, or state: *Mortgage rates declined, then reached a plateau.* **—plateau** *intr.v.* **-teaued, -teau·ing, -teaus.** To reach a stable level; level off: *"The tension seemed to grow by degrees, then it plateaued"* (Tom Clancy). [French, from Old French *platel,* platter, from *plat,* flat. See PLATE.]

plat·ed (plā′tĭd) *adj.* **1.** Coated with a thin adherent layer of

ă pat	oi boy
ā pay	ou out
âr care	o͝o took
ä father	o͞o boot
ĕ pet	ŭ cut
ē be	ûr urge
ĭ pit	th thin
ī pie	*th* this
îr pier	hw which
ŏ pot	zh vision
ō toe	ə about, item
ô paw	♦ regionalism

Stress marks: ′ (primary); ′ (secondary), as in **dictionary** (dĭk′shə-nĕr′ē)

metal. Often used in combination: *a gold-plated ceramic bowl; a silver-plated pen.* **2.** Covered with protective plates or sheets of metal. Often used in combination: *an armor-plated truck; a steel-plated safe.* **3.** Knitted with two kinds of yarn, one on the face and one on the back.

plate·ful (plāt′fo͝ol′) *n., pl.* **-fuls. 1.** The amount that a plate can hold. **2.** A generous portion of food.

plate glass *n.* A strong rolled and polished glass containing few impurities, used for mirrors and large windows.

plate·let (plāt′lĭt) *n.* A minute, disklike cytoplasmic body found in the blood plasma of mammals that promotes blood clotting. Also called *blood platelet, thrombocyte.*

plat·en (plăt′n) *n.* **1.** The roller in a typewriter that serves as the backing for the paper against which the type bars strike. **2.** *Computer Science.* The roller in a computer printer against which the print head strikes. **3.** A flat plate or rolling cylinder in a printing press that positions the paper and holds it against the inked type. [Middle English *plateine,* paten, from Old French *platine,* metal plate, from *plat,* flat. See PLATE.]

plate proof *n. Printing.* A proof taken from a master plate.

plate tectonics *n.* **1.** *(used with a sing. verb).* A theory of global dynamics having to do with the movement of a small number of semirigid sections of the earth's crust, with seismic activity and volcanism occurring primarily at the margins of these sections. This movement has resulted in continental drift and changes in the shape and size of ocean basins and continents. **2.** *(used with a sing. or pl. verb).* The dynamics of plate movement. **—plate′-tec·ton′ic** (plāt′tĕk-tŏn′ĭk) *adj.*

plat·form (plăt′fôrm′) *n. Abbr.* **plat. 1.a.** A horizontal surface raised above the level of the adjacent area, as a stage for public speaking or a landing alongside railroad tracks. **b.** A vessel, such as a submarine or an aircraft carrier, from which weapons can be deployed. **c.** An oil platform. **2.** A place, a means, or an opportunity for public expression of opinion: *a journal that served as a platform for radical views.* **3.** A vestibule at the end of a railway car. **4.** A formal declaration of the principles on which a group, such as a political party, makes its appeal to the public. **5.a.** A thick layer, as of leather, between the inner and outer soles of a shoe, giving added height. **b.** A shoe having such a construction. [French *plate-forme,* diagram, from Old French : *plat,* flat; see PLATE + *forme,* form (from Latin *forma*).]

platform bed *n.* A bed consisting of a mattress on a platform supported off the floor by legs, with the floor space beneath the platform used for living space or storage.

platform scale *n.* An industrial weighing instrument consisting of a platform coupled to an automatic system of levers and adjustable weights, used to weigh large or heavy objects.

platform tennis *n. Sports.* An outdoor court game played with paddles and a rubber ball on a raised and fenced wooden floor that is smaller than a tennis court.

Plath (plăth), **Sylvia.** 1932–1963. American writer. Her poems, collected in *Colossus* (1960) and *Ariel* (1965), are noted for their technical excellence and their disturbing images of alienation. Plath's other works include the semiautobiographical novel *The Bell Jar* (1963).

platin– *pref.* Variant of **platino–.**

pla·ti·na (plə-tē′nə) *n.* Platinum, especially as found naturally in impure form. [Spanish, diminutive of *plata,* silver, plate, from Vulgar Latin **plattus.* See PLATE.]

plat·ing (plā′tĭng) *n.* **1.** A thin layer of metal, such as gold or silver, deposited on or applied to a surface. **2.** A coating of metal sheets or plates.

platini– *pref.* Variant of **platino–.**

pla·tin·ic (plə-tĭn′ĭk) *adj.* Of, relating to, or containing platinum, especially with valence 4.

plat·i·nize (plăt′n-īz′) *tr.v.* **-nized, -niz·ing, -niz·es.** To electroplate with platinum.

platino– or **platini–** or **platin–** *pref.* Platinum: *platinotype.* [From PLATINUM.]

plat·i·no·cy·a·nide (plăt′n-ō-sī′ə-nīd′) *n.* A double salt of platinous cyanide and another cyanide.

plat·i·noid (plăt′n-oid′) *adj.* Resembling platinum. **—platinoid** *n.* **1.** An alloy of copper, nickel, tungsten, and zinc, formerly used in electric coils. **2.** A metal chemically resembling platinum, especially osmium, iridium, or palladium.

plat·i·no·type (plăt′n-ō-tīp′) *n.* **1.** A process formerly used for making photographic prints, using a finely precipitated platinum salt and an iron salt in the sensitizing solution to produce prints in platinum black. **2.** A print produced by platinotype.

plat·i·nous (plăt′n-əs) *adj.* Of, relating to, or containing platinum, especially with valence 2.

plat·i·num (plăt′n-əm) *n.* **1.** *Symbol* **Pt** A silver-white metallic element occurring worldwide, usually mixed with other metals such as iridium, osmium, or nickel. It is ductile and malleable, does not oxidize in air, and is used as a catalyst and in electrical components, jewelry, dentistry, and electroplating. Atomic number 78; atomic weight 195.09; melting point 1,772°C; boiling point 3,827°C; specific gravity 21.45; valence 2, 3, 4. See table at **element. 2.** *Color.* A medium to light gray. [New Latin, from Spanish *platina,* platinum. See PLATINA.]

platinum black *n.* A fine black powder of metallic platinum, used as a catalyst and as a gas absorbent.

platinum blond *n.* **1.** A very light silver-blond hair color, especially when artificially produced. **2.** A person having hair of this color.

plat·i·tude (plăt′ĭ-to͞od′, -tyo͞od′) *n.* **1.** A trite or banal remark or statement, especially one expressed as if it were original or significant. See Synonyms at **cliché. 2.** Lack of originality; triteness. [French, from *plat,* flat, from Old French. See PLATE.] **—plat′i·tu′di·nous** (-to͞od′n-əs, -tyo͞od′-), **plat′i·tu′di·nal** (-to͞od′n-əl, -tyo͞od′-) *adj.* **—plat′i·tu′di·nous·ly** *adv.*

plat·i·tu·di·nar·i·an (plăt′ĭ-to͞od′n-âr′ē-ən, -tyo͞od′-) *n.* One who habitually uses platitudes. [PLATITUDIN(OUS) + -ARIAN.]

plat·i·tu·di·nize (plăt′ĭ-to͞od′n-īz′, -tyo͞od′-) *intr.v.* **-nized, -niz·ing, -niz·es.** To use platitudes.

Pla·to (plā′tō). 427?–347? B.C. Greek philosopher. A follower of Socrates, he founded the Academy (386), where he taught and wrote for much of the rest of his life. Plato presented his ideas in the form of dramatic dialogues, as in *The Republic.*

Pla·ton·ic (plə-tŏn′ĭk, plā-) *adj.* **1.** Often **Pla·ton·i·cal** (-ĭ-kəl). Of, relating to, or characteristic of Plato or his philosophy: *Platonic dialogues; Platonic ontology.* **2.** Often **platonic.** Transcending physical desire and tending toward the purely spiritual or ideal: *platonic love.* **3.** Often **platonic.** Speculative or theoretical. [After PLATO.] **—Pla·ton′i·cal·ly** *adv.*

WORD HISTORY: Plato did not invent the term or the concept that bears his name, but he did see sexual desire as the germ for higher loves. Marsilio Ficino, a Renaissance follower of Plato, used the terms *amor socraticus* and *amor platonicus* interchangeably for a love between two human beings that was preparatory for the love of God. From Ficino's usage *Platonic* (already present in English as an adjective to describe what related to Plato and first recorded in 1533) came to be used for a spiritual love between persons of opposite sexes. In our own century *Platonic* has been used of relationships between members of the same sex. Though the concept is an elevated one, the term has perhaps more often been applied in ways that led Samuel Richardson to have one of his characters in *Pamela* say, "I am convinced, and always was, that Platonic love is Platonic nonsense."

Pla·to·nism (plāt′n-ĭz′əm) *n. Philosophy.* The philosophy of Plato, especially insofar as it asserts ideal forms as an absolute and eternal reality of which the phenomena of the world are an imperfect and transitory reflection. **—Pla′to·nist** *n.* **—Pla′to·nis′tic** *adj.*

pla·toon (plə-to͞on′) *n.* **1.** *Abbr.* **plat.** A subdivision of a company of troops consisting of two or more sections and usually commanded by a lieutenant. **2.** A group of people working, traveling, or assembled together: *a platoon of firefighters; buses carrying platoons of tourists.* **3.** *Sports.* A group of players within a team, especially a football team, that is trained and sent into or withdrawn from play as a unit: *the defensive platoon.* **—platoon** *v.* **-tooned, -toon·ing, -toons.** *Sports.* *—tr.* To play (a player) in alternation with another player in the same position: *platooned the two catchers.* *—intr.* **1.** To use alternate players at the same position. **2.** To take turns playing a position with another player. [French *peloton,* from Old French, diminutive of *pelote,* ball. See PELLET.]

platoon sergeant *n.* The senior noncommissioned officer in an army platoon or comparable unit.

Platt·deutsch (plät′doich′) *n.* See **Low German** (sense 1). [German (partial translation of Dutch *Platduits,* Low German) : Dutch *plat,* low, flat (from Middle Dutch, from Old French; see PLATE) + German *Deutsch,* German (from Middle High German *diutsch,* from Old High German *diutisc,* of the people; see **teutā-** in Appendix).]

Platte (plăt). A river, about 499 km (310 mi) long, of central Nebraska formed by the confluence of the North Platte and South Platte rivers and flowing eastward to the Missouri River at the Iowa border below Omaha.

plat·ter (plăt′ər) *n.* **1.** A large shallow dish or plate, used especially for serving food. **2.** A meal or course served on a platter. **3.** *Slang.* A phonograph record. **—*idiom.* on a platter.** Without exertion; effortlessly: *always got what they wanted on a platter.* [Middle English *plater,* from Anglo-Norman, from Old French *plate,* plate. See PLATE.]

Platts·burgh (plăts′bûrg′). A city of extreme northeast New York on Lake Champlain northwest of Burlington, Vermont. During the War of 1812 an American fleet defeated the British in a naval battle here on September 11, 1814. Population, 21,057.

plat·y¹ (plā′tē) *adj.* **-i·er, -i·est.** Designating soil or minerals occurring in flaky layers.

plat·y² (plăt′ē) *n., pl.* **-ys** or **-ies.** Any of several small freshwater live-bearing fishes of the genus *Xiphophorus* of southern North America, especially *X. maculatus* and *X. variatus,* popular in aquariums for their bright and variable colors. Also called *platyfish.* [Short for New Latin *Platypoecilus,* former genus name : PLATY– + Greek *poikilos,* many-colored; see **peig-** in Appendix.]

platy– *pref.* Flat: *platyhelminth.* [Greek *platu-,* from *platus.* See **plat-** in Appendix.]

plat·y·fish (plăt′ē-fĭsh′) *n., pl.* **platyfish** or **-fish·es.** See **platy².**

plat·y·hel·minth (plăt′ĭ-hĕl′mĭnth) *n.* See **flatworm.** [From New Latin *Platyhelminthes,* phylum name : PLATY– +

platform
Subway platform, Miami, Florida

Sylvia Plath
Photographed in 1955

Plato
Copy of a mid fourth-century B.C. herma attributed to Silanion (fl. 360–330 B.C.)

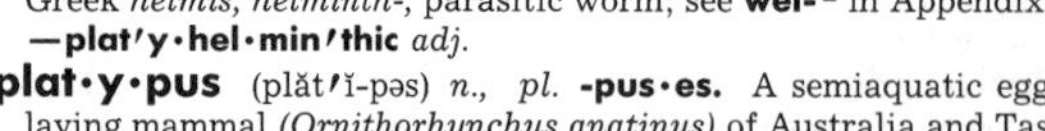

Greek *helmis, helminth-,* parasitic worm; see **wel-**[2] in Appendix.] **—plat′y·hel·min′thic** *adj.*

plat·y·pus (plăt′ĭ-pəs) *n., pl.* **-pus·es.** A semiaquatic egg-laying mammal *(Ornithorhynchus anatinus)* of Australia and Tasmania, having a broad flat tail, webbed feet, and a snout resembling a duck's bill. Also called *duckbill, duck-billed platypus.* [New Latin, from Greek *platupous,* flat-footed : *platu-,* platy- + *pous,* foot; see **ped-** in Appendix.]

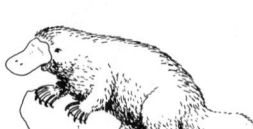

platypus
Ornithorhynchus anatinus

plat·yr·rhine (plăt′ĭ-rīn′) also **plat·yr·rhin·i·an** (plăt′ĭ-rĭn′ē-ən) *—adj.* **1.** Having a broad, flat nose. **2.** Of or designating the New World monkeys, distinguished from the Old World monkeys by widely separated nostrils that generally open to the side. *—n.* **1.** A platyrrhine person. **2.** A platyrrhine monkey. [New Latin *Platyrrhina,* group name, from Greek *platurrhis,* broad-nosed : *platu-,* platy- + *rhis, rhin-,* nose.] **—plat′yr·rhi′ny** (-rī′nē) *n.*

plau·dit (plô′dĭt) *n.* Enthusiastic expression of praise or approval: *a new play that opened to the plaudits of the critics.* [Short for Latin *plaudite,* pl. imperative of *plaudere,* to applaud.]

Plau·en (plou′ən). A city of east-central Germany south-southwest of Leipzig. Founded by Slavs in the 12th century, it passed to Bohemia in 1327 and to Saxony in 1466 and became a textile-milling center in the 15th century. Population, 78,797.

plau·si·ble (plô′zə-bəl) *adj.* **1.** Seemingly or apparently valid, likely, or acceptable; credible: *a plausible excuse.* **2.** Giving a deceptive impression of truth, acceptability, or reliability; specious: *the plausible talk of a crafty salesperson.* [Latin *plausibilis,* deserving applause, from *plausus,* past participle of *plaudere,* to applaud.] **—plau′si·bil′i·ty, plau′si·ble·ness** *n.* **—plau′si·bly** *adv.*

SYNONYMS: *plausible, believable, colorable, credible.* The central meaning shared by these adjectives is "appearing to merit belief or acceptance": *a plausible pretext; a believable excuse; a colorable explanation; a credible assertion.*
ANTONYM: *implausible.*

plau·sive (plô′zĭv, -sĭv) *adj.* **1.** Showing or expressing praise or approbation; applauding. **2.** *Obsolete.* Plausible. [From Latin *plaudere, plaus-,* to applaud.]

Plau·tus (plô′təs), **Titus Maccius.** 254?–184 B.C. Roman comic playwright whose works influenced Shakespeare and Molière.

play (plā) *v.* **played, play·ing, plays.** *—intr.* **1.** To occupy oneself in amusement, sport, or other recreation: *children playing with toys.* **2.a.** *Games.* To take part in a game: *No minors are eligible to play.* **b.** To participate in betting; gamble. **3.** To act in jest or sport: *They're not quarreling in earnest, they're just playing.* **4.** To deal or behave carelessly or indifferently; toy. See Synonyms at **flirt. 5.** To behave or converse in a sportive or playful way. **6.** To act or conduct oneself in a specified way: *play fair; an investor who plays cautiously.* **7.** To act, especially in a dramatic production. **8.** *Music.* **a.** To perform on an instrument: *play on an accordion.* **b.** To emit sound or be sounded in performance: *The band is playing.* **9.** To be performed, as in a theater or on television: *A good movie is playing tonight.* **10.** To be received or accepted: *a speech that played poorly with the voters.* **11.** To move or seem to move quickly, lightly, or irregularly: *The breeze played on the water.* **12.** To function or discharge uninterruptedly: *The fountains played in the courtyard.* **13.** To move or operate freely within a bounded space, as machine parts do. *—tr.* **1.a.** To perform or act (a role or part) in a dramatic performance. **b.** To assume the role of; act as: *played the peacemaker at the conference.* **2.** To perform (a theatrical work) on or as if on the stage. **3.** To present a theatrical performance in (a given place): *The company played Detroit last week.* **4.** To pretend to be; mimic the activities of: *played cowboy; played the star.* **5.** *Sports & Games.* **a.** To engage in (a game or sport): *play hockey; play chess.* **b.** To compete against in a game or sport. **c.** To occupy or work at (a position) in a game: *Lou Gehrig played first base.* **d.** To employ (a player) in a game or position: *Let's play her at first base.* **e.** To use or move (a card, piece, or ball) in a game or sport: *play the queen of hearts.* **f.** To make (a shot or stroke), as in tennis: *played a strong backhand.* **6.** *Games.* **a.** To bet; wager: *played five dollars on the roan horse.* **b.** To make bets on: *play the races.* **7.** To perform or put into effect, especially as a jest or deception: *play a joke on a friend.* **8.** To handle; manage: *played the matter quietly.* **9.** To use or manipulate, especially for one's own interests: *He played his two opponents against each other.* **10.** *Music.* **a.** To perform on (an instrument): *play the guitar.* **b.** To perform (a piece) on instruments or an instrument. **11.** To cause (a record or phonograph, for example) to emit recorded sounds. **12.** To discharge or direct in or as if in a continuous stream: *play a hose on a fire.* **13.** To cause to move rapidly, lightly, or irregularly: *play lights over the dance floor.* **14.** To exhaust (a hooked fish) by allowing it to pull on the line. **—play** *n.* **1.a.** A literary work written for performance on the stage; a drama. **b.** The performance of such a work. **2.** Activity engaged in for enjoyment or recreation. **3.** Fun or jesting: *It was all done in play.* **4.** *Sports & Games.* **a.** The act or manner of engaging in a game or sport: *After a time-out, play resumed. The golf tournament featured expert play.* **b.** The act or manner of using a card, piece, or ball in a game or sport: *my partner's play of the last trump; his clumsy play of the rebound.* **c.** A move or an action in a game: *It's your play. The runner was thrown out in a close play.* **5.** *Games.* Participation in betting; gambling. **6.** Manner of dealing with others; conduct: *fair play.* **7.** An attempt to obtain something; a bid: *a play for sympathy.* **8.a.** Action, motion, or use: *the play of the imagination.* **b.** Freedom or occasion for action; scope: *give full play to an artist's talents.* See Synonyms at **room. 9.** Movement or space for movement, as of mechanical parts. **10.** Quick, often irregular movement or action, especially of light or color: *the play of color on iridescent feathers.* ***—phrasal verbs.*** **play along.** *Informal.* To cooperate or pretend to cooperate: *decided to play along with the robbers for a while.* **play at. 1.** To participate in; engage in. **2.** To do or take part in half-heartedly. **play back.** To replay (a recently recorded tape, for example). **play down.** To minimize the importance of; make little of: *played down the defect to protect the troops' morale.* **play off. 1.** *Sports.* **a.** To establish the winner of (a tie) by playing in an additional game or series of games. **b.** To participate in a playoff. **2.** To set (one individual or party) in opposition to another so as to advance one's own interests: *a parent who played off one child against another.* **play on** (or **upon**). To take advantage of (another's attitudes or feelings) for one's own interests: *demagogues who play on popular fears.* **play out.** To use up; exhaust: *Our strength was played out early in the contest.* **play up.** To emphasize or publicize: *She played up her experience during the employment interview.* ***—idioms.*** **in play. 1.** *Sports.* In a position to be legally or feasibly played: *The ball is now in play.* **2.** In a position, or rumored to be in a position of possible corporate takeover: *The company's stock rose in price when news stories stated that it was in play.* **out of play.** *Sports.* Not in a position to be legally or feasibly played. **play ball.** *Slang.* To cooperate: *The opposing attorneys refused to play ball with us.* **play both ends against the middle.** To set opposing parties or interests against one another so as to advance one's own goals. **play fast and loose.** To behave in a recklessly irresponsible or deceitful manner: *played fast and loose with the facts.* **play for time.** To use delaying tactics; temporize. **play games.** *Slang.* To be evasive or deceptive: *Quit playing games and tell me what you want.* **play in Peoria.** *Slang.* To be acceptable to average constituents or consumers: *an elitist political campaign that could never play in Peoria.* **play into the hands of.** To act or behave so as to give an advantage to (an opponent). **play (one's) cards.** *Informal.* To use the resources or strategies at one's disposal: *played her cards right and got promoted.* **play possum.** To pretend to be sleeping or dead. **play the field.** To date more than one person. **play the game.** *Informal.* To behave according to the accepted customs or standards. **play up to.** To curry favor with. **play with fire.** To take part in a dangerous or risky undertaking. **play with (oneself).** *Vulgar Slang.* To masturbate. [Middle English *playen,* from Old English *plegian.*] **—play′a·bil′i·ty** *n.* **—play′a·ble** *adj.*

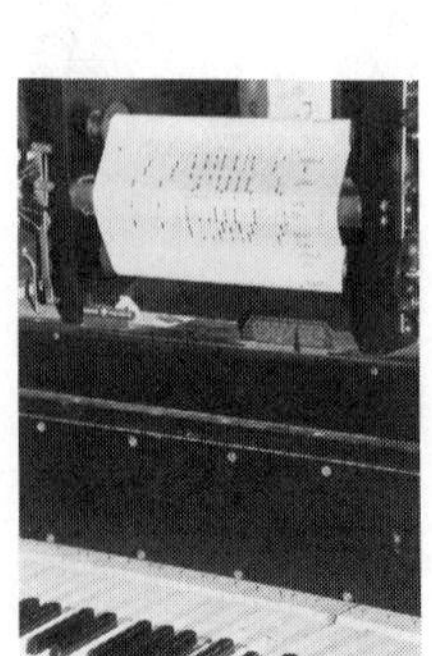

player piano

pla·ya (plī′ə) *n.* A nearly level area at the bottom of an undrained desert basin, sometimes temporarily covered with water. [Spanish, from Late Latin *plagia,* hillside, shoreline, probably from Greek, sides, from neuter pl. of *plagios,* oblique, sideways, from *plagos,* side. See **plāk-**[1] in Appendix.]

play-act (plā′ăkt′) *intr.v.* **-act·ed, -act·ing, -acts. 1.** To play a role in a dramatic performance. **2.** To make believe. **3.** To behave in an overdramatic or artificial manner.

play·back (plā′băk′) *n.* **1.** The act or process of replaying a newly made record or tape. **2.** A method of or an apparatus for reproducing sound recordings: *"switches on the playback of a telephone-answering machine"* (Vanity Fair).

play·bill (plā′bĭl′) *n.* A poster announcing a theatrical performance.

Play·bill (plā′bĭl′). A trademark used for a program of a theatrical performance. This trademark often occurs in lowercase in print: *"The typical hot, humid night . . . had most of the audience fanning themselves with their playbills"* (Washington Times). *"The playbill somehow listed the movement headings for the wrong Beethoven symphony"* (Los Angeles Times).

play·book (plā′bo͝ok′) *n.* **1.** A book containing the scripts of dramatic plays. **2.** *Sports.* A notebook containing descriptions and diagrams of the plays of a team, especially a football team.

play·boy (plā′boi′) *n.* A man who is devoted to the pursuit of pleasurable activities.

play-by-play (plā′bī-plā′) *adj.* Being or giving a detailed running account of the action of an event, especially a sports event, as it occurs. **—play-by-play** *n.* A detailed commentary of an event as it unfolds.

play·er (plā′ər) *n.* **1.** One that plays, especially: **a.** *Sports & Games.* One who participates in a game or sport. **b.** A gambler. **c.** One who performs in theatrical roles. **d.** *Music.* One who plays an instrument. **2.** An active participant: *a major player in world affairs.* **3.** *Music.* The mechanism actuating a player piano. **4.** A phonograph.

player piano *n. Music.* A mechanically operated piano that uses a perforated paper roll to actuate the keys.

play·ful (plā′fəl) *adj.* **1.** Full of fun and high spirits; frolicsome or sportive: *a playful kitten.* **2.** Humorous; jesting: *"He meant to be conversationally playful but his voice had no tone"* (Saul Bellow). **—play′ful·ly** *adv.* **—play′ful·ness** *n.*

SYNONYMS: *playful, mischievous, impish, waggish, frolicsome.* These adjectives mean inclined to or marked by lighthearted fun. *Playful,* the most general, suggests high spirits, gaiety, and often lively humor: *"the playful children just let loose from school"* (Oliver Goldsmith). *Mischievous* usually implies naughty and sometimes annoying or embarrassing playfulness: *"A mischievous ex-*

citability is the most obvious expression of [his face]. *If he were a horse, nobody would buy him; with that eye no one could answer for his temper"* (Walter Bagehot). *Impish* suggests an appealingly bold and devilish or rascally quality: *"teasing and worrying with impish laughter half suppressed"* (Thomas Hardy). *Waggish* stresses wittiness or jocularity: *"Muskrat Castle, as the house had been facetiously named by some waggish officer"* (James Fenimore Cooper). *Frolicsome* suggests high-spirited, carefree, and uninhibited merriment: *Frolicsome students celebrated their graduation with parties and practical jokes.*

play·girl (plā′gûrl′) *n.* A woman devoted to the pursuit of pleasurable activities.

play·go·er (plā′gō′ər) *n.* One who attends the theater. **—play′go′ing** *n.*

play·ground (plā′ground′) *n.* **1.** An outdoor area set aside for recreation and play, especially one containing equipment such as seesaws and swings. **2.** A field or sphere of unrestricted pleasurable activity: *"Foreign affairs had been T.R.'s personal playground during his Presidency"* (John Dos Passos).

play·house (plā′hous′) *n., pl.* **-hous·es** (-hou′zĭz, -sĭz). **1.** A theater. **2.** A small house for children to play in. **3.** A child's toy house; a doll house.

play·ing card (plā′ĭng) *n. Games.* A card marked with its rank and suit and belonging to any of several decks used in playing various games.

playing field *n. Sports.* A field for games such as football and soccer.

play·let (plā′lĭt) *n.* A short play.

play·mak·er (plā′mā′kər) *n. Sports.* A player, especially a guard in basketball, who calls the signals for and initiates offensive plays. **—play′mak′ing** *n.*

play·mate (plā′māt′) *n.* A companion in play or recreation.

play·off also **play-off** (plā′ôf′, -ŏf′) *n. Sports.* **1.** A final game or series of games played to break a tie. **2.** A series of games played to determine a championship.

play·pen (plā′pĕn′) *n.* A portable enclosure in which a baby or young child can be safely left to play.

play·room (plā′ro͞om′, -ro͝om′) *n.* A room designed or set aside for recreation or playing.

play·suit (plā′so͞ot′) *n.* A woman's or child's play outfit consisting of shorts and a blouse, sometimes in one piece.

play therapy *n.* A form of psychotherapy used with children to help them express or act out their experiences, feelings, and problems by playing, as with dolls or toys, under the guidance or observation of a therapist. **—play therapist** *n.*

play·thing (plā′thĭng′) *n.* **1.** Something to play with; a toy. **2.** One treated as a toy: *a plaything of fate.*

play·wear (plā′wâr′) *n.* Garments suitable for recreational activities.

play·wright (plā′rīt′) *n.* One who writes plays; a dramatist.

pla·za (plä′zə, plăz′ə) *n.* **1.** A public square or similar open area in a town or city. **2. a.** A widened roadway forming the approach to tollbooths on a highway. **b.** A parking or service area next to a highway. **3.** A shopping center. [Spanish, from Vulgar Latin **plattea,* from Latin *platea,* broad street. See PLACE.]

plea (plē) *n.* **1.** An earnest request; an appeal: *spoke out in a plea for greater tolerance.* **2.** An excuse; a pretext: *"necessity,/ The Tyrant's plea"* (John Milton). **3.** *Law.* **a.** An allegation offered in pleading a case. **b.** A defendant's answer to the declaration made by the plaintiff in a civil action. **c.** The answer of the accused to a criminal charge or indictment: *entered a plea of not guilty.* **d.** A special answer depending on or demonstrating one or more reasons why a suit should be delayed, dismissed, or barred in equity law. **e.** An action or a suit. [Middle English *plai,* lawsuit, from Old French *plai, plaid,* from Late Latin *placitum,* decree, from Latin, from neuter past participle of *placēre,* to please. See **plăk-**[1] in Appendix.]

plea-bar·gain (plē′bär′gən) *intr.v.* **-gained, -gain·ing, -gains.** *Law.* To make an agreement in which a defendant pleads guilty to a lesser charge and the prosecutor in return drops more serious charges. **—plea′-bar′gain·ing** *n.*

pleach (plēch, plăch) *tr.v.* **pleached, pleach·ing, pleach·es. 1.** To plait or interlace (branches or vines, for example), especially in making a hedge or an arbor. **2.** To shade or border with interlaced branches or vines. [Middle English *plechen,* from Old North French *plechier,* probably from Latin *plectere.* See **plek-** in Appendix.]

plead (plēd) *v.* **plead·ed** or **pled** (plĕd), **plead·ing, pleads.** *—intr.* **1.** To appeal earnestly; beg: *plead for more time.* **2.** To offer reasons for or against something; argue earnestly: *plead against a bill.* **3.** To provide an argument or appeal: *Your youth and simplicity plead for you in this instance.* **4.** *Law.* **a.** To put forward a plea of a specific nature in court: *plead guilty.* **b.** To make or answer an allegation in a legal proceeding. **c.** To address a court as a lawyer or an advocate. *—tr.* **1.** To assert as defense, vindication, or excuse; claim as a plea: *plead illness.* **2.** *Law.* **a.** To present as an answer to a charge, an indictment, or a declaration made against one. **b.** To argue or present (a case) in a court or similar tribunal. [Middle English *pleden, plaiden,* from Old French *plaidier,* from Medieval Latin *placitāre,* to appeal to the law, from Late Latin *placitum,* decree, opinion. See PLEA.] **—plead′a·ble** *adj.* **—plead′er** *n.* **—plead′ing·ly** *adv.*

USAGE NOTE: In strict legal usage, one is said to *plead guilty* or *plead not guilty* but not to *plead innocent.* In nonlegal contexts, however, *plead innocent* is well established.

plead·ing (plē′dĭng) *n.* **1.** A plea; an entreaty. **2.** *Law.* Advocacy of causes in court. **3.** *Law.* **a.** A formal statement, generally written, propounding the cause of action or the defense in a case. **b. pleadings.** The consecutive statements, allegations, and counter allegations made in turn by plaintiff and defendant, or prosecutor and accused, in a legal proceeding.

pleas·ance (plĕz′əns) *n.* **1.** A secluded garden or landscaped area. **2.** *Archaic.* Pleasure or a source of pleasure.

pleas·ant (plĕz′ənt) *adj.* **-er, -est. 1.** Giving or affording pleasure or enjoyment; agreeable: *a pleasant scene; pleasant sensations.* **2.** Pleasing in manner, behavior, or appearance. See Synonyms at **amiable. 3.** Fair and comfortable: *pleasant weather.* **4.** Merry; lively. [Middle English *plesaunt,* from Old French *plaisant,* present participle of *plaisir,* to please, from Latin *placēre.* See **plăk-**[1] in Appendix.] **—pleas′ant·ly** *adv.* **—pleas′ant·ness** *n.*

Pleas·ant Hill (plĕz′ənt). A city of western California northeast of Berkeley. It is mainly residential. Population, 25,124.

Pleasant Island. See **Nauru.**

Pleas·an·ton (plĕz′ən-tən). A city of western California southeast of Oakland. It is a residential and processing center in a grape-growing region. Population, 35,160.

pleas·ant·ry (plĕz′ən-trē) *n., pl.* **-ries. 1.** A humorous remark or act; a jest. **2.** A polite social utterance; a civility: *exchanged pleasantries before getting down to business.* **3.** A good-humored or playful manner in conversation or social relations. [French *plaisanterie,* from Old French *plesanterie,* from *plaisant,* pleasant. See PLEASANT.]

please (plēz) *v.* **pleased, pleas·ing, pleas·es.** *—tr.* **1.** To give enjoyment, pleasure, or satisfaction to; make glad or contented. **2.** To be the will or desire of: *May it please the court to admit this firearm as evidence. —intr.* **1.** To give satisfaction or pleasure; be agreeable: *waiters who try hard to please.* **2.** To have the will or desire; wish: *Do as you please. Sit down, if you please.* **—please** *adv.* **1.** If it is your desire or pleasure; if you please. Used in polite requests: *Please stand back. Pay attention, please.* **2.** Yes. Used in polite affirmative replies to offers: *May I help you? Please.* [Middle English *plesen,* from Old French *plaisir,* from Latin *placēre.* See **plăk-**[1] in Appendix.] **—pleas′er** *n.*

SYNONYMS: *please, delight, gladden, gratify, tickle.* The central meaning shared by these verbs is "to give pleasure to": *was pleased by their success; a gift that would delight any child; praise that gladdens the spirit; progress that gratified all concerned; compliments that tickle their vanity.*
ANTONYM: *displease.*

pleas·ing (plē′zĭng) *adj.* Giving pleasure or enjoyment; agreeable. **—pleas′ing·ly** *adv.* **—pleas′ing·ness** *n.*

pleas·ur·a·ble (plĕzh′ər-ə-bəl) *adj.* Agreeable; gratifying. **—pleas′ur·a·bil′i·ty, pleas′ur·a·ble·ness** *n.* **—pleas′ur·a·bly** *adv.*

pleas·ure (plĕzh′ər) *n.* **1.** The state or feeling of being pleased or gratified. **2.** A source of enjoyment or delight: *The graceful skaters were a pleasure to watch.* **3.** Amusement, diversion, or worldly enjoyment: *"Pleasure . . . is a safer guide than either right or duty"* (Samuel Butler). **4.** Sensual gratification or indulgence. **5.** One's preference or wish: *What is your pleasure?* **—pleasure** *v.* **-ured, -ur·ing, -ures.** *—tr.* To give pleasure or enjoyment to; gratify: *Our host pleasured us with his company. —intr.* **1.** To take pleasure; delight: *The hiker paused, pleasuring in the sounds of the forest.* **2.** To go in search of pleasure or enjoyment. [Middle English, from Old French *plaisir,* from *plaisir,* to please. See PLEASE.] **—pleas′ure·less** *adj.*

SYNONYMS: *pleasure, enjoyment, delight, delectation, joy.* These nouns denote a pleasant feeling, as of happiness or personal satisfaction, evoked by something that is to one's liking. *Pleasure* is the least specific: *"One of the greatest pleasures of life is conversation"* (Sydney Smith). *"Pleasure without joy is as hollow as passion without tenderness"* (Alan Jay Lerner). *Enjoyment* suggests pleasure, often abiding pleasure, arising from something gratifying or beneficial: *Books are her major source of enjoyment. "Was it* [ornament] *done with enjoyment—was the carver happy while he was about it?"* (John Ruskin). *Delight* and *delectation* imply keen but sometimes transitory pleasure: *"There is delight in singing"* (Walter Savage Landor). *"Certified 'masterpieces' by dead composers, manipulated by charismatic star performers for the delectation of an increasingly passive and uninquisitive audience"* (Will Crutchfield). *Joy* suggests an intense and especially an ecstatic or exultant state; the word is often associated with sharing, self-realization, or high-mindedness: *"The deep joy we take in the company of people with whom we have just recently fallen in love is undisguisable"* (John Cheever). *"The rule of joy and the law of duty seem to me all one"* (Oliver Wendell Holmes, Jr.).

ă pat	oi boy
ā pay	ou out
âr care	o͝o took
ä father	o͞o boot
ĕ pet	ŭ cut
ē be	ûr urge
ĭ pit	th thin
ī pie	*th* this
îr pier	hw which
ŏ pot	zh vision
ō toe	ə about, item
ô paw	♦ regionalism

Stress marks: ′ (primary); ′ (secondary), as in **dictionary** (dĭk′shə-nĕr′ē)

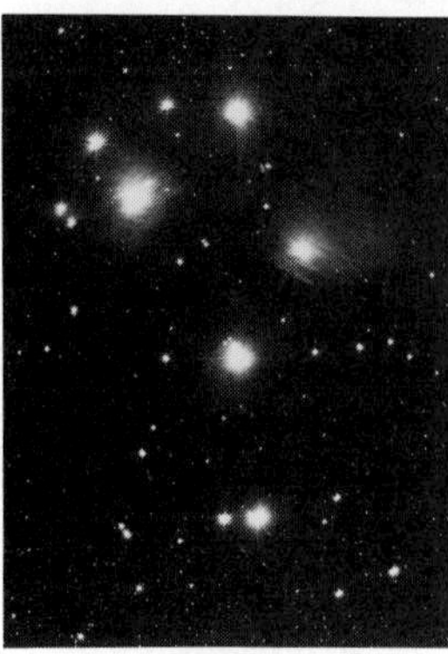

Pleiades
Pleiades cluster

pleasure principle *n.* In psychoanalysis, the tendency or drive to achieve pleasure and avoid pain as the chief motivating force in behavior.

pleat (plēt) *n.* A fold in cloth made by doubling the material upon itself and then pressing or stitching it into place. **—pleat** *tr.v.* **pleat·ed, pleat·ing, pleats.** To press or arrange in pleats: *pleat a skirt; pleat curtains.* [Middle English *plet,* variant of *plait,* pleat, fold. See PLAIT.] **—pleat′er** *n.*

pleb (plĕb) *n.* **1.** A commoner; a plebeian. **2.** A freshman; a plebe. [Short for PLEBEIAN, or perhaps from PLEBS (taken as pl.).]

plebe (plēb) also **pleb** (plĕb) *n.* A first-year student at the U.S. Military Academy or the U.S. Naval Academy. [Probably short for PLEBEIAN.]

ple·be·ian (plĭ-bē′ən) *adj.* **1.** Of or relating to the common people of ancient Rome: *a plebeian magistrate.* **2.** Of, belonging to, or characteristic of commoners. **3.** Unrefined or coarse in nature or manner; common or vulgar: *plebeian tastes.* **—plebeian** *n.* **1.** One of the common people of ancient Rome. **2.** A member of the lower classes. **3.** A vulgar or coarse person. [From Latin *plēbius,* from *plēbs, plēb-,* the common people. See **pelə-**[1] in Appendix.] **—ple·be′ian·ism** *n.* **—ple·be′ian·ly** *adv.*

ple·bes (plē′bēz) *n.* Plural of **plebs.**

pleb·i·scite (plĕb′ĭ-sīt′, -sĭt) *n.* **1.** A direct vote in which the entire electorate is invited to accept or refuse a proposal: *"a new constitution, which his people dutifully ratified in a plebiscite"* (New York Times). **2.** A vote in which a population exercises the right of national self-determination. [French *plébiscite,* from Latin *plēbiscītum* : *plēbis,* genitive of *plēbs,* the people; see **pelə-**[1] in Appendix + *scītum,* decree, from neuter past participle of *scīscere,* to vote for, inchoative of *scīre,* to know; see **skei-** in Appendix.] **—ple·bis′ci·tar′y** (plə-bĭs′ĭ-tĕr′ē, plĕb′ĭ-sĭt′ə-rē) *adj.*

plebs (plĕbz) *n., pl.* **ple·bes** (plē′bēz). **1.** The common people of ancient Rome: *the plebs and the patricians.* **2.** The common people; the populace. [Latin *plēbs.* See **pelə-**[1] in Appendix.]

ple·cop·ter·an (plĭ-kŏp′tər-ən) *n.* See **stonefly.** [From New Latin *Plecoptera,* order name : Greek *plekein,* to plait, twist; see **plek-** in Appendix + Greek *pteron,* wing; see **pet-** in Appendix.] **—ple·cop′ter·an** *adj.*

plec·tog·nath (plĕk′tŏg-năth′) *n.* Any of various tropical marine fishes of the order Tetraodontiformes or Plectognathi, which includes the triggerfishes, puffers, and trunkfishes. [From New Latin *Plectognathī,* order name : Greek *plektos,* twisted; see **plek-** in Appendix + Greek *gnathos,* jaw; see –GNATHOUS.] **—plec′tog·nath′** *adj.*

plec·trum (plĕk′trəm) *n., pl.* **-trums** or **-tra** (-trə). *Music.* A small, thin piece of metal, plastic, bone, or similar material, used to pluck the strings of certain instruments, such as the guitar or lute. [Latin *plēctrum,* from Greek *plēktron,* from *plēssein, plēg-,* to strike. See **plāk-**[2] in Appendix.]

pled (plĕd) *v.* A past tense and a past participle of **plead.**

pledge (plĕj) *n.* **1.** A solemn binding promise to do, give, or refrain from doing something: *signed a pledge never to reveal the secret; a pledge of money to a charity.* **2.a.** Something given or held as security to guarantee payment of a debt or fulfillment of an obligation. **b.** The condition of something thus given or held: *put an article in pledge.* **3.** *Law.* **a.** Delivery of goods or personal property as security for a debt or an obligation: *a loan that required a pledge of property.* **b.** The contract by which such delivery is made. **4.** A token or sign: *"fair pledges of a fruitful tree"* (Robert Herrick). **5.** A person who has been accepted for membership in a fraternity or similar organization and has promised to join but has not yet been initiated. **6.** The act of drinking in honor of someone; a toast. **7.** A vow to abstain from alcoholic liquor: *ex-drinkers who have taken the pledge.* **—pledge** *v.* **pledged, pledg·ing, pledg·es.** *—tr.* **1.** To offer or guarantee by a solemn binding promise: *pledge loyalty to a nation; pledged their cooperation.* See Synonyms at **devote. 2.** See Synonyms at **promise. 3.** To bind or secure by or as if by a pledge: *pledged themselves to the cause.* **4.** To deposit as security; pawn. **5.a.** To promise to join (a fraternity or similar organization). **b.** To accept as a prospective member of such an organization. **6.** To drink a toast to. *—intr.* **1.** To make a solemn binding promise; swear. **2.** To drink a toast. [Middle English, from Old French *plege,* probably from Late Latin *plevium,* a security, of Germanic origin.]

pledg·ee (plĕj-ē′) *n.* **1.** A person to whom something is pledged. **2.** A person with whom something is deposited as a pledge.

pledge·or (plĕj′ər, plĕj-ôr′) *n. Law.* Variant of **pledgor.**

pledg·er (plĕj′ər) *n.* One who makes or gives a pledge.

pled·get (plĕj′ĭt) *n.* A small, flat absorbent pad used to medicate, drain, or protect a wound or sore. [Origin unknown.]

pledg·or also **pledge·or** (plĕj′ər, plĕj-ôr′) *n. Law.* A person who deposits property as a pledge.

-plegia *suff.* Paralysis: *monoplegia.* [Greek *-plēgia,* from *plēgē,* a blow, from *plēssein, plēg-,* to strike. See **plāk-**[2] in Appendix.]

Ple·iad (plē′əd, -ăd′, plī′-) *n., pl.* **Ple·ia·des** (plē′ə-dēz′, plī′-). **1.** One of the Pleiades. **2.** Often **pleiad.** A group of seven illustrious persons. [Back-formation from PLEIADES.]

Ple·ia·des (plē′ə-dēz′, plī′-) *pl.n.* **1.** *Greek Mythology.* The seven daughters of Atlas (Maia, Electra, Celaeno, Taygeta, Merope, Alcyone, and Sterope), who were metamorphosed into stars. **2.** An open star cluster in Taurus, consisting of several hundred stars, of which six are visible to the naked eye. [Middle English *Pliades,* from Latin *Plēïades,* from Greek *Pleiades.*]

pleio– *pref.* Variant of **pleo–.**

plei·o·tax·y (plī′ə-tăk′sē) *n. Botany.* An increase in the number of whorls in an inflorescence. [Greek *pleiōn,* more; see **pelə-**[1] in Appendix + –TAXY.]

plei·ot·ro·pism (plī-ŏt′rə-pĭz′əm) also **plei·ot·ro·py** (-pē) *n.* The control by a single gene of several distinct and seemingly unrelated phenotypic effects. [Greek *pleiōn,* more; see **pelə-**[1] in Appendix + –TROPISM.] **—plei′o·tro′pic** (plī′ə-trō′pĭk, -trŏp′ĭk) *adj.* **—plei′o·tro′pi·cal·ly** *adv.*

Pleis·to·cene (plī′stə-sēn′) *adj.* Of, belonging to, or designating the geologic time, rock series, and sedimentary deposits of the earlier of the two epochs of the Quaternary Period, characterized by the alternate appearance and recession of northern glaciation and the appearance of the progenitors of human beings. See table at **geologic time. —Pleistocene** *n.* The Pleistocene Epoch or system of deposits. [Greek *pleistos,* most; see **pelə-**[1] in Appendix + –CENE.]

Ple·kha·nov (plĭ-kä′nôf′, -KHä′nəf), **Georgi Valentinovich.** 1857–1918. Russian revolutionary and political philosopher. The founder of the Marxist movement in Russia, he was also a leading Menshevik.

ple·na (plē′nə, plĕn′ə) *n.* A plural of **plenum.**

ple·na·ry (plē′nə-rē, plĕn′ə-) *adj.* **1.** Complete in all respects; unlimited or full: *a diplomat with plenary powers.* **2.** Fully attended by all qualified members: *a plenary session of the council.* [Late Latin *plēnārius,* from Latin *plēnus,* full. See **pelə-**[1] in Appendix.] **—ple′na·ri·ly** *adv.* **—ple′na·ri·ness** *n.*

plenary indulgence *n. Roman Catholic Church.* An indulgence that remits the full temporal punishment incurred by a sinner.

plen·i·po·ten·ti·ar·y (plĕn′ə-pə-tĕn′shē-ĕr′ē, -shə-rē) *adj.* Invested with or conferring full powers: *a plenipotentiary deputy.* **—plenipotentiary** *n., pl.* **-ies.** A diplomatic agent, such as an ambassador, fully authorized to represent his or her government. [Medieval Latin *plēnipotentiārius,* from Late Latin *plēnipotēns, plēnipotent-,* invested with full power : Latin *plēnus,* full; see **pelə-**[1] in Appendix + Latin *potēns,* powerful; see POTENT.]

plen·i·tude (plĕn′ĭ-to͞od′, -tyo͞od′) *n.* **1.** An ample amount or quantity; an abundance: *this midsummer plenitude of fruits and vegetables.* **2.** The condition of being full, ample, or complete: *granaries filled to plenitude.* [Middle English, from Old French, from Latin *plēnitūdō,* from *plēnus,* full. See **pelə-**[1] in Appendix.] **—plen′i·tu′di·nous** (-to͞od′n-əs, -tyo͞od′-) *adj.*

plen·te·ous (plĕn′tē-əs) *adj.* **1.** Abundant; copious. **2.** Producing or yielding in abundance. See Synonyms at **plentiful.** [Middle English, alteration of *plentivous,* from Old French *plentiveus,* from *plentif,* from *plente,* plenty. See PLENTY.] **—plen′te·ous·ly** *adv.* **—plen′te·ous·ness** *n.*

plen·ti·ful (plĕn′tĭ-fəl) *adj.* **1.** Existing in great quantity or ample supply. **2.** Providing or producing an abundance: *a plentiful harvest.* **—plen′ti·ful·ly** *adv.* **—plen′ti·ful·ness** *n.*

SYNONYMS: *plentiful, abundant, ample, copious, plenteous.* The central meaning shared by these adjectives is "being fully as much as one needs or desires": *a plentiful supply of stationery; her abundant talent; ample space; copious provisions; a plenteous crop of wheat.*
ANTONYM: *scant.*

plen·ty (plĕn′tē) *n.* **1.** A full or completely adequate amount or supply: *plenty of time.* **2.** A large quantity or amount; an abundance: *"Awards and honors came to her in plenty"* (Joyce Carol Oates). **3.** A condition of general abundance or prosperity: *"fruitful regions gladdened by plenty and lulled by peace!"* (Samuel Johnson). **—plenty** *adj.* Plentiful; abundant: *"Ships were then not so plenty in those waters as now"* (Herman Melville). **—plenty** *adv. Informal.* Sufficiently; very: *It's plenty hot.* [Middle English, from Old French *plente,* from Latin *plēnitās,* from *plēnus,* full. See **pelə-**[1] in Appendix.]

ple·num (plē′nəm, plĕn′əm) *n., pl.* **ple·nums** or **ple·na** (plē′nə, plĕn′ə). **1.** An assembly or a meeting with all members present. **2.** A condition, space, or enclosure in which air or other gas is at a pressure greater than that of the outside atmosphere. **3.** The condition of being full; fullness. **4.** A space completely filled with matter. [Latin *plēnum (spatium),* full (space), neuter of *plēnus.* See **pelə-**[1] in Appendix.]

pleo– or **pleio–** or **plio–** *pref.* More: *pleopod.* [From Greek *pleiōn, pleōn,* more. See **pelə-**[1] in Appendix.]

ple·och·ro·ism (plē-ŏk′rō-ĭz′əm) *n.* The property possessed by some crystals of exhibiting different colors, especially three different colors, when viewed along different axes. [PLEO– + Greek *khrōs,* color + –ISM.] **—ple′o·chro′ic** (plē′ə-krō′ĭk) *adj.*

ple·o·mor·phism (plē′ə-môr′fĭz′əm) *n.* **1.** *Chemistry.* See **polymorphism** (sense 2). **2.** *Biology.* The occurrence of two or more structural forms during a life cycle, especially of certain plants. **—ple′o·mor′phic** *adj.*

ple·o·nasm (plē′ə-năz′əm) *n.* **1.a.** The use of more words than are required to express an idea; redundancy. **b.** An instance

ă pat	oi boy
ā pay	ou out
âr care	o͝o took
ä father	o͞o boot
ĕ pet	ŭ cut
ē be	ûr urge
ĭ pit	th thin
ī pie	*th* this
îr pier	hw which
ŏ pot	zh vision
ō toe	ə about, item
ô paw	♦ regionalism

Stress marks: **′** (primary); ′ (secondary), as in **dictionary** (dĭk′shə-nĕr′ē)

of pleonasm. **2.** A superfluous word or phrase. [Late Latin *pleonasmus,* from Greek *pleonasmos,* from *pleonazein,* to be excessive, from *pleōn,* more. See **pelə-**[1] in Appendix.] **—ple′o·nas′tic** (-năs′tĭk) *adj.* **—ple′o·nas′ti·cal·ly** *adv.*

ple·o·pod (plē′ə-pŏd′) *n.* See **swimmeret.**

ple·ro·cer·coid (plîr′ō-sûr′koid′) *n.* The infective larva of some tapeworms, characterized by its solid elongated body. [Greek *plērēs,* full, infected; see **pelə-**[1] in Appendix + *kerkos,* tail + -OID.]

ple·si·o·saur (plē′sē-ə-sôr′, plē′zē-) also **ple·si·o·sau·rus** (plē′sē-ə-sôr′əs, plē′zē-) *n., pl.* **-saurs** also **-saur·i** (-sôr′ī). *Paleontology.* A large extinct marine reptile having paddlelike limbs that was common in Europe and North America during the Mesozoic Era. [New Latin *Plesiosaurus,* type genus : Greek *plēsios,* near; see **pel-**[5] in Appendix + New Latin *saurus,* lizard; see SAURIAN.]

ples·sim·e·ter (plĕ-sĭm′ĭ-tər) *n.* See **pleximeter.** [Greek *plēssein,* to strike; see PLEXOR + -METER.]

ples·sor (plĕs′ər) *n.* Variant of **plexor.**

pleth·o·ra (plĕth′ər-ə) *n.* **1.** A superabundance; an excess. **2.** An excess of blood in the circulatory system or in one organ or area. [Late Latin *plēthōra,* from Greek, from *plēthein,* to be full. See **pelə-**[1] in Appendix.]

ple·thor·ic (plĕ-thôr′ĭk, -thŏr′-, plĕth′ə-rĭk) *adj.* **1.a.** Excessive in quantity; superabundant: *"this successful industry of England, with its plethoric wealth"* (Thomas Carlyle). **b.** Excessive in style; turgid: *plethoric prose.* **2.** Characterized by an overabundance of blood. **—ple·thor′i·cal·ly** *adv.*

ple·thys·mo·gram (plē-thĭz′mə-grăm′, plə-) *n.* A record or tracing produced by a plethysmograph.

ple·thys·mo·graph (plĕ-thĭz′mə-grăf′, plə-) *n.* An instrument that measures variations in the size of an organ or body part on the basis of the amount of blood passing through or present in the part. [Greek *plēthusmos,* increase (from *plēthunein,* to increase, from *plēthus,* quantity, from *plēthein,* to be full; see **pelə-**[1] in Appendix) + -GRAPH.] **—ple·thys′mo·graph′ic** *adj.* **—ple·thys′mo·graph′i·cal·ly** *adv.* **—pleth′ys·mog′ra·phy** (plĕth′ĭz-mŏg′rə-fē) *n.*

pleur– *pref.* Variant of **pleuro–.**

pleu·ra[1] (plo͝or′ə) *n., pl.* **pleu·rae** (plo͝or′ē). A thin serous membrane in mammals that envelops each lung and folds back to make a lining for the chest cavity. [Middle English, from Medieval Latin, from Greek, side, rib.] **—pleu′ral** *adj.*

pleu·ra[2] (plo͝or′ə) *n.* Plural of **pleuron.**

pleu·rae (plo͝or′ē) *n.* Plural of **pleura**[1]**.**

pleu·ri·sy (plo͝or′ĭ-sē) *n.* Inflammation of the pleura, usually occurring as a complication of a disease such as pneumonia, accompanied by accumulation of fluid in the pleural cavity, chills, fever, and painful breathing and coughing. [Middle English *pluresy,* from Old French *pleuresie,* from Late Latin *pleurisis,* alteration of Latin *pleurītis,* from Greek *pleuritis* : *pleura,* side + *-itis,* -itis.] **—pleu·rit′ic** (plo͝o-rĭt′ĭk) *adj.*

pleurisy root *n.* See **butterfly weed.**

pleuro– or **pleur–** *pref.* **1.** Side; lateral: *pleurodont.* **2.** Pleura; pleural: *pleurotomy.* [Greek, from *pleura,* side, rib.]

pleu·ro·dont (plo͝or′ə-dŏnt′) *adj.* Having the teeth attached by their sides to the inner side of the jaw, as in some lizards. **—pleurodont** *n.* A lizard with pleurodont teeth.

pleu·ro·dyn·i·a (plo͝or′ə-dĭn′ē-ə) *n.* **1.** Paroxysmal pain and soreness of the muscles between the ribs. **2.** An epidemic disease caused by a coxsackievirus, characterized by paroxysmal pain in the lower chest and accompanied by fever, headache, and malaise. [New Latin : PLEUR(O)- + Greek *odunē,* pain; see **ed-** in Appendix + -IA[1].]

pleu·ron (plo͝or′ŏn′) *n., pl.* **pleu·ra** (plo͝or′ə). An external, lateral part of the body segments of arthropods. [New Latin, from Greek, side, rib.]

pleu·ro·pneu·mo·nia (plo͝or′ō-no͞o-mōn′yə, -nyo͞o-) *n.* **1.** Inflammation of the pleura and lungs; pneumonia aggravated by pleurisy. **2.** An infectious febrile disease of cattle, caused by a mycoplasma and characterized by inflammation of the pleura and lungs.

pleu·ro·pneu·mo·nia-like organism (plo͝or′ō-no͞o-mōn′yə-līk′, -nyo͞o-) *n. Abbr.* **PPLO** See **mycoplasma.**

pleu·rot·o·my (plo͝o-rŏt′ə-mē) *n., pl.* **-mies.** Surgical incision of the pleura.

pleus·ton (plo͞o′stən, -stŏn′) *n.* Plants that float on the surface of bodies of fresh water. [Greek *pleusis,* sailing; see **pleu-** in Appendix + (PLANK)TON.] **—pleus·ton′ic** (plo͞o-stŏn′ĭk) *adj.*

Plev·en (plĕv′ən, -ĕn) or **Plev·na** (-nə, -nä). A city of northern Bulgaria northeast of Sofia. Settled by Thracians, it was ruled by Turkey from the 15th to the 19th century. Population, 144,000.

plex·i·form (plĕk′sə-fôrm′) *adj.* Similar to or having the form of a plexus: *the plexiform layers of the retina.* [PLEX(US) + -FORM.]

Plex·i·glas (plĕk′sĭ-glăs′). A trademark used for a light, transparent, weather-resistant thermoplastic. This trademark, which often occurs in attributive contexts, also occurs in many instances lowercased and spelled *plexiglass*: *"The emergency room receptionist laments the construction of a Plexiglas divider at her counter"* (New York Times). *"The display pieces are double sealed inside plexiglass cases"* (Los Angeles Times). *"The tower was operating with interim lighting, no ceiling and a pane of plexiglass"* (Aviation Week & Space Technology).

plex·im·e·ter (plĕk-sĭm′ĭ-tər) *n.* A small, thin plate held against the body and struck with a plexor in diagnosis by percussion. Also called *plessimeter.* [Greek *plēxis,* a blow; see PLEXOR + -METER.] **—plex′i·met′ric** (plĕk′sə-mĕt′rĭk) *adj.* **—plex·im′e·try** *n.*

plex·or (plĕk′sər) also **ples·sor** (plĕs′ər) *n.* A small, rubber-headed hammer used in examination or diagnosis by percussion. [From Greek *plēxis,* a blow, from *plēssein, plēg-,* to strike. See **plāk-**[2] in Appendix.]

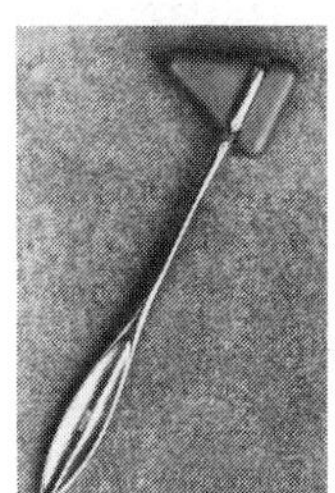
plexor

plex·us (plĕk′səs) *n., pl.* **plexus** or **-us·es. 1.** A structure in the form of a network, especially of nerves, blood vessels, or lymphatics: *the cardiac plexus; the pelvic plexus.* **2.** A combination of interlaced parts; a network. [New Latin, from Latin, braid, from past participle of *plectere,* to plait. See **plek-** in Appendix.]

plf. *abbr. Law.* Plaintiff.

pli·a·ble (plī′ə-bəl) *adj.* **1.** Easily bent or shaped. See Synonyms at **malleable. 2.** Receptive to change; adaptable: *pliable attitudes.* **3.** Easily influenced, persuaded, or swayed; tractable. [Middle English, from Old French, from *plier,* to bend. See PLIANT.] **—pli′a·bil′i·ty, pli′a·ble·ness** *n.* **—pli′a·bly** *adv.*

pli·ant (plī′ənt) *adj.* **1.** Easily bent or flexed; pliable. See Synonyms at **malleable. 2.** Easily altered or modified to fit conditions; adaptable. **3.** Yielding readily to influence or domination; compliant. [Middle English, from Old French, present participle of *plier,* to fold, bend, from Latin *plicāre.* See **plek-** in Appendix.] **—pli′an·cy, pliant·ness** *n.* **—pli′ant·ly** *adv.*

pli·ca (plī′kə) *n., pl.* **pli·cae** (plī′sē, -kē). A fold or ridge, as of skin, membrane, or shell. [Medieval Latin, fold, from Latin *plicāre,* to fold. See **plek-** in Appendix.] **—pli′cal** *adj.*

pli·cate (plī′kāt′) also **pli·cat·ed** (-kā′tĭd) *adj.* Arranged in folds like those of a fan; pleated. [Latin *plicātus,* past participle of *plicāre,* to fold. See **plek-** in Appendix.] **—pli′cate′ly** *adv.* **—pli′cate′ness** *n.*

pli·ca·tion (plī-kā′shən) also **plic·a·ture** (plĭk′ə-cho͝or′) *n.* **1.a.** The act or process of folding. **b.** The state of being folded. **2.** A fold.

pli·é (plē-ā′) *n.* A movement in ballet performance and exercise, in which the knees are bent while the back is held straight. [French, from past participle of *plier,* to fold, bend, from Old French. See PLIANT.]

plied[1] (plīd) *v.* Past tense and past participle of **ply**[1]**.**

plied[2] (plīd) *v.* Past tense and past participle of **ply**[2]**.**

pli·er also **ply·er** (plī′ər) *n.* **1.** One who plies a trade. **2. pliers.** A variously shaped hand tool having a pair of pivoted jaws, used for holding, bending, or cutting.

plies[1] (plīz) *v.* Third person singular present tense of **ply**[1]**. —plies** *n.* Plural of **ply**[1]**.**

plies[2] (plīz) *v.* Third person singular present tense of **ply**[2]**.**

plight[1] (plīt) *n.* A situation, especially a bad or unfortunate one. See Synonyms at **predicament.** [Middle English, alteration (influenced by *plight,* risky promise or pledge) of *plit,* fold, wrinkle, situation, from Anglo-Norman, from Latin *plicitum,* neuter past participle of *plicāre,* to fold. See **plek-** in Appendix.]

plight[2] (plīt) *tr.v.* **plight·ed, plight·ing, plights. 1.** To promise or bind by a solemn pledge, especially to betroth. See Synonyms at **promise. 2.** To give or pledge (one's word or oath, for example). **—plight** *n.* A solemn pledge, as of faith. ***—idiom.*** **plight (one's) troth. 1.** To become engaged to marry. **2.** To give one's solemn oath. [Middle English *plighten,* from Old English *plihtan,* to endanger, put at risk, from *pliht,* danger, risk.] **—plight′er** *n.*

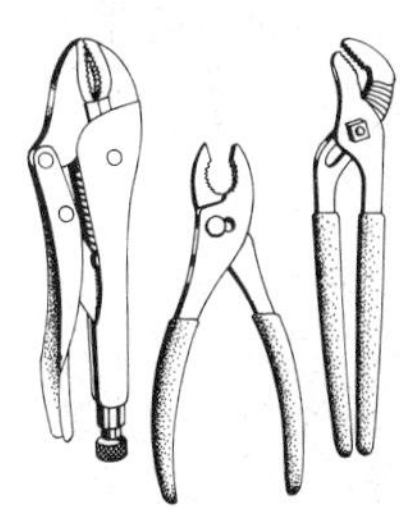
pliers
Left to right: Locking-grip, slip-joint, and multiple-joint pliers

plim·soll (plĭm′səl, -sôl′) also **plim·sol** or **plim·sole** (-sōl′) *n. Chiefly British.* A rubber-soled cloth shoe; a sneaker. [Probably from the resemblance of its mudguard to a PLIMSOLL MARK.]

Plim·soll (plĭm′səl, -sôl′), **Samuel.** 1824–1898. British merchant and shipping reformer. He introduced the Merchant Shipping Act of 1876, establishing safe load limits for cargo ships.

Plimsoll mark *n. Nautical.* Any of a set of lines on the hull of a merchant ship that indicate the depth to which it may be legally loaded under specified conditions. Also called *load line, Plimsoll line.* [After Samuel PLIMSOLL.]

plink (plĭngk) *v.* **plinked, plink·ing, plinks.** *—tr.* **1.** To cause to make a soft, sharp, metallic sound; clink. **2.** To shoot at casually. *—intr.* **1.** To make a soft, sharp, metallic sound. **2.** To shoot casually at random targets. [Imitative.]

plinth (plĭnth) *n.* **1.** *Architecture.* A block or slab on which a pedestal, column, or statue is placed. **2.** The base block at the intersection of the baseboard and the vertical trim around an opening. **3.** A continuous course of stones supporting a wall. Also called *plinth course.* **4.** A square base, as for a vase. [French *plinthe,* from Latin *plinthus,* from Greek *plinthos,* tile, plinth.]

Plin·y[1] (plĭn′ē). Known as "the Elder." A.D. 23–79. Roman scholar and naturalist. He wrote the *Historia Naturalis.*

Plin·y[2] (plĭn′ē). Known as "the Younger." A.D. 62?–113? Roman consul and writer, the nephew of Pliny the Elder. His letters provide valuable information about Roman life.

plio– *pref.* Variant of **pleo–.**

Pli·o·cene (plī′ə-sēn′) *Geology. adj.* Of, belonging to, or designating the geologic time, rock series, and sedimentary deposits of the last of the five epochs of the Tertiary Period, characterized by the appearance of distinctly modern animals. See table at **ge-**

plinth

ologic time. —**Pliocene** *n.* The Pliocene Epoch or its system of deposits. [Greek *pleiōn,* more; see **pelə-**[1] in Appendix + -CENE.]

plis·sé also **plis·se** (plĭ-sā′) *n.* **1.** A puckered finish given to fabric by treating it with a caustic soda. **2.** Fabric having such a finish. [French, from past participle of *plisser,* to pleat, from Old French, from *pli,* fold, from *plier,* to fold, from Latin *plicāre.* See **plek-** in Appendix.]

pln. *abbr.* Plain.

PLO *abbr.* Palestine Liberation Organization.

Plock (pwôtsk). A city of central Poland on the Vistula River west-southwest of Warsaw. Known since the tenth century, it passed to Prussia in 1793 and to Russia in 1815. It reverted to Poland after World War I. Population, 114,500.

plod (plŏd) *v.* **plod·ded, plod·ding, plods.** —*intr.* **1.** To move or walk heavily or laboriously; trudge: *"donkeys that plodded wearily in a circle round a gin"* (D.H. Lawrence). **2.** To work or act perseveringly or monotonously; drudge: *plodding through a mountain of paperwork.* —*tr.* To trudge along or over. —**plod** *n.* **1.** The act of moving or walking heavily and slowly. **2.** The sound made by a heavy step. [Perhaps imitative.] —**plod′der** *n.* —**plod′ding·ly** *adv.*

plover
Great thick-knee plover
Esacus recuvirostris

Plo·eş·ti (plô-yĕsht′, -yĕsh′tē). See **Ploieşti.**

-ploid *suff.* Having a number of chromosomes that has a specified relationship to, or is a multiple of, the basic number of chromosomes of a group: *heteroploid.* [From DIPLOID and HAPLOID.]

ploi·dy (ploi′dē) *n.* A multiple of the basic number of chromosomes in a cell. [From DIPLOIDY and HAPLOIDY.]

Plo·ieş·ti or **Plo·eş·ti** (plô-yĕsht′, -yĕsh′tē). A city of southeast-central Romania north of Bucharest. Founded in 1596, it is the center of a major oil-producing region. Population, 229,915.

plonk[1] (plŏngk, plŭngk) *v., n., & adv.* Variant of **plunk.**

plonk[2] (plŏngk) *n. Chiefly British.* Cheap or inferior wine. [Short for earlier *plink-plonk,* perhaps alteration of French *vin blanc,* white wine : *vin,* wine (from Old French; see VINEGAR) + *blanc,* white (from Old French; see BLANK).]

plop (plŏp) *v.* **plopped, plop·ping, plops.** —*intr.* **1.** To fall with a sound like that of an object falling into water without splashing. **2.** To let the body drop heavily: *Exhausted, I plopped into the armchair.* —*tr.* To drop or set heavily, with or as if with a plopping sound. —**plop** *n.* A plopping sound or movement. [Imitative.] —**plop** *adv.*

plo·sion (plō′zhən) *n. Linguistics.* **1.** The articulation of a plosive sound. **2.** The sudden release of occluded air characteristically occurring in the articulation of certain stop consonants. Also called *explosion.* [From EXPLOSION.]

plo·sive (plō′sĭv, -zĭv) *Linguistics. adj.* Of, relating to, or being a speech sound produced by complete closure of the oral passage and subsequent release accompanied by a burst of air, as in the sound (p) in *pit* or (d) in *dog.* —**plosive** *n.* A plosive speech sound. Also called *stop.* [From EXPLOSIVE.]

plot (plŏt) *n.* **1.a.** A small piece of ground, generally used for a specific purpose: *a garden plot; a cemetery plot.* **b.** A measured area of land; a lot. **2.** A ground plan, as for a building; a diagram. **3.** See **graph**[1] (sense 1). **4.** The plan of events or main story in a narrative or drama. **5.** A secret plan to accomplish a hostile or illegal purpose; a scheme. See Synonyms at **conspiracy.** —**plot** *v.* **plot·ted, plot·ting, plots.** —*tr.* **1.** To represent graphically, as on a chart: *plot a ship's course.* **2.** *Mathematics.* **a.** To locate (points or other figures) on a graph by means of coordinates. **b.** To draw (a curve) connecting points on a graph. **3.** To conceive and arrange the action and incidents of: *"I began plotting novels at about the time I learned to read"* (James Baldwin). **4.** To form a plot for; prearrange secretly or deviously: *plot an assassination.* —*intr.* **1.** To be located by means of coordinates, as on a chart or with data. **2.** To form or take part in a plot; scheme. [Middle English, from Old English.] —**plot′less·ness** *n.*

plow
Top: Moldboard plow
Bottom: Chisel plow

Plo·ti·nus (plō-tī′nəs). A.D. 205–270. Egyptian-born Roman philosopher who founded Neo-Platonism. His writings are collected in *The Enneads.*

plot line or **plot·line** (plŏt′līn′) *n.* **1.** A literary or dramatic plot; a story line. **2.** Often **plot lines.** Dialogue essential to the development of a plot in a drama.

plot·tage (plŏt′ĭj) *n.* The area of land in a plot or group of plots.

plot·ter (plŏt′ər) *n. Computer Science.* A computer output device that draws graphs or pictures, usually by moving a pen. Also called *plotting board, plotting table.*

plot·ting board (plŏt′ĭng) *n. Computer Science.* See **plotter.**

plotting table *n. Computer Science.* See **plotter.**

plough (plou) *n. & v.* Variant of **plow.**

Plov·div (plôv′dĭf′). A city of south-central Bulgaria on the Maritsa River southeast of Sofia. Originally built by Thracians, it fell to Macedonia in 341 B.C. and to Rome in 46. The city changed hands frequently in the Middle Ages and was controlled by Russia from 1877 to 1885. Population, 378,000.

plov·er (plŭv′ər, plō′vər) *n., pl.* **plover** or **-ers.** **1.** Any of various widely distributed wading birds of the family Charadriidae, having rounded bodies, short tails, and short bills. **2.** Any of various similar or related birds. [Middle English, from Anglo-Norman, from Vulgar Latin **pluviārius,* from Latin *pluvia,* rain. See PLUVIAL.]

plow also **plough** (plou) —*n.* **1.** A farm implement consisting of a heavy blade at the end of a beam, usually hitched to a draft team or motor vehicle and used for breaking up soil and cutting furrows in preparation for sowing. **2.** An implement of similar function, such as a snowplow. —*v.* **plowed, plow·ing, plows** also **ploughed, plough·ing, ploughs.** —*tr.* **1.a.** To break and turn over (earth) with a plow. **b.** To form (a furrow, for example) with a plow. **c.** To form furrows in with or as if with a plow: *plow a field.* **2.** To make or form with driving force: *I plowed my way through the crowd.* **3.** To cut through (water): *plow the high seas.* —*intr.* **1.** To break and turn up earth with a plow. **2.** To admit of plowing: *Rocky earth plows poorly.* **3.** To move or progress with driving force: *The attackers formed a wedge and plowed through the enemy line.* **4.** To proceed laboriously: plod: *plowed through the backlog of work.* —***phrasal verbs.*** **plow back.** To reinvest (earnings or profits) in one's business. **plow into.** *Informal.* **1.** To strike with force. **2.** To undertake (a task, for example) with eagerness and vigor. **plow under.** **1.** To cause to vanish under something piled up. **2.** To overwhelm, as with burdens. [Middle English *plough, plouw,* from Old English *plōh, plōg,* plow, plowland.] —**plow′a·ble** *adj.* —**plow′er** *n.*

Plow (plou) *n.* See **Big Dipper.**

plow·back (plou′băk′) *n.* **1.** Reinvestment of profits in the business that earned them. **2.** An amount of profits thus reinvested.

plow·boy (plou′boi′) *n.* **1.** A boy who leads or guides a team of animals in plowing. **2.** A country boy.

plow·man (plou′mən) *n.* **1.** A man who plows. **2.** A farmer or rustic.

plow·share (plou′shâr′) *n.* The cutting blade of a plow; a share.

plow steel *n.* A high-strength steel having a carbon content of 0.5 to 0.95 percent and used primarily to make wire rope.

ploy (ploi) *n.* An action calculated to frustrate an opponent or gain an advantage indirectly or deviously; a maneuver: *"A typical ploy is to feign illness, procure medicine, then sell it on the black market"* (Jill Smolowe). [Perhaps from EMPLOY, employment (obsolete).]

PLSS *abbr.* Portable life-support system.

plu. *abbr.* Plural.

pluck (plŭk) *v.* **plucked, pluck·ing, plucks.** —*tr.* **1.** To remove or detach by grasping and pulling abruptly with the fingers; pick: *pluck a flower; pluck feathers from a chicken; plucked a rabbit from the hat.* **2.** To pull out the hair or feathers of: *pluck a chicken.* **3.** To remove abruptly or forcibly: *plucked the child from school in midterm.* **4.** To give an abrupt pull to; tug at: *pluck a sleeve.* **5.** *Music.* To sound (the strings of an instrument) by pulling and releasing them with the fingers or a plectrum. —*intr.* To give an abrupt pull; tug. —**pluck** *n.* **1.** The act or an instance of plucking. **2.** Resourceful courage and daring in the face of difficulties; spirit. **3.** The heart, liver, windpipe, and lungs of a slaughtered animal. [Middle English *plukken,* from Old English *pluccian,* probably from Vulgar Latin **piluccāre,* ultimately from Latin *pilāre,* from *pilus,* hair.] —**pluck′er** *n.*

pluck·y (plŭk′ē) *adj.* **-i·er, -i·est.** Having or showing courage and spirit in trying circumstances. See Synonyms at **brave.** —**pluck′i·ly** *adv.* —**pluck′i·ness** *n.*

plug (plŭg) *n.* **1.** An object, such as a cork or a wad of cloth, used to fill a hole tightly; a stopper. **2.** A dense mass of material that obstructs a passage. **3.** A usually cylindrical or conic piece cut from something larger, often as a sample. **4.** *Electricity.* **a.** A fitting, commonly with two metal prongs for insertion in a fixed socket, used to connect an appliance to a power supply. **b.** A spark plug. **5.** A hydrant. **6.a.** A flat cake of pressed or twisted tobacco. **b.** A piece of chewing tobacco. **7.** *Geology.* A mass of igneous rock filling the vent of a volcano. **8.** *Informal.* A favorable public mention of a commercial product, business, or performance, especially when broadcast. **9.** *Slang.* Something inferior, useless, or defective, especially an old, worn-out horse. **10.** *Slang.* A gunshot or bullet: *a plug in the back.* **11.** *Sports.* A lure to which hooks are attached, used especially in angling. —**plug** *v.* **plugged, plug·ging, plugs.** —*tr.* **1.** To fill (a hole) tightly with or as if with a plug; stop up. **2.** To insert (something) as a plug: *plugged a cork in the bottle.* **3.** *Slang.* **a.** To hit with a bullet; shoot. **b.** To hit with the fist; punch. **4.** *Informal.* To publicize (a product, for example) favorably, as by mentioning on a broadcast: *authors who plug their latest books on TV talk shows.* —*intr.* **1.** To become stopped up or obstructed: *alveoli that plug up with phlegm.* **2.** *Informal.* To work doggedly and persistently: *"You may plug along fifty years before you get anywhere"* (Saul Bellow). —***phrasal verbs.*** **plug in.** **1.** To connect (an appliance) to an electrical outlet. **2.** To function by being connected to an electrical outlet: *a power drill that plugs in.* **plug into.** **1.** To connect or be connected to in the manner of an electrical appliance: *The local system is plugged into the national telephone network. This computer plugs into a data bank.* **2.** *Slang.* To cause to be closely attuned or responsive to: *connoisseurs who are plugged into the current art scene.* [Dutch, from Middle Dutch *plugge.*] —**plug′ger** *n.*

plug board *n.* **1.** A control panel or wiring panel. **2.** *Computer Science.* A removable panel in a computing device that may be rewired at will to sort data by a prescribed pattern.

plug-com·pat·i·ble (plŭg′kəm-păt′ə-bəl) *adj. Computer*

Science. Capable of being connected peripherally to a computer without modification. Used of hardware.

plug-in (plŭg′ĭn′) *adj.* Designed to be plugged in to an electric circuit: *a plug-in game.*

plug-ug·ly (plŭg′ŭg′lē) *n., pl.* **-lies.** *Slang.* A gangster or ruffian. [From the *Plug Uglies,* a gang active in several East Coast cities in the 1850's.]

plum[1] (plŭm) *n.* **1.a.** Any of several shrubs or small trees of the genus *Prunus,* bearing smooth-skinned, fleshy, edible fruit with a single hard-shelled stone that encloses the seed. **b.** The fruit of any of these trees. **2.a.** Any of several trees bearing plumlike fruit. **b.** The fruit of such a tree. **3.** A raisin, when added to a pudding or cake. **4.** A sugarplum. **5.** *Color.* A dark purple to deep reddish purple. **6.** An especially desirable position, assignment, or reward: *an ambassadorship granted as a political plum.* [Middle English, from Old English *plūme,* from Vulgar Latin **prūna,* from neuter pl. of Latin *prūnum.*]

plum[2] (plŭm) *adv.* Variant of **plumb** (sense 3). **—plum** *adj.* Variant of **plumb** (sense 2).

Plum (plŭm). A borough of southwest Pennsylvania, a suburb of Pittsburgh. Population, 25,390.

plum·age (plo͞o′mĭj) *n.* **1.** The covering of feathers on a bird. **2.** Feathers used ornamentally. **3.** Elaborate dress; finery. [Middle English, from Old French, from *plume,* plume, from Latin *plūma.*] **—plum′aged** *adj.*

plu·mate (plo͞o′māt′) *adj.* Resembling a plume or feather. [Latin *plūmātus,* feathered, from *plūma,* feather.]

plumb (plŭm) *n.* **1.** A weight on the end of a line, used to determine water depth. **2.** A weight on the end of a line, used especially by masons and carpenters to establish a true vertical. **—plumb** *adv.* **1.** In a vertical or perpendicular line. **2.** *Informal.* Directly; squarely: *fell plumb in the middle of the puddle.* **3.** Also **plum.** *Informal.* Utterly; completely: *plumb worn out.* **—plumb** *adj.* **1.** Exactly vertical. See Synonyms at **vertical. 2.** Also **plum.** *Informal.* Utter; absolute; sheer: *a plumb fool.* **—plumb** *v.* **plumbed, plumb·ing, plumbs.** *—tr.* **1.** To determine the depth of with a plumb; sound. **2.** To test the verticality or alignment of with a plumb. **3.** To straighten or make perpendicular: *plumb up the wall.* **4.** To examine closely or deeply; probe: *"Shallow ideas are plumbed and discarded"* (Gilbert Highet). **5.** To seal with lead. *—intr.* To work as a plumber. **—*idiom.* out of** (or **off**) **plumb.** Not vertical. [Middle English, lead, a plumb, from Old French *plomb,* from Latin *plumbum,* lead.] **—plumb′a·ble** *adj.*

plum·ba·go (plŭm-bā′gō) *n., pl.* **-gos. 1.** See **graphite. 2.** Any of various plants of the genus *Plumbago;* leadwort. [Latin *plumbāgō,* lead ore, from *plumbum,* lead.]

plumb bob *n.* A usually conical metal weight attached to the end of a plumb line.

plumb·er (plŭm′ər) *n.* **1.** One that installs and repairs pipes and plumbing. **2.** *Slang.* An employee assigned to investigate and stop leaks of sensitive information: *"The plumbers pushed the departments to investigate with interviews and polygraph tests"* (Richard M. Nixon). [Middle English *plummer,* from Old French *plomier,* from Latin *plumbārius,* lead worker, from Latin *plumbum,* lead.]

plumb·er's helper (plŭm′ərz) *n.* See **plunger** (sense 2).

plumber's snake *n.* See **snake** (sense 3).

plumb·er·y (plŭm′ə-rē) *n., pl.* **-ies. 1.** A plumber's workshop or place of business. **2.** A plumber's work; plumbing.

plum·bif·er·ous (plŭm-bĭf′ər-əs) *adj.* Containing lead. [Latin *plumbum,* lead + -FEROUS.]

plumb·ing (plŭm′ĭng) *n.* **1.** The pipes, fixtures, and other apparatus of a water, gas, or sewage system in a building. **2.** The work or trade of a plumber.

plum·bism (plŭm′bĭz′əm) *n.* Chronic lead poisoning. [From Latin *plumbum,* lead.]

plumb line *n.* **1.** A line from which a weight is suspended to determine verticality or depth. **2.** A line regarded as directed exactly toward the earth's center of gravity.

plumb rule *n.* A narrow strip of wood with a plumb line and bob attached, used to test verticality.

plume (plo͞om) *n.* **1.** A feather, especially a large and showy one: *the long plumes of a heron in the breeding season.* **2.** A large feather or cluster of feathers worn as an ornament or symbol of rank, as on a helmet. **3.** A token of honor or achievement. **4.** A structure or form that is like a long feather: *a plume of smoke.* **5.** *Ecology.* A space in air, water, or soil containing pollutants released from a point source. **6.** *Geology.* An upwelling of molten material from the earth's mantle. **—plume** *tr.v.* **plumed, plum·ing, plumes. 1.** To decorate, cover, or supply with or as if with plumes. **2.** To smooth (feathers); preen. **3.** To congratulate (oneself) in a self-satisfied way: *plumed himself on his victory.* [Middle English, from Old French, from Latin *plūma.*]

plume·let (plo͞om′lĭt) *n.* A small plume.

plum·met (plŭm′ĭt) *n.* **1.** A plumb bob. **2.** Something that weighs down or oppresses; a burden. **—plummet** *intr.v.* **-met·ed, -met·ing, -mets. 1.** To fall straight down; plunge. **2.** To decline suddenly and steeply: *Stock prices plummeted.* [Middle English *plomet,* from Old French, ball of lead, diminutive of *plom, plomb,* sounding lead, from Latin *plumbum.*]

plum·my (plŭm′ē) *adj.* **-mi·er, -mi·est. 1.a.** Filled with plums. **b.** Smelling or tasting of plums. **2.** Choice; desirable: *a plummy leading role; a plummy job.* **3.** Exceedingly or affectedly mellow and rich: *a radio announcer's plummy voice.*

plu·mose (plo͞o′mōs′) *adj.* **1.** Having feathers or featherlike growths; feathered. **2.** Resembling a plume; feathery. [Latin *plūmōsus,* from *plūma,* feather.] **—plu′mose′ly** *adv.* **—plu·mos′i·ty** (-mŏs′ĭ-tē) *n.*

plump[1] (plŭmp) *adj.* **plump·er, plump·est. 1.** Well-rounded and full in form; chubby. See Synonyms at **fat. 2.** Abundant; ample: *a plump reward.* **—plump** *v.* **plumped, plump·ing, plumps.** *—tr.* To make well-rounded or full in form: *plumped up the pillows.* *—intr.* To become well-rounded, chubby, or full in form. [Middle English, dull, probably from Middle Low German *plomp,* blunt, thick.] **—plump′ish** *adj.* **—plump′ly** *adv.* **—plump′ness** *n.*

plump[2] (plŭmp) *v.* **plumped, plump·ing, plumps.** *—intr.* **1.** To drop abruptly or heavily: *plumped into the easy chair.* **2.** To give full support or praise: *plumped for the candidate throughout the state.* *—tr.* To throw down or drop (something) abruptly or heavily: *plumped the books onto the table.* **—plump** *n.* **1.** A heavy or abrupt fall or collision. **2.** The sound of a heavy fall or collision. **—plump** *adj.* Blunt; direct. **—plump** *adv.* **1.** With a heavy or abrupt drop: *We dropped the rock plump into the water.* **2.** Straight down: *The anchor fell plump into the sea.* **3.** Without qualification; bluntly: *spoke out plump for the tax bill.* [Middle English *plumpen,* to immerse quickly, perhaps from Middle Low German, probably of imitative origin.]

plum pudding *n.* A rich boiled or steamed pudding made with flour, suet, raisins, currants, citron, and spices.

plum tomato *n.* A form of the cherry tomato, having somewhat oblong fruit.

plu·mule (plo͞om′yo͞ol) *n.* **1.** A down feather. **2.** *Botany.* The rudimentary bud of a plant embryo. [Latin *plūmula,* diminutive of *plūma,* feather.] **—plu′mu·lose′** (plo͞om′yə-lōs′) *adj.*

plum·y (plo͞o′mē) *adj.* **-i·er, -i·est. 1.** Consisting of or covered with feathers. **2.** Resembling a feather or plume.

plun·der (plŭn′dər) *v.* **-dered, -der·ing, -ders.** *—tr.* **1.** To rob of goods by force, especially in time of war; pillage. **2.** To seize wrongfully or by force; steal. *—intr.* To take booty; rob. **—plunder** *n.* **1.** The act or practice of plundering. **2.** Property stolen by fraud or force; booty. [German *plündern,* from Middle High German *plundern,* from Middle Low German *plunder,* household goods.] **—plun′der·a·ble** *adj.* **—plun′der·er** *n.* **—plun′der·ous** *adj.*

plunge (plŭnj) *v.* **plunged, plung·ing, plung·es.** *—tr.* **1.** To thrust or throw forcefully into a substance or place: *"Plunge the lobsters, head first, into a large pot of rapidly boiling salted water"* (Craig Claiborne). **2.** To cast suddenly, violently, or deeply into a given state or situation: *"The street was plunged in cool shadow"* (Richard Wright). *—intr.* **1.** To fall or throw oneself into a substance or place: *We plunged into the icy mountain lake.* **2.** To throw oneself earnestly or wholeheartedly into an activity or a situation: *The students plunged into their examinations.* **3.** To enter or move headlong through something: *The hunting dogs plunged into the forest in pursuit of game.* **4.** To descend steeply; fall precipitously: *a cliff that plunges to the sea.* **5.** To move forward and downward violently: *The disabled aircraft plunged to the ground and burst into flames.* **6.** To speculate or gamble extravagantly. **—plunge** *n.* **1.** The act or an instance of plunging. **2.a.** A place or an area, such as a swimming pool, for diving or plunging. **b.** A swim; a dip. **—*idiom.* take the plunge.** *Informal.* To begin an unfamiliar venture, especially after hesitating: *After a three-year engagement, they're finally taking the plunge.* [Middle English *plungen,* from Old French *plongier,* from Vulgar Latin **plumbicāre,* to heave a sounding lead, from Latin *plumbum,* lead.]

plung·er (plŭn′jər) *n.* **1.** One who plunges or dives. **2.** A device consisting of a rubber suction cup attached to the end of a stick, used to clean out clogged drains and pipes. Also called *plumber's helper.* **3.** A machine part, such as a piston, that operates with a thrusting or plunging movement.

plunk (plŭngk) also **plonk** (plŏngk, plŭngk) *—v.* **plunked, plunk·ing, plunks** also **plonked, plonk·ing, plonks.** *—tr.* **1.** To throw or place heavily or abruptly: *plunked the money down on the counter.* **2.** *Music.* To strum or pluck (a stringed instrument). *—intr.* **1.** To drop or fall abruptly or heavily; plump: *plunked into the armchair with a sigh of relief.* **2.** To emit a hollow, twanging sound. *—n.* **1.** *Informal.* A heavy blow or stroke. **2.** A short, hollow, twanging sound. *—adv. Informal.* **1.** With a short, hollow thud. **2.** Exactly; precisely: *The dart landed plunk in the center of the target.* [Imitative.] **—plunk′er** *n.* **—plunk′y** *adj.*

plu·per·fect (plo͞o-pûr′fĭkt) *adj.* **1.** *Grammar.* Of, relating to, or being a verb tense used to express action completed before a specified or implied past time. **2.** More than perfect; supremely accomplished; ideal: *"He has won a reputation as* [a] *pluperfect bureaucrat"* (New York Times). **—pluperfect** *n.* *Grammar.* **1.** The pluperfect tense, formed in English with the past participle of a verb and the auxiliary *had,* as *had learned* in the sentence *He had learned to type by the time the semester was over.* Also called *past perfect.* **2.** A verb or form in the pluperfect tense. [Middle English *pluperfyth,* alteration of Latin *plūs quam perfectum,* more than perfect : *plūs,* more; see **pelə-[1]** in Appendix + *quam,* than + *perfectum,* neuter past participle of *perficere,* to complete; see PERFECT.]

plum[1]

plunger

ă pat	oi boy
ā pay	ou out
âr care	o͝o took
ä father	o͞o boot
ĕ pet	ŭ cut
ē be	ûr urge
ĭ pit	th thin
ī pie	*th* this
îr pier	hw which
ŏ pot	zh vision
ō toe	ə about, item
ô paw	♦ regionalism

Stress marks: **′** (primary); ′ (secondary), as in **dictionary** (dĭk′shə-nĕr′ē)

plu·ral (plo͝or′əl) *adj.* **1.** Relating to or composed of more than one member, set, or kind: *the plural societies of the world.* **2.** *Abbr.* **pl., plu.** *Grammar.* Of, relating to, or being a grammatical form that designates more than one of the things specified. —**plural** *n. Abbr.* **pl., plu.** *Grammar.* **1.** The plural number or form. **2.** A word or term in the plural form. [Middle English *plurel,* from Old French, from Latin *plūrālis,* from *plūs, plūr-,* more. See **pelə-**[1] in Appendix.] —**plu′ral·ly** *adv.*

plu·ral·ism (plo͝or′ə-lĭz′əm) *n.* **1.** The condition of being plural. **2.** A condition of society in which numerous distinct ethnic, religious, or cultural groups coexist within one nation. **3.** *Ecclesiastical.* The holding by one person of two or more positions or offices, especially two or more ecclesiastical benefices, at the same time. **4.** *Philosophy.* **a.** The doctrine that reality is composed of many ultimate substances. **b.** The belief that no single explanatory system or view of reality can account for all the phenomena of life.

plu·ral·ist (plo͝or′ə-lĭst) *n.* **1.** *Ecclesiastical.* A person who holds two or more offices, especially two or more benefices, at the same time. **2.** *Philosophy.* One who adheres to pluralism. —**plu′ral·is′tic** *adj.* —**plu′ral·is′ti·cal·ly** *adv.*

plu·ral·i·ty (plo͞o-răl′ĭ-tē) *n., pl.* **-ties. 1.** The state or fact of being plural. **2.** A large number or amount; a multitude. **3.** *Ecclesiastical.* **a.** Pluralism. **b.** The offices or benefices held by a pluralist. **4. a.** In a contest of more than two choices, the number of votes cast for the winning choice if this number is not more than one half of the total votes cast. **b.** The number by which the vote of the winning choice in such a contest exceeds that of the closest opponent. **5.** The larger or greater part.

plu·ral·ize (plo͝or′ə-līz′) *v.* **-ized, -iz·ing, -iz·es.** —*tr.* **1.** To make plural. **2.** *Grammar.* To express in the plural. —*intr.* **1.** To become plural. **2.** *Ecclesiastical.* To hold more than one position or benefice at one time. —**plu′ral·i·za′tion** (plo͝or′ə-lĭ-zā′shən) *n.*

plural marriage *n.* See **polygamy** (sense 1).

plus (plŭs) *conj.* **1.** *Mathematics.* Increased by the addition of: *Two plus two is four.* **2.** Added to; along with: *Their strength plus their spirit makes them formidable. Intelligence plus wit makes for an interesting person.* **3.** *Usage Problem.* And: "[He] *is a committed man, plus he has imagination, vitality and national stature"* (Merv Griffin). —**plus** *adj.* **1.** Positive or on the positive part of a scale: *a plus value; a temperature of plus five degrees.* **2.** Added or extra: *a plus benefit.* **3.** *Informal.* Increased to a further degree or number: *"At 70 plus,* [he] *is old enough to be metaphysical"* (Anatole Broyard). **4.** Ranking on the higher end of a designated scale: *a grade of C plus.* **5.** *Physics.* Positive. —**plus** *n., pl.* **plus·es** or **plus·ses. 1.** *Mathematics.* The plus sign (+). **2.** A positive quantity. **3.** A favorable condition or factor: *The clear weather was a plus for the golf tournament.* [Latin *plūs,* more. See **pelə-**[1] in Appendix.]

USAGE NOTE: Philosophers of mathematics have long debated the proper analysis of the relation denoted by the + sign in equations such as 2 + 2 = 4, so it is not surprising that the syntactic status of its natural language equivalent, the word *plus,* should be similarly problematic—though to be sure, the questions are primarily of theoretical interest. When mathematical equations are pronounced as English sentences, the verb is usually in the singular: *Two plus two is* (or *equals*) *four.* By the same token, subjects containing two noun phrases joined by *plus* are usually construed as singular: *The construction slowdown plus the bad weather has made for a weak market.* This observation has suggested to some that *plus* should be regarded as a preposition in these uses, on the model of expressions such as *together with* or *in addition to.* But the phrases introduced by *plus* do not behave like prepositional phrases in other respects. They cannot be moved to the beginning of the sentence, for example. We do not say *Plus the bad weather, the construction slowdown has made for a weak market* (contrast the acceptable sentence beginning with *Together with the bad weather*). What is more, subjects containing two noun phrases connected by *plus* are usually singular even when the first noun phrase is plural: *Our contacts plus their capital* makes (more common than *make*) *for a formidable marketing organization* (compare *Two cows plus two cows* makes *four cows*). This situation suggests that *plus* in these uses should be regarded as a particular kind of conjunction, which joins two elements that are taken together as a single entity, the way the conjunction *and* does in a sentence such as *Peas and carrots* is *Sophie's favorite combination.* • The usage of *plus* in *The construction industry has been hurt by the rise in rates. Plus which, bad weather has affected housing starts* is not well established in formal writing, nor is the use of *plus* introducing an independent clause, as in *She has a great deal of talent, plus she is willing to work hard.*

plus fours

plus fours *pl.n.* Loose knickers bagging below the knees, worn formerly for sports. [From the fact that they were four inches longer than ordinary knickers.]

plush (plŭsh) *n.* A fabric of silk, rayon, cotton, or other material, having a thick, deep pile. —**plush** *adj.* **plush·er, plush·est. 1.** Made of or covered with plush. **2.** Luxurious. [French *pluche,* variant of *peluche,* from *pelucher,* to become fluffy, shed, from Old French *peluchier,* to pluck, probably from Vulgar Latin **piluccāre.* See PLUCK.] —**plush′ly** *adv.* —**plush′ness** *n.*

plush·y (plŭsh′ē) *adj.* **-i·er, -i·est. 1.** Resembling plush in texture. **2.** *Informal.* Ostentatiously luxurious: *a plushy office.* —**plush′i·ly** *adv.* —**plush′i·ness** *n.*

plus sign *n. Mathematics.* The symbol (+), as in 2 + 2 = 4, that is used to indicate addition or a positive quantity.

Plu·tarch (plo͞o′tärk′). A.D. 46?–120? Greek biographer and philosopher. He wrote *Parallel Lives,* a collection of biographies that Shakespeare used in his Roman plays. —**Plu·tarch′an** (-tär′kən), **Plu·tarch′i·an** (-tär′kē-ən) *adj.*

Plu·to (plo͞o′tō) *n.* **1.** *Roman Mythology.* The god of the dead and the ruler of the underworld. **2.** The ninth and usually farthest planet from the sun, having a sidereal period of revolution about the sun of 248.4 years, 4.5 billion kilometers or 2.8 billion miles distant at perihelion and 7.4 billion kilometers or 4.6 billion miles at aphelion, and a diameter less than half that of Earth. [Latin *Plūtō, Plūtōn-,* from Greek *Ploutōn,* from *ploutos,* wealth. See **pleu-** in Appendix.]

plu·toc·ra·cy (plo͞o-tŏk′rə-sē) *n., pl.* **-cies. 1.** Government by the wealthy. **2.** A wealthy class that controls a government. **3.** A government or state in which the wealthy rule. [Greek *ploutokratia* : *ploutos,* wealth; see **pleu-** in Appendix + *-kratia,* -cracy.] —**plu′to·crat′** (plo͞o′tə-krăt′) *n.* —**plu′to·crat′ic, plu′to·crat′i·cal** *adj.* —**plu′to·crat′i·cal·ly** *adv.*

plu·tog·ra·phy (plo͞o-tŏg′rə-fē) *n.* Depiction of the lives of the very rich, as in writing, in dramatic productions, or on television: *"It is the age of plutography, where the acts of the rich turn them into great stars"* (Tom Wolfe). [Greek *ploutos,* wealth; see **pleu-** in Appendix + -GRAPHY.] —**plu′to·graph′ic** (-tə-grăf′ĭk) *adj.*

plu·ton (plo͞o′tŏn′) *n.* A body of igneous rock formed beneath the surface of the earth by consolidation of magma. [German, back-formation from *plutonisch,* plutonic, from Latin *Plūtō, Plūtōn-,* Pluto. See PLUTO.]

Plu·to·ni·an (plo͞o-tō′nē-ən) also **Plu·ton·ic** (-tŏn′ĭk) *adj.* **1.** Of or relating to the god Pluto or the underworld; infernal. **2.** Of or relating to the planet Pluto.

plu·ton·ic (plo͞o-tŏn′ĭk) *adj.* Of deep igneous origin: *plutonic rocks.* [From Latin *Plūtō, Plūtōn-,* Pluto. See PLUTO.]

Plu·ton·ic (plo͞o-tŏn′ĭk) *adj.* Variant of **Plutonian.**

plu·to·ni·um (plo͞o-tō′nē-əm) *n. Symbol* **Pu** A naturally radioactive, silvery, metallic transuranic element, occurring in uranium ores and produced artificially by neutron bombardment of uranium. Its longest-lived isotope is Pu 244 with a half-life of 76 million years. It is a radiological poison, specifically absorbed by bone marrow, and is used, especially the highly fissionable isotope Pu 239, as a reactor fuel and in nuclear weapons. Atomic number 94; melting point 640°C; boiling point 3,235°C; specific gravity 19.84; valence 3, 4, 5, 6. See table at **element.** [After the planet PLUTO (from the fact that it follows neptunium in the periodic table).]

plu·vi·al (plo͞o′vē-əl) *adj.* **1.** Of or relating to rain; rainy. **2.** *Geology.* Caused by rain. [Latin *pluviālis,* from *pluvia,* rain. See PLUVIOUS.]

plu·vi·om·e·ter (plo͞o′vē-ŏm′ĭ-tər) *n.* See **rain gauge.** [Probably from French *pluviomètre* : Latin *pluvia,* rain; see PLUVIOUS + *-mètre,* -meter.] —**plu′vi·o·met′ric** (-ə-mĕt′rĭk), **plu′vi·o·met′ri·cal** (-rĭ-kəl) *adj.* —**plu′vi·o·met′ri·cal·ly** *adv.* —**plu′vi·om′e·try** *n.*

plu·vi·ous (plo͞o′vē-əs) also **plu·vi·ose** (-ōs′) *adj.* Characterized by heavy rainfall; rainy. [Middle English, from Old French *pluvieus,* from Latin *pluviōsus,* from *(aqua) pluvia,* rain (water), feminine of *pluvius,* of rain, from *pluere,* to rain. See **pleu-** in Appendix.] —**plu′vi·os′i·ty** (-ŏs′ĭ-tē) *n.*

ply[1] (plī) *tr.v.* **plied** (plīd), **ply·ing, plies** (plīz). **1.** To join together, as by molding or twisting. **2.** To double over (cloth, for example). —**ply** *n., pl.* **plies** (plīz). **1.** A layer, as of doubled-over cloth or of paperboard. **2.** One of the sheets of wood glued together to form plywood. **3.** One of the strands twisted together to make yarn, rope, or thread. Often used in combination: *three-ply cord.* **4.** A bias; an inclination. [Middle English *plien,* from Old French *plier,* alteration of *pleier,* from Latin *plicāre,* to fold. See **plek-** in Appendix.]

ply[2] (plī) *v.* **plied** (plīd), **ply·ing, plies** (plīz). —*tr.* **1.** To use diligently; wield: *plies a needle.* **2.** To engage in diligently; practice: *plies the carpenter's trade.* See Synonyms at **handle. 3.** To traverse or sail over regularly: *Trading ships plied the routes between coastal ports.* **4.** To continue supplying or offering to: *plied their guests with excellent food.* **5.** To assail vigorously. —*intr.* **1.** To traverse a route or course regularly: *The boat plies between the islands on a weekly schedule.* **2.** To perform or work diligently or regularly: *a person who had plied at the weaver's trade for 20 years.* **3.** *Nautical.* To work against the wind by a zigzag course; tack. [Middle English *plien,* from *applien,* to apply. See APPLY.]

ply·er (plī′ər) *n.* Variant of **plier.**

Plym·outh (plĭm′əth). **1.** A borough of southwest England on **Plymouth Sound,** an inlet of the English Channel. A major port, it was the embarkation point for the fleet that fought the Spanish Armada (1588) and for Drake, Raleigh, and several other early explorers. Population, 250,300. **2.** A town of southeast Massachusetts on **Plymouth Bay,** an inlet of the Atlantic Ocean, southeast of Boston. Founded in 1620 by Pilgrims, who supposedly set foot on **Plymouth Rock** when disembarking from the *Mayflower,* it was the center of **Plymouth Colony.** The colony was governed under precepts laid down in the Mayflower Compact until 1691, when it was absorbed by the royal colony of Massachusetts. Population, 35,913. **3.** A city of southeast Minnesota, a suburb of Minneapolis–St. Paul. Population, 31,615.

Plymouth Rock *n.* Any of an American breed of medium-sized domestic fowl raised for both meat and eggs. [After *Plymouth Rock,* legendary landing place of the Pilgrims in 1620.]

ply·wood (plī′wo͝od′) *n.* A structural material made of layers of wood glued together, usually with the grains of adjoining layers at right angles to each other. [PLY[1] + WOOD[1].]

Plzeň (pəl′zĕn′, -zĕn′yə). A city of western Czechoslovakia west-southwest of Prague. Famed for its beer, it was part of the Austro-Hungarian Empire until its inclusion in newly formed Czechoslovakia in 1918. Population, 174,555.

pm also **p-m** *abbr.* Phase modulation.

Pm The symbol for the element **promethium.**

PM or **P.M.** *abbr.* **1.** Past master. **2.** Police magistrate. **3. a.** Postmaster. **b.** Postmistress. **4.** Prime minister. **5.** Provost marshal.

pm. *abbr.* Premium.

p.m. also **P.M.** *abbr.* Postmortem.

P.M. also **p.m.** or **P.M.** *abbr.* Post meridiem. See Usage Note at **ante meridiem.**

P-mark·er (pē′mär′kər) *n. Grammar.* A phrase marker.

P.M.G. *abbr.* Postmaster general.

pmk. *abbr.* Postmark.

PMS *abbr.* Premenstrual syndrome.

pmt. *abbr.* Payment.

p.n. or **P/N** *abbr.* Promissory note.

pneum. *abbr.* Pneumatic; pneumatics.

pneum– *pref.* Variant of **pneumo–.**

pneu·ma (no͞o′mə, nyo͞o′-) *n.* The soul or vital spirit. [Greek. See **pneu-** in Appendix.]

pneumat– *pref.* Variant of **pneumato–.**

pneu·mat·ic (no͝o-măt′ĭk, nyo͝o-) also **pneu·mat·i·cal** (-ĭ-kəl) *adj. Abbr.* **pneum. 1.** Of or relating to air or other gases. **2.** Of or relating to pneumatics. **3. a.** Run by or using compressed air: *a pneumatic drill.* **b.** Filled with air, especially compressed air: *a pneumatic tire.* **4.** *Zoology.* Having cavities filled with air, as the bones of certain birds. **5.** *Theology.* Of or relating to the pneuma; spiritual. [French *pneumatique,* from Latin *pneumaticus,* from Greek *pneumatikos,* from *pneuma, pneumat-,* wind. See **pneu-** in Appendix.] **—pneu·mat′i·cal·ly** *adv.* **—pneu′ma·tic′i·ty** (no͞o′mə-tĭs′ĭ-tē, nyo͞o′-) *n.*

pneu·mat·ics (no͝o-măt′ĭks, nyo͝o-) *n.* *(used with a sing. verb). Abbr.* **pneum.** The study of the mechanical properties of air and other gases.

pneumato– or **pneumat–** *pref.* **1.** Air; gas: *pneumatolysis.* **2.** Breath; respiration: *pneumatometer.* [From Greek *pneuma, pneumat-,* wind, breath. See **pneu-** in Appendix.]

pneu·mat·o·graph (no͝o-măt′ə-grăf′, nyo͝o-) *n.* Variant of **pneumograph.**

pneu·ma·tol·o·gy (no͞o′mə-tŏl′ə-jē, nyo͞o′-) *n.* **1.** The doctrine or study of spiritual beings and phenomena, especially the belief in spirits intervening between human beings and God. **2.** The Christian doctrine of the Holy Ghost. **—pneu′ma·to·log′ic** (-tə-lŏj′ĭk), **pneu′ma·to·log′i·cal** (-ĭ-kəl) *adj.* **—pneu′ma·tol′o·gist** *n.*

pneu·ma·tol·y·sis (no͞o′mə-tŏl′ĭ-sĭs, nyo͞o′-) *n.* A process of rock alteration or mineral formation brought about by the action of gases emitted from solidifying magma. **—pneu′ma·to·lyt′ic** (-tə-lĭt′ĭk) *adj.*

pneu·ma·tom·e·ter (no͞o′mə-tŏm′ĭ-tər, nyo͞o′-) *n.* An instrument for measuring the force or volume of inspiration or expiration in the lungs. **—pneu′ma·tom′e·try** *n.*

pneu·mat·o·phore (no͝o-măt′ə-fôr′, -fōr′, nyo͝o-, no͞o′mə-tə-, nyo͞o′-) *n.* **1.** A gas-filled sac serving as a float in some colonial marine hydrozoans, such as the Portuguese man-of-war. **2.** *Botany.* A specialized respiratory root structure in certain aquatic plants, such as the bald cypress. **—pneu·mat′o·phor′ic** (-fôr′ĭk, -fōr′-) *adj.*

pneu·mec·to·my (no͝o-mĕk′tə-mē, nyo͝o-) *n.* Variant of **pneumonectomy.**

pneumo– or **pneum–** *pref.* **1.** Air; gas: *pneumothorax.* **2.** Lung; pulmonary: *pneumoconiosis.* **3.** Respiration: *pneumograph.* **4.** Pneumonia: *pneumococcus.* [From Greek *pneuma,* wind, breath; see **pneu-** in Appendix, and from Greek *pneumōn,* alteration (influenced by *pneuma*) of *pleumōn,* lung. See **pleu-** in Appendix.]

pneu·mo·ba·cil·lus (no͞o′mō-bə-sĭl′əs, nyo͞o′-) *n., pl.* **-cil·li** (-sĭl′ī′). A nonmotile, gram-negative bacterium *(Klebsiella pneumoniae)* that causes a severe form of pneumonia and is associated with other respiratory infections.

pneu·mo·coc·cus (no͞o′mə-kŏk′əs, nyo͞o′-) *n., pl.* **-coc·ci** (-kŏk′sī′, -kŏk′ī′). A nonmotile, gram-positive bacterium *(Streptococcus pneumoniae)* that is the most common cause of bacterial pneumonia, associated with meningitis and other infectious diseases. **—pneu′mo·coc′cal** (-kŏk′əl) *adj.*

pneu·mo·co·ni·o·sis (no͞o′mō-kō′nē-ō′sĭs, nyo͞o′-) *n.* A disease of the lungs, such as asbestosis or silicosis, caused by long-continued inhalation of dusts, especially mineral or metallic dusts. [PNEUMO– + Greek *konis, konia,* dust + –OSIS.] **—pneu′mo·co′ni·ot′ic** (-ŏt′ĭk) *adj. & n.*

pneu·mo·cys·tis (no͞o′mə-sĭs′tĭs, nyo͞o′-) *n.* A severe lung infection caused by the parasitic protozoan *Pneumocystis pneumonia* and affecting primarily individuals with an immunodeficiency disease, such as AIDS. Also called *pneumocystis pneumonia.* [From New Latin *Pneumocystis,* genus name : PNEUMO– + New Latin *cystis,* cyst; see CYST.]

pneu·mo·gas·tric (no͞o′mō-găs′trĭk, nyo͞o′-) *adj.* Of, relating to, or involving the lungs and the stomach.

pneumogastric nerve *n.* See **vagus nerve.**

pneu·mo·graph (no͞o′mə-grăf′, nyo͞o′-) also **pneu·mat·o·graph** (no͝o-măt′ə-grăf′, nyo͝o-) *n.* A device for recording the force and speed of chest movements during respiration. **—pneu′mo·graph′ic** *adj.*

pneu·mo·nec·to·my (no͞o′mə-nĕk′tə-mē, nyo͞o′-) also **pneu·mec·to·my** (no͝o-mĕk′tə-mē, nyo͝o-) *n., pl.* **-mies.** Surgical removal of all or part of a lung. [Greek *pneumōn,* lung; see PNEUMONIC + –ECTOMY.]

pneu·mo·nia (no͝o-mōn′yə, nyo͝o-) *n.* An acute or chronic disease marked by inflammation of the lungs and caused by viruses, bacteria, or other microorganisms and sometimes by physical and chemical irritants. [New Latin, from Greek, lung disease, alteration (influenced by *pneuma,* breath) of *pleumonia,* from *pleumōn,* lung. See **pleu-** in Appendix.]

pneu·mon·ic (no͝o-mŏn′ĭk, nyo͝o-) *adj.* **1.** Of, affecting, or relating to the lungs; pulmonary. **2.** Relating to, affected by, or similar to pneumonia. [New Latin *pneumonicus,* from Greek *pneumonikos,* of the lungs, from *pneumōn,* lung. See **pleu-** in Appendix.]

pneu·mo·ni·tis (no͞o′mə-nī′tĭs, nyo͞o′-) *n.* Inflammation of lung tissue. [Greek *pneumōn,* lung; see PNEUMONIC + –ITIS.]

pneu·mo·stome (no͞o′mə-stōm′, nyo͞o′-) *n.* A small opening in the mantle of a gastropod through which air passes. [From New Latin *pneumostoma* : PNEUMO– + STOMA.]

pneu·mo·tach·o·gram (no͞o′mə-tăk′ə-grăm′, nyo͞o′-) *n.* A record produced by a pneumotachograph.

pneu·mo·tach·o·graph (no͞o′mə-tăk′ə-grăf′, nyo͞o′-) *n.* An apparatus for recording the rate of airflow to and from the lungs. [PNEUMO– + Greek *takhos,* speed + –GRAPH.] **—pneu′mo·tach′o·graph′ic** *adj.* **—pneu′mo·ta·chog′ra·phy** (-tə-kŏg′rə-fē) *n.*

pneu·mo·tho·rax (no͞o′mō-thôr′ăks′, -thōr′-, nyo͞o′-) *n.* Accumulation of air or gas in the pleural cavity, occurring as a result of disease or injury, or sometimes induced to collapse the lung in the treatment of tuberculosis and other lung diseases.

po or **p.o.** *abbr. Baseball.* Putout.

Po[1] (pō). A river of northern Italy flowing about 652 km (405 mi) generally eastward to the Adriatic Sea. The Po Valley is a major industrial and agricultural area.

Po[2] The symbol for the element **polonium.**

PO or **P.O.** *abbr.* **1.** Personnel officer. **2.** Petty officer. **3.** Postal order. **4.** Also **p.o.** Post office.

poach[1] (pōch) *tr.v.* **poached, poach·ing, poach·es.** To cook in a boiling or simmering liquid: *Poach the fish in wine.* [Back-formation from Middle English *poched,* poached, from *poche,* dish of poached eggs, from Old French, from past participle of *pochier,* to poach eggs, from *poche,* pocket, bag (from their appearance), of Germanic origin.] **—poach′a·ble** *adj.*

poach[2] (pōch) *v.* **poached, poach·ing, poach·es.** *—intr.* **1.** To trespass on another's property in order to take fish or game. **2.** To take fish or game in a forbidden area. **3.** To become muddy or broken up from being trampled. Used of land. **4.** To sink into soft earth when walking. **5. a.** To take or appropriate something unfairly or illegally. **b.** *Sports.* To play a ball out of turn or in another's territory, as in doubles tennis. *—tr.* **1.** To trespass on (another's property) for fishing or hunting. **2.** To take (fish or game) illegally. **3.** To make (land) muddy or broken up by trampling. **4. a.** To take or appropriate unfairly or illegally. **b.** *Sports.* To play (a ball) out of turn or in another's territory. [Obsolete French *pocher,* to poke, thrust, intrude, from Old French *pochier,* to poke, gouge, of Germanic origin.] **—poach′a·ble** *adj.*

poach·er[1] (pō′chər) *n.* A vessel or dish designed for the poaching of food, such as eggs or fish.

poach·er[2] (pō′chər) *n.* **1.** One who hunts or fishes illegally on the property of another. **2.** Any of various elongated marine fishes of the family Agonidae, chiefly of northern Pacific waters, having an external covering of bony plates.

Po·be·da Peak (pō-bĕd′ə, pə-byĕ′də). A mountain, 7,443.8 m (24,406 ft) high, of the Tien Shan on the border between eastern Kirghiz and western China.

po·bla·no pepper (pō-blä′nō) *n.* A mild or fairly pungent dark green pepper with a thick, leathery skin. [American Spanish, of the village, from *pueblo,* people, village. See PUEBLO.]

Po·ca·hon·tas (pō′kə-hŏn′təs). 1595?–1617. Powhatan princess who befriended the English colonists at Jamestown and is said to have saved Capt. John Smith from execution by her people.

Po·ca·tel·lo (pō′kə-tĕl′ō, -tĕl′ə). A city of southeast Idaho south-southwest of Idaho Falls. It has been a railroad junction since 1882 and is the seat of Idaho State University (founded 1901). Population, 46,340.

po·chard (pō′chərd) *n.* Any of various diving ducks of the genus *Aythya,* especially *A. ferina* of Europe and Asia, which has gray and black plumage and a reddish head. [Origin unknown.]

Plymouth Rock
Rooster

Pocahontas
Portrait based on a 1616 engraving by Simon de Passe (1595?–1647)

ă pat	oi boy
ā pay	ou out
âr care	o͝o took
ä father	o͞o boot
ĕ pet	ŭ cut
ē be	ûr urge
ĭ pit	th thin
ī pie	*th* this
îr pier	hw which
ŏ pot	zh vision
ō toe	ə about, item
ô paw	♦ regionalism

Stress marks: ′ (primary); ′ (secondary), as in **dictionary** (dĭk′shə-nĕr′ē)

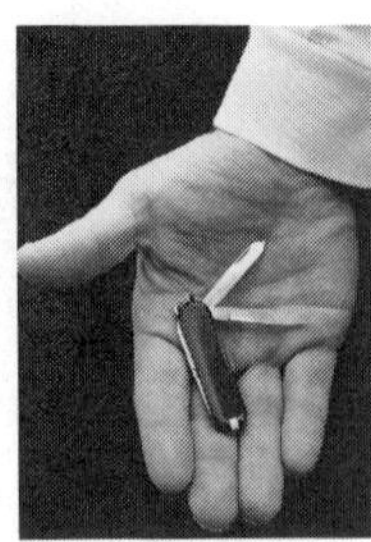

pocketknife

pock (pŏk) *n.* **1.** A pustule caused by smallpox or a similar eruptive disease. **2.** A mark or scar left in the skin by such a pustule; a pockmark. —**pock** *tr.v.* **pocked, pock•ing, pocks.** To mark with pocks; pit. [Middle English *pokke,* from Old English *pocc.*] —**pock′y** *adj.*

pock•et (pŏk′ĭt) *n.* **1.** A small baglike attachment forming part of a garment and used to carry small articles, as a flat pouch sewn inside a pair of pants or a piece of material sewn on its sides and bottom to the outside of a shirt. **2.** A small sack or bag. **3.** A receptacle, a cavity, or an opening. See Synonyms at **hole. 4.** Financial means; money supply: *The cost of the trip must come out of your own pocket.* **5.a.** A small cavity in the earth, especially one containing ore. **b.** A small body or accumulation of ore. **6.** A pouch in an animal body, such as the cheek pouch of a rodent or the abdominal pouch of a marsupial. **7.** *Games.* One of the pouchlike receptacles at the corners and sides of a billiard or pool table. **8.** *Sports.* A racing position in which a contestant has no room to pass a group of contestants immediately to his or her front or side. **9.** A small, isolated, or protected area or group. **10.** An air pocket. **11.** A bin for storing ore, grain, or other materials. —**pocket** *adj.* **1.** Suitable for or capable of being carried in one's pocket: *a pocket handkerchief; a pocket edition of a dictionary.* **2.** Small; miniature: *a pocket backyard; a pocket museum.* —**pocket** *tr.v.* **-et•ed, -et•ing, -ets. 1.** To place in or as if in a pocket. **2.** To take possession of for oneself, especially dishonestly: *pocketed the receipts from the charity dance.* **3.a.** To accept or tolerate (an insult, for example). **b.** To conceal or suppress: *I pocketed my pride and asked for a raise.* **4.** To prevent (a bill) from becoming law by failing to sign until the adjournment of the legislature. **5.** *Sports.* To hem in (a competitor) in a race. **6.** *Games.* To hit (a ball) into a pocket of a pool or billiard table. —***idioms.*** **in (one's) pocket.** In one's power, influence, or possession: *The defendant had the jury in his pocket.* **in pocket. 1.** Having funds. **2.** Having gained or retained funds of a specified amount: *was a hundred dollars in pocket after a day at the races.* **line (one's) pockets.** To make a profit, especially by illegitimate means. [Middle English, pouch, small bag, from Anglo-Norman *pokete,* diminutive of Old North French *poke,* bag, of Germanic origin.] —**pock′et•a•ble** *adj.* —**pock′et•less** *adj.*

pocket billiards *pl.n.* *(used with a sing. or pl. verb).* *Games.* See **pool²** (sense 7).

pock•et•book (pŏk′ĭt-bo͝ok′) *n.* **1.** A pocket-sized folder or case used to hold money and papers; a billfold. **2.** A purse; a handbag. **3.** Financial resources; money supply: *prices to fit your pocketbook.* **4.** Often **pocket book.** A pocket-sized, usually paperbound book. In this sense, also called *pocket edition.*

WORD HISTORY: The link between the senses "billfold, purse," and "pocket-sized book" of the word *pocketbook* can be clarified with a little historical information. The compound is first recorded in 1617 in the sense of "a small book designed to be carried in a pocket." It is only recently that such books have looked like the paperbound books we are familiar with; these early paperbacks were bound like any book but were smaller in size. The next recorded use of *pocketbook* (1685) is again for a book designed to fit in the pocket but this time used for notes or memoranda. The same word was then applied to a case that was shaped like a book and in which money or papers could be kept. Finally, the word *pocketbook* was transferred to yet another container for keeping things, a purse or handbag, rarely fitting in the pocket and not necessarily shaped like a book.

podium
Mother Teresa speaking at commencement exercises

pocket borough *n.* A borough in England, before the parliamentary reform of 1832, whose representation was controlled by a single person or family.

pocket bread *n.* See **pita¹.**

pocket calculator *n.* A small calculator designed to be carried in a pocket.

pocket edition *n.* See **pocketbook** (sense 4).

pock•et•ful (pŏk′ĭt-fo͝ol′) *n., pl.* **pock•et•fuls** or **pock•ets•ful** (pŏk′ĭts-fo͝ol′). The amount that a pocket can hold.

pocket gopher *n.* See **gopher** (sense 1).

pock•et•knife (pŏk′ĭt-nīf′) *n.* A small knife with blades or a blade that can fold into the handle when not in use.

pocket money *n.* Money for incidental or minor expenses.

pocket mouse *n.* Any of various small, nocturnal North American burrowing rodents of the genus *Perognathus,* related to the kangaroo rat and having fur-lined external cheek pouches, small ears, and a very long tail.

pocket park *n.* See **minipark.**

pock•ets•ful (pŏk′ĭts-fo͝ol′) *n.* A plural of **pocketful.**

pock•et-sized (pŏk′ĭt-sīzd′) or **pock•et•size** (-sīz′) *adj.* **1.** Of a size suitable to be carried in a pocket: *a pocket-sized radio.* **2.** Small: *"a pocket-sized riot in the Lower House"* (Terence Smith).

pocket veto *n.* **1.** The President's indirect veto of a bill that has been presented to him within ten days of adjournment, by the retention of the bill unsigned until Congress adjourns. **2.** A similar action exercised by a state governor or other chief executive. —**pock′et-ve′to** (pŏk′ĭt-vē′tō) *v.*

pock•mark (pŏk′märk′) *n.* **1.** A pitlike scar left on the skin by smallpox or another eruptive disease. **2.** A small pit on a surface: *The gophers left the lawn covered with pockmarks.* —**pockmark** *tr.v.* **-marked, -mark•ing, -marks.** To cover with pockmarks; pit. —**pock′marked′** *adj.*

po•co (pō′kō) *adv.* *Music.* To a slight degree or amount; somewhat. Used chiefly as a direction. [Italian, from Latin *paucus.* See **pau-** in Appendix.]

po•co a po•co (pō′kō ä pō′kō) *adv.* *Music.* Little by little; gradually. Used chiefly as a direction. [Italian : *poco,* little + *a,* by + *poco,* little.]

po•co•cu•ran•te (pō′kō-ko͞o-răn′tē, -rän′tē) *adj.* Indifferent; apathetic. —**pococurante** *n.* One who does not care. [Italian : *poco,* little; see POCO + *curante,* present participle of *curare,* to care for (from Latin *cūrāre,* from *cūra,* care).] —**po′co•cu•ran′tism** *n.*

Po•co•no Mountains (pō′kə-nō′). A range of the Appalachian system in northeast Pennsylvania rising to about 488 m (1,600 ft). The Poconos are a popular year-round resort area.

♦**po•co•sin** (pə-kō′sĭn) *n.* *Chiefly South Atlantic U.S.* A swamp in an upland coastal region. Also called ♦*dismal.* [Possibly of Virginia Algonquian origin.]

♦ ***REGIONAL NOTE:*** In coastal Virginia, Maryland, Delaware, and the Carolinas, a swamp or marsh can be called a *pocosin* or a *dismal,* the second term illustrated in the name of the Dismal Swamp on the border of North Carolina and Virginia. The word *pocosin* possibly comes from Virginia Algonquian. The early settlers used *pocosin* as a designation for low, swampy ground, especially a wooded swamp.

pod¹ (pŏd) *n.* **1.** *Botany.* **a.** A dehiscent fruit of a leguminous plant such as the pea. **b.** A dry, several-seeded, dehiscent fruit. Also called *seedpod.* **2.** *Zoology.* A protective covering that encases the eggs of some insects and fish. **3.** A casing or housing forming part of a vehicle, as: **a.** A streamlined external housing that encloses engines, machine guns, or fuel. **b.** *Aerospace.* A detachable compartment on a spacecraft for carrying personnel or instrumentation. **4.** Something resembling a pod, as in compactness. —**pod** *v.* **pod•ded, pod•ding, pods.** —*intr.* **1.** To bear or produce pods. **2.** To expand or swell like a pod. —*tr.* To remove (seeds) from a pod. [Origin unknown.]

pod² (pŏd) *n.* A school of marine mammals, such as seals, whales, or dolphins. See Synonyms at **flock¹.** [Origin unknown.]

pod³ (pŏd) *n.* **1.** The lengthwise groove in certain boring tools such as augers. **2.** The socket for holding the bit in a boring tool. [Origin unknown.]

-pod or **-pode** *suff.* Foot; footlike part: *pleopod.* [From New Latin *-podium* (from Greek *podion;* see PODIUM) and from New Latin *-poda* (from Greek, pl. of *pous, pod-,* foot; see **ped-** in Appendix).]

po•dag•ra (pə-dăg′rə) *n.* Gout, especially of the big toe. [Middle English, from Latin, from Greek : *pous, pod-,* foot; see **ped-** in Appendix + *agra,* trap, seizing; see **ag-** in Appendix.] —**po•dag′ral, po•dag′ric** *adj.*

-pode *suff.* Variant of **-pod.**

po•des•ta (pō-dĕs′tə, pō′dĕ-stä′) *n.* The chief magistrate in any of the republics of medieval Italy. [Italian *podestà,* from Old Italian *podestate,* from Latin *potestās,* power, from *potis,* powerful, able. See **poti-** in Appendix.]

po•de•ti•um (pə-dē′shē-əm, -shəm) *n., pl.* **-ti•a** (-shē-ə, -shə). **1.** A stalklike outgrowth of the thallus of certain lichens, bearing the apothecium. **2.** A stalklike growth or process. [New Latin, from Greek *pous, pod-,* foot. See -POD.]

Pod•gor•ny (pŏd-gôr′nē), **Nikolai Viktorovich.** 1903–1983. Soviet politician who was president of the U.S.S.R. from 1965 to 1977, when he was displaced by Leonid Brezhnev.

po•di•a (pō′dē-ə) *n.* A plural of **podium.**

po•di•a•try (pə-dī′ə-trē) *n.* The branch of medicine that deals with the diagnosis, treatment, and prevention of diseases of the human foot. Also called *chiropody.* [Greek *pous, pod-,* foot; see **ped-** in Appendix + -IATRY.] —**po′di•at′ric** (pō′dē-ăt′rĭk) *adj.* —**po•di′a•trist** *n.*

pod•ite (pŏd′īt′) *n.* A segment of the limb of an arthropod. [Greek *pous, pod-,* foot; see **ped-** in Appendix + -ITE¹.] —**po•dit′ic** (pə-dĭt′ĭk) *adj.*

po•di•um (pō′dē-əm) *n., pl.* **-di•a** (-dē-ə) or **-di•ums. 1.** An elevated platform, as for an orchestra conductor or a public speaker. **2.** A stand for holding the notes of a public speaker; a lectern. **3.** *Architecture.* **a.** A low wall serving as a foundation. **b.** A wall circling the arena of an ancient amphitheater. **4.** *Biology.* A structure resembling or functioning as a foot. [Latin, from Greek *podion,* base, diminutive of *pous, pod-,* foot. See **ped-** in Appendix.]

pod•o•phyl•lin (pŏd′ə-fĭl′ĭn) *n.* A bitter-tasting resin obtained from the dried root of the May apple and used in medicine as a cathartic and caustic. [From New Latin *Podophyllum,* genus name : Greek *pous, pod-,* foot; see **ped-** in Appendix + Greek *phullon,* leaf; see **bhel-³** in Appendix.]

-podous *suff.* Having a specified kind or number of feet or footlike parts: *polypodous.*

pod•sol (pŏd′sôl′) *n.* Variant of **podzol.**

pod•sol•i•za•tion (pŏd′sô-lĭ-zā′shən) *n.* Variant of **podzolization.**

Po•dunk (pō′dŭngk′) *n.* *Slang.* A small isolated town, region, or place that is regarded as unimportant. [After *Podunk,* name of two New England towns, of southern New England Algonquian origin.]

pod·zol (pŏd′zôl′) also **pod·sol** (-sôl′) *n.* A leached soil formed mainly in cool, humid climates. [Russian : *pod,* under; see **ped-** in Appendix + *zola,* ashes; see **ghel-**[2] in Appendix.] —**pod·zol′ic** *adj.*

pod·zol·i·za·tion (pŏd′zô-lĭ-zā′shən) also **pod·sol·i·za·tion** (pŏd′sô-) *n.* **1.** The process by which soils are depleted of bases and become acidic. **2.** The development of a podzol.

Poe (pō), **Edgar Allan.** 1809–1849. American writer known especially for his macabre poems, such as "The Raven" (1845), and short stories, including "The Fall of the House of Usher" (1839).

POE or **P.O.E.** *abbr.* Port of entry.

po·em (pō′əm) *n.* **1.** A verbal composition designed to convey experiences, ideas, or emotions in a vivid and imaginative way, characterized by the use of condensed language chosen for its sound and suggestive power and by the use of literary techniques such as meter, metaphor, and rhyme. **2.** A composition in verse rather than in prose. **3.** A literary composition written with an intensity or beauty of language more characteristic of poetry than of prose. **4.** A creation, an object, or an experience having beauty suggestive of poetry. [French *poème,* from Old French, from Latin *poēma,* from Greek *poiēma,* from *poiein,* to create. See **kʷei-**[2] in Appendix.]

poe·nol·o·gy (pē-nŏl′ə-jē) *n.* Variant of **penology.**

po·e·sy (pō′ĭ-zē, -sē) *n., pl.* **-sies. 1.** Poetical works; poetry. **2.** The art or practice of composing poems. **3.** The inspiration involved in composing poetry. [Middle English *poesie,* from Old French, from Latin *poēsis,* from Greek *poiēsis,* from *poiein,* to create. See **kʷei-**[2] in Appendix.]

po·et (pō′ĭt) *n.* **1.** A writer of poems. **2.** One who demonstrates great imaginative power, insight, or beauty of expression: *a poet of the classical ballet.* [Middle English, from Old French *poete,* from Latin *poēta,* from Greek *poiētēs,* maker, composer, from *poiein,* to create. See **kʷei-**[2] in Appendix.]

SYNONYMS: *poet, bard, versifier, rhymer, rhymester, poetaster.* These nouns denote persons who write verse. *Poet* is the most inclusive but usually applies to one who writes poetry of merit, as in being eloquent in expression, imaginative, and creative: *"Every man, that writes in verse is not a Poet"* (Ben Jonson). *Bard* in its original meaning denoted a Celtic poet who composed and sang verses dealing with legendary heroes or events; now the term applies especially to a lyric poet: *In reading their verse aloud, few bards can compare to Dylan Thomas. Versifier, rhymer,* and *rhymester* refer principally to minor or inferior poets: *He dismissed her work as that of a mere versifier. How could the critics praise such a rhymer? This rhymster has written mainly doggerel. Poetaster,* the most pejorative of these terms, applies to a writer of insignificant, meretricious, or shoddy verse: *His verse has the sing-song rhythm of a poetaster.*

poet. *abbr.* Poetic; poetical; poetry.

po·et·as·ter (pō′ĭt-ăs′tər) *n.* A writer of insignificant, meretricious, or shoddy poetry. See Synonyms at **poet.** [New Latin : Latin *poēta,* poet; see POET + Latin *-aster,* pejorative suff.]

po·et·ess (pō′ĭ-tĭs) *n.* A woman who writes poems.

po·et·ic (pō-ĕt′ĭk) *adj. Abbr.* **poet. 1.** Of or relating to poetry: *poetic works.* **2.** Having a quality or style characteristic of poetry: *poetic diction.* **3.** Suitable as a subject for poetry: *a poetic romance.* **4.** Of, relating to, or befitting a poet: *poetic insight.* **5.** Characterized by romantic imagery: *"Turner's vision of the rainbow . . . was poetic, and he knew it"* (Lawrence Gowing). —**poetic** *n.* The theory or practice of writing poetry; poetics. [Latin *poēticus,* from Greek *poiētikos,* inventive, from *poiein,* to make. See **kʷei-**[2] in Appendix.]

po·et·i·cal (pō-ĕt′ĭ-kəl) *adj. Abbr.* **poet. 1.** Poetic. **2.** Fancifully depicted or embellished; idealized: *a poetical description of the jungle.* —**po·et′i·cal·ly** *adv.* —**po·et′i·cal·ness, po·et′i·cal′i·ty** (-kăl′ĭ-tē) *n.*

po·et·i·cism (pō-ĕt′ĭ-sĭz′əm) *n.* A poetic expression that is hackneyed, archaic, or excessively artificial.

po·et·i·cize (pō-ĕt′ĭ-sīz′) *v.* **-cized, -ciz·ing, -ciz·es.** —*tr.* To describe or express in poetry or in a poetic manner. —*intr.* To write poetry.

poetic justice *n.* An outcome in which virtue is rewarded and vice punished, often in an especially appropriate or ironic manner.

poetic license *n.* The liberty taken by an artist or a writer in deviating from conventional form or fact to achieve an effect.

po·et·ics (pō-ĕt′ĭks) *n. (used with a sing. or pl. verb).* **1.** Literary criticism that deals with the nature, forms, and laws of poetry. **2.** A treatise on or study of poetry or aesthetics. **3.** The practice of writing poetry; poetic composition.

po·et·ize (pō′ĭ-tīz′) *v.* **-ized, -iz·ing, -iz·es.** —*tr.* To describe or express in poetry or a poetic manner. —*intr.* To write poetry. —**po′et·iz′er** *n.*

poet laureate *n., pl.* **poets laureate** or **poet laureates. 1.** A poet appointed for life by a British monarch as a member of the royal household and formerly expected to write poems celebrating occasions of national importance and honoring the royal family. **2.** A poet appointed to a similar honorary position or honored for artistic excellence. **3.** A poet acclaimed as the most excellent or most representative of a locality or group.

po·et·ry (pō′ĭ-trē) *n. Abbr.* **poet. 1.** The art or work of a poet. **2.a.** Poems regarded as forming a division of literature. **b.** The poetic works of a given author, group, nation, or kind. **3.** A piece of literature written in meter; verse. **4.** Prose that resembles a poem in some respect, as in form or sound. **5.** The essence or characteristic quality of a poem. **6.** The quality of a poem, as possessed by an object, act, or experience: *the poetry of the dance movements.* [Middle English *poetrie,* from Old French, from Medieval Latin *poētria,* from Latin *poēta,* poet. See POET.]

po·go·ni·a (pə-gō′nē-ə, -gōn′yə) *n.* Any of various small terrestrial orchids of the genus *Pogonia,* of the North Temperate Zone, having pink or whitish flowers. [New Latin *Pōgōnia,* genus name, from Greek *pōgōn,* beard.]

pog·o·nip (pŏg′ə-nĭp′) *n.* See **ice fog.** [Shoshone *pakenappeh.*]

po·go·noph·o·ran (pō′gə-nŏf′ər-ən) also **po·gon·o·phore** (pō-gŏn′ə-fôr′, -fōr′) *n.* Any of various wormlike marine invertebrates of the phylum Pogonophora that grow in upright chitin tubes, usually at depths greater than 100 meters (330 feet), have tentacles attached to the head region, and lack a digestive system. [From New Latin *Pōgōnophora,* phylum name : Greek *pōgōn,* beard + Greek *-phora,* neuter pl. of *-phoros,* -phore.] —**po′go·noph′o·ran, po′go·noph′o·rous** *adj.*

po·go stick (pō′gō) *n. Sports & Games.* A strong stick with footrests and a heavy spring set into the bottom end, used to propel oneself along the ground by hopping. [From *Pogo,* a former trademark.]

pogo stick

po·grom (pə-grŏm′, pō′grəm) *n.* An organized, often officially encouraged massacre or persecution of a minority group, especially one conducted against Jews. [Russian, outrage, havoc, from *pogromit',* to wreak havoc : *po-,* adverbial pref. (from *po,* next to; see **apo-** in Appendix) + *gromit',* to outrage, wreak havoc (from *grom,* thunder).] —**po·grom′** *v.*

po·gy (pō′gē) *n., pl.* **pogy** or **-gies.** See **menhaden.** [Alteration of dialectal *poghaden,* perhaps of Eastern Abenaki origin.]

Po Hai (bō′ hī′). See **Bo Hai.**

Po·hang (pō′hăng′). A city of southeast South Korea on an inlet of the Sea of Japan north-northeast of Pusan. It is a processing center with heavy industries. Population, 200,500.

poi (poi) *n.* A Hawaiian food made from taro corm that is cooked, pounded to a paste, and fermented. [Hawaiian.]

-poiesis *suff.* Production; creation; formation: *hematopoiesis.* [From Greek *poiēsis,* creation, from *poiein,* to make. See **kʷei-**[2] in Appendix.]

-poietic *suff.* Productive; formative: *galactopoietic.* [From Greek *poiētikos,* creative, from *poiētēs,* maker, from *poiein,* to make. See **kʷei-**[2] in Appendix.]

poign·ant (poin′yənt) *adj.* **1.a.** Physically painful: *"Keen, poignant agonies seemed to shoot from his neck downward"* (Ambrose Bierce). **b.** Keenly distressing to the mind or feelings: *poignant anxiety.* **c.** Profoundly moving; touching: *a poignant memory.* See Synonyms at **moving. 2.** Piercing; incisive: *poignant criticism.* **3.a.** Neat, skillful, and to the point: *poignant illustrations supplementing the text.* **b.** Astute and pertinent; relevant: *poignant suggestions.* **4.** Agreeably intense or stimulating: *poignant delight.* **5.** *Archaic.* **a.** Sharp or sour to the taste; piquant. **b.** Sharp or pungent to the smell. [Middle English *poinaunt,* from Old French *poignant,* present participle of *poindre,* to prick, from Latin *pungere.* See **peuk-** in Appendix.] —**poign′ance, poign′an·cy** *n.* —**poign′ant·ly** *adv.*

poi·kil·o·therm (poi-kĭl′ə-thûrm′) *n.* An organism, such as a fish or reptile, having a body temperature that varies with the temperature of its surroundings; an ectotherm. [Greek *poikilos,* spotted, various; see **peig-** in Appendix + -THERM.]

poi·ki·lo·ther·mic (poi′kə-lō-thûr′mĭk) also **poi·ki·lo·ther·mal** (-məl) also **poi·ki·lo·ther·mous** (-məs) *adj.* Of or relating to an organism having a body temperature that varies with the temperature of its surroundings; cold-blooded. —**poi′ki·lo·ther′mi·a, poi′ki·lo·ther′mism** *n.*

poi·lu (pwä-lü′) *n. Slang.* A French soldier, especially in World War I. [French, hairy, tough, poilu, from Old French *pelu,* hairy, from Vulgar Latin **pilūtus,* from Latin *pilus,* hair.]

Poin·ca·ré (pwăN-kä-rā′), **Jules Henri.** 1854–1912. French mathematician and physicist who made a number of contributions to the field of celestial mechanics.

Poincaré, Raymond. 1860–1934. French politician who served as president (1913–1920) and premier (1912–1913, 1922–1923, and 1926–1929).

poin·ci·an·a (poin′sē-ăn′ə, -ä′nə) *n.* See **royal poinciana.** [New Latin *Poinciana,* genus name, after M. De *Poinci,* 17th-century governor of French West Indies.]

Poin·sett (poin′sĕt′, -sĭt), **Joel Roberts.** 1779–1851. American diplomat who served as minister to Mexico (1825–1829) and U.S. secretary of war (1837–1841).

poin·set·ti·a (poin-sĕt′ē-ə, -sĕt′ə) *n.* A tropical American shrub *(Euphorbia pulcherrima)* that has showy, usually scarlet bracts beneath the small yellow flowerlike inflorescences. [New Latin, after Joel Roberts POINSETT.]

point (point) *n. Abbr.* **pt. 1.** A sharp or tapered end: *the point of a knife; the point of the antenna.* **2.** An object having a sharp or tapered end: *a stone projectile point.* **3.** A tapering extension of land projecting into water; a peninsula, cape, or promontory.

ă pat	oi boy
ā pay	ou out
âr care	o͝o took
ä father	o͞o boot
ĕ pet	ŭ cut
ē be	ûr urge
ĭ pit	th thin
ī pie	*th* this
îr pier	hw which
ŏ pot	zh vision
ō toe	ə about, item
ô paw	♦ regionalism

Stress marks: ′ (primary); ′ (secondary), as in **dictionary** (dĭk′shə-nĕr′ē)

pointer
Hunting dog

pointillism
Detail of
The Channel at Gravelines, Evening, 1890,
by Georges Seurat

4. A mark formed by or as if by a sharp end. **5.** A mark or dot used in printing or writing for punctuation, especially a period. **6.** A decimal point. **7.** *Linguistics.* A vowel point. **8.** One of the protruding marks used in certain methods of writing and printing for the sightless. **9.** *Mathematics.* A dimensionless geometric object having no properties except location. **10.a.** A place or locality considered with regard to its position: *connections to Chicago and points west.* **b.** A narrowly particularized and localized position or place; a spot: *The troops halted at a point roughly 1,000 yards from the river.* **11.** A specified degree, condition, or limit, as in a scale or course: *the melting point of a substance.* **12.a.** Any of the 32 equal divisions marked at the circumference of a mariner's compass card that indicate direction. **b.** The interval of 11°15′ between any two adjacent markings. **13.a.** A distinct condition or degree: *finally reached the point of exhaustion.* **b.** The interval of time immediately before a given occurrence; the verge: *on the point of resignation; at the point of death.* **14.** A specific moment in time: *At this point, we are ready to proceed.* **15.** An objective or a purpose to be reached or achieved, or one that is worth reaching or achieving: *What is the point of discussing this issue further?* **16.** The major idea or essential part of a concept or narrative: *You have missed the whole point of the novel.* **17.** A significant, outstanding, or effective idea, argument, or suggestion: *Your point is well taken.* **18.** A separate, distinguishing item or element; a detail: *Diplomacy is certainly not one of his strong points. Your weak point is your constant need for approval.* **19.** A quality or characteristic that is important or distinctive, especially a standard characteristic used to judge an animal. **20.** A single unit, as in counting, rating, or measuring. **21.a.** A unit of academic credit usually equal to one hour of class work per week during one semester. **b.** A numerical unit of academic achievement equal to a letter grade. **22.** *Sports & Games.* A unit of scoring or counting. **23.a.** A unit equal to one dollar, used to quote or state variations in the current prices of stocks or commodities. **b.** A unit equal to one percent, used to quote or state interest rates or shares in gross profits. **24.** One percent of the total principal of a loan, paid up front to the lender and considered separately from the interest. **25.** *Music.* A phrase, such as a fugue subject, in contrapuntal music. **26.** *Printing.* A unit of type size equal to 0.01384 inch, or approximately 1/72 of an inch. **27.** A jeweler's unit of weight equal to 2 milligrams or 0.01 carat. **28.a.** The act or an instance of pointing. **b.** The stiff and attentive stance taken by a hunting dog. **29.a.** Needlepoint. **b.** See **bobbin lace. 30.a.** A reconnaissance or patrol unit that moves ahead of an advance party or guard, or that follows a rear guard. **b.** The position occupied by such a unit or guard: *A team of Rangers were walking point at the outset of the operation.* **31.a.** An electrical contact, especially one in the distributor of an automobile engine. **b.** *Chiefly British.* An electrical socket or outlet. **32. points.** The extremities of an animal, such as a horse or dog. **33.a.** A movable rail, tapered at the end, such as that used in a railroad switch. **b.** The vertex of the angle created by the intersection of rails in a frog or switch. **34.** A ribbon or cord with a metal tag at the end, used to fasten clothing in the 16th and 17th centuries. **—point** *v.* **point·ed, point·ing, points.** —*tr.* **1.** To direct or aim: *point a weapon.* See Synonyms at **aim. 2.** To bring (something) to notice: *pointed out an error in their reasoning.* **3.** To indicate the position or direction of: *pointed out the oldest buildings on the skyline.* **4.** To sharpen (a pencil, for example); provide with a point. **5.** To separate with decimal points: *pointing off the hundredths place in a column of figures.* **6.** To mark (text) with points; punctuate. **7.** *Linguistics.* To mark (a consonant) with a vowel point. **8.** To give emphasis to; stress: *comments that simply point up flawed reasoning.* **9.** To indicate the presence and position of (game) by standing immobile and directing the muzzle toward it. Used of a hunting dog. **10.** To fill and finish the joints of (masonry) with cement or mortar. —*intr.* **1.** To direct attention or indicate position with or as if with the finger. **2.** To turn the mind or thought in a particular direction or to a particular conclusion: *All indications point to an early spring.* **3.** To be turned or faced in a given direction; aim. **4.** To indicate the presence and position of game. Used of a hunting dog. **5.** *Nautical.* To sail close to the wind. ***—idioms.* beside the point.** Irrelevant to the matter at hand. **in point.** Having relevance or pertinence. **in point of.** With reference to; in the matter of: *In point of fact, I never lived at the address stated on the form.* **make a point of.** To consider or treat (an action or activity) as indispensable: *made a point of visiting their niece on the way home.* **stretch a point.** To make an exception. **to the point.** Concerning or with relevance to the matter at hand: *remarks that were to the point; rambled and would not speak to the point.* [Middle English, partly from Old French *point,* prick, mark, moment (from Vulgar Latin **punctum,* from Latin *pūnctum,* from neuter past participle of *pungere,* to prick) and partly from Old French *pointe,* sharp end (from Vulgar Latin **puncta,* from Latin *pūncta,* feminine past participle of *pungere,* to prick; see **peuk-** in Appendix).]

point-and-shoot (point′ən-sho͞ot′) *adj.* Of, relating to, or being a camera that adjusts settings such as focus and exposure automatically.

point-blank (point′blăngk′) *adj.* **1.** Aimed straight at the mark or target without allowing for the drop in a projectile's course. **2.a.** So close to a target that a weapon may be aimed directly at it: *point-blank range.* **b.** Close enough so that missing the target is unlikely or impossible: *a point-blank shot.* **3.** Straightforward; blunt: *a point-blank accusation.* **—point-blank** *adv.* **1.** With a straight aim; directly: *fired point-blank at the intruder.* **2.** Without hesitation, deliberation, or equivocation: *answered point-blank.* [Perhaps from French *point (de tir),* (firing) point, or *point (visé),* (aiming) point (from Old French; see POINT) + French *blanc,* bullseye, target (from Old French, white; see BLANK).]

point defect *n.* A departure from symmetry in the alignment of atoms in a crystal that affects only one or two lattice sites.

point-de·vice (point′dĭ-vīs′) *adj.* Scrupulously correct or neat; precise or meticulous. [Middle English *at point devis,* probably from Old French **a point devis* : *a,* to + *point,* point, moment + *devis,* fixed, arranged.] **—point′-de·vice′** *adv.*

pointe (pwănt) *n.* In ballet, dancing that is performed on the tips of the toes. [From French *pointe (des pieds),* point (of the feet), tiptoe. See POINT.]

Pointe aux Trem·bles (pwănt ō trän′blə). A city of southern Quebec, Canada, a residential suburb of Montreal on northeast Montreal Island. Population, 36,270.

Pointe Claire (point′ klâr′, pwănt). A city of southern Quebec, Canada, a suburb of Montreal on southwest Montreal Island. It is mainly residential. Population, 24,571.

point·ed (poin′tĭd) *adj.* **1.** Having an end coming to a point: *a pointed stick.* **2.** Sharp; cutting: *a pointed critique.* **3.** Obviously directed at or making reference to a particular person or thing: *a pointed comment.* **4.** Clearly evident or conspicuous; marked: *a pointed lack of interest.* **5.** Characterized by the use of a pointed crown, as in Gothic architecture: *a pointed arch.* **—point′ed·ly** *adv.* **—point′ed·ness** *n.*

point·er (poin′tər) *n.* **1.** One that directs, indicates, or points. **2.** A scale indicator on a watch, balance, or other measuring instrument. **3.** A long, tapered stick for indicating objects, as on a chart or blackboard. **4.** Any of a breed of hunting dogs that points game, typically having a smooth, short-haired coat that is usually white with black or brownish spots. **5.a.** A piece of advice; a suggestion. **b.** A piece of indicative information: *interest rates and other pointers in the economic forecast.* **6.** *Computer Science.* A word that gives the address of a core storage location. **7.** Either of the two stars in the Big Dipper that are aligned so as to point to Polaris.

poin·til·lism (pwăn′tē-ĭz′əm, point′l-ĭz′-) *n.* A postimpressionist school of painting exemplified by Georges Seurat and his followers in late 19th-century France, characterized by the application of paint in small dots and brush strokes. [French *pointillisme,* from *pointiller,* to paint small dots, stipple, from Old French **pointille,* engraved with small dots, from *point,* point, from Latin *pūnctum,* from neuter past participle of *pungere,* to prick. See **peuk-** in Appendix.] **—poin′til·list** *adj. & n.*

poin·til·lis·tic (pwăn′tē-ĭs′tĭk, point′l-ĭs′-) *adj.* **1.** Of or relating to pointillism. **2.** Minutely particularized: *a pointillistic short story; pointillistic piano music.*

point lace *n.* See **needlepoint** (sense 2).

point·less (point′lĭs) *adj.* **1.** Lacking meaning; senseless. See Synonyms at **meaningless. 2.** Ineffectual: *pointless attempts to rescue the victims of the raging fire.* **—point′less·ly** *adv.* **—point′less·ness** *n.*

point man *n.* **1.** A soldier who is assigned to a position some distance ahead of a patrol as a lookout. **2.** A man who has a crucial, often hazardous role in the forefront of an enterprise: "[He] *has traditionally been the administration's point man on affirmative-action issues, making frequent public appearances to present and clarify the administration's views*" (Christian Science Monitor).

point mutation *n.* A mutation that affects only one or a few nucleotides in a gene.

point of accumulation *n. Mathematics.* See **limit** (sense 6).

point of honor *n., pl.* **points of honor.** A matter that affects one's honor or reputation.

point of no return *n.* **1.** The point in a course of action beyond which reversal is not possible. **2.** The point in the flight of an aircraft beyond which there is insufficient fuel for return to the starting point.

point of order *n., pl.* **points of order.** A question as to whether the present proceedings are in order or allowed by the rules of parliamentary procedure.

point-of-sale (point′əv-sāl′) *adj. Abbr.* **POS** Of, relating to, or being the physical place where an item or service is purchased: *a point-of-sale questionnaire.*

point of view *n., pl.* **points of view. 1.** A manner of viewing things; an attitude. **2.a.** A position from which something is observed or considered; a standpoint. **b.** The attitude or outlook of a narrator or character in a piece of literature, a movie, or another art form.

Point Pleas·ant (point plĕz′ənt). A borough of eastern New Jersey near the Atlantic Ocean south of Asbury Park. It is a residential and resort community. Population, 17,747.

point source *n.* A source, especially of pollution or radiation, occupying a very small area and having a concentrated output.

Point Suc·cess (sək-sĕs′). A peak, 4,318.2 m (14,158 ft) high, in the Cascade Range of west-central Washington near Mount Rainier.

point system *n.* **1.** A system of evaluating academic achievement based on grade points. **2.** Any of various systems of printing or writing for sightless people, as Braille, that uses an alphabet of raised symbols or dots that correspond to letters. **3.**

ă **pat**	oi **boy**
ā **pay**	ou **out**
âr **care**	o͝o **took**
ä **father**	o͞o **boot**
ĕ **pet**	ŭ **cut**
ē **be**	ûr **urge**
ĭ **pit**	th **thin**
ī **pie**	*th* **this**
îr **pier**	hw **which**
ŏ **pot**	zh **vision**
ō **toe**	ə **about, item**
ô **paw**	♦ **regionalism**

Stress marks: **′** (primary); ′ (secondary), as in **dictionary** (dĭk′shə-nĕr′ē)

Printing. A system of graduating sizes of type in multiples of the point. **4.** A system of penalizing drivers of motor vehicles for traffic violations by assigning points for each type of violation and revoking the driver's license if a certain number of points are accrued.

point woman *n.* A woman who has a crucial, often hazardous role in the forefront of an enterprise: *"They are the point men and women in the industry's drive to sell wine"* (New York Times).

point•y (poinʹtē) *adj.* **-i•er, -i•est.** Having an end tapering to a point.

point•y-head (poinʹtē-hĕdʹ) *n. Slang.* An intellectual. **—pointʹy-headʹed** *adj.*

poise¹ (poiz) *v.* **poised, pois•ing, pois•es.** *—tr.* To carry or hold in equilibrium; balance. *—intr.* To be balanced or held in suspension; hover. **—poise** *n.* **1.** A state of balance or equilibrium; stability. See Synonyms at **balance. 2.** Freedom from affectation or embarrassment; composure. **3.** The bearing or deportment of the head or body; mien. **4.** A state or condition of hovering or being suspended. [Middle English *poisen,* to balance, weigh, from Old French *peser, pois-,* from Vulgar Latin **pēsāre,* from Latin *pēnsāre.* See **(s)pen-** in Appendix.]

poise² (poiz) *n.* A centimeter-gram-second unit of dynamic viscosity equal to one dyne-second per square centimeter. [French, after Jean Louis Marie *Poiseuille* (1799–1869), French physician and physiologist.]

poi•son (poiʹzən) *n.* **1.** A substance that causes injury, illness, or death, especially by chemical means. **2.** Something destructive or fatal. **3.** *Chemistry & Physics.* A substance that inhibits another substance or a reaction: *a catalyst poison.* **—poison** *tr.v.* **-soned, -son•ing, -sons. 1.** To kill or harm with poison. **2.** To put poison on or into: *poisoning arrows; poisoned the drink.* **3. a.** To pollute: *Noxious fumes poison the air.* See Synonyms at **contaminate. b.** To have a harmful influence on; corrupt: *Jealousy poisoned their friendship.* **4.** *Chemistry & Physics.* To inhibit (a substance or reaction). **—poison** *adj.* Poisonous. [Middle English, from Old French, from Latin *pōtiō, pōtiōn-,* drink. See **pō(i)-** in Appendix.] **—poiʹson•er** *n.*

WORD HISTORY: The phrase *poison potion* besides being alliterative also consists of doublets, that is, two words that go back ultimately to the same source in another language. The source for both words is Latin *pōtiō,* which meant "the act of drinking, a drink, or a liquid dose, as of a medicine or poison." Our word *potion* retains the form of the Latin word (actually the form of the stem *pōtiōn–*) and the "dose" sense, although it passed through Old French (*pocion*) on its way to Middle English (*pocion*), first recorded in a work composed around 1300. In Old French *pocion* is a learned borrowing, one that was deliberately taken from Latin in a form corresponding to the Latin form. But the Latin word had also passed through Vulgar Latin into Old French in the different form *poison.* This word meant "beverage," "liquid dose," and also "poison beverage, poison." The word *poison* is first recorded in Middle English in a work composed around 1200.

poison elder *n.* See **poison sumac.**

poison gas *n.* A gas or vapor used especially in chemical warfare to injure, disable, or kill upon inhalation or contact.

poison hemlock *n.* A deadly poisonous European plant *(Conium maculatum)* widely naturalized in North America, having bipinnately compound leaves and compound umbels of small, white flowers.

poison ivy *n.* A North American shrub or vine *(Rhus radicans)* that has compound leaves with three leaflets, small green flowers, and whitish berries and that causes a rash on contact. Also called *poison oak.*

poison oak *n.* **1.** Either of two shrubs, *Rhus toxicodendron* of the southeast United States or *R. diversiloba* of western North America, related to poison ivy and causing a rash on contact. **2.** See **poison ivy.**

poi•son•ous (poiʹzə-nəs) *adj.* **1.** Having the capability of harming or killing by or as if by poison; toxic or venomous. **2.** Containing a poison. **3.** Marked by apparent ill will: *"poisonous hate . . . in his eyes"* (Ernest Hemingway). **—poiʹson•ous•ly** *adv.* **—poiʹson•ous•ness** *n.*

SYNONYMS: *poisonous, mephitic, pestilent, pestilential, toxic, venomous, virulent.* The central meaning shared by these adjectives is "having the destructive or fatal effect of a poison": *a poisonous snake; a mephitic vapor; a pestilent agitator; pestilential jungle mists; toxic fumes; venomous jealousy; a virulent form of cancer.*

poi•son-pen letter (poiʹzən-pĕnʹ) *n.* A usually anonymous letter or note containing abusive or malicious statements or accusations about the recipient or a third party.

poison pill *n. Informal.* A plan or tactic intended to make a hostile corporate takeover prohibitively expensive, as one in which a company's stockholders are offered shares of stock at a bargain price in the event that a single suitor acquires a high percentage of the stock.

poison sumac *n.* A swamp shrub *(Rhus vernix)* of the southeast United States, having compound leaves and greenish-white berries and causing an itching rash on contact with the skin. Also called *poison elder.*

poi•son•wood (poiʹzən-wo͝odʹ) *n.* A poisonous dioecious tree *(Metopium toxiferum)* of southern Florida and the West Indies, having pinnately compound leaves, yellow-green flowers clustered in axillary panicles, and yellow-orange drupes. It causes a rash on contact.

Pois•son distribution (pwä-sôɴʹ) *n.* A probability distribution that can be applied to distributions that are not continuous. [After Siméon Denis *Poisson* (1781–1840), French mathematician.]

Poi•tier (pwäʹtyā), **Sidney.** Born 1927. American actor and director whose film credits include *The Defiant Ones* (1958) and *Lilies of the Field* (1963).

Poi•tiers (pwä-tyāʹ). A city of west-central France east-southeast of Nantes. Settled by a Gallic people, it was an early Christian center with important monasteries. Nearby, Edward the Black Prince defeated and captured John II of France on September 19, 1356. Population, 79,350.

Poi•tou (pwä-to͞oʹ). A historical region of west-central France bordering on the Bay of Biscay. A part of the Roman province of Aquitania, it fell to the Visigoths (A.D. 418) and the Franks (507) and was frequently contested by France and England until the end of the Hundred Years' War, when it was incorporated into the French crown lands.

poke¹ (pōk) *v.* **poked, pok•ing, pokes.** *—tr.* **1.** To push or jab at, as with a finger or an arm; prod. **2.** To make (a hole or pathway, for example) by or as if by prodding, elbowing, or jabbing: *I poked my way to the front of the crowd.* **3.** To push; thrust: *A seal poked its head out of the water.* **4.** To stir (a fire) by prodding the wood or coal with a poker or stick. **5.** *Slang.* To strike; punch. *—intr.* **1.** To make thrusts or jabs, as with a stick or poker. **2.** To pry or meddle; intrude: *poking into another's business.* **3.** To search or look curiously in a desultory manner: *poked about in the desk.* **4.** To proceed in a slow or lazy manner; putter: *just poked along all morning.* **5.** To thrust forward; appear: *The child's head poked from under the blankets.* **—poke** *n.* **1.** A push, thrust, or jab. **2.** *Slang.* A punch or blow with the fist: *a poke in the jaw.* **3.** One who moves slowly or aimlessly; a dawdler. ***—idiom.* poke fun at.** To ridicule in a mischievous manner; tease. [Middle English *poken,* probably from Middle Low German or Middle Dutch.]

poke² (pōk) *n.* **1.** A projecting brim at the front of a bonnet. **2.** A large bonnet having a projecting brim. [From POKE¹.]

♦**poke³** (pōk) *n. Chiefly Southern U.S.* A sack; a bag. [Middle English, probably from Old North French. See POCKET.]

♦***REGIONAL NOTE:*** A *pig in a poke* is concealed in a sack from the buyer. The noun *poke*—meaning a bag or sack—dates from the 14th century in English. In many parts of Scotland *poke* means a little paper bag for carrying purchases or a cone-shaped piece of paper for an ice-cream cone. The *Oxford English Dictionary* gives similar forms in other languages: Icelandic *poki,* Gaelic *poc* or *poca,* and French *poche. Pouch* and *pocket* are undoubtedly cognates.

poke⁴ (pōk) *n.* Pokeweed. [Short for dialectal *pocan,* of Virginia Algonquian origin; akin to *puccoon.*]

poke•ber•ry (pōkʹbĕrʹē) *n.* **1.** The blackish-red berry of the pokeweed. **2.** See **pokeweed.**

pok•er¹ (pōʹkər) *n.* One that pokes, especially a metal rod used to stir a fire.

pok•er² (pōʹkər) *n. Games.* Any of various card games played by two or more players who bet on the value of their hands. [Origin unknown.]

poker face *n.* A face lacking any interpretable expression, as that of an expert poker player. **—pokʹer•facedʹ** (pōʹkər-fāstʹ) *adj.*

poke•root (pōkʹro͞otʹ, -ro͝otʹ) *n.* See **pokeweed.**

♦**poke sal•lit** (sălʹĭt) *n. Chiefly Southern U.S.* Greens of the wild pokeweed eaten boiled. [Variant of *poke salad.*]

poke•weed (pōkʹwēdʹ) *n.* A tall North American plant *(Phytolacca americana)* having small white flowers, blackish-red berries clustered on long, drooping racemes, and a poisonous root. Also called *pokeberry, pokeroot.* [POKE⁴ + WEED¹.]

po•key¹ also **po•ky** (pōʹkē) *n., pl.* **-keys** also **-kies.** *Slang.* A jail or prison. [Origin unknown.]

poke•y² (pōʹkē) *adj. Informal.* Variant of **poky¹.**

pok•y¹ also **poke•y** (pōʹkē) *adj.* **pok•i•er, pok•i•est.** *Informal.* **1.** Dawdling; slow: *a lazy, poky person.* **2.** Frumpish; shabby: *poky old clothes.* **3.** Small and cramped: *a poky apartment.* [From POKE¹.] **—pokʹi•ly** *adv.* **—pokʹi•ness** *n.*

po•ky² (pōʹkē) *n. Slang.* Variant of **pokey¹.**

pol (pŏl) *n. Informal.* A politician.

pol. *abbr.* Political; politics.

Pol. *abbr.* Poland; Polish.

Po•lack (pōʹlŏkʹ, -lăkʹ) *n.* **1.** *Offensive Slang.* Used as a disparaging term for a person of Polish birth or descent. **2.** *Obsolete.* A native of Poland; a Pole. [Polish *Polak,* from Slavic *polje,* field. See **pelə-²** in Appendix.]

Po•land (pōʹlənd). *Abbr.* **Pol.** A country of central Europe bordering on the Baltic Sea. Unified as a kingdom in the 10th century, it was a major power in the 15th and 16th centuries but was carved up among other states in three partitions (1772, 1793, and 1795) and then disappeared as a geographic entity until its recon-

poison ivy
Rhus radicans

Sidney Poitier
Photographed in the late 1980's

Poland

Poland China
Sow

polar bear
Ursus maritimus

pole vault

stitution as a republic in 1918. Its present boundaries date from the end of World War II. Warsaw is the capital and the largest city. Population, 37,063,000.

Poland China *n.* Any of a breed of large black-and-white hogs developed in North America.

po·lar (pō′lər) *adj.* **1.a.** Of or relating to a pole. **b.** Measured from or referred to a pole: *polar distance; polar diameter.* **2.** Relating to, connected with, or located near the North Pole or South Pole. **3.a.** Passing over a planet's north and south poles: *a polar orbit.* **b.** Traveling in an orbit that passes over a planet's north and south poles. **4.** Serving as a guide, as a polestar or a pole of the earth. **5.** Occupying or characterized by opposite extremes: *"In creative territory* [they] *make a strange yet ineluctable couple, more complementary, even polar, than twin-like"* (Josh Rubins). **6.** Central or pivotal. **7.** *Chemistry.* Having to do with or characterized by a dipole: *a polar molecule.*

polar angle *n. Mathematics.* The angle formed by the polar axis and the radius vector in a polar coordinate system.

polar axis *n. Mathematics.* The fixed reference axis from which the polar angle is measured in a polar coordinate system.

polar bear *n.* A large, white-furred bear *(Ursus maritimus* or *Thalarctos maritimus)* living in Arctic regions. Also called *white bear.*

polar body *n.* A minute cell produced and ultimately discarded in the development of an oocyte, containing little or no cytoplasm but having one of the nuclei derived from the first or second meiotic division.

polar cap *n.* **1.a.** Either of the regions around the poles of the earth that are permanently covered with ice. **b.** A high-altitude icecap. **2.** *Astronomy.* Either of the regions around the poles of Mars that are covered with frozen carbon dioxide and water.

polar circle *n.* **1.** The Arctic Circle. **2.** The Antarctic Circle.

polar coordinate *n. Mathematics.* Either of two coordinates, the radius vector or the polar angle, that together specify the position of a point in a plane.

po·lar·im·e·ter (pō′lə-rĭm′ĭ-tər) *n.* An instrument used to measure the rotation of the plane of polarization of polarized light passing through an optical structure or sample. **—po′lar·i·met′ric** (-lər-ə-mĕt′rĭk) *adj.* **—po′lar·im′e·try** *n.*

Po·lar·is (pə-lăr′ĭs) *n.* A star of the second magnitude, at the end of the handle of the Little Dipper and almost at the north celestial pole. Also called *North Star, polar star, polestar.* [New Latin *(Stella) Polāris,* polar (star), from Latin *polus,* pole. See POLE[1].]

po·lar·i·scope (pō-lăr′ĭ-skōp′) *n.* An instrument for ascertaining, measuring, or exhibiting the properties of polarized light or for studying the interactions of polarized light with optically transparent media.

po·lar·i·ty (pō-lăr′ĭ-tē, pə-) *n., pl.* **-ties. 1.** Intrinsic polar separation, alignment, or orientation, especially of a physical property: *magnetic polarity; ionic polarity.* **2.** An indicated polar extreme: *an electric terminal with positive polarity.* **3.** The possession or manifestation of two opposing attributes, tendencies, or principles: *political polarity.*

po·lar·i·za·tion (pō′lər-ĭ-zā′shən) *n.* **1.** The production or condition of polarity, as: **a.** A process or state in which rays of light exhibit different properties in different directions, especially the state in which all the vibration takes place in one plane. **b.** *Chemistry & Physics.* The partial or complete polar separation of positive and negative electric charge in a nuclear, atomic, molecular, or chemical system. **2.** A concentration, as of groups, forces, or interests, about two conflicting or contrasting positions.

po·lar·ize (pō′lə-rīz′) *v.* **-ized, -iz·ing, -iz·es.** *—tr.* **1.** To induce polarization in; impart polarity to. **2.** To cause to concentrate about two conflicting or contrasting positions. *—intr.* **1.** To acquire polarity. **2.** To cause polarization of light. **—po′lar·iz′a·ble** *adj.* **—po′lar·iz′er** *n.*

po·lar·iz·ing microscope (pō′lə-rī′zĭng) *n.* A microscope in which the object viewed is illuminated by polarized light.

polar nucleus *n. Botany.* Either of two nuclei located centrally in a flowering plant embryo sac that eventually fuse to form the endosperm nucleus.

po·lar·og·ra·phy (pō′lə-rŏg′rə-fē) *n. Chemistry.* An electrochemical method of quantitative or qualitative analysis based on the relationship between an increasing current passing through the solution being analyzed and the increasing voltage used to produce the current. [POLAR(IZATION) + -GRAPHY.] **—po·lar′o·graph′ic** (-lăr′ə-grăf′ĭk) *adj.* **—po·lar′o·graph′i·cal·ly** *adv.*

Po·lar·oid (pō′lə-roid′). **1.** A trademark used for a specially treated, transparent plastic capable of polarizing light passing through it, used in glare-reducing optical devices. **2.** A trademark used for a camera and film that produce instant photographs.

Po·lar Regions (pō′lər). The various lands and waters surrounding the North Pole and the South Pole, known respectively as the **North Polar Region** and the **South Polar Region.**

polar star *n.* See **Polaris.**

pol·der (pōl′dər) *n.* An area of low-lying land. especially in the Netherlands, that has been reclaimed from a body of water and is protected by dikes. [Dutch, from Middle Dutch.]

pole[1] (pōl) *n. Abbr.* **p. 1.** Either extremity of an axis through a sphere. **2.** *Geography.* Either of the regions contiguous to the extremities of the earth's rotational axis, the North Pole or the South Pole. **3.** *Physics.* A magnetic pole. **4.** Either of two oppositely charged terminals, as in an electric cell or battery. **5.** *Astronomy.* A celestial pole. **6.** *Biology.* **a.** Either extremity of the main axis of a nucleus, a cell, or an organism. **b.** Either end of the spindle formed in a cell during mitosis. **c.** The point on a nerve cell where a process originates. **7.** Either of two antithetical ideas, propensities, forces, or positions: *"the moral poles of modern medicine: on the one hand, a tinkering with procreation with at best ambiguous, at worst monstrous moral possibilities. On the other hand, scientific skill and cunning unambiguously in the service of hope"* (Charles Krauthammer). **8.** A fixed point of reference. **9.** *Mathematics.* The origin in a polar coordinate system; the vertex of a polar angle. [Middle English, from Old French, from Latin *polus,* from Greek *polos,* axis, sky. See **k^{w}el-**[1] in Appendix.]

pole[2] (pōl) *n.* **1.** A long, relatively slender, generally rounded piece of wood or other material. **2.** The long, tapering wooden shaft extending up from the front axle of a vehicle to the collars of the animals drawing it; a tongue. **3.a.** See **rod** (sense 6a). **b.** A unit of area equal to a square rod. **4.** *Nautical.* A small or light spar. **5.** *Sports.* The inside position on the starting line of a racetrack: *qualified in the time trials to start on the pole.* **—pole** *v.* **poled, pol·ing, poles.** *—tr.* **1.a.** *Nautical.* To propel with a pole: *boatmen poling barges up a placid river.* **b.** To propel (oneself) or make (one's way) by the use of ski poles: *"We ski through the glades on corn snow, then pole our way over a long one-hour runout to a road"* (Frederick Selby). **2.** To support (plants) with a pole. **3.** To strike, poke, or stir with a pole. *—intr.* **1.** *Nautical.* To propel a boat or raft with a pole. **2.** *Sports.* To use ski poles to maintain or gain speed. [Middle English, from Old English *pāl,* from Latin *pālus,* stake. See **pag-** in Appendix.]

Pole (pōl) *n.* **1.** A native or inhabitant of Poland. **2.** A person of Polish descent.

Pole, Reginald. 1500–1558. English prelate. The last Roman Catholic archbishop of Canterbury (1556), he was a leading figure in the Counter Reformation.

pole·ax or **pole·axe** (pōl′ăks′) *—n.* **1.** An ax having a hammer face opposite the blade, used to slaughter cattle. **2.** A battle-ax used in the Middle Ages consisting of a long shaft ending in an ax or a combination of an ax, a hammer, and a pick. *—tr.v.* **-axed, -ax·ing, -ax·es.** To strike or fell with or as if with a poleax: *"When a gang of doves circled above the flowing water and swooped in to feed, he poleaxed the leader with a clean head shot"* (William Hoffman). [Middle English, alteration (influenced by *pole,* long piece of wood) of *pollax* : *poll,* head; see POLL + *ax,* ax; see AX.]

pole bean *n.* Any of various cultivated climbing beans that grow on poles or supports.

pole·cat (pōl′kăt′) *n.* **1.a.** A chiefly nocturnal European carnivorous mammal *(Mustela putorius)* of the weasel family that ejects a malodorous fluid to mark its territory and ward off enemies. Also called *fitch.* **b.** Any of various related mammals of Asia, especially *Mustela eversmanni* of central Asia. **2.** See **skunk** (sense 1a). [Middle English *polcat* : possibly Old French *poll, poule,* fowl, hen; see PULLET + *cat,* cat; see CAT.]

pole horse *n.* A horse harnessed to the pole of a vehicle.

po·leis (pō′lās′) *n.* Plural of **polis.**

pole jump *n. Sports.* See **pole vault** (sense 1). **—pole′-jump′** (pōl′jŭmp′) *v.* **—pole′-jump′er** *n.*

pole lamp *n.* A lighting unit consisting of a usually spring-loaded pole extending from the ceiling to the floor and having attached lamp fixtures.

po·lem·ic (pə-lĕm′ĭk) *n.* **1.** A controversial argument, especially one refuting or attacking a specific opinion or doctrine. **2.** A person engaged in or inclined to controversy, argument, or refutation. **—polemic** also **po·lem·i·cal** (-ĭ-kəl) *adj.* Of or relating to a controversy, an argument, or a refutation. [French *polémique,* from Greek *polemikos,* hostile, from *polemos,* war.] **—po·lem′i·cal·ly** *adv.*

po·lem·i·cist (pə-lĕm′ĭ-sĭst) also **po·lem·ist** (pə-lĕm′ĭst, pŏl′ə-mĭst) *n.* A person skilled or involved in polemics.

po·lem·i·cize (pə-lĕm′ĭ-sīz′) *intr.v.* **-cized, -ciz·ing, -ciz·es.** To write or deliver an argument; engage in disputation or controversy.

po·lem·ics (pə-lĕm′ĭks) *n. (used with a sing. or pl. verb).* **1.** The art or practice of argumentation or controversy. **2.** The practice of theological controversy to refute errors of doctrine.

po·lem·ist (pə-lĕm′ĭst, pŏl′ə-mĭst) *n.* Variant of **polemicist.**

po·len·ta (pō-lĕn′tə) *n.* A thick mush made of cornmeal boiled in water or stock. [Italian, from Latin, crushed grain, barley meal.]

pol·er (pō′lər) *n.* **1.** One that propels, supports, conveys, or strikes with a pole. **2.** A pole horse.

pole·star (pōl′stär′) *n.* **1.** See **Polaris. 2.** A guiding principle.

pole vault *n. Sports.* **1.** A field event in which the contestant jumps or vaults over a high crossbar with the aid of a long pole. Also called *pole jump.* **2.** A vault made with the aid of a long pole. **—pole′-vault′** (pōl′vôlt′) *v.* **—pole′-vault′er** *n.*

po·lice (pə-lēs′) *n., pl.* **police. 1.** The governmental department charged with the regulation and control of the affairs of a community, now chiefly the department established to maintain order, enforce the law, and prevent and detect crime. **2.a.** A body of persons making up such a department, trained in methods of law enforcement and crime prevention and detection and given the authority to maintain the peace, safety, and order of the community. **b.** A body of persons having similar organization and function: *campus police.* Also called *police force.* **3.** *(used with a pl. verb).* Police officers considered as a group. **4.** Regulation and control of the affairs of a community, especially with respect to maintenance of order, law, health, morals, safety, and other matters affecting the public welfare. **5.a.** The cleaning of a military base or other military area: *Police of the barracks must be completed before inspection can take place.* **b.** The soldier or soldiers assigned to a specified maintenance duty. *—attributive.* Often used to modify another noun: *police uniforms; the police department.* **—police** *tr.v.* **-liced, -lic·ing, -lic·es. 1.** To regulate, control, or keep in order with or as if with a law enforcement agency. **2.** To make (a military area, for example) neat in appearance: *policed the barracks; policing up one's room.* [French, from Old French *policie,* civil organization, from Late Latin *polītīa,* from Latin, the State, from Greek *politeia,* from *politēs,* citizen, from *polis,* city. See **pelə-**[3] in Appendix.] **—po·lice′a·ble** *adj.* **—po·lic′er** *n.*

police action *n.* A localized military action undertaken without a formal declaration of war.

police court *n. Law.* An inferior court having the power to prosecute minor criminal offenses and to hold for trial persons charged with more serious offenses.

police dog *n.* **1.** A dog trained to aid the police, as in tracking criminals or detecting controlled substances. **2.** See **German shepherd.**

police force *n.* See **police** (sense 2).

po·lice·man (pə-lēs′mən) *n.* A man who is a member of a police force.

police officer *n.* A policeman or policewoman.

police power *n.* The inherent authority of a government to impose restrictions on private rights for the sake of public welfare, order, and security.

police procedural *n.* A story or drama about the investigation of a crime by the police.

police reporter *n.* A newspaper reporter whose assignment is to obtain and cover news in a local police department.

police state *n.* A state in which the government exercises rigid and repressive controls over the social, economic, and political life of the people, especially by means of a secret police force.

police station *n.* The headquarters of a unit of a police force, where those under arrest are first charged.

po·lice·wom·an (pə-lēs′wo͝om′ən) *n.* A woman who is a member of a police force.

pol·i·clin·ic (pŏl′ē-klĭn′ĭk) *n.* The department of a hospital or health care facility that treats outpatients. [German *Poliklinik* : Greek *polis,* city; see **pelə-**[3] in Appendix + *Klinik,* clinic (from Greek *klinikos,* of a bed; see CLINIC).]

pol·i·cy[1] (pŏl′ĭ-sē) *n., pl.* **-cies. 1.** A plan or course of action, as of a government, political party, or business, intended to influence and determine decisions, actions, and other matters: *American foreign policy; the company's personnel policy.* **2.a.** A course of action, guiding principle, or procedure considered expedient, prudent, or advantageous: *Honesty is the best policy.* **b.** Prudence, shrewdness, or sagacity in practical matters. *—attributive.* Often used to modify another noun: *policy statements; policy issues.* [Middle English *policie,* art of government, civil organization, from Old French. See POLICE.]

pol·i·cy[2] (pŏl′ĭ-sē) *n., pl.* **-cies. 1.** A written contract or certificate of insurance. **2.** A numbers game. [Obsolete *police,* from French, contract, bill of lading, from Old French, from Old Italian *polizza,* alteration of Medieval Latin *apodixa,* receipt, from Medieval Greek *apodeixis,* from Greek, proof, from *apodeiknunai,* to prove : *apo-,* intensive pref.; see APO– + *deiknunai,* to show; see **deik-** in Appendix.]

pol·i·cy·hol·der (pŏl′ĭ-sē-hōl′dər) *n.* One that holds an insurance contract or policy.

pol·i·cy·mak·ing or **pol·i·cy-mak·ing** (pŏl′ĭ-sē-mā′kĭng) *—n.* High-level development of policy, especially official government policy. *—adj.* Of, relating to, or involving the making of high-level policy: *policymaking committees; policymaking decisions.* **—pol′i·cy·mak′er** *n.*

po·li·o (pō′lē-ō′) *n.* Poliomyelitis.

po·li·o·my·e·li·tis (pō′lē-ō-mī′ə-lī′tĭs) *n.* A highly infectious viral disease that chiefly affects children and, in its acute forms, causes inflammation of motor neurons of the spinal cord and brainstem, leading to paralysis, muscular atrophy, and often deformity. Through vaccination, the disease is preventable. Also called *infantile paralysis.* [New Latin : Greek *polios,* gray; see **pel-**[1] in Appendix + MYELITIS.] **—po′li·o·my′e·lit′ic** (-lĭt′ĭk) *adj.*

po·li·o·vi·rus (pō′lē-ō-vī′rəs) *n., pl.* **-rus·es.** An enterovirus, separable into three serotypes, that is the causative agent of poliomyelitis.

po·lis (pō′lĭs) *n., pl.* **-leis** (-lās′). A city-state of ancient Greece. [Greek. See **pelə-**[3] in Appendix.]

pol·ish (pŏl′ĭsh) *v.* **-ished, -ish·ing, -ish·es.** *—tr.* **1.** To make smooth and shiny by rubbing or chemical action: *polished the silver and the brass.* **2.** To remove the outer layers from (grains of rice) by rotation in drums. **3.** To free from coarseness; refine: *Four years of prep school should polish those children.* **4.** To remove flaws from; perfect or complete: *polishing one's piano technique; polished up the lyrics.* *—intr.* **1.** To become smooth or shiny by or as if by being rubbed: *The surface on our dining table polishes easily.* **2.** To become perfect or refined. **—polish** *n.* **1.** Smoothness or shininess of surface or finish: *satin with a polish.* **2.** A substance containing chemical agents or abrasive particles and applied to smooth or shine a surface. **3.** The act or process of polishing. **4.** Elegance of style or manner. See Synonyms at **elegance.** ***—phrasal verb.*** **polish off.** *Informal.* To finish or dispose of quickly and easily. [Middle English *polisshen,* from Old French *polir, poliss-,* from Latin *polīre.* See **pel-**[5] in Appendix.] **—pol′ish·er** *n.*

Po·lish (pō′lĭsh) *adj. Abbr.* **Pol.** Of or relating to Poland or its people, their language, or culture. **—Polish** *n.* The Slavic language of the Poles.

Polish Corridor. A former strip of land between the German territories of Pomerania and East Prussia awarded to Poland by the Treaty of Versailles (1919) to afford access to the Baltic Sea. Friction over control of the area was an immediate cause of the German invasion of Poland (September 1, 1939) that marked the beginning of World War II.

pol·ished (pŏl′ĭsht) *adj.* **1.a.** Made shiny and smooth by or as if by rubbing or chemical action. **b.** Naturally shiny and smooth. **2.** Having the husk or outer layers removed. Used of grains of rice. **3.** Refined; cultured: *a polished manner.* **4.** Having no imperfections or errors; flawless: *a polished oration.*

polit. *abbr.* Political; politics.

pol·it·bu·ro (pŏl′ĭt-byo͝or′ō, pə-lĭt′-) *n., pl.* **-ros.** The chief political and executive committee of a Communist party. [Russian, contraction of *Polit(icheskoe) Buro,* political bureau.]

po·lite (pə-līt′) *adj.* **-lit·er, -lit·est. 1.** Marked by or showing consideration for others, tact, and observance of accepted social usage. **2.** Refined; elegant: *polite society.* [Middle English *polit,* polished, from Latin *polītus,* past participle of *polīre,* to polish. See POLISH.] **—po·lite′ly** *adv.* **—po·lite′ness** *n.*

SYNONYMS: *polite, mannerly, civil, courteous, genteel.* All these adjectives mean mindful of, conforming to, or marked by good manners. *Polite* and *mannerly* imply consideration for others and the adherence to conventional social standards expected of a well-bred person: *"The English are busy; they don't have time to be polite"* (Montesquieu). *"It costs nothing to be polite"* (Winston S. Churchill). *The child was scolded by his grandmother for not being more mannerly. Civil* suggests only the barest observance of accepted social usages; it often means merely neither polite nor rude: *"'Always be civil to the girls, you never know who they may marry' is an aphorism which has saved many an English spinster from being treated like an Indian widow"* (Nancy Mitford). *Courteous* implies courtliness and dignity: *"If a man be gracious and courteous to strangers, it shows he is a citizen of the world"* (Francis Bacon). *Genteel,* which originally meant well-bred and refined, now usually suggests excessive and affected refinement: *"A man, indeed, is not genteel when he gets drunk; but most vices may be committed very genteelly"* (James Boswell).

pol·i·tesse (pŏl′ĭ-tĕs′, pô′lē-) *n.* Courteous formality; politeness: *"the soul of uptown refinement and . . . politesse"* (Russell Baker). [French, from Old French, cleanliness, from Italian *pulitezza, politezza,* from *pulire,* to polish, clean, from Latin *polīre.* See POLITE.]

Po·li·tian (pə-lĭsh′ən, pō-). 1454–1494. Italian scholar and poet who translated Homer's *Iliad* into Latin and wrote *Orfeo* (1475), the first play in Italian.

pol·i·tic (pŏl′ĭ-tĭk) *adj.* **1.** Using or marked by prudence, expedience, and shrewdness; artful. See Synonyms at **suave. 2.** Using, displaying, or proceeding from policy; judicious: *a politic decision.* **3.** Crafty; cunning. [Middle English *politik,* from Old French *politique,* from Latin *polīticus,* political, from Greek *politikos,* from *politēs,* citizen, from *polis,* city. See **pelə-**[3] in Appendix.] **—pol′i·tic·ly** *adv.*

po·lit·i·cal (pə-lĭt′ĭ-kəl) *adj. Abbr.* **pol., polit. 1.** Of, relating to, or dealing with the structure or affairs of government, politics, or the state. **2.** Relating to, involving, or characteristic of politics, parties, or politicians: *"Calling a meeting is a political act in itself"* (Daniel Goleman). **3.** Having or marked by a definite or organized policy or structure with regard to government: *the union's political machine; political pressure.* **4.** Relating to or involving acts regarded as damaging to a government or state: *political crimes.* **—po·lit′i·cal·i·za′tion** (-ĭzā′shən) *n.* **—po·lit′i·cal·ize′** (-kə-līz′) *v.* **—po·lit′i·cal·ly** *adv.*

political action committee *n.* A committee formed by business, labor, or other special-interest groups to raise money and make contributions to the campaigns of political candidates whom they support.

political economy *n.* **1.** The social science that deals with political science and economics as a unified subject; the study of the interrelationships between political and economic processes. **2.** The early science of economics through the 19th century.

political science *n.* The study of the processes, principles, and structure of government and of political institutions; politics.

political terrorism *n.* **1.** Violent acts, such as kidnappings, arson, bombings, or assassinations, undertaken for political rea-

ă pat	oi boy
ā pay	ou out
âr care	o͝o took
ä father	o͞o boot
ĕ pet	ŭ cut
ē be	ûr urge
ĭ pit	th thin
ī pie	*th* this
îr pier	hw which
ŏ pot	zh vision
ō toe	ə about, item
ô paw	♦ regionalism

Stress marks: ′ (primary); ′ (secondary), as in **dictionary** (dĭk′shə-nĕr′ē)

sons especially by a person, group, or state seeking the overthrow of a government. **2.** *Informal.* Intimidation or verbal abuse used by a politician to frighten another politician or other politicians. **—political terrorist** *n.*

pol·i·ti·cian (pŏl′ĭ-tĭsh′ən) *n.* **1.a.** One who is actively involved in politics, especially party politics. **b.** One who holds or seeks a political office. **2.** One who seeks personal or partisan gain, often by scheming and maneuvering: *"Mothers may still want their favorite sons to grow up to be President, but . . . they do not want them to become politicians in the process"* (John F. Kennedy). **3.** One who is skilled or experienced in the science or administration of government.

po·lit·i·cize (pə-lĭt′ĭ-sīz′) *v.* **-cized, -ciz·ing, -ciz·es.** *—intr.* To engage in or discuss politics. *—tr.* To make political: *"The mayor was given authority to appoint police commissioners and by virtue of that power was able to politicize the department"* (Connie Paige). **—po·lit′i·ci·za′tion** (-sĭ-zā′shən) *n.*

pol·i·tick (pŏl′ĭ-tĭk) *intr.v.* **-ticked, -tick·ing, -ticks.** To engage in or discuss politics. **—pol′i·tick′er** *n.*

po·lit·i·co (pə-lĭt′ĭ-kō′) *n., pl.* **-cos.** A politician. [From Italian or from Spanish *político,* both from Latin *polīticus,* political. See POLITIC.]

pol·i·tics (pŏl′ĭ-tĭks) *n. Abbr.* **pol., polit. 1.** *(used with a sing. verb).* **a.** The art or science of government or governing, especially the governing of a political entity, such as a nation, and the administration and control of its internal and external affairs. **b.** Political science. **2.** *(used with a sing. or pl. verb).* **a.** The activities or affairs engaged in by a government, politician, or political party: *"All politics is local"* (Thomas P. O'Neill, Jr.). *"Politics have appealed to me since I was at Oxford because they are exciting morning, noon, and night"* (Jeffrey Archer). **b.** The methods or tactics involved in managing a state or government: *The politics of the former regime were rejected by the new government leadership. If the politics of the conservative government now borders on the repressive, what can be expected when the economy falters?* **3.** *(used with a sing. or pl. verb).* Political life: *studied law with a view to going into politics; felt that politics was a worthwhile career.* **4.** *(used with a sing. or pl. verb).* Intrigue or maneuvering within a political unit or a group in order to gain control or power: *Partisan politics is often an obstruction to good government. Office politics are often debilitating and counterproductive.* **5.** *(used with a sing. or pl. verb).* Political attitudes and positions: *His politics on that issue is his own business. Your politics are clearly more liberal than mine.* **6.** *(used with a sing. or pl. verb).* The often internally conflicting interrelationships among people in a society.

USAGE NOTE: *Politics,* although etymologically plural, takes a singular verb when used to refer to the art or science of governing or to political science: *Politics has been a concern of philosophers since Plato.* But in its other senses *politics* can take either a singular or plural verb. Many other nouns that end in *–ics* behave similarly, and the user is advised to consult specific entries for precise information.

James K. Polk

pol·i·ty (pŏl′ĭ-tē) *n., pl.* **-ties. 1.** The form of government of a nation, a state, a church, or an organization. **2.** An organized society, such as a nation, having a specific form of government: *"His alien philosophy found no roots in the American polity"* (New York Times). [Obsolete French *politie,* from Old French, from Late Latin *polītīa,* the Roman government. See POLICE.]

Polk (pōk), **James Knox.** 1795–1849. The 11th President of the United States (1845–1849), whose term was marked by the establishment of the 49th parallel as the northern border (1846).

pol·ka (pōl′kə, pō′kə) *n.* **1.** A lively round dance originating in Bohemia and performed by couples. **2.** Music for this dance, having duple meter. *—intr.* **-kaed, -ka·ing, -kas.** To dance the polka. [Czech, probably from Polish, from *Polka,* Polish woman, feminine of *Polak,* Pole, from Slavic *polje,* field. See **pele-**[2] in Appendix.]

pol·ka dot (pō′kə) *n.* **1.** One of a number of dots or round spots forming a pattern, as on cloth. **2.** A pattern or fabric with such dots.

poll (pōl) *n.* **1.** The casting and registering of votes in an election. **2.** The number of votes cast or recorded. **3.** Often **polls.** The place where votes are cast and registered. Used with *the.* **4.** A survey of the public or of a sample of public opinion to acquire information. **5.** The head, especially the top of the head where hair grows. **6.** The blunt or broad end of a tool such as a hammer or an ax. **—poll** *v.* **polled, poll·ing, polls.** *—tr.* **1.** To receive (a given number of votes). **2.** To receive or record the votes of: *polling a jury.* **3.** To cast (a vote or ballot). **4.** To question in a survey; canvass. **5.** To cut off or trim (hair, horns, or wool, for example); clip. **6.** To trim or cut off the hair, wool, branches, or horns of: *polled the sheep; polled the trees.* *—intr.* To vote at the polls in an election. [Middle English *pol,* head, from Middle Low German or Middle Dutch.] **—poll′er** *n.*

pol·lack also **pol·lock** (pŏl′ək) *n.* A marine food fish *(Pollachius virens)* of northern Atlantic waters, related to the cod. [Alteration of Scots *podlok.*]

pol·lard (pŏl′ərd) *n.* **1.** A tree whose top branches have been cut back to the trunk so that it may produce a dense growth of new shoots. **2.** An animal, such as an ox, a goat, or a sheep, that no longer has its horns. **—pollard** *tr.v.* **-lard·ed, -lard·ing, -lards.** To convert or make into a pollard. [From POLL.]

polled (pōld) *adj.* Having no horns; hornless.

pol·len (pŏl′ən) *n.* The fine, powderlike material consisting of pollen grains that is produced by the anthers of seed plants. [Latin, fine flour.]

pol·len·ate (pŏl′ə-nāt′) *v.* Variant of **pollinate.**

pollen count *n.* The average number of pollen grains, usually of ragweed, in a cubic yard or other standard volume of air over a 24-hour period at a specified time and place.

pollen grain *n.* A microspore of seed plants, containing a male gametophyte.

pol·len·if·er·ous (pŏl′ə-nĭf′ər-əs) *adj.* Variant of **polliniferous.**

pollen mother cell *n.* The microspore mother cell of a seed plant.

pol·len·o·sis (pŏl′ə-nō′sĭs) *n.* Variant of **pollinosis.**

pollen sac *n.* The microsporangium of a seed plant in which pollen is produced.

pollen tube *n.* The slender tube formed by the pollen grain that penetrates an ovule and releases the male gametes.

pol·lex (pŏl′ĕks′) *n., pl.* **pol·li·ces** (pŏl′ĭ-sēz′). See **thumb** (sense 1). [Latin, thumb, big toe.]

pollin– *pref.* Variant of **pollini–.**

pol·li·nate also **pol·len·ate** (pŏl′ə-nāt′) *tr.v.* **-li·nat·ed, -li·nat·ing, -li·nates** also **-len·at·ed, -len·at·ing, -len·ates.** To transfer pollen from an anther to the stigma of (a flower). [New Latin *pollen, pollin-,* pollen (from Latin, fine flour) + –ATE[1].] **—pol′li·na′tion** *n.* **—pol′li·na′tor** *n.*

pollini– or **pollin–** *pref.* Pollen: *polliniferous.* [From New Latin *pollen, pollin-,* pollen. See POLLINATE.]

pol·lin·i·a (pŏ-lĭn′ē-ə) *n.* Plural of **pollinium.**

pol·li·nif·er·ous also **pol·len·if·er·ous** (pŏl′ə-nĭf′ər-əs) *adj.* **1.** Producing or yielding pollen. **2.** Adapted for carrying pollen.

pol·lin·i·um (pŏ-lĭn′ē-əm) *n., pl.* **-i·a** (-ē-ə). A mass of coherent pollen grains, found in the flowers of orchids and milkweeds. [New Latin, from *pollen, pollin-,* pollen. See POLLINATE.]

pol·li·nize (pŏl′ə-nīz′) *tr.v.* **-nized, -niz·ing, -niz·es.** To pollinate. **—pol′li·ni·za′tion** (-nĭ-zā′shən) *n.* **—pol′li·niz′er** *n.*

pol·li·no·sis also **pol·len·o·sis** (pŏl′ə-nō′sĭs) *n.* See **hay fever.**

pol·li·wog also **pol·ly·wog** (pŏl′ē-wŏg′, -wôg′) *n.* See **tadpole.** [Variant of *polliwig,* from Middle English *polwigle* : *pol,* head; see POLL + *wiglen,* to wiggle; see WIGGLE.]

pol·lock (pŏl′ək) *n.* Variant of **pollack.**

Pol·lock (pŏl′ək), **Jackson.** 1912–1956. American artist. Using his drip technique of painting, he became a leader of abstract expressionism in America.

poll·ster (pōl′stər) *n.* One that takes public-opinion surveys. Also called *polltaker.*

WORD HISTORY: An understanding of the history of the *–ster* in *pollster* may perhaps raise more questions than it answers. In the first place a *pollster* does not have to be a woman, despite the fact that the suffix *–ster,* originally *–estre* in Old English, was used to form feminine agent nouns. *Hoppestere,* for example, meant "female dancer." But in Old English *–estre* was occasionally applied to men, although perhaps largely or completely in the case of translations of Latin masculine nouns denoting occupations that were held by women in Anglo-Saxon society. An example is *bæcester,* "baker," glossing Latin *pistor;* it survives as the Modern English name *Baxter.* In Middle English the suffix was still largely feminine in the south of England but masculine and feminine in the north, a tendency that became general in English starting with the 16th century. As an example of this tendency *seamster* was remade into the feminine *seamstress.* In Modern English the suffix is usually derogatory. This use probably arose from the occurrence of the suffix with ambiguous verbs, such as *game,* "to play at sports, to play at sex," or with pejorative verbs, such as *rime* or *rhyme.* In some modern formations on neutral words *–ster* is not derogatory, as in *youngster* (1589), but in most cases, as with *pollster* (1939), *–ster* has pejorative force.

poll·tak·er (pōl′tā′kər) *n.* See **pollster.**

poll tax *n.* A tax levied on people rather than on property, often as a requirement for voting.

pol·lut·ant (pə-lo͞ot′nt) *n.* Something that pollutes, especially a waste material that contaminates air, soil, or water.

pol·lute (pə-lo͞ot′) *tr.v.* **-lut·ed, -lut·ing, -lutes. 1.** To make unfit for or harmful to living things, especially by the addition of waste matter. See Synonyms at **contaminate. 2.** To make less suitable for an activity, especially by the introduction of unwanted factors: *The stadium lights polluted the sky around the observatory.* **3.** To render impure or morally harmful; corrupt. **4.** To make ceremonially impure; profane: *"Churches and altars were polluted by atrocious murders"* (Edward Gibbon). [Middle English *polluten,* from Latin *polluere, pollūt-.*] **—pol·lut′er** *n.*

pol·lu·tion (pə-lo͞o′shən) *n.* **1.** The act or process of polluting or the state of being polluted, especially the contamination of soil, water, or the atmosphere by the discharge of harmful substances. **2.** Something that pollutes; a pollutant or a group of pollutants: *Pollution in the air reduced the visibility near the airport.*

Pol·lux (pŏl′əks) *n. Greek Mythology.* **1.** One of the Dioscuri. **2.** A bright star in the constellation Gemini. [*Latin,* from Greek *Poludeukēs.*]

Pol·ly·an·na (pŏl′ē-ăn′ə) *n.* A person regarded as being foolishly or blindly optimistic. [After the heroine of the novel *Pollyanna,* by Eleanor Hodgman Porter (1868–1920), American writer.]

pol·ly·wog (pŏl′ē-wŏg′, -wôg′) *n.* Variant of **polliwog.**

po·lo (pō′lō) *n. Sports.* **1.** A game played by two teams of three or four players on horseback who are equipped with long-handled mallets for driving a small wooden ball through the opponents' goal. **2.** Water polo. [Anglo-Indian *polo,* of Tibeto-Burman origin.] **—po′lo·ist** *n.*

Po·lo (pō′lō), **Marco.** 1254–1324. Venetian traveler who explored Asia from 1271 to 1295. His *Travels of Marco Polo* was the only account of the Far East available to Europeans until the 17th century.

polo coat *n.* A loose-fitting, tailored overcoat made from camel's hair or a similar material.

pol·o·naise (pŏl′ə-nāz′, pō′lə-) *n.* **1.** A stately, marchlike Polish dance, primarily a promenade by couples. **2.** Music for or in the style of this dance, having triple meter. **3.** A woman's dress of the 18th century, having a fitted bodice and draped cutaway skirt, worn over an elaborate underskirt. [French, from feminine of *polonais,* Polish, from Medieval Latin *Polōnia,* Poland.]

po·lo·ni·um (pə-lō′nē-əm) *n. Symbol* **Po** A naturally radioactive metallic element, occurring in minute quantities as a product of radium disintegration and produced by bombarding bismuth or lead with neutrons. It has 27 isotopes ranging in mass number from 192 to 218, of which Po 210, with a half-life of 138.39 days, is the most readily available. Atomic number 84; melting point 254°C; boiling point 962°C; specific gravity 9.32; valence 2, 4. See table at **element.** [From Medieval Latin *Polōnia,* Poland.]

polo shirt *n.* A pullover sport shirt of knitted cotton.

Pol Pot (pŏl pŏt′). Born 1928. Cambodian political leader whose Khmer Rouge movement overthrew the Cambodian government in 1975. He fled the capital in 1979 when Vietnamese forces overthrew his government.

Pol·ta·va (pəl-tä′və). A city of central Ukraine west-southwest of Kharkov. Probably settled by Slavic peoples in the 8th or 9th century, it was a Cossack stronghold in the 17th century. Population, 302,000.

pol·ter·geist (pōl′tər-gīst′) *n.* A ghost that manifests itself by noises, rappings, and the creation of disorder. [German : *poltern,* to make noises (from Middle High German *boldern*) + *Geist,* ghost (from Middle High German, from Old High German).]

pol·troon (pŏl-tro͞on′) *n.* A base coward: *"Every moment of the fashion industry's misery is richly deserved by the designers . . . and magazine poltroons who perpetuate this absurd creation"* (Nina Totenberg). [French *poltron,* from Old Italian *poltrone,* coward, idler, perhaps augmentative of *poltro,* unbroken colt (from Vulgar Latin **pulliter,* from Latin *pullus,* young animal; see **pau-** in Appendix) or from *poltro,* bed, lazy.]

pol·y (pŏl′ē) *n.* **1.** Polyester. **2.** Polyethylene.

poly– *pref.* **1.** More than one; many; much: *polyatomic.* **2.** More than usual; excessive; abnormal: *polydipsia.* **3.** Polymer; polymeric: *polyethylene.* [Greek *polu-,* from *polus,* much, many. See **pelə-**[1] in Appendix.]

pol·y·a·cryl·a·mide (pŏl′ē-ə-krĭl′ə-mīd′) *n.* A white polyamide, $(=CH_2CHCONH_2=)$, related to acrylic acid. [POLY– + ACRYL(IC ACID) + AMIDE.]

polyacrylamide gel *n.* A hydrated polyacrylamide of stiff consistency used as a medium for electrophoresis because of its white coloring and thickening action in water-based solutions.

pol·y·ad·e·nyl·ic acid (pŏl′ē-ăd′n-ĭl′ĭk) *n.* A polymer of adenylic acid attached to messenger RNA that stabilizes the molecule before transport from the nucleus into the cytoplasm.

pol·y·al·co·hol (pŏl′ē-ăl′kə-hôl′, -hŏl′) *n.* An alcohol, such as glycerol, containing more than two hydroxy groups.

pol·y·am·ide (pŏl′ē-ăm′īd′) *n.* A polymer containing repeated amide groups, as in various kinds of nylon.

pol·y·a·mine (pŏl′ē-ə-mēn′, -ăm′ēn) *n.* Any of a group of organic compounds that contain two or more amino groups.

pol·y·an·drous (pŏl′ē-ăn′drəs) *adj.* **1.** Relating to, characterized by, or practicing polyandry. **2.** *Botany.* Having an indefinite number of stamens.

pol·y·an·dry (pŏl′ē-ăn′drē) *n.* **1.** The condition or practice of having more than one husband at one time. **2.** *Zoology.* A mating pattern in which a female mates with more than one male in a single breeding season. **3.** *Botany.* The condition of being polyandrous. **—pol′y·an′dric** *adj.*

pol·y·an·thus (pŏl′ē-ăn′thəs) *n., pl.* **-thus·es.** Any of a group of hybrid garden primroses having clusters of variously colored flowers. [New Latin, from Greek *poluanthos,* having many flowers : *polu-,* poly- + *anthos,* flower.]

polyanthus narcissus *n.* A bulbous Mediterranean plant *(Narcissus tazetta)* having clusters of fragrant flowers with white perianths and yellow coronas.

pol·y·a·tom·ic (pŏl′ē-ə-tŏm′ĭk) *adj.* Of or relating to a molecule that has three or more atoms as constituents.

pol·y·ba·sic (pŏl′ē-bā′sĭk) *adj.* Of or relating to an acid that has two or more hydrogen atoms that can be replaced by basic atoms or radicals.

pol·y·ba·site (pŏl′ē-bā′sīt′) *n.* A black mineral with a metallic luster, essentially $(Ag,Cu)_{16}Sb_2S_{11}$, that is an ore of silver. [POLY– + BAS(IS) + –ITE[1].]

Po·lyb·i·us (pə-lĭb′ē-əs). 200?–118? B.C. Greek historian. Only five books of his 40-volume history of Rome are extant.

pol·y·car·bon·ate (pŏl′ē-kär′bə-nāt′) *n.* Any of a family of thermoplastics characterized by a high-impact strength, used in making unbreakable windows.

Pol·y·carp (pŏl′ē-kärp′), Saint. A.D. 69?–155? Christian martyr. A student of the Apostle John, he was burned at the stake during a period of persecution of Christians in Smyrna.

pol·y·car·pel·lar·y (pŏl′ē-kär′pə-lĕr′ē) *adj. Botany.* Having or consisting of many carpels.

pol·y·car·pous (pŏl′ē-kär′pəs) also **po·ly·car·pic** (-pĭk) *adj. Botany.* Having fruit or pistils with two or more carpels. **—pol′y·car′py** *n.*

pol·y·cen·tric (pŏl′ē-sĕn′trĭk) *adj.* **1.** Having many centers, especially of authority or control: *the shift from Soviet-American hegemony to a polycentric world.* **2.** Having several central parts, such as centrosomes or chromatids. **—polycentric** *n.* A polycentric chromosome. **—pol′y·cen′trism** *n.*

pol·y·chete also **pol·y·chaete** (pŏl′ĭ-kēt′) *n.* Any of various annelid worms of the class Polychaeta, including mostly marine worms such as the lugworm, and characterized by fleshy paired appendages tipped with bristles on each body segment. [New Latin *Polychaeta,* class name, from Greek *polukhaitēs,* with much hair : *polu-,* poly- + *khaitē,* long hair.] **—pol′y·chaete′, pol′y·chae′tous** *adj.*

pol·y·chlo·rin·at·ed biphenyl (pŏl′ē-klôr′ə-nā′tĭd, -klōr′-) *n.* PCB.

pol·y·chro·mat·ic (pŏl′ē-krō-măt′ĭk) also **pol·y·chro·mic** (-krō′mĭk) or **pol·y·chro·mous** (-krō′məs) *adj.* **1.** Having or exhibiting many colors. **2.** Of or composed of radiation of more than one wavelength: *polychromatic light.*

pol·y·chro·mat·o·phil·i·a (pŏl′ē-krō-măt′ə-fĭl′ē-ə) also **pol·y·chro·mo·phil·i·a** (-krō′mə-fĭl′ē-ə) *n.* Affinity for more than one type of stain, especially for both basic and acidic stains. **—pol′y·chro·mat′o·phil′ic** (-fĭl′ĭk), **pol′y·chro·mat′o·phile′** *adj.*

pol·y·chrome (pŏl′ē-krōm′) *adj.* **1.** Having many or various colors; polychromatic. **2.** Made or decorated in many or various colors: *polychrome tiles.* **—polychrome** *n.* An object or a work composed of or decorated in many colors.

pol·y·chro·mic (pŏl′ē-krō′mĭk) or **pol·y·chro·mous** (-məs) *adj.* Variants of **polychromatic.**

pol·y·chro·mo·phil·i·a (pŏl′ē-krō′mə-fĭl′ē-ə) *n.* Variant of **polychromatophilia.**

pol·y·chro·my (pŏl′ē-krō′mē) *n.* The use of many colors in decoration, especially in architecture and sculpture.

Pol·y·clei·tus (pŏl′ĭ-klī′təs). See **Polyclitus.**

pol·y·clin·ic (pŏl′ē-klĭn′ĭk) *n.* A clinic, hospital, or health care facility that treats various types of diseases and injuries. [Alteration of POLICLINIC.]

Pol·y·cli·tus or **Pol·y·clei·tus** (pŏl′ĭ-klī′təs). fl. fifth century B.C. Greek sculptor and architect known for his bronze and marble statues of athletes.

pol·y·clone (pŏl′ē-klōn′) *n.* A clone descended from one or more small groups of cells, especially ones of genetically different origins. **—pol′y·clo′nal** *adj.* **—pol′y·clo′nal·ly** *adv.*

pol·y·con·ic projection (pŏl′ē-kŏn′ĭk) *n.* A conic map projection having distances between meridians along every parallel equal to those distances on a globe. The central geographic meridian is a straight line, whereas the others are curved and the parallels are arcs of circles.

pol·y·cot·y·le·don (pŏl′ē-kŏt′l-ēd′n) also **pol·y·cot** (-kŏt′) *n.* A plant whose seed contains more than two cotyledons. **—pol′y·cot′y·le′don·ous** *adj.*

pol·y·cy·clic (pŏl′ĭ-sī′klĭk, -sĭk′lĭk) *adj. Chemistry.* Having two or more atomic rings in a molecule.

pol·y·cys·tic (pŏl′ē-sĭs′tĭk) *adj.* Having or containing many cysts: *polycystic kidney disease.*

pol·y·cy·the·mi·a (pŏl′ē-sī-thē′mē-ə) *n.* A condition marked by an abnormally large number of red blood cells in the circulatory system.

pol·y·dac·tyl (pŏl′ē-dăk′təl) also **pol·y·dac·ty·lous** (-tə-ləs) *Biology.* —*adj.* Having more than the normal number of digits. —*n.* A person or an animal having more than the normal number of digits. **—pol′y·dac′tyl·ism, pol′y·dac′ty·ly** *n.*

pol·y·dem·ic (pŏl′ē-dĕm′ĭk) *adj.* Occurring in or inhabiting two or more regions: *polydemic species.* [POLY– + (EN)DEMIC.]

pol·y·dip·si·a (pŏl′ē-dĭp′sē-ə) *n.* Excessive or abnormal thirst. [POLY– + Greek *dipsa,* thirst + –IA[1].] **—pol′y·dip′sic** *adj.*

pol·y·e·lec·tro·lyte (pŏl′ē-ĭ-lĕk′trə-līt′) *n.* An electrolyte, such as a protein or polysaccharide, having a high molecular weight.

pol·y·em·bry·o·ny (pŏl′ē-ĕm′brē-ə-nē, -ĕm-brī′-) *n.* Development of more than one embryo from a single egg or ovule. **—pol′y·em′bry·on′ic** (-brē-ŏn′ĭk) *adj.*

polo

ă pat	oi boy
ā pay	ou out
âr care	o͝o took
ä father	o͞o boot
ĕ pet	ŭ cut
ē be	ûr urge
ĭ pit	th thin
ī pie	*th* this
îr pier	hw which
ŏ pot	zh vision
ō toe	ə about, item
ô paw	♦ regionalism

Stress marks: ′ (primary); ′ (secondary), as in **dictionary** (dĭk′shə-nĕr′ē)

pol•y•ene (pŏl′ē-ēn′) *n.* An organic compound containing many double bonds.

pol•y•es•ter (pŏl′ē-ĕs′tər, pŏl′ē-ĕs′tər) *n.* **1.** Any of numerous synthetic polymers produced chiefly by reaction of dibasic acids with dihydric alcohols and used primarily as light, strong, weather-resistant resins in boat hulls, swimming pools, textile fibers, adhesives, and molded parts. **2.** A wrinkle-resistant fabric of fibers made from any of these resins. **—pol′y•es′ter** *adj.* **—pol′y•es′ter•i•fi•ca′tion** (-ə-fĭ-kā′shən) *n.*

pol•y•es•trous (pŏl′ē-ĕs′trəs) *adj.* **1.** Having several estrous cycles during a single breeding season. **2.** Ovulating more than once a year.

pol•y•e•ther (pŏl′ē-ē′thər) *n.* A polymer in which the repeating unit contains two carbon atoms linked by an oxygen atom.

pol•y•eth•yl•ene (pŏl′ē-ĕth′ə-lēn′) *n.* A polymerized ethylene resin, used especially for containers, kitchenware, and tubing, or in the form of films and sheets for packaging.

polyethylene glycol *n.* Any of a family of colorless liquids with high molecular weight that are soluble in water and in many organic solvents and are used in detergents and as emulsifiers and plasticizers.

po•lyg•a•la (pə-lĭg′ə-lə) *n.* Any of various plants of the genus *Polygala,* which constitutes the milkworts. [New Latin *Polygala,* genus name, from Greek *polugalon,* milkwort : *polu-,* poly- + *gala,* milk; see **melg-** in Appendix.]

po•lyg•a•mist (pə-lĭg′ə-mĭst) *n.* One who practices polygamy.

po•lyg•a•mous (pə-lĭg′ə-məs) *adj.* **1.** Relating to, characterized by, or practicing polygamy. **2.** *Botany.* Having both hermaphroditic and unisexual flowers on the same plant or on separate plants of the same species. **—po•lyg′a•mous•ly** *adv.*

po•lyg•a•my (pə-lĭg′ə-mē) *n.* **1.** The condition or practice of having more than one spouse at one time. Also called *plural marriage.* **2.** *Zoology.* A mating pattern in which a single individual mates with more than one individual of the opposite sex. [French *polygamie,* from Late Latin *polygamia,* from Greek *polugamia* : *polu-,* poly- + *-gamia,* -gamy.]

pol•y•gene (pŏl′ē-jēn′) *n.* Any of a group of nonallelic genes, each having a small quantitative effect, that together produce a wide range of phenotypic variation. Also called *multiple factor, quantitative gene.*

pol•y•gen•e•sis (pŏl′ē-jĕn′ĭ-sĭs) *n.* Derivation of a species or type from more than one ancestor or germ cell. **—pol′y•gen′e•sist** *n.*

pol•y•gen•et•ic (pŏl′ē-jə-nĕt′ĭk) *adj.* **1.** Of or relating to polygenesis; polyphyletic. **2.** Having more than one origin.

pol•y•gen•ic (pŏl′ē-jĕn′ĭk) *adj.* Of, relating to, or determined by polygenes: *polygenic inheritance.* **—pol′y•gen′i•cal•ly** *adv.*

pol•y•glot (pŏl′ē-glŏt′) *adj.* Speaking, writing, written in, or composed of several languages. **—polyglot** *n.* **1.** A person having a speaking, reading, or writing knowledge of several languages. **2.** A book, especially a Bible, containing several versions of the same text in different languages. **3.** A mixture or confusion of languages. [French *polyglotte,* from Greek *poluglōttos* : *polu-,* poly- + *glōtta,* tongue, language.] **—pol′y•glot′ism, pol′y•glot′tism** *n.*

pol•y•gon (pŏl′ē-gŏn′) *n.* A closed plane figure bounded by three or more line segments. **—po•lyg′o•nal** (pə-lĭg′ə-nəl) *adj.* **—po•lyg′o•nal•ly** *adv.*

po•lyg•o•num (pə-lĭg′ə-nəm) *n.* Any of numerous plants of the widely distributed genus *Polygonum,* characterized by stems with knotlike joints and conspicuous sheathlike stipules. [New Latin *Polygonum,* genus name, from Greek *polugonon,* knotgrass : *polu-,* poly- + *gonu,* knee; see **genu-**[1] in Appendix.]

pol•y•graph (pŏl′ē-grăf′) *n.* An instrument that simultaneously records changes in physiological processes such as heartbeat, blood pressure, and respiration, often used as a lie detector. **—polygraph** *tr.v.* **-graphed, -graph•ing, -graphs.** To test (a criminal suspect, for example) with a polygraph. **—po•lyg′ra•pher** (pə-lĭg′rə-fər), **po•lyg′ra•phist** (-fĭst) *n.* **—pol′y•graph′ic** *adj.*

po•lyg•y•ny (pə-lĭj′ə-nē) *n.* **1.** The condition or practice of having more than one wife at one time. **2.** *Zoology.* A mating pattern in which a male mates with more than one female in a single breeding season. **—po•lyg′y•nous** *adj.*

pol•y•he•dra (pŏl′ē-hē′drə) *n.* A plural of **polyhedron.**

polyhedral angle *n.* *Mathematics.* A shape formed by three or more planes intersecting at a common point.

pol•y•he•dron (pŏl′ē-hē′drən) *n., pl.* **-drons** or **-dra** (-drə). A solid bounded by polygons. **—pol′y•he′dral** *adj.*

pol•y•he•dro•sis (pŏl′ē-hē-drō′sĭs) *n., pl.* **-ses** (-sēz). Any of several diseases of insect larvae, caused by infestation with polyhedral virus particles.

pol•y•his•tor (pŏl′ē-hĭs′tər) *n.* A person with broad knowledge. [Latin *Polyhistōr,* from Greek *poluistōr,* very learned : *polu-,* poly- + *histōr,* learned; see **weid-** in Appendix.] **—pol′y•his•tor′ic** (-hĭ-stôr′ĭk, -stŏr′-) *adj.*

pol•y•hy•dric (pŏl′ē-hī′drĭk) *adj.* *Chemistry.* Containing at least two hydroxyl groups.

Pol•y•hym•ni•a (pŏl′ē-hĭm′nē-ə) also **Po•lym•ni•a** (pə-lĭm′nē-ə) *n.* *Greek Mythology.* The Muse of sacred song and oratory.

pol•y I:C (pŏl′ē ī′sē′) *n.* A synthetic chemical that resembles the RNA of infectious viruses and is used to stimulate the production of interferon by the immune system. [POLY– + *i(nosinic acid)* (Greek *inos,* genitive of *is,* sinew; see INOSITOL + –INE[2] + –IC) + *c(ytidylic acid)* (CYTIDINE + –YL + –IC).]

pol•y•im•ide (pŏl′ē-ĭm′īd′) *n.* A synthetic polymeric resin of a class resistant to high temperatures, wear, and corrosion, used primarily as a coating or film on a substrate substance.

pol•y•math (pŏl′ē-măth′) *n.* A person of great or varied learning. [Greek *polumathēs* : *polu-,* poly- + *manthanein, math-,* to learn; see **mendh-** in Appendix.] **—pol′y•math′, pol′y•math′ic** *adj.* **—po•ly′ma•thy** (pə-lĭm′ə-thē) *n.*

pol•y•mer (pŏl′ə-mər) *n.* Any of numerous natural and synthetic compounds of usually high molecular weight consisting of up to millions of repeated linked units, each a relatively light and simple molecule.

pol•y•mer•ase (pŏl′ə-mə-rās′, -rāz′) *n.* Any of various enzymes that catalyze the formation of polynucleotides of DNA or RNA using an existing strand of DNA or RNA as a template.

pol•y•mer•ic (pŏl′ə-mĕr′ĭk) *adj.* Of, relating to, or consisting of a polymer. **—pol′y•mer′i•cal•ly** *adv.* **—po•lym′er•ism** (pə-lĭm′ə-rĭz′əm, pŏl′ə-mə-) *n.*

po•lym•er•i•za•tion (pə-lĭm′ər-ĭ-zā′shən, pŏl′ə-mər-) *n.* **1.** The bonding of two or more monomers to form a polymer. **2.** A chemical process that effects this bonding.

pol•y•mer•ize (pŏl′ə-mə-rīz′, pə-lĭm′ə-) *intr. & tr.v.* **-ized, -iz•ing, -iz•es.** To undergo or subject to polymerization.

po•lym•er•ous (pə-lĭm′ər-əs) *adj.* *Biology.* Consisting of numerous parts, members, or segments.

Po•lym•ni•a (pə-lĭm′nē-ə) *n.* *Greek Mythology.* Variant of **Polyhymnia.**

pol•y•morph (pŏl′ē-môrf′) *n.* **1.** *Biology.* An organism characterized by polymorphism. **2.** *Chemistry.* A specific crystalline form of a compound that can crystallize in different forms.

pol•y•mor•phism (pŏl′ē-môr′fĭz′əm) *n.* **1.** *Biology.* The occurrence of different forms, stages, or types in individual organisms or in organisms of the same species, independent of sexual variations. **2.** *Chemistry.* Crystallization of a compound in at least two distinct forms. In this sense, also called *pleomorphism.* **—pol′y•mor′phic, pol′y•mor′phous** *adj.* **—pol′y•mor′phous•ly** *adv.*

pol•y•mor•pho•nu•cle•ar (pŏl′ē-môr′fə-no͞o′klē-ər, -nyo͞o′-) *adj.* Having a lobed nucleus. Used especially of neutrophil white blood cells. **—polymorphonuclear** *n.* A polymorphonuclear cell.

polymorphous perverse *adj.* Characterized by or displaying sexual tendencies that have no specific direction, as in an infant or a young child, but that may evolve into acts that are regarded as perversions in adults.

pol•y•myx•in (pŏl′ē-mĭk′sĭn) *n.* Any of various mainly toxic antibiotics derived from strains of the soil bacterium *Bacillus polymyxa* and used to treat various infections with gram-negative bacteria. [New Latin *polymyxa,* species name (POLY– + Greek *muxa,* slime) + –IN.]

Pol•y•ne•sia (pŏl′ə-nē′zhə, -shə). A division of Oceania including scattered islands of the central and southern Pacific Ocean roughly between New Zealand, Hawaii, and Easter Island. The larger islands are volcanic, the smaller ones generally coral formations.

Pol•y•ne•sian (pŏl′ə-nē′zhən, -shən) *adj.* Of or relating to Polynesia or its peoples, languages, or cultures. **—Polynesian** *n.* **1.** A native or inhabitant of Polynesia. **2.** A subfamily of the Austronesian language family spoken in Polynesia.

pol•y•neu•ri•tis (pŏl′ē-no͝o-rī′tĭs, -nyo͝o-) *n.* See **multiple neuritis.** **—pol′y•neu•rit′ic** (-rĭt′ĭk) *adj.*

Pol•y•ni•ces (pŏl′ə-nī′sēz) *n.* *Greek Mythology.* A son of Oedipus for whom an expedition against Thebes was raised.

pol•y•no•mi•al (pŏl′ē-nō′mē-əl) *adj.* Of, relating to, or consisting of more than two names or terms. **—polynomial** *n.* **1.** A taxonomic designation consisting of more than two terms. **2.** *Mathematics.* **a.** An algebraic expression consisting of one or more summed terms, each term consisting of a constant multiplier and one or more variables raised to integral powers. For example, $x^2 - 5x + 6$ and $2p^3q + y$ are polynomials. Also called *multinomial.* **b.** An expression of two or more terms. [POLY– + (BI)NOMIAL.]

pol•y•nu•cle•o•tide (pŏl′ē-no͞o′klē-ə-tīd′, -nyo͞o′-) *n.* A polymeric compound consisting of a number of nucleotides.

po•lyn•ya (pŏl′ən-yä′, pə-lĭn′yə) *n.* An area of open water surrounded by sea ice. [Russian *polyn'ya,* from *polyĭ,* open, hollow. See **pelə-**[2] in Appendix.]

pol•y•o•ma (pŏl′ē-ō′mə) *n.* A small form of the papovavirus that contains DNA and is associated with the formation of various tumors in rodents. Also called *polyoma virus.*

pol•yp (pŏl′ĭp) *n.* **1.** A coelenterate, such as a hydra or coral, having a cylindrical body and an oral opening usually surrounded by tentacles. **2.** A usually nonmalignant growth or tumor protruding from the mucous lining of an organ such as the nose, bladder, or intestine, often causing obstruction. [Middle English *polip,* nasal tumor, from Old French *polipe,* from Latin *pōlypus,* cuttlefish, nasal tumor, from Greek *polupous* (probably by folk etymology from *polus,* many; see POLY–, and *pous,* foot; see **ped-** in Appendix).] **—pol′yp•oid′** *adj.*

pol·y·par·y (pŏl′ə-pĕr′ē) also **pol·y·par·i·um** (pŏl′ə-pâr′ē-əm) *n., pl.* **-ies** also **-i·a** (-ē-ə). The common supporting framework of a colony of polyps, especially of coral.

pol·y·pep·tide (pŏl′ē-pĕp′tīd′) *n.* A peptide containing many molecules of amino acids, typically between 10 and 100.

pol·y·pet·al·ous (pŏl′ē-pĕt′l-əs) *adj.* Having separate petals, as on the corolla of a rose or carnation.

pol·y·pha·gi·a (pŏl′ē-fā′jē-ə, -jə) **po·lyph·a·gy** (pə-lĭf′ə-jē) *n.* **1.** An excessive or pathological desire to eat. **2.** *Zoology.* The habit of feeding on many different kinds of food. **—pol′y·pha′gi·an** *adj.*

po·lyph·a·gous (pə-lĭf′ə-gəs) *adj.* Feeding on many different kinds of food: *polyphagous insects or birds.*

Pol·y·phe·mus (pŏl′ə-fē′məs) *n. Greek Mythology.* The Cyclops who confined Odysseus and his companions in a cave until Odysseus blinded him and escaped. [Latin, from Greek *Poluphēmos.*]

pol·y·phe·mus moth (pŏl′ə-fē′məs) *n.* A large North American silkworm moth *(Antheraea polyphemus)* having an eyelike spot on each hind wing. [After POLYPHEMUS, from the ocellus on its hind wings.]

pol·y·phone (pŏl′ē-fōn′) *n. Linguistics.* A written character or combination of characters having two or more phonetic values, such as the English letter *a.*

pol·y·phon·ic (pŏl′ē-fŏn′ĭk) *adj.* **1.** *Music.* Of, relating to, or characterized by polyphony. **2.** *Linguistics.* Having two or more phonetic values. **—pol′y·phon′i·cal·ly** *adv.*

po·lyph·o·ny (pə-lĭf′ə-nē) *n., pl.* **-nies.** *Music.* Music with two or more independent melodic parts sounded together. **—po·lyph′o·nous** *adj.* **—po·lyph′o·nous·ly** *adv.*

pol·y·phy·let·ic (pŏl′ē-fī-lĕt′ĭk) *adj.* Relating to or characterized by development from more than one ancestral type. **—pol′y·phy·let′i·cal·ly** *adv.*

pol·y·ploid (pŏl′ē-ploid′) *Genetics. adj.* Having one or more extra sets of chromosomes: *a polyploid species; a polyploid cell.* **—polyploid** *n.* An organism with more than two sets of chromosomes. **—pol′y·ploi′dy** *n.*

pol·yp·ne·a (pŏl′ĭp-nē′ə) *n.* Very rapid breathing; panting. [New Latin : POLY– + Greek *pnoia, pnoē,* breath, breathing (from *pnein,* to breathe; see **pneu-** in Appendix).] **—pol′yp·ne′ic** (-nē′ĭk) *adj.*

pol·y·pod (pŏl′ē-pŏd′) also **po·lyp·o·dous** (pə-lĭp′ə-dəs) *adj. Biology.* Having numerous feet.

pol·y·po·dy (pŏl′ē-pō′dē) *n., pl.* **-dies.** Any of various ferns of the widely distributed genus *Polypodium,* having simple or compound fronds, round sori arranged in one or more rows along the midrib, and creeping rootstocks. [Middle English *polypodie,* from Latin *polypodium,* from Greek *polupodion,* from diminutive of *polupous,* many-footed : *polu-,* poly- + *pous, pod-,* foot; see –POD.]

pol·y·pore (pŏl′ē-pôr′, -pōr′) *n.* See **pore fungus.**

pol·yp·o·sis (pŏl′ə-pō′sĭs) *n., pl.* **-ses** (-sēz). A hereditary disease in which numerous polyps erupt in a part of the body, especially on the lining of the colon and rectum, and often become malignant.

pol·y·pro·pyl·ene (pŏl′ē-prō′pə-lēn′) *n.* **1.** Any of various thermoplastic resins that are polymers of propylene. They are hard and tough, and are used to make molded articles and fibers. **2.** A fabric of fibers made from any of these resins. **—pol′y·pro′pyl·ene′** *adj.*

pol·y·pro·tic (pŏl′ē-prō′tĭk) *adj.* **1.** Of or relating to an acid that can donate more than one proton to a base. **2.** Of or relating to a base that can accept more than one proton. [POLY– + PROT(ON) + –IC.]

pol·yp·tych (pŏl′ĭp-tĭk′) *n.* A work consisting of four or more painted or carved panels that are hinged together. [From Late Latin *polyptycha,* registers, account books, from Greek *poluptukha,* from neuter pl. of *poluptukhos,* having many folds : *polu-,* poly- + *ptukhē,* fold; see DIPTYCH.]

pol·y·rhythm (pŏl′ē-rĭth′əm) *n. Music.* The use or an instance of simultaneous contrasting rhythms. **—pol′y·rhyth′mic** *adj.*

pol·y·ri·bo·nu·cle·o·tide (pŏl′ē-rī′bō-no͞o′klē-ə-tīd′, -nyo͞o′-) *n.* A polynucleotide consisting of a number of ribonucleotides.

pol·y·ri·bo·some (pŏl′ē-rī′bə-sōm′) *n.* A cluster of ribosomes connected by a strand of messenger RNA and functioning as a unit in protein synthesis. Also called *polysome.*

pol·y·sac·cha·ride (pŏl′ē-săk′ə-rīd′) also **pol·y·sac·cha·rid** (-rĭd) or **pol·y·sac·cha·rose** (-rōs′, -rōz′) *n.* Any of a class of carbohydrates, such as starch and cellulose, consisting of a number of monosaccharides joined by glycosidic bonds.

pol·y·se·mous (pŏl′ē-sē′məs) *adj. Linguistics.* Having or characterized by many meanings. [From Late Latin *polysēmus,* from Greek *polusēmos* : *polu-,* poly- + *sēma,* sign.] **—pol′y·se′my** (pŏl′ē-sē′mē, pə-lĭs′ə-) *n.*

pol·y·sep·al·ous (pŏl′ē-sĕp′ə-ləs) *adj. Botany.* Having separate sepals.

pol·y·some (pŏl′ē-sōm′) *n.* See **polyribosome.**

pol·y·so·mic (pŏl′ē-sō′mĭk) *Genetics. adj.* Having an extra copy of one or more chromosomes: *a polysomic individual; a polysomic cell.* **—polysomic** *n.* A polysomic organism or cell. [POLY– + (CHROMO)SOM(E) + –IC.]

pol·y·sor·bate (pŏl′ē-sôr′bāt′) *n.* Any of a class of emulsifiers used in food preparation and in some pharmaceuticals. [POLY– + *sorbate,* salt or ester of sorbitol (SORB(ITOL) + –ATE[2]).]

pol·y·sper·my (pŏl′ē-spûr′mē) *n.* The entry of several sperm into one ovum during fertilization. **—pol′y·sper′mic** *adj.*

po·lys·ti·chous (pə-lĭs′tĭ-kəs) *adj. Botany.* Arranged in two or more series or rows. [Greek *polustikhos,* of many lines : *polu-,* poly- + from *stikhos,* row; see STICH.]

pol·y·sty·rene (pŏl′ē-stī′rēn) *n.* A rigid, clear thermoplastic polymer that can be molded into objects or made into a foam that is used to insulate refrigerators. **—pol′y·sty′rene** *adj.*

pol·y·sul·fide (pŏl′ē-sŭl′fīd) *n.* A sulfide compound containing at least two sulfur atoms per molecule.

pol·y·syl·lab·ic (pŏl′ē-sĭ-lăb′ĭk) *adj. Linguistics.* **1.** Having more than three syllables. **2.** Characterized by words having more than three syllables. **—pol′y·syl·lab′i·cal·ly** *adv.*

pol·y·syl·la·ble (pŏl′ē-sĭl′ə-bəl) *n. Linguistics.* A word of more than three syllables.

pol·y·syn·ap·tic (pŏl′ē-sĭ-năp′tĭk) *adj.* Of or involving two or more synapses in the nervous system: *a polysynaptic reflex.*

pol·y·syn·de·ton (pŏl′ē-sĭn′dĭ-tŏn′) *n.* The repetition of conjunctions in close succession for rhetorical effect, as in the phrase *here and there and everywhere.* [Late Greek *polusundeton,* neuter of *polusundetos,* using many connectives : Greek *polu-,* poly- + Greek *sundetos,* bound together; see SYNDETIC.]

pol·y·syn·thet·ic (pŏl′ē-sĭn-thĕt′ĭk) *adj. Linguistics.* Of or relating to a language such as Eskimo or Mohawk, characterized by long, morphologically complex words with a large number of affixes that express syntactic relationships and meanings usually expressed as phrases or sentences in other languages.

pol·y·tech·nic (pŏl′ē-tĕk′nĭk) *adj.* Offering, receiving, or dealing with instruction in many industrial arts and applied sciences: *a polytechnic institute.* **—polytechnic** *n.* A school specializing in the teaching of industrial arts and applied sciences.

pol·y·tene (pŏl′ē-tēn′) *adj.* Relating to or having large, multistranded chromosomes whose corresponding chromomeres are in contact. [POLY– + Latin *taenia,* band (from Greek *tainia,* ribbon; see **ten-** in Appendix).] **—pol′y·te′nic** *adj.* **—pol′y·te′ny** *n.*

pol·y·tet·ra·fluor·o·eth·yl·ene (pŏl′ē-tĕt′rə-flo͝or′ō-ĕth′ə-lēn′, -flôr′-, -flōr′-) *n.* A thermoplastic resin, $(C_2F_4)_n$, that is resistant to heat and chemicals, has an extremely low coefficient of friction, and is used as a coating on cookware, gaskets, seals, and hoses.

pol·y·the·ism (pŏl′ē-thē-ĭz′əm, pŏl′ē-thē′ĭz-əm) *n.* The worship of or belief in more than one god. [French *polythéisme,* from Greek *polutheos,* polytheistic : *polu-,* poly- + *theos,* god; see **dhēs-** in Appendix.] **—pol′y·the′ist** *n.* **—pol′y·the·is′tic** *adj.*

pol·y·thene (pŏl′ə-thēn′) *n. Chiefly British.* Variant of **polyethylene.**

po·lyt·o·cous (pə-lĭt′ə-kəs) *adj.* Producing many offspring in a single birth. [Greek *polutokos,* bearing many offspring : *polu-,* poly- + *tokos,* offspring, birth; see **tek-** in Appendix.]

pol·y·to·nal·i·ty (pŏl′ē-tō-năl′ĭ-tē) *n. Music.* Simultaneous use of two or more tonalities in a composition. **—pol′y·to′nal** (-tō′nəl) *adj.* **—pol′y·to′nal·ly** *adv.*

pol·y·tro·phic (pŏl′ē-trō′fĭk, -trŏf′ĭk) *adj.* Subsisting on various types of organic material. Used of certain bacteria.

pol·y·typ·ic (pŏl′ē-tĭp′ĭk) also **pol·y·typ·i·cal** (-ĭ-kəl) *adj.* Having several variant forms, especially subspecies or varieties. [POLY– + TYP(E) + –IC.]

pol·y·un·sat·u·rat·ed (pŏl′ē-ŭn-săch′ə-rā′tĭd) *adj.* Of or relating to long-chain carbon compounds, especially fats, having many unsaturated bonds.

pol·y·ur·e·thane (pŏl′ē-yo͝or′ə-thān′) *n.* Any of various resins, widely varying in flexibility, used in tough chemical-resistant coatings, adhesives, and foams. **—pol′y·ur′·e·thane′** *adj.*

pol·y·u·ri·a (pŏl′ē-yo͝or′ē-ə) *n.* Excessive passage of urine, as in diabetes. **—pol′y·u′ric** *adj.*

pol·y·va·lent (pŏl′ē-vā′lənt) *adj.* **1.** Acting against or interacting with more than one kind of antigen, antibody, toxin, or microorganism. **2.** *Chemistry.* **a.** Having more than one valence. **b.** Having a valence of 3 or higher. **—pol′y·va′lence, pol′y·va′len·cy** *n.*

pol·y·vi·nyl (pŏl′ē-vī′nəl) *adj. Abbr.* **PV.** Designating any of a group of polymerized thermoplastic vinyls, such as polyvinyl chloride.

polyvinyl chloride *n.* PVC.

pol·y·zo·an (pŏl′ē-zō′ən) *n.* See **bryozoan.** [From New Latin *Polyzoa,* phylum name : POLY– + *–zoa,* pl. of *–zoon;* see –ZOON.] **—pol′y·zo′an** *adj.*

pol·y·zo·ar·i·um (pŏl′ē-zō-âr′ē-əm) also **pol·y·zo·a·ry** (-zō′ə-rē) *n., pl.* **-ar·i·a** (-âr′ē-ə) also **-a·ries.** A bryozoan colony or its supporting skeletal structure. [New Latin : *Polyzoa,* phylum name; see POLYZOAN + –ARIUM.]

pol·y·zo·ic (pŏl′ē-zō′ĭk) *adj. Biology.* **1.** Forming or consisting of a colony of zooids. **2.** Containing numerous sporozoites.

pom·ace (pŭm′ĭs, pŏm′-) *n.* **1.** The pulpy material remaining after the juice has been pressed from fruit, such as apples. **2.** Pulpy material remaining after the extraction of oil from nuts,

Polyphemus
c. 150 B.C. Greek marble sculpture

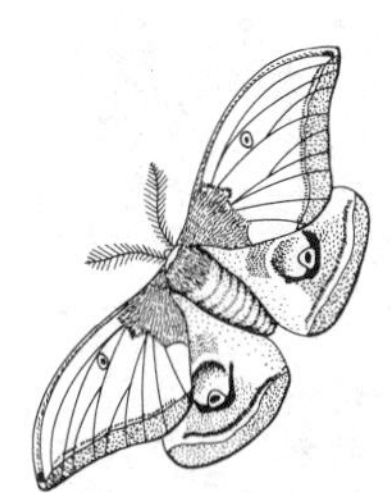

polyphemus moth
Antheraea polyphemus

ă pat	oi boy
ā pay	ou out
âr care	o͝o took
ä father	o͞o boot
ĕ pet	ŭ cut
ē be	ûr urge
ĭ pit	th thin
ī pie	*th* this
îr pier	hw which
ŏ pot	zh vision
ō toe	ə about, item
ô paw	♦ regionalism

Stress marks: ′ (primary); ′ (secondary), as in **dictionary** (dĭk′shə-nĕr′ē)

pomegranate
Punica granatum

seeds, or fish. [Middle English *pomis,* from Medieval Latin *pōmācium,* cider, from Vulgar Latin *pōma, apple, fruit. See POME.]

pomace fly *n.* See **fruit fly** (sense 1).

po·ma·ceous (pō-mā′shəs) *adj.* Of, relating to, bearing, or characteristic of apples or pomes. [From New Latin *pōmāceus,* from Late Latin *pōmum,* apple, fruit. See POME.]

po·made (pō-mād′, -mäd′, pŏ-) *n.* A perfumed ointment, especially one used to groom the hair. **—pomade** *tr.v.* **-mad·ed, -mad·ing, -mades.** To anoint with pomade. [French *pommade,* from Italian *pomata,* from *pomo,* apple, from Late Latin *pōmum.* See POME.]

po·man·der (pō′măn′dər, pō-măn′-) *n.* **1.** A mixture of aromatic substances enclosed in a bag or box as a protection against odor or infection, formerly worn on one's person but now usually placed in a dresser drawer or closet. **2.** A case, box, or bag for holding this mixture. [Middle English *pomendambre,* alteration of Old French *pome d'embre,* apple of amber, from Medieval Latin *pōmum dē ambrā* : *pōmum,* apple, ball (from Latin, fruit) + Latin *dē,* of; see DE– + *ambrā,* ablative of *ambra,* amber; see AMBER.]

pome (pōm) *n.* A fleshy fruit, such as an apple, a pear, or a quince, having several seed chambers and an outer fleshy part largely derived from the hypanthium. Also called *false fruit.* [Middle English, from Old French, apple, fruit, from Vulgar Latin *pōma, from neuter pl. of Late Latin *pōmum,* from Latin, fruit.]

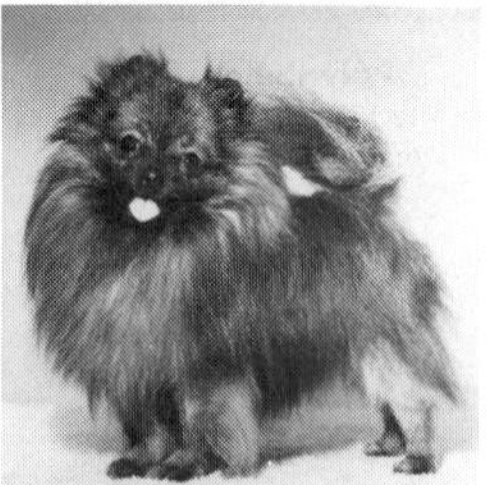
Pomeranian

pome·gran·ate (pŏm′grăn′ĭt, pŏm′ĭ-, pŭm′-, pŭm′ĭ-) *n.* **1.** A deciduous shrub or small tree *(Punica granatum)* native to Asia and widely cultivated for its edible fruit. **2.** The fruit of this tree, having a tough reddish rind, and containing many seeds, each enclosed in a juicy, mildly acidic, red pulp. [Middle English *pome granate,* from Old French *pome grenate* : *pome,* apple; see POME + *grenate,* having many seeds (from Latin *grānātus,* from *grānum,* grain, seed; see **gr̥ə-no-** in Appendix).]

pom·e·lo (pŏm′ə-lō′) *n., pl.* **-los.** See **shaddock.** [Alteration of POMPELMOUS.]

Pom·er·a·ni·a (pŏm′ə-rā′nē-ə, -rān′yə). A historical region of north-central Europe bordering on the Baltic Sea in present-day northwest Poland and northeast Germany. It was inhabited by Slavic tribes in the 10th century and conquered by Poland in the 12th century. The territory was later split up and controlled by various powers, including the Holy Roman Empire, Prussia, Sweden, Denmark, and Germany.

Pom·er·a·ni·an (pŏm′ə-rā′nē-ən, -rān′yən) *adj.* Of or relating to Pomerania or its people. **—Pomeranian** *n.* **1.** A native or inhabitant of Pomerania. **2.** Any of a breed of small dogs having long, silky hair, a foxlike face, pointed ears, and a hairy tail curling over the back.

po·mi·cul·ture (pō′mĭ-kŭl′chər) *n.* The cultivation of fruit. [Latin *pōmum,* fruit + CULTURE.]

po·mif·er·ous (pō-mĭf′ər-əs) *adj.* Bearing pomes. [Latin *pōmifer,* fruit-bearing (*pōmum,* fruit + *-fer,* -fer) + –OUS.]

Madame de Pompadour
Portrait by
François Boucher

pom·mel (pŭm′əl, pŏm′-) *tr.v.* **-meled, -mel·ing, -mels** also **-melled, -mel·ling, -mels.** To beat; pummel. **—pommel** *n.* **1.** The upper front part of a saddle; a saddlebow. **2.** A knob on the hilt of a sword or similar weapon. [From Middle English *pomel,* a pommel, from Old French, diminutive of *pom,* ball, fruit, from Latin *pōmum,* fruit.]

pom·my or **pom·mie** (pŏm′ē) *n., pl.* **-mies.** *Australian & New Zealand.* Used as a disparaging term for a British person, especially a recent immigrant. [Short for *pomegranate,* alteration of *Pummy Grant,* probably alteration of *immigrant.*]

Po·mo (pō′mō) *n., pl.* **Pomo** or **-mos. 1.a.** A group of Native American peoples inhabiting an area of the Coast Ranges of northern California. **b.** A member of this group. **2.** Any of the seven languages of the Pomo.

po·mol·o·gy (pō-mŏl′ə-jē) *n.* The scientific study and cultivation of fruit. [Latin *pōmum,* fruit + –LOGY.] **—po′mo·log′i·cal** (pō′mə-lŏj′ĭ-kəl) *adj.* **—po′mo·log′i·cal·ly** *adv.* **—po·mol′o·gist** *n.*

Po·mo·na (pə-mō′nə). A city of southern California, a residential and industrial suburb of Los Angeles. Population, 92,742.

pomp (pŏmp) *n.* **1.** Dignified or magnificent display; splendor: *the solemn pomp of a military funeral.* **2.** Vain or ostentatious display. See Synonyms at **display.** [Middle English, from Old French *pompe,* from Latin *pompa,* pomp, procession, from Greek *pompē,* procession, from *pempein,* to send.]

pom·pa·dour (pŏm′pə-dôr′, -dōr′) *n.* **1.** A woman's hairstyle formed by sweeping the hair up from the forehead. **2.** A man's hairstyle formed by brushing the hair up from the forehead. [After the Marquise de POMPADOUR.]

Pom·pa·dour (pŏm′pə-dôr′, -dōr′, -do͞or′, pôɴ-pä-do͞or′), Marquise de. Title of Jeanne Antoinette Poisson. 1721–1764. The lover of Louis XV of France. She was blamed for establishing France's alliance with Austria, which led to the Seven Years' War (1756–1763).

pom·pa·no (pŏm′pə-nō′) *n., pl.* **pompano** or **-nos.** Any of several marine food fishes of the genus *Trachinotus,* especially *T. carolinus,* of tropical and temperate Atlantic waters, having a flattened, oblong body with a bluish back and a yellowish breast. [American Spanish *pámpano,* any of several kinds of fish, from Spanish, vine tendril, a kind of fish with golden markings, from Latin *pampinus,* vine tendril.]

Pom·pa·no Beach (pŏm′pə-nō′). A city of southeast Florida on the Atlantic coast north of Miami. It is a resort community in a citrus and vegetable area. Population, 52,618.

Pompeian red *n. Color.* A grayish to moderate red. [From its similarity to the color found on house walls at Pompeii.]

Pom·pe·ii (pŏm-pā′, -pā′ē). An ancient city of southern Italy southeast of Naples. Founded in the sixth or early fifth century B.C., it was a Roman colony by 80 B.C. and became a prosperous port and resort with many noted villas, temples, theaters, and baths. Pompeii was destroyed by an eruption of Mount Vesuvius in A.D. 79. The incredibly well-preserved ruins were rediscovered in 1748 and have been extensively excavated. **—Pom·pe′ian, Pom·pei′ian** *adj. & n.*

pom·pel·mous (pŏm′pəl-mo͞os′) *n.* See **shaddock.** [Dutch *pompelmoes* (influenced by *pompoen,* gourd, and Portuguese *limoes,* lemon), probably ultimately from Tamil *pampalimāsu.*]

Pom·pey (pŏm′pē). Known as "the Great." 106–48 B.C. Roman general and political leader. With Caesar and Crassus he formed a ruling triumvirate (60–50) but was later defeated by Caesar and murdered in Egypt.

Pom·pi·dou (pŏm′pĭ-do͞o′, pôɴ-pē-do͞o′), **Georges Jean Raymond.** 1911–1974. French politician who served as premier (1962–1968) and president (1969–1974).

pom·pon or **pom-pon** (pŏm′pŏn′) also **pom-pom** or **pom·pom** (pŏm′-pŏm′) *n.* **1.** A tuft or ball of wool, feathers, or other material used as a decoration, especially on shoes, caps, and curtains. **2.** A small buttonlike flower of some chrysanthemums and dahlias. [French.]

pom·pous (pŏm′pəs) *adj.* **1.** Characterized by excessive self-esteem or exaggerated dignity; pretentious: *pompous officials who enjoy giving orders.* **2.** Full of high-sounding phrases; bombastic: *a pompous proclamation.* **3.** Characterized by pomp or stately display; ceremonious: *a pompous occasion.* [Middle English, from Old French *pompeux,* from Late Latin *pompōsus,* from Latin *pompa,* pomp. See POMP.] **—pom·pos′i·ty** (-pŏs′ĭ-tē), **pom′pous·ness** (-pəs-nĭs) *n.* **—pom′pous·ly** *adv.*

Pon·ca (pŏng′kə) *n., pl.* **Ponca** or **-cas. 1.a.** A Native American people formerly inhabiting northeast Nebraska near the Niobrara River, with present-day populations in Oklahoma and Nebraska. The Ponca are closely related to the Omaha in language and history. **b.** A member of this people. **2.** The Siouan language of the Ponca, dialectally related to Omaha.

Ponca City. A city of northern Oklahoma on the Arkansas River north-northeast of Oklahoma City. It was founded in 1893 after the opening of the Cherokee Strip. Population, 26,238.

Pon·ce (pôn′sā, -sĕ). A city of southern Puerto Rico southwest of San Juan. It is an agricultural trade and distribution center. Population, 161,739.

Ponce de Le·ón (pŏns′ də lē′ən, lē-ōn′, pôn′thĕ *thĕ* lĕ-ôn′, pôn′sĕ), **Juan.** 1460–1521. Spanish explorer who sailed with Columbus on his second voyage (1493–1494) and explored Florida (1513) while looking for the legendary Fountain of Youth.

Pon·chiel·li (pông-kyĕl′lē), **Amilcare.** 1834–1886. Italian composer. Among his works are the ballet *Clarina* (1873) and the opera *La Gioconda* (1876).

pon·cho (pŏn′chō) *n., pl.* **-chos. 1.** A blanketlike cloak having a hole in the center for the head. **2.** A similar garment having a hood used as a raincoat. [American Spanish, from Spanish, cape, perhaps variant of *pocho,* faded, discolored.]

pond (pŏnd) *n.* A still body of water smaller than a lake, often of artificial origin. [Middle English *ponde,* from Old English *pund-,* enclosure.]

pond apple *n.* An evergreen tree *(Annona glabra)* of Florida and tropical America, having yellow flowers with red markings and ovoid yellow fruit.

pond cypress *n.* A small variety of the bald cypress *(Taxodium distichum* var. *nutans)* native to the southeast United States.

pon·der (pŏn′dər) *v.* **-dered, -der·ing, -ders.** *—tr.* To weigh in the mind with thoroughness and care. *—intr.* To reflect or consider with thoroughness and care. [Middle English *ponderen,* from Old French *ponderer,* from Latin *ponderāre.* See **(s)pen-** in Appendix.] **—pon′der·er** *n.*

SYNONYMS: *ponder, meditate, deliberate, ruminate, mull, muse.* These verbs mean to consider something carefully and at length. To *ponder* is to weigh in the mind with painstaking thoroughness and care: *"He and the council had already pondered the list of members returned to the parliament"* (John Morley). *"The Doctor had been pondering, and had made up his mind to a certain course"* (Henry Kingsley). *Meditate* implies serious consideration, as of undertaking a course of action or of implementing a plan; the term can also denote engagement in deep reflection: *"The King struck the blow he had for some time meditated"* (William E.H. Lecky). *"He quitted her presence to meditate upon revenge"* (Frederick Marryat). To *deliberate* is to think attentively and usually slowly, as about a choice or decision to be made: *The jury deliberated for two days before returning a verdict. Ruminate* and *mull* imply turning a matter over and over again in the mind: *"The old warrior king was . . . ruminating on his gloomy fortunes"* (Washington Irving). *I sat mulling over my problem without finding a solution.* To *muse* is to be absorbed in one's thoughts; the word often connotes an abstracted quality: *"And musing there an hour alone,/I dreamed that Greece might still be free"* (Byron).

pon·der·a·ble (pŏn′dər-ə-bəl) *adj.* Considerable enough to be weighed or assessed; appreciable: *ponderable results; ponderable issues.* **—pon′der·a·bil′i·ty** *n.*

pon·der·o·sa pine (pŏn′də-rō′sə) *n.* A tall timber tree *(Pinus ponderosa)* of western North America, having long, dark green needles grouped in fascicles of three. [Translation of New Latin *Pīnus ponderōsa* : Latin *pīnus,* pine-tree + Latin *ponderōsa,* feminine of *ponderōsus,* heavy; see PONDEROUS.]

pon·der·ous (pŏn′dər-əs) *adj.* **1.** Having great weight. **2.** Unwieldy from weight or bulk. **3.** Lacking grace or fluency; labored and dull: *a ponderous speech.* See Synonyms at **heavy.** [Middle English, from Old French *pondereux,* from Latin *ponderōsus,* from *pondus, ponder-,* weight. See **(s)pen-** in Appendix.] **—pon′der·ous·ly** *adv.* **—pon′der·ous·ness, pon′der·os′i·ty** (-ŏs′ĭ-tē) *n.*

Pon·di·cher·ry (pŏn′dĭ-chĕr′ē, -shĕr′ē). A city of southeast India on the Bay of Bengal south-southwest of Madras. It consists of four former French coastal settlements whose administration was transferred to India in 1954. Population, 162,636.

pond lily *n.* See **water lily.**

pond scum *n.* Any of various freshwater algae that form a usually greenish film on the surface of stagnant water.

pond·weed (pŏnd′wēd′) *n.* Any of various submerged or floating aquatic plants of the genus *Potamogeton* having inconspicuous flowers borne in small spikes.

♦ **pone** (pōn) *n. Chiefly Southern U.S.* See **johnnycake.** See Regional Note at **johnnycake.** [Virginia Algonquian *poan, appoans,* cornbread.]

♦ ***REGIONAL NOTE:*** A staple of the early American colonies from New England southward to Virginia was *pone,* a bread made by Native Americans from flat cakes of cornmeal dough baked in ashes. Derived from an Algonquian word meaning "to roast" or "to bake," *pone* is one of several Virginia Algonquian words (including *hominy* and *tomahawk*) borrowed into the English of the Atlantic seaboard. The word *pone,* usually in the compound *cornpone,* is now used mainly in the South, where it means cakes of cornbread baked on a griddle or in hot ashes—as the Native Americans originally cooked it.

pon·gee (pŏn-jē′, pŏn′jē) *n.* A soft, thin cloth woven from Chinese or Indian raw silk or an imitation thereof. [Chinese (Mandarin) *bě zhī* : *běn,* one's own + *zhī,* to weave, spin.]

pon·gid (pŏn′jĭd) *n.* An anthropoid ape of the family Pongidae, which includes the chimpanzee, gorilla, and orangutan. **—pongid** *adj.* Of or belonging to the family Pongidae. [From New Latin *Pongidae,* family name, from *Pongo,* type genus, of African origin.]

pon·iard (pŏn′yərd) *n.* A dagger typically having a slender square or triangular blade. **—poniard** *tr.v.* **-iard·ed, -iard·ing, -iards.** To stab with such a dagger. [French *poignard,* from *poing,* fist, from Old French, from Latin *pugnus.* See **peuk-** in Appendix.]

pons (pŏnz) *n., pl.* **pon·tes** (pŏn′tēz). **1.** A slender tissue joining two parts of an organ. **2.** The pons Varolii. [Latin *pōns,* bridge. See **pent-** in Appendix.]

pons as·i·no·rum (pŏnz′ ăs′ə-nôr′əm, -nōr′əm) *n.* A problem that severely tests the ability of an inexperienced person. [New Latin *pōns asinōrum* : Latin *pōns,* bridge + Latin *asinōrum,* genitive pl. of *asinus,* ass, fool.]

Pon·selle (pŏn-sĕl′), **Rosa Melba.** 1897–1981. American soprano who was a leading performer with the Metropolitan Opera in the 1920's and 1930's.

pons Va·ro·li·i (pŏnz′ və-rō′lē-ī′) *n.* A band of nerve fibers on the ventral surface of the brain stem that links the medulla oblongata and the cerebellum with upper portions of the brain. [New Latin *pōns Varoliī,* bridge of Varoli, after Costanzo *Varolio* (1543?–1575), Italian anatomist.]

Pon·ta Del·ga·da (pŏn′tə dĕl-gä′də, pôɴ′-). A city of southwest Sao Miguel Island in the Azores. It is the chief commercial city of the island group. Population, 21,187.

Pont·char·train (pŏn′chər-trān′), **Lake.** A lake of southeast Louisiana north of New Orleans. A causeway links New Orleans with the region north of the lake.

pon·tes (pŏn′tēz) *n.* Plural of **pons.**

Pon·ti·ac[1] (pŏn′tē-ăk′). 1720?–1769. Ottawa leader who led a large Native American revolt against the British in the Great Lakes region (1763–1766).

Pon·ti·ac[2] (pŏn′tē-ăk′). A city of southeast Michigan northwest of Detroit. Its carriage-making industry of the 1880's was replaced by automobile manufacturing in the early 20th century. Population, 76,715.

Pon·ti·a·nak (pŏn′tē-ä′näk). A city of western Borneo, Indonesia, at the northern edge of the Kapuas River delta. Capital of a sultanate founded in 1772, it later became a major gold-exporting center. Population, 304,778.

pon·ti·fex (pŏn′tə-fĕks′) *n., pl.* **pon·tif·i·ces** (pŏn-tĭf′ĭ-sēz′). A man on the highest council of priests in ancient Rome. [Latin. See **pent-** in Appendix.]

pon·tiff (pŏn′tĭf) *n.* **1.a.** The pope. **b.** A bishop. **2.** A pontifex. [French *pontife,* from Old French *pontif,* from Latin *pontifex,* pontifex. See **pent-** in Appendix.]

pon·tif·i·cal (pŏn-tĭf′ĭ-kəl) *adj.* **1.** Relating to, characteristic of, or suitable for a pope or a bishop. **2.** Having the dignity, pomp, or authority of a pontiff or a bishop. **3.** Pompously dogmatic or self-important; pretentious. **—pontifical** *n.* **1. pontificals.** The vestments and insignia of a pontiff or a bishop. **2.** A book of forms for ceremonies performed by a bishop. [Middle English, from Old French, from Latin *pontificālis,* of a pontifex, from *pontifex, pontific-,* pontifex. See PONTIFEX.] **—pon·tif′i·cal·ly** *adv.*

Pon·tif·i·cal Mass (pŏn-tĭf′ĭ-kəl) *n. Ecclesiastical.* A celebration of the Eucharist performed by a bishop in all Roman Catholic churches, many Anglican churches, and some Lutheran churches.

pon·tif·i·cate (pŏn-tĭf′ĭ-kĭt, -kāt′) *n.* The office or term of office of a pontiff. **—pontificate** (-kāt′) *intr.v.* **-cat·ed, -cat·ing, -cates. 1.** To express opinions or judgments in a dogmatic way. **2.** To administer the office of a pontiff. [Latin *pontificātus,* from *pontifex, pontific-,* pontifex. See PONTIFEX. V., from Medieval Latin *pontificāre, pontificāt-,* to act as an ecclesiastic, from Latin *pontifex,* pontifex.] **—pon·tif′i·ca′tion** *n.* **—pon·tif′i·ca′tor** *n.*

pon·tif·i·ces (pŏn-tĭf′ĭ-sēz′) *n.* Plural of **pontifex.**

pon·til (pŏn′tĭl) *n.* See **punty.** [French, possibly from Italian *puntello,* diminutive of *punto,* point, from Latin *pūnctum,* from neuter past participle of *pungere,* to prick. See **peuk-** in Appendix.]

pon·tine (pŏn′tīn′, -tēn′) *adj.* **1.** Of or relating to bridges. **2.** Of or relating to a pons, especially the pons Varolii. [Latin *pōns, pont-,* bridge; see **pent-** in Appendix + -INE[1].]

Pon·tine Marshes (pŏn′tēn, -tīn). An area of central Italy between the Tyrrhenian Sea and the Apennine foothills. Formerly a malarial breeding ground, the land was drained during the 1930's to produce fertile farmland.

Pon·tius Pi·late (pŏn′chəs pī′lət). See Pontius **Pilate.**

Pont l'É·vêque (pŏnt′ lə-vĕk′, pôɴ′ lā-vĕk′) *n.* A mild, soft-centered French cheese made of whole milk. [After *Pont l'Évêque,* a town of northwest France.]

pon·to·nier (pŏn′tə-nîr′) *n.* One who is in charge of pontoons or is engaged in the construction of pontoon bridges. [French *pontonnier,* from Old French, from *ponton,* pontoon. See PONTOON.]

pon·toon (pŏn-to͞on′) *n.* **1.** A floating structure, such as a flat-bottomed boat, that is used to support a bridge. **2.** A floating structure serving as a dock. **3.** A float on a seaplane. [French *ponton,* from Old French, from Latin *pontō, pontōn-,* floating bridge, from *pōns, pont-,* bridge. See **pent-** in Appendix.]

pontoon bridge *n.* A temporary floating bridge that uses pontoons for support. Also called *bateau bridge.*

Pon·top·pi·dan (pŏn-tŏp′ĭ-dăn′, -dän′), **Henrik.** 1857–1943. Danish writer known for his series *The Promised Land* (1891–1895). He shared the 1917 Nobel Prize for literature.

Pon·tus (pŏn′təs). An ancient country of northeast Asia Minor along the southern coast of the Black Sea. Established in the fourth century B.C., it flourished under Mithridates VI until his defeat by Pompey of Rome in 66. **—Pon′tic** (-tĭk) *adj.*

Pon·ty·pool (pŏn′tə-po͞ol′). An urban district of southeast Wales north-northeast of Cardiff. Its iron and tin industries began in the late 16th century. Population, 90,300.

po·ny (pō′nē) *n., pl.* **-nies. 1.** Any of several types or breeds of horses that are small in size when full grown, such as the Shetland pony. **2.a.** *Informal.* A racehorse. **b.** *Sports.* A polo horse. **3.** Something small for its kind, especially a small glass for beer or liqueur. **4.** A word-for-word translation of a foreign language text, especially one used secretly by students as an aid in studying or test-taking. Also called *crib, trot.* **5.** *Chiefly British.* The sum of 25 pounds. **—pony** *tr. & intr.v.* **-nied, -ny·ing, -nies.** To study with the aid of a pony: *pony a lesson; ponied all night before the exam.* **—*phrasal verb.* pony up.** *Slang.* To pay (money owed or due). [Probably from obsolete French *poulenet,* diminutive of *poulain,* colt, from Late Latin *pullāmen,* young of an animal, from Latin *pullus.* See **pau-** in Appendix.]

pony express

pony express *n.* A system of rapid mail transportation by relays of horses that operated from St. Joseph, Missouri, to Sacramento, California, in 1860–1861.

po·ny·tail (pō′nē-tāl′) *n.* A hairstyle in which the hair is held back so as to hang down like a pony's tail. **—po′ny·tailed′** *adj.*

Pon·zi scheme (pŏn′zē) *n.* An investment swindle in which high profits are promised from fictitious sources and early investors are paid off with funds raised from later ones. [After Charles *Ponzi* (1882?–1949), Italian-born speculator who organized such a scheme (1919–1920).]

pooch (po͞och) *n. Slang.* A dog. [Origin unknown.]

pood (po͞od) *n.* A Russian unit of weight equivalent to about 16.4 kilograms (36.1 pounds) avoirdupois. [Russian *pud,* from Old Norse *pund,* pound, ultimately from Latin *pondō.* See POUND[1].]

poo·dle (po͞od′l) *n.* Any of a breed of dogs originally developed in Europe as hunting dogs, having thick, curly hair of varying color, and classified by shoulder height into standard, miniature, and toy varieties. [German *Pudel,* short for *Pudelhund* : Low German *pudeln,* to splash about (from *pudel,* puddle) + *Hund,* dog; see DACHSHUND.]

pooh (po͞o) *interj.* Used to express disdain or disbelief.

Pooh-Bah or **pooh-bah** (po͞o′bä′) *n.* **1.** A pompous, ostentatious official, especially one who, holding many offices, fulfills none of them. **2.** A person who holds high office. [After *Pooh-*

ă pat	oi boy
ā pay	ou out
âr care	o͝o took
ä father	o͞o boot
ĕ pet	ŭ cut
ē be	ûr urge
ĭ pit	th thin
ī pie	*th* this
îr pier	hw which
ŏ pot	zh vision
ō toe	ə about, item
ô paw	♦ regionalism

Stress marks: ′ (primary); ′ (secondary), as in **dictionary** (dĭk′shə-nĕr′ē)

Bah, Lord-High-Everything-Else, a character in *The Mikado* by W.S. Gilbert and Arthur Sullivan.]

pooh-pooh (po͞o′po͞o′) *tr.v.* **-poohed, -pooh·ing, -poohs.** *Informal.* To express contempt for or impatience about; make light of: *"British actors have long pooh-poohed the Method"* (Stephen Schiff). [Reduplication of POOH.]

pool[1] (po͞ol) *n.* **1.** A small body of still water. **2.** An accumulation of standing liquid; a puddle: *a pool of blood.* **3.** A deep or still place in a stream. **4.** A swimming pool. **5.** An underground accumulation of petroleum or gas in porous sedimentary rock. **—pool** *intr.v.* **pooled, pool·ing, pools. 1.** To form pools or a pool: *The receding tide pooled in hollows along the shore.* **2.** To accumulate in a body part: *preventing blood from pooling in the limbs.* [Middle English, from Old English *pōl.*]

pool[2] (po͞ol) *n.* **1.** *Games.* **a.** A game of chance, resembling a lottery, in which the contestants put staked money into a common fund that is later paid to the winner. **b.** A fund containing all the money bet in a game of chance or on the outcome of an event. **2.** A grouping of resources for the common advantage of the participants: *a pool of implements for the use of all the workers on the estate; forming a pool of our talents.* **3.** An available supply, the use of which is shared by a group. **4.** A group of journalists who cover an event and then by agreement share their reports with participating news media: *the White House press pool.* **5.a.** A mutual fund established by a group of stockholders for speculating in or manipulating prices of securities. **b.** The persons or parties participating in such a fund. **6.** An agreement between competing business concerns to establish controls over production, market, and prices for common profit. **7.** Any of several games played on a six-pocket billiard table usually with 15 object balls and a cue ball. In this sense, also called *pocket billiards.* **—pool** *v.* **pooled, pool·ing, pools.** *—tr.* To put into a fund for use by all: *Let's pool our resources to finish the project quickly.* *—intr.* To join or form a pool. [French *poule,* hen, stakes, booty, from Old French, hen, young chicken, from Latin *pullus,* young of an animal. See **pau-** in Appendix.] **—pool′er** *n.*

Poole (po͞ol). A municipal borough of southern England west-southwest of Southhampton on **Poole Bay,** an inlet of the English Channel. Chartered in 1248, Poole is a port and shipbuilding center with varied industries. Population, 120,000.

pool·room (po͞ol′ro͞om′, -ro͝om′) *n. Games.* A commercial establishment or room for the playing of pool or billiards.

pool·side (po͞ol′sīd′) *n.* The area next to or around a swimming pool. *—attributive.* Often used to modify another noun: *poolside furniture; a poolside party.*

pool table *n. Games.* A six-pocket billiards table on which pool is played.

poon (po͞on) *n.* Any of several trees of the genus *Calophyllum,* of southern Asia, having light, hard wood used for masts and spars. [Singhalese *pūna,* perhaps of Dravidian origin.]

Poo·na (po͞o′nə). A city of west-central India east-southeast of Bombay. It was a Maratha capital in the 17th and 18th centuries and passed to the British in 1818. Population, 1,203,351.

poop[1] (po͞op) *Nautical. n.* **1.** A superstructure at the stern of a ship. **2.** A poop deck. **—poop** *tr.v.* **pooped, poop·ing, poops. 1.** To break over the stern of (a ship). **2.** To take (a wave) over the stern. [Middle English *poupe,* from Old French, from Latin *puppis.*]

poop[2] (po͞op) *tr.v.* **pooped, poop·ing, poops.** *Slang.* To cause to become fatigued; tire: *"Many people stop here, pooped by the short, steep climb"* (Sierra Club Guides to the National Parks). ***—phrasal verb.*** **poop out.** *Slang.* **1.** To quit because of exhaustion: *poop out of a race.* **2.** To decide not to participate, especially at the last moment. [Origin unknown.]

poop[3] (po͞op) *n. Slang.* Inside information: *She gave me all the poop on the company party.* [Origin unknown.]

poop[4] (po͞op) *n. Slang.* A person regarded as very disagreeable. [Perhaps short for NINCOMPOOP.]

poop[5] (po͞op) *Slang. n.* Excrement. **—poop** *intr.v.* **pooped, poop·ing, poops.** To defecate. [Possibly from obsolete *poop,* to break wind, from Middle English *poupen,* to blow a horn, toot, of imitative origin.]

poop deck *n. Nautical.* An exposed, partial deck on the stern superstructure of a ship.

poop·er-scoop·er (po͞o′pər sko͞o′pər) *n.* A scoop for picking up and removing the feces of a dog or other pet. [From POOP[5] + SCOOP.]

poor (po͝or) *adj.* **poor·er, poor·est. 1.** Having little or no wealth and few or no possessions. **2.** Lacking in a specified resource or quality: *an area poor in timber and coal; a diet poor in calcium.* **3.** Not adequate in quality; inferior: *a poor performance.* **4.a.** Lacking in value; insufficient: *poor wages.* **b.** Lacking in quantity: *poor attendance.* **5.** Lacking fertility: *poor soil.* **6.** Undernourished; lean. **7.** Humble: *a poor spirit.* **8.** Eliciting or deserving pity; pitiable: *couldn't rescue the poor fellow.* **—poor** *n. (used with a pl. verb).* People with little or no wealth and possessions considered as a group: *The urban poor are in need of homes.* [Middle English *poure,* from Old French *povre,* from Latin *pauper.* See **pau-** in Appendix.] **—poor′ness** *n.*

SYNONYMS: *poor, indigent, needy, impecunious, penniless, impoverished, poverty-stricken, destitute.* These adjectives mean lacking the money or the means requisite to an adequate or comfortable life. *Poor* is the most general: *"Resolve not to be poor: whatever you have, spend less. Poverty is a great enemy to human happiness"* (Samuel Johnson). *Indigent* and *needy* refer to one in need or want: *The town government is responsible for assistance to indigent people. Local politicians used to distribute Thanksgiving turkeys to needy families. Impecunious* and *penniless* mean having little or no money: *"Certainly an impecunious Subaltern was not a catch"* (Rudyard Kipling). *If the breadwinner deserts the family, it will be left penniless.* One who is *impoverished* has been reduced to poverty: *The dictator, whose greed and excesses had produced an impoverished citizenry, fled the country. Poverty-stricken* means suffering from poverty and miserably poor: *"The poverty-stricken exiles contributed far more, in proportion . . . than the wealthy merchants"* (John Lothrop Motley). *Destitute* means lacking any means of subsistence: *Some nations have no middle class; one group is rich, while the other is destitute.*

USAGE NOTE: In informal speech *poor* is sometimes used as an adverb, as in *They never played poorer.* In formal usage *more poorly* would be required in this example.

poor box *n.* A box, such as one to be found in a church, used for collecting alms.

♦**poor boy** *n. New Orleans.* See **submarine** (sense 2). See Regional Note at **submarine.**

poor farm *n.* A farm that houses, supports, and employs the poor at public expense.

poor·house (po͝or′hous′) *n.* An establishment maintained at public expense as housing for the homeless.

poo·ri also **pu·ri** (po͝or′ē) *n., pl.* **-ris.** A light, flat wheat cake of Pakistan and northern India, usually fried in deep fat. [Hindi *puri,* from Sanskrit *pūraḥ,* cake. See **pele-**[1] in Appendix.]

poor·ish (po͝or′ĭsh) *adj.* Somewhat poor.

poor law *n.* A law or system of laws providing for public relief and support of the poor.

♦**poor·ly** (po͝or′lē) *adv.* In a poor manner. See Usage Note at **poor. —poorly** *adj. Chiefly Southern U.S.* In poor health; ill: *feeling poorly.* See Usage Note at **bad**[1]**.**

poor·mouth (po͝or′mouth′, -mouth′) *v.* **-mouthed, -mouth·ing, -mouths.** *—tr.* To speak ill of. *—intr.* To claim poverty as an excuse or a defense: *always poormouths when asked to donate to charity.* **—poormouth** *n.* An exaggerated assertion of poverty.

poor white *n. Offensive.* Used as a disparaging term for a member of a class of low-income white farmers and laborers, especially in the southern United States.

♦**pop**[1] (pŏp) *v.* **popped, pop·ping, pops.** *—intr.* **1.** To make a short, sharp, explosive sound. **2.** To burst open with a short, sharp, explosive sound. **3.** To move quickly or unexpectedly; appear abruptly: *At last the cottage popped into view.* **4.** To open wide suddenly: *The child's eyes popped with astonishment.* **5.** *Baseball.* To hit a short high fly ball, especially one that can be caught by an infielder: *popped out to shortstop.* **6.** To shoot a firearm, such as a pistol. *—tr.* **1.** To cause to make a sharp bursting sound. **2.** To cause to explode with a sharp bursting sound: *popped the balloon.* **3.** To put or thrust suddenly or unexpectedly: *"popping a crisp plump shrimp into her mouth"* (Kathleen Winsor). **4.a.** To discharge (a firearm). **b.** To fire at; shoot. **5.** To hit or strike: *popped me on the head.* **6.** *Baseball.* To hit (a ball) high in the air but not far. **7.** *Slang.* **a.** To take (drugs), especially orally: *"To calm a case of the jitters . . . the bride popped Valium"* (People). **b.** To have (a drink): *popped a few beers after work.* **—pop** *n.* **1.** A sudden sharp, explosive sound. **2.** A shot with a firearm. **3.** *Chiefly Midwestern U.S.* See **soft drink.** See Regional Note at **tonic. 4.** *Baseball.* A pop fly. **—pop** *adv.* **1.** With a popping sound. **2.** Abruptly or unexpectedly. **3.** *Slang.* Apiece; each: *Tickets to the benefit were $50 a pop.* ***—phrasal verb.*** **pop off.** *Informal.* **1.** To leave abruptly or hurriedly. **2.** To die suddenly. **3.** To speak thoughtlessly in a burst of released anger. ***—idiom.*** **pop the question.** *Informal.* To propose marriage. [Middle English *poppen,* from *pop,* a blow, stroke, of imitative origin.]

pop[2] (pŏp) *n. Informal.* Father. [Short for PAPA.]

pop[3] (pŏp) *Informal. adj.* **1.** Of or for the general public; popular or popularized: *pop culture; pop psychology.* **2.** Of, relating to, or specializing in popular music: *a pop singer.* **3.** Of or suggestive of pop art: *a pop style.* **—pop** *n.* **1.** Popular music. **2.** Pop art.

POP *abbr.* Proof of purchase.

pop. *abbr.* **1.** Popular. **2.** Population.

pop art *n.* A form of art that depicts objects or scenes from everyday life and employs techniques of commercial art and popular illustration.

pop·corn (pŏp′kôrn′) *n.* **1.a.** A variety of corn, *Zea mays everta,* having hard kernels that burst to form white, irregularly shaped puffs when heated. **b.** The edible, popped kernels of this variety of corn. **2.** A small piece, as of polystyrene, used in quantity to protect items during packaging and shipment. [Contraction of *popped corn.*]

WORD HISTORY: Popcorn is very much an American institution. Particularly enjoyed by people in the United States, it is grown as a native product and denoted by a word that is an Americanism, a word or expression that was first used in English in the United States. *Popcorn,* from the verb *pop* and the noun *corn,* fits these criteria because the first recorded use of the word is found in *Memorable Days in America,* an account written by the British

pop art
Campbell's Soup, 1965, by Andy Warhol. *Oil silkscreened on canvas, 36⅛" × 24". The Museum of Modern Art, New York. Philip Johnson Fund.*

traveler William Faux and published in London in 1823: "I crossed the Big Wabash . . . at La Valette's ferry, where is beautiful land . . . and two lonely families of naked-legged French settlers from whom I received two curious ears of poss corn." Notice that either Faux misunderstood the term or the French settlers mispronounced it. This type of corn, introduced to the settlers by Native Americans, was long grown by them, little knowing that their benefaction would one day be consumed by countless moviegoers while watching Westerns.

popcorn flower *n.* Any of several plants of the genus *Plagiobothrys,* of western North America, having cymose clusters of small flowers with a white salverform corolla.

pope (pōp) *n.* **1.** Often **Pope.** *Roman Catholic Church.* The bishop of Rome and head of the Roman Catholic Church on earth. **2.** *Eastern Orthodox Church.* The patriarch of Alexandria. **3.** The Coptic patriarch of Alexandria. **4.** The male head of some non-Christian religions: *the Taoist pope.* **5.** A person considered to have unquestioned authority: *the pope of surrealism.* [Middle English, from Old English *pāpa,* from Late Latin, from Latin, father (title of bishops), from Greek *pappas.* See **papa** in Appendix.]

Pope, Alexander. 1688–1744. English writer best remembered for his satirical mock-epic poems *The Rape of the Lock* (1712) and *The Dunciad* (1728).

Pope, John. 1822–1892. American Union general in the Civil War who was defeated by Gen. Robert E. Lee at the Second Battle of Bull Run (1862).

pope·dom (pōp′dəm) *n.* The office, jurisdiction, or tenure of a pope; the papacy.

pop·er·y (pō′pə-rē) *n. Offensive.* The doctrines, practices, and rituals of the Roman Catholic Church.

pope's nose (pōps) *n. Informal.* The tail of a cooked fowl. Also called *parson's nose.*

pop·eyed (pŏp′īd′) *adj.* **1.** Having bulging eyes. **2.** Amazed; astonished: *popeyed with wonder.*

pop fly *n. Baseball.* A short high fly ball. Also called *pop-up.*

pop·gun (pŏp′gŭn′) *n.* A toy gun that makes a popping noise.

pop·in·jay (pŏp′ĭn-jā′) *n.* A vain, talkative person. [Middle English, parrot, from Old French *papegai,* from Spanish *papagayo* or Old Provençal *papagai,* both from Arabic *babġā', babaġā',* from Persian *babbaghā.*]

pop·ish (pō′pĭsh) *adj. Offensive.* Of or relating to the popes or the Roman Catholic Church. **—pop′ish·ly** *adv.* **—pop′ish·ness** *n.*

pop·lar (pŏp′lər) *n.* **1.a.** Any of several fast-growing deciduous trees of the genus *Populus* having unisexual flowers borne in catkins. **b.** The wood of these trees. **2.** See **tulip tree** (sense 1). [Middle English *popler,* from Old French *poplier,* from *pouple,* from Latin *pōpulus.*]

Pop·lar Bluff (pŏp′lər). A city of southeast Missouri near the Arkansas border south of St. Louis. It is a trade, shipping, and manufacturing center in a farming area. Population, 17,139.

pop·lin (pŏp′lĭn) *n.* A ribbed fabric of silk, rayon, wool, or cotton, used in making clothing and upholstery. [Obsolete French *papeline,* perhaps from Provençal *papalino,* feminine of *papalin,* papal (so called because it was first made at the papal town of Avignon), from Medieval Latin *pāpālis,* from Late Latin *pāpa,* pope. See POPE.]

pop·lit·e·al (pŏp-lĭt′ē-əl, pŏp′lĭ-tē′əl) *adj.* Of or relating to the hollow part of the leg behind the knee joint. [From New Latin *popliteus,* from Latin *poples, poplit-,* ham of the knee.]

Po·po·ca·té·petl (pō′pə-kăt′ə-pĕt′l, pô′pô-kä-tĕ′pĕt′l). A volcano, 5,455.5 m (17,887 ft) high, in central Mexico west of Puebla. It has been dormant since 1702 but occasionally emits large puffs of steam.

pop·o·ver (pŏp′ō′vər) *n.* A very light, hollow muffin made with eggs, milk, and flour.

pop·pa (pä′pə) *n.* Variant of **papa.**

pop·per (pŏp′ər) *n.* **1.** One that pops. **2.** A container or pan for making popcorn. **3.** *Slang.* An ampoule of amyl nitrite or butyl nitrite used as a stimulant drug.

Pop·per (pŏp′ər), Sir **Karl Raimund.** Born 1902. British philosopher known for his contributions to the understanding of scientific reasoning and his attacks on historicism. His works include *The Open Society and Its Enemies* (1945).

pop·pet (pŏp′ĭt) *n.* **1.** A poppet valve. **2.** *Nautical.* **a.** A small wooden strip on a gunwale that forms or supports an oarlock. **b.** One of the beams of a launching cradle supporting a ship's hull. **3.** *Chiefly British.* A darling. [Middle English *popet,* small child, doll, puppet. See PUPPET.]

poppet valve *n.* An intake or exhaust valve, operated by springs and cams, that plugs and unplugs its opening by axial motion.

pop·ple¹ (pŏp′əl) *intr.v.* **-pled, -pling, -ples.** To move in a tossing, bubbling, or rippling manner, as choppy water. **—popple** *n.* **1.** Choppy water. **2.** The motion or sound of boiling liquid. [Middle English *poplen,* probably of Middle Dutch origin.]

pop·ple² (pŏp′əl) *n. Informal.* A poplar. [Middle English *popel* (perhaps from Old English *popul-*), from Latin *pōpulus.*]

pop·py (pŏp′ē) *n., pl.* **-pies. 1.** Any of numerous plants of the genus *Papaver,* having nodding buds with four crumpled petals, showy red, orange, or white flowers, a milky juice, and capsules that dehisce through terminal pores. **2.** Any of several similar or related plants, such as the California poppy. **3.** An extract from the sap of unripe poppy seedpods, used in medicine and narcotics. **4.** *Color.* A vivid red to reddish orange. [Middle English *popi,* from Old English *popig,* probably alteration of Vulgar Latin **papāvum,* alteration of Latin *papāver.*]

poppy
Prickly poppy
Argemone mexicana

pop·py·cock (pŏp′ē-kŏk′) *n.* Senseless talk; nonsense. [Dutch dialectal *pappekak* : *pap,* pap (from Middle Dutch *pappe,* perhaps from Latin *pappa,* food) + *kak,* dung (from *kakken,* to defecate, from Middle Dutch *kacken,* from Latin *cacāre;* see **kakka-** in Appendix).]

Pop·si·cle (pŏp′sĭ-kəl, -sĭk′əl). A trademark used for a colored, flavored ice confection with one or two flat sticks for a handle. This trademark sometimes occurs in lowercase in print: *"The roast duck . . . is best avoided; it is the color of an orange popsicle and flabby"* (Washington Post). It occurs in the plural: *"The neighborhood children cavorted in the street buying snow cones and Popsicles"* (Chicago Tribune). The trademark also occurs in figurative contexts: "[He] *likes blue and lavender lighting and finds lots of excuses to use it in the neon Popsicle landscape whose unrealness he celebrates"* (Boston Globe).

pop-top (pŏp′tŏp′) *n.* **1.** The tab of a container that can be pulled off to make an opening. **2.** A container having such a tab. **—pop-top** *adj.* Having a tab that can be pulled up or off to make an opening in a container: *pop-top beer cans.*

pop·u·lace (pŏp′yə-lĭs) *n.* **1.** The general public; the masses. **2.** A population. [French, from Italian *popolaccio,* rabble, from *popolo,* the people, from Latin *populus.* See POPULAR.]

pop·u·lar (pŏp′yə-lər) *adj. Abbr.* **pop. 1.** Widely liked or appreciated: *a popular resort.* **2.** Liked by acquaintances; sought after for company: *"Beware of over-great pleasure in being popular or even beloved"* (Margaret Fuller). **3.** Of, representing, or carried on by the people at large: *the popular vote.* **4.** Fit for, adapted to, or reflecting the taste of the people at large: *popular entertainment; popular science.* **5.** Accepted by or prevalent among the people in general: *a popular misunderstanding of the issue.* **6.** Suited to or within the means of ordinary people: *popular prices.* **7.** Originating among the people: *popular legend.* [Middle English *populer,* from Old French *populaire,* from Latin *populāris,* of the people, from *populus,* the people, of Etruscan origin.] **—pop′u·lar·ly** *adv.*

popular front *n.* A political coalition of leftist parties against fascism, such as that formed among European countries during the 1930's.

pop·u·lar·i·ty (pŏp′yə-lăr′ĭ-tē) *n.* The quality or state of being popular, especially the state of being widely admired, accepted, or sought after.

pop·u·lar·ize (pŏp′yə-lə-rīz′) *tr.v.* **-ized, -iz·ing, -iz·es. 1.** To make popular: *A famous dancer popularized the new hairstyle.* **2.** To present in a widely understandable or acceptable form: *popularize technical material for a general audience.* **—pop′u·lar·i·za′tion** (-lər-ĭ-zā′shən) *n.* **—pop′u·lar·iz′er** *n.*

pop·u·late (pŏp′yə-lāt′) *tr.v.* **-lat·ed, -lat·ing, -lates. 1.** To supply with inhabitants, as by colonization; people. **2.** To live in; inhabit: *creatures that populate the ocean depths.* [Medieval Latin *populāre, populāt-,* from Latin *populus,* the people. See POPULAR.]

pop·u·la·tion (pŏp′yə-lā′shən) *n. Abbr.* **pop., p. 1.a.** All of the people inhabiting a specified area. **b.** The total number of such people. **2.** The total number of inhabitants constituting a particular race, class, or group in a specified area. **3.** The act or process of furnishing with inhabitants. **4.** *Ecology.* All the organisms that constitute a specific group or occur in a specified habitat. **5.** *Statistics.* The set of individuals, items, or data from which a statistical sample is taken. In this sense, also called *universe.*

population control *n.* A government program to limit or slow population growth, as by birth control education, the wide availability of contraceptives, and economic incentives.

population explosion *n.* The geometric expansion of a biological population, especially the unchecked growth in human population resulting from a decrease in infant mortality and an increase in longevity.

population genetics *n. (used with a sing. verb).* The branch of genetics that deals with the genetic makeup of populations.

pop·u·lism (pŏp′yə-lĭz′əm) *n.* **1.a.** A political philosophy supporting the rights and power of the people in their struggle against the privileged elite. **b.** The movement organized around this philosophy. **2. Populism.** The philosophy of the Populist Party.

pop·u·list (pŏp′yə-lĭst) *n.* **1.** A supporter of the rights and power of the people. **2. Populist.** A supporter of the Populist Party. **—populist** *adj.* **1.** Of, relating to, or characteristic of populism or its advocates: *a populist aversion to business monopolies.* **2. Populist.** Of or relating to the Populist Party.

Populist Party *n.* A U.S. political party that sought to represent the interests of farmers and laborers in the 1890's, advocating increased currency issue, free coinage of gold and silver, public ownership of railroads, and a graduated federal income tax. Also called *People's Party.*

pop·u·lous (pŏp′yə-ləs) *adj.* Containing many people or inhabitants; having a large population. [Middle English, from Latin *populōsus,* from *populus,* the people. See POPULAR.] **—pop′u·lous·ly** *adv.* **—pop′u·lous·ness** *n.*

ă pat	oi boy
ā pay	ou out
âr care	o͝o took
ä father	o͞o boot
ĕ pet	ŭ cut
ē be	ûr urge
ĭ pit	th thin
ī pie	*th* this
îr pier	hw which
ŏ pot	zh vision
ō toe	ə about, item
ô paw	♦ regionalism

Stress marks: ′ (primary); ′ (secondary), as in **dictionary** (dĭk′shə-nĕr′ē)

porcelain
c. 1760–1770 Derby figure

porcupine
African porcupine
Hystrix cristata

porcupine fish
Diodon hystrix

porringer

pop-up (pŏp′ŭp′) *adj.* **1.** Emerging quickly from a recessed or concealed position when activated: *pop-up gun emplacements.* **2.** Rising to form a three-dimensional structure when a page is opened: *pop-up illustrations in a children's book.* **—pop-up** *n.* **1.** A device or an illustration that pops up. **2.** *Baseball.* See **pop fly.**

pop wine *n.* A sweet, often fruit-flavored, inexpensive wine.

por. *abbr.* Portrait.

por·bea·gle (pôr′bē′gəl) *n.* A mackeral shark *(Lamna nasus)* of temperate Atlantic waters. [Cornish *porbugel.*]

por·ce·lain (pôr′sə-lĭn, pōr′-, pôrs′lĭn, pōrs′-) *n.* **1.** A hard, white, translucent ceramic made by firing a pure clay and then glazing it with variously colored fusible materials; china. **2.** An object made of this substance. *—attributive.* Often used to modify another noun: *porcelain teacups; a doll with a porcelain face.* [French *porcelaine,* cowry shell, porcelain, from Old French, from Old Italian *porcellana,* from feminine of *porcellano,* of a young sow (from the shell's resemblance to a pig's back), from *porcella,* young sow, diminutive of *porca,* sow, from Latin, feminine of *porcus,* pig. See **porko-** in Appendix.] **—por′ce·la′ne·ous** (-lā′nē-əs) *adj.*

porcelain enamel *n.* A glass coating fired on metal. Also called *vitreous enamel.*

porcelain flower *n.* See **hoya.**

porch (pôrch, pōrch) *n.* **1.** A covered platform, usually having a separate roof, at an entrance to a building. **2.** An open or enclosed gallery or room attached to the outside of a building; a verandah. **3.** *Obsolete.* A portico or covered walk. [Middle English *porche,* from Old French, from Latin *porticus,* portico, from *porta,* gate. See **per-[2]** in Appendix.]

por·cine (pôr′sīn′) *adj.* Of or resembling swine or a pig: *"a bald porcine old man"* (Vladimir Nabokov). [Middle English, from Old French *porcin,* from Latin *porcīnus,* from *porcus,* pig. See **porko-** in Appendix.]

por·cu·pine (pôr′kyə-pīn′) *n.* Any of various rodents of the Old World family Hystricidae or the New World family Erethizontidae, having long, sharp, erectile quills interspersed with coarse hair. [Middle English *porke despine,* from Old French *porc espin* : Latin *porcus,* pig; see **porko-** in Appendix + Latin *spīna,* thorn, spine.]

porcupine fish *n.* Any of various tropical marine fishes of the family Diodontidae, having strong, sharp spines on the body and capable of inflating themselves when attacked.

Por·cu·pine River (pôr′kyə-pīn′). A river, about 721 km (448 mi) long, rising in northwest Yukon Territory, Canada, and flowing north then west to the Yukon River in northeast Alaska.

pore[1] (pôr, pōr) *intr.v.* **pored, por·ing, pores. 1.** To read or study carefully and attentively: *pored over the classified ads in search of a new job.* **2.** To gaze intently; stare. **3.** To meditate deeply; ponder: *pored on the matter.* [Middle English *pouren.*]

pore[2] (pôr, pōr) *n.* **1.** A minute opening in tissue, as in the skin of an animal, serving as an outlet for perspiration, or in a plant leaf or stem, serving as a means of absorption and transpiration. **2.** A space in rock, soil, or unconsolidated sediment that is not occupied by mineral matter and that allows the passage or absorption of fluids: *Water seeped into the pores of the rock.* [Middle English, from Old French, from Late Latin *porus,* passage, from Greek *poros.* See **per-[2]** in Appendix.]

pore fungus *n.* Any of various basidiomycetous fungi of the families Boletaceae and Polyporaceae, whose basidia line the inside of tubes that lead to exterior pores. Also called *polypore.*

por·gy (pôr′gē) *n., pl.* **porgy** or **-gies. 1.** Any of various deep-bodied marine food fishes of the family Sparidae, especially a common species *Pagrus pagrus* of Mediterranean and Atlantic waters. **2.** Any of several fishes similar to the porgy. [Alteration of Spanish and Portuguese *pargo,* both alteration of Latin *phager,* a kind of fish, from Greek *phagros,* sea bream.]

Po·ri (pôr′ē). A city of southwest Finland on an inlet of the Gulf of Bothnia northwest of Helsinki. Chartered in 1564, it was initially dominated by the Hanseatic League. Population, 78,933.

po·rif·er·an (pə-rĭf′ər-ən) *n.* Any of various members of the phylum Porifera constituting the sponges. [From New Latin *Porifera,* phylum name : Latin *porus,* passage; see PORE[2] + Latin *-fera,* neuter pl. of *-fer,* -fer.] **—po·rif′er·al, po·rif′er·an** *adj.*

po·rif·er·ous (pə-rĭf′ər-əs) *adj.* **1.** Having pores. **2.** Of or relating to the poriferans. [Latin *porus,* passage; see PORE[2] + –FEROUS.]

pork (pôrk, pōrk) *n.* **1.** The flesh of a pig or hog used as food. **2.** *Slang.* Government funds, appointments, or benefits dispensed or enacted by politicians to gain favor with their constituents. [Middle English, from Old French *porc,* pig, from Latin *porcus.* See **porko-** in Appendix.]

pork barrel *n. Slang.* A government project or appropriation that yields jobs or other benefits to a specific locale and patronage opportunities to its political representative.

pork belly *n.* A side of fresh pork.

pork·er (pôr′kər, pōr′-) *n.* A fattened young pig.

pork·pie (pôrk′pī′, pōrk′-) *n.* A man's hat having a low, flat crown and a flexible brim. Also called *porkpie hat.*

por·ky (pôr′kē, pōr′-) *n., pl.* **-kies.** *Informal.* A porcupine. [Shortening and alteration of PORCUPINE.]

porn (pôrn) also **por·no** (pôr′nō) *Slang.—n.* Pornography. *—adj.* Pornographic. **—porn′y** *adj.*

por·nog·ra·phy (pôr-nŏg′rə-fē) *n.* **1.** Pictures, writing, or other material that is sexually explicit and sometimes equates sex with power and violence. **2.** The presentation or production of this material. [French *pornographie,* from *pornographe,* pornographer, from Late Greek *pornographos,* writing about prostitutes : *pornē,* prostitute; see **per-[5]** in Appendix + *graphein,* to write; see –GRAPHY.] **—por·nog′ra·pher** *n.* **—por′no·graph′ic** (pôr′nə-grăf′ĭk) *adj.* **—por′no·graph′i·cal·ly** *adv.*

po·ro·mer·ic (pôr′ə-mĕr′ĭk, pōr′-) *n.* Any of several tough, porous leather substitutes. [Greek *poros,* passage; see **per-[2]** in Appendix + (POLY)MERIC.]

po·ros·i·ty (pə-rŏs′ĭ-tē, pô-) *n., pl.* **-ties. 1.** The state or property of being porous. **2.** A structure or part that is porous. **3.** The ratio of the volume of all the pores in a material to the volume of the whole. [Middle English *porosite,* from Old French, from Medieval Latin *porōsitās,* from *porōsus,* porous. See POROUS.]

po·rous (pôr′əs, pōr′-) *adj.* **1.** Full of or having pores. **2.** Admitting the passage of gas or liquid through pores or interstices. **3.** Easily crossed or penetrated. [Middle English, from Old French *poreux, poros,* from Medieval Latin *porōsus,* from Latin *porus,* passage. See PORE[2].] **—po′rous·ly** *adv.* **—po′rous·ness** *n.*

por·phyr·i·a (pôr-fîr′ē-ə) *n.* Any of several disorders of porphyrin metabolism, usually hereditary, characterized by the presence of large amounts of porphyrins in the blood and urine. [New Latin : PORPHYR(IN) + –IA[1].] **—por·phyr′ic** *adj.*

por·phy·rin (pôr′fə-rĭn) *n.* Any of various nitrogen-containing organic compounds, derived from pyrrole, occurring universally in protoplasm and providing the foundation structure for hemoglobin, chlorophyll, and certain enzymes. [Greek *porphura,* purple; see PURPLE + –IN.]

por·phy·rit·ic (pôr′fə-rĭt′ĭk) also **por·phy·rit·i·cal** (-ĭ-kəl) *adj.* **1.** Of or containing porphyry. **2.** Containing relatively large isolated crystals in a mass of fine texture.

por·phy·roid (pôr′fə-roid′) *n.* Metamorphic rock having porphyritic texture.

por·phy·rop·sin (pôr′fə-rŏp′sĭn) *n.* A purple pigment similar to rhodopsin, found in the rods of the retinas of freshwater fishes and certain frogs. [Greek *porphura,* purple + OPSIN.]

por·phy·ry (pôr′fə-rē) *n., pl.* **-ries.** Rock containing relatively large conspicuous crystals, especially feldspar, in a fine-grained igneous matrix. [Middle English *porphiri, porfurie,* from Old French *porfire,* from Italian *porfiro,* from Medieval Latin *porphyrium,* from Latin *porphyrītēs,* from Greek *porphuritēs,* from *porphura,* purple (from its color). See PURPLE.]

por·poise (pôr′pəs) *n., pl.* **porpoise** or **-pois·es. 1.** Any of several gregarious toothed whales of the genus *Phocaena* and related genera, of oceanic waters, characteristically having a blunt snout and a triangular dorsal fin. Also called *sea hog.* **2.** Any of several related aquatic mammals, such as the dolphin. [Middle English *porpeis,* from Old French (probably translation of a Germanic compound meaning sea-pig) : *porc,* pig (from Latin *porcus;* see **porko-** in Appendix) + *peis,* fish (from Latin *piscis*).]

por·rect (pə-rĕkt′, pô-) *adj. Zoology.* Stretched out or forth; extended, especially forward: *porrect mandibles.* [Latin *porrēctus,* past participle of *porrigere,* to stretch out : *por-,* forward, out; see **per[1]** in Appendix + *regere,* to direct, rule; see DIRECT.]

por·ridge (pôr′ĭj, pŏr′-) *n.* A soft food made by boiling oatmeal or another meal in water or milk. [Alteration of POTTAGE (influenced by obsolete *porray,* vegetable soup, from Middle English *porreie,* from Old French *poree,* leek soup, from *por,* leek, from Latin *porrum*).] **—por′ridg·y** *adj.*

por·rin·ger (pôr′ĭn-jər, pŏr′-) *n.* A shallow cup or bowl with a handle. [Middle English, alteration of *potinger, potager,* from Old French *potager,* from *potage,* soup. See POTTAGE.]

port[1] (pôrt, pōrt) *n. Abbr.* **pt. 1.a.** A place on a waterway with facilities for loading and unloading ships. **b.** A city or town on a waterway with such facilities. **c.** The waterfront district of a city. **2.** A place along a coast that gives ships and boats protection from storms and rough water; a harbor. **3.** A port of entry. **4.** *Computer Science.* **a.** An entrance to or exit for a data network. **b.** A connection point for a peripheral device. [Middle English, from Old English, from Latin *portus.* See **per-[2]** in Appendix.]

port[2] (pôrt, pōrt) *Nautical. n.* The left-hand side of a ship or aircraft facing forward. Also called *larboard.* **—port** *adj.* Of, relating to, or on the port. **—port** *tr. & intr.v.* **port·ed, port·ing, ports.** To turn (a craft) or make a shift to the port side: *port the helm; ported sharply to avoid a shoal.* [Probably from *port side,* from PORT[1].]

port[3] (pôrt, pōrt) *n.* **1.** *Nautical.* **a.** A porthole. **b.** *Archaic.* A cover for a porthole. **2.** An opening, as in a cylinder or valve face, for the passage of steam or fluid. **3.** A hole in an armored vehicle or a fortified structure for viewing or for firing weapons. **4.** *Scots.* A gateway or portal, as to a town. [Middle English, gate, porthole, from Old French *porte,* gate, from Latin *porta.* See **per-[2]** in Appendix.]

port[4] also **Port** (pôrt, pōrt) *n.* A rich sweet fortified wine. [After OPORTO.]

port[5] (pôrt, pōrt) *tr.v.* **port·ed, port·ing, ports.** To carry (a weapon) diagonally across the body, with the muzzle or blade near the left shoulder. **—port** *n.* **1.** The position of a rifle or other weapon when ported. **2.** The manner in which one carries oneself; bearing. [French *porter,* to carry, from Old French, from

Latin *portāre.* See **per-²** in Appendix. N., Middle English *porte,* from Old French *port,* from *porter,* to carry.]

Port. *abbr.* Portugal; Portuguese.

port·a·ble (pôr′tə-bəl, pōr′-) *adj.* **1.** Carried or moved with ease: *a portable typewriter; a portable generator.* **2.** *Obsolete.* Bearable; endurable. **—portable** *n.* Something, such as a light or small typewriter, that can be carried or moved with ease. [Middle English, from Old French, from Late Latin *portābilis,* from Latin *portāre,* to carry. See **per-²** in Appendix.] **—port′a·bil′i·ty, port′a·ble·ness** *n.* **—port′a·bly** *adv.*

port·age (pôr′tĭj, pōr′-, pôr-täzh′) *n.* **1.a.** The act or an instance of carrying. **b.** A charge for carrying. **2.** *Nautical.* **a.** The carrying of boats and supplies overland between two waterways or around an obstacle to navigation. **b.** A track or route used for such carrying. **—portage** *tr. & intr.v.* **-aged, -ag·ing, -ag·es.** *Nautical.* To transport or travel by portage: *canoed and portaged the goods; portaging around the rapids.* [Middle English, from Old French, from *porter,* to carry, from Latin *portāre.* See **per-²** in Appendix.]

Por·tage (pôr′tĭj, pōr′-). **1.** A city of northwest Indiana, an industrial suburb of Gary on Lake Michigan. Population, 27,409. **2.** A city of southwest Michigan south of Kalamazoo. It is a manufacturing center. Population, 38,157.

por·tal (pôr′tl, pōr′-) *n.* **1.** A doorway, an entrance, or a gate, especially one that is large and imposing. **2.** An entrance or a means of entrance: *the local library, a portal of knowledge.* **3.** The portal vein. **—portal** *adj.* **1.** Of or relating to the portal vein or the portal system. **2.** Of or relating to a point of entrance to an organ, especially the transverse fissure of the liver, through which the blood vessels enter. [Middle English, from Old French, from Medieval Latin *portāle,* city gate, from neuter of *portālis,* of a gate, from Latin *porta,* gate. See **per-²** in Appendix. N., sense 3 and adj., from New Latin *porta (hepatis),* transverse fissure (of the liver), from Latin, gate.]

Port Al·ber·ni (ăl-bûr′nē). A city of southwest British Columbia, Canada, on southeast-central Vancouver Island. It is a fishing port with wood-products industries. Population, 19,892.

portal system *n.* A system of blood vessels that begins and ends in capillaries.

por·tal-to-por·tal (pôr′tl-tə-pôr′tl, pōr′tl-tə-pōr′tl) *adj.* Of or based on the time a worker spends on the employer's property, calculated from the moment of arrival to that of departure: *portal-to-portal pay.*

portal vein *n.* A vein that conducts blood from the digestive organs, spleen, pancreas, and gall bladder to the liver.

por·ta·men·to (pôr′tə-mĕn′tō, pōr′-) *n., pl.* **-ti** (-tē) or **-tos.** *Music.* A smooth, uninterrupted glide in passing from one tone to another, especially with the voice or a bowed stringed instrument. [Italian, from *portare,* to carry, from Latin *portāre.* See **per-²** in Appendix.]

Port An·ge·les (ăn′jə-lĭs). A city of northwest Washington on the Strait of Juan de Fuca south of Victoria, British Columbia, Canada. Population, 17,311.

Port Ar·thur (är′thər). A city of extreme southeast Texas on Sabine Lake near the Louisiana border. It is a major deep-water port connected by channel with the Gulf of Mexico. Population, 61,195.

por·ta·tive (pôr′tə-tĭv, pōr′-) *adj.* **1.** Portable. **2.** Capable of or used in carrying. [Middle English *portatif,* from Old French, from Latin *portāre,* to carry. See **per-²** in Appendix.]

Port-au-Prince (pôrt′ō-prĭns′, pōrt′-, pôr′tō-präɴs′). The capital and largest city of Haiti, in the southwest part of the country on an arm of the Caribbean Sea. Founded by French sugar planters in 1749, it became the colonial capital in 1770 and the capital of independent Haiti in 1804. Population, 684,284.

Port Ches·ter (chĕs′tər). A village of southeast New York on Long Island Sound near the Connecticut border. It is an industrial and residential community. Population, 23,565.

Port Col·borne (kōl′bûrn′). A city of southeast Ontario, Canada, on Lake Erie at the southern end of the Welland Ship Canal west of Buffalo, New York. It is a manufacturing and transshipment center. Population, 19,225.

Port Co·quit·lam (kō-kwĭt′ləm). A city of southwest British Columbia, Canada, on the Fraser River east of Vancouver. It is a trade center in a farming region. Population, 27,535.

port·cul·lis (pôrt-kŭl′ĭs, pōrt-) *n.* A grating of iron or wooden bars or slats, suspended in the gateway of a fortified place and lowered to block passage. [Middle English *port-colice,* from Old French *porte coleice,* sliding gate : *porte,* gate (from Latin *porta;* see **per-²** in Appendix) + *coleice,* feminine of *coleis,* sliding (from Vulgar Latin **cōlātīcius,* from Latin *cōlātus,* past participle of *cōlāre,* to filter, strain, from *cōlum,* sieve).]

Port du Sa·lut (pôrt′ də să-lo͞o′, pōrt′, pôr′ dü sä-lü′) *n.* Variant of **Port Salut.**

Porte (pôrt, pōrt) *n.* The government of the Ottoman Empire. [French, short for *la Sublime Porte,* the High Gate, from Old French *porte,* gate. See PORT³.]

porte bouquet (pôrt, pōrt) *n.* See **bouquetier.** [French : *porter,* to carry, hold + *bouquet,* bouquet.]

porte-co·chère or **porte-co·chere** (pôrt′kō-shâr′, pōrt′-) *n.* **1.** A carriage entrance leading through a building or well into an enclosed courtyard. **2.** An enclosure over a driveway at the entrance of a building to provide shelter. [French *porte cochère* : *porte,* door + *cochère,* for coaches.]

Port E·liz·a·beth (ĭ-lĭz′ə-bəth). A city of southeast South Africa on an inlet of the Indian Ocean. It grew rapidly after the completion of the railroad to Kimberley in 1873. Population, 281,600.

por·tend (pôr-tĕnd′, pōr-) *tr.v.* **-tend·ed, -tend·ing, -tends.** **1.** To serve as an omen or a warning of; presage: *black clouds that portend a storm.* **2.** To indicate by prediction; forecast: *leading economic indicators that portend a recession.* [Middle English *portenden,* from Latin *portendere.* See **ten-** in Appendix.]

por·tent (pôr′tĕnt′, pōr′-) *n.* **1.** An indication of something important or calamitous about to occur; an omen. **2.** Prophetic or threatening significance: *signs full of portent.* **3.** Something amazing or marvelous; a prodigy. [Latin *portentum,* from neuter past participle of *portendere,* to portend. See PORTEND.]

por·ten·tous (pôr-tĕn′təs, pōr-) *adj.* **1.** Of the nature of or constituting a portent; foreboding: *"The present aspect of society is portentous of great change"* (Edward Bellamy). **2.** Full of unspecifiable significance; exciting wonder and awe: *"Such a portentous and mysterious monster roused all my curiosity"* (Herman Melville). **3.** Marked by pompousness; pretentiously weighty. **—por·ten′tous·ly** *adv.* **—por·ten′tous·ness** *n.*

por·ter¹ (pôr′tər, pōr′-) *n.* **1.** A person employed to carry burdens, especially an attendant who carries travelers' baggage at a hotel or transportation station. **2.** A railroad employee who waits on passengers in a sleeping car or parlor car. **3.** A maintenance worker for a building or an institution. [Middle English *portour,* from Anglo-Norman, from Late Latin *portātor,* from Latin *portāre,* to carry. See **per-²** in Appendix.]

por·ter² (pôr′tər, pōr′-) *n.* *Chiefly British.* One in charge of a gate or door. [Middle English, from Anglo-Norman, from Late Latin *portārius,* from Latin *porta,* gate. See **per-²** in Appendix.]

por·ter³ (pôr′tər, pōr′-) *n.* A dark beer resembling light stout, made from malt browned or charred by drying at a high temperature. [Short for *porter's ale.*]

Por·ter (pôr′tər, pōr′-), **Cole Albert.** 1891?–1964. American composer and lyricist remembered for his witty and sophisticated Broadway scores.

Porter, Sir **George.** Born 1920. British chemist. He shared a 1967 Nobel Prize for research on high-speed chemical reactions.

Porter, Katherine Anne. 1890–1980. American writer known for her carefully crafted short stories as well as her novel *Ship of Fools* (1962).

Porter, Rodney Robert. Born 1917. British biochemist. He shared a 1972 Nobel Prize for research on the chemical structure and nature of antibodies.

Porter, William Sydney. Pen name O. Henry. 1862–1910. American writer whose short stories are collected in a number of volumes, including *Cabbages and Kings* (1904) and *The Four Million* (1906).

por·ter·age (pôr′tər-ĭj, pōr′-) *n.* **1.** The carrying of burdens or goods as done by porters. **2.** The charge for this activity.

por·ter·ess (pôr′tər-ĭs, pōr′-) *n.* Variant of **portress.**

por·ter·house (pôr′tər-hous′, pōr′-) *n.* **1.** A cut of beef taken from the thick end of the short loin, having a T-bone and a sizable piece of tenderloin. Also called *porterhouse steak.* **2.** *Archaic.* An alehouse or a chophouse.

Por·ter·ville (pôr′tər-vĭl′, pōr′-). A city of south-central California north of Bakersfield. Founded in 1859 on the Los Angeles–San Francisco stage route, it is chiefly residential. Population, 19,707.

port·fo·li·o (pôrt-fō′lē-ō′, pōrt-) *n., pl.* **-os.** **1.a.** A portable case for holding material, such as loose papers, photographs, or drawings. **b.** The materials collected in such a case, especially when representative of a person's work: *a photographer's portfolio; an artist's portfolio of drawings.* **2.** The office or post of a cabinet member or minister of state. **3.** A group of investments. [Italian *portafoglio* : *porta,* imperative sing. of *portare,* to carry (from Latin *portāre;* see **per-²** in Appendix) + *foglio,* sheet (from Latin *folium,* leaf; see **bhel-³** in Appendix).]

Port Har·court (här′kərt). A city of southern Nigeria in the Niger River delta southeast of Ibadan. Laid out by the British in 1912, it is a rail terminus and manufacturing center. Population, 288,900.

port·hole (pôrt′hōl′, pōrt′-) *n.* **1.** *Nautical.* A small, usually circular window in a ship's side. **2.** An opening in a fortified wall; an embrasure.

Port Hue·ne·me (wī-nē′mē). A town of southern California west of Los Angeles. It was a naval training base during World War II. Population, 17,803.

Port Hu·ron (hyo͝or′ən, -ŏn′). A city of southeast Michigan on Lake Huron at the mouth of the St. Clair River north-northeast of Detroit. First settled as a French fort in 1686, it grew as a lumbering town in the 19th century and is now a port of entry with diversified industries. Population, 33,981.

por·ti·co (pôr′tĭ-kō′, pōr′-) *n., pl.* **-coes** or **-cos.** A porch or walkway with a roof supported by columns, often leading to the entrance of a building. [Italian, from Latin *porticus,* from *porta,* gate. See **per-²** in Appendix.] **—por′ti·coed′** *adj.*

por·tière or **por·tiere** (pôr-tyâr′, pōr-) *n.* A heavy curtain hung across a doorway. [French, feminine of *portier,* porter, from

portcullis

portico

ă pat	oi boy
ā pay	ou out
âr care	o͝o took
ä father	o͞o boot
ĕ pet	ŭ cut
ē be	ûr urge
ĭ pit	th thin
ī pie	*th* this
îr pier	hw which
ŏ pot	zh vision
ō toe	ə about, item
ô paw	♦ regionalism

Stress marks: ′ (primary); ′ (secondary), as in **dictionary** (dĭk′shə-nĕr′ē)

Old French, from Late Latin *portārius,* from Latin *porta,* gate. See **per-²** in Appendix.]

por·tion (pôr′shən, pōr′-) *n.* **1.** A section or quantity within a larger thing; a part of a whole. **2.** A part separated from a whole. **3.** A part that is allotted to a person or group, as: **a.** A helping of food. **b.** The part of an estate received by an heir. **c.** A woman's dowry. **4.** A person's lot or fate. See Synonyms at **fate.** —**portion** *tr.v.* **-tioned, -tion·ing, -tions. 1.** To divide into parts or shares for distribution; parcel. **2.** To provide with a share, an inheritance, or a dowry. [Middle English, from Old French, from Latin *portiō, portiōn-.* See **perə-²** in Appendix.] —**por′tion·a·ble** *adj.* —**por′tion·er** *n.* —**por′tion·less** *adj.*

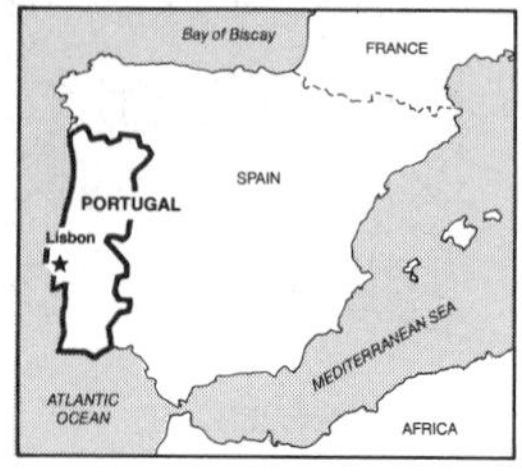

Portugal

Port·land (pôrt′lənd, pōrt′-). **1.** A city of southwest Maine on an arm of the Gulf of Maine south of Lewiston. Settled c. 1632, it became a commercial center in the 17th century and was state capital from 1820 to 1832. It is the largest city in the state. Population, 61,572. **2.** The largest city of Oregon, in the northwest part of the state on the Willamette River near its junction with the Columbia River. Founded in 1845, it grew as a lumber-exporting port and supply point for the California and Alaska goldfields. Population, 366,383. —**Port′land·er** *n.*

Portland cement or **port·land cement** (pôrt′lənd, pōrt′-) *n.* A hydraulic cement made by heating a mixture of limestone and clay in a kiln and pulverizing the resulting material. [After *Portland,* an urban district of southern England.]

Port Lou·is (lo͞o′ĭs, lo͞o′ē, lo͞o-ē′). The capital and largest city of Mauritius, in the northwest part of the island on the Indian Ocean. It was founded c. 1735. Population, 136,812.

port·ly (pôrt′lē, pōrt′-) *adj.* **-li·er, -li·est. 1.** Comfortably stout; corpulent. See Synonyms at **fat. 2.** *Archaic.* Stately; majestic; imposing. [From PORT⁵.] —**port′li·ness** *n.*

port·man·teau (pôrt-măn′tō, pōrt-, pôrt′măn-tō′, pōrt′-) *n., pl.* **-teaus** or **-teaux** (-tōz, -tōz′). A large leather suitcase that opens into two hinged compartments. [French *portemanteau* : *porte,* imperative of *porter,* to carry (from Old French; see PORT⁵) + *manteau,* cloak (from Old French *mantel,* from Latin *mantellum*).]

portmanteau word *n.* A word formed by merging the sounds and meanings of two different words; for example, *slithy,* from *lithe* and *slimy; chortle,* from *chuckle* and *snort.*

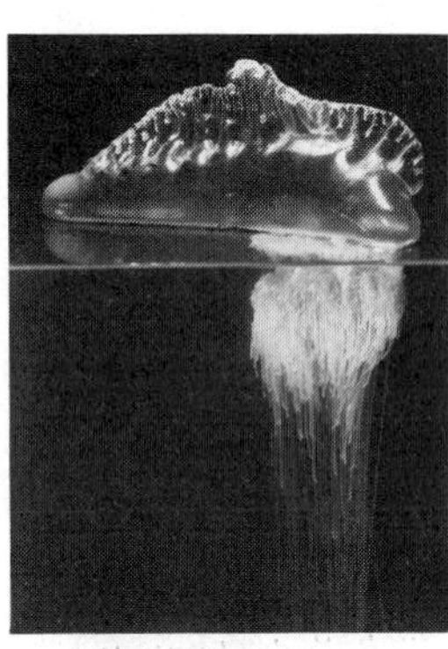

Portuguese man-of-war
Physalia physalis

Port Mores·by (môrz′bē, mōrz′-). The capital and largest city of Papua New Guinea, on southeast New Guinea and the Gulf of Papua. Population, 123,624.

Por·to or **Pôr·to** (pôr′to͞o). See **Oporto.**

Pôrto A·le·gre (ə-lĕ′grə). A city of southeast Brazil at the northern end of a large lagoon near the Atlantic Ocean. It was founded c. 1742 by emigrants from the Azores. Population, 1,125,477.

port of call *n., pl.* **ports of call.** A port where ships dock in the course of voyages to load or unload cargo, obtain supplies, or undergo repairs.

port of entry *n., pl.* **ports of entry.** *Abbr.* **POE, P.O.E.** A place where travelers or goods may enter or leave a country under official supervision.

Port of Spain (spān) or **Port-of-Spain** (pôrt′əv-spān′, pōrt′-). The capital of Trinidad and Tobago, on the northwest coast of Trinidad on an arm of the Atlantic Ocean. It is a commercial center and major port. Population, 65,906.

Por·to-No·vo (pôr′tō-nō′vō, pōr′-). The capital of Benin, in the southeast part of the country on an inlet of the Gulf of Guinea. Probably founded in the 16th century, it was settled as a slave-trading center by the Portuguese in the 17th century. Population, 123,000.

Port Or·ange (ôr′ĭnj, ŏr′-). A city of northeast Florida on the Atlantic coast south-southeast of Daytona Beach. It is in a citrus-growing area. Population, 18,756.

Port Or·ford cedar (ôr′fərd) *n.* A tall evergreen coniferous tree *(Chamaecyparis lawsoniana)* native to southwest Oregon and northwest California, having drooping, flattened branches and opposite, scalelike leaves with white markings. [After *Port Orford,* a town of southwest Oregon.]

Pôrto Vel·ho (vĕl′yo͞o). A city of northwest Brazil on the Madeira River near the Bolivian border. Its economy is based on rubber and Brazil nuts. Population, 101,162.

Port Phil·lip Bay (fĭl′əp). A large deep-water inlet of Bass Strait on the southeast coast of Australia.

por·trait (pôr′trĭt, -trāt′, pōr′-) *n.* **1.** *Abbr.* **por.** A likeness of a person, especially one showing the face, that is created by a painter or photographer, for example. **2.** A verbal picture or description, especially of a person. [French, from Old French, image, from past participle of *portraire,* to portray. See PORTRAY.]

por·trait·ist (pôr′trə-tĭst, pōr-) *n.* A person who makes portraits, especially a painter or photographer.

por·trai·ture (pôr′trĭ-cho͝or′, pōr′-) *n.* **1.** The art or practice of making portraits. **2.** A portrait. **3.** Portraits considered as a group.

por·tray (pôr-trā′, pōr-) *tr.v.* **-trayed, -tray·ing, -trays. 1.** To depict or represent pictorially; make a picture of. **2.** To depict or describe in words. **3.** To represent dramatically, as on the stage. See Synonyms at **represent.** [Middle English *portraien,* from Old French *portraire* : *por-,* forth (from Latin *prō-;* see PRO–¹) + *traire,* to draw (from Latin *trahere,* to drag).] —**por·tray′a·ble** *adj.* —**por·tray′er** *n.*

por·tray·al (pôr-trā′əl, pōr-) *n.* **1.** The act or process of depicting or portraying. **2.** A representation or description.

por·tress (pôr′trĭs, pōr′-) also **por·ter·ess** (-tər-ĭs) *n.* A woman doorkeeper or porter, especially in a convent.

Port Roy·al (roi′əl). See **Annapolis Royal.**

Port Sa·id (sä-ēd′). A city of northeast Egypt on the Mediterranean Sea at the northern entrance to the Suez Canal. It was founded in 1859 by the builders of the canal and was once an important coaling station. Population, 374,000.

Port Sa·lut (pôr′ să-lo͞o′, -lü′) also **Port du Sa·lut** (pôrt′ də să-lo͞o′, pōrt′, pôr dü să-lü′) *n.* A semihard fermented cheese, made originally by Trappist monks in France. [After Notre Dame de *Port-du-Salut,* a Trappist abbey in northwest France.]

port·side (pôrt′sīd′, pōrt′-) *adv. & adj.* **1.** On the waterfront of a port: *taking a stroll portside; a portside restaurant.* **2.** *Nautical.* On the port side of a ship or boat: *skirting a lighthouse portside; the portside oar.*

Ports·mouth (pôrt′sməth, pōrt′-). **1.** A borough of southern England on the English Channel opposite the Isle of Wight. Chartered in 1194, it is a major naval base. Population, 187,900. **2.** A city of southeast New Hampshire on the Atlantic Ocean. The Treaty of Portsmouth, ending the Russo-Japanese War, was signed at the naval base here in 1905. Population, 26,254. **3.** A city of southern Ohio on the Ohio River south of Columbus. An important industrial and rail center, it has prehistoric mounds and earthworks nearby. Population, 25,943. **4.** A city of southeast Virginia opposite Norfolk. It has been a major naval base since pre-Revolutionary times. Population, 104,577.

Port Stan·ley (stăn′lē). See **Stanley.**

Port Su·dan (so͞o-dăn′). A city of northeast Sudan on the Red Sea northeast of Khartoum. It was established after 1905 as a railroad terminus. Population, 206,727.

Por·tu·gal (pôr′chə-gəl, pōr′-). *Abbr.* **Port.** A country of southwest Europe on the western Iberian Peninsula. It includes the Madeira Islands and the Azores in the northern Atlantic Ocean. Originally inhabited by a Celtic people, the mainland area was conquered by the Romans in the 2nd century B.C. and subsequently held by the Visigoths and Moors. An independent kingdom was recognized in 1143 and soon flourished as a maritime and colonial power with holdings stretching from Africa to the Far East and Brazil in the New World. Much of its empire was lost to the British and the Dutch in the 17th and 18th centuries, and the remaining colonies in Africa became independent in the 20th century. Lisbon is the capital and the largest city. Population, 9,933,000.

Por·tu·ga·le·te (pôr′tə-gə-lā′tē, pōr′-, pôr′to͞o-gä-lĕ′tĕ). A city of northern Spain, a suburb of Bilbao on the Bay of Biscay. Population, 59,307.

Por·tu·guese (pôr′chə-gēz′, -gēs′, pōr′-) *adj. Abbr.* **Pg., Port.** Of or relating to Portugal or its people, language, or culture. —**Portuguese** *n., pl.* **Portuguese.** *Abbr.* **Pg., Port. 1.a.** A native or inhabitant of Portugal. **b.** A person of Portuguese descent. **2.** The Romance language of Portugal and Brazil. [*português,* from Vulgar Latin **portugalensis,* ultimately from Late Latin *Portus Cale,* the ancient port of Gaya (Oporto).]

Portuguese man-of-war *n.* A complex colonial siphonophore of the genus *Physalia,* of warm seas, having a bluish, bladderlike float with a broad saillike crest from which hang numerous long stinging tentacles.

Portuguese water dog *n.* Any of a breed of strong, medium-sized dog developed in Portugal that is able to swim long distances and is characterized by webbed feet and a curved tail.

por·tu·lac·a (pôr′chə-lăk′ə, pōr′-) *n.* Any of various fleshy plants of the genus *Portulaca,* especially *P. grandiflora* of South America, cultivated for its showy, colorful flowers that open only in sunlight. Also called *rose moss.* [Middle English, from Latin *portulāca,* purslane, from *portula,* diminutive of *porta,* gate (from the gatelike covering of the seed capsule). See **per-²** in Appendix.]

POS *abbr.* Point-of-sale.

pos. *abbr.* **1.** Position. **2.** Positive.

po·sa·da (pō-sä′də, pô-sä′*th*ä) *n.* A Christmas festival originating in Latin America that dramatizes the search of Joseph and Mary for lodging. [American Spanish, from Spanish, lodging, from *posar,* to lodge, rest, from Late Latin *pausāre,* to rest, from Latin *pausa,* pause. See PAUSE.]

pose¹ (pōz) *v.* **posed, pos·ing, pos·es.** —*intr.* **1.** To assume or hold a particular position or posture, as in sitting for a portrait. **2.** To affect a particular mental attitude. **3.** To represent oneself falsely; pretend to be other than what one is. —*tr.* **1.** To place (a model, for example) in a specific position. **2.** To set forth in words; propound: *pose a question.* **3.** To put forward; present: *pose a threat.* See Synonyms at **propose.** —**pose** *n.* **1.** A bodily attitude or position, especially one assumed for an artist or a photographer. See Synonyms at **posture. 2.** A studied attitude assumed for effect. See Synonyms at **affectation.** [Middle English *posen,* to place, from Old French *poser,* from Vulgar Latin **pausāre,* from Late Latin *pausāre,* to rest, from Latin *pausa,* pause. See PAUSE.] —**pos′a·ble** *adj.*

pose² (pōz) *tr.v.* **posed, pos·ing, pos·es.** To puzzle, confuse, or baffle. [Short for *appose,* to examine closely (from Middle English *apposen,* alteration of *opposen;* see OPPOSE) and from French *poser,* to assume (obsolete) (from Old French; see POSE¹).]

Po·sei·don (pō-sīd′n, pə-) *n. Greek Mythology.* The god of the waters, earthquakes, and horses, and brother of Zeus.

pos·er¹ (pō′zər) *n.* One who poses.

pos·er² (pō′zər) *n.* A baffling question or problem.

po·seur (pō-zœr′) *n.* One who affects a particular attitude, character, or manner to impress others. [French, from *poser,* to pose, from Old French. See POSE¹.]

posh (pŏsh) *adj.* Smart and fashionable. See Synonyms at **fashionable.** [Perhaps *posh,* halfpenny, money, dandy, from Romany *pāšh.*] **—posh′ly** *adv.* **—posh′ness** *n.*

WORD HISTORY: "Oh yes, Mater, we had a posh time of it down there." So in *Punch* for September 25, 1918, do we find the first recorded instance of that mysterious word *posh,* meaning "smart and fashionable," although in a 1903 book by P.G. Wodehouse, *Tales of St. Austin's,* there is a mention of a waistcoat that was "push." The latter may be a different word, but in either case the dates of occurrence are important because they are part of the objection to deriving *posh* from the initials of "Port Out, Starboard Home." This was the cooler, and thus more expensive, side of ships traveling between England and India in the mid-19th century, and the acronym *POSH* was supposedly stamped on the tickets of first-class passengers traveling on that side of ships owned by the Peninsular and Oriental Steam Navigation Company. No evidence is definitely known to exist for this theory, however. The *Oxford English Dictionary Supplement* may have found a possible source or sources for *posh.* Another word *posh* was 19th- and early 20th-century British slang for "money," specifically "a halfpenny, cash of small value." This word is borrowed from the common Romany word *pāšh,* "half," which was used in combinations such as *pāšhera,* "halfpenny." *Posh,* also meaning "a dandy," is recorded in two dictionaries of slang published in 1890 and 1902, although this particular *posh* may be still another word. This word or these words, however, are much more likely to be the source of *posh* than "Port Out, Starboard Home," although the latter source certainly has caught the public's etymological fancy.

pos·i·grade (pŏz′ĭ-grād′) *adj.* Of, relating to, or being an auxiliary rocket on a multistage spacecraft that is fired in the direction of the spacecraft's motion to separate the sections. [POSI(TIVE) + (RETRO)GRADE.]

pos·it (pŏz′ĭt) *tr.v.* **-it·ed, -it·ing, -its. 1.** To affirm or assume the existence of; postulate. See Synonyms at **presume. 2.** To put forward, as for consideration or study; suggest: *"If a book is hard going, it ought to be good. If it posits a complex moral situation, it ought to be even better"* (Anthony Burgess). **3.** To place firmly in position. [From Latin *positus,* past participle of *pōnere,* to place. See POSITION.]

po·si·tion (pə-zĭsh′ən) *n. Abbr.* **pos. 1.** A place or location. **2.a.** The right or appropriate place: *The bands were in position for the start of the parade.* **b.** An area occupied by members of a force for a strategic purpose: *The troops took up positions along the main road.* **3.a.** The way in which something is placed: *the position of the hands on the clock.* **b.** The arrangement of body parts; posture: *a standing position.* **4.** An advantageous place or location: *jockeys maneuvering for position.* **5.** A situation as it relates to the surrounding circumstances: *in a position to bargain.* **6.** A point of view or attitude on a certain question: *the senator's position on arms control.* **7.** Social standing or status; rank. **8.** A post of employment; a job. **9.a.** *Sports.* The area for which a particular player is responsible. **b.** *Games.* The arrangement of the pieces at any particular time in a game such as chess, checkers, or backgammon. **10.a.** The act or process of positing. **b.** A principle or proposition posited. **11.a.** A commitment to buy or sell a given amount of securities or commodities. **b.** The amount of securities or commodities held by a person, firm, or institution. **c.** The ownership status of a person's or an institution's investments. **—position** *tr.v.* **-tioned, -tion·ing, -tions. 1.** To put in place or position. **2.** To determine the position of; locate. [Middle English *posicioun,* from Old French *posicion,* from Latin *positiō, positiōn-,* from *positus,* past participle of *pōnere,* to place. See **apo-** in Appendix.] **—po·si′tion·al** *adj.* **—po·si′tion·al·ly** *adv.* **—po·si′tion·er** *n.*

positional notation *n.* A system of writing numbers in which the position of a digit affects its value.

position effect *n.* Variation in the expression of a gene resulting from changes in its position along a chromosome.

position paper *n.* **1.** A detailed policy report that usually explains, justifies, or recommends a particular course of action. **2.** See **aide-mémoire** (sense 1).

pos·i·tive (pŏz′ĭ-tĭv) *adj. Abbr.* **pos. 1.** Characterized by or displaying certainty, acceptance, or affirmation: *a positive answer; positive criticism.* **2.** Measured or moving forward or in a direction of increase or progress. **3.** Explicitly or openly expressed or laid down: *a positive demand.* **4.** Admitting of no doubt; irrefutable: *positive proof.* **5.a.** Very sure; confident: *I'm positive he's right.* See Synonyms at **sure. b.** Overconfident; dogmatic. **6.** Formally or arbitrarily determined; prescribed. **7.** Concerned with practical rather than theoretical matters. **8.** Composed of or characterized by the presence of particular qualities or attributes; real. **9.** *Philosophy.* **a.** Of or relating to positivism. **b.** Of or relating to laws imposed by human authority rather than by nature or reason alone: *"the glaring discrepancy between American positive law and natural rights"* (David Brion Davis). **c.** Of or relating to religion based on revelation rather than on nature or reason alone. **10.** *Informal.* Utter; absolute: *a positive darling.* **11.** *Mathematics.* **a.** Relating to or designating a quantity greater than zero. **b.** Relating to or designating the sign (+). **c.** Relating to or designating a quantity, number, angle, or direction opposite to another designated as negative. **12.** *Physics.* Relating to or designating electric charge of a sign opposite to that of an electron. **13.** *Medicine.* Indicating the presence of a particular disease, condition, or organism: *a positive test for pregnancy.* **14.** *Biology.* Indicating or characterized by response or motion toward the source of a stimulus, such as light: *positive tropism.* **15.** Having the areas of light and dark in their original and normal relationship, as in a photographic print made from a negative. **16.** *Grammar.* Of, relating to, or being the simple uncompared degree of an adjective or adverb, as opposed to either the comparative or superlative. **17.** Driven by or generating power directly through intermediate machine parts having little or no play: *positive drive.* **—positive** *n.* **1.** An affirmative element or characteristic. **2.** *Philosophy.* Something perceptible to the senses. **3.** *Mathematics.* A quantity greater than zero. **4.** *Physics.* A positive electric charge. **5.** A photographic image in which the lights and darks appear as they do in nature. **6.** *Grammar.* **a.** The uncompared degree of an adjective or adverb. **b.** A word in this degree. **7.** *Music.* A division of some pipe organs, similar in sound to the great but smaller and less powerful. [Middle English, having a specified quality, from Old French *positif,* from Latin *positīvus,* formally laid down, from *positus,* past participle of *pōnere,* to place. See **apo-** in Appendix.] **—pos′i·tive·ly** *adv.* **—pos′i·tive·ness, pos′i·tiv′i·ty** *n.*

positive prescription *n. Law.* See **prescription** (sense 4).

pos·i·tiv·ism (pŏz′ĭ-tĭ-vĭz′əm) *n.* **1.** *Philosophy.* **a.** A doctrine contending that sense perceptions are the only admissible basis of human knowledge and precise thought. **b.** The application of this doctrine in logic, epistemology, and ethics. **c.** The system of Auguste Comte designed to supersede theology and metaphysics and depending on a hierarchy of the sciences, beginning with mathematics and culminating in sociology. **d.** Any of several doctrines or viewpoints, often similar to Comte's, that stress attention to actual practice over consideration of what is ideal: *"Positivism became the 'scientific' base for authoritarian politics, especially in Mexico and Brazil"* (Raymond Carr). **2.** The state or quality of being positive. **—pos′i·tiv·ist, pos′i·tiv·is′tic** *adj.* **—pos′i·tiv·ist** *n.*

pos·i·tron (pŏz′ĭ-trŏn′) *n.* The antiparticle of the electron. Also called *antielectron.* [POSI(TIVE) + (ELEC)TRON.]

positron emission tomography *n. Abbr.* **PET** Tomography in which a computer-generated image of a biological activity within the body is produced through the detection of gamma rays that are emitted when introduced radionuclides decay and release positrons.

pos·i·tro·ni·um (pŏz′ĭ-trō′nē-əm) *n.* A short-lived association of an electron and a positron bound together in a configuration resembling the hydrogen atom.

po·sol·o·gy (pə-sŏl′ə-jē, pō-) *n.* The medical or pharmacological study of the dosages of medicines and drugs. [Greek *posos,* what quantity + –LOGY.]

poss. *abbr.* **1.** Possession. **2.** Possessive. **3.** Possible.

pos·se (pŏs′ē) *n.* **1.** A group of people summoned by a sheriff to aid in law enforcement. **2.** A search party. **3.** A Jamaican gang involved in crimes such as running guns and illegal narcotics trafficking. [Short for *posse comitatūs* : Medieval Latin *posse,* power, body of men (from Latin, to be able; see POTENT) + *comitātūs,* genitive of *comitātus,* county.]

pos·sess (pə-zĕs′) *tr.v.* **-sessed, -sess·ing, -sess·es. 1.** To have as property; own. **2.** To have as a quality, characteristic, or other attribute: *possessed great tact.* **3.** To acquire mastery of or have knowledge of: *possess valuable data.* **4.a.** To gain or exert influence or control over; dominate: *Fury possessed me.* **b.** To control or maintain (one's nature) in a particular condition: *I possessed my temper despite the insult.* **5.** To cause to own, hold, or master something, such as property or knowledge: *She possessed herself of the unclaimed goods.* **6.** To cause to be influenced or controlled, as by an idea or emotion: *The thought of getting rich possessed him.* **7.** *Obsolete.* To gain or seize. [Middle English *possessen,* from Old French *possesser,* from Latin *possidēre, possess-* : *pos-,* as master; see **poti-** in Appendix + *sedēre,* to sit; see **sed-** in Appendix.] **—pos·ses′sor** *n.*

pos·sessed (pə-zĕst′) *adj.* **1.** Owning or mastering something. Used with *of*: *He is possessed of great wealth.* **2.** Controlled by or as if by a spirit or other force; obsessed: *She is by love possessed.* **3.** Calm; collected: *a strong person who was able to remain possessed even in times of great trial.*

USAGE NOTE: *Possessed* is often followed by the prepositions *of, by,* or *with.* Mere possession of a thing or an attribute is indicated by *of*: *possessed of property; possessed of a sharp tongue.* When the term indicates obsession or lack of self-control, *by* and *with* are more often used: *possessed by* (or *with*) *an urge to kill.*

pos·ses·sion (pə-zĕsh′ən) *n. Abbr.* **poss. 1.a.** The act or fact of possessing. **b.** The state of being possessed. **2.** Something owned or possessed. **3. possessions.** Wealth or property. **4.** *Law.* Actual holding or occupancy with or without rightful ownership. **5.** A territory subject to foreign control. **6.** Self-control. **7.** The state of being dominated by or as if by evil spirits or by an obsession. **8.** *Sports.* **a.** Physical control of the ball or puck by

ă pat	oi boy
ā pay	ou out
âr care	o͝o took
ä father	o͞o boot
ĕ pet	ŭ cut
ē be	ûr urge
ĭ pit	th thin
ī pie	*th* this
îr pier	hw which
ŏ pot	zh vision
ō toe	ə about, item
ô paw	♦ regionalism

Stress marks: **′** (primary); ′ (secondary), as in **dictionary** (dĭk′shə-nĕr′ē)

a player or team. **b.** The condition of being on offense: *The home team was in possession during most of the fourth quarter.* **—pos·ses′sion·al** *adj.*

pos·ses·sive (pə-zĕs′ĭv) *adj. Abbr.* **poss. 1.** Of or relating to ownership or possession. **2.** Having or manifesting a desire to control or dominate: *a possessive parent.* **3.** *Grammar.* Of, relating to, or being a noun or pronoun case that indicates possession. **—possessive** *n. Abbr.* **poss.** *Grammar.* **1.** The possessive case. **2.** A possessive form or construction. **—pos·ses′sive·ly** *adv.* **—pos·ses′sive·ness** *n.*

possessive adjective *n. Grammar.* A pronominal adjective expressing possession.

possessive pronoun *n. Grammar.* One of several pronouns designating possession and capable of substituting for noun phrases.

pos·ses·so·ry (pə-zĕs′ə-rē) *adj.* **1.** Of, relating to, or having possession. **2.** *Law.* Depending on or arising from possession: *possessory interest.*

pos·set (pŏs′ĭt) *n.* A spiced drink of hot sweetened milk curdled with wine or ale. [Middle English *poshet, possot* : perhaps Old French **posce* (Latin *pōsca,* drink of vinegar and water, from *potāre,* to drink; see POTABLE + Latin *esca,* food, from *edere,* to eat; see EDIBLE) + Middle English *hot,* hot; see HOT.]

pos·si·bil·i·ty (pŏs′ə-bĭl′ĭ-tē) *n., pl.* **-ties. 1.** The fact or state of being possible. **2.** Something that is possible. **3. possibilities.** Potentiality for favorable or interesting results: *The idea has tremendous possibilities.*

pos·si·ble (pŏs′ə-bəl). *Abbr.* **poss.** *adj. Abbr.* **poss. 1.** Capable of happening, existing, or being true without contradicting proven facts, laws, or circumstances. **2.** Capable of occurring or being done without offense to character, nature, or custom. **3.** Capable of favorable development; potential: *a possible site for the new capital.* **4.** Of uncertain likelihood. [Middle English, from Old French, from Latin *possibilis,* from *posse,* to be able. See **poti-** in Appendix.] **—pos′si·bly** *adv.*

SYNONYMS: *possible, workable, practicable, feasible, viable.* These adjectives signify capable of occurring or of being done. *Possible* indicates that something may happen, exist, be true, or be realizable: *"I beseech you . . . think it possible you may be mistaken"* (Oliver Cromwell). *"Only the initiated know and honor those* [scientists] *whose patient integrity and devotion to exact observation have made the last step possible"* (Hans Zinsser). *Workable* is used of something that can be put into effective operation: *Assuming that the scheme is workable, how will you begin to implement it?* Something that is *practicable* is capable of being effected, done, or put into practice: *"As soon as it was practicable, he would wind up his business"* (George Eliot). *Feasible* refers to what can be accomplished, brought about, or carried out: Making cars by hand is possible but not economically feasible. Something *viable* is both practicable and workable; the term often implies capacity for continuing effectiveness or success: *"How viable are the ancient legends as vehicles for modern literary themes?"* (Richard Kain).

POSSLQ *abbr.* Person of the opposite sex sharing living quarters.

♦**pos·sum** (pŏs′əm) *n. Chiefly Southern U.S.* An opossum. [Short for OPOSSUM.]

♦***REGIONAL NOTE:*** Since English is a language that stresses some syllables and not others, weakly stressed syllables, especially those preceding strong stresses, are dropped at times. This process, called aphesis when it occurs at the beginning of a word, is more common in regional American dialects than in the more conservative Standard English, which tends to retain in pronunciation anything reflected in spelling. Although many American dialects feature aphesis, it is most famous in the dialects of the South, where it yields pronunciations such as *count of* for *(on) account of, tater* for *potato, possum* for *opossum,* and *skeeter* for *mosquito.*

possum haw *n.* **1.** A deciduous holly *(Ilex decidua)* of the southeast United States, having bright red fruit and dull green toothed leaves. **2.** A deciduous shrub *(Viburnum nudum)* of the eastern United States, having white or yellowish flowers and bluish-black fruit. **3.** See **dockmackie.**

post[1] (pōst) *n.* **1.** A long piece of wood or other material set upright into the ground to serve as a marker or support. **2.** A similar vertical support or structure, as: **a.** A support for a beam in the framework of a building. **b.** A terminal of a battery. **3.** *Sports.* A goal post. **4.** The starting point at a racetrack. **5.** An earring attached by a short bar or stud that passes through the ear and fits into a cap in the back. **—post** *tr.v.* **post·ed, post·ing, posts. 1.a.** To display (an announcement) in a place of public view. **b.** To cover (a wall, for example) with posters. **2.** To announce by or as if by posters: *post banns.* **3.** To put up signs on (property) warning against trespassing. **4.** To denounce publicly: *post a man as a thief.* **5.** To publish (a name) on a list. **6.** *Games.* To gain (points or a point) in a game or contest; score. [Middle English, from Old English, from Latin *postis.* See **stā-** in Appendix.]

post[2] (pōst) *n.* **1.a.** A military base. **b.** The grounds and buildings of a military base. **2.** A local organization of military veterans. **3.** Either of two bugle calls in the British Army, sounded in the evening as a signal to retire to quarters. **4.** An assigned position or station, as of a guard or sentry. **5.** A position of employment, especially an appointed public office. **6.** A place to which someone is assigned for duty. **7.** A trading post. **—post** *tr.v.* **post·ed, post·ing, posts. 1.** To assign to a specific position or station: *post a sentry at the gate.* **2.** To appoint to a naval or military command. **3.** To put forward; present: *post bail.* [French *poste,* from Italian *posto,* from Old Italian, from Vulgar Latin **postum,* from Latin *positum,* neuter past participle of *pōnere,* to place. See **apo-** in Appendix.]

post[3] (pōst) *n.* **1.a.** A delivery of mail. **b.** The mail delivered. **2.** *Chiefly British.* **a.** A governmental system for transporting and delivering the mail. **b.** A post office. **3.a.** *Archaic.* One of a series of relay stations along a fixed route, furnishing fresh riders and horses for the delivery of mail on horseback. **b.** *Obsolete.* A rider on such a mail route; a courier. **—post** *v.* **post·ed, post·ing, posts.** *—tr.* **1.** To mail (a letter or package). **2.** To send by mail in a system of relays on horseback. **3.** To inform of the latest news: *Keep us posted.* **4.a.** To transfer (an item) to a ledger in bookkeeping. **b.** To make the necessary entries in (a ledger). **5.** *Computer Science.* To enter (a unit of information) on a record or into a section of storage. *—intr.* **1.** To travel in stages or relays. **2.** To travel with speed or in haste. **3.** To bob up and down in the saddle in rhythm with a horse's trotting gait. **—post** *adv.* **1.** By mail. **2.** With great speed; rapidly. **3.** By post horse. [French *poste,* from Old French, relay station for horses, from Old Italian *posta,* from Vulgar Latin **posta,* station, from Latin *posita,* feminine past participle of *pōnere,* to place. See **apo-** in Appendix.]

Post (pōst), **Emily Price.** 1872–1960. American etiquette authority. She wrote *Etiquette: The Blue Book of Social Usage* (1922) and a popular syndicated newspaper column.

Post, Wiley. 1899–1935. American aviator who made the first solo flight around the world (1933).

post– *pref.* **1.** After; later: *postmillennial.* **2.** Behind; posterior to: *postaxial.* [Latin, from *post,* behind, after. See **apo-** in Appendix.]

post·age (pō′stĭj) *n.* **1.** The charge for mailing an item. **2.** The stamps, labels, or printing placed on an item to be mailed as evidence of payment of this charge.

postage meter *n.* A machine used in bulk mailing to print the correct amount of postage for each piece of mail, either directly on the piece or on a label to be put on the piece.

postage stamp *n.* A small, usually adhesive label issued by a government and sold in various denominations to be affixed to items of mail as evidence of the payment of postage.

post·age-stamp (pō′stĭj-stămp′) *adj.* Very small: *postage-stamp villages; a postage-stamp farm.*

post·al (pō′stəl) *adj.* Of or relating to a post office or mail service. **—post′al·ly** *adv.*

postal card *n.* An unadorned card printed with the image of a postage stamp, issued by a government and used for sending messages. Also called *post card.*

postal order *n. Abbr.* **PO, P.O.** *Chiefly British.* A money order.

postal service *n.* See **post office** (sense 1).

post·ax·i·al (pōst-ăk′sē-əl) *adj. Anatomy.* Located behind an axis of the body, as the lateral aspect of the lower leg or the medial aspect of the upper arm. **—post·ax′i·al·ly** *adv.*

post·bel·lum (pōst-bĕl′əm) *adj.* Belonging to the period after a war, especially the U.S. Civil War: *postbellum houses; postbellum governments.* [Latin *post,* after + *bellum,* war.]

post-boost phase (pōst′bo͞ost′) *n.* The period during which warheads and decoys are released from the last stage of a ballistic missile.

post·box also **post box** (pōst′bŏks′) *n.* See **mailbox** (sense 1).

post card also **post·card** (pōst′kärd′) *n. Abbr.* **p.c. 1.** A commercially printed card with space on one side for an address and a postage stamp, used for sending a short message through the mail. **2.** See **postal card.**

post·ca·va (pōst-kā′və) *n.* A large vein that returns blood to the heart from the lower half of the body; the inferior vena cava. **—post·ca′val** *adj.*

post chaise *n.* A closed, four-wheeled, horse-drawn carriage, formerly used to transport mail and passengers.

post·clas·si·cal (pōst-klăs′ĭ-kəl) *adj.* Of, relating to, or being a time following a classical period, as in art or literature.

post·co·lo·ni·al (pōst′kə-lō′nē-əl) *adj.* Of, relating to, or being the time following the establishment of independence in a colony: *postcolonial economics.*

post·cra·ni·al (pōst-krā′nē-əl) *adj.* **1.** Situated behind the cranium. **2.** Consisting of the parts or structures behind the cranium: *the postcranial skeleton of an animal.* **—post·cra′ni·al·ly** *adv.*

post·date (pōst-dāt′, pōst′-) *tr.v.* **-dat·ed, -dat·ing, -dates. 1.** To put a date on (a check, for example) that is later than the actual date. **2.** To occur later than; follow in time.

post·di·lu·vi·an (pōst′dĭ-lo͞o′vē-ən) also **post·di·lu·vi·al** (-əl) *Bible.* *—adj.* Existing or occurring after the Flood. *—n.* A person or thing living after the Flood. [POST– + Latin *dīluvium,* flood; see DILUVIAL + –AN[1].]

post·doc·tor·al (pōst-dŏk′tər-əl) also **post·doc·tor·ate**

(-ĭt) *adj.* Of, relating to, or engaged in academic study beyond the level of a doctoral degree.

post•em•bry•on•ic (pōst′ĕm-brē-ŏn′ĭk) *adj.* Following the embryonic stage of development.

post•er¹ (pō′stər) *n.* **1.a.** A large, usually printed placard, bill, or announcement, often illustrated, that is posted to advertise or publicize something. **b.** An artistic work, often a reproduction of an original painting or photograph, printed on a large sheet of paper. **2.** One that posts bills or notices.

post•er² (pō′stər) *n. Archaic.* One that travels in speed or with haste.

poster color *n.* See **tempera** (sense 1).

poste res•tante (pōst′ rĕ-stänt′) *n.* A notation written on a letter indicating that the letter should be held at the post office until claimed by the addressee. [French : *poste,* mail + *restante,* feminine present participle of *rester,* to remain.]

pos•te•ri•or (pŏ-stîr′ē-ər, pō-) *adj.* **1.** Located behind a part or toward the rear of a structure. **2.** Relating to the caudal end of the body in quadrupeds or the dorsal side in human beings and other primates. **3.** *Botany.* Next to or facing the main stem or axis. **4.** Coming after in order; following. **5.** Following in time; subsequent. **—posterior** *n.* The buttocks. [Latin, comparative of *posterus,* coming after, from *post,* afterward. See **apo-** in Appendix.] **—pos•te′ri•or•ly** *adv.*

pos•te•ri•or•i•ty (pŏ-stîr′ē-ôr′ĭ-tē, -ŏr′-, pō-) *n.* The condition of being posterior in location or time.

pos•ter•i•ty (pŏ-stĕr′ĭ-tē) *n.* **1.** Future generations: *"Everything he writes is consigned to posterity"* (Joyce Carol Oates). **2.** All of a person's descendants. [Middle English *posterite,* from Old French, from Latin *posteritās,* from *posterus,* coming after. See POSTERIOR.]

pos•tern (pō′stərn, pŏs′tərn) *n.* A small rear gate, especially one in a fort or castle. **—postern** *adj.* Situated in the back or at the side. [Middle English *posterne,* from Old French, alteration of *posterle,* from Late Latin *posterula,* diminutive of Latin *posterus,* behind. See POSTERIOR.]

poster paint *n.* See **tempera** (sense 1).

Post Exchange A service mark used for a store on a military base that sells goods to military personnel and their families or to authorized civilians. This service mark often occurs in lowercase in print: *"A chateau in southern France, a cabaret in Land Hesse, a post exchange—all of these have a taste and smell"* (Christian Science Moniter).

post•ex•il•ic (pōst′ĕg-zĭl′ĭk, -ĕk-sĭl′-) also **post•ex•il•i•an** (-ĕg-zĭl′ē-ən, -zĭl′yən, -ĕk-sĭl′ē-ən, -sĭl′yən) *adj.* Of or relating to the period of Jewish history following the Babylonian captivity (after 586 B.C.).

post•fix (pōst-fĭks′) *Linguistics. tr.v.* **-fixed, -fix•ing, -fix•es.** To suffix. **—postfix** (pōst′fĭks′) *n.* A suffix. **—post•fix′al, post•fix′i•al** *adj.*

post•fron•tal (pōst-frŭn′tl) *adj.* **1.** At the back of the frontal bone; behind the forehead: *a postfrontal suture.* **2.** Toward the rear of the frontal lobe.

post•gan•gli•on•ic (pōst′găng-glē-ŏn′ĭk) *adj.* Located posterior or distal to a ganglion.

post•gla•cial (pōst-glā′shəl) *adj.* Relating to or occurring during the time following a glacial period.

post•grad•u•ate (pōst-grăj′o͞o-ĭt, -āt′) *adj. Abbr.* **P.G.** Of, relating to, or pursuing advanced study after graduation from high school or college. **—postgraduate** *n. Abbr.* **P.G.** One who is engaged in postgraduate study.

post•haste (pōst′hāst′) *adv.* With great speed; rapidly. **—posthaste** *n. Archaic.* Great speed; rapidity. [From the phrase *haste, post, haste,* a direction on letters.]

post hoc (hŏk, hōk) *adv. & adj.* In or of the form of an argument in which one event is asserted to be the cause of a later event simply by virtue of having happened earlier: *coming to conclusions post hoc; post hoc reasoning.* [Latin, after this : *post,* after + *hoc,* this.]

post•hole (pōst′hōl′) *n.* A hole dug in the ground to hold a fence post.

post•hu•mous (pŏs′chə-məs) *adj.* **1.** Occurring or continuing after one's death: *a posthumous award.* **2.** Published after the writer's death: *a posthumous book.* **3.** Born after the death of the father: *a posthumous child.* [Middle English *posthumus,* from Late Latin, alteration (perhaps influenced by Latin *humus,* earth, or *humāre,* to bury) of *postumus,* superlative of *posterus,* coming after. See POSTERIOR.] **—post′hu•mous•ly** *adv.* **—post′hu•mous•ness** *n.*

WORD HISTORY: The word *posthumous* is associated with death, both in meaning and in form. Our word goes back to the Latin word *postumus,* meaning "last born, born after the death of one's father, born after the making of a will," and "last, final." *Postumus* was largely used with respect to events occurring after death but not exclusively so, since the word was simply one of the superlative forms of the adverb *post,* "subsequently, afterward." Because of its use in connection with death, however, later Latin writers decided that the last part of the word must have to do with *humus,* "earth," or *humāre,* "to bury," and began spelling the word *posthumus.* This form of the Latin word was borrowed into English, being first recorded in a work composed before 1464. Perhaps the most telling use of the word appears in the poet Robert Southey's comment on the rewards of an author: "It was well we should be contented with posthumous fame, but impossible to be so with posthumous bread and cheese."

post•hyp•not•ic suggestion (pōst′hĭp-nŏt′ĭk) *n.* A suggestion made to a hypnotized person that specifies an action to be performed after awakening, often in response to a cue.

pos•tiche (pô-stēsh′, pŏ-) *n.* **1.** Something false; a sham. **2.** A small hairpiece; a toupee. [French, from Italian *posticcio,* from *posto,* added (from Latin *positus,* past participle of *pōnere,* to place) or from Vulgar Latin **appostīcius* (alteration of Latin *appositus,* past participle of *appōnere,* to place by, to add : *ad-,* ad- + *pōnere,* to place; see **apo-** in Appendix).]

pos•til•ion also **pos•til•lion** (pō-stĭl′yən, pŏ-) *n.* One who rides the near horse of the leaders to guide the horses drawing a coach. [French *postillon,* from Italian *postiglione,* from *posta,* mail, from Old Italian, mail station. See POST³.]

post•im•pres•sion•ism (pōst′ĭm-prĕsh′ə-nĭz′əm) *n.* A school of painting in France in the late 19th century that rejected the objective naturalism of impressionism and used form and color in more personally expressive ways. **—post′im•pres′sion•ist** *n.* **—post′im•pres′sion•is′tic** *adj.*

postimpressionism
Woman with Mango, 1892, by Paul Gauguin

post•in•dus•tri•al (pōst′ĭn-dŭs′trē-əl) *adj.* Of or relating to a period in the development of an economy or a nation in which the relative importance of manufacturing lessens and that of services, information, and research grows.

post•lude (pōst′lo͞od′) *n.* **1.** *Music.* **a.** An organ voluntary played at the end of a church service. **b.** A concluding piece. **2.** A final chapter or phase. [POST– + (PRE)LUDE.]

post•man (pōst′mən) *n.* See **mailman.**

post•mark (pōst′märk′) *n. Abbr.* **pmk.** An official mark printed over a postage stamp, especially one that cancels the stamp and records the date and place of mailing. **—postmark** *tr.v.* **-marked, -mark•ing, -marks.** To stamp with such a mark.

post•mas•ter (pōst′măs′tər) *n. Abbr.* **PM, P.M.** A man who is in charge of the operations of a local post office. **—post′mas′ter•ship′** *n.*

postmaster general *n., pl.* **postmasters general.** *Abbr.* **P.M.G.** The executive head of a national postal service.

post•men•o•paus•al (pōst′mĕn-ə-pô′zəl) *adj.* Of or occurring in the time following menopause.

post•men•stru•al (pōst-mĕn′stro͞o-əl) *adj.* Of or occurring in the time following menstruation.

post•me•rid•i•an (pōst′mə-rĭd′ē-ən) *adj.* Of, relating to, or taking place in the afternoon.

post me•rid•i•em (mə-rĭd′ē-əm) *adv. & adj. Abbr.* **P.M., p.m.** After noon. Used chiefly in the abbreviated form to specify the hour: *10:30 P.M.; a P.M. appointment.* See Usage Note at **ante meridiem.** [Latin *post merīdiem* : *post,* after + *merīdiem,* accusative of *merīdiēs,* midday.]

post•mil•le•nar•i•an (pōst′mĭl-ə-nâr′ē-ən) *adj.* Of or relating to postmillennialism. **—postmillenarian** *n.* One who believes in postmillennialism.

post•mil•le•nar•i•an•ism (pōst′mĭl-ə-nâr′ē-ə-nĭz′əm) *n.* Postmillennialism.

post•mil•len•ni•al (pōst′mə-lĕn′ē-əl) also **post•mil•len•ni•an** (-ən) *adj.* Happening or existing after the millennium.

post•mil•len•ni•al•ism (pōst′mə-lĕn′ē-ə-lĭz′əm) *n.* The doctrine that Jesus's Second Coming will follow the millennium. **—post′mil•len′ni•al•ist** *n.*

post•mis•tress (pōst′mĭs′trĭs) *n. Abbr.* **PM, P.M.** A woman who is in charge of the operations of a local post office.

post•mod•ern or **post-mod•ern** (pōst-mŏd′ərn) *adj.* Of or relating to art, architecture, or literature that reacts against earlier modernist principles, as by reintroducing traditional or classical elements of style or by carrying modernist styles or practices to extremes: *"the post-modern mode of tapering the tops of buildings"* (Jane Holtz Kay). **—post•mod′ern•ism** *n.* **—post•mod′ern•ist** *adj.*

post•mor•tem (pōst-môr′təm) *adj. Abbr.* **p.m., P.M. 1.** Occurring or done after death. **2.** Of or relating to a medical examination of a dead body. **—postmortem** *n.* **1.** *Abbr.* **p.m., P.M.** See **autopsy** (sense 1). **2.** *Informal.* An analysis or review of a completed event. [Latin *post mortem* : *post,* afterward; see POST– + *mortem,* accusative of *mors,* death; see **mer-** in Appendix.] **—post mor′tem** *adv.*

postmortem examination *n.* See **autopsy** (sense 1).

post•na•sal (pōst-nā′zəl) *adj.* Located or occurring posterior to the nose.

postnasal drip *n.* The chronic secretion of mucus from the posterior nasal cavities, often caused by a cold or an allergy.

post•na•tal (pōst-nāt′l) *adj.* Of or occurring after birth, especially during the period immediately after birth. **—post•na′tal•ly** *adv.*

post•nup•tial (pōst-nŭp′shəl, -chəl) *adj.* Belonging to the period after marriage. **—post•nup′tial•ly** *adv.*

post office *n. Abbr.* **PO, P.O., p.o. 1.** The public department responsible for the transportation and delivery of the mails. Also called *postal service.* **2.** A local office where mail is received, sorted, and delivered, and where stamps and other postal mate-

ă pat	oi boy
ā pay	ou out
âr care	o͝o took
ä father	o͞o boot
ĕ pet	ŭ cut
ē be	ûr urge
ĭ pit	th thin
ī pie	*th* this
îr pier	hw which
ŏ pot	zh vision
ō toe	ə about, item
ô paw	♦ regionalism

Stress marks: **′** (primary); ′ (secondary), as in **dictionary** (dĭk′shə-nĕr′ē)

rials are sold. **3.** A game in which kisses are exchanged for pretended letters.

post office box *n.* A container, such as a pigeonhole, at a central mailing location, in which a patron's incoming mail is held until picked up by the patron.

post·op·er·a·tive (pōst-ŏp′ər-ə-tĭv, -ŏp′rə-, -ŏp′ə-rā′-) *adj.* Happening or done after a surgical operation. **—post·op′er·a·tive·ly** *adv.*

post·or·bi·tal (pōst-ôr′bĭ-tl) *adj.* Situated behind the socket of the eye: *a postorbital bone.*

post·o·vu·la·to·ry (pōst-ō′vyə-lə-tôr′ē, -tōr′ē, -ŏv′yə-) *adj.* Of or occurring in the period shortly after ovulation.

post·paid (pōst′pād′) *adj. Abbr.* **p.p., P.P., ppd.** With the postage having been paid in advance.

post·par·tum (pōst-pär′təm) *adj.* Of or occurring in the period shortly after childbirth: *postpartum complications.* [Latin *post partum* : *post,* after; see POST– + *partum,* accusative of *partus,* birth, from past participle of *parere,* to beget; see **pere-**[1] in Appendix.]

post-po·li·o syndrome (pōst-pō′lē-ō′) *n.* A condition affecting poliomyelitis patients several decades after the initial attack, characterized by fatigue, muscular deterioration, pain in the joints, and respiratory problems.

post·pone (pōst-pōn′, pōs-pōn′) *tr.v.* **-poned, -pon·ing, -pones. 1.** To delay until a future time; put off. See Synonyms at **defer**[1]. **2.** To place after in importance; subordinate. [Latin *postpōnere* : *post-,* post- + *pōnere,* to put; see POST[2].] **—post·pon′a·ble** *adj.* **—post·pone′ment** *n.* **—post·pon′er** *n.*

post·pose (pōst-pōz′) *v.* **-posed, -pos·ing, -pos·es.** *Linguistics. —tr.* To place (a word or phrasal constituent) after other constituents in a sentence, as the direct object noun phrase *all the interesting places he had visited* in the sentence *He described to them all the interesting places he had visited. —intr.* To become postposed. [Back-formation from POSTPOSITION.]

post·po·si·tion (pōst′pə-zĭsh′ən) *n. Linguistics.* **1.** The placing of a word or suffixed element after the word to which it is grammatically related. **2.** A word or element placed postpositionally, as a preposition placed after its object. **—post′po·si′tion·al** *adj.* **—post′po·si′tion·al·ly** *adv.*

post·pos·i·tive (pōst-pŏz′ĭ-tĭv) *Linguistics. adj.* Placed after or suffixed to another word. **—postpositive** *n.* An appended or suffixed word or word element; a postposition. [Late Latin *postpositīvus,* from Latin *postpositus,* past participle of *postpōnere,* to put after. See POSTPONE.] **—post·pos′i·tive·ly** *adv.*

post·pran·di·al (pōst-prăn′dē-əl) *adj.* Following a meal, especially dinner: *took a postprandial walk through the woods.* **—post·pran′di·al·ly** *adv.*

post·pro·duc·tion (pōst′prə-dŭk′shən) *n.* A final stage in the production of a film or a television program, occurring after the action has been filmed or videotaped and typically involving editing and the addition of soundtracks.

post·script (pōst′skrĭpt′, pōs′skrĭpt′) *n. Abbr.* **P.S., p.s., PS 1.** A message appended at the end of a letter after the writer's signature. **2.** Additional information appended to the manuscript, as of a book or an article. [Medieval Latin **postscriptum,* from neuter past participle of Latin *postscrībere,* to write after : *post-,* post- + *scrībere,* to write; see **skrībh-** in Appendix.]

post-sea·son (pōst′sē′zən) *adv. & adj. Sports.* In, of, or relating to games played after the regular season: *ran great defense post-season; a poor post-season record.*

post·syn·ap·tic (pōst′sĭ-năp′tĭk) *adj.* Situated behind or occurring after a synapse: *postsynaptic neurons.* **—post′syn·ap′ti·cal·ly** *adv.*

post·test (pōst′tĕst′) *n.* A test given after a unit of instruction to ascertain what the students have learned. Results of a posttest are typically compared with those of a pretest.

post time *n. Sports.* The time set immediately before the official start of a race after which point no further betting is allowed.

post·tran·scrip·tion·al (pōst′trăn-skrĭp′shə-nəl) *adj.* Occurring or formed after genetic transcription.

post·trans·fu·sion (pōst′trăns-fyo͞o′zhən) *adj.* Occurring after or as a consequence of blood transfusion.

post·trans·la·tion·al (pōst′trăns-lā′shə-nəl, -trănz-) *adj.* Occurring or formed after genetic translation: *a posttranslational amino acid.*

post·trau·mat·ic (pōst′trou-măt′ĭk, -trô-) *adj.* Following injury or resulting from it: *posttraumatic amnesia.*

posttraumatic stress disorder *n. Abbr.* **PTSD** A psychological disorder affecting individuals who have experienced profound emotional trauma, such as torture or rape, characterized by recurrent flashbacks of the traumatic event, nightmares, eating disorders, anxiety, fatigue, forgetfulness, and social withdrawal.

pos·tu·lant (pŏs′chə-lənt) *n.* **1.** A person submitting a request or application; a petitioner. **2.** A candidate for admission into a religious order. [French, from Old French, from Latin *postulāns, postulant-,* present participle of *postulāre,* to request. See POSTULATE.] **—pos′tu·lan·cy, pos′tu·lant·ship′** *n.*

pos·tu·late (pŏs′chə-lāt′) *tr.v.* **-lat·ed, -lat·ing, -lates. 1.** To make claim for; demand. **2.** To assume or assert the truth, reality, or necessity of, especially as a basis of an argument. **3.** To assume as a premise or axiom; take for granted. See Synonyms at **presume. —postulate** (pŏs′cho͞o-lĭt, -lāt′) *n.* **1.** Something assumed without proof as being self-evident or generally accepted, especially when used as a basis for an argument: *"the postulate that there is little moral difference between the superpowers"* (Henry A. Kissinger). **2.** A fundamental element; a basic principle. **3.** *Mathematics.* An axiom. **4.** A requirement; a prerequisite. [Medieval Latin *postulāre, postulāt-,* to nominate to a bishopric, to assume, from Latin, to request. See **prek-** in Appendix.] **—pos′tu·la′tion** *n.*

pos·tu·la·tor (pŏs′chə-lā′tər) *n.* **1.** One who postulates. **2.** *Roman Catholic Church.* A church official who presents a plea for canonization or beatification.

pos·ture (pŏs′chər) *n.* **1.a.** A position of the body or of body parts: *a sitting posture.* **b.** An attitude; a pose: *assumed a posture of angry defiance.* **2.** A characteristic way of bearing one's body; carriage: *stood with good posture.* **3.** Relative placement or arrangement: *the posture of the buildings on the land.* **4.** A stance or disposition with regard to something: *"Those bases are essential to our military posture in the Middle East"* (Gerard Smith). **5.** A frame of mind affecting one's thoughts or behavior; an overall attitude. **—posture** *v.* **-tured, -tur·ing, -tures.** *—intr.* **1.** To assume an exaggerated or unnatural pose or mental attitude; attitudinize. **2.** To assume a pose. *—tr.* To put into a specific posture; pose. [French, from Italian *postura,* from Latin *positūra,* position, from *positus,* past participle of *pōnere,* to place. See **apo-** in Appendix.] **—pos′tur·al** *adj.* **—pos′tur·er, pos′tur·ist** *n.*

SYNONYMS: *posture, attitude, carriage, pose, stance.* The central meaning shared by these nouns is "a position of the body and limbs": *erect posture; an attitude of prayer; dignified carriage; a defiant pose; the alert stance of a batter in baseball.*

post·ver·te·bral (pōst-vûr′tə-brəl, pōst′vər-tē′-) *adj.* Situated behind the vertebrae: *postvertebral muscles.*

post·vo·cal·ic (pōst′vō-kăl′ĭk) *adj. Linguistics.* **1.** Designating a consonant or consonantal sound directly following a vowel. **2.** Of, relating to, or being a form of a linguistic element, such as a suffix or word, that occurs only after vowels.

post·war (pōst′wôr′) *adj.* Belonging to the period after a war: *postwar resettlement; a postwar house.*

po·sy (pō′zē) *n., pl.* **-sies. 1.** A flower or bunch of flowers; a nosegay. See Synonyms at **bouquet. 2.** *Archaic.* A brief verse or sentimental phrase, especially one inscribed on a trinket. [Alteration of POESY, motto or line of verse (archaic).]

pot[1] (pŏt) *n.* **1.** Any of various usually domestic containers made of pottery, metal, or glass, as: **a.** A round, fairly deep cooking vessel with a handle and often a lid. **b.** A short, round container for storing or serving food: *a jam pot; a mustard pot.* **c.** A coffeepot. **d.** A teapot. **2.a.** Such a container and its contents: *a pot of stew; brewed a pot of coffee.* **b.** A potful. **3.a.** A large drinking cup; a tankard. **b.** A drink of liquor contained in such a cup. **4.** An artistic or decorative ceramic vessel of any shape. **5.** A flowerpot. **6.** Something, such as a chimney pot or a chamber pot, that resembles a round cooking vessel in appearance or function. **7.** A trap for eels, other fish, or crustaceans, typically consisting of a wicker or wire basket or cage. **8.** *Games.* **a.** The total amount staked by all the players in one hand at cards. See Synonyms at **bet. b.** The area on a card table where stakes are placed. **c.** A shot in billiards or related games intended to send a ball into a pocket. **9.** *Informal.* A common fund to which members of a group contribute. **10.** Often **pots.** *Informal.* A large amount: *made pots of money on their investment.* **11.** *Computer Science.* A section of storage reserved for storing accumulated data. **12.** *Informal.* A potshot. **13.** *Informal.* A potbelly. **14.** *Informal.* A potty or toilet. **15.** See **potentiometer** (sense 2). **—pot** *v.* **pot·ted, pot·ting, pots.** *—tr.* **1.** To place or plant in a pot: *pot a geranium.* **2.** To preserve (food) in a pot. **3.** To cook in a pot. **4.** To shoot (game) for food rather than for sport. **5.** *Informal.* To shoot with a potshot. **6.** *Informal.* To win or capture; bag. **7.** *Games.* To hit (a ball) into a pocket. *—intr. Informal.* To take a potshot. [Middle English, from Old English *pott,* from Vulgar Latin **pottus.*]

pot[2] (pŏt) *n. Slang.* Marijuana. [Origin unknown.]

pot. *abbr.* Potential.

po·ta·ble (pō′tə-bəl) *adj.* Fit to drink. **—potable** *n.* A beverage, especially an alcoholic beverage: *wine and other potables.* [Middle English, from Old French, from Late Latin *pōtābilis,* from Latin *pōtāre,* to drink, from *pōtus,* a drink. See **pō(i)-** in Appendix.] **—po′ta·bil′i·ty, po′ta·ble·ness** *n.*

po·tage (pō-täzh′) *n.* A thick, often creamy soup. [French, from Old French. See POTTAGE.]

pot·a·mo·plank·ton (pŏt′ə-mō-plăngk′tən) *n.* The plankton of rivers or streams. [Greek *potamos,* river; see HIPPOPOTAMUS + PLANKTON.]

Po·ta·ro (pə-tär′ō, pô-tä′rô). A river, about 161 km (100 mi) long, of central Guyana. It has gold deposits and is known for its Kaieteur Falls.

pot·ash (pŏt′ăsh′) *n.* **1.** See **potassium carbonate. 2.** See **potassium hydroxide. 3.** Any of several compounds containing potassium, especially soluble compounds such as potassium oxide, potassium chloride, and various potassium sulfates, used chiefly in fertilizers. [Sing. of obsolete *pot ashes,* translated from obsolete Dutch *potaschen* (from the fact that this substance was originally obtained by leaching wood ashes and evaporating the leach in a pot).]

potash feldspar *n.* See **orthoclase.**

potash mu·ri·ate (myo͝or′ē-ĭt, -āt′) *n.* See **potassium chloride.**

po·tas·si·um (pə-tăs′ē-əm) *n. Symbol* **K** A soft, silver-white, highly or explosively reactive metallic element that occurs in nature only in compounds. It is obtained by electrolysis of its common hydroxide and found in, or converted to, a wide variety of salts used especially in fertilizers and soaps. Atomic number 19; atomic weight 39.102; melting point 63.65°C; boiling point 774°C; specific gravity 0.862; valence 1. See table at **element.** [From POTASH (from which it was first obtained).] **—po·tas′sic** *adj.*

po·tas·si·um-ar·gon (pə-tăs′ē-əm-är′gŏn′) *adj.* Of, relating to, or being a geologic dating method relying on the percentage of potassium in a specimen that has radioactively decayed to argon.

potassium bicarbonate *n.* A compound, $KHCO_3$, in the form of a white powder or colorless crystals, used in baking powder and as an antacid medicine.

potassium bitartrate *n.* A white, acid, crystalline solid or powder, $KHC_4H_4O_6$, used in baking powder, in the tinning of metals, and as a component of laxatives. Also called *cream of tartar.*

potassium bromide *n.* A white crystalline solid or powder, KBr, used as a sedative, in photographic emulsion, and in lithography.

potassium carbonate *n.* A transparent, white, deliquescent, granular powder, K_2CO_3, used in making glass, enamels, and soaps. Also called *potash.*

potassium chlorate *n.* A poisonous crystalline compound, $KClO_3$, used as an oxidizing agent, a bleach, and a disinfectant and in making explosives, matches, and fireworks.

potassium chloride *n.* A colorless crystalline solid or powder, KCl, used in fertilizers and in the preparation of potassium compounds. Also called *potash muriate, potassium muriate.*

potassium cyanide *n.* An extremely poisonous white compound, KCN, used in the extraction of gold and silver from ores, electroplating, and photography, and as a fumigant and insecticide.

potassium dichromate *n.* A bright yellowish-red crystalline compound, $K_2Cr_2O_7$, used as an oxidizing agent, and in pyrotechnics, explosives, and safety matches.

potassium hydroxide *n.* A caustic white solid, KOH, used as a bleach and in the manufacture of soaps, dyes, alkaline batteries, and many potassium compounds. Also called *caustic potash, lye, potash.*

potassium iodide *n.* A white crystalline compound, KI, used in photography and medicine and as an analytical reagent.

potassium mu·ri·ate (myo͝or′ē-ĭt, -āt′) *n.* See **potassium chloride.**

potassium nitrate *n.* A transparent white crystalline compound, KNO_3, used to pickle meat and in the manufacture of pyrotechnics, explosives, matches, rocket propellants, and fertilizers. Also called *saltpeter.*

potassium permanganate *n.* A dark purple crystalline compound, $KMnO_4$, used as an oxidizing agent and disinfectant and in deodorizers and dyes.

potassium sodium tartrate *n.* A colorless efflorescent crystalline compound, $KNaC_4H_4O_6{\cdot}4H_2O$, used in making mirrors, in electronics, and as a laxative. Also called *Rochelle salt.*

potassium sulfate *n.* A colorless or white crystalline compound, K_2SO_4, used in glassmaking and fertilizers and as a reagent in analytical chemistry.

po·ta·tion (pō-tā′shən) *n.* **1.** The act of drinking. **2.** A drink, especially of an alcoholic beverage. [Middle English *potacion,* from Old French, from Latin *pōtātiō, pōtātiōn-,* a drinking party, from *pōtātus,* past participle of *pōtāre,* to drink, from *pōtus,* a drink. See **pō(i)-** in Appendix.]

♦**po·ta·to** (pə-tā′tō) *n., pl.* **-toes. 1.** A South American plant *(Solanum tuberosum)* widely cultivated for its starchy, edible tubers. **2.** A tuber of this plant. **3.** A sweet potato. **4.** See Regional Note at **possum.** [Spanish *patata,* alteration (probably influenced by Quechua *papa,* white potato) of Taino *batata,* sweet potato.]

potato beetle *n.* The Colorado potato beetle.

potato blight *n.* Any of various highly destructive fungus diseases of the potato.

potato bug *n.* The Colorado potato beetle.

potato chip *n.* A thin slice of potato fried in deep fat until crisp and then salted. Often used in the plural.

po·ta·to·ry (pō′tə-tôr′ē, -tōr′ē) *adj.* Of, relating to, or given to drinking. [Late Latin *pōtātōrius,* from Latin *pōtātus,* past participle of *pōtāre,* to drink, from *pōtus,* a drink. See **pō(i)-** in Appendix.]

potato skin *n.* An appetizer made with a slice of baked potato skin, spread with a topping such as cheese or meat, and usually broiled or baked. Often used in the plural.

potato yam *n.* See **air potato.**

pot-au-feu (pô-tō-fœ′) *n., pl.* **pot-au-feu.** A French dish of boiled meats and vegetables. [French : *pot,* pot + *au,* on the + *feu,* fire.]

Pot·a·wat·o·mi (pŏt′ə-wŏt′ə-mē) *n., pl.* **Potawatomi** or **-mis. 1.a.** A Native American people variously located in Michigan, Wisconsin, northern Illinois, and northern Indiana in the 17th to the 19th century, with present-day populations in Oklahoma, Kansas, Michigan, and Ontario. **b.** A member of this people. **2.** The Algonquian language of the Potawatomi.

pot·bel·lied stove (pŏt′bĕl′ēd) *n.* See **potbelly stove.**

pot·bel·ly (pŏt′bĕl′ē) *n., pl.* **-lies. 1.** A protruding abdominal region. **2.** A potbelly stove. **—pot′bel′lied** *adj.*

potbelly stove *n.* A short rounded stove in which wood or coal is burned. Also called *potbellied stove.*

pot·boil (pŏt′boil′) *intr.v.* **-boiled, -boil·ing, -boils.** To produce potboilers. [Back-formation from POTBOILER.]

pot·boil·er (pŏt′boi′lər) *n.* A literary or artistic work of poor quality, produced quickly for profit. [From the phrase *boil the pot,* to provide one's livelihood.]

pot·bound (pŏt′bound′) *adj.* Having grown too large for its container, resulting in matting or tangling of the roots. Used of a potted plant.

pot·boy (pŏt′boi′) *n. Chiefly British.* A boy or man who works in an inn or a public house serving customers and doing chores.

pot cheese *n.* See **cottage cheese.**

po·teen (pō-tēn′) *n.* Unlawfully distilled Irish whiskey. [Irish Gaelic *poitín,* small pot, poteen, from *pota,* pot, from POT[1].]

Po·tem·kin (pō-tĕm′kĭn, pə-, pə-tyôm′-), **Grigori Aleksandrovich.** 1739–1791. Russian army officer and politician. The lover of Catherine II, he helped her seize power in 1762.

Potemkin village *n.* Something that appears elaborate and impressive but in actual fact lacks substance: *"the Potemkin village of this country's borrowed prosperity"* (Lewis H. Lapham). [After Grigori Aleksandrovich POTEMKIN, who had elaborate fake villages constructed for Catherine the Great's tours of the Ukraine and the Crimea.]

po·tence (pōt′ns) *n.* Potency.

po·ten·cy (pōt′n-sē) *n., pl.* **-cies. 1.** The quality or condition of being potent. **2.** Inherent capacity for growth and development; potentiality.

po·tent (pōt′nt) *adj.* **1.** Possessing inner or physical strength; powerful. **2.a.** Exerting or capable of exerting strong physiological or chemical effects: *potent liquor; a potent toxin.* **b.** Exerting or capable of exerting strong influence; cogent: *potent arguments.* **3.** Having great control or authority: *"The police were potent only so long as they were feared"* (Thomas Burke). **4.** Able to perform sexual intercourse. Used of a male. [Middle English, from Latin *potēns, potent-,* present participle of *posse,* to be able. See **poti-** in Appendix.] **—po′tent·ly** *adv.* **—po′tent·ness** *n.*

po·ten·tate (pōt′n-tāt′) *n.* **1.** One who has the power and position to rule over others; a monarch. **2.** One who dominates or leads a group or an endeavor: *industrial potentates.* [Middle English *potentat,* from Old French, from Late Latin *potentātus,* from Latin, power, from *potēns,* present participle of *posse,* to be able. See POTENT.]

po·ten·tial (pə-tĕn′shəl) *adj. Abbr.* **pot. 1.** Capable of being but not yet in existence; latent: *a potential problem.* **2.** Having possibility, capability, or power. **3.** *Grammar.* Of, relating to, or being a verbal construction with auxiliaries such as *may* or *can;* for example, *it may snow.* **—potential** *n. Abbr.* **pot. 1.** The inherent ability or capacity for growth, development, or coming into being. **2.** Something possessing the capacity for growth or development. **3.** *Grammar.* A potential verb form. **4.** *Physics.* The work required to bring a unit electric charge, magnetic pole, or mass from an infinitely distant position to a designated point in a static electric, magnetic, or gravitational field, respectively. **5.** *Symbol* **V** *Electricity.* The potential energy of a unit charge at any point in an electric circuit measured with respect to a specified reference point in the circuit or to ground; voltage. [Middle English *potencial,* from Old French *potenciel,* from Late Latin *potentiālis,* powerful, from Latin *potentia,* power, from *potēns, potent-,* present participle of *posse,* to be able. See POTENT.] **—po·ten′tial·ly** *adv.*

potential energy *n.* The energy of a particle or system of particles derived from position, or condition, rather than motion. A raised weight, coiled spring, or charged battery has potential energy.

po·ten·ti·al·i·ty (pə-tĕn′shē-ăl′ĭ-tē) *n., pl.* **-ties. 1.** The state of being potential. **2.a.** Inherent capacity for growth, development, or coming into existence. **b.** Something possessing such capacity.

po·ten·ti·ate (pə-tĕn′shē-āt′) *tr.v.* **-at·ed, -at·ing, -ates. 1.** To make potent or powerful. **2.** To enhance or increase the effect of (a drug). **3.** To promote or strengthen (a biochemical or physiological action or effect). [From Latin *potentia,* power. See POTENTIAL.] **—po·ten′ti·a′tion** *n.*

po·ten·til·la (pōt′n-tĭl′ə) *n.* Any of numerous herbs or shrubs of the genus *Potentilla,* of the North Temperate Zone, having pinnately or palmately compound leaves and yellow, white, or red flowers with many pistils. [Medieval Latin, garden valerian, from Latin *potēns, potent-,* present participle of *posse,* to be able. See POTENT.]

po·ten·ti·om·e·ter (pə-tĕn′shē-ŏm′ĭ-tər) *n.* **1.** An instrument for measuring an unknown voltage by comparison to a standard voltage. **2.** A three-terminal resistor with an adjustable center connection, widely used for volume control in radio and

potato
Solanum tuberosum

potbelly stove

ă pat	oi boy
ā pay	ou out
âr care	o͝o took
ä father	o͞o boot
ĕ pet	ŭ cut
ē be	ûr urge
ĭ pit	th thin
ī pie	*th* this
îr pier	hw which
ŏ pot	zh vision
ō toe	ə about, item
ô paw	♦ regionalism

Stress marks: ′ (primary); ′ (secondary), as in **dictionary** (dĭk′shə-nĕr′ē)

television receivers. In this sense, also called *pot.* [POTENTI(AL) + -METER.] **—po·ten′ti·o·met′ric** (-ə-mĕt′rĭk) *adj.*

pot·ful (pŏt′fo͝ol′) *n.* **1.** The amount that a pot can hold. **2.** *Informal.* A large amount: *made a potful of money on the horses.*

pot·head (pŏt′hĕd′) *n. Slang.* One who habitually smokes marijuana.

poth·er (pŏ*th*′ər) *n.* **1.** A commotion; a disturbance. **2.** A state of nervous activity; a fuss. **3.** A cloud of smoke or dust that chokes or smothers. **—pother** *v.* **-ered, -er·ing, -ers.** *—tr.* To make confused; trouble; worry. *—intr.* To be overly concerned with trifles; fuss. [Origin unknown.]

pot·herb (pŏt′ûrb′, -hûrb′) *n.* A plant whose leaves, stems, or flowers are cooked and eaten or used as seasoning.

pot·hold·er (pŏt′hōl′dər) *n.* A small fabric pad used to handle hot cooking utensils.

♦**pot·hole** (pŏt′hōl′) *n.* **1.** A hole or pit, especially one in a road surface. Also called *chuckhole.* **2.** A deep, round hole worn in rock by loose stones whirling in strong rapids or waterfalls. **3.** *Western U.S.* A place filled with mud or quicksand that is a hazard to cattle. **—pot′holed′** *adj.*

pot·hook (pŏt′ho͝ok′) *n.* **1.** A bent or hooked piece of iron for hanging a pot or kettle over a fire. **2.** A curved iron rod with a hooked end used for lifting hot pots, irons, or stove lids. **3.** A curved, S-shaped mark made in writing. **4.** Often **pothooks. a.** Illegible handwriting or aimless scribbling. **b.** *Informal.* Stenographic writing.

potter's wheel

pot·house (pŏt′hous′) *n. Chiefly British.* A tavern.

pot·hunt·er (pŏt′hŭn′tər) *n.* **1.** One who hunts game for food, ignoring the rules of sport. **2.** One who participates in contests simply to win prizes. **3.** A nonprofessional archaeologist. **—pot′hunt′ing** *n.*

po·tiche (pô-tēsh′) *n.* A vase or jar with a round or polygonal body tapering at the neck and having a removable cover. [French, from *pot,* pot, from Old French, from Vulgar Latin **pottus.*]

Pot·i·dae·a (pŏt′ĭ-dē′ə). An ancient city of northeast Greece in Macedonia. Founded as a Corinthian colony in 609 B.C., it revolted against Athens in 432 but was reconquered in 429 after a two-year siege. Philip of Macedon destroyed the city in 356.

po·tion (pō′shən) *n.* A liquid dose, especially one of medicinal, magic, or poisonous content. [Middle English *pocion,* from Old French, from Latin *pōtiō, pōtiōn-.* See **pō(i)-** in Appendix.]

pot·latch (pŏt′lăch′) *n.* A ceremonial feast among certain Native American peoples of the northwest Pacific coast, as in celebration of a marriage or an accession, at which the host distributes gifts according to each guest's rank or status. Between rival groups the potlatch could involve extravagant or competitive giving and destruction by the host of valued items as a display of superior wealth. [Chinook Jargon, from Nootka *p'achitl,* to make a potlatch gift.]

pot·luck (pŏt′lŭk′) *n.* **1.** Whatever food happens to be available for a meal, especially when offered to a guest: *Having arrived unannounced for supper, we had to take potluck.* **2.** A meal at which each guest brings food that is then shared by all. Also called *potluck supper.* **3.** Whatever is available at a particular time: *The scheduled flight was canceled and passengers had to take potluck on the other airlines.*

pot marigold *n.* See **calendula.**

pot marjoram *n.* Marjoram.

Po·to·mac (pə-tō′mək). A community of central Maryland, a residential suburb of Washington, D.C. Population, 22,800.

Potomac River. A river of the east-central United States rising in northeast West Virginia and flowing about 459 km (285 mi) along the Virginia-Maryland border to Chesapeake Bay. It is navigable for large ships to Washington, D.C.

Po·to·sí (pō-tə-sē′, pô-tô-). A city of south-central Bolivia southwest of Sucre in the Andes at an altitude of about 4,203 m (13,780 ft). It was founded after silver was discovered in 1545 and was once a fabled source of riches. Population, 113,380.

pot·pie (pŏt′pī′) *n.* **1.** A mixture of meat or poultry and vegetables covered with a pastry crust and baked in a deep dish. **2.** A meat or poultry stew with dumplings.

pot·pour·ri (pō′po͞o-rē′) *n., pl.* **-ris.** **1.** A combination of incongruous things: *"In the minds of many, the real and imagined causes for Russia's defeats quickly mingled into a potpourri of terrible fears"* (W. Bruce Lincoln). **2.** A miscellaneous anthology or collection: *a potpourri of short stories and humorous verse.* **3.** A mixture of dried flower petals and spices used to scent the air. [French *pot pourri* (translation of Spanish *olla podrida;* see OLLA PODRIDA) : *pot,* pot; see POTICHE + *pourri,* past participle of *pourrir,* to rot (from Old French *purir,* from Vulgar Latin **putrīre,* from Latin *putrēscere;* see PUTRID).]

pot roast *n.* A cut of beef that is browned and then cooked until tender, often with vegetables, in a covered pot.

Pots·dam (pŏts′dăm′). A city of northeast Germany on the Havel River near Berlin. First mentioned in the 10th century, it became in the 18th century a favorite residence of Frederick the Great, who built the rococo palace of Sans Souci here (1745–1747). The city was the site of the Potsdam Conference (July–August 1945), at which American, British, and Soviet leaders drew up preliminary plans for the postwar administration of Germany and assigned various captured territories to Poland. Population, 135,922.

pot·sherd (pŏt′shûrd′) also **pot·shard** (-shärd′) *n.* A fragment of broken pottery, especially one found in an archaeological excavation.

pot·shot also **pot shot** (pŏt′shŏt′) *n.* **1.** A random or easy shot. **2.** A criticism made without careful thought and aimed at a handy target for attack: *reporters taking potshots at the mayor.* [So called because such a shot is fired by a hunter whose main purpose is to get food for the pot.]

pot·stone (pŏt′stōn′) *n.* A variety of steatite once used to make cooking vessels.

pot·tage (pŏt′ĭj) *n.* **1.** A thick soup or stew of vegetables and sometimes meat. **2.** *Archaic.* Porridge. [Middle English *potage,* from Old French, from *pot,* pot. See POTICHE.]

pot·ted (pŏt′ĭd) *adj.* **1.a.** Placed in a pot. **b.** Grown in a pot: *many potted plants in the study.* **2.** Preserved in a pot, can, or jar. **3.** *Slang.* **a.** Intoxicated; drunk. **b.** Under the influence of a hallucinogenic drug.

pot·ter¹ (pŏt′ər) *n.* One who makes pottery.

pot·ter² (pŏt′ər) *v. Chiefly British.* Variant of **putter².**

Pot·ter (pŏt′ər), **Beatrix.** 1866–1943. British writer and illustrator. Her animal stories include *The Tale of Peter Rabbit* (1900) and *The Tailor of Gloucester* (1902).

Potter, Paul or **Paulus.** 1625–1654. Dutch painter noted for his landscapes and animal paintings, such as *Horses at Pasture* (1649).

Pot·ter·ies (pŏt′ə-rēz). A district of west-central England in the Trent River valley. It has been a center of the manufacture of china and earthenware since the 16th century.

pot·ter's clay (pŏt′ərz) *n.* A clay free of iron, suitable for making pottery or for modeling. Also called *potter's earth.*

potter's field *n.* A place for the burial of unknown or indigent persons. [From the potter's field mentioned in Matthew 27:7.]

potter's wheel *n.* A revolving, often treadle-operated horizontal disk on which clay is shaped manually.

potter wasp *n.* Any of various small black and yellow solitary wasps of the genus *Eumenes,* characteristically building pot-shaped nests of clay. Also called ♦*dirt dauber,* ♦*mud wasp.*

pot·ter·y (pŏt′ə-rē) *n., pl.* **-ies.** **1.** Ware, such as vases, pots, bowls, or plates, shaped from moist clay and hardened by heat. **2.** The craft or occupation of a potter. **3.** The place where a potter works. [French *poterie,* from Old French, from *potier,* potter, from *pot,* pot. See POTICHE.]

pot·tle (pŏt′l) *n.* **1.** A pot or drinking vessel with a capacity of 2.0 quarts (1.9 liters). **2.** The liquid contained in this type of pot or drinking vessel. **3.** An old English liquid measure equal to 2.0 quarts (1.9 liters). [Middle English *potel,* from Old French, from *pot,* pot. See POTICHE.]

pot·to (pŏt′ō) *n., pl.* **-tos.** Any of several small nocturnal African primates of the genera *Perodicticus* and *Arctocebus,* having a pointed snout, large eyes and ears, and a stumplike index finger and tail. [Of Niger-Congo origin; perhaps akin to Wolof *pata,* a tailless monkey, or Akan (Twi) *apɔsɔ,* a fierce monkeylike animal.]

Pott's disease (pŏts) *n.* Partial destruction of the vertebral bones, usually caused by a tuberculous infection and often producing curvature of the spine. [After Percival *Pott* (1714–1788), British surgeon.]

Potts·town (pŏts′toun′). A borough of southeast Pennsylvania on the Schuylkill River east-southeast of Reading. Its first ironworks were established in 1715. Population, 22,729.

Potts·ville (pŏts′vĭl′). A city of east-central Pennsylvania west-northwest of Allentown. Once a coal-mining town, it is now a trade and industrial center. Population, 18,195.

pot·ty¹ (pŏt′ē) *adj.* **-ti·er, -ti·est.** *Chiefly British.* **1.** Of little importance; trivial. **2.** Slightly intoxicated. **3.** Somewhat silly or crazy; addlebrained. [Possibly from POT¹.]

pot·ty² (pŏt′ē) *n., pl.* **-ties.** A small pot for use as a toilet by an infant or young child.

pot·ty-chair (pŏt′ē-châr′) *n.* A small chair with an opening in the seat and a receptacle beneath, used for toilet-training young children.

pouch (pouch) *n.* **1.** A small bag often closing with a drawstring and used especially for carrying loose items in one's pocket. **2.** A bag or sack used to carry mail or diplomatic dispatches. **3.** A leather bag or case for carrying powder or small-arms ammunition. **4.** A sealed plastic or foil container used in packaging frozen or dehydrated food. **5.** Something resembling a bag in shape: *one's pouches under one's eyes.* **6.** *Zoology.* A saclike structure, such as the cheek pockets of the gopher or the external abdominal pocket in which marsupials carry their young. **7.** *Anatomy.* A pocketlike space in the body: *the pharyngeal pouch.* **8.** *Scots.* A pocket. **9.** *Archaic.* A purse for small coins. **—pouch** *v.* **pouched, pouch·ing, pouch·es.** *—tr.* **1.** To place in or as if in a pouch; pocket. **2.** To cause to resemble a pouch. **3.** To swallow. Used of certain birds or fishes. *—intr.* To assume the form of a pouch or pouchlike cavity. [Middle English, from Old French, of Germanic origin.] **—pouch′y** *adj.*

pouched (poucht) *adj.* Having a pouch, as a gopher, pelican, or marsupial.

pouf (po͞of) *n.* **1.** A woman's hairstyle popular in the 18th century, characterized by high rolled puffs. **2.** A part of a garment, such as a dress, that is gathered into a puff. **3.** A rounded ottoman. [French, from Old French, interjection used for a fall, of imitative origin.] **—pouf′fy** *adj.*

Pough·keep·sie (pə-kĭp′sē, pō-). A city of southeast New

York on the Hudson River north of New York City. Settled by the Dutch in 1687, Poughkeepsie is the seat of Vassar College (chartered 1861). Population, 29,757.

pouil·ly-fuis·sé (po͞o-yē′fwē-sā′) *n.* A dry white Burgundy wine. [After *Solutré-Pouilly* and *Fuissé,* villages of east-central France.]

pou·lard also **pou·larde** (po͞o-lärd′) *n.* A young hen that has been spayed for fattening. [French *poularde,* from *poule,* hen, from Old French, from Latin *pulla,* feminine of *pullus,* young of an animal, chicken. See **pau-** in Appendix.]

Pou·lenc (po͞o-lăNk′), **Francis.** 1899–1963. French composer and pianist whose works include the piano piece *Trois Mouvements Perpétuels* (1918) and the ballet *Les Biches* (1924).

poult (pōlt) *n.* A young fowl, especially a turkey, chicken, or pheasant. [Middle English *pult,* short for *polet,* from Old French *poulet,* diminutive of *poule, polle,* hen. See POULARD.]

poul·ter's measure (pōl′tərz) *n.* A metrical pattern employing couplets in which the first line is in iambic hexameter and the second is in iambic heptameter. [From obsolete *poulter,* a poultry dealer (from the practice of giving a few extra eggs in the dozen), from Middle English *pulter,* from Old French *pouletier,* from *poulet,* pullet. See PULLET.]

poul·tice (pōl′tĭs) *n.* A soft, moist mass of bread, meal, clay, or other adhesive substance, usually heated, spread on cloth, and applied to warm, moisten, or stimulate an aching or inflamed part of the body. Also called *cataplasm.* **—poultice** *tr.v.* **-ticed, -tic·ing, -tic·es.** To apply a poultice to. [Middle English *pultes,* from Medieval Latin *pultēs,* thick paste, from Latin, pl. of *puls, pult-,* pottage. See PULSE[2].]

poul·try (pōl′trē) *n.* Domestic fowls, such as chickens, turkeys, ducks, or geese, raised for meat or eggs. [Middle English *pultrie,* from Old French *pouletrie,* from *pouletier,* poulterer. See POULTER'S MEASURE.]

pounce[1] (pouns) *v.* **pounced, pounc·ing, pounc·es.** —*intr.* **1.** To spring or swoop with intent to seize someone or something: *a cat that pounced on a mouse; watched the falcon pounce on the baby rabbit.* **2.** To attack suddenly: *irregular troops who pounced on the convoy at a narrow pass; a colleague who pounced on me because of a mistake in my report.* **3.** To seize something swiftly and eagerly: *pounce on an opportunity.* —*tr.* To seize with or as if with talons. **—pounce** *n.* **1.** The act or an instance of pouncing. **2.** The talon or claw of a bird of prey. [From Middle English, pointed tool, talon of a hawk, perhaps variant of *ponson,* pointed tool. See PUNCHEON[1].] **—pounc′er** *n.*

pounce[2] (pouns) *n.* **1.** A fine powder formerly used to smooth and finish writing paper and soak up ink. **2.** A fine powder, such as pulverized charcoal, dusted over a stencil to transfer a design to an underlying surface. **—pounce** *tr.v.* **pounced, pounc·ing, pounc·es. 1.** To sprinkle, smooth, or treat with pounce. **2.** To transfer (a stenciled design) with pounce. [French *ponce,* from Old French, from Vulgar Latin **pōmex, pōmic-,* from Latin *pūmex,* pumice.] **—pounc′er** *n.*

pounce[3] (pouns) *tr.v.* **pounced, pounc·ing, pounc·es.** To ornament (metal, for example) by perforating from the back with a pointed implement. [Middle English *pouncen,* probably from Old French *poinssonner,* from *poinson,* pointed tool. See PUNCHEON[1].]

pounce box *n.* A small box with a perforated top, formerly used to sprinkle sand or pounce on writing paper to dry the ink.

poun·cet box (poun′sĭt) *n.* A small perfume box with a perforated top. [Perhaps alteration of **pounced-box,* from POUNCE[3].]

pound[1] (pound) *n., pl.* **pound** or **pounds. 1.** *Abbr.* **lb. a.** A unit of weight equal to 16 ounces (453.592 grams). **b.** A unit of apothecary weight equal to 12 ounces (373.242 grams). See table at **measurement. 2.** A unit of weight differing in various countries and times. **3.** A British unit of force equal to the weight of a standard one-pound mass where the local acceleration of gravity is 9.817 meters (32.174 feet) per second per second. **4.a.** The basic monetary unit of the United Kingdom, worth 20 shillings or 240 old pence before the decimalization of 1971. Also called *pound sterling.* **b.** See table at **currency. 5.** A monetary unit of Scotland before the Union. In this sense, also called *pound scots.* [Middle English, from Old English *pund,* from West Germanic **punda-,* from Latin *(lībra) pondō,* (a pound) by weight. See **(s)pen-** in Appendix.]

pound[2] (pound) *v.* **pound·ed, pound·ing, pounds.** —*tr.* **1.** To strike repeatedly and forcefully. See Synonyms at **beat. 2.** To beat to a powder or pulp; pulverize or crush. **3.** To instill by persistent, emphatic repetition: *pounded knowledge into the students' heads.* **4.** To assault with heavy gunfire. —*intr.* **1.** To strike vigorous, repeated blows: *He pounded on the table.* **2.** To move along heavily and noisily: *The children pounded up the stairs.* **3.** To pulsate rapidly and heavily; throb: *Her heart pounded.* **4.** To move or work laboriously: *a ship that pounded through heavy seas.* **—pound** *n.* **1.** A heavy blow. **2.** The sound of a heavy blow; a thump. **3.** The act of pounding. **—*idiom.* pound the pavement.** *Slang.* To travel the streets on foot, especially in search of work. [Middle English *pounden,* alteration of *pounen,* from Old English *pūnian.*] **—pound′er** *n.*

pound[3] (pound) *n.* **1.** A public enclosure for the confinement of stray dogs or livestock. **2.** A place in which impounded property is held until redeemed. **3.** An enclosure in which animals or fish are trapped or kept. **4.** A place of confinement for lawbreakers. **—pound** *tr.v.* **pound·ed, pound·ing, pounds.** To confine in or as if in a pound; impound. [Middle English, from Old English *pund-,* enclosure, as in *pundfald,* pen.]

Pound (pound), **Ezra Loomis.** 1885–1972. American writer who exerted great influence on the development of modern literature through his poetic works, such as the unfinished *Cantos* (1925–1960), his critical works, including *ABC of Reading* (1934), his voluminous contributions to literary magazines, and his tutelage of writers such as T.S. Eliot and Ernest Hemingway.

Pound, Roscoe. 1870–1964. American jurist who was dean of Harvard Law School (1916–1936) and wrote several influential books, including *The Spirit of the Common Law* (1921).

pound·age[1] (poun′dĭj) *n.* **1.** A tax or commission based on value per pound sterling. **2.** A rate or charge based on weight in pounds. **3.** Weight measured in pounds.

pound·age[2] (poun′dĭj) *n.* **1.** Confinement of animals in a pound. **2.** A fee charged for the redemption of impounded animals or other property.

pound·al (poun′dl) *n.* A unit of force in the foot-pound-second system of measurement, equal to the force required to accelerate a standard one-pound mass one foot per second per second (approximately 0.138 newton). [POUND[1] + *-al* (as in QUINTAL).]

pound cake *n.* A rich, finely textured yellow cake containing a large proportion of eggs, flour, butter, and sugar. [From the original recipe, calling for a pound each of butter, sugar, and flour.]

pound-fool·ish (pound′fo͞o′lĭsh) *adj.* Unwise in dealing with large sums of money or large matters. [From the phrase *penny-wise, pound-foolish.*]

pound of flesh *n., pl.* **pounds of flesh.** A debt harshly insisted upon. [From Antonio's debt to Shylock in *The Merchant of Venice* by Shakespeare.]

pound scots *n.* See **pound[1]** (sense 5).

pound sterling *n.* See **pound[1]** (sense 4a).

pour (pôr, pōr) *v.* **poured, pour·ing, pours.** —*tr.* **1.** To make (a liquid or granular solid) stream or flow, as from a container. **2.** To send forth, produce, express, or utter copiously, as if in a stream or flood: *poured money into the project; poured out my inner thoughts.* —*intr.* **1.** To stream or flow continuously or profusely. **2.** To rain hard or heavily. **3.** To pass or proceed in large numbers or quantity: *Students poured into the auditorium.* **4.** To serve a beverage, such as tea or coffee, to a gathering: *We need someone to pour.* **—pour** *n.* A pouring or flowing forth, especially a downpour of rain. [Middle English *pouren,* probably from Old North French *purer,* to sift, pour out, from Latin *pūrāre,* to purify, from *pūrus,* pure. See **peuə-** in Appendix.] **—pour′er** *n.*

pour·boire (po͝or-bwär′) *n.* Money given as a gratuity; a tip. [French, from *pour boire,* for drinking : *pour,* for (from Old French, from Latin *prō;* see PRO–[1]) + *boire,* to drink (from Old French *boivre,* from Latin *bibere;* see BEVERAGE).]

pour·par·ler (po͝or′pär-lā′) *n.* Conversation or discussion preliminary to negotiation. [French, from Old French, to discuss with the aim of reaching agreement, conversation preliminary to an agreement : *pour,* for, before (from Old French, from Latin *prō;* see PRO–[1]) + *parler,* to talk; see PARLEY.]

pour point *n.* The lowest temperature at which an oil or other liquid will pour under given conditions.

pousse-ca·fé (po͞os′kă-fā′) *n.* **1.** A drink consisting of several liqueurs of different densities, poured to form differently colored layers. **2.** A brandy or liqueur served after dinner with coffee. [French : *pousse,* third person sing. present tense of *pousser,* to push (from Old French; see POUSSETTE) + *café,* coffee; see CAFÉ.]

pous·sette (po͞o-sĕt′) *n.* A country-dance figure in which couples or a couple join hands and swing around the floor. [French, pushpin, diminutive of obsolete *pousse,* a push, from *pousser,* to push, from Old French *poulser, pousser,* to push, from Latin *pulsāre,* frequentative of *pellere,* to push. See **pel-[5]** in Appendix.]

Pous·sin (po͞o-săN′), **Nicolas.** 1594–1665. French painter whose landscapes and historical and religious paintings, such as *Holy Family on the Steps* (1648), are among the greatest examples of the classical style.

pout[1] (pout) *v.* **pout·ed, pout·ing, pouts.** —*intr.* **1.** To exhibit displeasure or disappointment; sulk. **2.** To protrude the lips in an expression of displeasure or sulkiness. **3.** To project or protrude. —*tr.* **1.** To push out or protrude (the lips). **2.** To utter or express with a pout. **—pout** *n.* **1.** A protrusion of the lips, especially as an expression of sullen discontent. **2.** Often **pouts.** A fit of petulant sulkiness. Often used with *the.* [Middle English *pouten,* perhaps of Scandinavian origin.] **—pout′y** *adj.*

pout[2] (pout) *n., pl.* **pout** or **pouts.** Any of various freshwater or marine fishes, especially an eelpout or hornpout. [Middle English **poute,* from Old English *-pūte,* as in *ǣlepūte,* eelpout.]

pout·er (pou′tər) *n.* **1.** One that pouts. **2.** One of a breed of pigeons capable of distending the crop until the breast becomes puffed out.

pov·er·ty (pŏv′ər-tē) *n.* **1.** The state of being poor; lack of the means of providing material needs or comforts. **2.** Deficiency in amount; scantiness: *"the poverty of feeling that reduced her soul"* (Scott Turow). **3.** Unproductiveness; infertility: *the poverty of the soil.* **4.** Renunciation made by a member of a religious order of the right to own property. [Middle English *poverte,* from Old

ă pat	oi boy
ā pay	ou out
âr care	o͝o took
ä father	o͞o boot
ĕ pet	ŭ cut
ē be	ûr urge
ĭ pit	th thin
ī pie	*th* this
îr pier	hw which
ŏ pot	zh vision
ō toe	ə about, item
ô paw	♦ regionalism

Stress marks: ′ (primary); ′ (secondary), as in **dictionary** (dĭk′shə-nĕr′ē)

French, from Latin *paupertās,* from *pauper,* poor. See **pau-** in Appendix.]

poverty grass *n.* Any of several North American grasses that grow in poor or sandy soil.

poverty level *n.* A minimum income level below which a person is officially considered to lack adequate subsistence and to be living in poverty. Also called *poverty line.*

pov·er·ty-strick·en (pŏv′ər-tē-strĭk′ən) *adj.* Suffering from poverty; miserably poor. See Synonyms at **poor.**

POW (pē′ō-dŭb′əl-yo͞o, -yo͝o) *n., pl.* **POW's** also **POWs.** A prisoner of war.

Pow·ay (pou′ā). A community of southern California north of San Diego. It is near a large naval air base. Population, 33,300.

pow·der (pou′dər) *n.* **1.** A substance consisting of ground, pulverized, or otherwise finely dispersed solid particles. **2.** Any of various preparations in the form of powder, as certain cosmetics and medicines. **3.** An explosive mixture, such as gunpowder. **4.** Light, dry snow. **—powder** *v.* **-dered, -der·ing, -ders.** *—tr.* **1.** To reduce to powder; pulverize. **2.** To dust or cover with or as if with powder. **3.** *Slang.* To defeat handily or decisively. *—intr.* **1.** To become pulverized; turn into powder. **2.** To use powder as a cosmetic. ***—idioms.*** **keep (one's) powder dry.** To be ready for a challenge with little warning. **take a powder.** To make a quick departure; run away. [Middle English *poudre,* from Old French, from Latin *pulvis, pulver-.*] **—pow′der·er** *n.*

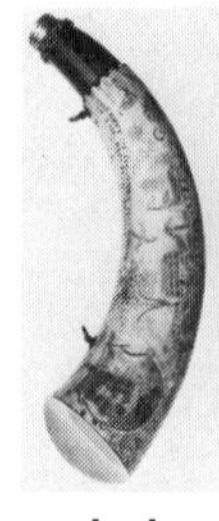

powder horn
1767 American

powder blue *n. Color.* A moderate to pale blue or purplish blue. [From the color of powdered smalt.]

powder horn *n.* An animal's horn capped at the open end, used to carry gunpowder.

powder keg *n.* **1.** A small cask for holding gunpowder or other explosives. **2.** A potentially explosive situation or thing.

Pow·der·ly (pou′dər-lē), **Terence Vincent.** 1849–1924. American labor leader who directed the Knights of Labor, a secret organization that disavowed strikes, during its period of greatest influence (1879–1893).

powder metallurgy *n.* The technology of powdered metals, especially the production and utilization of metallic powders for fabricating massive materials and shaped objects.

powder monkey *n. Slang.* One who carries or sets explosives.

powder puff *n.* A soft pad for applying powder to the skin.

pow·der-puff (pou′dər-pŭf′) *adj.* Of, relating to, or being a usually competitive activity in which only women take part: *powder-puff baseball.*

Pow·der River (pou′dər). A river rising in several branches in the Bighorn Mountains of central Wyoming and flowing about 782 km (486 mi) generally northeast into southern Montana.

powder room *n.* **1.** A lavatory for women. **2.** A lavatory for guests in a private home.

pow·der·y (pou′də-rē) *adj.* **1.** Composed of or similar to powder. **2.** Dusted or covered with or as if with powder. **3.** Easily made into powder; friable.

powdery mildew *n.* **1.** Any of various fungi, especially of the family Erysiphaceae, that produce powdery conidia on the host surface. **2.** A plant disease caused by any of these fungi.

Pow·ell (pou′əl), **Adam Clayton, Jr.** 1908–1972. American politician. A U.S. representative from New York (1945–1967 and 1969–1971), he was an outspoken advocate of civil rights.

Powell, Anthony. Born 1905. British writer best known for *A Dance to the Music of Time* (1951–1975), a cycle of 12 satirical novels.

Powell, Cecil Frank. 1903–1969. British physicist. He won a 1950 Nobel Prize for discovering methods of photographing atomic nuclei and for his study of mesons.

Powell, John Wesley. 1834–1902. American geologist and ethnologist who directed the U.S. Geological Survey (1881–1894) and classified many Native American languages.

Powell, Lewis Franklin, Jr. Born 1907. American jurist who served as an associate justice of the U.S. Supreme Court (1971–1987).

pow·er (pou′ər) *n. Abbr.* **pwr. 1.** The ability or capacity to perform or act effectively. **2.** Often **powers.** A specific capacity, faculty, or aptitude: *her powers of concentration.* **3.** Strength or force exerted or capable of being exerted; might. See Synonyms at **strength. 4.** The ability or official capacity to exercise control; authority. **5.** A person, group, or nation having great influence or control over others: *the western powers.* **6.** The might of a nation, political organization, or similar group. **7.** Forcefulness; effectiveness: *a novel of unusual power.* **8.** *Chiefly Upper Southern U.S.* A large number or amount. See Regional Note at **powerful. 9.a.** The energy or motive force by which a physical system or machine is operated: *turbines turned by steam power; a sailing ship driven by wind power.* **b.** The capacity of a system or machine to operate: *a vehicle that runs under its own power.* **c.** Electrical or mechanical energy, especially as used to assist or replace human energy. **d.** Electricity supplied to a home, building, or community: *a storm that cut off power to the whole region.* **10.** *Physics.* The rate at which work is done, expressed as the amount of work per unit time and commonly measured in units such as the watt and horsepower. **11.** *Electricity.* **a.** The product of applied potential difference and current in a direct-current circuit. **b.** The product of the effective values of the voltage and current with the cosine of the phase angle between current and voltage in an alternating-current circuit. **12.** *Mathematics.* **a.** See **exponent** (sense 3). **b.** The number of elements in a finite set. **13.** *Statistics.* The probability of rejecting the null hypothesis where it is false. **14.** A measure of the magnification of an optical instrument, such as a microscope or telescope. **15. powers.** *Theology.* The sixth of the nine orders of angels. **16.** *Archaic.* An armed force. **—power** *adj.* **1.** Of or relating to political, social, or economic control: *a power struggle; a power base.* **2.** Operated with mechanical or electrical energy in place of bodily exertion: *a power tool; power car windows.* **3.** Of or relating to the generation or transmission of electricity: *power companies; power lines.* **4.** *Informal.* Of or relating to influential business or professional practices: *a pinstriped suit with a power tie; met with high-level executives at a power breakfast.* **—power** *tr.v.* **-ered, -er·ing, -ers.** To supply with power, especially mechanical power. ***—idiom.*** **powers that be.** Those who hold effective power in a system or situation: *a plan vetoed by the powers that be.* [Middle English, from Old French *poeir,* to be able, power, from Vulgar Latin **potēre,* to be able, from *potis,* able, powerful. See **poti-** in Appendix.]

pow·er·boat (pou′ər-bōt′) *n.* See **motorboat.**

power brake *n.* A motor vehicle brake assisted by a power mechanism operated by the engine that amplifies pressure applied to the brake pedal.

power broker or **pow·er·brok·er** (pou′ər-brō′kər) *n.* A person who exerts strong political or economic influence, especially by virtue of the individuals and votes he or she controls: *"A power broker is someone who can assemble a number of favors due from a coterie of powerful people and then use that agglomeration of . . . favors to work a deal"* (William H. Hallahan).

power dive *n.* A downward plunge of an aircraft accelerated by both gravity and engine power. **—pow′er-dive′** (pou′ər-dīv′) *v.*

power drill *n.* **1.** A portable electric drill. **2.** A large drilling machine having a vertical, motorized drill set in a table stand.

♦**pow·er·ful** (pou′ər-fəl) *adj.* **1.** Having or capable of exerting power. **2.** Effective or potent: *a powerful drug.* **3.** *Computer Science.* Fast, versatile, or able to handle large tasks. Used of hardware or software. **4.** *Chiefly Upper Southern U.S.* Great: *The storm did a powerful lot of harm.* **—powerful** *adv. Chiefly Upper Southern U.S.* Very: *It was powerful humid.* **—pow′er·ful·ly** *adv.* **—pow′er·ful·ness** *n.*

♦***REGIONAL NOTE:*** In the upper southern United States the words *powerful* and *mighty* are intensives used frequently like the adverb *very*: *Your boy's grown powerful big. The new baby is mighty purty. Powerful* is used as an adjective in some expressions: *The storm did a powerful lot of harm.* In the same dialect region the noun *power* has, in addition to its standard meaning, the sense of "a large number or amount." This sense appears in the *Oxford English Dictionary* as common in dialectal British English of the 18th and 19th centuries: *"It has done a power of work"* (Charles Dickens). All these derivative senses of *power* and *might* take advantage of the notion of strength inherent in these nouns, making them natural intensives. Colloquial English is always on the lookout for ways to make language more vivid with new intensives. We think of the upper southern part of the United States as linguistically conservative, but in fact it has preserved uses of *power, powerful,* and *mighty* that were innovative in their time.

pow·er·house (pou′ər-hous′) *n.* **1.** See **power plant** (sense 2). **2.** One that possesses great force or energy: *She is an editorial powerhouse.*

pow·er·less (pou′ər-lĭs) *adj.* **1.** Lacking strength or power; helpless and totally ineffectual. **2.** Lacking legal or other authority. **—pow′er·less·ly** *adv.* **—pow′er·less·ness** *n.*

pow·er·lift·ing (pou′ər-lĭf′tĭng) *n. Sports.* A weightlifting competition in which participants compete in the squat, dead lift, and bench press.

power mower *n.* A lawn mower that is powered by a gasoline or electric motor.

power of appointment *n., pl.* **powers of appointment.** *Law.* Authority granted to one person by another to transfer property upon the death of the latter.

power of attorney *n., pl.* **powers of attorney.** *Abbr.* **P.A., P/A** *Law.* A legal instrument authorizing one to act as another's attorney or agent.

power pack *n.* A usually compact, portable device that converts supply current to direct or alternating current as required by specific equipment.

power plant *n.* **1.** All the equipment, including structural members, that constitutes a unit power source: *the power plant of a truck.* **2.** A complex of structures, machinery, and associated equipment for generating electric energy from another source of energy, such as nuclear reactions or a hydroelectric dam. In this sense, also called *powerhouse, power station.*

power play *n.* **1.** *Sports.* **a.** An offensive maneuver in a team game, especially in football, in which a massive concentration of players is applied in a certain area. **b.** A situation in ice hockey in which one team has a temporary numerical advantage because the other team has one or more players in the penalty box. **2.** A strategic maneuver, as in politics, diplomacy, or business, based on the use or threatened use of power as a means of coercion.

power politics *n. (used with a sing. or pl. verb).* International diplomacy in which each nation uses or threatens to use military or economic power to further its own interests: *"The Cold War undermined the Wilsonian dream of a world beyond power politics"* (Arthur M. Schlesinger, Jr.). [Translation of German *Machtpolitik.*]

Pow·ers (pouʹərz), **Hiram.** 1805–1873. American sculptor whose important works, all in the neoclassical style, include *Greek Slave* (1843) and busts of American leaders.

power series *n. Mathematics.* A sum of successively higher integral powers of a variable or combination of variables, each multiplied by a constant coefficient.

power shovel *n.* A large, usually mobile earthmoving machine having a boom and a hinged bucket for excavating. Also called *steam shovel.*

power station *n.* See **power plant** (sense 2).

power steering *n.* A device driven by the engine of a vehicle that facilitates the turning of the steering wheel by the driver.

power structure *n.* **1.** An elite group constituted by people holding influential positions within a government, a society, or an organization. **2.** A hierarchy of managerial authority: *sought to advance within the company's power structure.*

power takeoff *n. Abbr.* **PTO** A mechanism attached to a motor vehicle engine that supplies power to a nonvehicular device, such as a pump or pneumatic hammer.

power train *n.* An assembly of gears and associated parts by which power is transmitted from an engine to a driving axle.

power trip *n. Slang.* An action undertaken chiefly for the gratification associated with the exercise of power over another or others: *"He was giving orders, and people were taking them. He was on a power trip"* (Nelson DeMille). **—powʹer-tripʹ** (pouʹər-trĭpʹ) *v.* **—power tripper** *n.*

Pow·er·Walk·ing (pouʹər-wô′kĭng) *n. Sports.* See **race walking.**

Pow·ha·tan[1] (pouʹə-tănʹ, pou-hătʹn). Originally Wahunsonacock. 1550?–1618. Algonquian leader who founded the Powhatan confederacy and maintained peaceful relations with English colonists after the marriage of his daughter Pocahontas to John Rolfe (1614).

Pow·ha·tan[2] (pouʹə-tănʹ, pou-hătʹn) *n., pl.* **Powhatan** or **-tans. 1.a.** A confederacy of Native American peoples of eastern Virginia in the 16th and 17th centuries, with present-day descendants in the same area. **b.** A member of this confederacy. **2.** The Algonquian language of the Powhatan, a dialect of Virginia Algonquian. [After POWHATAN[1].]

pow·wow (pouʹwouʹ) *n.* **1.** A council or meeting with or of Native Americans. **2.a.** A Native American shaman. **b.** A ceremony conducted by a shaman, as in the performance of healing or hunting rituals. **3.** *Informal.* A conference or gathering. **—powwow** *intr.v.* **-wowed, -wow·ing, -wows.** *Informal.* To hold a powwow. [Narragansett *powwaw,* shaman.]

WORD HISTORY: Because trances were so important to the Native American shaman as a means of getting in touch with spiritual forces beyond the ken of the normal person, the title *powwaw,* literally meaning "one who has visions," was accorded him. One of the occurrences of this word in an early piece of propaganda designed to bring more settlers to New England represents fairly well the Puritan attitudes to the religion of the native inhabitants of the New World: "The office and dutie of the Powah is to be exercised principally in calling upon the Devil; and curing diseases of the sicke or wounded." The word whose spelling was eventually settled in English as *powwow* was also used as the name for ceremonies and councils, probably because of the important role played by the shaman in both. After the native peoples had been dealt with and the fear of devil worship was somewhat diminished, the newcomers decided that they could have powwows too, the first reference to one of these being recorded in the Salem, Massachusetts, *Gazette* of 1812: "The Warriors of the Democratic Tribe will hold a powwow at Agawam on Tuesday next." The verb *powwow,* "to confer," was recorded even earlier, in 1780.

Pow·ys (pōʹĭs). Family of British writers, comprising the brothers **John Cowper Powys** (1872–1963), whose novels, such as *Wolf Solent* (1929), glorify nature; **Theodore Francis Powys** (1875–1953), who lived reclusively and wrote allegorical novels, such as *Mr. Weston's Good Wine* (1927); and **Llewelyn Powys** (1884–1939), known primarily for his essays.

pox (pŏks) *n.* **1.** A disease such as chickenpox or smallpox, characterized by purulent skin eruptions that may leave pockmarks. **2.** Syphilis. **3.** *Archaic.* Misfortune and calamity. [Alteration of *pocks,* from Middle English, pl. of *pocke, pokke.* See POCK.]

pox·vi·rus (pŏksʹvīʹrəs) *n., pl.* **-rus·es.** Any of a group of DNA-containing viruses, including those that cause smallpox, cowpox, and other poxlike diseases in vertebrates.

Po·yang (pōʹyängʹ). A lake of eastern China southeast of Wuhan. It is connected to the Yangtze River (Chang Jiang) by canal.

Poz·nań (pōzʹnănʹ, -nänʹ, pôzʹnän′yə). A city of west-central Poland west of Warsaw. Dating from before the tenth century, it passed to Prussia in 1793 and reverted to Poland after World War I. Population, 579,100.

poz·zuo·la·na (pŏtʹswə-läʹnə) also **poz·zo·la·na** (pŏtʹsə-) *n.* **1.** A siliceous volcanic ash used to produce hydraulic cement. **2.** Any of various artificially produced substances resembling pozzuolana ash. [Italian *pozzolana,* after POZZUOLI.] **—poz′zuo·laʹnic** *adj.*

Poz·zuo·li (pôt-swôʹlē). A city of southern Italy west of Naples on the **Bay of Pozzuoli,** a section of the Bay of Naples. The city was founded by Greek exiles c. 529 B.C. and was an important commercial center during the Roman Empire. Population, 61,300.

power shovel

pp or **pp.** *abbr. Music.* Pianissimo.

pp. *abbr.* **1.** Pages. **2.** Or **PP.** Prepaid.

p.p.[1] *abbr. Latin.* Per procurationem (by proxy).

p.p.[2] or **P.P.** *abbr.* **1.** Parcel post. **2.** Parish priest. **3.** Or **pp.** Past participle. **4.** Postpaid.

PPA *abbr.* Phenylpropanolamine.

p.p.a. *abbr. Law.* Per power of attorney.

ppb *abbr.* Parts per billion.

ppd. *abbr.* **1.** Postpaid. **2.** Prepaid.

pph. *abbr.* Pamphlet.

PPLO *abbr.* Pleuropneumonia-like organism.

ppm *abbr.* Parts per million.

PPO *abbr.* Preferred provider organization.

P.P.S. also **p.p.s.** *abbr. Latin.* Post postscriptum (additional postscript).

ppt *abbr.* **1.** Parts per thousand. **2.** Parts per trillion. **3.** Or **ppt.** Precipitate.

pptn. *abbr.* Precipitation.

PQ *abbr.* Quebec.

p.q. or **P.Q.** *abbr.* Previous question.

Pr[1] The symbol for the element **praseodymium.**

Pr[2] *abbr.* **1.** Propyl. **2.** *Bible.* Proverbs.

PR *abbr.* **1.** Payroll. **2.** Also **P.R.** or **p.r.** Public relations. **3.** Or **P.R.** Puerto Rico.

pr. *abbr.* **1.** Pair. **2.** *Grammar.* Present. **3.** Price. **4.a.** Printed. **b.** Printing. **5.** *Grammar.* Pronoun.

Pr. *abbr.* **1.** Priest. **2.** Prince.

P.R. *abbr.* Proportional representation.

♦**praam** (präm) *n. New England, Chiefly British & Nautical.* Variant of **pram[2].**

prac·ti·ca·ble (prăkʹtĭ-kə-bəl) *adj.* **1.** Capable of being effected, done, or put into practice; feasible. See Synonyms at **possible. 2.** Usable for a specified purpose: *a practicable way of entry.* [Medieval Latin *practicābilis,* capable of being used, from *practicāre,* to practice, from *prāctica,* practice, from Late Latin *prāctice,* practical as against contemplative life, from Greek *praktikē,* feminine of *praktikos,* practical. See PRACTICAL.] **—prac′ti·ca·bilʹi·ty** *n.* **—pracʹti·ca·bly** *adv.*

USAGE NOTE: *Practicable* means "feasible" as well as "usable" and hence overlaps in meaning to some extent with *practical,* which can mean "useful." However, *practicable* does not share any other senses with *practical.*

prac·ti·cal (prăkʹtĭ-kəl) *adj.* **1.** Of, relating to, governed by, or acquired through practice or action, rather than theory, speculation, or ideals: *gained practical experience of sailing as a deck hand.* **2.** Manifested in or involving practice: *practical applications of calculus.* **3.** Actually engaged in a specified occupation or a certain kind or work; practicing. **4.** Capable of being used or put into effect; useful: *practical knowledge of Japanese.* See Usage Note at **practicable. 5.** Intended to serve a purpose without elaboration: *practical low-heeled shoes.* **6.** Concerned with the production or operation of something useful: *Woodworking is a practical art.* **7.** Level-headed, efficient, and unspeculative. **8.** Being actually so in almost every respect; virtual: *a practical disaster.* [Middle English *practicale,* from Medieval Latin *practicālis,* from Late Latin *prācticus,* from Greek *praktikos,* from *prassein,* to make, do.] **—prac′ti·calʹi·ty** (-kălʹĭ-tē), **pracʹti·cal·ness** *n.*

practical joke *n.* A mischievous trick played on a person, especially one that causes the victim to experience embarrassment, indignity, or discomfort. **—practical joker** *n.*

prac·ti·cal·ly (prăkʹtĭk-lē) *adv.* **1.** In a way that is practical. **2.** For all practical purposes; virtually. **3.** All but; nearly; almost.

USAGE NOTE: *Practically* is used unexceptionally in its primary sense of "in a way that is practical." Its use in the sense "for all practical purposes" is perfectly acceptable. Thus, a person whose liabilities exceed his or her assets may be said to be *practically bankrupt,* even though that person has not been legally declared insolvent. By a slight extension of this meaning, however, *practically* is often used to mean "all but" or "nearly": *He had practically finished his meal when I arrived.* This use of *practically,* sometimes considered informal, is widely encountered in reputable writing.

practical nurse *n.* **1.** A licensed practical nurse. **2.** A person who has had practical experience in nursing care but who is not a graduate of a degree program in nursing.

prac·tice (prăkʹtĭs) *v.* **-ticed, -tic·ing, -tic·es.** *—tr.* **1.** To do or perform habitually or customarily; make a habit of: *She prac-*

ă pat	oi boy
ā pay	ou out
âr care	o͝o took
ä father	o͞o boot
ĕ pet	ŭ cut
ē be	ûr urge
ĭ pit	th thin
ī pie	*th* this
îr pier	hw which
ŏ pot	zh vision
ō toe	ə about, item
ô paw	♦ regionalism

Stress marks: ʹ (primary); ′ (secondary), as in **dictionary** (dĭkʹshə-nĕr′ē)

prairie dog
Black-tailed prairie dog
Cynomys ludovicianus

ticed restraint in her friendships. **2.** To do or perform (something) repeatedly in order to acquire or polish a skill: *practice a dance step.* **3.** To give lessons or repeated instructions to; drill: *practiced the students in handwriting.* **4.** To work at, especially as a profession: *practice law.* **5.** To carry out in action; observe: *She practices her religion piously.* **6.** *Obsolete.* To plot (something evil). —*intr.* **1.** To do or perform something habitually or repeatedly. **2.** To do something repeatedly in order to acquire or polish a skill. **3.** To work at a profession. **4.** *Archaic.* To intrigue or plot. **—practice** *n.* **1.** A habitual or customary action or way of doing something: *makes a practice of being punctual.* **2. a.** Repeated performance of an activity in order to learn or perfect a skill: *Practice will make you a good musician.* **b.** *Archaic.* The skill so learned or perfected. **c.** The condition of being skilled through repeated exercise: *out of practice.* **3.** The act or process of doing something; performance or action: *a theory that is difficult to put into practice.* **4.** Exercise of an occupation or a profession: *the practice of law.* **5.** The business of a professional person: *an obstetrician with her own practice.* **6.** A habitual or customary action or act. Often used in the plural: *That company engages in questionable business practices. Facial tattooing is a standard practice among certain peoples.* **7.** *Law.* The methods of procedure used in a court of law. **8.** *Archaic.* **a.** The act of tricking or scheming, especially with malicious intent. **b.** A trick, a scheme, or an intrigue. [Middle English *practisen,* from Old French *practiser,* alteration of *practiquer,* from *practique,* practice, from Late Latin *prācticē,* practical. See PRACTICABLE.] **—prac′tic·er** *n.*

SYNONYMS: *practice, drill, exercise, rehearse.* The central meaning shared by these verbs is "to do or cause to do again and again in order to acquire proficiency": practice the shot put; drill pupils in the multiplication tables; exercising one's wits; an actor rehearsing a role. See also Synonyms at **habit.**

prac·ticed (prăk′tĭst) *adj.* **1.** Skilled or expert; proficient: *He is practiced in the art of design. She is a practiced lecturer.* **2.** Acquired or brought to perfection by practice: *greeted the guests with practiced courtesy.*

practice teacher *n.* See **student teacher. —prac′tice-teach′** (prăk′tĭs-tēch′) *v.* **—practice teaching** *n.*

prac·tic·ing (prăk′tĭ-sĭng) *adj.* Actively working in, engaged in, or observing, especially a particular profession or religion: *a practicing attorney; a practicing Catholic.*

prac·ti·cum (prăk′tĭ-kəm) *n.* A school or college course, especially one in a specialized field of study, that is designed to give students supervised practical application of previously studied theory: *advanced practicums in teaching reading.* [German *Praktikum,* from Late Latin *prācticum,* neuter of *prācticus,* practical. See PRACTICAL.]

prac·tise (prăk′tĭs) *v. & n. Chiefly British.* Variant of **practice. —prac′tis·er** *n.*

prac·ti·tion·er (prăk-tĭsh′ə-nər) *n.* **1.** One who practices something, especially an occupation, a profession, or a technique. **2.** *Christian Science.* A person engaged in the public ministry of spiritual healing. [Alteration of *practician,* from Old French *practicien,* from *practiser,* to practice. See PRACTICE.]

prae·di·al also **pre·di·al** (prē′dē-əl) *adj.* **1.** Relating to, containing, or possessing land; landed. **2.** Attached to, bound to, or arising from the land: *praedial serfs.* [Middle English, from Medieval Latin *praediālis,* of an estate, from Latin *praedium,* estate, from *praes, praed-,* surety, bondsman : *prae-,* pre- + *vas-,* guarantor.]

prae·mu·ni·re (prē′myo͞o-nī′rē) *n. Law.* **1.** The offense under English law of appealing to or obeying a foreign court or authority, thus challenging the supremacy of the Crown. **2.** The writ charging this offense. **3.** The penalty for this offense. [Short for Middle English *premunire facias,* from Medieval Latin *praemūnīre faciās : praemūnīre,* to warn (from Latin, to fortify : *prae-,* pre- + *mūnīre,* to defend) + Latin *faciās,* that you cause, second person sing. present subjunctive of *facere,* to do (words used in the writ).]

prae·no·men (prē-nō′mən) *n., pl.* **-no·mens** or **-nom·i·na** (-nŏm′ə-nə, -nō′mə-). **1.** A first or given name. **2.** The first name of a citizen of ancient Rome, as *Gaius* in *Gaius Julius Caesar.* [Latin *praenōmen : prae-,* pre- + *nōmen,* name; see **nō-men-** in Appendix.] **—prae·nom′i·nal** (-nŏm′ə-nəl) *adj.*

prae·tor also **pre·tor** (prē′tər) *n.* An annually elected magistrate of the ancient Roman Republic, ranking below but having approximately the same functions as a consul. [Middle English *pretor,* from Old French, from Latin *praetor,* perhaps from *praeīre,* to go before : *prae-,* pre- + *īre,* to go; see **ei-** in Appendix.] **—prae·to′ri·al** (prē-tôr′ē-əl, -tōr′-) *adj.* **—prae′tor·ship′** *n.*

prae·to·ri·an also **pre·to·ri·an** (prē-tôr′ē-ən, -tōr′-) —*adj.* **1.** Of or relating to a praetor or the praetorship. **2. Praetorian.** Of or belonging to the Praetorian Guard. **3.** Venal; corruptible: *"A large praetorian bureaucracy, filled with ambitious, possessive . . . and often sycophantic people, makes work and makes trouble"* (Arthur M. Schlesinger, Jr.). —*n.* **1.** A praetor or an ex-praetor. **2. Praetorian.** A member of the Praetorian Guard.

Praetorian Guard *n.* **1.** The elite bodyguard of a Roman emperor, approximately the size of a legion. **2.** A member of this bodyguard. [Originally the bodyguard of a praetor or a general.]

prag·mat·ic (prăg-măt′ĭk) *adj.* **1.** Dealing or concerned with facts or actual occurrences; practical. **2.** *Philosophy.* Of or relating to pragmatism. **3.** Relating to or being the study of cause and effect in historical or political events with emphasis on the practical lessons to be learned from them. **4.** *Archaic.* **a.** Active; busy. **b.** Active in an officious or meddlesome way. **c.** Dogmatic; dictatorial. **—pragmatic** *n.* **1.** A pragmatic sanction. **2.** *Archaic.* A meddler; a busybody. [Latin *prāgmaticus,* skilled in business, from Greek *pragmatikos,* from *pragma, pragmat-,* deed, from *prassein,* to do.] **—prag·mat′i·cal** *adj.* **—prag·mat′i·cal·ly** *adv.*

prag·mat·ics (prăg-măt′ĭks) *n.* *(used with a sing. verb). Linguistics.* The study of language as it is used in a social context and affects the interlocutors and their behavior.

pragmatic sanction *n.* An edict or a decree issued by a sovereign that becomes part of the fundamental law of the land. [Translation of Late Latin *pragmatica, sanctiō,* imperial decree referring to the affairs of a community : Latin *pragmatica,* relating to civil affairs + Latin *sanctiō,* ordinance.]

prag·ma·tism (prăg′mə-tĭz′əm) *n.* **1.** *Philosophy.* A movement consisting of varying but associated theories, originally developed by Charles S. Peirce and William James and distinguished by the doctrine that the meaning of an idea or a proposition lies in its observable practical consequences. **2.** A practical, matter-of-fact way of approaching or assessing situations or of solving problems. **—prag′ma·tist** *n.* **—prag′ma·tis′tic** *adj.*

Prague (präg). The capital and largest city of Czechoslovakia, in the western part of the country on the Vltava River. Known since the 9th century, it was a leading cultural and commercial center by the 14th century and came under Hapsburg rule in 1526. In 1618 citizens of Prague expressed their dissatisfaction of Hapsburg rule by throwing several royal officials out of the windows of the Hradčany Castle in the so-called Defenestration of Prague. The city became the capital of newly formed Czechoslovakia in 1918. Population, 1,189,828.

pra·hu (prä′o͞o) *n. Nautical.* Variant of **proa.**

Prai·a (prī′ə). The capital of Cape Verde, on the southeast coast of São Tiago Island. Population, 37,480.

prai·rie (prâr′ē) *n.* An extensive area of flat or rolling, predominantly treeless grassland, especially the large tract or plain of central North America. [French, from Old French *praierie,* from Latin *prāta,* meadow.]

prairie chicken *n.* Either of two birds *(Tympanuchus cupido* or *T. pallidicinctus)* of the grouse family, found in western North America and having deep-chested bodies and mottled brownish plumage.

prairie dog *n.* Any of several burrowing rodents of the genus *Cynomys* in the squirrel family, having light brown fur and a warning call similar to a dog's bark. The prairie dog lives in large colonies, chiefly in the Great Plains of North America.

prairie falcon *n.* A large, square-headed falcon *(Falco mexicanus)* of western North America, having dark brown back feathers with pale edges and faintly spotted whitish underparts.

♦ **prairie oyster** *n.* **1.** *Slang.* A drink made from a whole raw egg yolk, Worcestershire sauce, hot sauce, salt, and pepper that is taken as a palliative for a hangover or as a cure for hiccups. **2.** *Regional.* The testis of a calf, cooked and served as food.

prairie potato *n.* See **breadroot.**

Prai·rie Provinces (prâr′ē). The Canadian provinces of Manitoba, Saskatchewan, and Alberta.

prairie schooner *n.* A covered wagon, drawn by horses or oxen, that was used by pioneers in crossing the North American prairies and plains.

Prairie Village. A city of northeast Kansas, a suburb of Kansas City. Population, 24,657.

prairie wolf *n.* See **coyote** (sense 1).

praise (prāz) *n.* **1.** Expression of approval, commendation, or admiration. **2.** The extolling or exaltation of a deity, ruler, or hero. **3.** *Archaic.* A reason for praise; merit. **—praise** *tr.v.* **praised, prais·ing, prais·es. 1.** To express warm approbation of, commendation for, or admiration for. **2.** To extol or exalt; worship. [Middle English *preise,* from *preisen,* to praise, from Old French *preisier,* from Late Latin *pretiāre,* to prize, from Latin *pretium,* price. See **per-[5]** in Appendix.] **—prais′er** *n.*

SYNONYMS: *praise, acclaim, commend, extol, laud.* These verbs mean to express approval or admiration. To *praise* is to voice approbation, commendation, or esteem: *"I come to bury Caesar, not to praise him"* (Shakespeare). *"She was enthusiastically praising the beauties of Gothic architecture"* (Francis Marion Crawford). *Acclaim* usually implies hearty approbation warmly and publicly expressed: *The restoration of the frescoes is being widely but not universally acclaimed by art historians. Commend* suggests moderate or restrained approval, as that accorded by a superior: *The judge commended the jury for their patience and hard work.* To *extol* is to praise highly; the term suggests exaltation or glorification: *"that sign of old age, extolling the past at the expense of the present"* (Sydney Smith). *Laud* connotes respectful or lofty, often inordinate praise: *"aspirations which are lauded up to the skies"* (Charles Kingsley).

praise·wor·thy (prāz′wûr′thē) *adj.* **-thi·er, -thi·est.** Meriting praise; highly commendable. **—praise′wor′thi·ly** *adv.* **—praise′wor′thi·ness** *n.*

ă pat	oi boy
ā pay	ou out
âr care	o͝o took
ä father	o͞o boot
ĕ pet	ŭ cut
ē be	ûr urge
ĭ pit	th thin
ī pie	*th* this
îr pier	hw which
ŏ pot	zh vision
ō toe	ə about, item
ô paw	♦ regionalism

Stress marks: ′ (primary); ′ (secondary), as in **dictionary** (dĭk′shə-nĕr′ē)

Pra·ja·dhi·pok (prə-chä′tĭ-pŏk′). See **Rama VII.**

Pra·krit (prä′krĭt) *n.* **1.** Any of the vernacular and literary Indic languages recorded from the third century B.C. to the fourth century A.D., as opposed to Sanskrit. **2.** Any of the modern Indic languages. [Sanskrit *prākṛtam, prākṛta-*, natural, vulgar, vernacular : *pra-*, before, forward; see **per**[1] in Appendix + *karoti*, it makes; see SANSKRIT.] —**Pra·krit′ic** *adj.*

pra·line (prä′lēn′, prā′-) *n.* A confection made of nut kernels, especially almonds or pecans, stirred in boiling sugar syrup until crisp and brown. [French, after César de Choiseul, Comte du Plessis-*Praslin* (1598–1675), French army officer.]

prall·tril·ler (präl′trĭl′ər) *n. Music.* A trill consisting of alternation between a written note and the note immediately above it. Also called *inverted mordent.* [German : *prallen*, to rebound (alteration of Middle High German *prellen*) + *Triller*, trill (from Italian *trillo*, from *trillare*, to trill, probably of imitative origin).]

pram[1] (prăm) *n. Chiefly British.* A baby carriage. [Shortening and alteration of PERAMBULATOR.]

♦**pram**[2] also **praam** (präm) *n.* **1.** *New England & Chiefly British.* A small dinghy having a flat, snub-nosed bow. **2.** *Nautical.* A flat-bottomed boat used chiefly in the Baltic Sea as a barge. [Dutch *praam*, flat-bottomed boat, from Middle Dutch *praem*, from Czech *prám.* See **per**[1] in Appendix.]

prance (prăns) *v.* **pranced, pranc·ing, pranc·es.** —*intr.* **1.a.** To spring forward on the hind legs. Used of a horse. **b.** To spring or bound forward in a manner reminiscent of a spirited horse. **2.** To ride a horse moving in such a fashion. **3.** To walk or move about in a spirited manner; strut. —*tr.* To cause (a horse) to prance. —**prance** *n.* The act or an instance of prancing. [Middle English *prauncen.*] —**pranc′er** *n.* —**pranc′ing·ly** *adv.*

pran·di·al (prăn′dē-əl) *adj.* Of or relating to a meal. [From Latin *prandium*, a late breakfast. See **ed-** in Appendix.] —**pran′di·al·ly** *adv.*

prang (prăng) *tr.v.* **pranged, prang·ing, prangs.** *Chiefly British.* **1.** To crash (an airplane, for example). **2.** To damage by colliding with (a car, for example). **3.** To bomb from the air. [Origin unknown.]

prank[1] (prăngk) *n.* A mischievous trick or practical joke. [Origin unknown.]

prank[2] (prăngk) *v.* **pranked, prank·ing, pranks.** —*tr.* To decorate or dress ostentatiously or gaudily. —*intr.* To make an ostentatious display. [From Middle English *pranken*, to show off, perhaps from Middle Dutch *pronken* (from *pronk*, show, display) and from Middle Low German *prunken* (from *prank*, display).]

prank·ish (prăng′kĭsh) *adj.* Given to or characterized by impishness or playfulness; mischievous. —**prank′ish·ly** *adv.* —**prank′ish·ness** *n.*

prank·ster (prăngk′stər) *n.* One who plays tricks or pranks.

prase (prāz) *n.* A light green or light grayish-green variety of translucent chalcedony. [French, from Latin *prasius*, from Greek *prasios.* See PRASEODYMIUM.]

pra·se·o·dym·i·um (prā′zē-ō-dĭm′ē-əm, prā′sē-) *n. Symbol* **Pr** A soft, silvery, malleable, ductile rare-earth element that develops a characteristic green tarnish in air. It occurs naturally with other rare earths in monazite and is used to color glass and ceramics yellow, as a core material for carbon arcs, and in metallic alloys. Atomic number 59; atomic weight 140.907; melting point 935°C; boiling point 3,127°C; specific gravity 6.8; valence 3, 4. See table at **element.** [New Latin : from Greek *prasios*, leek-green (from *prason*, leek) + (DI)DYMIUM.]

prat (prăt) *n. Slang.* The buttocks. [Origin unknown.]

prate (prāt) *v.* **prat·ed, prat·ing, prates.** —*intr.* To talk idly and at length; chatter. —*tr.* To utter idly or to little purpose. —**prate** *n.* Empty, foolish, or trivial talk; idle chatter. [Middle English *praten*, from Middle Dutch *prāten.*] —**prat′er** *n.* —**prat′ing·ly** *adv.*

prat·fall (prăt′fôl′) *n.* **1.** A fall on the buttocks. **2.** A humiliating error, failure, or defeat: *"His characters not only survive their snarled problems and pratfalls but learn from their experiences"* (Joyce Carol Oates).

prat·in·cole (prăt′n-kōl′, prāt′-, prăt′ĭng-, prā′tĭng-) *n.* Any of several Old World shore birds of the genus *Glareola*, having brown and black plumage, long pointed wings, a forked tail, and a tapered bill. [New Latin *prātincola* : Latin *prātum*, meadow + Latin *incola*, inhabitant; see **kʷel-**[1] in Appendix.]

pra·tique (pră-tēk′) *n. Nautical.* Clearance granted to a ship to proceed into port after compliance with health regulations or quarantine. [French, from Old French *practique*, from Medieval Latin *prāctica*, ultimately from Greek *praktikē*, from feminine of *praktikos*, practical. See PRACTICAL.]

Pra·to (prä′tō). A city of central Italy northwest of Florence. It has been a textile center since the 13th century. Population, 158,797.

prat·tle (prăt′l) *v.* **-tled, -tling, -tles.** —*intr.* To talk or chatter idly or meaninglessly; babble or prate. —*tr.* To utter or express by chattering foolishly or babbling. —**prattle** *n.* **1.** Idle or meaningless chatter; babble. **2.** A sound suggestive of such chattering; a babbling noise. [Frequentative of PRATE.] —**prat′tler** *n.* —**prat′tling·ly** *adv.*

Pratt·ville (prăt′vĭl′, -vəl). A city of central Alabama, an industrial suburb of Montgomery. Population, 18,647.

prau (prou) *n. Nautical.* Variant of **proa.**

prawn (prôn) *n.* Any of various edible crustaceans similar to but larger than the shrimps. —**prawn** *intr.v.* **prawned, prawn·ing, prawns.** To fish for prawns. [Middle English *praine, prane.*] —**prawn′er** *n.*

prax·e·ol·o·gy also **prax·i·ol·o·gy** (prăk′sē-ŏl′ə-jē) *n.* The study of human conduct. [PRAX(IS) + -LOGY.] —**prax′e·o·log′i·cal** *adj.*

prax·is (prăk′sĭs) *n., pl.* **prax·es** (prăk′sēz′). **1.** Practical application or exercise of a branch of learning. **2.** Habitual or established practice; custom. [Medieval Latin *prāxis*, from Greek *praxis*, from *prassein*, to do.]

Prax·it·e·les (prăk′sĭt′l-ēz′). fl. fourth century B.C. Greek sculptor whose few surviving works include *Hermes Carrying Dionysius*, discovered at Olympia (1877).

pray (prā) *v.* **prayed, pray·ing, prays.** —*intr.* **1.** To utter or address a prayer or prayers to God, a god, or another object of worship. **2.** To make a fervent request or an entreaty. —*tr.* **1.** To utter or say a prayer or prayers to; address by prayer. **2.** To ask (someone) imploringly; beseech. Now often used elliptically for *I pray you* to introduce a request or an entreaty: *Pray be careful.* **3.** To make a devout or earnest request for: *I pray your permission to speak.* **4.** To move or bring by prayer or entreaty. [Middle English *preien*, from Old French *preier*, from Latin *precārī*, from **prex*, prayer. See **prek-** in Appendix.]

prayer rug
19th-century Turkish

prayer[1] (prâr) *n.* **1.a.** A reverent petition made to God, a god, or another object of worship. **b.** The act of making a reverent petition to God, a god, or another object of worship. **2.** An act of communion with God, a god, or another object of worship, such as in devotion, confession, praise, or thanksgiving: *One evening a week, the family would join together in prayer.* **3.** A specially worded form used to address God, a god, or another object of worship. **4. prayers.** A religious observance in which praying predominates: *morning prayers.* **5.a.** A fervent request: *Her prayer for rain was granted at last.* **b.** The thing requested: *His safe arrival was their only prayer.* **6.** The slightest chance or hope: *In a storm the mountain climbers won't have a prayer.* **7.** *Law.* **a.** The request of a complainant, as stated in a complaint or in equity, that the court grant the aid or relief solicited. **b.** The section of the complaint or bill that contains this request. [Middle English *preiere*, from Old French, from Medieval Latin *precāria*, from feminine of Latin *precārius*, obtained by entreaty, from *precārī*, to entreat, from **prex*, prayer. See **prek-** in Appendix.]

pray·er[2] (prā′ər) *n.* One who prays.

prayer beads (prâr) *pl.n.* A string of beads for keeping count of the prayers one is saying; a rosary.

prayer book (prâr) *n. Abbr.* **P.B. 1.** A book containing religious prayers. **2. Prayer Book.** The Book of Common Prayer.

prayer·ful (prâr′fəl) *adj.* **1.** Inclined or given to praying frequently; devout. **2.** Typical or indicative of prayer, as a mannerism, gesture, or facial expression. —**prayer′ful·ly** *adv.* —**prayer′ful·ness** *n.*

prayer meeting (prâr) *n.* An evangelical service, especially one held on a weekday evening, in which the laypersons participate by singing, praying, or testifying their faith.

prayer rug (prâr) *n.* A small rug used by Moslems to kneel and prostrate themselves upon during devotions.

prayer shawl (prâr) *n. Judaism.* See **tallith.**

prayer wheel (prâr) *n.* A cylinder containing or inscribed with prayers or litanies that is revolved on its axis in devotions, especially by Tibetan Buddhists.

prayer wheel
Brass Tibetan prayer wheel

pray·ing mantis (prā′ĭng) *n.* A green or brownish predatory insect *(Mantis religiosa)* that while at rest folds its front legs as if in prayer.

pra·zo·sin (prā′zō-sĭn) *n.* A crystalline vasodilator, $C_{19}H_{21}N_5O_4$, used in the form of its hydrochloride to treat hypertension. [By shortening and rearrangement of the chemical name *aminodimethoxyquinazolinylfuranylcarbonylpiperazine.*]

pre- *pref.* **1.a.** Earlier; before; prior to: *prehistoric.* **b.** Preparatory; preliminary: *premedical.* **c.** In advance: *prepay.* **2.** Anterior; in front of: *preaxial.* [Middle English, from Old French, from Latin *prae-*, from *prae*, before, in front. See **per**[1] in Appendix.]

preach (prēch) *v.* **preached, preach·ing, preach·es.** —*tr.* **1.** To proclaim or put forth in a sermon: *preached the gospel.* **2.** To advocate or exhort, especially to urge acceptance of or compliance with: *preached tolerance and peaceful coexistence.* **3.** To deliver (a sermon). —*intr.* **1.** To deliver a sermon. **2.** To give religious or moral instruction, especially in a tedious manner. [Middle English *prechen*, from Old French *preechier*, from Late Latin *praedicāre*, from Latin, to proclaim : *prae-*, pre- + *dicāre*, to proclaim; see **deik-** in Appendix.] —**preach′ing·ly** *adv.*

♦**preach·er** (prē′chər) *n.* **1.** One who preaches, especially one who publicly proclaims the gospel for an occupation. **2.** *Alaska.* A fallen tree or log submerged in a river and creating a hazard for boats.

♦***REGIONAL NOTE:*** River navigation in America has its own lexicon, including words for hazards encountered in riverboat travel. Large uprooted trees that had drifted down the river and become stuck in the riverbed were sometimes known by their peculiar and dangerous characteristics. John McPhee writes for the *New Yorker*: "One kind . . . known as a *sawyer*, sawed up and down with the vagaries of the current . . . In the Yukon River, such logs—

praying mantis
Mantis religiosa

eternally bowing—are known as *preachers.* In the Mississippi . . . they were all *snags.*"

preach·i·fy (prē′chə-fī′) *intr.v.* **-fied, -fy·ing, -fies.** *Informal.* To preach tediously and didactically. **—preach′i·fi·ca′tion** (-fĭ-kā′shən) *n.*

preach·ment (prēch′mənt) *n.* **1.** The act of preaching. **2.** A tiresome or unwelcome moral lecture or discourse; tedious sermonizing.

preach·y (prē′chē) *adj.* **-i·er, -i·est.** Inclined or given to tedious and excessive moralizing; didactic. **—preach′i·ly** *adv.* **—preach′i·ness** *n.*

pre·ad·ap·ta·tion (prē′ăd-ăp-tā′shən, -əp-) *n.* A characteristic evolved by an ancestral species or population that serves an adaptive though different function in a descendant species or population.

pre·ad·o·les·cence (prē′ăd-l-ĕs′əns) *n.* The period between childhood and the onset of puberty, often designated as between the ages of 10 and 12 in girls and 11 and 13 in boys. **—pre′ad·o·les′cent** *adj.* & *n.*

pre·a·dult (prē′ə-dŭlt′) *adj.* Of or relating to the period preceding adulthood or the adult stage of the life cycle: *preadult anxieties; the preadult morph.*

pre·ag·ri·cul·tur·al (prē′ăg-rĭ-kŭl′chər-əl) *adj.* Of, relating to, or being a society or population before the advent of agriculture as a means of subsistence.

pre·am·ble (prē′ăm′bəl, prē-ăm′-) *n.* **1.** A preliminary statement, especially the introduction to a formal document that serves to explain its purpose. **2.** An introductory occurrence or fact; a preliminary. [Middle English, from Old French *preambule,* from Medieval Latin *preambulum,* from neuter of *praeambulus,* walking in front : *prae-,* pre- + *ambulāre,* to walk; see AMBULATE.] **—pre·am′bu·lar′y** (-byə-lĕr′ē) *adj.*

pre·amp (prē′ămp) *n. Informal.* A preamplifier.

pre·am·pli·fi·er (prē-ăm′plə-fī′ər) *n.* An electronic circuit or device that strengthens weak signals, as in a radio receiver, for subsequent, more powerful amplification stages.

pre·ar·range (prē′ə-rānj′) *tr.v.* **-ranged, -rang·ing, -rang·es.** To arrange in advance. **—pre′ar·range′ment** *n.*

pre·a·tom·ic (prē′ə-tŏm′ĭk) *adj.* Of, relating to, or being the time preceding the use of, existence of, or capability for atomic energy or weapons.

pre·ax·i·al (prē-ăk′sē-əl) *adj. Anatomy.* Situated in front of or superior to the median axis of the body or a body part. **—pre·ax′i·al·ly** *adv.*

preb·end (prĕb′ənd) *n.* **1.** A stipend drawn from the endowment or revenues of an Anglican cathedral or church by a presiding member of the clergy; a cathedral or church benefice. **2.** The property or tithe providing the endowment for such a stipend. **3.** A prebendary. [Middle English *prebende,* from Old French, from Medieval Latin *praebenda,* from Late Latin, state allowance, from Latin, neuter pl. gerundive of *praebēre,* to grant, from *praehibēre* : *prae-,* pre- + *habēre,* to hold; see **ghabh-** in Appendix.] **—pre·ben′dal** (prĭ-bĕn′dl, prĕb′ən-dəl) *adj.*

preb·en·dar·y (prĕb′ən-dĕr′ē) *n., pl.* **-ies. 1.** An Anglican cleric holding the honorary title of prebend without a stipend. **2.** A member of the Anglican clergy who is the holder of a cathedral or church benefice; a prebend.

pre·bi·o·log·i·cal (prē′bī-ə-lŏj′ĭ-kəl) *adj.* Of, relating to, or being the time before the appearance of living things: *prebiological organic chemicals.* **—pre′bi·ol′o·gist** (-ŏl′ə-jĭst) *n.* **—pre′bi·ol′o·gy** *n.*

pre·bi·ot·ic (prē′bī-ŏt′ĭk) *adj.* Prebiological.

pre·built (prē′bĭlt′) *adj.* Of, relating to, or constituting a structure or a portion of a structure that is constructed or assembled before being transported to its site of installation; prefabricated: *a prebuilt home.*

prec. *abbr.* Preceding.

pre·cal·cu·lus (prē-kăl′kyə-ləs) *n. Mathematics.* A course of study taken as a prerequisite for the study of calculus. **—pre·cal′cu·lus** *adj.*

Pre·cam·bri·an (prē-kăm′brē-ən) *adj.* Of, belonging to, or being the oldest and largest division of geologic time, preceding the Cambrian Period, often subdivided into the Archeozoic and Proterozoic eras, and characterized by the appearance of primitive forms of life. See table at **geologic time.** **—Precambrian** *n.* The Precambrian Era.

pre·can·cel (prē-kăn′səl) *tr.v.* **-celed, -cel·ing, -cels** or **-celled, -cel·ling, -cels.** To cancel (a postage stamp, as on an envelope) before mailing. **—precancel** *n.* A precanceled stamp or envelope. **—pre′can·cel·la′tion** *n.*

pre·can·cer (prē′kăn′sər) *n.* A precancerous condition.

pre·can·cer·ous (prē-kăn′sər-əs) *adj.* Of, relating to, or being a condition that typically precedes or develops into a cancer: *a precancerous growth.*

pre·car·i·ous (prĭ-kâr′ē-əs) *adj.* **1.** Dangerously lacking in security or stability: *a precarious posture; precarious footing on the ladder.* **2.** Subject to chance or unknown conditions: *"His kingdom was still precarious; the Danes far from subdued"* (Christopher Brooke). **3.** Based on uncertain, unwarranted, or unproved premises: *a precarious solution to a difficult problem.* **4.** *Archaic.* Dependent on the will or favor of another. [From Latin *precārius,* obtained by entreaty, uncertain, from *precārī,* to entreat, from **prex,* prayer. See **prek-** in Appendix.] **—pre·car′i·ous·ly** *adv.* **—pre·car′i·ous·ness** *n.*

pre·cast (prē-kăst′) *adj.* Relating to or being a structural member, especially of concrete, that has been cast into form before being transported to its site of installation. **—pre·cast′** *v.*

prec·a·to·ry (prĕk′ə-tôr′ē, -tōr′ē) also **prec·a·tive** (-tĭv) *adj.* Relating to or expressing entreaty or supplication. [Late Latin *precātōrius,* from Latin *precārī,* to entreat. See PRECARIOUS.]

pre·cau·tion (prĭ-kô′shən) *n.* **1.** An action taken in advance to protect against possible danger or failure; a safeguard: *He took every precaution but still got a bad deal on that used car.* **2.** Caution practiced in advance; forethought or circumspection: *Precaution was impossible in those dire circumstances.* [Late Latin *praecautiō, praecautiōn-,* from *praecautus,* past participle of Latin *praecavēre,* to guard against : *prae-,* pre- + *cavēre,* to beware.]

pre·cau·tion·ar·y (prĭ-kô′shə-nĕr′ē) also **pre·cau·tion·al** (-shə-nəl) *adj.* Of, relating to, or constituting a precaution: *taking precautionary measures; gave precautionary advice.*

pre·ca·va (prē-kā′və, -kä′-) *n., pl.* **-vae** (-vē). The superior vena cava. [PRE– + (VENA) CAVA.] **—pre·ca′val** *adj.*

pre·cede (prĭ-sēd′) *v.* **-ced·ed, -ced·ing, -cedes.** —*tr.* **1.** To come, exist, or occur before in time. **2.** To come before in order or rank; surpass or outrank. **3.** To be in a position in front of; go in advance of. **4.** To preface; introduce: *He preceded his lecture with a humorous anecdote.* —*intr.* To come or go before in time, order, rank, or position. [Middle English *preceden,* from Old French *preceder,* from Latin *praecēdere* : *prae-,* pre- + *cēdere,* to go; see **ked-** in Appendix.]

prec·e·dence (prĕs′ĭ-dəns, prĭ-sēd′ns) also **prec·e·den·cy** (prĕs′ĭ-dən-sē, prĭ-sēd′n-sē) *n.* **1.** The fact, state, or right of preceding; priority: *Those applications arriving first will receive precedence.* **2.** Priority claimed or received because of preeminence or superiority: *Our company will continue to assert its precedence as the world's leading manufacturer of pharmaceuticals.* **3.** A ceremonial order of rank or preference, especially as observed on formal occasions: *Recipients of military honors were called in order of precedence—highest ranking officers first.*

prec·e·dent (prĕs′ĭ-dənt) *n.* **1.a.** An act or instance that may be used as an example in dealing with subsequent similar instances. **b.** *Law.* A judicial decision that may be used as a standard in subsequent similar cases: *a landmark decision that set a legal precedent.* **2.** Convention or custom arising from long practice: *The President followed historical precedent in forming the Cabinet.* **—precedent** (prĭ-sēd′nt, prĕs′ĭ-dənt) *adj.* Preceding. [Middle English, from Old French, from Latin *praecēdēns, praecēdent-,* present participle of *praecēdere,* to go before. See PRECEDE.]

prec·e·den·tial (prĕs′ĭ-dĕn′shəl) *adj.* **1.** Of, relating to, or constituting a precedent. **2.** Having precedence.

pre·ced·ing (prĭ-sē′dĭng) *adj. Abbr.* **prec.** Existing or coming before another or others in time, place, rank, or sequence; previous.

pre·cen·tor (prĭ-sĕn′tər) *n.* A cleric who directs the choral services of a church or cathedral. [Latin *praecentor,* from *praecentus,* past participle of *praecinere,* to sing before : *prae-,* pre- + *canere,* to sing; see **kan-** in Appendix.] **—pre′cen·to′ri·al** (prē′sĕn-tôr′ē-əl, -tōr′-) *adj.*

pre·cept (prē′sĕpt′) *n.* **1.** A rule or principle prescribing a particular course of action or conduct. **2.** *Law.* An authorized direction or order; a writ. [Middle English, from Old French, from Latin *praeceptum,* from neuter past participle of *praecipere,* to advise, teach : *prae-,* pre- + *capere,* to take; see **kap-** in Appendix.]

pre·cep·tive (prĭ-sĕp′tĭv) *adj.* **1.** Of, relating to, or expressing a rule or principle that prescribes a particular course of action or conduct. **2.** Instructive; didactic. **—pre·cep′tive·ly** *adv.*

pre·cep·tor (prĭ-sĕp′tər, prē′sĕp′tər) *n.* **1.** A teacher; an instructor. **2.** An expert or a specialist, such as a physician, who gives practical experience and training to a student, especially of medicine or nursing. **3.** The head of a preceptory. [Middle English, from Latin *praeceptor,* from *praecipere,* to teach. See PRECEPT.] **—pre′cep·to′ri·al** (prē′sĕp-tôr′ē-əl, -tōr′-) *adj.* **—pre′cep·to′ri·al·ly** *adv.*

pre·cep·tor·ship (prĭ-sĕp′tər-shĭp′) *n.* A period of practical experience and training for a student, especially of medicine or nursing, that is supervised by an expert or a specialist in a particular field.

pre·cep·to·ry (prĭ-sĕp′tə-rē, prē′sĕp-) *n., pl.* **-ries.** A community of medieval Knights Templars located on a provincial estate and subordinate to the main temples at Paris and London.

pre·cess (prē-sĕs′, prē′sĕs′) *intr.v.* **-cessed, -cess·ing, -cess·es.** *Physics & Astronomy.* To move in or be subjected to precession. [Back-formation from PRECESSION.]

pre·ces·sion (prē-sĕsh′ən) *n.* **1.** The act or state of preceding; precedence. **2.** *Physics.* The motion of the axis of a spinning body, such as the wobble of a spinning top, when there is an external force acting on the axis. **3.** *Astronomy.* **a.** Precession of the equinoxes. **b.** A slow gyration of Earth's axis around the pole of the ecliptic, caused mainly by the gravitational pull of the sun, moon, and other planets on Earth's equatorial bulge. [Late Latin *praecessiō, praecessiōn-,* from Latin *praecessus,* past participle of *praecēdere,* to go before. See PRECEDE.] **—pre·ces′sion·al** *adj.*

precession of the equinoxes *n. Astronomy.* A slow westward shift of the equinoxes along the plane of the ecliptic, resulting from precession of Earth's axis of rotation, and causing the equinoxes to occur earlier each sidereal year. The precession of the equinoxes occurs at a rate of 50.27 seconds of arc a year; a complete precession requires 25,800 years.

pre-Chris·tian (prē-krĭs′chən) *adj.* Of, relating to, or being the time before the beginning of the Christian era.

pre·cinct (prē′sĭngkt′) *n.* **1.a.** A subdivision or district of a city or town under the jurisdiction of or patrolled by a specific unit of its police force. **b.** The police station situated in and having jurisdiction over such a district. **2.** An election district of a city or town. **3.** Often **precincts. a.** A place or an enclosure marked off by definite limits, such as walls: *the mysterious precincts of the old monastery.* **b.** A boundary: *Hunting is not allowed within the precincts of the estate.* **4. precincts.** The neighborhood or surrounding area; the environs. **5. precincts.** An area of thought or action; a province or domain: *"It was in these spacious precincts that Dryden's imagination was most at home"* (Mark Van Doren). [Middle English *precincte,* a defined district or area, from Medieval Latin *praecinctum,* from Latin, neuter past participle of *praecingere,* to encircle : *prae-,* pre- + *cingere,* to gird; see **kenk-** in Appendix.]

pre·ci·os·i·ty (prĕsh′ē-ŏs′ĭ-tē, prĕs′-) *n., pl.* **-ties. 1.** Extreme meticulousness or overrefinement, as in language, taste, or style. **2.** An instance of extreme meticulousness or overrefinement. [Middle English *preciousite,* preciousness, from Old French *preciosite,* from Latin *pretiōsitās,* from *pretiōsus,* precious, from *pretium,* price. See PRECIOUS.]

pre·cious (prĕsh′əs) *adj.* **1.** Of high cost or worth; valuable. **2.** Highly esteemed; cherished. **3.** Dear; beloved. **4.** Affectedly dainty or overrefined: *precious mannerisms.* **5.** *Informal.* Thoroughgoing; unmitigated: *a precious mess.* **—precious** *n.* One who is dear or beloved; a darling. **—precious** *adv.* Used as an intensive: *"He had precious little right to complain"* (James Agee). [Middle English, from Old French *precios,* from Latin *pretiōsus,* from *pretium,* price. See **per-**[5] in Appendix.] **—pre′cious·ly** *adv.* **—pre′cious·ness** *n.*

precious stone *n.* Any of several gems, including the diamond, emerald, ruby, and sapphire, that have high economic value because of their rarity or appearance.

prec·i·pice (prĕs′ə-pĭs) *n.* **1.** An overhanging or extremely steep mass of rock, such as a crag or the face of a cliff. **2.** The brink of a dangerous or disastrous situation: *on the precipice of defeat.* [French *précipice,* from Latin *praecipitium,* from *praeceps, praecipit-,* headlong. See PRECIPITATE.]

pre·cip·i·ta·ble (prĭ-sĭp′ĭ-tə-bəl) *adj. Chemistry.* Capable of being precipitated.

pre·cip·i·tan·cy (prĭ-sĭp′ĭ-tən-sē) also **pre·cip·i·tance** (-təns) *n.* **1.** The quality of being precipitant. **2.** Action or thought marked by impulsiveness or rash haste.

pre·cip·i·tant (prĭ-sĭp′ĭ-tənt) *adj.* **1.** Rushing or falling headlong. **2.** Acting with or marked by impulsiveness in thought or action; rash. See Usage Note at **precipitate. 3.** Abrupt or unexpected; sudden. **—precipitant** *n. Chemistry.* A substance that causes a precipitate to form when it is added to a solution. [Latin *praecipitāns, praecipitant-,* present participle of *praecipitāre,* to throw headlong. See PRECIPITATE.] **—pre·cip′i·tant·ly** *adv.*

pre·cip·i·tate (prĭ-sĭp′ĭ-tāt′) *v.* **-tat·ed, -tat·ing, -tates.** *—tr.* **1.** To throw from or as if from a great height; hurl downward: *"The finest bridge in all Peru broke and precipitated five travelers into the gulf below"* (Thornton Wilder). **2.** To cause to happen, especially suddenly or prematurely. See Synonyms at **speed. 3.** *Meteorology.* To cause (water vapor) to condense and fall from the air as rain, snow, sleet, or hail. **4.** *Chemistry.* To cause (a solid substance) to be separated from a solution. *—intr.* **1.** *Meteorology.* To condense and fall from the air as rain, snow, sleet, or hail. **2.** *Chemistry.* To be separated from a solution as a solid. **3.** To fall or be thrown headlong: *An already ailing economy precipitated into ruin despite foreign intervention.* **—precipitate** (-tĭt) *adj.* **1.** Moving rapidly and heedlessly; speeding headlong. **2.** Acting with or marked by excessive haste and lack of due deliberation. See Synonyms at **impetuous, reckless. 3.** Occurring suddenly or unexpectedly. **—precipitate** (-tāt′, -tĭt) *n. Abbr.* **ppt, ppt. 1.** *Chemistry.* A solid or solid phase separated from a solution. **2.** A product resulting from a process, an event, or a course of action. [Latin *praecipitāre, praecipitāt-,* to throw headlong, from *praeceps, praecipit-,* headlong : *prae-,* pre- + *caput, capit-,* head; see **kaput-** in Appendix.] **—pre·cip′i·tate·ly** (-tĭt-lē) *adv.* **—pre·cip′i·tate·ness** *n.* **—pre·cip′i·ta′tive** *adj.* **—pre·cip′i·ta′tor** *n.*

USAGE NOTE: The adjective *precipitate* and the adverb *precipitately* were once applied to physical steepness but are now used primarily of rash, headlong actions: *They made a precipitate decision. He withdrew precipitately from the race. Precipitous* currently means "steep" in both literal and figurative senses: *the precipitous rapids of the upper river; a precipitous drop in commodity prices.* But *precipitous* and *precipitously* are also frequently used to mean "abrupt, hasty," which takes them into territory that would ordinarily belong to *precipitate* and *precipitately: their precipitous decision to leave.* This usage is a natural extension of the use of *precipitous* to describe a rise or fall in a quantity over time: *a precipitous increase in reports of measles* is also an abrupt or sudden event. Though this extended use of *precipitous* is well attested in the work of reputable writers, it is still widely regarded as an error.

pre·cip·i·ta·tion (prĭ-sĭp′ĭ-tā′shən) *n.* **1.** A headlong fall or rush. **2.** Abrupt or impulsive haste. **3.** A hastening or an acceleration, especially one that is sudden or unexpected: *He is responsible for the precipitation of his own demise.* **4.** *Abbr.* **pptn.** *Meteorology.* **a.** Any form of water, such as rain, snow, sleet, or hail, that falls to the earth's surface. **b.** The quantity of such water falling in a specific area within a specific period. **5.** *Chemistry.* The process of separating a substance from a solution as a solid.

pre·cip·i·tin (prĭ-sĭp′ĭ-tĭn) *n.* An antibody that reacts with a specific soluble antigen to produce a precipitate.

pre·cip·i·tin·o·gen (prĭ-sĭp′ĭ-tĭn′ə-jən) *n.* An antigen that induces the production of a precipitin.

pre·cip·i·tous (prĭ-sĭp′ĭ-təs) *adj.* **1.** Resembling a precipice; extremely steep. See Synonyms at **steep**[1]. **2.** Having several precipices: *a precipitous bluff.* **3.** *Usage Problem.* Extremely rapid, hasty, or abrupt; precipitate: *"The change has included a precipitous collapse of Communist authority"* (New York Times). See Usage Note at **precipitate.** [Probably from *precipitious,* from Latin *praecipitium,* precipice. See PRECIPICE.] **—pre·cip′i·tous·ly** *adv.* **—pre·cip′i·tous·ness** *n.*

pré·cis (prā′sē, prā-sē′) *n., pl.* **pré·cis** (prā′sēz, prā-sēz′). A concise summary of a book, an article, or another text; an abstract. **—précis** *tr.v.* **-cised, -cis·ing, -cis·es.** To make a précis of. [French, from Old French *precis,* condensed. See PRECISE.]

pre·cise (prĭ-sīs′) *adj.* **1.** Clearly expressed or delineated; definite: *The victim was able to give a precise description of the suspect.* **2.** Exact, as in performance, execution, or amount; accurate or correct: *a precise measurement; a precise instrument.* **3.** Strictly distinguished from others; very: *at that precise moment.* **4.** Distinct and correct in sound or meaning: *precise pronunciation; precise prose.* **5.** Conforming strictly to rule or proper form: *"The setting up of this Maypole was a lamentable spectacle to the precise separatists that lived at New Plymouth"* (Thomas Morton). [Middle English, exact, from Old French *precis,* condensed, precisely fixed, from Latin *praecīsus,* past participle of *praecīdere,* to shorten : *prae-,* pre- + *caedere,* to cut; see **kae-id-** in Appendix.] **—pre·cise′ness** *n.*

pre·cise·ly (prĭ-sīs′lē) *adv.* **1.** In a precise manner. **2.** Used as an intensive: *Inferior equipment was precisely the reason some hikers refused to continue the climb.*

pre·ci·sian (prĭ-sĭzh′ən) *n.* **1.** One who is strict and precise in adherence to established rules, forms, or standards, especially with regard to religious observance or moral behavior. **2.** A Puritan. [From PRECISE.] **—pre·ci′sian·ism** *n.*

pre·ci·sion (prĭ-sĭzh′ən) *n.* **1.** The state or quality of being precise; exactness. **2.** *Mathematics.* The exactness with which a number is specified; the number of significant digits with which a number is expressed. **—precision** *adj.* **1.** Used or intended for accurate or exact measurement: *a precision tool.* **2.** Made so as to vary minimally from a set standard: *precision components.* **3.** Of or characterized by accurate action: *precision bombing.* [Latin *praecīsiō, praecīsiōn-,* a cutting off, from *praecīsus,* past participle of *praecīdere,* to cut off. See PRECISE.]

pre·ci·sion·ism also **Pre·ci·sion·ism** (prĭ-sĭzh′ə-nĭz′əm) *n.* A style of early 20th-century painting in which depicted scenes or objects are reduced or simplified to elemental structural forms and rendered by a combination of abstractionism and realism.

pre·ci·sion·ist (prĭ-sĭzh′ə-nĭst) *n.* **1.** One who values precision; a purist. **2.** Often **Precisionist.** A painter whose work is marked by precisionism.

pre·clin·i·cal (prē-klĭn′ĭ-kəl) *adj.* Of or relating to the period of a disease before the appearance of symptoms.

pre·clude (prĭ-klo͞od′) *tr.v.* **-clud·ed, -clud·ing, -cludes. 1.** To make impossible, as by action taken in advance; prevent. See Synonyms at **prevent. 2.** To exclude or prevent (someone) from a given condition or activity: *Modesty precludes me from accepting the honor.* [Latin *praeclūdere* : *prae-,* pre- + *claudere,* to close.] **—pre·clu′sion** (-klo͞o′zhən) *n.* **—pre·clu′sive** (-klo͞o′sĭv, -zĭv) *adj.* **—pre·clu′sive·ly** *adv.*

pre·co·cial (prĭ-kō′shəl) *adj.* Covered with down and capable of moving about when hatched. Used of wading birds and domestic fowl. [From New Latin *Praecocēs,* precocial birds, from Latin, pl. of *praecox,* premature. See PRECOCIOUS.]

pre·co·cious (prĭ-kō′shəs) *adj.* **1.** Manifesting or characterized by unusually early development or maturity, especially in mental aptitude. **2.** *Botany.* Blossoming before the appearance of leaves. [From Latin *praecox, praecoc-,* premature, from *praecoquere,* to boil before, ripen fully : *prae-,* pre- + *coquere,* to cook, ripen; see **pekʷ-** in Appendix.] **—pre·co′cious·ly** *adv.* **—pre·coc′i·ty** (-kŏs′ĭ-tē), **pre·co′cious·ness** *n.*

pre·cog·ni·tion (prē′kŏg-nĭsh′ən) *n.* Knowledge of something in advance of its occurrence, especially by extrasensory perception; clairvoyance. **—pre·cog′ni·tive** *adj.*

pre·co·lo·ni·al or **pre-co·lo·ni·al** (prē′kə-lō′nē-əl) *adj.* Of, relating to, or being the period of time before colonization of a region or territory.

pre-Co·lum·bi·an (prē′kə-lŭm′bē-ən) *adj.* Of, relating to, or originating in the Americas before the arrival of Columbus: *pre-Columbian art.*

pre·con·ceive (prē′kən-sēv′) *tr.v.* **-ceived, -ceiv·ing, -ceives.** To form an opinion or a conception of (something) be-

precipice

pre-Columbian
Gold pendant from west-central Colombia

ă pat	oi boy
ā pay	ou out
âr care	o͝o took
ä father	o͞o boot
ĕ pet	ŭ cut
ē be	ûr urge
ĭ pit	th thin
ī pie	*th* this
îr pier	hw which
ŏ pot	zh vision
ō toe	ə about, item
ô paw	♦ regionalism

Stress marks: ′ (primary); ′ (secondary), as in **dictionary** (dĭk′shə-nĕr′ē)

fore possessing full or adequate knowledge or experience.

pre·con·cep·tion (prē′kən-sĕp′shən) *n.* An opinion or a conception formed in advance of full or adequate knowledge or experience; a prejudice or bias: *"His vision, unobstructed by ideological preconception, was continually reformed by experience"* (Doris Kearns Goodwin).

pre·con·cert (prē′kən-sûrt′) *tr.v.* **-cert·ed, -cert·ing, -certs.** To agree on, settle, or arrange in advance.

pre·con·di·tion (prē′kən-dĭsh′ən) *n.* A condition that must exist or be established before something can occur or be considered; a prerequisite. **—precondition** *tr.v.* **-tioned, -tion·ing, -tions.** To condition, train, or accustom in advance.

pre·con·scious (prē-kŏn′shəs) *n.* The memories or feelings that are not part of one's immediate awareness but that can be recalled through conscious effort. **—pre·con′scious** *adj.* **—pre·con′scious·ly** *adv.*

pre·con·tract (prē-kŏn′trăkt) *n.* An existing contract that obviates the making of another contract of the same kind: *a precontract of marriage.* **—pre′con·tract′** (-kən-trăkt′) *v.*

pre·cook (prē-ko͝ok′) *tr.v.* **-cooked, -cook·ing, -cooks.** To cook in advance or partially.

pre·cool (prē-ko͞ol′) *tr.v.* **-cooled, -cool·ing, -cools.** To reduce the temperature of (produce or meat, for example) by artificial means before packaging or shipping.

pre·crit·i·cal (prē-krĭt′ĭ-kəl) *adj.* Coming before a critical state or phase.

pre·cur·sive (prĭ-kûr′sĭv) *adj.* Precursory.

pre·cur·sor (prĭ-kûr′sər, prē′kûr′sər) *n.* **1.** One that precedes and indicates, suggests, or announces someone or something to come: *Opposition by colonists to unfair taxation by the British was a precursor of the Revolution.* **2.** One that precedes another; a forerunner or predecessor: *Her precursor as school principal was an eminent educator.* **3.** A biochemical substance, such as an intermediate compound in a chain of enzymatic reactions, that gives rise to a more stable or definitive product: *a precursor of insulin.* [Middle English *precursoure,* from Old French *precurseur,* from Latin *praecursor,* from *praecursus,* past participle of *praecurrere,* to run before : *prae-,* pre- + *currere,* to run; see **kers-** in Appendix.]

pre·cur·so·ry (prĭ-kûr′sə-rē) *adj.* **1.** Preceding or preliminary; introductory: *a precursory statement.* **2.** Suggesting or indicating something to follow.

pre·cut (prē′kŭt′) *adj.* Cut into size or shape before being marketed, assembled, or used: *precut fillet of fish; precut construction materials.* **—precut** (prē-kŭt′) *tr.v.* **-cut, -cut·ting, -cuts.** To cut into size or shape before marketing, assembling, or using.

pred. *abbr. Grammar & Logic.* Predicate.

pre·da·cious also **pre·da·ceous** (prĭ-dā′shəs) *adj.* **1.** Living by seizing or taking prey; predatory. **2.** Given to victimizing, plundering, or destroying for one's own gain: *"the most vicious, predacious, esurient and desperate elements of this society"* (Claude Brown). [From Latin *praedārī,* to plunder. See PREDATORY.] **—pre·da′cious·ness, pre·da′ceous·ness**, **pre·dac′i·ty** (-dăs′ĭ-tē) *n.*

pre·date (prē-dāt′) *tr.v.* **-dat·ed, -dat·ing, -dates. 1.** To mark or designate with a date earlier than the actual one. *predated the check.* **2.** To precede in time; antedate.

pre·da·tion (prĭ-dā′shən) *n.* **1.** The act or practice of plundering or marauding. **2.** The capturing of prey as a means of maintaining life. [Middle English *predacion,* from Latin *praedātiō, praedātiōn-,* from *praedātus,* past participle of *praedārī,* to plunder. See PREDATORY.]

pred·a·tor (prĕd′ə-tər, -tôr′) *n.* **1.** An organism that lives by preying on other organisms. **2.** One that victimizes, plunders, or destroys, especially for one's own gain. [Latin *praedātor,* pillager, from *praedārī,* to plunder. See PREDATORY.]

pred·a·to·ry (prĕd′ə-tôr′ē, -tōr′ē) *adj.* **1.** Living by preying on other organisms: *a predatory bird; a predatory mammal; a predatory insect.* **2. a.** Of, relating to, or characterized by plundering, pillaging, or marauding. **b.** Living by or given to victimizing or destroying others for one's own gain. [Latin *praedātōrius,* plundering, from *praedārī,* to plunder, from *praeda,* booty. See **ghend-** in Appendix.] **—pred′a·to′ri·ly** *adv.* **—pred′a·to′ri·ness** *n.*

pre·dawn (prē′dôn′) *n.* The time just before dawn. **—pre′dawn′** *adj.*

pre·de·cease (prē′dĭ-sēs′) *tr.v.* **-ceased, -ceas·ing, -ceas·es.** To die before (another person).

pred·e·ces·sor (prĕd′ĭ-sĕs′ər, prē′dĭ-) *n.* **1.** One who precedes another in time, especially in holding an office or a position. **2.** Something that has been succeeded by another: *The new building is more spacious than its predecessor.* **3.** *Archaic.* An ancestor; a forebear. [Middle English *predecessoure,* from Old French *predecesseur,* from Late Latin *praedēcessor* : Latin *prae-,* pre- + Latin *dēcessor,* a retiring magistrate (from *dēcessus,* past participle of *dēcēdere,* to depart : *dē-,* away; see DE– + *cēdere,* to go; see **ked-** in Appendix).]

pre·des·ig·nate (prē-dĕz′ĭg-nāt′) *tr.v.* **-nat·ed, -nat·ing, -nates.** To designate in advance. **—pre′des·ig·na′tion** *n.*

pre·des·ti·nar·i·an (prē-dĕs′tə-nâr′ē-ən) *adj.* **1.** Of or relating to predestination. **2.** Believing in or based on the doctrine of predestination. **—predestinarian** *n.* One who believes in the doctrine of predestination. **—pre·des′ti·nar′i·an·ism** *n.*

pre·des·ti·nate (prē-dĕs′tə-nāt′) *tr.v.* **-nat·ed, -nat·ing, -nates. 1.** *Theology.* To predestine. **2.** *Archaic.* To destine or determine in advance; foreordain. **—predestinate** (-nĭt, -nāt′) *adj.* Foreordained; predestined. [Middle English *predestinaten,* from Late Latin *praedēstināre, praedēstināt-.* See PREDESTINE.]

pre·des·ti·na·tion (prē-dĕs′tə-nā′shən) *n.* **1.** The act of predestining or the condition of being predestined. **2.** *Theology.* **a.** The doctrine that God has foreordained all things, especially that God has elected certain souls to eternal salvation. **b.** The divine decree foreordaining all souls to either salvation or damnation. **c.** The act of God foreordaining all things gone before and to come. **3.** Destiny; fate.

pre·des·tine (prē-dĕs′tĭn) *tr.v.* **-tined, -tin·ing, -tines. 1.** To fix upon, decide, or decree in advance; foreordain. **2.** *Theology.* To foreordain or elect by divine will or decree. [Middle English *predestinen,* from Old French *predestiner,* from Late Latin *praedēstināre* : Latin *prae-,* pre- + Latin *dēstināre,* to determine; see DESTINE.]

pre·de·ter·mine (prē′dĭ-tûr′mĭn) *v.* **-mined, -min·ing, -mines.** —*tr.* **1.** To determine, decide, or establish in advance: *"These factors predetermine to a large extent the outcome"* (Jessica Mitford). **2.** To influence or sway toward an action or opinion; predispose. —*intr.* To determine or decide something in advance. **—pre′de·ter′mi·nate** (-mə-nĭt) *adj.* **—pre′de·ter′mi·na′tion** *n.*

pre·de·ter·min·er (prē′dĭ-tûr′mə-nər) *n. Linguistics.* An adjectival word that can stand before an article, a possessive pronoun, or another determiner, as *all* in *all the flowers* or *both* in *both his children.*

pre·di·a·be·tes (prē′dī-ə-bē′tĭs, -tēz) *n.* The condition of having a hereditary tendency or high probability for developing diabetes mellitus, although neither symptoms nor test results confirm the presence of the disease. **—pre·di′a·bet′ic** (-bĕt′ĭk) *adj. & n.*

pre·di·al (prē′dē-əl) *adj.* Variant of **praedial.**

pred·i·ca·ble (prĕd′ĭ-kə-bəl) *adj.* That can be stated or predicated: *a predicable conclusion.* **—predicable** *n.* **1.** Something, such as a general quality or attribute, that can be predicated. **2.** *Logic.* One of five general attributes of a subject or class, traditionally including genus, species, property, differentia, and accident. [Late Latin *praedicābilis,* from Late Latin *praedicāre,* to proclaim publicly, preach, predicate. See PREACH.] **—pred′i·ca·bil′i·ty, pred′i·ca·ble·ness** *n.*

pre·dic·a·ment (prĭ-dĭk′ə-mənt) *n.* **1.** A situation, especially an unpleasant, troublesome, or trying one, from which extrication is difficult. See Usage Note at **dilemma. 2.** *Logic.* One of the basic states or classifications described by Aristotle into which all things can be placed; a category. [Middle English, class, category, from Old French, from Late Latin *praedicāmentum* (translation of Greek *katēgoria*), from Latin *praedicāre,* to proclaim publicly, predicate. See PREACH.] **—pre·dic′a·men′tal** (-mĕn′tl) *adj.* **—pre·dic′a·men′tal·ly** *adv.*

SYNONYMS: *predicament, plight, quandary, jam, fix, pickle.* These nouns all refer to a situation from which it is difficult to free oneself. A *predicament* is a problematic situation about which one does not know what to do: *"Werner finds himself suddenly in a most awkward a predicament"* (Thomas Carlyle). A *plight* is a bad or unfortunate situation: *The reporter wrote an article about the woeful plight of homeless people.* A *quandary* is a state of uncertainty or perplexity, especially about what course of action to take: *"Having captured our men, we were in a quandary how to keep them"* (Theodore Roosevelt). *Jam* and *fix* both refer to trying predicaments from which disengagement presents a problem: *The boys who broke the window are in a jam with the school authorities. "If we get left on this wreck we are in a fix"* (Mark Twain). A *pickle* is a disagreeable, embarrassing, or troublesome predicament: *"I could see no way out of the pickle I was in"* (Robert Louis Stevenson).

pred·i·cate (prĕd′ĭ-kāt′) *v.* **-cat·ed, -cat·ing, -cates.** —*tr.* **1.** To base or establish (a statement or an action, for example): *He predicates his argument on the facts.* **2.** To state or affirm as an attribute or a quality of something: *The sermon predicated the perfectibility of humankind.* **3.** To carry the connotation of; imply. **4.** *Logic.* To make (a term or an expression) the predicate of a proposition. **5.** To proclaim or assert; declare. —*intr.* To make a statement or an assertion. **—predicate** (-kĭt) *n. Abbr.* **pred. 1.** *Grammar.* One of the two main constituents of a sentence, modifying the subject and including the verb, objects, or phrases governed by the verb, as *opened the door* in *Jane opened the door* or *is very sleepy* in *The child is very sleepy.* **2.** *Logic.* That part of a proposition that is affirmed or denied about the subject. For example, in the proposition *We are mortal, mortal* is the predicate. **—predicate** (-kĭt) *adj.* **1.** *Grammar.* Of or belonging to the predicate of a sentence or clause. **2.** Stated or asserted; predicated. [Late Latin *praedicāre, praedicāt-,* from Latin, to proclaim : *prae-,* pre- + *dicāre,* to proclaim; see **deik-** in Appendix.] **—pred′i·ca′tion** *n.* **—pred′i·ca′tion·al** *adj.* **—pred′i·ca′tive** *adj.* **—pred′i·ca′tive·ly** *adv.*

predicate calculus *n. Logic.* The branch of symbolic logic that deals not only with relations between propositions as a whole but also with their internal structure, especially the relation between subject and predicate. Symbols are used to represent the subject and predicate of the proposition, and the existential or universal quantifier is used to denote whether the proposition is universal or particular in its application.

predicate nominative *n. Grammar.* A noun or pronoun that follows a linking verb and refers to the same person or thing as the subject of the verb.

pred·i·ca·to·ry (prĕd′ĭ-kə-tôr′ē, -tōr′ē) *adj.* Of, relating to, or characteristic of preaching or a preacher. [Late Latin *praedicātōrius,* praising, from Latin *praedicātor,* one who makes known, from *praedicāre,* to proclaim. See PREACH.]

pre·dict (prĭ-dĭkt′) *v.* **-dict·ed, -dict·ing, -dicts.** —*tr.* To state, tell about, or make known in advance, especially on the basis of special knowledge. —*intr.* To foretell something; prophesy. [Latin *praedīcere, praedict-* : *prae-,* pre- + *dīcere,* to say; see **deik-** in Appendix.] —**pre·dict′a·bil′i·ty** *n.* —**pre·dict′a·ble** *adj.* —**pre·dict′a·bly** *adv.* —**pre·dic′tive** *adj.* —**pre·dic′tive·ly** *adv.* —**pre·dic′tive·ness** *n.* —**pre·dic′tor** *n.*

SYNONYMS: *predict, call, forecast, foretell, prognosticate.* The central meaning shared by these verbs is "to tell about something in advance of its occurrence by means of special knowledge or inference": *predict an eclipse; couldn't call the outcome of the game; forecasting the weather; foretold the collapse of the government; prognosticating a rebellion.*

pre·dic·tion (prĭ-dĭk′shən) *n.* **1.** The act of predicting. **2.** Something foretold or predicted; a prophecy.

pre·di·gest (prē′dī-jĕst′, -dĭ-) *tr.v.* **-gest·ed, -gest·ing, -gests. 1.** To subject (food) to partial digestion, usually through an enzymatic or chemical process, before ingestion. **2.** To render in a simpler style or form. —**pre′di·ges′tion** *n.*

pred·i·lec·tion (prĕd′l-ĕk′shən, prēd′-) *n.* A partiality or disposition in favor of something; a preference. [French *prédilection,* from Old French, from Medieval Latin *predīlectus,* past participle of *predīligere,* to prefer : Latin *prae-,* pre- + Latin *dīligere,* to love; see DILIGENT.]

SYNONYMS: *predilection, bias, leaning, partiality, penchant, prejudice, proclivity, propensity.* The central meaning shared by these nouns is "a predisposition to favor a particular person, thing, point of view, or course of action": *a predilection for classical composers; a pro-American bias; conservative leanings; a partiality for liberal-minded friends; a penchant for exotic foods; a prejudice in favor of the underprivileged; a proclivity for self-assertiveness; a propensity for exaggeration.*

pre·dis·pose (prē′dĭ-spōz′) *tr.v.* **-posed, -pos·ing, -pos·es. 1.a.** To make (someone) inclined to something in advance: *His good manners predispose people in his favor.* See Synonyms at **incline. b.** To make susceptible or liable: *conditions that predispose miners to lung disease.* **2.** *Archaic.* To settle or dispose of in advance.

pre·dis·po·si·tion (prē′dĭs-pə-zĭsh′ən) *n.* The state of being predisposed; tendency, inclination, or susceptibility.

pred·nis·o·lone (prĕd-nĭs′ə-lōn′) *n.* A synthetic steroid, $C_{21}H_{28}O_5$, similar to hydrocortisone and used in various compounds as an anti-inflammatory, immunosuppressive, antiallergic, and anticancer drug. [Alteration of PREDNISONE.]

pred·ni·sone (prĕd′nĭ-sōn′,-zōn′) *n.* A synthetic steroid, $C_{21}H_{26}O_5$, similar to cortisone that is used as an antiallergic, immunosuppressive, and anticancer drug and as an anti-inflammatory agent in the treatment of rheumatoid arthritis. [*pre(gnane),* a derivative of cholesterol + D(I–)[1] + –(E)N(E) + (CORT)ISONE.]

pre·doc·tor·al (prē-dŏk′tər-əl) *adj.* Of, relating to, or engaged in advanced academic study in preparation for a doctorate: *predoctoral coursework; a predoctoral student.*

pre·dom·i·nance (prĭ-dŏm′ə-nəns) also **pre·dom·i·nan·cy** (-nən-sē) *n.* The state or quality of being predominant; preponderance.

pre·dom·i·nant (prĭ-dŏm′ə-nənt) *adj.* **1.** Having greatest ascendancy, importance, influence, authority, or force. See Synonyms at **dominant. 2.** Most common or conspicuous; main or prevalent: *the predominant color in a design.* [Medieval Latin *praedominăns, praedominant-,* present participle of *praedominārī,* to predominate. See PREDOMINATE.] —**pre·dom′i·nant·ly** *adv.*

pre·dom·i·nate (prĭ-dŏm′ə-nāt′) *v.* **-nat·ed, -nat·ing, -nates.** —*intr.* **1.** To have or gain controlling power or influence; prevail: *Good predominates over evil in many works of literature.* **2.** To be of or have greater quantity or importance; preponderate: *French-speaking people predominate in Quebec.* —*tr.* To dominate or prevail over. [Medieval Latin *prēdominārī, praedominăt-* : Latin *prae-,* pre- + Latin *dominārī,* to rule (from *dominus,* master; see **dem-** in Appendix).] —**pre·dom′i·nate·ly** (-nĭt-lē) *adv.* —**pre·dom′i·nat′ing·ly** *adv.* —**pre·dom′i·na′tion** *n.* —**pre·dom′i·na′tor** *n.*

pre·e·clamp·si·a (prē′ĭ-klămp′sē-ə) *n.* A condition of hypertension occurring in pregnancy, typically accompanied by edema and proteinuria. —**pre′e·clamp′tic** (-tĭk) *adj.*

pre·em·bry·o (prē-ĕm′brē-ō′) *n., pl.* **-os.** A fertilized ovum up to 14 days old, before it becomes implanted in the uterus. —**pre-em′bry·on′ic** (-ŏn′ĭk) *adj.*

pree·mie also **pre·mie** (prē′mē) *n. Informal.* A prematurely born infant. [Shortening and alteration of PREMATURE.]

pre·em·i·nent or **pre-em·i·nent** (prē-ĕm′ə-nənt) *adj.* Superior to or notable above all others; outstanding. See Synonyms at **dominant, noted.** [Middle English, from Latin *praeēminēns,* present participle of *praeēminēre,* to excel : *prae-,* pre- + *ēminēre,* to stand out; see EMINENT.] —**pre·em′i·nence** *n.* —**pre·em′i·nent·ly** *adv.*

pre·empt or **pre-empt** (prē-ĕmpt′) —*v.* **-empt·ed, -empt·ing, -empts.** —*tr.* **1.** To appropriate, seize, or take for oneself before others. See Synonyms at **appropriate. 2.a.** To take the place of; displace: *A special news program preempted the scheduled shows.* **b.** To have precedence or predominance over: *Discussion of the water shortage will preempt the other topics on this week's agenda.* **3.** To gain possession of by prior right or opportunity, especially to settle on (public land) so as to obtain the right to buy before others. —*intr. Games.* To make a preemptive bid in bridge. [Back-formation from PREEMPTION.] —**pre·emp′tor′** (-ĕmp′tôr′) *n.* —**pre·emp′to·ry** (-ĕmp′tə-rē) *adj.*

pre·emp·tion or **pre-emp·tion** (prē-ĕmp′shən) *n.* **1.a.** The right to purchase something before others, especially the right to purchase public land that is granted to one who has settled on that land. **b.** A purchase made by such a right. **2.** Prior seizure of, appropriation of, or claim to something, such as property. [PRE– + Latin *ēmptiō, ēmptiōn-,* buying (from *ēmptus,* past participle of Latin *emere,* to buy; see **em-** in Appendix).]

pre·emp·tive or **pre-emp·tive** (prē-ĕmp′tĭv) *adj.* **1.** Of, relating to, or characteristic of preemption. **2.** Having or granted by the right of preemption. **3.a.** Relating to or constituting a military strike made so as to gain the advantage when an enemy strike is believed to be imminent: *a preemptive nuclear attack.* **b.** Undertaken or initiated to deter or prevent an anticipated, usually unpleasant situation or occurrence: *The two companies organized a preemptive alliance against a possible takeover by another firm.* **4.** Having or marked by the power to preempt or take precedence: *a preemptive business offer; preemptive authority.* **5.** *Games.* Relating to or being a bid in bridge that is unnecessarily high and is intended to prevent the opposing players from bidding. —**pre·emp′tive·ly** *adv.*

preemptive right *n.* The right of certain stockholders to maintain ownership of a constant percentage of a firm's stock. Such stockholders have the first opportunity to purchase new stock in the firm proportionate to the percentage of shares already held.

preen (prēn) *v.* **preened, preen·ing, preens.** —*tr.* **1.a.** To smooth or clean (feathers) with the beak or bill. **b.** To trim or clean (fur) with the tongue, as cats do. **2.** To dress or groom (oneself) with elaborate care; primp. **3.** To take pride or satisfaction in (oneself); gloat. —*intr.* **1.** To dress up; primp. **2.** To swell with pride; gloat or exult. [Middle English *proinen, preinen,* blend of Old French *proignier,* to prune; see PRUNE[2], and Old French *poroindre,* to anoint before (*por-,* before, from Latin *prō-;* see PRO–[1] + *oindre,* to anoint, from Latin *unguere*).] —**preen′er** *n.*

pre·en·gi·neered or **pre-en·gi·neered** (prē′ĕn-jə-nîrd′) *adj.* Built of or using prefabricated sections or parts: *a preengineered building.*

pre·es·tab·lish or **pre-es·tab·lish** (prē′ĭ-stăb′lĭsh) *tr.v.* **-lished, -lish·ing, -lish·es.** To establish beforehand.

pre·ex·il·i·an or **pre-ex·il·i·an** (prē′ĕg-zĭl′ē-ən, -zĭl′yən, -ĕk-sĭl′ē-ən, -sĭl′yən) also **pre·ex·il·ic** or **pre-ex·il·ic** (-ĕg-zĭl′ĭk, -ĕk-sĭl′-) *adj.* Relating to the history of the Jews before their exile in Babylonia in the sixth century B.C..

pre·ex·ist or **pre-ex·ist** (prē′ĭg-zĭst′) *v.* **-ist·ed, -ist·ing, -ists.** —*tr.* To exist before (something); precede: *Dinosaurs preexisted human beings.* —*intr.* To exist beforehand. —**pre′ex·is′tence** *n.* —**pre′ex·is′tent** *adj.*

pref. *abbr.* **1.** Preface. **2.** Prefatory. **3.** Preference. **4.** Preferred. **5.** Prefix.

pre·fab (prē′făb′) *Informal. adj.* Prefabricated. —**prefab** *n.* Something prefabricated, especially a building or section of a building. —**pre′fab′** *v.*

pre·fab·ri·cate (prē-făb′rĭ-kāt′) *tr.v.* **-cat·ed, -cat·ing, -cates. 1.** To manufacture (a building or section of a building, for example) in advance, especially in standard sections that can be easily shipped and assembled. **2.** To make up, construct, or develop in an artificial, unoriginal, or stereotypic manner. —**pre·fab′ri·ca′tion** *n.* —**pre·fab′ri·ca′tor** *n.*

pref·ace (prĕf′ĭs) *n. Abbr.* **pref. 1.a.** A preliminary statement or essay introducing a book that explains its scope, intention, or background and is usually written by the author. **b.** An introductory section, as of a speech. **2.** Something introductory; a preliminary: *An informal brunch served as a preface to the three-day conference.* **3.** Often **Preface.** The words introducing the central part of the Eucharist in several Christian churches. —**preface** *tr.v.* **-aced, -ac·ing, -ac·es. 1.** To introduce by or provide with a preliminary statement or essay. **2.** To serve as an introduction to. [Middle English, from Old French, from Latin *praefātiō, praefātiōn-,* from *praefātus,* past participle of *praefārī,* to say before : *prae-,* pre- + *fārī,* to speak; see **bhā-**[2] in Appendix.] —**pref′ac·er** *n.*

pre·fad·ed (prē-fā′dĭd) *adj.* Given a faded, weathered, or aged appearance by artificial means. Used of clothing or fabric: *prefaded jeans.*

pref·a·to·ry (prĕf′ə-tôr′ē, -tōr′ē) *adj. Abbr.* **pref.** Of, relating to, or constituting a preface; introductory. See Synonyms at

prefab

ă pat	oi boy
ā pay	ou out
âr care	ŏŏ took
ä father	ōō boot
ĕ pet	ŭ cut
ē be	ûr urge
ĭ pit	th thin
ī pie	*th* this
îr pier	hw which
ŏ pot	zh vision
ō toe	ə about, item
ô paw	♦ regionalism

Stress marks: ′ (primary); ′ (secondary), as in **dictionary** (dĭk′shə-nĕr′ē)

prehensile
Opossum with prehensile tail

preliminary. [From Latin *praefātus,* past participle of *praefārī,* to say before. See PREFACE.] **—pref′a·to′ri·ly** *adv.*

pre·fect (prē′fĕkt′) *n.* **1.** A high administrative official or chief officer, as: **a.** Any of several high military or civil officials in ancient Rome. **b.** The chief of police of Paris, France. **c.** A chief administrative official of a department of France. **d.** The administrator in charge of discipline at a Jesuit school. **2.** A student monitor or officer, especially in a private school. [Middle English, from Old French, from Latin *praefectus,* from past participle of *praeficere,* to place at the head of : *prae-,* pre- + *facere,* to make; see **dhē-** in Appendix.]

prefect apostolic *n., pl.* **prefects apostolic.** *Roman Catholic Church.* A priest with broad jurisdiction in a missionary territory.

pre·fec·ture (prē′fĕk′chər) *n.* **1.** The district administered or governed by a prefect. **2.** The office or authority of a prefect. **3.** The residence or housing of a prefect. **—pre·fec′tur·al** (prĭ-fĕk′chər-əl) *adj.*

pre·fer (prĭ-fûr′) *tr.v.* **-ferred, -fer·ring, -fers. 1.** To choose or be in the habit of choosing as more desirable or as having more value: *prefers coffee to tea.* **2.** *Law.* **a.** To give priority or precedence to (a creditor). **b.** To file, prosecute, or offer for consideration or resolution before a magistrate, court, or other legal authority: *preferred the suit in a higher court.* **3.** *Archaic.* To recommend for advancement or appointment; promote. [Middle English *preferren,* from Old French *preferer,* from Latin *praeferre* : *prae-,* pre- + *ferre,* to carry; see **bher-**[1] in Appendix.] **—pre·fer′rer** *n.*

pref·er·a·ble (prĕf′ər-ə-bəl, prĕf′rə-) *adj.* More desirable or worthy than another; preferred: *Coffee is preferable to tea, I think.* **—pref′er·a·bil′i·ty, pref′er·a·ble·ness** *n.* **—pref′er·a·bly** *adv.*

pref·er·ence (prĕf′ər-əns, prĕf′rəns) *n. Abbr.* **pref. 1.a.** The selecting of someone or something over another or others. **b.** The right or chance to so choose. **c.** Someone or something so chosen. See Synonyms at **choice. 2.** The state of being preferred. **3.** *Law.* **a.** A priority of payment given to one or more creditors by an insolvent debtor. **b.** The right of a creditor to priority of payment. **4.** The granting of precedence or advantage to one country or group of countries in levying duties or in other matters of international trade. [Middle English *preferraunce,* preferment, from Old French *preference,* from *preferer,* to prefer. See PREFER.]

pref·er·en·tial (prĕf′ə-rĕn′shəl) *adj.* **1.** Of, relating to, or giving advantage or preference: *preferential treatment.* **2.** Manifesting or originating from partiality or preference: *preferential tariff rates.* **—pref′er·en′tial·ism** *n.* **—pref′er·en′tial·ist** *n.* **—pref′er·en′tial·ly** *adv.*

preferential shop *n.* A shop whose management gives priority or advantage to union members in hiring, promoting, or laying off.

preferential voting *n.* A system of voting in which the voter ranks candidates in order of preference.

pre·fer·ment (prĭ-fûr′mənt) *n.* **1.** The act of advancing to a higher position or office; promotion. **2.** A position, an appointment, or a rank giving advancement, as of profit or prestige. **3.** The act of preferring or the state of being preferred.

pre·ferred provider organization (prĭ-fûrd′) *n. Abbr.* **PPO** A medical insurance plan in which members receive more coverage if they choose health care providers approved by or affiliated with the plan.

preferred stock *n.* Stock having priority over a corporation's commonly held stock in the distribution of dividends and often of assets.

pre·fig·u·ra·tion (prē-fĭg′yə-rā′shən) *n.* **1.** The act of representing, suggesting, or imagining in advance. **2.** Something that prefigures; a foreshadowing.

pre·fig·ure (prē-fĭg′yər) *tr.v.* **-ured, -ur·ing, -ures. 1.** To suggest, indicate, or represent by an antecedent form or model; presage or foreshadow: *The paintings of Paul Cézanne prefigured the rise of cubism in the early 20th century.* **2.** To imagine or picture to oneself in advance. [Middle English *prefiguren,* from Old French *prefigurer,* from Late Latin *praefigūrāre* : Latin *prae-,* pre- + Latin *figūrāre,* to shape (from *figūra,* shape; see **dheigh-** in Appendix).] **—pre·fig′ur·a·tive** (-fĭg′yər-ə-tĭv) *adj.* **—pre·fig′ur·a·tive·ly** *adv.* **—pre·fig′ur·a·tive·ness** *n.* **—pre·fig′ure·ment** *n.*

pre·fin·ished (prē-fĭn′ĭsht) *adj.* Coated or treated before being sold or distributed: *prefinished wood paneling.*

pre·fix (prē′fĭks′) *tr.v.* **-fixed, -fix·ing, -fix·es. 1.** To put or attach before or in front of. **2.** (prē-fĭks′). To settle or arrange in advance. **3.** *Grammar.* **a.** To add as a prefix. **b.** To add a prefix to. **—prefix** *n. Abbr.* **pref. 1.** *Grammar.* An affix, such as *dis-* in *disbelieve,* put before a word to produce a derivative word or an inflected form. **2.** A title placed before a person's name. [Middle English *prefixen,* from Old French *prefixer* : *pre-,* before (from Latin *prae-;* see PRE–) + *fixer,* to place (from Latin *fīxus,* past participle of *fīgere,* to fasten). N., from New Latin *praefīxum,* from neuter sing. of Latin *praefīxus,* past participle of *praefīgere,* to fix in front : *prae-,* pre- + *fīgere,* to fasten; see **dhīgʷ-** in Appendix.] **—pre′fix′al** *adj.* **—pre′fix′al·ly** *adv.*

pre·flight (prē′flīt′) *adj.* Occurring before flight. **—preflight** *tr.v.* **-flight·ed, -flight·ing, -flights.** To check (an aircraft) for airworthiness before flight. **—pre′flight′** *n.*

pre·form (prē′fôrm′) *tr.v.* **-formed, -form·ing, -forms. 1.** To shape or form beforehand. **2.** To determine the shape or form of beforehand. **—preform** *n.* An object that has been subjected to preliminary, usually incomplete shaping or molding before undergoing complete or final processing.

pre·for·ma·tion (prē′fôr-mā′shən) *n.* **1.** The act of shaping or forming in advance; prior formation. **2.** A theory popular in the 18th century that all parts of an organism exist completely formed in the germ cell and develop only by increasing in size.

pre·fron·tal (prē-frŭn′tl) *adj.* **1.** Of, relating to, or situated in the anterior part of the frontal lobe. **2.** Situated anterior to the frontal bone.

prefrontal lobotomy *n.* A lobotomy in which the white fibers that connect the thalamus to the prefrontal and frontal lobes of the brain are severed, performed as a treatment for intense anxiety or violent behavior.

pre·gan·gli·on·ic (prē-găng′glē-ŏn′ĭk) *adj.* Of, relating to, or being the nerve fibers that supply a ganglion, especially a ganglion of the autonomic nervous system.

preg·na·ble (prĕg′nə-bəl) *adj.* Being such that attack, seizure, or capture is possible; vulnerable or assailable: *a pregnable fortress.* [Middle English *preignable, pregnabul,* from Old French *pregnauble,* from *prendre, pregn-,* to grasp, from Latin *prehendere.* See **ghend-** in Appendix.] **—preg′na·bil′i·ty** *n.*

preg·nan·cy (prĕg′nən-sē) *n., pl.* **-cies. 1.a.** The condition of being pregnant: *a test for pregnancy.* **b.** An instance of being pregnant: *Her second pregnancy was easy.* **c.** The period during which one is pregnant: *the first trimester of pregnancy.* **2.** The quality or condition of being rich in significance, import, or implication. **3.** Creativity; inventiveness.

preg·nant[1] (prĕg′nənt) *adj.* **1.** Carrying developing offspring within the body. **2.a.** Weighty or significant; full of meaning: *a conversation occasionally punctuated by pregnant pauses.* **b.** Of great or potentially great import, implication, or moment: *"It was a politically pregnant time in Poland"* (New York). **3.** Filled or fraught; replete: *"This was, from the Party's point of view, both deplorable in itself and pregnant with danger for the future"* (Robert Conquest). **4.** Having a profusion of ideas; creative or inventive. **5.** Producing results; fruitful: *a pregnant decision.* [Middle English, from Old French, from Latin *praegnāns, praegnant-,* variant of *praegnās.* See **genə-** in Appendix.] **—preg′nant·ly** *adv.*

preg·nant[2] (prĕg′nənt) *adj. Archaic.* Convincing; cogent. Used of an argument or a proof. [Middle English, probably from Old French *preignant,* present participle of *prembre,* to press, from Latin *premere.* See **per-**[4] in Appendix.]

pre·heat (prē-hēt′) *tr.v.* **-heat·ed, -heat·ing, -heats.** To heat (an oven, for example) beforehand. **—pre·heat′er** *n.*

pre·hen·sile (prē-hĕn′səl, -sīl′) *adj.* **1.** Adapted for seizing, grasping, or holding, especially by wrapping around an object: *a monkey's prehensile tail.* **2.** Having keen intellect; insightful. **3.** Greedy; grasping. [French *préhensile,* from Latin *prehēnsus,* past participle of *prehendere,* to grasp. See **ghend-** in Appendix.] **—pre′hen·sil′i·ty** (-sĭl′ĭ-tē) *n.*

pre·hen·sion (prē-hĕn′shən) *n.* **1.** The act of grasping or seizing. **2.a.** Apprehension by the senses. **b.** Understanding. [Latin *prehēnsiō, prehēnsiōn-,* from *prehēnsus,* past participle of *prehendere,* to seize. See **ghend-** in Appendix.]

pre·his·tor·ic (prē′hĭ-stôr′ĭk, -stŏr′-) also **pre·his·tor·i·cal** (-ĭ-kəl) *adj.* **1.** Of, relating to, or belonging to the era before recorded history. **2.** Of or relating to a language before it is first recorded in writing. **—pre′his·tor′i·cal·ly** *adv.*

pre·his·to·ry (prē-hĭs′tə-rē) *n., pl.* **-ries. 1.** History of humankind in the period before recorded history. **2.** The circumstances or developments leading up to or surrounding a current situation, event, or development; background: "[He] *then told me the curious prehistory of his obsessive interest in the seduction theory"* (Janet Malcolm). **—pre′his·tor′i·an** (-hĭ-stôr′ē-ən, -stŏr′-) *n.*

pre·hom·i·nid (prē-hŏm′ə-nĭd) *n.* Any of several extinct primates regarded as an immediate ancestor of the hominids. **—prehominid** *adj.* Of or relating to these extinct primates.

pre·ig·ni·tion (prē′ĭg-nĭsh′ən) *n.* The ignition of fuel in an internal-combustion engine before the spark passes through the fuel, resulting from a hot spot in the cylinder or from too great a compression ratio for the fuel.

pre·in·dus·tri·al (prē′ĭn-dŭs′trē-əl) *adj.* Of, relating to, or being a society or an economic system that is not or has not yet become industrialized.

pre·judge (prē-jŭj′) *tr.v.* **-judged, -judg·ing, -judg·es.** To judge beforehand without possessing adequate evidence. **—pre·judg′er** *n.* **—pre·judg′ment, pre·judge′ment** *n.*

prej·u·dice (prĕj′ə-dĭs) *n.* **1.a.** An adverse judgment or opinion formed beforehand or without knowledge or examination of the facts. See Synonyms at **predilection. b.** A preconceived preference or idea. **2.** The act or state of holding unreasonable preconceived judgments or convictions. **3.** Irrational suspicion or hatred of a particular group, race, or religion. **4.** Detriment or injury caused to a person by the preconceived, unfavorable conviction of another or others. **—prejudice** *tr.v.* **-diced, -dic·ing, -dic·es. 1.** To cause (someone) to judge prematurely and irrationally. **2.** To affect injuriously or detrimentally by a judgment or an act. See Synonyms at **bias.** [Middle English, from Old French, from Latin *praeiūdicium* : *prae-,* pre- + *iūdicium,* judgment (from *iūdex, iūdic-,* judge; see **deik-** in Appendix).]

prej·u·di·cial (prĕj′ə-dĭsh′əl) *adj.* **1.** Detrimental; injurious. **2.** Causing or tending to preconceived judgment or convictions: *Reporters were expelled from the courtroom after it was decided that their coverage had resulted in prejudicial publicity for the defendant.* **—prej′u·di′cial·ly** *adv.* **—prej′u·di′cial·ness** *n.*

prej·u·di·cious (prĕj′ə-dĭsh′əs) *adj.* Prejudicial. **—prej′u·di′cious·ly** *adv.*

prel·a·cy (prĕl′ə-sē) *n., pl.* **-cies. 1.a.** The office or station of a prelate. **b.** Prelates considered as a group. Also called *prelature.* **2.** Church government administrated by prelates.

pre·lap·sar·i·an (prē′lăp-sâr′ē-ən) *adj. Theology.* Of or relating to the period before the fall of Adam and Eve. [PRE– + Latin *lapsus,* fall; see LAPSE + –ARIAN.]

prel·ate (prĕl′ĭt) *n.* A high-ranking member of the clergy, especially a bishop. [Middle English *prelat,* from Old French, from Medieval Latin *praelātus,* from Latin, past participle of *praeferre,* to carry before, to prefer : *prae-,* pre- + *lātus,* brought; see **telə-** in Appendix.] **—pre·lat′ic** (prĭ-lăt′ĭk) *adj.*

prelate nul·li·us (no͞o-lē′əs) *n., pl.* **prelates nullius.** *Roman Catholic Church.* A prelate, usually a titular bishop, who has jurisdiction over a territory not in a diocese but subject directly to the Holy See. [PRELATE + New Latin *nullīus (dioecēsis),* of no (diocese) (from Latin, genitive sing. of *nullus,* none).]

prel·a·ture (prĕl′ə-chər, -cho͝or′) *n.* See **prelacy** (sense 1).

pre·launch (prē′lônch′, -lŏnch′) *adj.* Preparatory or preliminary to launch, especially of a spacecraft or missile.

pre·law (prē′lô′) *adj. Law.* Of, relating to, or being the studies that prepare one for the study of law.

pre·lect (prĭ-lĕkt′) *intr.v.* **-lect·ed, -lect·ing, -lects.** To lecture or discourse in public. [Latin *praelegere, praelect-* : *prae-,* pre- + *legere,* to read; see **leg-** in Appendix.] **—pre·lec′tion** *n.* **—pre·lec′tor** *n.*

pre·li·ba·tion (prē′lī-bā′shən) *n.* A foretaste. [Latin *praelībātiō, praelībātiōn-,* from *praelībātus,* past participle of *praelībāre,* to taste beforehand : *prae-,* pre- + *lībāre,* pour out, to taste.]

pre·lim (prē′lĭm′, prĭ-lĭm′) *n. Sports.* A preliminary: *Several top players were unexpectedly eliminated in the prelims.*

pre·lim·i·nar·y (prĭ-lĭm′ə-nĕr′ē) *adj.* Prior to or preparing for the main matter, action, or business; introductory or prefatory. **—preliminary** *n., pl.* **-ies. 1.** Something that precedes, prepares for, or introduces the main matter, action, or business. **2.** An academic test or examination that is preparatory to one that is longer, more complex, or more important. **3.** *Sports.* A contest to determine the finalists in a competition. **4.** *Sports.* An event that precedes the main event of a particular program, especially in boxing or wrestling. **5.** Often **preliminaries.** *Printing.* The front matter of a book. [From New Latin *praelīmināris* : Latin *prae-,* pre- + Latin *līmen, līmin-,* threshold.] **—pre·lim′i·nar′i·ly** (-nâr′ə-lē) *adv.*

SYNONYMS: *preliminary, introductory, prefatory, preparatory.* The central meaning shared by these adjectives is "going before and preparing the way for something else": *a preliminary investigation; introductory remarks; an author's prefatory notes; preparatory steps.*

pre·lit·er·ate (prē-lĭt′ər-ĭt) *adj.* Of, relating to, or being a culture not having a written language. **—preliterate** *n.* A person belonging to such a culture.

Pre·log (prĕl′ŏg′), **Vladimir.** Born 1906. Yugoslavian-born Swiss chemist. He shared a 1975 Nobel Prize for research on the structure of biological molecules.

prel·ude (prĕl′yo͞od′, prā′lo͞od′, prē′-) *n.* **1.** An introductory performance, event, or action preceding a more important one; a preliminary or preface. **2.** *Music.* An independent piece written for piano and usually based on a single, short thematic motif. **3.** *Music.* A piece or movement serving as an introduction to another section or composition, especially: **a.** An independent, relatively long piece that precedes a fugue. **b.** The first or opening section of a suite. **c.** The overture to an oratorio, opera, or act of an opera. **d.** A piece played before a church service; an introductory voluntary. **e.** A relatively short composition of the 15th and early 16th centuries written in a free style, usually for piano. **—prelude** *v.* **-ud·ed, -ud·ing, -udes.** *—tr.* **1.** To serve as a prelude to. **2.** To introduce with or as if with a prelude. *—intr.* To serve as a prelude or an introduction. [Medieval Latin *praelūdium,* from Latin *praelūdere,* to play beforehand : *prae-,* pre- + *lūdere,* to play (from *lūdus,* game; see **leid-** in Appendix).] **—prel′ud′er** *n.* **—pre·lu′di·al** (prĭ-lo͞o′dē-əl) *adj.*

pre·lu·sion (prĭ-lo͞o′zhən) *n.* A prelude or an introduction. [Latin *praelūsiō, praelūsiōn-,* from *praelūsus,* past participle of *praelūdere,* to play beforehand. See PRELUDE.]

pre·lu·sive (prĭ-lo͞o′sĭv) *adj.* Of or serving as a prelude; introductory. **—pre·lu′sive·ly** *adv.*

prem. *abbr.* Premium.

pre·ma·lig·nant (prē′mə-lĭg′nənt) *adj.* Precancerous.

pre·mar·i·tal (prē-măr′ĭ-tl) *adj.* Taking place or existing before marriage. **—pre·mar′i·tal·ly** *adv.*

pre·ma·ture (prē′mə-tyo͝or′, -to͝or′, -cho͝or′) *adj.* **1.** Occurring, growing, or existing before the customary, correct, or assigned time; uncommonly or unexpectedly early: *a premature end.* **2.** Born after a gestation period of less than the normal time: *a premature infant.* [Middle English, ripe, from Latin *praemātūrus,* ripe too early : *prae-,* pre- + *mātūrus,* ripe; see **mā-**[1] in Appendix.] **—pre′ma·ture′ly** *adv.* **—pre′ma·ture′ness, pre′ma·tu′ri·ty** *n.*

pre·max·il·la (prē′măk-sĭl′ə) *n., pl.* **-max·il·lae** (-măk-sĭl′ē). Either of two bones located in front of and between the maxillary bones in the upper jaw of vertebrates. **—pre·max′il·lar′y** (-măk′sə-lĕr′ē) *adj.*

pre·med (prē′mĕd′) *Informal. adj.* Premedical. **—premed** *n.* **1.** A premedical student. **2.** A premedical program of study.

pre·med·i·cal (prē-mĕd′ĭ-kəl) *adj.* Preparing for or relating to the studies that prepare one for the study of medicine: *a premedical student; premedical courses.*

pre·med·i·tate (prē-mĕd′ĭ-tāt′) *v.* **-tat·ed, -tat·ing, -tates.** *—tr.* To plan, arrange, or plot (a crime, for example) in advance. *—intr.* To reflect, ponder, or deliberate beforehand. **—pre·med′i·ta′tive** *adj.* **—pre·med′i·ta′tor** *n.*

pre·med·i·tat·ed (prē-mĕd′ĭ-tā′tĭd) *adj.* Characterized by deliberate purpose, previous consideration, and some degree of planning: *a premeditated crime.* **—pre·med′i·tat′ed·ly** *adv.*

pre·med·i·ta·tion (prē-mĕd′ĭ-tā′shən) *n.* **1.** The act of speculating, arranging, or plotting in advance. **2.** *Law.* The contemplation of a crime well enough in advance to show deliberate intent to commit the crime; forethought.

pre·me·no·paus·al (prē′mĕn-ə-pô′zəl) *adj.* Of or relating to the years or the stage of life immediately before the onset of menopause.

pre·men·stru·al (prē-mĕn′stro͞o-əl) *adj.* Of, relating to, or occurring in the period just before menstruation. **—pre·men′stru·al·ly** *adv.*

premenstrual syndrome *n. Abbr.* **PMS** A group of symptoms, including abdominal bloating, breast tenderness, headache, fatigue, irritability, and depression, that occur in many women from 2 to 14 days before the onset of menstruation.

pre·mie (prē′mē) *n. Informal.* Variant of **preemie.**

pre·mier (prĭ-mîr′, -myîr′, prē′mîr) *adj.* **1.** First in status or importance; principal or chief: *an architect of premier rank.* **2.** First to occur or exist; earliest. **—premier** (prĭ-mîr′) *n.* **1.** A prime minister. **2.** A chief administrative officer, as of a Canadian province. [Middle English *primier,* from Old French, from Latin *prīmārius,* from *prīmus,* first. See **per**[1] in Appendix.] **—pre·mier′ship′** *n.*

pre·mier dan·seur (prə-myā′ däɴ-sœr′) *n., pl.* **pre·miers dan·seurs** (prə-myā′ däɴ-sœr′). A man who is the principal dancer in a ballet company. [French : *premier,* first + *danseur,* dancer.]

pre·miere or **pre·mière** (prĭ-mîr′, -myâr′) *—n.* The first public performance, as of a movie or play. *—v.* **-miered, -mier·ing, -mieres** or **-mièred, -mièr·ing, -mières.** *—tr.* To present the first public performance of. *—intr.* **1.** To have the first public performance. **2.** To make a first appearance in a public performance. *—adj.* First or paramount; premier. [French, from feminine of *premier,* first. See PREMIER.]

USAGE NOTE: In entertainment contexts the verb *premiere* has by now become the standard way of saying "to introduce to the public," at least partly because of its ubiquitous use on television. Over the past 20 years this use has won the sometimes grudging acceptance of the Usage Panel. The example *The Philharmonic will premiere works by two young Americans* was acceptable to 51 percent of the Panelists in the most recent survey, up from 14 percent in 1969. But only 10 percent of the Panelists in the most recent survey accepted extension of the verb to nonentertainment contexts, as in *Last fall the school premiered new degree programs in word processing and accounting.*

pre·mière dan·seuse (prĭ-mîr′ däɴ-sœz′, -myâr′) *n., pl.* **pre·mières dan·seuses** (prĭ-myâr′ däɴ-sœz′). A woman who is the principal dancer in a ballet company. [French : *première,* feminine of *premier* + *danseuse,* feminine of *danseur,* dancer.]

pre·mil·le·nar·i·an (prē-mĭl′ə-nâr′ē-ən) *adj.* Of or relating to premillennialism. **—premillenarian** *n.* A person who believes in premillennialism. **—pre·mil′le·nar′i·an·ism** *n.*

pre·mil·len·ni·al (prē′mĭ-lĕn′ē-əl) *adj.* Of or happening in the time before the millennium. **—pre′mil·len′ni·al·ly** *adv.*

pre·mil·len·ni·al·ism (prē′mĭ-lĕn′ē-ə-lĭz′əm) *n.* The belief that the Second Coming of Jesus will immediately precede the millennium. **—pre′mil·len′ni·al·ist** *n.*

Prem·in·ger (prĕm′ĭn-jər), **Otto Ludwig.** 1906–1986. Austrian-born American film producer and director whose works include *Laura* (1944) and *Anatomy of a Murder* (1959).

prem·ise (prĕm′ĭs) also **prem·iss** (prĕm′ĭs) *n.* **1.** A proposition upon which an argument is based or from which a conclusion is drawn. **2.** *Logic.* **a.** One of the propositions in a deductive argument. **b.** Either the major or the minor proposition of a syllogism, from which the conclusion is drawn. **3. premises.** *Law.* The preliminary or explanatory statements or facts of a document, as in a deed. **4. premises. a.** Land and the buildings on it. **b.** A building or part of a building. **—premise** *v.* **-ised, -is·ing, -is·es.** *—tr.* **1.** To state in advance as an introduction or explanation. **2.** To state or assume as a proposition in an argument. *—intr.* To make a premise. [Middle English *premisse,* from Old French, from Medieval Latin *praemissa (prōpositiō),* (the proposition) put before, premise, from Latin, feminine past participle of *praemittere,* to set in front : *prae-,* pre- + *mittere,* to send.]

ă pat	oi boy
ā pay	ou out
âr care	o͝o took
ä father	o͞o boot
ĕ pet	ŭ cut
ē be	ûr urge
ĭ pit	th thin
ī pie	*th* this
îr pier	hw which
ŏ pot	zh vision
ō toe	ə about, item
ô paw	♦ regionalism

Stress marks: ′ (primary); ′ (secondary), as in **dictionary** (dĭk′shə-nĕr′ē)

WORD HISTORY: Why do we call a single building *the premises*? To answer this question, we must go back to the Middle Ages. But first, let it be noted that *premises* comes from the past participle *praemissa,* which is both a feminine singular and a neuter plural form of the Latin verb *praemittere,* "to send in advance, utter by way of preface, place in front, prefix." In Medieval Latin the feminine form *praemissa* was used as a term in logic, for which we still use the term *premise* descended from the Medieval Latin word (first recorded in a work composed before 1380). Medieval Latin *praemissa* in the plural meant "things mentioned before" and was used in legal documents, almost always in the plural, a use that was followed in Old French and Middle English, both of which borrowed the word from Latin. A more specific legal sense in Middle English, "that property, collectively, which is specified in the beginning of a legal document and which is conveyed, as by grant," was also always in the plural in Middle English and later Modern English. And so it remained when this sense was extended to mean "a house or building with its grounds or appurtenances," a usage first recorded before 1730.

pre·mi·um (prē′mē-əm) *n. Abbr.* **pm., prem. 1.** A prize or an award. **2.** Something offered free or at a reduced price as an inducement to buy something else. **3.** A sum of money or bonus paid in addition to a regular price, salary, or other amount. **4.** The amount paid, often in addition to the interest, to obtain a loan. See Synonyms at **bonus. 5.** The amount paid or payable, often in installments, for an insurance policy. **6.** The amount at which something is valued above its par or nominal value, as money or securities. **7.** The amount at which a securities option is bought or sold. **8.** Payment for training in a trade or profession. **9.** An unusual or high value: *Employers put a premium on honesty and hard work.* **—premium** *adj.* Of superior quality or value: *premium gasoline.* **—*idiom.* at a premium.** More valuable than usual, as from scarcity: *Fresh water was at a premium after the reservoir was contaminated.* [Latin *praemium,* inducement, reward : *prae-,* pre- + *emere,* to take, buy; see **em-** in Appendix.]

pre·mix (prē′mĭks′) *n.* Something that is mixed or blended from two or more ingredients or elements before being marketed, used, or mixed further: *a premix of the dry ingredients in cake batter; a premix of a multitrack recording.* **—premix** *tr.v.* **-mixed, -mix·ing, -mix·es.** To mix or blend beforehand.

pre·mod·ern (prē-mŏd′ərn) *adj.* Existing or coming before a modern period or time: *the feudal system of premodern Japan; a premodern assembly line.*

pre·mo·lar (prē-mō′lər) *n.* One of eight bicuspid teeth located in pairs on each side of the upper and lower jaws behind the canines and in front of the molars. **—pre·mo′lar** *adj.*

pre·mo·ni·tion (prē′mə-nĭsh′ən, prĕm′ə-) *n.* **1.** A presentiment of the future; a foreboding. **2.** A warning in advance; a forewarning. [Late Latin *praemonitiō, praemonitiōn-,* from Latin *praemonitus,* past participle of *praemonēre,* to forewarn : *prae-,* pre- + *monēre,* to warn; see **men-**[1] in Appendix.] **—pre·mon′i·to′ri·ly** (-mŏn′ĭ-tôr′ə-lē, -tōr′-) *adv.* **—pre·mon′i·to′ry** *adj.*

pre·morse (prĭ-môrs′) *adj.* Abruptly truncated, as though bitten or broken off: *a premorse leaf.* [Latin *praemorsus,* past participle of *praemordēre,* to bite off in front : *prae-,* pre- + *mordēre,* to bite; see **mer-** in Appendix.]

pre·mu·ni·tion (prē′myo͞o-nĭsh′ən) *n.* Relative immunity to severe infection by a particular pathogen as a result of a chronic low-grade infection induced earlier by the same pathogen. [French *prémunition,* from Latin *praemūnītiō, praemūnītiōn-,* fortification beforehand, from *praemūnītus,* past participle of *praemūnīre,* to fortify in advance : *prae-,* pre- + *mūnīre,* to fortify (from *moene, moenia,* defensive walls of a town).] **—pre·mune′** (prē-myo͞on′) *adj.*

pre·name (prē′nām′) *n.* A forename.

pre·na·tal (prē-nāt′l) *adj.* Existing or occurring before birth: *prenatal medical care.* **—pre·na′tal·ly** *adv.*

pren·tice (prĕn′tĭs) *n. Archaic.* An apprentice.

pre·nup·tial (prē-nŭp′shəl, -chəl) *adj.* Before marriage or a wedding: *a prenuptial celebration.*

pre·oc·cu·pan·cy (prē-ŏk′yə-pən-sē) *n.* **1.** The act or right of occupying a place beforehand or in advance. **2.** The state of being preoccupied or engrossed; preoccupation.

pre·oc·cu·pa·tion (prē-ŏk′yə-pā′shən) *n.* **1.** The state of being preoccupied; absorption of the attention or intellect. **2.** Something that preoccupies or engrosses the mind: *Money was their chief preoccupation.* **3.** Occupation of a place in advance; preoccupancy.

pre·oc·cu·pied (prē-ŏk′yə-pīd′) *adj.* **1.a.** Absorbed in thought; engrossed. **b.** Excessively concerned with something; distracted. **2.** Formerly or already occupied. **3.** Already used and therefore unavailable for further use. Used of taxonomic names.

pre·oc·cu·py (prē-ŏk′yə-pī′) *tr.v.* **-pied, -py·ing, -pies. 1.** To occupy completely the mind or attention of; engross. See Synonyms at **monopolize. 2.** To occupy or take possession of in advance or before another.

pre·op·er·a·tive (prē-ŏp′ər-ə-tĭv, -ŏp′rə-, -ŏp′ə-rā′-) *adj.* Occurring before surgery: *preoperative preparations.* **—pre·op′er·a·tive·ly** *adv.*

pre·o·ral (prē-ôr′əl, -ōr′-) *adj.* Situated in front of the mouth.

pre·or·bit·al (prē-ôr′bĭ-tl) *adj. Aerospace.* Occurring before orbit has been established.

pre·or·dain (prē′ôr-dān′) *tr.v.* **-dained, -dain·ing, -dains.** To appoint, decree, or ordain in advance; foreordain. **—pre′or·dain′ment** *n.* **—pre·or′di·na′tion** (-ôr′dn-ā′shən) *n.*

pre·owned (prē-ōnd′) *adj.* Previously owned or used; secondhand: *a preowned car.*

prep (prĕp) *adj. Informal.* Preparatory: *a college prep course; did extensive prep work for the interview.* **—prep** *n.* **1.** *Informal.* A preparatory school. **2.** *Informal.* Preparation: *Daily practices are the best prep for the upcoming track meet.* **3.** *Chiefly British.* The preparing of lessons; homework. **4.** *Informal.* A preppie. **—prep** *v.* **prepped, prep·ping, preps.** *Informal.* —*intr.* **1.** To be enrolled in and attend a preparatory school. **2.** To study or train in preparation for something. —*tr.* **1.** To prepare (someone) for a medical examination or surgical procedure. **2.** To prepare or prime: *prep a surface for painting.*

prep. *abbr.* **1.** Preparation. **2.** Preparatory. **3.** Prepare. **4.** *Grammar.* Preposition.

pre·pack·age (prē-păk′ĭj) *tr.v.* **-aged, -ag·ing, -ag·es.** To wrap or package (a product) before marketing.

prep·a·ra·tion (prĕp′ə-rā′shən) *n. Abbr.* **prep., prepn. 1.** The act or process of preparing. **2.** The state of having been made ready beforehand; readiness. **3.** A preliminary measure that serves to make ready for something. Often used in the plural: *preparations for the wedding.* **4.** A substance, such as a medicine, prepared for a particular purpose. **5.** *Music.* **a.** The anticipation of a dissonant tone by its introduction as a consonant tone in the preceding chord. **b.** The dissonant tone so anticipated.

pre·par·a·tive (prĭ-păr′ə-tĭv, -pâr′-) *adj.* Serving or tending to prepare or make ready; preliminary. **—preparative** *n.* Something that prepares for or acts as a preliminary to something following. **—pre·par′a·tive·ly** *adv.*

pre·par·a·tor (prĭ-păr′ə-tər, -pâr′-) *n.* One who prepares specimens or exhibits for scientific study or display, as in a museum.

pre·par·a·to·ry (prĭ-păr′ə-tôr′ē, -tōr′ē, -pâr′-, prĕp′ər-ə-) *adj. Abbr.* **prep. 1.** Serving to make ready or prepare; introductory. See Synonyms at **preliminary. 2.** Relating to or engaged in study or training that serves as preparation for advanced education: *a preparatory college course; preparatory students.* **—preparatory** *adv.* In preparation for. Used with *to*: *A thorough cleaning of the house took place preparatory to our departure.* **—pre·par′a·to′ri·ly** *adv.*

preparatory school *n.* **1.** A usually private secondary school that prepares students for college. **2.** A usually private elementary school in Great Britain that prepares students for public school.

pre·pare (prĭ-pâr′) *v.* **-pared, -par·ing, -pares.** *Abbr.* **prep.** —*tr.* **1.** To make ready beforehand for a specific purpose, as for an event or occasion: *The teacher prepared the students for the exams.* **2.** To put together or make by combining various elements or ingredients; manufacture or compound: *prepared a meal; prepared the lecture.* **3.** To fit out; equip: *prepared the ship for an arctic expedition.* **4.** *Music.* To lead up to and soften (a dissonance or its impact) by means of preparation. —*intr.* **1.** To make things or oneself ready. **2.** To study or complete a course of study at a preparatory school. [Middle English *preparen,* from Old French *preparer,* from Latin *praeparāre* : *prae-,* pre- + *parāre,* prepare, equip; see **pere-**[1] in Appendix.] **—pre·par′ed·ly** (-pâr′ĭd-lē) *adv.* **—pre·par′er** *n.*

pre·par·ed·ness (prĭ-pâr′ĭd-nĭs) *n.* The state of being prepared, especially military readiness for combat.

pre·pay (prē-pā′) *tr.v.* **-paid, -pay·ing, -pays.** To pay or pay for beforehand. **—pre·pay′ment** *n.*

prepd. *abbr.* Prepared.

pre·pense (prĭ-pĕns′) *adj.* Contemplated or arranged in advance; premeditated: *malice prepense.* [From Middle English, past participle of *purpensen,* to premeditate, from Anglo-Norman *purpenser* : *pur-,* before (from Latin *pro-;* see PRO–[1]) + *penser,* to think (from Latin *pēnsāre;* see **(s)pen-** in Appendix).] **—pre·pense′ly** *adv.*

prepn. *abbr.* Preparation.

pre·pon·der·ance (prĭ-pŏn′dər-əns) also **pre·pon·der·an·cy** (-ən-sē) *n.* Superiority in weight, force, importance, or influence.

pre·pon·der·ant (prĭ-pŏn′dər-ənt) *adj.* Having superior weight, force, importance, or influence. See Synonyms at **dominant. —pre·pon′der·ant·ly** *adv.*

pre·pon·der·ate (prĭ-pŏn′də-rāt′) *intr.v.* **-at·ed, -at·ing, -ates. 1.** To exceed something else in weight. **2.** To be greater than something else, as in power, force, quantity, or importance; predominate: *"In balancing his faults with his perfections, the latter seemed rather to preponderate"* (Henry Fielding). **—preponderate** (-dər-ĭt) *adj.* Preponderant. [Latin *praeponderāre, praeponderāt-* : *prae-,* pre- + *ponderāre,* to weigh; see **(s)pen-** in Appendix.] **—pre·pon′der·ate·ly** *adv.* **—pre·pon′der·a′tion** *n.*

prep·o·si·tion[1] (prĕp′ə-zĭsh′ən) *n. Abbr.* **prep.** *Grammar.* **1.** In some languages, a word placed before a substantive and indicating the relation of that substantive to a verb, an adjective, or another substantive, as English *at, by, in, to, from,* and *with.* **2.** A word or construction similar in function to a preposition, such as *in regard to* or *concerning.* [Middle English *preposicioun,* from Old French *preposicion,* from Latin *praepositiō, praepositiōn-,* a putting before, preposition (translation of Greek *prothesis*), from *praepositus,* past participle of *praepōnere,* to put in front : *prae-,* pre- + *pōnere,* to put; see **apo-** in Appendix.]

USAGE NOTE: The doctrine that a preposition may not be used to end a sentence was first promulgated by Dryden, probably on the basis of a specious analogy to Latin, and was subsequently refined by 18th-century grammarians. The rule has since become one of the most venerated maxims of schoolroom grammatical lore. But sentences ending with prepositions can be found in the works of most of the great writers since the Renaissance. In fact, English syntax allows and sometimes requires final placement of the preposition. Such placement is the only possible one in sentences such as *We have much to be thankful for* or *That depends on what you believe in.* Efforts to rewrite such sentences to place the preposition elsewhere will have comically stilted results; for example: *We have much for which to be thankful* or *That depends on that in which you believe.* • Even sticklers for the traditional rule can have no grounds for criticizing sentences such as *I don't know where she will end up* or *It's the most curious book I've ever run across.* In these examples, *up* and *across* are used as adverbs, not prepositions, as demonstrated by the ungrammaticality of sentences such as *I don't know up where she will end* and *It's the most curious book across which I have ever run.*

pre·po·si·tion² also **pre-po·si·tion** (prē′pə-zĭsh′ən) *tr.v.* **-tioned, -tion·ing, -tions.** To position or place in position in advance: *prepositioned artillery at strategic points in the desert.*

prep·o·si·tion·al (prĕp′ə-zĭsh′ə-nəl) *adj. Grammar.* Relating to, composed of, or used as a preposition. **—prep′o·si′tion·al·ly** *adv.*

prepositional phrase *n. Grammar.* A phrase that consists of a preposition and its object and has adjectival or adverbial value, such as *in the house* in *the people in the house* or *by him* in *The book was written by him.*

pre·pos·i·tive (prĭ-pŏz′ĭ-tĭv) *Grammar. adj.* Put before; prefixed. **—prepositive** *n.* A word or particle put before another word. [Late Latin *praepositīvus,* from Latin *praepositus,* past participle of *praepōnere,* to put in front. See PREPOSITION¹.] **—pre·pos′i·tive·ly** *adv.*

pre·pos·sess (prē′pə-zĕs′) *tr.v.* **-sessed, -sess·ing, -sess·es. 1.** To preoccupy the mind of to the exclusion of other thoughts or feelings. **2. a.** To influence beforehand against or in favor of someone or something; prejudice. **b.** To impress favorably in advance.

pre·pos·sess·ing (prē′pə-zĕs′ĭng) *adj.* **1.** Serving to impress favorably; pleasing: *a prepossessing appearance.* **2.** *Archaic.* Causing prejudice. **—pre′pos·sess′ing·ly** *adv.* **—pre′pos·sess′ing·ness** *n.*

pre·pos·ses·sion (prē′pə-zĕsh′ən) *n.* **1.** A preconception or prejudice. **2.** The state of being preoccupied with thoughts, opinions, or feelings.

pre·pos·ter·ous (prĭ-pŏs′tər-əs) *adj.* Contrary to nature, reason, or common sense; absurd. See Synonyms at **foolish.** [From Latin *praeposterus,* inverted, unseasonable : *prae-,* pre- + *posterus,* coming behind (from *post,* behind; see **apo-** in Appendix).] **—pre·pos′ter·ous·ly** *adv.* **—pre·pos′ter·ous·ness** *n.*

pre·po·ten·cy (prē-pōt′n-sē) *n.* **1.** The condition of being greater in power, influence, or force than another or others; predominance. **2.** *Genetics.* The ability of one parent, variety, or strain to transmit individual traits to an offspring, apparently to the exclusion of the other parent, variety, or strain.

pre·po·tent (prē-pōt′nt) *adj.* **1.** Greater in power, influence, or force than another or others; predominant. **2.** *Genetics.* Of, having, or exhibiting prepotency. [Middle English, from Latin *praepotēns, praepotent-,* present participle of *praeposse,* to be more powerful : *prae-,* pre- + *posse,* to be able or powerful; see **poti-** in Appendix.] **—pre·po′tent·ly** *adv.*

prep·py or **prep·pie** (prĕp′ē) *n., pl.* **-pies.** *Informal.* **1.** A student or former student of a preparatory school. **2.** A person whose manner and dress are deemed typical of traditional preparatory schools. **—prep′pi·ly** *adv.* **—prep′pi·ness** *n.* **—prep′py, prep′pie** *adj.*

pre·pran·di·al also **pre-pran·di·al** (prē-prăn′dē-əl) *adj.* Before a meal, especially dinner: *took a preprandial walk in the woods.*

pre·pri·mar·y (prē-prī′mĕr′ē, -mə-rē) *adj.* Relating to or taking place in the time before a primary election: *preprimary conventions; preprimary support.*

pre·print (prē′prĭnt′) *n.* Something printed and often distributed in partial or preliminary form in advance of official publication: *a preprint of a scientific article.* **—preprint** (prē-prĭnt′) *tr.v.* **-print·ed, -print·ing, -prints.** To print in advance.

pre·proc·ess (prē-prŏs′ĕs′, -prō′sĕs′) *tr.v.* **-essed, -ess·ing, -ess·es.** *Computer Science.* To perform conversion, formatting, or other functions on (data) before further processing. **—pre·proc′es·sor** *n.*

pre·pro·duc·tion (prē′prə-dŭk′shən) *adj.* **1.** Taking place or existing before production: *preproduction planning.* **2.** Of, relating to, or being a prototype: *preproduction models of next year's automobiles.* **—preproduction** *n.* The preliminary arrangements, as concerning financing or personnel, that are made upon the inception of a project: *a movie in preproduction.*

pre·pro·fes·sion·al (prē′prə-fĕsh′ə-nəl) *adj.* Preparatory to the practice of a profession or to its specialized field of study.

pre·pro·gram (prē-prō′grăm′, -grəm) *tr.v.* **-grammed, -gram·ming, -grams** or **-gramed, -gram·ing, -grams.** To program in advance; preset.

prep school *n. Informal.* A preparatory school.

pre·pu·ber·ty (prē-pyōō′bər-tē) *n.* The period of life immediately before puberty, often marked by accelerated physical growth. **—pre·pu′ber·tal, pre·pu′ber·al** (-bər-əl) *adj.*

pre·pu·bes·cence (prē′pyōō-bĕs′əns) *n.* Prepuberty.

pre·pu·bes·cent (prē′pyōō-bĕs′ənt) *adj.* Of, relating to, or characteristic of prepuberty. **—prepubescent** *n.* A prepubescent child.

pre·pub·li·ca·tion (prē-pŭb′lĭ-kā′shən) *adj.* Of or relating to the time just before a publication date, especially of a book: *The marketing department was amazed by the number of prepublication orders.*

pre·puce (prē′pyōōs′) *n.* **1.** See **foreskin. 2.** A loose fold of skin covering the glans clitoridis. [Middle English, from Old French, from Latin *praepūtium* : possibly *prae-,* pre- + **pūtos,* penis.] **—pre·pu′tial** (-pyōō′shəl) *adj.*

pre·punch (prē-pŭnch′) *tr.v.* **-punched, -punch·ing, -punch·es.** *Computer Science.* To punch computer data cards or tape before an anticipated use.

pre·pu·pa (prē-pyōō′pə) *n., pl* **-pae** (-pē) or **-pas. 1.** An inactive stage just before the pupa in the development of certain insects. **2.** The form of an insect in this stage. **—pre·pu′pal** *adj.*

pre·quel (prē′kwəl) *n.* **1.** A literary, cinematic, or dramatic work taking place in or concerned with a time before the action of a preexisting work: *a prequel that featured the characters of the famous novel in their youth.* **2.** A literary, cinematic, or dramatic work that precedes, introduces, or leads up to a later work: *"The sequel takes up right where the prequel left off"* (Washington Post). [PRE– + (SE)QUEL.]

Pre-Raph·a·el·ite also **pre-Raph·a·el·ite** (prē-răf′ē-ə-līt′, -rā′fē-) —*n.* A painter or writer belonging to or influenced by the Pre-Raphaelite Brotherhood, a society founded in England in 1848 to advance the style and spirit of Italian painting before Raphael. —*adj.* Of, relating to, or characteristic of the Pre-Raphaelites. **—Pre-Raph′a·el·it′ism** *n.*

pre·re·cord (prē′rĭ-kôrd′) *tr.v.* **-cord·ed, -cord·ing, -cords.** To record (a television program, for example) at an earlier time for later presentation or use.

pre·reg·is·ter (prē-rĕj′ĭ-stər) *intr.v.* **-tered, -ter·ing, -ters.** To take part in preregistration.

pre·reg·is·tra·tion (prē′rĕj-ĭ-strā′shən) *n.* An early registration, as for returning college students, that takes place before general registration.

pre·re·lease (prē′rĭ-lēs′) *n.* Something released before an official or scheduled date. **—prerelease** *adj.* Of or relating to an interval preceding an official or scheduled release: *a prerelease demonstration of a product; a prison prerelease program.*

pre·req·ui·site (prē-rĕk′wĭ-zĭt) *adj.* Required or necessary as a prior condition: *Competence is prerequisite to promotion.* **—prerequisite** *n.* Something that is prerequisite.

pre·re·tire·ment (prē′rĭ-tīr′mənt) *adj.* Of or relating to the period preceding retirement: *workers of preretirement age; preretirement planning.* **—pre′re·tire′ment** *n.*

pre·rog·a·tive (prĭ-rŏg′ə-tĭv) *n.* **1.** An exclusive right or privilege held by a person or group, especially a hereditary or official right. See Synonyms at **right. 2.** The exclusive right and power to command, decide, rule, or judge: *the principal's prerogative to suspend a student.* **3.** A natural gift or advantage that confers superiority. **4.** Characteristic superiority; preeminence. **—prerogative** *adj.* Of, arising from, or exercising a prerogative. [Middle English, from Old French, from Latin *praerogātīva,* feminine of *praerogātīvus,* asked first, from *praerogātus,* past participle of *praerogāre,* to ask before : *prae-,* pre- + *rogāre,* to ask; see **reg-** in Appendix.] **—pre·rog′a·tived** *adj.*

pres. *abbr.* **1.** *Grammar.* Present. **2.** Also **Pres.** President.

pres·age (prĕs′ĭj) *n.* **1.** An indication or a warning of a future occurrence; an omen. **2.** A feeling or an intuition of what is going to occur; a presentiment. **3.** Prophetic significance or meaning. **4.** *Archaic.* A prediction. **—presage** (prĭ-sāj′, prĕs′ĭj) *v.* **-saged, -sag·ing, -sag·es.** —*tr.* **1.** To indicate or warn of in advance; portend. **2.** To have a presentiment of. **3.** To foretell or predict. —*intr.* To make or utter a prediction. [Middle English, from Latin *praesāgium,* from *praesāgīre,* to perceive beforehand : *prae-,* pre- + *sāgīre,* to perceive; see **sāg-** in Appendix.] **—pre·sage′ful** (prĭ-sāj′fəl) *adj.*

pre·sale (prē′sāl′) *n.* **1.** The period before something, such as a work of art, is available for sale to the public. **2.** An exclusive or private sale held before an advertised sale. —*attributive.* Often used to modify another noun: *presale estimates; presale exhibitions.*

Presb. *abbr.* Presbyterian.

Presby. *abbr.* Presbyterian.

pres·by·ope (prĕz′bē-ōp′, prĕs′-) *n.* A person affected with presbyopia.

pres·by·o·pi·a (prĕz′bē-ō′pē-ə, prĕs′-) *n.* Inability of the eye to focus sharply on nearby objects, resulting from loss of elas-

Pre-Raphaelite
Saint Cecilia by
Sir Edward Burne-Jones

ă pat	oi boy
ā pay	ou out
âr care	ŏŏ took
ä father	ōō boot
ĕ pet	ŭ cut
ē be	ûr urge
ĭ pit	th thin
ī pie	*th* this
îr pier	hw which
ŏ pot	zh vision
ō toe	ə about, item
ô paw	♦ regionalism

Stress marks: **′** (primary); ′ (secondary), as in **dictionary** (dĭk′shə-nĕr′ē)

ticity of the crystalline lens with advancing age. [New Latin : Greek *presbus,* old man; see **per**[1] in Appendix + –OPIA.] **—pres′by·op′ic** (-ŏp′ĭk, -ō′pĭk) *adj.*

pres·by·ter (prĕz′bĭ-tər, prĕs′-) *n.* **1.** A priest in various hierarchical churches. **2.a.** A teaching elder in the Presbyterian Church. **b.** A ruling elder in the Presbyterian Church. **3.** An elder of the congregation in the early Christian church. [Late Latin, from Greek *presbuteros,* from comparative of *presbus,* old man. See **per**[1] in Appendix.]

pres·byt·er·ate (prĕz-bĭt′ər-ĭt, -ə-rāt′, prĕs-) *n.* **1.** The office of a presbyter. **2.** A body or an order of presbyters.

pres·by·te·ri·al (prĕz′bĭ-tîr′ē-əl, prĕs′-) *adj.* Of or relating to a presbyter or the presbytery. **—pres′by·te′ri·al·ly** *adv.*

pres·by·te·ri·an (prĕz′bĭ-tîr′ē-ən, prĕs′-) *adj.* **1.** Of or relating to ecclesiastical government by presbyters. **2. Presbyterian.** *Abbr.* **Presb., Presby.** Of or relating to a Presbyterian Church. **—Presbyterian** *n. Abbr.* **Presb., Presby.** A member or an adherent of a Presbyterian Church. **—pres′by·te′ri·an·ism** *n.*

Presbyterian Church *n.* Any of various Protestant churches governed by presbyters and traditionally Calvinist in doctrine.

pres·by·ter·y (prĕz′bĭ-tĕr′ē, prĕs′-) *n., pl.* **-ies. 1.a.** A court composed of Presbyterian Church ministers and representative elders of a particular locality. **b.** The district represented by this court. **2.** Presbyters considered as a group. **3.** Government of a church by presbyters. **4.** The section of a church reserved for the clergy. **5.** *Roman Catholic Church.* The residence of a priest. [Middle English *presbetory,* priests' bench, from Late Latin *presbyterium,* council of elders, from Greek *presbuterion,* from *presbuteros,* elder. See PRESBYTER.]

pre·school (prē′sko͞ol′) *adj.* Of, relating to, intended for, or being the early years of childhood that precede the beginning of elementary school. **—preschool** (prē′sko͞ol′) *n.* A school for children who are not old enough to attend kindergarten; a nursery school.

pre·school·er (prē′sko͞o′lər) *n.* **1.** A child who is not old enough to attend kindergarten. **2.** A child who is enrolled in a preschool.

pre·school·ing (prē′sko͞o′lĭng) *n.* Early childhood education, especially when received at a preschool.

pre·sci·ence (prē′shē-əns, -shəns, prĕsh′ē-əns, prĕsh′əns) *n.* Knowledge of actions or events before they occur; foresight.

pre·sci·ent (prē′shē-ənt, -shənt, prĕsh′ē-ənt, prĕsh′ənt) *adj.* **1.** Of or relating to prescience. **2.** Possessing prescience. [French *prescient,* from Old French, from Latin *praesciēns, praescient-,* present participle of *praescīre,* to know beforehand : *prae-,* pre- + *scīre,* to know; see **skei-** in Appendix.] **—pre′sci·ent·ly** *adv.*

pre·sci·en·tif·ic (prē-sī′ən-tĭf′ĭk) *adj.* Of, relating to, or occurring at a time before the advent of modern science and the application of its methods.

pre·scind (prĭ-sĭnd′) *v.* **-scind·ed, -scind·ing, -scinds.** *—tr.* To separate or divide in thought; consider individually. *—intr.* To withdraw one's attention. [Latin *praescindere,* to cut off in front : *prae-,* pre- + *scindere,* to cut off, split; see **skei-** in Appendix.]

Pres·cott (prĕs′kət, -kŏt′). A city of central Arizona north-northwest of Phoenix. It was territorial capital from 1864 to 1867 and from 1877 to 1889 and is now a trade center and health resort. Population, 20,055.

Prescott, Samuel. 1751–1777? American Revolutionary patriot who on April 18, 1775, joined Paul Revere and William Dawes on their ride to spread the news of the British advance on Concord, Massachusetts. Because Revere was captured and Dawes was forced to retreat, only Prescott was able to warn the militias of Lincoln and Concord.

Prescott, William. 1726–1795. American Revolutionary commander who led the defense of Breed's Hill during the Battle of Bunker Hill (June 17, 1775).

Prescott, William Hickling. 1796–1859. American historian noted for his lively studies of the conquistadors, including *History of the Conquest of Mexico* (1843).

pre·screen (prē-skrēn′) *tr.v.* **-screened, -screen·ing, -screens. 1.** To view (a movie) before release for public showing. **2.** To examine or interview before further selection processes occur: *prescreen applicants for interviews.*

pre·scribe (prĭ-skrīb′) *v.* **-scribed, -scrib·ing, -scribes.** *—tr.* **1.** To set down as a rule or guide; enjoin. See Synonyms at **dictate. 2.** To order the use of (a medicine or other treatment). *—intr.* **1.** To establish rules, laws, or directions. **2.** To order a medicine or other treatment. **3.** *Law.* **a.** To assert a right or title to something on the grounds of prescription. **b.** To become invalidated or unenforceable by the process of prescription. [Middle English *prescriben,* from Latin *praescrībere* : *prae-,* pre- + *scrībere,* to write; see **skrībh-** in Appendix.] **—pre·scrib′er** *n.*

pre·script (prē′skrĭpt′) *n.* Something prescribed, especially a rule or regulation of conduct. **—prescript** (prē′skrĭpt′, prĭ-skrĭpt′) *adj.* Having been established as a rule; prescribed. [From Middle English, prescribed, from Latin *praescrīptum,* neuter past participle of *praescrībere,* to order, prescribe. See PRESCRIBE.]

pre·scrip·ti·ble (prĭ-skrĭp′tə-bəl) *adj.* **1.** That can be prescribed: *prescriptible regulations.* **2.** Requiring or derived from prescription. **—pre·scrip′ti·bil′i·ty** *n.*

present arms

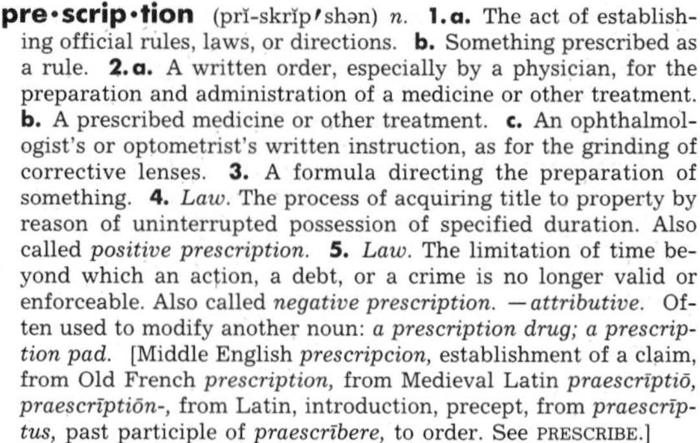

pre·scrip·tion (prĭ-skrĭp′shən) *n.* **1.a.** The act of establishing official rules, laws, or directions. **b.** Something prescribed as a rule. **2.a.** A written order, especially by a physician, for the preparation and administration of a medicine or other treatment. **b.** A prescribed medicine or other treatment. **c.** An ophthalmologist's or optometrist's written instruction, as for the grinding of corrective lenses. **3.** A formula directing the preparation of something. **4.** *Law.* The process of acquiring title to property by reason of uninterrupted possession of specified duration. Also called *positive prescription.* **5.** *Law.* The limitation of time beyond which an action, a debt, or a crime is no longer valid or enforceable. Also called *negative prescription. —attributive.* Often used to modify another noun: *a prescription drug; a prescription pad.* [Middle English *prescripcion,* establishment of a claim, from Old French *prescription,* from Medieval Latin *praescrīptiō, praescrīptiōn-,* from Latin, introduction, precept, from *praescrīptus,* past participle of *praescrībere,* to order. See PRESCRIBE.]

pre·scrip·tive (prĭ-skrĭp′tĭv) *adj.* **1.** Sanctioned or authorized by long-standing custom or usage. **2.** Making or giving injunctions, directions, laws, or rules. **3.** *Law.* Acquired by or based on uninterrupted possession. **—pre·scrip′tive·ly** *adv.* **—pre·scrip′tive·ness** *n.*

prescriptive grammar *n.* A grammar that attempts to establish norms or rules for correct usage and to characterize incorrect usage, as opposed to a grammar that simply describes how a language is used.

pre·scrip·tiv·ist (prĭ-skrĭp′tə-vĭst) *n.* One who supports or promotes prescriptive grammar.

pre·sea·son (prē′sē′zən) *n. Sports.* The period immediately before the start of a new season, in which athletes undergo intensive training and participate in exhibition games.

pre·se·lect (prē′sĭ-lĕkt′) *tr.v.* **-lect·ed, -lect·ing, -lects.** To select beforehand, usually according to a specific criterion. **—pre′se·lec′tion** *n.*

pre·sell (prē-sĕl′) *tr.v.* **-sold** (-sōld′), **-sell·ing, -sells. 1.** To sell (a house, for example) in advance of construction. **2.** To promote (a product not yet on the market) by means of advertising. **3.** To condition (a potential customer) in advance for later purchase of a product.

pres·ence (prĕz′əns) *n.* **1.** The state or fact of being present; current existence or occurrence. **2.** Immediate proximity in time or space. **3.** The area immediately surrounding a great personage, especially a sovereign. **4.** A person who is present. **5.a.** A person's bearing, especially when it commands respectful attention: *"He continues to possess the presence, mental as well as physical, of the young man"* (Brendan Gill). See Synonyms at **bearing. b.** The quality of self-assurance and effectiveness that permits a performer to achieve a rapport with the audience: *stage presence.* **6.** A supernatural influence felt to be nearby. **7.** The diplomatic, political, or military influence of a nation in a foreign country, especially as evidenced by the posting of its diplomats or its troops there: *"The American diplomatic presence in London began in 1785 when John Adams became our first minister"* (Nancy Holmes).

presence of mind *n.* The ability to think and act calmly and efficiently, especially in an emergency.

pres·ent[1] (prĕz′ənt) *n.* **1.** A moment or period in time perceptible as intermediate between past and future; now. **2.** *Abbr.* **pres., pr.** *Grammar.* **a.** The present tense. **b.** A verb form in the present tense. **3. presents.** *Law.* The document or instrument in question: *Be it known by these presents.* **—present** *adj.* **1.** Existing or happening now; current: *the present leader; present trends.* **2.a.** Being at hand or in attendance: *Thirty guests were present at the ceremony.* **b.** Existing in something specified: *Oxygen is present in the bloodstream.* **3.** Now being considered; actually here or involved: *the present subject; present company excepted.* **4.** *Abbr.* **pres., pr.** *Grammar.* Designating a verb tense or form that expresses current time. **5.** *Archaic.* Readily available; immediate. **6.** *Obsolete.* Alert to circumstances; attentive. *—idioms.* **at present.** At the present time; right now. **for the present.** For the time being; temporarily. [Middle English, from Old French, from Latin *praesēns, praesent-,* present participle of *praeesse,* to be present : *prae-,* pre- + *esse,* to be; see **es-** in Appendix.] **—pres′ent·ness** *n.*

pre·sent[2] (prĭ-zĕnt′) *tr.v.* **-sent·ed, -sent·ing, -sents. 1.a.** To introduce, especially with formal ceremony. **b.** To introduce (a young woman) to society with conventional ceremony. **2.** To bring before the public: *present a play.* **3.a.** To make a gift or an award of. **b.** To make a gift to. **4.** To offer for observation, examination, or consideration; show or display. See Synonyms at **offer. 5.** To salute with (a weapon, such as a rifle or saber). **6.** *Ecclesiastical.* To recommend (a cleric) for a benefice. **7.** *Law.* **a.** To offer to a legislature or court for consideration. **b.** To bring a charge or an indictment against. **—pres·ent** (prĕz′ənt) *n.* Something presented; a gift. [Middle English *presenten,* from Old French *presenter,* from Latin *praesentāre,* to show, from *praesēns, praesent-,* present participle of *praeesse,* to be in front of. See PRESENT[1].] **—pre·sent′er** *n.*

pre·sent·a·ble (prĭ-zĕn′tə-bəl) *adj.* **1.** That can be given, displayed, or offered: *presentable gifts; presentable attire.* **2.** Fit for introduction to others: *presentable relatives.* **—pre·sent′a·bil′i·ty, pre·sent′a·ble·ness** *n.* **—pre·sent′a·bly** *adv.*

pre·sent arms (prĭ-zĕnt′) *n.* **1.** A position in the military manual of arms in which the rifle is held vertically in front of the body. **2.** A command to assume present arms or to give a hand salute.

pres·en·ta·tion (prĕz′ən-tā′shən, prē′zən-) *n.* **1.a.** The act of presenting. **b.** The state of being presented. **2.** A performance, as of a drama. **3.a.** Something, such as an award or a gift, that is offered or given. **b.** Something, such as a lecture or speech, that is set forth for an audience: *gave a presentation on drug abuse.* **4.a.** A formal introduction. **b.** A social debut. **5.** *Ecclesiastical.* The act or right of naming a cleric to a benefice. **6.** The process of offering for consideration or display. **7.** *Medicine.* The position of the fetus in the uterus at birth with respect to the mouth of the uterus. **—pres′en·ta′tion·al** *adj.*

pre·sent·a·tive (prĭ-zĕn′tə-tĭv) *adj.* **1.** Having the capacity or function of bringing an idea or image to mind. **2.a.** Perceived or capable of being perceived directly rather than through association. **b.** Having the ability to so perceive. **3.** *Ecclesiastical.* Capable of naming or of being named to a benefice. **—pre·sent′a·tive·ness** *n.*

pres·ent-day (prĕz′ənt-dā′) *adj.* Now in existence or progress; current: *present-day attitudes about the family.*

pres·ent·ee (prĕz′ən-tē′, prĭ-zĕn′-) *n.* **1.** One who is presented. **2.** One to whom something is given.

pre·sen·tient (prē-sĕn′shənt, -shē-ənt) *adj.* Having a presentiment. [Latin *praesentiēns, praesentient-*, present participle of *praesentīre,* to feel beforehand. See PRESENTIMENT.]

pre·sen·ti·ment (prĭ-zĕn′tə-mənt) *n.* A sense that something is about to occur; a premonition. See Synonyms at **apprehension.** [Obsolete French, from *presentir,* to feel beforehand, from Latin *praesentīre* : *prae-,* pre- + *sentīre,* to feel; see **sent-** in Appendix.] **—pre·sen′ti·men′tal** (-mĕn′tl) *adj.*

pres·ent·ly (prĕz′ənt-lē) *adv.* **1.** In a short time; soon: *She will arrive presently.* **2.** *Usage Problem.* At this time or period; now: *He is presently staying with us.* **3.** *Archaic.* At once; immediately.

USAGE NOTE: An original meaning of *presently* was "at the present time; currently." That sense is said to have disappeared from the literary language in the 17th century, but it has survived in popular usage and is widely found nowadays in literate speech and writing. Still, there is a lingering prejudice against this use. In the most recent survey the sentence *General Walters is . . . presently the United States Ambassador to the United Nations* was acceptable to exactly 50 percent of the Usage Panel.

pre·sent·ment (prĭ-zĕnt′mənt) *n.* **1.a.** The act of presenting to view or to the mind. **b.** Something expressed, presented, or exhibited. **c.** The light in which something is presented. **2.** *Law.* **a.** The act of submitting or presenting a formal statement of a legal matter to a court or an authorized person. **b.** The report written by a grand jury concerning an offense and based on the jury's own knowledge and observation. **3.** The act of presenting a bill or note for payment.

pres·ent participle (prĕz′ənt) *n.* *Grammar.* A participle expressing present action, formed in English by the infinitive plus *-ing* and used to express present action in relation to the time indicated by the finite verb in its clause, to form progressive tenses with the auxiliary *be,* and to function as a verbal adjective.

pres·ent per·fect (prĕz′ənt pûr′fĭkt) *n.* *Grammar.* **1.** The verb tense expressing action completed at the present time, formed in English by combining the present tense of *have* with a past participle, as in *He has spoken.* **2.** A verb in the present perfect tense.

pres·ent tense (prĕz′ənt) *n.* *Grammar.* The verb tense expressing action in the present time, as in *She writes; she is writing.*

pres·er·va·tion·ist (prĕz′ər-vā′shə-nĭst) *n.* One who advocates preservation, especially of natural areas, historical sites, or endangered species. **—pres′er·va′tion·ism** *n.*

pre·ser·va·tive (prĭ-zûr′və-tĭv) *adj.* Tending to preserve or capable of preserving. **—preservative** *n.* Something used to preserve, especially a chemical added to foods to inhibit spoilage.

pre·serve (prĭ-zûrv′) *v.* **-served, -serv·ing, -serves.** *—tr.* **1.** To maintain in safety from injury, peril, or harm; protect. **2.** To keep in perfect or unaltered condition; maintain unchanged. **3.** To keep or maintain intact: *tried to preserve family harmony.* See Synonyms at **defend.** **4.** To prepare (food) for future use, as by canning or salting. **5.** To prevent (organic bodies) from decaying or spoiling. **6.** To keep or protect (game or fish) for one's private hunting or fishing. *—intr.* **1.** To treat fruit or other foods so as to prevent decay. **2.** To maintain a private area stocked with game or fish. **—preserve** *n.* **1.** Something that acts to preserve; a preservative. **2.** Often **preserves.** Fruit cooked with sugar to protect against decay or fermentation. **3.** An area maintained for the protection of wildlife or natural resources. **4.** Something considered as being the exclusive province of certain persons: *Ancient Greek is the preserve of scholars.* [Middle English *preserven,* from Old French *preserver,* from Medieval Latin *praeservāre,* from Late Latin, to observe beforehand : Latin *prae-,* pre- + Latin *servāre,* to guard, preserve; see **ser-[1]** in Appendix.] **—pre·serv′a·bil′i·ty** *n.* **—pre·serv′a·ble** *adj.* **—pres′er·va′tion** (prĕz′ər-vā′shən) *n.* **—pre·serv′er** *n.*

pre·set (prē-sĕt′) *tr.v.* **-set, -set·ting, -sets.** To set (an automatic control, for example) beforehand: *preset a microwave oven.* **—pre·set′ta·ble** *adj.*

pre·shrunk also **pre-shrunk** (prē′shrŭngk′) *adj.* Of, relating to, or being fabric or a garment that has undergone shrinking during manufacture to minimize subsequent shrinkage: *preshrunk jeans.*

pre·side (prĭ-zīd′) *intr.v.* **-sid·ed, -sid·ing, -sides.** **1.** To hold the position of authority; act as chairperson or president. **2.** To possess or exercise authority or control. **3.** *Music.* To be the featured instrumental performer: *presided at the keyboard.* [French *présider,* from Old French, from Latin *praesidēre* : *prae-,* pre- + *sedēre,* to sit; see **sed-** in Appendix.] **—pre·sid′er** *n.*

pres·i·den·cy (prĕz′ĭ-dən-sē, -dĕn′-) *n., pl.* **-cies.** **1.** The office, function, or term of a president. **2.a.** Often **Presidency.** The office of president of a republic. **b. Presidency.** The office of the President of the United States. **3.** *Mormon Church.* **a.** A governing body on a local level consisting of three men. **b.** Often **Presidency.** The chief administrative body of the church.

pres·i·dent (prĕz′ĭ-dənt, -dĕnt′) *n.* *Abbr.* **pres., Pres., p., P.** **1.** One appointed or elected to preside over an organized body of people, such as an assembly or a meeting. **2.a.** Often **President.** The chief executive of a republic. **b. President.** The chief executive of the United States, serving as both chief of state and chief political executive. **3.** The chief officer of a branch of government, a corporation, a board of trustees, a university, or a similar body. [Middle English, from Old French, from Latin *praesidēns, praesident-,* from present participle of *praesidēre,* to preside. See PRESIDE.] **—pres′i·dent·ship′** *n.*

pres·i·dent-e·lect (prĕz′ĭ-dənt-ĭ-lĕkt′) *n., pl.* **pres·i·dents-e·lect** (prĕz′ĭ-dənts-). A person who has been elected president but has not yet been inducted into office.

pres·i·den·tial (prĕz′ĭ-dĕn′shəl) *adj.* **1.a.** Of or relating to a president or presidency. **b.** Befitting a president, especially the office of the President of the United States: *criticized the candidate for not looking presidential.* **2.** Of or relating to a political system in which the chief officer is a president who is elected independently of the legislature for a fixed term: *a presidential government.* **—pres′i·den′tial·ly** *adv.*

president pro tem (prō tĕm′) *n., pl.* **presidents pro tem.** *Informal.* A president pro tempore.

president pro tem·po·re (prō tĕm′pə-rē) *n., pl.* **presidents pro tempore.** The senator who presides over the U.S. Senate in the absence of the Vice President.

Pres·i·dents' Day (prĕz′ĭ-dənts, -dĕnts) *n.* The third Monday in February, observed in the United States as a legal holiday in commemoration of the birthdays of George Washington and Abraham Lincoln.

pre·sid·i·a (prĭ-sĭd′ē-ə) *n.* A plural of **presidium.**

pre·sid·i·al (prĭ-sĭd′ē-əl) also **pre·sid·i·ar·y** (-ĕr′ē) *adj.* Of, relating to, possessing, or being a garrison.

pre·si·di·o (prĭ-sē′dē-ō′, -sĭd′ē-ō′) *n., pl.* **-os.** A garrison, especially a fortress of the kind established in the southwest United States by the Spanish to protect their holdings and missions. [Spanish, from Latin *praesidium,* guard, defense, from *praesidēre,* to guard. See PRESIDE.]

pre·sid·i·um (prĭ-sĭd′ē-əm) *n., pl.* **-i·a** (-ē-ə) or **-i·ums.** **1.** Any of various permanent executive committees in Communist countries having power to act for a larger governing body. **2. Presidium.** An executive committee of the Supreme Soviet headed by the president. [Russian *prezidium,* from Latin *praesidium,* garrison. See PRESIDIO.]

pre·sig·ni·fy (prē-sĭg′nə-fī′) *tr.v.* **-fied, -fy·ing, -fies.** To indicate or signify beforehand; foreshadow.

Pres·ley (prĕs′lē, prĕz′-), **Elvis Aron.** Known as "the King." 1935–1977. American singer whose numerous hit records, such as "Heartbreak Hotel," "Hound Dog," and "Don't Be Cruel," and charismatic manner greatly influenced American popular culture.

Elvis Presley

pre·soak (prē-sōk′) *tr.v.* **-soaked, -soak·ing, -soaks.** To soak (laundry) before washing. **—presoak** (prē′sōk′) *n.* **1.** The act or an instance of presoaking. **2.** A liquid preparation in which laundry is presoaked. **3.** A cycle on an automatic washing machine for presoaking laundry.

pre-So·crat·ic (prē′sō-krăt′ĭk, -sə-) *adj.* Of or relating to the Greek philosophers or philosophical systems of thought before Socrates. **—pre-Socratic** *n.* A pre-Socratic philosopher.

pre·sold (prē-sōld′) *v.* Past tense and past participle of **presell.**

pre·sort (prē-sôrt′) *tr.v.* **-sort·ed, -sort·ing, -sorts.** To sort (mail) according to ZIP codes before delivering to a post office.

♦ **press[1]** (prĕs) *v.* **pressed, press·ing, press·es.** *—tr.* **1.** To exert steady weight or force against; bear down on. **2.a.** To squeeze the juice or other contents from. **b.** To extract (juice, for example) by squeezing or compressing. **3.a.** To reshape or make compact by applying steady force; compress. **b.** To iron (clothing, for example). **4.** To clasp in fondness or politeness. **5.** To try to influence, as by insistent arguments; importune or entreat. **6.** To urge or force to action; impel. **7.** To place in trying or distressing circumstances; harass or oppress. See Synonyms at **urge.** **8.** To move (keys on a computer keyboard, for example) by applying pressure. **9.** To lay stress on; emphasize. **10.** To advance or carry on vigorously: *"Far from backing down, he pressed the attack"* (Justin Kaplan). **11.** To put forward importunately or insistently. **12.** To make (a phonograph record or videodisk) from a mold or matrix. **13.** *Sports.* To lift (a weight) to a position above the head without moving the legs. *—intr.* **1.** To exert force or pressure. **2.**

ă pat	oi boy
ā pay	ou out
âr care	o͝o took
ä father	o͞o boot
ĕ pet	ŭ cut
ē be	ûr urge
ĭ pit	th thin
ī pie	*th* this
îr pier	hw which
ŏ pot	zh vision
ō toe	ə about, item
ô paw	♦ regionalism

Stress marks: ′ (primary); ′ (secondary), as in **dictionary** (dĭk′shə-nĕr′ē)

To weigh heavily, as on the mind. **3.** To advance eagerly; push forward. **4.** To require haste; be urgent. **5.** To iron clothes or other material. **6.** To assemble closely and in large numbers; crowd. **7.** To employ urgent persuasion or entreaty. **8.** *Sports.* To raise or lift a weight in a press. **9.** *Basketball.* To employ a press. **—press** *n.* **1.** Any of various machines or devices that apply pressure. **2.** Any of various machines used for printing; a printing press. **3.** A place or an establishment where matter is printed. **4.** The art, method, or business of printing. **5.a.** The collecting and publishing or broadcasting of news; journalism in general. **b.** The entirety of media and agencies that collect, publish, transmit, or broadcast the news. **c.** The people involved in the media, as news reporters, photographers, publishers, and broadcasters. **d.** Commentary or coverage especially in newspapers or periodicals: *"Like the pool hall and the tattoo parlor, the motorcycle usually gets a bad press"* (R.Z. Sheppard). **6.** The act of gathering in large numbers or of pushing forward. **7.** A large gathering; a throng. See Synonyms at **crowd¹**. **8.a.** The act of applying pressure. **b.** The state of being pressed. **9.** The haste or urgency of business or matters. **10.** The set of proper creases in a garment or fabric, formed by ironing. **11.** *Chiefly Northeastern U.S.* An upright closet or case used for storing clothing, books, or other articles. **12.** A viselike device for keeping a racket from warping. **13.** *Sports.* A lift in weightlifting in which the weight is raised to shoulder level and then steadily pushed straight overhead without movement of the legs. **14.** *Basketball.* An aggressive defense tactic in which players guard opponents closely, often over the entire court. ***—idiom.* press the flesh.** *Informal.* To shake hands and mingle with many people, especially while campaigning for public office. [Middle English *pressen,* from Old French *presser,* from Latin *pressāre,* frequentative of *premere,* to press. See **per-⁴** in Appendix.]

press² (prĕs) *tr.v.* **pressed, press•ing, press•es. 1.** To force into service in the army or navy; impress. **2.a.** To take arbitrarily or by force, especially for public use. **b.** To use in a manner different from the usual or intended, especially in an emergency. **—press** *n.* **1.** Conscription or impressment into service, especially into the army or navy. **2.** *Obsolete.* An official warrant for impressing men into military service. [Alteration of obsolete *prest,* to hire for military service by advance payment, from Middle English, enlistment money, loan, from Old French, from *prester,* to lend, from Medieval Latin *praestāre,* from Latin, to furnish, from *praestō,* present, at hand.]

press agency *n.* See **news agency.**

press agent *n. Abbr.* **PA, P.A.** A person employed to arrange advertising and publicity, as for a performer or for a business. **—press agentry** *n.*

press association *n.* See **news agency.**

press•board (prĕs′bôrd′, -bōrd′) *n.* **1.** A heavy glazed paper or pasteboard used especially to cover the platen or cylinder of a printing press. **2.** A small ironing board.

press box *n.* A section for reporters, as in a stadium.

press conference *n.* An interview held for news reporters by a political figure or a famous person. Also called *news conference.*

press•er (prĕs′ər) *n.* **1.** One who presses clothes. **2.** Any of various devices that apply pressure to a product in manufacturing or canning.

press gang also **press•gang** (prĕs′găng′) *n.* A company of men under an officer detailed to force men into military or naval service.

press-gang (prĕs′găng′) *tr.v.* **-ganged, -gang•ing, -gangs. 1.** To force into military or naval service. **2.** To force or coerce: *"press-ganging a consumer into buying something he doesn't want"* (Feona McEwan).

press•ing (prĕs′ĭng) *adj.* **1.** Demanding immediate attention; urgent: *a pressing need.* See Synonyms at **urgent. 2.** Very earnest or persistent; insistent: *a pressing invitation.* **—pressing** *n.* **1.** The process or an instance of applying pressure by means of a press. **2.a.** A phonograph record pressed from a master mold or matrix. **b.** A number of recordings pressed at the same time. **3.** Urgent solicitation; insistence. **—press′ing•ly** *adv.*

press kit *n.* A packaged set of promotional materials, such as photographs and background information, for distribution to the press, as before the release of a new product.

press•man (prĕs′mən, -măn′) *n.* **1.** A man who operates a printing press. **2.** *Chiefly British.* A newspaper reporter.

press•mark (prĕs′märk′) *n.* **1.** *Printing.* A notation or figure in the margin of a printed sheet indicating the press on which it was printed. **2.** *Chiefly British.* A notation in or on a book indicating where it should be placed in a library.

press of sail *n. Nautical.* The greatest amount of sail that a ship can carry safely. Also called *press of canvas.*

pres•sor (prĕs′ôr′, -ər) *adj.* Causing an increase in blood pressure. [Late Latin, one who presses, from Latin *premere, press-,* to press. See PRESS¹.]

press release *n.* An announcement of an event, a performance, or other newsworthy item that is issued to the press.

press•room (prĕs′ro͞om′, -ro͝om′) *n.* The room in a printing or newspaper publishing establishment that contains the presses.

press run or **press•run** (prĕs′rŭn′) *n.* **1.** Continuous operation of a printing press for a specific job. **2.** The number of copies printed in one such continuous operation.

press secretary *n.* One who officially manages the public affairs and press conferences of a public figure.

pres•sure (prĕsh′ər) *n.* **1.a.** The act of pressing. **b.** The condition of being pressed. **2.** The application of continuous force by one body on another that it is touching; compression. **3.** *Abbr.* **P.** *Physics.* Force applied uniformly over a surface, measured as force per unit of area. **4.** *Meteorology.* Atmospheric pressure. **5.** A compelling or constraining influence, such as a moral force, on the mind or will: *pressure to conform; peer-group pressure.* **6.** Urgent claim or demand: *under the pressure of business; doesn't work well under pressure.* **7.** An oppressive condition of physical, mental, social, or economic distress. **8.** A physical sensation produced by compression of a part of the body. **9.** *Archaic.* A mark made by application of force or weight; an impression. **—pressure** *tr.v.* **-sured, -sur•ing, -sures. 1.** To force, as by overpowering influence or persuasion. **2.** To pressurize. **3.** To pressure-cook. [Middle English, from Old French, from Latin *pressūra,* from *pressus,* past participle of *premere,* to press. See **per-⁴** in Appendix.]

pressure cabin *n.* A pressurized section of an aircraft.

pres•sure-cook (prĕsh′ər-ko͝ok′) *tr.v.* **-cooked, -cook•ing, -cooks.** To cook in a pressure cooker.

pressure cooker *n.* **1.** An airtight metal pot that uses steam under pressure at high temperature to cook food quickly. **2.** *Informal.* A situation or an atmosphere of difficulty, stress, or anxiety: *"placing children into social, educational pressure cookers"* (Fred M. Hechinger).

pressure gauge *n.* **1.** A device for measuring the pressure of a gas or liquid. **2.** A device for measuring the pressure of explosions.

pressure group *n.* An interest group that endeavors to influence public policy and especially governmental legislation, regarding its particular concerns and priorities.

pressure point *n.* **1.** Any of several points on the body at which an underlying artery can be pressed against a bone to stop distal bleeding. **2.** An area on the skin that is highly sensitive to the application of pressure.

pressure suit *n.* A garment that is worn in high-altitude aircraft or in spacecraft to compensate for low-pressure conditions.

pres•sur•ize (prĕsh′ə-rīz′) *tr.v.* **-ized, -iz•ing, -iz•es. 1.** To maintain normal air pressure in (an enclosure, as an aircraft or a submarine). **2.** To put (gas or liquid) under a greater than normal pressure. **3.** To design to resist pressure. **4.** To pressure-cook. **5.** *Informal.* To subject to excessive stress, strain, or vexation: *an executive who was pressurized by a heavy workload.* **—pres′sur•i•za′tion** (-ər-ĭ-zā′shən) *n.* **—pres′sur•iz′er** *n.*

press•work (prĕs′wûrk′) *n.* **1.** Management or operation of a printing press. **2.** The matter printed by such a press.

Pres•ter John (prĕs′tər jŏn′) *n.* A legendary medieval Christian priest and king thought to have reigned over a Christian kingdom in the Far East or Ethiopia. [Middle English *prestre,* priest, from Old French, from Late Latin *presbyter.* See PRESBYTER.]

pre•ster•num (prē-stûr′nəm) *n.* See **manubrium** (sense 1).

pres•ti•dig•i•ta•tion (prĕs′tĭ-dĭj′ĭ-tā′shən) *n.* Manual skill and dexterity in the execution of tricks; sleight of hand. [French (influenced by *prestigiateur,* juggler, conjurer, from *prestige,* illusion; see PRESTIGE), from *prestidigitateur,* conjurer : *preste,* nimble (from Italian *presto;* see PRESTO) + Latin *digitus,* finger; see DIGIT.] **—pres′ti•dig′i•ta′tor** *n.*

pres•tige (prĕ-stēzh′, -stēj′) *n.* **1.** The level of respect at which one is regarded by others; standing. **2.** A person's high standing among others; honor or esteem. **3.** Widely recognized prominence, distinction, or importance: *a position of prestige in diplomatic circles.* —*attributive.* Often used to modify another noun: *a prestige address; the prestige groups in society.* [French, illusion, from Latin *praestīgiae,* tricks, probably alteration of **praestrīgiae,* from *praestringere,* to touch, blunt, blind : *prae-,* pre- + *stringere,* to draw tight; see **streig-** in Appendix.]

pres•ti•gious (prĕ-stē′jəs, -stĭj′əs) *adj.* Having prestige; esteemed. **—pres•ti′gious•ly** *adv.* **—pres•ti′gious•ness** *n.*

pres•tis•si•mo (prĕ-stĭs′ə-mō′) *Music. adv. & adj.* In as fast a tempo as possible. Used chiefly as a direction. **—prestissimo** *n., pl.* **-mos.** A prestissimo passage or movement. [Italian, superlative of *presto,* presto. See PRESTO.]

pres•to (prĕs′tō) *adv.* **1.** *Music.* In a very fast tempo, usually considered to be faster than allegro but slower than prestissimo. Used chiefly as a direction. **2.** So suddenly that magic seems involved; right away. **—presto** *n., pl.* **-tos.** *Music.* A passage or movement that is performed presto. [Italian, from Late Latin *praestus,* quick, from Latin *praestō,* at hand.] **—pres′to** *adj.*

Pres•ton (prĕs′tən). A borough of northwest England north-northeast of Liverpool. The Jacobites surrendered here after an uprising in 1715. Population, 125,800.

pre•sum•a•ble (prĭ-zo͞o′mə-bəl) *adj.* That can be presumed or taken for granted; reasonable as a supposition: *presumable causes of the disaster.* **—pre•sum′a•bly** *adv.*

pre•sume (prĭ-zo͞om′) *v.* **-sumed, -sum•ing, -sumes.** —*tr.* **1.** To take for granted as being true in the absence of proof to the contrary. **2.** To give reasonable evidence for assuming; appear to prove. **3.** To venture without authority or permission; dare: *He presumed to invite himself to dinner.* —*intr.* **1.** To act overconfidently; take liberties. **2.** To take unwarranted advantage of something; go beyond the proper limits: *Don't presume on their hospitality.* **3.** To take for granted that something is true or factual; suppose: *That's the new assistant, I presume.* [Middle English *presumen,* from Old French *presumer,* from Late Latin *praesūmere,* from Latin, to anticipate : *prae-,* pre- + *sūmere,* to take; see **em-** in Appendix.] **—pre·sum′ed·ly** (-zo͞o′mĭd-lē) *adv.* **—pre·sum′er** *n.*

SYNONYMS: *presume, presuppose, postulate, posit, assume.* These verbs signify to take something for granted or as being a fact. To *presume* is to suppose that something is reasonable, justifiable, sound, or possible in the absence of proof to the contrary: *"I presume you're tired after the long ride"* (Edith Wharton). *We cannot presume the existence of life on other planets. Presuppose* can mean merely to believe or suppose in advance; it can also mean to require as an antecedent condition: *It is unrealistic to presuppose a sophisticated knowledge of harmony and counterpoint in a beginning music student. The evolution of species presupposes a process of natural selection. Postulate* and *posit* denote the assertion of the existence, reality, necessity, or truth of something, as something considered to be self-evident or axiomatic, as the basis for reasoning or argument: *"We can see individuals, but we can't see providence; we have to postulate it"* (Aldous Huxley). *Historical linguists posit a common ancestor from which both Romance and Germanic languages descend.* To *assume* is to accept something as existing or being true without proof or on inconclusive grounds: *Why do you assume that I'm angry? "We must never assume that which is incapable of proof"* (G.H. Lewes).

pre·sum·ing (prĭ-zo͞o′mĭng) *adj.* Having or showing excessive and arrogant self-confidence; presumptuous. **—pre·sum′ing·ly** *adv.*

pre·sump·tion (prĭ-zŭmp′shən) *n.* **1.** Behavior or language that is boldly arrogant or offensive; effrontery. **2.** The act of presuming or accepting as true. **3.** Acceptance or belief based on reasonable evidence; assumption or supposition. **4.** A condition or basis for accepting or presuming. **5.** *Law.* A conclusion derived from a particular set of facts based on law, rather than probable reasoning. [Middle English *presumpcion,* from Old French, from Late Latin *praesūmptiō, praesūmptiōn-,* from Latin, anticipation, from *praesūmptus,* past participle of *praesūmere,* to anticipate. See PRESUME.]

pre·sump·tive (prĭ-zŭmp′tĭv) *adj.* **1.** Providing a reasonable basis for belief or acceptance. **2.** Founded on probability or presumption. **—pre·sump′tive·ly** *adv.*

pre·sump·tu·ous (prĭ-zŭmp′cho͞o-əs) *adj.* Going beyond what is right or proper; excessively forward. [Middle English, from Old French *presumptueux,* from Late Latin *presūmptuōsus,* variant of *praesūmptiōsus,* from *praesūmptiō,* presumption. See PRESUMPTION.] **—pre·sump′tu·ous·ly** *adv.* **—pre·sump′tu·ous·ness** *n.*

pre·sup·pose (prē′sə-pōz′) *tr.v.* **-posed, -pos·ing, -pos·es. 1.** To believe or suppose in advance. **2.** To require or involve necessarily as an antecedent condition. See Synonyms at **presume. —pre·sup′po·si′tion** (-sŭp′ə-zĭsh′ən) *n.* **—pre·sup′po·si′tion·al** *adj.*

pre·syn·ap·tic (prē′sĭ-năp′tĭk) *adj.* Situated in front of or occurring before a synapse: *a presynaptic nerve fiber; a presynaptic stimulus.*

pret. *abbr. Grammar.* Preterit.

prêt-à-por·ter (prĕt′ä-pôr-tā′, -pōr-) *n.* Ready-to-wear clothing. [French : *prêt,* ready + *à,* to + *porter,* to wear.]

pre·tax (prē′tăks′) *adj.* Existing before tax deductions: *pretax income.*

pre·teen (prē′tēn′) *adj.* **1.** Relating to or designed for children especially between the ages of 9 and 12: *preteen clothing.* **2.** Being a child especially between the ages of 9 and 12; preadolescent. **—preteen** *n.* A preadolescent boy or girl. Also called *subteen.*

pre·teen·ag·er (prē′tēn′ā′jər) *n.* A preteen.

pre·tence (prē′tĕns′, prĭ-tĕns′) *n. Chiefly British.* Variant of **pretense.**

pre·tend (prĭ-tĕnd′) *v.* **-tend·ed, -tend·ing, -tends.** *—tr.* **1.** To give a false appearance of; feign: *"You had to pretend conformity while privately pursuing high and dangerous nonconformism"* (Anthony Burgess). **2.** To claim or allege insincerely or falsely; profess: *doesn't pretend to be an expert.* **3.** To represent fictitiously in play; make believe: *pretended they were on a cruise.* **4.** To take upon oneself; venture: *I cannot pretend to say that you are wrong.* *—intr.* **1.** To feign an action or a character, as in play. **2.** To put forward a claim. **3.** To make pretensions: *pretends to gourmet tastes.* **—pretend** *adj. Informal.* Imitation; make-believe: *pretend money; pretend pearls.* [Middle English *pretenden,* from Old French *pretendre,* from Latin *praetendere* : *prae-,* pre- + *tendere,* to extend; see **ten-** in Appendix.]

SYNONYMS: *pretend, assume, affect, simulate, feign, fake, counterfeit.* These verbs all mean to take on a false or misleading appearance. *Pretend* often suggests a vain or transparent attempt to fool or deceive: *"My bedmate pretended to be asleep"* (George W. Cable). *Assume* may—but does not necessarily—connote dishonesty, insincerity, or trickery: *"Assume a virtue, if you have it not"* (Shakespeare). *I assumed an air of confidence that I was far from feeling. Affect* suggests an effort to give the appearance of something either out of personal preference or to make an impression: *"He affects the disdainful petulance of a rock star"* (Annalyn Swan). *Simulate* emphasizes the assumption of an appearance or a form that closely resembles reality: *"A . . . verdant scum upon the surface of deep pools simulated the turf that had been removed"* (John Lothrop Motley). The remaining terms—*feign, fake,* and *counterfeit*—all imply at least a measure of deliberate sham. *Feign* suggests false representation or fictitious fabrication: *The child feigned a look of innocence when his mother asked who had eaten the cake. Fake* implies fraudulent simulation: *He faked an interest in my work. Counterfeit* denotes a close imitation that can often pass for an original: *"Full well they laughed with counterfeited glee"* (Oliver Goldsmith).

pre·tend·ed (prĭ-tĕn′dĭd) *adj.* **1.** Not genuine or sincere; feigned: *a pretended interest in the proceedings.* **2.** Supposed; alleged: *the pretended heir to the throne.* **—pre·tend′ed·ly** *adv.*

pre·tend·er (prĭ-tĕn′dər) *n.* **1.** One who simulates, pretends, or alleges falsely; a hypocrite or dissembler. **2.** One who sets forth a claim, especially a claimant to a throne.

pre·tense (prē′tĕns′, prĭ-tĕns′) *n.* **1.** The act of pretending; a false appearance or action intended to deceive. **2.** A false or studied show; an affectation: *a pretense of nonchalance.* **3.** A professed but feigned reason or excuse; a pretext: *under false pretenses.* **4.** Something imagined or pretended. **5.** Mere show without reality; outward appearance. **6.** A right asserted with or without foundation; a claim. See Synonyms at **claim. 7.** The quality or state of being pretentious; ostentation. [Middle English, from Old French *pretensse,* from Medieval Latin **praetēnsa,* from Late Latin, feminine of *praetēnsus,* alteration of Latin *praetentus,* past participle of *praetendere,* to pretend, assert. See PRETEND.]

pre·ten·sion (prĭ-tĕn′shən) *n.* **1.** A specious allegation; a pretext. **2.** A claim to something, such as a privilege or right. See Synonyms at **claim. 3.** The advancing of a claim. **4.** Ostentatious display; pretentiousness.

pre·ten·tious (prĭ-tĕn′shəs) *adj.* **1.** Claiming or demanding a position of distinction or merit, especially when unjustified. **2.** Making or marked by an extravagant outward show; ostentatious. See Synonyms at **showy. —pre·ten′tious·ly** *adv.* **—pre·ten′tious·ness** *n.*

pret·er·it or **pret·er·ite** (prĕt′ər-ĭt) *Grammar.* *—adj. Abbr.* **pret., pt.** Of, relating to, or being the verb tense that describes a past action or state. *—n. Abbr.* **pret., pt. 1.** The verb form expressing or describing a past action or condition. **2.** A verb in the preterit form. [Middle English, from Old French, from Latin *(tempus) praeteritum,* past (tense), neuter past participle of *praeterīre,* to go by : *praeter,* beyond, comparative of *prae,* before; see **per**[1] in Appendix + *īre,* to go; see **ei-** in Appendix.]

pret·er·i·tion (prĕt′ə-rĭsh′ən) *n.* **1.** The act of passing by, disregarding, or omitting. **2.** *Law.* Neglect of a testator to mention a legal heir in his or her will. **3.** *Theology.* The Calvinist doctrine that God neglected to designate those who would be damned, positively determining only the elect. [Late Latin *praeteritiō, praeteritiōn-,* a passing over, from Latin *praeteritus,* past participle of *praeterīre,* to go by. See PRETERIT.]

pre·term (prē′tûrm′, prē-tûrm′) *adj.* Occurring or appearing before the expected time at the end of a full-term pregnancy: *preterm labor; a preterm infant.* **—preterm** *n.* An infant born prematurely.

pre·ter·mit (prē′tər-mĭt′) *tr.v.* **-mit·ted, -mit·ting, -mits. 1.** To disregard intentionally or allow to pass unnoticed or unmentioned. **2.** To fail to do or include; omit. **3.** To interrupt or terminate. [Latin *praetermittere* : *praeter,* beyond; see PRETERIT + *mittere,* to let go.] **—pre′ter·mis′sion** (-mĭsh′ən) *n.* **—pre′ter·mit′ter** *n.*

pre·ter·nat·u·ral (prē′tər-năch′ər-əl, -năch′rəl) *adj.* **1.** Out of or being beyond the normal course of nature; differing from the natural. **2.** Surpassing the normal or usual; extraordinary: *"Below his preternatural affability there is some acid and steel"* (George F. Will). **3.** Transcending the natural or material order; supernatural. [Medieval Latin *praeternātūrālis,* from Latin *praeter nātūrām,* beyond nature : *praeter,* beyond; see PRETERIT + *nātūra,* nature; see NATURE.] **—pre′ter·nat′u·ral·ism** *n.* **—pre′ter·nat′u·ral·ly** *adv.* **—pre′ter·nat′u·ral·ness** *n.*

pre·test (prē′tĕst′) *n.* **1.a.** A preliminary test given to determine whether students are sufficiently prepared for a more advanced course of studies. **b.** A test taken for practice. **2.** The advance testing of something, such as a questionnaire, a product, or an idea. **—pretest** (prē-tĕst′) *tr. & intr.v.* **-test·ed, -test·ing, -tests.** To subject to or conduct a pretest.

pre·text (prē′tĕkst′) *n.* **1.** An ostensible or professed purpose; an excuse. **2.** An effort or a strategy intended to conceal something. **—pretext** *tr.v.* **-text·ed, -text·ing, -texts.** To allege as an excuse. [Latin *praetextum,* from neuter past participle of *praetexere,* to disguise : *prae-,* pre- + *texere,* to weave; see **teks-** in Appendix.]

pre·tick·et or **pre-tick·et** (prē-tĭk′ĭt) *tr.v.* **-eted, -et·ing, -ets.** To issue or sell tickets to (passengers or customers) at a given time only or at a time before other tickets are sold.

pre·tor (prē′tər) *n.* Variant of **praetor.**

Pre·to·ri·a (prĭ-tôr′ē-ə, -tōr′-). The administrative capital of South Africa, in the northeast part of the country north of Johannesburg. Founded in 1855, it became the capital of Transvaal

ă pat	oi boy
ā pay	ou out
âr care	o͝o took
ä father	o͞o boot
ĕ pet	ŭ cut
ē be	ûr urge
ĭ pit	th thin
ī pie	*th* this
îr pier	hw which
ŏ pot	zh vision
ō toe	ə about, item
ô paw	♦ regionalism

Stress marks: ′ (primary); ′ (secondary), as in **dictionary** (dĭk′shə-nĕr′ē)

in 1860 and capital of South Africa in 1910. Population, 435,100.

pre·to·ri·an (prē-tôr′ē-ən, -tōr′-) *adj.* Variant of **praetorian.**

Pre·to·ri·us (prĭ-tôr′ē-əs, -tōr′-), **Andries Wilhelmus Jacobus.** 1798–1853. Afrikaner soldier and politician who led the defeat of the Zulus (1838) and negotiated the independence of the Transvaal (1852). His son **Marthinus Wessels Pretorius** (1819–1901) founded Pretoria (1855) and was president of the Transvaal (1857–1877) as well as the Orange Free State (1859–1863).

pre·treat (prē-trēt′) *tr.v.* **-treat·ed, -treat·ing, -treats.** To treat (wood or fabric, for example) beforehand. **—pre·treat′ment** *n.*

pre·tri·al (prē-trī′əl, -trīl′) *Law. n.* A proceeding held before an official trial, especially to clarify points of law and facts. **—pretrial** *adj.* **1.** Of or relating to a pretrial. **2.** Existing or occurring before a trial: *pretrial imprisonment; pretrial hearings.*

pret·ti·fy (prĭt′ĭ-fī′) *tr.v.* **-fied, -fy·ing, -fies.** To make pretty or prettier. **—pret′ti·fi·ca′tion** (-fĭ-kā′shən) *n.* **—pret′ti·fi′er** *n.*

pret·ty (prĭt′ē) *adj.* **-ti·er, -ti·est. 1.** Pleasing or attractive in a graceful or delicate way. See Synonyms at **beautiful. 2.** Clever; adroit: *a pretty maneuver.* **3.** Very bad; terrible: *in a pretty predicament; a situation that has reached a pretty pass.* **4.** Ostensibly or superficially attractive but lacking substance or conviction: *full of pretty phrases.* **5.** *Informal.* Considerable in size or extent: *a pretty fortune.* **—pretty** *adv.* **1.** To a fair degree; moderately: *a pretty good student.* **2.** In a pretty manner; prettily or pleasingly. **—pretty** *n., pl.* **-ties. 1.** One that is pretty. **2. pretties.** Delicate clothing, especially lingerie. **—pretty** *tr.v.* **-tied, -ty·ing, -ties.** To make pretty: *pretty up the house.* **—*idiom.* pretty much.** For the most part; mostly: *"The . . . matter was pretty much dying down"* (John Strahinich). [Middle English *prety,* clever, fine, handsome, from Old English *prættig,* cunning, from *prætt,* trick.] **—pret′ti·ly** *adv.* **—pret′ti·ness** *n.*

pretzel

pret·zel (prĕt′səl) *n.* A glazed, brittle biscuit that is salted on the outside and usually baked in the form of a loose knot or a stick. [German *Brezel, Pretzel,* from Middle High German *brēzel, prēzel,* from Old High German *brezitella,* from Medieval Latin **brāchitellum,* diminutive of Latin *bracchiātus,* branched, from *bracchium,* arm, from Greek *brakhiōn,* upper arm. See **mregh-u-** in Appendix.]

WORD HISTORY: It is probably well known or widely assumed that *pretzel* is a German word, since the food seems traditionally German, but the word ultimately has a Latin origin. The German word *Brezel* or *Pretzel,* which was borrowed into English (first being recorded in American English in a newspaper of March 1856) goes back to the assumed Medieval Latin word *brāchitellum.* This would accord with the story that a monk living in France or northern Italy first created the knotted shape of a pretzel, even though this type of biscuit had been enjoyed by the Romans. The monk wanted to symbolize arms folded in a prayer, hence the name derived from Latin *bracchiātus,* "having branches," itself from *bracchium,* "branch, arm."

prev. *abbr.* **1.** Previous. **2.** Previously.

pre·vail (prĭ-vāl′) *intr.v.* **-vailed, -vail·ing, -vails. 1.** To be greater in strength or influence; triumph: *prevailed against great odds.* **2.** To be or become effective; win out: *hoped justice would prevail.* **3.** To be most common or frequent; be predominant: *a region where snow and ice prevail.* **4.** To be in force, use, or effect; be current: *an ancient tradition that still prevails.* **5.** To use persuasion or inducement successfully. Often used with *on, upon,* or *with.* See Synonyms at **persuade.** [Middle English *prevailen,* from Old French *prevaloir, prevaill-,* from Latin *praevalēre,* to be stronger : *prae-,* pre- + *valēre,* to be strong; see **wal-** in Appendix.] **—pre·vail′er** *n.*

pre·vail·ing (prĭ-vā′lĭng) *adj.* **1.** Most frequent or common; predominant. **2.** Generally current; widespread. **—pre·vail′ing·ly** *adv.* **—pre·vail′ing·ness** *n.*

SYNONYMS: *prevailing, prevalent, current, rife.* These adjectives denote what exists or is encountered generally at a particular time. *Prevailing* applies to what is most frequent or common at a certain time or in a certain place: *The prevailing opinion seems to be that a trade war can be averted if both countries make concessions. Prevalent* suggests widespread existence or occurrence but does not imply predominance: *"The religion most prevalent in our northern colonies is a refinement on the principles of resistance: it is the dissidence of dissent"* (Edmund Burke). *Current* often stresses the present time; the term is frequently applied to what passes from one to another or to what is subject to frequent change: *Many current psychoanalytic theories diverge markedly from classical Freudian dogma. Rife* implies that something is current, plentiful, or rapidly spreading or increasing: *"The speculation which for some time was rife concerning* [the book's] *authorship made many turn to it"* (Samuel Butler). *"The drinking of tea . . . now . . . became very rife"* (John Galt).

prev·a·lence (prĕv′ə-ləns) *n.* **1.** The condition of being prevalent. **2.** *Medicine.* The total number of cases of a disease in a given population at a specific time.

prev·a·lent (prĕv′ə-lənt) *adj.* Widely or commonly occurring, existing, accepted, or practiced. See Synonyms at **prevailing.** [Middle English, very strong, from Latin *praevalēns, praevalent-,* present participle of *praevalēre,* to be stronger. See PREVAIL.] **—prev′a·lent·ly** *adv.*

pre·var·i·cate (prĭ-văr′ĭ-kāt′) *intr.v.* **-cat·ed, -cat·ing, -cates.** To stray from or evade the truth; equivocate. See Synonyms at **lie**[2]. [Latin *praevāricārī, praevāricāt-* : *prae-,* pre- + *vāricāre,* to straddle (from *vāricus,* straddling, from *vārus,* bent).] **—pre·var′i·ca′tion** *n.* **—pre·var′i·ca′tor** *n.*

pre·ven·ience (prĭ-vēn′yəns) *n.* **1.** The act or state of being antecedent or prevenient. **2.** Attention to another's needs.

pre·ven·ient (prĭ-vēn′yənt) *adj.* **1.** Coming before; preceding. **2.** Expectant; anticipatory. [Latin *praeveniēns, praevenient-,* present participle of *praevenīre,* to precede : *prae-,* pre- + *venīre,* to come; see **gʷā-** in Appendix.] **—pre·ven′ient·ly** *adv.*

pre·vent (prĭ-vĕnt′) *v.* **-vent·ed, -vent·ing, -vents.** *—tr.* **1.** To keep from happening: *took steps to prevent the strike.* **2.** To keep (someone) from doing something; impede: *prevented us from winning.* **3.** *Archaic.* To anticipate or counter in advance. **4.** *Archaic.* To come before; precede. *—intr.* To present an obstacle: *There will be a picnic if nothing prevents.* [Middle English *preventen,* to anticipate, from Latin *praevenīre, praevent-* : *prae-,* pre- + *venīre,* to come; see **gʷā-** in Appendix.] **—pre·vent′a·bil′i·ty, pre·vent′i·bil′i·ty** *n.* **—pre·vent′a·ble, pre·vent′i·ble** *adj.* **—pre·vent′er** *n.*

SYNONYMS: *prevent, preclude, avert, obviate, forestall.* These verbs mean to stop or hinder something from happening, especially by advance planning or action. *Prevent* implies anticipatory counteraction: *"The surest way to prevent war is not to fear it"* (John Randolph). To *preclude* is to exclude the possibility of the occurrence of an event or action: *"a tranquillity which . . . his wife's presence would have precluded"* (John Henry Newman). To *avert* is to ward off something about to happen: *Only quick thinking on the pilot's part averted a disastrous accident. Obviate* implies that something, such as a difficulty, has been anticipated and disposed of effectively: *"the objections . . . having . . . been obviated in the preceding chapter"* (Joseph Butler). *Forestall* usually suggests anticipatory measures taken to counteract, neutralize, or nullify the effects of something: *We installed an alarm system to forestall break-ins.*

pre·ven·ta·tive (prĭ-vĕn′tə-tĭv) *adj. & n.* Variant of **preventive.**

pre·ven·tion (prĭ-vĕn′shən) *n.* **1.** The act of preventing or impeding. **2.** A hindrance; an obstacle.

pre·ven·tive (prĭ-vĕn′tĭv) also **pre·ven·ta·tive** (-tə-tĭv) *—adj.* **1.** Intended or used to prevent or hinder; acting as an obstacle: *preventive measures.* **2.** Carried out to deter expected aggression by hostile forces. **3.** Preventing or slowing the course of an illness or a disease; prophylactic: *preventive medicine; preventive health care. —n.* **1.** Something that prevents; an obstacle. **2.** Something that prevents or slows the course of an illness or disease. **—pre·ven′tive·ly** *adv.* **—pre·ven′tive·ness** *n.*

preventive detention *n.* The pretrial imprisonment without the right to bail of a person accused of a felony and judged dangerous to society.

pre·verb (prē′vûrb′) *n. Linguistics.* A prefix or particle preceding the root or stem of a verb, as *for-* in *forget.* **—pre·verb′** *adj.*

pre·verb·al (prē-vûr′bəl) *adj.* **1.** *Grammar.* Preceding the verb. **2. a.** Having not yet learned to speak: *preverbal children.* **b.** Marked by the absence of spoken language: *preverbal sounds; the preverbal stage of development.*

pre·view also **pre·vue** (prē′vyo͞o′) *—n.* **1.** An advance showing, as of a movie or an art exhibition, to which a selected audience is invited before public presentation begins. **2.** An advance viewing or exhibition, especially the presentation of several scenes advertising a forthcoming movie; a trailer. **3.** An introductory or preliminary message, sample, or overview; a foretaste. *—tr.v.* **-viewed, -view·ing, -views** also **-vued, -vu·ing, -vues. 1.** To view or exhibit in advance. **2.** To provide a preliminary sample or overview of: *The professor previewed the course for us.*

pre·vi·ous (prē′vē-əs) *adj. Abbr.* **prev. 1.** Existing or occurring before something else in time or order; prior: *children by a previous marriage.* **2.** *Informal.* Acting, occurring, or done too soon; premature. [From Latin *praevius,* going before : *prae-,* pre- + *via,* way; see **wegh-** in Appendix.] **—pre′vi·ous·ly** *adv.* **—pre′vi·ous·ness** *n.*

previous question *n. Abbr.* **p.q., P.Q.** The motion in parliamentary procedure to take an immediate vote on the main question being considered or on any other questions so designated.

previous to *prep.* Prior to; before.

pre·vise (prĭ-vīz′) *tr.v.* **-vised, -vis·ing, -vis·es. 1.** To know in advance; foresee. **2.** To notify in advance; forewarn. [Middle English *previsen,* from Latin *praevidēre, praevīs-* : *prae-,* pre- + *vidēre,* to see; see **weid-** in Appendix.] **—pre·vi′sor** *n.*

pre·vi·sion (prĭ-vĭzh′ən) *n.* **1.** A knowing in advance; foresight. **2.** A prediction; a forecast. **—prevision** *tr.v.* **-sioned, -sion·ing, -sions.** To foresee. **—pre·vi′sion·al, pre·vi′sion·ar′y** (-vĭzh′ə-nĕr′ē) *adj.*

pre·vo·cal·ic (prē′vō-kăl′ĭk) *adj. Linguistics.* **1.** Preceding a vowel. **2.** Of or relating to a form of a linguistic element, such as a suffix, prefix, or word, that occurs only before a vowel.

ă pat	oi boy
ā pay	ou out
âr care	o͝o took
ä father	o͞o boot
ĕ pet	ŭ cut
ē be	ûr urge
ĭ pit	th thin
ī pie	*th* this
îr pier	hw which
ŏ pot	zh vision
ō toe	ə about, item
ô paw	♦ regionalism

Stress marks: **′** (primary); ′ (secondary), as in **dictionary** (dĭk′shə-nĕr′ē)

pre·vo·ca·tion·al (prē′vō-kā′shə-nəl) *adj.* Of or relating to instruction given in preparation for vocational school.

Pré·vost d'Ex·iles (prā-vō′ dĕg-zēl′), **Antoine François.** Known as "Abbé Prévost." 1697–1763. French writer and cleric who left the religious life to pursue worldly interests. His literary repute lies on the novel *Manon Lescaut* (1731).

pre·vue (prē′vyo͞o′) *n. & v.* Variant of **preview.**

pre·war (prē′wôr′) *adj.* Existing or occurring before a war.

pre·washed (prē′wŏsht′, -wôsht′) *adj.* Washed by the manufacturer so as to impart a softer texture or faded appearance. Used of textiles or clothing: *prewashed denim; prewashed jeans.*

pre·writ·ing (prē′rī′tĭng) *n.* The creation and arrangement of ideas preliminary to writing.

prex·y (prĕk′sē) *n., pl.* **-ies.** *Slang.* A president, especially of a college or university. [Shortening and alteration of PRESIDENT.]

prey (prā) *n.* **1.** An animal hunted or caught for food; quarry. **2.** One that is defenseless, especially in the face of attack; a victim. **3.** The act or practice of preying. **—prey** *intr.v.* **preyed, prey·ing, preys. 1.** To hunt, catch, or eat as prey: *Owls prey on mice.* **2.** To victimize or make a profit at someone else's expense. **3.** To plunder or pillage. **4.** To exert a baneful or injurious effect: *Remorse preyed on his mind.* [Middle English *preie,* from Old French, from Latin *praeda,* booty, prey. See **ghend-** in Appendix.] **—prey′er** *n.*

PRF *abbr.* **1.** Pulse recurrence frequency. **2.** Pulse repetition frequency.

prf. *abbr. Printing.* Proof.

Pri·am (prī′əm) *n. Greek Mythology.* The father of Paris, Hector, and Cassandra and king of Troy, who was killed when his city fell to the Greeks.

pri·a·pic (prī-ā′pĭk, -ăp′ĭk) also **pri·a·pe·an** (prī′ə-pē′ən) *adj.* **1.** Of, relating to, or resembling a phallus; phallic. **2.** Relating to or overly concerned with masculinity. [From PRIAPUS.]

pri·a·pism (prī′ə-pĭz′əm) *n.* Persistent, usually painful erection of the penis, especially as a consequence of disease and not related to sexual arousal. [French *priapisme,* from Late Latin *priāpismus,* from Greek *priapismos,* from *priapizein,* to have an erection, from *Priapos,* Priapus.]

pri·a·pus (prī-ā′pəs) *n.* **1. Priapus.** *Greek & Roman Mythology.* The god of procreation, guardian of gardens and vineyards, and personification of the erect phallus. **2.** An image of this god, often used as a scarecrow in ancient gardens. **3.** A representation of a phallus. [Latin *Priāpus,* from Greek *Priapos.*]

Prib·i·lof Islands (prĭb′ə-lôf′). A group of islands off southwest Alaska in the Bering Sea. First visited by a Russian explorer in 1786, they are noted as a breeding ground for seals.

price (prīs) *n. Abbr.* **pr. 1.** The amount as of money or goods, asked for or given in exchange for something else. **2.** The cost at which something is obtained: *believes that the price of success is hard work.* **3.** The cost of bribing someone: *maintained that every person has a price.* **4.** A reward offered for the capture or killing of a person: *a felon with a price on his head.* **5.** *Archaic.* Value or worth. **—price** *tr.v.* **priced, pric·ing, pric·es. 1.** To fix or establish a price for: *shoes that are priced at nine dollars.* **2.** To find out the price of: *spent the day pricing dresses.* ***—idiom.*** **price out of the market.** To charge so much for goods or services that people no longer buy or use them. [Middle English *pris,* from Old French, from Latin *pretium.* See **per-**[5] in Appendix.] **—price′a·ble** *adj.* **—pric′er** *n.*

SYNONYMS: *price, charge, cost, expense.* These nouns signify an amount given or asked for in payment for goods or services. *Price* is the amount of money needed to purchase something offered for sale: *The house didn't sell because the price was too high. Charge* is the sum asked especially for the rendering of a service: *There is a nominal charge for postage and handling. Cost,* a more inclusive term, generally applies to the total spent or to be spent, including money, time, and labor: *Sales more than offset production costs. Expense* suggests cost in the aggregate: *Litigation often entails enormous expense.*

Price (prīs), **(Mary) Leontyne.** Born 1927. American operatic soprano who performed with the New York Metropolitan Opera (1961–1985).

price-cut·ting (prīs′kŭt′ĭng) *n.* Reduction of retail prices to a level low enough to eliminate competition. **—price′-cut′ter** *n.*

price-earn·ings ratio (prīs′ûr′nĭngz) *n.* The ratio of the market price of a common stock to its earnings per share.

price fix·ing also **price-fix·ing** (prīs′fĭk′sĭng) *n.* **1.** The setting of commodity prices artificially by a government. **2.** The result of an unlawful agreement between manufacturers or dealers to set and maintain specified prices on typically competing products.

price index *n.* A number relating prices of a group of commodities to their prices during an arbitrarily chosen base period.

price·less (prīs′lĭs) *adj.* **1.** Of inestimable worth; invaluable. **2.** Highly amusing, absurd, or odd: *a priceless remark.* **—price′less·ly** *adv.*

price support *n.* Maintenance of prices, as of a raw material or commodity, at a certain level usually through public subsidy or government intervention.

price tag *n.* **1.** A label attached to a piece of merchandise indicating its price. **2.** The cost of something.

price war *n.* A period of intense competition among businesses in which each competitor tries to cut retail prices below those of the others.

pric·ey also **pric·y** (prī′sē) *adj.* **-i·er, -i·est.** *Informal.* Expensive: *a pricey restaurant.* **—pric′ey·ness** *n.* **—pric′i·ly** *adv.*

Leontyne Price

Prich·ard (prĭch′ərd). A city of southwest Alabama, an industrial suburb of Mobile. Population, 39,541.

prick (prĭk) *n.* **1.a.** The act of piercing or pricking. **b.** The sensation of being pierced or pricked. **2.a.** A persistent or sharply painful feeling of sorrow or remorse. **b.** A small, sharp, local pain, such as that made by a needle or a bee sting. **3.** A small mark or puncture made by a pointed object. **4.** A pointed object, such as an ice pick, a goad, or a thorn. **5.** A hare's track or footprint. **6.** *Vulgar Slang.* A penis. **7.** *Vulgar Slang.* A person regarded as highly unpleasant. **—prick** *v.* **pricked, prick·ing, pricks.** *—tr.* **1.** To puncture lightly. **2.** To affect with a mental or emotional pang, as of sorrow or remorse: *Her conscience began to prick her.* **3.** To impel as if with a spur; urge on. See Synonyms at **urge. 4.** To mark or delineate on a surface by means of small punctures: *prick a pattern on a board.* **5.** *Nautical.* To measure with dividers on a chart. **6.** To pierce the quick of (a horse's hoof) while shoeing. **7.** To transplant (seedlings, for example) before final planting. **8.** To cause to stand erect or point upward: *The dogs pricked their ears.* *—intr.* **1.** To pierce or puncture something or cause a pricking feeling. **2.** To feel a pang or twinge from or as if from being pricked. **3.a.** To spur a horse on. **b.** To ride at a gallop. **4.** To stand erect; point upward: *The dog's ears pricked at the noise.* ***—idiom.*** **prick up (one's) ears.** To listen with attentive interest. [Middle English, from Old English *prica,* puncture.]

prick·er (prĭk′ər) *n.* **1.** One, such as a pricking tool, that pierces or pricks. **2.** A prickle or thorn.

prick·et (prĭk′ĭt) *n.* **1.a.** A small point or spike for holding a candle upright. **b.** A candlestick having such a spike. **2.** A buck in its second year, before the antlers branch. [Middle English *priket,* diminutive of *prik, prick,* prick. See PRICK.]

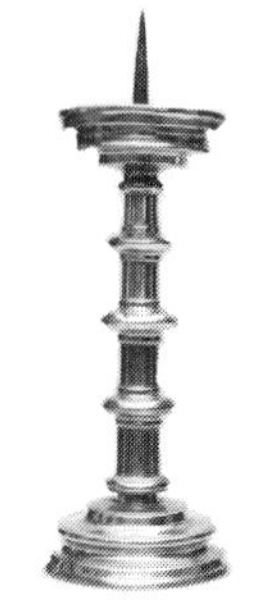

pricket
15th- or 16th-century bronze pricket

prick·le (prĭk′əl) *n.* **1.** A small sharp point, spine, or thorn. **2.** A tingling or pricking sensation. **—prickle** *v.* **-led, -ling, -les.** *—tr.* **1.** To prick as if with a thorn. **2.** To cause a tingling or pricking sensation in. *—intr.* **1.** To feel a tingling or pricking sensation. **2.** To rise or stand up like prickles. [Middle English *prikel,* from Old English *pricel.*]

prick·ly (prĭk′lē) *adj.* **-li·er, -li·est. 1.** Having prickles. **2.** Marked by prickling or tingling or smarting: *a prickly sensation in my foot.* **3.a.** Causing trouble or vexation; thorny: *a prickly situation.* **b.** Bristling or irritable: *"In consequence, he became rebarbative, prickly, spiteful"* (Robert Craft). **—prick′li·ness** *n.*

prickly ash *n.* **1.** Any of numerous cosmopolitan, deciduous or evergreen shrubs or trees of the genus *Zanthoxylum,* having aromatic bark and alternate, mostly pinnate leaves. **2.** See **Hercules' club** (sense 1).

prickly heat *n.* See **heat rash.**

prickly pear *n.* **1.** Any of various cacti of the genus *Opuntia,* having bristly, flattened or cylindrical joints, showy, usually yellow flowers, and ovoid, sometimes edible fruit. **2.** The fruit of any of these plants.

prickly pear
Plains prickly pear
Opuntia polyacantha

prickly poppy *n.* Any of various plants of the genus *Argemone,* chiefly of tropical America, having large yellow, lavender, or white flowers and prickly leaves, stems, and pods.

prick·y (prĭk′ē) *adj.* **-i·er, -i·est.** Prickly.

pride (prīd) *n.* **1.** A sense of one's own proper dignity or value; self-respect. **2.** Pleasure or satisfaction taken in an achievement, a possession, or an association: *parental pride.* **3.** Arrogant or disdainful conduct or treatment; haughtiness. **4.a.** A cause or source of pleasure or satisfaction; the best of a group or class: *These soldiers were their country's pride.* **b.** The most successful or thriving condition; prime: *the pride of youth.* **5.** An excessively high opinion of oneself; conceit. **6.** Mettle or spirit in horses. **7.** A company of lions. See Synonyms at **flock**[1]. **8.** A flamboyant or impressive group: *a pride of acrobats.* **—pride** *tr.v.* **prid·ed, prid·ing, prides.** To indulge (oneself) in a feeling of pleasure or satisfaction: *I pride myself on this beautiful garden.* [Middle English, from Old English *prȳde,* from *prūd,* proud. See PROUD.]

Pride (prīd), **Thomas.** Died 1658. English Parliamentarian who led a regiment to Parliament and expelled Presbyterian and Royalist members who opposed the condemnation of Charles I (1648). He was a signatory of Charles's death warrant.

pride·ful (prīd′fəl) *adj.* **1.** Arrogant; disdainful. **2.** Highly pleased; elated. **—pride′ful·ly** *adv.* **—pride′ful·ness** *n.*

pride of place *n.* The highest or most important position: *The crystal vase enjoyed pride of place on the grand piano.*

pried[1] (prīd) *v.* Past tense and past participle of **pry**[1].

pried[2] (prīd) *v.* Past tense and past participle of **pry**[2].

prie-dieu (prē-dyœ′) *n., pl.* **-dieus** or **-dieux** (-dyœz′). **1.** A narrow, desklike kneeling bench with space above for a book or the elbows, for use by a person at prayer. **2.** An armless, upholstered chair with a high, straight back and a low seat. [French *prie-Dieu : prier,* to pray (from Old French, from Latin *precārī;* see PRAY) + *Dieu,* God (from Old French; see ADIEU).]

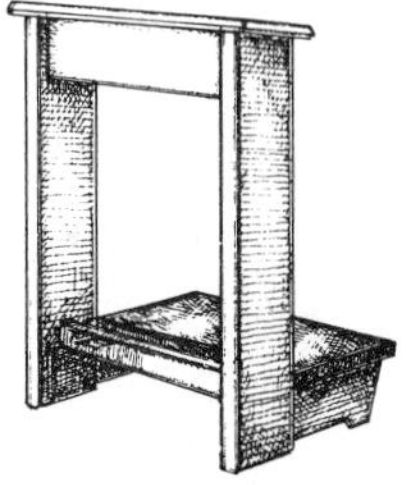

prie-dieu

pri·er also **pry·er** (prī′ər) *n.* One who pries, especially a person who is unduly interested in the affairs of others.

pries[1] (prīz) *v.* Third person singular present tense of **pry[1]**. —**pries** *n.* Plural of **pry[1]**.

pries[2] (prīz) *v.* Third person singular present tense of **pry[2]**. —**pries** *n.* Plural of **pry[2]**.

priest (prēst) *n. Abbr.* **Pr., P. 1.** In many Christian churches, a member of the second grade of clergy ranking below a bishop but above a deacon and having authority to administer the sacraments. **2.** A person having the authority to perform and administer religious rites. **3.** *Informal.* One whose role is considered comparable to that of a priest: *computers and their priests.* —**priest** *tr.v.* **priest·ed, priest·ing, priests.** To ordain or admit to the priesthood. [Middle English *preost,* from Old English *prēost,* perhaps from Vulgar Latin *prester (from Late Latin *presbyter;* see PRESBYTER) or from West Germanic *prēvost (from Latin *praepositus,* superintendent; see PROVOST).]

priest·ess (prē′stĭs) *n.* A woman who presides over especially pagan rites.

priest·hood (prēst′ho͝od′) *n.* **1.** The character, office, or vocation of a priest. **2.** The clergy.

Priest·ley (prēst′lē), **J(ohn) B(oynton).** 1894–1984. British writer of more than 100 novels, numerous dramas, and critical works on literature and social issues.

Priestley, Joseph. 1733–1804. British chemist noted for work on the isolation of gases and his discovery of oxygen (1774).

priest·ly (prēst′lē) *adj.* **-li·er, -li·est. 1.** Of or relating to a priest or the priesthood. **2.** Characteristic of or suitable for a priest. —**priest′li·ness** *n.*

prig (prĭg) *n.* **1.** A person who demonstrates an exaggerated conformity or propriety, especially in an irritatingly arrogant or smug manner. **2.** *Chiefly British.* A petty thief or pickpocket. **3.** *Archaic.* A conceited dandy; a fop. —**prig** *tr.v.* **prigged, prig·ging, prigs.** *Chiefly British.* To steal or pilfer. [Origin unknown.] —**prig′ger·y** *n.* —**prig′gish** *adj.* —**prig′gish·ly** *adv.* —**prig′gish·ness** *n.*

Pri·go·gine (prĭ-gô′zhən, -gô-zhēn′), **Ilya.** Born 1917. Russian-born Belgian chemist. He won a 1977 Nobel Prize for his contributions to nonequilibrium thermodynamics.

prim[1] (prĭm) *adj.* **prim·mer, prim·mest. 1.a.** Precise or proper to the point of affectation; excessively decorous. **b.** Strait-laced; prudish. **2.** Neat and trim: *a prim hedgerow.* —**prim** *v.* **primmed, prim·ming, prims.** —*tr.* **1.** To fix (the face or mouth) in a prim expression. **2.** To make prim, as in dress or appearance. —*intr.* To assume a prim expression. [Possibly from obsolete *prim,* formal or demure person, perhaps from Old French *prin,* first, delicate. See PRIME.] —**prim′ly** *adv.* —**prim′ness** *n.*

prim[2] (prĭm) *n.* A privet. [Short for obsolete *primprint,* of unknown origin.]

prim. *abbr.* **1.** Primary. **2.** Primitive.

pri·ma ballerina (prē′mə) *n.* The leading woman dancer in a ballet company. [Italian : *prima,* feminine of *primo,* first + *ballerina,* ballerina.]

pri·ma·cy (prī′mə-sē) *n., pl.* **-cies. 1.** The state of being first or foremost. **2.** *Ecclesiastical.* The office, rank, or province of primate. [Middle English *primacie,* from Old French, from Medieval Latin *prīmātia,* office of church primate, from Latin *prīmās, prīmāt-,* of first rank. See PRIMATE.]

pri·ma donna (prē′mə, prĭm′ə) *n.* **1.** The leading woman soloist in an opera company. **2.** A temperamental, conceited person. [Italian : *prima,* feminine of *primo,* first + *donna,* lady.]

pri·ma fa·cie (prī′mə fā′shē, -shē-ē, fā′shə) *adv.* At first sight; before closer inspection: *They had, prima facie, a legitimate complaint.* —**prima facie** *adj.* **1.** True, authentic, or adequate at first sight; ostensible: *prima facie credibility.* **2.** Evident without proof or reasoning; obvious: *a prima facie violation of the treaty.* [Middle English, manifestly, from Latin *prīmā faciē* : *prīmā,* feminine ablative of *prīmus,* first + *faciē,* ablative of *faciēs,* shape, face.]

prima facie case *n. Law.* A case in which the evidence presented is sufficient for a judgment to be made unless the evidence is contested.

prima facie evidence *n. Law.* Evidence that would, if uncontested, establish a fact or raise a presumption of a fact.

pri·mal (prī′məl) *adj.* **1.** Being first in time; original; primeval. **2.** Of first importance; primary. [Medieval Latin *prīmālis,* from Latin *prīmus,* first. See **per[1]** in Appendix.] —**pri·mal′i·ty** (-măl′ĭ-tē) *n.*

primal therapy *n.* A method of psychotherapy that treats neurosis by teaching patients to relive early traumatic experiences and to express feelings through angry screaming and other verbal or physical acts of aggression. Also called *primal scream therapy.* —**primal therapist** *n.*

pri·mar·i·ly (prī-mâr′ə-lē, -mĕr′-) *adv.* **1.** Chiefly; mainly: *a scholastic program primarily for seniors; a primarily middle-class neighborhood.* **2.** At first; originally.

pri·mar·y (prī′mĕr′ē, -mə-rē) *adj. Abbr.* **prim. 1.** First or highest in rank, quality, or importance; principal. **2.** Being or standing first in a list, series, or sequence. **3.** Occurring first in time or sequence; earliest. **4.** Being or existing as the first or earliest of a kind; primitive. **5.** *Geology.* Characteristic of or existing in a rock at the time of its formation. **6.** Serving as or being an essential component, as of a system; basic. **7.a.** Immediate; direct: *a primary effect; a primary information source.* **b.** Preliminary to a later stage in a continuing process: *primary training.* **c.** Of or relating to a primary school: *the primary grades.* **8.** *Color.* Of or relating to a primary color or colors. **9.** *Linguistics.* **a.** Having a word root or other linguistic element as a basis that cannot be further analyzed or broken down. Used of the derivation of a word or word element. **b.** Referring to present or future time. Used as a collective designation for various present and future verb tenses in Latin, Greek, and Sanskrit. **10.** *Electronics.* Of, relating to, or constituting an inducting current, circuit, or coil. **11.** Of, relating to, or designating the main flight feathers projecting along the outer edge of a bird's wing. **12.** Of or relating to agriculture, forestry, the industries that extract natural materials from the earth, or the products so obtained: *a primary commodity.* **13.** *Chemistry.* **a.** Relating to the replacement of one of several atoms or radicals in a compound by another atom or radical. **b.** Having a carbon atom attached solely to one other carbon atom in a molecule. **14.** *Biochemistry.* Of, relating to, or being the sequence of amino acids in a protein. **15.** *Botany.* Of, relating to, or being growth or tissue derived solely from apical meristems present in the embryo: *primary meristem; primary xylem.* —**primary** *n., pl.* **-ies. 1.a.** One that is first in time, order, or sequence. **b.** One that is first or best in degree, quality, or importance. **c.** One that is fundamental, basic, or elemental. **2.a.** A meeting of the registered voters of a political party for the purpose of nominating candidates and for choosing delegates to their party convention. **b.** A preliminary election in which the registered voters of a political party nominate candidates for office. **3.** *Color.* A primary color. **4.** One of the main flight feathers projecting along the outer edge of a bird's wing. **5.** *Electronics.* An inducting current, circuit, or coil. **6.** *Astronomy.* **a.** A celestial body, especially a star, relative to other bodies in orbit around it. **b.** The brighter of two stars that make up a double star. [Middle English, from Latin *prīmārius,* chief, from *prīmus,* first. See **per[1]** in Appendix.]

primary accent *n. Linguistics.* **1.** The strongest degree of stress placed on a syllable in the pronunciation of a word. **2.** The mark (′) used to indicate the strongest degree of stress.

primary atypical pneumonia *n.* An acute infectious respiratory disease caused by the bacterium *Mycoplasma pneumoniae,* often in association with a virus, and characterized by fever, coughing, sore throat, and muscle pain.

primary care *n.* The medical care a patient receives upon first contact with the health care system, before referral elsewhere within the system.

primary cell *n.* A cell in which an irreversible chemical reaction generates electricity; a cell that cannot be recharged. Also called *galvanic cell, voltaic cell.*

primary coil *n.* A coil to which the input voltage is applied in an inductively coupled circuit, especially a transformer.

primary color *n. Color.* A color belonging to any of three groups each of which is regarded as generating all colors, with the groups being: **a.** Additive, physiological, or light primaries red, green, and blue. Lights of red, green, and blue wavelengths may be mixed to produce all colors. **b.** Subtractive or colorant primaries magenta, yellow, and cyan. Substances that reflect light of one of these wavelengths and absorb other wavelengths may be mixed to produce all colors. **c.** Psychological primaries red, yellow, green, and blue, plus the achromatic pair black and white. All colors may be subjectively conceived as mixtures of these.

primary consumer *n. Ecology.* An animal that eats grass and other green plants in a food chain; an herbivore.

primary election *n.* A preliminary election in which voters nominate party candidates for office.

primary growth *n. Botany.* Growth originating from the apical meristems of roots and shoots and resulting chiefly in extension of the plant body.

primary meristem *n.* A type of plant tissue derived from the apical meristem of a root or stem.

primary school *n.* **1.** A school usually including the first three or four grades of elementary school and sometimes kindergarten. **2.** See **elementary school.**

primary syphilis *n.* The first stage of syphilis, characterized by formation of a painless chancre at the point of infection and hardening and swelling of adjacent lymph nodes.

primary tooth *n.* See **milk tooth.**

primary wall *n.* The wall layer of a plant cell deposited during cell expansion.

primary wave *n.* An earthquake wave in which rock particles vibrate parallel to the direction of wave travel. It can travel through solids and liquids.

primary xylem *n. Botany.* A type of xylem tissue derived from the procambium.

pri·mate (prī′mĭt, -māt′) *n.* **1.** (prī′māt′). A mammal of the order Primates, which includes the anthropoids and prosimians, characterized by refined development of the hands and feet, a shortened snout, and a large brain. **2.** A bishop of highest rank in a province or country. [From New Latin *Prīmātes,* order name, from Latin *prīmātēs,* pl. of *prīmās,* principal, of first rank, from *prīmus,* first. See **per[1]** in Appendix. Sense 2, from Middle English *primat,* from Old French, from Medieval Latin *prīmās, prīmāt-,* from Latin.] —**pri·ma′tial** (-mā′shəl) *adj.*

pri·ma·tol·o·gy (prī′mə-tŏl′ə-jē) *n.* The branch of zoology that deals with the study of primates. —**pri′ma·to·log′i·cal** (-tl-ŏj′ĭ-kəl) *adj.* —**pri′ma·tol′o·gist** *n.*

pri·ma·ve·ra¹ or **pri·ma ve·ra** (prē′mə-vĕr′ə) *n.* **1.** A tree *(Cybistax donnellsmithii)* of Mexico and Guatemala, having opposite, palmately compound leaves, yellow flowers, and close-grained, light-colored wood. **2.** The wood of this tree, used in cabinetry. In this sense, also called *white mahogany.* [Spanish, spring, primavera, from Late Latin *prīma vēra,* early spring, pl. of *prīmum vēr* : Latin *prīmus,* first; see **per¹** in Appendix + Latin *vēr,* spring; see **wesr̥** in Appendix.]

pri·ma·ve·ra² (prē′mə-vĕr′ə) *adj.* Made with different kinds of sliced or diced vegetables: *pasta primavera; shrimp in a primavera sauce.* [From Italian *(alla) primavera,* (in the) spring (style), from Late Latin *prīma vēra.* See PRIMAVERA¹.]

prime (prīm) *adj.* **1.** First in excellence, quality, or value. See Usage Note at **perfect. 2.** First in degree or rank; chief. **3.** First or early in time, order, or sequence; original. **4.** Of the highest U.S. government grade of meat. **5.** *Mathematics.* Of, relating to, or being a prime number. —**prime** *n.* **1.** The earliest hours of the day; dawn. **2.** The first season of the year; spring. **3.** The age of ideal physical perfection and intellectual vigor. **4.** The period or phase of ideal or peak condition. See Synonyms at **bloom¹. 5.** The first position of thrust and parry in fencing. **6.** A mark (′) appended above and to the right of a character, especially: **a.** One used to distinguish different values of the same variable in a mathematical expression. **b.** One used to represent a unit of measurement, such as feet or minutes in latitude and longitude. **7.** *Ecclesiastical.* **a.** The second of the seven canonical hours. No longer in ecclesiastical use. **b.** The time appointed for this service, the first hour of the day or 6 A.M. **8.** *Mathematics.* A prime number. **9.** A prime rate. —**prime** *v.* **primed, prim·ing, primes.** —*tr.* **1.** To make ready; prepare: *guard dogs primed for attack.* **2.** To prepare (a gun or mine) for firing by inserting a charge of gunpowder or a primer. **3.** To prepare for operation, as by pouring water into a pump or gasoline into a carburetor. **4.** To prepare (a surface) for painting by covering with size, primer, or an undercoat. **5.** To inform or instruct beforehand; coach. —*intr.* To become prepared for future action or operation. —***idiom.* prime the pump.** *Informal.* To encourage the growth or action of something. [Middle English, first in occurrence, from Old French, feminine of *prin,* from Latin *prīmus.* N., sense 7, from Middle English, from Old English *prīm,* from Late Latin *prīma (hora),* first (hour), from Latin, feminine of *prīmus.* See **per¹** in Appendix.] —**prime′ly** *adv.* —**prime′ness** *n.*

prime interest rate *n.* See **prime rate.**

prime meridian *n.* The zero meridian (0°), used as a reference line from which longitude east and west is measured. It passes through Greenwich, England.

prime minister *n. Abbr.* **PM, P.M. 1.** A chief minister appointed by a ruler. **2.** The head of the cabinet and often also the chief executive of a parliamentary democracy. —**prime ministerial** *adj.* —**prime ministership, prime ministry** *n.*

prime mover *n.* **1. a.** Something regarded as the initial source of energy directed toward a goal: *Patriotism was the prime mover of the revolution.* **b.** The initial force, such as electricity, wind, or gravity, that engages or moves a machine. **c.** A machine or mechanism that converts natural energy into work. Also called *primum mobile.* **2.** Any of various heavy-duty trucks or tractors. **3.** *Philosophy.* In Aristotelian philosophy, the self-moved being that causes all motion.

prime number *n. Mathematics.* A whole number not divisible without a remainder by any whole number other than itself and one.

prim·er¹ (prĭm′ər) *n.* **1.** An elementary textbook for teaching children to read. **2.** A book that covers the basic elements of a subject. [Middle English, from Norman French, from Medieval Latin *prīmārium,* from neuter of *prīmārius,* first, from Latin, from *prīmus.* See PRIME.]

prim·er² (prī′mər) *n.* **1.** A cap or tube containing a small amount of explosive used to detonate the main explosive charge of a firearm or mine. **2.** An undercoat of paint or size applied to prepare a surface, as for painting.

prime rate *n.* The lowest rate of interest on bank loans at a given time and place, offered to preferred borrowers. Also called *prime interest rate.*

pri·me·ro (prĭ-mâr′ō) *n. Games.* A gambling card game, popular in Elizabethan England. [Alteration of Spanish *primera,* feminine of *primero,* first, from Latin *prīmārius,* principal, from *prīmus,* first. See PRIME.]

prime time *n.* The evening hours, generally between 7 and 11 P.M., when the largest television audience is available. —**prime′-time′** (prīm′tīm′) *adj.*

pri·me·val (prī-mē′vəl) *adj.* Belonging to the first or earliest age or ages; original or ancient: *a primeval forest.* [From Latin *prīmaevus,* early in life : *prīmus,* first; see **per¹** in Appendix + *aevum,* age; see **aiw-** in Appendix.] —**pri·me′val·ly** *adv.*

pri·mi (prē′mē) *n. Music.* A plural of **primo.**

prim·ing (prī′mĭng) *n.* **1.** The act of one that primes. **2.** The explosive used to ignite a charge. **3.** A preliminary coat of paint or size applied to a surface.

pri·mip·a·ra (prī-mĭp′ər-ə) *n., pl.* **-a·ras** or **-a·rae** (-ə-rē′). **1.** A woman who is pregnant for the first time. **2.** A woman who has given birth to only one child. [Latin *prīmipara* : *prīmus,* first; see **per¹** in Appendix + *-para,* -para.] —**pri′mi·par′i·ty** (-mĭ-păr′ĭ-tē) *n.* —**pri·mip′a·rous** *adj.*

prim·i·tive (prĭm′ĭ-tĭv) *adj. Abbr.* **prim. 1.** Not derived from something else; primary or basic. **2. a.** Of or relating to an earliest or original stage or state; primeval. **b.** Being little evolved from an early ancestral type. **3.** Characterized by simplicity or crudity; unsophisticated: *primitive weapons.* See Synonyms at **rude. 4.** *Anthropology.* Of or relating to a nonindustrial, often tribal culture, especially one that is characterized by a low level of economic complexity: *primitive societies.* **5.** *Linguistics.* **a.** Serving as the basis for derived or inflected forms: Pick *is the primitive word from which* picket *is derived.* **b.** Being a protolanguage: *primitive Germanic.* **6.** *Mathematics.* An algebraic or geometric expression from which another expression is derived. **7.** Relating to or belonging to forces of nature; elemental: *primitive passions.* **8. a.** Of or created by an artist without formal training; simple or naive in style. **b.** Of or relating to the work of an artist from a nonindustrial, often tribal culture, especially a culture that is characterized by a low level of economic complexity. **9.** Of or relating to late medieval or pre-Renaissance European painters or sculptors. **10.** *Biology.* Occurring in or characteristic of an early stage of development or evolution. —**primitive** *n.* **1.** *Anthropology.* A person belonging to a nonindustrial, often tribal society, especially a society characterized by a low level of economic complexity. **2.** An unsophisticated person. **3.** One that is at a low or early stage of development. **4. a.** One belonging to an early stage in the development of an artistic trend, especially a painter of the pre-Renaissance period. **b.** An artist having or affecting a simple, direct, unschooled style, as of painting. **c.** A self-taught artist. **d.** A work of art created by a primitive artist. **5.** *Linguistics.* A word or word element from which another word is derived by morphological or historical processes or from which inflected forms are derived. **6.** *Computer Science.* A basic or fundamental unit of machine instruction or translation. [Middle English, from Old French *primitif, primitive,* from Latin *prīmitīvus,* from *prīmitus,* at first, from *prīmus,* first. See **per¹** in Appendix.] —**prim′i·tive·ly** *adv.* —**prim′i·tive·ness, prim′i·tiv′i·ty** *n.*

prim·i·tiv·ism (prĭm′ĭ-tĭ-vĭz′əm) *n.* **1.** The condition or quality of being primitive. **2.** The style characteristic of a primitive artist. **3. a.** A belief that it is best to live simply and in a natural environment. **b.** A belief that the acquisitions of civilization are evil or that the earliest period of human history was the best. —**prim′i·tiv·ist** *adj. & n.* —**prim′i·tiv·is′tic** *adj.*

pri·mo (prē′mō) *n., pl.* **-mi** (-mē) also **-mos** (-mōz). *Music.* The principal part in a duet or ensemble composition. —**primo** *adj.* **1.** First. **2.** *Slang.* **a.** Exceptionally good of its kind; first-class. **b.** Highly or most valuable. [Italian, from Old Italian, first, from Latin *prīmus.* See **per¹** in Appendix.]

Pri·mo de Ri·ve·ra y Or·ba·ne·ja (prē′mō dā rĭ-vĕr′ə, ē ôr′bə-nā′hä, *thĕ* rē-vĕ′rä ē ôr′vä-nĕ′hä), **Miguel.** Marqués de Estella. 1870–1930. Spanish general and politician who seized power and ruled as dictator (1923–1930). His son **José Antonio Primo de Rivera** (1903–1936) founded the Spanish Fascist Party (1933) and was executed by Loyalists during the Civil War.

pri·mo·gen·i·tor (prī′mō-jĕn′ĭ-tər) *n.* **1.** The earliest ancestor. **2.** An ancestor or a forefather. [Late Latin *prīmōgenitor* : Latin *prīmō,* at first (from *prīmus,* first; see **per¹** in Appendix) + Latin *genitor,* begetter (from *gignere, genit-,* to beget; see **gene-** in Appendix).]

pri·mo·gen·i·ture (prī′mō-jĕn′ĭ-cho͝or′) *n.* **1.** The state of being the first-born or eldest child of the same parents. **2.** *Law.* The right of the eldest child, especially the eldest son, to inherit the entire estate of one or both parents. [Late Latin *prīmōgenitūra* : Latin *prīmō,* at first (from *prīmus,* first; see **per¹** in Appendix) + Latin *genitūra,* birth (from *gignere, genit-,* to beget; see **gene-** in Appendix).] —**pri′mo·gen′i·tar′y** (-jĕn′ĭ-tĕr′ē), **pri′mo·gen′i·tal** (-təl) *adj.*

pri·mor·di·al (prī-môr′dē-əl) *adj.* **1.** Being or happening first in sequence of time; original. **2.** Primary or fundamental: *play a primordial role.* **3.** *Biology.* Belonging to or characteristic of the earliest stage of development of an organism or a part: *primordial cells.* —**primordial** *n.* A basic principle. [Middle English, from Late Latin *prīmōrdiālis,* from Latin *prīmōrdium,* origin : *prīmus,* first; see **per¹** in Appendix + *ōrdīrī,* to begin to weave; see **ar-** in Appendix.] —**pri·mor′di·al·ly** *adv.*

pri·mor·di·um (prī-môr′dē-əm) *n., pl.* **-di·a** (-dē-ə). An organ or a part in its most rudimentary form or stage of development. [Latin *prīmōrdium.* See PRIMORDIAL.]

primp (prĭmp) *v.* **primped, primp·ing, primps.** —*tr.* To dress or groom (oneself) with meticulous or excessive attention to detail. —*intr.* To dress or groom oneself with elaborate care; preen. [Perhaps alteration of PRIM¹.]

prim·rose (prĭm′rōz′) *n.* **1.** Any of numerous plants of the genus *Primula,* having well-developed basal leaves and tubular, variously colored flowers grouped in umbels or heads with a funnel-shaped or salverlike corolla and a tube much longer than the calyx. **2.** An evening primrose. [Middle English *primerose,* from Old French, from Medieval Latin *prīma rosa,* first rose : Latin *prīmum,* neuter of *prīmus,* first; see PRIME + Latin *rosa,* rose.]

primrose path *n.* **1.** A way of life of worldly ease or pleasure. **2.** A course of action that seems easy and appropriate but can actually end in calamity.

pri·mum mo·bi·le (prī′məm mō′bə-lē′, prē′məm mō′bĭ-lā′) *n.* **1.** The tenth and outermost concentric sphere of the universe thought in Ptolemaic astronomy to revolve around Earth from east to west in 24 hours and believed to cause the other nine spheres to revolve with it. **2.** See **prime mover** (sense 1). [Me-

ă pat	oi boy
ā pay	ou out
âr care	o͝o took
ä father	o͞o boot
ĕ pet	ŭ cut
ē be	ûr urge
ĭ pit	th thin
ī pie	*th* this
îr pier	hw which
ŏ pot	zh vision
ō toe	ə about, item
ô paw	♦ regionalism

Stress marks: ′ (primary); ′ (secondary), as in **dictionary** (dĭk′shə-nĕr′ē)

dieval Latin *prīmum mōbile* : *prīmum,* neuter of *prīmus,* first + *mōbile,* from neuter of *mōbilis,* movable (translation of Arabic *al-muḥarrik al-awwal*).]

pri·mus (prī′məs) *n., pl.* **-mus·es.** Often **Primus.** The first in rank of the bishops of Scotland. [Medieval Latin *prīmus,* from Latin, first. See **per**[1] in Appendix.]

pri·mus in·ter pa·res (prī′məs ĭn′tər pâr′ēz, prē′mo͝os ĭn′tər pä′rēs′) *n., pl.* **pri·mi inter pares** (-mī, -mē). The first among equals. [Latin *prīmus inter parēs* : *prīmus,* first + *inter,* among + *parēs,* pl. of *pār,* equal.]

prin. *abbr.* **1.** Principal. **2.** Principle.

prince (prĭns) *n. Abbr.* **p., P., Pr. 1.** A male member of a royal family other than the monarch, especially a son of the monarch. **2.a.** The ruler of a principality. **b.** A hereditary ruler; a king. **3.** A nobleman of varying status or rank. **4.** An outstanding man, especially in a particular group or class: *a merchant prince.* [Middle English, from Old French, from Latin *prīnceps.* See **per**[1] in Appendix.] **—prince′ship′** *n.*

Prince Al·bert[1] (prĭns ăl′bərt). A city of central Saskatchewan, Canada, on the North Saskatchewan River north-northeast of Saskatoon. It was founded in 1866. Population, 31,380.

Prince Al·bert[2] (prĭns ăl′bərt) *n.* A man's long, double-breasted frock coat. [After *Prince Albert* Edward, later Edward VII.]

Prince Charm·ing also **prince charm·ing** (chär′mĭng) *n.* **1.** A man who fulfills all the romantic expectations of a woman. **2.** A man who ardently seeks the company and affection of women. [After *Prince Charming,* hero of the fairy tale *Cinderella.*]

prince consort *n.* The husband of a sovereign queen.

prince·dom (prĭns′dəm) *n.* **1.** The territory, jurisdiction, sovereignty, rank, or estate of a prince. **2. princedoms.** *Theology.* See **principality** (sense 3).

Prince Ed·ward Island (ĕd′wərd). *Abbr.* **PE, P.E.I.** A province of southeast Canada consisting of **Prince Edward Island** in the southern Gulf of St. Lawrence. It joined the confederacy in 1873. The island was discovered by Jacques Cartier in 1534 and named Île St. Jean by Samuel de Champlain in 1603. It was renamed in 1798 after Edward, Duke of Kent (1767–1820), the father of Queen Victoria. Charlottetown is the capital and the largest city. Population, 122,506.

Prince George (jôrj). A city of central British Columbia, Canada, at the confluence of the Fraser and Nechako rivers. Originally a fur-trading post called Fort George (established in 1807), it is now a distributing center for a lumbering region. Population, 67,559.

prince·ling (prĭns′lĭng) *n.* A prince judged to be of minor status or importance.

prince·ly (prĭns′lē) *adj.* **-li·er, -li·est. 1.** Of or relating to a prince; royal. **2.** Befitting a prince; as: **a.** Noble: *a princely bearing.* **b.** Munificent; lavish: *inherited a princely sum.* **—prince′li·ness** *n.* **—prince′ly** *adv.*

Prince of Wales (wālz) *n.* **1.** The male heir to the British throne. **2.** Used as the title for the male heir to the British throne, conferred by the sovereign.

Prince of Wales Island. 1. An island of northern Northwest Territories, Canada, in the Arctic Ocean northeast of Victoria Island. **2.** An island of extreme southeast Alaska in the Alexander Archipelago. It is the largest island in the group.

prince regent *n., pl.* **prince regents** or **princes regent.** A prince who rules during the minority, absence, or incapacity of a sovereign.

Prince Ru·pert (ro͞o′pərt). A city of western British Columbia, Canada, on the Pacific Ocean near the Alaska border. A railroad and highway terminus and ice-free port, it is a processing and shipping center. Population, 16,197.

prince's feather (prĭn′sĭz) *n.* **1.** A tall plant *(Polygonum orientale)* of Asia and Australia, having hairy stems, broadly ovate leaves, and long spikes of pink or rose flowers. **2.** Either of two plants *(Amaranthus hybridus* var. *erythrostachys* or *A. cruentus)* having reddish foliage and panicles of brownish-red flowers.

prince's pine *n.* See **pipsissewa.**

prin·cess (prĭn′sĭs, -sĕs′, prĭn-sĕs′) *n.* **1.** A woman who is ruler of a principality. **2.** A woman member of a royal family other than the monarch, especially a daughter of a monarch. **3.** A noblewoman of varying status or rank. **4.** The wife of a prince. **5.** A woman regarded as having the status or qualities of a princess. **6.** *Archaic.* A hereditary woman ruler; a queen. **—princess** *adj.* Designed to hang in smooth, close-fitting, unbroken lines from shoulder to flared hem: *a princess dress.* [Middle English *princesse,* from Old French, feminine of *prince,* prince. See PRINCE.]

prin·cesse (prĭn-sĕs′) *adj.* Princess: *a gown cut on princesse lines.* [French, from Old French, princess. See PRINCESS.]

princess royal *n.* **1.** The eldest daughter of a British sovereign, who has had the title conferred on her for life by the sovereign. **2.** Used as the title for such a woman.

princess tree *n.* See **paulownia.** [After *Princess* Anna Paulovna (1795–1865), queen of William II of the Netherlands.]

Prince·ton (prĭn′stən). A borough of central New Jersey north-northeast of Trenton. Founded by Quakers in 1696, it is the seat of Princeton University (established in 1746 as the College of New Jersey and renamed in 1896). George Washington defeated the British here in January 1777. Population, 12,035.

Princeton, Mount. A mountain, 4,330 m (14,197 ft) high, in the Sawatch Range of the Rocky Mountains in central Colorado.

Prince Wil·liam Sound (wĭl′yəm). An arm of the Gulf of Alaska east of the Kenai Peninsula. The worst oil spill in U.S. history occurred here in March 1989.

prin·ci·pal (prĭn′sə-pəl) *adj. Abbr.* **prin. 1.** First, highest, or foremost in importance, rank, worth, or degree; chief. **2.** Of, relating to, or being financial principal, or a principal in a financial transaction. **—principal** *n. Abbr.* **prin. 1.** One who holds a position of presiding rank, especially the head of an elementary school or high school. **2.** A main participant in a situation. **3.** A person having a leading or starring role. **4.a.** The capital or main body of an estate or a financial holding as distinguished from the interest or revenue from it. **b.** A sum of money owed as a debt, upon which interest is calculated. **5.** *Law.* **a.** A person who empowers another to act as his or her representative. **b.** The person having prime responsibility for an obligation as distinguished from one who acts as surety or as an endorser. **c.** One who commits or is an accomplice to a crime. **6.** The main truss or rafter that supports and gives form to a roof. [Middle English, from Old French, from Latin *prīncipālis,* from *prīnceps, prīncip-,* leader, emperor. See **per**[1] in Appendix.] **—prin′ci·pal·ly** *adv.* **—prin′ci·pal·ship′** *n.*

USAGE NOTE: *Principal* and *principle* are often confused but have no meanings in common. *Principle* is only a noun, and most of its senses refer to that which is basic or to rules and standards. *Principal* is both a noun and an adjective. As a noun (aside from its specialized meanings in law and finance) it generally denotes a person who holds a high position or plays an important role: *a meeting among all the principals in the transaction.* As an adjective it has the sense of "chief" or "leading."

principal diagonal *n. Mathematics.* The diagonal in a square matrix that goes from the upper left corner to the lower right corner.

principal focus *n.* A focal point.

prin·ci·pal·i·ty (prĭn′sə-păl′ĭ-tē) *n., pl.* **-ties. 1.** A territory ruled by a prince or from which a prince derives his title. **2.** The position, authority, or jurisdiction of a prince; sovereignty. **3. principalities.** *Theology.* The seventh of the nine orders of angels. In this sense, also called *princedoms.*

principal parts *pl.n. Grammar.* **1.** In traditional grammars of inflected languages, the forms of the verb that are considered basic and from which all forms of the verb are derived. **2.** In English, the present infinitive (*play, eat, put*), the past tense (*played, ate, put*), and the present participle (*playing, eating, putting*).

Prín·ci·pe (prĭn′sə-pə, prēɴ′sĭ-). An island of western Africa in the Gulf of Guinea, part of São Tomé and Príncipe.

prin·cip·i·um (prĭn-sĭp′ē-əm) *n., pl.* **-i·a** (-ē-ə). A principle, especially a basic one. [Latin *prīncipium.* See PRINCIPLE.]

prin·ci·ple (prĭn′sə-pəl) *n. Abbr.* **prin. 1.** A basic truth, law, or assumption: *the principles of democracy.* **2.a.** A rule or standard, especially of good behavior: *a man of principle.* **b.** The collectivity of moral or ethical standards or judgments: *a decision based on principle rather than expediency.* **3.** A fixed or predetermined policy or mode of action. **4.** A basic or essential quality or element determining intrinsic nature or characteristic behavior: *the principle of self-preservation.* **5.** A rule or law concerning the functioning of natural phenomena or mechanical processes: *the principle of jet propulsion.* **6.** *Chemistry.* One of the elements that compose a substance, especially one that gives some special quality or effect. **7.** A basic source. See Usage Note at **principal. 8. Principle.** *Christian Science.* God. ***—idioms.*** **in principle.** With regard to the basics: *an idea that is acceptable in principle.* **on principle.** According to or because of principle. [Middle English, alteration of Old French *principe,* from Latin *prīncipium,* from *prīnceps, prīncip-,* leader, emperor. See **per**[1] in Appendix.]

WORD HISTORY: Despite generations of spelling lessons, the words *principle* and *principal* are still commonly confused. Perhaps an understanding of their history will help in keeping them straight. Both words go back to the same Latin word, *prīnceps,* meaning "first, as in time, position, or authority." The split that has caused all the trouble occurred in the next stage of development. From *prīnceps* were derived the noun *prīncipium,* "start, origin, guiding principle," the adjective *prīncipālis,* "first in importance or esteem," and the noun *prīncipālis,* "a leading citizen." Clearly the latter two words with the *ā* between the *p* and the *l* have given us the adjective *principal* (first recorded around 1300) and the noun *principal* (also first recorded in a work composed around 1300). Perhaps it should not be mentioned that one Middle English spelling for the noun was *principle.* On the other hand, the Latin word *prīncipium* and its Old French descendant *principe* were involved in the creation of the word *principle* in Middle English, first recorded in a work written around 1380. Words like *manciple* and *participle* influenced the spelling of this new word, but again perhaps we should keep silent about the fact that we also find the word spelled *principal* and *prinsipal* in Middle English. A key point to remember about these seemingly aberrant Middle English spellings is that in Middle English spelling was not nearly as fixed as it usually is today, a development that was much furthered by the invention of printing. When we interchange spellings for *principle* and *principal,* we are doing something that would have been less of a fault in the days before the conformity imposed on us by this marvelous invention.

---

prin·ci·pled (prĭnʹsə-pəld) *adj.* Based on, marked by, or manifesting principle: *a principled decision; a principled person.*

prink (prĭngk) *v.* **prinked, prink·ing, prinks.** —*tr.* To adorn (oneself) in a showy manner. —*intr.* To dress or groom oneself with elaborate care or vanity; primp. [Probably alteration of PRANK[2].] —**prinkʹer** *n.*

print (prĭnt) *n.* **1.** A mark or an impression made in or on a surface by pressure: *the print of footsteps in the sand.* See Synonyms at **impression. 2.a.** A device or an implement, such as a stamp, die, or seal, used to press markings onto or into a surface. **b.** Something formed or marked by such a device. **3.a.** Lettering or other impressions produced in ink from type by a printing press or other means. **b.** Matter so produced; printed material. **c.** Printed state or form. **4.a.** A printed publication, such as a magazine or newspaper. **b.** Printed matter. **5.** A design or picture transferred from an engraved plate, wood block, lithographic stone, or other medium. **6.** A photographic image transferred to paper or a similar surface, usually from a negative. **7.** A copy of a film or movie. **8.a.** A fabric or garment with a dyed pattern that has been pressed onto it, usually by engraved rollers. **b.** The pattern itself. —**print** *v.* **print·ed, print·ing, prints.** —*tr.* **1.** To press (a mark or design, for example) onto or into a surface. **2.a.** To make an impression on or in (a surface) with a device such as a stamp, seal, or die. **b.** To press (a stamp or similar device) onto or into a surface to leave a marking. **3.a.** To produce by means of pressed type on a paper surface, with or as if with a printing press. **b.** To offer in printed form; publish. **4.** To write (something) in characters similar to those commonly used in print. **5.** To impress firmly in the mind or memory. **6.** To produce a photographic image from (a negative, for example) by passing light through film onto a photosensitive surface, especially sensitized paper. —*intr.* **1.a.** To work as a printer. **b.** To produce printed material. **2.** To produce something in printed form by means of a printing press or other reproduction process. **3.** To write characters similar to those commonly used in print. **4.** To produce or receive an impression, a marking, or an image. —**print** *adj.* Of, relating to, writing for, or constituting printed publications: *a print journalist; print coverage.* —***phrasal verb.* print out.** *Computer Science.* To print as a function; produce printout. —***idioms.* in print. 1.** In printed or published form: *denials that were to be found in print.* **2.** Offered for sale by a publisher: *books that are still in print.* **out of print.** No longer offered for sale by a publisher: *books that are out of print.* [Middle English *preinte,* from Old French, from feminine past participle of *preindre,* to press, alteration of *prembre,* from Latin *premere.* See **per-**[4] in Appendix.]

print. *abbr.* Printing.

print·a·ble (prĭnʹtə-bəl) *adj.* **1.** Capable of being printed or of producing a print: *printable negatives.* **2.** Fit for publication: *printable language.* —**printʹa·bilʹi·ty** *n.*

print bar *n.* A mechanism in a printing device that carries the template of the final form of the alphanumeric characters to be printed.

print·ed circuit (prĭnʹtĭd) *n.* An electric circuit in which the conducting connections have been printed or otherwise deposited in predetermined patterns on an insulating base.

printed matter *n.* Printed material, such as a book or magazine, that is not considered first-class mail and qualifies for a special postal rate.

print·er (prĭnʹtər) *n.* **1.** One that prints, especially one whose occupation is printing. **2.** A device used for printing, especially a photographic machine from which a duplicate of a master print can be made. **3.** *Computer Science.* The part of a system that produces printed matter.

print·er's devil (prĭnʹtərz) *n.* An apprentice in a printing establishment.

print head *n.* *Computer Science.* The element of a printer that applies the mark or image to the paper.

print·ing (prĭnʹtĭng) *n.* *Abbr.* **print., pr., ptg. 1.** The art, process, or business of producing printed material by means of inked type and a printing press or by similar means. **2.a.** The act of one that prints. **b.** Matter that is printed. **3.** All the copies of a publication, such as a book, that are printed at one time. **4.** Written characters not connected to one another and resembling those appearing in print.

printing ink *n.* Ink made especially for use in printing.

printing office *n.* An establishment where printed material is produced, especially one that is officially authorized.

printing press *n.* A machine that transfers lettering or images by contact with various forms of inked surface onto paper or similar material fed into it in various ways.

print·mak·ing (prĭntʹmāʹkĭng) *n.* The artistic design and manufacture of prints, such as woodcuts or silk-screens. —**printʹmakʹer** *n.*

print·out (prĭntʹoutʹ) *n.* *Computer Science.* Printed output.

print wheel *n.* A disk-shaped mechanism in a printing device that carries the template of the characters to be printed around its rim and prints one character at a time, revolving after each character to the proper position for the next.

pri·on (prēʹŏn) *n.* A microscopic protein particle similar to a virus but lacking nucleic acid, thought to be the infectious agent responsible for scrapie and certain other degenerative diseases of the nervous system. [*proteinaceous* (PROTEIN + –ACEOUS) + I(NFECTIOUS) + –ON[1].]

pri·or[1] (prīʹər) *adj.* **1.** Preceding in time or order: "[They] *insist that foreign vessels seeking access obtain prior approval*" (Seymour M. Hersh). **2.** Preceding in importance or value: *a prior consideration.* [Latin. See PRIOR[2].] —**priʹor·ly** *adv.*

pri·or[2] (prīʹər) *n.* **1.** A monastic officer in charge of a priory or ranking next below the abbot of an abbey. **2.** One of the ruling magistrates of the medieval Italian republic of Florence. [Middle English *priour,* from Old English and Old French *prior,* both from Medieval Latin, from Latin, superior. See **per**[1] in Appendix.] —**priʹor·ate** (-ĭt), **priʹor·shipʹ** (-shĭpʹ) *n.*

Pri·or (prīʹər), **Matthew.** 1664–1721. English poet and diplomat known for his epigrams and light satirical verse.

pri·or·ess (prīʹər-ĭs) *n.* A nun in charge of a priory or ranking next below the abbess of an abbey. [Middle English *prioresse,* from Old French, feminine of *prior,* a prior. See PRIOR[2].]

pri·or·i·tize (prī-ôrʹĭ-tīzʹ, -ŏrʹ-) *v.* **-tized, -tiz·ing, -tiz·es.** *Usage Problem.* —*tr.* To arrange or deal with in order of importance. —*intr.* To put things in order of importance: *"Everyone should take time to be alone, to prioritize and meditate"* (Art Linkletter). [PRIORIT(Y) + –IZE.] —**pri·orʹi·ti·zaʹtion** (-tĭ-zāʹshən) *n.*

USAGE NOTE: It can be argued that *prioritize* serves a useful function in providing a single word to mean "arrange according to priority," but like many other recent formations with *-ize,* it is widely regarded as corporate or bureaucratic jargon. In an earlier survey, *prioritize* was unacceptable to the great majority of the Usage Panel. See Usage Note at **–ize.**

---

pri·or·i·ty (prī-ôrʹĭ-tē, -ŏrʹ-) *n., pl.* **-ties. 1.** Precedence, especially established by order of importance or urgency. **2.a.** An established right to precedence. **b.** An authoritative rating that establishes such precedence. **3.** A preceding or coming earlier in time. **4.** Something afforded or deserving prior attention. [Middle English *priorite,* from Old French, from Medieval Latin *priōritās,* from Latin *prior,* first. See PRIOR[2].]

prior to *prep.* Preceding, before: *"prior to the changes of ownership and editorship"* (Brendan Gill).

pri·or·y (prīʹə-rē) *n., pl.* **-ies.** A monastery governed by a prior or a convent governed by a prioress.

Prip·et (prĭpʹĕt) or **Pri·pyat** (prēʹpyət). A river, about 708 km (440 mi) long, of northern Ukraine and southern Belorussia, flowing generally eastward through the **Pripet Marshes** to the Dnieper River north of Kiev.

Pris·cian (prĭshʹən, -ē-ən). fl. A.D. 500. Latin grammarian at Constantinople whose text *Institutiones Grammaticae* was used throughout medieval Europe.

prise (prīz) *v. & n.* Variant of **prize**[3].

prism (prĭzʹəm) *n.* **1.** A solid figure whose bases or ends have the same size and shape and are parallel to one another, and each of whose sides is a parallelogram. **2.** A transparent body of this form, often of glass and usually with triangular ends, used for separating white light passed through it into a spectrum or for reflecting beams of light. **3.** A cut-glass object, such as a pendant of a chandelier. **4.** A crystal form consisting of three or more similar faces parallel to a single axis. **5.** A medium that misrepresents whatever is seen through it. [Late Latin *prīsma,* from Greek *prisma,* thing sawed off, prism, from *priein, prizein,* to saw.]

pris·mat·ic (prĭz-mătʹĭk) also **pris·mat·i·cal** (-ĭ-kəl) *adj.* **1.** Of, relating to, resembling, or being a prism. **2.** Formed by refraction of light through a prism. Used of a spectrum of light. **3.** Brilliantly colored; iridescent. [Greek *prisma, prismat-,* prism; see PRISM + –IC.] —**pris·matʹi·cal·ly** *adv.*

pris·ma·toid (prĭzʹmə-toidʹ) *n.* A polyhedron all of whose vertices lie in one of two parallel planes. [Greek *prisma, prismat-,* prism + –OID.] —**prisʹma·toiʹdal** (-toidʹl) *adj.*

pris·moid (prĭzʹmoidʹ) *n.* A prismatoid having polygons with the same number of sides as bases, and faces that are parallelograms or trapezoids. —**pris·moiʹdal** (-moidʹl) *adj.*

pris·on (prĭzʹən) *n.* **1.** A place where persons convicted or accused of crimes are confined; a penitentiary or a jail. **2.** A place or condition of confinement or forcible restraint. **3.** A state of imprisonment or captivity. —**prison** *tr.v.* **-oned, -on·ing, -ons.** To confine in a prison; imprison. [Middle English, from Old French, alteration (influenced by Old French *pris,* taken) of Latin *prēnsiō, prēnsiōn-,* a seizing, from **prehēnsiō,* from *prehēnsus,* past participle of *prehendere,* to seize. See **ghend-** in Appendix.]

WORD HISTORY: The word *prison* has its origins not in the notions of what such a place is but rather in the notion of how one gets there. *Prison* can be traced back to the Latin word *prēnsiō,* "the action or power of making an arrest." This in turn is derived from the verb *prehendere* or *prendere,* which meant "to take hold of, take into custody, arrest." *Prēnsiō* then dives into the obscurity of the time when Romance languages such as French were being formed from Vulgar Latin and resurfaces in the Old French of the 12th century with the form *prison* and the senses "capture" and

printed circuit
On a floppy disk drive

ă pat	oi boy
ā pay	ou out
âr care	ŏŏ took
ä father	ōō boot
ĕ pet	ŭ cut
ē be	ûr urge
ĭ pit	th thin
ī pie	*th* this
îr pier	hw which
ŏ pot	zh vision
ō toe	ə about, item
ô paw	♦ regionalism

Stress marks: ʹ (primary); ʹ (secondary), as in **dictionary** (dĭkʹshə-nĕrʹē)

"place of imprisonment." This new sense could have already been developed in Latin and not been recorded, but we have to wait until the 12th century to see it, the sense "captivity" being added in the same century. From Old French as well as the Medieval Latin word *priso,* "prison," derived from Old French, came our Middle English word *prisoun,* first recorded in a work written before 1121 in the sense "imprisonment." The sense "place of imprisonment" is recorded shortly afterward in a text copied down before 1225 but perhaps actually written in the Old English period before the Norman Conquest.

---

prison camp *n.* **1.** A camp for prisoners of war. **2.** A minimum security facility for the internment of prisoners. In this sense, also called *work camp.*

pris·on·er (prĭzʹə-nər, prĭzʹnər) *n.* **1.** A person held in custody, captivity, or a condition of forcible restraint, especially while on trial or serving a prison sentence. **2.** One deprived of freedom of expression or action: *"He was a prisoner of his own personality—of that given set of traits that . . . predisposed him to see the world in a certain way, to make certain moves, certain choices"* (William H. Hallahan).

prisoner of war *n., pl.* **prisoners of war.** A person taken by or surrendering to enemy forces in wartime.

Prisoner of War Medal *n.* A congressional decoration featuring a bald eagle surrounded by barbed wire and bayonet points, that is awarded to any American prisoner of war held captive by enemy troops after April 5, 1917.

pris·on·er's base (prĭzʹə-nərz, prĭzʹnərz) *n. Games.* A children's game in which two teams try to capture opposing players by tagging them and bringing them to a base.

prison fever *n.* See **typhus.** [So called because it formerly prevailed in prisons.]

pris·sy (prĭsʹē) *adj.* **-si·er, -si·est.** Excessively or affectedly prim and proper. [Perhaps blend of PRI(M)¹ and (SI)SSY.] **—prisʹsi·ly** *adv.* **—prisʹsi·ness** *n.*

pris·tine (prĭsʹtēnʹ, prĭ-stēnʹ) *adj.* **1.a.** Remaining in a pure state; uncorrupted by civilization. **b.** Remaining free from dirt or decay; clean: *pristine mountain snow.* **2.** Of, relating to, or typical of the earliest time or condition; primitive or original. [Latin *prīstinus.* See **per¹** in Appendix.] **—pris·tineʹly** *adv.*

Pritch·ett (prĭchʹĭt), Sir **V(ictor) S(awdon).** Born 1900. British writer of novels, literary criticism, and most notably, short stories.

prith·ee (prĭthʹē, prĭthʹē) *interj. Archaic.* Used to express a polite request. [Alteration of *(I) pray thee.*]

priv. *abbr.* **1.** Private. **2.** *Grammar.* Privative.

pri·va·cy (prīʹvə-sē) *n.* **1.a.** The quality or condition of being secluded from the presence or view of others. **b.** The state of being free from unsanctioned intrusion: *a person's right to privacy.* **2.** The state of being concealed; secrecy.

pri·vate (prīʹvĭt) *adj. Abbr.* **priv., pvt. 1.a.** Secluded from the sight, presence, or intrusion of others: *a private hideaway.* **b.** Designed or intended for one's exclusive use: *a private room.* **2.a.** Of or confined to the individual; personal: *a private joke; private opinions.* **b.** Undertaken on an individual basis: *private studies; private research.* **c.** Of, relating to, or receiving special hospital services and privileges: *a private patient.* **3.** Not available for public use, control, or participation: *a private club; a private party.* **4.a.** Belonging to a particular person or persons, as opposed to the public or the government: *private property.* **b.** Conducted and supported primarily by private individuals or by a nongovernmental agency or corporation: *a private college; a private sanatorium.* **c.** Of, relating to, or derived from nongovernment sources: *private funding.* **5.** Not holding an official or public position: *a former President who is now a private citizen.* **6.a.** Not for public knowledge or disclosure; secret: *private papers; a private communication.* **b.** Not appropriate for use or display in public; intimate: *private behavior; a private tragedy.* **c.** Placing a high value on personal privacy: *a retiring, private individual.* **—private** *n.* **1.** *Abbr.* **PVT, Pvt a.** A noncommissioned rank in the U.S. Army or Marine Corps that is below private first class. **b.** One who holds this rank or a similar rank in a military or paramilitary organization. **2. privates.** Private parts. Often used with *the.* **—*idioms.* go private.** To take a publicly owned company into private ownership, as by a leveraged buyout. **in private.** Not in public; secretly or confidentially. [Middle English *privat,* from Latin *prīvātus,* not in public life, past participle of *prīvāre,* to release, deprive, from *prīvus,* single, alone. See **per¹** in Appendix.] **—priʹvate·ly** *adv.* **—priʹvate·ness** *n.*

private detective *n.* A privately employed detective. Also called *private eye, private investigator.*

private enterprise *n.* **1.** Business activities unregulated by state ownership or control; privately owned business. **2.** A privately owned business enterprise, especially one operating under a system of free enterprise or laissez-faire capitalism.

pri·va·teer (prīʹvə-tîrʹ) *n.* **1.** A ship privately owned and manned but authorized by a government during wartime to attack and capture enemy vessels. **2.** The commander or one of the crew of such a ship. **—privateer** *intr.v.* **-teered, -teer·ing, -teers.** To sail as a privateer.

private eye *n.* See **private detective.**

private first class *n., pl.* **privates first class.** *Abbr.* **PFC, Pfc 1.** A noncommissioned rank in the U.S. Army that is above private and below corporal or in the U.S. Marine Corps that is above private and below lance corporal. **2.** One who holds this rank.

private investigator *n. Abbr.* **PI** See **private detective.**

private law *n.* The branch of law that deals with the legal rights and relationships of private individuals.

private member *n. Chiefly British.* A member of Parliament who does not hold office in the government or in his or her party.

private parts *pl.n.* The external organs of sex and excretion.

private school *n.* A secondary or elementary school run and supported by private individuals or a corporation rather than by a government or public agency.

pri·va·tion (prī-vāʹshən) *n.* **1.a.** Lack of the basic necessities or comforts of life. **b.** The condition resulting from such lack. **2.** An act, condition, or result of deprivation or loss. [Middle English *privacion,* from Old French, from Latin *prīvātiō, prīvātiōn-,* from *prīvātus,* past participle of *prīvāre,* to deprive. See PRIVATE.]

pri·vat·ism (prīʹvə-tĭzʹəm) *n.* The social position of being noncommittal to or uninvolved with anything other than one's own immediate interests and lifestyle. **—priʹva·tist** *adj. & n.* **—priʹva·tisʹtic** *adj.*

priv·a·tive (prĭvʹə-tĭv) *adj.* **1.** Causing deprivation, lack, or loss. **2.** *Abbr.* **priv.** *Grammar.* Altering the meaning of a term from positive to negative. **—privative** *n. Abbr.* **priv.** *Grammar.* A privative prefix or suffix, such as *a-, non-, un-,* or *-less.* [Middle English *privatif,* from Latin *prīvātīvus,* from *prīvātus,* past participle of *prīvāre,* to deprive. See PRIVATE.] **—privʹa·tive·ly** *adv.*

pri·va·tize (prīʹvə-tīzʹ) *tr.v.* **-tized, -tiz·ing, -tiz·es.** *Usage Problem.* To change (an industry or a business, for example) from governmental or public ownership or control to private enterprise: *"The strike . . . was called to protest the . . . government's plans to break up and privatize the deficit-ridden national railway system"* (Christian Science Monitor). See Usage Note at **-ize. —priʹva·ti·zaʹtion** (-tĭ-zāʹshən) *n.*

priv·et (prĭvʹĭt) *n.* **1.** Any of several shrubs of the genus *Ligustrum,* especially *L. vulgare* or *L. ovalifolium,* having opposite leaves and clusters of white flowers and widely used for hedges. **2.** Any of several similar or related plants. [Origin unknown.]

priv·i·lege (prĭvʹə-lĭj, prĭvʹlĭj) *n.* **1.a.** A special advantage, immunity, permission, right, or benefit granted to or enjoyed by an individual, a class, or a caste. See Synonyms at **right. b.** Such an advantage, an immunity, or a right held as a prerogative of status or rank, and exercised to the exclusion or detriment of others. **2.** The principle of granting and maintaining a special right or immunity: *a society based on privilege.* **3.** *Law.* The right to privileged communication in a confidential relationship, as between client and attorney, patient and physician, or communicant and priest. **4.** An option to buy or sell a stock, including put, call, spread, and straddle. **—privilege** *tr.v.* **-leged, -leg·ing, -leg·es. 1.** To grant a privilege to. **2.** To free or exempt. [Middle English, from Old French, from Latin *prīvilēgium,* a law affecting one person : *prīvus,* single, alone; see **per¹** in Appendix + *lēx, lēg-,* law; see **leg-** in Appendix.]

priv·i·leged (prĭvʹə-lĭjd, prĭvʹlĭjd) *adj.* **1.** Enjoying a privilege or having privileges: *privileged students.* **2.** Confined to an exclusive or chosen group of individuals: *privileged information.* **—privileged** *n. (used with a sing. or pl. verb).* Those enjoying a privilege or having privileges: *tax laws that favored the privileged at the expense of the disadvantaged.*

privileged communication *n. Law.* **1.** A confidential communication that one cannot be forced to divulge. **2.** A communication that is not subject to charges of slander or libel.

priv·i·ly (prĭvʹə-lē) *adv.* In a privy manner; privately or secretly.

priv·i·ty (prĭvʹĭ-tē) *n., pl.* **-ties. 1.** Knowledge of something private or secret shared between individuals, especially with the implication of approval or consent. **2.** *Law.* **a.** A relation between parties that is held to be sufficiently close and direct to support a legal claim on behalf of or against another person with whom this relation exists. **b.** A successive or mutual interest in or relationship to the same property. [Middle English *privete,* secrecy, privacy, from Old French, from Medieval Latin *prīvitās,* from Latin *prīvus,* single, alone. See **per¹** in Appendix.]

priv·y (prĭvʹē) *adj.* **1.** Made a participant in knowledge of something private or secret: *was privy to government secrets.* **2.** Belonging or proper to a person, such as the British sovereign, in a private rather than official capacity. **3.** Secret; concealed. **—privy** *n., pl.* **-ies. 1.a.** An outdoor toilet; an outhouse. **b.** A toilet. **2.** *Law.* One of the parties having an interest in the same matter. [Middle English *prive,* from Old French, from Latin *prīvātus,* private, from *prīvus,* single, alone. See **per¹** in Appendix.]

Priv·y Council (prĭvʹē) *n. Abbr.* **P.C. 1.** A council of the British sovereign that until the 17th century was the supreme legislative body, that now consists of cabinet ministers ex officio and others appointed for life, and that has no important function except through its Judicial Committee, which in certain cases acts as a supreme appellate court in the Commonwealth. **2. privy council.** An advisory council to an executive. **—privy councilor** *n.*

prix fixe (prēʹ fēksʹ) *n., pl.* **prix fixes** (prēʹ fēksʹ). **1.** A complete meal of several courses, sometimes with choices permitted, offered by a restaurant at a fixed price. **2.** A fixed price charged for such a meal. **3.** See **table d'hôte** (sense 2). [French : *prix,* price + *fixe,* fixed.]

prize¹ (prīz) *n.* **1.** Something offered or won as an award for superiority or victory, as in a contest or competition. See Synonyms at **bonus.** **2.** Something worth striving for; a highly desirable possession. **—prize** *adj.* **1.** Offered or given as a prize: *a prize cup.* **2.** Given a prize, or likely to win a prize: *a prize cow.* **3.** Worthy of a prize; first-class: *our prize azaleas.* **—prize** *tr.v.* **prized, priz·ing, priz·es. 1.** To value highly; esteem or treasure. See Synonyms at **appreciate. 2.** To estimate the worth of; evaluate. [Alteration of Middle English *pris,* value, price, reward. See PRICE.]

prize² (prīz) *n.* **1.** *Nautical.* Something seized by force or taken as booty, especially an enemy ship and its cargo captured at sea during wartime. **2.** The act of seizing; capture. [Alteration of Middle English *prise,* from Old French, from feminine past participle of *prendre,* from Latin *prehendere, prendere,* to seize. See **ghend-** in Appendix.]

♦ **prize³** also **prise** (prīz) *—tr.v.* **prized, priz·ing, priz·es** also **prised, pris·ing, pris·es.** To move or force with or as if with a lever; pry. *—n.* **1.** Leverage. **2.** *Chiefly Southern U.S.* Something used as a lever or for prying. [From Middle English *prise,* instrument for prying, probably from *prise,* the taking of something. See PRIZE².]

prize·fight (prīz′fīt′) *n. Sports.* A match fought between professional boxers for money. **—prize′fight′er** *n.* **—prize′fight′ing** *n.*

prize ring *n. Sports.* **1.** A platform enclosed by ropes on which contending boxers meet. **2.** Professional boxing.

prize·win·ner (prīz′wĭn′ər) *n.* One that wins a prize.

prize·win·ning also **prize-win·ning** (prīz′wĭn′ĭng) *adj.* Having won or worthy of winning a prize: *a prizewinning wine.*

p.r.n. or **PRN** *abbr. Latin.* Pro re nata (as the situation demands).

pro¹ (prō) *n., pl.* **pros.** *Abbr.* **p. 1.** An argument or a consideration in favor of something: *weighing the pros and cons.* **2.** One who supports a proposal or takes the affirmative side in debate. **—pro** *adv.* In favor; affirmatively: *arguing pro and con.* **—pro** *adj.* Affirmative; supporting: *a pro vote.* [Middle English, from Latin *prō,* for. See **per¹** in Appendix.]

pro² (prō) *Informal. n., pl.* **pros. 1.** A professional, especially in sports. **2.** An expert in a field of endeavor. **—pro** *adj.* Professional: *pro football.*

PRO also **P.R.O.** *abbr.* Public relations officer.

pro–¹ *pref.* **1.** Acting in the place of; substituting for: *pronoun.* **2.** Supporting; favoring: *prorevolutionary.* [Middle English, from Old French, from Latin *pro-, prō-,* from *prō,* for. See **per¹** in Appendix.]

pro–² *pref.* **1.a.** Earlier; before; prior to: *procambium.* **b.** Rudimentary: *pronucleus.* **2.** Anterior; in front of: *procephalic.* [Middle English, from Old French, from Greek, from *pro,* before, in front. See **per¹** in Appendix.]

pro·a (prō′ə) also **prau** (prou) or **prah·u** (prä′o͞o) *n. Nautical.* A swift Malayan sailboat with a triangular sail and a single outrigger. [Malay *pĕrāhū,* probably from Marathi *paḍāv.*]

pro-a·bor·tion (prō′ə-bôr′shən) *adj.* Favoring or supporting legalized abortion. **—pro′a·bor′tion·ist** *n.*

pro·ac·tive or **pro-ac·tive** (prō-ăk′tĭv) *adj.* Acting in advance to deal with an expected difficulty; anticipatory: *not reactive, but proactive steps to combat terrorism.* **—pro·ac′tion** *n.* **—pro·ac′tive·ly** *adv.*

pro-am (prō′ăm′) *Sports. n.* A sports event, such as a golf tournament, in which professionals compete with or against amateurs. **—pro-am** *adj.* Of, relating to, or constituting a sports event participated in by professionals and amateurs. [PRO(FESSIONAL) + AM(ATEUR).]

prob. *abbr.* **1.** Probable; probably. **2.** *Law.* Probate. **3.** Problem.

prob·a·bi·lism (prŏb′ə-bə-lĭz′əm) *n.* **1.** *Philosophy.* The doctrine that probability is a sufficient basis for belief and action, since certainty in knowledge is unattainable. **2.** *Roman Catholic Church.* The system of casuistry that, in those cases in which expert opinions on ethics are in doubt concerning the licitness of an act, allows an actor to follow the solidly probable opinion that favors the actor's personal liberty even though an opposing opinion, favoring law, may be more probable. **—prob′a·bi·list** *adj. & n.*

prob·a·bil·is·tic (prŏb′ə-bə-lĭs′tĭk) *adj.* **1.** Of, relating to, or based on probabilism: *the probabilistic system of ethics.* **2.** Of, based on, or affected by probability, randomness, or chance: *"The Big Bang universe is . . . exemplified in the probabilistic and indeterminate interactions of the smallest known physical properties"* (Frederick Turner). **—prob′a·bil·ist′i·cal·ly** *adv.*

prob·a·bil·i·ty (prŏb′ə-bĭl′ĭ-tē) *n., pl.* **-ties. 1.** The quality or condition of being probable; likelihood. **2.** A probable situation, condition, or event. **3.a.** The likelihood that a given event will occur: *a great probability of rain this evening.* **b.** *Statistics.* A number expressing the likelihood that a specific event will occur, expressed as the ratio of the number of actual occurrences to the number of possible occurrences. **—*idiom.* in all probability.** Most probably; very likely.

probability density *n. Statistics.* **1.** A function whose integral over a given interval gives the probability that the value of a random variable specified by its values will fall within the interval. **2.** The calculated value of a probability density. Also called *probability distribution.*

probability distribution *n. Statistics.* **1.** See **probability density. 2.** A function of a discrete random variable yielding the probability that the variable will have a given value.

probability theory *n.* The branch of mathematics that studies the likelihood of occurrence of random events in order to predict the behavior of defined systems.

prob·a·ble (prŏb′ə-bəl) *adj. Abbr.* **prob. 1.** Likely to happen or to be true: *War seemed probable in 1938. The home team, far ahead, is the probable winner.* **2.** Likely but uncertain; plausible. **3.** *Theology.* Of or relating to opinions and actions in ethics and morals for whose lawfulness intrinsic reasons or extrinsic authority may be adduced. [Middle English, plausible, from Old French, from Latin *probābilis,* from *probāre,* to prove. See PROVE.]

probable cause *n. Law.* Reasonable grounds for belief that an accused person may be subject to arrest or the issuance of a warrant. **—prob′a·ble-cause′** (prŏb′ə-bəl-kôz′) *adj.*

probable error *n. Abbr.* **P.E.** *Statistics.* The amount by which the arithmetic mean of a sample is expected to vary because of chance alone.

prob·a·bly (prŏb′ə-blē) *adv. Abbr.* **prob.** Most likely; presumably.

pro·bang (prō′băng′) *n.* A long, slender, flexible rod having a tuft or sponge at the end, used to remove foreign bodies from or apply medication to the larynx or esophagus. [Alteration (probably influenced by PROBE) of *provang.*]

pro·bate (prō′bāt′) *Law. n. Abbr.* **prob. 1.** The process of legally establishing the validity of a will before a judicial authority. **2.** Judicial certification of the validity of a will. **3.** An authenticated copy of a will so certified. **—probate** *tr.v.* **-bat·ed, -bat·ing, -bates.** To establish the validity of (a will) by probate. [Middle English *probat,* from Latin *probātum,* neuter past participle of *probāre,* to prove. See PROVE.]

probate court *n. Law.* A court limited to the jurisdiction of probating wills and administering estates.

pro·ba·tion (prō-bā′shən) *n.* **1.** A process or period in which a person's fitness, as for membership in a working or social group, is tested. **2.a.** *Law.* The act of suspending the sentence of a person convicted of a criminal offense and granting that person provisional freedom on the promise of good behavior. **b.** A discharge for a person from commitment as an insane person on condition of continued sanity and of being recommitted upon the reappearance of insanity. **3.** A trial period in which a student is given time to try to redeem failing grades or bad conduct. **4.** The status of a person on probation. [Middle English *probacion,* a testing, from Old French, from Latin *probātiō, probātiōn-,* from *probātus,* past participle of *probāre,* to test. See PROVE.] **—pro·ba′tion·al** *adj.* **—pro·ba′tion·al·ly** *adv.* **—pro·ba′tion·ar′y** *adj.*

pro·ba·tion·er (prō-bā′shə-nər) *n.* A person on probation.

probation officer *n. Law.* **1.** An official usually attached to a juvenile court and charged with the care of juvenile delinquents. **2.** An official charged with supervising convicts at large on suspended sentence or probation.

pro·ba·tive (prō′bə-tĭv) also **pro·ba·to·ry** (-tôr′ē, -tōr′ē) *adj.* **1.** Serving to test, try, or prove: *a probative period.* **2.** Furnishing evidence or proof.

probe (prōb) *n.* **1.** An exploratory action, expedition, or device, especially one designed to investigate and obtain information on a remote or unknown region: *electronic probes into the crust of the earth.* **2.** A slender, flexible surgical instrument used to explore a wound or body cavity. **3.** The act of exploring or searching with or as if with a device or an instrument. **4.** An investigation into unfamiliar matters or questionable activities; a penetrating inquiry: *a congressional probe into price fixing.* See Synonyms at **inquiry. 5.** A space probe. **—probe** *v.* **probed, prob·ing, probes.** *—tr.* **1.** To explore with or as if with a probe: *probe a wound to find its extent; probing the anthill with a stick.* **2.** To delve into; investigate. *—intr.* To conduct an exploratory investigation; search. [Middle English, examination, from Medieval Latin *proba,* from Late Latin, proof, from Latin *probāre,* to test, from *probus,* good. See **per¹** in Appendix.] **—prob′er** *n.* **—prob′ing·ly** *adv.*

pro·ben·e·cid (prō-bĕn′ĭ-sĭd) *n.* A uricosuric drug, $C_{13}H_{19}NO_4S$, derived from benzoic acid and used chiefly in the treatment of gout. [PRO(PYL) + BEN(ZOIC) (A)CID.]

pro·bi·ty (prō′bĭ-tē) *n.* Complete and confirmed integrity; uprightness: *"He was a gentlemanly Georgian, a person of early American probity"* (Mary McGrory). See Synonyms at **honesty.** [Middle English *probite,* from Old French, from Latin *probitās,* from *probus,* upright, good. See **per¹** in Appendix.]

prob·lem (prŏb′ləm) *n. Abbr.* **prob. 1.** A question to be considered, solved, or answered: *math problems; the problem of how to hem a skirt evenly.* **2.** A situation, matter, or person that presents perplexity or difficulty: *urban problems such as traffic congestion and smog; the philosophical problem of evil.* See Usage Note at **dilemma. —problem** *adj.* **1.** Difficult to deal with or control: *a problem child; problem customers.* **2.** Dealing with a moral or social problem: *a problem play.* [Middle English *probleme,* from Old French, from Latin *problēma, problēmat-,* from Greek, from *proballein,* to throw before, put forward : *pro-,* before; see PRO–² + *ballein, blē-,* to throw; see **gʷelə-** in Appendix.]

prob·lem·at·ic (prŏb′lə-măt′ĭk) also **prob·lem·at·i·cal** (-ĭ-kəl) *adj.* **1.** Posing a problem; difficult to solve: *a problematic situation in the home.* **2.** Open to doubt; debatable: *"if you ever get married, which seems to me extremely problematic"* (Oscar

ă pat	oi boy
ā pay	ou out
âr care	o͝o took
ä father	o͞o boot
ĕ pet	ŭ cut
ē be	ûr urge
ĭ pit	th thin
ī pie	*th* this
îr pier	hw which
ŏ pot	zh vision
ō toe	ə about, item
ô paw	♦ regionalism

Stress marks: **′** (primary); ′ (secondary), as in **dictionary** (dĭk′shə-nĕr′ē)

Wilde). **3.** Not settled; unresolved or dubious: *a problematic future.* —**prob′lem·at′i·cal·ly** *adv.*

prob·lem-o·ri·ent·ed language (prŏb′ləm-ôr′ē-ĕn′tĭd, -ōr′-) *n. Computer Science.* A programming language intended for use in solving a particular set of problems.

pro bo·no (prō bō′nō) *adj.* Done without compensation for the public good: *a lawyer's pro bono work.* [Latin *prō bonō (pūblicō),* for the (public) good : *prō,* for + *bonō,* ablative of *bonum,* the good.]

pro·bos·ci·de·an (prō-bŏs′ĭ-dē′ən) *adj. & n.* Variant of **proboscidian.**

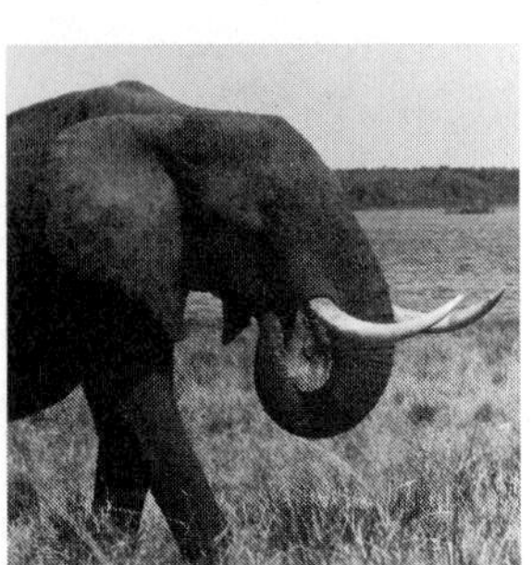

proboscis
African elephant eating grass

pro·bos·ci·des (prō-bŏs′ĭ-dēz′) *n.* A plural of **proboscis.**

pro·bos·cid·i·an (prō′bə-sĭd′ē-ən) also **pro·bos·ci·de·an** (prō-bŏs′ĭ-dē′ən) —*n.* A mammal of the order Proboscidea, such as the elephant or its extinct relatives, having a long trunk, large tusks, and a massive body. —*adj.* Of or belonging to the order Proboscidea. [From New Latin *Proboscidea,* order name, from Latin *proboscis, proboscid-,* proboscis. See PROBOSCIS.]

pro·bos·cis (prō-bŏs′ĭs) *n., pl.* **-bos·cis·es** or **-bos·ci·des** (-bŏs′ĭ-dēz′). **1.** A long, flexible snout or trunk, as of an elephant. **2.** The slender, tubular feeding and sucking organ of certain invertebrates, such as insects, worms, and mollusks. **3.** A human nose, especially a prominent one. [Latin, from Greek *proboskis* : *pro-,* in front; see PRO–[2] + *boskein,* to feed.]

pro-bus·ing (prō-bŭs′ĭng) *adj.* Favoring or supporting the busing of children to schools outside their neighborhoods as a means of achieving racial integration.

proc. *abbr.* **1.** Proceeding. **2.** Process.

pro·caine (prō′kān′) *n.* A white crystalline powder, $C_{13}H_{20}N_2O_2$, used chiefly in its hydrochloride form as a local anesthetic in medicine and dentistry. [PRO–[1] + (CO)CAINE.]

pro·cam·bi·um (prō-kăm′bē-əm) *n.* A type of undifferentiated plant tissue that gives rise to vascular tissue. —**pro·cam′bi·al** (-əl) *adj.*

pro·car·ba·zine (prō-kär′bə-zēn) *n.* A potent antineoplastic drug, $C_{12}H_{19}N_3O$, used to treat advanced Hodgkin's disease. [PRO(PYL) + CARB(O)– + AZINE.]

pro·car·y·ote (prō-kăr′ē-ōt′) *n.* Variant of **prokaryote.**

pro·ce·dur·al (prə-sē′jər-əl) *adj.* Of or concerning procedure, especially of a court of law or parliamentary body. —**procedural** *n.* A police procedural. —**pro·ce′dur·al·ly** *adv.*

pro·ce·dure (prə-sē′jər) *n.* **1.** A manner of proceeding; a way of performing or effecting something: *complained to the manager, and by this procedure got the money back.* **2.** A series of steps taken to accomplish an end: *a long therapeutic procedure.* **3.** A set of established forms or methods for conducting the affairs of a business, legislative body, or court of law. [French *procédure,* from Old French, from *proceder,* to proceed. See PROCEED.]

pro·ceed (prō-sēd′, prə-) *intr.v.* **-ceed·ed, -ceed·ing, -ceeds. 1.** To go forward or onward, especially after an interruption; continue: *proceeded to his destination; paused to clear her throat, then proceeded.* **2.** To begin to carry on an action or a process: *looked surprised, then proceeded to roar with laughter.* **3.** To move on in an orderly manner: *Business proceeded as usual.* **4.** To come from a source; originate or issue: *behavior proceeding from hidden motives.* See Synonyms at **stem**[1]. **5.** *Law.* To institute and conduct legal action: *proceeded against the defaulting debtor.* —**pro·ceeds** (prō′sēdz′) *n.* The amount of money derived from a commercial or fundraising venture; the yield. [Middle English *proceden,* from Old French *proceder,* from Latin *prōcēdere* : *prō-,* forward; see PRO–[1] + *cēdere,* to go; see **ked-** in Appendix.] —**pro·ceed′er** *n.*

pro·ceed·ing (prō-sē′dĭng, prə-) *n.* **1.** A course of action; a procedure. **2. proceedings.** A sequence of events occurring at a particular place or occasion: *watched the proceedings from a ringside seat.* **3. proceedings.** *Abbr.* **proc.** A record of business carried on by a society or other organization; minutes. **4.** Often **proceedings.** *Law.* **a.** Legal action; litigation. **b.** The instituting or conducting of legal action.

pro·ce·phal·ic (prō′sə-făl′ĭk) *adj.* Of, relating to, or located on or near the front of the head.

pro·cer·coid (prō-sûr′koid) *n.* A larval stage of certain tapeworms that typically develops in the body cavity of a copepod. [PRO–[2] + Greek *kerkos,* tail + –OID.]

proc·ess[1] (prŏs′ĕs′, prō′sĕs′) *n., pl.* **proc·ess·es** (prŏs′ĕs′ĭz, prō′sĕs′-, prŏs′ĭ-sēz′, prō′sĭ-). *Abbr.* **proc. 1.** A series of actions, changes, or functions bringing about a result: *the process of digestion; the process of obtaining a driver's license.* **2.** A series of operations performed in the making or treatment of a product: *a manufacturing process; leather dyed during the tanning process.* **3.** Progress; passage: *the process of time; events now in process.* **4.** *Law.* The entire course of a judicial proceeding. **5.** *Law.* **a.** A summons or writ ordering a defendant to appear in court. **b.** The total quantity of summonses or writs issued in a particular proceeding. **6.** *Biology.* An outgrowth of tissue; a projecting part: *a bony process.* **7.** Any of various photomechanical or photoengraving methods. **8.** See **conk**[3]. —**process** *tr.v.* **-essed, -ess·ing, -ess·es. 1.** To put through the steps of a prescribed procedure: *processing newly arrived immigrants; received the order, processed it, and dispatched the goods.* **2.** To prepare, treat, or convert by subjecting to a special process: *process ore to obtain minerals.* **3.** *Law.* **a.** To serve with a summons or writ. **b.** To institute legal proceedings against; prosecute. **4.** *Computer Science.* To perform operations on (data). **5.** To straighten (hair) by a chemical process; conk. —**process** *adj.* **1.** Prepared or converted by a special process: *process cheese.* **2.** Made by or used in any of several photomechanical or photoengraving processes: *a process print.* [Middle English *proces,* from Old French, development, from Latin *prōcessus,* from past participle of *prōcēdere,* to advance. See PROCEED.]

USAGE NOTE: In recent years there has been a tendency to pronounce the plural ending *–es* of *processes* as (-ēz), perhaps by analogy with words of Greek origin such as *analysis* and *neurosis.* But *process* is not of Greek origin, and there is no etymological justification for this pronunciation of its plural. The pronunciation may someday become so widespread as to be a standard variant, but it still strikes some listeners as a bungled affectation.

pro·cess[2] (prə-sĕs′) *intr.v.* **-cessed, -cess·ing, -cess·es.** To move along in or as if in a procession: *"The man in the panama hat offered his arm and . . . they processed into the dining room"* (Anita Brookner). [Back-formation from PROCESSION.]

pro·ces·sion (prə-sĕsh′ən) *n.* **1.** The act of moving along or forward; progression. **2.** Origination; emanation; rise. **3. a.** A group of persons, vehicles, or objects moving along in an orderly, formal manner. **b.** The movement of such a group. **4.** An orderly succession: *the procession of the seasons.* —**procession** *intr.v.* **-sioned, -sion·ing, -sions.** To form or go in a procession. [Middle English, from Old French, from Late Latin *prōcessiō, prōcessiōn-,* from Latin, an advance, from *prōcessus,* past participle of *prōcēdere,* to advance. See PROCEED.]

pro·ces·sion·al (prə-sĕsh′ə-nəl) *adj.* Of, relating to, or suitable for a procession. —**processional** *n.* **1.** A book containing the rituals observed during a religious procession. **2.** *Music.* **a.** A piece played or sung when the clergy enter a church at the beginning of a service. **b.** Music intended to be played or sung during a procession. —**pro·ces′sion·al·ly** *adv.*

proc·es·sor (prŏs′ĕs′ər, prō′sĕs′-) *n.* **1.** One that processes, especially an apparatus for preparing, treating, or converting material: *a wood pulp processor.* **2.** *Computer Science.* **a.** A computer. **b.** A central processing unit. **c.** A program that translates another program into a form acceptable by the computer being used.

proc·ess printing (prŏs′ĕs′, prō′sĕs′) *n.* Printing from multiple halftone images, each inked with a different color such that the composite impression will reproduce the colors of the original.

pro·cès-ver·bal (prō-sā′vĕr-bäl′) *n., pl.* **-ver·baux** (-vĕr-bō′). A detailed official record of diplomatic, deliberative, or legal proceedings. [French : *procès,* proceedings + *verbal,* oral (originally used of oral evidence given by illiterate police officers of the lower ranks).]

pro-choice (prō-chois′) *adj.* Favoring or supporting the legal right of women and girls to choose whether or not to continue a pregnancy to term.

pro·claim (prō-klām′, prə-) *tr.v.* **-claimed, -claim·ing, -claims. 1.** To announce officially and publicly; declare. See Synonyms at **announce. 2.** To indicate conspicuously; make plain: *wearing a button that proclaimed my choice for president.* **3.** To praise; extol. [Middle English *proclamen, proclaimen* (influenced by *claimen,* to claim), from Old French *proclamer,* from Latin *prōclāmāre* : *prō-,* forward; see PRO–[1] + *clāmāre,* to cry out; see **kelə-**[2] in Appendix.] —**pro·claim′er** *n.* —**pro·clam′a·to′ry** (prō-klăm′ə-tôr′ē, -tōr′ē) *adj.*

proc·la·ma·tion (prŏk′lə-mā′shən) *n.* **1.** The act of proclaiming or the condition of being proclaimed. **2.** Something proclaimed, especially an official public announcement.

pro·clit·ic (prō-klĭt′ĭk) *Linguistics. adj.* Forming an accentual unit with the following word and thus having no independent accent. —**proclitic** *n.* A proclitic word. [New Latin *procliticus* : PRO–[2] + Late Latin *encliticus,* enclitic; see ENCLITIC.]

pro·cliv·i·ty (prō-klĭv′ĭ-tē) *n., pl.* **-ties.** A natural propensity or inclination; predisposition. See Synonyms at **predilection.** [Latin *prōclīvitās,* from *prōclīvis,* inclined : *prō-,* forward; see PRO–[1] + *clīvus,* slope; see **klei-** in Appendix.]

Pro·clus (prō′kləs, prŏk′ləs). A.D. 410?–485. Greek philosopher and the last major Neo-Platonic teacher. He maintained that reality is fundamentally mental rather than material.

Proc·ne (prŏk′nē) *n. Greek Mythology.* An Athenian princess who avenged the betrayal and cruelty of her husband, Tereus, by killing their son. She and her sister Philomela were changed into swallows as Tereus pursued them.

pro·co·ag·u·lant (prō′kō-ăg′yə-lənt) *n.* **1.** The precursor of any of various blood factors necessary for coagulation. **2.** An agent that promotes the coagulation of blood.

pro·con·sul (prō-kŏn′səl) *n.* **1.** A provincial governor of consular rank in the Roman Republic and Roman Empire. **2.** A high administrator in one of the modern colonial empires. [Middle English, from Latin *prōcōnsul,* from *prō cōnsule,* in place of the consul : *prō,* instead of; see PRO–[1] + *cōnsule,* ablative of *cōnsul,* consul; see CONSUL.] —**pro·con′su·lar** (-sə-lər) *adj.* —**pro·con′su·late** (-sə-lĭt) *n.* —**pro·con′sul·ship′** *n.*

Pro·co·pi·us (prə-kō′pē-əs). fl. sixth century A.D. Byzantine historian during the reign of Justinian I.

pro·cras·ti·nate (prō-krăs′tə-nāt′, prə-) *v.* **-nat·ed, -nat·ing, -nates.** —*intr.* To put off doing something, especially out of habitual carelessness or laziness. —*tr.* To postpone or delay needlessly. [Latin *prōcrāstināre, prōcrāstināt-* : *prō-*, forward; see PRO–[1] + *crāstinus*, of tomorrow (from *crās*, tomorrow).] **—pro·cras′ti·na′tion** *n.* **—pro·cras′ti·na′tor** *n.*

pro·cre·ate (prō′krē-āt′) *v.* **-at·ed, -at·ing, -ates.** —*tr.* **1.** To beget and conceive (offspring). **2.** To produce or create; originate. —*intr.* To beget and conceive offspring; reproduce. [Latin *prōcreāre, prōcreāt-* : *prō-*, forward; see PRO–[1] + *creāre*, to create; see **ker-**[2] in Appendix.] **—pro′cre·ant** (-ənt) *adj.* **—pro′cre·a′tion** *n.* **—pro′cre·a′tor** *n.*

pro·cre·a·tive (prō′krē-ā′tĭv) *adj.* **1.** Capable of reproducing; generative. **2.** Of or directed to procreation: *the procreative instinct.*

Pro·crus·te·an also **pro·crus·te·an** (prō-krŭs′tē-ən) *adj.* Exhibiting merciless disregard for individual differences or special circumstances: *a private club with Procrustean standards for the admission of new members.* [After *Procrustes*, a mythical Greek giant who stretched or shortened captives to make them fit his beds, from Latin *Procrustēs*, from Greek *Prokroustēs*, from *prokrouein*, hammer out, to stretch out : *pro-*, forth; see PRO–[2] + *krouein*, to beat.]

Procrustean bed also **procrustean bed** *n.* An arbitrary standard to which exact conformity is forced.

pro·cryp·tic (prō-krĭp′tĭk) *adj. Zoology.* Having a pattern or coloration adapted for natural camouflage. [Probably PRO(TECTIVE) + CRYPTIC.]

proc·ti·tis (prŏk-tī′tĭs) *n.* Inflammation of the rectum or anus. [Greek *prōktos*, anus + –ITIS.]

proc·to·de·um also **proc·to·dae·um** (prŏk′tə-dē′əm) *n.*, *pl.* **-de·a** (-dē′ə) or **-de·ums** also **-dae·a** (-dē′ə) or **-dae·ums.** An inward fold on the surface of the embryonic ectoderm that develops into part of the anal passage. [New Latin : Greek *prōktos*, anus + New Latin *-odeum* (probably from Greek *hodaion*, neuter of *hodaios*, on the way, from *hodos*, way).]

proc·tol·o·gy (prŏk-tŏl′ə-jē) *n.* The branch of medicine that deals with the diagnosis and treatment of disorders affecting the colon, rectum, and anus. [Greek *prōktos*, anus + –LOGY.] **—proc′to·log′ic** (-tə-lŏj′ĭk), **proc′to·log′i·cal** (-ĭ-kəl) *adj.* **—proc′to·log′i·cal·ly** *adv.* **—proc·tol′o·gist** *n.*

proc·tor (prŏk′tər) *n.* A dormitory and examination supervisor in a school. **—proctor** *tr.v.* **-tored, -tor·ing, -tors.** To supervise (an examination). [Middle English *procutor*, *proctour*, university officer, manager, from *procuratour*. See PROCURATOR.] **—proc·to′ri·al** (-tôr′ē-əl, -tōr′-) *adj.* **—proc′tor·ship′** *n.*

proc·to·scope (prŏk′tə-skōp′) *n.* An instrument consisting of a tube or speculum equipped with a light, used to examine the rectum. [Greek *prōktos*, anus + –SCOPE.] **—proc′to·scop′ic** (-skŏp′ĭk) *adj.* **—proc·tos′co·py** (-tŏs′kə-pē) *n.*

pro·cum·bent (prō-kŭm′bənt) *adj.* **1.** Lying face down; prone. **2.** *Botany.* Trailing along the ground but not rooting: *a procumbent vine.* [Latin *prōcumbēns, prōcumbent-*, present participle of *prōcumbere*, to bend down : *prō-*, forward; see PRO–[1] + *-cumbere*, to lie down.]

proc·u·ra·tor (prŏk′yə-rā′tər) *n.* **1.** One authorized to manage the affairs of another; an agent. **2.** An employee of the Roman emperor in civil affairs, especially in finance and taxes, in management of imperial estates and properties, and in governing minor provinces. [Middle English *procuratour*, from Old French, from Latin *prōcūrātor*, from *prōcūrāre*, to take care of. See PROCURE.] **—proc′u·ra·to′ri·al** (-yər-ə-tôr′ē-əl, -tōr′-) *adj.*

pro·cure (prō-kyŏŏr′, prə-) *v.* **-cured, -cur·ing, -cures.** —*tr.* **1.** To get by special effort; obtain or acquire: *managed to procure a pass.* **2.** To bring about; effect: *procure a solution to a knotty problem.* **3.** To obtain for another (a person) for sex acts. —*intr.* To obtain sexual partners for others. [Middle English *procuren*, from Old French *procurer*, to take care of, from Latin *prōcūrāre*, to take care of : *prō-*, for; see PRO–[1] + *cūrāre*, to care for (from *cūra*, care; see CURE).] **—pro·cur′a·ble** *adj.* **—pro·cur′ance, pro·cure′ment** *n.*

pro·cur·er (prō-kyŏŏr′ər, prə-) *n.* **1.** One that procures: *a procurer of free tickets to concerts.* **2.** A pander.

Pro·cy·on (prō′sē-ŏn′) *n.* A binary star in the constellation Canis Minor. Also called *Dog Star.* [Latin *Procyōn*, from Greek *Prokuōn* : *pro-*, before; see PRO–[2] + *kuōn*, dog; see **kwon-** in Appendix.]

prod (prŏd) *tr.v.* **prod·ded, prod·ding, prods.** **1.** To jab or poke, as with a pointed object. **2.** To goad to action; incite. See Synonyms at **urge.** **—prod** *n.* **1.** A pointed object used to prod: *a cattle prod.* **2.** An incitement; a stimulus. [Origin unknown.] **—prod′der** *n.*

Prod or **prod** (prŏd) *n. Offensive Slang.* Used as a disparaging term for a Protestant.

prod. *abbr.* **1.** Produce. **2.** Produced. **3.** Product. **4.** Production.

prod·i·gal (prŏd′ĭ-gəl) *adj.* **1.** Rashly or wastefully extravagant: *They are prodigal in their expenditures.* **2.** Marked by rash or wasteful extravagance: *a prodigal life.* **3.** Giving or given in abundance; lavish or profuse: *prodigal praise.* See Synonyms at **profuse.** **—prodigal** *n.* One who is given to wasteful luxury or extravagance. [Probably back-formation from PRODIGALITY.] **—prod′i·gal·ly** *adv.*

prod·i·gal·i·ty (prŏd′ĭ-găl′ĭ-tē) *n.*, *pl.* **-ties.** **1.** Extravagant wastefulness. **2.** Profuse generosity. **3.** Extreme abundance; lavishness. [Middle English *prodigalite*, from Old French, from Late Latin *prōdigālitās*, from **prōdigālis*, prodigal, from Latin *prōdigus*, prodigal, from *prōdigere*, drive away, to squander : *prōd-*, *prō-*, forth; see PRO–[1] + *agere*, to drive; see **ag-** in Appendix.]

pro·di·gious (prə-dĭj′əs) *adj.* **1.** Impressively great in size, force, or extent; enormous: *a prodigious storm.* **2.** Extraordinary; marvelous: *the young Mozart's prodigious talents.* **3.** *Obsolete.* Portentous; ominous. [Latin *prōdigiōsus*, portentous, monstrous, from *prōdigium*, omen.] **—pro·di′gious·ly** *adv.* **—pro·di′gious·ness** *n.*

WORD HISTORY: No one would now say, as did a character in Fanny Burney's *Evelina* (1778), "You are prodigiously kind!" But this utterance, exclamation point and all, illustrates two important points about intensives, linguistic elements, such as *extremely* or *awfully*, that provide force or emphasis. One point is that we press words that originally had other meanings into service as intensives. *Prodigiously* is an adverb formed on *prodigious*, which meant such things as "ominous, amazing, enormous," going back to the Latin *prōdigiōsus*, "portentous, marvelous, unnatural." *Prodigiously*, first recorded in 1595, meant "portentously, ominously," and was later used to mean "wonderfully, astonishingly," therefore making a perfect candidate for use as an intensive. The other point about intensives illustrated by *prodigiously* is that they go in and out of fashion. The character in *Evelina* used *prodigiously* in a way that was no doubt very stylish; no one would find it so today. Perhaps the main reason for such shifts in the use of these intensives is that once they have been used for a while they no longer intensify.

prod·i·gy (prŏd′ə-jē) *n.*, *pl.* **-gies.** **1.** A person with exceptional talents or powers: *a prodigy who had learned several foreign languages by the age of five.* **2.** An act or event so extraordinary or rare as to inspire wonder. See Synonyms at **wonder.** **3.** A portentous sign or event; an omen. [Middle English *prodige*, portent, from Latin *prōdigium*.]

pro·drome (prō′drōm′) *n.*, *pl.* **-dromes** or **-dro·ma·ta** (-drō′mə-tə). An early symptom indicating the onset of an attack or a disease. [French, from Latin *prodromus*, precursor, from Greek *prodromos*, precursor : *pro-*, forward; see PRO–[2] + *dromos*, running.] **—pro·dro′mal** (-drō′məl), **pro·drom′ic** (-drŏm′ĭk) *adj.*

pro·drug (prō′drŭg′) *n.* An inactive precursor of a drug, converted into its active form in the body by normal metabolic processes.

pro·duce (prə-dōōs′, -dyōōs′, prō-) *v.* **-duced, -duc·ing, -duc·es.** —*tr.* **1.** To bring forth; yield: *produce offspring.* **2. a.** To create by physical or mental effort: *produce a tapestry; produce a poem.* **b.** To manufacture: *factories that produce cars and trucks.* **3.** To cause to occur or exist; give rise to: *chemicals that produce a noxious vapor when mixed.* **4.** To bring forth; exhibit: *reached into a pocket and produced a packet of matches; failed to produce an eyewitness to the crime.* **5.** To supervise and finance the making and public presentation of: *produce a stage play; produce a videotape.* **6.** *Mathematics.* To extend (an area or volume) or lengthen (a line). —*intr.* **1.** To make or yield products or a product: *an apple tree that produces well.* **2.** To manufacture or create economic goods and services. **—produce** (prŏd′ōōs, prō′dōōs) *n. Abbr.* **prod.** **1.** Something produced; a product. **2.** Farm products, especially fresh fruits and vegetables. [Middle English *producen*, to proceed, extend, from Latin *prōdūcere*, to extend, bring forth : *prō-*, forward; see PRO–[1] + *dūcere*, to lead; see **deuk-** in Appendix.] **—pro·duc′i·ble, pro·duce′a·ble** *adj.*

SYNONYMS: *produce, bear, yield.* The central meaning shared by these verbs is "to bring forth as a product": *a mine producing gold; a seed that finally bore fruit; a plant that yields a medicinal oil.*

pro·duc·er (prə-dōō′sər, -dyōō′-, prō-) *n.* **1.** One that produces, especially a person or an organization that produces goods or services for sale. **2.** One who finances and supervises the making and public presentation of a play, film, program, or similar work. **3.** A furnace that manufactures producer gas. **4.** *Ecology.* A photosynthetic green plant or chemosynthetic bacterium, constituting the first trophic level in a food chain; an autotrophic organism.

producer gas *n.* A combustible mixture of nitrogen, carbon monoxide, and hydrogen, generated by passing air with steam over burning coke or coal in a furnace and used as fuel. Also called *air gas.*

producer goods *pl.n.* Goods, such as raw materials and tools, used to make consumer goods.

prod·uct (prŏd′əkt) *n. Abbr.* **prod.** **1.** Something produced by human or mechanical effort or by a natural process. **2.** A direct result; a consequence: *"Is history the product of impersonal social and economic forces?"* (Anthony Lewis). **3.** *Chemistry.* A substance resulting from a chemical reaction. **4.** *Mathematics.* **a.** The number or quantity obtained by multiplying two or more numbers together. **b.** A scalar product. **c.** A vector product. [Middle English, result of multiplication, produced, from Medieval Latin *prōductum*, result of multiplication, from neuter past participle of Latin *prōdūcere*, to bring forth. See PRODUCE.]

ă pat	oi boy
ā pay	ou out
âr care	ŏŏ took
ä father	ōō boot
ĕ pet	ŭ cut
ē be	ûr urge
ĭ pit	th thin
ī pie	*th* this
îr pier	hw which
ŏ pot	zh vision
ō toe	ə about, item
ô paw	♦ regionalism

Stress marks: **′** (primary); ′ (secondary), as in **dictionary** (dĭk′shə-nĕr′ē)

pro·duc·tion (prə-dŭk′shən, prō-) *n.* *Abbr.* **prod.** **1.a.** The act or process of producing: *timber used for the production of lumber and paper.* **b.** The fact or process of being produced: *a movie going into production.* **2.** The creation of value or wealth by producing goods and services. **3.** Something produced; a product. **4.** An amount or quantity produced; output. **5.a.** A work of art or literature. **b.** A work produced for the stage, screen, television, or radio. **c.** A staging or presentation of a theatrical work: *a new Broadway production of a musical.* **6.** An exaggerated spectacle or display: *proposed on his knees, making a real production of it.* **—pro·duc′tion·al** *adj.*

production line *n.* See **assembly line** (sense 1).

pro·duc·tive (prə-dŭk′tĭv, prō-) *adj.* **1.** Producing or capable of producing. **2.** Producing abundantly; fertile. See Synonyms at **fertile.** **3.** Yielding favorable or useful results; constructive. **4.** *Economics.* Of or involved in the creation of goods and services to produce wealth or value. **5.** Effective in achieving specified results; originative: *policies productive of much harm.* **6.** *Medicine.* **a.** Producing mucus or sputum: *a productive cough.* **b.** Forming new tissue: *a productive inflammation.* **7.** *Linguistics.* Of or relating to the linguistic skills of speaking and writing. **—pro·duc′tive·ly** *adv.* **—pro·duc′tive·ness** *n.*

pro·duc·tiv·i·ty (prō′dŭk-tĭv′ĭ-tē, prŏd′ək-) *n.* **1.** The quality of being productive. **2.** *Economics.* The rate at which goods or services are produced especially output per unit of labor. **3.** *Ecology.* The rate at which radiant energy is used by producers to form organic substances as food for consumers.

pro·em (prō′ĕm′) *n.* An introduction; a preface. [Middle English *proheme,* from Old French, from Latin *prooemium,* from Greek *prooimion* : *pro-,* before; see PRO–[2] + *oimē,* song.] **—pro·e′mi·al** (prō-ē′mē-əl, -ĕm′ē-) *adj.*

pro·en·zyme (prō-ĕn′zīm′) *n.* The inactive or nearly inactive precursor of an enzyme, converted into an active enzyme by proteolysis. Also called *zymogen.*

pro·es·trus (prō-ĕs′trəs) *n.* The period immediately before estrus in most female mammals, characterized by development of the endometrium and ovarian follicles.

prof (prŏf) *n.* *Informal.* A professor.

prof. *abbr.* Professional.

prof·a·na·tion (prŏf′ə-nā′shən) *n.* The act or an instance of profaning; desecration.

pro·fane (prō-fān′, prə-) *adj.* **1.** Marked by contempt or irreverence for what is sacred: *profane words.* **2.** Nonreligious in subject matter, form, or use; secular: *sacred and profane music.* **3.** Not admitted into a body of secret knowledge or ritual; uninitiated. **4.** Vulgar; coarse. **—profane** *tr.v.* **-faned, -fan·ing, -fanes.** **1.** To treat with irreverence: *profane the name of God.* **2.** To put to an improper, unworthy, or degrading use; abuse. [Middle English *prophane,* from Old French, from Latin *profānus,* from *prō fānō,* in front of the temple : *prō-,* before, outside; see PRO–[1] + *fānō,* ablative of *fānum,* temple; see **dhēs-** in Appendix.] **—pro·fan′a·to′ry** (prō-făn′ə-tôr′ē, -tōr′ē, prə-) *adj.* **—pro·fane′ly** *adv.* **—pro·fane′ness** *n.* **—pro·fan′er** *n.*

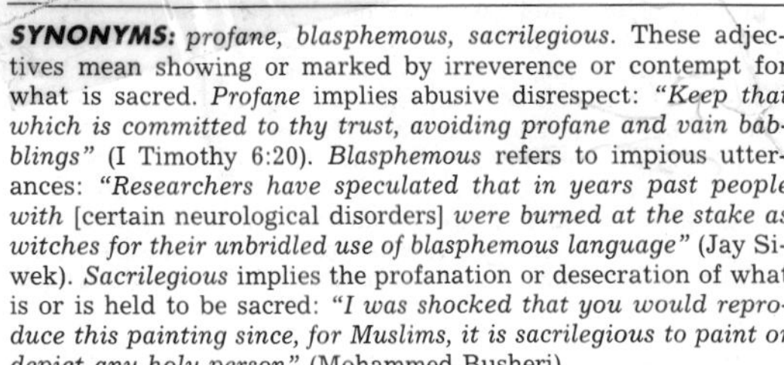

SYNONYMS: *profane, blasphemous, sacrilegious.* These adjectives mean showing or marked by irreverence or contempt for what is sacred. *Profane* implies abusive disrespect: *"Keep that which is committed to thy trust, avoiding profane and vain babblings"* (I Timothy 6:20). *Blasphemous* refers to impious utterances: *"Researchers have speculated that in years past people with* [certain neurological disorders] *were burned at the stake as witches for their unbridled use of blasphemous language"* (Jay Siwek). *Sacrilegious* implies the profanation or desecration of what is or is held to be sacred: *"I was shocked that you would reproduce this painting since, for Muslims, it is sacrilegious to paint or depict any holy person"* (Mohammed Busheri).

profile
Portrait of Bianca Maria Sforza by Giovanni de Predis (1450?–1520?)

pro·fan·i·ty (prō-făn′ĭ-tē, prə-) *n.,* *pl.* **-ties.** **1.** The condition or quality of being profane. **2.a.** Abusive, vulgar, or irreverent language. **b.** The use of such language.

pro·fess (prə-fĕs′, prō-) *v.* **-fessed, -fess·ing, -fess·es.** *—tr.* **1.** To affirm openly; declare or claim: *"I profess both to learn and to teach anatomy, not from books but from dissections"* (William Harvey). **2.** To make a pretense of; pretend: *"He professed to despise everything that had happened since 1850"* (Louis Auchincloss). **3.** To claim skill in or knowledge of: *profess medicine.* **4.** To affirm belief in: *profess Catholicism.* **5.** To receive into a religious order or congregation. *—intr.* **1.** To make an open affirmation. **2.** To take the vows of a religious order or congregation. [Middle English *professen,* to take vows, from Old French *profes,* that has taken a religious vow (from Medieval Latin *professus,* avowed) and from Medieval Latin *professāre,* to administer a vow, both from Latin *professus,* past participle of *profitērī,* to affirm openly : *pro-,* forth; see PRO–[1] + *fatērī,* to acknowledge; see **bhā-**[2] in Appendix.] **—pro·fess′ed·ly** (-fĕs′ĭd-lē) *adv.*

pro·fes·sion (prə-fĕsh′ən) *n.* **1.** An occupation requiring considerable training and specialized study: *the professions of law, medicine, and engineering.* **2.** The body of qualified persons in an occupation or field: *members of the teaching profession.* **3.** An act or instance of professing; a declaration. **4.** An avowal of faith or belief. **5.** A faith or belief: *believers of various professions.*

pro·fes·sion·al (prə-fĕsh′ə-nəl) *adj.* *Abbr.* **prof.** **1.a.** Of, relating to, engaged in, or suitable for a profession: *a professional field such as law; professional training.* **b.** Conforming to the standards of a profession: *professional ethics.* **2.** Engaging in a given activity as a source of livelihood or as a career: *amateur and professional actors.* **3.** Performed by persons receiving pay: *professional football.* **4.** Having or showing great skill; expert: *a thoroughly professional repair job.* **—professional** *n.* *Abbr.* **prof.** **1.** A person following a profession, especially a learned profession. **2.** One who earns a living in a given or implied occupation: *hired a professional to decorate the house.* **3.** A skilled practitioner; an expert. **—pro·fes′sion·al·ly** *adv.*

pro·fes·sion·al·ism (prə-fĕsh′ə-nə-lĭz′əm) *n.* **1.** Professional status, methods, character, or standards. **2.** The use of professional performers, as in athletics or in the arts.

pro·fes·sion·al·ize (prə-fĕsh′ə-nə-līz′) *tr.v.* **-ized, -iz·ing, -iz·es.** To make professional. **—pro·fes′sion·al·i·za′tion** (prə-fĕsh′ə-nə-lĭ-zā′shən) *n.*

pro·fes·sor (prə-fĕs′ər) *n.* **1.a.** A college or university teacher who ranks above an associate professor. **b.** A teacher or an instructor. **2.** One who professes. [Middle English *professour,* from Old French *professeur,* from Latin *professor,* from *professus,* past participle of *profitērī,* to profess. See PROFESS.] **—pro′fes·so′ri·al** (prō′fĭ-sôr′ē-əl, -sōr′-, prŏf′ĭ-) *adj.* **—pro′fes·so′ri·al·ly** *adv.* **—pro·fes′sor·ship′** *n.*

pro·fes·so·ri·ate or **pro·fes·so·ri·at** (prō′fĭ-sôr′ē-ət, -sōr′-, prŏf′ĭ-) *n.* **1.** The rank or office of a professor. **2.** College or university professors considered as a group.

prof·fer (prŏf′ər) *tr.v.* **-fered, -fer·ing, -fers.** To offer for acceptance; tender. See Synonyms at **offer.** **—proffer** *n.* The act of proffering; an offer. [Middle English *profren,* from Old French *poroffrir, profrir* : *por-,* forth (from Latin *prō-;* see PRO–[1]) + *offrir,* to offer (from Latin *offerre;* see OFFER).] **—prof′fer·er** *n.*

pro·fi·cien·cy (prə-fĭsh′ən-sē) *n.,* *pl.* **-cies.** The state or quality of being proficient; competence.

pro·fi·cient (prə-fĭsh′ənt) *adj.* Having or marked by an advanced degree of competence, as in an art, vocation, profession, or branch of learning. **—proficient** *n.* An expert; an adept. [Latin *prōficiēns, prōficient-,* present participle of *prōficere,* to make progress. See PROFIT.] **—pro·fi′cient·ly** *adv.*

SYNONYMS: *proficient, adept, skilled, skillful, expert.* These adjectives mean having or showing knowledge, ability, or skill, as in a vocation, profession, or branch of learning. *Proficient* implies an advanced degree of competence acquired through training: *A proficient surgeon is the product of lengthy training and experience.* *Adept* suggests a natural aptitude improved by practice: *The dress designer was adept at draping and cutting the fabric without using a pattern.* *Skilled* implies sound, thorough competence and often mastery, as in an an art, a craft, or a trade: *Only the most skilled gymnasts are accepted for the Olympic team.* *Skillful* adds to *skilled* the idea of natural dexterity in performance or achievement: *The crafts teacher is skillful in knitting, crocheting, embroidery, and the use of the hand loom.* *Expert* applies to one with consummate skill and command: *A virtuoso is one who is expert in playing a musical instrument.*

pro·file (prō′fīl′) *n.* **1.a.** A side view of an object or a structure, especially of the human head. **b.** A representation of an object or a structure seen from the side. See Synonyms at **form.** **2.** An outline of an object. See Synonyms at **outline.** **3.** Degree of exposure to public notice; visibility: *kept a low profile until the controversy had abated.* **4.** A biographical essay presenting the subject's most noteworthy characteristics and achievements. **5.** A formal summary or analysis of data, often in the form of a graph or table, representing distinctive features or characteristics: *a psychological profile of a job applicant; a biochemical profile of blood.* **6.** *Geology.* A vertical section of soil or rock showing the sequence of the various layers. **—profile** *tr.v.* **-filed, -fil·ing, -files.** **1.** To draw or shape a profile of. **2.** To produce a profile of. [Italian *profilo,* from *profilare,* to draw in outline : *pro-,* forward (from Latin *prō-;* see PRO–[1]) + *filare,* to draw a line (from Late Latin *filāre,* to spin, from Latin *fīlum,* thread; see **g^{w}hi-** in Appendix).] **—pro′fil·er** *n.*

prof·it (prŏf′ĭt) *n.* **1.** An advantageous gain or return; benefit. **2.** The return received on a business undertaking after all operating expenses have been met. **3.** Often **profits.** **a.** The return received on an investment after all charges have been paid. **b.** The rate of increase in the net worth of a business enterprise in a given accounting period. **c.** Income received from investments or property. **d.** The amount received for a commodity or service in excess of the original cost. **—profit** *v.* **-it·ed, -it·ing, -its.** *—intr.* **1.** To make a gain or profit. **2.** To derive advantage; benefit: *profiting from the other team's mistakes.* See Synonyms at **benefit.** *—tr.* To be beneficial to. [Middle English, from Old French, from Latin *prōfectus,* from past participle of *prōficere,* make progress, to profit : *prō-,* forward; see PRO–[1] + *facere,* to make; see **dhē-** in Appendix.] **—prof′it·less** *adj.*

prof·it·a·ble (prŏf′ĭ-tə-bəl) *adj.* Yielding profit; advantageous or lucrative. See Synonyms at **beneficial.** **—prof′it·a·bil′i·ty, prof′it·a·ble·ness** *n.* **—prof′it·a·bly** *adv.*

profit and loss *n.* *Abbr.* **P and L, p. and l.** *Accounting.* An account showing net profit and loss over a given period.

prof·it·eer (prŏf′ĭ-tîr′) *n.* One who makes excessive profits on goods in short supply. **—profiteer** *intr.v.* **-eered, -eer·ing, -eers.** To make excessive profits on goods in short supply.

pro·fit·er·ole (prə-fĭt′ə-rōl′) *n.* A small round cream puff. [French, perhaps diminutive of *profiter,* to profit, from Old French, from *profit,* profit. See PROFIT.]

profit shar·ing (shâr′ĭng) *n.* A system by which employees receive a share of the profits of a business enterprise.

prof·li·gate (prŏf′lĭ-gĭt, -gāt′) *adj.* **1.** Given over to dissipation; dissolute. **2.** Recklessly wasteful; wildly extravagant. **—profligate** *n.* A profligate person; a wastrel. [Latin *prōflīgātus,* past participle of *prōflīgāre,* to ruin, cast down : *prō-,* forward; see PRO–[1] + *-flīgāre,* intensive of *flīgere,* to strike down.] **—prof′li·ga·cy** (-gə-sē) *n.* **—prof′li·gate·ly** *adv.*

pro for·ma (prō fôr′mə) *adj.* **1.** Done as a formality; perfunctory: *one-candidate, pro forma elections.* **2.** Provided in advance so as to prescribe form or describe items: *a pro forma copy of a document.* [New Latin *prō formā* : *prō,* for the sake of + *formā,* ablative of *forma,* form.]

pro·found (prə-found′, prō-) *adj.* **-er, -est. 1.** Situated at, extending to, or coming from a great depth; deep. See Synonyms at **deep. 2.** Coming as if from the depths of one's being: *profound contempt.* **3.** Thoroughgoing; far-reaching: *profound social changes.* **4.** Penetrating beyond what is superficial or obvious: *a profound insight.* **5.** Unqualified; absolute: *a profound silence.* [Middle English *profounde,* from Old French *profond,* from Latin *profundus* : *prō-,* before; see PRO–[1] + *fundus,* bottom.] **—pro·found′ly** *adv.* **—pro·found′ness** *n.*

pro·fun·di·ty (prə-fŭn′dĭ-tē, prō-) *n., pl.* **-ties. 1.** Great depth. **2.** Depth of intellect, feeling, or meaning. **3.** Something profound or abstruse. [Middle English *profundite,* from Old French, from Late Latin *profunditās,* from Latin *profundus,* deep. See PROFOUND.]

pro·fuse (prə-fyo͞os′, prō-) *adj.* **1.** Plentiful; copious: *a field profuse with wildflowers.* **2.** Giving or given freely and abundantly; extravagant: *were profuse in their compliments.* [Middle English, lavish, from Latin *profūsus,* past participle of *profundere,* to pour forth : *pro-,* forth; see PRO–[1] + *fundere,* to pour; see **gheu-** in Appendix.] **—pro·fuse′ly** *adv.* **—pro·fuse′ness** *n.*

SYNONYMS: *profuse, exuberant, lavish, lush, luxuriant, prodigal, riotous.* The central meaning shared by these adjectives is "given with, giving with, or marked by unrestrained abundance": *profuse apologies; an exuberant growth of moss; lavish praise; lush vegetation; luxuriant hair; a prodigal party giver; a riotous growth of ferns.*
ANTONYM: *spare.*

pro·fu·sion (prə-fyo͞o′zhən, prō-) *n.* **1.** The state of being profuse; abundance. **2.** Lavish or unrestrained expense; extravagance. **3.** A profuse outpouring or quantity: *a profusion of helpful suggestions.*

pro·gen·i·tor (prō-jĕn′ĭ-tər) *n.* **1.** A direct ancestor. See Synonyms at **ancestor. 2.** An originator of a line of descent; a precursor. **3.** An originator; a founder: *progenitors of the new music.* [Middle English *progenitour,* from Old French *progeniteur,* from Latin *prōgenitor,* from *prōgenitus,* past participle of *prōgignere,* to beget : *prō-,* forward; see PRO–[1] + *gignere, gen-,* to beget; see **gene-** in Appendix.]

prog·e·ny (prŏj′ə-nē) *n., pl.* **progeny** or **-nies. 1.a.** One born of, begotten by, or derived from another; an offspring or a descendant. **b.** Offspring or descendants considered as a group. **2.** A result of creative effort; a product. [Middle English *progeni,* from Old French *progenie,* from Latin *prōgeniēs,* from *prōgignere,* to beget. See PROGENITOR.]

pro·ger·i·a (prō-jîr′ē-ə) *n.* A rare congenital disorder of childhood that is characterized by rapid onset of the physical changes typical of old age, usually resulting in death before the age of 20. Also called *Hutchinson-Gilford syndrome.* [PRO–[2] + Greek *gēras,* old age; see GERIATRICS + –IA[1].]

pro·ges·ta·tion·al (prō′jĕs-tā′shə-nəl) *adj.* **1.** Of or relating to the phase of the menstrual cycle immediately following ovulation, characterized by secretion of progesterone. **2.a.** Of or relating to progesterone and its actions. **b.** Having actions similar to progesterone. Used of a drug.

pro·ges·ter·one (prō-jĕs′tə-rōn′) *n.* **1.** A steroid hormone, $C_{21}H_{30}O_2$, secreted by the corpus luteum of the ovary and by the placenta, that acts to prepare the uterus for implantation of the fertilized ovum, to maintain pregnancy, and to promote development of the mammary glands. **2.** A drug prepared from natural or synthetic progesterone, used to prevent miscarriage and to treat menstrual disorders. [PRO–[1] + GEST(ATION) + (ST)ER(OL) + –ONE.]

pro·ges·tin (prō-jĕs′tĭn) *n.* **1.** A natural or synthetic progestational substance that mimics some or all of the actions of progesterone. **2.** A crude hormone of the corpus luteum from which progesterone can be isolated in pure form. No longer in scientific use. [PRO–[1] + GEST(ATION) + –IN.]

pro·ges·to·gen (prō-jĕs′tə-jən) *n.* Any of various substances having progestational effects; a progestin. [PRO–[1] + GEST(ATION) + –GEN.]

pro·glot·tid (prō-glŏt′ĭd) also **pro·glot·tis** (-glŏt′ĭs) *n., pl.* **-glot·tids** also **-glot·ti·des** (-glŏt′ĭ-dēz′). One of the segments of a tapeworm, containing both male and female reproductive organs. [Greek *proglōttis, proglōttid-,* tip of the tongue (from its shape) : *pro-,* before; see PRO–[2] + *glōtta,* tongue.] **—pro·glot′tic, pro′glot·ti·de′an** (-glŏt-ĭ-dē′ən, -glŏ-tĭd′ē-ən) *adj.*

prog·na·thous (prŏg′nə-thəs, prŏg-nā′-) also **prog·nath·ic** (prŏg-năth′ĭk, -nā′thĭk) *adj.* Having jaws that project forward to a marked degree. **—prog′na·thism** (-nə-thĭz′əm) *n.*

prog·no·sis (prŏg-nō′sĭs) *n., pl.* **-ses** (-sēz). **1.a.** A prediction of the probable course and outcome of a disease. **b.** The likelihood of recovery from a disease. **2.** A forecast or prediction: *a gloomy prognosis for economic recovery.* [Late Latin *prognōsis,* from Greek, from *progignōskein,* to foreknow : *pro-,* before; see PRO–[2] + *gignōskein,* to know; see **gnō-** in Appendix.]

prog·nos·tic (prŏg-nŏs′tĭk) *adj.* **1.** Of, relating to, or useful in prognosis. **2.** Of or relating to prediction; predictive. **—prognostic** *n.* **1.** A sign or symptom indicating the future course of a disease. **2.** A sign of a future happening; a portent. [Middle English *pronostik,* prognosticating, omen, from Medieval Latin *prognōsticus,* prognosticating, and from Latin *prognōsticum,* omen, from neuter of *prognōsticus,* from Greek *prognōstikos,* from *prognōsis,* foreknowledge. See PROGNOSIS.]

prog·nos·ti·cate (prŏg-nŏs′tĭ-kāt′) *tr.v.* **-cat·ed, -cat·ing, -cates. 1.** To predict according to present indications or signs; foretell. See Synonyms at **predict. 2.** To foreshadow; portend: *urban architectural renewal that prognosticates a social and cultural renaissance.* [Middle English *pronosticaten,* from Medieval Latin *prognōsticāre, prognōsticāt-,* from Latin *prognōsticum,* sign of the future, from Greek *prognōstikon,* from neuter of *prognōstikos,* foreknowing. See PROGNOSTIC.] **—prog·nos′ti·ca′tion** *n.* **—prog·nos′ti·ca′tive** *adj.* **—prog·nos′ti·ca′tor** *n.*

pro·gram (prō′grăm′, -grəm) *n.* **1.a.** A listing of the order of events and other pertinent information for a public presentation. **b.** The presentation itself: *a program of piano pieces.* **2.** A scheduled radio or television show. **3.** An ordered list of events to take place or procedures to be followed; a schedule: *a program of physical therapy for a convalescent.* **4.** A system of services, opportunities, or projects, usually designed to meet a social need: *"Working parents rely on the center's after-school latchkey program"* (New York Times). **5.a.** A course of academic study; a curriculum. **b.** A plan or system of academic and related or ancillary activities: *a work-study program.* **c.** A plan or system of nonacademic extracurricular activities: *the football program.* **6.** A set of coded instructions for insertion into a machine, in accordance with which the machine performs a desired sequence of operations. **7.** *Computer Science.* **a.** A procedure for solving a problem that involves collection of data, processing, and presentation of results. **b.** Such a procedure coded for a computer. **8.** An instruction sequence in programmed instruction. **—program** *tr.v.* **-grammed, -gram·ming, -grams** or **-gramed, -gram·ing, -grams. 1.** To include or schedule in a program: *program a new musical composition.* **2.** To design a program for; schedule the activities of. **3.** To provide (a machine) with a set of coded working instructions. **4.** *Computer Science.* To provide (a computer) with a set of instructions for solving a problem or processing data. **5.** To train to perform automatically in a desired way, as if programming a machine: *crudely programming children to make the right responses.* **6.** To prepare an instructional sequence for (material to be taught) in programmed instruction. [Late Latin *programma,* public notice, from Greek *programma, programmat-,* from *prographein,* to write publicly : *pro-,* forth; see PRO–[2] + *graphein,* to write; see **gerbh-** in Appendix.] **—pro·gram′ma·bil′i·ty** *n.* **—pro′gram′ma·ble** *adj.*

program director *n.* A radio or television station director responsible for selecting, planning, and scheduling programs.

pro·gramed (prō′grămd′, -grəmd) *adj.* Variant of **programmed.**

pro·gram·er (prō′grăm′ər) *n.* Variant of **programmer.**

pro·gram·ing (prō′grăm′ĭng, -grə-mĭng) *n.* Variant of **programming.**

pro·gram·mat·ic (prō′grə-măt′ĭk) *adj.* **1.** Of, relating to, or having a program. **2.** Following an overall plan or schedule: *a step-by-step, programmatic approach to problem solving.* **3.** *Music.* Of, resembling, or constituting program music. **—pro′gram·mat′i·cal·ly** *adv.*

pro·gramme (prō′grăm′, -grəm) *n. & v. Chiefly British.* Variant of **program.**

pro·grammed or **pro·gramed** (prō′grămd′, -grəmd) *adj.* Of, relating to, or resulting from programmed instruction: *programmed learning.*

programmed instruction *n.* A method of teaching in which the information to be learned is presented in discrete units, with a correct response to each unit required before the learner may advance to the next unit.

pro·gram·mer or **pro·gram·er** (prō′grăm′ər) *n.* One who programs, especially: **a.** One who writes computer programs. **b.** One who prepares or writes instructional programs.

pro·gram·ming or **pro·gram·ing** (prō′grăm′ĭng, -grə-mĭng) *n.* The designing, scheduling, or planning of a program.

program music *n.* Compositions intended to depict or suggest definite incidents, scenes, or images.

program trading *n.* Large-scale, computer-assisted trading of stocks or other securities according to systems in which decisions to buy and sell are triggered automatically by fluctuations in price. **—program trader** *n.*

prog·ress (prŏg′rĕs′, -rəs, prō′grĕs′) *n.* **1.** Movement, as toward a goal; advance. **2.** Development or growth: *pupils who show progress.* **3.** Steady improvement, as of a society or civilization: *a believer in human progress.* See Synonyms at **develop-**

ă pat	oi boy
ā pay	ou out
âr care	o͝o took
ä father	o͞o boot
ĕ pet	ŭ cut
ē be	ûr urge
ĭ pit	th thin
ī pie	*th* this
îr pier	hw which
ŏ pot	zh vision
ō toe	ə about, item
ô paw	♦ regionalism

Stress marks: **′** (primary); ′ (secondary), as in **dictionary** (dĭk′shə-nĕr′ē)

ment. 4. A ceremonial journey made by a sovereign through his or her realm. **—pro•gress** (prə-grĕs′) *intr.v.* **-gressed, -gress•ing, -gress•es. 1.** To advance; proceed: *Work on the new building progressed at a rapid rate.* **2.** To advance toward a higher or better stage; improve steadily: *as technology progresses.* **—*idiom.* in progress.** Going on; under way: *artistic works that are in progress.* [Middle English *progresse,* from Latin *prōgressus,* from past participle of *prōgredī,* to advance : *prō-,* forward; see PRO–[1] + *gradī,* to go, walk; see **ghredh-** in Appendix.]

pro•gres•sion (prə-grĕsh′ən) *n.* **1.** The process of progressing; progress. **2.** Movement from one member of a continuous series to the next. **3.** A continuous series; a sequence. See Synonyms at **series. 4.** *Mathematics.* A series of numbers or quantities in which there is always the same relation between each quantity and the one succeeding it. **5.** *Music.* **a.** A succession of tones or chords. **b.** A series of repetitions of a phrase, each in a new position on the scale. **—pro•gres′sion•al** *adj.*

pro•gres•sive (prə-grĕs′ĭv) *adj.* **1.** Moving forward; advancing. **2.** Proceeding in steps; continuing steadily by increments: *progressive change.* **3.** Promoting or favoring progress toward better conditions or new policies, ideas, or methods: *a progressive politician; progressive business leadership.* **4. Progressive.** Of or relating to a Progressive Party: *the Progressive platform of 1924.* **5.** Of or relating to progressive education: *a progressive school.* **6.** Increasing in rate as the taxable amount increases: *a progressive income tax.* **7.** *Pathology.* Tending to become more severe or wider in scope: *progressive paralysis.* **8.** *Grammar.* Designating a verb form that expresses an action or condition in progress. **—progressive** *n.* **1.** A person who actively favors or strives for progress toward better conditions, as in society or government. **2. Progressive.** A member or supporter of a Progressive Party. **3.** *Grammar.* A progressive verb form. **—pro•gres′sive•ly** *adv.* **—pro•gres′sive•ness** *n.*

Pro•gres•sive-Con•ser•va•tive Party (prə-grĕs′ĭv-kən-sûr′və-tĭv) *n. Abbr.* **PCP** A major political party in Canada advocating economic nationalism and close ties with Great Britain and the Commonwealth.

progressive education *n.* A set of reformist educational philosophies and methods that emphasize individual instruction, informality in the classroom, and the use of group discussions and laboratories as instructional techniques.

Progressive Party *n.* **1.** A U.S. political party that was organized by Republican insurgents in 1911 and supported the presidential candidacy of Theodore Roosevelt in 1912. Also called *Bull Moose Party.* **2.** A U.S. political party organized in 1924 that supported the presidential candidacy of Robert M. La Follette and was active in Wisconsin until 1946. **3.** A U.S. political party formed in 1948 to support the presidential candidacy of Henry A. Wallace.

Prohibition
Federal officers destroying barrels of beer

pro•gres•siv•ism (prə-grĕs′ĭ-vĭz′əm) *n.* **1.** The principles and practices of political progressives. **2.** Progressive education. **—pro•gres′siv•ist** *n.* **—pro•gres′siv•is′tic** *adj.*

pro•gres•siv•i•ty (prō′grĕ-sĭv′ĭ-tē, prŏg′rĕ-) *n., pl.* **-ties.** The quality or degree of being progressive: *"Proponents of progressivity often argue that higher-income people should pay higher taxes because they benefit more from government"* (National Review).

pro•hib•it (prō-hĭb′ĭt) *tr.v.* **-it•ed, -it•ing, -its. 1.** To forbid by authority: *Smoking is prohibited in most theaters.* See Synonyms at **forbid. 2.** To prevent; preclude: *Modesty prohibits me from saying what happened.* [Middle English *prohibiten,* from Latin *prohibēre, prohibit-* : *pro-,* in front; see PRO–[1] + *habēre,* to hold; see **ghabh-** in Appendix.]

pro•hi•bi•tion (prō′ə-bĭsh′ən) *n.* **1.** The act of prohibiting or the condition of being prohibited. **2.** A law, order, or decree that forbids something. **3. a.** The forbidding by law of the manufacture, transportation, sale, and possession of alcoholic beverages. **b. Prohibition.** The period (1920–1933) during which the 18th Amendment forbidding the manufacture and sale of alcoholic beverages was in force in the United States.

pro•hi•bi•tion•ist (prō′ə-bĭsh′ə-nĭst) *n.* **1.** One in favor of outlawing the manufacture and sale of alcoholic beverages. **2.** Often **Prohibitionist.** A member or supporter of the Prohibition Party. **—pro′hi•bi′tion•ism** *n.*

Prohibition Party *n.* A minor U.S. political party organized in 1869 that advocated prohibition.

pro•hib•i•tive (prō-hĭb′ĭ-tĭv) also **pro•hib•i•to•ry** (-tôr′ē, -tōr′ē) *adj.* **1.** Prohibiting; forbidding: *took prohibitive measures.* **2.** So high or burdensome as to discourage purchase or use: *prohibitive prices.* **3.** So likely to win as to discourage competition: *the prohibitive favorite to win the nomination.* **—pro•hib′i•tive•ly** *adv.* **—pro•hib′i•tive•ness** *n.*

pro•in•su•lin (prō-ĭn′sə-lĭn) *n.* A single-chain polypeptide that is the precursor of insulin, converted into insulin by enzymatic action.

proj•ect (prŏj′ĕkt′, -ĭkt) *n.* **1.** A plan or proposal; a scheme. See Synonyms at **plan. 2.** An undertaking requiring concerted effort: *a community cleanup project; a government-funded irrigation project.* **3.** An extensive task undertaken by a student or group of students to apply, illustrate, or supplement classroom lessons. **4.** A housing project. **— pro•ject** (prə-jĕkt′) *v.* **-ject•ed, -ject•ing, -jects.** *—tr.* **1.** To thrust outward or forward: *project one's jaw in defiance.* **2.** To throw forward; hurl: *project an arrow.* **3.** To send out into space; cast: *project a light beam.* **4.** To cause (an image) to appear on a surface: *projected the slide onto a screen.* **5.** *Mathematics.* To produce (a projection). **6.** To direct (one's voice) so as to be heard clearly at a distance. **7.** *Psychology.* To externalize and attribute (an emotion, for example) to someone or something else. **8.** To convey an impression of to an audience or to others: *a posture that projects defeat; projected a positive corporate image.* **9.** To form a plan or an intention for: *project a new business enterprise.* **10.** To calculate, estimate, or predict (something in the future), based on present data or trends: *projecting next year's expenses and income.* *—intr.* **1.** To extend forward or out; jut out: *beams that project beyond the eaves.* See Synonyms at **bulge. 2.** To direct one's voice so as to be heard clearly at a distance. [Middle English *projecte,* from Latin *prōiectum,* projecting structure, from neuter past participle of *prōicere,* to throw out : *prō-,* forth; see PRO–[1] + *iacere,* to throw; see **yē-** in Appendix.] **—pro•ject′a•ble** *adj.*

pro•jec•tile (prə-jĕk′təl, -tīl′) *n.* **1.** A fired, thrown, or otherwise propelled object, such as a bullet, having no capacity for self-propulsion. **2.** A self-propelled missile, such as a rocket. **—projectile** *adj.* **1.** Capable of being impelled or hurled forward. **2.** Driving forward; impelling: *a projectile force.* **3.** *Zoology.* Capable of being thrust outward; protrusile. [New Latin *proiectile,* neuter of *prōiectilis,* that can be thrown, from Latin *prōiectus,* past participle of *prōicere,* to throw out. See PROJECT.]

pro•jec•tion (prə-jĕk′shən) *n.* **1.** The act of projecting or the condition of being projected. **2.** A thing or part that extends outward beyond a prevailing line or surface: *spiky projections on top of a fence; a projection of land along the coast.* **3.** A plan for an anticipated course of action: *"facilities* [that] *are vital to the projection of U.S. force . . . in the Pacific"* (Alan D. Romberg). **4.** A prediction or an estimate of something in the future, based on present data or trends. **5. a.** The process of projecting a filmed image onto a screen or other viewing surface. **b.** An image so projected. **6.** *Mathematics.* The image of a geometric figure reproduced on a line, plane, or surface. **7.** A system of intersecting lines, such as the grid of a map, on which part or all of the globe or another spherical surface is represented as a plane surface. **8.** *Psychology.* **a.** The attribution of one's own attitudes, feelings, or suppositions to others: *"Even trained anthropologists have been guilty of unconscious projection—of clothing the subjects of their research in theories brought with them into the field"* (Alex Shoumatoff). **b.** The attribution of one's own attitudes, feelings, or desires to someone or something as a naive or unconscious defense against anxiety or guilt. **—pro•jec′tion•al** *adj.*

projection booth *n.* A booth, as in a theater, in which a movie projector is operated.

pro•jec•tion•ist (prə-jĕk′shə-nĭst) *n.* **1.** One who operates a movie projector. **2.** A maker of map projections.

pro•jec•tive (prə-jĕk′tĭv) *adj.* **1.** Extending outward; projecting. **2.** Relating to or made by projection. **3.** *Mathematics.* Designating a property of a geometric figure that does not vary when the figure undergoes projection. **—pro•jec′tive•ly** *adv.*

projective geometry *n.* *Mathematics.* The study of geometric properties that are invariant under projection.

projective test *n.* A psychological test in which a subject's responses to ambiguous or unstructured standard stimuli, such as a series of cartoons, abstract patterns, or incomplete sentences, are analyzed in order to determine underlying personality traits, feelings, or attitudes.

pro•jec•tor (prə-jĕk′tər) *n.* **1.** A device for projecting a beam of light. **2.** A machine for projecting an image onto a screen. **3.** One who devises plans or projects.

pro•kar•y•ote also **pro•car•y•ote** (prō-kăr′ē-ōt′) *n.* An organism of the kingdom Prokaryotae, constituting the bacteria and cyanobacteria, characterized by the absence of a nuclear membrane and by DNA that is not organized into chromosomes. [French *procaryote* : Greek *pro-,* before; see PRO–[2] + Greek *karuōtos,* having nuts (from *karuon,* nut; see KARYO–).] **—pro•kar′y•ot′ic** (-ŏt′ĭk) *adj.*

Pro•kho•rov (prô′KHə-rôf′), **Aleksandr Mikhailovich.** Born 1916. Russian physicist. He shared a 1964 Nobel Prize for developing the maser and laser principle of producing high-intensity radiation.

Pro•kof•iev (prə-kô′fē-ĕf, -əf, -kō′-, -kôf′yĭf), **Sergei Sergeyevich.** 1891–1953. Russian composer whose works include ballets, operas, and the symphonic fairy tale *Peter and the Wolf* (1936).

Pro•ko•pyevsk (prə-kôp′yəfsk). A city of south-central Russia east-southeast of Novosibirsk. It is a manufacturing and processing center in a major coal-mining region. Population, 274,000.

pro•lac•tin (prō-lăk′tĭn) *n.* A pituitary hormone that stimulates and maintains the secretion of milk.

pro•la•mine also **pro•la•min** (prō′lə-mĭn, -mēn′) *n.* Any of a class of simple proteins found in the seeds of wheat, rye, and other grains. [PROL(INE) + AM(MONIA) + –INE[2].]

pro•lan (prō′lăn′) *n.* **1.** Human chorionic gonadotropin. No longer in scientific use. **2.** Either of two hormones of the pituitary gland, luteinizing hormone and follicle-stimulating hormone. No longer in scientific use. [German, from Latin *prōlēs,* offspring. See **al-[2]** in Appendix.]

pro•lapse (prō-lăps′) *Medicine. intr.v.* **-lapsed, -laps•ing, -laps•es.** To fall or slip out of place. **—prolapse** (prō′lăps′, prō-lăps′) also **pro•lap•sus** (prō-lăp′səs) *n.* The falling down or slipping out of place of an organ or part, such as the uterus. [Latin *prōlābī, prōlāps-,* to fall down : *prō-,* forward; see PRO–[1] + *lābī,* to fall.]

pro·late (prō′lāt′) *adj.* **1.** Having the shape of a spheroid generated by rotating an ellipse about its longer axis. **2.** Having the polar axis longer than the equatorial diameter: *a prolate spheroid.* [Latin *prōlātus,* past participle of *prōferre,* to stretch out : *prō-,* forth; see PRO–[1] + *lātus,* brought; see **tele-** in Appendix.] **—pro′late′ly** *adv.* **—pro′late′ness** *n.*

prole (prōl) *n.* A proletarian: *"If there is hope . . . it lies in the proles"* (George Orwell).

pro·leg (prō′lĕg′) *n.* One of the stubby limbs on the abdominal segments of caterpillars and certain other insect larvae.

pro·le·gom·e·non (prō′lĭ-gŏm′ə-nŏn′, -nən) *n., pl.* **-na** (-nə). **1.** A preliminary discussion, especially a formal essay introducing a work of considerable length or complexity. **2. prolegomena.** *(used with a sing. or pl. verb).* Prefatory remarks or observations. [Greek, from neuter of present passive participle of *prolegein,* to say beforehand : *pro-,* before; see PRO–[2] + *legein,* to speak; see **leg-** in Appendix.] **—pro′le·gom′e·nous** *adj.*

pro·lep·sis (prō-lĕp′sĭs) *n., pl.* **-ses** (-sēz). **1.** The anachronistic representation of something as existing before its proper or historical time, as in *the precolonial United States.* **2.a.** The assignment of something, such as an event or a name, to a time that precedes it, as in *If you tell the cops, you're a dead man.* **b.** The use of a descriptive word in anticipation of the act or circumstances that would make it applicable, as *dry* in *They drained the lake dry.* **3.** The anticipation and answering of an objection or argument before one's opponent has put it forward. [Late Latin *prolēpsis,* from Greek *prolēpsis,* from *prolambanein,* to anticipate : *pro-,* before; see PRO–[2] + *lambanein, lēp-,* to take.] **—pro·lep′tic** (-lĕp′tĭk), **pro·lep′ti·cal** (-tĭ-kəl) *adj.*

pro·le·tar·i·an (prō′lĭ-târ′ē-ən) *adj.* Of, relating to, or characteristic of the proletariat. **—proletarian** *n.* A member of the proletariat; a worker. [From Latin *prōlētārius,* belonging to the lowest class of Roman citizens (viewed as contributing to the state only through having children), from *prōlēs,* offspring. See **al-**[2] in Appendix.] **—pro′le·tar′i·an·ism** *n.*

pro·le·tar·i·at (prō′lĭ-târ′ē-ĭt) *n.* **1.a.** The class of industrial wage earners who, possessing neither capital nor production means, must earn their living by selling their labor. **b.** The poorest class of working people. **2.** The propertyless class of ancient Rome, constituting the lowest class of citizens. [French *prolétariat,* from Latin *prōlētārius,* belonging to the lowest class of Roman citizens. See PROLETARIAN.]

pro-life (prō-līf′) *adj.* Advocating full legal protection of human embryos or fetuses, especially by opposing legalized abortion. **—pro-lif′er** *n.*

pro·lif·er·ate (prə-lĭf′ə-rāt′) *v.* **-at·ed, -at·ing, -ates.** *—intr.* **1.** To grow or multiply by rapidly producing new tissue, parts, cells, or offspring. **2.** To increase or spread at a rapid rate: *fears that nuclear weapons might proliferate.* *—tr.* To cause to grow or increase rapidly. [Back-formation from PROLIFERATION, the act of proliferating, from French *prolifération,* from *prolifère,* procreative : Latin *prōlēs, prōl-,* offspring; see PROLIFEROUS + Latin *-fer,* -fer.] **—pro·lif′er·a′tion** *n.* **—pro·lif′er·a′tive** *adj.* **—pro·lif′er·a′tor** *n.*

pro·lif·er·ous (prə-lĭf′ər-əs) *adj.* **1.** *Zoology.* Reproducing freely by means of buds and side branches, as corals do. **2.** *Botany.* Freely producing buds or offshoots, especially from unusual places, as shoots from flowers or fruits from fruits. [From Medieval Latin *prōlifer* : Latin *prōlēs, prōl-,* offspring; see **al-**[2] in Appendix + *-fer,* -fer.] **—pro·lif′er·ous·ly** *adv.*

pro·lif·ic (prə-lĭf′ĭk) *adj.* **1.** Producing offspring or fruit in great abundance; fertile. **2.** Producing abundant works or results: *a prolific artist.* See Synonyms at **fertile.** [French *prolifique,* from Medieval Latin *prōlificus* : Latin *prōlēs, prōl-,* offspring; see **al-**[2] in Appendix + Latin *-ficus,* -fic.] **—pro·lif′i·ca·cy** (-ĭ-kə-sē), **pro·lif′ic·ness** (-ĭk-nĭs) *n.* **—pro·lif′i·cal·ly** *adv.*

pro·line (prō′lēn′) *n.* An amino acid, C_4H_8NCOOH, that is found in most proteins and is a major constituent of collagen. [Short for *pyrrolidine* : PYRROLE + –ID(E) + –INE[2].]

pro·lix (prō-lĭks′, prō′lĭks′) *adj.* **1.** Tediously prolonged; wordy: *editing a prolix manuscript.* **2.** Tending to speak or write at excessive length. See Synonyms at **wordy.** [Middle English, from Old French *prolixe,* from Latin *prōlixus,* poured forth, extended.] **—pro·lix′i·ty** (-lĭk′sĭ-tē) *n.* **—pro·lix′ly** *adv.*

pro·log (prō′lôg′, -lŏg′) *n.* Variant of **prologue.**

Pro·log (prō′lôg′, -lŏg′) *n.* *Computer Science.* A programming language used for writing programs that model human thinking. [*pro(gramming in) log(ic).*]

pro·logue also **pro·log** (prō′lôg′, -lŏg′) *n.* **1.** An introduction or a preface, especially a poem recited to introduce a play. **2.** An introduction or introductory chapter, as to a novel. **3.** An introductory act, event, or period. [Middle English *prolog,* from Old French *prologue,* from Latin *prologus,* from Greek *prologos* : *pro-,* before; see PRO–[2] + *logos,* speech; see **leg-** in Appendix.]

pro·long (prə-lông′, -lŏng′) *tr.v.* **-longed, -long·ing, -longs.** **1.** To lengthen in duration; protract. **2.** To lengthen in extent. [Middle English *prolongen,* from Old French *prolonguer,* from Late Latin *prōlongāre* : Latin *prō-,* forth; see PRO–[1] + Latin *longus,* long; see **del-**[1] in Appendix.] **—pro·long′er** *n.*

pro·lon·gate (prə-lông′gāt′, -lŏng′-, prō-) *tr.v.* **-gat·ed, -gat·ing, -gates.** To prolong. **—pro′lon·ga′tion** (prō′lông-gā′shən, -lŏng-) *n.*

pro·lu·sion (prō-lo͞o′zhən) *n.* **1.** A preliminary exercise. **2.** An essay written as a preface to a more detailed work. [Latin *prōlūsiō, prōlūsiōn-,* from *prōlūsus,* past participle of *prōlūdere,* to practice beforehand : *prō-,* before; see PRO–[1] + *lūdere,* to play; see **leid-** in Appendix.] **—pro·lu′so·ry** (-sə-rē, -zə-) *adj.*

prom (prŏm) *n.* A formal dance held for a high-school or college class typically at or near the end of the academic year. [Short for PROMENADE.]

PROM (prŏm) *n.* *Computer Science.* A memory that can be programmed only once. [*p(rogrammable) r(ead-)o(nly) m(emory).*]

prom. *abbr.* Promontory.

prom·e·nade (prŏm′ə-nād′, -näd′) *n.* **1.a.** A leisurely walk, especially one taken in a public place as a social activity. **b.** A public place for such walking. **2.a.** A formal dance; a ball. **b.** A march of all the guests at the opening of a ball. **3.** A square-dance figure in which couples march counterclockwise in a circle. **—promenade** *v.* **-nad·ed, -nad·ing, -nades.** *—intr.* **1.** To go on a leisurely walk. **2.** To execute a promenade at a ball or in square dancing. *—tr.* **1.** To take a promenade along or through. **2.** To take or display on or as if on a promenade. [French, from *promener,* to take for a walk, from Latin *prōmināre,* to drive forward : *prō-,* forward; see PRO–[1] + *mināre,* to drive with shouts (from *minārī,* to threaten, from *minae,* threats; see **men-**[2] in Appendix).] **—prom′e·nad′er** *n.*

promenade deck *n.* *Nautical.* The upper deck or a section of the upper deck on a passenger ship where the passengers can promenade.

Pro·me·the·an (prə-mē′thē-ən) *adj.* **1.** *Greek Mythology.* Relating to or suggestive of Prometheus. **2.** Boldly creative; defiantly original. **—Promethean** *n.* One who is boldy creative or defiantly original in behavior or actions.

Pro·me·the·us (prə-mē′thē-əs, -thyo͞os′) *n.* *Greek Mythology.* A Titan who stole fire from Olympus and gave it to humankind, for which Zeus chained him to a rock and sent an eagle to eat his liver, which grew back daily. [Latin *Promētheus,* from Greek.]

pro·me·thi·um (prə-mē′thē-əm) *n.* *Symbol* **Pm** A radioactive rare-earth element prepared by fission of uranium or by neutron bombardment of neodymium, having 14 isotopes with mass numbers ranging from 141 to 154 and used as a source of beta rays. Atomic number 61; melting point 1,168°C; boiling point 2,460°C; valence 3. See table at **element.** [From PROMETHEUS.]

prom·i·nence (prŏm′ə-nəns) *n.* **1.** The quality or condition of being prominent. **2.** Something prominent, especially an area of land raised above its surroundings. **3.** *Anatomy.* A small projection or protuberance. **4.** *Astronomy.* A tonguelike cloud of flaming gas rising from the sun's surface, visible as part of the corona during a total solar eclipse.

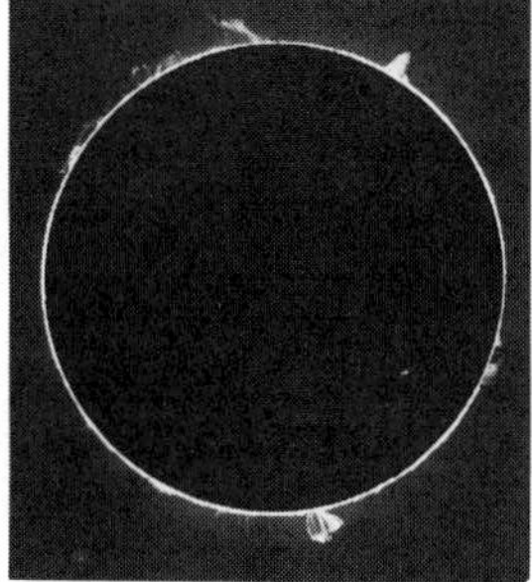

prominence
Solar prominences visible during a total eclipse

prom·i·nen·cy (prŏm′-ə-nən-sē) *n.* Prominence: *a former secretary who rose to a position of prominency as an ambassador.*

prom·i·nent (prŏm′ə-nənt) *adj.* **1.** Projecting outward or upward from a line or surface; protuberant. **2.** Immediately noticeable; conspicuous. See Synonyms at **noticeable.** **3.** Widely known; eminent. [Middle English, from Latin *prōminēns, prōminent-,* present participle of *prōminēre,* to jut out : *prō-,* forth; see PRO–[1] + *-minēre,* to jut, threaten; see **men-**[2] in Appendix.] **—prom′i·nent·ly** *adv.*

prom·is·cu·i·ty (prŏm′ĭ-skyo͞o′ĭ-tē, prō′mĭ-) *n., pl.* **-ties.** **1.** The state or character of being promiscuous. **2.** Promiscuous sexual relations. **3.** A mixture of diverse or unrelated parts or individuals; a hodgepodge.

pro·mis·cu·ous (prə-mĭs′kyo͞o-əs) *adj.* **1.** Indiscriminate in the choice of sexual partners. **2.** Lacking standards of selection; indiscriminate. **3.** Casual; random. **4.** Consisting of diverse, unrelated parts or individuals; confused: *"Throngs promiscuous strew the level green"* (Alexander Pope). [From Latin *prōmiscuus,* possessed equally : *prō-,* intensive pref.; see PRO–[1] + *miscēre,* to mix; see **meik-** in Appendix.] **—pro·mis′cu·ous·ly** *adv.* **—pro·mis′cu·ous·ness** *n.*

prom·ise (prŏm′ĭs) *n.* **1.a.** A declaration assuring that one will or will not do something; a vow. **b.** Something promised. **2.** Indication of something favorable to come; expectation: *a promise of spring in the milder air.* **3.** Indication of future excellence or success: *a young player of great promise.* **—promise** *v.* **-ised, -is·ing, -is·es.** *—tr.* **1.** To commit oneself by a promise to do or give; pledge: *promised a quick answer; left early but promised to return.* **2.** To afford a basis for expecting: *thunderclouds that promise rain.* *—intr.* **1.** To make a declaration assuring that something will or will not be done. **2.** To afford a basis for expectation: *an enterprise that promises well.* [Middle English *promis,* from Old French *promise,* from Medieval Latin *prōmissa,* alteration of Latin *prōmissum,* from neuter past participle of *prōmittere,* to send forth, promise : *prō-,* forth; see PRO–[1] + *mittere,* to send.] **—prom′is·er** *n.*

SYNONYMS: *promise, covenant, engage, pledge, plight, swear, vow.* The central meaning shared by these verbs is "to declare solemnly that one will perform or refrain from a particular course of action": *promise to write soon; covenanting to exchange their prisoners of war; engaged to reorganize the department; pledged*

ă **pat**	oi **boy**
ā **pay**	ou **out**
âr **care**	o͝o **took**
ä **father**	o͞o **boot**
ĕ **pet**	ŭ **cut**
ē **be**	ûr **urge**
ĭ **pit**	th **thin**
ī **pie**	*th* **this**
îr **pier**	hw **which**
ŏ **pot**	zh **vision**
ō **toe**	ə **about, item**
ô **paw**	♦ **regionalism**

Stress marks: **′** (primary); ′ (secondary), as in **dictionary** (dĭk′shə-nĕr′ē)

promontory
In southwest Oregon

pronghorn
Male pronghorn
Antilocapra americana

ă pat oi boy
ā pay ou out
âr care ŏŏ took
ä father ōō boot
ĕ pet ŭ cut
ē be ûr urge
ĭ pit th thin
ī pie *th* this
îr pier hw which
ŏ pot zh vision
ō toe ə about, item
ô paw ♦ regionalism

Stress marks: **′** (primary); ′ (secondary), as in **dictionary** (dĭk′shə-nĕr′ē)

to uphold the law; plighted their loyalty to the king; swore to get revenge; vowed they would never surrender.

Prom·ised Land (prŏm′ĭst) *n.* **1.** *Bible.* The land of Canaan, promised by the Lord to Abraham's descendants in the Old Testament. **2. promised land.** A longed-for place where complete satisfaction and happiness will be achieved.

prom·is·ee (prŏm′ĭ-sē′) *n. Law.* The party to which a promise is made.

prom·is·ing (prŏm′ĭ-sĭng) *adj.* Likely to develop in a desirable manner. **—prom′is·ing·ly** *adv.*

prom·i·sor (prŏm′ĭ-sôr′) *n. Law.* One that makes a promise.

prom·is·so·ry (prŏm′ĭ-sôr′ē, -sōr′ē) *adj.* **1.** Containing, involving, or having the nature of a promise. **2.** Indicating how the provisions of an insurance contract will be carried out after it has been signed. [Medieval Latin *prōmissōrius,* from Latin *prōmissor,* one who promises, from *prōmissus,* past participle of *prōmittere,* to promise. See PROMISE.]

promissory note *n. Abbr.* **P/N, p.n.** A written promise to pay or repay a specified sum of money at a stated time or on demand. Also called *note of hand.*

pro·mo (prō′mō) *n., pl.* **-mos.** *Informal.* A promotional presentation, such as a television spot, radio announcement, or personal appearance. *—attributive.* Often used to modify another noun: *a promo piece; an author's promo tour.*

prom·on·to·ry (prŏm′ən-tôr′ē, -tōr′ē) *n., pl.* **-ries. 1.** *Abbr.* **prom.** A high ridge of land or rock jutting out into a body of water; a headland. **2.** *Anatomy.* A projecting part. [Latin *prōmontorium,* alteration (influenced by *mōns, mont-,* mount; see MOUNT[2]) of *prōmunturium,* probably from *prominēre,* to jut out. See PROMINENT.]

pro·mote (prə-mōt′) *tr.v.* **-mot·ed, -mot·ing, -motes. 1.a.** To raise to a more important or responsible job or rank. **b.** To advance (a student) to the next higher grade. **2.** To contribute to the progress or growth of; further. See Synonyms at **advance. 3.** To urge the adoption of; advocate: *promote a constitutional amendment.* **4.** To attempt to sell or popularize by advertising or publicity: *commercials promoting a new product.* **5.** To help to establish or organize (a new enterprise), as by securing financial backing: *promote a Broadway show.* [Middle English *promoten,* from Old French *promoter,* from Latin *prōmovēre, prōmōt-* : *prō-,* forward; see PRO–[1] + *movēre,* to move; see **meuə-** in Appendix.] **—pro·mot′a·bil′i·ty** *n.* **—pro·mot′a·ble** *adj.*

pro·mot·er (prə-mō′tər) *n.* **1.** One that promotes, especially an active supporter or advocate. **2.** A financial and publicity organizer, as of a boxing match or an artistic performance. **3.** *Genetics.* A DNA molecule to which RNA polymerase binds, initiating the transcription of messenger RNA.

pro·mo·tion (prə-mō′shən) *n.* **1.** The act of promoting or the fact of being promoted. **2.** Advancement in rank or responsibility. **3.** Encouragement of the progress, growth, or acceptance of something; furtherance. **4.** Advertising; publicity. **—pro·mo′tion·al** *adj.* **—pro·mo′tion·al·ly** *adv.*

pro·mo·tive (prə-mō′tĭv) *adj.* Tending to promote. **—pro·mo′tive·ness** *n.*

prompt (prŏmpt) *adj.* **prompt·er, prompt·est. 1.** Being on time; punctual. **2.** Carried out or performed without delay: *a prompt reply.* **—prompt** *tr.v.* **prompt·ed, prompt·ing, prompts. 1.** To move to act; spur; incite: *A noise prompted the guard to go back and investigate.* **2.** To give rise to; inspire: *The accident prompted a review of school safety policy.* **3.** To assist with a reminder; remind. **4.** To assist (an actor or a reciter) by providing the next words of a forgotten passage; cue. **—prompt** *n.* **1.a.** The act of prompting or giving a cue. **b.** A reminder or cue. **2.** *Computer Science.* A symbol that appears on a monitor to indicate that the computer is ready to receive input. **3.** *Business.* **a.** A prompt note. **b.** The time limit stipulated in a prompt note. [Middle English, ready, from Old French, from Latin *prōmptus,* from past participle of *prōmere,* to bring forth : *prō-,* forth; see PRO–[1] + *emere,* to take, obtain; see **em-** in Appendix.] **—prompt′er** *n.* **—promp′ti·tude′** (prŏmp′tĭ-to͞od′, -tyo͞od′), **prompt′ness** (prŏmpt′nĭs) *n.* **—prompt′ly** *adv.*

prompt·book (prŏmpt′bo͝ok′) *n.* An annotated script used by a theater prompter.

prompt note *n.* A notice sent to the purchaser of goods as a reminder of the amount that is due the seller and the date that it is due.

prom·ul·gate (prŏm′əl-gāt′, prō-mŭl′gāt′) *tr.v.* **-gat·ed, -gat·ing, -gates. 1.** To make known (a decree, for example) by public declaration; announce officially. See Synonyms at **announce. 2.** To put (a law) into effect by formal public announcement. [Latin *prōmulgāre, prōmulgāt-.*] **—prom′ul·ga′tion** (prŏm′əl-gā′shən, prō′məl-) *n.* **—prom′ul·ga′tor** *n.*

pron. *abbr.* **1.** *Grammar.* Pronominal; pronoun. **2.** Pronounced. **3.** Pronunciation.

pro·na·tal·ism (prō-nāt′l-ĭz′əm) *n.* An attitude or a policy that encourages childbearing. **—pro·na′tal·ist** *n.* **—pro·na′tal·is′tic** *adj.*

pro·nate (prō′nāt′) *v.* **-nat·ed, -nat·ing, -nates.** *—tr.* **1.a.** To turn or rotate (the hand or forearm) so that the palm faces down or back. **b.** To turn or rotate (the sole of the foot) by abduction and eversion so that the inner edge of the sole bears the body's weight. **2.** To turn or rotate (a limb) so that the inner surface faces down or back. Used of a vertebrate animal. **3.** To place in a prone position. *—intr.* **1.** To become pronated. **2.** To assume a prone position. [Late Latin *prōnāre, prōnāt-,* to bend forward, from *prōnus,* turned forward. See PRONE.]

pro·na·tion (prō-nā′shən) *n.* **1.** The act of pronating. **2.** The condition of being pronated, especially the condition of having flat feet.

pro·na·tor (prō′nā′tər) *n.* A muscle that effects or assists in pronation.

prone (prōn) *adj.* **1.** Lying with the front or face downward. **2.** Having a tendency; inclined: *paper that is prone to yellowing; children who are prone to mischief.* **—prone** *adv.* In a prone manner: *The patient was lying prone on the bed.* [Middle English, inclined, disposed, from Latin *prōnus,* leaning forward. See **per**[1] in Appendix.] **—prone′ly** *adv.* **—prone′ness** *n.*

SYNONYMS: *prone, supine, prostrate, recumbent.* These adjectives mean lying down, as on the ground. *Prone* refers to lying face downward with the front of the body facing the surface on which it rests: *The spaniel lay prone on the floor, his long ears draped over his extended front legs. Supine* means lying down on the back: *The victim was supine on the stretcher. Prostrate* denotes lying down flat or at full length: *"the prostrate trunk of a coconut tree"* (Herman Melville). The word often implies that a prone or a supine position has been assumed out of humiliation, submission, helplessness, or physical or emotional incapacity: *"Heselrigge, as he lay prostrate . . . implored for life"* (Jane Porter). *Recumbent* means lying down in a position of comfort or rest: *The picnickers were recumbent on thick moss under a big tree.*

pro·neph·ros (prō-nĕf′rəs, -rŏs′) *n., pl.* **-roi** (-roi) or **-ra** (-rə). A kidneylike organ, being either part of the most anterior pair of three pairs of organs in a vertebrate embryo, disappearing early in the embryonic development of higher vertebrates, but functioning as a kidney in some simple vertebrates, such as the lamprey. [PRO–[2] + Greek *nephros,* kidney.] **—pro·neph′ric** (-rĭk) *adj.*

prong (prông, prŏng) *n.* **1.** A thin, pointed, projecting part: *a pitchfork with four prongs.* **2.** A branch; a fork: *the two prongs of a river.* **—prong** *tr.v.* **pronged, prong·ing, prongs.** To pierce with or as if with a thin, pointed, projecting part. [Middle English *pronge,* pointed instrument, pain, from Medieval Latin *pronga,* of Germanic origin.]

prong·horn (prông′hôrn′, prŏng′-) *n., pl.* **pronghorn** or **-horns.** A small ruminant mammal *(Antilocapra americana)* resembling an antelope and having small forked horns, found on western North American plains. Also called *pronghorn antelope.*

pro·no·grade (prō′nə-grād′) *adj.* Walking with the long axis of the body parallel to the ground. Used of quadrupeds. [Latin *prōnus,* leaning forward; see PRONE + *-gradus,* walking (from *gradī,* to move; see RETROGRADE).]

pro·nom·i·nal (prō-nŏm′ə-nəl) *adj. Abbr.* **pron., pronom.** *Grammar.* **1.** Of, relating to, or functioning as a pronoun. **2.** Resembling a pronoun, as by specifying a person, place, or thing, while functioning primarily as another part of speech. *His* in *his choice* is a pronominal adjective. [Late Latin *prōnōminālis,* from Latin *prōnōmen, prōnōmin-,* pronoun : *prō-,* in place of; see PRO–[1] + *nōmen,* name; see NOUN.] **—pro·nom′i·nal·ly** *adv.*

pro·noun (prō′noun′) *n. Abbr.* **pron., pr.** *Grammar.* One of a class of words that function as substitutes for nouns or noun phrases and designate persons or things asked for, previously specified, or understood from the context.

pro·nounce (prə-nouns′) *v.* **-nounced, -nounc·ing, -nounc·es.** *—tr.* **1.a.** To use the organs of speech to make heard (a word or speech sound); utter. **b.** To say clearly, correctly, or in a given manner: *learning to pronounce French; pronounced my name wrong.* **2.** To represent (a word) in phonetic symbols. **3.** To declare officially or formally: *pronounced the legislature to be in session; was pronounced dead on arrival. —intr.* **1.** To say words; speak. **2.** To declare one's opinion; make a pronouncement: *pronouncing on the issues of the day.* [Middle English *pronouncen,* from Old French *prononcier,* from Latin *prōnūntiāre* : *prō-,* forth; see PRO–[1] + *nūntiāre,* to announce (from *nūntius,* messenger; see **neu-** in Appendix).] **—pro·nounce′a·ble** *adj.* **—pro·nounc′er** *n.*

pro·nounced (prə-nounst′) *adj.* **1.** *Abbr.* **pron.** Spoken; voiced. **2.** Strongly marked; distinct: *walks with a pronounced limp.* **—pro·nounc′ed·ly** (-noun′sĭd-lē) *adv.* **—pro·nounc′ed·ness** *n.*

pro·nounce·ment (prə-nouns′mənt) *n.* **1.** A formal expression of opinion; a judgment. **2.** An authoritative statement.

pro·nounc·ing (prə-noun′sĭng) *adj.* Relating to, designed for, or showing pronunciation: *a pronouncing dictionary.*

pron·to (prŏn′tō) *adv. Informal.* Without delay; quickly. [Spanish, from Latin *prōmptus.* See PROMPT.]

pro·nu·cle·us (prō-no͞o′klē-əs, -nyo͞o′-) *n., pl.* **-cle·i** (-klē-ī′). The haploid nucleus of a sperm or egg before fusion of the nuclei in fertilization. **—pro·nu′cle·ar** *adj.*

pro·nun·ci·a·men·to (prō-nŭn′sē-ə-mĕn′tō) *n., pl.* **-tos** or **-toes.** An official or authoritarian declaration; a proclamation or an edict. [Spanish *pronunciamiento,* from *pronunciar,* to pronounce, from Latin *prōnūntiāre.* See PRONOUNCE.]

pro·nun·ci·a·tion (prə-nŭn′sē-ā′shən) *n. Abbr.* **pron. 1.** The act or manner of pronouncing words; utterance of speech. **2.** A way of speaking a word, especially a way that is accepted or generally understood. **3.** A graphic representation of the way a word is spoken, using phonetic symbols. [Middle English, from Old French *prononciation,* from Latin *prōnūntiātiō, prōnūntiātiōn-,* from *prōnūntiātus,* past participle of *prōnūntiāre,* to pronounce. See PRONOUNCE.] **—pro·nun′ci·a′tion·al** *adj.*

proof (pro͞of) *n. Abbr.* **prf. 1.** The evidence or argument that compels the mind to accept an assertion as true. **2.a.** The validation of a proposition by application of specified rules, as of induction or deduction, to assumptions, axioms, and sequentially derived conclusions. **b.** A statement or an argument used in such a validation. **3.a.** Convincing or persuasive demonstration: *was asked for proof of his identity; an employment history that was proof of her dependability.* **b.** The state of being convinced or persuaded by consideration of evidence. **4.** Determination of the quality of something by testing; trial: *put one's beliefs to the proof.* **5.** *Law.* The result or effect of evidence; the establishment or denial of a fact by evidence. **6.** The alcoholic strength of a liquor, expressed by a number that is twice the percentage by volume of alcohol present. **7.** *Printing.* **a.** A trial sheet of printed material that is made to be checked and corrected. Also called *proof sheet.* **b.** A trial impression of a plate, stone, or block taken at any of various stages in engraving. **8.a.** A trial photographic print. **b.** Any of a limited number of newly minted coins or medals struck as specimens and for collectors from a new die on a polished planchet. **9.** *Archaic.* Proven impenetrability: *"I was clothed in Armor of proof"* (John Bunyan). **—proof** *adj.* **1.** Fully or successfully resistant; impervious. Often used in combination: *waterproof watches; a fireproof cellar door.* **2.** Of standard alcoholic strength. **3.** Used in proving or making corrections. **—proof** *v.* **proofed, proof·ing, proofs.** *—tr.* **1.** *Printing.* **a.** To make a trial impression of (printed or engraved matter). **b.** To proofread (copy). **2.a.** To activate (dormant dry yeast) by adding water. **b.** To work (dough) into proper lightness. **3.** To treat so as to make resistant: *proof a fabric against shrinkage.* *—intr.* **1.** *Printing.* To proofread. **2.** To become properly light for cooking: *The batter proofed overnight.* [Middle English *prove, preve,* from Anglo-Norman *prove* and from Old French *prueve,* both from Late Latin *proba,* from Latin *probāre,* to prove. See PROVE.] **—proof′er** *n.*

proof-of-pur·chase (pro͞of′əv-pûr′chĭs) *n., pl.* **proofs-of-pur·chase** (pro͞ofs′-). A document, such as a sales slip or a product label, that is valid evidence for claiming a refund or a premium. **—proof′-of-pur′chase** *adj.*

proof of the pudding *n. Informal.* The ultimate evidence attesting the true nature of something: *The proof of the pudding is not to be found in preelection polls; rather, it lies in the results of the election.* [From the proverb *The proof of the pudding is in the eating.*]

proof·read (pro͞of′rēd′) *v.* **-read** (-rĕd′), **-read·ing, -reads.** *Printing.* *—tr.* To read (copy or proof) in order to find errors and mark corrections. *—intr.* To read copy or proof for purposes of error detection and correction. **—proof′read′er** *n.*

proof sheet *n. Printing.* See **proof** (sense 7a).

proofs-of-pur·chase (pro͞ofs′əv-pûr′chĭs) *n.* Plural of **proof-of-purchase.**

proof spirit *n.* An alcohol-water mixture or a beverage containing a standard amount of alcohol, the U.S. standard being 100 proof, or 50 percent, of ethyl alcohol by volume at 60°F (approximately 15.6°C).

prop¹ (prŏp) *n.* **1.** An object placed beneath or against a structure to keep it from falling or shaking; a support. **2.** One that serves as a support or stay: *my children, my props in old age.* **—prop** *tr.v.* **propped, prop·ping, props.** To support by placing something beneath or against; shore up. [Middle English *proppe,* probably from Middle Dutch.]

prop² (prŏp) *n.* A theatrical property.

prop³ (prŏp) *n. Informal.* A propeller.

prop. *abbr.* **1.** Proper. **2.** Properly. **3.** Property. **4.** Proposition. **5.** Proprietary. **6.** Proprietor; proprietress.

prop– *pref.* Related to or derived from propionic acid: *propane.* [From PROPIONIC ACID.]

pro·pae·deu·tic (prō′pĭ-do͞o′tĭk, -dyo͞o′-) *adj.* Providing introductory instruction. **—propaedeutic** *n.* Preparatory instruction. [From Greek *propaideuein,* to teach beforehand : *pro-,* before; see PRO–² + *paideuein,* to teach (from *pais, paid-,* child; see PEDO–²).]

prop·a·gan·da (prŏp′ə-găn′də) *n.* **1.** The systematic propagation of a doctrine or cause or of information reflecting the views and interests of those people advocating such a doctrine or cause. **2.** Material disseminated by the advocates of a doctrine or cause: *the selected truths, exaggerations, and lies of wartime propaganda.* **3. Propaganda.** *Roman Catholic Church.* A division of the Roman Curia that has authority in the matter of preaching the gospel, of establishing the Church in non-Christian countries, and of administering Church missions in territories where there is no properly organized hierarchy. [New Latin, short for *Sacra Congregātiō dē Prōpagandā Fide,* Sacred Congregation for Propagating the Faith (established 1622), from ablative feminine gerundive of Latin *prōpāgāre,* to propagate. See PROPAGATE.] **—prop′a·gan′dism** *n.* **—prop′a·gan′dist** *n.* **—prop′a·gan·dis′tic** *adj.* **—prop′a·gan·dis′ti·cal·ly** *adv.*

prop·a·gan·dize (prŏp′ə-găn′dīz′) *v.* **-dized, -diz·ing, -diz·es.** *—tr.* **1.** To engage in propaganda for (a doctrine or cause). **2.** To subject (a person or group) to propaganda. *—intr.* To spread propaganda: *propagandizing for nuclear disarmament.* **—prop′a·gan′diz′er** *n.*

PROOFREADERS' MARKS

INSTRUCTION	MARK IN MARGIN	MARK ON PROOF	CORRECTED TYPE
GENERAL			
Delete	ℓ	the ~~good~~ word	the word
Delete and close up space	ℓ (closed)	the wo(o)rd	the word
Insert indicated material	good	the ^ word	the good word
Let it stand	(stet)	the ~~good~~ word (dotted)	the good word
Spell out	(sp)	(2) words	two words
PARAGRAPHING			
New paragraph	¶	"Where is it?" / "It's on the shelf."	"Where is it?" "It's on the shelf."
Flush paragraph	[¶	"Where is it?" / "It's on the shelf."	"Where is it?" "It's on the shelf."
POSITION AND SPACING			
Transpose	(tr)	the (word/good)	the good word
Move left	⊏	⊏the word	the word
Move right	⊐	the word	the word
Move down	⊔	the word	the word
Move up	⊓	the word	the word
Align	‖	‖the word / the word	the word / the word
Straighten line	═	the word	the word
Insert space	#	the^word	the word
Equalize space	(eq #)	the^good^word	the good word
Close up	⁀	the wo⁀rd	the word
en space	1/N	^the word	the word
em space	1/M	^the word	the word
PUNCTUATION			
period	⊙	This is the word^	This is the word.
comma	^,^	words^words, words	words, words, words
hyphen	=/	word^for^word test	word-for-word test
colon	(:)	The following words^	The following words:
semicolon	;^	Scan the words/skim the words.	Scan the words; skim the words.
apostrophe	’	John^s words	John's words
double quotation marks	“ / ”	the word^word^	the word "word"
single quotation marks	‘ / ’	the "good^word^"	the "good 'word'"
brackets	[/]	He read from the Word ^in the Bible^	He read from the Word [in the Bible].
en dash	1/N	1964^1972	1964–1972
em dash	1/M	The dictionary^how often it is needed^belongs in every home.	The dictionary—how often it is needed—belongs in every home.
asterisk	*	word^	word*
dagger	†	a word^	a word†
double dagger	‡	words and words^	words and words‡
section symbol	§	^Book Reviews	§Book Reviews
virgule (slash)	/	either/or	either/or
three ellipses	⊙|⊙|⊙	the^word	the...word
four ellipses	⊙|⊙|⊙|⊙	the word^	the word....
STYLE OF TYPE			
uppercase	(uc)	the word (triple underline)	The Word
lowercase	(lc)	The Word (slashed)	the word
small capitals	(sc)	the word (double underline)	THE WORD
italic	(ital)	the entry word (underlined)	the entry *word*
roman	(rom)	the entry (word)	the entry word
boldface	(bf)	the entry word (wavy underline)	the entry **word**
lightface	(lf)	(**the entry word**)	the entry word
superior	2 (superior)	2^2 = 4	$2^2 = 4$
inferior	2 (inferior)	H^2O	H_2O

prop·a·gate (prŏp′ə-gāt′) *v.* **-gat·ed, -gat·ing, -gates.** *—tr.* **1.** To cause (an organism) to multiply or breed. **2.** To breed (offspring). **3.** To transmit (characteristics) from one generation to another. **4.** To cause to extend to a broader area or larger number; spread: *missionaries who propagate the faith.* **5.** To make widely known; publicize: *propagate a rumor.* **6.** *Physics.* To cause (a wave, for example) to move in some direction or through a medium; transmit. —*intr.* **1.** To have offspring; multiply. **2.** To extend to a broader area or larger number; spread. **3.** *Physics.* To move through a medium. [Latin *prōpāgāre, prōpāgāt-*. See **pag-** in Appendix.] **—prop′a·ga·ble** (-gə-bəl) *adj.* **—prop′a·ga′tive** *adj.* **—prop′a·ga′tor** *n.*

prop·a·ga·tion (prŏp′ə-gā′shən) *n.* **1.** Multiplication or increase, as by natural reproduction. **2.** The process of spreading to a larger area or greater number; dissemination. **3.** *Physics.* The act or process of propagating, especially the process by which a disturbance, such as the motion of electromagnetic or sound waves, is transmitted through a medium such as air or water. **—prop′a·ga′tion·al** *adj.*

prop·a·gule (prŏp′ə-gyo͞ol′) *n.* Any of various usually vegetative portions of a plant, such as a bud or other offshoot, that aid in dispersal of the species and from which a new individual may develop. [New Latin *prōpāgulum,* diminutive of Latin *prōpāgō,* shoot, from *prōpāgāre,* to propagate. See PROPAGATE.]

pro·pane (prō′pān′) *n.* A colorless gas, C_3H_8, found in natural gas and petroleum and widely used as a fuel.

pro·pa·no·ic acid (prō′pə-nō′ĭk) *n.* See **propionic acid.**

pro·pa·nol (prō′pə-nôl′, -nōl′, -nŏl′) *n.* See **propyl alcohol.**

pro·pel (prə-pĕl′) *tr.v.* **-pelled, -pel·ling, -pels.** To cause to move forward or onward. See Synonyms at **push.** [Middle English *propellen,* from Latin *prōpellere* : *prō-,* forward; see PRO–[1] + *pellere,* to drive; see **pel-**[5] in Appendix.]

propeller

pro·pel·lant also **pro·pel·lent** (prə-pĕl′ənt) —*n.* **1.** Something, such as an explosive charge or a rocket fuel, that propels or provides thrust. **2.** A compressed inert gas, such as a fluorocarbon, that acts as a vehicle for discharging the contents of an aerosol container. —*adj.* Serving to propel; propelling.

pro·pel·ler also **pro·pel·lor** (prə-pĕl′ər) *n.* A machine for propelling an aircraft or a boat, consisting of a power-driven shaft with radiating blades that are placed so as to thrust air or water in a desired direction when spinning.

pro·pend (prō-pĕnd′) *intr.v.* **-pend·ed, -pend·ing, -pends.** *Obsolete.* To have a propensity; incline or tend. [Latin *prōpendēre* : *prō-,* forward; see PRO–[1] + *pendēre,* to hang; see **(s)pen-** in Appendix.]

pro·pene (prō′pēn′) *n.* See **propylene.**

pro·pen·si·ty (prə-pĕn′sĭ-tē) *n., pl.* **-ties.** An innate inclination; a tendency. See Synonyms at **predilection.** [From *propense,* inclined, from Latin *prōpēnsus,* past participle of *prōpendēre,* to be inclined. See PROPEND.]

prop·er (prŏp′ər) *adj. Abbr.* **prop. 1.** Characterized by appropriateness or suitability; fitting: *the proper knife for cutting bread; not a proper moment for a joke.* See Synonyms at **fit**[1]. **2.** Called for by rules or conventions; correct: *the proper form for a business letter.* **3.** Strictly following rules or conventions, especially in social behavior; seemly: *a proper lady; a proper gentleman.* **4.a.** Belonging to one; own: *restored to his proper shape by the magician.* **b.** Characteristically belonging to the being or thing in question; peculiar: *an optical effect proper to fluids.* **5.** Being within the strictly limited sense, as of a term designating something: *the town proper, excluding the suburbs.* **6.** *Ecclesiastical.* For use in the liturgy of a particular feast or season of the year. **7.** *Mathematics.* Of or relating to a subset of a given set when the set has at least one element not in the subset. **8.** Worthy of the name; true: *wanted a proper dinner, not just a snack.* **9.** Out-and-out; thorough: *a proper whipping.* **—proper** *adv.* Thoroughly: *beat the eggs good and proper.* **—proper** also **Proper** *n.* *Ecclesiastical.* The parts of the liturgy that vary according to the particular feast or season of the year. [Middle English *propre,* from Old French, from Latin *proprius.* See **per**[1] in Appendix.] **—prop′er·ly** *adv.* **—prop′er·ness** *n.*

proper adjective *n. Grammar.* An adjective formed from a proper noun.

pro·per·din (prō-pûr′dn) *n.* A natural protein in human blood serum that participates in the body's immune response by working in conjunction with the complement system. [Probably PRO–[1] + Latin *perdere,* to destroy; see PERDITION + –IN.]

proper fraction *n. Mathematics.* **1.** A numerical fraction in which the numerator is less than the denominator. **2.** A polynomial fraction in which the numerator is of a lower degree than the denominator.

proper noun *n. Grammar.* A noun belonging to the class of words used as names for unique individuals, events, or places and usually having few possibilities for modification. Also called *proper name.*

prop·er·tied (prŏp′ər-tēd) *adj.* Owning land or securities as a principal source of revenue.

Pro·per·tius (prō-pûr′shəs, -shē-əs), **Sextus.** 50?–15? B.C. Roman elegiac poet whose extant works include *Cynthia,* an elegy on his former lover.

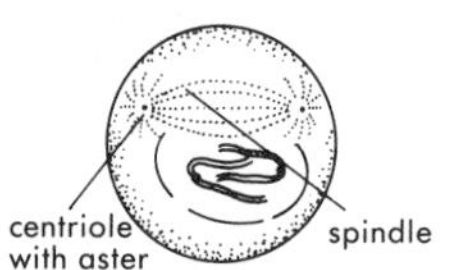

prophase

prop·er·ty (prŏp′ər-tē) *n., pl.* **-ties.** *Abbr.* **prop. 1.a.** Something owned; a possession. **b.** A piece of real estate: *my country property.* **c.** Something tangible or intangible to which its owner has legal title: *properties such as copyrights and trademarks.* **d.** Possessions considered as a group. **2.** The right of ownership; title. **3.** An article, except costumes and scenery, that appears on the stage or on screen during a dramatic performance. **4.a.** A characteristic trait or peculiarity, especially one serving to define or describe its possessor. **b.** A characteristic attribute possessed by all members of a class. See Synonyms at **quality. 5.** A special capability or power; a virtue: *a medicine with special properties.* [Middle English, from Old French *propriete,* from Latin *proprietās,* ownership (translation of Greek *idiotēs;* see IDIOT) from *proprius,* one's own. See **per**[1] in Appendix.] **—prop′er·ty·less** *adj.*

property damage insurance *n.* Liability insurance for claims brought against a person who causes damage to another's property, as by an automobile accident.

property tax *n.* A tax levied against the owner of real or personal property.

pro·phage (prō′fāj′) *n.* The latent form of a bacteriophage in which the viral genes are incorporated into the bacterial chromosomes without causing disruption of the bacterial cell. [Short for French *probactériophage* : Greek *pro-,* before; see PRO–[2] + New Latin *bacterium,* bacterium; see BACTERIO– + Greek *-phagos,* -phage.]

pro·phase (prō′fāz′) *n.* **1.** The first stage of mitosis, during which the chromosomes condense and become visible, the nuclear membrane breaks down, and the spindle apparatus forms at opposite poles of the cell. **2.** The first stage of meiosis, constituted by a series of events that include DNA replication, the synapsis of homologous chromosomes, crossing over, the formation of chiasmata, and contraction of the chromosomes. **—pro·pha′sic** (-fā′zĭk) *adj.*

proph·e·cy (prŏf′ĭ-sē) *n., pl.* **-cies** (-sēz). **1.a.** An inspired utterance of a prophet, viewed as a revelation of divine will. **b.** A prediction of the future, made under divine inspiration. **c.** Such an inspired message or prediction transmitted orally or in writing. **2.** The vocation or condition of a prophet. **3.** A prediction. [Middle English *prophecie,* from Old French, from Latin *prophētīa,* from Greek *prophēteia,* from *prophētēs,* prophet. See PROPHET.]

proph·e·sy (prŏf′ĭ-sī′) *v.* **-sied** (-sīd′), **-sy·ing** (-sī′ĭng), **-sies** (-sīz′). —*tr.* **1.** To reveal by divine inspiration. **2.** To predict with certainty as if by divine inspiration. See Synonyms at **foretell. 3.** To prefigure; foreshow. —*intr.* **1.** To reveal the will or message of God. **2.** To predict the future as if by divine inspiration. **3.** To speak as a prophet. [Middle English *prophecien,* from Old French *prophecier,* from *prophecie,* prophecy. See PROPHECY.] **—proph′e·si′er** *n.*

proph·et (prŏf′ĭt) *n.* **1.** A person who speaks by divine inspiration or as the interpreter through whom the will of a god is expressed. **2.** A person gifted with profound moral insight and exceptional powers of expression. **3.** A predictor; a soothsayer. **4.** The chief spokesperson of a movement or cause. **5. Prophets** *(used with a sing. or pl. verb). Bible.* The second of the three divisions of the Hebrew Scriptures, comprising the books of Joshua, Judges, Samuel, Kings, Isaiah, Jeremiah, Ezekiel, and the Twelve. See table at **Bible.** [Middle English *prophete,* from Old French, from Latin *prophēta,* from Greek *prophētēs* : *pro-,* before; see PRO–[2] + *-phētēs,* speaker (from *phanai,* to speak; see **bhā-**[2] in Appendix).] **—proph′et·hood′** *n.*

proph·et·ess (prŏf′ĭ-tĭs) *n.* **1.** A woman who speaks by divine inspiration or as the interpreter through whom the will of a god is expressed. **2.** A woman predictor; a woman soothsayer. **3.** The chief spokeswoman of a movement or cause.

pro·phet·ic (prə-fĕt′ĭk) also **pro·phet·i·cal** (-ĭ-kəl) *adj.* **1.** Of, belonging to, or characteristic of a prophet or prophecy: *prophetic books.* **2.** Foretelling events as if by divine inspiration: *casual words that proved prophetic.* **—pro·phet′i·cal·ly** *adv.* **—pro·phet′i·cal·ness** *n.*

pro·phy·lac·tic (prō′fə-lăk′tĭk, prŏf′ə-) *adj.* Acting to defend against or prevent something, especially disease; protective. **—prophylactic** *n.* **1.** A prophylactic agent, device, or measure, such as a vaccine or drug. **2.** A contraceptive device, especially a condom. [French *prophylactique,* from Greek *prophulaktikos,* from *prophulassein,* to take precautions against : *pro-,* before; see PRO–[2] + *phulassein,* to protect (from *phulax,* guard).] **—pro′phy·lac′ti·cal·ly** *adv.*

pro·phy·lax·is (prō′fə-lăk′sĭs, prŏf′ə-) *n., pl.* **-lax·es** (-lăk′sēz′). Prevention of or protective treatment for disease. [New Latin, from Greek *prophulaktikos,* prophylactic. See PROPHYLACTIC.]

pro·pin·qui·ty (prə-pĭng′kwĭ-tē) *n.* **1.** Proximity; nearness. **2.** Kinship. **3.** Similarity in nature. [Middle English *propinquite,* from Old French, from Latin *propinquitās,* from *propinquus,* near. See **per**[1] in Appendix.]

pro·pi·on·al·de·hyde (prō′pē-ŏn-ăl′də-hīd′) *n.* A flammable liquid, C_2H_5CHO, used in the manufacture of plastics and rubber chemicals. [PROPION(IC ACID) + ALDEHYDE.]

pro·pi·o·nate (prō′pē-ə-nāt′) *n.* A salt or an ester of propionic acid. [PROPION(IC ACID) + –ATE[2].]

pro·pi·on·ic acid (prō′pē-ŏn′ĭk) *n.* A liquid fatty acid, CH_3CH_2COOH, found naturally in sweat, in milk products, and as a product of bacterial fermentation. Prepared synthetically from ethyl alcohol and carbon monoxide, it is used chiefly in the form of its propionates as a mold inhibitor in bread and as an ingredient in perfume. Also called *propanoic acid.* [From Greek *pro-,* first; see PRO–[2] + Greek *piōn,* fat (from the fact that it is first in order among the fatty acids); see **peie-** in Appendix.]

pro·pi·ti·ate (prō-pĭsh′ē-āt′) *tr.v.* **-at·ed, -at·ing, -ates.** To conciliate (an offended power); appease: *propitiate the gods with a sacrifice.* [Latin *propitiāre, propitiāt-,* from *propitius,* propitious. See PROPITIOUS.] **—pro·pi′ti·a·ble** (-pĭsh′ē-ə-bəl, -pĭsh′ə-bəl) *adj.* **—pro·pi′ti·at′ing·ly** *adv.* **—pro·pi′ti·a′tive** *adj.* **—pro·pi′ti·a′tor** *n.*

pro·pi·ti·a·tion (prō-pĭsh′ē-ā′shən) *n.* **1.** The act of propitiating. **2.** Something that propitiates, especially a conciliatory offering to a god.

pro·pi·ti·a·to·ry (prō-pĭsh′ē-ə-tôr′ē, -tōr′ē, -pĭsh′ə-) *adj.* Of or offered in propitiation; conciliatory. **—pro·pi′ti·a·to′ri·ly** *adv.*

pro·pi·tious (prə-pĭsh′əs) *adj.* **1.** Presenting favorable circumstances; auspicious. See Synonyms at **favorable. 2.** Kindly; gracious. [Middle English *propicius,* from Old French *propicieux,* from Latin *propitius.* See **pet-** in Appendix.] **—pro·pi′tious·ly** *adv.* **—pro·pi′tious·ness** *n.*

prop·jet (prŏp′jĕt′) *n.* See **turboprop.**

pro·plas·tid (prō-plăs′tĭd) *n.* A cytoplasmic organelle from which a plastid develops.

prop·o·lis (prŏp′ə-lĭs) *n.* A resinous substance collected from the buds of certain trees by bees and used as a cement or sealant in the construction of their hives. [Latin, from Greek, suburb, bee glue (from the fact that it was originally the name of a structure around the opening into the hive) : *pro-,* before; see PRO–[2] + *polis,* city; see **pelə-**[3] in Appendix.]

pro·po·nent (prə-pō′nənt) *n.* One who argues in support of something; an advocate. [Latin *prōpōnēns, prōpōnent-,* present participle of *prōpōnere,* to set forth. See PROPOSE.]

pro·por·tion (prə-pôr′shən, -pōr′-) *n.* **1.** A part considered in relation to the whole. **2.** A relationship between things or parts of things with respect to comparative magnitude, quantity, or degree: *the proper proportion between oil and vinegar in the dressing.* **3.** A relationship between quantities such that if one varies then another varies in a manner dependent on the first: *"We do not always find visible happiness in proportion to visible virtue"* (Samuel Johnson). **4.** Agreeable or harmonious relation of parts within a whole; balance or symmetry. **5.** Often **proportions.** Dimensions; size. **6.** *Mathematics.* A statement of equality between two ratios. Four quantities, *a, b, c, d,* are said to be in proportion if $a/b = c/d$. **—proportion** *tr.v.* **-tioned, -tion·ing, -tions. 1.** To adjust so that proper relations between parts are attained. **2.** To form the parts of with balance or symmetry. [Middle English *proporcion,* from Old French *proportion,* from Latin *prōportiō, prōportiōn-,* from *prō portiōne,* according to (each) part : *prō,* according to; see PRO–[1] + *portiōne,* ablative of *portiō,* part; see **perə-**[2] in Appendix.] **—pro·por′tion·a·ble** *adj.* **—pro·por′tion·a·bly** *adv.* **—pro·por′tion·er** *n.* **—pro·por′tion·ment** *n.*

SYNONYMS: *proportion, harmony, symmetry, balance.* These nouns are compared as they mean aesthetic arrangement, as in a design, marked by proper distribution of elements. *Proportion* is the agreeable or harmonious relation of parts within a whole: *The house, of Spanish colonial design, has rooms with graciousness of proportion and beautiful details. Harmony* is the pleasing interaction or appropriate combination of elements: *The harmony of her face is not diminished by her imperfect nose. Symmetry* and *balance* both imply an arrangement of parts and details on either side of a dividing line, but *symmetry* frequently emphasizes exact or mirror-image correspondence of parts, while *balance* often suggests dissimilar parts that offset each other to make a harmonious and satisfying whole: *Beds of iris were set out in perfect symmetry around a pool filled with water lilies. "In all perfectly beautiful objects, there is found the opposition of one part to another, and a reciprocal balance"* (John Ruskin).

pro·por·tion·al (prə-pôr′shə-nəl, -pōr′-) *adj. Abbr.* **P.R. 1.** Forming a relationship with other parts or quantities; being in proportion. **2.** Properly related in size, degree, or other measurable characteristics; corresponding: *Punishment ought to be proportional to the crime.* **3.** *Mathematics.* Having the same or a constant ratio. **—proportional** *n.* One of the quantities in a mathematical proportion. **—pro·por′tion·al′i·ty** (-shə-năl′ĭ-tē) *n.* **—pro·por′tion·al·ly** *adv.*

proportional representation *n. Abbr.* **P.R.** Representation of all parties in a legislature in proportion to their popular vote.

pro·por·tion·ate (prə-pôr′shə-nĭt, -pōr′-) *adj.* Being in due proportion; proportional. **—proportionate** (-shə-nāt′) *tr.v.* **-at·ed, -at·ing, -ates.** To make proportionate. **—pro·por′tion·ate·ly** *adv.* **—pro·por′tion·ate·ness** *n.*

pro·pos·al (prə-pō′zəl) *n.* **1.** The act of proposing. **2.** A plan that is proposed. **3.** An offer of marriage.

pro·pose (prə-pōz′) *v.* **-posed, -pos·ing, -pos·es.** *—tr.* **1.** To put forward for consideration, discussion, or adoption; suggest: *propose a change in the law.* **2.** To recommend (a person) for a position, office, or membership; nominate. **3.** To offer (a toast to be drunk). **4.** To make known as one's intention; purpose or intend: *proposed to buy and run a farm. —intr.* To form or make a proposal, especially of marriage. [Middle English *proposen,* from Old French *proposer,* alteration (influenced by *poser,* to put, place; see POSE[1]) of Latin *prōpōnere* : *prō-,* forth; see PRO–[1] + *pōnere,* to put; see **apo-** in Appendix.]

SYNONYMS: *propose, pose, propound, submit.* The central meaning shared by these verbs is "to present something for consideration or discussion": *propose a solution to a problem; a situation posing many questions and problems; propound a theory; submitting a plan.*

prop·o·si·tion (prŏp′ə-zĭsh′ən) *n. Abbr.* **prop. 1.** A plan suggested for acceptance; a proposal. **2.** *Informal.* A matter to be dealt with; a task: *Finding an affordable apartment will be a difficult proposition.* **3.** *Informal.* An offer of a private bargain, especially a request for sexual relations. **4.** A subject for discussion or analysis. **5.** *Logic.* **a.** A statement in which the subject is affirmed or denied by the predicate. **b.** Something that is expressed in a statement, as opposed to the way it is expressed. **c.** A statement containing only logical constants and having a fixed truth-value. **—proposition** *tr.v.* **-tioned, -tion·ing, -tions.** *Informal.* To propose a private bargain to, especially to propose sexual relations with. [Middle English *proposicion,* from Old French *proposition,* from Latin *prōpositiō, prōpositiōn-,* setting out in words, from *prōpositus,* past participle of *prōpōnere,* to set forth. See PROPOSE.] **—prop′o·si′tion·al** *adj.* **—prop′o·si′tion·al·ly** *adv.*

propositional calculus *n. Logic.* The branch of symbolic logic that deals with the relationships formed between propositions by connectives such as *and, or,* and *if* as opposed to their internal structure.

propositional function *n. Logic.* An expression having the form of a proposition but containing undefined symbols for the substantive elements and becoming a proposition when appropriate values are assigned to the symbols.

pro·pos·i·tus (prō-pŏz′ĭ-təs) *n., pl.* **-ti** (-tī′). The person immediately concerned about or affected by an action. [Latin *prōpositus,* past participle of *prōpōnere,* to set forth. See PROPOSE.]

pro·pound (prə-pound′) *tr.v.* **-pound·ed, -pound·ing, -pounds.** To put forward for consideration; set forth. See Synonyms at **propose.** [Alteration of *propoune,* from Middle English *proponen,* from Latin *prōpōnere,* to set forth. See PROPOSE.] **—pro·pound′er** *n.*

pro·pox·y·phene (prō-pŏk′sə-fēn′) *n.* A nonnarcotic analgesic drug, $C_{22}H_{29}NO_2$. [PROP– + OXY– + *-phene* (alteration of PHENYL).]

propr. *abbr.* Proprietor; proprietress.

pro·prae·tor (prō-prē′tər) *n.* An ancient Roman official, appointed to be the chief administrator of a province after serving his term of office as praetor. [Latin *prōpraetor* : *prō-,* for; see PRO–[1] + *praetor,* praetor; see PRAETOR.] **—pro′prae·to′ri·al** (prō′prĭ-tôr′ē-əl, -tōr′-), **pro′prae·to′ri·an** (-ən) *adj.*

pro·pran·o·lol (prō-prăn′ə-lôl′, -lōl′, -lŏl′) *n.* A drug, $C_{16}H_{21}NO_2$, that blocks beta-adrenergic activity, used to treat hypertension, angina pectoris, and cardiac arrhythmia. [PRO(PYL) + PR(OP)ANOL (PROPAN(E) + –OL[1]) + –OL[1].]

pro·pri·e·tar·y (prə-prī′ĭ-tĕr′ē) *adj. Abbr.* **prop., pty. 1.** Of or relating to a proprietor or to proprietors as a group: *proprietary rights.* **2.** Exclusively owned; private: *a proprietary hospital.* **3.** Befitting an owner: *a proprietary air.* **4.** Owned by a private individual or corporation under a trademark or patent: *a proprietary drug.* **—proprietary** *n., pl.* **-ies.** *Abbr.* **prop., pty. 1.** A proprietor. **2.** A group of proprietors. **3.** Ownership; proprietorship. **4.** A proprietary medicine. **5.** One granted ownership of a proprietary colony. [From Middle English *proprietarie,* owner of property, from Old French *proprietaire* and from Medieval Latin *proprietārius,* both from Late Latin, of a property owner, from Latin *proprietās,* ownership. See PROPERTY.] **—pro·pri′e·tar′i·ly** *adv.*

proprietary colony *n.* Any of certain early North American colonies, such as Carolina and Pennsylvania, organized in the 17th century in territories granted by the English Crown to one or more proprietors who had full governing rights.

pro·pri·e·tor (prə-prī′ĭ-tər) *n. Abbr.* **prop., propr. 1.** One who has legal title to something; an owner. **2.** One who owns or owns and manages a business or other such establishment. [Probably alteration of Middle English *proprietarie.* See PROPRIETARY.] **—pro·pri′e·to′ri·al** (-tôr′ē-əl, -tōr′-) *adj.* **—pro·pri′e·to′ri·al·ly** *adv.* **—pro·pri′e·tor·ship′** *n.*

pro·pri·e·tress (prə-prī′ĭ-trĭs) *n. Abbr.* **prop., propr. 1.** A woman who has legal title to something; an owner. **2.** A woman who owns or owns and manages a business or other such establishment.

pro·pri·e·ty (prə-prī′ĭ-tē) *n., pl.* **-ties. 1.** The quality of being proper; appropriateness. **2.** Conformity to prevailing customs and usages. See Synonyms at **etiquette. 3. proprieties.** The usages and customs of polite society. [Middle English *propriete,* particular character, ownership, from Old French. See PROPERTY.]

pro·pri·o·cep·tion (prō′prē-ō-sĕp′shən) *n.* The unconscious perception of movement and spatial orientation arising from stimuli within the body itself. [Latin *proprius,* one's own; see **per**[1] in Appendix + (RE)CEPTION.]

pro·pri·o·cep·tor (prō′prē-ō-sĕp′tər) *n.* A sensory receptor, found chiefly in muscles, tendons, joints, and the inner ear, that detects the motion or position of the body or a limb by re-

ă pat	oi boy
ā pay	ou out
âr care	ŏŏ took
ä father	ōō boot
ĕ pet	ŭ cut
ē be	ûr urge
ĭ pit	th thin
ī pie	*th* this
îr pier	hw which
ŏ pot	zh vision
ō toe	ə about, item
ô paw	♦ regionalism

Stress marks: **′** (primary); ′ (secondary), as in **dictionary** (dĭk′shə-nĕr′ē)

prop root

sponding to stimuli arising within the organism. [Latin *proprius,* one's own; see **per**[1] in Appendix + (RE)CEPTOR.] **—pro′pri·o·cep′tive** *adj.*

prop root *n.* An adventitious root that arises from the stem, penetrates the soil, and helps to support the stem, as in corn. Also called *brace root.*

prop·to·sis (prŏp-tō′sĭs) *n., pl.* **-ses** (-sēz). Forward displacement of an organ, especially an eyeball. [Late Latin *proptōsis,* prolapse, from Greek, from *propiptein,* to fall forward : *pro-,* forward; see PRO–[2] + *piptein,* to fall; see **pet-** in Appendix.]

pro·pul·sion (prə-pŭl′shən) *n.* **1.** The process of driving or propelling. **2.** A driving or propelling force. [Medieval Latin *prōpulsiō, prōpulsiōn-,* onslaught, urging on, from Latin *prōpulsus,* past participle of *prōpellere,* to drive forward. See PROPEL.] **—pro·pul′sive, pro·pul′so·ry** (-sə-rē) *adj.*

pro·pyl (prō′pĭl) *n. Abbr.* **Pr** A univalent organic radical with composition C_3H_7, derived from propane. **—pro·pyl′ic** *adj.*

prop·y·la (prŏp′ə-lə, prō′pə-) *n.* Plural of **propylon.**

prop·y·lae·um (prŏp′ə-lē′əm, prō′pə-) *n., pl.* **-lae·a** (-lē′ə). *Architecture.* An entrance or vestibule to a temple or group of buildings. Also called *propylon.* [Latin, from Greek *propulaion* : *pro-,* before; see PRO–[2] + *pulē,* gate.]

propyl alcohol *n.* A clear colorless liquid, $CH_3CH_2CH_2OH$, used as a solvent and as an antiseptic. Also called *propanol.*

pro·pyl·ene (prō′pə-lēn′) *n.* A flammable gas, $CH_3CH{:}CH_2$, derived from petroleum hydrocarbon cracking and used in organic synthesis. Also called *propene.*

propylene glycol *n.* A colorless viscous hygroscopic liquid, $CH_3CHOHCH_2OH$, used in antifreeze solutions, in hydraulic fluids, and as a solvent.

prop·y·lon (prŏp′ə-lŏn′, prō′pə-) *n., pl.* **-la** (-lə). *Architecture.* See **propylaeum.** [Greek *propulon* : *pro-,* before; see PRO–[2] + *pulē,* gate.]

pro ra·ta (prō rā′tə, răt′ə, rä′tə) *adv.* In proportion, according to a factor that can be calculated exactly. [Latin *prō ratā (parte),* according to the calculated (share) : *prō,* according to + *ratā,* feminine ablative of *rātus,* calculated.]

pro·rate (prō-rāt′, prō′rāt′) *v.* **-rat·ed, -rat·ing, -rates.** *—tr.* To divide, distribute, or assess proportionately. *—intr.* To settle affairs on the basis of proportional distribution. [From PRO RATA.] **—pro·rat′a·ble** *adj.* **—pro·ra′tion** *n.*

pro·rogue (prō-rōg′) *tr.v.* **-rogued, -rogu·ing, -rogues. 1.** To discontinue a session of (a parliament, for example). **2.** To postpone; defer. [Middle English *prorogen,* from Old French *proroguer,* to postpone, from Latin *prōrogāre* : *pro-,* forward; see PRO–[1] + *rogāre,* to ask; see **reg-** in Appendix.] **—pro′ro·ga′tion** *n.*

pros. *abbr.* Prosody.

pros– *pref.* **1.** Near; toward: *prosenchyma.* **2.** In front of: *prosencephalon.* [Greek, from *pros,* near, at. See **per**[1] in Appendix.]

pro·sa·ic (prō-zā′ĭk) *adj.* **1.a.** Consisting or characteristic of prose. **b.** Matter-of-fact; straightforward. **2.** Lacking in imagination and spirit; dull. [Late Latin *prōsaicus,* from Latin *prōsa,* prose. See PROSE.] **—pro·sa′i·cal·ly** *adv.* **—pro·sa′ic·ness** *n.*

pro·sa·ism (prō′zā-ĭz′əm) *n.* **1.** A quality or style that is prosaic. **2.** A prosaic word, phrase, or other expression.

Pros. Atty. *abbr. Law.* Prosecuting attorney.

pro·sce·ni·um (prō-sē′nē-əm, prə-) *n.* **1.** *pl.* **-ni·ums.** The area of a modern theater that is located between the curtain and the orchestra. **2.** *pl.* **-ni·a** (-nē-ə). The stage of an ancient theater, located between the background and the orchestra. [Latin *proscēnium,* from Greek *proskēnion* : *pro-,* before; see PRO–[2] + *skēnē,* buildings at the back of the stage.]

pro·sciut·to (prō-sho͞o′tō) *n., pl.* **-ti** (-tē) or **-tos.** An aged, dry-cured, spiced Italian ham that is usually sliced thin and is served without cooking. [Italian, alteration (probably influenced by *prosciugare,* to dry out) of *presciutto,* from Vulgar Latin **perexsūctus,* thoroughly dried up : Latin *per-,* per- + Latin *exsūctus,* past participle of *exsūgere,* to suck out (*ex-,* ex- + *sūgere,* to suck; see SUCTION).]

pro·scribe (prō-skrīb′) *tr.v.* **-scribed, -scrib·ing, -scribes. 1.** To denounce or condemn. **2.** To prohibit; forbid. See Synonyms at **forbid. 3.a.** To banish or outlaw (a person). **b.** To publish the name of (a person) as outlawed. [Middle English *proscriben,* from Latin *prōscrībere,* to put up someone's name as outlawed : *prō-,* in front; see PRO–[1] + *scrībere,* to write; see **skrībh-** in Appendix.] **—pro·scrib′er** *n.*

pro·scrip·tion (prō-skrĭp′shən) *n.* **1.** The act of proscribing; prohibition. **2.** The condition of having been proscribed; outlawry. [Middle English *proscripcion,* from Latin *prōscrīptiō, prōscrīptiōn-,* public notice of outlawry, from *prōscrīptus,* past participle of *prōscrībere,* to proscribe. See PROSCRIBE.] **—pro·scrip′tive** *adj.* **—pro·scrip′tive·ly** *adv.*

prose (prōz) *n.* **1.** Ordinary speech or writing, without metrical structure. **2.** Commonplace expression or quality. **3.** *Roman Catholic Church.* A hymn of irregular meter sung after the gradual. **—prose** *v.* **prosed, pros·ing, pros·es.** *intr.* **1.** To write prose. **2.** To speak or write in a dull, tiresome style. [Middle English, from Old French, from Latin *prōsa (ōrātiō),* straightforward (discourse), feminine of *prōsus,* alteration of *prōrsus,* from *prōversus,* past participle of *prōvertere,* to turn forward : *prō-,* forward; see PRO–[1] + *vertere,* to turn; see **wer-**[2] in Appendix.]

Proserpina
The Rape of Proserpina by Giovanni Lorenzo Bernini

pro·sec·tor (prō-sĕk′tər) *n.* One who dissects cadavers for anatomical instruction or pathological examination. [Latin *prōsector,* anatomist, from *prōsecāre,* to cut off, up : *prō-,* before; see PRO–[1] + *secāre,* to cut; see SECTOR.]

pros·e·cute (prŏs′ĭ-kyo͞ot′) *v.* **-cut·ed, -cut·ing, -cutes.** *—tr.* **1.** *Law.* **a.** To initiate civil or criminal court action against. **b.** To seek to obtain or enforce by legal action. **2.a.** To pursue (an undertaking, for example) until completion; follow to the very end. **b.** To chase or pursue (a vessel): *"He held a dispatch saying that* [they] *had prosecuted and probably killed an Echo-class missile submarine"* (Tom Clancy). **3.** To carry on, engage in, or practice. *—intr. Law.* **1.** To initiate and conduct legal proceedings. **2.** To act as prosecutor. [Middle English *prosecuten,* from Latin *prōsequī, prōsecūt-* : *prō-,* forward; see PRO–[1] + *sequī,* to follow; see **sekʷ-**[1] in Appendix.] **—pros′e·cut′a·ble** *adj.*

pros·e·cut·ing attorney (prŏs′ĭ-kyo͞o′tĭng) *n. Abbr.* **Pros. Atty., PA, P.A.** *Law.* A lawyer empowered to prosecute cases on behalf of a government and its people. Also called *prosecution, prosecutor.*

pros·e·cu·tion (prŏs′ĭ-kyo͞o′shən) *n.* **1.** The act of prosecuting. **2.** *Law.* The institution and conduct of a legal proceeding. **3.** *Law.* See **prosecuting attorney.**

pros·e·cu·tor (prŏs′ĭ-kyo͞o′tər) *n.* **1.** One that prosecutes. **2.** *Law.* One that initiates and carries out a legal action, especially criminal proceedings. **3.** *Law.* See **prosecuting attorney.**

pros·e·cu·to·ri·al (prŏs′ĭ-kyo͞o-tôr′ē-əl, -tōr′-) *adj.* Of, relating to, or concerned with prosecution: *"a huge investigative and prosecutorial effort"* (Lucian K. Truscott IV).

pros·e·lyte (prŏs′ə-līt′) *n.* A new convert to a doctrine or religion. **—proselyte** *v.* **-lyt·ed, -lyt·ing, -lytes.** *—tr.* To proselytize (a person). *—intr.* To engage in proselytization. [Middle English *proselite,* from Old French, from Late Latin *prosēlytus,* from Greek *prosēlutos,* stranger, proselyte, from *prosēluth-,* aorist stem of *proserkhesthai,* to go to : *pros-,* pros- + *erkhesthai,* to go.] **—pros′e·lyt′er** *n.*

pros·e·ly·tism (prŏs′ə-lĭ-tĭz′əm, -lī-) *n.* **1.** The practice of proselytizing. **2.** The state of being a proselyte. **—pros′e·lyt′i·cal** (-lĭt′ĭ-kəl) *adj.*

pros·e·ly·tize (prŏs′ə-lĭ-tīz′) *v.* **-tized, -tiz·ing, -tiz·es.** *—intr.* **1.** To induce someone to convert to one's own religious faith. **2.** To induce someone to join one's own political party or to espouse one's doctrine. *—tr.* To convert (a person) from one belief, doctrine, cause, or faith to another. **—pros′e·ly·ti·za′tion** (-tĭ-zā′shən) *n.* **—pros′e·ly·tiz′er** *n.*

pro·sem·i·nar (prō-sĕm′ə-när′) *n.* A course of study for graduate and advanced undergraduate students in a college or university, conducted in the manner of a seminar. [PRO–[2] + SEMINAR.]

pros·en·ceph·a·lon (prŏs′ĕn-sĕf′ə-lŏn′) *n.* The forebrain. **—pros′en·ce·phal′ic** (-sə-făl′ĭk) *adj.*

pros·en·chy·ma (prŏ-sĕng′kĭ-mə) *n.* A type of plant tissue consisting of elongated cells with tapering ends, occurring in supporting and conducting tissue. **—pros′en·chym′a·tous** (-kĭm′ə-təs) *adj.*

prose poem *n.* A prose work that has poetic characteristics such as vivid imagery and concentrated expression.

Pro·ser·pi·na (prō-sûr′pə-nə) also **Pros·er·pi·ne** (prō-sûr′pə-nē, prŏs′ər-pīn′) *n. Roman Mythology.* The daughter of Ceres who became the goddess of the underworld when Pluto carried her away and made her his wife.

pro·sim·i·an (prō-sĭm′ē-ən) *adj.* Of or belonging to the Prosimii, a suborder of primates that includes the lemurs, lorises, and tarsiers. **—prosimian** *n.* A primate of the suborder Prosimii. [From New Latin *Prosīmiī,* suborder name : Latin *pro-,* before; see PRO–[1] + Latin *sīmiī,* pl. of *sīmius,* ape (variant of *sīmia;* see SIMIAN).]

pro·sit (prōst, prō′zĭt) or **prost** (prōst) *interj.* Used as a toast to someone's health while drinking. [German, from Latin, may it benefit, third person sing. subjunctive of *prodesse,* to benefit. See PROUD.]

pro·slav·er·y (prō-slā′və-rē, -slāv′rē) *adj.* Advocating the practice of slavery.

pros·o·dy (prŏs′ə-dē) *n., pl.* **-dies.** *Abbr.* **pros. 1.** The study of the metrical structure of verse. **2.** A particular system of versification. [Middle English *prosodie,* from Latin *prosōdia,* accent, from Greek *prosōidia,* song sung to music, accent : *pros-,* pros- + *ōidē,* song; see ODE.] **—pro·sod′ic** (prə-sŏd′ĭk) *adj.* **—pro·sod′i·cal·ly** *adv.* **—pros′o·dist** *n.*

pro·so·ma (prō-sō′mə) *n.* The anterior or cephalic portion of the body of certain invertebrates, such as arachnids, in which segmentation is not evident. [PRO–[2] + Greek *sōma,* body; see **teuə-** in Appendix.] **—pro·so′mal** *adj.*

pros·o·pog·ra·phy (prŏs′ə-pŏg′rə-fē) *n.* A study, often using statistics, that identifies and draws relationships between various characters or people within a specific historical, social, or literary context: *"an authentic tour de force of historical writing: part intellectual history, part cultural history, part prosopography"* (Josiah Bunting III). [Greek *prosōpon,* character; see PROSOPOPEIA + –GRAPHY.] **—pros′o·po·graph′i·cal** (-pə-grăf′ĭ-kəl) *adj.*

pro·so·po·pe·ia also **pro·so·po·poe·ia** (prə-sō′pə-pē′ə) *n.* **1.** A figure of speech in which an absent or imaginary person is represented as speaking. **2.** See **personification** (sense 3). [Latin *prosōpopoeia,* from Greek *prosōpopoiia* : *prosōpon,* face, mask, dramatic character (*pros-,* pros- + *ōpon,* face, from *ōps,* eye; see MYOPIA) + *poiein,* to make; see **kʷei-**[2] in Appendix.] **—pro·so'po·pe'ial** *adj.*

pros·pect (prŏs'pĕkt') *n.* **1.** Something expected; a possibility. **2. prospects. a.** Chances. **b.** Financial expectations, especially of success. **3. a.** A potential customer, client, or purchaser. **b.** A candidate deemed likely to succeed. **4.** The direction in which an object, such as a building, faces; an outlook. **5.** Something presented to the eye; a scene: *a pleasant prospect.* **6.** The act of surveying or examining. **7. a.** The location or probable location of a mineral deposit. **b.** An actual or probable mineral deposit. **c.** The mineral yield obtained by working an ore. **—prospect** *v.* **-pect·ed, -pect·ing, -pects.** *—tr.* To search for or explore (a region) for mineral deposits or oil. *—intr.* To explore for mineral deposits or oil. [Middle English *prospecte,* from Latin *prōspectus,* distant view, from past participle of *prōspicere,* to look out : *prō-,* forward; see PRO–[1] + *specere,* to look at; see **spek-** in Appendix.]

pro·spec·tive (prə-spĕk'tĭv) *adj.* **1.** Likely or expected to happen. **2.** Likely to become or be: *prospective clients.* **—pro·spec'tive·ly** *adv.*

pros·pec·tor (prŏs'pĕk'tər) *n.* One who explores an area for mineral deposits or oil.

pro·spec·tus (prə-spĕk'təs) *n.* **1.** A formal summary of a proposed venture or project: *She rewrote the prospectus of her dissertation three times before it was approved.* **2.** A document describing the chief features of something, such as a business, an educational program, or especially a stock offering or mutual fund, for prospective buyers, investors, or participants. [Latin *prōspectus,* distant view. See PROSPECT.]

pros·per (prŏs'pər) *intr.v.* **-pered, -per·ing, -pers.** To be fortunate or successful, especially in terms of one's finance's; thrive. [Middle English *prosperen,* from Old French *prosperer,* from Latin *prosperāre,* to render fortunate, from *prosperus,* favorable. See **spē-** in Appendix.]

pros·per·i·ty (prŏ-spĕr'ĭ-tē) *n.* The condition of being prosperous.

pros·per·ous (prŏs'pər-əs) *adj.* **1.** Having success; flourishing: *a prosperous new business.* **2.** Well-to-do; well-off: *a prosperous family.* **3.** Propitious; favorable: *a prosperous moment to make a decision.* **—pros'per·ous·ly** *adv.* **—pros'per·ous·ness** *n.*

prost (prōst) *interj.* Variant of **prosit.**

pros·ta·cy·clin (prŏs'tə-sī'klĭn) *n.* A prostaglandin produced in the walls of blood vessels that acts as a vasodilator and inhibits platelet aggregation. [PROSTA(TE) + CYCL(IC) + –IN.]

pros·ta·glan·din (prŏs'tə-glăn'dĭn) *n.* Any of a group of hormonelike substances produced in various mammalian tissues that are derived from amino acids and mediate a wide range of physiological functions, such as metabolism, smooth muscle activity, and nerve transmission. [PROSTA(TE) + GLAND[1] + –IN.]

pros·tate (prŏs'tāt') *n.* The prostate gland. **—prostate** *adj.* Of or relating to the prostate gland. [New Latin *prostata,* from Greek *prostatēs (adēn),* prostate (gland), from *proistanai,* to set before : *pro-,* in front; see PRO–[2] + *histanai,* to set, place; see **stā-** in Appendix.] **—pro·stat'ic** (prŏ-stăt'ĭk) *adj.*

pros·ta·tec·to·my (prŏs'tə-tĕk'tə-mē) *n., pl.* **-mies.** Surgical removal of all or part of the prostate gland.

prostate gland *n.* A gland in male mammals surrounding the urethra at the base of the bladder that controls release of urine from the bladder and secretes a fluid which is a major constituent of semen.

pros·ta·tism (prŏs'tə-tĭz'əm) *n.* A disorder characterized by decreased force of urination and dysuria, usually resulting from enlargement of the prostate gland.

pros·ta·ti·tis (prŏs'tə-tī'tĭs) *n.* Inflammation of the prostate gland.

pros·the·sis (prŏs-thē'sĭs) *n., pl.* **-ses** (-sēz). **1.** An artificial device used to replace a missing body part, such as a limb, a tooth, an eye, or a heart valve. **2.** Replacement of a missing body part with such a device. [Greek, addition, from *prostithenai,* to add : *pros-,* pros- + *tithenai,* to put; see **dhē-** in Appendix.]

pros·thet·ic (prŏs-thĕt'ĭk) *adj.* **1.** Serving as or relating to a prosthesis. **2.** Of or relating to prosthetics. **—pros·thet'i·cal·ly** *adv.*

prosthetic group *n. Biochemistry.* The nonprotein component of a conjugated protein, as the heme group in hemoglobin.

pros·thet·ics (prŏs-thĕt'ĭks) *n. (used with a sing. verb).* The branch of medicine or surgery that deals with the production and application of artificial body parts. **—pros'the·tist** (prŏs'thĭ-tĭst) *n.*

pros·tho·don·tia (prŏs'thə-dŏn'shə) *n.* Prosthodontics. [PROSTH(ESIS) + –ODONTIA.]

pros·tho·don·tics (prŏs'thə-dŏn'tĭks) *n. (used with a sing. verb).* The branch of dentistry that deals with the replacement of missing teeth and related mouth or jaw structures by bridges, dentures, or other artificial devices. [PROSTH(ESIS) + –ODONT(IA) + –ICS.] **—pros'tho·don'tic** *adj.* **—pros'tho·don'tist** *n.*

pros·ti·tute (prŏs'tĭ-to͞ot', -tyo͞ot') *n.* **1.** One who solicits and accepts payment for sex acts. **2.** One who sells one's abilities, talent, or name for an unworthy purpose. **—prostitute** *tr.v.* **-tut·ed, -tut·ing, -tutes.** **1.** To offer (oneself or another) for sexual hire. **2.** To sell (oneself or one's talent, for example) for an unworthy purpose. [Latin *prōstitūta,* from feminine past participle of *prōstituere,* to prostitute : *prō-,* in front; see PRO–[1] + *statuere,* to cause to stand; see **stā-** in Appendix.] **—pros'ti·tu'tor** *n.*

pros·ti·tu·tion (prŏs'tĭ-to͞o'shən, -tyo͞o'-) *n.* **1.** The act or practice of engaging in sex acts for hire. **2.** The act or an instance of offering or devoting one's talent to an unworthy use or cause.

pro·sto·mi·um (prō-stō'mē-əm) *n., pl.* **-mi·a** (-mē-ə). The portion of the head in earthworms and other annelids that is situated anterior to the mouth. [New Latin, from Greek *prostomion,* mouth, lips : Greek *pro-,* in front of; see PRO–[2] + Greek *stomion,* diminutive of *stoma,* mouth.] **—pro·sto'mi·al** (-əl) *adj.*

pros·trate (prŏs'trāt') *tr.v.* **-trat·ed, -trat·ing, -trates.** **1.** To make (oneself) bow or kneel down in humility or adoration. **2.** To throw down flat. **3.** To lay low; overcome. **—prostrate** *adj.* **1.** Lying face down, as in submission or adoration. **2.** Lying down at full length. See Synonyms at **prone. 3.** Physically or emotionally incapacitated; overcome. **4.** *Botany.* Growing flat along the ground. [Middle English *prostraten,* from *prostrat,* prostrate, from Latin *prōstrātus,* past participle of *prōsternere,* to throw down : *pro-,* forward; see PRO–[1] + *sternere,* to spread, cast down; see **ster-**[2] in Appendix.] **—pros'tra'tor** *n.*

pros·tra·tion (prŏ-strā'shən) *n.* **1. a.** The act of prostrating oneself. **b.** The state of being prostrate. **2.** Total exhaustion or weakness; collapse.

pro·style (prō'stīl') *adj. Architecture.* Having a row of columns across the front only, as in some Greek temples. [Latin *prostȳlos,* from Greek *prostulos* : *pro-,* in front; see PRO–[2] + *stulos,* pillar; see **stā-** in Appendix.]

pros·y (prō'zē) *adj.* **-i·er, -i·est.** **1.** Matter-of-fact and dry; prosaic. **2.** Dull; commonplace. [From PROSE.] **—pros'i·ly** *adv.* **—pros'i·ness** *n.*

Prot. *abbr.* Protestant.

prot– *pref.* Variant of **proto–.**

pro·tac·tin·i·um (prō'tăk-tĭn'ē-əm) *n. Symbol* **Pa** A rare, extremely toxic, radioactive element chemically similar to uranium, having 13 known isotopes, the most common of which is protactinium 231 with a half-life of 32,480 years. Atomic number 91; melting point 1,230°C; specific gravity 15.37; valence 4, 5. See table at **element.** [PROT(O)– + ACTINIUM (so called because it disintegrates into actinium).]

pro·tag·o·nist (prō-tăg'ə-nĭst) *n.* **1.** The main character in a drama or other literary work. **2.** In ancient Greek drama, the first actor to engage in dialogue with the chorus, in later dramas playing the main character and some minor characters as well. **3. a.** A leading or principal figure. **b.** The leader of a cause; a champion. **4.** *Usage Problem.* A proponent; an advocate. [Greek *prōtagōnistēs* : *prōto-,* proto- + *agōnistēs,* actor, combatant (from *agōnizesthai,* to contend, from *agōnia,* contest, from *agōn,* from *agein,* to drive, lead; see **ag-** in Appendix).]

USAGE NOTE: The *protagonist* of a Greek drama was its leading actor, of whom there could be but one in any play. This is an etymological nicety that many modern writers continue to observe when using the word to refer to the main character of a drama or other fiction. Thus when the members of the Usage Panel were asked "How many protagonists are there in *Othello*?" the great majority answered "One" and offered substitutes such as *antagonist, villain, principal,* and *deuteragonist* to describe Desdemona and Iago. But there is reputable precedent from the 17th century on for using *protagonist* to mean simply "important actor" or "principal party," with no implication of uniqueness, as in *There are three protagonists in this sluggish novel. Smith and Jones were the protagonists in the struggle over the future of the computer company.* Thus, while some writers may prefer to confine the word to a singular sense in their own usage, it is pedantic to insist that the looser use is incorrect. • The use of *protagonist* to refer to a proponent has become common only in the 20th century and may have been influenced by a misconception that the first syllable of the word represents the prefix *pro–,* "favoring." In sentences such as *He was an early protagonist of nuclear power,* this use is likely to strike many readers as an error and can usually be replaced by *advocate* or *proponent* with no loss of sense.

Pro·tag·o·ras (prō-tăg'ər-əs). fl. fifth century B.C. Greek philosopher. Considered the first Sophist, he taught a philosophy based on his maxim "Man is the measure of all things." **—Pro·tag'o·re'an** (-ə-rē'ən) *adj.*

pro·ta·mine (prō'tə-mēn', -mĭn) also **pro·ta·min** (-mĭn) *n.* Any of a group of simple proteins found in fish sperm that are strongly basic, are soluble in water, are not coagulated by heat, and yield chiefly arginine upon hydrolysis. In purified form, they are used in a long-acting formulation of insulin and to neutralize the anticoagulant effects of heparin.

pro·tan·drous (prō-tăn'drəs) *adj. Botany.* Of or relating to a flower in which the anthers release their pollen before the stigma of the same flower is receptive. **—pro·tan'dry** (-drē) *n.*

pro·ta·no·pi·a (prō'tə-nō'pē-ə) *n.* A form of colorblindness characterized by defective perception of red and confusion of red with green or bluish green. [PROT(O)– + AN– + –OPIA (from the blindness to red, which is considered the first of the primary colors).] **—pro'ta·nop'ic** (-nŏp'ĭk) *adj.*

prot·a·sis (prŏt'ə-sĭs) *n., pl.* **-ses** (-sēz'). **1.** *Grammar.* The

prospector
Panning for gold

prosthesis
Jeff Keith near the completion of his Run Across America in 1985

ă pat	oi boy
ā pay	ou out
âr care	o͝o took
ä father	o͞o boot
ĕ pet	ŭ cut
ē be	ûr urge
ĭ pit	th thin
ī pie	*th* this
îr pier	hw which
ŏ pot	zh vision
ō toe	ə about, item
ô paw	♦ regionalism

Stress marks: **'** (primary); ' (secondary), as in **dictionary** (dĭk'shə-nĕr'ē)

subordinate clause of a conditional sentence, as *if it rains* in *The game will be canceled if it rains.* **2.** The first part of an ancient Greek or Roman drama, in which the characters and subject are introduced. [Late Latin, proposition, first part of a play, from Greek, premise of a syllogism, conditional clause, from *proteinein,* to propose : *pro-,* forward; see PRO–[2] + *teinein,* to stretch; see **ten-** in Appendix.] **—pro·tat′ic** (prŏ-tăt′ĭk, prō-) *adj.*

prote– *pref.* Variant of **proteo–.**

pro·te·an (prō′tē-ən, prō-tē′-) *adj.* **1.** Readily taking on varied shapes, forms, or meanings. **2.** Exhibiting considerable variety or diversity: *"He loved to show off his protean talent"* (William A. Henry III). [From PROTEUS.]

pro·te·ase (prō′tē-ās′, -āz′) *n.* Any of various enzymes, including the proteinases and peptides, that catalyze the hydrolytic breakdown of proteins.

protec. *abbr.* Protectorate.

pro·tect (prə-tĕkt′) *tr.v.* **-tect·ed, -tect·ing, -tects. 1.** To keep from being damaged, attacked, stolen, or injured; guard. See Synonyms at **defend. 2.** To help (domestic industry) with tariffs or quotas on imported goods. **3.** To assure payment of (drafts or notes, for example) by setting aside funds. [Middle English *protecten,* from Latin *prōtegere, prōtēct-* : *prō-,* in front; see PRO–[1] + *tegere,* to cover; see **(s)teg-** in Appendix.] **—pro·tect′ing·ly** *adv.*

pro·tec·tant (prə-tĕk′tənt) *n.* One that protects: *applied a protectant to the raw wood.*

pro·tect·er (prə-tĕk′tər) *n.* Variant of **protector.**

pro·tec·tion (prə-tĕk′shən) *n.* **1.a.** The act of protecting. **b.** The condition of being protected. **2.** One that protects. **3.** A pass guaranteeing safe-conduct to travelers. **4.** A system of tariffs or other measures protecting domestic producers from foreign competition. **5.** *Slang.* **a.** Money extorted by racketeers threatening violence for nonpayment. **b.** Bribes paid to officials by racketeers for immunity from prosecution. **—pro·tec′tion·al** *adj.*

pro·tec·tion·ism (prə-tĕk′shə-nĭz′əm) *n.* The advocacy, system, or theory of protecting domestic producers by impeding or limiting, as by tariffs or quotas, the importation of foreign goods and services. **—pro·tec′tion·ist** *n.*

pro·tec·tive (prə-tĕk′tĭv) *adj.* Adapted or intended to afford protection. **—protective** *n.* Something that protects. **—pro·tec′tive·ly** *adv.* **—pro·tec′tive·ness** *n.*

pro·tec·tor also **pro·tect·er** (prə-tĕk′tər) *n.* **1.** One who protects; a guardian. **2.** A device that protects; a guard. **3. Protector. a.** A person who rules a kingdom during the minority of a sovereign. **b.** The head of the Commonwealth of England, Scotland, and Ireland from 1653 to 1659. **—pro·tec′tor·al** *adj.* **—pro·tec′tor·ship′** *n.*

pro·tec·tor·ate (prə-tĕk′tər-ĭt) *n. Abbr.* **protec. 1.a.** A relationship of protection and partial control assumed by a superior power over a dependent country or region. **b.** The protected country or region. **2. Protectorate. a.** The government, office, or term of a protector. **b.** The government of England under Oliver Cromwell and his son Richard, ruling as Lord Protector of the Commonwealth.

pro·tec·to·ry (prə-tĕk′tə-rē) *n., pl.* **-ries.** An institution providing for the welfare of homeless, destitute, or delinquent children.

pro·té·gé (prō′tə-zhā′, prō′tə-zhā′) *n.* One whose welfare, training, or career is promoted by an influential person. [French, from past participle of *protéger,* to protect, from Old French, from Latin *prōtegere.* See PROTECT.]

pro·té·gée (prō′tə-zhā′, prō′tə-zhā′) *n.* A woman or girl whose welfare, training, or career is promoted by an influential person. [French, feminine of *protégé,* protégé. See PROTÉGÉ.]

pro·te·i (prō′tē-ī′) *n.* Plural of **proteus.**

pro·te·id (prō′tē-ĭd) *n.* A protein. No longer in scientific use.

pro·tein (prō′tēn′, -tē-ĭn) *n.* Any of a group of complex organic macromolecules that contain carbon, hydrogen, oxygen, nitrogen, and usually sulfur and are composed of one or more chains of amino acids. Proteins are fundamental components of all living cells and include many substances, such as enzymes, hormones, and antibodies, that are necessary for the proper functioning of an organism. They are essential in the diet of animals for the growth and repair of tissue and can be obtained from foods such as meat, fish, eggs, milk, and legumes. *—attributive.* Often used to modify another noun: *protein compounds; protein diets.* [French *protéine,* from Late Greek *prōteios,* of the first quality, from Greek *prōtos,* first. See **per**[1] in Appendix.] **—pro′tein·a′ceous** (prōt′n-ā′shəs, prō′tē-nā′-), **pro′te·in′ic** (prō′tē-ĭn′ĭk) *adj.*

pro·tein·ase (prōt′n-ās′, -āz′, prō′tē-nās′, -nāz′) *n.* A protease that begins the hydrolytic breakdown of proteins usually by splitting them into polypeptide chains.

pro·tein·oid (prōt′n-oid′, prō′tē-noid′) *n.* A proteinlike polypeptide formed abiotically from amino acid mixtures in the presence of heat, thought to resemble early evolutionary forms of protein.

pro·tein·u·ri·a (prōt′n-o͝or′ē-ə, -yo͝or′-, prō′tē-no͝or′-, -nyo͝or′-) *n.* The presence of excessive amounts of protein in the urine.

pro tem (prō tĕm′) *adv.* Pro tempore.

pro tem·po·re (prō tĕm′pə-rē) *adv. Abbr.* **p.t.** For the time being; temporarily. [Latin *prō tempore* : *prō,* for + *tempore,* ablative of *tempus,* time.]

proteo– or **prote–** *pref.* Protein: *proteolysis.* [From PROTEIN.]

pro·te·o·clas·tic (prō′tē-ō-klăs′tĭk) *adj.* Of, relating to, or causing proteolysis; proteolytic. [PROTEO– + Greek *klastos,* broken (from *klan,* to break) + –IC.]

pro·te·ol·y·sis (prō′tē-ŏl′ĭ-sĭs) *n.* The hydrolytic breakdown of proteins into simpler, soluble substances, as occurs in digestion.

pro·te·o·lyt·ic (prō′tē-ə-lĭt′ĭk) *adj.* Relating to, characterized by, or promoting proteolysis. **—pro′te·o·lyt′i·cal·ly** *adv.*

pro·te·ose (prō′tē-ōs′, -ōz′) *n.* Any of various water-soluble compounds that are produced during digestion by the hydrolytic breakdown of proteins.

Prot·er·o·zo·ic (prŏt′ər-ə-zō′ĭk, prō′tər-) *adj.* Of, belonging to, or being the later of two divisions of Precambrian time, during which sponges, sea worms, and other forms of sea life appeared. **—Proterozoic** *n.* The Proterozoic Era. [Greek *proteros,* earlier, former; see **per**[1] in Appendix + –ZOIC.]

pro·test (prə-tĕst′, prō-, prō′tĕst′) *v.* **-test·ed, -test·ing, -tests.** *—tr.* **1.** To object to, especially in a formal statement. See Synonyms at **object. 2.** To promise or affirm with earnest solemnity: *"He continually protested his profound respect"* (Frank Norris). **3.** *Law.* To declare (a bill) dishonored or refused. **4.** *Archaic.* To proclaim or make known: *"unrough youths that even now/Protest their first of manhood"* (Shakespeare). *—intr.* **1.** To express strong objection. **2.** To make an earnest avowal or affirmation. **—protest** (prō′tĕst′) *n.* **1.** A formal declaration of disapproval or objection issued by a concerned person, group, or organization. **2.** An individual or collective gesture or display of disapproval. **3.** *Law.* **a.** A formal statement drawn up by a notary for a creditor declaring that the debtor has refused to accept or honor a bill. **b.** A formal declaration made by a taxpayer stating that the tax demanded is illegal or excessive and reserving the right to contest it. [Middle English *protesten,* from Old French *protester,* from Latin *prōtestārī* : *prō-,* forth; see PRO–[1] + *testārī,* to testify (from *testis,* witness; see **trei-** in Appendix).] **—pro·test′er** *n.* **—pro·test′ing·ly** *adv.*

Prot·es·tant (prŏt′ĭ-stənt) *n. Abbr.* **Prot.** *Theology.* **1.** A member of a Western Christian church whose faith and practice are founded on the principles of the Protestant Reformation, especially in the acceptance of the Bible as the sole source of revelation, in justification by faith alone, and in the universal priesthood of all the believers. **2.** A member of a Western Christian church adhering to the theologies of Luther, Calvin, or Zwingli. **3.** One who supported the protestation presented by the German Lutheran states against the revocation of the decree of the Diet of Speyer (1529). **4. protestant** (*also* prə-tĕs′tənt). One who makes a declaration or an avowal. **—Protestant** *adj. Abbr.* **Prot.** Of or relating to Protestants or Protestantism. [French, from German, from Latin *prōtestāns, prōtestant-,* present participle of *prōtestārī,* to protest. See PROTEST.]

Protestant Episcopal Church *n.* The Episcopal Church.

Prot·es·tant·ism (prŏt′ĭ-stən-tĭz′əm) *n.* **1.** Adherence to the religion and beliefs of a Protestant church. **2.** The religion and religious beliefs fostered by the Protestant movement. **3.** Protestants considered as a group.

prot·es·ta·tion (prŏt′ĭ-stā′shən, prō′tĭ-, -tĕ-) *n.* **1.** An emphatic declaration. **2.** A strong or formal expression of dissent.

pro·te·us (prō′tē-əs) *n., pl.* **-te·i** (-tē-ī′). Any of various gram-negative, rod-shaped bacteria of the genus *Proteus,* certain species of which are associated with human enteritis and urinary tract infections. [New Latin *Prōteus,* genus name, from Latin, Proteus. See PROTEUS.]

Pro·te·us (prō′tē-əs, -tyo͞os′) *n. Greek Mythology.* A sea god who could change his shape at will. [Latin *Prōteus,* from Greek.]

pro·tha·la·mi·on (prō′thə-lā′mē-ən, -ŏn′) *n., pl.* **-mi·a** (-mē-ə). *Music.* A song in celebration of a wedding; an epithalamium. [PRO–[2] + Greek *epithalamion,* epithalamium; see EPITHALAMIUM.]

pro·thal·lus (prō-thăl′əs) or **pro·thal·li·um** (-thăl′ē-əm) *n., pl.* **-thal·li** (-thăl′ī) or **-thal·li·a** (-thăl′ē-ə). A small, flat, delicate structure produced by a germinating spore and bearing sex organs. It is the gametophyte of ferns and some other plants. [New Latin : PRO–[2] + Greek *thallos,* shoot (from *thallein,* to sprout).] **—pro·thal′li·al** (-lē-əl) *adj.*

proth·e·sis (prŏth′ĭ-sĭs) *n., pl.* **-ses** (-sēz′). *Linguistics.* The addition of a phoneme or syllable at the beginning of a word, as in Spanish *espina,* "thorn," from Latin *spina.* [Greek, prefixing, from *protithenai,* to put before : *pro-,* before; see PRO–[2] + *tithenai,* to put; see **dhē-** in Appendix.] **—pro·thet′ic** (prō-thĕt′ĭk) *adj.* **—pro·thet′i·cal·ly** *adv.*

pro·thon·o·tar·y (prō-thŏn′ə-tĕr′ē, prō′thə-nō′tə-rē) also **pro·ton·o·tar·y** (prō-tŏn′ə-tĕr′ē, prō′tə-nō′tə-rē) *n., pl.* **-ies. 1.** The principal clerk in certain courts of law. **2.** *Roman Catholic Church.* One of a college of 12 ecclesiastics charged with the registry of important pontifical proceedings. [Middle English *prothonotarie,* from Medieval Latin *prōthonotārius,* from Late Latin *prōtonotārius* : Greek *prōto-,* proto- + Latin *notārius,* secretary (from *nota,* mark; see **gnō-** in Appendix).] **—pro·thon′o·tar′i·al** (prō-thŏn′ə-târ′ē-əl, prō′thə-nō-târ′-) *adj.*

prothonotary warbler *n.* A small North American bird *(Protonotaria citrea)* having a deep yellow head and breast and inhabiting wooded swamps. [Probably from the bright yellow robes worn by ecclesiastics at important meetings.]

pro·tho·ra·ces (prō-thôr′ə-sēz′, -thōr′-) *n.* A plural of **prothorax.**

prothoracic gland *n.* Either of a pair of endocrine glands located in the prothorax of certain insects and regulating molting.

pro·tho·rax (prō-thôr′ăks′, -thōr′-) *n., pl.* **-tho·rax·es** or **-tho·ra·ces** (-thôr′ə-sēz′, -thōr′-). The anterior division of the thorax of an insect, bearing the first pair of legs. **—pro′tho·rac′ic** (prō′thə-răs′ĭk) *adj.*

pro·throm·bin (prō-thrŏm′bĭn) *n.* A plasma protein that is converted into thrombin during blood clotting.

pro·tist (prō′tĭst) *n.* Any of the eukaryotic, unicellular organisms of the former kingdom Protista, which includes protozoans, slime molds, and certain algae. The protists now belong to the kingdom Protoctista, a new classification in most modern taxonomic systems. [From New Latin *Protista,* former kingdom name, from Greek *prōtista,* neuter pl. of *prōtistos,* the very first, superlative of *prōtos,* first. See **per**[1] in Appendix.] **—pro·tis′tan** (-tĭs′tən) *adj. & n.* **—pro′tis·tol′o·gy** (prō′tĭ-stŏl′ə-jē) *n.*

pro·ti·um (prō′tē-əm, prō′shē-) *n.* The most abundant isotope of hydrogen, H_1, with atomic mass 1.

proto– or **prot–** *pref.* **1.** First in time; earliest: *protolithic.* **2.** First formed; primitive; original: *protohuman.* **3. Proto–.** Being a form of a language that is the ancestor of a language or group of related languages: *Proto-Germanic.* **4.** Having the least amount of a specified element or radical: *protoporphyrin.* [Greek *prōto-,* from *prōtos.* See **per**[1] in Appendix.]

Pro·to-Al·gon·qui·an (prō′tō-ăl-gŏng′kwē-ən, -kē-ən) *n.* The reconstructed protolanguage of the Algonquian family of languages.

pro·to·col (prō′tə-kôl′, -kōl′, -kŏl′) *n.* **1.a.** The forms of ceremony and etiquette observed by diplomats and heads of state. **b.** A code of correct conduct: *a violation of safety protocols; academic protocol.* See Synonyms at **etiquette. 2.** The first copy of a treaty or other such document before its ratification. **3.** A preliminary draft or record of a transaction. **4.** The plan for a course of medical treatment or for a scientific experiment. **5.** *Computer Science.* A standard procedure for regulating data transmission between computers. **—protocol** *intr.v.* **-coled, -col·ing, -cols** or **-colled, -col·ling, -cols.** To form or issue protocols. [French *protocole,* from Old French *prothocolle,* draft of a document, from Medieval Latin *prōtocollum,* from Late Greek *prōtokollon,* table of contents, first sheet : Greek *prōto-,* proto- + Greek *kollēma,* sheets of a papyrus glued together (from *kollan,* to glue together, from *kolla,* glue).] **—pro′to·col′ar** (-kŏl′ər), **pro′to·col′a·ry** (-kŏl′ə-rē) *adj.*

pro·to·con·ti·nent (prō′tō-kŏn′tə-nənt) *n.* **1.** A landmass, actual or hypothetical, that could develop into a major continent. **2.** See **supercontinent.**

pro·toc·tist (prə-tŏk′tĭst) *n.* Any of the unicellular protists and their descendant multicellular organisms, considered as a separate taxonomic kingdom in most modern classification systems. [From New Latin *Prōtoctista,* kingdom name : Greek *prōto-,* proto- + Greek *ktistos,* produced, created (from *ktizein,* to create, establish).]

pro·to·derm (prō′tə-dûrm′) *n. Botany.* See **dermatogen. —pro′to·derm′al** *adj.*

Pro·to-Ger·man·ic (prō′tō-jûr-măn′ĭk) *n.* The reconstructed prehistoric ancestor of the Germanic languages.

pro·to·gy·nous (prō′tə-jī′nəs, -gī′-) *adj.* Of or relating to a flower in which the stigma is receptive before the pollen is shed from the anthers of the same flower. **—pro·tog′y·ny** (prō-tŏj′ə-nē) *n.*

pro·to·his·to·ry (prō′tō-hĭs′tə-rē, -hĭs′trē) *n.* The study of a culture just before the time of its earliest recorded history. **—pro′to·his·tor′i·an** (-hĭ-stôr′ē-ən, -stŏr′-) *n.* **—pro′to·his·tor′ic** (-hĭ-stôr′ĭk, -stŏr′-) *adj.*

pro·to·hu·man (prō′tō-hyo͞o′mən) *adj.* Of or relating to various extinct hominids or other primates that resemble modern human beings. **—protohuman** *n.* A protohuman primate.

Pro·to-In·do-Eur·o·pe·an (prō′tō-ĭn′dō-yo͝or′ə-pē′ən) *n.* The reconstructed language that was the ancestor of the Indo-European languages. **—Proto-Indo-European** *adj.* Of, relating to, or being Proto-Indo-European or one of its reconstructed linguistic features.

pro·to·lan·guage (prō′tō-lăng′gwĭj) *n.* A language that is the recorded or hypothetical ancestor of another language or group of languages. Also called *Ursprache.*

pro·to·lith·ic (prō′tə-lĭth′ĭk) *adj.* Of, relating to, or characteristic of the very beginning of the Stone Age; Eolithic.

pro·to·mar·tyr (prō′tō-mär′tər) *n.* The first martyr in a cause. Used especially of the first Christian martyr, Saint Stephen.

pro·to·mor·phic (prō′tə-môr′fĭk) *adj.* Primitive in structure or form. **—pro′to·morph′** *n.*

pro·ton (prō′tŏn′) *n. Abbr.* **p** *Physics.* A stable, positively charged subatomic particle in the baryon family having a mass 1,836 times that of the electron. See table at **subatomic particle.** [From Greek *prōton,* neuter of *prōtos,* first. See **per**[1] in Appendix.] **—pro·ton′ic** *adj.*

pro·to·ne·ma (prō′tə-nē′mə) *n., pl.* **-ne·ma·ta** (-nē′mə-tə, -nĕm′ə-). The green, filamentous growth that arises from spore germination in liverworts and mosses and eventually gives rise to a mature gametophyte. [PROTO– + Greek *nēma,* thread; see **(s)nē-** in Appendix.] **—pro′to·ne′mal** (-nē′məl), **pro′to·ne′ma·tal** (-nē′mə-təl, -nĕm′ə-) *adj.*

pro·ton·o·tar·y (prō-tŏn′ə-tĕr′ē, prō′tə-nō′tə-rē) *n.* Variant of **prothonotary.**

proton synchrotron *n. Physics.* A ring-shaped synchrotron that accelerates protons to energies of several billion electron volts.

pro·to-on·co·gene (prō′tō-ŏn′kə-jēn′, -ŏng′kə-) *n.* A normal gene that has the potential to become an oncogene.

pro·to·path·ic (prō′tə-păth′ĭk) *adj.* Sensing pain, pressure, heat, or cold in a nonspecific manner, usually without localizing the stimulus. Used especially of certain sensory nerves. [From Medieval Greek *prōtopathēs,* affected first, from Greek *prōtopathein,* to feel first : *prōto-,* proto- + *paskhein,* to feel.] **—pro·top′a·thy** (-tŏp′ə-thē) *n.*

pro·to·plasm (prō′tə-plăz′əm) *n.* The complex, semifluid, translucent substance that constitutes the living matter of plant and animal cells and manifests the essential life functions of a cell. Composed of proteins, fats, and other molecules suspended in water, it includes the nucleus and cytoplasm. **—pro′to·plas′mic** (-plăz′mĭk), **pro′to·plas′mal** (-plăz′məl), **pro′to·plas·mat′ic** (-plăz-măt′ĭk) *adj.*

pro·to·plast (prō′tə-plăst′) *n.* **1.** *Biology.* The living material of a plant or bacterial cell, including the protoplasm and plasma membrane after the cell wall has been removed. **2.** One that is the first made or formed; a prototype. [French *protoplaste,* from Old French, the first man, from Late Latin *prōtoplastus,* from Greek *prōtoplastos* : *prōto-,* proto- + *plastos,* formed, molded; see –PLAST.] **—pro′to·plas′tic** *adj.*

pro·to·por·phy·rin (prō′tō-pôr′fə-rĭn) *n.* A metal-free porphyrin, $C_{32}H_{32}N_4(COOH)_2$, that combines with iron to form the heme of hemoglobin, myoglobin, cytochrome, and other iron-containing proteins.

pro·to·stele (prō′tə-stēl′, prō′tə-stē′lē) *n. Botany.* A stele that has a solid core of vascular tissue. **—pro′to·ste′lic** (-stē′lĭk) *adj.*

pro·to·tro·phic (prō′tə-trō′fĭk, -trŏf′ĭk) *adj. Microbiology.* Having the same metabolic capabilities and nutritional requirements as the wild type parent strain: *prototrophic bacteria.* **—pro′to·troph′, pro′to·troph′y** *n.*

pro·to·type (prō′tə-tīp′) *n.* **1.** An original type, form, or instance that serves as a model on which later stages are based or judged. **2.** An early, typical example. **3.** *Biology.* A primitive or ancestral form or species. [French, from Greek *prōtotupon,* from neuter of *prōtotupos,* original : *prōto-,* proto- + *tupos,* model.] **—pro′to·typ′al** (-tī′pəl), **pro′to·typ′ic** (-tĭp′ĭk), **pro′to·typ′i·cal** (-ĭ-kəl) *adj.*

pro·to·xy·lem (prō′tə-zī′ləm) *n. Botany.* The first formed xylem that differentiates from the procambium.

pro·to·zo·an (prō′tə-zō′ən) also **pro·to·zo·on** (-ŏn′) *n., pl.* **-zo·ans** or **-zo·a** (-zō′ə) also **-zo·ons.** Any of a large group of single-celled, usually microscopic, eukaryotic organisms, such as amoebas, ciliates, flagellates, and sporozoans. [From New Latin *Protozoa,* former subkingdom name : PROTO– + New Latin *-zoa,* pl. of *-zoon,* -zoon.] **—pro′to·zo′an, pro′to·zo′al, pro′to·zo′ic** *adj.*

pro·to·zo·ol·o·gy (prō′tə-zō-ŏl′ə-jē) *n.* The biological study of protozoans. **—pro′to·zo′o·log′i·cal** (-zō′ə-lŏj′ĭ-kəl) *adj.* **—pro′to·zo·ol′o·gist** *n.*

pro·to·zo·on (prō′tə-zō′ŏn′) *n.* Variant of **protozoan.**

pro·tract (prō-trăkt′, prə-) *tr.v.* **-tract·ed, -tract·ing, -tracts. 1.** To draw out or lengthen in time; prolong: *disputants who needlessly protracted the negotiations.* **2.** *Mathematics.* To draw to scale by means of a scale and protractor; plot. **3.** *Anatomy.* To extend or protrude (a body part). [Latin *prōtrahere, prōtrāct-* : *prō-,* forth; see PRO–[1] + *trahere,* to drag.] **—pro·tract′ed·ly** (-trăk′tĭd-lē) *adv.* **—pro·tract′ed·ness** *n.* **—pro·trac′tive** *adj.*

pro·trac·tile (prō-trăk′təl, -tīl′, prə-) also **pro·tract·i·ble** (-tə-bəl) *adj.* That can be protracted; extensible: *protractile limbs and claws.* **—pro′trac·til′i·ty** (prō′trăk-tĭl′ĭ-tē) *n.*

pro·trac·tion (prō-trăk′shən, prə-) *n.* **1.a.** The act of protracting. **b.** The state of being protracted. **2.** *Linguistics.* The irregular lengthening of a normally short syllable.

pro·trac·tor (prō-trăk′tər, prə-) *n.* **1.** *Mathematics.* A semicircular instrument for measuring and constructing angles. **2.** An adjustable pattern used by tailors. **3.** *Anatomy.* A muscle that extends a limb or other part.

pro·trude (prō-tro͞od′) *v.* **-trud·ed, -trud·ing, -trudes.** —*tr.* To push or thrust outward. —*intr.* To jut out; project. See Synonyms at **bulge.** [Latin *prōtrūdere* : *prō-,* forward; see PRO–[1] + *trūdere,* to thrust; see **treud-** in Appendix.] **—pro·trud′ent** (-tro͞od′nt) *adj.*

pro·tru·sile (prō-tro͞o′səl, -sīl′) also **pro·tru·si·ble** (-sə-bəl) *adj.* Capable of being thrust outward, as the proboscis of many insects. [Latin *prōtrūsus,* past participle of *prōtrūdere,* to protrude; see PROTRUDE + –ILE[1].] **—pro′tru·sil′i·ty** (prō′tro͞o-sĭl′ĭ-tē) *n.*

pro·tru·sion (prō-tro͞o′zhən) *n.* **1.a.** The act of protruding. **b.** The state of being protruded. **2.** Something that protrudes. [Latin *prōtrūsus,* past participle of *prōtrūdere,* to protrude; see PROTRUDE + –ION.]

pro·tru·sive (prō-tro͞o′sĭv, prə-) *adj.* **1.** Tending to protrude;

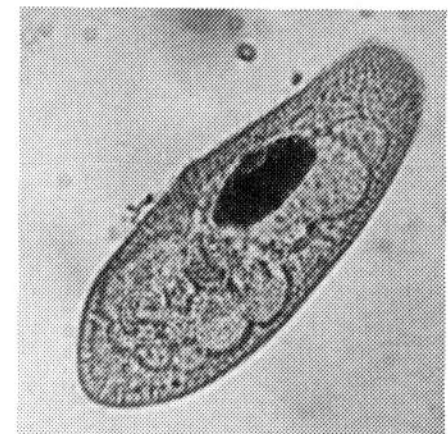

protozoan
Paramecium

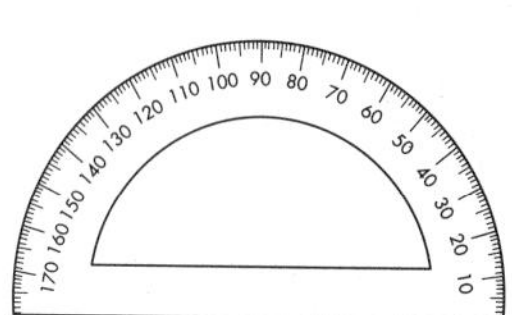

protractor
Mathematical instrument

ă pat	oi boy
ā pay	ou out
âr care	o͝o took
ä father	o͞o boot
ĕ pet	ŭ cut
ē be	ûr urge
ĭ pit	th thin
ī pie	*th* this
îr pier	hw which
ŏ pot	zh vision
ō toe	ə about, item
ô paw	♦ regionalism

Stress marks: ′ (primary); ′ (secondary), as in **dictionary** (dĭk′shə-nĕr′ē)

protruding. **2.** Unduly or disagreeably conspicuous; obtrusive. **—pro·tru′sive·ly** *adv.* **—pro·tru′sive·ness** *n.*

pro·tu·ber·ance (prō-to͞o′bər-əns, -tyo͞o′-, prə-) *n.* **1.** Something, such as a bulge, knob, or swelling, that protrudes. **2.** The condition of being protuberant.

pro·tu·ber·an·cy (prō-to͞o′bər-ən-sē, -tyo͞o′-, prə-) *n., pl.* **-cies. 1.** Protuberance. **2.** Something that is protuberant.

pro·tu·ber·ant (prō-to͞o′bər-ənt, -tyo͞o′-, prə-) *adj.* Swelling outward; bulging. [Late Latin *prōtūberāns, prōtūberant-,* present participle of *prōtūberāre,* to bulge out. See PROTUBERATE.] **—pro·tu′ber·ant·ly** *adv.*

pro·tu·ber·ate (prō-to͞o′bə-rāt′, -tyo͞o′-, prə-) *intr.v.* **-at·ed, -at·ing, -ates.** To swell or bulge. [Late Latin *prōtūberāre, prōtūberāt-* : Latin *prō-,* forth; see PRO–[1] + Latin *tūber,* a swelling; see **teue-** in Appendix.] **—pro·tu′ber·a′tion** *n.*

proud (proud) *adj.* **proud·er, proud·est. 1.** Feeling pleasurable satisfaction over an act, a possession, a quality, or a relationship by which one measures one's stature or self-worth: *proud of one's child; proud to serve one's country.* **2.** Occasioning or being a reason for pride: *"On January 1, 1900, Americans and Europeans greeted the twentieth century in the proud and certain belief that the next hundred years would make all things possible"* (W. Bruce Lincoln). **3.** Feeling or showing justifiable self-respect. **4.** Filled with or showing excessive self-esteem. **5.** Of great dignity; honored: *a proud name.* **6.** Majestic; magnificent: *proud alpine peaks.* **7.** Spirited. Used of an animal: *proud steeds.* [Middle English, from Old English *prūd,* from Old French *prou, prud,* brave, virtuous, oblique case of *prouz,* from Vulgar Latin ***prōdis,* from Late Latin *prōde,* advantageous, from Latin *prōdesse,* to be good : *prōd-,* for (variant of *prō-;* see PRO–[1]) + *esse,* to be; see **es-** in Appendix.] **—proud′ly** *adv.* **—proud′ness** *n.*

SYNONYMS: *proud, arrogant, haughty, disdainful, supercilious.* These adjectives mean filled with or marked by a high opinion of oneself and disdain for what one views as being unworthy. *Proud* can suggest dignity or justifiable self-respect or self-satisfaction, but it often implies conceit or vanity: *"There is such a thing as a man being too proud to fight"* (Woodrow Wilson). *"I pray God to keep me from being proud"* (Samuel Pepys). One who is *arrogant* is overbearingly proud and demands more power or consideration than is warranted: *"All sensibly gave him wide berth, for he was a dangerous-looking man, chewing a toothpick with the arrogant sullenness of one who is willing to commit violence"* (Stephen Hunter). *Haughty* suggests lofty, condescending pride, as by reason of high birth or station: *"We hardly know an instance of the strength and weakness of human nature so striking and so grotesque as the character of this haughty, vigilant, resolute, sagacious blue-stocking* [Frederick the Great]*"* (Macaulay). *Disdainful* emphasizes scorn or contempt: *"Nor* [let] *grandeur hear with a disdainful smile,/The short and simple annals of the poor"* (Thomas Gray). *Supercilious* implies haughty disdain: *"His mother eyed me in silence with a supercilious air"* (Tobias Smollett).

proud flesh *n. Pathology.* The swollen flesh that surrounds a healing wound, caused by excessive granulation. [From its swelling up.]

Prou·dhon (pro͞o-dôN′), **Pierre Joseph.** 1809–1865. French anarchist who believed that human moral development would ultimately eliminate the need for laws and government.

Proust (pro͞ost), **Marcel.** 1871–1922. French writer whose seven-part novel *Remembrance of Things Past* (1913–1927) is among the great works of modern literature. **—Proust′i·an** *adj.*

prov. *abbr.* **1.** Province; provincial. **2.** Provisional. **3.** Provost.

Prov. *abbr.* **1.** Provençal. **2.** *Bible.* Proverbs.

prove (pro͞ov) *v.* **proved** or **prov·en** (pro͞o′vən), **prov·ing, proves.** *—tr.* **1.** To establish the truth or validity of by presentation of argument or evidence. **2.** *Law.* To establish the authenticity of (a will). **3.** To determine the quality of by testing; try out. **4.** *Mathematics.* **a.** To demonstrate the validity of (a hypothesis or proposition). **b.** To verify (the result of a calculation). **5.** *Printing.* To make a sample impression of (type). **6.** *Archaic.* To find out or learn (something) through experience. *—intr.* To be shown to be such; turn out: *a theory that proved impractical in practice.* ***—phrasal verb.*** **prove out.** To turn out well; succeed. [Middle English *proven,* from Old French *prover,* from Latin *probāre,* to test, from *probus,* good. See **per**[1] in Appendix.] **—prov′a·bil′i·ty, prov′a·ble·ness** *n.* **—prov′a·ble** *adj.* **—prov′a·bly** *adv.* **—prov′er** *n.*

USAGE NOTE: *Proved* is actually the older form of the past participle; *proven* is a Scottish variant that was first introduced into wider usage in legal contexts: *The jury ruled that the charges were not proven.* Both forms are now well established in written English as participles: *He has proved* (or *proven*) *his point. The claims have not been proved* (or *proven*). However, *proven* is more common when the word is used as an adjective before a noun: *a proven talent.*

prov·en (pro͞o′vən) *v.* A past tense and a past participle of **prove.** **—proven** *adj.* Having been demonstrated or verified without doubt: *"a Soviet leader of proven shrewdness and prescience"* (Joyce Carol Oates). See Usage Note at **prove.** **—prov′en·ly** *adv.*

prov·e·nance (prŏv′ə-nəns, -näns′) *n.* **1.** Place of origin; derivation. **2.** Proof of authenticity or of past ownership. Used of art works and antiques. [French, from *provenant,* present participle of *provenir,* to originate, from Old French, from Latin *prōvenīre* : *prō-,* forth; see PRO–[1] + *venīre,* to come; see **gʷā-** in Appendix.]

Pro·ven·çal (prō′vən-säl′, -vän-, prŏv′ən-) *adj.* Of or relating to Provence or its people, language, or culture. **—Provençal** *n. Abbr.* **Prov. 1.** The Romance language of Provence. **2.** *pl.* **-çals** or **-çaux** (-sō′). A native or inhabitant of Provence. [French, from Latin *prōvinciālis,* from *prōvincia,* province.]

Pro·vence (prə-väns′, prô-vänsʹ). A historical region and former province of southeast France bordering on the Mediterranean Sea. It was settled c. 600 B.C. by Greeks and later by Phoenician merchants and was colonized by Rome in the second century B.C. Provence became part of the kingdom of Arles in 933 A.D. and later passed to the Angevin dynasty (1246) and to France (1486).

prov·en·der (prŏv′ən-dər) *n.* **1.** Dry food, such as hay, used as feed for livestock. **2.** Food or provisions. [Middle English *provendre,* from Old French, alteration of *provende,* from Vulgar Latin **prōvenda,* alteration (influenced by Latin *prōvidēre,* to provide) of Late Latin *praebenda.* See PREBEND.]

pro·ve·nience (prə-vēn′yəns, -vē′nē-əns) *n.* A source or an origin. [Alteration of PROVENANCE.]

pro·ven·tric·u·lus (prō′vĕn-trĭk′yə-ləs) *n., pl.* **-li** (-lī′). **1.** The division of the stomach in birds that secretes digestive enzymes and passes food from the crop to the gizzard. **2.** A similar digestive chamber in certain insects and worms. [PRO–[2] + Latin *ventriculus,* stomach, diminutive of *venter,* belly.] **—pro′ven·tric′u·lar** (-lər) *adj.*

prov·erb (prŏv′ûrb′) *n.* **1.** A short, pithy saying in frequent and widespread use that expresses a basic truth or practical precept. See Synonyms at **saying.** **2. Proverbs** *(used with a sing. verb). Abbr.* **Prov., Pr** *Bible.* See table at **Bible.** [Middle English *proverbe,* from Old French, from Latin *prōverbium* : *prō-,* forth; see PRO–[1] + *verbum,* word; see **wer-**[5] in Appendix.]

pro·ver·bi·al (prə-vûr′bē-əl) *adj.* **1.** Of the nature of a proverb. **2.** Expressed in a proverb. **3.** Widely referred to, as if the subject of a proverb; famous. **—pro·ver′bi·al·ly** *adv.*

pro·vide (prə-vīd′) *v.* **-vid·ed, -vid·ing, -vides.** *—tr.* **1.** To furnish; supply: *provide food and shelter for a family.* **2.** To make available; afford: *a room that provides ample sunlight through French windows.* **3.** To set down as a stipulation: *an agreement that provides deadlines for completion of the work.* **4.** *Archaic.* To make ready ahead of time; prepare. *—intr.* **1.** To take measures in preparation: *provided for the common defense of the states in time of war.* **2.** To supply means of subsistence: *She provides for her family by working in a hospital.* **3.** To make a stipulation or condition: *The Constitution provides for a bicameral legislature.* [Middle English *providen,* from Latin *prōvidēre,* to provide for : *prō-,* forward; see PRO–[1] + *vidēre,* to see; see **weid-** in Appendix.]

pro·vid·ed (prə-vī′dĭd) *conj.* On the condition; if: *will pay the bonus provided the job is completed on time.* See Usage Note at **providing.**

prov·i·dence (prŏv′ĭ-dəns, -dĕns′) *n.* **1.** Care or preparation in advance; foresight. **2.** Prudent management; economy. **3.** The care, guardianship, and control exercised by a deity; divine direction: *"Some sought the key to history in the working of divine providence"* (William Ebenstein). **4. Providence.** God.

Providence. The capital and largest city of Rhode Island, in the northeast part of the state on Narragansett Bay. It was founded by Roger Williams in 1636 as a haven for religious dissenters and became prosperous as a port in the 18th century. Providence was joint capital with Newport until 1900. Population, 156,804.

prov·i·dent (prŏv′ĭ-dənt, -dĕnt′) *adj.* **1.** Providing for future needs or events. **2.** Frugal; economical. [Middle English, from Latin *prōvidēns, prōvident-,* present participle of *prōvidēre,* to provide for. See PROVIDE.] **—prov′i·dent·ly** *adv.*

prov·i·den·tial (prŏv′ĭ-dĕn′shəl) *adj.* **1.** Of or resulting from divine providence. **2.** Happening as if through divine intervention; opportune. See Synonyms at **happy.** **—prov′i·den′tial·ly** *adv.*

pro·vid·er (prə-vī′dər) *n.* **1.** One who supplies a means of subsistence: *parents who were good providers.* **2.** One that makes something, such as a service, available: *health care providers.*

pro·vid·ing (prə-vī′dĭng) *conj.* On the condition; provided.

USAGE NOTE: In the past some critics have maintained that *provided* is preferable to *providing* as a conjunction meaning "on condition that." The use of *providing* has ample precedent, however, and cannot be considered incorrect.

prov·ince (prŏv′ĭns) *n. Abbr.* **prov. 1.** A territory governed as an administrative or political unit of a country or an empire. **2.** *Ecclesiastical.* A division of territory under the jurisdiction of an archbishop. **3. provinces.** Areas of a country situated away from the capital or population center. **4.** A comprehensive area of knowledge, activity, or interest: *a topic falling within the province of ancient history.* See Synonyms at **field.** **5.** The range of one's proper duties and functions; scope or jurisdiction. **6.** *Ecology.* An area of land, less extensive than a region, having a characteristic plant and animal population. **7.** Any of various lands outside Italy conquered by the Romans and administered by them as self-contained units. [Middle English, from Old French, from Latin *prōvincia.*]

Prov·ince·town (prŏv′ĭns-toun′). A town of southeast Massachusetts on the tip of Cape Cod. Pilgrims first landed on the site in 1620 before sailing on to Plymouth. Population, 3,536.

pro·vin·cial (prə-vĭn′shəl) *adj. Abbr.* **prov. 1.** Of or relating to a province. **2.** Of or characteristic of people from the provinces; not fashionable or sophisticated: *"Well-educated professional women . . made me feel uncomfortably provincial"* (J.R. Salamanca). **3.** Limited in perspective; narrow and self-centered. **—provincial** *n. Abbr.* **prov. 1.** A native or inhabitant of the provinces. **2.** A person who has provincial ideas or habits. **—pro·vin′cial·ism, pro·vin′ci·al′i·ty** (-shē-ăl′ĭ-tē) *n.* **—pro·vin′cial·ly** *adv.*

pro·vin·cial·ize (prə-vĭn′shə-līz′) *tr.v.* **-ized, -iz·ing, -iz·es.** To make provincial. **—pro·vin′cial·i·za′tion** (-shə-lĭ-zā′shən) *n.*

prov·ing ground (pro͞o′vĭng) *n.* A place for testing new devices, weapons, or theories.

pro·vi·rus (prō′vī′rəs, prō-vī′-) *n., pl.* **-rus·es.** The precursor or latent form of a virus that is capable of being integrated into the genetic material of a host cell and being replicated with it. **—pro′vi′ral** (-rəl) *adj.*

pro·vi·sion (prə-vĭzh′ən) *n.* **1.** The act of supplying or fitting out. **2.** Something provided. **3.** A preparatory action or measure. **4. provisions.** A stock of necessary supplies, especially food. **5.** A stipulation or qualification, especially a clause in a document or an agreement. **—provision** *tr.v.* **-sioned, -sion·ing, -sions.** To supply with provisions. [Middle English, from Old French, forethought, from Latin *prōvīsiō, prōvīsiōn-,* from *prōvīsus,* past participle of *prōvidēre,* to foresee, provide for. See PROVIDE.] **—pro·vi′sion·er** *n.*

pro·vi·sion·al (prə-vĭzh′ə-nəl) *adj. Abbr.* **prov.** Provided or serving only for the time being; temporary. See Synonyms at **temporary. —provisional** *n.* **1.** A person hired temporarily for a job, typically before having taken an examination qualifying the person for permanent employment: *police and fire department provisionals.* **2. Provisional.** A member of the extremist faction of the Irish Republican Army established in 1970. **—pro·vi′sion·al·ly** *adv.*

pro·vi·so (prə-vī′zō) *n., pl.* **-sos** or **-soes.** A clause in a document making a qualification, condition, or restriction. [Middle English, from Medieval Latin *prōvīsō (quod),* provided (that), from Latin *prōvīsō,* ablative of *prōvīsus,* past participle of *prōvidēre,* to provide. See PROVIDE.]

pro·vi·so·ry (prə-vī′zə-rē) *adj.* Depending on a proviso; conditional. [French *provisoire,* from Old French, from Medieval Latin *prōvīsōrius,* from Latin *prōvīsus,* past participle of *prōvidēre,* to provide for. See PROVIDE.] **—pro·vi′so·ri·ly** *adv.*

pro·vi·ta·min (prō-vī′tə-mĭn) *n.* A vitamin precursor that the body converts to its active form through normal metabolic processes. Carotene, for example, is a provitamin of vitamin A.

Pro·vo[1] (prō′vō). A city of north-central Utah south-southeast of Salt Lake City. It was settled by Mormons in 1849 and is the seat of Brigham Young University (established 1875). Population, 73,907.

Pro·vo[2] (prō′vō) *n., pl.* **-vos.** One of the members of the extremist faction of the Irish Republican Army. [Shortening and alteration of *Provisional (Wing),* name of the faction.]

pro·vo·ca·teur (prō-vŏk′ə-tûr′) *n.* An agent provocateur.

prov·o·ca·tion (prŏv′ə-kā′shən) *n.* **1.** The act of provoking or inciting. **2.** Something that provokes. [Middle English *provocacioun,* from Old French *provocation,* from Latin *prōvocātiō, prōvocātiōn-,* a challenging, from *prōvocātus,* past participle of *prōvocāre,* to challenge. See PROVOKE.]

pro·voc·a·tive (prə-vŏk′ə-tĭv) *adj.* Tending to provoke. **—pro·voc′a·tive** *n.* **—pro·voc′a·tive·ly** *adv.* **—pro·voc′a·tive·ness** *n.*

pro·voke (prə-vōk′) *tr.v.* **-voked, -vok·ing, -vokes. 1.** To incite to anger or resentment. **2.** To stir to action or feeling. **3.** To give rise to; evoke: *provoke laughter.* **4.** To bring about deliberately; induce: *provoke a fight.* [Middle English *provoken,* from Old French *provoquer,* from Latin *prōvocāre,* to challenge : *prō-,* forth; see PRO–[1] + *vocāre,* to call; see **wek**ʷ**-** in Appendix.] **—pro·vok′ing·ly** *adv.*

SYNONYMS: *provoke, incite, excite, stimulate, arouse, rouse, stir.* These verbs are compared in the sense of moving a person to action or feeling or summoning something into being by moving a person in this way. *Provoke,* the least explicit with respect to means, frequently does little more than state the consequences produced: *"Let my presumption not provoke thy wrath"* (Shakespeare). *"A situation which in the country would have provoked meetings"* (John Galsworthy). To *incite* is to provoke and urge on: *The insurrection was incited by members of the outlawed opposition. Excite* especially implies the provoking of a strong reaction or powerful emotion: *The play is bound to fail; the plot excites little interest or curiosity.* To *stimulate* is to excite to activity or to renewed vigor of action as if by spurring or goading: *"Our vigilance was stimulated by our finding traces of a large . . . encampment"* (Francis Parkman). *Arouse* and *rouse* suggest awakening, as from inactivity or apathy; *rouse,* the stronger term, often implies incitement to vigorous or animated activity or excitement of strong emotion: *"In a democratic society like ours, relief must come through an aroused popular conscience that sears the conscience of the people's representatives"* (Felix Frankfurter). *"His mother . . . endeavored to rouse him from this passive state"* (Washington Irving). *"The oceangoing steamers . . . roused in him wild and painful longings"* (Arnold Bennett). To *stir* is to prompt to activity, to arouse strong but usually agreeable feelings, or to provoke trouble or commotion: *"It was him as stirred up th' young woman to preach last night"* (George Eliot). *"I have seldom been so . . . stirred by any piece of writing"* (Mark Twain). *"Men blame you that you have stirred a quarrel up"* (William Butler Yeats). See also Synonyms at **annoy.**

pro·vok·ing (prə-vō′kĭng) *adj.* Troubling the nerves or peace of mind, as by repeated vexations: *a provoking delay at the airport.* **—pro·vok′ing·ly** *adv.*

pro·vo·lo·ne (prō′və-lō′nē) *n.* A hard, usually smoked Italian cheese. [Italian, augmentative of *provola,* a kind of cheese.]

pro·vost (prō′vōst′, -vəst, prŏv′əst) *n. Abbr.* **prov. 1.** A university administrator of high rank. **2.** The highest official in certain cathedrals or collegiate churches. **3.** The keeper of a prison. **4.** The chief magistrate of certain Scottish cities. [Middle English, from Old English *profost* and Old French *provost,* both from Medieval Latin *prōpositus,* alteration of Latin *praepositus,* person placed over others, superintendent, from past participle of *praepōnere,* to place over : *prae-,* pre- + *pōnere,* to put; see **apo-** in Appendix.]

pro·vost marshal (prō′vō) *n. Abbr.* **PM, P.M.** The head of a unit of military police.

prow (prou) *n.* **1.** *Nautical.* The forward part of a ship's hull; the bow. **2.** A projecting forward part, such as the front end of a ski. [French *proue,* from Old French, from Italian dialectal *prua,* from Vulgar Latin **prōda,* alteration of Latin *prōra,* from Greek *prōira.* See **per**[1] in Appendix.]

prow
Of the *Queen Elizabeth 2*

prow·ess (prou′ĭs) *n.* **1.** Superior skill or ability. **2.** Superior strength, courage, or daring, especially in battle. [Middle English *prowesse,* from Old French *proesse,* from *prud, prou,* brave. See PROUD.]

prowl (proul) *v.* **prowled, prowl·ing, prowls.** *—tr.* To roam through stealthily, as in search of prey or plunder: *prowled the alleys of the city after dark.* *—intr.* To rove furtively or with predatory intent: *cats prowling through the neighborhood.* **—prowl** *n.* The act or an instance of prowling. **—*idiom.* on the prowl.** Actively looking for something: *salespeople on the prowl for better jobs.* [Middle English *prollen,* to move about.] **—prowl′er** *n.*

prowl car *n.* See **squad car.**

prox. *abbr.* Proximo.

prox·e·mics (prŏk-sē′mĭks) *n.* *(used with a sing. verb).* The study of the cultural, behavioral, and sociological aspects of spatial distances between individuals. [PROX(IMITY) + *-emics* (as in PHONEMICS).] **—prox·e′mic** *adj.*

prox·i·mal (prŏk′sə-məl) *adj.* **1.** Nearest; proximate. **2.** *Anatomy.* Nearer to a point of reference such as an origin, a point of attachment, or the midline of the body: *the proximal end of a bone.* [From Latin *proximus,* nearest. See PROXIMATE.] **—prox′i·mal·ly** *adv.*

prox·i·mate (prŏk′sə-mĭt) *adj.* **1.** Closely related in space, time, or order; very near. See Synonyms at **close. 2.** Approximate. [Latin *proximātus,* past participle of *proximāre,* to come near, from *proximus,* nearest. See **per**[1] in Appendix.] **—prox′i·mate·ly** *adv.* **—prox′i·mate·ness** *n.*

prox·im·i·ty (prŏk-sĭm′ĭ-tē) *n.* The state, quality, sense, or fact of being near or next; closeness: *"Swift's major writings have a proximity and a relevance that is splendidly invigorating"* (M.D. Aeschliman). See Usage Notes at **close, redundancy.** [Middle English, from Old French *proximite,* from Latin *proximitās,* from *proximus,* nearest. See PROXIMATE.]

proximity fuze *n.* An electronic device for detonating a warhead as it approaches a target, used in antiaircraft shells. Also called *VT fuze.*

prox·i·mo (prŏk′sə-mō′) *adv. Abbr.* **prox.** *Archaic.* Of or in the following month. [Latin *proximō (mēnse),* in the next (month), from *proximō,* ablative of *proximus,* nearest, next. See PROXIMATE.]

prox·y (prŏk′sē) *n., pl.* **-ies. 1.** A person authorized to act for another; an agent or a substitute. **2.** The authority to act for another. **3.** The written authorization to act in place of another. *—attributive.* Often used to modify another noun: *a proxy vote; proxy troops for a world power.* [Middle English *proccy,* contraction of earlier *procracie,* annual payment to a prelate, from Anglo-Norman *procuracie,* from Medieval Latin *prōcūrātia,* alteration of Latin *prōcūrātiō,* from *prōcūrātus,* past participle of *prōcūrāre,* to take care of. See PROCURE.]

prude (pro͞od) *n.* One who is excessively concerned with being or appearing to be proper, modest, or righteous. [French, short for *prude femme,* virtuous woman : Old French *prude,* feminine of *prud,* virtuous; see PROUD + French *femme,* woman (from Latin *fēmina;* see FEMININE).]

WORD HISTORY: Being a prude has never been widely considered a good thing, but if we dig further into the history of the word *prude,* we will find that it had a noble past. The change for the worse took place in French. French *prude* first had a good sense, "wise woman," but apparently a woman could be too wise

ă pat	oi boy
ā pay	ou out
âr care	o͝o took
ä father	o͞o boot
ĕ pet	ŭ cut
ē be	ûr urge
ĭ pit	th thin
ī pie	*th* this
îr pier	hw which
ŏ pot	zh vision
ō toe	ə about, item
ô paw	♦ regionalism

Stress marks: **′** (primary); ′ (secondary), as in **dictionary** (dĭk′shə-nĕr′ē)

or, in the eyes of some, too observant of decorum and propriety, and so *prude* took on the sense in French that was brought into English along with the word, first recorded in 1704. The French word first meant "wise woman" because *prude* was a shortened form of *prude femme* (earlier in Old French *prode femme*), a word that was modeled on earlier *preudomme,* "a man of experience and integrity." The second part of this word is, of course, *homme,* "man." Old French *prod,* meaning "wise, prudent," is from Vulgar Latin *prōdis* with the same sense. *Prōdis* in turn comes from Late Latin *prōde,* "advantageous," derived from the verb *prodesse,* "to be good." We can see that the history of *prude* is filled with usefulness, profit, wisdom, and integrity, but in spite of all this, things did not turn out that well.

pru·dence (pro͞od′ns) *n.* **1.** The state, quality, or fact of being prudent. **2.** Careful management; economy.

SYNONYMS: *prudence, discretion, foresight, forethought, circumspection.* These nouns are compared as they refer to the exercise of good judgment and common sense, especially in the conduct of practical matters. *Prudence,* the most comprehensive, implies not only caution but also the capacity for judging in advance the probable results of one's actions: *"She had been forced into prudence in her youth, she learned romance as she grew older"* (Jane Austen). *Discretion* suggests prudence coupled with wise self-restraint, as in resisting the impulse to take rash action: *"The better part of valor is discretion"* (Shakespeare). *Foresight* implies the ability to foresee and make provision for what may happen: *She had the foresight to realize that once the ugly rumor had begun to circulate, only the truth could put it to rest. Forethought* suggests advance consideration of future eventualities: *An empty refrigerator illustrates a lack of forethought. Circumspection* implies discretion together with prudent heed for possible consequences, as out of concern for moral or social repercussions: *"The necessity of the times, more than ever, calls for our utmost circumspection, deliberation, fortitude and perseverance"* (Samuel Adams).

pru·dent (pro͞od′nt) *adj.* **1.** Wise in handling practical matters; exercising good judgment or common sense. **2.** Careful in regard to one's own interests; provident. **3.** Careful about one's conduct; circumspect. [Middle English, from Old French, from Latin *prūdēns, prūdent-,* contraction of *prōvidēns,* present participle of *prōvidēre,* to provide for. See PROVIDE.] **—pru′dent·ly** *adv.*

pru·den·tial (pro͞o-dĕn′shəl) *adj.* **1.** Arising from or characterized by prudence. **2.** Exercising prudence, good judgment, or common sense. **—pru·den′tial·ly** *adv.*

prud·er·y (pro͞o′də-rē) *n., pl.* **-ies. 1.** The state or quality of being prudish. **2.** An instance of prudish behavior or talk. [French *pruderie,* from *prude,* prude. See PRUDE.]

Prud·hoe Bay (pro͞od′hō, prŭd′-). An inlet of the Arctic Ocean on the northern coast of Alaska east of the Colville River delta. Extensive oil reserves were discovered here in 1968.

prud·ish (pro͞o′dĭsh) *adj.* Marked by or exhibiting the characteristics of a prude; priggish. **—prud′ish·ly** *adv.* **—prud′ish·ness** *n.*

pru·i·nose (pro͞o′ə-nōs′) *adj. Botany.* Having a white, powdery covering or bloom. [Latin *pruīnōsus,* frosty, from *pruīna,* hoarfrost. See **preus-** in Appendix.]

prune¹ (pro͞on) *n.* **1.a.** The partially dried fruit of any of several varieties of the common plum, *Prunus domestica.* **b.** Any kind of plum that can be dried without spoiling. **2.** *Slang.* An ill-tempered, stupid, or incompetent person. **—prune** *intr.v.* **pruned, prun·ing, prunes.** *Slang.* To make a facial expression exhibiting ill temper or disgust: *"Their faces prune at the slightest provocation"* (James Wolcott). [Middle English, from Old French, from Vulgar Latin *prūna, from Latin *prūnum,* plum.]

prune² (pro͞on) *v.* **pruned, prun·ing, prunes.** *—tr.* **1.** To cut off or remove dead or living parts or branches of (a plant, for example) to improve shape or growth. **2.** To remove or cut out as superfluous. **3.** To reduce: *prune a budget.* *—intr.* To remove what is superfluous or undesirable. [Middle English *prouinen,* from Old French *proignier,* perhaps from Vulgar Latin **prōretundiāre* : Latin *prō-,* in front; see PRO–¹ + Latin *rotundus,* round (from *rota,* wheel; see **ret-** in Appendix).] **—prun′er** *n.*

pru·nel·la (pro͞o-nĕl′ə) also **pru·nel·lo** (-nĕl′ō) *n., pl.* **-las** also **-los.** A strong, heavy fabric of worsted twill, used chiefly for shoe uppers, clerical robes, and academic gowns. [Alteration of French *prunelle,* sloe, from Old French, diminutive of *prune,* prune. See PRUNE¹.]

pru·nelle (pro͞o-nĕl′) *n.* A brownish sloe-flavored French liqueur. [French. See PRUNELLA.]

pru·nel·lo (pro͞o-nĕl′ō) *n.* Variant of **prunella.**

prun·ing hook (pro͞o′nĭng) *n.* A long pole with a curved saw blade and usually a clipping mechanism on one end, used especially for pruning small trees.

pru·ri·ent (pro͝or′ē-ənt) *adj.* **1.** Inordinately interested in matters of sex; lascivious. **2.a.** Characterized by an inordinate interest in sex: *prurient thoughts.* **b.** Arousing or appealing to an inordinate interest in sex: *prurient literature.* [Latin *prūriēns, prūrient-,* present participle of *prūrīre,* to yearn for, itch. See **preus-** in Appendix.] **—pru′ri·ence, pru′ri·en·cy** *n.* **—pru′ri·ent·ly** *adv.*

pru·ri·go (pro͞o-rī′gō) *n.* A chronic skin disease having various causes, marked by the eruption of pale, dome-shaped papules that itch severely. [Latin *prūrīgō,* an itching, from *prūrīre,* to itch. See **preus-** in Appendix.] **—pru·rig′i·nous** (-rĭj′ə-nəs) *adj.*

pru·ri·tus (pro͞o-rī′təs) *n.* Severe itching, often of undamaged skin. [Latin *prūrītus,* from past participle of *prūrīre,* to itch. See **preus-** in Appendix.] **—pru·rit′ic** (-rĭt′ĭk) *adj.*

Prus·sia (prŭsh′ə). A historical region and former kingdom of north-central Europe including present-day northern Germany and Poland. Its ancient inhabitants, of Baltic stock, were conquered by the Teutonic Knights in the 13th century. West Prussia was ceded to Poland in 1466, and East Prussia became a Polish fief that passed to Brandenburg in 1618. The kingdom of Prussia was proclaimed in 1701 and was greatly expanded and fortified by Emperor Frederick II (reigned 1740–1786). Prussia was instrumental in the unification of Germany, and in 1871 its king was declared Emperor William I of Germany. The state became a republic in 1918 and was formally abolished after World War II.

Prus·sian (prŭsh′ən) *adj.* **1.** Of or relating to Prussia or its Baltic or German inhabitants. **2.** Suggestive of or resembling the Junkers and the military class of Prussia. **—Prussian** *n.* **1.** Any of the western Balts inhabiting the region between the Vistula and Neman rivers in ancient times. **2.** A Baltic inhabitant of Prussia. **3.** A German inhabitant of Prussia.

Prussian blue *n.* **1.** An insoluble dark blue pigment and dye, ferric ferrocyanide or one of its modifications. **2.** See **iron blue. 3.** *Color.* A moderate to strong blue or deep greenish blue.

prus·si·ate (prŭs′ē-āt′) *n.* **1.** A ferrocyanide or ferricyanide. **2.** A salt of hydrocyanic acid; cyanide. [PRUSSI(C ACID) + –ATE².]

prus·sic acid (prŭs′ĭk) *n.* See **hydrocyanic acid.** [So called because it was first obtained from Prussian blue.]

Prut (pro͞ot). A river rising in southwest Ukraine and flowing about 885 km (550 mi) generally southeast along the Romania-Moldavia border to the Danube River.

pru·tah (pro͞o-tä′) *n., pl.* **-toth** or **-tot** (-tōt′). A coin formerly used in Israel, equal to one thousandth of a pound. [Modern Hebrew *pĕrūṭâ.*]

pry¹ (prī) *intr.v.* **pried** (prīd), **pry·ing, pries** (prīz). To look or inquire closely, curiously, or inquisitively, often in a furtive manner; snoop: *always prying into the affairs of others.* **—pry** *n., pl.* **pries** (prīz). **1.** The act of prying. **2.** An excessively inquisitive person; a snoop. [Middle English *prien.*] **—pry′ing·ly** *adv.*

pry² (prī) *tr.v.* **pried** (prīd), **pry·ing, pries** (prīz). **1.** To raise, move, or force open with a lever. **2.** To obtain with effort or difficulty: *pried a confession out of the suspect.* **—pry** *n., pl.* **pries** (prīz). Something, such as a crowbar, that is used to apply leverage. [Alteration of PRIZE³.]

pry·er (prī′ər) *n.* Variant of **prier.**

Prynne (prĭn), **William.** 1600–1669. English politician and pamphleteer whose attack on the theater, *Histrio-Mastix* (1633), resulted in his imprisonment and the amputation of his ears.

Ps or **Ps.** *abbr. Bible.* **1.** Psalm. **2.** Psalms.

p.s. *abbr.* Passenger steamer.

P.S. *abbr.* **1.** Permanent secretary. **2.** Police Sergeant. **3.** Also **PS** or **p.s.** Postscript. **4.** Public school.

psalm (säm) *n. Abbr.* **Ps, Ps. 1.** A sacred song; a hymn. **2. Psalms** *(used with a sing. verb). Bible.* See table at **Bible. —psalm** *tr.v.* **psalmed, psalm·ing, psalms.** To sing of or celebrate in psalms. [Middle English, from Old English, from Latin *psalmus,* from Greek *psalmos,* from *psallein,* to play the harp. See **pōl-** in Appendix.]

psalm·ist (sä′mĭst) *n.* A writer or composer of psalms.

psalm·o·dy (sä′mə-dē, săl′mə-) *n., pl.* **-dies. 1.** The act or practice of singing psalms in divine worship. **2.** The composition or arranging of psalms for singing. **3.** A collection of psalms. [Middle English *psalmodie,* from Late Latin *psalmōdia,* from Greek, singing to the harp : *psalmos,* psalm; see PSALM + *ōidē, aoidē,* song; see ODE.] **—psalm′o·dist** *n.*

Psal·ter also **psal·ter** (sôl′tər) *n.* A book containing the Book of Psalms or a particular version of, musical setting for, or selection from it. [Middle English, from Old English *psaltere* and Old French *psaultier,* both from Late Latin *psaltērium,* from Latin, psaltery, from Greek *psaltērion.* See PSALTERY.]

psal·te·ri·um (sôl-tîr′ē-əm) *n., pl.* **-te·ri·a** (-tîr′ē-ə). The omasum. [Late Latin *psaltērium,* psalter (so called because when slit open its folds fall apart like the leaves of a book). See PSALTER.] **—psal·te′ri·al** *adj.*

psal·ter·y (sôl′tə-rē) also **psal·try** (sôl′trē) *n., pl.* **-ter·ies** also **-tries.** *Music.* An ancient stringed instrument played by plucking the strings with the fingers or a plectrum. [Middle English *psalterie,* from Old French, from Latin *psaltērium,* from Greek *psaltērion,* from *psallein,* to play the harp. See **pōl-** in Appendix.]

p's and q's (pēz′ ən kyo͞oz′) *pl.n.* **1.** Socially correct behavior; manners. **2.** The way one acts; conduct: *was told to watch his p's and q's or he would be fired.*

PSAT *abbr.* Preliminary Scholastic Aptitude Test.

psec. *abbr.* Picosecond.

pse·phol·o·gy (sē-fŏl′ə-jē) *n.* The study of political elections. [Greek *psēphos,* pebble, ballot (from the ancient Greeks' use of pebbles for voting) + -LOGY.] **—pse′pho·log′i·cal** (sē′fə-lŏj′ĭ-kəl) *adj.* **—pse·phol′o·gist** *n.*

pseud. *abbr.* Pseudonym.

pseud– *pref.* Variant of **pseudo–.**

pseud·ax·is (so͞o-dăk′sĭs) *n. Botany.* See **sympodium.**

pseud·e·pig·ra·pha (so͞o′dĭ-pĭg′rə-fə) *pl.n.* **1.** Spurious writings, especially writings falsely attributed to biblical characters or times. **2.** A body of texts written between 200 B.C. and A.D. 200 and spuriously ascribed to various prophets and kings of Hebrew Scriptures. [Greek, from neuter pl. of *pseudepigraphos,* falsely ascribed : *pseudēs,* false; see PSEUDO– + *epigraphein,* to inscribe (*epi-,* epi- + *graphein,* to write; see **gerbh-** in Appendix).] **—pseud′e·pig′ra·phal** (-rə-fəl), **pseud′ep·i·graph′ic** (so͞o′dĕp-ĭ-grăf′ĭk), **pseud′ep·i·graph′i·cal** (-ĭ-kəl), **pseud′-e·pig′ra·phous** (-rə-fəs) *adj.*

pseudo– or **pseud–** *pref.* **1.** False; deceptive; sham: *pseudoscience.* **2.** Apparently similar: *pseudocoel.* [Greek, from *pseudēs,* false, from *pseudein,* to lie.]

pseu·do·bulb (so͞o′dō-bŭlb′) *n.* A thickened, bulblike, fleshy stem located above the ground, as in many orchids.

pseu·do·carp (so͞o′də-kärp′) *n.* See **accessory fruit.** **—pseu′do·car′pous** *adj.*

pseu·do·coel (so͞o′də-sēl′) also **pseu·do·coe·lom** (so͞o′də-sē′ləm) *n.* An internal body cavity of some primitive invertebrates, similar to a coelom but lacking a mesodermal lining.

pseu·do·coe·lo·mate (so͞o′dō-sē′lə-māt′) *adj.* Having a pseudocoel. **—pseudocoelomate** *n.* An animal having a pseudocoel.

pseu·do·cy·e·sis (so͞o′dō-sī-ē′sĭs) *n.* A usually psychosomatic condition in which physical symptoms of pregnancy, such as weight gain and amenorrhea, are manifested without conception. Also called *pseudopregnancy.* [PSEUDO– + New Latin *cyēsis,* pregnancy (from Greek *kuēsis,* from *kuein,* to swell; see **keuə-** in Appendix).]

pseu·do-e·vent (so͞o′dō-ĭ-vĕnt′) *n. Informal.* An event that has been caused to occur or staged to engender press coverage and public interest: *"Polls have become the quintessential pseudo-events of the preprimary campaign"* (Edward M. Kennedy).

pseu·do·gene (so͞o′də-jēn′) *n.* A segment of DNA resembling a gene but lacking a genetic function.

pseu·do·her·maph·ro·dite (so͞o′dō-hər-măf′rə-dīt′) *n.* One that possesses the internal reproductive organs of one sex while exhibiting some of the external physical characteristics of the opposite sex. **—pseu′do·her·maph′ro·dit′ic** (-dĭt′ĭk) *adj.* **—pseu′do·her·maph′ro·dit·ism** *n.*

pseu·do·mo·nad (so͞o′də-mō′năd′) *n.* **1.** Any of various gram-negative, rod-shaped, mostly aerobic flagellated bacteria of the phylum Pseudomonad, commonly found in soil, water, and decaying matter and including some plant and animal pathogens. **2.** A pseudomonad of the large genus *Pseudomonas,* some species of which are opportunistic pathogens in human beings. In this sense, also called *pseudomonas.* [From New Latin *Pseudomonas,* genus name : PSEUDO– + Latin *monas, monad-,* unit (from Greek, from *monos,* single; see **men-**[4] in Appendix).]

pseu·do·mo·nas (so͞o′də-mō′nəs, so͞o-dŏm′ə-nəs) *n., pl.* **-mon·a·des** (-mŏn′ə-dēz′). See **pseudomonad** (sense 2).

pseu·do·morph (so͞o′də-môrf′) *n.* **1.** A false, deceptive, or irregular form. **2.** *Mineralogy.* A mineral that has the crystalline form of another mineral rather than the form normally characteristic of its own composition. **—pseu′do·mor′phic, pseu′-do·mor′phous** *adj.* **—pseu′do·mor′phism** *n.*

pseu·do·nym (so͞od′n-ĭm′) *n. Abbr.* **pseud.** A fictitious name assumed by an author; a pen name. [French *pseudonyme,* from Greek *pseudōnumon,* neuter of *pseudōnumos,* falsely named : *pseudēs,* false; see PSEUDO– + *onuma,* name; see **nō-men-** in Appendix.] **—pseu·don′y·mous** (so͞o-dŏn′ə-məs) *adj.* **—pseu·don′y·mous·ly** *adv.* **—pseu·don′y·mous·ness** *n.*

pseu·do·pod (so͞o′də-pŏd′) *n.* A temporary projection of the cytoplasm of certain cells, such as phagocytes, or of certain unicellular organisms, especially amoebas, that serves in locomotion and phagocytosis. **—pseu·dop′o·dal** (-dŏp′ə-dl), **pseu′do·po′di·al** (-pō′dē-əl) *adj.*

pseu·do·po·di·um (so͞o′də-pō′dē-əm) *n., pl.* **-po·di·a** (-pō′dē-ə). A pseudopod.

pseu·do·preg·nan·cy (so͞o′dō-prĕg′nən-sē) *n., pl.* **-cies. 1.** See **pseudocyesis. 2.** A condition resembling pregnancy that occurs in some mammals, marked by persistence of the corpus luteum and usually following infertile copulation. **—pseu′do·preg′nant** *adj.*

pseu·do·ran·dom (so͞o′dō-răn′dəm) *adj. Mathematics.* Of, relating to, or being random numbers generated by a definite, nonrandom computational process.

pseu·do·sci·ence (so͞o′dō-sī′əns) *n.* A theory, methodology, or practice that is considered to be without scientific foundation. **—pseu′do·sci′en·tif′ic** (-ən-tĭf′ĭk) *adj.* **—pseu′do·sci′en·tist** *n.*

psf. or **p.s.f.** *abbr.* Pounds per square foot.

pshaw (shô) *interj.* Used to indicate impatience, irritation, disapproval, or disbelief.

psi[1] (sī, psī) *n.* The 23rd letter of the Greek alphabet. See table at **alphabet.** [Middle English, from Late Greek, from Greek *psei.*]

psi[2] or **p.s.i.** *abbr.* Pounds per square inch.

psil·o·cin (sĭl′ə-sĭn, sī′lə-) *n.* A potent hallucinogenic compound, $C_{12}H_{16}N_2O$, related to psilocybin. [PSILOC(YBIN) + -IN.]

psil·o·cy·bin (sĭl′ə-sī′bĭn, sī′lə-) *n.* A hallucinogenic compound, $C_{13}HN_2O_3P_2$, obtained from the mushroom *Psilocybe mexicana.* [New Latin *Psilocybe,* genus name (Greek *psilos,* bare + Greek *kubē,* head) + -IN.]

psi·lom·e·lane (sī-lŏm′ə-lān′) *n.* A mixture of black manganese oxide minerals. [Greek *psilos,* bare + Greek *melas, melan-,* black.]

psi particle *n.* See **J particle.**

psit·ta·cine (sĭt′ə-sīn′) *adj.* **1.** Relating to, resembling, or characteristic of parrots. **2.** Of or belonging to the family Psittacidae, which includes the parrots, macaws, and parakeets. [Latin *psittacīnus,* from *psittacus,* parrot, from Greek *psittakos.*]

psit·ta·co·sis (sĭt′ə-kō′sĭs) *n.* An infectious disease of parrots and related birds caused by the bacterium *Chlamydia psittaci,* that is communicable to human beings, in whom it produces high fever, severe headache, and symptoms similar to pneumonia. Also called *parrot fever.* [New Latin *psittacōsis* : Latin *psittacus,* parrot (from Greek *psittakos*) + -OSIS.] **—psit′ta·cot′ic** (-kŏt′ĭk, -kō′tĭk) *adj.*

Pskov (pə-skôf′, pskôf). A city of west-central Russia south-southwest of Leningrad. Dating from the eighth century, it became an important trade center and was annexed by Moscow in 1510. Population, 194,000.

pso·as (sō′əs) *n.* Either of two muscles of the loin that rotate the hip joint and flex the spine. [New Latin, from Greek *psoa.*]

pso·cid (sō′sĭd, sŏs′ĭd) *n.* Any of various small, soft-bodied, sometimes winged insects of the order Psocoptera, which includes the booklice. [From New Latin *Psōcidae,* family name, from *Psōcus,* type genus, from Greek *psōkhos,* dust.]

pso·ra·len (sôr′ə-lən) *n.* Any of a group of chemical compounds found naturally in certain plants that are used in the treatment of psoriasis and vitiligo. [From New Latin *Psōralea,* plant genus, from Greek *psōralea,* neuter pl. of *psōraleos,* mangy (from the appearance of the plants' leaves), from *psōra,* itch.]

pso·ri·a·sis (sə-rī′ə-sĭs) *n.* A noncontagious inflammatory skin disease characterized by recurring reddish patches covered with silvery scales. [Greek *psōriasis,* itch, mange, from *psōrian,* to have the itch, from *psōra,* itch.] **—pso′ri·at′ic** (sôr′ē-ăt′ĭk, sōr′-) *adj.*

PST or **P.S.T.** *abbr.* Pacific Standard Time.

psych (sīk) *Informal. n.* Psychology. **—psych** also **psyche** *v.* **psyched, psych·ing, psyches.** *—tr.* **1.a.** To put into the right psychological frame of mind: *The coach psyched the team before the game.* **b.** To excite emotionally: *She had psyched herself up so much for the camping trip that she forgot her sleeping bag.* **2.** To undermine the confidence of by psychological means; intimidate: *"Depending on whose personality is stronger, one can more easily psych the other"* (Harold C. Schonberg). **3.a.** To analyze, solve, or comprehend. **b.** To anticipate or guess the intentions of: *"Most others could never approach* [his] *ability . . . to psyche out the opposition's thinking so consistently"* (Steven Brill). **4.** *Informal.* To analyze and treat by psychoanalysis. *—intr.* To become confused or mentally deranged.

psych. *abbr.* Psychological; psychologist; psychology.

psych– *pref.* Variant of **psycho–.**

psy·chas·the·ni·a (sī′kəs-thē′nē-ə) *n.* A neurotic disorder characterized by phobias, obsessions, compulsions, or excessive anxiety. No longer in scientific use. **—psy′chas·then′ic** (-thĕn′ĭk) *adj.*

psy·che (sī′kē) *n.* **1.** The spirit or soul. **2.** *Psychiatry.* The mind functioning as the center of thought, emotion, and behavior and consciously or unconsciously adjusting or mediating the body's responses to the social and physical environment. [Latin *psȳchē,* from Greek *psukhē,* soul. See **bhes-** in Appendix.]

Psy·che (sī′kē) *n. Greek Mythology.* A young woman who loved and was loved by Eros and was united with him after Aphrodite's jealousy was overcome. She subsequently became the personification of the soul.

psy·che·de·li·a (sī′kĭ-dē′lē-ə, -dēl′yə) *n.* The subculture associated with psychedelic drugs.

psy·che·del·ic (sī′kĭ-dĕl′ĭk) *adj.* Of, characterized by, or generating hallucinations, distortions of perception, altered states of awareness, and occasionally states resembling psychosis. **—psychedelic** *n.* A drug, such as LSD or mescaline, that produces such effects. [PSYCHE + Greek *dēloun,* to make visible (from *dēlos,* clear, visible; see **deiw-** in Appendix) + -IC.] **—psy′che·del′i·cal·ly** *adv.*

psychiatric hospital *n.* A hospital for the care and treatment of patients affected with acute or chronic mental illness. Also called *mental hospital.*

psy·chi·a·trist (sĭ-kī′ə-trĭst, sī-) *n.* A physician who specializes in psychiatry.

psy·chi·a·try (sĭ-kī′ə-trē, sī-) *n.* The branch of medicine that deals with the diagnosis, treatment, and prevention of mental and emotional disorders. **—psy′chi·at′ric** (sī′kē-ăt′rĭk), **psy′chi·at′ri·cal** (-rĭ-kəl) *adj.* **—psy′chi·at′ri·cal·ly** *adv.*

psy·chic (sī′kĭk) *n.* **1.** A person apparently responsive to psychic forces. **2.** See **medium** (sense 5). **—psychic** also **psy·chi·cal** (-kĭ-kəl) *adj.* **1.** Of, relating to, affecting, or influenced by the human mind or psyche; mental: *psychic trauma; psychic energy.*

Psyche
Cupid and Psyche by Claude Michel Clodion (1738–1814)

ă pat	oi boy
ā pay	ou out
âr care	o͝o took
ä father	o͞o boot
ĕ pet	ŭ cut
ē be	ûr urge
ĭ pit	th thin
ī pie	*th* this
îr pier	hw which
ŏ pot	zh vision
ō toe	ə about, item
ô paw	♦ regionalism

Stress marks: ′ (primary); ′ (secondary), as in **dictionary** (dĭk′shə-nĕr′ē)

ptarmigan
White-tailed ptarmigan
Lagopus leucurus

2.a. Capable of extraordinary mental processes, such as extrasensory perception and mental telepathy. **b.** Of or relating to such mental processes. [From Greek *psukhikos,* of the soul, from *psukhē,* soul. See **bhes-** in Appendix.] **—psy′chi·cal·ly** *adv.*

psychic energizer *n.* An antidepressant drug.

psy·cho (sī′kō) *Slang. n., pl.* **-chos.** A psychopath. **—psycho** *adj.* Crazy; insane.

psycho– or **psych–** *pref.* **1.a.** Mind; mental: *psychogenic.* **b.** Mental activities or processes: *psychomotor.* **2.** Psychology; psychological: *psychohistory.* [Greek *psukho-,* soul, life, from *psukhē.* See **bhes-** in Appendix.]

psy·cho·a·cous·tics (sī′kō-ə-ko͞o′stĭks) *n. (used with a sing. verb).* The scientific study of the perception of sound. **—psy′cho·a·cous′tic, psy′cho·a·cous′ti·cal** *adj.*

psy·cho·ac·tive (sī′kō-ăk′tĭv) *adj.* Affecting the mind or mental processes. Used of a drug.

psy·cho·a·nal·y·sis (sī′kō-ə-năl′ĭ-sĭs) *n., pl.* **-ses** (-sēz′). **1.a.** The method of psychiatric therapy originated by Sigmund Freud in which free association, dream interpretation, and analysis of resistance and transference are used to explore repressed or unconscious impulses, anxieties, and internal conflicts. **b.** The theory of personality developed by Freud that focuses on repression and unconscious forces and includes the concepts of infantile sexuality, resistance, transference, and division of the psyche into the id, ego, and superego. **2.** Psychiatric treatment incorporating this method and theory. **—psy′cho·an′a·lyst** (-ăn′ə-lĭst) *n.* **—psy′cho·an′a·lyt′ic** (-ăn′ə-lĭt′ĭk), **psy′cho·an′a·lyt′i·cal** (-ĭ-kəl) *adj.* **—psy′cho·an′a·lyt′i·cal·ly** *adv.*

psy·cho·an·a·lyze (sī′kō-ăn′ə-līz′) *tr.v.* **-lyzed, -lyz·ing, -lyz·es.** To analyze and treat by psychoanalysis.

psy·cho·bab·ble (sī′kō-băb′əl) *n.* Psychological jargon, especially that of psychotherapy: *"There is . . . too much talk, psychobabble that gets in the way of the book"* (Michael M. Thomas). **—psy′cho·bab′bler** *n.*

psy·cho·bi·og·ra·phy (sī′kō-bī-ŏg′rə-fē, -bē-) *n., pl.* **-phies. 1.** A biography that analyzes the psychological makeup, character, or motivations of its subject: *"We are given a kind of psychobiography which ultimately pictures a deeply egotistical individual, unable to tolerate anyone else's success"* (Leon Botstein). **2.** A character analysis. **—psy′cho·bi·og′ra·pher** *n.* **—psy′cho·bi′o·graph′ic** (-bī′ə-grăf′ĭk), **psy′cho·bi·o·graph′i·cal** (-ĭ-kəl) *adj.*

psy·cho·bi·ol·o·gy (sī′kō-bī-ŏl′ə-jē) *n.* **1.** The study of the biological foundations of the mind, emotions, and mental processes. Also called *biopsychology.* **2.** The school of psychiatry that interprets personality, behavior, and mental illness in terms of adaptive responses to biological, social, cultural, and environmental factors. **—psy′cho·bi′o·log′ic** (-bī′ə-lŏj′ĭk), **psy′cho·bi′o·log′i·cal** (-ĭ-kəl) *adj.* **—psy′cho·bi′o·log′i·cal·ly** *adv.* **—psy′cho·bi·ol′o·gist** *n.*

psy·cho·chem·i·cal (sī′kō-kĕm′ĭ-kəl) *n.* A psychoactive drug or substance. **—psychochemical** *adj.* Of or relating to psychochemicals.

psy·cho·dra·ma (sī′kə-drä′mə, -drăm′ə) *n.* **1.** A psychotherapeutic and analytic technique in which people are assigned roles to be played spontaneously within a dramatic context devised by a therapist. **2.** A dramatization in which this technique is employed. **—psy′cho·dra·mat′ic** (-drə-măt′ĭk) *adj.*

psy·cho·dy·nam·ics (sī′kō-dī-năm′ĭks, -dĭ-) *n.* **1.** *(used with a sing. or pl. verb).* The interaction of various conscious and unconscious mental or emotional processes, especially as they influence personality, behavior, and attitudes. **2.** *(used with a sing. verb).* The study of personality and behavior in terms of such processes. **—psy′cho·dy·nam′ic** *adj.* **—psy′cho·dy·nam′i·cal·ly** *adv.*

psy·cho·gen·e·sis (sī′kə-jĕn′ĭ-sĭs) *n.* **1.** The origin and development of psychological processes, personality, or behavior. **2.** Development of a physical disorder or illness resulting from psychic, rather than physiological, factors. **—psy′cho·ge·net′ic** (-jə-nĕt′ĭk) *adj.* **—psy′cho·ge·net′i·cal·ly** *adv.*

psy·cho·gen·ic (sī′kə-jĕn′ĭk) *adj.* Originating in the mind or in mental or emotional processes; having a psychological rather than a physiological origin. Used of certain disorders. **—psy′cho·gen′i·cal·ly** *adv.*

psy·cho·graph (sī′kə-grăf′) *n.* A graphic representation or chart of the personality traits of an individual or a group. **—psy′cho·graph′ic** *adj.*

psy·cho·graph·ics (sī′kə-grăf′ĭks) *n.* **1.** *(used with a sing. verb).* The use of demographics to study and measure attitudes, values, lifestyles, and opinions, as for marketing purposes. **2.** *(used with a pl. verb).* The data obtained from such study. [PSYCHO– + (DEMO)GRAPHICS.]

psy·cho·his·to·ry (sī′kō-hĭs′tə-rē) *n., pl.* **-ries.** A psychological or psychoanalytic interpretation or study of historical events or persons: *the psychohistory of the Nazi era.* **—psy′cho·his·tor′i·an** (-hĭ-stôr′ē-ən, -stŏr′-) *n.* **—psy′cho·his·tor′i·cal** (-hĭ-stôr′ĭ-kəl, -stŏr′-) *adj.*

psy·cho·ki·ne·sis (sī′kō-kĭ-nē′sĭs, -kī-) *n., pl.* **-ses** (-sēz). *Abbr.* **PK 1.** The production or control of motion, especially in inanimate and remote objects, purportedly by the exercise of psychic powers. **2.** *Psychiatry.* An uncontrolled, maniacal outburst, resulting from defective inhibition. **—psy′cho·ki·net′ic** (-kĭ-nĕt′ĭk, -kī-) *adj.* **—psy′cho·ki·net′i·cal·ly** *adv.*

psychol. *abbr.* Psychological; psychologist; psychology.

psy·cho·lin·guis·tics (sī′kō-lĭng-gwĭs′tĭks) *n. (used with a sing. verb).* The study of the influence of psychological factors on the development, use, and interpretation of language. **—psy′cho·lin′guist** *n.* **—psy′cho·lin·guis′tic** *adj.*

psy·cho·log·i·cal (sī′kə-lŏj′ĭ-kəl) also **psy·cho·log·ic** (-lŏj′ĭk) *adj. Abbr.* **psych., psychol. 1.** Of or relating to psychology: *psychological research; psychological jargon.* **2.** Of, relating to, or arising from the mind or emotions. **3.** Influencing or intended to influence the mind or emotions: *psychological warfare.* **4.** *Color.* Of or being any of certain primary colors whose mixture may be subjectively conceived as producing other colors. **—psy′cho·log′i·cal·ly** *adv.*

psychological moment *n.* The time at which the mental state of a person is most likely to produce a desired response.

psy·chol·o·gist (sī-kŏl′ə-jĭst) *n. Abbr.* **psych., psychol.** A person trained and educated to perform psychological research, testing, and therapy.

psy·chol·o·gize (sī-kŏl′ə-jīz′) *v.* **-gized, -giz·ing, -giz·es.** *—tr.* To explain (behavior) in psychological terms. *—intr.* To investigate, reason, or speculate in psychological terms.

psy·chol·o·gy (sī-kŏl′ə-jē) *n., pl.* **-gies.** *Abbr.* **psych., psychol. 1.** The science that deals with mental processes and behavior. **2.** The emotional and behavioral characteristics of an individual, a group, or an activity: *the psychology of war.* **3.** Subtle tactical action or argument used to manipulate or influence another: *He used poor psychology on his employer when trying to make the point.* **4.** *Philosophy.* The branch of metaphysics that studies the soul, the mind, and the relationship of life and mind to the functions of the body.

psy·cho·met·rics (sī′kə-mĕt′rĭks) *n. (used with a sing. verb).* The branch of psychology that deals with the design, administration, and interpretation of quantitative tests for the measurement of psychological variables such as intelligence, aptitude, and personality traits. Also called *psychometry.* **—psy′cho·met′ric, psy′cho·met′ri·cal** *adj.* **—psy′cho·met′ri·cal·ly** *adv.* **—psy·chom′e·tri′cian** (sī-kŏm′ĭ-trĭsh′ən), **psy·chom′e·trist** (sī-kŏm′ĭ-trĭst) *n.*

psy·chom·e·try (sī-kŏm′ĭ-trē) *n.* **1.** See **psychometrics. 2.** The ability or art of divining information about people or events associated with an object solely by touching or being near to it.

psy·cho·mo·tor (sī′kō-mō′tər) *adj.* Of or relating to movement or muscular activity associated with mental processes.

psy·cho·neu·ro·sis (sī′kō-no͝o-rō′sĭs, -nyo͝o-) *n., pl.* **-ses** (-sēz). Neurosis. **—psy′cho·neu·rot′ic** (-rŏt′ĭk) *adj. & n.*

psy·cho·path (sī′kə-păth′) *n.* A person with an antisocial personality disorder, especially one manifested in aggressive, perverted, criminal, or amoral behavior. [Back-formation from PSYCHOPATHIC.]

psy·cho·path·ic (sī′kə-păth′ĭk) *adj.* **1.** Of, relating to, or characterized by psychopathy. **2.** Relating to or affected with an antisocial personality disorder that is usually characterized by aggressive, perverted, criminal, or amoral behavior. **—psy′cho·path′i·cal·ly** *adv.*

psy·cho·pa·thol·o·gy (sī′kō-pə-thŏl′ə-jē, -pă-) *n.* The study of the origin, development, and manifestations of mental or behavioral disorders. **—psy′cho·path′o·log′i·cal** (-păth′ə-lŏj′ĭ-kəl), **psy′cho·path′o·log′ic** (-lŏj′ĭk) *adj.* **—psy′cho·pa·thol′o·gist** *n.*

psy·chop·a·thy (sī-kŏp′ə-thē) *n.* Mental disorder, especially when manifested by antisocial behavior.

psy·cho·phar·ma·col·o·gy (sī′kō-fär′mə-kŏl′ə-jē) *n.* The branch of pharmacology that deals with the study of the actions and effects of psychoactive drugs. **—psy′cho·phar′ma·co·log′ic** (-kə-lŏj′ĭk), **psy′cho·phar′ma·co·log′i·cal** (-ĭ-kəl) *adj.* **—psy′cho·phar′ma·col′o·gist** *n.*

psy·cho·phys·ics (sī′kō-fĭz′ĭks) *n. (used with a sing. verb).* The branch of psychology that deals with the relationships between physical stimuli and sensory response. **—psy′cho·phys′i·cal** *adj.* **—psy′cho·phys′i·cal·ly** *adv.* **—psy′cho·phys′i·cist** (-fĭz′ĭ-sĭst) *n.*

psy·cho·phys·i·ol·o·gy (sī′kō-fĭz′ē-ŏl′ə-jē) *n.* The study of correlations between the mind, behavior, and bodily mechanisms. Also called *physiological psychology.* **—psy′cho·phys′i·o·log′i·cal** (-fĭz′ē-ə-lŏj′ĭ-kəl), **psy′cho·phys′i·o·log′ic** (-lŏj′ĭk) *adj.* **—psy′cho·phys′i·ol′o·gist** *n.*

psy·cho·sex·u·al (sī′kō-sĕk′sho͞o-əl) *adj.* Of or relating to the mental and emotional aspects of sexuality. **—psy′cho·sex′u·al′i·ty** (-ăl′ĭ-tē) *n.* **—psy′cho·sex′u·al·ly** *adv.*

psy·cho·sis (sī-kō′sĭs) *n., pl.* **-ses** (-sēz). A severe mental disorder, with or without organic damage, characterized by derangement of personality and loss of contact with reality and causing deterioration of normal social functioning.

psy·cho·so·cial (sī′kō-sō′shəl) *adj.* Involving aspects of social and psychological behavior: *a child's psychosocial development.* **—psy′cho·so′cial·ly** *adv.*

psy·cho·so·mat·ic (sī′kō-sō-măt′ĭk) *adj.* **1.** Of or relating to a disorder having physical symptoms but originating from mental or emotional causes. **2.** Relating to or concerned with the influence of the mind on the body, especially with respect to disease: *psychosomatic medicine.* **—psy′cho·so·mat′i·cal·ly** *adv.*

psy·cho·sur·ger·y (sī′kō-sûr′jə-rē) *n., pl.* **-ies.** Brain surgery used to treat severe, intractable mental or behavioral dis-

ă pat	oi boy
ā pay	ou out
âr care	o͝o took
ä father	o͞o boot
ĕ pet	ŭ cut
ē be	ûr urge
ĭ pit	th thin
ī pie	*th* this
îr pier	hw which
ŏ pot	zh vision
ō toe	ə about, item
ô paw	♦ regionalism

Stress marks: ′ (primary); ′ (secondary), as in **dictionary** (dĭk′shə-nĕr′ē)

orders. **—psy′cho·sur′geon** (-sûr′jən) *n.* **—psy′cho·sur′gi·cal** (-jĭ-kəl) *adj.*

psy·cho·tech·nics (sī′kō-tĕk′nĭks) *n. (used with a sing. verb).* The practical or technological application of psychology, as in analysis of social or economic problems. **—psy′cho·tech′ni·cal** *adj.* **—psy′cho·tech·ni′cian** (-tĕk-nĭsh′ən) *n.*

psy·cho·ther·a·peu·tics (sī′kō-thĕr′ə-pyo͞o′tĭks) *n. (used with a sing. verb).* Psychotherapy.

psy·cho·ther·a·py (sī′kō-thĕr′ə-pē) *n., pl.* **-pies.** The treatment of mental and emotional disorders through the use of psychological techniques designed to encourage communication of conflicts and insight into problems, with the goal being personality growth and behavior modification. **—psy′cho·ther′a·peu′tic** (-pyo͞o′tĭk) *adj.* **—psy′cho·ther′a·peu′ti·cal·ly** *adv.* **—psy′cho·ther′a·pist** *n.*

psy·chot·ic (sī-kŏt′ĭk) *adj.* Of, relating to, or affected by psychosis. **—psychotic** *n.* A person affected by psychosis. [PSYCH(OSIS) + -OTIC.] **—psy·chot′i·cal·ly** *adv.*

psy·chot·o·mi·met·ic (sī-kŏt′ō-mə-mĕt′ĭk, -mī-) *adj.* Tending to induce hallucinations, delusions, or other symptoms of a psychosis. Used of a drug. **—psychotomimetic** *n.* A psychotomimetic drug, such as LSD. [Alteration of *psychosomimetic* (influenced by PSYCHOTIC) : PSYCHOS(IS) + MIMETIC.] **—psy·chot′o·mi·met′i·cal·ly** *adv.*

psy·cho·tro·pic (sī′kə-trō′pĭk, -trŏp′ĭk) *adj.* Having an altering effect on perception or behavior. Used especially of a drug. **—psychotropic** *n.* A psychotropic drug or other agent.

psych-out (sīk′out′) *n. Informal.* The act or an instance of undermining someone's confidence by psychological means.

psychro– *pref.* Cold: *psychrophilic.* [Greek *psukhro-*, from *psukhros*, cold.]

psy·chrom·e·ter (sī-krŏm′ĭ-tər) *n.* An instrument that uses the difference in readings between two thermometers, one having a wet bulb and the other having a dry bulb, to measure the moisture content or relative humidity of air.

psy·chro·phil·ic (sī′krō-fĭl′ĭk) *adj. Biology.* Thriving at relatively low temperatures. Used of certain bacteria. **—psy′chro·phile′** (-fīl′) *n.*

psyl·la (sĭl′ə) also **psyl·lid** (sĭl′ĭd) *n.* Any of various jumping plant lice of the family Psyllidae, especially of the genus *Psylla*, which includes several species that infest fruit trees. [New Latin *Psylla*, type genus, from Greek *psulla*, flea.]

psyl·li·um (sĭl′ē-əm) *n.* **1.** An annual Eurasian plant *(Plantago psyllium)* having opposite leaves and small flowers borne in dense spikes. **2.** The seeds of this plant, widely used as a mild bulk laxative and sometimes added to foods as a dietary source of soluble fiber. [New Latin, from Greek *psullion*, diminutive of *psulla*, flea (from the plant's use against fleas).]

Pt The symbol for the element **platinum** (sense 1).

PT *abbr.* Patrol torpedo.

pt. *abbr.* **1.** Part. **2.** Payment. **3.** Pint. **4.** Point. **5.** Port. **6.** *Grammar.* Preterit.

p.t. *abbr.* Pro tempore.

P.T. *abbr.* **1.** Also **PT.** Pacific Time. **2.** Physical therapy. **3.** Physical training.

PTA or **P.T.A.** *abbr.* Parent Teacher Association.

pta. *abbr.* Peseta.

ptar·mi·gan (tär′mĭ-gən) *n., pl.* **ptarmigan** or **-gans.** Any of various grouses of the genus *Lagopus*, inhabiting arctic, subarctic, and alpine regions of the Northern Hemisphere and having feathered legs and feet and plumage that is brown or gray in summer and white in winter. [Alteration (influenced by the spelling *pt* in Greek words like *pteron*, wing) of Scottish Gaelic *tàrmachan*.]

PT boat (pē-tē′) *n.* A fast, maneuverable, lightly armed vessel, 60 to 100 feet (18 to 30 meters) in length, used to torpedo enemy shipping. [P(ATROL) + T(ORPEDO) BOAT.]

PTC *abbr.* Phenylthiocarbamide.

–pter *suff.* Wing; winglike part: *ornithopter.* [From Greek *pteron*, feather, wing. See **pet-** in Appendix.]

pter·i·dol·o·gy (tĕr′ĭ-dŏl′ə-jē) *n.* The study of ferns. [Greek *pteris, pterid-*, fern (from *pteron*, feather, wing; see **pet-** in Appendix) + -LOGY.] **—pter′i·do·log′i·cal** (-də-lŏj′ĭ-kəl) *adj.* **—pter′i·dol′o·gist** *n.*

pte·rid·o·phyte (tə-rĭd′ə-fīt′, tĕr′ĭ-dō-) *n.* Any of various vascular plants that reproduce by means of spores rather than by seeds, including the ferns and related plants, such as club mosses and horsetails. [From New Latin *Pteridophyta*, former division name : Greek *pteris, pterid-*, fern; see PTERIDOLOGY + Greek *phuton*, plant; see -PHYTE.] **—pte·rid′o·phyt′ic** (tə-rĭd′ə-fĭt′ĭk, tĕr′ĭ-dō-), **pter′i·doph′y·tous** (tĕr′ĭ-dŏf′ĭ-təs) *adj.*

pter·o·dac·tyl (tĕr′ə-dăk′təl) *n.* Any of various small, mostly tailless, extinct flying reptiles of the order Pterosauria that existed during the Jurassic and Cretaceous periods. [New Latin *Pterodactylus*, reptile genus : Greek *pteron*, feather, wing; see -PTER + Greek *daktulos*, finger.] **—pter′o·dac′ty·loid′** *adj.* **—pter′o·dac′ty·lous** *adj.*

pter·o·pod (tĕr′ə-pŏd′) *n.* Any of various small marine gastropod mollusks of the subclass Opisthobranchia that have winglike lobes on the feet. Also called *sea butterfly.* [From New Latin *Pteropoda*, order name : Greek *pteron*, feather, wing; see -PTER + New Latin *-poda*, -pod.] **—pter′o·pod′** *adj.* **—pte·rop′o·dan** (tə-rŏp′ə-dən) *adj. & n.*

pter·o·saur (tĕr′ə-sôr′) *n.* Any of various extinct flying reptiles of the order Pterosauria, including the pterodactyls, of the Jurassic and Cretaceous periods, characterized by wings consisting of a flap of skin supported by the very long fourth digit on each forelimb. [From New Latin *Pterosauria*, order name : Greek *pteron*, feather, wing; see -PTER + Greek *sauros*, lizard.]

pterodactyl
Pterodactylus

pter·o·yl·glu·tam·ic acid (tĕr′ō-ĭl-glo͞o-tăm′ĭk) *n.* Folic acid. [*ptero(ic acid)*, an amino acid + -YL + GLUTAMIC ACID.]

pte·ryg·i·um (tə-rĭj′ē-əm) *n., pl.* **-i·ums** or **-i·a** (-ē-ə). An abnormal mass of tissue arising from the conjunctiva of the inner corner of the eye that obstructs vision by growing over the cornea. [New Latin, from Greek *pterugion*, diminutive of *pterux, pterug-*, wing. See PTERYGOID.] **—pte·ryg′i·al** (-əl) *adj.*

pter·y·goid (tĕr′ĭ-goid′) *adj. Anatomy.* **1.** Of, relating to, or located in the region of the sphenoid bone; a pterygoid muscle. **2.** Resembling a wing; winglike. **—pterygoid** *n.* Either of two processes descending from the body of the sphenoid bone. [Greek *pterugoeidēs*, winglike : *pterux, pterug-*, wing; see **pet-** in Appendix + *-oeidēs*, -oid.]

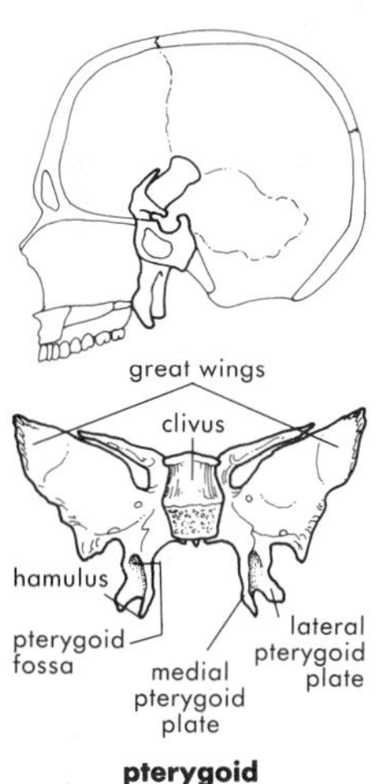

pterygoid

pter·y·la (tĕr′ə-lə) *n., pl.* **-lae** (-lē′, -lī′). An area on the skin of a bird from which feathers grow. [New Latin : Greek *pteron*, wing, feather; see -PTER + Greek *hulē*, forest, matter.]

ptg. *abbr.* Printing.

PTH *abbr.* Parathyroid hormone.

ptis·an (tĭz′ən, tĭ-zăn′) *n.* A medicinal infusion, such as sweetened barley water. [Middle English *tisane*, peeled barley, barley water, from Old French, from Latin *ptisana, tisana*, from Greek *ptisanē*, from *ptissein*, to crush.]

PTO *abbr.* **1.** Parent Teacher Organization. **2.** Power takeoff.

p.t.o. or **PTO** *abbr.* Please turn over.

Ptol·e·ma·ic (tŏl′ə-mā′ĭk) *adj.* **1.** Of or relating to the astronomer Ptolemy. **2.** Of or relating to the Ptolemies or to Egypt during their rule.

Ptolemaic system *n.* The astronomical system of Ptolemy, in which Earth is at the center of the universe with the sun, moon, planets, and stars revolving about it in circular orbits.

Ptol·e·ma·ist (tŏl′ə-mā′ĭst) *n.* An adherent of or a believer in the Ptolemaic system.

Ptol·e·my[1] (tŏl′ə-mē). An Egyptian dynasty of Macedonian kings (323–30 B.C.). The Ptolemies included **Ptolemy I** (367?–283?), a general in Alexander the Great's army who succeeded him as ruler of Egypt (323–285), and **Ptolemy XV** (47–30), who ruled as coregent (44–30) with his mother, Cleopatra.

Ptol·e·my[2] (tŏl′ə-mē). fl. second century A.D. Alexandrian astronomer, mathematician, and geographer who based his astronomy on the belief that all heavenly bodies revolve around the earth.

pto·maine (tō′mān′, tō-mān′) *n.* A basic nitrogenous organic compound produced by bacterial putrefaction of protein. [Italian *ptomaina*, from Greek *ptōma*, corpse, from *piptein*, to fall. See **pet-** in Appendix.]

ptomaine poi·son·ing (poi′zə-nĭng) *n.* Food poisoning, erroneously believed to be the result of ptomaine ingestion. Not in scientific use.

pto·sis (tō′sĭs) *n., pl.* **-ses** (-sēz). Abnormal lowering or drooping of an organ or a part, especially a drooping of the upper eyelid caused by muscle weakness or paralysis. [Greek *ptōsis*, fall, from *piptein*, to fall. See **pet-** in Appendix.] **—pto′tic** (-tĭk) *adj.*

PTSD *abbr.* Posttraumatic stress disorder.

PTV *abbr.* **1.** Pay television. **2.** Public television.

pty. *abbr.* Proprietary.

pty·a·lin (tī′ə-lĭn) *n.* A form of amylase in the saliva of human beings and some animals that catalyzes the hydrolysis of starch into maltose and dextrin. [Greek *ptualon*, saliva (from *ptuein*, to spit) + -IN.]

pty·a·lism (tī′ə-lĭz′əm) *n.* Excessive flow of saliva. [Greek *ptualismos*, salivation, from *ptualizein*, to salivate, from *ptualon*, saliva, from *ptuein*, to spit.]

Pu The symbol for the element **plutonium.**

pub (pŭb) *n.* A place of business where alcoholic beverages are sold and drunk. [Short for PUBLIC HOUSE.]

pub. *abbr.* **1.** Public. **2.** Publication. **3.** Published. **4.** Publisher.

pub-crawl (pŭb′krôl′) *intr.v.* **-crawled, -crawl·ing, -crawls.** *Slang.* To visit a series of bars.

pu·ber·ty (pyo͞o′bər-tē) *n.* **1.** The stage of adolescence in which an individual becomes physiologically capable of sexual reproduction. **2.** The approach to maturity: *"Mankind will not reach puberty for another hundred thousand years"* (René Dubos). [Middle English *puberte*, from Old French, from Latin *pūbertās*, from *pūbēs, pūber-*, adult.] **—pu′ber·tal, pu′ber·al** (-bər-əl) *adj.*

pu·ber·u·lent (pyo͞o-bĕr′yə-lənt, -bĕr′ə-) also **pu·ber·u·lous** (-bĕr′yə-ləs, -bĕr′ə-) *adj.* Covered with minute hairs or very fine down; finely pubescent. [Latin *pūber*, downy, adult + *-ulentus*, abounding in.]

pu·bes (pyo͞o′bēz) *n., pl.* **pubes. 1.** The lower part of the abdomen, especially the region surrounding the external genitalia.

Ptolemaic system

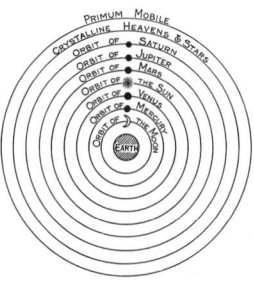

2. The hair that appears on this region at puberty. **3.** Plural of **pubis.** [Latin *pūbēs.*]

pu·bes·cence (pyo͞o-bĕs′əns) *n.* **1.** The state of being pubescent. **2.** The attainment or onset of puberty. **3.** A covering of soft down or short hairs, as on certain plants and insects.

pu·bes·cent (pyo͞o-bĕs′ənt) *adj.* **1.** Reaching or having reached puberty. **2.** Covered with short hairs or soft down. [Latin *pūbēscēns, pūbēscent-,* present participle of *pūbēscere,* to reach puberty, from *pūbēs,* adult.]

pu·bic (pyo͞o′bĭk) *adj.* Of, relating to, or located in the region of the pubis or the pubes. [From PUBES and PUBIS.]

pu·bis (pyo͞o′bĭs) *n., pl.* **-bes** (-bēz). The forward portion of either of the hipbones, at the juncture forming the front arch of the pelvis. Also called *pubic bone.* [Short for New Latin *(os) pūbis,* (bone) of the groin, from Latin, genitive of *pūbēs,* groin.]

publ. *abbr.* **1.** Publication. **2.** Published. **3.** Publisher.

pub·lic (pŭb′lĭk) *adj. Abbr.* **pub. 1.** Of, concerning, or affecting the community or the people: *the public good.* **2.** Maintained for or used by the people or community: *a public park.* **3.** Capitalized in shares of stock that can be traded on the open market: *a public company.* **4.** Participated in or attended by the people or community: *"Opinions are formed in a process of open discussion and public debate"* (Hannah Arendt). **5.** Connected with or acting on behalf of the people, community, or government: *public office.* **6.** Open to the knowledge or judgment of all: *a public scandal.* **—public** *n. Abbr.* **pub. 1.** The community or the people as a whole. **2.** A group of people sharing a common interest: *the reading public.* **3.** Admirers or followers, especially of a famous person. See Usage Note at **collective noun.** ***—idioms.*** **go public.** To become publicly owned, by launching shares of stock onto the open market: *The company went public after having been closely held for 12 years.* **go public with.** *Informal.* To reveal to the public a previously unknown or secret piece of information: *The president finally had to go public with the scandal.* **in public.** In such a way as to be visible to the scrutiny of the people: *"A career is born in public—talent in privacy"* (Marilyn Monroe). [Middle English *publik,* from Old French *public,* from Latin *pūblicus,* alteration (influenced by *pūbēs,* adult population; see PUBERTY) of *poplicus,* from *populus,* people, of Etruscan origin.] **—pub′lic·ness** *n.*

public access *n.* The availability of television or radio broadcast facilities, as provided by law, for use by the public for presentation of programs, as those of community interest.

pub·lic-ad·dress system (pŭb′lĭk-ə-drĕs′) *n. Abbr.* **PA** An electronic amplification apparatus installed and used for broadcasting in public areas.

public affairs *pl.n.* Issues, questions, and responses involving social, economic, governmental, military, scientific, or corporate activities that are of concern to the people at large. *—attributive.* Often used to modify another noun: *a public affairs officer for NASA; public affairs staff.*

pub·li·can (pŭb′lĭ-kən) *n.* **1.** *Chiefly British.* The keeper of a public house or tavern. **2.** A collector of public taxes or tolls in the ancient Roman Empire. **3.** A collector of taxes or tribute from the public. [Middle English, tax collector, from Old French, from Latin *pūblicānus,* from *pūblicum,* public revenue, from neuter of *pūblicus,* public. See PUBLIC.]

public assistance *n.* Aid, such as money or food, given to homeless and other financially needy people, the aged, or the inhabitants of a disaster-stricken area; relief.

pub·li·ca·tion (pŭb′lĭ-kā′shən) *n. Abbr.* **pub., publ. 1.** The act or process of publishing printed matter. **2.** An issue of printed material offered for sale or distribution. **3.** Communication of information to the public. [Middle English *publicacioun,* act of making public, from Old French *publicacion,* from Latin *pūblicātiō, pūblicātiōn-,* from *pūblicātus,* past participle of *pūblicāre,* to make public, from *pūblicus,* public. See PUBLIC.]

public defender *n. Law.* An attorney or a staff of attorneys, usually publicly appointed, having responsibility for the defense of those unable to afford or obtain legal assistance.

public domain *n. Law.* **1.** Land owned and controlled by the state or federal government. **2.** The status of publications, products, and processes that are not protected under patent or copyright.

public eye *n.* Public attention and scrutiny.

public figure *n.* A famous person, such as a politician or performer, whose life and behavior are the focus of intense public interest and scrutiny.

public health *n. Abbr.* **PH, P.H.** The science and practice of protecting and improving the health of a community, as by preventive medicine, health education, control of communicable diseases, application of sanitary measures, and monitoring of environmental hazards.

public house *n. Chiefly British.* A place, such as a tavern or bar, that is licensed to sell alcoholic beverages.

public housing *n.* Housing that is built, operated, and owned by a government and that is typically provided at nominal rent to the needy.

public interest *n.* **1.** The well-being of the general public; the commonweal. **2.** The attention of the people with respect to events or occurrences.

pub·li·cist (pŭb′lĭ-sĭst) *n.* One who publicizes, especially a press or publicity agent.

pub·lic·i·ty (pŭ-blĭs′ĭ-tē) *n.* **1.a.** Information that concerns a person, a group, an event, or a product and that is disseminated through various media to attract public notice. **b.** Public interest, notice, or notoriety achieved by the spreading of such information. **c.** The act, process, or occupation of disseminating information to gain public interest. **2.** The quality or condition of being public. *—attributive.* Often used to modify another noun: *publicity programs; a publicity department.* [French *publicité,* from *public,* public, from Old French. See PUBLIC.]

pub·li·cize (pŭb′lĭ-sīz′) *tr.v.* **-cized, -ciz·ing, -ciz·es.** To give publicity to.

public law *n.* **1.** The branch of law that deals with the state or government and its relationships with individuals or other governments. **2.** A law affecting the public.

public library *n.* A noncommercial library often supported with public funds, intended for use by the general public.

public life *n.* Public service or a term of public service by an appointed or elected official.

pub·lic·ly (pŭb′lĭk-lē) *adv.* **1.** In a public manner; openly. **2.** By or with consent of the public.

public offering *n.* The sale of a new securities issue to the public by way of an underwriter, a transaction that must be registered with the Securities and Exchange Commission.

public opinion *n.* Public consensus, as with respect to an issue or a situation. **—pub′lic-o·pin′ion** (pŭb′lĭk-ə-pĭn′yən) *adj.*

public policy *n.* The basic policy or set of policies forming the foundation of public laws, especially such policy not yet formally enunciated.

public prosecutor *n. Law.* A government official who prosecutes criminal actions on behalf of the state or community.

public relations *pl.n. Abbr.* **PR, p.r., P.R. 1.** *(used with a sing. verb).* The art or science of establishing and promoting a favorable relationship with the public. **2.** *(used with a pl. verb).* The methods and activities employed to establish and promote a favorable relationship with the public. **3.** *(used with a sing. or pl. verb).* The degree of success obtained in achieving a favorable relationship with the public.

public sale *n.* An auction of property or merchandise.

public school *n.* **1.** *Abbr.* **P.S.** An elementary or secondary school in the United States supported by public funds and providing free education for children of a community or district. **2.** A private boarding school in Great Britain for pupils between the ages of 13 and 18.

public servant *n.* A person who holds a government position by election or appointment.

public service *n.* **1.** Employment within a governmental system, especially within the civil service. **2.** A service performed for the benefit of the public, especially by a nonprofit organization. **3.** The business of supplying an essential commodity, such as water or electricity, or a service, such as communications or transportation, to the public. **—pub′lic-serv′ice** (pŭb′lĭk-sûr′vĭs) *adj.*

public-service corporation *n.* A corporation providing essential services, such as water or electricity, to the public.

public speaking *n.* The act, art, or process of making effective speeches before an audience. **—public speaker** *n.*

pub·lic-spir·it·ed (pŭb′lĭk-spĭr′ĭ-tĭd) *adj.* Motivated by or exhibiting devotion to the public welfare. **—pub′lic-spir′it·ed·ness** *n.*

public television *n. Abbr.* **PTV** Noncommercial television that provides programs, especially of an educational nature, for the public. Also called *educational television.*

public utility *n.* **1.** A private business organization, subject to governmental regulation, that provides an essential commodity or service, such as water, electricity, transportation, or communication, to the public. **2.** Often **public utilities.** Stock shares issued by a company providing essential public services.

public works *pl.n.* Construction projects, such as highways or dams, financed by public funds and constructed by a government for the benefit or use of the general public.

pub·lish (pŭb′lĭsh) *v.* **-lished, -lish·ing, -lish·es.** *—tr.* **1.** To prepare and issue (printed material) for public distribution or sale. **2.** To bring to the public attention; announce. See Synonyms at **announce.** *—intr.* **1.** To issue a publication. **2.** To be the writer or author of published works or a work. [Middle English *publicen, publishen,* to make known publicly, from Old French *publier,* from Latin *pūblicāre.* See PUBLICATION.] **—pub′lish·a·ble** *adj.*

pub·lish·er (pŭb′lĭ-shər) *n. Abbr.* **pub., publ.** One that is engaged in publishing printed material.

Puc·ci·ni (po͞o-chē′nē), **Giacomo.** 1858–1924. Italian operatic composer whose works include *La Bohème* (1896) and *Madame Butterfly* (1904).

puc·coon (pə-ko͞on′) *n.* **1.a.** Any of several North American plants of the genus *Lithospermum,* having orange or yellow flowers and roots that yield a red dye. **b.** Any of several plants, such as the bloodroot, whose roots yield a reddish dye. Also called *gromwell.* **2.** The dye from any of these plants. [Of Virginia Algonquian origin.]

puce (pyo͞os) *n. Color.* A deep red to dark grayish purple. [French *(couleur) puce,* flea (color), puce, from Old French, variant of *pulce,* flea, from Latin *pūlex, pūlic-.*] **—puce** *adj.*

ă pat	oi boy
ā pay	ou out
âr care	ŏŏ took
ä father	o͞o boot
ĕ pet	ŭ cut
ē be	ûr urge
ĭ pit	th thin
ī pie	*th* this
îr pier	hw which
ŏ pot	zh vision
ō toe	ə about, item
ô paw	♦ regionalism

Stress marks: ′ (primary); ′ (secondary), as in **dictionary** (dĭk′shə-nĕr′ē)

puck (pŭk) *n.* *Sports.* A hard rubber disk used in ice hockey as the playing and scoring medium. [Perhaps from dialectal *puck,* to strike.]

Puck (pŭk) *n.* A mischievous sprite in English folklore. [Middle English *pouke,* goblin, from Old English *pūca.*]

puck·a (pŭk′ə) *adj.* Variant of **pukka.**

puck·er (pŭk′ər) *v.* **-ered, -er·ing, -ers.** —*tr.* To gather into small wrinkles or folds. —*intr.* To become gathered, contracted, and wrinkled. —**pucker** *n.* A wrinkle or wrinkled part, as in tightly stitched cloth. [Probably frequentative of dialectal *pock,* bag, sack, variant of POKE[3].]

puck·ish (pŭk′ĭsh) *adj.* Mischievous; impish: *a puckish grin; puckish wit.* —**puck′ish·ly** *adv.* —**puck′ish·ness** *n.*

pud·ding (po͝od′ĭng) *n.* **1.a.** A sweet dessert, usually containing flour or a cereal product, that has been boiled, steamed, or baked. **b.** A mixture with a soft, puddinglike consistency. **2.** A sausagelike preparation made with minced meat or various other ingredients stuffed into a bag or skin and boiled. [Middle English, a kind of sausage, from Old French *boudin.*]

pud·ding·stone (po͝od′ĭng-stōn′) *n.* *Geology.* A conglomerate.

pud·dle (pŭd′l) *n.* **1.a.** A small pool of water, especially rainwater. **b.** A small pool of a liquid. **2.** A tempered paste of wet clay and sand that serves as waterproofing when dry. —**puddle** *v.* **-dled, -dling, -dles.** —*tr.* **1.** To make muddy. **2.** To work (clay or sand) into a thick, watertight paste. **3.** To process (impure metal) by puddling. —*intr.* To splash or dabble in or as if in a pool of liquid. [Middle English *podel,* diminutive of Old English *pudd,* ditch.] —**pud′dly** *adj.*

pud·dler (pŭd′lər) *n.* One that puddles iron or clay.

pud·dling (pŭd′lĭng) *n.* **1.** Purification of impure metal, especially pig iron, by heating and stirring in an oxidizing atmosphere. **2.** Compaction of wet material, such as clay, in order to make a watertight paste.

pu·den·cy (pyo͞od′n-sē) *n.* Modesty. [Late Latin *pudentia,* from Latin *pudēre,* to make or be ashamed.]

pu·den·dum (pyo͞o-dĕn′dəm) *n., pl.* **-da** (-də). The human external genitalia, especially of a woman. Often used in the plural. [Latin, neuter gerundive of *pudēre,* to make or be ashamed.] —**pu·den′dal** (-dĕn′dəl) *adj.*

pudg·y (pŭj′ē) *adj.* **-i·er, -i·est.** Short and fat; chubby: *pudgy fingers.* See Synonyms at **fat.** [From *pudge,* something thick and short.] —**pudg′i·ness** *n.*

Pueb·la (pwĕb′lä). A city of east-central Mexico east-southeast of Mexico City. Founded by the Spanish in 1532, it is an agricultural, commercial, and manufacturing center and a popular resort. Population, 835,759.

pueb·lo (pwĕb′lō) *n., pl.* **-los. 1. Pueblo** *pl.* **Pueblo** or **-los a.** Any of some 25 Native American peoples, including the Hopi, Zuñi, and Taos, living in established villages in northern and western New Mexico and northeast Arizona. The Pueblo are descendants of the cliff-dwelling Anasazi peoples and are noted for their skilled craft in pottery, basketry, weaving, and metalworking. **b.** A member of any of these peoples. **2.** A permanent village or community of any of the Pueblo peoples, typically consisting of multilevel adobe or stone apartment dwellings of terraced design clustered around a central plaza. [Spanish, people, pueblo, from Latin *populus,* people. See PUBLIC.]

WORD HISTORY: The identity of the Pueblo peoples is undeniably connected to the stone and adobe dwellings they have occupied for more than 700 years—especially from an etymological point of view. Originally coming from the Latin word *populus,* "people, nation," the Spanish word *pueblo,* meaning "town, village," as well as "nation, people," was naturally applied by 16th-century Spanish explorers to villages that they discovered or founded in the Southwest. The English word *pueblo* is first recorded in an American text in this sense in 1808, marking it as an Americanism. The distinctive adobe or stone villages of the Pueblo peoples, with some buildings rising as high as five stories, must have impressed the Spaniards considerably, because *pueblo* came to be transferred from a name for the village to a name for its inhabitants, perhaps in honor of their architectural achievements or simply as an obvious way to distinguish the Pueblo from other Native American peoples. The first recorded usage of this sense is found in 1834.

Pueblo. A city of southeast-central Colorado south-southeast of Colorado Springs. It is a shipping and industrial center for an irrigated agricultural region. Population, 101,686.

pu·er·ile (pyo͞o′ər-əl, pyo͝or′əl, -īl′) *adj.* **1.** Belonging to childhood; juvenile. **2.** Immature; childish. See Synonyms at **young.** [Latin *puerīlis,* from *puer,* child, boy. See **pau-** in Appendix.] —**pu′er·ile·ly** *adv.* —**pu′er·il′i·ty** (-ĭl′ĭ-tē), **pu′er·ile·ness** (-əl-nĭs, -īl-) *n.*

pu·er·il·ism (pyo͞o′ər-ə-lĭz′əm, pyo͝or′ə-) *n.* Childish behavior in an adult, especially as a symptom of mental illness.

pu·er·per·al (pyo͞o-ûr′pər-əl) *adj.* Relating to, connected with, or occurring during childbirth or the period immediately following childbirth. [From Latin *puerper,* a woman in childbed : *puer,* child, boy; see **pau-** in Appendix + *parere,* to bear; see -PAROUS.]

puerperal fever *n.* An illness resulting from infection of the endometrium following childbirth or abortion, marked by fever and septicemia and usually caused by unsterile technique. Also called *childbed fever.*

pu·er·pe·ri·um (pyo͞o′ər-pîr′ē-əm) *n., pl.* **-pe·ri·a** (-pîr′ē-ə). **1.** The state of a woman during childbirth or immediately thereafter. **2.** The approximate six-week period lasting from childbirth to the return of normal uterine size. [Latin, childbirth, from *puerpera,* a woman in childbed. See PUERPERAL.]

Puer·to Ca·bel·lo (pwĕr′tō kä-bā′ō, -vĕ′yō). A city of northern Venezuela on the Caribbean Sea west of Caracas. Population, 94,000.

Puer·to Ri·co (pwĕr′tə rē′kō, pôrt′ə, pōrt′ə, pwĕr′tō). *Abbr.* **PR, P.R.** A self-governing island commonwealth of the United States in the Caribbean Sea east of Hispaniola. Discovered by Columbus in 1493, it was colonized by the Spanish in the 16th century and ceded to the United States in 1898 after the Spanish-American War. Commonwealth status was proclaimed in 1952 and has been upheld by various plebiscites since the 1960's. San Juan is the capital and the largest city. Population, 3,196,520. —**Puer′to Ri′can** *adj. & n.*

Puer·to Val·lar·ta (pwĕr′tō vä-yär′tə, -tä, pwĕr′tô). A city of west-central Mexico on the Pacific Ocean west of Guadalajara. It is a popular coastal resort. Population, 38,645.

puff (pŭf) *n.* **1.a.** A short, forceful exhalation of breath. **b.** A short, sudden gust of wind. **c.** A brief, sudden emission of air, vapor, or smoke. **d.** A short, sibilant sound produced by a puff. **2.** An amount of vapor, smoke, or similar material released in a puff. **3.** An act of drawing in and expelling the breath, as in smoking tobacco. **4.** A swelling or rounded protuberance. **5.** Puff pastry. **6.** A light, soft pad for applying powder or lotion. **7.** A gathered, protruding portion of fabric. **8.** A light, padded bed covering. **9.a.** An approving or flattering recommendation. **b.** A piece of writing, as on the jacket of a book, containing often exaggerated praise, used for promotional purposes. **10.** *Genetics.* A localized region of swelling in certain chromosomes indicating the active synthesis of DNA and RNA. —**puff** *v.* **puffed, puff·ing, puffs.** —*intr.* **1.** To blow in puffs. **2.** To come forth in puffs: *steam puffing from an engine.* **3.** To breathe forcefully and rapidly: *huffed and puffed up the stairs.* **4.** To emit puffs. **5.** To take puffs on smoking material: *puffing on a cigar.* **6.** To swell or seem to swell, as with pride or air. Often used with *up: He puffed up and glared at the importuning questioner.* —*tr.* **1.** To emit or give forth in puffs. **2.** To impel with puffs. **3.** To smoke (a cigar, for example). **4.** To inflate or distend. **5.** To fill with pride or conceit. **6.** To publicize with often exaggerated praise: *publishers who puff their new books.* [From Middle English *puffen,* to puff, from Old English *pyffan,* perhaps of imitative origin.] —**puff′i·ly** *adv.* —**puff′i·ness** *n.* —**puff′y** *adj.*

puff adder *n.* **1.** A venomous African viper *(Bitis arietans)* having crescent-shaped yellowish markings. **2.** See **hognose snake.** [So called because it inflates its body when excited.]

puff·ball (pŭf′bôl′) *n.* **1.** Any of various fungi of the genus *Lycoperdon* and related genera, having a ball-shaped fruiting body that when pressed or struck releases the enclosed spores in puffs of dust. **2.** *Informal.* The rounded head of a dandelion that has gone to seed.

puffed-up (pŭft′ŭp′) *adj.* Displaying exaggerated dignity or self-importance; pompous.

puff·er (pŭf′ər) *n.* Any of various prickly, often poisonous, chiefly marine fishes of the family Tetraodontidae that are capable of puffing up by swallowing water or air. Also called *blowfish, swellfish.*

puff·er·y (pŭf′ə-rē) *n.* Flattering, often exaggerated praise and publicity, especially when used for promotional purposes.

puf·fin (pŭf′ĭn) *n.* Any of several sea birds of the genera *Fratercula* and *Lunda* of northern regions, characteristically having black and white plumage and a vertically flattened, triangular bill that is brightly colored during breeding season. [Middle English *poffoun, puffon,* perhaps from *puf,* puff. See PUFF.]

puff pastry *n.* A light, flaky, inflated pastry that is formed by rolling and folding the dough in layers so that it expands when baked.

pug[1] (pŭg) *n.* **1.** A small sturdy dog of an ancient breed originating in China, having a snub nose, a wrinkled face, a squarish body, short smooth hair, and a curled tail. **2.** A pug nose. [Origin unknown.]

pug[2] (pŭg) *n.* **1.** Clay ground and kneaded with water into a plastic consistency for forming bricks or pottery. **2.** A machine for grinding and mixing clay. —**pug** *tr.v.* **pugged, pug·ging, pugs. 1.** To work or knead (clay) with water. **2.** To fill in with clay or mortar. **3.** To make soundproof by covering or packing with clay, mortar, sawdust, or felt. [Origin unknown.]

pug[3] (pŭg) *n.* A footprint, track, or trail, especially of an animal; a pugmark. [Hindi *pag,* probably from Sanskrit *padakam,* footstep, foot, from *padam.* See **ped-** in Appendix.]

pug[4] (pŭg) *n.* *Slang.* A fighter, especially a boxer. [Short for PUGILIST, boxer, from Latin *pugil.* See PUGILISM.]

Pu·get Sound (pyo͞o′jĭt). A deep inlet of the Pacific Ocean in western Washington extending south from the Strait of Juan de Fuca through Admiralty Inlet. It was explored and named by Capt. George Vancouver for his aide, Peter Puget, in 1792.

pug·gree (pŭg′rē) also **pug·ga·ree** or **pug·a·ree** (pŭg′ə-rē) *n.* A cloth band or scarf wrapped around the crown of a hat

pueblo
Taos, New Mexico

puffball
Gem puffball
Lycoperdon perlatum

puffin
Horned puffin
Fratercula corniculata

pug[1]

Joseph Pulitzer

or sun helmet. [Hindi *pagrī,* turban, from Sanskrit *parikara,* girdle for a garment.]

pu·gi·lism (pyo͞o′jə-lĭz′əm) *n. Sports.* The skill, practice, and sport of fighting with the fists; boxing. [From Latin *pugil,* pugilist. See **peuk-** in Appendix.] **—pu′gi·list** *n.* **—pu′gi·lis′tic** *adj.*

pu·gil stick (pyo͞o′jəl) *n.* A long pole with padded ends used in the armed forces to simulate bayonet fighting. [Latin *pugil,* pugilist; see **peuk-** in Appendix + STICK.]

Pu·glia (po͞o′lyä). See **Apulia.**

pug·mark (pŭg′märk′) *n.* The mark, print, track, or trail of an animal; a pug.

pug·na·cious (pŭg-nā′shəs) *adj.* Combative in nature; belligerent. See Synonyms at **belligerent.** [From Latin *pugnāx, pugnāc-,* from *pugnāre,* to fight, from *pugnus,* fist. See **peuk-** in Appendix.] **—pug·na′cious·ly** *adv.* **—pug·na′cious·ness, pug·nac′i·ty** (-năs′ĭ-tē) *n.*

pug nose *n.* A short nose that is somewhat flattened and turned up at the end. [From PUG[1], ape (obsolete), pug.] **—pug′-nosed′** (pŭg′nōzd′) *adj.*

puis·ne (pyo͞o′nē) *Chiefly British. adj.* Lower in rank; junior. **—puisne** *n.* One of lesser rank than another, especially an associate judge. [Old French *puisne* : *puis,* afterward (ultimately from Latin *post;* see **apo-** in Appendix) + *ne,* born (from Latin *nātus,* past participle of *nāscī,* to be born; see **gene-** in Appendix).]

puis·sance (pwĭs′əns, pyo͞o′ĭ-səns, pyo͞o-ĭs′əns) *n.* Power; might. [Middle English, from Old French, from *poissant,* powerful, present participle of *pooir,* to be able. See POWER.] **—puis′sant** *adj.* **—puis′sant·ly** *adv.*

puke (pyo͞ok) *Slang. intr. & tr.v.* **puked, puk·ing, pukes.** To vomit (ingested matter) or experience vomiting. **—puke** *n.* **1.** The act of vomiting. **2.** Vomit. [Perhaps imitative.]

puk·ka also **puck·a** (pŭk′ə) *adj.* **1.** Genuine; authentic. **2.** Superior; first-class. [Hindi *pakkā,* cooked, ripe, from Sanskrit *pakva-,* from *pacati,* he cooks. See **pekʷ-** in Appendix.]

pul (po͞ol) *n., pl.* **puls** or **pu·li** (po͞o′lē). See table at **currency.** [Persian *pūl,* perhaps from Late Greek *phollis,* bellows, money bag, from Latin *follis.* See FOOL.]

pu·la (po͞o′lä) *n.* See table at **currency.**

Pu·las·ki (po͞o-lăs′kē, pə-), **Casimir** or **Kazimierz.** 1747–1779. Polish patriot and general who aided American forces in the Revolutionary War, commanding the defense of Charleston (1779) and leading a cavalry brigade in the siege of Savannah, during which he was mortally wounded.

pul·chri·tude (pŭl′krĭ-to͞od′, -tyo͞od′) *n.* Great physical beauty and appeal. [Middle English *pulcritude,* from Latin *pulchritūdō,* from *pulcher, pulchr-,* beautiful.]

pul·chri·tu·di·nous (pŭl′krĭ-to͞od′n-əs, -tyo͞od′-) *adj.* Characterized by or having great physical beauty and appeal.

pule (pyo͞ol) *intr.v.* **puled, pul·ing, pules.** To whine; whimper. [Perhaps from French *piauler,* of imitative origin.] **—pul′er** *n.*

pu·li[1] (po͞ol′ē, pyo͞o′lē) *n., pl.* **pu·lis** or **pu·lik** (po͞ol′ēk, pyo͞o′lēk). A long-haired sheepdog of a Hungarian breed. [Hungarian.]

pu·li[2] (po͞o′lē) *n.* A plural of **pul.**

pu·lik (po͞ol′ēk, pyo͞o′lēk) *n.* A plural of **puli[1].**

Pu·lit·zer (po͝ol′ĭt-sər, pyo͞o′lĭt-), **Joseph.** 1847–1911. Hungarian-born American journalist and newspaper publisher who owned newspapers in St. Louis and New York City and established and endowed the Pulitzer Prizes.

Pulitzer Prize *n.* Any of several awards established by Joseph Pulitzer and conferred annually for accomplishment in various fields of American journalism, literature, and music.

pull (po͝ol) *v.* **pulled, pull·ing, pulls.** *—tr.* **1.** To apply force to so as to cause or tend to cause motion toward the source of the force. **2.** To remove from a fixed position; extract: *The dentist pulled the tooth.* **3.** To tug at; jerk or tweak. **4.** To rip or tear; rend. **5.** To stretch (taffy, for example) repeatedly. **6.** To strain (a muscle, for example) injuriously. **7.** *Informal.* To attract; draw: *a performer who pulls large crowds.* **8.** *Slang.* To draw out (a weapon) in readiness for use: *pull a gun; pulled a knife on me.* **9.** *Informal.* To remove: *pulled the engine; pulled the tainted meat product from the stores.* **10.** *Baseball.* To hit (a ball) in the direction one is facing when the swing is carried through. **11.** *Nautical.* **a.** To operate (an oar) in rowing. **b.** To transport or propel by rowing. **c.** To be rowed by: *That boat pulls six oars.* **12.** To rein in (a horse) to keep it from winning a race. **13.** *Printing.* To produce (a print or an impression) from type. *—intr.* **1.** To exert force in moving something toward that force. **2.** To drink or inhale deeply: *pulled on the cold beer with gusto; pull on a cigarette.* **3.** *Nautical.* To row a boat. **4.** *Informal.* To express or feel great sympathy or empathy: *We're pulling for our new President.* **—pull** *n.* **1.** The act or process of pulling. **2.** Force exerted in pulling or required to overcome resistance in pulling. **3.** A sustained effort: *a long pull across the mountains.* **4.** Something, such as a knob on a drawer, that is used for pulling. **5.** A deep inhalation or draft, as on a cigarette or of a beverage. **6.** *Slang.* A means of gaining special advantage; influence: *The lobbyist has pull with the senator.* **7.** *Informal.* Ability to draw or attract; appeal: *a star with pull at the box office.* ***—phrasal verbs.*** **pull away. 1.** To move away or backward; withdraw: *The limousine pulled away from the curb.* **2.** To move ahead: *The horse pulled away and took the lead in the race.* **pull back.** To execute an orderly withdrawal, especially of troops. **pull down. 1.** To demolish; destroy: *pull down an old office building.* **2.** To reduce to a lower level. **3.** To depress, as in spirits or health. **4.** *Informal.* To draw (money) as wages: *pulls down a hefty salary.* **pull in. 1.** To arrive at a destination: *We pulled in at midnight.* **2.** To rein in; restrain. **3.** To arrest (a criminal suspect, for example). **pull off.** *Informal.* To perform in spite of difficulties or obstacles; bring off: *pulled off a last-minute victory.* **pull out. 1.** To leave or depart: *The train pulls out at noon.* **2.** To withdraw, as from a situation or commitment: *After the crash, many Wall Street investors pulled out.* **pull over. 1.** To bring a vehicle to a stop at a curb or at the side of a road: *We pulled over to watch the sunset.* **2.** To instruct or force (a motorist) to bring his or her vehicle to a stop at a curb or at the side of a road: *The state trooper pulled the speeding motorist over.* **pull round.** To restore or be restored to sound health. **pull through.** To come or bring successfully through trouble or illness. **pull up. 1.** To bring or come to a halt. **2.** To move to a position or place ahead, as in a race. ***—idioms.*** **pull a fast one.** *Informal.* To play a trick or perpetrate a fraud. **pull (oneself) together.** To regain one's composure. **pull (one's) punch** (or **punches).** To refrain from deploying all the resources or force at one's disposal: *didn't pull any punches during the negotiations.* **pull (one's) weight.** To do one's own share, as of work. **pull out all the stops.** *Informal.* To deploy all the resources or force at one's disposal: *The Inaugural Committee pulled out all the stops when arranging the ceremonies.* **pull (someone's) leg.** To play a joke on; tease. **pull strings** (or **wires).** *Informal.* To exert secret control or influence in order to gain an end. **pull the plug on.** *Slang.* To remove all restraints on: *"The federal government pulled the plug on deficit spending"* (Christian Science Monitor). **pull the rug (out) from under.** *Informal.* To remove all support and assistance from, usually suddenly. **pull the wool over (someone's) eyes.** To deceive; hoodwink. **pull together.** To make a joint effort. **pull up stakes.** To clear out; leave: *She pulled up stakes in New England and moved to the desert.* [Middle English *pullen,* from Old English *pullian.*] **—pull′er** *n.*

SYNONYMS: *pull, drag, draw, haul, tow, tug.* The central meaning shared by these verbs is "to cause something to move toward the source of an applied force": *pull a sled up a hill; drag furniture across the floor; draw up a chair; hauling wood from the forest; a car towing a trailer; tugging at the oars.*
ANTONYM: *push.*

pull·back (po͝ol′băk′) *n.* **1.** The act or process of pulling back, especially an orderly troop withdrawal. **2.** A device for holding or drawing back: *a pullback for heavy draperies.*

pull date *n.* A date stamped on a perishable item of food, such as milk, after which it should not be sold.

pul·let (po͝ol′ĭt) *n.* A young domestic hen, usually one that is less than one year old. [Middle English *pulet,* from Old French *polet,* diminutive of *poul,* cock, and *poule,* hen, both from Latin *pullus,* young animal, chicken. See **pau-** in Appendix.]

pul·ley (po͝ol′ē) *n., pl.* **-leys. 1.** A simple machine consisting essentially of a wheel with a grooved rim in which a pulled rope or chain can run to change the direction of the pull and thereby lift a load. **2.** A wheel turned by or driving a belt. [Middle English *poley,* from Old French *polie* and from Medieval Latin *poliva,* both ultimately from Greek *polos,* axis. See **kʷel-[1]** in Appendix.]

pull·man (po͝ol′mən) *adj.* Small, long, and narrow in architectural design: *a pullman hall; a pullman kitchen.* [From its resemblance to a PULLMAN[2].]

Pull·man[1] (po͝ol′mən). A city of southeast Washington south of Spokane. An agricultural trade center, it is the seat of Washington State University (founded 1890). Population, 23,579.

Pullman[2] (po͝ol′mən) *n.* **1.** A railroad parlor car or sleeping car. Also called *Pullman car.* **2.** A large suitcase. Also called *Pullman case.* [After George Mortimer *Pullman* (1831–1897), American industrialist and inventor.]

pull-on (po͝ol′ŏn′, -ôn′) *n.* A garment, such as a sweater or pair of pants, designed to be easily pulled on.

pul·lo·rum disease (pə-lôr′əm, -lōr′-) *n.* A contagious, often fatal diarrheal disease of young poultry, caused by the bacterium *Salmonella pullorum* and usually transmitted by infected hens through their eggs. [New Latin *pullōrum,* specific epithet of *Salmonella pullōrum,* from Latin, genitive plural of *pullus,* young fowl. See PULLET.]

pull·out (po͝ol′out′) *n.* **1.** A withdrawal, especially of troops. **2.** Change from a dive to level flight. Used of an aircraft. **3.** An object designed to be pulled out.

pull·o·ver (po͝ol′ō′vər) *n.* A garment, such as a sweater, that is put on by being drawn over the head.

pull-tab (po͝ol′tăb′) *n.* A metal ring that is pulled off the top of a can to provide an opening for drinking, pouring, or serving. **—pull-tab** *adj.* Configured with a tab that is pulled off to effect opening: *pull-tab cans.*

pul·lu·late (pŭl′yə-lāt′) *intr.v.* **-lat·ed, -lat·ing, -lates. 1.** To put forth sprouts or buds; germinate. **2.** To breed rapidly or abundantly. **3.** To teem; swarm: *a lagoon that pullulated with tropical fish.* [Latin *pullulāre, pullulāt-,* from *pullulus,* diminutive of *pullus,* young fowl. See PULLET.] **—pul′lu·la′tion** *n.* **—pul′lu·la′tive** *adj.*

pull-up (po͝ol′ŭp′) *n. Sports.* See **chin-up.**

pul·mo·nar·y (po͝ol′mə-nĕr′ē, pŭl′-) *adj.* **1.** Of, relating to, or affecting the lungs: *pulmonary tuberculosis.* **2.** Having lungs or lunglike organs. [Latin *pulmōnārius,* from *pulmō, pulmōn-,* lung. See **pleu-** in Appendix.]

pulmonary artery *n.* An artery that carries venous blood from the right ventricle of the heart to the lungs.

pulmonary vein *n.* A vein that carries oxygenated blood from the lungs to the left atrium of the heart.

pul·mo·nate (po͝ol′mə-nāt′, pŭl′-) *adj.* **1.** Having lungs or lunglike organs. **2.** Of or belonging to the Pulmonata, a subclass of gastropods including terrestrial snails and slugs and certain freshwater snails that are capable of breathing air through lunglike sacs. **—pulmonate** *n.* A gastropod of the subclass Pulmonata. [From Latin *pulmō, pulmōn-,* lung. See PULMONARY.]

pul·mon·ic (po͝ol-mŏn′ĭk, pŭl-) *adj.* Of or relating to the lungs; pulmonary.

pulp (pŭlp) *n.* **1.** A soft, moist, shapeless mass of matter. **2.** The soft, moist part of fruit. **3.** A mass of pressed vegetable matter: *apple pulp.* **4.** The soft pith forming the contents of the stem of a plant. **5.** A mixture of cellulose material, such as wood, paper, and rags, ground up and moistened to make paper. **6.** The soft tissue forming the inner structure of a tooth and containing nerves and blood vessels. **7.** A mixture of crushed ore and water. **8.** A publication, such as a magazine or book, containing lurid subject matter. **—pulp** *v.* **pulped, pulp·ing, pulps.** *—tr.* **1.** To reduce to pulp. See Synonyms at **crush. 2.** To remove the pulp from. *—intr.* To be reduced to a pulpy consistency. [Middle English, from Latin *pulpa,* fleshy parts of the body, fruit pulp.] **—pulp′i·ness** *n.* **—pulp′ous** (pŭl′pəs), **pulp′y** *adj.*

pul·pit (po͝ol′pĭt, pŭl′-) *n.* **1.** An elevated platform, lectern, or stand used in preaching or conducting a religious service. **2.a.** Clerics considered as a group. **b.** The ministry of preaching. **3.** An elevated platform, such as one used by harpooners in a whaling boat. [Middle English, from Old French, from Late Latin *pulpitum,* from Latin *pulpitum,* wooden platform.]

pulp·wood (pŭlp′wo͝od′) *n.* Soft wood, such as spruce, aspen, or pine, used in making paper.

pul·que (po͞ol′kā′, -kē, po͞ol′-) *n.* A thick, fermented alcoholic beverage made in Mexico from various species of agave. [American Spanish, from Nahuatl *poliuhqui,* decomposed, lost.]

pul·sar (pŭl′sär′) *n. Astronomy.* Any of several celestial radio sources emitting short, intense bursts of radio waves, x-rays, or visible electromagnetic radiation at regular intervals, generally believed to be rotating neutron stars. [*puls(ating st)ar.*]

pul·sate (pŭl′sāt′) *intr.v.* **-sat·ed, -sat·ing, -sates. 1.** To expand and contract rhythmically; beat. **2.** To quiver; vibrate. [Latin *pulsāre, pulsāt-,* frequentative of *pellere,* to beat. See **pel-**[5] in Appendix.]

SYNONYMS: *pulsate, pulse, beat, palpitate, throb.* These verbs mean to exhibit recurrent rhythmical movements of or like those involved in the periodic expansion and contraction of the heart. *Pulsate, pulse,* and *beat* imply regular, vigorous movement: *The emergency room pulsated with activity. Waves of excitement pulsed through us as the race began. The patient's heart continued to beat strongly.* To *palpitate* is to pulsate with excessive rapidity and often arrhythmically, as a malfunctioning heart might; the term may also denote a trembling, shaking, or quivering movement: *"fountains palpitating in the heat"* (Henry Wadsworth Longfellow). *Throb* suggests strong, sometimes violent pulsation; the word is especially associated with emotional states such as agitation, exhilaration, anxiety, or stress: *"Although her temples throbbed, she tried to analyze the letter"* (Winston Churchill). *"His lonely heart throbbed at the warm, firm grasp of this friend's hand"* (Owen Wister).

pul·sa·tile (pŭl′sə-təl, -tīl′) *adj.* Undergoing pulsation; vibrating. [Medieval Latin *pulsātilis,* from Latin *pulsātus,* past participle of *pulsāre,* frequentative of *pellere,* to beat. See PULSATE.]

pul·sa·tion (pŭl-sā′shən) *n.* **1.** The act of pulsating. **2.** A single beat, throb, or vibration.

pul·sa·tor (pŭl′sā′tər, pŭl-sā′-) *n.* A pulsating device or machine.

pul·sa·to·ry (pŭl′sə-tôr′ē, -tōr′ē) *adj.* Having rhythmical vibration or movement.

pulse[1] (pŭls) *n.* **1.** The rhythmical throbbing of arteries produced by the regular contractions of the heart, especially as palpated at the wrist or in the neck. **2.a.** A regular or rhythmical beating. **b.** A single beat or throb. **3.** *Physics.* **a.** A brief, sudden change in a normally constant quantity: *a pulse of current; a pulse of radiation.* **b.** Any of a series of intermittent occurrences characterized by a brief, sudden change in a quantity. **4.** The perceptible emotions or sentiments of a group of people: *"a man who had . . . his finger on the pulse of America"* (Thomas P. O'Neill, Jr.). **—pulse** *intr.v.* **pulsed, puls·ing, puls·es. 1.** To pulsate; beat: *"The nation pulsed with music and proclamation, with rages and moral pretensions"* (Lance Morrow). See Synonyms at **pulsate. 2.** *Physics.* To undergo a series of intermittent occurrences characterized by brief, sudden changes in a quantity. ***—idiom.*** **take the pulse of.** To judge the mood or views of (a political electorate, for example): *The politician was able to take the pulse of the grassroots voters without becoming overly absorbed.* [Middle English, from Old French, from Latin *pulsus,* from past participle of *pellere,* to beat. See **pel-**[5] in Appendix.]

pulse[2] (pŭls) *n.* **1.** The edible seeds of certain pod-bearing plants, such as peas and beans. **2.** A plant yielding these seeds. [Middle English *pols,* from Old French, from Latin *puls,* pottage of meal and pulse, probably ultimately from Greek *poltos.*]

pulse·jet (pŭls′jĕt′) *n.* A jet engine in which air intake and combustion occur intermittently, producing rapid periodic bursts of thrusts.

pulse modulation *n.* A system of modulation in which pulses are altered and controlled in order to represent the message to be communicated.

pul·som·e·ter (pŭl-sŏm′ĭ-tər) *n.* A pump without pistons that operates by means of pulsed condensation of steam. Also called *vacuum pump.*

pul·ver·a·ble (pŭl′vər-ə-bəl) *adj.* That can be pulverized: *pulverable stone.*

pul·ver·ize (pŭl′və-rīz′) *v.* **-ized, -iz·ing, -iz·es.** *—tr.* **1.** To pound, crush, or grind to a powder or dust. **2.** To demolish. *—intr.* To be ground or reduced to powder or dust. [Middle English *pulverizen,* from Late Latin *pulverizāre,* from Latin *pulvis, pulver-,* dust.] **—pul′ver·iz′a·ble** *adj.* **—pul′ver·i·za′tion** (-vər-ĭ-zā′shən) *n.* **—pul′ver·iz′er** *n.*

pul·ver·u·lent (pŭl-vĕr′yə-lənt, -vĕr′ə-) *adj.* **1.** Made of, covered with, or crumbling to fine powder or dust. **2.** Dusty; crumbly. [Latin *pulverulentus* : from *pulvis, pulver-,* dust + *-ulentus,* abounding in.]

pul·vil·lus (pŭl-vĭl′əs) *n., pl.* **-vil·li** (-vĭl′ī′). A soft, cushionlike pad on the foot of an insect, such as the housefly, by which it clings to a surface. [Latin, short for *pulvīnulus,* diminutive of *pulvīnus,* cushion.]

pul·vi·nate (pŭl′və-nāt′) also **pul·vi·nat·ed** (-nā′tĭd) *adj.* **1.** Shaped like a cushion. **2.** *Botany.* Having a swelling at the base. Used of a leafstalk. [Latin *pulvīnātus,* from *pulvīnus,* cushion.]

pul·vi·nus (pŭl-vī′nəs, -vē′-) *n., pl.* **-ni** (-nī′). A cushionlike swelling at the base of the stalk of a leaf or leaflet. [Latin *pulvīnus,* cushion.]

pu·ma (pyo͞o′mə, po͞o′-) *n.* See **mountain lion.** [Spanish, from Quechua *puma.*]

pum·e·lo (pŭm′ə-lō′) *n., pl.* **-los.** See **shaddock.** [Variant of POMELO.]

pum·ice (pŭm′ĭs) *n.* A light, porous, glassy lava, used in solid form as an abrasive and in powdered form as a polish and an abrasive. **—pumice** *tr.v.* **-iced, -ic·ing, -ic·es.** To clean, polish, or smooth with pumice. [Middle English, from Anglo-Norman *pomis,* from Late Latin *pōmex,* from Latin *pūmex,* alteration of *spūma,* foam.] **—pu·mi′ceous** (pyo͞o-mĭsh′əs, pə-) *adj.* **—pum′ic·er** *n.*

pum·mel (pŭm′əl) *tr.v.* **-meled, -mel·ing, -mels** also **-melled, -mel·ling, -mels.** To beat, as with the fists; pommel: *The thief was pushed and pummeled by an angry crowd.* See Synonyms at **beat. —pummel** *n.* The act of beating, as with the fists. [Alteration of POMMEL.]

pump[1] (pŭmp) *n.* **1.** A machine or device for raising, compressing, or transferring fluids. **2.** *Physiology.* A molecular mechanism for the active transport of ions or molecules across a cell membrane. **3.** *Physics.* Electromagnetic radiation used to raise atoms or molecules to a higher energy level. **—pump** *v.* **pumped, pump·ing, pumps.** *—tr.* **1.** To raise or cause to flow by means of a pump. **2.** To draw, deliver, or pour forth as if with a pump: *pumped new life into the economy.* **3.** To remove the water from: *pump out a flooded basement.* **4.** To cause to move with the up-and-down motion of a pump handle: *a bicyclist pumping the pedals.* **5.** To propel, eject, or insert with or as if with a pump. **6.** *Physics.* To raise atoms or molecules to a higher energy level by exposing them to electromagnetic radiation at a resonant frequency. **7.** *Physiology.* To transport (ions or molecules) against a concentration gradient by the expenditure of chemically stored energy. **8.** To question closely or persistently: *pump a witness for secret information.* *—intr.* **1.** To operate a pump. **2.** To raise or move gas or liquid with a pump. **3.** To move up and down in the manner of a pump handle. ***—phrasal verb.*** **pump up. 1.** To inflate with gas by means of a pump: *pump up a tire.* **2.** *Slang.* To fill with enthusiasm, strength, and energy: *The lively debate really pumped us up.* **3.** *Sports.* To be actively involved in a bodybuilding program: *I saw him pumping up at the gym.* ***—idiom.*** **pump iron.** *Sports.* To lift weights. [Middle English *pumpe.*] **—pump′er** *n.*

pump[2] (pŭmp) *n.* A woman's shoe that has medium or high heels and no fastenings. [Origin unknown.]

pumped storage (pŭmpt) *n.* A system of generating electricity with hydroelectric power, in which the electricity is generated during hours of peak consumption by using water that has been pumped into an elevated reservoir during the hours of low consumption.

pum·per·nick·el (pŭm′pər-nĭk′əl) *n.* A dark, sourish bread made from whole, coarsely ground rye. [German, probably from dialectal, term of abuse : obsolete *Pumper,* breaking wind (from dialectal *pumpern,* to break wind, from Middle High German, to knock, frequentative of *pumpen,* of imitative origin) + German *Nickel,* goblin; see NICKEL.]

pump·kin (pŭmp′kĭn, pŭm′-, pŭng′-) *n.* **1.a.** A coarse, trailing vine *(Cucurbita pepo)* widely cultivated for its fruit. **b.** The

pulpit

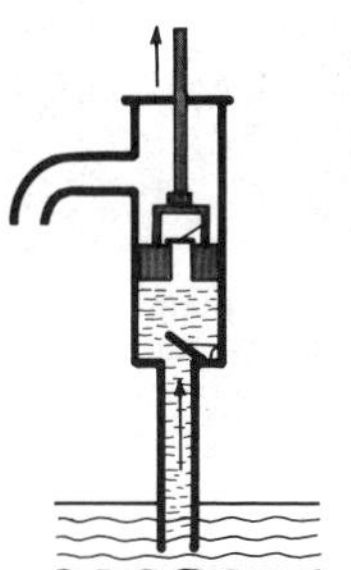

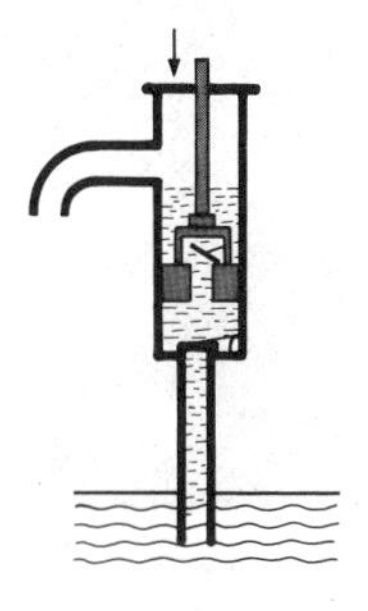

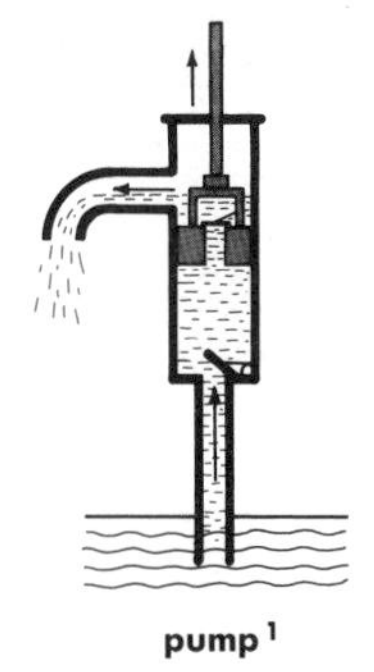

pump[1]

ă pat	oi boy
ā pay	ou out
âr care	o͝o took
ä father	o͞o boot
ĕ pet	ŭ cut
ē be	ûr urge
ĭ pit	th thin
ī pie	*th* this
îr pier	hw which
ŏ pot	zh vision
ō toe	ə about, item
ô paw	♦ regionalism

Stress marks: ′ (primary); ′ (secondary), as in **dictionary** (dĭk′shə-nĕr′ē)

large pulpy round fruit of this plant, having a thick, orange-yellow rind and numerous seeds. **c.** Any of several other vines of the genus *Cucurbita*, especially *C. maxima* or *C. moschata*, bearing large pumpkinlike squashes. **2.** *Color.* A moderate to strong orange. [Alteration (influenced by -KIN) of obsolete *pumpion*, from obsolete French *pompon, popon*, from Old French *pepon*, from Late Latin *pepōn*, from Latin, watermelon or gourd, from Greek, ripe, large melon. See **pekʷ-** in Appendix.]

pumpkinseed
Lepomis gibbosus

pump·kin·seed (pŭmp′kĭn-sēd′, pŭm′-, pŭng′-) *n.* **1.** The seed of a pumpkin. **2.** A North American sunfish *(Lepomis gibbosus)* having a rounded, mostly orange body with a bright red spot on each gill cover.

pun (pŭn) *n.* A play on words, sometimes on different senses of the same word and sometimes on the similar sense or sound of different words. **—pun** *intr.v.* **punned, pun·ning, puns.** To make puns or a pun. [Origin unknown.] **—pun′ning·ly** *adv.*

WORD HISTORY: The origin of the word *pun* is lost in obscurity, perhaps deservedly so in the eyes of those who consider the pun the feeblest form of wit. The word *pun* is first recorded in a work of 1662 written by John Dryden. In a slightly later passage of 1676 we find the word *pun* in the company of the words *pundigrion* and *punnet* with the same sense. *Punnet* is probably a diminutive of *pun*, as are the later *punlet* (used by Samuel Taylor Coleridge in 1819) and *punkin* (Henry James, 1866). But *pundigrion*, although recorded later, may have been around earlier than *pun* and might be its source. *Pundrigrion* in turn might be an alteration of the obsolete Italian word *puntiglio*, "fine point," which we have in English as *punctilio*. In any case, the word *pun* has given birth to some derivatives of its own, including *punnigram*, modeled on *epigram*, and *punnology*.

punt[1]
c. 1935 American work punt

punch[1] (pŭnch) *n.* **1.** A tool for circular or other piercing: *a leather punch.* **2.** A tool for forcing a pin, bolt, or rivet in or out of a hole. **3.** A tool for stamping a design on a surface. **4.** A tool for making a countersink. **—punch** *intr. & tr.v.* **punched, punch·ing, punch·es.** To use a punch or use a punch on. [Middle English *pounce, punche*, from Old French *poinçon, ponchon*. See PUNCHEON[1]. V., from Middle English *pouncen, punchen*, to prick, from Old French *poinçoner, ponchoner*, to emboss with a punch. See PUNCH[2].]

♦**punch**[2] (pŭnch) *tr.v.* **punched, punch·ing, punch·es. 1.** To hit with a sharp blow of the fist. **2.a.** To poke or prod with a stick. **b.** *Western U.S.* To herd (cattle). **3.** To depress (a key or button, for example) in order to activate a device or perform an operation: *punched the "repeat" key; punched in the number on the computer.* **—punch** *n.* **1.** A blow with the fist. **2.** Vigor or drive. See Synonyms at **vigor.** ***—phrasal verbs.*** **punch in.** To check in formally at a job upon arrival. **punch out. 1.** To check out formally at a job upon departure. **2.** *Slang.* To eject from a military aircraft. ***—idiom.*** **beat to the punch.** To make the first decisive move: *a marketing team that beat all the competitors to the punch.* [Middle English *punchen*, to thrust, prod, prick, from Old French *poinçonner, ponchonner*, to emboss with a punch, from *poinçon, ponchon*, pointed tool. See PUNCHEON[1].] **—punch′less** *adj.*

punty
Held in artisan's left hand

punch[3] (pŭnch) *n.* A beverage of fruit juices and sometimes carbonated water or soda, often spiced and mixed with a wine or liquor base. [Perhaps from Hindi *pañc-*, five-, from Sanskrit *pañca* (from the hypothesis that it was originally prepared from five ingredients). See **penkʷe** in Appendix.]

Punch (pŭnch) *n.* The quarrelsome hook-nosed husband of Judy in the comic puppet show *Punch and Judy.* ***—idiom.*** **pleased as Punch.** Highly pleased; gratified. [Short for PUNCHINELLO.]

punch·board (pŭnch′bord′, -bōrd′) *n. Games.* A small, usually rectangular board, used as a game of chance, that contains many holes each filled with a folded slip of paper that when punched out indicates a designated prize, win, or loss.

punch bowl *n.* A large bowl for serving a beverage, such as punch.

punch card also **punched card** (pŭncht) *n. Computer Science.* A medium for feeding data into a computer, essentially a card punched with holes or notches to represent letters and numbers or with a pattern of holes to represent related data. Also called *Hollerith card.*

punch-drunk (pŭnch′drŭngk′) *adj.* **1.** Showing signs of brain damage caused by repeated blows to the head. Used especially of a boxer. **2.** Behaving in a bewildered, confused, or dazed manner.

punched card (pŭncht) *n. Computer Science.* Variant of **punch card.**

pun·cheon[1] (pŭn′chən) *n.* **1.** A short wooden upright used in structural framing. **2.** A piece of broad, heavy, roughly dressed timber with one face finished flat. **3.** A punching, perforating, or stamping tool, especially one used by a goldsmith. [Middle English *punchon*, from Old French *ponçon, ponchon*, from Vulgar Latin *pūnctiō, pūnctiōn-, punch, from *pūnctiāre, to pierce, from Latin *pūnctus*, past participle of *pungere*, to prick. See **peuk-** in Appendix.]

pun·cheon[2] (pŭn′chən) *n.* **1.** A cask with a capacity of from 72 to 120 gallons (273 to 454 liters). **2.** The amount of liquid contained in a puncheon. [Middle English *ponchon*, from Old French *poinçon, poinchon*, punch, cask (probably because cask was inspected and marked with a punch). See PUNCHEON[1].]

punch·er (pŭn′chər) *n.* A cowpuncher.

Pun·chi·nel·lo (pŭn′chə-nĕl′ō) *n., pl.* **-los** or **-loes. 1.** The short, fat buffoon or clown in an Italian puppet show. **2.** One who is felt to resemble a short, fat clown. [Variant of *Polichinello*, from Italian dialectal *Pollecinella*, diminutive of *pollecena*, turkey pullet (from the resemblance between its beak and Punchinello's nose), ultimately from Latin *pullus*, young chicken. See PULLET.]

punch·ing bag (pŭn′chĭng) *n. Sports.* A stuffed or inflated leather bag that is usually suspended so that it can be punched with the fists for exercise.

punch line *n.* The climax of a joke or humorous story.

punch-out (pŭnch′out′) *n.* A section of material, such as cardboard, that is scored or perforated so it may easily be pushed out.

punch press *n.* A power press that can be fitted with various dies, as for metalworking.

punch tape *n. Computer Science.* A paper ribbon in which holes representing data to be processed by a computer are punched.

punch-up (pŭnch′ŭp′) *n. Chiefly British.* A fistfight.

punch·y (pŭn′chē) *adj.* **-i·er, -i·est. 1.** Characterized by vigor or drive: *"He speaks in short, punchy sentences, using plain, populist words that excite"* (Washington Post). **2.** Groggy or dazed from or as if from a punch or series of punches; punch-drunk. **—punch′i·ly** *adv.* **—punch′i·ness** *n.*

punc·tate (pŭngk′tāt′) also **punc·tat·ed** (-tā′tĭd) *adj.* Having tiny spots, points, or depressions. [From Latin *pūnctum*, prick mark, from neuter past participle of *pungere*, to prick. See PUNCTUATE.] **—punc·ta′tion** *n.*

punc·til·i·o (pŭngk-tĭl′ē-ō′) *n., pl.* **-os. 1.** A fine point of etiquette. **2.** Precise observance of formalities. [Obsolete Italian *punctiglio*, from Spanish *puntillo*, diminutive of *punto*, point, from Latin *pūnctum*, from neuter past participle of *pungere*, to prick. See PUNGENT.]

punc·til·i·ous (pŭngk-tĭl′ē-əs) *adj.* **1.** Strictly attentive to minute details of form in action or conduct. See Synonyms at **meticulous. 2.** Precise; scrupulous. **—punc·til′i·ous·ly** *adv.* **—punc·til′i·ous·ness** *n.*

punc·tu·al (pŭngk′cho͞o-əl) *adj.* **1.** Acting or arriving exactly at the time appointed; prompt. **2.** Paid or accomplished at or by the appointed time. **3.** Precise; exact. **4.** Confined to or having the nature of a point in space. [Middle English, sharp-pointed, from Medieval Latin *pūnctuālis*, from Latin *pūnctum*, point, from neuter past participle of *pungere*, to prick. See PUNGENT.] **—punc′tu·al′i·ty** (-ăl′ĭ-tē), **punc′tu·al·ness** (-əl-nĭs) *n.* **—punc′tu·al·ly** *adv.*

punc·tu·ate (pŭngk′cho͞o-āt′) *v.* **-at·ed, -at·ing, -ates.** *—tr.* **1.** To provide (a text) with punctuation marks. **2.** To interrupt periodically: *"lectures punctuated by questions and discussions"* (Gilbert Highet). "[There is] *a great emptiness in America's West punctuated by Air Force bases"* (Alfred Kazin). **3.** To stress or emphasize. *—intr.* To use punctuation. [Medieval Latin *pūnctuāre, pūnctuāt-*, from Latin *pūnctum*, point, from neuter past participle of *pungere*, to prick. See **peuk-** in Appendix.] **—punc′tu·a′tive** *adj.* **—punc′tu·a′tor** *n.*

punc·tu·a·tion (pŭngk′cho͞o-ā′shən) *n.* **1.a.** The use of standard marks and signs in writing and printing to separate words into sentences, clauses, and phrases in order to clarify meaning. **b.** The marks so used. **2.** The act or an instance of punctuating.

punctuation mark *n.* One of a set of marks or signs, such as the comma (,) or the period (.), used to punctuate texts.

punc·ture (pŭngk′chər) *v.* **-tured, -tur·ing, -tures.** *—tr.* **1.** To pierce with a pointed object. **2.** To make (a hole) by piercing. **3.** To cause to collapse by piercing. **4.** To depreciate or deflate: *cutting remarks that punctured my ego.* *—intr.* To be pierced or punctured. **—puncture** *n.* **1.** The act or an instance of puncturing. **2.** A hole or depression made by a sharp object, especially a hole in an automotive tire. [From Middle English, a pricking, from Late Latin *pūnctūra*, from *pūnctus*, past participle of *pungere*, to prick. See **peuk-** in Appendix.] **—punc′tur·a·ble** *adj.*

puncture weed *n.* A prostrate weed *(Tribulus terrestris)* native to the Old World, having opposite, pinnately compound leaves and woody fruit with stout, divergent spines. Also called *puncture vine.* [From the fact that the fruit can puncture tires.]

pun·dit (pŭn′dĭt) *n.* **1.** A source of opinion; a critic: *a political pundit.* **2.** A learned person. **3.** *Hinduism.* Variant of **pandit.** [Hindi *paṇḍit*, learned man, from Sanskrit *paṇḍitaḥ*, learned; scholar, perhaps of Dravidian origin.] **—pun′dit·ry** *n.*

♦**pung** (pŭng) *n. New England.* A low, one-horse box sleigh. [Short for dialectal *tom-pung*, from an Algonquian language of southern New England.]

pun·gent (pŭn′jənt) *adj.* **1.** Affecting the organs of taste or smell with a sharp, acrid sensation. **2.a.** Penetrating, biting, or caustic: *pungent satire.* **b.** To the point; sharp: *pungent talks during which the major issues were confronted.* **3.** Pointed: *a pungent leaf.* [Latin *pungēns, pungent-*, present participle of *pungere*, to sting. See **peuk-** in Appendix.] **—pun′gen·cy** *n.* **—pun′gent·ly** *adv.*

Pu·nic (pyo͞o′nĭk) *adj.* **1.** Of or relating to ancient Carthage, its inhabitants, or their language. **2.** Having the character of treachery attributed to the Carthaginians by the Romans. **—Punic** *n.* The dialect of Phoenician spoken in ancient Carthage. [Latin

ă pat	oi boy
ā pay	ou out
âr care	o͝o took
ä father	o͞o boot
ĕ pet	ŭ cut
ē be	ûr urge
ĭ pit	th thin
ī pie	*th* this
îr pier	hw which
ŏ pot	zh vision
ō toe	ə about, item
ô paw	♦ regionalism

Stress marks: ′ (primary); ′ (secondary), as in **dictionary** (dĭk′shə-nĕr′ē)

Poenicus, Pūnicus, from *Poenus,* a Carthaginian, from Greek *Phoinix,* Phoenician.]

pun·ish (pŭn′ĭsh) *v.* **-ished, -ish·ing, -ish·es.** —*tr.* **1.** To subject to a penalty for an offense, a sin, or a fault. **2.** To inflict a penalty for (an offense). **3.** To handle roughly; hurt: *My boots were punished by our long trek through the desert.* —*intr.* To exact or mete out punishment. [Middle English *punissen, punishen,* from Old French *punir, puniss-,* from Latin *poenīre, pūnīre,* from *poena,* punishment, from Greek *poinē.* See **kʷei-**[1] in Appendix.] **—pun′ish·a·bil′i·ty** *n.* **—pun′ish·a·ble** *adj.* **—pun′ish·er** *n.*

SYNONYMS: *punish, correct, chastise, discipline, castigate, penalize.* These verbs mean to subject a person to a penalty, such as loss, pain, or confinement, for an offense, a sin, or a fault. *Punish* is the least specific: *"The individual who refuses to defend his rights when called by his Government . . . must be punished as an enemy of his country and friend to her foe"* (Andrew Jackson). To *correct* is to punish so that the offender will mend his or her ways: *Regulations formerly permitted prison wardens to correct unruly inmates. Chastise* implies punishment, such as corporal punishment or a verbal rebuke, as a means of effecting improvement in behavior: *chastise a bully by giving him a thrashing; was roundly chastised for insolence. Discipline* stresses punishment inflicted by an authority in order to control an offender or to eliminate or reform unacceptable conduct: *The worker was disciplined for insubordination. Castigate* means to censure or criticize severely, often in public: *The judge castigated the attorney for badgering the witness. Penalize* usually implies a monetary penalty or the forfeiture of a privilege or gain because rules or regulations have been broken: *Those who file their income-tax returns after April 15 will be penalized.*

pun·ish·ment (pŭn′ĭsh-mənt) *n.* **1.a.** The act or an instance of punishing. **b.** The condition of being punished. **2.** A penalty imposed for wrongdoing: *"The severity of the punishment must . . . be in keeping with the kind of obligation which has been violated"* (Simone Weil). **3.** Rough handling; mistreatment: *These old skis have taken a lot of punishment over the years.*

pu·ni·tive (pyo͞o′nĭ-tĭv) *adj.* Inflicting or aiming to inflict punishment; punishing. [Medieval Latin *pūnītīvus,* from Latin *poenīre, pūnīre,* to punish. See PUNISH.] **—pu′ni·tive·ly** *adv.* **—pu′ni·tive·ness** *n.*

punitive damages *pl.n. Law.* Damages awarded by a court against a defendant as a deterrent or punishment to redress an egregious wrong perpetrated by the defendant.

pu·ni·to·ry (pyo͞o′nĭ-tôr′ē, -tōr′ē) *adj.* Inflicting or intended to inflict punishment. [From Latin *pūnītus,* from past participle of *pūnīre,* to punish. See PUNISH.]

Pun·jab (pŭn′jäb′, pŭn-jäb′). A historical region of northwest India and northern Pakistan bounded by the Indus and Jumna rivers. It was a center of the prehistoric Indus Valley civilization and after c. 1500 B.C. the site of early Aryan settlements. The Moguls brought the region to cultural eminence. The Punjab was controlled by Sikhs from 1799 to 1849, when it was annexed by Great Britain. It was partitioned between India and Pakistan in 1947.

Pun·ja·bi also **Pan·ja·bi** (pŭn-jä′bē, -jăb′ē) —*adj.* Of or relating to the Punjab or the Punjabi language. —*n., pl.* **-bis. 1.** A native or inhabitant of the Punjab. **2.** An Indic language spoken in the Punjab.

pun·ji stick (po͞on′jē, pŭn′-) *n.* A very sharp bamboo stake that is concealed at an angle in high grass or in deep mud, often coated with excrement, and planted to wound and infect the feet of enemy soldiers. Also called *punji stake.* [Origin unknown.]

punk (pŭngk) *n.* **1.** *Slang.* **a.** A young person, especially a member of a rebellious counterculture group. **b.** An inexperienced young man. **2.** *Music.* **a.** Punk rock. **b.** A punk rocker. **3.a.** *Slang.* A young man who is the sexual partner of an older man. **b.** *Archaic.* A prostitute. **4.** Dry, decayed wood, used as tinder. **5.** Any of various substances that smolder when ignited, used to light fireworks. **6.** Chinese incense. **—punk** *adj. Slang.* **1.** Of or relating to a style of dress worn by punk rockers and often characterized by unusual clothing, hairstyles, and makeup. **2.** Of poor quality; worthless. **3.** Weak in spirits or health. [Origin unknown.] **—punk′er** *n.*

pun·ka or **pun·kah** (pŭng′kə) *n.* A fan used especially in India, made of a palm frond or strip of cloth hung from the ceiling and moved by a servant. [Hindi *pankhā,* from Sanskrit *pakṣakaḥ,* fan, from *pakṣaḥ,* wing.]

punk·ie also **punk·y** (pŭng′kē) *n., pl.* **-ies.** Any of various minute, biting flies of the family Ceratopogonidae. Also called *biting midge, no-see-um.* [Of North American Dutch origin, from Munsee (Delaware language) *pónkwəs.*]

pun·kin (pŭng′kĭn) *n. Informal.* Variant of **pumpkin.**

punk rock *n. Music.* A form of hard-driving rock music characterized by harsh lyrics attacking conventional society and popular culture and often expressing alienation and anger.

punk rocker *n. Music.* A performer or follower of punk rock music.

punk·y (pŭng′kē) *n.* Variant of **punkie.**

pun·ster (pŭn′stər) *n.* A maker of puns.

punt[1] (pŭnt) *Nautical. n.* An open, flat-bottomed boat with squared ends, propelled by a long pole and used in shallow waters. **—punt** *v.* **punt·ed, punt·ing, punts.** —*tr.* **1.** To propel (a boat) with a pole. **2.** To carry in a punt. —*intr.* To go in a punt. [Probably Middle English **punt,* from Old English *punt,* from Latin *pontō, pontōn-,* pontoon, flat-bottomed boat, from *pōns, pont-,* bridge. See **pent-** in Appendix.] **—punt′er** *n.*

punt[2] (pŭnt) *Football. n.* A kick in which the ball is dropped from the hands and kicked before it touches the ground. **—punt** *v.* **punt·ed, punt·ing, punts.** —*tr.* To propel (a ball) by means of a punt. —*intr.* To execute a punt. [Perhaps from dialectal *punt,* to strike, push, perhaps alteration of *bunt.*] **—punt′er** *n.*

punt[3] (pŭnt) *intr.v.* **punt·ed, punt·ing, punts. 1.** *Games.* To lay a bet against the bank, as in roulette. **2.** *Chiefly British.* To gamble. [French *ponter,* from obsolete *pont,* past participle of *pondre,* to put (obsolete), to lay an egg, from Old French, to lay an egg, from Latin *pōnere.* See PROPOSE.] **—punt′er** *n.*

punt[4] (pŭnt) *n.* The indentation in the bottom of a champagne or wine bottle. [Perhaps from *punty,* iron rod used in glass blowing, probably from French *pontil,* from *pointe,* from Old French. See POINT.]

Pun·ta A·re·nas (po͞on′tə ə-rĕn′əs, po͞on′tä ä-rĕ′näs). A city of southern Chile on the Strait of Magellan. Founded in the 1840's, it is the southernmost city in the world. Population, 95,332.

pun·ty (pŭn′tē) *n., pl.* **-ties.** An iron rod on which molten glass is handled when being shaped and worked. Also called *pontil.* [Probably from French *pontil.* See PUNT[4].]

Punx·su·taw·ney (pŭngk′sə-tô′nē). A city of west-central Pennsylvania northeast of Pittsburgh. It is an industrial center noted for its annual observance of Groundhog Day, February 2, when "Punxsutawney Phil" emerges from its burrow and is carefully watched for a shadow, thus supposedly presaging six more weeks of winter weather. Population, 7,479.

♦**pu·ny** (pyo͞o′nē) *adj.* **-ni·er, -ni·est. 1.** Of inferior size, strength, or significance; weak: *a puny physique; puny excuses.* **2.** *Chiefly Southern U.S.* Sickly; ill. [Variant of PUISNE.] **—pu′ni·ly** *adv.* **—pu′ni·ness** *n.*

pup (pŭp) *n.* **1.a.** A young dog; a puppy. **b.** The young of various other canine animals, such as the wolf or fox. **c.** The young of certain other animals, such as the seal. **2.** An inexperienced or conceited young person: *a mere pup who had to be put in her place.* **—pup** *intr.v.* **pupped, pup·ping, pups.** To give birth to pups. [Short for PUPPY.]

pu·pa (pyo͞o′pə) *n., pl.* **-pae** (-pē) or **-pas.** The nonfeeding stage between the larva and adult in the metamorphosis of holometabolous insects, during which the larva typically undergoes complete transformation within a protective cocoon or hardened case. [Latin, girl, doll.] **—pu′pal** *adj.*

pu·pate (pyo͞o′pāt′) *intr.v.* **-pat·ed, -pat·ing, -pates. 1.** To become a pupa. **2.** To undergo a pupal stage. **—pu·pa′tion** *n.*

pup·fish (pŭp′fĭsh′) *n., pl.* **pupfish** or **-fish·es.** Any of various small killfishes of the genus *Cyprinodon,* inhabiting desert springs and streams of Mexico and the southwest United States.

pu·pil[1] (pyo͞o′pəl) *n.* **1.** A student under the direct supervision of a teacher or professor. **2.** *Law.* A minor under the supervision of a guardian. [Middle English *pupille,* orphan, from Old French, from Latin *pūpillus,* diminutive of *pūpus,* boy.]

pu·pil[2] (pyo͞o′pəl) *n.* The apparently black circular opening in the center of the iris of the eye, through which light passes to the retina. [Middle English, from Old French *pupille,* from Latin *pūpilla,* little doll, pupil of the eye (from the tiny image reflected in it). See PUPIL[1].] **—pu′pi·lar** *adj.*

pu·pil·age also **pu·pil·lage** (pyo͞o′pə-lĭj) *n.* The state or period of being a pupil.

pu·pil·lar·y[1] (pyo͞o′pə-lĕr′ē) *adj.* Of or relating to a student or ward.

pu·pil·lar·y[2] (pyo͞o′pə-lĕr′ē) *adj.* Of or affecting the pupil of the eye.

Pu·pin (pyo͞o-pēn′, po͞o′pēn), **Michael Idvorsky.** 1858–1935. Hungarian-born American physicist and inventor whose works improved the telegraph and telephone and increased the safety and effectiveness of x-ray photography.

pu·pip·a·rous (pyo͞o-pĭp′ər-əs) *adj.* Producing well-developed young that are ready to pupate. Used of an insect.

pup·pet (pŭp′ĭt) *n.* **1.** A small figure of a person or an animal, having a cloth body and hollow head, designed to be fitted over and manipulated by the hand. **2.** A figure having jointed parts animated from above by strings or wires; a marionette. **3.** A toy representing a human figure; a doll. **4.** One whose behavior is determined by the will of others: *a political puppet.* —*attributive.* Often used to modify another noun: *a puppet show; a puppet government.* [Middle English *poppet,* doll, possibly from Anglo-Norman *poppe,* doll. See PUPPY.]

pup·pet·eer (pŭp′ĭ-tîr′) *n.* One who entertains with and operates puppets or marionettes.

pup·pet·ry (pŭp′ĭ-trē) *n., pl.* **-ries. 1.** The art of making puppets and presenting puppet shows. **2.** The actions of puppets. **3.** A stilted or artificial dramatic performance.

Pup·pis (pŭp′ĭs) *n.* A constellation in the Southern Hemisphere near Canis Major and Pyxis. [Latin *puppis,* stern, poop.]

pup·py (pŭp′ē) *n., pl.* **-pies. 1.** A young dog; a pup. **2.** An inexperienced young person; a pup. [Middle English *popi,* small pet dog, perhaps from Anglo-Norman *poppe,* doll, from Vulgar Latin **puppa,* from Latin *pūpa,* girl, doll.]

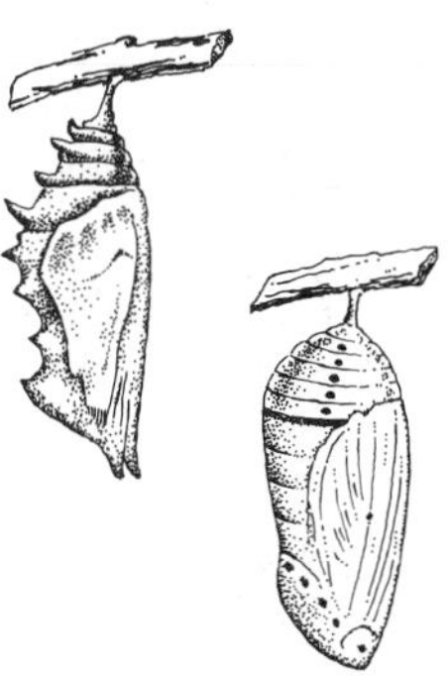

pupa
Top: Of a mourning cloak butterfly
Bottom: Of a monarch butterfly

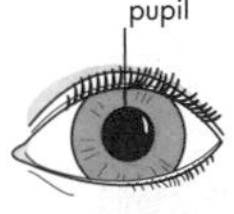

pupil[2]

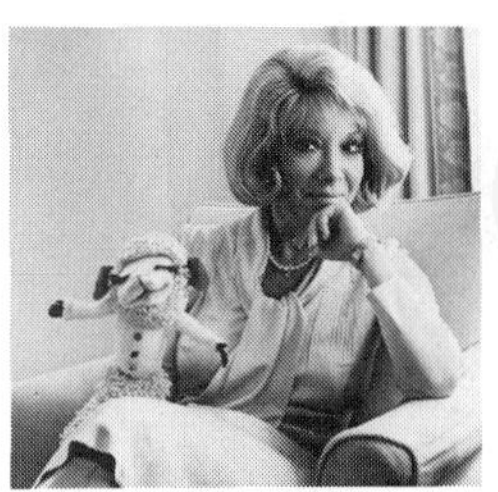

puppet
"Lamb Chop" and puppeteer Shari Lewis

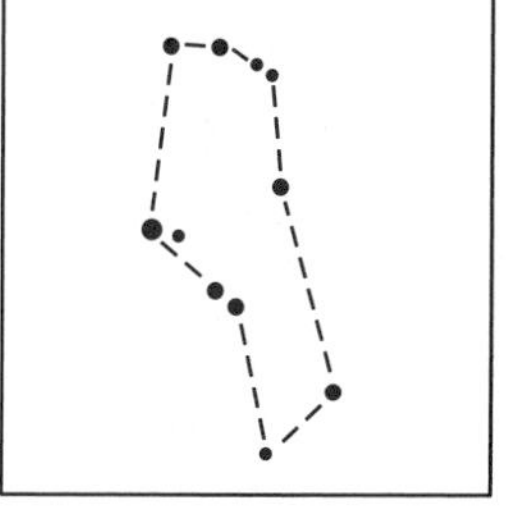

Puppis

pup·py·ish (pŭp′ē-ĭsh) *adj.* Resembling or characteristic of a puppy.

puppy love *n.* Adolescent love or infatuation.

pup tent *n.* See **shelter tent.**

Pu·ra·cé (po͝or′ə-sē′, po͞o-rä-sĕ′). A volcano, 4,758 m (15,600 ft) high, in the Andes of southwest Colombia. It erupted in 1827 and again on May 26, 1949.

pur·blind (pûr′blīnd′) *adj.* **1.** Having poor vision; nearly or partly blind. **2.** Slow in understanding or discernment; dull: *"a purblind oligarchy that flatly refused to see that history was condemning it to the dustbin"* (Jasper Griffin). **3.** *Obsolete.* Completely blind. [Middle English *pur blind,* totally blind, nearsighted : *pur,* pure; see PURE + *blind,* blind; see BLIND.] **—pur′blind′ly** *adv.* **—pur′blind′ness** *n.*

Pur·cell (pûr-sĕl′), **Edward Mills.** Born 1912. American physicist. He shared a 1952 Nobel Prize for work concerning the measurement of magnetic fields in atomic nuclei.

Pur·cell (pûr′səl, pûr-sĕl′), **Henry.** 1659?–1695. English composer and the leading musical figure of the baroque style in England.

pur·chas·a·ble (pûr′chĭ-sə-bəl) *adj.* **1.** That can be bought: *purchasable goods.* **2.** Capable of being bribed; venal: *a purchasable senator.* **—pur′chas·a·bil′i·ty** *n.*

pur·chase (pûr′chĭs) *tr.v.* **-chased, -chas·ing, -chas·es. 1.** To obtain in exchange for money or its equivalent; buy. **2.** To acquire by effort; earn. **3.** To move or hold with a mechanical device, such as a lever or wrench. **—purchase** *n.* **1. a.** The act or an instance of buying. **b.** Something bought. **c.** Acquisition through the payment of money or its equivalent. **2.** A grip applied manually or mechanically to move something or prevent it from slipping. **3.** A device, such as a tackle or lever, used to obtain mechanical advantage. **4.** A position, as of a lever or one's feet, affording means to move or secure a weight. **5. a.** A means of increasing power or influence. **b.** An advantage that is used in exerting one's power. [Middle English *purchasen,* to pursue, purchase, from Old French *purchacier* : *pur-,* forth (from Latin *prō-;* see **per**[1] in Appendix) + *chacier,* to chase; see CHASE[1].] **—pur′chas·er** *n.*

pur·chas·ing power (pûr′chĭ-sĭng) *n.* **1.** The ability to purchase, generally measured by income. **2.** The value of a particular monetary unit in terms of the goods or services that can be purchased with it.

pur·dah (pûr′də) *n.* **1. a.** A curtain or screen, used mainly in India to keep women separate from men or strangers. **b.** The Hindu or Moslem system of sex segregation, practiced especially by keeping women in seclusion. **2.** Social seclusion: *"Never have artists been more separate: their inordinate fame, wealth, drug use have driven them into luxurious purdah"* (D. Keith Mano). [Urdu *pardah,* veil, from Persian *pardah,* from Middle Persian *pardak,* from Old Persian **paridaka-,* from *pari-dā-,* to place over : *pari,* around, over; see **per**[1] in Appendix + *dā-,* to place; see **dhē-** in Appendix.]

pure (pyo͝or) *adj.* **pur·er, pur·est. 1.** Having a homogeneous or uniform composition; not mixed: *pure oxygen.* **2.** Free from adulterants or impurities: *pure chocolate.* **3.** Free of dirt, defilement, or pollution: *"A memory without blot or contamination must be . . . an inexhaustible source of pure refreshment"* (Charlotte Brontë). **4.** Free of foreign elements. **5.** Containing nothing inappropriate or extraneous: *a pure literary style.* **6.** Complete; utter: *pure folly.* **7.** Having no faults; sinless: *"I felt pure and sweet as a new baby"* (Sylvia Plath). **8.** Chaste; virgin. **9.** Of unmixed blood or ancestry. **10.** *Genetics.* Produced by self-fertilization or continual inbreeding; homozygous: *a pure line.* **11.** *Music.* Free from discordant qualities: *pure tones.* **12.** *Linguistics.* Articulated with a single unchanging speech sound; monophthongal: *a pure vowel.* **13.** Theoretical: *pure science.* **14.** *Philosophy.* Free of empirical elements: *pure reason.* [Middle English *pur,* from Old French, from Latin *pūrus.* See **peue-** in Appendix.] **—pure′ly** *adv.* **—pure′ness** *n.*

SYNONYMS: *pure, absolute, sheer, simple, unadulterated.* The central meaning shared by these adjectives is "free of extraneous elements": *pure gold; absolute alcohol; sheer wine; a simple substance; unadulterated coffee.*

pure·blood (pyo͝or′blŭd′) also **pure·blood·ed** (-blŭd′ĭd) *adj.* Of unmixed ancestry; purebred. **—pure′blood′** *n.*

pure·bred (pyo͝or′brĕd′) *adj.* Of or belonging to a recognized strain established by breeding individuals of unmixed lineage over many generations. **—purebred** (pyo͝or′brĕd′) *n.* A purebred animal.

pure democracy *n.* A democracy in which the power to govern lies directly in the hands of the people rather than being exercised through their representatives.

pu·rée (pyo͝o-rā′, pyo͝or′ā) *tr.v.* **-réed, -réing, -rées.** To rub through a strainer or process (food) in a blender. **—purée** *n.* Food prepared by straining or blending. [From French, pureé, from Old French, from feminine past participle of *purer,* to strain, clean, from Latin *pūrāre,* to purify, from *pūrus,* clean. See PURE.]

pur·fle (pûr′fəl) *tr.v.* **-fled, -fling, -fles.** To finish or decorate the border or edge of. **—purfle** also **pur·fling** (-flĭng) *n.* An ornamental border or edging. [Middle English *purfilen,* from Old French *porfiler,* from Vulgar Latin **prōfilāre* : Latin *prō-,* forth; see PRO-[1] + Latin *fīlum,* thread; see **gʷhī-** in Appendix.]

pur·ga·tion (pûr-gā′shən) *n.* The act of purging or purifying.

pur·ga·tive (pûr′gə-tĭv) *adj.* Tending to cleanse or purge, especially causing evacuation of the bowels. **—purgative** *n.* A purgative agent or medicine; a cathartic.

Pur·ga·toire (pûr′gə-twär′, -tôr′ē, -tōr′ē). A river, about 299 km (186 mi) long, of southeast Colorado flowing northeast to the Arkansas River.

pur·ga·to·ri·al (pûr′gə-tôr′ē-əl, -tōr′-) *adj.* **1.** Serving to purify of sin; expiatory. **2.** Of or resembling purgatory.

pur·ga·to·ry (pûr′gə-tôr′ē, -tōr′ē) *n., pl.* **-ries. 1.** *Roman Catholic Church.* A state in which the souls of those who have died in grace must expiate their sins. **2.** A place or condition of suffering, expiation, or remorse: *a purgatory of drug abuse.* **—purgatory** *adj.* Tending to cleanse or purge. [Middle English *purgatorie,* from Old French *purgatoire,* from Medieval Latin *pūrgātōrium,* from Late Latin, means of purgation, from neuter of *pūrgātōrius,* cleansing, from Latin *pūrgāre,* to cleanse. See PURGE.]

purge (pûrj) *v.* **purged, purg·ing, purg·es.** *—tr.* **1. a.** To free from impurities; purify. **b.** To remove (impurities and other elements) by or as if by cleansing. **2.** To rid of sin, guilt, or defilement. **3.** *Law.* To clear (a person) of a charge or an imputation. Often used with respect to contempt of court. **4. a.** To rid (a nation or political party, for example) of people considered undesirable. **b.** To get rid of (people considered undesirable). See Synonyms at **eliminate. 5.** *Medicine.* **a.** To cause evacuation of (the bowels). **b.** To induce evacuation of the bowels in an individual. *—intr.* **1.** To become pure or clean. **2.** *Medicine.* To undergo or cause an emptying of the bowels. **—purge** *n.* **1.** The act or process of purging. **2.** Something that purges, especially a medicinal purgative. [Middle English *purgen,* from Old French *purgier,* from Latin *pūrgāre,* from *pūrus,* pure. See **peue-** in Appendix.] **—purg′er** *n.*

pu·ri (po͝or′ē) *n.* Variant of **poori.**

pu·ri·fi·ca·tion (pyo͝or′ə-fĭ-kā′shən) *n.* The act or an instance of cleansing or purifying.

pu·ri·fi·ca·tor (pyo͝or′ə-fĭ-kā′tər) *n.* *Ecclesiastical.* A cloth used to clean the chalice after the celebration of the Eucharist.

pu·ri·fy (pyo͝or′ə-fī′) *v.* **-fied, -fy·ing, -fies.** *—tr.* **1.** To rid of impurities; cleanse. **2.** To rid of foreign or objectionable elements. **3.** To free from sin, guilt, or other defilement. *—intr.* To become clean or pure. [Middle English *purifien,* from Old French *purifier,* from Latin *pūrificāre* : *pūrus,* clean; see PURE + *-ficāre,* -fy.] **—pu·rif′i·ca·to′ry** (pyo͝o-rĭf′ĭ-kə-tôr′ē, -tōr′ē) *adj.* **—pu′ri·fi′er** *n.*

Pu·rim (po͝or′ĭm, po͞o-rēm′) *n.* *Judaism.* The 14th of Adar, observed in celebration of the deliverance of the Jews from massacre by Haman. [Hebrew *pûrîm,* pl. of *pûr,* lot (from the lots Haman cast to decide the day of the massacre, Esther 9:24–26), from Akkadian *pūru,* lot.]

pu·rine (pyo͝or′ēn′) *n.* **1.** A colorless crystalline organic base, $C_5H_4N_4$, that is the parent compound of various biologically important derivatives. **2.** Any of a group of organic compounds derived from or structurally related to purine, including uric acid, caffeine, and the nucleic acid constituents adenine and guanine. [German *Purin* : Latin *pūrus,* clean; see PURE + New Latin *uricus, uricum,* uric (from Greek *ouron,* urine) + *-in,* n. suff. (from French *-ine;* see -IN).]

pur·ism (pyo͝or′ĭz′əm) *n.* **1.** Strict observance of or insistence on traditional correctness, especially of language: *"By purism is to be understood a needless and irritating insistence on purity or correctness of speech"* (H.W. Fowler). **2.** An example of purism.

pur·ist (pyo͝or′ĭst) *n.* One who practices or urges strict correctness, especially in the use of words. **—pu·ris′tic** (pyo͝o-rĭs′tĭk) *adj.* **—pu·ris′ti·cal·ly** *adv.*

Pu·ri·tan (pyo͝or′ĭ-tn) *n.* **1.** A member of a group of English Protestants who in the 16th and 17th centuries advocated strict religious discipline along with simplification of the ceremonies and creeds of the Church of England. **2. puritan.** One who lives in accordance with Protestant precepts, especially one who regards pleasure or luxury as sinful. **—Puritan** *adj.* **1.** Of or relating to the Puritans or Puritanism. **2. puritan.** Characteristic of a puritan; puritanical. [From Late Latin *pūritās,* purity (on the model of Medieval Latin *Kathari,* "the Pure Ones," a third-century sect of rigorist heretics), from Latin *pūrus,* pure. See **peue-** in Appendix.]

pu·ri·tan·i·cal (pyo͝or′ĭ-tăn′ĭ-kəl) *adj.* **1.** Rigorous in religious observance; marked by stern morality. **2. Puritanical.** Of, relating to, or characteristic of the Puritans. **—pu′ri·tan′i·cal·ly** *adv.* **—pu′ri·tan′i·cal·ness** *n.*

Pu·ri·tan·ism (pyo͝or′ĭ-tn-ĭz′əm) *n.* **1.** The practices and doctrines of the Puritans. **2. puritanism.** Scrupulous moral rigor, especially hostility to social pleasures and indulgences: *"Puritanism is the source of our greatest hypocrisies and most crippling illusions"* (Molly Haskell).

pu·ri·ty (pyo͝or′ĭ-tē) *n.* **1.** The quality or condition of being pure. **2.** A quantitative assessment of homogeneity or uniformity. **3.** Freedom from sin or guilt; innocence; chastity: *"Teach your children . . . the belief in purity of body, mind and soul"* (Emmeline Pankhurst). **4.** The absence in speech or writing of slang or other elements deemed inappropriate to good style. **5.** *Color.* The degree to which a color is free from being mixed with other colors.

Pur·kin·je cell (pûr-kĭn′jē) *n.* A large, drop-shaped, densely branching neuron that is the characteristic cell of the cerebellar cortex. [After Johannes Evangelista von *Purkinje* (1787–1869), Bohemian physiologist.]

Purkinje fiber *n.* One of the specialized cardiac muscle fibers, part of the impulse-conducting network of the heart, that rapidly transmit impulses from the atrioventricular node to the ventricles. [After Johannes Evangelista von *Purkinje* (1787–1869), Bohemian physiologist.]

purl[1] (pûrl) *intr.v.* **purled, purl·ing, purls.** To flow or ripple with a murmuring sound. **—purl** *n.* The sound made by rippling water. [Probably of Scandinavian origin.]

purl[2] also **pearl** (pûrl) *—v.* **purled, purl·ing, purls** also **pearled, pearl·ing, pearls.** *Abbr.* **p.** *—tr.* **1.** To knit (yarn) with a purl stitch. **2.** To edge or finish (a handkerchief, for example) with lace or embroidery. *—intr.* **1.** To do knitting with a purl stitch. **2.** To edge or finish with lace or embroidery. *—n. Abbr.* **p. 1.** Inversion of a knit stitch; purl stitch. **2.** A decorative edging of lace or embroidery. **3.** Gold or silver wire used in embroidery. [Origin unknown.]

pur·lieu (pûrl′yo͞o, pûr′lo͞o) *n.* **1.** An outlying or neighboring area. **2. purlieus.** Outskirts; the environs. **3.** A place that one frequents. [Middle English *purlewe,* piece of land on the edge of a forest, probably alteration (influenced by Old French *lieu,* place) of *porale, purale,* royal perambulation, from Old French *porale,* from *poraler,* to traverse : *por-,* forth (from Latin *prō-;* see PRO–[1]) + *aler, aller,* to go; see ALLEY[1].]

pur·lin also **pur·line** (pûr′lĭn) *n.* One of several horizontal timbers supporting the rafters of a roof. [Middle English.]

pur·loin (pər-loin′, pûr′loin′) *v.* **-loined, -loin·ing, -loins.** *—tr.* To steal, often in a violation of trust. See Synonyms at **steal.** *—intr.* To commit theft. [Middle English *purloinen,* to remove, from Anglo-Norman *purloigner* : *pur-,* away (from Latin *prō-;* see PRO–[1]) + *loign,* far (from Latin *longē,* from *longus,* long; see **del-[1]** in Appendix).] **—pur·loin′er** *n.*

purl stitch *n.* An inverted knitting stitch, often alternated with the knit stitch to produce a ribbed effect.

pu·ro·my·cin (pyo͝or′ə-mī′sĭn) *n.* An antibiotic, $C_{22}H_{29}N_7O_5$, obtained from the soil bacterium *Streptomyces alboniger,* that is used experimentally as an inhibitor of protein synthesis. [PUR(INE) + –MYCIN.]

pur·ple (pûr′pəl) *n.* **1.** *Color.* Any of a group of colors with a hue between that of violet and red. **2.** Cloth of a color between violet and red, formerly worn as a symbol of royalty or high office. **3.** Imperial power; high rank: *born to the purple.* **4.** *Roman Catholic Church.* **a.** The rank or office of a cardinal. **b.** The rank or office of a bishop. **—purple** *adj.* **1.** *Color.* Of the color purple. **2.** Royal or imperial; regal. **3.** Elaborate and ornate: *purple prose.* **—purple** *tr. & intr.v.* **-pled, -pling, -ples.** To make or become purple. [Middle English, from Old English *purpul,* from *purpure,* purple garment, from Latin *purpura,* shellfish yielding purple dye, purple cloth, purple, from Greek *porphura,* a shellfish yielding purple dye.]

purple gallinule *n.* **1.** A colorful gallinule *(Porphyrula martinica)* of South America and the southeast United States, having a purple head, neck, and underpart, a greenish-bronze back, yellow legs, and yellow-tipped red bill. **2.** A related Old World gallinule *(Porphyrio porphyrio)* having dark, bluish-purple plumage and red legs.

purple grackle *n.* The common grackle *(Quiscalus quiscula)* of eastern North America, having iridescent blackish-purple plumage and a long, keel-shaped tail.

pur·ple·heart (pûr′pəl-härt′) *n.* **1.** A tropical tree *(Peltogyne paniculata)* native to Guiana and Trinidad, having very hard, durable brown wood that turns a purple color on exposure. **2.** The purplish heartwood of this tree, used in furniture and turnery.

Pur·ple Heart (pûr′pəl) *n. Abbr.* **PH, P.H.** A U.S. military decoration awarded to members of the armed forces who have been wounded in action.

purple loosestrife *n.* An Old World marsh plant *(Lythrum salicaria)* having long spikes of purple flowers.

purple martin *n.* A large North American swallow *(Progne subis)* having glossy, blue-black plumage and, in the female, a light-colored breast.

pur·plish (pûr′plĭsh) *adj. Color.* Somewhat purple.

pur·port (pər-pôrt′, -pōrt′) *tr.v.* **-port·ed, -port·ing, -ports. 1.** To have or present the often false appearance of being or intending; profess: *selfish behavior that purports to be altruistic.* **2.** To have the intention of doing; purpose. **—purport** (pûr′pôrt′, -pōrt′) *n.* **1.** Meaning presented, intended, or implied; import. See Synonyms at **substance. 2.** Intention; purpose. [Middle English *purporten,* to set forth, from Anglo-Norman *purporter* : *pur-,* forth (from Latin *prō-;* see PRO–[1]) + *porter,* to carry (from Latin *portāre;* see **per-[2]** in Appendix).]

pur·port·ed (pər-pôr′tĭd, -pōr′-) *adj.* Assumed to be such; supposed: *the purported author of the story.* **—pur·port′ed·ly** *adv.*

pur·pose (pûr′pəs) *n.* **1.** The object toward which one strives or for which something exists; an aim or a goal: *"And ever those, who would enjoyment gain/Must find it in the purpose they pursue"* (Sarah Josepha Hale). **2.** A result or an effect that is intended or desired; an intention. See Synonyms at **intention. 3.** Determination; resolution: *He was a man of purpose.* **4.** The matter at hand; the point at issue. **—purpose** *tr.v.* **-posed, -pos·ing, -pos·es.** To intend or resolve to perform or accomplish. ***—idioms.* on purpose.** Intentionally; deliberately. **to good purpose.** With good results. **to little** (or **no**) **purpose.** With few or no results. [Middle English *purpos,* from Anglo-Norman, from *purposer,* to intend : *pur-,* forth (from Latin *prō-;* see PRO–[1]) + *poser,* to put; see POSE[1].]

pur·pose·ful (pûr′pəs-fəl) *adj.* **1.** Having a purpose; intentional: *a purposeful musician.* **2.** Having or manifesting purpose; determined: *entered the room with a purposeful look.* **—pur′pose·ful·ly** *adv.* **—pur′pose·ful·ness** *n.*

pur·pose·less (pûr′pəs-lĭs) *adj.* Lacking a purpose; meaningless or aimless. See Synonyms at **meaningless. —pur′pose·less·ly** *adv.* **—pur′pose·less·ness** *n.*

pur·pose·ly (pûr′pəs-lē) *adv.* With specific purpose.

pur·po·sive (pûr′pə-sĭv) *adj.* **1.** Having or serving a purpose. **2.** Purposeful: *purposive behavior.* **—pur′po·sive·ly** *adv.* **—pur′po·sive·ness** *n.*

pur·pu·ra (pûr′pə-rə, -pyə-) *n.* A condition characterized by hemorrhages in the skin and mucous membranes that result in the appearance of purplish spots or patches. [Latin, purple. See PURPLE.] **—pur·pu′ric** (-pyo͝or′ĭk) *adj.*

pur·pu·rin (pûr′pyə-rĭn′) *n.* A reddish crystalline compound, $C_{14}H_5O_2(OH)_3$, that is isolated from madder root for use as a biological stain and commercial dye. [Latin *purpura,* purple; see PURPLE + –IN.]

purr (pûr) *n.* **1.** The soft vibrant sound made by a cat. **2.** A sound similar to that made by a cat: *the purr of an engine.* **—purr** *v.* **purred, purr·ing, purrs.** *—intr.* To make or utter a soft, vibrant sound: *The cat purred. The sewing machine purred.* *—tr.* To express by a soft, vibrant sound. [Imitative.]

purse (pûrs) *n.* **1.** A woman's bag for carrying keys, a wallet, and other personal items; a handbag. **2.** A small bag or pouch for carrying money. **3.** Something that resembles a bag or pouch. **4.** Available wealth or resources; money. **5.** A sum of money collected as a present or offered as a prize. **—purse** *tr.v.* **pursed, purs·ing, purs·es.** To gather or contract (the lips or brow) into wrinkles or folds; pucker. [Middle English, from Old English, from Late Latin *bursa.* See BURSA.] **—purse′like′** *adj.*

purse crab *n.* Either of two sand-dwelling brachyuran crabs *(Persephona mediterranea* or *P. punctata)* of the U.S. Atlantic coast, the Gulf of Mexico, and the West Indies, having a rounded body and, in the female, a purselike chamber for eggs.

purs·er (pûr′sər) *n.* The officer in charge of money matters on board a ship or commercial aircraft. [Middle English, from *purse,* purse. See PURSE.]

purse seine *n.* A fishing seine that is drawn into the shape of a bag to enclose the catch.

purse strings or **purse·strings** (pûrs′strĭngz′) *pl.n.* Financial support or resources, or control over them: *the politicians who control federal purse strings; tightened the corporate purse strings.*

purs·lane (pûrs′lĭn, -lān′) *n.* A trailing Asian weed *(Portulaca oleracea)* having small yellow flowers, reddish stems, and fleshy obovate leaves that are sometimes cooked as a vegetable or used in salads. [Middle English, from Anglo-Norman **purcelane,* alteration of Latin *portulāca, porcilāca.* See PORTULACA.]

pur·su·ance (pər-so͞o′əns) *n.* A carrying out or putting into effect; prosecution.

pur·su·ant (pər-so͞o′ənt) *adj.* Proceeding from and conformable to; in accordance with. **—pursuant** *adv.* Accordingly; consequently. [Probably from Middle English *pursuant,* aspirant, from Anglo-Norman, present participle of *pursure,* to pursue. See PURSUE.]

pur·sue (pər-so͞o′) *v.* **-sued, -su·ing, -sues.** *—tr.* **1.** To follow in an effort to overtake or capture; chase: *a fox that was pursued by hounds.* **2.** To strive to gain or accomplish: *pursue lofty political goals.* **3.** To proceed along the course of; follow: *a ship that pursued the southern course.* **4.** To carry further; advance: *Let's not pursue this argument.* **5.** To be engaged in (a vocation or hobby, for example). **6.** To court: *a lady who was pursued by many suitors.* **7.** To continue to torment or afflict; haunt: *was pursued by the demons of lust and greed.* *—intr.* **1.** To follow in an effort to overtake or capture; chase. **2.** To carry on; continue. [Middle English *pursuen,* from Anglo-Norman *pursure,* from Vulgar Latin **prōsequere,* from Latin *prōsequī.* See PROSECUTE.] **—pur·su′a·ble** *adj.* **—pur·su′er** *n.*

pur·suit (pər-so͞ot′) *n.* **1.** The act or an instance of chasing or pursuing. **2.** The act of striving: *the pursuit of higher education.* **3.** An activity, such as a vocation or hobby, engaged in regularly. [Middle English, from Anglo-Norman *pursuite,* from *pursure,* to pursue. See PURSUE.]

pursuit plane *n.* A high-speed fighter plane designed and equipped to pursue and attack enemy aircraft.

pur·sui·vant (pûr′swĭ-vənt) *n.* **1.** An officer in the British Colleges of Heralds who ranks below a herald. **2.** A follower or an attendant. [Middle English *pursevant,* attendant, from Old French *poursuivant,* from present participle of *poursuivre,* to follow, from Vulgar Latin **prōsequere.* See PURSUE.]

pur·te·nance (pûr′tn-əns) *n.* An animal's viscera or internal organs, especially the heart, liver, and lungs. [Middle English *pertenaunce, purtenaunce,* adjunct, from Old French *partenance,* pertinence, from *partenir,* to pertain. See PERTAIN.]

♦**pur·ty** (pûr′tē) *adj. Regional.* **pretty.**

Purple Heart

ă pat	oi boy
ā pay	ou out
âr care	o͝o took
ä father	o͞o boot
ĕ pet	ŭ cut
ē be	ûr urge
ĭ pit	th thin
ī pie	*th* this
îr pier	hw which
ŏ pot	zh vision
ō toe	ə about, item
ô paw	♦ regionalism

Stress marks: ′ (primary); ′ (secondary), as in **dictionary** (dĭk′shə-nĕr′ē)

♦ ***REGIONAL NOTE:*** *Purty* is probably the most common American example of metathesis, a linguistic process in which two adjacent sounds are reversed in order. Metathesis in English often involves the consonant *r* and a vowel, since the phonetic properties of *r* are so vowellike. For example, the word *third* used to be *thrid,* and *bird, brid.* By the same process, English *pretty* often came to be realized as *purty* in regional speech. Most such words stabilized because of the influence of printing and the resultant standardized spelling, but *purty* for *pretty* has survived in regional American dialects.

pu·ru·lence (pyo͝or′ə-ləns, pyo͝or′yə-) *n.* **1.** The condition of containing or discharging pus. **2.** Pus.

pu·ru·lent (pyo͝or′ə-lənt, pyo͝or′yə-) *adj.* Containing, discharging, or causing the production of pus: *a purulent infection.* [Middle English *purulente,* from Old French *purulent,* from Latin *pūrulentus,* from *pūs, pūr-,* pus. See **pū-** in Appendix.] **—pu′ru·lent·ly** *adv.*

Pu·rus (pə-ro͞os′, po͞o-). A river of east-central Peru and western Brazil flowing about 3,379 km (2,100 mi) generally northeast to the Amazon River.

pur·vey (pər-vā′, pûr′vā′) *tr.v.* **-veyed, -vey·ing, -veys. 1.** To supply (food, for example); furnish. **2.** To advertise or circulate. [Middle English *purveien,* from Anglo-Norman *purveier,* from Latin *prōvidēre.* See PROVIDE.] **—pur·vey′ance** *n.*

pur·vey·or (pər-vā′ər) *n.* **1.** One that furnishes provisions, especially food. **2.** One that promulgates something: *a purveyor of lies.*

pur·view (pûr′vyo͞o′) *n.* **1.** The extent or range of function, power, or competence; scope. See Synonyms at **range. 2.** Range of vision, comprehension, or experience; outlook. **3.** *Law.* The body, scope, or limit of a statute. [Alteration (influenced by VIEW) of Middle English *purveu,* proviso, from Anglo-Norman *purveu est,* it is provided (from the use of this word to introduce a proviso), past participle of *purveier,* to provide. See PURVEY.]

pushup

pus (pŭs) *n.* A generally viscous, yellowish-white fluid formed in infected tissue, consisting of white blood cells, cellular debris, and necrotic tissue. [Latin *pūs.* See **pū-** in Appendix.]

Pu·san (po͞o′sän′) also **Fu·san** (fo͞o′-). A city of extreme southeast South Korea on Korea Strait southeast of Seoul. It developed into a major port during the Japanese occupation of Korea (1910–1945). Population, 3,517,000.

Pu·sey (pyo͞o′zē), **Edward Bouverie.** 1800–1882. British theologian who led the Oxford movement after John Henry Newman's conversion to Roman Catholicism (1845).

Pu·sey·ism (pyo͞o′zē-ĭz′əm, pyo͞o′sē-) *n.* Tractarianism. [After Edward Bouverie PUSEY.] **—Pu′sey·ite′** (-īt′) *n.*

push (po͝osh) *v.* **pushed, push·ing, push·es.** —*tr.* **1.** To apply pressure against for the purpose of moving: *push a shopping cart through the aisles of a market.* **2.** To move (an object) by exerting force against it; thrust or shove. **3.** To force (one's way): *We pushed our way through the crowd.* **4.** To urge forward or urge insistently; pressure: *push a child to study harder.* **5.** To bear hard upon; press. **6.** To exert downward pressure on (a button or keyboard, for example); press. **7.** To extend or enlarge: *push society past the frontier.* **8.** *Slang.* **a.** To promote or sell (a product): *The author pushed her latest book by making appearances in bookstores.* **b.** To sell (a narcotic) illegally: *push drugs.* —*intr.* **1.** To exert outward pressure or force against something. **2.** To advance despite difficulty or opposition; press forward. **3.** To expend great or vigorous effort. **—push** *n.* **1.** The act of pushing; thrust: *gave the door a swift push.* **2.** A vigorous or insistent effort toward an end; a drive: *a push to democracy.* **3.** A provocation to action; a stimulus. **4.** *Informal.* Persevering energy; enterprise. ***—phrasal verbs.*** **push around.** *Informal.* To treat or threaten to treat roughly; intimidate. **push off.** *Informal.* To set out; depart: *The infantry patrol pushed off before dawn.* **push on.** To continue or proceed along one's way: *The path was barely visible, but we pushed on.* ***—idioms.*** **push paper.** *Informal.* To have one's time taken up by administrative, often seemingly petty, paperwork: *She spent the afternoon pushing paper for her boss.* **when** (or **if**) **push comes to shove.** At a point when or if all else has been taken into account and matters must be confronted, one way or another: *"We extol the virtues of motherhood and bestow praise on the self-sacrificing homemaker but when push comes to shove, we give her little recognition for what she does"* (Los Angeles Times). [Middle English *pusshen,* from Old French *poulser, pousser,* from Latin *pulsāre,* frequentative of *pellere,* to strike, push. See **pel-**[5] in Appendix.]

pussy willow
American pussy willow
Salix discolor

SYNONYMS: *push, propel, shove, thrust.* The central meaning shared by these verbs is "to press against something in order to move it forward or aside": *push a baby carriage; wind propelling a sailboat; shove a tray across a table; thrust the package into her hand.* See also Synonyms at **campaign.**
ANTONYM: *pull.*

push·back (po͝osh′băk′) *n.* **1.** A device or mechanism that affords movement of another object backwards: *the pushback on a subway door.* **2.** Forced movement of troops back from the line.

push·ball (po͝osh′bôl′) *n.* *Sports.* **1.** A game in which two opposing teams attempt to push a heavy ball, 6 feet (1.8 meters) in diameter, across a goal. **2.** The ball used in this game.

push broom *n.* A broom having a wide brush perpendicular to the end of a long handle, designed to be pushed in sweeping.

push button or **push·but·ton** (po͝osh′bŭt′n) *n.* A small button that activates an electric circuit when pushed.

push-but·ton or **push·but·ton** (po͝osh′bŭt′n) *adj.* Equipped with or operated by a push button.

push·cart (po͝osh′kärt′) *n.* A light cart pushed by hand.

push·down (po͝osh′doun′) *n.* *Computer Science.* A set of data stored in a computer, in which the first item to be retrieved is the one most recently stored.

push·er (po͝osh′ər) *n.* *Slang.* One who sells drugs illegally.

push·ful (po͝osh′fo͝ol′) *adj.* Pushing. **—push′ful·ness** *n.*

push·ing (po͝osh′ĭng) *adj.* **1.** Energetic; enterprising. **2.** Aggressive; forward; presuming. **—push′ing·ly** *adv.*

Push·kin (po͝osh′kĭn, po͝osh′-), **Aleksandr Sergeyevich.** 1799–1837. Russian writer who wrote the novel *Eugene Onegin* (1831), the play *Boris Godunov* (1831), and many narrative and lyrical poems and short stories.

push·o·ver (po͝osh′ō′vər) *n.* **1.** One that is easily defeated or taken advantage of. **2.** Something that is easily done or attained. See Synonyms at **breeze**[1]**.**

push·pin (po͝osh′pĭn′) *n.* **1.** A tacklike pin with a large head that is easily inserted into a wall or board. **2.** *Games.* A game played by children with pins.

push·rod also **push rod** (po͝osh′rŏd′) *n.* A rod moved by a cam to operate the valves in an internal-combustion engine.

Push·tu (pŭsh′to͞o) *n.* Variant of **Pashto.**

push·up (po͝osh′ŭp′) *n.* **1.** *Sports.* An exercise for strengthening arm muscles performed by lying face down with the palms on the floor, and pushing the body up and down with the arms. **2.** *Computer Science.* A set of stored data in which the first item to be retrieved is the one stored earliest.

push·y (po͝osh′ē) *adj.* **-i·er, -i·est.** Disagreeably aggressive or forward. **—push′i·ly** *adv.* **—push′i·ness** *n.*

pu·sil·la·nim·i·ty (pyo͞o′sə-lə-nĭm′ĭ-tē) *n.* The state or quality of being pusillanimous; cowardice.

pu·sil·lan·i·mous (pyo͞o′sə-lăn′ə-məs) *adj.* Lacking courage; cowardly. [Middle English *pusillanimus,* from Late Latin *pusillanimis* : Latin *pusillus,* weak, diminutive of *pullus,* young of an animal; see **pau-** in Appendix + *animus,* reason, mind; see **anə-** in Appendix.] **—pu′sil·lan′i·mous·ly** *adv.*

puss[1] (po͝os) *Informal. n.* **1.** A cat. **2.** A girl or young woman. [Probably of Germanic origin.]

puss[2] (po͝os) *n.* *Slang.* **1.** The mouth. **2.** The human face. See Synonyms at **face.** [Irish Gaelic *pus,* mouth, from Middle Irish *bus,* lip.]

puss·ley (pŭs′lē) *n.* Purslane. [Alteration of *pursley,* alteration of PURSLANE.]

puss·y[1] (po͝os′ē) *n., pl.* **-ies. 1.** *Informal.* A cat. **2.** *Botany.* A fuzzy catkin, especially of the pussy willow. **3.** *Vulgar Slang.* The vulva. **4.** *Offensive Slang.* Used as a disparaging term for a woman.

pus·sy[2] (pŭs′ē) *adj.* **-si·er, -si·est.** Containing or resembling pus.

puss·y·cat (po͝os′ē-kăt′) *n.* **1.** A cat. **2.** *Informal.* One who is regarded as easygoing, mild-mannered, or amiable.

puss·y·foot (po͝os′ē-fo͝ot′) *intr.v.* **-foot·ed, -foot·ing, -foots. 1.** To move stealthily or cautiously. **2.** *Informal.* To act or proceed cautiously or timidly to avoid committing oneself. **—puss′y·foot′er** *n.*

puss·y·toes (po͝os′ē-tōz′) *pl.n.* *(used with a sing. or pl. verb).* Any of several low-growing perennial plants of the genus *Antennaria,* having leaves with whitish down and clusters of small, white flower heads. [From the cluster's resemblance to a cat's paw.]

puss·y willow (po͝os′ē) *n.* **1.** A deciduous North American shrub or small tree *(Salix discolor)* having large silky catkins. **2.** Any of several willows similar to this plant.

pus·tu·lant (pŭs′chə-lənt, pŭs′tyə-) *adj.* Causing the formation of pustules. **—pustulant** *n.* A pustulant agent.

pus·tu·lar (pŭs′chə-lər, pŭs′tyə-) *adj.* Of, relating to, or consisting of pustules.

pus·tu·late (pŭs′chə-lāt′, pŭs′tyə-) *v.* **-lat·ed, -lat·ing, -lates.** —*tr.* To cause to form pustules. —*intr.* To form pustules. **—pustulate** (*also* -lĭt) *adj.* Covered with pustules.

pus·tu·la·tion (pŭs′chə-lā′shən, pŭs′tyə-) *n.* The formation or appearance of pustules.

pus·tule (pŭs′cho͞ol, pŭs′tyo͞ol) *n.* **1.** A small inflamed elevation of the skin that is filled with pus; a pimple. **2.** A small swelling similar to a blister or pimple. **3.** Something likened to an inflamed, pus-filled lesion: *"a cool glimpse of green between hot pustules of sooty sprawl"* (Nicholas Proffitt). [Middle English, from Old French, from Latin *pustula,* blister.]

put (po͝ot) *v.* **put, put·ting, puts.** —*tr.* **1.** To place in a specified location; set: *She put the books on the table.* **2.** To cause to be in a specified condition: *His gracious manners put me at ease.* **3.** To cause (one) to undergo something; subject: *The interrogators put the prisoner to torture.* **4.** To assign; attribute: *They put a false interpretation on events.* **5.** To estimate: *We put the time at five o'clock.* **6.** To impose or levy: *The governor has put a tax on cigarettes.* **7.** *Games.* To wager (a stake); bet: *put $50 on a horse.* **8.** *Sports.* To hurl with an overhand pushing motion: *put the shot.*

9. To bring up for consideration or judgment: *put a question to the judge.* **10.** To express; state: *I put my objections bluntly.* **11.** To render in a specified language or literary form: *put prose into verse.* **12.** To adapt: *The lyrics had been put to music.* **13.** To urge or force to an action: *a mob that put the thief to flight.* **14.** To apply: *We must put our minds to it.* —*intr.* **1.** To begin to move, especially in a hurry. **2.** *Nautical.* To proceed: *The ship put into the harbor.* —**put** *n.* **1.** *Sports.* An act of putting the shot. **2.** An option to sell a stipulated amount of stock or securities within a specified time and at a fixed price. —**put** *adj. Informal.* Fixed; stationary: *stay put.* —***phrasal verbs.*** **put about.** *Nautical.* To change or cause to change direction; go or cause to go from one tack to another. **put across. 1.** To state so as to be understood clearly or accepted readily: *tried to put her views across during the hearing.* **2.** To attain or carry through by deceit or trickery. **put away. 1.** To renounce; discard: *put all negative thoughts away.* **2.** *Informal.* To consume (food or drink) readily and quickly: *put away the dinner in just a few minutes.* **3.** *Informal.* To confine to a mental health facility. **4. a.** *Informal.* To kill: *The injured cat was put away.* **b.** To bury. **put by.** To save for later use: *My grandmother puts by her fresh vegetables.* **put down. 1. a.** To write down. **b.** To enter in a list. **2. a.** To bring to an end; repress: *put down a rebellion.* **b.** To render ineffective: *put down rumors.* **3.** To subject (an animal) to euthanasia. **4.** *Slang.* **a.** To criticize: *Her parents put her down for failing the course.* **b.** To belittle; disparage: *He tried to put down her knowledge of literature.* **c.** To humiliate: *"Many status games seem designed to put down others"* (Alvin F. Poussaint). **5. a.** To assign to a category: *Just put him down as a sneak.* **b.** To attribute: *Let's put this disaster down to experience.* **6.** To consume (food or drink) readily; put away: *puts down three big meals a day.* **put forth. 1.** To grow: *Plants put forth new growth in the spring.* **2.** To bring to bear; exert: *At least put forth a semblance of effort when you scrub the floor.* **3.** To offer for consideration: *put forth an idea.* **put forward.** To propose for consideration: *put forward a new plan.* **put in. 1.** To make a formal offer of: *put in a plea of guilty.* **2.** To interpose: *He put in a good word for me.* **3.** To spend (time) at a location or job: *The inmate had put in six years at hard labor. She put in eight hours behind a desk.* **4.** To plant: *We put in 20 rows of pine trees.* **5.** *Nautical.* To enter a port or harbor: *The freighter puts in at noon.* **put off. 1. a.** To delay; postpone: *put off paying the bills.* **b.** To persuade to delay further action: *managed to put off the creditors for another week.* **2.** To take off; discard: *put off a sweater.* **3.** To repel or repulse, as from bad manners: *His indifferent attitude has put us off.* **4.** To pass (money) or sell (merchandise) fraudulently. **put on. 1.** To clothe oneself with; don: *put on a coat; put socks on.* **2.** To apply; activate: *put on the brakes.* **3.** To assume affectedly: *put on an English accent.* **4.** *Slang.* To tease or mislead (another): *You're putting me on!* **5.** To add: *put on weight.* **6.** To produce; perform: *put on a variety show.* **put out. 1.** To extinguish: *put out a fire.* **2.** *Nautical.* To leave, as a port or harbor; depart. **3.** To expel: *put out a drunk.* **4.** To publish: *put out a weekly newsletter.* **5. a.** To inconvenience: *Did our early arrival put you out?* **b.** To offend or irritate: *I was put out by his attention to the television set.* **6.** *Baseball.* To retire a runner. **7.** *Vulgar Slang.* To be sexually active. Used of a woman. **put over. 1.** To postpone; delay. **2.** To put across, especially to deceive: *tried to put a lie over, but to no avail.* **put through. 1.** To bring to a successful end: *put the project through on time; put through a number of new laws.* **2.** To cause to undergo: *He put me through a lot of trouble.* **3. a.** To make a telephone connection for: *The operator put me through on the office line.* **b.** To obtain a connection for (a telephone call). **put to.** *Nautical.* To head for shore. **put together.** To construct; create: *put together a new bookcase; put together a tax package.* **put up. 1.** To erect; build. **2.** To preserve; can: *put up six jars of jam.* **3.** To nominate: *put up a candidate at a convention.* **4.** To provide (funds) in advance: *put up money for the new musical.* **5.** To provide lodgings for: *put a friend up for the night.* **6.** *Sports.* To startle (game animals) from cover: *put up grouse.* **7.** To offer for sale: *put up his antiques.* **8. a.** To make a display or the appearance of: *put up a bluff.* **b.** To engage in; carry on: *put up a good fight.* **put upon.** To impose on; overburden: *He was always being put upon by his friends.* —***idioms.*** **put down roots.** To establish a permanent residence in a locale. **put it to (someone).** *Slang.* **1.** To overburden with tasks or work. **2.** To put blame on. **3.** To take unfair advantage of. **4.** To lay out the facts of a situation to (another) in a forceful, candid manner. **put (one) in mind.** To remind: *You put me in mind of your grandmother.* **put (one's) finger on.** To identify: *I can't put my finger on the person in that photograph.* **put (one's) foot down.** To take a firm stand. **put (one's) foot in (one's) mouth.** To make a tactless remark. **put paid to.** *Chiefly British.* To finish off; put to rest: *"We've given up saying we only kill to eat; Kraft dinner and freeze-dried food have put paid to that one"* (Margaret Atwood). **put (someone) through (someone's) paces.** To cause to demonstrate ability or skill; test: *The drama coach put her students through their paces before the first performance.* **put (someone) up to.** To cause to commit a funny, mischievous, or malicious act: *My older brother put me up to making a prank telephone call.* **put the arm** (or **bite** or **squeeze) on.** *Slang.* To ask another for money. **put the finger on.** *Slang.* To inform on: *The witness put the finger on the killer.* **put the make on.** *Slang.* To make sexual advances to. **put the screws to** (or **on).** *Slang.* To pressure (another) in an extreme manner. **put the skids on.** *Slang.* To bring to a halt: *"Sacrificing free speech to put the skids on prurient printed matter is not the correct path, the courts said"* (Curtis J. Sitomer). **put to bed.** *Informal.* **1.** To make final preparations for the printing of (a newspaper, for example). **2.** To make final preparations for completing (a project). **put to it.** To cause extreme difficulty for: *We were put to it to finish the book on time.* **put two and two together.** To draw the proper conclusions from existing evidence or indications. **put up or shut up.** *Slang.* To have to endure (something unpleasant) without complaining or take the action necessary to remove the source of the unpleasantry. **put up with.** To endure without complaint: *We had to put up with the inconvenience.* [Middle English *putten,* back-formation from Old English **pūtte,* past tense of *pȳtan,* to put out.]

pu·ta·men (pyo͞o-tā′mən) *n., pl.* **-tam·i·na** (-tăm′ə-nə). A hard, shell-like covering, such as that enclosing the kernel of a peach. [Latin *putāmen,* that which falls off in pruning, shell, husk, from *putāre,* to prune. See **peu-** in Appendix.] —**pu·tam′i·nous** (-tăm′ə-nəs) *adj.*

pu·ta·tive (pyo͞o′tə-tĭv) *adj.* Generally regarded as such; supposed. See Synonyms at **supposed.** [Middle English, from Old French *putatif,* from Late Latin *putātīvus,* from Latin *putāre,* to prune, think. See **peu-** in Appendix.] —**pu′ta·tive·ly** *adv.*

put·down or **put-down** (po͝ot′doun′) *n. Slang.* **1.** A dismissal or rejection, especially in the form of a critical or slighting remark: *"Such answers were, perhaps still are, a . . . form of put-down to the questions of white people"* (Lillian Hellman). **2.** A typically good-natured parody, especially in theater: *"The comedy fodder ranged from putdowns of British Royalty to . . . Sophie Tuckerisms"* (Variety).

put·down·a·ble (po͝ot′dou′nə-bəl) *adj. Informal.* So poorly written and unentertaining as to be easily put down. Used especially of a book.

Put-in-Bay (po͝ot′ĭn-bā′). A bay of western Lake Erie in an island off Ohio. The U.S. Navy under Oliver Hazard Perry defeated a British fleet here on September 10, 1813, in the War of 1812.

put·log (po͝ot′lôg′, -lŏg′, pŭt′-) *n.* One of the short pieces of lumber supporting the floor of a scaffold. [Alteration (influenced by LOG[1]) of obsolete *putlock* : perhaps PUT + LOCK[1].]

Put·nam (pŭt′nəm), **Israel.** 1718–1790. American soldier active in the French and Indian War and the Revolutionary War. During the Battle of Bunker Hill (June 17, 1775), he supposedly issued the order, "Don't one of you shoot until you see the whites of their eyes."

Putnam, Rufus. 1738–1824. American Revolutionary soldier who organized the batteries on Dorchester Heights that forced the British to evacuate Boston (1775).

put·off (po͝ot′ôf′, -ŏf′) *n.* A pretext for inaction; an excuse.

put-on (po͝ot′ŏn′, -ôn′) *adj.* Pretended; feigned. —**put-on** *n. Slang.* **1.** A deceptive outward appearance. **2.** The act of teasing or misleading someone, especially for amusement. **3.** Something, such as a prank, intended as a hoax or joke; a spoof.

Pu·tong·hua also **Pu tong hua** (po͞o′tông′hwä′, -wä′, -tŏng′-) *n.* See **Mandarin** (sense 4). [Chinese (Mandarin) *pǔ tōnghuà* : *pǔ,* general, widespread + *tōng,* through + *huà,* words.]

put·out (po͝ot′out′) *abbr. Abbr.* **po, p.o.** *Baseball.* A play in which a batter or base runner is retired.

put-put (pŭt′pŭt′) *n. Slang.* **1.** A small gasoline engine. **2.** A vehicle, such as a boat, that is operated by a small gasoline engine. [Imitative of a running engine.]

pu·tre·fac·tion (pyo͞o′trə-făk′shən) *n.* **1.** Decomposition of organic matter, especially protein, by microorganisms, resulting in production of foul-smelling matter. **2.** Putrefied matter. **3.** The condition of being putrefied. [Middle English *putrefaccioun,* from Late Latin *putrefactiō, putrefactiōn-,* from *putrefactus,* past participle of Latin *putrefacere,* to make rotten. See PUTREFY.]

pu·tre·fac·tive (pyo͞o′trə-făk′tĭv) *adj.* **1.** Bringing about putrefaction. **2.** Of, relating to, or characterized by putrefaction.

pu·tre·fy (pyo͞o′trə-fī′) *v.* **-fied, -fy·ing, -fies.** —*tr.* **1.** To cause to decay and have a foul odor. See Synonyms at **decay. 2.** To make gangrenous. —*intr.* **1.** To become decayed and have a foul odor. **2.** To become gangrenous. [Middle English *putrefien,* from Old French *putrefier,* from Latin *putrefacere* : *puter, putr-,* rotten; see **pŭ-** in Appendix + *facere,* to make; see **dhē-** in Appendix.]

pu·tres·cence (pyo͞o-trĕs′əns) *n.* **1.** A putrescent character or condition. **2.** Putrid matter.

pu·tres·cent (pyo͞o-trĕs′ənt) *adj.* **1.** Becoming putrid. **2.** Of or relating to putrefaction. [Latin *putrēscēns, putrēscent-,* present participle of *putrēscere,* inchoative of *putrēre,* to be rotten, from *puter, putr-,* rotten. See **pŭ-** in Appendix.]

pu·tres·ci·ble (pyo͞o-trĕs′ə-bəl) *adj.* Subject to putrefaction. [French, from Old French, from Late Latin *putrēscibilis,* from Latin *putrēscere,* to rot. See PUTRESCENT.]

pu·tres·cine (pyo͞o-trĕs′ēn) *n.* A colorless, foul-smelling ptomaine, $NH_2(CH_2)_4NH_2$, produced in decaying animal tissue by the decarboxylation of ornithine. [Latin *putrēscere,* to rot; see PUTRESCENT + -INE[2].]

pu·trid (pyo͞o′trĭd) *adj.* **1.** Decomposed and foul-smelling; rotten. **2.** Proceeding from, relating to, or exhibiting putrefaction. **3.** Morally rotten; corrupt: *"and all the while scarlet thoughts, putrid fantasies, and no love"* (Louis Auchincloss). **4.** Extremely objectionable; vile. [Middle English *putred,* from Old French *putride,* from Latin *putridus,* from *putrēre,* to be rotten, from *puter,*

ă **pat**	oi **boy**
ā **pay**	ou **out**
âr **care**	o͝o **took**
ä **father**	o͞o **boot**
ĕ **pet**	ŭ **cut**
ē **be**	ûr **urge**
ĭ **pit**	th **thin**
ī **pie**	*th* **this**
îr **pier**	hw **which**
ŏ **pot**	zh **vision**
ō **toe**	ə **a**bout, **i**tem
ô **paw**	♦ regionalism

Stress marks: ′ (primary); ′ (secondary), as in **dictionary** (dĭk′shə-nĕr′ē)

putr-, rotten. See **pū-** in Appendix.] **—pu·trid′i·ty** (-trĭd′ĭ-tē), **pu′trid·ness** (-trĭd-nĭs) *n.* **—pu′trid·ly** *adv.*

putsch also **Putsch** (po͝och) *n.* A sudden attempt by a group to overthrow a government. [German, from German dialectal, from Middle High German, thrust, of imitative origin.] **—putsch′ist** *n.*

putting green

putt (pŭt) *Sports. n.* A light golf stroke made on the putting green in an effort to place the ball into the hole. **—putt** *v.* **putt·ed, putt·ing, putts.** *—tr.* To hit (a golf ball) with a light stroke on the green. *—intr.* To putt a golf ball. [Variant of PUT.]

put·tee (pŭ-tē′, pŭt′ē) *n.* **1.** A strip of cloth wound spirally around the leg from ankle to knee. Often used in the plural. **2.** A gaiter covering the lower leg. Often used in the plural. [Hindi *paṭṭī*, from Sanskrit *paṭṭikā*, feminine of *paṭṭakaḥ*, bandage, ribbon, from *paṭṭaḥ*, strip of cloth.]

put·ter¹ (pŭt′ər) *n. Sports.* **1.** A short golf club used for putting. **2.** A golfer who is putting.

put·ter² (pŭt′ər) *v.* **-tered, -ter·ing, -ters.** *—intr.* To occupy oneself in an aimless or ineffective manner. *—tr.* To waste (time) in idling: *puttered away the hours in the garden.* [Probably alteration of POTTER², probably frequentative of Middle English *poten,* to poke, push, from Old English *potian.*] **—put′ter·er** *n.*

putt·ing green (pŭt′ĭng) *n. Sports.* **1.** The area at the end of a golf course fairway in which the hole is placed, having more closely mowed turf than the rest of the course. **2.** An area in which to practice putting.

put·ty (pŭt′ē) *n., pl.* **-ties. 1.a.** A doughlike cement made by mixing whiting and linseed oil, used to fill holes in woodwork and secure panes of glass. **b.** A substance with a similar consistency or function. **2.** A fine lime cement used as a finishing coat on plaster. **3.** *Color.* A yellowish or light brownish gray to grayish yellow or light grayish brown. **—putty** *tr.v.* **-tied, -ty·ing, -ties.** To fill, cover, or secure with putty. [French *potée,* polishing powder, from Old French, a potful, from *pot,* pot, from Vulgar Latin **pottus.*]

put·ty·root (pŭt′ē-ro͞ot′, -ro͝ot′) *n.* A North American orchid *(Aplectrum hyemale)* bearing a single leaf and yellowish-brown flowers clustered in a raceme. Also called *Adam-and-Eve.* [From the use of the sticky substance in its corm as a cement.]

Pu·tu·ma·yo (po͞o′tə-mī′ō, po͞o′to͞o-mä′yô). A river of northwest South America rising in southwest Colombia and flowing about 1,609 km (1,000 mi) along the Colombia-Peru border to the Amazon River in northwest Brazil.

pygmy
Pygmy chimpanzee
Pan paniscus

put-up (po͝ot′ŭp′) *adj. Informal.* Planned or prearranged secretly: *The theft was a put-up job.*

putz (pŭts) *n.* **1.** *Slang.* A fool; an idiot. **2.** *Vulgar Slang.* A penis. **—putz** *intr.v.* **putzed, putz·ing, putz·es.** *Slang.* To behave in an idle manner; putter. [Yiddish *pots,* penis, fool.]

Pu·vis de Cha·vannes (pyo͞o-vē′ də shä-vän′, -vēs′, pü-vē′), **Pierre.** 1824–1898. French artist noted for his decorative and allegorical murals, such as *Work* (1863).

Puy·al·lup (pyo͞o-ăl′əp). A city of west-central Washington east-southeast of Tacoma. It is the site of an annual daffodil festival and fair. Population, 18,251.

puz·zle (pŭz′əl) *v.* **-zled, -zling, -zles.** *—tr.* **1.** To baffle or confuse mentally by presenting or being a difficult problem or matter. **2.** To clarify or solve (something confusing) by reasoning or study: *He puzzled out the significance of the statement.* *—intr.* **1.** To be perplexed. **2.** To ponder over a problem in an effort to solve or understand it. **—puzzle** *n.* **1.a.** A jigsaw puzzle. **b.** Something, such as a toy or game, that tests one's ingenuity. **2.** Something that baffles or confuses. **3.** The condition of being perplexed; bewilderment. [Origin unknown.] **—puz′zler** *n.*

SYNONYMS: *puzzle, perplex, mystify, bewilder, confound.* These verbs mean to cause bafflement or confusion. *Puzzle* suggests a problem or matter that is difficult to solve or interpret or that puts one at a loss: *"The poor creature puzzled me once . . . by a question merely natural and innocent, that I scarce knew what to say"* (Daniel Defoe). *Perplex* stresses puzzlement resulting in uncertainty or anxiety, as over attaining comprehension, reaching a decision, or finding a solution: *"It is not worth while to perplex the reader with inquiries into the abstract nature of evidence"* (Joseph Butler). To *mystify* is to perplex by defying or seeming to defy comprehension: *The author's imagery mystifies me. Bewilder* emphasizes both perplexity and extreme mental confusion: *"The old know what they want; the young are sad and bewildered"* (Logan Pearsall Smith). To *confound* is to bewilder and astonish so that one becomes immobilized or loses one's equanimity: *"God hath chosen the foolish things of the world to confound the wise"* (I Corinthians 1:27).

pylon

puz·zle·ment (pŭz′əl-mənt) *n.* The state of being confused or baffled; perplexity.

puzzle palace *n. Slang.* A place where high-level decisions are made in seclusion and great secrecy: *"the notion that Washington amounts to a puzzle palace on the Potomac, divorced from the genuine desires of the voters"* (David A. Stockman).

PV *abbr.* Polyvinyl.

PVC (pē′vē-sē′) *n.* A common thermoplastic resin, used in a wide variety of manufactured products, including rainwear, garden hoses, phonograph records, and floor tiles. [P(OLY)V(INYL) C(HLORIDE).]

PVO *abbr.* Private voluntary organization.

PVT or **Pvt** or **pvt.** *abbr.* Private.

PWA *abbr.* **1.** Person with AIDS. **2.** Also **P.W.A.** Public Works Administration.

pwr. *abbr.* Power.

pwt. *abbr.* Pennyweight.

pxt. *abbr. Latin.* Pinxit (He, or she, painted this).

py– *pref.* Variant of **pyo–.**

py·a (pē-ä′) *n.* See table at **currency.** [Burmese.]

pyc·nid·i·um (pĭk-nĭd′ē-əm) *n., pl.* **-i·a** (-ē-ə). A flask-shaped asexual structure containing conidia, found in certain fungi. [New Latin : Greek *puknos,* thick + Latin *-idium,* diminutive suff. (from Greek *-idion*).] **—pyc·nid′i·al** *adj.*

pyc·nog·o·nid (pĭk-nŏg′ə-nĭd, pĭk′nə-gŏn′ĭd) *n.* See **sea spider.** [From New Latin *Pycnogonidae,* family name, from *Pycnogonum,* type genus : Greek *puknos,* thick + Greek *gonu,* knee; see **genu-¹** in Appendix.]

pyc·nom·e·ter (pĭk-nŏm′ĭ-tər) *n.* A standard vessel used in measuring the density or specific gravity of materials. [Greek *puknos,* dense + –METER.]

pye-dog also **pi-dog** (pī′dôg′, -dŏg′) *n.* A stray dog. [Perhaps Hindi *pāhi,* outsider.]

py·e·li·tis (pī′ə-lī′tĭs) *n.* Acute inflammation of the pelvis of the kidney, caused by bacterial infection. [New Latin : Greek *puelos,* basin; see **pleu-** in Appendix + –ITIS.] **—py′e·lit′ic** (-lĭt′ĭk) *adj.*

py·e·lo·gram (pī′ə-lə-grăm′) *n.* An x-ray obtained by pyelography. [Greek *puelos,* basin; see PYELITIS + –GRAM.]

py·e·log·ra·phy (pī′ə-lŏg′rə-fē) *n.* X-ray photography of the pelvis of the kidney and associated structures after injection with a radiopaque dye. [Greek *puelos,* basin; see PYELITIS + –GRAPHY.] **—py′e·lo·graph′ic** (-lə-grăf′ĭk) *adj.*

py·e·lo·ne·phri·tis (pī′ə-lō-nĭ-frī′tĭs) *n.* Inflammation of the kidney and its pelvis, caused by bacterial infection. [New Latin : Greek *puelos,* basin; see PYELITIS + NEPHRITIS.] **—py′e·lo·ne·phrit′ic** (-frĭt′ĭk) *adj.*

py·e·mi·a (pī-ē′mē-ə) *n.* Septicemia caused by pyogenic microorganisms in the blood, often resulting in the formation of multiple abscesses. **—py·e′mic** *adj.*

py·gid·i·um (pī-jĭd′ē-əm) *n., pl.* **-i·a** (-ē-ə). The posterior body region or caudal segment of certain insects and other invertebrates. [New Latin, from Greek *pugidion,* diminutive of *pugē,* buttocks.] **—py·gid′i·al** (-ē-əl) *adj.*

pyg·mae·an or **pyg·me·an** (pĭg-mē′ən, pĭg′mē-) *adj.* Pygmy. [From Latin *pygmaeus,* sing. of *Pygmaeī,* the Pygmies. See PYGMY.]

Pyg·ma·lion (pĭg-māl′yən, -mā′lē-ən) *n. Greek Mythology.* A king of Cyprus who carved and then fell in love with a statue of a woman, which Aphrodite brought to life as Galatea.

pyg·me·an (pĭg-mē′ən, pĭg′mē-) *adj.* Variant of **pygmaean.**

pyg·moid (pĭg′moid′) *adj.* Resembling or characteristic of a Pygmy.

Pyg·my also **Pig·my** (pĭg′mē) *—n., pl.* **-mies. 1.** *Greek Mythology.* A member of a race of dwarfs. **2.** Also **pygmy.** *Anthropology.* A member of any of various peoples, especially of equatorial Africa and parts of southeast Asia, having an average height less than 5 feet (127 centimeters). **3. pygmy. a.** An individual of unusually small size. **b.** An individual considered to be of little or no importance. *—adj.* **1.** Also **pygmy.** *Anthropology.* Of or relating to the Pygmies. **2. pygmy. a.** Unusually or atypically small. **b.** Unimportant; trivial. [Middle English *pigmie,* from Latin *Pygmaeī,* the Pygmies, from Greek *Pugmaioi,* from *pugmē,* cubit, fist. See **peuk-** in Appendix.]

py·ja·ma (pə-jä′mə, -jăm′ə) *n. Chiefly British.* Variant of **pajama.**

pyk·nic (pĭk′nĭk) *adj.* Having a short, stocky physique. [From Greek *puknos,* compact.] **—pyk′nic** *n.*

Pyle (pīl), **Ernest Taylor.** Known as "Ernie." 1900–1945. American journalist noted for his stories about American soldiers on the European and North African fronts during World War II.

py·lon (pī′lŏn′) *n.* **1.** A steel tower supporting high-tension wires. **2.** A tower marking a turning point in a race among aircraft. **3.** A large structure or group of structures marking an entrance or approach. **4.** A monumental gateway in the form of a pair of truncated pyramids serving as the entrance to an ancient Egyptian temple. [Greek *pulōn,* gateway, from *pulē,* gate.]

py·lo·rus (pī-lôr′əs, -lōr′-, pĭ-) *n., pl.* **-lo·ri** (-lôr′ī′, -lōr′ī′). The passage at the lower end of the stomach that opens into the duodenum. [Late Latin *pylōrus,* from Greek *pulōros* : *pulē,* gate + *ouros,* guard; see **wer-³** in Appendix.] **—py·lo′ric** (-ĭk) *adj.*

Pym (pĭm), **John.** 1584–1643. English Parliamentarian who moved for the impeachment of the advisers to Charles I. The king's effort to arrest Pym in the House of Commons (1642) precipitated the English Civil War.

Pyn·chon (pĭn′chən), **Thomas.** Born 1937. American writer whose dark, pessimistic novels of life in a technologically advanced society include *Gravity's Rainbow* (1973).

pyo– or **py–** *pref.* Pus: *pyoderma.* [Greek *puo-,* from *puon,* pus. See **pū-** in Appendix.]

py·o·der·ma (pī′ə-dûr′mə) *n.* A pyogenic skin disease. **—py′o·der′mic** *adj.*

py·o·gen·e·sis (pī′ə-jĕn′ĭ-sĭs) *n.* Formation of pus.

py·o·gen·ic (pī′ə-jĕn′ĭk) *adj.* **1.** Producing pus. **2.** Of, relating to, or characterized by pyogenesis.

py·oid (pī′oid) *adj.* Of or resembling pus.

Pyong·yang (pyŭng′yäng′, -yăng′, pyông′-). The capital and largest city of North Korea, in the southwest-central part of the country. It was an important cultural center and Chinese colony after 108 B.C., later fell to the Japanese, and became capital of North Korea in 1948. Population, 1,283,000.

py·or·rhe·a or **py·or·rhoe·a** (pī′ə-rē′ə) *n.* **1.** Purulent inflammation of the gums and tooth sockets, often leading to loosening of the teeth. **2.** A discharge of pus. **—py′or·rhe′al** *adj.*

py·o·sis (pī-ō′sĭs) *n.* Pyogenesis.

pyr– *pref.* Variant of **pyro–**.

py·ra·can·tha (pī′rə-kăn′thə) *n.* A shrub of the genus *Pyracantha*; the fire thorn. [Latin, from Greek *purakantha,* a shrub : *pur,* fire; see PYRE + *akantha,* thorn.]

py·ral·id (pī-răl′ĭd, pĭr′ə-lĭd) also **py·ral·i·did** (pī-răl′ĭ-dĭd) —*n.* Any of numerous small or medium-sized moths of the diverse, widely distributed family Pyralidae. —*adj.* Of or belonging to the family Pyralidae. [From New Latin *Pyralidae,* family name, from *Pyralis,* type genus, from Greek *puralis, puralid-,* an insect said to live in fire, from *pur,* fire. See PYRE.]

pyr·a·mid (pĭr′ə-mĭd) *n.* **1.a.** A solid figure with a polygonal base and triangular faces that meet at a common point. **b.** Something shaped like this polyhedron. **2.a.** A massive monument of ancient Egypt having a rectangular base and four triangular faces culminating in a single apex, built over or around a crypt or tomb. **b.** Any of various similar constructions, especially a four-sided Mayan temple having stepped sides and a flat top surmounted by ceremonial chambers. **3.** The transactions involved in pyramiding stock. **4.** *Anatomy.* A structure or part suggestive of a pyramid in shape. **—pyramid** *v.* **-mid·ed, -mid·ing, -mids.** —*tr.* **1.** To place or build in the shape of a pyramid. **2.** To build (an argument or a thesis, for example) progressively from a basic general premise. **3.** To speculate in (stock) by making a series of buying and selling transactions in which paper profits are used as margin for buying more stock. —*intr.* **1.** To assume the shape of a pyramid. **2.** To increase rapidly and on a widening base. **3.** To pyramid stocks. [Latin *pȳramis, pȳramid-,* from Greek *puramis,* probably from Egyptian *pimar.*] **—py·ram′i·dal** (pĭ-răm′ĭ-dl), **pyr′a·mid′ic** (-mĭd′ĭk), **pyr′a·mid′i·cal** (-ĭ-kəl) *adj.* **—py·ram′i·dal·ly** *adv.*

Pyr·a·mid Peak (pĭr′ə-mĭd). A mountain, 4,275.5 m (14,018 ft) high, in the Elk Mountains of west-central Colorado.

pyramidal tract *n.* A major pathway of the central nervous system, originating in the sensorimotor areas of the cerebral cortex and generally descending through the brainstem to the spinal cord. The fibers of the pyramidal tract transmit motor impulses that function in the control of voluntary movement.

Pyr·a·mus (pĭr′ə-məs) *n.* *Roman Mythology.* A Babylonian youth who committed suicide when he mistakenly thought his lover Thisbe was dead.

py·ran (pī′răn′) *n.* Either of two isomeric compounds with the formula C_5H_6O, having a ring of five carbon atoms and one oxygen atom. [*pyrone,* heterocyclic compound (PYR(O)– + –ONE) + –AN[2].]

py·rar·gy·rite (pī-rär′jə-rīt′, pī-) *n.* A deep red to black silver ore with composition Ag_3SbS_3. [German *Pyrargyrit* : Greek *puro-,* pyro- + Greek *arguros,* silver; see ARGENT.]

pyre (pīr) *n.* **1.** A heap of combustibles for burning a corpse as a funeral rite. **2.** A pile of combustibles. [Latin *pyra,* from Greek *pura,* from *pur,* fire. See **pūr-** in Appendix.]

py·rene (pī′rēn′, pī-rēn′) *n.* The stone of certain fruits, such as the cherry. [New Latin *pȳrēna,* from Greek *purēn.*]

Pyr·e·nees (pîr′ə-nēz′). A mountain range of southwest Europe extending along the French-Spanish border from the Bay of Biscay to the Mediterranean Sea. It rises to 3,406.2 m (11,168 ft) at Pico de Aneto. **—Pyr′e·ne′an** *adj.*

py·re·noid (pī-rē′noid′, pī′rə-) *n.* A proteinaceous structure found within the chloroplast of certain algae and hornworts. It is considered to be associated with starch deposition. [New Latin *pȳrēna,* fruit stone; see PYRENE + –OID.]

py·re·thrin (pī-rē′thrĭn, -rĕth′rĭn) *n.* Either of two viscous liquid esters, $C_{21}H_{28}O_3$ or $C_{22}H_{28}O_5$, that are extracted from pyrethrum flowers and used as insecticides. [PYRETHR(UM) + –IN.]

py·re·throid (pī-rē′throid, -rĕth′roid) *n.* Any of several synthetic compounds similar to pyrethrin, used as an insecticide.

py·re·thrum (pī-rē′thrəm, -rĕth′rəm) *n.* **1.** Any of several Old World plants of the genus *Chrysanthemum,* such as *C. coccineum,* cultivated for their showy flower heads. **2.** An insecticide made from the dried flower heads of *Chrysanthemum cinerariifolium* or *C. coccineum.* [Latin, pellitory, from Greek *purethron,* feverfew, from *pur,* fire (from its warming effect). See PYRETIC.]

py·ret·ic (pī-rĕt′ĭk) *adj.* Relating to, producing, or affected by fever. [New Latin *pyreticus,* from Greek *puretos,* fever, from *pur,* fire. See **pūr-** in Appendix.]

Py·rex (pī′rĕks′). A trademark used for any of various types of heat-resistant and chemical-resistant glass. This trademark often occurs in attributive contexts in print: *"The water is mixed with titanium dioxide, which serves as a catalyst, and is pumped through Pyrex tubes"* (Scientific American). *"The physicist sets the ice sample in an empty Pyrex beaker"* (Smithsonian).

py·rex·i·a (pī-rĕk′sē-ə) *n.* Fever. [New Latin, from Greek *purexis,* from *puressein,* to have a fever, from *puretos,* fever. See PYRETIC.] **—py·rex′i·al, py·rex′ic** *adj.*

pyr·he·li·om·e·ter (pîr′hē-lē-ŏm′ĭ-tər, pĭr′-) *n.* Any of various devices that measure all the intensity of solar radiation received at the earth. **—pyr′he·li·o·met′ric** (-ə-mĕt′rĭk) *adj.*

py·ric (pī′rĭk, pĭr′ĭk) *adj.* Of, relating to, or resulting from burning.

pyr·i·dine (pĭr′ĭ-dēn′) *n.* A flammable, colorless or yellowish liquid base, C_5H_5N, having a penetrating odor and serving as the parent compound of many biologically important derivatives. It is used as a solvent and waterproofing agent and in the manufacture of various drugs and vitamins. **—py·rid′ic** (pī-rĭd′ĭk) *adj.*

pyr·i·dox·al (pĭr′ĭ-dŏk′səl) *n.* An aldehyde, $C_8H_9NO_3$, one of several active forms of pyridoxine, important in amino acid synthesis. [PYRIDOX(INE) + –AL[3].]

pyr·i·dox·a·mine (pĭr′ĭ-dŏk′sə-mēn′) *n.* A crystalline amine, $C_8H_{12}N_2O_2$, one of several active forms of pyridoxine, important in protein metabolism. [PYRIDOX(INE) + –AMINE.]

pyr·i·dox·ine (pĭr′ĭ-dŏk′sēn, -sĭn) also **pyr·i·dox·in** (-dŏk′sĭn) *n.* A pyridine derivative, $C_{18}H_{11}NO_3$, occurring especially in cereals, yeast, liver, and fish and serving as a coenzyme in amino acid synthesis. Also called *vitamin B_6.* [PYRID(INE) + OX(O)– + –INE[2].]

pyr·i·form (pĭr′ə-fôrm′) *adj.* Shaped like a pear. [Medieval Latin *pyrum,* pear (alteration of Latin *pirum*) + –FORM.]

pyramid
The Temple of Inscriptions at Palenque, Mexico

py·ri·meth·a·mine (pī′rə-mĕth′ə-mēn′, -mĭn) *n.* A drug, $C_{12}H_{13}ClN_4$, used principally in the prophylactic treatment of malaria. [PYRIM(IDINE) + ETH(YL) + AMINE.]

py·rim·i·dine (pī-rĭm′ĭ-dēn′, pĭ-) *n.* **1.** A crystalline organic base, $C_4H_4N_2$, that is the parent substance of various biologically important derivatives. **2.** Any of several basic compounds derived from or structurally related to pyrimidine, especially the nucleic acid constituents uracil, cytosine, and thymine. [Alteration of PYRIDINE.]

py·rite (pī′rīt′) *n.* A brass-colored mineral, FeS_2, occurring widely and used as an iron ore and in producing sulfur dioxide for sulfuric acid. Also called *fool's gold, iron pyrites.* [Middle English *perides, pirite,* from Old French *pirite,* from Latin *pyrītēs,* flint. See PYRITES.] **—py·rit′ic** (-rĭt′ĭk), **py·rit′i·cal** (-ĭ-kəl) *adj.*

py·ri·tes (pī-rī′tēz, pī′rīts′) *n., pl.* **pyrites.** Any of various natural metallic sulfide minerals, especially of iron. [Latin *pyrītēs,* from Greek *puritēs (lithos),* fire (stone), flint, from *pur,* fire. See **pūr-** in Appendix.]

pyro. *abbr.* Pyrotechnics.

pyro– or **pyr–** *pref.* **1.** Fire; heat: *pyrotechnic.* **2.** Relating to the action of fire or heat: *pyrography.* **3.** Fever: *pyrogen.* **4.** Derived from an acid by the loss of a water molecule: *pyrosulfuric acid.* [New Latin, from Greek *puro-,* from *pur,* fire. See **pūr-** in Appendix.]

py·ro·cel·lu·lose (pī′rō-sĕl′yə-lōs′, -lōz′) *n.* A cellulose nitrate used as a component of smokeless powder.

py·ro·chem·i·cal (pī′rō-kĕm′ĭ-kəl) *adj.* Relating to or designating chemical activity at elevated temperatures. **—py′ro·chem′i·cal·ly** *adv.*

py·ro·clas·tic (pī′rō-klăs′tĭk) *adj.* Composed chiefly of rock fragments of volcanic origin.

py·ro·e·lec·tric (pī′rō-ĭ-lĕk′trĭk) *adj.* Relating to or exhibiting pyroelectricity. **—pyroelectric** *n.* A pyroelectric material.

py·ro·e·lec·tric·i·ty (pī′rō-ĭ-lĕk-trĭs′ĭ-tē, -ē′lĕk-) *n.* Generation of electric charge on a crystal by change of temperature.

py·ro·gal·lic acid (pī′rō-găl′ĭk, -gô′lĭk) *n.* See **pyrogallol.**

py·ro·gal·lol (pī′rō-găl′ôl′, -ōl′, -ŏl′, -gô′lôl′, -lōl′, -lŏl′) *n.* A white, toxic crystalline phenol, $C_6H_3(OH)_3$, used as a photographic developer and to treat certain skin diseases. Also called *pyrogallic acid.* [PYRO– + GALL(IC ACID) + –OL[1].] **—py′ro·gal′lic** (-găl′ĭk, -gô′lĭk) *adj.*

py·ro·gen (pī′rə-jən) *n.* A substance that produces fever.

py·ro·gen·ic (pī′rō-jĕn′ĭk) also **py·rog·e·nous** (pī-rŏj′ə-nəs) *adj.* **1.** Producing or produced by fever. **2.** Caused by or generating heat. **3.** Of or relating to solid rock formed from molten rock; igneous. **—py′ro·ge·nic′i·ty** (-rō-jə-nĭs′ĭ-tē) *n.*

py·rog·ra·phy (pī-rŏg′rə-fē) *n., pl.* **-phies. 1.** The process or art of producing designs on wood, leather, or other materials by using heated tools or a fine flame. **2.** A design made by this process. **—py′ro·graph′** (pī′rə-grăf′) *n.* **—py·rog′ra·pher** *n.* **—py′ro·graph′ic** *adj.*

py·ro·lig·ne·ous (pī′rō-lĭg′nē-əs) *adj.* Made by the destructive distillation of wood.

pyroligneous acid *n.* A reddish-brown wood distillate containing acetic acid, methyl alcohol, acetone, and a tarry residue. Also called *wood vinegar.*

py·ro·lu·site (pī′rō-lo͞o′sīt) *n.* A soft, black to dark gray mineral, MnO_2, the commonest and most important secondary ore of manganese. [German *Pyrolusit* : Greek *puro-,* pyro- + Greek *lousis,* a washing (from *louein,* to wash; see **leu(ə)-** in Appendix).]

py·rol·y·sis (pī-rŏl′ĭ-sĭs) *n.* Decomposition or transformation of a compound caused by heat. **—py′ro·lyt′ic** (-rə-lĭt′ĭk) *adj.* **—py′ro·lyt′i·cal·ly** *adv.*

py·ro·lyze (pī′rə-līz′) *tr.v.* **-lyzed, -lyz·ing, -lyz·es.** To subject (something) to pyrolysis.

py·ro·man·cy (pī′rə-măn′sē) *n.* Divination by fire or

ă pat	oi boy
ā pay	ou out
âr care	o͝o took
ä father	o͞o boot
ĕ pet	ŭ cut
ē be	ûr urge
ĭ pit	th thin
ī pie	*th* this
îr pier	hw which
ŏ pot	zh vision
ō toe	ə about, item
ô paw	♦ regionalism

Stress marks: **′** (primary); ′ (secondary), as in **dictionary** (dĭk′shə-nĕr′ē)

pyrrhuloxia
Pyrrhuloxia sinuata

python
Ball python
Python regius

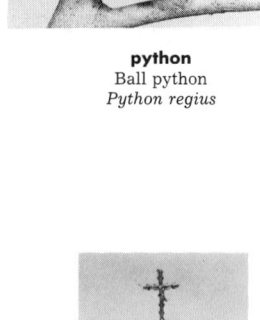

pyx
15th-century
Spanish silver

ă pat	oi boy
ā pay	ou out
âr care	o͝o took
ä father	o͞o boot
ĕ pet	ŭ cut
ē be	ûr urge
ĭ pit	th thin
ī pie	*th* this
îr pier	hw which
ŏ pot	zh vision
ō toe	ə about, item
ô paw	♦ regionalism

Stress marks: **ʹ** (primary); ʹ (secondary), as in **dictionary** (dĭkʹshə-nĕrʹē)

flames. [Middle English *piromance,* from Old French *pyromancie,* from Late Latin *pyromantīa,* from Greek *puromanteia* : *puro-,* pyro- + *manteia,* divination; see –MANCY.] **—pyʹro·manʹtic** (-mănʹtĭk) *adj.*

py·ro·ma·ni·a (pīʹrō-māʹnē-ə, -mānʹyə) *n. Psychiatry.* An uncontrollable impulse to start fires. **—pyʹro·maʹni·acʹ** (-māʹnē-ăkʹ) *adj. & n.* **—pyʹro·ma·niʹa·cal** (-mə-nīʹə-kəl) *adj.*

py·ro·met·al·lur·gy (pīʹrō-mĕtʹl-ûrʹjē) *n., pl.* **-gies.** An ore-refining process, such as smelting, dependent on the action of heat. **—pyʹro·metʹal·lurʹgi·cal** (-mĕtʹl-ûrʹjĭ-kəl) *adj.*

py·rom·e·ter (pī-rŏmʹĭ-tər) *n.* Any of various thermometers used for measuring high temperatures. **—pyʹro·metʹric** (-rə-mĕtʹrĭk), **pyʹro·metʹri·cal** (-rĭ-kəl) *adj.* **—pyʹro·metʹri·cal·ly** *adv.* **—py·romʹe·try** *n.*

py·ro·mor·phite (pīʹrə-môrʹfītʹ) *n.* A green, brown, or yellow mineral, $Pb_5(PO_4)_3Cl$, a minor ore of lead. [German *Pyromorphit* : Greek *puro-,* pyro- + Greek *morphē,* form.]

py·ro·nine (pīʹrə-nēnʹ) *n.* Any of a group of red dyes used as a biological stain, especially to detect the presence of RNA. [German *Pyronin,* originally a trademark.]

py·rope (pīʹrōpʹ) *n.* A deep red garnet, $Mg_3Al_2Si_3O_{12}$, used as a gem. [Middle English *pirope,* from Old French, from Latin *pyrōpum,* gold-bronze alloy, from Greek *purōpos,* fiery, kind of red bronze : *puro-,* pyro- + *ōps,* eye, face; see **okʷ-** in Appendix.]

py·ro·phor·ic (pīʹrə-fôrʹĭk, -fŏrʹ-) *adj.* **1.** Spontaneously igniting in air. **2.** Producing sparks by friction. [From *pyrophorus,* substance that ignites spontaneously : from Greek *purophoros,* fire-bearing : *puro-,* pyro- + *-phoros,* -phorous.]

py·ro·phos·phate (pīʹrə-fŏsʹfātʹ) *n.* A salt or an ester of pyrophosphoric acid. **—pyʹro·phos·phatʹic** (-fātʹĭk) *adj.*

py·ro·phos·phor·ic acid (pīʹrō-fŏs-fôrʹĭk, -fŏrʹ-) *n.* A syrupy viscous liquid, $H_4P_2O_7$, used as a catalyst and in organic chemical manufacture.

py·ro·phyl·lite (pīʹrō-fĭlʹītʹ, pī-rŏfʹə-lītʹ) *n.* A silvery white or pale green aluminum silicate mineral, $Al_2Si_4O_{10}(OH)_2$, occurring naturally in soft, compact masses.

py·ro·sis (pī-rōʹsĭs) *n.* See **heartburn.** [New Latin, from Greek *purōsis,* a burning, from *puroun,* to burn, from *pur,* fire. See **pūr-** in Appendix.]

py·ro·stat (pīʹrə-stătʹ) *n.* **1.** An automatic sensing device that activates an alarm or extinguisher in case of fire. **2.** A high-temperature thermostat.

py·ro·sul·fate (pīʹrō-sŭlʹfātʹ) *n.* A salt of pyrosulfuric acid. [PYROSULF(URIC ACID) + –ATE[2].]

py·ro·sul·fu·ric acid (pīʹrō-sŭl-fyo͝orʹĭk) *n.* A heavy, oily, colorless to dark brown liquid, $H_2S_2O_7$, produced by adding sulfur trioxide to concentrated sulfuric acid and used in petroleum refining and the manufacture of explosives.

py·ro·tech·nic (pīʹrə-tĕkʹnĭk) also **py·ro·tech·ni·cal** (-nĭ-kəl) *adj.* **1.** Of or relating to fireworks. **2. pyrotechnic.** Resembling fireworks; brilliant: *a pyrotechnic wit; pyrotechnic keyboard virtuosity.* **—pyʹro·techʹni·cal·ly** *adv.*

py·ro·tech·nics (pīʹrə-tĕkʹnĭks) *n. (used with a sing. verb). Abbr.* **pyro. 1.** The art of manufacturing or setting off fireworks. Also called *pyrotechny.* **2.** A fireworks display. **3.** A brilliant display, as of rhetoric or wit, or of virtuosity in the performing arts. **—pyʹro·techʹnist** *n.*

py·ro·tech·ny (pīʹrə-tĕkʹnē) *n.* See **pyrotechnics** (sense 1). [New Latin *pyrotechnia* : Greek *puro-,* pyro- + Greek *tekhnē,* craft; see TECHNIQUE.]

py·rox·ene (pī-rŏkʹsēnʹ) *n.* Any of a group of crystalline silicate minerals common in igneous and metamorphic rocks and containing two metallic oxides, as of magnesium, iron, calcium, sodium, or aluminum. [French *pyroxène* : Greek *puro-,* pyro- + Greek *xenos,* stranger (originally viewed as a foreign substance when found in igneous rocks); see **ghos-ti-** in Appendix.] **—pyʹrox·enʹic** (pīʹrŏk-sēʹnĭk, -sĕnʹĭk) *adj.*

py·rox·e·nite (pī-rŏkʹsə-nītʹ) *n.* An igneous rock consisting chiefly of pyroxenes. **—py·roxʹe·nitʹic** (-nĭtʹĭk) *adj.*

py·rox·y·lin (pī-rŏkʹsə-lĭn) also **py·rox·y·line** (-lēnʹ, -lĭn) *n.* A highly flammable nitrocellulose used in the manufacture of collodion, plastics, and lacquers.

pyr·rhic (pĭrʹĭk) *n.* A metrical foot having two short or unaccented syllables. **—pyrrhic** *adj.* Of or characterized by pyrrhics. [Latin *pyrrhicius,* from Greek *purrikhios,* from *purrikhē,* a war dance, perhaps from *Purrikhos,* supposed inventor of the dance.]

Pyr·rhic victory (pĭrʹĭk) *n.* A victory that is offset by staggering losses. [After PYRRHUS.]

pyr·rho·tite (pĭrʹə-tītʹ) also **pyr·rho·tine** (-tīnʹ) *n.* A brownish-bronze iron sulfide mineral, FeS, characterized by weak magnetic properties and used as an iron ore and in the manufacture of sulfuric acid. Also called *magnetic pyrites.* [Alteration (influenced by –ITE[1]) of German *Pyrrhotin,* from Greek *purrotēs,* redness, from *purros,* fiery, from *pur,* fire. See **pūr-** in Appendix.]

pyr·rhu·lox·i·a (pĭrʹə-lŏkʹsē-ə, pĭrʹyə-) *n.* A large, crested finch *(Pyrrhuloxia sinuata)* of Mexico and the southwest United States, having gray and red plumage and a short, thick bill. [New Latin *Pyrrhuloxia,* genus name : *Pyrrhula,* finch genus (from Greek *purroulas,* red-colored bird, from *purros,* red, from *pur,* fire; see PYRE) + *Loxia,* crossbill genus (from Greek *loxos,* oblique).]

Pyr·rhus (pĭrʹəs). 319–272 B.C. King of Epirus (306–302 and 297–272) who defeated the Romans at Heraclea (280) and Asculum (279) despite his own staggering losses.

pyr·role (pîrʹōlʹ) *n.* A five-membered heterocyclic ring compound, C_4H_5N, having an odor similar to chloroform. It is the parent compound of hemoglobin, chlorophyll, and many other complex, biologically active substances. [Greek *purros,* red (from *pur,* fire; see PYRE) + –OLE.] **—pyr·roʹlic** (pĭ-rōʹlĭk) *adj.*

py·ru·vate (pī-ro͞oʹvāt, pĭ-) *n.* A salt or an ester of pyruvic acid.

py·ru·vic acid (pī-ro͞oʹvĭk, pĭ-) *n.* A colorless organic liquid, $CH_3COCOOH$, formed as a fundamental intermediate in protein and carbohydrate metabolism. [PYR(O)– + Latin *ūva,* grape (from its being produced by the dry distillation of racemic acid, originally derived from grapes) + –IC.]

Py·thag·o·ras (pĭ-thăgʹər-əs). fl. sixth century B.C. Greek philosopher and mathematician who founded in southern Italy a school that emphasized the study of musical harmony and geometry. He proved the universal validity of the Pythagorean theorem and is considered the first true mathematician.

Py·thag·o·re·an·ism (pĭ-thăgʹə-rēʹə-nĭzʹəm) *n. Philosophy.* The syncretistic philosophy expounded by Pythagoras, distinguished chiefly by its description of reality in terms of arithmetical relationships. **—Py·thagʹo·reʹan** *adj. & n.*

Pythagorean theorem *n. Mathematics.* The theorem that the sum of the squares of the lengths of the sides of a right triangle is equal to the square of the length of the hypotenuse.

Pyth·i·an (pĭthʹē-ən) also **Pyth·ic** (pĭthʹĭk) *adj.* **1.** *Greek Mythology.* Of or relating to Delphi, the temple of Apollo at Delphi, or its oracle. **2.** Of or relating to the Pythian games. [From Latin *Pȳthius,* from Greek *Puthios,* from *Puthō,* ancient name of Delphi.]

Pythian games *pl.n.* A pan-Hellenic festival of athletic tournaments held every four years at Delphi in honor of Apollo.

Pyth·i·as (pĭthʹē-əs) *n.* A Greek who rescued his friend Damon, who stood bail for Pythias when he was condemned to die.

Pyth·ic (pĭthʹĭk) *adj.* Variant of **Pythian.**

py·thon (pīʹthŏnʹ, -thən) *n.* Any of various nonvenomous snakes of the family Pythonidae, found chiefly in Asia, Africa, and Australia, that coil around and suffocate their prey. Pythons often attain lengths of 6 meters (20 feet) or more. [Probably French, from Latin *Pȳthōn,* mythical serpent killed by Apollo near Delphi. See PYTHON.]

Py·thon (pīʹthŏnʹ, -thən) *n.* **1.** *Greek Mythology.* A dragon or serpent that was the tutelary demon of the oracular cult at Delphi until killed and expropriated by Apollo. **2. python. a.** A soothsaying spirit or demon. **b.** A person possessed by such a spirit. [Latin *Pȳthōn,* from Greek *Puthōn.*]

py·tho·ness (pīʹthə-nĭs, pĭthʹə-) *n.* **1.** *Greek Mythology.* A priestess of Apollo at Delphi. **2.** A prophetess. [Middle English *phitonesse,* from Old French *phitonise,* from Late Latin *pythonissa,* from Greek *Puthōn,* Python.]

py·thon·ic (pī-thŏnʹĭk) *adj.* **1.** Of, relating to, or resembling a python. **2.** Of or resembling an oracle; prophetic. **3.** Of extraordinary size and power.

py·u·ri·a (pī-yo͝orʹē-ə) *n.* The presence of pus in the urine, usually a sign of urinary tract infection.

pyx also **pix** (pĭks) *n.* **1.** *Ecclesiastical.* **a.** A container in which wafers for the Eucharist are kept. **b.** A container in which the Eucharist is carried to the sick. **2.** A chest in a mint in which specimen coins are placed to await assay. [Middle English *pyxe,* from Latin *pyxis,* box, from Greek *puxis.*]

pyx·i·des (pĭkʹsĭ-dēzʹ) *n.* Plural of **pyxis.**

pyx·id·i·um (pĭk-sĭdʹē-əm) *n., pl.* **-i·a** (-ē-ə). A pyxis. [New Latin, from Greek *puxidion,* diminutive of *puxis,* box.]

pyx·ie (pĭkʹsē) *n.* A creeping evergreen shrub *(Pyxidanthera barbulata)* having small white or pinkish flowers, native to pine barrens of the eastern United States. [Shortening and alteration of New Latin *Pyxidanthera,* genus name : Greek *puxis, puxid-,* box + Greek *anthera,* pollen; see ANTHER.]

pyx·is (pĭkʹsĭs) *n., pl.* **pyx·i·des** (pĭkʹsĭ-dēzʹ). *Botany.* A capsule dehiscing transversely by a lid that falls off to release the seeds. [Latin *pyxis,* box, from Greek *puxis.*]

Pyx·is (pĭkʹsĭs) *n.* A constellation in the Southern Hemisphere, near Antlia and Puppis. [New Latin *Pyxis (nautica),* (mariner's) compass, from Greek *puxis,* box.]

q¹ or **Q** (kyōō) *n., pl.* **q's** or **Q's. 1.** The 17th letter of the modern English alphabet. **2.** Any of the speech sounds represented by the letter *q*. **3.** The 17th in a series. **4.** Something shaped like the letter Q.

q² *Physics.* The symbol for **charge** (sense 13).

Q *abbr.* **1.** *Games.* Queen (chess). **2.** Quetzal.

q. *abbr.* **1.** Quart. **2.** Quarter. **3.** Quarterly. **4.** Also **Q.** Quarto. **5.** Query. **6.** Question. **7.** Quintal. **8.** Quire.

Qad·da·fi or **Qa·dha·fi** or **Kad·da·fi** or **Kha·da·fy** (kə-dä′fē) or **Gad·da·fi** (gə-), **Muammar al-** or **el-.** Born 1942. Libyan political leader who seized power in a military coup d'état against the Libyan monarchy (1969) and imposed socialist policies and Islamic orthodoxy on the country.

q and a *abbr.* Question and answer.

Qan·da·har (kŭn′də-här′, kän′-). See **Kandahar.**

Qa·tar (kä′tär′, kə-tär′). A country of eastern Arabia on a peninsula in the southwest Persian Gulf. It was under British protection from 1916 until 1971, when it became independent. Oil was first produced commercially in 1949. Doha is the capital. Population, 220,000. **—Qa·tar′i** *adj. & n.*

Qat·ta·ra Depression (kə-tär′ə). A desert basin of northwest Egypt in the Libyan Desert. Its lowest point is about 134 m (440 ft) below sea level.

Qaz·vin also **Kaz·vin** (kăz-vēn′). A city of northwest Iran northwest of Tehran. Founded in the fourth century A.D., it was captured by the Arabs in 644 and was the capital of Persia from 1548 to 1598. Population, 244,000.

qb *abbr. Football.* Quarterback.

QB *abbr. Games.* Queen's bishop (chess).

Q.B. *abbr. Law.* Queen's Bench.

Q.C. *abbr.* **1.** Also **QC** Quality control. **2.** *Law.* Queen's Counsel.

Q.E.D. *abbr. Latin.* Quod erat demonstrandum (which was to be demonstrated.).

Q.E.F. *abbr. Latin.* Quod erat faciendum (which was to have been done).

QF *abbr.* Quick-firing.

Q fever *n.* An infectious disease caused by the rickettsia *Coxiella burnetii* that is characterized by fever, malaise, and muscular pains. [Q(UERY) + FEVER.]

Qian·long (chyän′lŏŏng′) also **Ch'ien-lung** (chyĕn′lŏŏng′). 1711–1799. Chinese emperor (1735–1796) of the Qing dynasty who subdued the Turkish and Mongolian threats to northern China, expanded the empire, and was a patron of the arts.

q.i.d. *abbr. Latin.* Quater in die (four times a day).

Qi·lian Shan (chē′lyän′ shän′) also **Nan Shan** (nän′). A mountain range of north-central China extending northwest to southeast and having peaks rising from 5,490 m (18,000 ft) to more than 6,100 m (20,000 ft).

Qin also **Ch'in** (chĭn). A Chinese dynasty (221–206 B.C.) that established the first centralized imperial government in China. Much of the Great Wall of China was built during the rule of this dynasty.

qin·dar·ka (kĭn-där′kə) *n.* See table at **currency.** [Albanian *qindarka,* definite sing. of *qindarkë,* from *qintar,* from *qint, qind,* hundred, from Latin *centum.* See CENT.]

Qing also **Ch'ing** (chĭng). Also called Manchu. A Chinese dynasty (1644–1912) during which increasing Western influence and trade led to the Opium War (1839–1842) with Britain and the Boxer Rebellion (1898–1900). The dynasty, China's last, was overthrown by nationalist revolutionaries.

Qing·dao (chĭng′dou′) also **Tsing·tao** (tsĭng′tou′). A city of eastern China on the Yellow Sea north-northwest of Shanghai. It is a leading industrial and tourist center. The city was leased in 1898 to the Germans, who established a famed brewery. Population, 1,250,000.

Qing·hai also **Ching·hai** (chĭng′hī′) or **Tsing·hai** (tsĭng′). A province of northwest-central China. Its northern border is the Qilian Shan. Xining is the capital. Population, 4,070,000.

Qinghai Hu (hōō) also **Ko·ko Nor** (kō′kō′ nôr′, nōr′). A salt lake of north-central China south of the Qilian Shan. The largest lake in China, it is at an altitude of more than 3,050 m (10,000 ft).

Qin·huang·dao (chĭn′hwäng′dou′) also **Chin·wang·tao** (chĭn′wäng′tou′). A city of northeast China on the Gulf of Bo Hai east of Beijing. It was formerly a treaty port. Population, 300,000.

qin·tar (kĭn-tär′) *n.* A coin formerly used in Albania and worth one one-hundredth of a lek. [Albanian. See QINDARKA.]

Qi·qi·har (chē′chē′här′) also **Tsi·tsi·har** (tsē′tsē′-). A city of northeast China in Manchuria northwest of Harbin. Founded as a fortress in 1691, it is a processing center. Population, 955,200.

qi·vi·ut (kē′vē-ət, -ōōt′) *n.* The soft wool lying beneath the long coat of the musk ox, valued for its use as a fiber. [Inupiaq.]

QKt *abbr. Games.* Queen's knight (chess).

ql. *abbr.* Quintal.

qlty. *abbr.* Quality.

QM *abbr.* Quartermaster.

Q.M. *abbr. Latin.* Quaque mane (every morning).

QMC *abbr.* Quartermaster Corps.

QMG *abbr.* Quartermaster General.

qn. *abbr.* Question.

Qom (kōm) also **Qum** (kōōm). A city of west-central Iran south-southwest of Tehran. It has been a Shiite Moslem center since early Islamic times and a pilgrimage site since the 17th century. Population, 424,000.

qoph (kôf) *n.* The 19th letter of the Hebrew alphabet. See table at **alphabet.** [Hebrew *qôp.*]

QP *abbr. Games.* Queen's pawn (chess).

q.p. *abbr. Latin.* Quantum placet (as much as you please).

qq. *abbr.* Questions.

qq.v. *abbr. Latin.* Quae vide (which [things] see).

QR *abbr. Games.* Queen's rook (chess).

qr. *abbr.* **1.** Quarter. **2.** Quarterly. **3.** Quire.

q.s. *abbr. Latin.* Quantum sufficit (as much as suffices).

qt or **qt.** *abbr.* Quart.

qt. *abbr.* Quantity.

q.t. (kyōō′tē′) *n. Slang.* Quiet: *told me the story strictly on the q.t.* [Short for QUIET.]

Q-Tip (kyōō′tĭp′). A trademark used for a cotton-tipped swab. This trademark often occurs in print in the plural and with a lowercase *t*: *"They scrubbed for two hours straight, using rolls of paper towels, sponges, Q-tips (for hard to reach places) . . . and lots of elbow grease"* (Washington Post). *"With a surgical scalpel,* [he] *cut away most of the epoxy under a microscope; then, using a Q-tip . . . he cleaned the edges"* (Smithsonian).

qto. *abbr.* Quarto.

qty. *abbr.* Quantity.

qu. *abbr.* **1.** Queen. **2.** Query. **3.** Question.

qua (kwā, kwä) *prep.* In the capacity or character of; as: *The President qua head of the party mediated the dispute.* [Latin *quā,* feminine ablative sing. of *quī,* who. See **kʷo-** in Appendix.]

Quaa·lude (kwā′lōōd′). A trademark formerly used for methaqualone.

WORD HISTORY: The former trademark *Quaalude* for the sedative and hypnotic agent methaqualone is an example of how a product name is carefully chosen for a positive public response. Methaqualone was developed in the 1960's by William H. Rorer, Inc. At that time, the company's best-known product was Maalox, a digestive aid that derived its name from its ingredients, *mag*nesium and *al*uminum hydr*ox*ides. To enhance the product recognition of their new sedative drug, the company incorporated the *aa* of *Maalox* into the name *Quaalude.* The other elements of the name are presumed to be a contraction of the phrase *quiet interlude,* a soothing, even poetic description of the drug's effect.

quack¹ (kwăk) *n.* The characteristic sound uttered by a duck. **—quack** *intr.v.* **quacked, quack·ing, quacks.** To utter the characteristic sound of a duck. [Middle English *quek,* of imitative origin.] **—quack′y** *adj.*

Phoenician

The Semitic languages distinguish in writing between the consonant *k* and the similar-sounding velar stop *q*, called *qōph.*

Early Greek

In adapting the Phoenician alphabet the Greeks at first retained the letter they called *koppa* to stand for a *k* before *o* or *u.* In the East Greek dialects, which furnished the classical Greek alphabet, this usage was soon abandoned in favor of *kappa.*

Roman

But the practice survived in West Greek, so that the Roman heirs to that tradition continued to use the letter Q for the sound of *k* before *u.*

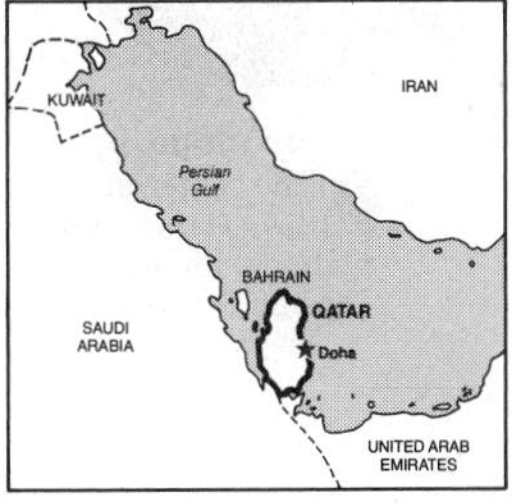

Qatar

quack² (kwăk) *n.* **1.** An untrained person who pretends to be a physician and dispenses medical advice and treatment. **2.** A charlatan; a mountebank. See Synonyms at **imposter.** —**quack** *adj.* Relating to or characteristic of a quack: *a quack cure.* —**quack** *intr.v.* **quacked, quack·ing, quacks.** To act as a medical quack or a charlatan. [Short for QUACKSALVER.] —**quack′er·y** *n.* —**quack′ish** *adj.* —**quack′ish·ly** *adv.*

quack grass *n.* See **couch grass.** [Variant of QUITCH GRASS.]

quack·sal·ver (kwăk′săl′vər) *n. Archaic.* A quack or charlatan. [Obsolete Dutch : Middle Dutch *quac-*, unguent, or *quacken,* to quack, boast + Middle Dutch *salven,* to salve.]

quad¹ (kwŏd) *n.* A quadrangle: *cadets forming up in the barracks quad.*

quad² (kwŏd) *n. Printing.* See **quadrat** (sense 1).

quad³ (kwŏd) *n.* A quadruplet.

quad⁴ (kwŏd) *adj.* Quadraphonic.

quad. *abbr.* **1.** Quadrangle. **2.** Quadrant. **3.** Quadrilateral.

quadr– *pref.* Variant of **quadri–.**

quad·ran·gle (kwŏd′răng′gəl) *n. Abbr.* **quad. 1.** *Mathematics.* A plane figure consisting of four points, no three of which are collinear, connected by straight lines. **2.a.** A rectangular area surrounded on all four sides by buildings. **b.** The buildings bordering this area. **3.** The area of land shown on one atlas sheet charted by the U.S. Geological Survey. [Middle English, from Old French, from Late Latin *quadrangulum,* from Latin, neuter of *quadrangulus,* four-cornered : *quadri-*, quadri- + *angulus,* angle.] —**quad·ran′gu·lar** (-răng′gyə-lər) *adj.* —**quad·ran′gu·lar·ly** *adv.* —**quad·ran′gu·lar·ness** *n.*

quad·rant (kwŏd′rənt) *n. Abbr.* **quad. 1.** *Mathematics.* **a.** A circular arc of 90°; one fourth of the circumference of a circle. **b.** The plane area bounded by such an arc and two perpendicular radii. **c.** Any of the four areas into which a plane is divided by the reference axes in a Cartesian coordinate system, designated *first, second, third,* and *fourth,* counting counterclockwise from the area in which both coordinates are positive. **2.** A machine part or other mechanical device that is shaped like a quarter circle. **3.** An early instrument for measuring altitude of celestial bodies, consisting of a 90° graduated arc with a movable radius for measuring angles. [Middle English, quarter of a day, from Latin *quadrāns, quadrant-*, a fourth part. See **kʷetwer-** in Appendix.]

quad·ra·phon·ic also **quad·ri·phon·ic** (kwŏd′rə-fŏn′ĭk) *adj.* Of or for a four-channel sound system in which speakers are positioned at all four corners of the listening space, reproducing signals that are independent of each other. —**qua·draph′o·ny** (kwŏ-drăf′ə-nē) *n.*

quad·ra·son·ic (kwŏd′rə-sŏn′ĭk) *adj.* Quadraphonic.

quad·rat (kwŏd′rət, -răt′) *n.* **1.** *Printing.* A piece of type metal lower than the raised typeface, used for filling spaces and blank lines. Also called *quad.* **2.** *Ecology.* Any of a group of small, usually rectangular plots of land arranged for close study of the distribution of plants or animals in an area. [Middle English, a square geometric instrument, rectangular area. See QUADRATE.]

quad·rate (kwŏd′rāt′, -rĭt) *n.* **1.a.** A square or cube. **b.** An approximately square or cubic area, space, or object. **2.** *Zoology.* A bone or cartilaginous structure of the skull, joining the upper and lower jaws in birds, fish, reptiles, and amphibians. —**quadrate** *adj.* **1.** Having four sides and four angles; square or rectangular. **2.** *Zoology.* Designating the quadrate bone or cartilage. —**quadrate** *intr.v.* **-rat·ed, -rat·ing, -rates.** *Archaic.* To correspond; agree. [Middle English *quadrat,* something square, from Latin *quadrātum,* from neuter past participle of *quadrāre,* to make square, from *quadrum,* square. See **kʷetwer-** in Appendix.]

quad·rat·ic (kwŏ-drăt′ĭk) *adj. Mathematics.* Of, relating to, or containing quantities of the second degree. [From QUADRATE.] —**quad·rat′ic** *n.* —**quad·rat′i·cal·ly** *adv.*

quadratic equation *n. Mathematics.* An equation in which one or more of the terms is squared but raised to no higher power, having the general form $ax^2 + bx + c = 0$, where *a, b,* and *c* are constants.

quadratic formula *n. Mathematics.* The formula $x = [-b \pm \sqrt{(b^2 - 4ac)}]/2a$, used to compute the roots of a quadratic equation.

quad·rat·ics (kwŏ-drăt′ĭks) *n.* (*used with a sing. verb*). *Mathematics.* The branch of algebra that deals with quadratic equations.

quad·ra·ture (kwŏd′rə-cho͝or′) *n.* **1.** The process of making something square. **2.** *Mathematics.* The process of constructing a square equal in area to a given surface. **3.** *Astronomy.* A configuration in which the position of one celestial body is 90° from another celestial body, as measured from a third.

quad·ren·ni·a (kwô-drĕn′ē-ə) *n.* A plural of **quadrennium.**

quad·ren·ni·al (kwŏ-drĕn′ē-əl) *adj.* **1.** Happening once in four years. **2.** Lasting for four years. —**quad·ren′ni·al** *n.* —**quad·ren′ni·al·ly** *adv.*

quad·ren·ni·um (kwŏ-drĕn′ē-əm) *n., pl.* **quad·ren·ni·ums** or **quad·ren·ni·a** (kwô-drĕn′ē-ə). A period of four years. [Latin *quadriennium* : *quadri-*, quadri- + *-ennium* (from *annus,* year; see **at-** in Appendix).]

quadri– or **quadru–** or **quadr–** *pref.* **1.** Four: *quadrilateral.* **2.** Square: *quadrate.* [Middle English, from Latin. See **kʷetwer-** in Appendix.]

quad·ric (kwŏd′rĭk) *adj. Mathematics.* Of or relating to geometric surfaces that are defined by quadratic equations.

quadriga
In the center of a c. 1810 earthenware plate attributed to Josiah Spode II

quad·ri·cen·ten·ni·al (kwŏd′rĭ-sĕn-tĕn′ē-əl) *n.* A 400th anniversary. —**quad′ri·cen·ten′ni·al** *adj.*

quad·ri·ceps (kwŏd′rĭ-sĕps′) *n.* The large four-part extensor muscle at the front of the thigh. [QUADRI– + (BI)CEPS.] —**quad′ri·cip′i·tal** (-sĭp′ĭ-tl) *adj.*

quad·ri·ga (kwŏd′rī-gə) *n., pl.* **-gae** (-gē). A two-wheeled chariot drawn by four horses abreast. [Latin *quadrīga,* sing. of *quadrīgae,* team of four horses, contraction of *quadriiugae,* feminine pl. of *quadriiugus,* of a team of four : *quadri-*, quadri- + *iugum,* yoke; see JUGUM.]

quad·ri·lat·er·al (kwŏd′rə-lăt′ər-əl) *n. Abbr.* **quad.** *Mathematics.* A plane figure with four sides and four angles. —**quadrilateral** *adj. Abbr.* **quad.** Having four sides.

qua·drille¹ (kwŏ-drĭl′, kwə-, kə-) *n.* **1.** A square dance of French origin composed of five figures and performed by four couples. **2.** Music for this dance in 6/8 and 2/4 time. [French, from *quadrille,* team, crew, one of four groups of horsemen, from Spanish *cuadrilla,* probably diminutive of *cuadro,* square, from Latin *quadrum.* See **kʷetwer-** in Appendix.]

qua·drille² (kwŏ-drĭl′, kwə-, kə-) *n. Games.* A card game popular during the 18th century, played by four people with a deck of 40 cards. [French, perhaps from Spanish *cuartillo,* diminutive of *cuarto,* fourth, from Latin *quārtus.* See **kʷetwer-** in Appendix.]

quad·ril·lion (kwŏ-drĭl′yən) *n.* **1.** The cardinal number equal to 10^{15}. **2.** *Chiefly British.* Septillion. [QUADR(I)– + (M)ILLION.] —**quad·ril′lion** *adj.*

quad·ril·lionth (kwŏ-drĭl′yənth) *n.* **1.** The ordinal number matching the number quadrillion in a series. **2.** One of a quadrillion equal parts. —**quad·ril′lionth** *adv. & adj.*

quad·ri·par·tite (kwŏd′rə-pär′tīt′) *adj.* **1.** Consisting of or divided into four parts. **2.** Involving four participants.

quad·ri·phon·ic (kwŏd′rə-fŏn′ĭk) *adj.* Variant of **quadraphonic.** —**quad′ri·phon′y** *n.*

quad·ri·ple·gi·a (kwŏd′rə-plē′jē-ə, -jə) *n.* Paralysis of the body from the neck down. —**quad′ri·ple′gic** *adj. & n.*

quad·ri·va·lent (kwŏd′rə-vā′lənt) *adj. Chemistry.* **1.** Having four valences. **2.** Having a valence of four; tetravalent. —**quad′ri·va′lence, quad′ri·va′len·cy** *n.*

quad·riv·i·um (kwŏ-drĭv′ē-əm) *n., pl.* **-i·a** (-ē-ə). The higher division of the seven liberal arts in the Middle Ages, composed of geometry, astronomy, arithmetic, and music. [Late Latin, from Latin, place where four roads meet : *quadri-*, quadri- + *via,* road; see VIA.]

quad·roon (kwŏ-dro͞on′) *n.* A person having one-quarter Black ancestry. [Alteration of Spanish *cuarterón,* from *cuarto,* quarter, from Latin *quārtus.* See **kʷetwer-** in Appendix.]

quadru– *pref.* Variant of **quadri–.**

quad·ru·ma·nous (kwŏ-dro͞o′mə-nəs) also **quad·ru·ma·nal** (-nəl) *adj. Zoology.* Having four feet with opposable first digits, as primates other than human beings. [QUADRU– + Latin *manus,* hand; see **man-²** in Appendix + –OUS.]

quad·rum·vi·rate (kwŏ-drŭm′vər-ĭt) *n.* A group of four people joined in authority or office, especially a government of four people: "[Chiang Kai-shek] *was . . . the last survivor of the World War II quadrumvirate that included Roosevelt, Churchill and Stalin*" (Newsweek). [QUADR(I)– + (TRI)UMVIRATE.]

quad·ru·ped (kwŏd′rə-pĕd′) *n.* A four-footed animal. —**quadruped** *adj.* Four-footed: *a quadruped mammal.* —**quad·ru′pe·dal** (kwŏ-dro͞o′pə-dəl, kwŏd′rə-pĕd′l) *adj.*

quad·ru·ple (kwŏ-dro͞o′pəl, -drŭp′əl, kwŏd′ro͞o-pəl) *adj.* **1.** Having four parts or members. **2.** Multiplied by four; fourfold. **3.** *Music.* Having four beats to the measure. —**quadruple** *n.* A number four times as great as another. —**quadruple** *tr. & intr.v.* **-pled, -pling, -ples.** To multiply or be multiplied by four: *quadrupled the order; quadrupled in size.* [From Middle English *quadriple,* fourfold amount, and *quadruple,* tooth with four roots, both from Old French *quadruple,* from Latin *quadruplum,* from neuter of *quadruplus,* fourfold : *quadru-*, *quadri-*, quadri- + *-plus,* -fold; see **pel-²** in Appendix.] —**quad·ru′ply** *adv.*

quad·ru·plet (kwŏ-drŭp′lĭt, -dro͞o′plĭt, kwŏd′rə-plĭt) *n.* **1.** One of four offspring born in a single birth. **2.** A group or combination of four associated by common properties or behavior.

quad·ru·pli·cate (kwŏ-dro͞o′plĭ-kĭt) *adj.* **1.** Multiplied by four; quadruple. **2.** Fourth in a group of four identical things. —**quadruplicate** *n.* One of a group of four identical things. —**quadruplicate** (-kāt′) *tr. & intr.v.* **-cat·ed, -cat·ing, -cates.** To multiply or be multiplied four times. [Latin *quadruplicātus,* past participle of *quadruplicāre,* to multiply by four, from *quadruplex,* fourfold : *quadru-*, *quadri-*, quadri- + *-plex,* -fold; see DUPLEX.] —**quad·ru′pli·cate·ly** (-kĭt-lē) *adv.* —**quad·ru′pli·ca′tion** *n.*

quaes·tor (kwĕs′tər, kwē′stər) *n.* Any of various public officials in ancient Rome responsible for finance and administration in various areas of government and the military. [Middle English *questor,* from Latin *quaestor,* from *quaerere, quaest-*, to inquire.] —**quaes·to′ri·al** (kwĕ-stôr′ē-əl, -stōr′-, kwē-) *adj.* —**quaes′tor·ship′** *n.*

quaff (kwŏf, kwăf, kwôf) *v.* **quaffed, quaff·ing, quaffs.** —*tr.* To drink (a beverage) heartily: *quaffed the ale with gusto.* —*intr.* To drink a liquid heartily: *quaffed from the spring.* —**quaff** *n.* A hearty draft of liquid. [Origin unknown.] —**quaff′er** *n.*

quag (kwăg, kwŏg) *n.* A quagmire. [Perhaps variant of Middle English *quabbe,* from Old English **cwabba.*]

quag·ga (kwăg′ə, kwŏg′ə) *n.* A zebralike mammal *(Equus quagga)* of southern Africa, extinct since the late 19th century. [Afrikaans, from Nguni (Xhosa) *(i-)qwaxa,* something striped, perhaps from Khoikhoin *!ua-xa.*]

quag·gy (kwăg′ē, kwŏg′ē) *adj.* **-gi·er, -gi·est. 1.** Resembling a marsh; soggy. **2.** Soft and flabby.

quag·mire (kwăg′mīr′, kwŏg′-) *n.* **1.** Land with a soft, muddy surface. **2.** A difficult or precarious situation; a predicament.

qua·hog also **qua·haug** (kwô′hôg′, -hŏg′, kwō′-, kō′-) *n.* An edible clam *(Venus mercenaria)* of the Atlantic coast of North America, having a hard, rounded shell. Also called *hard-shell clam, round clam.* [Narragansett *poquaûhock.*]

quaich also **quaigh** (kwāKH) *n. Scots.* A two-handled drinking cup. [Scottish Gaelic *cuach,* from Old Irish *cúach,* alteration of *cuăch.*]

Quai d'Or·say (kā′ dôr-sā′, kē′, kĕ dôr-sĕ′). A street paralleling the southern bank of the Seine River in Paris, France, notable for its governmental ministries. The name is used figuratively to refer to the French foreign office.

quail[1] (kwāl) *n., pl.* **quail** or **quails. 1.** Any of various Old World chickenlike birds of the genus *Coturnix,* especially *C. coturnix,* small in size and having mottled brown plumage and a short tail. **2.** Any of various similar or related New World birds, such as the bobwhite. [Middle English *quaille,* from Old French, perhaps from Vulgar Latin **coacula,* of imitative origin.]

quail[2] (kwāl) *intr.v.* **quailed, quail·ing, quails.** To shrink back in fear; cower. See Synonyms at **recoil.** [Middle English *quailen,* to give way, probably from Middle Dutch *quelen,* to suffer, be ill. See **g^{w}ele-** in Appendix.]

quaint (kwānt) *adj.* **quaint·er, quaint·est. 1.** Odd, especially in an old-fashioned way: *"There is something almost quaint in the image of Irish organized crime, something that calls to mind old movies with Jimmy Cagney"* (James Traub). **2.** Unfamiliar or unusual; strange: *quaint dialect words.* See Synonyms at **strange.** [Middle English, clever, cunning, peculiar, from Old French *queinte, cointe,* from Latin *cognitus,* past participle of *cognōscere,* to learn. See COGNITION.] **—quaint′ly** *adv.* **—quaint′ness** *n.*

quake (kwāk) *intr.v.* **quaked, quak·ing, quakes. 1.** To shake, as from instability or shock. **2.** To shiver, as with cold or from strong emotion. See Synonyms at **shake. —quake** *n.* **1.** An instance of quaking. **2.** An earthquake. [Middle English *quaken,* from Old English *cwacian.*] **—quak′y** *adj.*

quake·proof (kwāk′pro͞of′) *adj.* Designed or constructed to withstand or resist the effects of an earthquake. **—quakeproof** *tr.v.* **-proofed, -proof·ing, -proofs.** To make quakeproof.

Quak·er (kwā′kər) *n.* A member of the Society of Friends. [From QUAKE (from an early leader's admonishment to "tremble at the word of the Lord.").] **—Quak′er·ism** *n.* **—Quak′er·ly** *adv. & adj.*

Quaker gun *n.* A dummy gun made of wood. [From the Quakers' opposition to war.]

Quak·er-la·dies (kwā′kər-lā′dēz) *pl.n.* See **bluets.**

quak·ing aspen (kwā′kĭng) *n.* A North American deciduous tree *(Populus tremuloides)* having broadly ovate, finely toothed leaves with a truncate base.

qual. *abbr.* Qualitative.

qua·le (kwä′lē) *n., pl.* **-li·a** (-lē-ə). A property, such as whiteness, considered independently from things having the property. [From Latin *quāle,* neuter of *quālis,* of what kind. See QUALITY.]

qual·i·fi·ca·tion (kwŏl′ə-fĭ-kā′shən) *n.* **1.** The act of qualifying or the condition of being qualified. **2.** A quality, an ability, or an accomplishment that makes a person suitable for a particular position or task. **3.** A condition or circumstance that must be met or complied with: *fulfilled the qualifications for registering to vote in the presidential election.* **4.** A restriction or modification: *an offer with a number of qualifications.*

qual·i·fied (kwŏl′ə-fīd′) *adj.* **1.** Having the appropriate qualifications for an office, a position, or a task. **2.** Limited, restricted, or modified: *a qualified plan for expansion.* **—qual′i·fied′ly** (-fīd′lē, -fī′ĭd-lē) *adv.*

qual·i·fi·er (kwŏl′ə-fī′ər) *n.* **1.** One that qualifies, especially one that has or fulfills all appropriate qualifications, as for a position, an office, or a task. **2.** *Grammar.* A word or phrase that qualifies, limits, or modifies the meaning of another word or phrase.

qual·i·fy (kwŏl′ə-fī′) *v.* **-fied, -fy·ing, -fies.** —*tr.* **1.** To describe by enumerating the characteristics or qualities of; characterize. **2.** To make competent or eligible for an office, a position, or a task. **3.a.** To declare competent or capable; certify. **b.** To make legally capable; license. **4.** To modify, limit, or restrict, as by giving exceptions. **5.** To make less harsh or severe; moderate. See Synonyms at **moderate. 6.** *Grammar.* To modify the meaning of (a noun, for example). —*intr.* **1.** To be or become qualified. **2.** To reach the later stages of a selection process or contest by competing successfully in earlier rounds. [From French *qualifier* (from Old French) and from Middle English *qualifien,* to specify the time and place of a document's execution, both from Medieval Latin *quālificāre,* to attribute a quality to : Latin *quālis,* of such a kind; see QUALITY + Latin *-ficāre,* -fy.]

qual·i·ta·tive (kwŏl′ĭ-tā′tĭv) *adj. Abbr.* **qual.** Of, relating to, or concerning quality. [Middle English, producing a primary quality, from Medieval Latin *quālitātīvus,* from Late Latin, qualitative, from Latin *quālitās, quālitāt-,* quality. See QUALITY.] **—qual′i·ta′tive·ly** *adv.*

qualitative analysis *n.* The testing of a substance or mixture to determine its chemical constituents.

qual·i·ty (kwŏl′ĭ-tē) *n., pl.* **-ties.** *Abbr.* **qlty. 1.a.** An inherent or distinguishing characteristic; a property. **b.** A personal trait, especially a character trait: *someone with few redeeming qualities.* **2.** Essential character; nature: *Mahogany has the quality of being durable.* **3.a.** Superiority of kind: *an intellect of unquestioned quality.* **b.** Degree or grade of excellence: *yard goods of low quality.* **4.a.** High social position. **b.** Those in a high social position. **5.** *Music.* Timbre, as determined by overtones: *a voice with a distinctive metallic quality.* **6.** *Linguistics.* The character of a vowel sound determined by the size and shape of the oral cavity and the amount of resonance with which the sound is produced. **7.** *Logic.* The positive or negative character of a proposition. **—quality** *adj.* Having a high degree of excellence: *"He settled in to read Edmund Wilson . . . It was quality time"* (Margaret Truman). [Middle English *qualite,* from Old French, from Latin *quālitās, quālitāt-,* from *quālis,* of what kind. See **k^{w}o-** in Appendix.]

SYNONYMS: *quality, property, attribute, character, trait.* These nouns all signify a feature that distinguishes or identifies someone or something. *Quality* is the most inclusive: *"The spring of water . . . entirely lost the deliciousness of its pristine quality"* (Nathaniel Hawthorne). *"From now on an artist will be judged only by the resonance of his solitude or the quality of his despair"* (Cyril Connolly). *"The most vital quality a soldier can possess is self-confidence"* (George S. Patton). A *property* is a basic or essential quality possessed by all members of a class: *Resilience is a property of rubber.* An *attribute* is a quality that is ascribed to someone or something: *"God and all the attributes of God are eternal"* (Spinoza). *Character* in this comparison is a distinctive feature of a group or category: *"Natural Selection, entailing Divergence of Character and the Extinction of less-improved forms"* (Charles Darwin). A *trait* is a single, clearly delineated characteristic, as of a person or group of people: *"This reliance on authority is a fundamental primitive trait"* (James Harvey Robinson).

quality circle *n.* A group of employees who perform similar duties and meet at periodic intervals, often with management, to discuss work-related issues and to offer suggestions and ideas for improvements, as in production methods or quality control.

quality control *n. Abbr.* **QC, Q.C.** A system for ensuring the maintenance of proper standards in manufactured goods, especially by periodic random inspection of the product. **—qual′i·ty-con·trol′** (kwŏl′ĭ-tē-kən-trōl′) *adj.*

quality of life *n.* The degree of emotional, intellectual, or cultural satisfaction in a person's everyday life as distinct from the degree of material comfort: *"programs that . . . make a big difference in the quality of life here in the city"* (Henry Geldzahler).

qualm (kwäm, kwôm) *n.* **1.** A sudden feeling of sickness, faintness, or nausea. **2.** A sudden disturbing feeling: *qualms of homesickness.* **3.** An uneasy feeling about the propriety or rightness of a course of action. [Origin unknown.] **—qualm′ish** *adj.* **—qualm′ish·ly** *adv.*

SYNONYMS: *qualm, scruple, compunction, misgiving.* These nouns denote a feeling of uncertainty about the fitness or correctness of an action. *Qualm* is a disturbing, often queasy feeling of uneasiness and self-doubt: *"an ignorant ruffianly gaucho, who . . . would . . . fight, steal, and do other naughty things without a qualm"* (W.H. Hudson). *Scruple* is an uneasy feeling arising from conscience or principle about the decency, propriety, or appropriateness of a course of action: *"My father's old-fashioned notions boggled a little at first to this arrangement . . . but his scruples were in the end overruled"* (John Galt). *Compunction* implies a prick or twinge of conscience aroused by wrongdoing or the prospect of wrongdoing: *He stole the money without the slightest compunction. Misgiving* suggests often sudden apprehension: *"The British Empire and the United States will have to be somewhat mixed up together . . . for mutual and general advantage. For my own part . . . I do not view the process with any misgivings"* (Winston S. Churchill).

quam·ash (kwŏm′ăsh′) *n.* See **camas** (sense 1). [New Latin, species name, variant of Chinook Jargon *kamass.* See CAMAS.]

quan·da·ry (kwŏn′də-rē, -drē) *n., pl.* **-ries.** A state of uncertainty or perplexity. See Synonyms at **predicament.** [Origin unknown.]

Quan·da·ry Peak (kwän′də-rē, -drē). A mountain, 4,350.8 m (14,265 ft) high, in the Park Range of the Rocky Mountains in central Colorado.

quan·dong also **quan·dang** (kwŏn′dŏng′) *n.* **1.** An Australian root-parasitic tree or shrub *(Santalum acuminatum)* bearing shiny red drupes with edible flesh used for jam or as a dessert. **2.** An Australian tree *(Elaeocarpus angustifolius)* having dark glossy green leaves, greenish-white flowers, and globular, shiny, bright blue drupes. [Wiradhuri (Aboriginal language of southeast Australia) *guwandhaŋ.*]

quan·go (kwăng′gō) *n., pl.* **-gos.** An organization or agency

quagga
Equus quagga

quail[1]
Male California quail
Lophortyx californicus

ă **pat**	oi **boy**
ā **pay**	ou **out**
âr **care**	o͝o **took**
ä **father**	o͞o **boot**
ĕ **pet**	ŭ **cut**
ē **be**	ûr **urge**
ĭ **pit**	th **thin**
ī **pie**	*th* **this**
îr **pier**	hw **which**
ŏ **pot**	zh **vision**
ō **toe**	ə **about, item**
ô **paw**	♦ **regionalism**

Stress marks: **′** (primary); ′ (secondary), as in **dictionary** (dĭk′shə-nĕr′ē)

quarrel²

that is financed by a government but that acts independently of it. [*qua(si) n(on-)g(overnmental) o(rganization)*.]

quant (kwŏnt) *n. Slang.* An expert in the use of mathematics and related subjects, particularly in investment management and stock trading. [Probably short for QUANTITATIVE.]

quant. *abbr.* Quantitative.

quan·ta (kwŏn′tə) *n.* Plural of **quantum.**

quan·tal (kwŏn′tl) *adj.* **1.** *Physics.* **a.** Of or relating to a quantum or a quantized system. **b.** Existing in only one of two possible states. **2.** *Biology.* Of or designating an all-or-none response or effect: *a quantal reaction.* **—quan′tal·ly** *adv.*

quan·ta·some (kwŏn′tə-sōm′) *n.* One of numerous particles located on the inner lamellar surface of a chloroplast and sometimes considered to be the functional unit of photosynthesis. [QUANTA + –SOME³.]

quan·tic (kwŏn′tĭk) *n. Mathematics.* A homogeneous polynomial having two or more variables. [Latin *quantus,* how much; see QUANTITY + –IC.]

Quan·ti·co (kwän′tĭ-kō′). A town of northwest Virginia on the Potomac River south-southwest of Alexandria. A U.S. Marine Corps base was established nearby in 1918. Population, 621.

quan·ti·fy (kwŏn′tə-fī′) *tr.v.* **-fied, -fy·ing, -fies. 1.** To determine or express the quantity of. **2.** *Logic.* To limit the variables of (a proposition) by prefixing an operator such as *all* or *some.* [Medieval Latin *quantificāre* : Latin *quantus,* how great; see QUANTITY + Latin *-ficāre,* -fy.] **—quan′ti·fi′a·ble** *adj.* **—quan′ti·fi·ca′tion** (-fĭ-kā′shən) *n.* **—quan′ti·fi′er** *n.*

quan·ti·tate (kwŏn′tĭ-tāt′) *tr.v.* **-tat·ed, -tat·ing, -tates.** To determine or measure the quantity of. [Back-formation from QUANTITATIVE (ANALYSIS).] **—quan′ti·ta′tion** *n.*

quan·ti·ta·tive (kwŏn′tĭ-tā′tĭv) *adj. Abbr.* **quant. 1.a.** Expressed or expressible as a quantity. **b.** Of, relating to, or susceptible of measurement. **c.** Of or relating to number or quantity. **2.** Of or relating to a metrical system based on the duration of syllables rather than on stress. Used especially of classical Greek and Latin verse. [Medieval Latin *quantitātīvus,* from Latin *quantitās, quantitāt-,* quantity, from *quantus,* how great. See QUANTITY.] **—quan′ti·ta′tive·ly** *adv.* **—quan′ti·ta′tive·ness** *n.*

quantitative analysis *n.* The testing of a substance or mixture to determine the amounts and proportions of its chemical constituents.

quantitative gene *n. Genetics.* See **polygene.**

quan·ti·ty (kwŏn′tĭ-tē) *n., pl.* **-ti·ties.** *Abbr.* **qt., qty. 1.a.** A specified or indefinite number or amount. **b.** A considerable amount or number: *sells drugs wholesale and in quantity.* **c.** An exact amount or number. **2.** The measurable, countable, or comparable property or aspect of a thing. **3.** *Mathematics.* Something that serves as the object of an operation. **4.a.** *Linguistics.* The relative amount of time needed to pronounce a vowel, consonant, or syllable. **b.** The duration of a syllable in quantitative verse. **5.** *Logic.* The exact character of a proposition in reference to its universality, singularity, or particularity. [Middle English *quantite,* from Old French, from Latin *quantitās, quantitāt-,* from *quantus,* how great. See **kʷo-** in Appendix.]

quan·tize (kwŏn′tīz′) *tr.v.* **-tized, -tiz·ing, -tiz·es.** *Physics.* **1.** To limit the possible values of (a magnitude or quantity) to a discrete set of values by quantum mechanical rules. **2.** To apply quantum mechanics or the quantum theory to. **—quan′ti·za′tion** (-tĭ-zā′shən) *n.*

Quan·trill (kwŏn′trĭl′), **William Clarke.** 1837–1865. American desperado who led a guerrilla band that sporadically supported the Confederacy during the Civil War.

quan·tum (kwŏn′təm) *n., pl.* **-ta** (-tə). **1.** A quantity or an amount. **2.** A specified portion. **3.** Something that can be counted or measured. **4.** *Physics.* **a.** The smallest amount of a physical quantity that can exist independently, especially a discrete quantity of electromagnetic radiation. **b.** This amount of energy regarded as a unit. *—attributive.* Often used to modify another noun: *quantum advances in technology.* [Latin, from neuter of *quantus,* how great. See QUANTITY.]

quantum chromodynamics *n. (used with a sing. verb).* Chromodynamics.

quantum electrodynamics *n. (used with a sing. verb). Physics.* The quantum theory of the properties and behavior of electrons and the electromagnetic field.

quantum jump *n.* **1.** *Physics.* Abrupt change from one energy level to another, especially such a change in the orbit of an electron with the loss or gain of a quantum of energy. **2.** A quantum leap.

quantum leap *n.* An abrupt change or step, especially in method, information, or knowledge: *"War was going to take a quantum leap; it would never be the same"* (Garry Wills).

quantum mechanics *n. (used with a sing. or pl. verb). Physics.* Quantum theory, especially the quantum theory of the structure and behavior of atoms and molecules.

quantum number *n. Physics.* Any of a set of real numbers assigned to a physical system that individually characterize the properties and collectively specify the state of a particle or of the system.

quantum state *n. Physics.* Any of the possible states of a system described by quantum theory.

quantum theory *n. Physics.* The theory that radiant energy is transmitted in the form of discrete units.

quarry²
Marble quarry

Qua·paw (kwô′pô) *n., pl.* **Quapaw** or **-paws. 1.a.** A Native American people formerly inhabiting parts of Arkansas along the Arkansas River, with a present-day population in Oklahoma. **b.** A member of this people. **2.** The Siouan language of the Quapaw.

Qu'Ap·pelle (kwə-pĕl′). A river, about 434 km (270 mi) long, of southern Saskatchewan and southwest Manitoba, Canada, flowing east to the Assiniboine River.

quar. *abbr.* **1.** Quarter. **2.** Quarterly.

quar·an·tine (kwôr′ən-tēn′, kwŏr′-) *n.* **1.a.** A period of time during which a vehicle, person, or material suspected of carrying a contagious disease is detained at a port of entry under enforced isolation to prevent disease from entering a country. **b.** A place for such detention. **2.** Enforced isolation or restriction of free movement imposed to prevent the spread of contagious disease. **3.** A condition of enforced isolation. **4.** A period of 40 days. **—quarantine** *tr.v.* **-tined, -tin·ing, -tines. 1.** To isolate in or as if in quarantine. **2.** To isolate politically or economically. [Italian *quarantina,* from *quaranta (giorni),* forty (days), from Latin *quadrāgintā.* See **kʷetwer-** in Appendix.] **—quar′an·tin′a·ble** *adj.*

quark¹ (kwôrk, kwärk) *n.* Any of a group of hypothetical elementary particles having electric charges of magnitude one-third or two-thirds that of the electron, regarded as constituents of all hadrons. See table at **subatomic particle.** [Possibly from *Three quarks for Muster Mark!,* a line in *Finnegans Wake* by James Joyce.]

WORD HISTORY: *"Three quarks for Muster Mark!/Sure he hasn't got much of a bark/And sure any he has it's all beside the mark."* This passage of James Joyce's *Finnegans Wake* is part of a scurrilous 13-line poem directed against King Mark, the cuckolded husband in the Tristan legend. The poem and the accompanying prose are packed with names of birds and words suggestive of birds, and the poem is a squawk, like the cawing of a crow, against King Mark. Thus, Joyce uses the word *quark,* which comes from the standard English verb *quark,* meaning "to caw, croak," and also from the dialectal verb *quawk,* meaning "to caw, screech like a bird." But Joyce's *quark* was not what it has become: "any of a group of hypothetical subatomic particles proposed as the fundamental units of matter." Murray Gell-Mann, the physicist who proposed these particles, in a private letter of June 27, 1978, to the editor of the *Oxford English Dictionary,* said that he had actually been influenced by Joyce's word in naming the particle, although the influence was subconscious at first. Gell-Mann was thinking of using the pronunciation (kwôrk) for the particle, possibly something he had picked up from *Finnegans Wake,* which he "had perused from time to time since it appeared in 1939. . . . The allusion to three quarks seemed perfect" (originally there were only three subatomic quarks). Gell-Mann, however, wanted to pronounce the word with (ô) not (ä), as Joyce seemed to indicate by rhyming words in the vicinity such as *Mark.* Gell-Mann got around that "by supposing that one ingredient of the line 'Three quarks for Muster Mark' was a cry of 'Three quarts for Mister . . . ' heard in H.C. Earwicker's pub."

quark² (kwôrk, kwärk) *n.* A soft, creamy acid-cured cheese of central Europe made from whole milk. [German, from Middle High German *quarc,* of Slavic origin.]

Quarles (kwärlz, kwôrlz), **Francis.** 1592–1644. English Metaphysical poet whose book *Emblems, Divine and Moral* (1635) was influential in its time.

quar·rel¹ (kwôr′əl, kwŏr′-) *n.* **1.** An angry dispute; an altercation. **2.** A cause of a dispute or an argument: *We have no quarrel with the findings of the committee.* **—quarrel** *intr.v.* **-reled, -rel·ing, -rels** or **-relled, -rel·ling, -rels. 1.** To engage in a quarrel; dispute angrily. See Synonyms at **argue. 2.** To disagree; differ: *I quarrel with your conclusions.* **3.** To find fault; complain. [Middle English *querele,* from Old French, complaint, from Latin *querella, querēla,* from *querī,* to complain. See **kwes-** in Appendix.] **—quar′rel·er, quar′rel·ler** *n.*

quar·rel² (kwôr′əl, kwŏr′-) *n.* **1.** A bolt for a crossbow. **2.** A tool, such as a stonemason's chisel, that has a squared head. **3.** A small diamond-shaped or square pane of glass in a latticed window. [Middle English *quarel,* from Old French, from Vulgar Latin **quadrellus,* diminutive of Late Latin *quadrus,* square, from Latin *quadrum.* See **kʷetwer-** in Appendix.]

quar·rel·some (kwôr′əl-səm, kwŏr′-) *adj.* **1.** Given to quarreling; contentious. See Synonyms at **argumentative. 2.** Marked by quarreling. See Synonyms at **belligerent.**

quar·ry¹ (kwôr′ē, kwŏr′ē) *n., pl.* **-ries. 1.a.** A hunted animal; prey. **b.** Hunted animals considered as a group; game. **2.** An object of pursuit: *The police lost their quarry in the crowd.* [Middle English *querre,* entrails of a deer given to hounds as a reward, from Old French *cuiriee,* alteration (influenced by *cuir,* skin) of *coree,* from Vulgar Latin **corāta,* viscera, from Latin *cor,* heart. See **kerd-** in Appendix.]

quar·ry² (kwôr′ē, kwŏr′ē) *n., pl.* **-ries. 1.** An open excavation or pit from which stone is obtained by digging, cutting, or blasting. **2.** A rich or productive source: *found the book an indispensable quarry of information.* **—quarry** *tr.v.* **-ried, -ry·ing, -ries. 1.** To obtain (stone) from a quarry, as by cutting, digging, or blasting. **2.** To extract (facts, for example) by long, careful searching: *finally quarried out the genealogy from hundreds of sources.* **3.** To use (land) as a quarry. [Middle English *quarey,* from Medieval Latin *quareria, quareia,* alteration of Old French *quarriere,* from **quarre,* cut stone, from Latin *quadrum,* square. See **kʷetwer-** in Appendix.] —**quar′ri·er** *n.*

quar·ry3 (kwôr′ē, kwŏr′ē) *n., pl.* **-ries. 1.** A square or diamond shape. **2.** A pane of glass having this shape. [Variant of QUARREL2.]

quart (kwôrt) *n. Abbr.* **q., qt, qt. 1.a.** A unit of volume or capacity in the U.S. Customary System, used in liquid measure, equal to ¼ gallon or 32 ounces (0.946 liter). **b.** A unit of volume or capacity in the U.S. Customary System, used in dry measure, equal to ⅛ peck or 2 pints (1.101 liters). **c.** A unit of volume or capacity in the British Imperial System, used in liquid and dry measure, equal to 1.201 U.S. liquid quarts or 1.032 U.S. dry quarts (1.136 liters). See table at **measurement. 2.a.** A container having a capacity of one quart. **b.** The contents of such a container. [Middle English, from Old French *quarte,* from Latin *quārta,* feminine of *quārtus,* fourth. See **kʷetwer-** in Appendix.]

quar·tan (kwôrt′n) *adj.* Occurring every fourth day, counting inclusively, or every 72 hours. Used of a fever. —**quartan** *n.* A malarial fever recurring every 72 hours. [Middle English *quartaine,* from Old French, from Latin *quārtāna,* from *quārtānus,* of the fourth, from *quārtus,* fourth. See **kʷetwer-** in Appendix.]

quar·ter (kwôr′tər) *n. Abbr.* **q., qr., quar. 1.** One of four equal parts. **2.** A coin equal to one fourth of the dollar of the United States and Canada. **3.** One fourth of an hour; 15 minutes. **4.a.** One fourth of a year; three months: *Sales were up in the second quarter.* **b.** An academic term lasting approximately three months. **5.** *Astronomy.* **a.** One fourth of the period of the moon's revolution around Earth. **b.** One of the four phases of the moon: *the first quarter; the third quarter.* **6.** *Sports.* One of four equal periods of playing time into which some games, such as football and basketball, are divided. **7.** One fourth of a yard; nine inches. **8.** One fourth of a mile; two furlongs. **9.** One fourth of a pound; four ounces. **10.** One fourth of a ton; 500 pounds. Used as a measure of grain. **11.** *Chiefly British.* A measure of grain equal to approximately eight bushels. **12.a.** One fourth of a hundredweight; 25 pounds. **b.** One fourth of a British hundredweight; 28 pounds. **13.a.** One of the four major divisions of the compass. **b.** One fourth of the distance between any two of the 32 divisions of the compass. **c.** One of the four major divisions of the horizon as determined by the four major points of the compass. **d.** A region or an area of the earth thought of as falling into such a specific division of the compass. **e.** *Nautical.* The general direction on either side of a ship located 45° off the stern. **14.** *Nautical.* **a.** The upper portion of the after side of a ship, usually between the aftermost mast and the stern. **b.** The part of a yard between the slings and the yardarm. **15.** *Heraldry.* Any of four equal divisions of a shield. **16.** One leg of an animal's carcass, usually including the adjoining parts. **17.** Either side of a horse's hoof. **18.** The part of the side of a shoe between the heel and the vamp. **19. quarters.** A place of residence, especially the buildings or barracks used to house military personnel or their dependents. **20.** Often **quarters.** A proper or assigned station or place, as for officers and crew on a warship. **21.** Often **Quarter.** A specific district or section, as of a city: *the French Quarter.* **22.** Often **quarters.** An unspecified person or group: *information from the highest quarters.* **23.** Mercy or clemency, especially when displayed or given to an enemy. —**quarter** *adj.* **1.** Being one of four equal or equivalent parts. **2.** Being one fourth of a standard or usual value. —**quarter** *v.* **-tered, -ter·ing, -ters.** —*tr.* **1.a.** To divide into four equal or equivalent parts. **b.** To quartersaw. **2.** To divide or separate into a number of parts. **3.** To dismember (a human body) into four parts. **4.** *Heraldry.* To divide (a shield) into four equal areas with vertical and horizontal lines. **5.a.** To mark or place (holes, for example) a fourth of a circle apart. **b.** To locate and adjust (one machine part) at right angles to its connecting part within the machine. **6.** To furnish with housing: *quarter troops.* **7.** To traverse (an area of ground) laterally back and forth while slowly advancing forward. —*intr.* **1.** To take up or be assigned lodgings. **2.** To cover an area of ground by ranging over it from side to side. [Middle English, from Old French *quartier,* from Latin *quārtārius,* from *quārtus,* fourth. See **kʷetwer-** in Appendix.]

USAGE NOTE: When referring to the time of day, the article *a* is optional in phrases such as *(a) quarter to* (or *of, before,* or *till*) *nine; (a) quarter after* (or *past*) *ten.*

quar·ter·age (kwôr′tər-ĭj) *n.* A monetary allowance, wage, or payment made or received quarterly.

quar·ter·back (kwôr′tər-băk′) *n. Abbr.* **qb** *Football.* The backfield player whose position is behind the line of scrimmage and who usually calls the signals for the plays. —**quarterback** *v.* **-backed, -back·ing, -backs.** —*tr.* **1.** *Football.* To direct the offense of. **2.** *Slang.* To lead or direct the operations of: *"needed someone to quarterback the* [brain trust] *for the first U.S. ICBM program"* (Forbes). —*intr. Football.* To play quarterback.

quarter day *n.* Any of the four days of the year regarded as the beginning of a new season or quarter, when most quarterly payments are due.

quar·ter·deck (kwôr′tər-dĕk′) *n. Nautical.* The after part of the upper deck of a ship, usually reserved for officers.

quar·ter·fi·nal (kwôr′tər-fī′nəl) *adj. Sports & Games.* Of or relating to one of four competitions in a tournament, whose winners go on to play in semifinal competitions. —**quarterfinal** *n.* **1. quarterfinals.** A quarterfinal round. **2.** A quarterfinal match. —**quar′ter·fi′nal·ist** *n.*

quarter horse *n.* One of a breed of strong saddle horses developed in the western United States. [From its formerly being trained for races up to a quarter mile.]

quar·ter-hour also **quar·ter hour** (kwôr′tər-our′) *n.* **1.** Fifteen minutes. **2.** The point on a clock's face marking either 15 minutes after or 15 minutes before an hour.

quar·ter·ly (kwôr′tər-lē) *adj. Abbr.* **q., qr., quar. 1.** Made up of four parts. **2.** Being one of four parts. **3.** Occurring or appearing at three-month intervals: *a quarterly magazine; a quarterly payment.* **4.** *Heraldry.* Having four sections. Used of a shield. —**quarterly** *n., pl.* **-lies.** *Abbr.* **q., qr., quar. 1.** A publication issued regularly every three months. **2.** An examination given regularly every three months in some colleges. —**quarterly** *adv.* In or by quarters.

quar·ter·mas·ter (kwôr′tər-măs′tər) *n. Abbr.* **QM 1.** An officer responsible for the food, clothing, and equipment of troops. **2.** A petty officer responsible for the navigation of a ship.

quar·tern (kwôr′tərn) *n.* **1.** One fourth of something, especially of some weights and measures. **2.** *Chiefly British.* A loaf of bread weighing about 4 pounds (1.81 kilograms). [Middle English *quartron,* from Old French *quarteron,* from *quartier,* quarter. See QUARTER.]

quarter note *n. Music.* A note having one-fourth the time value of a whole note. Also called *crotchet.*

quar·ter-phase (kwôr′tər-fāz′) *adj. Electricity.* Two-phase.

quar·ter·saw (kwôr′tər-sô′) *tr.v.* **-sawed, -sawed** or **-sawn** (-sôn′), **-saw·ing, -saws.** To saw (a log) into quarters lengthwise along its axis.

quarter section *n.* A land unit equal to a quarter of a section and measuring ½ of a mile on a side.

quarter sessions *pl.n. Law.* **1.** A British local court of limited jurisdiction that sits quarterly. **2.** A local court in the United States with criminal jurisdiction and sometimes administrative functions.

quar·ter·staff (kwôr′tər-stăf′) *n., pl.* **-staves** (-stāvz′). A long wooden staff formerly used as a weapon.

quar·ter·tone (kwôr′tər-tōn′) *n. Music.* Half a semitone.

quar·tet also **quar·tette** (kwôr-tĕt′) *n.* **1.** *Music.* **a.** A composition for four voices or instruments. **b.** A group of four performing musicians. **2.** A set of four persons or things. [French *quartette,* from Italian *quartetto,* diminutive of *quarto,* fourth, from Latin *quārtus.* See QUART.]

quar·tic (kwôr′tĭk) *adj. Mathematics.* Of or relating to the fourth degree. [Latin *quārtus,* fourth; see QUART + -IC.] —**quar′tic** *n.*

quar·tile (kwôr′tīl′, -tĭl) *n. Statistics.* The value of the boundary at the 25th, 50th, or 75th percentiles of a frequency distribution divided into four parts, each containing a quarter of the population. [Middle English, ninety degrees apart (of the relative position of two celestial bodies), from Old French *quartil,* from Medieval Latin *quārtīlis,* of a quartile, from Latin *quārtus,* fourth. See QUART.]

quar·to (kwôr′tō) *n., pl.* **-tos.** *Abbr.* **q., Q., qto. 1.** The page size obtained by folding a whole sheet into four leaves. **2.** A book composed of pages of this size. [Short for Middle English *(in) quarto,* (in) the fourth part (of a sheet), from Medieval Latin *(in) quārtō,* from Latin, ablative of *quārtus,* fourth. See **kʷetwer-** in Appendix.]

quartz (kwôrts) *n.* A very hard mineral composed of silica, SiO_2, found worldwide in many different types of rocks, including sandstone and granite. Varieties of quartz include agate, chalcedony, chert, flint, opal, and rock crystal. [German *Quarz,* from Middle High German *quarc,* of Slavic origin.] —**quartz′ose′** (kwôrt′sōs′) *adj.*

quartz crystal *n.* A small crystal of quartz accurately cut along certain axes so that it can be vibrated at a particular frequency, used for its piezoelectric properties to produce an electric signal of constant known frequency.

quartz glass *n.* A clear vitreous solid, formed by melting pure quartz, that can withstand high temperatures and is extremely transparent to infrared, visible, and ultraviolet radiations. Also called *fused quartz, fused silica.*

quartz·if·er·ous (kwôrt-sĭf′ər-əs) *adj.* Containing quartz.

quartz·ite (kwôrt′sīt′) *n.* A rock formed from the metamorphism of quartz sandstone.

quartz lamp *n.* A mercury-vapor lamp enclosed by an envelope made from quartz rather than glass.

qua·sar (kwā′zär′, -sär′, -zər, -sər) *n.* A starlike object that has a large red shift and emits powerful blue light and often radio waves. [QUAS(I) + (ST)AR.]

quash1 (kwŏsh) *tr.v.* **quashed, quash·ing, quash·es.** To set aside or annul, especially by judicial action. [Middle English *quassen,* from Old French *casser, quasser,* from Medieval Latin *quassāre,* alteration (influenced by *quassāre,* to shatter; see QUASH2) of *cassāre,* from Latin *cassus,* empty, void. See **kes-** in Appendix.]

quash2 (kwŏsh) *tr.v.* **quashed, quash·ing, quash·es.** To put down or suppress forcibly and completely: *quash a rebellion.* [Middle English *quashen,* from Old French *quasser,* from Medieval Latin *quassāre,* to shatter, from Latin. See SQUASH2.]

quarter horse

ă pat	oi boy
ā pay	ou out
âr care	ŏŏ took
ä father	ōō boot
ĕ pet	ŭ cut
ē be	ûr urge
ĭ pit	th thin
ī pie	*th* this
îr pier	hw which
ŏ pot	zh vision
ō toe	ə about, item
ô paw	♦ regionalism

Stress marks: ′ (primary); ′ (secondary), as in **dictionary** (dĭk′shə-nĕr′ē)

quatrefoil
Stained-glass window above an entrance to a church

qua•si (kwā′zī′, -sī′, kwä′zē, -sē) *adj.* Having a likeness to something; resembling: *a quasi success.* [Middle English, as if, from Old French, from Latin *quasi* : *quam,* as; see **k^{w}o-** in Appendix + *sī,* if; see **swo-** in Appendix.]

quasi– *pref.* To some degree; in some manner: *quasi-stellar object.* [Latin *quasi,* as if. See QUASI.]

Qua•si•mo•do (kwä′zē-mō′dō), **Salvatore.** 1901–1968. Italian poet whose early nostalgic works contrast with his later socially concerned poetry. He won the 1950 Nobel Prize for literature.

qua•si-stel•lar object (kwā′zī-stĕl′ər, -sī′-, kwä′zē-, -sē-) *n.* A quasar.

quas•sia (kwŏsh′ə) *n.* **1.a.** A tropical American shrub or small tree *(Quassia amara)* having bright scarlet flowers and yielding a valuable, lustrous, fine-grained, yellowish-white wood. **b.** The wood of this plant. **2.** A bitter substance obtained from the wood of this plant, used in medicine and as an insecticide. [New Latin, after Graman *Quassi,* an 18th-century Surinamese.]

qua•ter•cen•ten•a•ry (kwŏt′ər-sĕn-tĕn′ə-rē, -sĕn′tə-nĕr′ē) *n., pl.* **-ries.** A quadricentennial. [Latin *quater,* four times; see QUATERNARY + CENTENARY.]

qua•ter•nar•y (kwŏt′ər-nĕr′ē, kwə-tûr′nə-rē) *adj.* **1.** Consisting of four; in fours. **2. Quaternary.** *Geology.* Of, belonging to, or designating the geologic time, system of rocks, and sedimentary deposits of the second period of the Cenozoic Era, from the end of the Tertiary Period through the present, characterized by the appearance and development of human beings and including the Pleistocene Epoch and the Holocene Epoch. See table at **geologic time. 3.** *Chemistry.* Relating to an atom bonded to four carbon atoms: *a quarternary nitrogen atom.* **—quaternary** *n., pl.* **-nar•ies. 1.** The number four. **2.** The member of a group that is fourth in order. **3. Quaternary.** *Geology.* The second period of the Cenozoic Era and its system of deposits. [Latin *quaternārius,* from *quaternī,* by fours, from *quater,* four times. See **k^{w}etwer-** in Appendix.]

queen
Chess piece

quaternary ammonium compound *n.* Any of a group of compounds in which a central nitrogen atom is joined to four organic radicals and one acid radical, used as antiseptics, solvents, and emulsifying agents.

qua•ter•ni•on (kwə-tûr′nē-ən) *n.* **1.** A set of four persons or items. **2.** *Mathematics.* An expression that is the sum of a real number and a vector and that contains four terms, one real and three imaginary. [Middle English *quaternioun,* from Late Latin *quaterniō, quaterniōn-,* from Latin *quaternī,* by fours, from *quater,* four times. See **k^{w}etwer-** in Appendix.]

quat•rain (kwŏt′rān′, kwŏ-trān′) *n.* A stanza or poem of four lines. [French, from Old French, from *quatre,* four, from Latin *quattuor.* See **k^{w}etwer-** in Appendix.]

quat•re•foil (kăt′ər-foil′, kăt′rə-) *n.* **1.** A representation of a flower with four petals or a leaf with four leaflets, especially in heraldry. **2.** *Architecture.* Tracery or an ornament with four foils or lobes. [Middle English *quaterfoile* : Old French *quatre,* four; see QUATRAIN + Old French *foil,* leaf; see FOIL[2].]

quat•tro•cen•to (kwŏt′rō-chĕn′tō) *n.* The 15th-century period of Italian art and literature. [Italian, short for *(mil) quattrocento,* one thousand four hundred : *quattro,* four (from Latin *quattuor;* see **k^{w}etwer-** in Appendix) + *cento,* hundred (from Latin *centum;* see **dekm̥** in Appendix).]

Queen Anne
Mid 18th-century American side chair

qua•ver (kwā′vər) *v.* **-vered, -ver•ing, -vers.** *—intr.* **1.** To quiver, as from weakness; tremble. **2.** To speak in a quivering voice; utter a quivering sound. **3.** *Music.* To produce a trill on an instrument or with the voice. *—tr.* To utter or sing in a trilling voice. **—quaver** *n.* **1.** A quivering sound. **2.** A trill. **3.** *Chiefly British.* An eighth note. [Middle English *quaveren,* probably frequentative of *cwavien, quaven,* to tremble.] **—qua′ver•ing•ly** *adv.* **—qua′ver•y** *adj.*

quay (kē, kā) *n.* A wharf or reinforced bank where ships are loaded or unloaded. [Middle English *keye,* from Old North French *cai,* of Celtic origin.]

quay•age (kē′ĭj) *n.* **1.** A charge for the use of a quay. **2.** A system or group of quays. **3.** The space available on a system of quays.

Quayle (kwāl), **James Danforth.** Born 1947. Vice President of the United States (since 1989) under George Bush.

quay•side (kē′sīd′) *n.* The area adjacent to a quay or wharf or a system of quays, especially in a port city.

Que. *abbr.* Quebec.

quean (kwēn) *n.* **1.** A woman regarded as being disreputable, especially a prostitute. **2.** *Scots.* A young woman. [Middle English *quene,* from Old English *cwene,* woman. See **g^{w}en-** in Appendix.]

Queen Anne's lace
Daucus carota var. *carota*

quea•sy also **quea•zy** (kwē′zē) *adj.* **-si•er, -si•est** also **-zi•er, -zi•est. 1.** Experiencing nausea; nauseated. **2.** Easily nauseated. **3.** Causing nausea; sickening: *the queasy lurch of an airplane during a storm.* **4.a.** Causing uneasiness. **b.** Uneasy; troubled. **5.a.** Easily troubled. **b.** Ill at ease; squeamish: *"He is not queasy about depicting mass violence, in some circumstances, as a legitimate instrument of social transformation"* (Shaul Bakhash). [Middle English *coisy,* perhaps of Scandinavian origin.] **—quea′si•ly** *adv.* **—quea′si•ness** *n.*

Que•bec (kwĭ-bĕk′) or **Qué•bec** (kā-). **1.** *Abbr.* **PQ, P.Q., Que.** A province of eastern Canada. It joined the confederacy in 1867. The region was first explored and claimed for France by Jacques Cartier (1534) and Samuel de Champlain (1608) and was made a royal colony, known as New France, by Louis XIV in 1663. Conflict between the French and British for control of the territory ended in 1763 when Great Britain was given sovereignty, but the French influence has remained dominant. Quebec is the capital and Montreal the largest city. Population, 6,438,403. **2.** Also **Quebec City** or **Québec City.** The capital of Quebec, Canada, in the southern part of the province on the St. Lawrence River. Champlain established a colony in its Lower Town in 1608. British forces under General Wolfe defeated the French forces led by General Montcalm at the Plains of Abraham here in 1759. The city is today a popular tourist center. Population, 166,474. **—Que•beck′er, Que•bec′er** *n.*

Qué•be•cois or **Que•be•cois** (kā′bĕ-kwä′) *—adj.* Of or relating to Quebec and especially to its French-speaking inhabitants or their culture. *—n., pl.* **Québecois** or **Quebecois.** A native or inhabitant of Quebec, especially a French-speaking one. [French *québecois,* from *Québec,* Quebec.]

que•bra•cho (kā-brä′chō) *n., pl.* **-chos. 1.** Either of two South American trees, *Aspidosperma quebracho-blanco* whose bark is used in medicine, or *Schinopsis lorentzii* whose wood is one of the richest sources of tannin. **2.** The bark or wood of either of these trees. [Spanish, alteration of *quiebrahacha* : *quebrar,* to break (from Latin *crepāre,* to crack) + *hacha,* ax (from French *hache,* from Old French, of Germanic origin).]

Que•chan (kĕch′ən) *n.* See **Yuma[1].** [Yuma *k^{w}aćán,* those who descended (from the sacred mountain of creation).]

Quech•ua also **Kech•ua** (kĕch′wə, -wä′) *n., pl.* **Quechua** or **-uas** also **Kechua** or **-uas. 1.** The Quechuan language of the Inca empire, now widely spoken throughout the Andes highlands from southern Colombia to Chile. **2.a.** A member of a South American Indian people originally constituting the ruling class of the Inca empire. **b.** A speaker of the Quechua language. [Spanish, from Quechua *kkechuwa,* plunderer.]

Quech•uan (kĕch′wən) *n.* A subgroup of the Quechumaran languages, the most important language being Quechua. **—Quechuan** *adj.* Of or relating to the Quechua or their language or culture.

Quech•u•mar•an (kĕch′o͞o-mä-rän′) *n.* A group of languages found mostly in the Andes highlands from southern Colombia to northern Chile and Argentina, composed of the Quechuan and Aymaran languages.

queen (kwēn) *n.* **1.** *Abbr.* **qu. a.** The wife or widow of a king. **b.** A woman sovereign. **2.** Something having eminence or supremacy in a given domain and personified as a woman: *Paris is regarded as the queen of cities.* **3.** *Games.* **a.** *Abbr.* **Q** The most powerful chess piece, able to move in any direction in a straight line. **b.** *Abbr.* **qu.** A playing card bearing the figure of a queen, ranking above the jack and below the king. **4.** *Abbr.* **qu.** The fertile, fully developed female in a colony of social bees, ants, or termites. **5.** *Offensive Slang.* Used as a disparaging term for a gay or homosexual man. **—queen** *v.* **queened, queen•ing, queens.** *—tr.* **1.** To make (a woman) a queen. **2.** *Games.* To raise (a pawn) to queen in chess. *—intr. Games.* To become a queen in chess. **—*idiom.* queen it.** To act like a queen; domineer: *queens it over the whole family.* [Middle English *quene,* from Old English *cwēn.* See **g^{w}en-** in Appendix.]

Queen Anne (kwēn ăn′) *n.* The style in English architecture and furniture typical of the reign of Queen Anne (1702–1714).

Queen Anne's lace (ănz) *n.* A widely naturalized Eurasian herb *(Daucus carota* var. *carota)* having white, nonfleshy, fusiform compound umbels of small white or yellowish flowers. Also called *wild carrot.*

Queen Char•lotte Islands (shär′lət). An archipelago off the western coast of British Columbia, Canada, separated from Vancouver Island to the southeast by **Queen Charlotte Sound,** an inlet of the Pacific Ocean.

queen consort *n., pl.* **queens consort.** The wife of a reigning king.

queen cup *n.* A perennial stemless plant *(Clintonia uniflora)* of Pacific North America, having a solitary white flower and a blue berry.

Queen E•liz•a•beth Islands (ĭ-lĭz′ə-bəth). A group of islands of northern Northwest Territories, Canada, in the Arctic Archipelago north of Parry Channel.

queen•ly (kwēn′lē) *adj.* **-li•er, -li•est. 1.** Having the status or rank of queen. **2.** Of, resembling, or befitting a queen; majestic and regal. **—queenly** *adv.* In a royal way; regally. **—queen′li•ness** *n.*

Queen Maud Land (môd). A region of Antarctica between the Weddell Sea and Enderby Land. It was claimed by Norway in 1939.

Queen Maud Mountains. A mountain range of Antarctica near the South Pole. It extends some 805 km (500 mi).

queen mother *n.* A dowager queen who is the mother of a reigning monarch.

queen-of-the-prai•rie (kwēn′əv-*th*ə-prâr′ē) *n.* A rhizomatous plant *(Filipendula rubra)* of the prairies and meadows of the eastern and central United States, having aromatic, pinnately compound leaves and showy panicles of small pink flowers.

queen olive *n.* A large, edible variety of olive not used as a source of oil.

queen post *n.* One of two upright supporting posts set vertically between the rafters and the tie beam at equal distances from the apex of a roof.

queen regnant *n., pl.* **queens regnant.** A queen reigning in her own right.

Queens (kwēnz). A borough of New York City in southeast New York on western Long Island. It was first settled by the Dutch in 1635 and became part of Greater New York in 1898. Population, 1,891,325.

Queen's Bench (kwēnz) *n. Abbr.* **Q.B.** *Law.* A division of the British superior courts system that hears criminal and civil cases. Used when the sovereign is a woman.

Queens·ber·ry (kwēnz′bĕr′ē, -bə-rē), Eighth Marquis of. Title of Sir John Sholto Douglas. 1844–1900. British aristocrat and boxing promoter who formulated the Marquis of Queensbury rules (1867) to govern boxing.

Queensberry rules *pl.n.* Marquis of Queensberry rules.

Queen's Counsel *n. Abbr.* **Q.C.** *Law.* A barrister appointed as counsel to the British crown. Used when the sovereign is a woman.

Queen's English *n.* English speech or usage that is considered standard or accepted; Received Standard English.

queen·ship (kwēn′shĭp′) *n.* **1.** The rank or state of being a queen. **2.** A noble or regal quality, as of a queen.

queen·side (kwēn′sīd′) *n. Games.* The side of the chessboard that is nearest to the queen's opening position. **—queen′side′** *adv. & adj.*

queen-size (kwēn′sīz′) also **queen-sized** (-sīzd′) *adj.* **1.** Extra large in size: *queen-size pantyhose.* **2.a.** Measuring about 60 inches by 80 inches (1.5 meters by 2.0 meters). Used of a bed. **b.** Being of a size that will fit such a bed: *queen-size fitted sheets.*

Queens·land arrowroot (kwēnz′lănd′, -lənd) *n.* See **edible canna** (sense 1). [After *Queensland*, a state of northeast Australia.]

queen substance *n.* A pheromone secreted by queen bees and given to worker bees to prevent them from producing more queens.

queen truss *n.* A building truss using queen posts.

queer (kwîr) *adj.* **queer·er, queer·est. 1.** Deviating from the expected or normal; strange: *a queer situation.* **2.** Odd or unconventional, as in behavior; eccentric. See Synonyms at **strange. 3.** Of a questionable nature or character; suspicious. **4.** *Slang.* Fake; counterfeit. **5.** Feeling slightly ill; queasy. **6.** *Offensive Slang.* Gay; homosexual. **—queer** *n. Offensive Slang.* Used as a disparaging term for a gay or homosexual person. **—queer** *tr.v.* **queered, queer·ing, queers.** *Slang.* **1.** To ruin or thwart: *"might try to queer the Games with anything from troop movements . . . to a bomb attack"* (Newsweek). **2.** To put (someone) in a bad position. [Perhaps from Low German, oblique, off-center, from Middle Low German *dwer.* See **terkʷ-** in Appendix.] **—queer′ish** *adj.* **—queer′ly** *adv.* **—queer′ness** *n.*

Queer Street (kwîr) *n. Chiefly British.* Difficulties, especially financial ones.

que·le·a (kwē′lē-ə) *n.* An African weaverbird of the genus *Quelea,* especially *Q. quelea,* a small red-billed bird that is extremely destructive to grain crops. [New Latin *Quelea,* genus name, perhaps alteration of Medieval Latin *qualea,* quail, ultimately from Vulgar Latin **coacula,* of imitative origin.]

quell (kwĕl) *tr.v.* **quelled, quell·ing, quells. 1.** To put down forcibly; suppress: *Police quelled the riot.* **2.** To pacify; quiet: *finally quelled the children's fears.* [Middle English *quellen,* to kill, from Old English *cwellan.* See **gʷelə-** in Appendix.]

Que·moy (kĭ-moi′). In Pinyin **Jin·men** (jĭn′mœn′). An island and group of 2 islands and 12 islets off southeast China in Taiwan Strait. The islands are heavily fortified and have been administered by Taiwan since the Chinese Revolution of 1949.

quench (kwĕnch) *tr.v.* **quenched, quench·ing, quench·es. 1.** To put out (a fire, for example); extinguish. **2.** To suppress; squelch: *The disapproval of my colleagues quenched my enthusiasm for the plan.* **3.** To put an end to; destroy. **4.** To slake; satisfy: *Mineral water quenched our thirst.* **5.** To cool (hot metal) by thrusting into water or other liquid. [Middle English *quenchen,* from Old English *ācwencan.*] **—quench′a·ble** *adj.* **—quench′er** *n.* **—quench′less** *adj.*

que·nelle (kə-nĕl′) *n.* A ball or dumpling of finely chopped meat or seafood bound with eggs and poached in stock or water. [French, from German *Knödel,* from Middle High German, diminutive of *knode,* knot, knob, from Old High German *knodo.*]

quer·ce·tin (kwûr′sĭ-tĭn) *n.* A yellow, powdered crystalline compound, $C_5H_{15}O_2(OH)_5$, synthesized or occurring as a glycoside in the rind and bark of numerous plants, and used medicinally to treat abnormal capillary fragility. [Latin *quercētum,* oak forest (from *quercus,* oak; see **perkʷu-** in Appendix) + -IN.]

quer·ci·tron (kwûr′sĭ-trən, -trŏn′, kwər-sĭt′rən) *n.* **1.** The bright orange inner bark of the black oak, from which a yellow dye is obtained. **2.** The dye obtained from this bark. [Blend of Latin *quercus,* oak; see **perkʷu-** in Appendix, and CITRON.]

Que·ré·ta·ro (kə-rĕt′ə-rō′, kĕ-rĕ′tä-rō′). A city of central Mexico northwest of Mexico City. An ancient pre-Aztec settlement, it was conquered by the Spanish in 1531. Emperor Maximilian was executed nearby in 1867. Population, 215,976.

que·rist (kwîr′ĭst) *n.* One who asks questions; an inquirer. [From obsolete *quere,* question. See QUERY.]

quern (kwûrn) *n.* A primitive hand-turned grain mill. [Middle English *querne,* from Old English *cweorn.* See **gʷerə-¹** in Appendix.]

quer·u·lous (kwĕr′ə-ləs, kwĕr′yə-) *adj.* **1.** Given to complaining; peevish. **2.** Expressing a complaint or grievance; grumbling: *a querulous voice; querulous comments.* [Middle English *querulose,* litigious, quarrelsome, from Old French *querelos,* from Late Latin *querulōsus,* querulous, from Latin *querulus,* from *querī,* to complain. See **kwes-** in Appendix.] **—quer′u·lous·ly** *adv.* **—quer′u·lous·ness** *n.*

que·ry (kwîr′ē) *n., pl.* **-ries. 1.** A question; an inquiry. **2.** A doubt in the mind; a mental reservation. **3.** *Abbr.* **q., qu.** A notation, usually a question mark, calling attention to an item in order to question its validity or accuracy. **—query** *tr.v.* **-ried, -ry·ing, -ries. 1.** To express doubt or uncertainty about; question: *query someone's motives.* **2.** To put a question to (a person). See Synonyms at **ask. 3.** To mark (an item) with a notation in order to question its validity or accuracy. [Alteration of obsolete *quaere, quere,* from Latin, imperative of *quaerere,* to ask, to seek.] **—que′ri·er** *n.*

ques. *abbr.* Question.

Ques·nay (kā-nā′, kĕ-), **François.** 1694–1774. French physician and pioneer political economist who emphasized the primary economic importance of land and agriculture.

quest (kwĕst) *n.* **1.** The act or an instance of seeking or pursuing something; a search. **2.** An expedition undertaken in medieval romance by a knight in order to perform a prescribed feat: *the quest for the Holy Grail.* **3.** *Archaic.* A jury of inquest. **—quest** *v.* **quest·ed, quest·ing, quests.** —*intr.* **1.** To go on a quest. **2.** To search for game. —*tr.* To search for; seek. See Synonyms at **seek.** [Middle English *queste,* from Old French, ultimately from Latin *quaesta,* feminine past participle of *quaerere,* to seek, ask.] **—quest′er** *n.*

ques·tion (kwĕs′chən) *n. Abbr.* **q., qn., qu., ques. 1.a.** An expression of inquiry that invites or calls for a reply. **b.** An interrogative sentence, phrase, or gesture. **2.** A subject or point open to controversy; an issue. **3.** A difficult matter; a problem: *a question of ethics.* **4.** A point or subject under discussion or consideration. **5.a.** A proposition brought up for consideration by an assembly. **b.** The act of bringing a proposal to vote. **6.** Uncertainty; doubt: *There is no question about the validity of the enterprise.* **—question** *v.* **-tioned, -tion·ing, -tions.** —*tr.* **1.** To put a question to. See Synonyms at **ask. 2.** To examine (a witness, for example) by questioning; interrogate. **3.** To express doubt about; dispute. **4.** To analyze; examine. —*intr.* To ask questions. —***idiom.* out of the question.** Not worth considering; impossible: *Starting over is out of the question.* [Middle English, from Old French, legal inquiry, from Latin *quaestiō, quaestiōn-,* from **quaestus,* past participle of *quaerere,* to ask, seek.] **—ques′tion·er** *n.* **—ques′tion·ing·ly** *adv.*

ques·tion·a·ble (kwĕs′chə-nə-bəl) *adj.* **1.a.** Open to doubt or challenge; problematic. **b.** Not yet determined or specified. See Synonyms at **doubtful. 2.** Of dubious morality or respectability: *a questionable reputation.* **—ques′tion·a·ble·ness, ques′tion·a·bil′i·ty** *n.* **—ques′tion·a·bly** *adv.*

question mark *n.* A punctuation symbol (?) written at the end of a sentence or phrase to indicate a direct question. Also called *interrogation point.*

ques·tion·naire (kwĕs′chə-nâr′) *n.* A printed form containing a set of questions, especially one addressed to a statistically significant number of subjects as a way of gathering information for a survey. [French, from *questionner,* to ask, from Old French, from *question,* legal inquiry. See QUESTION.]

Quet·ta (kwĕt′ə). A city of west-central Pakistan west-southwest of Lahore. Ringed by mountains, it commands the entrance through the strategic Bolan Pass into Afghanistan. Population, 243,000.

quet·zal (kĕt-säl′) *n., pl.* **-zals** or **-za·les** (-sä′lās). **1.** A Central American bird *(Pharomachrus mocino)* that has brilliant bronze-green and red plumage and, in the male, long flowing tail feathers. **2.** *Abbr.* **Q** See table at **currency.** [American Spanish, from Nahuatl *quetzalli,* large brilliant tail feather.]

quetzal
Male resplendent quetzal
Pharomachrus mocino

Quet·zal·co·a·tl (kĕt-säl′kō-ät′l) *n. Mythology.* A god of the Toltecs and Aztecs, represented as a plumed serpent.

queue (kyōō) *n.* **1.** A line of waiting people or vehicles. **2.** A long braid of hair worn hanging down the back of the neck; a pigtail. **3.** *Computer Science.* A sequence of stored data or programs awaiting processing. **—queue** *intr.v.* **queued, queu·ing, queues.** To get in line: *queue up at the box office.* [French, from Old French *cue,* tail, from Latin *cauda, cōda.*]

Que·zon City (kā′sôn′, -sŏn′). A city of central Luzon, Philippines, adjoining Manila. Chiefly residential with a textile industry, it was the official capital of the Philippines from 1948 to 1976. Population, 1,165,865.

Quezon y Mo·li·na (ē mə-lē′nə, mô-lē′nä), **Manuel Luis.** 1878–1944. Philippine politician. The first president of the Philippine Commonwealth (1935–1944), he was forced to flee his country after the Japanese conquest of the Philippine Islands (1941) but continued to lead the government in exile.

quib·ble (kwĭb′əl) *intr.v.* **-bled, -bling, -bles. 1.** To evade the truth or importance of an issue by raising trivial distinctions and objections. **2.** To find fault or criticize for petty reasons; cavil. **—quibble** *n.* **1.** A petty distinction or an irrelevant objection. **2.** *Archaic.* A pun. [Probably diminutive of obsolete *quib,* equivocation, perhaps from Latin *quibus,* dative and abla-

ă pat	oi boy
ā pay	ou out
âr care	ŏŏ took
ä father	ōō boot
ĕ pet	ŭ cut
ē be	ûr urge
ĭ pit	th thin
ī pie	*th* this
îr pier	hw which
ŏ pot	zh vision
ō toe	ə about, item
ô paw	♦ regionalism

Stress marks: ′ (primary); ′ (secondary), as in **dictionary** (dĭk′shə-nĕr′ē)

tive pl. of *quī*, who, what (from its frequent use in legal documents). See **kʷo-** in Appendix.] —**quib′bler** *n.*

SYNONYMS: *quibble, carp, cavil, niggle, nitpick, pettifog.* The central meaning shared by these verbs is "to raise petty or frivolous objections or complaints": *quibbling about minor points of grammar; an art critic who constantly carped; caviling about the price of a cup of coffee; an editor who niggled about commas; tried to get her to stop nitpicking all the time; pettifogging about a trivial clause in a contract.*

quiche (kēsh) *n.* A rich unsweetened custard baked in a pastry shell often with other ingredients such as vegetables or seafood. [French, from German dialectal *Küche*, diminutive of German *Kuchen*, cake. See KUCHEN.]

Qui·ché (kē-chā′) *n., pl.* **Quiché** or **-chés.** **1.** A member of a Mayan people of Guatemala. **2.** The Mayan language of the Quiché.

quiche Lor·raine (lə-rān′, lô-) *n.* A quiche made with cheese and pieces of bacon. [French, after LORRAINE.]

quick (kwĭk) *adj.* **quick·er, quick·est.** **1.** Moving or functioning rapidly and energetically; speedy. **2.** Learning, thinking, or understanding with speed and dexterity; bright: *a quick mind.* See Synonyms at **nimble.** **3.a.** Perceiving or responding with speed and sensitivity; keen. **b.** Reacting immediately and sharply: *a quick temper.* **4.a.** Occurring or achieved in a relatively brief period of time: *a quick rise through the ranks.* **b.** Done or occurring immediately: *a quick inspection.* See Synonyms at **fast**[1]. **5.** Tending to react hastily: *quick to find fault.* **6.** *Archaic.* **a.** Alive. **b.** Pregnant. —**quick** *n.* **1.** Sensitive or raw exposed flesh, as under the fingernails. **2.** The most personal and sensitive aspect of the emotions. **3.** The living: *the quick and the dead.* **4.** The vital core; the essence: *got to the quick of the matter.* —**quick** *adv.* Quickly; promptly. [Middle English, alive, lively, quick, from Old English *cwicu*, alive. See **gʷei-** in Appendix.] —**quick′ly** *adv.* —**quick′ness** *n.*

USAGE NOTE: In speech *quick* is commonly used as an adverb in phrases such as *Come quick.* In formal writing, however, *quickly* is required.

quilt

quick-and-dirt·y (kwĭk′ən-dûr′tē) *adj.* Cheaply made or done; of inferior quality: *a quick-and-dirty construction project; a quick-and-dirty research report.*

quick assets *pl.n.* Liquid assets, including cash on hand and assets readily convertible to cash.

quick bread *n.* A bread made with a leavening agent, such as baking powder, that expands during baking and requires no leavening period beforehand.

quick·en (kwĭk′ən) *v.* **-ened, -en·ing, -ens.** —*tr.* **1.** To make more rapid; accelerate. **2.** To make alive; vitalize. **3.** To excite and stimulate; stir. **4.** To make steeper. —*intr.* **1.** To become more rapid. See Synonyms at **speed.** **2.** To come or return to life: *"And the weak spirit quickens"* (T.S. Eliot). **3.** To reach the stage of pregnancy when the fetus can be felt to move. —**quick′en·er** *n.*

quick fix *n.* *Slang.* A hastily contrived remedy that alleviates a problem for the time being: *"Conversion of sexist English into nonsexist English is not a quick fix—it is anything but mechanical"* (Douglas R. Hofstadter). —**quick′-fix′** (kwĭk′fĭks′) *adj.*

quick-freeze (kwĭk′frēz′) *tr.v.* **-froze** (-frōz′), **-froz·en** (-frō′zən), **-freez·ing, -freez·es.** To freeze (food) by a process sufficiently rapid to retain natural flavor, nutritional value, or other properties.

quick·ie (kwĭk′ē) *n.* *Informal.* Something done rapidly.

quick·lime (kwĭk′līm′) *n.* See **lime**[3] (sense 1b). [Middle English *qwike lime* : *quick*, live; see QUICK + *lime*, lime; see LIME[3] (translation of Latin *calx vīva* : *calx*, lime + *vīva*, live).]

quick·sand (kwĭk′sănd′) *n.* **1.** A bed of loose sand mixed with water forming a soft, shifting mass that yields easily to pressure and tends to engulf any object resting on its surface. **2.** Often **quicksands.** A place or situation into which entry can be swift and sudden but from which extrication can be difficult or impossible: *"This theory of the future entrapped* [them] *in the quicksands of Vietnam"* (Arthur M. Schlesinger, Jr.).

quick·set (kwĭk′sĕt′) *n.* *Chiefly British.* **1.** Cuttings or slips of a plant suitable for hedges. **2.** A hedge consisting of these plant cuttings or slips. [QUICK, alive + SET[1].]

quick·sil·ver (kwĭk′sĭl′vər) *n.* See **mercury** (sense 1). —**quicksilver** *adj.* Unpredictable; mercurial: *"a quicksilver character, cool and willful at one moment, utterly fragile the next"* (Sven Birkerts). [Middle English, from Old English *cwicseolfor* : *cwic, cwicu*, alive; see **gʷei-** in Appendix + *seolfor*, silver; see SILVER (translation of Latin *argentum vīvum*).]

quilting

quick·step (kwĭk′stĕp′) *n.* *Music.* A march for accompanying quick time.

quick study *n.* One who is able to memorize something easily and quickly or is able to understand and deal with something easily and successfully.

quick-tem·pered (kwĭk′tĕm′pərd) *adj.* Easily aroused to anger.

quick time *n.* A military marching pace of 120 steps per minute.

quick-wit·ted (kwĭk′wĭt′ĭd) *adj.* Mentally alert and sharp; keen. See Synonyms at **intelligent.** —**quick′-wit′ted·ly** *adv.* —**quick′-wit′ted·ness** *n.*

quid[1] (kwĭd) *n.* A cut, as of chewing tobacco. [Middle English *quide*, cud, from Old English *cwidu*.]

quid[2] (kwĭd) *n., pl.* **quid** or **quids.** *Chiefly British.* A pound sterling. [Possibly from Latin, something, what. See QUIDDITY.]

Quid·de (kvĭd′ə), **Ludwig.** 1858–1941. German politician and pacifist. He shared the 1927 Nobel Peace Prize.

quid·di·ty (kwĭd′ĭ-tē) *n., pl.* **-ties.** **1.** The real nature of a thing; the essence. **2.** A hairsplitting distinction; a quibble. [Medieval Latin *quidditās*, from Latin *quid*, what. See **kʷo-** in Appendix.]

quid·nunc (kwĭd′nŭngk′) *n.* A nosy person; a busybody. [Latin *quid nunc?* what now : *quid*, what; see **kʷo-** in Appendix + *nunc*, now; see **nu-** in Appendix.]

quid pro quo (kwĭd′ prō kwō′) *n., pl.* **quid pro quos** or **quids pro quo.** An equal exchange or substitution. [Latin *quid prō quō* : *quid*, what + *prō*, for + *quō*, ablative of *quid*, what?]

qui·es·cent (kwē-ĕs′ənt, kwī-) *adj.* Being quiet, still, or at rest; inactive. See Synonyms at **latent.** [Latin *quiēscēns, quiēscent-*, present participle of *quiēscere*, to rest, from *quiēs*, quiet. See QUIET.] —**qui·es′cence** *n.* —**qui·es′cent·ly** *adv.*

qui·et (kwī′ĭt) *adj.* **-et·er, -et·est.** **1.** Making no noise; silent: *a quiet audience at the concert.* **2.** Free of noise; hushed: *a quiet place for studying.* **3.** Calm and unmoving; still: *floating on quiet waters.* **4.** Free of turmoil and agitation; untroubled. See Synonyms at **still**[1]. **5.** Restful; soothing: *a quiet afternoon nap; a warm, quiet bath.* **6.** Tranquil; serene: *a quiet manner.* **7.** Not showy or garish; restrained: *a room decorated in quiet colors.* —**quiet** *n.* The quality or condition of being quiet: *"A menacing quiet fills the empty streets"* (Time). —**quiet** *v.* **-et·ed, -et·ing, -ets.** —*tr.* **1.** To cause to become quiet. **2.** *Law.* To make (a title) secure by freeing from all questions or challenges. —*intr.* To become quiet: *The child wouldn't quiet down for me.* [Middle English, from Old French, from Latin *quiētus*, from past participle of *quiēscere*, to rest, from *quiēs*, quiet. See **kʷeiə-** in Appendix.] —**qui′et·ly** *adv.* —**qui′et·ness** *n.*

qui·et·en (kwī′ĭ-tn) *tr. & intr.v.* **-ened, -en·ing, -ens.** To make or become quiet.

qui·et·ism (kwī′ĭ-tĭz′əm) *n.* **1.** A form of Christian mysticism enjoining passive contemplation and the beatific annihilation of the will. **2.** A state of quietness and passivity. —**qui′et·ist** *n.* —**qui′et·is′tic** *adj.*

qui·e·tude (kwī′ĭ-to͞od′, -tyo͞od′) *n.* Tranquillity. [Late Latin *quiētūdō*, from Latin *quiētus*, resting, from past participle of *quiēscere*, to rest. See QUIET.]

qui·e·tus (kwī-ē′təs) *n.* **1.** Something that serves to suppress, check, or eliminate. **2.** Release from life; death. **3.** A final discharge, as of a duty or debt. [Short for Middle English *quietus (est)*, (he is) discharged (of an obligation), from Medieval Latin *quiētus (est)*, from Latin, (he is) at rest. See QUIET.]

quiff[1] (kwĭf) *n.* *Chiefly British.* A tuft of hair, especially a forelock. [Origin unknown.]

quiff[2] (kwĭf) *n.* A woman regarded as promiscuous. [Origin unknown.]

quill (kwĭl) *n.* **1.** The hollow stemlike main shaft of a feather. Also called *calamus.* **2.** Any of the larger wing or tail feathers of a bird. **3.** A writing pen made from the shaft of a feather. **4.** *Music.* **a.** A plectrum for a stringed instrument of the clavichord type. **b.** A pipe having a hollow stem. **5.** A toothpick made from the stem of a feather. **6.** One of the sharp hollow spines of a porcupine or hedgehog. **7.** A spindle or bobbin around which yarn is wound in weaving. **8.** A hollow shaft that rotates on a solid shaft when gears are engaged. —**quill** *tr.v.* **quilled, quill·ing, quills.** **1.** To wind (thread or yarn) onto a quill. **2.** To make or press small ridges in (fabric). [Middle English *quil.*]

quill·back (kwĭl′băk′) *n., pl.* **quillback** or **-backs.** A North American freshwater fish *(Carpiodes cyprinus)* that has one ray of the dorsal fin extending conspicuously beyond the others.

Quil·ler-Couch (kwĭl′ər-ko͞och′), Sir **Arthur Thomas.** Pen name "Q." 1863–1944. British writer and editor of *The Oxford Book of English Verse* (1900) and other anthologies.

quill·work (kwĭl′wûrk′) *n.* Decorative articles made with overlaid porcupine quills by Native Americans.

quill·wort (kwĭl′wûrt′, -wôrt′) *n.* Any of several vascular, spore-bearing, aquatic or marsh plants of the genus *Isoetes* having short rhizomes and quill-like leaves.

Quil·mes (kēl′mĕs′). A city of eastern Argentina, a suburb of Buenos Aires on the Río de la Plata. Population, 445,662.

quilt (kwĭlt) *n.* **1.** A coverlet or blanket made of two layers of fabric with a layer of cotton, wool, feathers, or down in between, all stitched firmly together, usually in a decorative crisscross design. **2.** A thick protective cover similar to or suggestive of a quilt. —**quilt** *v.* **quilt·ed, quilt·ing, quilts.** —*tr.* **1.** To make into a quilt by stitching (layers of fabric) together. **2.** To construct like a quilt: *quilt a skirt.* **3.** To pad and stitch ornamentally. —*intr.* **1.** To make a quilt. **2.** To do quilted work. [Middle English *quilte*, from Anglo-Norman, from Latin *culcita*, mattress.] —**quilt′er** *n.*

quilt·ing (kwĭl′tĭng) *n.* **1.** The process of doing quilted work. **2.a.** Material used to make quilts. **b.** Material that has been quilted.

Quim·per (kăɴ-pĕr′). A city of northwest France near the Bay of Biscay south-southeast of Brest. It is noted for its pottery, known as Quimper ware. Population, 56,907.

quin– *pref.* Variant of **quino–.**

quin·a·crine hydrochloride (kwĭn′ə-krēn′) *n.* A bright yellow, bitter, crystalline compound, $C_{23}H_{30}ClN_3O$, used primarily to treat malaria. [QUIN– + ACR(ID)INE.]

quin·a·liz·a·rin (kwĭn′ə-lĭz′ə-rĭn) *n.* A red crystalline compound, $C_{14}H_8O_6$, used to dye cotton.

qui·nate (kwī′nāt′) *adj.* Arranged in groups of five: *quinate leaflets.* [Latin *quīnī,* five each; see **penkʷe** in Appendix + –ATE [1].]

quince (kwĭns) *n.* **1.** A western Asian shrub or tree *(Cydonia oblonga)* having white flowers and hard applelike fruit. **2.** The aromatic, many-seeded fruit of this plant, edible only when cooked. [Middle English *quynce,* pl. of *quyn,* quince, from Old French *cooin,* from Latin *cotōneum (mālum),* quince (fruit), probably variant of *cydōnium,* from Greek *kudōnion (malon),* alteration (influenced by *Kudōniā,* Cydonia, an ancient city of northwest Crete) of *Kodumalon.*]

quin·cun·cial also **quin·cunx·ial** (kwĭn-kŭn′shəl) *adj.* Of, relating to, or forming a quincunx. **—quin·cun′cial·ly** *adv.*

quin·cunx (kwĭn′kŭngks′) *n.* An arrangement of five objects with one at each corner of a rectangle or square and one at the center. [Latin *quincunx, quincunc-,* five twelfths : *quīnque,* five; see **penkʷe** in Appendix + *uncia,* twelfth part of a unit; see OUNCE [1].]

quin·cunx·ial (kwĭn-kŭn′shəl) *adj.* Variant of **quincuncial.**

Quin·cy. 1. (kwĭn′sē). A city of western Illinois on a bluff above the Mississippi River. It is a trade, industrial, and distributing center. Population, 42,352. **2.** (kwĭn′zē). A city of eastern Massachusetts, an industrial suburb of Boston. John and John Quincy Adams were born here; the Adams homestead is now a national historic site. Population, 84,743.

Quin·cy (kwĭn′zē, -sē), **Josiah.** 1744–1775. American Revolutionary patriot who traveled to England to present the colonists' grievances (1774–1775). His son **Josiah** (1772–1864) was a U.S. representative from Massachusetts (1804–1813) who opposed involvement in the War of 1812 and served as mayor of Boston (1823–1829) and president of Harvard University (1829–1845).

quin·de·cen·ni·al (kwĭn′dĭ-sĕn′ē-əl) *adj.* **1.** Occurring once every 15 years. **2.** Lasting 15 years. **—quindecennial** *n.* A 15th anniversary. [From Latin *quīndecim,* fifteen; see **penkʷe** in Appendix + Latin *-ennium* (from *annus,* year; see **at-** in Appendix).]

qui·nel·la (kwĭ-nĕl′ə, kē-) also **qui·nie·la** (kēn-yĕl′ə) *n. Games.* A system of betting in which the bettor, in order to win, must pick the first two finishers of a race, but not necessarily in the correct sequence. [American Spanish *quiniela,* diminutive of Spanish *quina,* keno, from French *quine.* See KENO.]

quin·i·dine (kwĭn′ĭ-dēn′) *n.* A colorless crystalline alkaloid, $C_{20}H_{24}N_2O_2$, resembling quinine and used in treating malaria and certain heart disorders.

qui·nie·la (kēn-yĕl′ə) *n. Games.* Variant of **quinella.**

qui·nine (kwī′nīn′) *n.* **1.** A bitter, colorless, amorphous powder or crystalline alkaloid, $C_{20}H_{24}N_2O_2 \cdot 3H_2O$, derived from certain cinchona barks and used in medicine to treat malaria. **2.** Any of various compounds or salts of quinine.

quinine water *n.* A carbonated beverage flavored with quinine.

quin·nat salmon (kwĭn′ăt′) *n.* See **Chinook salmon.** [Chinook *ikwanat.*]

quino– or **quin–** *pref.* **1.** Cinchona; cinchona bark: *quinoidine.* **2.** Quinone: *quinoid.* [From Spanish *quina,* cinchona bark, from Quechua *kina.*]

qui·no·a (kĭ-nō′ə, kēn′wä) *n.* A goosefoot *(Chenopodium quinoa)* native to the Andes and cultivated for its edible seeds. [American Spanish *quínoa,* from Quechua *kinua, kinoa.*]

quin·oid (kwĭn′oid′) *n.* A substance resembling quinone in structure or physical properties.

qui·noi·dine (kwĭ-noi′dēn′, -dĭn) *n.* A brownish-black mixture of alkaloids remaining after extraction of crystalline alkaloids from cinchona bark, used as a quinine substitute.

quin·o·line (kwĭn′ə-lēn′, -lĭn) *n.* An aromatic organic base, C_9H_7N, having a pungent tarlike odor, synthesized or obtained from coal tar, and used as a food preservative and in making antiseptics and dyes.

qui·none (kwĭ-nōn′, kwĭn′ōn′) *n.* Any of a class of aromatic compounds found widely in plants, especially the yellow crystalline form, $CO(CHCH)_2CO$, used in making dyes, tanning hides, and photography.

quin·o·noid (kwĭn′ə-noid′, kwĭ-nō′-) *adj.* Of or containing quinone or resembling it in structure or properties.

quin·qua·ge·nar·i·an (kwĭng′kwə-jə-nâr′ē-ən) *n.* A person 50 years old, or in his or her fifties. **—quinquagenarian** *adj.* Of or characteristic of a person in his or her fifties. [From Latin *quīnquāgēnārius,* containing fifty, from *quīnquāgēnī,* fifty each, from *quīnquāginta,* fifty. See **penkʷe** in Appendix.]

Quin·qua·ges·i·ma (kwĭng′kwə-jĕs′ə-mə) *n.* Shrove Sunday. [Medieval Latin, from Latin, fiftieth, from *quīnquāginta,* fifty. See **penkʷe** in Appendix.]

quinque– *pref.* Five: *quinquevalent.* [Latin *quīnque-,* from *quīnque,* five. See **penkʷe** in Appendix.]

quin·quen·ni·a (kwĭn-kwĕn′ē-ə) *n.* A plural of **quinquennium.**

quin·quen·ni·al (kwĭn-kwĕn′ē-əl, kwĭng-) *adj.* **1.** Happening once every five years. **2.** Lasting for five years. **—quinquennial** *n.* **1.** A fifth anniversary. **2.** A period of five years. **—quin·quen′ni·al·ly** *adv.*

quin·quen·ni·um (kwĭn-kwĕn′ē-əm, kwĭng-) *n., pl.* **-quen·ni·ums** or **-quen·ni·a** (-kwĕn′ē-ə). A period of five years. [Latin *quīnquennium* : *quīnque,* quinque- + *-ennium* (from *annus,* year; see **at-** in Appendix).]

quin·que·va·lent (kwĭng′kwə-vā′lənt) *adj.* Pentavalent. **—quin′que·va′lence** *n.*

quin·sy (kwĭn′zē) *n.* Acute inflammation of the tonsils and the surrounding tissue, often leading to the formation of an abscess. [Middle English, from Medieval Latin *quinancia* and Old French *quinancie,* both from Greek *kunankhē,* dog quinsy, dog-collar : *kuōn, kun-,* dog; see **kwon-** in Appendix + *ankhein,* to squeeze; see **angh-** in Appendix.]

quint[1] (kwĭnt) *n. Games.* A sequence of five cards of the same suit in one hand in piquet. [French *quinte,* from Old French, interval of a fifth (in music), feminine of *quint,* fifth, from Latin *quīntus,* fifth. See **penkʷe** in Appendix.]

quint[2] (kwĭnt) *n.* A quintuplet.

quin·tain (kwĭn′tən) *n.* A post or an object mounted on a post, used as a target in tilting exercises. [Middle English *quintaine,* from Old French, probably from Latin *quīntāna (via),* fifth (street in a Roman camp, supposedly used for military exercises), from *quīntus,* fifth. See **penkʷe** in Appendix.]

quin·tal (kwĭnt′l) *n. Abbr.* **q., ql. 1.** A unit of mass in the metric system equal to 100 kilograms. **2.** See **hundredweight** (sense 2). [Middle English, a unit of weight, from Old French, from Medieval Latin *quintāle,* from Arabic *qinṭār,* from Late Greek *kentēnarion,* from Late Latin *centēnārium (pondus),* hundred(weight), from Latin *centēnārius,* of a hundred. See CENTENARY.]

Quin·te·ro (kēn-tĕ′rō), **Serafín Álvarez.** See Serafín **Álvarez Quintero.**

quin·tes·sence (kwĭn-tĕs′əns) *n.* **1.** The pure, highly concentrated essence of a thing. **2.** The purest or most typical instance: *the quintessence of evil.* **3.** In ancient and medieval philosophy, the fifth and highest essence after the four elements of earth, air, fire, and water, thought to be the substance of the heavenly bodies and latent in all things. [Middle English, from Old French *quinte essence,* fifth essence, from Medieval Latin *quīnta essentia* : Latin *quīnta,* feminine of *quīntus,* fifth; see **penkʷe** in Appendix + Latin *essentia,* essence; see ESSENCE (translation of Greek *pemptē ousia*).]

quin·tes·sen·tial (kwĭn′tə-sĕn′shəl) *adj.* Of, relating to, or having the nature of a quintessence; being the most typical: *"Liszt was the quintessential romantic"* (Musical Heritage Review). **—quin′tes·sen′tial·ly** *adv.*

quin·tet also **quin·tette** (kwĭn-tĕt′) *n.* **1.** *Music.* **a.** A composition for five voices or instruments. **b.** A group of five performing musicians. **2.** A set of five persons or things. [Probably from Italian *quintetto,* diminutive of *quinto,* fifth, from Latin *quīntus.* See **penkʷe** in Appendix.]

quin·tile (kwĭn′tīl′, kwĭnt′l) *n.* **1.** The astrological aspect of planets distant from each other by 72° or one fifth of the zodiac. **2.** *Statistics.* The portion of a frequency distribution containing one fifth of the total sample. [Latin *quīntus,* fifth; see **penkʷe** in Appendix + *-ile,* as in QUARTILE.]

Quin·til·ian (kwĭn-tĭl′yən, -ē-ən). Originally Marcus Fabius Quintilianus. First century A.D. Roman rhetorician whose major work, the *Institutio Oratorio,* discusses the complete education and career of an orator.

quin·til·lion (kwĭn-tĭl′yən) *n.* **1.** The cardinal number equal to 10^{18}. **2.** *Chiefly British.* The cardinal number equal to 10^{30}. [Latin *quīntus,* fifth; see **penkʷe** in Appendix + (M)ILLION.] **—quin·til′lion** *adj.*

quin·til·lionth (kwĭn-tĭl′yənth) *n.* **1.** The ordinal number matching the number quintillion in a series. **2.** One of a quintillion equal parts. **—quin·til′lionth** *adj.*

quin·tu·ple (kwĭn-to͞o′pəl, -tyo͞o′-, -tŭp′əl, kwĭn′tə-pəl) *adj.* **1.** Consisting of five parts or units. **2.** Five times as much, as many, or as large. **—quintuple** *n.* A fivefold amount or number. **—quintuple** *v.* **-pled, -pling, -ples.** —*tr.* To multiply by five. —*intr.* To be multiplied fivefold. [French, from Old French : from Latin *quīntus,* fifth; see **penkʷe** in Appendix + *-ple,* -fold (from Latin *-plus;* see **pel-**[2] in Appendix).]

quin·tu·plet (kwĭn-tŭp′lĭt, -to͞o′plĭt, -tyo͞o′-, kwĭn′tə-plĭt) *n.* **1.** One of five offspring born in a single birth. **2.** A group or combination of five associated by common properties or behavior. [From QUINTUPLE.]

quin·tu·pli·cate (kwĭn-to͞o′plĭ-kĭt, -tyo͞o′-) *adj.* **1.** Multiplied by five; fivefold. **2.** Being the fifth of a set of five identical copies. **—quintuplicate** *n.* **1.** One of a set of five identical things. **2.** A set of five copies. **—quintuplicate** (-kāt′) *tr.v.* **-cat·ed, -cat·ing, -cates.** To make five copies of. [Latin *quīntus,* fifth; see QUINTUPLE + (QUADRU)PLICATE.]

quip (kwĭp) *n.* **1.** A clever, witty remark often prompted by the occasion. **2.** A clever, often sarcastic remark; a gibe. See Synonyms at **joke. 3.** A petty distinction or objection; a quibble. **4.** Something curious or odd. **—quip** *intr.v.* **quipped, quip·ping,**

quince
Cydonia oblonga

Josiah Quincy
1796 engraving by Charles Balthazar Julien Fevret de Saint-Memin (1770?–1852?)

ă **pat**	oi **boy**
ā **pay**	ou **out**
âr **care**	o͝o **took**
ä **father**	o͞o **boot**
ĕ **pet**	ŭ **cut**
ē **be**	ûr **urge**
ĭ **pit**	th **thin**
ī **pie**	*th* **this**
îr **pier**	hw **which**
ŏ **pot**	zh **vision**
ō **toe**	ə **about, item**
ô **paw**	♦ **regionalism**

Stress marks: **′** (primary); ′ (secondary), as in **dictionary** (dĭk′shə-nĕr′ē)

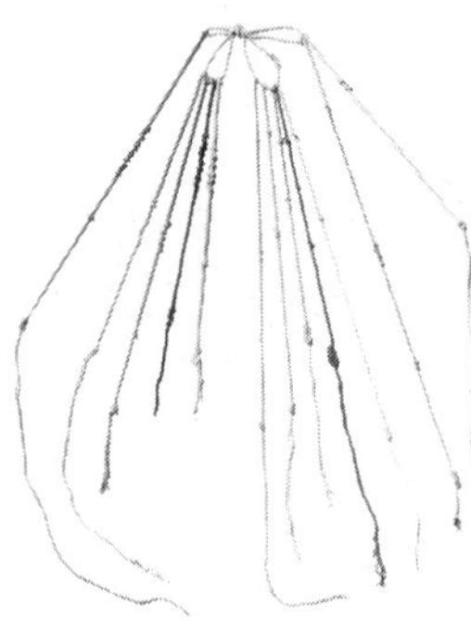
quipu
Peruvian

quips. To make quips or a quip. [Alteration of obsolete *quippy,* perhaps from Latin *quippe,* indeed, from *quid,* what. See **kʷo-** in Appendix.] **—quip′py** *adj.*

quip·ster (kwĭp′stər) *n.* One given to or known for making quips.

qui·pu (kē′po͞o) *n.* A record-keeping device of the Inca empire consisting of a series of variously colored strings attached to a base rope and knotted so as to encode information, used especially for accounting purposes. [American Spanish, from Quechua *kipu.*]

quire¹ (kwīr) *n. Abbr.* **q., qr. 1.** A set of 24 or sometimes 25 sheets of paper of the same size and stock; one twentieth of a ream. **2.** A collection of leaves of parchment or paper, folded one within the other, in a manuscript or book. [Middle English *quayer,* four double sheets of paper, from Old French *quaer,* from Vulgar Latin **quaternus,* from Latin *quaternī,* set of four, four each, from *quater,* four times. See **kʷetwer-** in Appendix.]

quire² (kwīr) *n. & v. Archaic.* Variant of **choir.**

Quir·i·nal (kwĭr′ə-nəl). One of the seven hills of ancient Rome, traditionally occupied by the Sabines. A papal palace was built here in the 16th century and served as the residence of Italian kings from 1870 to 1946. **—Quir′i·nal** *adj.*

quirk (kwûrk) *n.* **1.** A peculiarity of behavior; an idiosyncrasy. See Synonyms at **eccentricity. 2.** An unpredictable or unaccountable act or event; a vagary: *a quirk of fate.* **3.** A sudden sharp turn or twist. **4.** An equivocation; a quibble. **5.** *Architecture.* A lengthwise groove on a molding between the convex upper part and the soffit. [Origin unknown.] **—quirk′i·ly** *adv.* **—quirk′i·ness** *n.* **—quirk′y** *adj.*

quirt (kwûrt) *n.* A riding whip with a short handle and a lash of braided rawhide. [Probably from American Spanish *cuarta,* whip, ultimately from Latin *quārta,* fourth. See QUART.]

quiver²
Apache

quis·ling (kwĭz′lĭng) *n.* A traitor who serves as the puppet of the enemy occupying his or her country. [After Vidkun *Quisling* (1887–1945), head of Norway's government during the Nazi occupation (1940–1945).]

quit (kwĭt) *v.* **quit** or **quit·ted** (kwĭt′ĭd), **quit·ting, quits.** *—tr.* **1.** To depart from; leave: *"You and I are on the point of quitting the theater of our exploits"* (Horatio Nelson). **2.** To leave the company of: *had to quit the gathering in order to be home by midnight.* **3.** To give up; relinquish: *quit a job.* **4.** To abandon or put aside; forsake: *advised them to quit their dissipated ways.* **5.** To cease or discontinue: *asked them to quit talking.* **6.a.** To rid oneself of by paying: *quit a debt.* **b.** To release from a burden or responsibility. **7.** To conduct (oneself) in a specified way: *Quit yourselves like adults.* *—intr.* **1.** To cease performing an action. See Synonyms at **stop. 2.** To give up, as in defeat; stop. **3.** To leave a job. **—quit** *adj.* Absolved of a duty or an obligation; free. [Middle English *quiten,* to release, from Old French *quiter,* from Medieval Latin *quiētāre, quītāre,* from Latin *quiētus,* at rest. See QUIET.]

quitch grass (kwĭch) *n.* Couch grass. [Middle English *quich,* from Old English *cwice.* See **gʷei-** in Appendix.]

quit·claim (kwĭt′klām′) *Law. n.* The transfer of a title, right, or claim to another. **—quitclaim** *tr.v.* **-claimed, -claim·ing, -claims.** To renounce all claim to (a possession or right). [Middle English *quitclaime,* from Anglo-Norman *quiteclame,* from *quiteclamer,* to release : *quite,* free (from Latin *quiētus,* freed of; see QUIET) + *clamer,* to proclaim (from Latin *clāmāre;* see CLAIM).]

quite (kwīt) *adv.* **1.** To the greatest extent; completely: *quite alone; not quite finished.* See Usage Note at **perfect. 2.** Actually; really: *I'm quite positive about it.* **3.** To a degree; rather: *quite soon; quite tasty.* [Middle English, from *quite,* clear, free, from Old French, from Latin *quiētus,* freed. See QUIET.]

Qui·to (kē′tō). The capital of Ecuador, in the north-central part of the country. Settled by the Quito people, it was captured by the Incas in 1487 and held by the Spanish from 1534 until 1822. The city has frequently been damaged by earthquakes. Population, 890,355.

quit·rent (kwĭt′rĕnt′) *n.* A rent paid by a freeman in lieu of the services required by feudal custom. [Middle English *quiterent* : *quite,* free; see QUITE + *rent,* rent; see RENT¹.]

quits (kwĭts) *adj.* On even terms with by payment or requital: *I am finally quits with the loan.* [Middle English, probably alteration (influenced by Medieval Latin *quittus, quītus,* past participle of *quītāre,* to free) of *quit,* rid of a debt, from Old French *quiter.* See QUIT.]

quoin

quit·tance (kwĭt′ns) *n.* **1.a.** Release from a debt, an obligation, or a penalty. **b.** A document or receipt certifying such release. **2.** Something given as requital or recompense; a repayment. [Middle English *quitance,* from Old French, from *quiter,* to free. See QUIT.]

quit·ter (kwĭt′ər) *n.* One who gives up easily.

quit·tor (kwĭt′ər) *n.* An inflammation of the hoof cartilage of horses and other solid-hoofed animals, characterized by degeneration of hoof tissue, formation of a slough, and fistulous sores. [Middle English *quiture,* perhaps from Old French, act of boiling, from Latin *coctūra,* boiling liquid, from *coctus,* past participle of *coquere,* to cook. See **pekʷ-** in Appendix.]

quiv·er¹ (kwĭv′ər) *intr.v.* **-ered, -er·ing, -ers.** To shake with a slight, rapid, tremulous movement. See Synonyms at **shake.** **—quiver** *n.* The act or motion of quivering. [Middle English *quiveren,* perhaps from *quiver,* nimble (from Old English *cwifer-.* See **gʷei-** in Appendix.)] **—quiv′er·y** *adj.*

quiv·er² (kwĭv′ər) *n.* **1.** A portable case for holding arrows. **2.** A case full of arrows. [Middle English, from Anglo-Norman *quiveir,* variant of Old French *cuivre,* from Old Low Franconian *cocar,* probably from Medieval Latin *cucurum,* probably from Hunnish; akin to Mongolian *kökür.*]

qui vive (kē vēv′) *n.* A sentinel's challenge. **—*idiom.* on the qui vive.** On the alert; vigilant: *"a loathsome Dublin politico who is on the qui vive for . . . terrorists"* (Julian Moynahan). [French, (long) live who? (a sentry's challenge to determine a person's political sympathies) : *qui,* who + *vive,* third person sing. present subjunctive of *vivre,* to live.]

quix·ot·ic (kwĭk-sŏt′ĭk) also **quix·ot·i·cal** (-ĭ-kəl) *adj.* **1.** Caught up in the romance of noble deeds and the pursuit of unreachable goals; idealistic without regard to practicality. **2.** Capricious; impulsive: *"At worst his scruples must have been quixotic, not malicious"* (Louis Auchincloss). [From English *Quixote,* a visionary, after *Don Quixote,* hero of a romance by Miguel de Cervantes.] **—quix·ot′i·cal·ly** *adv.* **—quix′o·tism** (kwĭk′sə-tĭz′əm) *n.*

quiz (kwĭz) *tr.v.* **quizzed, quiz·zing, quiz·zes. 1.** To question closely or repeatedly; interrogate. **2.** To test the knowledge of by posing questions. See Synonyms at **ask. 3.** *Chiefly British.* To poke fun at; mock. **—quiz** *n., pl.* **quiz·zes. 1.** A questioning or an inquiry. **2.** A short oral or written test. **3.** A practical joke. [Origin unknown.] **—quiz′zer** *n.*

WORD HISTORY: Although we do not know the origin of the word *quiz,* just as we may not know the answers to all the questions on a quiz, we can say that its first recorded sense has to do with people, not tests. The term, first recorded in 1782, meant "an odd or eccentric person." From the noun in this sense came a verb meaning "to make sport or fun of" and "to regard mockingly." In English dialects and probably in American English the verb *quiz* acquired senses relating to interrogation and questioning. This presumably occurred because *quiz* was associated with *question, inquisitive,* or perhaps the English dialect verb *quiset,* "to question" (probably itself short for obsolete *inquisite,* "to investigate"). From this new area of meaning came the noun and verb senses all too familiar to students. The second recorded instance of the noun sense occurs in the writings of no less an educator than William James, who in a December 26, 1867, letter proffers the hope that "perhaps giving 'quizzes' in anatomy and physiology . . . may help along."

quiz show *n.* A television or radio program in which the contestants' knowledge is tested by questioning, with some contestants winning money or prizes.

quiz·zi·cal (kwĭz′ĭ-kəl) *adj.* **1.** Suggesting puzzlement; questioning. **2.** Teasing; mocking: *"His face wore a somewhat quizzical almost impertinent air"* (Lawrence Durrell). **3.** Eccentric; odd. **—quiz′zi·cal′i·ty** (-kăl′ĭ-tē) *n.* **—quiz′zi·cal·ly** *adv.*

Qum (ko͝om). See **Qom.**

Qum·ran (ko͝om-rän′) also **Khir·bet Qumran** (kîr′bĕt). An ancient village of Palestine on the northwest shore of the Dead Sea in the West Bank east of Jerusalem. It is noted for the caves in which the Dead Sea Scrolls were found.

quod·li·bet (kwŏd′lə-bĕt′) *n.* **1.a.** A theological or philosophical issue presented for formal argument or disputation. **b.** Formal disputation of such an issue. **2.** *Music.* A usually humorous medley. [Middle English, from Medieval Latin *quodlibetum,* from Latin *quod libet,* anything at all : *quod,* what; see **kʷo-** in Appendix + *libet,* it pleases, third person sing. present of *libēre,* to be pleasing; see **leubh-** in Appendix.]

quoin also **coign** (koin, kwoin) *—n.* **1.a.** An exterior angle of a wall or other piece of masonry. **b.** A stone serving to form such an angle; a cornerstone. **2.** A keystone. **3.** *Printing.* A wedge-shaped block used to lock type in a chase. **4.** A wedge used to raise the level of a gun. *—tr.v.* **quoined, quoin·ing, quoins** also **coigned, coign·ing, coigns.** To provide, secure, or raise with a quoin or quoins. [Variant of COIN.]

♦ **quoit** (kwoit, koit) *n.* **1. quoits.** *(used with a sing. verb). Upper Northern U.S.* A game in which flat rings of iron or rope are pitched at a stake, with points awarded for encircling it. **2.** One of the rings used in this game. [Middle English *coyte,* flat stone, quoit, from Old French *coilte, coite,* from Latin *culcita,* cushion.]

♦ ***REGIONAL NOTE:*** The game *quoits* derives its name from *quoit,* specifically denoting a heavy iron ring slightly convex on the outside and concave inside, configured so as to give it an edge for cutting into the ground. Both the game and the term are associated almost exclusively with the Upper North (the northernmost tier of states from New York State westward to North Dakota). In fact, *quoits* is one of a dozen terms that are most reliable for delineating the Upper North dialect boundary.

quok·ka (kwŏk′ə) *n.* A small short-tailed wallaby *(Setonix brachyurus)* living in coastal areas of southwest Australia. [Nyungar (Aboriginal language of southwest Australia) *kwaka.*]

quon·dam (kwŏn′dəm, -dăm′) *adj.* That once was; former: *"the quondam drunkard, now perfectly sober"* (Bret Harte). [Latin, from *quom,* when. See **kʷo-** in Appendix.]

Quon·set (kwŏn′sĭt). A trademark used for a prefabricated portable hut having a semicircular roof of corrugated metal that curves down to form walls. This trademark often occurs in attributive contexts in print: *"a Quonset building that once stored grain"* (Chicago Tribune); *"an unassuming assemblage of clapboard buildings, Quonset storage huts, and docks"* (Christian Science Monitor). It sometimes occurs in lowercase: *"wooden frame shacks, auto trailers, abandoned Air Force quonsets"* (Washington Post).

quo•rum (kwôr′əm, kwōr′-) *n.* **1.** The minimal number of officers and members of a committee or an organization, usually a majority, who must be present for valid transaction of business. **2.** A select group. [Middle English, quorum of justices of the peace, from Latin *quōrum,* of whom, from the wording of a commission naming certain persons as members of a body, genitive pl. of *quī,* who. See **k^{w}o-** in Appendix.]

quot. *abbr.* Quotation.

quo•ta (kwō′tə) *n.* **1.** A proportional share, as of goods, assigned to a group or to each member of a group; an allotment. **2.** A production assignment. **3.** The maximum number, especially of people, that may be admitted to a nation, a group, or an institution. [Medieval Latin, from Latin *quota (pars),* how large (a part), feminine of *quotus,* of what number. See QUOTE.]

quot•a•ble (kwō′tə-bəl) *adj.* Suitable for or worthy of quoting: *a quotable slogan; a quotable pundit.* **—quot′a•bil′i•ty** *n.*

quo•ta•tion (kwō-tā′shən) *n. Abbr.* **quot. 1.** The act of quoting. **2.** A passage quoted. **3.** An explicit reference or allusion in an artistic work to a passage or element from another, usually well-known work: *"Direct quotations from other paintings are fairly sparse"* (Robert Hughes). **4. a.** The quoting of current prices and bids for securities and goods. **b.** The prices or bids cited. **—quo•ta′tion•al** *adj.* **—quo•ta′tion•al•ly** *adv.*

quotation mark *n.* Either of a pair of punctuation marks used to mark the beginning and end of a passage attributed to another and repeated word for word. They appear in the form of double quotation marks (" ") and single quotation marks (' '). Single quotation marks are usually reserved for setting off a quotation within another quotation.

quote (kwōt) *v.* **quot•ed, quot•ing, quotes.** *—tr.* **1.** To repeat or copy the words of (another), usually with acknowledgment of the source. **2.** To cite or refer to for illustration or proof. **3.** To repeat a brief passage or excerpt from: *The saxophonist quoted a Duke Ellington melody in his solo.* **4.** To state (a price) for securities, goods, or services. *—intr.* To give a quotation, as from a book. **—quote** *n.* **1.** *Informal.* A quotation. **2.** A quotation mark. **3.** Used by a speaker to indicate the beginning of a quotation. **4.** *Usage Problem.* A dictum; a saying. [Middle English *coten,* to mark a book with numbers or marginal references, from Old French *coter,* from Medieval Latin *quotāre,* to number chapters, from Latin *quotus,* of what number, from *quot,* how many. See **k^{w}o-** in Appendix.] **—quot′er** *n.*

USAGE NOTE: As a transitive verb *quote* is appropriately used to describe the use of an exact wording drawn from another source. When the original source is paraphrased or alluded to, the more general term *cite* is usually preferable. • The noun *quote* is well established as a truncation of *quotation,* though many critics regard it as unduly journalistic or breezy. As such, it is best avoided in formal literary discussions. The use of the noun was acceptable to only 38 percent of the Usage Panel in the sentence *He began the chapter with a* quote *from the Bible.* But the usage is less objectionable in informal contexts or in reference to less august sources; the word was acceptable to 53 percent of the Panel in the sentence *He lightened up his talk by throwing in* quotes *from Marx Brothers movies.* • The noun *quote* is sometimes used as a synonym for "dictum, saying," as in *His career is just one more validation of Andy Warhol's* quote *that "in the future, everybody will be famous for fifteen minutes."* This example was unacceptable to 76 percent of the Usage Panel.

quoth (kwōth) *tr.v. Archaic.* Uttered; said. Used only in the first and third persons, with the subject following: *"Quoth the Raven, 'Nevermore!'"* (Edgar Allan Poe). [Middle English, from Old English *cwæth,* third person sing. past tense of *cwethan,* to say. See **g^{w}et-** in Appendix.]

quo•tha (kwō′thə) *interj. Archaic.* Used to express surprise or sarcasm, after quoting the word or phrase of another. [Alteration of *quoth he.*]

quo•tid•i•an (kwō-tĭd′ē-ən) *adj.* **1.** Everyday; commonplace: *"There's nothing quite like a real . . . train conductor to add color to a quotidian commute"* (Anita Diamant). **2.** Recurring daily. Used especially of attacks of malaria. [Middle English *cotidien,* from Old French, from Latin *quōtīdiānus,* from *quōtīdiē,* each day : *quot,* how many, as many as; see **k^{w}o-** in Appendix + *diē,* genitive and dative of *diēs,* day; see **deiw-** in Appendix.]

quo•tient (kwō′shənt) *n. Mathematics.* The number obtained by dividing one quantity by another. In $45 \div 3 = 15$, 15 is the quotient. [Middle English *quocient,* alteration of Latin *quotiēns,* how many times, from *quot,* how many. See **k^{w}o-** in Appendix.]

Qur•'an (kə-răn′, -rän′, kô-, kō-) *n.* Variant of **Koran.**

Qur•net es Sau•da (ko͝or′nĭt ĕs sou′də, -dä). A peak, 3,090 m (10,131 ft) high, of the Lebanon Mountains in northern Lebanon. It is the highest elevation in the country.

qu•rush (ko͞o′rəsh) *n., pl.* **qurush** or **-es.** See table at **currency.** [Arabic *qurūš,* pl. of *qirš.*]

q.v. *abbr. Latin.* Quod vide (which see).

QWER•TY (kwûr′tē) *adj.* Of, relating to, or designating the traditional configuration of typewriter or computer keyboard keys. [From the first six letters at the upper left.]

ă **pat**	oi **boy**
ā **pay**	ou **out**
âr **care**	o͝o **took**
ä **father**	o͞o **boot**
ĕ **pet**	ŭ **cut**
ē **be**	ûr **urge**
ĭ **pit**	th **thin**
ī **pie**	*th* **this**
îr **pier**	hw **which**
ŏ **pot**	zh **vision**
ō **toe**	ə **about, item**
ô **paw**	♦ **regionalism**

Stress marks: **′** (primary); ′ (secondary), as in **dictionary** (dĭk′shə-nĕr′ē)

Rr

9 ⦗

Phoenician

In the Phoenician alphabet this letter represented the initial sound in *rōsh* (later *rēsh*), "head."

4

Greek

It was adopted by the Greeks, who called it *rhō*.

R

Roman

In borrowing the Greek letter the Romans added the beard that still distinguishes it from P.

Ra [1]

rabbit

r[1] or **R** (är) *n., pl.* **r's** or **R's.** **1.** The 18th letter of the modern English alphabet. **2.** Any of the speech sounds represented by the letter *r.* **3.** The 18th in a series.

r[2] *abbr.* **1.** Or **R.** *Mathematics.* Radius. **2.** Or **R.** *Electricity.* Resistance. **3.** Or **r.** *Baseball.* Run.

R[1] (är) *n.* A movie rating that allows admission only to persons of a certain age, usually 17, unless accompanied by a parent or guardian. —*attributive.* Often used to modify another noun: *an R movie.* [Short for RESTRICTED.]

R[2] **1.** The symbol for **gas constant. 2.** The symbol for **radical.**

R[3] *abbr.* **1.** Or **R.** Réaumur (scale). **2.** Registered trademark. **3.** *Ecclesiastical.* Response. **4.** Or **r.** Roentgen. **5.** *Games.* Rook (chess).

r. *abbr.* **1.** Or **R.** Railroad; railway. **2.** Or **R.** Range. **3.** Rare. **4.** Retired. **5.** Or **R.** Right. **6.** Or **R.** River. **7.** Or **R.** Road. **8.** Rod (unit of length). **9.** *Games.* Rubber. **10.** Ruble. **11.** Or **R.** Rupee.

R. *abbr.* **1.** Rabbi. **2.** Rector. **3.** Republican. **4.** Royal.

Ra[1] (rä) also **Re** (rā) *n. Mythology.* The ancient Egyptian sun god, the supreme deity represented as a man with the head of a hawk crowned with a solar disk and uraeus.

Ra[2] The symbol for the element **radium.**

Ra. *abbr.* Range.

R.A. *abbr.* **1.** Or **RA.** Rear admiral. **2.** Or **RA.** Regular army. **3.** *Astronomy.* Right ascension. **4.** Royal Academy; Royal Academician.

ra·bat (răb′ē, rə-băt′) *n.* A piece of cloth fitted to the collar and covering the shirt front, worn chiefly by Roman Catholic and Anglican clergy. [French, from Old French. See REBATO.]

Ra·bat (rə-bät′, rä-). The capital of Morocco, on the Atlantic Ocean northeast of Casablanca. Settled in ancient times, it became a Moslem fortress c. 700. Rabat was the capital of the French protectorate of Morocco from 1912 until independence was achieved in 1956. Population, 518,616.

ra·ba·to (rə-bä′tō) *n.* Variant of **rebato.**

rab·bet (răb′ĭt) also **re·bate** (rē′bāt′, răb′ĭt) —*n.* **1.** A cut or groove along or near the edge of a piece of wood that allows another piece to fit into it to form a joint. **2.** A joint so made. —*v.* **-bet·ed, -bet·ing, -bets** also **-bat·ed, -bat·ing, -bates.** —*tr.* **1.** To cut a rabbet in. **2.** To join by a rabbet. —*intr.* To be joined by a rabbet. [Middle English *rabet,* from Old French *rabat,* recess in a wall, act of beating down, from *rabattre,* to beat down again. See REBATE[1].]

rab·bi (răb′ī) *n., pl.* **-bis. 1.** *Abbr.* **R.** A person trained in Jewish law, ritual, and tradition and ordained for leadership of a Jewish congregation, especially one serving as chief religious official of a synagogue. **2.** A scholar qualified to interpret Jewish law. [Middle English *rabi,* from Old French, from Late Latin *rabbī,* master, from Greek *rhabbi,* from Hebrew *rabbî* : *rab,* master + *-ī,* my.]

rab·bin·ate (răb′ə-nāt′, -nĭt) *n.* **1.** The office or function of a rabbi. **2.** Rabbis considered as a group.

rab·bin·i·cal (rə-bĭn′ĭ-kəl) also **rab·bin·ic** (-ĭk) *adj.* Of, relating to, or characteristic of rabbis. [From obsolete *rabbin,* rabbi, from French, from Old French *rabain,* probably from Aramaic *rabbīn,* pl. of *rab,* master.] —**rab·bin′i·cal·ly** *adv.*

Rab·bin·ic Hebrew (rə-bĭn′ĭk) *n.* See **Mishnaic Hebrew.**

rab·bin·ism (răb′ə-nĭz′əm) *n.* Rabbinical teachings and traditions.

rab·bin·ist (răb′ə-nĭst) *n.* A strict observer of the Talmud and of rabbinical traditions. —**rab′bin·is′tic, rab′bin·it′ic** (-ĭt′ĭk) *adj.*

rab·bit (răb′ĭt) *n., pl.* **-bits** or **rabbit. 1.** Any of various long-eared, short-tailed, burrowing mammals of the family Leporidae, as the commonly domesticated Old World species *Oryctolagus cuniculus* or the cottontail. **2.** A hare. **3.** The fur of a rabbit or hare. **4.** *Sports.* A runner who intentionally sets a fast pace for a teammate during a long-distance race. —**rabbit** *intr.v.* **-bit·ed, -bit·ing, -bits.** To hunt rabbits or hares. [Middle English *rabet,* young rabbit, probably from Old French, from Middle Dutch *robbe,* rabbit.] —**rab′bit·er** *n.*

rabbit ears *pl.n. Informal.* An indoor television antenna consisting of two usually adjustable rods connected to a base and swiveling apart at a V-shaped angle.

rabbit fever *n.* See **tularemia.**

rabbit food *n. Informal.* Raw vegetables, especially those eaten in salads.

rab·bit-foot clover (răb′ĭt-fo͝ot′) *n.* An annual clover *(Trifolium arvense)* native to the Old World, having white or pale pink furlike flowers resembling rabbits' paws.

rabbit punch *n.* A chopping blow to the back of the neck. —**rab′bit-punch′** (răb′ĭt-pŭnch′) *v.*

rab·ble[1] (răb′əl) *n.* **1.** A tumultuous crowd; a mob: *an aristocrat who was killed in the street by rabble.* **2.** The lowest or coarsest class of people: *aristocrats who regarded the rabble with deep contempt.* [Middle English.]

rab·ble[2] (răb′əl) *n.* **1.** An iron bar with one end bent like a rake, used to stir and skim molten iron in puddling. **2.** Any of various similar tools or mechanically operated devices used in roasting or refining furnaces. —**rabble** *tr.v.* **-bled, -bling, -bles.** To stir or skim (molten iron) with an iron bar. [French *râble,* fire shovel, from Old French *roable,* from Medieval Latin *rotābulum,* from Latin *rutābulum,* from *rutus,* past participle of *ruere,* to rake up, tumble down.] —**rab′bler** *n.*

rab·ble-rous·er (răb′əl-rou′zər) *n.* A leader or speaker who stirs up the passions of the masses; a demagogue.

Ra·be·lais (răb′ə-lā′, răb′ə-lā′, räb-lĕ′), **François.** 1494?–1553. French humanist and writer of satirical attacks on medieval scholasticism and superstition, most notably *Pantagruel* (1532) and *Gargantua* (1534).

Rab·e·lai·si·an (răb′ə-lā′zē-ən, -zhən) *adj.* **1.** Of, relating to, or characteristic of Rabelais or his works: *a Rabelaisian catalogue.* **2.** Characterized by coarse humor, exuberant learning, or bold caricature.

Ra·bi (rŭ′bē) also **Ra·bi·a** (rə-bē′ə) *n.* Either the third or the fourth month of the year in the Moslem calendar. See table at **calendar.** [Arabic *rabī',* spring.]

Ra·bi (rä′bē), **Isidor Isaac.** 1898–1988. Austrian-born American physicist. He won a 1944 Nobel Prize for his study of magnetic movement of atomic particles.

rab·id (răb′ĭd) *adj.* **1.** Of or affected by rabies. **2.** Raging; uncontrollable: *rabid thirst.* **3.** Extremely zealous or enthusiastic; fanatical: *a rabid football fan.* [Latin *rabidus,* from *rabere,* to rave.] —**ra·bid′i·ty** (rə-bĭd′ĭ-tē, ră-), **rab′id·ness** (răb′ĭd-nĭs) *n.* —**rab′id·ly** *adv.*

ra·bies (rā′bēz) *n.* An acute, infectious, often fatal viral disease of most warm-blooded animals, especially wolves, cats, and dogs, that attacks the central nervous system and is transmitted by the bite of infected animals. [Latin *rabiēs,* rage, from *rabere,* to rave.] —**ra′bi·et′ic** (-ĕt′ĭk) *adj.*

Ra·bin (rä-bēn′), **Itzhak** or **Yitzhak.** Born 1922. Israeli military and political leader who commanded Israeli forces in the Six-Day War (1967) and served as prime minister (1974–1977).

rac·coon also **ra·coon** (ră-ko͞on′) *n., pl.* **rac·coons** or **raccoon** also **ra·coons** or **racoon. 1.** A carnivorous North American mammal *(Procyon lotor)* having grayish-brown fur, black masklike facial markings, and a black-ringed bushy tail. **2.** The fur of this mammal. **3.** Any of various similar or related animals. [Of Virginia Algonquian origin.]

Rac·coon River (ră-ko͞on′). A river rising in northwest Iowa and flowing about 322 km (200 mi) southeast to the Des Moines River near the city of Des Moines.

race[1] (rās) *n.* **1.** A local geographic or global human population distinguished as a more or less distinct group by genetically transmitted physical characteristics. **2.** A group of people united or classified together on the basis of common history, nationality, or geographic distribution: *the German race.* **3.** A genealogical line; a lineage. **4.** Human beings considered as a group. **5.** *Biology.* **a.** A population of organisms differing from others of the same species in the frequency of hereditary traits; a subspecies. **b.** A breed or strain, as of domestic animals. **6.** A distinguishing or characteristic quality, such as the flavor of a wine. [French, from Old French, from Old Italian *razza,* race, lineage.]

race² (rās) *n.* **1.** *Sports.* **a.** A competition of speed, as in running or riding. **b. races.** A series of such competitions held at a specified time on a regular course: *attending the dog races.* **2.** An extended competition in which participants struggle like runners to be the winner: *the presidential race.* **3.** Steady or rapid onward movement: *the race of time.* **4. a.** A strong or swift current of water. **b.** The channel of such a current. **c.** An artificial channel built to transport water and use its energy; a raceway. **5.** A groovelike part of a machine in which a moving part slides or rolls. **6.** See **slipstream** (sense 1). **—race** *v.* **raced, rac•ing, rac•es.** *—intr.* **1.** *Sports.* To compete in a contest of speed. **2.** To move rapidly or at top speed: *raced home in time.* **3.** To run too rapidly because of decreased resistance or a lighter load: *an engine that was racing.* *—tr.* **1.** *Sports.* **a.** To compete against in a race. **b.** To cause to compete in a race; enter in a contest: *The monarch raced her horses in the derby each year.* **2.** To transport rapidly or at top speed; rush: *raced the injured motorist to the hospital.* **3.** To cause (an engine with the gears disengaged, for example) to run swiftly or too swiftly. [Middle English *ras,* from Old Norse *rās,* rush, running. See **ers-** in Appendix.]

Race (rās), **Cape.** A promontory of southeast Newfoundland, Canada, on the coast of the Avalon Peninsula.

race•car (rās′kär′) *n.* *Sports.* An automobile used for racing.

race•course (rās′kôrs′, -kōrs′) *n.* *Sports.* A course laid out for racing.

race•horse (rās′hôrs′) *n.* A horse bred and trained to race.

ra•ceme (rā-sēm′, rə-) *n.* *Botany.* An inflorescence having stalked flowers arranged singly along an elongated, unbranched axis, as in the lily of the valley. [Latin *racēmus,* a bunch of grapes.]

ra•ce•mic (rā-sē′mĭk, -sĕm′ĭk, rə-) *adj.* Of or relating to a chemical compound that contains equal quantities of dextrorotatory and levorotatory forms and therefore does not rotate the plane of incident polarized light.

racemic acid *n.* An optically inactive form of tartaric acid, $C_2H_4O_2(COOH)_2 \cdot H_2O$, that can be separated into dextrorotatory and levorotatory components and is sometimes found in grape juice during the making of wine.

ra•ce•mi•form (rā-sē′mə-fôrm′) *adj.* *Botany.* Having the form of a raceme.

rac•e•mism (răs′ə-mĭz′əm, rā-sē′-) *n.* *Chemistry.* The condition or state of being racemic.

rac•e•mi•za•tion (răs′ə-mĭ-zā′shən) *n.* *Chemistry.* Conversion of an optically active substance to a racemic form.

rac•e•mose (răs′ə-mōs′) *adj.* **1.** *Botany.* Resembling or borne in a raceme. **2.** *Anatomy.* Having a structure of clustered parts. Used of glands. **—rac′e•mose′ly** *adv.*

rac•er (rā′sər) *n.* **1.** One that engages in races or is capable of great speed: *a dog bred as a racer.* **2.** Any of various fast-moving North American snakes of the genus *Coluber.*

race riot *n.* A riot caused by racial hatred or dissension.

race•run•ner (rās′rŭn′ər) *n.* Any of several fast-moving New World lizards of the genus *Cnemidophorus.*

race•track (rās′trăk′) *n.* *Sports.* A usually oval, specially surfaced course on which races are held.

race-walk (rās′wôk′) *intr.v.* **-walked, -walk•ing, -walks.** *Sports.* To engage in race walking.

race walking *n.* *Sports.* The sport of walking for speed, the rules of which require the racer to maintain continual foot contact with the ground and to keep the supporting leg straight at the knee when that leg is directly below the body. Also called *health walking, heel-and-toeing, PowerWalking, speed walking.* **—race walker** *n.*

race•way (rās′wā′) *n.* **1.** *Sports.* A course or track for racing, especially harness racing. **2.** A tube that encloses and protects electric wires. **3.** A race: *the raceway beside the old mill.*

Ra•chel (rā′chəl). In the Old Testament, the second wife of Jacob and the mother of Joseph and Benjamin.

rach•i•des (răk′ĭ-dēz′, rā′kĭ-) *n.* *Biology.* A plural of **rachis.**

ra•chil•la (rə-kĭl′ə) *n., pl.* **-chil•lae** (-kĭl′ē). *Botany.* A diminutive axis of a spikelet that bears the florets, as in grasses and sedges. [New Latin, diminutive of RACHIS.]

ra•chis (rā′kĭs) *n., pl.* **ra•chis•es** or **rach•i•des** (răk′ĭ-dēz′, rā′kĭ-). *Biology.* A main axis or shaft, such as the main stem of an inflorescence, the stalk of a pinnately compound leaf, or the spinal column. [New Latin, from Greek *rhakhis,* spine, ridge.] **—ra′chi•al** *adj.*

ra•chi•tis (rə-kī′tĭs) *n.* See **rickets.** [Greek *rhakhis,* spine + -ITIS.] **—ra•chit′ic** (-kĭt′ĭk) *adj.*

Rach•ma•ni•noff (răk-mä′nə-nôf′, räkн-, rəkн-mä′nyĭ-nəf), **Sergei Vasilievich.** 1873–1943. Russian-born composer. A virtuoso pianist, he excelled at the interpretation of the late romantic composers. His own work is largely a continuation of that genre.

ra•cial (rā′shəl) *adj.* **1.** Of, relating to, or characteristic of race or races. **2.** Arising from or based on differences among human racial groups: *racial conflict; racial discrimination.* **—ra′cial•ly** *adv.*

ra•cial•ism (rā′shə-lĭz′əm) *n.* *Chiefly British.* Variant of **racism.** **—ra′cial•ist** *adj. & n.* **—ra′cial•is′tic** *adj.*

Ra•ci•bórz (rät-sē′bo͞osh′). A city of southern Poland on the Oder River near the Czechoslovakian border. First mentioned in the 12th century, it was later the capital of an independent principality and passed to Bohemia and Prussia before being incorporated into Poland in 1945. Population, 59,800.

Ra•cine (rə-sēn′, rā-). A city of southeast Wisconsin on Lake Michigan south of Milwaukee. It is a port and manufacturing center. Population, 85,725.

Ra•cine (rə-sēn′, rä-), **Jean Baptiste.** 1639–1699. French playwright. The greatest tragedian of the French classical period, he based his works, such as *Britannicus* (1669) and *Phèdre* (1677), on classical Greek and Roman themes.

rac•ing form (rā′sĭng) *n.* *Sports.* An information sheet about horseraces.

racing skate *n.* *Sports.* See **speed skate.**

ra•cism (rā′sĭz′əm) *n.* **1.** The belief that race accounts for differences in human character or ability and that a particular race is superior to others. **2.** Discrimination or prejudice based on race. **—rac′ist** *adj. & n.*

rack¹ (răk) *n.* **1. a.** A framework or stand in or on which to hold, hang, or display various articles: *a trophy rack; a rack for baseball bats in the dugout; a drying rack for laundry.* **b.** *Games.* A triangular frame for arranging billiard balls at the start of a game. **c.** A receptacle for livestock feed. **d.** A frame for holding bombs in an aircraft. **2.** *Slang.* **a.** A bunk; a bed. **b.** Sleep: *was finally able to get some rack.* **3.** A toothed bar that meshes with a gearwheel, a pinion, or another toothed machine part. **4. a.** A state of intense anguish. **b.** A cause of intense anguish. **5.** An instrument of torture on which the victim's body was stretched. **6.** A pair of antlers: *a buck with a handsome rack.* **—rack** *tr.v.* **racked, rack•ing, racks. 1.** *Sports.* To place (billiard balls, for example) in a rack. **2.** To cause great physical or mental suffering to: *Pain racked his entire body.* See Synonyms at **afflict. 3.** To torture by means of the rack. ***—phrasal verbs.* rack out.** *Slang.* To go to sleep or get some sleep. **rack up.** *Informal.* To accumulate or score: *rack up points.* ***—idiom.* on the rack.** Under great stress. [Middle English *rakke,* probably from Middle Dutch *rec,* framework. See **reg-** in Appendix.] **—rack′er** *n.*

rack² (răk) *n.* A fast, flashy, four-beat gait of a horse in which each foot touches the ground separately and at equal intervals. **—rack** *intr.v.* **racked, rack•ing, racks.** To go or move in a rack. [Origin unknown.]

rack³ (răk) *n.* A thin mass of wind-driven clouds. **—rack** *intr.v.* **racked, rack•ing, racks.** To be driven by the wind; scud: *as clouds racked by.* [Middle English *rak,* probably of Scandinavian origin; akin to Swedish *rak,* wreckage.]

rack⁴ (răk) *n.* Variant of **wrack¹.**

♦ **rack⁵** (răk) *n. & v.* Variant of **wrack².**

rack⁶ (răk) *tr.v.* **racked, rack•ing, racks.** To drain (wine or cider) from the dregs. [Middle English *rakken,* from Old Provençal *arracar,* from *raca,* stems and husks of grapes.]

rack⁷ (răk) *n.* **1. a.** A wholesale rib cut of lamb or veal between the shoulder and the loin. **b.** A retail rib cut of lamb or veal, prepared for roasting or for rib chops. **2.** The neck and upper spine of mutton, pork, or veal. [Probably from RACK¹.]

rack and pinion *n.* A device for the conversion of rotary and linear motion, consisting of a pinion and a mated rack. **—rack′-and-pin′ion** (răk′ən-pĭn′yən) *adj.*

rack•et¹ also **rac•quet** (răk′ĭt) *n.* *Sports.* **1.** A device consisting of an oval frame with a tight interlaced network of strings and a handle, used to strike a ball or shuttlecock in various games. **2.** A wooden paddle, as one used in table tennis. [Middle English *raket,* a kind of handball, from Old French *rachette,* palm of the hand, racket, from Medieval Latin *rascheta,* palm, from Arabic *rāḥet,* variant of *rāḥah.*]

rack•et² (răk′ĭt) *n.* **1.** A loud, distressing noise. See Synonyms at **noise. 2.** A dishonest business or practice, especially one that obtains money through fraud or extortion. **3. a.** An easy, profitable means of livelihood. **b.** *Slang.* A business or an occupation. **—racket** *intr.v.* **-et•ed, -et•ing, -ets. 1.** To make or move with a loud, distressing noise. **2.** To lead an active social life. [Origin unknown.]

rack•et•eer (răk′ĭ-tîr′) *n.* A person who commits crimes such as extortion, loansharking, bribery, and obstruction of justice in furtherance of illegal business activities. **—racketeer** *intr.v.* **-eered, -eer•ing, -eers.** To carry on illegal business activities that involve crimes.

rack•ets (răk′ĭts) *pl.n.* *(used with a sing. verb).* *Sports.* Variant of **racquets.**

rack•et•y (răk′ĭ-tē) *adj.* Noisy; raucous.

Rack•ham (răk′əm), **Arthur.** 1867–1939. British artist known for his ethereal illustrations for children's books.

rack railway *n.* See **cog railway.**

rack-rent (răk′rĕnt′) *n.* Exorbitant rent. **—rack-rent** *tr.v.* **-rent•ed, -rent•ing, -rents.** To exact exorbitant rent for or from. [From RACK¹.] **—rack′-rent′er** *n.*

ra•clette (rä-klĕt′, rā-) *n.* **1.** A Swiss dish consisting of cheese melted and served on boiled potatoes or bread. **2.** A firm cheese used in making this dish. [French, from *racler,* to rake, scrape, from Provençal *rasclar,* to rake, from Old Provençal, from Vulgar Latin **rāsculāre,* from **rāsculum,* diminutive of Latin *rāstrum,* rake. See **rēd-** in Appendix.]

rac•on•teur (răk′ŏn-tûr′) *n.* One who tells stories and anecdotes with skill and wit. [French, from *raconter,* to relate, from

François Rabelais
17th-century portrait by an unknown artist

raccoon
Procyon lotor

Sergei Rachmaninoff

racket¹
Top: Tennis racket
Center: Squash racket
Bottom: Badminton racket

ă pat	oi boy
ā pay	ou out
âr care	o͝o took
ä father	o͞o boot
ĕ pet	ŭ cut
ē be	ûr urge
ĭ pit	th thin
ī pie	*th* this
îr pier	hw which
ŏ pot	zh vision
ō toe	ə about, item
ô paw	♦ regionalism

Stress marks: ′ (primary); ′ (secondary), as in **dictionary** (dĭk′shə-nĕr′ē)

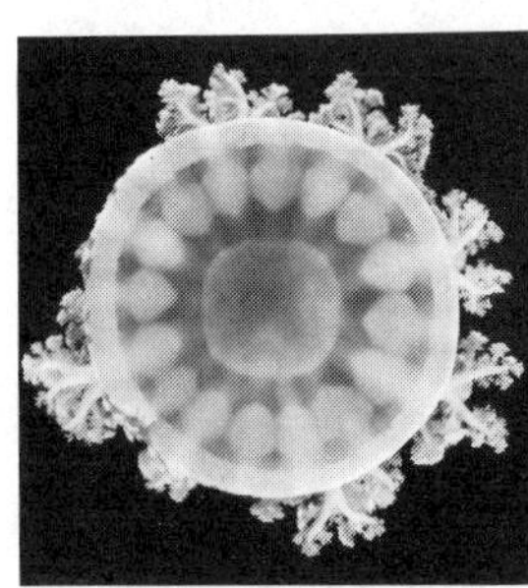
radial symmetry
Jellyfish

Old French : *re-*, re- + *aconter,* to count up, reckon; see ACCOUNT.]

ra·coon (rä-ko͞on′) *n.* Variant of **raccoon.**

rac·quet (răk′ĭt) *n. Sports.* Variant of **racket**[1].

rac·quet·ball (răk′ĭt-bôl′) *n. Sports.* A game played on a four-walled handball court by two or four players with short-handled rackets and a hollow rubber ball 2¼ inches (5.7 centimeters) in diameter.

rac·quets also **rack·ets** (răk′ĭts) *pl.n. (used with a sing. verb). Sports.* A game played on a large, netless, four-walled court by two or four players with long-handled rackets and a hard, fast-moving ball 1 inch (2.5 centimeters) in diameter.

rac·y (rā′sē) *adj.* **-i·er, -i·est. 1.** Having a distinctive and characteristic quality or taste. **2.** Strong and sharp in flavor or odor; piquant or pungent. **3.** Risqué; ribald. **4.** Vigorous; lively. [From RACE[1].] **—rac′i·ly** *adv.* **—rac′i·ness** *n.*

rad[1] (răd) *n. Physics.* A unit of energy absorbed from ionizing radiation, equal to 100 ergs per gram or 0.01 joule per kilogram of irradiated material. [Short for RADIATION.]

rad[2] (răd) *adj. Slang.* **1.** Radical: *rad moves on a skateboard.* **2.** Wonderful; marvelous.

rad[3] *abbr. Mathematics.* Radian.

rad. *abbr.* **1.** *Mathematics.* Radical. **2.** Radio. **3.** *Mathematics.* Radius. **4.** *Mathematics.* Radix.

ra·dar (rā′där) *n.* **1.** A method of detecting distant objects and determining their position, velocity, or other characteristics by analysis of very high frequency radio waves reflected from their surfaces. **2.** The equipment used in such detection. *—attributive.* Often used to modify another noun: *radar technology; a radar installation.* [RA(DIO) + D(ETECTING) + A(ND) + R(ANGING).]

radar astronomy *n.* The branch of astronomy that studies bodies in the solar system by analyzing the reflections of radio waves sent from Earth.

radar beacon *n.* A fixed device that sends or receives, amplifies, alters, and returns a radar signal, permitting a distant receiver to determine its bearing and sometimes its range.

ra·dar·scope (rā′där-skōp′) *n.* The oscilloscope viewing screen of a radar receiver.

radar telescope *n.* A large radar antenna used in radar astronomy.

Rad·cliffe (răd′klĭf′), **Ann Ward.** 1764–1823. British writer of Gothic novels, including *The Mysteries of Udolpho* (1794).

rad·dle[1] (răd′l) *tr.v.* **-dled, -dling, -dles.** To twist together; interweave. [From dialectal *raddle,* stick interwoven with others in a fence, from Anglo-Norman *reidele,* stout pole, possibly from Middle High German *reidel,* rod. See **reidh-** in Appendix.]

rad·dle[2] (răd′l) *n. & v.* Variant of **ruddle.**

rad·dled (răd′ld) *adj.* Worn-out and broken-down. [Origin unknown.]

radi– *pref.* Variant of **radio–.**

ra·di·al (rā′dē-əl) *adj.* **1.a.** Of, relating to, or arranged like rays or radii. **b.** Radiating from or converging to a common center. **c.** Having or characterized by parts so arranged or so radiating. **2.** Moving or directed along a radius. **3.** *Anatomy.* Of, relating to, or near the radius or forearm. **4.** Developing symmetrically about a central point. **—radial** *n.* **1.** A radial part, such as a ray, spoke, or radius. **2.** A radial tire. [Middle English, from Medieval Latin *radiālis,* from Latin *radius,* ray.] **—ra′di·al·ly** *adv.*

radial engine *n.* An internal-combustion engine, formerly used in propeller-driven aircraft, with cylinders arranged radially around the crankshaft.

radially symmetrical *adj.* Having radial symmetry; actinomorphic.

radial symmetry *n.* Symmetrical arrangement of constituents, especially of radiating parts, about a central point.

radial tire *n.* A pneumatic tire in which the ply cords extending to beads are laid at approximately right angles to the center line of the tread.

ra·di·an (rā′dē-ən) *n. Abbr.* **rad** *Mathematics.* A unit of angular measure equal to the angle subtended at the center of a circle by an arc equal in length to the radius of the circle, approximately 57°17′44.6″. See table at **measurement.** [RADI(US) + -AN[1].]

ra·di·ance (rā′dē-əns) also **ra·di·an·cy** (-ən-sē) *n.* **1.** The quality or state of being radiant. **2.** *Physics.* The radiant energy emitted per unit time in a specified direction by a unit area of an emitting surface.

ra·di·ant (rā′dē-ənt) *adj.* **1.** Emitting heat or light. **2.** Consisting of or emitted as radiation: *radiant heat.* **3.a.** Filled with light; bright. **b.** Glowing; beaming. See Synonyms at **bright. —radiant** *n.* **1.** An object or a point from which light or heat rays are emitted. **2.** *Astronomy.* The apparent celestial origin of a meteoric shower. [Middle English, from Latin *radiāns, radiant-,* present participle of *radiāre,* to radiate. See RADIATE.] **—ra′di·ant·ly** *adv.*

radiant energy *n. Physics.* Energy transferred by radiation, especially by an electromagnetic wave.

radiant flux *n. Physics.* The rate of flow of radiant energy.

ra·di·ate (rā′dē-āt′) *v.* **-at·ed, -at·ing, -ates.** *—intr.* **1.** To send out rays or waves. **2.** To issue or emerge in rays or waves: *Heat radiated from the stove.* **3.** To extend in straight lines from or toward a center; diverge or converge like rays: *Spokes radiate from a wheel hub.* **4.** *Ecology.* To spread into new habitats and thereby diverge or diversify. Used of a group of organisms. *—tr.* **1.** To emit (light, for example) in or as if in rays. **2.** To send or spread out from or as if from a center: *a cactus that radiates spines.* **3.** To irradiate or illuminate (an object). **4.** To manifest in a glowing manner: *a leader who radiates confidence.* **—radiate** (-ĭt) *adj.* **1.** *Botany.* Having rays or raylike parts, as in the flower heads of daisies. **2.** *Biology.* Characterized by radial symmetry. **3.** Surrounded with rays: *a radiate head on a coin.* [Latin *radiāre, radiāt-,* to emit beams, from *radius,* ray.] **—ra′di·a′tive** *adj.*

ra·di·a·tion (rā′dē-ā′shən) *n.* **1.** The act or process of radiating: *the radiation of heat and light from a burning body.* **2.** *Physics.* **a.** Emission and propagation of energy in the form of rays or waves. **b.** Energy radiated or transmitted in the form of rays, waves, or particles. **c.** A stream of particles or electromagnetic waves emitted by the atoms and molecules of a radioactive substance as a result of nuclear decay. **3.** *Anatomy.* Radial arrangement of parts, as of a group of nerve fibers connecting different areas of the brain. **4.a.** *Ecology.* The spread of a group of organisms into new habitats. **b.** Adaptive radiation.

ra·di·a·tion·al cool·ing (rā′dē-ā′shə-nəl ko͞o′lĭng) *n.* The cooling of the earth's surface and the air near the surface, occurring chiefly at night and caused by heat loss engendered by terrestrial radiation.

radiation sickness *n.* Illness induced by ionizing radiation, ranging in severity from nausea, vomiting, headache, and diarrhea to loss of hair and teeth, reduction in red and white blood cell counts, extensive hemorrhaging, sterility, and death.

ra·di·a·tor (rā′dē-ā′tər) *n.* **1.** A heating device consisting of a series of connected pipes, typically inside an upright metal structure, through which steam or hot water is circulated so as to radiate heat into the surrounding space. **2.** A cooling device, as in automotive engines, through which water or other fluids circulate as a coolant. **3.** *Physics.* A body that emits radiation. **4.** A transmitting antenna.

rad·i·cal (răd′ĭ-kəl) *adj.* **1.** Arising from or going to a root or source; basic: *a radical flaw in a plan; chose the radical solution of starting all over again.* **2.** Departing markedly from the usual or customary; extreme: *radical opinions on education.* **3.** Favoring or effecting fundamental or revolutionary changes in current practices, conditions, or institutions: *radical political views.* **4.** *Linguistics.* Of or being a root: *a radical form.* **5.** *Botany.* Arising from the root or its crown: *radical leaves.* **—radical** *n.* **1.** One who advocates fundamental or revolutionary changes in current practices, conditions, or institutions: *radicals seeking to overthrow the social order.* **2.** *Abbr.* **rad.** *Mathematics.* The root of a quantity as indicated by the radical sign. **3.** *Symbol* **R** An atom or a group of atoms with at least one unpaired electron. **4.** *Abbr.* **rad.** *Linguistics.* See **root**[1] (sense 8). [Middle English, of a root, from Late Latin *rādīcālis,* having roots, from Latin *rādīx, rādīc-,* root. See **wrād-** in Appendix.] **—rad′i·cal·ly** *adv.* **—rad′i·cal·ness** *n.*

radical expression *n. Mathematics.* An expression or form in which radical signs appear.

rad·i·cal·ism (răd′ĭ-kə-lĭz′əm) *n.* **1.** The doctrines or practices of radicals. **2.** The quality of being radical.

rad·i·cal·ize (răd′ĭ-kə-līz′) *tr.v.* **-ized, -iz·ing, -iz·es.** To make radical or more radical: *"Many, probably most, of those have been radicalized by their experiences among the poor"* (Conor Cruise O'Brien). **—rad′i·cal·i·za′tion** (-kə-lĭ-zā′shən) *n.*

radical sign *n. Mathematics.* **1.** The sign $\surd$ placed before a quantity, indicating extraction of the root designated by a raised integer. When extracting a square root, the raised integer is customarily omitted. **2.** The radical sign together with a horizontal bar extending from its top to the end of the expression from which a root is to be extracted.

rad·i·cand (răd′ĭ-kănd′) *n. Mathematics.* The quantity under a radical sign. For example, 3 is the radicand of $\sqrt{3}$. [Latin *rādīcandum,* neuter gerundive of *rādīcāre,* to take root, from *rādīx, rādīc-,* root. See RADICAL.]

ra·dic·chi·o (rə-dē′kē-ō, rä-) *n., pl.* **-os.** Any of several prized varieties of chicory, having red or red-spotted leaves that form globose or elongated heads. [Italian, from Old Italian, chicory, from Vulgar Latin **rādīculum,* from Latin *rādīcula,* diminutive of *rādīx, rādīc-,* root. See RADISH.]

rad·i·ces (răd′ĭ-sēz′, rā′dĭ-) *n.* A plural of **radix.**

rad·i·cle (răd′ĭ-kəl) *n.* **1.** *Botany.* The part of a plant embryo that develops into a root. **2.** *Anatomy.* A small structure, such as a fibril of a nerve, that resembles a root. [Latin *rādīcula,* diminutive of *rādīx, rādīc-,* root. See **wrād-** in Appendix.]

ra·di·i (rā′dē-ī′) *n.* A plural of **radius.**

ra·di·o (rā′dē-ō) *n., pl.* **-os.** *Abbr.* **rad. 1.** The wireless transmission through space of electromagnetic waves in the approximate frequency range from 10 kilohertz to 300,000 megahertz. **2.** Communication of audible signals encoded in electromagnetic waves. **3.** Transmission of programs for the public by radio broadcast. **4.a.** An apparatus used to transmit radio signals; a transmitter. **b.** An apparatus used to receive radio signals; a receiver. **c.** A complex of equipment capable of transmitting and receiving radio signals. **5.a.** A station for radio transmitting. **b.** A radio broadcasting organization or network of affiliated organizations. **c.** The radio broadcasting industry. **6.** A message sent by radio. *—attributive.* Often used to modify an-

ă pat	oi boy
ā pay	ou out
âr care	o͝o took
ä father	o͞o boot
ĕ pet	ŭ cut
ē be	ûr urge
ĭ pit	th thin
ī pie	*th* this
îr pier	hw which
ŏ pot	zh vision
ō toe	ə about, item
ô paw	♦ regionalism

Stress marks: **′** (primary); ′ (secondary), as in **dictionary** (dĭk′shə-nĕr′ē)

other noun: *radio stations; radio programs.* —**radio** *v.* **-oed, -o·ing, -os.** —*tr.* **1.** To transmit by radio: *radio a message to headquarters.* **2.** To transmit a message to by radio: *radioed the spacecraft.* —*intr.* To transmit messages or a message by radio: *a ship radioing for help.* [Short for RADIOTELEGRAPHY.]

radio– or **radi–** *pref.* **1.** Radiation; radiant energy: *radiometer.* **2.** Radioactive: *radiochemistry.* **3.** Radio: *radiotelephone.* [From RADIATION.]

ra·di·o·ac·tive (rā′dē-ō-ăk′tĭv) *adj.* Of or exhibiting radioactivity. —**ra′di·o·ac′tive·ly** *adv.*

radioactive decay *n.* Spontaneous disintegration of a radioactive substance accompanied by emission of ionizing radiation in the form of particles and gamma rays.

radioactive series *n.* A group of isotopes representing various stages of radioactive decay in which the heavier members of the group are transformed into successively lighter ones, the lightest being stable.

ra·di·o·ac·tiv·i·ty (rā′dē-ō-ăk-tĭv′ĭ-tē) *n.* **1.** Spontaneous emission of radiation, either directly from unstable atomic nuclei or as a consequence of a nuclear reaction. **2.** The radiation, including alpha particles, nucleons, electrons, and gamma rays, emitted by a radioactive substance.

radio astronomy *n.* The branch of astronomy that deals with detection and study of celestial objects and phenomena by means of the radio waves emitted by these objects and phenomena. —**radio astronomer** *n.*

radio beacon *n.* A fixed radio transmitter that broadcasts distinctive signals as a navigational aid.

radio beam *n.* A focused beam of radio signals transmitted by a radio beacon to guide aircraft or ships.

ra·di·o·bi·ol·o·gy (rā′dē-ō-bī-ŏl′ə-jē) *n.* **1.** The study of the effects of radiation on living organisms. **2.** The use of radioactive tracers to study biological processes. —**ra′di·o·bi′o·log′i·cal** (-ə-lŏj′ĭ-kəl) *adj.* —**ra′di·o·bi·ol′o·gist** *n.*

ra·di·o·broad·cast (rā′dē-ō-brôd′kăst′) *tr. & intr.v.* **-cast** or **-cast·ed, -cast·ing, -casts.** To broadcast or be broadcast by radio. —**ra′di·o·broad′cast′er** *n.*

ra·di·o·car·bon (rā′dē-ō-kär′bən) *n.* A radioactive isotope of carbon, especially carbon 14.

radiocarbon dating *n.* Carbon dating.

ra·di·o·chem·is·try (rā′dē-ō-kĕm′ĭ-strē) *n.* The chemistry of radioactive materials. —**ra′di·o·chem′i·cal** (-ĭ-kəl) *adj.*

radio compass *n.* A navigational aid consisting of an automatic radio receiver that determines the transmission direction of incoming radio waves.

ra·di·o·e·col·o·gy (rā′dē-ō-ĭ-kŏl′ə-jē) *n.* The study of the effects of radiation and radioisotopes on an ecological population or community. —**ra′di·o·ec′o·log′i·cal** (-ĕk′ə-lŏj′ĭ-kəl) *adj.* —**ra′di·o·e·col′o·gist** *n.*

ra·di·o·el·e·ment (rā′dē-ō-ĕl′ə-mənt) *n.* A naturally occurring or artificially produced radioactive element.

radio frequency *n. Abbr.* **RF 1.** The frequency of the waves transmitted by a specific radio station. **2.** A frequency in the range within which radio waves may be transmitted, from about 10 kilocycles per second to about 300,000 megacycles per second. The radio frequency groups are: very low frequency (vlf), 10 to 30 kilohertz; low frequency (lf), 30 to 300 kilohertz; medium frequency (mf), 300 to 3,000 kilohertz; high frequency (hf), 3,000 to 30,000 kilohertz; very high frequency (vhf), 30 to 300 megahertz; ultrahigh frequency (uhf), 300 to 3,000 megahertz; superhigh frequency (shf), 3,000 to 30,000 megahertz; extremely high frequency (ehf), 30,000 to 300,000 megahertz.

radio galaxy *n.* A galaxy emitting large amounts of radio energy.

ra·di·o·ge·nic (rā′dē-ō-jĕn′ĭk) *adj.* Relating to or caused by radioactivity.

ra·di·o·gram (rā′dē-ō-grăm′) *n.* **1.** A message transmitted by wireless telegraphy. **2.** A radiograph.

ra·di·o·graph (rā′dē-ō-grăf′) *n.* An image produced on a radiosensitive surface, such as a photographic film, by radiation other than visible light, especially by x-rays passed through an object or by photographing a fluoroscopic image. Also called *shadowgraph, skiagram, skiagraph.* —**radiograph** *tr.v.* **-graphed, -graph·ing, -graphs.** To make a radiograph of. —**ra′di·og′ra·pher** (-ŏg′rə-fər) *n.* —**ra′di·o·graph′ic** *adj.* —**ra′di·o·graph′i·cal·ly** *adv.*

ra·di·og·ra·phy (rā′dē-ŏg′rə-fē) *n.* The process by which radiographs are made. Also called *skiagraphy.*

ra·di·o·im·mu·no·as·say (rā′dē-ō-ĭm′yə-nō-ăs′ā, -ĭm-yo͞o′-) *n. Abbr.* **RIA** The immunoassay of a radiolabeled substance, such as a hormone or an enzyme.

ra·di·o·im·mu·nol·o·gy (rā′dē-ō-ĭm′yə-nŏl′ə-jē) *n.* The study of immunity by radiolabeling and other radiological methods. —**ra′di·o·im′mu·no·log′i·cal** (-nə-lŏj′ĭ-kəl) *adj.*

ra·di·o·i·o·dine (rā′dē-ō-ī′ə-dīn′) *n.* A radioactive isotope of iodine widely used as a tracer in medical diagnosis.

ra·di·o·i·so·tope (rā′dē-ō-ī′sə-tōp′) *n.* A naturally or artificially produced radioactive isotope of an element.

ra·di·o·la·bel (rā′dē-ō-lā′bəl) *tr.v.* **-beled, -bel·ing, -bels** or **-belled, -bel·ling, -bels.** To tag (a hormone, an enzyme, or other substance) with a radioactive tracer. —**radiolabel** *n.* A radioactive isotope used as a tracer; a radiotracer.

ra·di·o·lar·i·an (rā′dē-ō-lâr′ē-ən) *n.* Any of various marine protozoans of the order Radiolaria, having rigid siliceous skeletons and spicules. [From New Latin *Radiolāria,* order name, from Late Latin *radiolus,* diminutive of *radius,* ray.]

ra·di·o·lo·ca·tion (rā′dē-ō-lō-kā′shən) *n.* Detection of distant objects, such as ships or aircraft, by radar.

ra·di·ol·o·gy (rā′dē-ŏl′ə-jē) *n.* **1.** The branch of medicine that deals with the use of radioactive substances in diagnosis and treatment of disease. **2.** The use of ionizing radiation for medical diagnosis, especially the use of x-rays in medical radiography or fluoroscopy. **3.** The use of radiation for the scientific examination of material structures; radioscopy. —**ra′di·o·log′i·cal** (-ə-lŏj′ĭ-kəl), **ra′di·o·log′ic** (-lŏj′ĭk) *adj.* —**ra′di·o·log′i·cal·ly** *adv.* —**ra′di·ol′o·gist** *n.*

ra·di·o·lu·cent (rā′dē-ō-lo͞o′sənt) *adj.* Allowing the passage of x-rays or other radiation; not radiopaque. —**ra′di·o·lu′cen·cy** *n.*

ra·di·ol·y·sis (rā′dē-ŏl′ĭ-sĭs) *n., pl.* **-ses** (-sēz′). Molecular decomposition of a substance as a result of radiation. —**ra′di·o·lyt′ic** (-ə-lĭt′ĭk) *adj.*

ra·di·o·man (rā′dē-ō-măn′) *n.* A radio technician or operator.

ra·di·om·e·ter (rā′dē-ŏm′ĭ-tər) *n.* **1.** A device that measures the intensity of radiant energy, consisting of a partially evacuated glass bulb containing lightweight vertical vanes, each blackened on one side, suspended radially about a central vertical axis to permit their revolution about the axis as a result of incident radiation. **2.** An instrument that detects electromagnetic radiation. —**ra′di·om′e·try** *n.*

ra·di·o·mi·met·ic (rā′dē-ō-mĭ-mĕt′ĭk) *adj.* Having effects on living tissue similar to those produced by radiation: *a radiomimetic chemical.*

ra·di·o·nu·clide (rā′dē-ō-no͞o′klīd′, -nyo͞o′-) *n.* A nuclide that exhibits radioactivity.

ra·di·o·paque (rā′dē-ō-pāk′) *adj.* Not transparent to x-rays or other radiation. —**ra′di·o·pac′i·ty** (-ō-păs′ĭ-tē) *n.*

ra·di·o·phar·ma·ceu·ti·cal (rā′dē-ō-fär′mə-so͞o′tĭ-kəl) *n.* A radioactive compound used in radiotherapy or diagnosis. —**ra′di·o·phar′ma·ceu′ti·cal** *adj.*

ra·di·o·phone (rā′dē-ō-fōn′) *n.* A radiotelephone. —**ra′di·o·phon′ic** (-fŏn′ĭk) *adj.*

ra·di·o·pho·to (rā′dē-ō-fō′tō) *n.* A radiophotograph.

ra·di·o·pho·to·graph (rā′dē-ō-fō′tə-grăf′) *n.* A photograph transmitted by radio waves, each image point being reproduced by a received electric impulse. —**ra′di·o·pho·tog′ra·phy** (-fə-tŏg′rə-fē) *n.*

ra·di·o·pro·tec·tion (rā′dē-ō-prə-tĕk′shən) *n.* Protection against the harmful effects of radiation. —**ra′di·o·pro·tec′tive** *adj.*

ra·di·os·co·py (rā′dē-ŏs′kə-pē) *n.* Examination of the inner structure of optically opaque objects by x-rays or other penetrating radiation; radiology. —**ra′di·o·scop′ic** (-ō-skŏp′ĭk), **ra′di·o·scop′i·cal** (-ĭ-kəl) *adj.*

ra·di·o·sen·si·tive (rā′dē-ō-sĕn′sĭ-tĭv) *adj.* Sensitive to the action of radiation. Used especially of living structures. —**ra′di·o·sen′si·tiv′i·ty** *n.*

ra·di·o·sonde (rā′dē-ō-sŏnd′) *n.* An instrument carried aloft, chiefly by balloon, to gather and transmit meteorological data. [RADIO + French *sonde,* sounding line (from Old French, from Old English *sund(rāp),* sounding (line), from *sund,* sea).]

radio spectrum *n.* The entire range of electromagnetic communications frequencies, including those used for radio, radar, and television; radio-frequency spectrum.

ra·di·o·tel·e·graph (rā′dē-ō-tĕl′ĭ-grăf′) *n.* Transmission of messages by radiotelegraphy. —**ra′di·o·tel′e·graph′ic** *adj.*

ra·di·o·te·leg·ra·phy (rā′dē-ō-tə-lĕg′rə-fē) *n.* Telegraphy in which messages are transmitted by radio instead of wire.

ra·di·o·tel·e·phone (rā′dē-ō-tĕl′ə-fōn′) *n. Abbr.* **RT** A telephone in which audible communication is established by use of a two-way radio transmitter and receiver. Also called *wireless telephone.* —**ra′di·o·tel′e·phon′ic** (-fŏn′ĭk) *adj.* —**ra′di·o·te·leph′o·ny** (-tə-lĕf′ə-nē) *n.*

radio telescope *n.* A device used in radio astronomy for detecting and recording radio waves coming from stars and other celestial objects, consisting of a radio receiver with an antenna fixed on a wide bowl-shaped reflector that collects the waves.

ra·di·o·ther·a·py (rā′dē-ō-thĕr′ə-pē) *n., pl.* **-pies.** Treatment of disease with radiation, especially by selective irradiation with x-rays or other ionizing radiation and by ingestion of radioisotopes. —**ra′di·o·ther′a·pist** *n.*

ra·di·o·tho·ri·um (rā′dē-ō-thôr′ē-əm, -thōr′-) *n.* A radioactive isotope of thorium with mass number 228.

ra·di·o·tox·ic (rā′dē-ō-tŏk′sĭk) *adj.* Of, relating to, or being a radioactive substance that is toxic to living cells or tissues: *the radiotoxic effects of radium on bone.* —**ra′di·o·tox·ic′i·ty** (-tŏk-sĭs′ĭ-tē) *n.*

ra·di·o·trac·er (rā′dē-ō-trā′sər) *n.* A radioactive tracer.

radio wave *n.* An electromagnetic wave within the range of radio frequencies.

rad·ish (răd′ĭsh) *n.* **1.** A Eurasian plant *(Raphanus sativus)* having a fleshy, edible root and white to purple flowers clustered in a terminal raceme. **2.** The pungent root of this plant, eaten raw

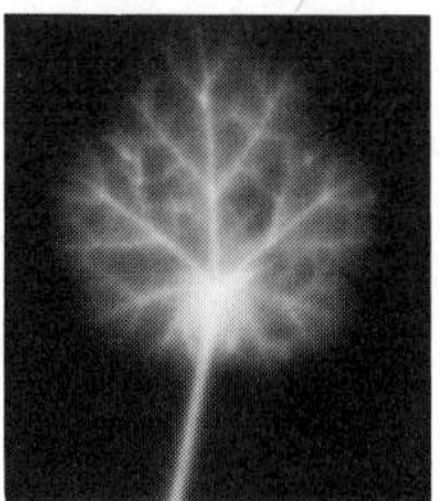

radiograph
Of a coral-bells leaf

radiometer

radio telescope
National Radio Astronomy Observatory, Green Bank, West Virginia

radish
Raphanus sativus

as an appetizer and in salads. [Middle English *radiche,* from Old English *rædic,* from Latin *rādīx, rādīc-,* root. See **wrād-** in Appendix.]

Rad•is•son (rä-dē-sôɴ′), **Pierre Esprit.** 1636?–1710? French explorer whose expedition to Hudson Bay and subsequent reports of the economic opportunity there led to the chartering of the Hudson Bay Company (1670).

ra•di•um (rā′dē-əm) *n. Symbol* **Ra** A rare, brilliant white, luminescent, highly radioactive metallic element found in very small amounts in uranium ores, having 13 isotopes with mass numbers between 213 and 230, of which radium 226 with a half-life of 1,622 years is the most common. It is used in cancer radiotherapy, as a neutron source for some research purposes, and as a constituent of luminescent paints. Atomic number 88; melting point 700°C; boiling point 1,737°C; valence 2. See table at **element.** [Latin *radius,* ray + –IUM.]

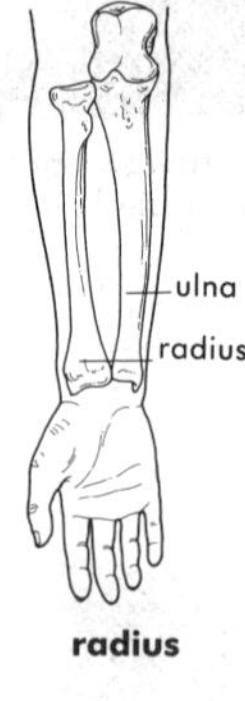

radius

radium therapy *n.* The use of radium in radiotherapy, especially in treating cancer.

ra•di•us (rā′dē-əs) *n., pl.* **-di•i** (-dē-ī′) or **-di•us•es. 1.** *Abbr.* **R, r, rad.** *Mathematics.* **a.** A line segment that joins the center of a circle with any point on its circumference. **b.** A line segment that joins the center of a sphere with any point on its surface. **c.** A line segment that joins the center of a regular polygon with any of its vertices. **d.** The length of any such line segment. **2.** A circular area measured by a given radius: *every family within a radius of 25 miles of the city center.* **3.** A bounded range of effective activity or influence: *the operating radius of a helicopter.* **4.** A radial part or structure, such as a mechanically pivoted arm or the spoke of a wheel. **5.** *Anatomy.* **a.** A long, prismatic, slightly curved bone, the shorter and thicker of the two forearm bones, located on the lateral side of the ulna. **b.** A similar bone in many vertebrates. [Latin, ray.]

radius vector *n.* **1.** *Mathematics.* **a.** A line segment that joins the origin and a variable point in a system of polar or spherical coordinates. **b.** The length of such a line segment. **2.** *Astronomy.* A straight line connecting the center of the sun or another body with the center of a planet, comet, or another body orbiting around it.

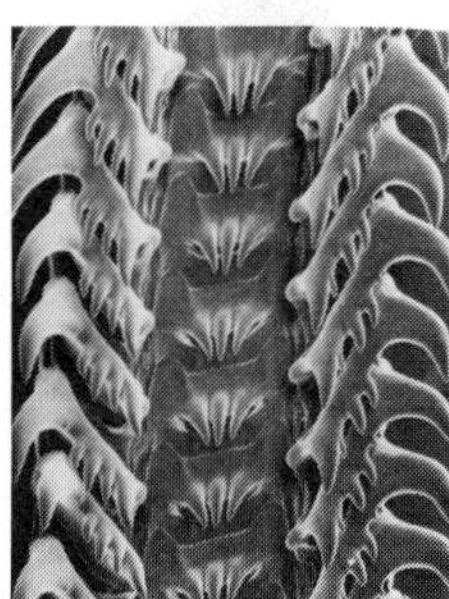
radula
Magnified image of a snail's radulae

ra•dix (rā′dĭks) *n., pl.* **rad•i•ces** (răd′ĭ-sēz′, rā′dĭ-) or **ra•dix•es. 1.** *Biology.* A root or point of origin. **2.** *Abbr.* **rad.** *Mathematics.* The base of a system of numbers, such as 2 in the binary system and 10 in the decimal system. [Latin *rādīx,* root. See **wrād-** in Appendix.]

RADM or **R.Adm.** *abbr.* Rear admiral.

Ra•dom (rä′dôm). A city of east-central Poland south of Warsaw. Founded in the 14th century, it passed to Austria in 1795 and to Russia in 1815, reverting to Poland after World War I. Population, 213,500.

ra•dome (rā′dōm) *n.* A domelike shell transparent to radio-frequency radiation, used to house a radar antenna. [RA(DAR) + DOME.]

ra•don (rā′dŏn) *n. Symbol* **Rn** A colorless, radioactive, inert gaseous element formed by the radioactive decay of radium. It is used as a radiation source in radiotherapy and to produce neutrons for research. Its most stable isotope is Rn 222 with a half-life of 3.82 days. Atomic number 86; melting point –71°C; boiling point –61.8°C; specific gravity (solid) 4. See table at **element.** [RAD(IUM) + –ON[2].]

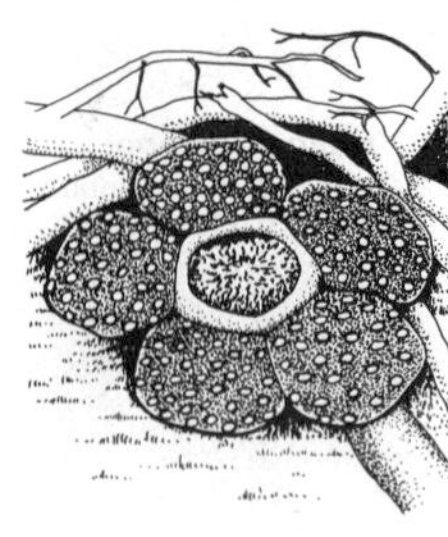
rafflesia

rad•u•la (răj′o͞o-lə) *n., pl.* **-lae** (-lē′). *Zoology.* A flexible tonguelike organ in certain mollusks, having rows of horny teeth on the surface. [Latin *rādula,* scraper, from *rādere,* to scrape. See **rēd-** in Appendix.] **—rad′u•lar** *adj.*

Rae (rā), **John.** 1813–1893. British explorer who charted much of the Canadian Arctic coast.

Rae•burn (rā′bərn), Sir **Henry.** 1756–1823. British portrait painter whose many subjects included Sir Walter Scott, David Hume, and James Boswell.

Rae•der (rā′dər), **Erich.** 1876–1960. German admiral who commanded the German navy (1928–1943) and advocated submarine warfare during World War II.

RAF also **R.A.F.** *abbr.* Royal Air Force.

raf•fi•a also **raph•i•a** (răf′ē-ə) *n.* **1.** An African palm tree *(Raphia ruffia)* having large leaves that yield a useful fiber. **2.** The leaf fibers of this plant, used for mats, baskets, and other products. [Malagasy *rafia.*]

raf•fi•nate (răf′ə-nāt′) *n.* The portion of an original liquid that remains after other components have been dissolved by a solvent. [French *raffiner,* to refine; see RAFFINOSE + –ATE[2].]

raf•fi•nose (răf′ə-nōs′) *n.* A white crystalline sugar, $C_{18}H_{32}O_{16}\cdot 5H_2O$, obtained from cottonseed meal, sugar beets, and molasses. [French, from *raffiner,* to refine : *re-,* again (from Old French; see RE–) + *affiner,* to refine (*a-,* to, from Latin *ad-;* see AD– + *fin,* fine, from Old French; see FINE[1]).]

raff•ish (răf′ĭsh) *adj.* **1.** Cheaply or showily vulgar in appearance or nature; tawdry. **2.** Characterized by a carefree or fun-loving unconventionality; rakish. [Probably from dialectal *raff,* rubbish, from Middle English *raf,* perhaps of Scandinavian origin.] **—raff′ish•ly** *adv.* **—raff′ish•ness** *n.*

raft[1]

raf•fle[1] (răf′əl) *Games. n.* A lottery in which a number of persons buy chances to win a prize. [Middle English *rafle,* a game using dice, from Old French, act of seizing, dice game, perhaps of Germanic origin.] **—raf′fle** *v.* **—raf′fler** *n.*

raf•fle[2] (răf′əl) *n.* Rubbish; debris. [Probably from French *rafle,* act of seizing, from Old French. See RAFFLE[1].]

Raf•fles (răf′əlz), Sir **Thomas Stamford.** 1781–1826. British colonial administrator who acquired Singapore for the East India Company (1819) and founded a settlement there.

raf•fle•sia (ră-flē′zhə) *n.* Any of various parasitic plants of the genus *Rafflesia* of tropical Asia, having small, brownish, scale-like leaves and fleshy, apetalous, foul-smelling flowers of various sizes. The species *R. arnoldii* has the largest flowers among all flowering plants, often measuring up to 1 meter (40 inches) in diameter. [New Latin, genus name, after Sir Thomas Stamford RAFFLES.]

Ra•fi•nesque (rä-fē-nĕsk′) also **Ra•fi•nesque-Schmaltz** (-shmälts), **Constantine Samuel.** 1783–1840. French-American naturalist whose thoughts on the origin of plant species presaged Darwin's theory of evolution.

raft[1] (răft) *n.* **1.** A flat structure, typically made of planks, logs, or barrels, that floats on water and is used for transport or as a platform for swimmers. **2.** A flat-bottomed inflatable craft for floating or drifting on water: *shooting the rapids in a rubber raft.* **—raft** *v.* **raft•ed, raft•ing, rafts.** *—tr.* **1.** To convey on a raft. **2.** To make into a raft. *—intr.* To travel by raft. [Middle English, from Old Norse *raptr,* beam, rafter.]

raft[2] (răft) *n. Informal.* A great number, amount, or collection: *asked a raft of questions.* [Alteration of dialectal *raff,* rubbish, from Middle English *raf.* See RAFFISH.]

raft•er[1] (răf′tər) *n.* One who travels by raft.

raf•ter[2] (răf′tər) *n.* One of the sloping beams that supports a pitched roof. [Middle English, from Old English *ræfter.*] **—raf′tered** *adj.*

rag[1] (răg) *n.* **1.a.** A scrap of cloth. **b.** A piece of cloth used for cleaning, washing, or dusting. **2. rags.** Threadbare or tattered clothing. **3.** Cloth converted to pulp for making paper. **4.** A scrap; a fragment. **5.** *Slang.* A newspaper, especially one specializing in sensationalism or gossip. **6.** The stringy central portion and membranous walls of a citrus fruit. [Middle English *ragge,* from Old English *ragg, from Old Norse *rögg, woven tuft of wool.]

rag[2] (răg) *tr.v.* **ragged, rag•ging, rags. 1.** *Slang.* To tease or taunt. See Synonyms at **banter. 2.** *Slang.* To berate; scold. **3.** *Chiefly British.* To play a joke on. **—rag** *n. Chiefly British.* A practical joke; a prank. [Origin unknown.]

rag[3] (răg) *n.* **1.** A roofing slate with one rough surface. **2.** *Chiefly British.* A coarsely textured rock. [Origin unknown.]

rag[4] (răg) *Music. tr.v.* **ragged, rag•ging, rags.** To compose or play (a piece) in ragtime. **—rag** *n.* A piece written in ragtime. [Perhaps from RAGGED.]

ra•ga (rä′gə) *n. Music.* A traditional form in Hindu music, consisting of a theme that expresses an aspect of religious feeling and sets forth a tonal system on which variations are improvised within a prescribed framework of typical progressions, melodic formulas, and rhythmic patterns. [Sanskrit *rāgaḥ,* color, musical mode.]

rag•a•muf•fin (răg′ə-mŭf′ĭn) *n.* A shabbily clothed, dirty child. [Middle English *Ragamuffyn,* a personal name : probably *raggi,* ragged (from *ragge,* rag; see RAG[1]) + Middle Dutch *moffel, muffe,* mitten; see MUFF[2].]

WORD HISTORY: Perhaps *ragamuffin* should be seen as an example of melioration, or improvement in the sense of a word, since it can now be used rather affectionately of children who are normally far from dirty or unkempt. In any event, even its use for an unkempt child or man represents something of an improvement over one of its earliest uses. *Ragamuffin* was a name given to a demon in *Piers Plowman,* an allegorical poem of the 14th century. This name was once thought to be the source of our word, but researches at the *Middle English Dictionary* have shown that the word was used as the last name of a woman, Isabella Ragamuffyn, earlier in the 14th century (1344), before the poem was composed. The word even then had the sense "ragged lout, tattered oaf," though it was found only in names. The element *raga–* is probably from the Middle English adjective *raggi,* "ragged," also used of the devil in the sense "shaggy" and as a name. The element *–muffin* is probably from Middle Dutch *moffel* or *muffe,* "mitten."

rag•bag (răg′băg′) *n.* **1.** A bag for storing rags. **2.** A motley collection; a hodgepodge.

rage (rāj) *n.* **1.a.** Violent, explosive anger. See Synonyms at **anger. b.** A fit of anger. **2.** Furious intensity, as of a storm or disease. **3.** A burning desire; a passion. **4.** A current, eagerly adopted fashion; a fad or craze: *when torn jeans were all the rage.* **—rage** *intr.v.* **raged, rag•ing, rag•es. 1.** To speak or act in violent anger: *raged at the mindless bureaucracy.* **2.** To move with great violence or intensity: *A storm raged through the mountains.* **3.** To spread or prevail forcefully: *The plague raged for months.* [Middle English, from Old French, from Late Latin *rabia,* from Latin *rabiēs,* from *rabere,* to be mad.]

rag•ged (răg′ĭd) *adj.* **1.** Tattered, frayed, or torn: *clothes as ragged as a scarecrow's.* **2.** Dressed in tattered or threadbare clothes: *a ragged tramp.* **3.** Unkempt or shaggy. **4.** Having an irregular surface or edge; uneven or jagged in outline: *a column of text set with a ragged right margin.* **5.** Imperfect; uneven: *a ragged performance.* **6.** Harsh; rasping: *a ragged cough.* [Middle

English, from *ragge,* rag. See RAG[1].] **—rag′ged·ly** *adv.* **—rag′ged·ness** *n.*

ragged edge *n.* **1.** The edge of a cliff. **2.** A dangerous or precarious position; a brink: *"the gray, grainy, complex nature of existence and the ragged edges of our lives as we actually live them"* (A. Bartlett Giamatti).

ragged robin *n.* A European perennial plant *(Lychnis flos-cuculi)* having opposite, clasping leaves, and panicles of reddish or white flowers with deeply lobed petals. Also called *cuckooflower.*

rag·ged·y (răg′ĭ-dē) *adj.* **-i·er, -i·est.** Tattered or worn-out; ragged.

ra·gi (răg′ē) *n., pl.* **ra·gis.** See **finger millet.** [Hindi *rāgī,* from Sanskrit, perhaps of Dravidian origin.]

rag·lan (răg′lən) *adj.* Having or being a sleeve that extends in one piece to the neckline of the garment, with slanted seams from the armhole to the neck. **—raglan** *n.* A garment, such as an overcoat or a sweater, that has raglan sleeves. [After Fitzroy James Henry Somerset (1788–1855), First Baron *Raglan,* British field marshal.]

rag·man (răg′măn′) *n.* A man who collects and sells rags.

ra·gout (ră-go͞o′) *n.* A well-seasoned meat or fish stew, usually with vegetables. [French *ragoût,* from *ragoûter,* to revive the taste, from Old French *ragouster* : *re-,* re- + *a,* to (from Latin *ad;* see AD–) + *gost,* taste (from Latin *gustus;* see **geus-** in Appendix).]

rag picker *n.* One who makes a living scavenging rags and other refuse.

rag·tag (răg′tăg′) *adj.* **1.** Shaggy or unkempt; ragged. **2.** Diverse and disorderly in appearance or composition: *"They're a small ragtag army of racketeers, bandits, and murderers"* (Thomas P. O'Neill, Jr.).

ragtag and bobtail *n.* The lowest social class; the rabble.

rag·time (răg′tīm′) *n. Music.* A style of jazz characterized by elaborately syncopated rhythm in the melody and a steadily accented accompaniment. [From RAG[4].]

rag·top (răg′tŏp′) *n. Slang.* A convertible automobile.

rag trade *n. Slang.* The garment industry.

Ra·gu·sa (rə-go͞o′zə, rä-go͞o′zä). **1.** A city of southeast Sicily, Italy, south-southwest of Messina. It is a manufacturing and food-processing center. Population, 53,000. **2.** See **Dubrovnik.**

rag·weed (răg′wēd′) *n.* **1.** Any of various weeds of the genus *Ambrosia* having small, greenish, unisexual flower heads and producing abundant pollen that is one of the chief causes of hay fever. **2.** *Chiefly British.* Ragwort. [From the ragged shape of its leaves.]

rag·wort (răg′wûrt′, -wôrt′) *n.* Any of several plants of the very large genus *Senecio* in the composite family, having yellow flower heads, especially *S. aureus* of eastern North America and *S. jacobaea* of Europe. [From the ragged shape of its leaves.]

rah (rä) *interj.* Used as an exclamation of approval or encouragement. [Short for HURRAH.]

rah-rah (rä′rä′) *adj. Informal.* Ardently enthusiastic. [Reduplication of RAH.]

Rah·way (rô′wā′). A city of northeast New Jersey south-southwest of Elizabeth on the **Rahway River.** Settled c. 1720, Rahway is a manufacturing center. Population, 26,723.

Ra·ia·te·a (rī′ə-tā′ə). A volcanic island of the southern Pacific Ocean west-northwest of Tahiti. It is the largest of the Leeward group of the Society Islands in French Polynesia. Migration of its people to Hawaii, the Cook Islands, and New Zealand is believed to have begun some 600 years ago.

raid (rād) *n.* **1.** A surprise attack by a small armed force. **2.** Sudden, forcible entry into a place by police: *a raid on a gambling den.* **3.** An entrance into another's territory for the purpose of seizing goods or valuables. **4.** A predatory operation mounted against a competitor, especially an attempt to lure away the personnel or membership of a competing organization. **5.** An attempt to seize control of a company, as by acquiring a majority of its stock. **6.** An attempt by speculators to drive stock prices down by coordinated selling. **—raid** *v.* **raid·ed, raid·ing, raids.** *—tr.* To make a raid on. *—intr.* To conduct a raid or participate in one. [Scots, raid on horseback, from Middle English *rade,* from Old English *rād,* a riding, road. See **reidh-** in Appendix.] **—raid′er** *n.*

WORD HISTORY: The members of an army traveling on a particular *road* to carry out a *raid* probably would not draw a connection between the two words. However, *raid* and *road* descend from the same Old English word *rād.* The *ai* in *raid* represents the standard development in the northern dialects of Old English long *a,* while the *oa* in *road* represents the standard development of Old English long *a* in the rest of the English dialects. Old English *rād* meant "the act of riding" and "the act of riding with a hostile intent; that is, a raid," senses that no longer exist for our word *road.* It was left to Sir Walter Scott to revive the Scots form *raid* with the sense "a military expedition on horseback." The Scots weren't making all the raids, however. Others seem to have returned the favor, for we find these words in the Middle English *Coventry Leet Book*: "aftur a Rode . . . made uppon the Scottes at thende of this last somer." The "Rode" was led by the non-Scottish Duke of Gloucester, who was later crowned as Richard III, and Henry Percy, Duke of Northumberland.

rail[1] (rāl) *n.* **1.a.** A bar extending horizontally between supports, as in a fence. **b.** A structure made of such bars and supports and forming a barrier or guard; a railing. **2.** A steel bar used, usually in pairs, as a track for railroad cars or other wheeled vehicles. **3.** The railroad as a means of transportation: *goods transported by rail.* **4.** A horizontal piece of wood in a door or in paneling. **—rail** *tr.v.* **railed, rail·ing, rails.** To supply or enclose with rails or a rail. [Middle English *raile,* from Old French *reille,* from Latin *rēgula,* straight piece of wood, ruler. See **reg-** in Appendix.]

rail[2] (rāl) *n.* Any of various marsh birds of the family Rallidae, characteristically having brownish plumage and short wings adapted only for short flights. [Middle English *raile,* from Old French *raale,* perhaps from Old French *raler, racler,* to scrape, from Old Provençal *rasclar.* See RACLETTE.]

rail[3] (rāl) *intr.v.* **railed, rail·ing, rails.** To express objections or criticisms in bitter, harsh, or abusive language. See Synonyms at **scold.** [Middle English *railen,* from Old French *railler,* to tease, joke, from Old Provençal *ralhar,* to chat, joke, from Vulgar Latin **ragulāre,* to bray, from Late Latin *ragere.*] **—rail′er** *n.*

rail·bird (rāl′bûrd′) *n. Slang.* A horseracing enthusiast, especially one who watches races at the outer rail of the track.

rail·car (rāl′kär′) *n.* A railroad car.

rail fence *n.* A fence of split logs secured to stakes or laid across each other at an angle.

rail·head (rāl′hĕd′) *n.* **1.** The farthest point on a railroad to which rails have been laid. **2.** A place on a railroad where military supplies are unloaded.

rail·ing (rā′lĭng) *n.* **1.a.** A structure made of rails and upright members that is used as a guard or barrier or for support. **b.** The upper rail of such a structure. **2.** Rails considered as a group.

rail·ler·y (rā′lə-rē) *n., pl.* **-ies.** **1.** Good-natured teasing or ridicule; banter. **2.** An instance of bantering or teasing. [French *raillerie,* from Old French *railler,* to tease. See RAIL[3].]

rail·road (rāl′rōd′) *n. Abbr.* **RR, R.R., r., R.** **1.** A road composed of parallel steel rails supported by ties and providing a track for locomotive-drawn trains or other wheeled vehicles. **2.** A system of railroad track, together with the land, stations, rolling stock, and other related property under one management. *—attributive.* Often used to modify another noun: *railroad lines; railroad ties.* **—railroad** *v.* **-road·ed, -road·ing, -roads.** *—tr.* **1.** To transport by railroad. **2.** To supply (an area) with railroads. **3.** *Informal.* **a.** To rush or push (something) through quickly in order to prevent careful consideration and possible criticism or obstruction: *railroad a special-interest bill through Congress.* **b.** To convict (an accused person) without a fair trial or on trumped-up charges. *—intr.* To work for a railroad company. **—rail′road′er** *n.*

railroad flat *n.* An apartment in which the rooms are connected in a line.

rail·road·ing (rāl′rō′dĭng) *n.* The construction or operation of railroads.

rail-split·ter (rāl′splĭt′ər) *n.* One that splits logs for fences.

rail·way (rāl′wā′) *n. Abbr.* **rwy., ry., r., R.** **1.** A railroad, especially one operated over a limited area: *a commuter railway.* **2.** A track providing a runway for wheeled equipment. *—attributive.* Often used to modify another noun: *railway stops; railway lines.*

rai·ment (rā′mənt) *n.* Clothing; garments. [Middle English, short for *araiment,* from Old French *areement,* array, from *areer, arrayer,* to array. See ARRAY.]

rain (rān) *n.* **1.a.** Water condensed from atmospheric vapor and falling in drops. **b.** A fall of such water; a rainstorm. **c.** The descent of such water. **d.** Rainy weather. **e. rains.** A rainy season. **2.** A heavy or abundant fall: *a rain of fluffy cottonwood seeds; a rain of insults.* **—rain** *v.* **rained, rain·ing, rains.** *—intr.* **1.** To fall in drops of water from the clouds. **2.** To fall like rain: *Praise rained down on the composer.* **3.** To release rain. *—tr.* **1.** To send or pour down. **2.** To give abundantly; shower: *rain gifts; rain curses upon their heads.* ***—phrasal verb.*** **rain out.** To force the cancellation or postponement of (an outdoor event) because of rain. ***—idiom.*** **rain cats and dogs.** *Informal.* To rain very heavily. [Middle English, from Old English *rēn, regn.*] **—rain′less** *adj.*

rain·bow (rān′bō′) *n.* **1.a.** An arc of all seven spectral colors appearing in the sky opposite the sun as a result of the refractive dispersion of sunlight in drops of rain or mist. **b.** A similar arc or band, as one produced by a prism or by iridescence. **c.** A graded display of colors. **2.** An illusory hope: *chasing the rainbow of overnight success.* **3.** A diverse assortment or collection. [Middle English, from Old English *rēnboga* : *rēn,* rain + *boga,* bow; see BOW[3].]

rainbow cactus *n.* Either of two tall, spiny, cylindrical varieties of cactus of the southwest United States and Mexico, *Echinocereus pectinatus* var. *neomexicanus* having yellow flowers or *E. pectinatus* var. *rigidissimus* having showy magenta flowers.

rainbow trout *n.* A North American food fish *(Salmo gairdneri)* having a reddish longitudinal band and black spots.

rain check *n.* **1.** A ticket stub entitling the holder to admission to a future event if the scheduled event is canceled because of rain. **2.** An assurance to a customer that an item on sale that is sold out or out of stock may be purchased later at the sale price. **3.** A promise that an unaccepted offer will be renewed in the

rainbow trout
Salmo gairdneri

ă pat	oi boy
ā pay	ou out
âr care	o͝o took
ä father	o͞o boot
ĕ pet	ŭ cut
ē be	ûr urge
ĭ pit	th thin
ī pie	*th* this
îr pier	hw which
ŏ pot	zh vision
ō toe	ə about, item
ô paw	♦ regionalism

Stress marks: ′ (primary); ′ (secondary), as in **dictionary** (dĭk′shə-nĕr′ē)

future: *declined the invitation to dinner, but asked for a rain check.*

rain·coat (rān′kōt′) *n.* A waterproof or water-resistant coat.

rain date *n.* A second date scheduled for an outdoor event in case rain forces cancellation of the first date.

rain·drop (rān′drŏp′) *n.* A drop of rain.

Rai·ney (rā′nē), **Gertrude Pridgett.** Known as "Ma Rainey." 1886–1939. American singer considered the first great blues vocalist.

rain·fall (rān′fôl′) *n.* **1.** A shower or fall of rain. **2.** The quantity of water, expressed in inches, precipitated as rain, snow, hail, or sleet in a specified area and time interval.

rain forest *n.* A dense evergreen forest occupying a tropical region with an annual rainfall of at least 2.5 meters (100 inches).

rain gauge also **rain gage** *n.* A device for measuring rainfall. Also called *pluviometer, udometer.*

Rai·nier III (rā-nîr′, rĕ-, rə-, rĕ-nyā′). Born 1923. Prince of Monaco (since 1949) who married the American actress Grace Kelly in 1956.

Rai·nier (rə-nîr′, rā-), **Mount.** A volcanic peak, 4,395.1 m (14,410 ft) high, of the Cascade Range in west-central Washington. It is the highest point in the range and the highest elevation in the state.

rain lily *n.* See **zephyr lily.**

rain·mak·er (rān′mā′kər) *n.* **1.** *Slang.* One who is known for achieving excellent results, as in business or politics. **2.** One who is supposedly capable of producing rain.

rain·mak·ing (rān′mā′kĭng) *n.* **1.** The process of producing or attempting to produce rain, as by magic. **2.** *Informal.* Cloud seeding.

rain·out (rān′out′) *n.* An event, such as an athletic contest, that has been rained out.

♦**rain·spout** (rān′spout′) *n. Chiefly Pennsylvania & New Jersey.* See **gutter** (sense 2). See Regional Note at **gutter.**

rain·squall (rān′skwôl′) *n.* A squall accompanied by rain.

rain·storm (rān′stôrm′) *n.* A storm accompanied by rain.

rain-wash (rān′wŏsh′, -wôsh′) *Geology. n.* Rock debris transported downhill by rain. **—rain-wash** *tr.v.* **-washed, -wash·ing, -wash·es.** To wash (material) down a slope by rain.

rain·wat·er (rān′wô′tər, -wŏt′ər) *n.* Water that has fallen as rain and contains little dissolved mineral matter.

Rain·wat·er (rān′wô′tər, -wŏt′ər), **L(eo) James.** 1917–1986. American physicist. He shared a 1975 Nobel Prize for discovering the asymmetry of atomic nuclei.

rain·wear (rān′wâr′) *n.* Waterproof clothing.

rain·y (rā′nē) *adj.* **-i·er, -i·est.** Characterized by, full of, or bringing rain. **—rain′i·ness** *n.*

Rain·y Lake (rā′nē). A lake of northern Minnesota and southwest Ontario, Canada, drained by the **Rainy River,** which flows about 129 km (80 mi) generally westward along the U.S.-Canadian border to Lake of the Woods.

rainy day *n.* A time of need or trouble.

Rai·pur (rī′pŏŏr). A city of east-central India east of Nagpur. It is a trade and processing center in an agricultural district. Population, 338,245.

raise (rāz) *v.* **raised, rais·ing, rais·es.** *—tr.* **1.** To move to a higher position; elevate: *raised the loads with a crane.* See Synonyms at **lift. 2.** To set in an upright or erect position: *raise a flagpole.* **3.** To erect or build: *raise a new building.* **4.** To cause to arise, appear, or exist: *The slap raised a welt.* **5.** To increase in size, quantity, or worth: *raise an employee's salary.* **6.** To increase in intensity, degree, strength, or pitch: *raised his voice.* **7.** To improve in rank or dignity; promote: *raised her to management level.* **8. a.** To grow, especially in quantity; cultivate: *raise corn and soybeans.* **b.** To breed and care for to maturity: *raise cattle.* **c.** To bring up; rear: *raise children.* **9.** To put forward for consideration: *raised an important question.* See Synonyms at **broach¹. 10.** To voice; utter: *raise a shout.* **11. a.** To awaken; arouse: *noise that would raise the dead.* **b.** To stir up; instigate: *raise a revolt.* **c.** To bring about; provoke: *remarks intended to raise a laugh.* **12.** To make contact with by radio: *couldn't raise the control tower after midnight.* **13.** To gather together; collect: *raise money from the neighbors for a charity.* **14.** To cause (dough) to puff up. **15.** To end (a siege) by withdrawing troops or forcing the enemy troops to withdraw. **16.** To remove or withdraw (an order). **17.** *Games.* **a.** To increase (a poker bet). **b.** To bet more than (a preceding bettor in poker). **c.** To increase the bid of (one's bridge partner). **18.** *Nautical.* To bring into sight by approaching nearer: *raised the Cape.* **19.** To alter and increase fraudulently the written value of (a check, for example). **20.** To cough up (phlegm). **21.** *Scots.* To make angry; enrage. *—intr. Games.* To increase a poker bet or a bridge bid. **—raise** *n.* **1.** The act of raising or increasing. **2.** An increase in salary. ***—idioms.*** **raise Cain** (or **the devil** or **hell**). **1.** To behave in a rowdy or disruptive fashion. **2.** To reprimand someone angrily. **raise eyebrows.** To cause surprise or mild disapproval. **raise the stakes.** To increase one's commitment or involvement. [Middle English *raisen,* from Old Norse *reisa.*] **—rais′er** *n.*

raised (rāzd) *adj.* **1.** Projecting from a flat background; in relief; embossed: *a raised design.* **2.** Made light and high by yeast or other leaven.

rai·sin (rā′zĭn) *n.* A sweet grape dried either in the sun or by artificial means. [Middle English, from Old French, grape, from Vulgar Latin **racīmus,* from Latin *racēmus,* bunch of grapes.]

rake¹
Leaf rake

Sir Walter Raleigh

rai·son d'ê·tre (rā′zōn dĕt′rə, rĕ-zôN) *n., pl.* **rai·sons d'ê·tre** (rā′zōn, rĕ-zôN). Reason or justification for existing. [French : *raison,* reason + *de,* of, for + *être,* to be.]

raj (räj) *n.* Dominion or rule, especially the British rule over India (1757–1947). [Hindi *rāj,* from Sanskrit *rājā,* king. See **reg-** in Appendix.]

ra·ja (rä′jə) *n.* Variant of **rajah.**

Raj·ab (rŭj′əb) *n.* The seventh month of the year in the Moslem calendar. See table at **calendar.** [Arabic *rajab.*]

Ra·ja·go·pa·la·cha·ri (rä′jə-gō-pä′lä-chär′ē), **Chakravarti.** 1879–1972. Indian politician who served as India's first native-born governor-general (1948–1950).

ra·jah or **ra·ja** (rä′jə) *n.* A prince, chief, or ruler in India or the East Indies. [Hindi *rājā,* from Sanskrit, king. See **reg-** in Appendix.]

Ra·jah·mun·dry (rä′jə-mŏŏn′drē). A city of eastern India on the Godavari River east of Hyderabad. A pilgrimage center, it has timber and tobacco industries. Population, 203,358.

Raj·kot (räj′kōt′). A city of western India west-southwest of Ahmadabad. Formerly the capital of a princely state, it is now an educational center and a transportation hub. Population, 445,076.

Raj·put also **Raj·poot** (räj′pŏŏt) *n.* A member of any of several powerful Hindu landowning and military lineages inhabiting northern and central India. [Hindi *rājpūt,* from Sanskrit *rājaputraḥ,* king's son : *rājā,* king; see RAJAH + *putraḥ,* son.]

rake¹ (rāk) *n.* **1.** A long-handled implement with a row of projecting teeth at its head, used especially to gather leaves or to loosen or smooth earth. **2.** A device that resembles such an implement. **—rake** *v.* **raked, rak·ing, rakes.** *—tr.* **1.** To gather or move with or as if with a rake: *rake leaves; rake in the gambling chips.* **2.** To smooth, scrape, or loosen with a rake or similar implement: *rake the soil for planting.* **3.** *Informal.* To gain in abundance: *suddenly began raking in the money.* **4.** To search or examine thoroughly; ransack. **5.** To scrape; scratch. **6.** To aim heavy gunfire along the length of. *—intr.* **1.** To use a rake. **2.** To conduct a thorough search: *raked through the files for the misplaced letter.* ***—phrasal verb.*** **rake up.** To revive or bring to light; uncover: *rake up old gossip.* [Middle English, from Old English *raca.* See **reg-** in Appendix.] **—rak′er** *n.*

rake² (rāk) *n.* An immoral or dissolute person; a libertine. [Short for RAKEHELL.]

rake³ (rāk) *intr. & tr.v.* **raked, rak·ing, rakes.** To slant or cause to incline from the perpendicular: *propeller blades that rake backward from the shaft; rake a ship's mast.* **—rake** *n.* **1.** Inclination from the perpendicular: *the rake of a jet plane's wings.* **2.** The angle between the cutting edge of a tool and a plane perpendicular to the working surface to which the tool is applied. [Origin unknown.]

rak·ee (răk′ē, rä′kē, rä′kə) *n.* Variant of **raki.**

rake·hell (rāk′hĕl′) *n.* A dissolute person; a rake. [Possibly by folk-etymology from obsolete *rackle,* headstrong, from Middle English *rakel,* perhaps from *raken,* to go.]

rake-off (rāk′ôf′, -ŏf′) *n. Informal.* A percentage or share of the profits of an enterprise, especially one given or accepted as a bribe. [From the rake used by a croupier in a gambling house.]

rak·i also **rak·ee** (răk′ē, rä′kē, rä′kə) *n., pl.* **-is** also **-ees.** A brandy of Turkey and the Balkans, distilled from grapes or plums and flavored with anise. [Turkish *rāqī,* from Arabic *'araq,* arrack.]

rak·ish¹ (rā′kĭsh) *adj.* **1.** *Nautical.* Having a trim, streamlined appearance: *"We were schooner-rigged and rakish, with a long and lissome hull"* (John Masefield). **2.** Dashingly or sportingly stylish; jaunty. [Probably from RAKE³ (from the raking masts of pirate ships).]

rak·ish² (rā′kĭsh) *adj.* Of the character of a rake; dissolute.

rale also **râle** (räl) *n.* An abnormal or pathological respiratory sound. [French *râle,* from *râler,* to make a rattling sound in the throat, from Old French *racler,* to scrape, rattle. See RACLETTE.]

Ra·leigh (rô′lē, rä′-). The capital of North Carolina, in the east-central part of the state southeast of Durham. Selected as the capital in 1788, the city was laid out in 1792. Population, 149,771.

Raleigh or **Ra·legh** (rô′lē, rä′-), Sir **Walter.** 1552?–1618. English courtier, navigator, colonizer, and writer. A favorite of Elizabeth I, he campaigned in Ireland and Cádiz, explored Guiana, colonized Virginia, and introduced tobacco and the potato to Europe. Convicted of treason by James I, he was released for another expedition to Guiana and executed after its failure. His literary works include poetry, memoirs, and a world history.

Ra·lik Chain (rä′lĭk). The western group of the Marshall Islands in the western Pacific Ocean. The chain comprises 3 coral islands and 15 atolls, including Eniwetok.

ral·len·tan·do (răl′ən-tăn′dō, räl′lĕn-tän′dō) *Music. adv. & adj. Abbr.* **rall.** Gradually slackening in tempo; ritardando. Used chiefly as a direction. **—rallentando** *n., pl.* **-dos.** A rallentando passage or movement. [Italian, present participle of *rallentare,* to slow down : *re-,* intensive pref. (from Latin; see RE–) + *allentare,* to slow down (from Late Latin *allentāre* : Latin *ad-,* ad- + Latin *lentus,* slow).]

ral·li·form (răl′ə-fôrm′) *adj.* Relating to or resembling the rail, a marsh bird. [New Latin *Rallus,* rail genus (from French *râle,* rail, from Old French *raale;* see RAIL²) + –FORM.]

ral·ly¹ (răl′ē) *v.* **-lied, -ly·ing, -lies.** —*tr.* **1.** To call together for a common purpose; assemble: *rally troops at a parade ground.* **2.** To reassemble and restore to order: *rally scattered forces.* **3.** To rouse or revive from inactivity or decline: *paused to refresh themselves and rally their strength.* —*intr.* **1.** To come together for a common purpose. **2.** To join in an effort for a common cause: *"In the terror and confusion of change, society rallied round the kings"* (Garrett Mattingly). **3.** To recover abruptly from a setback or disadvantage: *The stock market declined, then rallied. The home team rallied in the ninth inning to win the game.* **4.** To show sudden improvement in health or spirits. **5.** *Sports.* To exchange several strokes before a point is won, as in tennis. —**rally** *n., pl.* **-lies. 1.** A gathering, especially one intended to inspire enthusiasm for a cause: *a political rally.* **2.a.** A reassembling, as of dispersed troops. **b.** The signal ordering this reassembly. **3.** An abrupt recovery from a setback or disadvantage. **4.** A sharp improvement in health, vigor, or spirits. **5.** A notable rise in stock market prices and trading volume after a decline. **6.** *Sports.* **a.** An exchange of several strokes, before a point is won, as in tennis. **b.** A competition in which automobiles are driven over public roads and under normal traffic regulations but with specified rules as to speed, time, and route. [French *rallier,* from Old French *ralier* : *re-,* re- + *alier,* to unite, ally; see ALLY.]

ral·ly² (răl′ē) *v.* **-lied, -ly·ing, -lies.** —*tr.* To tease good-humoredly; banter. —*intr.* To engage in good-humored teasing or jesting. [French *railler,* from Old French, to tease. See RAIL³.]

ralph (rălf) *intr.v.* **ralphed, ralph·ing, ralphs.** *Slang.* To vomit. [Imitative.]

ram (răm) *n.* **1.** A male sheep. **2.** Any of several devices used to drive, batter, or crush by forceful impact, especially: **a.** A battering ram. **b.** The weight that drops in a pile driver or steam hammer. **c.** The plunger or piston of a force pump or hydraulic press. **3.** A hydraulic ram. **4.a.** A projection on the prow of a warship, used to batter or cut into enemy vessels. **b.** A ship having such a projection. —**ram** *tr.v.* **rammed, ram·ming, rams. 1.** To strike or drive against with a heavy impact; butt: *rammed the door with a sledgehammer until it broke open.* **2.** To force or press into place. **3.** To cram; stuff: *rammed the clothes into the suitcase.* **4.** To force passage or acceptance of: *rammed the project through the city council despite local opposition.* [Middle English, from Old English *ramm.*] —**ram′mer** *n.*

Ram (răm) *n.* See **Aries.**

RAM *abbr.* **1.** *Computer Science.* Random-access memory. **2.** Also **R.A.M.** Royal Academy of Music.

Ra·ma (rä′mə) *n.* *Hinduism.* A deified hero worshiped as an incarnation of Vishnu.

Rama VII. Originally **Pra·ja·dhi·pok** (prə-chä′tĭ-pŏk′). 1893–1941. King of Siam (1925–1935) who abdicated after failing to suppress the newly formed constitutional government.

♦ **ra·ma·da** (rə-mä′də) *n.* *Southwestern U.S.* **1.** An open porch. **2.** An openwork trellis, constructed over a walkway, onto which climbing plants are trained. [Spanish, from *rama,* branch, from Vulgar Latin **rāma,* from Latin *rāmus.* See RAMIFY.]

♦ ***REGIONAL NOTE:*** One of the words Spanish contributed to the English of the American Southwest is *ramada,* a term for an open porch. *Ramada* can also mean an openwork trellis constructed over a walkway onto which climbing plants are trained; this sense illustrates the derivation of the word from Spanish *rama,* meaning "branch"—hence *ramada,* "arbor, mass of branches." The suffix *-ada* in Spanish denotes "a place characterized by (something)." *Ramada* might have remained a relatively obscure regional word were it not for its adoption in the name of a national chain of motels.

Ram·a·dan (răm′ə-dän′, răm′ə-dän′) *n.* **1.** The ninth month of the year in the Moslem calendar. See table at **calendar. 2.** A fast, held from sunrise to sunset, that is carried out during this period. [Arabic *Ramaḍān,* from *ramaḍ,* dryness.]

Ra·man (rä′mən), Sir **Chandrasekhara Venkata.** 1888–1970. Indian physicist. He won a 1930 Nobel Prize for his discovery of the Raman effect.

Raman effect *n.* *Physics.* The alteration in frequency and random alteration in phase of light passing through a transparent medium. [After Sir Chandrasekhara Venkata RAMAN.]

Ra·ma's Bridge (rä′məz). See **Adam's Bridge.**

ra·mate (rā′māt′) *adj.* Having branches; branched. [Latin *rāmus,* branch; see RAMUS + -ATE¹.]

Ra·mat Gan (rə-mät′ gän′, rä′mät). A city of west-central Israel, a suburb of Tel Aviv–Jaffa. Its diamond exchange was founded in 1921. Population, 116,500.

ram·ble (răm′bəl) *intr.v.* **-bled, -bling, -bles. 1.** To move about aimlessly. See Synonyms at **wander. 2.** To walk about casually or for pleasure. **3.** To follow an irregularly winding course of motion or growth. **4.** To speak or write at length and with many digressions. —**ramble** *n.* A leisurely, sometimes lengthy walk. [Probably from Middle Dutch **rammelen,* to wander about in a state of sexual desire, from *rammen,* to copulate with.]

ram·bler (răm′blər) *n.* **1.** One that rambles: *tourists and Sunday ramblers on the village streets; a conversational rambler.* **2.** A climbing rose having numerous red, pink, or white flowers.

ram·bling (răm′blĭng) *adj.* **1.** Often or habitually roaming; wandering. **2.** Extended over an irregular area; sprawling: *a large rambling country estate.* **3.** Lengthy and digressive: *a rambling speech.* —**ram′bling·ly** *adv.*

Ram·bo (răm′bō) *n., pl.* **-bos.** *Slang.* An extremely aggressive person who feels no qualms about defying rules, regulations, or the law in order to right a perceived wrong. —*attributive.* Often used to modify another noun: *a Rambo mentality; Rambo motorists.* [After John *Rambo,* character in American films.]

Ram·bouil·let (răm′bo͞o-lā, räm′bo͞o-yā′) *n.* Any of a breed of merino sheep of French origin, raised for wool and meat. [After *Rambouillet,* a town of north-central France.]

ram·bunc·tious (răm-bŭngk′shəs) *adj.* Boisterous and disorderly. [Probably alteration of *robustious, rumbustious,* from ROBUST.] —**ram·bunc′tious·ly** *adv.* —**ram·bunc′tious·ness** *n.*

WORD HISTORY: The origins of *rambunctious* are not clearly established, a situation that may be better understood after looking at the evidence. The development that is generally accepted is from the word *robustious,* derived from *robust* and first recorded in a work written before 1548, to *rumbustious,* first recorded in 1778, to *rambunctious,* first recorded in 1830, all three words having more or less the same meaning. But how did *robustious* lead to *rumbustious?* It has been suggested that the word *rumble* played a part in this, although the word *rumbustion,* meaning "the alcoholic beverage rum," might also have been involved. The first form in which *rambunctious* is recorded is *rumbunctious,* showing how *rumbustious* was involved in the alteration of *robustious* to *rambunctious,* but how the sound indicated by *s* became that indicated by *nc* or why the first *u* became *a* is a mystery.

ram·bu·tan (răm-bo͞ot′n) *n.* **1.** A tree *(Nephelium lappaceum)* of southeast Asia, bearing edible oval red fruit with soft spines. **2.** The fruit of this tree. [Malay, from *rambut,* hair (from its hairy covering).]

Ra·meau (rä-mō′), **Jean Philippe.** 1683–1764. French composer and music theorist known for his treatise on harmony (1722) and his ballets and operas, including *Castor et Pollux* (1737).

Ra·mée (rə-mā′), **Marie Louise de la.** Pen name Ouida. 1839–1908. British writer whose romantic novels include *Under Two Flags* (1867).

ram·e·kin also **ram·e·quin** (răm′ĭ-kĭn) *n.* **1.** A cheese preparation made with eggs and bread crumbs or unsweetened puff pastry, baked and served in individual dishes. **2.** A small dish used for baking and serving. [French *ramequin,* perhaps from Dutch dialectal *rammeken,* toasted bread or from Low German *ramken,* diminutive of *ram,* cream (from Middle Low German *rōme*).]

Rameses II
XIX Dynasty quartzite portrait bust

Ram·e·ses II also **Ram·es·ses II** (răm′ĭ-sēz′) or **Ram·ses II** (răm′sēz′). Known as "Rameses the Great." 14th–13th century B.C. King of Egypt (1304–1237 B.C.) whose reign was marked by the building of numerous monuments. He was probably king during the Jewish exodus from Egypt.

ra·met (rā′mĭt) *n.* An individual member of a clone. [Latin *rāmus,* branch; see RAMUS + -ET.]

ra·mi (rā′mī′) *n.* *Biology & Anatomy.* Plural of **ramus.**

ram·ie (răm′ē, rā′mē) *n.* **1.** A tropical Asian perennial herb *(Boehmeria nivea)* having broad leaves and densely branched panicles of small, unisexual, apetalous flowers. **2.** The flaxlike fiber from the stem of this plant, used in making fabrics and cordage. [Malay *rami.*]

ram·i·fi·ca·tion (răm′ə-fĭ-kā′shən) *n.* **1.** A development or consequence growing out of and sometimes complicating a problem, plan, or statement: *the ramifications of a court decision.* **2.a.** The act or process of branching out or dividing into branches. **b.** A subordinate part extending from a main body; a branch. **c.** An arrangement of branches or branching parts.

ram·i·form (răm′ə-fôrm′) *adj.* Branching or branchlike. [Latin *rāmus,* branch; see RAMUS + -FORM.]

ramp¹
Airplane ramp

ram·i·fy (răm′ə-fī′) *v.* **-fied, -fy·ing, -fies.** —*intr.* **1.** To have complicating consequences or outgrowths: *The problem merely ramified after the unsuccessful meeting.* **2.** To send out branches or subordinate branchlike parts. —*tr.* To divide into or cause to extend in branches or subordinate branchlike parts. [Middle English *ramifien,* from Old French *ramifier,* from Medieval Latin *rāmificāre* : Latin *rāmus,* branch; see **wrād-** in Appendix + Latin *-ficāre,* -fy.]

ram·jet (răm′jĕt′) *n.* A jet engine that propels aircraft by igniting fuel mixed with air taken and compressed by the engine in a fashion that produces greater exhaust than intake velocity.

ra·mo·na (rə-mō′nə) *n.* See **sage²** (sense 1a). [Possibly after *Ramona,* heroine of a novel by Helen Hunt Jackson.]

Ra·món y Ca·jal (rä-môn′ ē kä-häl′), **Santiago.** 1852–1934. Spanish histologist. He shared a 1906 Nobel Prize for research on the structure of the nervous system.

ra·mose (rā′mōs′, rə-mōs′) *adj.* Having many branches. [Latin *rāmōsus,* from *rāmus,* branch. See **wrād-** in Appendix.]

ra·mous (rā′məs) *adj.* **1.** Of or resembling branches. **2.** Branching; ramose. [From Latin *rāmōsus,* ramose. See RAMOSE.]

ramp¹ (rămp) *n.* **1.** An inclined surface or roadway connecting different levels. **2.** A mobile staircase by which passengers board and leave an aircraft. **3.** A concave bend of a handrail where a sharp change in level or direction occurs, as at a stair landing.

ă pat	oi boy
ā pay	ou out
âr care	o͝o took
ä father	o͞o boot
ĕ pet	ŭ cut
ē be	ûr urge
ĭ pit	th thin
ī pie	*th* this
îr pier	hw which
ŏ pot	zh vision
ō toe	ə about, item
ô paw	♦ regionalism

Stress marks: ′ (primary); ′ (secondary), as in **dictionary** (dĭk′shə-nĕr′ē)

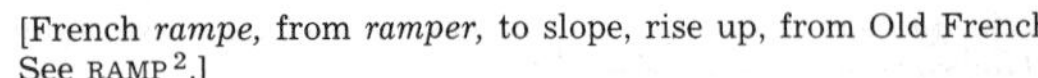

[French *rampe,* from *ramper,* to slope, rise up, from Old French. See RAMP^{2}.]

ramp^{2} (rămp) *intr.v.* **ramped, ramp·ing, ramps. 1.** To act threateningly or violently; rage. **2.** To assume a threatening stance. **3.** *Heraldry.* To stand in the rampant position. [Middle English *rampen,* from Old French *ramper,* to rear, rise up, of Germanic origin.] **—ramp** *n.*

ram·page (răm′pāj′) *n.* A course of violent, frenzied action or behavior. **—rampage** (*also* răm-pāj′) *intr.v.* **-paged, -pag·ing, -pag·es.** To move about wildly or violently. [Scots, possibly from RAMP^{2}.] **—ram·pag′er** *n.*

rampant
Coat of arms of the Duke of Dover

ram·pa·geous (răm-pā′jəs) *adj.* Raging; frenzied: *"the hot rampageous horses of my will"* (W.H. Auden). **—ram·pa′geous·ly** *adv.* **—ram·pa′geous·ness** *n.*

ram·pant (răm′pənt) *adj.* **1.** Extending unchecked; unrestrained: *a rampant growth of weeds in the neglected yard.* **2.** Occurring without restraint and frequently, widely, or menacingly; rife: *a rampant epidemic; rampant corruption in city government.* **3. a.** Rearing on the hind legs. **b.** *Heraldry.* Rearing on the left hind leg with the forelegs elevated, the right above the left, and usually with the head in profile. **4.** *Architecture.* Springing from a support or an abutment that is higher at one side than at the other: *a rampant arch.* [Middle English *rampaunt,* from Old French *rampant,* present participle of *ramper,* to ramp. See RAMP^{2}.] **—ram′pan·cy** *n.* **—ram′pant·ly** *adv.*

ram·part (răm′pärt′, -pərt) *n.* **1.** A fortification consisting of an embankment, often with a parapet built on top. **2.** A means of protection or defense; a bulwark. See Synonyms at **bulwark. —rampart** *tr.v.* **-part·ed, -part·ing, -parts.** To defend with a rampart. [French *rempart,* from Old French, from *remparer,* to fortify : *re-,* re- + *emparer,* to fortify, take possession of (from Old Provençal *amparar,* from Vulgar Latin **ante parāre,* to prepare : Latin *ante-,* ante- + Latin *parāre,* to prepare; see **perə-^{1}** in Appendix).]

ram·pike (răm′pīk′) *n.* A standing dead tree or tree stump, especially one killed by fire. [Origin unknown.]

ram·pi·on (răm′pē-ən) *n.* **1.** A biennial Eurasian plant *(Campanula rapunculus)* having rosette leaves with winged stalks, panicles of lilac-colored flowers, and an edible root used in salads. **2.** Any of various similar plants of the genus *Phyteuma.* [Probably alteration of French *raiponce,* from Old French *responce,* from Old Italian *raponzo,* probably from *rapa,* turnip, from Latin *rāpum.*]

Ram·pur (räm′po͝or). A city of north-central India east of Delhi. It is a processing and manufacturing center known for its library containing a fine collection of Mogul miniature paintings. Population, 204,610.

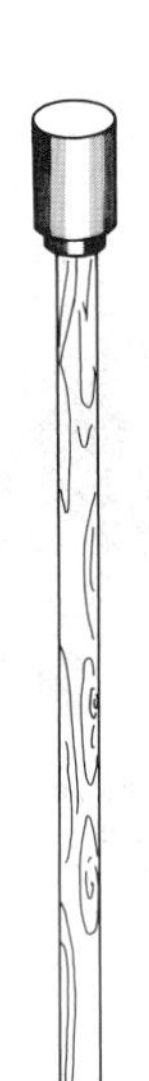

ramrod

ram·rod (răm′rŏd′) *n.* **1.** A rod used to force the charge into a muzzleloading firearm. **2.** A rod used to clean the barrel of a firearm. **3.** A harshly demanding overseer; a disciplinarian. **—ramrod** *tr.v.* **-rod·ded, -rod·ding, -rods. 1.** To exert strict control over; supervise closely. **2.** To force passage or acceptance of: *a group that ramrodded the bill through Congress.*

Ram·say (răm′zē), **Allan.** 1686–1758. Scottish poet noted for his patriotic and pastoral works, including the drama *The Gentle Shepherd* (1725).

Ramsay, James Andrew Brown. See Tenth Earl and First Marquis of **Dalhousie.**

Ramsay, Sir **William.** 1852–1916. British chemist. He won a 1904 Nobel Prize for discovering the inert gases argon, helium, neon, xenon, and krypton.

Ram·ses II (răm′sēz′). See **Rameses II.**

Ram·sey (răm′zē), **Arthur Michael.** 1904–1988. British prelate and archbishop of Canterbury (1961–1974).

ram·shack·le (răm′shăk′əl) *adj.* So poorly constructed or kept up that disintegration is likely; rickety: *a ramshackle cabin in the woods.* [Back-formation from obsolete *ranshackled,* ramshackle, alteration of *ransackled,* past participle of *ransackle,* to ransack, frequentative of Middle English *ransaken,* to pillage. See RANSACK.]

ram's horn (rămz) *n. Judaism.* A shofar.

ram·son (răm′zən, -sən) *n.* A Eurasian garlic *(Allium ursinum)* having broad, stalked, oblong to lance-shaped leaves and bulbous roots used in salads and relishes. Often used in the plural. [Middle English *ramsyn,* from Old English *hramsan,* pl. of *hramsa.*]

ram·til (răm′tĭl) or **ram·til·la** (răm-tĭl′ə) *n.* An Ethiopian plant *(Guizotia abyssinica)* having opposite leaves and rayed, yellow flower heads, grown for its oil-rich seeds. [Hindi *rāmtil* : Sanskrit *rāma-,* dark + Sanskrit *tilaḥ,* sesame.]

ram·u·lose (răm′yə-lōs′) *adj.* Having numerous small branches. [Latin *rāmulōsus,* from *rāmulus,* diminutive of *rāmus,* branch. See RAMUS.]

ra·mus (rā′məs) *n., pl.* **-mi** (-mī′). **1.** *Biology.* A branch, as of a plant, nerve, or blood vessel. **2.** *Anatomy.* A bony process extending like a branch from a larger bone, especially the ascending part of the lower jaw that makes a joint at the temple. [Latin *rāmus,* branch. See **wrād-** in Appendix.]

ranch house

ran (răn) *v.* Past tense of **run.**

Ran (răn) *n. Mythology.* The Norse goddess of the sea.

Ran·ca·gua (rän-kä′gwä, räng-). A city of central Chile south of Santiago. It is primarily an agricultural center in a copper-mining area. Population, 139,925.

ranch (rănch) *n.* **1.** An extensive farm, especially in the western United States, on which large herds of cattle, sheep, or horses are raised. **2.** A large farm on which a particular crop or kind of animal is raised: *a mink ranch.* **3.** A house in which the owner of an extensive farm lives. **—ranch** *intr.v.* **ranched, ranch·ing, ranch·es.** To manage or work on a ranch. [American Spanish *rancho,* small farm, from Spanish, hut, group of people who eat together, from Old Spanish *rancharse,* to be billeted, from Old French *se ranger,* to be arranged, from *renc, reng,* row, line, of Germanic origin. See **sker-^{2}** in Appendix.]

ranch·er (răn′chər) *n.* **1.** One that owns or manages a ranch. **2.** A rectangular house of one story; a ranch house.

♦ **ran·che·ri·a** (răn′chə-rē′ə) *n. Southwestern U.S.* **1. a.** A Mexican herdsman's hut. **b.** A village of these huts. **2.** A rural Native American settlement. [American Spanish *ranchería,* from *rancho,* small farm. See RANCH.]

♦ **ran·che·ro** (răn-châr′ō) *n., pl.* **-ros.** *Southwestern U.S.* A ranch owner; a rancher. [American Spanish, from *rancho,* small ranch. See RANCH.]

ranch house *n.* **1.** The building on a ranch occupied by its operator. **2.** A rectangular, one-story house with a low-pitched roof.

Ran·chi (rän′chē). A city of northeast India west-northwest of Calcutta. It is a manufacturing center and health resort. Population, 489,626.

ranch·man (rănch′mən) *n.* The owner or manager of a ranch; a rancher.

ranch mink *n.* A mink bred in captivity from Alaskan and Labrador strains for special pelt colors and qualities.

♦ **ran·cho** (răn′chō) *n., pl.* **-chos.** *Southwestern U.S.* **1.** A hut or group of huts for housing ranch workers. **2.** A ranch. [American Spanish, small ranch. See RANCH.]

Ran·cho Cor·do·va (răn′chō kôr-dō′və, kôr′də-). A community of north-central California, a suburb of Sacramento. Population, 42,881.

Rancho Cu·ca·mon·ga (ko͞o′kə-mŭng′gə, -mŏng′-). An unincorporated community of southwest California west of San Bernadino. It is in a wine-producing area. Population, 55,250.

Rancho Pal·os Ver·des (păl′ōs vûr′dēz, păl′əs). A city of southern California on a channel of the Pacific Ocean west of Long Beach. Population, 36,577.

ran·cid (răn′sĭd) *adj.* **1.** Having the disagreeable odor or taste of decomposing oils or fats; rank. **2.** Repugnant; nasty: *rancid remarks.* [Latin *rancidus,* past participle of *rancēre,* to stink, be rotten.] **—ran·cid′i·ty, ran′cid·ness** *n.*

ran·cor (răng′kər) *n.* Bitter, long-lasting resentment; deep-seated ill will. See Synonyms at **enmity.** [Middle English, from Old French, from Late Latin, rancid smell, from Latin *rancēre,* to stink, be rotten.] **—ran′cor·ous** *adj.* **—ran′cor·ous·ly** *adv.* **—ran′cor·ous·ness** *n.*

ran·cour (răng′kər) *n. Chiefly British.* Variant of **rancor.**

rand (rănd, ränd) *n.* See table at **currency.** [Afrikaans, after (WITWATERS)RAND.]

Rand (rănd). See **Witwatersrand.**

Rand, Ayn. 1905–1982. Russian-born American writer primarily known for her polemical novels, such as *The Fountainhead* (1943), which defend political conservatism.

Ran·dalls·town (răn′dlz-toun′). A community of north-central Maryland, a suburb of Baltimore. Population, 20,500.

ran·dan (răn′dăn′) *n. Nautical.* **1.** A boat designed to be rowed by three persons. **2.** The method of rowing such a boat, in which the persons fore and aft use one oar each and the person amidships uses two. [Origin unknown.]

r & b or **R & B** *abbr. Music.* Rhythm and blues.

R & D *abbr.* Research and development.

Rand·ers (rä′nərs). A city of northern Denmark in the eastern part of the Jutland Peninsula north-northwest of Århus. It is a trade and manufacturing center in an agricultural and salmon-fishing area. Population, 61,410.

Ran·dolph (răn′dŏlf′). A town of eastern Massachusetts south-southwest of Quincy. It is mainly residential. Population, 22,218.

Randolph, Edmund Jennings. 1753–1813. American Revolutionary leader and public official. A member of the Constitutional Convention (1787), he later served as U.S. attorney general (1789–1794) and secretary of state (1794–1795).

Randolph, John. Called "Randolph of Roanoke." 1773–1833. American politician known for his brilliant oratory and eccentric behavior during his tenure as a U.S. representative (12 terms between 1799 and 1829) and senator (1825–1827) from Virginia.

ran·dom (răn′dəm) *adj.* **1.** Having no specific pattern, purpose, or objective: *random movements; a random choice.* See Synonyms at **chance. 2.** *Statistics.* Of or relating to the same or equal chances or probability of occurrence for each member of a group. **—*idiom.* at random.** Without a design, method, or purpose; unsystematically: *chose a card at random from the deck.* [From *at random,* by chance, at great speed, from Middle English *randon,* speed, violence, from Old French, from *randir,* to run, of Germanic origin.] **—ran′dom·ly** *adv.* **—ran′dom·ness** *n.*

ran·dom-ac·cess memory (răn′dəm-ăk′sĕs) *adj. Abbr.* **RAM** *Computer Science.* A memory device in which information can be accessed in any order.

ran·dom·ize (răn′də-mīz′) *tr.v.* **-ized, -iz·ing, -iz·es.** To make random in arrangement, especially in order to control the variables in an experiment. **—ran′dom·i·za′tion** (-də-mĭ-zā′shən) *n.* **—ran′dom·iz′er** *n.*

random variable *n. Statistics.* A variable whose values are distributed according to a probability distribution.

random walk *n. Statistics.* A series of sequential movements in which the direction and size of each move is randomly determined.

R and R *abbr.* Rest and recreation.

ran·dy (răn′dē) *adj.* **-di·er, ran·di·est. 1.a.** Lascivious; lecherous. **b.** Of or characterized by frank, uninhibited sexuality. **2.** *Scots.* Ill-mannered. [Possibly from obsolete *rand,* to rant, from obsolete Dutch *randen, ranten.*]

ra·nee (rä′nē) *n.* Variant of **rani.**

rang (răng) *v.* Past tense of **ring²**.

range (rānj) *n. Abbr.* **Ra., r., R. 1.a.** Extent of perception, knowledge, experience, or ability. **b.** The area or sphere in which an activity takes place. **c.** The full extent covered: *within the range of possibilities.* **2.a.** An amount or extent of variation: *a wide price range.* **b.** *Music.* The gamut of tones that a voice or an instrument is capable of producing. **3.a.** The maximum extent or distance limiting operation, action, or effectiveness, as of a projectile, an aircraft, a radio signal, or a sound. **b.** The maximum distance that can be covered by a vehicle with a specified payload before its fuel supply is exhausted. **c.** The distance between a projectile weapon and its target. **4.** A place equipped for practice in shooting at targets. **5.** *Aerospace.* A testing area at which rockets and missiles are launched and tracked. **6.** An extensive area of open land on which livestock wander and graze. **7.** The geographic region in which a plant or an animal normally lives or grows. **8.** The act of wandering or roaming over a large area. **9.** *Mathematics.* The set of all values a given function may take on. **10.** *Statistics.* The difference or interval between the smallest and largest values in a frequency distribution. **11.** A class, a rank, or an order: *The candidate had broad support from the lower ranges of the party.* **12.** An extended group or series, especially a row or chain of mountains. **13.** One of a series of double-faced bookcases in a library stack room. **14.** A north-south strip of townships, each six miles square, numbered east and west from a specified meridian in a U.S. public land survey. **15.** A stove with spaces for cooking a number of things at the same time. **—range** *v.* **ranged, rang·ing, rang·es.** *—tr.* **1.** To arrange or dispose in a particular order, especially in rows or lines. **2.** To assign to a particular category; classify. **3.** To align (a gun, for example) with a target. **4.a.** To determine the distance of (a target). **b.** To be capable of reaching (a maximum distance). **5.** To pass over or through (an area or a region). **6.** To turn (livestock) onto an extensive area of open land for grazing. **7.** *Nautical.* To uncoil (an anchor cable) on deck so the anchor may descend easily. *—intr.* **1.** To vary within specified limits: *ages that ranged from two to five.* **2.** To extend in a particular direction: *a river that ranges to the east.* **3.** To extend or lie in the same direction: *"Whatsoever comes athwart his affection ranges evenly with mine"* (Shakespeare). **4.** To pass over or through an area or a region in or as if in exploration. **5.** To wander freely; roam. **6.** To live or grow within a particular region. [Middle English, row, rank, from Old French, from *rangier,* to put in a row, from *rang, reng,* line, of Germanic origin. See **sker-²** in Appendix.]

SYNONYMS: *range, ambit, compass, orbit, purview, reach, scope, sweep.* The central meaning shared by these nouns is "an area within which something acts, operates, or has power or control": *the range of a supersonic jet; the ambit of municipal legislation; information not within the compass of this article; countries within the political orbit of a world power; hospital regulations under the purview of the department of health; outside the reach of the law; issues within the scope of an investigation; outside the sweep of federal authority.* See also Synonyms at **wander.**

range finder also **range·find·er** (rānj′fīn′dər) *n.* Any of various optical, electronic, or acoustical instruments used to determine the distance of an object. **—range′find′er** *adj.*

range·land (rānj′lănd′, -lənd) *n.* An expanse of land suitable for livestock to wander and graze on.

Range·ley Lake (rānj′lē). A lake of west-central Maine near the New Hampshire border. It and other nearby lakes form a popular resort area.

rang·er (rān′jər) *n.* **1.** A wanderer; a rover. **2.** A member of an armed troop employed in patrolling a specific region. **3. Ranger.** A member of a group of U.S. soldiers specially trained for making raids either on foot, in ground vehicles, or by airlift. **4.a.** A warden employed to maintain and protect a forest or other natural area. **b.** *Chiefly British.* The keeper of a royal forest or park.

Ran·goon (răn-gōōn′, răng-). Officially (since 1989) **Yan·gon** (yän′gôn′). The capital and largest city of Burma, in the southern part of the country on the **Rangoon River** near its outlet in the Irrawaddy River delta. It was a small fishing village until it became the capital of Burmese kings after the 1750's. Further growth was spurred by the British occupation of the city in 1852. Population, 2,458,712.

rang·y (rān′jē) *adj.* **-i·er, -i·est. 1.** Having long, slender limbs. **2.** Inclined to rove. **3.** Providing ample range; roomy.

ra·ni also **ra·nee** (rä′nē) *n., pl.* **-nis** also **-nees. 1.** The wife of a rajah. **2.** A reigning Hindu princess or queen. [Hindi *rānī,* from Sanskrit *rājñī,* feminine of *rājā,* rajah. See RAJAH.]

Ran·jit Singh (rŭn′jĭt sĭng′). Known as "the Lion of the Punjab." 1780–1839. Indian leader of the Sikhs who founded a kingdom uniting the Sikh provinces and maintained an alliance with the British.

rank¹ (răngk) *n.* **1.a.** A relative position in a society. **b.** An official position or grade: *the rank of sergeant.* **c.** A relative position or degree of value in a graded group. **d.** High or eminent station or position: *persons of rank.* **2.** A row, line, series, or range. **3.a.** A line of soldiers, vehicles, or equipment standing side by side in close order. **b. ranks.** The armed forces. **c. ranks.** Personnel, especially enlisted military personnel. **4. ranks.** A body of people classed together; numbers: *joined the ranks of the unemployed.* **5.** *Games.* Any of the horizontal lines of squares on a chessboard. **—rank** *v.* **ranked, rank·ing, ranks.** *—tr.* **1.** To place in a row or rows. **2.** To give a particular order or position to; classify. **3.** To outrank or take precedence over. *—intr.* **1.** To hold a particular rank: *ranked first in the class.* **2.** To form or stand in a row or rows. **3.** *Slang.* **a.** To complain. **b.** To engage in carping criticism. Often used with *on*: *Stop ranking on me all the time.* ***—idiom.*** **pull rank.** To use one's superior rank to gain an advantage. [Middle English, line, row, from Old French *ranc, renc,* of Germanic origin. See **sker-²** in Appendix.]

rank² (răngk) *adj.* **rank·er, rank·est. 1.** Growing profusely or with excessive vigor: *rank vegetation in the jungle.* **2.** Yielding a profuse, often excessive crop; highly fertile: *rank earth.* **3.** Strong and offensive in odor or flavor. **4.** Conspicuously offensive: *rank treachery.* See Synonyms at **flagrant. 5.** Absolute; complete: *a rank amateur; a rank stranger.* [Middle English *ranc,* from Old English, strong, overbearing. See **reg-** in Appendix.] **—rank′ly** *adv.* **—rank′ness** *n.*

rank and file *n.* **1.** The enlisted troops, excluding noncommissioned officers, in an army. **2.** Those who form the major portion of a group or an organization, excluding the leaders and officers.

rank-and-file (răngk′ən-fīl′) *adj.* **1.** Made up of or coming from the ordinary members of a group, excluding leaders and officers: *rank-and-file committees; rank-and-file grievances.* **2.** Made up of or coming from the common people: *a rank-and-file pressure group; political candidates seeking rank-and-file support.*

Ran·ke (räng′kə), **Leopold von.** 1795–1886. German historian who pioneered the modern methods of rigorously analyzing first-hand documentation. His written works include *The History of the Popes* (1834–1836).

rank·er (răng′kər) *n. Chiefly British.* **1.** An enlisted soldier. **2.** A commissioned officer who has been promoted from enlisted status.

Jeannette Rankin

Ran·kin (răng′kĭn), **Jeannette.** 1880–1973. American reformer and politician. A leader in the women's suffrage movement in Montana, her home state, she later was the first woman U.S. representative (1917–1919 and 1941–1943) and the only legislator to oppose U.S. involvement in both World Wars.

Ran·kine scale (răng′kĭn) *n.* A scale of absolute temperature using Fahrenheit degrees, in which the freezing point of water is 491.69° and the boiling point of water is 671.69°. [After William John Macquorn *Rankine* (1820–1872), Scottish engineer and physicist.]

rank·ing (răng′kĭng) *adj.* Of the highest rank; preeminent.

ran·kle (răng′kəl) *v.* **-kled, -kling, -kles.** *—intr.* **1.** To cause persistent irritation or resentment. **2.** To become sore or inflamed; fester. *—tr.* To embitter; irritate. [Middle English *ranclen,* from Old French *rancler,* alteration of *draoncler,* from *draoncle,* festering sore, from Latin *dracunculus,* diminutive of *dracō, dracōn-,* serpent. See DRAGON.]

WORD HISTORY: A persistent resentment, a festering sore, and a little snake are all coiled together in the history of the word *rankle.* "A little snake" is the sense of the Latin word *dracunculus* to which *rankle* can be traced, *dracunculus* being a diminutive of *dracō,* "snake." The Latin word passed into Old French, as *draoncle,* having probably already developed the sense "festering sore," because some of these sores resembled little snakes in their shape or bite. The verb *draoncler,* "to fester," was then formed in Old French. The noun and verb developed alternate forms without the *d*–, and both were borrowed into Middle English, the noun *rancle* being recorded in a work written around 1190, the verb *ranclen,* in a work probably composed about 1300. Both words had literal senses having to do with festering sores. The noun is not recorded after the 16th century, but the verb went on to develop the figurative senses having to do with resentment and bitterness with which we are all too familiar.

Rann of Kutch (rŭn; kŭch). An extensive salt marsh of western India and southeast Pakistan between the Gulf of Kutch and the Indus River delta. It was the scene of major border disputes in 1965 and 1971.

ran·sack (răn′săk′) *tr.v.* **-sacked, -sack·ing, -sacks. 1.** To search or examine thoroughly. **2.** To search carefully for plunder; pillage. [Middle English *ransaken,* from Old Norse *rannsaka* : *rann,* house + *saka, to search, seek; see **sāg-** in Appendix.] **—ran′sack′er** *n.*

ă pat	oi boy
ā pay	ou out
âr care	ŏŏ took
ä father	ōō boot
ĕ pet	ŭ cut
ē be	ûr urge
ĭ pit	th thin
ī pie	*th* this
îr pier	hw which
ŏ pot	zh vision
ō toe	ə about, item
ô paw	♦ regionalism

Stress marks: ′ (primary); ′ (secondary), as in **dictionary** (dĭk′shə-nĕr′ē)

ran·som (răn′səm) *n.* **1.a.** The release of property or a person in return for payment of a demanded price. **b.** The price or payment demanded or paid for such release. **2.** *Theology.* A redemption from sin and its consequences. **—ransom** *tr.v.* **-somed, -som·ing, -soms. 1.a.** To obtain the release of by paying a certain price. **b.** To release after receiving such a payment. **2.** *Theology.* To deliver from sin and its consequences. [Middle English *ransome,* from Old French *rançon,* from Latin *redēmptiō, redēmptiōn-,* a buying back. See REDEMPTION.] **—ran′som·er** *n.*

Ran·som (răn′səm), **John Crowe.** 1888–1974. American poet and critic. The founder and editor (1939–1959) of the *Kenyon Review,* he was a leading proponent of New Criticism. His collections of poetry include *Chills and Fevers* (1924).

rant (rănt) *v.* **rant·ed, rant·ing, rants.** *—intr.* To speak or declaim in a violent, loud, or vehement manner; rave. *—tr.* To utter with violence or extravagance: *a dictator who ranted his vitriol onto a captive audience.* **—rant** *n.* **1.** Violent, loud, or extravagant speech. See Synonyms at **bombast. 2.** *Chiefly British.* Wild or uproarious merriment. [Probably from obsolete Dutch *ranten.*] **—rant′er** *n.*

Ran·toul (răn-to͞ol′). A village of east-central Illinois north of Champaign. A U.S. military air technical school was established here in 1917. Population, 20,161.

ran·u·la (răn′yə-lə) *n.* A cyst on the underside of the tongue caused by the obstruction of a duct of a salivary gland. [Latin *rānula,* swelling on the tongue, diminutive of *rāna,* frog. See RANUNCULUS.]

ra·nun·cu·lus (rə-nŭng′kyə-ləs) *n., pl.* **-lus·es** or **-li** (-lī′). Any of numerous plants of the genus *Ranunculus,* including the buttercups. [New Latin *Rānunculus,* genus name, from Latin *rānunculus,* a kind of medicinal plant, diminutive of *rāna,* frog, perhaps of imitative origin.]

rap¹ (răp) *v.* **rapped, rap·ping, raps.** *—tr.* **1.** To hit sharply and swiftly; strike: *rapped the table with his fist.* **2.** To utter sharply: *rap out a complaint.* **3.** To criticize or blame. *—intr.* To strike a quick, light blow: *rapped on the door.* **—rap** *n.* **1.** A quick, light blow or knock. **2.** A knocking or tapping sound. **3.** *Slang.* **a.** A reprimand. **b.** A sentence to serve time in prison. **4.** *Slang.* A negative quality or characteristic associated with a person or an object. **—*idioms.* beat the rap.** *Slang.* To escape punishment or be acquitted of a charge. **take the rap.** *Slang.* To accept punishment or take the blame for an offense or error. [Middle English *rappen,* possibly of imitative origin.]

rap² (răp) *tr.v.* **rapt** or **rapped** (răpt), **rap·ping, raps.** *Archaic.* **1.** *past participle* **rapt.** To enchant or seize with rapture. **2.** To snatch. [Back-formation from RAPT.]

rap³ (răp) *n. Informal.* The least bit: *I don't give a rap about office politics. I don't care a rap what you do.* [From obsolete *rap,* 18th-century Irish counterfeit halfpenny, from Irish Gaelic, alteration (possibly influenced by *rap,* piece, bit) of *ropaire.*]

rap⁴ (răp) *n.* **1.** *Slang.* A talk, conversation, or discussion. **2.** *Music.* A form of popular music characterized by spoken or chanted rhyming lyrics with a syncopated, repetitive rhythmic accompaniment. **—rap** *intr.v.* **rap·ped, rap·ping, raps. 1.** *Slang.* To discuss freely and at length. **2.** *Music.* To perform rap. [Possibly from RAP¹.]

Ra·pa (rä′pə). An island of the southern Pacific Ocean in southern French Polynesia south-southeast of Tahiti. It was much visited by whalers in the early 19th century.

ra·pa·cious (rə-pā′shəs) *adj.* **1.** Taking by force; plundering. **2.** Greedy; ravenous. See Synonyms at **voracious. 3.** Subsisting on live prey. [From Latin *rapāx, rapāc-,* from *rapere,* to seize. See **rep-** in Appendix.] **—ra·pa′cious·ly** *adv.* **—ra·pac′i·ty** (rə-păs′ĭ-tē), **ra·pa′cious·ness** *n.*

Ra·pal·lo (rə-pä′lō, rä-päl′-). A city of northwest Italy on the Ligurian Sea. It is a resort on the Italian Riviera. The treaty proclaiming Fiume (now Rijeka) an independent city was signed here by Italy and Yugoslavia in November 1920. Population, 28,318.

Rapa Nu·i (no͞o′ē). See **Easter Island.**

rape¹ (rāp) *n.* **1.** The crime of forcing another person to submit to sex acts, especially sexual intercourse. **2.** The act of seizing and carrying off by force; abduction. **3.** Abusive or improper treatment; violation: *a rape of justice.* **—rape** *tr.v.* **raped, rap·ing, rapes. 1.** To force (another person) to submit to sex acts, especially sexual intercourse; commit rape on. **2.** To seize and carry off by force. **3.** To plunder or pillage. [Middle English, from *rapen,* to rape, from Old French *raper,* to abduct, from Latin *rapere,* to seize. See **rep-** in Appendix.] **—rap′er** *n.*

WORD HISTORY: Although three senses are listed in our entry for the verb *rape,* it is unlikely that many people think of the word as having more than one sense. The Latin word *rapere* from which *rape* comes had an even wider range of meanings, including "to ravish." It must be kept in mind, however, that most of its senses had to do with the notion of seizing or carrying off and that sexual violation was confined to the one sense. In the case of the Middle English word *rapen,* taken from Latin *rapere,* fewer senses existed, but some of them differed quite significantly from any in which we would use the word today. It could mean "to fix or set a certain time" ("*The tyme he wild* [would] *not rape*") or "to carry off somebody to heaven from earth" ("*the visions of seynt poul wan* [when] *he was rapt in to paradys*"). The past participle *rapt* has survived in Modern English, where it has become a separate word referring to states of deep delight or absorption, far removed from the hideous cruelties of *rape.* The sense involving these cruelties was probably present in Middle English and has largely taken over the word.

rappel

rape² (rāp) *n.* A European plant *(Brassica napus)* of the mustard family, cultivated as fodder and for its seed that yields a valuable oil. Also called *colza, oil-seed rape.* [Middle English, from Old French, from Latin *rāpa,* turnip.]

rape³ (rāp) *n.* The refuse of grapes left after the extraction of the juice in winemaking. [French *râpe,* grape stalk, from Old French, from *rasper,* to scrape. See RASP.]

rape oil *n.* The edible oil extracted from rapeseed, also used as a lubricant and in the manufacture of various products. Also called *rapeseed oil.*

rape·seed (rāp′sēd′) *n.* The seed of the rape plant.

rapeseed oil *n.* See **rape oil.**

rape shield law *n.* A law that prohibits the defense in a rape case from cross-examination regarding the plaintiff's prior sexual conduct.

ra·phae (rā′fē′) *n.* Plural of **raphe.**

Raph·a·el¹ (răf′ē-əl, rā′fē-, rä′fē-ĕl′) *n.* One of the archangels of Hebrew tradition.

Raph·a·el² (răf′ē-əl, rā′fē-, rä′fē-ĕl′). 1483–1520. Italian painter whose works, including religious subjects, portraits, and frescoes, exemplify the ideals of the High Renaissance.

ra·phe also **rha·phe** (rā′fē) *n., pl.* **-phae** (-fē′). **1.** *Anatomy.* A seamlike line or ridge between two similar parts of a body organ, as in the scrotum. **2.** *Botany.* The portion of the funiculus that is united to the ovule wall, commonly visible as a line or ridge on the seed coat. **3.** The median groove of a diatom valve. [New Latin, from Greek *rhaphē,* seam, suture, from *rhaptein,* to sew. See **wer-²** in Appendix.]

raph·i·a (răf′ē-ə) *n.* Variant of **raffia.**

ra·phide (rā′fīd) also **ra·phis** (-fĭs) *n., pl.* **raph·i·des** (răf′ĭ-dēz′). *Botany.* One of a bundle of needlelike crystals of calcium oxalate occurring in many plant cells. [French, sing. of *raphides,* from New Latin, from Greek *rhaphides,* pl. of *rhaphis,* needle, from *rhaptein,* to sew. See **wer-²** in Appendix.]

rap·id (răp′ĭd) *adj.* **-er, -est.** Moving, acting, or occurring with great speed; swift. See Synonyms at **fast¹. —rapid** *n.* An extremely fast-moving part of a river, caused by a steep descent in the riverbed. Often used in the plural. [Latin *rapidus,* from *rapere,* to seize. See **rep-** in Appendix.] **—ra·pid′i·ty** (rə-pĭd′ĭ-tē), **rap′id·ness** (răp′ĭd-nĕs) *n.* **—rap′id·ly** *adv.*

Rap·id City (răp′ĭd). A city of southwest South Dakota west-southwest of Pierre in the eastern part of the Black Hills. It is a trade, transportation, and tourist center. Population, 46,492.

rapid eye movement *n.* REM.

rap·id-fire (răp′ĭd-fīr′) *adj.* **1.** Designed to fire shots in rapid succession: *a rapid-fire machine gun.* **2.** Marked by continuous, rapid occurrence: *rapid-fire questions.*

rapid transit *n.* An urban passenger transportation system using elevated or underground trains or a combination of both.

ra·pi·er (rā′pē-ər, rāp′yər) *n.* **1.** A long, slender, two-edged sword with a cuplike hilt, used in the 16th and 17th centuries. **2.** A light, sharp-pointed sword lacking a cutting edge and used only for thrusting. [French *rapière,* from Old French *(espee) rapiere,* rapier (sword).]

rap·ine (răp′ĭn) *n.* Forcible seizure of another's property; plunder. [Middle English, from Old French, from Latin *rapīna,* from *rapere,* to seize. See **rep-** in Appendix.]

rap·ist (rā′pĭst) *n.* One who commits the crime of rape.

Rapp (răp, räp), **George.** 1757–1847. German-born American religious leader who founded utopian communities in Pennsylvania and Indiana.

Rap·pa·han·nock (răp′ə-hăn′ək). A river of northeast Virginia rising in the Blue Ridge and flowing about 341 km (212 mi) generally southeast to form a long estuary that empties into Chesapeake Bay.

rap·pa·ree (răp′ə-rē′) *n.* **1.** A freebooting soldier of 17th-century Ireland. **2.** A bandit or robber. [Irish Gaelic *rapaire,* variant of *ropaire,* cutpurse, from *ropaid,* he stabs.]

rap·pee (ră-pē′) *n.* A strong snuff made from a dark, coarse tobacco. [From French *(tabac) râpé,* grated (tobacco), past participle of *râper,* to grate, from Old French *rasper,* to scrape. See RASP.]

rap·pel (ră-pĕl′) *n.* The act or method of descending from a mountainside or cliff by means of a belayed rope that is passed under one thigh and over the opposite shoulder so that it can be payed out smoothly and gradually. **—rappel** *intr.v.* **-pelled, -pel·ling, -pels.** To descend from a steep height by this method. [French, recall, return, rappel, from Old French, recall, from *rapeler,* to recall : *re-,* re- + *apeler,* to summon; see APPEAL.]

rap·pen (rä′pən) *n., pl.* **rappen.** A Swiss centime. [German, from *Rappe,* raven (in joking reference to the eagle on the original coin), from Middle High German, alteration of *raben,* from Old High German *hraban.*]

rap·per¹ (răp′ər) *n.* One that raps or strikes, especially a door knocker.

rap·per² (răp′ər) *n. Music.* One who performs rap.

rap·port (ră-pôr′, -pōr′, rə-) *n.* Relationship, especially one of mutual trust or emotional affinity. [French, from Old French, from *raporter,* to bring back : *re-,* re- + *aporter,* to bring (from Latin *apportāre* : *ad-,* ad- + *portāre,* to carry; see **per-²** in Appendix).]

rap·por·teur (răp′ôr-tûr′, -tœr′) *n.* One who is designated to give a report, as at a meeting. [Middle English *raportour,* judge, from Old French *raporteur,* from *raporter,* to bring back. See RAPPORT.]

rap·proche·ment (rä′prôsh-mäɴ′) *n.* **1.** A reestablishing of cordial relations, as between two countries. **2.** The state of reconciliation or of cordial relations. [French, from *rapprocher,* to bring together : *re-,* re- + *approcher,* to approach (from Old French *aprochier;* see APPROACH).]

rap·scal·lion (răp-skăl′yən) *n.* A rascal; a scamp. [Alteration of obsolete *rascallion,* from RASCAL.]

rap session *n. Slang.* An informal discussion held especially by a group of people with similar concerns.

rap sheet *n. Slang.* A police arrest record.

rapt (răpt) *v.* Past participle of **rap²** (sense 1). —**rapt** *adj.* **1.** Deeply moved or delighted; enraptured: *listened to the speaker with rapt admiration.* **2.** Deeply absorbed; engrossed: *was rapt in thought all evening.* [Middle English, carried away, from Latin *raptus,* past participle of *rapere,* to seize. See **rep-** in Appendix.] —**rapt·ly** *adv.*

rap·tor (răp′tər) *n.* A bird of prey. [Latin, one who seizes, from *rapere,* to seize. See RAPT.]

rap·to·ri·al (răp-tôr′ē-əl, -tōr′-) *adj.* **1.** Subsisting by seizing prey; predatory. **2.** Adapted for the seizing of prey. **3.** Of, relating to, or characteristic of birds of prey.

rap·ture (răp′chər) *n.* **1.** The state of being transported by a lofty emotion; ecstasy. **2.** Often **raptures.** An expression of ecstatic feeling. See Synonyms at **ecstasy.** **3.** The transporting of a person from one place to another, especially to heaven. —**rapture** *tr.v.* **-tured, -tur·ing, -tures.** To enrapture. [Obsolete French *rapture,* abduction, carrying off, from *rapt,* carried away, from Old French *rat,* from Latin *raptus.* See RAPT.]

rap·tur·ous (răp′chər-əs) *adj.* Filled with great joy or rapture; ecstatic. —**rap′tur·ous·ly** *adv.* —**rap′tur·ous·ness** *n.*

ra·ra a·vis (râr′ə ā′vĭs) *n., pl.* **ra·ra a·vis·es** or **ra·rae a·ves** (râr′ē ā′vēz). A rare or unique person or thing. [Latin *rāra avis* : *rāra,* feminine of *rārus,* rare + *avis,* bird.]

rare¹ (râr) *adj.* **rar·er, rar·est.** *Abbr.* **r.** **1.** Infrequently occurring; uncommon: *a rare event; a plant that is rare in this region.* **2.** Excellent; extraordinary: *a rare sense of honor; a rare friend.* **3.** Thin in density: rarefied: *rare air.* [Middle English, from Old French, from Latin *rārus.*] —**rare′ness** *n.*

rare² (râr) *adj.* **rar·er, rar·est.** Cooked a short time to retain juice and redness: *a rare steak.* [Middle English *rere,* lightly boiled, from Old English *hrēr.* See **kere-** in Appendix.] —**rare′ness** *n.*

rare·bit (râr′bĭt) *n.* Welsh rabbit. [Probably alteration of (WELSH) RABBIT.]

rare earth *n.* **1.** Any of various oxides of the rare-earth elements. **2.** A rare-earth element.

rare-earth element (râr′ûrth′) *n.* Any of the abundant metallic elements of atomic number 57 through 71. Also called *lanthanide.* [So called because they were originally thought to be rare.]

rar·ee show (râr′ē) *n.* **1.** See **peepshow** (sense 1). **2.** A street show. [Alteration of RARE¹ + SHOW.]

rar·e·fac·tion (râr′ə-făk′shən) *n.* **1.** A decrease in density and pressure in a medium, such as air, caused by the passage of a sound wave. **2.** The region in which this occurs. —**rar′e·fac′tive** *adj.*

rar·e·fied also **rar·i·fied** (râr′ə-fīd′) *adj.* **1.** Belonging to or reserved for a small, select group; esoteric. **2.** Elevated in character or style; lofty.

rar·e·fy also **rar·i·fy** (râr′ə-fī′) —*v.* **-fied, -fy·ing, -fies.** —*tr.* **1.** To make thin, less compact, or less dense. **2.** To purify or refine. —*intr.* To become thin or less compact or dense. [Middle English *rarefien,* from Old French *rarefier,* from Medieval Latin *rārificāre,* alteration of Latin *rārēfacere* : *rārus,* rare + *facere,* to make; see **dhē-** in Appendix.] —**rar′e·fi′a·ble** *adj.*

rare·ly (râr′lē) *adv.* **1.** Not often; infrequently: *"The truth is rarely pure and never simple"* (Oscar Wilde). **2.** In an unusual degree; exceptionally. **3.** With uncommon excellence.

USAGE NOTE: Strictly speaking, the use of *ever* after *rarely* and *seldom* is redundant; *She rarely ever watches television* adds nothing to *She rarely watches television.* In an earlier survey a large majority of the Usage Panel found this construction unacceptable in formal writing. But *ever* has been used as an intensive with *rarely* for several hundred years, and the construction is common in informal contexts. By contrast, the constructions *rarely (or seldom) if ever* and *rarely (or seldom) or never* are unexceptionable, as in: *She rarely if ever watches television. She rarely or never watches television.* See Usage Notes at **hardly, redundancy.**

rare·ripe (râr′rīp′) *adj.* Ripening early. —**rareripe** *n.* A fruit or vegetable that ripens early. [Dialectal *rare,* early (variant of RATHE) + RIPE.]

rar·i·fied (râr′ə-fīd′) *adj.* Variant of **rarefied.**

rar·i·fy (râr′ə-fī′) *v.* Variant of **rarefy.**

rar·ing (râr′ĭng) also **rar·in′** (-ĭn) *adj. Informal.* Full of eagerness; enthusiastic. [Present participle of dialectal *rare,* to rear, variant of REAR².]

Rar·i·tan (răr′ĭ-tən). A river, about 129 km (80 mi) long, formed by the confluence of two tributaries in north-central New Jersey and flowing eastward to **Raritan Bay,** the western arm of Lower New York Bay, at Perth Amboy.

rar·i·ty (râr′ĭ-tē) *n., pl.* **-ties.** **1.** Something rare. **2.** The quality or state of being rare; infrequency of occurrence.

Rar·o·ton·ga (răr′ə-tŏng′gə). A volcanic island of the southern Pacific Ocean in the southwest Cook Islands. Discovered in the early 1820's by English missionaries, it is the largest and most important island in the group.

ras·bo·ra (răz-bôr′ə, -bōr′ə) *n.* Any of various tropical fishes of the genus *Rasbora,* of which several brightly colored species are kept in home aquariums. [New Latin *Rasbora,* genus name, from a native word in the East Indies.]

rasp
Half-rounded wood rasp

ras·cal (răs′kəl) *n.* **1.** One that is playfully mischievous. **2.** An unscrupulous, dishonest person; a scoundrel. —**rascal** *adj. Archaic.* Made up of, belonging to, or relating to the common people: *"Nor shall the Rascal Rabble here have Peace"* (John Dryden). [Middle English *rascaile,* rabble, commoners, from Old French *rascaille,* probably from *rasque,* mud, from Vulgar Latin **rāsicāre,* to scrape. See RASH².] —**ras′cal·ly** *adj.*

ras·cal·i·ty (răs-kăl′ĭ-tē) *n., pl.* **-ties.** **1.** Behavior or character typical of a rascal. **2.** A base or mischievous act.

Ras Da·shan (räs də-shän′). A mountain, 4,623.2 m (15,158 ft) high, in northern Ethiopia. Of volcanic origin, it is the highest peak in the country.

rase¹ (rāz) *tr.v.* **rased, ras·ing, ras·es.** To erase. [Middle English *rasen,* to scrape off, erase. See RAZE.]

rase² (rāz) *v.* Variant of **raze.**

rash¹ (răsh) *adj.* **rash·er, rash·est.** **1.** Characterized by or resulting from ill-considered haste or boldness. See Synonyms at **reckless.** **2.** *Archaic.* Quick in producing a strong or marked effect. [Middle English *rasche,* active, perhaps from Old English *-raesc* (in *līgræsc,* lightning) or from Middle Dutch or Middle Low German *rasch.*] —**rash′ly** *adv.* —**rash′ness** *n.*

rash² (răsh) *n.* **1.** A skin eruption. **2.** An outbreak of many instances within a brief period: *a rash of burglaries.* [Possibly from obsolete French *rache,* a sore, from Old French *rasche,* scurf, from *raschier,* to scrape, scratch, from Vulgar Latin **rāsicāre,* from Latin *rāsus,* past participle of *rādere.* See **rēd-** in Appendix.]

rash·er (răsh′ər) *n.* **1.** A thin slice of fried or broiled bacon. **2.** A dish or an order of thin slices of fried or broiled bacon. [Origin unknown.]

Rasht (räsht) also **Resht** (rĕsht). A city of northwest Iran near the Caspian Sea east-southeast of Tabriz. It is a trade and silk-producing center. Population, 260,000.

Rask (răsk, räsk), **Rasmus Christian.** 1787–1832. Danish philologist who was a founder of comparative linguistics.

Ras·mus·sen (răs′mə-sən, räs′mo͞os-ən), **Knud Johan Victor.** 1879–1933. Danish ethnologist and Arctic explorer who conducted extensive research on Eskimo culture and heritage.

ra·so·ri·al (rə-zôr′ē-əl, -zōr′-, -sôr′-, -sōr′-) *adj.* Characteristically scratching the ground for food. Used of chickens and similar birds. [From Late Latin *rāsōr,* scraper, from Latin *rāsus,* past participle of *rādere,* to scrape. See **rēd-** in Appendix.]

rasp (răsp) *v.* **rasped, rasp·ing, rasps.** —*tr.* **1.** To file or scrape with a coarse file having sharp projections. **2.** To utter in a grating voice. **3.** To grate on (nerves or feelings). —*intr.* **1.** To scrape harshly; grate. **2.** To make a harsh, grating sound. —**rasp** *n.* **1.** A coarse file with sharp, raised, pointed projections. **2.** The act of filing with a rasp. **3.** A harsh, grating sound. [Middle English *raspen,* from Middle Dutch *raspen* and Old French *rasper,* of Germanic origin.] —**rasp′er** *n.* —**rasp′ing·ly** *adv.*

Rasputin

rasp·ber·ry (răz′bĕr′ē) *n.* **1.** Any of various shrubby, usually prickly plants of the genus *Rubus* in the rose family, such as *R. idaeus* var. *strigosus* of eastern North America and *R. idaeus* of Europe, that bear edible fruit. **2.** The aggregate fruit of any of these plants, consisting of many small, fleshy, usually red drupelets. **3.** *Color.* A moderate to dark or deep purplish red. **4.** *Slang.* A derisive or contemptuous sound made by vibrating the extended tongue and the lips while exhaling. [Obsolete *raspis,* raspberry + BERRY. Sense 4, possibly short for *raspberry tart,* rhyming slang for FART.]

Ras·pu·tin (răs-pyo͞o′tĭn, rə-spo͞o′tyĭn), **Grigori Efimovich.** 1872?–1916. Russian starets whose magnetic personality and relative success in the treatment of the czarevich's hemophilia gained him favor in the court of Nicholas II. He was assassinated by noblemen who feared that his licentious manner and ignorance would undermine the monarchy.

rasp·y (răs′pē) *adj.* **-i·er, -i·est.** Rough; grating.

Ras·ta (rä′stə, răs′tə) *n.* **1.** A Rastafarian. **2.** Rastafarianism. —**Rasta** *adj.* Rastafarian.

Ras·ta·far·i·an (räs′tə-fär′ē-ən, răs′tə-făr′-) *n.* An adherent of Rastafarianism. —**Rastafarian** *adj.* Of or relating to Rastafarianism or its adherents.

Ras·ta·fa·ri·an·ism (rä′stə-fär′ē-ə-nĭz′əm, răs′tə-fâr′-) *n.* A religious sect originating in Jamaica whose members worship Haile Selassie as savior and regard Africa, especially Ethiopia, as the Promised Land. [After *Ras Tafari,* former name of Haile Selassie : Amharic *ras,* head, prince + Amharic *tafari,* to be feared.]

ă pat	oi boy
ā pay	ou out
âr care	o͝o took
ä father	o͞o boot
ĕ pet	ŭ cut
ē be	ûr urge
ĭ pit	th thin
ī pie	*th* this
îr pier	hw which
ŏ pot	zh vision
ō toe	ə about, item
ô paw	♦ regionalism

Stress marks: ′ (primary); ′ (secondary), as in **dictionary** (dĭk′shə-nĕr′ē)

rat (răt) *n.* **1.a.** Any of various long-tailed rodents resembling mice but larger, especially one of the genus *Rattus.* **b.** Any of various animals similar to one of these long-tailed rodents. **2.** *Informal.* A despicable, sneaky person, especially one who betrays or informs upon associates. **3.** A pad of material, typically hair, worn as part of a woman's coiffure to puff out her own hair. **—rat** *intr.v.* **rat·ted, rat·ting, rats. 1.** To hunt for or catch rats, especially with the aid of dogs. **2.** *Slang.* To desert or betray one's comrades by giving information: *ratted on his best friend to the police.* [Middle English, from Old English *ræt.*]

rat·a·ble (rā′tə-bəl) *adj.* **1.** That can be rated, estimated, or appraised: *ratable income.* **2.** Proportional. **3.** *Chiefly British.* Liable to assessment; taxable. **—rat′a·bil′i·ty, rat′a·ble·ness** *n.* **—rat′a·bly** *adv.*

rat·a·bles (rā′tə-bəlz) *pl.n.* **1.** Income from property taxes: *netted the city over $30 million in new ratables.* **2.** Properties or buildings, especially those used for commercial purposes, that provide tax income for local government: *constructed a total of $10 million in new ratables.*

rat·a·fi·a (răt′ə-fē′ə) also **rat·a·fee** (-ə-fē′) *n.* **1.** A sweet cordial flavored with fruit kernels or almonds. **2.** A biscuit flavored with ratafia. [French, perhaps of West Indian Creole origin.]

Ra·tak Chain (rä′täk′). The eastern group of the Marshall Islands in the western Pacific Ocean. The chain comprises 2 coral islands and 14 atolls, including Bikini.

rat·a·plan (răt′ə-plăn′) *n.* A tattoo, as of a drum, the hoofs of a galloping horse, or machine-gun fire. [French, of imitative origin.]

rat-a-tat-tat (răt′ə-tăt′tăt′) *n.* A series of short, sharp sounds, as that made by knocking on a door. [Imitative.]

ra·ta·tou·ille (răt′ə-to͞o′ē, rä′tä-) *n.* A vegetable stew, usually made with eggplant, tomatoes, zucchini, peppers, and onions, seasoned with herbs and garlic, and served hot or cold. [French, from alteration of *toillier, touiller,* to stir, mix. See TOIL[1].]

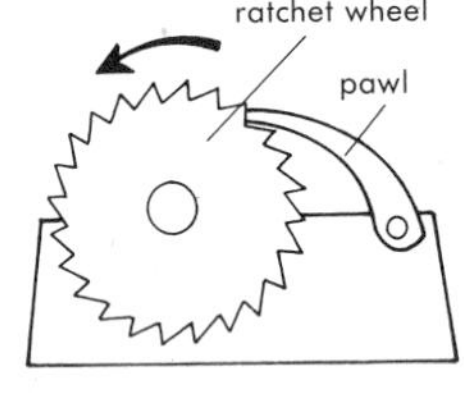

ratchet

rat-bite fever (răt′bīt′) *n.* Either of two infectious diseases contractible from the bite of a rat, specifically: **a.** A disease caused by the bacterium *Streptobacillus moniliformis* and characterized by skin inflammation, back and joint pains, headache, and vomiting. **b.** A disease caused by the bacterium *Spirillum minus* and characterized by ulceration at the site of the bite, a purplish rash, and recurrent fever.

rat cheese *n.* Cheddar.

ratch·et (răch′ĭt) *n.* **1.** A mechanism consisting of a pawl that engages the sloping teeth of a wheel or bar, permitting motion in one direction only. **2.** The pawl, wheel, or bar of this mechanism. **—ratchet** *tr.v.* **-et·ed, -et·ing, -ets.** To increase or decrease by increments. Often used with *up, upward, down,* or *downward*: *"Some companies . . . may make things worse if they seek to ratchet down their medical expenses by limiting benefits for psychological or psychiatric care"* (Newsweek). [French *rochet,* from Old French *rocquet,* head of a lance (from the shape of the teeth), of Germanic origin.]

rate[1] (rāt) *n.* **1.** A quantity measured with respect to another measured quantity: *a rate of speed of 60 miles an hour.* **2.** A measure of a part with respect to a whole; a proportion: *the mortality rate; a tax rate.* **3.** The cost per unit of a commodity or service: *postal rates.* **4.** A charge or payment calculated in relation to a particular sum or quantity: *interest rates.* **5.** Level of quality. **6.** Often **rates.** *Chiefly British.* A locally assessed property tax. **—rate** *v.* **rat·ed, rat·ing, rates.** *—tr.* **1.** To calculate the value of; appraise. See Synonyms at **estimate. 2.** To place in a particular rank or grade. **3.** To regard or account: *rated the movie excellent.* **4.** To value for purposes of taxation. **5.** To set a rate for (goods to be shipped). **6.** To specify the performance limits of (a machine, for example): *This fuse is rated at 50 amperes.* **7.** *Informal.* To merit or deserve: *people that rate special treatment.* See Synonyms at **earn[1].** *—intr.* **1.** To be ranked in a particular class. **2.** *Informal.* To have status, importance, or influence. ***—idiom.* at any rate. 1.** Whatever the case may be. **2.** At least. [Middle English, from Old French, from Medieval Latin *rata,* proportion, short for Latin *(prō) ratā (parte),* (according to a) fixed (part), from feminine ablative past participle of *rērī,* to consider, reckon. See **ar-** in Appendix.]

rate[2] (rāt) *v.* **rat·ed, rat·ing, rates.** *—tr.* To berate. *—intr.* To express reproof. [Middle English *raten,* perhaps of Scandinavian origin.]

ratel
Mellivora capensis

ra·tel (rāt′l, rät′l) *n.* A carnivorous mammal *(Mellivora capensis)* of Africa and Asia, having short legs and a thick coat that is dark below and whitish above. Also called *honey badger.* [Afrikaans, from Middle Dutch, rattle, honeycomb (either from its cry or its taste for honey).]

rate·mak·ing (rāt′mā′kĭng) *n.* The practice of establishing rates of payment, as for public transportation or utilities. **—rate′mak′ing** *adj.*

rate of exchange *n., pl.* **rates of exchange.** The ratio at which the unit of currency of one country is or may be exchanged for the unit of currency of another country.

rate·pay·er (rāt′pā′ər) *n.* One that pays rates: *utility ratepayers.*

rat·er (rā′tər) *n.* **1.** One that rates, especially one that establishes a rating. **2.** One having an indicated rank or rating. Often used in combination: *a third-rater; a first-rater.*

rat·fink (răt′fĭngk′) *n. Slang.* A person regarded as contemptible, obnoxious, or otherwise undesirable.

rat·fish (răt′fĭsh′) *n., pl.* **ratfish** or **-fish·es.** A fish *(Hydrolagus collei)* of Pacific waters, having a long narrow tail.

rathe (rāth, răth) *adj. Archaic.* Appearing or ripening early in the year, as flowers or fruit. [Middle English, quick, from Old English *hræd, hræth.*]

rath·er (răth′ər, rä′thər) *adv.* **1.** More readily; preferably: *I'd rather go to the movies.* **2.** With more reason, logic, wisdom, or other justification. **3.** More exactly; more accurately: *He's my friend, or rather he was my friend.* **4.** To a certain extent; somewhat: *rather cold.* **5.** On the contrary. **6.** (răth′ûr′, rä′-). *Chiefly British.* Most certainly. Used as an emphatic affirmative reply. [Middle English, from Old English *hrathor,* comparative of *hræthe,* quickly, soon, from *hræth,* quick.]

USAGE NOTE: In expressions of preference *rather* is commonly preceded by *would* or in formal style *should*: *We would rather rent the house than buy it outright. I should rather my daughter attended a public school.* The use of *had* in these constructions may now be more infrequent than it once was but is still encountered in reputable writing: *I had rather be dead than be a slave.* This use of *had* was once widely criticized as a mistake, the result of a misanalysis of the contraction in sentences such as *I'd rather stay.* But it is in fact a survival of the subjunctive form *had* that appears in constructions like *had better* and *had best,* as in *We had better leave her alone.* (Notice that in these constructions *would* and *should* cannot be used.) This use of *had* shows an unbroken line of usage running back to Middle English, and traditional criticisms of these constructions are unfounded. • Before an unmodified noun only *rather a* is used: *It was rather a disaster.* When the noun is preceded by an adjective, however, both *rather a* and *a rather* are found: *It was rather a boring party. It was a rather boring party.* When *a rather* is used in this construction, *rather* can be construed as qualifying only the adjective, whereas with *rather a* it can be construed as qualifying either the adjective or the entire noun phrase. Thus *a rather long ordeal* can mean only "an ordeal that is rather long," whereas *rather a long ordeal* can also mean roughly "a long process that is something of an ordeal." *Rather a* is the only possible choice when the adjective itself does not permit modification: *The horse was rather a long shot* (not *The horse was a rather long shot*). See Usage Notes at **better[1], should.**

raths·kel·ler (rät′skĕl′ər, răt′-, răth′-) *n.* A restaurant or tavern, usually below street level, that features the serving of beer. [Obsolete German, restaurant in the city hall basement : German *Rat,* council, counsel (from Middle High German *rāt,* from Old High German *rāt*; see **ar-** in Appendix) + German *Keller,* cellar (from Middle High German, from Old High German *kellāri,* from Latin *cellārium;* see CELLAR).]

rat·i·fi·ca·tion (răt′ə-fĭ-kā′shən) *n.* The act of ratifying or the condition of being ratified.

rat·i·fy (răt′ə-fī′) *tr.v.* **-fied, -fy·ing, -fies.** To approve and give formal sanction to; confirm. See Synonyms at **approve.** [Middle English *ratifien,* from Old French *ratifier,* from Medieval Latin *ratificāre* : Latin *ratus,* fixed, past participle of *rērī,* to reckon, consider; see RATE[1] + Latin *-ficāre,* -fy.] **—rat′i·fi′er** *n.*

rat·i·né (răt′ə-nā′) *n.* A loosely woven fabric with a rough, nubby texture. [French, past participle of *ratiner,* to adorn, from *ratine,* ratteen. See RATTEEN.]

rat·ing[1] (rā′tĭng) *n.* **1.** A position assigned on a scale; a standing. **2.a.** A classification according to specialty or proficiency, as of a member of the armed forces. **b.** *Chiefly British.* An enlisted person in the navy. **3.** An evaluation of the financial status of a business or person: *a credit rating.* **4.** A specified performance limit, as of capacity, range, or operational capability: *the power rating of a light fixture.* **5.** The popularity of a television or radio program as estimated by a poll of segments of the audience.

rat·ing[2] (rā′tĭng) *n.* A harsh scolding.

Ra·ting·en (rä′tĭng-ən). A city of west-central Germany north of Düsseldorf. Chartered in 1276, it is a manufacturing center. Population, 87,710.

ra·tio (rā′shō, rā′shē-ō′) *n., pl.* **-tios. 1.** Relation in degree or number between two similar things. **2.** The relative value of silver and gold in a currency system that is bimetallic. **3.** *Mathematics.* The relation between two quantities expressed as the quotient of one divided by the other: *The ratio of 7 to 4 is written 7:4 or 7/4.* [Latin *ratiō,* calculation, from *ratus,* past participle of *rērī,* to reckon, consider. See **ar-** in Appendix.]

ra·ti·oc·i·nate (răsh′ē-ŏs′ə-nāt′) *intr.v.* **-nat·ed, -nat·ing, -nates.** To reason methodically and logically. [Latin *ratiōcinārī, ratiōcināt-,* from *ratiō,* calculation. See RATIO.] **—ra′ti·oc′i·na′tion** *n.* **—ra′ti·oc′i·na′tor** *n.*

ra·ti·oc·i·na·tive (răsh′ē-ŏs′ə-nā′tĭv) *adj.* Of, relating to, marked by, or skilled in methodical and logical reasoning. See Synonyms at **logical.**

ra·tion (răsh′ən, rā′shən) *n.* **1.** A fixed portion, especially an amount of food allotted to persons in military service or to civilians in times of scarcity. **2. rations.** Food issued or available to members of a group. **—ration** *tr.v.* **-tioned, -tion·ing, -tions. 1.** To supply with rations. **2.** To distribute as rations: *rationed out flour and sugar.* See Synonyms at **distribute. 3.** To restrict to limited allotments, as during wartime. [French, from Latin *ratiō, ratiōn-,* calculation. See RATIO.]

ra·tion·al (răsh′ə-nəl) *adj.* **1.** Having or exercising the ability to reason. **2.** Of sound mind; sane. **3.** Consistent with or based on reason; logical: *rational behavior.* See Synonyms at **logical. 4.** *Mathematics.* Capable of being expressed as a quotient of integers. [Middle English *racional,* from Old French *racionel,* from Latin *ratiōnālis,* from *ratiō, ratiōn-,* reason. See REASON.] **—ra′tion·al·ly** *adv.* **—ra′tion·al·ness** *n.*

ra·tion·ale (răsh′ə-năl′) *n.* **1.** Fundamental reasons; the basis. **2.** An exposition of principles or reasons. [Late Latin *ratiōnāle,* from neuter of Latin *ratiōnālis,* rational. See RATIONAL.]

rational function *n. Mathematics.* A function that can be expressed as a quotient of polynomials.

rational horizon *n. Astronomy.* See **celestial horizon.**

ra·tion·al·ism (răsh′ə-nə-lĭz′əm) *n.* **1.** Reliance on reason as the best guide for belief and action. **2.** *Philosophy.* The theory that the exercise of reason, rather than the acceptance of empiricism, authority, or spiritual revelation, provides the only valid basis for action or belief and that reason is the prime source of knowledge and of spiritual truth. **—ra′tion·al·ist** *n.* **—ra′tion·al·is′tic** *adj.* **—ra′tion·al·is′ti·cal·ly** *adv.*

ra·tion·al·i·ty (răsh′ə-năl′ĭ-tē) *n., pl.* **-ties. 1.** The quality or condition of being rational. **2.** A rational belief or practice.

ra·tion·al·i·za·tion (răsh′ə-nə-lĭ-zā′shən) *n.* **1.** The act, process, or practice of rationalizing. **2.** An instance of rationalizing.

ra·tion·al·ize (răsh′ə-nə-līz′) *v.* **-ized, -iz·ing, -iz·es.** *—tr.* **1.** To make rational. **2.** To interpret from a rational standpoint. **3.** To devise self-satisfying but incorrect reasons for (one's behavior). **4.** *Mathematics.* To remove radicals without changing the value of (an expression) or roots of (an equation). **5.** *Chiefly British.* To bring modern, efficient methods to (an industry, for example). *—intr.* **1.** To think in a rational or rationalistic way. **2.** To devise self-satisfying but incorrect reasons for one's behavior. **—ra′tion·al·iz′er** *n.*

rational number *n. Mathematics.* A number capable of being expressed as an integer or a quotient of integers, excluding zero as a denominator.

Rat Islands (răt). A group of islands in the western Aleutian Islands of southwest Alaska. Kiska and **Rat Island** are included in the group.

rat·ite (răt′īt′) *adj.* Relating to or being any of a group of flightless birds having a flat breastbone without the keellike prominence characteristic of most flying birds. **—ratite** *n.* A ratite bird, such as the ostrich or emu. [From Latin *ratītus,* marked with the figure of a raft, from *ratis,* raft.]

rat·line also **rat·lin** (răt′lĭn) *n. Nautical.* **1.** Any of the small ropes fastened horizontally to the shrouds of a ship and forming a ladder for going aloft. **2.** The material used for these ropes. [Middle English *rathelinge (line),* wattling, ratline (cord).]

ra·toon also **rat·toon** (ră-to͞on′) *—n.* A shoot sprouting from a plant base, as in the banana, pineapple, or sugar cane. *—v.* **-tooned, -toon·ing, -toons.** *—intr.* To produce or grow as a ratoon. *—tr.* To propagate (a crop) from ratoons. [Spanish *retoño,* sprout, from *retoñar,* to sprout : *re-,* again (from Latin; see RE–) + *otoñar,* to grow in autumn (from *otoño,* autumn, from Latin *autumnus;* see AUTUMN).]

rat pack *n. Slang.* A closely knit group of people sharing interests: *a rat pack of popular singers who were friendly with high government officials.*

rat race *n. Informal.* A difficult, tiring, often competitive activity or routine.

rats·bane (răts′bān′) *n.* **1.** Rat poison. **2.** Arsenic trioxide.

rat snake *n.* Any of several nonvenomous snakes of the genus *Elaphe* that eat rats and other rodents. Also called *chicken snake.*

rat's tail cactus (răts) *n.* Variant of **rattail cactus.**

rat-tail (răt′tāl′) *n.* See **grenadier** (sense 2). **—rat-tail** also **rat·tailed** (-tāld′) or **rat·tail** (răt′tāl′) *adj.* Shaped like or having a part shaped like a rat's tail: *a rat-tail file; a rattail comb.*

rattail cactus or **rat's tail cactus** (răts) *n.* A Mexican cactus *(Aporocactus flagelliformis)* having thin, creeping or hanging stems and brilliant crimson-pink flowers.

rat·tan (ră-tăn′, rə-) *n.* **1.** Any of various climbing palms of the genera *Calamus, Daemonorops,* or *Plectomia* of tropical Asia, having long, tough, slender stems. **2. a.** The stems of any of these palms, used to make wickerwork, canes, and furniture. **b.** Work made of the stems of these palms. **3.** A switch or cane made from these palms. [Malay *rōtan* (perhaps from *raut,* to pare or trim for use).]

rat·teen (ră-tēn′) *n. Archaic.* A thick, twilled woolen cloth. [French *ratine,* from Old French *rastin,* from **raster,* to scrape, ultimately from Latin *rādere.* See RASH[2].]

rat·ter (răt′ər) *n.* **1.** One that catches or kills rats: *Many terriers are good ratters.* **2.** *Slang.* One who betrays or deserts another.

Rat·ti·gan (răt′ĭ-gən), Sir **Terence Mervyn.** 1911–1977. British playwright whose works include *The Winslow Boy* (1946) and *Separate Tables* (1954).

rat·tle[1] (răt′l) *v.* **-tled, -tling, -tles.** *—intr.* **1. a.** To make or emit a quick succession of short percussive sounds. **b.** To move with such sounds: *A train rattled along the track.* **2.** To talk rapidly and at length, usually without much thought: *rattled on about this and that.* *—tr.* **1.** To cause to make a quick succession of short percussive sounds: *rattled the dishes in the kitchen.* **2.** To utter or perform rapidly or effortlessly: *rattled off a list of complaints.* **3.** *Informal.* To fluster; unnerve: *The accident rattled me.* See Synonyms at **embarrass. —rattle** *n.* **1.** A rapid succession of short percussive sounds. **2.** A device, such as a baby's toy, that produces short percussive sounds. **3.** A rattling sound in the throat caused by obstructed breathing, especially near the time of death. **4.** The series of horny structures at the end of a rattlesnake's tail. **5.** Loud or rapid talk; chatter. [Middle English *ratelen,* perhaps from Middle Dutch, probably of imitative origin.]

WORD HISTORY: A large proportion (86 percent) of the Usage Panel approved the use of the verb *rattle* in the sense "to unnerve" in the first edition of *The American Heritage Dictionary,* published in 1969. But we may ask how the verb *rattle* came to have such a sense. The earliest use of the word is found in a name, *Johannes Ratellebagg,* recorded in a document of around 1273; the earliest use of the word as a common noun (in the sense "to flap, used of a banner") is found in a work written about 1300 and copied in manuscript around 1330. It is thought that the word probably comes from Middle Dutch *ratelen,* which may be imitative in origin. In any case, the word *ratelen* was used mainly in intransitive senses such as "to make a rattling sound." Already in Middle English, however, the transitive sense "to babble something" existed, and other transitive senses, as in "to make something rattle," "to stir up, rouse," "to drive in a rapid, rattling manner," came into existence from the 16th century on. The transitive sense "to unnerve," that is, "to make somebody rattle," is first found in an American work of 1869.

rat·tle[2] (răt′l) *tr.v.* **-tled, -tling, -tles.** *Nautical.* To secure ratlines to (shrouds). [Back-formation from *rattling,* ratline, variant of RATLINE.]

rat·tle·box (răt′l-bŏks′) *n.* Any of various plants of the genus *Crotalaria,* having inflated pods containing seeds that rattle when the stem is moved.

rat·tle·brained (răt′l-brānd′) *adj.* Giddy and talkative; foolish. **—rat′tle·brain′** (-brān′) *n.*

rat·tler (răt′lər) *n.* **1.** One that rattles: *a rattler of pots and pans.* **2.** A rattlesnake. **3.** *Informal.* A freight train.

rat·tle·snake (răt′l-snāk′) *n.* Any of various venomous New World snakes of the genera *Crotalus* and *Sistrurus,* having at the end of the tail a series of loosely attached, horny segments that can be vibrated to produce a rattling or buzzing sound.

rattlesnake
Southwest speckled rattlesnake
Crotalus mitchellii pyrrhus

rattlesnake flag *n.* Any of several U.S. flags bearing the motto "Don't Tread on Me" and a picture of a rattlesnake, used during the French and Indian War and the Revolutionary War.

rattlesnake master *n.* Any of several plants, such as *Eryngium yuccifolium* of the eastern United States, supposedly effective against the venom of rattlesnakes and having narrow leaves with spiny margins and whitish flower heads. Also called *button snakeroot.*

rattlesnake plantain *n.* Any of various rhizomatous orchids of the genus *Goodyera,* having mottled or striped leaves and spikes of small whitish flowers. [From the resemblance of its leaves to a rattlesnake's skin.]

rattlesnake root *n.* Any of various plants of the genus *Prenanthes,* having bitter-tasting tuberous roots and white to purple ligulate flower heads. [From the belief that the root cured a rattlesnake's bite.]

rattlesnake weed *n.* A North American plant *(Hieracium venosum)* having basal leaves with reddish-purple veins and yellow flower heads borne in open corymbose panicles.

rat·tle·trap (răt′l-trăp′) *n.* A rickety, worn-out vehicle.

rat·tling (răt′lĭng) *adj. Informal.* Animated; brisk: *A rattling conversation about politics.* **—rattling** *adv.* Used as an intensive: *"the guiltless gust of a rattling good yarn"* (Anthony Burgess).

rat·tly (răt′l-ē) *adj.* Rattling or likely to rattle; clattering.

rat·toon (ră-to͞on′) *n. & v.* Variant of **ratoon.**

rat·trap (răt′trăp′) *n.* **1.** A device for trapping rats. **2.** *Informal.* A dilapidated or unsanitary dwelling.

rat·ty (răt′ē) *adj.* **-ti·er, -ti·est. 1.** Of or characteristic of rats. **2.** Infested with rats. **3.** Dilapidated; shabby.

rau·cous (rô′kəs) *adj.* **1.** Rough-sounding and harsh: *raucous laughter.* **2.** Boisterous and disorderly: *"the raucous give and take of American democracy"* (Charles Kuralt). [From Latin *raucus.*] **—rau′cous·ly** *adv.* **—rau′cous·ness, rau′ci·ty** (rô′sĭ-tē) *n.*

raunch (rônch, ränch) *n. Slang.* **1.** Lewdness; vulgarity; obscenity. **2.** Material or a performance that is sexually explicit or evocative: *"Audiences are still astonished when she goes for the raunch"* (Katrine Ames). [Back-formation from RAUNCHY.]

raun·chy (rôn′chē, rän′-) *adj.* **-chi·er, -chi·est.** *Slang.* **1. a.** Obscene, lewd, or vulgar: "[He] *uses language so aggressively raunchy that he seems to be insisting his choice of vocabulary, at least, is no sin"* (Wall Street Journal). **b.** Sexually explicit. **c.** Exhibiting lust. **2.** Grimy; unkempt. [Origin unknown.] **—raun′chi·ly** *adv.* **—raun′chi·ness** *n.*

Raur·ke·la or **Rour·ke·la** (rôr-kā′lə). A town of eastern India west of Calcutta. It has important iron and steel plants. Population, 206,821.

Rausch·en·berg (rou′shən-bûrg′), **Robert.** Born 1925.

ă pat	oi boy
ā pay	ou out
âr care	o͝o took
ä father	o͞o boot
ĕ pet	ŭ cut
ē be	ûr urge
ĭ pit	th thin
ī pie	*th* this
îr pier	hw which
ŏ pot	zh vision
ō toe	ə about, item
ô paw	♦ regionalism

Stress marks: ′ (primary); ′ (secondary), as in **dictionary** (dĭk′shə-nĕr′ē)

American artist noted for his collages, photomontages, and paintings that incorporate photographs and real objects.

Rau·schen·busch (rou′shən-bo͝osh′), **Walter.** 1861–1918. American religious leader who sought solutions to social and economics problems through the application of Christian and socialist ideals.

rau·wol·fi·a (rou-wo͝ol′fē-ə, rô-) *n.* Any of various tropical trees and shrubs of the genus *Rauvolfia,* especially *R. serpentina,* of southeast Asia, the root of which is the source of tranquilizing alkaloid drugs such as reserpine. [New Latin *Rauwolfia,* genus name, after Leonhard *Rauwolf* (died 1596), German botanist.]

rav·age (răv′ĭj) *v.* **-aged, -ag·ing, -ages.** —*tr.* **1.** To bring heavy destruction on; devastate: *A tornado ravaged the countryside.* **2.** To pillage; sack: *Enemy soldiers ravaged the village.* —*intr.* To wreak destruction. —**ravage** *n.* **1.** The act or practice of pillaging, destroying, or devastating. **2.** Grievous damage; havoc: *the ravages of disease.* [French *ravager,* from Old French, to uproot, from *ravir,* to ravish. See RAVISH.] —**rav′ag·er** *n.*

rave (rāv) *v.* **raved, rav·ing, raves.** —*intr.* **1.** To speak wildly, irrationally, or incoherently. **2.** To roar; rage: *The storm raved along the coast.* **3.** To speak with wild enthusiasm: *He raved about the new play.* —*tr.* To utter in a frenzied manner. —**rave** *n.* **1.** The act or an instance of raving. **2.** *Informal.* An extravagantly enthusiastic opinion or review: *The play received raves.* —**rave** *adj. Informal.* Relating to or being an extravagantly enthusiastic opinion or review. [Middle English *raven,* from Old North French *raver,* variant of *resver,* to dream, wander, rave.]

rav·el (răv′əl) *v.* **-eled, -el·ing, -els** also **-elled, -el·ling, -els.** —*tr.* **1.** To separate the fibers or threads of (cloth, for example); unravel. **2.** To clarify by separating the aspects of. **3.** To tangle or complicate. —*intr.* **1.** To become separated into its component threads; unravel or fray. **2.** To become tangled or confused. —**ravel** *n.* **1.** A raveling. **2.** A broken or discarded thread. **3.** A tangle. [Obsolete Dutch *ravelen,* from *ravel,* loose thread.] —**rav′el·er** *n.*

WORD HISTORY: To say that we will ravel the history of *ravel* is an ambiguous statement, given that history. *Ravel* comes from the obsolete Dutch verb *ravelen,* "to tangle, fray out, unweave," which comes in turn from the noun *ravel,* "a loose thread." We can see the ambiguity of *ravel* already in the notion of a loose thread, because threads can be loose when they are tangled or when they are untangling. The Dutch verb has both notions present in it, denoting both tangling and unweaving. In one of its earliest recorded uses in English (before 1585) the verb means "to become entangled or confused," and in 1598 we find a use in the sense "to entangle." But in 1611 the word is used with reference to a fabric in the sense "to fray out," and in 1607 in the sense "to unwind, unweave, or unravel." In 1582 we already have an author using the word in a figurative way to mean "to take to pieces or disentangle," while in a work written before 1656 we have a figurative instance of the sense "to entangle or confuse." Clearly there was a need for the word *unravel,* which is first found in 1603, but strangely enough it did not solve the problem, *ravel* retaining up to this day both "entangling" and "disentangling" senses.

ray[2]

Ra·vel (rə-vĕl′, rä-), **Maurice Joseph.** 1875–1937. French composer of impressionistic operas, ballets, orchestral works, such as *Boléro* (1928), and piano works, including *Le Tombeau de Couperin* (1917).

rav·el·ing also **rav·el·ling** (răv′ə-lĭng) *n.* A thread or fiber that has become separated from a woven material.

rav·el·ment (răv′əl-mənt) *n.* Confusion or complexity.

ra·ven¹ (rā′vən) *n.* A large bird *(Corvus corax)* having black plumage and a croaking cry. —**raven** *adj.* Black and shiny: *raven tresses.* [Middle English, from Old English *hræfn.*]

rav·en² (răv′ən) *v.* **-ened, -en·ing, -ens.** —*tr.* **1.** To consume greedily; devour. **2.** To seek or seize as prey or plunder. —*intr.* **1.** To seek or seize prey or plunder. **2.** To eat ravenously. —**raven** *n.* Variant of **ravin.** [From Middle English *ravin, raven,* rapine, plunder, prey. See RAVIN.] —**rav′en·er** *n.*

rav·en·ing (răv′ə-nĭng) *adj.* Greedily predacious; voracious or rapacious. —**ravening** *n.* The action of one that ravens. —**rav′en·ing·ly** *adv.*

Ra·ven·na (rə-vĕn′ə, rä-vĕn′nä). A city of northeast Italy near the Adriatic Sea northeast of Florence. An important naval station in Roman times, it was an Ostrogoth capital in the fifth and sixth centuries A.D. and the center of Byzantine power in Italy from the late sixth century until c. 750, when it was conquered by the Lombards. Ravenna eventually became part of the papal dominions and was included in the kingdom of Italy in 1860. Population, 101,000.

rav·en·ous (răv′ə-nəs) *adj.* **1.** Extremely hungry; voracious. **2.** Rapacious; predatory. **3.** Greedy for gratification: *ravenous for power.* See Synonyms at **voracious.** [Middle English, from Old French *ravineux,* from *raviner,* to take by force, from Vulgar Latin **rapīnāre,* from Latin *rapīna,* plunder. See RAPINE.] —**rav′en·ous·ly** *adv.* —**rav′en·ous·ness** *n.*

rave-up (rāv′ŭp′) *n.* **1.** *Music.* A wild or vigorous musical performance. **2.** *Chiefly British.* A raucous party or gathering.

Ra·vi (rä′vē). A river, about 764 km (475 mi) long, of northwest India and northeast Pakistan. Rising in the Himalaya Mountains, it is one of the five rivers of the Punjab.

ra·vi·gote also **ra·vi·gotte** (rä-vē-gôt′) *n.* A vinegar sauce seasoned with minced onion, capers, and herbs, used with boiled meats or fish. [French, from *ravigoter,* to add new vigor, alteration of obsolete *ravigorer,* from Old French : *re-,* re- + *a-,* to (from Latin *ad-;* see AD–) + *vigeur,* vigor; see VIGOR.]

rav·in also **rav·en** (răv′ən) *n.* **1.** Voracity; rapaciousness. **2.** Something taken as prey. **3.** The act or practice of preying. [Middle English *ravin, raven,* from Old French *ravine,* rapine, from Latin *rapīna,* from *rapere,* to seize. See **rep-** in Appendix.]

ra·vine (rə-vēn′) *n.* A deep, narrow valley or gorge in the earth's surface worn by running water. [French, from Old French, violent rush, from Latin *rapīna,* rapine. See RAVIN.]

rav·ing (rā′vĭng) *adj.* **1.** Talking or behaving irrationally; wild: *a raving maniac.* **2.** Exciting admiration: *a raving beauty.* —**raving** *n.* Delirious, irrational speech. —**rav′ing·ly** *adv.*

ra·vi·o·li (răv′ē-ō′lē, rä′vē-) *n., pl.* **ravioli** or **-lis.** **1.** A small casing of pasta with various fillings, such as chopped meat or cheese. **2.** A dish made with ravioli. [Italian, pl. of dialectal *raviolo.*]

rav·ish (răv′ĭsh) *tr.v.* **-ished, -ish·ing, -ish·es.** **1.** To seize and carry away by force. **2.** To rape; violate. **3.** To overwhelm with emotion; enrapture. See Synonyms at **enrapture.** [Middle English *ravisshen,* from Old French *ravir, raviss-,* from Vulgar Latin **rapīre,* from Latin *rapere,* to seize. See **rep-** in Appendix.] —**rav′ish·er** *n.*

rav·ish·ing (răv′ĭ-shĭng) *adj.* Extremely attractive; entrancing. —**rav′ish·ing·ly** *adv.*

rav·ish·ment (răv′ĭsh-mənt) *n.* **1.** The act of seizing by force. **2.** Sexual rape. **3.** Rapture; entrancement.

raw (rô) *adj.* **raw·er, raw·est.** **1.** Uncooked: *raw meat.* **2.a.** Being in a natural condition; not processed or refined: *raw wool.* See Synonyms at **crude. b.** Not finished, covered, or coated: *raw wood.* See Synonyms at **rude. c.** Not having been subjected to adjustment, treatment, or analysis: *raw data; the raw cost of production.* **3.** Untrained and inexperienced: *raw recruits.* **4.** Recently finished; fresh: *raw plaster.* **5.** Having subcutaneous tissue exposed: *a raw wound.* **6.** Inflamed; sore: *a raw throat.* **7.** Unpleasantly damp and chilly: *raw weather.* **8.** Cruel and unfair: *a raw punishment.* **9.** Outspoken; crude: *a raw portrayal of truth.* **10.** Powerfully impressive; stark: *raw beauty; raw talent.* **11.** Nude; naked. —***idiom.*** **in the raw. 1.** In a crude or unrefined state: *nature in the raw.* **2.** Nude; naked. [Middle English, from Old English *hrēaw.* See **kreuə-** in Appendix.] —**raw′ly** *adv.* —**raw′ness** *n.*

Ra·wal·pin·di (rä′wəl-pĭn′dē). A city of northeast Pakistan north-northwest of Lahore. Settled by Sikhs in 1765, it was interim capital of Pakistan from 1959 to 1970. Population, 452,000.

raw·boned (rô′bōnd′) *adj.* Having a lean, gaunt frame with prominent bones. See Synonyms at **lean².**

raw·hide (rô′hīd′) *n.* **1.** The untanned hide of cattle or other animals. **2.** A whip or rope made of rawhide. —**rawhide** *tr.v.* **-hid·ed, -hid·ing, -hides.** To beat with a rawhide whip.

ra·win·sonde (rā′wĭn-sŏnd′) *n.* A radiosonde used to observe the velocity and direction of upper-air winds and tracked by a radio direction-finding instrument or radar. [RA(DAR) + WIN(D)¹ + (RADIO)SONDE.]

Raw·lings (rô′lĭngz), **Marjorie Kinnan.** 1896–1953. American writer known for her novel *The Yearling* (1938).

Raw·lin·son (rô′lĭn-sən), Sir **Henry Creswicke.** 1810–1895. British diplomat and scholar who deciphered cuneiform texts from ancient Persia.

raw material *n.* **1.** An unprocessed natural product used in manufacture. **2.** Unprocessed material of any kind: *These data are the raw material for the analysis.*

raw sienna *n.* **1.** A brownish-yellow pigment. **2.** *Color.* A brownish orange to light brown.

raw silk *n.* **1.** Untreated silk as reeled from a cocoon. **2.** Fabric or yarn made from untreated silk.

ray¹ (rā) *n.* **1.a.** A thin line or narrow beam of light or other radiant energy. **b.** A graphic or other representation of such a line. **2.** Radiance; light. **3.** A small amount; a trace: *not a ray of hope left.* **4.** *Mathematics.* A straight line extending from a point. Also called *half-line.* **5.** A structure or part having the form of a straight line extending from a point. **6.** Any of the bright streaks that are seen radiating from some craters on the moon. **7.** *Botany.* **a.** A ray flower or the corolla of a ray flower. **b.** A branch of an umbel. **8.** *Zoology.* **a.** One of the bony spines supporting the membrane of a fish's fin. **b.** One of the arms of a starfish or other radiate animal. **9. rays.** *Slang.* Sunshine: *Let's go to the beach and catch some rays.* —**ray** *tr.v.* **rayed, ray·ing, rays.** **1.** To send out as rays; emit. **2.** To supply with rays or radiating lines. **3.** To cast rays on; irradiate. [Middle English, from Old French *rai,* from Latin *radius.*]

ray² (rā) *n.* Any of various marine fishes of the order Rajiformes or Batoidei, having cartilaginous skeletons, horizontally flattened bodies, and narrow tails. [Middle English *raye,* from Old French *raie,* from Latin *raia.*]

Ray (rā), **Cape.** A promontory of extreme southwest Newfoundland, Canada, on Cabot Strait.

Ray, John. 1627–1705. English naturalist who was the first to use anatomy to distinguish between specific plants and animals and established "species" as the basic classification of living things.

Ray, Man. 1890–1976. American artist. A founder of Dada in

New York, he is known for his photographs, paintings, sculpture, films, and later experiments with surrealism.

Ray (rī), **Satyajit.** 1921–1992. Bengali filmmaker whose works, especially the trilogy including *The World of Apu* (1958), offer a contemplative depiction of Bengali life.

Ray·burn (rā′bûrn′), **Samuel Taliaferro.** 1882–1961. American politician. A U.S. representative from Texas (1913–1961), he served as Speaker of the House (17 terms between 1940 and 1961) and was a major advocate of Franklin D. Roosevelt's New Deal.

ray flower *n.* A flower with a flat, strap-shaped corolla, found in members of the composite family, as the units of a flower head of the dandelion or the marginal units of a flower head of the daisy.

ray gun *n.* A gun that fires a ray of energy, especially one depicted as a destructive weapon in science fiction.

Ray·leigh (rā′lē), Third Baron. Title of John William Strutt. 1842–1919. British physicist. He won a 1904 Nobel Prize for investigating the density of gases and for discovering argon with Sir William Ramsay.

Rayleigh scattering *n.* The scattering of electromagnetic radiation by particles with dimensions much smaller than the wavelength of the radiation, resulting in angular separation of colors and responsible for the reddish color of sunset and the blue of the sky. [After Third Baron RAYLEIGH.]

ray·less (rā′lĭs) *adj.* **1.** Lacking rays: *a rayless flower.* **2.** Lacking light: *"Hid by a rayless night"* (Percy Bysshe Shelley).

Ray·mond (rā′mənd), **Henry Jarvis.** 1820–1869. American journalist and politician who founded the *New York Times* (1851).

Ray·naud's phenomenon (rā-nōz′) *n.* A circulatory disorder that affects the hands and feet, caused by insufficient blood supply to these parts and resulting in cyanosis, numbness, pain, and, in extreme cases, gangrene. [After Maurice *Raynaud* (1834–1881), French physician.]

ray·on (rā′ŏn) *n.* **1.** Any of several synthetic textile fibers produced by forcing a cellulose solution through fine spinnerets and solidifying the resulting filaments. **2.** A fabric so woven or knit. [Perhaps from French *rayon,* ray of light (from its sheen), from *rai,* from Old French. See RAY[1].]

Ray·on·ism (rā′ə-nĭz′əm) *n.* A style of abstract painting allied to futurism, developed about 1911, in which forms are depicted as emitting rays of light. [French *rayonisme,* from *rayon,* ray (translation of Russian *luchizm,* from *luch,* ray). See RAYON.] **—Ray′on·ist** *adj. & n.* **—Ray′on·is′tic** *adj.*

Ray·town (rā′toun′). A city of western Missouri, a residential suburb surrounded by Kansas City. Population, 31,759.

raze also **rase** (rāz) *tr.v.* **razed, raz·ing, raz·es** also **rased, ras·ing, ras·es. 1.** To level to the ground; demolish. See Synonyms at **ruin. 2.** To scrape or shave off. **3.** *Archaic.* To erase. [Middle English *rasen,* to scrape off, from Old French *raser,* from Vulgar Latin **rāsāre,* frequentative of Latin *rādere.* See RASH[2].]

ra·zor (rā′zər) *n.* **1.** A sharp-edged cutting instrument used especially for shaving the face or removing other body hair. **2.** A device for holding a razorblade, with guards to prevent cutting of the skin. Also called *safety razor.* **3.** An electric instrument with vibrating or rotating blades used for shaving. [Middle English *rasor,* from Old French, from *raser,* to scrape. See RAZE.]

ra·zor·back (rā′zər-băk′) *n.* **1.** A semiwild hog of the southeast United States, having a narrow body with a ridged back. **2.** See **rorqual. 3.** A sharp, ridged hill.

ra·zor·bill (rā′zər-bĭl′) *n.* A razor-billed auk.

ra·zor-billed auk (rā′zər-bĭld′) *n.* A sea bird *(Alca torda)* of the northern Atlantic, having black-and-white plumage and a white-ringed, flattened bill.

ra·zor·blade also **ra·zor blade** (rā′zər-blād′) *n.* A thin, sharp-edged piece of steel that can be fitted into a razor.

razor clam *n.* Any of various clams of the family Solenidae, characteristically having long narrow shells.

razor wire *n.* A sharp-edged wire used for fences and barriers.

razz (răz) *Slang. n.* A raspberry sound; a Bronx cheer. **—razz** *tr.v.* **razzed, razz·ing, razz·es.** To deride, heckle, or tease. See Synonyms at **banter.** [Shortening and alteration of RASPBERRY.]

raz·zle-daz·zle (răz′əl-dăz′əl) *n. Informal.* Dazzling excitement. [Reduplication of DAZZLE.]

razz·ma·tazz (răz′mə-tăz′) *n. Slang.* **1.** A flashy action or display intended to bewilder, confuse, or deceive. **2.** Ambiguous or evasive language; double talk. **3.** Ebullient energy; vim. [Perhaps alteration of RAZZLE-DAZZLE.]

Rb The symbol for the element **rubidium.**

RBC or **rbc** *abbr.* **1.** Red blood cell. **2.** Red blood cell count.

RBE or **rbe** *abbr.* Relative biological effectiveness.

RBI also **rbi** *abbr. Baseball.* Run batted in; runs batted in.

RC *abbr.* **1.** Red Cross. **2.** Roman Catholic.

RCAF also **R.C.A.F.** *abbr.* Royal Canadian Air Force.

R.C.Ch. *abbr.* Roman Catholic Church.

RCMP also **R.C.M.P.** *abbr.* Royal Canadian Mounted Police.

R.C.P. *abbr.* Royal College of Physicians.

rcpt. *abbr.* Receipt.

R.C.S. *abbr.* Royal College of Surgeons.

rct. *abbr.* Recruit.

rd *abbr.* **1.** Rod (unit of measure). **2.** Rutherford.

RD *abbr.* Rural delivery.

rd. *abbr.* **1.** Or **Rd.** Road. **2.** Round.

RDA *abbr.* Recommended daily allowance.

RDF *abbr.* Radio direction finder.

re[1] (rā) *n. Music.* The second tone of the diatonic scale in solfeggio. [Middle English, from Medieval Latin. See GAMUT.]

re[2] (rē) *prep.* In reference to; in the case of; concerning. [Latin *rē,* ablative of *rēs,* thing. See **rē-** in Appendix.]

Re[1] (rā) *n. Mythology.* Variant of **Ra[1].**

Re[2] The symbol for the element **rhenium.**

Re. *abbr.* Rupee.

R.E. or **RE** *abbr.* Real estate.

re– *pref.* **1.** Again; anew: *rebuild.* **2.** Backward; back: *react.* **3.** Used as an intensive: *refine.* [Middle English, from Old French, from Latin. See **re-** in Appendix.]

're Are: *They're not at home.*

re·ab·sorb (rē′əb-sôrb′, -zôrb′) *v.* **-sorbed, -sorb·ing, -sorbs.** *—tr.* **1.** To absorb again. **2.** To accommodate or accept again, as into a group or category. *—intr.* To undergo resorption. **—re′ab·sorp′tion** (-sôrp′shən, -zôrp′-) *n.*

re·ac·cred·i·ta·tion (rē′ə-krĕd′ĭ-tā′shən) *n.* **1.** The process of reviewing the accreditation of an institution. **2.** Renewal of accreditation status.

reach (rēch) *v.* **reached, reach·ing, reach·es.** *—tr.* **1.** To stretch out or put forth (a body part); extend: *reached out an arm.* **2.** To touch or grasp by stretching out or extending: *couldn't reach the shelf.* **3.** To arrive at; attain: *reached a conclusion; reached their destination.* **4.a.** To succeed in getting in contact with or communicating with: *They reached us by telephone. Our newsletter reaches a very specialized readership.* **b.** To succeed in having an effect on: *No one seems able to reach her anymore.* **5.a.** To extend as far as: *The property reaches the shore.* **b.** To project as far as: *A distant cry reached our ears.* **c.** To travel as far as: *a long fly ball that reached the wall of the stadium.* **6.** To aggregate or amount to: *Sales reached the thousands.* **7.** *Informal.* To grasp and hand over to another: *Reach me the sugar.* *—intr.* **1.** To thrust out or extend something. **2.** To try to grasp or touch something: *reached for a book.* **3.a.** To have extension in space or time: *a coat that reaches to the knee; shrubbery reaching up to the eaves; a career that reached over several decades.* **b.** To be extensive in influence or effect. **4.** To make an excessive effort, as in drawing a conclusion or making a joke; overreach. **5.** *Nautical.* To sail with the wind abeam. **—reach** *n.* **1.** The act or an instance of stretching or thrusting out. **2.** The extent or distance something can reach. **3.a.** Range of understanding; comprehension: *a subject beyond my reach.* **b.** Range or scope of influence or effect. **4.** An expanse: *a reach of prairie; the lower reaches of the food chain.* **5.** A pole connecting the rear axle of a vehicle with the front. **6.** *Nautical.* The tack of a sailing vessel with the wind abeam. **7.** The stretch of water visible between bends in a river or channel. [Middle English *rechen,* from Old English *rǣcan.* See **reig-** in Appendix.] **—reach′a·ble** *adj.* **—reach′er** *n.*

SYNONYMS: *reach, achieve, attain, gain, compass.* All of these verbs mean to succeed in arriving at a goal or an objective. *Reach,* the least specific, like the other terms connotes the expenditure of effort: *reached shelter before the storm broke; reach an understanding; reach perfection. Achieve* suggests in addition the application of skill or initiative: *achieved international recognition. Attain* often implies the impelling force of ambition, principle, or ideals: *trying to attain self-confidence. Gain* connotes considerable effort in surmounting obstacles: *gained the confidence of the workers. Compass* implies circumvention of impediments to success: *couldn't compass the assigned task.* See also Synonyms at **range.**

re·act (rē-ăkt′) *intr.v.* **-act·ed, -act·ing, -acts. 1.** To act in response to or under the influence of a stimulus or prompting: *reacted strongly to the sarcastic tone of the memorandum.* **2.** To act in opposition to a former condition or act: *composers who reacted against romanticism.* **3.** To act reciprocally or in return. **4.** *Chemistry.* To undergo a reaction: *Methane reacts with hydroxyl to produce formaldehyde.*

re·ac·tance (rē-ăk′təns) *n. Symbol* **X** *Electricity.* Opposition to the flow of alternating current caused by the inductance and capacitance in a circuit rather than by resistance.

re·ac·tant (rē-ăk′tənt) *n.* A substance participating in a chemical reaction, especially a directly reacting substance present at the initiation of the reaction.

re·ac·tion (rē-ăk′shən) *n.* **1.a.** A response to a stimulus. **b.** The state resulting from such a response. **2.** A reverse or opposing action. **3.a.** A tendency to revert to a former state. **b.** Opposition to progress or liberalism; extreme conservatism. **4.** *Chemistry.* A change or transformation in which a substance decomposes, combines with other substances, or interchanges constituents with other substances. **5.** *Physics.* A nuclear reaction. **6.** *Physics.* An equal and opposite force exerted by a body against a force acting upon it. **7.** The response of cells or tissues to an antigen, as in a test for immunization. **8.** *Psychology.* A pattern of behavior constituting a mental disorder or personality type.

re·ac·tion·ar·y (rē-ăk′shə-nĕr′ē) *adj.* Characterized by reaction, especially opposition to progress or liberalism; extremely conservative. **—reactionary** *n., pl.* **-ar·ies.** An opponent of progress or liberalism; an extreme conservative.

ă pat	oi boy
ā pay	ou out
âr care	o͝o took
ä father	o͞o boot
ĕ pet	ŭ cut
ē be	ûr urge
ĭ pit	th thin
ī pie	*th* this
îr pier	hw which
ŏ pot	zh vision
ō toe	ə about, item
ô paw	♦ regionalism

Stress marks: ′ (primary); ′ (secondary), as in **dictionary** (dĭk′shə-nĕr′ē)

Nancy Reagan
Photographed by
Lord Snowdon
(Antony Armstrong Jones)

Ronald Reagan
Photographed in 1976

reaction engine *n.* An engine that develops thrust by the focused expulsion of matter, especially ignited fuel gases.

reaction formation *n. Psychology.* A defense mechanism by which an objectionable impulse is expressed in an opposite or contrasting factor.

reaction time *n.* The interval of time between application of a stimulus and detection of a response.

re·ac·ti·vate (rē-ăk′tə-vāt′) *tr.v.* **-vat·ed, -vat·ing, -vates. 1.** To make active again. **2.** To restore the ability to function or the effectiveness of. **—re·ac′ti·va′tion** *n.*

re·ac·tive (rē-ăk′tĭv) *adj.* **1.** Tending to be responsive or to react to a stimulus. **2.** Characterized by reaction. **3.** *Chemistry & Physics.* Tending to participate readily in reactions. **—re·ac′tive·ly** *adv.* **—re·ac′tive·ness, re′ac·tiv′i·ty** *n.*

re·ac·tor (rē-ăk′tər) *n.* **1.** One that reacts to a stimulus. **2.** *Electronics.* A circuit element, such as a coil, used to introduce reactance. **3.** *Physics.* A nuclear reaction.

read (rēd) *v.* **read** (rĕd), **read·ing, reads.** *—tr.* **1.** To examine and grasp the meaning of (written or printed characters, words, or sentences). **2.** To utter or render aloud (written or printed material): *She read her poems to the students.* **3.** To have the ability to examine and grasp the meaning of (written or printed material in a given language or notation): *reads Chinese; reads music.* **4.a.** To examine and grasp the meaning of (language in a form other than written or printed characters, words, or sentences): *reading Braille; reading sign language.* **b.** To examine and grasp the meaning of (a graphic representation): *reading a map.* **5.a.** To discern and interpret the nature or significance of through close examination or sensitive observation: *The tracker read the trail for signs of game.* **b.** To discern or anticipate through examination or observation; descry: *"I can read abandonment in a broken door or shattered window"* (William H. Gass). **6.** To determine the intent or mood of: *I can read your mind like a book. He's a hard person to read.* **7.a.** To attribute a certain interpretation or meaning to: *She read a different meaning into what he had said.* **b.** To consider (something written or printed) as having a particular meaning or significance: *I read the novel as a parable.* **8.** To foretell or predict (the future). **9.** To receive or comprehend (a radio message, for example): *I read you loud and clear.* **10.** To study or make a study of: *She read history as an undergraduate.* **11.** To learn or get knowledge of from something written or printed: *He read that interest rates would continue to rise.* **12.** To proofread. **13.** To have or use as a preferred reading in a particular passage: *For change read charge.* **14.** To indicate, register, or show: *The dial reads 32°.* **15.** *Computer Science.* To obtain information from a storage medium, such as a magnetic disk. *—intr.* **1.** To examine and grasp the meaning of printed or written characters, as of words or music. **2.** To speak aloud the words that one is reading: *He reads to his children every night.* **3.** To learn by reading: *We read about the storm in the paper today.* **4.** To study. **5.** To have a particular wording: *Recite the poem exactly as it reads.* **6.** To contain a specific meaning: *As the law reads, the defendant is guilty.* **7.** To indicate, register, or show a measurement or figure: *How does your new watch read?* **8.** To have a specified character or quality for the reader: *His poems read well.* **—read** *n. Informal.* Something that is read: *"The book is a page-turner as well as a very satisfying read"* (Frank Conroy). **—read** (rĕd) *adj.* Informed by reading; learned: *He was only sparsely read in fields outside his profession.* ***—phrasal verbs.*** **read out.** To read aloud: *Please read out the names on the list.* **read up.** To study or learn by reading: *Read up on the places you plan to visit before you travel.* ***—idioms.*** **read a lecture** (or **lesson**)**.** To issue a reprimand: *Mother read us a lecture after the principal telephoned her.* **read between the lines.** To perceive or detect an obscure or unexpressed meaning: *learned to read between the lines of corporate annual reports to discern areas of fiscal weakness.* **read out of.** To expel by proclamation from a social, political, or other group: *He was read out of the secretariat after the embarrassing incident.* [Middle English *reden,* from Old English *rǣdan,* to advise. See **ar-** in Appendix.]

Read (rēd), **George.** 1733–1798. American Revolutionary leader, politician, and jurist. Delaware's delegate to the Constitutional Convention (1787), he championed the rights of small states and later served as a U.S. senator (1789–1793).

Read (rēd), Sir **Herbert.** 1893–1968. British writer known for his imagistic poetry and works of literary and art criticism.

read·a·ble (rē′də-bəl) *adj.* **1.** Easily read; legible: *a readable typeface.* **2.** Pleasurable or interesting to read: *a readable story.* **—read′a·bil′i·ty, read′a·ble·ness** *n.* **—read′a·bly** *adv.*

Reade (rēd), **Charles.** 1814–1884. British writer whose work includes *The Cloister and the Hearth* (1861), a historical novel.

read·er (rē′dər) *n.* **1.** One that reads. **2.** One who publicly recites literary works. **3.a.** A person employed by a publisher to read and evaluate manuscripts. **b.** One who corrects printers' proofs; a proofreader. **4.** A teaching assistant who reads and grades examination papers. **5.** *Chiefly British.* A university teacher, especially one ranking next below a professor. **6.a.** A textbook of reading exercises. **b.** An anthology, especially a literary anthology. **7.** A layperson or minor cleric who recites lessons or prayers in church services.

read·er·ship (rē′dər-shĭp′) *n.* **1.** The readers of a publication considered as a group. **2.** *Chiefly British.* The office of a reader at a university.

read·i·ly (rĕd′ə-lē, rĕd′l-ē) *adv.* **1.** In a prompt, timely manner; promptly. **2.** In a cooperative manner; willingly. **3.** In a manner indicating or connoting ease; easily.

read·ing (rē′dĭng) *n.* **1.** The act or activity of one that reads. **2.** The act or practice of rendering aloud written or printed matter: *skilled at forensic reading.* **3.** An official or public recitation of written material: *the reading of a will; a reading by the poet of her own works.* **4.a.** The specific form of a particular passage in a text: *an unusual reading of the old manuscript.* **b.** The distinctive interpretation of a work of performing art given by the person or persons performing it. **5.** A personal interpretation or appraisal: *He gave us his reading of the situation.* **6.** Written or printed material. **7.** The information indicated by a gauge or graduated instrument.

Read·ing (rĕd′ĭng). **1.** A borough of south-central England west of London. Occupied by the Danes in 871, it was chartered in 1253. Population, 136,200. **2.** A town of northeast Massachusetts, a primarily residential suburb of Boston. Population, 22,678. **3.** A city of southeast Pennsylvania on the Schuykill River northwest of Philadelphia. Settled in 1748, it is an important commercial, industrial, and transportation center. Population, 78,686.

Read·ing (rĕd′ĭng), First Marquis of. Title of Rufus Daniel Isaacs. 1860–1935. British politician, diplomat, and colonial administrator who served as the lord chief justice of England (1913–1921) and viceroy of India (1921–1926).

read·ing desk (rē′dĭng) *n.* A desk or stand, usually with a slanted top, for holding a book or papers for a standing reader.

re·ad·just (rē′ə-jŭst′) *tr.v.* **-just·ed, -just·ing, -justs.** To adjust or arrange again. **—re′ad·just′er** *n.* **—re′ad·just′ment** *n.*

read-on·ly memory (rĕd′ōn′lē) *n. Abbr.* **ROM** *Computer Science.* A small memory that allows fast access to permanently stored data but prevents addition to or modification of the data.

read·out or **read-out** (rēd′out′) *n. Computer Science.* Presentation of data, usually in digital form, from calculations or storage.

read·y (rĕd′ē) *adj.* **-i·er, -i·est. 1.** Prepared or available for service, action, or progress: *I am ready to work. The soup will be ready in a minute. The pupils are ready to learn to read.* **2.** Mentally disposed; willing: *He was ready to believe her.* **3.** Likely or about to do something: *She is ready to resign.* **4.** Prompt in apprehending or reacting: *a ready intelligence; a ready response.* **5.** Available: *ready money.* **—ready** *tr.v.* **read·ied, read·y·ing, read·ies.** To cause to be ready. ***—idioms.*** **at the ready.** Available for immediate use: *soldiers with machine guns at the ready; students with notebooks at the ready.* **make ready.** To make preparations. [Middle English *redy,* from Old English *rǣde.* See **reidh-** in Appendix.] **—read′i·ness** *n.*

read·y-made or **read·y·made** (rĕd′ē-mād′) *adj.* **1.** Already made, prepared, or available: *ready-made clothes.* **2.** Preconceived: *a raft of ready-made excuses.*

read·y-mix (rĕd′ē-mĭks′) *n.* A mixture in proper proportions of two or more ingredients, as of concrete or a food product, marketed for convenience; a premix. **—ready-mix, ready-mixed** *adj.*

read·y-to-wear (rĕd′ē-tə-wâr′) *adj. Abbr.* **RTW 1.** Marketed in a finished condition in standard sizes. Used of clothing. **2.** Of, relating to, or doing business in ready-to-wear clothing. **—ready-to-wear** *n.* Clothing marketed in a finished condition in standard sizes.

re·af·firm (rē′ə-fûrm′) *tr.v.* **-firmed, -firm·ing, -firms.** To affirm or assert again. **—re′af·fir·ma′tion** (rē′ăf-ər-mā′shən) *n.*

Rea·gan (rā′gən), **Nancy Davis.** Born 1921. First Lady of the United States (1981–1989) as the wife of President Ronald Reagan. She established a nationwide antidrug campaign.

Reagan, Ronald Wilson. Born 1911. The 40th President of the United States (1981–1989). An actor turned politician, he was governor of California (1967–1975) and defeated the incumbent Jimmy Carter in the 1980 presidential election. His administration was marked by economic recovery, military involvement in Grenada, Central America, Lebanon, and Libya, and improved relations with the Soviet Union.

re·a·gent (rē-ā′jənt) *n.* A substance used in a chemical reaction to detect, measure, examine, or produce other substances.

re·a·gin (rē-ā′jĭn) *n.* **1.** An antibody found in the blood of individuals having a genetic predisposition to allergies such as asthma and hay fever. **2.** A substance present in the blood of individuals having a positive serological test for syphilis. [REAG(ENT) + -IN.] **—re′a·gin′ic** (rē′ə-jĭn′ĭk) *adj.* **—re′a·gin′i·cal·ly** *adv.*

re·al¹ (rē′əl, rēl) *adj.* **1.a.** Being or occurring in fact or actuality; having verifiable existence: *real objects; a real illness.* **b.** True and actual; not imaginary, alleged, or ideal: *real people, not ghosts; a real problem; a film based on real life.* **c.** Of or founded on practical matters and concerns: *a recent graduate experiencing the real world for the first time.* **2.** Genuine and authentic; not artificial or spurious: *real mink; real humility.* **3.** Being no less than what is stated; worthy of the name: *a real friend.* **4.** Free of pretense, falsehood, or affectation: *tourists wishing for a real experience while on the guided tour.* **5.** Not to be taken lightly; serious: *We're in real trouble.* **6.** *Philosophy.* Existing objectively in the world regardless of subjectivity or conventions of thought or language. **7.** Relating to, being, or having value reckoned by actual purchasing power: *real income; real growth.* **8.** *Physics.* Of, relating to, or being an image formed by light rays that converge in space. **9.** *Mathematics.* Of, relating to, or being a real number. **10.** *Law.* Of or relating to stationary or fixed property, such as buildings or land. **—real** *adv. Informal.* Very: *I'm real sorry about that.* **—real** *n.* **1.** A thing or whole having actual existence. Often used with *the*: *theories beyond the realm of the real.* **2.** *Mathematics.* A real number. ***—idiom.* for real.** *Slang.* Truly so in fact or actuality: *"Is this place for real? A wolf in a . . . leisure suit and a cow in a print dress wait patiently on the couch in the lobby"* (Teresa Carson). [Middle English, from Old French, from Late Latin *reālis*, from Latin *rēs*, thing. See **rē-** in Appendix.] **—real′ness** *n.*

SYNONYMS: *real, actual, true, existent.* These adjectives are compared as they mean not imaginary but having verifiable existence. *Real* implies that something is genuine or authentic or that what it seems or purports to be tallies with fact: *Don't lose the bracelet; it's made of real gold. My mother showed real sympathy for my predicament. "The general, in a well-feigned or real ecstasy, embraced him"* (William Hickling Prescott). *Actual* means existing and not merely potential or possible: *"rocks, trees . . . the actual world"* (Henry David Thoreau); *"what the actual things were which produced the emotion that you experienced"* (Ernest Hemingway). *True* implies that something is consistent with fact, reality, or the actual state of things: *"It is undesirable to believe a proposition when there is no ground whatever for supposing it true"* (Bertrand Russell). *Existent* applies to what has life or being: *Much of the beluga caviar existent in the world is found in the Soviet Union and Iran.* See also Synonyms at **authentic.**

re·al² (rā-äl′) *n., pl.* **-als** or **-al·es** (-ä′lĕs). A silver coin formerly used in Spain and Latin America. [Spanish, royal, real, from Latin *rēgālis*, royal, from *rēx, rēg-*, king. See **reg-** in Appendix.]

re·al³ (rā-äl′) *n., pl.* **reals** or **reis** (rās). Either of two monetary units formerly used in Portugal and Brazil. [Portuguese, royal, real, from Latin *rēgālis*, royal. See REAL².]

re·al estate (rē′əl, rēl) *n. Abbr.* **R.E., RE** Land, including all the natural resources and permanent buildings on it. **—re′al-es·tate′** (rē′əl-ĭ-stāt′, rēl′-) *adj.*

re·al·gar (rē-ăl′gär′, -gər) *n.* A soft orange-red arsenic ore, As_2S_2, used in pyrotechnics and tanning and as a pigment. [Middle English, from Medieval Latin, from Catalan, from Arabic *rahj al-ġār*, powder (of) the mine or cave : *rahj*, powder + *al*, the + *ġār*, cave.]

re·a·lign (rē′ə-līn′) *tr.v.* **-ligned, -lign·ing, -ligns. 1.** To put back into proper order or alignment. **2.** To make new groupings of or working arrangements between. **—re′a·lign′ment** *n.*

re·al·ism (rē′ə-lĭz′əm) *n.* **1.** An inclination toward literal truth and pragmatism. **2.** The representation in art or literature of objects, actions, or social conditions as they actually are, without idealization or presentation in abstract form. **3.** *Philosophy.* **a.** The scholastic doctrine, opposed to nominalism, that universals exist independently of their being thought. **b.** The modern philosophical doctrine, opposed to idealism, that physical objects exist independently of their being perceived.

re·al·ist (rē′ə-lĭst) *n.* **1.** One who is inclined to literal truth and pragmatism. **2.** A practitioner of artistic or philosophic realism.

re·al·is·tic (rē′ə-lĭs′tĭk) *adj.* **1.** Tending to or expressing an awareness of things as they really are: *She gave us a realistic appraisal of our chances.* **2.** Of or relating to the representation of objects, actions, or social conditions as they actually are: *a realistic novel about ghetto life.* See Synonyms at **graphic.** **—re′al·is′ti·cal·ly** *adv.*

re·al·i·ty (rē-ăl′ĭ-tē) *n., pl.* **-ties. 1.** The quality or state of being actual or true. **2.** One, such as a person, an entity, or an event, that is actual: *"the weight of history and political realities"* (Benno C. Schmidt, Jr.). **3.** The totality of all things possessing actuality, existence, or essence. **4.** That which exists objectively and in fact: *Your observations do not seem to be about reality.* **5.** *Philosophy.* That which has necessary existence and not contingent existence. ***—idiom.* in reality.** In fact; actually.

reality principle *n. Psychiatry.* Awareness of and adjustment to environmental demands in a manner that assures ultimate satisfaction of instinctual needs.

re·al·i·za·tion (rē′ə-lĭ-zā′shən) *n.* **1.** The act of realizing or the condition of being realized. **2.** The result of realizing.

re·al·ize (rē′ə-līz′) *v.* **-ized, -iz·ing, -iz·es.** *—tr.* **1.** To comprehend completely or correctly. **2.** To make real; fulfill: *He finally realized his lifelong ambition to learn how to play the violin.* **3.** To make realistic. **4.** To obtain or achieve, as gain or profit: *She realized a substantial return on the investment.* **5.** To bring in (a sum) as profit by sale. *—intr.* To exchange holdings or goods for money. [French *réaliser*, from Old French, from *real*, real. See REAL¹.] **—re′al·iz′a·ble** *adj.* **—re′al·iz′er** *n.*

re·al·ly (rē′ə-lē, rē′lē) *adv.* **1.** In actual truth or fact: *The horseshoe crab isn't really a crab at all.* **2.** Truly; genuinely: *That was a really enjoyable evening.* **3.** Indeed: *Really, you shouldn't have done it.*

realm (rĕlm) *n.* **1.** A kingdom. **2.** A field, sphere, or province: *the realm of science.* See Synonyms at **field.** [Middle English *realme*, from Old French, alteration (influenced by Old French *reial*, royal) of Latin *regimen*, government, from *regere*, to rule. See **reg-** in Appendix.]

re·al number (rē′əl, rēl) *n. Mathematics.* A number that is rational or irrational, not imaginary.

re·al·po·li·tik (rā-äl′pō′lĭ-tēk′) *n.* A usually expansionist national policy having as its sole principle advancement of the national interest. [German : *real*, practical (from Late Latin *reālis*, real; see REAL¹) + *Politik*, politics (from French *politique*, political, policy; see POLITIC).] **—re·al′po′li·tik′er** *n.*

re·al time (rē′əl, rēl) *n. Computer Science.* **1.** The actual time in which a physical process under computer study or control occurs. **2.** The time required for a computer to solve a problem, measured from the time data are fed in to the time a solution is received.

re·al-time (rē′əl-tīm′, rēl′-) *adj. Computer Science.* Of or relating to computer systems that update information at the same rate as they receive data, enabling them to direct or control a process such as an automatic pilot.

Re·al·tor (rē′əl-tər, -tôr′). A service mark used for a real-estate agent affiliated with the National Association of Realtors. This service mark often occurs in print in lowercase and in the plural as well: *"None of the realtors who worked on the deal would comment"* (Los Angeles Times). *"The economic aftershocks are already rippling through the area's non-defense businesses, from realtors to pizzerias"* (New York Times). *"Since virtually every other industry publicizes its top performers, the Realtors should be proud of theirs, too"* (Chicago Tribune).

re·al·ty (rē′əl-tē) *n., pl.* **-ties.** Real estate.

ream¹ (rēm) *n. Abbr.* **rm. 1.** A quantity of paper, formerly 480 sheets, now 500 sheets or, in a printer's ream, 516 sheets. **2.** Often **reams.** A very large amount: *reams of work to do.* [Middle English *reme*, from Old French *reime*, from Old Spanish *resma*, from Arabic *rizmah*, bundle.]

ream² (rēm) *tr.v.* **reamed, ream·ing, reams. 1.** To form, shape, taper, or enlarge (a hole) with or as if with a reamer. **2.** To remove (material) by this process. **3.** To squeeze the juice out of (fruit) with a reamer. [Possibly from Middle English *remen*, to make room, variant of *rimen*, from Old English *rȳman*. See **reue-** in Appendix.]

ream·er (rē′mər) *n.* **1.** Any of various tools used to shape or enlarge holes. **2.** A utensil with a conical, ridged projection, used for extracting citrus-fruit juice.

reamer
Top: Fluted (left) and pipe (right) reamers for enlarging holes
Bottom: Juice reamer

re·an·i·mate (rē-ăn′ə-māt′) *tr.v.* **-mat·ed, -mat·ing, -mates. 1.** To give new life to: *Her dancing reanimates the classical style.* **2.** To bring to life; evoke powerfully or effectively: *a book that reanimates the Mayan civilization.*

reap (rēp) *v.* **reaped, reap·ing, reaps.** *—tr.* **1.** To cut (grain or pulse) for harvest with a scythe, sickle, or reaper. **2.** To harvest (a crop). **3.** To harvest a crop from: *reaping a field.* **4.** To obtain as a result of effort: *She reaped large profits from her unique invention.* *—intr.* **1.** To cut or harvest grain or pulse. **2.** To obtain a return or reward. [Middle English *repen*, from Old English *rīpan*.]

reap
Cutting hay with a scythe

SYNONYMS: *reap, garner, gather, glean, harvest.* The central meaning shared by these verbs is "to collect": *reap grain; garner compliments; gathering mushrooms; glean information; harvested rich rewards.*

reap·er (rē′pər) *n.* One that reaps, especially a machine for harvesting grain or pulse crops.

re·ap·por·tion (rē′ə-pôr′shən) *tr.v.* **-tioned, -tion·ing, -tions.** To distribute anew.

re·ap·por·tion·ment (rē′ə-pôr′shən-mənt) *n.* **1.** The act of reapportioning or the state of being reapportioned. **2.** Redistribution of representation in a legislative body, especially the periodic reallotment of U.S. congressional seats according to changes in the census figures as required by the Constitution.

re·ap·prais·al (rē′ə-prā′zəl) *n.* A new appraisal or evaluation.

re·ap·praise (rē′ə-prāz′) *tr.v.* **-praised, -prais·ing, -prais·es.** To make a fresh appraisal or evaluation of.

rear¹ (rîr) *n.* **1.** A hind part. **2.** The point or area farthest from the front: *the rear of the hall.* **3.** The part of a military deployment usually farthest from the fighting front. **4.** *Informal.* The buttocks. **—rear** *adj.* Of, at, or located in the rear. [Middle English *rere*, rear of an army, short for *rerewarde*, rear guard. See REARWARD².]

rear² (rîr) *v.* **reared, rear·ing, rears.** *—tr.* **1.** To care for (children or a child) during the early stages of life; bring up. **2.** To lift upright; raise. **3.** To build; erect. See Synonyms at **lift. 4.** To tend (growing plants or animals). *—intr.* **1.** To rise on the hind legs, as a horse. **2.** To rise high in the air; tower. [Middle English *reren*, to raise, from Old English *rǣran*.] **—rear′er** *n.*

rear admiral *n. Abbr.* **RADM, R.A., RA, R. Adm. 1.** A commissioned rank in the U.S. Navy or Coast Guard that is above commodore and below vice admiral. **2.** One who holds this rank.

rear end *n.* **1.** The rear part: *the rear end of a car.* **2.** *Informal.* The buttocks.

rear-end (rîr′ĕnd′) *tr.v.* **-end·ed, -end·ing, -ends.** *Slang.* To run into (another motor vehicle) from behind: *My car was rear-ended by a truck.* **—rear′-end′er** *n.*

rear guard *n.* A detachment of troops that protects the rear of

ă **pat**	oi **boy**
ā **pay**	ou **out**
âr **care**	ŏŏ **took**
ä **father**	ōō **boot**
ĕ **pet**	ŭ **cut**
ē **be**	ûr **urge**
ĭ **pit**	th **thin**
ī **pie**	*th* **this**
îr **pier**	hw **which**
ŏ **pot**	zh **vision**
ō **toe**	ə **about, item**
ô **paw**	♦ **regionalism**

Stress marks: **′** (primary); ′ (secondary), as in **dictionary** (dĭk′shə-nĕr′ē)

a military force. [Middle English *reregarde,* from Old French : *rere,* backward (from Latin *retrō;* see **re-** in Appendix) + *guarde,* guard (from *guarder,* to defend; see GUARD).]

rear-guard (rîr′gärd′) *adj.* **1.** Of or relating to a rear guard. **2.** Of or relating to economic, political, or social resistance: *mounting a rear-guard effort to prevent tax increases.*

re·ar·gue (rē-är′gyo͞o) *tr.v.* **-gued, -gu·ing, -gues. 1.** To argue again or repeatedly. **2.** To debate again or present additional arguments for (a case or an issue, for example), especially in a court of law: *filed a motion to reargue the case.*

re·arm (rē-ärm′) *v.* **-armed, -arm·ing, -arms.** —*tr.* **1.** To arm again. **2.** To equip with better weapons. —*intr.* To arm oneself again. **—re·ar′ma·ment** (rē-är′mə-mənt) *n.*

rear·most (rîr′mōst′) *adj.* Farthest in the rear; last.

re·ar·range (rē′ə-rānj′) *tr.v.* **-ranged, -rang·ing, -rang·es.** To change the arrangement of. **—re′ar·range′ment** *n.*

rear-view mirror or **rear·view mirror** also **rear view mirror** (rîr′vyo͞o′) *n.* A mirror, such as one attached to a motor vehicle, that provides a view of what is behind.

rear·ward[1] (rîr′wərd) *adv.* Toward, to, or at the rear. **—rearward** *adj.* At or in the rear. **—rearward** *n.* A rearward direction, point, or position. **—rear′wards** *adv.*

rear·ward[2] (rîr′wôrd′) *n.* The rear guard of an armed force. [Middle English *rerewarde,* from Anglo-Norman : *rere,* behind (from Latin *retrō;* see **re-** in Appendix) + *warde,* guard (of Germanic origin; see **wer-[3]** in Appendix).]

rea·son (rē′zən) *n.* **1.** The basis or motive for an action, a decision, or a conviction. See Usage Notes at **because, why. 2.** A declaration made to explain or justify an action, a decision, or a conviction: *inquired about her reason for leaving.* **3.** An underlying fact or cause that provides logical sense for a premise or an occurrence: *There is reason to believe that the accused did not commit this crime.* **4.** The capacity for logical, rational, and analytic thought; intelligence. **5.** Good judgment; sound sense. **6.** A normal mental state; sanity: *He has lost his reason.* **7.** *Logic.* A premise, usually the minor premise, of an argument. **—reason** *v.* **-soned, -son·ing, -sons.** —*intr.* **1.** To use the faculty of reason; think logically. **2.** To talk or argue logically and persuasively. **3.** *Obsolete.* To engage in conversation or discussion. —*tr.* **1.** To determine or conclude by logical thinking: *reasoned out a solution to the problem.* **2.** To persuade or dissuade (someone) with reasons. —***idioms.*** **by reason of.** Because of. **in reason.** With good sense or justification; reasonably. **within reason.** Within the bounds of good sense or practicality. **with reason.** With good cause; justifiably. [Middle English, from Old French *raison,* from Latin *ratiō, ratiōn-,* from *ratus,* past participle of *rērī,* to consider, think. See **ar-** in Appendix.] **—rea′son·er** *n.*

SYNONYMS: *reason, intuition, understanding, judgment.* These nouns refer to the intellectual faculty by means of which human beings seek or attain knowledge or truth. *Reason* is the power to think rationally and logically and to draw inferences: *"the rationalist whose reason is not sufficient to teach him those limitations of the powers of conscious reason"* (Friedrich August von Hayek). *"Mere reason is insufficient to convince us of its* [the Christian religion's] *veracity"* (David Hume). *Intuition* is perception or comprehension, as of truths or facts, without the use of the rational process: *"Because of their age-long training in human relations—for that is what feminine intuition really is—women have a special contribution to make to any group enterprise"* (Margaret Mead). *Understanding* is the faculty by which one understands, often together with the comprehension resulting from its exercise: *"So long as the human heart is strong and the human reason weak, Royalty will be strong because it appeals to diffused feeling, and Republics weak because they appeal to the understanding"* (Walter Bagehot). *"The greatest dangers to liberty lurk in insidious encroachment by men of zeal, well-meaning but without understanding"* (Louis D. Brandeis). *Judgment* is the ability to assess situations or circumstances and draw sound conclusions: *"my salad days,/When I was green in judgment"* (Shakespeare). *"At twenty years of age, the will reigns; at thirty, the wit; and at forty, the judgment"* (Benjamin Franklin). See also Synonyms at **cause, mind, think.**

rea·son·a·ble (rē′zə-nə-bəl) *adj.* **1.** Capable of reasoning; rational: *a reasonable person.* **2.** Governed by or being in accordance with reason or sound thinking: *a reasonable solution to the problem.* **3.** Being within the bounds of common sense: *arrive home at a reasonable hour.* **4.** Not excessive or extreme; fair: *reasonable prices.* **—rea′son·a·bil′i·ty, rea′son·a·ble·ness** *n.* **—rea′son·a·bly** *adv.*

rea·son·ing (rē′zə-nĭng) *n.* **1.** Use of reason, especially to form conclusions, inferences, or judgments. **2.** Evidence or arguments used in thinking or argumentation.

re·as·sem·ble (rē′ə-sĕm′bəl) *v.* **-bled, -bling, -bles.** —*tr.* **1.** To bring or gather together again: *reassembled the cast for an anniversary performance of the musical.* **2.** To fit or joint the parts of (something) together again: *took the entire artifact apart and reassembled it at the museum.* —*intr.* To gather together again, especially in a different place: *The crowd reassembled in front of the state house.*

re·as·sign (rē′ə-sīn′) *tr.v.* **-signed, -sign·ing, -signs.** To assign to a new position, distribution, or function: *reassigned the ambassador to a new post; reassigned the job to more experienced workers.* **—re·as·sign′ment** *n.*

re·as·sure (rē′ə-sho͝or′) *tr.v.* **-sured, -sur·ing, -sures. 1.** To restore confidence to. **2.** To assure again. **3.** To reinsure. **—re′as·sur′ance** *n.* **—re′as·sur′ing·ly** *adv.*

re·a·ta (rē-ä′tə) *n.* Variant of **riata.**

Ré·au·mur or **Re·au·mur** (rā′ō-myo͝or′) *adj. Abbr.* **R, R.** Relating to, being, or indicated on a thermometer scale that registers the freezing point of water as 0° and the boiling point as 80°. [After René Antoine Ferchault de RÉAUMUR.]

Ré·au·mur (rā′ə-myo͝or′, -ō-, rā-ō-mür′), **René Antoine Ferchault de.** 1683–1757. French physicist who invented the alcohol thermometer and devised the Réaumur scale.

reave[1] (rēv) *v.* **reaved** or **reft** (rĕft), **reav·ing, reaves.** *Archaic.* —*tr.* **1.** To seize and carry off forcibly. **2.** To deprive (one) of something; bereave. —*intr.* To rob, plunder, or pillage. [Middle English *reven,* to plunder, from Old English *rēafian.* See **reup-** in Appendix.]

reave[2] (rēv) *tr.v.* **reaved** or **reft** (rĕft), **reav·ing, reaves.** *Archaic.* To break or tear apart. [Middle English *reven,* possibly alteration (influenced by *reven,* to plunder) of Old Norse *rīfa,* to rive.]

Reb[1] also **reb** (rĕb) *n. Informal.* A Confederate soldier. [Short for REBEL.]

Reb[2] (rĕb) *n. Judaism.* Used as a title of respect for a man. Used with the given name. [Yiddish, from Hebrew *rabbî,* my master. See RABBI.]

re·bar·ba·tive (rē-bär′bə-tĭv) *adj.* Tending to irritate; repellent: *"He became rebarbative, prickly, spiteful"* (Robert Craft). [French *rébarbatif,* from Old French, from *(se) rebarber,* to confront : *re-,* re- + *barbe,* beard (from Latin *barba;* see **bhardh-ā-** in Appendix).]

re·bate[1] (rē′bāt′) *n.* A deduction from an amount to be paid or a return of part of an amount given in payment. **—rebate** (rē′bāt′, rĭ-bāt′) *tr.v.* **-bat·ed, -bat·ing, -bates. 1.** To deduct or return (an amount) from a payment or bill. **2.** To lessen; diminish. [From Middle English *rebaten,* to deduct, from Old French *rabattre, rebattre,* to reduce, to beat down again : *re-,* re- + *abbattre,* to beat down; see ABATE.] **—re′bat·er** *n.*

re·bate[2] (rē′bāt′, răb′ĭt) *n. & v.* Variant of **rabbet.**

re·ba·to (rĭ-bä′tō) also **ra·ba·to** (rə-) *n., pl.* **-tos.** A stiff, flaring collar of lace or other fabric, worn early in the 17th century. [Obsolete French *rebateau,* alteration of French *rabat,* from Old French, from *rabattre,* to turn down again, reduce. See REBATE[1].]

reb·be (rĕb′ə, rĕb′ē) *n.* A Jewish spiritual leader or rabbi, especially of a Hasidic sect. [Yiddish, from Hebrew *rabbî,* rabbi. See RABBI.]

re·bec also **re·beck** (rē′bĕk′) *n. Music.* A pear-shaped, two-stringed or three-stringed medieval instrument, played with a bow. [French, from Old French, alteration (influenced by *bec,* beak, from its shape) of *rebebe,* from Old Provençal *rebeb,* from Arabic *rabāb.*]

Re·bec·ca also **Re·bek·ah** (rĭ-bĕk′ə). In the Old Testament, the wife of Isaac and the mother of Jacob and Esau.

re·bel (rĭ-bĕl′) *intr.v.* **-belled, -bel·ling, -bels. 1.** To refuse allegiance to and oppose by force an established government or ruling authority. **2.** To resist or defy an authority or a generally accepted convention. **3.** To feel or express strong unwillingness or repugnance: *She rebelled at the unwelcome suggestion.* **— reb·el** (rĕb′əl) *n.* One who rebels or is in rebellion: *"He is the perfect recruit for fascist movements: a rebel not a revolutionary, contemptuous yet envious of the rich and involved with them"* (Stanley Hoffman). —*attributive.* Often used to modify another noun: *rebel troops; a rebel army.* [Middle English *rebellen,* from Old French *rebeller,* from Latin *rebellāre* : *re-,* re- + *bellāre,* to make war (from *bellum,* war). N., Middle English, rebellious, rebel, from Old French *rebelle,* from Latin *rebellis,* from *rebellāre,* to rebel.]

re·bel·lion (rĭ-bĕl′yən) *n.* **1.** Open, armed, and organized resistance to a constituted government. **2.** An act or a show of defiance toward an authority or established convention. [Middle English, from Old French, from Latin *rebelliō, rebelliōn-,* from *rebellāre,* to rebel. See REBEL.]

SYNONYMS: *rebellion, revolution, revolt, mutiny, insurrection, uprising.* These nouns denote acts of violence intended to change or overthrow an existing order or authority. *Rebellion* is open, armed, organized resistance to constituted political authority that often fails of its purpose: *A rebellion in the officer corps led to chaos in the armed forces.* A *revolution* is the overthrow of one government and its replacement with another: *The 20th century has seen several major revolutions, which in turn have altered the balance of power among nations. Revolt* is rejection of and rebellion against a prevailing state of affairs or a controlling authority: *Fearing a taxpayers' revolt, the legislature passed a less confiscatory revenue bill. Mutiny* is revolt against constituted authority, especially by sailors: *The sailprs, who had received low pay and poor rations, were finally in a state of mutiny. Insurrection* and *uprising* apply to popular revolts that are sometimes limited or are viewed as being the first indications of a more extensive rebellion: *The freedom fighters withdrew into the mountains, from which* *they mounted an insurrection against the junta. The 1956 uprising in Hungary was soon quelled by ruthless Soviet military action.*

re·bel·lious (rĭ-bĕl′yəs) *adj.* **1.** Prone to or participating in a rebellion: *rebellious students.* **2.** Of, relating to, or characteristic of a rebel or rebellion: *rebellious behavior.* **3.** Resisting treatment or control; unruly. See Synonyms at **insubordinate.** —**re·bel′lious·ly** *adv.* —**re·bel′lious·ness** *n.*

♦**rebel yell** *n. Chiefly Southern U.S.* See **wahoo**[4].

re·bid (rē-bĭd′) *v.* **-bid, -bid·den** (-bĭd′n), or **-bid, -bid·ding, -bids.** —*tr.* **1.** *Games.* To bid (a previously bid suit) again in bridge. **2.** To offer a revised bid for (a contract). —*intr.* **1.** *Games.* To bid again in the auction of a deal in bridge. **2.** To offer a revised bid for a contract. —**re′bid′** *n.*

re·bind (rē-bīnd′) *tr.v.* **-bound** (-bound′), **-bind·ing, -binds.** To bind again, especially to put a new binding on (a book). —**rebind** (rē′bīnd′) *n.* A book that has been rebound.

re·birth (rē-bûrth′, rē′bûrth′) *n.* **1.** A second or new birth; reincarnation. **2.** A renaissance; a revival: *a rebirth of classicism in architecture.*

re·book (rē-bo͝ok′) *v.* **-booked, -book·ing, -books.** —*tr.* **1.** To book again. **2.** To change a booking for (a performance or reservation). —*intr.* To make a new booking: *rebooked on another airline.*

re·boot (rē-bo͞ot′) *tr.v.* **-boot·ed, -boot·ing, -boots.** *Computer Science.* To turn a computer off and then on again; restart the operating system.

re·born (rē-bôrn′) *adj.* Emotionally or spiritually revived or regenerated.

re·bound[1] (rē′bound′, rĭ-) *v.* **-bound·ed, -bound·ing, -bounds.** —*intr.* **1.** To spring or bounce back after hitting or colliding with something. **2.** To recover, as from depression or disappointment. **3.** To reecho; resound. **4.** *Basketball.* To retrieve and gain possession of the ball as it bounces off the backboard or rim after an unsuccessful shot. —*tr.* To cause to rebound. —**rebound** (rē′bound′, rĭ-bound′) *n.* **1.** A springing or bounding back; a recoil. **2.a.** *Sports.* A rebounding or caroming ball or hockey puck. **b.** *Basketball.* The act or an instance of taking possession of a rebounding ball. **3.** A quick recovery from or reaction to disappointment or depression. [Middle English *rebounden,* from Old French *rebondir* : *re-,* re- + *bondir,* to leap; see BOUND[1].] —**re·bound′er** *n.*

re·bound[2] (rē-bound′) *v.* Past tense and past participle of **rebind.**

re·bo·zo (rĭ-bō′sō, rĕ-bô′thô) *n., pl.* **-zos.** A long scarf worn over the head and shoulders chiefly by Mexican women. [Spanish, from *rebosar,* to muffle with a shawl : *re-,* back (from Latin; see RE–) + *bozo,* muzzle, mouth (from Vulgar Latin **bucceum,* from Latin *bucca,* cheek).]

re·broad·cast (rē-brôd′kăst′) *tr.v.* **-cast** or **-cast·ed, -cast·ing, -casts.** **1.** To repeat the broadcast of (a program). **2.** To receive and send out (a broadcast) again. —**rebroadcast** *n.* A broadcast that is repeated or that is relayed from another station.

re·buff (rĭ-bŭf′) *n.* **1.** A blunt or abrupt repulse or refusal, as to an offer. **2.** A check or an abrupt setback to progress or action. —**rebuff** *tr.v.* **-buffed, -buff·ing, -buffs.** **1.** To reject bluntly, often disdainfully; snub. See Synonyms at **refuse**[1]. **2.** To repel or drive back. [From obsolete French *rebuffer,* to reject, from Italian *ribuffare,* from *ribuffo,* reprimand : *ri-,* back (from Latin *re-;* see RE–) + *buffo,* gust, puff (of imitative origin).]

re·build (rē-bĭld′) *tr.v.* **-built** (-bĭlt′), **-build·ing, -builds.** **1.** To build again. **2.** To make extensive structural repairs on. **3.** To remodel or make extensive changes in: *tried to rebuild society.*

re·buke (rĭ-byo͞ok′) *tr.v.* **-buked, -buk·ing, -bukes.** **1.** To criticize or reprove sharply; reprimand. See Synonyms at **admonish.** **2.** To check or repress. —**rebuke** *n.* A sharp reproof. [Middle English *rebuken,* from Old North French *rebuker* : *re-,* back (from Latin; see RE–) + **buker,* to strike, chop·wood (variant of Old French *buschier,* from *busche,* firewood, of Germanic origin).]

re·bus (rē′bəs) *n.* **-bus·es.** A representation of words in the form of pictures or symbols, often presented as a puzzle. [Latin *rēbus,* ablative pl. of *rēs,* thing. See **rē-** in Appendix.]

re·but (rĭ-bŭt′) *v.* **-but·ted, -but·ting, -buts.** —*tr.* **1.** To refute, especially by offering opposing evidence or arguments, as in a legal case. **2.** To repel. —*intr.* To present opposing evidence or arguments. [Middle English *reboten, rebutte,* to rebuke, repel, from Old French *rebouter* : *re-,* re- + *bouter,* to push (of Germanic origin; see **bhau-** in Appendix).]

re·but·tal (rĭ-bŭt′l) *n.* **1.** The act of rebutting. **2.** A statement made in rebutting.

re·but·ter (rĭ-bŭt′ər) *n.* One who refutes or rebuts.

rec (rĕk) *n. Informal.* Recreation. —*attributive.* Often used to modify another noun: *a rec room; a rec hall.*

rec. *abbr.* **1.** Receipt. **2.** Record; recording. **3.** Recreation.

re·cal·ci·trant (rĭ-kăl′sĭ-trənt) *adj.* Marked by stubborn resistance to and defiance of authority or guidance. See Synonyms at **unruly.** —**recalcitrant** *n.* A recalcitrant person. [Late Latin *recalcitrāns, recalcitrant-,* present participle of *recalcitrāre,* to be disobedient, from Latin, to deny access : *re-,* re- + *calcitrāre,* to kick (from *calx, calc-,* heel).] —**re·cal′ci·trance, re·cal′ci·tran·cy** *n.*

re·cal·cu·late (rē-kăl′kyə-lāt′) *tr.v.* **-lat·ed, -lat·ing, -lates.** To calculate again, especially in order to eliminate errors or to incorporate additional data. —**re′cal·cu·la′tion** *n.*

re·ca·les·cence (rē′kə-lĕs′əns) *n.* A sudden glowing in a cooling metal caused by liberation of the latent heat of transformation. [From Latin *recalēscēns, recalēscent-,* present participle of *recalēscere,* to grow warm again : *re-,* re- + *calēscere,* to become warm, inchoative of *calēre,* to be warm; see **kelə-**[1] in Appendix.] —**re′ca·les′cent** *adj.*

re·call (rĭ-kôl′) *tr.v.* **-called, -cal·ling, -calls.** **1.** To ask or order to return: *recalled all workers who had been laid off.* **2.** To summon back to awareness of or concern with the subject or situation at hand. **3.** To remember; recollect. See Synonyms at **remember.** **4.** To cancel, take back, or revoke. **5.** To bring back; restore. **6.** To request return (of a product) to the manufacturer, as for necessary repairs or adjustments. —**recall** (*also* rē′kôl′) *n.* **1.** The act of recalling or summoning back, especially an official order to return. **2.** A signal, such as a bugle call, used to summon troops back to their posts. **3.** The ability to remember information or experiences. **4.** The act of revoking. **5.a.** The procedure by which a public official may be removed from office by popular vote. **b.** The right to employ this procedure. **6.** A request by the manufacturer of a product that has been identified as defective to return it, as for necessary repairs or adjustments. —**re·call′a·ble** *adj.*

Ré·ca·mi·er (rā′kəm-yā′, rā-käm-), **Jeanne Françoise Julie Adélaïde Bernard.** 1777–1849. French socialite whose Parisian salon attracted noted literary and political figures.

re·cant (rĭ-kănt′) *v.* **-cant·ed, -cant·ing, -cants.** —*tr.* To make a formal retraction or disavowal of (a statement or belief to which one has previously committed oneself). —*intr.* To make a formal retraction or disavowal of a previously held statement or belief. [Latin *recantāre* : *re-,* re- + *cantāre,* to sing, frequentative of *canere;* see **kan-** in Appendix.] —**re′can·ta′tion** (rē′kăn-tā′shən) *n.* —**re·cant′er** *n.*

re·cap[1] (rē-kăp′) *tr.v.* **-capped, -cap·ping, -caps.** **1.** To replace a cap or caplike covering on: *recapped the bottle.* **2.** To restore (a used tire of a motor vehicle) to usable condition by bonding new rubber onto the worn tread and lateral surface. —**recap** (rē′kăp′) *n.* A tire that has been recapped.

re·cap[2] (rē′kăp′) *Informal. tr.v.* **-capped, -cap·ping, -caps.** To recapitulate: *recapped the headlines at the end of the news broadcast.* —**recap** *n.* A recapitulation, as of a news report.

re·cap·i·tal·ize (rē-kăp′ĭ-tl-īz′) *tr.v.* **-ized, -iz·ing, -iz·es.** To change the capital structure of (a corporation). —**re·cap′i·tal·i·za′tion** (-ĭ-zā′shən) *n.*

re·ca·pit·u·late (rē′kə-pĭch′ə-lāt′) *v.* **-lat·ed, -lat·ing, -lates.** —*tr.* **1.** To repeat in concise form. **2.** *Biology.* To appear to repeat (the evolutionary stages of the species) during the embryonic development of the individual organism. —*intr.* To make a summary. [Latin *recapitulāre, recapitulāt-* : *re-,* re- + *capitulum,* main point, heading, diminutive of *caput, capit-,* head; see **kaput-** in Appendix.] —**re·ca·pit′u·la′tive, re·ca·pit′u·la·to′ry** (-lə-tôr′ē, -tōr′ē) *adj.*

re·ca·pit·u·la·tion (rē′kə-pĭch′ə-lā′shən) *n.* **1.** The act or process of recapitulating. **2.** A summary or concise review. **3.** See **biogenesis** (sense 4). **4.** *Music.* Restatement of the exposition that constitutes the third section of the typical sonata form.

recapitulation theory *n.* See **biogenetic law.**

re·cap·ture (rē-kăp′chər) *n.* **1.a.** The act of retaking or recovering. **b.** The condition of having been retaken or recovered. **2.** *Law.* The act or an instance of retaking booty or goods. **3.** Something recaptured. **4.** The lawful taking by a government of a fixed amount of the profits of a public-service corporation in excess of a stipulated rate of return. —**recapture** *tr.v.* **-tured, -tur·ing, -tures.** **1.** To capture again. **2.** To recall: *an attempt to recapture the past.* **3.** To acquire by the government procedure of recapture.

re·cast (rē-kăst′) *tr.v.* **-cast, -cast·ing, -casts.** **1.** To mold again: *recast a bell.* **2.** To set down or present (ideas, for example) in a new or different arrangement: *recast a sentence.* **3.** To change the cast of (a theatrical production). —**recast** (rē′kăst′) *n.* **1.** The act or process of recasting. **2.** Something produced by recasting.

rec·ce (rĕk′ē) *n. Slang.* Reconnaissance. —**rec′ce** *adj.*

recd. *abbr.* Received.

re·cede (rĭ-sēd′) *intr.v.* **-ced·ed, -ced·ing, -cedes.** **1.** To move back or away from a limit, point, or mark: *The flood waters finally receded.* **2.** To slope backward. **3.** To become or seem to become fainter or more distant: *With the passage of time, my unhappy memories of the place receded.* **4.** To withdraw or retreat. [Middle English *receden,* from Old French *receder,* from Latin *recēdere* : *re-,* re- + *cēdere,* to go; see **ked-** in Appendix.]

SYNONYMS: *recede, ebb, retract, retreat, retrograde.* The central meaning shared by these verbs is "to move backward": *a hairline that had receded; waters ebbing at low tide; a turtle retracting its head into its shell; a retreating army; academic standards that have retrograded.*
ANTONYM: *advance.*

re-cede (rē-sēd′) *tr.v.* **-ced·ed, -ced·ing, -cedes.** To yield or grant to one formerly in possession; cede (something) back.

re·ceipt (rĭ-sēt′) *n. Abbr.* **rcpt., rec., rect.** **1.a.** The act of receiving: *We are in receipt of your letter.* **b.** The fact of being or

ă pat	oi boy
ā pay	ou out
âr care	o͝o took
ä father	o͞o boot
ĕ pet	ŭ cut
ē be	ûr urge
ĭ pit	th thin
ī pie	*th* this
îr pier	hw which
ŏ pot	zh vision
ō toe	ə about, item
ô paw	♦ regionalism

Stress marks: **′** (primary); ′ (secondary), as in **dictionary** (dĭk′shə-nĕr′ē)

having been received: *They denied receipt of the shipment.* **2.** Often **receipts.** A quantity or amount received: *cash receipts.* **3.** A written acknowledgment that a specified article, sum of money, or shipment of merchandise has been received. **4.** A recipe. **—receipt** *v.* **-ceipt·ed, -ceipt·ing, -ceipts.** *—tr.* **1.** To mark (a bill) as having been paid. **2.** To give or write a receipt for (money paid or goods or services delivered). *—intr.* To give a receipt. [Middle English *receite,* from Old North French, from Medieval Latin *recepta,* medical prescription, money received, from Latin, feminine past participle of *recipere,* to receive. See RECEIVE.]

re·ceiv·a·ble (rĭ-sēʹvə-bəl) *adj.* **1.** Suitable for being received or accepted, especially as payment. **2.** Awaiting or requiring payment; due or collectible. **—receivable** *n.* A business asset due to one business from another. Often used in the plural.

re·ceive (rĭ-sēvʹ) *v.* **-ceived, -ceiv·ing, -ceives.** *—tr.* **1.** To take or acquire (something given, offered, or transmitted); get. **2.** To hear or see (information, for example): *receive bad news; received a good report of the group's activities.* **3.** To have (a title, for example) bestowed on oneself. **4.** To meet with; experience: *receive sympathetic treatment.* **5.** To have inflicted or imposed on oneself: *receive a penalty.* **6.** To bear the weight or force of; support: *The beams receive the full weight of the walls and roof.* **7.** To take or intercept the impact of (a blow, for example). **8.** To take in, hold, or contain: *a tank that receives rainwater.* **9.** To admit: *receive new members.* **10.** To greet or welcome: *receive guests.* **11.** To perceive or acquire mentally: *receive a bad impression.* **12.** To regard with approval or disapproval: *essays that were received well.* **13.** To listen to and acknowledge formally and authoritatively: *The judge received their oath of allegiance.* *—intr.* **1.** To acquire or get something; be a recipient. **2.** To admit or welcome guests or visitors: *The couple are not receiving this winter.* **3.** To partake of the Eucharist. **4.** *Electronics.* To convert incoming electromagnetic waves into visible or audible signals. **5.** *Football.* To catch or take possession of a kicked ball. [Middle English *receiven,* from Old North French *receivre,* from Latin *recipere* : *re-,* re- + *capere,* to take; see **kap-** in Appendix.]

re·ceived (rĭ-sēvdʹ) *adj.* Having been accepted as true or worthy: *"Received political wisdom says not. Surveys show otherwise"* (Economist).

Re·ceived Pronunciation (rĭ-sēvdʹ) *n. Abbr.* **R.P.** The pronunciation of British English that reflects the social and cultural predominance of southern English speech, that was at one time characteristic of the English spoken at the public schools and Oxford and Cambridge Universities, and that was accepted as the standard form of English used in broadcasting. Also called *BBC English, Southern Educated Standard.*

Received Standard English *n.* British English characterized especially by Received Pronunciation.

re·ceiv·er (rĭ-sēʹvər) *n.* **1.** One that receives something: *a receiver of many compliments.* **2.** *Electronics.* A device, such as a part of a radio, television set, or telephone, that receives incoming radio signals and converts them to perceptible forms, such as sound or light. **3.** An official appointed to receive and account for money due. **4.** *Law.* A person appointed by a court administrator to take into custody the property or funds of others, pending litigation. **5.** A person who knowingly buys or receives stolen goods. **6.** A receptacle intended for a specific purpose. **7. a.** *Football.* A member of the offensive team eligible to catch a forward pass. **b.** *Baseball.* The catcher.

re·ceiv·er·ship (rĭ-sēʹvər-shĭpʹ) *n. Law.* **1.** The office or functions of a receiver. **2.** The state of being held by a receiver: *The company went into receivership.*

re·ceiv·ing blanket (rĭ-sēʹvĭng) *n.* A lightweight blanket used to wrap a baby especially after a bath.

receiving line *n.* A line of people formed to greet arriving guests individually, as at a formal gathering.

re·cen·sion (rĭ-sĕnʹshən) *n.* **1.** A critical revision of a text incorporating the most plausible elements found in varying sources. **2.** A text so revised. [Latin *recēnsiō, recēnsiōn-,* a reviewing, from *recēnsēre,* to review : *re-,* re- + *cēnsēre,* to estimate; see **kens-** in Appendix.]

re·cent (rēʹsənt) *adj.* **1.** Of, belonging to, or occurring at a time immediately before the present. **2.** Modern; new. **3. Recent.** *Geology.* Of, belonging to, or denoting the Holocene Epoch. See table at **geologic time.** [Middle English, new, fresh, from Latin *recēns, recent-.* See **ken-** in Appendix.] **—reʹcen·cy, reʹcent·ness** *n.* **—reʹcent·ly** *adv.*

re·cep·ta·cle (rĭ-sĕpʹtə-kəl) *n.* **1.** A container that holds items or matter. **2.** *Botany.* The expanded tip of a flower stalk or axis that bears the floral organs or the group of flowers in a head. **3.** *Electronics.* A fitting connected to a power supply and equipped to receive a plug. [Middle English, from Old French, from Latin *receptāculum,* from *receptāre,* to receive again, frequentative of *recipere,* to receive. See RECEIVE.]

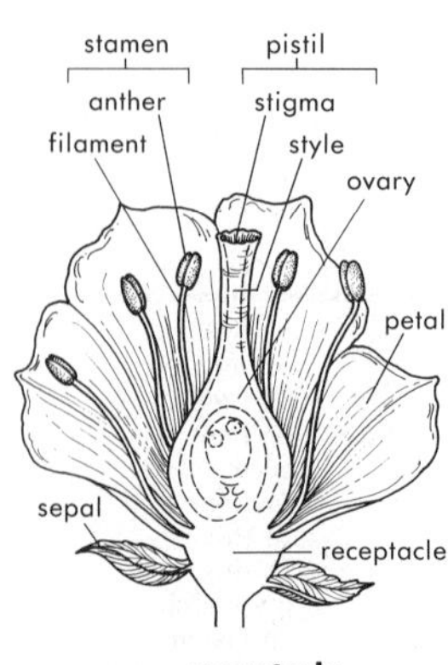

receptacle

re·cep·tion (rĭ-sĕpʹshən) *n.* **1.** The act or process of receiving or of being received. **2.** A welcome, greeting, or acceptance: *a friendly reception.* **3.** A social function, especially one intended to provide a welcome or greeting: *a wedding reception.* **4.** Mental approval or acceptance: *the reception of a new theory.* **5.** *Electronics.* **a.** Conversion of transmitted radio waves or electric signals into perceptible forms, such as sound or light, by means of antennas and electronic equipment. **b.** The condition or quality of the waves or signals so received. [Middle English *recepcion,* from Old French *reception,* from Latin *receptiō, receptiōn-,* from *receptus,* past participle of *recipere,* to receive. See RECEIVE.]

re·cep·tion·ist (rĭ-sĕpʹshə-nĭst) *n.* An office worker employed chiefly to receive visitors and answer the telephone.

re·cep·tive (rĭ-sĕpʹtĭv) *adj.* **1.** Capable of or qualified for receiving. **2.** Ready or willing to receive favorably: *receptive to their proposals.* **3.** *Linguistics.* Of or relating to the skills of listening and reading. **—re·cepʹtive·ly** *adv.* **—reʹcep·tivʹi·ty, re·cepʹtive·ness** *n.*

re·cep·tor (rĭ-sĕpʹtər) *n.* **1.** *Physiology.* A specialized cell or group of nerve endings that responds to sensory stimuli. **2.** *Biochemistry.* A molecular structure or site on the surface or interior of a cell that binds with substances such as hormones, antigens, drugs, or neurotransmitters.

re·cer·ti·fy (rē-sûrʹtə-fīʹ) *tr.v.* **-fied, -fy·ing, -fies.** To renew the certification of, especially certification given by a licensing board. **—reʹcer·ti·fi·caʹtion** (-fĭ-kāʹshən) *n.*

re·cess (rēʹsĕsʹ, rĭ-sĕsʹ) *n.* **1. a.** A temporary cessation of the customary activities of an engagement, occupation, or pursuit. **b.** The period of such cessation. See Synonyms at **pause.** **2.** Often **recesses.** A remote, secret, or secluded place. **3. a.** An indentation or small hollow. **b.** An alcove. **—recess** *v.* **-cessed, -cess·ing, -cess·es.** *—tr.* **1.** To place in a recess. **2.** To create or fashion a recess in: *recessed a portion of the wall.* **3.** To suspend for a recess: *The committee chair recessed the hearings.* *—intr.* To take a recess: *The investigators recessed for lunch.* [Latin *recessus,* retreat, from past participle of *recēdere,* to recede. See RECEDE.]

re·ces·sion (rĭ-sĕshʹən) *n.* **1.** The act of withdrawing or going back. **2.** An extended decline in general business activity, typically three consecutive quarters of falling real gross national product. **3.** The withdrawal in a line or file of participants in a ceremony, especially clerics and choir members after a church service. [Latin *recessiō, recessiōn-,* from *recessus,* past participle of *recēdere,* to recede. See RECEDE.]

re·ces·sion (rē-sĕshʹən) *n. Law.* The act of restoring possession to a former owner.

re·ces·sion·al (rĭ-sĕshʹə-nəl) *n.* **1.** *Music.* A hymn that accompanies the exit of the clergy and choir after a service. **2.** A recession from a church. **—recessional** *adj.* Of or relating to a recession.

re·ces·sive (rĭ-sĕsʹĭv) *adj.* **1.** Tending to go backward or recede. **2. a.** *Genetics.* Of, relating to, or designating an allele that does not produce a characteristic effect when present with a dominant allele. **b.** Of or relating to a trait that is expressed only when the determining allele is present in the homozygous condition. **—recessive** *n. Genetics.* **1.** A recessive allele or trait. **2.** An organism having a recessive trait. **—re·cesʹsive·ly** *adv.* **—re·cesʹsive·ness** *n.*

re·charge (rē-chärjʹ) *tr.v.* **-charged, -charg·ing, -charg·es.** To charge again, especially to reenergize a storage battery. **—reʹchargeʹ** *n.* **—re·chargeʹa·ble** *adj.* **—re·chargʹer** *n.*

ré·chauf·fé (rāʹshō-fāʹ) *n.* **1.** Warmed leftover food. **2.** Old material reworked or rehashed. [French, past participle of *réchauffer,* to reheat, warm over, from Old French *rechaufer* : *re-,* re- + *echaufer,* to warm (from Vulgar Latin **excalefāre* : Latin *ex-,* intensive pref.; see EX– + Latin *calefacere,* to warm; see CHAFE).]

re·cher·ché (rə-shĕrʹshāʹ) *adj.* **1.** Uncommon; rare. **2.** Exquisite; choice. **3.** Overrefined; forced. **4.** Pretentious; overblown. [French, past participle of *rechercher,* to research, from Old French *recercher.* See RESEARCH.]

re·cid·i·vism (rĭ-sĭdʹə-vĭzʹəm) *n.* A tendency to lapse into a previous pattern of behavior, especially a tendency to return to criminal habits. [From *recidivist,* from French *récidiviste,* from *récidiver,* to relapse, from Medieval Latin *recidīvāre,* from Latin *recidīvus,* falling back, from *recidere,* to fall back : *re-,* re- + *cadere,* to fall; see **kad-** in Appendix.] **—re·cidʹi·vist** *n.* **—re·cidʹi·visʹtic, re·cidʹi·vous** *adj.*

Re·ci·fe (rə-sēʹfə). A city of northeast Brazil on the Atlantic Ocean south of Natal. First settled in 1535, it was plundered by English privateers in 1595 and occupied by the Dutch from 1630 to 1654. Population, 1,203,899.

recip. *abbr.* Reciprocal; reciprocity.

rec·i·pe (rĕsʹə-pēʹ) *n.* **1.** A set of directions with a list of ingredients for making or preparing something, especially food. **2.** A formula for or means to a desired end: *a recipe for success.* **3.** A medical prescription. [Latin, imperative of *recipere,* to take, receive. See RECEIVE.]

re·cip·i·ence (rĭ-sĭpʹē-əns) also **re·cip·i·en·cy** (-ən-sē) *n.* Capacity to receive; receptivity.

re·cip·i·ent (rĭ-sĭpʹē-ənt) *adj.* Functioning as a receiver; receptive. **—recipient** *n.* **1.** One that receives or is receptive. **2.** One who receives blood, tissue, or an organ from a donor. [Latin *recipiēns, recipient-,* present participle of *recipere,* to receive. See RECEIVE.]

re·cip·ro·cal (rĭ-sĭpʹrə-kəl) *adj. Abbr.* **recip.** **1.** Concerning each of two or more persons or things. **2.** Interchanged, given, or owed to each other: *reciprocal agreements to abolish customs duties; a reciprocal invitation to lunch.* **3.** Performed, experienced, or felt by both sides: *reciprocal respect.* **4.** Interchangeable; complementary: *reciprocal electric outlets.* **5.** *Grammar.* Expressing mutual action or relationship. Used of some verbs and compound pronouns. **6.** *Mathematics.* Of or relating to the reciprocal of a quantity. **7.** *Physiology.* Of or relating to a neuromuscular phenomenon in which the excitation of one group of muscles is accompanied by the inhibition of another. **8.** *Genetics.* Of or designating a pair of crosses in which the male parent in one cross is of the same genotype or phenotype as the female parent in the other cross. **—reciprocal** *n. Abbr.* **recip. 1.** Something that is reciprocal to something else. **2.** *Mathematics.* A number related to another in such a way that when multiplied together their product is 1. For example, the reciprocal of 7 is 1/7; the reciprocal of 2/3 is 3/2. [From Latin *reciprocus,* alternating. See **per**[1] in Appendix.] **—re·cip′ro·cal′i·ty** (-kăl′ĭ-tē), **re·cip′ro·cal·ness** (-kəl-nĭs) *n.* **—re·cip′ro·cal·ly** *adv.*

reciprocal pronoun *n. Grammar.* A pronoun or pronominal phrase, such as *each other,* that expresses mutual action or relationship.

re·cip·ro·cate (rĭ-sĭp′rə-kāt′) *v.* **-cat·ed, -cat·ing, -cates.** *—tr.* **1.** To give or take mutually; interchange. **2.** To show, feel, or give in response or return. *—intr.* **1.** To move back and forth alternately. **2.** To give and take something mutually. **3.** To make a return for something given or done. **4.** To be complementary or equivalent. [Latin *reciprocāre, reciprocāt-,* to move back and forth, from *reciprocus,* alternating. See RECIPROCAL.] **—re·cip′ro·ca′tive** *adj.* **—re·cip′ro·ca′tor** *n.*

SYNONYMS: *reciprocate, requite, return.* The central meaning shared by these verbs is "to give, take, or feel reciprocally": *doesn't reciprocate favors; consideration requited with callous disregard; return a compliment.*

re·cip·ro·cat·ing engine (rĭ-sĭp′rə-kā′tĭng) *n.* An engine in which the crankshaft is turned by pistons moving up and down in a cylinder.

re·cip·ro·ca·tion (rĭ-sĭp′rə-kā′shən) *n.* **1.** An alternating back-and-forth movement. **2.** The act or fact of reciprocating; interchange.

rec·i·proc·i·ty (rĕs′ə-prŏs′ĭ-tē) *n., pl.* **-ties.** *Abbr.* **recip. 1.** A reciprocal condition or relationship. **2.** A mutual or cooperative interchange of favors or privileges, especially the exchange of rights or privileges of trade between nations.

re·ci·sion (rĭ-sĭzh′ən) *n.* The act of rescinding; annulment or cancellation. [Obsolete French, from Old French, annulment of a judgment, from Latin *recīsiō, recīsiōn-,* from *recīsus,* past participle of *recīdere,* to cut back : *re-,* re- + *caedere,* to cut; see **kaə-id-** in Appendix.]

re·cit·al (rĭ-sīt′l) *n.* **1.** The act of reading or reciting in a public performance. **2.** A very detailed account or report of something; a narration. **3.** A public performance of music or dance, especially by a solo performer. **—re·ci′tal·ist** *n.*

rec·i·ta·tion (rĕs′ĭ-tā′shən) *n.* **1.a.** The act of reciting memorized materials in a public performance. **b.** The material so presented. **2.a.** Oral delivery of prepared lessons by a pupil. **b.** The class period within which this delivery occurs.

rec·i·ta·tive[1] (rĕs′ĭ-tā′tĭv, rĭ-sī′tə-tĭv) *adj.* Of, relating to, or having the character of a recital or recitation.

rec·i·ta·tive[2] (rĕs′ĭ-tə-tēv′) *n. Music.* **1.** A style used in operas, oratorios, and cantatas in which the text is declaimed in the rhythm of natural speech with slight melodic variation. **2.** A passage rendered in this style. Also called *recitativo.* [Italian *recitativo,* from *recitare,* to recite, from Latin *recitāre.* See RECITE.]

re·ci·ta·ti·vo (rĕs′ĭ-tə-tē′vō, rĕ′chē-tä-) *n., pl.* **-vi** (-vē) or **-vos** (-vōz). *Music.* See **recitative**[2]. [Italian. See RECITATIVE[2].]

re·cite (rĭ-sīt′) *v.* **-cit·ed, -cit·ing, -cites.** *—tr.* **1.** To repeat or utter aloud (something rehearsed or memorized), especially before an audience. **2.** To relate in detail. See Synonyms at **describe. 3.** To list or enumerate. *—intr.* **1.** To deliver a recitation. **2.** To repeat lessons prepared or memorized. [Middle English *reciten,* from Old French *reciter,* from Latin *recitāre,* to read out : *re-,* re- + *citāre,* to quote; see CITE.] **—re·cit′er** *n.*

reck (rĕk) *tr. & intr.v.* **recked, reck·ing, recks.** To take heed of or to have caution. [Middle English *recken,* from Old English *reccan.* See **reg-** in Appendix.]

reck·less (rĕk′lĭs) *adj.* **1.a.** Heedless or careless. **b.** Headstrong; rash. **2.** Indifferent to or disregardful of consequences: *a reckless driver.* [Middle English *reckeles,* from Old English *rēcelēas.* See **reg-** in Appendix.] **—reck′less·ly** *adv.* **—reck′less·ness** *n.*

SYNONYMS: *reckless, rash, precipitate, foolhardy, temerarious.* These adjectives are compared as they mean given to or marked by unthinking boldness. *Reckless* suggests brazen indifference to or defiant disregard for consequences: *"James . . . became the fiercest and most reckless of partisans"* (Macaulay). *Rash* implies haste, impetuousness, and insufficient consideration: *"Take calculated risks. That is quite different from being rash"* (George S. Patton). *Precipitate* connotes headlong haste without due deliberation: *"destroyed in a precipitate burning of his papers a few days before his death"* (James Boswell). *Foolhardy* implies injudicious or imprudent boldness: *One of the hostages was foolhardy enough to try to wrest the gun from the hijacker's hand. Temerarious* suggests reckless presumption: *"the temerarious use of Christian names"* (H.G. Wells).

Reck·ling·hau·sen (rĕk′lĭng-hou′zən). A city of west-central Germany southwest of Münster. Originally a Saxon settlement, it was held by the archbishop of Cologne after 1236 and passed to Prussia in 1815. Population, 117,989.

reck·on (rĕk′ən) *v.* **-oned, -on·ing, -ons.** *—tr.* **1.** To count or compute: *reckon the cost.* See Synonyms at **calculate. 2.** To consider as being; regard as. See Synonyms at **consider. 3.** *Informal.* To think or assume. *—intr.* **1.** To make a calculation; figure. **2.** To rely with confident expectancy. See Synonyms at **rely.** *—phrasal verb.* **reckon with.** To come to terms or settle accounts with. [Middle English *reknen,* from Old English *gerecenian,* to recount, arrange. See **reg-** in Appendix.]

reck·on·er (rĕk′ə-nər) *n.* A handbook of mathematical tables used to facilitate computation.

reck·on·ing (rĕk′ə-nĭng) *n.* **1.** The act of counting or computing. **2.** An itemized bill or statement of a sum due. **3.** A settlement of accounts: *a day of reckoning.* **4.a.** The act or process of calculating the position of a ship or an aircraft. **b.** The position so calculated.

re·claim (rĭ-klām′) *tr.v.* **-claimed, -claim·ing, -claims. 1.** To bring into or return to a suitable condition for use, as cultivation or habitation: *reclaim marshlands, reclaim strip-mined land.* **2.** To procure (usable substances) from refuse or waste products. **3.** To bring back, as from error, to a right or proper course; reform. See Synonyms at **save**[1]. **4.** To tame (a falcon, for example). [Middle English *reclamen,* to call back, from Old French *reclamer,* to entreat, from Latin *reclāmāre* : *re-,* re- + *clāmāre,* to cry out; see **kelə-**[2] in Appendix.] **—re·claim′a·ble** *adj.* **—re·claim′ant, re·claim′er** *n.*

re-claim (rē-klām′) *tr.v.* **-claimed, -claim·ing, -claims.** To demand the restoration or return of (a possession, for example); claim again or back.

rec·la·ma·tion (rĕk′lə-mā′shən) *n.* **1.** The act or process of reclaiming. **2.** A restoration, as to productivity, usefulness, or morality. [Middle English *reclamacion,* from Old French *reclamation,* from Latin *reclāmātiō, reclāmātiōn-,* cry of opposition, from *reclāmātus,* past participle of *reclāmāre,* to exclaim against. See RECLAIM.]

ré·clame (rā-kläm′) *n.* **1.** Public acclaim. **2.** A taste or flair for publicity. [French, advertising, from *réclamer,* to claim, beg for, from Old French *reclamer,* to exclaim against. See RECLAIM.]

rec·li·nate (rĕk′lə-nāt′) *adj. Botany.* Bent or turned downward toward the base. [Latin *reclīnātus,* past participle of *reclīnāre,* to recline. See RECLINE.]

re·cline (rĭ-klīn′) *v.* **-clined, -clin·ing, -clines.** *—tr.* To cause to assume a leaning or prone position. *—intr.* To lie back or down. [Middle English *reclinen,* from Old French *recliner,* from Latin *reclīnāre* : *re-,* re- + *-clīnāre,* to bend; see **klei-** in Appendix.] **—rec′li·na′tion** (rĕk′lə-nā′shən) *n.*

re·clin·er (rĭ-klī′nər) *n.* One that reclines, as an armchair that reclines when the sitter lowers the chair's back and raises its front.

recliner

re·cluse (rĕk′lo͞os′, rĭ-klo͞os′) *n.* A person who withdraws from the world to live in seclusion and often in solitude. **—recluse** *adj.* Withdrawn from the world; reclusive. [Middle English, from Old French *reclus,* from Latin *reclūsus,* past participle of *reclūdere,* to shut up : *re-,* re- + *claudere,* to close.]

re·clu·sion (rĭ-klo͞o′zhən) *n.* **1.** The condition of being a recluse. **2.** The state of being in solitary confinement.

re·clu·sive (rĭ-klo͞o′sĭv, -zĭv) *adj.* **1.** Seeking or preferring seclusion or isolation. **2.** Providing seclusion: *a reclusive hut.* **—re·clu′sive·ly** *adv.* **—re·clu′sive·ness** *n.*

rec·og·ni·tion (rĕk′əg-nĭsh′ən) *n.* **1.** The act of recognizing or condition of being recognized. **2.** An awareness that something perceived has been perceived before. **3.** An acceptance as true or valid, as of a claim: *a recognition of their civil rights.* **4.** Attention or favorable notice: *She received recognition for her many achievements.* **5.** Official acceptance of the national status of a new government by another nation. **6.** *Biology.* The ability of one molecule to attach itself to another molecule having a complementary shape, as in enzyme-substrate and antibody-antigen interactions. [Middle English *recognicion,* knowledge of an event, from Old French *recognition,* from Latin *recognitiō, recognitiōn-,* act of recognizing, from *recognitus,* past participle of *recognōscere,* to recognize. See RECOGNIZE.] **—re·cog′ni·to′ry** (rĭ-kŏg′nĭ-tôr′ē, -tōr′ē), **re·cog′ni·tive** (-tĭv) *adj.*

re·cog·ni·zance (rĭ-kŏg′nĭ-zəns, -kŏn′ĭ-) *n.* **1.** *Law.* **a.** An obligation of record that is entered into before a court or magistrate, containing a condition to perform a particular act, such as making a court appearance. **b.** A sum of money pledged to assure the performance of such an act. **2.** A recognition. **3.** *Archaic.* A pledge; a token. [Middle English *recognisanze,* from Old French *recognuissance,* alteration (influenced by Medieval Latin *recognizāre,* to recognize) of *reconoissance,* from *reconoistre, reconoiss-,* to recognize. See RECOGNIZE.] **—re·cog′ni·zant** *adj.*

rec·og·nize (rĕk′əg-nīz′) *tr.v.* **-nized, -niz·ing, -niz·es. 1.** To know to be something that has been perceived before: *recognize a face.* **2.** To know or identify from past experience or knowledge: *recognize hostility.* **3.** To perceive or show acceptance of the validity or reality of: *recognizes the concerns of the tenants.* **4.** To permit to address a meeting: *The club's president recognized the new member.* **5.** To accept officially the national status of as a new government. **6.** To show awareness of; approve of or appreciate: *recognize services rendered.* **7.** To admit the acquaintance of, as by salutation: *recognize an old friend with a cheerful greeting.* **8.** *Law.* To enter into a recognizance. **9.** *Bi-*

ă pat	oi boy
ā pay	ou out
âr care	o͝o took
ä father	o͞o boot
ĕ pet	ŭ cut
ē be	ûr urge
ĭ pit	th thin
ī pie	*th* this
îr pier	hw which
ŏ pot	zh vision
ō toe	ə about, item
ô paw	♦ regionalism

Stress marks: **′** (primary); ′ (secondary), as in **dictionary** (dĭk′shə-nĕr′ē)

ology. To exhibit recognition for (an antigen or a substrate, for example). [Middle English *recognisen,* to resume possession of land, alteration (influenced by Medieval Latin *recognizāre,* to recognize) of Old French *reconoistre, reconoiss-,* to know again, from Latin *recognōscere* : *re-,* re- + *cognōscere,* to get to know; see **gnō-** in Appendix.] **—rec′og·niz′a·ble** *adj.* **—rec′og·niz′a·bly** *adv.* **—rec′og·niz′er** *n.*

re·coil (rĭ-koil′) *intr.v.* **-coiled, -coil·ing, -coils. 1.** To spring back, as upon firing. **2.** To shrink back, as in fear or repugnance. **3.** To fall back; return: *"Violence does, in truth, recoil upon the violent"* (Arthur Conan Doyle). **—recoil** (*also* rē′koil′) *n.* **1.** The backward action of a firearm upon firing. **2.** The act or state of recoiling; reaction. [Middle English *recoilen,* from Old French *reculer* : *re-,* re- + *cul,* buttocks (from Latin *cūlus;* see **(s)keu-** in Appendix).] **—re·coil′er** *n.*

SYNONYMS: *recoil, blench, quail, shrink, flinch.* These verbs all mean to draw back involuntarily, as through fright, timidity, or abhorrence. To *recoil* is to spring back; the term can imply a physical motion or an emotional withdrawal or retreat: *"Those who had felt his strength recoiled from his presence"* (Sir Walter Scott). *"With a sudden revulsion his heart recoiled from its purpose"* (Henry Wadsworth Longfellow). *Blench* suggests shying away, as to evade something unpleasant or threatening: *"split-second dealmaking and risks that would make a currency dealer blench"* (Financial Times). *Quail* implies cringing loss of courage, as that resulting from being intimidated: *"She made Barnes quail before her by the shafts of contempt which she flashed at him"* (Thackeray). To *shrink* is to start back instinctively, as in avoidance: *"These are the times that try men's souls. The summer soldier and the sunshine patriot will, in this crisis, shrink from the service of their country"* (Thomas Paine). *Flinch* denotes a shrinking away from what is unpleasant or difficult; it often implies a faint-hearted retreat, as from a necessary undertaking: *"We did not flinch but gave our lives to save Greece"* (Simonides).

re·coil·less (rĭ-koil′lĭs, rē′koil′-) *adj.* Of or being a weapon designed to minimize the effect of recoil: *a recoilless rifle.*

rec·ol·lect (rĕk′ə-lĕkt′) *v.* **-lect·ed, -lect·ing, -lects.** *—tr.* To recall to mind. See Synonyms at **remember.** *—intr.* To have a recollection. [Medieval Latin *recolligere, recollēct-,* from Latin, to gather up : *re-,* re- + *colligere,* to collect; see COLLECT[1].] **—rec′ol·lec′tive** *adj.* **—rec′ol·lec′tive·ly** *adv.*

re-col·lect (rē′kə-lĕkt′) *tr.v.* **-lect·ed, -lect·ing, -lects. 1.** To collect again: *re-collect monies owed.* **2.** To calm or control (oneself).

rec·ol·lec·tion (rĕk′ə-lĕk′shən) *n.* **1.** The act or power of recollecting. **2.** Something recollected. See Synonyms at **memory.**

re·com·bi·nant (rē-kŏm′bə-nənt) *Genetics. n.* **1.** An organism or a cell in which genetic recombination has taken place. **2.** Genetic material produced by gene-splicing. **—recombinant** *adj.* **1.** Formed by or showing recombination: *a recombinant chromosome.* **2.** Of or relating to recombinant DNA: *recombinant fragments; recombinant technology.* **—re·com′bi·nant** *adj.*

recombinant DNA *n.* Genetically engineered DNA prepared by transplanting or splicing genes from one species into the cells of a host organism of a different species. Such DNA becomes part of the host's genetic makeup and is replicated.

re·com·bi·nase (rē-kŏm′bə-nās′, -nāz′) *n.* An enzyme that catalyzes genetic recombination.

re·com·bi·na·tion (rē′kŏm-bə-nā′shən) *n.* The natural formation in offspring of genetic combinations not present in parents, by the processes of crossing over or independent assortment.

re·com·bine (rē′kəm-bīn′) *v.* **-bined, -bin·ing, -bines.** *—tr.* To combine (things) again. *—intr.* **1.** To combine again. **2.** *Genetics.* To undergo or cause recombination; form new combinations.

rec·om·mend (rĕk′ə-mĕnd′) *v.* **-mend·ed, -mend·ing, -mends.** *—tr.* **1.** To praise or commend (one) to another as being worthy or desirable; endorse: *recommended him for the job; recommended a sedan instead of a station wagon.* **2.** To make (the possessor, as of an attribute) attractive or acceptable: *Honesty recommends any person.* **3.** To commit to the charge of another; entrust. **4.** To advise or counsel: *She recommended that we avoid giving offense.* See Synonyms at **advise.** *—intr.* To give advice or counsel: *"recommended against signing an international agreement"* (Time). [Middle English *recommenden,* from Medieval Latin *recommendāre* : Latin *re-,* re- + Latin *commendāre,* to entrust, commend; see COMMEND.] **—rec′om·mend′a·ble** *adj.* **—rec′om·mend′er** *n.*

rec·om·men·da·tion (rĕk′ə-mĕn-dā′shən) *n.* **1.** The act of recommending. **2.** Something that recommends, especially a favorable statement concerning character or qualifications. **3.** Something, such as a course of action, that is recommended. See Synonyms at **advice.** **—rec′om·men′da·to′ry** (-də-tôr′ē, -tōr′ē) *adj.*

re·com·mit (rē′kə-mĭt′) *tr.v.* **-mit·ted, -mit·ting, -mits. 1.** To commit again. **2.** To refer (proposed legislation, for example) to a committee again. **—re′com·mit′ment, re′com·mit′tal** (-mĭt′l) *n.*

rec·om·pense (rĕk′əm-pĕns′) *tr.v.* **-pensed, -pens·ing, -pens·es. 1.** To award compensation to: *recompensed the victims of the accident.* **2.** To award compensation for; make a return for: *recompensed their injuries.* **—recompense** *n.* **1.** Amends made, as for damage or loss. **2.** Payment in return for something, such as a service. [Middle English *recompensen,* from Old French *recompenser,* from Late Latin *recompēnsāre* : Latin *re-,* re- + Latin *compēnsāre,* to compensate; see COMPENSATE.]

re·com·pose (rē′kəm-pōz′) *tr.v.* **-posed, -pos·ing, -pos·es. 1.** To compose again; reorganize or rearrange. **2.** To restore to composure. **—re′com·po·si′tion** (rē′kŏm-pə-zĭsh′ən) *n.*

re·con[1] (rē′kŏn′) *n.* The smallest genetic unit capable of recombination. [REC(OMBINATION) + -ON[1].]

re·con[2] (rē′kŏn′) *n. Informal.* Reconnaissance. **—re′con′** *adj.*

rec·on·cil·a·ble (rĕk′ən-sī′lə-bəl, rĕk′ən-sī′-) *adj.* Capable of or qualified for reconciliation: *reconcilable differences.* **—rec′on·cil′a·bil′i·ty, rec′on·cil′a·ble·ness** *n.* **—rec′on·cil′a·bly** *adv.*

rec·on·cile (rĕk′ən-sīl′) *v.* **-ciled, -cil·ing, -ciles.** *—tr.* **1.** To reestablish a close relationship between. **2.** To settle or resolve. **3.** To bring (oneself) to accept: *He finally reconciled himself to the change in management.* **4.** To make compatible or consistent: *reconcile my way of thinking with yours.* See Synonyms at **adapt.** *—intr.* **1.** To reestablish a close relationship, as in marriage: *The estranged couple reconciled after a year.* **2.** To become compatible or consistent: *The figures would not reconcile.* [Middle English *reconcilen,* from Old French *reconcilier,* from Latin *reconciliāre* : *re-,* re- + *conciliāre,* to conciliate; see CONCILIATE.] **—rec′on·cile′ment** *n.* **—rec′on·cil′er** *n.* **—rec′on·cil′i·a·to′ry** (-sĭl′ē-ə-tôr′ē, -tōr′ē) *adj.*

rec·on·cil·i·a·tion (rĕk′ən-sĭl′ē-ā′shən) *n.* **1.** The act of reconciling. **2.** The condition of being reconciled. **3.** See **penance** (sense 2). [Middle English *reconsiliacion,* from Old French *reconciliation,* from Latin *reconciliātiō, reconciliātiōn-,* from *reconciliātus,* past participle of *reconciliāre,* to reconcile. See RECONCILE.]

rec·on·dite (rĕk′ən-dīt′, rĭ-kŏn′dīt′) *adj.* **1.** Not easily understood; abstruse. See Synonyms at **ambiguous. 2.** Concerned with or treating something abstruse or obscure: *recondite scholarship.* **3.** Concealed; hidden. [Latin *reconditus,* past participle of *recondere,* to put away : *re-,* re- + *condere,* to put together, preserve; see **dhē-** in Appendix.] **—rec′on·dite′ly** *adv.* **—rec′on·dite′ness** *n.*

re·con·di·tion (rē′kən-dĭsh′ən) *tr.v.* **-tioned, -tion·ing, -tions.** To restore to good condition, especially by repairing, renovating, or rebuilding.

re·con·firm (rē′kən-fûrm′) *tr.v.* **-firmed, -firm·ing, -firms.** To confirm again, especially to establish or support more firmly: *reconfirmed the reservations.* **—re′con·fir·ma′tion** (rē′kŏn-fər-mā′shən) *n.*

re·con·nais·sance also **re·con·nois·sance** (rĭ-kŏn′ə-səns, -zəns) *n.* An inspection or exploration of an area, especially one made to gather military information. [French, from Old French *reconoissance,* recognition, from *reconoistre, reconoiss-,* to recognize. See RECOGNIZE.]

re·con·noi·ter (rē′kə-noi′tər, rĕk′ə-) *v.* **-tered, -ter·ing, -ters.** *—tr.* To make a preliminary inspection of, especially in order to gather military information. *—intr.* To make a reconnaissance. [Obsolete French *reconnoître,* from Old French *reconoistre,* to recognize. See RECOGNIZE.] **—re′con·noi′ter·er** *n.*

re·con·sid·er (rē′kən-sĭd′ər) *v.* **-ered, -er·ing, -ers.** *—tr.* **1.** To consider again, especially with intent to alter or modify a previous decision. **2.** To take up for reconsideration, as a matter previously acted on by a legislature. *—intr.* To consider again. **—re′con·sid′er·a′tion** *n.*

re·con·sti·tute (rē-kŏn′stĭ-to͞ot′, -tyo͞ot′) *tr.v.* **-tut·ed, -tut·ing, -tutes. 1.** To provide with a new structure: *The parks commission has been reconstituted.* **2.** To bring (a liquid in concentrated or powder form) to normal strength by adding water.

re·con·struct (rē′kən-strŭkt′) *tr.v.* **-struct·ed, -struct·ing, -structs. 1.** To construct again. **2.** To cause to adapt to social or economic change. **—re′con·struc′ti·ble** *adj.*

re·con·struc·tion (rē′kən-strŭk′shən) *n.* **1.** The act or result of reconstructing. **2. Reconstruction.** The period (1865–1877) during which the states of the Confederacy were controlled by the federal government before being readmitted to the Union. **—re′con·struc′tive** *adj.*

Re·con·struc·tion·ism (rē′-kən-strŭk′shə-nĭz′əm) *n. Judaism.* The branch of Judaism founded in the United States in the 20th century that regards Judaism as a religious civilization and questions the doctrine that the Jews are God's chosen people. **—Re′con·struc′tion·ist** *adj.* & *n.*

re·con·vert (rē′kən-vûrt′) *intr.* & *tr.v.* **-vert·ed, -vert·ing, -verts.** To undergo or cause to undergo conversion to a previous state or condition. **—re′con·ver′sion** (-vûr′zhən, -shən) *n.*

re·con·vey (rē′kən-vā′) *tr.v.* **-veyed, -vey·ing, -veys.** To convey to a former owner or place. **—re′con·vey′ance** *n.*

re·cord (rĭ-kôrd′) *v.* **-cord·ed, -cord·ing, -cords.** *—tr.* **1.** To set down for preservation in writing or other permanent form. **2.** To register or indicate: *The clerk recorded the votes.* **3.a.** To register (sound or images) in permanent form by mechanical or electrical means for reproduction. **b.** To register the words, sound, appearance, or performance of by such means: *recorded the oldest townspeople on tape; recorded the violin concerto.* *—intr.* To record something. **—rec·ord** (rĕk′ərd) *n. Abbr.* **rec.**

1.a. An account, as of information or facts, set down especially in writing as a means of preserving knowledge. **b.** Something on which such an account is based. **c.** Something that records: *a fossil record.* **2.** Information or data on a particular subject collected and preserved: *the coldest day on record.* **3.** The known history of performance, activities, or achievement: *your academic record; hampered by a police record.* **4.** An unsurpassed measurement: *a world record in weightlifting; a record for cold weather.* **5.** *Computer Science.* A collection of related, often adjacent items of data, treated as a unit. **6.** *Law.* **a.** An account officially written and preserved as evidence or testimony. **b.** An account of judicial or legislative proceedings written and preserved as evidence. **c.** The documents or volumes containing such evidence. **7.a.** A disk designed to be played on a phonograph. **b.** Something, such as magnetic tape, on which sound or visual images have been recorded. **—*idioms.* go on record.** To embrace a certain position publicly: *go on record in favor of the mayor's reelection.* **off the record.** Not for publication: *The senator told the reporters that his remarks were strictly off the record.* **on record.** Known to have been stated or to have taken a certain position: *The senator's opposition to the new legislation is on record.* [Middle English *recorden,* from Old French *recorder,* from Latin *recordārī,* to remember : *re-,* re- + *cor, cord-,* heart; see **kerd-** in Appendix.]

rec·ord changer (rĕk′ərd) *n.* A device on a phonograph that automatically plays each in turn of a group of records stacked on the spindle.

re·cord·er (rĭ-kôr′dər) *n.* **1.** One, such as a tape recorder, that makes recordings or records. **2.** *Law.* A judge who has criminal jurisdiction in a city. **3.** *Music.* A flute with eight finger holes and a whistlelike mouthpiece. [Sense 3, probably from RECORD, to practice a tune, warble.]

re·cord·ing (rĭ-kôr′dĭng) *n.* *Abbr.* **rec.** **1.** Something on which sound or visual images have been recorded. **2.** A recorded sound or picture.

re·cord·ist (rĭ-kôr′dĭst) *n.* One that records sound electronically, as for films or at concerts.

re·count (rĭ-kount′) *tr.v.* **-count·ed, -count·ing, -counts. 1.** To narrate the facts or particulars of. See Synonyms at **describe. 2.** To enumerate. [Middle English *recounten,* from Old French *reconter* : *re-,* re- + *conter,* relate; see COUNT[1].] **—re·count′al** *n.*

re-count (rē-kount′) *tr.v.* **-count·ed, -count·ing, -counts.** To count again. **—re-count** (*also* rē′kount′) *n.* An additional count, especially a second count of votes cast in an election.

re·coup (rĭ-ko͞op′) *v.* **-couped, -coup·ing, -coups.** *—tr.* **1.** To receive an equivalent for; make up for: *recoup a loss.* See Synonyms at **recover. 2.** To return as an equivalent for; reimburse. **3.** *Law.* To deduct or withhold (part of something due) for an equitable reason. *—intr.* To regain a former favorable position. **—recoup** *n.* The act of recouping. [Middle English *recoupen,* from Old French *recouper,* to cut back : *re-,* re- + *couper,* to cut (from *coup,* blow; see COUP).] **—re·coup′a·ble** *adj.* **—re·coup′ment** *n.*

re·course (rē′kôrs′, -kōrs′, rĭ-kôrs′, -kōrs′) *n.* **1.** The act or an instance of turning or applying to a person or thing for aid or security: *have recourse to the courts.* **2.** One that is turned or applied to for aid or security: *His only recourse was the police.* **3.** *Law.* The right to demand payment from the endorser of a commercial paper when the first party liable fails to pay. [Middle English *recours,* from Old French, from Latin *recursus,* a running back, from past participle of *recurrere,* to run back : *re-,* re- + *currere,* to run; see **kers-** in Appendix.]

re·cov·er (rĭ-kŭv′ər) *v.* **-ered, -er·ing, -ers.** *—tr.* **1.** To get back; regain. **2.** To restore (oneself) to a normal state: *He recovered himself after a slip on the ice.* **3.** To compensate for: *She recovered her losses.* **4.** To procure (usable substances, such as metal) from unusable substances, such as ore or waste. **5.** To bring under observation again: *"watching the comet since it was first recovered—first spotted since its 1910 visit"* (Christian Science Monitor). *—intr.* **1.** To regain a normal or usual condition, as of health. **2.** To receive a favorable judgment in a lawsuit. [Middle English *recoveren,* from Old French *recoverer,* from Latin *recuperāre.* See RECUPERATE.] **—re·cov′er·a·ble** *adj.* **—re·cov′er·er** *n.*

SYNONYMS: *recover, regain, recoup, retrieve.* These verbs are compared as they mean to get back something lost or taken away. *Recover* is the least specific: *The police recovered the stolen car. "In a few days Mr. Barnstaple had recovered strength of body and mind"* (H.G. Wells). *"He . . . stood in the porch a minute to recover his composure"* (John Galsworthy). *Regain* suggests success in recovering something that has been taken from one: *"hopeful to regain/Thy Love"* (John Milton); *"regain'd my freedom with a sigh"* (Byron). To *recoup* is to get back the equivalent of something lost: *The teacher, who had bought the book for the school library, felt entitled to recoup her expenses. Retrieve* pertains to the effortful recovery of something (*retrieved the ball from the end zone*) or to the rectification of unfavorable consequences or the making good of something gone amiss or awry: *"a false step that he was never able to retrieve"* (John Morley). *"By a brilliant coup he has retrieved . . . a rather serious loss"* (Samuel Butler).

re-cov·er (rē-kŭv′ər) *tr.v.* **-ered, -er·ing, -ers.** To cover anew: *re-cover an armchair.*

recoverable error *n.* *Computer Science.* A program error that does not prevent execution.

re·cov·er·y (rĭ-kŭv′ə-rē) *n., pl.* **-ies. 1.** The act, process, duration, or an instance of recovering. **2.** A return to a normal condition. **3.** Something gained or restored in recovering. **4.** The act of obtaining usable substances from unusable sources.

recovery room *n.* A hospital room equipped for the care and observation of patients immediately following surgery.

rec·re·ant (rĕk′rē-ənt) *adj.* **1.** Unfaithful or disloyal to a belief, duty, or cause. See Synonyms at **faithless. 2.** Craven or cowardly. **—recreant** *n.* **1.** A faithless or disloyal person. **2.** A coward. [Middle English, from Old French, present participle of *recroire,* to remember, from Medieval Latin *recrēdere,* to yield, pledge : Latin *re-,* re- + Latin *crēdere,* to believe; see **kerd-** in Appendix.] **—rec′re·ance, rec′re·an·cy** *n.* **—rec′re·ant·ly** *adv.*

rec·re·ate (rĕk′rē-āt′) *v.* **-at·ed, -at·ing, -ates.** *—tr.* To impart fresh life to; refresh mentally or physically. *—intr.* To take recreation. [Middle English *recreaten,* from Latin *recreāre, recreāt-* : *re-,* re- + *creāre,* to create; see CREATE.] **—rec′re·a′tive** *adj.*

re-cre·ate (rē′krē-āt′) *tr.v.* **-at·ed, -at·ing, -ates.** To create anew.

rec·re·a·tion (rĕk′rē-ā′shən) *n.* *Abbr.* **rec.** Refreshment of one's mind or body after work through activity that amuses or stimulates; play.

rec·re·a·tion·al (rĕk′rē-ā′shə-nəl) *adj.* **1.** Of or relating to recreation: *recreational swimming.* **2.** Of or relating to the occasional use, asserted not to be addictive, of narcotics: *"You can't accept recreational drug use and expect to control the drug problem"* (Lacy Thornburg). **—rec′re·a′tion·al·ly** *adv.*

recreational vehicle *n.* *Abbr.* **RV** A vehicle, such as a camper or a motor home, used for traveling and recreational activities.

recreation room *n.* A room in a house or an institution suited for games, dancing, or other kinds of recreation.

rec·re·ment (rĕk′rə-mənt) *n.* Waste matter; dross. [Latin *recrēmentum* : *re-,* re- + *cernere, crē-,* to separate; see **krei-** in Appendix.] **—rec′re·men′tal** (-mĕn′tl) *adj.*

re·crim·i·nate (rĭ-krĭm′ə-nāt′) *v.* **-nat·ed, -nat·ing, -nates.** *—tr.* To accuse in return. *—intr.* To counter one accusation with another. [Medieval Latin *recrīmināri, recrīmināt-* : Latin *re-,* re- + *crīmināre,* to accuse (from *crīmen, crīmin-,* accusation, crime; see **krei-** in Appendix).] **—re·crim′i·na′tive, re·crim′i·na·to′ry** (-nə-tôr′ē, -tōr′ē) *adj.* **—re·crim′i·na′tor** *n.*

re·crim·i·na·tion (rĭ-krĭm′ə-nā′shən) *n.* **1.** The act of recriminating. **2.** A countercharge.

rec room (rĕk) *n.* *Informal.* A recreation room.

re·cru·desce (rē′kro͞o-dĕs′) *intr.v.* **-desced, -desc·ing, -desc·es.** To break out anew or come into renewed activity, as after a period of quiescence. See Synonyms at **return.** [Latin *recrūdēscere,* to grow raw again : *re-,* re- + *crūdēscere,* to get worse (from *crūdus,* raw; see **kreuə-** in Appendix).] **—re′cru·des′cence** *n.* **—re′cru·des′cent** *adj.*

re·cruit (rĭ-kro͞ot′) *v.* **-cruit·ed, -cruit·ing, -cruits.** *—tr.* **1.** To engage (persons) for military service. **2.** To strengthen or raise (an armed force) by enlistment. **3.** To supply with new members or employees. **4.** To enroll or seek to enroll: *colleges recruiting minority students.* **5.** To replenish. **6.** To renew or restore the health, vitality, or intensity of. *—intr.* **1.** To raise a military force. **2.** To obtain replacements for or new supplies of something lost, wasted, or needed. **3.** To regain lost health or strength; recover. **—recruit** *n.* *Abbr.* **rct. 1.** A newly engaged member of a military force, especially one of the lowest rank or grade. **2.** A new member of an organization or a body. [French *recruter,* from obsolete *recrute,* recruit, variant of *recrue,* from feminine past participle of *recroître,* to grow again, from Old French *recroistre* : *re-,* re- + *croistre,* to grow (from Latin *crēscere;* see **ker-**[2] in Appendix).] **—re·cruit′er** *n.* **—re·cruit′ment** *n.*

rec. sec. *abbr.* Recording secretary.

rect. *abbr.* **1.** Receipt. **2.** Rectangle; rectangular. **3.** Rectified. **4.** Rector; rectory.

rec·ta (rĕk′tə) *n.* A plural of **rectum.**

rec·tal (rĕk′təl) *adj.* Of, relating to, or situated near the rectum. **—rec′tal·ly** *adv.*

rec·tan·gle (rĕk′tăng′gəl) *n.* *Abbr.* **rect.** A four-sided plane figure with four right angles. [French, from Medieval Latin *rēctangulum,* a right triangle, from Late Latin *rēctiangulum* : Latin *rēctus,* right; see **reg-** in Appendix + Latin *angulus,* angle.]

rec·tan·gu·lar (rĕk-tăng′gyə-lər) *adj.* *Abbr.* **rect. 1.** Having the shape of a rectangle. **2.** Having one or more right angles. **3.** Designating a geometric coordinate system with mutually perpendicular axes. **—rec·tan′gu·lar′i·ty** (-lăr′ĭ-tē) *n.* **—rec·tan′gu·lar·ly** *adv.*

rectangular coordinate *n.* *Mathematics.* A coordinate in a rectangular Cartesian coordinate system.

rec·ti (rĕk′tī′) *n.* Plural of **rectus.**

rec·ti·fi·er (rĕk′tə-fī′ər) *n.* **1.** One that rectifies: *a rectifier of many wrongs.* **2.** *Electronics.* A device, such as a diode, that converts alternating current to direct current. **3.** A worker who blends or dilutes whiskey or other alcoholic beverages.

rec·ti·fy (rĕk′tə-fī′) *tr.v.* **-fied, -fy·ing, -fies. 1.** To set right; correct. **2.** To correct by calculation or adjustment. See Syn-

recorder

ă pat	oi boy
ā pay	ou out
âr care	o͝o took
ä father	o͞o boot
ĕ pet	ŭ cut
ē be	ûr urge
ĭ pit	th thin
ī pie	*th* this
îr pier	hw which
ŏ pot	zh vision
ō toe	ə about, item
ô paw	♦ regionalism

Stress marks: ′ (primary); ′ (secondary), as in dictionary (dĭk′shə-nĕr′ē)

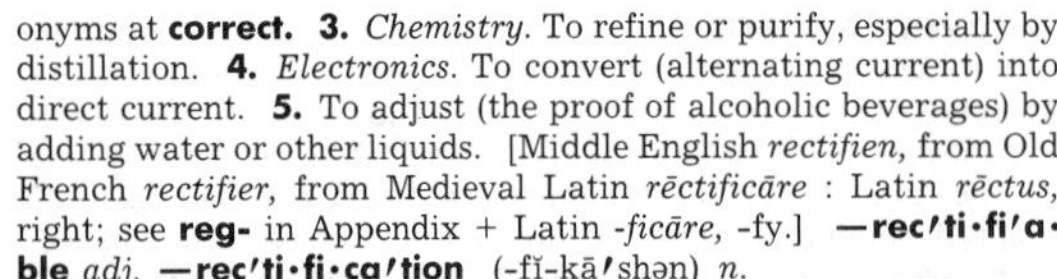

onyms at **correct.** **3.** *Chemistry.* To refine or purify, especially by distillation. **4.** *Electronics.* To convert (alternating current) into direct current. **5.** To adjust (the proof of alcoholic beverages) by adding water or other liquids. [Middle English *rectifien,* from Old French *rectifier,* from Medieval Latin *rēctificāre* : Latin *rēctus,* right; see **reg-** in Appendix + Latin *-ficāre,* -fy.] **—rec′ti·fi′a·ble** *adj.* **—rec′ti·fi·ca′tion** (-fĭ-kā′shən) *n.*

recycle

rec·ti·lin·e·ar (rĕk′tə-lĭn′ē-ər) *adj.* Moving in, consisting of, bounded by, or characterized by a straight line or lines: *following a rectilinear path; rectilinear patterns in wallpaper.* [From Late Latin *rēctilīneus* : Latin *rēctus,* right; see **reg-** in Appendix + Latin *līnea,* line; see LINE[1].] **—rec′ti·lin′e·ar·ly** *adv.*

rec·ti·tude (rĕk′tĭ-to͞od′, -tyo͞od′) *n.* **1.** Moral uprightness; righteousness. See Synonyms at **honesty.** **2.** The quality or condition of being correct in judgment. **3.** The quality of being straight. [Middle English, from Old French, from Late Latin *rēctitūdō,* from Latin *rēctus,* straight. See **reg-** in Appendix.] **—rec′ti·tu′di·nous** *adj.*

rec·to (rĕk′tō) *n., pl.* **-tos.** *Printing.* A right-hand page of a book or the front side of a leaf, on the other side of the verso. [From Latin *(foliō) rēctō,* (the leaf) being right, ablative of *rēctus,* straight, right. See **reg-** in Appendix.]

rec·tor (rĕk′tər) *n. Abbr.* **R., rect.** **1.** A cleric in charge of a parish in the Protestant Episcopal Church. **2.** An Anglican cleric who has charge of a parish and owns the tithes from it. **3.** A Roman Catholic priest appointed to be managerial as well as spiritual head of a church or other institution, such as a seminary or university. **4.** The principal of certain schools, colleges, and universities. [Middle English, from Old French, from Latin *rēctor,* director, from *regere, rēct-,* to rule. See **reg-** in Appendix.] **—rec′tor·ate** (-ĭt) *n.* **—rec·to′ri·al** (rĕk-tôr′ē-əl, -tōr′-) *adj.*

Red Cloud
Photographed in 1880

rec·to·ry (rĕk′tə-rē) *n., pl.* **-ries.** *Abbr.* **rect.** **1.** The house in which a parish priest or minister lives. **2. a.** An Anglican rector's dwelling. **b.** An Anglican rector's office and benefice.

rec·trix (rĕk′trĭks) *n., pl.* **rec·tri·ces** (rĕk′trĭ-sēz′, rĕk-trī′sēz). One of the stiff main feathers of a bird's tail, used to control the direction of flight. [Latin *rēctrīx,* feminine of *rēctor,* director. See RECTOR.]

rec·tum (rĕk′təm) *n., pl.* **-tums** or **-ta** (-tə). The terminal portion of the large intestine, extending from the sigmoid flexure to the anal canal. [Middle English, from Latin *(intestīnum) rēctum,* straight (intestine), neuter of *rēctus.* See **reg-** in Appendix.]

rec·tus (rĕk′təs) *n., pl.* **-ti** (-tī′). Any of various straight muscles, as of the abdomen, eye, neck, and thigh. [New Latin *(mūsculus) rēctus,* from Latin, straight (muscle). See RECTUM.]

re·cum·bent (rĭ-kŭm′bənt) *adj.* **1.** Lying down, especially in a position of comfort or rest; reclining. See Synonyms at **prone.** **2.** Resting; idle. **3.** *Biology.* Resting on the surface from which it arises. Used of an organ or other structure. [Latin *recumbēns, recumbent-,* present participle of *recumbere,* to lie down : *re-,* re- + *cumbere,* to lie.] **—re·cum′bence, re·cum′ben·cy** *n.* **—re·cum′bent·ly** *adv.*

re·cu·per·ate (rĭ-ko͞o′pə-rāt′, -kyo͞o′-) *v.* **-at·ed, -at·ing, -ates.** *—intr.* **1.** To return to health or strength; recover. **2.** To recover from financial loss. *—tr.* **1.** To restore to health or strength. **2.** To regain. [Latin *recuperāre, recuperāt-* : *re-,* re- + *capere,* to take; see **kap-** in Appendix.] **—re·cu′per·a′tion** *n.* **—re·cu′per·a′tive** (-pə-rā′tĭv, -pər-ə-tĭv), **re·cu′per·a·to′ry** (-pər-ə-tôr′ē, -tōr′ē) *adj.*

re·cur (rĭ-kûr′) *intr.v.* **-curred, -cur·ring, -curs.** **1.** To happen, come up, or show up again or repeatedly. See Synonyms at **return.** **2.** To return to one's attention or memory. **3.** To return in thought or discourse. **4.** To have recourse: *recur to the use of force.* [Latin *recurrere* : *re-,* re- + *currere,* to run; see **kers-** in Appendix.] **—re·cur′rence** *n.*

re·cur·rent (rĭ-kûr′ənt, -kŭr′-) *adj.* **1.** Occurring or appearing again or repeatedly. **2.** *Anatomy.* Turning in a reverse direction. Used of blood vessels and nerves. **—re·cur′rent·ly** *adv.*

recurrent fever *n.* See **relapsing fever.**

re·cur·ring decimal (rĭ-kûr′ĭng, -kŭr′-) *n. Mathematics.* See **repeating decimal.**

re·cur·sion (rĭ-kûr′zhən) *n. Mathematics.* **1.** An expression, such as a polynomial, each term of which is determined by application of a formula to preceding terms. **2.** A formula that generates the successive terms of a recursion. [Late Latin *recursiō, recursiōn-,* a running back, from Latin *recursus,* past participle of *recurrere,* to run back. See RECUR.] **—re·cur′sive** *adj.*

re·cur·vate (rĭ-kûr′vāt′, -vĭt) *adj.* Bent or curved backward.

re·curve (rē-kûrv′) *tr. & intr.v.* **-curved, -curv·ing, -curves.** To curve (something) backward or downward or become curved backward or downward. [Latin *recurvāre* : *re-,* re- + *curvāre,* to curve (from *curvus,* curve; see CURVE).] **—re′cur·va′tion** (rē′kûr-vā′shən) *n.*

rec·u·sant (rĕk′yə-zənt, rĭ-kyo͞o′-) *n.* **1.** One of the Roman Catholics in England who incurred legal and social penalties in the 16th century and afterward for refusing to attend services of the Church of England. **2.** A dissenter; a nonconformist. **—rec′u·san·cy** *n.* **—rec′u·sant** *adj.*

Red Cross

re·cuse (rĭ-kyo͞oz′) *tr.v.* **-cused, -cus·ing, -cus·es.** To disqualify or seek to disqualify from participation in a decision on grounds such as prejudice or personal involvement. [Middle English *recusen,* from Old French *recuser,* from Latin *recūsāre* : *re-,* re- + *causa,* cause.]

re·cy·cle (rē-sī′kəl) *tr.v.* **-cled, -cling, -cles.** **1.** To put or pass through a cycle again, as for further treatment. **2.** To start a different cycle in. **3. a.** To extract useful materials from (garbage or waste). **b.** To extract and reuse (useful substances found in waste). **4. a.** To use again, especially to reprocess: *recycle aluminum cans; recycle old jokes.* **b.** To recondition and adapt to a new use or function: *recycling old warehouses as condominiums.* **—re·cy′cla·ble** *adj. & n.* **—re·cy′cler** *n.*

red (rĕd) *n.* **1. a.** *Color.* The hue of the long-wave end of the visible spectrum, evoked in the human observer by radiant energy with wavelengths of approximately 630 to 750 nanometers; any of a group of colors that may vary in lightness and saturation and whose hue resembles that of blood; one of the additive or light primaries; one of the psychological primary hues. **b.** A pigment or dye having a red hue. **c.** Something that has a red hue. **2. a.** *Often* **Red.** A Communist. **b.** A revolutionary activist. **—red** *adj.* **red·der, red·dest.** **1.** *Color.* Having a color resembling that of blood. **2.** Reddish in color or having parts that are reddish in color: *a red dog; a red oak.* **3. a.** Having a reddish or coppery skin color. **b.** *Often* **Red.** *Offensive.* Of or being a Native American. **4.** Having a ruddy or flushed complexion: *red with embarrassment.* **5.** often **Red.** Communist. **—*idiom.* in the red.** Operating at a loss; in debt. [Middle English, from Old English *rēad.* See **reudh-** in Appendix.] **—red′ly** *adv.* **—red′ness** *n.*

red. *abbr.* **1.** Reduced. **2.** Reduction.

re·dact (rĭ-dăkt′) *tr.v.* **-dact·ed, -dact·ing, -dacts.** **1.** To draw up or frame (a proclamation, for example). **2.** To make ready for publication; edit or revise. [Middle English *redacten,* from Latin *redigere, redāct-,* to drive back : *re-, red-,* re- + *agere,* to drive; see ACT.] **—re·dac′tor** (-dăk′tər, -tôr′) *n.*

re·dac·tion (rĭ-dăk′shən) *n.* **1.** The act or process of editing or revising a piece of writing; preparation for publication. **2.** An edited work; a new edition or revision.

red alga *n.* Any of various predominantly marine algae of the division Rhodophyta, characteristically red or reddish in color. Often used in the plural.

red·bait (rĕd′bāt′) *tr.v.* **-bait·ed, -bait·ing, -baits.** To accuse, denounce, or attack (a person, for example) as a Communist or a Communist sympathizer. **—red′bait′er** *n.* **—red′bait′ing** *n.*

red·bird (rĕd′bûrd′) *n.* Any of various birds with red plumage, as the cardinal or scarlet tanager.

red blood cell *n. Abbr.* **RBC, rbc** A cell in the blood of vertebrates that transports oxygen and carbon dioxide to and from the tissues. In mammals, the red blood cell is disk-shaped and biconcave, contains hemoglobin, and lacks a nucleus. Also called *erythrocyte, red cell, red corpuscle.*

red-blood·ed (rĕd′blŭd′ĭd) *adj.* Strong and highly spirited.

red·breast (rĕd′brĕst′) *n.* **1.** A bird, such as the robin, that has a red breast. **2.** A freshwater sunfish *(Lepomis auritus)* of the eastern United States, having a reddish belly.

red·brick (rĕd′brĭk′) *adj.* Of, relating to, or being the British universities other than Oxford and Cambridge. [So-called because many of the buildings of such universities were built of red bricks.]

red·bud (rĕd′bŭd′) *n.* Any of several shrubs or small trees of the genus *Cercis,* having flat pods and pinkish flowers that bloom before the leaves appear. Also called *Judas tree.*

red bug also **red·bug** (rĕd′bŭg′) *n.* See **chigger** (sense 1).

red·cap (rĕd′kăp′) *n.* A porter, usually in a railroad station.

Red·car (rĕd′kär′). A municipal borough of northeast England on the North Sea northeast of Middlesbrough. It is a seaside resort and has iron and steel industries. Population, 85,600.

red carpet *n.* A carpet laid down for important visitors. **—*idiom.* roll out the red carpet.** To welcome with great hospitality or ceremony.

red cedar *n.* **1.** An evergreen, coniferous, eastern North American tree *(Juniperus virginiana)* having fleshy, purplish-black seed cones. **2.** A tall, evergreen, Pacific North American tree *(Thuja plicata)* having flattened branches, scalelike opposite leaves, and small, ovoid seed-bearing cones. **3.** The reddish, aromatic, durable wood of either of these trees.

red cell *n.* See **red blood cell.**

red cent *n. Informal.* Insignificant value: *not worth a red cent.*

Red Cloud (kloud). 1822–1909. Oglala Sioux leader of the resistance against the development of a trail through Wyoming and Montana by the U.S. government (1865–1867).

Red·cloud Peak (rĕd′kloud′). A mountain, 4,280.4 m (14,034 ft) high, in the San Juan Mountains of southwest Colorado.

red clover *n.* A Eurasian plant *(Trifolium pratense)* having trifoliate leaves and globular heads of fragrant rose-purple flowers, widely naturalized in North America and frequently planted as a forage or cover crop.

red·coat (rĕd′kōt′) *n.* A British soldier, especially one serving during the American Revolution.

red corpuscle *n.* See **red blood cell.**

Red Crescent *n.* **1.** A branch of the Red Cross organization operating in a Moslem country. **2.** The crescent-shaped emblem of such a branch.

Red Cross *n. Abbr.* **RC** **1. a.** An international organization that cares for the wounded, sick, and homeless in wartime, according to the terms of the Geneva Convention of 1864, and now also during and following natural disasters. **b.** A national branch of this organization. **2.** The emblem of this organization, a Geneva cross or a red Greek cross on a white background.

♦**redd** (rĕd) *tr.v.* **redd·ed** or **redd, redd·ing, redds.** *Chiefly Pennsylvania.* To clear: *redd the dinner table.* —***phrasal verb.*** **redd up.** To tidy: *She redded up the front room.* [Middle English dialectal *redden,* to clear an area (influenced by Middle English *redden,* to rescue, free from, from Old English *hreddan*), from Old Norse *rydhja.* See RID.]

♦***REGIONAL NOTE:*** The terms *redd* and *redd up* came to the American Midlands from the many Scottish immigrants who settled there. Meaning "to clear an area or to make it tidy," *redd* is still used in Scotland and Northern Ireland; in the United States it is especially common in Pennsylvania as the phrasal verb *redd up.* The term, which goes back to Old Norse *rydhja,* can be traced from the 15th century to the present, particularly in dialects of Scotland and the North of England.

red deer *n.* **1.** A common deer *(Cervus elaphus)* of Europe and Asia, having a reddish-brown coat. **2.** The summer morph of the white-tailed deer, having a reddish coat.

Red Deer (dîr). A city of south-central Alberta, Canada, on the Red Deer River north of Calgary. It is a trade center in a farm and dairy region. Population, 46,393.

Red Deer River. A river rising in the Rocky Mountains of southwest Alberta, Canada, and flowing about 619 km (385 mi) northeast then southeast and east across the province and into the South Saskatchewan River just across the Saskatchewan border.

red·den (rĕd′n) *tr. & intr.v.* **-dened, -den·ing, -dens.** To make or become red.

Red·ding (rĕd′ĭng). A city of northern California on the Sacramento River south of Shasta Lake. It is a resort and has lumbering and food-processing industries. Population, 41,995.

red·dish (rĕd′ĭsh) *adj. Color.* Mixed or tinged with red; somewhat red. —**red′dish·ness** *n.*

red·dle (rĕd′l) *n. & v.* Variant of **ruddle.**

red-dog (rĕd′dôg′, -dŏg′) *Football. n.* See **blitz** (sense 3). —**red-dog** *v.* **-dogged, -dog·ging, -dogs.** —*tr.* To rush (the quarterback) in a blitz. —*intr.* To carry out a blitz.

red drum *n.* A large food fish *(Sciaenops ocellata)* of the Atlantic coastal waters of North America. Also called *channel bass.*

rede (rēd) *tr.v.* **red·ed, red·ing, redes. 1.** To give advice to; counsel. **2.** To interpret; explain. —**rede** *n.* **1.** Advice or counsel. **2.** *Archaic.* A narration. [Middle English *reden,* from Old English *rǣdan.* See **ar-** in Appendix.]

re·dec·o·rate (rē-dĕk′ə-rāt′) *v.* **-rat·ed, -rat·ing, -rates.** —*tr.* To change the appearance or furnishings of; refurbish. —*intr.* To change a decorative scheme. —**re·dec′o·ra′tion** *n.* —**re·dec′o·ra′tor** *n.*

re·deem (rĭ-dēm′) *tr.v.* **-deemed, -deem·ing, -deems. 1.** To recover ownership of by paying a specified sum. **2.** To pay off (a promissory note, for example). **3.** To turn in (coupons, for example) and receive something in exchange. **4.** To fulfill (a pledge, for example). **5.** To convert into cash: *redeem stocks.* **6.** To set free; rescue or ransom. **7.** To save from a state of sinfulness and its consequences. See Synonyms at **save**[1]. **8.** To make up for: *The low price of the clothes dryer redeems its lack of special features.* **9.** To restore the honor, worth, or reputation of: *You botched the last job but can redeem yourself on this one.* [Middle English *redemen,* from Old French *redimer,* from Latin *redimere* : *re-, red-,* re- + *emere,* to buy; see **em-** in Appendix.] —**re·deem′a·ble** *adj.*

re·deem·er (rĭ-dē′mər) *n.* **1.** One who redeems. **2. Redeemer.** Jesus.

red eft *n.* The bright red terrestrial stage in the life cycle of a newt *(Notophthalmus viridescens)* of the eastern United States. Also called *red-spotted eft.*

re·de·liv·er (rē′dĭ-lĭv′ər) *tr.v.* **-ered, -er·ing, -ers. 1.** To deliver again. **2.** To deliver in return; give back.

re·demp·tion (rĭ-dĕmp′shən) *n.* **1.** The act of redeeming or the condition of having been redeemed. **2.** Recovery of something pawned or mortgaged. **3.** The payment of an obligation, as a government's payment of the value of its bonds. **4.** Deliverance upon payment of ransom; rescue. **5.** *Theology.* Salvation from sin through Jesus's sacrifice. [Middle English *redempcioun,* from Old French *redemption,* from Latin *redēmptiō, redēmptiōn-,* from *redēmptus,* past participle of *redimere,* to redeem. See REDEEM.] —**re·demp′tion·al, re·demp′tive, re·demp′to·ry** (-tə-rē) *adj.*

re·demp·tion·er (rĭ-dĕmp′shə-nər) *n.* A colonial emigrant from Europe to America who paid for the voyage by serving for a specified period as a bondservant.

Re·demp·tor·ist (rĭ-dĕmp′tər-ĭst) *n.* A member of the Congregation of the Most Holy Redeemer, a Roman Catholic order founded in 1732 by Saint Alphonsus Liguori (1696–1787). [French *rédemptoriste,* from Late Latin *redēmptor,* redeemer, from Latin, contractor, from *redimere,* to buy back. See REDEEM.]

re·de·ploy (rē′dĭ-ploi′) *tr.v.* **-ployed, -ploy·ing, -ploys. 1.** To move (military forces) from one combat zone to another. **2.** To shift (something) from one place or use to another for greater effectiveness: *redeploy the company's resources.* —**re′de·ploy′ment** *n.*

re·de·sign (rē′dĭ-zīn′) *tr.v.* **-signed, -sign·ing, -signs.** To make a revision in the design of. —**re′de·sign′** *n.*

re·de·vel·op (rē′dĭ-vĕl′əp) *v.* **-oped, -op·ing, -ops.** —*tr.* **1.** To develop (something) again. **2.** To tone or intensify (a photographic print, for example) by a second developing process. **3.** To restore (buildings or neighborhoods, for example) to a better condition: *redeveloped the waterfront.* —*intr.* To develop again. —**re′de·vel′op·er** *n.* —**re′de·vel′op·ment** *n.*

red·eye (rĕd′ī′) *n.* **1.** *Informal.* A danger signal on a railroad. **2.** *Slang.* A late-night or overnight flight: *caught the redeye from Los Angeles to New York.* **3.** Any of several fishes with red eyes, as the rock bass. **4.** *Slang.* Inferior whiskey.

redeye gravy *n.* Gravy made from the juices of a cooked ham.

red-faced (rĕd′fāst′) *adj.* Embarrassed: *"They were caught red-handed, and now they are red-faced"* (Margaret Thatcher).

red fir *n.* **1.** An evergreen tree *(Abies magnifica)* of California and Oregon, having reddish wood valued as timber. **2.** The wood of this tree.

red fire *n.* Any of various combustible compounds, especially salts of lithium or strontium, that burn bright red and are used in flares and fireworks.

red·fish (rĕd′fĭsh′) *n., pl.* **redfish** or **-fish·es.** Any of several fishes that are reddish in color, as the red drum and the rosefish.

Red·ford (rĕd′fərd). A community of southeast Michigan, a suburb of Detroit. Population, 58,441.

red fox *n.* A fox of the genus *Vulpes,* characteristically having reddish fur, especially *V. fulva* of North America and *V. vulpes* of Europe.

red fox
Vulpes fulva

Red·grave (rĕd′grāv′), Sir **Michael.** 1908–1985. British actor noted for his Shakespearean and motion-picture roles. His daughters **Vanessa** (born 1937) and **Lynn** (born 1943) are both versatile actresses.

red giant *n.* A star of great size and brightness that has a relatively low surface temperature.

red grouse *n.* A grouse *(Lagopus lagopus* subsp. *scoticus)* of the British Isles that has chestnut plumage and inhabits open fields. Also called *moorfowl.*

Red Guard *n.* **1.** A member of an activist youth movement in China, prominent during the Chinese Cultural Revolution of the late 1960's, that espoused Maoist principles. **2.** A member of a radical political group with Maoist leanings. [Translation of Chinese (Mandarin) *hóng wèi bīng* : *hóng,* red + *wèi bīng,* guard.]

red gum[1] *n.* Any of several Australian evergreen trees of the genus *Eucalyptus,* especially *E. camaldulensis* or *E. calophylla,* having lance-shaped, aromatic leaves.

red gum[2] *n.* See **strophulus.**

red-hand·ed (rĕd′hăn′dĭd) *adv. & adj.* In the act of committing something wrong. —**red′-hand′ed·ly** *adv.*

red·head (rĕd′hĕd′) *n.* **1.** A person with red hair. **2.** A North American duck *(Aythya americana),* the male of which has black and gray plumage and a reddish head.

red·head·ed (rĕd′hĕd′ĭd) *adj.* **1.** Having red hair. **2.** Having a red head: *a redheaded woodpecker.*

red heat *n.* **1.** The temperature of a red-hot substance. **2.** The physical condition of a red-hot substance.

red herring *n.* **1.** A smoked herring having a reddish color. **2.** Something that draws attention away from the central issue. [From its use to distract hunting dogs from the trail.]

red hind *n.* A reddish-brown grouper *(Epinephelus guttatus)* of the West Indies and the Gulf of Mexico, having dark red-brown spots.

redingote

red-hot (rĕd′hŏt′) *adj.* **1.** Glowing hot; very hot. **2.** Heated, as with excitement, anger, or enthusiasm: *a red-hot speech.* **3.** Very recent; new: *red-hot information.* —**red-hot** *n.* **1.** See **hot dog. 2.** A small, usually round red candy strongly flavored with cinnamon.

re·di·a (rē′dē-ə) *n., pl.* **-di·ae** (-dē-ē′). A larva of certain trematodes that is produced within the sporocyst and that can give rise to additional rediae or to cercariae. [New Latin, after Francesco *Redi* (1626–1697), Italian naturalist.]

re·did (rē-dĭd′) *v.* Past tense of **redo.**

re·dif·fer·en·ti·a·tion (rē′dĭf-ə-rĕn′shē-ā′shən) *n. Biology.* A process by which a group of once differentiated cells return to their original specialized form.

red·in·gote (rĕd′ĭng-gōt′) *n.* **1.** A man's long double-breasted topcoat with full skirt. **2.** A woman's full-length unlined coat or dress open down the front to show a dress or underdress. [French, alteration of English *riding coat.*]

red ink *n.* **1.** A financial loss in business. **2.** The condition of showing a fiscal deficit: *a firm drowning in red ink.* [From the use of red ink to record debits and losses in financial records.]

red·in·te·gra·tion (rĕd-ĭn′tĭ-grā′shən, rĭ-dĭn′-) *n. Psychology.* Evocation of a particular state of mind resulting from the recurrence of one of the elements that made up the original experience. [Middle English *redintegracion,* from Latin *redintegrātiō, redintegrātiōn-,* from *redintegrātus,* past participle of *redintegrāre,* to make whole again : *re-, red-,* re- + *integer,* whole, entire; see INTEGER.] —**red·in′te·gra′tive** *adj.* —**red·in′te·gra′tor** *n.*

re·di·rect (rē′dĭ-rĕkt′, -dī-) *tr.v.* **-rect·ed, -rect·ing, -rects.** To change the direction or course of. —**redirect** (rē′dĭ-rĕkt′, -dī-) *n. Law.* A redirect examination. —**re′di·rec′tion** *n.*

ă pat	oi boy
ā pay	ou out
âr care	ŏŏ took
ä father	ōō boot
ĕ pet	ŭ cut
ē be	ûr urge
ĭ pit	th thin
ī pie	*th* this
îr pier	hw which
ŏ pot	zh vision
ō toe	ə about, item
ô paw	♦ regionalism

Stress marks: **′** (primary); ′ (secondary), as in **dictionary** (dĭk′shə-nĕr′ē)

redirect examination *n. Law.* Further examination of a witness after cross-examination, carried out by the party that first called the witness.

re·dis·count (rē-dĭs′kount′) *tr.v.* **-count·ed, -count·ing, -counts.** To discount again. **—rediscount** *n.* **1.** The act of rediscounting. **2.** Often **rediscounts.** Commercial paper that is discounted a second time.

re·dis·trib·ute (rē′dĭ-strĭb′yo͞ot) *tr.v.* **-ut·ed, -ut·ing, -utes.** To distribute again in a different way; reallocate.

re·dis·tri·bu·tion (rē′dĭs-trə-byo͞o′shən) *n.* **1.** The act or process of redistributing. **2.** An economic theory or policy that advocates reducing inequalities in the distribution of wealth. **—re′dis·tri·bu′tion·ist** *adj. & n.*

re·dis·trict (rē-dĭs′trĭkt) *tr.v.* **-trict·ed, -trict·ing, -tricts.** To divide again into districts, especially to give new boundaries to administrative or election districts.

red·i·vi·vus (rĕd′ə-vī′vəs, -vē′-) *adj.* Come back to life; revived: *"defenders of the Imperial Presidency redivivus"* (Arthur M. Schlesinger, Jr.). [Late Latin *redivīvus,* from Latin, renewed : *re-, red-,* re- + *vīvus,* living; see VIVIFY.]

Red Jack·et (jăk′ĭt). 1756?–1830. Seneca leader who advocated peace with the United States while resisting the geographic and cultural encroachment of settlers.

Red·lands (rĕd′ləndz). A city of southern California in the San Bernardino Valley. It is primarily residential with varied light industries. Population, 43,619.

red lead (lĕd) *n.* A poisonous bright red powder, Pb_3O_4, used in paints, glass, pottery, and packing for pipe joints.

red-let·ter (rĕd′lĕt′ər) *adj.* Memorably happy: *a red-letter day.* [From the practice of marking in red the holy days in church calendars.]

red light *n.* **1.** The red-colored light that signals traffic to stop. **2.** *Informal.* A command to stop.

red-light district (rĕd′lĭt′) *n.* A neighborhood containing many brothels.

red·line (rĕd′līn′) *v.* **-lined, -lin·ing, -lines. —redline** *intr.* To refuse home mortgages or home insurance to areas or neighborhoods deemed poor financial risks. *—tr.* **1.** To discriminate against by refusing to grant loans, mortgages, or insurance to. **2.** To remove from operational status because of mechanical defects or the need for scheduled maintenance: *redlined three fighter aircraft.*

red maple *n.* A medium-sized eastern North American maple *(Acer rubrum)* having reddish twigs and buds.

red meat *n.* Meat, especially beef, that is dark-colored before being cooked.

Red·mond (rĕd′mənd). A city of west-central Washington, a residential and industrial suburb of Seattle east of Lake Washington. Population, 23,318.

Redmond, John Edward. 1856–1918. Irish nationalist politician who succeeded Charles Parnell as the principal advocate of Irish home rule. His support for Britain during World War I and his opposition to Sinn Fein undermined his influence.

red mulberry *n.* A deciduous eastern North American tree *(Morus rubra)* having irregularly lobed leaves and edible, fleshy, red to purple, multiple fruit.

red mullet *n.* See **goatfish.**

red·neck (rĕd′nĕk′) *n. Offensive Slang.* **1.** Used as a disparaging term for a member of the white rural laboring class, especially in the southern United States. **2.** One who is regarded as having a provincial, conservative, often bigoted sociopolitical attitude.

re·do (rē-do͞o′) *tr.v.* **-did** (-dĭd′), **-done** (-dŭn′), **-do·ing, -does** (-dŭz′). **1.** To do over again. **2.** To redecorate: *redo a living area in yellow.*

red oak *n.* Either of two eastern North American deciduous trees *(Quercus rubra* or *Q. falcata)* having deeply and acutely lobed leaves and a saucer-shaped cup enclosing the lower third of the nut.

red ocher *n.* A form of hematite used as a red pigment.

red·o·lence (rĕd′l-əns) also **red·o·len·cy** (-l-ən-sē) *n.* The quality or state of being redolent. See Synonyms at **fragrance.**

red·o·lent (rĕd′l-ənt) *adj.* **1.** Having or emitting fragrance; aromatic. **2.** Suggestive; reminiscent: *a campaign redolent of machine politics.* [Middle English, from Old French, from Latin *redolēns, redolent-,* present participle of *redolēre,* to smell : *re-, red-,* re- + *olēre,* to smell.] **—red′o·lent·ly** *adv.*

Re·don (rə-dôn′, -dôN′), **Odilon.** 1840–1916. French artist and forerunner of surrealism whose works include eerie lithographs and floral paintings.

Re·don·do Beach (rĭ-dŏn′dō). A city of southern California, a residential suburb of Los Angeles on the Pacific Ocean. Population, 57,102.

re·done (rē-dŭn′) *v.* Past participle of **redo.**

red osier *n.* North American shrub *(Cornus sericea)* often growing in dense clumps and having red branches, white flowers, and bluish-white drupes.

re·dou·ble (rē-dŭb′əl) *v.* **-bled, -bling, -bles.** *—tr.* **1.** To double. **2.** To repeat. **3.** *Games.* To double the doubling bid of (an opponent) in bridge. *—intr.* **1.** To become twice as great. **2.** *Games.* To double a double in bridge.

re·doubt (rĭ-dout′) *n.* **1.** A small, often temporary defensive fortification. **2.** A reinforcing earthwork or breastwork within a permanent rampart. **3.** A protected place of refuge or defense. [French *redoute,* from Italian *ridotto,* from Medieval Latin *reductus,* concealed place, from Latin, past participle of *redūcere,* to withdraw, lead back. See REDUCE.]

Re·doubt (rē′dout′), **Mount.** A volcano, 3,111 m (10,200 ft) high, of southern Alaska. The highest peak of the Aleutian Range, it erupted in 1989 for the first time in 25 years.

re·doubt·a·ble (rĭ-dou′tə-bəl) *adj.* **1.** Arousing fear or awe; formidable. **2.** Worthy of respect or honor. [Middle English *redoutabel,* from Old French *redoutable,* from *redouter,* to dread : *re-,* re- + *douter,* to doubt, fear; see DOUBT.] **—re·doubt′a·bly** *adv.*

re·dound (rĭ-dound′) *intr.v.* **-dound·ed, -dound·ing, -dounds.** **1.** To have an effect or consequence: *deeds that redound to one's discredit.* **2.** To return; recoil: *Glory redounds upon the brave.* **3.** To contribute; accrue. [Middle English *redounden,* to abound, from Old French *redonder,* from Latin *redundāre,* to overflow. See REDUNDANT.]

red·out (rĕd′out′) *n.* A sudden reddening of the visual field accompanied by severe headache and caused by engorgement of the blood vessels of the head when a person is subjected to a negative force of gravity, as in stunt flying.

re·dox (rē′dŏks′) *n.* Oxidation-reduction. [RED(UCTION) + OX(IDATION).]

red panda *n.* See **panda** (sense 2).

red-pen·cil (rĕd′pĕn′səl) *tr.v.* **-ciled, -cil·ing, -cils** also **-cilled, -cil·ling, -cils.** To censor, cut, revise, or correct with or as if with a red pencil.

red pepper *n.* **1.** The pungent, red, podlike fruit of any of several cultivars of the pepper plants, *Capsicum frutescens* and *C. annum.* **2.** See **cayenne pepper.**

red pine *n.* An evergreen timber tree *(Pinus resinosa)* of northeast North America, having long, flexible, glossy leaves grouped in fascicles of two. Also called *Norway pine.*

red·poll (rĕd′pōl′) *n.* Any of several small finches of the genus *Carduelis* of northern North America and Eurasia, especially *C. flammea,* having a red crown and black chin.

Red Poll or **Red Polled** (pōld) *n.* Any of a breed of reddish, hornless cattle developed in England and raised for milk and meat.

red puccoon *n.* See **bloodroot.**

re·dress (rĭ-drĕs′) *tr.v.* **-dressed, -dress·ing, -dress·es.** **1.** To set right; remedy or rectify. **2.** To make amends to. **3.** To make amends for. See Synonyms at **correct.** **4.** To adjust (a balance, for example). **—redress** (*also* rē′drĕs) *n.* **1.** Satisfaction for wrong or injury; reparation. See Synonyms at **reparation.** **2.** Correction or reformation. [Middle English *redressen,* from Old French *redrecier* : *re-,* re- + *drecier,* to arrange; see DRESS.] **—re·dress′er, re·dres′sor** *n.*

red ribbon *n.* An emblem, a badge, or a rosette made of red ribbon that is awarded as the second prize in a competition.

Red River. **1.** Or in China **Yu·an Jiang** (yo͞o-än′ jyäng′, yüän′), **Hong Ha** (hông′ hä′) or **Song Hong** (sông′ hông′). A river of southeast Asia rising in southern China and flowing about 1,175 km (730 mi) generally south through northern Vietnam to a fertile delta on the Gulf of Tonkin. **2.** A river of the south-central United States rising in two branches in the Texas Panhandle and flowing about 1,638 km (1,018 mi) eastward along the Texas-Oklahoma border and into Arkansas, where it changes direction and flows southward into Louisiana and then southeast to the Mississippi River. **3.** Also **Red River of the North.** A river of the north-central United States and south-central Canada formed by the confluence of two tributaries in west-central Minnesota and flowing about 499 km (310 mi) north along the Minnesota–North Dakota border into southeast Manitoba, Canada, where it empties into Lake Winnipeg. The **Red River Valley** is a fertile region for growing wheat, flax, and barley.

red·root (rĕd′ro͞ot′, -ro͝ot′) *n.* **1.** An eastern North American bog plant *(Lachnanthes caroliana)* having red roots and woolly yellow flowers. **2.** See **pigweed** (sense 2). **3.** See **ceanothus.**

red salmon *n.* See **sockeye salmon.**

Red Sea. A long, narrow sea between northeast Africa and the Arabian Peninsula. It is linked with the Mediterranean to the north through the Gulf of Suez and the Suez Canal and with the Gulf of Aden and the Arabian Sea to the south through the strait of Bab el Mandeb.

red·shank (rĕd′shăngk′) *n.* An Old World wading bird *(Tringa totanus)* having long red legs.

red shift *n.* An increase in the wavelength of radiation emitted by a celestial body as a consequence of the Doppler effect. [From the fact that the longer wavelengths of light are at the red end of the visible spectrum.]

red·shirt (rĕd′shûrt′) *tr.v.* **-shirt·ed, -shirt·ing, -shirts.** *Sports.* To keep (a college or school athlete) out of varsity competition for one year in order to extend the athlete's period of eligibility. [From the red jerseys worn by such athletes to distinguish them from the regular players.] **—red′shirt′** *adj. & n.*

red·should·ered hawk (rĕd′shō′dərd) *n.* A medium-sized North American hawk *(Buteo lineatus),* having rufous shoulder feathers and found typically in wet woodlands and savannas.

redshouldered hawk
Buteo lineatus

red·skin (rĕd′skĭn′) *n. Offensive Slang.* Used as a disparaging term for a Native American.

red snapper *n.* Any of several marine food fishes of the genus *Lutjanus,* of tropical and semitropical waters, having red or reddish bodies.

red snow *n.* Snow on which red-pigmented algae has grown, commonly found in Arctic and Alpine regions.

red spider *n.* Any of various small red mites of the family Tetranychidae that feed on vegetation, causing damage to the leaves. Also called *spider mite.*

red-spot·ted eft (rĕd′spŏt′ĭd) *n.* See **red eft.**

Red Square. A large open area in central Moscow bordered by the Kremlin, Lenin's tomb, St. Basil's Cathedral, and the GUM department store.

red squill *n.* **1.** See **sea onion** (sense 1). **2.** A powder prepared from the bulbs of the red squill and used as a rat poison.

red squirrel *n.* A North American squirrel *(Tamiasciurus hudsonicus)* having reddish or tawny fur.

red·start (rĕd′stärt′) *n.* **1.** A small North American bird *(Setophaga ruticilla),* the male of which has black plumage with orange patches on the wings and tail. **2.** A European bird *(Phoenicurus phoenicurus)* having grayish plumage and a rust-red breast and tail. [RED + obsolete *start,* tail (from Middle English *stert,* from Old English *steort;* see **ster-**[1] in Appendix).]

red-tailed hawk (rĕd′tāld′) *n.* A heavy-bodied North American hawk *(Buteo jamaicensis)* that feeds primarily on rodents and has a conspicuous reddish-brown tail in the male.

red tape *n.* Official forms and procedures, especially when oppressively complex and time consuming. [From its former use in tying British official documents.]

red tide *n.* A bloom of dinoflagellates that causes reddish discoloration of coastal ocean waters. Certain dinoflagellates of the genus *Gonyamlax* produce toxins that kill fish and contaminate shellfish.

red·top (rĕd′tŏp′) *n.* A widely cultivated Eurasian grass *(Agrostis gigantea)* having reddish flower clusters.

re·duce (rĭ-do͞os′, -dyo͞os′) *v.* **-duced, -duc·ing, -duc·es.** —*tr.* **1.** To bring down, as in extent, amount, or degree; diminish. See Synonyms at **decrease. 2.** To bring to a humbler, weaker, difficult, or forced state or condition; especially: **a.** To gain control of; conquer: *"a design to reduce them under absolute despotism"* (Declaration of Independence). **b.** To subject to destruction: *Enemy bombers reduced the city to rubble.* **c.** To weaken bodily: *was reduced almost to emaciation.* **d.** To sap the spirit or mental energy of. **e.** To compel to desperate acts: *The Depression reduced many to begging on street corners.* **f.** To lower in rank or grade; demote. See Synonyms at **demote. g.** To powder or pulverize. **h.** To thin (paint) with a solvent. **3.** To lower the price of: *The store has drastically reduced winter coats.* **4.** To put in order or arrange systematically: *reduce a complex tax situation.* **5.** To separate into orderly components by analysis. **6.** *Chemistry.* **a.** To decrease the valence of (an atom) by adding electrons. **b.** To remove oxygen from (a compound). **c.** To add hydrogen to (a compound). **d.** To change to a metallic state by removing nonmetallic constituents; smelt. **7.** *Mathematics.* To simplify the form of (an expression, such as a fraction) without changing the value. **8.** *Medicine.* To restore (a fractured or displaced body part) to a normal condition or position. —*intr.* **1.** To become diminished. **2.** To lose weight, as by dieting. **3.** *Biology.* To undergo meiosis. [Middle English *reducen,* to bring back, from Old French *reducier,* from Latin *redūcere* : *re-,* re- + *dūcere,* to lead; see **deuk-** in Appendix.] —**re·duc′er** *n.* —**re·duc′i·bil′i·ty** *n.* —**re·duc′i·ble** *adj.* —**re·duc′i·bly** *adv.*

re·duc·ing agent (rĭ-do͞o′sĭng, -dyo͞o′-) *n.* A substance that chemically reduces other substances, especially by donating an electron or electrons.

re·duc·tant (rĭ-dŭk′tənt) *n.* A reducing agent. [REDUCT(ION) + -ANT.]

re·duc·tase (rĭ-dŭk′tās′, -tāz′) *n.* An enzyme that promotes reduction of an organic compound. [REDUCT(ION) + -ASE.]

re·duc·ti·o ad ab·sur·dum (rĭ-dŭk′tē-ō ăd əb-sûr′dəm, -zûr′-, -shē-ō) *n., pl.* **-o·nes ad absurdum** (-ō′nēz, -nās). Disproof of a proposition by showing the absurdity of its inevitable conclusion. [Medieval Latin *reductiō ad absurdum* : Latin *reductiō,* a bringing back, reduction + Latin *ad,* to + Latin *absurdum,* absurdity, from neuter of *absurdus,* absurd.]

re·duc·tion (rĭ-dŭk′shən) *n. Abbr.* **red. 1.** The act or process of reducing. **2.** The result of reducing: *a reduction in absenteeism.* **3.** The amount by which something is lessened or diminished: *a reduction of 12 percent in violent crime.* **4.** *Biology.* The first meiotic division, in which the chromosome number is reduced. Also called *reduction division.* **5.** *Chemistry.* **a.** A decrease in positive valence or an increase in negative valence by the gaining of electrons. **b.** A reaction in which hydrogen is combined with a compound. **c.** A reaction in which oxygen is removed from a compound. **6.** *Mathematics.* **a.** The canceling of common factors in the numerator and denominator of a fraction. **b.** The converting of a fraction to its decimal equivalent. **c.** The converting of an expression or equation to its simplest form. [Middle English *reduccion,* restoration, from Old French *reduction,* from Latin *reductiō, reductiōn-,* from *reductus,* past participle of *redūcere,* to bring back. See REDUCE.] —**re·duc′tion·al** *adj.*

re·duc·tion·ism (rĭ-dŭk′shə-nĭz′əm) *n.* An attempt or a tendency to explain complex phenomena or structures by relatively simple principles, as by asserting that life processes or mental acts are instances of chemical and physical laws: *"Our educational system has had a dangerous predilection for reductionism—an addiction to the primary, the elementary"* (Frederick Turner). —**re·duc′tion·ist** *adj. & n.* —**re·duc′tion·is′tic** *adj.*

re·duc·tive (rĭ-dŭk′tĭv) *adj.* **1.** Of or relating to reduction. **2.** Relating to, being an instance of, or exhibiting reductionism. **3.** Relating to or being an instance of reductivism. —**re·duc′tive·ly** *adv.*

re·duc·tiv·ism (rĭ-dŭk′tə-vĭz′əm) *n.* See **minimalism** (sense 1). —**re·duc′tiv·ist** *n.*

re·dun·dan·cy (rĭ-dŭn′dən-sē) *n., pl.* **-cies. 1.** The state of being redundant. **2.** A superfluity; an excess. **3.** Unnecessary repetition. **4.** *Electronics.* Duplication or repetition of elements in electronic equipment to provide alternative functional channels in case of failure. **5.** Repetition of parts or all of a message to circumvent transmission errors.

USAGE NOTE: The usages that critics have condemned as redundancies fall into several classes. In some cases, such as *consensus of opinion, close proximity, hollow tube,* and *refer back,* the use of what is regarded as an unnecessary modifier or qualifier can sometimes be justified on the grounds that it in fact makes a semantic contribution. Thus a *hollow tube* can be distinguished from one that has been blocked up with deposits, and a *consensus of opinion* can be distinguished from a consensus of judgments or practice. In other cases the use of the qualifier is harder to defend. Thus there is no way to *revert* without *reverting back* and no *consensus* that is not *general.* • Sometimes recognition of redundancy may require familiarity with a foreign language. The expressions *Sierra Mountains* and *Rio Grande River* are indeed redundant for those who know Spanish, but the use of the words *mountains* and *river* may still serve some purpose when one is addressing an English-speaking audience. Occasionally, what originates as a redundant element may, through long use, become part of the established name of a thing. Thus a reference to the site of a famous World War II battle as "the El Alamein" incorporates three versions of the definite article, in English, Spanish, and Arabic. See Usage Notes at **close, consensus, cross section, mental telepathy, rarely, refer.**

re·dun·dant (rĭ-dŭn′dənt) *adj.* **1.** Exceeding what is necessary or natural; superfluous. **2.** Needlessly repetitive; verbose. **3.** *Electronics.* Of or involving redundancy in electronic equipment. **4.** Of or involving redundancy in the transmission of messages. [Latin *redundāns, redundant-,* present participle of *redundāre,* to overflow : *re-, red-,* re- + *undāre,* to surge (from *unda,* wave; see **wed-**[1] in Appendix).] —**re·dun′dant·ly** *adv.*

re·du·pli·cate (rĭ-do͞o′plə-kāt′, -dyo͞o′-) *v.* **-cat·ed, -cat·ing, -cates.** —*tr.* **1.** To repeat over and over again; redouble. **2.** *Linguistics.* **a.** To double (the initial syllable or all of a root word) to produce an inflectional or derivational form. **b.** To form (a new word) by doubling all or part of a word. —*intr.* To be doubled. —**reduplicate** (-plə-kĭt) *adj.* Doubled. [Late Latin *reduplicāre, reduplicāt-* : Latin *re-,* re- + *duplicāre,* to duplicate; see DUPLICATE.]

re·du·pli·ca·tion (rĭ-do͞o′plĭ-kā′shən, -dyo͞o′-) *n.* **1.** The act of reduplicating or the state of being reduplicated. **2.** The product or result of reduplicating. **3.** *Linguistics.* **a.** A word formed by or containing a reduplicated element. **b.** The added element in a word form that is reduplicated. —**re·du′pli·ca′tive** *adj.* —**re·du′pli·ca′tive·ly** *adv.*

re·du·vi·id (rĭ-do͞o′vē-ĭd, -dyo͞o′-) *n.* See **assassin bug.** [From New Latin *Reduviidae,* family name, from *Reduvius,* type genus, from Latin *reduvia,* hangnail, fragment. See **eu-**[1] in Appendix.]

re·dux (rē-dŭks′) *adj.* Brought back; returned. Used postpositively. [Latin : *re-,* re- + *dux,* leader; see DUKE.]

red valerian *n.* A Mediterranean perennial plant *(Centranthus ruber)* having glabrous, ovate leaves and fragrant crimson to pale red flowers borne in dense terminal clusters.

red·wing (rĕd′wĭng′) *n.* **1.** See **red-winged blackbird. 2.** A European thrush *(Turdus iliacus)* having reddish feathers under the wings and a white eye stripe.

red-winged blackbird (rĕd′wĭngd′) *n.* A North American blackbird *(Agelaius phoeniceus),* the male of which has scarlet patches on the wings. Also called *redwing.*

red wolf *n.* A small reddish wolf *(Canis rufus)* of the southeast United States, having gray or black highlights and existing almost exclusively in captivity.

red·wood (rĕd′wo͝od′) *n.* **1.a.** A very tall, evergreen, coniferous tree *(Sequoia sempervirens)* native to the coastal ranges of southern Oregon and central and northern California, having small, seed-bearing cones with peltate scales and unflattened branches. **b.** The soft, reddish wood of this tree. Also called *sequoia.* **2.** Any of various woods having a reddish color or yielding a red dye.

Red·wood City (rĕd′wo͝od′). A city of western California northwest of Palo Alto. It is a residential community with an electronics industry. Population, 54,965.

re·ech·o also **re-ech·o** (rĭ-ĕk′ō) —*v.* **-oed, -o·ing, -oes.** —*intr.* To sound back or reverberate. —*tr.* To echo back; repeat. See Synonyms at **echo.**

reed (rēd) *n.* **1.a.** Any of various tall perennial grasses, espe-

red squirrel
Tamiasciurus hudsonicus

red-tailed hawk
Buteo jamaicensis

reed
Reed boat on Lake Titicaca

ă pat	oi boy
ā pay	ou out
âr care	o͝o took
ä father	o͞o boot
ĕ pet	ŭ cut
ē be	ûr urge
ĭ pit	th thin
ī pie	*th* this
îr pier	hw which
ŏ pot	zh vision
ō toe	ə about, item
ô paw	♦ regionalism

Stress marks: **′** (primary); ′ (secondary), as in **dictionary** (dĭk′shə-nĕr′ē)

cially of the genera *Phragmites* or *Arundo,* having hollow stems, broad leaves, and large plumelike terminal panicles. **b.** The stalk of any of these plants. **c.** A collection of these stalks: *reed for making baskets.* **2.** *Music.* A primitive wind instrument made of a hollow reed stalk. **3.** *Music.* **a.** A flexible strip of cane or metal set into the mouthpiece or air opening of certain instruments to produce tone by vibrating in response to a stream of air. **b.** An instrument, such as an oboe or a clarinet, that is fitted with a reed. **4.** A narrow, movable frame fitted with reed or metal strips that separate the warp threads in weaving. **5.** *Architecture.* A reading. [Middle English *rede,* from Old English *hrēod.*]

Reed (rēd), **John.** 1887–1920. American journalist. A World War I correspondent, he was in Petrograd during the October Revolution (1917), an experience he recounted in *Ten Days That Shook the World* (1919). In 1919 he founded the American Communist Labor Party. Reed is buried in the Kremlin in Moscow.

Reed, Stanley Forman. 1884–1980. American jurist who served as an associate justice of the U.S. Supreme Court (1938–1957).

Reed, Thomas Brackett. 1839–1902. American politician. A U.S. representative from Maine (1877–1899), he twice served as Speaker of the House (1889–1891 and 1895–1899).

Reed, Walter. 1851–1902. American physician and army surgeon who proved that yellow fever was transmitted by the *Aedes aegypti* mosquito.

reed•bird (rēd′bûrd′) *n.* See **bobolink.**

reed•buck (rēd′bŭk′) *n.* Any of several African antelopes of the genus *Redunca,* having long hoofs, small horns that curve forward, and a short bushy tail. [Translation of Afrikaans *rietbok.*]

reed•ing (rē′dĭng) *n.* **1.** *Architecture.* A convex decorative molding having parallel strips resembling thin reeds. **2.** Parallel grooves cut into the edge of a coin at right angles to the faces.

reed•ling (rēd′lĭng) *n.* A small Eurasian marsh bird *(Panurus biarmicus),* the male of which has mustachelike black markings.

reed mace *n.* See **cattail.**

reed•man (rēd′măn′) *n. Music.* A player of reeds, especially a jazz saxophonist or jazz clarinetist.

reed organ *n. Music.* A harmonium.

reed pipe *n. Music.* An organ pipe with a reed that vibrates and produces a tone when air is forced through it.

reed stop *n. Music.* A stop on an organ made up of or controlling reed pipes.

re•ed•u•cate also **re-ed•u•cate** (rē-ĕj′ə-kāt′) *tr.v.* **-cat•ed, -cat•ing, -cates.** **1.** To instruct again. **2.** To retrain (a person) to function effectively; rehabilitate. **—re•ed′u•ca′tion** *n.*

reed•y (rē′dē) *adj.* **-i•er, -i•est.** **1.** Full of reeds. **2.** Made of reeds. **3.** Resembling a reed, especially in being thin or fragile: *"reedy businessmen in severe three-piece business suits"* (Jimmy Breslin). **4.** *Music.* Having a tone like that of a reed instrument. **—reed′i•ness** *n.*

reef¹ (rēf) *n. Abbr.* **rf.** **1.** A strip or ridge of rocks, sand, or coral that rises to or near the surface of a body of water. **2.** A vein of ore. [Obsolete Dutch *rif,* possibly from Old Norse, ridge.] **—reef′y** *adj.*

reef² (rēf) *Nautical. n.* A portion of a sail rolled and tied down to lessen the area exposed to the wind. **—reef** *tr.v.* **reefed, reef•ing, reefs.** **1.** To reduce the size of (a sail) by tucking in a part and tying it to or rolling it around a yard. **2.** To shorten (a topmast or bowsprit) by taking part of it in. [Middle English *riff,* from Old Norse *rif,* ridge, reef.]

reef•er¹ (rē′fər) *n.* **1.** A short, heavy, close-fitting, double-breasted jacket. **2.** A close-fitting, single-breasted or double-breasted coat. **3.** *Nautical.* A person, such as a midshipman, who reefs.

reef•er² (rē′fər) *n. Slang.* Marijuana, especially a marijuana cigarette. [Origin unknown.]

ree•fer³ (rē′fər) *n. Slang.* **1.** A conveyance, such as a railroad car or truck trailer, that carries cargo under refrigeration. **2.** A refrigerator. [Alteration of REFRIGERATOR.]

reef knot *n. Nautical.* A square knot used in reefing sails.

reek (rēk) *v.* **reeked, reek•ing, reeks.** *—intr.* **1.** To smoke, steam, or fume. **2.** To be pervaded by something unpleasant: *"This document . . . reeks of self-pity and self-deception"* (Christopher Hitchens). **3.** To give off or become permeated with a strong, unpleasant odor: *"Grandma, who reeks of face powder and lilac water"* (Garrison Keillor). *—tr.* **1.** To emit or exude (smoke, for example). **2.** To process or treat by exposing to the action of smoke. **—reek** *n.* **1.** A strong, offensive odor; a stench. See Synonyms at **stench.** **2.** Vapor; steam. [Middle English *reken,* to smoke, from Old English *rēocan,* to emit smoke, and *rēcan,* to expose to smoke; see **reug-** in Appendix.] **—reek′er** *n.* **—reek′y** *adj.*

WORD HISTORY: *Reek* is a word that can be said to have been degraded by the company that it has kept. The Old English word *rēocan,* one of two ancestors of our word, meant "to emit vapor, steam, or smoke," while the other Old English ancestor, *rēcan,* meant "to fumigate, expose to smoke," or "to cause to emit smoke, burn incense." Burning incense and fumigating are certainly a far cry from the sort of thing now denoted by the verb *reek.* But at least in one case Old English *rēocan* did mean "to stink," hardly a surprise when one considers how bad some smoke smells. Middle English *reken,* the descendant of these two Old English words, never meant "to stink," but it could refer to a stench while meaning "to rise, ascend." It would seem that the various exhalations of heated persons and animals, of freshly shed blood, and of smoke referred to by Middle English *reken* and its Modern English descendant *reek* eventually overwhelmed the word, so that as far as concrete senses are concerned, we largely think of it as meaning "to stink."

reel¹
Film reels

reel¹ (rēl) *n.* **1.** A device, such as a cylinder, spool, or frame, that turns on an axis and is used for winding and storing rope, tape, film, or other flexible materials. **2.** A cylindrical device attached to a fishing rod to let out or wind up the line. **3.** The quantity of wire, film, or other material wound on one reel. **4.** A set of curved lawn-mower blades that rotate around a bar parallel to the ground, cutting grass while moving against a stationary straight blade. **—reel** *tr.v.* **reeled, reel•ing, reels.** **1.** To wind on or let out from a reel. **2.** To recover by winding on a reel: *reel in a large fish.* ***—phrasal verb.*** **reel off.** To recite fluently and usually at length: *reeled off a long list of names and dates.* [Middle English, from Old English *hrēol.*] **—reel′a•ble** *adj.*

reel² (rēl) *v.* **reeled, reel•ing, reels.** *—intr.* **1.** To be thrown off balance or fall back: *reeled from the sharp blow.* **2.** To stagger, lurch, or sway, as from drunkenness: *reeled down the alley.* **3.** To go round and round in a whirling motion: *gulls reeling and diving.* **4.** To feel dizzy: *My head reeled with the facts and figures.* *—tr.* To cause to reel. **—reel** *n.* **1.** A staggering, swaying, or whirling movement. **2. a.** A fast dance of Scottish origin. **b.** The Virginia reel. **c.** The music for one of these dances. [Middle English *relen,* to whirl about, probably from *reel,* spool. See REEL¹.] **—reel′er** *n.*

♦ **reel³** *n. Maine.* A hand-held hammer used in a quarry for shaping granite blocks. See Regional Note at **reeling.** [Origin unknown.]

re•e•lect also **re-e•lect** (rē′ĭ-lĕkt′) *tr.v.* **-lect•ed, -lect•ing, -lects.** To elect again. **—re′e•lec′tion** *n.*

♦ **reel•ing** (rē′lĭng) *n. Maine.* Sustained noise, as from hammering: *"Hark that reeling, now, you'll wake the baby!"* (Anonymous).

♦ ***REGIONAL NOTE:*** In the granite quarries of Maine, stones for paving were once shaped by men using small hammers called *reels.* Crews of 30 men at a time would use these hammers. The resulting "shattering noise as the pieces of the granite were shaped. . . . gave Mainers a word for any sustained hubbub—*reelin'* " (John Gould). *Reeling* can denote noise made by humans as well: *She told the children to hush their reeling.*

reel-to-reel (rēl′tə-rēl′) *adj.* Designating sound recording equipment or sound recordings that use magnetic tape which must be threaded through the equipment and onto an empty reel.

re•en•act also **re-en•act** (rē′ĕn-ăkt′, -ə-năkt′) *tr.v.* **-act•ed, -act•ing, -acts.** **1.** To enact again: *reenact a law.* **2.** To perform again: *reenact the first two scenes.* **3.** To go through a second time: *reenacted the events leading up to the accident.* **—re′en•act′ment** *n.*

re•en•force or **re-en•force** (rē′ĭn-fôrs′, -fōrs′) *v.* Variants of **reinforce.**

re•en•ter also **re-en•ter** (rē-ĕn′tər) *—v.* **-tered, -ter•ing, -ters.** *—intr.* To come in or enter again. *—tr.* To record again on a list or ledger. **—re•en′trance** *n.*

re•en•trant also **re-en•trant** (rē-ĕn′trənt) *—adj.* Reentering; pointing inward. *—n.* A reentrant angle or part.

reentrant angle also **re-entrant angle** *n. Mathematics.* In an irregular polygon, an interior angle that is greater than 180° and whose apex faces into the polygon.

re•en•try also **re-en•try** (rē-ĕn′trē) *n., pl.* **-tries.** **1.** The act of reentering. **2.** *Law.* The recovery of possession under a right reserved in a previous property transaction. **3.** *Games.* **a.** The act of regaining the lead by taking a trick in bridge and whist. **b.** The card that will take a trick and thus regain the lead. **4.** *Aerospace.* The return of a missile or spacecraft into Earth's atmosphere.

reentry vehicle *n. Abbr.* **RV** The part of a spacecraft or missile that reenters Earth's atmosphere.

Reese (rēs), **Lizette Woodworth.** 1856–1935. American poet and educator whose works include *A Handful of Lavender* (1891) and *White April* (1930).

reeve¹ (rēv) *n.* **1.** The elected president of a town council in some parts of Canada. **2.** Any of various minor officers of parishes or other local authorities. **3.** A bailiff or steward of a manor in the later medieval period. **4.** A high officer of local administration appointed by the Anglo-Saxon kings. [Middle English, from Old English *gerēfa.*]

reeve² (rēv) *tr.v.* **reeved** or **rove** (rōv), **reev•ing, reeves.** *Nautical.* **1.** To pass (a rope or rod) through a hole, ring, pulley, or block. **2.** To fasten by passing through or around. **3.** To pass a rope or rod through (a hole, ring, pulley, or block). [Origin unknown.]

reeve³ (rēv) *n.* The female ruff. [Probably alteration of RUFF¹.]

re•ex•am•ine also **re-ex•am•ine** (rē′ĭg-zăm′ĭn) *tr.v.* **-ined, -in•ing, -ines.** **1.** To examine again or anew; review. **2.** *Law.* To question (a witness) again after cross-examination. **—re′ex•am′i•na′tion** *n.*

ref (rĕf) *n. Sports & Games.* A referee.

ref. *abbr.* **1.** Reference. **2.** Referred. **3.** Refining. **4.** Reformation; reformed. **5.** Refunding.

re·fect (rĭ-fĕkt′) *tr.v.* **-fect·ed, -fect·ing, -fects.** *Archaic.* To refresh with food and drink. [Latin *reficere, refect-,* to refresh : *re-,* re- + *facere,* to make; see **dhē-** in Appendix.]

re·fec·tion (rĭ-fĕk′shən) *n.* **1.** Refreshment with food and drink. **2.** A light meal or repast.

re·fec·to·ry (rĭ-fĕk′tə-rē) *n., pl.* **-ries.** A room where meals are served, especially in a college or other institution.

refectory table *n.* A long table with straight, heavy legs.

re·fer (rĭ-fûr′) *v.* **-ferred, -fer·ring, -fers.** —*tr.* **1.** To direct to a source for help or information: *referred her to a heart specialist; referred me to his last employer for a recommendation.* **2.** To assign or attribute to; regard as originated by. **3.** To assign to or regard as belonging within a particular kind or class. **4.** To submit (a matter in dispute) to an authority for arbitration, decision, or examination. **5.** To direct the attention of: *refer him to his duties.* —*intr.* **1.** To pertain; concern: *questions referring to yesterday's lecture.* **2.** To make mention or reference. **3.** To have recourse; turn: *refer to a dictionary.* [Middle English *referren,* from Old French *referer,* from Latin *referre* : *re-,* re- + *ferre,* to carry; see **bher-**[1] in Appendix.] —**ref′er·a·ble** (rĕf′ər-ə-bəl, rĭ-fûr′-) *adj.* —**re·fer′ral** *n.* —**re·fer′rer** *n.*

SYNONYMS: *refer, advert, mention.* The central meaning shared by these verbs is "to call or direct attention to something": *referred to my indiscretion; adverting to childhood experiences; often mentions his old friend.* See also Synonyms at **attribute, resort.**

USAGE NOTE: It is sometimes believed that the phrase *refer back* is redundant, since the prefix *re–* means "back," but the objection is misplaced. In fact, an expression can refer either to something that has already been mentioned or to something that is yet to be mentioned, and the distinction between *refer back* and *refer ahead* may thus be required for clarification. For example, the sentence *Jones promised that if he was elected to the council, Harris would be made the council president* is ambiguous, because the pronoun *he* may either refer back or refer ahead. See Usage Notes at **allude, redundancy.**

ref·e·ree (rĕf′ə-rē′) *n.* **1.** One to whom something is referred, especially for settlement, decision, or an opinion as to the thing's quality. **2.** *Sports & Games.* An official supervising the play; an umpire. **3.** *Law.* A person appointed by a court to make a determination of a case or to investigate and make a report on it. See Synonyms at **judge.** —**referee** *v.* **-reed, -ree·ing, -rees.** —*tr.* To judge as referee. —*intr.* To act as referee.

ref·er·ence (rĕf′ər-əns, rĕf′rəns) *n. Abbr.* **ref. 1.** An act of referring: *My careful writing results from many references to a dictionary.* **2. a.** Significance in a specified context: *Her speeches have special reference to the African situation.* **b.** Meaning or denotation. **3.** The state of being related or referred: *with reference to; in reference to.* **4.** A mention of an occurrence or a situation: *She made frequent references to her promotion.* **5. a.** A note in a publication referring the reader to another passage or source. **b.** The passage or source so referred to. **c.** A work frequently used as a source. **d.** A mark or footnote used to direct a reader elsewhere for additional information. **6.** *Law.* **a.** Submission of a case to a referee. **b.** Legal actions conducted before or by a referee. **7. a.** A person who is in a position to recommend another or to vouch for his or her fitness, as for a job. **b.** A statement about a person's qualifications, character, and dependability. —**reference** *tr.v.* **-enced, -enc·ing, -ences. 1.** To supply references to: *"Our memories are addressed and referenced . . . by significant fragments of their own content"* (Frederick Turner). **2.** To mention in a reference; refer to: *He referenced her book in his speech.* See Usage Note at **allude.** —**ref′er·enc·er** *n.* —**ref′er·en′tial** (-ə-rĕn′shəl) *adj.* —**ref′er·en′tial·ly** *adv.*

reference book *n.* **1.** A book, such as a dictionary or an encyclopedia, to which one can refer for authoritative information. **2.** See **passbook** (sense 3).

ref·er·en·dum (rĕf′ə-rĕn′dəm) *n., pl.* **-dums** or **-da** (-də). **1. a.** The submission of a proposed public measure or actual statute to a direct popular vote. **b.** Such a vote. **2.** A note from a diplomat to the diplomat's government requesting instructions. [Latin, neuter gerundive of *referre,* to refer. See REFER.]

ref·er·ent (rĕf′ər-ənt, rĭ-fûr′ənt) *n.* **1.** Something that refers, especially a linguistic item in its capacity of referring to a meaning. **2.** Something referred to.

re·ferred pain (rĭ-fûrd′) *n.* Pain that is felt in a part of the body at a distance from the area of pathology, as pain in the right shoulder derived from the presence of a gallstone in the bladder.

re·fill (rē-fĭl′) *tr.v.* **-filled, -fill·ing, -fills.** To fill again. —**refill** (rē′fĭl′) *n.* **1.** A product packaged to replace the used contents of a container. **2.** A second or subsequent filling.

re·fin·ance (rē′fə-năns′, rē-fī′năns′) *intr. & tr.v.* **-nanced, -nanc·ing, -nanc·es.** To provide new financing or new financing for, as by discharging a mortgage with the proceeds from a new mortgage obtained at a lower interest rate. —**re·fi′nance′** *n.* —**re′fi·nan′cer, re′fin·an·cier′** (-fĭn-ən-sîr′, -fə-năn′-) *n.*

re·fine (rĭ-fīn′) *v.* **-fined, -fin·ing, -fines.** —*tr.* **1.** To reduce to a pure state; purify. **2.** To remove by purifying. **3.** To free from coarse, unsuitable, or immoral characteristics: *refined his manners; refined her speaking style.* —*intr.* **1.** To become free of impurities. **2.** To acquire polish or elegance. **3.** To use precise distinctions and subtlety in thought or speech. —**re·fin′er** *n.*

re·fined (rĭ-fīnd′) *adj.* **1.** Free from coarseness or vulgarity; polite. **2.** Free of impurities; purified. **3.** Precise to a fine degree.

re·fine·ment (rĭ-fīn′mənt) *n.* **1.** The act of refining. **2.** The result of refining; an improvement or elaboration. **3.** The state or quality of being refined; cultivation, as in manners or taste. **4.** A keen or precise phrasing; a subtle distinction.

re·fin·er·y (rĭ-fī′nə-rē) *n., pl.* **-ies.** An industrial plant for purifying a crude substance, such as petroleum or sugar.

re·fin·ish (rē-fĭn′ĭsh) *tr.v.* **-ished, -ish·ing, -ish·es.** To put a new finish on (furniture). —**re·fin′ish·er** *n.*

re·fit (rē-fĭt′) *v.* **-fit·ted, -fit·ting, -fits.** —*tr.* To prepare and equip for additional use. —*intr.* To be made fit again. —**refit** (rē′fĭt′, rē-fĭt′) *n.* **1.** Repair of damage or wear: *"a house . . . in need of a major refit"* (Nancy Holmes). **2.** A secondary or subsequent preparation of supplies and equipment.

refl. *abbr.* **1.** Reflection; reflective. **2.** Reflex; reflexive.

re·flag (rē-flăg′) *tr.v.* **-flagged, -flag·ging, -flags.** To give a new registered nationality to (a ship or an aircraft).

re·flect (rĭ-flĕkt′) *v.* **-flect·ed, -flect·ing, -flects.** —*tr.* **1.** To throw or bend back (light, for example) from a surface. See Synonyms at **echo. 2.** To form an image of (an object); mirror: *"Baseball reflects America's history"* (Roslyn A. Mazer). **3.** To manifest as a result of one's actions: *Her work reflects intelligence.* **4.** *Archaic.* To bend back. —*intr.* **1.** To be bent back. **2.** To give back a likeness. **3. a.** To think seriously. See Synonyms at **think. b.** To express carefully considered thoughts. —***phrasal verb.*** **reflect on. 1.** To form or express carefully considered thoughts about: *reflects on her country's place in history.* **2.** To give evidence of the qualities of (one): *The hasty preparation of this report reflects on you.* **3.** To give evidence that (one) has acted in a given way: *The excuses you gave reflect disappointingly on you.* [Middle English *reflecten,* from Old French *reflecter,* from Latin *reflectere,* to bend back : *re-,* re- + *flectere,* to bend.]

re·flec·tance (rĭ-flĕk′təns) *n.* The ratio of the total amount of radiation, as of light, reflected by a surface to the total amount of radiation incident on the surface.

re·flect·ing telescope (rĭ-flĕk′tĭng) *n.* A telescope in which light from the object is gathered and focused by a concave mirror, with the resulting image magnified by the eyepiece.

re·flec·tion (rĭ-flĕk′shən) *n. Abbr.* **refl. 1.** The act of reflecting or the state of being reflected. **2.** Something, such as light, radiant heat, sound, or an image, that is reflected. **3. a.** Mental concentration; careful consideration. **b.** A thought or an opinion resulting from such consideration. **4.** An indirect expression of censure or discredit: *a reflection on his integrity.* **5.** A manifestation or result: *Her achievements are a reflection of her courage.* **6.** *Anatomy.* **a.** The folding of a membrane from the wall of a cavity over an organ and back to the wall. **b.** The folds so made. —**re·flec′tion·al** *adj.*

re·flec·tive (rĭ-flĕk′tĭv) *adj. Abbr.* **refl. 1. a.** Of, relating to, produced by, or resulting from reflection. **b.** Capable of or producing reflection: *a reflective surface.* **2.** Characterized by or given to meditation or contemplation; thoughtful. See Synonyms at **pensive.** —**re·flec′tive·ly** *adv.* —**re·flec′tive·ness** *n.*

re·flec·tiv·i·ty (rē′flĕk-tĭv′ĭ-tē) *n., pl.* **-ties. 1.** The quality of being reflective. **2.** The ability to reflect. **3.** *Physics.* The ratio of the intensity of a wave reflected from a surface to the energy possessed by the wave striking the surface.

re·flec·tom·e·ter (rē′flĕk-tŏm′ĭ-tər) *n.* An instrument for measuring the reflectance of a surface.

re·flec·tor (rĭ-flĕk′tər) *n.* **1.** Something, such as a surface, that reflects. **2.** A reflecting telescope.

re·flec·tor·ize (rĭ-flĕk′tə-rīz′) *tr.v.* **-ized, -iz·ing, -iz·es.** To cause (a surface, for example) to reflect light, as by chemical treatment.

re·flex (rē′flĕks′) *adj. Abbr.* **refl. 1.** Bent, turned, or thrown back; reflected. **2.** *Physiology.* Being an involuntary action or response, such as a sneeze, blink, or hiccup. **3.** Produced as an automatic response or reaction: *reflex opposition to change.* —**reflex** *n. Abbr.* **refl. 1. a.** Something, such as light or heat, that is reflected. **b.** An image produced by reflection. **c.** A copy or reproduction. **2.** *Physiology.* An involuntary response to a stimulus. **3.** *Psychology.* An unlearned or instinctive response to a stimulus. **4.** *Linguistics.* A form or feature that reflects or represents an earlier, often reconstructed, form or feature having undergone phonetic or other change. —**reflex** (rĭ-flĕks′) *tr.v.* **-flexed, -flex·ing, -flex·es.** *Abbr.* **refl. 1.** To bend, turn back, or reflect. **2.** To cause to undergo a reflex process. [From Middle English *reflexen,* to refract light, bend back, from Latin *reflexus,* past participle of *reflectere,* to bend back. See REFLECT.]

reflex angle *n. Mathematics.* An angle greater than 180° and less than 360°.

reflex arc *n. Physiology.* The neural path of a reflex.

reflex camera *n.* A camera fitted with a mirror that reflects the image of an object or a scene onto a viewing screen so that focus, lighting, and composition may be evaluated.

re·flex·ion (rĭ-flĕk′shən) *n. Chiefly British.* Variant of **reflection.**

re·flex·ive (rĭ-flĕk′sĭv) *adj. Abbr.* **refl. 1.** Directed back on

referee

ă pat	oi boy
ā pay	ou out
âr care	ŏŏ took
ä father	ōō boot
ĕ pet	ŭ cut
ē be	ûr urge
ĭ pit	th thin
ī pie	*th* this
îr pier	hw which
ŏ pot	zh vision
ō toe	ə about, item
ô paw	♦ regionalism

Stress marks: **′** (primary); ′ (secondary), as in **dictionary** (dĭk′shə-nĕr′ē)

itself. **2.** *Grammar.* **a.** Of, relating to, or being a verb having an identical subject and direct object, as *dressed* in the sentence *She dressed herself.* **b.** Of, relating to, or being the pronoun used as the direct object of a reflexive verb, as *herself* in *She dressed herself.* **3.** Of or relating to a reflex. **4.** Elicited automatically; spontaneous: *"a bid for . . . reflexive left-wing approval"* (Marshall Delaney). **—reflexive** *n. Abbr.* **refl.** *Grammar.* A reflexive verb or pronoun. See Usage Note at **myself.** **—re·flex′ive·ly** *adv.* **—re·flex′ive·ness, re′flex·iv′i·ty** (rē′flĕk-sĭv′ĭ-tē) *n.*

re·flex·ol·o·gy (rē′flĕk-sŏl′ə-jē) *n.* **1.** The study of reflex responses, especially as they affect behavior. **2.** A method of massage that relieves nervous tension through the application of finger pressure, especially to the feet. **—re′flex·ol′o·gist** *n.*

ref·lu·ent (rĕf′lo͞o-ənt) *adj.* Flowing back; ebbing. [Latin *refluēns, refluent-,* present participle of *refluere,* to flow back : *re-,* re- + *fluere,* to flow; see FLUENT.] **—ref′lu·ence** *n.*

re·flux (rē′flŭks′) *n.* **1.** A flowing back; ebb. **2.** *Chemistry.* The process of refluxing. **—reflux** *v.* **-fluxed, -flux·ing, -flux·es.** *—tr. Chemistry.* To boil (a liquid) in a vessel attached to a condenser so that the vapors continuously condense for reboiling. *—intr.* To be boiled in such a way. [Medieval Latin *refluxus* : Latin *re-,* re- + *fluxus,* flow, from past participle of *fluere,* to flow; see **bhleu-** in Appendix.]

re·for·est (rē-fôr′ĭst, -fŏr′ĭst) *tr.v.* **-est·ed, -est·ing, -ests.** To replant (an area) with forest cover. **—re′for·es·ta′tion** *n.*

re·form (rĭ-fôrm′) *v.* **-formed, -form·ing, -forms.** *—tr.* **1.** To improve by alteration, correction of error, or removal of defects; put into a better form or condition. **2.a.** To abolish abuse or malpractice in: *reform the government.* **b.** To put an end to (a wrong). See Synonyms at **correct.** **3.** To cause (a person) to give up harmful or immoral practices; persuade to adopt a better way of life. *—intr.* To change for the better. **—reform** *n.* **1.** A change for the better; an improvement. **2.** Correction of evils, abuses, or errors. **3.** Action to improve social or economic conditions without radical or revolutionary change. **—reform** *adj.* **1.** Relating to or favoring reform: *a reform candidate for mayor.* **2.** **Reform.** Of or relating to Reform Judaism. [Middle English *reformen,* from Old French *reformer,* from Latin *refōrmāre* : *re-,* re- + *fōrmāre* (from *fōrma,* form).] **—re·form′a·bil′i·ty** *n.* **—re·form′a·ble** *adj.* **—re·form′er** *n.*

re-form (rē-fôrm′) *v.* **-formed, -form·ing, -forms.** *—tr.* To form again. *—intr.* To become formed again.

ref·or·ma·tion (rĕf′ər-mā′shən) *n.* **1.** *Abbr.* **ref.** The act of reforming or the state of being reformed. **2.** **Reformation.** A 16th-century movement in Western Europe that aimed at reforming some doctrines and practices of the Roman Catholic Church and resulted in the establishment of the Protestant churches. **—ref′or·ma′tion·al** *adj.*

re·for·ma·tive (rĭ-fôr′mə-tĭv) *adj.* Serving to induce reform.

re·for·ma·to·ry (rĭ-fôr′mə-tôr′ē, -tōr′ē) *n., pl.* **-ries.** A penal institution for the discipline, reformation, and training of young or first offenders. Also called *reform school.* **—reformatory** *adj.* Reformative.

re·formed (rĭ-fôrmd′) *adj. Abbr.* **ref.** **1.** Improved by the removal of faults or abuses. **2.** Improved in conduct or character. **3.** **Reformed.** Relating to or being the Protestant churches that follow the teachings of John Calvin and Ulrich Zwingli.

re·form·ism (rĭ-fôr′mĭz′əm) *n.* A doctrine or movement of reform. **—re·form′ist** *n.*

Reform Judaism *n.* The branch of Judaism introduced in the 19th century that seeks to reconcile historical Judaism with modern life and does not require strict observance of traditional religious law and ritual.

reform school *n.* See **reformatory.**

re·fract (rĭ-frăkt′) *tr.v.* **-fract·ed, -fract·ing, -fracts.** **1.** To deflect (light, for example) from a straight path by refraction. **2.** To alter by viewing through a medium: *"In the Quartet reality is refracted through a variety of eyes"* (Elizabeth Kastor). **3.** *Medicine.* To determine the refraction of (an eye, for example). [Latin *refringere, refrāct-,* to break up : *re-,* re- + *frangere,* to break; see **bhreg-** in Appendix.]

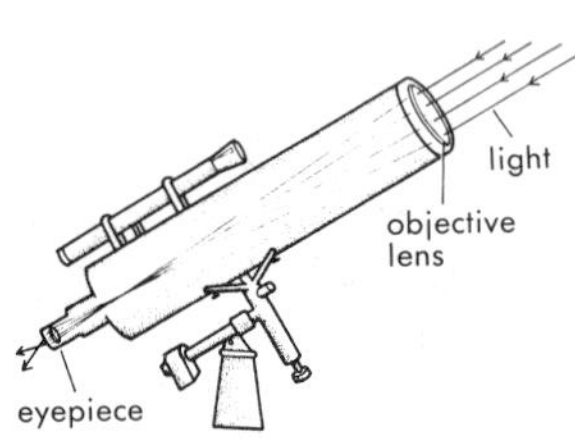

refracting telescope

re·fract·ing telescope (rĭ-frăk′tĭng) *n.* A telescope in which light from an object is gathered and focused by lenses, with the resulting image magnified by the eyepiece.

re·frac·tion (rĭ-frăk′shən) *n.* **1.** The turning or bending of any wave, such as a light or sound wave, when it passes from one medium into another of different density. **2.** *Astronomy.* The apparent change in position of celestial objects caused by the bending of light rays entering Earth's atmosphere. **3.** *Medicine.* **a.** The ability of the eye to bend light so that an image is focused on the retina. **b.** Determination of the refractive characteristics of the eye. **—re·frac′tion·al, re·frac′tive** *adj.* **—re·frac′tive·ly** *adv.* **—re·frac′tive·ness, re′frac·tiv′i·ty** (rē′frăk-tĭv′ĭ-tē) *n.*

refractive index *n. Physics.* See **index of refraction.**

re·frac·tom·e·ter (rē′frăk-tŏm′ĭ-tər) *n.* Any of several instruments used to measure the index of refraction of a substance.

re·frac·tor (rĭ-frăk′tər) *n.* **1.** One that refracts. **2.** A refracting telescope.

re·frac·to·ry (rĭ-frăk′tə-rē) *adj.* **1.** Obstinately resistant to authority or control. See Synonyms at **unruly.** **2.** Difficult to melt or work; resistant to heat: *a refractory material such as silica.* **3.** Resistant to treatment: *a refractory case of acne.* **—refractory** *n., pl.* **-ries.** **1.** One that is refractory. **2.** Material that has a high melting point. [Alteration (influenced by adjectives in -ORY) of obsolete *refractary,* from Latin *refrāctārius,* from *refrāctus,* past participle of *refringere,* to break up. See REFRACT.] **—re·frac′to·ri·ly** *adv.* **—re·frac′to·ri·ness** *n.*

re·frain¹ (rĭ-frān′) *v.* **-frained, -frain·ing, -frains.** *—intr.* To hold oneself back; forbear: *refrained from swearing. —tr. Archaic.* To restrain or hold back; curb. [Middle English *refreinen,* from Old French *refrener,* to restrain, from Latin *refrēnāre* : *re-,* re- + *frēnāre,* to restrain (from *frēnum,* bridle, from *frendere,* to grind; see **ghrendh-** in Appendix).] **—re·frain′er** *n.* **—re·frain′ment** *n.*

SYNONYMS: *refrain, abstain, forbear.* The central meaning shared by these verbs is "to keep or prevent oneself from doing or saying something": *refrained from commenting; abstained from smoking; can't forbear criticizing their ineptitude.*

re·frain² (rĭ-frān′) *n.* **1.a.** A phrase, verse, or group of verses repeated at intervals throughout a song or poem, especially at the end of each stanza. **b.** Music for the refrain of a poem. **2.** A song or melody. **3.** A repeated utterance or theme. [Middle English *refrein,* from Old French *refrain,* alteration of *refrait,* past participle of *refraindre,* to break off, repeat, from Vulgar Latin **refrangere,* to break off, alteration of Latin *refringere.* See REFRACT.]

re·fran·gi·ble (rĭ-frăn′jə-bəl) *adj.* That can be refracted: *refrangible rays of light.* [From Latin *refringere,* to refract (influenced by REFRACT).] **—re·fran′gi·bil′i·ty, re·fran′gi·ble·ness** *n.*

re·fresh (rĭ-frĕsh′) *v.* **-freshed, -fresh·ing, -fresh·es.** *—tr.* **1.** To revive with or as if with rest, food, or drink; give new vigor or spirit to. **2.** To give new freshness or brightness to; restore. **3.** To make cool, clean, or moist; freshen up. **4.** To renew by stimulation: *refresh one's memory.* **5.** To fill up again; replenish: *refresh a drink. —intr.* **1.** To take refreshment. **2.** To become fresh again; revive. [Middle English *refresshen,* from Old French *refreschir* : *re-,* re- + *fres, fresche,* fresh (of Germanic origin).]

re·fresh·en (rĭ-frĕsh′ən) *tr. & intr.v.* **-fresh·ened, -fresh·en·ing, -fresh·ens.** To refresh or become refreshed.

re·fresh·er (rĭ-frĕsh′ər) *n.* **1.** One that refreshes: *a lemon refresher imbibed on a hot day.* **2.** Instruction that serves to reacquaint one with material previously studied or to bring one's knowledge or skills up to date.

re·fresh·ing (rĭ-frĕsh′ĭng) *adj.* **1.** Serving to refresh. **2.** Pleasantly fresh and different: *"common sense of a most refreshing sort"* (William Raspberry). **—re·fresh′ing·ly** *adv.*

re·fresh·ment (rĭ-frĕsh′mənt) *n.* **1.** The act of refreshing or the state of being refreshed. **2.** Something, such as food or drink, that refreshes. **3.** **refreshments.** A snack or light meal and drinks.

re·fried beans (rē′frīd′) *pl.n.* Beans that have been cooked and then mashed and fried with seasonings. [Translation of Spanish *frijoles refritos* : *frijoles,* pl. of *frijol,* bean + *refritos,* pl. past participle of *refreír,* to refry.]

re·frig·er·ant (rĭ-frĭj′ər-ənt) *adj.* **1.** Cooling or freezing; refrigerating. **2.** *Medicine.* Reducing fever. **—refrigerant** *n.* **1.** A substance, such as air, ammonia, water, or carbon dioxide, used to provide cooling either as the working substance of a refrigerator or by direct absorption of heat. **2.** *Medicine.* An agent used to reduce fever.

re·frig·er·ate (rĭ-frĭj′ə-rāt′) *tr.v.* **-at·ed, -at·ing, -ates.** **1.** To cool or chill (a substance). **2.** To preserve (food) by chilling. [Latin *refrīgerāre, refrīgerāt-* : *re-,* re- + *frīgerāre,* to make cool (from *frīgus, frīgor-,* coldness).] **—re·frig′er·a′tion** *n.* **—re·frig′er·a′tive, re·frig′er·a·to′ry** (-ər-ə-tôr′ē, -tōr′ē) *adj.*

re·frig·er·a·tor (rĭ-frĭj′ə-rā′tər) *n.* An appliance, a cabinet, or a room for storing food or other substances at a low temperature.

re·frin·gence (rĭ-frĭn′jəns) *n.* Refractive power.

re·frin·gent (rĭ-frĭn′jənt) *adj.* Of, relating to, or producing refraction; refractive. [Latin *refringēns, refringent-,* present participle of *refringere,* to break up. See REFRACT.]

reft¹ (rĕft) *v.* A past tense and a past participle of **reave¹.**

reft² (rĕft) *v.* A past tense and a past participle of **reave².**

re·fu·el (rē-fyo͞o′əl) *v.* **-eled, -el·ing, -els** also **-elled, -el·ling, -els.** *—tr.* To supply again with fuel. *—intr.* To take on a fresh supply of fuel.

ref·uge (rĕf′yo͞oj) *n.* **1.** Protection or shelter, as from danger or hardship. **2.** A place providing protection or shelter. **3.** A source of help, relief, or comfort in times of trouble. See Synonyms at **shelter.** **—refuge** *v.* **-uged, -ug·ing, -ug·es.** *Archaic. —tr.* To give refuge to. *—intr.* To take refuge. [Middle English, from Old French, from Latin *refugium,* from *refugere,* to run away : *re-,* re- + *fugere,* to flee.]

ref·u·gee (rĕf′yo͞o-jē′) *n.* One who flees in search of refuge, as in times of war, political oppression, or religious persecution. [French *réfugié,* from past participle of *réfugier,* to take refuge, from Old French, from *refuge,* refuge. See REFUGE.]

re·fu·gi·um (rĭ-fyo͞o′jē-əm) *n., pl.* **-gi·a** (-jē-ə). *Ecology.* An area that has escaped ecological changes occurring elsewhere and so provides a suitable habitat for relict species. [Latin, refuge. See REFUGE.]

re·ful·gent (rĭ-fo͝ol′jənt, -fŭl′-) *adj.* Shining radiantly; resplendent. [Latin *refulgēns, refulgent-,* present participle of *re-*

fulgēre, to flash back : *re-,* re- + *fulgēre,* to flash; see **bhel-**[1] in Appendix.] **—re·ful′gence, re·ful′gen·cy** *n.* **—re·ful′gent·ly** *adv.*

re·fund (rĭ-fŭnd′, rē′fŭnd′) *v.* **-fund·ed, -fund·ing, -funds.** *—tr.* To give back, especially money; return or repay: *refunded the purchase price.* *—intr.* To make repayment. **—refund** (rē′-fŭnd′) *n. Abbr.* **rf. 1.** A repayment of funds. **2.** An amount repaid. [Middle English *refunden,* from Old French *refunder,* from Latin *refundere* : *re-,* re- + *fundere,* to pour; see **gheu-** in Appendix.] **—re·fund′a·ble** *adj.* **—re·fund′er** *n.* **—re·fund′ment** *n.*

re-fund (rē-fŭnd′) *tr.v.* **-fund·ed, -fund·ing, -funds. 1.** To fund anew. **2.** To pay back (a debt) with new borrowing, especially to replace (a bond issue) with a new issue.

re·fur·bish (rē-fûr′bĭsh) *tr.v.* **-bished, -bish·ing, -bish·es.** To make clean, bright, or fresh again; renovate. **—re·fur′bish·ment** *n.*

re·fus·al (rĭ-fyo͞o′zəl) *n.* **1.** The act or an instance of refusing. **2.** The opportunity or right to accept or reject something before it is offered elsewhere.

re·fuse[1] (rĭ-fyo͞oz′) *v.* **-fused, -fus·ing, -fus·es.** *—tr.* **1.a.** To indicate unwillingness to do, accept, give, or allow: *She was refused admittance. He refused treatment.* **b.** To indicate unwillingness (to do something): *refused to leave.* **2.** To decline to jump (an obstacle). Used of a horse. *—intr.* To decline to do, accept, give, or allow something. [Middle English *refusen,* from Old French *refuser,* from Vulgar Latin **refūsāre,* probably blend of Latin *recūsāre,* to refuse; see RECUSE, and *refūtāre;* see REFUTE.] **—re·fus′er** *n.*

SYNONYMS: *refuse, decline, reject, spurn, rebuff.* These verbs all mean to be unwilling to accept, consider, or receive someone or something. *Refuse* usually implies determination and often brusqueness: *"The commander . . . refused to discuss questions of right"* (George Bancroft). *"I'll make him an offer he can't refuse"* (Mario Puzo). To *decline* is to refuse courteously: *"I declined election to the National Institute of Arts and Letters some years ago, and now I must decline the Pulitzer Prize"* (Sinclair Lewis). *Reject* suggests the discarding of someone or something as unsatisfactory, defective, or useless; it implies categoric refusal: *"He again offered himself for enlistment and was again rejected"* (Arthur S.M. Hutchinson). *"Emphasize your choice by utter ignoring of all that you reject"* (Ralph Waldo Emerson). To *spurn* is to reject scornfully or contemptuously: *"The more she spurns my love,/ The more it grows"* (Shakespeare). *Rebuff* pertains to blunt, often disdainful rejection: *"He had . . . forgotten himself, had gone too far in his advances, and had been rebuffed"* (Robert Louis Stevenson).

ref·use[2] (rĕf′yo͞os) *n.* Items or material discarded or rejected as useless or worthless; trash or rubbish. [Middle English, from Old French *refus,* rejection, refuse, from *refuser,* to refuse. See REFUSE[1].]

re·fuse·nik **re·fused·nik** (rĭ-fyo͞oz′nĭk) *n.* A Soviet citizen who has been denied the right to emigrate.

ref·u·ta·tion (rĕf′yo͞o-tā′shən) also **re·fut·al** (rĭ-fyo͞ot′l) *n.* **1.** The act of refuting. **2.** Something, such as an argument, that refutes someone or something.

re·fute (rĭ-fyo͞ot′) *tr.v.* **-fut·ed, -fut·ing, -futes. 1.** To prove to be false or erroneous; overthrow by argument or proof: *refute testimony.* **2.** To deny the accuracy or truth of: *refuted the results of the poll.* [Latin *refūtāre.* See **bhau-** in Appendix.] **—re·fut′a·bil′i·ty** (rĭ-fyo͞o′tə-bĭl′ĭ-tē, rĕf′yə-tə-) *n.* **—re·fut′a·ble** (rĭ-fyo͞o′tə-bəl, rĕf′yə-tə-) *adj.* **—re·fut′a·bly** *adv.*

reg. *abbr.* **1.** Regent. **2.** Regiment. **3.** Region. **4.** Register; registered. **5.** Registrar. **6.** Registry. **7.a.** Regular. **b.** Regularly. **8.** Regulation. **9.** Regulator.

re·gain (rē-gān′) *tr.v.* **-gained, -gain·ing, -gains. 1.** To recover possession of; get back again: *regain one's strength.* See Synonyms at **recover. 2.** To manage to reach again: *regained the summit.* **—re·gain′er** *n.*

re·gal (rē′gəl) *adj.* **1.** Of or relating to a monarch; royal. **2.** Belonging to or befitting a monarch: *regal attire.* **3.** Magnificent; splendid. [Middle English, from Old French, from Latin *rēgālis,* from *rēx, rēg-,* king. See **reg-** in Appendix.] **—re·gal′i·ty** (rĭ-găl′ĭ-tē) *n.* **—re′gal·ly** *adv.*

re·gale (rĭ-gāl′) *v.* **-galed, -gal·ing, -gales.** *—tr.* **1.** To provide with great enjoyment; entertain. See Synonyms at **amuse. 2.** To entertain sumptuously with food and drink; provide a feast for. *—intr.* To feast. **—regale** *n.* **1.** A great feast. **2.** A choice food; a delicacy. **3.** Refreshment. [French *régaler,* from Old French *regal,* feast, from *gale* (influenced by *se rigoler,* to amuse oneself), from *galer,* to make merry.] **—re·gale′ment** *n.*

re·ga·lia (rĭ-găl′yə, -gā′lē-ə) *pl.n. (used with a sing. or pl. verb).* **1.** The emblems and symbols of royalty, such as the crown and scepter. **2.** The rights and privileges of royalty. **3.** The distinguishing symbols of a rank, office, order, or society. **4.** Magnificent attire; finery. [Medieval Latin *rēgālia,* from Latin, neuter pl. of *rēgālis,* regal. See REGAL.]

re·gard (rĭ-gärd′) *v.* **-gard·ed, -gard·ing, -gards.** *—tr.* **1.** To look at attentively; observe closely. **2.** To look upon or consider in a particular way: *I regard him as a fool.* **3.** To hold in esteem or respect: *She regards her teachers highly.* **4.** To relate or refer to; concern: *This item regards their liability.* **5.** To take into account; consider. **6.** *Obsolete.* To take care of. *—intr.* **1.** To look or gaze. **2.** To give heed; pay attention. **—regard** *n.* **1.** A look or gaze. **2.** Careful thought or attention; heed: *She gives little regard to her appearance.* **3.a.** Respect, affection, or esteem: *He has high regard for your work.* **b. regards.** Good wishes expressing such sentiment: *Give the family my best regards.* **4.** A particular point or aspect; respect: *She was lucky in that regard.* **5.** Basis for action; motive. **6.** *Obsolete.* Appearance or aspect. **—*idioms.* as regards.** Concerning. **in** (or **with**) **regard to.** With respect to. [Middle English *regarden,* from Old French *regarder* : *re-,* re- + *guarder,* to guard (of Germanic origin; see GUARD).]

SYNONYMS: *regard, esteem, admiration, respect.* These nouns refer to a feeling based on perception of and a measure of approval for the worth of a person or thing. *Regard* is the least forceful and most general: *Please give your parents my warmest regards. "I once thought you had a kind of regard for her"* (George Borrow). *Esteem* connotes considered appraisal and positive regard: *"The near-unanimity of esteem he enjoyed during his lifetime has by no means been sustained since"* (Will Crutchfield). *Admiration* is a feeling of keen approbation: *"Greatness is a spiritual condition worthy to excite love, interest, and admiration"* (Matthew Arnold). *Respect* implies appreciative, often deferential regard resulting from careful assessment: *"I have a great respect for any man who makes his own way in life"* (Winston Churchill). See also Synonyms at **consider.**

USAGE NOTE: *Regard* is traditionally used in the singular in the phrase *in regard* (not *in regards*) *to. Regarding* and *as regards* are also standard in the sense "with reference to." In the same sense *with respect to* is acceptable, but *respecting* is not. • *Respects* is sometimes considered preferable to *regards* in the sense of "particulars": *In some respects* (not *regards*) *the books are alike.*

re·gar·dant (rĭ-gär′dnt) *adj. Heraldry.* Looking backward in profile: *a lion regardant.* [Middle English, from Old French, present participle of *regarder,* to regard. See REGARD.]

re·gard·ful (rĭ-gärd′fəl) *adj.* **1.** Showing attention; heedful. **2.** Showing deference; respectful. **—re·gard′ful·ly** *adv.* **—re·gard′ful·ness** *n.*

re·gard·ing (rĭ-gär′dĭng) *prep.* In reference to; with respect to; concerning. See Usage Note at **regard.**

re·gard·less (rĭ-gärd′lĭs) *adv.* In spite of everything; anyway: *continues to work regardless.* **—regardless** *adj.* Heedless; unmindful. **—re·gard′less·ly** *adv.* **—re·gard′less·ness** *n.*

regardless of *prep.* **1.** In spite of: *We will persevere regardless of past failures.* **2.** With no heed to: *freedom for all, regardless of race or creed.*

re·gat·ta (rĭ-gä′tə, -găt′ə) *n. Nautical.* A boat race or a series of boat races. [Italian dialectal, a contention, regatta, from *regattare,* to contend, perhaps from *recatare,* to sell again, compete, from Vulgar Latin **recaptāre,* to contend : Latin *re-,* re- + Latin *captāre,* to seek to catch, frequentative of *capere,* to seize; see CATCH.]

regd. *abbr.* Registered.

re·ge·late (rē′jə-lāt′, rē′jə-lāt′) *intr.v.* **-lat·ed, -lat·ing, -lates.** To undergo regelation. [RE– + Latin *gelāre, gelāt-,* to freeze; see GELATION.]

re·ge·la·tion (rē′jə-lā′shən) *n.* **1.** The fusion of two blocks of ice by pressure. **2.** Successive melting under pressure and freezing when pressure is relaxed at the interface of two blocks of ice.

re·gen·cy (rē′jən-sē) *n., pl.* **-cies. 1.** A person or group selected to govern in place of a monarch or other ruler who is absent, disabled, or still in minority. **2.** The period during which a regent governs. **3.** The office, area of jurisdiction, or government of regents or a regent. **—regency** *adj.* **1. Regency.** Of, relating to, or characteristic of the style, especially in furniture, prevalent in England during the regency (1811–1820) of George, Prince of Wales (later George IV). **2. Regency.** Of, relating to, or characteristic of the style prevalent in France during the regency (1715–1723) of Philippe, Duc d'Orléans (1674–1723). **3.** Of or relating to a regency: *regency policies and appointments that were later rescinded.*

re·gen·er·a·cy (rĭ-jĕn′ər-ə-sē) *n.* The state of being regenerated.

re·gen·er·ate (rĭ-jĕn′ə-rāt′) *v.* **-at·ed, -at·ing, -ates.** *—tr.* **1.** To reform spiritually or morally. **2.** To form, construct, or create anew, especially in an improved state. **3.** To give new life or energy to; revitalize. **4.** *Biology.* To replace (a lost or damaged organ or part) by formation of new tissue. *—intr.* **1.** To become formed or constructed again. **2.** To undergo spiritual conversion or rebirth; reform. **3.** To effect regeneration. **—regenerate** (-ər-ĭt) *n.* **1.** One who is spiritually reborn. **2.** *Biology.* A regenerated organ or part. **—regenerate** (-ər-ĭt) *adj.* **1.** Spiritually or morally reformed. **2.** Formed or created anew. **3.** Restored to a better state, refreshed or renewed. [Latin *regenerāre, regenerāt-,* to reproduce : *re-,* re- + *generāre,* to beget; see GENERATE.] **—re·gen′er·a·ble** (-ər-ə-bəl) *adj.* **—re·gen′er·ate·ly** *adv.* **—re·gen′er·a′tor** *n.*

re·gen·er·a·tion (rĭ-jĕn′ə-rā′shən) *n.* **1.** The act or process of regenerating or the state of being regenerated. **2.** Spiritual or moral revival or rebirth. **3.** *Biology.* Regrowth of lost or destroyed parts or organs.

ă pat	oi boy
ā pay	ou out
âr care	o͝o took
ä father	o͞o boot
ĕ pet	ŭ cut
ē be	ûr urge
ĭ pit	th thin
ī pie	*th* this
îr pier	hw which
ŏ pot	zh vision
ō toe	ə about, item
ô paw	♦ regionalism

Stress marks: **′** (primary); ′ (secondary), as in **dictionary** (dĭk′shə-nĕr′ē)

re·gen·er·a·tive (rĭ-jĕn′ə-rā′tĭv, -ər-ə-tĭv) *adj.* **1.** Of, relating to, or marked by regeneration. **2.** Tending to regenerate. **—re·gen′er·a′tive·ly** *adv.*

Re·gens·burg (rā′gənz-bûrg′, -gəns-bo͝ork′). A city of southeast Germany on the Danube River north-northeast of Munich. An ancient Celtic settlement, it was an important Roman frontier station and later a free imperial city before passing to Bavaria in 1810. Population, 126,681.

re·gent (rē′jənt) *n. Abbr.* **reg., regt. 1.** One who rules during the minority, absence, or disability of a monarch. **2.** One acting as a ruler or governor. **3.** A member of a board that governs an institution, such as a state university. [Middle English, from Old French, from Latin *regēns, regent-,* ruler, from present participle of *regere,* to rule. See **reg-** in Appendix.] **—re′gent·al** (-jən-tl) *adj.*

reg·gae (rĕg′ā) *n. Music.* Popular music of Jamaican origin having elements of calypso, soul, and rock 'n' roll and characterized by a strongly accentuated offbeat. [Jamaican English, ultimately from *rege-rege,* ragged clothing, probably from RAG[1].]

Reg·gio di Ca·la·bri·a (rĕj′ē-ō dē kä-lä′brē-ä, rĕd′jō) also **Reggio** or **Reggio Calabria.** A city of extreme southern Italy on the Strait of Messina opposite Sicily. Founded by Greek colonists in the late eighth century B.C., it suffered frequent invasions because of its strategic location. Earthquakes have also caused extensive damage. Population, 171,324.

Reggio nell'E·mi·lia (nĕl′ĕ-mēl′yä) also **Reggio** or **Reggio Emilia.** A city of north-central Italy west-northwest of Bologna. Founded by Romans in the second century B.C., it was ruled by the Este family for many centuries. Population, 129,893.

reg·i·cide (rĕj′ĭ-sīd′) *n.* **1.** The killing of a king. **2.** One who kills a king. [Latin *rēx, rēg-,* king; see **reg-** in Appendix + –CIDE.] **—reg′i·ci′dal** (-sīd′l) *adj.*

re·gime also **ré·gime** (rā-zhēm′, rĭ-) *n.* **1.a.** A form of government: *a fascist regime.* **b.** A government in power; administration: *suffered under the new regime.* **2.** A prevailing social system or pattern. **3.** The period during which a particular administration or system prevails. **4.** A regulated system, as of diet and exercise; a regimen. [French *régime,* from Old French, from Latin *regimen,* from *regere,* to rule. See **reg-** in Appendix.]

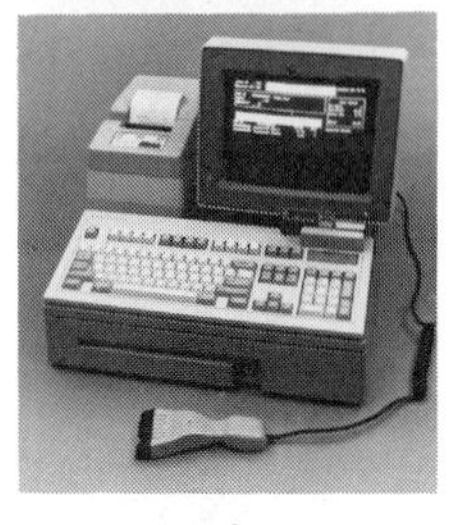

register
Top: Hand-cranked
Bottom: Electronic

reg·i·men (rĕj′ə-mən, -mĕn′) *n.* **1.** Governmental rule or control. **2.** The systematic procedure of a natural phenomenon or process. **3.a.** A regulated system, as of diet, therapy, or exercise, intended to promote health or achieve another beneficial effect. **b.** A course of intense physical training. [Middle English, from Latin. See REGIME.]

reg·i·ment (rĕj′ə-mənt) *n. Abbr.* **reg., regt. 1.** A military unit of ground troops consisting of at least two battalions, usually commanded by a colonel. **2.** A large group of people. **—regiment** (rĕj′ə-mĕnt′) *tr.v.* **-ment·ed, -ment·ing, -ments. 1.** To form into a regiment. **2.** To put into systematic order; systematize. **3.** To subject to uniformity and rigid order. [Middle English, government, rule, from Old French, from Late Latin *regimentum,* rule, from Latin *regere,* to rule. See **reg-** in Appendix.] **—reg′i·men′tal** (-mĕn′tl) *adj.* **—reg′i·men′tal·ly** *adv.* **—reg′i·men·ta′tion** *n.*

reg·i·men·tals (rĕj′ə-mĕnt′lz) *pl.n.* **1.** The uniform and insignia of a particular regiment. **2.** Military dress.

Re·gi·na (rĭ-jī′nə). The capital and largest city of Saskatchewan, Canada, in the southern part of the province southeast of Saskatoon. It was the capital of the Northwest Territories until the province of Saskatchewan was created in 1905. Population, 162,613.

Re·gi·o·mon·ta·nus (rē′jē-ō-mŏn-tā′nəs, -tä′-, -tăn-əs, rĕj′ē-). See Johann **Müller.**

re·gion (rē′jən) *n. Abbr.* **reg. 1.** A large, usually continuous segment of a surface or space; area. **2.** A large, indefinite portion of the earth's surface. **3.** A specified district or territory. **4.** An area of interest or activity; a sphere. **5.** *Ecology.* A part of the earth characterized by distinctive animal or plant life. **6.** An area of the body having natural or arbitrarily assigned boundaries: *the abdominal region.* See Synonyms at **area.** [Middle English, from Old French, from Latin *regiō, regiōn-,* from *regere,* to rule. See **reg-** in Appendix.]

re·gion·al (rē′jə-nəl) *adj.* **1.** Of or relating to a large geographic region. **2.** Of or relating to a particular region or district. **3.** Of or characteristic of a form of a language that is distributed in identifiable geographic areas and differs in pronunciation, grammar, or vocabulary from the standard form; dialectal. **—regional** *n.* Something, such as a magazine or a company branch, that serves a region: *"earlier attempts to launch glossy regionals for women"* (Business Week). **—re′gion·al·ly** *adv.*

re·gion·al·ism (rē′jə-nə-lĭz′əm) *n.* **1.a.** Political division of an area into partially autonomous regions. **b.** Advocacy of such a political system. **2.** Loyalty to the interests of a particular region. **3.** A feature, such as an expression, a pronunciation, or a custom, that is characteristic of a geographic area. **4.** The use of regional characteristics, as of locale, custom, or speech, in literature or art. **5.** A policy whereby the interests of a nation in world affairs are defined in terms of particular countries or regions. **—re′gion·al·ist** *adj. & n.* **—re′gion·al·is′tic** *adj.*

re·gion·a·lize (rē′jə-nə-līz′) *tr.v.* **-ized, -iz·ing, -iz·es.** To divide into regions, especially for administrative purposes. **—re′gion·al·i·za′tion** (rē′jə-nə-lĭ-zā′shən) *n.*

ré·gis·seur (rā′zhē-sûr′, -sœr′) *n., pl.* **-seurs** (-sûr′, -sœr′). A stage director, especially of a ballet. [French, from *régir, régiss-,* to direct, from Old French *regir,* from Latin *regere.* See REGENT.]

reg·is·ter (rĕj′ĭ-stər) *n. Abbr.* **reg. 1.a.** A formal or official recording of items, names, or actions. **b.** A book for such entries. **c.** An entry in such a record. **2.** The act of registering. **3.** A device that automatically records a quantity or number. **4.** *Computer Science.* A part of the central processing unit where groups of binary digits are stored as the computer is processing them. **5.** An adjustable, grill-like device through which heated or cooled air is released into a room. **6.** A state of proper alignment: *to be in register.* **7.** *Printing.* **a.** Exact alignment of the lines and margins on the opposite sides of a leaf. **b.** Proper positioning of colors in color printing. **8.** *Music.* **a.** The range of an instrument or a voice. **b.** A part of such a range. **c.** A group of matched organ pipes; a stop. **9.** A variety of language used in a specific social setting: *speaking in an informal register; writing in a scientific register.* **—register** *v.* **-tered, -ter·ing, -ters.** —*tr.* **1.a.** To enter in an official register. **b.** To enroll officially or formally, especially in order to vote or attend classes. **2.** To set down in writing; record: *"It is for the historian to discover and register what actually happened"* (Robert Conquest). **3.** To indicate on or as if on an instrument or a scale. **4.** To give outward signs of; express: *Her face registered surprise.* **5.** To attain or achieve: *registered a new high in sales.* **6.** To cause (mail) to be officially recorded and specially handled by payment of a fee. **7.** To adjust so as to be properly aligned. —*intr.* **1.** To place or cause placement of one's name in a register. **2.** To have one's name officially placed on a list of eligible voters. **3.** To enroll as a student. **4.** To be indicated on or as if on an instrument or a scale. **5.** To be shown or expressed, as on the face. **6.** To make an impression; be recorded in the mind: *The warning failed to register.* **7.** To be in proper alignment. [Middle English *registre,* from Old French, from Medieval Latin *registrum,* alteration of Late Latin *regesta,* from Latin, neuter pl. past participle of *regerere,* to record : *re-,* re- + *gerere,* to carry.] **—reg′is·ter·er** *n.* **—reg′is·tra·ble** (-ĭ-strə-bəl) *adj.*

reg·is·tered (rĕj′ĭ-stərd) *adj. Abbr.* **reg., regd. 1.** Having the owner's name listed in a register: *registered bonds.* **2.** Having the pedigree recorded and verified by an authorized association of breeders: *a registered golden retriever.* **3.** Officially qualified or certified: *a registered pharmacist.*

registered mail *n.* Mail that is recorded by the post office when sent and at each point on its route so as to assure safe delivery.

registered nurse *n. Abbr.* **RN, R.N.** A graduate trained nurse who has passed a state registration examination and has been licensed to practice nursing.

reg·is·trant (rĕj′ĭ-strənt) *n.* One who registers or is registered.

reg·is·trar (rĕj′ĭ-strär′, rĕj′ĭ-strär′) *n. Abbr.* **reg. 1.** One who is in charge of official records. **2.** An officer in a college or university who keeps the records of enrollment and academic standing. **3.** An officer of a corporation responsible for maintaining records of ownership of its securities. **4.** An admitting officer in a hospital. [Probably from *registrary,* from Medieval Latin *registrārius,* from *registrum,* register. See REGISTER.]

reg·is·tra·tion (rĕj′ĭ-strā′shən) *n.* **1.** The act of registering: *voter registration.* **2.** The number of persons registered; enrollment. **3.** An entry in a register. **4.** A document certifying an act of registering. **5.** *Music.* **a.** A combination of organ stops selected to be used in playing a piece. **b.** The technique of selecting and adjusting organ stops.

reg·is·try (rĕj′ĭ-strē) *n., pl.* **-tries.** *Abbr.* **reg. 1.** The act of registering; registration. **2.** The registered nationality of a ship. **3.** A place for registering. **4.a.** A book for official records. **b.** The place where such records are kept.

re·gius professor (rē′jəs, -jē-əs) *n.* One holding a professorship established by royal subsidy at any of certain older British universities. [From Latin *rēgius,* royal, from *rēx, rēg-,* king. See **reg-** in Appendix.]

reg·let (rĕg′lĭt) *n.* **1.** *Architecture.* A narrow, flat molding. **2.** *Printing.* A flat piece of wood used to separate lines of type. [French *réglet,* from Old French, diminutive of *regle,* ruler, from Latin *rēgula,* rod. See **reg-** in Appendix.]

reg·nal (rĕg′nəl) *adj.* Being a specified year of a monarch's reign calculated from the date of accession: *in her 12th regnal year.* [Medieval Latin *rēgnālis,* royal, from Latin *rēgnum,* reign. See REIGN.]

reg·nant (rĕg′nənt) *adj.* **1.** Reigning; ruling: *a queen regnant.* **2.** Predominant. **3.** Widespread; prevalent. [Probably from Middle English, a sovereign, from Old French, from Latin *rēgnāns, rēgnant-,* present participle of *rēgnāre,* to reign, from *rēgnum,* reign. See REIGN.]

reg·o·lith (rĕg′ə-lĭth′) *n.* The layer of loose rock resting on bedrock, constituting the surface of most land. Also called *mantle rock.* [Greek *rhēgos,* blanket + –LITH.]

re·gorge (rē-gôrj′) *tr.v.* **-gorged, -gorg·ing, -gorg·es.** To disgorge. [French *regorger,* from Old French : *re-,* re- + *gorger,* to gorge (from *gorge,* throat; see GORGE).]

re·gress (rĭ-grĕs′) *v.* **-gressed, -gress·ing, -gress·es.** —*intr.* **1.** To go back; move backward. **2.** To return to a previous, usually worse or less developed state. **3.** To have a tendency to approach or go back to a statistical mean. —*tr. Psy-*

chology. To induce a state of regression in. **—regress** (rē′grĕs′) *n.* **1.a.** The act of going or coming back; return. **b.** Passage back; reentry. **2.** The act of reasoning backward from an effect to a cause. [Latin *regredī, regress-* : *re-*, re- + *gradī*, to go; see **ghredh-** in Appendix.] **—re·gres′sor** *n.*

re·gres·sion (rĭ-grĕsh′ən) *n.* **1.** Reversion; retrogression. **2.** Relapse to a less perfect or developed state. **3.** *Psychology.* Reversion to an earlier or less mature pattern of feeling or behavior. **4.** *Biology.* The return of a population to an earlier or less complex physical type in successive generations. **5.** *Statistics.* The relationship between the mean value of a random variable and the corresponding values of one or more independent variables. **6.** *Astronomy.* Retrograde motion of a celestial body.

re·gres·sive (rĭ-grĕs′ĭv) *adj.* **1.** Tending to return or revert. **2.** Characterized by regression or a tendency to regress. **3.** Decreasing proportionately as the amount taxed increases. *a regressive tax.* **—re·gres′sive·ly** *adv.* **—re·gres′sive·ness** *n.*

re·gret (rĭ-grĕt′) *v.* **-gret·ted, -gret·ting, -grets.** *—tr.* **1.** To feel sorry, disappointed, or distressed about. **2.** To remember with a feeling of loss or sorrow; mourn. *—intr.* To feel regret. **—regret** *n.* **1.** A sense of loss and longing for someone or something gone. **2.** A feeling of disappointment or distress about something that one wishes could be different. **3. regrets.** A courteous expression of regret, especially at having to decline an invitation. [Middle English *regretten*, to lament, from Old French *regreter* : *re-*, re- + *-greter*, to weep (perhaps of Germanic origin).] **—re·gret′ter** *n.*

SYNONYMS: *regret, sorrow, grief, anguish, woe, heartache, heartbreak.* All of these nouns denote mental distress. *Regret* has the broadest range, from mere disappointment to a painful sense of loss, dissatisfaction, self-reproach, or longing, as over something lost, gone, done, or left undone: *He had hoped that our policy of not dealing with terrorists would be an example to other countries but soon realized, to his regret, that we didn't practice what we preached. She looked back with regret on the pain she had caused her family. Sorrow* connotes sadness caused by misfortune, affliction, or loss; it can also imply contrition: *"sorrow for his women, for his kinfolk, for his children, who needed his protection, and whom he could not protect"* (James Baldwin). *Grief* is deep, acute personal sorrow, as that arising from irreplaceable loss: *"Grief fills the room up of my absent child,/Lies in his bed, walks up and down with me"* (Shakespeare). *Anguish* implies agonizing, excruciating mental pain: *"I pray that our heavenly Father may assuage the anguish of your bereavement"* (Abraham Lincoln). *Woe* is intense, often prolonged wretchedness or misery: *"the deep, unutterable woe/Which none save exiles feel"* (W.E. Aytoun). *Heartache* most often applies to sustained private sorrow: *The child's devastating problems are a source of untold heartache to the parents. Heartbreak* is overwhelming grief: *"Better a little chiding than a great deal of heartbreak"* (Shakespeare).

re·gret·ful (rĭ-grĕt′fəl) *adj.* Full of regret; sorrowful or sorry. **—re·gret′ful·ly** *adv.* **—re·gret′ful·ness** *n.*

re·gret·ta·ble (rĭ-grĕt′ə-bəl) *adj.* Eliciting or deserving regret: *a regrettable lack of funds; regrettable remarks.*

re·gret·ta·bly (rĭ-grĕt′ə-blē) *adv.* **1.** To an extent deserving of regret: *a regrettably brief career.* **2.** As a matter of regret: *Regrettably, the book is not available.*

re·group (rē-gro͞op′) *v.* **-grouped, -group·ing, -groups.** *—tr.* To arrange in a new grouping. *—intr.* **1.** To come back together in a tactical formation, as after a dispersal in a retreat. **2.** To reorganize for renewed effort, as after a temporary setback.

regt. *abbr.* **1.** Regent. **2.** Regiment.

reg·u·lar (rĕg′yə-lər) *adj. Abbr.* **reg. 1.** Customary, usual, or normal: *the train's regular schedule.* **2.** Orderly, even, or symmetrical: *regular teeth.* **3.** In conformity with a fixed procedure, principle, or discipline. **4.** Well-ordered; methodical: *regular habits.* **5.** Occurring at fixed intervals; periodic: *regular payments.* See Synonyms at **normal. 6.a.** Occurring with normal or healthy frequency. **b.** Having bowel movements or menstrual periods with normal or healthy frequency. **7.** Not varying; constant. **8.** Formally correct; proper. **9.** Having the required qualifications for an occupation: *not a regular lawyer.* **10.** *Informal.* Complete; thorough: *a regular scoundrel.* **11.** *Informal.* Good; nice: *a regular guy.* **12.** *Botany.* Having symmetrically arranged parts of similar size and shape: *regular flowers.* **13.** *Grammar.* Conforming to the usual pattern of inflection, derivation, or word formation. **14.** *Ecclesiastical.* Belonging to a religious order and bound by its rules: *the regular clergy.* **15.** *Mathematics.* **a.** Having equal sides and equal angles. Used of polygons. **b.** Having faces that are congruent regular polygons and congruent polyhedral angles. Used of polyhedrons. **16.** Belonging to or constituting the permanent army of a nation. **—regular** *n.* **1.** *Ecclesiastical.* A member of the clergy or of a religious order. **2.** A soldier belonging to a regular army. **3.** A dependable, loyal person: *one of the party regulars.* **4.** A clothing size designed for persons of average height. **5.** A habitual customer. [Middle English *reguler*, living under religious rule, from Old French, from Late Latin *rēgulāris*, according to rule, from Latin *rēgula*, rod, rule. See **reg-** in Appendix.] **—reg′u·lar′i·ty** (-lăr′ĭ-tē) *n.* **—reg′u·lar·ly** *adv.*

regular army *n. Abbr.* **R.A., RA** The permanent standing army of a nation or state.

reg·u·lar·ize (rĕg′yə-lə-rīz′) *tr.v.* **-ized, -iz·ing, -iz·es.** To make regular; cause to conform. **—reg′u·lar·i·za′tion** (-lər-ĭ-zā′shən) *n.* **—reg′u·lar·iz′er** *n.*

regular year *n.* An ordinary year of 354 days or a leap year of 384 days in the Jewish calendar.

reg·u·late (rĕg′yə-lāt′) *tr.v.* **-lat·ed, -lat·ing, -lates. 1.** To control or direct according to rule, principle, or law. **2.** To adjust to a particular specification or requirement: *regulate temperature.* **3.** To adjust (a mechanism) for accurate and proper functioning. **4.** To put or maintain in order: *regulate one's eating habits.* [Middle English, from Late Latin *rēgulāre, rēgulāt-*, from Latin *rēgula*, rod, rule. See **reg-** in Appendix.] **—reg′u·la′tive, reg′u·la·to′ry** (-lə-tôr′ē, -tōr′ē) *adj.*

reg·u·la·tion (rĕg′yə-lā′shən) *n. Abbr.* **reg. 1.** The act of regulating or the state of being regulated. **2.** A principle, rule, or law designed to control or govern conduct. **3.** A governmental order having the force of law. Also called *executive order.* **4.** *Embryology.* The capacity of an embryo to continue normal development following injury to or alteration of a structure.

reg·u·la·tor (rĕg′yə-lā′tər) *n. Abbr.* **reg. 1.** One that regulates, as: **a.** The mechanism in a watch by which its speed is governed. **b.** A highly accurate clock used as a standard for timing other clocks. **c.** A device used to maintain uniform speed in a machine; a governor. **d.** A device used to control the flow of gases, liquids, or electric current. **2.** One, such as the member of a governmental regulatory agency, that ensures compliance with laws, regulations, and established rules: *banking regulators; price regulators.*

regulator gene *n.* A gene that represses the activity of another gene in an operon. Also called *regulatory gene.*

re·gu·lus (rĕg′yə-ləs) *n., pl.* **-li** (-lī) or **-lus·es. 1.** The metallic mass that sinks to the bottom of a furnace or crucible during smelting. **2.** A relatively impure intermediate product of various ores in smelting. [Latin *rēgulus*, diminutive of *rēx, rēg-*, king. See **reg-** in Appendix.] **—reg′u·line** (rĕg′yə-lĭn, -līn′) *adj.*

Reg·u·lus (rĕg′yə-ləs) *n.* A bright double star in the constellation Leo. [Latin *rēgulus*, diminutive of *rēx, rēg-*, king. See REGULUS.]

Regulus, Marcus Atilius. Died c. 250 B.C. Roman general and politician who was captured by the Carthaginians (255). Giving his word to return to Carthage, he was sent to Rome to negotiate a peace treaty but instead convinced the Romans to reject the Carthaginian terms. He subsequently returned to Carthage, where he died in prison.

re·gur·gi·tate (rē-gûr′jĭ-tāt′) *v.* **-tat·ed, -tat·ing, -tates.** *—intr.* To rush or surge back. *—tr.* To cause to pour back, especially to cast up (partially digested food). [Medieval Latin *regurgitāre, regurgitāt-*, to overflow : Latin *re-*, re- + Late Latin *gurgitāre*, to engulf, flood (from Latin *gurges, gurgit-*, whirlpool).] **—re·gur′gi·tant** (-tənt) *adj.* **—re·gur′gi·ta′tion** *n.* **—re·gur′gi·ta·tive** *adj.*

re·hab (rē′hăb′) *Informal. n.* **1.** Rehabilitation. **2.** Something, especially a building, that has undergone rehabilitation. *—attributive.* Often used to modify another noun: *rehab programs; rehab sites.* **—rehab** *tr.v.* **-habbed, -hab·bing, -habs.** To rehabilitate: *"purchased and rehabbed eight units of housing"* (Hatfield MA Valley Advocate).

re·ha·bil·i·tant (rē′hə-bĭl′ĭ-tənt) *n.* One who is undergoing rehabilitation, as for a disability.

re·ha·bil·i·tate (rē′hə-bĭl′ĭ-tāt′) *tr.v.* **-tat·ed, -tat·ing, -tates. 1.** To restore to good health or useful life, as through therapy and education. **2.** To restore to good condition, operation, or capacity. **3.** To reinstate the good name of. **4.** To restore the former rank, privileges, or rights of. [Medieval Latin *rehabilitāre, rehabilitāt-*, to restore to a former rank : Latin *re-*, re- + Late Latin *habilitāre*, to enable; see HABILITATE.] **—re′ha·bil′i·tat′a·ble** *adj.* **—re′ha·bil′i·ta′tion** *n.* **—re′ha·bil′i·ta′tive** *adj.*

re·hash (rē-hăsh′) *tr.v.* **-hashed, -hash·ing, -hash·es. 1.** To bring forth again in another form without significant alteration: *rehashing old ideas.* **2.** To discuss again. **—rehash** (rē′-hăsh′) *n.* The act or result of rehashing: *a rehash of an old plot.*

re·hear (rē-hîr′) *tr.v.* **-heard** (-hûrd′), **-hear·ing, -hears. 1.** To hear again. **2.** *Law.* To give a new hearing to (a case) by the same court.

re·hear·ing (rē-hîr′ĭng) *n. Law.* A new hearing of a case by the same court or other administrative tribunal in which it was originally heard.

re·hears·al (rĭ-hûr′səl) *n.* **1.** The act of practicing in preparation for a public performance. **2.** A session of practice for a performance, as of a play. **3.** A detailed enumeration or repetition: *a long rehearsal of his woes.*

re·hearse (rĭ-hûrs′) *v.* **-hearsed, -hears·ing, -hears·es.** *—tr.* **1.a.** To practice (a part in a play, for example) in preparation for a public performance. **b.** To direct in rehearsal: *rehearsed the orchestra.* **2.** To perfect or cause to perfect (an action) by repetition. See Synonyms at **practice. 3.a.** To retell or recite. **b.** To list or enumerate: *rehearsed her complaints in a letter.* See Synonyms at **describe.** *—intr.* To practice something, such as a speech, before presenting it publicly. [Middle English *rehercen*, to repeat, from Old French *rehercier* : *re-*, re- + *hercier*, to harrow (from *herce*, harrow; see HEARSE).] **—re·hears′er** *n.*

Rehn·quist (rĕn′kwĭst′), **William Hubbs.** Born 1924. American jurist who served as an associate justice of the U.S. Supreme Court (1972–1986) and was appointed chief justice in 1986.

ă pat	oi boy
ā pay	ou out
âr care	o͝o took
ä father	o͞o boot
ĕ pet	ŭ cut
ē be	ûr urge
ĭ pit	th thin
ī pie	*th* this
îr pier	hw which
ŏ pot	zh vision
ō toe	ə about, item
ô paw	♦ regionalism

Stress marks: ′ (primary); ′ (secondary), as in **dictionary** (dĭk′shə-nĕr′ē)

re·house (rē-houz′) *tr.v.* **-housed, -hous·ing, -hous·es.** To provide with new, usually improved housing.

re·hy·drate (rē-hī′drāt′) *tr.v.* **-drat·ed, -drat·ing, -drates. 1.** To cause (something dehydrated) to take up fluid. **2.** To replenish the body fluids of. **—re′hy·dra′tion** *n.*

Reich (rīk, rīKH), **Wilhelm.** 1897–1957. Austrian psychoanalyst who theorized that sexual repression is the source of many psychological and social problems.

reichs·mark (rīks′märk′, rīKHs′-) *n., pl.* **reichsmark** or **-marks.** *Abbr.* **RM, Rm.** A monetary unit of Germany from 1925 to 1948. [German : *Reichs,* genitive of *Reich,* realm (from Middle High German *rīch,* from Old High German *rīchi;* see **reg-** in Appendix) + *Mark,* unit of currency (from Middle High German *marke;* see MARK[2]).]

Reich·stein (rīk′stīn′, rīKH′shtīn′), **Tadeus.** Born 1897. Polish-born Swiss chemist. He shared a 1950 Nobel Prize for discoveries concerning the hormones of the adrenal cortex.

Reid (rēd), **Thomas.** 1710–1796. Scottish philosopher who founded a philosophy of common sense largely as a reaction to the ideas of David Hume.

Reid, Whitelaw. 1837–1912. American editor and diplomat who was publisher of the *New York Tribune* (1872–1912), U.S. minister to France (1889–1892), and ambassador to Great Britain (1905–1912).

re·i·fy (rē′ə-fī′, rā′-) *tr.v.* **-fied, -fy·ing, -fies.** To regard or treat (an abstraction) as if it had concrete or material existence. [Latin *rēs, rē-,* thing; see **rē-** in Appendix + -FY.] **—re′i·fi·ca′tion** (-fĭ-kā′shən) *n.* **—re′i·fi′er** *n.*

Rei·gate (rī′gĭt). A municipal borough of southern England, a residential suburb of London. Population, 116,700.

reign (rān) *n.* **1.** Exercise of sovereign power, as by a monarch. **2.** The period during which a monarch rules. **3.** Dominance or widespread influence: *the reign of reason.* **—reign** *intr.v.* **reigned, reign·ing, reigns. 1.** To exercise sovereign power. **2.** To hold the title of monarch, but with limited authority. **3.** To be predominant or prevalent: *Panic reigned as the fire spread.* [Middle English *reigne,* from Old French, from Latin *rēgnum,* from *rēx, rēg-,* king. See **reg-** in Appendix.]

Reign of Terror (rān) *n.* **1.** The period (1793–1794) of the French Revolution during which thousands of people were executed. **2. reign of terror.,** *pl.* **reigns of terror.** A period of brutal suppression or intimidation by those in power.

re·im·burse (rē′ĭm-bûrs′) *tr.v.* **-bursed, -burs·ing, -burs·es. 1.** To repay (money spent); refund. **2.** To pay back or compensate (another party) for money spent or losses incurred. [RE- + *imburse,* to put in a purse, pay (from French *embourser,* from Old French : *en-,* in, from Latin *in-;* see IN-[2] + *borser,* to get money, from *borse,* purse, from Late Latin *bursa,* bag; see BURSA).] **—re′im·burs′a·ble** *adj.* **—re′im·burse′ment** *n.*

re·im·port (rē′ĭm-pôrt′, -pōrt′, rē-ĭm′pôrt′, -pōrt′) *tr.v.* **-port·ed, -port·ing, -ports.** To bring back into a country (goods made from its exported raw materials). **—re·im′port** (rē-ĭm′-pôrt, -pōrt) *n.* **—re′im·por·ta′tion** *n.*

re·im·pres·sion (rē′ĭm-prĕsh′ən) *n.* *Printing.* A second impression, as of a book, that is identical to the original; a reprint.

Reims (rēmz, răNs). See **Rheims.**

rein (rān) *n.* **1.** Often **reins.** A long, narrow leather strap attached to each end of the bit of a bridle and used by a rider or driver to control a horse or other animal. **2.** A means of restraint, check, or guidance. **3.** Often **reins.** A means or an instrument by which power is exercised: *the reins of government.* **—rein** *v.* **reined, rein·ing, reins.** *—tr.* **1.** To check or hold back by or as if by the use of reins. Often with *in, back,* or *up.* **2.** To restrain or control. *—intr.* To control a horse, for example, with reins. ***—idioms.*** **draw in the reins.** To slow down or stop by or as if by pressure on the reins. **give (free** or **full) rein to.** To release from restraints; allow to go unchecked: *gave rein to her emotions.* **tight rein.** Close control: *kept expenses on a tight rein.* [Middle English, from Old French *resne, reine,* from Vulgar Latin **retina,* from Latin *retinēre,* to retain. See RETAIN.]

re·in·car·nate (rē′ĭn-kär′nāt) *tr.v.* **-nat·ed, -nat·ing, -nates.** To cause to be reborn in another body; incarnate again.

re·in·car·na·tion (rē′ĭn-kär-nā′shən) *n.* **1.a.** Rebirth of the soul in another body. **b.** Belief in this rebirth. **2.** A rebirth in another form; a new embodiment.

reindeer
Rangifer tarandus

rein·deer (rān′dîr′) *n., pl.* **reindeer** or **-deers.** A large deer *(Rangifer tarandus)* of the Arctic and northern regions of Eurasia and North America, having branched antlers in both sexes. [Middle English *reindere* : Old Norse *hreinn,* reindeer; see **ker-**[1] in Appendix + Middle English *der,* animal; see DEER.]

WORD HISTORY: Although Saint Nick uses reins on his reindeer and reindeer are used to pull sleds in Lapland and northern Siberia, the word *reindeer* has nothing to do with reins. The element *-deer* is indeed our word *deer,* but the *rein-* part is borrowed from another language, specifically from the Scandinavian languages spoken by the chiefly Danish and Norwegian invaders and settlers of England from the 9th to the 11th century. Even though the Old Icelandic language in which much of Old Norse literature is written is not the same variety of Old Norse spoken by these settlers of England, it is close enough to give us an idea of the words that were borrowed into English. Thus we can cite the Old Icelandic word *hreinn,* which means "reindeer," as the source of the first part of the English word. The word *reindeer* is first recorded in Middle English in a work composed before 1400.

Rein·deer Lake (rān′dîr′). A lake of northeast Saskatchewan and northwest Manitoba, Canada. It is drained by the **Reindeer River,** which flows about 230 km (143 mi) southward to the Churchill River.

reindeer moss *n.* An erect, grayish, branching lichen *(Cladonia rangiferina)* of Arctic regions, constituting the chief source of food for reindeer and several other herbivores.

re·in·fec·tion (rē′ĭn-fĕk′shən) *n.* A second infection that follows recovery from a previous infection by the same causative agent.

re·in·force also **re·en·force** or **re·ën·force** (rē′ĭn-fôrs′, -fōrs′) *tr.v.* **-forced, -forc·ing, -forc·es. 1.** To give more force or effectiveness to; strengthen: *The news reinforced her hopes.* **2.** To strengthen (a military force) with additional personnel or equipment. **3.** To strengthen by adding extra support or material. **4.** To increase the number or amount of; augment. **5.** *Psychology.* **a.** To reward (an experimental subject, for example) with a reinforcer subsequent to a desired response or performance. **b.** To stimulate (a response) by means of a reinforcer. [RE- + *inforce* (variant of ENFORCE).] **—re′in·force′a·ble** *adj.*

re·in·forced concrete (rē′ĭn-fôrst′, -fōrst′) *n.* Poured concrete containing steel bars or metal netting to increase its tensile strength. Also called *ferroconcrete.*

re·in·force·ment (rē′ĭn-fôrs′mənt, -fōrs′-) *n.* **1.** The act or process of reinforcing or the state of being reinforced. **2.** Something that reinforces. **3.** Often **reinforcements.** Additional personnel or equipment sent to support a military action. **4.** *Psychology.* **a.** The occurrence or experimental introduction of an unconditioned stimulus along with a conditioned stimulus. **b.** The strengthening of a conditioned response by such means. **c.** An event, a circumstance, or a condition that increases the likelihood that a given response will recur in a situation like that in which the reinforcing condition originally occurred.

re·in·forc·er (rē′ĭn-fôr′sər, -fōr′-) *n.* *Psychology.* A stimulus, such as a reward, that in operant conditioning maintains or strengthens a desired response.

Rein·hardt (rīn′härt′), **Max.** 1873–1943. Austrian theatrical director and manager whose experimental, large-scale productions included *Oedipus Rex* and *The Miracle.*

reins (rānz) *pl.n.* **1.** The kidneys, loins, or lower back. **2.** The seat of the affections and passions. [Middle English, from Old French, from Latin *rēnēs.*]

re·in·state (rē′ĭn-stāt′) *tr.v.* **-stat·ed, -stat·ing, -states. 1.** To bring back into use or existence. **2.** To restore to a previous condition or position. **—re′in·state′ment** *n.*

re·in·sure (rē′ĭn-shŏor′) *tr.v.* **-sured, -sur·ing, -sures.** To insure again, especially by transferring in whole or in part a risk or contingent liability already covered under an existing contract. **—re′in·sur′ance** *n.* **—re′in·sur′er** *n.*

re·in·te·grate (rē-ĭn′tĭ-grāt′) *tr.v.* **-grat·ed, -grat·ing, -grates.** To restore to a condition of integration or unity. **—re′in·te·gra′tion** *n.* **—re·in′te·gra′tive** *adj.*

re·in·ter·pret (rē′ĭn-tûr′prĭt) *tr.v.* **-pret·ed, -pret·ing, -prets.** To interpret again or anew. **—re′in·ter′pre·ta′tion** (-tûr′prĭ-tā′shən) *n.*

re·in·vent (rē′ĭn-vĕnt′) *tr.v.* **-vent·ed, -vent·ing, -vents. 1.** To make over completely: *She kept trying to reinvent herself as an actress.* **2.** To bring back into existence or use: *reinvented the concept of neighborliness.* ***—idiom.*** **reinvent the wheel. 1.** To do something again, from the beginning, especially in a needless or inefficient effort: *"School districts need not reinvent the wheel every time they try to improve their schools"* (Washington Post). **2.** To recast something familiar or old into a different form: *"Call it reinventing the wheel or recasting old ideas, but these contemporary versions have a spirit and style all their own"* (New York Times).

re·in·vest (rē′ĭn-vĕst′) *tr.v.* **-vest·ed, -vest·ing, -vests.** To invest (capital or earnings) again, especially to invest (income from securities or funds) in additional shares. **—re′in·vest′ment** *n.*

re·in·vig·o·rate (rē′ĭn-vĭg′ə-rāt′) *tr.v.* **-rat·ed, -rat·ing, -rates.** To give new life or energy to. **—re′in·vig′o·ra′tion** *n.* **—re′in·vig′o·ra′tor** *n.*

reis (rās) *n.* A plural of **real**[3]**.**

re·is·sue (rē-ĭsh′o͞o) *v.* **-sued, -su·ing, -sues.** *—tr.* To issue again, especially to make available again. *—intr.* To come forth again. **—reissue** *n.* **1.** A second or subsequent issue, as of a book. **2.** A reprinting of postage stamps from unchanged plates.

Rei·sters·town (rī′stərz-toun′). A community of north-central Maryland, a suburb of Baltimore. Population, 19,385.

REIT *abbr.* Real estate investment trust.

re·it·er·ate (rē-ĭt′ə-rāt′) *tr.v.* **-at·ed, -at·ing, -ates.** To say or do again or repeatedly. See Synonyms at **repeat. —re·it′er·a′tion** *n.* **—re·it′er·a′tive** (-ə-rā′tĭv, -ər-ə-tĭv) *adj.* **—re·it′er·a′tive·ly** *adv.* **—re·it′er·a′tor** *n.*

re·ject (rĭ-jĕkt′) *tr.v.* **-ject·ed, -ject·ing, -jects. 1.** To refuse to accept, submit to, believe, or make use of. **2.** To refuse to consider or grant; deny. **3.** To refuse to recognize or give affection to (a person). See Synonyms at **refuse**[1]**. 4.** To discard as defective or useless; throw away. **5.** To spit out or vomit. **6.**

Medicine. To resist immunologically the introduction of (a transplanted organ or tissue); fail to accept as part of one's own body. **—reject** (rē′jĕkt) *n.* One that has been rejected: *a reject from the varsity team; a tire that is a reject.* [Middle English *rejecten,* from Latin *rēicere, rēiect-* : *re-,* re- + *iacere,* to throw; see **yē-** in Appendix.] **—re·ject′er, re·jec′tor** *n.* **—re·jec′tive** *adj.*

re·jec·tion (rĭ-jĕk′shən) *n.* **1.** The act of rejecting or the state of being rejected. **2.** Something rejected. **3.** *Medicine.* The failure of a recipient's body to accept a transplanted tissue or organ as the result of immunological incompatability; immunological resistance to foreign tissue.

rejection slip *n.* A printed note accompanying a manuscript rejected for publication and returned to the author.

rejective art *n.* See **minimalism** (sense 1). **—re·jec′tiv·ist** *adj.*

re·jig (rē-jĭg′) *tr.v.* **-jigged, -jig·ging, -jigs.** *Informal.* To rejigger: *"a series of measures to . . . rejig the monetary system"* (Christian Science Monitor).

re·jig·ger (rē-jĭg′ər) *tr.v.* **-gered, -ger·ing, -gers.** *Informal.* To readjust or rearrange.

re·joice (rĭ-jois′) *v.* **-joiced, -joic·ing, -joic·es.** *—intr.* To feel joyful; be delighted: *rejoiced at the news; rejoiced in her friend's good fortune.* *—tr.* To fill with joy; gladden. ***—phrasal verb.* rejoice in.** To have or possess: *rejoices in a keen mind.* [Middle English *rejoicen,* from Old French *rejoir, rejoiss-* : *re-,* re- + *joir,* to be joyful (from Vulgar Latin **gaudīre,* from Latin *gaudēre;* see **gāu-** in Appendix).] **—re·joic′er** *n.*

re·join¹ (rĭ-join′) *v.* **-joined, -join·ing, -joins.** *—tr.* To say in reply, especially in sharp response to a reply. *—intr.* To reply. [Middle English *rejoinen,* from Old French *rejoindre, rejoin-* : *re-,* re- + *joindre,* to join; see JOIN.]

re·join² (rē-join′) *v.* **-joined, -join·ing, -joins.** *—tr.* **1.** To come again into the company of: *rejoined his regiment.* **2.** To join together again; reunite. *—intr.* To become joined again.

re·join·der (rĭ-join′dər) *n.* An answer, especially to a reply. [Middle English, from Old French *rejoindre,* to answer, rejoin. See REJOIN¹.]

re·ju·ve·nate (rĭ-jo͞o′və-nāt′) *tr.v.* **-nat·ed, -nat·ing, -nates.** **1.** To restore to youthful vigor or appearance; make young again. **2.** To restore to an original or new condition: *rejuvenate an old sofa.* **3.a.** To stimulate (a stream) to renewed erosive activity, as by uplift of the land. **b.** To develop youthful topographic features in (a previously leveled area). [From RE– + Latin *iuvenis,* young; see **yeu-** in Appendix.] **—re·ju′ve·na′tion** *n.* **—re·ju′ve·na′tor** (-tər) *n.*

re·ju·ve·nes·cence (rĭ-jo͞o′və-nĕs′əns) *n.* A renewal of youthful appearance or character. **—re·ju′ve·nes′cent** *adj.*

re·kin·dle (rē-kĭn′dl) *tr.v.* **-dled, -dling, -dles.** **1.** To relight (a fire). **2.** To revive or renew: *rekindled an old interest in the sciences.*

rel. *abbr.* **1.** Relating. **2.** Relative. **3.** Relatively. **4.** Released. **5.** Religion; religious.

re·laid (rē-lād′) *v.* Past tense and past participle of **re-lay.**

re·lapse (rĭ-lăps′) *intr.v.* **-lapsed, -laps·ing, -laps·es.** **1.** To fall or slide back into a former state. **2.** To regress after partial recovery from illness. **3.** To slip back into bad ways; backslide. **—relapse** (rē′lăps, rĭ-lăps′) *n.* A falling back into a former state, especially after apparent improvement. [Middle English *relapsen,* to forswear, from Latin *relābī, relāps-,* to fall back gradually : *re-,* re- + *lābī,* to slide.] **—re·laps′er** *n.*

re·laps·ing fever (rĭ-lăp′sĭng) *n.* Any of several infectious diseases characterized by chills and fever and caused by spirochetes transmitted by lice and ticks. Also called *recurrent fever.*

re·late (rĭ-lāt′) *v.* **-lat·ed, -lat·ing, -lates.** *—tr.* **1.** To narrate or tell. See Synonyms at **describe. 2.** To bring into or link in logical or natural association. See Synonyms at **join. 3.** To establish or demonstrate a connection between. *—intr.* **1.** To have connection, relation, or reference: *The symbols relate to an earlier system.* **2.** To have or establish a reciprocal relationship; interact: *She doesn't relate well to her peers.* **3.** To react in response, especially favorably: *I just can't relate to these new fashions.* [Obsolete French *relater,* from Old French, from Latin *relātus,* past participle of *referre* : *re-,* re- + *lātus,* brought; see **tela-** in Appendix.] **—re·lat′a·ble** *adj.* **—re·lat′er** *n.*

re·lat·ed (rĭ-lā′tĭd) *adj.* **1.** Being connected; associated. **2.** Connected by kinship, common origin, or marriage. **3.** *Music.* Having a close harmonic connection. **—re·lat′ed·ly** *adv.* **—re·lat′ed·ness** *n.*

re·la·tion (rĭ-lā′shən) *n.* **1.** A logical or natural association between two or more things; relevance of one to another; connection: *the relation between smoking and heart disease.* **2.** The connection of people by blood or marriage; kinship. **3.** A person connected to another by blood or marriage; a relative. **4.** The way in which one person or thing is connected with another: *the relation of parent to child.* **5. relations. a.** The mutual dealings or connections of persons, groups, or nations in social, business, or diplomatic matters: *international relations.* **b.** Sexual intercourse. **6.** Reference; regard: *in relation to your inquiry.* **7.a.** The act of telling or narrating. **b.** A narrative; an account. **8.** *Law.* The principle whereby an act done at a later date is considered to have been done on a prior date.

re·la·tion·al (rĭ-lā′shə-nəl) *adj.* **1.** Of or arising from kinship. **2.** Indicating or constituting relation. **3.** *Grammar.* Of, relating to, or being a word or particle, such as a conjunction or preposition, that expresses a syntactic relation between elements in a phrase or sentence. **—re·la′tion·al·ly** *adv.*

re·la·tion·ship (rĭ-lā′shən-shĭp′) *n.* **1.** The condition or fact of being related; connection or association. **2.** Connection by blood or marriage; kinship. **3.** A particular type of connection existing between people related to or having dealings with each other: *has a close relationship with his siblings.* **4.** A romantic or sexual involvement.

rel·a·tive (rĕl′ə-tĭv) *adj. Abbr.* **rel. 1.** Having pertinence or relevance; connected or related. **2.** Considered in comparison with something else: *the relative quiet of the suburbs.* **3.** Dependent on or interconnected with something else; not absolute. See Synonyms at **dependent. 4.** *Grammar.* Referring to or qualifying an antecedent, as the pronoun *who* in *the man who was on TV* or *that* in *the dictionary that I use.* **5.** *Music.* Having the same key signature. Used of major and minor scales and keys: *C major is the relative major of A minor.* **—relative** *n.* **1.** One related by kinship, common origin, or marriage. **2.** Something having a relation or connection to something else. **3.** *Grammar.* A relative pronoun. [Middle English, from Old French *relatif,* from Late Latin *relātīvus,* from Latin *relātus,* past participle of *referre,* to relate. See RELATE.] **—rel′a·tive·ness** *n.*

relative biological effectiveness *n. Abbr.* **RBE, rbe** A measure of the capacity of a specific ionizing radiation to produce a specific biological effect, expressed relative to a reference radiation, such as radium gamma rays or 200-volt x-rays.

relative clause *n. Grammar.* A dependent clause introduced by a relative pronoun, as *which is downstairs* in *The dining room, which is downstairs, is too dark.*

relative humidity *n. Abbr.* **r.h.** The ratio of the amount of water vapor in the air at a specific temperature to the maximum amount that the air could hold at that temperature, expressed as a percentage.

rel·a·tive·ly (rĕl′ə-tĭv-lē) *adv. Abbr.* **rel.** In a relative manner; in comparison with something else: *a relatively minor problem.* See Usage Note at **perfect.**

relative permittivity *n. Physics.* See **permittivity.**

relative pitch *n. Music.* **1.** The pitch of a tone as determined by its position in a scale. **2.** The ability to recognize or produce a tone by mentally establishing a relationship between its pitch and that of a recently heard tone.

relative pronoun *n. Grammar.* A pronoun that introduces a relative clause and has reference to an antecedent, as *who* in *the child who is wearing a hat* or *that* in *the house that you live in.*

relative to *prep.* With regard to; concerning: *questions relative to the deficit.*

rel·a·tiv·ism (rĕl′ə-tĭ-vĭz′əm) *n. Philosophy.* A theory that conceptions of truth and moral values are not absolute but are relative to the persons or groups holding them.

rel·a·tiv·ist (rĕl′ə-tĭ-vĭst) *n.* **1.** *Philosophy.* A proponent of relativism. **2.** A physicist who specializes in the theories of relativity.

rel·a·tiv·is·tic (rĕl′ə-tĭ-vĭs′tĭk) *adj.* **1.** Of or relating to relativism. **2.** *Physics.* **a.** Of, relating to, or resulting from speeds approaching the speed of light: *relativistic increase in mass.* **b.** Having to do with or based on the theory of relativity: *relativistic mechanics.*

rel·a·tiv·i·ty (rĕl′ə-tĭv′ĭ-tē) *n.* **1.** The quality or state of being relative. **2.** *Philosophy.* Existence dependent solely on relation to a thinking mind. **3.** A state of dependence in which the existence or significance of one entity is solely dependent on that of another. **4.** *Physics.* **a.** Special relativity. **b.** General relativity.

re·la·tor (rĭ-lā′tər) *n.* **1.** One who relates or narrates: *a relator of stories for children.* **2.** *Law.* A beneficially interested person on whose behalf an action is maintained by a sovereign power or a state.

re·lax (rĭ-lăks′) *v.* **-laxed, -lax·ing, -lax·es.** *—tr.* **1.** To make lax or loose: *relax one's grip.* **2.** To make less severe or strict: *relax a curfew.* **3.** To reduce in intensity; slacken: *relax one's efforts.* **4.** To relieve from tension or strain: *The warm bath relaxed me.* *—intr.* **1.** To take one's ease; rest. **2.** To become lax or loose. **3.** To become less severe or strict. **4.** To become less restrained or tense. [Middle English *relaxen,* from Old French *relaxer,* from Latin *relaxāre* : *re-,* re- + *laxāre,* to loosen (from *laxus,* loose; see **slēg-** in Appendix).] **—re·lax′a·ble** *adj.*

re·lax·ant (rĭ-lăk′sənt) *n.* Something, such as a drug or therapeutic treatment, that relaxes or relieves muscular or nervous tension. **—relaxant** *adj.* Tending to relax or to relieve tension.

re·lax·a·tion (rē′lăk-sā′shən) *n.* **1.** The act of relaxing or the state of being relaxed. **2.** Refreshment of body or mind; recreation: *played golf for relaxation.* See Synonyms at **rest¹. 3.** A loosening or slackening. **4.** A reduction in strictness or severity. **5.** *Physiology.* The lengthening of inactive muscle or muscle fibers. **6.** *Physics.* The return or adjustment of a system to equilibrium following displacement or abrupt change. **7.** *Mathematics.* A method of solving equations in which the errors resulting from an initial approximation are reduced by succeeding approximations until all errors are within specified limits.

relaxation time *n. Physics.* The time required for an exponential variable to decrease to $1/e$ (0.368) of its initial value.

re·laxed (rĭ-lăkst′) *adj.* **1.** Not rigorous or strict. **2.** Free

ă pat	oi boy
ā pay	ou out
âr care	o͝o took
ä father	o͞o boot
ĕ pet	ŭ cut
ē be	ûr urge
ĭ pit	th thin
ī pie	*th* this
îr pier	hw which
ŏ pot	zh vision
ō toe	ə about, item
ô paw	♦ regionalism

Stress marks: ′ (primary); ′ (secondary), as in **dictionary** (dĭk′shə-nĕr′ē)

from strain or tension. **3.** Easy and informal in manner.

re·lax·er (rĭ-lăk′sər) *n.* One that relaxes, as a chemical solution used on tightly curled hair to soften or loosen the curls.

re·lax·in (rĭ-lăk′sĭn) *n.* A female hormone secreted by the corpus luteum that helps soften the cervix and relax the pelvic ligaments in childbirth.

re·lay (rē′lā) *n.* **1.** An act of passing something along from one person, group, or station to another. **2.** *Sports.* **a.** A relay race. **b.** A division of a relay race. **3.** *Electronics.* A device that responds to a small current or voltage change by activating switches or other devices in an electric circuit. **4.** A crew of workers who relieve another crew; a shift. **5.** A fresh team, as of horses or dogs, to relieve weary animals in a hunt, task, or journey. **—relay** (rē′lā, rĭ-lā′) *tr.v.* **-layed, -lay·ing, -lays. 1.** To pass along by or as if by relay: *relayed the message to his boss.* **2.** To supply with fresh relays. **3.** *Electronics.* To control or retransmit by means of a relay. [Middle English *relai,* fresh team of dogs for a hunt, from Old French, from *relaier,* to relay : *re-,* re- + *laier,* to leave (of Germanic origin; see **leip-** in Appendix).]

relay race
Runner passing baton to a teammate

re-lay (rē-lā′) *tr.v.* **-laid** (-lād′), **-lay·ing, -lays.** To lay again: *re-laid the carpet.*

relay race *n. Sports.* A race between two or more teams, in which each team member runs only a set part of the race and is then relieved by another member of the team.

re·leas·a·ble (rĭ-lē′sə-bəl) *adj.* **1.** That can be released: *releasable documents; releasable prisoners.* **2.** Intended or configured to release: *releasable ski bindings.* **—re·leas·a·bil′i·ty** *n.* **—re·leas′a·bly** *adv.*

re·lease (rĭ-lēs′) *tr.v.* **-leased, -leas·ing, -leas·es. 1.** To set free from confinement, restraint, or bondage: *released the prisoners.* **2.** To free from something that binds, fastens, or holds back; let go: *released the balloons; released a flood of questions.* **3.** To dismiss, as from a job. **4.** To relieve of debt or obligation. **5.** To relieve of care and suffering. **6. a.** To issue for performance, sale, publication, or distribution. **b.** To make known or available. **7.** To relinquish (a right or claim). **—release** *n.* **1.** A deliverance or liberation, as from confinement, restraint, or suffering. **2.** An authoritative discharge, as from an obligation or from prison. **3.** An unfastening or letting go of something caught or held fast. **4.** A device or catch for locking or releasing a mechanism. **5. a.** The act or an instance of issuing something for publication, use, or distribution. **b.** Something thus released: *a press release.* **6.** *Law.* **a.** Relinquishment to another of a right, title, or claim. **b.** The document authorizing such relinquishment. [Middle English *relesen,* from Old French *relaissier,* alteration of *relacher,* from Latin *relaxāre.* See RELAX.]

relief
Top: Low relief of a ram from the Ptolemaic period
Center: Detail of a first–second century A.D. Roman half relief of a woman holding a fan
Bottom: High relief of a woman on a c. 400 B.C. Greek grave stele

re-lease (rē-lēs′) *tr.v.* **-leased, -leas·ing, -leas·es.** To lease again: *re-leased the car.*

re·leas·er (rĭ-lē′sər) *n.* **1.** One that releases: *a releaser of shipments; a releaser of prisoners.* **2.** *Zoology.* A stimulus that releases a specific behavior pattern in an animal.

re·leas·ing factor (rĭ-le′sĭng) *n.* Any of several hormones secreted by the hypothalamus that stimulate the anterior part of the pituitary gland to release certain hormones.

rel·e·gate (rĕl′ĭ-gāt′) *tr.v.* **-gat·ed, -gat·ing, -gates. 1.** To assign to an obscure place, position, or condition. **2.** To assign to a particular class or category; classify. See Synonyms at **commit. 3.** To refer or assign (a matter or task, for example) for decision or action. **4.** To send to a place of exile; banish. [Middle English *relegaten,* to banish, from Latin *relēgāre, relēgāt-* : *re-,* re- + *lēgāre,* to send, depute; see **leg-** in Appendix.] **—rel′e·ga′tion** *n.*

re·lent (rĭ-lĕnt′) *v.* **-lent·ed, -lent·ing, -lents.** —*intr.* To become more lenient, compassionate, or forgiving. See Synonyms at **yield.** —*tr. Obsolete.* **1.** To cause to slacken or abate. **2.** To cause to soften in attitude or temper. [Middle English *relenten,* to melt, from Anglo-Norman *relenter,* from *relent,* damp : Latin *re-,* re- + Latin *lentus,* sticky, slow.]

re·lent·less (rĭ-lĕnt′lĭs) *adj.* **1.** Unyielding in severity or strictness; unrelenting: *relentless persecution.* **2.** Steady and persistent; unremitting: *the relentless beat of the drums.* **—re·lent′less·ly** *adv.* **—re·lent′less·ness** *n.*

rel·e·vance (rĕl′ə-vəns) also **rel·e·van·cy** (-vən-sē) *n.* **1.** Pertinence to the matter at hand. **2.** Applicability to social issues: *a governmental policy lacking relevance.* **3.** *Computer Science.* The capability of an information retrieval system to select and retrieve data appropriate to a user's needs.

rel·e·vant (rĕl′ə-vənt) *adj.* Having a bearing on or connection with the matter at hand. [Medieval Latin *relevāns, relevant-,* from Latin, present participle of *relevāre,* to relieve, raise up. See RELIEVE.] **—rel′e·vant·ly** *adv.*

SYNONYMS: *relevant, pertinent, germane, material, apposite, apropos.* These adjectives all describe what relates to and has a direct bearing on the matter at hand. Something *relevant* is connected with a subject or issue: *The scientist corresponds with colleagues in order to learn about matters relevant to her own research. Pertinent* suggests a logical, precise relevance: *The professor has given the students a list of articles pertinent to the topic under discussion. Germane* implies close kinship and appropriateness: *"He's a serious student of the issues, always inquisitive about the facts, and aggressive in their pursuit. . . . he asks questions that are germane and central to the issue"* (Marlin Fitzwater). Something *material* is not only relevant but also crucial to a matter: *"Facts, the statement of which may reasonably be presumed likely to have such an influence on the judgment of the underwriter are called material facts"* (Joseph Arnould). *Apposite* implies a striking appropriateness and pertinence: *The successful copywriter is a master of apposite and evocative verbal images.* Something *apropos* is both to the point and opportune: *The thought may have been apropos, but I suppressed its expression out of consideration of their feelings.*
ANTONYM: *irrelevant.*

re·li·a·ble (rĭ-lī′ə-bəl) *adj.* Capable of being relied on; dependable: *a reliable assistant; a reliable car.* **—re·li′a·bil′i·ty, re·li′a·ble·ness** *n.* **—re·li′a·bly** *adv.*

SYNONYMS: *reliable, dependable, responsible, trustworthy, trusty.* The central meaning shared by these adjectives is "worthy of reliance or trust": *a reliable source of information; a dependable worker; a responsible used-car dealer; a trustworthy report; a trusty servant of the state.*

re·li·ance (rĭ-lī′əns) *n.* **1.** The act of relying or the state of being reliant. **2.** The faith, confidence, or trust felt by one who relies; dependence. See Synonyms at **trust. 3.** One relied on; a mainstay.

re·li·ant (rĭ-lī′ənt) *adj.* Having or exhibiting reliance; dependent: *reliant on medication.* **—re·li′ant·ly** *adv.*

rel·ic (rĕl′ĭk) *n.* **1.** Something that has survived the passage of time, especially an object or a custom whose original culture has disappeared: *"Corporal punishment was a relic of barbarism"* (Cyril Connolly). **2.** Something cherished for its age or historic interest. **3.** An object kept for its association with the past; a memento. **4.** An object of religious veneration, especially a piece of the body or a personal item of a saint. **5.** Or **relics.** A corpse; remains. [Middle English *relik,* object of religious veneration, from Old French *relique,* from Late Latin *reliquiae,* sacred relics, from Latin, remains, from *reliquus,* remaining, from *relinquere, relīq-,* to leave behind. See RELINQUISH.]

rel·ict (rĕl′ĭkt, rĭ-lĭkt′) *n.* **1.** *Ecology.* An organism or a species of an earlier time surviving in an environment that has undergone considerable change. **2.** Something that has survived; a remnant. **3.** A widow. **—relict** *adj. Geology.* Of or relating to something that has survived, as structures or minerals after destructive processes. [From Middle English *relicte,* left undisturbed, from Latin *relictus,* past participle of *relinquere,* to leave behind. See RELINQUISH. Sense 2, Middle English *relicte,* widow, from Medieval Latin *relicta,* from Latin, feminine past participle of *relinquere,* to leave behind.]

re·lic·tion (rĭ-lĭk′shən) *n. Geology.* Gradual recession of water in a sea, lake, or stream, leaving permanently dry land.

re·lief (rĭ-lēf′) *n.* **1.** The easing of a burden or distress, such as pain, anxiety, or oppression. **2.** Something that alleviates pain or distress. **3. a.** Public assistance. **b.** Aid in time of danger, especially rescue from siege. **4. a.** Release from a post or duty, as that of sentinel. **b.** One who releases another by taking over a post or duty. **5.** A pleasant or amusing change; a diversion. **6. a.** The projection of figures or forms from a flat background, as in sculpture, or such a projection that is apparent only, as in painting. **b.** A work of art featuring such projection. Also called *relievo.* **7.** *Geology.* The variations in elevation of an area of the earth's surface. **8.** Distinction or prominence due to contrast: *"The light brought the white church . . . into relief from the flat ledges"* (Willa Cather). **9.** *Law.* Redress awarded by a court. **10.** A payment made by the heir of a deceased tenant to a feudal lord for the privilege of succeeding to the tenant's estate. **—*idiom.* on relief.** Receiving public assistance because of need or poverty. [Middle English, from Old French, from *relever,* to relieve. See RELIEVE. Senses 6, 7, and 8, French, from Italian *rilievo.* See BAS-RELIEF.]

relief map *n.* A map that depicts land configuration, usually with contour lines.

relief pitcher *n. Baseball.* A pitcher who replaces another during a game.

re·lieve (rĭ-lēv′) *tr.v.* **-lieved, -liev·ing, -lieves. 1.** To cause a lessening or alleviation of: *relieved all his symptoms; relieved the tension.* **2.** To free from pain, anxiety, or distress. **3.** To furnish assistance or aid to. **4.** To rescue from siege. **5.** To release (a person) from an obligation, a restriction, or a burden, as by law or legislation. **6.** To free from a specified duty by providing or acting as a substitute. **7.** To make less tedious, monotonous, or unpleasant: *Only one small candle relieved the gloom.* **8.** To make prominent or effective by contrast; set off. **9.** *Informal.* To rob or deprive: *Pickpockets relieved him of his money.* **—*idiom.* relieve oneself.** To urinate or defecate. [Middle English *releven,* from Old French *relever,* from Latin *relevāre* : *re-,* re- + *levāre,* to raise; see **legʷh-** in Appendix.] **—re·liev′a·ble** *adj.* **—re·liev′er** *n.*

SYNONYMS: *relieve, allay, alleviate, assuage, lighten, mitigate, palliate.* All of these verbs mean to make something less severe or more bearable. To *relieve* is to ease and make more endurable something causing discomfort or distress: *"that misery which he strives in vain to relieve"* (Henry David Thoreau). *"The counselor relieved her fears"* (Sir Walter Scott). *Allay* suggests relief at least for the time being from what is burdensome or painful: *"This music crept by me upon the waters,/Allaying both their fury and my passion/With its sweet air"* (Shakespeare). *Alleviate* connotes temporary lessening of distress without removal of its cause: *"No *arguments shall be wanting on my part that can alleviate so severe a misfortune"* (Jane Austen). To *assuage* is to soothe or make milder: *"What shall assuage the unforgotten pain/And teach the unforgetful to forget?"* (Dante Gabriel Rossetti). *Lighten* in this comparison signifies to make less heavy or oppressive: *Congress endeavored to lighten the taxpayers' burden. Mitigate* and *palliate* connote moderating the severity, force, or intensity of something that causes suffering: *"I . . . prayed to the Lord to mitigate a calamity which seemed to me past the capacity of man to remedy"* (John Galt). *"His well-known financial ability made men turn to him in the hour of distress, as of all statesmen the most fitted to palliate it"* (William E.H. Lecky).

re•lie•vo (rĭ-lē′vō) *n., pl.* **-vos.** See **relief** (sense 6). [Italian *rilievo.* See BAS-RELIEF.]

re•lig•ion (rĭ-lĭj′ən) *n. Abbr.* **rel., relig. 1.a.** Belief in and reverence for a supernatural power or powers regarded as creator and governor of the universe. **b.** A personal or institutionalized system grounded in such belief and worship. **2.** The life or condition of a person in a religious order. **3.** A set of beliefs, values, and practices based on the teachings of a spiritual leader. **4.** A cause, a principle, or an activity pursued with zeal or conscientious devotion. **—*idiom.* get religion.** *Informal.* To accept a higher power as a controlling influence for the good in one's life. [Middle English *religioun,* from Old French *religion,* from Latin *religiō, religiōn-,* perhaps from *religāre,* to tie fast. See RELY.]

re•lig•ion•ism (rĭ-lĭj′ə-nĭz′əm) *n.* Excessive or affected religious zeal. **—re•lig′ion•ist** *n.*

re•li•gi•ose (rĭ-lĭj′ē-ōs′) *adj.* Excessively religious, especially in a conspicuous or sentimental manner.

re•lig•i•os•i•ty (rĭ-lĭj′ē-ŏs′ĭ-tē) *n.* **1.** The quality of being religious. **2.** Excessive or affected piety.

re•lig•ious (rĭ-lĭj′əs) *adj. Abbr.* **rel. 1.** Having or showing belief in and reverence for God or a deity. **2.** Of, concerned with, or teaching religion: *a religious text.* **3.** Extremely scrupulous or conscientious: *religious devotion to duty.* **—religious** *n., pl.* **religious.** A member of a monastic order, especially a nun or monk. [Middle English, from Old French, from Latin *religiōsus,* from *religiō,* religion. See RELIGION.] **—re•lig′ious•ly** *adv.* **—re•lig′ious•ness** *n.*

SYNONYMS: *religious, devout, pious, sanctimonious.* These adjectives mean having or showing a belief in and veneration for God or a divine power, especially as it is reflected in the practice of religion. *Religious* implies adherence to religion in both belief and practice: *The cathedral at Chartres is an expression of the religious fervor of the Middle Ages. "To know that what is impenetrable to us really exists . . . is at the center of true religiousness. In this sense, and in this sense only, I belong to the ranks of the devoutly religious men"* (Albert Einstein). *Devout* connotes ardent faith and sincere devotion: *Devout Moslems observe Ramadan punctiliously. Pious* stresses dutiful, reverential discharge of religious duties: *Her mother, a pious woman, attends Mass every morning.* When the term refers to insincere piety, however, it is derogatory: *"It is . . . well stored with pious frauds, and . . . much better calculated for the private advantage of the preacher than the edification of the hearers"* (Edmund Burke). *Sanctimonious* in its modern usage always implies a hypocritical pretense of sanctity: *"Thou conclud'st like the sanctimonious pirate, that went to sea with the Ten Commandments, but scrap'd one* [Thou shalt not steal] *out of the table"* (Shakespeare).

re•line (rē-līn′) *tr.v.* **-lined, -lin•ing, -lines. 1.** To make new lines on. **2.** To put a new lining in.

re•lin•quish (rĭ-lĭng′kwĭsh) *tr.v.* **-quished, -quish•ing, -quish•es. 1.** To retire from; give up or abandon. **2.** To put aside or desist from (something practiced, professed, or intended). **3.** To let go; surrender. **4.** To cease holding physically; release: *relinquish a grip.* [Middle English *relinquisshen,* from Old French *relinquir, relinquiss-,* from Latin *relinquere* : *re-,* re- + *linquere,* to leave; see **leikʷ-** in Appendix.] **—re•lin′quish•er** *n.* **—re•lin′quish•ment** *n.*

SYNONYMS: *relinquish, yield, resign, abandon, surrender, cede, waive, renounce.* These verbs have in common the sense of letting something go or giving something up. *Relinquish,* the least specific, sometimes connotes unwillingness or regret: *can't bear to relinquish the idea. Yield* implies giving way, as to pressure or superior authority, often in the hope that such action will be temporary: *gradually had to yield ground. Resign* suggests unresisting submission or acquiescence, as that arising from hopelessness: *was forced by the scandal to resign the office to which he had been elected. Abandon* and *surrender* agree in implying no expectation of returning to or recovering what is given up, but the terms differ in that *surrender* implies the operation of compulsion, demand, or force: *abandoned all hope; refusing to surrender control. Cede* connotes formal transfer, as of rights or territory: *a province ceded by treaty. Waive* implies a voluntary decision to dispense with something, such as a claim or right: *waived all privileges.* To *renounce* is to relinquish something formally and usually as a matter of principle: *renounced his claim to the estate.*

rel•i•quar•y (rĕl′ĭ-kwĕr′ē) *n., pl.* **-ies.** A receptacle, such as a coffer or shrine, for keeping or displaying sacred relics. [French *reliquaire,* from Old French from *relique,* relic, from Late Latin *reliquiae,* sacred relics. See RELIC.]

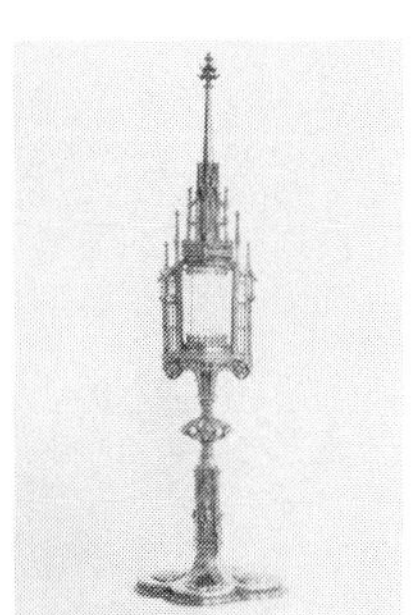

reliquary
15th-century German

rel•ique (rĕl′ĭk) *n. Archaic.* Variant of **relic.**

re•liq•ui•ae (rĭ-lĭk′wē-ē′) *pl.n.* Remains, as of fossil organisms. [Latin, remains. See RELIC.]

rel•ish (rĕl′ĭsh) *n.* **1.** An appetite for something; a strong appreciation or liking: *a relish for luxury.* **2.a.** Hearty enjoyment; zest. See Synonyms at **zest. b.** Something that lends pleasure or zest. **3.a.** A spicy or savory condiment or appetizer, such as chutney or olives. **b.** A condiment of chopped sweet pickle. **4.** The flavor of a food, especially when appetizing. See Synonyms at **taste. 5.** A trace or suggestion of a pleasurable quality. **—relish** *v.* **-ished, -ish•ing, -ish•es.** *—tr.* **1.** To take keen or zestful pleasure in. See Synonyms at **like[1]. 2.** To enjoy the flavor of. **3.** To give spice or flavor to. *—intr.* To have a pleasing or distinctive taste. [Alteration of Middle English *reles,* taste, from Old French, something remaining, from *relaissier,* to leave behind. See RELEASE.]

re•live (rē-lĭv′) *v.* **-lived, -liv•ing, -lives.** *—tr.* To undergo or experience again, especially in the imagination. *—intr.* To live again.

re•lo•cate (rē-lō′kāt) *v.* **-cat•ed, -cat•ing, -cates. —relocate** *tr. & intr.v.* To move or be moved to a new place: *relocated the business; plan to relocate in the suburbs.* **—re′lo•ca′tion** *n.*

re•lu•cent (rĭ-lo͞o′sənt) *adj.* Reflecting light; shining. [Latin *relūcēns, relūcent-,* present participle of *relūcēre,* to shine back : *re-,* re- + *lūcēre,* to shine; see **leuk-** in Appendix.]

re•luct (rĭ-lŭkt′) *intr.v.* **-luct•ed, -luct•ing, -lucts.** To show reluctance or repugnance. [Latin *reluctārī* : *re-,* re- + *luctārī,* to struggle.]

re•luc•tance (rĭ-lŭk′təns) also **re•luc•tan•cy** (-tən-sē) *n.* **1.** The state of being reluctant; unwillingness. **2.** *Physics.* A measure of the opposition to magnetic flux, analogous to electric resistance.

re•luc•tant (rĭ-lŭk′tənt) *adj.* **1.** Unwilling; disinclined: *reluctant to help.* **2.** Exhibiting or marked by unwillingness: *a reluctant smile.* **3.** Offering resistance; opposing. [Latin *reluctāns, reluctant-,* present participle of *reluctārī,* to reluct. See RELUCT.] **—re•luc′tant•ly** *adv.*

rel•uc•tiv•i•ty (rĕl′ək-tĭv′ĭ-tē) *n. Physics.* A measure of the resistance of a material to the establishment of a magnetic field within it, equal to the ratio of the intensity of the magnetic field to the magnetic induction of the material. [RELUCT(ANCE) + (CONDUCT)IVITY.]

re•lume (rĭ-lo͞om′) *tr.v.* **-lumed, -lum•ing, -lumes.** To make bright or clear again; illuminate again. [RE– + (IL)LUME.]

re•ly (rĭ-lī′) *intr.v.* **-lied, -ly•ing, -lies. 1.** To be dependent for support, help, or supply: *relies on her parents for tuition.* **2.** To place or have faith or confidence: *relied on them to tell him the truth.* [Middle English *relien,* to rally, from Old French *relier,* from Latin *religāre,* to bind fast : *re-,* re- + *ligāre,* to bind; see **leig-** in Appendix.] **—re•li′er** *n.*

SYNONYMS: *rely, trust, depend, reckon.* These verbs share the meaning "to place or have faith or confidence in someone or something." *Rely* implies complete confidence: *"You are the only woman I can rely on to be interested in her"* (John Galsworthy). *Trust* stresses confidence arising from belief that is often based on inconclusive evidence: *"We must try to trust one another. Stay and cooperate"* (Jomo Kenyatta). *"I don't think I could trust myself to speak to him about it"* (Booth Tarkington). *Prepare yourself thoroughly for the performance; then trust in your talent to carry you through. Depend* implies confidence in the help or support of another: *Synthetic fuels should be developed; it is foolhardy to depend on Middle Eastern countries for our oil supplies. Reckon* implies a sense of confident expectancy: *"He reckons on finding a woman as big a fool as himself"* (George Meredith).

rem (rĕm) *n. Physics.* **1.** The amount of ionizing radiation required to produce the same biological effect as one rad of high-penetration x-rays. **2.** A unit for measuring absorbed doses of radiation, equivalent to one roentgen of x-rays or gamma rays. [*r(oentgen) e(quivalent in) m(an).*]

REM (rĕm) *n.* The rapid, periodic, jerky movement of the eyes during certain stages of the sleep cycle when dreaming takes place. [R(APID) E(YE) M(OVEMENT).]

rem. *abbr.* Remittance.

re•made (rē-mād′) *v.* Past tense and past participle of **remake.**

re•main (rĭ-mān′) *intr.v.* **-mained, -main•ing, -mains. 1.** To continue in the same state or condition: *These matters remain in doubt.* **2.** To continue to be in the same place; stay or stay behind: *We are remaining at home.* **3.** To be left after the removal, loss, passage, or destruction of others: *Only a few trees remain.* See Synonyms at **stay[1]. 4.** To be left as still to be dealt with: *A cure remains to be found.* **5.** To endure or persist. [Middle English *remainen,* from Old French *remainer, remaindre,* from Latin *remanēre* : *re-,* re- + *manēre,* to remain; see **men-[3]** in Appendix.]

re•main•der (rĭ-mān′dər) *n.* **1.** Something left over after other parts have been taken away. **2.** *Mathematics.* **a.** The number left over when one integer is divided by another. The remainder plus the product of the quotient times the divisor equals the dividend. **b.** The number obtained when one number is subtracted

ă pat	oi boy
ā pay	ou out
âr care	o͝o took
ä father	o͞o boot
ĕ pet	ŭ cut
ē be	ûr urge
ĭ pit	th thin
ī pie	*th* this
îr pier	hw which
ŏ pot	zh vision
ō toe	ə about, item
ô paw	♦ regionalism

Stress marks: ′ (primary); ′ (secondary), as in **dictionary** (dĭk′shə-nĕr′ē)

from another; the difference. **3.** *Law.* An estate in land that is conveyed only after the termination of a preceding estate created at the same time. **4.** A book that remains with a publisher after sales have fallen off, usually sold at a reduced price. **—remainder** *tr.v.* **-dered, -der·ing, -ders.** To dispose of as a remainder. [Middle English, second party's right of ownership, from Anglo-Norman, from *remeindre,* to remain, variant of Old French *remaindre, remainer.* See REMAIN.]

SYNONYMS: *remainder, rest, balance, residue, residuum, remnant, leavings, remains.* These nouns are compared as they denote what is left after a part has been used or subtracted. *Remainder* and *rest,* used interchangeably, are the least specific: *ate some of the candy and gave the remainder* (or *rest*) *away; will spend the remainder* (or *rest*) *of the day relaxing. Balance,* which often specifically refers to an amount of money left in a bank account after withdrawals and to an unpaid amount due on a charge account, in its general sense is synonymous with *remainder* and *rest*: *A few discriminating listeners heard the flaws in the performance; the balance of the audience cheered. Residue* and *residuum* refer especially to what is left after something has undergone dissolution, depletion, or diminution: *"The residue of the conquered people fled"* (Daniel Defoe). *"After elimination of all verbiage, this fact was the only residuum"* (John Lothrop Motley). *Remnant* denotes a small piece or quantity remaining after the major part has been used: *"The sum exceeded the remnant of his savings"* (Samuel Butler). *"I saw his brindled cow feeding on fish remnants"* (Herman Melville). *Leavings* are the culls remaining after what is valuable has been taken away: *The untouched leavings from the banquet made a fine meal for the kitchen staff.* Although *remains* often specifically refers to a corpse, it also applies to remnants, fragments, and relics, as of times past: *fossil remains; remains of an ancient Greek temple; dispose of the remains of dinner.*

Rembrandt
Self-portrait

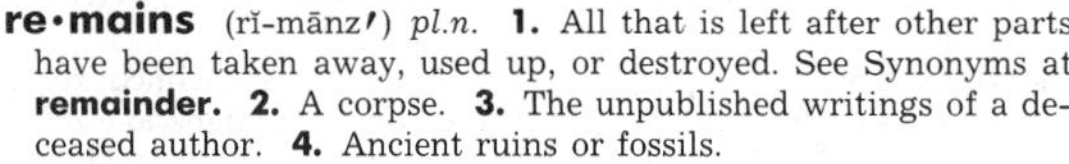

re·mains (rĭ-mānz′) *pl.n.* **1.** All that is left after other parts have been taken away, used up, or destroyed. See Synonyms at **remainder. 2.** A corpse. **3.** The unpublished writings of a deceased author. **4.** Ancient ruins or fossils.

re·make (rē-māk′) *tr.v.* **-made** (-mād′), **-mak·ing, -makes.** To make again or anew. **—remake** (rē′māk′) *n.* **1.** The act of remaking. **2.** Something in remade form, especially a new version of an old movie.

re·man (rē-măn′) *tr.v.* **-manned, -man·ning, -mans. 1.** To supply with new personnel: *reman a ship.* **2.** To imbue with new manliness or courage.

re·mand (rĭ-mănd′) *tr.v.* **-mand·ed, -mand·ing, -mands. 1.** To send or order back. **2.** *Law.* **a.** To send back to custody. **b.** To send back (a case) to a lower court with instructions about further proceedings. [Middle English *remaunden,* from Old French *remander,* from Late Latin *remandāre,* to send back word : Latin *re-,* re- + Latin *mandāre,* to order; see **man-**[2] in Appendix.] **—re·mand′** *n.* **—re·mand′ment** *n.*

Frederic Remington

rem·a·nence (rĕm′ə-nəns) *n. Physics.* The magnetic induction that remains in a material after removal of the magnetizing force. [From Middle English *remanent,* remaining, from Latin *remanēns, remanent-,* present participle of *remanēre,* to remain. See REMAIN.] **—rem′a·nent** *adj.*

re·mark (rĭ-märk′) *v.* **-marked, -mark·ing, -marks.** —*tr.* **1.** To express briefly and casually as a comment. **2.** To take notice of; observe. See Synonyms at **see**[1]. —*intr.* To make a comment or an observation: *remarked on her good taste.* **—remark** *n.* **1.** The act of noticing or observing: *a place worthy of remark.* **2.** A casual or brief expression of opinion; a comment. See Synonyms at **comment.** [Alteration (influenced by MARK[1]) of French *remarquer* : Old French *re-,* re- + Old French *marquer,* to mark (ultimately from *merc,* sign, from Old Norse *merki,* mark; see **merg-** in Appendix).] **—re·mark′er** *n.*

re·mark·a·ble (rĭ-mär′kə-bəl) *adj.* **1.** Worthy of notice. **2.** Attracting notice as being unusual or extraordinary. See Synonyms at **noticeable. —re·mark′a·ble·ness** *n.* **—re·mark′a·bly** *adv.*

re·marque (rĭ-märk′) *n.* **1.** A small mark or sketch engraved in the margin of a plate to indicate its stage of development prior to completion. **2.** A print or proof from a plate carrying such a mark. [French, from *remarquer,* to remark. See REMARK.]

Re·marque (rə-märk′), **Erich Maria.** 1898–1970. German-born American writer best known for *All Quiet on the Western Front* (1929), a novel based on his experiences in World War I.

re·match (rē-măch′, rē′măch′) *n.* A second contest between the same opponents.

Rem·brandt van Rijn or **Rem·brandt van Ryn** (rĕm′brănt′ vän rīn′, -bränt′). 1606–1669. Dutch painter whose works are unmatched in their portrayal of subtle human emotions. His masterpieces include historical and religious scenes, group portraits, such as *The Anatomy Lesson of Dr. Tulp* (1632) and *The Night Watch* (1642), as well as a series of self-portraits.

re·me·di·a·ble (rĭ-mē′dē-ə-bəl) *adj.* Possible to remedy: *remediable problems; a remediable setback.* **—re·me′di·a·ble·ness** *n.* **—re·me′di·a·bly** *adv.*

re·me·di·al (rĭ-mē′dē-əl) *adj.* **1.** Supplying a remedy. **2.** Intended to correct or improve deficient skills in a specific subject: *remedial reading.* **—re·me′di·al·ly** *adv.*

re·me·di·a·tion (rĭ-mē′dē-ā′shən) *n.* The act or process of correcting a fault or deficiency: *remediation of a learning disability.* **—re·me′di·ate′** *v.*

rem·e·dy (rĕm′ĭ-dē) *n., pl.* **-dies. 1.** Something, such as medicine or therapy, that relieves pain, cures disease, or corrects a disorder. **2.** Something that corrects an evil, a fault, or an error. **3.** *Law.* A legal order of preventing or redressing a wrong or enforcing a right. **4.** The allowance by a mint for deviation from the standard weight or quality of coins. —*tr.* **-died, -dy·ing, -dies. 1.** To relieve or cure (a disease or disorder). **2.** To set right; remove, rectify, or counteract. See Synonyms at **correct. 3.** See Synonyms at **cure.** [Middle English *remedie,* from Old French, from Latin *remedium* : *re-,* re- + *medērī,* to heal; see **med-** in Appendix.]

re·mem·ber (rĭ-mĕm′bər) *v.* **-bered, -ber·ing, -bers.** —*tr.* **1.** To recall to the mind; think of again. **2.** To recall to the mind with effort: *finally remembered the address.* **3.** To retain in the memory: *Remember your appointment.* **4.** To keep (someone) in mind as worthy of consideration or recognition. **5.** To reward with a gift or tip. **6.** To give greetings from: *Remember me to your family.* **7.** *Engineering.* To return to (an original shape or form) after being deformed or altered. **8.** *Electronics.* To carry out (a programmed or preset activity). **9.** *Archaic.* To remind. —*intr.* To have or use the power of memory. [Middle English *remembren,* from Old French *remembrer,* from Latin *rememorārī,* to remember again : *re-,* re- + *memor,* mindful; see **(s)mer-**[1] in Appendix.] **—re·mem′ber·a·bil′i·ty** *n.* **—re·mem′ber·a·ble** *adj.* **—re·mem′ber·er** *n.*

SYNONYMS: *remember, bethink, recall, recollect.* The central meaning shared by these verbs is "to bring an image or a thought back to the mind": *can't remember his name; bethought herself of her responsibilities; recalling her kindness; recollect how the accident happened.*
ANTONYM: *forget.*

re·mem·brance (rĭ-mĕm′brəns) *n.* **1. a.** The act or process of remembering. See Synonyms at **memory. b.** The state of being remembered: *holds him in fond rememberance.* **2.** Something serving to celebrate or honor the memory of a person or an event; a memorial. **3.** The length of time over which one's memory extends. **4.** Something remembered; a reminiscence. **5.** A souvenir. **6.** A greeting or token expressive of affection. [Middle English, from Old French, from *remembrer,* to remember. See REMEMBER.]

Re·mem·brance Day (rĭ-mĕm′brəns) *n.* The Sunday closest to November 11, observed in Canada and Great Britain in commemoration of those killed in the World Wars.

re·mem·branc·er (rĭ-mĕm′brən-sər) *n.* **1.** One that causes another to remember something. **2. Remembrancer. a.** An officer of the British judiciary responsible for collecting debts owed to the Crown. **b.** An official who represents the City of London, as on ceremonial occasions.

re·mex (rē′mĕks′) *n., pl.* **rem·i·ges** (rĕm′ə-jēz′). A quill or flight feather of a bird's wing. [Latin *rēmex,* rower : *rēmus,* oar; see **erə-** in Appendix + *agere, ēg-,* to drive; see ACT.] **—re·mig′i·al** (rĭ-mĭj′ē-əl) *adj.*

re·mil·i·ta·rize (rē-mĭl′ĭ-tə-rīz′) *tr.v.* **-rized, -riz·ing, -riz·es.** To equip again for war. **—re·mil′i·ta·ri·za′tion** (-tər-ĭ-zā′shən) *n.*

re·mind (rĭ-mīnd′) *tr.v.* **-mind·ed, -mind·ing, -minds.** To cause to remember; put in mind: *must remind him to call; reminded her of college days.* **—re·mind′er** *n.*

Rem·ing·ton (rĕm′ĭng-tən), **Eliphalet.** 1793–1861. American firearms manufacturer whose company was a major munitions supplier to the U.S. government and under his son **Philo** (1816–1889) an important manufacturer of sewing machines and typewriters.

Remington, Frederic. 1861–1909. American artist and journalist best known for his sculptures and paintings of the American West.

rem·i·nisce (rĕm′ə-nĭs′) *intr.v.* **-nisced, -nisc·ing, -nisc·es.** To recollect and tell of past experiences or events. [Back-formation from REMINISCENCE.] **—rem′i·nis′cer** *n.*

rem·i·nis·cence (rĕm′ə-nĭs′əns) *n.* **1.** The act or process of recollecting past experiences or events. **2.** An experience or event recollected. See Synonyms at **memory. 3.** Often **reminiscences.** A narration of past experiences. **4.** An event that brings to mind a similar, former event.

rem·i·nis·cent (rĕm′ə-nĭs′ənt) *adj.* **1.** Having the quality of or containing reminiscence. **2.** Inclined to engage in reminiscence. **3.** Tending to recall or suggest something in the past: *an evening reminiscent of happier times.* [Latin *reminīscēns, reminīscent-,* present participle of *reminīscī,* to recollect. See **men-**[1] in Appendix.] **—rem′i·nis′cent·ly** *adv.*

re·mint (rē-mĭnt′) *tr.v.* **-mint·ed, -mint·ing, -mints.** To make into new coin by melting down and reprocessing.

re·mise (rĭ-mīz′) *tr.v.* **-mised, -mis·ing, -mis·es.** *Law.* To relinquish a claim to; surrender by deed. [Middle English *remisen,* from Old French *remis,* past participle of *remettre,* to remit, from Latin *remittere.* See REMIT.]

re·miss (rĭ-mĭs′) *adj.* **1.** Lax in attending to duty; negligent. **2.** Exhibiting carelessness or slackness. See Synonyms at **negligent.** [Middle English, from Latin *remissus,* past participle of *remittere,* to remit, slacken. See REMIT.] **—re·miss′ly** *adv.* **—re·miss′ness** *n.*

re·mis·si·ble (rĭ-mĭs′ə-bəl) *adj.* Being such that forgiveness is possible: *a remissible sin.* **—re·mis′si·bil′i·ty** *n.* **—re·mis′si·bly** *adv.*

re·mis·sion (rĭ-mĭsh′ən) *n.* **1. a.** The act of remitting. **b.** A condition or period in which something is remitted. **2.** A lessening of intensity or degree; abatement. **3. a.** *Medicine.* Abatement or subsiding of the symptoms of a disease. **b.** The period during which the symptoms of a disease abate or subside. **4. a.** Release, as from a debt, a penalty, or an obligation. **b.** Forgiveness; pardon. [Middle English, from Old French, from Latin *remissiō, remissiōn-,* from *remissus,* past participle of *remittere,* to let go. See REMIT.]

re·mit (rĭ-mĭt′) *v.* **-mit·ted, -mit·ting, -mits.** *—tr.* **1.** To transmit (money) in payment. **2. a.** To refrain from exacting (a tax or penalty, for example); cancel. **b.** To pardon; forgive: *remitted their sins.* **3.** To restore to a former condition or position. **4.** *Law.* **a.** To refer (a case) to another court for further consideration or action. **b.** To refer (a matter) to a committee or an authority for decision. **5.** To allow to slacken: *The storm remitted its fury.* **6.** To desist from; give up. **7.** To put off; postpone. *—intr.* **1.** To transmit money. **2.** To diminish; abate. **—remit** (rĭ-mĭt′, rē′mĭt) *n.* **1.** The act of remitting, especially the referral of a case to another court. **2.** A matter remitted for further consideration. [Middle English *remitten,* to send back, from Latin *remittere* : *re-,* re- + *mittere,* to send.] **—re·mit′ment** *n.* **—re·mit′ta·ble** *adj.* **—re·mit′ter** *n.*

re·mit·tal (rĭ-mĭt′l) *n.* Remission.

re·mit·tance (rĭ-mĭt′ns) *n. Abbr.* **rem. 1.** The sending of money to someone at a distance. **2.** The sum of money sent.

re·mit·tent (rĭ-mĭt′nt) *adj.* Characterized by temporary abatement in severity. Used especially of diseases. **—re·mit′tence, re·mit′ten·cy** *n.* **—re·mit′tent·ly** *adv.*

rem·nant (rĕm′nənt) *n.* **1.** Something left over; a remainder. **2.** A leftover piece of fabric remaining after the rest has been used or sold. **3.** A surviving trace or vestige: *a remnant of his past glory.* See Synonyms at **remainder. 4.** Often **remnants.** A small surviving group of people. [Middle English *remanant, remnant,* from Old French *remanant,* from present participle of *remaindre,* to remain. See REMAIN.]

re·mod·el (rē-mŏd′l) *tr.v.* **-eled, -el·ing, -els** also **-elled, -el·ling, -els.** To make over in structure or style; reconstruct. **—re·mod′el·er** *n.*

re·mon·e·tize (rē-mŏn′ĭ-tīz′, -mŭn′-) *tr.v.* **-tized, -tiz·ing, -tiz·es.** To restore to use as legal tender: *remonetize silver.* **—re·mon′e·ti·za′tion** (-tĭ-zā′shən) *n.*

re·mon·strance (rĭ-mŏn′strəns) *n.* **1.** The act of remonstrating. **2.** An expression of protest, complaint, or reproof, especially a formal statement of grievances.

re·mon·strant (rĭ-mŏn′strənt) *adj.* Characterized by remonstrance; expostulatory. **—remonstrant** *n.* **1.** One that remonstrates. **2. Remonstrant.** One of the Dutch Arminians who, in 1610, formally stated the grounds of their dissent from strict Calvinism. **—re·mon′strant·ly** *adv.*

re·mon·strate (rĭ-mŏn′strāt′) *v.* **-strat·ed, -strat·ing, -strates.** *—tr.* To say or plead in protest, objection, or reproof. *—intr.* To reason or plead in protest; present an objection. See Synonyms at **object.** [Medieval Latin *remōnstrāre, remōnstrāt-,* to demonstrate : Latin *re-,* re- + Latin *mōnstrāre,* to show (from *mōnstrum,* portent; see MONSTER).] **—re′mon·stra′tion** (rē′mŏn-strā′shən, rĕm′ən-) *n.* **—re·mon′stra·tive** (rĭ-mŏn′strə-tĭv) *adj.* **—re·mon′stra·tive·ly** *adv.* **—re·mon′stra′tor** *n.*

rem·o·ra (rĕm′ər-ə) *n.* Any of several marine fishes of the family Echeneidae, having on the head a sucking disk with which they attach themselves to sharks, whales, sea turtles, or the hulls of ships. Also called *shark sucker, suckerfish, suckfish.* [Latin, delay (from the belief that they could slow ships down), from *remorārī,* to delay : *re-,* re- + *morārī,* to delay (from *mora,* delay).]

re·morse (rĭ-môrs′) *n.* **1.** Moral anguish arising from repentance for past misdeeds; bitter regret. See Synonyms at **penitence. 2.** *Obsolete.* Compassion. [Middle English *remors,* from Old French, from Medieval Latin *remorsum,* from neuter past participle of Latin *remordēre,* to torment : *re-,* re- + *mordēre,* to bite; see **mer-** in Appendix.]

re·morse·ful (rĭ-môrs′fəl) *adj.* Marked by or filled with remorse. **—re·morse′ful·ly** *adv.* **—re·morse′ful·ness** *n.*

re·morse·less (rĭ-môrs′lĭs) *adj.* **1.** Having no pity or compassion; merciless. **2.** Unyielding; relentless. **—re·morse′less·ly** *adv.* **—re·morse′less·ness** *n.*

re·mote (rĭ-mōt′) *adj.* **-mot·er, -mot·est. 1. a.** Located far away; distant in space. **b.** Hidden away; secluded: *a remote hamlet.* **2.** Distant in time: *the remote past.* See Synonyms at **distant. 3.** Faint; slight: *a remote possibility; had not the remotest interest.* **4.** Far removed in connection or relevance: *a cause remote from everyday concerns.* **5.** Distantly related by blood or marriage: *a remote cousin.* **6.** Distant in manner; aloof. **7.** Operating or controlled from a distance: *remote sensors.* **8.** *Computer Science.* Of, relating to, or being a computer device or system situated at some distance from a central computer and communicating with it often by means of cables. **—remote** *n.* **1.** A radio or television broadcast originating from a point outside a studio. **2.** Remote control. [Middle English, from Old French *remot,* from Latin *remōtus,* past participle of *removēre,* to remove. See REMOVE.] **—re·mote′ly** *adv.* **—re·mote′ness** *n.*

remote control *n.* **1.** The control of an activity, a process, or a machine from a distance, as by radioed instructions or coded signals. **2.** A device used to control an apparatus or a machine from a distance. **—re·mote′-con·trol′** (rĭ-mōt′kən-trōl′), **re·mote′-con·trolled′** (-trōld′) *adj.*

re·mo·tion (rĭ-mō′shən) *n.* **1.** The act of removing; removal. **2.** The state of being remote. **3.** *Obsolete.* Departure. [Middle English *remocion,* from Latin *remōtiō, remōtiōn-,* from *remōtus,* past participle of *removēre,* to remove. See REMOVE.]

ré·mou·lade (rā′mōō-läd′) *n.* A piquant cold sauce made with mayonnaise, chopped pickles, capers, anchovies, and herbs. [French, from dialectal *rémola,* large black radish, from Latin *armoracia,* wild radish.]

re·mount (rē-mount′) *tr.v.* **-mount·ed, -mount·ing, -mounts. 1.** To mount again. **2.** To supply with a fresh horse. **—remount** (rē′mount′, rē-mount′) *n.* A fresh horse.

re·mov·a·ble (rĭ-mōō′və-bəl) *adj.* That can be removed: *a removable cord; removable plugs.* **—re·mov′a·bil′i·ty, re·mov′a·ble·ness** *n.* **—re·mov′a·bly** *adv.*

re·mov·al (rĭ-mōō′vəl) *n.* **1. a.** The act of removing. **b.** The fact of being removed. **2.** Relocation, as of a residence or business. **3.** Dismissal, as from office.

re·move (rĭ-mōōv′) *v.* **-moved, -mov·ing, -moves.** *—tr.* **1.** To move from a place or position occupied: *removed the dishes from the table.* **2.** To transfer or convey from one place to another: *removed the family to the West Coast.* **3.** To take off: *removed her jewelry.* **4.** To take away; withdraw: *removed his name from consideration.* **5.** To do away with; eliminate: *remove a stain.* **6.** To dismiss from office. *—intr.* **1.** To change one's place of residence or business; move: *"In 1751, I removed from the country to the town"* (David Hume). **2.** To go away; depart. **3.** To be removable: *paint that removes with water.* **—remove** *n.* **1.** The act of removing; removal. **2.** Distance or degree of separation or remoteness: *"to spill, though at a safe remove, the blood of brave men"* (Anthony Burgess). [Middle English *removen,* from Old French *remouvoir,* from Latin *removēre* : *re-,* re- + *movēre,* to move; see MOVE.] **—re·mov′er** *n.*

re·moved (rĭ-mōōvd′) *adj.* **1.** Distant in space, time, or nature; remote. See Synonyms at **distant. 2.** Separated in relationship by a given degree of descent: *A first cousin's child is one's first cousin once removed.* **—re·mov′ed·ly** (-mōō′vĭd-lē) *adv.* **—re·mov′ed·ness** *n.*

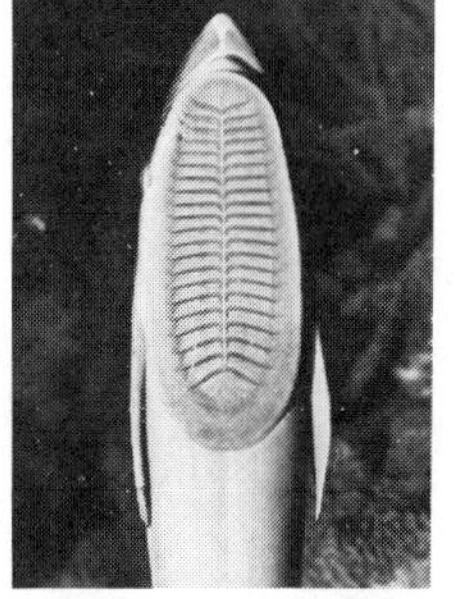

remora
Suction disk on the head of a remora

Rem·scheid (rĕm′shīt′). A city of west-central Germany northeast of Cologne. It is a center of the German tool and hardware industry. Population, 121,830.

Rem·sen (rĕm′sən), **Ira.** 1846–1927. American chemist who discovered the sweetening agent saccharin.

REM sleep *n.* A stage in the normal sleep cycle during which dreams occur and the body undergoes marked changes including rapid eye movement, loss of reflexes, and increased pulse rate and brain activity. Also called *paradoxical sleep.*

♦ **re·mu·da** (rĭ-mōō′də) *n. Southwestern U.S.* A herd of horses from which ranch hands select their mounts. [American Spanish, change of horses, remuda, from Spanish, exchange, from *remudar,* to exchange : *re-,* in return (from Latin; see RE–) + *mudar,* to change (from Latin *mūtāre;* see **mei-**[1] in Appendix).]

re·mu·ner·ate (rĭ-myōō′nə-rāt′) *tr.v.* **-at·ed, -at·ing, -ates. 1.** To pay (a person) a suitable equivalent in return for goods provided, services rendered, or losses incurred; recompense. **2.** To compensate for; make payment for: *remunerate his efforts.* [Latin *remūnerārī, remūnerāt-* : *re-,* re- + *mūnerārī,* to give (from *mūnus, mūner-,* gift; see **mei-**[1] in Appendix).] **—re·mu′ner·a·bil′i·ty** (-nər-ə-bĭl′ĭ-tē) *n.* **—re·mu′ner·a·ble** *adj.* **—re·mu′ner·a′tor** *n.*

re·mu·ner·a·tion (rĭ-myōō′nə-rā′shən) *n.* **1.** The act of remunerating. **2.** Something, such as a payment, that remunerates.

re·mu·ner·a·tive (rĭ-myōō′nər-ə-tĭv, -nə-rā′tĭv) *adj.* **1.** Yielding suitable recompense; profitable. **2.** Serving to remunerate. **—re·mu′ner·a·tive·ly** *adv.*

Re·mus (rē′məs) *n. Roman Mythology.* The twin brother of Romulus.

ren·ais·sance (rĕn′ĭ-säns′, -zäns′, rĕn′ĭ-säns′, -zäns′, rĭ-nā′səns) *n.* **1.** A rebirth or revival. **2. Renaissance. a.** The humanistic revival of classical art, architecture, literature, and learning that originated in Italy in the 14th century and later spread throughout Europe. **b.** The period of this revival, roughly the 14th through the 16th century, marking the transition from medieval to modern times. **3.** Often **Renaissance. a.** A revival of intellectual or artistic achievement and vigor: *the Celtic Renaissance.* **b.** The period of such a revival. **—Renaissance** *adj.* **1.** Of, relating to, or characteristic of the Renaissance or its artistic and intellectual works and styles. **2.** Of or being the neoclassic style of architecture and decoration that originated in Italy in the 15th century. [French, from Old French, from *renaistre,* to be born again, from Vulgar Latin *renāscere, from Latin *renāscī* : *re-,* re- + *nāscī,* to be born; see **gena-** in Appendix.]

Renaissance man *n.* A man who has broad intellectual interests and is accomplished in areas of both the arts and the sciences.

Renaissance woman *n.* A woman who has broad intellectual interests and is accomplished in areas of both the arts and the

ă pat	oi boy
ā pay	ou out
âr care	ŏŏ took
ä father	ōō boot
ĕ pet	ŭ cut
ē be	ûr urge
ĭ pit	th thin
ī pie	*th* this
îr pier	hw which
ŏ pot	zh vision
ō toe	ə about, item
ô paw	♦ regionalism

Stress marks: **′** (primary); ′ (secondary), as in **dictionary** (dĭk′shə-nĕr′ē)

sciences: *"In an age of specialists and technocrats,* [she] *was a Renaissance woman. The incisiveness of her mind in which there was not room for cant, was matched by the generosity of her spirit and by the grace of her style"* (Smith Hempstone).

re•nal (rē′nəl) *adj.* Of, relating to, or in the region of the kidneys. [Late Latin *rēnālis,* from Latin *rēnēs,* kidneys.]

renal clearance *n. Physiology.* The volume of plasma completely cleared of a specific compound per unit time and measured as a test of kidney function.

renal corpuscle *n. Anatomy.* See **Malpighian corpuscle** (sense 1).

renal pelvis *n. Anatomy.* See **pelvis** (sense 2).

Re•nan (rə-näN′), **Joseph Ernest.** 1823–1892. French philologist, philosopher, and historian who wrote the series *History of the Origins of Christianity* (1863–1881).

re•nas•cence (rĭ-năs′əns, -nā′səns) *n.* **1.** A new birth or life; a rebirth. **2.** A cultural revival; a renaissance. **3. Renascence.** Renaissance.

re•nas•cent (rĭ-năs′ənt, -nā′sənt) *adj.* Coming again into being; showing renewed growth or vigor. [Latin *renāscēns, renāscent-,* present participle of *renāscī,* to be born again. See RENAISSANCE.]

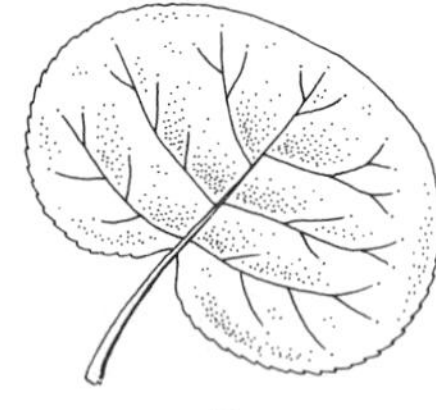

reniform

Re•nault (rə-nō′), **Jean Louis.** 1843–1918. French jurist who represented France at The Hague Conference of 1907. He shared the 1907 Nobel Peace Prize.

ren•coun•ter (rĕn-koun′tər) *Archaic. n.* **1.** An unplanned meeting. **2.** A hostile encounter or contest. **—rencounter** *tr. & intr.v.* **-tered, -ter•ing, -ters.** To meet unexpectedly or have an unexpected meeting. [French *rencontre,* from Old French, from *rencontrer,* to meet : *re-,* re- + *encontrer,* to meet; see ENCOUNTER.]

rend (rĕnd) *v.* **rent** (rĕnt), or **rend•ed, rend•ing, rends.** *—tr.* **1.** To tear or split apart or into pieces violently. See Synonyms at **tear**[1]. **2.** To tear (one's garments or hair) in anguish or rage. **3.** To tear away forcibly; wrest. **4.** To pull, split, or divide as if by tearing: *"Chip was rent between the impulse to laugh wildly and a bitterness that threatened hot tears"* (Louis Auchincloss). **5.** To pierce or disturb with sound: *a scream rent the silence.* **6.** To cause pain or distress to: *tales that rend the heart.* *—intr.* To become torn or split; come apart. [Middle English *renden,* from Old English *rendan.*]

ren•der (rĕn′dər) *tr.v.* **-dered, -der•ing, -ders. 1.** To submit or present, as for consideration, approval, or payment: *render a bill.* **2.** To give or make available; provide: *render assistance.* **3.** To give what is due or owed: *render thanks; rendered homage.* **4.** To give in return or retribution: *He had to render an apology for his rudeness.* **5.** To surrender or relinquish; yield. **6. a.** To represent in verbal form; depict: *"Joyce has attempted . . . to render . . . what our participation in life is like"* (Edmund Wilson). **b.** To represent in a drawing or painting, especially in perspective. **7.** To perform an interpretation of (a musical piece, for example). **8.** To express in another language or form; translate. **9.** To deliver or pronounce formally: *The jury has rendered its verdict.* **10.** To cause to become; make: *The news rendered her speechless.* **11.** To reduce, convert, or melt down (fat) by heating. **12.** To coat (brick, for example) with plaster or cement. **—render** *n.* A payment in kind, services, or cash from a tenant to a feudal lord. [Middle English *rendren,* from Old French *rendre,* to give back, from Vulgar Latin **rendere,* alteration of Latin *reddere* (influenced by *prēndere,* to grasp) : *red-, re-,* re- + *dare,* to give; see **dō-** in Appendix.] **—ren′der•a•ble** *adj.* **—ren′der•er** *n.*

ren•der•ing (rĕn′dər-ĭng) *n.* **1.** A depiction or an interpretation, as in painting or music. **2.** A drawing in perspective of a proposed structure. **3.** A translation: *a rendering of Cicero's treatises into English.* **4.** A coat of plaster or cement applied to a masonry surface.

ren•dez•vous (rän′dā-vo͞o′, -də-) *n., pl.* **ren•dez•vous** (-vo͞oz′). **1.** A meeting at a prearranged time and place. See Synonyms at **engagement. 2.** A prearranged meeting place, especially an assembly point for troops or ships. **3.** A popular gathering place: *The café is a favorite rendezvous for artists.* **4.** *Aerospace.* The process of bringing two spacecraft together. **—rendezvous** *tr. & intr.v.* **-voused** (-vo͞od′), **-vous•ing** (-vo͞o′ĭng), **-vous** (-vo͞oz′). To cause to assemble or to assemble at a prearranged time and place. [French, from the phrase *rendez vous,* present yourselves, from Old French : *rendez,* second person pl. imperative of *rendre,* to present; see RENDER + *vous,* yourselves, you (from Latin *vōs,* you; see **wōs** in Appendix).]

WORD HISTORY: A word that refers to the process of bringing two spacecraft together and to a meeting between lovers might be thought to have a source having to do with connection. The history of *rendezvous,* however, had originally to do with the process of getting to a meeting place. The French word *rendezvous,* which English borrowed, is made up of the second person plural imperative of the verb *rendre,* meaning in this case "to present or betake," and *vous,* the second person plural reflexive pronoun meaning "yourselves." The word *rendezvous* in French denoted the place at which you were supposed to present yourselves or the meeting you were to attend. The first recorded use of the word in English (1591) is for a place where troops are to assemble.

ren•di•tion (rĕn-dĭsh′ən) *n.* **1.** The act of rendering. **2.** An interpretation of a musical score or a dramatic piece. **3.** A performance of a musical or dramatic work. **4.** A translation, often interpretive. **5.** A surrender. [Obsolete French, from Old French *rendre,* to give back. See RENDER.]

ren•dzi•na (rĕn-jē′nə) *n.* A dark soil that develops under grass on limestone and chalk. [Polish *rędzina.*]

ren•e•gade (rĕn′ĭ-gād′) *n.* **1.** One who rejects a religion, a cause, an allegiance, or a group for another; a deserter. **2.** An outlaw; a rebel. **—renegade** *adj.* Of, relating to, or resembling a renegade; traitorous. **—renegade** *intr.v.* **-gad•ed, -gad•ing, -gades.** To become a deserter or an outlaw. [Spanish *renegado,* from Medieval Latin *renegātus,* past participle of *renegāre,* to deny : Latin *re-,* re- + Latin *negāre,* to deny; see **ne** in Appendix.]

re•nege (rĭ-nĭg′, -nĕg′, -nēg′) *v.* **-neged, -neg•ing, -neges.** *—intr.* **1.** To fail to carry out a promise or commitment: *reneged on the contract at the last minute.* **2.** *Games.* To fail to follow suit in cards when able and required by the rules to do so. *—tr.* To renounce; disown. **—renege** *n.* The act of reneging. [Medieval Latin *renegāre,* to deny. See RENEGADE.] **—re•neg′er** *n.*

re•ne•go•ti•ate (rē′nĭ-gō′shē-āt′) *tr.v.* **-at•ed, -at•ing, -ates. 1.** To negotiate anew. **2.** To revise the terms of (a contract) so as to limit or regain excess profits gained by the contractor. **—re′ne•go′ti•a•ble** (-shē-ə-bəl, -shə-bəl) *adj.* **—re′ne•go•ti•a′tion** *n.*

re•new (rĭ-no͞o′, -nyo͞o′) *v.* **-newed, -new•ing, -news.** *—tr.* **1.** To make new or as if new again; restore: *renewed the antique chair.* **2.** To take up again; resume: *renew an old friendship; renewed the argument.* **3.** To repeat so as to reaffirm: *renew a promise.* **4.** To regain or restore the physical or mental vigor of; revive: *I renewed my spirits in the country air.* **5. a.** To arrange for the extension of: *renew a contract; renew a magazine subscription.* **b.** To arrange to extend the loan of: *renewed the library books before they were overdue.* **6.** To replenish: *renewed the water in the humidifier.* **7.** To bring into being again; reestablish. *—intr.* **1.** To become new again. **2.** To start over. [Middle English *renewen* : *re-,* re- + *newen,* to renew (from *new,* new; see NEW).] **—re•new′er** *n.*

re•new•a•ble (rĭ-no͞o′ə-bəl, -nyo͞o′-) *adj.* **1.** That can be renewed: *a renewable membership; renewable subscriptions.* **2.** Designating a commodity or resource, such as solar energy or firewood, that is inexhaustible or replaceable by new growth. **—re•new′a•bil′i•ty** (-bĭl′ĭ-tē) *n.* **—re•new′a•bly** *adv.*

re•new•al (rĭ-no͞o′əl, -nyo͞o′-) *n.* **1.** The act of renewing or the state of having been renewed. **2.** Something renewed.

re•new•ed•ly (rĭ-no͞o′ĭd-lē, -nyo͞o′-) *adv.* Over again; anew.

Re•ni (rā′nē), **Guido.** 1575–1642. Italian painter whose lyrical, idealistic works include the *Crucifixion of Saint Peter* (1603) and the *Aurora* fresco (1613–1614).

ren•i•form (rĕn′ə-fôrm′, rē′nə-) *adj.* Shaped like a kidney: *a reniform leaf.* [Latin *rēnēs,* kidneys + –FORM.]

ren•in (rĕn′ĭn) *n.* A protein-digesting enzyme that is released by the kidney and acts to raise blood pressure by activating angiotensin. [Latin *rēnēs,* kidneys + –IN.]

ren•i•tent (rĕn′ĭ-tənt, rĭ-nīt′nt) *adj.* **1.** Resistant to physical pressure; not pliant. **2.** Reluctant to yield or be swayed; recalcitrant. [Latin *renītēns, renītent-,* present participle of *renītī,* to resist : *re-,* re- + *nītī,* to press forward.] **—ren′i•tence, ren′i•ten•cy** *n.*

Ren•ner (rĕn′ər), **Karl.** 1870–1950. Austrian politician who was chancellor of the Austrian Republic (1918–1920) and president of Austria from 1945 until his death.

Rennes (rĕn). A city of northwest France north of Nantes. It was an important Gallo-Roman town and became capital of Brittany in 1196. Population, 117,234.

ren•net (rĕn′ĭt) *n.* **1.** The inner lining of the fourth stomach of calves and other young ruminants. **2.** A dried extract made from the stomach lining of a ruminant, used in cheesemaking to curdle milk. **3.** See **rennin.** [Middle English, probably from Old English **rynet.* See **rei-** in Appendix.]

ren•nin (rĕn′ĭn) *n.* A milk-coagulating enzyme found in the gastric juice of the fourth stomach of young ruminants, used in making cheeses and junkets. Also called *chymosin, rennet.* [REN-N(ET) + –IN.]

ren•nin•o•gen (rĕ-nĭn′ə-jən) *n.* The zymogenic precursor of rennin.

Re•no (rē′nō′). A city of western Nevada near the California border. Developed after the coming of the Union Pacific Railroad in 1868, it is a famous resort that was once noted primarily as a divorce center. Population, 100,756.

re•no•gram (rē′nə-grăm′) *n.* **1.** A graphic record of the passage of radiation through the renal system after injection of a radioactive tracer. **2.** A radiograph of a kidney. [Latin *rēnēs,* kidneys + –GRAM.] **—re′nog′ra•phy** (rē-nŏg′rə-fē) *n.*

Ren•oir (rĕn′wär′, rən-wär′), **Jean.** 1894–1979. French filmmaker who won acclaim for the artistry of films such as *La Grande Illusion* (1937) and *Rules of the Game* (1939).

Renoir, Pierre Auguste. 1841–1919. French impressionist painter whose warm, luminous works include *Child with Watering Can* (1876) and *Luncheon of the Boating Party* (1881).

re•nom•i•nate (rē-nŏm′ə-nāt′) *tr.v.* **-nat•ed, -nat•ing, -nates.** To nominate again, especially for a subsequent term. **—re′nom•i•na′tion** *n.*

re•nor•mal•ize (rē-nôr′mə-līz′) *tr.v.* **-ized, -iz•ing, -iz•es.** To bring into a normal or more normal state once again. **—re•nor′mal•i•za′tion** (-mə-lĭ-zā′shən) *n.*

re•nounce (rĭ-nouns′) *v.* **-nounced, -nounc•ing, -nounc•es.** —*tr.* **1.** To give up (a title, for example), especially by formal announcment. See Synonyms at **relinquish. 2.** To reject; disown. —*intr. Games.* To revoke in cards. **—renounce** *n. Games.* A revoke in cards. [Middle English *renouncen,* from Old French *renoncer,* from Latin *renūntiāre,* to report : *re-,* re- + *nūntiāre,* to announce (from *nūntius,* messenger; see **neu-** in Appendix).] **—re•nounce′ment** *n.* **—re•nounc′er** *n.*

ren•o•vate (rĕn′ə-vāt′) *tr.v.* **-vat•ed, -vat•ing, -vates. 1.** To restore to an earlier condition, as by repairing or remodeling. **2.** To impart new vigor to; revive. [Latin *renovāre, renovāt-* : *re-,* re- + *novāre,* to make new (from *novus,* new; see **newo-** in Appendix).] **—ren′o•va′tion** *n.* **—ren′o•va′tor** *n.*

re•nown (rĭ-noun′) *n.* **1.** The quality of being widely honored and acclaimed; fame. **2.** *Obsolete.* Report; rumor. [Middle English *renoun,* from Anglo-Norman, from *renomer,* to make famous : *re-,* repeatedly (from Latin; see RE–) + *nomer,* to name (from Latin *nōmināre,* from *nōmen, nōmin-,* name; see **nō-men-** in Appendix).]

re•nowned (rĭ-nound′) *adj.* Having renown; famous. See Synonyms at **noted.**

rent¹ (rĕnt) *n.* **1.a.** Payment, usually of an amount fixed by contract, made by a tenant at specified intervals in return for the right to occupy or use the property of another. **b.** A similar payment made for the use of a facility, equipment, or service provided by another. **2.** The return derived from cultivated or improved land after deduction of all production costs. **3.** The revenue yielded by a piece of land in excess of that yielded by the poorest or least favorably located land under equal market conditions. In this sense, also called *economic rent.* **—rent** *v.* **rent•ed, rent•ing, rents.** —*tr.* **1.** To obtain occupancy or use of (another's property) in return for regular payments. **2.** To grant temporary occupancy or use of (one's own property or a service) in return for regular payments: *rents out TV sets.* —*intr.* To be for rent: *The cottage rents for $200 a month.* **—*idiom.* for rent.** Available for use or service in return for payment. [Middle English *rente,* from Old French, from Vulgar Latin **rendita,* from feminine past participle of **rendere,* to yield, return. See RENDER.] **—rent′a•bil′i•ty** *n.* **—rent′a•ble** *adj.*

rent² (rĕnt) *v.* A past tense and a past participle of **rend. —rent** *n.* **1.** An opening made by rending; a rip. **2.** A breach of relations between persons or groups; a rift.

rent-a-car (rĕnt′ə-kär′) *n.* **1.** A rented car. **2.** An agency that offers cars and vans for rent.

rent•al (rĕn′tl) *n.* **1.** An amount paid out or taken in as rent. **2.** Property available for renting: *summer rentals by the beach.* **3.** The act of renting. **4.** An agency that rents something. **5.** A list of tenants and schedule of rents. In this sense, also called *rent-roll.* **—rental** *adj.* Of, relating to, or available for rent: *rental income; rental properties.*

rent control *n.* Governmental control and regulation of the amounts charged for rented housing.

rent•er (rĕn′tər) *n.* **1.** One that receives payment in exchange for the use of one's property by another. **2.** One that pays rent for the use of another's property; a tenant.

rent-free (rĕnt′frē′) *adj.* Not being subject to rent. **—rent-free** *adv.* Not having to pay or not paying rent.

Ren•ton (rĕn′tən). A city of west-central Washington, a suburb of Seattle. It has an extensive aircraft industry. Population, 30,612.

rent-roll (rĕnt′rōl′) *n.* See **rental** (sense 5).

rent strike *n.* An agreement among tenants to refuse to pay rent, often in protest of poor services.

re•num•ber (rē-nŭm′bər) *tr.v.* **-bered, -ber•ing, -bers.** To number again or in a different order.

re•nun•ci•a•tion (rĭ-nŭn′sē-ā′shən) *n.* **1.** The act or an instance of renouncing: *the renunciation of all earthly pleasures.* **2.** A declaration in which something is renounced. [Middle English, from Anglo-Norman *renunciacion,* from Latin *renūntiātiō, renūntiātiōn-,* from *renūntiātus,* past participle of *renūntiāre,* to renounce. See RENOUNCE.] **—re•nun′ci•a′tive, re•nun′ci•a•to′ry** (-ə-tôr′ē, -tōr′ē) *adj.*

Ren•wick (rĕn′wĭk), **James.** 1818–1895. American architect who designed the Smithsonian Institution in Washington, D.C. (1848), and Saint Patrick's Cathedral in New York City (1853).

re•o•pen (rē-ō′pən) *tr. & intr.v.* **-pened, -pen•ing, -pens. 1.** To open or be opened again: *Officials reopened the airport after the snow was cleared. Schools reopen in September.* **2.** To take up again or be taken up again; resume.

re•or•der (rē-ôr′dər) *v.* **-dered, -der•ing, -ders.** —*tr.* **1.** To order (the same goods) again. **2.** To straighten out or put in order again. **3.** To rearrange. —*intr.* To order the same goods again. **—reorder** *n.* A further order of goods from the same supplier.

re•or•gan•i•za•tion (rē-ôr′gə-nĭ-zā′shən) *n.* **1.** The act or process of organizing again or differently. **2.** A thorough alteration of the structure of a business corporation. **—re•or′gan•i•za′tion•al** *adj.*

re•or•gan•ize (rē-ôr′gə-nīz′) *v.* **-ized, -iz•ing, -iz•es.** —*tr.* To organize again or anew. —*intr.* To undergo or effect changes in organization. **—re•or′gan•iz′er** *n.*

re•o•vi•rus (rē′ō-vī′rəs) *n., pl.* **-rus•es.** Any of a group of viruses that contain double-stranded RNA and are associated with various diseases in animals, including human respiratory and gastrointestinal infections. [R(ESPIRATORY) + E(NTERIC) + O(RPHAN) + VIRUS.]

rep¹ also **repp** (rĕp) *n.* A ribbed or corded fabric of various materials, such as cotton, wool, or silk. [Alteration of French *reps,* from English *ribs,* pl. of RIB.]

rep² (rĕp) *n. Informal.* A representative.

rep³ (rĕp) *n. Physics.* A unit of absorbed radiation dose, equal to the amount of ionizing radiation that will transfer 93 ergs of energy to 1 gram of water or living tissue. [R(OENTGEN) + E(QUIVALENT) + P(HYSICAL).]

rep⁴ (rĕp) *n. Informal.* **1.** A repertory company. **2.** A repertory theater.

rep⁵ (rĕp) *n. Informal.* Reputation: *"Modern British royalty began with Queen Victoria, who still has a bad rep for being stodgy, straitlaced and—well, Victorian"* (Anthony Holden).

rep. *abbr.* **1.** Repair. **2.** Repetition. **3.** Report. **4.** Reporter. **5.** Or **Rep.** Representative. **6.** Reprint. **7.** Or **Rep.** Republic.

Rep. *abbr.* Republican.

re•pack•age (rē-păk′ĭj) *tr.v.* **-aged, -ag•ing, -ag•es.** To package again or anew, especially in a more attractive package. **—re•pack′ag•er** *n.*

re•paid (rĭ-pād′) *v.* Past tense and past participle of **repay.**

re•pair¹ (rĭ-pâr′) *v.* **-paired, -pair•ing, -pairs.** —*tr.* **1.** To restore to sound condition after damage or injury; fix: *repaired the broken watch.* **2.** To set right; remedy: *repair an oversight.* **3.** To renew or revitalize. **4.** To make up for or compensate for (a loss or wrong, for example). —*intr.* To make repairs. **—repair** *n. Abbr.* **rep. 1.a.** The work, act, or process of repairing. **b.** An instance of repairing. **2.** General condition after use or repairing: *in good repair.* **3.** Something that has been repaired. [Middle English *reparen, repairen,* from Old French *reparer,* from Latin *reparāre* : *re-,* re- + *parāre,* to prepare, put in order; see **perə-¹** in Appendix.] **—re•pair′a•bil′i•ty** *n.* **—re•pair′a•ble** *adj.* **—re•pair′a•bly** *adv.* **—re•pair′er** *n.*

re•pair² (rĭ-pâr′) *intr.v.* **-paired, -pair•ing, -pairs. 1.** To betake oneself; go: *repair to the dining room.* **2.** To go frequently or habitually: *repairs to the restaurant every week.* **—repair** *n.* **1.** An act of going or sojourning: *our annual repair to the mountains.* **2.** A place to which one goes frequently or habitually; a haunt. [Middle English *repairen,* to return, from Old French *repairier,* from Late Latin *repatriāre,* to return to one's country. See REPATRIATE.]

re•pair•man (rĭ-pâr′măn′, -mən) *n.* A man whose occupation is making repairs.

re•pair•per•son (rĭ-pâr′pûr′sən) *n., pl.* **-per•sons** or **-peo•ple** (-pē′pəl). A repairman or repairwoman.

re•pair•wom•an (rĭ-pâr′wo͝om′ən) *n.* A woman whose occupation is making repairs.

re•pand (rĭ-pănd′) *adj. Botany.* Having a somewhat wavy margin: *a repand leaf.* [Latin *repandus,* bent backward : *re-,* re- + *pandus,* past participle of *pandere,* to spread out; see **petə-** in Appendix.]

rep•a•ra•ble (rĕp′ər-ə-bəl) *adj.* Possible to repair: *reparable damage to the car; reparable wrongs.* [French *réparable,* from Latin *reparābilis,* from *reparāre,* to repair. See REPAIR¹.] **—rep′a•ra•bil′i•ty** *n.* **—rep′a•ra•bly** *adv.*

rep•a•ra•tion (rĕp′ə-rā′shən) *n.* **1.** The act or process of repairing or the condition of being repaired. **2.** The act or process of making amends; expiation. **3.** Something done or paid to compensate or make amends. **4. reparations.** Compensation or remuneration required from a defeated nation as indemnity for damage or injury during a war. [Middle English *reparacion,* from Old French, from Late Latin *reparātiō, reparātiōn-,* restoration, from Latin *reparātus,* past participle of *reparāre,* to repair. See REPAIR¹.]

SYNONYMS: *reparation, redress, amends, restitution, indemnity.* All of these nouns refer to something given in compensation for loss, suffering, or damage. *Reparation* implies recompense given to one who has suffered injury, harm, or wrong at the hands of another: *"reparation for our rights at home, and security against the like future violations"* (William Pitt). *Redress* involves setting right what is wrong or providing relief from injustice; the term may imply retaliation or punishment: *"The people, whose privileges he has invaded, call aloud for redress"* (Jane Porter). *"There is no grievance that is a fit object of redress by mob law"* (Abraham Lincoln). *Amends,* less forceful than *redress,* usually implies the giving of satisfaction for a minor grievance or lesser injury: *How can I make amends for losing my temper? Restitution* is the restoration of something taken illegally or its equivalent: *"He attempted to enforce the restitution of the Roman lands and cities"* (George P.R. James). *Indemnity* implies reimbursement for loss or damage sustained: *The innocent victims of the riot demanded indemnity for the lawless violence to which they had been subjected.*

re•par•a•tive (rĭ-păr′ə-tĭv) also **re•par•a•to•ry** (-tôr′ē, -tōr′ē) *adj.* **1.** Tending to repair. **2.** Of, relating to, or of the nature of reparations.

rep•ar•tee (rĕp′ər-tē′, -tā′, -är-) *n.* **1.** A swift, witty reply. **2.** Conversation marked by the exchange of witty retorts. See Synonyms at **wit¹.** [French *repartie,* from feminine past participle of *repartir,* to retort, from Old French, to retort, to depart again : *re-,* re- + *partir,* to depart (from Latin *partīre,* to divide, from *pars, part-,* part; see **perə-²** in Appendix).]

ă pat	oi boy
ā pay	ou out
âr care	o͝o took
ä father	o͞o boot
ĕ pet	ŭ cut
ē be	ûr urge
ĭ pit	th thin
ī pie	*th* this
îr pier	hw which
ŏ pot	zh vision
ō toe	ə about, item
ô paw	♦ regionalism

Stress marks: **′** (primary); ′ (secondary), as in **dictionary** (dĭk′shə-nĕr′ē)

re·par·ti·tion (rē′pär-tĭsh′ən) *n.* **1.** Distribution; apportionment. **2.** A partitioning again or in a different way. **—repartition** *tr.v.* **-tioned, -tion·ing, -tions.** To partition again; redivide.

re·pass (rē-păs′) *v.* **-passed, -pass·ing, -pass·es.** *—tr.* **1.** To pass (something) again. **2.** To cause to pass again in the opposite direction. *—intr.* To pass again; go by again. **—re·pas′sage** (-ĭj) *n.*

re·past (rĭ-păst′) *n.* A meal or the food eaten or provided at a meal. **—repast** *v.* **-past·ed, -past·ing, -pasts.** *—intr.* To eat or feast. *—tr. Obsolete.* To give food to. [Middle English, from Old French, from Late Latin *repāstus,* from past participle of *repāscere,* to feed : *re-,* re- + Latin *pāscere,* to feed; see **pā-** in Appendix.]

re·pa·tri·ate (rē-pā′trē-āt′) *tr.v.* **-at·ed, -at·ing, -ates.** To restore or return to the country of birth, citizenship, or origin: *repatriate war refugees.* **—repatriate** (-ĭt, -āt′) *n.* One who has been repatriated. [Late Latin *repatriāre, repatriāt-,* to return to one's country : *re-,* re- + *patria,* native country; see EXPATRIATE.] **—re·pa′tri·a′tion** *n.*

re·pay (rĭ-pā′) *v.* **-paid** (-pād′), **-pay·ing, -pays.** *—tr.* **1.** To pay back: *repaid a debt.* **2.** To give back, either in return or in compensation: *repay kindness with kindness.* **3.** To make a return or compensation for: *a company that repays hard work with bonuses.* **4.** To make or do in return: *repay a call.* *—intr.* To make repayment or requital. **—re·pay′a·ble** *adj.* **—re·pay′ment** *n.*

re·peal (rĭ-pēl′) *tr.v.* **-pealed, -peal·ing, -peals.** **1.** To revoke or rescind, especially by an official or formal act. **2.** *Obsolete.* To summon back or recall, especially from exile. **—repeal** *n.* The act or process of repealing. [Middle English *repelen, repealen,* from Anglo-Norman *repeler,* alteration of Old French *rapeler* : *re-,* re- + *apeler,* to appeal; see APPEAL.] **—re·peal′a·ble** *adj.* **—re·peal′er** *n.*

re·peat (rĭ-pēt′) *v.* **-peat·ed, -peat·ing, -peats.** *—tr.* **1.** To say again: *repeat a question.* **2.** To utter in duplication of another's utterance. **3.** To recite from memory. **4.** To tell to another. **5.** To do, experience, or produce again: *repeat past successes.* **6.** To express (oneself) in the same way or words: *repeats himself constantly.* *—intr.* **1.** To do or say something again. **2.** To commit the fraudulent offense of voting more than once in a single election. **—repeat** *n. Abbr.* **rpt. 1.** An act of repeating. **2.** Something repeated: *a repeat of a television program.* **3.** *Music.* **a.** A passage or section that is repeated. **b.** A sign usually consisting of two vertical dots, indicating a passage to be repeated. **—repeat** *adj.* Of, relating to, or being something that repeats or is repeated: *a repeat offender; a repeat performance of the play.* [Middle English *repeten,* from Old French *repeter,* from Latin *repetere,* to seek again : *re-,* re- + *petere,* to seek; see **pet-** in Appendix.] **—re·peat′a·bil′i·ty** *n.* **—re·peat′a·ble** *adj.*

SYNONYMS: *repeat, iterate, reiterate, restate.* The central meaning shared by these verbs is "to state again": *repeated the warning; iterate a demand; reiterating a question; restated the obvious.*

re·peat·ed (rĭ-pē′tĭd) *adj.* Said, done, or occurring again and again: *We heard repeated knocks on the door.*

re·peat·ed·ly (rĭ-pē′tĭd-lē) *adv.* More than once; again and again.

re·peat·er (rĭ-pē′tər) *n.* **1.** One that repeats: "[The] *tourists are mainly repeaters from the United States and Canada who come for the peace and quiet"* (James Kerr). **2.** A watch or clock with a pressure-activated mechanism that strikes the hour. **3.** A repeating firearm. **4.** A student who repeats a course, usually one that has been failed. **5.** One who fraudulently votes more than once in a single election. **6.** One who has been convicted of wrongdoing more than once, especially for the same offense.

re·peat·ing decimal (rĭ-pē′tĭng) *n. Mathematics.* A decimal in which a pattern of one or more digits is repeated indefinitely, for example, 0.3333 . . . Also called *circulating decimal, recurring decimal.*

repeating firearm *n.* A firearm capable of firing several times without being reloaded.

re·pel (rĭ-pĕl′) *v.* **-pelled, -pel·ling, -pels.** *—tr.* **1.** To ward off or keep away; drive back: *repel insects.* **2.** To offer resistance to; fight against: *repel an invasion.* **3.** To refuse to accept; reject: *a company that was trying to repel a hostile takeover.* **4.** To turn away from; spurn. **5.** To cause aversion or distaste in: *Her rudeness repels everyone.* See Synonyms at **disgust.** See Usage Note at **repulse. 6.** To be resistant to; be incapable of absorbing or mixing with: *Oil repels water.* **7.** *Physics.* To present an opposing force to; push back or away by a force: *Electric charges of the same sign repel one another.* *—intr.* **1.** To offer a resistant force to something. **2.** To cause aversion or distaste: *behavior that repels.* [Middle English *repellen,* from Old French *repeller,* from Latin *repellere* : *re-,* re- + *pellere,* to drive; see **pel-**[5] in Appendix.] **—re·pel′ler** *n.*

re·pel·lent also **re·pel·lant** (rĭ-pĕl′ənt) *—adj.* **1. a.** Serving or tending to repel. **b.** Able to repel. **2.** Inspiring aversion or distaste; repulsive. See Synonyms at **hateful, offensive. 3.** Resistant or impervious to a substance. Often used in combination: *a water-repellent fabric.* *—n.* **1.** One that repels. **2. a.** A substance used to repel insects. **b.** A substance or treatment for making a fabric or surface impervious or resistant to something else. **—re·pel′lence, re·pel′len·cy** *n.* **—re·pel′lent·ly** *adv.*

re·pent[1] (rĭ-pĕnt′) *v.* **-pent·ed, -pent·ing, -pents.** *—intr.* **1.** To feel remorse, contrition, or self-reproach for what one has done or failed to do; be contrite. **2.** To feel such regret for past conduct as to change one's mind regarding it: *repented of intemperate behavior.* **3.** To make a change for the better as a result of remorse or contrition for one's sins. *—tr.* **1.** To feel regret or self-reproach for: *repent one's sins.* **2.** To cause to feel remorse or regret. [Middle English *repenten,* from Old French *repentir* : *re-,* re- + *pentir,* to be sorry (from Vulgar Latin **paenitīre,* from Latin *paenitēre*).] **—re·pent′er** *n.*

re·pent[2] (rē′pənt) *adj. Biology.* Creeping along the ground; prostrate. [Latin *rēpēns, rēpent-,* present participle of *rēpere,* to creep.]

re·pen·tance (rĭ-pĕn′təns) *n.* **1.** The act or process of repenting. **2.** Remorse or contrition for past conduct or sin. See Synonyms at **penitence.**

re·pen·tant (rĭ-pĕn′tənt) *adj.* Characterized by or demonstrating repentance; penitent. **—re·pen′tant·ly** *adv.*

Re·pen·ti·gny (rə-päɴ-tē-nyē′). A town of southern Quebec, Canada, a residential suburb of Montreal. Population, 34,419.

re·per·cus·sion (rē′pər-kŭsh′ən, rĕp′ər-) *n.* **1.** An often indirect effect, influence, or result that is produced by an event or action. See Synonyms at **impact. 2.** A recoil, rebounding, or reciprocal motion after impact. **3.** A reflection, especially of sound. [Middle English *repercussioun,* from Old French *repercussion,* from Latin *repercussiō, repercussiōn-,* from *repercussus,* past participle of *repercutere,* to cause to rebound : *re-,* re- + *percutere,* to strike; see PERCUSS.] **—re′per·cus′sive** *adj.*

rep·er·toire (rĕp′ər-twär′) *n.* **1.** The stock of songs, plays, operas, readings, or other pieces that a player or company is prepared to perform. **2.** The range or number of skills, aptitudes, or special accomplishments of a particular person or group. [French *répertoire,* from Old French, from Late Latin *repertōrium.* See REPERTORY.]

rep·er·to·ry (rĕp′ər-tôr′ē, -tōr′ē) *n., pl.* **-ries. 1.** A repertoire. **2. a.** A theater in which a resident company presents works from a specified repertoire, usually in alternation. **b.** A repertory company. **3. a.** A place, such as a storehouse, where a stock of things is kept; a repository. **b.** Something stored in or as if in such a place; a stock or collection. [Late Latin *repertōrium,* from Latin *repertus,* past participle of *reperīre,* to find out : *re-,* re- + *parīre,* to get, beget; see **perə-**[1] in Appendix.] **—rep′er·to′ri·al** *adj.*

repertory company *n.* A company that presents and performs a number of different plays or other works during a season, usually in alternation.

rep·e·tend (rĕp′ĭ-tĕnd′, rĕp′ĭ-tĕnd′) *n.* **1.** A word, sound, or phrase that is repeated; a refrain. **2.** *Mathematics.* The digit or group of digits that repeats infinitely in a repeating decimal. [From Latin *repetendum,* neuter gerundive of *repetere,* to repeat. See REPEAT.]

rep·e·ti·tion (rĕp′ĭ-tĭsh′ən) *n. Abbr.* **rep. 1.** The act or process or an instance of repeating or being repeated. **2.** A recitation or recital, especially of prepared or memorized material. [Middle English *repeticioun,* from Old French *repeticion,* from Latin *repetītiō, repetītiōn-,* from *repetītus,* past participle of *repetere,* to repeat. See REPEAT.] **—rep′e·ti′tion·al** *adj.*

rep·e·ti·tious (rĕp′ĭ-tĭsh′əs) *adj.* Filled with repetition, especially needless or tedious repetition. **—rep′e·ti′tious·ly** *adv.* **—rep′e·ti′tious·ness** *n.*

re·pet·i·tive (rĭ-pĕt′ĭ-tĭv) *adj.* Given to or characterized by repetition. **—re·pet′i·tive·ly** *adv.* **—re·pet′i·tive·ness** *n.*

re·phrase (rē-frāz′) *tr.v.* **-phrased, -phras·ing, -phras·es.** To phrase again, especially to state in a new, clearer, or different way.

re·pine (rĭ-pīn′) *intr.v.* **-pined, -pin·ing, -pines. 1.** To be discontented or low in spirits; complain or fret. **2.** To yearn after something: *Immigrants who repined for their homeland.* [Middle English *repinen,* to be aggrieved : *re-,* re- + *pinen,* to yearn; see PINE[2].] **—re·pin′er** *n.*

repl. *abbr.* Replace; replacement.

re·place (rĭ-plās′) *tr.v.* **-placed, -plac·ing, -plac·es.** *Abbr.* **repl. 1.** To put back into a former position or place. **2.** To take or fill the place of. **3.** To be or provide a substitute for. **4.** To pay back or return; refund. **—re·place′a·ble** *adj.* **—re·plac′er** *n.*

SYNONYMS: *replace, supplant, supersede.* These verbs are compared as they mean to turn someone or something out and place another in his, her, or its stead. To *replace* is to be or furnish an equivalent or a substitute in the place of another, especially another that has been lost, depleted, worn out, or discharged: *"A conspiracy was carefully engineered to replace the Directory by three Consuls"* (H.G. Wells). *"I succeed him* [Benjamin Franklin, as envoy to France]*; no one could replace him"* (Thomas Jefferson). *Supplant* often suggests the use of intrigue or underhanded tactics to take another's place: *"The rivaling poor Jones, and supplanting him in her affections, added another spur to his pursuit"* (Henry Fielding). The term does not, however, invariably have this connotation: *"The steam engine began to supplant the muscular power of men and animals"* (James Harvey Robinson). To *supersede* is to replace one person or thing by another held to be superior, more valuable or useful, or less antiquated: *"In our island* *the Latin appears never to have superseded the old Gaelic speech"* (Macaulay). *"Each of us carries his own life-form—an indeterminable form which cannot be superseded by any other"* (Carl Jung).

---

re·place·ment (rĭ-plās′mənt) *n.* *Abbr.* **repl.** **1.** The act or process of replacing or of being replaced; substitution. **2.** One that replaces, especially a person assigned to a vacant military position.

replacement therapy *n.* Administration of a body substance to compensate for the loss, as from disease or surgery, of a gland or tissue that would normally produce the substance.

re·plant (rē-plănt′) *tr.v.* **-plant·ed, -plant·ing, -plants. 1.** To plant (something) again or in a new place: *separated and replanted the perennials.* **2.** To supply with new plants: *replant a window box.* **3.** To reattach (an organ or limbs, for example) surgically to the original site. **—replant** (rē′plănt′) *n.* Something replanted. **—re′plan·ta′tion** *n.*

re·play (rē-plā′) *tr.v.* **-played, -play·ing, -plays.** To play over again: *replay a tennis match; replay a tape; replay history.* **—replay** (rē′plā′) *n.* **1.** The act or process of replaying. **2.** Something replayed. **3.** An instant replay.

re·plen·ish (rĭ-plĕn′ĭsh) *v.* **-ished, -ish·ing, -ish·es.** *—tr.* **1.** To fill or make complete again; add a new stock or supply to: *replenish the larder.* **2.** To inspire or nourish: *The music will replenish my weary soul.* *—intr.* To become full again. [Middle English *replenisshen,* from Old French *replenir, repleniss-* : *re-,* re- + *plenir,* to fill (from *plein,* full, from Latin *plēnus;* see **pelə-[1]** in Appendix).] **—re·plen′ish·er** *n.* **—re·plen′ish·ment** *n.*

re·plete (rĭ-plēt′) *adj.* **1.** Abundantly supplied; abounding: *a stream replete with trout; an apartment replete with Empire furniture.* **2.** Filled to satiation; gorged. **3.** *Usage Problem.* Complete: *a computer system replete with color monitor, printer, and software.* [Middle English, from Old French, from Latin *replētus,* past participle of *replēre,* to refill : *re-,* re- + *plēre,* to fill; see **pelə-[1]** in Appendix.] **—re·plete′ness** *n.*

USAGE NOTE: *Replete* means "abundantly supplied" and is not generally accepted as a synonym for *complete.*

---

re·ple·tion (rĭ-plē′shən) *n.* **1.** The condition of being fully supplied or completely filled. **2.** A state of excessive fullness.

re·plev·i·a·ble (rĭ-plĕv′ē-ə-bəl) *adj.* *Law.* Recoverable by replevin: *repleviable property.*

re·plev·in (rĭ-plĕv′ĭn) *Law. n.* **1.** An action to recover personal property said or claimed to be unlawfully taken. **2.** The writ or procedure of such an action. **—replevin** *tr.v.* **-ined, -in·ing, -ines.** To replevy. [Middle English, from Anglo-Norman *replevine,* from *replevir,* to give as a security : *re-,* re- + *plevir,* to pledge (from Late Latin *plebere,* of Germanic origin).]

re·plev·y (rĭ-plĕv′ē) *Law. tr.v.* **-ied, -y·ing, -ies.** To regain possession of by a writ of replevin. **—replevy** *n., pl.* **-ies.** A replevin. [Anglo-Norman *replevir.* See REPLEVIN.]

rep·li·ca (rĕp′lĭ-kə) *n.* **1.** A copy or reproduction of a work of art, especially one made by the original artist. **2.** A copy or reproduction, especially one on a scale smaller than the original. [Italian, from *replicare,* to repeat, from Late Latin *replicāre,* from Latin, to fold back. See REPLICATE.]

rep·li·case (rĕp′lĭ-kās′, -kāz′) *n.* An enzyme that promotes the synthesis of a complementary RNA molecule from an RNA template. [REPLIC(ATE) + –ASE.]

rep·li·cate (rĕp′lĭ-kāt′) *v.* **-cat·ed, -cat·ing, -cates.** *—tr.* **1.** To duplicate, copy, reproduce, or repeat. **2.** *Biology.* To reproduce or make an exact copy or copies of (genetic material, a cell, or an organism). **3.** To fold over or bend back. *—intr.* To become replicated; undergo replication. **—replicate** (-kĭt) also **rep·li·cat·ed** (-kā′tĭd) *adj.* Folded over or bent back upon itself: *a replicate leaf.* **—replicate** (-kĭt)*n.* A repetition of an experiment or a procedure. [Middle English *replicaten,* from Late Latin *replicāre, replicāt-,* to repeat, from Latin, to fold back : *re-,* re- + *plicāre,* to fold; see **plek-** in Appendix.] **—rep′li·ca′tive** *adj.*

rep·li·ca·tion (rĕp′lĭ-kā′shən) *n.* **1.** A fold or a folding back. **2.** A reply to an answer; a rejoinder. **3.** *Law.* The plaintiff's response to the defendant's answer or plea. **4.** An echo or a reverberation. **5.** A copy or reproduction. **6.** The act or process of duplicating or reproducing something. **7.** *Biology.* The act or process by which genetic material, a cell, or an organism reproduces or makes an exact copy of itself.

rep·li·con (rĕp′lĭ-kŏn′) *n.* A genetic element that undergoes replication as an autonomous unit. [REPLIC(ATION) + –ON[1].]

re·ply (rĭ-plī′) *v.* **-plied, -ply·ing, -plies.** *—intr.* **1.** To give an answer in speech or writing. **2.** To respond by an action or a gesture. **3.** To echo. **4.** To return gunfire or an attack: *The big guns replied.* **5.** *Law.* To respond to a defendant's plea. *—tr.* To say or give as an answer: *I replied that I was unable to help them.* See Synonyms at **answer. —reply** *n., pl.* **-plies. 1.** A response in speech or writing. **2.** A response by action or gesture. **3.** *Law.* A plaintiff's formal response in answer to that of a defendant. [Middle English *replien,* from Old French *replier,* from Latin *replicāre,* to fold back. See REPLICATE.] **—re·pli′er** *n.*

re·po[1] (rē′pō′) *n., pl.* **-pos.** *Informal.* A repurchase agreement. [Shortening and alteration of REPURCHASE AGREEMENT.]

re·po[2] (rē′pō′) *n., pl.* **-pos.** *Informal.* **1.** Repossession of merchandise or property from a buyer who has defaulted on payment. **2.** Repossessed merchandise or property.

re·po·lar·i·za·tion (rē-pō′lər-ĭ-zā′shən) *n.* The restoration of a polarized state across a membrane, as in a muscle fiber following contraction.

re·po·lar·ize (rē-pō′lə-rīz′) *intr.v.* **-ized, -iz·ing, -iz·es.** To return to a polarized state; undergo repolarization.

re·port (rĭ-pôrt′ -pōrt′) *n.* *Abbr.* **rep., rept., rpt. 1.** An account presented usually in detail. **2.** A formal account of the proceedings or transactions of a group. **3.** Often **reports.** *Law.* A published collection of authoritative accounts of court cases or of judicial decisions. **4.** Common talk; rumor or gossip: *According to report, they eloped.* **5.** Reputation; repute: *a person of bad report.* **6.** An explosive noise: *the report of a rifle.* **—report** *v.* **-port·ed, -port·ing, -ports.** *—tr.* **1.** To make or present an often official, formal, or regular account of. **2.** To relate or tell about; present: *report one's findings.* See Synonyms at **describe. 3.** To write or provide an account or a summation of for publication or broadcast: *report the news.* **4.** To submit or relate the results of considerations concerning: *The committee reported the bill.* **5.** To carry back and repeat to another: *reported the rumor of a strike.* **6.** To complain about or denounce: *reported them to the principal.* *—intr.* **1.** To make a report. **2.** To serve as a reporter for a publication, broadcasting company, or other news media. **3.** To present oneself: *report for duty.* **4.** To be accountable: *She reports directly to the board of directors.* ***—phrasal verb.*** **report out.** To return after deliberation to a legislative body for action: *The committee reported the new tax bill out.* ***—idiom.*** **on report.** Subject to disciplinary action. [Middle English *report,* from Old French, from *reporter,* to report, from Latin *reportāre* : *re-,* re- + *portāre,* to carry; see **per-[2]** in Appendix.] **—re·port′a·ble** *adj.*

re·port·age (rĕp′ər-täzh′, rĭ-pôr′tĭj, -pōr′-) *n.* **1.** The reporting of news or information of general interest. **2.** Something reported. [French, from *reporter,* to report, from Old French. See REPORT.]

report card *n.* A report of a student's progress presented periodically to a parent or guardian.

re·port·ed·ly (rĭ-pôr′tĭd-lē, -pōr′-) *adv.* By report; supposedly.

re·port·er (rĭ-pôr′tər, -pōr′-) *n.* *Abbr.* **rep. 1.** A writer, an investigator, or a presenter of news stories. **2.** *Law.* A person who is authorized to write and issue official accounts of judicial or legislative proceedings. **—rep′or·to′ri·al** (rĕp′ər-tôr′ē-əl, -tōr′-, rē′pər-) *adj.* **—rep′or·to′ri·al·ly** *adv.*

re·pose[1] (rĭ-pōz′) *n.* **1.** The act of resting or the state of being at rest. **2.** Freedom from worry; peace of mind. **3.** Calmness; tranquillity. See Synonyms at **rest[1]**. **—repose** *v.* **-posed, -pos·ing, -pos·es.** *—tr.* **1.** To lay (oneself) down. **2.** To rest or relax (oneself). *—intr.* **1.** To lie at rest. **2.** To lie dead: *repose in a grave.* **3.** To lie while being supported by something. [From Middle English *reposen,* to be at rest, from Old French *reposer,* from Late Latin *repausāre,* to cause to rest : Latin *re-,* re- + *pausāre,* to rest (from Latin *pausa,* rest; see PAUSE).] **—re·pos′al** *n.* **—re·pos′er** *n.*

re·pose[2] (rĭ-pōz′) *tr.v.* **-posed, -pos·ing, -pos·es.** To place (trust, for example) in: *The nation had reposed its hopes in a single man.* [Middle English *reposen,* to replace, from Latin *repōnere, repos-,* to put away. See REPOSIT.]

re·pose·ful (rĭ-pōz′fəl) *adj.* Marked by, conducive to, or expressing repose. **—re·pose′ful·ly** *adv.* **—re·pose′ful·ness** *n.*

re·pos·it (rĭ-pŏz′ĭt) *tr.v.* **-it·ed, -it·ing, -its.** To put away; store. [Latin *repōnere, reposit-* : *re-,* re- + *pōnere,* to place; see **apo-** in Appendix.] **—re′po·si′tion** (rē′pə-zĭsh′ən, rĕp′ə-) *n.*

re·pos·i·to·ry (rĭ-pŏz′ĭ-tôr′ē, -tōr′ē) *n., pl.* **-ries. 1.** A place where things may be put for safekeeping. **2.** A warehouse. **3.** A museum. **4.** A burial vault; a tomb. **5.** One that contains or is a store of something specified: *"Bone marrow is also the repository for some leukemias and lymphomas"* (Seth Rolbein). **6.** One who is entrusted with secrets or confidential information.

re·pos·sess (rē′pə-zĕs′) *tr.v.* **-sessed, -sess·ing, -sess·es. 1.a.** To regain possession of. **b.** To reclaim possession of for failure to pay installments due. **2.** To give back possession to. **—re′pos·ses′sion** (-zĕsh′ən) *n.*

re·pous·sé (rə-po͞o-sā′) *adj.* **1.** Shaped or decorated with patterns in relief formed by hammering and pressing on the reverse side. Used especially of metal. **2.** Raised in relief. **—repoussé** *n.* **1.** A design in relief. **2.** The technique of hammering and pressing designs in relief. [French, past participle of *repousser,* to push back, from Old French : *re-,* re- + *pousser,* to push (from Latin *pulsāre,* to beat, frequentative of *pellere,* to push; see REPEL).]

repp (rĕp) *n.* Variant of **rep[1]**.

rep·re·hend (rĕp′rĭ-hĕnd′) *tr.v.* **-hend·ed, -hend·ing, -hends.** To reprove; censure. See Synonyms at **criticize.** [Middle English *reprehenden,* from Latin *reprehendere* : *re-,* re- + *prehendere,* to seize; see **ghend-** in Appendix.]

rep·re·hen·si·ble (rĕp′rĭ-hĕn′sə-bəl) *adj.* Deserving rebuke or censure; blameworthy. See Synonyms at **blameworthy.** [Middle English, from Old French, from Late Latin *reprehēnsibilis,* from Latin *reprehēnsus,* past participle of *reprehendere,* to reprehend. See REPREHEND.] **—rep′re·hen′si·bil′i·ty, rep′re·hen′si·ble·ness** *n.* **—rep′re·hen′si·bly** *adv.*

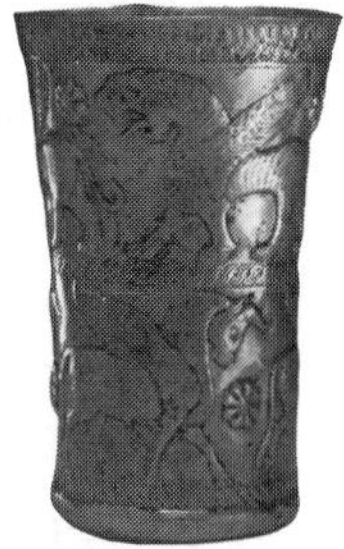

repoussé
c. eighth-century B.C.
Persian gold beaker

ă pat	oi boy
ā pay	ou out
âr care	o͝o took
ä father	o͞o boot
ĕ pet	ŭ cut
ē be	ûr urge
ĭ pit	th thin
ī pie	*th* this
îr pier	hw which
ŏ pot	zh vision
ō toe	ə about, item
ô paw	♦ regionalism

Stress marks: **′** (primary); ′ (secondary), as in **dictionary** (dĭk′shə-nĕr′ē)

rep·re·hen·sion (rĕp′rĭ-hĕn′shən) *n.* The act of rebuking or censuring; reproval.

rep·re·sent (rĕp′rĭ-zĕnt′) *tr.v.* **-sent·ed, -sent·ing, -sents. 1.a.** To stand for; symbolize: *The bald eagle represents the United States.* **b.** To indicate or communicate by signs or symbols: *Letters of the alphabet represent sounds.* **2.a.** To depict in art; portray. **b.** To describe or present in words; set forth. **3.** To present clearly to the mind. **4.** To draw attention to by way of remonstrance or protest: *Our parents represented to us the need for greater caution.* **5.** To describe or put forward (a person or thing) as an embodiment of a specified quality. **6.a.** To serve as the official and authorized delegate or agent for. **b.** To act as a spokesperson for. **7.** To serve as an example of: *The museum had several paintings representing the artist's early style.* **8.** To be the equivalent of. **9.a.** To stage (a play, for example); produce. **b.** To act the part or role of. [Middle English *representen,* from Old French *representer,* from Latin *repraesentāre,* to show : *re-,* re- + *praesentāre,* to present; see PRESENT[2].] **—rep′re·sent′a·bil′i·ty** *n.* **—rep′re·sent′a·ble** *adj.* **—rep′re·sent′er** *n.*

SYNONYMS: *represent, delineate, depict, limn, picture, portray.* The central meaning shared by these verbs is "to render or present a realistic image or likeness of": *a statue representing a king; cave paintings that delineate horses and hunters; a cartoon depicting a sea monster; the personality of a great leader limned in words; a country landscape pictured in soft colors; a book portraying life in the Middle Ages.*

rep·re·sen·ta·tion (rĕp′rĭ-zĕn-tā′shən, -zən-) *n.* **1.** The act of representing or the state of being represented. **2.** Something that represents. **3.a.** An account or a statement, as of facts, allegations, or arguments. **b.** An expostulation; a protest. **4.** A presentation or production, as of a play. **5.** The state or condition of serving as an official delegate, agent, or spokesperson. **6.** The right or privilege of being represented by delegates having a voice in a legislative body. **7.** *Law.* A statement of fact made by one party in order to induce another party to enter into a contract.

rep·re·sen·ta·tion·al (rĕp′rĭ-zĕn-tā′shə-nəl, -zən-) *adj.* Of or relating to representation, especially to realistic graphic representation. **—rep′re·sen·ta′tion·al·ism** *n.*

rep·re·sen·ta·tive (rĕp′rĭ-zĕn′tə-tĭv) *n. Abbr.* **rep., Rep. 1.** One that serves as an example or a type for others of the same classification. **2.** One that serves as a delegate or an agent for another. **3.a.** A member of a governmental body, usually legislative, chosen by popular vote. **b.** A member of the U.S. House of Representatives or of the lower house of a state legislature. **—representative** *adj.* **1.** Representing, depicting, or portraying or able to do so. **2.** Authorized to act as an official delegate or agent. **3.** Of, relating to, or characteristic of government by representation. **4.** Like or typical of others of the same class. See Usage Note at **cross section. —rep′re·sen′ta·tive·ly** *adv.* **—rep′re·sen′ta·tive·ness** *n.*

re·press (rĭ-prĕs′) *v.* **-pressed, -press·ing, -press·es.** *—tr.* **1.** To hold back by an act of volition: *couldn't repress a smirk.* See Synonyms at **suppress. 2.** To put down by force, usually before total control has been lost; quell: *repress a rebellion.* **3.** *Psychology.* To exclude (painful or unpleasant memories, for example) from the conscious mind. *—intr.* To take repressive action. [Middle English *repressen,* from Latin *reprimere, repress-* : *re-,* re- + *premere,* to press; see **per-**[4] in Appendix.] **—re·press′i·bil′i·ty** *n.* **—re·press′i·ble** *adj.*

re·press·er (rĭ-prĕs′ər) *n.* Variant of **repressor** (sense 1).

re·pres·sion (rĭ-prĕsh′ən) *n.* **1.** The act of repressing or the state of being repressed. **2.** *Psychology.* The unconscious exclusion of painful impulses, desires, or fears from the conscious mind. **—re·pres′sion·ist** *adj.*

re·pres·sive (rĭ-prĕs′ĭv) *adj.* Causing or inclined to cause repression: *a repressive dictatorship.* **—re·pres′sive·ly** *adv.* **—re·pres′sive·ness** *n.*

re·pres·sor (rĭ-prĕs′ər) *n.* **1.** Also **re·press·er.** One that represses. **2.** *Genetics.* A protein that binds to an operator, blocking transcription of an operon and the enzymes for which the operon codes.

re·prieve (rĭ-prēv′) *tr.v.* **-prieved, -priev·ing, -prieves. 1.** To postpone or cancel the punishment of. **2.** To bring relief to. **—reprieve** *n.* **1.a.** Postponement or cancellation of a punishment. **b.** A warrant for such an action. **2.** Temporary relief, as from danger or pain. [Alteration (influenced by Middle English *repreven,* to contradict, variant of *reproven,* to rebuke; see REPROVE) of Middle English *reprien,* probably from Old French *repris,* past participle of *reprendre,* to take back, from Latin *reprehendere,* to hold back. See REPREHEND.] **—re·priev′a·ble** *adj.*

rep·ri·mand (rĕp′rə-mănd′) *tr.v.* **-mand·ed, -mand·ing, -mands.** To reprove severely, especially in a formal or official way. See Synonyms at **admonish. —reprimand** *n.* A severe, formal, or official rebuke or censure. [French *réprimander,* from *réprimande,* a reprimand, alteration (influenced by *mander,* to order) of obsolete *reprimende,* from Latin *reprimenda (culpa),* (fault) to be repressed, feminine gerundive of *reprimere,* to restrain. See REPRESS.]

re·print (rē′prĭnt′) *n. Abbr.* **rep. 1.** Something that has been printed again, especially: **a.** A new printing that is identical to an original; a reimpression. **b.** A separately printed excerpt; an offprint. **2.** A facsimile of a postage stamp printed after the original issue of the stamp has been discontinued. **—reprint** (rē-prĭnt′) *tr.v.* **-print·ed, -print·ing, -prints.** To make a new copy or edition of; print again. **—re·print′er** *n.*

re·pri·sal (rĭ-prī′zəl) *n.* **1.** Retaliation for an injury with the intent of inflicting at least as much injury in return. **2.** Forcible seizure of an enemy's goods or subjects in retaliation for injuries inflicted. **3.** The practice of using political or military force without actually resorting to war. [Middle English *reprisail,* from Old French *reprisaille,* from Old Italian *ripresaglia,* from *ripreso,* past participle of *riprendere,* to take back, from Latin *reprendere, reprehendere,* to take hold of. See REPREHEND.]

re·prise (rĭ-prēz′) *n.* **1.** *Music.* **a.** A repetition of a phrase or verse. **b.** A return to an original theme. **2.** A recurrence or resumption of an action. **—reprise** *tr.v.* **-prised, -pris·ing, -pris·es.** To repeat or resume an action; make a reprise of. [Middle English, act of taking back, from Old French, from feminine past participle of *reprendre,* to take back. See REPRIEVE.]

re·pro (rē′prō) *n., pl.* **-pros.** *Printing.* A reproduction proof.

re·proach (rĭ-prōch′) *tr.v.* **-proached, -proach·ing, -proach·es. 1.** To express disapproval of, criticism of, or disappointment in (someone). See Synonyms at **admonish. 2.** To bring shame upon; disgrace. **—reproach** *n.* **1.** Blame; rebuke. **2.** One that causes rebuke or blame. **3.** Disgrace; shame. ***—idiom.*** **beyond reproach.** So good as to preclude any possibility of criticism. [Middle English *reprochen,* from Old French *reprochier,* from Vulgar Latin **repropiāre* : Latin *re-,* re- + Latin *prope,* near; see **per**[1] in Appendix.] **—re·proach′a·ble** *adj.* **—re·proach′a·ble·ness** *n.* **—re·proach′a·bly** *adv.* **—re·proach′er** *n.*

re·proach·ful (rĭ-prōch′fəl) *adj.* Expressing reproach or blame. **—re·proach′ful·ly** *adv.* **—re·proach′ful·ness** *n.*

rep·ro·bate (rĕp′rə-bāt′) *n.* **1.** A morally unprincipled person. **2.** *Theology.* One who is predestined to damnation. **—reprobate** *adj.* **1.** Morally unprincipled; shameless. **2.** *Theology.* Rejected by God and without hope of salvation. **—reprobate** *tr.v.* **-bat·ed, -bat·ing, -bates. 1.** To disapprove of; condemn. **2.** *Theology.* To abandon to eternal damnation. [From Middle English, condemned, from Late Latin *reprobātus,* past participle of *reprobāre,* to reprove : Latin *re-,* opposite; see RE– + *probāre,* to approve; see PROVE.] **—rep′ro·ba′tion** *n.* **—rep′ro·ba′tive** *adj.*

re·proc·ess (rē-prŏs′ĕs′, -prō′sĕs′) *tr.v.* **-essed, -ess·ing, -ess·es.** To cause to undergo special or additional processing before reuse.

re·pro·duce (rē′prə-do͞os′, -dyo͞os′) *v.* **-duced, -duc·ing, -duc·es.** *—tr.* **1.** To produce a counterpart, an image, or a copy of. **2.** *Biology.* To generate (offspring) by sexual or asexual means. **3.** To produce again or anew; re-create. **4.** To bring (a memory, for example) to mind again. *—intr.* **1.** To generate offspring. **2.** To undergo copying: *graphics that reproduce well.* **—re′pro·duc′er** *n.* **—re′pro·duc′i·bil′i·ty** *n.* **—re′pro·duc′i·ble** *adj.*

re·pro·duc·tion (rē′prə-dŭk′shən) *n.* **1.** The act of reproducing or the condition or process of being reproduced. **2.** Something reproduced, especially in the faithfulness of its resemblance to the form and elements of the original: *the realistic quality of the sound reproduction; a fine reproduction of an Adams mantel.* **3.** *Biology.* The sexual or asexual process by which organisms generate others of the same kind.

reproduction proof *n. Printing.* A proof of typeset material made for reproduction through a photographic process such as photo-offset lithography.

re·pro·duc·tive (rē′prə-dŭk′tĭv) *adj.* **1.** Of or relating to reproduction: *legal and political questions concerning reproductive rights.* **2.** Tending to reproduce. **—reproductive** *n. Zoology.* A reproductive organism, especially a sexually mature social insect. **—re′pro·duc′tive·ly** *adv.* **—re′pro·duc′tive·ness** *n.*

re·pro·gram (rē-prō′grăm′) *tr.v.* **-grammed, -gram·ming, -grams** or **-gramed, -gram·ing, -grams.** To program again. **—re′pro·gram′ma·bil′i·ty** *n.* **—re·pro′gram·ma·ble** *adj.*

re·pro·graph·ics (rē′prə-grăf′ĭks) *n.* **1.** *(used with a sing. verb).* The technique of reprography. **2.** *(used with a sing. or pl. verb).* The materials, equipment, and processes used in reprography.

re·prog·ra·phy (rĭ-prŏg′rə-fē) *n.* The process of reproducing, reprinting, or copying graphic material especially by mechanical, photographic, or electronic means. [REPRO(DUCTION) + -GRAPHY.] **—re·prog′ra·pher** *n.* **—re′pro·graph′ic** (rē′prə-grăf′ĭk, rĕp′rə-) *adj.*

re·proof (rĭ-pro͞of′) *n.* The act, an instance, or an expression of reproving; a rebuke. [Middle English *reprof,* variant of *reprove, repreve,* from Old French *repruеve,* from *reprover,* to find fault with. See REPROVE.]

re·prove (rĭ-pro͞ov′) *tr.v.* **-proved, -prov·ing, -proves. 1.** To voice or convey disapproval of; rebuke. See Synonyms at **admonish. 2.** To find fault with. [Middle English *reproven,* from Anglo-Norman *repruver,* variant of Old French *reprover,* from Late Latin *reprobāre,* to disapprove. See REPROBATE.] **—re·prov′a·ble** *adj.* **—re·prov′er** *n.* **—re·prov′ing·ly** *adv.*

rept. *abbr.* Report.

rep·tant (rĕp′tənt) *adj. Biology.* Creeping or crawling; repent. [Latin *rēptāns, rēptant-,* present participle of *rēptāre,* to creep, frequentative of *rēpere.*]

rep·tile (rĕp′tĭl, -tīl′) *n.* **1.** Any of various cold-blooded, usually egg-laying vertebrates of the class Reptilia, such as a snake, lizard, crocodile, turtle, or dinosaur, having an external covering of scales or horny plates and breathing by means of lungs. **2.** A person regarded as despicable or treacherous. [Middle English *reptil,* from Old French *reptile,* from Late Latin *rēptile,* from neuter of Latin *rēptilis,* creeping, from *rēptus,* past participle of *rēpere,* to creep.]

rep·til·i·an (rĕp-tĭl′ē-ən, -tĭl′yən) *adj.* **1.** Of or relating to reptiles. **2.** Resembling or characteristic of a reptile. **3.** Despicable; treacherous. **—reptilian** *n.* A reptile.

rep·til·i·um (rĕp-tĭl′ē-əm) *n., pl.* **-i·a** (-ē-ə). A building or an enclosure housing reptiles for public display.

Repub. *abbr.* **1.** Republic. **2.** Republican.

re·pub·lic (rĭ-pŭb′lĭk) *n. Abbr.* **rep., Rep., Repub. 1.a.** A political order whose head of state is not a monarch and in modern times is usually a president. **b.** A nation that has such a political order. **2.a.** A political order in which the supreme power lies in a body of citizens who are entitled to vote for officers and representatives responsible to them. **b.** A nation that has such a political order. **3.** Often **Republic.** A specific republican government of a nation: *the Fourth Republic of France.* **4.** An autonomous or partially autonomous political and territorial unit belonging to a sovereign federation. **5.** A group of people working as equals in the same sphere or field: *the republic of letters.* [French *république,* from Old French, from Latin *rēspūblica* : *rēs,* thing; see **rē-** in Appendix + *pūblica,* feminine of *pūblicus,* of the people; see PUBLIC.]

re·pub·li·can (rĭ-pŭb′lĭ-kən) *adj.* **1.** Of, relating to, or characteristic of a republic. **2.** Being in favor of a republic as the best form of government. **3. Republican.** *Abbr.* **R., Rep., Repub.** Of, relating to, characteristic of, or belonging to the Republican Party of the United States. **—republican** *n.* **1.** One who favors a republic as the best form of government. **2. Republican.** *Abbr.* **R., Rep., Repub.** A member of the Republican Party of the United States. **—re·pub′li·can·ism** *n.*

re·pub·li·can·ize (rĭ-pŭb′lĭ-kə-nīz′) *tr.v.* **-ized, -iz·ing, -iz·es.** To make republican. **—re·pub′li·can·i·za′tion** (-kə-nĭ-zā′shən) *n.*

Republican Party *n.* **1.** One of the two primary political parties of the United States, organized in 1854 to oppose slavery. **2.** The Democratic-Republican Party, a former political party of the United States, organized in 1792 by Thomas Jefferson.

Republican River. A river, about 676 km (420 mi) long, rising in eastern Colorado and flowing northeast and east across southern Nebraska then southeast through northeast-central Kansas, where it joins the Smoky Hill River to form the Kansas River.

re·pub·li·ca·tion (rē-pŭb′lĭ-kā′shən) *n.* **1.** The act or process of republishing. **2.** Something republished.

re·pub·lish (rē-pŭb′lĭsh) *tr.v.* **-lished, -lish·ing, -lish·es. 1.** To publish again. **2.** *Law.* To revive (a libel or a canceled will). **—re·pub′lish·er** *n.*

re·pu·di·ate (rĭ-pyo͞o′dē-āt′) *tr.v.* **-at·ed, -at·ing, -ates. 1.** To reject the validity or authority of: *"Chaucer . . . not only came to doubt the worth of his extraordinary body of work, but repudiated it"* (Joyce Carol Oates). **2.** To reject emphatically as unfounded, untrue, or unjust: *repudiated the accusation.* **3.** To refuse to recognize or pay: *repudiate a debt.* **4.a.** To disown (a child, for example). **b.** To refuse to have any dealings with. [Latin *repudiāre, repudiāt-,* from *repudium,* divorce.] **—re·pu′di·a′tive** *adj.* **—re·pu′di·a′tor** *n.*

re·pu·di·a·tion (rĭ-pyo͞o′dē-ā′shən) *n.* **1.** The act of repudiating or the state of being repudiated. **2.** The refusal, especially by public authorities, to acknowledge a contract or debt. **—re·pu′di·a′tion·ist** *n.*

re·pugn (rĭ-pyo͞on′) *v.* **-pugned, -pugn·ing, -pugns.** *—tr.* To oppose or contend against. *—intr. Archaic.* To be opposed; conflict. [Middle English *repugnen,* from Old French *repugner,* from Latin *repugnāre,* to fight against : *re-,* re- + *pugnāre,* to fight with the fist; see **peuk-** in Appendix.]

re·pug·nance (rĭ-pŭg′nəns) *n.* **1.** Extreme dislike or aversion. **2.** *Logic.* The relationship of contradictory terms; inconsistency.

re·pug·nan·cy (rĭ-pŭg′nən-sē) *n., pl.* **-cies.** Repugnance.

re·pug·nant (rĭ-pŭg′nənt) *adj.* **1.** Arousing disgust or aversion; offensive or repulsive: *morally repugnant behavior.* **2.** *Logic.* Contradictory; inconsistent. [Middle English, antagonistic, from Old French, from Latin *repugnāns, repugnant-,* present participle of *repugnāre,* to fight against. See REPUGN.] **—re·pug′nant·ly** *adv.*

re·pulse (rĭ-pŭls′) *tr.v.* **-pulsed, -puls·ing, -puls·es. 1.** To drive back; repel. **2.** To rebuff or reject with rudeness, coldness, or denial. **3.** *Usage Problem.* To cause repugnance or distaste in. **—repulse** *n.* **1.** The act of repulsing or the state of being repulsed. **2.** Rejection; refusal. [Middle English *repulsen,* from Latin *repellere, repuls-.* See REPEL.] **—re·puls′er** *n.*

USAGE NOTE: A number of critics have maintained that *repulse* should only be used to mean "to drive away, spurn," as in *He rudely repulsed their overtures,* and not to mean "to cause repulsion in," as in *Their hypocrisy repulsed me.* In recent years, however, there has been an increasing tendency to use *repulse* in the sense "cause repulsion in." Reputable literary precedent exists for this usage, and the confusion is understandable, given that the stigmatized use of *repulse* is parallel to the unexceptionable uses of *repulsion* and *repulsive.* Still, writers who want to stay on the safe side may prefer to use only *repel* when the intended sense is "cause repulsion in."

re·pul·sion (rĭ-pŭl′shən) *n.* **1.** The act of repulsing or the condition of being repulsed. **2.** Extreme aversion. **3.** *Physics.* The tendency of particles or bodies of the same electric charge or magnetic polarity to separate.

re·pul·sive (rĭ-pŭl′sĭv) *adj.* **1.** Causing repugnance or aversion; disgusting. See Synonyms at **offensive. 2.** Tending to repel or drive off. **3.** *Physics.* Opposing in direction: *a repulsive force.* **—re·pul′sive·ly** *adv.* **—re·pul′sive·ness** *n.*

re·pur·chase agreement (rē-pûr′chĭs) *n.* A contract giving the seller of an asset the right or obligation to buy back the asset at a specified price on a given date.

rep·u·ta·ble (rĕp′yə-tə-bəl) *adj.* Having a good reputation; honorable. **—rep′u·ta·bil′i·ty** *n.* **—rep′u·ta·bly** *adv.*

rep·u·ta·tion (rĕp′yə-tā′shən) *n.* **1.** The general estimation in which a person is held by the public. **2.** The state or situation of being held in high esteem. **3.** A specific characteristic or trait ascribed to a person or thing: *a reputation for courtesy.* [Middle English *reputacioun,* from Latin *reputātiō, reputātiōn-,* a reckoning, from *reputātus,* past participle of *reputāre,* to reckon, think over. See REPUTE.]

re·pute (rĭ-pyo͞ot′) *tr.v.* **-put·ed, -put·ing, -putes. 1.** To ascribe a particular fact or characteristic to. **2.** To consider; suppose. **—repute** *n.* **1.** Reputation. **2.** A good reputation. [Middle English *reputen,* from Old French *reputer,* from Latin *reputāre,* to think over : *re-,* re- + *putāre,* to think over; see **peu-** in Appendix.]

re·put·ed (rĭ-pyo͞o′tĭd) *adj.* Generally supposed to be such. See Synonyms at **supposed. —re·put′ed·ly** *adv.*

req. *abbr.* **1.** Require; required. **2.** Requisition.

reqd. *abbr.* Required.

re·quest (rĭ-kwĕst′) *tr.v.* **-quest·ed, -quest·ing, -quests. 1.** To express a desire for; ask for. **2.** To ask (a person) to do something. **—request** *n.* **1.** The act of asking. **2.** Something asked for. **—*idioms.* by request.** In response to an expressed desire: *We are offering these scarves for sale again by request.* **in request.** In great demand: *a pianist in great request.* **on** (or **upon**) **request.** When asked for: *References are available on request.* [From Middle English *requeste,* the act of requesting, from Old French, from Vulgar Latin **(rēs) requaesīta,* (thing) requested, from Latin, feminine past participle of *requīrere,* to ask for. See REQUIRE.] **—re·quest′er** *n.*

req·ui·em (rĕk′wē-əm, rē′kwē-) *n.* **1. Requiem.** *Roman Catholic Church.* **a.** A mass for a deceased person. **b.** A musical composition for such a mass. **2.** A hymn, composition, or service for the dead. [Middle English, from Latin, accusative of *requiēs,* rest, the first word of the mass for the dead : *re-,* re- + *quiēs,* quiet; see **k^{w}eiə-** in Appendix.]

req·ui·es·cat (rĕk′wē-ĕs′kăt′, -kät′) *n.* A prayer for the repose of the souls of the dead. [Latin, third person sing. present subjunctive of *requiēscere,* to rest. See **k^{w}eiə-** in Appendix.]

re·quire (rĭ-kwīr′) *tr.v.* **-quired, -quir·ing, -quires.** *Abbr.* **req. 1.** To have as a requisite; need: *Most plants require sunlight.* **2.** To call for as obligatory or appropriate; demand. See Synonyms at **demand. 3.** To impose an obligation on; compel: *Students are required to attend classes.* [Middle English *requiren,* from Old French *requerre,* from Vulgar Latin **requaerere,* alteration (influenced by *quaerere,* to seek) of Latin *requīrere* : *re-,* re- + *quaerere,* to seek.] **—re·quir′a·ble** *adj.* **—re·quir′er** *n.*

re·quired (rĭ-kwīrd′) *adj. Abbr.* **req., reqd. 1.** Needed; essential. **2.** Obligatory: *required reading.*

re·quire·ment (rĭ-kwīr′mənt) *n.* **1.** Something that is required; a necessity. **2.** Something obligatory; a prerequisite.

req·ui·site (rĕk′wĭ-zĭt) *adj.* Required; essential. See Synonyms at **indispensable. —requisite** *n.* Something indispensable; a requirement. See Synonyms at **need.** [Middle English, from Latin *requīsītus,* past participle of *requīrere,* to require. See REQUIRE.] **—req′ui·site·ly** *adv.* **—req′ui·site·ness** *n.*

req·ui·si·tion (rĕk′wĭ-zĭsh′ən) *n. Abbr.* **req. 1.** A formal written request for something needed. **2.** A necessity; a requirement. **3.** The state or condition of being needed or put into service. **4.** *Law.* A formal request of one government to another demanding the return of a criminal or fugitive. **—requisition** *tr.v.* **-tioned, -tion·ing, -tions. 1.** To demand, as for military needs. **2.** To make demands of.

re·quit·al (rĭ-kwīt′l) *n.* **1.** The act of requiting. **2.** Return, as for an injury or a friendly act.

re·quite (rĭ-kwīt′) *tr.v.* **-quit·ed, -quit·ing, -quites. 1.** To make repayment or return for: *requite another's love.* See Synonyms at **reciprocate. 2.** To avenge. [Middle English *requiten* : *re-,* re- + *quiten,* to pay; see QUIT.] **—re·quit′a·ble** *adj.* **—re·quit′er** *n.*

re·ra·di·ate (rē-rā′dē-āt′) *tr.v.* **-at·ed, -at·ing, -ates.** To emit (absorbed radiation) anew: *"Different organic materials in the soil reradiate the sun's heat at different rates"* (Lori Oliwenstein).

re·ra·di·a·tion (rē-rā′dē-ā′shən) *n. Physics.* Radiation emission following the absorption of incident radiation.

re·ran (rē-răn′) *v.* Past tense and past participle of **rerun.**

ă pat	oi boy
ā pay	ou out
âr care	o͝o took
ä father	o͞o boot
ĕ pet	ŭ cut
ē be	ûr urge
ĭ pit	th thin
ī pie	*th* this
îr pier	hw which
ŏ pot	zh vision
ō toe	ə about, item
ô paw	♦ regionalism

Stress marks: **′** (primary); ′ (secondary), as in **dictionary** (dĭk′shə-nĕr′ē)

rere·dos (rîr′dŏs′, rîr′ĭ-, rĕr′ĭ-) *n.* **1.** A decorative screen or facing on the wall at the back of an altar; a retable. **2.** The back of an open hearth of a fireplace. [Middle English, from Anglo-Norman, from *areredos* : *arere,* behind (Latin *ad-*, ad- + *retrō,* backward; see **re-** in Appendix) + *dos,* back (from Latin *dorsum*).]

re·re·lease (rē′rĭ-lēs′) *tr.v.* **-leased, -leas·ing, -leas·es.** To release (a movie, for example) again. **—re′re·lease′** *n.*

re·run (rē′rŭn′) *n.* The act or an instance of repeating a recorded movie or a recorded television performance. **—rerun** (rē-rŭn′) *tr.v.* **-ran** (-răn′), **-run, -run·ning, -runs.** To present a rerun of.

RES *abbr.* Reticuloendothial system.

res. *abbr.* **1.** Research. **2.** Reservation. **3.** Reserve. **4.** Reservoir. **5.** Residence; resident. **6.** Resolution.

res ad·ju·di·ca·ta (rēz′ ə-jo͞o′dĭ-kä′tə, rās′) *n. Law.* Variant of **res judicata.**

re·sale (rē′săl′, rē-săl′) *n.* The act of selling again. *—attributive.* Often used to modify another noun: *resale value; resale potential.* **—re·sal′a·ble** *adj.*

re·sched·ule (rē-skĕj′o͞ol) *tr.v.* **-uled, -ul·ing, -ules.** To schedule again or anew: *rescheduled the meeting for the following week; rescheduled the debts of many developing nations.*

re·scind (rĭ-sĭnd′) *tr.v.* **-scind·ed, -scind·ing, -scinds.** To make void; repeal or annul. [Latin *rescindere* : *re-*, re- + *scindere,* to split; see **skei-** in Appendix.] **—re·scind′a·ble** *adj.* **—re·scind′er** *n.* **—re·scind′ment** *n.*

re·scis·sion (rĭ-sĭzh′ən) *n.* The act of rescinding. [Latin *rescissiō, rescissiōn-*, from *rescissus,* past participle of *rescindere,* to rescind. See RESCIND.]

re·scis·so·ry (rĭ-sĭz′ə-rē, -sĭs′-) *adj.* Of, relating to, or having the power of rescission.

re·script (rē′skrĭpt′) *n.* **1.a.** The act of rewriting. **b.** Something that has been rewritten. **2.** A formal decree or edict. **3.** *Roman Catholic Church.* A response from the pope or another ecclesiastical superior to a question regarding discipline or doctrine. **4.** A reply from a Roman emperor to a magistrate's query about a point of law. [Latin *rescrīptum,* from neuter past participle of *rescrībere,* to write back : *re-*, re- + *scrībere,* to write; see **skrībh-** in Appendix.]

res·cue (rĕs′kyo͞o) *tr.v.* **-cued, -cu·ing, -cues. 1.** To set free, as from danger or imprisonment; save. See Synonyms at **save[1]. 2.** *Law.* To take from legal custody by force. **—rescue** *n.* **1.** An act of rescuing; a deliverance. **2.** *Law.* Removal from legal custody by force. *—attributive.* Often used to modify another noun: *a rescue team; a rescue mission.* [Middle English *rescouen,* from Old French *rescourre* : *re-*, re- + *escourre,* to shake (from Latin *escutere* : *ex-*, ex- + *quatere,* to shake; see **kwēt-** in Appendix).] **—res′cu·a·ble** *adj.* **—res′cu·er** *n.*

rescue grass *n.* A tall South American grass *(Bromus unioloides)* cultivated in warm regions for hay. [Probably alteration of FESCUE.]

re·search (rĭ-sûrch′, rē′sûrch′) *n. Abbr.* **res. 1.** Scholarly or scientific investigation or inquiry. See Synonyms at **inquiry. 2.** Close, careful study. *—attributive.* Often used to modify another noun: *a research grant; research assistants.* **—research** *v.* **-searched, -search·ing, -search·es.** *—intr.* To engage in or perform research. *—tr.* **1.** To study (something) thoroughly so as to present in a detailed, accurate manner: *researching the effects of acid rain.* **2.** To do research for: *carefully researched the historical novel.* [Obsolete French *recerche,* from *recercher,* to search closely, from Old French : *re-*, re- + *cerchier,* to search; see SEARCH.] **—re·search′a·ble** *adj.* **—re·search′er** *n.*

USAGE NOTE: Some critics have objected to the use of *research* as a transitive verb, but the usage has ample historical precedent and is common in reputable writing. In the most recent survey 81 percent of the Usage Panel accepted the sentence *He spent a week at a funeral home researching mortuary procedures for his new novel,* and 91 percent accepted *The chapters on the internment are both readable and well researched.*

re·search-in·ten·sive (rĭ-sûrch′ĭn-tĕn′sĭv, rē′sûrch-) *adj.* Having or requiring a relatively large expenditure on research and development in comparison to capital and labor: *the research-intensive field of biotechnology.*

re·seat (rē-sēt′) *tr.v.* **-seat·ed, -seat·ing, -seats. 1.** To provide with a new or different seat. **2.** To fit (a valve, for example) in a new seating.

ré·seau or **re·seau** (rā-zō′, rĭ-) *n., pl.* **-seaus** or **-seaux** (-zōz′, -zō′). **1.** A net or mesh foundation for lace. **2.** *Astronomy.* A reference grid of fine lines forming uniform squares on a photographic plate or print, used to aid in measurement. **3.** A mosaic screen of fine lines of three colors, used in color photography. [French, from Old French *reseuil,* diminutive of *raiz,* net, from Latin *rēte.*]

réseau

re·sect (rĭ-sĕkt′) *tr.v.* **-sect·ed, -sect·ing, -sects.** To perform a resection on. [Latin *resecāre, resect-*, to cut back : *re-*, re- + *secāre,* to cut; see **sek-** in Appendix.] **—re·sect′a·bil′i·ty** *n.* **—re·sect′a·ble** *adj.*

re·sec·tion (rĭ-sĕk′shən) *n.* Surgical removal of part of an organ or a structure.

re·sec·to·scope (rĭ-sĕk′tə-skōp′) *n.* A surgical instrument for performing a resection without an opening or incision other than that made by the instrument.

re·se·da (rĭ-sē′də, -sĕd′ə) *n.* **1.** Any of various Mediterranean plants of the genus *Reseda,* including the mignonette, having densely flowered terminal racemes and divided petals. **2.** *Color.* A grayish or dark green to yellow green or light olive. [New Latin *Resēda,* genus name, from Latin *resēda,* a kind of plant used to reduce tumors.] **—re·se′da** *adj.*

re·seg·re·ga·tion (rē-sĕg′rĭ-gā′shən) *n.* Renewal of segregation, as in a school system, after a period of desegregation.

re·sem·blance (rĭ-zĕm′bləns) *n.* **1.** The state or quality of resembling, especially similarity in appearance or in external or superficial details. See Synonyms at **likeness. 2.** Something that resembles another.

re·sem·ble (rĭ-zĕm′bəl) *tr.v.* **-bled, -bling, -bles.** To exhibit similarity or likeness to. [Middle English *resemblen,* from Old French *resembler* : *re-*, re- + *sembler,* to appear (from Latin *simulāre,* to imitate, from *similis,* like; see **sem-[1]** in Appendix).] **—re·sem′bler** *n.*

re·sent (rĭ-zĕnt′) *tr.v.* **-sent·ed, -sent·ing, -sents.** To feel indignantly aggrieved at. [French *ressentir,* to be angry, from Old French *resentir,* to feel strongly : *re-*, re- + *sentir,* to feel (from Latin *sentīre;* see **sent-** in Appendix).]

WORD HISTORY: When we read the statement "Should we not be monstrously ingratefull if we did not deeply resent such kindness?" (from the *Sermons* of Isaac Barrow, written before 1677), we may be pardoned for momentarily thinking we are in never-never land. For a time ranging roughly from the last part of the 17th century to the second half of the 18th, the word *resent* did refer to gratefulness and appreciation as well as injury and insult. *Resent* has also been used in other senses that seem strange to us, such as "to feel pain" or "to perceive by smell." The thread that ties the senses together is the notion of feeling or perceiving. The Old French source of our word, *resentir,* "to feel strongly," is made up of the prefix *re–*, acting in this case as an intensive, and *sentir,* "to feel or perceive." There is much that one can feel, but at least for now this word has narrowed its focus to a feeling of indignation.

re·sent·ful (rĭ-zĕnt′fəl) *adj.* Full of, characterized by, or inclined to feel indignant ill will. **—re·sent′ful·ly** *adv.* **—re·sent′ful·ness** *n.*

re·sent·ment (rĭ-zĕnt′mənt) *n.* Indignation or ill will felt as a result of a real or imagined grievance. See Synonyms at **anger.**

re·ser·pine (rĭ-sûr′pēn′, -pĭn, rĕs′ər-pĭn, -pēn′, rĕz′-) *n.* A white to yellowish powder, $C_{33}H_{40}N_2O_9$, isolated from the roots of certain species of rauwolfia and used as a sedative and an antihypertensive. [German *Reserpin,* from alteration of New Latin *Rauwolfia serpentīna,* species of snakeroot : RAUWOLFIA + Late Latin *serpentīna,* feminine of *serpentīnus,* serpentine; see SERPENTINE.]

res·er·va·tion (rĕz′ər-vā′shən) *n. Abbr.* **res. 1.** The act of reserving; a keeping back or withholding. **2.** Something that is kept back or withheld. **3.** A limiting qualification, condition, or exception: *has reservations about the proposal.* **4.** A tract of land set apart by the federal government for a special purpose, especially one for the use of a Native American people. **5.a.** An arrangement by which accommodations are secured in advance, as in a hotel or on an airplane. **b.** The accommodations so secured. **c.** The record or promise of such an arrangement. **—res′er·va′tion·ist** *n.*

re·serve (rĭ-zûrv′) *tr.v.* **-served, -serv·ing, -serves. 1.** To keep back, as for future use or for a special purpose. **2.** To set or cause to be set apart for a particular person or use. See Synonyms at **book. 3.** To keep or secure for oneself; retain: *I reserve the right to disagree.* See Synonyms at **keep. —reserve** *n. Abbr.* **res. 1.** Something kept back or saved for future use or a special purpose. **2.** The act of reserving. **3.** The keeping of one's feelings, thoughts, or affairs to oneself. **4.** Self-restraint in expression; reticence: *"One feels it everywhere, a quality of reserve, something held back"* (Rollene W. Saal). **5.** Lack of enthusiasm; skeptical caution. **6.** An amount of capital held back from investment in order to meet probable or possible demands. **7.** A reservation of public land: *a forest reserve.* **8.** An amount of a mineral, fossil fuel, or other resource known to exist in a particular location and to be exploitable: *the discovery of oil reserves.* **9.** Often **reserves. a.** A fighting force kept uncommitted until strategic need arises. **b.** The part of a country's armed forces not on active duty but subject to call in an emergency. **—reserve** *adj.* Held in or forming a reserve: *a reserve supply of food.* **—*idiom.* in reserve.** Kept back, set aside, or saved. [Middle English *reserven,* from Old French *reserver,* from Latin *reservāre,* to keep back : *re-*, re- + *servāre,* to keep; see **ser-[1]** in Appendix.] **—re·serv′a·ble** *adj.* **—re·serv′er** *n.*

reserve bank *n.* **1.** A central bank that holds the reserves of other banks. **2.** One of the 12 main banks of the U.S. Federal Reserve System.

reserve currency *n.* Currency kept in reserve by a government for the paying of international debts.

re·served (rĭ-zûrvd′) *adj.* **1.** Held in reserve; kept back or set aside. **2.** Marked by self-restraint and reticence. See Synonyms at **silent. —re·serv′ed·ly** (-zûr′vĭd-lē) *adv.* **—re·serv′ed·ness** *n.*

reserve price *n.* The price fixed and announced as the minimum at which property will be sold at an auction.

re·serv·ist (rĭ-zûr′vĭst) *n.* A member of a military reserve.

res·er·voir (rĕz′ər-vwär′, -vwôr′, -vôr′) *n. Abbr.* **res. 1.** A natural or artificial pond or lake used for the storage and regulation of water. **2.** A receptacle or chamber for storing a fluid. **3.** An underground accumulation of petroleum or natural gas. **4.** *Anatomy.* See **cisterna** (sense 1). **5.** A large or extra supply; a reserve: *a reservoir of gratitude.* **6.** *Medicine.* An organism or a population that directly or indirectly transmits a pathogen while being virtually immune to its effects. [French *réservoir,* from *réserver,* to reserve, from Old French *reserver.* See RESERVE.]

re·set (rē-sĕt′) *tr.v.* **-set, -set·ting, -sets. 1.** To set again: *reset a broken bone.* **2.** To change the reading of: *reset a clock.* **—reset** (rē′sĕt′) *n.* **1.** The act of setting again. **2.** Something set again. **—re·set′ta·ble** *adj.* **—re·set′ter** *n.*

res ges·tae (rās′ gĕs′tī′, rēz′ jĕs′tē) *pl.n.* **1.** Things done; deeds. **2.** *Law.* The facts that are admissible in evidence as the surrounding circumstances of the event to be proved. [Latin *rēs gestae* : *rēs,* pl. of *rēs,* thing + *gestae,* feminine pl. past participle of *gerere,* to carry, show.]

resh (rĕsh) *n.* The 20th letter of the Hebrew alphabet. See table at **alphabet.** [Aramaic *rēš,* head.]

re·shape (rē-shāp′) *tr.v.* **-shaped, -shap·ing, -shapes.** To shape, form, or organize again or anew: *"media consultants whose TV ads reshape candidates' images to suit ephemeral public tastes"* (New Republic). **—re·shap′er** *n.*

Resht (rĕsht). See **Rasht.**

re·shuf·fle (rē-shŭf′əl) *tr.v.* **-fled, -fling, -fles. 1.** To shuffle again: *reshuffle cards.* **2.** To arrange or organize anew: *The president reshuffled the advisory committee.* **—re·shuf′fle** *n.*

re·sid (rĭ-zĭd′) *n. Informal.* Residual oil.

re·side (rĭ-zīd′) *intr.v.* **-sid·ed, -sid·ing, -sides. 1.** To live in a place permanently or for an extended period. **2.** To be inherently present; exist: *the potential energy that resides in flowing water.* **3.** To be vested, as a power or right: *The authority of governance resided in the monarchy.* [Middle English *residen,* from Old French *resider,* from Latin *residēre,* to remain behind, reside : *re-,* re- + *sedēre,* to sit; see **sed-** in Appendix.] **—re·sid′er** *n.*

res·i·dence (rĕz′ĭ-dəns, -dĕns′) *n. Abbr.* **res. 1.** The place in which one lives; a dwelling. **2.** The act or a period of residing in a place. **3.** A medical residency. **4.** The official home or location of a corporation. ***—idiom.*** **in residence.** Committed to live and work in a specific place, often for a certain length of time: *an artist in residence at a college.*

res·i·den·cy (rĕz′ĭ-dən-sē, -dĕn′-) *n., pl.* **-cies. 1.** The period during which a physician receives specialized clinical training. **2. a.** The house of a colonial resident. **b.** The sphere of authority of a colonial resident. **3.** Residence.

res·i·dent (rĕz′ĭ-dənt, -dĕnt′) *n. Abbr.* **res. 1.** A physician serving a period of residency. **2.** One who resides in a particular place permanently or for an extended period, as: **a.** A diplomatic official residing in a foreign seat of government. **b.** A colonial official acting as adviser to the ruler of a protected state, often having quasi-gubernatorial powers. **c.** A member of an intelligence-gathering or nonuniformed law enforcement agency who resides and oversees operations in a certain locale: *the KGB resident in New York City; the FBI resident in Boston.* **3.** A nonmigratory bird or other animal. **—resident** *adj.* **1.** Dwelling in a particular place; residing: *resident aliens.* **2.** Living somewhere in connection with duty or work. **3.** Inherently present: *resident anxieties.* **4.** Nonmigratory: *resident fauna.*

res·i·den·tial (rĕz′ĭ-dĕn′shəl) *adj.* **1.** Of, relating to, or having residence: *a residential college.* **2.** Of, suitable for, or limited to residences: *residential zoning.* **—res′i·den′tial·ly** *adv.*

res·i·den·ti·ar·y (rĕz′ĭ-dĕn′shē-ĕr′ē, -shə-rē) *adj.* **1.** Having a residence, especially an official one. **2.** Involving or requiring official residence. **—residentiary** *n., pl.* **-ies. 1.** One who resides in a certain place; a resident. **2.** A member of the clergy required to live in an official residence.

re·sid·u·a (rĭ-zĭj′o͞o-ə) *n.* Plural of **residuum.**

re·sid·u·al (rĭ-zĭj′o͞o-əl) *adj.* **1.** Of, relating to, or characteristic of a residue. **2.** Remaining as a residue. **—residual** *n.* **1.** The quantity left over at the end of a process; a remainder. **2.** Often **residuals.** A payment made to a performer, writer, or director for each repeat showing of a recorded television show or commercial. **—re·sid′u·al·ly** *adv.*

residual oil *n.* The low-grade oil products that remain after the distillation of petroleum, used in adhesives, roofing compounds, and asphalt manufacture.

re·sid·u·ar·y (rĭ-zĭj′o͞o-ĕr′ē) *adj.* **1.** Of, relating to, or constituting a residue. **2.** *Law.* Entitled to the residue of an estate.

res·i·due (rĕz′ĭ-do͞o′, -dyo͞o′) *n.* **1.** The remainder of something after removal of parts or a part. See Synonyms at **remainder. 2.** Matter remaining after completion of an abstractive chemical or physical process, such as evaporation, combustion, distillation, or filtration; residuum. **3.** *Law.* The remainder of a testator's estate after all claims, debts, and bequests are satisfied. In this sense, also called *residuum.* [Middle English, from Old French *residu,* from Latin *residuum,* neuter of *residuus,* remaining, from *residēre,* to remain behind. See RESIDE.]

re·sid·u·um (rĭ-zĭj′o͞o-əm) *n., pl.* **-u·a** (-o͞o-ə). **1.** Something remaining after removal of a part; a residue. See Synonyms at **remainder. 2.** *Law.* See **residue** (sense 3). [Latin, residue. See RESIDUE.]

re·sign (rĭ-zīn′) *v.* **-signed, -sign·ing, -signs.** *—tr.* **1.** To submit (oneself) passively; accept as inevitable: *I resigned myself to a long wait in line.* **2.** To give up (a position, for example), especially by formal notification. **3.** To relinquish (a privilege, right, or claim). See Synonyms at **relinquish.** *—intr.* To give up one's job or office; quit, especially by formal notification: *resign from a board of directors.* [Middle English *resignen,* from Old French *resigner,* from Latin *resignāre,* to unseal : *re-,* re- + *signāre,* to seal (from *signum,* mark, seal; see **sekʷ-¹** in Appendix).] **—re·sign′er** *n.*

re-sign (rē-sīn′) *tr.v.* **-signed, -sign·ing, -signs.** To sign again: *re-signed the lease.*

res·ig·na·tion (rĕz′ĭg-nā′shən) *n.* **1.** The act or an instance of resigning. **2.** An oral or written statement that one is resigning a position or an office. **3.** Unresisting acceptance of something as inescapable; submission. See Synonyms at **patience.**

re·signed (rĭ-zīnd′) *adj.* Feeling or marked by resignation; acquiescent: *"I like trees because they seem more resigned to the way they have to live than other things do"* (Willa Cather). **—re·sign′ed·ly** (-zī′nĭd-lē) *adv.* **—re·sign′ed·ness** *n.*

re·sile (rĭ-zīl′) *intr.v.* **-siled, -sil·ing, -siles. 1.** To spring back, especially to resume a former position or structure after being stretched or compressed. **2.** To draw back; recoil. [Obsolete French *resilir,* from Latin *resilīre,* to leap back : *re-,* re- + *salīre,* to leap; see **sel-** in Appendix.]

re·sil·ience (rĭ-zĭl′yəns) *n.* **1.** The ability to recover quickly from illness, change, or misfortune; buoyancy. **2.** The property of a material that enables it to resume its original shape or position after being bent, stretched, or compressed; elasticity.

re·sil·ien·cy (rĭ-zĭl′yən-sē) *n.* Resilience.

re·sil·ient (rĭ-zĭl′yənt) *adj.* **1.** Marked by the ability to recover readily, as from misfortune. **2.** Capable of returning to an original shape or position, as after having been compressed. See Synonyms at **flexible.** [Latin *resiliēns, resilient-,* present participle of *resilīre,* to leap back. See RESILE.] **—re·sil′ient·ly** *adv.*

res·i·lin (rĕz′ə-lĭn) *n.* An elastic substance consisting of cross-linked protein chains, found in the cuticles of many insects. [RESIL(E) + -IN.]

res·in (rĕz′ĭn) *n.* **1.** Any of numerous clear to translucent yellow or brown, solid or semisolid, viscous substances of plant origin, such as copal, rosin, and amber, used principally in lacquers, varnishes, inks, adhesives, synthetic plastics, and pharmaceuticals. **2.** Any of numerous physically similar polymerized synthetics or chemically modified natural resins including thermoplastic materials such as polyvinyl, polystyrene, and polyethylene and thermosetting materials such as polyesters, epoxies, and silicones that are used with fillers, stabilizers, pigments, and other components to form plastics. **—resin** *tr.v.* **-ined, -in·ing, -ines.** To treat or rub with resin. [Middle English, from Old French *resine,* from Latin *rēsīna,* from Greek dialectal **rhēsina,* variant of Greek *rhētinē.*] **—res′in·ous** (rĕz′ə-nəs) *adj.*

res·in·ate (rĕz′ə-nāt′) *tr.v.* **-at·ed, -at·ing, -ates.** To impregnate, permeate, or flavor with resin.

resin canal *n.* An intercellular tube lined with resin-secreting cells, found in the wood and leaves of many gymnosperms. Also called *resin duct.*

res·in·if·er·ous (rĕz′ə-nĭf′ər-əs) *adj.* Yielding resin.

res·in·oid (rĕz′ə-noid′) *adj.* Relating to, resembling, or containing resin. **—resinoid** *n.* A synthetic resin, especially a thermosetting resin.

re·sist (rĭ-zĭst′) *v.* **-sist·ed, -sist·ing, -sists.** *—tr.* **1.** To strive to fend off or offset the actions, effects, or force of. **2.** To remain firm against the actions, effects, or force of; withstand: *a bacterium that resisted the antibiotic.* **3.** To keep from giving in to or enjoying. *—intr.* To offer resistance. See Synonyms at **oppose. —resist** *n.* A substance that can cover and protect a surface, as from corrosion. [Middle English *resisten,* from Old French *resister,* from Latin *resistere* : *re-,* re- + *sistere,* to place; see **stā-** in Appendix.] **—re·sist′er** *n.*

re·sis·tance (rĭ-zĭs′təns) *n.* **1.** The act or an instance of resisting or the capacity to resist. **2.** A force that tends to oppose or retard motion. **3.** Often **Resistance.** An underground organization engaged in a struggle for national liberation in a country under military or totalitarian occupation. **4.** *Psychology.* A process in which the ego opposes the conscious recall of unpleasant experiences. **5.** *Biology.* **a.** The capacity of an organism to defend itself against a disease. **b.** The capacity of an organism or a tissue to withstand the effects of a harmful environmental agent. **6.** *Abbr.* **r, R** *Electricity.* The opposition of a body or substance to current passing through it, resulting in a change of electrical energy into heat or another form of energy. **—re·sis′tant** *adj.*

resistance transfer factor *n.* R factor.

Re·sis·ten·cia (rĕs′ĭ-stĕn′sē-ə, rĕ′sēs-tĕn′syä). A city of northeast Argentina on the Paraná River opposite Corrientes. It is a major trade and shipping center. Population, 220,104.

re·sist·i·ble (rĭ-zĭs′tə-bəl) *adj.* Possible to resist: *resistible impulses.* **—re·sist′i·bil′i·ty** *n.* **—re·sist′i·bly** *adv.*

re·sis·tive (rĭ-zĭs′tĭv) *adj.* Of, tending toward, or marked by resistance: *a person resistive to change.* **—re·sis′tive·ly** *adv.* **—re·sis′tive·ness** *n.*

ă pat	oi boy
ā pay	ou out
âr care	o͝o took
ä father	o͞o boot
ĕ pet	ŭ cut
ē be	ûr urge
ĭ pit	th thin
ī pie	*th* this
îr pier	hw which
ŏ pot	zh vision
ō toe	ə about, item
ô paw	♦ regionalism

Stress marks: ′ (primary); ′ (secondary), as in **dictionary**

re·sis·tiv·i·ty (rē′zĭs-tĭv′ĭ-tē) *n., pl.* **-ties. 1.** The capacity for or tendency toward resistance. **2.** *Electricity.* The resistance per unit length of a substance with uniform cross section.

re·sist·less (rĭ-zĭst′lĭs) *adj.* **1.** Impossible to resist; irresistible: *resistless impulses.* **2.** Powerless to resist; unresisting: *resistless hostages.* **—re·sist′less·ly** *adv.* **—re·sist′less·ness** *n.*

re·sis·tor (rĭ-zĭs′tər) *n.* A device used to control current in an electric circuit by providing resistance.

Re·şi·ţa (rĕ′shē-tsä′). A city of western Romania in the western Transylvanian Alps west-northwest of Bucharest. It has an important iron and steel industry. Population, 101,902.

res ju·di·ca·ta (rēz′ jo͞o′dĭ-kä′tə, rās′) also **res ad·ju·di·ca·ta** (ə-jo͞o′-) *n. Law.* An adjudicated precedent. [Latin *rēs iūdicāta,* thing decided : *rēs,* thing + *iūdicāta,* feminine past participle of *iūdicāre,* to judge.]

re·sole (rē-sōl′) *tr.v.* **-soled, -sol·ing, -soles.** To put a new sole on (a shoe).

re·sol·u·ble (rĭ-zŏl′yə-bəl) *adj.* Possible to resolve; resolvable: *resoluble differences in opinion.* [Late Latin *resolūbilis,* from Latin *resolvere,* to resolve. See RESOLVE.] **—re·sol′u·bil′i·ty, re·sol′u·ble·ness** *n.*

res·o·lute (rĕz′ə-lo͞ot′) *adj.* Firm or determined; unwavering. [Middle English, dissolved, dissolute, from Latin *resolūtus,* relaxed, past participle of *resolvere,* to relax, untie. See RESOLVE.] **—res′o·lute′ly** *adv.* **—res′o·lute′ness** *n.*

res·o·lu·tion (rĕz′ə-lo͞o′shən) *n. Abbr.* **res. 1.** The state or quality of being resolute; firm determination. **2.** A resolving to do something. **3.** A course of action determined or decided on. **4.** A formal statement of a decision or expression of opinion put before or adopted by an assembly such as the U.S. Congress. **5.** *Physics & Chemistry.* The act or process of separating or reducing something into its constituent parts: *the prismatic resolution of sunlight into its spectral colors.* **6.** The fineness of detail that can be distinguished in an image, as on a video display terminal. **7.** *Medicine.* The subsiding or termination of an abnormal condition, such as a fever or an inflammation. **8.** *Law.* A court decision. **9.a.** An explanation, as of a problem or puzzle; a solution. **b.** The part of a literary work in which the complications of the plot are resolved or simplified. **10.** *Music.* **a.** The progression of a dissonant tone or chord to a consonant tone or chord. **b.** The tone or chord to which such a progression is made. **11.** The substitution of one metrical unit for another, especially the substitution of two short syllables for one long syllable in quantitative verse.

re·solve (rĭ-zŏlv′) *v.* **-solved, -solv·ing, -solves.** *—tr.* **1.** To make a firm decision about. **2.** To cause (a person) to reach a decision. See Synonyms at **decide. 3.** To decide or express by formal vote. **4.** To separate (something) into constituent parts. See Synonyms at **analyze. 5.** To change or convert: *My resentment resolved itself into resignation.* **6.** To find a solution to; solve. See Synonyms at **solve. 7.** To remove or dispel (doubts). **8.** To bring to a usually successful conclusion: *resolve a conflict.* **9.** *Medicine.* To cause reduction of (an inflammation, for example). **10.** *Music.* To cause (a tone or chord) to progress from dissonance to consonance. **11.** *Chemistry.* To separate (an optically inactive compound or mixture) into its optically active constituents. **12.** To render parts of (an image) visible and distinct. **13.** *Mathematics.* To separate (a vector, for example) into coordinate components. **14.** To melt or dissolve (something). *—intr.* **1.** To reach a decision or make a determination: *resolve on a course of action.* **2.** To become separated or reduced to constituents. **3.** *Music.* To undergo resolution. **—resolve** *n.* **1.** Firmness of purpose; resolution. **2.** A determination or decision; a fixed purpose. **3.** A formal resolution made by a deliberative body. [Middle English *resolven,* to dissolve, from Old French *resolver,* from Latin *resolvere,* to untie : *re-,* re- + *solvere,* to untie; see **leu-** in Appendix.] **—re·solv′a·bil′i·ty, re·solv′a·ble·ness** *n.* **—re·solv′a·ble** *adj.* **—re·solv′ed·ly** (-zŏl′vĭd-lē) *adv.* **—re·solv′er** *n.*

re·sol·vent (rĭ-zŏl′vənt) *adj.* Causing or able to cause separation into constituents; solvent. **—resolvent** *n.* A resolvent substance, especially a medicine that reduces inflammation or swelling.

res·o·nance (rĕz′ə-nəns) *n.* **1.** The quality or condition of being resonant: *"It is home and family that give resonance . . . to life"* (George Gilder). *"Israel, gateway to Mecca, is of course a land of religious resonance and geopolitical significance"* (James Wolcott). **2.** *Physics.* The increase in amplitude of oscillation of an electric or mechanical system exposed to a periodic force whose frequency is equal or very close to the natural undamped frequency of the system. **3.** *Acoustics.* Intensification and prolongation of sound, especially of a musical tone, produced by sympathetic vibration. **4.** *Linguistics.* Intensification of vocal tones during articulation, as by the air cavities of the mouth and nasal passages. **5.** *Medicine.* The sound produced by diagnostic percussion of the normal chest. **6.** *Chemistry.* The property of a compound having simultaneously the characteristics of two or more structural forms that differ only in the distribution of electrons. Such compounds are highly stable and cannot be properly represented by a single structural formula.

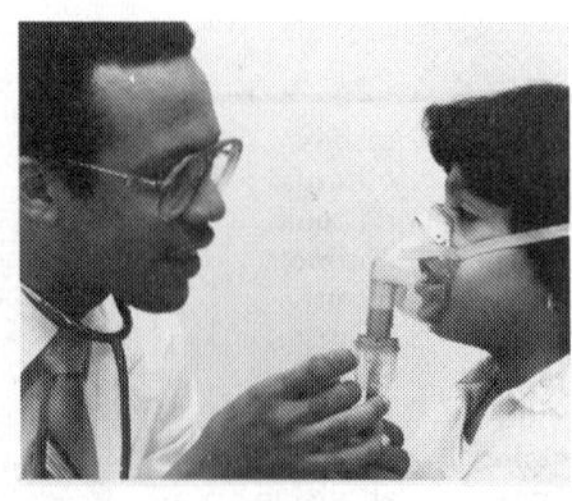

respirator

res·o·nant (rĕz′ə-nənt) *adj.* **1.a.** Strong and deep in tone; resounding: *a resonant voice.* **b.** Continuing to sound in the ears or memory; echoing: *resonant words of exhortation.* **c.** Having a prolonged, subtle, or stimulating effect beyond the initial impact: *"While her husband . . . travels far less, they find her life on the run a resonant stress factor in her home"* (Robert Berry). **2.** Producing or exhibiting resonance: *resonant frequency excitation.* **3.** Resulting from or as if from resonance: *resonant amplification.* [Latin *resonāns, resonant-,* present participle of *resonāre,* to resound. See RESOUND.] **—res′o·nant·ly** *adv.*

resonant circuit *n.* An electric circuit with inductance and capacitance chosen to allow the greatest flow of current at a certain frequency.

res·o·nate (rĕz′ə-nāt′) *v.* **-nat·ed, -nat·ing, -nates.** *—intr.* **1.** To exhibit or produce resonance or resonant effects. **2.** To resound: *"It is a demonology* [that] *seems to resonate among secular and religious voters alike"* (Tamar Jacoby). *—tr.* To cause to resound. [Latin *resonāre, resonāt-.* See RESOUND.] **—res′o·na′tion** *n.*

res·o·na·tor (rĕz′ə-nā′tər) *n.* **1.** A resonating system. **2.** A hollow chamber or cavity with dimensions chosen to permit internal resonant oscillation of electromagnetic or acoustical waves of specific frequencies. **3.** A resonant circuit.

re·sorb (rē-sôrb′, -zôrb′) *v.* **-sorbed, -sorb·ing, -sorbs.** *—tr.* **1.** To absorb again. **2.** *Biology.* To dissolve and assimilate (bone tissue, for example). *—intr.* To undergo resorption. [Latin *resorbēre,* to suck back : *re-,* re- + *sorbēre,* to suck up.]

res·or·cin·ol (rĭ-zôr′sə-nôl′, -nōl′, -nŏl′) also **res·or·cin** (rĭ-zôr′sĭn) *n.* A white crystalline compound, $C_6H_4(OH)_2$, used to treat certain skin diseases and in dyes, resin adhesives, and pharmaceuticals. [RES(IN) + ORC(HIL) + –IN + –OL[1].]

re·sorp·tion (rē-sôrp′shən, -zôrp′-) *n.* The act or process of resorbing.

re·sort (rĭ-zôrt′) *intr.v.* **-sort·ed, -sort·ing, -sorts. 1.** To have recourse: *The government resorted to censorship of the press.* **2.** To go customarily or frequently; repair. **—resort** *n.* **1.** A place frequented by people for relaxation or recreation: *a tropical resort.* **2.** A customary or frequent going or gathering: *a popular place of resort.* **3.** The act of turning to for aid or relief; recourse. **4.** One turned to for aid or relief. [Middle English *resorten,* to return, from Old French *resortir,* to go out again : *re-,* re- + *sortir,* to go out.]

SYNONYMS: *resort, apply, go, refer, turn.* The central meaning shared by these verbs is "to repair to or fall back on someone or something in time of need": *never resorted to corporal punishment; apply to a bank for a loan; went to her parents for comfort; referred to his notes to refresh his memory; has no friends to turn to.* See also Synonyms at **makeshift.**

re-sort (rē-sôrt′) *tr.v.* **-sort·ed, -sort·ing, -sorts.** To sort again.

re·sort·er (rĭ-zôr′tər) *n.* One who frequents resorts for vacations or recreation.

re·sound (rĭ-zound′) *v.* **-sound·ed, -sound·ing, -sounds.** *—intr.* **1.** To be filled with sound; reverberate: *The school yard resounded with the laughter of children.* **2.** To make a loud, long, or reverberating sound: *Rolls of thunder resounded in the valley.* **3.** To sound loudly; ring. **4.** To become famous, celebrated, or extolled: *Picasso—a name to resound for ages in art history.* *—tr.* **1.** To send back (sound). See Synonyms at **echo. 2.** To utter or emit loudly. **3.** To celebrate or praise, as in verse or song. [Alteration (influenced by SOUND[1]) of Middle English *resounen,* from Old French *resoner,* from Latin *resonāre* : *re-,* re- + *sonāre,* to sound; see **swen-** in Appendix.] **—re·sound′ing** *adj.* **—re·sound′ing·ly** *adv.*

re·source (rē′sôrs′, -sōrs′, -zôrs′, -zōrs′, rĭ-sôrs′, -sōrs′, -zôrs′, -zōrs′) *n.* **1.** Something that can be used for support or help: *The local library is a valuable resource.* **2.** Often **resources.** An available supply that can be drawn on when needed. **3.** The ability to deal with a difficult or troublesome situation effectively; initiative: *a person of resource.* **4.** Often **resources.** Means that can be used to cope with a difficult situation: *needed all my intellectual resources for the exam.* **5.a. resources.** The total means available for economic and political development, such as mineral wealth, labor force, and armaments. **b. resources.** The total means available to a company for increasing production or profit, including plant, labor, and raw material; assets. **c.** Such means considered individually. [Obsolete French, from Old French, from feminine past participle of *resourdre,* to rise again, from Latin *resurgere* : *re-,* re- + *surgere,* to rise; see SURGE.]

re·source·ful (rĭ-sôrs′fəl, -sōrs′-, -zôrs′-, -zōrs′-) *adj.* Able to act effectively or imaginatively, especially in difficult situations. **—re·source′ful·ly** *adv.* **—re·source′ful·ness** *n.*

resp. *abbr.* **1.** Respective; respectively. **2.** Respiration.

re·spect (rĭ-spĕkt′) *tr.v.* **-spect·ed, -spect·ing, -spects. 1.** To feel or show deferential regard for; esteem. **2.** To avoid violation of or interference with: *respect the speed limit.* **3.** To relate or refer to; concern. **—respect** *n.* **1.** A feeling of appreciative, often deferential regard; esteem. See Synonyms at **regard. 2.** The state of being regarded with honor or esteem. **3.** Willingness to show consideration or appreciation. **4. respects.** Polite expressions of consideration or deference: *pay one's respects.* **5.** A particular aspect, feature, or detail: *In many respects this is an important decision.* **6.** *Usage Problem.* Relation; reference. See Usage Note at **regard.** [From Middle English, regard, from Old French, from Latin *respectus,* from past participle of *respicere,* to look back at, regard : *re-,* re- + *specere,* to look at; see **spek-** in Appendix.] **—re·spect′er** *n.*

re·spect·a·bil·i·ty (rĭ-spĕk′tə-bĭl′ĭ-tē) *n.* The quality, state, or characteristic of being respectable.

re·spect·a·ble (rĭ-spĕk′tə-bəl) *adj.* **1.** Meriting respect or esteem; worthy. **2.** Of or appropriate to good or proper behavior or conventional conduct. **3.** Of moderately good quality: *respectable work.* **4.** Considerable in amount, number, or size: *a respectable sum of money.* **5.** Acceptable in appearance; presentable: *a respectable hat.* **—re·spect′a·ble·ness** *n.* **—re·spect′a·bly** *adv.*

re·spect·ful (rĭ-spĕkt′fəl) *adj.* Showing or marked by proper respect. **—re·spect′ful·ly** *adv.* **—re·spect′ful·ness** *n.*

re·spect·ing (rĭ-spĕk′tĭng) *prep. Usage Problem.* With respect to; concerning. See Usage Note at **regard.**

re·spec·tive (rĭ-spĕk′tĭv) *adj. Abbr.* **resp.** Relating to two or more persons or things regarded individually; particular: *successful in their respective fields.* **—re·spec′tive·ness** *n.*

re·spec·tive·ly (rĭ-spĕk′tĭv-lē) *adv. Abbr.* **resp.** Singly in the order designated or mentioned: *I'm referring to each of you respectively.*

re·spell (rē-spĕl′) *tr.v.* **-spelled** or **-spelt** (-spĕlt′), **-spell·ing, -spells.** To spell again or in a new way, especially by using a phonetic alphabet.

Re·spi·ghi (rĕ-spē′gē), **Ottorino.** 1879–1936. Italian composer known for his symphonic poems, such as *The Fountains of Rome* (1917) and *Roman Festivals* (1929).

res·pi·ra·ble (rĕs′pər-ə-bəl, rĭ-spīr′-) *adj.* **1.** Fit for breathing: *respirable air.* **2.** Capable of undergoing respiration: *respirable organisms.* **—res′pi·ra·bil′i·ty** *n.*

res·pi·ra·tion (rĕs′pə-rā′shən) *n. Abbr.* **resp. 1.a.** The act or process of inhaling and exhaling; breathing. **b.** The act or process by which an organism without lungs, such as a fish or plant, exchanges gases with its environment. **2.a.** The oxidative process occurring within living cells by which the chemical energy of organic molecules is released in a series of metabolic steps involving the consumption of oxygen and the liberation of carbon dioxide and water. **b.** Any of various analogous metabolic processes by which certain organisms, such as fungi and anaerobic bacteria, obtain energy from organic molecules. **—res′pi·ra′tion·al** *adj.*

res·pi·ra·tor (rĕs′pə-rā′tər) *n.* **1.** A device that supplies oxygen or a mixture of oxygen and carbon dioxide for breathing, used especially in artificial respiration. Also called *inhalator.* **2.** A screenlike device worn over the mouth or nose or both to protect the respiratory tract.

res·pi·ra·to·ry (rĕs′pər-ə-tôr′ē, -tōr′ē, rĭ-spīr′ə-) *adj.* Of, relating to, used in, or affecting respiration.

respiratory distress syndrome *n.* A respiratory disease of newborn babies, especially premature babies, characterized by distressful breathing, cyanosis, and the formation of a glassy membrane over the alveoli of the lungs. Also called *hyaline membrane disease.*

respiratory enzyme *n.* An enzyme, such as oxidase, that transfers electrons from its substrate to molecular oxygen during cellular respiration.

respiratory pigment *n.* Any of various colored conjugated proteins, such as hemoglobin, that occur in living organisms and function in oxygen transfer in cellular respiration.

respiratory quotient *n. Abbr.* **R.Q.** The ratio of the volume of carbon dioxide released to the volume of oxygen consumed by a body tissue or an organism in a given period.

respiratory system *n.* The integrated system of organs involved in the intake and exchange of oxygen and carbon dioxide between an organism and the environment.

re·spire (rĭ-spīr′) *v.* **-spired, -spir·ing, -spires.** *—intr.* **1.** To breathe in and out; inhale and exhale. **2.** To undergo the metabolic process of respiration. **3.** To breathe easily again, as after a period of exertion or trouble. *—tr.* To inhale and exhale (air); breathe. [Middle English *respiren,* to breathe again, from Latin *respīrāre* : *re-,* re- + *spīrāre,* to breathe.]

res·pi·rom·e·ter (rĕs′pə-rŏm′ĭ-tər) *n.* An instrument for measuring the degree and nature of respiration. **—res′pi·ro·met′ric** (-rō-mĕt′rĭk) *adj.* **—res′pi·rom′e·try** *n.*

res·pite (rĕs′pĭt) *n.* **1.** A usually short interval of rest or relief. See Synonyms at **pause. 2.** *Law.* Temporary suspension of a death sentence; a reprieve. **—respite** *tr.v.* **-pit·ed, -pit·ing, -pites.** To delay; postpone. [Middle English, from Old French *respit,* from Latin *respectus,* refuge, looking back. See RESPECT.]

re·splen·dent (rĭ-splĕn′dənt) *adj.* Splendid or dazzling in appearance; brilliant. [Middle English, from Old French, from Latin *resplendēns, resplendent-,* present participle of *resplendēre,* to shine brightly : *re-,* re- + *splendēre,* to shine.] **—re·splen′dence, re·splen′den·cy** *n.* **—re·splen′dent·ly** *adv.*

re·spond (rĭ-spŏnd′) *v.* **-spond·ed, -spond·ing, -sponds.** *—intr.* **1.** To make a reply; answer. See Synonyms at **answer. 2.** To act in return or in answer. **3.** To react positively or favorably: *The patient has responded rapidly to the treatment.* *—tr.* To give as a reply; answer. **—respond** *n. Architecture.* A pilaster supporting an arch. [Middle English *responden,* from Old French *respondre,* from Latin *respondēre* : *re-,* re- + *spondēre,* to promise; see **spend-** in Appendix.] **—re·spond′er** *n.*

re·spon·dent (rĭ-spŏn′dənt) *adj.* **1.** Giving or given as an answer; responsive. **2.** *Law.* Being a defendant. **—respondent** *n.* **1.** One who responds. **2.** *Law.* A defendant, especially in a divorce or equity case. **—re·spon′dence, re·spon′den·cy** *n.*

re·sponse (rĭ-spŏns′) *n.* **1.** The act of responding. **2.** A reply or an answer. **3.** A reaction, as that of an organism or a mechanism, to a specific stimulus. **4.a.** *Abbr.* **R** *Ecclesiastical.* Something that is spoken or sung by a congregation or choir in answer to the officiating minister or priest. **b.** A responsory. [Middle English *respons,* from Old French, from Latin *respōnsum,* from neuter past participle of *respondēre,* to respond. See RESPOND.]

re·spon·si·bil·i·ty (rĭ-spŏn′sə-bĭl′ĭ-tē) *n., pl.* **-ties. 1.** The state, quality, or fact of being responsible. See Synonyms at **obligation. 2.** Something for which one is responsible; a duty, an obligation, or a burden.

re·spon·si·ble (rĭ-spŏn′sə-bəl) *adj.* **1.** Liable to be required to give account, as of one's actions or of the discharge of a duty or trust. **2.** Involving personal accountability or ability to act without guidance or superior authority: *a responsible position within the company.* **3.** Being a source or cause. **4.** Able to make moral or rational decisions on one's own and therefore answerable for one's behavior. **5.** Able to be trusted or depended upon; reliable. **6.** Based on or characterized by good judgment or sound thinking: *responsible journalism.* **7.** Having the means to pay debts or fulfill obligations. **8.** Required to render account; answerable: *The cabinet is responsible to the parliament.* [Obsolete French, corresponding to, from Latin *respōnsus,* past participle of *respondēre,* to respond. See RESPOND.] **—re·spon′si·ble·ness** *n.* **—re·spon′si·bly** *adv.*

SYNONYMS: *responsible, answerable, liable, accountable, amenable.* These adjectives share the meaning obliged to answer, as for one's actions, to an authority that may impose a penalty for failure. *Responsible* often implies the satisfactory performance of duties, the adequate discharge of obligations, or the trustworthy care for or disposition of possessions: *"I am responsible for the ship's safety"* (Robert Louis Stevenson). *"The people had given him his command, and to the people alone he was responsible"* (J.A. Froude). *Answerable* suggests a moral or legal responsibility subject to review by a higher authority: *The court held the parents answerable for their minor child's acts of vandalism. Liable* may refer to a legal obligation, as to pay damages, or to a responsibility to do something, as to perform jury duty, if called on: *Wage earners are liable to income tax. During the war men between the ages of 18 and 35 were liable for military conscription. Accountable* especially emphasizes the requirement to give an account of one's discharge of a responsibility entrusted to one: *"The liberal philosophy holds that enduring governments must be accountable to someone beside themselves; that a government responsible only to its own conscience is not for long tolerable"* (Walter Lippmann). *Amenable* implies the condition of being subject to the control of an authority and therefore the absence of complete autonomy: *"The sovereign of this country is not amenable to any form of trial"* (Letters of Junius). See also Synonyms at **reliable.**

USAGE NOTE: Some critics have maintained that *responsible* should not be used to describe things, since only persons can be held accountable. The application to things is justifiable, however, when *responsible* is used to mean "being the source or cause of." In an earlier survey, a majority of the Usage Panel accepted the sentence *Faulty construction was responsible for the crash.* • In recent years, many people have objected to the use of the phrase *claim responsibility* with reference to the authors of terrorist acts, as in *A small separatist group claimed responsibility for the explosion, in which 30 passengers were killed.* It is true that the phrase is not entirely felicitous, inasmuch as it does not convey the speaker's conviction that the action is deplorable. But alternatives such as *admit* or *take the blame* cannot be recommended either, since they would imply misleadingly that the instigators had themselves acknowledged that the action was wrongful.

re·spon·sive (rĭ-spŏn′sĭv) *adj.* **1.** Answering or replying; responding. **2.** Readily reacting to suggestions, influences, appeals, or efforts: *a responsive student.* **3.** Containing or using responses: *responsive reading; responsive liturgy.* **—re·spon′sive·ly** *adv.* **—re·spon′sive·ness** *n.*

re·spon·so·ry (rĭ-spŏn′sə-rē) *n., pl.* **-ries.** *Ecclesiastical.* A chant or an anthem recited or sung after a reading in a church service. [Middle English *responsorie,* from Late Latin *respōnsōrium,* from Latin *respōnsus,* past participle of *respondēre,* to respond. See RESPOND.] **—re·spon·so′ri·al** (-sôr′ē-əl, -sōr′-) *adj.*

res pub·li·ca (rēz pŭb′lĭ-kə, rās po͞o′blē-kä′) *n., pl.* **-cae** (-kā, -kī). **1.** A state, republic, or commonwealth. **2.** The general public good or welfare. [Latin *rēs pūblica.* See REPUBLIC.]

res·sen·ti·ment (rə-säɴ′tē-mäɴ′) *n.* A generalized feeling of resentment and often hostility harbored by one individual or group against another, especially chronically and with no means of direct expression. [French, resentment, from Old French *ressentement,* from *resentir,* to feel strongly. See RESENT.]

rest[1] (rĕst) *n.* **1.** Cessation of work, exertion, or activity. **2.** Peace, ease, or refreshment resulting from sleep or the cessation of an activity. **3.** Sleep or quiet relaxation. **4.** The repose of death: *eternal rest.* **5.** Relief or freedom from disquiet or disturbance. **6.** Mental or emotional tranquillity. **7.** Termination or absence of motion. **8.** *Music.* **a.** An interval of silence corresponding to one of the possible time values within a measure. **b.** The mark or symbol indicating such a pause and its length. **9.** A short pause in a line of poetry; a caesura. **10.** A device used as a support: *a*

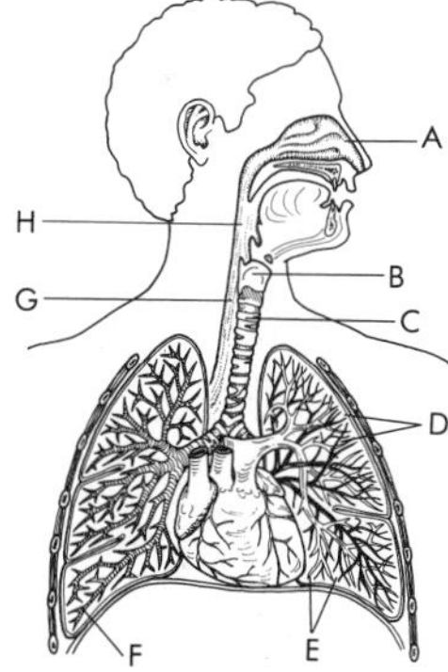

respiratory system
A. Nasal passages
B. Larynx
C. Trachea
D. Veins
E. Arteries
F. Bronchus
G. Esophagus
H. Throat

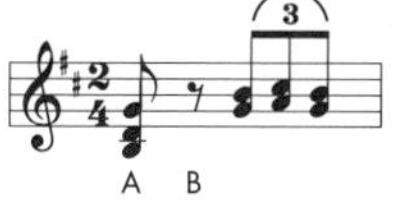

rest[1]
A. Note
B. Rest

ă pat	oi boy
ā pay	ou out
âr care	o͝o took
ä father	o͞o boot
ĕ pet	ŭ cut
ē be	ûr urge
ĭ pit	th thin
ī pie	*th* this
îr pier	hw which
ŏ pot	zh vision
ō toe	ə about, item
ô paw	♦ regionalism

Stress marks: ′ (primary); ′ (secondary), as in **dictionary** (dĭk′shə-nĕr′ē)

back rest. **11.** *Games.* See **bridge**[1] (sense 7a). **—rest** *v.* **rest·ed, rest·ing, rests.** *—intr.* **1.** To cease motion, work, or activity. **2.** To lie down, especially to sleep. **3.** To be at peace or ease; be tranquil. **4.** To be, become, or remain temporarily still, quiet, or inactive: *Let the issue rest here.* **5.** To be supported or based; lie, lean, or sit: *The ladder rests firmly against the tree.* **6.** To be imposed or vested, as a responsibility or burden: *The final decision rests with the chairperson.* **7.** To depend or rely: *That argument rests on a false assumption.* **8.** To be located or be in a specified place: *The original manuscript rests in the museum.* **9.** To be fixed or directed on something: *"His brown eyes rested on her for a moment"* (John le Carré). **10.** To remain; linger. **11.** *Law.* To cease voluntarily the presentation of evidence in a case: *The defense rests.* *—tr.* **1.** To give rest or repose to: *rested my eyes.* **2.** To place, lay, or lean for ease, support, or repose. **3.** To base or ground: *I rested my conclusion on that fact.* **4.** To fix or direct (the gaze, for example). **5.** To bring to rest; halt. **6.** *Law.* To cease voluntarily the introduction of evidence in (a case). ***—idioms.*** **at rest. 1.a.** Asleep. **b.** Dead. **2.** Motionless; inactive. **3.** Free from anxiety or distress. **lay** (or **put**) **to rest. 1.** To bury (a dead body); inter. **2.** To settle (an issue, for example), especially so as to be free of it: *The judge's ruling put to rest the dispute between the neighbors.* [Middle English, from Old English.] **—rest′er** *n.*

SYNONYMS: *rest, relaxation, repose, leisure, ease, comfort.* All of these nouns mean freedom or relief from labor, responsibility, or strain. *Rest,* the least specific, suggests mental or physical recuperation: *Try to get a good night's rest. "Absence of occupation is not rest"* (William Cowper). *Relaxation* implies release from tension or fatigue: *"We hold the period of youth sacred to education, and the period of maturity, when the physical forces begin to flag, equally sacred to ease and agreeable relaxation"* (Edward Bellamy). *Repose* connotes rest and peace of mind: *"when you're lying awake with a dismal headache, and repose is tabooed by anxiety"* (W.S. Gilbert). *Leisure* implies freedom from work or duty and latitude in choosing a pastime or an activity: *"Do you know that conversation is one of the greatest pleasures in life? But it wants leisure"* (W. Somerset Maugham). *Ease* connotes freedom from toil or worry, absence of constraint, and a relaxed frame of mind: *"It is the interest of every man to live as much at his ease as he can"* (Adam Smith). *Comfort* suggests ease, well-being, and contentment: *"They knew luxury; they knew beggary; but they never knew comfort"* (Macaulay).

rest[2] (rĕst) *n.* **1.** The part that is left over after something has been removed; remainder. See Synonyms at **remainder. 2.** That or those remaining: *The beginning was boring, but the rest was interesting. The rest are arriving later.* **—rest** *intr.v.* **rest·ed, rest·ing, rests. 1.** To be or continue to be; remain: *Rest assured that we will finish on time.* **2.** To remain or be left over. [Middle English, from Old French *reste,* from *rester,* to remain, from Latin *restāre,* to stay behind : *re-,* re- + *stāre,* to stand; see **stā-** in Appendix.]

rest[3] (rĕst) *n.* A support for a lance on the side of the breastplate of medieval armor. [Middle English *reste,* short for *areste,* a stopping, holding, from Old French, from *arester,* to stop. See ARREST.]

rest area *n.* A designated area, usually along a major highway, where motorists can pause to relax. Also called *rest stop.*

re·start (rē-stärt′) *v.* **-start·ed, -start·ing, -starts.** *—tr.* To start again or anew: *restarted the engine after it stalled.* *—intr.* To begin operation again. **—re′start′** *n.* **—re·start′a·ble** *adj.*

re·state (rē-stāt′) *tr.v.* **-stat·ed, -stat·ing, -states.** To state again or in a new form. See Synonyms at **repeat. —re·state′ment** *n.*

res·tau·rant (rĕs′tər-ənt, -tə-ränt′) *n.* A place where meals are served to the public. [French, from present participle of *restaurer,* to restore, from Old French *restorer.* See RESTORE.]

res·tau·ra·teur (rĕs′tər-ə-tûr′) also **res·tau·ran·teur** (-tə-rän-tûr′) *n.* The manager or owner of a restaurant. [French, from *restaurer,* to restore. See RESTAURANT.]

rest energy *n.* The energy equivalent of the rest mass of a body, equal to the rest mass multiplied by the speed of light squared.

rest·ful (rĕst′fəl) *adj.* **1.** Affording, marked by, or suggesting rest; tranquil. See Synonyms at **comfortable. 2.** Being at rest; quiet. **—rest′ful·ly** *adv.* **—rest′ful·ness** *n.*

rest·har·row (rĕst′hăr′ō) *n.* Any of several Old World plants of the genus *Ononis,* having woody stems, axillary pink or purplish flowers, and trifoliate leaves with dentate leaflets. [Obsolete *rest,* to check (short for Middle English *aresten;* see ARREST) + HARROW[1].]

rest home *n.* An establishment where the elderly or frail are housed and cared for.

res·ti·form body (rĕs′tə-fôrm′) *n.* A large cordlike bundle of nerve fibers lying on either side of the medulla oblongata and connecting it with the cerebellum. [Latin *restis,* rope + -FORM.]

rest·ing (rĕs′tĭng) *adj.* **1.a.** In a state of inactivity or rest. **b.** Dead. **2.** *Botany.* Dormant. Used especially of spores that germinate after a prolonged period.

resting cell *n.* A cell that is not actively in the process of dividing.

res·ti·tute (rĕs′tĭ-to͞ot′, -tyo͞ot′) *v.* **-tut·ed, -tut·ing, -tutes.** *—tr.* **1.** To bring back to a former condition; restore. **2.** To refund. *—intr.* To undergo restitution. [Latin *restituere, restitūt-* : *re-,* re- + *statuere,* to set up (from *stāre,* to stand; see **stā-** in Appendix).]

res·ti·tu·tion (rĕs′tĭ-to͞o′shən, -tyo͞o′-) *n.* **1.** The act of restoring to the rightful owner something that has been taken away, lost, or surrendered. See Synonyms at **reparation. 2.** The act of making good or compensating for loss, damage, or injury; indemnification. **3.** A return to or restoration of a previous state or position.

res·tive (rĕs′tĭv) *adj.* **1.** Uneasily impatient under restriction, opposition, criticism, or delay. **2.** Resisting control; difficult to control. **3.** Refusing to move. Used of a horse or other animal. [Middle English *restif,* stationary, from Old French, from *rester,* to remain, from Latin *restāre,* to keep back : *re-,* re- + *stāre,* to stand; see **stā-** in Appendix.] **—res′tive·ly** *adv.* **—res′tive·ness** *n.*

USAGE NOTE: *Restive* is properly applied to the impatience or uneasiness induced by external coercion or restriction and is not a general synonym for *restless: The government has done nothing to ease export restrictions, and domestic manufacturers are growing restive* (not *restless*). *The atmosphere in the office was congenial, but after five years she began to grow restless* (not *restive*).

rest·less (rĕst′lĭs) *adj.* **1.** Marked by a lack of quiet, repose, or rest: *spent a restless night.* **2.** Not able to rest, relax, or be still: *a restless child.* **3.** Never still or motionless: *the restless sea.* See Usage Note at **restive. —rest′less·ly** *adv.* **—rest′less·ness** *n.*

rest mass *n.* The physical mass of a body when it is regarded as being at rest.

re·stock (rē-stŏk′) *tr.v.* **-stocked, -stock·ing, -stocks.** To furnish new stock for; stock again.

Res·ton (rĕs′tən). A community of northeast Virginia, a suburb of the Washington, D.C.–Alexandria, Virginia, area. Population, 32,000.

Reston, James Barrett. Known as "Scotty." Born 1909. Scottish-born American journalist. Associated with the *New York Times* since 1939, he was awarded the Pulitzer Prize in 1945 and in 1957 for his reporting.

res·to·ra·tion (rĕs′tə-rā′shən) *n.* **1.a.** An act of restoring: *damage too great for restoration.* **b.** An instance of restoring or of being restored: *Restoration of the sculpture was expensive.* **c.** The state of being restored. **2.** Something, such as a renovated building, that has been restored. **3. Restoration. a.** The return of a constitutional monarchy to Great Britain in 1660 under Charles II. **b.** The period between the crowning of Charles II and the Revolution of 1688.

re·stor·a·tive (rĭ-stôr′ə-tĭv, -stōr′-) *adj.* **1.** Of or relating to restoration. **2.** Tending or having the power to restore: *a restorative tonic.* **—restorative** *n.* **1.** Something that restores. **2.** A medicine or other agent that helps to restore health, strength, or consciousness. **—re·stor′a·tive·ly** *adv.* **—re·stor′a·tive·ness** *n.*

re·store (rĭ-stôr′, -stōr′) *tr.v.* **-stored, -stor·ing, -stores. 1.** To bring back into existence or use; reestablish: *restore law and order.* **2.** To bring back to an original condition: *restore a building.* See Synonyms at **revive. 3.** To put (someone) back in a former position: *restore the emperor to the throne.* **4.** To make restitution of; give back: *restore the stolen funds.* [Middle English *restoren,* from Old French *restorer,* from Latin *restaurāre.* See **stā-** in Appendix.] **—re·stor′er** *n.*

re·strain (rĭ-strān′) *tr.v.* **-strained, -strain·ing, -strains. 1.a.** To hold back or keep in check; control: *couldn't restrain the tears.* **b.** To hold (a person) back; prevent: *restrained them from going.* **2.** To deprive of freedom or liberty. **3.** To limit or restrict. [Middle English *restreinen,* from Old French *restraindre, restreign-,* from Latin *restringere,* to bind back. See RESTRICT.] **—re·strain′a·ble** *adj.* **—re·strain′ed·ly** (-strā′nĭd-lē) *adv.* **—re·strain′er** *n.*

SYNONYMS: *restrain, curb, check, bridle, inhibit.* These verbs are compared as they mean to hold back or keep under control. *Restrain* implies restriction or limitation, as on one's freedom of action: *"a wise and frugal government, which shall restrain men from injuring one another"* (Thomas Jefferson). *He had difficulty restraining his curiosity.* To *curb* is to restrain as if with reins: *"You might curb your magnanimity"* (John Keats). *Check* implies arresting or stopping, often suddenly or forcibly: *"a light to guide, a rod/To check the erring"* (William Wordsworth). To *bridle* is often to hold in or govern one's emotions or passions: *She tried with all her might to bridle her resentment. Inhibit* usually connotes a check, either self-imposed or involuntary, on one's actions, desires, thoughts, or emotions: *For the compliant child parental disapproval is as strong an inhibiting force as the threat of punishment.*

re·straint (rĭ-strānt′) *n.* **1.** The act of restraining or the condition of being restrained. **2.** Loss or abridgment of freedom. **3.** An influence that inhibits or restrains; a limitation. **4.** An instrument or a means of restraining. **5.** Control or repression of feelings; constraint. [Middle English *restreinte,* from Old French *restrainte,* from feminine past participle of *restraindre,* to restrain. See RESTRAIN.]

restraint of trade *n., pl.* **restraints of trade.** An action or a condition that tends to prevent free competition in business, as the creation of a monopoly or the limiting of a market.

re•strict (rĭ-strĭkt′) *tr.v.* **-strict•ed, -strict•ing, -stricts.** To keep or confine within limits. See Synonyms at **limit.** [Latin *restringere, restrict-* : *re-*, re- + *stringere,* to draw tight; see **streig-** in Appendix.] **—re•stric′tor, re•strict′er** *n.*

re•strict•ed (rĭ-strĭk′tĭd) *adj.* **1.** Kept within certain limits; limited: *on a restricted diet.* **2.** Excluding or unavailable to certain groups: *a restricted area.* **3.** Of, relating to, or being information available only to authorized persons. **—re•strict′ed•ly** *adv.*

re•stric•tion (rĭ-strĭk′shən) *n.* **1.a.** The act of restricting. **b.** The state of being restricted. **2.** Something that restricts; a regulation or limitation.

restriction enzyme *n.* Any of a group of enzymes that cleave DNA at specific sites to produce discrete fragments, used especially in gene-splicing. Also called *restriction endonuclease.*

re•stric•tion•ism (rĭ-strĭk′shə-nĭz′əm) *n.* A viewpoint or policy approving the imposing of restrictions, as on immigration or trade. **—re•stric′tion•ist** *n.*

re•stric•tive (rĭ-strĭk′tĭv) *adj.* **1.a.** Of or relating to restriction. **b.** Tending or serving to restrict; limiting. **2.** *Grammar.* Of, relating to, or being a subordinate clause or phrase that identifies the noun, phrase, or clause it modifies and limits or restricts its meaning, as the clause *who live in glass houses* in *People who live in glass houses shouldn't throw stones.* **—re•stric′tive•ly** *adv.* **—re•stric′tive•ness** *n.*

re•strike (rē′strīk′) *n.* A coin or medal freshly minted from an original die at a time after the first issue. **—re′strike′** *v.*

rest•room (rĕst′ro͞om′, -ro͝om′) *n.* A room equipped with toilets and lavatories for public use.

re•struc•ture (rē-strŭk′chər) *v.* **-tured, -tur•ing, -tures.** *—tr.* **1.** To alter the makeup or pattern of: *"serious efforts to restructure third world debt"* (Felix Rohatyn). **2.** To make a basic change in (an organization or a system, for example). *—intr.* To alter the structure of something.

rest stop *n.* See **rest area.**

re•sult (rĭ-zŭlt′) *intr.v.* **-sult•ed, -sult•ing, -sults. 1.** To come about as a consequence. See Synonyms at **follow. 2.** To end in a particular way: *Their profligate lifestyle resulted in bankruptcy.* **—result** *n.* **1.a.** The consequence of a particular action, operation, or course; an outcome. See Synonyms at **effect. b.** Often **results.** A favorable or concrete outcome or effect: *started studying and got immediate results.* **2.** *Mathematics.* The quantity or expression obtained by calculation. [Middle English *resulten,* from Medieval Latin *resultāre,* from Latin, to leap back, frequentative of *resilīre* : *re-*, re- + *salīre,* to leap; see **sel-** in Appendix.] **—re•sult′ful** *adj.* **—re•sult′ful•ness** *n.* **—re•sult′less** *adj.*

re•sul•tant (rĭ-zŭl′tənt) *adj.* Issuing or following as a consequence or result. **—resultant** *n.* **1.** Something that results; an outcome. **2.** *Mathematics.* A single vector that is the equivalent of a set of vectors. **—re•sul′tant•ly** *adv.*

re•sume (rĭ-zo͞om′) *v.* **-sumed, -sum•ing, -sumes.** *—tr.* **1.** To begin or take up again after interruption: *resumed our dinner.* **2.** To assume, take, or occupy again: *The dog resumed its post by the door.* **3.** To take on or take back again: *resumed my original name.* *—intr.* To begin again or continue after interruption. [Middle English *resumen,* from Old French *resumer,* from Latin *resūmere* : *re-*, re- + *sūmere,* to take; see **em-** in Appendix.] **—re•sum′a•ble** *adj.* **—re•sum′er** *n.*

ré•su•mé or **re•su•me** or **re•su•mé** (rĕz′o͝o-mā′, rĕz′o͝o-mā′) *n.* **1.** A brief account of one's professional or work experience and qualifications, often submitted with an employment application. **2.** A summary: *a résumé of the facts of the case.* [French, from past participle of *résumer,* to summarize, from Old French *resumer,* to resume. See RESUME.]

re•sump•tion (rĭ-zŭmp′shən) *n.* The act or an instance of resuming; a beginning again: *resumption of negotiations.* [Middle English, from Old French, from Late Latin *resūmptiō, resūmptiōn-*, recovery, from Latin *resūmptus,* past participle of *resūmere,* to resume. See RESUME.]

re•su•pi•nate (rĭ-so͞o′pə-nāt′, -nĭt) *adj.* *Biology.* Inverted or seemingly turned upside down, as the flowers of most orchids. [Latin *resupīnātus,* past participle of *resupīnāre,* to bend back : *re-*, re- + *supīnus,* supine; see SUPINE.] **—re•su′pi•na′tion** *n.*

re•su•pine (rĕs′ə-pīn′) *adj.* Lying on the back; supine. [Latin *resupīnus* : *re-*, re- + *supīnus,* supine; see SUPINE.]

re•sup•ply (rē′sə-plī′) *tr.v.* **-plied, -ply•ing, -plies.** To provide with fresh supplies, as of weapons and ammunition. **—re′sup•ply′** *n.*

re•sur•face (rē-sûr′fəs) *v.* **-faced, -fac•ing, -fac•es.** *—tr.* To cover with a new surface: *resurfacing a road; resurfaced the floor.* *—intr.* To come to the surface again; reappear: *The rumor has resurfaced.* **—re•sur′fac•er** *n.*

re•surge (rĭ-sûrj′) *intr.v.* **-surged, -surg•ing, -surg•es. 1.** To rise again; experience resurgence. **2.** To sweep or surge back again. [Latin *resurgere* : *re-*, re- + *surgere,* to rise; see SURGE.]

re•sur•gence (rĭ-sûr′jəns) *n.* **1.** A continuing after interruption; a renewal. **2.** A restoration to use, acceptance, activity, or vigor; a revival.

re•sur•gent (rĭ-sûr′jənt) *adj.* **1.** Experiencing or tending to bring about renewal or revival. **2.** Sweeping or surging back again.

res•ur•rect (rĕz′ə-rĕkt′) *v.* **-rect•ed, -rect•ing, -rects.** *—tr.* **1.** To bring back to life; raise from the dead. **2.** To bring back into practice, notice, or use. *—intr.* *Theology.* To rise from the dead; return to life. [Back-formation from RESURRECTION.] **—res′ur•rec′tor** *n.*

res•ur•rec•tion (rĕz′ə-rĕk′shən) *n.* **1.** The act of rising from the dead or returning to life. **2.** The state of one who has returned to life. **3.** The act of bringing back to practice, notice, or use; revival. **4. Resurrection.** *Theology.* **a.** The rising again of Jesus on the third day after the Crucifixion. **b.** The rising again of the dead at the Last Judgment. [Middle English, from Old French, from Late Latin *resurrēctiō, resurrēctiōn-*, from Latin *resurrēctus,* past participle of *resurgere,* to rise again. See RESURGE.] **—res′ur•rec′tion•al** *adj.*

resurrection fern *n.* An epiphytic, creeping American fern *(Polypodium polypodioides)* of warm regions, having fronds that curl up and appear dead in prolonged dry weather and expand under moist conditions.

res•ur•rec•tion•ist (rĕz′ə-rĕk′shə-nĭst) *n.* **1.** One who steals bodies from graves in order to sell them for dissection; a body snatcher. **2.** One who brings something back into use or notice again.

resurrection plant *n.* See **rose of Jericho.**

re•sur•vey (rē′sər-vā′, rē-sûr′vā) *tr.v.* **-veyed, -vey•ing, -veys.** To survey or study anew. **—resurvey** (rē-sûr′vā) *n.* A new survey or study.

re•sus•ci•tate (rĭ-sŭs′ĭ-tāt′) *v.* **-tat•ed, -tat•ing, -tates.** *—tr.* To restore consciousness, vigor, or life to. See Synonyms at **revive.** *—intr.* To regain consciousness. [Latin *resuscitāre, resuscitāt-* : *re-*, re- + *suscitāre,* to stir up (*sub-*, sub- + *citāre,* to move violently, frequentative of *ciēre,* to set in motion; see **kei-**[2] in Appendix).] **—re•sus′ci•ta•ble** (-tə-bəl) *adj.* **—re•sus′ci•ta′tion** *n.* **—re•sus′ci•ta′tive** *adj.*

re•sus•ci•ta•tor (rĭ-sŭs′ĭ-tā′tər) *n.* One that resuscitates, as an apparatus that forces oxygen or a mixture of oxygen and carbon dioxide into the lungs of a person who has undergone partial asphyxiation.

ret (rĕt) *v.* **ret•ted, ret•ting, rets.** *—tr.* To moisten or soak (flax, for example) in order to soften and separate the fibers by partial rotting. *—intr.* To become so moistened or soaked. [Middle English *reten,* probably from Middle Dutch *reeten.*]

ret. *abbr.* **1.** Retain. **2.** Retired. **3.** Return.

re•ta•ble (rē′tā′bəl, rĕt′ə-) *n.* A structure forming the back of an altar, especially: **a.** An overhanging shelf for lights and ornaments. **b.** A frame enclosing painted panels. [French, from Spanish *retablo* : Latin *retro-*, retro- + *tabula,* tablet, board.]

re•tail (rē′tāl′) *n.* The sale of goods or commodities in small quantities directly to consumers. **—retail** *adj.* Of, relating to, or engaged in the sale of goods or commodities at retail. **—retail** *adv.* **1.** In retail quantities. **2.** At a retail price. **—retail** *v.* **-tailed, -tail•ing, -tails.** *—tr.* **1.** To sell in small quantities directly to consumers. **2.** (*also* rĭ-tāl′). To tell or repeat (gossip or stories, for example) to others. *—intr.* To sell at retail. [Middle English, from Anglo-Norman, variant of Old French, piece cut off, from *retaillier,* to cut up : *re-*, re- + *tailler,* to cut; see TAILOR.] **—re′tail′er** *n.*

re•tail•ing (rē′tā′lĭng) *n.* The functions and activities involved in the selling of commodities directly to consumers.

re•tain (rĭ-tān′) *tr.v.* **-tained, -tain•ing, -tains.** *Abbr.* **ret. 1.** To maintain possession of. See Synonyms at **keep. 2.** To keep or hold in a particular place, condition, or position. **3.** To keep in mind; remember. **4.** To hire (an attorney, for example) by the payment of a fee. **5.** To keep in one's service or pay. [Middle English *retainen,* from Old French *retenir,* from Latin *retinēre* : *re-*, re- + *tenēre,* to hold; see **ten-** in Appendix.] **—re•tain′a•bil′i•ty** *n.* **—re•tain′a•ble** *adj.* **—re•tain′ment** *n.*

re•tained object (rĭ-tānd′) *n.* *Grammar.* An object in a passive construction that is identical to the object in the corresponding active construction, as *story* in *Susan was told the story by John.*

retaining wall

re•tain•er[1] (rĭ-tā′nər) *n.* **1.** One that retains, as a device, frame, or groove that restrains or guides. **2.** *Dentistry.* An appliance used to hold teeth in position after orthodontic treatment. **3.a.** An employee, typically a long-term employee. **b.** A servant or an attendant, especially one in the household of a person of high rank.

re•tain•er[2] (rĭ-tā′nər) *n.* **1.** The act of engaging the services of a professional adviser, such as an attorney, a counselor, or a consultant. **2.** The fee paid to retain a professional adviser.

re•tain•ing wall (rĭ-tā′nĭng) *n.* A wall built to support or prevent the advance of a mass of earth or water.

re•take (rē-tāk′) *tr.v.* **-took** (-to͝ok′), **-tak•en** (-tā′kən), **-tak•ing, -takes. 1.** To take back or again. **2.** To recapture. **3.** To photograph, film, or record again. **—retake** (rē′tāk′) *n.* **1.** A taking again. **2.** The act or an instance of photographing, filming, or recording again.

re•tal•i•ate (rĭ-tăl′ē-āt′) *v.* **-at•ed, -at•ing, -ates.** *—intr.* To return like for like, especially evil for evil. *—tr.* To pay back (an injury) in kind. [Late Latin *retāliāre, retāliāt-* : Latin *re-*, re- + Latin *tāliō,* punishment in kind; see **tele-** in Appendix.] **—re•tal′i•a′tion** *n.* **—re•tal′i•a′tive, re•tal′i•a•to′ry** (-ə-tôr′ē, -tōr′ē) *adj.* **—re•tal′i•a′tor** *n.*

re•tard (rĭ-tärd′) *v.* **-tard•ed, -tard•ing, -tards.** *—tr.* To

ă pat	oi boy
ā pay	ou out
âr care	o͝o took
ä father	o͞o boot
ĕ pet	ŭ cut
ē be	ûr urge
ĭ pit	th thin
ī pie	*th* this
îr pier	hw which
ŏ pot	zh vision
ō toe	ə about, item
ô paw	♦ regionalism

Stress marks: ′ (primary); ′ (secondary), as in **dictionary** (dĭk′shə-nĕr′ē)

cause to move or proceed slowly; delay or impede. —*intr.* To be delayed. See Synonyms at **delay.** —**retard** *n.* **1.** A slowing down or hindering of progress; a delay. **2.** *Music.* A slackening of tempo. **3.** (rē′tärd′). *Offensive Slang.* Used as a disparaging term for a mentally retarded person. [Middle English *retarden,* from Old French *retarder,* from Latin *retardāre* : *re-,* re- + *tardāre,* to delay (from *tardus,* slow).] —**re·tard′er** *n.*

re·tar·dant (rĭ-tär′dnt) *adj.* Acting or tending to retard. Often used in combination: *flame-retardant pajamas for children; a fire-retardant security chest.* —**re·tar′dant** *n.*

re·tar·date (rĭ-tär′dāt′, -dĭt) *n.* A mentally retarded person.

re·tar·da·tion (rē′tär-dā′shən) *n.* **1. a.** The act or process of retarding. **b.** The condition of being retarded. **2.** The extent to which something is held back or delayed. **3.** Something that retards; a delay or hindrance. **4.** Mental retardation. **5.** *Music.* A diminishing of tempo; a retard.

re·tard·ed (rĭ-tär′dĭd) *Offensive. adj.* **1.** Affected with mental retardation. **2.** Relatively slow in mental, emotional, or physical development. —**retarded** *n.* *(used with a pl. verb).* Persons affected with mental retardation considered as a group. Often used with *the.*

re·tar·get (rē-tär′gĭt) *tr.v.* **-get·ed, -get·ing, -gets. 1.** To direct toward a different target: *retargeting strategic missiles.* **2.** To change the target or goal of: *federal monies retargeted for youth job training.*

retch (rĕch) *v.* **retched, retch·ing, retch·es.** —*intr.* To try to vomit. —*tr.* To vomit. [Alteration of Middle English *rechen,* from Old English *hrǣcan.*] —**retch** *n.*

re·te (rē′tē) *n., pl.* **re·ti·a** (rē′tē-ə, rē′shə). An anatomical mesh or network, as of veins, arteries, or nerves. [Latin *rēte,* net.]

re·tell (rē-tĕl′) *tr.v.* **-told** (-tōld′), **-tell·ing, -tells. 1.** To relate or tell again or in a different form. **2.** To count again.

re·tell·ing (rē-tĕl′ĭng) *n.* A new account or an adaptation of a story: *a retelling of a Roman myth.*

re·tene (rē′tēn′, rĕt′ēn′) *n.* A crystalline compound, $C_{18}H_{18}$, derived from pine tar, fossil resins, and tar oils. [From Greek *rhētinē,* resin.]

re·ten·tion (rĭ-tĕn′shən) *n.* **1. a.** The act of retaining. **b.** The condition of being retained. **2.** Capacity or power of retaining. **3.** An ability to recall or recognize what has been learned or experienced; memory. **4.** Something retained. **5.** *Medicine.* Involuntary withholding of wastes or secretions that are normally eliminated. [Middle English *retencioun,* from Old French *retention,* from Latin *retentiō, retentiōn-,* from *retentus,* past participle of *retinēre,* to retain. See RETAIN.]

re·ten·tive (rĭ-tĕn′tĭv) *adj.* **1.** Having the quality, power, or capacity of retaining. **2.** Having the ability or capacity to retain knowledge or information with ease: *a retentive memory.* —**re·ten′tive·ly** *adv.* —**re·ten′tive·ness** *n.*

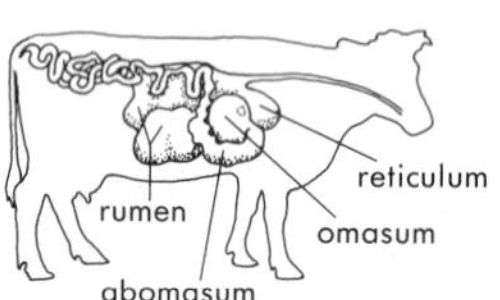

reticulum

re·ten·tiv·i·ty (rē′tĕn-tĭv′ĭ-tē) *n.* **1. a.** The quality or state of being retentive. **b.** Capacity or power of retaining. **2.** *Physics.* The capacity for remaining magnetized after cessation of the magnetizing force.

re·test (rē′tĕst′) *tr.v.* **-test·ed, -test·ing, -tests.** To test again. —**retest** *n.* A second or repeated test.

re·think (rē-thĭngk′) *tr. & intr.v.* **-thought** (-thôt′), **-think·ing, -thinks.** To reconsider (something) or to involve oneself in reconsideration. —**re′think′** *n.* —**re·think′er** *n.*

Re·thondes (rə-tôɴd′). A village of northern France west-northwest of Rheims. The armistice ending World War I was signed here on November 11, 1918.

re·ti·a (rē′tē-ə, rē′shə) *n.* Plural of **rete.**

re·ti·ar·y (rē′shē-ĕr′ē) *adj.* Of, resembling, or forming a net or web. [From Latin *rēte,* net.]

ret·i·cence (rĕt′ĭ-səns) *n.* **1.** The state or quality of being reticent; reserve. **2.** The state or quality of being reluctant; unwillingness. **3.** An instance of being reticent.

ret·i·cent (rĕt′ĭ-sənt) *adj.* **1.** Inclined to keep one's thoughts, feelings, and personal affairs to oneself. See Synonyms at **silent. 2.** Restrained or reserved in style. **3.** Reluctant; unwilling. [Latin *reticēns, reticent-,* present participle of *reticēre,* to keep silent : *re-,* re- + *tacēre,* to be silent.] —**ret′i·cent·ly** *adv.*

ret·i·cle (rĕt′ĭ-kəl) *n.* A grid or pattern placed in the eyepiece of an optical instrument, used to establish scale or position. [Latin *rēticulum,* diminutive of *rēte,* net.]

retinoscope

re·tic·u·la (rĭ-tĭk′yə-lə) *n.* Plural of **reticulum.**

re·tic·u·lar (rĭ-tĭk′yə-lər) *adj.* **1.** Resembling a net in form; netlike: *reticular tissue.* **2.** Marked by complexity; intricate. [From Latin *rēticulum,* diminutive of *rēte,* net.]

reticular formation *n.* A diffuse network of nerve fibers and cells in parts of the brainstem, important in regulating consciousness or wakefulness.

re·tic·u·late (rĭ-tĭk′yə-lĭt, -lāt′) *adj.* Resembling or forming a net or network: *reticulate veins of a leaf.* —**reticulate** (-lāt′) *v.* **-lat·ed, -lat·ing, -lates.** —*tr.* **1.** To make a net or network of. **2.** To mark with lines resembling a network. —*intr.* To form a net or network. [Latin *rēticulātus,* from *rēticulum,* diminutive of *rēte,* net.] —**re·tic′u·late·ly** *adv.* —**re·tic′u·la′tion** *n.*

ret·i·cule (rĕt′ĭ-kyo͞ol′) *n.* **1.** A woman's drawstring handbag or purse. **2.** A reticle. [French *réticule,* from Latin *rēticulum,* diminutive of *rēte,* net.]

re·tic·u·lo·cyte (rĭ-tĭk′yə-lō-sīt′) *n.* An immature red blood cell that contains a network of basophilic filaments. [RETICU-L(UM) + -CYTE.] —**re·tic′u·lo·cyt′ic** (-sĭt′ĭk) *adj.*

re·tic·u·lo·en·do·the·li·al (rĭ-tĭk′yə-lō-ĕn′də-thē′lē-əl) *n.* Of, relating to, or being the widely diffused bodily system constituting all phagocytic cells except certain white blood cells. [RETICUL(UM) + ENDOTHELIAL.]

re·tic·u·lum (rĭ-tĭk′yə-ləm) *n., pl.* **-la** (-lə). **1.** A netlike formation or structure; a network. **2.** *Zoology.* The second compartment of the stomach of ruminant mammals, lined with a membrane having honeycombed ridges. [Latin *rēticulum,* diminutive of *rēte,* net.]

Re·tic·u·lum (rĭ-tĭk′yə-ləm) *n.* A constellation in the Southern Hemisphere near Dorado and Horologium. [Latin *rēticulum,* diminutive of *rēte,* net.]

re·ti·form (rē′tə-fôrm′, rĕt′ə-) *adj.* Arranged like a net; reticulate. [Latin *rēte,* net + -FORM.]

retin– *pref.* Variant of **retino–.**

ret·i·na (rĕt′n-ə) *n., pl.* **ret·i·nas** or **ret·i·nae** (rĕt′n-ē′). A delicate, multilayered, light-sensitive membrane lining the inner eyeball and connected by the optic nerve to the brain. [Middle English, from Medieval Latin *rētina,* from Latin *rēte,* net.] —**ret′i·nal** *adj.*

ret·i·nac·u·lum (rĕt′n-ăk′yə-ləm) *n., pl.* **-la** (-lə). *Biology.* A band or bandlike structure that holds an organ or a part in place. [Latin *retināculum,* band, tether : *retinēre,* to restrain; see RETAIN + *-culum,* suff. denoting instruments.] —**ret′i·nac′u·lar** (-lər) *adj.*

ret·i·nae (rĕt′n-ē′) *n.* A plural of **retina.**

ret·i·nal (rĕt′n-ăl′, -ôl′) *n.* See **retinene.**

ret·i·nene (rĕt′n-ēn′) *n.* Either of two yellow to red retinal pigments, formed by oxidation of vitamin A alcohols. Also called *retinal.*

ret·i·ni·tis (rĕt′n-ī′tĭs) *n.* Inflammation of the retina.

retinitis pig·men·to·sa (pĭg′mĕn-tō′sə, -mən-) *n.* A hereditary degenerative disease of the retina, characterized by night blindness, pigmentary changes within the retina, a narrowing of the visual field, and eventual loss of vision. [New Latin *pigmentōsa,* feminine of *pigmentōsus,* pigmented.]

retino– or **retin–** *pref.* Retina: *retinoscopy.* [From RETINA.]

ret·i·no·blas·to·ma (rĕt′n-ō-blă-stō′mə) *n., pl.* **-mas** or **-ma·ta** (-mə-tə). A hereditary malignant tumor of the retina, transmitted as a dominant trait and occurring chiefly among infants.

ret·i·nol (rĕt′n-ôl′, -ōl′, -ŏl′) *n.* See **vitamin A.**

ret·i·nop·a·thy (rĕt′n-ŏp′ə-thē) *n., pl.* **-thies.** A pathological disorder of the retina. —**ret′i·no·path′ic** (-ō-păth′ĭk) *adj.*

ret·i·no·scope (rĕt′n-ə-skōp′) *n.* An optical instrument for examining refraction of light in the eye. Also called *skiascope.*

ret·i·nos·co·py (rĕt′n-ŏs′kə-pē) *n., pl.* **-pies.** Medical examination and analysis of the refractive properties of the eye. Also called *skiascopy.* —**ret′i·no·scop′ic** (-ə-skŏp′ĭk) *adj.*

ret·i·nue (rĕt′n-o͞o′, -yo͞o′) *n.* The retainers or attendants accompanying a high-ranking person. [Middle English *retenue,* from Old French, from feminine past participle of *retenir,* to retain. See RETAIN.]

re·tin·u·la (rĭ-tĭn′yə-lə) *n., pl.* **-lae** (-lē). A cluster of pigmented sensory cells in the compound eye of an arthropod. [New Latin *rētinula,* diminutive of Medieval Latin *rētina,* retina. See RETINA.] —**re·tin′u·lar** *adj.*

re·tire (rĭ-tīr′) *v.* **-tired, -tir·ing, -tires.** —*intr.* **1.** To withdraw, as for rest or seclusion. **2.** To go to bed. **3.** To withdraw from one's occupation, business, or office; stop working. **4.** To fall back or retreat, as from battle. **5.** To move back or away; recede. —*tr.* **1.** To cause to withdraw from one's usual field of activity: *retired all executives at 55.* **2.** To lead (troops, for example) away from action; withdraw. **3.** To take out of circulation: *retired the bonds.* **4.** To withdraw from use or active service: *retiring an old battleship.* **5.** *Baseball.* **a.** To put out (a batter). **b.** To cause (the opposing team) to end a turn at bat. [French *retirer,* to retreat, from Old French, to take back : *re-,* re- + *tirer,* to draw; see TIER [1].]

WORD HISTORY: Despite the upbeat books written about retiring and the fact that it is a well-earned time of relaxation from the daily rigors of work, many people do not find it a particularly pleasant prospect. Perhaps the etymology of *retire* may hint at why. The ultimate source of our word is the Old French word *retirer,* made up of the prefix *re–,* meaning in this case "back," and the verb *tirer,* "to draw," together meaning "to take back or withdraw." The first use of the English word *retire* is recorded in 1533 in reference to a military force that withdraws. It is not until 1667 that we find the word used to mean "to withdraw from a position for more leisure." In regard to the sting in all this we need to look at the source of *tirer,* "to draw, draw out, endure," which ultimately may be from Old French *martir,* "a martyr," probably reflecting the fact that martyrs had to endure the torture of being stretched up to and beyond the point of dislocating their bones.

re·tired (rĭ-tīrd′) *adj. Abbr.* **ret., r. 1.** Withdrawn from one's occupation, business, or office; having finished one's active working life. **2.** Received by a person in retirement: *retired pay.* **3.** Withdrawn; secluded. —**retired** *n.* *(used with a pl. verb).* Retired people considered as a group. Used with *the.* **—re·tired·ly** *adv.* **—re·tired′ness** *n.*

re·tir·ee (rĭ-tīr′ē′) *n.* One who has retired from active working life.

re·tire·ment (rĭ-tīr′mənt) *n.* **1.** The act of retiring. **2.** The state of being retired. **3.** Withdrawal from one's occupation, business, or office. **4.** Withdrawal into privacy or seclusion. **5.** A place of privacy or seclusion; a retreat. See Synonyms at **solitude.** *—attributive.* Often used to modify another noun: *a retirement program; a retirement community.*

re·tir·ing (rĭ-tīr′ĭng) *adj.* Shy and reserved; modest. **—re·tir′ing·ly** *adv.* **—re·tir′ing·ness** *n.*

re·told (rē-tōld′) *v.* Past tense and past participle of **retell.**

re·took (rē-to͝ok′) *v.* Past tense of **retake.**

re·tool (rē-to͞ol′) *v. —tr.* **-tooled, -tool·ing, -tools. 1.** To fit out (a factory, for example) with a new set of machinery and tools for making a different product. **2.** To revise and reorganize, especially for the purpose of updating or improving: *had to retool the city's economy. —intr.* To fit out a factory with a new set of machinery and tools.

re·tor·sion or **re·tor·tion** (rĭ-tôr′shən) *n. Law.* An act perpetrated by one nation upon another in retaliation or reprisal for a similar act perpetrated by the other nation. [Probably French *rétorsion,* from Latin *retortus* (influenced by Late Latin *torsiō,* a twisting, wringing; see TORSION), past participle of *retorquēre,* to cast back. See RETORT[1].]

re·tort[1] (rĭ-tôrt′) *v.* **-tort·ed, -tort·ing, -torts.** *—tr.* **1. a.** To reply, especially to answer in a quick, caustic, or witty manner. See Synonyms at **answer. b.** To present a counterargument to. **2.** To return in kind; pay back. *—intr.* **1.** To make a reply, especially a quick, caustic, or witty one. **2.** To present a counterargument. **3.** To return like for like; retaliate. **—retort** *n.* **1.** A quick, incisive reply, especially one that turns the first speaker's words to his or her own disadvantage. **2.** The act or an instance of retorting. [Latin *retorquēre, retort-,* to bend back, retort : *re-,* re- + *torquēre,* to bend, twist; see **terkʷ-** in Appendix.] **—re·tort′er** *n.*

re·tort[2] (rĭ-tôrt′, rē′tôrt′) *n.* A closed laboratory vessel with an outlet tube, used for distillation, sublimation, or decomposition by heat. [French *retorte,* from Medieval Latin *retorta,* from feminine of Latin *retortus,* past participle of *retorquēre,* to bend back. See RETORT[1].]

retort[2]

re·tor·tion (rĭ-tôr′shən) *n. Law.* Variant of **retorsion.**

re·touch (rē-tŭch′) *v.* **-touched, -touch·ing, -touch·es.** *—tr.* **1.** To add new details or touches to for correction or improvement. **2.** To improve or change (a photographic negative or print), as by adding details or removing flaws. **3.** To color (recent growth of hair) to match hair that was tinted, dyed, or bleached at an earlier date. *—intr.* To give or make retouches. **—retouch** (rē′tŭch′, rē-tŭch′) *n.* The act, process, or an instance of retouching. **—re·touch′er** *n.*

re·trace (rē-trās′) *tr.v.* **-traced, -trac·ing, -trac·es.** To trace again or back: *retraced their steps.* **—re·trace′a·ble** *adj.* **—re·trace′ment** *n.* **—re·trac′er** *n.*

re·tract (rĭ-trăkt′) *v.* **-tract·ed, -tract·ing, -tracts.** *—tr.* **1.** To take back; disavow: *refused to retract the statement.* **2.** To draw back or in: *a plane retracting its landing gear.* See Synonyms at **recede. 3.** *Linguistics.* **a.** To utter (a sound) with the tongue drawn back. **b.** To draw back (the tongue). *—intr.* **1.** To take something back or disavow it. **2.** To draw back. [Latin *retractāre, retract-,* to revoke, frequentative of *retrahere,* to draw back : *re-,* re- + *trahere,* to draw. V., tr., senses 2 and 3, and v., intr., sense 2, Middle English *retracten,* from Old French *retracter,* from Latin *retractus,* past participle of *retrahere,* to draw back.] **—re·tract′a·bil′i·ty, re·tract′i·bil′i·ty** *n.* **—re·tract′a·ble, re·tract′i·ble** *adj.* **—re′trac·ta′tion** (rē′trăk-tā′shən) *n.*

re·trac·tile (rĭ-trăk′tĭl, -tīl′) *adj.* That can be drawn back or in: *the retractile claws of a cat.* **—re′trac·til′i·ty** (rē′trăk-tĭl′ĭ-tē) *n.*

re·trac·tion (rĭ-trăk′shən) *n.* **1.** The act of retracting or the state of being retracted. **2. a.** The act of recanting or disavowing a previously held statement or belief. **b.** A formal statement of disavowal. **c.** Something recanted or disavowed. **3.** The power of drawing back or of being drawn back.

re·trac·tive (rĭ-trăk′tĭv) *adj.* Tending or serving to retract. **—re·trac′tive·ly** *adv.* **—re·trac′tive·ness** *n.*

re·trac·tor (rĭ-trăk′tər) *n.* One that retracts, as: **a.** *Anatomy.* A muscle, such as a flexor, that retracts an organ or a part. **b.** *Medicine.* A surgical instrument used to hold back organs or the edges of an incision.

re·train (rē-trān′) *tr. & intr.v.* **-trained, -train·ing, -trains.** To train or undergo training again. **—re·train′a·ble** *adj.*

re·train·ee (rē′trā-nē′) *n.* One who is being or has been retrained.

re·tral (rē′trəl, rĕt′rəl) *adj.* **1.** Situated at, located close to, or directed toward the back. **2.** Backward; reverse. [From Latin *retrō,* back. See **re-** in Appendix.] **—re′tral·ly** *adv.*

re·trans·late (rē′trăns-lāt′, -trănz-, rē-trăns′lāt′, -trănz′-) *v.* *—tr.* **-lat·ed, -lat·ing, -lates. 1.** To translate (something already translated) into a different language. **2.** To change the form of (something) into something new. *—intr.* To retranslate material. **—re′trans·la′tion** *n.*

re·tread (rē-trĕd′) *tr.v.* **-tread·ed, -tread·ing, -treads. 1.** To fit (a worn automotive tire) with a new tread. **2.** To make or do over again, especially with minimal revision; rehash: *retreading a familiar story line.* **—retread** (rē′trĕd′) *n.* **1.** A tire that has been fitted with a new tread. **2.** A revision or reworking; a remake or rehash: *a trite retread of an old musical.* **3.** *Informal.* A person who has been retrained for work.

re-tread (rē-trĕd′) *tr. & intr.v.* **-trod** (-trŏd′), **-trod·den** (-trŏd′n), or **-trod, -tread·ing, -treads.** To tread upon or engage in treading again.

re·treat (rĭ-trēt′) *n.* **1. a.** The act or process of withdrawing, especially from something hazardous, formidable, or unpleasant. **b.** The process of going backward or receding from a position or condition gained. **2.** A place affording peace, quiet, privacy, or security. See Synonyms at **shelter. 3. a.** A period of seclusion, retirement, or solitude. **b.** A period of group withdrawal for prayer, meditation, and study: *a religious retreat.* **4. a.** Withdrawal of a military force from a dangerous position or from an enemy attack. **b.** The signal for such withdrawal. **c.** A bugle call or drumbeat signaling the lowering of the flag at sunset, as on a military base. **d.** The military ceremony of lowering the flag. **—retreat** *v.* **-treat·ed, -treat·ing, -treats.** *—intr.* **1.** To fall or draw back; withdraw or retire. See Synonyms at **recede. 2.** To slope backward. *—tr. Games.* To move (a chess piece) back. [Middle English *retret,* from Old French *retrait, retret,* from past participle of *retraire, retrere,* to draw back, from Latin *retrahere.* See RETRACT.] **—re·treat′er** *n.*

re·treat·ant (rĭ-trēt′nt) *n.* One who participates in a religious retreat.

re·trench (rĭ-trĕnch′) *v.* **-trenched, -trench·ing, -trench·es.** *—tr.* **1.** To cut down; reduce. **2.** To remove, delete, or omit. *—intr.* To curtail expenses; economize. [Obsolete French *retrencher,* from Old French *retrenchier* : *re-,* re- + *trenchier,* to cut; see TRENCH.] **—re·trench′er** *n.*

re·trench·ment (rĭ-trĕnch′mənt) *n.* **1.** A cutting down or back; reduction. **2.** A curtailment of expenses.

re·tri·al (rē-trī′əl, -trīl′, rē′trī′əl, -trīl′) *n.* A second trial, as of a legal case.

ret·ri·bu·tion (rĕt′rə-byo͞o′shən) *n.* **1.** Something justly deserved; recompense. **2.** Something given or demanded in repayment, especially punishment. **3.** *Theology.* Punishment or reward distributed in a future life based on performance in this one. [Middle English *retribucion,* from Old French *retribution,* from Latin *retribūtiō, retribūtiōn-,* from *retribūtus,* past participle of *retribuere,* to pay back : *re-,* re- + *tribuere,* to grant; see TRIBE.]

re·trib·u·tive (rĭ-trĭb′yə-tĭv) *adj.* Of, involving, or characterized by retribution; retributory. **—re·trib′u·tive·ly** *adv.*

re·trib·u·to·ry (rĭ-trĭb′yə-tôr′ē, -tōr′ē) *adj.* Retributive.

re·tried (rē-trīd′) *v.* Past tense and past participle of **retry.**

re·tries (rē-trīz′) *v.* Third person singular present tense of **retry.**

re·triev·al (rĭ-trē′vəl) *n.* **1.** The act or process of retrieving. **2.** *Computer Science.* The process of accessing information from memory or other storage devices. **3.** The possibility of being retrieved or restored: *lost possessions beyond retrieval.*

retriever

re·trieve (rĭ-trēv′) *v.* **-trieved, -triev·ing, -trieves.** *—tr.* **1.** To get back; regain. **2. a.** To rescue or save. **b.** *Sports.* To make a difficult but successful return of (a ball or shuttlecock, as in tennis or badminton). **3.** To bring back again; revive or restore. **4.** To rectify the unfavorable consequences of; remedy. See Synonyms at **recover. 5.** To recall to mind; remember. **6.** To find and carry back; fetch. *—intr.* To find and bring back game: *a dog trained to retrieve.* **—retrieve** *n.* **1.** The act of retrieving; retrieval. **2.** *Sports.* A difficult but successful return of a ball or shuttlecock. [Middle English *retreven,* from Old French *retrover, retruev-* : *re-,* re- + *trover,* to find; see TROVER.] **—re·triev′a·bil′i·ty** *n.* **—re·triev′a·ble** *adj.* **—re·triev′a·bly** *adv.*

re·triev·er (rĭ-trē′vər) *n.* One that retrieves, especially any one of several breeds of dog that were developed and trained to retrieve game.

ret·ro (rĕt′rō) *adj.* **1.** Retroactive: *retro pay.* **2.** Involving, relating to, or reminiscent of things past; retrospective: *"As is often the case in retro fashion, historical accuracy is somewhat beside the point"* (New York Times). **—retro** *n., pl.* **-ros.** A fashion, decor, design, or style reminiscent of things past.

retro– *pref.* **1.** Backward; back: *retrorocket.* **2.** Situated behind: *retrolental.* [Latin *retrō-,* from *retrō,* backward, behind. See **re-** in Appendix.]

ret·ro·ac·tion (rĕt′rō-ăk′shən) *n.* **1.** An action, as of a law, that influences or applies to a prior time. **2.** An opposing or reciprocal action; a reaction. **—ret′ro·act′** *v.*

ret·ro·ac·tive (rĕt′rō-ăk′tĭv) *adj.* Influencing or applying to a period prior to enactment: *a retroactive pay increase.* [French *rétroactif,* from Latin *retroāctus,* past participle of *retroagere,* to drive back : *retrō-,* retro- + *agere,* to drive; see **ag-** in Appendix.] **—ret′ro·ac′tive·ly** *adv.* **—ret′ro·ac·tiv′i·ty** *n.*

ret·ro·cede (rĕt′rō-sēd′) *v.* **-ced·ed, -ced·ing, -cedes.** *—intr.* To go back; recede. *—tr.* To cede or give back (a territory, for example); return. [Latin *retrōcēdere* : *retrō-,* retro- + *cēdere,* to go; see **ked-** in Appendix.] **—ret′ro·ces′sion** (-sĕsh′ən) *n.*

re-trod (rē-trŏd′) *v.* Past tense and a past participle of **re-tread.**

re-trod·den (rē-trŏd′n) *v.* A past participle of **re-tread.**

ă pat	oi boy
ā pay	ou out
âr care	o͝o took
ä father	o͞o boot
ĕ pet	ŭ cut
ē be	ûr urge
ĭ pit	th thin
ī pie	*th* this
îr pier	hw which
ŏ pot	zh vision
ō toe	ə about, item
ô paw	♦ regionalism

Stress marks: ′ (primary); ′ (secondary), as in **dictionary** (dĭk′shə-nĕr′ē)

ret·ro·fire (rĕt′rō-fīr′) *v.* **-fired, -fir·ing, -fires.** —*tr.* To ignite or fire (a retrorocket). —*intr.* To become ignited or fired. Used of a retrorocket.

ret·ro·fit (rĕt′rō-fĭt′) *v.* **-fit·ted, -fit·ting, -fits.** —*tr.* **1.** To provide (a jet, an automobile, a computer, or a factory, for example) with parts, devices, or equipment not in existence or available at the time of original manufacture. **2.** To install or fit (a device or system, for example) for use in or on an existing structure, especially an older dwelling. —*intr.* **1.** To fit into or onto equipment already in existence or service. **2.** To substitute new or modernized parts or systems for older equipment: *an industrial plant that was retrofitting to meet new safety regulations.* **—retrofit** *n.* **1.** Something that has been retrofitted or that has undergone retrofitting. **2.** An instance of modernizing or expanding with new or modified parts, devices, systems, or equipment: *a retrofit for the heating system.* **—retrofit** *adj.* Relating to or being a retrofit: *a retrofit kit for the homeowner; an energy-saving retrofit program; a large retrofit market.* **—ret′ro·fit′ta·ble** *adj.* **—ret′ro·fit′ter** *n.*

ret·ro·flex (rĕt′rə-flĕks′) also **ret·ro·flexed** (-flĕkst′) *adj.* **1.** Bent, curved, or turned backward. **2.** *Linguistics.* Pronounced with the tip of the tongue turned back against the roof of the mouth. **—retroflex** *n. Linguistics.* A sound pronounced with the tongue in retroflex position, as the sound (r) in some varieties of English. [Latin **retrōflexus,* past participle of *retrōflectere,* to bend back : *retrō,* retro- + *flectere,* to bend.] **—ret′ro·flex′ion, ret′ro·flec′tion** *n.*

ret·ro·grade (rĕt′rə-grād′) *adj.* **1.** Moving or tending backward. **2.** Opposite to the usual order; inverted or reversed. **3.** Reverting to an earlier or inferior condition. **4.** *Astronomy.* **a.** Of or relating to the orbital revolution or axial rotation of a planetary or other celestial body that moves clockwise from east to west, in the direction opposite to most celestial bodies. **b.** Of or relating to the brief, regularly occurring, apparently backward movement of a planetary body in its orbit as viewed against the fixed stars, caused by the differing orbital velocities of Earth and the body observed. **5.** *Archaic.* Opposed; contrary. **—retrograde** *intr.v.* **-grad·ed, -grad·ing, -grades. 1.** To move or seem to move backward. See Synonyms at **recede. 2.** To decline to an inferior state; degenerate. [Middle English, from Latin *retrōgradus,* from *retrōgradī,* to go back : *retrō-,* retro- + *-gradus,* walking (from *gradī,* to go; see **ghredh-** in Appendix).] **—ret′ro·gra·da′tion** (-rō-grā-dā′shən) *n.* **—ret′ro·grade′ly** *adv.*

ret·ro·gress (rĕt′rə-grĕs′, rĕt′rə-grĕs′) *intr.v.* **-gressed, -gress·ing, -gress·es. 1.** To return to an earlier, inferior, or less complex condition. **2.** To go or move backward. [Latin *retrōgradī,* **retrōgress-* : *retrō-,* retro- + *gradī,* to go; see **ghredh-** in Appendix.] **—ret′ro·gres′sive** *adj.* **—re′tro·gres′sive·ly** *adv.*

ret·ro·gres·sion (rĕt′rə-grĕsh′ən) *n.* **1.** The act or process of deteriorating or declining. **2.** *Biology.* A return to a less complex or more primitive state or stage.

ret·ro·len·tal (rĕt′rō-lĕn′tl) *adj.* Situated or occurring behind a lens, as of the eye. [RETRO– + New Latin *lēns, lent-,* lens; see LENS + –AL[1].]

ret·ro·oc·u·lar (rĕt′rō-ŏk′yə-lər) *adj.* Situated behind the eye.

ret·ro·per·i·to·ne·al (rĕt′rō-pĕr′ĭ-tn-ē′əl) *adj.* Situated behind the peritoneum.

ret·ro·pha·ryn·ge·al (rĕt′rō-fə-rĭn′jē-əl, -jəl, -făr′ĭn-jē′əl) *adj.* Situated or occurring behind the pharynx.

ret·ro·rock·et (rĕt′rō-rŏk′ĭt) *n.* A rocket engine used to retard, arrest, or reverse the motion of a vehicle, such as an aircraft, a missile, or a spacecraft.

re·trorse (rĭ-trôrs′, rē′trôrs′) *adj.* Directed or turned backward or downward. [Latin *retrōrsus,* from *retrōversus* : *retrō-,* retro- + *versus,* past participle of *vertere,* to turn; see **wer-**[2] in Appendix.] **—re·trorse′ly** *adv.*

ret·ro·spect (rĕt′rə-spĕkt′) *n.* A review, survey, or contemplation of things in the past. **—retrospect** *v.* **-spect·ed, -spect·ing, -spects.** —*intr.* **1.** To contemplate the past. **2.** To refer back. —*tr.* To look back on or contemplate (things past). **—*idiom.* in retrospect.** Looking backward or reviewing the past. [From Latin **retrōspectus,* past participle of *retrōspicere,* to look back at : *retrō-,* retro- + *specere,* to look at; see **spek-** in Appendix.] **—ret′ro·spec′tion** *n.*

ret·ro·spec·tive (rĕt′rə-spĕk′tĭv) *adj.* **1.** Looking back on, contemplating, or directed to the past. **2.** Looking or directed backward. **3.** Applying to or influencing the past; retroactive. **4.** Of, relating to, or being a retrospective: *a retrospective art exhibition.* **—retrospective** *n.* An extensive exhibition or performance of the work of an artist over a period of years. **—ret′ro·spec′tive·ly** *adv.*

re·trous·sé (rə-trōō-sā′, rĕt′rōō-) *adj.* Turned up at the end. Used of the nose. [French, past participle of *retrousser,* to turn back, from Old French : *re-,* re- + *torser, trousser,* to tie in a bundle (probably from Vulgar Latin **torsāre,* from **torsus,* twisted, variant of Latin *tortus,* past participle of *torquēre,* to twist; see TORQUE[1]).]

ret·ro·ver·sion (rĕt′rō-vûr′zhən, -shən) *n.* **1.** A turning or tilting backward. **2.** The state of being turned or tilted back. [From Latin *retrōversus,* retrorse. See RETRORSE.]

ret·ro·vi·rus (rĕt′rō-vī′rəs, rĕt′rə-vī′-) *n., pl.* **-rus·es.** Any of a group of viruses, many of which produce tumors, that contain RNA and reverse transcriptase, including the virus that causes AIDS. **—ret′ro·vi′ral** *adj.*

re·try (rē-trī′) *tr.v.* **-tried** (-trīd′), **-try·ing, -tries** (-trīz′). To try again.

ret·si·na (rĕt′sĭ-nə, rĕt-sē′nə) *n.* A Greek wine flavored with pine resin. [Modern Greek, probably from Italian *resina,* resin, from Latin *rēsīna.* See RESIN.]

re·turn (rĭ-tûrn′) *v.* **-turned, -turn·ing, -turns.** —*intr.* **1.** To go or come back, as to an earlier condition or place. **2.** To revert in speech, thought, or practice. **3.** To revert to a former owner. **4.** To answer or respond. —*tr.* **1.** To send, put, or carry back: *We return bottles to the store.* **2. a.** To give or send back in reciprocation: *She returned his praise.* **b.** To give back to the owner: *He returned her book.* **c.** To reflect or send back: *The echo was returned by the canyon wall.* **3.** To produce or yield (profit or interest) as a payment for labor, investment, or expenditure. **4.** *Law.* **a.** To submit (an official report, for example) to a judge or other person in authority. **b.** To render or deliver (a writ or verdict, for example) to the proper officer or court of law. **5.** To elect or reelect, as to a legislative body. **6.** *Games.* To respond to (a partner's lead) by leading the same suit in cards. **7.** *Architecture.* To turn away from or place at an angle to the previous line of direction. **8. a.** *Sports.* To send back (a tennis ball, for example) to one's opponent. **b.** *Football.* To run with (the ball) after a kickoff, a punt, an interception, or a fumble. **—return** *n. Abbr.* **ret. 1. a.** The act or condition of going, coming, bringing, or sending back. **b.** The act of bringing or sending something back to a previous place, condition, or owner. **2. a.** Something brought or sent back. **b. returns.** Merchandise returned, as to a retailer by a consumer or to a wholesaler by a retailer. **c.** Something that goes or comes back. **3.** A recurrence, as of a periodic occasion or event: *the return of spring.* **4.** Something exchanged for that received; repayment. **5.** A reply; a response. **6. a.** The profit made on an exchange of goods. **b.** Often **returns.** A profit or yield, as from labor or investments. **c.** Output or yield per unit rather than cost per unit, as in the manufacturing of a particular product. **7. a.** A report, list, or set of statistics, especially one that is formal or official. **b.** Often **returns.** A report on the vote in an election. **c.** *Chiefly British.* An election. **8.** *Games.* A lead in certain card games that responds to the lead of one's partner. **9.** *Sports.* In tennis and certain other sports: **a.** The act of sending the ball back to one's opponent. **b.** The ball thus sent back. **10.** *Football.* **a.** The act of running back the ball after a kickoff, a punt, an interception, or a fumble. **b.** The yardage so gained. **11.** *Architecture.* **a.** The extension of a molding, projection, or other part at an angle (usually 90°) to the main part. **b.** A part of a building set at an angle to the façade. **12. a.** A turn, bend, or similar reversal of direction, as in a stream or road. **b.** A pipe or conduit for carrying something, especially water, back to its starting point. **13.** The key or mechanism on a machine, such as a typewriter or computer, that positions the carriage, cursor, or printing element at the beginning of a new line. **14.** *Chiefly British.* A roundtrip ticket. **15.** *Law.* **a.** The bringing or sending back of a writ, subpoena, or other document, generally with a short written report on it, by a sheriff or other officer to the court from which it was issued. **b.** A certified report by an assessor, an election officer, a collector, or another official. **16.** A formal tax statement on the required official form indicating taxable income, allowed deductions, exemptions, and the computed tax that is due. In this sense, also called *income tax return, tax return.* **—return** *adj.* **1.** Of, relating to, or bringing about a going or coming back to a place or situation: *the return voyage; a return envelope.* **2.** Given, sent, or done in reciprocation or exchange: *a return volley; a return invitation.* **3.** Performed, presented, or taking place again: *a return engagement of the ballet; a return tennis match.* **4.** Used on or for returning: *a return route.* **5.** Returning or affording return or recirculation: *a return plumbing pipe; a return valve.* **6.** Relating to or being a roundtrip ticket. **7. a.** Reversing or changing direction. **b.** Having or formed by a reversal or change in direction; returning on itself, as a bend in a road or stream. **—*idiom.* in return.** In repayment or reciprocation. [Middle English *retornen,* from Old French *retourner,* from Vulgar Latin **retornāre* : Latin *re-,* re- + Latin *tornāre,* to turn in a lathe; see TURN.] **—re·turn′er** *n.*

SYNONYMS: *return, revert, recur, recrudesce.* These verbs refer to coming or going back, as to a place, position, or condition. *Return* is the least specific: *"Thus with the year/Seasons return"* (John Milton). *"Not the poem which we have read, but that to which we* return . . . *possesses the genuine power, and claims the name of* essential poetry" (Samuel Taylor Coleridge). *"I shall return"* (Douglas MacArthur). *Revert* refers to returning to an earlier, often less desirable condition, practice, subject, or belief: *"Part of them . . . reverted to their former prejudices in regard to Lincoln"* (Baron Charnwood). *Recur* means to occur or come up again, often repeatedly: *We thought we had disposed of the problem, but it kept recurring.* To *recrudesce* is to come into renewed activity after a period of quiescence: *"It* [a visual art genre] *has wilted in latter decades, but recrudesced in recent years"* (Earl W. Count). See also Synonyms at **reciprocate.**

re·turn·a·ble (rĭ-tûr′nə-bəl) *adj.* **1.** That can be returned or brought back: *returnable bottles and cans; returnable merchandise.* **2.** *Law.* Required to be returned within a specified time: *a returnable writ.* **—returnable** *n.* An empty beverage container that may be returned for refund of a deposit.

re·turn·ee (rĭ-tûr′nē′) *n.* **1.** One who returns, as from a journey or to school after a long absence. **2.** A person returning from military duty overseas. See Usage Note at **-ee**[1].

re·tuse (rĭ-to͞os′, -tyo͞os′) *adj. Botany.* Having a rounded or obtuse apex with a central shallow notch: *a retuse leaf.* [Latin *retūsus,* past participle of *retundere,* to beat back : *re-,* re- + *tundere,* to beat.]

Retz (rĕts), Cardinal de. Title of Jean François Paul de Gondi. 1614–1679. French politician, prelate, and writer who was active in the Fronde, a French civil war (1648–1653) that ultimately strengthened the monarchy.

Reu·ben[1] (ro͞o′bən). In the Old Testament, a son of Jacob and Leah and the forebear of one of the tribes of Israel.

Reu·ben[2] (ro͞o′bən) *n.* A hot sandwich consisting of corned beef, Swiss cheese, and sauerkraut usually served on rye bread. [From the name *Reuben.*]

Reuch·lin (roik′lən, roiKH′lēn, roiKH-lēn′), **Johann.** 1455–1522. German humanist and scholar who wrote *On the Fundamentals of Hebrew* (1506), a classic text on Hebrew grammar and language.

re·u·ni·fy (rē-yo͞o′nə-fī′) *tr.v.* **-fied, -fy·ing, -fies.** To cause (a group, party, state, or sect) to become unified again after being divided. **—re·u′ni·fi·ca′tion** (-fĭ-kā′shən) *n.*

re·un·ion (rē-yo͞on′yən) *n.* **1.a.** The act of reuniting. **b.** The state of being reunited. **2.** A gathering of the members of a group who have been separated: *a high school reunion.*

Ré·un·ion (rē-yo͞on′yən, rā-ü-nyôN′). An island of France in the western Indian Ocean southwest of Mauritius. Visited by the Portuguese in the early 16th century, it was first colonized by the French in the mid-1600's as the Isle de Bourbon. Renamed Réunion in 1793, it became an overseas department in 1946.

re·un·ion·ist (rē-yo͞on′yə-nĭst) *n.* One who advocates reunion, as of divided parties or sects, especially an advocate of the reunion of the Anglican Church with the Roman Catholic Church. **—re·un′ion·ism** *n.* **—re·un′ion·is′tic** *adj.*

re·u·nite (rē′yo͞o-nīt′) *tr. & intr.v.* **-nit·ed, -nit·ing, -nites.** To bring or come together again.

re-up (rē-ŭp′) *intr.v.* **-upped, -up·ping, -ups.** *Informal.* **1.** To enlist again for military service. **2.** To sign a renewed contract for employment or service.

Reus (rĕ′o͞os). A city of northeast Spain near the Mediterranean Sea west of Barcelona. Founded c. 13th century, it is a trade and industrial center. Population, 82,354.

re·use (rē-yo͞oz′) *tr.v.* **-used, -us·ing, -us·es.** To use again, especially after salvaging or special treatment or processing. **—re·us′a·bil′i·ty** *n.* **—re·us′a·ble** *adj. & n.* **—re·use′** (-yo͞os′) *n.*

Reu·ter (roi′tər), Baron **Paul Julius von.** 1816–1899. German-born British journalist who founded (1848) Reuter's, one of the first international news agencies.

Reu·ther (ro͞o′thər), **Walter Philip.** 1907–1970. American labor leader who was president of the United Auto Workers (1946–1970) and of the Congress of Industrial Organizations (1952–1955).

Reut·ling·en (roit′lĭng-ən). A city of southwest Germany south of Stuttgart. It was a free imperial city from 1240 to 1802 and is now a manufacturing center with an important textile industry. Population, 96,337.

rev (rĕv) *Informal. n.* A revolution, as of a motor. **—rev** *v.* **revved, rev·ving, revs.** *—tr.* **1.a.** To increase the speed of (a motor, for example): *revved the engine.* **b.** To accelerate or increase: *orders to rev up factory output.* **2.** To make livelier or more productive: *revving ourselves up for the game; efforts to rev the economy.* *—intr.* **1.** To operate at an increased speed: *heard the motors revving.* **2.** To accelerate in quantity or activity.

rev. *abbr.* **1.** Revenue. **2.** Reverse. **3.** Reversed. **4.** Review. **5.** Reviewed. **6.** Revise; revision. **7.** Revolution.

Rev. *abbr.* **1.** *Bible.* Revelation. **2.** Reverend.

re·val·i·date (rē-văl′ĭ-dāt′) *tr.v.* **-dat·ed, -dat·ing, -dates.** To declare valid again. **—re·val′i·da′tion** *n.*

re·val·u·ate (rē-văl′yo͞o-āt′) *tr.v.* **-at·ed, -at·ing, -ates. 1.** To make a new valuation of. **2.** To increase the exchange value of (a nation's currency). **—re·val′u·a′tion** *n.*

re·val·ue (rē-văl′yo͞o) *tr.v.* **-ued, -u·ing, -ues. 1.** To revise the value of (a nation's currency). **2.** To evaluate anew; reappraise.

re·vamp (rē-vămp′) *tr.v.* **-vamped, -vamp·ing, -vamps. 1.** To patch up or restore; renovate. **2.** To revise or reconstruct (a manuscript, for example). **3.** To vamp (a shoe) anew. **—revamp** *n.* The act or an instance of revamping; a complete reorganization or revision. **—re·vamp′ment** *n.*

re·vanche (rə-vänch′, -vänsh′) *n.* **1.** The act of retaliating; revenge. **2.** A usually political policy, as of a nation or an ethnic group, intended to regain lost territory or standing. [French, from Old French *revancher,* to revenge : *re-,* re- + *vengier, vencher,* to avenge; see REVENGE.] **—re·vanch′ism** (-vän′chĭz-əm, -vän′-shĭz-) *n.* **—re·vanch′ist** *adj. & n.* **—re·vanch·is′tic** *adj.*

re·veal[1] (rĭ-vēl′) *tr.v.* **-vealed, -veal·ing, -veals. 1.a.** To make known (something concealed or secret): *revealed a confidence.* **b.** To bring to view; show. **2.** To make known by supernatural or divine means: *"For the wrath of God is revealed from heaven"* (Romans 1:18). [Middle English *revelen,* from Old French *reveler,* from Latin *revēlāre* : *re-,* re- + *vēlāre,* to cover (from *vēlum,* veil).] **—re·veal′a·ble** *adj.* **—re·veal′er** *n.* **—re·veal′ment** *n.*

SYNONYMS: *reveal, expose, disclose, divulge, betray.* These verbs signify to make known what has been or ought to be kept from the knowledge of others. *Reveal* suggests uncovering what has been concealed: *"He was glad it was to him she had revealed her secret"* (Edith Wharton). To *expose* is to lay bare to public scrutiny: *In a slip of the tongue the schemer exposed his true motivation. Disclose* means to make known as if by removing a cover: *The journalist refused to disclose the source of her information. Divulge* often implies the improper revelation of something private or secret: *"And whatsoever I shall see or hear in the course of my profession . . . if it be what should not be published abroad, I will never divulge, holding such things to be holy secrets"* (Hippocratic Oath). To *betray* is to make known in a breach of trust or confidence: *"A servant . . . betrayed their presence . . . to the Germans"* (William Styron). The term can also mean to reveal against one's desire or will: *Her comment betrayed annoyance.*

re·veal[2] (rĭ-vēl′) *n.* **1.a.** The part of the side of a window or door opening that is between the outer surface of a wall and the window or door frame. **b.** The whole side of such an opening; the jamb. **2.** The framework of a motor vehicle window. [From Middle English *revalen,* to lower, from Old French *revaler* : *re-,* re- + *avaler,* to lower (from *a val,* down : *a,* to, from Latin *ad;* see AD– + *val,* valley; see VALE[1]).]

re·vealed religion (rĭ-vēld′) *n.* A religion founded primarily on the revelations of God to humankind.

re·veal·ing (rĭ-vē′lĭng) *adj.* Permitting an elucidating glimpse or a perception of something intimate or concealed: *a very revealing biography; a revealing gown.* **—re·veal′ing·ly** *adv.*

re·veg·e·tate (rē-vĕj′ĭ-tāt′) *v.* **-tat·ed, -tat·ing, -tates.** *—tr.* To cause (eroded land, for example) to bear a new cover of vegetation. *—intr.* To bear a new cover of vegetation. **—re·veg′e·ta′tion** *n.*

rev·eil·le (rĕv′ə-lē) *n.* **1.a.** The sounding of a bugle early in the morning to awaken and summon people in a camp or garrison. **b.** This bugle call or its equivalent. **c.** The first military formation of the day. **2.** A signal to get up out of bed. [Alteration of French *réveillez,* second person imperative pl. of *réveiller,* to wake, from Old French *resveiller* : *re-,* re- + *esveiller,* to awake, from Vulgar Latin **exvigilāre* (Latin *ex-,* ex- + Latin *vigilāre,* to stay awake) from *vigil,* awake. See **weg-** in Appendix.]

rev·el (rĕv′əl) *intr.v.* **-eled, -el·ing, -els** also **-elled, -el·ling, -els. 1.** To take great pleasure or delight: *She reveled in her unaccustomed leisure.* **2.** To engage in uproarious festivities; make merry. **—revel** *n.* A boisterous festivity or celebration; merrymaking. Often used in the plural. [Middle English *revelen,* to carouse, from Old French *reveler,* to rebel, carouse, from Latin *rebellāre,* to rebel. See REBEL.] **—rev′el·ler, rev′el·er** *n.*

rev·e·la·tion (rĕv′ə-lā′shən) *n.* **1.a.** The act of revealing or disclosing. **b.** Something revealed, especially a dramatic disclosure of something not previously known or realized. **2.** *Theology.* A manifestation of divine will or truth. **3. Revelation.** *Abbr.* **Rev., Rv.** *Bible.* See table at **Bible.** [Middle English *revelacion,* from Old French *revelation,* from Latin *revēlātiō, revēlātiōn-,* from *revēlātus,* past participle of *revēlāre,* to reveal. See REVEAL[1].]

rev·e·la·tor (rĕv′ə-lā′tər) *n.* One who reveals, especially one who reveals divine will.

rev·e·la·to·ry (rĕv′ə-lə-tôr′ē, -tōr′ē, rĭ-vĕl′ə-) *adj.* Of, relating to, or containing a revelation: *"the distinction between Mrs. and Miss and its concomitant revelatory features"* (Mario Pei).

rev·el·ry (rĕv′əl-rē) *n., pl.* **-ries.** Boisterous merrymaking. **—rev′el·rous** (-rəs) *adj.*

rev·e·nant (rĕv′ə-nənt) *n.* **1.** One that returns after a lengthy absence. **2.** One who returns after death. [French, from present participle of *revenir,* to return, from Old French, from Latin *revenīre* : *re-,* re- + *venīre,* to come; see **g^wā-** in Appendix.]

re·venge (rĭ-vĕnj′) *tr.v.* **-venged, -veng·ing, -veng·es. 1.** To inflict punishment in return for (injury or insult). **2.** To seek or take vengeance for (oneself or another person); avenge. **—revenge** *n.* **1.** The act of taking vengeance for injuries or wrongs; retaliation. **2.** Something done in vengeance; a retaliatory measure. **3.** A desire for revenge; spite or vindictiveness. **4.** An opportunity to retaliate, as by a return sports match after a defeat. [Middle English *revengen,* from Old French *revengier* : *re-,* re- + *vengier,* to take revenge (from Latin *vindicāre,* to avenge, from *vindex, vindic-,* avenger; see **deik-** in Appendix).] **—re·veng′er** *n.*

re·venge·ful (rĭ-vĕnj′fəl) *adj.* Full of or given to revenge. See Synonyms at **vindictive.** **—re·venge′ful·ly** *adv.* **—re·venge′ful·ness** *n.*

rev·e·nue (rĕv′ə-no͞o, -nyo͞o) *n. Abbr.* **rev. 1.** The income of a government from all sources appropriated for the payment of the public expenses. **2.** Yield from property or investment; income. **3.** All the income produced by a particular source. **4.** A governmental department set up to collect public funds. [Middle English, from Old French, from feminine past participle of *revenir,* to return, from Latin *revenīre* : *re-,* re- + *venīre,* to come; see **g^wā-** in Appendix.]

revenue bond *n.* A bond issued by an agency commissioned to finance the building or improving of a public property, such as

ă pat	oi boy
ā pay	ou out
âr care	o͝o took
ä father	o͞o boot
ĕ pet	ŭ cut
ē be	ûr urge
ĭ pit	th thin
ī pie	*th* this
îr pier	hw which
ŏ pot	zh vision
ō toe	ə about, item
ô paw	♦ regionalism

Stress marks: ′ (primary); ′ (secondary), as in **dictionary** (dĭk′shə-nĕr′ē)

a bridge or toll road, the revenue from which will pay for the bond.

rev·e·nu·er (rĕv′ə-no͞o′ər, -nyo͞o′-) *n. Informal.* **1.** A government agent in charge of collecting revenue, especially one responsible for halting the unlawful distilling or bootlegging of alcohol. **2.** *Nautical.* A lightly armed motorboat used by revenuers.

revenue shar·ing (shâr′ĭng) *n.* Distribution of a portion of federal tax revenues to state and municipal governments. **—rev′e·nue-shar′ing** (rĕv′ə-no͞o-shâr′ĭng, -nyo͞o-) *adj.*

revenue stamp *n.* A stamp affixed to an item as proof that a government tax has been paid.

revenue tariff *n.* A tariff imposed chiefly to generate public revenue.

re·verb (rĭ-vûrb′) *Informal. n.* **1.** A reverberative effect produced in recorded music by electronic means. **2.** A device used for producing this effect. **—reverb** *intr. & tr.v.* **-verbed, -verb·ing, -verbs.** To reverberate or cause to reverberate.

re·ver·ber·ant (rĭ-vûr′bər-ənt) *adj.* **1.** Having a tendency to reverberate. **2.** Characterized by reverberation; resounding. **—re·ver′ber·ant·ly** *adv.*

re·ver·ber·ate (rĭ-vûr′bə-rāt′) *v.* **-at·ed, -at·ing, -ates.** *—intr.* **1.** To resound in or as if in a succession of echoes; reecho. **2.** To be repeatedly reflected, as sound waves, heat, or light. **3.** To be forced or driven back; recoil or rebound. *—tr.* **1.** To reecho (a sound). See Synonyms at **echo.** **2.** To reflect (heat or light) repeatedly. **3.** To drive or force back; repel. **4.** To subject (a metal, for example) to treatment in a reverberatory furnace. [Latin *reverberāre, reverberāt-,* to repel : *re-,* re- + *verberāre,* to beat (from *verber,* whip; see **wer-**[2] in Appendix).] **—re·ver′ber·a·tor** *n.*

re·ver·ber·a·tion (rĭ-vûr′bə-rā′shən) *n.* **1.a.** The act of reverberating. **b.** The condition of being reverberated. **2.a.** Something reverberated. **b.** An echolike force or effect; a repercussion: *Reverberations from the stock market crash were still being felt months later.*

reverberation pedal *n. Music.* See **sustaining pedal.**

re·ver·ber·a·tive (rĭ-vûr′bə-rā′tĭv, -bər-ə-) *adj.* **1.** Having the nature of reverberation. **2.** Tending to reverberate; reverberant. **—re·ver′ber·a·tive·ly** *adv.*

re·ver·ber·a·to·ry (rĭ-vûr′bər-ə-tôr′ē, -tōr′ē) *adj.* **1.** Produced or operating by reverberation; deflected or diverted, as flame or heat, onto material being treated. **2.** Of, relating to, or being a reverberatory furnace. **—reverberatory** *n., pl.* **-ies.** A reverberatory furnace.

reverberatory furnace *n.* A furnace or kiln in which the material under treatment is heated indirectly by means of a flame deflected downward from the roof.

re·vere[1] (rĭ-vîr′) *tr.v.* **-vered, -ver·ing, -veres.** To regard with awe, deference, and devotion. [French *révérer,* from Old French *reverer,* from Latin *reverērī* : *re-,* re- + *verērī,* to respect; see **wer-**[3] in Appendix.]

SYNONYMS: *revere, worship, venerate, adore, idolize.* These verbs all mean to regard with the deepest respect, deference, and esteem. *Revere* suggests awe coupled with profound honor: *"At least one third of the population . . . reveres every sort of holy man"* (Rudyard Kipling). *Worship* implies reverent love and homage rendered to God or a god: *The ancient Egyptians, who were polytheists, worshiped a number of gods and sacred animals.* In a more general sense *worship* connotes an often uncritical but always very admiring regard: *"She had worshiped intellect"* (Charles Kingsley). *Venerate* connotes reverence accorded by virtue especially of dignity, character, or age: *"I venerate the memory of my grandfather"* (Horace Walpole). To *adore* is to worship with deep, often rapturous love: *"O come, let us adore him, Christ the Lord!"* ("Adeste Fideles"). *A number of the students detested the subject but adored the teacher. Idolize* implies worship like that accorded an object of religious devotion: *He idolizes his wife and doesn't care who knows it.*

re·vere[2] (rĭ-vîr′, -vâr′) *n.* Variant of **revers.**

Re·vere (rĭ-vîr′). A city of eastern Massachusetts, a mainly residential suburb of Boston on Massachusetts Bay. Population, 42,423.

Revere, Paul. 1735–1818. American silversmith, engraver, and Revolutionary hero. On April 18, 1775, he made his famous ride, celebrated in a poem by Longfellow, to warn of the British advance on Lexington and Concord, Massachusetts.

rev·er·ence (rĕv′ər-əns) *n.* **1.** A feeling of profound awe and respect and often love; veneration. See Synonyms at **honor.** **2.** An act showing respect, especially a bow or curtsy. **3.** The state of being revered. **4. Reverence.** Used as a form of address for certain members of the Christian clergy: *Your Reverence.* **—reverence** *tr.v.* **-enced, -enc·ing, -enc·es.** To consider or treat with profound awe and respect. **—rev′er·enc·er** *n.*

rev·er·end (rĕv′ər-ənd) *adj.* **1.** Deserving reverence. **2.** Relating to or characteristic of the clergy; clerical. **3. Reverend.** *Abbr.* **Rev.** Used as a title and form of address for certain clerics in many Christian churches. In formal usage, preceded by *the*: *the Reverend Jane Doe; Reverend John Jones.* **—reverend** *n. Informal.* A cleric or minister. Used with *the.* [Middle English, from Old French, from Latin *reverendus,* gerundive of *reverērī,* to revere. See REVERE[1].]

rev·er·ent (rĕv′ər-ənt) *adj.* Marked by, feeling, or expressing reverence. [Middle English, from Old French, from Latin *reverēns, reverent-,* present participle of *reverērī,* to revere. See REVERE[1].] **—rev′er·ent·ly** *adv.*

rev·er·en·tial (rĕv′ə-rĕn′shəl) *adj.* **1.** Expressing reverence; reverent. **2.** Inspiring reverence. **—rev′er·en′tial·ly** *adv.*

rev·er·ie (rĕv′ə-rē) *n.* **1.** A state of abstracted musing; daydreaming. **2.** A daydream: *"I felt caught up in a reverie of years long past"* (William Styron). [Middle English, revelry, from Old French, from *rever,* to dream, rave.]

re·vers also **re·vere** (rĭ-vîr′, -vâr′) *n., pl.* **revers** also **-veres** (-vîrz′, -vârz′). A part of a garment, such as a lapel, turned back to show the reverse side. [French, from Old French, reverse. See REVERSE.]

re·ver·sal (rĭ-vûr′səl) *n.* **1.a.** The act or an instance of reversing. **b.** The state of being reversed. **2.** A usually adverse change in fortune: *financial reversals.* **3.** *Law.* The act or an instance of changing or setting aside a lower court's decision by a higher court.

re·verse (rĭ-vûrs′) *adj. Abbr.* **rev.** **1.a.** Turned backward in position, direction, or order. **b.** Having the back showing or in view of the observer. **2.** Moving, acting, or organized in a manner contrary to the usual. **3.** Causing backward movement: *a reverse gear.* **4.** *Printing.* Printed in such a way that the normally colored part appears white against a colored or black background. **—reverse** *n. Abbr.* **rev.** **1.** The opposite or contrary: *All along we thought Sue was older than Bill, but just the reverse was true.* **2.a.** The back or rear part. **b.** The side of a coin or medal that does not carry the principal design; the verso. **3.** A change to an opposite position, condition, or direction. **4.** A change in fortune from better to worse; a setback: *suffered financial reverses.* **5.a.** A mechanism, such as a gear in a motor vehicle, that is used to reverse movement. **b.** The position or operating condition of such a mechanism. **c.** Movement in an opposite direction. **6.** *Football.* An offensive play in which a back running in one direction executes a handoff to a back running in the opposite direction. **—reverse** *v.* **-versed, -vers·ing, -vers·es.** *—tr.* **1.** To turn around to the opposite direction. **2.** To turn inside out or upside down. **3.** To exchange the positions of; transpose. **4.** *Law.* To revoke or annul (a decision or decree, for example). **5.a.** To cause to adopt a contrary viewpoint. **b.** To change to the opposite: *reversed their planned course of action.* **6.** To cause (an engine or a mechanism) to function in reverse. *—intr.* **1.** To turn or move in the opposite direction. **2.** To reverse the action of an engine. ***—idiom.*** **reverse (one's) field.** To turn and proceed in the opposite direction. [Middle English *revers,* from Old French, from Latin *reversus,* past participle of *revertere,* to turn back. See REVERT.] **—re·verse′ly** *adv.* **—re·vers′er** *n.*

SYNONYMS: *reverse, invert, transpose.* These verbs are compared as they mean to change to the opposite position, direction, or course. *Reverse* implies a complete turning about to a contrary position: *reversed the paintings for a more satisfying effect.* To *invert* is basically to turn something upside down or inside out, but the term may imply placing something in a reverse order: *inverted and aired the mattress; inverting subject and verb to form an interrogative. Transpose* applies to altering position in a sequence by reversing or changing the order: *often misspells* receive *by transposing the* e *and the* i.

reverse discrimination *n.* Discrimination against members of a dominant group, especially such discrimination resulting from policies established to correct discrimination against members of minority groups.

reverse osmosis *n.* A method of producing pure water by forcing saline or waste water through a semipermeable membrane through which the salts or waste products cannot pass.

reverse transcriptase *n.* A polymerase that catalyzes the formation of DNA on an RNA template, found in oncogenic viruses containing RNA, especially the retroviruses.

re·vers·i·ble (rĭ-vûr′sə-bəl) *adj.* **1.** That can be reversed, as: **a.** Finished so that either side can be used: *a reversible fabric.* **b.** Wearable with either side turned outward: *a reversible skirt; a reversible vest.* **2.** *Chemistry & Physics.* Capable of successively assuming or producing either of two states: *a reversible cell; a reversible reaction.* **—reversible** *n.* A reversible fabric or item of clothing. **—re·vers′i·bil′i·ty, re·vers′i·ble·ness** *n.* **—re·vers′i·bly** *adv.*

re·ver·sion (rĭ-vûr′zhən) *n.* **1.** A return to a former condition, belief, or interest. **2.** A turning away or in the opposite direction; a reversal. **3.** *Genetics.* A return to the normal phenotype, usually by a second mutation. **4.** *Law.* **a.** The return of an estate to the grantor or to the grantor's heirs or successor after the grant has expired. **b.** The estate thus returned. **c.** The right to succeed to an estate.

re·ver·sion·ar·y (rĭ-vûr′zhə-nĕr′ē) also **re·ver·sion·al** (-zhə-nəl) *adj. Law.* Of or connected with the reversion of an estate.

re·ver·sion·er (rĭ-vûr′zhə-nər) *n. Law.* A party entitled to receive an estate in reversion.

re·vert (rĭ-vûrt′) *intr.v.* **-vert·ed, -vert·ing, -verts.** **1.** To return to a former condition, practice, subject, or belief. See Synonyms at **return.** See Usage Note at **redundancy.** **2.** *Law.* To return to the former owner or to the former owner's heirs. Used of money or property. **3.** *Genetics.* To undergo reversion. [Middle

English *reverten,* from Old French *revertir,* from Vulgar Latin **revertīre,* variant of Latin *revertere* : *re-,* re- + *vertere,* to turn; see **wer-**[2] in Appendix.] **—re·vert′er** *n.* **—re·vert′i·ble** *adj.* **—re·ver′tive** *adj.*

re·ver·tant (rĭ-vûr′tnt) *Genetics. adj.* Having reverted to the normal phenotype, usually by a second mutation: *a revertant mutant; revertant cells.* **—revertant** *n.* A revertant organism, cell, or strain.

re·vest (rē-vĕst′) *tr.v.* **-vest·ed, -vest·ing, -vests. 1.** To invest (someone) again with power or ownership; reinstate. **2.** To vest (power, for example) once again in a person or an agency.

re·vet (rĭ-vĕt′) *v.* **-vet·ted, -vet·ting, -vets.** *—tr.* To retain (an embankment, for example) with a layer of stone, concrete, or other supporting material; provide with a revetment. *—intr.* To construct a revetment. [French *revêtir,* from Old French *revestir,* to clothe again, from Latin *revestīre* : *re-,* re- + *vestīre,* to clothe (from *vestis,* garment; see **wes-**[2] in Appendix).]

re·vet·ment (rĭ-vĕt′mənt) *n.* **1.** A facing, as of masonry, used to support an embankment. **2.** A barricade against explosives.

re·view (rĭ-vyo͞o′) *v.* **-viewed, -view·ing, -views.** *—tr.* **1.** To look over, study, or examine again. **2.** To consider retrospectively; look back on. **3.** To examine with an eye to criticism or correction: *reviewed the research findings.* **4.** To write or give a critical report on (a new work or performance, for example). **5.** *Law.* To reexamine (an action or a determination) judicially, especially in a higher court, in order to correct possible errors. **6.** To subject to a formal inspection, especially a military inspection. *—intr.* **1.** To go over or restudy material: *reviewing for a final exam.* **2.** To write critical reviews, especially for a newspaper or magazine. **—review** *n. Abbr.* **rev. 1.** A reexamination or reconsideration. **2.** A retrospective view or survey. **3.a.** A restudying of subject matter. **b.** An exercise for use in restudying material. **4.** An inspection or examination for the purpose of evaluation. **5.a.** A report or an essay giving a critical estimate of a work or performance. **b.** A periodical devoted to articles and essays on current affairs, literature, or art. **6.a.** A formal military inspection. **b.** A formal military ceremony held in honor of a person or an occasion. **7.** *Law.* A judicial reexamination, especially by a higher court, of an action or a determination. **8.** A musical show consisting of often satirical skits, songs, and dances; a revue. [Probably from Middle English, inspection of military forces, from Old French *revue,* review, from feminine past participle of *reveeir,* to see again, from Latin *revidēre* : *re-,* re- + *vidēre,* to see; see **weid-** in Appendix.] **—re·view′a·ble** *adj.*

re·view·er (rĭ-vyo͞o′ər) *n.* One who reviews, especially one who writes critical reviews, as for a newspaper or magazine.

re·vile (rĭ-vīl′) *v.* **-viled, -vil·ing, -viles.** *—tr.* To assail with abusive language; vituperate. See Synonyms at **scold.** *—intr.* To use abusive language. [Middle English *revilen,* from Old French *reviler* : *re-,* re- + *vil,* vile; see VILE.] **—re·vile′ment** *n.* **—re·vil′er** *n.* **—re·vil′ing·ly** *adv.*

Re·vil·la·gi·ge·do Islands also **Re·vil·la Gi·ge·do Islands** (rĭ-vē′ə-hĭ-hā′dō, rĕ-vē′yä-hē-hĕ′thô). An island group of Mexico in the Pacific Ocean south of Baja California. The rocky islands are surrounded by good fishing grounds.

re·vis·al (rĭ-vī′zəl) *n.* The act or an instance of revising; a revision.

re·vise (rĭ-vīz′) *tr.v.* **-vised, -vis·ing, -vis·es. 1.** To prepare a newly edited version of (a text). **2.** To reconsider and change or modify: *I have revised my opinion of him.* See Synonyms at **correct. —revise** (rē′vīz′, rĭ-vīz′) *n. Abbr.* **rev.** *Printing.* A proof made from an earlier proof on which corrections have been made. [Latin *revīsere,* to visit again, look at again : *re-,* re- + *vīsere,* frequentative of *vidēre,* to see; see REVIEW.] **—re·vis′a·ble** *adj.* **—re·vis′er, re·vi′sor** *n.*

Re·vised Standard Version (rĭ-vīzd′) *n. Abbr.* **RSV, R.S.V.** A modern American version of the English Bible, a revision of the American Standard Version, completed in 1952.

Revised Version *n. Abbr.* **Rev. Ver., RV, R.V.** A British and American revision of the King James Version of the Bible, completed in 1885.

re·vi·sion (rĭ-vĭzh′ən) *n. Abbr.* **rev. 1.** The act or process of revising. **2.** A revised or new version, as of a book or other written material. **—re·vi′sion·ar′y** *adj.*

re·vi·sion·ism (rĭ-vĭzh′ə-nĭz′əm) *n.* **1.** Advocacy of the revision of an accepted, usually long-standing view, theory, or doctrine, especially a revision of historical events and movements. **2.** A recurrent tendency within the Communist movement to revise Marxist theory in such a way as to provide justification for a retreat from the revolutionary to the reformist position. **—re·vi′sion·ist** *adj. & n.*

re·vis·it (rē-vĭz′ĭt) *tr.v.* **-it·ed, -it·ing, -its.** To visit again. **—revisit** *n.* A second or repeated visit. **—re′vis·i·ta′tion** *n.*

re·vi·so·ry (rĭ-vī′zə-rē) *adj.* Of, relating to, effecting, or having the power of revision.

re·vi·tal·ize (rē-vīt′l-īz′) *tr.v.* **-ized, -iz·ing, -iz·es.** To impart new life or vigor to: *plans to revitalize inner-city neighborhoods; tried to revitalize a flagging economy.* **—re·vi′tal·i·za′tion** (-ĭ-zā′shən) *n.*

re·viv·al (rĭ-vī′vəl) *n.* **1.a.** The act or an instance of reviving. **b.** The condition of being revived. **2.** A restoration to use, acceptance, activity, or vigor after a period of obscurity or quiescence. **3.** A new presentation of an old play, movie, opera, ballet, or similar vehicle. **4.a.** A time of reawakened interest in religion. **b.** A meeting or series of meetings for the purpose of reawakening religious faith, often characterized by impassioned preaching and public testimony. **5.** *Law.* Renewal of validity or effect, as of a contract or judicial decision.

re·viv·al·ism (rĭ-vī′və-lĭz′əm) *n.* **1.** The spirit or activities characteristic of religious revivals. **2.** A desire or an inclination to revive what belongs to an earlier time.

re·viv·al·ist (rĭ-vī′və-lĭst) *n.* **1.** One who promotes or leads religious revivals. **2.** One who revives practices or ideas of an earlier time. **—re·viv′al·ist** *adj.* **—re·viv′al·is′tic** *adj.*

re·vive (rĭ-vīv′) *v.* **-vived, -viv·ing, -vives.** *—tr.* **1.** To bring back to life or consciousness; resuscitate. **2.** To impart new health, vigor, or spirit to. **3.** To restore to use, currency, activity, or notice. **4.** To restore the validity or effectiveness of. **5.** To renew in the mind; recall. **6.** To present (an old play, for example) again. *—intr.* **1.** To return to life or consciousness. **2.** To regain health, vigor, or good spirits. **3.** To return to use, currency, or notice. **4.** To return to validity, effectiveness, or operative condition. [Middle English *reviven,* from Old French *revivre,* from Latin *revīvere,* to live again : *re-,* re- + *vīvere,* to live; see **gʷei-** in Appendix.] **—re·viv′a·ble** *adj.* **—re·viv′er** *n.*

SYNONYMS: *revive, restore, resuscitate, revivify.* The central meaning shared by these verbs is "to give renewed well-being, vitality, or strength to": *rains that revive lawns and flowers; an invalid restored by quiet and fresh air; resuscitating old hopes and aspirations; a celebration that revivified our spirits.*

re·viv·i·fy (rē-vĭv′ə-fī′) *tr.v.* **-fied, -fy·ing, -fies.** To impart new life, energy, or spirit to. See Synonyms at **revive.** [French *revivifier,* from Old French, to come back to life, from Latin **revīvificāre,* to revivify : Latin *re-,* re- + Latin *vīvificāre,* to vivify; see VIVIFY.] **—re·viv′i·fi·ca′tion** (-fĭ-kā′shən) *n.*

rev·o·ca·ble (rĕv′ə-kə-bəl) also **re·vok·a·ble** (rĭ-vō′-) *adj.* That can be revoked: *a revocable order; a revocable vote.*

rev·o·ca·tion (rĕv′ə-kā′shən) *n.* The act or an instance of revoking. [Middle English *revocacion,* from Old French, from Latin *revocātiō, revocātiōn-,* from *revocātus,* past participle of *revocāre,* to call back. See REVOKE.] **—rev′o·ca·to′ry** (rĕv′ə-kə-tôr′ē, -tōr′ē) *adj.*

re·vok·a·ble (rĭ-vō′kə-bəl) *adj.* Variant of **revocable.**

re·voke (rĭ-vōk′) *v.* **-voked, -vok·ing, -vokes.** *—tr.* To void or annul by recalling, withdrawing, or reversing: *Her license was revoked.* *—intr. Games.* To fail to follow suit in cards when required and able to do so. **—revoke** *n. Games.* Failure to follow suit in a card game. [Middle English *revoken,* from Old French *revoquer,* from Latin *revocāre* : *re-,* re- + *vocāre,* to call; see **wekʷ-** in Appendix.] **—re·vok′er** *n.*

re·volt (rĭ-vōlt′) *v.* **-volt·ed, -volt·ing, -volts.** *—intr.* **1.** To attempt to overthrow the authority of the state; rebel. **2.** To oppose or refuse to accept something: *revolting against high taxes.* **3.a.** To feel disgust or repugnance: *to revolt at a public display of cruelty.* **b.** To turn away in revulsion or abhorrence: *They revolted from the sight.* *—tr.* To fill with disgust or abhorrence; repel. See Synonyms at **disgust. —revolt** *n.* **1.** An uprising, especially against state authority; a rebellion. See Synonyms at **rebellion. 2.** An act of protest or rejection. **3.** The state of a person or persons in rebellion: *students in revolt over administrative policies.* [French *revolter,* from Italian *rivoltare,* to turn round, from Vulgar Latin **revolvitāre,* frequentative of Latin *revolvere,* to turn over. See REVOLVE.] **—re·volt′er** *n.*

re·volt·ing (rĭ-vōl′tĭng) *adj.* Causing abhorrence or disgust. See Synonyms at **offensive. —re·volt′ing·ly** *adv.*

rev·o·lute (rĕv′ə-lo͞ot′) *adj. Botany.* Rolled backward from the tip or margins to the undersurface: *a revolute leaf.* [Latin *revolūtus,* past participle of *revolvere,* to roll back. See REVOLVE.]

rev·o·lu·tion (rĕv′ə-lo͞o′shən) *n. Abbr.* **rev. 1.a.** Orbital motion about a point, especially as distinguished from axial rotation: *the planetary revolution about the sun.* **b.** A turning or rotational motion about an axis. **c.** A single complete cycle of such orbital or axial motion. **2.** The overthrow of one government and its replacement with another. See Synonyms at **rebellion. 3.** A sudden or momentous change in a situation: *the revolution in computer technology.* **4.** *Geology.* A time of major crustal deformation, when folds and faults are formed. [Middle English *revolucioun,* from Old French *revolution,* from Late Latin *revolūtiō, revolūtiōn-,* from Latin *revolūtus,* past participle of *revolvere,* to turn over. See REVOLVE.]

rev·o·lu·tion·ar·y (rĕv′ə-lo͞o′shə-nĕr′ē) *adj.* **1.a.** Often **Revolutionary.** Of, relating to, or being a revolution: *revolutionary war; a museum of the Revolutionary era.* **b.** Bringing about or supporting a political or social revolution: *revolutionary pamphlets.* **2.** Characterized by or resulting in radical change: *a revolutionary discovery.* **—revolutionary** *n., pl.* **-ies. 1.** A militant in the struggle for revolution. **2.** A supporter of revolutionary principles. **—rev′o·lu′tion·ar′i·ly** *adv.* **—rev′o·lu′tion·ar′i·ness** *n.*

rev·o·lu·tion·ist (rĕv′ə-lo͞o′shə-nĭst) *n.* One who favors or is engaged in a revolution. **—rev′o·lu′tion·ist** *adj.*

rev·o·lu·tion·ize (rĕv′ə-lo͞o′shə-nīz′) *tr.v.* **-ized, -iz·ing, -iz·es. 1.** To bring about a radical change in: *Television has revolutionized news coverage.* **2.** To subject to a political or social revolution. **3.** To fill with revolutionary principles. **—rev′o·lu′tion·iz′er** *n.*

revetment

ă pat	oi boy
ā pay	ou out
âr care	o͝o took
ä father	o͞o boot
ĕ pet	ŭ cut
ē be	ûr urge
ĭ pit	th thin
ī pie	*th* this
îr pier	hw which
ŏ pot	zh vision
ō toe	ə about, item
ô paw	♦ regionalism

Stress marks: **′** (primary); ′ (secondary), as in **dictionary** (dĭk′shə-nĕr′ē)

revolver

revolving door

re·volve (rĭ-vŏlv′) *v.* **-volved, -volv·ing, -volves.** —*intr.* **1.** To orbit a central point. **2.** To turn on an axis; rotate. See Synonyms at **turn. 3.** To recur in cycles or at periodic intervals. **4.** To be held in the mind and considered in turn. **5.** To be centered: *Their troubles revolve around money management.* —*tr.* **1.** To cause to revolve. **2.** To ponder or reflect on. [Middle English *revolven,* to change direction, from Old French *revolver,* to reflect upon, from Latin *revolvere,* to turn over, roll back, reflect upon : *re-,* re- + *volvere,* to roll; see **wel-**[2] in Appendix.] —**re·volv′a·ble** *adj.*

re·volv·er (rĭ-vŏl′vər) *n.* **1.** A pistol having a revolving cylinder with several cartridge chambers that may be fired in succession. **2.** One that revolves, as a part of a mechanism.

re·volv·ing (rĭ-vŏl′vĭng) *adj.* **1.** Tending to revolve or happen repeatedly. **2.** Available at regular intervals.

revolving charge account *n.* A charge account that features revolving credit, monthly repayments, and a carrying charge.

revolving credit *n.* Credit repeatedly available up to a specified amount as periodic repayments are made.

revolving door *n.* **1.** A door, as in the entrance of an office or apartment building, usually consisting of four rigid upright sections interconnected at right angles and rotating about a central, upright pivot. **2.** *Informal.* An organization, an institution, or a place whose members, personnel, or population remain only a short time before going elsewhere. —**re·volv′ing-door′** (rĭ-vŏl′vĭng-dôr′, -dōr′) *adj.*

revolving fund *n.* A fund established for a certain purpose, such as making loans, with the stipulation that repayments to the fund may be used anew for the same purpose.

re·vue (rĭ-vyo͞o′) *n.* A musical show consisting of skits, songs, and dances, often satirizing current events, trends, and personalities. [French, from Old French, review. See REVIEW.]

re·vulsed (rĭ-vŭlst′) *adj.* Affected with or having experienced revulsion.

re·vul·sion (rĭ-vŭl′shən) *n.* **1.** A sudden, strong change or reaction in feeling, especially a feeling of violent disgust or loathing. **2.** A withdrawing or turning away from something. **3.** *Medicine.* Counterirritation used to reduce inflammation or increase the blood supply to the affected area. [Latin *revulsiō, revulsiōn-,* from *revulsus,* past participle of *revellere,* to tear back : *re-,* re- + *vellere,* to tear.] —**re·vul′sive** *adj.*

Rev. Ver. *abbr. Bible.* Revised Version.

re·wake (rē-wāk′) *v.* **-woke** (-wōk′), or **-waked, -waked** or **-wok·en** (-wō′kən), **-wak·ing, -wakes.** —*tr.* To waken again. —*intr.* To become awake again.

re·wak·en (rē-wā′kən) *tr. & intr.v.* **-ened, -en·ing, -ens.** To rewake (another) or to become awake again.

re·ward (rĭ-wôrd′) *n.* **1.** Something given or received in recompense for worthy behavior or in retribution for evil acts. **2.** Money offered or given for some special service, such as the return of a lost article or the capture of a criminal. See Synonyms at **bonus. 3.** A satisfying return or result; profit. **4.** *Psychology.* The return for performance of a desired behavior; positive reinforcement. —**reward** *tr.v.* **-ward·ed, -ward·ing, -wards. 1.** To give a reward to or for. **2.** To satisfy or gratify; recompense. [Middle English *reward,* from Anglo-Norman, reward, from *rewarder,* to take notice of : *re-,* intensive pref. (from Latin; see RE– + *warder,* to guard, watch over, of Germanic origin; see **wer-**[3] in Appendix).] —**re·ward′a·ble** *adj.* —**re·ward′er** *n.*

re·ward·ing (rĭ-wôr′dĭng) *adj.* **1.** Offering or likely to offer satisfaction or gratification: *a very rewarding career as a paramedic.* **2.** Affording profit; remunerative: *a rewarding business venture.* **3.** Constituting a reward: *a rewarding hug.* —**re·ward′ing·ly** *adv.*

re·wind (rē-wīnd′) *tr.v.* **-wound** (-wound′), **-wind·ing, -winds. 1.** To wind again or anew. **2.** To reverse the winding of (recording tape or camera film). —**rewind** (rē′wīnd′, rē-wīnd′) *n.* **1.** The act or process of rewinding. **2.** Something that rewinds or is rewound. **3.** A control mechanism for rewinding (tape or film). —**re·wind′er** *n.*

re·wire (rē-wīr′) *v.* **-wired, -wir·ing, -wires.** —*tr.* To provide with new wiring: *rewired the old house.* —*intr.* To install new wiring.

re·woke (rē-wōk′) *v.* A past tense of **rewake.**

re·wok·en (rē-wō′kən) *v.* A past participle of **rewake.**

re·word (rē-wûrd′) *tr.v.* **-word·ed, -word·ing, -words. 1.a.** To change the wording of. **b.** To state or express again in different words. **2.** To state or express again in the same words; repeat.

re·work (rē-wûrk′) *tr.v.* **-worked, -work·ing, -works. 1.** To work over again; revise. **2.** To subject to a repeated or new process. —**rework** (rē′wûrk′) *n.* Something reworked: *just a rework of an old speech.*

re·wound (rē-wound′) *v.* Past tense and past participle of **rewind.**

re·write (rē-rīt′) *v.* **-wrote** (-rōt′), **-writ·ten** (-rĭt′n), **-writ·ing, -writes.** —*tr.* **1.** To write again, especially in a different or improved form; revise. **2.** To put (material submitted to a newspaper or magazine) in a form suitable for publishing. —*intr.* To make revisions in written material. —**rewrite** (rē′rīt′) *n.* **1.** The act or an instance of rewriting. **2.** Something rewritten. —**re·writ′er** *n.*

Rex·roth (rĕks′rôth′), **Kenneth.** 1905–1982. American writer and translator known especially for his poetry, collected in volumes such as *The Phoenix and the Tortoise* (1944) and *In Defense of Earth* (1956).

Reyes (rāz), **Point.** A promontory on the western central California coast northwest of San Francisco. It is reported to be the windiest and foggiest place on the western coast of the continental United States, with an average of 137 foggy days a year.

Reye's syndrome (rīz, rāz) *n.* An acute encephalopathy characterized by fever, vomiting, fatty infiltration of the liver, disorientation, and coma, occurring mainly in children and usually following a viral infection, such as chicken pox or influenza. [After Ralph Douglas Kenneth *Reye* (1912–1978), Australian pediatrician.]

Rey·kja·vík (rā′kyə-vēk′, -vĭk′). The capital and largest city of Iceland, in the southwest part of the island. Traditionally founded in 874, it became capital of the country in 1918 after Denmark recognized Iceland's sovereignty. Population, 88,745.

Rey·mont (rā′mŏnt′, -mônt′), **Wladyslaw Stanislaw.** 1867–1925. Polish writer whose novels include *The Comedienne* (1896) and *The Peasants* (1904–1909). He won the 1924 Nobel Prize for literature.

Rey·nard or **rey·nard** (rā′nərd, -närd′, rĕn′ərd) *n.* A fox. [Middle English *Renard, Reynard,* from Old French *Renart* and Middle Dutch *Reynaert,* the name of the fox in the beast epic *Roman de Renart.*]

Reyn·olds (rĕn′əldz), Sir **Joshua.** 1723–1792. British portrait painter and critic considered one of the most important figures in the history of English painting.

Rey·nolds·burg (rĕn′əldz-bûrg′). A city of central Ohio, a suburb of Columbus in an agricultural area. Population, 20,661.

Rey·no·sa (rā-nō′sə). A city of eastern Mexico on the Rio Grande east-northeast of Monterrey. It is a processing and shipping center in an agricultural region. Population, 194,693.

re·zone (rē-zōn′) *tr.v.* **-zoned, -zon·ing, -zones.** To change the zoning classification of (a neighborhood or property, for example). —**re′zone′** *n.*

RF *abbr.* **1.** Radio frequency. **2.** Right field; right fielder.

rf. *abbr.* **1.** Reef. **2.** Refund.

R factor *n.* A genetic factor of bacteria that transmits resistance to antibiotics from one bacterium to another by conjugation. [R(ESISTANCE).]

RFD also **R.F.D.** *abbr.* Rural free delivery.

Rh[1] (är′āch′) *adj.* Of or relating to the Rh factor: *an Rh antigen; the Rh blood group; Rh incompatibility.*

Rh[2] The symbol for the element **rhodium.**

r.h. *abbr.* **1.** Relative humidity. **2.** Also **RH.** Right-hand.

rhab·dom (răb′dəm, -dŏm′) *n.* A transparent rod in the center of each ommatidium in the compound eye of an arthropod. [From Greek *rhabdōma,* bundle of rods, from Greek *rhabdos,* rod. See RHABDOMANCY.]

rhab·do·man·cy (răb′də-măn′sē) *n.* Divination with a wand or rod, especially for discovering underground water or ores. [Late Greek *rhabdomanteia* : Greek *rhabdos,* rod; see **wer-**[2] in Appendix + Greek *-manteia,* -mancy.] —**rhab′do·man′cer** *n.*

rhab·do·my·o·ma (răb′dō-mī-ō′mə) *n., pl.* **-mas** or **-ma·ta** (-mə-tə). *Pathology.* A tumor in striated muscle fibers. [Greek *rhabdos,* rod; see RHABDOMANCY + MYOMA.]

rhab·do·vi·rus (răb′də-vī′rəs) *n., pl.* **-rus·es.** Any of a group of RNA-containing plant and animal viruses, which includes the rabies virus. [Greek *rhabdos,* rod; see **wer-**[2] in Appendix + VIRUS.]

Rhad·a·man·thine (răd′ə-măn′thĭn, -thīn′) *adj.* Strictly and uncompromisingly just. [From RHADAMANTHUS.]

Rhad·a·man·thus also **Rhad·a·man·thys** (răd′ə-măn′thəs) *n. Greek Mythology.* A son of Zeus and Europa who, in reward for his exemplary sense of justice, was made a judge of the underworld after his death. [Latin, from Greek *Rhadamanthos.*]

Rhae·ti·a (rē′shē-ə, -shə). An ancient Roman province that included present-day eastern Switzerland and western Austria. It was added to the Roman Empire during the reign of Augustus. —**Rhae′tian** *adj. & n.*

Rhaetian Alps. A range of the central Alps primarily in eastern Switzerland and along the Italian and Austrian borders. It rises to Piz Bernina, 4,051.6 m (13,284 ft) high, in the Bernina section of the range on the Italian border.

Rhae·to-Ro·mance (rē′tō-rō-măns′) *n.* A group of three Romance dialects, including Romansch, spoken in southern Switzerland, northern Italy, and the Tyrol. [Latin *Rhaetus,* of Rhaetia, a Roman province + ROMANCE.]

Rha·gae (rā′jē). An ancient city of Media southeast of modern Tehran in north-central Iran. One of the greatest cities of ancient times, it was traditionally founded in 3000 B.C. and flourished until the Middle Ages. The city was finally destroyed by Tartars in the 12th century A.D.

rha·phe (rā′fē) *n.* Variant of **raphe.**

rhap·sod·ic (răp-sŏd′ĭk) also **rhap·sod·i·cal** (-ĭ-kəl) *adj.* **1.** Of, resembling, or characteristic of a rhapsody. **2.** Immoderately impassioned or enthusiastic; ecstatic. —**rhap·sod′i·cal·ly** *adv.*

rhap·so·dist (răp′sə-dĭst) *n.* **1.** One who uses extravagantly enthusiastic or impassioned language. **2.** One who recited epic and other poetry, especially professionally, in ancient Greece.

rhap·so·dize (răp′sə-dīz′) *v.* **-dized, -diz·ing, -diz·es.** —*intr.* To express oneself in an immoderately enthusiastic manner. —*tr.* To recite (something) in the manner of a rhapsody.

rhap·so·dy (răp′sə-dē) *n., pl.* **-dies. 1.** Exalted or excessively enthusiastic expression of feeling in speech or writing. **2.** A literary work written in an impassioned or exalted style. **3.** A state of elated bliss; ecstasy. **4.** *Music.* A composition of irregular form and often improvisatory character. **5.** An ancient Greek epic poem or a portion of one suitable for uninterrupted recitation. [Latin *rhapsōdia,* section of an epic poem, from Greek *rhapsōidia,* from *rhapsōidein,* to recite poems : *rhaptein, rhaps-,* to sew; see **wer-**[2] in Appendix + *ōidē,* song; see **wed-**[2] in Appendix.]

rhat·a·ny (răt′n-ē) *n., pl.* **-nies. 1.** Either of two South American shrubs *(Krameria lappacea* or *K. argentea)* having bilaterally symmetrical flowers, spiny globose fruits, and thick roots. **2.** The dried root of either of these plants, formerly used as an astringent and now used in various dental preparations, such as toothpaste and mouthwash. [American Spanish *ratania,* possibly from Quechua *ratana,* to thin, unite.]

rhbdr. *abbr.* Rhombohedron.

rhe·a (rē′ə) *n.* Any of several flightless South American birds of the genus *Rhea,* resembling the ostrich but somewhat smaller and having three toes instead of two. [New Latin *Rhea,* genus name, probably from Latin, the wife of Cronus. See RHEA.]

Rhe·a (rē′ə) *n.* **1.** *Greek Mythology.* The sister and wife of Cronus and the mother of Demeter, Hades, Hera, Hestia, Poseidon, and Zeus. **2.** *Astronomy.* The satellite of Saturn that is 13th in distance from the planet. [Latin, from Greek.]

Rhee (rē), **Syngman.** 1875–1965. Korean politician who became president of South Korea in 1948. His dictatorial rule ended in 1960, when he was forced out of office and into exile.

Rheims or **Reims** (rēmz, răɴs). A city of northeast France east-northeast of Paris. One of the most important cities of Roman Gaul, it was long the site of the coronation of French kings. In World War II the unconditional German surrender was signed at Allied headquarters here on May 7, 1945. Population, 194,656.

Rhen·ish (rĕn′ĭsh) *adj.* Of or relating to the Rhine River or the lands bordering on it. —**Rhenish** *n.* See **Rhine wine** (sense 1). [Ultimately from Latin *Rhēnus,* the Rhine.]

rhe·ni·um (rē′nē-əm) *n. Symbol* **Re** A rare, dense, silvery-white metallic element with a very high melting point used for electrical contacts and with tungsten for high-temperature thermocouples. Atomic number 75; atomic weight 186.2; melting point 3,180°C; boiling point 5,627°C; specific gravity 21.02; valence 1, 2, 3, 4, 5, 6, 7. See table at **element.** [From Latin *Rhēnus,* the Rhine.]

rheo. *abbr.* Rheostat.

rheo– *pref.* Current; flow: *rheotaxis.* [From Greek *rheos,* stream, from *rhein,* to flow. See **sreu-** in Appendix.]

rhe·ol·o·gy (rē-ŏl′ə-jē) *n.* The study of the deformation and flow of matter. —**rhe′o·log′i·cal** (rē′ə-lŏj′ĭ-kəl) *adj.* —**rhe′o·log′i·cal·ly** *adv.* —**rhe·ol′o·gist** *n.*

rhe·om·e·ter (rē-ŏm′ĭ-tər) *n.* An instrument for measuring the flow of viscous liquids, such as blood.

rhe·o·stat (rē′ə-stăt′) *n. Abbr.* **rheo.** A continuously variable electrical resistor used to regulate current. —**rhe′o·stat′ic** *adj.*

rhe·o·tax·is (rē′ə-tăk′sĭs) *n.* Movement of an organism in response to a current of water or air. —**rhe′o·tac′tic** (-tăk′tĭk) *adj.*

rhe·sus (rē′səs) *n.* A rhesus monkey. [Latin *Rhēsus,* a mythical king of Thrace, from Greek *Rhēsos.*]

Rhe·sus factor (rē′səs) *n.* Rh factor.

rhesus monkey *n.* A brownish monkey *(Macaca mulatta)* of India, used extensively in biological and medical research.

rhet. *abbr.* Rhetoric.

rhe·tor (rē′tôr′, -tər) *n.* **1.** A teacher of rhetoric. **2.** An orator. [Middle English *rether,* from Latin *rhētor,* from Greek *rhētōr.* See **wer-**[5] in Appendix.]

rhet·o·ric (rĕt′ər-ĭk) *n. Abbr.* **rhet. 1.a.** The art or study of using language effectively and persuasively. **b.** A treatise or book discussing this art. **2.** Skill in using language effectively and persuasively. **3.a.** A style of speaking or writing, especially the language of a particular subject: *fiery political rhetoric.* **b.** Language that is elaborate, pretentious, insincere, or intellectually vacuous: *His offers of compromise were mere rhetoric.* **4.** Verbal communication; discourse. [Middle English *rethorik,* from Old French *rethorique,* from Latin *rhētoricē, rhētorica,* from Greek *rhētorikē (tekhnē),* rhetorical (art), feminine of *rhētorikos,* rhetorical, from *rhētōr, rhētor-,* rhetor. See RHETOR.]

USAGE NOTE: The word *rhetoric* was once primarily the name of an important branch of philosophy and an art deserving of serious study. In recent years the word has come to be used chiefly in a pejorative sense to refer to inflated language and pomposity. Deprecation of the term may result from a modern linguistic puritanism, which holds that language used in legitimate persuasion should be plain and free of artifice—itself a tendentious rhetorical doctrine, though not often recognized as such. But many writers still prefer to bear in mind the traditional meanings of the word. Thus, according to the newer use of the term, the phrase *empty rhetoric,* as in *The politicians talk about solutions, but they usually offer only empty rhetoric,* might be construed as redundant. But in fact only 35 percent of the Usage Panel judged this example to be redundant. Presumably, it can be maintained that rhetoric can be other than empty.

rhe·tor·i·cal (rĭ-tôr′ĭ-kəl, -tŏr′-) *adj.* **1.** Of or relating to rhetoric. **2.** Characterized by overelaborate or bombastic rhetoric. **3.** Used for persuasive effect: *a speech punctuated by rhetorical pauses.* —**rhe·tor′i·cal·ly** *adv.*

rhetorical question *n.* A question to which no answer is expected, often used for rhetorical effect.

rhet·o·ri·cian (rĕt′ə-rĭsh′ən) *n.* **1.** An expert in or teacher of rhetoric. **2.** An eloquent speaker or writer. **3.** A person given to verbal extravagance.

rheum (ro͞om) *n.* A watery or thin mucous discharge from the eyes or nose. [Middle English *reume,* from Old French, from Late Latin *rheuma,* from Greek, a flowing, rheum. See **sreu-** in Appendix.] —**rheum′y** *adj.*

rheu·mat·ic (ro͞o-măt′ĭk) *adj.* Of, relating to, or suffering from rheumatism. —**rheumatic** *n.* **1.** One who is affected by rheumatism. **2. rheumatics.** *Informal.* Pains caused by rheumatism. [Middle English *reumatik,* of rheum, from Old French *reumatique,* from Latin *rheumaticus,* suffering from rheum, from Greek *rheumatikos,* from *rheuma, rheumat-,* stream. See RHEUM.]

rheumatic fever *n.* A severe infectious disease occurring chiefly in children, characterized by fever and painful inflammation of the joints and frequently resulting in permanent damage to the valves of the heart.

rheumatic heart disease *n.* Permanent damage to the valves of the heart caused especially by repeated attacks of rheumatic fever.

rheu·ma·tism (ro͞o′mə-tĭz′əm) *n.* **1.** Any of several pathological conditions of the muscles, tendons, joints, bones, or nerves, characterized by discomfort and disability. **2.** Rheumatoid arthritis. [Latin *rheumatismus,* rheum, from Greek *rheumatismos,* from *rheumatizesthai,* to suffer from rheum, from *rheuma, rheumat-,* rheum. See RHEUM.]

rheu·ma·toid (ro͞o′mə-toid′) also **rheu·ma·toi·dal** (ro͞o′mə-toid′l) *adj.* **1.** Of or resembling rheumatism. **2.** Suffering from rheumatism. —**rheu′ma·toi′dal·ly** *adv.*

rheumatoid arthritis *n.* A chronic disease marked by stiffness and inflammation of the joints, weakness, loss of mobility, and deformity.

rheumatoid factor *n.* An immunoglobulin present in the blood serum of many individuals affected by rheumatoid arthritis, used as a means of diagnosing the disease.

rheu·ma·tol·o·gy (ro͞o′mə-tŏl′ə-jē) *n.* The medical science that deals with the study and treatment of rheumatic diseases. —**rheu′ma·tol′o·gist** *n.*

Rh factor *n.* Any of several substances on the surface of red blood cells that induce a strong antigenic response in individuals lacking the substance. [From RH(ESUS MONKEY), from its being first detected in the blood of this animal.]

rhin– *pref.* Variant of **rhino–.**

rhi·nal (rī′nəl) *adj.* Of or relating to the nose; nasal.

Rhine (rīn). A river of western Europe formed by the confluence of two tributaries in eastern Switzerland and flowing about 1,319 km (820 mi) north and northwest through Germany and the Netherlands to its two-pronged outlet on the North Sea. It is a major commercial shipping waterway linked by canals to other important European rivers and passes through a number of scenic valleys.

Rhine, Joseph Banks. 1895–1980. American psychologist noted for his pioneering work in parapsychology.

Rhine·land (rīn′lănd′, -lənd). A region along the Rhine River in western Germany. It includes noted vineyards and highly industrial sections north of Bonn and Cologne.

rhi·nen·ceph·a·lon (rī′nĕn-sĕf′ə-lŏn′, -lən) *n., pl.* **-la** (-lə). The olfactory region of the brain, located in the cerebrum. —**rhi′nen·ce·phal′ic** (-sə-făl′ĭk) *adj.*

rhine·stone (rīn′stōn′) *n.* A colorless artificial gem of paste or glass, often with facets that sparkle in imitation of a diamond. [After the RHINE (translation of French *caillou du Rhin* : *caillou,* pebble + *du,* of the + *Rhin,* Rhine).] —**rhine′stoned′** *adj.*

WORD HISTORY: Although rhinestones are inseparably associated with the costumes of country and western singers and Las Vegas showgirls, the word originally had European associations. The Rhine in *rhinestone* is the Rhine River, and *rhinestone* is a translation into English of the French phrase *caillou du Rhin.* Originally a rhinestone was a kind of rock crystal that was found in or near the Rhine and given a fancy name, as have other types of rock crystal such as Cornish diamond. Such stones could be made to imitate diamonds; hence the name *rhinestone* was applied to artificial gems made from paste, glass, or gem quartz. Rhinestones have spread far beyond the Rhine, becoming a central ingredient of certain aspects of Americana. Cornish diamonds have not shared the same fate.

Rhine wine *n.* **1.** Any of several dry white wines produced in

rhea
Gray rhea
Rhea americana

rhesus monkey
Macaca mulatta

ă **pat**	oi **boy**
ā **pay**	ou **out**
âr **care**	o͝o **took**
ä **father**	o͞o **boot**
ĕ **pet**	ŭ **cut**
ē **be**	ûr **urge**
ĭ **pit**	th **thin**
ī **pie**	*th* **this**
îr **pier**	hw **which**
ŏ **pot**	zh **vision**
ō **toe**	ə **about, item**
ô **paw**	♦ **regionalism**

Stress marks: ′ (primary); ′ (secondary), as in **dictionary** (dĭk′shə-nĕr′ē)

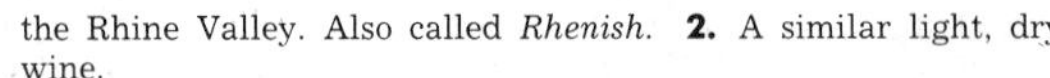

the Rhine Valley. Also called *Rhenish.* **2.** A similar light, dry wine.

rhi·ni·tis (rī-nī′tĭs) *n.* Inflammation of the nasal mucous membranes.

rhi·no[1] (rī′nō) *n., pl.* **-nos.** *Informal.* A rhinoceros.

rhi·no[2] (rī′nō) *n., pl.* **rhino.** *Chiefly British.* Money; cash. [Origin unknown.]

rhino– or **rhin–** *pref.* Nose; nasal: *rhinitis.* [Greek, from *rhis, rhin-,* nose.]

rhinoceros
Black rhinoceros
Diceros bicornis

rhi·noc·er·os (rī-nŏs′ər-əs) *n., pl.* **rhinoceros** or **-os·es.** Any of several large, thick-skinned, herbivorous mammals of the family Rhinocerotidae, of Africa and Asia, having one or two upright horns on the snout. [Middle English *rinoceros,* from Latin *rhīnocerōs,* from Greek *rhinokerōs* : *rhino-,* rhino- + *keras,* horn; see **ker-[1]** in Appendix.]

rhinoceros beetle *n.* Any of various large scarabaeid beetles of the genus *Dynastes* and related genera, characterized by horns on the head and thorax and found in tropical regions.

rhi·nol·o·gy (rī-nŏl′ə-jē) *n.* The anatomy, physiology, and pathology of the nose. **—rhi·nol′o·gist** *n.*

rhi·no·phar·yn·gi·tis (rī′nō-făr′ĭn-jī′tĭs) *n.* Inflammation of the nasal and pharyngeal mucous membranes.

rhi·no·plas·ty (rī′nō-plăs′tē, -nə-) *n., pl.* **-ties.** Plastic surgery of the nose. **—rhi′no·plas′tic** *adj.*

rhi·nos·co·py (rī-nŏs′kə-pē) *n., pl.* **-pies.** Examination of the nasal passages by means of a speculum or similar instrument.

rhi·no·vi·rus (rī′nō-vī′rəs) *n., pl.* **-rus·es.** Any of a group of picornaviruses that are causative agents of disorders of the respiratory tract, such as the common cold.

rhiz– *pref.* Variant of **rhizo–.**

rhi·zan·thous (rī-zăn′thəs) *adj. Botany.* Bearing flowers directly from the root.

rhizo– or **rhiz–** *pref.* Root: *rhizogenic.* [Greek, from *rhiza,* root. See **wrād-** in Appendix.]

Rhodesian ridgeback

rhi·zo·bi·um (rī-zō′bē-əm) *n., pl.* **-bi·a** (-bē-ə). Any of various nitrogen-fixing bacteria of the genus *Rhizobium* that form nodules on the roots of leguminous plants, such as clover and beans. [New Latin *Rhizobium,* genus name : RHIZO– + Greek *bios,* life; see **gʷei-** in Appendix.]

rhi·zo·ceph·a·lan (rī′zō-sĕf′ə-lən) *n.* Any of various small aquatic crustaceans of the order Rhizocephala that are parasitic on other crustaceans. [From New Latin *Rhizocephala,* order name : RHIZO– + Greek *kephalē,* head; see CEPHALO–.] **—rhi′zo·ceph′a·lous** (-ləs) *adj.*

rhi·zo·gen·ic (rī′zō-jĕn′ĭk) also **rhi·zo·ge·net·ic** (-jə-nĕt′ĭk) *adj. Botany.* Giving rise to or producing roots: *rhizogenic tissue.*

rhi·zoid (rī′zoid′) *n.* **1.** A slender rootlike filament by which mosses, liverworts, and fern gametophytes attach to the substratum and absorb nourishment. **2.** A rootlike extension of the thallus of a fungus. **—rhi′zoid′, rhi·zoi′dal** (-zoid′l) *adj.*

rhi·zome (rī′zōm′) *n.* A horizontal, usually underground stem that often sends out roots and shoots from its nodes. Also called *rootstalk, rootstock.* [Greek *rhizōma,* mass of roots, from *rhizoun,* to cause to take root, from *rhiza,* root. See **wrād-** in Appendix.] **—rhi·zom′a·tous** (-zŏm′ə-təs, -zō′mə-) *adj.* **—rhi·zom′ic** *adj.*

rhi·zoph·a·gous (rī-zŏf′ə-gəs) *adj.* Feeding on roots.

rhi·zo·pod (rī′zō-pŏd′, -zə-) *n.* A protozoan of the phylum Rhizopoda, such as an amoeba or a radiolarian, characteristically moving and taking in food by means of pseudopods. [From New Latin *Rhizopoda,* phylum name : RHIZO– + New Latin *-poda,* -pod.] **—rhi·zop′o·dan** (-zŏp′ə-dən) *adj. & n.* **—rhi·zop′o·dous** *adj.*

rhi·zo·pus (rī′zō-pəs, -zə-) *n.* Any of various rot-causing fungi of the genus *Rhizopus,* such as *R. nigricans,* the common bread mold. [New Latin *Rhizopus,* genus name : RHIZO– + Greek *pous, pod-,* foot; see –POD.]

rhi·zo·sphere (rī′zə-sfîr′) *n.* The soil zone that surrounds and is influenced by the roots of plants.

rhi·zot·o·my (rī-zŏt′ə-mē) *n., pl.* **-mies.** Surgical severance of spinal nerve roots to relieve pain or hypertension.

Rh-neg·a·tive (är′āch-nĕg′ə-tĭv) *adj.* Lacking an Rh factor.

rho (rō) *n.* The 17th letter of the Greek alphabet. See table at **alphabet.** [Greek *rhō,* of Phoenician origin; akin to Hebrew *rēsh.*]

Rho (rō). A city of northern Italy, an industrial suburb of Milan. Population, 50,740.

rhod– *pref.* Variant of **rhodo–.**

rho·da·mine (rō′də-mēn′) *n.* Any of several synthetic red to pink dyes having brilliant fluorescent qualities.

rhododendron

Rhode Island[1] (rōd). An island of Rhode Island at the entrance to Narragansett Bay. Originally known as Aquidneck Island, it was renamed Rhode Island in 1644, probably after the isle of Rhodes.

Rhode Island[2] (rōd). *Abbr.* **RI, R.I.** A state of the northeast United States on the Atlantic Ocean. It was admitted as one of the original Thirteen Colonies in 1790. Rhode Island was settled by religious exiles from Massachusetts, including Roger Williams, who founded Providence in 1636. It was granted a royal charter in 1663 and after the American Revolution began the industrialization that is still a major part of the state's economy. Providence is the capital and the largest city. Population, 947,154. **—Rhode Is′land·er** *n.*

Rhode Island Red *n.* Any of an American breed of domestic fowls having dark reddish-brown feathers.

Rhodes (rōdz). An island of southeast Greece in the Aegean Sea off southwest Turkey. It is the largest of the Dodecanese Islands and was colonized by Dorians from Argos before 1000 B.C. and strongly influenced by the Minoan culture of Crete. The ancient city of **Rhodes,** on the northeast end of the island near the present-day city of **Rhodes,** was founded c. 408 B.C. Its harbor was the site of the Colossus of Rhodes, a bronze statue erected 292–280 B.C. that was one of the Seven Wonders of the World. The modern city has a population of 40,392.

Rhodes, Cecil John. 1853–1902. British financier and colonizer who became prime minister of Cape Colony in 1890 but was forced to resign in 1896 after attempting to overthrow the Boer regime in the Transvaal. He later helped colonize the territory now called Zimbabwe.

Rhodes, James Ford. 1848–1927. American historian known for his seven-volume *History of the United States from the Compromise of 1850* (1893–1906).

Rho·de·sia (rō-dē′zhə). **1.** A region of south-central Africa south of Zaire and comprising modern-day Zambia and Zimbabwe. Probably inhabited since ancient times, it was formerly administered by the British South Africa Company. **2.** See **Zimbabwe[2].** **—Rho·de′sian** *adj. & n.*

Rhodesia and Ny·as·a·land (nī-ăs′ə-lănd′, nyä′sä-). A former colonial federation (1953–1963) of south-central Africa that included the present-day countries of Zimbabwe, Zambia, and Malawi.

Rhodesian man *n.* A fossil human *(Homo rhodesiensis* or *Cyphanthropus rhodesiensis)* found in south-central Africa, having a large low skull with massive brow ridges and skeletal bones like those of modern human beings.

Rhodesian ridgeback *n.* Any of a breed of large dog developed in Africa, having short, yellowish-tan hair that forms a ridge along the back.

Rhodes scholar *n.* A student who holds a scholarship established by the will of Cecil J. Rhodes that permits attendance at Oxford University for a period of two or three years. **—Rhodes scholarship** *n.*

rho·di·um (rō′dē-əm) *n. Symbol* **Rh** A hard, durable, silvery-white metallic element that is used to form high-temperature alloys with platinum and is plated on other metals to produce a durable corrosion-resistant coating. Atomic number 45; atomic weight 102.905; melting point 1,966°C; boiling point 3,727°C; specific gravity 12.41; valence 2, 3, 4, 5, 6. See table at **element.** [Greek *rhodo-,* rhodo- + –IUM.]

rhodo– or **rhod–** *pref.* Rose; rosy; red: *rhodolite.* [Greek, from *rhodon,* rose.]

rho·do·chro·site (rō′də-krō′sīt′) *n.* A mineral consisting mainly of manganese carbonate, $MnCO_3$, light pink to rose-red in color with a pearly or vitreous luster, used as a manganese ore. [From German *Rhodochrosit,* from Greek *rhodokhrōs,* rose-colored : *rhodo-,* rhodo- + *khrōs,* color.]

rho·do·den·dron (rō′də-dĕn′drən) *n.* Any of numerous usually evergreen ornamental shrubs of the genus *Rhododendron* of the North Temperate Zone, having clusters of variously colored, often bell-shaped flowers. [Latin, oleander, from Greek : *rhodo-,* rhodo- + *dendron,* tree; see **deru-** in Appendix.]

rho·do·lite (rōd′l-īt′) *n.* A rose-red or pink variety of garnet, a silicate mineral used as a gem.

rho·do·mon·tade (rŏd′ə-mŏn-tād′, -täd′, rō′də-) *n.* Variant of **rodomontade.**

rho·do·nite (rōd′n-īt′) *n.* A pink to rose-red mineral, essentially a glassy crystalline manganese silicate, $MnSiO_3$, used as an ornamental stone. [From Greek *rhodon,* rose.]

Rhod·o·pe Mountains (rŏd′ə-pē, rŏ-dō′-). A range in the Balkan Peninsula of southeast Europe extending southeast from southwest Bulgaria to northeast Greece and rising to 2,926.8 m (9,596 ft). In Roman times the range marked the boundary between Thrace and Macedonia.

rho·dop·sin (rō-dŏp′sĭn) *n.* The pigment sensitive to red light in the retinal rods of the eyes, consisting of opsin and retinene. Also called *visual purple.* [RHOD(O)– + Greek *opsis,* sight; see –OPSIS + –IN.]

rho·do·ra (rō-dôr′ə, -dōr′ə) *n.* A deciduous shrub *(Rhododendron canadense)* of northeast North America, having rose-purple, two-lipped flowers that bloom before the leaves appear. [Latin *rhodōra,* variant of *rōdarum,* a kind of plant, of Gaulish origin.]

rhomb. *abbr.* Rhombic.

rhomb– *pref.* Variant of **rhombo–.**

rhom·ben·ceph·a·lon (rŏm′bĕn-sĕf′ə-lŏn′, -lən) *n.* The portion of the embryonic brain from which the metencephalon and myelencephalon develop. Also called *hindbrain.* **—rhom′ben·ce·phal′ic** (-sə-făl′ĭk) *adj.*

rhom·bi (rŏm′bī) *n.* A plural of **rhombus.**

rhom·bic (rŏm′bĭk) *adj. Abbr.* **rhomb. 1.** Shaped like a rhombus. **2.** Orthorhombic.

rhombo– or **rhomb–** *pref.* Rhombus: *rhombohedron.* [Greek, from *rhombos.* See RHOMBUS.]

rhom·bo·he·dron (rŏm′bō-hē′drən) *n., pl.* **-drons** or

-dra (-drə). *Abbr.* **rhbdr.** A prism with six faces, each a rhombus. **—rhom′bo·he′dral** (-drəl) *adj.*

rhom·boid (rŏm′boid′) *n.* A parallelogram with unequal adjacent sides. **—rhomboid** also **rhom·boi·dal** (-boid′l) *adj.* Shaped like a rhombus or rhomboid.

rhom·bus (rŏm′bəs) *n., pl.* **-bus·es** or **-bi** (-bī). An equilateral parallelogram. [Late Latin, from Latin, flatfish, magician's circle, from Greek *rhombos,* rhombus. See **wer-²** in Appendix.]

rhon·chus (rŏng′kəs) *n., pl.* **-chi** (-kī). A coarse rattling sound somewhat like snoring, usually caused by secretion in a bronchial tube. [Latin, a snoring, from Greek **rhonkhos,* variant of *rhenkos, rhenkhos,* from *rhenkein,* to snore.] **—rhon′chal** (-kəl), **rhon′chi·al** (-kē-əl) *adj.*

Rhon·dda (rŏn′də, hrŏn′thä). A municipal borough of southern Wales northwest of Cardiff. Coal mining was particularly important to its economy in the 1920's and 1930's. Population, 81,700.

Rhone or **Rhône** (rōn). A river rising in the Alps of south-central Switzerland and flowing about 813 km (505 mi) west-southwest and northwest to Lake Geneva then into eastern France, where it joins the Saône River at Lyons and continues southward to the Mediterranean Sea.

rhp or **r.h.p.** *abbr.* Rated horsepower.

Rh-pos·i·tive (är′āch-pŏz′ĭ-tĭv) *adj.* Containing an Rh factor.

rhu·barb (ro͞o′bärb′) *n.* **1.** Any of several plants of the genus *Rheum,* especially *R. rhubarbarum,* having long, green or reddish acidic leafstalks that are edible when sweetened and cooked. Also called *pie plant.* **2.** The dried, bitter-tasting rhizome and roots of *Rheum palmatum* or *R. officinale* of eastern Asia, used as a laxative. **3.** *Informal.* A quarrel, fight, or heated discussion. [Middle English *rubarbe,* from Old French, from Late Latin *reubarbarum,* probably alteration (influenced by Greek *rhēon*) of *rhabarbarum* : *rha,* rhubarb (from Greek, perhaps from *Rha,* the Volga River) + Latin *barbarum,* neuter of *barbarus,* barbarian, foreign; see BARBAROUS.]

WORD HISTORY: The word *rhubarb* may contain two hidden references to its origins. The first of these is in the *rhu–* part of the word, which can be traced back to the Greek word *rha,* meaning "rhubarb." According to the Late Latin historian Ammianus Marcellinus, rhubarb was named *rha* because it grew near the river named *Rha,* which we know as the Volga. The *–barb* part of *rhubarb* was actually added first to Late Latin *rha,* descended from Greek *rha,* in the form *rhabarbarum, barbarum* being the neuter form of *barbarus,* "foreign." Another Greek word for rhubarb, *rhēon,* influenced the Late Latin word *rhabarbarum,* giving us *reubarbarum,* which yielded Old French *reubarbe.* The Old French form gave us Middle English *rubarbe,* first recorded in a work written around 1390. In imitation of the way the Greek word *rha* is spelled, an *h* was added, completing the long journey of this word into English from the banks of the Volga in classical times.

rhumb (rŭm, rŭmb) *n. Nautical.* **1.** A rhumb line. **2.** One of the points of the mariner's compass. [Possibly from Spanish or Portuguese *rumbo,* course, direction, ultimately from Latin *rhombus,* rhombus. See RHOMBUS.]

rhum·ba (rŭm′bə, ro͝om′-, ro͞om′-) *n.* Variant of **rumba.**

rhumb line *n. Nautical.* The path of a ship that maintains a fixed compass direction, shown on a map as a line crossing all meridians at the same angle. Also called *loxodromic curve.*

rhyme also **rime** (rīm) *—n.* **1.** Correspondence of terminal sounds of words or of lines of verse. **2.a.** A poem or verse having a regular correspondence of sounds, especially at the ends of lines. **b.** Poetry or verse of this kind. **3.** A word that corresponds with another in terminal sound, as *behold* and *cold.* *—v.* **rhymed, rhym·ing, rhymes** also **rimed, rim·ing, rimes.** *—intr.* **1.** To form a rhyme. **2.** To compose rhymes or verse. **3.** To make use of rhymes in composing verse. *—tr.* **1.** To put into rhyme or compose with rhymes. **2.** To use (a word or words) as a rhyme. [Alteration (influenced by RHYTHM) of Middle English *rime,* from Old French, of Germanic origin. See **ar-** in Appendix.]

rhym·er also **rim·er** (rī′mər) *n.* One who composes rhymes. See Synonyms at **poet.**

rhyme royal *n.* **1.** A form of verse having stanzas with seven lines in iambic pentameter rhyming *ababbcc.* **2.** One of these stanzas.

rhyme scheme *n.* The arrangement of rhymes in a poem or stanza.

rhyme·ster also **rime·ster** (rīm′stər) *n.* **1.** One who composes light verse. **2.** A minor or inferior poet. See Synonyms at **poet.**

rhy·ming slang (rī′mĭng) *n.* Slang in which a word is replaced by a word or phrase that rhymes with it, as *kiss* by *hit or miss.*

rhyn·cho·ce·pha·lian (rĭng′kō-sə-fāl′yən) *adj.* Of or belonging to the Rhynchocephalia, an order of mostly extinct lizardlike reptiles. **—rhynchocephalian** *n.* A rhynchocephalian reptile. [From New Latin *Rhynchocephalia,* order name : Greek *rhunkhos,* beak + Greek *kephalē,* head; see CEPHALIC.]

rhy·o·lite (rī′ə-līt′) *n.* A fine-grained extrusive volcanic rock, similar to granite in composition and usually exhibiting flow lines. [Greek *rhuax,* stream (from *rhein,* to flow; see **sreu-** in Appendix) + –LITE.]

Rhys (rēs), **Jean.** 1894–1979. West Indian-born British writer known for *Wide Sargasso Sea* (1966), a novel based on the character of the first Mrs. Rochester in Charlotte Brontë's *Jane Eyre.*

rhythm (rĭth′əm) *n.* **1.** Movement or variation characterized by the regular recurrence or alternation of different quantities or conditions: *the rhythm of the tides.* **2.** The patterned, recurring alternations of contrasting elements of sound or speech. **3.** *Music.* **a.** A regular pattern formed by a series of notes of differing duration and stress. **b.** A specific kind of such a pattern: *a waltz rhythm.* **c.** A group of instruments supplying the rhythm in a band. **4.a.** The pattern or flow of sound created by the arrangement of stressed and unstressed syllables in accentual verse or of long and short syllables in quantitative verse. **b.** The similar but less formal sequence of sounds in prose. **c.** A specific kind of metrical pattern or flow: *iambic rhythm.* **5.a.** The sense of temporal development created in a work of literature or a film by the arrangement of formal elements such as the length of scenes, the nature and amount of dialogue, or the repetition of motifs. **b.** A regular or harmonious pattern created by lines, forms, and colors in painting, sculpture, and other visual arts. **6.** The pattern of development produced in a literary or dramatic work by repetition of elements such as words, phrases, incidents, themes, images, and symbols. **7.** Procedure or routine characterized by regularly recurring elements, activities, or factors: *the rhythm of civilization; the rhythm of the lengthy negotiations.* [Latin *rhythmus,* from Greek *rhuthmos.* See **sreu-** in Appendix.]

SYNONYMS: *rhythm, meter, cadence.* These nouns are compared as they denote the regular patterned ebb and rise of accented and unaccented sounds, especially in music, speech, or verse. *Rhythm,* the most comprehensive, suggests the recurring flow of alternating elements: *the rhythm of the seasons; the rhythms of life.* *"Rhythm was described by Schopenhauer as melody deprived of its pitch"* (Edith Sitwell). *Meter* applies in poetry to any of various measured rhythmic patterns (*elegiac meter*) and in music to the combining of rhythmic pulses into measures of equal time value (*duple meter*). *Cadence* refers especially to the fall of the voice in speech (*end a sentence with a cadence*) and to balanced rhythmic flow, as in poetry (*the cadence of the sea*).

rhythm and blues *pl.n.* (*used with a sing. or pl. verb*). *Abbr.* **r & b, R & B** *Music.* A kind of music developed by Black Americans that combines blues and jazz, characterized by a strong backbeat and repeated variations on syncopated instrumental phrases.

rhyth·mic (rĭth′mĭk) also **rhyth·mi·cal** (-mĭ-kəl) *adj.* Of, relating to, or having rhythm; recurring with measured regularity. **—rhyth′mi·cal·ly** *adv.*

rhyth·mics (rĭth′mĭks) *n.* (*used with a sing. verb*). *Music.* The study of rhythm.

rhyth·mist (rĭth′mĭst) *n.* **1.** One who is an expert in or has a keen sense of rhythm. **2.** *Music.* One who studies or produces rhythm.

rhythm method *n.* A birth-control method dependent on abstinence during the period of ovulation.

rhy·ti·dec·to·my (rĭt′ĭ-dĕk′tə-mē) *n., pl.* **-mies.** See **face-lift** (sense 1). [Greek *rhutis, rhutid-,* wrinkle + –ECTOMY.]

RI or **R.I.** *abbr.* Rhode Island.

RIA *abbr.* Radioimmunoassay.

ri·al¹ (rē-ôl′, -äl′) *n.* See table at **currency.** [Persian, from Arabic *riyāl,* from Spanish *real.* See REAL².]

ri·al² (rē-ôl′, -äl′) *n.* Variant of **riyal.**

ri·al·to (rē-ăl′tō, rā-äl′-) *n., pl.* **-tos.** **1.** A theatrical district. **2.** A marketplace. [After *Rialto,* an island of Venice where a market was situated.]

Ri·al·to (rē-ăl′tō). A city of southern California, a residential suburb of San Bernardino. Population, 37,474.

ri·a·ta also **re·a·ta** (rē-ä′tə) *n.* A lariat; a lasso. [Spanish *reata,* lasso, lariat. See LARIAT.]

Ri·au Archipelago (rē′ou). An island group of western Indonesia off the southeast end of the Malay Peninsula. It is separated from Singapore by Singapore Strait.

rib (rĭb) *n.* **1.** *Anatomy.* **a.** One of a series of long, curved bones occurring in 12 pairs in human beings and extending from the spine to or toward the sternum. **b.** A similar bone in most vertebrates. **2.** A part or piece similar to a rib and serving to shape or support: *the rib of an umbrella.* **3.** A cut of meat enclosing one or more rib bones. **4.** *Nautical.* One of many curved members attached to a boat or ship's keel and extending upward and outward to form the framework of the hull. **5.** One of many transverse pieces that provide an airplane wing with shape and strength. **6.** *Architecture.* **a.** An arch or a projecting arched member of a vault. **b.** One of the curved pieces of an arch. **7.** A raised ridge or wale in knitted material or in cloth. **8.** *Botany.* The main vein or any of the prominent veins of a leaf or other plant organ. **9.** *Slang.* A teasing remark or action; a joke. **—rib** *tr.v.* **ribbed, rib·bing, ribs.** **1.** To shape, support, or provide with a rib or ribs. **2.** To make with ridges or raised markings. **3.** *Informal.* To tease or make fun of. See Synonyms at **banter.** [Middle English, from Old English *ribb.*]

rib·ald (rĭb′əld, rī′bôld′) *adj.* Characterized by or indulging in vulgar, lewd humor. See Synonyms at **coarse.** **—ribald** *n.* A vul-

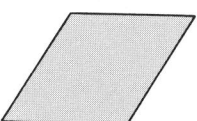

rhombus

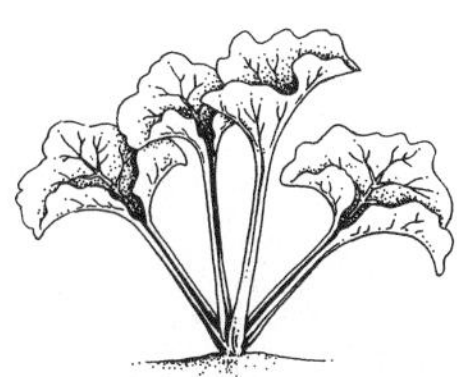

rhubarb
Rheum rhubarbarum

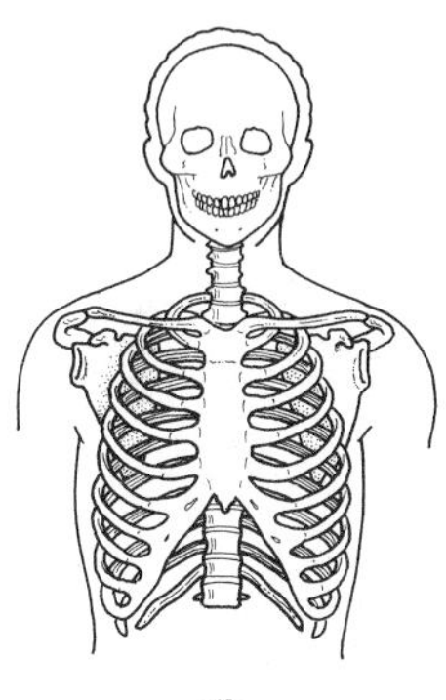

rib

ă pat	oi boy
ā pay	ou out
âr care	o͝o took
ä father	o͞o boot
ĕ pet	ŭ cut
ē be	ûr urge
ĭ pit	th thin
ī pie	*th* this
îr pier	hw which
ŏ pot	zh vision
ō toe	ə about, item
ô paw	♦ regionalism

Stress marks: **′** (primary); ′ (secondary), as in **dictionary** (dĭk′shə-nĕr′ē)

gar, lewdly funny person. [From Middle English *ribaud*, ribald person, from Old French, from *riber*, to be wanton, of Germanic origin. See **wer-**[2] in Appendix.]

rib·ald·ry (rĭb′əl-drē, rī′-) *n., pl.* **-ries.** Vulgar, lewdly humorous language or joking or an instance of it.

rib·and (rĭb′ənd) *n.* A ribbon, especially one used as a decoration. [Middle English, variant of *riban*. See RIBBON.]

ri·ba·vi·rin (rī′bə-vī′rĭn) *n.* A synthetic, antiviral ribonucleoside, $C_8H_{12}N_4O_5$, that inhibits the replication of DNA and RNA. [Probably RIB(ONUCLEIC) A(CID) + VIR(US) + –IN.]

rib·band (rĭb′ănd, -ənd, -ən) *n. Nautical.* A length of flexible wood or metal used to hold the ribs of a ship in place while the exterior planking or plating is being applied. [RIB + BAND[1].]

ribbing
Of a boat under construction

Rib·ben·trop (rĭb′ən-trŏp′, -trô′), **Joachim von.** 1893–1946. German diplomat who as minister of foreign affairs (1938–1945) helped negotiate the German-Soviet Nonaggression Pact of 1939. He was convicted of war crimes at Nuremberg and hanged.

rib·bing (rĭb′ĭng) *n.* **1.** Ribs considered as a group. **2.** An arrangement of ribs, as in a boat. **3.** *Informal.* The act or an instance of joking or teasing.

rib·bon (rĭb′ən) *n.* **1.** A narrow strip or band of fine fabric, such as satin or velvet, finished at the edges and used for trimming, tying, or finishing. **2. a.** Something, such as a tape measure, that resembles a ribbon. **b.** A long, thin strip: *a ribbon of land along the shore.* **3. ribbons.** Tattered or ragged strips: *a dress torn to ribbons.* **4.** An inked strip of cloth used for making an impression, as in a typewriter. **5. a.** A band of colored cloth signifying membership in an order or the award of a prize. **b.** A strip of colored cloth worn on the left breast of a uniform to indicate the award of a medal or decoration. **6. ribbons.** *Informal.* Reins for driving horses. **7.** See **ledger board** (sense 2). **—ribbon** *tr.v.* **-boned, -bon·ing, -bons. 1.** To decorate or tie with ribbons. **2.** To tear into ribbons or shreds. [Middle English *ribban, riban*, from Old French *ruban*, probably of Germanic origin. See **bhendh-** in Appendix.] **—rib′bon·y** *adj.*

rib·bon·fish (rĭb′ən-fĭsh′) *n., pl.* **ribbonfish** or **-fish·es.** Any of several marine fishes, chiefly of the genus *Trachipterus*, having long, narrow, compressed bodies.

ribbon grass *n.* A grass *(Phalaris arundinacea* var. *picta)* of the Northern Hemisphere that has leaf blades striped with white and is cultivated for ornament.

ribbon snake
Thamnophis sauritus

ribbon snake *n.* A nonvenomous North American snake *(Thamnophis sauritus)* having yellow or reddish stripes along the body.

ribbon worm *n.* See **nemertean.**

rib cage *n.* The enclosing structure formed by the ribs and the bones to which they are attached.

Ri·bei·rão Prê·to (rē′bā-rouN′ prĕ′to͞o). A city of southeast Brazil north-northwest of São Paulo. It is a processing center in an agricultural region. Population, 300,828.

Ri·be·ra (rē-bĕr′ə, -bĕ′rä), **José** or **Jusepe de.** 1588–1652. Spanish baroque painter whose works include *Martyrdom of Saint Bartholomew* (1630) and *The Immaculate Conception* (1635).

rib eye *n.* A cut of meat taken from the outside of the rib.

rib·grass (rĭb′grăs′) *n.* A weedy Eurasian plant *(Plantago lanceolata)* having lance-shaped, ribbed leaves and a dense spike of small whitish flowers. Also called *English plantain, ripplegrass.*

rib·let (rĭb′lĭt) *n.* **1.** A cut of meat from a rib end of veal or lamb. **2.** One of a series of microscopic grooves, each a few thousandths of an inch wide, inscribed on the surface of an adhesive-backed tape and used on airplanes and boat hulls to reduce drag.

ri·bo·fla·vin (rī′bō-flā′vĭn, -bə-) *n.* An orange-yellow crystalline compound, $C_{17}H_{20}N_4O_6$, the principal growth-promoting factor in the vitamin B complex, naturally occurring in milk, leafy vegetables, fresh meat, and egg yolks. Also called *lactoflavin, vitamin* B_2. [RIBO(SE) + FLAVIN.]

ri·bo·nu·cle·ase (rī′bō-no͞o′klē-ās′, -āz′,-nyo͞o′-) *n.* Any of various enzymes that break down RNA. Also called *RNase.*

ri·bo·nu·cle·ic acid (rī′bō-no͞o-klē′ĭk, -klā′-, -nyo͞o-) *n.* See **RNA.** [RIBO(SE) + NUCLEIC ACID.]

ri·bo·nu·cle·o·pro·tein (rī′bō-no͞o′klē-ō-prō′tēn, -tē-ĭn, -nyo͞o′-) *n. Abbr.* **RNP** A nucleoprotein that contains RNA. [RIBO(NUCLEIC ACID) + NUCLEOPROTEIN.]

ri·bo·nu·cle·o·side (rī′bō-no͞o′klē-ə-sīd′, -nyo͞o′-) *n.* A nucleoside that contains ribose as its sugar component. [RIBO(SE) + NUCLEOSIDE.]

ri·bo·nu·cle·o·tide (rī′bō-no͞oklē-ə-tīd′, -nyo͞o′-) *n.* A nucleotide that contains ribose as its sugar and in an immediate component of RNA. [RIBO(SE) + NUCLEOTIDE.]

ri·bose (rī′bōs′) *n.* A pentose sugar, $C_5H_{10}O_5$, occurring as a component of riboflavin, nucleotides, and nucleic acids. [German, alteration of English *arabinuse*, a kind of sugar : (GUM) ARAB(IC) + –IN + –OSE[2].]

ribosomal RNA *n. Abbr.* **rRNA** The RNA that is a permanent structural part of a ribosome.

Richard the Lion-Hearted
Statue near the Houses of Parliament, London, England

ri·bo·some (rī′bə-sōm′) *n.* A minute, round particle composed of RNA and protein found in the cytoplasm of living cells and active in the synthesis of proteins. [RIBO(SE) + –SOME[3].] **—ri·bo·so′mal** (-sō′məl) *adj.*

rib roast *n.* A cut of red meat, such as beef or venison, containing the sizable piece located along the outside of the rib.

rib·wort (rĭb′wûrt′, -wôrt′) *n.* See **plantain**[1].

Ri·car·do (rĭ-kär′dō), **David.** 1772–1823. British economist whose major work, *Principles of Political Economy and Taxation* (1817), supported the laws of supply and demand in a free market.

rice (rīs) *n.* **1.** A cereal grass *(Oryza sativa)* that is cultivated extensively in warm climates and is a staple food throughout the world. **2.** The starchy edible seed of this plant. *—attributive.* Often used to modify another noun: *rice paddies; rice pudding.* **—rice** *tr.v.* **riced, ric·ing, ric·es.** To sieve (food) to the consistency of rice. [Middle English, from Old French *ris*, from Old Italian *riso*, from Latin *oryza*, from Greek *oruza*, of Indo-Iranian origin.]

Rice (rīs), **Elmer Leopold.** 1892–1967. American playwright noted for *The Adding Machine* (1923) and *Street Scene* (1929).

♦ **rice·bird** (rīs′bûrd′) *n.* **1.** *Chiefly Southern U.S.* See **bobolink. 2.** Any of various birds that frequent rice fields.

rice paper *n.* A thin paper made chiefly from the pith of the rice-paper plant.

rice-pa·per plant (rīs′pā′pər) *n.* A Chinese shrub or small tree *(Tetrapanax papyriferus)* grown as a source of fiber for rice paper. Also called *rice-paper tree.*

ric·er (rī′sər) *n.* A kitchen utensil used for ricing soft foods by extrusion through small holes.

rice rat *n.* A hardy, agile rat of the genus *Oryzomys*, found in rice fields and marshy areas of Mexico and the southern United States.

rice weevil *n.* A small destructive insect *(Sitophilus oryzae)* that infests stored grain and cereal products.

rich (rĭch) *adj.* **rich·er, rich·est. 1.** Possessing great material wealth: *"Now that he was rich he was not thought ignorant any more, but simply eccentric"* (Mavis Gallant). **2.** Having great worth or value: *a rich harvest of grain.* **3.** Magnificent; sumptuous: *a rich brocade.* **4. a.** Having an abundant supply: *rich in ideas.* **b.** Abounding, especially in natural resources: *rich land.* **5.** Meaningful and significant: *"a rich sense of the transaction between writer and reader"* (William Zinsser). **6.** Very productive and therefore financially profitable: *rich seams of coal.* **7. a.** Containing a large amount of choice ingredients, such as butter, sugar, or eggs, and therefore unusually heavy or sweet: *a rich dessert.* **b.** Having or exuding a strong or pungent aroma: *"Texas air is so rich you can nourish off it like it was food"* (Edna Ferber). **8. a.** Pleasantly full and mellow: *a rich tenor voice.* **b.** Warm and strong in color: *a rich brown velvet.* **9.** Containing a large proportion of fuel to air: *a rich gas mixture.* **10.** *Informal.* Highly amusing. **—rich** *n.* *(used with a pl. verb).* Wealthy people considered as a group. Often used with *the*: *"Were there, indeed, a sure appeal to the mercies of the rich, the calamities of the poor might be less intolerable"* (Charlotte Smith). [Middle English *riche*, from Old French (of Germanic origin) and from Old English *rīce*, strong, powerful; see **reg-** in Appendix.] **—rich′ly** *adv.* **—rich′ness** *n.*

SYNONYMS: *rich, affluent, flush, loaded, moneyed, wealthy.* The central meaning shared by these adjectives is "having an abundant supply of money, property, or possessions of value": *a rich philanthropist; an affluent banker; a speculator flush with cash; not merely rich but loaded; moneyed aristocrats; wealthy corporations.*
ANTONYM: *poor.*

Rich·ard I (rĭch′ərd). Known as "Coeur de Lion" or **"the Lion-Hearted."** 1157–1199. King of England (1189–1199). A leader of the Third Crusade (1190–1192), he was captured in Austria (1192) and held as a prisoner by Holy Roman Emperor Henry VI until England ransomed him in 1194.

Richard II. 1367–1400. King of England (1377–1399). He quelled the Peasants' Revolt in 1381 but spent the rest of his reign at odds with the baronial opposition in Parliament.

Richard III. 1452–1485. King of England (1483–1485) who claimed the throne after imprisoning the sons of his deceased brother Edward IV. Richard's death at the Battle of Bosworth Field brought an end to the Wars of the Roses.

Richard Roe (rō) *n.* A name used in legal proceedings to designate a fictitious or unidentified person.

Rich·ards (rĭch′ərdz), **Dickinson Woodruff.** 1895–1973. American physician. He shared a 1956 Nobel Prize for developing new techniques for treating heart disease.

Richards, I(vor) A(rmstrong). 1893–1979. British literary critic who helped Charles Ogden develop Basic English and was a founder of the New Criticism movement.

Richards, Theodore William. 1868–1928. American chemist. He won a 1914 Nobel Prize for determining the atomic weight of more than 50 elements.

Rich·ard·son (rĭch′ərd-sən). A city of northeast Texas, a residential and agricultural suburb of Dallas. Population, 72,496.

Richardson, Henry Hobson. 1838–1886. American architect whose Romanesque designs include Trinity Church in Boston (1872–1877) and the Marshall Field Warehouse in Chicago (1885–1887).

Richardson, Sir **Ralph David.** 1902–1983. British actor noted for his strong characterizations in classic roles as well as in contemporary works, such as Pinter's *No Man's Land* (1975).

Richardson, Samuel. 1689–1761. English writer whose epistolary novels include *Pamela* (1740), often considered the first modern English novel, and *Clarissa Harlowe* (1747–1748).

Rich•ard•son's ground squirrel (rĭch′ərd-sənz) *n.* A ground squirrel *(Citellus richardsoni)* of the northwest United States and Canada. Also called *flickertail.* [After Sir John *Richardson* (1787–1865), Scottish naturalist.]

Ri•che•lieu (rĭsh′ə-lo͞o′). A river of southern Quebec, Canada, flowing about 121 km (75 mi) north from Lake Champlain to the St. Lawrence River.

Ri•che•lieu (rĭsh′ə-lo͞o′, rē-shə-lyœ′), Duc de. Title of Armand Jean du Plessis. 1585–1642. French prelate and politician. As chief minister of Louis XIII he worked to strengthen the authority of the monarchy and directed France during the Thirty Years' War (1618–1648).

rich•en (rĭch′ən) *tr.v.* **-ened, -en•ing, -ens.** To make rich.

rich•es (rĭch′ĭz) *pl.n.* **1.** Abundant wealth: *"the impassable gulf that lies between riches and poverty"* (Elizabeth Cady Stanton). **2.** Valuable or precious possessions. [Middle English *richesse,* wealth, from Old French, from *riche,* wealthy. See RICH.]

Rich•field (rĭch′fēld′). A city of southeast Minnesota, a residential suburb of Minneapolis. Population, 37,851.

Rich•land (rĭch′lənd). A city of southeast Washington on the Columbia River west-northwest of Walla Walla. It was developed in 1943–1945 to house employees of the nearby Hanford Atomic Works. Federal management of the city was relinquished in 1958. Population, 33,578.

Rich•ler (rĭch′lər), **Mordecai.** Born 1931. Canadian writer whose novels, based on his working-class Jewish background, include *The Apprenticeship of Duddy Kravitz* (1959) and *Saint Urbain's Horseman* (1971).

Rich•mond (rĭch′mənd). **1.** A community of southwest British Columbia, Canada, a suburb of Vancouver on the Strait of Georgia. Population, 96,154. **2.** A city of western California on an inlet of San Francisco Bay north-northwest of Oakland. It is a port and industrial center. Population, 74,676. **3.** A city of eastern Indiana east of Indianapolis. Settled in 1806 by Quakers, it is primarily an industrial center. Population, 41,349. **4.** A city of east-central Kentucky south-southeast of Lexington. It is a tobacco and livestock market in the Bluegrass. Population, 21,705. **5.** The capital of Virginia, in the east-central part of the state on the James River north of Petersburg. Settled in the 17th century, it became the capital of Virginia in 1779 and was strategically important in the American Revolution and the Civil War, during which it was the capital of the Confederacy. The evacuation of Richmond by Confederate troops on April 3, 1865, led to Gen. Robert E. Lee's surrender to Gen. Ulysses S. Grant on April 9. Population, 219,214. **6.** See **Staten Island.**

Richmond High•lands (hī′ləndz). A community of west-central Washington, a residential suburb of Seattle. Population, 20,300.

Richmond Hill. A city of southeast Ontario, Canada, north of Toronto. It is mainly residential. Population, 37,778.

Rich•ter (rĭk′tər), **Burton.** Born 1931. American physicist. He shared a 1976 Nobel for discovering a subatomic particle.

Rich•ter (rĭk′tər, rĭkн′-), **Jean Paul Friedrich.** Pen name Jean Paul. 1763–1825. German writer whose humorous and sentimental novels include *Titan* (1800–1803) and *Years of Indiscretion* (1804–1805).

Rich•ter scale (rĭk′tər) *n.* A logarithmic scale ranging from 1 to 10, used to express the total amount of energy released by an earthquake. In this scale an increase of 1 represents a 32-fold increase in released energy. [After Charles Francis *Richter* (1900–1985), American seismologist.]

rich•weed (rĭch′wēd′) *n.* See **clearweed.**

ri•cin (rī′sĭn, rĭs′ĭn) *n.* A poisonous protein extracted from the castor bean and used as a biochemical reagent. [From Latin *ricinus,* castor-oil plant.]

ric•in•o•le•ic acid (rĭs′ĭn-ō-lē′ĭk) *n.* An unsaturated fatty acid, $C_{18}H_{34}O_3$, prepared from castor oil and used in making soaps and in textile finishing. [Latin *ricinus,* castor-oil plant + OLEIC.]

rick (rĭk) *n.* A stack of hay, straw, or similar material, especially when covered or thatched for protection from the weather. **—rick** *tr.v.* **ricked, rick•ing, ricks.** To pile into ricks. [Middle English *reke,* from Old English *hrēac.*]

Rick•en•back•er (rĭk′ĭn-băk′ər), **Edward Vernon.** Known as "Eddie." 1890–1973. American aviator who was the most decorated combat pilot of World War I and later became president (1938–1963) of Eastern Airlines.

rick•ets (rĭk′ĭts) *n. (used with a sing. or pl. verb).* A deficiency disease resulting from a lack of vitamin D or calcium and from insufficient exposure to sunlight, characterized by defective bone growth and occurring chiefly in children. Also called *rachitis.* [Origin unknown.]

rick•ett•si•a (rĭ-kĕt′sē-ə) *n., pl.* **-si•ae** (-sē-ē′). Any of various bacteria of the genus *Rickettsia,* carried as parasites by many ticks, fleas, and lice, that cause diseases such as typhus, scrub typhus, and Rocky Mountain spotted fever in human beings. [New Latin *Rickettsia,* genus name, after Howard Taylor *Ricketts* (1871–1910), American pathologist.] **—rick•ett′si•al** *adj.*

rick•ett•si•o•sis (rĭ-kĕt′sē-ō′sĭs) *n., pl.* **-ses** (-sēz). Infection with or disease caused by rickettsiae.

rick•et•y (rĭk′ĭ-tē) *adj.* **-i•er, -i•est. 1.** Likely to break or fall apart; shaky. **2.** Feeble with age; infirm. **3.** Of, having, or resembling rickets. [From RICKETS.] **—rick′et•i•ness** *n.*

rick•ey (rĭk′ē) *n., pl.* **-eys.** A drink of soda water, lime or lemon juice, sugar, and usually gin. [Probably from the name *Rickey.*]

Rick•o•ver (rĭk′ō′vər), **Hyman George.** 1900–1986. American admiral who advocated and greatly contributed to the development of nuclear submarines and ships. He was also an outspoken critic of the American educational system.

rick•rack (rĭk′răk′) *n.* A flat, narrow braid woven in zigzag form, used as a trimming for clothing or curtains. [Reduplication of RACK[1].]

rick•sha or **rick•shaw** (rĭk′shô) *n.* A jinriksha. [Short for JINRIKSHA.]

RICO *abbr.* Racketeer Influenced and Corrupt Organizations Act of 1970.

ric•o•chet (rĭk′ə-shā′, rĭk′ə-shā′) *intr.v.* **-cheted** (-shād′), **-chet•ing** (-shā′ĭng), **-chets** (-shāz′). To rebound at least once from a surface. **—ricochet** *n.* The act or an instance of ricocheting. [French, from Old French, give-and-take.]

ri•cot•ta (rĭ-kŏt′ə, rē-kôt′tä) *n.* **1.** A soft Italian cheese that resembles cottage cheese. **2.** A similar soft cheese made in the United States. [Italian, from Latin *recocta,* feminine past participle of *recoquere,* to cook again : *re-,* re- + *coquere,* to cook; see **pekʷ-** in Appendix.]

ric•tus (rĭk′təs) *n., pl.* **rictus** or **-tus•es. 1.** The expanse of an open mouth, a bird's beak, or similar structure. **2.** A gaping grimace: *"his mouth gaping in a kind of rictus of startled alarm"* (Richard Adams). [Latin, from past participle of *ringī,* to gape.] **—ric′tal** *adj.*

rid (rĭd) *tr.v.* **rid** or **rid•ded, rid•ding, rids.** To free from: *He was finally able to rid himself of all financial worries.* [Middle English *ridden,* from Old Norse *rydhja,* to clear land, from *hrjōdha,* to strip, clear.] **—rid′der** *n.*

rid•dance (rĭd′ns) *n.* **1.** A deliverance from or removal of something unwanted or undesirable: *"Compeyson took it easy as a good riddance for both sides"* (Charles Dickens). **2.** The act of ridding: *riddance of household pests.*

rid•den (rĭd′n) *v.* Past participle of **ride. —ridden** *adj.* Dominated, harassed, or obsessed by. Often used in combination: *disease-ridden; grief-ridden.*

rid•dle[1] (rĭd′l) *tr.v.* **-dled, -dling, -dles. 1.** To pierce with numerous holes; perforate: *riddle a target with bullets.* **2.** To spread throughout: *"Election campaigns have always been riddled with demagogy and worse"* (New Republic). **3.** To put (gravel, for example) through a coarse sieve. **—riddle** *n.* A coarse sieve, as for gravel. [Middle English *riddlen,* to sift, from *riddil,* sieve, alteration of Old English *hriddel.* See **krei-** in Appendix.] **—rid′dler** *n.*

rid•dle[2] (rĭd′l) *n.* **1.** A question or statement requiring thought to answer or understand; a conundrum. **2.** One that is perplexing; an enigma. **—riddle** *v.* **-dled, -dling, -dles.** *—tr.* To solve or explain. *—intr.* **1.** To propound or solve riddles. **2.** To speak in riddles. [Middle English *redels,* from Old English *rǣdels.* See **ar-** in Appendix.] **—rid′dler** *n.*

ride (rīd) *v.* **rode** (rōd), **rid•den** (rĭd′n), **rid•ing, rides.** *—intr.* **1.** To be carried or conveyed, as in a vehicle or on horseback. **2.** To travel over a surface: *This car rides well.* **3.** To move by way of an intangible force or impetus; move as if on water: *The President rode into office on a tide of discontent.* **4.** *Nautical.* To lie at anchor: *battleships riding at the mouth of the estuary.* **5.** To seem to float: *The moon was riding among the clouds.* **6.** To be sustained or supported on a pivot, an axle, or another point. **7.** To be contingent; depend: *The final outcome rides on the results of the election.* **8.** To continue without interference: *Let the matter ride.* **9.** To work or move from the proper place, especially on the body: *pants that ride up.* *—tr.* **1.** To sit on and move in a given direction: *rode a motorcycle to town; ride a horse to the village.* **2.** To travel over, along, or through: *ride the highways.* **3.** To be supported or carried on: *a swimmer riding the waves.* **4.** To take part in or do by riding: *He rode his last race.* **5.** To cause to ride, especially to cause to be carried. **6.** *Nautical.* To keep (a vessel) at anchor. **7.** *Informal.* **a.** To tease or ridicule. **b.** To harass with persistent carping and criticism. **8.** To keep partially engaged by slightly depressing a pedal with the foot: *Don't ride the clutch or the brakes.* **—ride** *n.* **1.** The act or an instance of riding, as in a vehicle or on an animal. **2.** A path made for riding on horseback, especially through woodlands. **3.** A device, such as one at an amusement park, that one rides for pleasure or excitement. **4.** A means of transportation: *waiting for her ride to come.* ***—phrasal verb.*** **ride out.** To survive or outlast: *rode out the storm.* ***—idioms.*** **ride for a fall.** To court danger or disaster. **ride herd on.** To keep watch or control over. **ride high.** To experience success. **ride roughshod over.** To take a course of action without regard for the feelings, opinions, or welfare of others. **ride shotgun. 1.** To guard a person or thing while in transit. **2.** *Slang.* To ride in the front passenger seat of a car or truck. **take for a ride.** *Slang.* **1.** To deceive or swindle: *an author who tried to take his publisher for a ride.* **2.** To transport to a place and kill. [Middle English *riden,* from Old English *rīdan.* See **reidh-** in Appendix.]

Ride (rīd), **Sally.** Born 1951. American astronaut who in 1983 became the first U.S. woman to enter outer space.

Ri•deau Canal (rĭ-dō′). A waterway, about 203 km (126 mi)

Richard III
Portrait by an unknown artist

Duc de Richelieu
1636 portrait by Philippe de Champaigne (1602–1674)

Sally Ride
Photographed in 1983

ă pat	oi boy
ā pay	ou out
âr care	o͝o took
ä father	o͞o boot
ĕ pet	ŭ cut
ē be	ûr urge
ĭ pit	th thin
ī pie	*th* this
îr pier	hw which
ŏ pot	zh vision
ō toe	ə about, item
ô paw	♦ regionalism

Stress marks: ′ (primary); ′ (secondary), as in **dictionary** (dĭk′shə-nĕr′ē)

long, of southeast Ontario, Canada, connecting the Ottawa River at Ottawa with Lake Ontario at Kingston. It follows the course of the **Rideau River** for much of its length and was constructed in 1826 to 1832.

rid·er (rī′dər) *n.* **1.** One that rides, especially one who rides horses. **2.a.** A clause, usually having little relevance to the main issue, that is added to a legislative bill. **b.** An amendment or addition to a document or record. **3.** Something, such as the top rail of a fence, that rests on or is supported by something else.

rid·er·ship (rī′dər-shĭp′) *n.* The number of passengers who ride a public transport system.

ride·shar·ing (rīd′shâr′ĭng) *n.* The act or an instance of sharing motor vehicle transportation with another or others, especially among commuters. **—ride′shar′ing** *adj.*

ridge (rĭj) *n.* **1.** A long narrow upper section or crest: *the ridge of a wave.* **2.** A long narrow chain of hills or mountains. Also called *ridgeline.* **3.** A long narrow elevation on the ocean floor. **4.** *Meteorology.* An elongated zone of relatively high atmospheric pressure. Also called *wedge.* **5.** A long, narrow, or crested part of the body: *the ridge of the nose.* **6.** The horizontal line formed by the juncture of two sloping planes, especially the line formed by the surfaces at the top of a roof. **7.** A narrow, raised strip, as in cloth or on plowed ground. **—ridge** *v.* **ridged, ridg·ing, ridg·es.** *—tr.* To mark with, form into, or provide with ridges. *—intr.* To form ridges. [Middle English *rigge,* from Old English *hrycg.* See **sker-**[2] in Appendix.]

ridge·back (rĭj′băk′) *n.* A Rhodesian ridgeback.

Ridge·field (rĭj′fēld′). A town of southwest Connecticut near the New York border north-northeast of Stamford. It is mainly residential. Population, 20,120.

ridge·line (rĭj′līn′) *n.* See **ridge** (sense 2).

ridge·ling also **ridg·ling** (rĭj′lĭng) *n.* A male animal with one or two undescended testicles. [From obsolete *ridgel,* perhaps from RIDGE (from the belief that the undescended testicles remained near the animal's back).]

ridge·pole (rĭj′pōl′) *n.* **1.** A horizontal beam at the ridge of a roof to which the rafters are attached. **2.** The horizontal pole at the top of a tent.

Ridge·wood (rĭj′wŏŏd′). A village of northeast New Jersey north-northeast of Paterson. Both British and American troops had encampments here during the Revolution. Population, 25,208.

ridg·ling (rĭj′lĭng) *n.* Variant of **ridgeling.**

Ridg·way (rĭj′wā′), **Matthew Bunker.** Born 1895. American army officer who commanded airborne divisions in Europe during World War II. He was supreme commander of United Nations forces in Korea (1951–1952) and of NATO forces in Europe (1951–1953) and served as chief of staff of the U.S. Army (1953–1955).

ridg·y (rĭj′ē) *adj.* **-i·er, -i·est.** Having or forming ridges.

rid·i·cule (rĭd′ĭ-kyōōl′) *n.* Words or actions intended to evoke contemptuous laughter at or feelings toward a person or thing: *"I know that ridicule may be a shield, but it is not a weapon"* (Dorothy Parker). **—ridicule** *tr.v.* **-culed, -cul·ing, -cules.** To expose to ridicule; make fun of. [French, from Latin *rīdiculum,* joke, from neuter of *rīdiculus,* laughable. See RIDICULOUS.] **—rid′i·cul′er** *n.*

riding habit

SYNONYMS: *ridicule, mock, taunt, twit, deride, gibe.* These verbs refer to making another the butt of amusement or mirth. *Ridicule* implies purposeful disparagement: *"My father discouraged me by ridiculing my performances"* (Benjamin Franklin). To *mock* is to poke fun at someone, often by mimicking and caricaturing his or her speech or actions: *"Seldom he smiles, and smiles in such a sort/As if he mock'd himself, and scorn'd his spirit"* (Shakespeare). *Taunt* suggests mocking, insulting, or scornful reproach: *"taunting him with want of courage to leap into the great pit"* (Daniel Defoe). To *twit* is to taunt by calling attention to something embarrassing: *"The schoolmaster was twitted about the lady who threw him over"* (J.M. Barrie). *Deride* implies scorn and contempt: *Musical snobs often deride the harmonica as a serious instrument.* To *gibe* is to make taunting, heckling, or jeering remarks: *The child's classmates gibed at him for his timidity.*

ri·dic·u·lous (rĭ-dĭk′yə-ləs) *adj.* Deserving or inspiring ridicule; absurd, preposterous, or silly. See Synonyms at **foolish.** [Latin *rīdiculus,* laughable, from *rīdēre,* to laugh.] **—ri·dic′u·lous·ly** *adv.* **—ri·dic′u·lous·ness** *n.*

rid·ing[1] (rī′dĭng) *n.* **1.** The act of riding. **2.** Horseback riding.

rid·ing[2] (rī′dĭng) *n.* **1.** An administrative division or electoral division in Canada. **2.** Any one of three former administrative divisions of Yorkshire, England. [Middle English, alteration of *trithing,* from Old English **thrithing,* from Old Norse *thridhjungr,* third part, from *thridhi,* third. See **trei-** in Appendix.]

riding habit *n.* The outfit typically worn by a horseback rider.

rid·ley (rĭd′lē) *n., pl.* **-leys. 1.** A marine turtle *(Lepidochelys kempii)* of the Gulf of Mexico and Atlantic coastal waters. **2.** A related species *(Lepidochelys olivaceae)* of the Pacific and Indian oceans. [Origin unknown.]

rifle[1]
With a telescopic site

Rid·ley (rĭd′lē), **Nicholas.** 1500?–1555. English prelate who was executed for refusing to renounce his Protestantism after the accession of the Catholic Mary I.

ri·el (rē-ĕl′) *n.* See table at **currency.** [Origin unknown.]

Ri·el (rē-ĕl′), **Louis.** 1844–1885. Canadian insurrectionist who organized the métis settlers of the Red River valley in a rebellion over their land rights (1869). After leading a similar uprising in Saskatchewan (1884–1885), he was captured and executed by Canadian authorities.

Rie·mann (rē′mən, -män′), **Georg Friedrich Bernhard.** 1826–1866. German mathematician who was a pioneer of non-Euclidean geometry.

Rie·mann·ian geometry (rē-män′ē-ən) *n. Mathematics.* A non-Euclidean system of geometry based on the postulate that within a plane every pair of lines intersects. [After Georg Friedrich Bernhard RIEMANN.]

Ri·en·zi (rē-ĕn′zē) or **Ri·en·zo** (-zō), **Cola di.** 1313?–1354. Italian revolutionary leader who installed himself as dictator of Rome (1347) but was quickly ousted at the bidding of the pope. In his second attempt to rule (1354), he was killed by a mob.

Ries·ling (rēs′lĭng, rēz′-) *n.* A dry to sweet white wine similar to Rhine wine. [German, alteration of obsolete *Rüssling.*]

Ries·man (rēs′mən), **David, Jr.** Born 1909. American sociologist whose best-known work is *The Lonely Crowd* (1950).

Rif (rĭf). See **Er Rif.**

ri·fam·pin (rĭ-făm′pĭn) also **ri·fam·pi·cin** (-pĭ-sĭn) *n.* A semisynthetic antibiotic derived from a form of rifamycin that interferes with the synthesis of RNA and is used to treat bacterial and viral diseases. [Blend of *rifam(yc)in* and P(IPERAZINE).]

rif·a·my·cin (rĭf′ə-mī′sĭn) *n.* Any of a group of antibiotics originally isolated from a strain of the soil microorganism *Streptomyces mediterranei,* used in the treatment of leprosy, tuberculosis, and other bacterial diseases. [Alteration of *rifomycin,* probably from : Italian *riformare,* to reform (*ri-,* again, from Latin *re-;* see RE– + *formare,* to form, from Latin *formāre;* see REFORM) + –MYCIN.]

rife (rīf) *adj.* **rif·er, rif·est. 1.** In widespread existence, practice, or use; increasingly prevalent. **2.** Abundant or numerous. See Synonyms at **prevailing.** [Middle English, from Old English *rȳfe.*]

riff (rĭf) *n.* **1.** *Music.* A short rhythmic phrase, especially one that is repeated in improvisation. **2.** Rapid, clever, often rhythmic speech, as by a disc jockey: *"Those little riffs that had seemed to have such sparkle over drinks by the . . . pool look all too embarrassing in cold print"* (John Richardson). **—riff** *intr.v.* **riffed, riff·ing, riffs.** *Music.* To play riffs. [Origin unknown.]

Riff or **Rif** (rĭf) *n., pl.* **Riff** or **Riffs** also **Rif·fi** (rĭf′ē) or **Rif** or **Rifs. 1.** A member of any of several Berber peoples inhabiting Er Rif. **2.** The Berber language of this people. **—Rif′fi·an** *adj. & n.*

rif·fle (rĭf′əl) *n.* **1.a.** A rocky shoal or sandbar lying just below the surface of a waterway. **b.** A stretch of choppy water caused by such a shoal or sandbar; a rapid. **2.a.** In mining, the sectional stone or wood bottom lining of a sluice, arranged for trapping mineral particles, as of gold. **b.** A groove or block in such a lining. **3.** *Games.* The act or an instance of shuffling cards. **—riffle** *v.* **-fled, -fling, -fles.** *—tr.* **1.** *Games.* To shuffle (playing cards) by holding part of a deck in each hand and raising up the edges before releasing them to fall alternately in one stack. **2.** To thumb through (the pages of a book, for example). *—intr.* **1.** *Games.* To shuffle cards. **2.** To become choppy, as water. [Possibly blend of RIPPLE[1] and RUFFLE[1].]

riff·raff (rĭf′răf′) *n.* **1.** People regarded as disreputable or worthless. **2.** Rubbish; trash. [Middle English *riffe raffe,* from *rif and raf,* one and all, from Anglo-Norman *rif et raf, rifle et rafle* : Old French *rifler,* to rifle; see RIFLE[2] + Old French *raffler,* to carry off (from *raffle,* act of seizing; see RAFFLE[1]).]

ri·fle[1] (rī′fəl) *n.* **1.a.** A firearm with a rifled bore, designed to be fired from the shoulder. **b.** An artillery piece or naval gun with such spiral grooves. **2. rifles.** Troops armed with rifles. **—rifle** *tr.v.* **-fled, -fling, -fles.** To cut spiral grooves within (a gun barrel, for example). [From *rifle,* to cut spiral grooves in, from French *rifler,* from Old French, to plunder, scratch. See RIFLE[2].]

ri·fle[2] (rī′fəl) *v.* **-fled, -fling, -fles.** *—tr.* **1.** To search with intent to steal. **2.** To ransack or plunder; pillage. **3.** To rob: *rifle a safe.* *—intr.* To search vigorously: *rifling through my drawers to find matching socks.* [Middle English *riflen,* to plunder, from Old French *rifler,* probably of Germanic origin.] **—ri′fler** *n.*

ri·fle·bird (rī′fəl-bûrd′) *n.* Any of several birds of paradise of the genera *Craspedophora* and *Ptiloris* of Australia and New Guinea.

ri·fle·man (rī′fəl-mən) *n.* **1.** A soldier equipped with a rifle. **2.** A man who shoots a rifle skillfully.

ri·fle·ry (rī′fəl-rē) *n.* **1.** The skill and practice of shooting a gun. **2.** Rifle fire: *the sound of distant riflery.*

ri·fle·scope (rī′fəl-skōp′) *n.* A telescopic sight for a rifle.

ri·fling (rī′flĭng) *n.* **1.** The process or operation of cutting spiral grooves in a rifle barrel. **2.** Grooves cut in a rifle barrel.

rift[1] (rĭft) *n.* **1.** A narrow fissure in rock. **2.** A break in friendly relations: *a rift between siblings.* **—rift** *v.* **rift·ed, rift·ing, rifts.** *—intr.* To split open; break. *—tr.* To cause to split open or break. [Middle English, of Scandinavian origin.]

rift[2] (rĭft) *n.* **1.** A shallow area in a waterway. **2.** The backwash of a wave that has broken upon a beach. [Probably alteration of dialectal *riff,* reef, from Dutch *rif, riffe.* See REEF[1].]

rift valley *n.* A deep fracture or break, about 25–50 km (15–30 miles) wide, extending along the crest of a mid-ocean ridge.

rift zone *n.* A large area of the earth in which plates of the earth's crust are moving away from each other, forming an extensive system of fractures and faults.

♦**rig** (rĭg) *tr.v.* **rigged, rig·ging, rigs. 1.** To provide with a harness or equipment; fit out. **2.** *Nautical.* **a.** To equip (a ship) with sails, shrouds, and yards. **b.** To fit (sails or shrouds, for example) to masts and yards. **3.** *Informal.* To dress, clothe, or adorn: *They rigged out their daughter in her best dress.* **4.** To make or construct in haste or in a makeshift manner: *rig up a tent for the night.* **5.** To manipulate dishonestly for personal gain: *rig a prizefight; rig stock prices.* **—rig** *n.* **1.** *Nautical.* The arrangement of masts, spars, and sails on a sailing vessel. **2.** Special equipment or gear used for a particular purpose. See Synonyms at **equipment. 3.a.** A truck or tractor. **b.** A tractor-trailer. **c.** A vehicle with one or more horses harnessed to it. **4.** The special apparatus used for drilling oil wells. **5.** *Western U.S.* See **saddle** (sense 1a). **6.** *Informal.* A costume or an outfit: *wore an outlandish rig to the office.* **7.** Fishing tackle. [Middle English *riggen,* probably of Scandinavian origin; akin to Norwegian *rigga,* to bind.]

Ri·ga (rē′gə). The capital and largest city of Latvia, in the central part on the **Gulf of Riga,** an inlet of the Baltic Sea bordering on Latvia and Estonia. Founded as a trading post on a site originally inhabited by Baltic tribes, the city became a member of the Hanseatic League in 1282 and later passed to Poland (1581), Sweden (1621), and Russia (1710). Population, 883,000.

rig·a·doon (rĭg′ə-do͞on′) *n.* **1.** A lively jumping quickstep for one couple. **2.** Music for this dance, usually in rapid duple meter. [French *rigaudon,* possibly from the name *Rigaud.*]

rig·a·ma·role (rĭg′ə-mə-rōl′) *n.* Variant of **rigmarole.**

rig·a·to·ni (rĭg′ə-tō′nē) *n.* Large, ribbed macaroni, slightly curved and cut into short lengths. [Italian, from *rigato,* past participle of *rigare,* to draw a line, from *riga,* line, of Germanic origin.]

Ri·gel (rī′jəl) *n.* A bright double star in the constellation Orion. [Arabic *rijl,* foot.]

rig·ger (rĭg′ər) *n.* **1.** One that rigs: *oil and gas riggers.* **2.** *Nautical.* A ship with a specific kind of rigging.

rig·ging (rĭg′ĭng) *n.* **1.** *Nautical.* The system of ropes, chains, and tackle used to support and control the masts, sails, and yards of a sailing vessel. **2.** The supporting material for construction work.

Riggs' disease (rĭgz) *n.* Inflammation of the tissues surrounding and supporting the teeth. [After John Mankey *Riggs* (1810–1885), American dentist.]

♦**right** (rīt) *adj.* **right·er, right·est.** *Abbr.* **r., R., rt. 1.** Conforming with or conformable to justice, law, or morality: *do the right thing and confess.* **2.** In accordance with fact, reason, or truth; correct: *the right answer.* **3.** Fitting, proper, or appropriate: *It is not right to leave the party without saying goodbye.* **4.** Most favorable, desirable, or convenient: *the right time to act.* **5.** In or into a satisfactory state or condition: *put things right.* **6.** In good mental or physical health or order. **7.** Intended to be worn or positioned facing outward or toward an observer: *the right side of the dress; made sure that the right side of the fabric was visible.* **8.a.** Of, belonging to, located on, or being the side of the body to the south when the subject is facing east. **b.** Of, relating to, directed toward, or located on the right side. **c.** Located on the right side of a person facing downstream: *the right bank of a river.* **9.** Often **Right.** Of or belonging to the political or intellectual Right. **10.** *Mathematics.* **a.** Formed by or in reference to a line or plane that is perpendicular to another line or plane. **b.** Having the axis perpendicular to the base: *right cone.* **11.** Straight; uncurved; direct: *a right line.* **12.** *Archaic.* Not spurious; genuine. **—right** *n.* **1.** That which is just, morally good, legal, proper, or fitting. **2.a.** The direction or position on the right side. **b.** The right side. **c.** The right hand. **d.** A turn in the direction of the right hand or side. **3.** Often **Right. a.** The people and groups who advocate the adoption of conservative or reactionary measures, especially in government and politics. Also called *right wing.* **b.** The opinion of those advocating such measures. **4.** *Sports.* A blow delivered by a boxer's right hand. **5.** *Baseball.* Right field. **6.** Something that is due to a person or governmental body by law, tradition, or nature: *"Certain rights can never be granted to the government, but must be kept in the hands of the people"* (Eleanor Roosevelt). **7.** A just or legal claim or title. **8.a.** A stockholder's privilege of buying additional stock in a corporation at a special price, usually at par or at a price below the current market value. **b.** The negotiable certificate on which this privilege is indicated. **c.** Often **rights.** A privilege of subscribing for a particular stock or bond. **—right** *adv.* **1.** Toward or on the right. **2.** In a straight line; directly: *went right to school.* **3.** In the proper or desired manner; well: *The jacket doesn't fit right.* **4.** Exactly; just: *The accident happened right over there.* **5.** Immediately: *called me right after dinner.* **6.** Completely; quite: *The icy wind blew right through me.* **7.** According to law, morality, or justice. **8.** Accurately; correctly: *answered the question right.* **9.** *Chiefly Southern U.S.* Considerably; very: *They have a right nice place.* **10.** Used as an intensive: *kept right on going.* **11.** Used in titles: *The Right Reverend Jane Smith.* **—right** *v.* **right·ed, right·ing, rights.** *—tr.* **1.** To put in or restore to an upright or proper position: *They righted their boat.* **2.** To put in order or set right; correct: *measures designed to right generations of unfair labor practices.* **3.** To make reparation or amends for; redress: *right a wrong.* *—intr.* To regain an upright or proper position. ***—idioms.*** **by rights.** In a just or proper manner; justly. **in (one's) own right.** Through the force of one's own skills or qualifications. **right and left.** From all directions or on every side: *criticism coming right and left; questions raised from right and left.* **to rights.** In a satisfactory or orderly condition: *set the place to rights.* [Middle English, from Old English *riht.* See **reg-** in Appendix.] **—right′er** *n.*

SYNONYMS: *right, privilege, prerogative, perquisite, birthright.* These nouns apply to something, such as a power or possession, to which one has an established claim. *Right* refers to a legally, morally, or traditionally just claim: *"I'm a champion for the Rights of Woman"* (Maria Edgeworth). *"An unconditional right to say what one pleases about public affairs is what I consider to be the minimum guarantee of the First Amendment"* (Hugo L. Black). *"Our children are not individuals whose rights and tastes are casually respected from infancy, as they are in some primitive societies"* (Ruth Benedict). *Privilege* usually suggests a right not enjoyed by everyone: *"When the laws undertake to . . . grant . . . exclusive privileges, to make the rich richer and the potent more powerful, the humble members of society . . . have a right to complain of the injustice of their government"* (Andrew Jackson). *Prerogative* denotes an exclusive right or privilege, as one based on custom, law, office, or recognition of precedence: *It is my prerogative to change my mind.* A *perquisite* is a privilege or advantage accorded to one by virtue of one's position or the needs of one's employment: *"The wardrobe of her niece was the perquisite of her* [maid]*"* (Tobias Smollett). A *birthright* is a right to which one is entitled by birth: *Many view gainful employment as a birthright.*

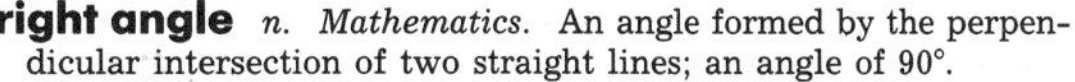

right angle *n.* *Mathematics.* An angle formed by the perpendicular intersection of two straight lines; an angle of 90°.

right-an·gled (rīt′ăng′gəld) *adj.* Forming or containing one or more right angles: *a right-angled bend.*

right ascension *n.* *Abbr.* **R.A.** *Astronomy.* The angular distance of a celestial body or point on the celestial sphere, measured eastward from the vernal equinox along the celestial equator to the hour circle of the body or point and expressed in degrees or hours.

right away *adv.* Without delay; at once.

Right Bank. A district of Paris on the northern, or right, bank of the Seine River. The Arc de Triomphe, the Elysée Palace, the Louvre, fashionable shopping boulevards, and the picturesque area of Montmarte are on the Right Bank.

right brain *n.* The cerebral hemisphere to the right of the corpus callosum, controlling the left side of the body.

right circular cone *n.* *Mathematics.* The surface generated by a generator passing through a vertex that lies on the perpendicular axis of a circular directrix.

right·eous (rī′chəs) *adj.* **1.** Morally upright; without guilt or sin: *a righteous woman.* **2.** In accordance with virtue or morality: *a righteous judgment.* **3.** Morally justifiable: *righteous anger.* See Synonyms at **moral. —righteous** *n.* Righteous people considered as a group. [Middle English *ryghtuous,* alteration of *rihtwise,* from Old English *rihtwīs* : *riht,* right; see RIGHT + *-wīse,* -wise.] **—right′eous·ly** *adv.* **—right′eous·ness** *n.*

right face *n.* A military command to turn 90 degrees to the right.

right field *n.* *Abbr.* **RF** *Baseball.* **a.** The third of the outfield that is to the right, looking from home plate. **b.** The position played by the right fielder.

right fielder *n.* *Abbr.* **RF** *Baseball.* The player who defends right field.

right·ful (rīt′fəl) *adj.* **1.** Right or proper; just. **2.** Having a just or proper claim: *Return this dog to its rightful owner.* **3.** Held or owned by just or proper claim: *This land is my rightful property.* **—right′ful·ly** *adv.* **—right′ful·ness** *n.*

right-hand (rīt′hănd′) *adj.* *Abbr.* **r.h., RH 1.** Of, relating to, or located on the right. **2.** Relating to, designed for, or done with the right hand. **3.** Most helpful or reliable: *my right-hand assistant.*

right-hand·ed (rīt′hăn′dĭd) *adj.* **1.a.** Using the right hand more skillfully or easily than the left. **b.** *Sports.* Swinging from the right to the left: *a right-handed batter.* **2.a.** Done with the right hand. **b.** Intended for wear on or use by the right hand: *a right-handed pair of scissors.* **3.** Turning or spiraling from left to right; clockwise. **—right-handed** *adv.* **1.** With the right hand. **2.** *Sports.* From left to right: *swings right-handed.* **—right′-hand′ed·ly** *adv.* **—right′-hand′ed·ness** *n.*

right-hand·er (rīt′hăn′dər) *n.* One who is right-handed.

right·ish (rī′tĭsh) *adj.* Tending toward the political right.

right·ism also **Right·ism** (rī′tĭz′əm) *n.* **1.** The ideology of the political right. **2.** Belief in or support of the tenets of the political right. **—right′ist** *n.*

right·ly (rīt′lē) *adv.* **1.** In a correct manner; properly: *act rightly.* **2.** With honesty; justly. **3.** *Informal.* Really: *I don't rightly know.*

right-mind·ed (rīt′mīn′dĭd) *adj.* Having ideas and views based on what is right or intended to be right. **—right′-mind′ed·ness** *n.*

right·most (rīt′mōst′) *adj.* Farthest to the right: *in the rightmost lane of the highway.*

right·ness (rīt′nĭs) *n.* The state or quality of being right.

rig
Offshore drilling rig

rigging
Replica of the H.M.S. *Bounty* used in MGM's 1962 version of *Muting on the Bounty*

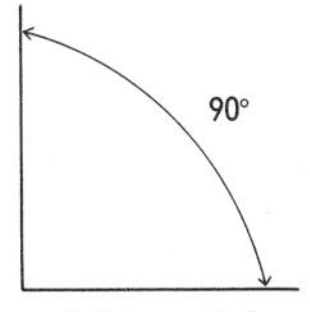

right angle

ă pat	oi boy
ā pay	ou out
âr care	o͝o took
ä father	o͞o boot
ĕ pet	ŭ cut
ē be	ûr urge
ĭ pit	th thin
ī pie	*th* this
îr pier	hw which
ŏ pot	zh vision
ō toe	ə about, item
ô paw	♦ regionalism

Stress marks: **′** (primary); ′ (secondary), as in **dictionary** (dĭk′shə-nĕr′ē)

right of asylum *n., pl.* **rights of asylum.** *Law.* The right of receiving protection within a foreign embassy or other place recognized by custom, law, or treaty.

right off *adv.* Right away; immediately.

right of search *n., pl.* **rights of search.** *Law.* The right of a warring nation to stop a neutral vessel on the high seas and search it for contraband.

right of way also **right-of-way** (rīt′əv-wā′) *n., pl.* **rights of way** or **right of ways** also **rights-of-way** (rīts′-) or **right-of-ways** (-wāz′). **1.** *Law.* **a.** The right to pass over property owned by another party. **b.** The path or thoroughfare on which such passage is made. **2.** The strip of land over which facilities such as highways, railroads, or power lines are built. **3.** The customary or legal right of a person, vessel, or vehicle to pass in front of another.

right on *interj. Slang.* Used as an exclamation of encouragement, support, or enthusiastic agreement.

right-on (rīt′ŏn′, -ôn′) *adj. Slang.* **1.** Up-to-date and sophisticated. **2.** Absolutely right; perfectly true.

♦ **right-out** (rīt′out′) *adj. Chiefly Southern U.S.* Outright. See Regional Note at **everwhere.**

right-side up (rīt′sīd′) *adv. & adj.* **1.a.** With the top facing upward: *Keep this box right-side up.* **b.** In or into the correct orientation: *Turn the slides right-side up in the projector.* **2.** In or into a condition of order: *Get this house right-side up before any guests arrive. The President wants to put the economy right-side up.*

right stuff *n. Informal.* Essential or requisite qualities, such as self-confidence, courage, stability, dependability, organizational skills, and technical knowledge, appropriate for application in a given field or situation: *"Passengers as well as pilots need the right stuff"* (Jonathan Dahl). *"We have the right stuff—a liberal arts, undergraduate, teaching-centered institution of higher education"* (Robert A. Spivey).

right-to-die (rīt′tə-dī′) *adj.* Advocating or expressing, as in a living will, a person's right to refuse extraordinary life-sustaining measures intended to prolong life artificially when the person is deemed by his or her physicians to be terminally or incurably ill.

right-to-know (rīt′tə-nō′) *adj.* Of or relating to policies and laws that make some governmental records and other information available to a person who can demonstrate a right or need to know the contents.

right-to-life (rīt′tə-līf′) *adj.* Pro-life.

right-to-lif·er (rīt′tə-lī′fər) *n.* One whose beliefs or actions are informed by a pro-life philosophy.

right-to-work law (rīt′tə-wûrk′) *n.* A state law that prohibits required union membership of workers.

right triangle *n. Mathematics.* A triangle containing an angle of 90°.

right·ward (rīt′wərd) *adv. & adj.* To or on the right.

right whale *n.* Any of several whales of the family Balaenidae, characterized by a large head, whalebone plates in the mouth, and absence of a dorsal fin.

right wing *n.* **1.** The conservative or reactionary faction of a group. **2.** See **right** (sense 3a). **—right′-wing′** (rīt′wĭng′) *adj.* **—right′-wing′er** *n.*

right·y (rī′tē) *Informal. n., pl.* **-ies. 1.** A right-handed person. **2.** An advocate or a member of the political right. **—righty** *adv.* With the right hand or in a right-handed manner: *throws righty; eats righty.*

rig·id (rĭj′ĭd) *adj.* **1.** Not flexible or pliant; stiff. **2.** Not moving; fixed. **3.** Marked by a lack of flexibility; rigorous and exacting: *"We have watered down a rigid training . . . until we now have an educational diet in many of our public high schools that nourishes neither the classes nor the masses"* (Agnes Meyer). **4.** Scrupulously maintained or performed: *rigid discipline.* See Synonyms at **stiff.** [Middle English *rigide,* from Latin *rigidus,* from *rigēre,* to be stiff. See **reig-** in Appendix.] **—rig′id·ly** *adv.* **—rig′id·ness** *n.*

ri·gid·i·ty (rĭ-jĭd′ĭ-tē) *n., pl.* **-ties. 1.** The quality or state of being rigid. **2.** An instance of being rigid.

rig·ma·role (rĭg′mə-rōl′) also **rig·a·ma·role** (-ə-mə-rōl′) *n.* **1.** Confused, rambling, or incoherent discourse; nonsense. **2.** A complicated, petty set of procedures. [Alteration of obsolete *ragman roll,* catalogue, from Middle English *ragmane rolle,* scroll used in Ragman, a game of chance, perhaps from : Anglo-Norman *Ragemon le bon,* Ragemon the Good, title of a set of verses about a character of this name + Middle English *rolle,* list (from Old French, from Latin *rotula,* wheel; see ROLL).]

ring-billed gull
Larus delawarensis

rig·or (rĭg′ər) *n.* **1.** Strictness or severity, as in temperament, action, or judgment. **2.** A harsh or trying circumstance; hardship. See Synonyms at **difficulty. 3.** A harsh or cruel act. **4.** *Medicine.* Shivering or trembling, as caused by a chill. **5.** *Physiology.* A state of rigidity in living tissues or organs that prevents response to stimuli. **6.** *Obsolete.* Stiffness or rigidity. [Middle English *rigour,* from Old French, from Latin *rigor,* from *rigēre,* to be stiff. See **reig-** in Appendix.]

rig·or·ism (rĭg′ə-rĭz′əm) *n.* Harshness or strictness in conduct, judgment, or practice. **—rig′or·ist** *n.* **—rig′or·is′tic** *adj.*

rigor mor·tis (môr′tĭs) *n.* Muscular stiffening following death. [Latin : *rigor,* stiffness + *mortis,* genitive of *mors,* death.]

rig·or·ous (rĭg′ər-əs) *adj.* **1.** Characterized by or acting with rigor: *a rigorous program to restore physical fitness.* **2.** Full of rigors; harsh: *a rigorous climate.* **3.** Rigidly accurate; precise. See Synonyms at **burdensome. —rig′or·ous·ly** *adv.* **—rig′or·ous·ness** *n.*

rig·our (rĭg′ər) *n. Chiefly British.* Variant of **rigor.**

Rig-Ve·da (rĭg-vā′də, -vē′də) *n.* The most ancient collection of Hindu sacred verses. [Sanskrit *ṛgvedaḥ* : *ṛk,* verse, sacred text + *vedaḥ,* knowledge, veda; see **weid-** in Appendix.]

Riis (rēs), **Jacob August.** 1849–1914. Danish-born American journalist and reformer whose reports on living conditions in city slums led to improvements in housing and education.

Ri·je·ka (rē-yĕk′ə). Formerly **Fi·u·me** (fyo͞o′mā, -mĕ). A city of northwest Yugoslavia on the Adriatic Sea west-southwest of Zagreb. Held at various times by Austria, Croatia, France, and Hungary, it was seized by Italian irregulars in 1919. The Treaty of Rapallo between Italy and Yugoslavia (1920) guaranteed its status as an independent city, although it was formally annexed by Italy four years later. In 1947 the city was officially transferred to Yugoslavia. Population, 160,300.

rijst·taf·fel also **rijs·ta·fel** or **rijs·taf·fel** (rīs′tä′fəl) *n.* A dish originating in Indonesia in which a wide variety of foods and sauces are served with rice. [Dutch : Middle Dutch *rijs* (from Old French *ris;* see RICE) + Dutch *tafel,* table (from Middle Dutch *tafele,* from Vulgar Latin **tavola,* from Latin *tabula,* tablet, board).]

Rijs·wijk (rīs′vīk) also **Rys·wick** (rĭz′wĭk). A city of western Netherlands, a suburb of The Hague. The Treaty of Ryswick (1697) ended the War of the Grand Alliance between England and France and acknowledged William of Orange as William III of England. Population, 49,790.

Riks·mål (rĭks′môl′, rēks′-) *n.* See **Dano-Norwegian.** [Norwegian : *riks,* genitive of *rik,* realm (from Old Norse *rīki;* see **reg-** in Appendix) + *mål,* speech (from Old Norse *māl*).]

rile (rīl) *tr.v.* **riled, ril·ing, riles. 1.** To stir to anger. See Synonyms at **annoy. 2.** To stir up (liquid); roil. [Variant of ROIL.]

ril·ey (rī′lē) *adj.* **1.** Stirred up emotionally; upset. **2.** Roiled; turbid.

Ri·ley (rī′lē), **James Whitcomb.** 1849–1916. American poet whose most famous works, "Little Orphant Annie" (1885) and "The Raggedy Man" (1890), were written in an Indiana dialect.

Ril·ke (rĭl′kə), **Rainer Maria.** 1875–1926. German poet whose verse, often marked by a mystic lyricism and precise imagery, profoundly influenced 20th-century German literature. His collections include *The Book of Hours* (1905) and *The Duino Elegies* (1923).

rill also **rille** (rĭl) *n.* **1.** A small brook; a rivulet. **2.** A long, narrow, straight valley on the moon's surface. [Low German *rille* or Dutch *ril,* running stream; see **rei-** in Appendix.]

rill·et (rĭl′ĭt) *n.* A small rill.

rim (rĭm) *n.* **1.** The border, edge, or margin of an object. See Synonyms at **border. 2.** The circular outer part of a wheel, furthest from the axle. **3.** A circular metal structure around which a wheel tire is fitted. —*tr.* **rimmed, rim·ming, rims. 1.** To furnish with a rim. **2.** *Sports.* To roll around the rim of (a basket or golf cup, for example) without falling in. [Middle English, from Old English *rima.*]

Rim·baud (răm-bō′, răɴ-), **Jean Nicholas Arthur.** 1854–1891. French poet whose hallucinatory work had a strong influence on the surrealists.

rime[1] (rīm) *n.* **1.** A coating of ice, as on grass and trees, formed when extremely cold water droplets freeze almost instantly on a cold surface. **2.** A coating, as of mud or slime, likened to a frosty film: *"A meal couldn't leave us feeling really full unless it laid down a rime of fat globules in our mouths and stomachs"* (James Fallows). **—rime** *tr.v.* **rimed, rim·ing, rimes.** To cover with or as if with frost or ice: *"had identical shoes, heavy and rimed with mud and cement, because they had come from the building site"* (Seamus Deane). [Middle English *rim,* from Old English *hrīm.*] **—rim′y** *adj.*

rime[2] (rīm) *n. & v.* Variant of **rhyme.**

rim·er (rī′mər) *n.* Variant of **rhymer.**

rime riche (rēm rēsh′) *n., pl.* **rimes riches** (rēm rēsh′). Rhyme using words or parts of words that are pronounced identically but have different meanings, for example, *write-right* or *port-deport.* Also called *identical rhyme.* [French : *rime,* rhyme + *riche,* rich.]

rime·ster (rīm′stər) *n.* Variant of **rhymester.**

Ri·mi·ni (rĭm′ə-nē). A city of northern Italy on the Adriatic Sea south-southeast of Ravenna. Founded by Umbrians, it became a strategic Roman military base after the third century B.C. Rimini was ruled as part of the Papal States from 1509 to 1860. Population, 126,949.

Rim·i·ni (rĭm′ĭ-nē, rē′mē-), **Francesca da.** See **Francesca da Rimini.**

ri·mose (rī′mōs′, rī-mōs′) *adj.* Full of chinks, cracks, or crevices. [Latin *rīmōsus,* from *rīma,* fissure.] **—ri′mose·ly** *adv.* **—ri·mos′i·ty** (-mŏs′ĭ-tē) *n.*

Ri·mous·ki (rĭ-mo͞o′skē). A city of southern Quebec, Canada, on the St. Lawrence River northeast of Quebec. It is a port and processing center. Population, 29,120.

rim·ple (rĭm′pəl) *n.* A fold; a wrinkle. **—rimple** *tr. & intr.v.* **-pled, -pling, -ples.** To wrinkle or form wrinkles. [Middle English *rimpil,* from Old English *hrympel.*]

Rim·ski-Kor·sa·kov or **Rim·sky-Kor·sa·kov** (rĭm′skē-kôr′sə-kôf′), **Nikolai Andreyevich.** 1844–1908. Russian composer whose operas and orchestral works were heavily influenced by traditional folk music.

rind (rīnd) *n.* A tough outer covering such as bark, the skin of some fruits, or the coating on cheese or bacon. [Middle English, from Old English.]

rin·der·pest (rĭn′dər-pĕst′) *n.* An acute, often fatal, contagious viral disease, chiefly of cattle, characterized by ulceration of the alimentary tract and resulting in diarrhea. [German : *Rinder,* genitive pl. of *Rind,* head of cattle, ox (from Middle High German *rint,* from Old High German *hrind;* see **ker-**[1] in Appendix) + *Pest,* plague (from Latin *pestis*).]

Rine·hart (rīn′härt′), **Mary Roberts.** 1876–1958. American writer known for her mysteries, including *The Circular Staircase* (1908) and *The Door* (1930).

rin·for·zan·do (rēn′fôr-tsän′dō) *adj. Music.* With a sudden increase of emphasis. Used chiefly as a direction. [Italian, present participle of *rinforzare,* to reinforce, strengthen : *ri-,* again (from Latin *re-;* see RE–) + *inforzare,* to enforce, make strong (from Old French *enforcier;* see ENFORCE).]

ring[1] (rĭng) *n.* **1.** A circular object, form, or arrangement with a vacant circular center. **2.** A small circular band, generally made of precious metal and often set with jewels, worn on the finger. **3.** A circular band used for carrying, holding, or containing something: *a napkin ring.* **4.** A circular movement or course, as in dancing. **5.** An enclosed, usually circular area in which exhibitions, sports, or contests take place: *a circus ring.* **6.** *Sports.* **a.** A rectangular arena set off by stakes and ropes in which boxing or wrestling events are held. **b.** The sport of boxing. **7.** *Games.* **a.** An enclosed area in which bets are placed at a racetrack. **b.** Bookmakers considered as a group. **8.** An exclusive group of people acting privately or illegally to advance their own interests: *a drug ring.* **9.** A political contest; a race. **10.** *Botany.* An annual ring. **11.** *Mathematics.* The area between two concentric circles; annulus. **12.** *Mathematics.* A set of elements subject to the operations of addition and multiplication, in which the set is commutative under addition and associative under multiplication and in which the two operations are related by distributive laws. **13.** Any of the turns constituting a spiral or helix. **14.** *Chemistry.* A group of atoms linked by bonds that may be represented graphically in circular or triangular form. In this sense, also called *closed chain.* **—ring** *v.* **ringed, ring·ing, rings.** *—tr.* **1.** To surround with or as if with a ring; encircle. See Synonyms at **surround. 2.** To form into a ring or rings. **3.** To ornament or supply with a ring or rings: *ringed the door knocker with a wreath of holly.* **4.** To remove a circular strip of bark around the circumference of (a tree trunk or branch); girdle. **5.** To put a ring in the nose of (an animal). **6.** To hem in (animals) by riding in a circle around them. **7.** *Games.* To toss a ring over (a peg), as in horseshoes. *—intr.* **1.** To form a ring or rings: *Spectators ringed the intersection.* **2.** To move, run, or fly in a spiral or circular course. [Middle English, from Old English *hring.* See **sker-**[2] in Appendix.]

ring[2] (rĭng) *v.* **rang** (răng), **rung** (rŭng), **ring·ing, rings.** *—intr.* **1.** To give forth a clear, resonant sound. **2.** To cause something to ring. **3.** To sound a bell in order to summon someone: *I'll ring for the maid.* **4.** To have a sound or character suggestive of a particular quality: *a story that rings true.* **5.** To be filled with sound; resound: *The room rang with the laughter of happy children.* **6.** To hear a persistent humming or buzzing: *My ears were ringing from the sound of the blast.* **7.** To be filled with talk or rumor: *The whole town rang with the bad news.* *—tr.* **1.** To cause (a bell, for example) to ring. **2.** To produce (a sound) by or as if by ringing. **3.** To announce, proclaim, or signal by or as if by ringing: *a clock that rings the hour.* **4.** To call (someone) on the telephone: *She rang me at noon.* **5.** To test (a coin, for example) for quality by the sound it produces when struck against something. **—ring** *n.* **1.** The sound created by a bell or another sonorous, vibrating object. **2.** A loud sound, especially one that is repeated or continued. **3.** A telephone call: *Give me a ring when you have time.* **4.** A suggestion of a particular quality: *His offer has a suspicious ring.* **5.** A set of bells. **6.** The act or an instance of sounding a bell. ***—phrasal verb.* ring up. 1.** To record, especially by means of a cash register: *ring up a sale.* **2.** To accomplish or achieve; win: *rang up several consecutive victories.* ***—idioms.* ring a bell.** *Informal.* To arouse an often indistinct memory. **ring down the curtain.** To end a performance, an event, or an action. **ring (someone's) chimes** (or **bells**). *Slang.* To knock (an opponent) out by physical or other force. **ring up the curtain.** To begin a performance, an event, or an action. [Middle English *ringen,* from Old English *hringan.*]

ring-bill (rĭng′bĭl′) *n.* See **ring-necked duck.**

ring-billed gull (rĭng′bĭld′) *n.* A North American gull *(Larus delawarensis)* having a black ring around its bill.

ring·bolt (rĭng′bōlt′) *n.* A bolt having a ring fitted through its eye.

ring·bone (rĭng′bōn′) *n.* A bony growth on the fetlock, pastern, or coffin bone of a horse's foot, usually causing lameness.

ring buoy *n. Nautical.* A life preserver in the shape of a ring.

ring·dove (rĭng′dŭv′) *n.* **1.** An Old World pigeon *(Streptopelia risoria)* having black markings forming a half circle on the neck. **2.** See **wood pigeon.**

ringed (rĭngd) *adj.* **1.** Wearing or marked with a ring or rings. **2.** Encircled or surrounded by bands or rings. **3.** *Zoology.* Formed from segmented rings; annulate.

ringed plover *n.* A plump species of plover *(Charadrius hiaticula)* that breeds in northern regions of the world.

ringed seal *n.* An Arctic seal *(Phoca hispida)* having white, ring-shaped markings on the sides of the body.

rin·gent (rĭn′jənt) *adj. Biology.* Having gaping liplike parts, as the corolla of some flowers or the shells of certain bivalves. [Latin *ringēns, ringent-,* present participle of *ringī,* to gape.]

ring·er[1] (rĭng′ər) *n. Games.* A horseshoe or quoit thrown so that it encircles the peg.

ring·er[2] (rĭng′ər) *n.* **1.** One that rings, especially one that sounds a bell or chime. **2.** *Slang.* A contestant entered dishonestly into a competition. **3.** *Slang.* One who bears a striking resemblance to another: *a ringer for his father.*

Ring·er's solution (rĭng′ərz) also **Ring·er solution** (-ər) *n.* An aqueous solution of the chlorides of sodium, potassium, and calcium that is isotonic to animal tissue and is used topically as a physiological saline and, in experiments, to bathe animal tissues. [After Sydney *Ringer* (1835–1910), British physician.]

ring finger *n.* The third finger of the left hand.

ring·git (rĭng′gĭt) *n.* See table at **currency.** [Malay.]

ring·hals (rĭng′hăls′) *n., pl.* **-hals·es.** An African snake *(Hemachatus haemachatus)* that spits venom at the eyes of an attacker, sometimes causing blindness. Also called *spitting cobra.* [Obsolete Afrikaans : *ring,* ring (from Middle Dutch *rinc;* see **sker-**[2] in Appendix) + *hals,* neck (from Middle Dutch; see **k**ʷ**el-**[1] in Appendix).]

ring knocker *n. Slang.* A commissioned, nonreservist officer, especially in the U.S. Army, who is a graduate of the United States Military Academy at West Point.

ring·lead·er (rĭng′lē′dər) *n.* A person who leads others, especially in illicit or informal activities.

ring·let (rĭng′lĭt) *n.* **1.** A long, spirally curled lock of hair. **2.** A small circle or ring. **—ring′let·ed** *adj.*

Ring·ling (rĭng′lĭng), **Charles.** 1863–1926. American circus owner. With his brothers he formed (1882) a song-and-dance troop that evolved into the Ringling Brothers and Barnum & Bailey Circus (1907).

Charles Ringling

ring·mas·ter (rĭng′măs′tər) *n.* A person, especially a man, in charge of the performances in a circus ring.

Ring Nebula (rĭng) *n.* A planetary nebula in the constellation Lyra.

ring-necked duck (rĭng′nĕkt′) *n.* A North American duck *(Aythya collaris)* having a distinctive light ring behind the tip of the bill and, in the male, a light chestnut ring around the neck. Also called *ring-bill.*

ring-necked pheasant *n.* A widely distributed bird *(Phasianus colchicus)* native to the Old World, the male of which has a long pointed tail, brightly colored plumage, and a white ring around the neck.

ring-necked pheasant
Phasianus colchicus

ring·neck snake (rĭng′nĕk′) also **ring-necked snake** (-nĕkt′) *n.* Any of several small nonvenomous snakes of the genus *Diadophis,* having a bright reddish or yellowish underside and a yellow or orange ring around the neck, widespread in the United States and Central America.

Ring of Fire *n.* An extensive zone of volcanic and seismic activity that coincides roughly with the borders of the Pacific Ocean.

ring·side (rĭng′sīd′) *n.* **1.** *Sports.* The area or seats immediately outside an arena or a ring, as at a prizefight. **2.** A place providing a close view of a spectacle. *—attributive.* Often used as an attributive: *ringside tickets; a ringside seat.*

ring·tail (rĭng′tāl′) *n.* A ring-tailed animal, such as the cacomistle and the raccoon.

ring-tailed (rĭng′tāld′) *adj.* **1.** Having a tail with ringlike markings. **2.** Having a tail that curls to form a ring.

ring·worm (rĭng′wûrm′) *n.* Any of a number of contagious skin diseases caused by several related fungi, characterized by ring-shaped, scaly, itching patches on the skin.

rink (rĭngk) *n. Sports.* **1.** An area surfaced with smooth ice for skating, hockey, or curling. **2.** A smooth floor suited for roller-skating. **3.** A building that houses a surface prepared for skating. **4.** A section of a bowling green large enough for holding a match. **5.** A team of players in quoits, bowling, or curling. [Middle English *renk,* racecourse, from Old French *renc,* line, of Germanic origin. See **sker-**[2] in Appendix.]

rink

rin·ky-dink (rĭng′kē-dĭngk′) *Slang. adj.* **1.** Old-fashioned; worn-out. **2.** Insignificant; unimportant. **3.** Of cheap or poor quality; makeshift. **—rinky-dink** *n.* One that is regarded as old-fashioned, worn-out, insignificant, or cheap in quality. [Origin unknown.]

rinse (rĭns) *tr.v.* **rinsed, rins·ing, rins·es. 1.** To wash lightly with water. **2.** To remove (soap, for example) by washing lightly in water. **—rinse** *n.* **1.** The act of washing lightly. **2.** A solution, such as water, used in rinsing. **3.** A solution used in coloring or conditioning the hair. [Middle English *rincen,* from Old French *rincier,* from Vulgar Latin **recentiāre,* from Latin *recēns, recent-,* fresh. See RECENT.] **—rins′a·ble, rins′i·ble** *adj.* **—rins′er** *n.*

Rí·o or **Ri·o** (rē′ō). For names of South American rivers, see the specific element; for example, **Plata, Río de la,** or **Roosevelt, Rio.**

Ri·o·bam·ba (rē′ō-bäm′bə, -väm′bä). A city of central Ec-

ă pat	oi boy
ā pay	ou out
âr care	ŏŏ took
ä father	ōō boot
ĕ pet	ŭ cut
ē be	ûr urge
ĭ pit	th thin
ī pie	*th* this
îr pier	hw which
ŏ pot	zh vision
ō toe	ə about, item
ô paw	♦ regionalism

Stress marks: ′ (primary); ′ (secondary), as in **dictionary** (dĭk′shə-nĕr′ē)

uador in the Andes south of Quito. Ecuador's independence was proclaimed here in 1830. Population, 75,455.

Rí•o Bra•vo (rē′ō brä′vō). See **Rio Grande[1].**

Ri•o de Ja•nei•ro (rē′ō dā zhə-nâr′ō, dē-, rē′o͞o dĭ zhĭ-nā′-ro͞o). Familiarly known as "Rio." A city of southeast Brazil on Guanabara Bay, an arm of the Atlantic Ocean. According to tradition, it was first visited in January 1502 by Portuguese explorers who believed Guanabara Bay to be the mouth of a river and therefore named the city Rio de Janeiro ("River of January"). It became capital of the colony of Brazil in 1763, of the Brazilian empire in 1822, and of the independent country in 1889. In 1960 the capital was transferred to Brasília. Population, 5,090,700.

Rí•o de O•ro (rē′ō dē ôr′ō, *thē*). The southern part of Western Sahara in northwest Africa.

Ri•o Grande[1] (rē′ō grănd′, grăn′dē). Or in Mexico **Rí•o Bra•vo** (rē′ō brä′vō). A river, about 3,033 km (1,885 mi) long, rising in southwest Colorado and flowing generally south through central New Mexico to southwest Texas, where it turns southeast and forms the U.S.-Mexican border for the rest of its course. It empties into the Gulf of Mexico near Brownsville, Texas, and Matamoros, Mexico.

Ri•o Gran•de[2] (rē′ō grăn′də, rē′o͞o grăɴ′dĭ). A city of extreme southeast Brazil at the southern entrance of the Lagoa dos Patos. Founded in 1737, it is a major processing and shipping center. Population, 130,149.

Rí•o Mu•ni (rē′ō mo͞o′nē). The mainland part of Equatorial Guinea, on the Bight of Biafra in western Africa.

ri•ot (rī′ət) *n.* **1.** A wild or turbulent disturbance created by a large number of people. **2.** *Law.* A violent disturbance of the public peace by three or more persons assembled for a common purpose. **3.** An unrestrained outbreak, as of laughter or passions. **4.** A profusion: *The garden was a riot of colors in August.* **5.a.** Unrestrained merrymaking; revelry. **b.** Debauchery. **6.** *Slang.* An irresistibly funny person or thing: *Isn't she a riot?* **—riot** *v.* **-ot•ed, -ot•ing, -ots.** *—intr.* **1.** To take part in a riot. **2.** To live wildly or engage in uncontrolled revelry. **3.** To exhibit profusion: *a huge garden in which different flowers rioted during spring and summer.* *—tr.* To waste (money or time) in wild or wanton living: *"rioted his life out, and made an end"* (Tennyson). [Middle English, from Old French, dispute, from *rioter,* to quarrel, perhaps from *ruire,* to roar, from Latin *rūgīre.*] **—ri′ot•er** *n.*

Ri•ot Act (rī′ət) *n.* An English law, enacted in 1715, providing that if 12 or more people unlawfully assemble and disturb the public peace, they must disperse upon proclamation or be considered guilty of felony. ***—idiom.* read the riot act.** To warn or reprimand energetically or forcefully: *The teacher read the riot act to the rowdy class.*

ripple[2]

WORD HISTORY: The riot act has been read to far more people than it once covered, thanks to a figurative development in meaning of the original sense of the term. The official Riot Act was enacted by Parliament in 1715 to discourage unlawful assembly and disturbances of the peace. The act provided that if 12 or more people gathered unlawfully or for purposes of disturbing the peace, a portion of the Riot Act would be read to them, and if the assembled did not disperse by one hour after this reading, they would then be guilty of felony. The Riot Act, which was not repealed until 1973, became a part of the public consciousness literally (the term is first recorded in 1731) and then figuratively in the phrase *to read the riot act,* meaning "to warn forcefully." The first use of *riot act* in this way is found in a work published in 1819: "She has just run out to read the riot act in the Nursery."

ri•ot•ous (rī′ət-əs) *adj.* **1.** Of, relating to, or resembling a riot. **2.** Participating in or inciting to riot or uproar. **3.** Uproarious; boisterous: *a riotous party.* **4.** Dissolute; wanton: *riotous living.* **5.** Abundant or luxuriant: *a riotous growth.* See Synonyms at **profuse. —ri′ot•ous•ly** *adv.* **—ri′ot•ous•ness** *n.*

rip[1] (rĭp) *v.* **ripped, rip•ping, rips.** *—tr.* **1.** To cut, tear apart, or tear away roughly or energetically. See Synonyms at **tear[1]. 2.** To split or saw (wood) along the grain. **3.** *Informal.* To produce, display, or utter suddenly: *ripped out a vicious oath.* *—intr.* **1.** To become torn or split apart. **2.** *Informal.* To move quickly or violently. **—rip** *n.* **1.** The act of ripping. **2.** A torn or split place, especially along a seam. **3.** A ripsaw. ***—phrasal verbs.* rip into.** To attack or criticize vehemently: *ripped into her opponent's political record.* **rip off.** *Slang.* **1.** To steal from: *"I've ripped him off as much as I could possibly rip him off"* (Gary Fisketjon). **2.** To steal: *She ripped off a leather jacket while ostensibly trying on clothes.* **3.** To exploit, swindle, cheat, or defraud: *a false advertising campaign that ripped off a great many consumers.* [Middle English *rippen,* from Flemish *rippen.* See **reup-** in Appendix.] **—rip′per** *n.*

rip[2] (rĭp) *n.* **1.** A stretch of water in a river, an estuary, or a tidal channel made rough by waves meeting an opposing current. **2.** A rip current. [Probably from RIP[1].]

rip[3] (rĭp) *n.* **1.** A dissolute person. **2.** An old or worthless horse. [Possibly shortening and alteration of REPROBATE.]

R.I.P. *abbr. Latin.* Requiescat in pace (may he, or she, rest in peace).

ri•par•i•an (rĭ-pâr′ē-ən) *adj.* Of, on, or relating to the banks of a natural course of water. [From Latin *rīpārius,* from *rīpa,* bank.]

riparian right *n. Law.* The right, as to fishing or to the use of a riverbed, of one who owns riparian land.

rip•cord (rĭp′kôrd′) *n.* **1.** A cord pulled to release the pack of a parachute. **2.** A cord pulled to release gas from a balloon.

rip current *n.* A strong, narrow surface current that flows rapidly away from the shore, returning the water carried landward by waves. Also called *rip tide, tiderip.*

ripe (rīp) *adj.* **rip•er, rip•est. 1.** Fully developed; mature: *ripe peaches.* **2.** Resembling matured fruit, as in fullness. **3.** Sufficiently advanced in preparation or aging to be used or eaten: *ripe cheese.* **4.** Thoroughly matured, as by study or experience; seasoned: *ripe judgment.* **5.** Advanced in years: *the ripe age of 90.* **6.** Fully prepared to do or undergo something; ready: *"By 1965 the republic was ripe for a coup"* (Alex Shoumatoff). **7.** Sufficiently advanced; opportune: *The time is ripe for great societal changes.* **8.** Exhibiting overtones of or references to sex; scatological: *"The language on the stage was riper than anything I have heard in a lifetime of newspaper work"* (John Hughes). **9.** Emitting a foul odor, especially body odor. [Middle English, from Old English *rīpe.*] **—ripe′ly** *adv.* **—ripe′ness** *n.*

rip•en (rī′pən) *tr. & intr.v.* **-ened, -en•ing, -ens.** To make or become ripe or riper; mature. See Synonyms at **mature. —rip′-en•er** *n.*

Rip•ley (rĭp′lē), **George.** 1802–1880. American minister, scholar, and literary critic. An important figure in the New England Transcendentalist movement, he directed the utopian community at Brook Farm, near Boston (1841–1847), and was the literary critic of the *New York Tribune* (1849–1880).

rip-off (rĭp′ôf′, -ŏf′) *n. Slang.* **1.** A theft. **2.** A thief. **3.** An act of exploitation. **4.** Something, such as a film or story, that is clearly imitative of or based on something else.

ri•poste (rĭ-pōst′) *n.* **1.** *Sports.* A quick thrust given after parrying an opponent's lunge in fencing. **2.** A retaliatory action, maneuver, or retort. **—riposte** *intr.v.* **-post•ed, -post•ing, -postes. 1.** To make a return thrust. **2.** To retort quickly. [French, alteration of obsolete *risposte,* from Italian *risposta,* answer, from feminine past participle of *rispondere,* to answer, from Latin *respondēre.* See RESPOND.]

rip•ping (rĭp′ĭng) *adj. Informal.* Excellent; marvelous: *had a ripping time at the party.* [Probably from RIP[1].]

rip•ple[1] (rĭp′əl) *v.* **-pled, -pling, -ples.** *—intr.* **1.a.** To form or display little undulations or waves on the surface, as disturbed water does. **b.** To flow with such undulations or waves on the surface. **2.** To rise and fall gently in tone or volume. *—tr.* To cause to form small waves or undulations. **—ripple** *n.* **1.** A small wave. **2.** A wavelike motion; an undulation: *the ripple of a flag.* **3.** A sound like that made by rippling water: *a ripple of laughter.* [Middle English *ripplen,* to wrinkle, crease, perhaps of Scandinavian origin.] **—rip′pler** *n.* **—rip′pling•ly** *adv.*

rip•ple[2] (rĭp′əl) *n.* A comblike, toothed instrument for removing seeds from flax and other fibers. **—ripple** *tr.v.* **-pled, -pling, -ples.** To remove seeds from with a comblike, toothed instrument. [Middle English, from **ripelen,* to remove seeds; akin to Middle Low German *repelen.*]

ripple effect *n.* A gradually spreading effect or influence: *"Those deviations tend to have a ripple effect throughout the economy as a whole"* (Tom Clancy).

rip•ple•grass (rĭp′əl-grăs′) *n.* See **ribgrass.**

rip•plet (rĭp′lĭt) *n.* A little wave or ripple.

rip•ply (rĭp′lē) *adj.* **-pli•er, -pli•est.** Characterized by or sounding in ripples.

rip•rap (rĭp′răp′) *n.* **1.** A loose assemblage of broken stones erected in water or on soft ground as a foundation. **2.** The broken stones used for such a foundation. **—riprap** *tr.v.* **-rapped, -rap•ping, -raps. 1.** To construct a riprap in or on. **2.** To strengthen with a riprap. [Reduplication of RAP[1].]

rip-roar•ing (rĭp′rôr′ĭng, -rōr′-) also **rip-roar•i•ous** (rĭp′-rôr′ē-əs, -rōr′-) *adj. Informal.* Noisy, lively, and exciting. [From RIP[1] + (UP)ROAR(IOUS).] **—rip′-roar′•ing•ly** *adv.*

rip•saw (rĭp′sô′) *n.* A coarse-toothed saw used for cutting wood along the grain.

rip•snort•er (rĭp′snôr′tər) *n. Slang.* One that is remarkable for strength, intensity, or excellence. **—rip′snort′ing** *adj.*

rip tide *n.* See **rip current.**

Rip•u•ar•i•an (rĭp′yo͞o-âr′ē-ən) *adj.* Of, relating to, or being a group of Franks who settled along the Rhine, near Cologne, in the fourth century A.D. **—Ripuarian** *n.* A Ripuarian Frank. [From Medieval Latin *Ripuārius.*]

rise (rīz) *v.* **rose** (rōz), **ris•en** (rĭz′ən), **ris•ing, ris•es.** *—intr.* **1.** To assume a standing position after lying, sitting, or kneeling. **2.** To get out of bed: *rose at dawn.* **3.** To move from a lower to a higher position; ascend: *Hot air rises.* **4.** To increase in size, volume, or level: *The river is rising.* **5.** To increase in number, amount, or value: *Prices rose.* **6.** To increase in intensity, force, or speed: *The wind has risen.* **7.** To increase in pitch or volume: *The sound of their voices rose and fell.* **8.** To appear above the horizon: *The sun rises later in the fall.* **9.** To extend upward; be prominent: *The tower rose above the hill.* **10.** To slant or slope upward: *Mount McKinley rises to 6,197.6 meters (20,320 feet).* **11.** To come into existence; originate. **12.** To be erected: *New buildings are rising in the city.* **13.** To appear at the surface of the water or the earth; emerge. **14.** To puff up or become larger; swell up: *The bread dough should rise to double its original size.*

15. To become stiff and erect. **16.** To attain a higher status: *an officer who rose through the ranks.* **17.** To become apparent to the mind or senses: *Old fears rose to haunt me.* **18.** To uplift oneself to meet a demand or challenge: *She rose to the occasion and won the election.* **19.** To return to life. **20.** To rebel: *"the right to rise up, and shake off the existing government"* (Abraham Lincoln). **21.** To close a session of an official assembly; adjourn. —*tr.* **1.** To cause to rise. **2.** To cause (a distant object at sea) to become visible above the horizon by advancing closer. **—rise** *n.* **1.** The act of rising; ascent. **2.** The degree of elevation or ascent. **3.** The appearance of the sun or other celestial body above the horizon. **4.** An increase in height, as of the level of water. **5.** A gently sloped hill. **6.** A long, broad elevation that slopes gently from the earth's surface or the ocean floor. **7.** An origin, a beginning, or a source: *the rise of a river.* **8.** Occasion or opportunity: *facts that give rise to doubts about her motives.* **9.** The emergence of a fish seeking food or bait at the water's surface. **10.** An increase in price, worth, quantity, or degree. **11.** An increase in intensity, volume, or pitch. **12.** Elevation in status, prosperity, or importance: *the family's rise in New York society.* **13.** The height of a flight of stairs or of a single riser. **14.** *Chiefly British.* An increase in salary or wages; a raise. **15.** *Informal.* An angry or irritated reaction: *finally got a rise out of her.* [Middle English *risen,* from Old English *rīsan.*]

SYNONYMS: *rise, ascend, climb, soar, tower, mount, surge.* These verbs are compared as they mean to move upward from a lower to a higher position. *Rise* has the widest range of application: *We rose at dawn. The sun rises early in the summer. Fog was rising from the pond. Prices rise and fall. Ascend* frequently suggests a gradual step-by-step rise: *The plane took off and ascended steadily until it was out of sight. "Ascend above the restrictions and conventions of the world, but not so high as to lose sight of them"* (Richard Garnett). *Climb* connotes steady, often effortful progress, as against gravity: *"still climbing after knowledge infinite"* (Christopher Marlowe). *"You climb up through the little grades and then get to the top"* (John Updike). *Soar* implies effortless ascent to a great height: *A lone condor soared above the Andean peaks. "Well is it known that ambition can creep as well as soar"* (Edmund Burke). To *tower* is to attain a height or prominence exceeding that of anything in the surroundings: *"the tall Lombardy poplar . . . towering high above all other trees"* (W.H. Hudson). *Bach's gifts towered over those of his contemporaries. Mount* in this comparison connotes progressive climb to a higher level: *Water mounted in the ship's hold. The blood mounted to her cheeks. Our expenses mou..ted fearfully. Surge* implies a tumultuous swelling or heaving force like that of waves: *The crowd of pedestrians surged ahead when the light turned green. I could feel indignation surging up in me.* See also Synonyms at **beginning, stem[1].**

ris·er (rī′zər) *n.* **1.** One who rises, especially from sleep: *She is a late riser.* **2.** The vertical part of a stair step.

ris·i·bil·i·ty (rĭz′ə-bĭl′ĭ-tē) *n., pl.* **-ties. 1.** The ability or tendency to laugh. **2.** Often **risibilities.** A sense of the ludicrous or amusing. **3.** Laughter; hilarity.

ris·i·ble (rĭz′ə-bəl) *adj.* **1.** Relating to laughter or used in eliciting laughter. **2.** Eliciting laughter; ludicrous. **3.** Capable of laughing or inclined to laugh. [Late Latin *rīsibilis,* from Latin *rīsus,* past participle of *rīdēre,* to laugh.] **—ris′i·bly** *adv.*

ris·ing (rī′zĭng) *adj.* **1.** Ascending, sloping upward, or advancing: *a rising tide.* **2.** Coming to maturity; emerging: *the rising generation.* **—rising** *n.* **1.** The action of one that rises. **2.** An uprising; an insurrection. **3.** A prominence or projection. **4.** The leaven or yeast used to make dough rise in baking.

rising action *n.* The events of a dramatic or narrative plot preceding the climax.

rising rhythm *n.* A rhythmic pattern in which the stress falls on the last syllable of each foot, as in *"They danced by the light of the moon"* (Edward Lear). Also called *ascending rhythm.*

risk (rĭsk) *n.* **1.** The possibility of suffering harm or loss; danger. **2.** A factor, thing, element, or course involving uncertain danger; a hazard: *"the usual risks of the desert: rattlesnakes, the heat, and lack of water"* (Frank Clancy). **3. a.** The danger or probability of loss to an insurer. **b.** The amount that an insurance company stands to lose. **4. a.** The variability of returns from an investment. **b.** The chance of nonpayment of a debt. **5.** One considered with respect to the possibility of loss: *a poor risk.* —*attributive.* Often used to modify another noun: *risk factors; risk management.* **—risk** *tr.v.* **risked, risk·ing, risks. 1.** To expose to a chance of loss or damage; hazard. **2.** To incur the risk of: *His action risked a sharp reprisal.* See Synonyms at **endanger.** —***idiom.* at risk** or **at-risk.** Being endangered, as from exposure to disease or from a lack of parental or familial guidance and proper health care: *at risk youth in the inner cities; at-risk groups of children not having received the vaccine.* [French *risque,* from Italian *risco, rischio.*] **—risk′er** *n.*

risk arbitrage *n.* The simultaneous purchase and sale of assets that are potentially but not necessarily equivalent. **—risk arbitrageur** *n.*

risk capital *n.* See **venture capital.**

risk factor *n.* A factor that increases one's chances of contracting a particular disease: *"The report emphasizes that interaction of many risk factors is responsible for coronary heart disease in an individual"* (Science News).

risk·y (rĭs′kē) *adj.* **-i·er, -i·est.** Accompanied by or involving risk or danger; hazardous: *"Anything that promises to pay too much can't help being risky"* (Dorothy Canfield Fisher). **—risk′i·ness** *n.*

Ri·sor·gi·men·to (rĭ-sôr′jə-mĕn′tō, rē-zôr′jē-) *n.* The period of or the movement for the liberation and political unification of Italy, beginning about 1750 and lasting until 1870. [Italian, from *risorgere,* to rise again, from Latin *resurgere.* See RESURGE.]

ri·sot·to (rĭ-sô′tō, -sŏt′ō, rē-zôt′tô) *n., pl.* **-tos.** A dish of rice cooked in broth, usually with saffron, and served with grated cheese. [Italian, from *riso,* from Old Italian. See RICE.]

ris·qué (rĭs-kā′) *adj.* Suggestive of or bordering on indelicacy or impropriety. [French, from past participle of *risquer,* to risk, from *risque,* risk. See RISK.]

ris·sole (rĭ-sōl′, rĭs′ōl, rē-sôl′) *n.* A small, pastry-enclosed croquette of a minced meat or fish, usually fried in deep fat. [French, from Old French, from Vulgar Latin **russeola,* reddish paste, from Late Latin, feminine of *russeolus,* reddish, from Latin *russus,* red. See **reudh-** in Appendix.]

ris·so·lé (rē-sô-lā′) *adj.* Browned by frying. [French, from past participle of *rissoler,* to brown, from *rissole,* rissole. See RISSOLE.]

rit. *abbr. Music.* Ritardando.

Rit·a·lin (rĭt′l-ĭn). A trademark used for methylphenidate.

ri·tar·dan·do (rē′tär-dän′dō) *adv. & adj. Abbr.* **rit.** *Music.* Gradually slowing in tempo; retarding. Used chiefly as a direction. [Italian, present participle of *ritardare,* to slow down, from Latin *retardāre.* See RETARD.]

rite (rīt) *n.* **1.** The prescribed or customary form for conducting a religious or other solemn ceremony: *the rite of baptism.* **2.** A ceremonial act or series of acts: *fertility rites.* **3. Rite.** The liturgy or practice of a branch of the Christian church. [Middle English, from Latin *rītus.* See **ar-** in Appendix.]

rite of passage *n., pl.* **rites of passage.** A ritual or ceremony signifying an event in a person's life indicative of a transition from one stage to another, as from adolescence to adulthood.

ri·tor·nel·lo (rĕ′tôr-nĕl′lō) *n., pl.* **-li** (-lē) or **-los.** *Music.* **1.** An instrumental interlude recurring after each stanza in a vocal work. **2.** A passage for full orchestra in a baroque concerto grosso. **3.** An instrumental interlude in early 17th-century opera. **4.** The refrain of a rondo. [Italian, diminutive of *ritorno,* return, from *ritornare,* to return, from Vulgar Latin **retornāre.* See RETURN.]

Rit·ten·house (rĭt′n-hous′), **David.** 1732–1796. American astronomer, mathematician, and public official who is reputed to have built the first American-made telescope and was the first director of the U.S. Mint (1792–1795).

rit·ter (rĭt′ər) *n., pl.* **ritter.** A knight. [German, from Middle High German *riter,* from Middle Dutch *ridder,* from *rīden,* to ride. See **reidh-** in Appendix.]

Rit·ter (rĭt′ər), **Woodward Maurice.** Known as "Tex." 1907–1974. American singer and actor who played a singing cowboy in radio shows and motion-picture Westerns.

rit·u·al (rĭch′o͞o-əl) *n.* **1. a.** The prescribed order of a religious ceremony. **b.** The body of ceremonies or rites used in a place of worship. **2. a.** The prescribed form of conducting a formal secular ceremony: *the ritual of an inauguration.* **b.** The body of ceremonies used by a fraternal organization. **3.** A book of rites or ceremonial forms. **4. rituals. a.** A ceremonial act or a series of such acts. **b.** The performance of such acts. **5. a.** A detailed method of procedure faithfully or regularly followed: *My household chores have become a morning ritual.* **b.** A state or condition characterized by the presence of established procedure or routine: *"Prison was a ritual—reenacted daily, year in, year out. Prisoners came and went; generations came and went; and yet the ritual endured"* (William H. Hallahan). [From Latin *rītuālis,* of rites, from *rītus,* rite. See RITE.] **—rit′u·al·ly** *adv.*

rit·u·al·ism (rĭch′o͞o-ə-lĭz′əm) *n.* **1.** The practice or observance of religious ritual. **2.** Insistence on or adherence to ritual.

rit·u·al·ist (rĭch′o͞o-ə-lĭst) *n.* **1.** An authority on or a student of ritual. **2.** One who practices or advocates the observance of ritual.

rit·u·al·is·tic (rĭch′o͞o-ə-lĭs′tĭk) *adj.* **1.** Relating to ritual or ritualism. **2.** Advocating or practicing ritual. **—rit′u·al·is′ti·cal·ly** *adv.*

rit·u·al·ize (rĭch′o͞o-ə-līz′) *v.* **-ized, -iz·ing, -iz·es.** —*tr.* **1.** To make a ritual of. **2.** To force a ritual on. —*intr.* To engage in ritualism. **—rit′u·al·i·za′tion** (-ə-lĭ-zā′shən) *n.*

ritual murder *n.* **1.** The murder of a person as a human sacrifice to a deity. **2.** A murder committed in such a way as to resemble a sacrifice to a deity.

ritz (rĭts) *n. Informal.* Elegant, often ostentatious display. —***idiom.* put on the ritz.** *Informal.* To behave or live in an elegant, ostentatious manner. [Back-formation from RITZY.]

ritz·y (rĭt′sē) *adj.* **-i·er, -i·est.** *Informal.* Elegant; fancy. [After the *Ritz* hotels, established by César Ritz (1850–1918), Swiss hotelier.]

riv. *abbr.* River.

riv·age (rĭv′ĭj) *n. Archaic.* A coast, shore, or bank. [Middle English, from Old French, from *rive,* bank, from Latin *rīpa.*]

ri·val (rī′vəl) *n.* **1.** One who attempts to equal or surpass another, or who pursues the same object as another; a competitor. **2.** One that equals or almost equals another in a particular re-

ă pat	oi boy
ā pay	ou out
âr care	o͝o took
ä father	o͞o boot
ĕ pet	ŭ cut
ē be	ûr urge
ĭ pit	th thin
ī pie	*th* this
îr pier	hw which
ŏ pot	zh vision
ō toe	ə about, item
ô paw	♦ regionalism

Stress marks: ′ (primary); ′ (secondary), as in **dictionary** (dĭk′shə-nĕr′ē)

spect. **3.** *Obsolete.* A companion or an associate in a particular duty. —*attributive.* Often used to modify another noun: *rival companies; rival products; rival teams; rival schools.* —**rival** *v.* **-valed, -val·ing, -vals** or **-valled, -val·ling, -vals.** —*tr.* **1.** To attempt to equal or surpass. **2.** To be the equal of; match: *"They achieved more than they had ever dreamed, lending a magic to their family story that no tale or ordinary life could possibly rival"* (Doris Kearns Goodwin). —*intr.* To be a competitor or rival; compete. [Latin *rīvālis,* a rival, one using the same stream as another, from *rīvus,* stream. See **rei-** in Appendix.]

SYNONYMS: *rival, compete, vie, emulate.* These verbs mean to seek to equal or surpass another. *Rival* is the most general: *"His ambition led him to rival the career of Edmund Burke"* (Henry Adams). To *compete* is to contend with another or others to attain a goal, as gaining an advantage, victory in a contest, or a prize: *Local hardware stores can't compete with discount outlets. "She must learn to compete . . . not as a woman, but as a human being"* (Betty Friedan). *Vie,* often interchangeable with *compete,* sometimes stresses the challenge implicit in rivalry: *"No mortal could vie with Zeus"* (Homer). *Emulate* connotes imitation in an effort to match or outdo another: *"The whole world emulates Athens and Rome"* (David Hume).

ri·val·rous (rīʹvəl-rəs) *adj.* Characterized by or given to rivalry or competition.

ri·val·ry (rīʹvəl-rē) *n., pl.* **-ries. 1.** The act of competing or emulating. **2.** The state or condition of being a rival.

rive (rīv) *v.* **rived, riv·en** (rĭvʹən) also **rived, riv·ing, rives.** —*tr.* **1.** To rend or tear apart. **2.** To break into pieces, as by a blow; cleave or split asunder. **3.** To break or distress (the spirit, for example). —*intr.* To be or become split. [Middle English *riven,* from Old Norse *rīfa.*]

riv·er (rĭvʹər) *n. Abbr.* **r., R., riv. 1.** A large natural stream of water emptying into an ocean, a lake, or another body of water and usually fed along its course by converging tributaries. **2.** A stream or an abundant flow: *a river of tears.* —*attributive.* Often used to modify another noun: *a river cruise; river ice.* —***idiom.* up the river.** *Slang.* In or into prison. [Middle English *rivere,* from Anglo-Norman, from Vulgar Latin **rīpāria,* from Latin, feminine of *rīpārius,* of a bank, from *rīpa,* bank.]

Ri·ve·ra (rĭ-vĕrʹə, rē-vĕʹrä), **Diego.** 1886–1957. Mexican painter noted for his murals that exalt workers in a style derived from Mexican folk art.

Rivera y Or·ba·ne·ja (ē ôr'bä-nĕʹhä), **Miguel Primo de.** See Miguel **Primo de Rivera y Orbaneja.**

riv·er·bank (rĭvʹər-băngkʹ) *n.* The bank of a river. —*attributive.* Often used to modify another noun: *riverbank weeds; a riverbank cottage.*

river basin *n.* The land area drained by a river and its tributaries.

riv·er·bed (rĭvʹər-bĕdʹ) *n.* The area between the banks of a river ordinarily covered by water.

river birch *n.* A deciduous eastern North American tree *(Betula nigra)* having reddish-brown to silver-gray bark that peels off in papery flakes. Also called *black birch.*

river blindness *n.* See **onchocerciasis.**

riv·er·boat (rĭvʹər-bōtʹ) *n. Nautical.* A boat suitable for use on a river.

riv·er·front (rĭvʹər-frŭntʹ) *n.* The land or property along a river. —*attributive.* Often used to modify another noun: *riverfront property; riverfront houses.*

riv·er·head (rĭvʹər-hĕdʹ) *n.* The source of a river.

river horse *n.* See **hippopotamus** (sense 1). [Translation of Greek *hippopotamos.* See HIPPOPOTAMUS.]

riv·er·ine (rĭvʹə-rīnʹ, -rēnʹ) *adj.* **1.** Relating to or resembling a river. **2.** Located on or inhabiting the banks of a river; riparian: *"Members of a riverine tribe . . . were wading in the swamp, whose water they had impounded in a series of dams"* (Alex Shoumatoff). **3.** Operating on or equipped to operate on rivers: *riverine units of the Marine Corps.* —**riverine** *n.* An inland or coastal area constituting both land and water, characterized by limited landlines for communications, and extensive coastal waters and inland waterways providing natural routes for transport.

Riv·er Ridge (rĭvʹər). A community of southeast Louisiana, a suburb of New Orleans. Population, 17,146.

Riv·ers (rĭvʹərz), **Larry.** Born 1923. American artist whose complex paintings combine the bold brushwork of abstract expressionism with realistic images.

riv·er·side (rĭvʹər-sīdʹ) *n.* The bank or area alongside a river. —*attributive.* Often used to modify another noun: *riverside plant life; riverside cottages.*

Riv·er·side (rĭvʹər-sīdʹ). A city of southern California northeast of Santa Ana. The navel orange was introduced here in 1873, and the city still has an important citrus industry. Population, 170,876.

Riv·er·ton Heights (rĭvʹər-tən). A community of west-central Washington, a suburb of Seattle. Population, 33,500.

riv·er·ward (rĭvʹər-wərd) also **riv·er·wards** (-wərdz) *adv.* Toward a river.

riv·er·weed (rĭvʹər-wēdʹ) *n.* An eastern North American plant *(Podostemum ceratophyllum)* having olive-green foliage resembling seaweed and growing on rocks in rapidly flowing streams.

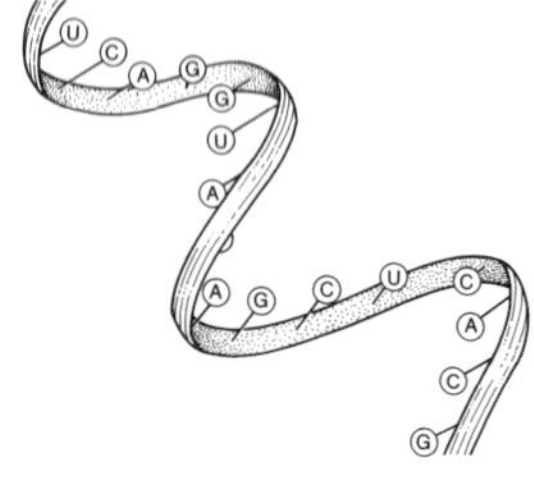

RNA

roadblock

riv·et (rĭvʹĭt) *n.* A metal bolt or pin having a head on one end, inserted through aligned holes in the pieces to be joined and then hammered on the plain end so as to form a second head. —**rivet** *tr.v.* **-et·ed, -et·ing, -ets. 1.** To fasten or secure with or as if with a rivet. **2.** To hammer the headless end of so as to form a head and fasten something. **3.** To fasten or secure firmly; fix. **4.** To engross or hold (the attention, for example). [Middle English, from Old French *river,* to attach.] —**rivʹet·er** *n.*

riv·et·ing (rĭvʹĭ-tĭng) *adj.* Wholly absorbing or engrossing one's attention; fascinating: *The last chapter was so riveting that I was reading past midnight.* —**rivʹet·ing·ly** *adv.*

Riv·i·er·a (rĭvʹē-ĕrʹə, rē-vyĕʹrä). A narrow coastal region between the Alps and the Mediterranean Sea extending from southeast France to northwest Italy. The Riviera, also known as the Côte d'Azur in France, is a popular resort area that is noted for its flowers grown for export and for use in perfumery.

Riviera Beach. A city of southeast Florida on the Atlantic Ocean north of West Palm Beach. It is a resort with varied industries. Population, 26,596.

ri·vière (rē-vyârʹ) *n.* A necklace of precious stones, generally set in one strand. [French *rivière (de diamants),* river (of diamonds), from Old French *rivere,* from Vulgar Latin **rīpāria.* See RIVER.]

riv·u·let (rĭvʹyə-lĭt) *n.* A small brook or stream; a streamlet. [Possibly from Italian *rivoletto,* diminutive of *rivolo,* small stream, from Latin *rīvulus,* diminutive of *rīvus,* stream. See **rei-** in Appendix.]

Ri·yadh (rē-yädʹ). The capital and largest city of Saudi Arabia, in the east-central part of the country east-northeast of Mecca. Situated in a desert oasis, it was formerly a walled city until the oil boom of the 1950's led to the demolition of older structures to make way for commercial expansion. Population, 1,250,000.

ri·yal also **ri·al** (rē-ôlʹ, -älʹ) *n.* See table at **currency.** [Arabic *riyāl,* from Spanish *real,* real. See REAL 2.]

ri·yal-o·man·i (rē-ôlʹō-mäʹnē, rē-älʹ-) *n., pl.* **ri·yals-o·man·i** (rē-ôlzʹ-, rē-älzʹ-). See table at **currency.** [Arabic *riyāl ʿumānī* : *riyāl,* riyal + *ʿumānī,* of Oman.]

Ri·zal (rĭ-zälʹ, rē-sälʹ), **José.** 1861–1896. Philippine national leader and writer. Having been exiled (1892–1896) for his political novels, he was arrested on his return, charged with sedition, and executed, an act that precipitated an insurrection against Spanish rule (1896–1898).

Riz·zio (rĭtʹsē-ōʹ, rĕtʹtsē-ôʹ), **David.** 1533?–1566. Italian musician and secretary to Mary Queen of Scots. His closeness to the queen prompted the jealous Lord Darnley and other Scottish noblemen to murder him.

RJ *abbr.* Road junction.

Rm *abbr. Bible.* Romans.

RM also **Rm.** *abbr.* Reichsmark.

rm. *abbr.* **1.** Ream. **2.** Room.

rms *abbr. Mathematics.* Root mean square.

RMS *abbr.* **1.** Railway Mail Service. **2.** Also **R.M.S.** Royal Mail Service. **3.** Also **R.M.S.** Royal Mail Steamship.

Rn The symbol for the element **radon.**

RN or **R.N.** *abbr.* **1.** Registered nurse. **2.** Royal Navy.

RNA (ärʹĕn-āʹ) *n.* A polymeric constituent of all living cells and many viruses, consisting of a long, usually single-stranded chain of alternating phosphate and ribose units with the bases adenine, guanine, cytosine, and uracil bonded to the ribose. The structure and base sequence of RNA are determinants of protein synthesis and the transmission of genetic information. Also called *ribonucleic acid.* [R(IBO)N(UCLEIC) A(CID).]

RNA·ase (ärʹĕn-āʹās', -āzʹ) *n.* Variant of **RNase.**

RNA polymerase *n.* A polymerase that catalyzes the synthesis of RNA from a DNA or RNA template.

RN·ase (ärʹĕn-ās', -āzʹ) also **RNA·ase** (ärʹĕn-āʹās', -āzʹ) *n.* See **ribonuclease.**

RNA virus *n.* An RNA-containing virus; retrovirus.

rnd. *abbr.* Round.

RNP *abbr.* Ribonucleoprotein.

ro. *abbr.* Rood.

roach¹ (rōch) *n., pl.* **roach** or **roach·es. 1.** A freshwater fish *(Rutilus rutilus)* of northern Europe. **2.** Any of various similar or related fishes, such as some North American sunfishes. [Middle English *roche,* from Old French *roce, roche.*]

roach² (rōch) *n., pl.* **roach·es. 1.** The cockroach. **2.** *Slang.* The butt of a marijuana cigarette.

roach³ (rōch) *n., pl.* **roach·es. 1.** A roll of hair brushed up from the forehead or temple. **2.** A hairstyle especially among certain Native American peoples in which the head is shaved except for a strip from front to back across the top. **3.** *Nautical.* An outward curve in the leech of a fore-and-aft sail. —*tr.* **roached, roach·ing, roach·es. 1.** To brush (hair) in a roach. **2.** To shave (the mane of a horse) to a short bristle. [Origin unknown.]

roach clip *n.* A device used to hold the butt of a marijuana cigarette.

road (rōd) *n. Abbr.* **rd., Rd., r., R. 1.a.** An open, generally public way for the passage of vehicles, people, and animals. **b.** The surface of a road; a roadbed. **2.** A course or path. **3.** A railroad. **4.** Often **roads.** *Nautical.* A roadstead. —***idiom.* on**

the road. **1.** On tour, as a theatrical company. **2.** Traveling, especially as a salesperson. **3.** Wandering, as a vagabond. [Middle English *rode, rade,* a riding, road, from Old English *rād.* See **reidh-** in Appendix.]

road agent *n.* A stagecoach robber; a bandit.

road•bed (rōd′bĕd′) *n.* **1.a.** The foundation upon which the ties, rails, and ballast of a railroad are laid. **b.** A layer of ballast directly under the ties. **2.** The foundation and surface of a road.

road•block (rōd′blŏk′) *n.* **1.** A barricade or an obstruction across a road set up to prevent the escape or passage, as of a fugitive or enemy troops. **2.** An obstruction in a road, as fallen rocks or trees. **3.** Something, such as a situation or condition, that prevents further progress toward an accomplishment.

road hog *n. Informal.* A motorist whose vehicle overlaps the traffic lane used by another motorist.

road•house (rōd′hous′) *n.* An inn, a restaurant, or a nightclub located on a road outside a town or city.

road•ie also **road•y** (rō′dē) *n.* A person engaged to load, unload, and set up equipment and to perform errands for rock musicians on tour.

road•less (rōd′lĭs) *adj.* **1.** Not containing or crossed by any roads: *roadless wilderness.* **2.** Forbidden by law to contain or be crossed by any roads or to be entered by any vehicles: *tracts of land designated by the government as roadless areas.*

road map or **road•map** (rōd′măp′) *n.* **1.** A map, especially one for motorists, showing and designating the roads of a region. **2.** A set of guidelines, instructions, or explanations: *wrote an ethics code as a road map for the behavior of elected officials.*

road metal *n.* Crushed or broken stone, cinders, or similar material used in the construction and repair of roads and roadbeds.

road•run•ner (rōd′rŭn′ər) *n.* A swift-running, crested bird *(Geococcyx californianus)* of southwest North America, having streaked brownish plumage and a long tail. Also called *chaparral bird, chaparral cock.*

road show *n.* **1.** A show presented by a troupe of theatrical performers on tour. **2.** A new movie shown at selected theaters usually for higher ticket prices. **3.** The repeated speeches and accompanying performances or events engaged in by politicians or members of a political organization on tour.

road•side (rōd′sīd′) *n.* The area bordering on the side of a road. —*attributive.* Often used to modify another noun: *roadside diners; roadside stops.*

road•stead (rōd′stĕd′) *n. Nautical.* A sheltered offshore anchorage area for ships. [Variant of *rodestead* : RODE[2] + *sted,* place (variant of STEAD).]

road•ster (rōd′stər) *n.* **1.** An open automobile having a single seat in the front for two or three people and a rumble seat or luggage compartment in the back. **2.** A horse for riding on a road.

road test *n.* **1.** A test of a motor vehicle's operating capability under actual road conditions. **2.** A test of driving ability on the road required of a candidate for a driver's license. **—road′-test′** (rōd′tĕst′) *v.*

Road Town (rōd). The capital of the British Virgin Islands, on Tortola Island in the West Indies east of Puerto Rico. It is a port of entry. Population, 2,479.

road•way (rōd′wā′) *n.* A road, especially the part over which vehicles travel.

road•work (rōd′wûrk′) *n.* **1.** *Sports.* Outdoor long-distance running as a form of physical exercise or conditioning. **2.** The activity of taking a band, typically a rock band, on extended tours. **3.** Highway construction.

road•wor•thy (rōd′wûr′thē) *adj.* **-thi•er, -thi•est.** Fit to be driven on the open road: *a roadworthy truck.*

roam (rōm) *v.* **roamed, roam•ing, roams.** —*intr.* To move about without purpose or plan; wander. See Synonyms at **wander.** —*tr.* To wander over or through: *roamed the streets.* **—roam** *n.* The act or an instance of roaming. [Middle English *romen.*] **—roam′er** *n.*

roan (rōn) *adj.* Having a chestnut, bay, or sorrel coat thickly sprinkled with white or gray: *a roan horse.* **—roan** *n.* **1.a.** The coloring of a roan horse. **b.** A roan horse or other animal. **2.** A soft, flexible sheepskin leather, often treated to resemble morocco and used in bookbinding. [Obsolete French, from Old French, from Old Spanish *roano,* probably of Germanic origin.]

Ro•a•noke (rō′ə-nōk′). An independent city of southwest Virginia west-southwest of Richmond. It grew with the coming of the railroad in 1882 and is today a tourist and industrial center. Population, 100,427.

Roanoke Island. An island of northeast North Carolina off the Atlantic coast between Albemarle and Pamlico sounds. Colonists dispatched by Sir Walter Raleigh founded the first English settlement in North America in August 1585 but returned to England the following year. A second group of colonists organized by Raleigh landed on the island in July 1587 but vanished without a trace sometime before 1591. The mystery of the Lost Colony has never been solved.

Roanoke River. A river rising in southwest Virginia and flowing about 660 km (410 mi) generally east and southeast to Albemarle Sound in northeast North Carolina.

roar (rôr, rōr) *v.* **roared, roar•ing, roars.** —*intr.* **1.** To utter a loud, deep, prolonged sound, especially in distress, rage, or excitement. **2.** To laugh loudly or excitedly. **3.** To make or produce a loud noise or din: *The engines roared.* **4.** To be disorderly or rowdy. **5.** To breathe with a rasping sound. Used of a horse. —*tr.* **1.** To utter or express with a loud, deep, and prolonged sound. **2.** To put, bring, or force into a specified state by roaring: *The crowd roared itself hoarse.* See Synonyms at **shout.** **—roar** *n.* **1.** A loud, deep, prolonged sound or cry, as of a person in distress or rage. **2.** The loud, deep cry of a wild animal. **3.** A loud, prolonged noise, such as that produced by waves. **4.** A loud burst of laughter. [Middle English *roren,* from Old English *rārian.*] **—roar′er** *n.*

roar•ing (rôr′ĭng, rōr′-) *adj.* **1.** Very lively or successful; thriving: *a roaring trade.* **2.** Used as an intensive: *roaring drunk.* **—roar′ing•ly** *adv.*

roast (rōst) *v.* **roast•ed, roast•ing, roasts.** —*tr.* **1.** To cook with dry heat, as in an oven or near hot coals. **2.** To dry, brown, or parch by exposing to heat. **3.** To expose to great or excessive heat. **4.** *Metallurgy.* To heat (ores) in a furnace in order to dehydrate, purify, or oxidize before smelting. **5.** *Informal.* To ridicule or criticize harshly. —*intr.* **1.** To cook food in an oven. **2.** To undergo roasting. **—roast** *n.* **1.a.** Something roasted. **b.** A cut of meat suitable or prepared for roasting. **2.a.** The act or process of roasting. **b.** The state of being roasted. **3.a.** Harsh ridicule or criticism. **b.** A facetious tribute, usually in the form of a banquet, in which the honoree's friends and acquaintances alternate short speeches of praise and insult. **—roast** *adj.* Roasted: *roast duck.* [Middle English *rosten,* from Old French *rostir,* of Germanic origin.]

roast•er (rō′stər) *n.* **1.** One that roasts. **2.** A special pan or apparatus for roasting. **3.** Something, especially a young chicken, that is fit for roasting.

rob (rŏb) *v.* **robbed, rob•bing, robs.** —*tr.* **1.** *Law.* To take property from (a person or persons) illegally by using or threatening to use violence or force; commit robbery upon. **2.** To take valuable or desired articles unlawfully from: *rob a bank.* **3.a.** To deprive unjustly of something belonging to, desired by, or legally due (someone): *robbed her of her professional standing.* **b.** To deprive of something injuriously: *a parasite that robs a tree of its sap.* **4.** To take as booty; steal. —*intr.* To engage in or commit robbery. **—*idioms.*** **rob (someone or something) blind.** To rob in an unusually deceitful or thorough way: *robbed the old couple blind while employed as a companion.* **rob the cradle.** *Informal.* To have a romantic or sexual relationship with someone significantly younger than oneself. [Middle English *robben,* from Old French *rober,* of Germanic origin. See **reup-** in Appendix.] **—rob′ber** *n.*

ro•ba•lo (rō-bä′lō) *n., pl.* **-los** or **robalo.** Any of various chiefly tropical marine food fishes of the family Centropomidae, such as the snook. [Spanish *róbalo,* haddock, probably alteration of Catalan *llobarro,* from *lobo,* wolf, from Latin *lupus.* See LOBO.]

Robbe-Gril•let (rôb-grē-yā′), **Alain.** Born 1922. French writer and exponent of the New Wave in French literature. His screenplays and novels, such as *The Erasers* (1953), subordinate plot to the treatment of space and time.

robber baron *n.* **1.** One of the American industrial or financial magnates of the latter 19th century who became wealthy by unethical means, such as questionable stock-market operations and exploitation of labor. **2.** A feudal lord who robbed travelers passing through his domain.

robber fly *n.* Any of various predatory flies of the family Asilidae, characteristically having long, bristly legs.

rob•ber•y (rŏb′ə-rē) *n., pl.* **-ies.** *Law.* The act or an instance of unlawfully taking the property of another by the use of violence or intimidation.

Rob•bins (rŏb′ĭnz), **Frederick Chapman.** Born 1916. American microbiologist. He shared a 1954 Nobel Prize for work on the cultivation of the polio virus.

Robbins, Jerome. Born 1918. American dancer and choreographer of ballets and musicals, including *West Side Story* (1957).

robe (rōb) *n.* **1.** A long, loose, flowing outer garment, especially: **a.** An official garment worn on formal occasions to show office or rank, as by a judge or high church official. **b.** An academic gown. **c.** A dressing gown or bathrobe. **2. robes.** Clothes; apparel. **3.** A blanket or covering made of material, such as fur or cloth: *a lap robe.* **—robe** *v.* **robed, rob•ing, robes.** —*tr.* To cover or dress in or as if in a robe. See Synonyms at **clothe.** —*intr.* To put on robes or a robe. [Middle English, from Old French, of Germanic origin. See **reup-** in Appendix.]

Rob•ert I[1] (rŏb′ərt). Known as "Robert the Devil." Died 1035. Duke of Normandy (1027–1035) who named as his heir his illegitimate son William, the future William I of England.

Rob•ert I[2] (rŏb′ərt). Known as "Robert the Bruce." 1274–1329. King of Scotland (1306–1329) who defied Edward I of England by having himself crowned and won Scottish independence from England in a battle at Bannockburn (1314).

Robert, Henry Martyn. 1837–1923. American army engineer and parliamentary authority. He designed the defenses for Washington, D.C., during the Civil War and later wrote *Robert's Rules of Order* (1876).

Ro•bert Guis•card (rô-bĕr′ gē-skär′). 1015?–1085. Norman military leader who conquered much of southern Italy and protected Pope Gregory VII from the invading armies of the Holy Roman Empire (1084).

Rob•erts (rŏb′ərts), Sir **Charles George Douglas.** 1860–1943.

roadrunner
Geococcyx californianus

robe
Mandan buffalo robe with painted sunburst design

ă pat	oi boy
ā pay	ou out
âr care	o͝o took
ä father	o͞o boot
ĕ pet	ŭ cut
ē be	ûr urge
ĭ pit	th thin
ī pie	*th* this
îr pier	hw which
ŏ pot	zh vision
ō toe	ə about, item
ô paw	♦ regionalism

Stress marks: ′ (primary); ′ (secondary), as in **dictionary** (dĭk′shə-nĕr′ē)

Paul Robeson

Robespierre
Detail of a portrait by Louis Léopold Boilly (1761–1845)

robin
Turdus migratorious

Jackie Robinson
Photographed in the early 1950's

Sugar Ray Robinson

Canadian writer whose poetry and other works established a literature based on Canadian themes and sources.

Roberts, Elizabeth Madox. 1886–1941. American writer whose works, including the novel *The Great Meadow* (1930), concern the pioneers and impoverished people of Kentucky and Virginia.

Roberts, Kenneth. 1885–1957. American writer noted for his historical novels about the Colonial period, including *Northwest Passage* (1937).

Roberts, Oral. Born 1918. American evangelist who has preached widely on tours and radio and television broadcasts.

Roberts, Owen Josephus. 1875–1955. American jurist who served as an associate justice of the U.S. Supreme Court (1930–1945).

Rob·ert·son (rŏb′ərt-sən), **William.** 1721–1793. British historian whose works include *History of Scotland 1542–1603* (1759).

Robe·son (rōb′sən), **Paul Bustill.** 1898–1976. American singer and actor who played the lead roles in *Othello* and in Eugene O'Neill's *The Emperor Jones* and sang "Ol' Man River" in *Showboat.* He was an outspoken critic of racism and a supporter of socialism.

Robes·pierre (rōbz′pîr, -pē-âr′, rô-bĕs-pyĕr′), **Maximilien François Marie Isidore de.** 1758–1794. French revolutionary. Leader of the Jacobins and architect of the Reign of Terror, he was known as an austere and incorruptible man. His laws permitting the confiscation of property and arrest of suspected traitors, many of whom were guillotined, led to his own arrest and execution without trial.

rob·in (rŏb′ĭn) *n.* **1.** A North American songbird *(Turdus migratorius)* having a rust-red breast and gray and black upper plumage. Also called *robin redbreast.* **2.** A small Old World bird *(Erithacus rubecula)* having an orange breast and a brown back. Also called *robin redbreast.* **3.** Any of various birds resembling a robin. [Short for *Robin Redbreast,* from Middle English *Robin,* personal name, from Old French, diminutive of Robert.]

Rob·in Good·fel·low (rŏb′ĭn go͝od′fĕl′ō) *n.* Puck.

Robin Hood *n.* A legendary English outlaw of the 12th century, famous for his courage, chivalry, and practice of robbing the rich to aid the poor.

robin redbreast *n.* See **robin** (senses 1, 2).

rob·in's-egg blue (rŏb′ĭnz-ĕg′) *n. Color.* A pale bluish green to greenish or grayish blue.

Rob·in·son (rŏb′ĭn-sən), **Edward G.** 1893–1973. American actor known for his portrayal of gangsters in motion pictures, including *Little Caesar* (1930).

Robinson, Edwin Arlington. 1869–1935. American poet whose works include long narratives and character studies of New Englanders, including "Miniver Cheevy" (1910).

Robinson, (Esmé Stuart) Lennox. 1886–1958. Irish playwright and manager of the Abbey Theater in Dublin (1910–1914 and 1919–1923). His own plays include *The Whiteheaded Boy* (1920).

Robinson, Jack Roosevelt. Known as "Jackie." 1919–1972. American baseball player. The first Black player in the major leagues, he was a second baseman for the Brooklyn Dodgers (1947–1956), had a lifetime batting average of .311, and was inducted into the Baseball Hall of Fame in 1962.

Robinson, James Harvey. 1863–1936. American historian who stressed the importance of social and intellectual events on the course of history. He was a founder of the New School for Social Research in New York City (1919).

Robinson, Ray. Known as "Sugar Ray." 1921–1989. American prizefighter who was world champion six times, once as a welterweight (1946–1951) and five times as a middleweight (1951–1960).

Robinson, Sir **Robert.** 1886–1975. British chemist. He won a 1947 Nobel Prize for his study of molecular structures in plants.

Robinson Cru·soe (kro͞o′sō) *n.* The hero of Daniel Defoe's novel *Robinson Crusoe* of 1719, a shipwrecked English sailor who, by virtue of his own ingenuity, survives for years on a small tropical island.

Rob·in's plantain (rŏb′ĭnz) *n.* An eastern North American plant *(Erigeron pulchellus)* having many-rayed purplish flower heads grouped in a corymb.

ro·ble (rō′blā) *n.* **1.** A Californian oak *(Quercus lobata)* having leathery leaves and slender, pointed acorns. Also called *white oak.* **2.** Any of various similar or related trees. [Spanish and Portuguese, oak, both from Latin *rōbur.* See **reudh-** in Appendix.]

rob·o·rant (rŏb′ər-ənt) *adj.* Restoring vigor or strength. **—roborant** *n.* A roborant drug; a restorative or tonic. [Latin *rōborāns, rōborant-,* present participle of *rōborāre,* to strengthen, from *rōbur, rōbor-,* oak, strength. See **reudh-** in Appendix.]

ro·bot (rō′bət, -bŏt′) *n.* **1.** A mechanical device that sometimes resembles a human being and is capable of performing a variety of often complex human tasks on command or by being programmed in advance. **2.** A machine or device that operates automatically or by remote control. **3.** A person who works mechanically without original thought, especially one who responds automatically to the commands of others. [Czech, from *robota,* drudgery. See **orbh-** in Appendix.] **—ro·bot′ic, ro′bot·is′tic** (-bə-tĭs′tĭk) *adj.*

robot bomb *n.* A small winged missile that is loaded with explosives, jet-propelled, and guided only by a gyroscopic device. Also called *buzz bomb, flying bomb.*

ro·bot·ics (rō-bŏt′ĭks) *n. (used with a sing. verb).* The science or study of the technology associated with the design, fabrication, theory, and application of robots.

ro·bot·ize (rō′bə-tīz′) *tr.v.* **-ized, -iz·ing, -iz·es. 1.** To convert (a system, for example) to automation by the application of advanced scientific technology. **2.** To make (a person) machinelike, as in giving responses or performing work. **—ro′bot·i·za′tion** (-bə-tĭ-zā′shən) *n.*

robot pilot *n.* See **automatic pilot.**

rob roy (rŏb roi′) *n.* A cocktail made with Scotch whisky, sweet vermouth, and bitters. [After Rob Roy.]

Rob Roy (rŏb roi′). Originally Robert MacGregor. 1671–1734. Scottish clan leader and outlaw whose banditry is the subject of Sir Walter Scott's novel *Rob Roy* (1817).

Rob·son (rŏb′sən), **Mount.** A mountain, 3,956.5 m (12,972 ft) high, of eastern British Columbia, Canada, on the border with Alberta. It is the highest elevation in the Canadian Rocky Mountains.

ro·bust (rō-bŭst′, rō′bŭst′) *adj.* **1.** Full of health and strength; vigorous. **2.** Powerfully built; sturdy. See Synonyms at **healthy. 3.** Requiring or suited to physical strength or endurance: *robust labor.* **4.** Rough or crude; boisterous: *a robust tale.* **5.** Marked by richness and fullness; full-bodied: *a robust wine.* [Latin *rōbustus,* from *rōbus, rōbur,* oak, strength. See **reudh-** in Appendix.] **—ro·bust′ly** *adv.* **—ro·bust′ness** *n.*

ro·bus·ta coffee (rō-bŭs′tə) *n.* **1.a.** A west African tropical shrub or small tree *(Coffea canephora)* having fragrant white flowers and red fruit. **b.** The seed of this plant. **2.** The coffee brewed from the seeds of this plant. [Latin *rōbusta,* feminine of *rōbustus,* strong. See robust.]

ro·bus·tious (rō-bŭs′chəs) *adj.* **1.** Boisterous; vigorous: *a robustious group of teenagers.* **2.** Rough, coarse, or crude: *a robustious comedy.* **—ro·bus′tious·ly** *adv.*

roc (rŏk) *n.* A mythical bird of prey having enormous size and strength. [Arabic *ruḫḫ,* probably from Persian *rukh.*]

Ro·ca (rō′kə, rô′-), **Cape.** A cape of western Portugal on the Atlantic Ocean west-northwest of Lisbon. It is the westernmost extremity of continental Europe.

roc·am·bole (rŏk′əm-bōl′) *n.* **1.** A European plant *(Allium sativum* var. *ophioscordon)* having a garliclike bulb. **2.** The bulb of this plant used as a seasoning. [French, from German *Rokenbolle* : *Rocken,* distaff (from Middle High German *rocke,* from Old High German *rocko*) + *Bolle,* bulb (from Middle High German *bolle,* from Old High German *bolla,* ball; see **bhel-²** in Appendix).]

Ro·cham·beau (rō′shăm-bō′, -shäN-), **Comte de.** Title of Jean Baptiste Donatien de Vimeur. 1725–1807. French army officer who commanded French forces in the American Revolution, most notably in the defeat of the British at Yorktown (1781).

Roch·dale (rŏch′dāl′). A borough of northwest England north-northeast of Manchester. It is a manufacturing center with an important textile industry. Population, 288,400.

Roche limit (rōsh) *n.* The smallest distance at which a natural satellite can orbit a celestial body without being torn apart by the larger body's gravitational force. The distance depends on the densities of the two bodies and the orbit of the satellite. [After Edouard Albert *Roche* (1820–1883), French mathematician.]

Ro·chelle salt or **Ro·chelle salts** (rə-shĕl′, rō-) *n.* See **potassium sodium tartrate.** [After (La) Rochelle.]

roche mou·ton·née (rôsh′ mo͞ot′n-ā′, mo͞o′tô-nā′) *n., pl.* **roches mou·ton·nées** (rôsh′ mo͞ot′n-ā′, -āz′, mo͞o′tô-nā′). An elongate mound of bedrock worn smooth and rounded by glacial abrasion. [French : *roche,* rock + *moutonné,* fleecy.]

Roch·es·ter (rŏch′ĭ-stər, -ĕs′tər). **1.** A municipal borough of southeast England east-southeast of London. It was an important Roman and Saxon settlement. Population, 56,030. **2.** A city of southeast Minnesota southeast of St. Paul. The Mayo Clinic (founded in 1889) is located here. Population, 57,855. **3.** A city of southeast New Hampshire north-northwest of Dover. Settled in 1728, it has diverse industries. Population, 21,560. **4.** A city of western New York east-northeast of Buffalo on the New York State Barge Canal near Lake Ontario. It was first settled c. 1812 and grew rapidly after the opening of the Erie Canal (1825). Population, 241,741.

roch·et (rŏch′ĭt) *n.* A white ceremonial vestment made of linen or lawn, worn by bishops and other church dignitaries. [Middle English, from Old French, of Germanic origin.]

rock¹ (rŏk) *n.* **1.** Relatively hard, naturally formed mineral or petrified matter; stone. **2.a.** A relatively small piece or fragment of such material. **b.** A relatively large body of such material, as a cliff or peak. **3.** A naturally formed aggregate of mineral matter constituting a significant part of the earth's crust. **4.** One that is similar to or suggestive of a mass of stone in stability, firmness, or dependability: *The family has been his rock during this difficult time.* **5. rocks.** *Slang.* Money. **6.** *Slang.* A large gem, especially a diamond. **7.** *Slang.* Crack cocaine. **8.a.** A varicolored stick candy. **b.** Rock candy. ***—idioms.*** **between a rock and a hard place.** Confronted with equally unpleasant alternatives and few or no opportunities to evade or circumvent them. **on the rocks. 1.** In a state of difficulty, destruction, or ruin: *Their marriage is on the rocks.* **2.** Without money; bankrupt: *Our accountant says* *the business is on the rocks.* **3.** Served over ice cubes: *Scotch on the rocks.* [Middle English, from Old North French *roque,* from Vulgar Latin *rocca.]

rock² (rŏk) *v.* **rocked, rock·ing, rocks.** —*intr.* **1.** To move back and forth or from side to side, especially gently or rhythmically. **2.** To sway violently, as from a blow or shock. See Synonyms at **swing.** **3.** To be washed and panned in a cradle or in a rocker. Used of ores. **4.** *Music.* To play or dance to rock 'n' roll. —*tr.* **1.** To move back and forth or from side to side, especially in order to soothe or lull to sleep. **2.** To cause to shake or sway violently. See Synonyms at **agitate.** **3.** To disturb the mental or emotional equilibrium of; upset: *News of the scandal rocked the town.* **4.** To wash or pan (ore) in a cradle or rocker. **5.** In mezzotint engraving, to roughen (a metal plate) with a rocker or roulette. —**rock** *n.* **1.a.** A rocking motion. **b.** The act of rocking. **2.** *Music.* Rock 'n' roll. —***idiom.*** **rock the boat.** *Slang.* To disturb the balance or routine of a situation: *He has an easygoing managerial style and won't rock the boat unless absolutely necessary.* [Middle English *rokken,* from Old English *roccian.*] —**rock′ing·ly** *adv.*

rock·a·bil·ly (rŏk′ə-bĭl′ē) *n. Music.* A form of popular music combining features of rock 'n' roll and country music. [ROCK ('N' ROLL) + (HILL)BILLY.]

rock-a-bye also **rock·a·bye** or **rock·a·by** (rŏk′ə-bī′) *interj.* Used to lull an infant or a child to sleep. [ROCK² + (LULL)ABY.]

rock-and-roll (rŏk′ən-rōl′) *n. Music.* Variant of **rock 'n' roll.**

rock and rye *n.* A liqueur made of whiskey blended with powdered rock candy and sometimes fruit. In the 19th century it was reputed to aid in digestion.

rock·a·way (rŏk′ə-wā′) *n.* A four-wheeled carriage with two seats and a standing top. [Probably after *Rockaway,* a town of northern New Jersey.]

rock bass (băs) *n.* **1.** A freshwater food and game fish *(Ambloplites rupestris)* of eastern and central North America. **2.** Any of various similar or related fishes.

rock bottom *n.* The lowest possible level or absolute bottom: *Prices have hit rock bottom.* —**rock′-bot′tom** (rŏk′bŏt′əm) *adj.*

rock·bound also **rock-bound** (rŏk′bound′) *adj.* Hemmed in by or bordered with rocks: *a rockbound lake.*

rock brake *n.* Any of several ferns of the genus *Crytogramma* that usually grow in rocky ground and have compound fronds and podlike fertile leaflets.

rock candy *n.* A hard confection that is made by cooling a concentrated sugar syrup into large, clear crystals around a piece of string or a stick.

Rock Cornish (rŏk) *n.* A small fowl of a breed developed by crossing white Plymouth Rock and Cornish strains, used especially as a roasting chicken. [(PLYMOUTH) ROCK + CORNISH.]

rock crab *n.* A crab found along rocky coasts, especially one of the genus *Cancer,* whose hindmost pair of legs is adapted for running.

rock crystal *n.* Colorless, transparent quartz, used in optical instruments and as a semiprecious gemstone.

rock dove *n.* A bird *(Columba livia)* native to Europe but widely distributed elsewhere, having variously colored plumage with iridescent markings on the neck. It is the common pigeon seen in cities and frequently domesticated. Also called *rock pigeon.*

Rock·e·fel·ler (rŏk′ə-fĕl′ər). American family, including **John Davison** (1839–1937), an oil magnate who amassed great wealth through the Standard Oil Company and spent about half of his fortune on philanthropic works. His son **John Davison, Jr.** (1874–1960), continued his father's work and had five sons, including **Nelson Aldrich** (1908–1979), who was governor of New York (1959–1973) and Vice President of the United States (1974–1977) under Gerald Ford.

rock elm *n.* **1.** A deciduous eastern North American tree *(Ulmus thomasii)* having corky branches and coarsely toothed leaves. **2.** The wood of this tree.

rock·er (rŏk′ər) *n.* **1.** One that rocks, as: **a.** A rocking chair. **b.** A rocking horse. **2.** One of the two curved pieces upon which a cradle, rocking chair, or similar device rocks. **3.** A cradle used for washing or panning ores. **4.** A small curved blade with a toothed edge used in mezzotint engraving to roughen the surface of the metal plate. **5.** An ice skate with a curved blade. **6.** A curved stripe at the bottom part of a chevron worn by noncommissioned officers below the rank of sergeant. **7.** *Music.* **a.** A rock 'n' roll song, singer, or musician. **b.** A fan of rock 'n' roll. —***idiom.*** **off (one's) rocker.** *Slang.* Out of one's mind; crazy.

rocker arm *n.* A pivoted lever used in an internal combustion engine to transfer cam or pushrod motion to a valve stem.

rocker cam *n.* A cam on a rockshaft.

rocker panel *n.* One of the sections of body paneling in a vehicle, such as an automobile, lying beneath the passenger compartment.

rock·er·y (rŏk′ə-rē) *n., pl.* **-ies.** See **rock garden** (sense 2).

rock·et¹ (rŏk′ĭt) *n.* **1.a.** A rocket engine. **b.** A vehicle or device propelled by one or more rocket engines, especially such a vehicle designed to travel through space. **2.** A projectile weapon carrying a warhead that is powered and propelled by rockets. **3.** A projectile firework having a cylindrical shape and a fuse that is lit from the rear. —**rocket** *v.* **-et·ed, -et·ing, -ets.** —*intr.* **1.** To move swiftly and powerfully, as a rocket. **2.** To fly swiftly straight up, as a game bird frightened from cover. **3.** To soar or rise rapidly: *The book rocketed to the top of the bestseller list.* —*tr.* **1.** To carry by means of a rocket. **2.** To assault with rockets. [Italian *rocchetta,* diminutive of *rocca,* spindle, distaff, of Germanic origin.]

rock·et² (rŏk′ĭt) *n.* **1.** A Mediterranean plant *(Eruca vesicaria* subsp. *sativa)* having flowers with purple-veined, yellowish-white petals and leaves that are sometimes used in salads. Also called *arugula, rocket salad, roquette.* **2.** Any of several plants of the mustard family, especially the dame's rocket and the sea rocket. [Middle English *rokette,* from Old French *roquette,* from Italian *rochetta,* variant of *ruchetta,* diminutive of *ruca,* a kind of cabbage, from Latin *ērūca.*]

rock·et·eer (rŏk′ĭ-tîr′) *n.* **1.** One who launches, rides in, or pilots rockets. **2.** One, such as a scientist, who is an expert in rocketry.

rocket engine *n.* A reaction engine that contains all the substances necessary for its operation and is not dependent on substances such as atmospheric oxygen, drawn from the surrounding medium, and thus is capable of operating in outer space. Also called *rocket motor.*

rocket plane *n.* **1.** An aircraft powered by one or more rocket engines. **2.** An aircraft designed to carry and launch rockets.

rock·et·ry (rŏk′ĭ-trē) *n.* The science and technology of rocket design, construction, and flight.

rocket salad *n.* See **rocket²** (sense 1).

rocket ship *n.* A spacecraft powered and propelled by rockets.

rocket sled *n.* A rocket-propelled sled that travels along rails and is used to study acceleration, deceleration, and crash survival techniques.

rock·et·sonde (rŏk′ĭt-sŏnd′) *n.* An instrument transported to the upper atmosphere by rocket, used to study meteorological conditions. [ROCKET¹ + (RADIO)SONDE.]

Rock fever *n.* See **brucellosis** (sense 1). [After the *Rock* of Gibraltar, where it is endemic.]

rock·fish (rŏk′fĭsh′) *n., pl.* **rockfish** or **-fish·es. 1.** Any of various fishes living among rocks. **2.** Any of various fishes, chiefly of the genus *Sebastes,* of Pacific waters. **3.** See **striped bass.**

rock flour *n.* Finely ground rock particles produced by glacial abrasion. Also called *glacier meal.*

Rock·ford (rŏk′fərd). A city of northern Illinois west-northwest of Chicago. Founded in 1834, it is a trade, processing, and shipping center. Population, 139,712.

rock garden *n.* **1.** A rocky area in which plants particularly adapted to such terrain are cultivated. **2.** A garden in which rocks are arranged and plants cultivated in a carefully designed, decorative scheme. In this sense, also called *rockery.*

Rock Hill. A city of northern South Carolina north of Columbia. It is a manufacturing and processing center with a textile industry. Population, 35,344.

rock hound *n. Informal.* **1.** One who specializes in geology. **2.** One who collects rocks and minerals, especially gemstones, as a hobby. —**rock′ hound′ing, rock′hound′ing** (rŏk′houn′dĭng) *n.*

rock house *n. Slang.* A crack house.

rock hyrax *n.* See **rock rabbit** (sense 1).

Rock·ies (rŏk′ēz). See **Rocky Mountains.**

rock·ing chair (rŏk′ĭng) *n.* A chair mounted on rockers or springs.

Rock·ing·ham (rŏk′ĭng-əm, -həm), Second Marquis of. Title of Charles Watson-Wentworth. 1730–1782. British politician who served as prime minister (1765–1766 and 1782), repealed the Stamp Act (1766), and favored American independence.

rocking horse *n.* A toy horse that is mounted on rockers or springs and is large enough for a child to ride. Also called *hobbyhorse.*

Rock Island. A city of northwest Illinois on the Mississippi River adjacent to Moline. It was the site of a Union prison during the Civil War. Population, 47,036.

rock·ling (rŏk′lĭng) *n., pl.* **rockling** or **-lings.** Any of various small marine fishes of the family Gadidae, of North Atlantic coastal waters.

rock lobster *n.* See **spiny lobster.**

rock maple *n.* **1.** See **sugar maple.** **2.** The tough, close-grained wood of the sugar maple.

Rock·ne (rŏk′nē), **Knute Kenneth.** 1888–1931. Norwegian-born American football coach at the University of Notre Dame (1918–1931). He revolutionized the sport with the use of the forward pass and other strategies requiring speed and agility.

rock 'n' roll or **rock-and-roll** (rŏk′ən-rōl′) —*n. Music.* A form of popular music arising from and incorporating a variety of musical styles, especially rhythm and blues, country music, and gospel. Originating in the United States in the 1950's, it is characterized by electronically amplified instrumentation, a heavily accented beat, and relatively simple phrase structure. —*attributive.* Often used to modify another noun: *rock 'n' roll music; rock 'n' roll records.* —**rock 'n' roller** *n.*

rock oil *n. Chiefly British.* Petroleum.

rock·oon (rŏ-ko͞on′) *n.* A device used for high-altitude sound-

robot

rocking chair

rocking horse
17th-century Dutch colonial

ă pat	oi boy
ā pay	ou out
âr care	o͝o took
ä father	o͞o boot
ĕ pet	ŭ cut
ē be	ûr urge
ĭ pit	th thin
ī pie	*th* this
îr pier	hw which
ŏ pot	zh vision
ō toe	ə about, item
ô paw	♦ regionalism

Stress marks: ′ (primary); ′ (secondary), as in **dictionary** (dĭk′shə-nĕr′ē)

ing, composed of a small, solid-propellant rocket that is launched from a balloon. [ROCK(ET)[1] + (BALL)OON.]

rock pigeon *n.* See **rock dove.**

rock rabbit *n.* **1.** A hyrax of the genus *Procavia* or *Dendrohyrax,* especially the African species *P. capensis.* Also called *rock hyrax.* **2.** See **pika.**

Norman Rockwell

rock-ribbed (rŏk′rĭbd′) *adj.* **1.** Having rocks or rock outcroppings; rocky. **2.** Firm and unyielding, especially with regard to one's principles or beliefs: *a rock-ribbed conservative.*

Rock River. A river rising in southeast Wisconsin and flowing about 459 km (285 mi) generally south and southwest to the Mississippi River in northwest Illinois.

rock·rose (rŏk′rōz′) *n.* Any of various plants of the genera *Cistus* or *Helianthemum* having small roselike yellow, white, or reddish flowers.

rock salt *n.* Sodium chloride occurring as extensive masses or rock.

rock·shaft (rŏk′shăft′) *n.* A shaft that oscillates or rocks upon its bearings but does not revolve.

rock·slide (rŏk′slīd′) *n.* **1.** The usually rapid downward movement of newly detached segments of bedrock. **2.** The rock mass that has reached its current position through such a movement.

rococo
Doors designed by Jean François de Cuvilliés (1695?–1768?)

Rock Springs. A city of southwest Wyoming north of the Utah border. It was a trading post and stagecoach station on the Oregon Trail in the 1860's. Population, 19,458.

rock squirrel *n.* A large ground squirrel *(Spermophilus variegatus)* with variegated black and white upper parts, found in rocky places in Mexico and the southwest United States.

Rock·ville (rŏk′vĭl′, -vəl). A city of central Maryland north-northwest of Washington, D.C. It is the site of several research laboratories. Population, 43,811.

Rockville Cen·tre (sĕn′tər). A village of southeast New York on southwest Long Island south-southwest of Hempstead. It is primarily residential. Population, 25,405.

rock wallaby *n.* Any of several small agile wallabies, chiefly of the genus *Petrogale,* that live in rocky areas and have thick-soled feet and a slender tail.

rock·weed (rŏk′wēd′) *n.* Any of several coarse, brownish seaweeds of the genera *Fucus* and *Ascophyllum* that grow on rocks in coastal areas.

Rock·well (rŏk′wĕl′), **Norman.** 1894–1978. American illustrator whose works, many of which appeared on the cover of the *Saturday Evening Post,* offer a nostalgic, idealized view of everyday American life.

rock wool *n.* See **mineral wool.**

rock·work (rŏk′wûrk′) *n.* **1.** A natural mass or pile of rocks. **2.** Stonework imitating the irregular surface of natural rock.

rock wren *n.* **1.** Any of several wrens of the genus *Salpinctes,* especially *S. obsoletus,* found in rocky regions of the western United States and Mexico. **2.** A small wren *(Xenicus gilviventris)* that inhabits New Zealand and feeds mostly on the ground among stones.

rodeo

rock·y[1] (rŏk′ē) *adj.* **-i·er, -i·est. 1.** Consisting of, containing, or abounding in rock or rocks. **2.a.** Resembling or suggesting rock; firm or hard. **b.** Steadfast or stubborn; unyielding: *her rocky heart.* **3.** Marked by obstructions or difficulties: *the rocky road to success.* **—rock′i·ness′** *n.*

rock·y[2] (rŏk′ē) *adj.* **-i·er, -i·est. 1.a.** Inclined or prone to sway or totter; unsteady or shaky: *a rocky shelf.* **b.** Appearing inclined to fail; discouraging or disappointing: *After a somewhat rocky start, the team went on to win the state championships.* **2.** Weak, dizzy, or nauseated, especially as a result of the excessive intake of alcohol or drugs. **—rock′i·ness′** *n.*

Rock·y Mount (rŏk′ē). A city of northeast North Carolina east-northeast of Raleigh. It is a manufacturing, processing, and shipping center in a rich agricultural region. Population, 41,283.

Rocky Mountain goat *n.* See **mountain goat.**

Rocky Mountains also **Rock·ies** (rŏk′ēz). A major mountain system of western North America extending more than 4,827 km (3,000 mi) from northwest Alaska to the Mexican border. The system includes numerous ranges and forms the Continental Divide. Its highest elevation is Mount Elbert, 4,402.1 m (14,433 ft), in central Colorado. In Canada the Rockies rise to 3,956.5 m (12,972 ft) at Mount Robson in eastern British Columbia. Sections of the mountains were explored in early times by Coronado, Lewis and Clark, Zebulon Pike, Sir Alexander Mackenzie, and Simon Fraser.

Auguste Rodin

Rocky Mountain sheep *n.* See **bighorn.**

Rocky Mountain spotted fever *n.* An acute infectious disease caused by a microorganism *(Rickettsia rickettsii)* transmitted by ticks, characterized by muscular pains, high fever, and skin eruptions, and endemic throughout North America.

Rocky Mountain States. A region of the western United States including Colorado, Idaho, Montana, Nevada, Utah, and Wyoming.

Rocky River. A city of northeast Ohio, a residential suburb of Cleveland. Population, 21,084.

ro·co·co (rə-kō′kō, rō′kə-kō′) *n.* **1.a.** Also **Rococo.** A style of art, especially architecture and decorative art, that originated in France in the early 18th century and is marked by elaborate ornamentation, as with a profusion of scrolls, foliage, and animal forms. **b.** A very ornate style of speech or writing. **2.** Also **Rococo.** *Music.* A style of composition arising in 18th-century Europe immediately following the baroque that is characterized by a certain lightness of form, largely the result of a high degree of ornamentation. **—rococo** *adj.* **1.** Also **Rococo.** Of or relating to the rococo. **2.** Immoderately elaborate. See Synonyms at **ornate.** [French, probably alteration of *rocaille,* rockwork, from *roc,* rock, variant of *roche,* from Vulgar Latin **rocca.*]

rod (rŏd) *n.* **1.** A thin straight piece or bar of material, such as metal or wood, often having a particular function or use, as: **a.** A fishing rod. **b.** A piston rod. **c.** An often expandable horizontal bar, especially of metal, used to suspend household items such as curtains or towels. **d.** A leveling rod. **e.** A lightning rod. **f.** A divining rod. **g.** A measuring stick. **2.** A shoot or stem cut from or growing as part of a woody plant. **3.a.** A stick or bundle of sticks or switches used to give punishment by whipping. **b.** Punishment; correction. **4.** A scepter, staff, or wand symbolizing power or authority. **5.** Power or dominion, especially of a tyrannical nature: *"under the rod of a cruel slavery"* (John Henry Newman). **6.** *Abbr.* **r., rd a.** A linear measure equal to 5.5 yards or 16.5 feet (5.03 meters). Also called *pole.* **b.** The square of this measure, equal to 30.25 square yards or 272.25 square feet (25.30 square meters). See table at **measurement. 7.** *Bible.* A line of family descent; a branch of a tribe. **8.** *Anatomy.* Any of various rod-shaped cells in the retina that respond to dim light. **9.** *Microbiology.* An elongated bacterium; a bacillus. **10.** *Slang.* A pistol or revolver. **11.** Often **rods.** A portion of the undercarriage of a train, especially the drawbar under a freight car: *ride the rods.* [Middle English *rodd,* from Old English.]

rode[1] (rōd) *v.* Past tense of **ride.**

rode[2] (rōd) *n. Nautical.* A rope, especially one attached to the anchor of a small boat. [From Middle English *at rode,* at an anchorage, from *rode,* a riding. See ROAD.]

ro·dent (rōd′nt) *n.* Any of various mammals of the order Rodentia, such as a mouse, rat, squirrel, or beaver, characterized by large incisors adapted for gnawing or nibbling. **—rodent** *adj.* **1.** Gnawing. **2.** Of or relating to rodents. [From New Latin *Rodentia,* order name, from Latin *rōdēns, rōdent-,* present participle of *rōdere,* to gnaw. See **rēd-** in Appendix.]

ro·den·ti·cide (rō-dĕn′tĭ-sīd′) *n.* A chemical substance used to kill rodents.

rodent ulcer *n.* A cancerous skin ulcer that derives from basal cells and usually occurs on the face. [Latin *rodēns, rodent-,* gnawing. See RODENT.]

ro·de·o (rō′dē-ō′, rō-dā′ō) *n., pl.* **-os. 1.** A public competition or exhibition in which skills such as riding broncos or roping calves are displayed. **2.** A cattle roundup. **3.** An enclosure for keeping cattle that have been rounded up. [Spanish, corral, rodeo, from *rodear,* to surround, from *rueda,* wheel, from Latin *rota.* See **ret-** in Appendix.]

Rod·gers (rŏj′ərz), **Richard.** 1902–1979. American composer known for his musical comedies, especially his collaborations with Oscar Hammerstein II, including *Oklahoma!* (1943), *South Pacific* (1949), and *The Sound of Music* (1959).

Ro·din (rō-dăn′, -dăN′), **François Auguste René.** 1840–1917. French sculptor whose innovative, sometimes controversial works include the lifelike *Bronze Age* (1877) and the uncompleted series *Gates of Hell,* comprising some of his best-known works, such as *The Thinker.*

rod·man (rŏd′mən) *n.* One who carries and employs a leveling rod under the supervision of a surveyor.

Rod·ney (rŏd′nē), **George Brydges.** First Baron Rodney. 1718–1792. British naval officer who won important victories over the European powers that supported the colonists during the American Revolution.

rod·o·mon·tade also **rho·do·mon·tade** (rŏd′ə-mŏn-tăd′, -täd′, rō′də-) —*n.* Pretentious boasting or bragging; bluster. See Synonyms at **bombast.** —*adj.* Pretentiously boastful or bragging. —*intr.v.* **-tad·ed, -tad·ing, -tades.** To boast or brag; bluster. [French, from Italian *rodomontada,* from *Rodomonte,* arrogant Saracen leader in *Orlando Innamorato* by Matteo Boiardo and *Orlando Furioso* by Ludovico Ariosto.]

roe[1] (rō) *n.* **1.** The eggs or the egg-laden ovary of a fish. **2.** The egg mass or spawn of certain crustaceans, such as the lobster. [Middle English *row,* from Middle Low German or Middle Dutch *roge.*]

roe[2] (rō) *n., pl.* **roe** or **roes.** The roe deer. [Middle English *ro,* from Old English *rā, rāha.*]

Roeb·ling (rō′blĭng), **John Augustus.** 1806–1869. German-born American engineer who designed and began the construction of the Brooklyn Bridge, a project completed (1883) by his son **Washington Augustus Roebling** (1837–1926).

roe·buck (rō′bŭk′) *n.* A male roe deer.

roe deer *n.* A rather small, delicately formed Eurasian deer *(Capreolus capreolus)* having short, branched antlers in the male and a brownish coat.

roent·gen also **rönt·gen** (rĕnt′gən, -jən, rŭnt′-) *n. Abbr.* **R, r** A unit of radiation exposure equal to the quantity of ionizing radiation that will produce one electrostatic unit of electricity in one cubic centimeter of dry air at 0°C and standard atmospheric pressure. [After Wilhelm Konrad ROENTGEN.] **—roent′gen** *adj.*

Roent·gen (rĕnt′gən, -jən, rŭnt′-) or **Rönt·gen** (rœnt′gən), **Wilhelm Konrad.** 1845–1923. German physicist who discovered x-rays and developed x-ray photography, revolutionizing medical diagnosis. He won a 1901 Nobel Prize.

roent·gen·ize (rĕnt′gə-nīz′, -jə-, rŭnt′-) *tr.v.* **-ized, -iz·ing, -iz·es.** To subject to the action of x-rays.

roentgeno– *pref.* X-ray: *roentgenography.* [From ROENTGEN.]

roent·gen·o·gram (rĕnt′gə-nə-grăm′, -jə-, rŭnt′-) *n.* A photograph made with x-rays. Also called *roentgenograph.*

roent·gen·o·graph (rĕnt′gə-nə-grăf′, -jə-, rŭnt′-) *n.* See **roentgenogram.**

roent·gen·og·ra·phy (rĕnt′gə-nŏg′rə-fē, -jə-, rŭnt′-) *n.* Photography with the use of x-rays. **—roent′gen·o·graph′ic** (-gə-nə-grăf′ĭk, -jə-) *adj.* **—roent′gen·o·graph′ic·al·ly** *adv.*

roent·gen·ol·o·gy (rĕnt′gə-nŏl′ə-jē, -jə-, rŭnt′-) *n.* Radiology employing x-rays. **—roent′gen·o·log′ic** (-ə-lŏj′ĭk), **roent′gen·o·log′i·cal** (-ĭ-kəl) *adj.* **—roent′gen·o·log′i·cal·ly** *adv.* **—roent′gen·ol′o·gist** *n.*

roent·gen·o·scope (rĕnt′gə-nə-skōp′, -jə-, rŭnt′-) *n.* See **fluoroscope. —roent′gen·o·scop′ic** (-skŏp′ĭk) *adj.* **—roent′gen·os′co·py** (-gə-nŏs′kə-pē, -jə-) *n.*

roent·gen·o·ther·a·py (rĕnt′gə-nə-thĕr′ə-pē, -jə-, rŭnt′-) *n., pl.* **-pies.** The therapeutic use of x-rays in treating disease.

roentgen ray *n.* See **x-ray** (sense 1).

Roe·rich (rûr′ĭk, ryô′rĭkh), **Nicholas Konstantin.** 1874–1947. Russian-born artist and archaeologist known especially for the sets he designed for Diaghilev's ballets.

Roeth·ke (rĕt′kē, -kə, rĕth′-), **Theodore.** 1908–1963. American poet whose short, lyrical works, often imbued with floral images, were published in *The Waking* (1953) and other collections.

ro·ga·tion (rō-gā′shən) *n.* **1.** Often **rogations.** *Ecclesiastical.* Solemn prayer or supplication, especially as chanted during the rites of Rogation Day. **2.a.** The formal proposal of a law in ancient Rome by a tribune or consul to the people for acceptance or rejection. **b.** A law proposed in this manner. [Middle English *rogacioun,* from Latin *rogātiō, rogātiōn-,* from *rogātus,* past participle of *rogāre,* to ask. See **reg-** in Appendix.]

Ro·ga·tion Day (rō-gā′shən) *n. Ecclesiastical.* One of the three days of prayer preceding Ascension Day.

ro·ga·to·ry (rō′gə-tôr′ē, -tōr′ē) *adj. Law.* Requesting information. Used especially of a request by one court of another, often foreign court for aid in obtaining desired information: *a rogatory letter.* [French *rogatoire,* from Medieval Latin *rogātōrius,* from Latin *rogātus,* past participle of *rogāre,* to ask. See **reg-** in Appendix.]

rog·er (rŏj′ər) *interj.* Used especially in radio communications to indicate receipt of a message. [From *Roger,* spoken representation of the letter *r,* short for RECEIVED.]

Rog·ers (rŏj′ərz). A city of northwest Arkansas north of Fayetteville. It is a processing center in a farming and tourist area. Population, 17,351.

Rogers, Bruce. 1870–1957. American book designer and typographer noted for his use of design to reflect a volume's subject matter.

Rogers, Carl. 1902–1987. American psychologist. A founder of humanistic psychology, he developed client-centered therapy, in which the client directs the focus and pace of each session.

Rogers, Ginger. Born 1911. American dancer and actress particularly noted for her partnership with Fred Astaire in several motion pictures, including *Swing Time* (1936).

Rogers, John. 1829–1904. American sculptor noted for his groups of small sculptures, such as "Checkers up at the Farm" and "The Slave Auction" (both 1859).

Rogers, Robert. 1731–1795. American soldier and frontiersman who led (1758–1763) the Rogers's Rangers on a series of daring missions during the French and Indian War.

Rogers, Roy. Born 1912. American singer and actor who played a singing cowboy in motion-picture Westerns.

Rogers, Samuel. 1763–1855. British poet whose works include *The Pleasures of Memory* (1792).

Rogers, William Penn Adair. Known as "Will." 1879–1935. American humorist noted for his wry, homespun commentary on American society and politics.

Ro·get (rō-zhā′, rō′zhā), **Peter Mark.** 1779–1869. British physician and scholar who compiled the *Thesaurus of English Words and Phrases* (1852).

rogue (rōg) *n.* **1.** An unprincipled, deceitful, and unreliable person; a scoundrel or rascal. **2.** One who is playfully mischievous; a scamp: *My little brother is such a rogue!* **3.** A wandering beggar; a vagrant. **4.** A vicious and solitary animal, especially an elephant that has separated itself from its herd. **5.** An organism, especially a plant, that shows an undesirable variation from a standard. **—rogue** *v.* **rogued, rogu·ing, rogues.** —*tr.* **1.** To defraud. **2.** To remove (diseased or abnormal specimens) from a group of plants of the same variety. —*intr.* To remove deviant plants. [Origin unknown.]

Rogue River (rōg). A river, about 322 km (200 mi) long, rising in the Cascade Range of southwest Oregon and flowing generally south and southwest to the Pacific Ocean.

rogu·er·y (rō′gə-rē) *n., pl.* **-ies. 1.** Behavior characteristic of a rogue. **2.** A mischievous act.

rogues' gallery (rōgz) *n.* A collection of pictures of known and suspected criminals maintained in police files and used for making identifications.

rogu·ish (rō′gĭsh) *adj.* **1.** Deceitful; unprincipled: *Set adrift by his roguish crew, the captain of the ship spent a week alone at sea.* **2.** Playfully mischievous: *a roguish grin.* **—rogu′ish·ly** *adv.* **—rogu′ish·ness** *n.*

Rohn·ert Park (rō′nərt). A city of western California, a suburb of Santa Rosa. Population, 22,965.

roil (roil) *v.* **roiled, roil·ing, roils.** —*tr.* **1.** To make (a liquid) muddy or cloudy by stirring up sediment. **2.** To displease or disturb; vex: *Some of her habits are off-putting but don't let them roil you.* —*intr.* To be in a state of turbulence or agitation. [Origin unknown.]

roil·y (roi′lē) *adj.* **-i·er, -i·est. 1.** Full of sediment; muddy or cloudy. **2.** Turbulent; agitated.

rois·ter (roi′stər) *intr.v.* **-tered, -ter·ing, -ters. 1.** To engage in boisterous merrymaking; revel noisily. **2.** To behave in a blustering manner; swagger. [From obsolete *roister,* roisterer, probably from Old French *rustre,* ruffian, alteration of *ruste,* from Latin *rūsticus,* rustic. See RUSTIC.] **—rois′ter·er** *n.* **—rois′ter·ous** *adj.* **—rois′ter·ous·ly** *adv.*

ro·la·mite (rō′lə-mīt′) *n.* A mechanism consisting of two or more hard, cylindrical rollers with a flexible nonstretching band looped around them, so that the rollers move against each other with very little friction. [ROL(L) + *-amite,* of unknown origin.]

Ginger Rogers

Ro·land (rō′lənd, rô-läɴ′) *n.* A French hero celebrated in medieval chansons de geste as the nephew of Charlemagne and defender of Christianity who was killed in battle against the Saracens at Roncesvalles in A.D. 778.

role also **rôle** (rōl) *n.* **1.** A character or part played by a performer. **2.** The characteristic and expected social behavior of an individual. **3.** A function or position. See Synonyms at **function.** [French *rôle,* from Old French *rolle,* roll of parchment (on which an actor's part was written), from Latin *rotula,* diminutive of *rota,* wheel. See ROLL.]

WORD HISTORY: Considering the various great roles in the theater, such as Hamlet or Lear, or the various roles we play, such as parent or teacher, employer or employee, it is difficult to think back to a time in the history of the word *role* when none of these important associations was present. *Role,* which is first recorded in English in 1606, came to us from French with the sense "a part one has to play." Obviously the development of the sense familiar to us had already occurred in French, where the word *rôle* in its earlier history (Old French *rolle*) had meant "a roll, as of parchment," particularly with reference to a manuscript roll. The word could also mean "a legal document" or "a list or register." From such use it also came to refer to the text from which an actor learned a part. This use brought the word into the world of the theater where it has played an important role ever since.

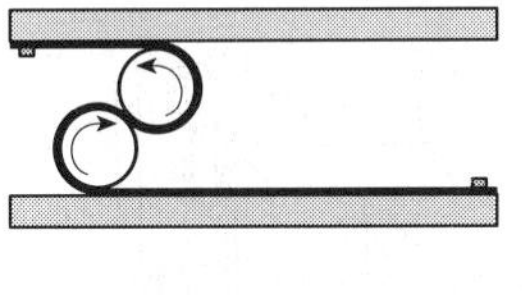

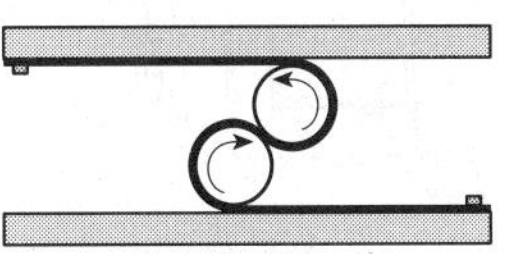

rolamite

role indicator *n. Computer Science.* In information retrieval, a code that is assigned to a key word to indicate the part of speech or function of the word in the text where it occurs.

role model *n.* A person who serves as a model in a particular behavioral or social role for another person to emulate.

role-play (rōl′plā′) *v.* **-played, -play·ing, -plays.** —*tr.* To assume deliberately the part or role of; act out: *"Participants are encouraged to pass on leads about jobs . . . and to role-play interview situations with each other"* (Hatfield MA Valley Advocate). —*intr.* To assume or act out a particular role: *"When I hire people I role-play with them . . . to see how they take pressure"* (Peter Schrag). **—role-play** *n.* Role-playing.

role-play·ing (rōl′plā′ĭng) *n.* **1.** *Psychology.* A therapeutic technique, designed to reduce the conflict inherent in various social situations, in which participants act out particular behavioral roles in order to expand their awareness of differing points of view. **2.** An instance or a situation in which one deliberately acts out or assumes a particular character or role.

Rolf (rŏlf). See **Rollo.**

Rolfe (rŏlf), **John.** 1585–1622. English colonist in America and husband of Pocahontas.

Rolf·ing (rôl′fĭng, rŏl′-). A service mark used for a technique of deep muscular manipulation and massage for the relief of bodily and emotional tension.

roll (rōl) *v.* **rolled, roll·ing, rolls.** —*intr.* **1.** To move forward along a surface by revolving on an axis or by repeatedly turning over. **2.** To travel or be moved on wheels or rollers: *rolled down the sidewalk on their scooters.* **3.** To travel around; wander: *roll from town to town.* **4.a.** To travel or be carried in a vehicle. **b.** To be carried on a stream: *The logs rolled down the cascading river.* **5.a.** To start to move or operate: *The press wouldn't roll.* **b.** To work or succeed in a sustained way; gain momentum: *The political campaign finally began to roll.* **6.** To go by; elapse: *The days rolled along.* **7.** To recur: *Summer has rolled around again.* **8.** To move in a periodic revolution, as a planet in its orbit. **9.** To turn over and over: *The puppy rolled in the mud.* **10.** To shift the gaze usually quickly and continually: *Her eyes rolled with fright.* **11.** To turn around or revolve on or as if on an axis. **12.** To move or advance with a rising and falling motion; undulate: *The waves rolled toward shore.* **13.** To extend or appear to extend in gentle rises and falls: *The dunes roll to the sea.* **14.** To move or rock from side to side: *The ship pitched and rolled in heavy seas.* **15.** To walk with a swaying, unsteady motion. **16.** To take the shape

ă pat	oi boy
ā pay	ou out
âr care	o͝o took
ä father	o͞o boot
ĕ pet	ŭ cut
ē be	ûr urge
ĭ pit	th thin
ī pie	*th* this
îr pier	hw which
ŏ pot	zh vision
ō toe	ə about, item
ô paw	♦ regionalism

Stress marks: ′ (primary); ′ (secondary), as in **dictionary** (dĭk′shə-nĕr′ē)

roller coaster

roller skate

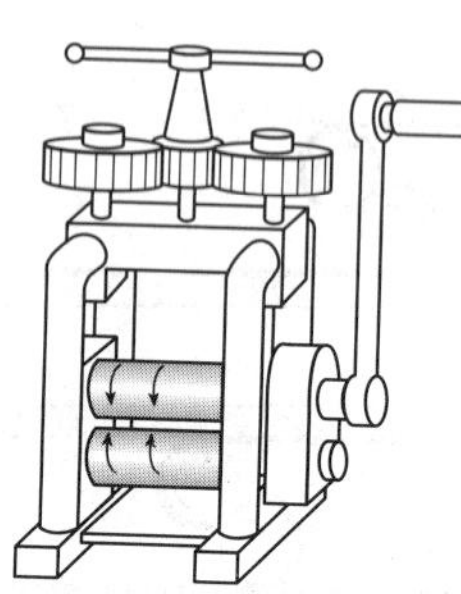

rolling mill

rolling pin

of a ball or cylinder: *Yarn rolls easily.* **17.** To become flattened by or as if by pressure applied by a roller. **18.** To make a deep, prolonged, surging sound: *Thunder rolled in the distance.* **19.** To make a sustained, trilling sound, as certain birds do. **20.** To beat a drum in a continuous series of short blows. **21.** To pour or flow in or as if in a continual stream: *tourists rolling into the city.* **22.** To enjoy ample amounts: *rolled in the money.* —*tr.* **1.** To cause to move forward along a surface by revolving on an axis or by repeatedly turning over. **2.** To move or push along on wheels or rollers: *rolled the plane out of the hangar.* **3.** To impel or send onward in a steady, swelling motion: *The sea rolls its waves onto the sand.* **4.** To impart a swaying, rocking motion to: *Heavy seas rolled the ship.* **5.** To turn around or partly turn around; rotate: *rolled his head toward the door.* **6.** To cause to begin moving or operating: *roll the cameras; roll the presses.* **7.** To extend or lay out: *rolled out a long rope.* **8.** To pronounce or utter with a trill: *You must roll your* r*'s in Spanish.* **9.** To utter or emit in full, swelling tones. **10.** To beat (a drum) with a continuous series of short blows. **11.** To wrap (something) round and round upon itself or around something else: *roll up a poster.* **12. a.** To envelop or enfold in a covering: *roll dirty laundry in a sheet.* **b.** To make by shaping into a ball or cylinder: *roll a cigarette.* **13.** To spread, compress, or flatten by applying pressure with a roller: *roll pastry dough.* **14.** *Printing.* To apply ink to (type) with a roller or rollers. **15.** *Games.* To throw (dice), as in craps. **16.** *Slang.* To rob (a drunken, sleeping, or otherwise helpless person). —**roll** *n.* **1.** The act or an instance of rolling. **2.** Something rolled up: *a roll of tape.* **3.** A quantity, as of cloth or wallpaper, rolled into a cylinder and often considered as a unit of measure. **4.** A piece of parchment or paper that may be or is rolled up; a scroll. **5.** A register or a catalogue. **6.** A list of names of persons belonging to a group. **7.** A mass in cylindrical or rounded form: *a roll of tobacco.* **8. a.** A small rounded portion of bread. **b.** A portion of food shaped like a tube with a filling. **9.** A rolling, swaying, or rocking motion. **10.** A gentle swell or undulation of a surface: *the roll of the plains.* **11.** A deep reverberation or rumble: *the roll of thunder.* **12.** A rapid succession of short sounds: *the roll of a drum.* **13.** A trill: *the roll of his* r*'s.* **14.** A resonant, rhythmical flow of words. **15.** A roller, especially a cylinder on which to roll something up or with which to flatten something. **16.** A maneuver in which an airplane makes a single complete rotation about its longitudinal axis without changing direction or losing altitude. **17.** *Slang.* Money, especially a wad of paper money. —***phrasal verbs.*** **roll back.** **1.** To reduce (prices or wages, for example) to a previous lower level. **2.** To cause to turn back or retreat. **roll out.** **1.** To get out of bed. **2.** *Football.* To execute a rollout. **roll over.** **1.** To defer or postpone payment of (an obligation). **2.** To renegotiate the terms of (a financial deal). **3.** To reinvest (funds from a maturing security) into a similar security. **roll up.** **1.** To arrive in a vehicle. **2.** To accumulate; amass: *rolled up quite a fortune.* —***idioms.*** **on a roll.** *Informal.* Undergoing or experiencing sustained, even increasing good fortune, or success: *"The stock market's on a roll"* (Karen Pennar). **roll in the hay.** *Slang.* Sexual intercourse. **roll the bones.** *Games.* To cast dice, especially in craps. **roll with the punches.** *Slang.* To cope with and withstand adversity, especially by being flexible. [Middle English *rollen,* from Old French *roler,* from Vulgar Latin **rotulāre,* from Latin *rotula,* diminutive of *rota,* wheel. See **ret-** in Appendix.]

Rol·land (rô-läɴ′), **Romain.** 1866–1944. French writer whose varied works include *Jean Christophe* (1904–1912), a series of satirical novels. He won the 1915 Nobel Prize for literature.

roll·a·way (rōl′ə-wā′) *adj.* Set on rollers or casters for easy moving and storing: *a rollaway bed.*

roll·back (rōl′băk′) *n.* **1.** A reduction, especially in prices or wages, to a previous lower level by governmental action or direction: *a price rollback; a rollback of military supplies.* **2.** A turning back or retreat, as from a previously held position or policy: *Conservatives hoped for a rollback of left-wing support for the controversial new legislation.*

roll bar *n.* A sturdy metal bar built into the inside roof of a motor vehicle to prevent or reduce injury in case of a rollover.

roll call *n.* **1.** The reading aloud of a list of names of people, as in a classroom or military post, to determine who is present or absent. **2.** The time fixed for such a reading.

roll·er¹ (rō′lər) *n.* **1.** One that rolls or performs a rolling operation or activity. **2.** Any of various cylindrical or spherical devices that roll or rotate, especially: **a.** A small, spokeless wheel, such as that of a roller skate or caster. **b.** An elongated cylinder on which something, such as a window shade or towel, is wound. **c.** A heavy, revolving cylinder that is used to level, crush, or smooth. **d.** *Printing.* A cylinder, usually of hard rubber, used to ink the type before the paper is impressed. **e.** A cylinder of wire mesh, foam rubber, or other material around which a strand of hair is wound to produce a soft curl or wave. **3.** A long, rolled bandage. **4.** A heavy, swelling wave that breaks on a coast. **5.** A tumbler pigeon.

rol·ler² (rō′lər) *n.* **1.** Any of various Old World birds of the family Coraciidae, having bright blue wings, stocky bodies, and hooked bills. They are noted for their aggressiveness and their habit of rolling and twisting in flight, especially during the breeding season. **2.** A canary that trills. [German, from *rollen,* to roll, burble. See ROLLMOPS.]

roller bearing *n.* A bearing using rollers to reduce friction between machine parts.

roller coaster *n.* **1.** A steep, sharply curving elevated railway with small open passenger cars that is operated at high speeds as a ride, especially in an amusement park. **2.** Something, such as an action or experience, that is marked by abrupt, extreme changes in circumstance or behavior: *"the demographic roller coaster caused by the baby boom"* (American Demographics).

roller hockey *n.* *Sports.* Hockey played on a hard surface in which two opposing teams of roller skaters, using curved sticks, try to drive a ball into the opponents' goal.

roller skate *n.* A shoe or boot with two or four wheels or casters attached to its sole for skating on hard surfaces.

roll·er-skate (rō′lər-skāt′) *intr.v.* **-skat·ed, -skat·ing, -skates.** To engage in roller skating. —**roller skater** *n.*

Rolle's theorem (rôlz, rōlz) *n.* *Mathematics.* A theorem stating that if a curve is continuous, has two x-intercepts, and has a tangent at every point between the intercepts, at least one of these tangents is parallel to the x-axis. [After Michel *Rolle* (1652–1719), French mathematician.]

roll film *n.* Photographic film rolled on a spool and encased before being loaded into a camera.

rol·lick (rŏl′ĭk) *intr.v.* **-licked, -lick·ing, -licks.** To behave or move in a carefree, frolicsome manner; romp. [Origin unknown.] —**rol′lick** *n.* —**rol′lick·some, rol′lick·y** *adj.*

rol·lick·ing (rŏl′ĭ-kĭng) *adj.* Carefree and high-spirited; boisterous: *a rollicking celebration.* —**rol′lick·ing·ly** *adv.*

Roll·ing Meadows (rō′lĭng). A city of northeast Illinois, a suburb of Chicago. Population, 20,167.

roll·ing mill (rō′lĭng) *n.* **1.** A factory in which metal is rolled into sheets, bars, or other forms. **2.** A machine used for rolling metal.

rolling pin *n.* A smooth cylinder, usually of wood, with a handle at each end, used for rolling out dough.

rolling stock *n.* The equipment available for use as transportation, as automotive vehicles, locomotives, or railroad cars, owned by a particular company or carrier.

roll·mops (rōl′mŏps′) *n., pl.* **rollmops.** A marinated fillet of herring wrapped around a pickle or an onion. [German : *rollen,* to roll (from Middle High German, from Old French *roler;* see ROLL) + *Mops,* blockhead, pug dog.]

Rol·lo (rŏl′ō). Also called **Hrolf** (hrŏlf, rŏlf) or **Rolf** (rŏlf). 860?–931? Norse chieftain and the first duke of Normandy.

roll-on (rōl′ŏn′, -ôn′) *adj.* Of or being a substance, such as a deodorant, that is dispensed from a container having a rolling ball at one end serving as an applicator. —**roll′-on′** *n.*

roll·out (rōl′out′) *n.* **1.** The inauguration or initial public exhibition of a new product, service, or policy: *The manufacturer's rollout of the new jet is scheduled for next month.* **2.** *Football.* A play in which the quarterback runs toward a sideline after receiving the snap with the intention of passing the ball.

roll·o·ver (rōl′ō′vər) *n.* **1.** The act or process of rolling over. **2.** An accident in which a motor vehicle overturns. **3.** *Economics.* Reinvestment of profits received from one often short-term security into another, similar security: *an IRA rollover.*

roll-top desk or **roll·top desk** (rōl′tŏp′) *n.* A desk fitted with a flexible sliding top made of parallel slats.

roll·way (rōl′wā′) *n.* A surface along which cylindrical objects or objects on rollers may be moved, especially a naturally or artificially inclined surface used by lumberjacks to slide logs into a waterway for transport.

Ro·lo·dex (rō′lə-dĕks′). A trademark used for a desktop rotary file of removable cards, usually used for names, addresses, and telephone numbers. This trademark often occurs in attributive contexts in print: *"He recently sent 1,000 journalists a set of four Rolodex cards, each featuring his picture and a list of his four committee assignments"* (National Journal). It also occurs in the plural: *"Their names can be found in Rolodexes all over town"* (New York Times).

Röl·vaag (rōl′väg′), **Ole Edvart.** 1876–1931. Norwegian-born American writer whose novels, especially the trilogy beginning with *Giants in the Earth* (1927), concern the Norwegian settlers of the American West.

ro·ly-po·ly (rō′lē-pō′lē) *adj.* Short and plump; pudgy. —**roly-poly** *n., pl.* **-lies.** **1.** A short, plump person or thing. **2.** *Chiefly British.* A pudding made of jam or fruit rolled up in pastry dough and baked or steamed until soft. [Alteration and reduplication of ROLL.]

rom also **rom.** *abbr.* *Printing.* Roman.

ROM *abbr.* *Computer Science.* Read-only memory.

Rom. *abbr.* **1.** Roman. **2.** Romance (languages). **3.** Romania. **4.** Romanian. **5.** *Bible.* Romans.

Ro·ma·gna (rō-män′yə, rô-mä′nyä). A historical region of north-central Italy. It was the center of Byzantine influence in Italy and later came under papal rule. The region now forms part of Emilia-Romagna.

Ro·ma·ic (rō-mā′ĭk) *n.* Modern Greek. [Modern Greek *Rhōmaikos,* from Greek, Roman, from *Rhōmē,* Rome, from Latin *Rōma.*] —**Ro·ma′ic** *adj.*

ro·maine (rō-mān′) *n.* A cultivar of lettuce *(Lactuca sativa)* having a slender head of oblong or obovate leaves with broad midribs. Also called *cos, cos lettuce.* [French, from feminine of *Romain,* Roman, from Old French, from Latin *Rōmānus,* from *Rōma,* Rome.]

Ro·mains (rō-măɴ′), **Jules.** Pen name of Louis Farigoule.

1885–1972. French writer whose poetry, drama, and fiction, including the novel cycle *Men of Good Will* (1932–1946), express the belief that an individual is unimportant unless associated with some group.

ro•man (rō-mäɴ′) *n.* **1.** A narrative poem or a prose tale in medieval French literature. **2.** A novel. [French, from Old French *romans,* romance. See ROMANCE.]

Ro•man (rō′mən) *adj.* **1.** *Abbr.* **Rom. a.** Of or relating to ancient or modern Rome or its people or culture. **b.** Of or relating to the Roman Empire. **2.** *Abbr.* **Rom. a.** Of, relating to, or composed in the Latin language. **b.** Of or using the Latin alphabet. **3.** *Abbr.* **Rom.** Of or relating to the Roman Catholic Church. **4.** *Abbr.* **Rom.** Of or being an architectural style developed by the ancient Romans and characterized by the round arch as chief structural element, the vault, concrete masonry construction, and classical ornamentation. **5. roman.** *Abbr.* **rom, rom.** Of or being a typestyle characterized by upright letters having serifs and vertical lines thicker than horizontal lines. **—Roman** *n.* **1.** *Abbr.* **Rom.** A native, inhabitant, or citizen of ancient or modern Rome. **2.** *Abbr.* **Rom.** The Italian language as spoken in Rome. **3.** *Abbr.* **Rom.** One belonging to the Roman Catholic Church. **4. roman.** *Abbr.* **rom, rom.** Roman print or typestyle. **5. Romans** *(used with a sing. verb). Abbr.* **Rom., Rm.** *Bible.* See table at **Bible.** [Middle English, from Old English *Rōmān* or from Old French *romain,* both from Latin *Rōmānus,* from *Rōma,* Rome.]

ro•man à clef (rō-mäɴ′ ä klā′) *n., pl.* **ro•mans à clef** (rōmäɴ′ zä klā′). A novel in which actual persons, places, or events are depicted in fictional guise. [French : *roman,* novel + *à,* with + *clef,* key.]

Roman alphabet *n.* See **Latin alphabet.**

Roman calendar *n.* The lunar calendar used by the ancient Romans until the introduction of the Julian calendar in 46 B.C.

Roman candle *n.* A cylindrical firework that emits balls of fire and a shower of sparks.

Roman Catholic *adj. Abbr.* **RC** Of, relating to, or being the Roman Catholic Church. **—Roman Catholic** *n.* A member of the Roman Catholic Church.

Roman Catholic Church *n. Abbr.* **R.C.Ch.** The Christian church characterized by an episcopal hierarchy with the pope as its head and belief in seven sacraments and the authority of tradition.

Roman Catholicism *n.* The doctrines, practices, and organization of the Roman Catholic Church.

ro•mance (rō-măns′, rō′măns′) *n.* **1.a.** A love affair. **b.** Ardent emotional attachment or involvement between people, especially that characterized by a high level of purity and devotion; love: *They kept the romance alive in their marriage for 35 years.* **c.** A strong, sometimes short-lived attachment, fascination, or enthusiasm for something: *a childhood romance with the sea.* **2.** A mysterious or fascinating quality or appeal, as of something adventurous, heroic, or strangely beautiful: *"These fine old guns often have a romance clinging to them"* (Richard Jeffries). **3.a.** A long medieval narrative in prose or verse that tells of the adventures and heroic exploits of chivalric heroes: *an Arthurian romance.* **b.** A long, fictitious tale of heroes and extraordinary or mysterious events. **c.** The class of literature constituted by such tales. **4.a.** An artistic work, such as a novel, story, or film, that deals with sexual love, especially in an idealized form. **b.** The class or style of such works. **5.** A fictitiously embellished account or explanation: *We have been given speculation and romance instead of the facts.* **6.** *Music.* A lyrical, tender, usually sentimental song or short instrumental piece. **7. Romance.** The Romance languages. **—Romance** *adj. Abbr.* **Rom.** Of, relating to, or being any of the languages that developed from Latin, the principal ones being Italian, French, Portuguese, Romanian, and Spanish. Other such languages are Catalan, Provençal, Rhaeto-Romanic, Sardinian, and Ladino. **—romance** (rō-măns′) *v.* **-manced, -manc•ing, -manc•es.** *—intr.* **1.** To invent, write, or tell romances. **2.** To think or behave in a romantic manner. *—tr. Informal.* **1.** To make love to; court or woo. **2.** To have a love affair with. [Middle English, from Old French *romans,* romance, work written in French, from Vulgar Latin **rōmānicē (scrībere),* (to write) in the vernacular, from Latin *Rōmānicus,* Roman, from *Rōmānus.* See ROMAN.] **—ro•manc′er** *n.*

Roman congregation *n. Roman Catholic Church.* Any department of the Curia dealing with rites, legal and administrative problems, questions of faith and morals, and other ecclesiastical matters.

Roman Empire. Also called **Rome** (rōm). An empire that succeeded the Roman Republic during the time of Augustus, who ruled from 27 B.C. to A.D. 14. At its greatest extent it encompassed territories stretching from Britain and Germany to North Africa and the Persian Gulf. After 395 it was split into the Byzantine Empire and the Western Roman Empire, which rapidly sank into anarchy under the onslaught of barbarian invaders from the north and east. The last emperor of the West, Romulus Augustulus (born c. 461), was deposed by Goths in 476, the traditional date for the end of the empire.

Ro•man•esque (rō′mə-nĕsk′) *adj.* **1.** Of, relating to, or being a style of European architecture containing both Roman and Byzantine elements, prevalent especially in the 11th and 12th centuries and characterized by thick walls, barrel vaults, and relatively unrefined ornamentation. **2.** Of, relating to, or being corresponding styles in painting and sculpture. **—Romanesque** *n.* A Romanesque style of architecture, painting, or sculpture.

ro•man-fleuve (rō-mäɴ′flœv′) *n., pl.* **ro•mans-fleuves** (rō-mäɴ′flœv′). A long novel, often in many volumes, chronicling the history of several generations of a family, community, or other group and often presenting an overall view of society during a particular epoch. Also called *saga novel.* [French : *roman,* novel + *fleuve,* river.]

Roman holiday *n.* **1.** Enjoyment or satisfaction derived from observing the suffering of others. **2.** A violent public spectacle or disturbance in which shame, degradation, or physical harm is intentionally inflicted on one person or group by another. [From the bloody gladiatorial contests staged as entertainment for the ancient Romans.]

Ro•ma•ni•a (rō-mā′nē-ə, -mān′yə) or **Ru•ma•ni•a** (ro͞o-). *Abbr.* **Rom.** A country of southeast Europe with a short coastline on the Black Sea. Originally a Roman province, the area was united in 1861 and became independent in 1878. Bucharest is the capital and the largest city. Population, 22,533,074.

Ro•ma•ni•an (rō-mā′nē-ən, -mān′yən) also **Ru•ma•ni•an** (ro͞o-) *—adj. Abbr.* **Rom.** Of or relating to Romania or its people, language, or culture. *—n. Abbr.* **Rom. 1.** A native or inhabitant of Romania. **2.** The Romance language of the Romanians.

Ro•man•ic (rō-măn′ĭk) *adj.* **1.** Of or derived from the ancient Romans. **2.** Of or relating to the Romance languages. **—Ro•man′ic** *n.*

Ro•man•ism (rō′mə-nĭz′əm) *n. Offensive.* Roman Catholicism.

Ro•man•ist (rō′mə-nĭst) *n.* **1.** *Offensive.* One who professes Roman Catholicism. **2.** A student of or authority on ancient Roman law, culture, and institutions.

Ro•man•ize (rō′mə-nīz′) *tr.v.* **-ized, -iz•ing, -iz•es. 1.** To convert (a person) to Roman Catholicism. **2.** To make Roman in character, allegiance, or style. **3.** Often **romanize.** To write or transliterate in the Latin alphabet. **—Ro′man•i•za′tion** (-mə-nĭ-zā′shən) *n.*

Roman law *n.* The legal system of ancient Rome which serves as the basis for modern civil law.

Roman nose *n.* A nose with a high, prominent bridge.

Roman numeral *n.* Any of the numerals formed with the characters I, V, X, L, C, D, and M in the ancient system of numeration.

Ro•ma•no (rə-mä′nō, rō-) *n.* A hard, sharp, dry cheese of Italian origin that is made from cow's milk and usually served grated as a garnish. [Italian, short for *(pecorino) romano,* Roman (sheep's milk cheese), from Latin *Rōmānus.*]

Ro•ma•nov also **Ro•ma•noff** (rō′mə-nôf′, rō-mä′nəf, rə-). Russian ruling dynasty (1613–1917) that began with the accession of Czar Michael (1596–1645; ruled 1613–1645) and ended with the abdication of Nicholas II during the Russian Revolution.

Ro•mansch also **Ro•mansh** (rō-mänsh′, -mănsh′) *n.* The Rhaeto-Romance dialect that is an official language of Switzerland. Also called *Ladin.* [Romansch *Romonsch,* from Latin *Rōmānicus,* Roman. See ROMANCE.]

ro•man•tic (rō-măn′tĭk) *adj.* **1.** Of, relating to, or characteristic of romance. **2.** Given to thoughts or feelings of romance. See Synonyms at **sentimental. 3.** Displaying, expressive of, or conducive to love: *a romantic atmosphere.* **4.** Imaginative but impractical; visionary: *romantic notions.* **5.** Not based on fact; imaginary or fictitious: *His memoirs were criticized as offering a fascinating but thoroughly romantic view of the past.* **6.** Often **Romantic.** Of or characteristic of romanticism in the arts. **—romantic** *n.* **1.** A romantic person. **2.** Often **Romantic.** A follower or adherent of romanticism. [French *romantique,* from obsolete *romant,* romance, from Old French *romans, romant-,* romance. See ROMANCE.] **—ro•man′ti•cal•ly** *adv.*

ro•man•ti•cism (rō-măn′tĭ-sĭz′əm) *n.* **1.** Often **Romanticism.** An artistic and intellectual movement originating in Europe in the late 18th century and characterized by a heightened interest in nature, emphasis on the individual's expression of emotion and imagination, departure from the attitudes and forms of classicism, and rebellion against established social rules and conventions. **2.** Romantic quality or spirit in thought, expression, or action. **—ro•man′ti•cist** *n.*

ro•man•ti•cize (rō-măn′tĭ-sīz′) *v.* **-cized, -ciz•ing, -ciz•es.** *—tr.* To view or interpret romantically; make romantic. *—intr.* To think in a romantic way. **—ro•man′ti•ci•za′tion** (-sĭ-zā′shən) *n.*

Rom•a•ny (rŏm′ə-nē, rō′mə-) *n., pl.* **-nies. 1.** A Gypsy. **2.** The Indic language of the Gypsies. Also called *Gypsy.* **—Romany** *adj.* Of or relating to the Gypsies or their language or culture. [Romany *romani,* feminine of *romano,* gypsy, from *rom,* man, from Prakrit *ḍoma,* man of a low caste, of Dravidian origin.]

ro•maunt (rō-mônt′, -mŏnt′) *n. Archaic.* A verse romance. [Middle English, from Old French *romans, romant-,* romance. See ROMANCE.]

Rom•bau•er (rŏm′bou′ər), **Irma von Starkloff.** 1877–1962. American cookery expert who wrote *The Joy of Cooking* (1931) and several of its revisions.

Rom•berg (rŏm′bərg), **Sigmund.** 1887–1951. Hungarian-born American composer of operettas, including *Blossom Time* (1921) and *The Student Prince* (1924).

Rom•blon Islands (rŏm-blōn′). An island group of the central Philippines in the Sibuyan Sea. Part of the Visayan Islands,

Romanesque
Campanile of the Duomo, Florence, Italy

Romania

romanticism
Detail of *Liberty Leading the People,* 1830, by Eugène Delacroix

ă **pat**	oi **boy**
ā **pay**	ou **out**
âr **care**	o͝o **took**
ä **father**	o͞o **boot**
ĕ **pet**	ŭ **cut**
ē **be**	ûr **urge**
ĭ **pit**	th **thin**
ī **pie**	*th* **this**
îr **pier**	hw **which**
ŏ **pot**	zh **vision**
ō **toe**	ə **about, item**
ô **paw**	♦ **regionalism**

Stress marks: ′ (primary); ′ (secondary), as in **dictionary** (dĭk′shə-nĕr′ē)

the group comprises 3 large islands, including **Romblon Island,** and about 30 smaller islands. They were visited by the Spanish at least as early as 1582.

Rome (rōm). **1.** The capital and largest city of Italy, in the west-central part of the country on the Tiber River. Traditionally founded by Romulus and Remus, it was ruled first by Etruscans, who were overthrown c. 500 B.C. The Roman Republic gradually extended its territory and expanded its influence, giving way to the Roman Empire during the reign of Augustus (27 B.C.–A.D. 14). As capital of the empire, Rome was considered the center of the known world, but the city declined when Constantine transferred his capital to Byzantium (323). Alaric I conquered the city in 410, leading to a lengthy period of devastation by barbarian tribes. In the Middle Ages the city revived as the spiritual and temporal power of the papacy increased. During the 1800's Rome was held at various times by the French until it became the capital of Italy in 1871. Vatican City remains an independent enclave within the confines of Rome. Population, 2,830,569. **2.** A city of northwest Georgia northwest of Atlanta. It was established in 1834 on the site of a Cherokee settlement. Population, 29,654. **3.** A city of central New York on the Mohawk River west-northwest Utica. Because of its location as a portage point, the city was strategically important during the French and Indian Wars and the American Revolution. Population, 43,826. **4.** See **Roman Empire.**

rook²
Chess piece

Ro·me·o (rō′mē-ō′) *n., pl.* **-os.** A man who is devoted to lovemaking or the pursuit of love. [After *Romeo,* the hero of Shakespeare's *Romeo and Juliet.*]

Rom·ish (rō′mĭsh) *adj. Offensive.* Of or relating to the Roman Catholic Church. **—Rom′ish·ly** *adv.* **—Rom′ish·ness** *n.*

Rom·mel (rŏm′əl), **Erwin.** Known as "the Desert Fox." 1891–1944. German general active in France, Italy, and northern Africa during World War II. After his implication in the July Plot (1944) to assassinate Hitler, he committed suicide.

Rom·ney (rŏm′nē), **George.** 1734–1802. British painter of portraits and historical scenes, such as *Death of General Wolfe* (1763).

romp (rŏmp) *intr.v.* **romped, romp·ing, romps. 1.** To play or frolic boisterously. **2.** To run or advance in a rapid or easy manner. **3.** *Slang.* To win a race or game easily. **—romp** *n.* **1.a.** Lively, merry play; frolic. **b.** Lively or frolicsome play that encompasses lovemaking. **2.** One, especially a girl, that sports and frolics. **3.** A rapid or easy pace. **4.** *Slang.* An easy win. [Alteration of RAMP².]

Edith Roosevelt

romp·er (rŏm′pər) *n.* **1.** One that romps. **2. rompers.** A loosely fitted, one-piece garment having short bloomers that is worn especially by small children for play.

Ro·mu·lo (rŏm′yo͞o-lō′, rô′mo͞o-lô′), **Carlos Pena.** 1899–1985. Philippine journalist and diplomat who supported the Allies during the Japanese invasion and occupation of the Philippines (1941–1945) and was later president of the United Nations General Assembly (1949–1950).

Rom·u·lus¹ (rŏm′yə-ləs) *n. Roman Mythology.* The son of Mars and eponymous founder of Rome who, with his twin brother, Remus, was reared and suckled by a wolf.

Rom·u·lus² (rŏm′yə-ləs). A city of southeast Michigan, a suburb of Detroit. Population, 24,857.

Ron·ces·valles (rŏn′sə-vălz′, rôn′thĕs-väl′yĕs). A mountain pass, 1,057.7 m (3,468 ft) high, through the western Pyrenees in northern Spain. It is the traditional site of the death of the hero Roland during the defeat of Charlemagne's army by the Saracens (778).

ron·deau (rŏn′dō, rŏn-dō′) *n., pl.* **-deaux** (-dōz, -dōz′). **1.** A lyrical poem of French origin having 13 or sometimes 10 lines with two rhymes throughout and with the opening phrase repeated twice as a refrain. **2.** *Music.* A medieval French song, either monophonic, as in the songs of the trouvères, or polyphonic. [French, alteration of Old French *rondel.* See RONDEL.]

ron·del (rŏn′dəl, rŏn-dĕl′) *n.* **1.** A poem similar to a rondeau, having 13 or 14 lines with two rhymes throughout. The first and second lines reappear in the middle and at the end, although sometimes only the first line appears at the end. **2.** Often **ron·delle** (rŏn-dĕl′). A rounded or circular object. [Middle English, from Old French, diminutive of *ronde,* circle, round. See ROUND¹.]

ron·de·let (rŏn′dl-ĕt′, -dl-ā′) *n.* A poem similar to a rondeau, usually having seven lines and always two rhymes, with the first line containing four syllables repeated as lines three and seven and the other lines containing eight syllables. [French, from Old French, diminutive of *rondel,* rondel. See RONDEL.]

Eleanor Roosevelt
Photographed in 1949 by Clara E. Sipprell (1885–1975)

ron·delle (rŏn-dĕl′) *n.* Variant of **rondel** (sense 2).

ron·do (rŏn′dō, rŏn-dō′) *n., pl.* **-dos.** *Music.* A composition having a principal theme that occurs at least three times in its original key between contrasting subordinate themes. [Italian *rondò,* from French *rondeau,* rondeau. See RONDEAU.]

ron·dure (rŏn′jər, -dyo͝or′) *n.* A circular or gracefully rounded object. [French *rondeur,* roundness, from Old French, from *ronde,* round. See ROUND¹.]

Ron·kon·ko·ma (rŏng-kŏng′kə-mə, rŏn-kŏn′-). A town of southeast New York on central Long Island. It is mainly residential. Population, 20,200.

Ron·ne Ice Shelf (rō′nə, rŏn′ə). An area of shelf ice in western Antarctica south of the Weddell Sea.

ron·nel (rŏn′əl) *n.* A solid, light brown compound, $C_8H_8Cl_3O_3PS$, used as an insecticide, especially against flies and cockroaches. [From *Ronnel,* a non-U.S. trademark.]

Ron·sard (rôN-sär′), **Pierre de.** 1524–1585. French poet whose lyrical love poems, including *Sonnets pour Hélène* (1578), are considered his best works.

rönt·gen (rĕnt′gən, -jən, rŭnt′-) *n.* Variant of **roentgen.**

Rönt·gen (rœnt′gən), **Wilhelm Konrad.** See Wilhelm Konrad **Roentgen.**

rood (ro͞od) *n.* **1.a.** A crucifix symbolizing the cross on which Jesus was crucified. **b.** A large crucifix or the representation of one over the altar screen of a medieval church. **2.** *Abbr.* **ro.** *Chiefly British.* A measure of length that varies from 5½ to 8 yards (5.0 to 7.3 meters). **3.** *Abbr.* **ro.** A measure of land equal to ¼ acre, or 40 square rods (0.10 hectare). [Middle English, from Old English *rōd.*]

rood screen *n.* An ornamented altar screen surmounted by a crucifix that separates the choir of a church from the nave.

roof (ro͞of, ro͝of) *n.* **1.a.** The exterior surface and its supporting structures on the top of a building. **b.** The upper exterior surface of a dwelling as a symbol of the home itself: *three generations living under one roof.* **2.** The top covering of something: *the roof of a car.* **3.** The upper surface of an anatomical structure, especially one having a vaulted inner structure: *the roof of the mouth.* **4.** The highest point or limit; the summit or ceiling: *A roof on prices is needed to keep our customers happy.* **—roof** *tr.v.* **roofed, roof·ing, roofs.** To furnish or cover with or as if with a roof. **—*idioms.* go through the roof.** *Slang.* **1.** To grow, intensify, or rise to an enormous, often unexpected degree: *Operating costs went through the roof last year.* **2.** To become extremely angry: *When I told her about breaking the window, she went through the roof.* **raise the roof.** *Slang.* **1.** To be extremely noisy and boisterous: *The participants plan to dance, drink, and generally raise the roof at tonight's party.* **2.** To complain loudly and bitterly: *Angry tenants finally raised the roof about their noisy neighbors.* [Middle English, from Old English *hrōf.*]

roof·er (ro͞o′fər, ro͝of′ər) *n.* One who lays or repairs roofs.

roof garden *n.* **1.** A garden on the roof of a building, especially one found in an urban setting. **2.** The roof or top floor of a building designed for use by the public that often contains outdoor seating or dining facilities.

roof·ing (ro͞o′fĭng, ro͝of′ĭng) *n.* **1.** Materials used in building a roof. **2.** A roof.

roof·less (ro͞of′lĭs, ro͝of′-) *adj.* **1.** Lacking a roof. **2.** Having no home or shelter; homeless or destitute.

roof·line (ro͞of′līn′, ro͝of′-) *n.* The profile of or silhouette made by a roof or series of roofs.

roof·top (ro͞of′tŏp′, ro͝of′-) *n.* The outer surface of a roof. *—attributive.* Often used to modify another noun: *rooftop gardens; rooftop tiles.*

roof·tree (ro͞of′trē′, ro͝of′-) *n.* **1.** The ridgepole of a roof. **2.** A roof.

rook¹ (ro͝ok) *n.* **1.** An Old World bird *(Corvus frugilegus)* that resembles the North American crow and nests in colonies near the tops of trees. **2.** A swindler or cheat, especially at games. **—rook** *tr.v.* **rooked, rook·ing, rooks.** To swindle; cheat: *Customers are afraid of being rooked by unscrupulous vendors.* [Middle English *rok,* from Old English *hrōc.*]

rook² (ro͝ok) *n. Abbr.* **R** *Games.* A chess piece that may move in a straight line over any number of empty squares in a rank or file. Also called *castle.* [Middle English *rok,* from Old French *roc,* from Arabic *ruḫḫ,* from Persian.]

rook·er·y (ro͝ok′ə-rē) *n., pl.* **-ies. 1.a.** A place where rooks nest or breed. **b.** A colony of rooks. **2.** The breeding ground of certain other birds or animals, such as penguins and seals. **3.** A crowded and dilapidated tenement.

rook·ie (ro͝ok′ē) *n.* **1.** *Slang.* **a.** An untrained or inexperienced recruit, as in the army or police. **b.** An inexperienced person; a novice. **2.** *Sports.* A first-year player, especially in a professional sport. [Perhaps alteration of RECRUIT.]

rook·y (ro͝ok′ē) *adj.* Of, characteristic of, or abounding in rooks.

room (ro͞om, ro͝om) *n. Abbr.* **rm. 1.** A space that is or may be occupied: *That easy chair takes up too much room.* **2.a.** An area separated by walls or partitions from other similar parts of the structure or building in which it is located: *the first room on the left; an unpainted room.* **b.** The people present in such an area: *The whole room laughed.* **3. rooms.** Living quarters; lodgings. **4.** Suitable opportunity; occasion. **—room** *intr.v.* **roomed, room·ing, rooms.** To occupy a room; lodge. [Middle English *roum,* from Old English *rūm.* See **reuə-** in Appendix.]

SYNONYMS: *room, elbowroom, latitude, leeway, margin, play, scope.* The central meaning shared by these nouns is "adequate space or opportunity for freedom of movement or action": *room for improvement; needed elbowroom to negotiate effectively; no latitude allowed in conduct or speech; allowed the chef leeway in choosing the menu; no margin for error; imagination given full play; permitting their talents free scope.*

room and board *n.* Lodging and meals earned, purchased for a set fee, or otherwise provided.

room·er (ro͞o′mər, ro͝om′ər) *n.* One who rents a room or rooms in which to live; a lodger.

room·ette (ro͞o-mĕt′, ro͝om-ĕt′) *n.* A small private compartment in a railroad sleeping car.

room·ful (ro͞om′fo͝ol′, ro͝om′-) *n., pl.* **-fuls. 1.a.** The amount that a room can hold: *a roomful of furniture.* **b.** The number of people that a room can hold: *a roomful of guests.* **2.** The number of people in a room, considered as a group: *The whole roomful gasped when he entered, wearing a bizarre costume.*

room·ing house (ro͞o′mĭng, ro͝om′ĭng) *n.* A house where lodgers may rent rooms.

room·mate (ro͞om′māt′, ro͝om′-) *n.* A person with whom one shares a room or rooms.

room temperature *n. Abbr.* **RT.** An indoor temperature of from 20 to 25°C (68 to 77°F).

room·y (ro͞o′mē, ro͝om′ē) *adj.* **-i·er, -i·est.** Having plenty of room; spacious. See Synonyms at **spacious. —room′i·ly** *adv.* **—room′i·ness** *n.*

roor·back (ro͝or′băk′) *n.* A false or slanderous story used for political advantage. [After Baron von *Roorback*, imaginary author of *Roorback's Tour Through the Western and Southern States*, from which a passage was purportedly quoted in an attempt to disparage presidential candidate James K. Polk in 1844.]

Roo·se·velt (rō′zə-vĕlt′, rōz′vĕlt′, -vəlt, ro͞o′-). An unincorporated community of southeast New York on western Long Island southeast of Hempstead. It is primarily residential. Population, 15,000.

Roosevelt, (Anna) Eleanor. 1884–1962. American diplomat, writer, and First Lady of the United States (1933–1945) as the wife of President Franklin D. Roosevelt. A delegate to the United Nations (1945–1952 and 1961–1962), she was an outspoken advocate of human rights. Her written works include *This I Remember* (1949).

Roosevelt, Edith Carow. 1861–1948. First Lady of the United States (1901–1909) as the wife of President Theodore Roosevelt. Known as a shrewd manager of the White House, she oversaw a major renovation (1902) and delegated many of the responsibilities traditionally belonging to the First Lady.

Roosevelt, Franklin Delano. 1882–1945. The 32nd President of the United States (1933–1945). Governor of New York (1929–1932), he ran for President with the promise of a New Deal for the American people. His administration was marked by relief programs, measures to increase employment and assist industrial and agricultural recovery from the Depression, and World War II. He was the only U.S. President to be reelected three times (1936, 1940, and 1944). He died in office.

Roosevelt, Rio. A river, about 644 km (400 mi) long, of northwestern Brazil. Originally known as the River of Doubt, it was renamed in honor of Theodore Roosevelt, who explored it in 1913.

Roosevelt, Theodore. 1858–1919. The 26th President of the United States (1901–1909). A hero of the Spanish-American War, he served as governor of New York (1899–1900) and U.S. Vice President (1901) under William McKinley. On McKinley's assassination (September 1901), he assumed the presidency. Roosevelt's administration was marked by the regulation of trusts, the building of the Panama Canal, and a foreign policy based on the motto "Speak softly and carry a big stick." He won the 1906 Nobel Peace Prize for his mediation in the Russo-Japanese War.

Roosevelt Island. 1. Formerly **Wel·fare Island** (wĕl′fâr′) An island in the East River off the coast of central Manhattan Island. It has long been the site of a municipal hospital and penal institution but is also being developed as a residential area. **2.** An island of Antartica in the eastern part of the Ross Ice Shelf. Robert E. Byrd discovered the ice-covered island in 1934.

roost (ro͞ost) *n.* **1.** A perch on which domestic fowl or other birds rest or sleep. **2.** A place with perches for fowl or other birds. **3.** A place for temporary rest or sleep. **—roost** *intr.v.* **roost·ed, roost·ing, roosts.** To rest or sleep on or as if on a perch or roost. **—*idioms.* come home to roost.** To have repercussions or aftereffects, especially unfavorable ones: *The consequences of her misdeeds eventually came home to roost.* **rule the roost.** *Informal.* To be in charge; dominate: *In this house grandfather rules the roost.* [Middle English *rooste*, from Old English *hrōst.*]

roost·er (ro͞o′stər) *n.* **1.a.** An adult male chicken. **b.** An adult male of other birds. **2.** A person regarded as cocky or pugnacious.

roost·er·fish (ro͞o′stər-fĭsh′) *n., pl.* **roosterfish** or **-fish·es.** A brightly colored food and game fish *(nematistius pectoralis)* found from the Gulf of California to Panama.

root¹ (ro͞ot, ro͝ot) *n.* **1.** The usually underground portion of a plant that lacks buds, leaves, or nodes and serves as support, draws minerals and water from the surrounding soil, and sometimes stores food. **2.** Any of various other underground plant parts, especially an underground stem such as a rhizome, corm, or tuber. **3.a.** The embedded part of an organ or structure such as a hair, tooth, or nerve, that serves as a base or support. **b.** A base or support: *We snipped the wires at the roots.* **4.** An essential part or element; the basic core: *I finally got to the root of the problem.* **5.** A primary source; an origin. See Synonyms at **origin. 6.** A progenitor or an ancestor from which a person or family is descended. **7.a.** Often **roots.** The condition of being settled and of belonging to a particular place or society: *Our roots in this town go back a long way.* **b. roots.** The state of having or establishing an indigenous relationship with or a personal affinity for a particular culture, society, or environment: *music with unmistakable African roots.* **8.** *Linguistics.* **a.** The element that carries the main component of meaning in a word and provides the basis from which a word is derived by adding affixes or inflectional endings or by phonetic change. **b.** Such an element reconstructed for a protolanguage. Also called *radical.* **9.** *Mathematics.* **a.** A number that when multiplied by itself an indicated number of times forms a product equal to a specified number. For example, a fourth root of 4 is $\sqrt{2}$. Also called *nth root.* **b.** A number that reduces a polynomial equation in one variable to an identity when it is substituted for the variable. **10.** *Music.* **a.** The note from which a chord is built. **b.** A triad or other chord that has such a note lowermost. **—root** *v.* **root·ed, root·ing, roots.** —*intr.* **1.** To grow roots or a root. **2.** To become firmly established, settled, or entrenched. **3.** To come into existence; originate. —*tr.* **1.** To cause to put out roots and grow. **2.** To implant by or as if by the roots. **3.** To furnish a primary source or origin to. **4.** To remove by or as if by the roots. Often used with *up* or *out*: *"declared that waste and fraud will be vigorously rooted out of Government"* (New York Times). **—*idiom.* root and branch.** Utterly; completely: *The organization has been transformed root and branch by its new leaders.* [Middle English *rot,* from Old English *rōt,* from Old Norse. See **wrād-** in Appendix.] **—root′er** *n.*

Franklin D. Roosevelt

root² (ro͞ot, ro͝ot) *v.* **root·ed, root·ing, roots.** —*tr.* To dig with or as if with the snout or nose. —*intr.* **1.** To dig in the earth with or as if with the snout or nose. **2.** To rummage for something. [Middle English *wroten,* from Old English *wrōtan.*] **—root′er** *n.*

Theodore Roosevelt

root³ (ro͞ot, ro͝ot) *intr.v.* **root·ed, root·ing, roots. 1.** To give audible encouragement or applause to a contestant or team; cheer. See Synonyms at **applaud. 2.** To lend support to someone or something. [Possibly alteration of ROUT³.] **—root′er** *n.*

Root (ro͞ot), **Elihu.** 1845–1937. American lawyer and public official who served as U.S. secretary of war (1899–1904), secretary of state (1905–1909), and senator from New York (1909–1915). He won the 1912 Nobel Peace Prize.

Root, John Wellborn. 1850–1891. American architect whose designs include the Monadnock Building (1889–1891) in Chicago, which employed steel framing instead of traditional solid-wall construction.

root·age (ro͞o′tĭj, ro͝ot′ĭj) *n.* **1.** A system or growth of roots. **2.** Establishment by or as if by roots.

root beer *n.* A carbonated soft drink made from extracts of certain plant roots and herbs.

root canal *n.* **1.** A pulp-filled channel in a root of a tooth. **2.** A treatment in which diseased tissue from this part of the tooth is removed and the resulting cavity is filled with an inert material.

root cap *n. Botany.* A thimble-shaped mass of cells that covers and protects the root tip.

root cellar *n.* An underground pit or cellar, usually covered with earth, used for the storage of root crops and other vegetables.

root climber *n.* A vine, such as the ivy, that clings to its support by means of adventitious roots.

root crop *n.* A crop, as of turnips or yams, grown for its edible roots.

root·ed·ness (ro͞o′tĭd-nĭs, ro͝ot′ĭd-) *n.* The quality or state of having roots, especially of being firmly established, settled, or entrenched: *"stories that give . . . a sense of rootedness and place"* (Pat Conroy).

rooster

root hair *n. Botany.* A thin, hairlike outgrowth of an epidermal cell of a plant root that absorbs water and minerals from the soil.

root·hold (ro͞ot′hōld′, ro͝ot′-) *n.* Support or stabilization of a plant in the soil through the spreading of its roots.

root knot *n.* A disease of plants characterized by protuberant enlargements on the roots caused by a nematode.

root·less (ro͞ot′lĭs, ro͝ot′-) *adj.* **1.** Having no roots. **2.** Not belonging to a particular place or society: *rootless refugees in a strange country.* **—root′less·ness** *n.*

root·let (ro͞ot′lĭt, ro͝ot′-) *n.* A small root or division of a root.

root mean square *n. Abbr.* **rms** *Statistics.* The square root of the average of the squares of a set of numbers.

root pressure *n.* Pressure exerted in the roots of plants as the result of osmosis, causing exudation from cut stems and guttation of water from leaves.

root·stalk (ro͞ot′stôk′, ro͝ot′-) *n.* See **rhizome.**

root·stock (ro͞ot′stŏk′, ro͝ot′-) *n.* **1.** See **rhizome. 2.** A root or part of a root used as a stock for plant propagation. **3.** A source or origin.

root system *n.* All the roots of a plant.

root·worm (ro͞ot′wûrm′, ro͝ot′-) *n.* Any of several beetles of the genus *Diabrotica*, the larvae of which feed on the roots of various crop plants, especially corn.

root·y (ro͞o′tē, ro͝ot′ē) *adj.* **-i·er, -i·est. 1.** Full or consisting of roots: *a rooty patch of soil.* **2.** Suggestive of or resembling roots. **—root′i·ness** *n.*

rope (rōp) *n.* **1.** A flexible, heavy cord of tightly intertwined hemp or other fiber. **2.** A string of items attached in one line by or as if by twisting or braiding: *a rope of onions.* **3.** A sticky glutinous formation of stringy matter in a liquid. **4.a.** A cord with a noose at one end for hanging a person. **b.** Execution or death by hanging: *to die by the rope.* **5.** A lasso or lariat. **6. ropes.** *Sports.* Several cords strung between poles to enclose a

ă pat	oi boy
ā pay	ou out
âr care	o͝o took
ä father	o͞o boot
ĕ pet	ŭ cut
ē be	ûr urge
ĭ pit	th thin
ī pie	*th* this
îr pier	hw which
ŏ pot	zh vision
ō toe	ə about, item
ô paw	♦ regionalism

Stress marks: **′** (primary); ′ (secondary), as in **dictionary** (dĭk′shə-nĕr′ē)

boxing or wrestling ring. **7. ropes.** *Informal.* Specialized procedures or details: *learn the ropes; know the ropes.* **—rope** *v.* **roped, rop·ing, ropes.** *—tr.* **1.** To tie or fasten with or as if with rope. **2.** To enclose, separate, or partition with or as if with a rope: *rope off the scene of the crime.* **3.** To catch with a rope or lasso. **4.** *Informal.* To trick or deceive: *An unscrupulous salesperson roped us into buying worthless property.* *—intr.* To become like a cord or rope. **—*idioms.* on the ropes. 1.** *Sports.* Knocked against the ropes that enclose a boxing ring. **2.** On the verge of defeat or collapse; hopeless or powerless. **the end of (one's) rope.** The limit of one's patience, endurance, or resources: *After six months on strike, the workers were at the end of their rope.* [Middle English, from Old English *rāp.*] **—rop′er** *n.*

rorqual
Piked whale
Balaenoptera acutorostrata

rope tow *n.* A continuous rope conveyor used to pull skiers up a slope; a ski tow.

rope·walk (rōp′wôk′) *n.* **1.** A long alley or covered pathway where strands of material, such as hemp fiber, are laid and twisted into rope. **2.** A long narrow building containing such a pathway.

rop·y also **rop·ey** (rō′pē) *adj.* **-i·er, -i·est. 1.** Resembling a rope or ropes. **2.** Forming sticky glutinous strings or threads, as some liquids. **—rop′i·ly** *adv.* **—rop′i·ness** *n.*

roque (rōk) *n. Sports.* A variation of croquet played with short-handled mallets on a hard court that is bounded by a concrete wall against which a ball may rebound and be retrieved. [Alteration of ROQUET.]

rosary

Roque·fort (rōk′fərt). A trademark used for a cheese that is made from ewes' milk and ripened in caves.

ro·que·laure (rō′kə-lôr′, -lōr′, rŏk′ə-) *n.* A knee-length cloak lined with brightly colored silk and often trimmed with fur that was worn by European men in the 18th century. [After Antoine Gaston Jean Baptiste, Duc de *Roquelaure* (1656–1738), French marshal.]

ro·quet (rō-kā′) *tr.v.* **-queted** (-kād′), **-quet·ing** (-kā′ĭng), **-quets** (-kāz′). *Sports.* To hit (another player's ball) in croquet. [Alteration of CROQUET.]

ro·quette (rō-kĕt′) *n. Botany.* See **rocket²** (sense 1).

Ro·rem (rôr′əm, rōr′-), **Ned.** Born 1923. American composer whose works include art songs, such as the cycle *War Scenes* (1969), and symphonies, including *Air Music* (1976).

ror·qual (rôr′kwəl) *n.* Any of several baleen whales of the family Balaenopteridae having longitudinal grooves on the throat and a small, pointed dorsal fin. Also called *razorback.* [French, from Norwegian *rørhval,* from Old Norse *reydharhvalr* : *reydhr,* rorqual (from *raudhr,* red; see **reudh-** in Appendix) + *hvalr,* whale.]

Ror·schach test (rôr′shäk′, -shäĸʜ′) *n. Psychology.* A projective test in which a subject's interpretations of ten standard inkblots are analyzed as a measure of emotional and intellectual functioning and integration. [After Hermann *Rorschach* (1884–1922), Swiss psychiatrist.]

Ro·sa (rō′zə, rô′zä), **Monte.** A mountain, 4,636.9 m (15,203 ft) high, in the Pennine Alps on the Swiss-Italian border. It is the highest elevation in the range.

rose¹
Compass card

ro·sa·ce·a (rō-zā′shē-ə) *n.* A chronic dermatitis of the face, especially of the nose and cheeks, characterized by a red or rosy coloration, caused by dilation of capillaries, and the appearance of acnelike pimples. Also called *acne rosacea.* [New Latin *(acne) rosācea,* rose-colored (acne), from Latin, feminine of *rosāceus,* made of roses. See ROSACEOUS.]

ro·sa·ceous (rō-zā′shəs) *adj.* **1.** *Botany.* Of or belonging to the rose family. **2.** Resembling the flower of a rose. [From Latin *rosāceus,* made of roses, from *rosa,* rose.]

ros·an·i·line also **ros·an·i·lin** (rō-zăn′ə-lĭn) *n.* A brownish-red crystalline organic compound, $C_{20}H_{21}N_3O$, derived from aniline and used in the manufacture of dyes and in Schiff's reagent. [ROS(E)¹ + ANILINE.]

ro·sar·i·an (rō-zâr′ē-ən) *n.* A person with expertise or a special interest in the cultivation of roses.

Ro·sa·ri·o (rō-zär′ē-ō′, -sär′-). A city of east-central Argentina on the Paraná River northwest of Buenos Aires. It grew rapidly as a port after 1870 with the development of the surrounding region. Population, 938,120.

Ro·sar·i·o Strait (rō-zâr′ē-ō). A strait in the San Juan Islands of northwest Washington connecting Admiralty Inlet with the Strait of Georgia.

rosemary
Rosmarinus officinalis

ro·sa·ry (rō′zə-rē) *n., pl.* **-ries. 1.** *Roman Catholic Church.* **a.** A form of devotion to the Virgin Mary, chiefly consisting of three sets of five decades each of the Hail Mary, each decade preceded by the Lord's Prayer and ending with a doxology. **b.** One of these sets of decades. **c.** A string of beads of 5 or 15 decades on which these prayers are counted. **2.** Similar beads used by other religious groups. [Middle English, rose garden, from Medieval Latin *rosārium,* rose garden, rosary, from Latin, rose garden, from neuter of *rosārius,* of roses, from *rosa,* rose.]

rosary pea *n.* A tropical woody vine *(Abrus precatorius)* widely naturalized in Florida, having scarlet and black poisonous seeds used as beads. Also called *crab's eye, Indian licorice.*

Ro·sas (rō′säs), **Juan Manuel de.** Duke of Caxias. 1793–1877. Argentine political leader who as governor of Buenos Aires (1829–1831 and 1835–1852) united the provinces of Argentina under a virtual dictatorship.

rose¹ (rōz) *n.* **1.** A member of the rose family. **2. a.** Any of numerous shrubs or vines of the genus *Rosa,* having prickly stems, pinnately compound leaves, and variously colored, often fragrant flowers. **b.** The flower of any of these plants. **c.** Any of various similar or related plants. **3.** *Color.* A dark pink to moderate red. **4.** An ornament, such as a decorative knot, resembling a rose in form; a rosette. **5.** A perforated nozzle for spraying water from a hose or sprinkling can. **6. a.** A form of gem cut marked by a flat base and a faceted, hemispheric upper surface. **b.** A gem, especially a diamond, cut in this manner. **7.** A rose window. **8.** A compass card or its representation, as on a map. **9. roses.** That which is marked by favor, success, or ease of execution: *Directing this play has been all roses since the new producer took over.* **—rose** *adj.* **1.** *Color.* Of the color rose. **2.** Relating to, containing, or used for roses. **3.** Scented or flavored with or as if with roses. **—*idioms.* come up roses.** To result favorably or successfully: *Those were difficult times but now everything's coming up roses.* **under the rose.** Sub rosa. [Middle English, from Old English, from Latin *rosa.*]

rose² (rōz) *v.* Past tense of **rise.**

Rose (rōz), **Billy.** 1899–1966. American impresario and songwriter who produced *Crazy Quilt* (1931) and other musical comedies and wrote several popular songs, including "Me and My Shadow."

ro·sé (rō-zā′) *n.* A light pink wine made from red grapes from which the skins are removed during fermentation as soon as the desired color has been attained. [French *(vin) rosé,* pink (wine), from Old French, from *rose,* rose. See ROSE¹.]

rose acacia *n.* A shrub *(Robinia hispida)* of the southeast United States, having bristly brittle branches and clusters of pale purple or rose flowers.

rose apple *n.* **1.** A southeast Asian evergreen tree *(Syzygium jambos)* widely cultivated for its showy flowers and fragrant, cream-yellow, ovoid fruits that are used for jellies and confections. **2.** The fruit of this plant.

ro·se·ate (rō′zē-ĭt, -āt′) *adj.* **1.** Rose-colored: *the roseate glow of dawn.* **2.** Cheerful or bright; optimistic: *a roseate outlook.* [From Latin *roseus,* rosy, from *rosa,* rose.] **—ro′se·ate·ly** *adv.*

roseate spoonbill *n.* A New World species of spoonbill *(Ajaia ajaja)* having rosy or pinkish plumage and, in the adult, a bare head.

Ro·seau (rō-zō′). The capital of Dominica, in the Windward Islands of the West Indies. It is a port on the southwest coast of the island. Population, 9,348.

rose·bay (rōz′bā′) *n.* **1.** Any of several shrubs of the genus *Rhododendron,* especially *R. maximum* of the southeast United States, having large glossy leaves and flowers with a rose-pink, bell-shaped corolla with green spots. Also called *great laurel.* **2.** See **oleander. 3.** *Chiefly British.* The willow herb.

rose beetle *n.* See **rose chafer.**

Rose·ber·y (rōz′bĕr′ē, -bə-rē), Fifth Earl of. Title of Archibald Philip Primrose. 1847–1929. British politician who served as prime minister (1894–1895) and supported imperialist policies.

rose-breast·ed grosbeak (rōz′brĕs′tĭd) *n.* A North American bird *(Pheucticus ludovicianus),* the male of which is black and white with a rose-red patch on the breast.

rose·bud (rōz′bŭd′) *n.* The bud of a rose.

rose bug *n.* See **rose chafer.**

Rose·burg (rōz′bûrg′). A city of southwest Oregon south-southwest of Eugene. Lumbering is its chief industry. Population, 16,644.

rose·bush (rōz′bo͝osh′) *n.* A flowering rose shrub.

rose campion *n.* A Eurasian plant *(Lychnis coronaria)* naturalized in northeast North America, having a dense cover of white, woolly down and rose-red flowers. Also called *mullein pink.*

rose chafer *n.* A long-legged gray North American beetle *(Macrodactylus subspinosus)* that causes damage to the roots, leaves, and blossoms of garden plants, especially roses. Also called *rose beetle, rose bug.*

rose cold *n.* See **rose fever.**

rose-col·ored (rōz′kŭl′ərd) *adj.* **1.** *Color.* Having the color rose. **2.** Cheerful or optimistic, especially to an excessive degree: *took a rose-colored view of the situation.* **—*idiom.* through rose-colored glasses.** With an unduly cheerful, optimistic, or favorable view of things: *see the world through rose-colored glasses.*

Rose·crans (rōz′krănz′), **William Starke.** 1819–1898. American Union general. After successful campaigns in West Virginia and Mississippi, he was defeated at Chickamauga, Georgia (1863), and relieved of his duties.

Rose·dale (rōz′dāl′). A community of north-central Maryland, a suburb of Baltimore. Population, 19,956.

rose family *n.* A large family of plants, the Rosaceae, characterized by showy flowers with five separated petals and numerous stamens borne on the margin of a cuplike structure, including important fruit plants such as the apple, cherry, peach, pear, plum, raspberry, and strawberry, as well as ornamentals such as the rose and spirea.

rose fever *n.* A spring or early summer hay fever. Also called *rose cold.*

rose·fish (rōz′fĭsh′) *n., pl.* **rosefish** or **-fish·es.** A bright red marine food fish *(Sebastes marinus)* of North Atlantic waters. Also called *ocean perch.*

rose geranium *n.* A woody plant *(Pelargonium graveolens)* having rose-pink flowers and fragrant, deeply palmately lobed leaves used for flavoring and in perfumery.

rose hip or **rose·hip** (rōz′hĭp′) *n.* The aggregate fruit of the rose plant, consisting of several dry fruitlets enclosed by the enlarged, fleshy, usually red, flavorful floral cup that is used for jelly or tea.

ro·selle (rō-zĕl′) *n.* A tropical African plant *(Hibiscus sabdariffa)* having flowers with yellow petals and a persistent, bright red calyx that has a pleasantly acid flavor and is used to make jelly and beverages. [Origin unknown.]

Ro·selle (rō-zĕl′). **1.** A city of northeast Illinois, a suburb of Chicago. Population, 16,948. **2.** A borough of northeast New Jersey, a residential suburb in the Newark-Elizabeth area. Thomas A. Edison had a laboratory here. Population, 20,641.

rose mallow *n.* A tall marsh plant *(Hibiscus moscheutos)* of eastern North America, having leaves covered with whitish down and flowers with white, pink, or rose petals with crimson bases.

rose·mar·y (rōz′mâr′ē) *n., pl.* **-ies.** An aromatic evergreen Mediterranean shrub *(Rosmarinus officinalis)* having light blue or pink flowers and grayish-green leaves that are used in cooking and perfumery. [Alteration of Middle English *rosmarine,* from Latin *rōs marīnus,* sea dew : *rōs,* dew + *marīnus,* of the sea; see MARINE.]

Rose·mead (rōz′mēd′). A city of southern California, a commercial and residential suburb of Los Angeles. Population, 42,604.

rose moss *n.* **1.** Any of the various mosses of the genus *Rhodobryum,* especially *R. roseum,* characterized by conspicuous terminal leaf rosettes. **2.** See **portulaca.**

Ro·sen·berg (rō′zən-bûrg′). A city of southeast Texas on the Brazos River west-southwest Houston. It was founded in 1883 with the coming of the railroad. Population, 17,995.

Ro·sen·berg (rō′zĭn-bûrg′, -bĕrg′, -bĕrk′), **Alfred.** 1893–1946. German political leader who expounded Nazi doctrine in *The Myth of the 20th Century* (1930). He was executed as a war criminal.

Ro·sen·berg (rō′zĭn-bûrg′), **Julius.** 1918–1953. American spy who with his wife, **Ethel** (1915–1953), was convicted of helping pass information concerning nuclear weaponry to the Soviets. Despite questions concerning the fairness of their trial and international pleas for clemency, the couple was executed.

rose of heaven *n.* A glabrous Mediterranean annual plant *(Lychnis coeli-rosa)* having opposite, linear, or lance-shaped leaves and large, rose-pink flowers.

rose of Jer·i·cho (jĕr′ĭ-kō′) *n.* Either of two desert plants, *Anastatica hierochuntica* of the mustard family, native to northern Africa and southwest Asia, or *Selaginella lepidophylla,* a fern ally distributed from Texas and Arizona south to El Salvador. Each plant forms a tight ball when dry and unfolds and grows under moist conditions. Also called *resurrection plant.*

rose of Shar·on (shăr′ən, shâr′-) *n.* **1.** A small eastern Asian tree or tall shrub *(Hibiscus syriacus)* having large reddish, purple, or white flowers and coarsely toothed leaves. Also called *althea.* **2.** A shrubby Eurasian evergreen plant *(Hypericum calycinum)* having oblong leaves and yellow flowers and usually grown as a ground cover. Also called *Aaron's beard.* [After the Plain of SHARON.]

ro·se·o·la (rō-zē′ə-lə, rō′zē-ō′lə) *n.* A rose-colored skin rash, sometimes occurring with diseases such as measles, syphilis, or scarlet fever. [New Latin, from diminutive of Latin *roseus,* rosy, from *rosa,* rose.] **—ro·se′o·lar** *adj.*

rose periwinkle *n.* See **Madagascar periwinkle.**

rose pink *n. Color.* A moderate to dark pink. **—rose′-pink′** (rōz′pĭngk′) *adj.*

rose quartz *n.* A pinkish variety of the mineral quartz, used as a gemstone or as an ornamental stone.

rose·root (rōz′ro͞ot′, -ro͝ot′) *n.* A perennial plant *(Sedum rosea)* of the Northern Hemisphere, having fleshy leaves and greenish-yellow or purple flowers.

rose slug *n.* The larva of either of two sawflies *(Cladius isomerus* or *Endelomyia aethiops)* that feeds destructively on the leaves of roses.

Ro·set·ta stone (rō-zĕt′ə) *n.* A basalt tablet bearing inscriptions in Greek and in Egyptian hieroglyphic and demotic scripts that was discovered in 1799 near Rosetta, a town of northern Egypt in the Nile River delta, and provided the key to the decipherment of Egyptian hieroglyphics.

ro·sette (rō-zĕt′) *n.* **1.** An ornament or a badge made of ribbon or silk that is pleated or gathered to resemble a rose and is used to decorate clothing or is worn in the buttonhole of civilian dress to indicate the possession of certain medals or honors. **2.** A roselike marking or formation, such as one of the clusters of spots on a leopard's fur. **3.** *Architecture.* A painted, carved, or sculptured ornament having a circular arrangement of parts radiating out from the center and suggesting the petals of a rose. **4.** *Botany.* A circular cluster of leaves that radiate from a center at or close to the ground, as in the dandelion. **5.** An ornamental, circular band surrounding the central hole of an acoustic guitar. [French, from Old French, diminutive of *rose,* rose. See ROSE[1].]

Rose·ville (rōz′vĭl′). **1.** A city of north-central California northeast of Sacramento in the foothills of the Sierra Nevada. It is a processing center in an agricultural region. Population, 24,347. **2.** A city of southeast Michigan, a residential suburb of Detroit. Population, 54,311. **3.** A city of southeast Minnesota, an industrial suburb of St. Paul. Population, 35,820.

rose water *n.* A fragrant preparation made by steeping or distilling rose petals in water, used in cosmetics, as toilet water, and in cookery.

rose window *n.* A circular window usually of stained glass with radiating tracery suggesting the form of a rose.

rose·wood (rōz′wo͝od′) *n.* **1.** Any of various tropical or semitropical leguminous trees of the genera *Tipuana, Pterocarpus,* or *Dalbergia,* having hard reddish or dark wood with a strongly marked grain. **2.** The wood of any of these trees, used in cabinetwork.

Rosh Ha·sha·nah also **Rosh Ha·sha·na** or **Rosh Ha·sho·na** or **Rosh Ha·sho·nah** (rôsh′ hə-shô′nə, -shä′-, hä-, hä-shä-nä′) *n.* The Jewish New Year, observed on the first day or the first and second days of Tishri and marked by solemnity as well as festivity. [Hebrew *rō'š haššānâ* : *rō'š,* head, beginning + *ha,* the + *šānâ,* year.]

Ro·si·cru·cian (rō′zĭ-kro͞o′shən, rŏz′ĭ-) *n.* **1.** A member of an international organization, especially the Ancient Mystic Order Rosae Crucis and the Rosicrucian Order, devoted to the study of ancient mystical, philosophical, and religious doctrines and concerned with the application of these doctrines to modern life. **2.** A member of any of several secret organizations or orders of the 17th and 18th centuries concerned with the study of religious mysticism and professing esoteric religious beliefs. **—Rosicrucian** *adj.* Of or relating to Rosicrucians or their philosophy. [From New Latin *(Frater) Rosae Crucis,* (Brother) of the Cross of the Rose, translation of German *Rosenkreutz,* surname of the traditional founder of the society.] **—Ro′si·cru′cian·ism** *n.*

Rosetta stone

ros·in (rŏz′ĭn) *n.* A translucent yellowish to dark brown resin derived from the stumps or sap of various pine trees and used to increase sliding friction, as on the bows of certain stringed instruments, and to manufacture products including varnishes, inks, linoleum, adhesives, and soldering compounds. **—rosin** *tr.v.* **-ined, -in·ing, -ins.** To coat or rub with rosin. [Middle English, variant of *resin.* See RESIN.] **—ros′in·y** *adj.*

rosin oil *n.* A white to brown viscous liquid obtained by fractional distillation of rosin and used in lubricants, adhesives, electrical insulation, and printing inks.

ros·in·weed (rŏz′ĭn-wēd′) *n.* Any of several North American plants of the genera *Grindelia* or *Silphium,* especially the compass plant, the cup plant, and the gum plant, having a resinous juice.

Ros·kil·de (rŭ′skē′lə). A city of eastern Denmark on Sjaelland Island west of Copenhagen. It was the capital of Denmark from the tenth century until 1443. Population, 49,110.

Ross (rôs, rŏs), **Betsy Griscom.** 1752–1836. American seamstress who, according to tradition, made the first American flag (June 1776) at the request of George Washington.

Ross, Harold Wallace. 1892–1951. American publisher who founded and edited (1925–1951) the *New Yorker* magazine.

Ross, Sir **James Clark.** 1800–1862. British polar explorer who located the north magnetic pole (1831). On an Antarctic expedition (1839–1843) he discovered Victoria Land and the Ross Sea.

Ross, John. Originally Coowescoowe or Kooweskoowe. 1790–1866. Cherokee leader who reluctantly directed the forced removal of the Cherokee from Georgia to the Oklahoma Territory (1838–1839) along a route called the Trail of Tears.

Ross, Sir **John.** 1777–1856. British naval officer and Arctic explorer whose expeditions (1818 and 1829–1833) in search of the Northwest Passage yielded several geographic discoveries.

rose window
In cathedral façade, Orvieto, Italy

Ross, Nellie Tayloe. 1876–1977. American politician who was elected (1924) to complete her deceased husband's term as governor of Wyoming (1925–1927), thereby becoming the first woman governor in the United States.

Ross, Sir **Ronald.** 1857–1932. British physician. He won a 1902 Nobel Prize for discovering that mosquitoes transmit malaria.

Ros·sel·li·ni (rô′sə-lē′nē, rŏs′ə-), **Roberto.** 1906–1977. Italian filmmaker whose works, such as *Rome, Open City* (1945), employ fictional characters to depict historical events.

Ros·set·ti (rō-zĕt′ē), **Dante Gabriel.** 1828–1882. British poet and painter. A founder (1848) of the Pre-Raphaelite Brotherhood, he is known for his portraits and his vividly detailed, mystic poems, including "The Blessed Damozel" (1850). His sister **Christina Georgina Rossetti** (1830–1894) wrote lyrical religious works and ballads, such as "Up-Hill" (1861).

Ross Ice Shelf. A vast area in Antarctica bordering on **Ross Sea,** an arm of the southern Pacific Ocean. In the western part of the sea is **Ross Island,** site of the active volcano Mount Erebus.

Ros·si·ni (rō-sē′nē, rô-), **Gioacchino Antonio.** 1792–1868. Italian composer whose numerous operas include *The Barber of Seville* (1816) and *William Tell* (1829).

Ros·tand (rôs-tăɴ′), **Edmond.** 1868–1918. French playwright known for his light, entertaining works, particularly *Cyrano de Bergerac* (1897).

ros·tel·la (rŏ-stĕl′ə) *n. Biology.* Plural of **rostellum.**

ros·tel·late (rŏs′tə-lāt′, rŏ-stĕl′ĭt) *adj.* Having a rostellum.

ros·tel·lum (rŏ-stĕl′əm) *n., pl.* **ros·tel·la** (rŏ-stĕl′ə). *Biology.* A small beaklike part, such as a projection on the stigma of an orchid, a tubular mouthpart on some insects, or the hooked projection on the head of a tapeworm. [Latin, diminutive of *rōstrum,* beak. See ROSTRUM.] **—ros·tel′lar** *adj.*

ros·ter (rŏs′tər, rô′stər) *n.* **1.** A list, especially of names. **2.** A

ă pat	oi boy
ā pay	ou out
âr care	o͝o took
ä father	o͞o boot
ĕ pet	ŭ cut
ē be	ûr urge
ĭ pit	th thin
ī pie	*th* this
îr pier	hw which
ŏ pot	zh vision
ō toe	ə about, item
ô paw	♦ regionalism

Stress marks: ′ (primary); ′ (secondary), as in **dictionary** (dĭk′shə-nĕr′ē)

list of the names of military officers and enlisted personnel enrolled for active duty. [Dutch *rooster,* gridiron, roster (from the ruled paper used for a roster), from *roosten,* to roast.]

WORD HISTORY: To be told that the word *roster* is related to a gridiron upon which one roasts meat might not come as a surprise, depending on what sort of rosters one's name has graced. The connection between the roster as we know it and a gridiron was made in Dutch, where the word *rooster,* meaning "gridiron" (from the verb *roosten,* "to roast"), was extended in sense to mean "a table, list." This extension was made because of the resemblance of a gridiron to a piece of paper divided by parallel lines that contains a list or table. The earliest use in English (first recorded in 1727) for the word *roster* borrowed from Dutch was military, referring to a list or plan that outlined when officers, men, and bodies of troops should perform their turn of duty. *Roster* is no longer exclusively military in usage, nor does it mean simply a list of rotating turns of duty; one could perhaps even have a roster of meats to be roasted at a barbecue.

Ros·tock (rŏs′tŏk′, rôs′tôk′). A city of northeast Germany near the Baltic Sea north-northwest of Berlin. Originally a Slavic fortress, it was chartered in 1218 and was an important member of the Hanseatic League in the 14th century. Population, 241,146.

Ros·tov (rə-stôf′) also **Ros·tov-on-Don** (-ŏn-dŏn′, -dôn′, -ôn-). A city of southwest Russia on the Don River near its outlet on an arm of the Sea of Azov. The city grew around a fortress built in 1761 and was chartered in 1797. It is now an important commercial center. Population, 986,000.

ros·tra (rŏs′trə, rô′strə) *n.* A plural of **rostrum.**

ros·trate (rŏs′trāt′, -trĭt, rô′strāt′, -strĭt) *adj.* Having a beaklike part. [Latin *rōstrātus,* from *rōstrum,* beak. See ROSTRUM.]

Ros·tro·po·vich (rŏs′trə-pō′vĭch, rə-strə-), **Mstislav.** Born 1927. Russian cellist and conductor of the National Symphony Orchestra in Washington, D.C. (since 1977).

ros·trum (rŏs′trəm, rô′strəm) *n., pl.* **ros·trums** or **ros·tra** (rŏs′trə, rô′strə). **1.** A dais, pulpit, or other elevated platform for public speaking. **2.a.** The curved, beaklike prow of an ancient Roman ship, especially a war galley. **b.** The speaker's platform in an ancient Roman forum, which was decorated with the prows of captured enemy ships. **3.** *Biology.* A beaklike or snoutlike projection. [Latin *rōstrum,* beak. See **rēd-** in Appendix.] **—ros′tral** (-trəl) *adj.*

Ros·well (rŏz′wĕl′, -wəl). **1.** A city of northwest Georgia, a residential suburb of Atlanta. Population, 23,337. **2.** A city of southeast New Mexico southeast of Albuquerque. It is a trade and processing center in an irrigated farming region. Population, 39,676.

ros·y (rō′zē) *adj.* **-i·er, -i·est. 1.a.** Having the characteristic pink or red color of a rose. **b.** Flushed with a healthy glow: *rosy cheeks.* **2.** Consisting of, decorated with, or suggestive of a rose or roses. **3.** Bright or cheerful; optimistic: *rosy predictions.* **—ros′i·ly** *adv.* **—ros′i·ness** *n.*

rot (rŏt) *v.* **rot·ted, rot·ting, rots.** *—intr.* **1.** To undergo decomposition, especially organic decomposition; decay. **2.a.** To become damaged, weakened, or useless because of decay: *The beams had rotted away.* **b.** To disappear or fall by decaying: *One could see the blackened areas where the branches had rotted off.* **3.** To languish; decline: *"He was thrown into one of Napoleon's dungeons and left to rot"* (Michael Massing). **4.** To decay morally; become degenerate. *—tr.* To cause to decompose or decay. See Synonyms at **decay. —rot** *n.* **1.** The process of rotting or the condition of being rotten: *The rot spread quickly, rendering the bridge unsafe even for pedestrians.* **2.** Foot rot. **3.** See **liver fluke** (sense 2). **4.** Any of several plant diseases characterized by the breakdown of tissue and caused by various bacteria or fungi. **5.** Pointless talk; nonsense: *She always talks such rot.* **6.** *Archaic.* Any disease causing the decay of flesh. **—rot** *interj.* Used to express annoyance, contempt, or impatience. [Middle English *roten,* from Old English *rotian.*]

rot. *abbr.* **1.** Rotating. **2.** Rotation.

ro·ta (rō′tə) *n.* **1.** *Chiefly British.* A roll call or roster of names. **2.** *Chiefly British.* A round or rotation of duties. **3. Rota.** *Roman Catholic Church.* A tribunal of prelates that serves as an ecclesiastical court. [Latin, wheel. See **ret-** in Appendix.]

Ro·ta (rō′tə, -tä). An island of the western Pacific Ocean in the southern Mariana Islands north of Guam. The Japanese used it as a base for their attack on Guam on December 11, 1941. Rota remained in Japanese hands until the end of the war.

Ro·tar·i·an (rō-târ′ē-ən) *n.* A member of a Rotary Club, a major national and international service club.

ro·ta·ry (rō′tə-rē) *adj.* Of, relating to, causing, or characterized by rotation, especially axial rotation. **—rotary** *n., pl.* **-ries. 1.** A part or device that rotates around an axis. **2.** A traffic circle. [Medieval Latin *rotārius,* from Latin *rota,* wheel. See **ret-** in Appendix.]

rotary engine *n.* An engine, such as a turbine, in which power is supplied directly to vanes or other rotary parts.

rotary harrow *n.* A harrow consisting of a series of freely turning wheels rimmed with spikes.

rotary plow *n.* A plow having a series of hoes arranged on a revolving power-driven shaft. Also called *rotary tiller.*

rotary press *n.* A printing press consisting of curved plates attached to a revolving cylinder that prints onto a continuous roll of paper.

rotary tiller *n.* See **rotary plow.**

ro·ta·ry-wing aircraft (rō′tə-rē-wĭng′) *n.* A rotorcraft.

ro·tate (rō′tāt) *v.* **-tat·ed, -tat·ing, -tates.** *—intr.* **1.** To turn around on an axis or center. **2.** To proceed in sequence; take turns or alternate: *Interns will rotate through the various departments.* *—tr.* **1.** To cause to turn on an axis or center. See Synonyms at **turn. 2.a.** To plant or grow (crops) in a fixed order of succession. **b.** To cause to alternate or proceed in sequence: *The coach rotates her players frequently near the end of the game.* **—rotate** *adj.* Having radiating parts; wheel-shaped. [Latin *rotāre, rotāt-,* from *rota,* wheel. See **ret-** in Appendix.] **—ro′tat′a·ble** *adj.*

ro·ta·tion (rō-tā′shən) *n. Abbr.* **rot. 1.a.** The act or process of turning around a center or an axis: *the axial rotation of the earth.* **b.** A single complete cycle of such motion. **2.** *Mathematics.* A transformation of a coordinate system in which the new axes have a specified angular displacement from their original position while the origin remains fixed. **3.** Regular and uniform variation in a sequence or series: *a rotation of personnel; crop rotation.* **4.** *Games.* An order of shooting balls in billiards in which the ball with the lowest number on the table is always pocketed first. **—ro·ta′tion·al** *adj.*

ro·ta·tive (rō′tā′tĭv) *adj.* **1.** Of, relating to, causing, or characterized by rotation. **2.** Characterized by or occurring in alternation or succession. **—ro′ta′tive·ly** *adv.*

ro·ta·tor (rō′tā′tər) *n.* **1.** One that rotates. **2.** *pl.* **ro·ta·tor·es** (rō′tə-tôr′ēz, -tōr-) *Anatomy.* A muscle that serves to rotate a part of the body.

rotator cuff *n.* A set of muscles and tendons that secures the arm to the shoulder joint and permits rotation of the arm.

ro·ta·to·ry (rō′tə-tôr′ē, -tōr′ē) *adj.* **1.** Of, relating to, causing, or characterized by rotation: *a rotary muscle.* **2.** Occurring or proceeding in alternation or succession.

ro·ta·vi·rus (rō′tə-vī′rəs) *n., pl.* **-rus·es.** Any of a group of wheel-shaped, RNA-contained viruses that cause gastroenteritis, especially in infants and newborn animals.

ROTC *abbr.* Reserve Officers' Training Corps.

rote[1] (rōt) *n.* **1.** A memorizing process using routine or repetition, often without full attention or comprehension: *learn by rote.* **2.** Mechanical routine. [Middle English.] **—rote** *adj.*

rote[2] (rōt) *n.* The sound of surf breaking on the shore. [Probably of Scandinavian origin; akin to Old Norse *rauta,* to roar.]

rote[3] (rōt) *n. Music.* A medieval stringed instrument variably identified with a lyre, lute, or harp. [Middle English, from Old French, probably of Germanic origin.]

ro·te·none (rōt′n-ōn′) *n.* A white crystalline compound, $C_{23}H_{22}O_6$, extracted from the roots of derris and cubé and used as an insecticide. [Japanese *rōten,* derris + -ONE.]

rot·gut (rŏt′gŭt′) *n. Slang.* Raw, inferior liquor.

Roth (rôth), **Philip Milton.** Born 1933. American writer whose witty and ironic fiction, including the comic novel *Portnoy's Complaint* (1969), concerns middle-class Jewish life.

Roth·er·ham (rŏth′ər-əm). A borough of northern England northeast of Sheffield. It is an industrial center. Population, 251,900.

Roth·ko (rŏth′kō), **Mark.** 1903–1970. Russian-born American abstract expressionist painter whose works are characterized by horizontal bands of subtle color with blurred edges.

Roth·schild (rŏth′chīld, rŏths′-, rôth′-, rôths′-, rōt′shĭlt′). German family of bankers, including **Mayer Amschel** (1743–1812), who founded a bank at Frankfurt am Main. His sons, most notably **Salomon** (1774–1855) and **Nathan Mayer** (1774–1836), established branches of the bank throughout Europe.

ro·ti·fer (rō′tə-fər) *n.* Any of various minute multicellular aquatic organisms of the phylum Rotifera, having at the anterior end a wheellike ring of cilia. [From New Latin *Rotifera,* phylum name : Latin *rota,* wheel; see ROTA + Latin *-fer,* -fer.] **—ro·tif′er·al** (-tĭf′ər-əl), **ro·tif′er·ous** (-ər-əs) *adj.*

ro·ti·form (rō′tə-fôrm′) *adj.* Shaped like a wheel. [Latin *rota,* wheel; see **ret-** in Appendix + -FORM.]

ro·tis·se·rie (rō-tĭs′ə-rē) *n.* **1.** A cooking device equipped with a rotating spit on which meat or other food is roasted. **2.** A shop or restaurant where meats are roasted to order. [French *rôtisserie,* from Old French *rostisserie,* from *rostir,* to roast, of Germanic origin.]

rot·l (rŏt′l) *n.* A unit of weight used in countries bordering on the Mediterranean and in nearby areas, varying in different regions from about 1 to 5 pounds (0.45 to 2.25 kilograms). [Arabic *raṭl, riṭl,* possibly from Greek *litra.*]

ro·to·gra·vure (rō′tə-grə-vyo͝or′) *n.* **1.** An intaglio printing process in which letters and pictures are transferred from an etched copper cylinder to a web of paper, plastic, or similar material in a rotary press. **2.** Printed material, such as a newspaper section, produced by this process. [Latin *rota,* wheel; see **ret-** in Appendix + GRAVURE.]

ro·tor (rō′tər) *n.* **1.** A rotating part of an electrical or mechanical device. **2.** An assembly of rotating horizontal airfoils, as that of a helicopter. [Contraction of ROTATOR.]

ro·tor·craft (rō′tər-krăft′) *n.* An aircraft, especially a helicopter, that is kept partially or completely airborne by airfoils rotating around a vertical axis.

rotor ship *n. Nautical.* A ship propelled by one or more tall cylindrical rotors operated by wind power.

ro·to·till (rō′tə-tĭl′) *tr.v.* **-tilled, -till·ing, -tills.** To cultivate or dig with a rototiller: *rototilled the garden before planting.*

ro·to·till·er (rō′tə-tĭl′ər) *n.* A motorized rotary cultivator. [ROT(ARY) + TILLER [1].]

rot·ten (rŏt′n) *adj.* **-er, -est. 1.** Being in a state of putrefaction or decay; decomposed. **2.** Having a foul odor resulting from or suggestive of decay; putrid. **3.** Made weak or unsound by rot: *rotten floorboards.* **4.** Morally corrupt or despicable: *She's rotten to the core.* **5.** Very bad; wretched: *rotten weather.* **—rotten** *adv.* To a very great degree: *The child is spoiled rotten.* [Middle English *roten,* from Old Norse *rotinn.*] **—rot′ten·ly** *adv.* **—rot′ten·ness** *n.*

rotten borough *n.* An election district having only a few voters but the same voting power as other more populous districts.

rot·ten·stone (rŏt′n-stōn′) *n.* A soft, decomposed limestone, used in powder form as a polishing material.

rot·ter (rŏt′ər) *n. Chiefly British.* A scoundrel.

Rot·ter·dam (rôt′ər-dăm′). A city of southwest Netherlands on the Rhine-Meuse delta south-southeast of The Hague. Chartered in 1328, it was a major commercial power during the 16th and 17th centuries and is today a thriving port accessible via canal to oceangoing vessels. The city was heavily bombed during World War II. Population, 555,341.

rott·wei·ler (rŏt′wī′lər, rôt′vī′-) *n.* Any of a German breed of dog having a stocky body, short black fur, and tan face markings. [German, after *Rottweil,* a city of southern Germany.]

ro·tund (rō-tŭnd′) *adj.* **1.** Rounded in figure; plump. See Synonyms at **fat. 2.** Having a full, rich sound; sonorous. [Latin *rotundus.* See **ret-** in Appendix.] **—ro·tun′di·ty** *n.* **—ro·tund′ly** *adv.* **—ro·tund′ness** *n.*

ro·tun·da (rō-tŭn′də) *n.* **1.** A circular building, especially one with a dome. **2. a.** A large area with a high ceiling, as in a hotel lobby. **b.** A large round room. [Italian *rotonda,* from feminine of *rotondo,* round, from Latin *rotundus.* See ROTUND.]

ro·tu·rier (rō-to͝or′ē-ā′, -tyo͝or′-) *n.* A commoner. [French, from Old French, from *roture,* newly cultivated land, from Latin *ruptūra,* action of breaking. See RUPTURE.]

Rou·ault (ro͞o-ō′), **Georges.** 1871–1958. French artist whose paintings, often of biblical figures, clowns, or prostitutes, are characterized by brilliant colors and black outlines.

Rou·baix (ro͞o-bĕ′). A city of northern France north-northeast of Lille near the Belgian border. It is an important textile center. Population, 101,602.

rou·ble (ro͞o′bəl) *n.* Variant of **ruble.**

rou·é (ro͞o-ā′) *n.* A lecherous, dissipated man. [French, from past participle of *rouer,* to break on a wheel (from the feeling that such a person deserves that punishment), from Old French, from Latin *rotāre,* to rotate. See ROTATE.]

Rou·en [1] (ro͞o-än′, -äɴ′). A city of northern France on the Seine River west-northwest of Paris. Of pre-Roman origin, it was repeatedly raided by the Norse in the ninth century, became the capital of medieval Normandy in the tenth century, and was held by the English from 1418 to 1449. Joan of Arc was burned at the stake here in 1431. Population, 101,945.

Rou·en [2] (ro͞o-än′, -äɴ′) *n.* Any of a breed of domestic ducks descended from and resembling the mallard. [After ROUEN [1].]

rouge (ro͞ozh) *n.* **1.** A red or pink cosmetic for coloring the cheeks or lips. **2.** A reddish powder, chiefly ferric oxide, used to polish metals or glass. **—rouge** *v.* **rouged, roug·ing, roug·es.** *—tr.* **1.** To put rouge onto: *rouged her cheeks.* **2.** To color as if with a facial cosmetic: *"Their job is to rouge up the war . . . to turn the horror into cheering press releases"* (Richard Corliss). *—intr.* To use rouge. [French, from Old French, red, from Latin *rubeus.* See **reudh-** in Appendix.]

Rou·get cell (ro͞o-zhā′) *n.* Any of numerous branching, contractile cells on the external wall of a capillary. [After Charles Marie Benjamin *Rouget* (1824–1904), French physiologist.]

Rouget de Lisle (də lēl′), **Claude Joseph.** 1760–1836. French soldier and songwriter who wrote "La Marseillaise" (1792), the French national anthem.

rough (rŭf) *adj.* **rough·er, rough·est. 1.** Having a surface marked by irregularities, protuberances, or ridges; not smooth. **2.** Coarse or shaggy to the touch: *a rough, scratchy blanket.* **3. a.** Difficult to travel over or through: *the rough terrain of the highlands.* **b.** Characterized by violent motion; turbulent: *rough waters.* **c.** Difficult to endure or live through, especially because of harsh or inclement weather: *a rough winter.* **d.** Unpleasant or difficult: *had a rough time during the exam.* **4. a.** Boisterous, unruly, uncouth, or rowdy: *ran with a rough crowd.* **b.** Lacking polish or finesse: *rough manners.* **5.** Characterized by carelessness or force, as in manipulating: *broke the crystal through rough handling.* **6.** Harsh to the ear: *a rough, raspy sound.* **7.** Being in a natural state: *rough diamonds.* **8.** Not perfected, completed, or fully detailed: *a rough drawing; rough carpentry.* **—rough** *n.* **1. a.** Rugged, overgrown terrain. **b.** *Sports.* The part of a golf course left unmowed and uncultivated. **2.** The difficult or disagreeable aspect, part, or side: *observed politics in the rough when working as an intern on Capitol Hill.* **3.** Something in an unfinished or hastily worked-out state. **4.** A crude, unmannered person; a rowdy. **—rough** *tr.v.* **roughed, rough·ing, roughs. 1. a.** To treat roughly or with physical violence: *roughed up his opponent.* **b.** *Sports.* To treat (an opposing player) with unnecessary roughness during a sport or game: *roughed the passer and was ejected from the game.* **2.** To prepare or indicate in an unfinished form: *rough out a house plan.* **—rough** *adv.* In a rough manner; roughly. **—*idiom.* rough it.** To live without the usual comforts and conveniences: *roughed it in a small hunting shack.* [Middle English, from Old English *rūh.*] **—rough′er** *n.* **—rough′ly** *adv.* **—rough′ness** *n.*

SYNONYMS: *rough, harsh, jagged, rugged, scabrous, uneven.* These adjectives apply to what is not smooth but has a coarse, irregular surface. *Rough* describes something that to the sight or touch has inequalities, as projections or ridges: *rough bark; rough, chapped hands; a rough homespun fabric.* Something *harsh* is unpleasantly rough, discordant, or grating: *harsh burlap; the harsh cry of a crow. Jagged* refers to an edge or a surface with irregular projections and indentations: *a jagged piece of glass. Rugged,* which often refers to strength or endurance, especially in people, can also apply to land surfaces characterized by irregular, often steep rises and slopes: *a rugged, rocky trail; rugged countryside. Scabrous* means rough and scaly to the tactile sense: *a granular, scabrous spot on his cheek. Uneven* describes lines or surfaces of which some parts are not level with others: *uneven ground; uneven handwriting.* See also Synonyms at **rude.**

rottweiler

rough·age (rŭf′ĭj) *n.* See **fiber** (sense 6).

rough-and-read·y (rŭf′ən-rĕd′ē) *adj.* Rough or crude but effective for a purpose or use.

rough-and-tum·ble (rŭf′ən-tŭm′bəl) *adj.* Characterized by roughness and disregard for order or rules: *rough-and-tumble politics.* **—rough-and-tumble** *n.* A condition marked by rough, disorderly struggle; infighting: *the rough-and-tumble of national politics.*

rough·back (rŭf′băk′) *n.* Any of several flatfish with rough skin, especially a species of dab *(Hippoglossoides platessoides).*

rough breathing *n. Linguistics.* **1.** An aspirate sound in ancient Greek like that of the sound (h) in English. **2.** The symbol (ʽ) written over some initial vowels and the letter rho in ancient Greek to indicate that a word begins with the sound (h). **3.** In ancient Greek, a word beginning with the sound (h) plus a vowel or diphthong.

rough·cast (rŭf′kăst′) *n.* **1.** A coarse plaster of lime, shells, and pebbles used for outside wall surfaces. **2.** A rough preliminary model or form. **—roughcast** *tr.v.* **-cast, -cast·ing, -casts. 1.** To plaster (a wall, for example) with roughcast. **2.** To shape or work into a rough or preliminary form. **—rough′cast′er** *n.*

rough collie *n.* A collie with a long, rough, mostly black-and-white coat.

rough-cut (rŭf′kŭt′) *n.* A print of a movie that has not been completely edited. **—rough-cut** *adj.* Lacking manners and finesse: *"a rough-cut man who drew his life with a broad stroke"* (Clif Garboden).

rough·dry (rŭf′drī′) *tr.v.* **-dried, -dry·ing, -dries.** To dry (laundry) without ironing or smoothing out. **—rough′dry′** *adj.*

rough·en (rŭf′ən) *tr. & intr.v.* **-ened, -en·ing, -ens.** To make or become rough.

rough fish *n.* A fish that is neither a sport fish nor an important food fish.

rough-hew (rŭf′hyo͞o′) *tr.v.* **-hewed, -hewed** or **-hewn** (-hyo͞on′), **-hew·ing, -hews. 1.** To hew or shape (timber, for example) roughly, without finishing. **2.** To make in rough form.

rotunda
At the New York Botanical Garden

rough·house (rŭf′hous′) *n.* Rowdy, uproarious behavior or play. **—roughhouse** (*also* rŭf′houz′) *v.* **-housed, -hous·ing, -hous·es.** *—intr.* To engage in rowdy, uproarious behavior or play. *—tr.* To handle or treat roughly, usually in fun.

rough-leg·ged hawk (rŭf′lĕg′ĭd) *n.* An Arctic hawk *(Buteo lagopus)* that has dark plumage and whitish feathers covering the legs and feeds mainly on small rodents.

rough·neck (rŭf′nĕk′) *n.* **1.** An uncouth person. **2.** A rowdy. **3.** A member of the crew of an oil rig other than the driller.

rough·rid·er (rŭf′rī′dər) *n.* **1.** A skilled rider of little-trained horses, especially one who breaks horses for riding. **2. Rough Rider.** A member of the First U.S. Volunteer Cavalry regiment under Theodore Roosevelt in the Spanish-American War.

rough·shod (rŭf′shŏd′) *adj.* **1.** Shod with horseshoes having projecting nails or points to prevent slipping. **2.** Marked by brutal force: *Stalin's roughshod treatment of the kulaks.* **—*idiom.* ride roughshod over.** To treat with brutal force: *a manager who rode roughshod over all opposition.*

rough sledding *n. Informal.* A difficult time or situation.

rough trade *n. Slang.* **1.** Violent, often brutal sex acts. **2.** A person, especially a male prostitute, who engages in or appears likely to engage in such acts.

rough-winged swallow (rŭf′wĭngd′) *n.* **1.** Either of two New World species of swallow *(Stelgidopteryx serripennis* or *S. ruficollis)* having outer primary feathers equipped with small barblike hooks. **2.** An African swallow of the genus *Psalidoprocne* having similarly barbed outer primaries.

rough·y (rŭf′ē) *n., pl.* **roughy** or **-ies. 1.** A perchlike food fish *(Arripis georgianus)* of Australia and New Zealand. **2.** A small fish *(Trachichthys australis)* with rough scales, found in shallow waters along the southeast coast of Australia. [Probably from ROUGH.]

ă pat	oi boy
ā pay	ou out
âr care	o͝o took
ä father	o͞o boot
ĕ pet	ŭ cut
ē be	ûr urge
ĭ pit	th thin
ī pie	*th* this
îr pier	hw which
ŏ pot	zh vision
ō toe	ə about, item
ô paw	♦ regionalism

Stress marks: ′ (primary); ′ (secondary), as in **dictionary** (dĭk′shə-nĕr′ē)

roulette

rou·lade (ro͞o-läd′) *n.* **1.** *Music.* **a.** An embellishment consisting of a rapid run of several notes sung to one syllable. **b.** A roll on a drum. **2.** A slice of meat rolled around a filling and cooked. [French, from *rouler,* to roll, from Old French *roler.* See ROLL.]

rou·leau (ro͞o-lō′) *n., pl.* **-leaux** or **-leaus** (-lōz′). A small roll, especially of coins wrapped in paper. [French, from Old French *rolel,* diminutive of *role,* roll, from Latin *rotula,* diminutive of *rota,* wheel. See ROTA.]

rou·lette (ro͞o-lĕt′) *n.* **1.** *Games.* A gambling game in which the players bet on which slot of a rotating disk a small ball will come to rest in. **2.a.** A small, toothed disk of tempered steel attached to a handle and used to make rows of dots, slits, or perforations, as in engraving or on a sheet of postage stamps. **b.** Short consecutive incisions made between individual stamps in a sheet for easy separation. **—roulette** *tr.v.* **-lett·ed, -lett·ing, -lettes.** To mark or divide with a roulette. [French, from Old French *ruelete,* feminine diminutive of *ruele,* diminutive of *roue,* wheel, from Latin *rota.* See **ret-** in Appendix.]

round[1] (round) *adj. Abbr.* **rd., rnd. 1.a.** Being such that every part of the surface or the circumference is equidistant from the center: *a round ball.* **b.** Moving in or forming a circle. **c.** Shaped like a cylinder; cylindrical. **d.** Rather rounded in shape: *the child's round face.* **e.** Full in physique; plump: *a round figure.* **2.a.** *Linguistics.* Formed or articulated with the lips in a rounded shape: *a round vowel.* **b.** Full in tone; sonorous. **3.** Whole or complete; full: *a round dozen.* **4.a.** *Mathematics.* Expressed or designated as a whole number or integer; not fractional. **b.** Not exact; approximate: *a round estimate.* **5.** Large; considerable: *a round sum of money.* **6.** Brought to satisfactory conclusion or completion; finished. **7.a.** Outspoken; blunt: *a round scolding.* **b.** Done with full force; unrestrained: *gave me a round thrashing.* **—round** *n.* **1.a.** Something, such as a circle, disk, globe, or ring, that is round. **b.** A circle formed of various things. **c.** Movement around a circle or about an axis. **2.** A rung or crossbar, as one on a ladder or chair. **3.** A cut of beef from the part of the thigh between the rump and the shank. **4.** An assembly of people; a group. **5.** A round dance. **6.a.** A complete course, succession, or series: *a round of parties; a round of negotiations.* **b.** Often **rounds.** A course of customary or prescribed actions, duties, or places: *physicians' rounds.* **7.** A complete range or extent. **8.** One drink for each person in a gathering or group: *Let me buy the next round.* **9.** A single outburst, as of applause or cheering. **10.a.** A single shot or volley. **b.** Ammunition for a single shot or volley. **11.** A specified number of arrows shot from a specified distance to a target in archery. **12.** *Sports & Games.* An interval of play that occupies a specified time, constitutes a certain number of plays, or allows each player a turn. **13.** *Music.* A composition for two or more voices in which each voice enters at a different time with the same melody. **—round** *v.* **round·ed, round·ing, rounds.** *—tr.* **1.** To make round. See Synonyms at **bend**[1]. **2.** To encompass; surround. **3.** To cause to proceed or move in a circular course. **4.** *Linguistics.* To pronounce with rounded lips; labialize. **5.** To fill out; make plump. **6.** To bring to completion or perfection; finish. **7.** *Mathematics.* To express as a round number: *The number 1.64 can be rounded to 1.6 or to 2.* **8.** To make a complete circuit of; go or pass around. **9.** To make a turn about or to the other side of: *rounded a bend in the road.* *—intr.* **1.** To become round. **2.** To take a circular course; complete or partially complete a circuit: *racecars rounding into the final lap.* **3.** To turn about, as on an axis; reverse. **4.** To become curved, filled out, or plump. **5.** To come to satisfactory completion or perfection. **—round** *adv.* **1.** In a circular progression or movement; around. **2.** With revolutions: *wheels moving round.* **3.** To a specific place or person: *called round for the pastor; sent round for the veterinarian.* **—round** *prep.* **1.** Around. **2.** From the beginning to the end of; throughout: *a plant that grows round the year.* ***—phrasal verbs.*** **round on.** To turn on and assail. **round up. 1.** To seek out and bring together; gather. **2.** To herd (cattle) together from various places. ***—idioms.*** **in the round. 1.** With the stage in the center of the audience. **2.** Fully shaped so as to stand free of a background: *a sculpture in the round.* **make** (or **go**) **the rounds. 1.** To go from place to place, as on business or for entertainment: *a delivery truck making the rounds; students going the rounds in the entertainment district.* **2.** To be communicated or passed from person to person: *The news quickly made the rounds. A piece of juicy gossip is going the rounds.* [Middle English, from Anglo-Norman *rounde,* variant of Old French *rond,* ultimately from Vulgar Latin **retundus,* from Latin *rotundus,* from *rota,* wheel. See **ret-** in Appendix.] **—round′ness** *n.*

round[2] (round) *tr.v.* **round·ed, round·ing, rounds.** *Archaic.* To whisper. [Middle English *rounden,* from Old English *rūnian,* from *rūn,* a secret.]

round·a·bout (round′ə-bout′) *adj.* Indirect; circuitous: *"This conclusion was reached in a roundabout but nevertheless perfectly reliable way"* (George Gamow). See Synonyms at **indirect. —roundabout** *n.* **1.** A short, close-fitting jacket. **2.** *Chiefly British.* A merry-go-round. **3.** *Chiefly British.* A traffic circle.

round clam *n.* See **quahog.**

round dance *n.* **1.** A folk dance performed with the dancers arranged in a circle. **2.** A ballroom dance in which couples proceed in a circular direction around the room.

round·ed (roun′dĭd) *adj.* **1.** Shaped into the form of a circle or sphere; made round. **2.** *Linguistics.* Pronounced with the lips shaped ovally; labialized. **3.** Complete; balanced: *a rounded meal.* **—round′ed·ness** *n.*

roun·del (roun′dəl) *n.* **1.** A curved form, especially a semicircular panel, window, or recess. **2.a.** A rondel. **b.** A rondeau. **c.** An English variation of the rondeau consisting of three triplets with a refrain after the first and third. [Middle English, from Old French *rondel,* diminutive of *rond,* circle, round. See ROUND[1].]

roun·de·lay (roun′də-lā′) *n.* A poem or song with a regularly recurring refrain. [Middle English, alteration (influenced by *lai,* poem, song; see LAY[3]) of Old French *rondelet,* diminutive of *rondel,* roundel. See ROUNDEL.]

round·er (roun′dər) *n.* **1.** One that rounds, especially a tool for rounding corners and edges. **2.** One, such as a security guard, who makes rounds. **3.** A dissolute person. **4.** *Sports.* **a.** A boxing match that goes on for a specified number of rounds. Often used in combination: *a five-rounder.* **b. rounders** *(used with a sing. verb).* An English ball game similar to baseball.

round hand *n.* A style of handwriting in which the letters are rounded and full rather than angular.

Round·head (round′hĕd′) *n.* A supporter of the Parliamentarians during the English Civil War and the Commonwealth. [From the close-cropped hair of the Puritans.]

round herring *n.* Any of the mostly tropical marine fishes of the family Dussumierlidae, similar to the clupeid herrings but having an abdomen that is rounded and smooth along the edges.

round·house (round′hous′) *n.* **1.** A circular building for housing and switching locomotives. **2.** *Nautical.* A cabin on the after part of the quarterdeck of a ship. **3.** *Games.* A meld of four kings and four queens in pinochle. **4.** *Slang.* A punch or swing delivered with a sweeping sidearm movement.

round·ish (roun′dĭsh) *adj.* Somewhat round. **—round′ish·ness** *n.*

round·let (round′lĭt) *n.* **1.** A little circle. **2.** A small circular object. [Middle English, from Old French *rondelet,* diminutive of *rondel,* roundel. See ROUNDEL.]

round·ly (round′lē) *adv.* **1.** In the form of a circle or sphere. **2.** With full force or vigor; thoroughly: *applauded roundly; was roundly criticized.*

round robin *n.* **1.** *Sports.* A tournament in which each contestant is matched in turn against every other contestant. **2.** A petition or protest on which the signatures are arranged in a circle in order to conceal the order of signing. **3.** A letter sent among members of a group, often with comments added by each person in turn.

round-shoul·dered (round′shōl′dərd) *adj.* Having the shoulders and upper back rounded.

rounds·man (roundz′mən) *n.* **1.** A police officer in charge of several other officers. **2.** One, such as a delivery person, who makes rounds.

round steak *n.* A lean, oval cut of beef from between the rump and shank.

round·ta·ble (round′tā′bəl) *n.* **1.** Often **round-ta·ble** (round′tā′bəl) or **round table.** A conference or discussion involving several participants. **2. Round Table. a.** In Arthurian legend, the circular table of King Arthur and his knights. **b.** The knights of King Arthur considered as a group.

round-the-clock (round′*th*ə-klŏk′) also **a·round-the-clock** (ə-round′-) *adj.* Lasting or continuing throughout the entire 24 hours of the day; continuous.

round·trip or **round-trip** also **round trip** (round′trĭp′) *—n.* A trip from one place to another and back, usually over the same route. *—attributive.* Often used to modify another noun: *roundtrip flights; round-trip tickets; round trip passengers.*

round·up (round′ŭp′) *n.* **1.a.** The herding together of cattle for inspection, branding, or shipping. **b.** The cattle so herded. **c.** The workers and horses employed in such herding. **2.** A gathering up, as of people under suspicion by the police. **3.** A summary: *a news roundup.*

round·worm (round′wûrm′) *n.* See **nematode.**

roup (ro͞op) *n.* An infectious disease of poultry and pigeons characterized by inflammation of and mucous discharge from the mouth and eyes. [Origin unknown.]

Rour·ke·la (rôr-kā′lə). See **Raurkela.**

Rous (rous), **Francis Peyton.** 1879–1970. American pathologist. He shared a 1966 Nobel Prize for his discovery of tumor-producing viruses.

rouse (rouz) *v.* **roused, rous·ing, rous·es.** *—tr.* **1.** To arouse from slumber, apathy, or depression. **2.** To excite, as to anger or action; stir up. See Synonyms at **provoke.** *—intr.* **1.** To awaken. **2.** To become active. **—rouse** *n.* The act or an instance of arousing. [Middle English *rousen,* to shake the feathers: used of a hawk, perhaps from Old French *reuser, ruser,* to repel, push back, from Vulgar Latin **recūsāre,* from Latin, to refuse. See RECUSE.] **—rous′er** *n.*

rous·ing (rou′zĭng) *adj.* **1.** Inducing enthusiasm or excitement; stirring: *a rousing sermon.* **2.** Lively; vigorous: *a rousing march tune.* **3.** Used as an intensive: *a rousing lie.* **—rous′ing·ly** *adv.*

Rous sarcoma *n.* A sarcoma produced in chickens by an RNA-containing virus. [After Francis Peyton ROUS.]

Rous·seau (ro͞o-sō′), **Henri.** Known as "Le Douanier Rousseau." 1844–1910. French primitive painter of portraits, still lifes, city scenes, and metaphorical works, such as *The Snake Charmer* (1907).

Rousseau, Jean Jacques. 1712–1778. French philosopher and writer who held that humanity is essentially good but corrupted by society. His written works include *The Social Contract* and the novel *Émile* (both 1762).

Rousseau, Théodore. 1812–1867. French landscape painter who was the leader of the Barbizon school. His works include *Descent of the Cattle* (c. 1834).

Rous·sil·lon (ro͞o-sē-yôɴ′). A historical region of southern France bordering on Spain and the Mediterranean Sea. Originally inhabited by Iberians, it became part of Roman Gaul after c. 121 B.C. and later changed hands many times, eventually becoming a Spanish possession that was transferred to France by the Treaty of the Pyrenees (1659).

roust (roust) *tr.v.* **roust·ed, roust·ing, rousts.** To rout, especially out of bed. [Probably alteration of ROUSE.]

roust·a·bout (rous′tə-bout′) *n.* **1.** A laborer employed for temporary or unskilled jobs, as in an oil field. **2.** A circus laborer. **3.** A deck or wharf laborer, especially on the Mississippi River.

rout¹ (rout) *n.* **1.a.** A disorderly retreat or flight following defeat. **b.** An overwhelming defeat. **2.a.** A disorderly crowd of people; a mob. **b.** People of the lowest class; rabble. **3.** A public disturbance; a riot. **4.** A company, as of knights or wolves, that are in movement. **5.** A fashionable gathering. **—rout** *tr.v.* **rout·ed, rout·ing, routs. 1.** To put to disorderly flight or retreat: *"the flock of starlings which Jasper had routed with his gun"* (Virginia Woolf). **2.** To defeat overwhelmingly. See Synonyms at **defeat.** [Middle English *route,* from Old French, troop, defeat, from Vulgar Latin **rupta,* from feminine of Latin *ruptus,* past participle of *rumpere,* to break. See **reup-** in Appendix.]

rout² (rout) *v.* **rout·ed, rout·ing, routs.** *—intr.* **1.** To dig with the snout; root. **2.** To poke around; rummage. *—tr.* **1.** To expose to view as if by digging; uncover. **2.** To hollow, scoop, or gouge out. **3.** To drive or force out as if by digging; eject: *rout out an informant.* **4.** *Archaic.* To dig up with the snout. [Variant of ROOT².]

rout³ (rout, ro͝ot) *intr.v.* **rout·ed, rout·ing, routs.** *Chiefly British.* To bellow. Used of cattle. [Middle English *routen,* to roar, from Old Norse *rauta.*]

route (ro͞ot, rout) *n. Abbr.* **rte. 1.a.** A road, course, or way for travel from one place to another. **b.** A highway. **2.** A customary line of travel. See Synonyms at **way. 3.** A fixed course or territory assigned to a salesperson or delivery person. **4.** A means of reaching a goal. **—route** *tr.v.* **rout·ed, rout·ing, routes. 1.** To send or forward by a specific route. See Synonyms at **send¹. 2.** To schedule the order of (a sequence of procedures). [Middle English, from Old French, from Latin *rupta (via),* broken (road), feminine past participle of *rumpere,* to break. See ROUT¹.]

rout·er¹ (rou′tər) *n.* One that routs, especially a machine tool that mills out the surface of metal or wood.

rout·er² (ro͞o′tər, rou′-) *n.* One that routes, especially one who prepares shipments for distribution and delivery.

rou·tine (ro͞o-tēn′) *n.* **1.** A prescribed, detailed course of action to be followed regularly; a standard procedure. **2.** A set of customary and often mechanically performed procedures or activities. See Synonyms at **method. 3.** A set piece of entertainment, especially in a nightclub or theater. **4.** *Slang.* A particular kind of behavior or activity: *She went into her hurt routine.* **5.** *Computer Science.* A set of programming instructions designed to perform a specific, limited task. **—routine** *adj.* **1.** In accord with established procedure: *a routine check of passports.* **2.** Habitual; regular: *made his routine trip to the store.* **3.** Having no special quality; ordinary: *a routine day.* [French, from *route,* route, from Old French. See ROUTE.] **—rou·tine′ly** *adv.* **—rou·tin′ism** *n.* **—rou·tin′ist** *n.*

rou·tin·ize (ro͞o-tē′nīz′, ro͞ot′n-īz′) *tr.v.* **-ized, -iz·ing, -iz·es. 1.** To establish a routine for. **2.** To reduce to a routine: *a government that routinized mass murder while carrying out its totalitarian policies.* **—rou·tin′i·za′tion** (-ĭ-zā′shən) *n.*

roux (ro͞o) *n., pl.* **roux.** A mixture of flour and fat cooked together and used as a thickening. [French *(beurre) roux,* browned (butter), from Old French *rous,* reddish brown, from Latin *russus,* red. See **reudh-** in Appendix.]

Rou·yn (ro͞o′ĭn, rwăɴ). A city of southwest Quebec, Canada, near the Ontario border west-northwest of Quebec City. It is a trade center in a mining region. Population, 17,224.

rove¹ (rōv) *v.* **roved, rov·ing, roves.** *—intr.* To wander about at random, especially over a wide area; roam. *—tr.* To roam or wander around, over, or through. See Synonyms at **wander. —rove** *n.* An act of wandering about, over, around, or through. [Middle English *roven,* to shoot arrows at a mark.]

rove² (rōv) *tr.v.* **roved, rov·ing, roves. 1.** To card (wool). **2.** To put (fibers) through an eye or opening. **3.** To stretch and twist (fibers) before spinning; ravel out. **—rove** *n.* A slightly twisted and extended fiber or sliver. [Origin unknown.]

rove³ (rōv) *v. Nautical.* A past tense and a past participle of **reeve².**

rove beetle *n.* Any of numerous beetles of the family Staphylinidae, often found in decaying matter and having slender bodies and short wing covers. Also called *staphylinid.* [Possibly from ROVE¹.]

rov·er¹ (rō′vər) *n.* **1.a.** One that roves; a wanderer. **b.** A crewed or uncrewed vehicle, used especially in exploring the terrain of a planet and its satellites. **2.** *Sports.* A mark in archery selected by chance.

ro·ver² (rō′vər) *n.* **1.** A pirate. **2.** A pirate vessel. [Middle English, from Middle Dutch or Middle Low German, robber, from *roven,* to rob. See **reup-** in Appendix.]

Rov·no (rôv′nə). A city of northwest Ukraine west of Kiev. It was annexed by Russia in 1793 and by Poland in 1921. The city was occupied by Soviet troops in 1939. Population, 221,000.

Ro·vu·ma (ro͞o-vo͞o′mə). See **Ruvuma.**

row¹ (rō) *n.* **1.** A series of objects placed next to each other, usually in a straight line. **2.** A succession without a break or gap in time: *won the title for three years in a row.* **3.** A continuous line of buildings along a street. **—row** *tr.v.* **rowed, row·ing, rows.** To place in a row. ***—idiom.* a tough row to hoe.** *Informal.* A difficult situation to endure. [Middle English, from Old English *rāw.*]

row² (rō) *v.* **rowed, row·ing, rows.** *—intr. Nautical.* To propel a boat with or as if with oars. *—tr.* **1.** *Nautical.* **a.** To propel (a boat) with or as if with oars. **b.** To carry in or on a boat propelled by oars. **c.** To use (a specified number of oars or people deploying them). **2.** To propel or convey in a manner resembling rowing of a boat. **3.** *Sports.* **a.** To pull (an oar) as part of a racing crew. **b.** To race against by rowing. **—row** *n. Nautical.* **1.a.** The act of rowing. **b.** A shift at the oars of a boat. **2.** A trip or an excursion in a rowboat. [Middle English *rowen,* from Old English *rōwan.* See **erə-** in Appendix.] **—row′er** *n.*

row³ (rou) *n.* **1.** A boisterous disturbance or quarrel; a brawl. See Synonyms at **brawl. 2.** An uproar; a great noise. **—row** *intr.v.* **rowed, row·ing, rows.** To take part in a quarrel, a brawl, or an uproar. [Origin unknown.]

row·an (rō′ən, rou′-) *n.* A small deciduous European tree *(Sorbus aucuparia)* of the rose family, having pinnately compound leaves, corymbs of white flowers, and orange-red berries. [Of Scandinavian origin. See **reudh-** in Appendix.]

row·boat (rō′bōt′) *n.* **1.** *Nautical.* A small boat propelled by oars. **2.** *Sports.* A rowing machine.

row·dy (rou′dē) *n., pl.* **-dies.** A rough, disorderly person. **—rowdy** *adj.* **-di·er, -di·est.** Disorderly; rough: *rowdy teenagers; a rowdy beer party.* [Probably from ROW³.] **—row′di·ly** *adv.* **—row′di·ness** *n.* **—row′dy·ism** *n.*

Rowe (rō), **Nicholas.** 1674–1718. English writer whose works include drama, poetry, and an edition of Shakespeare. He was appointed poet laureate in 1715.

row·el (rou′əl) *n.* A sharp-toothed wheel inserted into the end of the shank of a spur. [Middle English, from Old French *roelle,* diminutive of *roue,* wheel, from Latin *rota.* See **ret-** in Appendix.] **—row′el** *v.*

♦ **row·en** (rou′ən) *n. New England.* A second crop, as of hay, in a season. [Middle English *rowein,* from Anglo-Norman *rewain,* variant of Old French *regain* : *re-,* re- + *gaaignier,* to till; see GAIN¹.]

row house (rō) *n.* One of a series of identical houses situated side by side and joined by common walls.

row·ing machine (rō′ĭng) *n. Sports.* A fitness device with oarlike handles, pivoting footrests, and an adjustable sliding seat, used to provide a thorough workout of all major muscle groups in the body.

Row·land Heights (rō′lənd). A community of southern California, a suburb of the Los Angeles–Long Beach metropolitan area. Population, 28,252.

Row·land·son (rō′lənd-sən), **Thomas.** 1756–1827. British caricaturist and illustrator of works by Sterne, Goldsmith, and others.

row·lock (rō′lŏk′) *n. Chiefly British.* An oarlock.

Ro·xas y A·cu·ña (rô′häs ē ä-ko͞on′yə, -yä), **Manuel.** 1892–1948. Philippine politician who was the first president of the Republic of the Philippines (1946–1948).

Roy (roi). A city of northern Utah, a suburb of Ogden. Population, 19,694.

roy·al (roi′əl) *adj. Abbr.* **R. 1.** Of or relating to a monarch. **2.** Of the rank of a monarch. **3.** Of, relating to, or in the service of a kingdom. **4.** Issued or performed by a monarch: *a royal warrant; a royal visit.* **5.** Founded, chartered, or authorized by a monarch: *a royal society of musicians.* **6.** Befitting royalty; stately: *royal treatment.* **7.a.** Superior, as in size or quality. **b.** Used as an intensive: *"It would be a first-class royal mess"* (Sam Nunn). **—royal** *n.* **1.** *Informal.* A member of a monarch's family: *"Among the resort's distinguished visitors are Swedish and Spanish royals"* (Alistair Scott). **2.** *Nautical.* A sail set on the royalmast. **3.** A paper size, 20 by 25 inches for printing, 19 by 24 inches for writing. ***—idiom.* the royal road.** A way or method that presents no difficulties: *the royal road to success.* [Middle English, from Old French, from Latin *rēgālis,* from *rēx, rēg-,* king. See **reg-** in Appendix.] **—roy′al·ly** *adv.*

royal blue *n. Color.* A deep to strong blue. **—roy′al-blue′** (roi′əl-blo͞o′) *adj.*

royal fern *n.* A deep-rooted fern *(Osmunda regalis)* of worldwide distribution, having tall, upright, bipinnately compound fronds.

royal flush *n. Games.* A straight flush consisting of the five highest cards of one suit, ranked as the highest hand in certain games of poker.

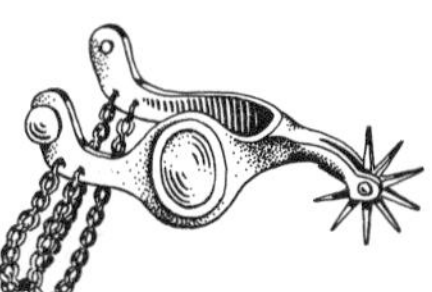

rowel

row house

ă pat	oi boy
ā pay	ou out
âr care	o͝o took
ä father	o͞o boot
ĕ pet	ŭ cut
ē be	ûr urge
ĭ pit	th thin
ī pie	*th* this
îr pier	hw which
ŏ pot	zh vision
ō toe	ə about, item
ô paw	♦ regionalism

Stress marks: ′ (primary); ′ (secondary), as in **dictionary** (dĭk′shə-nĕr′ē)

Roy·al Gorge (roiʹəl). A long, narrow canyon formed by the Arkansas River in south-central Colorado. Its near-vertical walls are more than 305 m (1,000 ft) high. The gorge was discovered by Zebulon Pike's expedition in 1806.

roy·al·ism (roiʹə-lĭzʹəm) *n.* Support of or adherence to the principle of rule by a monarch.

roy·al·ist (roiʹə-lĭst) *n.* **1.** A supporter of government by a monarch. **2. Royalist. a.** See **cavalier** (sense 3). **b.** An American loyal to British rule during the American Revolution; a Tory.

royal jelly *n.* A nutritious substance secreted by the pharyngeal glands of worker bees that serves as food for all young larvae and as the only food for larvae that will develop into queen bees.

Roy·all (roiʹəl), **Anne Newport.** 1769–1854. American writer known for her travel writing and muckraking journalism.

Royal Leam·ing·ton Spa (lĕmʹĭng-tən). See **Leamington.**

royal lily *n.* A western Chinese lily *(Lilium regale)* having umbels of very large, fragrant, horizontal, funnel-shaped flowers that are lilac or purple on the outside and white with a yellow base on the inside.

roy·al·mast also **roy·al mast** (roiʹəl-măstʹ) *n. Nautical.* The small mast immediately above the topgallant mast.

Royal Oak (ōk). A city of southeast Michigan, a residential suburb of Detroit. Population, 70,893.

royal palm *n.* Any of several tropical American palm trees of the genus *Roystonea* having a tall, naked trunk surmounted by a large tuft of pinnately compound leaves.

royal poinciana *n.* A tropical and semitropical tree *(Delonix regia)* native to Madagascar, having bipinnately compound leaves, clusters of large scarlet flowers, and long pods. Also called *flamboyant, poinciana.*

royal purple *n. Color.* A moderate or strong violet to deep purple or dark reddish purple. **—royʹal-purʹple** (roiʹəl-pûrʹpəl) *adj.*

roy·al·ty (roiʹəl-tē) *n., pl.* **-ties. 1.a.** A person of royal rank or lineage. **b.** Monarchs and their families considered as a group. **2.** The lineage or rank of a monarch. **3.** The power, status, or authority of a monarch. **4.** Royal quality or bearing. **5.** A kingdom or possession ruled by a monarch. **6.** A right or prerogative of the crown, as that of receiving a percentage of the proceeds from mines in the royal domain. **7.a.** The granting of a right by a monarch to a corporation or an individual to exploit specified natural resources. **b.** The payment for such a right. **8.a.** A share paid to a writer or composer out of the proceeds resulting from the sale or performance of his or her work. **b.** A share in the proceeds paid to an inventor or a proprietor for the right to use his or her invention or services. **9.** A share of the profit or product reserved by the grantor, especially of an oil or mining lease. In this sense, also called *override.*

Royce (rois), **Josiah.** 1855–1916. American philosopher. The leading American idealist of his day, he contributed to the fields of metaphysics, religion, logic, and mathematics.

R.P. *abbr.* Received Pronunciation.

RPG (ärʹpē-jēʹ) *n. Computer Science.* A programming language used for creating business reports. [*r(eport) p(rogram) g(enerator).*]

rpm or **r.p.m.** *abbr.* Revolutions per minute.

rps or **r.p.s.** *abbr.* Revolutions per second.

rpt. *abbr.* **1.** Repeat. **2.** Report.

R.Q. *abbr.* Respiratory quotient.

RR also **R.R.** *abbr.* **1.** Railroad. **2.** Rural route.

R.R. *abbr.* Right Reverend.

RRB *abbr.* Railroad Retirement Board.

-rrhagia *suff.* Abnormal or excessive flow or discharge: *menorrhagia.* [Greek *-rragia,* from *rhēgnunai, rhag-,* to burst forth.]

-rrhea or **-rrhoea** *suff.* Flow; discharge: *seborrhea.* [New Latin *-rrhoea,* from Greek *-rrhoia,* from *rhoia,* a flowing, from *rhein,* to flow. See **sreu-** in Appendix.]

rRNA *abbr.* Ribosomal RNA.

RS *abbr.* **1.** Recording secretary. **2.** Right side. **3.** Also **R.S.** Royal Society.

r selection *n. Ecology.* A form of selection that occurs in an environment with plentiful resources, favoring a reproductive strategy in which many offspring are produced. [*r(ate of increase).*]

RSFSR or **R.S.F.S.R.** *abbr.* Russian Soviet Federated Socialist Republic.

RSV or **R.S.V.** *abbr. Bible.* Revised Standard Version.

R.S.V.P. or **r.s.v.p.** *abbr. French.* Répondez s'il vous plaît (please reply).

RT *abbr.* **1.** Radiotelephone. **2.** Room temperature.

rt. *abbr.* Right.

Rt. *abbr. Bible.* Ruth.

RTA *abbr.* Ready to assemble.

rte. *abbr.* Route.

Rt. Hon. *abbr.* Right Honorable.

Rt. Rev. *abbr.* Right Reverend.

RTW *abbr.* Ready-to-wear.

Ru The symbol for the element **ruthenium.**

Ru·an·da (ro͞o-änʹdə). See **Rwanda.**

Ru·an·da-U·run·di (ro͞o-änʹdə-o͝o-ro͞onʹdē). A former colonial possession of central Africa. A German territory after the Conference of Berlin (1884–1885), it was mandated to Belgium by the League of Nations after World War I. When independence was achieved in 1962, the region split into the present-day countries of Rwanda and Burundi.

rub (rŭb) *v.* **rubbed, rub·bing, rubs.** *—tr.* **1.a.** To subject to the action of something that moves back and forth with friction and pressure. **b.** To cause to move along a surface with friction and pressure. **2.** To irritate; annoy: *His laziness was beginning to rub me.* *—intr.* **1.a.** To move along a surface with friction and pressure. **b.** To chafe with friction. **c.** To cause irritation or annoyance. **2.** To continue in a given situation, usually with some difficulty: *Despite all our problems, we continue to rub along.* **3.** To admit rubbing: *a blackboard that rubs clean easily.* **4.** To be transferred by contact or proximity: *wished some of her luck would rub off on me.* **—rub** *n.* **1.** The act of rubbing. **2.** The application of friction and pressure: *a back rub.* **3.** An unevenness on a surface. **4.** An act or a remark that annoys or hurts another. **5.** Difficulty: *"Ay, there's the rub"* (Shakespeare). ***—phrasal verbs.*** **rub down.** To perform a brisk rubbing of the body, as in massage. **rub in.** To harp on (an unpleasant matter). **rub out. 1.** To obliterate by or as if by rubbing. **2.** *Slang.* To kill; murder. ***—idioms.*** **rub elbows** (or **shoulders).** To mix or socialize closely: *diplomats rubbing elbows with heads of state.* **rub (one's) hands.** To experience or display pleased anticipation, self-satisfaction, or glee. **rub (someone's) nose in.** *Slang.* To bring repeatedly and forcefully to another's attention. **rub (someone) the wrong way.** To annoy; irritate: *"One can see . . . how* [his] *expression of his ideals and intentions must have rubbed many people the wrong way"* (Christopher Lehmann-Haupt). **rub up on.** To refresh one's knowledge of: *I have to rub up on my French.* [Middle English *rubben.*]

Rub al Kha·li (ro͝obʹ äl käʹlē, äl KHäʹlē). Sometimes called "the Empty Quarter." A desert region in the southeast interior of the Arabian Peninsula. Virtually without water and uninhabited, it was first visited by an English explorer in 1932 but has not yet been completely explored.

ru·basse (ro͞o-băsʹ, ro͞oʹbăsʹ) *n.* A variety of quartz colored ruby red by its iron-oxide content. [French *rubace,* from *rubis,* ruby. See RUBY.]

ru·ba·to (ro͞o-bäʹtō) *Music. n., pl.* **-tos.** Rhythmic flexibility within a phrase or measure; a relaxation of strict time. **—rubato** *adj.* Containing or characterized by rubato. [Italian *(tempo) rubato,* stolen (time), rubato, past participle of *rubare,* to rob, of Germanic origin. See **reup-** in Appendix.]

rub·ber¹ (rŭbʹər) *n.* **1.** A yellowish, amorphous, elastic material obtained from the milky sap or latex of various tropical plants, especially the rubber tree, and vulcanized, pigmented, finished, and modified into products such as electric insulation, elastic bands and belts, tires, and containers. Also called *caoutchouc, India rubber.* **2.** Any of numerous synthetic elastic materials of varying chemical composition with properties similar to those of natural rubber. **3.** A low overshoe made of rubber. **4.** *Baseball.* The oblong piece of hard rubber on which the pitcher must stand when delivering the ball. **5.** Something made of rubber, as: **a.** An eraser. **b.** A tire. **c.** A set of tires on a vehicle. **6.** *Slang.* A condom. **7.** One that rubs, especially one that gives a massage. [From RUB.]

rub·ber² (rŭbʹər) *n. Abbr.* **r.** *Games.* **1.** A series of games of which two out of three or three out of five must be won to terminate the play. **2.** An odd game played to break a tie. [Origin unknown.]

♦ **rubber band** *n.* An elastic loop of natural or synthetic rubber used to hold objects together. Also called ♦*gum band.*

rub·ber-base paint (rŭbʹər-bāsʹ) *n.* See **latex paint.**

rubber bullet *n.* A hard rubber bullet for a riot gun used especially by military personnel and law enforcement officers in crowd control.

rubber cement *n.* Nonvulcanized rubber in an organic solvent, used as an adhesive.

rubber check *n. Slang.* A check returned by a bank because of insufficient funds in the account on which it is drawn.

rub·ber-chick·en circuit (rŭbʹər-chĭkʹən) *n. Informal.* A monotonous series of events, such as lunches and dinners often featuring chicken, which politicians and heads of state feel compelled to attend.

rub·ber·ize (rŭbʹə-rīzʹ) *tr.v.* **-ized, -iz·ing, -iz·es.** To coat, treat, or impregnate with rubber.

rub·ber·neck (rŭbʹər-nĕkʹ) *Slang. intr.v.* **-necked, -neck·ing, -necks.** To look about or survey with unsophisticated wonderment or curiosity. **—rubberneck** *n.* A rubbernecker.

rub·ber·neck·er (rŭbʹər-nĕkʹər) *n. Slang.* A gawking onlooker.

rubber plant *n.* **1.** Any of several tropical plants yielding sap that can be coagulated to form crude rubber. **2.** A small tree *(Ficus elastica)* that has large, oblong, glossy, leathery leaves and is a popular house plant.

rubber stamp also **rub·ber·stamp** (rŭbʹər-stămpʹ) *n.* **1. rubber stamp.** A piece of rubber affixed to a handle and bearing raised characters used to make ink impressions, as of names or dates. **2.** A person or body that gives perfunctory approval or endorsement of a policy without assessing its merit. **3.** A perfunctory approval or endorsement.

rub·ber-stamp (rŭb′ər-stămp′) *tr.v.* **-stamped, -stamp·ing, -stamps. 1.** To mark with the imprint of a rubber stamp. **2.** To endorse, vote for, or approve without question or deliberation.

rubber tree *n.* A tropical South American tree *(Hevea brasiliensis)* widely cultivated throughout the Tropics and yielding a milky juice that is a major source of commercial rubber.

rub·ber·y (rŭb′ə-rē) *adj.* **-i·er, -i·est.** Of or resembling rubber; elastic.

rub·bing (rŭb′ĭng) *n.* **1.** The act of polishing, cleaning, or drying. **2.** A representation of a raised or indented surface made by placing paper over the surface and rubbing the paper gently with a marking agent such as charcoal or chalk.

rub·bish (rŭb′ĭsh) *n.* **1.** Refuse; garbage. **2.** Worthless material. **3.** Foolish discourse; nonsense. —*attributive.* Often used to modify another noun: *rubbish collection; a rubbish pail.* [Middle English *robishe.*]

rub·bish·y (rŭb′ĭ-shē) *adj.* **1.** Littered with rubbish. **2.** Of no value; worthless.

rub·ble (rŭb′əl) *n.* **1.** A loose mass of angular fragments of rock or masonry crumbled by natural or human forces. **2.a.** Irregular fragments or pieces of rock used in masonry. **b.** The masonry made with such rocks. [Middle English *rubel.*] **—rub′bly** *adj.*

rub·ble·work (rŭb′əl-wûrk′) *n.* Masonry made with rubble.

rub·down (rŭb′doun′) *n.* An energetic massage of the body.

rube (ro͞ob) *n. Slang.* An unsophisticated country fellow. [Probably from *Rube,* nickname for *Reuben.*]

ru·be·fa·cient (ro͞o′bə-fā′shənt) *adj.* Producing redness, as of the skin. **—rubefacient** *n.* A substance that irritates the skin, causing redness. [Latin *rubefaciēns, rubefacient-,* present participle of *rubefacere,* to make red : *rubeus,* red; see **reudh-** in Appendix + *facere,* to make; see **dhē-** in Appendix.] **—ru′be·fac′tion** (-făk′shən) *n.*

Rube Gold·berg (ro͞ob′ gōld′bûrg′) *adj.* Of, relating to, or being a contrivance that brings about by complicated means what apparently could have been accomplished simply. [After Reuben Lucius GOLDBERG.]

WORD HISTORY: When we are told in the November 9, 1978, issue of *Nature* that "Orchids are Rube Goldberg machines; a perfect engineer would certainly have come up with something better," we see a recent example of how a proper name has worked its way into the language as a common word. Reuben ("Rube") Lucius Goldberg (1883–1970) was an American cartoonist who delighted his readers with drawings of contrivances that used complicated means to perform what otherwise could be accomplished quite simply. For example, a device to shell an egg is tripped when one picks up the morning paper from the kitchen table. In doing so, one pulls a string that opens the door of a birdcage, releasing a bird that follows a trail of birdseed up a platform. The bird falling off the platform into a pitcher of water splashes water onto a flower that grows, pushing up a rod that causes a pistol to fire. A monkey scared by the shot hits his head against a bumper attached to a razor that cuts into the egg, loosening the shell, which falls into a saucer.

ru·bel·la (ro͞o-bĕl′ə) *n.* A mild, contagious, eruptive disease caused by a virus and capable of producing congenital defects in infants born to mothers infected during the first three months of pregnancy. Also called *German measles.* [From Latin, neuter pl. of *rubellus,* red, from *ruber.* See **reudh-** in Appendix.]

ru·bel·lite (ro͞o′bə-līt′, ro͞o-bĕl′īt) *n.* The red variety of tourmaline, used as a gemstone. [Latin *rubellus,* red; see RUBELLA + -ITE [1].]

Ru·bens (ro͞o′bənz), **Peter Paul.** 1577–1640. Flemish painter. A master of the baroque, he executed many portraits and exuberant works of allegorical, historical, and religious themes, including *Descent from the Cross* (1611–1614). **—Ru′ben·esque′** (ro͞o′bə-nĕsk′) *adj.*

ru·be·o·la (ro͞o-bē′ə-lə, ro͞o′bē-ō′lə) *n.* See **measles** (sense 1a). [From Latin, neuter pl. diminutive of *rubeus,* red. See **reudh-** in Appendix.] **—ru·be′o·lar** *adj.*

ru·bes·cent (ro͞o-bĕs′ənt) *adj.* Turning red; reddening. [Latin *rubēscēns, rubēscent-,* present participle of *rubēscere,* to grow red, inchoative of *rubēre,* to be red. See **reudh-** in Appendix.] **—ru·bes′cence** *n.*

Ru·bi·con (ro͞o′bĭ-kŏn′) *n.* A limit that when passed or exceeded permits of no return and typically results in irrevocable commitment. [Latin *Rubicō, Rubicōn-,* Rubicon, a short river of north-central Italy, the crossing of which by Julius Caesar and his army in 49 B.C. began a civil war.]

ru·bi·cund (ro͞o′bĭ-kənd) *adj.* Inclined to a healthy rosiness; ruddy. [Latin *rubicundus.* See **reudh-** in Appendix.] **—ru′bi·cun′di·ty** (-kŭn′dĭ-tē) *n.*

ru·bid·i·um (ro͞o-bĭd′ē-əm) *n. Symbol* **Rb** A soft silvery-white metallic element of the alkali group that ignites spontaneously in air and reacts violently with water, used in photocells and in the manufacture of vacuum tubes. Atomic number 37; atomic weight 85.47; melting point 38.89°C; boiling point 688°C; specific gravity (solid) 1.532; valence 1, 2, 3, 4. See table at **element.** [From Latin *rubidus,* red. See **reudh-** in Appendix.]

ru·big·i·nous (ro͞o-bĭj′ə-nəs) also **ru·big·i·nose** (-nōs′) *adj.* Rust-colored; reddish-brown. [Latin *rūbīginōsus,* from *rūbīgo, rūbīgin-,* rust, from *rōbus,* red. See **reudh-** in Appendix.]

Ru·bin·stein (ro͞o′bĭn-stīn′), **Anton Gregor.** 1829–1894. Russian pianist and composer who founded the St. Petersburg Conservatory (1862). His compositions include chamber music, operas, and six symphonies.

Rubinstein, Arthur or **Artur.** 1887–1982. Polish-born American pianist particularly known for his interpretations of the works of Chopin.

ru·bi·ous (ro͞o′bē-əs) *adj.* Of the color of a ruby; red.

ru·ble also **rou·ble** (ro͞o′bəl) *n. Abbr.* **r.** See table at **currency.** [Russian *rubl',* from Old Russian *rublĭ,* cut, piece (probably originally a piece cut from a silver bar), from *rubiti,* to chop, hew. See **reup-** in Appendix.]

rub·off or **rub-off** (rŭb′ôf′, -ŏf′) *n.* A repercussion.

rub·out (rŭb′out′) *n. Slang.* Murder; destruction.

ru·bre·dox·in (ro͞o′brĭ-dŏk′sĭn) *n.* An electron-carrying protein associated with oxidation-reduction reactions in anaerobic bacteria and eukaryotic cells. [Latin *ruber, rubr-,* red; see RUBRIC + REDOX + -IN.]

ru·bric (ro͞o′brĭk) *n.* **1.a.** A class or category: *"This mission is sometimes discussed under the rubric of 'horizontal escalation' . . . from conventional to nuclear war"* (Jack Beatty). **b.** A title; a name. **2.** A part of a manuscript or book, such as a title, a heading, or an initial letter, that appears in decorative red lettering or is otherwise distinguished from the rest of the text. **3.** A title or heading of a statute or chapter in a code of law. **4.** *Ecclesiastical.* A direction in a missal, hymnal, or other liturgical book. **5.** An authoritative rule or direction. **6.** A short commentary or explanation covering a broad subject. **7.** Red ocher. **—rubric** *adj.* **1.** *Color.* Red or reddish. **2.** Written in red. [Middle English *rubrike,* from Old French *rubrique,* from Latin *rūbrīca,* red chalk, from *ruber, rubr-,* red. See **reudh-** in Appendix.] **—ru′bri·cal** *adj.*

ru·bri·cate (ro͞o′brĭ-kāt′) *tr.v.* **-cat·ed, -cat·ing, -cates. 1.** To arrange, write, or print as a rubric. **2.** To provide with rubrics. **3.** To establish rules for. [Late Latin *rūbrīcāre, rūbrīcāt-,* to color red, from Latin *rūbrīcātus,* rubricated, from *rūbrīca,* rubric. See RUBRIC.] **—ru′bri·ca′tion** *n.* **—ru′bri·ca′tor** *n.*

ru·bri·cian (ro͞o-brĭsh′ən) *n. Ecclesiastical.* A person learned in the rubrics of ritual.

ru·by (ro͞o′bē) *n., pl.* **-bies. 1.** A deep red, translucent variety of the mineral corundum, highly valued as a precious stone. **2.** Something, such as a watch bearing, that is made from a ruby. **3.** *Color.* A dark or deep red to deep purplish red. **—ruby** *adj.* Of the color ruby. [Middle English, from Old French *rubi,* from Medieval Latin *rubīnus (lapis),* red (stone), ruby, from Latin *rubeus,* red. See **reudh-** in Appendix.]

ruby laser *n.* A laser that uses a ruby crystal to produce an intense, narrow beam of coherent red light, used in light-transmission communication and for localized heating.

ru·by-throat·ed hummingbird (ro͞o′bē-thrō′tĭd) *n.* A small bird *(Archilochus colubris)* of eastern North America, having metallic-green upper plumage and, in the male, a brilliant red throat.

ruche (ro͞osh) *n.* A ruffle or pleat of lace, muslin, or other fine fabric used for trimming women's garments. [French, from Old French *rusche,* beehive, from Medieval Latin *rūsca,* bark of a tree (used for making beehives), of Celtic origin.]

ruck¹ (rŭk) *n.* **1.a.** A multitude; a throng. **b.** The undistinguished crowd or ordinary run of persons or things. **2.** People who are followers, not leaders. [Middle English *ruke,* heap, probably of Scandinavian origin.]

ruck² (rŭk) *v.* **rucked, ruck·ing, rucks.** —*tr.* To make a fold in; crease. —*intr.* To become creased. **—ruck** *n.* A crease or pucker, as in cloth. [Ultimately from Old Norse *hrukka,* wrinkle, fold. See **sker-²** in Appendix.]

ruck·sack (rŭk′săk′, ro͝ok′-) *n.* A knapsack. [German : dialectal *Ruck,* back (from Middle High German *rück, ruck,* from Old High German *hrukki;* see **sker-²** in Appendix) + *Sack,* sack (from Middle High German *sac,* from Old High German, from Latin *saccus;* see SACK¹).]

ruck·us (rŭk′əs) *n.* A disturbance; a commotion: *"Little was heard by us in the upper regions of the considerable ruckus (and surely the heartbreak) being endured some floors below"* (Brendan Gill). [Perhaps blend of RUCTION and RUMPUS.]

ruc·tion (rŭk′shən) *n.* A riotous disturbance; a noisy quarrel. See Synonyms at **brawl.** [Possibly alteration of INSURRECTION.]

Ru·da Ślas·ka (ro͞o′də shlôɴ′skə). A city of south-central Poland, a suburb of Katowice in a mining area. Population, 164,600.

rudd (rŭd) *n.* A European freshwater fish *(Scardinius erythrophthalmus)* related to the carp and having a brownish body and red fins. [Probably from *rud,* red. See RUDDLE.]

rud·der (rŭd′ər) *n.* **1.a.** *Nautical.* A vertically hinged plate of metal, fiberglass, or wood mounted at the stern of a vessel for directing its course. **b.** A similar structure at the tail of an aircraft, used for effecting horizontal changes in course. **2.** A controlling agent or influence over direction; a guide. [Middle English *ruder,* from Old English *rōther,* steering oar. See **erə-** in Appendix.]

rud·der·fish (rud′ər-fĭsh′) *n., pl.* **rudderfish** or **-fish·es.** Any of several oval-shaped schooling fishes of the family Ky-

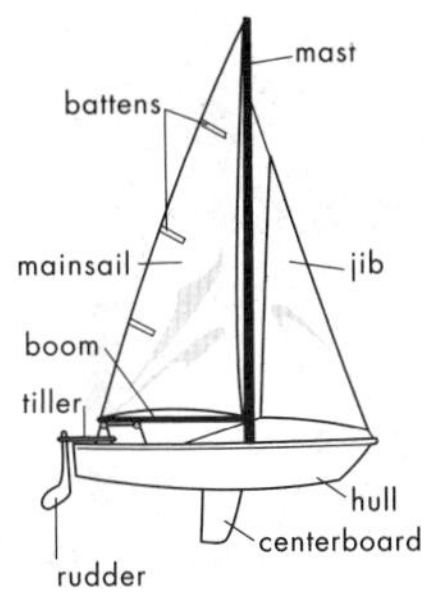

rudder
Bermuda-rigged sloop

ă pat	oi boy
ā pay	ou out
âr care	o͝o took
ä father	o͞o boot
ĕ pet	ŭ cut
ē be	ûr urge
ĭ pit	th thin
ī pie	*th* this
îr pier	hw which
ŏ pot	zh vision
ō toe	ə about, item
ô paw	♦ regionalism

Stress marks: ′ (primary); ′ (secondary), as in **dictionary** (dĭk′shə-nĕr′ē)

ruddy duck
Oxyura jamaicensis

ruffed lemur
Lemur variegatus

Rugby[2]

phosidae, found in tropical parts of the Atlantic and often sighted swimming behind ships.

rud·der·less (rŭd′ər-lĭs) *adj.* **1.** Lacking in direction, control, or coherence: *the confused and rudderless financial markets; characterized the administration's Central American policy as rudderless.* **2.** *Nautical.* Lacking a rudder or a crew member at the rudder.

rud·der·post (rŭd′ər-pōst′) *n.* See **rudderstock.**

rud·der·stock (rŭd′ər-stŏk′) *n.* The vertical shaft of a rudder that allows it to pivot when the tiller or steering gear is operated. Also called *rudderpost.*

rud·dle (rŭd′l) also **red·dle** (rĕd′l) or **rad·dle** (răd′l) *—n.* Red ocherous iron ore, used in dyeing and marking. *—tr.v.* **-dled, -dling, -dles.** To dye or mark with or as if with red ocher: *ruddle sheep.* [Probably diminutive of *rud,* red, from Middle English *rudde,* from Old English *rudu.* See **reudh-** in Appendix.]

rud·dock (rŭd′ək) *n. Chiefly British.* An Old World robin *(Erithacus rubecula)* having olive-brown upper plumage and a conspicuous orange breast. [Middle English *ruddok,* from Old English *rudduc.* See **reudh-** in Appendix.]

rud·dy (rŭd′ē) *adj.* **-di·er, -di·est. 1.a.** Having a healthy, reddish color. **b.** Reddish; rosy. **2.** *Chiefly British.* Used as an intensive: *"You ruddy liar!"* (John Galsworthy). [Middle English *rudi,* from Old English *rudig.* See **reudh-** in Appendix.] **—rud′di·ly** *adv.* **—rud′di·ness** *n.*

ruddy duck *n.* A North American duck *(Oxyura jamaicensis)* having stiff, pointed tail feathers and, in the male, brownish-red upper plumage and a black-and-white head. Also called *sprigtail.*

rude (ro͞od) *adj.* **rud·er, rud·est. 1.** Relatively undeveloped; primitive: *a rude and savage land; a rude agricultural implement.* **2.a.** Being in a crude, rough, unfinished condition: *a rude thatched hut.* **b.** Exhibiting a marked lack of skill or precision in work: *rude crafts.* **c.** In a natural, raw state: *bales of rude cotton.* **3.a.** Lacking the graces and refinement of civilized life; uncouth. **b.** Lacking education or knowledge; unlearned. **c.** Ill-mannered; discourteous: *rude behavior.* **4.** Vigorous, robust, and sturdy. **5.** Abruptly and unpleasantly forceful: *received a rude shock.* [Middle English, from Old French, from Latin *rudis.*] **—rude′ly** *adv.* **—rude′ness** *n.*

SYNONYMS: *rude, crude, primitive, raw, rough.* The central meaning shared by these adjectives is "marked by a lack of skill and finish": *a rude hut; a crude drawing; primitive kitchen facilities; a raw wooden canoe; a rough sketch.*

ru·der·al (ro͞o′dər-əl) *Botany. adj.* Growing in rubbish, poor land, or waste. **—ruderal** *n.* A plant that grows in rubbish, poor land, or waste. [New Latin *rūderālis,* from Latin *rūdus, rūder-,* rubbish.]

ru·di·ment (ro͞o′də-mənt) *n.* **1.** Often **rudiments.** A fundamental element, principle, or skill, as of a field of learning. **2.** Often **rudiments.** Something in an incipient or undeveloped form: *the rudiments of social behavior in children; the rudiments of a plan of action.* **3.** *Biology.* An imperfectly or incompletely developed organ or part. [Latin *rudīmentum,* from *rudis,* rough, unformed.] **—ru′di·men′tal** (-mĕn′tl) *adj.*

ru·di·men·ta·ry (ro͞o′də-mĕn′tə-rē, -mĕn′trē) *adj.* **1.** Of or relating to basic facts or principles; elementary. **2.** Being in the earliest stages of development; incipient. **3.** *Biology.* Imperfectly or incompletely developed; embryonic: *a rudimentary beak.* **—ru′di·men·tar′i·ly** (-târ′ə-lē) *adv.* **—ru′di·men′ta·ri·ness** *n.*

Ru·dolf (ro͞o′dŏlf). 1858–1889. Austrian crown prince. The controversially liberal heir to Francis Joseph I, he was found dead with his mistress in Mayerling, his hunting lodge near Vienna. Officially deemed a double suicide, the suspicious event was never fully investigated.

Rudolf I. 1218–1291. Holy Roman emperor (1273–1291) and founder of the Hapsburg dynasty.

Rudolf, Lake. See Lake **Turkana.**

Ru·dolph (ro͞o′dŏlf), **Wilma Glodean.** Born 1940. American athlete who won gold medals in the 1960 Olympics in the 100-meter dash, 200-meter dash, and 400-meter relay race.

rue[1] (ro͞o) *v.* **rued, ru·ing, rues.** *—tr.* To feel regret, remorse, or sorrow for. *—intr.* To feel regret, remorse, or sorrow. **—rue** *n.* Sorrow; regret: *"To their rue, the Social Democrats have to acknowledge that the Conservative-Liberal coalition has captured the center where elections are won"* (Elizabeth Pond). [Middle English *ruen,* from Old English *hrēowan,* to affect with grief, and *hrēowian,* to repent.] **—ru′er** *n.*

rue[2] (ro͞o) *n.* Any of various aromatic southwest Asian or Mediterranean plants of the genus *Ruta,* especially the ornamental *R. graveolens,* having bipinnately compound leaves that yield an acrid, volatile oil formerly used in medicine. [Middle English, from Old French, from Latin *rūta,* probably from Greek *rhutē.*]

rue anemone *n.* A small North American woodland plant *(Anemonella thalictroides)* having white or pinkish apetalous flowers grouped in umbels.

rue·ful (ro͞o′fəl) *adj.* **1.** Inspiring pity or compassion. **2.** Causing, feeling, or expressing sorrow or regret. **—rue′ful·ly** *adv.* **—rue′ful·ness** *n.*

ru·fes·cent (ro͞o-fĕs′ənt) *adj.* Tinged with red. [Latin *rūfēscēns, rūfēscent-,* present participle of *rūfēscere,* to become red, from *rūfus,* red, reddish. See **reudh-** in Appendix.] **—ru·fes′cence** *n.*

ruff[1] (rŭf) *n.* **1.** A stiffly starched frilled or pleated circular collar of lace, muslin, or other fine fabric, worn by men and women in the 16th and 17th centuries. **2.** A distinctive collarlike projection around the neck, as of feathers on a bird or of fur on a mammal. **3.** A Eurasian sandpiper *(Philomachus pugnax)* the male of which has collarlike, erectile feathers around the neck during the breeding season. [Perhaps short for RUFFLE[1].] **—ruffed** *adj.*

ruff[2] (rŭf) *Games. n.* **1.** The playing of a trump card when one cannot follow suit. **2.** An old game resembling whist. **—ruff** *tr. & intr.v.* **ruffed, ruff·ing, ruffs.** To trump or play a trump. [Obsolete French *ronfle, roffle,* a kind of card game, from Old French *ronfle,* from *renfler,* to rise : *re-,* re- + *enfler,* to cause to swell (from Latin *īnflāre;* see INFLATE).]

ruff[3] (rŭf) *n.* A small European freshwater fish *(Acerina cernua)* related to the perches. [Middle English *ruffe,* probably from Medieval Latin *rufus,* a kind of fish.]

ruffed grouse (rŭft) *n.* A chickenlike North American game bird *(Bonasa umbellus)* having mottled brownish plumage and noted for the drumming sounds the male makes with its wings. Also called *birch partridge.*

ruffed lemur *n.* A chiefly nocturnal lemur *(Lemur variegatus)* of Madagascar having a black and white coat with a fluffy white ruff and that makes nests.

ruf·fi·an (rŭf′ē-ən, rŭf′yən) *n.* **1.** A tough or rowdy fellow. **2.** A thug or gangster. [French, pimp, from Old French *rufien,* from Old Provençal *rufian,* from Old Italian *ruffiano.*] **—ruf′fi·an·ism** *n.* **—ruf′fi·an·ly** *adj.*

ruf·fle[1] (rŭf′əl) *n.* **1.** A strip of frilled or closely pleated fabric used for trimming or decoration. **2.** A ruff on a bird. **3.a.** A ruckus or fray. **b.** Annoyance; vexation. **4.** An irregularity or a slight disturbance of a surface. **—ruffle** *v.* **-fled, -fling, -fles.** *—tr.* **1.** To disturb the smoothness or regularity of; ripple. **2.** To pleat or gather (fabric) into a ruffle. **3.** To erect (the feathers). Used of birds. **4.** To discompose; fluster: *a book that is bound to ruffle some people.* **5.** To flip through (the pages of a book). **6.** *Games.* To shuffle (cards). *—intr.* **1.** To become irregular or rough. **2.** To flutter. **3.** To become flustered. [From Middle English *ruffelen,* to roughen.]

ruf·fle[2] (rŭf′əl) *Music. n.* A low continuous beating of a drum that is not as loud as a roll. **—ruffle** *tr.v.* **-fled, -fling, -fles.** To beat a ruffle on (a drum). [Perhaps from frequentative of *ruff,* a drum roll, perhaps of imitative origin.]

ruf·fle[3] (rŭf′əl) *intr.v.* **-fled, -fling, -fles.** To behave arrogantly or roughly; swagger. [Middle English *ruffelen,* to quarrel.] **—ruf′fler** *n.*

ru·fi·yaa (ro͞o′fē-yä′) *n.* See table at **currency.** [Hindi *rupayā, rupiyā,* from *rūpyam,* silver coin. See RUPEE.]

ru·fous (ro͞o′fəs) *adj. Color.* Strong yellowish pink to moderate orange; reddish. [From Latin *rūfus,* red. See **reudh-** in Appendix.]

rufous hummingbird *n.* A hummingbird *(Selasphorus rufus)* of western North America, distributed from Mexico to Alaska, having rufous upper parts in the male.

rug (rŭg) *n.* **1.** A heavy fabric used to cover a floor. **2.** An animal skin used as a floor covering. **3.** *Chiefly British.* A piece of thick, warm fabric or fur used as a coverlet or lap robe. **4.** *Slang.* A toupee. [Of Scandinavian origin.]

ru·ga (ro͞o′gə) *n., pl.* **-gae** (-gē′, -gī′). *Biology.* A fold, crease, or wrinkle, as in the lining of the stomach. Often used in the plural. [Latin *rūga.*] **—ru′gate′** (-gāt′) *adj.*

Rug·by[1] (rŭg′bē). A municipal borough of central England east-southeast of Birmingham. It is noted primarily as the site of Rugby School, opened in 1574, where the game of Rugby was developed in the 19th century. Population, 59,564.

Rug·by[2] (rŭg′bē) *n. Sports.* A form of football in which players on two competing teams may kick, dribble, or run with the ball and in which forward passing, substitution of players, and timeouts are not permitted. [After *Rugby* School, England.]

Rugby shirt *n.* A knit pullover sports shirt typically having long sleeves, a white collar and neckline, front button closure, and bold horizontal team stripes.

Rü·gen (ro͞o′gən, rü′-). An island of northeast Germany in the Baltic Sea. Separated from the mainland by a narrow channel, it was seized by Denmark in 1168, passed to Pomerania in 1325 and to Sweden in 1648, and became part of Prussia in 1815.

rug·ged (rŭg′ĭd) *adj.* **1.** Having a rough, irregular surface. See Synonyms at **rough. 2.** Having strong features marked with furrows or wrinkles: *the rugged face of the old sailor.* **3.** Having a sturdy build or strong constitution: *a rugged trapper who spent months in the wilderness.* **4.** Tempestuous; stormy: *the rugged weather of the North Atlantic.* **5.** Demanding great effort, ability, or endurance: *the rugged conditions of barracks life.* **6.** Lacking culture or polish; coarse and rude: *rugged manners and ribald wit.* [Middle English, shaggy, of Scandinavian origin.] **—rug′ged·ly** *adv.* **—rug′ged·ness** *n.*

rug·ger (rŭg′ər) *n. Chiefly British.* Rugby. [Alteration of RUGBY[2].]

ru·gose (ro͞o′gōs′) also **ru·gous** (-gəs) *adj.* **1.** Having many wrinkles or creases; ridged or wrinkled. **2.** *Botany.* Having a rough, wrinkled surface, as in certain prominently veined leaves.

[Latin *rūgōsus,* from *rūga,* wrinkle.] **—ru′gose′ly** *adv.* **—ru·gos′i·ty** (-gŏs′ĭ-tē) *n.*

Ruhr (ro͝or). A region of northwest Germany along and north of the **Ruhr River,** which flows about 233 km (145 mi) westward to the Rhine River near Duisburg. The industrial development of the region began in the 19th century.

ru·in (ro͞o′ĭn) *n.* **1.** Total destruction or disintegration, either physical, moral, social, or economic. **2.** A cause of total destruction. **3. a.** The act of destroying totally. **b.** A destroyed person, object, or building. **4.** Often **ruins.** The remains of something destroyed, disintegrated, or decayed: *studied the ruins of ancient Greece.* **—ruin** *v.* **-ined, -in·ing, -ins.** *—tr.* **1.** To destroy completely; demolish. **2.** To harm irreparably. **3.** To reduce to poverty or bankruptcy. **4.** To deprive of chastity. *—intr.* To fall into ruin. [Middle English *ruine,* from Old French, from Latin *ruīna,* from *ruere,* to rush, collapse.] **—ru′in·a·ble** *adj.* **—ru′in·er** *n.*

SYNONYMS: *ruin, raze, demolish, destroy, wreck.* These verbs mean to injure and deprive something—or, less often, someone—of usefulness, soundness, or value. *Ruin* usually implies irretrievable harm but not necessarily total destruction: *The fire ruined the books in the library. "You will ruin no more lives as you ruined mine"* (Arthur Conan Doyle). *Raze,* to level to the ground, *demolish,* to pull down or break to pieces, and the more general *destroy,* to tear down, can all imply reduction to ruins or even complete obliteration: *"raze what was left of the city from the surface of the earth"* (John Lothrop Motley). *The conquerors tried to raze the very name of the people's national hero from their memories. Both of the cars involved were demolished in the accident. The prosecutor demolished the opposition's argument. "It became necessary to destroy the town in order to save it"* (Anonymous major in Vietnam). *"I saw the best minds of my generation destroyed by madness"* (Allen Ginsberg). To *wreck* is to ruin in or as if in a violent collision: *"The Boers had just wrecked a British military train"* (Arnold Bennett). When *wreck* is used in its extended sense, as in referring to the ruination of a person or his or her hopes or reputation, it implies irreparable shattering: *"Coleridge, poet and philosopher wrecked in a mist of opium"* (Matthew Arnold).

ru·in·ate (ro͞o′ə-nāt′) *adj.* Having been ruined. [Medieval Latin *ruīnātus,* from Latin *ruīna,* ruin. See RUIN.]

ru·in·a·tion (ro͞o′ə-nā′shən) *n.* **1.** The act or ruining or the condition of being ruined. **2.** A cause of ruin.

ru·in·ous (ro͞o′ə-nəs) *adj.* **1.** Causing or apt to cause ruin; destructive. **2.** Falling to ruin; dilapidated or decayed. **—ru′in·ous·ly** *adv.* **—ru′in·ous·ness** *n.*

Ruis·dael or **Ruys·dael** (rīz′däl′, rīs′-, rois′-), **Jacob van.** 1628?–1682. Dutch landscape painter whose baroque works, such as *Windmill at Wijk* (c. 1665), depict the majesty of nature.

Ru·key·ser (ro͞o′kī-zər), **Muriel.** 1913–1980. American writer whose feminist poetry, including the collections *Beast in View* (1944) and *The Gates* (1976), often speaks out against racism and war.

rule (ro͞ol) *n.* **1. a.** Governing power or its possession or use; authority. **b.** The duration of such power. **2. a.** An authoritative, prescribed direction for conduct, especially one of the regulations governing procedure in a legislative body or a regulation observed by the players in a game, sport, or contest. **b.** The body of regulations prescribed by the founder of a religious order for governing the conduct of its members. **3.** A usual, customary, or generalized course of action or behavior: *"The rule of life in the defense bar ordinarily is to go along and get along"* (Scott Turow). **4.** A generalized statement that describes what is true in most or all cases: *In this office, hard work is the rule, not the exception.* **5.** *Mathematics.* A standard method or procedure for solving a class of problems. **6.** *Law.* **a.** A court order limited in application to a specific case. **b.** A subordinate regulation governing a particular matter. **7.** See **ruler** (sense 2). **8.** *Printing.* A thin metal strip of various widths and designs, used to print borders or lines, as between columns. **—rule** *v.* **ruled, rul·ing, rules.** *—tr.* **1.** To exercise control, dominion, or direction over; govern. **2.** To dominate by powerful influence. **3.** To decide or declare authoritatively or judicially; decree. See Synonyms at **decide. 4. a.** To mark with straight parallel lines. **b.** To mark (a straight line), as with a ruler. *—intr.* **1.** To be in total control or command; exercise supreme authority. **2.** To formulate and issue a decree or decision. **3.** To prevail at a particular level or rate: *Prices ruled low.* ***—phrasal verb.* rule out. 1.** To prevent; preclude: *The snowstorm ruled out their weekly meeting.* **2.** To remove from consideration; exclude: *The option of starting over has been ruled out.* ***—idiom.* as a rule.** In general; for the most part: *As a rule, we take the bus.* [Middle English *reule,* from Old French, from Vulgar Latin **regula,* from Latin *rēgula,* rod, principle. See **reg-** in Appendix.] **—rul′a·ble** *adj.*

ruled surface (ro͞old) *n.* A surface, such as a cone or cylinder, generated by the motion of a straight line.

rule of engagement *n., pl.* **rules of engagement.** A directive issued by competent military authority that delineates the limitations and circumstances under which forces will initiate and prosecute combat engagement with other forces encountered.

rule of the road *n., pl.* **rules of the road. 1.** A set of customary practices, especially for the operation of a motor vehicle, a boat, or an aircraft, established to promote efficiency and safety. Often used in the plural. **2.** A set of established rules or practices, usually unstated, intended to minimize confusion or conflict. Often used in the plural: *"Great powers . . . wishing to avoid war could resort to one of three tools: condominium, spheres of influence or rules of the road"* (Charles William Maynes).

rule of thumb *n., pl.* **rules of thumb.** A useful principle having wide application but not intended to be strictly accurate or reliable in every situation.

rul·er (ro͞o′lər) *n.* **1.** One, such as a monarch or dictator, that rules or governs. **2.** A straightedged strip, as of wood or metal, for drawing straight lines and measuring lengths. In this sense, also called *rule.*

rul·ing (ro͞o′lĭng) *adj.* **1.** Exercising control or authority: *the ruling junta; ruling circles of the government.* **2.** Predominant: *the ruling principle.* **—ruling** *n.* **1.** The act of governing or controlling. **2.** An authoritative or official decision: *a court ruling.*

rul·y (ro͞o′lē) *adj.* **-li·er, -li·est.** Neat and orderly: *"A small, ruly beard balances his hair"* (Whitney Balliett). [Back-formation from UNRULY.]

rum¹ (rŭm) *n.* **1.** An alcoholic liquor distilled from fermented molasses or sugar cane. **2.** Intoxicating beverages. [Probably short for obsolete *rumbullion.*]

rum² (rŭm) *adj.* **rum·mer, rum·mest.** *Chiefly British.* **1.** Odd; strange. **2.** Presenting danger or difficulty. [Origin unknown.]

ru·ma·ki (rə-mä′kē) *n., pl.* **-kis.** An appetizer of Japanese origin consisting of a marinated piece of chicken liver and a water chestnut wrapped in a slice of bacon and grilled or broiled. [Origin unknown.]

Ru·ma·ni·a (ro͞o-mā′nē-ə, -mān′yə). See **Romania.**

Ru·ma·ni·an (ro͞o-mā′nē-ən, -mān′yən) *adj. & n.* Variant of **Romanian.**

rum·ba also **rhum·ba** (rŭm′bə, ro͝om′-, ro͞om′-) *n.* **1.** A complex rhythmical dance that originated in Cuba. **2.** A modern ballroom adaptation of this dance. [American Spanish, from Spanish *rumbo,* ship's course, revelry, pomp. See RHUMB.] **—rum′ba** *v.*

rum·ble (rŭm′bəl) *v.* **-bled, -bling, -bles.** *—intr.* **1.** To make a deep, long, rolling sound. **2.** To move or proceed with a deep, long, rolling sound. **3.** *Slang.* To engage in a gang fight. *—tr.* **1.** To utter with a deep, long, rolling sound. **2.** To polish or mix (metal parts) in a tumbling box. **—rumble** *n.* **1.** A deep, long, rolling sound. **2.** A tumbling box. **3.** A luggage compartment or servant's seat in the rear of a carriage. **4.** *Slang.* **a.** Pervasive, widespread expression of unrest or dissatisfaction. **b.** A gang fight. [Middle English *romblen,* perhaps from Middle Dutch *rommelen* or from Middle Low German *rummeln.*] **—rum′bler** *n.* **—rum′bling·ly** *adv.* **—rum′bly** *adj.*

rumble seat *n.* An uncovered passenger seat that opens out from the rear of an automobile.

rum·bus·tious (rŭm-bŭs′chəs) *adj.* Uncontrollably exuberant; unruly: *"Common to both his illustrations and his independent paintings . . . and lurking below their rumbustious surface, is a sympathy for the vulnerability of the ordinary human being"* (Christopher Andreae). [Probably alteration of ROBUSTIOUS.] **—rum·bus′tious·ly** *adv.* **—rum·bus′tious·ness** *n.*

ru·men (ro͞o′mən) *n., pl.* **-mi·na** (-mə-nə) or **-mens.** The first division of the stomach of a ruminant animal, in which most food collects immediately after being swallowed and from which it is later returned to the mouth as cud for thorough chewing. Also called *paunch.* [Latin *rūmen,* throat.] **—ru′mi·nal** *adj.*

ru·mi·nant (ro͞o′mə-nənt) *n.* Any of various hoofed, even-toed, usually horned mammals of the suborder Ruminantia, such as cattle, sheep, goats, deer, and giraffes, characteristically having a stomach divided into four compartments and chewing a cud consisting of regurgitated, partially digested food. **—ruminant** *adj.* **1.** Characterized by the chewing of cud. **2.** Of or belonging to the Ruminantia. **3.** Meditative; contemplative. [From Latin *rūmināns, rūminant-,* present participle of *rūmināre,* to ruminate. See RUMINATE.]

ru·mi·nate (ro͞o′mə-nāt′) *v.* **-nat·ed, -nat·ing, -nates.** *—intr.* **1.** To turn a matter over and over in the mind. See Synonyms at **ponder. 2.** To chew cud. *—tr.* To reflect on over and over again. [Latin *rūmināre, rūmināt-,* from *rūmen, rūmin-,* throat.] **—ru′mi·na′tive** *adj.* **—ru′mi·na′tive·ly** *adv.* **—ru′mi·na′tor** *n.*

ru·mi·na·tion (ro͞o′mə-nā′shən) *n.* **1.** The act of pondering; meditation. **2.** The act or process of chewing cud.

rum·mage (rŭm′ĭj) *v.* **-maged, -mag·ing, -mag·es.** *—tr.* **1.** To search thoroughly by handling, turning over, or disarranging the contents of. **2.** To discover by searching thoroughly. *—intr.* To make an energetic, usually hasty search. **—rummage** *n.* **1.** A thorough search among a number of things. **2.** A confusion of miscellaneous articles. [From earlier *romage,* act of packing cargo, from French *arrumage,* from Old French, from *arumer,* to stow, from Old Provençal *arumar* : *a-,* to (from Latin *ad-;* see AD–) + perhaps *run,* ship's hold (of Germanic origin; see **reuə-** in Appendix).] **—rum′mag·er** *n.*

rummage sale *n.* **1.** A sale of assorted secondhand objects contributed by donors to raise money for a charity. **2.** A sale, especially of unclaimed or excess goods, as at a warehouse or wharf.

rum·mer (rŭm′ər) *n.* A large drinking cup or glass. [German *Römer,* from Dutch *roemer,* from *roem,* praise, from Middle Dutch.]

Rugby shirt

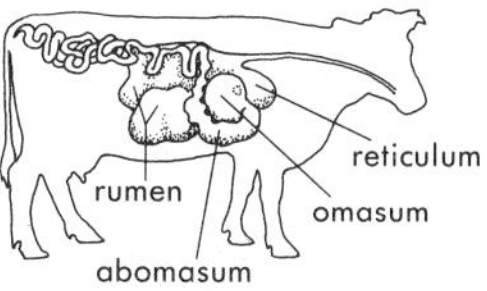

rumen

ă pat	oi boy
ā pay	ou out
âr care	o͝o took
ä father	o͞o boot
ĕ pet	ŭ cut
ē be	ûr urge
ĭ pit	th thin
ī pie	*th* this
îr pier	hw which
ŏ pot	zh vision
ō toe	ə about, item
ô paw	♦ regionalism

Stress marks: ′ (primary); ′ (secondary), as in **dictionary** (dĭk′shə-nĕr′ē)

rum·my[1] (rŭm′ē) *n. Games.* A card game, played in many variations, in which the object is to obtain sets of three or more cards of the same rank or suit. [Origin unknown.]

rum·my[2] (rŭm′ē) *n., pl.* **-mies.** *Slang.* A drunkard.

rum·my[3] (rŭm′ē) *adj.* **-mi·er, -mi·est.** *Chiefly British.* Odd, strange, or dangerous; rum.

ru·mor (ro͞o′mər) *n.* Unverified information of uncertain origin usually spread by word of mouth; hearsay. **—rumor** *tr.v.* **-mored, -mor·ing, -mors.** To spread or tell by rumor. [Middle English *rumour,* from Old French, from Latin *rūmor.*]

ru·mor·mon·ger (ro͞o′mər-mŭng′gər, -mŏng′-) *n.* One that spreads rumors. **—rumormonger** *intr.v.* **-gered, -ger·ing, -gers.** To engage in the spreading of rumors.

ru·mour (ro͞o′mər) *n. & v. Chiefly British.* Variant of **rumor.**

rump (rŭmp) *n.* **1.** The fleshy hindquarters of an animal. **2.** A cut of beef or veal from the rump. **3.** The buttocks. **4.** The part of a bird's back nearest the tail. **5.** The last or inferior part. **6.** A legislature having only a small part of its original membership and therefore being unrepresentative or lacking in authority. [Middle English *rumpe,* of Scandinavian origin.]

rum·ple (rŭm′pəl) *v.* **-pled, -pling, -ples.** *—tr.* To wrinkle or form into folds or creases. *—intr.* To become wrinkled or creased. **—rumple** *n.* An irregular or untidy crease. [Perhaps Dutch *rompelen,* from Middle Dutch *rumpelen.*] **—rum′ply** *adj.*

rum·pus (rŭm′pəs) *n.* A noisy clamor. [Origin unknown.]

rumpus room *n.* A room for play and parties.

rum·run·ner (rŭm′rŭn′ər) *n.* **1.** One who illegally transports liquor across a border. **2.** *Nautical.* A boat used to transport liquor illegally across a border.

Rum·sey (rŭm′zē), **James.** 1743–1792. American engineer and inventor of a practical steamboat (1787) and steam boiler.

♦**rum shop** *n. Caribbean.* A tavern, usually selling alcoholic beverages by the bottle as well as by the drink.

♦**run** (rŭn) *v.* **ran** (răn), **run, run·ning, runs.** *—intr.* **1.a.** To move swiftly on foot so that both feet leave the ground during each stride. **b.** To move at a fast gallop. Used of a horse. **2.** To retreat rapidly; flee: *seized the money and ran.* **3.a.** To move without hindrance or restraint: *dogs that always ran loose.* **b.** To keep company: *runs with a wild crowd.* **c.** To go or move about from place to place; roam: *I am always running about, looking for my glasses.* **4.** To migrate, especially to move in a shoal in order to spawn. Used of fish. **5.a.** To move or go quickly; hurry: *run for the police; ran for help.* **b.** To go when in trouble or distress: *He is always running to his lawyer.* **c.** To make a short, quick trip or visit: *ran next door to borrow a cup of sugar; ran down to the store.* **6.a.** To take part in a race or contest: *ran in the marathon; athletes who run for the gold medal.* **b.** To compete in a race for elected office: *ran for mayor.* **c.** To finish a race or contest in a specified position: *ran second.* **7.** To move freely, on or as if on wheels: *The car ran downhill. The drawer runs on small bearings.* **8.** To be in operation: *The engine is running.* **9.** To go back and forth especially on a regular basis; ply: *The ferry runs every hour.* **10.** *Nautical.* To sail or steer before the wind or on an indicated course: *run before a storm.* **11.a.** To flow, especially in a steady stream: *Fresh water runs from the spring. Turn on the faucet and let the water run.* **b.** To emit pus, mucus, or serous fluid: *Pollen makes my nose run.* **12.** To melt and flow: *A hot flame will make the solder run.* **13.** To spread or dissolve, as dyes in fabric: *Colorfast garments are not supposed to run.* **14.** To extend, stretch, or reach in a certain direction or to a particular point: *This road runs to the next town.* **15.** To extend, spread, or climb as a result of growing: *Ivy ran up the wall.* **16.** To spread rapidly: *disease that ran rampant.* **17.a.** To be valid in a given area: *The speed limit runs only to the town line.* **b.** To be present as a valid accompaniment: *Fishing rights run with ownership of the land.* **18.** To unravel along a line: *Her stocking ran.* **19.** To continue in effect or operation: *a lease with one year to run.* **20.** To pass: *Days ran into weeks.* **21.** To tend to persist or recur: *Stinginess seems to run in that family.* **22.a.** To accumulate or accrue: *The interest runs from the first of the month.* **b.** To become payable. **23.** To take a particular form, order, or expression: *My reasoning runs thus. The report runs as follows.* **24.** To tend or incline: *Their taste in art runs to the bizarre.* **25.** To occupy or exist in a certain range: *The sizes run from small to large.* **26.** To be presented or performed for a continuous period of time: *The play ran for six months.* **27.** To pass into a specified condition: *We ran into debt.* *—tr.* **1.a.** To travel over on foot at a pace faster than a walk: *ran the entire distance.* **b.** To cause (an animal) to move quickly or rapidly: *We run our hunting dogs every morning.* **2.** To allow to move without restraint. **3.** To do or accomplish by or as if by running: *run errands.* **4.** To hunt or pursue; chase: *dogs running deer.* **5.** To bring to a given condition by or as if by running: *The toddlers ran me ragged.* **6.** To cause to move quickly: *She ran her fingers along the keyboard.* **7.a.** To cause to compete in or as if in a race: *He ran two horses in the Kentucky Derby.* **b.** To present or nominate for elective office: *The party ran her for senator.* **8.** To cause to move or progress freely. **9.** To cause to function; operate: *run a machine.* **10.** To convey or transport: *Run me into town. Run the garbage over to the dump.* **11.** *Nautical.* To cause to move on a course: *We ran our boat into a cove.* **12.a.** To smuggle: *run guns.* **b.** To evade and pass through: *run a roadblock.* **13.** To pass over or through: *run the rapids.* **14.** To cause to flow: *run water into a tub.* **15.** To stream with: *The fountains ran champagne.* **16.** *Metallurgy.* **a.** To melt, fuse, or smelt (metal). **b.** To mold or cast (molten metal): *run gold into ingots.* **17.** To cause to extend or pass: *run a rope between the poles.* **18.** To mark or trace on a surface: *run a pencil line between two points.* **19.** To sew with a continuous line of stitches: *run a seam.* **20.** To cause to unravel along a line: *She ran her stocking on a splinter.* **21.a.** To cause to crash or collide: *ran the car into a fence.* **b.** To cause to penetrate: *I ran a pin into my thumb.* **22.** To continue to present or perform: *ran the film for a month.* **23.** To publish in a periodical: *run an advertisement.* **24.** To subject or be subjected to: *run a risk.* **25.** *Games.* **a.** To score (balls or points) consecutively in billiards: *run 15 balls.* **b.** To clear (the table) in pool by consecutive scores. **26.** To conduct or perform: *run an experiment.* **27.** *Computer Science.* To process or execute (a program or an instruction). **28.** To control, manage, or direct: *ran the campaign by himself; a bureau that runs espionage operations.* **—run** *n.* **1.a.** A pace faster than a walk. **b.** A fast gallop. Used of a horse. **2.** An act of running. **3.a.** A distance covered by or as if by running. **b.** The time taken to cover such a distance: *It is a two minutes' run from the subway.* **4.** A quick trip or visit: *a run into town.* **5.a.** *Sports.* A running race: *the winner of the mile run.* **b.** A campaign for public office: *She managed his successful senatorial run.* **6.** *Abbr.* **r, r.** *Baseball.* A point scored by advancing around the bases and reaching home plate safely. **7.** *Football.* A player's attempt to carry the ball past or through the opposing team, usually for a specified distance: *a 30-yard run.* **8.a.** The migration of fish, especially in order to spawn. **b.** A group or school of fish ascending a river in order to spawn. **9.** Unrestricted freedom or use: *I had the run of the library.* **10.** A stretch or period of riding, as in a race or to the hounds. **11.a.** A track or slope along or down which something can travel: *a logging run.* **b.** *Sports.* A particular type of passage down a hill or across country experienced by an athlete, especially a skier or bobsledder: *had two very good runs before the end of the day.* **12.** *Sports.* The distance a golf ball rolls after hitting the ground. **13.a.** A scheduled or regular route. **b.** The territory of a news reporter. **14.a.** A continuous period of operation, especially of a machine or factory. **b.** The production achieved during such a period: *a press run of 15,000 copies.* **15.a.** A movement or flow. **b.** The duration of such a flow. **c.** The amount of such a flow. **16.** A pipe or channel through which something flows. **17.** *Eastern Lower Northern U.S.* See **creek** (sense 1). **18.** A fall or slide, as of sand or mud. **19.** Continuous length or extent: *a five-foot run of tubing.* **20.** *Geology.* A vein or seam, as of ore or rock. **21.** The direction, configuration, or lie: *the run of the grain in leather.* **22.a.** A trail or way made or frequented by animals. **b.** An outdoor enclosure for domestic animals or poultry: *a dog run; a turkey run.* **23.a.** A length of torn or unraveled stitches in a knitted fabric. **b.** A blemish caused by excessive paint flow. **24.** An unbroken series or sequence: *a run of dry summers.* **25.** An unbroken sequence of theatrical performances. **26.** *Music.* A rapid sequence of notes; a roulade. **27.** A series of unexpected and urgent demands, as by depositors or customers: *a run on a bank.* **28.a.** A continuous set or sequence, as of playing cards in one suit. **b.** A successful sequence of shots or points. **29.** A sustained state or condition: *a run of good luck.* **30.** A trend or tendency: *the run of events.* **31.** The average type, group, or category: *The broad run of voters want the candidate to win.* **32.** *Computer Science.* An execution of a specific program or instruction. **33.** **runs.** *Slang.* Diarrhea. Often used with *the.* **—run** *adj.* **1.** Being in a melted or molten state: *run butter; run gold.* **2.** Completely exhausted from running. ***—phrasal verbs.*** **run across.** To find by chance; come upon. **run after.** **1.** To pursue; chase. **2.** To seek the company or attention of for purposes of courting: *He finally became tired of running after her.* **run against.** **1.** To encounter unexpectedly; run into. **2.** To work against; oppose: *found public sentiment running against him.* **run along.** To go away; leave. **run away.** **1.** To flee; escape. **2.** To leave one's home, especially to elope. **3.** To stampede. **run down.** **1.** To stop because of lack of force or power: *The alarm clock finally ran down.* **2.** To become tired. **3.a.** To collide with and knock down: *a pedestrian who was run down by a speeding motorist.* **b.** *Nautical.* To collide with and cause to sink. **4.** To chase and capture: *Detectives ran down the suspects.* **5.** To trace the source of: *The police ran down all possible leads in the missing-person case.* **6.** To disparage: *Don't run her down; she is very talented.* **7.** To go over; review: *run down a list once more.* **8.** *Baseball.* To put a runner out after trapping him or her between two bases. **run in.** **1.** To insert or include as something extra: *ran in an illustration next to the first paragraph.* **2.** *Printing.* To make a solid body of text without a paragraph or other break. **3.** *Slang.* To take into legal custody. **4.** To go to or seek out the company of in order to socialize; visit: *We ran in for an hour.* **run into.** **1.** To meet or find by chance: *ran into an old friend.* **2.** To encounter (something): *ran into trouble.* **3.** To collide with. **4.** To amount to: *His net worth runs into seven figures.* **run off.** **1.** To print, duplicate, or copy: *ran off 200 copies of the report.* **2.** To run away; elope. **3.** To flow off; drain away. **4.** To decide a contest or competition by a runoff. **5.** To force or drive off (trespassers, for example). **run on.** **a.** To keep going; continue. **b.** To talk volubly, persistently, and usually inconsequentially: *He is always running on about his tax problems.* **c.** To continue a text without a formal break. **run out.** **1.** To become used up; be exhausted: *Our supplies finally ran out.* **2.** To put out by force; compel to leave: *We ran him out of town.* **3.** To become void, especially through the passage of time or an omission: *an insurance policy that had run out.* **run over.** **1.** To collide with, knock down, and often pass over: *The car ran over a child.* **2.** To read or review quickly: *run over a speech before giving it.* **3.** To flow over. **4.** To go beyond a limit: *The meeting ran over by 30 minutes.* **run through. 1.** To pierce: *The soldier was run through by a bayonet.* **2.** To use up quickly: *She ran through all her money.* **3.** To rehearse quickly: *Let's run through the first act again.* **4.** To go over the salient points or facts of: *The crew ran through the preflight procedures. We ran through the witness's testimony before presenting it in court.* **run up.** To make or become greater or larger: *ran up huge bills; run up the price of the company's stock.* **run with.** To take as one's own; adopt: "[He] *was determined to run with the idea and go public before it had been researched*" (Betty Cuniberti). **—*idioms.* a run for (one's) money.** Strong competition. **in the long run.** In the final analysis or outcome. **in the short run.** In the immediate future. **on the run. 1.a.** In rapid retreat: *guerrillas on the run after an ambush.* **b.** In hiding: *fugitives on the run.* **2.** Hurrying busily from place to place: *executives always on the run from New York to Los Angeles.* **run a temperature.** To have a fever. **run away with. 1.a.** To make off with hurriedly. **b.** To steal. **2.** To be greater or bigger than others in (a performance, for example). **run foul** (or **afoul**) **of. 1.** To run into; collide with: *a sloop that had run foul of the submerged reef.* **2.** To come into conflict with: *a pickpocket who ran foul of the law.* **run in place.** To go through the movements of running without leaving one's original position. **run off with.** To capture or carry off: *ran off with the state championship.* **run (one's) eyes over.** To look at or read in a cursory manner. **run out of.** To exhaust the supply of: *ran out of fuel.* **run out of gas.** *Slang.* **1.** To exhaust one's energy or enthusiasm. **2.** To falter or come to a stop because of a lack of capital, support, or enthusiasm. **run out on.** To abandon: *has run out on the family.* **run rings around.** To be markedly superior to. **run scared.** *Informal.* To become intimidated or frightened. **run short.** To become scanty or insufficient in supply: *Fuel oil ran short during the winter.* **run short of.** To use up so that a supply becomes insufficient or scanty: *ran short of paper clips.* **run to earth** (or **ground**). To pursue and successfully capture: *Dogs ran the fox to earth. The police ran the terrorists to ground.* [Middle English *ernen, runnen,* from Old English *rinnan, eornan, earnan* and from Old Norse *rinna;* see **rei-** in Appendix.]

♦ ***REGIONAL NOTE:*** Terms for "a small, fast-flowing stream" vary throughout the eastern United States especially. Speakers in the eastern part of the Lower North (including Virginia, West Virginia, Delaware, Maryland, and southern Pennsylvania) use the word *run,* as in *Bull Run.* Speakers in New York State are liable to call such a stream a *kill* (a Dutch borrowing). *Brook* has come to be used throughout the Northeast. Southerners refer to a *branch,* and throughout the northern United States the term is *crick,* a variant of *creek.*

run·a·bout (rŭn′ə-bout′) *n.* **1.a.** *Nautical.* A small motorboat. **b.** A light aircraft. **c.** A small, open automobile or carriage. **2.** A vagabond or wanderer.

run·a·gate (rŭn′ə-gāt′) *n.* **1.** A renegade or deserter. **2.** A vagabond. [Alteration of obsolete *renegate,* renegade (influenced by RUN + *agate,* on the way, from Middle English, straight way : Middle English *a,* on, variant of *on;* see ON + Old Norse *gata,* way; see **ghē-** in Appendix), from Middle English, from Medieval Latin *renegātus.* See RENEGADE.]

run·a·round (rŭn′ə-round′) *n.* **1.** *Informal.* Deception, usually in the form of evasive excuses. **2.** *Printing.* Type set in a column narrower than the body of the text, as on either side of a picture.

run·a·way (rŭn′ə-wā′) *n.* **1.** A person who has run away. **2.** Something that has escaped control or proper confinement. **3.** *Informal.* An easy victory. **—runaway** *adj.* **1.** Escaping or having escaped restraint, captivity, or control: *runaway horses; runaway children.* **2.** Out of control: *a runaway car; runaway inflation.* **3.** Easily won: *a runaway victory.*

run·back (rŭn′băk′) *n.* *Football.* **1.** The act of returning a kickoff, a punt, or an intercepted forward pass. **2.** The distance so covered.

run·ci·ble spoon (rŭn′sə-bəl) *n.* A three-pronged fork, such as a pickle fork, curved like a spoon and having a cutting edge. [Coined by Edward Lear, perhaps alteration of *rounceval,* big woman, large pea, wart, monster, huge, from *Roncevaux* (Roncesvalles), site where giant bones were found.]

Run·cie (rŭn′sē), **Robert Alexander Kennedy.** Born 1921. British prelate and archbishop of Canterbury (1980–1991).

run·ci·nate (rŭn′sə-nāt′) *adj.* *Botany.* Having saw-toothed divisions directed backward: *runcinate leaves.* [Latin *runcinātus,* past participle of *runcināre,* to plane, from *runcina,* carpenter's plane, formerly taken to mean saw, alteration (influenced by *runcāre,* to weed, pluck) of Greek *rhukanē,* carpenter's plane.]

run·down (rŭn′doun′) *n.* **1.** A point-by-point summary. **2.** *Baseball.* A play in which a runner is trapped between bases and is pursued by fielders attempting to make the tag. **—rundown** also **run-down** (rŭn′doun′) *adj.* **1.a.** In poor physical condition; weak or exhausted. **b.** Dirty and dilapidated: *rundown housing projects.* **2.** Unwound and not running: *a run-down watch.*

Rund·stedt (ro͞on′stĕt′, ro͞ont′shtĕt′), **Karl Rudolf Gerd von.** 1875–1953. German general who took part in the invasions of Poland, France, and Russia during World War II and was commander in chief of the western front (1942–1945).

rune¹ (ro͞on) *n.* **1.a.** Any of the characters in several alphabets used by ancient Germanic peoples from the 3rd to the 13th century. **b.** A similar character in another alphabet, sometimes believed to have magic powers. **2.** A poem or an incantation of mysterious significance, especially a magic charm. [Possibly Old Norse or Old English *rūn.*] **—run′ic** *adj.*

rune² (ro͞on) *n.* A Finnish poem or section of a poem. [Finnish *runo,* of Germanic origin.]

rung¹ (rŭng) *n.* **1.** A rod or bar forming a step of a ladder. **2.** A crosspiece between the legs of a chair. **3.** The spoke in a wheel. **4.** *Nautical.* One of the spokes or handles on a ship's wheel. [Middle English, from Old English *hrung.*]

rung² (rŭng) *v.* Past participle of **ring².**

run-in (rŭn′ĭn′) *n.* **1.** A quarrel or an argument. **2.** *Printing.* Matter added to a text. **—run-in** *adj.* *Printing.* Having been added to or inserted into a text.

run·let (rŭn′lĭt) *n.* A rivulet.

run·nel (rŭn′əl) *n.* **1.** A rivulet; a brook. **2.** A narrow channel or course, as for water. [Middle English *rynel,* from Old English, from *rinnan,* to run. See **rei-** in Appendix.]

run·ner (rŭn′ər) *n.* **1.** *Sports.* One who competes in a race. **2.a.** *Baseball.* One who runs the bases. **b.** *Football.* One who carries the ball. **3.** A fugitive. **4.** One who carries messages or runs errands. **5.** One who serves as an agent or a collector, as for a bank or brokerage house. **6.** One who solicits business, as for a hotel or store. **7.** A smuggler: *a narcotics runner.* **8.** *Nautical.* A vessel engaged in smuggling. **9.** One who operates or manages something: *the runner of a series of gambling operations.* **10.** A device in or on which a mechanism slides or moves, as: **a.** The blade of a skate. **b.** The supports on which a drawer slides. **11.** A long narrow carpet. **12.** A long narrow tablecloth. **13.** A roller towel. **14.** *Metallurgy.* A channel along which molten metal is poured into a mold; a gate. **15.** *Botany.* **a.** A slender, creeping stem that puts forth roots from nodes spaced at intervals along its length. **b.** A plant, such as the strawberry, having such a stem. **c.** A twining vine, such as the scarlet runner. **16.** Any of several marine fishes of the family Carangidae, especially the blue runner *(Caranx crysos),* of temperate waters of the American Atlantic coast. Also called *blue runner.* **17.** *Sports.* See **flat¹** (sense 9).

runner

run·ner-up (rŭn′ər-ŭp′) *n., pl.* **run·ners-up** (rŭn′ərz-). One that takes second place, as in a game, sport, or other competition.

run·ning (rŭn′ĭng) *n.* **1.** The act or an instance of running. **2.** The power or ability to run. **3.** *Sports.* The exercise or sport of someone who runs. **—running** *adj.* Ongoing over a period of time: *a running conversation; a running joke among us.* **—running** *adv.* In a consecutive way: *four years running.* **—*idioms.* in the running. 1.** Entered as a contender in a competition. **2.** Having the possibility of winning or placing well in a competition. **out of the running. 1.** Not entered as a contender in a competition. **2.** Having no possibility of winning or placing well in a competition.

running back *n.* *Football.* An offensive back, such as a fullback or halfback, who is designated the responsibility of advancing the ball by running with it on plays from the line of scrimmage.

running board *n.* A narrow footboard extending under and beside the doors of some automobiles and other conveyances.

running board

running dog *n.* A servile follower or lackey. [Translation of Chinese (Mandarin) *zǒu gǒu* : *zǒu,* running + *gǒu,* dog.]

running gear *n.* The working parts of an automobile, a locomotive, or other vehicle.

running hand *n.* Handwriting done rapidly without lifting the pen from the paper.

running head *n.* *Printing.* A title printed at the top of every page or every other page, as in a book. Also called *running title.*

running knot *n.* See **slipknot.**

running light *n.* One of several lights on a vehicle, such as a ship, turned on between dusk and dawn to indicate position and size.

running mate *n.* **1.** The candidate or nominee for the lesser of two closely associated political offices. **2.** A companion. **3.** A horse used to set the pace in a race for another horse.

running noose *n.* See **noose** (sense 1).

running shoe *n.* *Sports.* A shoe in which to run for sport or exercise, especially one with a durable insole for support and comfort, a soft padded collar for reduced friction, and a resilient outer sole for cushioning and absorbing shock.

running start *n.* See **flying start.**

running stitch *n.* One of a series of small, even stitches.

running title *n.* *Printing.* See **running head.**

running track *n.* *Sports.* A course, indoors or outdoors, for engaging in the sport or exercise of running.

run·ny (rŭn′ē) *adj.* **-ni·er, -ni·est.** Inclined to run or flow: *runny icing; a runny nose.*

Run·ny·mede (rŭn′ē-mēd′). A meadow in southeast England on the Thames River west of London. King John accepted the Magna Carta here or on a nearby island in 1215.

run·off (rŭn′ôf′, -ŏf′) *n.* **1.a.** The overflow of fluid from a container. **b.** Rainfall not absorbed by soil. **2.** Eliminated waste products from manufacturing processes. **3.** An extra competition held to break a tie.

ă pat	oi boy
ā pay	ou out
âr care	o͝o took
ä father	o͞o boot
ĕ pet	ŭ cut
ē be	ûr urge
ĭ pit	th thin
ī pie	*th* this
îr pier	hw which
ŏ pot	zh vision
ō toe	ə about, item
ô paw	♦ regionalism

Stress marks: ′ (primary); ′ (secondary), as in **dictionary** (dĭk′shə-nĕr′ē)

runway
Logan Airport, Boston, Massachusetts

Mount Rushmore
Left to right: Portraits of Presidents Washington, Jefferson, Theodore Roosevelt, and Lincoln by Gutzon Borglum

rusine antler
Sambar buck
Cervus unicolor

run-of-the-mill (rŭn′əv-*thə*-mĭl′) *adj.* Not special or outstanding; average.

run-on (rŭn′ŏn′, -ôn′) *n. Printing.* Matter that is appended or added without a formal break. **—run′-on′** *adj.*

run-on sentence *n. Grammar.* A sentence in which two or more independent clauses are improperly joined, as by a comma fault.

run·out (rŭn′out′) *n.* **1.** The act or an instance of fleeing so as to evade undesirable consequences. **2.** The area where one curved surface merges with another: *a snowy runout at the bottom of the ski slope.* **3.** The act or an instance of expiring or having expired: *the runout of an executive contract.*

runt (rŭnt) *n.* **1.** An undersized animal, especially the smallest animal of a litter. **2.** *Offensive.* A short person. [Origin unknown.] **—runt′i·ness** *n.* **—runt′y** *adj.*

run-through (rŭn′thrōō′) *n.* A complete but rapid review or rehearsal of something, such as a theatrical work.

run-up or **run·up** (rŭn′ŭp′) *n.* An often sudden increase: *a run-up in interest rates; a run-up in food prices; a run-up in house values.*

run·way (rŭn′wā′) *n.* **1.** A strip of level, usually paved ground on which aircraft take off and land. **2.** A path, channel, or track over which something runs. **3.** The channel of a stream. **4.** A chute down which logs are skidded. **5.** *Sports.* A narrow track in a bowling lane on which balls are returned after they are bowled. **6.** A smooth ramp for wheeled vehicles. **7.** A narrow walkway extending from a stage into an auditorium.

Run·yon (rŭn′yən), **(Alfred) Damon.** 1884–1946. American writer known for his stylized, idiomatic stories about Broadway and the New York underworld, such as "Guys and Dolls" (1931). **—Run′yon·esque′** (rŭn′yə-nĕsk′) *adj.*

♦**run·za** (rĕn′zə) *n. Nebraska.* A pastry consisting of cabbage and usually pork or beef encased in yeast dough. [Origin unknown.]

ru·pee (rōō-pē′, rōō′pē) *n. Abbr.* **Re., r., R.** See table at **currency.** [Hindi *rupayā, rupyā,* from Sanskrit *rūpyam,* silver coin, from *rūpya-,* silver, from *rūpam,* shape.]

Ru·pert (rōō′pərt), Prince. 1619–1682. German-born English military and political leader who was the dominant Royalist figure during the English Civil War.

Rupert River. A river of west-central Quebec, Canada, rising in Lake Mistassini and flowing about 611 km (380 mi) westward to James Bay.

ru·pi·ah (rōō-pē′ə) *n., pl.* **rupiah** or **-ahs.** See table at **currency.** [Hindi *rupayā, rupiyā.* See RUPEE.]

ru·pic·o·lous (rōō-pĭk′ə-ləs) *adj.* Thriving among or inhabiting rocks. [Latin *rūpēs,* rock (from *ruptus,* past participle of *rumpere,* to break; see **reup-** in Appendix) + -COLOUS.]

rup·ture (rŭp′chər) *n.* **1.a.** The process of breaking open or bursting. **b.** The state of being broken open. **2.** A break in friendly relations. **3.** *Pathology.* **a.** A hernia, especially of the groin or intestines. **b.** A tear in bodily tissue. **—rupture** *v.* **-tured, -tur·ing, -tures.** *—tr.* To break open; burst. *—intr.* To undergo or suffer a rupture. [Middle English, from Old French, from Latin *ruptūra,* from *ruptus,* past participle of *rumpere,* to break. See **reup-** in Appendix.] **—rup′tur·a·ble** *adj.*

ru·ral (rŏŏr′əl) *adj.* **1.** Of, relating to, or characteristic of the country. **2.** Of or relating to people who live in the country: *rural households.* **3.** Of or relating to farming; agricultural. [Middle English, from Old French, from Latin *rūrālis,* from *rūs, rūr-,* country. See **reuə-** in Appendix.] **—ru′ral·ly** *adv.*

SYNONYMS: *rural, bucolic, rustic, pastoral.* These adjectives all mean of or typical of the country as distinguished from the city. *Rural* applies to sparsely settled or agricultural country: *"I do love quiet, rural England"* (George Meredith). *Bucolic* is often used pejoratively or facetiously of country people or their manners: *"The keenest of bucolic minds felt a whispering awe at the sight of the gentry"* (George Eliot). *Rustic* frequently suggests a lack of sophistication or elegance, but it may also connote artless and pleasing simplicity: *"some rustic phrases which I had learned at the farmer's house"* (Jonathan Swift). *The cottage has a rustic grace and beauty. Pastoral,* which evokes the image of shepherds, sheep, and verdant countryside, suggests the charm and serenity of the country: *We watched from the train window as the pastoral landscapes of Burgundy unfolded.*

rural free delivery *n. Abbr.* **RFD, R.F.D.** Free government delivery of mail in rural areas.

ru·ral·ism (rŏŏr′ə-lĭz′əm) *n.* Rurality.

ru·ral·ist (rŏŏr′ə-lĭst) *n.* **1.** One who resides in a rural area. **2.** An advocate of rural life.

ru·ral·i·ty (rōō-răl′ĭ-tē) *n., pl.* **-ties. 1.** The state or quality of being rural. **2.** A rural trait or characteristic.

ru·ral·ize (rŏŏr′ə-līz′) *tr. & intr.v.* **-ized, -iz·ing, -iz·es.** To make or become rural in character. **—ru′ral·i·za′tion** (rŏŏr′ə-lĭ-zā′shən) *n.*

rural route *n. Abbr.* **RR, R.R.** A rural mail route.

Ru·rik (rŏŏr′ĭk, rōō′rĭk). Died c. 879. Scandinavian warrior and the founder of the dynasty that ruled Russia until 1598.

Ru·ri·ta·ni·an (rŏŏr′ĭ-tā′nē-ən) *adj.* Of, relating to, or having the characteristics of a mythical place of high, typically comic-opera romance: *designed Ruritanian uniforms for the honor guard.* [After *Ruritania,* imaginary realm in the novel *The Prisoner of Zenda* by Anthony Hope.]

Rus. *abbr.* Russia; Russian.

ruse (rōōs, rōōz) *n.* A crafty stratagem; a subterfuge. See Synonyms at **artifice.** [Middle English, detour, dodging, from Old French, from *ruser,* to drive back. See RUSH [1].]

Ru·se (rōō′sā). A city of northeast Bulgaria on the Danube River south of Bucharest, Romania. Founded as a Roman fortress in the second century A.D., it is today a major port and industrial center. Population, 185,000.

rush[1] (rŭsh) *v.* **rushed, rush·ing, rush·es.** *—intr.* **1.** To move or act swiftly; hurry. **2.** To make a sudden or swift attack or charge. **3.** To flow or surge rapidly, often with noise: *Tons of water rushed over the falls.* **4.** *Football.* To move the ball by running. *—tr.* **1.** To cause to move or act with unusual haste or violence. **2.** To perform with great haste: *rushed completion of the project.* **3.** To attack swiftly and suddenly: *Infantry rushed the enemy after the artillery barrage.* **4.** To transport or carry hastily: *An ambulance rushed her to the hospital.* **5.** To entertain or pay great attention to: *They rushed him for their fraternity.* **6.** *Football.* To charge (a quarterback or passer) in order to block or prevent a play. **—rush** *n.* **1.** A sudden forward motion. **2.a.** Surging emotion: *a rush of shame.* **b.** An anxious and eager movement to get to or from a place: *a rush to the goldfields.* **c.** A sudden, very insistent, generalized demand: *a rush for gold coins.* **3.** General haste or busyness: *The office always operates in a rush.* **4.** A sudden attack; an onslaught. **5.** A rapid, often noisy flow or passage. See Synonyms at **flow. 6.** *Football.* **a.** An attempt to move the ball by running. **b.** An act of charging the offensive quarterback or passer in order to block or prevent a play. **7.** Often **rushes.** The first, unedited print of a movie scene. **8.a.** A time of attention, usually one in which extensive social activity occurs: *a rush of debutante parties.* **b.** A drive by a Greek society on a college campus to recruit new members: *a sorority rush.* **9.a.** The intensely pleasurable sensation experienced immediately after use of a stimulant or a mind-altering drug. **b.** A sudden, brief exhilaration: *A familiar rush overtook him each time the store announced a half-price special on expensive stereo equipment.* [Middle English *rushen,* from Anglo-Norman *russher,* variant of Old French *ruser,* to drive back, from Latin *recūsāre,* to reject : *re-,* re- + *causārī,* to give as a reason (from *causa,* cause).] **—rush′er** *n.*

rush[2] (rŭsh) *n.* **1.a.** Any of various stiff marsh plants of the genus *Juncus,* having pliant hollow or pithy stems and small flowers with scalelike perianths. **b.** Any of various similar, usually aquatic plants. **2.** The stem of one of these plants, used in making baskets, mats, and chair seats. [Middle English, from Old English *rysc.*]

Rush (rŭsh), **Benjamin.** 1745–1813. American physician, politician, and educator. A signer of the Declaration of Independence, he promoted the abolition of slavery and the humane treatment of the mentally handicapped.

rush candle *n.* See **rushlight.**

rush hour *n.* A period of heavy traffic. **—rush′-hour′** (rŭsh′our′) *adj.*

rush·light (rŭsh′līt′) *n.* A candle consisting of a rush wick in tallow. Also called *rush candle.*

Rush·more (rŭsh′môr′, -mōr′), **Mount.** A mountain, 1,708 m (5,600 ft) high, in the Black Hills of western South Dakota. Its monument with massive carved likenesses of Washington, Jefferson, Lincoln, and Theodore Roosevelt was carved under the direction of Gutzon Borglum.

rush·y (rŭsh′ē) *adj.* **-i·er, -i·est. 1.** Resembling or characteristic of rushes; rushlike. **2.** Abounding in rushes: *a rushy marsh.*

ru·sine antler (roo′sīn) *n.* An antler with three tines, as that of the sambar. [From New Latin *Rusa,* former genus name, from Malay *rusa,* a deer.]

rusk (rŭsk) *n.* **1.** A light, soft-textured sweetened biscuit. **2.** Sweet raised bread dried and browned in an oven. [Spanish or Portuguese *rosca,* coil, rusk, perhaps from Vulgar Latin **rotisca,* diminutive of Latin *rota,* wheel. See ROTATE.]

Rusk (rŭsk), **David Dean.** Born 1909. American public official. As U.S. secretary of state (1961–1969) he supported U.S. military involvement in Vietnam.

Rus·ka (rŭs′kə, rōōs′kä), **Ernst.** 1906–1988. German physicist. He shared a 1986 Nobel Prize for the development of the electron microscope.

Rus·kin (rŭs′kĭn), **John.** 1819–1900. British writer and art critic who considered a great painting to be one that conveys great ideas to the viewer. His works include *Modern Painters* (1843–1860). **—Rus′kin′i·an** *adj.*

Russ. *abbr.* Russia; Russian.

Rus·sell (rŭs′əl), **Bertrand Arthur William.** Third Earl Russell. 1872–1970. British philosopher, mathematician, social critic, and writer who had profound influence on the development of symbolic logic, logical positivism, and the set theory of mathematics. His written works include *Principia Mathematica* (1910–1913), written with Alfred North Whitehead, and *A History of Western Philosophy* (1945). He won the 1950 Nobel Prize for literature.

Russell, Charles Taze. 1852–1916. American religious leader who founded (1884) the sect now called Jehovah's Witnesses.

Rus·sell, **George William.** Pen name "A.E." 1867–1935. Irish writer and nationalist who was a leader of the Irish literary renaissance at the turn of the 20th century.

Rus·sell, **Henry Norris.** 1877–1957. American astronomer who developed a theory of stellar evolution and devised the Hertzsprung-Russell diagram.

Rus·sell, **John.** First Earl Russell. 1792–1878. British politician who served as prime minister (1846–1852 and 1865–1866) and advocated parliamentary reform.

Rus·sell, **Lillian.** 1861–1922. American entertainer known for her roles in comic operas.

Rus·sell, **Mount.** A peak, 4,296.8 m (14,088 ft) high, of the Sierra Nevada in eastern California.

Rus·sell, **William Felton.** Known as "Bill." Born 1934. American basketball player and coach. A center for the Boston Celtics (1956–1969), he led the team to 11 National Basketball Association championships (1957–1965 and 1968–1969).

Rus·sell's viper (rŭs′əlz) *n.* A venomous snake *(Vipera russellii)* of India and southeast Asia, characterized by large black-ringed spots on yellow, tan, or light brown skin. [After Patrick *Russell* (1727–1805), Scottish naturalist.]

Rüs·sels·heim (ro͞os′əls-hīm′, rü′səls-). A city of west-central Germany, a manufacturing suburb of Mainz on the Main River. Population, 58,167.

rus·set (rŭs′ĭt) *n.* **1.** *Color.* A moderate to strong brown. **2.** A coarse reddish-brown to brown homespun cloth. **3.** A winter apple with a rough reddish-brown skin. **—russet** *adj. Color.* Moderate to strong brown. [Middle English, from Old French *rousset,* from *rous,* red, from Latin *russus.* See **reudh-** in Appendix.]

Rus·sia (rŭsh′ə). *Abbr.* **Rus., Russ. 1.** A former empire of eastern Europe and northern Asia. Originally settled by Slavs from the 3rd to the 8th century, the region was long a conglomerate of independent principalities until Moscow gained ascendancy in the 14th, 15th, and 16th centuries. The empire achieved the height of its power and territorial influence under Peter the Great and Catherine the Great in the 17th and 18th centuries. The early 1800's were a period of reactionism, and although some liberal reforms were effected in the late 1800's, discontent remained and led directly to the Revolutions of 1905 and 1917, an internal power struggle, and the formation of the U.S.S.R. in 1922. **2.** A region of eastern Europe and northern Asia bordering in the west on Finland, the Baltic States, Belorussia, and the Ukraine and stretching eastward to the Pacific Ocean. The Russian Soviet Federated Republic, coextensive with the region, was proclaimed in 1917 after the Russian Revolution and became part of the U.S.S.R. in 1922. Moscow is the capital and the largest city. Population, 143,093,000. **3.** The Union of Soviet Socialist Republics.

Rus·sian (rŭsh′ən) *adj. Abbr.* **Rus., Russ. 1.** Of or relating to Russia or its people, language, or culture. **2.** Of or relating to the Soviet Union. **—Russian** *n.* **1.a.** A native or inhabitant of Russia. **b.** A person of Russian descent. **c.** A native or inhabitant of the Soviet Union. **2.** The Slavic language of the Russians that is the official language of the Soviet Union. [Medieval Latin *Russiānus,* from Old Russian *Rusĭ,* from Old Norse **rōdhsmenn,* seafarers, from *rōdhr,* rowing. See **erə-** in Appendix.]

Russian dressing *n.* Salad dressing, such as mayonnaise, with chili sauce or ketchup, chopped pickles, and pimientos.

Rus·sian·ize (rŭsh′ə-nīz′) *tr.v.* **-ized, -iz·ing, -iz·es.** To make Russian. **—Rus′sian·i·za′tion** (-ə-nĭ-zā′shən) *n.*

Russian olive *n.* See **oleaster.**

Russian Orthodox Church *n.* The Eastern Orthodox Church in Russia that until 1917 constituted the established church and has autonomous branches outside Russia.

Russian roulette *n.* **1.** A stunt in which one spins the cylinder of a revolver loaded with only one bullet, aims the muzzle at one's head, and pulls the trigger. **2.** An act of reckless bravado.

Russian thistle *n.* A red-stemmed, prickly Eurasian plant *(Salsola kali* var. *tenuifolia)* that is a troublesome weed in western North America.

Russian wolfhound *n.* See **borzoi.**

Russo– *pref.* Russia; Russian: *Russophobe.* [From RUSSIA.]

Rus·so·phile (rŭs′ə-fīl′) *n.* An admirer of Russia or its people, language, or culture. **—Rus′so·phil′i·a** (-fĭl′ē-ə) *n.*

Rus·so·phobe (rŭs′ə-fōb′) *n.* One who fears or dislikes Russia or its people or culture. **—Rus′so·pho′bi·a** *n.*

rust (rŭst) *n.* **1.** Any of various powdery or scaly reddish-brown or reddish-yellow hydrated ferric oxides formed on iron and iron-containing materials by low-temperature oxidation in the presence of water. **2.** Any of various metallic coatings, especially oxides, formed by corrosion. **3.** A stain or coating resembling iron rust. **4.** Deterioration, as of ability, resulting from inactivity or neglect. **5.** *Botany.* **a.** Rust fungus. **b.** A plant disease caused by a rust fungus, characterized by reddish or brownish spots on leaves, stems, and other parts. **6.** *Color.* A strong brown. **—rust** *v.* **rust·ed, rust·ing, rusts.** *—intr.* **1.** To become corroded. **2.** To deteriorate or degenerate through inactivity or neglect. **3.** To become the color of rust. **4.** *Botany.* To develop a disease caused by a rust fungus. *—tr.* **1.** To corrode or subject (a metal) to rust formation. **2.** To impair or spoil, as by misuse or inactivity. **3.** To color (something) a strong brown. [Middle English, from Old English *rūst.* See **reudh-** in Appendix.] **—rust** *adj.* **—rust′a·ble** *adj.*

Rus·ta·vi (ro͞o-stä′vē, -vyĭ). A city of southern Georgia southeast of Tbilisi. An ancient town on the site was destroyed c. 1400 by Tamerlane. Population, 143,000.

rust belt or **rust·belt** also **Rust Belt** (rŭst′bĕlt′) *n.* A heavily industrialized area containing older factories, particularly those that are marginally profitable or that have been closed. **—rust′-belt′** *adj.*

rust fungus *n.* Any of various fungi of the order Uredinales that are injurious to a wide variety of plants.

rus·tic (rŭs′tĭk) *adj.* **1.** Of, relating to, or typical of country life or country people. See Synonyms at **rural. 2.** Marked by a lack of sophistication or elegance. **3.** Appropriate for use in the country: *rustic gloves and boots.* **—rustic** *n.* **1.** A rural person. **2.** A person regarded as crude, coarse, or simple. [Middle English *rustik,* from Old French *rustique,* from Latin *rūsticus,* from *rūs,* country. See **reuə-** in Appendix.] **—rus′ti·cal·ly** *adv.*

rus·ti·cate (rŭs′tĭ-kāt′) *v.* **-cat·ed, -cat·ing, -cates.** *—intr.* To go to or live in the country. *—tr.* **1.** To send to the country. **2.** *Chiefly British.* To suspend (a student) from a university. **3.** To construct (masonry) with conspicuous, often beveled points. [Latin *rūsticārī, rūsticāt-,* from *rūsticus,* rustic. See RUSTIC.] **—rus′ti·ca′tion** *n.* **—rus′ti·ca′tor** *n.*

rus·tic·i·ty (rŭ-stĭs′ĭ-tē) *n., pl.* **-ties. 1.** The condition of being rustic. **2.** A rustic trait or mannerism.

Rus·tin (rŭs′tĭn), **Bayard.** 1910–1987. American civil rights leader and pacifist who organized the 1963 March on Washington.

rus·tle (rŭs′əl) *v.* **-tled, -tling, -tles.** *—intr.* **1.** To move with soft fluttering or crackling sounds. **2.** To move or act energetically or with speed. **3.** To forage food. **4.** To steal livestock, especially cattle. *—tr.* **1.** To cause to rustle. **2.** To obtain by rustling: *rustled up some food in the kitchen.* **3.** To steal (livestock, especially cattle). [Middle English *rustlen,* perhaps of imitative origin.] **—rus′tler** *n.* **—rus′tling·ly** *adv.*

rust·less (rŭst′lĭs) *adj.* **1.** Free from rust. **2.** Unlikely to rust; not rustable.

rust mite *n.* Any of various mites that cause a plant disease characterized by reddish or brownish spots on leaves and fruits.

Rus·ton (rŭs′tən). A city of northern Louisiana west of Monroe. It was settled in 1884 as a railroad town. Population, 20,585.

rust·proof (rŭst′pro͞of′) *adj.* Incapable of rusting. **—rust′-proof′** *v.*

rust·y (rŭs′tē) *adj.* **-i·er, -i·est. 1.** Covered with rust; corroded. **2.** Consisting of or produced by rust. **3.** *Color.* Of a yellowish-red or brownish-red color. **4.** Working or operating stiffly or incorrectly because of or as if because of rust. **5.** Weakened or impaired by neglect, disuse, or lack of practice. **—rust′i·ly** *adv.* **—rust′i·ness** *n.*

rusty blackbird *n.* A North American blackbird *(Euphagus carolinus),* the male of which has blue-black feathers in the spring that turn rust-colored in the fall.

rut[1] (rŭt) *n.* **1.** A sunken track or groove made by the passage of vehicles. **2.** A fixed, usually boring routine. **—rut** *tr.v.* **rut·ted, rut·ting, ruts.** To furrow. [Possibly alteration of ROUTE.]

rut[2] (rŭt) *n.* **1.** An annually recurring condition or period of sexual excitement and reproductive activity in male deer. **2.** A condition or period of mammalian sexual activity, such as estrus. **—rut** *intr.v.* **rut·ted, rut·ting, ruts.** To be in rut. [Middle English *rutte,* from Old French *rut,* from Vulgar Latin **rūgitus,* from **rūgere,* to roar, from Latin *rūgīre,* to roar.]

ru·ta·ba·ga (ro͞o′tə-bā′gə, ro͝ot′ə-, ro͞o′tə-bā′gə, ro͝ot′ə-) *n.* **1.** A European plant *(Brassica napus* var. *napobrassica)* having a thick bulbous root used as food and as livestock feed. **2.** The edible root of this plant. Also called *swede, Swedish turnip.* [Swedish dialectal *rotabagge* : *rot,* root (from Old Norse *rōt;* see **wrād-** in Appendix) + *bagge,* bag (from Old Norse *baggi*).]

ruth (ro͞oth) *n.* **1.** Compassion or pity for another. **2.** Sorrow or misery about one's own misdeeds or flaws. [Middle English *ruthe,* from Old Norse *hrygdh* (influenced by Old English *hrēow,* sorrow, regret).]

Ruth (ro͞oth) *n. Bible.* **1.** In the Old Testament, a Moabite widow who left home with her mother-in-law and went to Bethlehem, where she later married Boaz. **2.** *Abbr.* **Rt.** See table at **Bible.**

Ruth, **George Herman.** Called "Babe." 1895–1948. American baseball player. A pitcher for the Boston Red Sox (1915–1919) and outfielder for the New York Yankees (1920–1935), he hit 714 home runs, played in 10 World Series, and held 54 major-league records. Known as "the Sultan of Swat," he was inducted into the Baseball Hall of Fame in 1936.

Ru·the·nia (ro͞o-thēn′yə, -thē′nē-ə). A region in the western Ukraine south of the Carpathian Mountains. It was once a province of Czechoslovakia (1918–1939) and was annexed by the U.S.S.R. in 1945.

Ru·the·ni·an (ro͞o-thē′nē-ən, -thēn′yən) *adj.* Of or relating to Ruthenia, the Ruthenians, or their language or culture. **—Ruthenian** *n.* **1.** A native or inhabitant of Ruthenia. **2.** The variety of Ukrainian used by the Ruthenians.

ru·then·ic (ro͞o-thĕn′ĭk, -thē′nĭk) *adj.* Relating to or containing ruthenium with a high valence.

ru·the·ni·ous (ro͞o-thē′nē-əs) *adj.* Relating to or containing ruthenium with a low valence.

ru·the·ni·um (ro͞o-thē′nē-əm) *n. Symbol* **Ru** A hard white acid-resistant metallic element that is found in platinum ores and is used to harden platinum and palladium for jewelry and in

Lillian Russell
Photographed in 1889

rutabaga
Brassica napus var. *napobrassica*

Babe Ruth
Photographed in the 1930's

ă pat	oi boy
ā pay	ou out
âr care	o͝o took
ä father	o͞o boot
ĕ pet	ŭ cut
ē be	ûr urge
ĭ pit	th thin
ī pie	*th* this
îr pier	hw which
ŏ pot	zh vision
ō toe	ə about, item
ô paw	♦ regionalism

Stress marks: ′ (primary); ′ (secondary), as in **dictionary** (dĭk′shə-nĕr′ē)

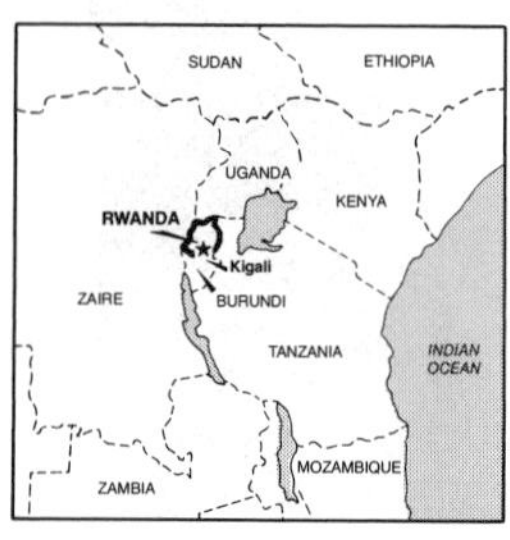

Rwanda

alloys for nonmagnetic wear-resistant instrument pivots and electrical contacts. Atomic number 44; atomic weight 101.07; melting point 2,310°C; boiling point 3,900°C; specific gravity 12.41; valence 0, 1, 2, 3, 4, 5, 6, 7, 8. See table at **element.** [From Medieval Latin *Ruthenia,* Russia, from Russian *Rutheni,* Russians, from Russian *Rusin,* from Old Russian *Rusĭ,* Russian. See RUSSIAN.]

ruth·er·ford (rŭth′ər-fərd) *n. Abbr.* **rd** A unit expressing the rate of decay of radioactive material, equal to one million disintegrations per second. [After Ernest RUTHERFORD.]

Ruth·er·ford (rŭth′ər-fərd, rŭth′-). A borough of northeast New Jersey, a residential suburb of the New York City metropolitan area. Population, 19,068.

Rutherford, Daniel. 1749–1819. British chemist and physician who is credited with the discovery of nitrogen.

Rutherford, Ernest. First Baron Rutherford of Nelson. 1871–1937. New Zealand-born British physicist who classified radiation into alpha, beta, and gamma types and discovered the atomic nucleus. He won the 1908 Nobel Prize in chemistry.

ruth·er·ford·i·um (rŭth′ər-fôr′dē-əm, -fōr′-) *n.* Element 104. [After Ernest RUTHERFORD.]

Rutherford scattering *n.* The scattering undergone by a stream of heavy charged particles fired at a sample of a heavy metal, caused by exposure to coulombic forces in the atomic nuclei of the sample.

ruth·ful (ro͞oth′fəl) *adj.* **1.** Full of sorrow; rueful. **2.** Causing sorrow or pity. **—ruth′ful·ly** *adv.* **—ruth′ful·ness** *n.*

ruth·less (ro͞oth′lĭs) *adj.* Having no compassion or pity; merciless: *ruthless cruelty; ruthless opportunism.* **—ruth′less·ly** *adv.* **—ruth′less·ness** *n.*

ru·ti·lant (ro͞ot′l-ənt) *adj.* Bright red. [Middle English *rutilaunt,* from Latin *rutilāns, rutilant-,* present participle of *rutilāre,* to make red, to be reddish, from *rutilus,* red, reddish. See **reudh-** in Appendix.]

ru·tile (ro͞o′tēl′, -tīl′) *n.* A lustrous red, reddish-brown, or black mineral, TiO_2, used as a gemstone, as an ore, and in paints and fillers. [French, from German *Rutil,* from Latin *rutilus,* red. See RUTILANT.]

Rut·land (rŭt′lənd). A city of central Vermont south-southwest of Montpelier. There are marble quarries in the area. Population, 18,436.

Rut·ledge (rŭt′lĭj), **John.** 1739–1800. American politician and jurist. Governor of South Carolina (1779–1782) and a delegate to the U.S. Constitutional Convention, he advocated slavery and a strong central government. He also served as an associate justice (1789–1791) and the chief justice (1795) of the U.S. Supreme Court.

Rutledge, Wiley Blount, Jr. 1894–1949. American jurist who served as an associate justice of the U.S. Supreme Court (1943–1949).

rut·tish (rŭt′ĭsh) *adj.* Lustful; libidinous. **—rut′tish·ly** *adv.* **—rut′tish·ness** *n.*

rut·ty (rŭt′ē) *adj.* **-ti·er, -ti·est.** Full of ruts: *rutty farm roads.* **—rut′ti·ness** *n.*

Ru·vu·ma also **Ro·vu·ma** (ro͞o-vo͞o′mə). A river of southeast Africa flowing about 724 km (450 mi) eastward along the Mozambique-Tanzania border to the Indian Ocean.

Ru·wen·zo·ri (ro͞o′wən-zôr′ē, -zōr′ē). A mountain range of east-central Africa on the Uganda-Zaire border. The range was explored in 1889 by Henry M. Stanley and has traditionally been associated with the geographer Ptolemy's Mountains of the Moon, the supposed source of the Nile River.

Ruys·dael (rīz′däl′, rīs′-, rois′-), **Jacob van.** See Jacob van **Ruisdael.**

Ru·žič·ka (ro͞o′zĭch-kə, ro͞o-zĭch′-, ro͞o′zhĕch-kä), **Leopold.** 1887–1976. Yugoslavian-born Swiss chemist. He won a 1939 Nobel Prize for his study of ringed molecules and terpenes.

RV *abbr.* **1.** Recreational vehicle. **2.** Reentry vehicle. **3.** Or **R.V.** *Bible.* Revised Version.

Rv. *abbr. Bible.* Revelations.

R-val·ue (är′văl′yo͞o) *n.* A measure of the capacity of a material, such as insulation, to impede heat flow, with increasing values indicating a greater capacity. [*r(esistance) value.*]

R.W. *abbr.* **1.** Right Worshipful. **2.** Right Worthy.

Rwan·da (ro͞o-än′də). Formerly **Ru·an·da** (ro͞o-än′də). A country of east-central Africa. Part of the colonial territory of Ruanda-Urundi administered by Germany and Belgium, it achieved independence in 1962. The southern portion of the territory became the country of Burundi. Kigali is the capital of Rwanda and its largest city. Population, 5,109,000. **—Rwan′dan** *adj. & n.*

rwy. *abbr.* Railway.

Rx (är′ĕks′) *n.* **1.** A prescription for medicine or a medical appliance. **2.** A remedy, cure, or solution for a disorder or problem. [Alteration of ℞, symbol used in prescriptions, abbreviation of Latin *recipe,* imperative of *recipere,* to take. See RECEIVE.]

ry. *abbr.* Railway.

—ry *suff.* Variant of **—ery.**

ry·a (rē′ə) *n.* **1.** A handwoven Scandinavian rug with a thick pile and usually colorful abstract designs. **2.** The weaving pattern characteristic of such rugs. [After *Rya,* a village of southwest Sweden.]

Rya·zan (ryĭ-zän′). A city of west-central Russia on the Oka River southeast of Moscow. Founded in 1095, it was the capital of an independent principality until it was annexed by Moscow in 1521. It is now a manufacturing and industrial center. Population, 494,000.

Ryb·nik (rĭb′nĭk). A town of southern Poland west-southwest of Katowice. Chartered in the 14th century, it passed to Poland in 1921 and is today a manufacturing and industrial center. Population, 135,500.

Ry·der (rī′dər), **Albert Pinkham.** 1847–1917. American painter known for his rhythmic allegorical works, landscapes, and marine scenes, such as *Toilers of the Sea* (c. 1884).

rye[1] (rī) *n.* **1.** A cereal grass *(Secale cereale)* widely cultivated for its grain. **2.** The grain of this plant, used in making flour and whiskey and for livestock feed. **3.** Whiskey made from the grains of this plant. [Middle English, from Old English *ryge.*]

rye[2] (rī) *n.* A Gypsy man. [Romany *rai,* from Sanskrit *rājā,* king. See RAJAH.]

Rye (rī). A city of southeast New York on Long Island Sound northeast of New York City. It is primarily residential. Population, 15,083.

rye bread *n.* Bread made partially or entirely from rye flour.

rye grass or **rye·grass** (rī′grăs′) *n.* See **darnel.** [Alteration of *raygrass* : *ray,* darnel (from Middle English *rai,* perhaps alteration of Old French *ivraie,* from Latin *ēbriaca,* from feminine of *ēbriācus,* drunk (from the plant's effects if ingested), from *ēbrius;* see INEBRIATE) + GRASS.]

Ryle (rīl), **Gilbert.** 1900–1976. British philosopher who regarded the linguistic misrepresentation of mental concepts as the root of philosophical problems and challenged Cartesian dualism in *The Concept of Mind* (1949).

Ryle, Sir **Martin.** 1918–1984. British astronomer. He shared a 1974 Nobel Prize for physics for using radio telescopes to probe outer space with great precision.

Rys·wick (rĭz′wĭk). See **Rijswijk.**

Ryu·kyu Islands (rē-o͞o′kyo͞o′, ryo͞o′-kyo͞o). An island group of southwest Japan extending about 1,046 km (650 mi) between Kyushu and Taiwan. The archipelago was incorporated into Japan in 1879 and returned to Japanese sovereignty in 1972 after occupation by U.S. forces following World War II.

Rze·szów (zhĕ′sho͝of′). A city of southeast Poland east of Cracow. Chartered in the 14th century, it passed to Austria in 1772 and reverted to Poland after World War I. Population, 138,000.

ă pat	oi boy
ā pay	ou out
âr care	o͝o took
ä father	o͞o boot
ĕ pet	ŭ cut
ē be	ûr urge
ĭ pit	th thin
ī pie	*th* this
îr pier	hw which
ŏ pot	zh vision
ō toe	ə about, item
ô paw	♦ regionalism

Stress marks: ′ (primary); ′ (secondary), as in **dictionary** (dĭk′shə-nĕr′ē)

Ss

s¹ or **S** (ĕs) *n., pl.* **s's** or **S's. 1.** The 19th letter of the modern English alphabet. **2.** Any of the speech sounds represented by the letter *s*. **3.** The 19th in a series. **4.** Something shaped like the letter S.

s² *abbr.* **1.** Second (unit of time). **2.** *Mathematics.* Second (of arc). **3.** Stere. **4.** *Physics.* Strange quark.

S¹ 1. The symbol for the element **sulfur. 2.** The symbol for **entropy** (sense 1).

S² *abbr.* **1.** *Bible.* Samuel. **2.** Or **s.** Siemens. **3.** Also **S.** or **s** or **s.** South; southern.

s. *abbr.* **1.** Or **S.** School. **2.** Or **S.** Sea. **3.** See. **4.** Shilling. **5.** *Grammar.* Singular. **6.** Sire. **7.** Sister. **8.** Small. **9.** Or **S.** Society. **10.** *Music.* Solo. **11.** Son. **12.** Or **S.** *Music.* Soprano. **13.** Sou. **14.** Stock. **15.** *Grammar.* Substantive. **16.** Surplus.

S. *abbr.* **1.** Sabbath. **2.** Saint. **3.** Saturday. **4.** Saxon. **5.** *Medicine.* Signature. **6.** Signor; signore. **7.** *Grammar.* Singular. **8.** Sunday.

–s¹ or **–es** *suff.* Used to form plural nouns: *letters.* [Middle English *-es, -s,* from Old English *-es, -as,* nominative and accusative pl. suff.]

–s² or **–es** *suff.* Used to form the third person singular present tense of all regular and most irregular verbs: *looks; holds.* [Middle English *-es, -s,* from Old English *-es, -as.*]

–s³ *suff.* Used to form adverbs: *They were caught unawares. He works nights.* [Middle English *-es, -s,* genitive sing. suff., from Old English *-es.*]

–'s *suff.* Used to form the possessive case of singular nouns, plural nouns that do not end in *s,* certain pronouns, and phrases that function as nouns or pronouns: *nation's; women's; another's; the girl next door's cat.* [Middle English *-s, -es,* from Old English *-es,* genitive sing. suff.]

's 1. Is: *She's here.* **2.** Has: *He's arrived.* **3.** Does: *What's he want?* **4.** Us: *Let's go.*

SA *abbr.* **1.** Salvation Army. **2.** Seventh Avenue (New York City garment district).

s.a. *abbr. Latin.* Sine anno (without date).

S.A. *abbr.* **1.** South Africa. **2.** South America.

Saa·le (zä'lə, sä'-). A river, about 426 km (265 mi) long, rising in central Germany and flowing north to the Elbe River.

Saa·nen (sä'nən, zä'-) *n.* A dairy goat of a breed developed in Switzerland, having a short-haired white coat and no horns. [After *Saanen,* a town of southwest Switzerland.]

Saar¹ (sär, zär). A river, about 241 km (150 mi) long, rising in northeast France and flowing north and north-northwest to the Moselle River in western Germany. The river's valley, also known as the **Saar Basin,** is a highly industrialized region.

Saar² (sär, zär). See **Saarland.**

Saar·brück·en (zär-bro͝ok'ən, sär-, zär-brük'-). A city of southwest Germany on the Saar River near the French border south of Bonn. Located on the site of earlier Celtic, Roman, and Frankish settlements, it was chartered in 1321. Population, 188,763.

Saa·re·maa also **Sa·re·ma** (sär'ə-mä'). An island of western Estonia in the Baltic Sea at the mouth of the Gulf of Riga. Long strategically important, it has been controlled by the Teutonic Knights and by Denmark, Sweden, Livonia, Russia, and Estonia.

Saa·ri·nen (sär'ə-nən, -nĕn'), **Eero.** 1910–1961. Finnish-born American architect whose designs include the Trans World Airlines terminal at Kennedy Airport in New York City (1962).

Saar·land (sär'lănd', zär'-, -länt') or **Saar** (sär, zär). A region of southwest Germany in the Saar River valley on the border with France. Because of its extensive coal deposits, it was long contested between Germany and France, especially after World War I, when the League of Nations assigned the administration of the newly formed **Saar Territory** to France. After a 1935 plebiscite Saarland became a German province, but it was again placed under French control in 1945. The notion of an autonomous Saarland was rejected by the populace in 1955, and the region officially became a state of West Germany in 1957. **—Saar'land'er** *n.*

Saa·ve·dra La·mas (sä-vā'drə lä'mäs, sä'ä-vĕ'*th*rä), **Carlos.** 1878?–1959. Argentinean diplomat. He won the 1936 Nobel Peace Prize for his part in negotiating an end to the Chaco War (1932–1935) between Bolivia and Paraguay.

Sab. *abbr.* Sabbath.

Sa·ba (sä'bə, -bä). An island of the northern Netherlands Antilles in the West Indies between St. Martin and St. Eustatius. First occupied by the Dutch in 1632, the island is the cone of an extinct volcano.

Sa·ba·dell (sä'bə-dĕl', sä'bä-*th*ĕl'). A city of northeast Spain, an industrial suburb of Barcelona. Population, 189,775.

sab·a·dil·la (săb'ə-dĭl'ə, -dē'ə) *n.* **1.** A Mexican and Central American plant *(Schoenocaulon officinale)* of the lily family, having very long, densely flowered spikelike racemes, straplike perianth segments, and brown seeds that are rich in veratrine. **2.** The seeds of this plant used in insecticides and formerly in medicine. [Spanish *cebadilla,* diminutive of *cebada,* barley, from Latin *cibātus,* from past participle of *cibāre,* to feed, from *cibus,* food.]

Sa·bah (sä'bä'). A region of Malaysia in northeast Borneo. Sabah was a British protectorate, originally controlled by the British North Borneo Company, from the early 1800's until it became part of Malaysia in 1963.

sa·bal (sā'băl) *n.* See **palmetto** (sense 1). [New Latin, genus name.]

Sab·a·oth (săb'ā-ŏth', sə-bā'ōth') *pl.n.* Hosts; armies: *the Lord of Sabaoth.* [Latin *sabaoth,* from Greek *sabaōth,* from Hebrew *sĕbā'ôt,* pl. of *ṣābā',* army.]

Sa·ba·tier (sä-bä-tyā'), **Paul.** 1854–1941. French chemist. He shared a 1912 Nobel Prize for developing methods of hydrogenating organic compounds.

sa·ba·yon (sä'bä-yôɴ') *n.* See **zabaglione.** [French, from Italian *zabaglione, zabaione.*]

sab·bat (săb'ət) *n.* Witches' Sabbath. [French, Sabbath, sabbat, from Old French, Sabbath. See SABBATH.]

Sab·ba·tar·i·an (săb'ə-târ'ē-ən) *n.* **1.** One who observes Saturday as the Sabbath, as in Judaism. **2.** One who believes in strict observance of the Sabbath. **—Sabbatarian** *adj.* Relating to the Sabbath or to Sabbatarians. [From Late Latin *sabbatārius,* from Latin *sabbatum,* Sabbath. See SABBATH.] **—Sab'ba·tar'i·an·ism** *n.*

Sab·bath (săb'əth) *n. Abbr.* **S., Sab. 1.** The seventh day of the week, Saturday, observed as the day of rest and worship by the Jews and some Christian sects. **2.** The first day of the week, Sunday, observed as the day of rest and worship by most Christians. [Middle English *sabath,* from Old French *sabbat* and Old English *sabat,* both from Latin *sabbatum,* from Greek *sabbaton,* from Hebrew *šabbāt,* from *šābat,* to rest.]

sab·bat·i·cal (sə-băt'ĭ-kəl) also **sab·bat·ic** (-ĭk) *—adj.* **1.** Relating to a sabbatical year. **2. Sabbatical, Sabbatic.** Relating or appropriate to the Sabbath as the day of rest. *—n.* A sabbatical year. [From Late Latin *sabbaticus,* from Greek *sabbatikos,* from *sabbaton,* Sabbath. See SABBATH.]

sabbatical year *n.* **1.** A leave of absence, often with pay, usually granted every seventh year, as to a college professor, for travel, research, or rest. **2.** Often **Sabbatical year.** A year during which land remained fallow, observed every seven years by the ancient Jews.

Sa·bel·li·an (sə-bĕl'ē-ən) *n.* **1.** A group of extinct Italic languages that includes Sabine. **2.** A speaker of one of these languages. [From Latin *Sabellus,* Sabine.] **—Sa·bel'li·an** *adj.*

sa·ber (sā'bər) *n.* **1.** A heavy cavalry sword with a one-edged, slightly curved blade. **2.** A light dueling or fencing sword having an arched guard covering the hand and a tapered flexible blade with a cutting edge on one side and on the tip. **—saber** *tr.v.* **-bered, -ber·ing, -bers.** To hit, injure, or kill with a saber. [French *sabre,* from obsolete German *sabel,* from Middle High German, from Hungarian *szablya,* from *szabni,* to cut.]

saber rattling *n.* **1.** A flamboyant display of military power. **2.** A threat or an implied threat to use military force.

Phoenician
In the Phoenician alphabet this sign represented the sound *sh.*

Early Greek
The Greeks assigned it to the sound *s,* changed its orientation, and renamed it *sigma,* possibly through confusion with the Semitic letter *samekh.*

Roman
The Romans altered its angular form to the S-curve familiar today.

saber-toothed tiger

sa·ber-toothed tiger (sā′bər-to͞otht′) *n.* Any of various extinct cats of the Oligocene to the Pleistocene Epoch, especially one of the larger members of the genus *Smilodon,* characterized by long upper canine teeth.

sa·bin (sā′bĭn) *n.* A unit of acoustic absorption equivalent to the absorption by one square foot of a surface that absorbs all incident sound. [After Wallace Clement Ware *Sabine* (1868–1919), American physicist.]

Sa·bin (sā′bĭn), **Albert Bruce.** Born 1906. American microbiologist and physician who developed a live-virus vaccine against polio (1957), replacing the killed-virus vaccine invented by Jonas Salk.

Sa·bine (sā′bīn′) *n.* **1.** A member of an ancient people of central Italy, conquered and assimilated by the Romans in 290 B.C. **2.** The Italic language of the Sabines. —**Sabine** *adj.* Of or relating to the Sabines or their language or culture. [Middle English *Sabyn,* from Latin *Sabīnus.*]

Sa·bine River (sə-bēn′). A river of eastern Texas rising northeast of Dallas and flowing about 925 km (575 mi) generally southeast and south to the Gulf of Mexico. Its lower course forms the Texas-Louisiana border and crosses **Sabine Lake** before entering the Gulf.

Sabin vaccine *n.* An oral vaccine consisting of live attenuated polio viruses, used to immunize against poliomyelitis. [After Albert Bruce SABIN.]

Sab·ine's gull (săb′īnz, -ĭnz, sā′bīnz) *n.* A gull *(Xema sabini)* of Arctic regions, having a forked tail with feathers rounded at the ends. [After Sir Edward *Sabine* (1788–1883), British astronomer and explorer.]

Sabine's gull
Xema sabini

sa·ble (sā′bəl) *n.* **1.a.** A carnivorous mammal *(Martes zibellina)* of northern Europe and Asia, having soft dark fur. **b.** The pelt or fur of this animal. **c.** The similar fur of other species of martens. **2.a.** The color black, especially in heraldry. **b. sables.** Black garments worn in mourning. **3.** *Color.* A grayish yellowish brown. **4.** A sablefish. —**sable** *adj.* **1.** *Color.* Of a grayish yellowish brown. **2.** Of the color black, as in heraldry or mourning. **3.** Dark; somber. **4.** Of the fur of the sable: *a sable coat.* [Middle English, from Old French, from Middle Low German *sabel,* from Old Russian *sobol',* ultimately from Persian *samōr.*]

Sa·ble (sā′bəl), **Cape. 1.** A promontory of extreme southern Nova Scotia, Canada. It is on an inlet south of **Sable Island,** a low, sandy island often called "the Graveyard of the Atlantic" because of its hazard to navigation. **2.** A cape at the southwest tip of Florida. Part of Everglades National Park, it is the southernmost extremity of the U.S. mainland.

sable antelope *n.* A large African antelope *(Hippotragus niger)* having backward-curving horns and a usually dark coat.

sa·ble·fish (sā′bəl-fĭsh′) *n., pl.* **sablefish** or **-fish·es.** A dark-colored marine food fish *(Anoplopoma fimbria)* of North American Pacific waters. Also called *black cod.*

sa·bot (să-bō′, săb′ō) *n.* **1.** A wooden shoe worn in some European countries. **2.** (săb′ət). A sandal or shoe having a band of leather or other material across the instep. **3.** A lightweight carrier in which a projectile of a smaller caliber is centered so as to permit firing the projectile within a larger caliber weapon. The carrier fills the bore of the weapon from which the projectile is fired; it is normally discarded a short distance from the muzzle. [French, from Old French *çabot,* alteration of *savate,* old shoe, probably of Turkish or Arabic origin.]

sabot
A pair of sabots

sab·o·tage (săb′ə-täzh′) *n.* **1.** Destruction of property or obstruction of normal operations, as by civilians or enemy agents in time of war. **2.** Treacherous action to defeat or hinder a cause or an endeavor; deliberate subversion. —**sabotage** *tr.v.* **-taged, -tag·ing, -tag·es.** To commit sabotage against. [French, from *saboter,* to walk noisily, bungle, sabotage, from *sabot,* sabot. See SABOT.]

sab·o·teur (săb′ə-tûr′) *n.* One that commits sabotage. [French, from *saboter,* to sabotage. See SABOTAGE.]

sa·bra (sä′brə) *n.* A native-born Israeli. [New Hebrew *ṣābār,* sabra, prickly pear.]

sabra cactus *n.* A Central American cactus *(Opuntia ficus-indica)* naturalized and cultivated in the warmer parts of the world for its prickly edible fruits and as a hedge plant.

sa·bre (sā′bər) *n.* & *v.* *Chiefly British.* Variant of **saber.**

sab·u·lous (săb′yə-ləs) also **sab·u·lose** (-lōs′) *adj.* Gritty; sandy. [From Latin *sabulōsus,* from *sabulum,* coarse sand.] —**sab′u·los′i·ty** (-lŏs′ĭ-tē) *n.*

sac (săk) *n.* A pouch or pouchlike structure in a plant or an animal, sometimes filled with fluid. [French, bag, from Old French, from Latin *saccus.* See SACK[1].]

Sac (săk, sôk) *n.* Variant of **Sauk.**

SAC *abbr.* Strategic Air Command.

Sac·a·ja·we·a (săk′ə-jə-wē′ə). 1787?–1812. Shoshone guide and interpreter who accompanied (1805–1806) the Lewis and Clark Expedition.

Sacajawea

sac·a·ton (săk′ə-tōn′) *n.* A tufted perennial grass *(Sporobolus wrightii)* of the southwest United States, used for pasture and hay in arid regions. [American Spanish *zacatón,* from *zacate,* coarse grass, from Nahuatl *zacatl,* grass, straw.]

sac·cade (să-käd′, sə-) *n.* A rapid intermittent eye movement, as that which occurs when the eyes fix on one point after another in the visual field. [French, twitch, from Old French, from Old North French *saquier,* to pull, from *sac,* sack. See SAC.] —**sac·cad′ic** *adj.*

sac·cate (săk′āt′) *adj.* **1.** Shaped like a pouch or sac. **2.** Having a pouch or sac. [Latin *saccus,* bag; see SACK[1] + –ATE[1].]

sacchar– *pref.* Variant of **saccharo–.**

sac·cha·rase (săk′ə-rās′, -rāz′) *n.* See **invertase.**

sac·cha·rate (săk′ə-rāt′) *n.* A salt or an ester of saccharic acid. [SACCHAR(IC ACID) + –ATE[2].]

sac·char·ic acid (sə-kăr′ĭk) *n.* A white crystalline acid, $COOH(CHOH)_4COOH$, formed by the oxidation of glucose, sucrose, or starch.

sac·cha·ride (săk′ə-rīd′) *n.* Any of a series of compounds of carbon, hydrogen, and oxygen in which the atoms of the latter two elements are in the ratio of 2:1, especially those containing the group $C_6H_{10}O_5$.

sac·char·i·fy (sə-kăr′ə-fī′, să-) *tr.v.* **-fied** (-fīd′), **-fy·ing, -fies** (-fīz′). To convert (starch, for example) into sugar. —**sac·char′i·fi·ca′tion** (-fĭ-kā′shən) *n.*

sac·cha·rim·e·ter (săk′ə-rĭm′ĭ-tər) *n.* **1.** A polarimeter that indicates the concentration of sugar in a solution. **2.** An instrument that determines the concentration of sugar in a fermenting solution from carbon dioxide measurements. —**sac′cha·rim′e·try** *n.*

sac·cha·rin (săk′ər-ĭn) *n.* A white crystalline powder, $C_7H_5NO_3S$, having a taste about 500 times sweeter than cane sugar, used as a calorie-free sweetener.

sac·cha·rine (săk′ər-ĭn, -ə-rēn′, -ə-rīn′) *adj.* **1.** Of, relating to, or characteristic of sugar or saccharin; sweet. **2.** Having a cloyingly sweet tone or character: *a saccharine smile.* **3.** Excessively sentimental: *"It was enough for him to rely on sentiment . . . and saccharine assertions about The Home"* (Kate Millett). —**sac′cha·rine·ly** *adv.* —**sac′cha·rin′i·ty** (-ə-rĭn′ĭ-tē) *n.*

saccharo– or **sacchar–** *pref.* Sugar: *saccharide.* [From Medieval Latin *saccharum,* sugar, from Latin *saccharon,* from Greek *sakkhar,* from Pali *sakkharā,* from Sanskrit *śarkarā.*]

sac·cha·roid (săk′ə-roid′) or **sac·cha·roi·dal** (-roid′l) *adj.* Having a texture similar to that of granulated sugar. Used of rocks and minerals.

sac·cha·rom·e·ter (săk′ə-rŏm′ĭ-tər) *n.* A hydrometer that determines the amount of sugar in a solution from density measurements.

sac·cha·ro·my·ces (săk′ə-rō-mī′sēz) *n., pl.* **saccharomyces.** Any of several single-celled yeasts belonging to the genus *Saccharomyces* that lack a true mycelium and many of which ferment sugar. [New Latin *Saccharomycēs,* genus name : SACCHARO– + Greek *mukēs,* fungus.]

sac·cha·ro·my·cete (săk′ə-rō-mī′sēt′) *n.* A yeast of the family Saccharomycetaceae, including the saccharomyces. —**sac′cha·ro·my·ce′tic** (-mī-sē′tĭk), **sac′cha·ro·my·ce′tous** *adj.*

sac·cha·rose (săk′ə-rōs′) *n.* See **sucrose.**

Sac·co (săk′ō, säk′kō), **Nicola.** 1891–1927. Italian-born American anarchist who with Bartolomeo Vanzetti was convicted of a double murder and sentenced to death (1921). Despite the circumstantial nature of the evidence against them and worldwide protest at the political overtones of the proceedings, the two were executed in 1927.

sac·cu·late (săk′yə-lāt′) or **sac·cu·lat·ed** (-lā′tĭd) also **sac·cu·lar** (-lər) *adj.* Formed of or divided into a series of saclike dilations or pouches.

sac·cule (săk′yo͞ol) also **sac·cu·lus** (-yə-ləs) *n., pl.* **sac·cules** also **sac·cu·li** (săk′yə-lī′). **1.** A small sac. **2.** The smaller of two membranous sacs in the vestibule of the inner ear. [Latin *sacculus,* diminutive of *saccus,* bag. See SACK[1].]

sac·er·do·tal (săs′ər-dōt′l, săk′-) *adj.* **1.** Of or relating to priests or the priesthood; priestly. **2.** Of or relating to sacerdotalism. [Middle English, from Old French, from Latin *sacerdōtālis,* from *sacerdōs, sacerdōt-,* priest. See **sak-** in Appendix.] —**sac′er·do′tal·ly** *adv.*

sac·er·do·tal·ism (săs′ər-dōt′l-ĭz′əm, săk′-) *n.* The belief that priests act as mediators between God and human beings.

SACEUR *abbr.* Supreme Allied Commander, Europe.

sac fungus *n.* *Botany.* See **ascomycete.**

sa·chem (sā′chəm) *n.* **1.a.** A chief of a Native American tribe or confederation, especially an Algonquian chief. **b.** A member of the ruling council of the Iroquois confederacy. **2.** A high official of the Tammany Society, a political organization in New York City. [Of Massachusett origin.]

sa·cher torte (sä′kər tôrt′, zä′KHər tôr′tə) *n.* A rich chocolate cake filled with apricot jam and topped with chocolate icing. [German *Sachertorte* : *Sacher,* surname of a family of 19th- and 20th-century hoteliers + *Torte,* torte; see TORTE.]

sa·chet (să-shā′) *n.* A small packet of perfumed powder used to scent clothes, as in trunks or closets. [French, from Old French, diminutive of *sac,* bag, from Latin *saccus.* See SACK[1].]

Sachs (zäks, săks), **Hans.** 1494–1576. German writer and Meistersinger noted for his many dramas, poems, and songs. His life inspired Wagner's opera *Die Meistersinger von Nürnberg* (1868).

Sachs, Nelly. 1891–1970. German writer whose work is based on the suffering of the Jewish people during World War II. She shared the 1966 Nobel Prize for literature.

sack¹ (săk) *n. Abbr.* **sk.** **1.a.** A large bag of strong, coarse material for holding objects in bulk. **b.** A similar container of paper or plastic. **c.** The amount that such a container can hold. **2.** Also **sacque.** A short, loose-fitting garment for women and children. **3.** *Slang.* Dismissal from employment: *finally got the sack after a year of ineptitude.* **4.** *Informal.* A bed, mattress, or sleeping bag. **5.** *Baseball.* A base. **6.** *Football.* A successful attempt at sacking the quarterback. **—sack** *tr.v.* **sacked, sack·ing, sacks.** **1.** To place into a sack. **2.** *Slang.* To discharge from employment. See Synonyms at **dismiss.** **3.** *Football.* To tackle (a quarterback attempting to pass the ball) behind the line of scrimmage. ***—phrasal verb.* sack out.** *Slang.* To sleep. [Middle English, from Old English *sacc,* from Latin *saccus,* from Greek *sakkos,* of Semitic origin.]

WORD HISTORY: The word *sack* may seem an odd candidate for preserving a few thousand years of history, but this word for an ordinary thing probably goes back to Middle Eastern antiquity. *Sack* owes its long history to the fact that it and its ancestors denoted an object that was used in trade between peoples. Thus the Greeks got their word *sakkos,* "a bag made out of coarse cloth or hair," from the Phoenicians with whom they traded. We do not know the Phoenician word, but we know words that are akin to it, such as Hebrew *saq* and Akkadian *saqqu.* The Greeks then passed the sack, as it were, to the Latin-speaking Romans, who transmitted their word *saccus,* "a large bag or sack," to the Germanic tribes with whom they traded, who gave it the form **sakkiz* (other peoples as well have taken this word from Greek or Latin, including speakers of Welsh, Russian, Polish, and Albanian). The speakers of Old English, a Germanic language, used two forms of the word, *sæc,* from **sakkiz,* and *sacc,* directly from Latin; the second Old English form is the ancestor of our *sack.*

sack² (săk) *tr.v.* **sacked, sack·ing, sacks.** To rob of goods or valuables, especially after capture. **—sack** *n.* **1.** The looting or pillaging of a captured city or town. **2.** Plunder; loot. [Probably from French *(mettre à) sac,* (to put in) a sack, from Old French *sac,* sack, from Latin *saccus,* sack, bag. See SACK¹.]

sack³ (săk) *n.* Any of various light, dry, strong wines from Spain and the Canary Islands, imported to England in the 16th and 17th centuries. [From French *(vin) sec,* dry (wine), from Old French, from Latin *siccus,* dry.]

sack·but (săk′bŭt′) *n. Music.* **1.** A medieval instrument resembling the trombone. **2.** An ancient triangular stringed instrument. [French *saquebute,* from Old French *saqueboute* : Old North French *saquier,* to pull; see SACCADE + Old French *bouter,* to push (of Germanic origin; see **bhau-** in Appendix). Sense 2, alteration of Aramaic *sabběka, from* Greek *sambukē.*]

sack·cloth (săk′klôth′, -klŏth′) *n.* **1.** Sacking. **2.a.** A rough cloth of camel's hair, goat hair, hemp, cotton, or flax. **b.** Garments made of this cloth, worn as a symbol of mourning or penitence.

sack·er (săk′ər) *n.* **1.** *Football.* A lineman skilled at sacking the quarterback. **2.** *Baseball.* A baseman. **3.** One who puts things into sacks: *a grocery sacker.*

sack·ing (săk′ĭng) *n.* A coarse, stout woven cloth, such as burlap or gunny, used for making sacks; sackcloth.

Sack·ville (săk′vĭl′), **Thomas.** First Earl of Dorset and Baron Buckhurst. 1536–1608. English political adviser and poet who collaborated with Thomas Norton (1532–1584) on the blank-verse drama *Gorboduc* (1561), the first tragedy written in English.

Sack·ville-West (săk′vĭl-wĕst′), **Victoria Mary.** Known as "Vita." 1892–1962. British writer whose novels include *The Edwardians* (1930) and *All Passion Spent* (1931).

Sa·co (sô′kō). A river, about 169 km (105 mi) long, rising in the White Mountains of northeast-central New Hampshire and flowing southeast through Maine to the Atlantic Ocean.

sacque (săk) *n.* Variant of **sack¹** (sense 2).

sacr– *pref.* Variant of **sacro–.**

sa·cra (sā′krə, săk′rə) *n.* Plural of **sacrum.**

sa·cral¹ (sā′krəl) *adj.* Of, near, or relating to the sacrum.

sa·cral² (sā′krəl) *adj.* Relating to sacred rites or observances. [From Latin *sacer, sacr-,* sacred. See SACRED.]

sac·ra·ment (săk′rə-mənt) *n. Theology.* **1.** A visible form of invisible grace, especially: **a.** In the Eastern, Roman Catholic, and some other Western Christian churches, any of the traditional seven rites that were instituted by Jesus and recorded in the New Testament and that confer sanctifying grace. **b.** In most other Western Christian churches, the two rites, Baptism and the Eucharist, that were instituted by Jesus to confer sanctifying grace. **2.** Often **Sacrament. a.** The Eucharist. **b.** The consecrated elements of the Eucharist, especially the bread or host. [Middle English, from Old French *sacrement,* from Late Latin *sacrāmentum,* from Latin, oath, from *sacrāre,* to consecrate, from *sacer, sacr-,* sacred. See SACRED.]

sac·ra·men·tal (săk′rə-mĕn′tl) *adj.* **1.** Of, relating to, or used in a sacrament. **2.** Consecrated or bound by or as if by a sacrament: *a sacramental duty.* **3.** Having the force or efficacy of a sacrament. **—sacramental** *n.* A rite, an act, or a sacred object used by some Christian churches in worship. **—sac′ra·men′tal·ly** *adv.*

sac·ra·men·tal·ism (săk′rə-mĕn′tl-ĭz′əm) *n.* **1.** The doctrine that observance of the sacraments is necessary for salvation and that such participation can confer grace. **2.** Emphasis on the efficacy of a sacramental. **—sac′ra·men′tal·ist** *n.*

Sac·ra·men·tar·i·an (săk′rə-mĕn-târ′ē-ən) *n.* One who regards the consecrated bread and wine of the Eucharist as only the metaphorical, and not the physical, body and blood of Jesus. **—Sacramentarian** *adj.* **1.** Of or relating to Sacramentarians. **2.** Of or relating to sacramentalism or sacramentalists. **—Sac′ra·men·tar′i·an·ism** *n.*

Sac·ra·men·to (săk′rə-mĕn′tō). The capital of California, in the north-central part of the state on the Sacramento River northeast of Oakland. Discovery of gold nearby in 1848 led to the growth of the original settlement as a trade and shipping center. It became the state capital in 1854. Population, 275,741.

Sacramento Mountains. A range of south-central New Mexico extending north and south to the Texas border and rising to 3,660.9 m (12,003 ft).

Sacramento River. A river of northern California rising near Mount Shasta and flowing about 611 km (380 mi) generally southward to an extension of San Francisco Bay.

sa·crar·i·um (sə-krâr′ē-əm, să-, sā-) *n., pl.* **-i·a** (-ē-ə). *Ecclesiastical.* **1.** The sanctuary or sacristy of a church. **2.** Piscina. [Medieval Latin *sacrārium,* from Latin, shrine, from *sacer, sacr-,* sacred. See SACRED.]

sa·cred (sā′krĭd) *adj.* **1.** Dedicated to or set apart for the worship of a deity. **2.** Worthy of religious veneration: *the sacred teachings of the Buddha.* **3.** Made or declared holy: *sacred bread and wine.* **4.** Dedicated or devoted exclusively to a single use, purpose, or person: *sacred to the memory of her sister; a private office sacred to the President.* **5.** Worthy of respect; venerable. **6.** Of or relating to religious objects, rites, or practices. [Middle English, past participle of *sacren,* to consecrate, from Old French *sacrer,* from Latin *sacrāre,* from *sacer, sacr-,* sacred. See **sak-** in Appendix.] **—sa′cred·ly** *adv.* **—sa′cred·ness** *n.*

sacred baboon *n.* See **hamadryas.** [From the fact that the ancient Egyptians revered it as the god Anubis.]

Sa·cred College (sā′krĭd) *n. Roman Catholic Church.* The College of Cardinals.

sacred cow *n.* One that is immune from criticism, often unreasonably so: *"The need for widespread secrecy has become a sacred cow"* (Bulletin of the Atomic Scientists). [From the veneration of the cow by Hindus.]

sacred ibis *n.* A large, short-legged ibis *(Threskiornis aethiopica)* of Africa and Asia, having white plumage and a sooty black, naked head and neck. [From the veneration of this ibis by the ancient Egyptians.]

sacred ibis
Threskiornis aethiopica

sac·ri·fice (săk′rə-fīs′) *n.* **1.a.** The act of offering something to a deity in propitiation or homage, especially the ritual slaughter of an animal or a person. **b.** A victim offered in this way. **2.a.** Forfeiture of something highly valued for the sake of one considered to have a greater value or claim. **b.** Something so forfeited. **3.a.** Relinquishment of something at less than its presumed value. **b.** Something so relinquished. **c.** A loss so sustained. **4.** *Baseball.* A sacrifice hit. **—sacrifice** *v.* **-ficed, -fic·ing, -fic·es.** *—tr.* **1.** To offer as a sacrifice to a deity. **2.** To forfeit (one thing) for another thing considered to be of greater value. **3.** To sell or give away at a loss. *—intr.* **1.** To make or offer a sacrifice. **2.** *Baseball.* To make a sacrifice hit. [Middle English, from Old French, from Latin *sacrificium* : *sacer,* sacred; see SACRED + *facere,* to make; see **dhē-** in Appendix.] **—sac′ri·fic′er** *n.*

sacrifice fly *n. Abbr.* **SF** *Baseball.* A fly ball enabling a runner to score after it is caught by a fielder.

sacrifice hit *n. Baseball.* A bunt that allows a runner to advance a base while the batter is retired.

sac·ri·fi·cial (săk′rə-fĭsh′əl) *adj.* Of, relating to, or concerned with a sacrifice: *a sacrificial offering.* **—sac′ri·fi′cial·ly** *adv.*

sacrificial anode *n. Metallurgy.* An anode that is attached to a metal object, such as a boat or an underground tank, to inhibit corrosion of the object. The anode is electrolytically decomposed while the object remains free of damage.

sac·ri·lege (săk′rə-lĭj) *n.* Desecration, profanation, misuse, or theft of something sacred. [Middle English, from Old French, from Latin *sacrilegium,* from *sacrilegus,* one who steals sacred things : *sacer,* sacred; see SACRED + *legere,* to gather; see **leg-** in Appendix.] **—sac′ri·le′gist** (săk′rə-lē′jĭst) *n.*

sac·ri·le·gious (săk′rə-lĭj′əs, -lē′jəs) *adj.* **1.** Grossly irreverent toward what is or is held to be sacred. See Synonyms at **profane.** **2.** Having committed sacrilege. **—sac′ri·le′gious·ly** *adv.* **—sac′ri·le′gious·ness** *n.*

USAGE NOTE: *Sacrilegious,* the adjective of *sacrilege,* is often misspelled through confusion with *religious.*

sac·ris·tan (săk′rĭ-stən) *n.* **1.** One who is in charge of a sacristy. **2.** A sexton. [Middle English, from Medieval Latin *sacristānus,* from *sacrista,* from Latin *sacer,* sacred. See SACRED.]

sac·ris·ty (săk′rĭ-stē) *n., pl.* **-ties.** A room in a church housing the sacred vessels and vestments; a vestry. [Middle English *sacriste,* from Anglo-Norman, from Medieval Latin *sacristia,* from *sacrista,* sacristan. See SACRISTAN.]

sacro– or **sacr–** *pref.* Sacrum: *sacrolumbar.*

sac·ro·coc·cyg·e·al (săk′rō-kŏk-sĭj′ē-əl, sā′krō-) *adj.* Of, relating to, or affecting the sacrum and coccyx.

sac·ro·il·i·ac (săk′rō-ĭl′ē-ăk′, sā′krō-) *adj.* Of, relating to,

ă pat	oi boy
ā pay	ou out
âr care	ŏŏ took
ä father	ōō boot
ĕ pet	ŭ cut
ē be	ûr urge
ĭ pit	th thin
ī pie	*th* this
îr pier	hw which
ŏ pot	zh vision
ō toe	ə about, item
ô paw	♦ regionalism

Stress marks: ′ (primary); ′ (secondary), as in **dictionary** (dĭk′shə-nĕr′ē)

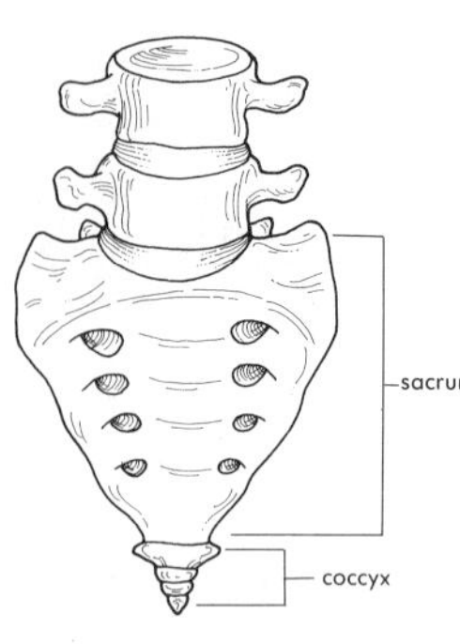

sacrum

or affecting the sacrum and ilium and their articulation or associated ligaments. **—sacroiliac** *n.* The sacroiliac region or cartilage.

sac·ro·lum·bar (săk′rō-lŭm′bər, -bär′, sā′krō-) *adj.* Of, relating to, or affecting the sacral and the lumbar region.

sac·ro·sanct (săk′rō-săngkt′) *adj.* Regarded as sacred and inviolable. [Latin *sacrōsānctus,* consecrated with religious ceremonies : *sacrum,* religious rite (from *sacer,* sacred; see SACRED) + *sānctus,* past participle of *sancīre,* to consecrate; see **sak-** in Appendix.] **—sac′ro·sanc′ti·ty** (-săngk′tĭ-tē) *n.*

sac·ro·sci·at·ic (săk′rō-sī-ăt′ĭk, sā′krō-) *adj.* Of, relating to, or affecting the sacrum and ischium.

sa·crum (sā′krəm, săk′rəm) *n., pl.* **sa·cra** (sā′krə, săk′rə). A triangular bone made up of five fused vertebrae and forming the posterior section of the pelvis. [New Latin, from Late Latin *(os) sacrum* (translation of Greek *hieron (osteon),* sacred bone : *hieros,* sacred + *osteon,* bone), from Latin *sacer,* sacred. See SACRED.]

sad (săd) *adj.* **sad·der, sad·dest. 1.** Affected or characterized by sorrow or unhappiness. **2.** Expressive of sorrow or unhappiness. **3.** Causing sorrow or gloom; depressing: *a sad movie; sad news.* **4.** Deplorable; sorry: *a sad state of affairs; a sad excuse.* **5.** Dark-hued; somber. [Middle English, weary, sorrowful, from Old English *sæd,* sated, weary. See **sā-** in Appendix.] **—sad′ly** *adv.* **—sad′ness** *n.*

SYNONYMS: *sad, melancholy, sorrowful, doleful, woebegone, desolate.* These adjectives all mean affected with or marked by unhappiness, as that caused by affliction. *Sad* is the most general: *"Better by far you should forget and smile/Than that you should remember and be sad"* (Christina Rossetti). *Melancholy* can refer to a lingering or habitual state of mind marked by somberness or sadness: *The patient's face, though it was melancholy, brightened at the arrival of the guests. Sorrowful* applies to mental pain such as that resulting from irreparable loss: *"Even in laughter the heart is sorrowful"* (Proverbs 14:13). *Doleful* describes what is mournful, morose, or gloomy: *The chastised child looked at her father with a pathetic, doleful expression. Woebegone* suggests grief or wretchedness, especially as it is reflected in a person's appearance: *"His sorrow . . . made him look . . . haggard and . . . woebegone"* (George du Maurier). *Desolate* applies to one that is sorrowful to the point of being beyond consolation: *"No one is so accursed by fate,/No one so utterly desolate,/But some heart, though unknown,/Responds unto his own"* (Henry Wadsworth Longfellow).

Anwar el-Sadat
Photographed in 1974

SAD *abbr.* Seasonal affective disorder.

Sa·dat (sə-dăt′, -dät′), **Anwar el-.** 1918–1981. Egyptian politician. President of Egypt (1970–1981), he shared the 1978 Nobel Peace Prize with Israeli Prime Minister Menachem Begin for negotiations that led to a historic peace treaty in 1979. Sadat was assassinated by Islamic fundamentalists.

sad·den (săd′n) *tr. & intr.v.* **-dened, -den·ing, -dens.** To make or become sad.

sad·dhu (sä′do͞o) *n. Hinduism.* Variant of **sadhu.**

♦ **sad·dle** (săd′l) *n.* **1.a.** A leather seat for a rider, secured on an animal's back by a girth. Also called ♦ *rig.* **b.** Similar tack used for attaching a pack to an animal. **c.** The padded part of a driving harness fitting over a horse's back. **d.** The seat of a bicycle, motorcycle, or similar vehicle. **e.** Something shaped like a saddle. **2.a.** A cut of meat consisting of part of the backbone and both loins. **b.** The lower part of a male fowl's back. **3.a.** A saddle-shaped depression in the ridge of a hill. **b.** A ridge between two peaks. **—saddle** *v.* **-dled, -dling, -dles.** *—tr.* **1.** To put a saddle onto. **2.** To load or burden; encumber: *They were saddled with heavy expenses. —intr.* **1.** To saddle a horse. **2.** To get into a saddle. ***—idiom.*** **in the saddle.** In control; dominant. [Middle English *sadel,* from Old English *sadol.* See **sed-** in Appendix.]

sad·dle·back (săd′l-băk′) *n.* Any of various birds, fishes, and other animals having saddle-shaped markings on the back.

saddleback caterpillar *n.* The brown and green larva of a moth *(Sibine stimulea)* of the southeast United States, having a brown saddle-shaped mark on its back and stinging spines that are mildly poisonous.

sad·dle·bag (săd′l-băg′) *n.* **1.** One of a pair of pouches hanging across the back of a horse behind the saddle. **2.** A pouch hanging from a saddle or over the rear wheel of a motorcycle or bicycle.

sad·dle-billed stork (săd′l-bĭld′) *n.* A large stork *(Ephippiorhynchus senegalensis)* of tropical Africa, having a white body and a very long black and red bill.

saddle blanket *n.* A blanket placed between a saddle and a horse's back to prevent galling.

sad·dle·bow (săd′l-bō′) *n.* The arched upper front part of a saddle.

sad·dle·cloth (săd′l-klôth′, -klŏth′) *n.* A cloth placed under the saddle of a racehorse and bearing its number.

saddle horse *n.* A horse bred or schooled for riding.

sad·dler (săd′lər) *n.* One that makes, repairs, or sells equipment for horses.

saddle roof *n.* A roof having a ridge and two gables.

sad·dler·y (săd′lə-rē) *n., pl.* **-ies. 1.** Equipment, such as saddles and harnesses, for horses. **2.** A shop that sells tack. **3.** The craft or business of one that makes or sells tack.

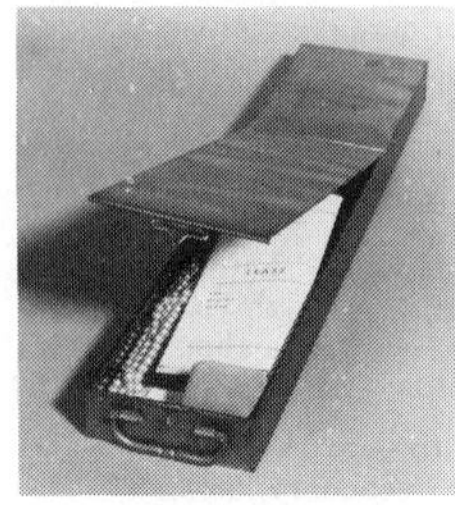
safe-deposit box

saddle shoe *n.* A flat casual shoe, usually white, having a band of leather in a contrasting color across the instep.

saddle soap *n.* A preparation containing mild soap and neat's-foot oil, used for cleaning and softening leather.

saddle sore *n.* **1.** A sore on a horse's back caused by an improperly fitted saddle. **2.** A sore on a rider caused by the chafing of a saddle.

saddle stitch *n.* **1.** A simple overcasting stitch, usually of a thread contrasting in color with the fabric, used primarily as ornament on clothing. **2.** A stitch used in sewing together the leaves of a book at the fold lines, either with thread or wire.

sad·dle·tree (săd′l-trē′) *n.* The frame of a saddle.

Sad·du·cee (săj′ə-sē′, săd′yə-) *n.* A member of a priestly, aristocratic Jewish sect founded in the second century B.C. that accepted only the written Mosaic law and that ceased to exist after the destruction of the Temple in 70 A.D. [Middle English *Saducee,* from Old English *Sadducēas,* Sadducees, from Late Latin *Saddūcaeī,* from Greek *Saddoukaioi,* from Hebrew *Ṣĕdûqî.*] **—Sad′du·ce′an** (-sē′ən) *adj.* **—Sad′du·cee′ism** *n.*

Sade (säd, săd), Comte **Donatien Alphonse François de.** Known as "Marquis de Sade." 1740–1814. French writer of novels, plays, and short stories characterized by a preoccupation with sexual violence.

sa·dhe (sä′də, tsä′-, -dē) also **tsa·de** (tsä′də, -dē) *n.* The 18th letter of the Hebrew alphabet. See table at **alphabet.** [Hebrew *ṣādē.*]

sa·dhu also **sad·dhu** (sä′do͞o) *n. Hinduism.* An ascetic holy man. [From Sanskrit *sādhu-,* right, holy.]

sa·dism (sā′dĭz′əm, săd′ĭz′-) *n.* **1.** *Psychology.* **a.** The act or an instance of deriving sexual gratification from infliction of pain on others. **b.** A psychological disorder in which sexual gratification is derived from infliction of pain on others. **2.** Delight in cruelty. **3.** Extreme cruelty. [After Comte Donatien Alphonse François de SADE.] **—sa′dist** *n.* **—sa·dis′tic** (sə-dĭs′tĭk) *adj.* **—sa·dis′ti·cal·ly** *adv.*

sa·do·mas·o·chism (sā′dō-măs′ə-kĭz′əm, săd′ō-) *n. Abbr.* **S-M, s-m, S&M, s&m** *Psychology.* The perversion of deriving pleasure, especially sexual pleasure, from simultaneous sadism and masochism. [SAD(ISM) + MASOCHISM.] **—sa′do·mas′o·chist** *n.* **—sa′do·mas′o·chis′tic** *adj.*

sad sack *n. Informal.* A person regarded as extremely inept or clumsy. [After a cartoon character created in 1942 by George Baker (1915–1975).]

Sa·far also **Sa·phar** (sə-fär′) *n.* The second month of the year in the Moslem calendar. See table at **calendar.** [Arabic *ṣafar.*]

sa·fa·ri (sə-fär′ē) *n., pl.* **-ris. 1.** An overland expedition, especially one for hunting or exploring in eastern Africa. **2.** A journey or trip: *a sightseeing safari.* [Arabic *safarī,* journey, from *safara,* to travel, set out.]

safari jacket *n.* A belted, often pleated shirt jacket with large patch pockets.

safe (sāf) *adj.* **saf·er, saf·est. 1.** Secure from danger, harm, or evil. **2.** Free from danger or injury; unhurt: *safe and sound.* **3.** Free from risk; sure: *a safe bet.* **4.** Affording protection: *a safe place.* **5.** *Baseball.* Having reached a base without being put out, as a batter or base runner. **—safe** *n.* **1.** A metal container usually having a lock, used for storing valuables. **2.** A repository for protecting stored items, especially a cooled compartment for perishable foods: *a cheese safe.* **3.** *Slang.* A condom. [Middle English *sauf,* from Old French, from Latin *salvus,* healthy. See **sol-** in Appendix.] **—safe′ly** *adv.* **—safe′ness** *n.*

safe-con·duct (sāf′kŏn′dŭkt) *n.* **1.** An official document or an escort assuring unmolested passage, as through enemy territory. **2.** The protection afforded by such a document.

safe·crack·er (sāf′krăk′ər) *n.* One who breaks into safes in order to steal items from them. **—safe′crack′ing** *n.*

safe-de·pos·it box (sāf′dĭ-pŏz′ĭt) *n.* A fireproof metal box, usually in a bank vault, for the safe storage of valuables.

safe·guard (sāf′gärd′) *n.* **1.a.** One that serves as protection or a guard. **b.** A mechanical device designed to prevent accidents. **c.** A safe-conduct. **2.a.** A protective stipulation, as in a contract. **b.** A precautionary measure. **—safeguard** *tr.v.* **-guard·ed, -guard·ing, -guards.** To ensure the safety of; protect. See Synonyms at **defend.**

safe house *n.* A house or an apartment used as a hiding place or secure refuge by the members of an organization, such as a secret service agency or an underground terrorist group.

safe·keep·ing (sāf′kē′pĭng) *n.* The act of keeping safe or the state of being kept safe; protection.

safe·light (sāf′līt′) *n.* A lamp having one or more color filters allowing moderate darkroom illumination without affecting photosensitive film or paper.

safe sex *n.* Sexual activity in which safeguards, such as the use of a condom, are taken to avoid acquiring or spreading a sexually transmitted disease. **—safe′-sex′** (sāf′sĕks′) *adj.*

safe·ty (sāf′tē) *n., pl.* **-ties. 1.** The condition of being safe; freedom from danger, risk, or injury. **2.** A device designed to prevent accidents, as a lock on a firearm preventing accidental firing. **3.** *Football.* **a.** A play in which a member of the offensive team downs the ball, willingly or unwillingly, behind his own goal line, resulting in two points for the defensive team. **b.** One of two defensive backs; a safetyman. **4.** *Slang.* A condom. *—attributive.*

Often used to modify another noun: *safety precautions; safety rules.*

safety belt *n.* **1.** A strap or belt worn as a safety precaution by a person working at great heights. **2.** See **seat belt.**

safety circuit *n.* An electronic circuit that prevents malfunction by either sounding an alert or activating a trip circuit on a protective device.

safety glass *n.* **1.** Glass that resists shattering, especially a composite of two sheets of glass with an intermediate layer of transparent plastic. Also called *shatterproof glass.* **2.** See **wire glass. 3.** Tempered glass that breaks into rounded grains instead of jagged shards.

safety island *n.* An area marked off within a roadway from which traffic is banned, especially to provide pedestrian safety.

safety lamp *n.* A miner's lamp with a protective wire gauze surrounding the flame to prevent ignition of flammable gases.

safe·ty·man (sāf′tē-măn′) *n. Football.* A safety.

safety match *n.* A match that can be lighted only by being struck against a chemically prepared friction surface.

safety net *n.* **1.** A large net for catching one that falls or jumps, as from a circus trapeze. **2.** A guarantee, as of professional, physical, or financial security: *"They cannot invoke the sacrifice of vital policies having to do with . . . terrorism as a safety net for their own careers"* (Moorhead Kennedy).

safety pin *n.* **1.** A pin in the form of a clasp, having a sheath to cover and hold the point. **2.** A pin that prevents the premature or accidental detonation of an explosive device, such as a bomb or grenade.

safety razor *n.* See **razor** (sense 2).

safety valve *n.* **1.** A valve in a pressure container, as in a steam boiler, that automatically opens when pressure reaches a dangerous level. **2.** An outlet for the release of repressed energy or emotion.

saf·flow·er (săf′lou′ər) *n.* **1.** A thistlelike Eurasian plant *(Carthamus tinctorius)* of the composite family, having heads of orange flowers that yield a dyestuff and produce seeds containing an oil used in cooking, cosmetics, paints, and medicine. **2.** The dried flowers of this plant. [Middle English *saflour,* from Old French *safleur,* from Old Italian *saffiore,* from Arabic *aṣfar,* yellow, a yellow plant.]

saf·fron (săf′rən) *n.* **1.a.** A corm-producing plant *(Crocus sativus)* native to the Old World, having purple or white flowers with orange stigmas. **b.** The dried aromatic stigmas of this plant, used to color foods and as a cooking spice and dyestuff. **2.** *Color.* A moderate or strong orange yellow to moderate orange. [Middle English *saffran,* from Old French *safran,* from Medieval Latin *safrānum,* from Arabic *za'farān.*]

Sa·fi (săf′ē). A city of western Morocco on the Atlantic Ocean west-northwest of Marrakesh. A Portuguese base in the early 16th century, it is today a fishing, processing, and shipping center. Population, 197,309.

S.Afr. *abbr.* South Africa.

saf·ra·nine (săf′rə-nēn′, -nĭn) also **saf·ra·nin** (-nĭn) *n.* Any of a family of dyes based on phenazine, used in the textile industry and as a biological stain. [French *safran,* saffron (from Old French; see SAFFRON) + –INE[2].]

saf·role (săf′rōl′) *n.* A colorless or pale yellow oily liquid, $C_{10}H_{10}O_2$, derived from oil of sassafras and other essential oils and used in making perfume and soap. [French *safran,* saffron; see SAFFRON + –OLE.]

sag (săg) *v.* **sagged, sag·ging, sags.** —*intr.* **1.** To sink, droop, or settle from pressure or weight. **2.** To lose vigor, firmness, or resilience: *My spirits sagged after I had been rejected for the job.* **3.** To decline, as in value or price: *Stock prices sagged after a short rally.* **4.** *Nautical.* To drift to leeward. —*tr.* To cause to sag. —**sag** *n.* **1.a.** The act or an instance of sagging. **b.** The degree or extent to which something sags. **2.** A sagging area; a depression. **3.** A temporary decline in monetary value. **4.** *Nautical.* A drift to leeward. [Middle English *saggen,* probably of Scandinavian origin; akin to Swedish *sacka,* to sink.]

sa·ga (sä′gə) *n.* **1.a.** A prose narrative usually written in Iceland between 1120 and 1400, dealing with the families that first settled Iceland and their descendants, with the histories of the kings of Norway, and with the myths and legends of early Germanic gods and heroes. **b.** A modern prose narrative that resembles a saga. **2.** A long, detailed report: *recounted the saga of their family problems.* [Old Norse. See **sekʷ-³** in Appendix.]

sa·ga·cious (sə-gā′shəs) *adj.* Having or showing keen discernment, sound judgment, and farsightedness. See Synonyms at **shrewd.** [From Latin *sagāx, sagāc-,* of keen perception. See **sāg-** in Appendix.] —**sa·ga′cious·ly** *adv.* —**sa·ga′cious·ness** *n.*

sa·gac·i·ty (sə-găs′ĭ-tē) *n.* The quality of being discerning, sound in judgment, and farsighted; wisdom. [French *sagacité,* from Old French *sagacite,* from Latin *sagācitās,* quickness of perception, from *sagāx, sagāc-,* of keen perception. See SAGACIOUS.]

Sa·ga·mi·ha·ra (sə-gä′mē-här′ə). A city of east-central Honshu, Japan, a suburb of Tokyo. Population, 482,778.

sag·a·more (săg′ə-môr′, -mōr′) *n.* A subordinate chief among the Algonquians of North America. [Eastern Abenaki *sàkəma.*].

Sa·gan (sā′gən), **Carl.** Born 1934. American astronomer noted for research on the possibility of extraterrestrial life and for speculation on the severity of a nuclear winter.

Sa·gan (sä-gäɴ′), **Françoise.** Born 1935. French writer best known for her first novel, *Bonjour Tristesse* (1954).

saga novel *n.* See **roman-fleuve.**

sage¹ (sāj) *n.* One venerated for experience, judgment, and wisdom. —**sage** *adj.* **sag·er, sag·est. 1.** Having or exhibiting wisdom and calm judgment. **2.** Proceeding from or marked by wisdom and calm judgment: *sage advice.* **3.** *Archaic.* Serious; solemn. [Middle English, from Old French, from Vulgar Latin **sapius,* from Latin *sapere,* to be wise. See **sep-** in Appendix.] —**sage′ly** *adv.* —**sage′ness** *n.*

sage² (sāj) *n.* **1.a.** Any of various plants of the genus *Salvia,* especially *S. officinalis,* having aromatic grayish-green, opposite leaves used as a cooking herb. Also called *ramona.* **b.** The leaves of this plant. **2.** Any of various similar or related plants in the mint family. **3.** Sagebrush. [Middle English *sauge,* from Old French, from Latin *salvia,* from *salvus,* healthy. See **sol-** in Appendix.]

sage·brush (sāj′brŭsh′) *n.* Any of several aromatic plants of the genus *Artemisia,* especially *A. tridentata,* a shrub of arid regions of western North America, having silver-green leaves and large clusters of small white flower heads.

sage cock *n.* The male sage grouse.

sage grouse *n.* A chickenlike bird *(Centrocercus urophasianus)* of western North America, having long, pointed tail feathers that can be spread like a fan.

sage hen *n.* The sage grouse, especially the female.

sage sparrow *n.* A small brownish-gray sparrow *(Amphispiza belli)* found in dry or desert regions of the southwest United States.

sage thrasher *n.* A light grayish-brown thrasher *(Oreoscoptes montanus)* that nests in low sage and cactus bushes in dry or desert regions of the western United States.

sag·ger also **sag·gar** (săg′ər) *n.* **1.** A protective casing of fire clay in which delicate ceramic articles are fired. **2.** Clay used to make ceramic casings. [Perhaps alteration of SAFEGUARD.]

Sag Harbor (săg). A village of southeast New York on the eastern end of Long Island on an inlet of Long Island Sound. A major whaling port in the early 19th century, it is today primarily a resort. Population, 2,581.

Sa·gi·naw (săg′ə-nô′). A city of east-central Michigan on the **Saginaw River,** which flows about 32 km (20 mi) into **Saginaw Bay,** a large inlet of Lake Huron. The city is a port of entry and an industrial center. Population, 77,508.

Sa·git·ta (sə-jĭt′ə) *n.* A constellation in the Northern Hemisphere near Aquila and Vulpecula. [Latin, *sagitta,* arrow.]

sag·it·tal (săj′ĭ-tl) *adj.* **1.** *Anatomy.* Of or relating to the suture uniting the two parietal bones of the skull. **2.** *Zoology.* Of or relating to the sagittal plane. [New Latin *sagittālis,* from Latin *sagitta,* arrow.] —**sag′it·tal·ly** *adv.*

sagittal plane *n. Zoology.* A longitudinal plane that divides the body of a bilaterally symmetrical animal into right and left sections.

Sag·it·tar·i·an (săj′ĭ-târ′ē-ən) *n.* One who is born under the sign of Sagittarius. —**Sag′it·tar′i·an** *adj.*

Sag·it·tar·i·us (săj′ĭ-târ′ē-əs) *n.* **1.** A constellation in the Southern Hemisphere near Scorpius and Capricorn. **2.a.** The ninth sign of the zodiac in astrology. **b.** One who is born under this sign. Also called *Archer.* [Middle English, from Latin *Sagittārius,* from *sagittārius,* archer, from *sagitta,* arrow.]

sag·it·tate (săj′ĭ-tāt′) *adj. Biology.* Having the shape of an arrowhead: *sagittate leaves; sagittate shells.* [Latin *sagitta,* arrow + –ATE¹.]

sa·go (sā′gō) *n., pl.* **-gos.** A powdery starch obtained from the trunks of certain sago palms and used in Asia as a food thickener and textile stiffener. [Malay *sagu,* mealy pith.]

sago palm *n.* **1.** Any of various palms of the genera *Metroxylon, Arenga,* and *Caryota* of tropical Asia. **2.** Either of two palmlike cycads *(Cycas circinalis* or *C. revoluta)* of eastern and tropical Asia.

sa·gua·ro (sə-gwär′ō, -wär′ō) also **sa·hua·ro** (sə-wär′ō) *n., pl.* **-ros. 1.** A very large cactus *(Carnegiea gigantea)* of the southwest United States and northern Mexico, having ribbed upward-curving branches, white funnel-shaped flowers, and edible red fruit. **2.** The fruit of this cactus. [American Spanish, probably of Piman origin.]

Sag·ue·nay (săg′ə-nā′). A river, about 201 km (125 mi) long, of southern Quebec, Canada, flowing from Lake St. John eastward to the St. Lawrence River.

Sa·gun·to (sə-go͝on′tō, sä-). A city of eastern Spain north-northeast of Valencia. Founded by Greek colonists and later allied with Rome, it was besieged and captured by Carthaginian forces led by Hannibal (219–218 B.C.), thus precipitating the Second Punic War. Population, 57,380.

Sa·hap·ti·an (sä-hăp′tē-ən) also **Sha·hap·ti·an** (shä-) *n.* **1.** A North American Indian language family spoken in Washington, Oregon, and Idaho and comprising the Sahaptin and Nez Perce languages. **2.** A speaker of a Sahaptian language. —**Sa·hap′ti·an** *adj.*

Sa·hap·tin (sä-hăp′tĭn) also **Sha·hap·tin** (shä-) *n., pl.* **Sahaptin** or **-tins** also **Shahaptin** or **-tins. 1.a.** Any of various Native American peoples of Idaho, Washington, and Oregon. **b.** A member of any of these peoples. **2.** The dialectally diverse

safety net
Beneath tightrope walkers

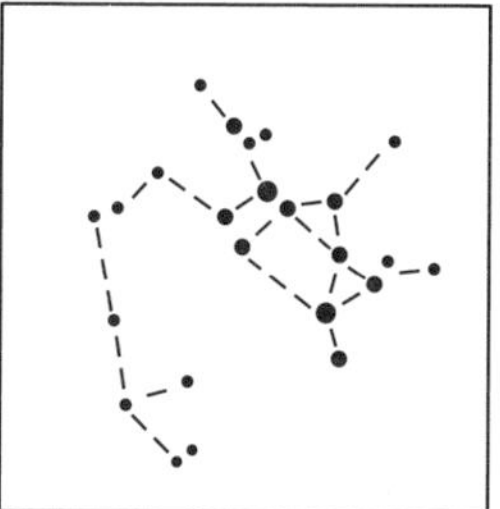

Sagittarius

saguaro
Carnegiea gigantea

ă pat	oi boy
ā pay	ou out
âr care	o͝o took
ä father	o͞o boot
ĕ pet	ŭ cut
ē be	ûr urge
ĭ pit	th thin
ī pie	*th* this
îr pier	hw which
ŏ pot	zh vision
ō toe	ə about, item
ô paw	♦ regionalism

Stress marks: ′ (primary); ′ (secondary), as in **dictionary** (dĭk′shə-nĕr′ē)

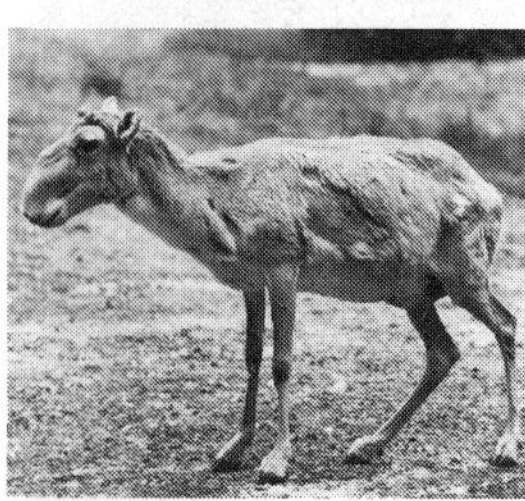

saiga
Saiga tatarica

Sahaptian language of the Sahaptin. [Southern Interior Salish *s'aptnx*.]

Sa·har·a (sə-hâr′ə, -hăr′ə, -hä′rə). A vast desert of northern Africa extending east from the Atlantic coast to the Nile Valley and south from the Atlas Mountains to the region of the Sudan. During the Ice Age (about 50,000 to 100,000 years ago), the Sahara was a region of extensive shallow lakes watering large areas of vegetation, most of which had disappeared by Roman times. Introduction of the camel (probably in the first century A.D.) led to occupation by nomadic tribes who moved from oasis to oasis in search of water. **—Sa·har′an** *adj.*

Sa·ha·ran·pur (sə-här′ən-pŏŏr′). A city of north-central India north-northeast of Delhi. It was once a summer resort for the Mogul court. Population, 295,355.

Sa·hel (sə-hāl′, -hēl′). A semiarid region of north-central Africa south of the Sahara Desert. **—Sa·hel′i·an** *adj.*

sa·hib (sä′ĭb, -ēb, -hĭb) *n.* Used formerly as a form of respectful address for a European man in colonial India. [Hindi *ṣāḥib*, master, from Arabic, companion, master.]

sa·hua·ro (sə-wär′ō) *n.* Variant of **saguaro.**

said (sĕd) *v.* Past tense and past participle of **say.** **—said** *adj. Law.* Named or mentioned before; aforementioned: *Said party has denied the charges.*

USAGE NOTE: The adjective *said* is seldom appropriate to any but legal or business writing, where it is equivalent to *aforesaid*: *the said tenant* (named in a lease); *said property.* In similar general contexts *said* is usually unnecessary, and *the tenant* or *the property* will suffice.

sai·ga (sī′gə) *n.* Either of two small antelopes *(Saiga tatarica* or *S. mongolia)* of the plains of northern Eurasia, having a stubby snout. [Russian *saĭga*, of Turkic origin.]

Sai·gon (sī-gŏn′). See **Ho Chi Minh City.**

sail (sāl) *n.* **1.** *Nautical.* **a.** A piece of fabric sewn together and fitted to the spars and rigging of a vessel so as to convert the force of the wind into forward motion of the vessel. **b.** The sails of a ship or boat. **c.** The superstructure of a submarine. **2.** *pl.* **sail** or **sails.** *Nautical.* A sailing vessel. **3.** *Nautical.* A trip or voyage in a sailing craft. **4.** Something, such as the blade of a windmill, that resembles a sail in form or function. **—sail** *v.* **sailed, sail·ing, sails.** *—intr.* **1.** *Nautical.* **a.** To move across the surface of water, especially by means of a sailing vessel. **b.** To travel by water in a vessel. **c.** To start out on such a voyage or journey. **d.** To operate a sailing craft, especially for sport. **2.** To move swiftly, smoothly, or effortlessly: *sailed through the examination.* *—tr. Nautical.* **1.** To navigate or manage (a vessel). **2.** To voyage upon or across: *sail the Pacific.* ***—phrasal verb.*** **sail into.** To attack or criticize vigorously. [Middle English, from Old English *segl*.]

sail·board (sāl′bôrd′, -bōrd′) *Nautical. n.* A small light sailboat with a flat hull. **—sailboard** *intr.v.* **-board·ed, -board·ing, -boards.** To engage in the activity or sport of sailing a small, flat-hulled sailboat. **—sail′board′er** *n.*

sail·boat (sāl′bōt′) *n. Nautical.* A small boat propelled partially or wholly by sail.

sail·cloth (sāl′klôth′, -klŏth′) *n.* A strong fabric, such as cotton canvas, suitable for making sails or tents.

sail·fish (sāl′fĭsh′) *n., pl.* **sailfish** or **-fish·es.** Any of various large marine fishes of the genus *Istiophorus,* having a large saillike dorsal fin and an upper jaw that is prolonged into a spearlike bone.

Saint Andrew's cross

sail·ing (sā′lĭng) *n. Nautical.* **1.** The skill required to operate and navigate a vessel; navigation. **2.** The sport of operating or riding in a sailboat. **3.** Departure or time of departure from a port.

sail·or (sā′lər) *n.* **1.** *Nautical.* One who serves in a navy or works on a ship. **2.** One who travels by water. **3.** A low-crowned straw hat with a flat top and flat brim.

sail·or's-choice (sā′lərz-chois′) *n., pl.* **sailor's-choice.** Any of various fishes of the North American Atlantic coast, as the pinfish or the grunt *Haemulon parrai* of southerly waters.

sail·plane (sāl′plăn′) *n.* A light glider used especially for soaring. **—sailplane** *intr.v.* **-planed, -plan·ing, -planes.** To fly a sailplane. **—sail′plan′er** *n.*

Sai·maa (sī′mä′), **Lake.** A lake of southeast Finland. It is the largest of the **Saimaa Lakes,** a group of more than 120 interconnected lakes.

sain·foin (săn′foin′, săn′-) *n.* A Eurasian plant *(Onobrychis viciifolia)* having pinnately compound leaves and pink or white flowers, often grown as a forage crop. [French, from Old French, from Medieval Latin *sānum faenum* : Latin *sānum,* neuter of *sānus,* healthy + Latin *faenum,* hay; see **dhē(i)-** in Appendix.]

saint (sānt) *n. Abbr.* **S., St.** **1.a.** *Theology.* A person officially recognized, especially by canonization, as being entitled to public veneration and capable of interceding for people on earth. **b.** A person who has died and gone to heaven. **c. Saint.** A member of any of various religious groups, especially a Latter-Day Saint. **2.** An extremely virtuous person. **—saint** *tr.v.* **saint·ed, saint·ing, saints.** To name, recognize, or venerate as a saint; canonize. [Middle English, from Old French, from Late Latin *sānctus,* from Latin, holy, past participle of *sancīre,* to consecrate. See **sak-** in Appendix.]

Saint Bernard

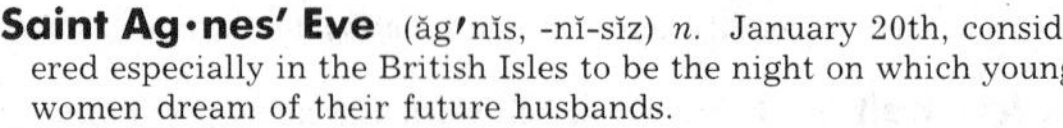

Saint Ag·nes' Eve (ăg′nĭs, -nĭ-sĭz) *n.* January 20th, considered especially in the British Isles to be the night on which young women dream of their future husbands.

Saint Al·bans (ôl′bənz). A municipal borough of southeast England north-northwest of London. On the site of the Roman settlement of Verulamium, it was founded as an abbey town in 793. Population, 125,400.

Saint Al·bert (ăl′bərt). A city of central Alberta, Canada, an industrial suburb of Edmonton. Population, 31,996.

Saint An·drews (ăn′drōōz). **1.** A burgh of eastern Scotland southeast of Dundee on **Saint Andrews Bay,** an inlet of the North Sea. Chartered in 1160, it was an important ecclesiastical center during the Middle Ages. It is now primarily a resort known for its golf courses. Population, 10,358. **2.** A community of southeast South Carolina, a suburb of Charleston. Population, 20,245.

Saint An·drew's cross (ăn′drōōz) *n.* **1.** A cross shaped like the letter X. **2.** A shrubby New World plant *(Hypericum hypericoides)* having four-petaled yellow flowers.

Saint An·tho·ny's cross (ăn′thə-nēz) *n.* See **tau cross.**

Saint Anthony's fire *n.* See **erysipelas.** [From the belief that Saint Anthony's intercession could cure it.]

Saint Au·gus·tine (ô′gə-stēn′). A city of northeast Florida on the Atlantic Ocean south-southeast of Jacksonville. Founded by the Spanish in 1565, it is the oldest permanent European settlement in the United States. Population, 11,985.

Saint-Bar·thél·e·my (săN-bär-tāl-mē′) or **Saint Bar·thol·o·mew** (sānt bär-thŏl′ə-myōō′). Familiarly known as **Saint Barts** (bärts). An island of the French overseas department of Guadeloupe in the Leeward Islands of the West Indies north-northwest of the island of Guadeloupe.

Saint Ber·nard (bər-närd′) *n.* Any of a breed of large, strong dog developed in Switzerland, having a thick brown and white coat, originally used by monks of the hospice of Saint Bernard in the Swiss Alps to help patrol the snow-covered region.

Saint Bru·no de Mon·tar·ville or **Saint-Bru·no-de-Mon·tar·ville** (sānt brōō′nō də mŏn′tər-vĭl′, săN brü-nô′ də môN-tär-vēl′). A town of southern Quebec, Canada, a suburb of Montreal on the St. Lawrence River. Population, 22,880.

Saint Cath·a·rines (sānt kăth′ə-rĭnz′, kăth′rĭnz). A city of southeast Ontario, Canada, on the Welland Ship Canal east-southeast of Hamilton. Founded in 1790, it is an industrial center. Population, 124,018.

Saint Charles (chärlz). **1.** A city of northeast Illinois west of Chicago. It is a manufacturing center in an agricultural area. Population, 17,492. **2.** A city of eastern Missouri on the Missouri River northwest of St. Louis. Settled by French traders in 1769, it was the state capital from 1821 to 1826. Population, 37,379.

Saint Chris·to·pher-Ne·vis (krĭs′tə-fər-nē′vĭs, -nĕv′ĭs) also **Saint Kitts and Ne·vis** (kĭts; nē′vĭs, nĕv′ĭs). An island country in the Leeward Islands of the West Indies east-southeast of Puerto Rico comprising **Saint Christopher,** the largest island of the group, and the islands of Nevis and Sombrero. The main islands were discovered by Columbus in 1493 and settled by the English in the early 1600's. They were part of the West Indies Federation from 1958 to 1962 and in 1967 joined in a short-lived association with Anguilla. St. Christopher-Nevis became independent in 1983. Basseterre, on St. Christopher, is the capital. Population, 44,404.

Saint Clair (sānt klâr), **Lake.** A lake between southwest Ontario, Canada, and southeast Michigan. It is connected with Lake Huron by the **Saint Clair River,** about 64 km (40 mi) long.

Saint Clair Shores. A city of southeast Michigan, a residential suburb of Detroit. Population, 76,210.

Saint Cloud (kloud). A city of central Minnesota on the Mississippi River northwest of Minneapolis. Granite has been quarried in the area since the 1860's. Population, 42,566.

Saint Croix (kroi). An island of the U.S. Virgin Islands in the West Indies east of Puerto Rico. Discovered by Columbus in 1493, it was controlled successively by Holland, England, Spain, France, and Denmark, which sold it to the United States in 1917.

Saint Croix River. **1.** A river, about 264 km (164 mi) long, rising in northwest Wisconsin and flowing generally south along the Minnesota border to the Mississippi River southeast of St. Paul. **2.** A river, about 121 km (75 mi) long, forming part of the boundary between eastern Maine and southwest New Brunswick, Canada. It rises in a series of lakes and flows generally southeast to Passamaquoddy Bay. In 1604 Samuel de Champlain established a colony on **Saint Croix Island** near the mouth of the river, but the settlement was abandoned in 1605.

Saint-Cyr-l'É·cole (săN-sîr-lā-kôl′). A town of north-central France west of Versailles. It was long noted as the site of a military academy founded by Napoleon I in 1808. Population, 14,996.

Saint Den·is (sānt dĕn′ĭs), **Ruth.** 1878–1968. American choreographer and pioneer of modern dance. With her husband Ted Shawn she founded (1915) the Denishawn Dance School.

Saint-De·nis (săN-də-nē′). **1.** A city of north-central France, an industrial suburb of Paris. Dating from early Christian times as a place of pilgrimage, it is the site of a Benedictine abbey founded in 626. The city's 12th-century Gothic cathedral contains the tombs of numerous French monarchs. Population, 90,829. **2.** The capital of Réunion, a port on the Indian Ocean. It was founded in the late 17th century as a way station on the route to the Orient. Population, 84,400.

saint•dom (sānt′dəm) *n.* The condition or quality of being a saint.

Sainte Anne de Beau•pré or **Sainte-Anne-de-Beau•pré** (sānt ăn′ də bō-prā′, săɴ-tăn). A village of southern Quebec, Canada, on the St. Lawrence River northeast of Quebec City. Its famous shrine was established by shipwrecked sailors in 1620.

Sainte-Beuve (săɴt-bœv′), **Charles Augustin.** 1804–1869. French literary critic and historian noted for his biographical approach to literature.

saint•ed (sān′tĭd) *adj.* **1.** Having been canonized. **2.** Of saintly character; holy.

Sainte Foy or **Sainte-Foy** (sānt foi′, săɴt fwä′). A city of southern Quebec, Canada, a suburb of Quebec City. Population, 68,883.

Saint E•li•as (sānt ĭ-lī′əs), **Mount.** A peak, 5,492.4 m (18,008 ft) high, in the **Saint Elias Mountains,** a section of the Coast Ranges on the border between eastern Alaska and southwest Yukon Territory, Canada. Mount Logan, rising to 5,954.8 m (19,524 ft), is the highest peak in the range.

Saint El•mo's fire (ĕl′mōz) *n.* A visible electric discharge on a pointed object, such as the mast of a ship or the wing of an airplane, during an electrical storm. Also called *corposant.* [After *Saint Elmo,* fourth-century A.D. patron saint of sailors.]

Sainte Thé•rèse or **Sainte-Thé•rèse** (sānt′ tə-rĕz′, săɴt tā-rĕz′). A city of southern Quebec, Canada, on the St. Lawrence River northwest of Montreal. Population, 18,750.

Saint-É•tienne (săɴ-tā-tyĕn′). A city of southeast-central France southwest of Lyons. It has been a textile-producing center since the 11th century. Population, 204,995.

Saint Eu•stache or **Saint-Eu•stache** (sānt′ o͞o-stăsh′, săɴ-tœ-stăsh′). A town of southern Quebec, Canada, west of Montreal. It is a residential and resort community. Population, 29,716.

Saint Eu•sta•ti•us (sānt yo͞o-stā′shəs, -shē-əs). An island of the Netherlands Antilles in the Leeward Islands of the West Indies northwest of St. Christopher. Settled originally by the French, it passed to the Dutch in 1632.

Saint-Ex•u•pé•ry (săɴ-tĕg-zo͞o-pā-rē′, -zü-), **Antoine de.** 1900–1944. French writer and aviator best known for his fairy tale *The Little Prince* (1943).

Saint Fran•cis River (frăn′sĭs). A river, about 756 km (470 mi) long, rising in southeast Missouri and flowing generally southward to the Mississippi River in eastern Arkansas.

Saint Gall (sānt gôl′, gäl′, săɴ gäl′). See **Sankt Gallen.**

Saint-Gau•dens (sānt-gôd′nz), **Augustus.** 1848–1907. Irish-born American sculptor noted for his heroic monuments, including the equestrian statue of Gen. William T. Sherman in New York City (1903).

Saint George's (sānt jôr′jəz). The capital of Grenada, on the southwest coast of the island in the Windward Islands of the West Indies. Population, 7,500.

Saint George's Channel. A strait between western Wales and southeast Ireland. It connects the Atlantic Ocean with the Irish Sea.

Saint Gott•hard (gŏt′ərd). A range of the Lepontine Alps in south-central Switzerland. It is crossed by **Saint Gotthard Pass,** 2,115.2 m (6,935 ft) high.

Saint He•le•na (hə-lē′nə). A volcanic island in the southern Atlantic Ocean west of Angola. Together with the islands of Ascension and Tristan da Cunha, it forms the British dependency of **Saint Helena** and has been occupied by the British since the mid-1600's. The island is best known as Napoleon's place of exile from 1815 until 1821. Jamestown is the capital. Population, 5,147.

Saint Hel•ens (hĕl′ənz). A borough of northwest England east-northeast of Liverpool. It is an important glassmaking center. Population, 190,000.

Saint Helens, Mount. An active volcanic peak of the Cascade Range in southwest Washington. Before its violent eruption on May 18, 1980, it was 2,949.7 m (9,671 ft) high. The eruption produced a smoke plume visible over much of western Washington and Oregon, set off fires and mud slides that killed at least 65 people, and covered a large area with a blanket of volcanic ash.

Saint Hel•ier (hĕl′yər). A town of Jersey, England, in the Channel Islands. Home to Victor Hugo from 1852 to 1855, it is now a resort and residential center. Population, 24,941.

saint•hood (sānt′ho͝od′) *n.* **1.** The status, character, or condition of being a saint. **2.** Saints considered as a group.

Saint Hu•bert or **Saint-Hu•bert** (sānt′ hyo͞o′bərt, săɴ ü-bĕr′). A town of southern Quebec, Canada, a suburb of Montreal east of the St. Lawrence River. Population, 60,573.

Saint Hy•a•cinthe or **Saint-Hy•a•cinthe** (sānt′ hī′ə-sĭnth, săɴ-tyä-săɴt′). A city of southern Quebec, Canada, east-northeast of Montreal. It is an industrial center. Population, 38,246.

Saint Jean or **Saint-Jean** (săɴ zhäɴ′) or **Saint Johns** (sānt jŏnz′). A city of southern Quebec, Canada, on the Richelieu River southeast of Montreal. Founded in 1666, it was an important British fortress in the 17th and 18th centuries. Population, 35,640.

Saint Jean or **Saint-Jean, Lake.** See Lake **Saint John.**

Saint Jé•rôme or **Saint-Jé•rôme** (sānt′ jə-rōm′, săɴ zhā-rōm′). A city of southern Quebec, Canada, northwest of Montreal. It is an industrial center. Population, 25,123.

Saint John[1] (sānt jŏn′). An island of the U.S. Virgin Islands in the West Indies east of Puerto Rico. It was discovered by Columbus in 1493 and passed to various European powers before being sold to the United States by Denmark in 1917.

Saint John[2] (sānt jŏn′). A city of southern New Brunswick, Canada, at the mouth of the St. John River on the Bay of Fundy. First settled as a French trading post in the 1630's, it was captured by the British in 1758 and was a refuge for Loyalists after the American Revolution. Population, 80,521.

Saint John, Henry. See First Viscount **Bolingbroke.**

Saint John (sānt jŏn′) or **Saint Jean** or **Saint-Jean** (săɴ zhäɴ′), **Lake.** A lake of south-central Quebec, Canada, connected by the Saguenay River with the St. Lawrence River.

Saint John River. A river, about 673 km (418 mi) long, rising in northern Maine and flowing northeast into New Brunswick, Canada, then generally southeast, south, east, and south into the Bay of Fundy. It was discovered in 1604 by Samuel de Champlain.

Saint Johns (jŏnz). **1.** See **Saint Jean. 2.** See **Saint John's** (sense 1).

Saint Johns (sānt jŏnz′, sĭnt), **Adela Rogers.** 1894–1988. American journalist who covered major stories for the Hearst newspapers for more than 60 years.

Saint John's (sānt jŏnz). **1.** Also **Saint Johns.** The capital of Antigua and Barbuda, on the northern coast of Antigua in the Leeward Islands of the West Indies. Tourism is important to its economy. Population, 24,359. **2.** The capital and largest city of Newfoundland, Canada, on the southeast coast of the island. One of the oldest settlements in North America, it was first colonized by the English in 1583 but did not come under permanent British control until 1762. Population, 83,770.

Saint John's Eve *n.* See **Midsummer Eve** (sense 2).

Saint Johns River. A river, about 459 km (285 mi) long, of northeast Florida flowing generally north to Jacksonville then east to the Atlantic Ocean.

Saint Johns•wort (jonz′wûrt′, -wôrt′) *n.* Any of various herbs or shrubs of the genus *Hypericum,* having yellow flowers with five petals and numerous stamens that are united at the base into three to five fascicles.

Saint Jo•seph (jō′zəf, -səf). A city of northwest Missouri on the Missouri River north-northwest of Kansas City. Laid out in 1843 on the site of a trading post founded in 1826, it became the eastern terminus of the Pony Express in 1860. Population, 76,691.

Saint-Just (săɴ-zho͞ost′, -zhüst′), **Louis Antoine Léon de.** 1767–1794. French revolutionary. Active during the Reign of Terror, he was tried and executed in 1794.

Saint Kitts and Ne•vis (kĭts; nē′vĭs, nĕv′ĭs). See **Saint Christopher-Nevis.**

Saint Lam•bert or **Saint-Lam•bert** (sānt lăm′bərt, săɴ läm-bĕr′). A city of southern Quebec, Canada, a residential suburb of Montreal on the St. Lawrence River. Population, 20,557.

Saint Lau•rent or **Saint-Lau•rent** (sānt′ lô-rĕnt′, săɴ lô-räɴ′). A city of southern Quebec, Canada, an industrial suburb of Montreal. Population, 65,900.

Saint Lau•rent (săɴ lô-räɴ′), **Louis Stephen.** 1882–1973. Canadian politician who served as prime minister (1948–1957).

Saint Law•rence (sānt lôr′əns, lŏr′-), **Gulf of.** An arm of the northwest Atlantic Ocean off southeast Canada bordered by New Brunswick, Nova Scotia, Newfoundland, and Quebec. It is connected with the Atlantic by Cabot Strait and the Straits of Canso and Belle Isle.

Saint Lawrence River. A river of southeast Canada flowing about 1,207 km (750 mi) northeast from Lake Ontario along the Ontario–New York border and through southern Quebec to the Gulf of St. Lawrence. The river was first sighted by Jacques Cartier in 1534; in 1535 he ascended it as far as the modern-day city of Montreal.

Saint Lawrence Seaway. An international waterway, about 3,781 km (2,350 mi) long, consisting of a system of canals, dams, and locks in the St. Lawrence River and connecting channels through the Great Lakes. Jointly developed by the United States and Canada, the seaway opened in 1959 and provides passage for oceangoing ships as far west as Lake Superior.

Saint Lé•o•nard or **Saint-Lé•o•nard** (sānt′ lĕn′ərd, săɴ lā-ō-när′). A city of southern Quebec, Canada, a residential suburb of Montreal. Population, 79,429.

Saint-Lô (sānt′lō′, săɴ-). A town of northwest France west of Caen. Its capture on July 18, 1945, played a pivotal role in the Allied invasion of Europe during World War II. Population, 23,212.

Saint Lou•is (sānt lo͞o′ĭs). An independent city of eastern Missouri on the Mississippi River just south of its confluence with the Missouri River. Settled by the French as a trading post in 1763–1764, it passed to Spain (1770), to France again (1800), and to the United States as part of the Louisiana Purchase (1803). It is the largest city in the state. Population, 453,085.

Saint-Lou•is (săɴ-lo͞o-ē′). A city of northwest Senegal at the mouth of the Senegal River. The oldest French colonial settlement in Africa, it was founded as a trading base c. 1658 and was the capital of French West Africa from 1895 to 1902. Dakar replaced it as the capital of Senegal in 1958. Population, 107,072.

Saint Lou•is encephalitis (sānt lo͞o′ĭs) *n.* A viral encephalitis occurring in parts of North America and transmitted by a culex mosquito. [After SAINT LOUIS, Missouri.]

Saint Louis Park. A city of southeast Minnesota, an industrial suburb of Minneapolis. Population, 42,931.

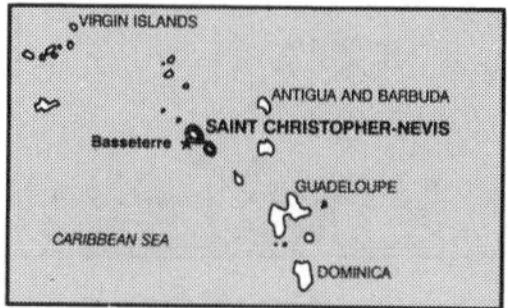

Saint Christopher-Nevis

ă pat	oi boy
ā pay	ou out
âr care	o͝o took
ä father	o͞o boot
ĕ pet	ŭ cut
ē be	ûr urge
ĭ pit	th thin
ī pie	*th* this
îr pier	hw which
ŏ pot	zh vision
ō toe	ə about, item
ô paw	♦ regionalism

Stress marks: ′ (primary); ′ (secondary), as in **dictionary** (dĭk′shə-nĕr′ē)

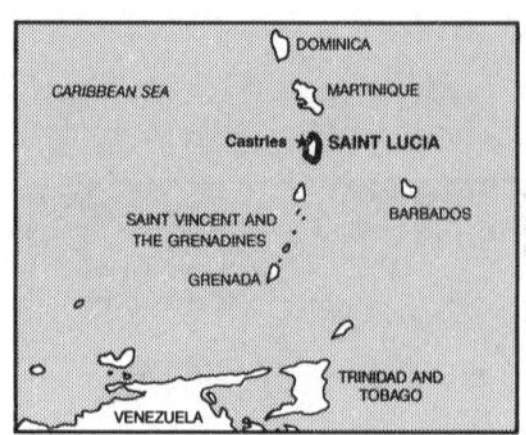

Saint Lucia

Saint Lu·cia (lo͞o′shə, lo͞o-sē′ə). An island country of the West Indies in the Windward Islands south of Martinique. The island was probably discovered by Columbus in 1502 and was first settled by the English in 1605. Its possession was contested by the French until the end of the Napoleonic Wars (1814), when it passed definitively to Great Britain. The country achieved independence in 1979. Castries is the capital. Population, 134,006.

saint·ly (sānt′lē) *adj.* **-li·er, -li·est.** Of, relating to, resembling, or befitting a saint. **—saint′li·ness** *n.*

Saint Maar·ten (mär′tn). See **Saint Martin.**

Saint-Ma·lo (săɴ-mə-lō′). A town of northwest France north-northwest of Nantes on the **Gulf of Saint-Malo,** an inlet of the English Channel. Founded on the site of a 6th-century A.D. monastery, it was a base for French corsairs in the 17th and 18th centuries. Population, 46,347.

Saint Mar·tin or **Saint Maar·ten** (mär′tn). An island of the West Indies in the western Leeward Islands. Administration of the island is divided between the French overseas department of Guadeloupe and the Netherlands Antilles. The French and Dutch first assumed joint control in 1648.

Saint Mar·ys River (mâr′ēz). **1.** A river, about 282 km (175 mi) long, rising in southeast Georgia in the Okefenokee Swamp and flowing eastward along the Georgia-Florida border to the Atlantic Ocean. **2.** A river, about 101 km (63 mi) long, rising in the eastern Upper Peninsula of Michigan and flowing generally south and southeast to the northern end of Lake Huron.

Saint-Maur-des-Fos·sés (săɴ-môr-dā-fô-sā′). A city of north-central France, a suburb of Paris. Population, 80,811.

Saint Mau·rice or **Saint-Mau·rice** (sānt′ môr′ĭs, -mŏr′-, săɴ mô-rēs′). A river, about 523 km (325 mi) long, of southern Quebec, Canada, flowing south and southeast to the St. Lawrence River at Trois Rivières.

Saint-Mi·hiel (sănt-mē-yĕl′, săɴ-). A village of northeast France on the Meuse River east of Paris. The World War I battle here (September 12–14, 1918) was the first major American offensive led by Gen. John J. Pershing and forced the Germans to relinquish a salient held since 1914.

Saint Mo·ritz (sānt′ mə-rĭts′, săɴ mô-rēts′). A city of southeast Switzerland on the Inn River south-southeast of Chur. It is noted as a skiing resort and was the site of the Winter Olympics in 1928 and 1948. Population, 5,900.

Saint-Na·zaire (săɴ-nä-zĕr′). A city of west-central France at the mouth of the Loire River west of Nantes. Built on the ruins of an ancient Gallo-Roman town, it was an important naval base during both World Wars. Population, 68,348.

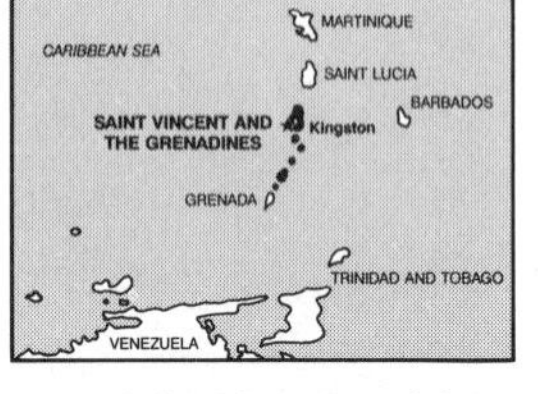

Saint Vincent and the Grenadines

Saint Nich·o·las (sānt nĭk′ə-ləs) or **Saint Nick** (nĭk) *n.* Santa Claus.

Saint Pat·rick's Day (păt′rĭks) *n.* March 17, observed in the United States and Ireland by some Christians in honor of Saint Patrick, the patron saint of Ireland.

Saint Paul (pôl). The capital of Minnesota, in the southeast part of the state on the Mississippi River adjacent to Minneapolis. Founded on the site of an early fur-trading post, it became territorial capital in 1849 and state capital in 1858. Population, 270,230.

Saint Pe·ters·burg (pē′tərz-bûrg′). **1.** A city of west-central Florida on Tampa Bay south-southwest of Tampa. Settled in the mid-1800's, it is a port of entry and popular resort. Population, 238,647. **2.** See **Leningrad.**

Saint Pi·erre or **Saint-Pi·erre** (sānt′ pîr′, pē-âr′, săɴ pyĕr′). The capital of St. Pierre and Miquelon, on St. Pierre Island in the northern Atlantic Ocean. Population, 5,371.

Saint Pierre and Mi·que·lon (sānt, săɴ; mĭk′ə-lŏn′, mē-klôɴ′). A French island group and overseas department in the northern Atlantic Ocean south of Newfoundland, Canada. The group consists of nine small islands, including **Saint Pierre Island,** site of the capital, and Miquelon, the largest of the islands. Probably first visited by Breton and Basque fishermen, the islands were colonized by France in 1604, taken by the British three times, and finally awarded to France in 1814. St. Pierre is the capital. Population, 6,041.

Saint-Quen·tin (sānt′kwĕn′tən, săɴ-käɴ-tăɴ′). A city of northern France on the Somme River north-northeast of Paris. Chartered in 1080, the city was an important center of the woolen industry during the Middle Ages. Population, 63,567.

Saint-Saëns (săɴ-säɴs′, -säɴ′), **Charles Camille.** 1835–1921. French composer whose works include symphonies, operas, such as *Samson et Dalila* (1877), and symphonic poems, including *Danse Macabre* (1874).

saint's day (sānts) *n., pl.* **saints' days.** A day in a liturgical calendar that is observed in honor of a saint.

Saint-Si·mon (săɴ-sē-môɴ′), Comte de. Title of Claude Henri de Rouvroy. 1760–1825. French philosopher who advocated a society governed by technocrats, in which poverty would be abolished and religion replaced by rationalism.

Saint-Simon, Duc de. Title of Louis de Rouvroy. 1675–1755. French diplomat and writer whose memoirs of the court of Louis XIV are a valuable historical source.

Andrei Sakharov
Photographed in 1988

Saint Tho·mas[1] (sānt tŏm′əs). An island of the U.S. Virgin Islands in the West Indies east of Puerto Rico. Named by Columbus in 1493, it was settled by the Dutch in 1657 and later passed to the Danes, who sold it to the United States in 1917.

Saint Tho·mas[2] (sānt tŏm′əs). A city of southern Ontario, Canada, near Lake Erie south of London. Population, 28,165.

Saint-Tro·pez (săɴ-trô-pā′). A town of southeast France on the Mediterranean coast of the French Riviera. It is a noted seaside resort. Population, 4,961.

Saint Val·en·tine's Day (sānt văl′ən-tīnz′) *n.* February 14, celebrated in various North American and European countries by the exchange of valentines or love tokens. Also called *Valentine's Day.* [Primarily after Saint VALENTINE.]

Saint Vin·cent (vĭn′sənt). An island of St. Vincent and the Grenadines in the central Windward Islands of the West Indies. Supposedly sighted by Columbus in 1498, the island was first settled by the British in the mid-1700's and was held by France from 1779 to 1783.

Saint Vincent, Cape. A promontory at the southwest extremity of Portugal. Prince Henry the Navigator established (c. 1420) an observatory and a school of navigation nearby.

Saint Vincent and the Gren·a·dines (grĕn′ə-dēnz′). An island country in the central Windward Islands of the West Indies. It comprises St. Vincent Island and the northern islets of the Grenadines. Part of the West Indies Federation from 1958 to 1962, the country gained its independence in 1979. Kingstown, on St. Vincent, is the capital. Population, 108,704.

Saint Vi·tus' dance also **Saint Vi·tus's dance** (vī′təs, -tə-sĭz) *n.* See **Sydenham's chorea.** [After *Saint Vitus,* third-century A.D. Christian martyr.]

Sai·pan (sī-păn′, -pän′, sī′păn). An island of the western Pacific Ocean in the southern Mariana Islands. It is part of the U.S. Trust Territory of the Pacific Islands and was held by Spain, Germany, and Japan before being captured by U.S. troops in July 1944. **—Sai′pa·nese′** (-nēz′, -nēs′) *adj. & n.*

Sa·ïs (sā′ĭs). A city of ancient Egypt in the west-central region of the Nile delta. It served as a royal residence during the XXVI Dynasty.

saith (sĕth, sā′ĭth) *v. Archaic.* A third person singular present tense of **say.**

Sai·va (sī′və, shī′-) *n. Hinduism.* One who worships Shiva. [Sanskrit *śaiva-,* belonging to Shiva, from *śivaḥ,* Shiva.] **—Sai′·vism** *n.*

Sa·ja·ma (sə-hä′mə). A mountain, 6,574.3 m (21,555 ft) high, in the Andes of western Bolivia near the Chilean border.

Sa·kai (sä′kī′). A city of southern Honshu, Japan, on Osaka Bay south of Osaka. It was a leading port from the 15th to the 17th century. Population, 818,368.

Sak·a·ka·we·a (săk′ə-kə-wē′ə), **Lake.** A reservoir in west-central North Dakota. It is a widening of the Missouri River and was created in 1956 when the Garrison Dam was completed.

sake[1] (sāk) *n.* **1.** Purpose; motive: *a quarrel only for the sake of argument.* **2.** Advantage; good: *for the sake of his health.* **3.** Personal benefit or interest; welfare: *for her own sake.* [Middle English, lawsuit, guilt, from Old English *sacu.* See **sāg-** in Appendix.]

sa·ke[2] also **sa·ki** (sä′kē, -kĕ) *n.* A Japanese wine made from fermented rice. [Japanese.]

sa·ker (sā′kər) *n.* A Eurasian falcon *(Falco cherrug)* having brown plumage and often trained for falconry. [Middle English *sagre,* from Old French *sacre,* from Arabic *ṣaqr.*]

Sa·kha·lin (săk′ə-lēn′, -lən, sä-ᴋʜə-lyēn′). An island of southeast Russia in the Sea of Okhotsk north of Hokkaido, Japan. Colonized by Russia and Japan in the 18th and 19th centuries, it passed under Russian control in 1875.

Sa·kha·rov (sä′kə-rôf′, săk′ə-, sä′ᴋʜə-rəf), **Andrei Dimitrievich.** 1921–1989. Soviet physicist and dissident who helped develop the first Soviet hydrogen bomb. An outspoken advocate of human rights and nuclear disarmament, he won the 1975 Nobel Peace Prize and was banished to Gorky from 1980 to 1986.

sa·ki (sä′kē, -kĕ) *n.* Variant of **sake**[2].

Sa·ki (sä′kē). See Hector Hugh **Munro.**

Sak·ka·ra (sə-kär′ə). See **Saqqara.**

sal (săl) *n.* Salt. [Middle English, from Old French, from Latin *sāl.* See **sal-** in Appendix.]

sa·laam (sə-läm′) *n.* **1.** A ceremonious act of deference or obeisance, especially a low bow performed while placing the right palm on the forehead. **2.** A respectful ceremonial greeting performed especially in Islamic countries. **—salaam** *tr. & intr.v.* **-laamed, -laam·ing, -laams.** To greet with or perform a salaam. [Arabic *salām,* peace, salaam, from *salima,* to be safe.]

sal·a·ble also **sale·a·ble** (sā′lə-bəl) *adj.* Offered or suitable for sale; marketable. **—sal′a·bil′i·ty, sal′a·ble·ness** *n.* **—sal′a·bly** *adv.*

sa·la·cious (sə-lā′shəs) *adj.* **1.** Appealing to or stimulating sexual desire; lascivious. **2.** Lustful; bawdy. [From Latin *salāx, salāc-,* fond of leaping, lustful, from *salīre,* to leap. See **sel-** in Appendix.] **—sa·la′cious·ly** *adv.* **—sa·la′cious·ness, sa·lac′i·ty** (sə-lăs′ĭ-tē) *n.*

sal·ad (săl′əd) *n.* **1.a.** A dish consisting of green, leafy raw vegetables, often with radish, cucumber, or tomato, served with a dressing. **b.** The course of a meal consisting of this dish. **2.** A cold dish of chopped fruit, meat, fish, eggs, or other food, usually prepared with a dressing, such as mayonnaise. **3.** A green vegetable or herb used in salad, especially lettuce. **4.** A varied mixture: *"The Declaration of Independence was . . . a salad of illusions"* (George Santayana). *—attributive.* Often used to modify another noun: *salad plates; salad makings.* [Middle English *salade,* from Old French, possibly from Old Provençal *salada,* from Vulgar Latin **salāta,* from feminine past participle of **salāre,* to salt, from Latin *sāl,* salt. See **sal-** in Appendix.]

WORD HISTORY: The word *salad* may have come to us from Vulgar Latin, the chiefly unrecorded common speech of the ancient Romans, which is distinguished from standard literary, or Classical, Latin. The word takes its origin from the fact that salt was and is an important ingredient of salad dressings. Hence the Vulgar Latin verb **salāre,* "to salt," from Latin *sāl,* "salt," in the past participial form **salāta,* "having been salted," came to mean "salad." The Vulgar Latin word passed into languages descending from it, such as Portuguese (*salada*) and Old Provençal (*salada*). Old French may have borrowed its word *salade* from Old Provençal. Medieval Latin also carried on the Vulgar Latin word in the form *salāta.* As in the case of so many culinary delights, the English borrowed the word and probably the dish from the French. The Middle English word *salade,* from Old French *salade* and Medieval Latin *salāta,* is first recorded in a recipe book composed before 1399.

salad bar *n.* A counter in a restaurant from which customers may serve themselves a variety of salad ingredients and dressings.

salad days *pl.n.* A time of youth, innocence, and inexperience: *"my salad days,/When I was green in judgment, cold in blood"* (Shakespeare).

salad dressing *n.* A sauce, such as one made of mayonnaise or of oil and vinegar, that is served on salad.

Sal•a•din (săl′ə-dĭn). 1137?–1193. Sultan of Egypt and Syria who captured (1187) Jerusalem and defended it during the Third Crusade (1189–1192).

Sa•la•do (sə-lä′dō, sä-lä′*thô*). **1.** Also **Salado del Nor•te** (dĕl nôr′tĕ). A river of northern Argentina rising in the Andes and flowing about 2,011 km (1,250 mi) southeast to the Paraná River. **2.** A river, about 1,368 km (850 mi) long, rising in western Argentina and flowing south-southeast to the Colorado River.

salad oil *n.* An edible vegetable oil, such as corn oil or olive oil, that can be used in salad dressings.

sa•lal (sə-lăl′) *n.* A small evergreen shrub *(Gaultheria shallon)* native to the Pacific coast of North America, having white or pink flowers clustered in racemes and edible purple-black berries. [Chinook Jargon *sallal,* from Chinook *sálal.*]

Sal•a•man•ca (săl′ə-măng′kə, sä′lä-mäng′kä). A city of west-central Spain west-northwest of Madrid. Conquered by Hannibal in 220 B.C., it was captured by Moors in the 8th century A.D. Population, 159,336.

sal•a•man•der (săl′ə-măn′dər) *n.* **1.** Any of various small lizardlike amphibians of the order Caudata, having porous scaleless skin and four, often weak or rudimentary legs. **2.** A mythical creature, generally resembling a lizard, believed capable of living in or withstanding fire. **3.** An object, such as a poker, used in fire or capable of withstanding heat. **4.** *Metallurgy.* A mass of solidified material, largely metallic, left in a blast-furnace hearth. **5.** A portable stove used to heat or dry buildings under construction. [Middle English *salamandre,* from Old French, from Latin *salamandra,* from Greek.] **—sal′a•man′drine** (-drĭn) *adj.*

sa•la•mi (sə-lä′mē) *n., pl.* **-mis.** A highly spiced and salted sausage, either hard or soft in consistency. [Italian, pl. of *salame,* salami, from Vulgar Latin **salāmen,* from **salāre,* to salt, from Latin *sāl,* salt. See **sal-** in Appendix.]

Sal•a•mis[1] (săl′ə-mĭs, sä′lä-mēs′). An island of Greece in the Saronic Gulf east of Athens. In an important naval battle off the island's northeast coast the Greeks, led by Themistocles, defeated the Persian fleet in 480 B.C.

Sal•a•mis[2] (săl′ə-mĭs, sä′lä-mēs′). An ancient city of eastern Cyprus. According to tradition, it was founded c. 1180 B.C. by Teucer, a hero of the Trojan War, and was visited by Saint Paul during his first missionary journey.

sal ammoniac *n.* See **ammonium chloride.** [Middle English *sal armoniak,* alteration of *sal amoniak,* from Latin *sāl ammōniacus,* salt of Amen : *sāl,* salt; see SAL + *ammōniacus,* of Amen; see AMMONIA.]

sal•a•ry (săl′ə-rē, săl′rē) *n., pl.* **-ries.** Fixed compensation for services, paid to a person on a regular basis. [Middle English *salarie,* from Anglo-Norman, from Latin *salārium,* money given to Roman soldiers to buy salt, from neuter of *salārius,* pertaining to salt, from *sāl,* salt. See **sal-** in Appendix.] **—sal′a•ried** *adj.*

Sa•la•zar (săl′ə-zär′, sä′lə-), **Antonio de Oliveira.** 1889–1970. Portuguese dictator (1932–1968) known for his programs of fiscal austerity and his attempts to repress growing opposition in Portugal's African colonies.

sal•bu•ta•mol (săl-byo͞o′tə-môl′, -mōl′, -mŏl′) *n.* A sympathomimetic agent, $C_{13}H_{21}NO_3$, used as a bronchodilator, especially in the treatment of asthma. [SAL(ICYLIC ACID) + BUT(YL) + AM(INO)– + –OL[1].]

Sal•can•tay (säl′kən-tī′, säl′kän-). A peak, 6,275.4 m (20,575 ft) high, of the Cordillera Oriental in southern Peru.

sal•chow (săl′kou′) *n. Sports.* A move in figure skating in which the skater jumps from one skate, completes a full rotation, and lands on the other skate. [After Ulrich *Salchow* (1877–1949), Swedish figure skater.]

sale (sāl) *n.* **1.** The exchange of goods or services for an amount of money or its equivalent; the act of selling. **2.** An instance of selling. **3.** An opportunity for selling or being sold; demand. **4.** Availability for purchase: *a store where pets are for sale.* **5.** A selling of property to the highest bidder; an auction. **6.** A special disposal of goods at lowered prices: *coats on sale this week.* **7. sales. a.** Activities involved in selling goods or services. **b.** Gross receipts. *—attributive.* Often used to modify another noun: *sale merchandise; sale advertising.* [Middle English, from Old English *sala,* from Old Norse.]

Sa•lé (sä-lā′) also **Sla** (slä). A city of northwest Morocco, a suburb of Rabat on the Atlantic Ocean. Population, 289,391.

sale•a•ble (sā′lə-bəl) *adj.* Variant of **salable.**

sale and leaseback *n., pl.* **sales and leasebacks.** See **leaseback.**

sale-lease•back (sāl′lēs′băk′) *n.* See **leaseback.**

Sa•lem (sā′ləm). **1.** A city of southern India southwest of Madras. It is a trade center with an important textile industry. Population, 361,394. **2.** A city of northeast Massachusetts northeast of Boston. Founded in 1626, it is noted as the site of witchcraft trials (1692) and of Nathaniel Hawthorne's House of the Seven Gables. Population, 38,220. **3.** A town of southeast New Hampshire east of Nashua. It was part of Haverhill, Massachusetts, until 1741. Population, 24,124. **4.** The capital of Oregon, in the northwest part of the state on the Willamette River south-southwest of Portland. Founded c. 1840, it became territorial capital in 1851 and state capital in 1859. Population, 89,233. **5.** An independent city of southwest Virginia, an industrial and residential suburb of Roanoke. Population, 23,958.

sal•ep (săl′əp) *n.* A starchy meal ground from the dried roots of various Old World orchids of the genera *Orchis* and *Eulophia,* used for food and formerly as medicine. [French or Spanish, both from Ottoman Turkish *sālep,* from Arabic *saḥlab,* a kind of orchid.]

sal•er•a•tus (săl′ə-rā′təs) *n.* Sodium or potassium bicarbonate used as a leavening agent; baking soda. [New Latin *sāl aerātus* : Latin *sāl,* salt; see SAL + New Latin *āerātus,* aerated (from Latin *āēr,* air; see AIR).]

Sa•ler•no (sə-lûr′nō, sä-lĕr′-). A city of southern Italy on the **Gulf of Salerno,** an inlet of the Tyrrhenian Sea. Originally a Greek settlement and later a Roman colony (founded in 197 B.C.), Salerno was the site of a noted medical school during the Middle Ages. Population, 157,243.

sales check (sālz) *n.* A slip of paper given by a store to serve as a record or receipt of a purchase or sale.

sales•clerk (sālz′klûrk′) *n.* One who is employed to sell goods in a store.

sales•girl (sālz′gûrl′) *n.* A saleswoman.

Sa•le•sian (sə-lē′zhən, -shən) *n.* A member of the Society of Saint Francis of Sales, a Roman Catholic congregation founded in Turin in 1845 and dedicated chiefly to education and missionary work. **—Salesian** *adj.* Of or relating to the Salesians.

sales•la•dy (sālz′lā′dē) *n.* A saleswoman.

sales•man (sālz′mən) *n.* A man who is employed to sell merchandise in a store or in a designated territory. **—sales′man•ship′** *n.*

sales•peo•ple (sālz′pē′pəl) *pl.n.* Persons who are employed to sell merchandise in a store or in a designated territory.

sales•per•son (sālz′pûr′sən) *n.* A salesman or a saleswoman.

sales•room (sālz′ro͞om′, -ro͝om′) *n.* A room in which items are displayed and offered for sale or auction.

sales tax *n.* A tax levied on the retail price of merchandise and collected by the retailer.

sales•wom•an (sālz′wo͝om′ən) *n.* A woman who is employed to sell merchandise in a store or in a designated territory.

Sal•ford (sôl′fərd). A borough of northwest England on the Manchester Ship Canal adjacent to Manchester. It was first chartered in 1230. Population, 247,400.

sali– *pref.* Salt: *salimeter.* [From Latin *sāl, sal-,* salt. See **sal-** in Appendix.]

Sa•li•an (sā′lē-ən, sāl′yən) *adj.* Of or relating to a tribe of Franks who settled in the Rhine region of the Netherlands in the fourth century A.D. **—Salian** *n.* A Salian Frank. [From Late Latin *Saliī,* the Salian Franks.]

sal•ic (săl′ĭk) *adj.* Of or relating to certain minerals, such as quartz and the feldspars, that commonly occur in igneous rocks and contain large amounts of silica and alumina. [S(ILICA) + AL(UMINA) + –IC.]

Sa•lic (sā′lĭk, săl′ĭk) also **Sa•lique** (sā′lĭk, săl′ĭk, sə-lēk′) *adj.* **1.** Of or relating to the Salian Franks. **2.** Of or relating to the Salic law or to the legal code of the Salian Franks. [French *salique,* from Medieval Latin *Salicus,* from Late Latin *Salii,* the Salian Franks.]

sal•i•cin (săl′ĭ-sĭn) *n.* A bitter glucoside, $C_{13}H_{18}O_7$, obtained mainly from the bark of poplar and willow trees and formerly used as an analgesic. [French *salicine,* from Latin *salix, salic-,* willow.]

Salic law *n.* **1.** The legal code of the Salian Franks. **2.** A law, thought to derive from the code of laws of the Salian Franks, prohibiting a woman from succeeding to a throne.

sa•lic•y•late (sə-lĭs′ə-lāt′, -lĭt, săl′ə-sĭl′ĭt) *n.* A salt or an ester of salicylic acid. [SALICYL(IC ACID) + –ATE[2].]

sal•i•cyl•ic acid (săl′ĭ-sĭl′ĭk) *n.* A white crystalline acid, $C_6H_4(OH)(COOH)$, used in making aspirin, as a preservative, and in the external treatment of skin conditions such as eczema.

salamander
Spotted salamander
Ambystoma maculatum

Antonio de Oliveira Salazar
Photographed in 1951

ă pat	oi boy
ā pay	ou out
âr care	o͝o took
ä father	o͞o boot
ĕ pet	ŭ cut
ē be	ûr urge
ĭ pit	th thin
ī pie	*th* this
îr pier	hw which
ŏ pot	zh vision
ō toe	ə about, item
ô paw	♦ regionalism

Stress marks: ′ (primary); ′ (secondary), as in **dictionary** (dĭk′shə-nĕr′ē)

J.D. Salinger

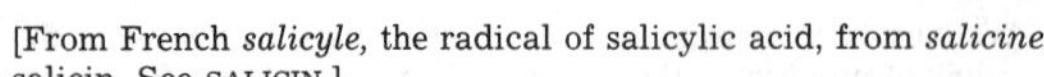

[From French *salicyle,* the radical of salicylic acid, from *salicine,* salicin. See SALICIN.]

sal·i·cyl·ism (săl′ĭ-sə-lĭz′əm) *n.* A toxic syndrome caused by excessive doses of salicylic acid or salicylates. [SALICYL(IC ACID) + -ISM.]

sa·li·ence (sā′lē-əns, săl′yəns) also **sa·li·en·cy** (sā′lē-ən-sē, săl′yən-) *n., pl.* **-en·ces** also **-en·cies. 1.** The quality or condition of being salient. **2.** A pronounced feature or part; a highlight.

sa·li·ent (sā′lē-ənt, săl′yənt) *adj.* **1.** Projecting or jutting beyond a line or surface; protruding. **2.** Strikingly conspicuous; prominent. See Synonyms at **noticeable. 3.** Springing; jumping: *salient tree toads.* **—salient** *n.* **1.** The area of a military defense, such as a battle line, that projects closest to the enemy. **2.** A projecting angle or part. [Latin *saliēns, salient-,* present participle of *salīre,* to leap. See **sel-** in Appendix.] **—sa′li·ent·ly** *adv.* **—sa′li·ent·ness** *n.*

sa·li·en·tian (sā′lē-ĕn′shən) *n.* An amphibian of the order Salientia (formerly Anura or Batrachia), which includes the frogs and toads. Also called *anuran.* **—salientian** *adj.* Of or belonging to the Salientia. [From New Latin *Salientia,* order name, from Latin *saliēns, salient-,* present participle of *salīre,* to leap. See SALIENT.]

sa·lif·er·ous (sə-lĭf′ər-əs) *adj.* Containing or yielding salt.

sa·lim·e·ter (sə-lĭm′ĭ-tər) or **sa·lom·e·ter** (-lŏm′-) *n.* A specially graduated hydrometer that directly indicates the concentration of salt in a solution. Also called *salinometer.* **—sal′i·met′ric** (săl′ə-mĕt′rĭk) *adj.* **—sa·lim′e·try** *n.*

sa·li·na (sə-lī′nə, -lē′-) *n.* **1.** A salt marsh, spring, pond, or lake. **2.** An area of land encrusted with salt. **3.** A saltworks. [Spanish, from Latin *salīnae,* salt pits, from feminine pl. of *salīnus,* of salt. See SALINE.]

Sa·li·na (sə-lī′nə). A city of central Kansas north-northwest of Wichita. It is a manufacturing center. Population, 41,843.

Sa·li·nas (sə-lē′nəs). A city of western California east-northeast of Monterey on the **Salinas River,** about 241 km (150 mi) long, near its outlet on Monterey Bay. The city is a processing center and the birthplace of John Steinbeck, who based many of his stories on the migratory farm workers of the Salinas Valley. Population, 80,479.

sa·line (sā′lēn′, -līn′) *adj.* **1.** Of, relating to, or containing salt; salty. **2.** Of or relating to chemical salts. **—saline** *n.* **1.** A salt of magnesium or of the alkalis, used in medicine as a cathartic. **2.** A saline solution, especially one that is isotonic with blood and is used in medicine and surgery. [Latin *salīnus,* from *sāl,* salt. See **sal-** in Appendix.] **—sa·lin′i·ty** (sə-lĭn′ĭ-tē) *n.*

Sal·in·ger (săl′ĭn-jər), **J(erome) D(avid).** Born 1919. American writer whose works, most notably his novel *The Catcher in the Rye* (1951), often concern troubled, sensitive adolescents.

sal·i·nize (săl′ə-nīz′) *tr.v.* **-nized, -niz·ing, -niz·es.** To treat with salt. **—sal′i·ni·za′tion** (-nĭ-zā′shən) *n.*

sal·i·nom·e·ter (săl′ə-nŏm′ĭ-tər) *n.* **1.** An instrument that uses electrical conductivity to measure the concentration of salt in a solution. **2.** See **salimeter. —sal′i·no·met′ric** (-nə-mĕt′rĭk) *adj.* **—sal′i·nom′e·try** *n.*

Sa·lique (sā′lĭk, săl′ĭk, să-lēk′) *adj.* Variant of **Salic.**

Salis·bur·y (sôlz′bĕr′ē, -brē). **1.** A municipal borough of southern England northwest of Southampton on the edge of **Salisbury Plain,** a chalky plateau that is the site of Stonehenge. The city was chartered in 1220 and developed around its noted cathedral. Population, 35,700. **2.** A city of southeast Maryland on the Eastern Shore south of Dover, Delaware. It is a processing and manufacturing center. Population, 16,429. **3.** A city of central North Carolina south-southwest of Winston-Salem. During the Civil War the city was the site of one of the largest Confederate prisons. Population, 22,677. **4.** See **Harare.**

Salisbury steak *n.* A patty of ground beef mixed with eggs, milk, onions, and various seasonings and broiled, fried, or baked. [After James Henry *Salisbury* (1823–1905), American physician.]

Sa·lish (sā′lĭsh) also **Sa·lish·an** (-lĭ-shən) *n.* **1.** A family of Native American languages of the northwest United States and British Columbia. **2.** The group of Native American peoples speaking languages of the Salish family. [Southern Interior Salish *se′lish,* Flatheads.] **—Sa′lish·an** *adj.*

sa·li·va (sə-lī′və) *n.* The watery mixture of secretions from the salivary and oral mucous glands that lubricates chewed food, moistens the oral walls, and contains ptyalin. [Latin *salīva.*]

sal·i·var·y (săl′ə-vĕr′ē) *adj.* **1.** Of, relating to, or producing saliva. **2.** Of or relating to a salivary gland.

salivary gland *n.* A gland that secretes saliva, especially any of three pairs of large glands, the parotid, submaxillary, and sublingual, whose secretions enter the mouth and mingle in saliva.

sal·i·vate (săl′ə-vāt′) *v.* **-vat·ed, -vat·ing, -vates.** *—intr.* To secrete or produce saliva. *—tr.* To produce excessive salivation in. [Latin *salīvāre, salīvāt-,* from *salīva,* saliva.]

sal·i·va·tion (săl′ə-vā′shən) *n.* **1.** The act or process of secreting saliva. **2.** An abnormally abundant flow of saliva.

Salk (sôlk), **Jonas Edward.** Born 1914. American microbiologist who developed the first effective killed-virus vaccine against polio (1954).

Salk vaccine *n.* A vaccine consisting of inactivated polioviruses, used to immunize against poliomyelitis. [After Jonas Edward SALK.]

sallet
Late 15th-century German

Salome
Painting by Lucas Cranach the Elder

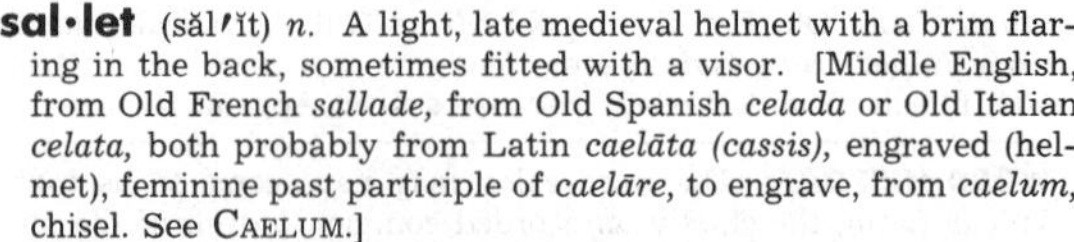

sal·let (săl′ĭt) *n.* A light, late medieval helmet with a brim flaring in the back, sometimes fitted with a visor. [Middle English, from Old French *sallade,* from Old Spanish *celada* or Old Italian *celata,* both probably from Latin *caelāta (cassis),* engraved (helmet), feminine past participle of *caelāre,* to engrave, from *caelum,* chisel. See CAELUM.]

sal·low¹ (săl′ō) *adj.* **-er, -est.** Of a sickly yellowish hue or complexion. **—sallow** *tr.v.* **-lowed, -low·ing, -lows.** To make sallow. [Middle English *salowe,* from Old English *salo.*] **—sal′low·ly** *adv.* **—sal′low·ness** *n.*

sal·low² (săl′ō) *n.* A broad-leaved European willow *(Salix caprea)* having large catkins that appear before the leaves and tough wood used as a source of charcoal. [Middle English, from Old English *sealh.*]

Sal·lust (săl′əst). 86?–34? B.C. Roman politician and historian known for his account of the conspiracy of Catiline.

sal·ly (săl′ē) *intr.v.* **-lied, -ly·ing, -lies. 1.** To rush out or leap forth suddenly. **2.** To issue suddenly from a defensive or besieged position to attack an enemy. **3.** To set out on a trip or an excursion: *sallied forth to see the world.* **—sally** *n., pl.* **-lies. 1.** A sudden rush forward; a leap. **2.** An assault from a defensive position; a sortie. **3.** A sudden emergence into action or expression; an outburst. **4.** A sudden quick witticism; a quip. See Synonyms at **joke. 5.** A venturing forth; a jaunt. [From French *saillie,* a sally, from Old French, from feminine past participle of *salir,* to rush forward, from Latin *salīre,* to leap. See **sel-** in Appendix.]

sal·ly lunn (săl′ē lŭn′) *n.* A somewhat sweet bread leavened with yeast. [After *Sally Lunn,* 18th-century British baker.]

sally port *n.* A gate in a fortification designed for sorties.

Sal·ma·cis (săl-mā′sĭs) *n. Greek Mythology.* A nymph who fell in love with Hermaphroditus and became united with him in one body.

sal·ma·gun·di (săl′mə-gŭn′dē) *n., pl.* **-dis. 1.** A salad of chopped meat, anchovies, eggs, and onions, often arranged in rows on lettuce and served with vinegar and oil. **2.** A mixture or an assortment; a potpourri. [French *salmigondis* : probably from Old French *salemine,* salted food (from Vulgar Latin **salāmen;* see SALAMI) + Old French *condir,* to season (from Latin *condīre;* see CONDIMENT).]

sal·mi (săl′mē) *n., pl.* **-mis.** A highly spiced dish consisting of roasted game birds minced and stewed in wine. [French *salmis,* short for *salmigondis,* salmagundi. See SALMAGUNDI.]

salm·on (săm′ən) *n., pl.* **salmon** or **-ons. 1.** Any of various large food and game fishes of the genera *Salmo* and *Oncorhynchus,* of northern waters, having delicate pinkish flesh and characteristically swimming from salt to fresh water to spawn. **2.** *Color.* A moderate, light, or strong yellowish pink to a moderate reddish orange or light orange. [Middle English, from Old French *saumon,* from Latin *salmō, salmōn-.* See **sel-** in Appendix.]

salm·on·ber·ry (săm′ən-bĕr′ē) *n.* **1.** Any of several prickly shrubs of the genus *Rubus,* especially *R. spectabilis* of western North America, having trifoliate leaves and fragrant reddish flowers. **2.** The salmon-colored, raspberrylike fruit of this plant.

sal·mo·nel·la (săl′mə-nĕl′ə) *n., pl.* **-nel·lae** (-nĕl′ē) or **-nel·las** or **salmonella.** Any of various rod-shaped bacteria of the genus *Salmonella,* many of which are pathogenic, causing food poisoning, typhoid, and paratyphoid fever in human beings and other infectious diseases in domestic animals. [New Latin *Salmonella,* genus name, after Daniel Elmer *Salmon* (1850–1914), American pathologist.]

sal·mo·nel·lo·sis (săl′mə-nĕ-lō′sĭs) *n., pl.* **-ses** (-sēz′). Infection with salmonellae, characterized by intestinal problems and fever and caused especially by eating certain improperly stored or undercooked foods.

salm·o·nid (săm′ə-nĭd, săl′mə-) *adj.* Of, belonging to, or characteristic of the family Salmonidae, which includes the salmon, trout, and whitefish. [From New Latin *Salmōnidae,* family name, from *Salmō,* type genus, from Latin *salmō, salmōn-,* salmon. See SALMON.] **—salm′o·nid** *n.*

salm·o·noid (săm′ə-noid′, săl′mə-) *adj.* Of, belonging to, or characteristic of the suborder Salmonoidea. **—salm′o·noid′** *n.*

Sal·mon River (săm′ən, săl′mən). A river of central Idaho rising in the **Salmon River Mountains** and flowing about 684 km (425 mi) to the Snake River. The mountain range rises to 3,153.7 m (10,340 ft) at Twin Peaks.

salmon trout *n.* Any of various large trouts, especially the lake trout, the sea trout, or the steelhead.

sal·ol (săl′ôl′, -ōl′, -ŏl′) *n.* A white crystalline powder, $C_{13}H_{10}O_3$, derived from salicylic acid and used in the manufacture of plastics and suntan oils and medicinally as an analgesic and antipyretic. [Originally a trademark.]

Sa·lo·me (sə-lō′mē, săl′ə-mē′). In the New Testament, the daughter of Herodias and niece of Herod Antipas, who granted her the head of John the Baptist in return for her dancing.

sa·lom·e·ter (sə-lŏm′ĭ-tər) *n.* Variant of **salimeter.**

Sal·o·mon (săl′ə-mən), **Haym.** 1740?–1785. Polish-born American financier who helped fund the Continental Army during the American Revolution.

sa·lon (sə-lŏn′, săl′ŏn′, să-lôN′) *n.* **1.** A large room, such as a drawing room, used for receiving and entertaining guests. **2.** A periodic gathering of people of social or intellectual distinction. **3.** A hall or gallery for the exhibition of works of art. **4.** A commercial establishment offering a product or service related to fashion: *a beauty salon.* [French, from Italian *salone,* augmentative of *sala,* hall, of Germanic origin.]

Sa·lo·ni·ka (sə-lŏn′ĭ-kə, săl′ə-nē′kə). See **Thessaloníki.**

sa·loon (sə-lo͞on′) *n.* **1.** A place where alcoholic drinks are sold and drunk; a tavern. **2.** A large room or hall for receptions, public entertainment, or exhibitions. **3.** *Nautical.* **a.** The officers' dining and social room on a cargo ship. **b.** A large social lounge on a passenger ship. **4.** *Chiefly British.* A sedan automobile. [French *salon,* salon. See SALON.]

sa·loon·keep·er (sə-lo͞on′kē′pər) *n.* One that owns or operates a drinking saloon.

sa·loop (sə-lo͞op′) *n. Archaic.* A hot drink, sometimes used medicinally, made from salep, sassafras, or similar aromatic herbs. [Alteration of SALEP.]

salp (sălp) also **sal·pa** (săl′pə) *n.* Any of various free-swimming chordates of the genus *Salpa,* of warm seas, having a translucent, somewhat flattened, keglike body. [From New Latin *Salpa,* genus name, from Latin, a kind of stockfish, from Greek *salpē.*] **—sal′pi·form′** (săl′pə-fôrm′) *adj.*

salping– *pref.* Salpinx: *salpingitis.* [From Greek *salpinx, salping-,* trumpet.]

sal·pin·gec·to·my (săl′pĭn-jĕk′tə-mē) *n., pl.* **-mies.** Surgical removal of the fallopian tube. Also called *tubectomy.*

sal·pin·ges (săl-pĭn′jēz) *n.* Plural of **salpinx.**

sal·pin·gi·tis (săl′pĭn-jī′tĭs) *n.* Inflammation of the fallopian or eustachian tube.

sal·pinx (săl′pĭngks) *n., pl.* **sal·pin·ges** (săl-pĭn′jēz). **1.** The fallopian tube. **2.** The eustachian tube. [New Latin, from Greek *salpinx,* trumpet.] **—sal·pin′gi·an** (-pĭn′jē-ən, -jən) *adj.*

♦**sal·sa** (säl′sə) *n.* **1.** Also **sar·sa** (sär′sə). *Chiefly Southwestern U.S.* A spicy sauce made of tomatoes, onions, and chili peppers, eaten with tortilla chips or other Mexican food. **2.** *Music.* A popular form of Latin-American dance music, characterized by Afro-Caribbean rhythms, Cuban big-band dance melodies, and elements of jazz and rock. [American Spanish, from Spanish, sauce, from Old Spanish, from Vulgar Latin *salsa. See SAUCE.]

♦**sal·si·fy** (săl′sə-fē, -fī′) *n., pl.* **-fies. 1.** A European plant *(Tragopogon porrifolius)* having grasslike leaves, purple flower heads, and an edible taproot. **2.** The root of this plant, eaten as a vegetable. Also called ♦*oyster plant,* ♦*vegetable oyster.* [French *salsifis,* from obsolete Italian *(erba) salsifica.*]

sal soda *n.* A hydrated sodium carbonate used as a general cleanser.

salt (sôlt) *n.* **1.** A colorless or white crystalline solid, chiefly sodium chloride, used extensively as a food seasoning and preservative. Also called *common salt, table salt.* **2.** A chemical compound formed by replacing all or part of the hydrogen ions of an acid with metal ions or electropositive radicals. **3. salts.** Any of various mineral salts used as laxatives or cathartics. **4. salts.** Smelling salts. **5.** Often **salts.** Epsom salts. **6.** An element that gives flavor or zest. **7.** Sharp, lively wit. **8.** *Informal.* A sailor, especially when old or experienced. **9.** A saltcellar. **—salt** *adj.* **1.** Containing or filled with salt: *a salt spray, salt tears.* **2.** Having a salty taste or smell: *breathed the salt air.* **3.** Preserved in salt or a salt solution: *salt mackerel.* **4. a.** Flooded with seawater. **b.** Found in or near such a flooded area: *salt grasses* **—salt** *tr.v.* **salt·ed, salt·ing, salts. 1.** To add, treat, season, or sprinkle with salt. **2.** To cure or preserve by treating with salt or a salt solution. **3.** To provide salt for (deer or cattle). **4.** To add zest or liveliness to: *salt a lecture with anecdotes.* **5.** To give an appearance of value to by fraudulent means, especially to place valuable minerals in (a mine) for the purpose of deceiving. ***—phrasal verbs.*** **salt away.** To put aside; save. **salt out.** To separate (a dissolved substance) by adding salt to the solution. ***—idiom.*** **worth (one's) salt.** Efficient and capable. [Middle English, from Old English *sealt.* See **sal-** in Appendix.]

SALT *abbr.* Strategic Arms Limitation Talks.

Sal·ta (säl′tə, -tä). A city of northwest Argentina north-northeast of Córdoba. Founded in 1582, it is a processing and shipping center in an agricultural region. Population, 260,744.

salt-and-pep·per (sôlt′ən-pĕp′ər) *adj.* Pepper-and-salt.

sal·ta·rel·lo (săl′tə-rĕl′ō, sôl′-) *n., pl.* **-rel·los** or **-rel·li** (-rĕl′ē). A lively Italian dance with a skipping step at the beginning of each measure. [Italian, from *saltare,* to leap, from Latin *saltāre.* See SALTATION.]

sal·ta·tion (săl-tā′shən, sôl-) *n.* **1.** The act of leaping, jumping, or dancing. **2.** Discontinuous movement, transition, or development; advancement by leaps. **3.** *Genetics.* A single mutation that drastically alters the phenotype. [Latin *saltātiō, saltātiōn-,* from *saltātus,* past participle of *saltāre,* to leap, frequentative of *salīre,* to jump. See SALIENT.]

sal·ta·to·ri·al (săl′tə-tôr′ē-əl, -tōr′-, sôl′-) *adj.* **1.** Of or relating to leaping or dancing. **2.** Adapted for or characterized by leaping.

sal·ta·to·ry (săl′tə-tôr′ē, -tōr′ē, sôl′-) *adj.* **1.** Of, relating to, or adapted for leaping or dancing. **2.** Proceeding by leaps rather than by smooth, gradual transitions.

salt·box (sôlt′bŏks′) *n.* A frame house with two stories in front and one in back, topped by a roof with a long, often broken, rear slope.

salt·bush (sôlt′bo͝osh′) *n.* Any of several salt-tolerant plants of the genus *Atriplex,* especially *A. hortensis* of Asia, grown for greens and ornament.

salt cake *n.* Impure sodium sulfate used in making paper pulp, soaps and detergents, glass, ceramic glazes, and dyes.

salt·cel·lar (sôlt′sĕl′ər) *n.* A small dish for holding and dispensing salt. [Alteration of Middle English *salt saler* : *salt,* salt; see SALT + *saler,* saltcellar (from Old French *saliere,* from Medieval Latin *salāria,* from Latin, feminine of *salārius,* of salt, from *sāl, sal-,* salt; see **sal-** in Appendix).]

salt dome *n. Geology.* An anticlinal fold with a columnar salt plug at its core.

salt·er (sôl′tər) *n.* **1.** One that manufactures or sells salt. **2.** One that treats meat, fish, or other foods with salt.

salt·ern (sôl′tərn) *n.* A saltworks. [Old English *sealtærn* : *sealt,* salt; see SALT + *ærn,* house.]

salt gland *n.* A specialized gland in marine animals that excretes the excess salt taken into the body.

salt grass *n.* Any of various grasses, especially North American perennial plants of the genus *Distichlis,* that grow in salt marshes and alkaline areas.

salt hay *n.* **1.** The wiry, tough stems of several species of salt-marsh rushes, especially *Juncus gerardi,* used as a garden mulch and packing material. **2.** Hay prepared from salt grass.

Sal·til·lo (säl-tē′yō). A city of northeast Mexico southwest of Monterrey. It was founded in 1575 and occupied by Zachary Taylor's forces during the Mexican War. Population, 284,937.

sal·tim·boc·ca (säl′tĭm-bō′kə) *n.* Scallops of veal, rolled and stuffed with sage, spiced ham, and cheese, sautéed and served with a wine sauce. [Italian, contraction of *salta in bocca,* it leaps into the mouth : *salta,* third person sing. of *saltare,* to leap (from Latin *saltāre,* to leap; see SALTATION) + *in,* into (from Latin; see IN–[2]) + *bocca,* mouth (from Latin *bucca,* cheek, mouthful).]

sal·tine (sôl-tēn′) *n.* A thin, crisp cracker sprinkled with coarse salt.

sal·tire (sôl′tîr′, -tīr′, săl′-) *n. Heraldry.* An ordinary in the shape of a Saint Andrew's cross, formed by the crossing of a bend and a bend sinister. [Middle English *sawtire,* from Old French *saultoir,* stile, from *saulter,* to jump, from Latin *saltāre.* See SALTATION.]

salt·ish (sôl′tĭsh) *adj.* Somewhat salty.

Salt Lake City (sôlt). The capital and largest city of Utah, in the north-central part of the state near Great Salt Lake. Brigham Young and his followers settled here in 1847 and established the community as the center of the Church of Jesus Christ of Latter-day Saints. Population, 163,033.

salt lick *n.* **1.** A natural deposit of exposed salt that animals lick. **2.** A block of salt or an artificial medicated saline preparation set out for cattle, sheep, or deer to lick.

salt marsh *n.* Low coastal grassland frequently overflowed by the tide.

salt-marsh caterpillar (sôlt′märsh′) *n.* The larva of a common tiger moth *(Estigmene acraea)* that feeds destructively on various grasses.

Sal·ton Sea (sôl′tən). A saline lake of southeast California in the Imperial Valley. It was a salt-covered depression known as the **Salton Sink** until 1905, when flood waters of the Colorado River formed the lake.

salt·pe·ter (sôlt′pē′tər) *n.* **1.** See **potassium nitrate. 2.** See **sodium nitrate. 3.** See **niter.** [Middle English *salpetre,* from Old French, from Medieval Latin *sālpetrae* : Latin *sāl,* salt; see **sal-** in Appendix + Latin *petrae,* genitive of *petra,* rock (from Greek).]

Salt River. 1. A river, about 322 km (200 mi) long, rising in eastern Arizona and flowing generally west to the Gila River near Phoenix. **2.** A river rising in northeast Missouri and flowing about 322 km (200 mi) southeast to the Mississippi River.

salt·shak·er (sôlt′shā′kər) *n.* A container with a perforated top for sprinkling table salt.

salt·wa·ter or **salt-wa·ter** (sôlt′wô′tər, -wŏt′ər) *adj.* **1.** Relating to, consisting of, or containing salt water: *a saltwater solution.* **2.** Inhabiting or occurring in seawater or salt water: *saltwater fish; the saltwater crocodile.* **3.** Done or used in salt water: *saltwater fishing; saltwater lures.*

salt·works (sôlt′wûrks′) *pl.n. (used with a sing. or pl. verb).* A place where salt is produced commercially.

salt·wort (sôlt′wûrt′, -wôrt′) *n.* **1.** Any of several plants of the genus *Salsola,* especially *S. kali,* native to the Old World, having stiff, awl-shaped prickly leaves and growing on sandy seashores. **2.** A strong-smelling succulent shrub *(Batis maritima)* native to warm coastal regions of the New World, having unisexual flowers and thick leaves that are flattened on the upper surface.

salt·y (sôl′tē) *adj.* **-i·er, -i·est. 1.** Of, containing, or seasoned with salt. **2.** Suggestive of the sea or sailing life. **3.** Witty; pungent: *salty humor.* **—salt′i·ly** *adv.* **—salt′i·ness** *n.*

sa·lu·bri·ous (sə-lo͞o′brē-əs) *adj.* Conducive or favorable to health or well-being. [From Latin *salūbris,* from *salūs,* health. See **sol-** in Appendix.] **—sa·lu′bri·ous·ly** *adv.* **—sa·lu′bri·ous·ness, sa·lu′bri·ty** (-brĭ-tē) *n.*

Sa·lu·da (sə-lo͞o′də). A river, about 322 km (200 mi) long, of west-central South Carolina rising in the Blue Ridge and flowing southeast across the Piedmont to the Broad River.

saltbox

saltcellar
By Pierre Reymond
(1513–1584)

saltire

ă pat	oi boy
ā pay	ou out
âr care	o͝o took
ä father	o͞o boot
ĕ pet	ŭ cut
ē be	ûr urge
ĭ pit	th thin
ī pie	*th* this
îr pier	hw which
ŏ pot	zh vision
ō toe	ə about, item
ô paw	♦ regionalism

Stress marks: **′** (primary); ′ (secondary), as in **dictionary** (dĭk′shə-nĕr′ē)

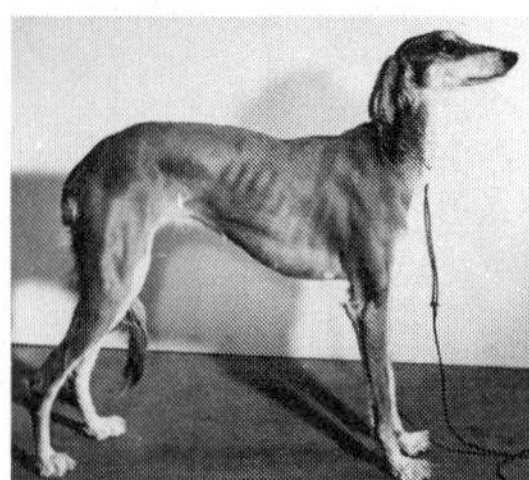
saluki

salver
c. 1740–1750 American silver salver by Jacob Hurd (1703–1758)

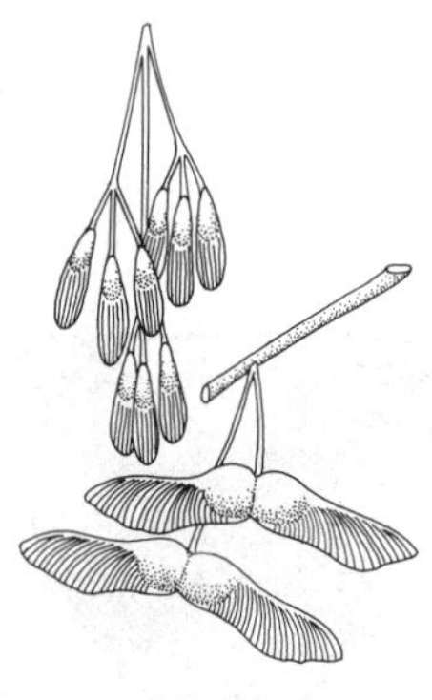
samara
Top: Field maple
Acer campestre
Bottom: Flowering ash
Fraxinus ornus

ă pat oi boy
ā pay ou out
âr care o͝o took
ä father o͞o boot
ĕ pet ŭ cut
ē be ûr urge
ĭ pit th thin
ī pie *th* this
îr pier hw which
ŏ pot zh vision
ō toe ə about, item
ô paw ♦ regionalism

Stress marks: **ʹ** (primary); ʹ (secondary), as in **dictionary** (dĭkʹshə-nĕrʹē)

sa•lu•ki (sə-lo͞oʹkē) *n., pl.* **-kis.** Any of an ancient breed of tall, slender dog developed in Arabia and Egypt and having a smooth, silky, variously colored coat. [Arabic *salūqīy,* of Saluq, an ancient city of southern Arabia.]

sal•u•ret•ic (săl'yə-rĕtʹĭk) *n.* A drug that promotes excretion of salt in the urine. **—saluretic** *adj.* Relating to or causing excretion of salt.

sal•u•tar•y (sălʹyə-tĕr'ē) *adj.* **1.** Effecting or designed to effect an improvement; remedial: *salutary advice.* **2.** Favorable to health; wholesome: *a salutary climate.* [Middle English, from Old French *salutaire,* from Latin *salūtāris,* from *salūs, salūt-,* health. See **sol-** in Appendix.] **—sal'u•tarʹi•ly** (-târʹə-lē) *adv.* **—sal'u•tarʹi•ness** *n.*

sal•u•ta•tion (săl'yə-tāʹshən) *n.* **1.a.** A polite expression of greeting or goodwill. **b. salutations.** Greetings indicating respect and affection; regards. **2.** A gesture of greeting, such as a bow or kiss. **3.** A word or phrase of greeting used to begin a letter. **—sal'u•taʹtion•al** *adj.*

sa•lu•ta•to•ri•an (sə-lo͞o'tə-tôrʹē-ən, -tōrʹ-) *n.* The student with the second highest academic rank in a class who delivers the salutatory at graduation exercises.

sa•lu•ta•to•ry (sə-lo͞oʹtə-tôr'ē, -tōr'ē) *n., pl.* **-ries.** An opening or welcoming statement or address, especially one delivered at graduation exercises. **—salutatory** *adj.* Of, relating to, or expressing a salutation.

sa•lute (sə-lo͞otʹ) *v.* **-lut•ed, -lut•ing, -lutes.** *—tr.* **1.** To greet or address with an expression of welcome, goodwill, or respect. **2.** To recognize (a superior) with a gesture prescribed by military regulations, as by raising the hand to the cap. **3.a.** To honor formally and ceremoniously. **b.** To express warm approval of; commend: *salute an organization for its humanitarian work.* **4.** To become noticeable to: *A foul smell saluted our nostrils. —intr.* To make a gesture of greeting or respect. **—salute** *n.* **1.** An act of greeting; a salutation. **2.a.** An act or a gesture of welcome, honor, or courteous recognition: *a musical salute to the composer's 90th birthday.* **b.** The position of the hand or rifle or the bodily posture of a person saluting a military superior. **3.** A formal military display of honor or greeting, such as the firing of cannon. [Middle English *saluten,* from Latin *salūtāre,* from *salūs, salūt-,* health. See **sol-** in Appendix.] **—sa•lutʹer** *n.*

sal•va•ble (sălʹvə-bəl) *adj.* That can be salvaged or saved: *salvable merchandise that survived the fire.* [From Late Latin *salvāre,* to save. See SALVAGE.]

Sal•va•dor (sălʹvə-dôr', săl'və-dôrʹ). Formerly **Ba•hi•a** (bə-hēʹə, bä-ēʹə). A city of eastern Brazil on the Atlantic Ocean south-southwest of Recife. Founded in 1549, it was the capital of the Portuguese possessions in the New World until 1763. Population, 1,501,981.

Sal•va•do•ran (săl'və-dôrʹən, -dōrʹ-) or **Sal•va•do•ri•an** (-dôrʹēən, -dōrʹ-) *—adj.* Of or relating to El Salvador or its people or culture. *—n.* A native or inhabitant of El Salvador.

sal•vage (sălʹvĭj) *n.* **1.a.** The rescue of a ship, its crew, or its cargo from fire or shipwreck. **b.** The ship, crew, or cargo so rescued. **c.** Compensation given to those who voluntarily aid in such a rescue. **2.a.** The act of saving imperiled property from loss. **b.** The property so saved. **3.** Something saved from destruction or waste and put to further use. **—salvage** *tr.v.* **-vaged, -vag•ing, -vag•es.** **1.** To save from loss or destruction. **2.** To save (discarded or damaged material) for further use. [Obsolete French, from Old French *salvaige,* right of salvage, from Late Latin *salvāre,* from Latin *salvus,* safe. See **sol-** in Appendix.] **—sal'vage•a•bilʹi•ty** *n.* **—salʹvage•a•ble** *adj.* **—salʹvag•er** *n.*

sal•va•tion (săl-vāʹshən) *n.* **1.a.** Preservation or deliverance from destruction, difficulty, or evil. **b.** A source, means, or cause of such preservation or deliverance. **2.** *Theology.* **a.** Deliverance from the power or penalty of sin; redemption. **b.** The agent or means that brings about such deliverance. **3.** *Christian Science.* The realization and demonstration of Life, Truth, and Love as supreme over all, carrying with it the destruction of the illusions of sin, sickness, and death. [Middle English, from Old French, from Late Latin *salvātiō, salvātiōn-,* from *salvātus,* past participle of *salvāre,* to save. See SALVAGE.] **—sal•vaʹtion•al** *adj.*

Sal•va•tion Army (săl-vāʹshən) *n. Abbr.* **SA** An international evangelical and charitable organization founded in 1865 by William Booth as a London revival society and renamed in 1878.

sal•va•tion•ism (săl-vāʹshə-nĭz'əm) *n.* Religious doctrine stressing salvation of the soul.

Sal•va•tion•ist (săl-vāʹshə-nĭst) *n.* **1.** A member of the Salvation Army. **2. salvationist.** One who preaches salvation; an evangelist. **—sal•vaʹtion•ist** *adj.*

salve¹ (săv, säv) *n.* **1.** An analgesic or medicinal ointment. **2.** Something that soothes or heals; a balm. **3.** Flattery or commendation. **—salve** *tr.v.* **salved, salv•ing, salves.** **1.** To soothe or heal with or as if with salve. **2.** To ease the distress or agitation of; assuage: *salved my conscience by apologizing.* [Middle English, from Old English *sealf.*]

salve² (sălv) *tr.v.* **salved, salv•ing, salves.** To salvage. [Back-formation from SALVAGE or SALVABLE.] **—salʹvor** *n.*

sal•ver (sălʹvər) *n.* A tray for serving food or drinks. [Alteration of French *salve,* from Spanish *salva,* tasting of food to detect poison, salver, from *salvar,* to save, taste food to detect poison, from Late Latin *salvāre,* to save. See SALVAGE.]

sal•ver•form (sălʹvər-fôrm') *adj. Botany.* Of, relating to, or being a gamopetalous corolla having a slender tube and an abruptly expanded limb, as in phlox.

sal•vi•a (sălʹvē-ə) *n.* Any of various plants of the genus *Salvia* in the mint family, having opposite leaves, a two-lipped corolla, and two stamens. [Latin *salvia,* sage. See SAGE².]

sal•vif•ic (săl-vĭfʹĭk) *adj.* Having the intention or power to bring about salvation or redemption: *"the doctrine that only a perfect male form can incarnate God fully and be salvific"* (Rita N. Brock). [Late Latin *salvificus* : Latin *salvus,* safe; see SAFE + Latin *-ficus,* -fic.] **—sal•vifʹi•cal•ly** *adv.*

sal•vo¹ (sălʹvō) *n., pl.* **-vos** or **-voes.** **1.a.** A simultaneous discharge of firearms. **b.** The simultaneous release of a rack of bombs from an aircraft. **c.** The projectiles or bombs thus released. **2.** Something resembling a release or discharge of bombs or firearms, as: **a.** A sudden outburst, as of cheers or praise. **b.** A forceful verbal or written assault. [Italian *salva,* from French *salve,* from Latin *salvē,* hail, imperative of *salvēre,* to be in good health, from *salvus,* safe. See **sol-** in Appendix.]

sal•vo² (sălʹvō) *n., pl.* **-vos.** **1.** A mental provision or reservation. **2.** *Law.* A saving clause. **3.** An expedient for protecting one's reputation or for soothing one's conscience. [Latin *salvō* (as in Medieval Latin *salvō jure,* saving the right), ablative of *salvus,* safe. See SAFE.]

sal vo•la•ti•le (vō-lătʹl-ē) *n.* A solution of ammonium carbonate in alcohol or ammonia water, used in smelling salts. [New Latin : Latin *sāl,* salt + Latin *volātile,* flying.]

Sal•ween (sălʹwēnʹ). A river of southeast Asia rising in eastern Tibet and flowing about 2,816 km (1,750 mi) east then south through Burma into the Gulf of Martaban.

Salz•burg (sôlzʹbûrg', sälzʹ-, zältsʹbo͝ork'). A city of west-central Austria near the German border southwest of Linz. Originally a Celtic settlement, it was later a Roman colony and is now a major music center and tourist resort. Population, 139,426.

Salz•git•ter (zältsʹgĭt'ər). A city of central Germany southeast of Hanover. First mentioned c. 1000, it is an important metallurgical center in a rich iron ore region. Population, 107,023.

SAM *abbr.* Surface-to-air missile.

Sam. *abbr. Bible.* Samuel.

Sa•ma (säʹmä) *n.* An Austronesian language spoken in the Sulu Archipelago. Also called *Samal.*

Sa•mal (sä-mälʹ) *n.* See **Sama.**

Sa•mar (säʹmär'). An island of east-central Philippines in the Visayan Islands northeast of Leyte in the **Samar Sea,** an arm of the Pacific Ocean.

sam•a•ra (sămʹər-ə, sə-mârʹə, -märʹə) *n. Botany.* A dry, indehiscent, winged, often one-seeded fruit, as of the ash, elm, or maple. Also called *key fruit.* [Latin, elm seed.]

Sa•mar•i•a (sə-mărʹē-ə, -mârʹ-). An ancient city of central Palestine in present-day northwest Jordan. It was founded in the ninth century B.C. as the capital of the northern kingdom of Israel, also known as **Samaria.** Conquered by Sargon II in 721, it was destroyed in the second century and rebuilt by Herod the Great.

Sa•mar•i•tan (sə-mărʹĭ-tn) *n.* **1.** A native or inhabitant of Samaria. **2.** Often **samaritan.** A Good Samaritan. **—Samaritan** *adj.* Of or relating to Samaria or to Samaritans. [Middle English, from Old English, from Late Latin *Samaritānus,* from Greek *Samaritēs,* from *Samareia,* Samaria.]

sa•mar•i•um (sə-mârʹē-əm, -mărʹ-) *n. Symbol* **Sm** A silvery or pale gray metallic rare-earth element found in monazite and bastnaesite and used as a dopant for laser materials, in infrared absorbing glass, and as a neutron absorber in certain nuclear reactors. Atomic number 62; atomic weight 150.35; melting point 1,072°C; boiling point 1,791°C; specific gravity (approximately) 7.50; valence 2, 3. See table at **element.** [SAMAR(SKITE) + -IUM.]

Sam•ar•kand (sămʹər-kănd', sə-mər-käntʹ). A city of southern Uzbekistan southwest of Tashkent. Dating from the third or fourth millennium B.C., the city was conquered by Alexander the Great in 329, taken by the Arabs in the eighth century A.D., and destroyed by Genghis Khan c. 1220. It was rebuilt as a fabled center of great splendor and opulence when it became (c. 1370) the capital of Tamerlane's empire. Population, 371,000.

sa•mar•skite (sə-märʹskīt', sămʹər-) *n.* A velvet-black mineral that is a complex mixture of several rare-earth metals with niobium and tantalum oxide. [After Col. M. von *Samarski,* 19th-century Russian mining official.]

sam•ba (sămʹbə, sämʹ-) *n.* **1.** A Brazilian ballroom dance of African origin. **2.** Music in 4/4 time for performing this dance. **—samba** *intr.v.* **-baed, -ba•ing, -bas.** To perform this dance. [Portuguese, possibly of African origin.]

sam•bal (sämʹbäl) *n.* A very spicy condiment or side dish of southeast Asia that is usually seasoned with hot chili peppers. [Malay, from Tamil *sambhar,* from Prakrit *saṃbhārei,* he gathers, from Sanskrit *saṃbhārayati,* he causes to be brought together : *sam,* together; see SANSKRIT + *bharati,* he carries, brings; see **bher-¹** in Appendix.]

sam•bar also **sam•bur** (sămʹbər, sämʹ-) *n.* A large deer *(Cervus unicolor)* of southern Asia, having three-tined antlers and a reddish-brown coat. [Hindi *sāmbar,* from Sanskrit *śambaraḥ.*]

Sam Browne belt (sămʹ brounʹ) *n.* A belt having a shoulder strap that runs diagonally across the chest, worn as part of a military or police uniform. [After Sir *Samuel* James *Browne* (1824–1901), British general.]

sam•bu•ca (săm-bo͞oʹkə, säm-bo͞oʹkä) *n.* An Italian liqueur made from elderberries and flavored with licorice. [Italian, from feminine of *sambuco,* elder, from Latin *sambūcus.*]

sam·bur (săm′bər, säm′-) *n.* Variant of **sambar.**

same (sām) *adj.* **1.** Being the very one; identical: *the same boat we rented before.* **2.** Similar in kind, quality, quantity, or degree. **3.** Conforming in every detail: *according to the same rules as before.* **4.** Being the one previously mentioned or indicated; aforesaid. **—same** *adv.* In the same way. **—same** *pron.* **1.** Someone or something identical with another. **2.** Someone or something previously mentioned or described. [Middle English, from Old Norse *samr.* See **sem-**[1] in Appendix.]

SYNONYMS: *same, identical, selfsame, very.* The central meaning shared by these adjectives is "not different in identity or nature from another or others": *wore the same dress twice; gave identical answers; saw the selfsame quotation in two newspapers; the very person who should have warned us.*
ANTONYM: *different.*
USAGE NOTE: The expressions *same* and *the same* are sometimes used in place of pronouns such as *it* or *one,* as in *When you have filled out the form, please remit same to this office.* As this example suggests, the usage is associated chiefly with commercial and legal language, and some critics have suggested that it should be reserved for such contexts. But though the usage often does sound stilted, it occurs with some frequency in informal writing, particularly in the phrase *lack of same,* as in *It is a question of money, or lack of same.* And blind conformity to the critical injunction would have deprived us of the famously laconic radio message sent by a U.S. Navy officer during World War II: *"Sighted sub, sank same."*

sa·mekh (sä′mĕk, -məKH) *n.* The 15th letter of the Hebrew alphabet. See table at **alphabet.** [Hebrew *sāmek.*]

same·ness (sām′nĭs) *n.* **1.** The quality or condition of being the same. **2.** A lack of variety or change; monotony.

sam hill also **Sam Hill** (săm′ hĭl′) *n. Slang.* Used as an intensive: *What in sam hill is going on?* [Origin unknown.]

Sa·mi (sä′mē) *n., pl.* **Sami** or **-mis.** See **Lapp** (sense 1).

sam·iel (săm-yĕl′) *n.* See **simoom.** [Turkish *samyeli* : *sam,* poisonous + *yel,* wind.]

sam·i·sen (săm′ĭ-sĕn′) *n. Music.* A Japanese instrument resembling a banjo, having a very long neck and three strings played with a plectrum. [Japanese : *sami,* three + *sen,* string.]

sam·ite (săm′īt′, sā′mīt′) *n.* A heavy silk fabric, often interwoven with gold or silver, worn in the Middle Ages. [Middle English *samit,* from Old French, from Medieval Latin *examitum,* from Medieval Greek *hexamiton,* from Greek, neuter of *hexamitos,* of six threads : *hexa-,* hexa- + *mitos,* warp thread.]

sa·miz·dat (sä′mĭz-dät′, sə-myĭz-dät′) *n.* **1.a.** The secret publication and distribution of government-banned literature in the Soviet Union. **b.** The literature produced by this system. **2.** An underground press. [Russian : *sam,* self; see **sem-**[1] in Appendix + *izdatel'stvo,* publishing house (from *izdat',* to publish, on the model of *Gosizdát,* State Publishing House : *iz,* from, out of; see **eghs** in Appendix + *dat',* to give; see **dō-** in Appendix).]

sam·let (săm′lĭt) *n.* A young salmon. [SA(L)M(ON) + –LET.]

Sam·ni·um (săm′nē-əm). An ancient country of central and southern Italy. The expansionist desires of its rulers led to the Samnite Wars (343–290 B.C.) and the ultimate defeat of Samnium by Rome. **—Sam′nite** (săm′nīt′) *adj. & n.*

Sa·mo·a (sə-mō′ə). An island group of the southern Pacific Ocean east-northeast of Fiji, divided between **American Samoa** and **Western Samoa.** The islands were originally populated by Polynesians perhaps as early as 1000 B.C. and were first sighted by European explorers in 1722. Dual administration of the archipelago was established by treaty in 1899.

Sa·mo·an (sə-mō′ən) *adj.* Of or relating to Samoa or its people, language, or culture. **—Samoan** *n.* **1.** A native or inhabitant of Samoa. **2.** The Polynesian language of Samoa.

Sa·mos (sā′mŏs′, săm′ōs, sä′môs). An island of eastern Greece in the Aegean Sea off the western coast of Turkey. First inhabited in the Bronze Age, it was later colonized by Ionian Greeks and became an important commercial and maritime power in the sixth century B.C. Subsequently controlled by Persia, Athens, Sparta, Rome, Byzantium, and the Ottoman Empire, the island became part of modern-day Greece in 1913.

sa·mo·sa (sə-mō′sə, sä-mō′sä) *n.* A small fried turnover of Indian origin that is filled with seasoned vegetables or meat and served hot. [Urdu.]

Sam·o·set (săm′ə-sĕt′). Died c. 1653. Native American leader and friend of the early colonists. He was the first to sell land to the Pilgrims (1625).

Sam·o·thrace (săm′ə-thrās′) or **Sam·o·thrá·ki** (sä′mô-thrä′kē). An island of northeast Greece in the northeast Aegean Sea off the coast of European Turkey. The famed *Winged Victory of Samothrace,* now at the Louvre in Paris, was sculpted c. 200 B.C. and found on the island in 1863.

sam·o·var (săm′ə-vär′) *n.* A metal urn with a chimney, a vertical compartment for hot charcoal, and a spigot, used especially by Russians to boil water for tea. [Russian : *samo,* self; see **sem-**[1] in Appendix + *varit',* to boil.]

Sam·o·yed also **Sam·o·yede** (săm′ə-yĕd′, -oi-ĕd′, sə-moi′ĭd) *n.* **1.** See **Nenets. 2.** Any of a breed of medium-sized dog originally developed in northern Eurasia, having a thick, long, white or cream-colored coat. [Obsolete Russian *samoyed* (*samo-,* self; see SAMOVAR + *-ed,* eater; see **ed-** in Appendix), alteration of Sami *sämm emmne,* land of the Sami.] **—Sam′o·yed′** *adj.* **—Sam′o·yed′ic** *adj.*

♦**samp** (sămp) *n. New England.* Cornmeal mush. [Narraganset *nasàump.*]

sam·pan (săm′păn′) *n. Nautical.* A flat-bottomed Asian skiff usually propelled by two oars. [Chinese (Mandarin) *sān bǎn* : *sān,* three + *bǎn,* board.]

sam·phire (săm′fīr′) *n.* **1.** See **glasswort. 2.** An Old World coastal plant *(Crithmum maritimum)* having fleshy compound leaves and small white flowers grouped in compound umbels. [Alteration of French *herbe de Saint Pierre,* from *Saint Pierre,* Saint Peter.]

sam·ple (săm′pəl) *n.* **1.a.** A portion, piece, or segment that is representative of a whole. **b.** An entity that is representative of a class; a specimen. See Synonyms at **example. 2.** *Statistics.* A set of elements drawn from and analyzed to estimate the characteristics of a population. In this sense, also called *sampling.* **—sample** *tr.v.* **-pled, -pling, -ples.** To take a sample of, especially to test or examine by a sample: *the restaurant critic who must sample a little of everything.* **—sample** *adj.* Serving as a representative or an example: *sample test questions; a sample piece of fabric.* [Partly Middle English (from Anglo-Norman) and partly short for Middle English *ensample* (from Anglo-Norman), both from Latin *exemplum.* See EXAMPLE.]

sam·pler (săm′plər) *n.* **1.** One who is employed to take and appraise samples, as of a food product. **2.** A mechanical device that is used to obtain and analyze samples. **3.** A decorative piece of cloth embroidered with various designs or mottoes in a variety of stitches, serving as an example of skill at needlework. **4.a.** A representative collection or selection: *a sampler of American short-story writers.* **b.** A variety; an assortment. [Senses 3 and 4, partly Middle English, model (from Anglo-Norman *essamplur), and partly short for Middle English *ensampler* (from Anglo-Norman *ensamplour*), both from Late Latin *exemplārium,* model, copy, from Latin *exemplārium,* copy. See EXEMPLAR.]

sam·pling (săm′plĭng) *n.* **1.** *Statistics.* See **sample** (sense 2). **2.a.** The act, process, or technique of selecting an appropriate sample. **b.** A small portion, piece, or segment selected as a sample.

sampling distribution *n. Statistics.* The distribution of a statistic, such as occurs when a number of sample means are calculated for a given population.

sampling gate *n. Electronics.* A circuit that produces an output only when first activated by a preliminary pulse.

Samp·son (sămp′sən), **Deborah.** 1760–1827. American Revolutionary soldier who fought disguised as a man (1782–1783) and was wounded twice before her secret was discovered.

sam·sa·ra (səm-sär′ə) *n. Hinduism & Buddhism.* The eternal cycle of birth, suffering, death, and rebirth. [Sanskrit *saṃsārah,* course of life, samsara : *sam,* together; see **sem-**[1] in Appendix + *sarati,* it flows.]

Sam·son[1] (săm′sən). In the Old Testament, the Israelite judge and warrior who was betrayed to the Philistines by Delilah.

Sam·son[2] (săm′sən) *n.* A man of great physical strength. **—Sam·so′ni·an** (săm-sō′nē-ən) *adj.*

Sam·sun (säm-so͞on′). A city of northern Turkey northeast of Ankara on **Samsun Bay,** an inlet of the Black Sea. In ancient times Samsun was an important Greek colony. Population, 198,749.

Sam·u·el (săm′yo͞o-əl) *n. Bible.* **1.** Hebrew judge and prophet of the 11th century B.C. who anointed Saul as king. **2.** *Abbr.* **Sam., S** See table at **Bible.**

sam·u·rai (săm′ə-rī′) *n., pl.* **samurai** or **-rais. 1.** The Japanese feudal military aristocracy. **2.** A professional warrior belonging to this class. [Japanese, warrior.]

san also **-san** (sän) *n.* Used as a courtesy title in Japanese-speaking areas as a suffix to the given name, surname, or title of the person being addressed, regardless of age or gender: *Yamamoto san; sensei-san.* [Japanese *-san.*]

San (sän) *n., pl.* **San** or **Sans. 1.** A member of a traditionally nomadic hunting people of southwest Africa. **2.** Any of the Khoisan languages of the San. Also called *Bushman.* [Khoikhoin (Nama) : *sa,* to pick up from the ground, gather + *-n,* common gender pl. suff.]

Sa·na or **Sa·n'a** or **Sa·naa** (sä-nä′). The capital of Yemen, in the western part of the country. Settled in ancient times, it became the capital of North Yemen in 1962 and the capital of united North Yemen and Southern Yemen in 1990. Population, 277,800.

San An·dre·as Fault (săn ăn-drā′əs). A major zone of fractures in the earth's crust extending along the coastline of California from the northwest part of the state to the Gulf of California.

San An·ge·lo (ăn′jə-lō′). A city of west-central Texas south-southwest of Abilene. A notorious frontier town in the 1870's, it grew after the coming of the railroad in 1888. Population, 73,240.

San An·to·ni·o (ăn-tō′nē-ō′). A city of south-central Texas southwest of Austin on the **San Antonio River,** flowing about 322 km (200 mi) southeast to **San Antonio Bay** on the Gulf of Mexico. The city was founded as a Franciscan mission in 1718 and is the

Sam Browne belt

samisen

samovar

Samoyed

sampan

George Sand

Carl Sandburg

sandcastle

site of the Alamo, which was besieged and captured by Mexican forces in February–March 1836. Population, 785,410.

san·a·tar·i·um (săn′ə-târ′ē-əm) *n.* Variant of **sanatorium.**

san·a·tive (săn′ə-tĭv) *adj.* Having the power to cure; healing or restorative: *a sanative environment of mountains and fresh air.* [Middle English *sanatif,* from Old French, from Late Latin *sānātīvus,* from Latin *sānātus,* past participle of *sānāre,* to heal. See SANATORIUM.]

san·a·to·ri·um (săn′ə-tôr′ē-əm, -tōr′-) also **san·a·tar·i·um** (-târ′ē-əm) *n., pl.* **-to·ri·ums** or **-to·ri·a** (-tôr′ē-ə, -tōr′-) also **-tar·i·ums** or **-tar·i·a** (-târ′ē-ə). **1.** An institution for the treatment of chronic diseases or for medically supervised recuperation. **2.** A resort for improvement or maintenance of health, especially for convalescents. Also called *sanitarium.* [From neuter of Late Latin *sānātōrius,* curative, from Latin *sānātus,* past participle of *sānāre,* to heal, from *sānus,* healthy.]

san·be·ni·to (săn′bə-nē′tō) *n., pl.* **-tos.** A garment of sackcloth worn at an auto-da-fé of the Spanish Inquisition by condemned heretics, being yellow with red crosses for the penitent and black with painted flames and devils for the impenitent. [Spanish *sambenito,* from SAN BENITO, Saint Benedict of Nursia (from its similarity to the scapular supposedly introduced by him).]

San Be·ni·to (bə-nē′tō). A city of extreme southern Texas north of Brownsville. It is a processing and shipping center and a winter resort. Population, 17,988.

San Ber·nar·di·no (bûr′nə-dē′nō, -nər-). A city of southern California at the foot of the San Bernardino Mountains east of Los Angeles. The site was first explored in 1772, named in 1810, and laid out as a city in the 1850's. Population, 118,794.

San Bernardino Mountains. A mountain range of southern California in the Coast Ranges south of the Mojave Desert.

San Blas (săn blăs′, sän bläs′), **Gulf of.** An inlet of the Caribbean Sea on the northern coast of Panama east of the Panama Canal.

San Bru·no (săn brōō′nō). A city of western California, a residential suburb of San Francisco on San Francisco Bay. Population, 35,417.

San Car·los (kär′ləs). A city of western California southeast of San Francisco. It is mainly residential. Population, 24,710.

San Cle·men·te (klə-mĕn′tē). A city of southern California on the Pacific Ocean southeast of Long Beach. It is a popular resort center. Population, 27,325.

San Cris·tó·bal (săn krĭs-tō′bəl, sän′ krē-stô′väl). A city of extreme western Venezuela in a mountainous region near the Colombian border south-southwest of Maracaibo. Founded in 1561, it was severely damaged by an earthquake in 1875. Population, 280,000.

sanc·ta (săngk′tə) *n.* A plural of **sanctum.**

sanc·ti·fy (săngk′tə-fī′) *tr.v.* **-fied, -fy·ing, -fies. 1.** To set apart for sacred use; consecrate. **2.** To make holy; purify. **3.** To give religious sanction to, as with an oath or a vow: *sanctify a marriage.* **4.** To give social or moral sanction to. **5.** To make productive of holiness or spiritual blessing. [Middle English *sanctifien,* alteration of *seintefien,* from Old French *saintifier,* from Late Latin *sānctificāre* : Latin *sānctus,* holy, from past participle of *sancīre,* to consecrate; see **sak-** in Appendix + Latin *-ficāre,* -fy.] **—sanc′ti·fi·ca′tion** (-fĭ-kā′shən) *n.* **—sanc′ti·fi′er** *n.*

sanc·ti·mo·ni·ous (săngk′tə-mō′nē-əs) *adj.* Feigning piety or righteousness. See Synonyms at **religious. —sanc′ti·mo′ni·ous·ly** *adv.* **—sanc′ti·mo′ni·ous·ness** *n.*

sanc·ti·mo·ny (săngk′tə-mō′nē) *n.* Feigned piety or righteousness; hypocritical devoutness or high-mindedness. [Obsolete French *sanctimonie,* from Latin *sānctimōnia,* sacredness, from *sānctus,* holy. See SANCTIFY.]

sanc·tion (săngk′shən) *n.* **1.** Authoritative permission or approval that makes a course of action valid. See Synonyms at **permission. 2.** Support or encouragement, as from public opinion or established custom. **3.** A consideration, an influence, or a principle that dictates an ethical choice. **4.a.** A law or decree. **b.** The penalty for noncompliance specified in a law or decree. **5.** A penalty, specified or in the form of moral pressure, that acts to ensure compliance or conformity. **6.** A coercive measure adopted usually by several nations acting together against a nation violating international law. **—sanction** *tr.v.* **-tioned, -tion·ing, -tions. 1.** To give official authorization or approval to: *"The president, we are told, has sanctioned greed at the cost of compassion"* (David Rankin). **2.** To encourage or tolerate by indicating approval. See Synonyms at **approve.** [Middle English, enactment of a law, from Old French, ecclesiastical decree, from Latin *sānctiō, sānctiōn-,* binding law, penal sanction, from *sānctus,* holy. See SANCTIFY.]

sanc·ti·ty (săngk′tĭ-tē) *n., pl.* **-ties. 1.** Holiness of life or disposition; saintliness. **2.** The quality or condition of being considered sacred; inviolability. **3.** Something considered sacred. [Middle English *saunctite,* from Old French *saintcite,* from Latin *sānctitās,* from *sānctus,* sacred. See SANCTIFY.]

sanc·tu·ar·y (săngk′chōō-ĕr′ē) *n., pl.* **-ies. 1.a.** A sacred place, such as a church, temple, or mosque. **b.** The holiest part of a sacred place, as the part of a Christian church around the altar. **2.a.** A sacred place, such as a church, in which fugitives formerly were immune to arrest. **b.** Immunity to arrest afforded by a sanctuary. **3.** A place of refuge or asylum. **4.** A reserved area in which birds and other animals, especially wild animals, are protected from hunting or molestation. See Synonyms at **shelter.** [Middle English, from Old French *sainctuarie,* from Late Latin *sānctuārium,* from Latin *sānctus,* sacred. See SANCTIFY.]

sanc·tum (săngk′təm) *n., pl.* **-tums** or **-ta** (-tə). **1.** A sacred or holy place. **2.** A private place where one is free from intrusion. [Late Latin *sānctum,* from Latin, neuter of *sānctus,* sacred. See SANCTIFY.]

sanctum sanc·to·rum (săngk-tôr′əm, -tōr′-) *n.* **1.** *Judaism.* The innermost shrine of a tabernacle and temple; the holy of holies. **2.** An inviolably private place: *The clubhouse was their sanctum sanctorum.* [Late Latin *sānctum sānctōrum* (translation of Greek *to hagion tōn hagiōn,* translation of Hebrew *qōdeš haqqodāšîm*) : *sānctum,* holy place + *sānctōrum,* genitive pl. of *sānctum,* holy place.]

Sanc·tus (săngk′təs) *n., pl.* **-tus·es.** A hymn of praise sung at the end of the Preface in many Eucharistic liturgies. [Middle English, from Late Latin *Sānctus,* from Latin *sānctus,* holy (from the first word of the hymn). See SANCTIFY.]

sand (sănd) *n.* **1.a.** Small, loose grains of worn or disintegrated rock. **b.** *Geology.* A sedimentary material, finer than a granule and coarser than silt, with grains between 0.06 and 2.0 millimeters in diameter. **2.** Often **sands.** A tract of land covered with sand, as a beach or desert. **3.a.** The loose, granular, gritty particles in an hourglass. **b. sands.** Moments of allotted time or duration: *"The sands are numb'red that makes up my life"* (Shakespeare). **4.** *Slang.* Courage; stamina; perseverance: *"She had more sand in her than any girl I ever see; in my opinion she was just full of sand"* (Mark Twain). **5.** *Color.* A light grayish brown to yellowish gray. **—sand** *tr.v.* **sand·ed, sand·ing, sands. 1.** To sprinkle or cover with or as if with sand. **2.** To polish or scrape with sand or sandpaper. **3.** To mix with sand. **4.** To fill up (a harbor) with sand. [Middle English, from Old English.]

Sand (sănd, säɴd), **George.** Pen name of Amandine Aurore Lucie Dupin, Baroness Dudevant. 1804–1876. French writer whose novels, plays, and essays concern the freedom and independence of women.

san·dal[1] (săn′dl) *n.* **1.** A shoe consisting of a sole fastened to the foot by thongs or straps. **2.** A low-cut shoe fastened to the foot by an ankle strap. **3.** A rubber overshoe cut very low and covering little more than the sole of the shoe. **4.** A strap or band for fastening a low shoe or slipper on the foot. [Middle English, from Old French *sandale,* from Latin *sandalium,* from Greek *sandalion,* diminutive of *sandalon,* sandal.] **—san′daled** *adj.*

san·dal[2] (săn′dl) *n.* Sandalwood. [Middle English, from Old French *sandale* (possibly via Late Greek *santalon*), from Arabic *ṣandal,* from Sanskrit *candanam.*]

san·dal·wood (săn′dl-wŏŏd′) *n.* **1.** Any of several tropical Asian trees of the genus *Santalum,* especially *S. album,* having aromatic yellowish heartwood used in cabinetmaking and wood carving and yielding an oil used in perfumery. **2.** Any of several tropical Asian trees of the genera *Adenanthera, Myroporum,* and *Pterocarpus.* **3.** The wood of any of these trees. **4.** *Color.* A light to moderate or grayish brown.

san·da·rac (săn′də-răk′) *n.* **1.** A coniferous evergreen tree *(Tetraclinis articulata)* of Spain and northern Africa, having flattened branches, scalelike leaves, and bark that yields a hard, brittle, translucent resin used in varnishes. **2.** The resin of this tree. [Middle English *sandaracha,* from Latin, red pigment, from Greek *sandarakē,* realgar.]

sand·bag (sănd′băg′) *n.* A bag filled with sand and used as ballast, in the formation of protective walls, or as a weapon. **—sandbag** *tr.v.* **-bagged, -bag·ging, -bags. 1.** To put sandbags in or around. **2.a.** To hit with or as if with a sandbag. **b.** *Slang.* To treat severely or unjustly. **c.** *Slang.* To force by crude means; coerce. **—sand′bag′ger** *n.*

sand·bank (sănd′băngk′) *n.* A ridge of sand forming a mound, shoal, or hillside.

sand·bar (sănd′bär′) *n.* A ridge of sand formed in a river or along a shore by the action of waves or currents.

sand·blast (sănd′blăst′) *n.* **1.a.** A blast of air or steam carrying sand at high velocity to etch glass or to clean stone or metal surfaces. **b.** A machine used to apply such a blast. **2.** A strong wind carrying sand along. **—sandblast** *tr.v.* **-blast·ed, -blast·ing, -blasts.** To apply a sandblast to (a building, for example). **—sand′blast′er** *n.*

sand-blind (sănd′blīnd′) *adj.* Having poor vision; partially blind. [Middle English, from Old English **sāmblind : sām-,* half; see **sēmi-** in Appendix + *blind,* blind; see BLIND.] **—sand′-blind′ness** *n.*

sand·box (sănd′bŏks′) *n.* **1.** A low box filled with sand for children to play in. **2.** A litter box, especially for a cat.

sandbox tree *n.* A tropical American tree *(Hura crepitans)* having an irritating milky juice, a spiny trunk, and large woody seed capsules that split explosively when ripe. [So called because the capsules were formerly used to hold sand for drying ink.]

sand·bur (sănd′bûr′) *n.* **1.** Any of several grasses of the genus *Cenchrus,* especially *C. tribuloides,* of the eastern United States and tropical America, having a spiny burlike envelope that surrounds several one-grained spikelets. **2.** The burlike envelope of any of these plants. Also called *sandspur.*

Sand·burg (sănd′bûrg′, săn′-), **Carl.** 1878–1967. American writer known for his free verse poems celebrating American people, geography, and industry and for his six-volume biography *Abraham Lincoln* (1926–1939).

sand-cast (sănd′kăst′) *tr.v.* **-cast, -cast·ing, -casts.** To make (a casting) by pouring molten metal into a sand mold.

sand casting *n.* A casting made in a mold of sand.

sand·cas·tle (sănd′kăs′əl) *n.* **1.** A castlelike structure built of wet sand, as by children at a beach. **2.** Something that lacks substance or significance.

sand crack *n.* A fissure in the side of a horse's hoof, often causing lameness.

sand dab *n.* Any of several small food fishes of the genus *Citharichthys* of Pacific waters, related to the flounders.

sand dollar *n.* Any of various thin, circular echinoderms of the class Echinoidea, especially *Echinarachnius parma,* of sandy ocean bottoms of the northern Atlantic and Pacific.

sand eel *n.* See **sand lance.**

sand·er (săn′dər) *n.* One that sands, especially: **a.** A device that spreads sand on roads. **b.** Such a device together with the truck that carries it. **c.** A machine having a powered abrasive-covered disk or belt, used for smoothing or polishing surfaces: *a floor sander.*

sand·er·ling (săn′dər-lĭng) *n.* A small shore bird *(Crocethia alba)* related to the sandpipers, having predominantly gray and white plumage. [Perhaps from SAND + –LING[1].]

sand·fish (sănd′fĭsh′) *n., pl.* **sandfish** or **-fish·es. 1.** Any of various marine fishes that live or burrow in sandy or muddy bottoms, as a scaleless fish of the family Trichodontidae of the northern Pacific. **2.** A slender fish *(Gonorhynchus gonorhynchus)* of the Pacific and Indian oceans, characterized by an angular snout. In this sense, also called *beaked salmon.*

sand flea *n.* **1.** Any of various small crustaceans living on sandy beaches. **2.** See **chigoe** (sense 1).

sand fly *n.* Any of various small biting flies of the genus *Phlebotomus* of tropical areas, some of which transmit diseases.

sand·fly fever (sănd′flī′) *n.* A mild viral disease transmitted by the bite of the sand fly *(Phlebotomus papatasii),* characterized by fever, malaise, eye pain, and headache. Also called *pappataci fever, phlebotomus fever.*

sand grouse *n.* Any of various pigeonlike birds of the genus *Pterocles* and related genera, of arid and semiarid regions of the Old World.

san·dhi (săn′dē, sän′-) *n.* *Linguistics.* Modification of the sound of a morpheme in certain phonetic contexts, as the difference between the pronunciation of *don't* in *don't you* and in *don't we.* [Sanskrit *saṃdhiḥ,* union, sandhi : *sam,* together; see **sem-**[1] in Appendix + *dadhāti, dhī-,* he places; see **dhē-** in Appendix.]

sand·hill crane (sănd′hĭl′) *n.* A North American crane *(Grus canadensis)* having gray plumage and a bald red forehead.

sand·hog (sănd′hôg′, -hŏg′) *n.* *Slang.* A laborer who works inside a caisson, as in the construction of underwater tunnels.

sand hopper *n.* See **beach flea.**

Sand·hurst (sănd′hûrst′). A village of south-central England southeast of Reading. Its famed Royal Military College (now Academy) was founded in the 1790's.

San Di·e·go (săn dē-ā′gō). A city of southern California on **San Diego Bay,** an inlet of the Pacific Ocean near the Mexican border. The bay was first explored by the Spanish in 1542 although the area was not settled until the 1700's. A noted zoological park is located in the city. Population, 875,504.

San Di·mas (dē′məs). A city of southern California east of Los Angeles. It is a residential community in a citrus-growing area. Population, 24,014.

S & L *abbr.* Savings and loan association.

sand lance *n.* Any of several small marine fishes of the genus *Ammodytes,* having a slender body with a forked tail fin and often burrowing in the sand of tidelands. Also called *launce, sand eel.*

sand lily *n.* A low-growing plant *(Leucocrinum montanum)* of the western United States, having grasslike leaves and fragrant, white, star-shaped flowers.

sand·lot (sănd′lŏt′) *n.* *Sports & Games.* A vacant lot used especially by children for unorganized sports and games. **—sandlot** *adj.* Of, relating to, or played in a sandlot: *sandlot baseball.* **—sand′lot′ter** *n.*

S & M or **s & m** *abbr.* *Psychology.* Sadomasochism.

sand·man (sănd′măn′) *n.* A character in fairy tales and folklore who makes children go to sleep by sprinkling sand in their eyes.

sand painting *n.* **1.** A ceremonial design of the Navajo and Pueblo peoples made by trickling fine colored sand, pollen, or powder onto a base of neutral sand. **2.** The art of making designs with colored sand.

sand·pa·per (sănd′pā′pər) *n.* Heavy paper coated on one side with sand or other abrasive material and used for smoothing surfaces. **—sandpaper** *tr.v.* **-pered, -per·ing, -pers.** To rub with or as if with sandpaper. **—sand′pa′per·y** *adj.*

sand pear *n.* **1.** A Chinese tree *(Pyrus pyrifolia)* of the rose family, having edible, globose, firm, juicy fruit. **2.** The fruit of this plant. Also called *Asian pear, Chinese pear.*

sand·pi·per (sănd′pī′pər) *n.* Any of various small wading birds of the family Scolopacidae, usually having a long, straight, sensitive bill with which it picks up insects, worms, and soft mollusks in mud and sand.

sand·pit (sănd′pĭt′) *n.* A large, deep pit in sandy ground from which sand is dug.

San·dring·ham (săn′drĭng-əm). A village of eastern England near the Wash west-northwest of Norwich. Sandringham House, a private royal residence, was purchased in 1861 by Victoria for her son the Prince of Wales, later King Edward VII, and extensively rebuilt in the 1890's.

sand shark *n.* A shark of the genus *Carcharias,* especially *C. taurus,* found mainly in shallow waters of the temperate and tropical Atlantic.

sand·spur (sănd′spûr′) *n.* See **sandbur.**

sand·stone (sănd′stōn′) *n.* A sedimentary rock formed by the consolidation and compaction of sand and held together by a natural cement, such as silica.

sand·storm (sănd′stôrm′) *n.* A strong wind carrying clouds of sand and dust through the air.

sand table *n.* **1.** A table with raised edges, used for holding sand with which children play. **2.** A table on which a relief model of terrain is built out of sand for the study of military maneuvers.

sand trap *n.* *Sports.* A hazard on a golf course consisting of a depression partly filled with sand.

San·dus·ky (sən-dŭs′kē, săn-). A city of northern Ohio west of Cleveland on **Sandusky Bay,** an inlet of Lake Erie. The **Sandusky River,** about 241 km (150 mi) long, flows west and north into the bay. Sandusky was founded in the early 1800's and is a port of entry and manufacturing center. Population, 31,360.

sand verbena *n.* Any of several herbs of the genus *Abronia,* of western North America, having fragrant, usually red, yellow, or white flowers that are grouped in long-stalked heads.

sand viper *n.* See **horned viper.**

sand·wich (sănd′wĭch, săn′-) *n.* **1.a.** Two or more slices of bread with a filling such as meat or cheese placed between them. **b.** A partly split long or round roll containing a filling. **c.** One slice of bread covered with a filling. **2.** Something resembling a sandwich. **—sandwich** *tr.v.* **-wiched, -wich·ing, -wich·es. 1.** To make into or as if into a sandwich. **2.** To insert (one thing) tightly between two other things of differing character or quality. **3.** To make room or time for: *sandwiched a trip to the store between the hours of one and three.* [After John Montagu, Fourth Earl of *Sandwich* (1718–1792), British politician.]

Sand·wich (sănd′wĭch′, săn′-). A municipal borough of southeast England north of Dover. One of the original Cinque Ports, it is now a resort and market center. Population, 4,227.

sandwich board *n.* Two large boards bearing placards, hinged at the top by straps for hanging over the shoulders with one board in front and the other behind, used for picketing or advertising.

sandwich coin *n.* A coin having a layer of one metal, such as copper, between exterior layers of a different metal, such as silver.

Sandwich Islands. See **Hawaiian Islands.**

sandwich man *n.* A man who pickets or advertises by carrying a sandwich board.

sand·worm (sănd′wûrm′) *n.* Any of various segmented worms, especially of the genera *Nereis* and *Arenicola,* generally inhabiting coastal mud or sand and often used as fishing bait.

sand·wort (sănd′wûrt′, -wôrt′) *n.* Any of numerous low-growing herbs of the genus *Arenaria,* having small, usually white flowers often grouped in cymose clusters.

sand·y (săn′dē) *adj.* **-i·er, -i·est. 1.** Covered with, full of, or consisting of sand. **2.** Having characteristics similar to sand. **3.** *Color.* Of the color of sand; light yellowish brown. **—sand′i·ness** *n.*

Sand·y or **Sand·y City** (săn′dē). A city of north-central Utah, a suburb of Salt Lake City. Population, 52,210.

Sandy Hook. A low peninsula of eastern New Jersey at the entrance to Lower New York Bay. It separates **Sandy Hook Bay** from the Atlantic Ocean and was first explored in 1609.

sane (sān) *adj.* **san·er, san·est. 1.** Of sound mind; mentally healthy: *"their protector, the strongest and sanest of them all"* (Pat Conroy). **2.** Having or showing sound judgment; reasonable. [Latin *sānus,* healthy.] **—sane′ly** *adv.* **—sane′ness** *n.*

San Fer·nan·do (săn fər-năn′dō). **1.** (*also* sän′ fĕr-nän′dô). A city of southern Spain, a seaport and suburb of Cádiz on the Gulf of Cádiz. Population, 76,101. **2.** A city of southern California in the San Fernando Valley surrounded by Los Angeles. It is a residential community with varied light industries. Population, 17,731.

San Fernando Valley. A fertile valley of southern California northwest of central Los Angeles. The valley, first explored by the Spanish in 1769, lies partly within the city limits of Los Angeles and includes many residential communities.

San·ford (săn′fərd). **1.** A city of central Florida north-northeast of Orlando. It is a manufacturing and agricultural trade center. Population, 23,176. **2.** A city of southwest Maine west of Biddeford. Formerly dependent on textile and clothing manufacturing, it now has diversified industries. Population, 18,020.

Sanford, Edward Terry. 1865–1930. American jurist who served as an associate justice of the U.S. Supreme Court (1923–1930).

Sanford, Mount. A mountain, 4,952.3 m (16,237 ft) high, of Alaska in the Wrangell Mountains northeast of Anchorage.

San·for·ized (săn′fə-rīzd′). A trademark used for fabric pre-

sand dollar
Five-holed keyhole urchin
Mellita quinquiesperforata

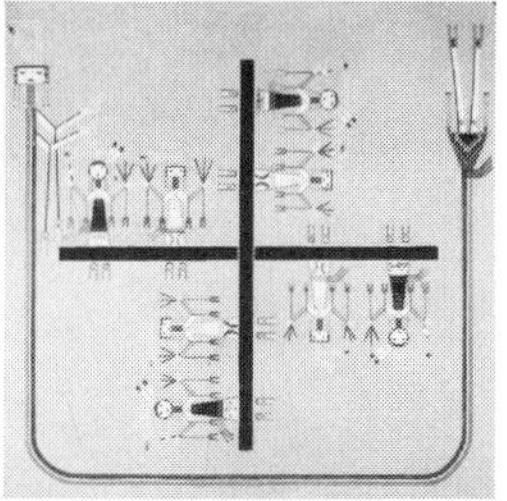

sand painting
Navajo sand painting entitled *Whirling Logs*

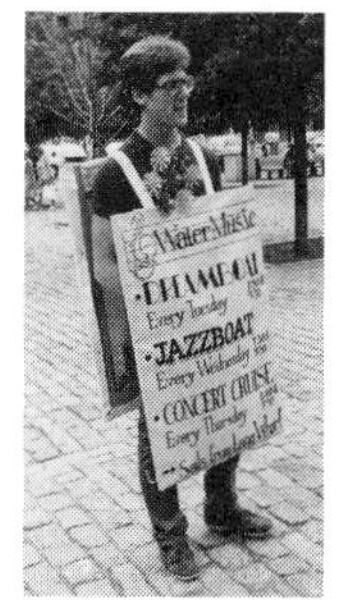

sandwich board

ă pat	oi boy
ā pay	ou out
âr care	o͝o took
ä father	o͞o boot
ĕ pet	ŭ cut
ē be	ûr urge
ĭ pit	th thin
ī pie	*th* this
îr pier	hw which
ŏ pot	zh vision
ō toe	ə about, item
ô paw	♦ regionalism

Stress marks: ′ (primary); ′ (secondary), as in **dictionary** (dĭk′shə-nĕr′ē)

Margaret Sanger

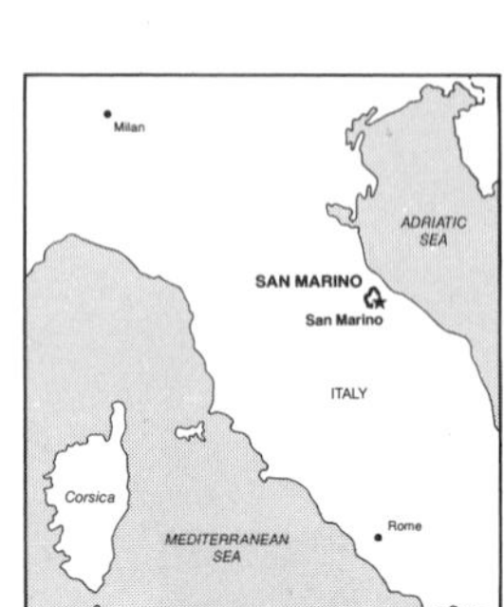

San Marino

ă pat	oi boy
ā pay	ou out
âr care	ŏŏ took
ä father	ōō boot
ĕ pet	ŭ cut
ē be	ûr urge
ĭ pit	th thin
ī pie	*th* this
îr pier	hw which
ŏ pot	zh vision
ō toe	ə about, item
ô paw	♦ regionalism

Stress marks: **ʹ** (primary); ʹ (secondary), as in **dictionary** (dĭkʹshə-nĕrʹē)

shrunk by a patented mechanical process so as to minimize later shrinkage.

San Fran·cis·co (frən-sĭsʹkō). A city of western California on a peninsula between the Pacific Ocean and **San Francisco Bay,** an inlet of the Pacific. A Spanish presidio and mission were founded here in 1776. The first settlement was known as Yerba Buena, and the name was changed to San Francisco after control of the town passed to the United States in 1846. Discovery of gold nearby in 1848 changed the city from a small community into a thriving boom town known for its lawlessness and bawdy amusements. The city was all but destroyed by a devastating earthquake and fire on April 18, 1906. Population, 678,974. **—San Fran·cisʹcan** (-kən) *n.*

San Francisco Peaks also **San Francisco Mountains.** A group of mountains in north-central Arizona north of Flagstaff. The range rises to 3,853.1 m (12,633 ft).

sang (săng) *v.* A past tense of **sing.**

San Ga·bri·el (gāʹbrē-əl). A city of southern California, a residential suburb of Los Angeles. Population, 30,072.

San Gabriel Mountains. A mountain range of southern California east and northeast of Los Angeles. It rises to 3,074.4 m (10,080 ft).

San·gal·lo (sän-gäʹlō, säng-), **Giuliano da.** 1445–1516. Italian architect and engineer noted especially for the works he executed under Medici patronage, including the Palazzo Gondi in Florence (1490).

San·ga·mon (săngʹgə-mən). A river, about 402 km (250 mi) long, of central Illinois flowing southwest and west to the Illinois River.

san·ga·ree (săng'gə-rēʹ) *n.* **1.** A sweet, chilled beverage made of wine or other alcoholic liquor and grated nutmeg. **2.** See **sangria.** [Origin unknown.]

Sang·er (săngʹər), **Frederick.** Born 1918. British biochemist. He won a 1958 Nobel Prize for determining the order of amino acids in the insulin molecule and shared a 1980 Nobel Prize for developing methods for mapping the structure of DNA.

Sanger, Margaret Higgins. 1883–1966. American nurse who campaigned widely for birth control and founded (1929) the organization that became the Planned Parenthood Federation (1942).

sang-froid (säɴ-frwäʹ) *n.* Coolness and composure, especially in trying circumstances. See Synonyms at **equanimity.** [French : *sang,* blood (from Old French, from Latin *sanguīs*) + *froid,* cold (from Old French, from Vulgar Latin **frigidus,* alteration of Latin *frīgidus;* see FRIGID).]

San·gre de Cris·to Mountains (săngʹgrē dē krĭsʹtō). A range of the southern Rocky Mountains extending about 354 km (220 mi) from south-central Colorado to north-central New Mexico. Blanca Peak, 4,375.2 m (14,345 ft), is the highest point.

san·gri·a (săng-grēʹə, sän-) *n.* A cold drink made of red or white wine mixed with brandy, sugar, fruit juice, and soda water. Also called *sangaree.* [Probably from Spanish *sangría,* act of bleeding, sangria, from *sangre,* blood, from Latin *sanguīs, sanguin-.*]

san·guic·o·lous (săng-gwĭkʹə-ləs) *adj.* Living in the blood: *a sanguicolous parasite.* [Latin *sanguīs,* blood + –COLOUS.]

san·gui·nar·i·a (săngʹgwə-nârʹē-ə) *n.* The bloodroot. [New Latin *Sanguinaria,* genus name, from Latin *(herba) sanguināria,* a plant that stanches blood, feminine of *sanguinārius,* sanguinary. See SANGUINARY.]

san·gui·nar·y (săngʹgwə-nĕrʹē) *adj.* **1.** Accompanied by bloodshed. See Synonyms at **bloody. 2.** Eager for bloodshed; bloodthirsty. **3.** Consisting of blood. [Latin *sanguinārius,* from *sanguīs, sanguin-,* blood.] **—san'gui·narʹi·ly** (-nârʹə-lē) *adv.*

san·guine (săngʹgwĭn) *adj.* **1.a.** *Color.* Of the color of blood; red. **b.** Of a healthy, reddish color; ruddy: *a sanguine complexion.* **2.** *Archaic.* **a.** Having blood as the dominant humor in terms of medieval physiology. **b.** Having the temperament and ruddy complexion formerly thought to be characteristic of a person dominated by this humor; passionate. **3.** Cheerfully confident; optimistic. [Middle English, from Old French *sanguin,* from Latin *sanguineus,* from *sanguīs, sanguin-,* blood.] **—sanʹguine·ly** *adv.* **—sanʹguine·ness, san·guinʹi·ty** *n.*

WORD HISTORY: Perhaps one has wondered what the connection between *sanguinary,* "bloodthirsty," and *sanguine,* "cheerfully optimistic," could be. The connection can be found in medieval physiology with its notion of the four humors (blood, bile, phlegm, and black bile). These four body fluids were thought to determine a person's temperament, or distinguishing mental and physical characteristics. Thus, if blood was the predominant humor, one had a ruddy face and a disposition marked by courage, hope, and a readiness to fall in love. Such a temperament was called *sanguine,* the Middle English ancestor of our word *sanguine.* The sources of the Middle English word were Old French *sanguin* and Latin *sanguineus,* the source of the French word. Both the Old French and Latin words meant "bloody," "blood-colored," Old French *sanguin* having the sense "sanguine in temperament" as well. Latin *sanguineus* in turn was derived from *sanguīs,* "blood," just as English *sanguinary* is. The English adjective *sanguine,* first recorded in Middle English before 1350, went on to refer simply to the cheerfulness and optimism that accompanied a sanguine temperament, no longer having any direct reference to medieval physiology.

san·guin·e·ous (săng-gwĭnʹē-əs) *adj.* **1.** Relating to or involving blood or bloodshed. See Synonyms at **bloody. 2.** *Color.* Having the color of blood; blood-red. [From Latin *sanguineus,* from *sanguīs, sanguin-,* blood.]

san·guin·o·lent (săng-gwĭnʹə-lənt) *adj.* Mixed or tinged with blood. [Latin *sanguinolentus,* full of blood : *sanguīs, sanguin-,* blood + *-olentus,* abounding in.]

San·hed·rin (săn-hĕdʹrĭn, -hēʹdrĭn, sän-) *n.* The highest judicial and ecclesiastical council of the ancient Jewish nation, composed of from 70 to 72 members. [Hebrew *sanhedhrîn,* from Greek *sunedrion,* council, from *sunedros,* sitting in council : *sun-,* syn- + *hedra,* seat; see **sed-** in Appendix.]

San·i·bel Island (sănʹə-bəl). An island of southwest Florida in the Gulf of Mexico southwest of Fort Myers. The island's beaches are popular with seashell collectors.

san·i·cle (sănʹĭ-kəl) *n.* Any of various plants of the genus *Sanicula,* having usually compound leaves and compound umbels of small yellow, purple, or greenish flowers, formerly used as an astringent. [Middle English, from Old French, from Medieval Latin *sānicula,* probably from Latin *sānus,* healthy.]

san·i·dine (sănʹĭ-dēnʹ, -dĭn) *n.* A glassy variety of orthoclase feldspar, known as moonstone when translucent. [Greek *sanis, sanid-,* board (from its flat crystals) + –INE[2].]

sa·ni·es (sāʹnē-ēzʹ) *n., pl.* **sanies.** A thin, fetid, greenish fluid consisting of serum and pus discharged from a wound, an ulcer, or a fistula. [Latin *saniēs.*] **—saʹni·ous** (-əs) *adj.*

San I·si·dro (sănʹ ĭ-sēʹdrō, sänʹ ē-sēʹ*th*rô). A city of eastern Argentina, a residential and industrial suburb of Buenos Aires. Population, 287,048.

sanit. *abbr.* **1.** Sanitary. **2.** Sanitation.

san·i·tar·i·a (sănʹĭ-târʹē-ə) *n.* A plural of **sanitarium.**

san·i·tar·i·an (sănʹĭ-târʹē-ən) *n.* A public health or sanitation expert.

san·i·tar·i·um (sănʹĭ-târʹē-əm) *n., pl.* **-i·ums** or **-i·a** (-ē-ə). See **sanatorium.** [New Latin, from Latin *sānitās,* health. See SANITY.]

san·i·tar·y (sănʹĭ-tĕrʹē) *adj. Abbr.* **sanit. 1.** Of or relating to health. **2.** Free from elements, such as filth or pathogens, that endanger health; hygienic: *sanitary conditions for the preparation of food.* [French *sanitaire,* from Latin *sānitās,* health. See SANITY.] **—sanʹi·tarʹi·ly** (-târʹə-lē) *adv.*

sanitary engineer *n.* An engineer specializing in the maintenance of urban environmental conditions conducive to the preservation of public health. **—sanitary engineering** *n.*

sanitary landfill *n.* Rehabilitated land in which garbage and trash have been buried; a landfill.

sanitary napkin *n.* A disposable pad of absorbent material worn to absorb menstrual flow.

san·i·ta·tion (sănʹĭ-tāʹshən) *n. Abbr.* **sanit. 1.** Formulation and application of measures designed to protect public health. **2.** Disposal of sewage. [SANIT(ARY) + –ATION.]

sanitation worker *n.* A person employed, as by a municipality or private company, to collect and dispose of garbage.

san·i·tize (sănʹĭ-tīzʹ) *tr.v.* **-tized, -tiz·ing, -tiz·es. 1.** To make sanitary, as by cleaning or disinfecting. **2.** To make more acceptable by removing unpleasant or offensive features from: *sanitized the language in adapting the novel for television.* **—sanʹi·ti·zaʹtion** (-tĭ-zāʹshən) *n.*

san·i·ty (sănʹĭ-tē) *n.* **1.** The quality or condition of being sane; soundness of mind. **2.** Soundness of judgment or reason. [Middle English *sanite,* health, from Old French, from Latin *sānitās,* from *sānus,* healthy.]

San Ja·cin·to (săn jə-sĭnʹtō). A river, about 209 km (130 mi) long, of southeast Texas flowing into Galveston Bay. The final battle of the Texas Revolution, in which insurgents under Sam Houston defeated the Mexican forces led by Santa Anna, was fought on its banks on April 21, 1836.

San Joa·quin (wô-kēnʹ, wä-). A river of central California, rising in the Sierra Nevada and flowing about 515 km (320 mi) west and northwest to form a large delta with the Sacramento River. The **San Joaquin Valley** is a rich agricultural region.

San Jo·se (hō-zāʹ). A city of western California southeast of San Francisco. Founded in 1777, it was the state capital from December 1849 to January 1852. Population, 636,550.

San Jo·sé (sänʹ hô-sĕʹ). The capital and largest city of Costa Rica, in the central part of the country. Settled c. 1736, it became the capital in 1823. Population, 277,800.

San Jose scale *n.* A destructive scale insect *(Aspidiotus perniciosus)* that damages fruit trees and fruit-bearing plants. [After SAN JOSE, California.]

San Juan (săn wänʹ, hwänʹ). **1.** A city of northwest Argentina west of Córdoba. Founded in 1562, it was moved to its present site in the 1590's. Population, 310,000. **2.** The capital and largest city of Puerto Rico, in the northeast part of the island on the Atlantic Ocean. First settled by Ponce de León in 1508–1509, it was attacked by English buccaneers in the 1590's and sacked by the Dutch in 1625. American forces took control of the city during the Spanish-American War (1898). Population, 424,700.

San Juan Cap·is·tra·no (kăpʹĭ-sträʹnō). A city of southern

California southeast of Santa Ana. Founded as a mission in 1776, it is famous for the swallows that supposedly return to the area every year on March 19 and depart on October 23, the date on which Saint John of Capistrano died in 1456. Population, 18,959.

San Juan Hill. An elevation in eastern Cuba near Santiago de Cuba. It was captured by Cuban and American forces on July 1, 1898, during the Spanish-American War. Theodore Roosevelt and his Rough Riders became famous for a charge up the hill during the battle.

San Juan Islands. An archipelago of northwest Washington off the southeast coast of Vancouver Island north of Puget Sound. The islands were discovered and named c. 1790 by Spanish explorers and were later claimed by both Great Britain and the United States. The boundary dispute was finally settled in 1872.

San Juan Mountains. A range of the Rocky Mountains in southwest Colorado extending northwest to southeast and rising to 4,364.2 m (14,309 ft) at Uncompahgre Peak.

San Juan River. A river rising in southern Colorado and flowing about 579 km (360 mi) into northwest New Mexico and southeast Utah, where it joins the Colorado River.

San Jus•to (săn ho͞o′stō, sän). A city of eastern Argentina, an industrial suburb of Buenos Aires. Population, 941,499.

sank (săngk) *v.* A past tense of **sink.**

San•khya (säng′kyə) *n. Hinduism.* A system of Hindu philosophy based on a dualism involving the ultimate principles of soul and potential matter. [Sanskrit *sāṁkhya-,* based on enumeration, Sankhya, from *saṁkhyā,* enumeration : *sam,* together; see SANDHI + *khyāti,* he tells.]

Sankt Gal•len (zängkt gä′lən) also **Saint Gall** (sānt gôl′, gäl′, săɴ gäl′). A city of northeast Switzerland east of Zurich. Developed around a Benedictine abbey founded by an Irish missionary in the seventh century, it joined the Swiss Confederation in 1454. Population, 73,500.

San•ku•ru (säng-ko͝or′o͞o). A river, about 1,207 km (750 mi) long, of southern and central Zaire flowing west-northwest to the Kasai River.

San Le•an•dro (săn lē-ăn′drō). A city of western California southeast of Oakland. It is a residential community with varied light industries. Population, 63,952.

San Lu•cas (săn lo͞o′kəs, sän lo͞o′käs), **Cape.** A cape of western Mexico at the southern tip of Baja California extending into the Pacific Ocean.

San Lu•is O•bis•po (săn lo͞o′ĭs ə-bĭs′pō). A city of southwest California northwest of Santa Barbara. A Franciscan mission was founded on the site in 1772. Population, 34,252.

San Luis Peak. A mountain, 4,274.3 m (14,014 ft) high, in the San Juan Mountains of southwest Colorado.

San Lu•is Po•to•sí (sän lo͞o-ēs′ pô′tô-sē′). A city of central Mexico northeast of León. Founded in the late 1500's, it is a mining, transportation, and industrial center. Population, 362,371.

San Mar•cos (săn mär′kəs). **1.** A city of southern California north-northwest of San Diego. It is a manufacturing center in an agricultural region. Population, 17,479. **2.** A city of south-central Texas northeast of San Antonio. Food processing is important to its economy. Population, 23,420.

San Ma•ri•no (mə-rē′nō). A country in the Apennines near the Adriatic Sea. It is surrounded by Italy and is the world's smallest republic. According to tradition, it was founded in the fourth century A.D. and has succeeded, with a few brief interruptions, in maintaining its independence because of its relative inaccessibility. The city of **San Marino** is its capital. The country's population is 21,537; the city's, 4,628.

San Mar•tín (săn mär-tēn′, sän), **José de.** 1778–1850. Argentine revolutionary leader who played a major part in expelling the Spanish from Chile (1818) and Peru (1821).

San Ma•te•o (săn mə-tā′ō). A city of western California south-southeast of San Francisco. Named by a Spanish expedition in 1776, it was the center of a Mexican colony from 1822 to 1846. Population, 77,561.

San Mi•guel de Tu•cu•mán (săn′ mĭ-gĕl′ də to͞o′kə-män′, sän′ mē-gĕl′ dĕ to͞o′ko͞o-män′) or **Tucumán.** A city of northern Argentina at the foot of an eastern range of the Andes north-northwest of Córdoba. The country's independence was proclaimed here in July 1816. Population, 392,751.

San Ni•co•lás de los Gar•zas (sän nē′kô-läs′ dĕ lôs gär′säs). A city of northern Mexico, a suburb of Monterrey in a citrus-growing area. Population, 280,696.

san•nup (săn′əp) *n.* A married Native American man. [Of Massachusett origin.]

sann•ya•si (sŭn-yä′sē) or **sann•ya•sin** (-sĭn) *n. Hinduism.* A wandering mendicant and ascetic. [Hindi *sannyāsī,* from Sanskrit *saṃnyāsī,* from *saṃnyasyati,* he renounces : *sam,* together; see SANSKRIT + *ni,* down + *asyati,* he throws.]

S-A node (ĕs′ā′) *n.* The sinoatrial node.

San Pab•lo (păb′lō). A city of western California north-northwest of Oakland near **San Pablo Bay,** a northern arm of San Francisco Bay. Population, 19,750.

san•pa•ku (săn-pä′ko͞o) *n.* A condition in which the white of the eye is visible below the iris as well as on either side, believed by some to indicate poor health remedied by a macrobiotic diet. [Japanese : *san,* three + *haku,* white.]

San Pe•dro Channel (pē′drō). A strait of southern California between the mainland and Santa Catalina Island. **San Pedro Bay** is an inlet of the channel.

San Pe•dro Su•la (săn pē′drō so͞o′lə, sän pĕ′*th*rô so͞o′lä). A city of northwest Honduras northwest of Tegucigalpa. It is a commercial center. Population, 344,500.

San Ra•fael (săn rə-fĕl′). A city of western California north-northwest of San Francisco. It is a residential community with varied light industries. Population, 44,700.

San Re•mo (rā′mō, rē′-). A city of northwest Italy on the Ligurian Sea east of Monaco. It is a fashionable resort on the Italian Riviera. Population, 50,200.

San River (sän). A river, about 451 km (280 mi) long, of southeast Poland flowing generally north-northwest from the Carpathian Mountains to the Vistula River.

sans (sănz, säɴ) *prep.* Without. [Middle English, from Old French, blend of Latin *sine* and *absentiā,* in the absence of, ablative of *absentia,* absence, from *absēns, absent-,* present participle of *abesse,* to be away. See ABSENT.]

San Sal•va•dor¹ (săn săl′və-dôr′, sän säl′və-dôr′). Formerly **Wat•lings Island** (wät′lĭngz). An island of the central Bahamas in the West Indies. It is generally identified as the first landfall of Christopher Columbus (October 12, 1492).

San Sal•va•dor² (săn săl′və-dôr′, sän säl′vä-*th*ôr′). The capital and largest city of El Salvador, in the west-central part of the country. Founded in the 16th century, it became the national capital in 1841. Population, 445,100.

sans-cu•lotte (sănz′kyo͞o-lŏt′, -ko͞o-, säɴ-kü-lôt′) *n.* **1.** An extreme radical republican during the French Revolution. **2.** A revolutionary extremist. [French : *sans,* without + *culotte,* breeches.] **—sans′-cu•lot′tic** (-lŏt′ĭk), **sans′-cu•lot′tish** (-lŏt′ĭsh) *adj.* **—sans′-cu•lot′tism** *n.* **—sans′-cu•lot′tist** *n.*

San Se•bas•tián (săn sə-băs′chĭn, sän′ sĕ-väs-tyän′). A city of northern Spain on the Bay of Biscay near the French border east of Bilbao. It is a fashionable seaside resort and has fishing and chemical industries. Population, 178,906.

San•sei (sän′sā′, sän-sā′) *n., pl.* **Sansei** or **-seis.** The U.S.-born grandchild of Japanese immigrants to America. [Japanese : *san,* three + *sei,* generation.]

san•se•vie•ri•a (săn′sə-vîr′ē-ə, -vē-ĕr′-) *n.* Any of various tropical Old World plants of the genus *Sansevieria,* having thick, lance-shaped leaves and often cultivated as a houseplant. [New Latin *Sanseveria,* genus name, after Raimondo di Sangro (1710–1771), Prince of *San Seviero,* Italy.]

sansevieria

San•skrit (săn′skrĭt′) *n. Abbr.* **Skr., Skt.** An ancient Indic language that is the language of Hinduism and the Vedas and is the classical literary language of India. [Sanskrit *saṃskṛtam,* from neuter of *saṃskṛta-,* perfected, refined : *sam,* together; see **sem-¹** in Appendix + *karoti,* he makes; see **kʷer-** in Appendix.] **—San′skrit′ist** *n.*

San•skrit•ic (săn-skrĭt′ĭk) *n.* See **Indic.** **—San•skrit′ic** *adj.*

sans ser•if (săn sĕr′ĭf) *n. Printing.* A typeface without serifs. Also called *gothic.* **—sans-ser′if** *adj.*

San•ta An•a¹ (săn′tə ăn′ə). **1.** (*also* sän′tä ä′nä). A city of western El Salvador northwest of San Salvador. It is an important commercial, industrial, and processing center. Population, 132,200. **2.** A city of southern California east of Long Beach in the fertile valley of the **Santa Ana River,** about 145 km (90 mi) long. Santa Ana is a manufacturing and trade center for a large metropolitan area. Population, 203,713.

San•ta An•a² (săn′tə ăn′ə) *n.* A strong, dry, hot wind blowing from the desert regions of southern California toward the Pacific coast usually in winter. [After the *Santa Ana* Canyon of southern California.]

San•ta An•na or **San•ta An•a** (săn′tä ăn′ə, sän′tə ä′nä), **Antonio López de.** 1795?–1876. Mexican military and political leader who tried to crush the Texan revolt. Victorious at the Alamo (1836), he was soon after defeated and captured by the Texans. In the Mexican War he lost several major battles (1846–1847) to Gen. Zachary Taylor.

Antonio López de Santa Anna
Detail of a c. 1858 portrait by Paul L'Ouvrier

San•ta Bar•ba•ra (săn′tə bär′bər-ə, bär′brə). A city of southern California on the Santa Barbara Channel west-northwest of Los Angeles. Site of an early Spanish presidio and mission, it is a residential and resort community with aerospace and electronics industries. Population, 74,542.

Santa Barbara Islands. A chain of islands and islets off southern California in the Pacific Ocean. The islands are separated from the mainland by **Santa Barbara Channel** in the north and San Pedro Channel in the south.

Santa Cat•a•li•na Island (kăt′l-ē′nə) or **Catalina Island.** An island off southern California in the southern Santa Barbara Islands. Discovered in 1542, it has been a noted resort center since the 1920's.

Santa Cla•ra (klăr′ə, klâr′ə). **1.** (*also* sän′tä klä′rä). A city of central Cuba east-southeast of Havana. Founded in 1689, it is a processing center and rail junction. Population, 172,652. **2.** A city of western California northwest of San Jose. It is a residential community with diversified light industries. Population, 87,746.

San•ta Claus (săn′tə klôz′) *n.* The personification of the spirit of Christmas, usually represented as a jolly, fat old man with a white beard and a red suit, who brings gifts to good children on Christmas Eve. [Probably alteration of Dutch *Sinterklaas,* from Middle Dutch *Sinterclaes,* St. Nicholas : *sint,* saint (from Middle

Santa Claus
Illustration from "A Visit from St. Nicholas" by Clement Clarke Moore

Dutch, from Old French *saint;* see SAINT) + *heer,* lord; see MYNHEER + *claes* (short for *Niclaes,* Nicholas).]

San·ta Co·lo·ma de Gra·ma·net (săn′tə kə-lō′mə də grä′mə-nĕt′, sän′tä kô-lô′mä *thĕ* grä′mä-nĕt′). A city of northeast Spain, a suburb of Barcelona. Population, 140,274.

San·ta Cruz (săn′tə kro͞oz′). **1.** (*also* sän′tä kro͞os′). A city of central Bolivia northeast of Sucre. Founded c. 1560, it is a trade and processing center. Population, 441,717. **2.** A city of western California on Monterey Bay south-southwest of San Jose. It is a tourist center with varied processing and manufacturing industries. Population, 41,483.

Santa Cruz de Te·ne·ri·fe (săn′tə kro͞oz′ də tĕn′ə-rē′fā, -rēf′, -rīf′, sän′tä kro͞oth′ *thĕ* tĕn′ĕ-rē′fĕ). A city of the Canary Islands on the northeast coast of Tenerife Island. It is a popular resort. Population, 185,899.

San·ta Cruz Island (săn′tə kro͞oz′). An island off southern California in the northern Santa Barbara Islands.

Santa Cruz Islands. An island group of the southwest Pacific Ocean in the southeast Solomon Islands.

San·ta Fe (săn′tə fā′). **1.** (*also* sän′tä fĕ′). A city of northeast Argentina on the Salado River northwest of Buenos Aires. Founded in 1573, it is a port with various light industries. Population, 291,966. **2.** The capital of New Mexico, in the north-central part of the state northeast of Albuquerque. The Spanish established a settlement here c. 1609 on the site of ancient Native American ruins and developed it as a trade center over the next 200 years. Occupied by U.S. forces in 1846, it became territorial capital in 1851 and state capital in 1912. Population, 48,899.

Santa Fe Trail. A trade route to the southwest United States extending about 1,287 km (800 mi) westward from Independence, Missouri, to Santa Fe, New Mexico. First traversed in 1821, it was the primary wagon and stage route to the Southwest until the coming of the railroad in 1880.

Santa Ger·tru·dis (gər-tro͞o′dĭs) *n., pl.* **Santa Gertrudis.** Any of a breed of large beef cattle that are highly resistant to heat and insects, developed in the United States by crossing Brahmans and shorthorns. [After the *Santa Gertrudis* section of the King Ranch in Kingsville, Texas.]

San·ta Is·a·bel (săn′tə ĭz′ə-bĕl′, sän′tä ē-sä-bĕl′). See **Malabo.**

san·ta·lol (săn′tə-lôl′, -lōl′, -lŏl′) *n.* A colorless liquid, $C_{15}H_{24}O$, obtained from sandalwood and used in perfumes. [New Latin *Santalum,* sandalwood genus (from Medieval Latin *santalum,* sandalwood; see SANDAL[2]) + –OL(E).]

San·ta Ma·ri·a (săn′tə mə-rē′ə). **1.** (*also* sän′tä mä-rē′ä). A city of southern Brazil west of Pôrto Alegre. It is a rail junction and processing center. Population, 151,156. **2.** A city of southern California northwest of Santa Barbara. Nearby Vandenberg Air Force Base is important to its economy. Population, 39,685.

San·ta Mar·ta (săn′tə mär′tə, sän′tä mär′tä). A city of northern Colombia on the Caribbean Sea east-northeast of Barranquilla. Founded in 1525, it is the oldest city in the country and an important processing and shipping center. Population, 193,160.

San·ta Mon·i·ca (săn′tə mŏn′ĭ-kə). A city of southern California on the Pacific Ocean west of Los Angeles. It is a residential community with varied industries. Population, 88,314.

San·tan·der (sän′tän-dĕr′). A city of northern Spain on the Bay of Biscay west-northwest of Bilbao. It was a major port after the discovery of America and is now a resort and industrial center. Population, 187,057.

Santa Pau·la (pô′lə). A city of southern California east of Santa Barbara. Food processing is important to its economy. Population, 20,552.

San·ta·rém (săn′tə-rĕm′, säɴ′tä-rāɴ′). A city of northern Brazil on the Amazon River east of Manaus. Founded in 1661, it is a major river port. Population, 102,181.

Santa Ro·sa (rō′zə). A city of western California north-northwest of San Francisco. Luther Burbank lived here, and his gardens are preserved as a memorial. Population, 83,205.

Santa Rosa Island. An island of southern California in the northwest Santa Barbara Islands separated from the mainland by the Santa Barbara Channel.

San·ta·ya·na (săn′tē-ă′nə, sän′tä-yä′nä), **George.** 1863–1952. Spanish-born American philosopher and writer primarily known for his theories of aesthetics, morality, and the spiritual life. In addition to his philosophical works, such as the four-volume *Realms of Being* (1927–1940), he wrote poetry and a novel, *The Last Puritan* (1935).

San·tee[1] (săn-tē′) *n., pl.* **Santee** or **-tees. 1.** The eastern branch of the Sioux, comprising the Mdewakanton, Sisseton, Wahpekute, and Wahpeton peoples, with present-day populations in Nebraska, Minnesota, the Dakotas, and Canada. **2.** A member of a people of this division. Also called *Eastern Sioux, Santee Dakota, Santee Sioux.*

San·tee[2] (săn-tē′). A community of southern California, a suburb of San Diego. Population, 40,313.

Santee Dakota *n.* See **Santee[1].**

Santee River. A river, about 230 km (143 mi) long, of central South Carolina flowing southeast to the Atlantic Ocean.

Santee Sioux *n.* See **Santee[1].**

San·ti·a·go (săn′tē-ä′gō, sän′-). **1.** The capital and largest city of Chile, in the central part of the country east-southeast of Valparaiso. On a plain in the foothills of the Andes, it was founded in 1541. Population, 425,924. **2.** Also **Santiago de los Ca·bal·le·ros** (dā′ lôs kä′bəl-yĕr′ōz, *thĕ* lôs kä′vä-yĕ′rôs). A city of northern Dominican Republic northwest of Santo Domingo. Settled c. 1500, it is a transportation hub in a fertile agricultural region. Population, 278,638. **3.** Also **Santiago de Com·pos·te·la** (də kŏm′pə-stĕl′ə, *thĕ* kôm′pôs-tĕ′lä). A city of northwest Spain south-southwest of La Coruña. The city grew around a shrine housing the reputed tomb of Saint James the Great and has long been a pilgrimage center. Population, 62,300.

Santiago de Cu·ba (də kyo͞o′bə, *thĕ* ko͞o′vä). A city of southeast Cuba on an inlet of the Caribbean Sea. Founded in 1514, it was a haven for buccaneers and smugglers during its early history. Population, 349,444.

Santiago del Es·te·ro (dĕl ə-stĕr′ō, *thĕl* ĕ-stĕ′rô). A city of north-central Argentina north of Córdoba. Originally founded in 1553, it is the oldest continuous settlement in the country. Population, 148,758.

san·tir (săn′tîr′) *n. Music.* An instrument of Persia that closely resembles a dulcimer. [Arabic *sanṭīr,* from Greek *psaltērion,* psaltery. See PSALTERY.]

San·to An·dré (säɴ′to͞o äɴ-drā′). A city of southern Brazil, an industrial suburb of São Paulo. Population, 549,546.

San·to Do·min·go (săn′tō də-mĭng′gō, sän′tô dô-). Formerly (1936–1961) **Ci·u·dad Tru·jil·lo** (sē′o͞o-däd′ tro͞o-hē′yō, syo͞o-*thäth*′). The capital and largest city of the Dominican Republic, in the southeast part of the island of Hispaniola on the Caribbean Sea. Founded in 1496 by Christopher Columbus's brother Bartholomew, it is the oldest continuously inhabited settlement in the Western Hemisphere. The name has also been used for a Spanish colony on Hispaniola and for the Dominican Republic. Population, 1,313,172.

san·ton·i·ca (săn-tŏn′ĭ-kə) *n.* **1.** A perennial or shrubby Eurasian plant *(Artemisia maritima)* having aromatic, bipinnately dissected leaves and numerous flower heads that yield santonin. **2.** The dried unopened flower heads of this plant. [New Latin, from Latin *(herba) santonica,* from feminine of *santonicus,* of the Santoni, a people of Aquitania.]

san·to·nin (săn′tə-nĭn) *n.* A colorless crystalline compound, $C_{15}H_{18}O_3$, obtained from species of wormwood, especially santonica, and used as an anthelmintic. [SANTON(ICA) + –IN.]

San·to·rin (săn′tə-rēn′). See **Thíra.**

San·tos (săn′təs, säɴ′to͞os). A city of southeast Brazil on an offshore island in the Atlantic Ocean southeast of São Paulo. Settled in the 1540's, it is a major port, especially for coffee. Population, 410,933.

São Ber·nar·do do Cam·po (souɴ bĕr-när′do͞o do͞o käɴ′po͞o). A city of southeast Brazil, an industrial suburb of São Paulo. Population, 381,097.

São Cae·ta·no do Sul (kī-tä′no͞o do͞o so͞ol′). A city of southeast Brazil, a suburb of São Paulo. Population, 163,082.

São Fran·cis·co (frən-sĭs′kō, fräɴ-sēs′ko͞o). A river of eastern Brazil flowing about 2,896 km (1,800 mi) generally north-northeast and east to the Atlantic Ocean.

São Gon·ça·lo (gôɴ-säl′o͞o). A city of southeast Brazil, an industrial suburb on Guanabara Bay opposite Rio de Janeiro. Population, 221,579.

São João de Me·ri·ti (zhwouɴ′ də mə-rē′tē, dĭ mĭ-rĭ-tē′). A city of southeast Brazil, a residential suburb of Rio de Janeiro. Population, 210,574.

São Jo·sé do Ri·o Prêt·o (zho͞o-zā′ do͞o rē′o͞o prĕt′o͞o). A city of southeast Brazil, an industrial suburb of São Paulo. Population, 172,127.

São José dos Cam·pos (do͞os käɴ′po͞os). A city of southeast Brazil east-northeast of São Paulo. It is a major center of Brazil's aircraft industry. Population, 268,034.

São Lu·is (lo͞o-ēs′). A city of northeast Brazil on an offshore island in the Atlantic Ocean east-southeast of Belém. It was founded by the French in 1612 and named in honor of Louis XIII. Population, 182,258.

São Mi·guel (mē-gĕl′). An island of the eastern Azores in the Atlantic Ocean. It is the largest island in the archipelago and a popular tourist center.

Saône (sōn). A river, about 431 km (268 mi) long, rising in the Vosges Mountains of northeast France and flowing generally south-southwest to the Rhone River at Lyons.

São Pau·lo (pou′lō, -lo͞o). A city of southeast Brazil west-southwest of Rio de Janeiro. Founded by Jesuits in 1554, it developed rapidly as an industrial and commercial center after the 1880's and is now the largest city in South America. Population, 8,493,226.

São Tia·go (tē-ä′go͞o, tyä′go͞o). An island of southern Cape Verde in the northern Atlantic Ocean. It is the largest island in the group and the site of the capital, Praia.

São To·mé (tə-mā′, to͞o-mĕ′). An island of São Tomé and Príncipe in the Gulf of Guinea off western Africa. The city of **São Tomé,** the capital of the country, is on the southeast coast. Its population is 17,380.

São Tomé and Prín·ci·pe (prĭn′sə-pə, prēɴ′sē-pə). An island country in the Gulf of Guinea off western Africa. It was an overseas province of Portugal from the early 16th century until it achieved independence in 1975. São Tomé is the capital. Population, 73,631.

São Vi·cen·te (vē-sĕɴ′tə). A city of southeast Brazil on an

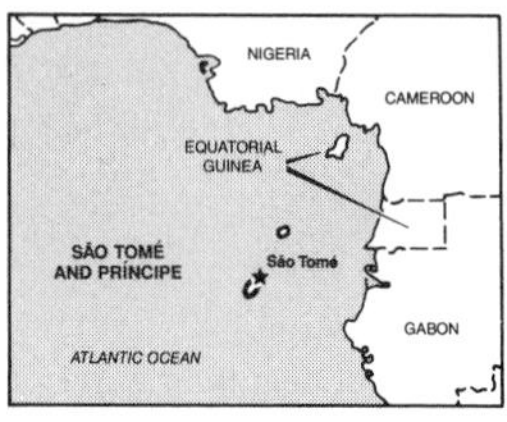

São Tomé and Príncipe

offshore island in the Atlantic Ocean west of Santos. Founded in 1532, it was sacked by English pirates in 1591. Population, 192,858.

sap¹ (săp) *n.* **1.a.** The watery fluid that circulates through a plant, carrying food and other substances to the various tissues. **b.** The fluid contents of a plant cell vacuole. **2.** An essential bodily fluid. **3.** Health and energy; vitality. **4.** *Slang.* A gullible person; a dupe. **5.** A leather-covered hand weapon; a blackjack. **—sap** *tr.v.* **sapped, sap·ping, saps. 1.** To drain of sap. **2.** To hit or knock out with a sap. [Middle English, from Old English *sæp.*]

sap² (săp) *n.* A covered trench or tunnel dug to a point within an enemy position. **—sap** *v.* **sapped, sap·ping, saps.** *—tr.* **1.** To undermine the foundations of (a fortification). **2.** To deplete or weaken gradually; devitalize. *—intr.* To dig a sap. [Obsolete French *sappe* or Italian *zappa,* hoe, from Old French and Old Italian, both from Late Latin *sappa.*]

s.ap. *abbr.* Apothecaries' scruple.

sap·a·jou (săp′ə-jo͞o) *n.* See **capuchin** (sense 3). [French.]

Sa·phar (sə-fär′) *n.* Variant of **Safar.**

sap·head (săp′hĕd′) *n. Slang.* A person regarded as gullible or foolish. **—sap′head′ed** *adj.*

sa·phe·na (sə-fē′nə) *n., pl.* **-nae** (-nē′). Either of two main superficial veins of the leg, one larger than the other, that begin at the foot. [Middle English, from Medieval Latin *saphēna,* from Arabic *ṣāfin.*] **—sa·phe′nous** *adj.*

sap·id (săp′ĭd) *adj.* **1.a.** Perceptible to the sense of taste; having flavor. **b.** Having a strong, pleasant flavor; savory. **2.** Pleasing to the mind; engaging. [Latin *sapidus,* from *sapere,* to taste. See **sep-** in Appendix.] **—sa·pid′i·ty** (să-pĭd′ĭ-tē, sə-) *n.*

sa·pi·ens (sā′pē-ənz, -ĕnz) *adj.* Of, relating to, or characteristic of *Homo sapiens.* **—sapiens** *n.* An early or prehistoric form of *Homo sapiens.* [Latin *sapiēns, sapient-,* present participle of *sapere,* to taste, be wise. See SAPIENT.]

sa·pi·ent (sā′pē-ənt) *adj.* Having great wisdom and discernment. [Middle English, from Old French, from Latin *sapiēns, sapient-,* present participle of *sapere,* to taste, be wise. See **sep-** in Appendix.] **—sa′pi·ence** *n.* **—sa′pi·ent·ly** *adv.*

Sa·pir (sə-pîr′), **Edward.** 1884–1939. American linguist and anthropologist noted for his studies of Native American languages and his theories on the ways in which language shapes our perceptions.

sap·less (săp′lĭs) *adj.* **1.** Devoid of sap; dry. **2.** Lacking spirit or energy. **—sap′less·ness** *n.*

sap·ling (săp′lĭng) *n.* **1.** A young tree. **2.** A youth.

sap·o·dil·la (săp′ə-dĭl′ə, -dē′yə) *n.* **1.** An evergreen tree *(Manilkara zapota)* of Mexico and Central America, having latex that yields chicle and edible fruit with sweet yellow-brown flesh. **2.** The fruit of this plant. Also called *naseberry.* [Spanish *zapotillo,* diminutive of *zapote,* sapodilla fruit, from Nahuatl *tzapotl.*]

sap·o·na·ceous (săp′ə-nā′shəs) *adj.* Having the qualities of soap. [Latin *sāpō, sāpōn-,* hair dye; see SAPONIN + –ACEOUS.] **—sap′o·na′ceous·ness** *n.*

sap·o·na·ted (săp′ə-nā′tĭd) *adj.* Combined or treated with a soap. [From Latin *sāpō, sāpōn-,* hair dye. See SAPONIN.]

sa·pon·i·fi·ca·tion (sə-pŏn′ə-fĭ-kā′shən) *n.* A reaction in which an ester is heated with an alkali, such as sodium hydroxide, producing a free alcohol and an acid salt, especially alkaline hydrolysis of a fat or an oil to make soap.

sa·pon·i·fy (sə-pŏn′ə-fī′) *v.* **-fied, -fy·ing, -fies.** *—tr.* **1.** To convert (an ester) by saponification. **2.** To convert (a fat or an oil) into soap. *—intr.* To undergo saponification. [French *saponifier,* from Latin *sāpō, sāpōn-,* hair dye. See SAPONIN.] **—sa·pon′i·fi′a·ble** *adj.* **—sa·pon′i·fi′er** *n.*

sap·o·nin (săp′ə-nĭn, sə-pō′-) *n.* Any of various plant glucosides that form soapy lathers when mixed and agitated with water, used in detergents, foaming agents, and emulsifiers. [From Latin *sāpō, sāpōn-,* hair dye (of Germanic origin).]

sap·o·nite (săp′ə-nīt′) *n.* A clay mineral that is a hydrous silicate of aluminum and magnesium and occurs in soft amorphous masses in the cavities of certain rocks. [Latin *sāpō, sāpōn-,* hair dye; see SAPONIN + –ITE¹.]

sa·por (sā′pər, -pôr′) *n.* A quality perceptible to the sense of taste; flavor. [Middle English, from Latin, from *sapere,* to taste. See **sep-** in Appendix.] **—sa′po·rif′ic** (sā′pə-rĭf′ĭk, săp′ə-), **sa′po·rous** (sā′pər-əs, săp′ər-) *adj.*

sa·po·te (sə-pō′tē, -tā) or **sa·po·ta** (-tə) *n.* **1.** A Mexican and Central American tree *(Poulteria sapota)* having edible, brown, oval fruit with very sweet reddish flesh. **2.** The fruit of this tree. Also called *marmalade plum.* [Spanish *zapota,* from Nahuatl *tzapotl.*]

sap·pan·wood (sə-păn′wo͝od′, săp′ăn-, -ən-) *n.* **1.** A tree *(Caesalpina sappan)* of tropical Asia, having wood that yields a red dye. **2.** The wood of this tree. [Malay *sapang* + WOOD¹.]

sap·per (săp′ər) *n.* **1.** A military engineer who specializes in sapping and other field fortification activities. **2.** A military engineer who lays, detects, and disarms mines. [From SAP².]

Sap·phic (săf′ĭk) *adj.* **1.** Of or relating to the Greek poet Sappho. **2.a.** Of, relating to, or being an Aeolic verse of 11 syllables, consisting of a first part of 4 syllables, a central choriamb, and a final part of 3 syllables. **b.** Relating to or being a stanza of three such verses followed by a verse consisting of a dactyl followed by a spondee or trochee. **c.** Relating to or being an ode made up of such stanzas. **d.** Of, relating to, or being a verse, stanza, or poem in accentual meter composed in imitation of Sapphic quantitative verse. **3.** Often **sapphic.** Of or relating to lesbianism. **—Sapphic** *n.* A Sapphic meter, verse, stanza, or ode.

sap·phire (săf′īr′) *n.* **1.** A clear, hard variety of corundum used as a gemstone that is usually blue but may be any color except red. **2.** A corundum gem. **3.** *Color.* The blue color of a gem sapphire. **—sapphire** *adj.* **1.** Made of or resembling a gem sapphire. **2.** *Color.* Having the color of a blue sapphire. [Middle English *saphir,* from Old French *safir,* from Latin *sapphīrus,* from Greek *sappheiros,* from Hebrew *sappîr,* a precious stone.]

sap·phi·rine (săf′ə-rīn′, -rēn′, sə-fīr′ĭn) *adj.* Of or resembling sapphire. **—sapphirine** *n.* A rare light blue or green aluminum-magnesium silicate mineral.

Sap·pho (săf′ō). fl. c. 600 B.C. Greek lyric poet considered one of the greatest poets of antiquity although only fragments of her romantic lyrics survive.

Sap·po·ro (sə-pôr′ō, -pōr′ō). A city of southwest Hokkaido, Japan, near the head of Ishikari Bay. A processing and commercial center, it was the site of the 1972 Winter Olympics. Population, 1,542,979.

sap·py (săp′ē) *adj.* **-pi·er, -pi·est. 1.** Full of sap; juicy. **2.** *Slang.* Excessively sentimental; mawkish. **3.** *Slang.* Silly or foolish. **—sap′pi·ly** *adv.* **—sap′pi·ness** *n.*

sapr– *pref.* Variant of **sapro–.**

sa·pre·mi·a also **sa·prae·mi·a** (sə-prē′mē-ə) *n.* Blood poisoning resulting from the absorption of the products of putrefaction. **—sa·pre′mic** *adj.*

sapro– or **sapr–** *pref.* **1.** Decay; putrefaction; decomposition: *saprogenic.* **2.** Dead or decaying organic material: *saprophyte.* [Greek, from *sapros,* rotten.]

sap·robe (săp′rōb′) *n.* An organism that derives its nourishment from nonliving or decaying organic matter. [SAPRO– + Greek *bios,* life; see **gʷei-** in Appendix.] **—sap·ro′bi·al** (să-prō′bē-əl), **sap·ro′bic** (-bĭk) *adj.* **—sa·pro′bi·cal·ly** *adv.*

sap·ro·bi·ol·o·gy (săp′rō-bī-ŏl′ə-jē) *n.* The study of decaying organisms or environments, especially as a branch of ecology. **—sap′ro·bi′o·log′i·cal** (-bī′ə-lŏj′ĭ-kəl) *adj.* **—sap′ro·bi·ol′o·gist** *n.*

sap·ro·gen·ic (săp′rə-jĕn′ĭk) also **sa·prog·e·nous** (sə-prŏj′ə-nəs) *adj.* Of, producing, or resulting from putrefaction. **—sap′ro·ge·nic′i·ty** (-jə-nĭs′ĭ-tē) *n.*

sap·ro·lite (săp′rə-līt′) *n.* Soft, partially decomposed rock rich in clay and remaining in its original place.

sap·ro·pel (săp′rə-pĕl′) *n.* **1.** A mud rich in organic matter formed at the bottom of a body of water. **2.** A fluid slime found in swamps as a product of putrefaction. [SAPRO– + Greek *pēlos,* mud.] **—sap′ro·pel′ic** (-pĕl′ĭk, -pē′lĭk) *adj.*

sa·proph·a·gous (să-prŏf′ə-gəs) *adj.* Feeding on decaying organic matter.

sap·ro·phyte (săp′rə-fīt′) *n.* An organism, especially a fungus or bacterium, that grows on and derives its nourishment from dead or decaying organic matter. **—sap′ro·phyt′ic** (-fĭt′ĭk) *adj.* **—sap′ro·phyt′i·cal·ly** *adv.*

sap·ro·zo·ic (săp′rə-zō′ĭk) *adj.* **1.** Obtaining nourishment by absorption of dissolved organic and inorganic materials, as in protozoans and some fungi. **2.** Feeding on dead or decaying animal matter.

sap·sa·go (săp-sā′gō, săp′sə-gō′) *n., pl.* **-gos.** A hard green cheese made from skim-milk curd, colored and flavored with sweet clover. [Alteration of German *Schabzieger* : *schaben,* to scrape (from Middle High German, from Old High German *skaban*) + *Zieger,* whey, whey cheese (from Middle High German *ziger,* probably of Celtic origin).]

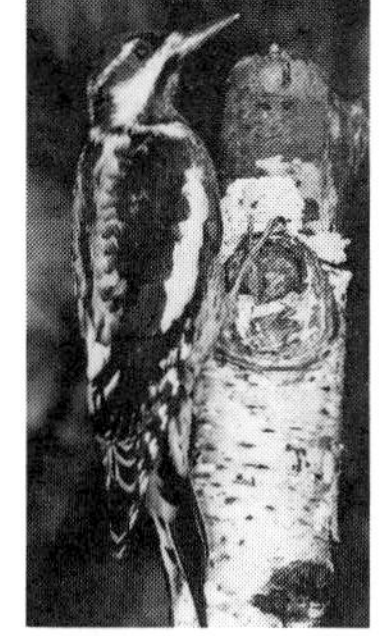
sapsucker

sap·suck·er (săp′sŭk′ər) *n.* Any of various small American woodpeckers of the genus *Sphyrapicus* that drill holes in certain trees to drink the sap and eat insects in them, especially *S. varius,* the common species in the eastern United States, and *S. thyrsoides,* found in the mountain regions of the western United States.

sap·wood (săp′wo͝od′) *n.* Newly formed outer wood that lies just inside the cambium of a tree trunk and is usually lighter in color and more active in water conduction than the heartwood.

Saq·qa·ra also **Sak·ka·ra** (sə-kär′ə). A village of northern Egypt near Cairo. It is the site of the oldest Egyptian pyramids, including the Step Pyramid built by Zoser during the III Dynasty (c. 2980–2900 B.C.).

SAR *abbr.* Sons of the American Revolution.

sar·a·band also **sar·a·bande** (săr′ə-bănd′) *n.* **1.** A stately court dance of the 17th and 18th centuries, in slow triple time. **2.** The music for this dance. [French *sarabande,* from Spanish *zarabanda.*]

Sar·a·cen (săr′ə-sən) *n.* **1.** A member of a pre-Islamic nomadic people of the Syrian-Arabian deserts. **2.** An Arab. **3.** A Moslem, especially of the time of the Crusades. [Middle English, from Old English, from Late Latin *Saracēnus,* from Late Greek *Sarakēnos,* ultimately from Arabic *šarq,* east.] **—Sar′a·cen′ic** (-sĕn′ĭk) *adj.*

Sar·a·gos·sa (săr′ə-gŏs′ə) also **Za·ra·go·za** (zăr′ə-gō′zə, thä′rä-gô′thä). A city of northeast Spain on the Ebro River northeast of Madrid. An important city under Roman rule, it was held by the Moors from 713 until 1118. Population, 601,235.

ă pat	oi boy
ā pay	ou out
âr care	o͝o took
ä father	o͞o boot
ĕ pet	ŭ cut
ē be	ûr urge
ĭ pit	th thin
ī pie	*th* this
îr pier	hw which
ŏ pot	zh vision
ō toe	ə about, item
ô paw	♦ regionalism

Stress marks: **′** (primary); ′ (secondary), as in **dictionary** (dĭk′shə-nĕr′ē)

sarcophagus
c. A.D. 160–165 Roman marble sarcophagus

sari

Sar·ah (sâr′ə). In the Old Testament, the wife of Abraham and mother of Isaac.

Sa·ra·je·vo (săr′ə-yā′vō, sär′ə-yĕ-vô′). A city of central Yugoslavia southwest of Belgrade. The assassination of Archduke Francis Ferdinand and his wife on June 28, 1914, triggered the outbreak of World War I. Population, 374,500.

sa·ran (sə-răn′) *n.* Any of various thermoplastic resins derived from vinyl compounds and used to make packaging films, fittings, and bristles and as a fiber in various heavy fabrics. [From *Saran,* a former U.S. trademark.]

Sar·a·nac Lakes (săr′ə-năk′). A group of three lakes in the Adirondack Mountains of northeast New York. They are linked by the **Saranac River,** which flows about 161 km (100 mi) generally northeast to Lake Champlain.

Sa·ransk (sə-ränsk′). A city of western Russia west of Ulyanovsk. Founded as a fort in the 1600's, it is a manufacturing and processing center. Population, 307,000.

sa·ra·pe (sə-rä′pē, -răp′ē) *n.* Variant of **serape.**

Sar·a·so·ta (săr′ə-sō′tə). A city of west-central Florida south of Tampa Bay on **Sarasota Bay,** an inlet of the Gulf of Mexico. A yachting and fishing resort with varied industries, Sarasota is the site of the Circus Hall of Fame. Population, 48,868.

Sar·a·to·ga (săr′ə-tō′gə). **1.** A city of western California southwest of San Jose. It is a residential community in a wine-producing region. Population, 29,261. **2.** A former village of eastern New York on the west bank of the Hudson River east of Saratoga Springs. The defeat and surrender of Gen. John Burgoyne's British army on October 17, 1777, marked the end of the hard-fought Saratoga Campaign (June–October) and was a major turning point in the American Revolution.

Saratoga Springs. A city of eastern New York in the foothills of the Adirondack Mountains north of Albany. The city's mineral springs led to its development as a health resort in the late 18th century. It has also been an important horseracing and sporting center since the 1860's. Population, 23,906.

Saratoga trunk *n.* A large traveling trunk having a rounded top. [After SARATOGA (SPRINGS).]

Sa·ra·tov (sə-rä′təf). A city of southwest Russia on the Volga River north-northeast of Volgorad. Founded on a nearby site in 1590, it is a major industrial center. Population, 899,000.

Sa·ra·wak (sə-rä′wäk, -wăk, -wä). A region of Malaysia on northwest Borneo. A British protectorate after 1888 and a crown colony after 1946, it joined Malaysia in 1963.

sarc– *pref.* Variant of **sarco–.**

sar·casm (sär′kăz′əm) *n.* **1.** A cutting, often ironic remark intended to wound. **2.** A form of wit that is marked by the use of sarcastic language and is intended to make its victim the butt of contempt or ridicule. **3.** The use of sarcasm. See Synonyms at **wit**[1]. [Late Latin *sarcasmus,* from Greek *sarkasmos,* from *sarkazein,* to bite the lips in rage, from *sarx, sark-,* flesh.]

sar·cas·tic (sär-kăs′tĭk) *adj.* **1.** Expressing or marked by sarcasm. **2.** Given to using sarcasm. [SARC(ASM) + *-astic,* as in ENTHUSIASTIC.] **—sar·cas′ti·cal·ly** *adv.*

SYNONYMS: *sarcastic, ironic, caustic, satirical, sardonic.* These adjectives mean having or marked by a feeling of bitterness and a biting or cutting quality. *Sarcastic* suggests sharp taunting and ridicule that wounds: *"a deserved reputation for sarcastic, acerbic and uninhibited polemics"* (Burke Marshall). *Ironic* implies a subtler form of mockery in which an intended meaning is conveyed obliquely: *"a man of eccentric charm, ironic humor, and—above all—profound literary genius"* (Jonathan Kirsch). *Caustic* means corrosive and bitingly trenchant: *"The caustic jokes . . . deal with such diverse matters as political assassination, talk-show hosts, medical ethics"* (Frank Rich). *Satirical* implies the exposure of something, especially vice or folly, to ridicule: *"on the surface a satirical look at commercial radio, but also a study of the misuse of telecommunications"* (Richard Harrington). *Sardonic* is associated with scorn, derision, mockery, and often cynicism: *"He was proud, sardonic, harsh to inferiority of every description"* (Charlotte Brontë).

sarce·net (särs′nĭt) *n.* A fine, soft silk cloth. [Middle English *sarsenet,* from Anglo-Norman *sarzinett,* perhaps from Old French *Saracin,* Saracen, from Late Latin *Saracēnus.* See SARACEN.]

sarco– or **sarc–** *pref.* **1.** Flesh: *sarcophagic.* **2.** Striated muscle: *sarcolemma.* [Greek *sarko-,* from *sarx, sark-,* flesh.]

sar·co·din·i·an (sär′kə-dĭn′ē-ən) *adj.* Of or belonging to the Sarcodina, a superclass of protozoans that includes the rhizopods. **—sarcodinian** *n.* A protozoan belonging to the superclass Sarcodina. [New Latin *Sarcodīna,* superclass name, from Greek *sarkōdēs,* fleshy, from *sarx, sark-,* flesh.]

sar·coid (sär′koid′) *adj.* Relating to or resembling flesh. **—sarcoid** *n.* **1.** See **sarcoidosis. 2.** A tumor resembling a sarcoma.

sar·coid·o·sis (sär′koi-dō′sĭs) *n., pl.* **-ses** (-sēz). A disease of unknown origin characterized by the formation of granulomatous lesions that appear especially in the liver, lungs, skin, and lymph nodes. Also called *sarcoid.*

sar·co·lac·tic acid (sär′kə-lăk′tĭk) *n.* An isomeric form of lactic acid produced by muscle tissue during the anaerobic metabolism of glucose.

sar·co·lem·ma (sär′kə-lĕm′ə) *n.* A thin membrane enclosing a striated muscle fiber. [SARCO– + Greek *lemma,* husk; see LEMMA[2].] **—sar′co·lem′mal** *adj.*

sar·co·ma (sär-kō′mə) *n., pl.* **-mas** also **-ma·ta** (-mə-tə). A malignant tumor arising from connective tissues. [New Latin, from Greek *sarkōma, sarkōmat-,* fleshy excrescence, from *sarkoun,* to produce flesh, from *sarx, sark-,* flesh.] **—sar·co′ma·toid′** (-mə-toid′), **sar·co′ma·tous** (-təs) *adj.*

sar·co·ma·to·sis (sär-kō′mə-tō′sĭs) *n.* Formation of numerous sarcomas in various parts of the body.

sar·co·mere (sär′kə-mîr′) *n.* One of the segments into which a fibril of striated muscle is divided.

sar·coph·a·gi (sär-kŏf′ə-jī′) *n.* A plural of **sarcophagus.**

sar·co·phag·ic (sär′kə-făj′ĭk, -fā′jĭk) also **sar·coph·a·gous** (sär-kŏf′ə-gəs) *adj.* Flesh-eating; carnivorous.

sar·coph·a·gus (sär-kŏf′ə-gəs) *n., pl.* **-gi** (-jī′) or **-gus·es.** A stone coffin, often inscribed or decorated with sculpture. [Latin, from Greek *sarkophagos,* coffin, from *(lithos) sarkophagos,* limestone that consumed the flesh of corpses laid in it : *sarx, sark-,* flesh + *-phagos,* -phagous.]

WORD HISTORY: A gruesome name befits a gruesome thing, as in the case of *sarcophagus,* our term for a stone coffin, often a decorated one, that is located above ground. The word comes to us from Latin and Greek, having been derived in Greek from *sarx,* "flesh," and *phagein,* "to eat." The Greek word *sarkophagos* meant "eating flesh," and in the phrase *lithos* ("stone") *sarcophagos* denoted a limestone that was thought to decompose the flesh of corpses placed in it. The Greek term used by itself as a noun then came to mean "coffin." The term was carried over into Latin, where *sarcophagus* was used in the phrase *lapis* ("stone") *sarcophagus,* referring to the same stone as in Greek. *Sarcophagus* used as a noun in Latin meant "coffin of any material." This Latin word was borrowed into English, first being recorded in 1601 with reference to the flesh-consuming stone and then in 1705 with reference to a stone coffin.

sar·co·plasm (sär′kə-plăz′əm) *n.* The cytoplasm of a striated muscle fiber. **—sar′co·plas·mat′ic** (-plăz-măt′ĭk), **sar′co·plas′mic** (-mĭk) *adj.*

sarcoplasmic reticulum *n.* The form of endoplasmic reticulum found in striated muscle fibers.

sar·cop·tic mange (sär-kŏp′tĭk) *n.* Mange caused by the mite *Sarcoptes scabiei.* [From New Latin *Sarcoptes,* genus name : SARCO– + Greek *koptein,* to cut.]

sar·co·some (sär′kə-sōm′) *n.* A large specialized mitochondrion found in striated muscle. **—sar′co·so′mal** *adj.*

sar·co·style (sär′kə-stīl′) *n.* See **myofibril.**

sar·cous (sär′kəs) *adj.* Of, relating to, or consisting of flesh or muscle tissue.

sard (särd) *n.* A clear or translucent, deep orange-red to brownish-red variety of chalcedony. Also called *sardius.* [Middle English *sarde,* from Old French, from Latin *sarda,* perhaps from *Sardīs,* Sardis, an ancient city of western Asia Minor.]

sar·dine (sär-dēn′) *n.* **1.** Any of various small or half-grown edible herrings or related fishes of the family Clupeidae, frequently canned in oil or water, especially the pilchard of European waters. **2.** Any of numerous small, silvery, edible freshwater or marine fishes unrelated to the sardine. **—sardine** *tr.v.* **-dined, -din·ing, -dines.** *Slang.* To pack tightly; cram: *"The bars are sardined with hungry hopefuls"* (Gael Greene). [Middle English *sardin,* from Old French *sardine,* from Latin *sardīna,* from *sarda,* a kind of fish, ultimately from Greek *Sardō,* Sardinia.]

Sar·din·i·a (sär-dĭn′ē-ə, -dĭn′yə). An island of Italy in the Mediterranean Sea south of Corsica. Settled by Phoenicians, Greeks, and Carthaginians before the sixth century B.C., the island was taken by Rome in 238 B.C. and later fell to the Vandals (fifth century A.D.) and the Byzantines (early sixth century). Numerous European powers controlled the island before 1720, when it passed to the House of Savoy and became the nucleus of the Kingdom of Sardinia. Victor Emmanuel II of Sardinia became the first king of Italy in 1861.

Sar·din·i·an (sär-dĭn′ē-ən, -yən) *adj.* Of or relating to Sardinia or its people, language, or culture. **—Sardinian** *n.* **1.** A native or inhabitant of Sardinia. **2.** The Romance language of the Sardinians.

Sar·dis (sär′dĭs). An ancient city of western Asia Minor northeast of modern-day Izmir, Turkey. As the capital of Lydia it was the political and cultural center of Asia Minor from 650 to c. 550 B.C. and remained an important city during Roman and Byzantine times. Sardis was destroyed by Tamerlane in 1402.

sar·di·us (sär′dē-əs) *n.* See **sard.** [Middle English, from Old English, from Latin, from *sarda.* See SARD.]

sar·don·ic (sär-dŏn′ĭk) *adj.* Scornfully or cynically mocking. See Synonyms at **sarcastic.** [French *sardonique,* from Greek *sardonios,* alteration of *sardanios.*] **—sar·don′i·cal·ly** *adv.* **—sar·don′i·cism** (-ĭ-sĭz′əm) *n.*

sar·don·yx (sär-dŏn′ĭks, sär′dn-ĭks′) *n.* An onyx with alternating brown and white bands of sard and other minerals. [Middle English *sardonix,* probably from Latin *sardonyx,* from Greek *sardonux* : *sardion,* sard; see SARD + *onux,* onyx, nail; see **nogh-** in Appendix.]

Sar·dou (sär-do͞o′), **Victorien.** 1831–1908. French playwright known especially for his light comedies, including *A Scrap of Paper* (1860) and *Peril* (1861).

Sa·re·ma (sär′ə-mä′). See **Saaremaa.**

sar·gas·so (sär-găs′ō) *n., pl.* **-sos.** See **gulfweed.** [Portuguese *sargaço.*]

Sar·gas·so Sea (sär-găs′ō). A part of the northern Atlantic Ocean between the West Indies and the Azores. The relatively calm sea is noted for the abundance of gulfweed floating on its surface.

sar·gas·sum (sär-găs′əm) *n.* See **gulfweed.** [New Latin *Sargassum,* genus name, from SARGASSO.]

sargassum fish *n.* A frogfish *(Histrio histrio)* found commonly among the gulfweed of the Atlantic and western Pacific.

sarge (särj) *n. Informal.* Sergeant.

Sar·gent (sär′jənt), **John Singer.** 1856–1925. American painter known for his elegant portraits and watercolor landscapes.

Sar·go·dha (sər-gō′də). A city of northeast Pakistan west-northwest of Lahore. It is an agricultural trade center with varied industries. Population, 235,000.

Sar·gon II (sär′gŏn′). Died 705 B.C. Assyrian king (721–705) who completed the conquest of the northern Jewish kingdom of Israel, later known as Samaria.

sa·ri (sä′rē) *n., pl.* **-ris.** An outer garment worn chiefly by women of India and Pakistan, consisting of a length of lightweight cloth with one end wrapped about the waist to form a skirt and the other draped over the shoulder or covering the head. [Hindi *sāṛī,* from Prakrit *sāḍī,* from Sanskrit *śāṭī.*]

Sark (särk). One of the Channel Islands in the English Channel east of Guernsey. It comprises **Great Sark** and **Little Sark,** which are joined by a causeway. **—Sark·ese′** (-ēz′, -ēs′) *adj. & n.*

Sar·ma·tia (sär-mā′shə, -shē-ə). An ancient region of eastern Europe northeast of the Black Sea. The Sarmatian people occupied the area after the fourth century B.C. and fled across the Carpathian Mountains and along the Danube River after the onslaught of the Huns. The term is also applied to the territory between the Vistula and Volga rivers during the time of the Roman Empire. **—Sar·ma′tian** *adj. & n.*

sar·men·tose (sär-mĕn′tōs′) *adj. Botany.* Having slender, prostrate stolons, as in the strawberry. [Latin *sarmentōsus,* full of twigs, from *sarmentum,* twigs.]

Sar·ni·a (sär′nē-ə). A city of southeast Ontario, Canada, at the southern end of Lake Huron west of London. Settled by the French in 1807 and the British in 1833, it is a port and manufacturing center. Population, 50,892.

Sar·noff (sär′nôf′), **David.** 1891–1971. American radio and television pioneer who proposed the first commercial radio receiver and in 1926 formed the National Broadcasting Company.

sa·rod or **sa·rode** (sə-rōd′) *n. Music.* A many-stringed lute of northern India that is played with a bow. [Urdu, from Persian *sarūd,* from Middle Persian *srōd,* from Old Iranian *srauta-.* See **kleu-** in Appendix.] **—sa·rod′ist** *n.*

sa·rong (sə-rông′, -rŏng′) *n.* **1.** A skirt consisting of a length of brightly colored cloth wrapped about the waist that is worn by men and women in Malaysia, Indonesia, and the Pacific islands. **2.** Cloth for such skirts. [Malay *(kain) sarong,* covering (cloth), sarong.]

Sa·ron·ic Gulf (sə-rŏn′ĭk). An arm of the Aegean Sea in southern Greece between Attica and the Peloponnesus east of Corinth. A canal links it with the Gulf of Corinth.

Sa·ros (sâr′ŏs′, sä′rôs), **Gulf of.** An inlet of the Aegean Sea indenting northwest European Turkey north of Gallipoli.

Sa·roy·an (sə-roi′ən), **William.** 1908–1981. American writer whose works include short stories, such as *The Daring Young Man on the Flying Trapeze* (1934), plays, most notably *The Time of Your Life* (1939), and novels.

Sar·pe·don (sär-pēd′n, -pē′dŏn) *n. Greek Mythology.* A son of Zeus and Europa who became king of Lycia and was killed by Patroclus in the Trojan War.

♦**sar·sa** (sär′sə) *n. Chiefly Southwestern U.S.* Variant of **salsa** (sense 1).

sar·sa·pa·ril·la (săs′pə-rĭl′ə, särs′-) *n.* **1.a.** Any of several tropical American plants of the genus *Smilax,* having fragrant roots used as a flavoring. **b.** The dried roots of any of these plants. **c.** A sweet soft drink flavored with these roots. **2.** Either of two North American plants *(Aralia hispida* or *A. nudicaulis)* having umbels of small white flowers and bipinnately compound leaves. [Spanish *zarzaparrilla* : *zarza,* bramble (from Arabic *šaraṣ*) + *parrilla,* diminutive of *parra,* vine.]

Sarthe (särt). A river, about 285 km (177 mi) long, of northwest France flowing generally south to Angers.

sar·to·ri·al (sär-tôr′ē-əl, -tōr′-) *adj.* Of or relating to a tailor, tailoring, or tailored clothing: *sartorial elegance.* [From Late Latin *sartor,* tailor. See SARTORIUS.] **—sar·to′ri·al·ly** *adv.*

sar·to·ri·us (sär-tôr′ē-əs, -tōr′-) *n., pl.* **-to·ri·i** (-tôr′ē-ī, -tōr′-). A flat, narrow thigh muscle, the longest of the human anatomy, crossing the front of the thigh obliquely from the hip to the inner side of the tibia. [New Latin, from Late Latin *sartor,* tailor (from its producing the cross-legged position of a tailor at work), from *sartus,* past participle of *sarcīre,* to mend.]

Sar·tre (sär′trə, särt), **Jean Paul.** 1905–1980. French writer and philosopher. A leading existentialist, he wrote literary works, such as the autobiographical novel *Nausea* (1938) and the play *No Exit* (1944), and philosophical volumes that include *Being and Nothingness* (1943). Sartre declined the 1957 Nobel Prize for literature.

sa·rus crane (sär′əs) *n.* A large crane *(Grus antigone)* of southern Asia, having a partly red head and neck. [Hindi *sāras,* from Sanskrit *sārasaḥ,* from *sārasa-,* of lakes, from *saraḥ,* lake, from *sarati,* it flows.]

SASE *abbr.* Self-addressed stamped envelope.

sash[1] (săsh) *n.* A band or ribbon worn about the waist, as for ornament, or over the shoulder as a symbol of rank. **—sash** *tr.v.* **sashed, sash·ing, sash·es.** To put a band or ribbon about (the waist). [Arabic *šāš,* muslin.]

sash[2] (săsh) *n.* A frame in which the panes of a window or door are set. **—sash** *tr.v.* **sashed, sash·ing, sash·es.** To furnish with a sash. [Alteration of French *châssis,* frame (taken as pl.). See CHASSIS.]

sa·shay (să-shā′) *Informal. intr.v.* **-shayed, -shay·ing, -shays. 1.a.** To walk or proceed, especially in an easy or casual manner. **b.** To strut or flounce in a showy manner: *"sashays in tight black pants and harlequin shoes across the patio"* (Tom Ashbrook). **2.** To perform the chassé in dancing. **3.** To move in a sideways manner. **—sashay** *n.* **1.** A chassé. **2.** An excursion; an outing. **3.** A figure in square dancing in which partners circle each other by taking sideways steps. [Alteration of CHASSÉ.]

sa·shi·mi (sä-shē′mē) *n., pl.* **-mis.** A Japanese dish consisting of very thin, bite-size slices of fresh raw fish, traditionally served with a sharp-tasting sauce. [Japanese.]

Sas·katch·e·wan (să-skăch′ə-wän′, -wən). *Abbr.* **SK, Sask.** A province of south-central Canada. It joined the Confederation in 1905. The French established trading posts in the area c. 1750, but the first permanent settlement was made by the Hudson's Bay Company in 1774. The region became part of the Northwest Territories in 1870. Regina is the capital and the largest city. Population, 968,313.

Saskatchewan River. A river, about 547 km (340 mi) long, of south-central Canada formed by the confluence of the North and South Saskatchewan rivers in central Saskatchewan and flowing eastward to Lake Winnipeg in Manitoba.

sas·ka·toon (săs′kə-to͞on′) *n.* **1.** A shrub *(Amelanchier alnifolia)* of northwest North America, having white flowers and edible dark purple fruit. **2.** The fruit of this plant. [From Cree *misaaskwatoomin,* saskatoon berry.]

Sas·ka·toon (săs′kə-to͞on′). A city of south-central Saskatchewan, Canada, on the South Saskatchewan River northwest of Regina. Settled in 1883, it is a trade and processing center. Population, 154,210.

Sas·quatch (săs′kwŏch, -kwăch) *n.* See **Bigfoot.** [Halkomelem (Salish language) *sɛ′sq′əč.*]

sass (săs) *Informal. n.* Impertinent, disrespectful speech; back talk. **—sass** *tr.v.* **sassed, sass·ing, sass·es.** To talk impudently to. [Back-formation from SASSY[1].]

sas·sa·by (săs′ə-bē) *n., pl.* **-bies.** A South African antelope *(Damaliscus lunatus)* having curved, ridged horns. [Sotho (Setswana) *tshêsêbê.*]

sas·sa·fras (săs′ə-frăs′) *n.* **1.** A deciduous eastern North American tree *(Sassafras albidum)* having irregularly lobed leaves and aromatic bark, leaves, and branches. **2.** The dried root bark of this plant, used as a flavoring and a source of a volatile oil. [Spanish *sasafrás,* from Late Latin *saxifragia,* kind of herb, variant of *(herba) saxifraga,* saxifrage. See SAXIFRAGE.]

Sas·sa·nid (săs′ə-nĭd, sə-sä′nĭd, -săn′ĭd) also **Sas·sa·ni·an** (sə-sā′nē-ən, să-) or **Sas·sa·nide** (săs′ə-nīd′, -nĭd). A Persian dynasty (A.D. 224–651) and the last line of Persian kings before the Arab conquest. The Sassanid era was marked by wars against Romans, Armenians, and Huns and by the revival of Zoroastrianism. **—Sas′sa·nid** *adj.*

Sas·sa·ri (sä′sə-rē′). A city of northwest Sardinia, Italy, north-northwest of Cagliari. An important trading center in the Middle Ages, it was held by the Genoese and Aragonese before passing to Piedmont in 1718. Population, 118,158.

Sas·soon (sə-so͞on′, să-), **Siegfried Lorraine.** 1886–1967. British writer known for his antiwar poems, based on his combat experience in World War I, and for his fictionalized three-volume autobiography, first published as *The Memoirs of George Sherston* (1928–1936).

sass·wood (săs′wo͝od′) *n.* See **sassy**[2]. [Alteration of *sassy-wood* : SASSY[2] + WOOD[1].]

sas·sy[1] (săs′ē) *adj.* **-si·er, -si·est. 1.** Rude and disrespectful; impudent. **2.** Lively and spirited; jaunty. **3.** Stylish; chic: *a sassy little hat.* [Alteration of SAUCY.] **—sas′si·ly** *adv.* **—sas′si·ness** *n.*

sas·sy[2] (săs′ē) *n., pl.* **-sies.** A western African tree *(Erythrophleum suaveolens)* of the pea family, having bark that yields a poison and wood that is used for construction. Also called *sasswood, sassy bark.* [Of West African origin; akin to Twi *ɔ-sésé,* plane tree, Ewe *séséwú,* timber tree, Gã *sèsè,* kind of tree.]

sas·tru·ga (să-stro͞o′gə, săs′trə-, sä′strə-) also **zas·tru·ga** (ză-stro͞o′gə, zä-) *n.* A long wavelike ridge of snow, formed by the wind and found on the polar plains. [Russian dialectal *zastruga* : *za,* beyond + *struga,* deep place into which one may fall; see **sreu-** in Appendix.]

sat (săt) *v.* Past tense and past participle of **sit.**

sarong

Jean Paul Sartre

ă pat	oi boy
ā pay	ou out
âr care	o͝o took
ä father	o͞o boot
ĕ pet	ŭ cut
ē be	ûr urge
ĭ pit	th thin
ī pie	*th* this
îr pier	hw which
ŏ pot	zh vision
ō toe	ə about, item
ô paw	♦ regionalism

Stress marks: ′ (primary); ′ (secondary), as in **dictionary** (dĭk′shə-nĕr′ē)

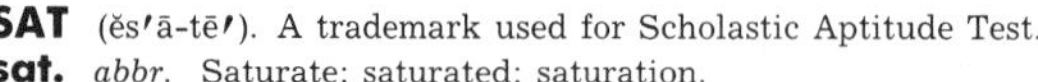

satellite
Syncom IV-5
communications satellite

Saturn
Photographed by
Voyager 2

SAT (ĕs′ā-tē′). A trademark used for Scholastic Aptitude Test.

sat. *abbr.* Saturate; saturated; saturation.

Sat. *abbr.* Saturday.

Sa·tan (sāt′n) *n. Theology.* The profoundly evil adversary of God and humanity, often identified with the leader of the fallen angels; the Devil. [Middle English, from Old English, from Late Latin *Satān,* from Greek *Satanas, Satan,* from Hebrew *śāṭān,* devil, adversary, from *śāṭan,* to accuse.]

sa·tang (sə-tăng′) *n., pl.* **satang.** See table at **currency.** [Thai *satān.*]

sa·tan·ic (sə-tăn′ĭk, sā-) or **sa·tan·i·cal** (-ĭ-kəl) *adj.* **1.** Relating to or suggestive of Satan or evil. **2.** Profoundly cruel or evil; fiendish. **—sa·tan′i·cal·ly** *adv.*

Sa·tan·ism (sāt′n-ĭz′əm) *n.* **1.** The worship of Satan characterized by a travesty of the Christian rites. **2. satanism.** Profound wickedness. **—Sa′tan·ist** *n.*

sa·tay also **sa·té** or **sa·te** (sä′tā) *n.* A dish of southeast Asia consisting of strips of marinated meat, poultry, or seafood grilled on skewers and dipped in peanut sauce. [Malay or Indonesian.]

satch·el (săch′əl) *n.* A small bag, often having a shoulder strap, used for carrying books or clothing. [Middle English *sachel,* from Old French, from Late Latin *saccellus,* from Latin *sacculus,* diminutive of *saccus,* bag. See SACK[1].] **—satch′eled** *adj.* **—satch′el·ful′** (-fo͝ol′) *n.*

satd. *abbr.* Saturated.

sate[1] (sāt) *tr.v.* **sat·ed, sat·ing, sates. 1.** To satisfy (an appetite) fully. **2.** To satisfy to excess. See Synonyms at **satiate.** [Probably alteration of Middle English *saden,* from Old English *sadian.* See **sā-** in Appendix.]

sate[2] (săt, sāt) *v. Archaic.* A past tense of **sit.**

sa·té or **sa·te** (sä′tā) *n.* Variants of **satay.**

sa·teen (să-tēn′) *n.* A cotton fabric with a satinlike finish. [Alteration (influenced by VELVETEEN) of SATIN.]

sat·el·lite (săt′l-īt′) *n.* **1.** *Astronomy.* A celestial body that orbits a planet; a moon. **2.** *Aerospace.* An object launched to orbit Earth or another celestial body. **3.** One who attends a powerful dignitary; a minion. **4.** A subservient follower; a sycophant. **5.** A nation dominated politically and economically by another nation. **6.** An urban or suburban community located near a big city. **7.** *Genetics.* A short segment of a chromosome separated from the rest by a constriction, typically associated with the formation of a nucleolus. **8.** *Microbiology.* A colony of microorganisms whose growth in culture medium is enhanced by certain substances produced by another colony in its proximity. *—attributive.* Often used to modify another noun: *satellite telecommunications; satellite countries in the Eastern Bloc.* [French, hanger-on, hireling, from Old French, from Latin *satelles, satellit-.*]

satellite cell *n. Anatomy.* Any of the cells that encapsulate the bodies of nerve cells in many ganglia.

satellite DNA *n.* A portion of DNA in animal cells whose density differs from that of the other DNA and that consists of short, repeating sequences of nucleotide pairs near the region of the centromere.

satellite station *n.* A radio or television station that rebroadcasts a received transmission immediately on a different wavelength.

sa·tem (sä′təm) *adj.* Designating those Indo-European languages, including the Indo-Iranian, Armenian, Albanian, and Balto-Slavic subfamilies, in which original velar stops became fricatives (as $k > s$ or *š*) and labiovelar stops became velars (as $kw > k$). [Avestan *satəm,* hundred (a word whose initial sound illustrates the sound change). See **dekm̥** in Appendix.]

sa·ti (sŭ-tē′, sŭt′ē′) *n.* Variant of **suttee.**

sa·tia·ble (sā′shə-bəl, -shē-ə-) *adj.* Possible to satisfy or sate: *satiable thirst; a satiable appetite.* **—sa′tia·bil′i·ty** *n.* **—sa′tia·bly** *adv.*

sa·ti·ate (sā′shē-āt′) *tr.v.* **-at·ed, -at·ing, -ates. 1.** To satisfy (an appetite or a desire) fully. **2.** To satisfy to excess. **—satiate** (-ĭt) *adj.* Filled to satisfaction. [Middle English *saciaten,* from Latin *satiāre, satiāt-,* from *satis,* sufficient. See **sā-** in Appendix.] **—sa′ti·a′tion** *n.*

SYNONYMS: *satiate, sate, cloy, glut, gorge, surfeit.* These verbs mean to fill or become filled to the utmost. *Satiate* and *sate,* which are generally interchangeable, can mean merely to satisfy fully, but usually both imply satisfaction beyond natural desire: *The actor is so vain that he can never be satiated with adulation. The novel she finished last night sated her appetite for fiction. Cloy* stresses the distaste or ennui produced by overindulgence: *The host served a dessert so sweet that it cloyed. Glut* emphasizes the sheer volume of oversupply: *Even the surrender of half of Europe failed to glut Hitler's ambition. Gorge* refers principally to greedy overstuffing with food: *The children gorged on potato chips. Surfeit* implies excess resulting in revulsion or illness: *I surfeited myself with chocolate.*

Sa·tie (sä-tē′), **Erik.** 1866–1925. French composer who rebelled against romanticism with his unorthodox and often whimsical compositions, such as *Socrate* (1918).

sa·ti·e·ty (sə-tī′ĭ-tē) *n.* The condition of being full or gratified beyond the point of satisfaction; surfeit. [French *satiete,* from Old French *saciete,* from Latin *satietās,* from *satis,* sufficient. See **sā-** in Appendix.]

sat·in (săt′n) *n.* **1.** A smooth fabric, as of silk or rayon, woven with a glossy face and a dull back. **2.** A garment made of this fabric. **—satin** *adj.* **1.** Made of or covered with satin. **2.** Glossy and smooth. [Middle English, from Old French, probably from Arabic *(′aṭlas) zaitūnīy,* (satin) of Zaitun, from *Zaitūn,* probably Tsinkiang (Quanzhou or Chuanchow), a city of southeast China.]

sat·in·et (săt′n-ĕt′) *n.* A thin inferior satin or an imitation satin, especially one containing cotton.

satin flower *n.* **1.** A plant *(Clarkia amoena)* of coastal California having showy, red-blotched flowers. **2.** See **honesty** (sense 4).

satin stitch *n.* An embroidery stitch worked in close parallel lines to give a solid satinlike finish.

satin weave *n.* A basic weave construction with the interlacing of the threads so arranged that the face of the cloth is covered with warp yarn or filling yarn and no twill line is distinguishable.

sat·in·wood (săt′n-wo͝od′) *n.* **1.** A deciduous tree *(Chloroxylon swietenia)* of India and Sri Lanka, having hard, yellowish, close-grained wood. **2.** A West Indian tree *(Zanthoxylum flavum)* having smooth, slightly oily, lustrous wood. **3.** The wood of either of these trees, used for furniture and cabinetwork.

sat·in·y (săt′n-ē) *adj.* Lustrous and smooth like satin. See Synonyms at **sleek.**

sat·ire (săt′īr′) *n.* **1. a.** A literary work in which human vice or folly is attacked through irony, derision, or wit. **b.** The branch of literature constituting such works. See Synonyms at **caricature. 2.** Irony, sarcasm, or caustic wit used to attack or expose folly, vice, or stupidity. [Latin *satira,* probably alteration (influenced by Greek *satur,* satyr, and *satyros,* burlesque of a mythical episode) of *(lanx) satura,* fruit (plate) mixture, from feminine of *satur,* sated, well-fitted. See **sā-** in Appendix.]

sa·tir·i·cal (sə-tîr′ĭ-kəl) or **sa·tir·ic** (-ĭk) *adj.* Of, relating to, or characterized by satire. See Synonyms at **sarcastic. —sa·tir′i·cal·ly** *adv.*

sat·i·rist (săt′ər-ĭst) *n.* One who is given to satire, especially a writer of satirical works.

sat·i·rize (săt′ə-rīz′) *tr.v.* **-rized, -riz·ing, -riz·es.** To ridicule or attack by means of satire.

sat·is·fac·tion (săt′ĭs-făk′shən) *n.* **1. a.** The fulfillment or gratification of a desire, a need, or an appetite. **b.** Pleasure or contentment derived from such gratification. **c.** A source or means of gratification. **2. a.** Compensation for injury or loss; reparation. **b.** The opportunity to avenge a wrong; vindication. **3.** Assurance beyond doubt or question; complete conviction. [Middle English, from Old French, from Latin *satisfactiō, satisfactiōn-,* amends, from *satisfactus,* past participle of *satisfacere,* to satisfy. See SATISFY.]

sat·is·fac·to·ry (săt′ĭs-făk′tə-rē) *adj.* Giving satisfaction sufficient to meet a demand or requirement; adequate. **—sat′is·fac′to·ri·ly** *adv.* **—sat′is·fac′to·ri·ness** *n.*

sat·is·fi·a·ble (săt′ĭs-fī′ə-bəl) *adj.* Capable of being satisfied: *satisfiable needs and desires.*

sat·is·fied (săt′ĭs-fīd′) *adj.* **1.** Filled with satisfaction; content: *a very satisfied customer.* **2.** Paid or discharged in full, as a debt or an obligation. **3.** Convinced beyond a doubt.

sat·is·fy (săt′ĭs-fī′) *v.* **-fied, -fy·ing, -fies.** *—tr.* **1.** To gratify the need, desire, or expectation of. **2.** To fulfill (a need or desire). **3. a.** To free from doubt or question; assure. **b.** To get rid of (a doubt or question); dispel. **4. a.** To discharge (a debt or an obligation, for example) in full. **b.** To discharge an obligation to (a creditor). **5.** To conform to the requirements of (a standard or rule); be sufficient to (an end). **6.** To make reparation for; redress. **7.** *Mathematics.* To make the left and right sides of an equation equal after substituting equivalent quantities for the unknown variables in the equation. *—intr.* **1.** To be sufficient or adequate. **2.** To give satisfaction. [Middle English *satisfien,* from Old French *satisfier,* from Latin *satisfacere* : *satis,* sufficient; see **sā-** in Appendix + *facere,* to make; see **dhē-** in Appendix.] **—sat′is·fi′er** *n.* **—sat′is·fy′ing·ly** *adv.*

SYNONYMS: *satisfy, answer, fill, fulfill, meet.* The central meaning shared by these verbs is "to supply fully or completely": *satisfied all requirements; answered our needs; filling a purpose; fulfilled their aspirations; meeting her obligations.*

Sa·to (sä′tō), **Eisaku.** 1901–1975. Japanese politician who served as prime minister (1964–1972). He won the 1974 Nobel Peace Prize for his efforts toward nuclear disarmament.

sa·to·ri (sä-tôr′ē, -tōr′ē, sə-) *n. Buddhism.* A state of spiritual enlightenment sought in Zen Buddhism. [Japanese.]

sa·trap (sā′trăp′, săt′răp′) *n.* **1.** A governor of a province in ancient Persia. **2.** A ruler. **3.** A subordinate bureaucrat or an official: *"The satraps of Capitol Hill will not sit idly by"* (David Nyhan). [Middle English *satrape,* from Old French, from Latin *satrapēs,* from Greek, from Old Persian *khshathrapāvā,* protector of the province : *khshathra-,* realm, province + *pāvā,* protector; see **pā-** in Appendix.]

sa·tra·py (sā′trə-pē, -trăp′ē, săt′rə-pē) *n., pl.* **-pies. 1.** The territory or sphere under the rule of a satrap. **2.** A nation, state, territory, or area controlled as if by a satrap: *"No military legions*

ă pat	oi boy
ā pay	ou out
âr care	o͝o took
ä father	o͞o boot
ĕ pet	ŭ cut
ē be	ûr urge
ĭ pit	th thin
ī pie	*th* this
îr pier	hw which
ŏ pot	zh vision
ō toe	ə about, item
ô paw	♦ regionalism

Stress marks: **′** (primary); ′ (secondary), as in **dictionary** (dĭk′shə-nĕr′ē)

from the West are going to liberate their Eastern European satrapies" (John Hughes).

sat·su·ma (săt-so͞o′mə, sä-tso͞o′mä, sä′tso͞o-mä′) *n.* **1.** A tangerine native to Japan and the hardiest commercial citrus fruit. **2. Satsuma.** A Japanese porcelain. In this sense, also called *Satsuma ware.* [After *Satsuma,* a peninsula of southwest Kyushu, Japan.]

Sa·tu-Ma·re also **Sa·tu Ma·re** (sä′to͞o-mär′ĕ). A city of northwest Romania near the Hungarian border northwest of Bucharest. It is a commercial, cultural, and industrial center. Population, 124,691.

sat·u·rant (săch′ər-ənt) *adj.* Serving to saturate. **—saturant** *n.* A substance used to saturate.

sat·u·rate (săch′ə-rāt′) *tr.v.* **-rat·ed, -rat·ing, -rates.** *Abbr.* **sat. 1.** To imbue or impregnate thoroughly: *"The recollection was saturated with sunshine"* (Vladimir Nabokov). See Synonyms at **charge. 2.** To soak, fill, or load to capacity. **3.** *Chemistry.* To cause (a substance) to unite with the greatest possible amount of another substance. **—saturate** (-rĭt) *adj.* Saturated. [Latin *saturāre, saturāt-,* to fill, from *satur,* sated. See **sā-** in Appendix.] **—sat′u·ra·ble** (săch′ər-ə-bəl) *adj.* **—sat′u·ra′tor** *n.*

sat·u·rat·ed (săch′ə-rā′tĭd) *adj. Abbr.* **sat., satd. 1.** Unable to hold or contain more; full. **2.** Soaked with moisture; drenched. **3.** *Chemistry.* **a.** Combined with or containing all the solute that can normally be dissolved at a given temperature. **b.** Having all available valence bonds filled. Used especially of organic compounds: *saturated fats.* **4.** *Geology.* Of or relating to minerals that can crystallize from magmas even in the presence of excess silica.

saturated fat *n.* A fat, most often of animal origin, whose fatty acid chains cannot incorporate additional hydrogen atoms. An excess of these fats in the diet is thought to raise the cholesterol level in the bloodstream.

sat·u·ra·tion (săch′ə-rā′shən) *n. Abbr.* **sat. 1.a.** The act or process of saturating. **b.** The condition of being saturated. **c.** The condition of being full to or beyond satisfaction; satiety. **2.** *Physics.* A state of a ferromagnetic substance in which an increase in applied magnetic field strength does not produce an increase in magnetic intensity. **3.** *Chemistry.* The state of a compound or solution that is fully saturated. **4.** *Meteorology.* A condition in which air at a specific temperature contains all the water vapor it can hold; 100 percent relative humidity. **5.** *Color.* Vividness of hue; degree of difference from a gray of the same lightness or brightness. Also called *intensity.* **6.** Intensive shelling or bombing of a military target to achieve total destruction. **7.** The flooding of a market with all of a commodity that consumers can purchase.

Sat·ur·day (săt′ər-dē, -dā′) *n. Abbr.* **S., Sat. 1.** The seventh day of the week. **2.** The Sabbath for many Jews. [Middle English, from Old English *Sæternesdæg,* translation of Latin *Sāturnī diēs* : *Sāturnī,* genitive of *Sāturnus,* Saturn + *diēs,* day.]

Saturday night special *n. Informal.* A cheap handgun easily obtained and concealed.

Sat·urn (săt′ərn) *n.* **1.** *Roman Mythology.* The god of agriculture. **2.** The sixth planet from the sun and the second largest in the solar system, having a sidereal period of revolution about the sun of 29.5 years at a mean distance of about 1,425,000,000 kilometers (886,000,000 miles), a mean diameter of approximately 119,000 kilometers (74,000 miles), and a mass 95 times that of Earth. [Middle English *Saturnus,* from Old English, from Latin *Sāturnus,* of Etruscan origin.]

sat·ur·na·li·a (săt′ər-nā′lē-ə, -nāl′yə) *pl.n.* **1. Saturnalia.** The ancient Roman seven-day festival of Saturn, which began on December 17. **2.** *(used with a sing. verb).* A celebration marked by unrestrained revelry and often licentiousness; an orgy. [Latin *Sāturnālia,* from neuter pl. of *Sāturnālis,* Saturnian, from *Sāturnus,* Saturn. See SATURN.]

Sa·tur·ni·an (să-tûr′nē-ən, sə-) *adj.* **1.** Of or relating to the planet Saturn or to its supposed astrological influence. **2.** *Archaic.* Of or relating to the god Saturn or his reign.

sa·tur·ni·id (să-tûr′nē-ĭd, sə-) *n.* Any of various often large and colorful moths of the family Saturniidae, such as the emperor moth. **—saturniid** *adj.* Of or belonging to the Saturniidae. [From New Latin *Sāturniidae,* family name, from *Sāturnia,* type genus, from Latin, daughter of Saturn, from feminine of *Sāturnius,* Saturnian, from *Sāturnus,* Saturn. See SATURN.]

sat·ur·nine (săt′ər-nīn′) *adj.* **1.** Having the temperament of one born under the supposed astrological influence of Saturn. **2.a.** Melancholy or sullen. **b.** Having or marked by a tendency to be bitter or sardonic: *a saturnine expression on his face.* See Synonyms at **glum. 3.** Produced by absorption of lead. **—sat′ur·nine′ly** *adv.*

sat·urn·ism (săt′ər-nĭz′əm) *n.* See **lead poisoning.** [From SATURN, lead (obsolete), with which alchemists associated the planet Saturn.]

Sa·tya·gra·ha (sə-tyä′grə-hə, sŭt′yə-grŭ′hə) *n.* The policy of nonviolent resistance initiated in India by Mahatma Gandhi as a means of pressing for political reform. [Sanskrit *satyāgrahaḥ* : *satyam,* truth (from *sat-, sant-,* existing, true; see **es-** in Appendix) + *āgrahaḥ,* determination, insistence (*ā-,* to + *grahaḥ,* act of seizing, from *gṛhṇāti,* he seizes; see **ghrebh-**[1] in Appendix).]

sa·tyr (sā′tər, săt′ər) *n.* **1.** Often **Satyr.** *Greek Mythology.* A woodland creature depicted as having the pointed ears, legs, and short horns of a goat and a fondness for unrestrained revelry. **2.** A licentious man; a lecher. **3.** A man who is affected by satyriasis. **4.** Any of various butterflies of the family Satyridae, having brown wings marked with eyelike spots. [Middle English *satire,* from Old French, from Latin *satyrus,* from Greek *saturos.*] **—sa·tyr′ic** (sā-tîr′ĭk, sə-), **sa·tyr′i·cal** (-ĭ-kəl) *adj.*

satyr

sa·ty·ri·a·sis (sā′tə-rī′ə-sĭs, săt′ə-) *n.* Excessive, often uncontrollable sexual desire in a man. [Late Latin, from Greek *saturiasis,* from *saturos,* satyr.]

sa·tyr·id (sā′tər-ĭd, săt′ər-, sə-tī′rĭd) *n.* A butterfly of the family Satyridae, including the satyrs and wood nymphs. **—satyrid** *adj.* Of or belonging to the Satyridae. [From New Latin *Satyridae,* family name, from *Satyrus,* type genus, from Latin *satyrus,* satyr. See SATYR.]

sauce (sôs) *n.* **1.** A flavorful seasoning or relish served as an accompaniment to food, especially a liquid dressing or topping for food. **2.** Stewed fruit, usually served with other foods. **3.** Something that adds zest, flavor, or piquancy. **4.** *Informal.* Impudent speech or behavior; impertinence or sauciness. **5.** *Slang.* Alcoholic liquor. **—sauce** *tr.v.* **sauced, sauc·ing, sauc·es. 1.** To season or flavor with sauce. **2.** To add piquancy or zest to. **3.** *Informal.* To be impertinent or impudent to. [Middle English, from Old French, from Vulgar Latin **salsa,* from Latin, feminine of *salsus,* past participle of *sallere,* to salt. See **sal-** in Appendix.]

sauce·boat (sôs′bōt′) *n.* A low, boat-shaped pitcher typically having a wide lip at one end and a handle at the other and used for serving sauces and gravies.

sauceboat
c. 1760–1770 American silver sauceboat by Benjamin Burt (1729–1805)

sauce·box (sôs′bŏks′) *n. Informal.* An impertinent person.

sauce·pan (sôs′păn′) *n.* A deep cooking pan with a handle.

sauce·pot (sôs′pŏt′) *n.* A cooking pot having a close-fitting lid and a handle on either side.

sau·cer (sô′sər) *n.* **1.** A small shallow dish having a slight circular depression in the center for holding a cup. **2.** An object similar in shape to a saucer. [Middle English, sauce dish, from Old French *saussier,* from *sauce,* sauce. See SAUCE.]

sauce suprême *n.* See **suprême** (sense 1). [French : *sauce,* sauce + *suprême,* suprême.]

sauc·y (sô′sē) *adj.* **-i·er, -i·est. 1.a.** Impertinent or disrespectful. **b.** Impertinent in an entertaining way; impossible to repress or control. **2.** Piquant; pert: *a saucy red bow tie.* **—sau′ci·ly** *adv.* **—sau′ci·ness** *n.*

Sa·ud (sä-o͞od′), **Abdul Aziz ibn.** 1901?–1969. Saudi Arabian king (1953–1964) who was unable to deal with his country's economic problems and was replaced by his brother Faisal in 1964.

Abdul Aziz ibn Saud

Sa·u·di A·ra·bi·a (sou′dē ə-rā′bē-ə, sô′dē, sä-o͞o′dē). A country occupying most of the Arabian Peninsula. Political agitation in the region began in the late 18th century and resulted in a dual kingdom formed in 1926 and a unified independent kingdom proclaimed in 1932. Riyadh is the capital and the largest city. Population, 9,320,000. **—Sa·u′di, Sa·u′di A·ra′bi·an** *adj. & n.*

sau·er·bra·ten (sour′brät′n) *n.* A pot roast of beef marinated in vinegar, water, wine, and spices before being cooked. [German : *sauer,* sour (from Middle High German *sūr,* from Old High German) + *Braten,* roast meat (from Middle High German *brāte,* edible meat, from Old High German *brāto;* see **bhreu-** in Appendix).]

sau·er·kraut (sour′krout′) *n.* Chopped or shredded cabbage salted and fermented in its own juice. [German : *sauer,* sour; see SAUERBRATEN + *Kraut,* cabbage (from Middle High German *krūt,* from Old High German).]

sau·ger (sô′gər) *n.* A small North American freshwater fish *(Stizostidion canadense)* having a spotted, spiny dorsal fin. [Origin unknown.]

Sau·gus (sô′gəs). A town of northeast Massachusetts, a residential and manufacturing suburb of Boston. Population 24,746.

Sauk (sôk) also **Sac** (săk, sôk) *n., pl.* **Sauk** or **Sauks** also **Sac** or **Sacs. 1.a.** A Native American people formerly inhabiting parts of Wisconsin, Illinois, and Iowa, with a present-day population mainly in Oklahoma. Sauk resistance to removal from their Illinois lands ended in 1832 with the Black Hawk War. **b.** A member of this people. **2.** The Algonquian language of the Sauk, dialectally related to Fox. [North American French *saki,* from Sauk *asaakiiha.*]

Sauk Cen·tre (sôk sĕn′tər). A city of central Minnesota west-northwest of Minneapolis. Sinclair Lewis was born here and used the community as the setting for a number of novels, including *Main Street* (1920). Population, 3,709.

Saul (sôl). fl. 11th century B.C. The first king of Israel. He defended Israel against numerous enemies, especially the Philistines, and was succeeded by David.

sault (so͞o) *n.* A waterfall or rapids. [Obsolete French, from Old French, leap, waterfall. See SOMERSAULT.]

Sault Sainte Ma·rie (so͞o′ sānt′ mə-rē′). A city of southern Ontario, Canada, at the falls of the St. Marys River opposite Upper Michigan. It is an industrial center in a resort area. Population, 82,698.

Saudi Arabia

Sault Sainte Marie Canals. Popularly called **Soo Canals** (so͞o). Three ship canals bypassing the rapids on the St. Marys River between Lakes Superior and Huron. The Canadian canal, opened in 1895, follows the route of the canal built around the rapids by a fur company in 1797–1798. The first American canal was completed in 1855 and was enlarged and split into two canals,

sauropod
Brachiosaurus

sausage tree
Kigelia pinnata

Savonarola
Portrait by
Fra Bartolommeo
(1472–1517)

opened in 1896 and 1919. Though often icebound in winter, the canals are vital links in the Great Lakes waterway system.

sau·na (sô′nə, sou′-) *n.* **1.a.** A Finnish steam bath in which the steam is produced by pouring water over heated rocks. **b.** A bathhouse or room for taking such a steam bath. **2.a.** A dry heat bath. **b.** A room or an enclosure for taking a dry heat bath. [Finnish.]

saun·ter (sôn′tər) *intr.v.* **-tered, -ter·ing, -ters.** To walk at a leisurely pace; stroll. **—saunter** *n.* **1.** A leisurely pace. **2.** A leisurely walk or stroll. [Probably from Middle English *santren,* to muse.] **—saun′ter·er** *n.*

sau·rel (sôr′əl, sô-rĕl′) *n.* **1.** A marine fish of the genus *Trachurus,* characterized by bony lateral lines, especially *T. trachurus* of eastern Atlantic waters. Also called *horse mackerel.* **2.** See **jack mackerel.** [French, from Late Latin *saurus,* horse mackerel, from Greek *sauros.*]

sau·ri·an (sôr′ē-ən) *n.* Any of various reptiles of the suborder Sauria, which includes the lizards and in former classifications also the crocodiles and dinosaurs. **—saurian** *adj.* Of, belonging to, or characteristic of the Sauria. [From New Latin *Sauria,* suborder name, from *saurus,* lizard, from Greek *sauros.*]

saur·is·chi·an (sô-rĭs′kē-ən) *n.* A dinosaur of the order Saurischia, having a pelvic girdle similar to that of modern reptiles. **—saurischian** *adj.* Of, belonging to, or characteristic of the order Saurischia. [From New Latin *Saurischia,* order name : *saurus,* lizard; see SAURIAN + Latin *ischium,* hip joint (possibly of Greek origin).]

sau·ro·pod (sôr′ə-pŏd′) *n.* Any of various large semiaquatic dinosaurs of the suborder Sauropoda, of the Jurassic and Cretaceous periods. **—sauropod** *adj.* Of, belonging to, or characteristic of the suborder Sauropoda. [From New Latin *Sauropoda,* suborder name : *saurus,* lizard; see SAURIAN + *-poda,* -pod.] **—sau·rop′o·dous** (sô-rŏp′ə-dəs) *adj.*

sau·ry (sôr′ē) *n., pl.* **-ries.** Any of several offshore marine fishes of the family Scomberesocidae, related to the needlefishes. [From New Latin *saurus,* lizard, from Greek *sauros.*]

sau·sage (sô′sĭj) *n.* Finely chopped and seasoned meat, especially pork, usually stuffed into a prepared animal intestine or other casing and cooked or cured. [Middle English *sausige,* from Anglo-Norman *sausiche,* from Vulgar Latin **salsīcia,* from Late Latin, neuter pl. of *salsīcius,* prepared by salting, from *salsus,* salted. See SAUCE.]

sausage tree *n.* A tropical African tree *(Kigelia pinnata)* having pinnately compound whorled leaves, large scarlet bell-shaped flowers borne on loose drooping clusters, and long gourdlike fruit suspended on stalks more than a meter long.

Sau·sa·li·to (sô′sə-lē′tō). A city of western California on San Francisco Bay at the northern terminus of the Golden Gate Bridge. It is a residential community, an artists' colony, and a popular boating resort. Population, 7,338.

Saus·sure (sō-sŏŏr′, -sür′), **Ferdinand de.** 1857–1913. Swiss linguist. The founder of structural linguistics, he declared that there is only an arbitrary relationship between a linguistic sign and that which it signifies.

sau·té (sō-tā′, sô-) *tr.v.* **-téed, -té·ing, -tés.** To fry lightly in fat in a shallow, open pan. **—sauté** *n.* A dish of food so prepared. [French, sautéed, from past participle of *sauter,* to leap, from Old French, from Latin *saltāre.* See SALTATION.]

WORD HISTORY: The term *sauté* is connected with lightness in several ways. One goes lighter on the use of fat when one sautés food. Also, sautéing food is one example of the lightened workload and expanded opportunities for the average cook after ranges with adjustable heat levels were invented (around the turn of the 19th century) and brought into wide use. Before the advent of the range, the ordinary cook could not sauté food; only a specialized member of a large staff had the time to do this kind of cooking. Perhaps this is why the term is first recorded in French (1812) and then, passing across the Channel, in English (1813). The last association with lightness is etymological. The French word comes from the past participle of *sauter,* "to jump," the reference being to the occasional tossing of food being sautéed.

Sau·ternes or **sau·ternes** (sō-tûrn′, sô-) *n., pl.* **Sauternes** or **sauternes. 1.** A delicate, sweet white wine from the Bordeaux region of France. **2.** Often **sau·terne** (-tûrn′)., *pl.* **sauternes.** A sweet to moderately dry white wine from California. [French, after *Sauternes,* a village of southwest France.]

Sa·va (sä′və, -vä). A river, about 933 km (580 mi) long, rising in two headstreams in the Julian Alps of northwest Yugoslavia and flowing generally eastward to the Danube River at Belgrade.

sav·age (săv′ĭj) *adj.* **1.** Not domesticated or cultivated; wild: *savage beasts of the jungle.* **2.** Not civilized; barbaric: *a savage people.* **3.** Ferocious; fierce: *in a savage temper.* **4.** Vicious or merciless; brutal: *a savage attack on a political rival.* See Synonyms at **cruel. 5.** Lacking polish or manners; rude. **—savage** *n.* **1.** A person regarded as primitive or uncivilized. **2.** A person regarded as brutal, fierce, or vicious. **3.** A rude person; a boor. **—savage** *tr.v.* **-aged, -ag·ing, -ag·es. 1.** To assault ferociously. **2.** To attack without restraint or pity: *The critics savaged the new play.* [Middle English *sauvage,* from Old French, from Late Latin *salvāticus,* from Latin *silvāticus,* of the woods, wild, from *silva,* forest.] **—sav′age·ly** *adv.* **—sav′age·ness** *n.*

sav·age·ry (săv′ĭj-rē) *n., pl.* **-ries. 1.** The quality or condition of being savage. **2.** An act of violent cruelty. **3.** Savage behavior or nature; barbarity.

Sa·vai·i or **Sa·vai′i** (sä-vī′ē). An island of Western Samoa in the southwest Pacific Ocean. It is the largest and most westerly of the Samoa Islands.

sa·van·na also **sa·van·nah** (sə-văn′ə) *n.* A flat grassland of tropical or subtropical regions. [Obsolete Spanish *çavana,* from Taino *zabana.*]

Sa·van·nah (sə-văn′ə). A city of southeast Georgia near the mouth of the Savannah River. Founded by James Oglethorpe in 1733, it is the oldest city in Georgia and has been a major port since the early 19th century. Population, 141,634.

Savannah River. A river, about 505 km (314 mi) long, rising in northwest South Carolina and flowing southeast along the South Carolina–Georgia border to the Atlantic Ocean.

sa·vant (să-vänt′) *n.* **1.** A learned person; a scholar. **2.** An idiot savant. [French, learned, savant, from Old French, present participle of *savoir,* to know, from Vulgar Latin **sapēre,* from Latin *sapere,* to be wise. See **sep-** in Appendix.]

sa·vate (sə-văt′, -vät′) *n. Sports.* A form of boxing in which kicking as well as punching is permitted. [French, from Old French, old shoe.]

save¹ (sāv) *v.* **saved, sav·ing, saves.** *—tr.* **1.a.** To rescue from harm, danger, or loss. **b.** To set free from the consequences of sin; redeem. **2.** To keep in a safe condition; safeguard. **3.** To prevent the waste or loss of; conserve. **4.** To set aside for future use; store. **5.** To treat with care by avoiding fatigue, wear, or damage; spare: *save one's eyesight.* **6.** To make unnecessary; obviate: *Your taking the trunk to the attic has saved me an extra trip.* **7.a.** *Sports.* To prevent (a goal, score, or win by an opponent). **b.** *Baseball.* To preserve (another pitcher's win) by protecting one's team's lead during a stint of relief pitching. **8.** *Computer Science.* To copy (a file) from a computer's main memory to a disk or other storage medium so that it can be used again. *—intr.* **1.** To avoid waste or expense; economize. **2.** To accumulate money: *saving for a vacation.* **3.** To preserve a person or thing from harm or loss. **—save** *n.* **1.** *Sports.* An act that prevents an opponent from scoring. **2.** *Baseball.* A preservation by a relief pitcher of another pitcher's win. ***—idiom.* save (one's) breath.** To refrain from a futile appeal: *Save your breath; you can't dissuade them.* [Middle English *saven,* from Old French *sauver,* from Late Latin *salvāre,* from Latin *salvus,* safe. See **sol-** in Appendix.] **—sav′a·ble, save′a·ble** *adj.* **—sav′er** *n.*

SYNONYMS: *save, rescue, reclaim, redeem, deliver.* These verbs are compared in the sense of freeing a person or thing from danger, evil, confinement, or servitude. *Save,* the most general, applies to an act of keeping safe or preserving from danger, harm, or the consequences of evil: *The smallpox vaccine has saved many lives. A police officer saved the tourist from being cheated. Rescue* usually implies saving from immediate harm or danger by direct action: *rescue a rare manuscript from a fire; rescued sailors from a torpedoed ship. Reclaim,* applied to people, means to bring back, as from error to virtue or to right or proper conduct; it can also mean to return a thing to usefulness or productivity: *"To reclaim me from this course of life was the sole cause of his journey to London"* (Henry Fielding). *"The foundations of the capital were gradually reclaimed from the watery element"* (William Hickling Prescott). To *redeem* is to free someone from captivity or the consequences of sin or error or to save something from pawn or from deterioration or destruction; the term can imply the expenditure of money or effort: *The price exacted by the hijackers for redeeming the hostages was extortionate. He redeemed his ring from the pawnbroker. Deliver* in this comparison applies to liberating people from something such as misery, peril, error, or evil: *"consigned to a state of wretchedness from which no human efforts will deliver them"* (George Washington).

save² (sāv) *prep.* With the exception of; except: *"No man enjoys self-reproach save a masochist"* (Philip Wylie). **—save** *conj.* **1.** Were it not; except: *The house would be finished by now, save that we had difficulty contracting a roofer.* **2.** Unless. [Middle English, from Old French *sauf,* from Latin *salvō,* ablative sing. of *salvus,* safe. See **sol-** in Appendix.]

save-all (sāv′ôl′) *n.* **1.** Any of various devices for preventing waste, damage, or loss. **2.** A receptacle for catching the waste products of a process for further use in manufacture.

sav·e·loy (săv′ə-loi′) *n.* A highly seasoned smoked pork sausage. [Alteration of obsolete French *cervelat,* from Italian *cervellato,* ultimately from dialectal *zervello,* brain, from Latin *cerebellum,* diminutive of *cerebrum,* brain. See **ker-¹** in Appendix.]

sav·in or **sav·ine** (săv′ĭn) *n.* **1.** An evergreen Eurasian shrub *(Juniperus sabina)* having brownish-blue seed-bearing cones and young shoots that yield an oil formerly used medicinally. **2.** Any of several related plants. [Middle English, from Old English *safine* and from Old French *savine,* both from Latin *(herba) Sabīna,* Sabine (plant), savin, feminine of *Sabīnus.*]

sav·ing (sā′vĭng) *n.* **1.** Rescue from harm, danger, or loss. **2.** Avoidance of excess expenditure; economy. **3.** A reduction in expenditure or cost. **4.** Something saved. **5. savings.** *Abbr.* **svgs.** Money saved: *a bank account for savings.* **6.** *Law.* An exception or reservation. **—saving** *prep.* With the exception of. **—saving** *conj.* Except; save.

ă pat	oi boy
ā pay	ou out
âr care	ŏŏ took
ä father	ōō boot
ĕ pet	ŭ cut
ē be	ûr urge
ĭ pit	th thin
ī pie	*th* this
îr pier	hw which
ŏ pot	zh vision
ō toe	ə about, item
ô paw	♦ regionalism

Stress marks: ′ (primary); ′ (secondary), as in **dictionary** (dĭk′shə-nĕr′ē)

USAGE NOTE: There is a widespread tendency to use the form *savings* as a singular, as reflected in compounds such as *savings account* and *savings bond* (note by contrast that one would not form compounds like *investments account,* using an unambiguous plural). But the phrase *a savings,* though increasingly common, remains unacceptable to 57 percent of the Usage Panel; *a saving* is the only uncontroversial form.

sav·ings account (sā′vĭngz) *n.* An account that draws interest at a bank.

savings and loan association *n. Abbr.* **S & L.** A financial institution, organized cooperatively or corporately, that holds the funds of its members or clients in interest-bearing accounts and certificates of deposit, invests these funds chiefly in home mortgage loans and may also offer checking accounts and other banking services.

savings bank *n.* A bank that receives and invests the savings of private depositors and pays interest on the deposits.

savings bond *n.* A nontransferable registered bond issued by the U.S. government in denominations of $50 to $10,000.

sav·ior (sāv′yər) *n.* **1.** A person who rescues another from harm, danger, or loss. **2. Savior.** Jesus. [Middle English *saviour,* from Old French *sauveour,* from Late Latin *salvātor,* from *salvāre,* to save. See SAVE[1].]

sav·iour (sāv′yər) *n. Chiefly British.* Variant of **savior.**

sa·voir-faire (săv′wär-fâr′) *n.* The ability to say or do the right or graceful thing. See Synonyms at **tact.** [French : *savoir,* to know how + *faire,* to do.]

Sa·vo·na (sə-vō′nə, sä-vô′nä). A city of northwest Italy on an arm of the Ligurian Sea west-southwest of Genoa. Known since early Roman times, it was an important commercial center in the Middle Ages. Population, 75,069.

Sa·vo·na·ro·la (săv′ə-nə-rō′lə, sä′vô-nä-), **Girolamo.** 1452–1498. Italian reformer. A Dominican friar, he gained a vast popular following and drove the Medici family out of Florence in 1494. He was later excommunicated and executed for criticizing Pope Alexander VI.

sa·vor (sā′vər) *n.* **1.** The taste or smell of something. **2.** A specific taste or smell. See Synonyms at **taste.** **3.** A distinctive quality or sensation: *enjoying the savor of victory.* **—savor** *v.* **-vored, -vor·ing, -vors.** *—intr.* **1.** To have a particular taste or smell: *a dish that savors of curry.* **2.** To exhibit a specified quality or characteristic; smack: *postures that savored of vanity.* *—tr.* **1.** To impart flavor or scent to; season: *savored the bland soup with salt.* **2.** To taste or smell, especially with pleasure: *savored each morsel of the feast.* **3.** To appreciate fully; enjoy or relish: *I want to savor this great moment of accomplishment.* [Middle English *savour,* from Old French, from Latin *sapor,* from *sapere,* to taste. See **sep-** in Appendix.] **—sa′vor·ous** *adj.*

sa·vor·y[1] (sā′və-rē) *adj.* **1.** Appetizing to the taste or smell: *a savory stew.* **2.** Piquant, pungent, or salty to the taste; not sweet. **3.** Morally respectable; inoffensive: *a past that was scarcely savory.* **—savory** *n., pl.* **-ies.** A dish of pungent taste, such as anchovies on toast or pickled fruit, sometimes served in Great Britain as an hors d'oeuvre or instead of a sweet dessert. [Middle English *savure,* from Old French *savoure,* past participle of *savourer,* to taste, from Late Latin *sapōrāre,* from Latin *sapor.* See SAVOR.] **—sa′vor·i·ly** *adv.* **—sa′vor·i·ness** *n.*

sa·vor·y[2] (sā′və-rē) *n., pl.* **-ies.** **1.** An annual Mediterranean aromatic herb *(Satureja hortensis)* of the mint family, having flowers with a pale lavender to white corolla. Also called *summer savory.* **2.** A related Mediterranean aromatic herb *(Satureja montana)* having flowers in a long, white or pink corolla. Also called *winter savory.* **3.** The leaves of either of these plants, used as seasoning. **4.** Any of several plants of the genus *Micromeria* in the mint family. [Middle English *saverey,* alteration of Old French *sarree,* alteration of Latin *saturēia.*]

sa·vour (sā′vər) *n. & v. Chiefly British.* Variant of **savor.**

sa·vour·y (sā′və-rē) *adj. & n. Chiefly British.* Variant of **savory**[1].

Sa·voy[1] (sə-voi′). A ruling house of Sardinia (1720–1861) and Italy (1861–1946).

Sa·voy[2] (sə-voi′). A historical region and former duchy of southeast France, western Switzerland, and northwest Italy. The region changed hands many times after its conquest by Julius Caesar and became a duchy in the early 15th century. In 1720 the duke of Savoy gained the title king of Sardinia, and in 1861 the Savoyard Victor Emmanuel II ascended the throne of the newly formed kingdom of Italy. Much of the original territory was ceded to France at the same time. **—Sa·voy′ard** (sə-voi′ärd′, săv′-oi-yärd′) *adj. & n.*

Savoy Alps. A range of the western Alps in southeast France rising to 4,810.2 m (15,771 ft) at Mont Blanc, the highest elevation in Europe.

sav·vy (săv′ē) *Informal. adj.* **-vi·er, -vi·est.** Well informed and perceptive; shrewd: *savvy Washington insiders.* **—savvy** *n.* Practical understanding or shrewdness: *a banker known for financial savvy.* **—savvy** *tr. & intr.v.* **sav·vied** (săv′ēd), **sav·vy·ing, sav·vies** (săv′ēz). To understand; comprehend. [From Spanish *sabe (usted),* (you) know, from *saber,* to know, from Old Spanish, from Vulgar Latin **sapēre,* from Latin *sapere,* to be wise. See **sep-** in Appendix.] **—sav′vi·ly** *adv.*

saw[1] (sô) *n.* Any of various tools, either hand-operated or power-driven, having a thin metal blade or disk with a sharp, usually toothed edge, used for cutting wood, metal, or other hard materials. **—saw** *v.* **sawed, sawed** or **sawn** (sôn), **saw·ing, saws.** *—tr.* **1.** To cut or divide with a saw. **2.** To produce or shape with a saw: *sawed a hole in the board.* **3.** To make back-and-forth motions through or on: *a speaker who saws the air with his arms.* *—intr.* **1.** To use a saw: *sawing along a penciled guideline.* **2.** To undergo cutting with a saw: *Pine wood saws easily.* [Middle English *sawe,* from Old English *sagu.* See **sek-** in Appendix.] **—saw′er** *n.*

saw[1]

saw[2] (sô) *n.* A familiar saying, especially one that has become trite through repetition. See Synonyms at **saying.** [Middle English *sawe,* from Old English *sagu,* speech. See **sek**^{w}**-**[3] in Appendix.]

saw[3] (sô) *v.* Past tense of **see**[1].

Sa·watch Range (sə-wŏch′). A range of the Rocky Mountains in central Colorado rising to 4,402.1 m (14,433 ft) at Mount Elbert.

saw·bones (sô′bōnz′) *n., pl.* **sawbones** or **-bones·es** (-bōn′zĭz). *Slang.* A physician, especially a surgeon.

saw·buck (sô′bŭk′) *n.* **1.** A sawhorse, especially one having a crossed pair of legs at each end. **2.** *Slang.* A ten-dollar bill.

saw·dust (sô′dŭst′) *n.* The small particles of wood or other material that fall from an object being sawed.

sawed-off (sôd′ôf′, -ŏf′) *adj.* **1.** Having one end sawed off: *a sawed-off shotgun.* **2.** *Slang.* Short; runty.

saw·fish (sô′fĭsh′) *n., pl.* **sawfish** or **-fish·es.** Any of various marine fishes of the genus *Pristis,* related to the rays and skates and having a bladelike snout with teeth along both sides.

sawfish
Largetooth sawfish
Pristis pristis

saw·fly (sô′flī′) *n.* Any of various hymenopterous insects, chiefly of the family Tenthredinidae, the females of which have sawlike ovipositors used for cutting into plant tissue to deposit their eggs.

saw grass *n.* A tall coastal or marshy sedge *(Cladium jamaicense)* of eastern North America, Mexico, and the West Indies, having leaves with sharp, minutely toothed margins.

saw·horse (sô′hôrs′) *n.* A frame with legs, used to support pieces of wood being sawed.

saw log *n.* A log of a size large enough to be sawed into boards.

saw·mill (sô′mĭl′) *n.* **1.** A plant where timber is sawed into boards. **2.** A large machine for sawing lumber.

sawn (sôn) *v.* A past participle of **saw**[1].

saw palmetto *n.* A small, creeping palm *(Serenoa repens)* of the southeast United States, having palmately divided leaves with one-ribbed segments and black, one-seeded fruit.

saw set *n.* An instrument used to give set to the teeth of a saw by bending each alternate tooth slightly outward.

saw-toothed (sô′to͞otht′) *adj.* **1.** Having teeth resembling the teeth of a saw: *saw-toothed sharks.* **2.** Often **saw·tooth** (-to͞oth′). Having a jagged or zigzag pattern, outline, or course; serrate: *a saw-toothed mountain range; a sawtooth curve.*

saw-whet owl (sô′hwĕt′, -wĕt′) *n.* A small brown and white owl *(Aegolius acadicus)* of North America, having no ear tufts. [From the resemblance of its call to the sound made in sharpening a saw.]

sawfly
Common sawfly
Tenthredo varipictus

♦ **saw·yer** (sô′yər) *n.* **1.** One that is employed in sawing wood. **2.** Any of several long-horned beetles of the genus *Monochamus* having larvae that bore large holes in living or dead wood. **3.** See **snag** (sense 1a). See Regional Note at **preacher.** [Middle English *sauere, sawier,* from *sawen,* to saw, from *sawe,* saw. See SAW[1].]

sax (săks) *n. Music.* A saxophone.

Sax. *abbr.* Saxon.

sax·a·tile (săk′sə-tīl′, -tĭl) *adj.* Saxicolous. [Latin *saxātilis,* from *saxum,* rock. See **sek-** in Appendix.]

Saxe-Co·burg (săks-kō′bûrg). A British royal house (1901–1910) whose only ruler was Edward VII.

sax·horn (săks′hôrn′) *n. Music.* Any of a family of valved brass wind instruments that resemble the bugle and have a full, even tone and wide compass. [After *Sax,* name of 19th-century Belgian instrument-making family.]

sax·ic·o·lous (săk-sĭk′ə-ləs) also **sax·ic·o·line** (-līn′) *adj.* Growing on or living among rocks: *saxicolous lichens.* [Latin *saxum,* stone; see **sek-** in Appendix + -COLOUS.]

sax·i·frage (săk′sə-frĭj, -frāj′) *n.* Any of numerous herbs of the genus *Saxifraga,* having small, variously colored flowers and leaves that often form a basal rosette. [Middle English, from Old French, from Late Latin *(herba) saxifraga,* maidenhair fern, from Latin *saxifragus,* rock-breaking (from its being found growing in rock crevices) : *saxum,* rock; see **sek-** in Appendix + *frangere, frāct-,* to break; see **bhreg-** in Appendix.]

sax·i·tox·in (săk′sĭ-tŏk′sĭn) *n.* A potent neurotoxin produced by certain dinoflagellates that accumulates in shellfish feeding on these organisms and consequently causes food poisoning in human beings who eat the shellfish. [New Latin *Saxidomus gigantēus,* clam species (Latin *saxum,* stone; see SAXATILE + Latin *domus,* house; see DOME + Latin *gigantēus,* giant) + TOXIN.]

Sax·o Gram·mat·i·cus (săk′sō grə-măt′ĭ-kəs). 1150?–1220? Danish historian whose *Gesta Danorum,* a chronicle of Danish kings, contains the story of Hamlet.

Sax·on (săk′sən) *n. Abbr.* **Sax., S.** **1.** A member of a West Germanic tribal group that inhabited northern Germany and invaded Britain in the fifth and sixth centuries A.D. with the Angles and Jutes. **2.** A person of English or Lowland Scots birth or

sawhorse

saxophone

descent as distinguished from one of Irish, Welsh, or Highland Scots birth or descent. **3.** A native or inhabitant of Saxony. **4.** The West Germanic language of any of the ancient Saxon peoples. **5.** The Germanic element of English as distinguished from the French and Latin elements. [Middle English, from Late Latin *Saxō, Saxon-,* of Germanic origin. See **sek-** in Appendix.] **—Sax′on** *adj.*

Sax·on·ism (săk′sə-nĭz′əm) *n.* An English word, phrase, or idiom of Anglo-Saxon origin.

sax·o·ny also **Sax·o·ny** (săk′sə-nē) *n., pl.* **-nies. 1.** A high-grade wool fabric originally made from the wool of sheep raised in Saxony. **2.** A fine soft woolen fabric similar in weave to tweed. **3.** A woven carpet having a cut pile of dense, erect tufts.

Saxony. A historical region of northern Germany. The original home of the Saxons, it was conquered by Charlemagne in the 8th century and became a duchy after his death. Its borders were eventually extended southeastward as the region was subdivided and redivided. The dukes of Saxony became electors of the Holy Roman Empire in 1356, and in 1806 the elector was elevated to kingship but lost half his territory to Prussia in 1815. A later kingdom of Saxony was part of the German Empire (1871–1918).

sax·o·phone (săk′sə-fōn′) *n. Music.* A woodwind instrument with a single-reed mouthpiece and a usually curved conical metal tube, including soprano, alto, tenor, and baritone sizes. [After *Sax,* name of 19th-century Belgian instrument-making family.] **—sax′o·phon′ist** *n.*

sax·tu·ba (săks′tōō′bə, -tyōō′-) *n. Music.* A large bass saxhorn. [SAX(HORN) + TUBA.]

say (sā) *v.* **said** (sĕd), **say·ing, says** (sĕz). *—tr.* **1.** To utter aloud; pronounce: *The children said, "Good morning."* **2.** To express in words: *Say what's on your mind.* **3.a.** To state as one's opinion or judgment; declare: *I say let's eat out.* **b.** To state as a determination of fact: *It's hard to say who is right in this matter.* **4.** To repeat or recite: *said grace.* **5.** To report or maintain; allege. **6.a.** To indicate; show: *The clock says half past two.* **b.** To give nonverbal expression to; signify or embody: *It was an act that said "devotion."* **7.** To suppose; assume: *Let's say that you're right.* *—intr.* To make a statement; express oneself: *The story must be true because the teacher said so.* **—say** *n.* **1.** A turn or chance to speak: *Having had my say, I sat down.* **2.** The right or power to influence or make a decision: *Citizens have a say in the councils of government. All I want is some say in the matter.* **3.** *Archaic.* Something said; a statement. **—say** *adv.* **1.** Approximately: *There were, say, 500 people present.* **2.** For instance: *a woodwind, say an oboe.* **—say** *interj.* Used to express surprise or appeal for someone's attention. ***—idioms.*** **I say. 1.** Used preceding an utterance to call attention to it: *I say, do you have the time?* **2.** Used as an exclamation of surprise, delight, or dismay. **that is to say.** In other words. **to say nothing of.** And there is no need to mention. Used to allude to things that fill out an idea or argument: *The yard is a mess, to say nothing of the house.* **you can say that again.** *Slang.* Used to express strong agreement with what has just been said. [Middle English *seien,* from Old English *secgan.* See **sekʷ-³** in Appendix.] **—say′er** *n.*

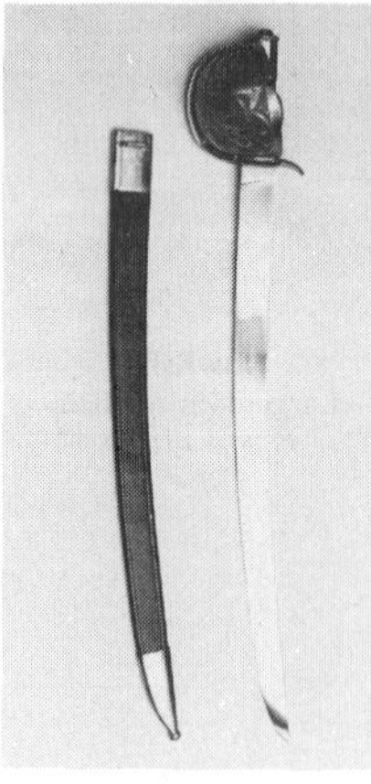
scabbard
With sword

Sa·yan Mountains (sä-yän′). A range of mountains in south-central Russia west of Lake Baikal. The mountains have important mineral deposits.

Say·ers (sā′ərz), **Dorothy L(eigh).** 1893–1957. British writer known for her detective stories, usually featuring the amateur investigator Lord Peter Wimsey.

say·ing (sā′ĭng) *n.* Something, such as an adage or a maxim, that is said.

SYNONYMS: *saying, maxim, adage, saw, motto, epigram, proverb, aphorism.* These nouns refer to concise verbal expressions setting forth wisdom or a truth. A *saying* is an often repeated and familiar expression: *She was fond of quoting the sayings of philosophers. Maxim* denotes particularly an expression of a general truth or a rule of conduct: *"For a wise man, he seemed to me . . . to be governed too much by general maxims"* (Edmund Burke). *Adage* applies to a saying that has gained credit through long use: *On his birthday the child gave no credence to the adage, "Good things come in small packages." Saw* often refers to a familiar saying that has become trite through frequent repetition: *My wise saws gave little comfort to the losing team.* A *motto* is a maxim that expresses the aims, character, or guiding principles of a person, a group, or an institution: *"Exuberance over taste" was her motto.* An *epigram* is a terse, witty expression, often paradoxical or satirical and neatly or brilliantly phrased: *In his epigram Samuel Johnson called remarriage a "triumph of hope over experience." Proverb* refers to an old and popular saying that illustrates something such as a basic truth or a practical precept: *"Slow and steady wins the race" is a proverb to live by. Aphorism,* a concise expression of a truth or principle, implies depth of content and stylistic distinction: *Few writers have coined more aphorisms than Benjamin Franklin.*

scaffold

sa·yo·na·ra (sī′ə-när′ə) *interj.* Good-bye. [Japanese.]

Say·re·ville (sā′ər-vĭl′, sâr′-). A borough of east-central New Jersey south-southwest of Perth Amboy. It is a manufacturing center. Population, 29,969.

say-so (sā′sō′) *n., pl.* **-sos.** *Informal.* **1.** An unsupported statement or assurance. **2.** An authoritative expression of permission or approval. **3.** The right or authority to decide.

say·yid (sä′yĭd) *n. Islam.* Used as a title and form of address for a male dignitary. [Arabic.]

Sb The symbol for the element **antimony.** [Latin *stibium.* See STIBNITE.]

SB *abbr.* Simultaneous broadcast.

sb. *abbr.* Substantive.

s.b. *abbr. Baseball.* Stolen base.

S.B. *abbr. Latin.* Scientiae Baccalaureus (Bachelor of Science).

SBA *abbr.* Small Business Administration.

SbE *abbr.* South by east.

'sblood (zblŭd) *interj. Archaic.* Used as an oath. [Alteration of *God's blood.*]

SBN *abbr.* Standard Book Number.

SbW *abbr.* South by west.

sc also **s.c.** *abbr. Printing.* Small capital.

Sc The symbol for the element **scandium.**

SC *abbr.* **1.** Security Council. **2.** Or **S.C.** South Carolina.

sc. *abbr.* **1.** Scale. **2.** Scene. **3.** Science. **4.** Scilicet. **5.** Scruple (unit of weight).

Sc. *abbr.* **1.** Scots; Scottish. **2.** Scotch.

S.C. *abbr. Law.* Supreme Court.

scab (skăb) *n.* **1.** A crust discharged from and covering a healing wound. **2.** Scabies or mange in domestic animals or livestock, especially sheep. **3.a.** Any of various plant diseases caused by fungi or bacteria and resulting in crustlike spots on fruit, leaves, or roots. **b.** The spots caused by such a disease. **4.** *Slang.* A person regarded as contemptible. **5.a.** A worker who refuses membership in a labor union. **b.** An employee who works while others are on strike; a strikebreaker. **c.** A person hired to replace a striking worker. **—scab** *intr.v.* **scabbed, scab·bing, scabs. 1.** To become covered with scabs or a scab. **2.** To work or take a job as a scab. [Middle English, from Old Norse *skabb.*]

scab·bard (skăb′ərd) *n.* A sheath, as for a dagger or sword. **—scabbard** *tr.v.* **-bard·ed, -bard·ing, -bards.** To put into or furnish with such a sheath. [Middle English *scauberc, scabbard,* from Old French *escauberc,* possibly of Germanic origin. See **sker-¹** in Appendix.]

scabbard fish *n.* Any of various marine fishes with a long, narrow, silvery body, especially a cutlass fish *(Trichiurus lepturus)* of the western Atlantic.

scab·ble (skăb′əl) *tr.v.* **-bled, -bling, -bles.** To work or dress (stone) roughly, preliminary to fine tooling. [Middle English *scaplen,* from Old North French *escapler,* to dress timber : *es-,* off (from Latin *ex-;* see EX–) + *capler,* to cut (from Late Latin **capulāre, cappulāre*).]

scab·by (skăb′ē) *adj.* **-bi·er, -bi·est. 1.** Having, consisting of, or covered with scabs. **2.** Affected with scab or scabies. **3.** *Informal.* Contemptible; vile: *scabby greed.* **—scab′bi·ly** *adv.* **—scab′bi·ness** *n.*

sca·bies (skā′bēz) *n., pl.* **scabies. 1.** A contagious skin disease caused by a parasitic mite *(Sarcoptes scabiei)* and characterized by intense itching. **2.** A similar disease in animals, especially sheep. [Middle English, from Latin *scabiēs,* from *scabere,* to scratch.]

sca·bi·et·ic (skā′bē-ĕt′ĭk) *adj.* Relating to or affected with scabies.

sca·bi·o·sa (skā′bē-ō′sə, -zə, skăb′ē-) *n.* See **scabious².** [New Latin *Scabiōsa,* genus name, from Medieval Latin *(herba) scabiōsa,* (herb) for scabies, scabious, feminine of Latin *scabiōsus,* mangy, from *scabiēs,* itch. See SCABIES.]

sca·bi·ous¹ (skā′bē-əs, skăb′ē-) *adj.* **1.** Of or relating to scabies. **2.** Having scabs. [From Latin *scabiōsus,* mangy. See SCABIOSA.]

sca·bi·ous² (skā′bē-əs) *n.* Any of various plants of the genus *Scabiosa,* especially *S. atropurpurea,* having opposite leaves and variously colored flower heads that are subtended by an involucre. Also called *scabiosa.* [Middle English *scabiose,* from Medieval Latin *(herba) scabiōsa,* (herb) for scabies, scabious. See SCABIOSA.]

scab·land (skăb′lănd′) *n.* An elevated area of barren, rocky land with little or no soil cover, often crossed by dry stream channels: *the scablands of eastern Washington.*

scab·rous (skăb′rəs, skā′brəs) *adj.* **1.** Having or covered with scales or small projections and rough to the touch. See Synonyms at **rough. 2.** Difficult to handle; knotty: *a scabrous situation.* **3.** Dealing with scandalous or salacious material: *a scabrous novel.* [Late Latin *scabrōsus,* from *scaber, scabr-,* scurfy.] **—scab′rous·ly** *adv.* **—scab′rous·ness** *n.*

scad¹ (skăd) *n., pl.* **scad** or **scads.** Any of several carangid fishes of the genus *Decapterus,* especially *D. punctatus* of the western Atlantic. [Origin unknown.]

scad² (skăd) *n. Informal.* A large number or amount. Often used in the plural: *Scads of people are in the hall.* [Origin unknown.]

Sca·fell Pike (skô′fĕl′). A mountain in the Cumbrian Mountains of northwest England. At 979.1 m (3,210 ft), it is the highest peak in the range and the highest elevation in England.

scaf·fold (skăf′əld, -ōld′) *n.* **1.** A temporary platform, either supported from below or suspended from above, on which workers sit or stand when performing tasks at heights above the ground. **2.** A raised wooden framework or platform. **3.** A platform used in the execution of condemned prisoners, as by hanging or beheading. **—scaffold** *tr.v.* **-fold·ed, -fold·ing, -folds. 1.** To provide or support with a raised framework or platform. **2.** To place on a raised framework or platform. [Middle English, from Medieval Latin *scaffaldus,* of Old French origin.]

scaf·fold·ing (skăf′əl-dĭng, skăf′ōl′-) *n.* **1.** A scaffold or system of scaffolds. **2.** Materials used for constructing scaffolds.

scag (skăg) *n. Slang.* Heroin. [Origin unknown.]

scagl·io·la (skăl-yō′lə, -yô′-) *n.* Plasterwork in imitation of ornamental marble, consisting of ground gypsum and glue colored with marble or granite dust. [Italian, diminutive of *scaglia,* chip, of Germanic origin. See **skel-**[1] in Appendix.]

sca·lade (skə-lād′, -läd′) also **sca·la·do** (-lā′dō, -lä′-) *n., pl.* **-lades** also **-la·dos.** *Archaic.* An act of scaling a wall; an escalade. [Alteration of Italian *scalata,* from *scala,* ladder. See ESCALADE.]

scal·age (skā′lĭj) *n.* **1.** An assessed percentage of the total price or measured amount of goods being shipped or stored, used to figure a deduction from the price or amount to reflect normal shrinkage or depletion of the goods. **2.** The estimated amount of lumber in logs being scaled.

sca·lar (skā′lər, -lär′) *n.* **1.** A quantity, such as mass, length, or speed, that is completely specified by its magnitude and has no direction. **2.** A device that yields an output equal to the input multiplied by a constant, as in a linear amplifier. **—scalar** *adj. Mathematics.* Having only magnitude. Used of numbers or quantities. [Latin *scālāris,* of a ladder, from *scālae,* ladder. See SCALE[2].]

sca·la·re (skə-lâr′ē, -lär′ē) *n.* See **angelfish** (sense 2). [Latin *scālāre,* neuter of *scālāris,* of a ladder (so-called from its parallel markings), from *scālae,* ladder. See SCALE[2].]

sca·lar·i·form (skə-lăr′ə-fôrm′) *adj. Biology.* Resembling the rungs of a ladder; ladderlike. Used of certain vessels and tissues. [Latin *scālāris,* of a ladder; see SCALARE + –FORM.] **—sca·lar′i·form′ly** *adv.*

scalar product *n. Mathematics.* The numerical product of the lengths of two vectors and the cosine of the angle between them. Also called *dot product, inner product.*

scal·a·wag (skăl′ə-wăg′) also **scal·ly·wag** (skăl′ē-) *n.* **1.** *Informal.* A reprobate; a rascal. **2.** A white Southerner working for or supporting the federal government during Reconstruction. [Origin unknown.]

scald[1] (skôld) *v.* **scald·ed, scald·ing, scalds.** *—tr.* **1.** To burn with or as if with hot liquid or steam. **2.** To subject to or treat with boiling water: *scalded the hide to remove the hair; scalded and peeled the tomatoes.* **3.** To heat (a liquid, such as milk) almost to the boiling point. **4.** To criticize harshly; excoriate. *—intr.* To become scalded. **—scald** *n.* **1.** A body injury caused by scalding. **2.** *Botany.* **a.** A superficial discoloration on fruit, vegetables, leaves, or tree trunks caused by sudden exposure to intense sunlight or the action of gases. **b.** A disease of some cereal grasses caused by a fungus of the genus *Rhynchosporium.* [Middle English *scalden,* from Old North French *escalder,* from Late Latin *excaldāre,* to wash in hot water : Latin *ex-,* ex- + Latin *calidus, caldus,* warm, hot; see **kele-**[1] in Appendix.]

scald[2] (skôld, skäld) *n.* Variant of **skald.**

scald[3] (skôld, skäld) *n.* Variant of **scall.**

scald·ing (skôl′dĭng) *adj.* **1.** Causing a burning sensation, as from contact with hot liquid. **2.** Boiling: *scalding water.* **3.** Scorching; searing: *scalding sunlight.* **4.** Harshly critical or denunciatory; scathing: *a scalding review of the play.* **—scald′ing·ly** *adv.*

scale[1] (skāl) *n.* **1. a.** One of the many small, platelike dermal or epidermal structures that characteristically form the external covering of fishes, reptiles, and certain mammals. **b.** A similar part, such as one of the minute structures overlapping to form the covering on the wings of butterflies and moths. **2.** *Pathology.* A dry, thin flake of epidermis shed from the skin. **3.** A small, thin piece. **4.** *Botany.* A small, thin, usually dry, often appressed plant structure, such as any of the protective leaves that cover a tree bud or the bract that subtends a flower in a sedge spikelet. **5. a.** A scale insect. **b.** A plant disease or infestation caused by scale insects. **6. a.** A flaky oxide film formed on a metal, as on iron, that has been heated to high temperatures. **b.** A flake of rust. **7.** A hard mineral coating that forms on the inside surface of boilers, kettles, and other containers in which water is repeatedly heated. **—scale** *v.* **scaled, scal·ing, scales.** *—tr.* **1.** To clear or strip of scale or scales: *Scale and clean the fish.* **2.** To remove in layers or scales: *scaled off the old paint.* **3.** To cover with scales; encrust. **4.** To throw (a thin, flat object) so that it soars through the air or skips along the surface of water. **5.** *Dentistry.* To remove (tartar) from tooth surfaces with a pointed instrument. **6.** *Australian.* **a.** To cheat; swindle. **b.** To ride on (a tram or train, for example) without paying the fare. *—intr.* **1.** To come off in scales or layers; flake. **2.** To become encrusted. [Middle English, from Old French *escale,* of Germanic origin. See **skel-**[1] in Appendix.] **—scale′like** *adj.*

scale[2] (skāl) *n. Abbr.* **sc. 1. a.** A system of ordered marks at fixed intervals used as a reference standard in measurement: *a ruler with scales in inches and centimeters.* **b.** An instrument or device bearing such marks. **c.** A standard of measurement or judgment; a criterion. **2. a.** A proportion used in determining the dimensional relationship of a representation to that which it represents: *a world map with a scale of 1:4,560,000.* **b.** A calibrated line, as on a map or an architectural plan, indicating such a proportion. **c.** Proper proportion: *a house that seemed out of scale with its surroundings.* **3.** A progressive classification, as of size, amount, importance, or rank: *judging divers' performances on a scale of 1 to 10; a family that ranks high on the social scale.* **4.** A relative level or degree: *entertained on a lavish scale.* **5.** A minimum wage fixed by contract: *musicians playing a benefit concert for scale.* **6.** *Mathematics.* A system of notation in which the values of numerical expressions are determined by their places relative to the chosen base of the system: *the decimal scale.* **7.** *Music.* An ascending or descending series of tones proceeding by a specified scheme of intervals and varying in pitch arrangement and interval size. **—scale** *v.* **scaled, scal·ing, scales.** *—tr.* **1.** To climb up or over; ascend: *scaled the peak.* **2.** To make in accord with a particular proportion or scale: *Scale the model to be one tenth of actual size.* **3.** To alter according to a standard or by degrees; adjust in calculated amounts: *scaled down their demands to fit reality; scaled back the scheduled pay increase.* **4.** To estimate or measure the quantity of lumber in (logs or uncut trees). *—intr.* **1.** To climb; ascend. **2.** To rise in steps or stages. [Middle English, from Latin *scālae,* ladder. See **skand-** in Appendix.] **—scal′a·ble** *adj.*

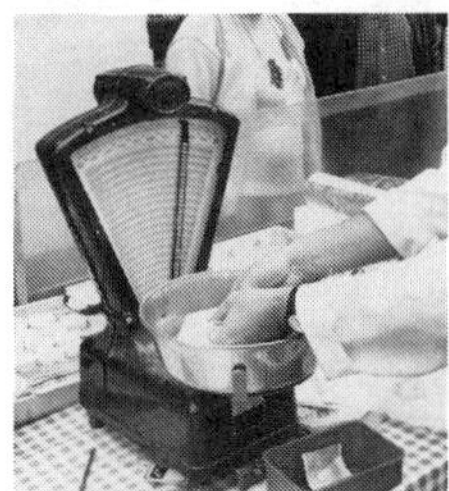

scale[3]

scale[3] (skāl) *n.* **1.** An instrument or a machine for weighing. Often used in the plural. **2.** Either of the pans, trays, or dishes of a balance. **—scale** *v.* **scaled, scal·ing, scales.** *—tr.* To weigh with scales. *—intr.* To have a given weight, as determined by a scale: *cargo that scales 14 metric tons.* [Middle English, bowl, balance, from Old Norse *skāl.* See **skel-**[1] in Appendix.]

scale insect *n.* Any of various small homopterous insects of the superfamily Coccoidea that suck the juices of plants and the females of which secrete and remain under waxy scales on plant tissue.

scale moss *n.* Any of various leafy liverworts of the order Jungermanniales.

sca·lene (skā′lēn′, skā-lēn′) *adj. Mathematics.* Having three unequal sides. Used of triangles. [Late Latin *scalēnus,* from Greek *skalēnos,* from *skallein,* to hoe, stir up. See **skel-**[1] in Appendix.]

scalene muscle *n.* Any of three muscles on each side of the neck that serve to bend and rotate the neck and that assist breathing by raising or fixing the first two ribs. Also called *scalenus.*

sca·le·nus (skā-lē′nəs) *n., pl.* **-ni** (-nī, -nē). See **scalene muscle.** [Late Latin *scalēnus,* scalene. See SCALENE.]

scal·er (skā′lər) *n.* An electronic circuit that records the aggregate of a specific number of signals that occur too rapidly to be recorded individually. [From SCALE[2].]

Scales (skālz) *pl.n. (used with a sing. verb).* See **Libra** (senses 1, 2a).

Sca·li·a (skə-lē′ə), **Antonin.** Born 1936. American jurist who was appointed an associate justice of the U.S. Supreme Court in 1986.

Scal·i·ger (skăl′ə-jər), **Julius Caesar.** 1484–1558. Italian physician and scholar noted for his scientific and philosophical writings. His son **Joseph Justus Scaliger** (1540–1609), a French scholar, pioneered the modern study of classical texts.

scall (skôl, skăl) also **scald** (skôld, skäld) *n.* A scaly eruption of the skin or scalp. [Middle English, from Old Norse *skalli,* a bald head. See **skel-**[1] in Appendix.]

scal·lion (skăl′yən) *n.* **1.** A young onion before the development of the bulb. **2.** Any of several onionlike plants, such as the leek or shallot. [Middle English *scaloun,* from Anglo-Norman *scalun,* from Vulgar Latin *_escalōnia,_ alteration of Latin *(caepa) Ascalōnia,* Ascalonian (onion), shallot, feminine of *Ascalōnius,* Ascalonian, from *Ascalō, Ascalōn-,* Ascalon (Ashqelon), an ancient city of southwest Palestine.]

scallop
Top: Bay scallop
Pecten irradians
Bottom: Border of a
c. 1752–1788 Chelsea dish

scal·lop (skŏl′əp, skăl′-) also **scol·lop** (skŏl′-) or **es·cal·lop** (ĭ-skŏl′-, ĭ-skăl′-) *—n.* **1. a.** Any of various free-swimming marine mollusks of the family Pectinidae, having fan-shaped bivalve shells with a radiating fluted pattern. **b.** The edible adductor muscle of this mollusk. **c.** A shell of this mollusk, or a dish in a similar shape, used for baking and serving seafood. **2.** One of a series of curved projections forming an ornamental border. **3.** A thin, boneless slice of meat. *—v.* **-loped, -lop·ing, -lops.** *—tr.* **1.** To edge (cloth, for example) with a series of curved projections. **2.** To bake in a casserole with milk or a sauce and often with bread crumbs: *scalloped potatoes.* **3.** To cut (meat) into thin, boneless slices. *—intr.* To gather scallops for eating or sale. [Middle English *scalop,* from Old French *escalope,* shell, of Germanic origin.] **—scal′lop·er** *n.*

scal·ly·wag (skăl′ē-wăg′) *n.* Variant of **scalawag.**

scal·o·gram (skā′lə-grăm′) *n. Psychology.* A scale for measuring attitude or opinion in which agreement with a given item implies agreement with the items lower in rank.

sca·lop·pi·ne also **sca·lop·pi·ni** (skăl′ə-pē′nē, skä′lə-) *n.* Small, thinly sliced pieces of meat, especially veal, dredged in flour, sautéed, and served in a sauce. [Italian, pl. of *scaloppina,* diminutive of *scaloppa,* thin slice, from French *escalope,* from Old French, shell (from the fillets being served curled like shells). See SCALLOP.]

scalp (skălp) *n.* **1.** The skin covering the top of the human head. **2.** A portion of this skin with its attached hair, cut from a body by certain Native American warriors as a battle trophy or by American settlers as proof in claiming a bounty. **3.** A piece of hide from the skull of certain animals, such as the fox, shown as proof of killing in order to collect a bounty. **4.** A trophy of victory. **5.** *Slang.* A quick profit made by buying and reselling

ă pat	oi boy
ā pay	ou out
âr care	o͝o took
ä father	o͞o boot
ĕ pet	ŭ cut
ē be	ûr urge
ĭ pit	th thin
ī pie	*th* this
îr pier	hw which
ŏ pot	zh vision
ō toe	ə about, item
ô paw	♦ regionalism

Stress marks: ′ (primary); ′ (secondary), as in **dictionary** (dĭk′shə-nĕr′ē)

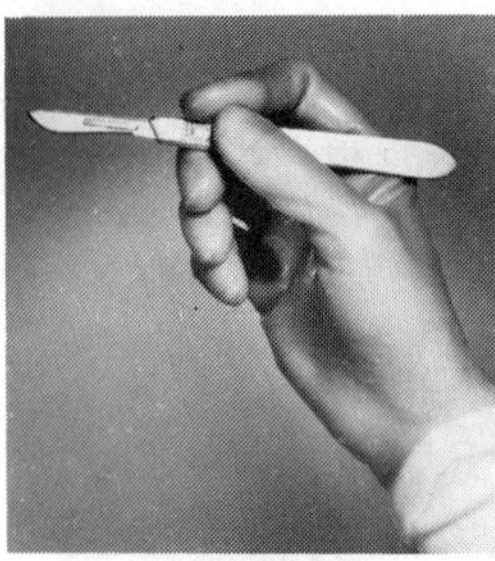
scalpel

something, especially tickets. **—scalp** *v.* **scalped, scalp·ing, scalps.** *—tr.* **1.** To cut or tear the scalp from. **2.** To deprive of top growth or a top layer: *land scalped by strip miners.* **3.** *Slang.* To resell at a price higher than the established value: *scalping tickets to a popular sports event.* **4.** *Slang.* To buy and sell (securities or commodities) in order to make small, quick profits. *—intr. Slang.* **1.** To engage in the reselling of something, such as tickets, at a price higher than the established value. **2.** To buy and sell securities or commodities for small, quick profits. [Middle English, top of the head, of Scandinavian origin. See **skel-**[1] in Appendix.] **—scalp′er** *n.*

scal·pel (skăl′pəl) *n.* A small, straight knife with a thin, sharp blade used in surgery and dissection. [Latin *scalpellum,* diminutive of *scalper, scalprum,* knife, from *scalpere,* to scratch, cut. See **skel-**[1] in Appendix.]

scalp lock *n.* A long lock of hair left on the top of the shaven head by certain Native American men.

scal·y (skā′lē) *adj.* **-i·er, -i·est. 1.** Covered or partially covered with scales. **2.** Shedding scales or flakes; flaking. **—scal′i·ness** *n.*

scaly anteater *n.* See **pangolin.**

scam (skăm) *Slang. n.* A fraudulent business scheme; a swindle. **—scam** *tr.v.* **scammed, scam·ming, scams.** To defraud; swindle. [Origin unknown.] **—scam′mer** *n.*

scam·mo·ny (skăm′ə-nē) *n., pl.* **-nies. 1.** An eastern Mediterranean plant *(Convolvulus scammonia)* having large roots that yield a resin formerly used as a cathartic. **2.** The resin obtained from this plant. **3.** A cathartic preparation made from this resin. [Middle English *scamonie,* from Old English *scammōniam* and from Old French *scamonie,* both from Latin *scammōnea,* from Greek *skammōnia.*]

scamp[1] (skămp) *n.* **1.** A rogue; a rascal. **2.** A mischievous youngster. [Probably from *scamp,* to go about idly, probably from obsolete Dutch *schampen,* to decamp, from Middle Dutch *ontscampen.* See SCAMPER.]

scamp[2] (skămp) *tr.v.* **scamped, scamp·ing, scamps.** To perform in a careless, superficial way. [Possibly of Scandinavian origin.] **—scamp′er** *n.*

scam·per (skăm′pər) *intr.v.* **-pered, -per·ing, -pers.** To run or go quickly and lightly: *children scampering off to play.* **—scamper** *n.* A quick light run or movement. [Probably from Flemish *schampeeren,* frequentative of obsolete Dutch *schampen,* to run away, decamp, from Middle Dutch *ontscampen,* from Old French *escamper,* from Old Italian *scampare,* from Vulgar Latin **excampāre,* from Latin *ex campō,* out of the field : *ex-,* away; see EX– + *campō,* ablative of *campus,* field.]

scam·pi (skăm′pē, skäm′-) *n., pl.* **scampi.** Large shrimp broiled or sautéed and served in a garlic and butter sauce. [Italian, pl. of *scampo,* a kind of lobster, from Greek *kampē,* bending (from its shape), perhaps from Greek *kamptein,* to bend.]

scan (skăn) *v.* **scanned, scan·ning, scans.** *—tr.* **1.** To examine closely. **2.** To look over quickly and systematically: *scanning the horizon for signs of land.* **3.** To look over or leaf through hastily: *scanned the morning papers while eating breakfast.* **4.** To analyze (verse) into metrical patterns. **5.** *Electronics.* **a.** To move a finely focused beam of light or electrons in a systematic pattern over (a surface) in order to reproduce or sense and subsequently transmit an image. **b.** To move a radar beam in a systematic pattern over (a sector of sky) in search of a target. **6.** *Computer Science.* To search (stored data) automatically for specific data. **7.** *Medicine.* To examine (a body or a body part) with a CAT scanner or similar scanning apparatus. *—intr.* **1.** To analyze verse into metrical patterns. **2.** To conform to a metrical pattern. **3.** *Electronics.* To undergo electronic scanning. **—scan** *n.* **1.** The act or an instance of scanning. **2.** Scope or field of vision. **3. a.** Examination of a body or bodily part by a CAT scanner or similar scanning apparatus. **b.** A picture or an image produced by this means. **4.** A single sweep of the beam of electrons across a television screen. [Middle English *scanden, scannen,* to scan a verse, from Latin *scandere,* to climb, scan a verse. See **skand-** in Appendix.] **—scan′na·ble** *adj.* **—scan′ner** *n.*

WORD HISTORY: In the 1969 edition of *The American Heritage Dictionary* a dead issue was buried by our Usage Panel, 85 percent of whom thought it was acceptable to use *scan* in the sense "to look over quickly," though the note stated that this was less formal usage. The usage issue was raised because *scan* in an earlier sense meant "to examine closely." From a historical perspective it is easy to see how these two opposite senses of *scan* developed. The source of our word, Latin *scandere,* which meant "to climb," came to mean "to scan a verse of poetry," because one could beat the rhythm by lifting and putting down one's foot. The Middle English verb *scannen,* derived from *scandere,* came into Middle English in this sense (first recorded in a text composed before 1398). In the 16th century this highly specialized sense having to do with the close analysis of verse developed other senses, such as "to criticize, examine minutely, interpret, perceive." From these senses having to do with examination and perception, it was an easy step to the sense "to look at searchingly" (first recorded in 1798), perhaps harking back still to the careful, detailed work involved in analyzing prosody. But a thorough search can change into a quick one, as it seems to have done in the case of the verb *scan.*

Scand. *abbr.* Scandinavia; Scandinavian.

scan·dal (skăn′dl) *n.* **1.** A publicized incident that brings about disgrace or offends the moral sensibilities of society: *a drug scandal that forced the mayor's resignation.* **2.** A person, thing, or circumstance that causes or ought to cause disgrace or outrage: *a politician whose dishonesty is a scandal; considered the housing shortage a scandal.* **3.** Damage to reputation or character caused by public disclosure of immoral or grossly improper behavior; disgrace. **4.** Talk that is damaging to one's character; malicious gossip. [French *scandale,* from Old French, cause of sin, from Latin *scandalum,* trap, stumbling block, temptation, from Greek *skandalon.* See **skand-** in Appendix.]

scan·dal·ize (skăn′dl-īz′) *tr.v.* **-ized, -iz·ing, -iz·es. 1.** To offend the moral sensibilities of: *a lurid incident that scandalized the whole town.* **2.** *Archaic.* To dishonor; disgrace. **—scan′dal·i·za′tion** (-ĭ-zā′shən) *n.* **—scan′dal·iz′er** *n.*

scan·dal·mon·ger (skăn′dl-mŭng′gər, -mŏng′-) *n.* One who spreads malicious gossip. **—scan′dal·mon′ger·ing** *n.*

scan·dal·ous (skăn′dl-əs) *adj.* **1.** Causing scandal; shocking: *scandalous behavior.* **2.** Containing material damaging to reputation; defamatory: *a scandalous exposé.* **—scan′dal·ous·ly** *adv.* **—scan′dal·ous·ness** *n.*

scandal sheet *n.* A periodical, such as a newspaper, that habitually prints gossip or scandalous stories.

scan·dent (skăn′dənt) *adj.* *Botany.* Climbing: *a scandent vine.* [Latin *scandēns, scandent-,* present participle of *scandere,* to climb. See **skand-** in Appendix.]

scan·di·a (skăn′dē-ə) *n.* See **scandium oxide.** [From SCANDIUM.]

Scan·di·a (skăn′dē-ə). An ancient and poetic name for Scandinavia or the Scandinavian Peninsula.

Scan·di·an (skăn′dē-ən) *adj.* Scandinavian. **—Scandian** *n.* A Scandinavian. [From Latin *Scandia,* Scandinavia.]

Scan·di·na·vi·a (skăn′də-nā′vē-ə, -nāv′yə). *Abbr.* **Scand.** A region of northern Europe consisting of Norway, Sweden, and Denmark. Finland, Iceland, and the Faeroe Islands are often included in the region.

Scan·di·na·vi·an (skăn′də-nā′vē-ən, -nāv′yən) *adj. Abbr.* **Scand.** Of or relating to Scandinavia or to its peoples, languages, or cultures. **—Scandinavian** *n. Abbr.* **Scand. 1.** A native or inhabitant of Scandinavia. **2.** See **North Germanic.**

Scandinavian Peninsula. A peninsula of northern Europe comprising Norway and Sweden.

scan·di·um (skăn′dē-əm) *n.* *Symbol* **Sc** A silvery-white metallic element found in various rare minerals and separated as a byproduct in the processing of certain uranium ores. An artificially produced radioactive isotope is used as a tracer in studies of oil wells and pipelines. Atomic number 21; atomic weight 44.956; melting point 1,540°C; boiling point 2,850°C; specific gravity 2.99; valence 3. See table at **element.** [From Latin *Scandia,* Scandinavia.] **—scan′dic** (-dĭk) *adj.*

scandium oxide *n.* A white amorphous powder, Sc_2O_3, used as a source of scandium and in the manufacture of ceramics. Also called *scandia.*

scan·ning electron microscope (skăn′ĭng) *n. Abbr.* **SEM** An electron microscope that forms a three-dimensional image on a cathode-ray tube by moving a beam of focused electrons across an object and reading both the electrons scattered by the object and the secondary electrons produced by it.

scan·sion (skăn′shən) *n.* Analysis of verse into metrical patterns. [Late Latin *scānsiō, scānsiōn-,* from Latin, act of climbing, from *scānsus,* past participle of *scandere,* to climb. See **skand-** in Appendix.]

scan·so·ri·al (skăn-sôr′ē-əl, -sōr′-) *adj.* *Zoology.* Adapted to or specialized for climbing. [From Latin *scānsōrius,* from *scānsus,* past participle of *scandere,* to climb. See **skand-** in Appendix.]

scant (skănt) *adj.* **scant·er, scant·est. 1.** Barely sufficient: *paid scant attention to the lecture.* **2.** Falling short of a specific measure: *a scant cup of sugar.* See Synonyms at **meager. 3.** Inadequately supplied; short: *We were scant of breath after the lengthy climb.* **—scant** *tr.v.* **scant·ed, scant·ing, scants. 1.** To give an inadequate portion or allowance to: *had to scant the older children in order to nourish the newborn.* **2.** To limit, as in amount or share; stint: *Our leisure time is scanted by this demanding job.* **3.** To deal with or treat inadequately or neglectfully; slight. [Middle English, from Old Norse *skamt,* neuter of *skammr,* short.] **—scant′ly** *adv.* **—scant′ness** *n.*

scant·ling (skănt′lĭng, -lĭn) *n.* **1.** A very small amount; a modicum. **2.** A small timber used in construction. **3.** The dimensions of a building material, especially the width and thickness of a timber. **4.** Often **scantlings.** *Nautical.* The dimensions of the structural parts of a vessel. [Alteration of Middle English *scantlon, scantilon,* carpenter's gauge, from Old French *escantillon,* alteration of **eschandillon,* from Late Latin **scandiculum,* alteration of *scandāculum,* ladder, gauge, from Latin *scandere,* to climb. See SCAN.]

scant·y (skăn′tē) *adj.* **-i·er, -i·est. 1.** Barely sufficient or adequate. **2.** Insufficient, as in extent or degree. See Synonyms at **meager. —scant′i·ly** *adv.* **—scant′i·ness** *n.*

Scap·a Flow (skăp′ə). A sheltered area of water in the Orkney Islands off northern Scotland. It was the site of the chief British naval base in both World Wars. The German fleet was scuttled here in June 1919 at the end of World War I.

ă pat	oi boy
ā pay	ou out
âr care	ŏŏ took
ä father	ōō boot
ĕ pet	ŭ cut
ē be	ûr urge
ĭ pit	th thin
ī pie	*th* this
îr pier	hw which
ŏ pot	zh vision
ō toe	ə about, item
ô paw	♦ regionalism

Stress marks: ′ (primary); ′ (secondary), as in **dictionary** (dĭk′shə-nĕr′ē)

scape¹ (skāp) *n.* **1.** *Botany.* A leafless flower stalk growing directly from the ground, as in the tulip. **2.** *Biology.* A stalklike part, such as a feather shaft or a segment of an insect's antenna. **3.** *Architecture.* The shaft of a column. [Latin *scāpus,* stalk, perhaps from Greek *skapos.*]

scape² (skāp) *v. & n. Archaic.* Variant of **escape.**

scape³ (skāp) *n.* A scene; a view. Often used in combination: *seascape; mindscape.* [From LANDSCAPE.]

scape•goat (skāp′gōt′) *n.* **1.** One that is made to bear the blame of others. **2.** *Bible.* A live goat over whose head Aaron confessed all the sins of the children of Israel on the Day of Atonement. The goat, symbolically bearing their sins, was then sent into the wilderness. **—scapegoat** *tr.v.* **-goat•ed, -goat•ing, -goats.** To make a scapegoat of. [*scape* (variant of ESCAPE) + GOAT (translation of Hebrew *'ăzā'zēl,* goat for Azazel, demon of the desert, misread as *'ēz 'ōzēl,* goat that escapes).]

scape•grace (skāp′grās′) *n.* A scoundrel; a rascal. [*scape* (variant of *escape*) + GRACE.]

scaph•o•ce•phal•ic (skăf′ō-sə-făl′ĭk) *adj.* Having an abnormally long, narrow skull. [Greek *skaphē,* boat + –CEPHALIC.] **—scaph′o•ceph′a•ly** (-ə-sĕf′ə-lē) *n.*

scaph•oid (skăf′oid′) *adj.* Shaped like a boat. **—scaphoid** *n. Anatomy.* See **navicular.** [New Latin *scaphoīdēs,* from Greek *skaphoeidēs,* like a bowl : *skaphē,* tub, boat + *-oeidēs,* -oid.]

scaph•o•pod (skăf′ə-pŏd′) *n.* See **tooth shell.** [From New Latin *Scaphopoda,* class name : Greek *skaphē,* boat + New Latin *-poda,* -pod.]

scap•o•lite (skăp′ə-līt′) *n.* Any of a series of variously colored, often fluorescent mineral silicates of aluminum, calcium, and sodium. Also called *wernerite.* [Latin *scāpus,* stalk; see SCAPE¹ + –LITE, stone (from the prismatic shape of its crystals).]

sca•pose (skā′pōs′) *adj.* Resembling or consisting of a scape: *a scapose column; scapose flowers.*

scap•u•la (skăp′yə-lə) *n., pl.* **-las** or **-lae** (-lē′). Either of two large, flat, triangular bones forming the back part of the shoulder. Also called *shoulder blade.* [Late Latin, shoulder, from Latin *scapulae,* the shoulder blades.]

scap•u•lar (skăp′yə-lər) *n.* **1.** A monk's sleeveless outer garment that hangs from the shoulders and sometimes has a cowl. **2.** A badge worn by affiliates of certain religious orders, consisting of two pieces of cloth joined by shoulder bands and worn under the clothing on the chest and back. **3.** One of the feathers covering the shoulder of a bird. **—scapular** also **scap•u•lar•y** (-lĕr′ē) *adj. Anatomy.* Of or relating to the shoulder or scapula. [Middle English *scapulare,* from Late Latin *scapulāre,* from neuter of *scapulāris,* pertaining to the shoulders or scapula, from *scapula,* shoulder. See SCAPULA.]

scap•u•lo•cla•vic•u•lar (skăp′yə-lō-klə-vĭk′yə-lər) *adj.* Of, relating to, or affecting both the scapula and the clavicle.

scar¹ (skär) *n.* **1.** A mark left on the skin after a surface injury or wound has healed. **2.** A lingering sign of damage or injury, either mental or physical: *nightmares, anxiety, and other enduring scars of wartime experiences.* **3.** *Botany.* A mark indicating a former attachment, as of a leaf to a stem. **4.** A mark, such as a dent, resulting from use or contact. **—scar** *v.* **scarred, scar•ring, scars.** *—tr.* **1.** To mark with a scar. **2.** To leave lasting signs of damage on: *a wretched childhood that scarred his psyche.* *—intr.* **1.** To form a scar: *The pustule healed and scarred.* **2.** To become scarred: *delicate skin that scars easily.* [Middle English, alteration of *escare,* from Old French, scab, from Late Latin *eschara,* from Greek *eskhara,* hearth, scab caused by burning.]

scar² (skär) *n.* **1.** A protruding, isolated rock. **2.** A bare, rocky place on a mountainside or other steep slope. [Middle English *skerre,* from Old Norse *sker,* low reef. See **sker-¹** in Appendix.]

scar•ab (skăr′əb) *n.* **1.** A scarabaeid beetle, especially *Scarabaeus sacer,* regarded as sacred by the ancient Egyptians. **2.** A representation of this beetle, such as a ceramic or stone sculpture or a cut gem, used in ancient Egypt as a talisman and a symbol of the soul. In this sense, also called *scarabaeus.* [French *scarabée,* from Latin *scarabaeus,* from Greek *karabos,* crab, beetle.]

scar•a•bae•i (skăr′ə-bē′ī′) *n.* A plural of **scarabaeus.**

scar•a•bae•id (skăr′ə-bē′ĭd) *n.* Any of the numerous stout-bodied, lamellicorn beetles of the family Scarabaeidae, which includes the June beetle and dung beetles. **—scarabaeid** *adj.* Of or belonging to the family Scarabaeidae. [From New Latin *Scarabaeidae,* family name, from *Scarabaeus,* type genus, from Latin *scarabaeus,* beetle. See SCARAB.]

scar•a•bae•us (skăr′ə-bē′əs) *n., pl.* **-bae•us•es** or **-bae•i** (-bē′ī′). See **scarab** (sense 2). [Latin. See SCARAB.]

scar•a•boid (skăr′ə-boid′) *adj.* Resembling or characteristic of a scarabaeid beetle.

Scar•a•mouch also **Scar•a•mouche** (skăr′ə-mo͞osh′, -mo͞och′, -mouch′) *n.* A stock character in commedia dell'arte and pantomime, depicted as a boastful coward or buffoon. [French *Scaramouche,* from Italian *Scaramuccia,* from *scaramuccia,* skirmish, perhaps of Germanic origin.]

Scar•bor•ough (skär′bûr′ō, -bŭr′ō, -bər-ə). A municipal borough of northeast England on the North Sea north of Hull. Site of a Bronze Age village and a fourth-century A.D. Roman signaling tower, it is a noted seaside resort. Population, 43,300.

scarce (skârs) *adj.* **scarc•er, scarc•est. 1.** Insufficient to meet a demand or requirement; short in supply: *Fresh vegetables were scarce during the drought.* **2.** Hard to find; absent or rare: *Steel pennies are scarce now except in coin shops.* **—scarce** *adv.* Barely or hardly; scarcely. **—*idiom.* make (oneself) scarce.** *Informal.* **1.** To stay away; be absent or elusive. **2.** To depart, especially quickly or furtively; abscond. [Middle English *scars,* from Old French *scars,* from Vulgar Latin **excarpsus,* narrow, cramped, from past participle of **excarpere,* to pluck out, alteration of Latin *excerpere,* to pick out. See EXCERPT.] **—scarce′ness** *n.*

WORD HISTORY: The phrase *scarce excerpt,* if it ever should occur to one, is an excellent example of how two intimately related words can diverge from one another in form while passing from one language to another over the centuries. Both words can be traced back to the Latin word *excerpo* (past participle stem *excerpt–*), meaning "to pick out," "to pick out mentally," and "to select a passage for quotation." This is clearly the ultimate source of our noun *excerpt* (first recorded before 1638) and verb (first recorded around 1536), a past participle usage already being recorded in the 15th century. A more tangled path leads to our word *scarce.* It is assumed that side by side with Latin *excerpere* existed the Vulgar Latin form **excarpere.* **Excarpsus,* an adjective formed with the past participle of **excarpere* in Vulgar Latin, meant "narrow, cramped," and from this Vulgar Latin form came the Old French word *échars,* "insufficient, cramped," and "stingy." The Old French word, which existed in a variety of forms in Old French, including *scars* and the chiefly Old North French form *escarse,* was borrowed into Middle English as *scarse,* being first recorded in a manuscript written around 1300.

scarce•ly (skârs′lē) *adv.* **1.** By a small margin; barely: *We scarely made it in time.* **2.** Almost not; hardly: *We scarcely ever used the reserve generator.* **3.** Certainly not: *They could scarcely complain after such good treatment.*

USAGE NOTE: *Scarcely* has the force of a negative and is therefore regarded as incorrectly used with another negative, as in *I couldn't scarcely believe it.* • A clause following *scarcely* is correctly introduced by *when* or *before;* the use of *than,* though common, is still unacceptable to some grammarians: *The meeting had scarcely begun when* (or *before* but not *than*) *it was interrupted.* See Usage Notes at **double negative, hardly.**

scar•ci•ty (skâr′sĭ-tē) *n., pl.* **-ties. 1.** Insufficiency of amount or supply; shortage: *"Having looked to Government for bread, on the first scarcity they will turn and bite the hand that fed them"* (Edmund Burke). **2.** Rarity of appearance or occurrence: *antiques that are valued for their scarcity.*

scare (skâr) *v.* **scared, scar•ing, scares.** *—tr.* To strike with sudden fear; alarm. See Synonyms at **frighten.** *—intr.* To become frightened: *a child who scares easily.* **—scare** *n.* **1.** A condition or sensation of sudden fear. **2.** A general state of alarm; a panic: *a bomb scare that necessitated evacuating the building.* **—scare** *adj.* Serving or intended to frighten people: *scare stories; scare tactics.* **—*phrasal verb.* scare up.** *Informal.* To gather or prepare with considerable effort or ingenuity: *managed to scare up some folding chairs for the unexpected crowd.* [Middle English *skerren, scaren,* from Old Norse *skirra,* from *skjarr,* timid.] **—scar′er** *n.*

scare•crow (skâr′krō′) *n.* **1.** A crude image or effigy of a person set up in a field to scare birds away from growing crops. **2.** Something frightening but not dangerous. **3.** A gaunt or haggard person.

scare•mon•ger (skâr′mŭng′gər, -mŏng′-) *n.* One who spreads frightening rumors. **—scare′mon′ger•ing** *n.*

scarf¹ (skärf) *n., pl.* **scarfs** (skärfs) or **scarves** (skärvz). **1.** A long piece of cloth worn about the head, neck, or shoulders. **2.** A decorative cloth for covering the top of a piece of furniture; a runner. **3.** A sash indicating military rank. **—scarf** *tr.v.* **scarfed, scarf•ing, scarfs. 1.** To dress, cover, or decorate with or as if with a scarf. **2.** To wrap (an outer garment) around one like a scarf. [French dialectal *escarpe,* sash, sling, from Old North French, variant of Old French *escherpe,* pilgrim's bag hung from neck, from Frankish **skirpja,* small rush, from Latin *scirpus,* rush.]

scarf² (skärf) *n., pl.* **scarfs** (skärfs). **1.** A joint made by cutting or notching the ends of two pieces correspondingly and strapping or bolting them together. Also called *scarf joint.* **2.** Either of the correspondingly cut or notched ends that fit together to form such a joint. **—scarf** *tr.v.* **scarfed, scarf•ing, scarfs. 1.** To join by means of a scarf. **2.** To cut a scarf in. [Middle English *skarf,* as in *scarfnail,* probably from Old Norse *skarfr,* end piece of a board cut off on the bias.]

scarf³ (skärf) *tr.v.* **scarfed, scarf•ing, scarfs.** *Slang.* To eat or drink voraciously; devour: *"Americans scarf down 50 million hot dogs on an average summer day"* (George F. Will). [Variant of SCOFF².] **—scarf′er** *n.*

scarf joint *n.* See **scarf²** (sense 1).

scarf•skin (skärf′skĭn′) *n.* The outermost layer of skin, especially that which forms the cuticle.

scar•i•fi•ca•tor (skăr′ə-fĭ-kā′tər) *n.* A surgical instrument with several spring-operated lancets, used to scarify the skin.

scar•i•fy¹ (skăr′ə-fī′) *tr.v.* **-fied, -fy•ing, -fies. 1.** To make shallow cuts in (the skin), as when vaccinating. **2.** To break up the surface of (topsoil). **3.** To distress deeply, as with severe criticism; lacerate. **4.** *Botany.* To slit or soften the outer coat of

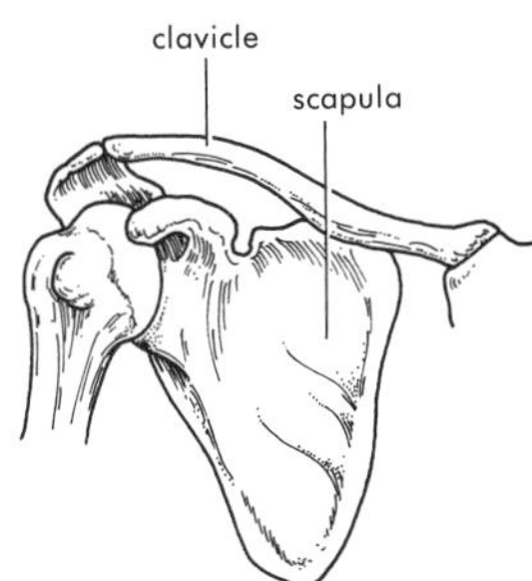

scapula

scarab
XVIII Dynasty Egyptian scarab with hieroglyphic inscription on reverse

scarecrow

scarf²

(seeds) in order to speed germination. [Middle English *scarifien,* from Old French *scarifier,* from Late Latin *scarīficāre,* alteration of Latin *scarīfāre,* from Greek *skariphasthai,* to sketch, scratch, from *skariphos,* pencil, stylus. See **skrībh-** in Appendix.] **—scar′i·fi·ca′tion** (-fĭ-kā′shən) *n.* **—scar′i·fi′er** *n.*

scar·i·fy² (skâr′ə-fī′) *tr.v.* **-fied, -fy·ing, -fies.** To scare.

scar·i·ous (skâr′ē-əs) also **scar·i·ose** (-ōs′) *adj.* Thin, membranous, and dry: *scarious bracts; a scarious tongue.* [New Latin *scariōsus.*]

scar·la·ti·na (skär′lə-tē′nə) *n.* See **scarlet fever.** [New Latin *(febris) scarlatina,* scarlet (fever), from Italian *scarlattina,* feminine of *scarlattino,* scarlet, diminutive of *scarlatto,* from Persian *saqirlāt.* See SCARLET.] **—scar′la·ti′nal** *adj.*

scar·la·ti·noid (skär′lə-tē′noid′) *adj.* Resembling scarlet fever or its rash.

Scar·lat·ti (skär-lä′tē), **Alessandro.** 1660–1725. Italian composer who influenced the development of modern opera. His son **Domenico** (1685–1757), a harpsichordist, wrote numerous works for the instrument.

scar·let (skär′lĭt) *n.* **1.** *Color.* A strong to vivid red or reddish orange. **2.** Scarlet-colored clothing or cloth. **—scarlet** *adj.* **1.** *Color.* Of a strong to vivid red or reddish orange. **2.** Flagrantly immoral or unchaste: *scarlet thoughts.* [Middle English, scarlet cloth, scarlet, from Old French *escarlate,* from Medieval Latin *scarlata,* scarlet cloth, from Persian *sāqirlāt,* rich cloth, scarlet cloth, variant of *siqillāt,* from Arabic, perhaps from Medieval Greek *sigillatos,* from Latin *sigillātus,* decorated with raised figures, from *sigilla,* little figures, pl. of *sigillum,* sigil. See SIGIL.]

scarlet fever *n.* An acute contagious disease caused by a hemolytic streptococcus, occurring predominantly among children and characterized by a scarlet skin eruption and high fever. Also called *scarlatina.*

scarlet tanager
Piranga olivacea

scarlet pimpernel *n.* The pimpernel.

scarlet runner *n.* A climbing tropical American bean plant *(Phaseolus coccineus)* having scarlet flowers and long pods with edible seeds.

scarlet sage *n.* A shrubby Brazilian plant *(Salvia splendens)* having showy scarlet flowers, red bracts, and opposite leaves.

scarlet tanager *n.* A New World bird *(Piranga olivacea)* the male of which has bright scarlet plumage with a black tail and wings.

scarp (skärp) *n.* An escarpment. **—scarp** *tr.v.* **scarped, scarp·ing, scarps.** To cut or make into an escarpment. [Italian *scarpa,* slope, perhaps of Germanic origin. See **sker-¹** in Appendix.]

Scar·ron (skă-rōN′), **Paul.** 1610–1660. French writer noted for his burlesque dramas and the picaresque novel *Le Roman Comique* (1651–1657).

Scars·dale (skärz′dāl′). A city of southeast New York, a residential suburb of New York City. Population, 17,650.

scar tissue *n.* Dense, fibrous connective tissue that forms over a healed wound or cut.

scarves (skärvz) *n.* A plural of **scarf¹.**

scar·y (skâr′ē) *adj.* **-i·er, -i·est. 1.** Causing fright or alarm. **2.** Easily scared; very timid. **—scar′i·ly** *adv.* **—scar′i·ness** *n.*

scat¹ (skăt) *intr.v.* **scat·ted, scat·ting, scats.** *Informal.* To go away hastily; leave at once. [Origin unknown.]

scat² (skăt) *Music. n.* Jazz singing in which improvised, meaningless syllables are sung to a melody. **—scat** *intr.v.* **scat·ted, scat·ting, scats.** To sing scat. [Origin unknown.]

scat³ (skăt) *n.* Excrement, especially of an animal; dung. [Perhaps from Greek *skōr, skat-,* excrement. See SCATO–.]

scathe (skāth) *tr.v.* **scathed, scath·ing, scathes. 1.** To harm or injure, especially by fire. **2.** To criticize or denounce severely; excoriate. **—scathe** *n.* Harm or injury. [Middle English *skathen,* from Old Norse *skadha.*]

scath·ing (skā′thĭng) *adj.* **1.** Bitterly denunciatory; harshly critical: *"a scathing tract on the uselessness of war"* (Pierre Brodin). **2.** Harmful or painful; injurious. **—scath′ing·ly** *adv.*

scato– *pref.* Excrement: *scatology.* [Greek *skato-,* from *skōr, skat-,* dung. See **sker-³** in Appendix.]

sca·tol·o·gy (skă-tŏl′ə-jē, skə-) *n., pl.* **-gies. 1.** The study of fecal excrement, as in medicine, paleontology, or biology. **2.a.** An obsession with excrement or excretory functions. **b.** The psychiatric study of such an obsession. **3.** Obscene language or literature, especially that dealing pruriently or humorously with excrement and excretory functions. **—scat′o·log′i·cal** (skăt′l-ŏj′ĭ-kəl), **scat′o·log′ic** (-ĭk) *adj.* **—sca·tol′o·gist** *n.*

scat·ter (skăt′ər) *v.* **-tered, -ter·ing, -ters.** —*tr.* **1.** To cause to separate and go in different directions. **2.** To distribute loosely by or as if by sprinkling; strew: *scattering confetti from the upper windows.* **3.** *Physics.* To deflect (radiation or particles). —*intr.* **1.** To separate and go in different directions; disperse. **2.** To occur or fall at widely spaced intervals. **—scatter** *n.* **1.** The act of scattering or the condition of being scattered. **2.** Something scattered. [Middle English *scateren.*] **—scat′ter·er** *n.*

SYNONYMS: *scatter, disperse, dissipate, dispel.* These verbs are compared as they mean to cause a mass or an aggregate to separate and go in different directions. *Scatter* usually refers to widespread, often haphazard distribution of components: *"the scattered driftwood, bleached and dry"* (Celia Laighton Thaxter). *Disperse* implies the complete breaking up of the mass or aggregate: *"only a few industrious Scots perhaps, who indeed are dispersed over the face of the whole earth"* (George Chapman). *Dissipate* usually suggests a reduction to nothing: *"Time dissipates to shining ether the solid angularity of facts"* (Ralph Waldo Emerson). *Dispel* suggests driving away or off by or as if by scattering: *"Truth is a torch that gleams through the fog without dispelling it"* (Claude Adrien Helvétius).

scat·ter·brain (skăt′ər-brān′) *n.* A person regarded as flighty, thoughtless, or disorganized. **—scat′ter·brained′** *adj.*

scat·ter·good (skăt′ər-go͝od′) *n.* A spendthrift; a wastrel.

scat·ter·gun (skăt′ər-gŭn′) *n.* See **shotgun** (sense 1).

scat·ter·ing (skăt′ər-ĭng) *n.* **1.** Something scattered, especially a small, irregularly occurring amount or quantity: *a scattering of applause.* **2.** *Physics.* The dispersal of a beam of particles or of radiation into a range of directions as a result of physical interactions. **—scattering** *adj.* Placed irregularly and far apart; scattered. **—scat′ter·ing·ly** *adv.*

scattering layer *n.* A concentrated layer of organisms in the ocean that reflects and scatters sound waves, as from sonar.

scatter pin *n.* A woman's small decorative brooch often worn in groups of two or three.

scatter rug *n.* A small rug for covering a part of a floor. Also called *throw rug.*

scat·ter·shot (skăt′ər-shŏt′) *adj.* Covering a wide range in a random way; indiscriminate: *"his habit of scattershot comment on whatever issue catches his eye"* (Howell Raines).

scat·ter-site (skăt′ər-sīt′) *adj.* Relating to or being publicly funded low-income housing units scattered throughout middle-income residential areas.

scat·ty (skăt′ē) *adj.* **-ti·er, -ti·est.** *Chiefly British.* Scatterbrained; flighty: *"the scatty, glancing quality of a hyperactive but unfocused intelligence"* (London Review of Books). [Probably SCATT(ERBRAIN) + –Y¹.]

scaup (skôp) *n., pl.* **scaup** or **scaups.** Either of two diving ducks *(Aythya marila* or *A. affinis)* having predominantly black and white plumage in the male. Also called *bluebill.* [Perhaps from Scots *scalp, scaup,* bed of mussels (from its feeding on shellfish).]

scav·enge (skăv′ənj) *v.* **-enged, -eng·ing, -eng·es.** —*tr.* **1.** To search through for salvageable material: *scavenged the garbage cans for food scraps.* **2.** To collect and remove refuse from: *The streets are periodically scavenged.* **3.** To collect (salvageable material) by searching. **4.a.** To expel (exhaust gases) from a cylinder of an internal-combustion engine. **b.** To expel exhaust gases from (such a cylinder). **5.** *Metallurgy.* To clean (molten metal) by chemically removing impurities. —*intr.* **1.** To search through refuse for useful material. **2.** To feed on dead or decaying matter. [Back-formation from SCAVENGER.]

scav·en·ger (skăv′ən-jər) *n.* **1.** One that scavenges, as a person who searches through refuse for food. **2.** An animal, such as a bird or an insect, that feeds on dead or decaying matter. **3.** *Chemistry.* A substance added to a mixture to remove or inactivate impurities. [Alteration of Middle English *scauager, schavager,* official charged with street maintenance, from Anglo-Norman *scawager,* toll collector, from *scawage,* a tax on the goods of foreign merchants, from Flemish *scauwen,* to look at, show. See **keu-** in Appendix.]

Sc.B. *abbr. Latin.* Scientiae Baccalaureus (Bachelor of Science).

SCC *abbr. Electronics.* Storage connecting circuit.

Sc.D. *abbr. Latin.* Scientiae Doctor (Doctor of Science).

sce·na (shā′nə) *n. Music.* An extended operatic vocal composition for one or more voices consisting of a recitative and arias or an aria. [Italian, from Latin *scaena,* stage. See SCENE.]

sce·nar·i·o (sĭ-nâr′ē-ō′, -när′-, -năr′-) *n., pl.* **-os. 1.** An outline of the plot of a dramatic or literary work. **2.** A screenplay. **3.** An outline or a model of an expected or a supposed sequence of events: *"In the scenario posed by many climatologists, decades of continued global warming would raise sea levels anywhere from 20 inches to more than 11 feet as the polar ice caps melt and the ocean's upper layers expand"* (San Francisco Chronicle). [Italian, from *scena,* scene, from Latin *scaena.* See SCENE.]

sce·nar·ist (sĭ-nâr′ĭst, -när′-, -năr′-) *n.* One who writes screenplays.

scend also **send** (sĕnd) *Nautical.* —*intr.v.* **scend·ed, scend·ing, scends** also **send·ed, send·ing, sends.** To heave upward on a wave or swell. —*n.* The rising movement of a ship on a wave or swell. [Probably alteration (influenced by DESCEND, or ASCEND) of SEND¹.]

scene (sēn) *n.* **1.** Something seen by a viewer; a view or prospect. **2.** The place where an action or event occurs: *the scene of the crime.* **3.** *Abbr.* **sc.** The place in which the action of a play, movie, novel, or other narrative occurs; a setting. **4.a.** A subdivision of an act in a dramatic presentation in which the setting is fixed and the time continuous. **b.** A shot or series of shots in a movie constituting a unit of continuous related action. **5.a.** The scenery and properties for a dramatic presentation. **b.** A theater stage. **6.** A real or fictitious episode, especially when described. **7.** A public display of passion or temper: *tried not to make a scene.* **8.a.** A sphere of activity: *observers of the political scene.* **b.** *Slang.* A situation or set of circumstances: *a bad scene; a wild scene.* **—*idiom.* behind the scenes. 1.** Backstage. **2.** In private. [French *scène,* stage, from Old French, from Latin *scaena,* from Greek *skēnē,* tent, stage.]

scen•er•y (sē′nə-rē) *n., pl.* **-ies. 1.** A view or views of natural features, especially in open country: *enjoying the varied mountain scenery.* **2.** The painted backdrops on a theatrical stage.

scene-steal•er (sēn′stē′lər) *n.* An actor who draws attention from or overshadows other actors in the same production, as by charm or quality of performance.

sce•nic (sē′nĭk) *adj.* **1.** Of or relating to the stage, stage scenery, or theatrical representation: *scenic design.* **2.** Constituting or affording pleasing views of natural features: *climbed a hill for a scenic panorama of the valley; a scenic drive along the crater rim.* **—scenic** *n.* A depiction of natural scenery. **—sce′ni•cal•ly** *adv.*

sce•no•graph•ic (sē′nə-grăf′ĭk) *adj.* Of, relating to, or characteristic of scenography: *"Contemporary design has a strongly scenographic appeal, as if modern rooms were meant to be stage sets"* (Los Angeles Times).

sce•nog•ra•phy (sē-nŏg′rə-fē) *n.* The art of representing objects in perspective, especially as applied in the design and painting of theatrical scenery. **—sce•nog′raph•er** *n.*

scent (sĕnt) *n.* **1.** A distinctive, often agreeable odor. See Synonyms at **fragrance, smell. 2.** A perfume: *an expensive French scent.* **3.** An odor left by the passing of an animal. **4.** The trail of a hunted animal or fugitive. **5.** The sense of smell: *a bear's keen scent.* **6.** A hint of something imminent; a suggestion: *caught the scent of a reconciliation.* **—scent** *v.* **scent•ed, scent•ing, scents.** *—tr.* **1.** To perceive or identify by the sense of smell: *dogs scenting their prey.* **2.** To suspect or detect as if by smelling: *scented danger.* **3.** To fill with a pleasant odor; perfume: *when blossoms scent the air.* *—intr.* To hunt prey by means of the sense of smell. Used of hounds. [Middle English *sent,* from *senten,* to scent, from Old French *sentir,* from Latin *sentīre,* to feel. See **sent-** in Appendix.] **—scent′less** *adj.*

scent gland *n.* A specialized apocrine gland found in many mammals that produces a strong-smelling substance.

scent strip *n.* A strip of paper impregnated with perfume, used by advertisers to acquaint potential buyers with the fragrance of the perfume.

scep•ter (sĕp′tər) *n.* **1.** A staff held by a sovereign as an emblem of authority. **2.** Ruling power or authority; sovereignty. **—scepter** *tr.v.* **-tered, -ter•ing, -ters.** To invest with royal authority. [Middle English *sceptre,* from Old French, from Latin *scēptrum,* from Greek *skēptron.*]

scep•tic (skĕp′tĭk) *n.* Variant of **skeptic.**

scep•ti•cal (skĕp′tĭ-kəl) *adj.* Variant of **skeptical.**

scep•ti•cism (skĕp′tĭ-sĭz′əm) *n.* Variant of **skepticism.**

scep•tre (sĕp′tər) *n. & v. Chiefly British.* Variant of **scepter.**

sch. *abbr.* School.

scha•den•freu•de (shäd′n-froi′də) *n.* Pleasure derived from the misfortunes of others. [German : *Schaden,* damage (from Middle High German *schade,* from Old High German *scado*) + *Freude,* joy (from Middle High German *vreude,* from Old High German *frewida,* from *frō,* happy).]

Schaer•beek (skär′bāk′, sᴋʜär′-). A city of central Belgium, an industrial suburb of Brussels. Population, 105,672.

Scha•pi•ro (shə-pîr′ō), **Miriam.** Born 1923. Canadian-born American artist who developed "femmage," a form of collage using such media as lace and fabric. With Judy Chicago she executed *Womanhouse* (1972), a project highlighting the traditional crafts and folk art of American women.

Schaum•burg (shäm′bûrg′). A village of northeast Illinois, a suburb of Chicago. Population, 53,305.

schav (shäv, shchäv) *n.* A chilled soup made with sorrel, onions, lemon juice, eggs, and sugar and served with sour cream. [Yiddish *shtshav,* from Polish *szczaw.*]

Schech•ter (shĕk′tər), **Solomon.** 1847–1915. Romanian-born Hebrew scholar who discovered the lost chapters of the biblical book Ecclesiasticus.

sched•ule (skĕj′o͞ol, -o͞o-əl, skĕj′əl) *n.* **1.** A list of times of departures and arrivals; a timetable: *a bus schedule; a schedule of guided tours.* **2.** A plan for performing work or achieving an objective, specifying the order and allotted time for each part: *finished the project on schedule.* **3.** A printed or written list of items in tabular form: *a schedule of postal rates.* **4. a.** A program of events or appointments expected in a given time: *Can you fit me into your schedule Tuesday afternoon?* **b.** A student's program of classes. **5.** A supplemental statement of details appended to a document. **—schedule** *tr.v.* **-uled, -ul•ing, -ules. 1.** To enter on a schedule: *calculate and schedule each tax deduction on the proper form.* **2.** To make up a schedule for: *I haven't scheduled the coming week yet.* **3.** To plan or appoint for a certain time or date: *scheduled a trip in June; was scheduled to arrive Monday.* [Middle English *sedule,* slip of parchment or paper, note, from Old French *cedule,* from Late Latin *schedula,* diminutive of *scheda,* variant of Latin *scida,* papyrus strip, from Greek *skhida, skhedē;* perhaps akin to *skhizein,* to split. See SCHIZO–.] **—sched′u•lar** *adj.* **—sched′u•ler** *n.*

Schee•le (shā′lə), **Karl Wilhelm.** 1742–1786. German-born Swedish chemist who independently discovered oxygen (c. 1772) before Joseph Priestley.

schee•lite (shā′līt′, shē′-) *n.* A variously colored mineral, $CaWO_4$, found in igneous rocks and used as an ore of tungsten. [After Karl Wilhelm SCHEELE.]

schef•fler•a (shĕf-lîr′ə, -lĕr′ə, shĕf′lər-ə) *n.* Any of numerous evergreen shrubs or small trees of the genus *Schefflera,* having palmately compound leaves and unisexual flowers that are grouped in umbels. It is widely grown indoors as a foliage plant. Also called *umbrella tree.* [New Latin, genus name, after J.C. *Scheffler,* 18th-century German botanist.]

Scheldt (skĕlt). A river rising in northern France and flowing about 434 km (270 mi) generally northeast across western Belgium and southwest Netherlands. It empties into the North Sea through two estuaries.

Schel•ling (shĕl′ĭng), **Friedrich Wilhelm Joseph von.** 1775–1854. German idealist philosopher whose theories of the self, nature, and art influenced romanticism and to a degree presaged existentialism.

sche•ma (skē′mə) *n., pl.* **sche•ma•ta** (skē-mä′tə, skĭ-măt′ə) or **sche•mas. 1.** A diagrammatic representation; an outline or a model. **2.** *Psychology.* A pattern imposed on complex reality or experience to assist in explaining it, mediate perception, or guide response. [Latin *schēma, schēmat-,* form. See SCHEME.]

sche•mat•ic (skē-măt′ĭk, skĭ-) *adj.* Of, relating to, or in the form of a scheme or diagram. **—schematic** *n.* A structural or procedural diagram, especially of an electrical or mechanical system. **—sche•mat′i•cal•ly** *adv.*

sche•ma•tism (skē′mə-tĭz′əm) *n.* The patterned disposition of constituents within a given system.

sche•ma•tize (skē′mə-tīz′) *tr.v.* **-tized, -tiz•ing, -tiz•es.** To express in or reduce to a scheme: *a diagram that schematizes the creation and consumption of wealth.* [Greek *skhēmatizein,* to give form to, from *skhēma, skhēmat-,* form. See SCHEME.] **—sche′ma•ti•za′tion** (-tĭ-zā′shən) *n.*

scheme (skēm) *n.* **1.** A systematic plan of action. **2.** A secret or devious plan; a plot. See Synonyms at **plan. 3.** An impractical or unrealistic plan: *"Your scheme yields no revenue; it yields nothing but discontent, disorder, disobedience"* (Edmund Burke). **4.** An orderly combination of related parts: *an irrigation scheme with dams, reservoirs, and channels.* **5.** A chart, a diagram, or an outline of a system or an object. **—scheme** *v.* **schemed, schem•ing, schemes.** *—tr.* **1.** To plot: *scheming their revenge.* **2.** To contrive a plan or scheme for. *—intr.* To make plans, especially secret or devious ones. [Latin *schēma,* figure, from Greek *skhēma.* See **segh-** in Appendix.] **—schem′er** *n.*

Sche•nec•ta•dy (skə-nĕk′tə-dē). A city of eastern New York on the Mohawk River northwest of Albany. First settled in 1661, it prospered after the opening of the Erie Canal and the coming of the railroad in the early 19th century. Population, 67,972.

scher•zan•do (skĕrt-sän′dō) *Music. adv. & adj.* In a light, playful manner. Used chiefly as a direction. **—scherzando** *n., pl.* **-dos.** A scherzando passage. [Italian, gerund of *scherzare,* to joke, from Old Italian. See SCHERZO.]

scher•zo (skĕr′tsō) *n., pl.* **-zos** or **-zi** (-tsē). *Music.* A lively movement, commonly in 3/4 time. [Italian, joke, scherzo, from Old Italian *scherzare,* to joke, perhaps of Germanic origin.]

Schia•pa•rel•li (skē-äp′ə-rĕl′ē, skăp′-, shăp′-, skyäp′ä-rĕl′lē), **Elsa.** 1896–1973. Italian-born fashion designer noted for her use of brilliant colors and synthetic materials in haute couture designs.

Schiaparelli, Giovanni Virginio. 1835–1910. Italian astronomer who first observed lines on the surface of Mars, which he described as canals.

Schick test (shĭk) *n.* A test to determine immunity to diphtheria by injection into the skin of dilute diptheria toxin. Inflammation of the injected area indicates a lack of immunity. [After Béla *Schick* (1877–1967), Hungarian-born American pediatrician.]

Schie•dam (skē-däm′, sᴋʜē-). A city of southwest Netherlands, an industrial suburb of Rotterdam. Chartered in 1275, it is noted for its gin distilleries. Population, 69,849.

Schiff's reagent (shĭfs) *n.* An aqueous solution of rosaniline and sulfurous acid used to test for the presence of aldehydes. [After Hugo *Schiff* (1834–1915), German chemist.]

schil•ler (shĭl′ər) *n.* A lustrous, colored reflection from certain planes in a mineral grain. [German, iridescence, from Middle High German *schilher,* iridescent taffeta, from *schilhen,* to twinkle, squint, from Old High German *scilihen,* to squint, wink.]

Schil•ler (shĭl′ər), **Johann Christoph Friedrich von.** 1759–1805. German writer. A leading romanticist, he is best known for his historical plays, such as *Don Carlos* (1787) and *Wallenstein* (1798–1799), and for his long, didactic poems.

schil•ling (shĭl′ĭng) *n.* See table at **currency.** [German, from Middle High German *schillinc,* from Old High German *skilling,* gold coin.]

schip•per•ke (skĭp′ər-kē, -kə) *n.* A small stocky dog of a breed developed in Belgium, having dense, long black fur and small pointed ears. [Flemish, diminutive of *schipper,* skipper (from the dog's use as a watchdog on a boat), from Middle Dutch. See SKIPPER[1].]

schism (sĭz′əm, skĭz′-) *n.* **1.** A separation or division into factions. **2. a.** A formal breach of union within a Christian church. **b.** The offense of attempting to produce such a breach. **3.** Disunion; discord. [Middle English *scisme,* from Old French, from Latin *schisma, schismat-,* from Greek *skhisma,* from *skhizein,* to split. See **skei-** in Appendix.]

scepter

schipperke

ă pat	oi boy
ā pay	ou out
âr care	o͝o took
ä father	o͞o boot
ĕ pet	ŭ cut
ē be	ûr urge
ĭ pit	th thin
ī pie	*th* this
îr pier	hw which
ŏ pot	zh vision
ō toe	ə about, item
ô paw	♦ regionalism

Stress marks: **′** (primary); ′ (secondary), as in **dictionary** (dĭk′shə-nĕr′ē)

schis·mat·ic (sĭz-măt′ĭk, skĭz-) *adj.* Of, relating to, or engaging in schism. **—schismatic** *n.* One who promotes or engages in schism. **—schis·mat′i·cal·ly** *adv.*

schist (shĭst) *n.* Any of various medium-grained to coarse-grained metamorphic rocks composed of laminated, often flaky parallel layers of chiefly micaceous minerals. [French *schiste,* from Latin *(lapis) schistos,* fissile (stone), a kind of iron ore, from Greek *skhistos,* split, divisible, from *skhizein,* to split. See **skei-** in Appendix.] **—schis′tose′** (shĭs′tōs′), **schis′tous** (-təs) *adj.*

schis·to·cyte (shĭs′tə-sīt′) *n.* **1.** A red blood cell undergoing fragmentation. **2.** A fragmented part of a red blood cell. [Greek *skhistos,* split; see SCHIST + –CYTE.]

schis·to·cy·to·sis (shĭs′tə-sī-tō′sĭs) *n.* **1.** Fragmentation of a red blood cell. **2.** The presence or accumulation of schistocytes in the blood.

schis·tor·rha·chis (shĭ-stôr′ə-kĭs) *n.* See **spina bifida.** [Greek *skhistos,* split; see SCHIST + Greek *rhakhis,* backbone.]

schis·to·some (shĭs′tə-sōm′) *n.* Any of several chiefly tropical trematode worms of the genus *Schistosoma,* many of which are parasitic in the blood of human beings and other mammals. Also called *bilharzia, blood fluke.* [New Latin *Schistosoma,* genus name : Greek *skhistos,* split; see SCHIST + Greek *soma,* body; see –SOME[3].] **—schis′to·som′al** (-sō′məl) *adj.*

schis·to·so·mi·a·sis (shĭs′tə-sə-mī′ə-sĭs) *n., pl.* **-ses** (-sēz′). Any of various generally tropical diseases caused by infestation with schistosomes, widespread in rural areas of Africa, Asia, and Latin America through use of contaminated water, and characterized by infection and gradual destruction of the tissues of the kidneys, liver, and other organs. Also called *bilharziasis, snail fever.*

schis·to·som·u·lum (shĭs′tə-sŏm′yə-ləm) *n., pl.* **-la** (-lə). The immature form of a parasitic schistosome after it has entered the blood vessels of its host. [New Latin, diminutive of *Schistosoma,* genus name. See SCHISTOSOME.]

schiz– *pref.* Variant of **schizo–.**

schiz·o (skĭt′sō) *n., pl.* **-os.** *Informal.* A schizophrenic person. **—schiz′o** *adj.*

schizo– or **schiz–** *pref.* **1.** Split; cleft: *schizocarp.* **2.** Cleavage; fission: *schizogenesis.* **3.** Schizophrenia: *schizoid.* [New Latin, from Greek *skhizo-,* from *skhizein,* to split. See **skei-** in Appendix.]

schiz·o·af·fec·tive (skĭt′sō-ə-fĕk′tĭv) *adj.* Showing symptoms of both schizophrenia and manic-depressive disorder.

schiz·o·carp (skĭz′ə-kärp′, skĭt′sə-) *n.* A dry fruit that splits at maturity into two or more closed, one-seeded parts, as in the carrot or mallow. **—schiz′o·car′pous, schiz′o·car′pic** *adj.*

schi·zog·a·my (skĭ-zŏg′ə-mē, skĭt-sŏg′-) *n. Biology.* Reproduction in which a sexual form is produced by fission from an asexual one, as in some annelid worms.

schiz·o·gen·e·sis (skĭz′ō-jĕn′ĭ-sĭs, skĭt′sō-) *n. Biology.* Reproduction by fission.

schi·zog·e·nous (skĭ-zŏj′ə-nəs, skĭt-sŏj′-) *adj.* **1.** Relating to or characterized by schizogenesis. **2.** Relating to or characterized by schizogony.

schi·zog·o·ny (skĭ-zŏg′ə-nē, skĭt-sŏg′-) *n.* Reproduction by multiple asexual fission, characteristic of many sporozoans. **—schi·zog′o·nous** *adj.*

schiz·oid (skĭt′soid′) *adj.* **1.** Schizophrenic. **2.** Of, relating to, or having a personality marked by extreme shyness, seclusiveness, and an inability to form close relationships. **—schizoid** *n.* A schizoid or schizophrenic person.

schiz·ont (skĭz′ŏnt′, skĭt′sŏnt′) *n.* A sporozoan cell produced by schizogony.

schiz·o·phrene (skĭt′sə-frēn′) *n.* A person having or predisposed to schizophrenia. [Probably back-formation from SCHIZOPHRENIA.]

schiz·o·phre·ni·a (skĭt′sə-frē′nē-ə, -frĕn′ē-ə) *n.* **1.** Any of a group of psychotic disorders usually characterized by withdrawal from reality, illogical patterns of thinking, delusions, and hallucinations, and accompanied in varying degrees by other emotional, behavioral, or intellectual disturbances. Schizophrenia, often associated with dopamine imbalances in the brain and defects of the frontal lobe, may have an underlying genetic cause. **2.** A condition that results from the coexistence of disparate or antagonistic qualities, identities, or activities: *the schizophrenia of the double espionage agent.*

schiz·o·phren·ic (skĭt′sə-frĕn′ĭk) *adj.* **1.** Of, relating to, or affected with schizophrenia. **2.** Of, relating to, or characterized by the coexistence of disparate or antagonistic elements. **—schizophrenic** *n.* One who is affected with schizophrenia. **—schiz′o·phren′i·cal·ly** *adv.*

schiz·o·phren·i·form (skĭt′sə-frĕn′ə-fôrm′) *adj.* Having the form of or resembling schizophrenia.

schiz·o·phre·no·gen·ic (skĭt′sə-frē′nə-jĕn′ĭk, -frĕn′ə-) *adj.* Tending to produce or develop schizophrenia.

schiz·o·pod (skĭz′ə-pŏd′, skĭt′sə-) *n.* Any of various shrimplike crustaceans of the orders Euphausiacea and Mysidacea (formerly included in the single order Schizopoda), consisting of the krill and the mysids. [From New Latin *Schizopoda,* former order name : SCHIZO– + New Latin *-poda,* -pod.] **—schiz·op′o·dous** (skĭ-zŏp′ə-dəs, skĭt-sŏp′-) *adj.*

schiz·o·thyme (skĭt′sə-thīm′) *n.* One who exhibits characteristics or symptoms of schizothymia. **—schizothyme** *adj.* Relating to, characterized by, or showing schizothymia. [Probably back-formation from SCHIZOTHYMIA.]

schiz·o·thy·mi·a (skĭt′sə-thī′mē-ə) *n.* Behavior or characteristics resembling schizophrenia in certain tendencies but remaining within the limits of normality. **—schiz′o·thy′mic** *adj.* & *n.*

schiz·y also **schiz·zy** (skĭt′sē) *adj.* **-i·er, -i·est.** *Informal.* Schizophrenic or schizoid. [Shortening and alteration of SCHIZOID.]

Schle·gel (shlā′gəl), **August Wilhelm von.** 1767–1845. German scholar who wrote influential criticism, translated several Shakespearean works, and composed poetry. He also edited a literary magazine with his brother **Friedrich** (1772–1829), a philosopher, poet, and critic whose essays formed the intellectual basis of German romanticism.

Schlei·er·ma·cher (shlī′ər-mä′kər, -KHər), **Friedrich Ernst Daniel.** 1768–1834. German philosopher and Protestant theologian who believed that the individual must develop a personal religious attitude.

schle·miel also **shle·miel** (shlə-mēl′) *n. Slang.* A habitual bungler; a dolt. [Yiddish *shlemíl,* perhaps from Hebrew *šəlumî'ēl,* Shelumiel, a character in the Bible (Numbers 7:36).]

schlep or **schlepp** also **shlep** (shlĕp) *Slang.* —*v.* **schlepped, schlep·ping, schleps** or **schlepped, schlepp·ing, schlepps.** —*tr.* To carry clumsily or with difficulty; lug: *schlepped a shopping bag around town.* —*intr.* To move slowly or laboriously: *schlepped around with the twins in a stroller.* —*n.* **1.** An arduous journey. **2.** A person regarded as clumsy or stupid. [Yiddish *shlepn,* to drag, pull, from Middle Low German *slēpen.* See **lei-** in Appendix.] **—schlep′per, schlepp′er, shlep′per** *n.*

Schles·in·ger (shlĕs′ĭn-jər), **Arthur Meier.** 1888–1965. American historian whose works include *The Rise of the City* (1933). His son **Arthur Meier, Jr.** (born 1917), also a historian, was an adviser to President John F. Kennedy, whose administration is chronicled in *A Thousand Days* (1965).

Schles·wig (shlĕs′wĭg, -wĭk, shlās′vĭk). A historical region and former duchy of northern Germany and southern Denmark in southern Jutland. The duchy was created in 1115 and passed, along with the duchy of Holstein, to Christian I of Denmark in 1460. After subdivisions caused by complex hereditary holdings, the duchies were once more reunited under the Danish crown in 1773. Denmark, Prussia, and Austria contended for the region until 1866, when it was annexed by Prussia. In 1920 the northern part of Schleswig was returned to Denmark by plebiscite. The southern portion became part of the West German state of Schleswig-Holstein after World War II.

Schley (slī), **Winfield Scott.** 1839–1911. American naval commander during the Spanish-American War (1898).

Schlie·mann (shlē′män′), **Heinrich.** 1822–1890. German archaeologist who discovered the ruins of ancient Troy (1871) and excavated Mycenae (1876).

schlie·ren (shlîr′ən) *pl.n.* **1.** *Geology.* Irregular dark or light streaks in plutonic igneous rock that differ in composition from the principal mass. **2.** Regions of a transparent medium, as of a flowing gas, that are visible because their densities are different from that of the bulk of the medium. [German, pl. of *Schliere,* from dialectal *Shliere,* streaks, from Middle High German *slier,* mud, slime, from Old High German *slierrun,* pieces, bits.]

schli·ma·zel (shlĭ-mä′zəl) *n. Slang.* An extremely unlucky or inept person; a habitual failure. [Yiddish *shlimázl,* bad luck, unlucky person : Middle High German *slimp,* wrong + *mázl,* luck (from Hebrew *mazzāl*).]

schlock also **shlock** (shlŏk) *Slang.* —*n.* Something, such as merchandise or literature, that is inferior or shoddy. —*adj.* Of inferior quality; cheap or shoddy. [Possibly from Yiddish *shlak,* apoplexy, stroke, wretch, evil, nuisance, from Middle High German *slag, slak,* stroke, from *slahen,* to strike, from Old High German *slahan.*] **—schlock′y** *adj.*

schlock·meis·ter (shlŏk′mī′stər) *n. Slang.* One who produces or deals in inferior or shoddy goods or material. [SCHLOCK + German *Meister,* master; see MEISTERSINGER.]

schmaltz also **schmalz** (shmälts) *n.* **1.** *Informal.* **a.** Excessively sentimental art or music. **b.** Maudlin sentimentality. **2.** Liquid fat, especially chicken fat. [Yiddish *shmalts,* animal fat, sentimentality, from Middle High German *smalz,* animal fat, from Old High German. See **mel-**[1] in Appendix.]

schmaltz·y also **schmalz·y** (shmält′sē) *adj.* **-i·er, -i·est.** *Informal.* Of or marked by excessive or maudlin sentimentality. See Synonyms at **sentimental.** **—schmaltz′i·ness** *n.*

schmalz (shmälts) *n.* Variant of **schmaltz.**

schmalz·y (shmält′sē) *adj. Informal.* Variant of **schmaltzy.**

schmeer also **schmear** or **shmear** (shmîr) *n. Slang.* A number of things that go together; an aggregate: *bought the whole schmeer.* [Yiddish *shmir,* smear, smudge, from *shmirn,* to smear, grease, from Middle High German *smiren,* from Old High German *smirwen.*]

Schmidt (shmĭt), **Helmut.** Born 1918. German politician who served as West German minister of defense (1969–1972), minister of finance (1972–1974), and chancellor (1974–1982).

Schmidt system *n.* A system consisting of a concave spherical mirror and a transparent plate of glass at its center of curvature, used in reflecting telescopes to offset spherical aberration and

Helmut Schmidt

coma. [After Bernhard Voldemar *Schmidt* (1879–1935), Estonian-born German optical scientist.]

schmo (shmō) *n., pl.* **schmoes** or **schmos.** *Slang.* A person regarded as stupid or obnoxious. [From Yiddish *shmok,* penis, fool. See SCHMUCK.]

schmooze or **schmoose** (shmo͞oz) *Slang.* —*intr.v.* **schmoozed, schmooz·ing, schmooz·es** or **schmoosed, schmoos·ing, schmoos·es.** To talk casually. —*n.* A chat. [Yiddish *shmúesn,* possibly from *shmúes,* a chat, pl. of *shmúe,* rumor; akin to Hebrew *šĕmû'â,* rumor.] —**schmooz′er** *n.*

schmuck also **shmuck** (shmŭk) *n. Slang.* A person regarded as clumsy or stupid; an oaf. [Yiddish *shmok,* penis, fool, probably from Polish *smok,* serpent, tail.]

Schna·bel (shnä′bəl), **Artur.** 1882–1951. Austrian-born American pianist and composer noted for his interpretations of Beethoven, Mozart, and Schubert.

schnap·per (shnăp′ər, snăp′-) *n.* A porgy *(Chrysophrys guttulatus)* of Australia, Tasmania, and New Zealand, having a large bony protuberance on the nape when fully grown and prized as a sport fish and food fish. Also called *snapper.* [Alteration (influenced by German *Schnapper,* snap, schnapper) of SNAPPER.]

schnapps (shnäps, shnăps) *n., pl.* **schnapps.** Any of various strong, dry liquors, such as a strong Dutch gin. [German *Schnaps,* mouthful, schnapps, from Low German *snaps,* from *snappen,* to snap, from Middle Low German, to snap at.]

schnau·zer (shnou′zər, shnou′tsər) *n.* Any of three German breeds of dog of a range of sizes, having a wiry pepper-and-salt or black coat and a blunt muzzle with wiry whiskers. [German, from *Schnauze,* snout, alteration of Middle Low German *snūte.*]

schnit·zel (shnĭt′səl) *n.* A thin cutlet of veal, usually seasoned, that is dipped in batter and fried. [German, from Middle High German *snitzel,* diminutive of *sniz,* slice, from *snitzen,* to carve, frequentative of *snīden,* to cut, from Old High German *snīdan.*]

Schnitz·ler (shnĭts′lər), **Arthur.** 1862–1931. Austrian writer known for his psychologically penetrating and sometimes erotic novels and plays, particularly *La Ronde* (1896).

schnook (shno͝ok) *n. Slang.* A stupid or easily victimized person; a dupe. [Yiddish *shnuk,* snout, schnook, from Lithuanian *snùkis,* mug, snout.]

schnor·rer (shnôr′ər, shnōr′-) *n. Slang.* One who habitually takes advantage of the generosity of others; a parasite. [Yiddish *shnorer,* beggar, sponger, from *shnorn,* to beg, from Middle High German *snurren,* to hum, whir (from the sound of the musical instrument played by beggars).]

schnoz (shnŏz) also **schnoz·zle** (shnŏz′əl) *n. Slang.* The human nose. [Probably alteration of Yiddish *snoyts,* snout, muzzle, from German *Schnauze.*]

schol·ar (skŏl′ər) *n.* **1.a.** A learned person. **b.** A specialist in a given branch of knowledge: *a classical scholar.* **2.** One who attends school or studies with a teacher; a student. **3.** A student who holds or has held a particular scholarship. [Middle English *scoler,* from Old French *escoler* and from Old English *scolere,* both from Medieval Latin *scholāris,* from Late Latin, of a school, from Latin *scola, schola,* school. See SCHOOL[1].]

schol·ar·ly (skŏl′ər-lē) *adj.* Of, relating to, or characteristic of scholars or scholarship: *scholarly pursuits; a scholarly edition with footnotes.* See Synonyms at **learned.** —**schol′ar·li·ness** *n.*

schol·ar·ship (skŏl′ər-shĭp′) *n.* **1.** The methods, discipline, and attainments of a scholar or scholars. **2.** Knowledge resulting from study and research in a particular field. See Synonyms at **knowledge. 3.** A grant of financial aid awarded to a student, as for the purpose of attending a college.

scho·las·tic (skə-lăs′tĭk) *adj.* **1.** Of or relating to schools; academic. **2.** Often **Scholastic.** Of, relating to, or characteristic of Scholasticism. **3.** Adhering rigidly to scholarly methods; pedantic. See Synonyms at **pedantic.** —**scholastic** *n.* **1.** Often **Scholastic.** A Scholastic philosopher or theologian. **2.** A dogmatist; a pedant. [Latin *scholasticus,* from Greek *skholastikos,* learned, studious, from *skholazein,* to study, from *skholē,* school. See **segh-** in Appendix.] —**scho·las′ti·cal·ly** *adv.*

scho·las·ti·cism (skə-lăs′tĭ-sĭz′əm) *n.* **1.** Often **Scholasticism.** The dominant western Christian theological and philosophical school of the Middle Ages, based on the authority of the Latin Fathers and of Aristotle and his commentators. **2.** Close adherence to the methods, traditions, and teachings of a sect or school. **3.** Scholarly conservatism or pedantry.

scho·li·a (skō′lē-ə) *n.* A plural of **scholium.**

scho·li·ast (skō′lē-ăst′) *n.* One of the ancient commentators who annotated the classical authors. [Medieval Greek *skholiastēs,* from *skholiazein,* to comment on, from Greek *skholion,* scholium. See SCHOLIUM.]

scho·li·um (skō′lē-əm) *n., pl.* **-li·ums** or **-li·a** (-lē-ə). **1.** An explanatory note or commentary, as on a Greek or Latin text. **2.** A note amplifying a proof or course of reasoning, as in mathematics. [New Latin, from Greek *skholion,* diminutive of *skholē,* lecture, school. See **segh-** in Appendix.]

Schön·berg (shœn′bûrg, shûrn′-, shœn′bĕrk′), **Arnold.** 1874–1951. Austrian composer who developed atonal composition. His works include operas, chamber music, symphonies, and vocal arrangements, such as *Pierrot Lunaire* (1912).

school[1] (sko͞ol) *n. Abbr.* **sch., s., S. 1.** An institution for the instruction of children or people under college age. **2.** An institution for instruction in a skill or business: *a secretarial school; a karate school.* **3.a.** A college or university. **b.** An institution within or associated with a college or university that gives instruction in a specialized field and recommends candidates for degrees. **c.** A division of an educational institution constituting several grades or classes: *advanced to the upper school.* **d.** The student body of an educational institution. **e.** The building or group of buildings housing an educational institution. **4.** The process of being educated formally, especially education constituting a planned series of courses over a number of years: *The children were put to school at home. What do you plan to do when you finish school?* **5.** A session of instruction: *School will start in three weeks. He had to stay after school today.* **6.a.** A group of people, especially philosophers, artists, or writers, whose thought, work, or style demonstrates a common origin or influence or unifying belief: *the school of Aristotle; the Venetian school of painters.* **b.** A group of people distinguished by similar manners, customs, or opinions: *aristocrats of the old school.* **7.** Close-order drill instructions or exercises for military units or personnel. **8.** *Australian.* A group of people gathered together for gambling. —**school** *tr.v.* **schooled, school·ing, schools. 1.** To educate in or as if in a school. **2.** To train or discipline: *She is well schooled in literature.* See Synonyms at **teach.** —**school** *adj.* Of or relating to school or education in schools: *school supplies; a school dictionary.* [Middle English *scole,* from Old English *scōl,* from Latin *schola, scola,* from Greek *skholē.* See **segh-** in Appendix.]

school[2] (sko͞ol) *n.* A large group of aquatic animals, especially fish, swimming together; a shoal. See Synonyms at **flock**[1]. —**school** *intr.v.* **schooled, school·ing, schools.** To swim in or form into a school. [Middle English *scole,* from Middle Dutch. See **skel-**[1] in Appendix.]

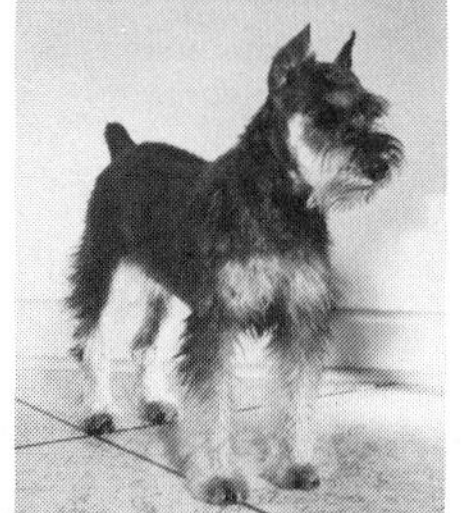

schnauzer
Miniature breed

school age *n.* The age at which a child is considered old enough to attend school. —**school′-age′** (sko͞ol′āj′) *adj.*

school bag or **school·bag** (sko͞ol′băg′) *n.* A bag for carrying textbooks and school supplies.

school board *n.* A local board that oversees public schools.

school·book (sko͞ol′bo͝ok′) *n.* A textbook or other book for use in school.

school·boy (sko͞ol′boi′) *n.* A boy attending school.

school bus *n.* A publicly or privately owned vehicle that is used for taking schoolchildren to and from school or school-related activities.

school·child also **school child** (sko͞ol′chīld′) *n.* A child attending school.

School·craft (sko͞ol′krăft′), **Henry Rowe.** 1793–1864. American geologist, ethnologist, and explorer who discovered the source of the Mississippi River (1832).

school day *n.* **1.** A day on which school is in session. **2.** The part of a day during which school is in session.

school district *n.* A geographic district, the public schools of which are administered together.

school·fel·low (sko͞ol′fĕl′ō) *n.* A schoolmate.

school figure *n. Sports.* A traditional pattern, such as a figure eight, performed as part of an ice-skating competition. Often used in the plural.

school·girl (sko͞ol′gûrl′) *n.* A girl attending school.

school·house (sko͞ol′hous′) *n.* A building used as a school.

school·ing (sko͞o′lĭng) *n.* **1.** Instruction or training given at school. **2.** Education obtained through experience or exposure: *Her tumultuous childhood was a unique schooling.* **3.** The training of a horse or a horse and rider in equitation.

school·ma'am (sko͞ol′mäm′, -măm′) *n.* Variant of **schoolmarm.**

school·man (sko͞ol′mən) *n.* **1.** A man who is a professional educator or scholar. **2. Schoolman.** A medieval Scholastic scholar or philosopher.

school·marm (sko͞ol′märm′) also **school·ma'am** (-mäm′, -măm′) *n.* A woman teacher, especially one who is regarded as strict, old-fashioned, or prudish. [SCHOOL[1] + dialectal *marm* (variant of MA'AM).] —**school′marm′ish** *adj.*

school·mas·ter (sko͞ol′măs′tər) *n.* **1.** A man who is a teacher. **2.** A headmaster of a school. **3.** One that educates, guides, or instructs. **4.** A grayish-brown snapper *(Lutjanus apodus)* of the tropical Atlantic and the Gulf of Mexico. —**school′mas′ter·ish** *adj.* —**school′mas′ter·ly** *adj.*

school·mate (sko͞ol′māt′) *n.* A companion or an associate in one's school.

school·mis·tress (sko͞ol′mĭs′trĭs) *n.* **1.** A woman who is a teacher. **2.** A headmistress of a school.

school of hard knocks *n. Informal.* The practical experiences of life, including hardships and disappointments, that serve to educate and temper a person: *"He hadn't grown up in the school of hard knocks. Politically he had lived an easy life"* (Thomas P. O'Neill, Jr.).

school of thought *n., pl.* **schools of thought.** The point of view held by a particular group: *"We have many schools of thought in the intelligence services"* (Tom Clancy).

school·room (sko͞ol′ro͞om′, -ro͝om′) *n.* A classroom.

school·teach·er (sko͞ol′tē′chər) *n.* A person who teaches in a school below the college level.

school·work (sko͞ol′wûrk′) *n.* Lessons done at school or to be done at home.

ă pat	oi boy
ā pay	ou out
âr care	o͝o took
ä father	o͞o boot
ĕ pet	ŭ cut
ē be	ûr urge
ĭ pit	th thin
ī pie	*th* this
îr pier	hw which
ŏ pot	zh vision
ō toe	ə about, item
ô paw	♦ regionalism

Stress marks: ′ (primary); ′ (secondary), as in **dictionary** (dĭk′shə-nĕr′ē)

schooner
The *Adventure*

school·yard (skōōl′yärd′) *n.* An open area next to a school building for play and outdoor activities.

school year *n.* The part of the year during which school is in session, typically from September to June.

schoo·ner (skōō′nər) *n.* **1.** *Nautical.* A fore-and-aft rigged sailing vessel with at least two masts, a foremast, and a mainmast stepped nearly amidships. **2.** A large beer glass, generally holding a pint or more. **3.** A prairie schooner. [Origin unknown.]

Scho·pen·hau·er (shō′pən-hou′ər), **Arthur.** 1788–1860. German philosopher who believed that the will to live is the fundamental reality and that this will, being a constant striving, is insatiable and ultimately yields only suffering.

schorl (shôrl) *n.* Tourmaline, especially black tourmaline. [German *Schörl.*] **—schor·la′ceous** (shôr-lā′shəs) *adj.*

schot·tische (shŏt′ĭsh, shŏ-tēsh′) *n.* **1.** A round dance in 2/4 time. **2.** A piece of music for this dance. [German, from *schottisch,* Scottish, from Middle High German *schottesch,* from *schotte,* a Scot, from Old High German *scotto,* from Late Latin *Scottus,* Irishman.]

Schou·ten Islands (skout′n). An island group of eastern Indonesia in the southern Pacific Ocean off the northern coast of New Guinea.

♦**schrod** (skrŏd) *n. New England.* Variant of **scrod.**

Schrö·ding·er (shrō′dĭng-ər, shrā′-, shrœ′-), **Erwin.** 1887–1961. Austrian physicist. He shared a 1933 Nobel Prize for new formulations of the atomic theory.

schtick (shtĭk) *n.* Variant of **shtick.**

Franz Schubert

Schu·bert (shōō′bərt, -bĕrt′), **Franz Peter.** 1797–1828. Austrian composer who perfected the form of the German art song in his more than 600 compositions for voice and piano. He also composed symphonies and chamber music.

Schulz (shōōlts), **Charles Monroe.** Born 1922. American cartoonist who created the *Peanuts* comic strip.

Schu·man (shōō′mən), **William Howard.** Born 1910. American composer whose works include symphonies, an opera, and the cantata *A Free Song* (1943), for which he received a Pulitzer Prize.

Schu·mann (shōō′män′, -mən), **Robert.** 1810–1856. German composer known particularly for his song cycles, piano works, and symphonies. A leading romanticist, he encouraged and influenced Chopin and Brahms.

Schu·mann-Heink (shōō′mən-hĭngk′), **Ernestine.** 1861–1936. American contralto noted for her roles in the operas of Wagner and Richard Strauss.

Schum·pe·ter (shōōm′pā-tər), **Joseph Alois.** 1883–1950. Czechoslovakian-born American economist known for his theories of the development of capitalism.

Schurz (shōōrts, shûrz), **Carl.** 1829–1906. German-born American army officer, politician, and editor. A U.S. senator from Missouri (1869–1875), he influenced Republican Party policy through his speeches and later newspaper editorials.

schuss (shōōs, shōōs) *Sports. intr.v.* **schussed, schuss·ing, schuss·es.** To make a fast straight downhill run in skiing. **—schuss** *n.* **1.** A fast straight downhill run in skiing. **2.** A straight, steep course for skiing. [From German, shot, schuss, from Middle High German *schuz,* shot, from Old High German *scuz.* See **skeud-** in Appendix.]

schuss·boom·er (shōōs′bōō′mər, shōōs′-) *n. Sports.* A skier who schusses well.

Schuy·ler (skī′lər), **Philip John.** 1733–1804. American Revolutionary general of American forces in New York State who was relieved of his command after the British capture of Fort Ticonderoga (1777).

Schuyl·kill (skōōl′kĭl′, skōō′kəl). A river, about 209 km (130 mi) long, of southeast Pennsylvania flowing generally southeast to the Delaware River at Philadelphia.

schwa (shwä) *n. Linguistics.* **1.** A mid-central neutral vowel, typically occurring in unstressed syllables, as the final vowel of English *sofa.* Also called *indeterminate vowel.* **2.** The symbol (ə) used to represent an unstressed neutral vowel and, in some systems of phonetic transcription, a stressed mid-central vowel, as in *but.* [German, from Hebrew *šĕwā',* probably from Syriac *šĕwayyā,* equal.]

Charles Schulz

Schwann (shvän), **Theodor.** 1810–1882. German physiologist and pioneer histologist who described the cell as the basic structure of animal tissue.

Schwann cell (shwän, shvän) *n.* Any of the cells that cover the nerve fibers in the peripheral nervous system and form the myelin sheath. [After Theodor SCHWANN.]

Schwarz·schild radius (shwôrts′chīld′, shvärts′shĭld) *n.* The radius of a collapsing celestial object at which gravitational forces exceed the ability of matter and energy to escape, resulting in a black hole. [After Karl *Schwarzschild* (1873–1916), German astronomer.]

Schweit·zer (shwīt′sər, shvīt′-), **Albert.** 1875–1965. French philosopher, physician, and musician who founded (1913) and spent much of his life at a missionary hospital in present-day Gabon. Schweitzer was a noted organist and wrote many philosophical and theological works. He won the 1952 Nobel Peace Prize.

Schwe·rin (shvā-rēn′). A city of north-central Germany on **Schwerin Lake** southwest of Rostock. Originally a Wendish settlement, it was chartered c. 1160 and today is a commercial, industrial, and transportation center. Population, 124,975.

sci. *abbr.* Science; scientific.

sci·ae·noid (sī-ē′noid) *adj.* Of or belonging to the Sciaenidae, a family of fishes that includes the drums and croakers. **—sciaenoid** *n.* A sciaenoid fish. [New Latin *Sciaena,* type genus (from Latin *sciaena,* a kind of fish, from Greek *skiaina*) + -OID.] **—sci·ae′nid** (-nĭd) *adj. & n.*

sci·at·ic (sī-ăt′ĭk) *adj.* **1.** Of or relating to the ischium or to the region of the hipbone in which it is located. **2.** Of or relating to sciatica. [French *sciatique,* from Old French, from Medieval Latin *sciaticus,* alteration of Latin *ischiadicus,* from Greek *iskhiadikos,* from *iskhias, iskhiad-,* sciatica, from *iskhion,* hip.]

sci·at·i·ca (sī-ăt′ĭ-kə) *n.* Pain along the sciatic nerve usually caused by a herniated disk of the lumbar region of the spine and radiating to the buttocks and to the back of the thigh. [Middle English, from Medieval Latin, from feminine of *sciaticus,* of the hip. See SCIATIC.]

sciatic nerve *n.* A sensory and motor nerve originating in the sacral plexus and running through the pelvis and upper leg.

SCID *abbr.* Severe combined immunodeficiency.

sci·ence (sī′əns) *n. Abbr.* **sc., sci. 1.a.** The observation, identification, description, experimental investigation, and theoretical explanation of phenomena. **b.** Such activities restricted to a class of natural phenomena. **c.** Such activities applied to an object of inquiry or study. **2.** Methodological activity, discipline, or study: *I've got packing a suitcase down to a science.* **3.** An activity that appears to require study and method: *the science of purchasing.* **4.** Knowledge, especially that gained through experience. **5. Science.** Christian Science. [Middle English, knowledge, learning, from Old French, from Latin *scientia,* from *sciēns, scient-,* present participle of *scīre,* to know. See **skei-** in Appendix.]

science fiction *n. Abbr.* **sf, SF** A literary or cinematic genre in which fantasy, typically based on speculative scientific discoveries or developments, environmental changes, space travel, or life on other planets, forms part of the plot or background.

sci·en·ter (sī-ĕn′tər) *adv. Law.* Deliberately or knowingly. [Latin, from *sciēns, scient-,* present participle of *scīre,* to know. See SCIENCE.]

sci·en·tial (sī-ĕn′shəl) *adj.* **1.** Of or producing knowledge or science. **2.** Capable; skillful.

sci·en·tif·ic (sī′ən-tĭf′ĭk) *adj. Abbr.* **sci.** Of, relating to, or employing the methodology of science. [Medieval Latin *scientificus,* producing knowledge : Latin *scientia,* knowledge; see SCIENCE + Latin *-ficus,* -fic.] **—sci′en·tif′i·cal·ly** *adv.*

scientific empiricism *n.* The philosophical view that there are no ultimate differences among the various sciences.

scientific method *n.* The principles and empirical processes of discovery and demonstration considered characteristic of or necessary for scientific investigation, generally involving the observation of phenomena, the formulation of a hypothesis concerning the phenomena, experimentation to demonstrate the truth or falseness of the hypothesis, and a conclusion that validates or modifies the hypothesis.

scientific notation *n. Mathematics.* A method of writing or displaying numbers in terms of a decimal number between 1 and 10 multiplied by a power of 10. The scientific notation of 10,492, for example, is 1.0492×10^4.

sci·en·tism (sī′ən-tĭz′əm) *n.* **1.** The theory that investigational methods used in the natural sciences should be applied in all fields of inquiry. **2.** The application of quasi-scientific techniques or justifications to unsuitable subjects or topics. **—sci′en·tis′tic** *adj.*

sci·en·tist (sī′ən-tĭst) *n.* **1.** A person having expert knowledge of one or more sciences, especially a natural or physical science. **2. Scientist.** A Christian Scientist.

sci-fi (sī′fī′) *n., pl.* **-fis.** *Informal.* Science fiction. **—sci-fi** *adj.* Of, relating to, being, or similar to science fiction: *a sci-fi movie; a sci-fi weapons system.*

scil·i·cet (sĭl′ĭ-sĕt′, skē′lĭ-kĕt′) *adv. Abbr.* **sc., scil., ss, ss.** That is to say; namely. [Middle English, from Latin *scīlicet,* contraction of *scīre licet,* it is permitted to know : *scīre,* to know; see **skei-** in Appendix + *licet,* third person sing. of *licēre,* to be permitted.]

Scil·ly Islands (sĭl′ē). An archipelago comprising more than 140 small islands and rocky islets off southwest England at the entrance to the English Channel west-southwest of Land's End.

scim·i·tar (sĭm′ĭ-tər, -tär′) *n.* A curved Asian sword with the edge on the convex side. [French *cimeterre* and Italian *scimitarra,* both perhaps ultimately from Persian *šimšīr.*]

scin·coid (sĭng′koid) *adj.* Of, belonging to, or resembling the skinks. **—scincoid** *n.* A scincoid lizard. [Latin *scincus,* skink; see SKINK + -OID.]

scin·ti·gram (sĭn′tĭ-grăm′) *n.* A two-dimensional record of the distribution of a radioactive tracer in a tissue or organ, obtained by means of a scanning scintillation counter. Also called *scintigraph, scintiscan.* [SCINTI(LLATION) + -GRAM.]

scin·ti·graph (sĭn′tĭ-grăf′) *n.* **1.** A device for producing a scintigram; a scintiscanner. **2.** See **scintigram. —scin′ti·graph′ic** *adj.* **—scin·ti·graph′i·cal·ly** *adv.* **—scin·tig′ra·phy** (sĭn-tĭg′rə-fē) *n.*

scin·til·la (sĭn-tĭl′ə) *n.* **1.** A minute amount; an iota or a trace. **2.** A spark; a flash. [Latin, spark.] **—scin′til·lant** *adj.*

scin·til·late (sĭn′tl-āt′) *v.* **-lat·ed, -lat·ing, -lates.** *—intr.* **1.** To throw off sparks; flash. **2.** To sparkle or shine. See Synonyms at **flash.** **3.** To be animated and brilliant: *dinner conversation that scintillated.* —*tr.* To give off (sparks or flashes). [Latin *scintillāre, scintillāt-,* from *scintilla,* spark.] —**scin′til·lat′ing·ly** *adv.*

scin·til·la·tion (sĭn′tl-ā′shən) *n.* **1.** The act of scintillating. **2.** A spark; a flash. **3.** *Astronomy.* Rapid variation in the light of a celestial body caused by turbulence in Earth's atmosphere; a twinkling. **4.** *Physics.* A flash of light produced in a phosphor by absorption of an ionizing particle or photon.

scintillation counter *n.* A device for detecting and counting scintillations produced by ionizing radiation.

scin·til·la·tor (sĭn′tl-ā′tər) *n.* A substance that glows when hit by high-energy particles or photons.

scin·ti·scan (sĭn′tĭ-skăn′) *n.* See **scintigram.** [SCINTI(LLATION) + SCAN.] —**scin′ti·scan′ner** *n.*

sci·o·lism (sī′ə-lĭz′əm) *n.* A pretentious attitude of scholarship; superficial knowledgeability. [From Late Latin *sciolus,* smatterer, diminutive of Latin *scius,* knowing, from *scīre,* to know. See **skei-** in Appendix.] —**sci′o·list** *n.* —**sci′o·lis′tic** *adj.*

sci·on (sī′ən) *n.* **1.** A descendant or an heir. **2.** Also **ci·on** (sī′ən). A detached shoot or twig containing buds from a woody plant, used in grafting. [Middle English, from Old French *cion,* possibly of Germanic origin.]

Sci·o·to (sī-ō′tə). A river, about 381 km (237 mi) long, rising in western Ohio and flowing east then south to the Ohio River in south-central Ohio.

Scip·io (sĭp′ē-ō′, skĭp′-), **Publius Cornelius.** Known as "Scipio the Younger." 185?–129 B.C. Roman general and politician who commanded the final destruction of Carthage (146) in the Third Punic War.

Scipio Af·ri·ca·nus (ăf-rĭ-kä′nəs), **Publius Cornelius.** Known as "Scipio the Elder." 236?–183? B.C. Roman general who invaded northern Africa, conquered Carthage, and brought to an end the Second Punic War by defeating Hannibal at Zama (202).

sci·re fa·ci·as (sī′rē fā′shē-əs, skē′rĕ fä′kē-äs′) *n. Law.* **1.** A writ requiring the party against which it is issued to appear and show cause why a judicial record should not be enforced, repealed, or annulled. **2.** A judicial proceeding under this writ. [Middle English, from Latin *scīre faciās,* you should cause (him) to know (a phrase that occurs in the writ) : *scīre,* to know + *faciās,* second person sing. present subjunctive of *facere,* to do, make.]

sci·roc·co (shə-rŏk′ō, sə-) *n.* Variant of **sirocco.**

scir·rhus (skĭr′əs, sĭr′-) *n., pl.* **scir·rhi** (skĭr′ī, sĭr′ī) or **scir·rhus·es.** A hard, dense cancerous growth usually arising from connective tissue. [New Latin, from Latin *scirros,* from Greek *skiros, skirros,* from *skiros,* hard.] —**scir′rhous, scir′rhoid′** *adj.*

scis·sile (sĭs′əl, -īl′) *adj.* Cut or split easily: *a scissile mineral; a scissile peptide bond.* [French, from Latin *scissilis,* from *scissus,* past participle of *scindere,* to cut. See SCISSION.]

scis·sion (sĭzh′ən, sĭsh′-) *n.* The act of cutting or severing; division or fission. [Middle English, from Old French, from Late Latin *scissiō, scissiōn-,* from Latin *scissus,* past participle of *scindere,* to cut, split. See **skei-** in Appendix.]

scis·sor (sĭz′ər) *tr.v.* **-sored, -sor·ing, -sors.** To cut or clip with scissors or shears. —**scissor** *n.* **1. scissors.** *(used with a sing. or pl. verb).* A cutting implement consisting of two blades joined by a swivel pin that allows the cutting edges to be opened and closed. **2.** Something resembling a two-bladed cutting implement: *wore a jeweled scissor on her lapel.* **3. scissors.** *(used with a sing. verb). Sports.* **a.** Any of various gymnastic exercises or jumps in which the movement of the legs suggests the opening and closing of scissors. **b.** A scissors hold. [From alteration (influenced by Latin *scissor,* cutter, from *scissus,* cut; see SCISSION) of Middle English *sisours,* scissors, from Old French *cisoires,* from Vulgar Latin **cīsōria,* from Late Latin, pl. of *cīsōrium,* cutting instrument, from Latin *caesus, -cīsus,* past participle of *caedere,* to cut. See **kae-id-** in Appendix.]

scis·sors hold (sĭz′ərz) *n. Sports.* A wrestling hold in which the legs of one opponent are locked about the head or body of another opponent.

scissors kick *n. Sports.* A swimming kick in which the legs are opened and closed like scissors.

scis·sor·tail (sĭz′ər-tāl′) *n.* A scissor-tailed flycatcher.

scissor-tailed flycatcher (sĭz′ər-tāld′) *n.* A flycatcher *(Muscivora forficata)* of the southwest United States, Mexico, and Central America, having a long forked tail.

scis·sure (sĭzh′ər, sĭsh′-) *n. Anatomy.* A split or opening in an organ or part. [Middle English, from Old French, from Latin *scissūra,* from *scissus,* past participle of *scindere,* to split. See SCISSION.]

Scit·u·ate (sĭch′o͞o-āt′, -ĭt). A town of eastern Massachusetts on Massachusetts Bay southeast of Boston. It is a residential community and summer resort. Population, 17,317.

sci·u·rid (sī′yo͞o-rĭd′) *adj.* Of, belonging to, or resembling the Sciuridae, a family of rodents that includes the squirrels and related mammals. —**sciurid** *n.* A sciurid rodent. [From New Latin *Sciūridae,* family name, from Latin *sciūrus,* squirrel. See SQUIRREL.] —**sci′u·rine** (-rīn′) *adj.* —**sci′u·roid** (sī′yo͞o-roid′, sī-yo͝or′oid) *adj.*

sclaff (sklăf) *v.* **sclaffed, sclaff·ing, sclaffs.** *Sports.* —*intr.* To scrape or strike the ground with a golf club behind the ball before hitting it. —*tr.* **1.** To strike (the ground) with a golf club before hitting the ball. **2.** To hit (a ball) in this manner. [Scots, to strike with a flat surface.] —**sclaff** *n.* —**sclaff′er** *n.*

SCLC *abbr.* Southern Christian Leadership Conference.

scler– *pref.* Variant of **sclero–.**

scle·ra (sklîr′ə) *n.* The tough, white, fibrous outer envelope of tissue covering all of the eyeball except the cornea. Also called *sclerotic, sclerotic coat.* [New Latin, from Greek, feminine of *sklēros,* hard.] —**scle′ral** *adj.*

scler·e·id (sklĕr′ē-ĭd) *n.* A thick-walled lignified plant cell that is often branched. [SCLERE(NCHYMA) + –ID.]

scle·ren·chy·ma (sklə-rĕng′kə-mə) *n.* A supportive plant tissue that consists of thick-walled, usually lignified cells. —**scle′ren·chym′a·tous** (sklîr′ən-kĭm′ə-təs, -kī′mə-) *adj.*

scle·rite (sklîr′īt′) *n.* A chitinous or calcareous plate, spicule, or similar part of an invertebrate, especially one of the hard outer plates forming part of the exoskeleton of an arthropod.

scle·ri·tis (sklə-rī′tĭs) *n.* Inflammation of the sclera. —**scle·rit′ic** (-rĭt′ĭk) *adj.*

sclero– or **scler–** *pref.* **1.** Hard: *sclerite.* **2.** Hardness: *sclerometer.* **3.** Sclera: *scleritis.* [Greek *sklēro-,* from *sklēros,* hard.]

scle·ro·der·ma (sklîr′ə-dûr′mə) *n.* A pathological thickening and hardening of the skin.

scle·ro·der·ma·tous (sklîr′ə-dûr′mə-təs) *adj.* **1.** Of, relating to, or affected by scleroderma. **2.** *Zoology.* Having an outer covering of hard plates or bony scales.

scle·roid (sklîr′oid′) *adj. Biology.* Hard or hardened; indurated.

scle·ro·ma (sklə-rō′mə) *n., pl.* **-mas** or **-ma·ta** (-mə-tə). An abnormally hard patch of body tissue especially in the upper respiratory tract. [New Latin, from Greek *sklērōma,* hardening, from *sklēroun,* to harden, from *sklēros,* hard.]

scle·rom·e·ter (sklə-rŏm′ĭ-tər) *n.* An instrument used to determine the relative hardness of a material by measuring the pressure required to penetrate the material with a standard diamond stylus.

scle·ro·pro·tein (sklîr′ō-prō′tēn′, -tē-ĭn) *n.* Any of a class of generally insoluble proteins, such as collagen, found in skeletal and connective tissue. Also called *albuminoid.*

scle·rosed (sklə-rōzd′, -rōst′) *adj.* **1.** Affected by sclerosis; hardened. **2.** *Botany.* Lignified. [From SCLEROSIS.]

scle·ro·sis (sklə-rō′sĭs) *n., pl.* **-ses** (-sēz). **1.a.** A thickening or hardening of a body part, as of an artery, especially from excessive formation of fibrous interstitial tissue. **b.** A disease characterized by this thickening or hardening. **2.** *Botany.* The hardening of cells by the formation of a secondary wall and the deposition of lignin. [Middle English *sclirosis,* from Medieval Latin *sclīrōsis,* from Greek *sklērōsis,* hardening, from *sklēroun,* to harden. See SCLEROMA.]

scle·ro·ti·a (sklə-rō′shē-ə, -shə) *n.* Plural of **sclerotium.**

scle·ro·ti·al (sklə-rō′shē-əl, -shəl) *adj.* Of or relating to sclerotia or a sclerotium.

scle·rot·ic (sklə-rŏt′ĭk) *adj.* **1.** Affected or marked by sclerosis. **2.** *Anatomy.* Of or relating to the sclera. —**sclerotic** *n.* See **sclera.**

sclerotic coat *n.* See **sclera.**

scler·o·tin (sklîr′ə-tĭn, sklĕr′-) *n.* An insoluble protein that hardens and darkens the cuticle of arthropods by a natural tanning process involving the cross-linkage of chitin protein molecules. [SCLERO– + *-tin* (as in KERATIN, or CHITIN).]

scle·ro·ti·um (sklə-rō′shē-əm, -shəm) *n., pl.* **-ti·a** (-shē-ə, -shə). A dense mass of branched hyphae, as in certain fungi, that contain stored food and are capable of remaining dormant for long periods. [New Latin, from Greek *sklērotēs,* hardness, from *sklēros,* hard.]

scler·o·ti·za·tion (sklĕr′ə-tĭ-zā′shən) *n.* The process by which the cuticle of an arthropod is hardened by formation of sclerotin. [Greek *sklērotēs,* hardness (from *sklēros,* hard) + –IZATION.]

scle·rot·o·my (sklə-rŏt′ə-mē) *n., pl.* **-mies.** Surgical incision of the sclera.

scle·rous (sklîr′əs, sklĕr′-) *adj.* Having been hardened; toughened.

scoff¹ (skŏf, skôf) *v.* **scoffed, scoff·ing, scoffs.** —*tr.* To mock at or treat with derision. —*intr.* To treat or express derisively; mock. —**scoff** *n.* An expression of derision or scorn. [Middle English *scoffen,* from *scof,* mockery, probably of Scandinavian origin; akin to Danish *skof,* jest, teasing.] —**scoff′er** *n.* —**scoff′ing·ly** *adv.*

scoff² (skŏf, skôf) *v.* **scoffed, scoff·ing, scoffs.** *Slang.* —*tr.* To eat (food) quickly and greedily. —*intr.* To eat greedily. [Alteration of obsolete *scaff.*] —**scoff′er** *n.*

scoff·law (skŏf′lô′, skôf′-) *n.* One who habitually violates the law or fails to answer court summonses.

scold (skōld) *v.* **scold·ed, scold·ing, scolds.** —*tr.* To reprimand or criticize harshly and usually angrily. —*intr.* To reprove or criticize openly. —**scold** *n.* One who persistently nags or criticizes: *"As a critic gets older, he or she usually grows more tetchy and . . . may even become a big-league scold"* (James Wolcott). [Middle English *scolden,* to rail at, from *scolde,* an abusive person, probably of Scandinavian origin. See **sekʷ-³** in Appendix.] —**scold′er** *n.* —**scold′ing·ly** *adv.*

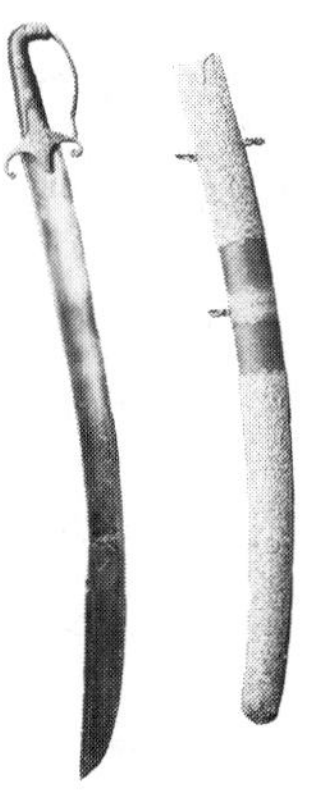

scimitar

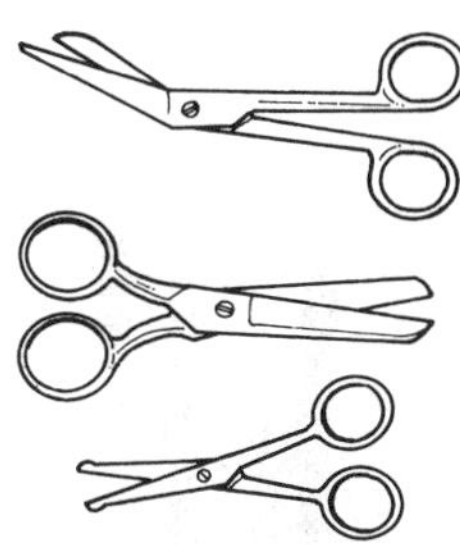

scissors
Top: Bandage scissors
Center: Safety-point scissors
Bottom: Nose and mustache scissors

ă pat	oi boy
ā pay	ou out
âr care	o͝o took
ä father	o͞o boot
ĕ pet	ŭ cut
ē be	ûr urge
ĭ pit	th thin
ī pie	*th* this
îr pier	hw which
ŏ pot	zh vision
ō toe	ə about, item
ô paw	♦ regionalism

Stress marks: **′** (primary); ′ (secondary), as in **dictionary** (dĭk′shə-nĕr′ē)

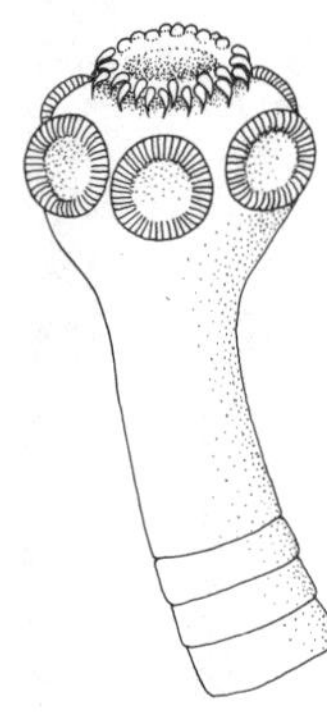
scolex

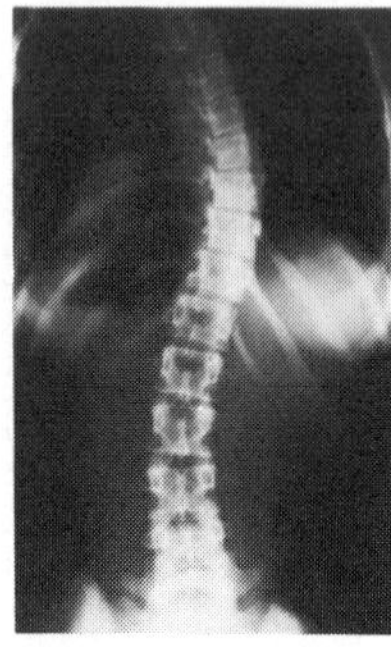
scoliosis

sconce[2]
Late 18th-century French

ă pat oi boy
ā pay ou out
âr care o͝o took
ä father o͞o boot
ĕ pet ŭ cut
ē be ûr urge
ĭ pit th thin
ī pie *th* this
îr pier hw which
ŏ pot zh vision
ō toe ə about, item
ô paw ♦ regionalism

Stress marks: **ʹ** (primary); ʹ (secondary), as in **dictionary** (dĭkʹshə-nĕrʹē)

SYNONYMS: *scold, upbraid, berate, revile, vituperate, rail.* These verbs mean to reprimand or criticize angrily or vehemently. *Scold* implies an annoyed or bad-tempered reproof: *The young woman's parents scolded her for questioning their authority. Upbraid* generally suggests a well-founded reproach, as one leveled by an authority: *"upbraided him for not having worn his overcoat"* (Arnold Bennett). *Berate* suggests scolding or rebuking angrily and at length: *The dissatisfied customer berated the florist. Revile* and *vituperate* especially stress the use of disparaging or abusive language: *Critics reviled the novel as unsophisticated pulp. "The incensed priests . . . continued to raise their voices, vituperating each other in bad Latin"* (Sir Walter Scott). *Rail* suggests bitter, harsh, or denunciatory language: *"Why rail at fate? The mischief is your own"* (John Greenleaf Whittier).

WORD HISTORY: A scold is no poet and a scolding is not poetry, at least to the one being scolded, but it seems that the word *scold* has a poetic background. It is probable that *scold,* which is first recorded in Middle English in a work probably composed around 1150, has a Scandinavian source that is related to the Old Icelandic word *skāld,* "poet." Middle English *scolde* may in fact mean "a minstrel," but of that we are not sure. However, its Middle English meanings, "a ribald, abusive person" and "a shrewish, chiding woman," may be related to *skāld,* as shown by the senses of some of the Old Icelandic words derived from *skāld.* Old Icelandic *skāldskapr,* for example, meant "poetry" in a good sense but also "a libel in verse," while *skāld-stöng* meant "a pole with imprecations or charms scratched on it." It would seem that libelous, cursing verse was a noted part of at least some poets' productions and that this association with poets passed firmly along with the Scandinavian borrowing into English.

scold·ing (skōlʹdĭng) *n.* A harsh or sharp reprimand.

sco·lex (skōʹlĕksʹ) *n., pl.* **-li·ces** (-lĭ-sēzʹ). The knoblike anterior end of a tapeworm, having suckers or hooklike parts that in the adult stage serve as organs of attachment to the host on which the tapeworm is parasitic. [New Latin, from Greek *skōlēx,* worm.]

sco·li·o·sis (skōʹlē-ōʹsĭs, skŏlʹē-) *n.* Abnormal lateral curvature of the spine. [Greek *skolios,* crooked + –OSIS.] **—scoʹli·otʹic** (-ŏtʹĭk) *adj.*

scol·lop (skŏlʹəp) *n. & v.* Variant of **scallop.**

scol·o·pen·drid (skŏlʹə-pĕnʹdrĭd) *n.* Any of numerous centipedes of the family Scolopendridae, especially the larger ones, such as *Scolopendra gigas* of the West Indies. [From New Latin *Scolopendridae,* family name, from Latin *scolopendra,* a kind of centipede, from Greek *skolopendra,* millipede.] **—scolʹo·penʹdrineʹ** (-drīnʹ, -drĭn) *adj.*

scom·broid (skŏmʹbroidʹ) *adj.* Of or belonging to the suborder Scombroidei, which includes marine fishes such as the mackerel. **—scombroid** *n.* A scombroid fish. [New Latin *Scombroidei,* suborder name, from Latin *scomber, scombr-,* mackerel, from Greek *skombros.*]

sconce[1] (skŏns) *n.* A small defensive earthwork or fort. [Dutch *schans,* from German *Schanze,* from Middle High German.]

sconce[2] (skŏns) *n.* **1.** A decorative wall bracket for holding candles or lights. **2.** A flattened candlestick that has a handle. **3.** *Slang.* The human head or skull. [Middle English, from Old French *esconse,* lantern, hiding place, from Medieval Latin *scōnsa,* from Latin *abscōnsa,* feminine past participle of *abscondere,* to hide away : *ab-, abs-,* away; see AB–[1] + *condere,* to preserve; see **dhē-** in Appendix.]

♦**scone** (skōn, skŏn) *n.* **1.** A small, rich, biscuitlike pastry or quick bread, sometimes baked on a griddle. **2.** *Utah.* Yeast bread dough, deep-fried and served with honey and butter or with a savory filling. [Perhaps from Dutch *schoonbrood,* fine white bread, from Middle Dutch *schoonbroot* : *schoon,* bright; see **keu-** in Appendix + *broot,* bread.]

Scone (sko͞on). A village of central Scotland northeast of Perth. The old part of the village was the coronation site of Scottish kings until 1651. The Stone of Scone, or Stone of Destiny, which served as a throne during the coronation rites, was taken to England by Edward I in the late 13th century and today rests in Westminster Abbey beneath the chair used during the crowning of British monarchs.

scoop (sko͞op) *n.* **1.a.** A shovellike utensil, usually having a deep, curved dish and a short handle: *a flour scoop.* **b.** The amount that such a utensil can hold. **2.a.** A thick-handled cuplike utensil for dispensing balls of ice cream or other semisoft food, often having a sweeping band in the cup that is levered by the thumb to free the contents. **b.** A portion of food gathered with this utensil. **3.** A ladle; a dipper. **4.** An implement for bailing water from a boat. **5.** A narrow, spoon-shaped instrument for surgical extraction in cavities or cysts. **6.** The bucket or shovel, as of a dredge or backhoe. **7.** A hollow area; a cavity. **8.** An opening, as on the body of a motor vehicle, by which a fluid is directed inward: *"The* [sports car] *has . . . enough scoops and spoilers to get you a citation just standing still"* (Mark Weinstein). **9.** A scooping movement or action. **10.** *Informal.* An exclusive news story acquired by luck or initiative before a competitor. **11.** *Informal.* Current information or details: *What's the scoop on the new neighbors?* **—scoop** *tr.v.* **scooped, scoop·ing, scoops. 1.** To take up or dip into with or as if with a scoop. **2.** To hollow out by digging. **3.** To gather or collect swiftly and unceremoniously; grab: *scoop up a handful of jelly beans.* **4.** *Informal.* To top or outmaneuver (a competitor) in acquiring and publishing an important news story. [Middle English *scope,* from Middle Dutch and Middle Low German *schōpe,* bucket for bailing water.] **—scoopʹer** *n.* **—scoopʹfulʹ** *n.*

scoop neck *n.* A rounded, usually low-cut neckline, as on a blouse or dress. Also called *scoop neckline.*

♦**scoot** (sko͞ot) *v.* **scoot·ed, scoot·ing, scoots.** *—intr.* To go suddenly and speedily; hurry. *—tr. Upper Southern U.S.* To squirt with water: *"I know I wouldn't scoot down no hog with no hose"* (Flannery O'Connor). ***—phrasal verb.*** **scoot over.** *Midland & Upper Southern U.S.* To move (a person or thing) to the side to make room: *Scoot that chair over.* [Scots, to eject, squirt, probably of Scandinavian origin; akin to Old Norse *skjōta,* to shoot.] **—scoot** *n.*

♦***REGIONAL NOTE:*** *Scoot* comes from a Scandinavian verb related to the verb *shoot* and, borrowed into Scots dialect, originally meant "to squirt with water." Two derived senses, both intransitive verbs, have become even more common: "to slide suddenly across a surface" and "to move quickly": *The mouse scooted across the floor.* In the American Midlands, there is a phrasal verb *scoot over,* meaning, in its transitive sense, "to push (someone or something) to the side to make room."

scoot·er (sko͞oʹtər) *n.* **1.** A child's vehicle consisting of a long footboard between two small end wheels, controlled by an upright steering handle attached to the front wheel. **2.** A motor scooter. **3.** *Nautical.* A flat-bottomed sailboat with runners that can skim over water or ice.

scop (shōp) *n.* An Old English poet or bard. [Old English.]

scope (skōp) *n.* **1.** The range of one's perceptions, thoughts, or actions. **2.** Breadth or opportunity to function. See Synonyms at **room. 3.** The area covered by a given activity or subject. See Synonyms at **range. 4.** The length or sweep of a mooring cable. **5.** *Informal.* A viewing instrument such as a periscope, microscope, or telescope. **—scope** *tr.v.* **scoped, scop·ing, scopes.** *Slang.* To examine or study carefully and in detail: "[He] *scopes the big picture of Israeli-Arab relations"* (James Wolcott). [Italian *scopo,* aim, purpose, from Greek *skopos,* target, aim. See **spek-** in Appendix.]

-scope *suff.* An instrument for viewing or observing: *bronchoscope.* [New Latin *-scopium,* from Greek *-skopion,* from *skopein,* to see. See **spek-** in Appendix.]

Scopes (skōps), **John Thomas.** 1900–1970. American teacher who violated a state law by teaching the theory of evolution in a Tennessee high school. His trial (July 1925) was a highly publicized confrontation between defense attorney Clarence Darrow and the director of the prosecution William Jennings Bryan. Scopes was found guilty and fined a nominal sum, but his conviction was later reversed on technical grounds.

sco·pol·a·mine (skə-pŏlʹə-mēnʹ, -mĭn) *n.* A thick, syrupy, colorless alkaloid, $C_{17}H_{21}NO_4$, extracted from plants such as henbane and used as a mydriatic, sedative, and truth serum. Also called *hyoscine.* [New Latin *Scopolia,* plant genus (after Giovanni Antonio *Scopoli* (1723–1788), Italian naturalist) + –AMINE.]

scop·u·la (skŏpʹyə-lə) *n., pl.* **-lae** (-lēʹ). A dense, brushlike tuft of hairs, as on the feet of certain insects. [Latin *scōpula,* small brush of twigs, diminutive of *scōpae,* branches, broom.] **—scopʹu·lateʹ** (-lātʹ) *adj.*

-scopy *suff.* Viewing; seeing; observation: *microscopy.* [Greek *-skopia,* from *skopein,* to see. See **spek-** in Appendix.]

scor·bu·tic (skôr-byo͞oʹtĭk) also **scor·bu·ti·cal** (-tĭ-kəl) *adj.* Of, relating to, resembling, or affected by scurvy. [New Latin *scorbūticus,* from *scorbūtus,* scurvy, perhaps of Germanic origin.] **—scor·buʹti·cal·ly** *adv.*

scorch (skôrch) *v.* **scorched, scorch·ing, scorch·es.** *—tr.* **1.** To burn superficially so as to discolor or damage the texture of. See Synonyms at **burn[1]. 2.** To wither or parch with intense heat. **3.** To destroy by or as if by fire (all land and buildings in one's path) so as to leave nothing salvageable to an enemy army. **4.** To subject to severe censure; excoriate. *—intr.* **1.** To become scorched or singed. **2.** To go or move at a very fast, often excessively fast rate. **—scorch** *n.* **1.** A slight or surface burn. **2.** A discoloration caused by heat. **3.** Brown spotting on plant leaves caused by fungi, heat, or lack of water. [Middle English *scorchen,* possibly of Scandinavian origin; akin to Old Norse *skorpna,* to shrink, be shriveled.] **—scorchʹing·ly** *adv.*

scorched-earth policy (skôrchtʹûrthʹ) *n.* The policy of devastating all land and buildings in the course of advancing or retreating troops so as to leave nothing salvageable to the enemy.

scorch·er (skôrʹchər) *n.* **1.** One that scorches: *an iron that was a scorcher.* **2.** *Informal.* An extremely hot day.

score (skôr, skōr) *n.* **1.** A notch or an incision, especially one that is made to keep a tally. **2.** *Sports & Games.* **a.** A usually numerical record of a competitive event: *keeping score.* **b.** The total number of points made by each competitor or side in a contest, either final or at a given stage: *The score stood tied in the bottom of the ninth inning.* **c.** The number of points attributed to a competitor or team. **3.** A result, usually expressed numerically, of a test or examination. **4.a.** An amount due; a debt. **b.** A grievance that is harbored and requires satisfaction: *settle an old score.* **5.** A ground; a reason. **6.** A group of 20 items. **7. scores.** Large numbers: *Scores of people attended the rally.* **8.** *Music.* **a.** The written form of a composition for orchestral or vocal parts, either complete or for a particular instrument or voice. **b.** A composition written for a musical comedy. **9.** *Slang.* **a.** The act of securing an advantage, especially a surprising or significant gain: *"He had dropped out of school and gone for that quick dollar, that big score"* (Peter Goldman). **b.** The act or an instance of buying illicit drugs. **c.** A successful robbery. **d.** A sexual conquest. **—score** *v.* **scored, scor·ing, scores.** *—tr.* **1.** To mark with lines or notches, especially for the purpose of keeping a record. **2.** To cancel or eliminate by or as if by superimposing lines. **3.** To mark the surface of (meat, for example) with usually parallel cuts. **4.** *Sports & Games.* **a.** To gain (a point) in a game or contest. **b.** To count or be worth as points. **5.** To achieve; win. **6.** To evaluate and assign a grade to. **7.** *Music.* **a.** To orchestrate. **b.** To arrange for a specific instrument. **8.** To criticize cuttingly; berate. **9.** *Slang.* **a.** To succeed in acquiring: *scored two tickets to the play.* **b.** To succeed in obtaining (an illicit drug): *"Aging punks try to impress her with tales of . . . the different drugs they've scored"* (Art Jahnke). *—intr.* **1.** *Sports & Games.* **a.** To make a point in a game or contest. **b.** To keep the score of a game or contest. **2.** *Slang.* **a.** To achieve a purpose or advantage, especially to make a surprising gain or coup: *"They . . . score in places like the bond market"* (Mike Barnicle). **b.** To succeed in seducing someone sexually. **c.** To succeed in buying or obtaining an illicit drug. [Middle English, from Old English *scoru, twenty, from Old Norse *skor.* See **sker-**[1] in Appendix.] **—scor′er** *n.*

score·board (skôr′bôrd′, skōr′bōrd′) *n.* *Sports & Games.* A large board that records and displays the score of a game or contest.

score·card (skôr′kärd′, skōr′-) *n.* *Sports & Games.* **1.** A printed program or card enabling a spectator to identify players and record the progress of a game or competition. **2.** A small card used to record one's own performance in sports such as golf.

score·keep·er (skôr′kē′pər, skōr′-) *n.* *Sports & Games.* An official who records the score throughout a game or competition. **—score′keep′ing** *adj. & n.*

score·less (skôr′lĭs, skōr′-) *adj.* *Sports & Games.* Having no points scored.

Scores·by Sound (skôrz′bē, skōrz′-). An arm of the Norwegian Sea indenting eastern Greenland.

sco·ri·a (skôr′ē-ə, skōr′-) *n., pl.* **sco·ri·ae** (skôr′ē-ē′, skōr′-). **1.** *Geology.* Porous cinderlike fragments of dark lava. Also called *cinders, slag.* **2.** *Metallurgy.* The refuse of a smelted metal or ore; slag. Also called *cinder.* [Middle English, dross, from Latin *scōria,* from Greek *skōria,* from *skōr,* excrement, dung. See **sker-**[3] in Appendix.] **—sco′ri·a′ceous** (-ā′shəs) *adj.*

sco·ri·fy (skôr′ə-fī′, skōr′-) *tr.v.* **-fied, -fy·ing, -fies.** To separate (an ore) into scoria and a precious metal. **—sco′ri·fi·ca′tion** (-fĭ-kā′shən) *n.* **—sco′ri·fi′er** *n.*

scorn (skôrn) *n.* **1.a.** Contempt or disdain felt toward a person or object considered despicable or unworthy. **b.** The expression of such an attitude in behavior or speech; derision. **2.** One spoken of or treated with contempt. **—scorn** *v.* **scorned, scorn·ing, scorns.** *—tr.* **1.** To consider or treat as contemptible or unworthy. **2.** To reject or refuse with derision. See Synonyms at **despise.** *—intr.* To express contempt; scoff. [Middle English, from Old French *escarn,* of Germanic origin.] **—scorn′er** *n.* **—scorn′ful** *adj.* **—scorn′ful·ly** *adv.* **—scorn′ful·ness** *n.*

scor·pae·noid (skôr-pē′noid′) *adj.* Of or belonging to the suborder Scorpaenoidei, which includes the scorpion fishes and rockfishes. **—scorpaenoid** *n.* A scorpaenoid fish. [From New Latin *Scorpaenoidei,* suborder name, from *Scorpaena,* type genus, from Latin, a kind of fish, from Greek *skorpaina,* feminine of *skorpios,* a sea fish, scorpion.] **—scor·pae′nid** (-nĭd) *adj. & n.*

Scor·pi·o (skôr′pē-ō′) *n.* **1.** Variant of **Scorpius. 2.a.** The eighth sign of the zodiac in astrology. **b.** One who is born under this sign. [Middle English, from Latin *Scorpiō,* from *scorpiō,* scorpion. See SCORPION.]

scor·pi·oid (skôr′pē-oid′) *adj.* **1.** Of, relating to, or resembling a scorpion. **2.** *Botany.* Like the tail of a scorpion; circinate: *a scorpioid cyme.* [Greek *skorpioeidēs,* scorpionlike : *skorpios,* scorpion + *-oeidēs,* -oid.]

scor·pi·on (skôr′pē-ən) *n.* Any of various arachnids of the order Scorpionida, of warm, dry regions, having a segmented body and an erectile tail tipped with a venomous sting. [Middle English, from Old French, from Latin *scorpiō, scorpiōn-,* alteration of *scorpius,* from Greek *skorpios.*]

Scor·pi·on (skôr′pē-ən) *n.* See **Scorpius.**

scorpion fish *n.* Any of numerous small, often brilliantly colored marine fishes of the family Scorpaenidae, most species of which have poisonous spines in the dorsal fin.

scorpion fly *n.* **1.** A mecopterous insect of the family Panorpidae, having in the male of most species a curved genital structure that resembles the sting of a scorpion. **2.** Any mecopterous insect; a mecopteran.

scorpion grass *n.* See **forget-me-not** (sense 1).

Scor·pi·us (skôr′pē-əs) also **Scor·pi·o** (-pē-ō′) *n.* A constellation in the Southern Hemisphere near Libra and Sagittarius, containing the bright red star Antares. Also called *Scorpion.* [Latin *scorpius,* scorpion, Scorpius. See SCORPION.]

scot (scŏt) *n.* Money assessed or paid. [Middle English, tax, partly from Old Norse *skot* and partly from Old French *escot,* of Germanic origin. See **skeud-** in Appendix.]

Scot (skŏt) *n.* **1.** A native or inhabitant of Scotland. **2.** A member of the ancient Gaelic tribe that migrated to the northern part of Britain from Ireland in about the sixth century A.D. See Usage Note at **Scottish.** [From Middle English *Scottes,* Scotsmen, from Old English *Scottas,* Scotsmen, Irishmen, from Late Latin *Scottī,* Irishmen.]

Scot. *abbr.* Scotch; Scotland; Scottish.

scot and lot *n.* A municipal tax formerly levied in Great Britain on the members of a community in proportion to their ability to pay. ***—idiom.*** **pay scot and lot.** To pay in full.

scotch[1] (skŏch) *tr.v.* **scotched, scotch·ing, scotch·es. 1.** To put an abrupt end to: *The prime minister scotched the rumors of her illness with a public appearance.* **2.** To injure so as to render harmless. **3.** To cut or score. **—scotch** *n.* **1.** A surface cut or abrasion. **2.** A line drawn on the ground, as one used in playing hopscotch. [Middle English *scocchen,* perhaps from Anglo-Norman *escocher,* to notch : *es-,* intensive pref. (from Latin *ex-;* see EX–) + Old French *coche,* notch (probably from Latin *coccum,* scarlet oak berry, from Greek *kokkos*).]

scotch[2] (skŏch) *tr.v.* **scotched, scotch·ing, scotch·es.** To block (a wheel, for example) with a prop to prevent rolling or slipping. **—scotch** *n.* A block or wedge used as a prop behind or under an object likely to roll. [Origin unknown.]

Scotch (skŏch) *n. Abbr.* **Sc., Scot. 1.** The people of Scotland. **2.** Scots English. **3.** Scotch whisky. **—Scotch** *adj.* **1.** Scottish. See Usage Note at **Scottish. 2.** Tight with one's money; frugal. [Contraction of SCOTTISH.]

Scotch egg *n.* A hard-boiled egg wrapped in sausage meat, coated with bread crumbs, and deep-fried.

Scotch-I·rish (skŏch′ī′rĭsh) *n.* The people of Scotland who settled in northern Ireland or their descendants, especially those who emigrated to America. **—Scotch-Irish** *adj.* Of or relating to the Scotch-Irish.

Scotch·man (skŏch′mən) *n.* A Scotsman. See Usage Note at **Scottish.**

Scotch pine *n.* **1.** A Eurasian pine tree *(Pinus sylvestris)* having twisted needles arranged in fascicles of two and yellow wood that is valued as timber. **2.** The wood of this tree.

Scotch Plains. A community of northeast New Jersey west of Elizabeth. It is primarily residential. Population, 20,774.

Scotch terrier *n.* See **Scottish terrier.**

Scotch verdict *n.* **1.** *Law.* A verdict permissible in certain criminal cases indicating only that guilt is not proven. **2.** An inconclusive judgment or pronouncement.

Scotch whisky *n.* A whiskey distilled in Scotland from malted barley.

Scotch·wom·an (skŏch′wo͝om′ən) *n.* A Scotswoman. See Usage Note at **Scottish.**

Scotch woodcock *n.* A savory dish consisting of scrambled eggs on toast with anchovies or anchovy paste.

sco·ter (skō′tər) *n.* Any of several dark-colored diving ducks of the genera *Oidemia* and *Melanitta,* of northern coastal areas. Also called *coot.* [Origin unknown.]

scot-free (skŏt′frē′) *adv.* **1.** Without having to pay: *got away from the restaurant scot-free.* **2.** Without incurring any penalty or punishment: *came away from the incident scot-free.* **—scot′-free′** *adj.*

sco·tia (skō′shə) *n.* *Architecture.* A hollow concave molding at or near the base of a column. [Latin, from Greek *skotia,* from feminine of *skotios,* dark, shadowy (from the shadow it casts), from *skotos,* darkness.]

Sco·tia (skō′shə). A medieval and poetic name for Scotland.

Scot·land (skŏt′lənd). *Abbr.* **Scot.** A constituent country of the United Kingdom comprising the northern part of the island of Great Britain and the Hebrides, Shetland Islands, and Orkney Islands. Inhabited by Picts in prehistoric times, the region was invaded but never conquered by the Romans and split into a variety of small kingdoms after the fifth century A.D.. In the ninth century most of Scotland was unified into one kingdom, but conflicts with the English to the south soon erupted, leading to a series of bloody wars. When Mary Queen of Scots's son James VI succeeded to the English throne in 1603, the two kingdoms were united. Scotland became a part of the kingdom of Great Britain by a parliamentary act of 1707. Edinburgh is the capital and Glasgow the largest city. Population, 5,149,500.

sco·to·ma (skə-tō′mə) *n., pl.* **-mas** or **-ma·ta** (-mə-tə). An area of diminished vision within the visual field. [New Latin *scotōma,* from Late Latin, dim sight, from Greek *skotōma,* dizziness, from *skotoun,* to darken, from *skotos,* darkness.] **—sco·to′ma·tous** *adj.*

sco·to·phil (skō′tə-fĭl′) also **sco·to·phil·ic** (skō′tə-fĭl′ĭk) *adj.* *Biology.* Growing or functioning best in darkness: *a scotophil phase in the circadian rhythm.* [Greek *skotos,* darkness + –PHIL(E).] **—sco·toph′i·ly** (skō-tŏf′ə-lē, skə-) *n.*

sco·to·pho·bin (skō′tə-fō′bĭn) *n.* A peptide isolated from the brain tissue of rats conditioned to fear darkness, claimed to have been used in its natural or synthesized form to induce a similar fear in untrained rats, thereby implying that a memory or a conditioned response can be chemically transferred. [Greek *skotos,* darkness + –PHOB(E) + –IN.] **—sco′to·pho′bic** *adj.*

sco·to·pi·a (skə-tō′pē-ə) *n.* The ability to see in darkness or dim light; dark-adapted vision. [Greek *skotos,* darkness + –OPIA.] **—sco·to′pic** (-tō′pĭk, -tŏp′ĭk) *adj.*

Scots (skŏts) *adj. Abbr.* **Sc.** Scottish. See Usage Note at **Scot-**

scoreboard

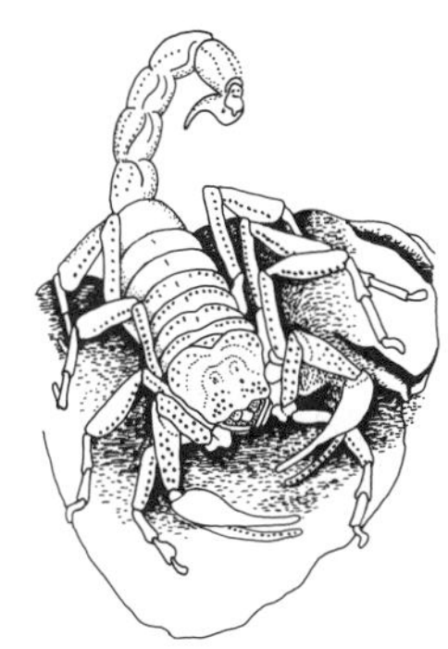
scorpion
Arizona scorpion
Centruroides sculpturatus

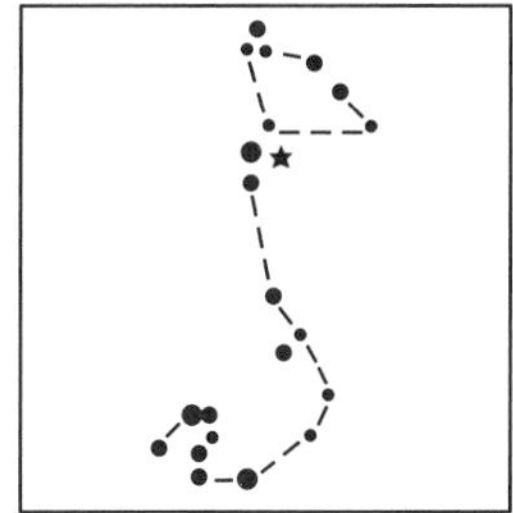
Scorpius

scotch[2]

Dred Scott
Detail of an 1881 oil on canvas portrait by Louis Schultze (after an 1858 photograph)

tish. **—Scots** *n.* The dialect of English used in the Lowlands of Scotland. [Middle English *scottis,* variant of *scottisc,* Scottish, from *Scotte,* sing. of *Scottes,* Scotsmen. See SCOT.]

Scots·man (skŏts′mən) *n.* A man who is a native or inhabitant of Scotland. See Usage Note at **Scottish.**

Scots·wom·an (skŏts′wo͝om′ən) *n.* A woman who is a native or inhabitant of Scotland. See Usage Note at **Scottish.**

Scott (skŏt), **Dred.** 1795?–1858. American slave who sued for his liberty after spending four years with his master in a territory where slavery had been banned by the Missouri Compromise. The resulting decision by the U.S. Supreme Court (1857) declared the Missouri Compromise unconstitutional because a slave could not be taken from a master without due process of law.

Scott, Robert Falcon. 1868–1912. British explorer who reached the South Pole (January 1912) only to find that Roald Amundsen had discovered the spot one month before.

Scott, Sir **Walter.** 1771–1832. British writer of ballads and historical novels, a genre he developed. His works include *Waverley* (1814) and *Ivanhoe* (1819).

Scott, Winfield. 1786–1866. American general. A hero of the War of 1812, he captured Veracruz, defeated Santa Anna, and captured Chapultepec during the Mexican War (1846–1848).

Scot·ti·cism (skŏt′ĭ-sĭz′əm) *n.* An idiom or other expression characteristic of Scottish English.

Scot·tie also **Scot·ty** (skŏt′ē) *n., pl.* **-ties.** A Scottish terrier.

Scot·tish (skŏt′ĭsh) *adj. Abbr.* **Sc., Scot.** Of or relating to Scotland or its people, language, or culture. **—Scottish** *n.* **1.** Scots English. **2.** The people of Scotland. [Middle English *scottisc.* See SCOTS.]

USAGE NOTE: *Scottish* is the full, original form of the adjective. *Scots* is an old Scottish variant of the form; *Scotch* is an English contraction of Scottish that at one time also came into use in Scotland (as in Burns's *"O thou, my Muse! guid auld Scotch drink!"*) but subsequently fell into disfavor. To some extent these facts can serve as a guide in choosing among the many variant forms of related words, such as *Scot, Scotsman* or *Scotswoman,* or *Scotchman* or *Scotchwoman,* for one of the people of Scotland; *Scots, (the) Scotch,* or, rarely, *(the) Scottish* for the people of Scotland; and *Scots, Scotch,* or *Scottish* for the dialect of English spoken in Scotland. The forms based on *Scotch* are English and disfavored in Scotland, while those involving the full form *Scottish* tend to be more formal. In the interest of civility, forms involving *Scotch* are best avoided in reference to people. But there is no sure rule for referring to things, since the history of variation in the use of these words has also left many expressions in which the choice is fixed, such as *Scotch broth, Scotch whisky, Scottish rite,* and *Scots Guards.*

Scottish deerhound *n.* See **deerhound.**

Scottish Gaelic *n.* The Goidelic language of Scotland. Also called *Erse.*

Scottish rite *n.* A ceremonial rite in a Masonic system.

Scottish terrier *n.* A terrier of a breed originating in Scotland, having a heavy-set body, short legs, a long head with small erect ears, and a hard, wiry coat. Also called *Scotch terrier.*

Scot·to (skŏt′ō, skôt′tô), **Renata.** Born 1934? Italian operatic soprano noted for her dramatic intensity and her roles in the works of Italian composers.

Scott Peak. A mountain, 3,474.9 m (11,393 ft) high, in the Bitterroot Range of eastern Idaho.

Scotts·dale (skŏts′dāl′). A city of south-central Arizona, a suburb of Phoenix. It is a noted resort area and retirement community. Population, 88,364.

Scot·ty (skŏt′ē) *n.* Variant of **Scottie.**

scoun·drel (skoun′drəl) *n.* A villain; a rogue. [Origin unknown.] **—scoun′drel·ly** *adj.*

scour[1] (skour) *v.* **scoured, scour·ing, scours.** *—tr.* **1.a.** To clean, polish, or wash by scrubbing vigorously: *scour a dirty oven.* **b.** To remove by scrubbing: *scour grease from a pan.* **2.** To remove dirt or grease from (cloth or fibers) by means of a detergent. **3.** To clean (wheat) before the milling process. **4.** To clear (an area) by freeing of weeds or other vegetation. **5.** To clear (a channel or pipe) by flushing. *—intr.* **1.** To scrub something in order to clean or polish it. **2.** To have diarrhea. Used of livestock. **—scour** *n.* **1.** A scouring action or effect. **2.** A place that has been scoured, as by flushing with water. **3.** A cleansing agent for wool. **4. scours.** *(used with a sing. or pl. verb).* Diarrhea in livestock. [Middle English *scouren,* from Middle Dutch *scūren,* from Old French *escurer,* from Late Latin *excūrāre,* to clean out : Latin *ex-,* ex- + Late Latin *cūrāre,* to clean (from Latin, to take care of, from *cūra,* care. See CURE).] **—scour′er** *n.*

scour[2] (skour) *v.* **scoured, scour·ing, scours.** *—tr.* **1.** To search through or over thoroughly: *The detective scoured the scene of the crime for clues.* **2.** To range over (an area) quickly and energetically. *—intr.* **1.** To range over or about an area, especially in a search. **2.** To move swiftly; scurry. [Middle English *scouren,* probably of Scandinavian origin; akin to Old Norse *skūr,* shower.] **—scour′er** *n.*

scourge (skûrj) *n.* **1.** A source of widespread, dreadful affliction and devastation such as that caused by pestilence or war. **2.** A means of inflicting severe suffering, vengeance, or punishment. **3.** A whip used to inflict punishment. **—scourge** *tr.v.* **scourged, scourg·ing, scourg·es. 1.** To afflict with severe or widespread suffering and devastation; ravage. **2.** To chastise severely; excoriate. **3.** To flog. [Middle English, from Anglo-Norman *escorge,* from Old French *escorgier,* to whip, from Vulgar Latin **excorrigiāre* : Latin *ex-,* intensive pref.; see EX– + Latin *corrigia,* thong (probably of Celtic origin).] **—scourg′er** *n.*

scour·ing rush (skour′ĭng) *n.* Any of several species of horsetail, especially *Equisetum hyemale,* having rough-ridged stems formerly used for scouring utensils.

scour·ings (skour′ĭngz) *pl.n.* **1.** The refuse that remains after scouring grain. **2.** Dregs; scum.

scouse (skous) *n.* **1.** A lobscouse. **2.a.** Also **scous·er** (skou′sər). A native or resident of Liverpool, England. **b.** Often **Scouse.** The dialect of English spoken in Liverpool. [Short for LOBSCOUSE.]

scout[1] (skout) *v.* **scout·ed, scout·ing, scouts.** *—tr.* **1.** To spy on or explore carefully in order to obtain information; reconnoiter. **2.** To observe and evaluate (a talented person) for possible hiring. *—intr.* **1.** To search: *scout around for some gossip.* **2.** To search for talented people: *She scouts for a professional basketball team.* **—scout** *n.* **1.a.** One that is dispatched from a main body to gather information, especially in preparation for military action. **b.** The act of reconnoitering. **2.** A watcher or sentinel. **3.** One who is employed to discover and recruit talented persons, especially in the fields of sports and entertainment. **4.** *Sports.* One who is employed to observe and report on the strategies and players of rival teams. **5.** Often **Scout. a.** A member of the Boy Scouts. **b.** A member of the Girl Scouts. **6.** *Informal.* A person: *a good scout.* **7.** *Chiefly British.* A student's male servant at Oxford University. [From Middle English *scoute,* act of watching or spying, from Old French *escoute,* from *escouter,* to listen, alteration of *ascouter,* from Vulgar Latin **ascultāre,* alteration of Latin *auscultāre.* See **ous-** in Appendix.] **—scout′er** *n.*

scout[2] (skout) *v.* **scout·ed, scout·ing, scouts.** *—tr.* To reject with disdain or derision. See Synonyms at **despise.** *—intr.* To treat another with derision; scoff. [Of Scandinavian origin. See **skeud-** in Appendix.]

scout·ing (skou′tĭng) *n.* **1.** The act of one that scouts. **2.** Often **Scouting.** The activities of the Boy Scouts or Girl Scouts.

scout·mas·ter (skout′măs′tər) *n.* The adult leader in charge of a troop of Boy Scouts.

scow (skou) *n. Nautical.* A large flat-bottomed boat with square ends, used chiefly for transporting freight. [Dutch *schouw,* from Middle Dutch *scouwe.*]

scowl (skoul) *v.* **scowled, scowl·ing, scowls.** *—intr.* To wrinkle or contract the brow as an expression of anger or disapproval. See Synonyms at **frown.** *—tr.* To express with a frowning facial expression. **—scowl** *n.* A look of anger or frowning disapproval. [Middle English *scoulen,* probably of Scandinavian origin.] **—scowl′er** *n.* **—scowl′ing·ly** *adv.*

SCP *abbr.* Single-cell protein.

SCPO *abbr.* Senior chief petty officer.

scr. *abbr.* Scruple (unit of weight).

scrab·ble (skrăb′əl) *v.* **-bled, -bling, -bles.** *—intr.* **1.** To scrape or grope about frenetically with the hands. **2.** To struggle by or as if by scraping or groping. **3.** To climb with scrambling, disorderly haste; clamber. **4.** To make hasty, disordered markings; scribble. *—tr.* **1.** To make or obtain by scraping together hastily. **2.** To scribble on or over. **—scrabble** *n.* **1.** The act or an instance of scrabbling. **2.** A scribble. [Dutch *schrabbelen,* from Middle Dutch, frequentative of *schrabben,* to scrape. See **sker-**[1] in Appendix.] **—scrab′bler** *n.* **—scrab′bly** *adj.*

scrab·bled (skrăb′əld) *adj.* Covered with sparse vegetation; scrubby: *"We can stand . . . and look out toward the scrabbled, snow-covered mountains in the west"* (Russell Banks).

scrag (skrăg) *n.* **1.** A bony or scrawny person or animal. **2.** A piece of lean or bony meat, especially a neck of mutton. **3.** *Slang.* The human neck. **—scrag** *tr.v.* **scragged, scrag·ging, scrags.** *Slang.* To wring the neck of; strangle. [Perhaps from dialectal *crag,* neck, from Middle English *cragge,* from Middle Dutch *crāghe,* throat.]

scrag·gly (skrăg′lē) *adj.* **-gli·er, -gli·est.** Ragged; unkempt.

scrag·gy (skrăg′ē) *adj.* **-gi·er, -gi·est. 1.** Jagged; rough: *scraggy cliffs.* **2.** Bony and lean: *a scraggy cat.* **—scrag′gi·ly** *adv.* **—scrag′gi·ness** *n.*

scram (skrăm) *Slang. intr.v.* **scrammed, scram·ming, scrams. 1.** To leave a scene at once; go abruptly. **2.** To shut down automatically. Used of a nuclear reactor. **—scram** *n.* A rapid shutting down of a nuclear reactor, especially in an emergency. [Perhaps short for SCRAMBLE.]

scram·ble (skrăm′bəl) *v.* **-bled, -bling, -bles.** *—intr.* **1.** To move or climb hurriedly, especially on the hands and knees. **2.** To struggle or contend frantically in order to get something: *scrambled for the best seats.* **3.** To take off with all possible haste, as to intercept enemy aircraft. **4.** *Football.* **a.** To run around with the ball behind the line of scrimmage while searching for an open receiver. **b.** To run forward with the ball when unable to complete an intended pass play. Used of a quarterback. *—tr.* **1.** To mix or throw together haphazardly. **2.** To gather together in a hurried or disorderly fashion. **3.** To cook (beaten eggs) until firm but with a soft consistency. **4.** *Electronics.* To distort or garble (a signal) so as to render it unintelligible without a special receiver. **5.** To cause (aircraft) to take off as fast as possible, as to intercept enemy aircraft. **—scramble** *n.* **1.** The act or an instance of scrambling. **2.** An arduous hike or climb over rough terrain. **3.** An unceremonious scuffle or struggle. **4.** *Sports.* A motorcycle race over rough terrain. **5.** A swift takeoff of military aircraft in response to an alert or an attack. [Perhaps blend of obsolete *scamble,* to struggle for, and *cramble,* to crawl.]

scram·bled eggs (skrăm′bəld) *pl.n.* **1.** Eggs with the yolks and whites beaten together and cooked to a firm but soft consistency. **2.** *Slang.* The gold braid worn on the bill of the cap of a field-grade officer in the armed services.

scram·bler (skrăm′blər) *n.* **1.** An electronic device that scrambles telecommunication signals to make them unintelligible to anyone without a special receiver. **2.** A motorcycle with thick ridged tires and strong suspension, designed for riding and racing across rough terrain.

scram·jet (skrăm′jĕt′) *n.* A ramjet airplane engine designed for hypersonic flight that burns fuel in the supersonic airstream produced by the plane. [S(UPERSONIC) + C(OMBUSTION) + RAMJET.]

Scran·ton (skrăn′tən). A city of northeast Pennsylvania northeast of Wilkes-Barre. Population, 88,117.

scrap¹ (skrăp) *n.* **1.** A small piece or bit; a fragment. **2. scraps.** Leftover bits of food. **3.** Discarded waste material, especially metal suitable for reprocessing. **4. scraps.** Crisp pieces of rendered animal fat; cracklings. **—scrap** *tr.v.* **scrapped, scrap·ping, scraps. 1.** To break down into parts for disposal or salvage. **2.** To discard as worthless; junk. [Middle English, from Old Norse *skrap,* trifles, pieces. See **sker-¹** in Appendix.]

scrap² (skrăp) *intr.v.* **scrapped, scrap·ping, scraps.** To fight, often with the fists. **—scrap** *n.* A fight or a scuffle. [Perhaps variant of SCRAPE.] **—scrap′per** *n.*

scrap·book (skrăp′bo͝ok′) *n.* A book with blank pages used for the mounting and preserving of pictures, clippings, or other mementos.

scrape (skrāp) *v.* **scraped, scrap·ing, scrapes.** *—tr.* **1.** To remove (an outer layer, for example) from a surface by forceful strokes of an edged or rough instrument: *scraped the wallpaper off before painting the wall.* **2.** To abrade or smooth by rubbing with a sharp or rough instrument. **3.** To rub (a surface) with considerable pressure, as with an edged instrument or a hard object. **4.** To draw (a hard or abrasive object) forcefully over a surface: *scraped my fingernails down the blackboard.* **5.** To injure the surface of by rubbing against something rough or sharp: *scraped my knee on the sidewalk.* **6.** To amass or produce with difficulty: *scrape together some cash.* *—intr.* **1.** To come into sliding, abrasive contact. **2.** To rub or move with a harsh grating noise. **3.** To give forth a harsh grating noise. **4.** To practice petty economies; scrimp. **5.** To succeed or manage with difficulty: *scraped through by a narrow margin.* **—scrape** *n.* **1.a.** The act of scraping. **b.** The sound of scraping. **2.** An abrasion on the skin. **3.a.** An embarrassing predicament. **b.** A fight; a scuffle. [Middle English *scrapen,* from Old Norse *skrapa.* See **sker-¹** in Appendix.]

scrap·er (skrā′pər) *n.* One that scrapes, especially a tool for scraping off paint or other adherent matter such as ice on a windshield.

scrap·er·board (skrā′pər-bôrd′, -bōrd′) *n.* See **scratchboard.**

scrap·heap also **scrap heap** (skrăp′hēp′) *n.* **1.** A pile or heap of waste material. **2.** A place for discarding useless or worthless material.

scra·pie (skrā′pē, skrăp′ē) *n.* A usually fatal disease of sheep and goats, marked by chronic itching, loss of muscular coordination, and progressive degeneration of the central nervous system. [From SCRAPE (from the scraping of itching parts of the skin against objects).]

scrap·ple (skrăp′əl) *n.* A mush of ground pork and cornmeal that is set in a mold and then sliced and fried. [Diminutive of SCRAP¹.]

scrap·py¹ (skrăp′ē) *adj.* **-pi·er, -pi·est.** Composed of scraps; fragmentary: *scrappy evidence.* **—scrap′pi·ly** *adv.* **—scrap′pi·ness** *n.*

scrap·py² (skrăp′ē) *adj.* **-pi·er, -pi·est. 1.** Quarrelsome; contentious. **2.** Full of fighting spirit. See Synonyms at **argumentative. —scrap′pi·ly** *adv.* **—scrap′pi·ness** *n.*

scratch (skrăch) *v.* **scratched, scratch·ing, scratch·es.** *—tr.* **1.** To make a thin, shallow cut or mark on (a surface) with a sharp instrument. **2.** To use the nails or claws to dig or scrape at. **3.** To rub or scrape (the skin) to relieve itching. **4.** To scrape or strike on an abrasive surface. **5.** To write or draw (something) by scraping a surface: *scratched their initials on a rock.* **6.** To write or draw hurriedly: *scratched off a thank-you note.* **7.a.** To strike out or cancel (a word, for example) by or as if by drawing lines through. **b.** *Slang.* To cancel (a project or a program, for example). **8.** *Sports & Games.* To withdraw (an entry) from a contest. *—intr.* **1.** To use the nails or claws to dig, scrape, or wound. **2.** To rub or scrape the skin to relieve itching. **3.** To make a harsh, scraping sound. **4.** To gather funds or produce a living with difficulty. **5.a.** *Sports & Games.* To withdraw from a contest. **b.** *Games.* To make a shot in billiards that results in a penalty, as when the cue ball falls into a pocket or jumps the cushion. **—scratch** *n.* **1.a.** A mark resembling a line that is produced by scratching. **b.** A slight wound. **2.** A hasty scribble. **3.** A sound made by scratching. **4.a.** *Sports.* The starting line for a race. **b.** *Sports & Games.* A contestant who has been withdrawn from a competition. **5.** *Games.* **a.** The act of scratching in billiards. **b.** A fluke or chance shot in billiards. **6.** Poultry feed. **7.** *Slang.* Money. **—scratch** *adj.* **1.** Done haphazardly or by chance. **2.** Assembled hastily or at random. **3.** *Sports.* Having no golf handicap. **—*idioms.* from scratch.** From the very beginning. **up to scratch.** *Informal.* **1.** Meeting the requirements. **2.** In fit condition. [Middle English *scracchen,* probably blend of *scratten,* to scratch, and *cracchen,* to scratch (possibly from Middle Dutch *cratsen*).] **—scratch′er** *n.*

scratch·board (skrăch′bôrd′, -bōrd′) *n.* A drawing board covered with white clay and a black surface layer that is scraped away with a scratching tool to produce black-and-white line drawings. Also called *scraperboard.*

scratch hit *n.* *Baseball.* A batted ball that is not squarely struck or cleanly fielded but is counted as a hit.

scratch line *n.* *Sports.* **1.** A starting line for a race. **2.** A line beyond which a contestant must not step.

scratch pad *n.* **1.** A pad of paper for preliminary or hasty writing, notes, or sketches. **2.** Also **scratch·pad** (skrăch′păd′). *Computer Science.* A usually high-speed internal register used for temporary storage of preliminary data or notes.

scratch·proof (scrăch′pro͞of′) *adj.* Resistant to or capable of withstanding scratches: *scratchproof glass.*

scratch sheet *n.* *Sports & Games.* A publication listing the horses withdrawn from a day's races and giving information and betting odds on the horses scheduled to race.

scratch test *n.* A test for allergy performed by scratching the skin and applying an allergen to the wound.

scratch·y (skrăch′ē) *adj.* **-i·er, -i·est. 1.** Marked by or consisting of scratches: *scratchy handwriting.* **2.** Making a harsh, scratching noise: *a scratchy voice; a scratchy record.* **3.** Harsh and irritating: *a scratchy fabric.* **4.** Irregular; uneven: *played a scratchy stroke.* **—scratch′i·ly** *adv.* **—scratch′i·ness** *n.*

scrawl (skrôl) *v.* **scrawled, scrawl·ing, scrawls.** *—tr.* To write hastily or illegibly. *—intr.* To write in a sprawling, irregular manner. **—scrawl** *n.* **1.** Irregular, often illegible handwriting. **2.** Something, such as a note, written hastily or illegibly. [Perhaps from obsolete *scrawl,* to gesticulate, sprawl, from Middle English *scrawlen,* probably blend of *sprawlen,* to sprawl; see SPRAWL, and *craulen,* to crawl; see CRAWL¹.] **—scrawl′er** *n.*

scraw·ny (skrô′nē) *adj.* **-ni·er, -ni·est.** Gaunt and bony. See Synonyms at **lean².** [Alteration of dialectal *scranny,* possibly of Scandinavian origin; akin to Norwegian *skran,* lean.] **—scraw′ni·ness** *n.*

screak (skrēk) *intr.v.* **screaked, screak·ing, screaks. 1.** To screech; shriek. **2.** To creak. **—screak** *n.* **1.** A screech; a shriek. **2.** A creak. [Middle English *skricken,* from Old Norse *skrækja.*]

scream (skrēm) *v.* **screamed, scream·ing, screams.** *—intr.* **1.** To utter a long, loud, piercing cry, as from pain or fear. **2.** To make a loud, piercing sound: *Jet planes screamed through the air.* **3.** To speak or write in a heated, hysterical manner. **4.** To have or produce a startling effect: *The outlandish costume screamed with clashing colors.* *—tr.* To utter or say in or as if in a screaming voice. **—scream** *n.* **1.** A long, loud, piercing cry or sound. **2.** *Informal.* One that is hilariously or ridiculously funny: *The new play was a scream.* [Middle English *screamen,* possibly of Scandinavian origin; akin to Old Norse *scræma.*] **—scream′ing·ly** *adv.*

SYNONYMS: *scream, shriek, screech.* These verbs mean to make or give voice to a loud, piercing sound. *Scream* generally denotes a prolonged penetrating sound indicative of physical suffering or emotion, such as fear: *"He immediately began to scream with pain"* (Francis Marion Crawford). *Shriek* differs from *scream* principally in implying a shrill, often frantic cry: *"In the midst of the confusion and uproar . . . Cicero could only shriek that he had saved his country"* (J.A. Froude). *Screech* stresses a high-pitched, strident, often annoying sound: *"'Leave me alone!' he screeched"* (Robert Louis Stevenson).

scream·er (skrē′mər) *n.* **1.** One that screams, especially one that sings in a harsh, strident manner. **2.** *Slang.* A sensational headline. **3.** *Slang.* One that evokes screams or laughter: *The comedian's act is a real screamer.* **4.** *Slang.* An exclamation point. **5.** *Baseball.* A hard-hit line drive. **6.** Any of several large aquatic birds of the family Anhimidae, of South America, that have a harsh, resonant call.

scream·ing mee·mies (skrē′mĭng mē′mēz) *pl.n.* *(Used with a sing. or pl. verb). Slang.* An attack of nerves; the jitters. [Expressive of nervousness.]

scree (skrē) *n.* **1.** Loose rock debris covering a slope. **2.** A slope of loose rock debris at the base of a steep incline or cliff. [Probably ultimately from Old Norse *skridha,* landslide, from *skrīdha,* to slide.]

screech (skrēch) *n.* **1.** A high-pitched, strident cry. **2.** A sound suggestive of this cry: *the screech of train brakes.* **—screech** *v.* **screeched, screech·ing, screech·es.** *—tr.* To utter in or as if in a screech. *—intr.* **1.** To cry out in a high-pitched, strident voice. See Synonyms at **scream. 2.** To make a sound suggestive of a screech: *Tires screeched on the wet pavement.* [Alteration of obsolete *scrich,* from Middle English *scrichen,* to screech, perhaps of Scandinavian origin; akin to Old Norse *skrækja.*] **—screech′er** *n.* **—screech′i·ness** *n.* **—screech′y** *adj.*

screech owl *n.* Any of various small owls of the genus *Otus,*

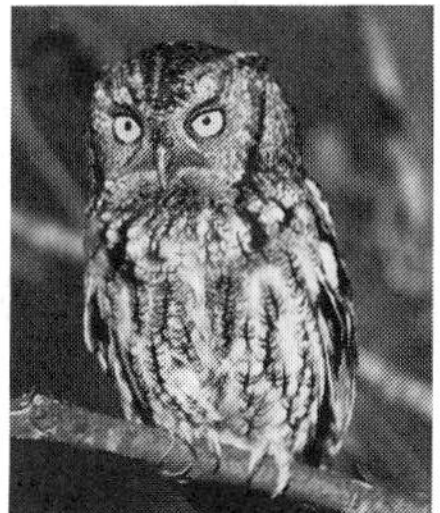

screech owl
Common screech owl
Otus asio

ă pat	oi boy
ā pay	ou out
âr care	o͝o took
ä father	o͞o boot
ĕ pet	ŭ cut
ē be	ûr urge
ĭ pit	th thin
ī pie	*th* this
îr pier	hw which
ŏ pot	zh vision
ō toe	ə about, item
ô paw	♦ regionalism

Stress marks: ′ (primary); ′ (secondary), as in **dictionary** (dĭk′shə-nĕr′ē)

screen

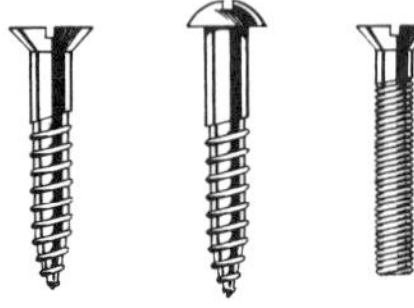

screw
Left to right: Flat head wood screw, round head wood screw, and flat head machine screw

scrimshaw
Scrimshawed tooth with Masonic emblems, 1866, by Henry R. Abbott

especially *O. asio,* of North America, having ear tufts and a quavering, whistlelike call.

screed (skrēd) *n.* **1.** A long, monotonous harangue or piece of writing. **2.a.** A strip of wood, plaster, or metal placed on a wall or pavement as a guide for the even application of plaster or concrete. **b.** A layer or strip of material used to level off a horizontal surface such as a floor. **c.** A smooth final surface of a substance, such as concrete, applied to a floor. [Middle English *screde,* fragment, strip of cloth, from Old English *scrēade,* shred.]

screen (skrēn) *n.* **1.** A movable device, especially a framed construction such as a room divider or a decorative panel, designed to divide, conceal, or protect. **2.** One that serves to protect, conceal, or divide: *Security guards formed a screen around the President. A screen of evergreens afforded privacy from our neighbors.* **3.** A coarse sieve used for sifting out fine particles, as of sand, gravel, or coal. **4.** A system for preliminary appraisal and selection of personnel as to their suitability for particular jobs. **5.** A window or door insertion of framed wire or plastic mesh used to keep out insects and permit air flow. **6.a.** The white or silver surface on which a picture is projected for viewing. **b.** The movie industry: *a star of stage and screen.* Also called *silver screen.* **7.a.** *Electronics.* The phosphorescent surface on which an image is displayed, as on a television, computer monitor, or radar receiver. **b.** *Computer Science.* The information or image displayed at a given time on a monitor, display, or video terminal: *printing a hard copy of the screen.* **8.** *Electronics.* The electrode placed between the anode and the control grid in a tetrode valve. Also called *screen grid.* **9.** *Printing.* A glass plate marked off with crossing lines, placed before the lens of a camera when photographing for halftone reproduction. **10.** A body of troops or ships sent in advance of or surrounding a larger body to protect or warn of attack. **11.a.** *Sports.* A block, set with the body, that impedes the vision or movement of an opponent. **b.** *Football.* A screen pass. **—screen** *tr.v.* **screened, screen·ing, screens. 1.** To provide with a screen: *screen a porch.* **2.a.** To conceal from view with or as if with a screen. See Synonyms at **block, hide**[1]. **b.** To protect, guard, or shield. **3.a.** To separate or sift out (fine particles of sand, for example) by means of a sieve or screen. **b.** To examine (a job applicant, for example) systematically in order to determine suitability. **4.** To show or project (a movie, for example) on a screen. **5.** To test or examine for the presence of disease or infection: *screen blood for the presence of a virus; screen patients in an epidemic zone.* **6.** *Sports.* **a.** To block the vision or movement of (an opponent) with the body. **b.** To obscure an opponent's view of (a shot) by positioning oneself between the opponent and the shooter. [Middle English *screne,* from Old North French *escren,* from Middle Dutch *scherm,* shield, screen. See **sker-**[1] in Appendix.] **—screen′a·ble** *adj.* **—screen′er** *n.*

screen dump *n. Computer Science.* The act or process of transferring data on a screen to a printer or storage medium.

screen grid *n. Electronics.* See **screen** (sense 8).

screen·ing (skrē′nĭng) *n.* **1. screenings.** *(used with a sing. or pl. verb).* Refuse, such as waste coal, separated by a screen. **2.** The mesh material used to make door or window screens. **3.** A presentation of a movie.

screen·land (skrēn′lănd′) *n.* The motion picture industry; Hollywood.

screen memory *n.* A memory of something that is unconsciously used to repress recollection of an associated but distressing event.

screen pass *n. Football.* A short forward pass to a receiver in the flat who is protected by a formation of blockers.

screen·play (skrēn′plā′) *n.* The script for a movie, including camera directions and descriptions of scenes.

screen-print (skrēn′prĭnt′) *tr.v.* **-print·ed, -print·ing, -prints.** To print using the silk-screen process.

screen-print·ing (skrēn′prĭnt′ĭng) *n.* See **silk-screen.**

screen test *n.* A brief movie sequence filmed to test the ability of an aspiring performer. **—screen′-test′** (skrēn′tĕst′) *v.*

screen·writ·er (skrēn′rī′tər) *n.* One who writes screenplays. **—screen′writ′ing** *n.*

screw (skro͞o) *n.* **1.a.** A cylindrical rod incised with one or more helical or advancing spiral threads, as a lead screw or worm screw. **b.** The tapped collar or socket that receives this rod. **2.** A metal pin with incised threads and a broad slotted head that can be driven as a fastener by turning with a screwdriver, especially: **a.** A tapered and pointed wood screw. **b.** A cylindrical and flat-tipped machine screw. **3.** A device having a helical form, such as a corkscrew. **4.** A propeller. **5.** A twist or turn of or as if of a screw. **6.** *Slang.* **a.** A prison guard. **b.** The turnkey of a jail. **7.** *Vulgar Slang.* The act or an instance of having sexual intercourse. **8.** *Chiefly British.* **a.** Salary; wages. **b.** A small paper packet, as of tobacco. **c.** An old broken-down horse. **d.** A stingy or crafty bargainer. **—screw** *v.* **screwed, screw·ing, screws.** *—tr.* **1.** To drive or tighten (a screw). **2.a.** To fasten, tighten, or attach by or as if by means of a screw. **b.** To attach (a tapped or threaded fitting or cap) by twisting into place. **c.** To rotate (a part) on a threaded axis. **3.** To contort (one's face). **4.** *Slang.* To take advantage of; cheat: *screwed me out of the most lucrative sales territory.* **5.** *Vulgar Slang.* To have sexual intercourse with. *—intr.* **1.** To turn or twist. **2.a.** To become attached by means of the threads of a screw. **b.** To be capable of such attachment. **3.** *Vulgar Slang.* To have sexual intercourse. ***—phrasal verbs.*** **screw around. 1.** *Slang.* To act or fool around aimlessly or in a confused way and accomplish nothing. **2.** *Vulgar Slang.* To be sexually promiscuous. **screw up. 1.** To muster or summon up: *screwed up my courage.* **2.** *Slang.* To make a mess of (an undertaking). **3.** *Slang.* To injure; damage: *Lifting those boxes really screwed up my back.* **4.** *Slang.* To make neurotic or anxious. ***—idiom.* have a screw loose.** *Slang.* **1.** To behave in an eccentric manner. **2.** To be insane. [Middle English *skrewe,* from Old French *escrove,* female screw, nut, perhaps from Medieval Latin *scrōfa,* from Latin, sow. See **sker-**[1] in Appendix.] **—screw′a·ble** *adj.* **—screw′er** *n.*

screw·ball (skro͞o′bôl′) *n.* **1.** *Baseball.* A pitched ball that curves in the direction opposite to that of a normal curve ball. **2.** *Slang.* A person who is regarded as eccentric, impulsively whimsical, or irrational. **—screwball** *adj. Slang.* Impulsively whimsical; eccentric: *That screwball proposal won't work.*

screw bean *n.* **1.** A shrub or small tree *(Prosopis pubescens)* of the southwest United States and adjacent areas of Mexico, having pinnately compound leaves, tiny yellowish-white flowers, and twisted pods used as fodder. **2.** The pod of this plant. Also called *tornillo.*

screw cap *n.* A cap that screws onto the threaded mouth of a container such as a bottle or jar.

screw·driv·er (skro͞o′drī′vər) *n.* **1.** A tool used for turning screws. **2.** A cocktail made with vodka and orange juice.

screw eye *n.* A wood screw with an eyelet in place of a head.

screw jack *n.* See **jackscrew.**

screw log *n. Nautical.* See **patent log.**

screw pine *n.* See **pandanus.**

screw propeller *n.* A propeller.

screw thread *n.* **1.** The continuous helical groove on a screw or on the inner surface of a nut. **2.** One complete turn of a screw thread.

screw·up also **screw-up** (skro͞o′ŭp′) *n. Slang.* **1.** One that makes a mess of an undertaking; a bungler. **2.** A blunder; a mess: *a managerial screwup.*

screw·worm (skro͞o′wûrm′) *n.* The larva of the screwworm fly.

screwworm fly *n.* A bluish fly *(Cochliomyia hominivorax)* of the New World that breeds in the living tissue of mammals, having penetrated chiefly through open wounds or the nostrils, and whose parasitic larvae cause serious injury or death to livestock.

screw·y (skro͞o′ē) *adj.* **-i·er, -i·est.** *Slang.* **1.** Eccentric; crazy. **2.** Ludicrously odd, unlikely, or inappropriate. **—screw′i·ness** *n.*

Scri·a·bin (skrē-ä′bĭn), **Alexander Nikolayevich.** 1872–1915. Russian composer of orchestral and piano works who incorporated visual arts into some of his compositions, such as *Prometheus* (1910), a tonal poem whose performance includes the projection of colored lights.

scrib·ble (skrĭb′əl) *v.* **-bled, -bling, -bles.** *—tr.* **1.** To write hurriedly without heed to legibility or style. **2.** To cover with scribbles, doodles, or meaningless marks. *—intr.* To write or draw in a hurried, careless way. **—scribble** *n.* **1.** Careless, hurried writing. **2.** Meaningless marks and lines. [Middle English *scriblen,* probably from *scriben,* to write, from Latin *scrībere,* to write. See **skrībh-** in Appendix.] **—scrib′bly** *adj.*

WORD HISTORY: It is not easy to think simultaneously of the carefully crafted writings of a trained scribe and the hastily scrawled jottings referred to by the word *scribble,* but the two words are related. *Scribe* goes back to the Latin *scrība,* meaning "one who has charge of things such as public records or accounts," *scrība,* in turn, coming from *scrībere,* "to write." The Latin word was borrowed into English directly as well as by way of Old French (*scribe*), giving us Middle English *scribe,* first recorded in a work written probably around 1200. People do not always write with great care, especially when pressed for time, as is shown by an early use of the verb *scribble* in a Middle English text: "Scribled in hast with mine owne hand in default of other helpe." Hence it is easy to see why the verb *scribble* came into existence. From Latin *scrībere* English had formed its own verb *scriben,* "to write," and probably from this verb with the addition of the suffix *-el,* denoting diminutive, repetitive, or intensive actions, came the Middle English word *scriblen* (first recorded around 1456), the ancestor of our word *scribble.*

scrib·bler (skrĭb′lər) *n.* One who scribbles, especially an author regarded as very minor, untalented, or disreputable: *a scribbler of sentimental verse.*

scribe (skrīb) *n.* **1.** A public clerk or secretary, especially in ancient times. **2.** A professional copyist of manuscripts and documents. **3.** A writer or journalist. **4.** See **scriber. —scribe** *v.* **scribed, scrib·ing, scribes.** *—tr.* **1.** To mark with a scriber. **2.** To write or inscribe. *—intr.* To work as a scribe. [Middle English, from Old French, from Late Latin *scrība,* from Latin, keeper of accounts, secretary, from *scrībere,* to write. See **skrībh-** in Appendix.] **—scrib′al** *adj.*

Scribe (skrēb), **Augustin Eugène.** 1791–1861. French playwright whose works include more than 300 comedies of manners, including *Une Chaine* (1841).

scrib·er (skrī′bər) *n.* A sharply pointed tool used for marking lines, as on wood, metal, or ceramic. Also called *scribe.*

scried (skrīd) *v.* Past tense and past participle of **scry.**

scries (skrīz) *v.* Third person singular present tense of **scry.**

scrim (skrĭm) *n.* **1.** A durable, loosely woven cotton or linen fabric used for curtains or upholstery lining or in industry. **2.** A transparent fabric used as a drop in the theater to create special effects of lights or atmosphere. [Origin unknown.]

scrim·mage (skrĭm′ĭj) *n.* **1.** *Football.* The contest between two teams from the time the ball is snapped until it is declared dead. **2.** *Sports.* A practice session or informal game, as between two units of the same team. **3. a.** A rough-and-tumble struggle; a tussle. **b.** A skirmish. **—scrimmage** *intr.v.* **-maged, -mag·ing, -mag·es.** *Sports.* To engage in a scrimmage. [Middle English, alteration of *skirmisshe, scrimish.* See SKIRMISH.]

scrimp (skrĭmp) *v.* **scrimped, scrimp·ing, scrimps.** *—intr.* To economize severely. *—tr.* **1.** To be excessively sparing with or of. **2.** To cut or make too small or scanty. [Perhaps of Scandinavian origin; akin to Swedish *skrympa,* to shrink.] **—scrimp′er** *n.* **—scrimp′i·ness** *n.* **—scrimp′y** *adj.*

scrim·shand·er (skrĭm′shăn′dər) *n.* One who carves scrimshaw. [Origin unknown.]

scrim·shaw (skrĭm′shô′) *n., pl.* **scrimshaw** or **-shaws. 1.** The art of carving or incising intricate designs on whalebone or whale ivory. **2.** A decorative article made by this art. **—scrimshaw** *tr. & intr.v.* **-shawed, -shaw·ing, -shaws.** To decorate (whale ivory or whalebone) with intricate designs or make such designs. [Probably from SCRIMSHANDER.]

scrip[1] (skrĭp) *n.* **1.** Paper money issued for temporary emergency use. **2.** A small scrap of paper, especially with a short list or schedule written on it. [Perhaps alteration (influenced by SCRAP[1]) of SCRIPT.]

scrip[2] (skrĭp) *n.* **1.** A provisional certificate entitling the holder to a fractional share of stock or of other jointly owned property. **2.** Such certificates considered as a group. [Short for *subscription receipt,* receipt for a portion of a loan.]

scrip[3] (skrĭp) *n. Archaic.* A wallet, small satchel, or bag. [Middle English *scrippe.*]

scrip issue *n.* An issue of shares made by a company free of charge to existing shareholders. Also called *bonus issue.*

Scripps (skrĭps). Family of American newspaper publishers, including **James Edmund** (1835–1906), who founded the *Detroit Evening News* (1873), and his half-brother **Edward Wyllis Scripps** (1854–1926), who established (1907) the news agency that became United Press International and organized the syndication of features and illustrations. James's sister **Ellen Browning Scripps** (1836–1932) invested heavily in the family's newspaper projects and founded Scripps College in Claremont, California (1926).

script (skrĭpt) *n.* **1. a.** Handwriting. **b.** A style of writing with cursive characters. **c.** A particular system of writing: *cuneiform script.* **2.** *Printing.* **a.** A style of type that imitates handwriting. **b.** The matter set in this type. **3. a.** The text of a play, broadcast, or movie. **b.** A copy of a text used by a director or performer. **4.** *Law.* An original document. **—script** *tr.v.* **script·ed, script·ing, scripts. 1.** To prepare (a text) for filming or broadcasting. **2.** To orchestrate (behavior or an event, for example) as if writing a script: *"the brilliant, charming, judicial moderate scripted by his White House fans"* (Ellen Goodman). [Middle English *skript,* a piece of writing, alteration of *scrite,* from Old French *escrit,* from Latin *scrīptum,* from neuter past participle of *scrībere,* to write. See **skrībh-** in Appendix.]

Script. *abbr.* Scriptural; Scripture.

scrip·to·ri·um (skrĭp-tôr′ē-əm, -tōr′-) *n., pl.* **-to·ri·ums** or **-to·ri·a** (-tôr′ē-ə, -tōr′-). A room in a monastery set aside for the copying, writing, or illuminating of manuscripts and records. [Medieval Latin *scrīptōrium,* from Latin *scrīptus,* past participle of *scrībere,* to write. See **skrībh-** in Appendix.]

scrip·tur·al (skrĭp′chər-əl) *adj.* **1.** Of or relating to writing; written. **2.** Often **Scriptural.** *Abbr.* **Script.** Of, relating to, based on, or contained in the Scriptures. **—scrip′tur·al·ly** *adv.*

Scrip·ture (skrĭp′chər) *n. Abbr.* **Script. 1. a.** A sacred writing or book. **b.** A passage from such a writing or book. **2.** Often **Scriptures.** The sacred writings of the Bible. Also called *Holy Scriptures.* **3. scripture.** A statement regarded as authoritative. [Middle English, from Late Latin *scrīptūra,* from Latin, act of writing, from *scrīptus,* past participle of *scrībere,* to write. See **skrībh-** in Appendix.]

script·writ·er (skrĭpt′rī′tər) *n.* One who writes copy to be used by an announcer, performer, or director in a film or broadcast. **—script′writ′ing** *n.*

scriv·en·er (skrĭv′ə-nər, skrĭv′nər) *n.* **1.** A professional copyist; a scribe: *"Gutenberg's invention of movable type . . . took words out of the sole possession of monastic scriveners and placed them before the wider public"* (Irvin Molotsky). **2.** A notary. [Middle English *scriveiner,* from *scrivein,* from Old French *escrivein,* from Vulgar Latin **scrība, scrībān-,* from Latin *scrība,* scribe. See SCRIBE.]

scro·bic·u·late (skrō-bĭk′yə-lĭt, -lāt′) *adj. Biology.* Marked with many shallow depressions, grooves, or pits. [Latin *scrobiculus,* diminutive of *scrobis,* trench; see **sker-**[1] in Appendix + -ATE[1].]

♦ **scrod** also **schrod** (skrŏd) *n., pl.* **scrod** also **schrod.** *New England.* A young cod or haddock, especially one split and boned for cooking as the catch of the day. [Possibly from obsolete Dutch *schrood,* slice, shred, from Middle Dutch *scrōde.*]

scrof·u·la (skrŏf′yə-lə) *n.* A form of tuberculosis affecting the lymph nodes, especially of the neck, that is most common in children and is usually spread by unpasteurized milk from infected cows. Also called *struma.* [Middle English *scrophula,* from Late Latin *scrōfulae,* swelling of the glands, diminutive of Latin *scrōfa,* sow. See **sker-**[1] in Appendix.]

scrof·u·lous (skrŏf′yə-ləs) *adj.* **1.** Of, affected with, or resembling scrofula. **2.** Morally degenerate: *"a scrofulous, grim, darkly funny burlesque on art, celebrity, and love"* (Stephen Schiff). **—scrof′u·lous·ly** *adv.* **—scrof′u·lous·ness** *n.*

scroll (skrōl) *n.* **1. a.** A roll, as of parchment or papyrus, used especially for writing a document. **b.** An ancient book or volume written on such a roll. **2.** A list or schedule of names. **3.** An ornament or ornamental design that resembles a partially rolled scroll of paper, as the volute in Ionic and Corinthian capitals. **4.** *Music.* The curved head on an instrument of the violin family. **5.** *Heraldry.* A ribbon inscribed with a motto. **—scroll** *v.* **scrolled, scroll·ing, scrolls.** *—tr.* **1.** To inscribe on a scroll. **2.** To roll up into a scroll. **3.** To ornament with a scroll. **4.** *Computer Science.* To cause (displayed text or graphics) to move vertically or horizontally across the screen so that a line of text or graphics appears at one edge of the screen for each line that moves off the opposite edge: *scroll a document; scroll a page of text.* *—intr.* *Computer Science.* **1.** To cause displayed text or graphics to move vertically or horizontally across the screen: *scrolled down to the end of the document.* **2.** To appear on screen and roll by: *"The information scrolls so fast it's unreadable"* (Creative Computing). [Middle English *scrowle,* alteration (influenced by *rolle,* roll, from *rollen,* to roll; see ROLL) of *scrowe,* from Old French *escroue, escroe,* strip of parchment, scroll, of Germanic origin.]

scroll saw *n.* A hand or power saw with a narrow ribbonlike blade for cutting curved or irregular shapes.

scroll·work (skrōl′wûrk′) *n.* Embellishment with a scroll motif, especially ornamentation executed in wood with a scroll saw.

scrooch also **scrootch** (skro͞och) *intr.v.* **scrooched, scrooch·ing, scrooch·es** also **scrootched, scrootch·ing, scrootch·es.** To hunch down; crouch: *"the hot kind of hot Indiana hot weather that sends the family dog scrooching under the pickup truck to enjoy the shade"* (John Skow). [Alteration (perhaps influenced by CROUCH, or *scrunch,* or HUNCH) of *scrooge, scrouge,* to squeeze, crowd, possibly blend of SCREW and SQUEEZE.]

Scrooge also **scrooge** (skro͞oj) *n.* A mean-spirited miserly person; a skinflint. [After Ebenezer *Scrooge,* miserly protagonist of *A Christmas Carol* by Charles Dickens.]

scroog·ie (skro͞o′jē) *n. Baseball.* A screwball. [Shortening and alteration of SCREWBALL.]

scrootch (skro͞och) *v.* Variant of **scrooch.**

scro·tum (skrō′təm) *n., pl.* **-ta** (-tə) or **-tums.** The external sac of skin enclosing the testes in most mammals. [Latin *scrōtum.*] **—scro′tal** (skrōt′l) *adj.*

scrounge (skrounj) *v.* **scrounged, scroung·ing, scroung·es.** *Slang.* *—tr.* **1.** To obtain (something) by begging or borrowing with no intention of reparation: *scrounged a few dollars off my brother.* **2.** To obtain by salvaging or foraging; round up. *—intr.* **1.** To seek to obtain something by begging or borrowing with no intention of reparation: *scrounge for a cigarette.* **2.** To forage about in an effort to acquire something at no cost: *scrounging around the kitchen for a late-night snack.* [Alteration of dialectal *scrunge,* to steal.] **—scroung′er** *n.*

scroung·y (skroun′jē) *adj.* **-i·er, -i·est.** *Slang.* Dirty or shabby: *a scroungy overcoat.*

scrub[1] (skrŭb) *v.* **scrubbed, scrub·bing, scrubs.** *—tr.* **1. a.** To rub hard in order to clean. **b.** To remove (dirt or stains) by hard rubbing. **2.** To remove impurities from (a gas) chemically. **3.** *Slang.* To cancel or abandon; drop: *We had to scrub our plans for vacation.* *—intr.* To clean or wash something by hard rubbing: *Don't forget to scrub behind your ears.* **—scrub** *n.* The act or an instance of scrubbing. ***—phrasal verb.* scrub up.** To wash the hands and arms thoroughly, as before performing or participating in surgery. [Middle English *scrobben,* to currycomb a horse, from Middle Dutch *schrobben,* to clean by rubbing, scrape. See **sker-**[1] in Appendix.] **—scrub′ba·ble** *adj.*

scrub[2] (skrŭb) *n.* **1.** A straggly, stunted tree or shrub. **2.** A growth or tract of stunted vegetation. **3.** An undersized or poorly developed domestic animal. **4.** An undersized or insignificant person. **5.** *Sports.* A player not on the varsity or first team. **6.** *Australian.* Remote rural land; the bush. [Middle English, variant of *shrubbe.* See SHRUB[1].]

scrub·ber (skrŭb′ər) *n.* One that scrubs, especially: **a.** One who cleans floors, for example, by scrubbing. **b.** A brush, appliance, or abrasive that is used in cleaning. **c.** An apparatus that is used for removing impurities from a gas.

scrub·by (skrŭb′ē) *adj.* **-bi·er, -bi·est. 1.** Covered with or consisting of scrub or underbrush. **2.** Straggly or stunted. **3.** Paltry or shabby; wretched. **—scrub′bi·ly** *adv.* **—scrub′bi·ness** *n.*

scrub fowl *n.* See **megapode.**

scrub jay *n.* A blue and gray jay *(Aphelocoma coerulescens)* with a long, slender body and no crest, found in dense brush or scrub especially in the Florida peninsula.

scrub·land (skrŭb′lănd′) *n.* An area of land that is uncultivated and covered with sparse, stunted vegetation.

scrub pine *n.* **1.** A straggly pine tree *(Pinus virginiana)* of the

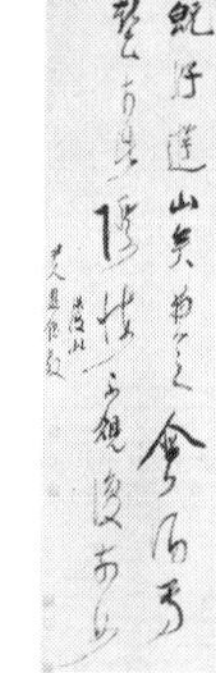

script
17th-century Chinese hanging scroll by Ch'en Hung-shou (1598–1652)

scriptorium

scroll
Of a double bass

ă pat	oi boy
ā pay	ou out
âr care	o͝o took
ä father	o͞o boot
ĕ pet	ŭ cut
ē be	ûr urge
ĭ pit	th thin
ī pie	*th* this
îr pier	hw which
ŏ pot	zh vision
ō toe	ə about, item
ô paw	♦ regionalism

Stress marks: **′** (primary); ′ (secondary), as in **dictionary** (dĭk′shə-nĕr′ē)

scuba diver

eastern United States, having prickly cones and drooping or spreading branches. Also called *spruce pine.* **2.** See **jack pine.**

scrub typhus *n.* An acute infectious disease common in Asia that is caused by the rickettsia *R. tsutsugamushi* transmitted by mites and that is characterized by sudden fever, painful swelling of the lymphatic glands, skin lesions, and skin rash. Also called *Japanese river fever, tsutsugamushi disease.*

scrub·wom·an (skrŭb′wo͝om′ən) *n.* A woman hired to clean.

scruff (skrŭf) *n.* The back of the neck; the nape. [Alteration of dialectal *scuft, scuff.*]

scruff·y (skrŭf′ē) *adj.* **-i·er, -i·est. 1.** Shabby; untidy. **2.** *Chiefly British.* Scaly; scabby. [From obsolete *scruff,* scurf, variant of *scurf.* See SCURF.] **—scruff′i·ly** *adv.* **—scruff′i·ness** *n.*

scrum (skrŭm) *Sports. n.* A scrummage. **—scrum** *intr.v.* **scrummed, scrum·ming, scrums.** To engage in a scrummage.

scrum·mage (skrŭm′ĭj) *Sports. n.* A Rugby formation in which the two sets of forwards mass together around the ball and, with their heads down, try to shoulder their opponents off the ball and kick it to their own team. **—scrummage** *intr.v.* **-maged, -mag·ing, -mag·es.** To engage in a scrummage. [Alteration of SCRIMMAGE.] **—scrum′mag·er** *n.*

scrump·tious (skrŭmp′shəs) *adj.* Splendid; delectable: *"Normandy . . . where the bosky landscape is enchanting* [and the pen] *inadequate to describe the scrumptious food and wine"* (Daily Telegraph). See Synonyms at **delicious.** [Perhaps alteration of SUMPTUOUS.] **—scrump′tious·ly** *adv.* **—scrump′tious·ness** *n.*

scrunch (skrŭnch, skro͝onch) *v.* **scrunched, scrunch·ing, scrunch·es.** *—tr.* **1.** To crush or crunch. **2.** To crumple or squeeze; hunch: *scrunched up their shoulders; scrunch one's nose against a window.* *—intr.* **1.** To hunch: *"The men scrunched closer"* (Susan Dworski). **2.** To move with or make a crunching sound: *scrunching along the gravel path.* **—scrunch** *n.* A crunching sound. [Probably alteration of CRUNCH.]

scru·ple (skro͞o′pəl) *n.* **1.** An uneasy feeling arising from conscience or principle that tends to hinder action. See Synonyms at **qualm. 2.** *Abbr.* **sc., scr.** A unit of apothecary weight equal to about 1.3 grams, or 20 grains. **3.** A minute part or amount. **—scruple** *intr.v.* **-pled, -pling, -ples.** To hesitate as a result of conscience or principle: *"A man who could make so vile a pun would not scruple to pick a pocket"* (John Dennis). [Middle English *scrupul,* from Old French *scrupule,* from Latin *scrūpulus,* small unit of measurement, scruple, diminutive of *scrūpus,* rough stone, scruple.]

scuffle[2]

scru·pu·lous (skro͞o′pyə-ləs) *adj.* **1.** Conscientious and exact; painstaking. See Synonyms at **meticulous. 2.** Having scruples; principled. [Middle English, from Old French *scrupuleux,* from Latin *scrūpulōsus,* from *scrūpulus,* scruple. See SCRUPLE.] **—scru′pu·los′i·ty** (-lŏs′ĭ-tē), **scru′pu·lous·ness** (-ləs-nĭs) *n.* **—scru′pu·lous·ly** *adv.*

scru·ta·ble (skro͞o′tə-bəl) *adj.* Capable of being understood through study and observation; comprehensible. [Late Latin *scrūtābilis,* searchable, from Latin *scrūtārī,* to search. See SCRUTINY.]

scru·ti·nize (skro͞ot′n-īz′) *tr.v.* **-nized, -niz·ing, -niz·es.** To examine or observe with great care; inspect critically. **—scru′ti·niz′er** *n.* **—scru′ti·niz′ing·ly** *adv.*

scru·ti·ny (skro͞ot′n-ē) *n., pl.* **-nies. 1.** A close, careful examination or study. **2.** Close observation; surveillance. [Middle English *scrutinie,* taking of a formal vote, from Latin *scrūtinium,* inquiry, search, from *scrūtārī,* to search, examine, from *scrūta,* trash.]

scry (skrī) *intr.v.* **scried** (skrīd), **scry·ing, scries** (skrīz). To see or predict the future by means of a crystal ball. [Short for DESCRY.]

SCSI (skŭz′ē) *n. Computer Science.* Small computer systems interface. *—attributive.* Often used to modify another noun: *SCSI port; SCSI technology.*

scu·ba (sko͞o′bə) *n.* A portable apparatus containing compressed air and used for breathing under water. [*s(elf) c(ontained) u(nderwater) b(reathing) a(pparatus).*]

WORD HISTORY: To go *scuba diving* sounds much more desirable than to go *self-contained underwater breathing apparatus diving.* In talking about such an apparatus, first successfully tested in 1943, it must have seemed much simpler to say *scuba,* taking the first letter of each word in the phrase and putting them together to form one word. *Scuba,* like other acronyms, as such words are called, has a vowel at a point that allows it to be pronounced like an English word. The word, first recorded in 1952, has been accepted to the extent that people probably rarely think of it as a collection of initials and furthermore have used it in forming other words, such as *scuba-dive.* In fact, a verb *scuba* was first recorded in 1973 and is still in use.

scuba diver *n.* One who uses scuba gear in underwater swimming. **—scu′ba-dive′** (sko͞o′bə-dīv′) *v.* **—scuba diving** *n.*

scud (skŭd) *intr.v.* **scud·ded, scud·ding, scuds. 1.** To run or skim along swiftly and easily: *dark clouds scudding by.* **2.** *Nautical.* To run before a gale with little or no sail set. **—scud** *n.* **1.** The act of scudding. **2.a.** Wind-driven clouds, mist, or rain. **b.** A gust of wind. **c.** Ragged low clouds, moving rapidly beneath another cloud layer. [Possibly from Middle English *scut,* rabbit, rabbit's tail. See SCUT.]

scu·do (sko͞o′dō) *n., pl.* **-di** (-dē). A monetary unit and coin formerly used in Italy and Sicily. [Italian, shield, scudo, from Latin *scūtum,* shield. See **skei-** in Appendix.]

scuff (skŭf) *v.* **scuffed, scuff·ing, scuffs.** *—intr.* To scrape the feet while walking; shuffle. *—tr.* **1.** To scrape with the feet. **2.** To shuffle or shift (the feet), as in embarrassment. **3.** To scrape and roughen the surface of. **—scuff** *n.* **1.** The act or sound of scraping especially with the feet. **2.** A worn or rough spot resulting from scraping. **3.** A flat, backless house slipper. [Probably of Scandinavian origin; akin to Old Norse *skūfa,* to push.] **—scuff′er** *n.*

scuf·fle[1] (skŭf′əl) *intr.v.* **-fled, -fling, -fles. 1.** To fight or struggle confusedly at close quarters. **2.** To shuffle. **—scuffle** *n.* A rough, disorderly struggle at close quarters. [Probably frequentative of *scuff.*] **—scuf′fler** *n.*

scuf·fle[2] (skŭf′əl) *n.* A hoe manipulated by pushing rather than pulling. Also called *Dutch hoe, scuffle hoe.* [Dutch *schoffel,* hoe for weeding, from Middle Dutch, hoe, shovel.]

♦ **sculch** (skŭlch) *n. New England.* Variant of **culch** (sense 3).

scull (skŭl) *Nautical. n.* **1.** A long oar mounted over the stern of a boat and moved from side to side to propel the boat forward. **2.** One of a pair of short-handled oars used by a single rower. **3.** A small, light racing boat for one, two, or four rowers. **—scull** *v.* **sculled, scull·ing, sculls.** *—tr.* To propel (a boat) with a scull. *—intr.* To use a scull to propel a boat. [Middle English *sculle.*] **—scull′er** *n.*

scul·ler·y (skŭl′ə-rē) *n., pl.* **-ies.** A small room adjoining a kitchen, in which dishwashing and other kitchen chores are done. [Middle English, from Old French *escuelerie,* from *escuelier,* keeper of dishes, from *escuele,* dish, from Vulgar Latin **scūtella,* alteration (influenced by *scūtum,* shield) of Latin *scutella,* salver, diminutive of *scutra,* platter.]

scul·lion (skŭl′yən) *n.* A servant employed to do menial tasks in a kitchen. [Middle English *sculyon,* probably from Old French *escouvillon,* dishcloth, diminutive of *escouve,* broom, from Latin *scōpa,* branches, broom.]

sculp. *abbr.* Sculptor; sculptress; sculpture.

scul·pin (skŭl′pĭn) *n., pl.* **-pins** or **sculpin. 1.** Any of various marine and freshwater fishes of the family Cottidae, having a large flattened head and prominent spines. **2.** A scorpion fish *(Scorpaena guttata)* of California coastal waters. In this sense, also called *sea scorpion.* [Origin unknown.]

sculpt (skŭlpt) *v.* **sculpt·ed, sculpt·ing, sculpts.** *—tr.* **1.** To sculpture (an object). **2.** To shape, mold, or fashion especially with artistry or precision: *"Zoning is a blunt instrument that can at best shape but should not try to sculpt cities"* (H. Claude Shostal). *—intr.* To be a sculptor. [French *sculpter,* from Old French, from Latin *sculpere, sculpt-,* to carve. See SCULPTURE.]

sculp·tor (skŭlp′tər) *n.* **1.** *Abbr.* **sculp.** One who produces sculptural artwork. **2.** One who shapes, molds, or fashions especially with artistry or precision. [Latin, from *sculpere,* to carve (See SCULPTURE).]

Sculp·tor (skŭlp′tər) *n.* A constellation in the Southern Hemisphere near Cetus and Phoenix. Also called *Sculptor's Workshop.*

Sculp·tor's Workshop (skŭlp′tərz) *n.* See **Sculptor.**

sculp·tress (skŭlp′trĭs) *n. Abbr.* **sculp.** *Usage Problem.* A woman who sculptures. See Usage Note at **-ess.**

sculp·ture (skŭlp′chər) *n. Abbr.* **sculp. 1.** The art or practice of shaping figures or designs in the round or in relief, as by chiseling marble, modeling clay, or casting in metal. **2.a.** A work of art created by sculpture. **b.** Such works of art considered as a group. **3.** Ridges, indentations, or other markings, as on a shell, formed by natural processes. **—sculpture** *v.* **-tured, -tur·ing, -tures.** *—tr.* **1.** To fashion (stone, bronze, or wood, for example) into a three-dimensional figure. **2.** To represent in sculpture. **3.** To ornament with sculpture. **4.** To change the shape or contour of, as by erosion. *—intr.* To make sculptures or a sculpture. [Middle English, from Latin *sculptūra,* from *sculptus,* past participle of *sculpere,* to carve. See **skel-[1]** in Appendix.] **—sculp′tur·al** *adj.* **—sculp′tur·al·ly** *adv.*

sculp·tur·esque (skŭlp′chə-rĕsk′) *adj.* Suggestive of or having the qualities of sculpture. **—sculp′tur·esque′ly** *adv.*

♦ **scultch** (skŭlch) *n. New England.* Variant of **culch** (sense 3).

scum (skŭm) *n.* **1.** A filmy layer of extraneous or impure matter that forms on or rises to the surface of a liquid or body of water. **2.** The refuse or dross of molten metals. **3.** Refuse or worthless matter. **4.** *Slang.* One, such as a person or an element of society, that is regarded as despicable or worthless. **—scum** *v.* **scummed, scum·ming, scums.** *—tr.* To remove the scum from. *—intr.* To become covered with scum. [Middle English, from Middle Dutch *schūm.* See **(s)keu-** in Appendix.] **—scum′mer** *n.* **—scum′mi·ly** *adv.* **—scum′mi·ness** *n.* **—scum′my** *adj.*

scum·bag (skŭm′băg′) *n. Slang.* A person regarded as despicable.

scum·ble (skŭm′bəl) *tr.v.* **-bled, -bling, -bles. 1.** To soften the colors or outlines of (a painting or a drawing) by covering with a film of opaque or semiopaque color or by rubbing. **2.** To blur the outlines of: *a writer who scumbled the line that divides history and fiction.* **—scumble** *n.* **1.** The effect produced by or as if by scumbling. **2.** Material used for scumbling. [Possibly from SCUM.]

scun·ner (skŭn′ər) *n.* A strong dislike; an aversion. [From

Middle English *skunner,* to shrink back in disgust, from *scurnen,* to flinch.]

scup (skŭp) *n., pl.* **scup** or **scups.** A porgy *(Stenotomus chrysops)* of the northern Atlantic coastal waters, important commercially as a food fish. [Short for Narragansett *mishcùp.*]

scup·per[1] (skŭp′ər) *n.* **1.** *Nautical.* An opening in the side of a ship at deck level to allow water to run off. **2.** An opening for draining off water, as from a floor or the roof of a building. [Middle English *scoper;* possibly akin to *scope,* scoop. See SCOOP.]

scup·per[2] (skŭp′ər) *tr.v.* **-pered, -per·ing, -pers. 1.** *Chiefly British.* To overwhelm or massacre. **2.** To ruin or destroy: *"The world oil glut combined with disastrous federal energy policies to scupper Alberta's economy"* (Christian Science Monitor). [Perhaps from SCUPPER[1].]

scup·per·nong (skŭp′ər-nông′, -nŏng′) *n.* **1.** See **muscadine. 2.a.** A cultivated variety of the muscadine grape with sweet, yellowish fruit. **b.** A wine made from this grape. [After the *Scuppernong* River in northeast North Carolina.]

scurf (skûrf) *n.* **1.** Scaly or shredded dry skin, such as dandruff. **2.** A loose, scaly crust coating a surface, especially of a plant. [Middle English, probably of Scandinavian origin. See **sker-**[1] in Appendix.] **—scurf′i·ness** *n.* **—scurf′y** *adj.*

scur·rile also **scur·ril** (skûr′əl, skŭr′-) *adj. Archaic.* Scurrilous. [French, from Old French, from Latin *scurrīlis,* jeering, from *scurra,* buffoon, possibly of Etruscan origin.]

scur·ril·i·ty (skə-rĭl′ĭ-tē) *n., pl.* **-ties. 1.** The quality of being vulgar, coarse, or abusive. **2.** A vulgar, coarse, or abusive remark or passage.

scur·ri·lous (skûr′ə-ləs, skŭr′-) *adj.* **1.** Given to the use of vulgar, coarse, or abusive language; foul-mouthed. **2.** Expressed in vulgar, coarse, and abusive language. **—scur′ri·lous·ly** *adv.* **—scur′ri·lous·ness** *n.*

scur·ry (skûr′ē, skŭr′ē) *intr.v.* **-ried, -ry·ing, -ries. 1.** To go with light running steps; scamper. **2.** To flurry or swirl about. **—scurry** *n., pl.* **-ries. 1.** The act of scurrying. **2.** The noise produced by scurrying. [Probably short for HURRY-SCURRY.]

scur·vy (skûr′vē) *n.* A disease caused by deficiency of vitamin C, characterized by spongy and bleeding gums, bleeding under the skin, and extreme weakness. **—scurvy** *adj.* **-vi·er, -vi·est.** Mean; contemptible. [From Middle English *scurfy,* characterized by scurf (influenced by French *scorbut,* scurvy, from Latin *scorbūtus;* see SCORBUTIC) from *scurf,* scurf. See SCURF.] **—scur′vi·ly** *adv.* **—scur′vi·ness** *n.*

scurvy grass *n.* **1.** Any of various plants of the genus *Cochlearia,* especially *C. officinalis,* of northern Europe, having pungent foliage and formerly used to cure scurvy. **2.** See **sea kale.**

scut (skŭt) *n.* A stubby erect tail, as that of a hare, rabbit, or deer. [Middle English, hare.]

scu·ta (skyo͞o′tə) *n.* Plural of **scutum.**

scu·tage (skyo͞o′tĭj) *n.* A tax paid in lieu of military service in feudal times. [Middle English, from Medieval Latin *scūtāgium,* from Latin *scūtum,* shield. See SCUTUM.]

Scu·ta·ri (sko͞o′tə-rē), **Lake.** A lake of southeast Europe on the border between southwest Yugoslavia and northwest Albania. It was once an inlet of the Adriatic but is now separated from the sea by an alluvial isthmus.

scu·tate (skyo͞o′tāt) *adj.* **1.** *Zoology.* Covered or protected by scutes. **2.** *Botany.* Shaped like a shield or buckler: *scutate leaves.* [Latin *scūtātus,* shield-bearing, from *scūtum,* shield. See SCUTUM.]

scutch (skŭch) *tr.v.* **scutched, scutch·ing, scutch·es.** To separate the valuable fibers of (flax, for example) from the woody parts by beating. **—scutch** *n.* An implement used for scutching. [Obsolete French *escoucher,* from Anglo-Norman *escucher,* from Vulgar Latin **excuticāre,* frequentative of Latin *excutere,* to shake out : *ex-,* ex- + *quatere,* to shake; see **kwēt-** in Appendix.] **—scutch′er** *n.*

scutch·eon (skŭch′ən) *n.* **1.** An escutcheon. **2.** A shield-shaped object, such as a scute.

scutch grass *n.* See **Bermuda grass.**

scute (skyo͞ot) *n.* A horny, chitinous, or bony external plate or scale, as on the shell of a turtle or the underside of a snake. Also called *scutum.* [From Latin *scūtum,* shield. See SCUTUM.]

scu·tel·la (skyo͞o-tĕl′ə) *n.* Plural of **scutellum.**

scu·tel·late (skyo͞o-tĕl′ĭt, skyo͞ot′l-āt′) also **scu·tel·lat·ed** (skyo͞ot′l-ā′tĭd) *adj.* **1.** *Zoology.* **a.** Covered with shieldlike bony plates or scales. **b.** Having a scutellum. **2.** *Botany.* Shaped like a shield or platter.

scu·tel·la·tion (skyo͞ot′l-ā′shən) *n.* An arrangement or a covering of scales, as that on a bird's leg.

scu·tel·lum (skyo͞o-tĕl′əm) *n., pl.* **-tel·la** (-tĕl′ə). **1.** *Zoology.* A shieldlike bony plate or scale, as on the thorax of some insects. **2.** *Botany.* Any of several shield-shaped structures, such as the cotyledon of a grass. [New Latin, from Latin, diminutive of *scūtum,* shield. See SCUTUM.] **—scu·tel′lar** (-tĕl′ər) *adj.*

scu·ti·form (skyo͞o′tə-fôrm′) *adj.* Shield-shaped: *scutiform leaves.* [Latin *scūtum,* shield; see SCUTUM + —FORM.]

scut·ter (skŭt′ər) *intr.v.* **-tered, -ter·ing, -ters.** To move with a clattering, scurrying sound: *"The gun scutters over the tiles and lands against the molding of the hallway with a thump"* (Scott Turow). [Alteration of SCUTTLE[3].]

scut·tle[1] (skŭt′l) *n.* **1.** A small opening or hatch with a movable lid in the deck or hull of a ship or in the roof, wall, or floor of a building. **2.** The lid or hatch of such an opening. **—scuttle** *tr.v.* **-tled, -tling, -tles. 1.** *Nautical.* **a.** To cut or open a hole or holes in (a ship's hull). **b.** To sink (a ship) by this means. **2.** *Informal.* To scrap; discard: *"a program* [the] *President . . . sought to scuttle"* (Christian Science Monitor). [Middle English *skottell,* from Old French *escoutille,* possibly from Spanish *escotilla.*]

scut·tle[2] (skŭt′l) *n.* **1.** A metal pail for carrying coal. **2.** A shallow open basket for carrying vegetables, flowers, or grain. [Middle English *scutel,* basket, from Old English, dish, from Latin *scutella.* See SCULLERY.]

scut·tle[3] (skŭt′l) *intr.v.* **-tled, -tling, -tles.** To run or move with short hurried movements; scurry. **—scuttle** *n.* A hurried run. [Middle English *scottlen;* possibly akin to SCUD.]

scut·tle·butt (skŭt′l-bŭt′) *n.* **1.** *Slang.* Gossip; rumor. **2.** *Nautical.* **a.** A drinking fountain on a ship. **b.** A cask on a ship used to hold the day's supply of drinking water. [SCUTTLE[1] + BUTT[5].]

scu·tum (skyo͞o′təm) *n., pl.* **-ta** (-tə). *Zoology.* See **scute.** [Latin *scūtum,* shield. See **skei-** in Appendix.]

scut·work (skŭt′wûrk′) *n. Informal.* Monotonous work or menial tasks that have to be done usually as part of a large, complex job or project. [From *scut,* worthless person, perhaps from SCOUT[2].]

scuz·zy (skŭz′ē) *adj.* **-zi·er, -zi·est.** *Slang.* **1.** Dirty; grimy: *scuzzy floors.* **2.** Disreputable; sleazy: *"ran a scuzzy operation"* (Myra MacPherson). [Possibly from blend of SCUM and FUZZ[1].]

Scyl·la (sĭl′ə) *n. Greek Mythology.* A female sea monster who devoured sailors. **—*idiom.* between Scylla and Charybdis.** In a position where avoidance of one danger exposes one to another danger.

scy·phis·to·ma (sī-fĭs′tə-mə) *n., pl.* **-mae** (-mē) or **-mas.** A larva of a scyphozoan, consisting of an elongated and deeply constricted polyp that successively splits off minute, free-swimming medusas. [New Latin : Greek *skuphos,* cup + Greek *stoma,* mouth.]

scy·pho·zo·an (sī′fə-zō′ən) *n.* Any of various marine coelenterates of the class Scyphozoa, which includes the large jellyfishes, characterized by the absence of a velum and by a polyp stage that is very small or lacking entirely. **—scyphozoan** *adj.* Of or belonging to the class Scyphozoa. [From New Latin *Scyphozoa,* class name : Greek *skuphos,* cup + Greek *zōia,* pl. of *zōion,* -zoon.]

Scy·ros (skī′rəs, skē′rôs). See **Skíros.**

scythe (sīth) *n.* An implement consisting of a long, curved single-edged blade with a long, bent handle, used for mowing or reaping. **—scythe** *tr.v.* **scythed, scyth·ing, scythes.** To cut with or as if with a scythe. [Middle English *sithe,* from Old English *sīthe,* sickle. See **sek-** in Appendix.]

Scyth·i·a (sĭth′ē-ə, sĭth′-). An ancient region of Eurasia extending from the mouth of the Danube River on the Black Sea to the territory east of the Aral Sea. The nomadic people of the region flourished from the eighth to the fourth century B.C. but were conquered by the Sarmatians in the second century and were soon subsumed into other cultures.

Scyth·i·an (sĭth′ē-ən, sĭth′-) *adj.* Of or relating to Scythia or its people, language, or culture. **—Scythian** *n.* **1.** A member of the ancient nomadic people inhabiting Scythia. **2.** The Iranian language of the Scythians.

Scyth·o-Dra·vid·i·an (sĭth′ō-drə-vĭd′ē-ən, sĭth′-) *adj.* Of or relating to an ethnic group of northwest India having mixed Iranian and Dravidian characteristics. [SCYTH(IAN) + DRAVIDIAN.]

SD *abbr.* **1.** Sight draft. **2.** Or **S.D.** South Dakota. **3.** Special delivery. **4.** *Statistics.* Standard deviation.

sd. *abbr.* Sound (body of water).

s.d. *abbr.* Sine die.

S.Dak. *abbr.* South Dakota.

SDI or **S.D.I.** *abbr.* Strategic Defense Initiative.

SDS *abbr.* Students for a Democratic Society.

Se The symbol for the element **selenium.**

SE *abbr.* **1.a.** Southeast. **b.** Southeastern. **2.** Stock exchange.

sea (sē) *n. Abbr.* **s., S. 1.a.** The continuous body of salt water covering most of the earth's surface, especially this body regarded as a geophysical entity distinct from earth and sky. **b.** A tract of water within an ocean. **c.** A relatively large body of salt water completely or partially enclosed by land. **d.** A relatively large landlocked body of fresh water. **2.** The condition of the ocean's surface with regard to its course, flow, swell, or turbulence: *a high sea.* **3.** Something that suggests the ocean in its overwhelming sweep or vastness: *a sea of controversy.* **4.** Seafaring as a way of life. **5.** *Astronomy.* A lunar mare. *—attributive.* Often used to modify another noun: *sea air; sea voyages.* **—*idiom.* at sea. 1.** On the sea, especially on a sea voyage. **2.** In a state of confusion or perplexity; at a loss. [Middle English *see,* from Old English *sǣ.*]

sea anchor *n. Nautical.* A drag, usually a canvas-covered conical frame, floating behind a vessel to prevent drifting or to maintain a heading into the wind. Also called *drogue.*

sea anemone *n.* Any of numerous flowerlike marine coelenterates of the class Anthozoa, having a flexible cylindrical body and tentacles surrounding a central mouth.

sea bass (băs) *n.* **1.** Any of various marine food fishes of the genus *Centropristes* and related genera, especially *C. striatus,* of

sculptor

scuttle[2]

scythe

ă pat	oi boy
ā pay	ou out
âr care	o͝o took
ä father	o͞o boot
ĕ pet	ŭ cut
ē be	ûr urge
ĭ pit	th thin
ī pie	*th* this
îr pier	hw which
ŏ pot	zh vision
ō toe	ə about, item
ô paw	♦ regionalism

Stress marks: ′ (primary); ′ (secondary), as in **dictionary** (dĭk′shə-nĕr′ē)

sea fan
Common sea fan
Gorgonia ventilina

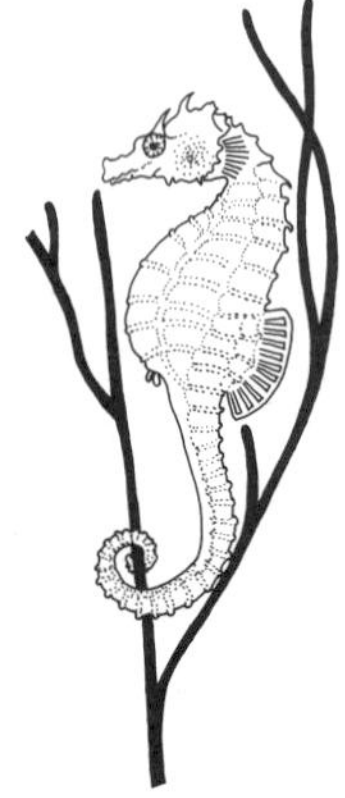

sea horse
Hippocampus hudsonius

seal[1]
Top: c. 1700 official seal of Marbletown, New York, by Jacob Boelen (1657–1729)
Bottom: Connecticut state seal

coastal Atlantic waters of the United States. **2.** Any of the various similar fishes of the family Serranidea.

sea·bed (sē′bĕd′) *n.* The floor of the sea or the ocean.

Sea·bee (sē′bē′) *n.* A member of one of the construction battalions in the U.S. Navy that builds naval aviation bases and facilities. [Alteration of *cee bee,* pronunciation of the initial letters of *construction battalion.*]

sea bird *n.* A bird, such as a petrel or an albatross, that frequents the ocean, especially far from shore.

sea biscuit *n.* See **hardtack.**

sea blubber *n.* A scyphozoan jellyfish of the genus *Cyanea,* especially the largest jellyfish, *C. arctica,* which usually grows to more than 3.6 meters (12 feet) wide and has tentacles over 30 meters (100 feet) long.

sea·board (sē′bôrd′, -bōrd′) *n.* **1.** A seacoast. **2.** Land near the sea.

Sea·borg (sē′bôrg′), **Glenn Theodore.** Born 1912. American chemist. He shared a 1951 Nobel Prize for the discovery of plutonium.

sea·borne (sē′bôrn′, -bōrn′) *adj.* **1.** Conveyed by sea; transported by ship. **2.** Carried on or over the sea.

sea bread *n.* See **hardtack.**

sea bream *n.* Any of various marine food fishes of the family Sparidae or Bramidae, especially a sparid fish *(Archosargus rhomboidalis)* of western Atlantic coastal waters.

sea breeze *n.* A cool breeze blowing from the sea toward the land.

Sea·bur·y (sē′bĕr′ē, -bə-rē), **Samuel.** 1729–1796. American religious leader who was the first bishop of the Protestant Episcopal Church in America (1784–1796).

sea butterfly *n.* See **pteropod.**

sea calf *n.* See **harbor seal.**

sea canary *n.* See **white whale.** [So called for the variety of melodious sounds it makes.]

sea captain *n. Nautical.* The captain of a ship, especially a merchant ship.

sea change *n.* **1.** A change caused by the sea: *"Of his bones are coral made:/Those are pearls that were his eyes:/Nothing of him that doth fade,/But doth suffer a sea change"* (Shakespeare). **2.** A marked transformation: *"The script suffered considerable sea changes, particularly in structure"* (Harold Pinter).

sea chest *n.* A box or trunk suitable for use by a sailor to store personal property.

sea·coast (sē′kōst′) *n.* Land bordering the sea. —*attributive.* Often used to modify another noun: *seacoast erosion; seacoast villages.*

sea·cock (sē′kŏk′) *n. Nautical.* A valve in the hull of a boat or ship that may be opened to let in water so as to flood a ballast tank, for example.

sea cow *n.* Any of several large, cylindrical, herbivorous marine mammals of the order Sirenia, having a paddlelike tail and rounded front flippers, including the manatee, dugong, and the very large species *Hydrodamalis stelleri* of the northern Pacific that became extinct in the late 1700's. Also called *sirenian.*

sea cradle *n.* See **chiton** (sense 1).

sea crayfish also **sea crawfish** *n.* See **spiny lobster.**

sea cucumber *n.* Any of various cucumber-shaped echinoderms of the class Holothuroidea, having a flexible body with tentacles surrounding the mouth.

sea devil *n.* See **manta** (sense 2).

sea dog *n.* **1.** Any of various seals or similar marine mammals. **2.** *Nautical.* A very experienced sailor. **3. sea·dog** (sē′dôg′, -dŏg′). See **fogbow.**

sea duck *n.* Any of various diving ducks, such as the eider or scoter, of coastal areas.

sea duty *n.* Duty at sea undertaken by personnel in the U.S. Navy.

sea eagle *n.* Any of various fish-eating eagles or similar birds, such as the bald eagle or the osprey.

sea elephant *n.* See **elephant seal.**

Sea Explorer (sē) *n.* A participant in a program designed to train Explorer Scouts in seamanship. Also called *Sea Scout.*

sea fan *n.* Any of various yellowish to reddish fan-shaped corals of the genus *Gorgonia,* especially *G. flabellum,* of coastal waters of Florida and the West Indies.

sea·far·er (sē′fâr′ər) *n. Nautical.* **1.** A sailor or mariner. **2.** One who travels by sea.

sea·far·ing (sē′fâr′ĭng) *Nautical. n.* A sailor's calling. —**seafaring** *adj.* **1.** Following a life at sea: *seafaring peoples of the world; seafaring nations.* **2.** Fit to travel on the sea; seagoing: *seafaring vessels.*

sea feather *n.* Any of several anthozoans of the family Pennatulidae, having a featherlike shape formed by an elongate shaft with paired lateral pinnules.

sea fire *n.* Bioluminescence produced by marine life.

sea floor also **sea·floor** (sē′flôr′, -flōr′) *n.* The bottom of a sea or an ocean.

sea-floor spread·ing (sē′flôr′ sprĕd′ĭng, -flōr′) *n.* In the theory of plate tectonics, the process by which the sea floor is being continuously formed and spread by upwellings from the earth's mantle along the mid-ocean ridges when crustal plates move apart.

sea·food (sē′fo͞od′) *n.* Edible fish or shellfish from the sea.

sea·fowl (sē′foul′) *n.* **1.** A sea bird. **2.** Sea birds considered as a group.

sea front *n.* A strip of land at the very edge of the sea, especially land desirable for a resort.

sea·girt (sē′gûrt′) *adj.* Surrounded by the sea.

sea·go·ing (sē′gō′ĭng) *adj. Nautical.* Made or used for ocean voyages; seafaring.

sea gooseberry *n.* A ctenophore of the genus *Pleurobrachia,* having two tentacles and a round, iridescent body.

sea grant college *n.* A state college or university that receives government grants for oceanographic research.

sea grape *n.* A small tropical American tree *(Coccolobis uvifera)* growing on sandy beaches and having large, glossy, leathery, rounded leaves and hard, purplish fruit arranged in grapelike clusters.

sea green *n. Color.* A medium green or bluish green.

sea gull also **sea·gull** (sē′gŭl′) *n.* A gull, especially one found near coastal areas.

sea hog *n.* See **porpoise** (sense 1).

sea holly *n.* A European seashore plant *(Eryngium maritimum)* having prickly, fleshy, bluish leaves and heads of blue or purplish flowers.

sea horse *n.* **1.** A small marine fish of the genus *Hippocampus,* characteristically swimming in an upright position and having a prehensile tail, a horselike head, and a body covered with bony plates. **2.** See **walrus. 3.** *Mythology.* An animal, half fish and half horse, ridden by Neptune and other sea gods. **4.** A large white-capped wave.

Sea Island cotton *n.* A tropical American species of cotton *(Gossypium barbadense)* widely cultivated for its fine, long-staple fibers. [After the SEA ISLANDS.]

Sea Islands. A chain of islands in the Atlantic Ocean off South Carolina, Georgia, and northern Florida. The Spanish discovered and first inhabited the islands in the 16th century but were displaced by English colonists after the 17th century.

sea·jack (sē′jăk′) *tr.v.* **-jacked, -jack·ing, -jacks.** To hijack a ship. [SEA + (HI)JACK.] —**sea′jack′er** *n.* —**sea′jack′ing** *n.*

sea kale *n.* A European seashore plant *(Crambe maritima)* of the mustard family, having edible, cabbagelike leaves. Also called *scurvy grass.*

sea king *n.* A Viking pirate chief of the early Middle Ages.

seal[1] (sēl) *n.* **1.a.** A die or signet having a raised or incised emblem used to stamp an impression on a receptive substance such as wax or lead. **b.** The impression so made. **c.** The design or emblem itself, belonging exclusively to the user: *a monarch's seal.* **d.** A small disk or wafer of wax, lead, or paper bearing such an imprint and affixed to a document to prove authenticity or to secure it. **2.** Something, such as a commercial hallmark, that authenticates, confirms, or attests. **3.** A substance, especially an adhesive agent such as wax or putty, used to close or secure something or to prevent seepage of moisture or air. **4.** A device that joins two systems or elements in such a way as to prevent leakage. **5.a.** An airtight closure. **b.** A closure, as on a package, used to prove that the contents have not been tampered with. **6.** A small decorative paper sticker. —**seal** *tr.v.* **sealed, seal·ing, seals. 1.** To affix a seal to in order to prove authenticity or attest to accuracy, legal weight, quality, or another standard. **2.a.** To close with or as if with a seal. **b.** To close hermetically. **c.** To make fast or fill up, as with plaster or cement. **d.** To apply a waterproof coating to: *seal a blacktop driveway.* **3.** To grant, certify, or designate under seal or authority. **4.** To establish or determine irrevocably: *Our fate was sealed.* **5.** *Mormon Church.* To make (a marriage, for example) binding for life; solemnize forever. —***phrasal verb.* seal off.** To close tightly or surround with a barricade or cordon: *An unused wing of the hospital was sealed off.* [Middle English, from Old French *seel,* from Vulgar Latin **sigellum,* from Latin *sigillum,* diminutive of *signum,* sign, seal. See **sekʷ-[1]** in Appendix.] —**seal′a·ble** *adj.*

seal[2] (sēl) *n.* **1.** Any of various aquatic, carnivorous mammals of the families Phocidae and Otariidae, found chiefly in the Northern Hemisphere and having a sleek, torpedo-shaped body and limbs that are modified into paddlelike flippers. **2.** The pelt or fur of one of these animals, especially a fur seal. **3.** Leather made from the hide of one of these animals. —**seal** *intr.v.* **sealed, seal·ing, seals.** To hunt seals. [Middle English *sele,* from Old English *seolh, sēol-.*]

sea lamprey *n.* A large marine lamprey *(Petromyzon marinus)* common in the Great Lakes and parasitic to freshwater fish.

sea-lane (sē′lān′) *n. Nautical.* A permanent or commonly used sea route.

seal·ant (sē′lənt) *n.* **1.** A substance, such as sealing wax, used to seal a surface to prevent passage of a liquid or gas. **2.** A plastic resin used in dentistry to coat the chewing surfaces of the back teeth to prevent the growth of cavity-causing bacteria.

sea lavender *n.* Any of several salt-marsh plants of the genus *Limonium,* having clusters of small lavender or pinkish flowers. Also called *statice.*

Seal Beach (sēl). A city of southern California on the Pacific Ocean south-southeast of Los Angeles. It is a resort community with various light industries. Population, 25,975.

sea legs *pl.n. Nautical.* The ability to walk on board ship with steadiness, especially in rough seas.

seal·er[1] (sē′lər) *n.* **1.** One that seals, as an undercoat of paint or varnish used to size a surface. **2.** An officer who inspects, tests, and certifies weights and measures.

seal·er[2] (sē′lər) *n.* One that is engaged in the hunting of seals.

sea lettuce *n.* Any of several green algae of the genus *Ulva,* having a membranous leaflike, irregularly shaped thallus sometimes used in salads.

sea level *n. Abbr.* **SL** The level of the ocean's surface, especially the level halfway between mean high and low tide, used as a standard in reckoning land elevation or sea depths.

sea·lift (sē′lĭft′) *tr.v.* **-lift·ed, -lift·ing, -lifts.** To transport (troops or supplies) by sea, as when ground or air routes are blocked. **—sealift** *n.* A system or an instance of such transport.

sea lily *n.* Any of various marine crinoids having a flowerlike body supported by a long stalk and usually anchored to the ocean floor in deep water.

seal·ing wax (sē′lĭng) *n.* A resinous preparation of shellac and turpentine that is soft and fluid when heated but solidifies upon cooling, used to seal letters, batteries, or jars.

sea lion *n.* Any of several large-eared seals with relatively long neck and limbs, especially *Zalophus californianus,* of the northern Pacific.

seal ring *n.* See **signet ring.**

seal·skin (sēl′skĭn′) *n.* **1.** The pelt or fur, especially the underfur, of a seal. **2.** A garment made of sealskin.

Sea·ly·ham terrier (sē′lē-hăm′, -lē-əm) *n.* A terrier of a breed developed in Wales, having a wiry white coat with brownish markings on the head and ears, a long head, powerful jaws, and short legs. [After *Sealyham,* a town of southwest Wales.]

seam (sēm) *n.* **1.a.** A line of junction formed by sewing together two pieces of material along their margins. **b.** A similar line, ridge, or groove made by fitting, joining, or lapping together two sections along their edges. **c.** A suture. **d.** A scar. **2.** A line across a surface, as a crack, fissure, or wrinkle. **3.** A thin layer or stratum, as of coal or rock. **—seam** *v.* **seamed, seam·ing, seams.** *—tr.* **1.** To put together with or as if with a seam. **2.** To mark with a groove, wrinkle, scar, or other seamlike line. **3.** To form ridges in by purling. *—intr.* **1.** To become fissured or furrowed; crack open. **2.** To purl. [Middle English *seme,* from Old English *sēam.* See **syū-** in Appendix.] **—seam′er** *n.*

sea-maid·en (sē′mād′n) also **sea-maid** (-mād′) *n. Mythology.* A mermaid or sea nymph.

sea·man (sē′mən) *n. Nautical.* **1.** A mariner or sailor. **2.** *Abbr.* **SMN a.** A noncommissioned rank in the U.S. Navy or Coast Guard that is above seaman apprentice and below petty officer. **b.** One who holds the rank of seaman, seaman apprentice, or seaman recruit.

Sea·man (sē′mən), **Elizabeth Cochrane.** Pen name Nellie Bly. 1867–1922. American journalist known for her muckraking articles in the *New York World,* particularly an exposé on conditions in mental institutions. She also wrote an account of her 72-day journey around the world.

seaman apprentice *n.* **1.** A noncommissioned rank in the U.S. Navy or Coast Guard that is above seaman recruit and below seaman. **2.** One who holds this rank.

seaman recruit *n.* **1.** The lowest noncommissioned rank in the U.S. Navy or Coast Guard. **2.** One who holds this rank.

sea·man·ship (sē′mən-shĭp′) *n. Nautical.* Skill in navigating or managing a boat or ship.

sea·mark (sē′märk′) *n. Nautical.* A landmark visible from the sea, used as a guide in navigation.

sea mew *n.* Any of various sea gulls, especially *Larus canus,* of Europe.

sea mile *n.* See **nautical mile.**

sea milkwort *n.* A succulent North American plant *(Glaux maritima)* of shores and brackish marshes, having pink or white flowers.

seam·less (sēm′lĭs) *adj.* **1.** Having no seams: *seamless stockings.* **2.** Perfectly consistent: *a seamless plot in the novel.* **—seam′less·ly** *adv.* **—seam′less·ness** *n.*

sea·mount (sē′mount′) *n.* An underwater mountain rising from the ocean floor and having a peaked or flat-topped summit below the surface of the sea.

sea mouse *n.* Any of various large marine polychete worms of the genus *Aphrodite,* especially *A. aculeata,* having a flattened elliptic body with overlapping scales covered by long hairs.

seam·ster (sēm′stər) *n.* A tailor. [Middle English *semester,* from Old English *sēamestre,* from *sēam,* seam. See SEAM.]

seam·stress (sēm′strĭs) *n.* A woman who sews, especially one who makes her living by sewing.

seam·y (sē′mē) *adj.* **-i·er, -i·est. 1.** Sordid; base: *"seamy tales of aberrant sexual practices, messy divorces, drug addiction, mental instability, and suicide attempts"* (Barbara Goldsmith). **2.** Having, marked with, or showing a seam. **—seam′i·ness** *n.*

sé·ance (sā′äns′, -äɴ′) *n.* **1.** A meeting of people to receive spiritualistic messages. **2.** A meeting, session, or sitting, as of a learned or legislative body. [French, a sitting, from Old French *seoir,* to sit, from Latin *sedēre.* See **sed-** in Appendix.]

WORD HISTORY: A gathering in which phenomena such as levitation, telepathy, and communication with the dead take place should seemingly have little in common with a session of an administrative body of a learned society, but the word *séance* can refer to both. *Séance* does not have the mysterious and exciting background one might expect for such a word but rather comes from French *séance,* "seat, session," from Old French *seoir,* "to sit." In French as in English the word came to be used specifically for a meeting of people to receive spiritualistic messages (a sense first recorded in English in 1845), but earlier in French and English the word had been used for meetings more generally. Certainly the second recorded use of the word in English in 1803 hardly seems to refer to an exciting spiritualistic meeting: "your séances . . . which I have a shrewd suspicion must be something dull."

sea nettle *n.* A stinging jellyfish, especially a scyphozoan *(Dactylometra quinquecirrha)* of the tropical Atlantic.

sea oats *pl.n. (used with a sing. or pl. verb).* A tall coastal grass *(Uniola paniculata)* of the southeast United States, Mexico, and the West Indies.

sea onion *n.* **1.** A Mediterranean plant *(Urginea maritima)* of the lily family, cultivated for its bulb that yields a powder used medicinally and as a rat poison. Also called *red squill, squill.* **2.** A small bulbous European plant *(Scilla verna)* having fragrant blue flowers.

sea otter *n.* A large marine otter *(Enhydra lutris)* of northern Pacific coastal waters, formerly hunted for its soft, dark brown fur.

sea palm *n.* A brown seaweed *(Postelsia palmaeformis)* found in the middle littoral zone along the Pacific coast of the United States, having a shape resembling a palm tree with numerous edible, toothed blades that crown the tip of a long stipe.

sea peach *n.* A tunicate *(Halocynthia pyriformis)* having a yellow or orange-red color and a sandpapery surface, found in shallow water along the northern Atlantic coast of North America.

sea pen *n.* Any of various marine anthozoans of the families Stylatulidae and Funiculinidae, resembling and related to the sea feathers. [From its resemblance to a quill pen.]

sea pigeon *n.* A guillemot *(Cepphus grylle)* of the North Atlantic.

sea·plane (sē′plān′) *n.* An aircraft equipped with floats for landing on or taking off from a body of water. Also called *hydroplane.*

sea·port (sē′pôrt′, -pōrt′) *n. Abbr.* **spt** A harbor or town having facilities for seagoing ships.

sea power *n.* **1.** A nation having significant naval strength. **2.** Naval strength.

sea purse *n.* The purse-shaped egg case of skates, rays, or certain sharks.

sea·quake (sē′kwāk′) *n.* An earthquake originating under the sea floor.

sear[1] (sîr) *v.* **seared, sear·ing, sears.** *—tr.* **1.** To char, scorch, or burn the surface of with or as if with a hot instrument. See Synonyms at **burn[1].** **2.** To cause to dry up and wither. *—intr.* To become withered or dried up. **—sear** *n.* A condition, such as a scar, produced by searing. [Middle English *seren,* from Old English *sēarian,* to wither, from *sēar,* withered.]

sear[2] (sîr) *n.* The catch in a gunlock that keeps the hammer halfcocked or fully cocked. [Probably French *serre,* something that grasps, from Old French, lock, from *serrer,* to grasp, from Vulgar Latin **serrāre,* from Late Latin *serāre,* to bolt, from Latin *sera,* bar, bolt. See **ser-[2]** in Appendix.]

sear[3] (sîr) *adj.* Variant of **sere[1].**

sea raven *n.* A large sculpin *(Hemitripterus americanus)* of the North Atlantic.

search (sûrch) *v.* **searched, search·ing, search·es.** *—tr.* **1.** To make a thorough examination of; look over carefully in order to find something; explore. See Synonyms at **seek.** **2.** To make a careful examination or investigation of; probe: *search one's conscience for the right solution to the problem.* **3.** *Law.* To make a thorough check of (a legal document); scrutinize: *search a title.* **4.a.** To examine in order to find something lost or concealed. **b.** To examine the person or personal effects of in order to find something lost or concealed. **5.** To come to know; learn. *—intr.* To conduct a thorough investigation; seek: *were searching for clues.* **—search** *n.* **1.** An act of searching. **2.** *Law.* The exercise of right of search. ***—idiom.*** **search me.** *Slang.* Used by a speaker to indicate that he or she does not have an answer to a question just asked. [Middle English *serchen,* from Anglo-Norman *sercher,* variant of Old French *cerchier,* from Latin *circāre,* to go around, from Latin *circus,* circle, from Greek *krikos, kirkos.* See **sker-[2]** in Appendix.] **—search′a·ble** *adj.* **—search′er** *n.*

search·ing (sûr′chĭng) *adj.* **1.** Examining closely or thoroughly; probing: *a searching investigation of their past dealings.* **2.** Keenly observant: *searching insights.* **—search′ing·ly** *adv.*

search·less (sûrch′lĭs) *adj.* Mysterious and inscrutable: *gave me a searchless look and then passed by.*

search·light (sûrch′līt′) *n.* **1.a.** An apparatus containing a light source and a reflector for projecting a high-intensity beam of approximately parallel rays of light. **b.** The beam of light so projected. **2.** A flashlight.

Sealyham terrier

Elizabeth Seaman
"Nellie Bly"
Illustration from the *New York World's Correspondent,* February 2, 1890

seaplane

ă pat	oi boy
ā pay	ou out
âr care	o͝o took
ä father	o͞o boot
ĕ pet	ŭ cut
ē be	ûr urge
ĭ pit	th thin
ī pie	*th* this
îr pier	hw which
ŏ pot	zh vision
ō toe	ə about, item
ô paw	♦ regionalism

Stress marks: **′** (primary); ′ (secondary), as in **dictionary** (dĭk′shə-nĕr′ē)

search warrant *n. Law.* A warrant giving legal authorization for a search.

sea robin *n.* Any of various marine fishes of the family Triglidae, having a bony head and extremely long pectoral fins with fingerlike rays that are used as feelers over the sea bottom, especially a gurnard of the genus *Prionotus* noted for its ability to produce sounds with its air bladder.

sea rocket *n.* Any of various succulent annual seashore herbs of the genus *Cakile,* of the mustard family, having pungent foliage and white to lavender flowers.

sea room *n. Nautical.* Space at sea adequate for maneuvering a ship.

sea rover *n. Nautical.* **1.** One that travels extensively by sea. **2.** A pirate. **3.** A pirate ship.

sea•scape (sē′skāp′) *n.* A view or picture of the sea.

sea scorpion *n.* See **sculpin** (sense 2).

Sea Scout *n.* See **Sea Explorer.**

sea serpent *n.* A large snakelike marine animal often reported by mariners since antiquity but never positively identified.

sea•shell (sē′shĕl′) *n.* The calcareous shell of a marine mollusk or similar marine organism.

sea•shore (sē′shôr′, -shōr′) *n.* **1.** Land by the sea. **2.** *Law.* Ground lying between high-water and low-water marks; the foreshore. —*attributive.* Often used to modify another noun: *seashore resorts; seashore plants.*

sea•sick•ness (sē′sĭk′nĭs) *n.* Motion sickness resulting from the pitching and rolling of a ship or boat in water, especially at sea. **—sea′sick′** *adj.*

sea•side (sē′sīd′) *n.* The seashore. —*attributive.* Often used to modify another noun: *seaside dwellings; seaside amusement parks.*

Sea•side (sē′sīd′). A city of western California on Monterey Bay west-southwest of Salinas. It is a resort and commercial center. Population, 36,567.

seaside sparrow *n.* A small sparrow *(Ammospiza maritima)* of the Atlantic coast of North America.

sea turtle

sea slug *n.* Any of various highly colorful marine gastropods of the suborder Nudibranchia, lacking a shell and gills but having fringelike projections that serve as respiratory organs. Also called *nudibranch.*

sea snail *n.* Any of various marine gastropods, such as a periwinkle, having a spiral shell.

sea snake *n.* Any of various venomous tropical snakes of the family Hydrophidae that are adapted to living in the sea, especially in the Pacific and Indian oceans, and that bear live offspring.

sea•son (sē′zən) *n.* **1.a.** One of the four natural divisions of the year, spring, summer, fall, and winter, in the North and South Temperate zones. Each season, beginning astronomically at an equinox or a solstice, is characterized by specific meteorological or climatic conditions. **b.** The two divisions of the year, rainy and dry, in some tropical regions. **2.** A recurrent period characterized by certain occurrences, occupations, festivities, or crops: *the holiday season; tomato season.* **3.** A suitable, natural, or convenient time: *a season for merriment.* **4.** A period of time: *gone for a season.* **—season** *v.* **-soned, -son•ing, -sons.** —*tr.* **1.** To improve or enhance the flavor of (food) by adding salt, spices, herbs, or other flavorings. **2.** To add zest, piquancy, or interest to: *seasoned the lecture with jokes.* **3.** To treat or dry (lumber, for example) until ready for use; cure. **4.** To render competent through trial and experience: *a lawyer who had been seasoned by years in the trial courts.* **5.** To accustom or inure; harden: *troops who had been seasoned in combat.* See Synonyms at **harden. 6.** To moderate; temper. —*intr.* To become usable, competent, or tempered. **—*idioms.* in season. 1.** Available or ready for eating or other use. **2.** Legally permitted to be caught or hunted during a specified period. **3.** At the right moment; opportunely. **4.** In heat. Used of animals. **out of season. 1.** Not available, permitted, or ready to be eaten, caught, or hunted. **2.** Not at the right or proper moment; inopportunely. [Middle English, from Old French *seison,* from Latin *satiō, satiōn-,* act of sowing, from *satus,* past participle of *serere,* to plant. See **sē-** in Appendix.]

sea•son•a•ble (sē′zə-nə-bəl) *adj.* **1.** In keeping with the time or the season. **2.** Occurring or performed at the proper time; timely. See Synonyms at **opportune.** See Usage Note at **seasonal. —sea′son•a•bly** *adv.*

sea•son•al (sē′zə-nəl) *adj.* Of or dependent on a particular season. **—sea′son•al′i•ty** (-zə-năl′ĭ-tē) *n.* **—sea′son•al•ly** *adv.*

USAGE NOTE: *Seasonal* and *seasonable,* though closely related, are differentiated in usage. *Seasonal* applies to what depends on or is controlled by the season of the year: *a seasonal rise in employment. Seasonable* applies to what is appropriate to the season (*seasonable clothing*) or timely (*seasonable intervention in the dispute*). Rains are *seasonal* if they occur at a certain time of the year. They are *seasonable* at any time if they save the crops.

seasonal affective disorder *n. Abbr.* **SAD** A mild form of depression occurring at certain seasons of the year, especially one recurring in winter that is characterized by loss of energy and sexual drive, restlessness, and often a craving for carbohydrates.

sea•son•er (sē′zə-nər) *n.* **1.** One that uses seasonings: *The cook is a heavy seasoner.* **2.** See **seasoning** (sense 1).

sea•son•ing (sē′zə-nĭng) *n.* **1.** Something, such as a spice or herb, used to flavor food. Also called *seasoner.* **2.** The act or process by which something is seasoned.

season ticket *n.* A ticket valid for a specified period of time, as for a series of performances or for transportation between designated points.

sea spider *n.* Any of various marine arthropods of the class Pycnogonida, having long legs and a relatively small body. Also called *pycnogonid.*

sea squirt *n.* Any of various sedentary marine animals of the class Ascidiacea, having a transparent sac-shaped body with two siphons. Also called *ascidian.* [From its habit of squirting water when disturbed.]

sea star *n.* See **starfish.**

sea•strand (sē′strănd′) *n.* A seashore.

sea swallow *n.* Any of various terns, especially a common tern *(Sterna hirundo)* that breeds within the Arctic Circle.

seat (sēt) *n.* **1.** Something, such as a chair or bench, that may be sat on. **2.a.** A place in which one may sit. **b.** The right to occupy such a place or a ticket indicating this right: *got seats for the concert.* **3.** The part on which one rests in sitting: *a bicycle seat.* **4.a.** The buttocks. **b.** The part of a garment that covers the buttocks. **5.a.** A part serving as the base of something else. **b.** The surface or part on which another part sits or rests. **6.a.** The place where something is located or based: *The heart is the seat of the emotions.* **b.** A center of authority; a capital: *the county seat.* See Synonyms at **center. 7.** A place of abode or residence, especially a large house that is part of an estate: *the squire's country seat.* **8.** Membership in an organization, such as a legislative body or stock exchange, that is obtained by appointment, election, or purchase. **9.** The manner of sitting on a horse: *a fox hunter with a good seat.* **—seat** *v.* **seat•ed, seat•ing, seats.** —*tr.* **1.a.** To place in or on a seat. **b.** To cause or assist to sit down: *The ushers will seat the members of the bride's family.* **2.** To provide with a particular seat: *The usher seated me in the back row.* **3.** To have or provide seats for: *We can seat 300 in the auditorium.* **4.** To install in a position of authority or eminence. **5.** To fix firmly in place: *seat an ammunition clip in an automatic rifle.* —*intr.* To rest on or fit into another part: *The O-rings had not seated correctly in their grooves.* **—*idiom.* by the seat of (one's) pants.** *Slang.* **1.** In a manner based on intuition and experience rather than method: *He ran the business by the seat of his pants.* **2.** Without the use of instruments: *an inexperienced pilot who had to fly the aircraft by the seat of her pants.* [Middle English *sete,* probably from Old Norse *sæti.* See **sed-** in Appendix.]

sea tangle *n.* Any of various brown algae, especially of the genus *Laminaria.*

seat•back also **seat back** (sēt′băk′) *n.* The back of a chair or other type of seating.

seat belt *n.* A safety strap or harness designed to hold a person securely in a seat, as in a motor vehicle or an aircraft. Also called *safety belt.*

seat•ing (sē′tĭng) *n.* **1.a.** The act of providing or furnishing with a seat or seats. **b.** The seats so provided or furnished: *seating for 500.* **2.** The arrangement of seats in a room, an auditorium, or a banquet hall: *a theater that offers semicircular seating.* **3.** The member or part on or within which another part is seated. **4.** Material for upholstering seats.

seat•mate (sēt′māt′) *n.* A person sitting next to another on a conveyance such as an airplane: *"His seatmate was a gray-haired woman with glasses"* (Anne Tyler).

SEATO *abbr.* Southeast Asia Treaty Organization.

seat-of-the-pants (sēt′əv-*thə*-pănts′) *adj. Slang.* **1.** Based on or using intuition and experience rather than a plan or method; improvised: *"Each has already moved beyond seat-of-the-pants management to more professional operating procedures"* (Business Week). **2.** Performed without using instruments: *a seat-of-the-pants landing of the aircraft.*

sea•train (sē′trān′) *n. Nautical.* A seagoing vessel capable of carrying a train of railroad cars.

sea trout *n.* **1.** Any of several marine fishes of the genus *Cynoscion,* especially the weakfish. **2.** Any of several trouts or similar fishes that live in the sea but migrate to fresh water to spawn.

Se•at•tle[1] (sē-ăt′l). Originally Seathl. 1786?–1866. Suquamish leader who befriended white settlers of the Pacific Northwest. The city of Seattle is named for him.

Se•at•tle[2] (sē-ăt′l). A city of west-central Washington bounded by Puget Sound and Lake Washington. First settled in the 1850's, it prospered after the coming of the railroad in 1884 and became a boom town during the Alaskan gold rush of 1897. It is now an important commercial, transportation, and industrial hub and a major port of entry. Population, 493,846.

sea turtle *n.* Any of various large marine turtles of the families Cheloniidae and Dermochelyidae, including the green turtle, loggerhead turtle, ridley, and leatherback, having the forelimbs modified into very large flippers and usually living in tropical and subtropical oceans.

seat•work (sēt′wûrk′) *n.* Lessons assigned to be done by students at their desks in the classroom.

sea urchin *n.* Any of various echinoderms of the class

Echinoidea, having a soft body enclosed in a round, symmetrical, calcareous shell covered with long spines.

sea wall also **sea•wall** (sē′wôl′) *n.* An embankment to prevent erosion of a shoreline.

sea walnut *n.* A walnut-shaped ctenophore, especially one of the genus *Mnemiopsis.*

sea•ward (sē′wərd) *adv. & adj.* Toward or at the sea. **—seaward** *n.* A seaward place or direction. **—sea′wards** (-wərdz) *adv.*

sea•ware (sē′wâr′) *n.* Sea wrack used as fertilizer. [Possibly Old English *sǣ wār* : *sǣ*, sea + *wār*, seaweed; see **wei-** in Appendix.]

sea wasp *n.* Any of various jellyfishes of the class Cubozoa, having a cube-shaped medusa and a venomous, sometimes fatal sting.

sea•wa•ter (sē′wô′tər, -wŏt′ər) *n.* The salt water in or coming from the sea or ocean.

sea•way (sē′wā′) *n. Nautical.* **1.** A sea route. **2.** An inland waterway for ocean shipping. **3.** The headway of a ship. **4.** A rough sea.

sea•weed (sē′wēd′) *n.* **1.** Any of numerous marine algae, such as a kelp, rockweed, or gulfweed. **2.** Any of various marine plants.

sea whip *n.* Any of various gorgonian corals forming flexible colonies with few or no branches and commonly found on coral reefs of the Atlantic.

sea•wor•thy (sē′wûr′thē) *adj.* **-thi•er, -thi•est.** *Nautical.* Fit to traverse the seas: *a seaworthy freighter; a seaworthy crew.* **—sea′wor′thi•ness** *n.*

sea wrack *n.* Material cast ashore, especially seaweed.

se•ba•ceous (sĭ-bā′shəs) *adj. Physiology.* **1.** Of, relating to, or resembling fat or sebum; fatty. **2.** Secreting fat or sebum. [Latin *sēbum*, tallow + –ACEOUS.]

sebaceous gland *n.* Any of various glands in the dermis of the skin that open into a hair follicle and produce and secrete sebum.

se•bac•ic acid (sĭ-băs′ĭk, -bā′sĭk) *n.* A white crystalline acid, $COOH(CH_2)_8COOH$, used in the manufacture of certain synthetic resins and fibers, various plasticizers, and polyester rubbers. [From SEBACEOUS (so called because it was originally obtained from melted suet).]

Se•bas•to•pol (sə-băs′tə-pōl′). See **Sevastopol.**

SEbE *abbr.* Southeast by east.

sebi– or **sebo–** *pref.* Fat; sebum: *sebiferous.* [From Latin *sēbum*, tallow.]

se•bif•er•ous (sĭ-bĭf′ər-əs) also **se•bip•a•rous** (-bĭp′-). Producing or secreting fatty, oily, or waxy matter; sebaceous.

sebo– *pref.* Variant of **sebi–.**

seb•or•rhe•a also **seb•or•rhoe•a** (sĕb′ə-rē′ə) *n.* A disease of the sebaceous glands characterized by excessive secretion of sebum or an alteration in its quality, resulting in an oily coating, crusts, or scales on the skin. **—seb′or•rhe′ic** *adj.*

SEbS *abbr.* Southeast by south.

se•bum (sē′bəm) *n.* The semifluid secretion of the sebaceous glands, consisting chiefly of fat, keratin, and cellular material. [Latin *sēbum*, tallow.]

sec¹ (sĕk) *adj.* Dry. Used of wines, especially champagne. [French, from Old French, from Latin *siccus.*]

sec² *abbr.* **1.** *Mathematics.* Secant. **2.** Second. **3.** Secondary.

SEC *abbr.* Securities and Exchange Commission.

sec. *abbr.* **1.** Second. **2.** Secondary. **3.** Secretary. **4.** Section. **5.** Sector. **6.** *Latin.* Secundum (according to). **7.** Security.

se•cant (sē′kănt′, -kənt) *n. Abbr.* **sec** *Mathematics.* **1.a.** A straight line intersecting a curve at two or more points. **b.** The straight line drawn from the center through one end of a circular arc and intersecting the tangent to the other end of the arc. **c.** The ratio of the length of this line to the length of the radius of the circle. **2.** The reciprocal of the cosine of an angle in a right triangle. [From Latin *secāns, secant-*, present participle of *secāre*, to cut. See **sek-** in Appendix.]

sec•co (sĕk′ō) *n., pl.* **-cos.** The art or an example of painting on dry plaster. **—secco** *adj. Music.* Of or being a kind of recitative in which the words are sung rapidly to minimal melody, usually with continuo. [Italian, from Latin *siccus*, dry.]

se•cede (sĭ-sēd′) *intr.v.* **-ced•ed, -ced•ing, -cedes.** To withdraw formally from membership in an organization, association, or alliance. [Latin *sēcēdere*, to withdraw : *sē-*, apart; see **s(w)e-** in Appendix + *cēdere*, to go; see **ked-** in Appendix.]

se•cern (sĭ-sûrn′) *tr.v.* **-cerned, -cern•ing, -cerns.** To discern as separate; discriminate. [Latin *sēcernere*, to sever : *sē-*, apart; see **s(w)e-** in Appendix + *cernere*, to separate; see **krei-** in Appendix.] **—se•cern′ment** *n.*

se•ces•sion (sĭ-sĕsh′ən) *n.* **1.** The act of seceding. **2.** Often **Secession.** The withdrawal of 11 Southern states from the Union in 1860–1861, precipitating the U.S. Civil War. [Latin *sēcessiō, sēcessiōn-*, from *sēcessus*, past participle of *sēcēdere*, to secede. See SECEDE.] **—se•ces′sion•al** *adj.*

se•ces•sion•ism (sĭ-sĕsh′ə-nĭz′əm) *n.* The policy of those maintaining the right of secession. **—se•ces′sion•ist** *n.*

Sech•ua•na (sĕch-wä′nə) *n.* Variant of **Setswana.**

Seck•el pear (sĕk′əl, sĭk′-) *n.* A variety of pear having small, sweet, reddish-brown fruit. [Perhaps from *Seckle*, the name of a Pennsylvania farmer.]

se•clude (sĭ-klo͞od′) *tr.v.* **-clud•ed, -clud•ing, -cludes. 1.** To set or keep apart, as from social contact with others. See Synonyms at **isolate. 2.** To screen from view; make private. [Middle English *secluden*, to shut off, from Latin *sēclūdere* : *sē-*, apart; see **s(w)e-** in Appendix + *claudere*, to shut.]

se•clud•ed (sĭ-klo͞o′dĭd) *adj.* **1.** Removed or remote from others; solitary. **2.** Screened from view; sequestered. **—se•clud′ed•ly** *adv.* **—se•clud′ed•ness** *n.*

se•clu•sion (sĭ-klo͞o′zhən) *n.* **1.a.** The act of secluding. **b.** The state of being secluded. See Synonyms at **solitude. 2.** A secluded place or abode. [Medieval Latin *sēclūsiō, sēclūsiōn-*, from Latin *sēclūsus*, past participle of *sēclūdere*, to seclude. See SECLUDE.]

se•clu•sive (sĭ-klo͞o′sĭv, -zĭv) *adj.* Of, fond of, or seeking seclusion. **—se•clu′sive•ly** *adv.* **—se•clu′sive•ness** *n.*

sec•o•bar•bi•tal (sĕk′ō-bär′bĭ-tôl′, -tăl′) *n.* A white, odorless barbiturate, $C_{12}H_{18}N_2O_3$, used in the form of its sodium salt as a sedative and hypnotic. [SECO(NDARY) + BARBITAL.]

sec•ond¹ (sĕk′ənd) *n.* **1.** *Abbr.* **sec, sec., s** A unit of time equal to one sixtieth of a minute. See table at **measurement. 2.** A brief interval of time; a moment. See Synonyms at **moment. 3.** *Abbr.* **s** *Mathematics.* A unit of angular measure equal to one sixtieth of a minute. [Middle English *seconde*, from Old French, from Medieval Latin *(pars minūta) secunda*, second (small part), feminine of Latin *secundus*, second, following. See SECOND².]

sec•ond² (sĕk′ənd) *adj. Abbr.* **sec. 1.** Coming next after the first in order, place, rank, time, or quality. **2.a.** Repeating an initial instance: *a second chance.* **b.** Reminiscent of one that is well known: *a second George Washington; a second Waterloo.* **c.** Alternate; other: *every second year.* **3.** Inferior to another; subordinate: *received the title of second vice president at the bank; a leader who is second to none.* **4.** *Music.* **a.** Having a lower pitch. **b.** Singing or playing a part having a lower range. **5.** Having the second-highest ratio. Used of gears in a sequence. **—second** *n. Abbr.* **sec. 1.a.** The ordinal number matching the number 2 in a series. **b.** One of two equal parts. **2.** One that is next in order, place, time, or quality after the first. **3.** Often **seconds.** An article of merchandise of inferior quality. **4.** The official attendant of a contestant in a duel or boxing match. See Synonyms at **assistant. 5.** *Music.* **a.** The interval between consecutive tones on the diatonic scale. **b.** A tone separated by this interval from another tone. **c.** A combination of two such tones in notation or in harmony. **d.** The second part, instrument, or voice in a harmonized composition. **6.** An utterance of endorsement, as to a parliamentary motion. **7.** The transmission gear or gear ratio used to produce forward speeds higher than those of first and lower than those of third in a motor vehicle. **8.** Or **seconds.** *Informal.* A second serving of food. **9.** *Baseball.* Second base. **—second** *tr.v.* **-ond•ed, -ond•ing, -onds. 1.** To attend (a duelist or a boxer) as an aide or assistant. **2.** To promote or encourage; reinforce. **3.** To endorse (a motion or nomination) as a required preliminary to discussion or vote. **4.** (sĭ-kŏnd′). *Chiefly British.* To transfer (a military officer, for example) temporarily. **—second** *adv. Abbr.* **sec. 1.** In the second order, place, or rank: *finished second.* **2.** But for one other; save one: *the second highest peak.* [Middle English, from Old French, from Latin *secundus.* See **sekʷ-¹** in Appendix.]

Sec•ond Advent (sĕk′ənd) *n.* See **Second Coming.**

sec•ond•ar•y (sĕk′ən-dĕr′ē) *adj. Abbr.* **sec, sec. 1.a.** Of the second rank; not primary. **b.** Inferior. **c.** Minor; lesser. **2.** Derived from what is primary or original: *a secondary source; a secondary infection.* **3.** Of, relating to, or being the shorter flight feathers projecting along the inner edge of a bird's wing. **4.** *Electricity.* Having an induced current that is generated by an inductively coupled primary. Used of a circuit or coil. **5.** *Chemistry.* Characterized or formed by replacement of two atoms or radicals within a molecule. Used of a compound. **6.** *Geology.* Produced from another mineral by decay or alteration. **7.** Of or relating to a secondary school: *secondary education.* **8.** Being a degree of health care intermediate between that offered in a physician's office and that available at a research hospital, as the care typically offered at a clinic or community hospital. **9.** *Botany.* Of, relating to, or being growth or tissue caused by activity of the cambium and resulting in wider branches and stems: *secondary xylem.* **—secondary** *n., pl.* **-ies.** *Abbr.* **sec, sec. 1.** One that acts in an auxiliary, subordinate, or inferior capacity. **2.** One of the shorter flight feathers projecting along the inner edge of a bird's wing. **3.** *Electricity.* A coil or circuit having an induced current. **4.a.** *Astronomy.* A celestial body that revolves around another; a satellite. **b.** The dimmer star of a binary star system. **5.** *Football.* The defensive backfield. **—sec′ond•ar′i•ly** (-dâr′ə-lē) *adv.* **—sec′ond•ar′i•ness** *n.*

secondary accent *n. Linguistics.* **1.** The degree of stress weaker than a primary accent placed on a syllable in the pronunciation of a word. **2.** The mark (′) used to indicate this degree of stress.

secondary battery *n. Electricity.* See **storage battery.**

secondary cell *n.* A rechargeable electric cell that converts chemical energy into electrical energy by a reversible chemical reaction. Also called *storage cell.*

secondary color *n. Color.* A color produced by mixing two primary colors in approximately equal proportions.

sea wall

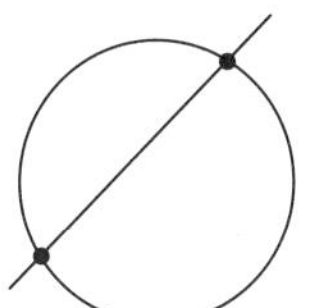

secant
Intersecting a curve

ă pat	oi boy
ā pay	ou out
âr care	o͝o took
ä father	o͞o boot
ĕ pet	ŭ cut
ē be	ûr urge
ĭ pit	th thin
ī pie	*th* this
îr pier	hw which
ŏ pot	zh vision
ō toe	ə about, item
ô paw	♦ regionalism

Stress marks: ′ (primary); ′ (secondary), as in **dictionary** (dĭk′shə-nĕr′ē)

secondary consumer *n. Ecology.* An animal that feeds on smaller plant-eating animals in a food chain.

secondary electron *n.* An electron produced in secondary emission.

secondary emission *n.* Emission of electrons from the surface of a substance as a result of bombardment by electrons or ions.

secondary offering *n.* The sale of a large block of outstanding stock through dealers outside a stock exchange.

secondary school *n.* A school that is intermediate in level between elementary school and college and that usually offers general, technical, vocational, or college-preparatory curricula.

secondary sex characteristic *n.* Any of various genetically transmitted anatomical, physiological, or behavioral characteristics, such as voice quality, abundance of facial hair, or breast development, that first appear in humans at puberty and differentiate between the sexes without having a direct reproductive function.

secondary syphilis *n.* The second and highly infectious stage of syphilis, appearing from seven to ten weeks after the initial exposure, characterized by a general skin rash accompanied by various symptoms of illness such as fatigue, headache, sore throat, muscle pain, and fever.

secondary wall *n.* The innermost wall of a plant cell that is deposited after cell elongation has ceased.

secondary wave *n.* An earthquake wave in which rock particles vibrate at right angles to the direction of wave travel. It can travel through solids but not through liquids.

second banana *n. Slang.* **1.** One, such as an assistant or a deputy, who is subordinate to another. **2.** One who serves as the straight man opposite the leading comedian in a burlesque.

second base *n. Baseball.* **1.** The base across the diamond from home plate, to be touched second by a runner. **2.** The position played by a second baseman.

second baseman *n. Baseball.* The infielder who is positioned near and to the first-base side of second base.

second best *n.* One that is next to the best. **—second best** *adv.* Next to the best. **—sec′ond-best′** (sĕk′ənd-bĕst′) *adj.*

second blessing *n.* Sanctification of a Christian believer, considered as a gift of the Holy Spirit given after conversion and sometimes thought of as rendering the believer incapable of committing sin.

second childhood *n.* Senility; dotage.

second class *n.* **1.** Travel accommodations ranking next below the highest or first class. **2.** Second-class mail.

sec•ond-class (sĕk′ənd-klăs′) *adj.* **1.** Of secondary status: *secondary issues.* **2.** Of or relating to travel accommodations ranking next below the highest or first class. **3.** Of or relating to a class of U.S. and Canadian mail consisting of newspapers and periodicals. **—second-class** *adv.* By means of second-class mail or second-class travel accommodations.

second-class citizen *n.* A person considered inferior in status or rights in comparison with some others: *"He believes women . . . are second-class citizens under the Constitution"* (Edward M. Kennedy).

Second Coming *n. Theology.* The return of Jesus as judge for the Last Judgment. Also called *Advent, Second Advent.*

second cousin *n.* The child of one's first cousin.

sec•ond-de•gree burn (sĕk′ənd-dĭ-grē′) *n.* A burn that blisters the skin and is more severe than a first-degree burn.

Second Empire *n.* A heavily ornate style of furniture, architecture, and decoration that was developed in France in the middle of the 19th century. [After *Second Empire,* the reign of Napoleon III, the next empire after that of Napoleon I.]

second fiddle *n. Informal.* **1.** A secondary role. **2.** One who plays a secondary role.

sec•ond-gen•er•a•tion (sĕk′ənd-jĕn′ə-rā′shən) *adj.* **1.** Of or relating to a person or persons whose parents are immigrants. **2.** Of or relating to a person or persons whose parents are citizens by birth and whose grandparents are immigrants. **3.** *Computer Science.* Of, relating to, or being the period of computer technology distinguished by the use of solid-state circuitry.

second growth *n.* Trees that cover an area after the removal of the original stand, as by cutting or fire.

sec•ond-guess (sĕk′ənd-gĕs′) *v.* **-guessed, -guess•ing, -guess•es.** *—tr.* **1.** To criticize or correct after an outcome is known. **2.a.** To outguess. **b.** To predict or anticipate: *"She can second-guess indictments"* (Scott Turow). *—intr.* To criticize a decision after its outcome is known. **—sec′ond-guess′er** *n.*

sec•ond•hand (sĕk′ənd-hănd′) *adj.* **1.** Previously used by another; not new. **2.** Dealing in previously used merchandise. **3.** Obtained, derived, or borrowed from another; not original. **—secondhand** *adv.* In an indirect manner; indirectly.

second hand[1] *n.* The hand of a timepiece that marks the seconds.

second hand[2] *n.* An intermediary person or source: *heard the news at second hand.*

secondhand smoke *n.* Cigarette, cigar, or pipe smoke that is inhaled unintentionally by nonsmokers and may be injurious to their health if inhaled regularly or continuously over a long period.

se•con•di (sĭ-kôn′dē) *n. Music.* Plural of **secondo.**

secretary

second lieutenant *n.* **1.** The lowest commissioned rank in the U.S. Army, Air Force, and Marine Corps. **2.** One who holds this rank.

sec•ond•ly (sĕk′ənd-lē) *adv.* In the second place; second.

second mortgage *n.* A mortgage taken out on property that already has one mortgage, with priority in settlement of claims given to the earlier mortgage.

second nature *n.* An acquired behavior or trait that is so long practiced as to seem innate. [From the proverb *Habit is second nature.*]

se•con•do (sĭ-kôn′dō) *n., pl.* **-di** (-dē). *Music.* The second part in a concert piece, especially the lower part in a piano duet. [Italian, from Latin *secundus,* second, following. See **sek**^{w}**-**[1] in Appendix.]

second person *n. Grammar.* The form of a pronoun or verb used in referring to the person addressed, as *you* and *shall* in *You shall not enter.*

sec•ond-rate (sĕk′ənd-rāt′) *adj.* Of inferior or mediocre quality or value. **—sec′ond-rate′ness** *n.* **—sec′ond-rat′er** *n.*

second sight *n.* Clairvoyance.

sec•ond•sto•ry man (sĕk′ənd-stôr′ē, -stōr′ē) *n. Informal.* A burglar adept at entering through upstairs windows.

sec•ond-strike (sĕk′ənd-strīk′) *adj.* Of, relating to, or constituting a nuclear-weapons force able to withstand nuclear attack and therefore capable of delivering a retaliatory attack.

sec•ond-string (sĕk′ənd-strĭng′) *adj.* Of, relating to, or being a substitute, as on a sports team. **—sec′ond-string′er** *n.*

second thought *n.* A reconsideration of a decision or opinion previously made.

second wind (wĭnd) *n.* **1.** The return of relative ease of breathing after the initial exhaustion that occurs during continued physical exertion. **2.** Restored energy or strength.

Second World *n.* The Communist nations of the world, especially as an economic and political bloc.

Second World War *n.* World War II.

se•cre•cy (sē′krĭ-sē) *n., pl.* **-cies. 1.** The quality or condition of being secret or hidden; concealment. **2.** The ability or habit of keeping secrets; closeness. [Alteration of Middle English *secretee,* from *secret,* secret. See SECRET.]

se•cret (sē′krĭt) *adj.* **1.** Kept hidden from knowledge or view; concealed. **2.** Dependably discreet. **3.** Operating in a hidden or confidential manner: *a secret agent.* **4.** Not expressed; inward: *their secret thoughts.* **5.** Not frequented; secluded: *wandered about the secret byways of Paris.* **6.** Known or shared only by the initiated: *secret rites.* **7.** Beyond ordinary understanding; mysterious. **8.** Containing information, the unauthorized disclosure of which poses a grave threat to national security. **—secret** *n.* **1.** Something kept hidden from others or known only to oneself or to a few. **2.** Something that remains beyond understanding or explanation; a mystery. **3.** A method or formula on which success is based: *The secret of this dish is in the sauce.* **4. Secret.** A variable prayer said after the Offertory and before the Preface in the Mass. [Middle English, from Old French, from Latin *sēcrētus,* from past participle of *sēcernere,* to set aside : *sē-,* apart; see **s(w)e-** in Appendix + *cernere,* to separate; see **krei-** in Appendix.] **—se′cret•ly** *adv.*

SYNONYMS: *secret, stealthy, covert, clandestine, furtive, surreptitious, underhand.* These adjectives mean deliberately hidden from view or knowledge. *Secret* is the most general: *a desk with a secret compartment; a secret marriage; secret negotiations. Stealthy* suggests quiet, cautious deceptiveness intended to escape notice: *heard stealthy footsteps on the stairs. Covert* describes something that is not overt but is concealed or disguised: *Students protested covert actions undertaken by the CIA. Clandestine* implies stealth and secrecy for the concealment of an often illegal or improper purpose: *a clandestine tryst; clandestine intelligence operations. Furtive* suggests the slyness, shiftiness, and evasiveness of a thief: *a menacing and furtive look to his eye.* Something *surreptitious* is stealthy, furtive, and often unseemly or unethical: *took a surreptitious glance at his watch; the surreptitious mobilization of troops in preparation for a sneak attack. Underhand* implies unfairness, deceit, fraud, or slyness as well as secrecy: *achieved success in business only by resorting to underhand methods.*

se•cre•ta (sĭ-krē′tə) *pl.n.* Substances secreted by a cell, a tissue, or an organ; the products of secretion. [Latin *sēcrēta,* neuter pl. past participle of *sēcernere,* to set aside. See SECRET.]

se•cre•ta•gogue (sĭ-krē′tə-gôg′, -gŏg′) *n.* A hormone or another agent that causes or stimulates secretion. [SECRET(ION)[1] + -AGOGUE.]

sec•re•tar•i•at (sĕk′rĭ-târ′ē-ĭt) *n.* **1.a.** The department administered by a governmental secretary, especially for an international organization. **b.** The office occupied by such a department. **2.** The office or position of a governmental secretary. [French *secrétariat,* from Old French, from Medieval Latin *sēcrētāriātus,* from *sēcrētārius,* secretary. See SECRETARY.]

sec•re•tar•y (sĕk′rĭ-tĕr′ē) *n., pl.* **-ies.** *Abbr.* **sec., secy. 1.** A person employed to handle correspondence, keep files, and do clerical work for another person or an organization. **2.** An officer who keeps records, takes minutes of the meetings, and answers correspondence, as for a company. **3.** An official who presides over an administrative department of state. **4.** A desk with a small bookcase on top. [Middle English *secretarie,* from Medieval Latin *sēcrētārius,* confidential officer, clerk, from Latin *sēcrētus,* secret. See SECRET.] **—sec′re·tar′i·al** (-târ′ē-əl) *adj.*

secretary bird *n.* A large African bird of prey *(Sagittarius serpentarius)* with long legs and a crest of quills at the back of the head.

secretary bird
Sagittarius serpentarius

sec·re·tar·y-gen·er·al (sĕk′rĭ-tĕr′ē-jĕn′ər-əl) *n., pl.* **sec·re·tar·ies-gen·er·al** (sĕk′rĭ-tĕr′ēz-). A principal executive officer, as in certain political parties or governmental bodies such as the United Nations.

secret ballot *n.* **1.** A type of voting in which each person's vote is kept secret, but the amassed votes of various groups are revealed publicly. **2.** See **Australian ballot.**

se·crete¹ (sĭ-krēt′) *tr.v.* **-cret·ed, -cret·ing, -cretes.** To generate and separate (a substance) from cells or bodily fluids: *secrete digestive juices.* [Back-formation from SECRETION¹.]

se·crete² (sĭ-krēt′) *tr.v.* **-cret·ed, -cret·ing, -cret·es. 1.** To conceal in a hiding place; cache. See Synonyms at **hide¹. 2.** To steal secretly; filch. [Probably alteration of obsolete *secret,* from SECRET.]

se·cret·er (sĭ-krē′tər) *n.* Variant of **secretor.**

se·cre·tin (sĭ-krēt′n) *n.* A polypeptide hormone produced in the duodenum, especially on contact with acid, to stimulate secretion of pancreatic juice. [SECRET(ION)¹ + -IN.]

se·cre·tion¹ (sĭ-krē′shən) *n.* **1.** The process of secreting a substance, especially one that is not a waste, from the blood or cells: *secretion of hormones; secretion of milk by the mammary glands.* **2.** A substance, such as saliva, mucus, tears, bile, or a hormone, that is secreted. [French *sécrétion,* from Old French, separation, from Latin *sēcrētiō, sēcrētiōn-,* from *sēcrētus,* past participle of *sēcernere,* to set aside. See SECERN.] **—se·cre′tion·ar′y** (-shə-nĕr′ē) *adj.*

se·cre·tion² (sĭ-krē′shən) *n.* **1.** The act of concealing something in a hiding place. **2.** The act of stealing something secretly. [From SECRETE².]

se·cre·tive (sē′krĭ-tĭv, sĭ-krē′tĭv) *adj.* Having or marked by an inclination to secrecy; not open, forthright, or frank. See Synonyms at **silent. —se′cre·tive·ly** *adv.* **—se′cre·tive·ness** *n.*

se·cre·tor also **se·cret·er** (sĭ-krē′tər) *n.* **1.** A cell, a tissue, or an organ that produces a secretion. **2.** A person whose saliva and other body fluids contain ABO antigens.

se·cre·to·ry (sĭ-krē′tə-rē) *adj. Physiology.* Relating to or performing secretion.

secret partner *n.* A partner whose participation in a business partnership is hidden from the public.

secret police *n.* A police force operating largely in secret and often using terror tactics to suppress dissent and political opposition.

secret service *n.* **1.a.** Intelligence-gathering activities conducted secretly by a government agency. **b.** A government agency engaged in intelligence-gathering activities. **2. Secret Service.** A branch of the U.S. Treasury Department concerned especially with protection of the President.

secret society *n.* An organization, such as a lodge, that requires its members to conceal certain activities, such as its rites of initiation, from outsiders.

sect (sĕkt) *n.* **1.** A group of people forming a distinct unit within a larger group by virtue of certain refinements or distinctions of belief or practice. **2.** A religious body, especially one that has separated from a larger denomination. **3.** A small faction united by common interests or beliefs. [Middle English *secte,* from Old French, from Latin *secta,* course, school of thought, from feminine past participle of *sequī,* to follow. See **sekʷ-¹** in Appendix.]

sect. *abbr.* **1.** Section. **2.** Sectional.

-sect *suff.* **1.** To cut; divide: *trisect.* **2.** Cut; divided: *pinnatisect.* [From Latin *sectus,* past participle of *secāre,* to cut. See **sek-** in Appendix.]

sec·tar·i·an (sĕk-târ′ē-ən) *adj.* **1.** Of, relating to, or characteristic of a sect. **2.** Adhering or confined to the dogmatic limits of a sect or denomination; partisan. **3.** Narrow-minded; parochial. **—sectarian** *n.* **1.** A member of a sect. **2.** One characterized by bigoted adherence to a factional viewpoint. **—sec·tar′i·an·ism** *n.*

sec·ta·ry (sĕk′tə-rē) *n., pl.* **-ries. 1.** A sectarian. **2.** A dissenter from an established church, especially a Protestant nonconformist. [Medieval Latin *sectārius,* from Latin *secta,* sect. See SECT.]

sec·tile (sĕk′təl, -tīl′) *adj.* Of or relating to a mineral that can be cut or severed smoothly by a knife but cannot withstand pulverization. [Latin *sectilis,* from *sectus,* past participle of *secāre,* to cut. See **sek-** in Appendix.] **—sec·til′i·ty** (-tĭl′ĭ-tē) *n.*

sec·tion (sĕk′shən) *n. Abbr.* **sec., sect. 1.** One of several components; a piece. **2.** A subdivision of a written work. **3.** *Law.* A division of a statute or code. **4.** A distinct portion of a newspaper: *the sports section.* **5.** A distinct area of a town, county, or country: *a residential section.* **6.** A land unit equal to one square mile (2.59 square kilometers), 640 acres, or 1⁄36 of a township. **7.** The act or process of separating or cutting, especially the surgical cutting or dividing of tissue. **8.** A thin slice, as of tissue, suitable for microscopic examination. **9.** A segment of a fruit, especially a citrus fruit. **10.** Representation of a solid object as it would appear if cut by an intersecting plane, so that the internal structure is displayed. **11.** *Music.* A group of instruments or voices in the same class considered as a division of a band, an orchestra, or a choir: *the rhythm section; the woodwind section.* **12.** A class or discussion group of students taking the same course: *She taught three sections of English composition.* **13.a.** A portion of railroad track maintained by a single crew. **b.** An area in a train's sleeping car containing an upper and a lower berth. **14.** An army tactical unit smaller than a platoon and larger than a squad. **15.** A unit of vessels or aircraft within a division of armed forces. **16.** One of two or more vehicles, such as a bus or train, given the same route and schedule, often used to carry extra passengers. **17.a.** The character (§) used in printing to mark the beginning of a section. **b.** This character used as the fourth in a series of reference marks for footnotes. **—section** *tr.v.* **-tioned, -tion·ing, -tions. 1.** To separate or divide into parts. **2.** To cut or divide (tissue) surgically. **3.** To shade or crosshatch (part of a drawing) to indicate sections. [Middle English *seccioun,* from Old French, from Latin *sectiō, sectiōn-,* from *sectus,* past participle of *secāre,* to cut. See **sek-** in Appendix.]

sec·tion·al (sĕk′shə-nəl) *adj. Abbr.* **sect. 1.** Of, relating to, or characteristic of a particular district. **2.** Composed of or divided into component sections. **—sectional** *n.* A piece of furniture made up of sections that can be used separately or together. **—sec′tion·al·ly** *adv.*

sec·tion·al·ism (sĕk′shə-nə-lĭz′əm) *n.* Excessive devotion to local interests and customs. **—sec′tion·al·ist** *n.*

sec·tion·al·ize (sĕk′shə-nə-līz′) *tr.v.* **-ized, -iz·ing, -iz·es.** To divide into sections, especially into geographic sections. **—sec′tion·al·i·za′tion** (sĕk′shə-nə-lĭ-zā′shən) *n.*

Sec·tion Eight (sĕk′shən) *n.* **1.** A U.S. Army discharge based on military assessment of unfitness or character traits deemed undesirable. **2.** *Slang.* A soldier given such a discharge. [After *Section VIII* of World War II U.S. Army Regulation 615–360, which provided for the discharge of those deemed unfit for military service.]

section gang *n.* A work crew assigned to a section of railroad track.

section hand *n.* A laborer assigned to a section gang.

sec·tor (sĕk′tər, -tôr′) *n. Abbr.* **sec. 1.** *Mathematics.* **a.** The portion of a circle bounded by two radii and the included arc. **b.** A measuring instrument consisting of two graduated arms hinged together at one end. **2.a.** A division of a defensive position for which one military unit is responsible. **b.** A division of an offensive military position. **3.** A part or division, as of a city or a national economy: *the manufacturing sector; the private sector.* **4.** *Computer Science.* A bit or a set of bits on a magnetic storage device making up the smallest addressable unit of information. **—sector** *tr.v.* **-tored, -tor·ing, -tors.** To divide (something) into sectors. [Late Latin, from Latin, cutter, from *sectus,* past participle of *secāre,* to cut. See **sek-** in Appendix.] **—sec·to′ri·al** (-tôr′ē-əl, -tōr′-) *adj.*

sec·u·lar (sĕk′yə-lər) *adj.* **1.** Worldly rather than spiritual. **2.** Not specifically relating to religion or to a religious body: *secular music.* **3.** Relating to or advocating secularism. **4.** Not bound by monastic restrictions, especially not belonging to a religious order. Used of the clergy. **5.** Occurring or observed once in an age or a century. **6.** Lasting from century to century. **—secular** *n.* **1.** A member of the secular clergy. **2.** A layperson. [Middle English, from Old French *seculer,* from Late Latin *saeculāris,* from Latin, of an age, from *saeculum,* generation, age.] **—sec′u·lar·ly** *adv.*

secular humanism *n.* **1.** An outlook or a philosophy that advocates human rather than religious values. **2.** Secularism. **—secular humanist** *adj. & n.*

sec·u·lar·ism (sĕk′yə-lə-rĭz′əm) *n.* **1.** Religious skepticism or indifference. **2.** The view that religious considerations should be excluded from civil affairs or public education. **—sec′u·lar·ist** *n.* **—sec′u·lar·is′tic** *adj.*

sec·u·lar·i·ty (sĕk′yə-lăr′ĭ-tē) *n., pl.* **-ties. 1.** The condition or quality of being secular. **2.** Something secular.

sec·u·lar·ize (sĕk′yə-lə-rīz′) *tr.v.* **-ized, -iz·ing, -iz·es. 1.** To transfer from ecclesiastical or religious to civil or lay use or ownership. **2.** To draw away from religious orientation; make worldly. **3.** To lift the monastic restrictions from (a member of the clergy). **—sec′u·lar·i·za′tion** (-lər-ĭ-zā′shən) *n.*

se·cund (sē′kŭnd′, sĭ-kŭnd′) *adj. Botany & Zoology.* Arranged on or turned to one side of an axis. [Latin *secundus,* following. See **sekʷ-¹** in Appendix.]

se·cun·dines (sē-kŭn′dīnz′, sĕk′ən-dīnz′) *pl.n.* The afterbirth. [Middle English *secundinas,* from Late Latin *secundīnae,* from *secundus,* following. See **sekʷ-¹** in Appendix.]

se·cure (sĭ-kyŏŏr′) *adj.* **-cur·er, -cur·est. 1.** Free from danger or attack: *a secure fortress.* **2.** Free from risk of loss; safe: *Her jewels were secure in the vault.* **3.** Free from the risk of being intercepted or listened to by unauthorized persons: *Only one telephone line in the embassy was secure.* **4.** Free from fear, anxiety, or doubt. **5.a.** Not likely to fail or give way; stable: *a secure stepladder.* **b.** Firmly fastened: *a secure lock.* **6.** Reliable; dependable: *secure investments.* **7.** Assured; certain: *With three goals in the first period they had a secure victory, but somehow they lost.* **8.** *Archaic.* Careless or overconfident. **—secure** *tr.v.* **-cured, -cur·ing, -cures. 1.** To guard from danger or risk of loss: *The troops secured the area before the civilians were allowed to return.* **2.** To make firm or tight; fasten. See Synonyms at **fasten. 3.** To make certain; ensure: *Despite making several good*

ă pat	oi boy
ā pay	ou out
âr care	ŏŏ took
ä father	ōō boot
ĕ pet	ŭ cut
ē be	ûr urge
ĭ pit	th thin
ī pie	*th* this
îr pier	hw which
ŏ pot	zh vision
ō toe	ə about, item
ô paw	♦ regionalism

Stress marks: **′** (primary); ′ (secondary), as in **dictionary** (dĭk′shə-nĕr′ē)

jokes, he could not secure the goodwill of the audience. **4.a.** To guarantee payment of (a loan, for example). **b.** To guarantee payment to (a creditor). **5.** To get possession of; acquire: *secured a job.* **6.** To capture or confine: *They secured the suspect in the squad car.* **7.** To bring about; effect: *secured release of the hostages.* **8.** To protect or ensure the privacy or secrecy of (a telephone line, for example). [Latin *sēcūrus* : *sē-*, without; see **s(w)e-** in Appendix + *cūra*, care; see CURE.] **—se·cur′a·ble** *adj.* **—se·cure′ly** *adv.* **—se·cure′ment** *n.* **—se·cure′ness** *n.* **—se·cur′er** *n.*

Se·cu·ri·ties and Exchange Commission (sĭ-kyo͝or′ĭ-tēz) *n. Abbr.* **SEC** A U.S. government agency that supervises the exchange of securities so as to protect investors against malpractice.

se·cu·ri·tize (sĭ-kyo͝or′ĭ-tīz′) *tr.v.* **-tized, -tiz·ing, -tiz·es.** To buy (loans, such as mortgages) from lenders, arrange them in groups, and issue bonds on the groups.

se·cu·ri·ty (sĭ-kyo͝or′ĭ-tē) *n., pl.* **-ties.** *Abbr.* **sec.** **1.** Freedom from risk or danger; safety. **2.** Freedom from doubt, anxiety, or fear; confidence. **3.** Something that gives or assures safety, as: **a.** A group or department of private guards: *Call building security if a visitor acts suspicious.* **b.** Measures adopted by a government to prevent espionage, sabotage, or attack. **c.** Measures adopted, as by a business or homeowner, to prevent a crime such as burglary or assault: *Security was lax at the firm's smaller plant.* **d.** Measures adopted to prevent escape: *Security in the prison is very tight.* **4.** *Computer Science.* **a.** The level to which a program or device is safe from unauthorized use. **b.** Prevention of unauthorized use of a program or device. **5.** Something deposited or given as assurance of the fulfillment of an obligation; a pledge. **6.** One who undertakes to fulfill the obligation of another; a surety. **7.** A document indicating ownership or creditorship; a stock certificate or bond. [Middle English *securite*, from Old French, from Latin *sēcūritās*, from *sēcūrus*, secure. See SECURE.]

security blanket *n.* **1.** A blanket or toy carried by a child to reduce anxiety. **2.** *Informal.* Something that dispels anxiety.

Se·cu·ri·ty Council (sĭ-kyo͝or′ĭ-tē) *n. Abbr.* **SC** The permanent peacekeeping organ of the United Nations, composed of five permanent members (China, France, the Soviet Union, the United Kingdom, and the United States) and ten elected members.

security guard *n.* A person hired by a private organization to guard a physical plant and maintain order.

secy. *abbr.* Secretary.

sed. *abbr.* **1.** Sediment. **2.** Sedimentation.

Se·da·lia (sĭ-dăl′yə). A city of central Missouri east-southeast of Kansas City. It is a processing center. Population, 20,927.

se·dan (sĭ-dăn′) *n.* **1.** A closed automobile having two or four doors and a front and rear seat. **2.** A portable enclosed chair for one person, having poles in the front and rear and carried by two other people. In this sense, also called *sedan chair.* [Origin unknown.]

Se·dan (sĭ-dăn′, sə-däN′). A town of northeast France on the Meuse River near the Belgian border. It was the site of the decisive defeat and surrender of Napoleon III (September 2, 1870) in the Franco-Prussian War. Population, 23,477.

Se·dar·im (sĭ-där′ĭm, sĕ-dä-rēm′) *n. Judaism.* A plural of **Seder.**

se·date¹ (sĭ-dāt′) *adj.* Serenely deliberate, composed, and dignified in character or manner. See Synonyms at **serious.** [Latin *sēdātus*, past participle of *sēdāre*, to settle, calm. See **sed-** in Appendix.] **—se·date′ly** *adv.* **—se·date′ness** *n.*

se·date² (sĭ-dāt′) *tr.v.* **-dat·ed, -dat·ing, -dates.** To administer a sedative to; calm or relieve by means of a sedative drug. [Back-formation from SEDATIVE and SEDATION.]

se·da·tion (sĭ-dā′shən) *n.* **1.** Reduction of anxiety, stress, irritability, or excitement by administration of a sedative agent or drug. **2.** The state or condition induced by a sedative. [Middle English *sedacioun*, from Old French *sedation*, from Latin *sēdātiō*, *sēdātiōn-*, from *sēdātus*, past participle of *sēdāre*, to calm. See SEDATE¹.]

sed·a·tive (sĕd′ə-tĭv) *adj.* Having a soothing, calming, or tranquilizing effect; reducing or relieving anxiety, stress, irritability, or excitement. **—sedative** *n.* An agent or a drug having a soothing, calming, or tranquilizing effect. [Middle English, from Old French *sedatif*, from Medieval Latin *sēdātīvus*, from Latin *sēdātus*, past participle of *sēdāre*, to calm. See SEDATE¹.]

sed·en·tar·y (sĕd′n-tĕr′ē) *adj.* **1.** Characterized by or requiring much sitting: *a sedentary job.* **2.** Accustomed to sitting or to taking little exercise. **3.** Remaining or living in one area, as certain birds; not migratory. **4.** Attached to a surface and not moving freely, as a barnacle. [French *sédentaire*, from Old French, from Latin *sedentārius*, from *sedēns*, *sedent-*, present participle of *sedēre*, to sit. See **sed-** in Appendix.] **—sed′en·tar′i·ly** (-târ′ə-lē) *adv.* **—sed′en·tar′i·ness** *n.*

Se·der (sā′dər) *n., pl.* **Se·ders** or **Se·dar·im** (sĭ-där′ĭm, sĕ-dä-rēm′). *Judaism.* The feast commemorating the exodus of the Jews from Egypt, celebrated on the first two nights of Passover. [Hebrew *sēder*, order, arrangement, Seder.]

Seder

se·der·unt (sə-dîr′ənt, -dĕr′-) *n.* A prolonged session, as for discussion. [From Latin *sēdērunt*, third person pl. perfect tense of *sedēre*, to sit. See **sed-** in Appendix.]

sedge (sĕj) *n.* Any of numerous grasslike plants of the family Cyperaceae, having solid stems, leaves in three vertical rows, and spikelets of inconspicuous flowers, with each flower subtended by a scalelike bract. [Middle English *segge*, from Old English *secg.* See **sek-** in Appendix.]

Sedge·moor (sĕj′mo͝or′, -môr′, -mōr′). A marshy tract in southwest England where the forces of James II defeated the Duke of Monmouth (June 6, 1685).

se·di·le (sĭ-dī′lē) *n., pl.* **se·di·lia** (-dĭl′yə, -dĭl′ē-ə). One of a set of seats, usually three, provided in some Roman Catholic and Anglican churches for the use of the presiding clergy, traditionally placed on the epistle side of the choir near the altar, and in Gothic-style churches often built into the wall. [Latin *sedīle*, seat, from *sedēre*, to sit. See **sed-** in Appendix.]

sed·i·ment (sĕd′ə-mənt) *n. Abbr.* **sed.** **1.** Material that settles to the bottom of a liquid; lees. **2.** Solid fragments of inorganic or organic material that come from the weathering of rock and are carried and deposited by wind, water, or ice. [Latin *sedimentum*, act of settling, from *sedēre*, to sit, settle. See **sed-** in Appendix.]

sed·i·men·ta·ry (sĕd′ə-mĕn′tə-rē, -mĕn′trē) also **sed·i·men·tal** (-mĕn′tl) *adj.* **1.** Of, containing, resembling, or derived from sediment. **2.** *Geology.* Of or relating to rocks formed by the deposition of sediment.

sed·i·men·ta·tion (sĕd′ə-mən-tā′shən, -mĕn-) *n. Abbr.* **sed.** The act or process of depositing sediment.

sed·i·men·tol·o·gy (sĕd′ə-mən-tŏl′ə-jē, -mĕn-) *n.* The science that deals with the description, classification, and origin of sedimentary rock. **—sed′i·men′to·log′ic** (-mĕn′tl-ŏj′ĭk), **sed′i·men′to·log′i·cal** (-ĭ-kəl) *adj.* **—sed′i·men·tol′o·gist** *n.*

se·di·tion (sĭ-dĭsh′ən) *n.* **1.** Conduct or language inciting rebellion against the authority of a state. **2.** Insurrection; rebellion. [Middle English *sedicioun*, violent party strife, from Old French *sedition*, from Latin *sēditiō*, *sēditiōn-* : *sēd-*, *sē-*, apart; see **s(w)e-** in Appendix + *itiō*, act of going (from *itus*, past participle of *īre*, to go; see **ei-** in Appendix).] **—se·di′tion·ist** *n.*

se·di·tious (sĭ-dĭsh′əs) *adj.* **1.** Of, relating to, or having the nature of sedition. **2.** Given to or guilty of engaging in or promoting sedition. See Synonyms at **insubordinate.** **—se·di′tious·ly** *adv.* **—se·di′tious·ness** *n.*

se·duce (sĭ-do͞os′, -dyo͞os′) *tr.v.* **-duced, -duc·ing, -duc·es.** **1.** To lead away from duty, principles, or proper conduct. See Synonyms at **lure.** **2.** To induce to engage in sex. **3.a.** To entice into a desired state or position. **b.** To win over; attract. [Middle English *seduisen*, from Old French *seduire*, *seduis-*, alteration (influenced by Medieval Latin *sēdūcere*, to lead astray, from Latin, to lead away : *sē-*, apart; see **s(w)e-** in Appendix + *dūcere*, to lead) of *suduire*, to seduce, from Latin *subdūcere*, to withdraw : *sub-*, sub- + *dūcere*, to lead; see **deuk-** in Appendix.] **—se·duce′a·ble, se·duc′i·ble** *adj.* **—se·duc′er** *n.*

se·duce·ment (sĭ-do͞os′mənt, -dyo͞os′-) *n.* **1.** Seduction. **2.** Something that seduces.

se·duc·tion (sĭ-dŭk′shən) *n.* **1.a.** The act of seducing. **b.** The condition of being seduced. **2.** Something that seduces or has the qualities to seduce; an enticement. [Latin *sēductiō*, *sēductiōn-*, from *sēductus*, past participle of *sēdūcere*, to lead astray. See SEDUCE.]

se·duc·tive (sĭ-dŭk′tĭv) *adj.* Tending to seduce: *"his sad and fastidious but ever seductive Irish voice"* (John Fowles). **—se·duc′tive·ly** *adv.* **—se·duc′tive·ness** *n.*

se·duc·tress (sĭ-dŭk′trĭs) *n.* A woman who seduces. See Usage Note at **-ess.**

sed·u·lous (sĕj′ə-ləs) *adj.* Persevering and constant in effort or application; assiduous. See Synonyms at **busy.** [From Latin *sēdulus*, from *sēdulō*, zealously : *sē*, without; see **s(w)e-** in Appendix + *dolō*, ablative of *dolus*, trickery (probably from Greek *dolos*, cunning; see **del-²** in Appendix).] **—sed′u·lous·ly** *adv.* **—sed′u·lous·ness, se·du′li·ty** (sĭ-do͞o′lĭ-tē, -dyo͞o′-) *n.*

se·dum (sē′dəm) *n.* Any of numerous plants of the genus *Sedum*, having thick, fleshy leaves. [Middle English *cedum*, from Latin *sedum*, houseleek.]

see¹ (sē) *v.* **saw** (sô), **seen** (sēn), **see·ing, sees.** —*tr.* **1.** To perceive with the eye. **2.a.** To apprehend as if with the eye. **b.** To detect by means analogous to use of the eye: *an electronic surveillance camera that saw the activity in the embassy yard.* **3.** To have a mental image of; visualize: *They could still see their hometown as it once was.* **4.** To understand; comprehend: *I see your point.* **5.** To consider to be; regard: *Many saw her as a world leader.* **6.** To believe possible; imagine: *I don't see him as a teacher.* **7.** To foresee: *I see great things for that child.* **8.** To know through firsthand experience; undergo: *"He saw some service on the king's side"* (Tucker Brooke). **9.** To give rise to or be characterized by: *"Her long reign saw the heyday of verbal humor"* (Richard Kain). *"The 1930s saw the development of sulfa drugs and penicillin"* (Gregg Easterbrook). **10.** To find out; ascertain: *Please see who's knocking.* **11.** *Abbr.* **s.** To refer to; read: *Persons interested in the book's history should see page one of the preface.* **12.** To take note of; recognize: *She sees only the good aspects of the organization.* **13.** To meet or be in the company of: *I saw all my aunts and uncles at the reunion.* **14.** To share the companionship of often or regularly: *He's been seeing the same woman for eight years.* **15.a.** To visit socially; call on. **b.** To visit for consultation: *You ought to see your doctor more frequently.* **16.** To admit or receive, as for consultation or a social visit: *The doctor will see you now.* **17.** To attend; view: *Let's see a* *movie.* **18.** To escort; attend: *I'm seeing Nellie home.* **19.** To make sure; take care: *See that it gets done right away.* **20.** *Games.* **a.** To meet (a bet) in card games. **b.** To meet the bet of (another player). —*intr.* **1.** To have the power to perceive with or as if with the eye. **2.** To understand; comprehend. **3.** To consider: *Let's see, which suitcase should we take?* **4. a.** To go and look: *She had to see for herself and went into the garage.* **b.** To ascertain; find out: *We probably can do it, but we'll have to see.* **5.** To have foresight: *"No man can see to the end of time"* (John F. Kennedy). **6.** To take note. ***—phrasal verbs.*** **see about. 1.** To attend to. **2.** To investigate. **see after.** To take care of: *Please see after the children while I'm gone.* **see off.** To take leave of (someone): *saw the guests off at the door; went to the airport to see us off.* **see out.** To escort (a guest) to the door: *Will you please see Ms. Smith out?* **see through. 1.** To understand the true character or nature of: *We saw through his superficial charm.* **2.** To provide unstinting support, cooperation, or management in good times and bad: *We'll see you through until you finish your college education. I saw the project through and then resigned.* **see to.** To attend to: *See to the chores, will you?* ***—idiom.*** **see red.** *Informal.* To be extremely angry. [Middle English *sen,* from Old English *sēon.* See **sek**[w]**-**[2] in Appendix.]

SYNONYMS: *see, behold, note, notice, espy, descry, observe, contemplate, survey, view, perceive, discern, remark.* These verbs refer to being or becoming visually or mentally aware of something. *See,* the most general, can mean merely to use the faculty of sight but more often implies recognition, understanding, or appreciation: *"We must . . . give the image of what we actually see"* (Paul Cézanne). *"If I have seen further (than . . . Descartes) it is by standing upon the shoulders of Giants"* (Isaac Newton). *Behold* more strongly implies awareness of what is seen: *"My heart leaps up when I behold/A rainbow in the sky"* (William Wordsworth). *Note* and *notice* suggest close observation and a rather detailed visual or mental impression; *note* in particular implies careful, systematic recording in the mind: *Be careful to note where the road turns left. I have noted and overridden your protests. She didn't notice the run in her stocking until she had arrived at the office. I notice that you're out of sorts. Espy* and *descry* both stress acuteness of sight that permits the detection of something distant, partially hidden, or obscure: *"espied the misspelled Latin word in* [the] *letter"* (Los Angeles Times); *"the lighthouse, which can be descried from a distance"* (Michael Strauss). *Observe* emphasizes careful, closely directed attention: *"I saw the pots . . . red-hot . . . and observed that they did not crack at all"* (Daniel Defoe). *Contemplate* implies looking attentively and thoughtfully: *"It is interesting to contemplate an entangled bank, clothed with many plants of many kinds, with birds singing on the bushes"* (Charles Darwin). *Survey* stresses detailed, often comprehensive examination: *"Strickland looked away and idly surveyed the ceiling"* (W. Somerset Maugham). *View* usually suggests examination with a particular purpose in mind or in a special way: *The medical examiner viewed the victim's body. "He* [man] *viewed the crocodile as a thing sometimes to worship, but always to run away from"* (Thomas De Quincey). *Perceive* and *discern* both imply not only visual recognition but also mental comprehension; *perceive* is especially associated with insight, and *discern,* with the ability to distinguish, discriminate, and make judgments: *"We perceived a little girl coming towards us"* (Frederick Marryat). *"I plainly perceive* [that] *some objections remain"* (Edmund Burke). *Even with a magnifying glass I couldn't discern any imperfections in the porcelain. Many in the audience lack the background and taste to discern a good performance of the sonata from a bad one. Remark* suggests close attention and often an evaluation of what is noticed: *"Their assemblies afforded me daily opportunities of remarking characters and manners"* (Samuel Johnson).

see[2] (sē) *n.* **1.** The official seat, center of authority, jurisdiction, or office of a bishop. **2.** *Obsolete.* A cathedra. [Middle English, from Old French *se,* from Vulgar Latin **sedem,* from Latin *sēdēs,* seat. See **sed-** in Appendix.]

see·catch (sē′kăch′) *n., pl.* **-catch·ie** (-kăch′ē). The adult male fur seal of Alaska. [Russian *sekach,* from *sech,* to cut.]

seed (sēd) *n., pl.* **seeds** or **seed. 1.** A ripened plant ovule containing an embryo. **2.** A propagative part of a plant, as a tuber or spore. **3.** Seeds considered as a group. **4.** The seed-bearing stage of a plant. **5.** Something that resembles a seed, as a tiny bubble in a piece of glass or a small crystal added to a solution to start crystallization. **6.** A source or beginning; a germ. **7.** Offspring; progeny. **8.** Family stock; ancestry. **9.** Sperm; semen. **10.** A seed oyster or oysters; spat. **11.** *Sports.* A player who has been seeded for a tournament, often at a given rank: *a top seed.* **—seed** *v.* **seed·ed, seed·ing, seeds.** —*tr.* **1.** To plant seeds in (land, for example); sow. **2.** To plant in soil. **3.** To remove the seeds from (fruit). **4.** *Meteorology.* To sprinkle (a cloud) with particles, as of silver iodide, in order to disperse it or produce rain. **5.** *Sports.* **a.** To arrange (the drawing for positions in a tournament) so that the more skilled contestants meet in the later rounds. **b.** To rank (a contestant) in this way. **6.** To help (a business, for example) in its early development. —*intr.* **1.** To sow seed. **2.** To go to seed. **—seed** *adj.* **1.** Set aside for planting a new crop: *seed corn; seed wheat.* **2.** Intended to help in early stages: *provided seed capital for a fledgling business.* ***—idiom.*** **go** (or **run**) **to seed. 1.** To pass into the seed-bearing stage. **2.** To become weak or devitalized; deteriorate: *The old neighborhood has gone to seed.* [Middle English, from Old English *sǣd, sēd.* See **sē-** in Appendix.]

seed·bed (sēd′bĕd′) *n.* **1.** A bed of soil cultivated for planting seeds. **2.** An area or source of growth or gradual manifestation: *a seedbed of revolution.*

seed cake *n.* A sweet cake or cookie containing aromatic seeds.

seed coat *n. Botany.* The outer protective covering of a seed.

seed·eat·er (sēd′ē′tər) *n.* Any bird that feeds primarily on seeds, especially a finch of the genus *Sporophila.*

seed·er (sē′dər) *n.* **1.** A machine or an implement used for planting seeds. **2.** A machine or implement used to remove the seeds from fruit. **3.** One that seeds clouds.

seed leaf *n. Botany.* See **cotyledon** (sense 1).

seed·ling (sēd′lĭng) *n.* A young plant that is grown from a seed.

seed oyster *n.* A young oyster, especially one suitable for transplanting to another bed; a spat.

seed pearl *n.* A very small, often imperfect pearl.

seed plant *n.* A seed-bearing plant.

seed·pod (sēd′pŏd′) *n.* See **pod**[1] (sense 1).

seed-snipe (sēd′snīp′) *n., pl.* **seed-snipe** or **-snipes.** Any of several short-legged South American birds of the family Thinocoridae, related to the plover and snipe but resembling a small quail.

seed stock *n.* **1.** A supply of seed for planting. **2.** A source of new entities: *a seed stock of salmon in the river.*

seed tick *n.* The tiny six-legged larva of a tick, smaller than the eight-legged nymph.

seed·time (sēd′tīm′) *n.* **1.** A time for planting seeds. **2.** A time of new growth or development.

seed weevil *n.* Any of various small beetles of the family Bruchidae whose larvae bore into and feed on the dried seeds of peas, beans, and similar plants.

seed·y (sē′dē) *adj.* **-i·er, -i·est. 1.** Having many seeds. **2.** Resembling seeds or a seed. **3.** Worn and shabby; unkempt: *"He was soiled and seedy and fragrant with gin"* (Mark Twain). **4.** Tired or sick; unwell. **5.** Somewhat disreputable; squalid: *a seedy hotel in a run-down neighborhood.* **—seed′i·ly** *adv.* **—seed′i·ness** *n.*

See·ger (sē′gər), **Alan.** 1888–1916. American poet best known for "I Have a Rendezvous with Death" (1916). He was killed in action in World War I.

Seeger, Peter. Known as "Pete." Born 1919. American folk singer who was largely responsible for the revival of American folk music in the 1950's and 1960's. His songs, many of which have social or political themes, include "Where Have All the Flowers Gone" and "If I Had a Hammer."

see·ing (sē′ĭng) *conj.* Inasmuch as; in view of the fact: *Seeing that you're already at the door, I suppose I must invite you inside.*

See·ing Eye (sē′ĭng). A trademark used for a dog trained to lead a sightless person.

seek (sēk) *v.* **sought** (sôt), **seek·ing, seeks.** —*tr.* **1.** To try to locate or discover; search for. **2.** To endeavor to obtain or reach: *seek a college education.* **3.** To go to or toward: *Water seeks its own level.* **4.** To inquire for; request: *seek directions from a police officer.* **5.** To try; endeavor: *seek to do good.* **6.** *Obsolete.* To explore. —*intr.* To make a search or an investigation: *Seek and you will find.* [Middle English *sechen, seken,* from Old English *sēcan.* See **săg-** in Appendix.]

SYNONYMS: *seek, hunt, quest, search.* The central meaning shared by these verbs is "to make an effort to find something": *seeking information; hunting through the telephone book for a number; questing after treasure; searched his face for his reaction.*

seek·er (sē′kər) *n.* **1.** One that seeks: *a seeker of the truth.* **2.** A device used in a moving object, especially a missile, that locates a target by detecting light, heat, or other radiation.

seel (sēl) *tr.v.* **seeled, seel·ing, seels.** To stitch closed the eyes of (a falcon). [Middle English *silen,* from Old French *cillier,* from Medieval Latin *ciliāre,* from Latin *cilium,* lower eyelid. See **kel-**[1] in Appendix.]

seem (sēm) *intr.v.* **seemed, seem·ing, seems. 1.** To give the impression of being; appear: *The child seems healthy, but the doctor is concerned.* **2.** To appear to one's own opinion or mind: *I can't seem to get the story straight.* **3.** To appear to be true, probable, or evident: *It seems you object to the plan. It seems like rain. He seems to have worked in sales for several years.* **4.** To appear to exist: *There seems no reason to postpone it.* [Middle English *semen,* from Old Norse *sœma,* to conform to, from *sœmr,* fitting. See **sem-**[1] in Appendix.]

SYNONYMS: *seem, appear, look.* The central meaning shared by these verbs is "to present the appearance of being": *seems angry; appears skeptical; looks happy.*

seem·ing (sē′mĭng) *adj.* Apparent; ostensible. **—seeming** *n.* Outward appearance; semblance. **—seem′ing·ly** *adv.* **—seem′ing·ness** *n.*

seem·ly (sēm′lē) *adj.* **-li·er, -li·est. 1.** Conforming to standards of conduct and good taste; suitable: *seemly behavior.* **2.** Of pleasing appearance; handsome. **—seemly** *adv.* In a seemly manner; suitably. [Middle English *semely,* from Old Norse *sœ-*

ă pat	oi boy
ā pay	ou out
âr care	ŏŏ took
ä father	ōō boot
ĕ pet	ŭ cut
ē be	ûr urge
ĭ pit	th thin
ī pie	*th* this
îr pier	hw which
ŏ pot	zh vision
ō toe	ə about, item
ô paw	♦ regionalism

Stress marks: **′** (primary); ′ (secondary), as in **dictionary** (dĭk′shə-nĕr′ē)

Andrés Segovia

miligr, from *sœmr,* fitting. See **sem-**[1] in Appendix.] **—seem′li·ness** *n.*

seen (sēn) *v.* Past participle of **see**[1].

seep (sēp) *intr.v.* **seeped, seep·ing, seeps. 1.** To pass slowly through small openings or pores; ooze. **2.** To enter, depart, or become diffused gradually. **—seep** *n.* **1.** A spot where water or petroleum trickles out of the ground to form a pool. **2.** Seepage. [Alteration of dialectal *sipe.*]

seep·age (sē′pĭj) *n.* **1.** The act or process of seeping. **2.** A quantity of something that has seeped.

seer (sîr) *n.* **1.** (sē′ər). One that sees: *an inveterate seer of sights.* **2.** A clairvoyant. **3.** A prophet.

seer·ess (sîr′ĭs) *n.* A woman who acts as a prophet or clairvoyant.

seer·suck·er (sîr′sŭk′ər) *n.* A light, thin fabric, generally cotton or rayon, with a crinkled surface and a usually striped pattern. [Hindi *śīrśakar* : *shīroshakar* : *shīr,* milk (from Middle Persian) + *o,* and (from Middle Persian *u,* from Old Persian *utā*) + *shakar,* sugar (from Sanskrit *śarkarā,* from the resemblance of its smooth and rough stripes to the smooth surface of milk and bumpy texture of sugar).]

WORD HISTORY: Through its name, seersucker, a lightweight fabric for summer suits and dresses, gives us a glimpse at the history of India. The facts of the word's history are that it came into English from the East Indian language Hindi (*śīrśakar*). The word in Hindi was borrowed from the Persian compound *shīroshakar,* meaning literally "milk and sugar" but used in a figurative way for a striped linen garment. The Persian word *shakar,* "sugar," in turn came from Sanskrit *śarkarā.* Persian, Indian, English—clearly we are dealing with multiple cultural borrowing here, and the Persians did indeed borrow sugar and the word for sugar from India in the 6th century. During and after Tamerlane's invasion of India in the late 14th century, the opportunity for borrowing Persian things and words such as *shīr-o-shakar* was present, since the Mongol Turk Tamerlane incorporated Persia as well as India into his empire. It then remained for the English during the 18th century, when the East India Company and England were moving toward supremacy in India, to borrow the material and its name *seersucker* (first recorded in 1722 in the form *Sea Sucker*) from an Indian language.

♦ **see·saw** (sē′sô′) *n.* **1.** A long plank balanced on a central fulcrum so that with a person riding on each end, one end goes up as the other goes down. Also called ♦*dandle,* ♦*dandle board,* ♦*teedle board,* ♦*teeter,* ♦*teeterboard,* ♦*teeter-totter,* ♦*tilt,* ♦*tilting board.* See Regional Note at **teeter-totter. 2.** The act or game of riding a seesaw. **3.** A back-and-forth or up-and-down movement, as of the lead between two contesting parties. **—seesaw** *intr.v.* **-sawed, -saw·ing, -saws. 1.** To play on a seesaw. **2.** To move back and forth or up and down. [Reduplication of SAW[1].]

seethe (sēth) *intr.v.* **seethed, seeth·ing, seethes. 1.** To churn and foam as if boiling. **2. a.** To be in a state of turmoil or ferment: *The nation seethed with suppressed revolutionary activity.* **b.** To be violently excited or agitated: *I seethed with anger over the insult.* See Synonyms at **boil**[1]. **3.** *Archaic.* To come to a boil. [Middle English *sethen,* to boil, from Old English *sēothan.*] **—seethe** *n.*

see-through (sē′thrōō′) *adj.* Transparent.

Se·fe·ri·a·des (sĕ-fĕ′rē-ä′*th*ēs), **Giorgos Stylianou.** Pen name George Seferis. 1900–1971. Greek poet and diplomat whose poetic works are imbued with references to Greek history and mythology. He won the 1963 Nobel Prize for literature.

Se·gal (sē′gəl), **George.** Born 1924. American sculptor known for his realistic plaster casts of people in ordinary situations.

Se·ges·ta (sĭ-jĕs′tə, sĕ-jĕs′tä). An ancient city of northwest Sicily near modern-day Alcamo. Traditionally a Trojan colony, it was a Carthaginian dependency after c. 400 B.C. but declined during the first century.

seg·ment (sĕg′mənt) *n.* **1.** Any of the parts into which something can be divided: *segments of the community; a segment of a television program.* **2.** *Mathematics.* **a.** The portion of a line between any two points on the line. **b.** The area bounded by a chord and the arc of a curve subtended by the chord. **c.** The portion of a sphere cut off by two parallel planes. **3.** *Biology.* A clearly differentiated subdivision of an organism or part, such as a metamere. **—segment** (sĕg-mĕnt′) *tr. & intr.v.* **-ment·ed, -ment·ing, -ments.** To divide or become divided into segments. [Latin *segmentum,* from *secāre,* to cut. See **sek-** in Appendix.] **—seg′men·tar′y** (-mən-tĕr′ē) *adj.*

seg·men·tal (sĕg-mĕn′tl) *adj.* **1.** Of or relating to segments. **2.** Divided or organized into segments. **—seg·men′tal·ly** *adv.*

seg·men·ta·tion (sĕg′mən-tā′shən, -mĕn-) *n.* **1.** Division into segments. **2.** *Embryology.* See **cleavage** (sense 4a).

segmentation cavity *n.* See **blastocoel.**

seg·ment·ed (sĕg′mĕn′tĭd, sĕg-mĕn′-) *adj.* Divided into or made up of distinct segments.

se·gno (sā′nyō) *n., pl.* **-gnos.** *Music.* A notational sign, especially the sign marking the beginning or the end of a repeat. [Italian, from Latin *signum,* sign. See **sekʷ-**[1] in Appendix.]

se·go (sē′gō) *n., pl.* **-gos.** The edible, succulent bulb of the sego lily. [Southern Paiute *sigho'o.*]

sego lily *n.* A western North American plant *(Calochortus nuttallii)* having showy, variously colored flowers.

Se·go·vi·a (sĭ-gō′vē-ə, sĕ-gô′vyä). A city of central Spain north-northwest of Madrid. An important Roman town, it was held sporadically by the Moors from 714 to 1079. Population, 53,005.

Segovia, Andrés. 1893?–1987. Spanish guitarist who spurred interest in the guitar as an instrument for classical music through his arrangements of the works of Bach and Handel.

seg·re·ga·ble (sĕg′rĭ-gə-bəl) *adj.* **1.** That can be segregated: *segregable items in a budget.* **2.** *Genetics.* Able to undergo segregation: *segregable characters.*

seg·re·gant (sĕg′rĭ-gənt) *Genetics. adj.* Differing from either parent as a result of segregation: *a segregant genotype.* **—segregant** *n.* A segregant type or organism. Also called *segregate.*

seg·re·gate (sĕg′rĭ-gāt′) *v.* **-gat·ed, -gat·ing, -gates.** *—tr.* **1.** To separate or isolate from others or from a main body or group. See Synonyms at **isolate. 2.** To impose the separation of (a race or class) from the rest of society. *—intr.* **1.** To become separated from a main body or mass. **2.** To practice a policy of racial segregation. **3.** *Genetics.* To undergo genetic segregation. **—segregate** (-gĭt, -gāt′) *adj.* Separated; isolated. **—segregate** (-gĭt, -gāt′) *n.* **1.** One that is or has been segregated. **2.** *Genetics.* See **segregant.** [Latin *sēgregāre, sēgregāt-* : *sē-,* apart; see **s(w)e-** in Appendix + *grex, greg-,* flock; see **ger-** in Appendix.] **—seg′re·ga′tive** *adj.* **—seg′re·ga′tor** *n.*

seg·re·ga·tion (sĕg′rĭ-gā′shən) *n.* **1.** The act or process of segregating or the condition of being segregated. **2.** The policy and practice of imposing the social separation of races, as in schools, housing, and industry, especially so as to practice discrimination against people of color in a predominantly white society. **3.** *Genetics.* The separation of paired alleles especially during meiosis, so that the members of each pair of alleles appear in different gametes.

seg·re·ga·tion·ist (sĕg′rĭ-gā′shə-nĭst) *n.* One that advocates or practices a policy of racial segregation. **—seg′re·ga′tion·ist** *adj.*

se·gue (sĕg′wā′, sā′gwā′) *intr.v.* **-gued, -gu·ing, -gues. 1.** *Music.* To make a transition directly from one section or theme to another. **2.** To move smoothly and unhesitatingly from one state, condition, situation, or element to another: *"Daylight segued into dusk"* (Susan Dworski). [From Italian, there follows, third-person sing. present tense of *seguire,* to follow, from Vulgar Latin **sequere,* from Latin *sequī.* See **sekʷ-**[1] in Appendix.]

se·gui·dil·la (sĕg′ə-dē′yə, -dēl′yə, sā′gə-, sĕ′gē-*th*ē′lyä) *n.* **1.** A Spanish stanza form of four to seven short verses. **2. a.** A lively Spanish dance. **b.** The music for this dance, in 3/4 time. [Spanish, diminutive of *seguida,* sequence, from feminine past participle of *seguir,* to follow, from Vulgar Latin **sequere,* from Latin *sequī.* See **sekʷ-**[1] in Appendix.]

Se·guin (sĭ-gēn′). A city of south-central Texas east-northeast of San Antonio. It was founded in 1831. Population, 17,854.

Se·gu·ra (sā-gŏŏr′ə, sĕ-gōō′rä). A river, about 322 km (200 mi) long, of southeast Spain flowing generally eastward to the Mediterranean Sea.

sei (sā) *n., pl.* **seis.** A sei whale. [From Norwegian *seihval* : *sei,* coalfish (from Old Norse *seidh*) + *hval,* whale (from Old Norse *hvalr*).]

sei·cen·to (sā-chĕn′tō) *n.* The 17th century with reference to Italian literature and art. [Italian, from *(mil)seicento,* (one thousand) six hundred : *sei,* six (from Latin *sex;* see **s(w)eks** in Appendix) + *cento,* hundred (from Latin *centum;* see **dekm̥** in Appendix).]

seiche (sāsh, sĕch) *n.* A wave that oscillates in lakes, bays, or gulfs from a few minutes to a few hours as a result of seismic or atmospheric disturbances. [French dialectal, exposed lake bottom, probably from French *sèche,* feminine of *sec,* dry. See SEC[1].]

sei·del (sīd′l, zīd′l) *n.* A beer mug. [German, from Middle High German *sīdel,* from Latin *situla,* bucket.]

Seid·litz powder also **Seid·litz powders** (sĕd′lĭts) *n.* A mixture of tartaric acid, sodium bicarbonate, and potassium sodium tartrate, used as a mild cathartic by dissolving in water and drinking. [After *Seidlitz* (Sedlec), a village of northwest Czechoslovakia that is a site of large mineral springs.]

Sei·fert (sī′fərt), **Jaroslav.** 1901–1986. Czech poet whose work often concerns political repression. He won the 1984 Nobel Prize for literature.

seign·eur (sān-yûr′, sĕn-) *n.* **1.** A man of rank, especially a feudal lord in the ancien régime. **2.** In Canada, a man who owned a large estate originally held by a feudal grant from the king of France. **3.** Used as a form of address for such a man. [French, from Old French *seignor,* from Vulgar Latin **senior.* See SEIGNIOR.] **—seign·eur′i·al** *adj.*

seign·eur·y (sān′yə-rē, sĕn′-) *n., pl.* **-ies.** The power, rank, or estate of a seigneur.

seign·ior (sān-yôr′, sān′yôr′) *n.* **1.** A man of rank, especially a feudal lord. **2.** Used as a form of address for such a man. [Middle English *segnour,* from Old French *seignor,* from Vulgar Latin **senior,* from Latin, older, comparative of *senex, sen-,* old. See **sen-** in Appendix.] **—sei·gnio′ri·al** *adj.*

seign·ior·age (sān′yər-ĭj) *n.* Revenue or a profit taken from the minting of coins, usually the difference between the value of the bullion used and the face value of the coin. [Middle English *seigneurage,* from Old French, from *seignor,* seignior. See SEIGNIOR.]

seign·ior·y (sān′yə-rē) *n., pl.* **-ies.** The power, rank, or estate of a feudal lord. Also called *signory.* [Middle English *seigniorie,* from Old French, from *seignor,* seignior. See SEIGNIOR.]

seine (sān) *n.* A large fishing net made to hang vertically in the water by weights at the lower edge and floats at the top. **—seine** *v.* **seined, sein·ing, seines.** *—intr.* To fish with such a net. *—tr.* To fish for or catch with such a net. [Middle English, from Old English *segne,* from Germanic **sagina,* from Latin *sagēna,* from Greek *sagēnē.*] **—sein′er** *n.*

Seine (sān, sĕn). A river of northern France flowing about 772 km (480 mi) generally northwest to the **Bay of the Seine,** an inlet of the English Channel, near Le Havre. It has been an important commercial waterway since Roman times.

seise (sēz) *v.* Variant of **seize** (sense 6).

sei·sin also **sei·zin** (sē′zĭn) *n. Law.* **1.** Legal possession of land, as a freehold estate. **2.a.** The act or an instance of taking legal possession of land. **b.** Property thus possessed. [Middle English *seisine,* from Old French *saisine,* from *seisir,* to seize. See SEIZE.]

seism (sī′zəm) *n.* See **earthquake.** [Greek *seismos,* from *seiein,* to shake.]

seism– *pref.* Variant of **seismo–.**

seis·mic (sīz′mĭk) *adj.* **1.** Of, subject to, or caused by an earthquake or earth vibration. **2.** Earthshaking: *an issue of seismic proportions and ramifications.* **—seis′mi·cal·ly** *adv.* **—seis·mic′i·ty** (-mĭs′ĭ-tē) *n.*

seis·mism (sīz′mĭz′əm) *n.* The phenomena involved in earthquakes.

seismo– or **seism–** *pref.* Earthquake: *seismograph.* [Greek, from *seismos,* seism. See SEISM.]

seis·mo·gram (sīz′mə-grăm′) *n.* The record of an earth tremor made by a seismograph.

seis·mo·graph (sīz′mə-grăf′) *n.* An instrument for automatically detecting and recording the intensity, direction, and duration of a movement of the ground, especially of an earthquake. **—seis·mog′ra·pher** (sīz-mŏg′rə-fər) *n.* **—seis′mo·graph′ic** (-grăf′ĭk), **seis′mo·graph′i·cal** (-ĭ-kəl) *adj.* **—seis·mog′ra·phy** *n.*

seis·mol·o·gy (sīz-mŏl′ə-jē) *n.* The geophysical science of earthquakes and the mechanical properties of the earth. **—seis′mo·log′ic** (-mə-lŏj′ĭk), **seis′mo·log′i·cal** (-ĭ-kəl) *adj.* **—seis′mo·log′i·cal·ly** *adv.* **—seis·mol′o·gist** *n.*

seis·mom·e·ter (sīz-mŏm′ĭ-tər) *n.* A detecting device that receives seismic impulses. **—seis′mo·met′ric** (-mə-mĕt′rĭk), **seis′mo·met′ri·cal** (-rĭ-kəl) *adj.*

seis·mom·e·try (sīz-mŏm′ĭ-trē) *n.* The scientific study and recording of earthquakes.

seis·mo·scope (sīz′mə-skōp′) *n.* An instrument that indicates the occurrence or time of occurrence of an earthquake. **—seis′mo·scop′ic** (-skŏp′ĭk) *adj.*

sei·sor (sē′zər, -zôr′) *n. Law.* Variant of **seizor.**

sei whale *n.* A rorqual *(Balaenoptera borealis)* that is blue-black above and white below, that grows up to about 55 feet (17 meters) in length, and that is found in all the oceans, with the greatest number living in Antarctic waters. [From Norwegian *seihval.* See SEI.]

seize (sēz) *v.* **seized, seiz·ing, seiz·es.** *—tr.* **1.** To grasp suddenly and forcibly; take or grab: *seize a sword.* **2.a.** To grasp with the mind; apprehend: *seize an idea and develop it to the fullest extent.* **b.** To possess oneself of (something): *seize an opportunity.* **3.a.** To have a sudden, overwhelming effect on: *a heinous crime that seized the minds and emotions of the populace.* **b.** To overwhelm physically: *a person who was seized with a terminal disease.* **4.** To take into custody; capture. **5.** To take quick and forcible possession of; confiscate: *seize a cache of illegal drugs.* **6.** Also **seise** (sēz). **a.** To put (one) into possession of something. **b.** To vest ownership of a feudal property in. **7.** *Nautical.* To bind with turns of small line. *—intr.* **1.** To lay sudden or forcible hold of. **2.a.** To cohere or fuse with another part as a result of high pressure or temperature and restrict or prevent further motion or flow. **b.** To come to a halt: *The talks seized up and were rescheduled.* [Middle English *seisen,* from Old French *seisir,* to take possession, of Germanic origin.] **—seiz′a·ble** *adj.* **—seiz′er** *n.*

sei·zin (sē′zĭn) *n. Law.* Variant of **seisin.**

seiz·ing (sē′zĭng) *n. Nautical.* A binding of larger lines made with multiple turns of smaller line.

sei·zor also **sei·sor** (sē′zər, -zôr′) *n. Law.* One that takes seisin.

sei·zure (sē′zhər) *n.* **1.** The act or an instance of seizing or the condition of being seized. **2.** A sudden attack, spasm, or convulsion, as in epilepsy or another disorder. **3.** A sudden onset or sensation of feeling or emotion.

Sek·on·di-Ta·ko·ra·di (sĕk′ən-dē′tä-kə-rä′dē). A city of southwest Ghana on the Gulf of Guinea west-southwest of Accra. The two parts of the city developed around Dutch and English forts built in the 17th century. Population, 93,882.

sel. *abbr.* Select; selected; selectivity.

se·la·chi·an (sĭ-lā′kē-ən) *adj.* Of or belonging to the order Selachii of elasmobranch fishes that includes the sharks and in some classifications also the rays and skates. **—selachian** *n.* A member of this order. [Probably from New Latin *Selachiī,* order name, from Greek *selakhios,* cartilaginous, from *selakhos,* cartilaginous fish.]

se·la·dang (sĭ-lä′däng) *n.* See **gaur.** [Malay.]

se·lag·i·nel·la (sə-lăj′ə-nĕl′ə) *n.* Any of numerous fernlike, usually prostrate plants of the genus *Selaginella,* having small scalelike leaves and bearing spores. [New Latin *Selāginella,* genus name, from Latin *selāgō, selāgin-,* a plant resembling the savin.]

se·lah (sē′lə, sĕl′ə) *interj.* Used to conclude a verse in the Psalms. [Hebrew *selā.*]

sel·dom (sĕl′dəm) *adv.* Not often; infrequently or rarely. See Usage Note at **rarely. —seldom** *adj. Archaic.* Infrequent; rare. [Middle English, from Old English *seldum,* alteration of *seldan.*] **—sel′dom·ness** *n.*

se·lect (sĭ-lĕkt′) *v.* **-lect·ed, -lect·ing, -lects.** *—tr.* To take as a choice from among several; pick out. *—intr.* To make a choice or selection. See Synonyms at **choose. —select** *adj. Abbr.* **sel. 1.** Singled out in preference; chosen: *a select few.* **2.** Of special quality or value; choice: *select peaches.* **3.** Of or relating to a lean grade of beef. **—select** *n. (used with a sing. or pl. verb).* One that is preferred or chosen in preference to others or because of special value. Often used with *the.* [Latin *sēligere, sēlēct-* : *sē-,* apart; see **s(w)e-** in Appendix + *legere,* to choose; see **leg-** in Appendix.] **—se·lec′ta·ble** *adj.* **—se·lect′ness** *n.*

se·lect·ee (sĭ-lĕk′tē′) *n.* One who is selected, especially for military service.

se·lec·tion (sĭ-lĕk′shən) *n.* **1.a.** The act or an instance of selecting or the fact of having been selected. **b.** One that is selected. **2.** A carefully chosen or representative collection of people or things. See Synonyms at **choice. 3.** A literary or musical text chosen for reading or performance. **4.** *Biology.* A natural or artificial process that favors or induces survival and perpetuation of one kind of organism over others that die or fail to produce offspring.

se·lec·tion·ist (sĭ-lĕk′shə-nĭst) or **se·lec·tion·al** (-shə-nəl) *adj.* Of or relating to the view that evolution or genetic variation occurs chiefly as a result of natural selection. **—selectionist** *n.* One who holds a selectionist view. **—se·lec′tion·ism** *n.*

se·lec·tive (sĭ-lĕk′tĭv) *adj.* **1.** Of or characterized by selection; discriminating. **2.** Empowered or tending to select. **3.** *Electronics.* Able to reject frequencies other than the one selected or tuned. **—se·lec′tive·ly** *adv.* **—se·lec′tive·ness** *n.*

selective service *n.* A system for calling up people for compulsory military service.

selective veto *n.* See **item veto.**

se·lec·tiv·i·ty (sĭ-lĕk′tĭv′ĭ-tē, sē′lĕk-) *n., pl.* **-ties. 1.** The state or quality of being selective. **2.** *Abbr.* **sel.** The degree to which an electronic receiver is selective.

se·lect·man (sĭ-lĕkt′măn′, -mən) *n.* One of a board of town officers chosen annually in New England communities to manage local affairs.

se·lec·tor (sĭ-lĕk′tər) *n.* One that selects: *the frequency selector of a radio.*

se·lect·wom·an (sĭ-lĕkt′wo͝om′ən) *n.* A woman who is one of a board of town officers chosen annually in New England communities to manage local affairs.

selen– *pref.* Variant of **seleno–.**

sel·e·nate (sĕl′ə-nāt′) *n.* A salt or ester of selenic acid. [SELEN(IC ACID) + –ATE[2].]

Se·len·e (sə-lē′nē) *n. Greek Mythology.* The goddess of the moon.

Se·len·ga (sĕl′ĕng-gä′). A river of northern Mongolia and southeast Russia flowing about 1,207 km (750 mi) east and north to Lake Baikal.

se·le·nic (sə-lē′nĭk, -lĕn′ĭk) *adj.* Of, relating to, or containing selenium.

selenic acid *n.* A highly corrosive hygroscopic white solid acid with composition H_2SeO_4.

sel·e·nif·er·ous (sĕl′ə-nĭf′ər-əs) *adj.* Containing selenium: *seleniferous soil.*

sel·e·nite (sĕl′ə-nīt′, sĭ-lē′-) *n.* Gypsum in the form of colorless clear crystals. [Latin *selēnītēs,* from Greek *selēnitēs (lithos),* moon (stone), selenite (so called because it was believed to wax and wane with the moon), from *selēnē,* moon. See SELENIUM.]

se·le·ni·um (sĭ-lē′nē-əm) *n. Symbol* **Se** A nonmetallic element, red in powder form, black in vitreous form, and metallic gray in crystalline form, resembling sulfur and obtained primarily as a byproduct of electrolytic copper refining. It is widely used in rectifiers, as a semiconductor, and in xerography. Its photovoltaic and photoconductive actions make it useful in photocells, photographic exposure meters, and solar cells. Atomic number 34; atomic weight 78.96; melting point (of gray selenium) 217°C; boiling point (gray) 684.9°C; specific gravity (gray) 4.79; (vitreous) 4.28; valence 2, 4, or 6. See table at **element.** [Greek *selēnē,* moon (from *selas,* light, brightness) + –IUM.]

selenium cell *n.* A photoconductive cell consisting of an insulated selenium strip between two suitable electrodes.

seleno– or **selen–** *pref.* **1.** Moon: *selenography.* **2.** Selenium: *selenosis.* [Greek *selēno-,* from *selēnē,* moon. See SELENIUM.]

seismograph

ă pat	oi boy
ā pay	ou out
âr care	o͝o took
ä father	o͞o boot
ĕ pet	ŭ cut
ē be	ûr urge
ĭ pit	th thin
ī pie	*th* this
îr pier	hw which
ŏ pot	zh vision
ō toe	ə about, item
ô paw	♦ regionalism

Stress marks: ′ (primary); ′ (secondary), as in **dictionary** (dĭk′shə-nĕr′ē)

sel·e·nog·ra·phy (sĕl′ə-nŏg′rə-fē) *n.* The study of the physical features of the moon. —**sel′e·nog′ra·pher, sel′e·nog′ra·phist** *n.* —**sel′e·no·graph′ic** (-nə-grăf′ĭk), **sel′e·no·graph′i·cal** (-ĭ-kəl) *adj.* —**sel′e·no·graph′i·cal·ly** *adv.*

sel·e·nol·o·gy (sĕl′ə-nŏl′ə-jē) *n.* The astronomical study of the moon. —**sel′e·no·log′i·cal** (-nə-lŏj′ĭ-kəl) *adj.* —**sel′e·nol′o·gist** *n.*

sel·e·no·sis (sĕl′ə-nō′sĭs) *n.* Poisoning, especially of livestock, caused by ingesting selenium found in some plants, in the soil, or in some microorganisms.

Se·leu·ci·a (sĭ-lo͞o′shē-ə, -shə). An ancient city of Mesopotamia on the Tigris River south-southeast of modern Baghdad. Founded c. 300 B.C., it was an important commercial center and the chief city of the empire founded by Seleucus I.

Se·leu·cid (sĭ-lo͞o′-sĭd). A Hellenistic dynasty founded by Seleucus I after the death of Alexander the Great. It ruled much of Asia Minor from 312 to 64 B.C. —**Se·leu′cid** *adj.*

Se·leu·cus I (sĭ-lo͞o′kəs). 358?–281 B.C. Macedonian general under Alexander the Great. He founded and ruled (312–281) the Seleucid dynasty after Alexander's death.

self (sĕlf) *n., pl.* **selves** (sĕlvz). **1.** The total, essential, or particular being of a person; the individual: *"An actor's instrument is the self"* (Joan Juliet Buck). **2.** The essential qualities distinguishing one person from another; individuality: *"He would walk a little first along the southern walls, shed his European self, fully enter this world"* (Howard Kaplan). **3.** One's consciousness of one's own being or identity; the ego: *"For some of us, the self's natural doubts are given in mesmerizing amplification by way of critics' negative assessments of our writing"* (Joyce Carol Oates). **4.** One's own interests, welfare, or advantage: *thinking of self alone.* **5.** *Immunology.* That which the immune system identifies as belonging to the body: *tissues no longer recognized as self.* —**self** *pron.* Myself, yourself, himself, or herself: *a living wage for self and family.* —**self** *adj.* **1.** Of the same character throughout. **2.** Of the same material as the article with which it is used: *a dress with a self belt.* **3.** *Obsolete.* Same or identical. [Middle English, selfsame, from Old English. See **s(w)e-** in Appendix.]

self– *pref.* **1.** Oneself; itself: *self-control.* **2.** Automatic; automatically: *self-loading.* [Middle English, from Old English, from *self,* self. See SELF.]

self-a·ban·doned (sĕlf′ə-băn′dənd) *adj.* Lacking self-restraint, especially having completely yielded to one's impulses. —**self′-a·ban′don·ment** *n.*

self-a·base·ment (sĕlf′ə-bās′mənt) *n.* Degradation or humiliation of oneself, especially because of feelings of guilt or inferiority.

self-ab·ne·ga·tion (sĕlf′ăb′nĭ-gā′shən) *n.* The setting aside of self-interest for the sake of others or for a belief or principle. —**self′-ab′ne·gat′ing** *adj.*

self-ab·sorbed (sĕlf′əb-sôrbd′, -zôrbd′) *adj.* Excessively self-involved. —**self′-ab·sorp′tion** (-sôrp′shən, -zôrp′-) *n.*

self-a·buse (sĕlf′ə-byo͞os′) *n.* **1.** Abuse of oneself or one's abilities. **2.** Masturbation.

self-act·ing (sĕlf′ăk′tĭng) *adj.* Able to act or work automatically.

self-ac·tu·al·ize (sĕlf′ăk′cho͞o-ə-līz′) *intr.v.* **-ized, -iz·ing, -iz·es.** To develop or achieve one's full potential. —**self′-ac′tu·al·i·za′tion** (-ə-lĭ-zā′shən) *n.* —**self′-ac′tu·al·iz′er** *n.*

self-ad·dressed (sĕlf′ə-drĕst′) *adj.* Addressed to oneself: *a self-addressed envelope.*

self-ad·he·sive (sĕlf′ăd-hē′sĭv) *adj.* Having a surface coated with an adhesive and not needing any substance, such as glue or paste, applied to form a bond: *self-adhesive wallpaper; self-adhesive labels.*

self-ad·min·is·ter (sĕlf′ăd-mĭn′ĭ-stər) *tr.v.* **-tered, -ter·ing, -ters.** To administer (something) to oneself or itself: *"Laboratory animals chose to self-administer cocaine, to the exclusion of food and water, until they collapsed"* (Ross Gelbspan). —**self′-ad·min′is·tra′tion** *n.*

self-ag·gran·dize·ment (sĕlf′ə-grăn′dĭz-mənt) *n.* The act or practice of enhancing or exaggerating one's own importance, power, or reputation. —**self′-ag·gran′diz′ing** (-ə-grăn′dī′zĭng) *adj.*

self-a·nal·y·sis (sĕlf′ə-năl′ĭ-sĭs) *n., pl.* **-ses** (-sēz′). An independent methodical attempt by one to study and comprehend one's own personality or emotions. —**self′-an′a·lyt′i·cal** (-ăn′ə-lĭt′ĭ-kəl), **self′-an′a·lyt′ic** (-ĭk) *adj.*

self-an·ni·hi·la·tion (sĕlf′ə-nī′ə-lā′shən) *n.* **1.** Self-destruction. **2.** Loss of self-awareness, as in a mystical state.

self-ap·point·ed (sĕlf′ə-poin′tĭd) *adj.* Designated or chosen by oneself rather than by due authority: *a self-appointed arbiter.*

self-as·sert·ing (sĕlf′ə-sûr′tĭng) *adj.* **1.** Asserting oneself or one's own rights or views. **2.a.** Self-confident. **b.** Overbearing; arrogant.

self-as·ser·tion (sĕlf′ə-sûr′shən) *n.* Determined advancement of one's own personality, wishes, or views. —**self′-as·ser′tive** *adj.* —**self′-as·ser′tive·ly** *adv.* —**self-as·ser′tive·ness** *n.*

self-as·sured (sĕlf′ə-sho͝ord′) *adj.* Having or showing confidence and poise. —**self′-as·sur′ance** (-sho͝or′əns) *n.*

self-a·ware (sĕlf′ə-wâr′) *adj.* Aware of oneself as an individual entity or personality. —**self′-a·ware′ness** *n.*

self-bast·ing (sĕlf′bā′stĭng) *adj.* Prepared so as to remain moist while being cooked: *a self-basting turkey.*

self-care (sĕlf′kâr′) *n.* The care of oneself without medical, professional, or other assistance or oversight.

self-cen·tered (sĕlf′sĕn′tərd) *adj.* Engrossed in oneself and one's own affairs; selfish. —**self′-cen′tered·ly** *adv.* —**self′-cen′tered·ness** *n.*

self-clean·ing (sĕlf′klē′nĭng) *adj.* Made or designed to clean itself, often automatically: *a self-cleaning oven.*

self-col·ored (sĕlf′kŭl′ərd) *adj.* **1.** Being in the natural or original color. **2.** Of only one color.

self-com·mand (sĕlf′kə-mănd′) *n.* Full presence of mind; self-confidence.

self-com·pat·i·ble (sĕlf′kəm-păt′ə-bəl) *adj. Botany.* Capable of self-fertilization. —**self′-com·pat′i·bil′i·ty** *n.*

self-com·pla·cent (sĕlf′kəm-plā′sənt) *adj.* Self-satisfied, often smugly so. —**self′-com·pla′cen·cy** *n.* —**self′-com·pla′cent·ly** *adv.*

self-con·cept (sĕlf′kŏn′sĕpt) *n.* The mental image or perception that one has of oneself.

self-con·cep·tion (sĕlf′kən-sĕp′shən) *n.* Self-concept.

self-con·cern (sĕlf′kən-sûrn′) *n.* Selfish or excessive concern for oneself. —**self′-con·cerned′** *adj.*

self-con·fessed (sĕlf′kən-fĕst′) *adj.* According to one's own admission: *a self-confessed plagiarist.*

self-con·fi·dence (sĕlf′kŏn′fĭ-dəns) *n.* Confidence in oneself or one's own abilities: *"Without self-confidence we are as babes in the cradle"* (Virginia Woolf). See Synonyms at **confidence.** —**self′-con′fi·dent** *adj.* —**self′-con′fi·dent·ly** *adv.*

self-con·scious (sĕlf′kŏn′shəs) *adj.* **1.** Aware of oneself as an individual or of one's own being, actions, or thoughts. **2.** Socially ill at ease: *a self-conscious teenager.* **3.** Excessively conscious of one's appearance or manner: *a young, self-conscious executive.* **4.** Showing the effects of self-consciousness; stilted: *self-conscious prose.* —**self′-con′scious·ly** *adv.* —**self′-con′scious·ness** *n.*

self-con·tained (sĕlf′kən-tānd′) *adj.* **1.** Constituting a complete and independent unit in and of itself: *a self-contained retirement community; a self-contained dictionary.* **2.a.** Not dependent on others; self-sufficient: *a self-contained settlement in the Arctic.* **b.** Keeping to oneself; reserved. —**self′-con·tain′ment** *n.*

self-con·tent (sĕlf′kən-tĕnt′) *adj.* Satisfied with oneself; complacent. —**self-content** *n.* Self-contentment. —**self′con·tent′ed·ly** *adv.*

self-con·tent·ment (sĕlf′kən-tĕnt′mənt) *n.* Self-satisfaction; complacency.

self-con·tra·dic·tion (sĕlf′kŏn′trə-dĭk′shən) *n.* **1.** The act, state, or fact of contradicting oneself or itself. **2.** An idea or statement containing contradictory elements. —**self′-con′tra·dic′to·ry** (-dĭk′tə-rē) *adj.*

self-con·trol (sĕlf′kən-trōl′) *n.* Control of one's emotions, desires, or actions by one's own will: *"You think yourself a miracle of sensibility; but self-control is what you need"* (Mary Boykin Chesnut). —**self′-con·trolled′** *adj.*

self-cor·rect·ing (sĕlf′kə-rĕk′tĭng) *adj.* **1.** Correcting its or one's own mistakes. **2.** Of or being a typewriter mechanism that allows for automatic correction of a typing error.

self-crit·i·cal (sĕlf′krĭt′ĭ-kəl) *adj.* Critical of oneself and one's faults and weaknesses: *"In my experience, no species of performing artist is as self-critical as a dancer"* (Susan Sontag). —**self′-crit′i·cal·ly** *adv.* —**self′-crit′i·cism** (-krĭt′ĭ-sĭz′əm) *n.*

self-de·ceit (sĕlf′dĭ-sēt′) *n.* Self-deception.

self-de·ceived (sĕlf′dĭ-sēvd′) *adj.* Deceived by one's own illusions or errors.

self-de·ceiv·ing (sĕlf′dĭ-sē′vĭng) *adj.* Given to or believing or fancying mistaken notions about oneself.

self-de·cep·tion (sĕlf′dĭ-sĕp′shən) *n.* The act of deceiving oneself or the state of being deceived by oneself. —**self′-de·cep′tive** *adj.* —**self′-de·cep′tive·ly** *adv.*

self-de·feat·ing (sĕlf′dĭ-fē′tĭng) *adj.* Injurious to one's or its own purposes or welfare: *"American officials will find it harder than ever to ward off self-defeating protectionist measures"* (George R. Packard).

self-de·fense (sĕlf′dĭ-fĕns′) *n.* **1.** Defense of oneself when physically attacked: *She was taking a course in self-defense.* **2.** Defense of what belongs to oneself, as one's works or reputation. **3.** *Law.* The right to protect oneself against violence or threatened violence with whatever force or means are reasonably necessary. —**self′-de·fen′sive** *adj.*

self-def·i·ni·tion (sĕlf′dĕf′ənĭsh′ən) *n.* Definition of one's identity, character, abilities, and attitudes, especially in relation to persons or things outside oneself or itself.

self-de·ni·al (sĕlf′dĭ-nī′əl) *n.* Sacrifice of one's own desires or interests. See Synonyms at **abstinence.** —**self′-de·ny′ing** (-nī′ĭng) *adj.* —**self′-de·ny′ing·ly** *adv.*

self-dep·re·cat·ing (sĕlf′dĕp′rĭ-kā′tĭng) *adj.* Tending to undervalue oneself and one's abilities. —**self′-dep′re·cat′ing·ly** *adv.*

self-dep·re·ca·to·ry (sĕlf′dĕp′rĭ-kə-tôr′ē, -tōr′ē) *adj.* Self-deprecating.

self-de·pre·ci·a·tion (sĕlf′dĭ-prē′shē-ā′shən) *n.* Disparagement or undervaluation of oneself and one's abilities.

self-de·scribed (sĕlf′dĭ-skrībd′) *adj.* **1.** As described by oneself about oneself. **2.** Self-styled. —**self′-de·scrip′tion** (-skrĭp′shən) *n.*

self-de·struct (sĕlf′dĭ-strŭkt′) *n.* A mechanism for causing a device to destroy itself. —**self-destruct** *intr.v.* **-struct·ed, -struct·ing, -structs.** To destroy oneself or itself: *"died at 28, wasted from years of self-destructing on drugs"* (Jack Knoll).

self-de·struc·tion (sĕlf′dĭ-strŭk′shən) *n.* **1.** The act or process of destroying oneself or itself. **2.** Suicide.

self-de·struc·tive (sĕlf′dĭ-strŭk′tĭv) *adj.* **1.** Tending to do harm to oneself. **2.** Marked by an impulse or tendency to harm or kill oneself. —**self′-de·struc′tive·ly** *adv.* —**self′-de·struc′tive·ness** *n.*

self-de·ter·mi·na·tion (sĕlf′dĭ-tûr′mə-nā′shən) *n.* **1.** Determination of one's own fate or course of action without compulsion; free will. **2.** Freedom of the people of a given area to determine their own political status; independence.

self-de·vel·op·ment (sĕlf′dĭ-vĕl′əp-mənt) *n.* Development of one's capabilities or potentialities.

self-de·vo·tion (sĕlf′dĭ-vō′shən) *n.* Devotion or dedication of oneself, especially to a service or an ideal. —**self′-de·vot′ed·ly** (-vō′tĭd-lē) *adv.* —**self′-de·vot′ed·ness** *n.*

self-di·ag·no·sis (sĕlf′dī′əg-nō′sĭs) *n., pl.* **-ses** (-sēz). Diagnosis of one's own illness or disease without professional medical consultation. —**self′-di′ag·nos′tic** (-nŏs′tĭk) *adj.*

self-di·ges·tion (sĕlf′dī-jĕs′chən, -dĭ-) *n. Biochemistry.* See **autolysis.**

self-di·rect·ed (sĕlf′dĭ-rĕk′tĭd, -dī-) *adj.* Directed or guided by oneself, especially as an independent agent: *the self-directed study of a language.* —**self′-di·rect′ing** *adj.* —**self′-di·rec′tion** *n.*

self-dis·ci·pline (sĕlf′dĭs′ə-plĭn) *n.* Training and control of oneself and one's conduct, usually for personal improvement.

self-dis·cov·er·y (sĕlf′dĭ-skŭv′ə-rē) *n., pl.* **-ies.** The act or process of achieving understanding or knowledge of oneself.

self-dis·trust (sĕlf′dĭs-trŭst′) *n.* Lack of faith or confidence in one's own abilities. —**self′-dis·trust′ful** *adj.*

self·dom (sĕlf′dəm) *n.* Selfhood.

self-doomed (sĕlf′do͞omd′) *adj.* Doomed by one's own feelings or actions: *"The romantic is self-doomed, deliberately inviting terminal illness"* (Margaret Spillane).

self-doubt (sĕlf′dout′) *n.* A lack of faith or confidence in oneself. —**self′-doubt′ing** *adj.*

self-ed·u·cat·ed (sĕlf′ĕj′ə-kā′tĭd) *adj.* Educated by one's own efforts rather than by formal instruction. —**self′-ed′u·ca′tion** *n.*

self-ef·fac·ing (sĕlf′ĭ-fā′sĭng) *adj.* Not drawing attention to oneself; modest. —**self′-ef·face′ment** (-fās′mənt) *n.*

self-e·lect·ed (sĕlf′ĭ-lĕk′tĭd) *adj.* Self-appointed.

self-em·ployed (sĕlf′ĕm-ploid′) *adj.* Earning one's livelihood directly from one's own trade or business rather than as an employee of another. —**self′-em·ploy′ment** *n.*

self-en·forc·ing (sĕlf′ĕn-fôr′sĭng, -fōr′-) *adj.* Holding within itself the means or a guarantee of its enforcement: *a self-enforcing peace settlement.*

self-en·rich·ment (sĕlf′ĕn-rĭch′mənt) *n.* **1.** The act or process of developing or augmenting one's intellectual powers or spiritual resources. **2.** The act or process of enriching oneself financially.

self-es·teem (sĕlf′ĭ-stēm′) *n.* Pride in oneself; self-respect.

self-e·val·u·a·tion (sĕlf′ĕ-văl′yo͞o-ā′shən) *n.* Evaluation or appraisal of oneself, especially in relation to certain objective standards.

self-ev·i·dent (sĕlf′ĕv′ĭ-dənt) *adj.* Requiring no proof or explanation. —**self′-ev′i·dence** *n.* —**self′-ev′i·dent·ly** *adv.*

self-ex·am·i·na·tion (sĕlf′ĭg-zăm′ə-nā′shən) *n.* **1.** An introspective consideration of one's own thoughts or emotions. **2.** Examination of one's own body for medical reasons: *a periodontal self-examination; a breast self-examination.*

self-ex·ile (sĕlf′ĕg′zīl, -ĕk′sīl) *n.* One exiled by his or her own decision or volition. —**self′-ex′iled** *adj.*

self-ex·plan·a·to·ry (sĕlf′ĭk-splăn′ə-tôr′ē, -tōr′ē) *adj.* Needing no explanation; obvious.

self-ex·pres·sion (sĕlf′ĭk-sprĕsh′ən) *n.* Expression of one's own personality, feelings, or ideas, as through speech or art: *"Self-expression must pass into communication for its fulfillment"* (Pearl S. Buck). —**self′-ex·press′** *v.* —**self′-ex·pres′sive** (-sprĕs′ĭv) *adj.*

self-ex·tin·guish·ing (sĕlf′ĭk-stĭng′gwĭ-shĭng) *adj.* Having or designed to have within itself a substance or device that extinguishes: *a self-extinguishing cigarette; a self-extinguishing light.*

self-fer·tile (sĕlf′fûr′tl) *adj.* Having the property of fertilizing itself; capable of self-fertilization.

self-fer·til·i·za·tion (sĕlf′fûr′tl-ĭ-zā′shən) *n.* Fertilization by sperm from the same animal, as in some hermaphrodites, or by pollen from the same flower. —**self′-fer′til·ized′** (-īzd′) *adj.* —**self′-fer′til·iz′ing** *adj.*

self-flag·el·la·tion (sĕlf′flăj′ə-lā′shən) *n.* **1.** The act of severely criticizing oneself. **2.** The act of punishing oneself.

self-ful·fill·ing (sĕlf′fo͝ol-fĭl′ĭng) *adj.* **1.** Achieving fulfillment as a result of having been expected or foretold: *a self-fulfilling prophecy.* **2.** Achieving self-fulfillment.

self-ful·fill·ment (sĕlf′fo͝ol-fĭl′mənt) *n.* Fulfillment of oneself.

self-giv·en (sĕlf′gĭv′ən) *adj.* **1.** Originating or derived from itself: *a self-given entity.* **2.** Given by oneself; self-appointed: *a self-given role.*

self-giv·ing (sĕlf′gĭv′ĭng) *adj.* Characterized by self-sacrificing behavior; unselfish.

self-gov·erned (sĕlf′gŭv′ərnd) *adj.* **1.** Not controlled or swayed by others. **2.** Characterized by self-discipline or self-control.

self-gov·ern·ing (sĕlf′gŭv′ər-nĭng) *adj.* **1.** Exercising control or rule over oneself or itself. **2.** Having the right or power of self-government; autonomous.

self-gov·ern·ment (sĕlf′gŭv′ərn-mənt) *n.* **1.** Political independence; autonomy. **2.** Popular or representative government; democracy. **3.** Self-control.

self-grat·i·fi·ca·tion (sĕlf′grăt′ə-fĭ-kā′shən) *n.* The act of giving oneself pleasure or of satisfying one's own desires.

self-hard·en·ing (sĕlf′här′dn-ĭng) *adj.* Of or relating to materials, such as certain steels, that harden without special treatment.

self-hate (sĕlf′hāt′) *n.* Self-hatred.

self-ha·tred (sĕlf′hā′trĭd) *n.* Hatred, disregard, and denigration of oneself.

self-heal (sĕlf′hēl′) *n.* Any of several plants reputed to have healing powers, especially *Prunella vulgaris,* a creeping Eurasian plant with deep violet-blue, two-lipped flowers.

self-heal

self-help (sĕlf′hĕlp′) *n.* The act or an instance of helping or improving oneself without assistance from others. —*attributive.* Often used to modify another noun: *self-help manuals; self-help programs.*

self·hood (sĕlf′ho͝od′) *n.* **1.** The state of having a distinct identity; individuality. **2.** The fully developed self; an achieved personality. **3.** Self-centeredness: *"the cult of selfhood that became fashionable in the 1960s"* (David Rankin). [Translation of German *Meinheit* : *mein,* my, mine + *-heit,* n. suff.]

self-hyp·no·sis (sĕlf′hĭp-nō′sĭs) *n.* See **autohypnosis.**

self-i·den·ti·fi·ca·tion (sĕlf′ī-dĕn′tə-fĭ-kā′shən) *n.* Identification of oneself with another person or thing.

self-i·den·ti·ty (sĕlf′ī-dĕn′tĭ-tē) *n.* **1.** Oneness of a thing with itself. **2.** Awareness of and identification with oneself as a separate individual.

self-im·age (sĕlf′ĭm′ĭj) *n.* The conception that one has of oneself, including an assessment of qualities and personal worth.

self-im·mo·la·tion (sĕlf′ĭm′ə-lā′shən) *n.* Deliberate sacrifice of oneself.

self-im·por·tance (sĕlf′ĭm-pôr′tns) *n.* Excessively high regard for one's own importance or station; conceit. —**self′-im·por′tant** *adj.* —**self′-im·por′tant·ly** *adv.*

self-im·posed (sĕlf′ĭm-pōzd′) *adj.* Imposed by oneself on oneself; voluntarily assumed or endured: *self-imposed exile.*

self-im·prove·ment (sĕlf′ĭm-pro͞ov′mənt) *n.* Improvement of one's condition through one's own efforts.

self-in·clu·sive (sĕlf′ĭn-klo͞o′sĭv, -zĭv) *adj.* **1.** Enclosing or including itself. **2.** Whole or complete in itself.

self-in·com·pat·i·ble (sĕlf′ĭn-kəm-păt′ə-bəl) *adj. Botany.* Incapable of self-fertilization. —**self′-in′com·pat′i·bil′i·ty** *n.*

self-in·crim·i·na·tion (sĕlf′ĭn-krĭm′ə-nā′shən) *n.* Incrimination of oneself, especially by one's own testimony in a criminal prosecution. —**self′-in·crim′i·nat′ing** *adj.* —**self′-in·crim′i·na·to′ry** (-nə-tôr′ē, -tōr′ē) *adj.*

self-in·duced (sĕlf′ĭn-do͞ost′, -dyo͞ost′) *adj.* **1.** Induced by oneself or itself: *self-induced vomiting.* **2.** *Electricity.* Produced by self-induction.

self-in·duct·ance (sĕlf′ĭn-dŭk′təns) *n. Electricity.* The ratio of the electromotive force produced in a circuit by self-induction to the rate of change of current producing it, expressed in henries. Also called *coefficient of self-induction.*

self-in·duc·tion (sĕlf′ĭn-dŭk′shən) *n. Electricity.* The generation by a changing current of an electromotive force in the same circuit. —**self′-in·duc′tive** *adj.*

self-in·dul·gence (sĕlf′ĭn-dŭl′jəns) *n.* Excessive indulgence of one's own appetites and desires. —**self′-in·dul′gent** *adj.* —**self′-in·dul′gent·ly** *adv.*

self-in·flict·ed (sĕlf′ĭn-flĭk′tĭd) *adj.* Inflicted or imposed on oneself: *died of a self-inflicted gunshot wound.*

self-in·struct·ed (sĕlf′ĭn-strŭk′tĭd) *adj.* Self-taught.

self-in·struc·tion·al (sĕlf′ĭn-strŭk′shə-nəl) *adj.* Of, relating to, or designed for independent study.

self-in·sur·ance (sĕlf′ĭn-sho͝or′əns) *n.* Insurance of oneself or one's possessions against possible loss by regularly setting aside funds. —**self′-in·sure′** *v.* —**self′-in·sured′** *adj.* —**self′-in·sur′er** *n.*

self-in·ter·est (sĕlf′ĭn′trĭst, -ĭn′tər-ĭst) *n.* **1.** Selfish or excessive regard for one's personal advantage or interest. **2.** Personal advantage or interest. —**self′-in′ter·est·ed** *adj.*

self-in·volved (sĕlf′ĭn-vŏlvd′) *adj.* Absorbed primarily in one's own interests or activities. —**self′-in·volve′ment** *n.*

ă pat	oi boy
ā pay	ou out
âr care	o͝o took
ä father	o͞o boot
ĕ pet	ŭ cut
ē be	ûr urge
ĭ pit	th thin
ī pie	*th* this
îr pier	hw which
ŏ pot	zh vision
ō toe	ə about, item
ô paw	♦ regionalism

Stress marks: ′ (primary); ′ (secondary), as in **dictionary** (dĭk′shə-nĕr′ē)

self·ish (sĕl′fĭsh) *adj.* **1.** Concerned chiefly or only with oneself: *"Selfish men were . . . trying to make capital for themselves out of the sacred cause of human rights"* (Maria Weston Chapman). **2.** Arising from, characterized by, or showing selfishness: *a selfish whim.* **—self′ish·ly** *adv.* **—self′ish·ness** *n.*

self-jus·ti·fy·ing (sĕlf′jŭs′tə-fī′ĭng) *adj.* **1.** Making excuses for oneself or one's behavior. **2.** Justifying itself automatically: *a self-justifying typewriter.* **—self′-jus′ti·fi·ca′tion** (-jŭs′tə-fĭ-kā′shən) *n.*

self-knowl·edge (sĕlf′nŏl′ĭj) *n.* Knowledge or understanding of one's own nature, abilities, and limitations; insight into oneself: *"The most elusive knowledge of all is self-knowledge"* (Mirra Komarovsky).

self·less (sĕlf′lĭs) *adj.* Having, exhibiting, or motivated by no concern for oneself; unselfish: *"Volunteers need both selfish and selfless motives to sustain their interest"* (Natalie de Combray). **—self′less·ly** *adv.* **—self′less·ness** *n.*

self-lim·it·ed (sĕlf-lĭm′ĭ-tĭd) *adj.* **1.** Limited by its or one's own characteristics rather than by external influences. **2.** Running a definite course within a specific period; little modified by treatment. Used of a disease.

self-lim·it·ing (sĕlf-lĭm′ĭ-tĭng) *adj.* **1.** Limiting oneself or itself. **2.** Self-limited. **—self′-lim′i·ta′tion** (-tā′shən) *n.*

self-liq·ui·dat·ing (sĕlf′lĭk′wĭ-dā′tĭng) *adj.* **1.** Involving goods convertible into cash in a short time. Used of business transactions. **2.** Producing a return equal to the sum invested to create or maintain something: *a self-liquidating toll-bridge project.* **—self′-liq′ui·da′tion** *n.*

self-load·ing (sĕlf′lō′dĭng) *adj.* Automatically ejecting a shell and chambering the next round from the magazine; automatic or semiautomatic. Used of a firearm.

self-loath·ing (sĕlf′lō′*th*ĭng) *n.* Self-hatred.

self-love (sĕlf′lŭv′) *n.* The instinct or desire to promote one's own well-being; regard for or love of one's self. **—self′-lov′ing** *adj.*

self-made (sĕlf′mād′) *adj.* **1.** Having achieved success or recognition by one's own efforts: *a self-made millionaire.* **2.** Made by itself or oneself: *a self-made pond.*

self-mail·er (sĕlf′mā′lər) *n.* A folder that can be mailed without being enclosed in an envelope. **—self′-mail′ing** *adj.*

self-mas·ter·y (sĕlf′măs′tə-rē) *n.* Self-command.

self-med·i·ca·tion (sĕlf′mĕd′ĭ-kā′shən) *n.* Medication of oneself without professional supervision to alleviate an illness or condition, as by using an over-the-counter drug or preparation.

self·ness (sĕlf′nĭs) *n.* **1.** The quality or state of being self-centered; selfishness. **2.** Individuality; selfhood.

self-ob·ser·va·tion (sĕlf′ŏb′zər-vā′shən) *n.* **1.** Observation of one's own countenance or appearance. **2.** Examination of one's own thoughts or emotions.

self-o·pin·ion (sĕlf′ə-pĭn′yən) *n.* An unduly high opinion of oneself.

self-o·pin·ion·at·ed (sĕlf′ə-pĭn′yə-nā′tĭd) *adj.* **1.** Obstinately insistent upon one's own opinions. **2.** Vain; conceited.

self-or·dained (sĕlf′ôr-dānd′) *adj.* Ordained by oneself rather than by others; practicing by one's own authority: *a self-ordained foreign policy expert.*

self-per·cep·tion (sĕlf′pər-sĕp′shən) *n.* An awareness of the characteristics that constitute one's self; self-knowledge.

self-per·pet·u·at·ing (sĕlf′pər-pĕch′o͞o-ā′tĭng) *adj.* Having the power to renew or perpetuate oneself or itself for an indefinite length of time. **—self′-per·pet′u·a′tion** *n.*

self-pit·y (sĕlf′pĭt′ē) *n.* Pity for oneself, especially exaggerated or self-indulgent pity. **—self′-pit′y·ing** *adj.* **—self′-pit′y·ing·ly** *adv.*

self-poised (sĕlf′poizd′) *adj.* **1.** In command of oneself. **2.** In a state of balance without need of support.

self-pol·li·na·tion (sĕlf′pŏl′ə-nā′shən) *n.* Transfer of pollen from an anther to a stigma of the same flower. **—self′-pol′li·nate′** *v.*

self-por·trait (sĕlf′pôr′trĭt, -trāt′, -pōr′-) *n.* A pictorial or literary portrait of oneself, created by oneself.

self-portrait
By Norman Rockwell

self-pos·ses·sion (sĕlf′pə-zĕsh′ən) *n.* Full command of one's faculties, feelings, and behavior. See Synonyms at **confidence.** **—self′-pos·sessed′** *adj.*

self-pres·er·va·tion (sĕlf′prĕz′ər-vā′shən) *n.* **1.** Protection of oneself from harm or destruction. **2.** The instinct for individual preservation; the innate desire to stay alive.

self-pro·claimed (sĕlf′prō-klāmd′, -prə-) *adj.* So called by oneself; self-styled.

self-pro·mo·tion (sĕlf′prə-mō′shən) *n.* Promotion, including advertising and publicity, of oneself effected by oneself: *A television talk show is an excellent vehicle for self-promotion.* **—self′-pro·mot′er** *n.*

self-pro·pelled (sĕlf′prə-pĕld′) *adj. Abbr.* **SP 1.** Containing its own means of propulsion: *a self-propelled golf cart.* **2.** Fired from or mounted on a moving vehicle: *a self-propelled howitzer.* **—self′-pro·pul′sion** (-pŭl′shən) *n.*

self-pro·tec·tive (sĕlf′prə-tĕk′tĭv) *adj.* Serving or designed to protect oneself. **—self′-pro·tec′tion** *n.* **—self′-pro·tec′tive·ly** *adv.*

self-pub·lished (sĕlf′pŭb′lĭshd) *adj.* Having one's writings published by oneself: *a self-published volume of memoirs; a self-published poet.*

self-pu·ri·fi·ca·tion (sĕlf′pyo͝or′ə-fĭ-kā′shən) *n.* **1.** Naturally produced purification: *self-purification of water.* **2.** Purification of oneself.

self-re·ac·tive (sĕlf′rē-ăk′tĭv) *adj.* Immunologically reactive to itself. Used of a cell or tissue.

self-re·al·i·za·tion (sĕlf′rē′ə-lĭ-zā′shən) *n.* Complete development or fulfillment of one's own potential.

self-re·cord·ing (sĕlf′rĭ-kôr′dĭng) *adj.* Automatically recording its own functions or operations. Used of a machine or an instrument.

self-re·crim·i·na·tion (sĕlf′rĭ-krĭm′ə-nā′shən) *n.* The act or an instance of blaming or censuring oneself.

self-ref·er·en·tial (sĕlf′rĕf′ə-rĕn′shəl) *adj.* Referring to oneself or itself: *The biographer's account of the poet's life was surprisingly self-referential.* **—self′-ref′er·ence** *n.* **—self′-ref′er·en′tial·ly** *adv.*

self-re·flec·tion (sĕlf′rĭ-flĕk′shən) *n.* Self-examination; introspection. **—self′-re·flec′tive** *adj.* **—self′-re·flec′tive·ly** *adv.*

self-re·gard (sĕlf′rĭ-gärd′) *n.* **1.** Consideration of oneself or one's interests. **2.** Self-respect.

self-reg·u·lat·ing (sĕlf′rĕg′yə-lā′tĭng) *adj.* **1.** Regulating oneself or itself. **2.** Regulating itself automatically. **—self′-reg·u·la′tion** *n.*

self-re·li·ance (sĕlf′rĭ-lī′əns) *n.* Reliance on one's own capabilities, judgment, or resources; independence. **—self′-re·li′ant** *adj.* **—self′-re·li′ant·ly** *adv.*

self-rep·li·cat·ing (sĕlf′rĕp′lĭ-kā′tĭng) *adj.* Replicating oneself or itself: *DNA is a self-replicating molecule.* **—self′-rep′li·ca′tion** *n.*

self-re·proach (sĕlf′rĭ-prōch′) *n.* The act or an instance of charging oneself with a fault or mistake. **—self′-re·proach′ful** *adj.* **—self′-re·proach′ful·ly** *adv.*

self-re·spect (sĕlf′rĭ-spĕkt′) *n.* Due respect for oneself, one's character, and one's conduct. **—self′-re·spect′ing** *adj.*

self-re·straint (sĕlf′rĭ-strānt′) *n.* Restraint of one's emotions, desires, or inclinations; self-control.

self-rev·e·la·tion (sĕlf′rĕv′ə-lā′shən) *n.* Revelation of one's own thoughts, emotions, or attitudes, especially unintentionally. **—self′-re·veal′ing** (-rĭ-vē′lĭng) *adj.*

self-right·eous (sĕlf′rī′chəs) *adj.* **1.** Piously sure of one's own righteousness; moralistic. **2.** Exhibiting pious self-assurance: *self-righteous remarks.* **—self′-right′eous·ly** *adv.* **—self′-right′eous·ness** *n.*

self-right·ing (sĕlf′rī′tĭng) *adj.* Capable of righting itself when overturned: *a self-righting boat.*

self-ris·ing flour (sĕlf′rī′zĭng) *n.* A commercially produced mixture of flour and leavening.

self-rule (sĕlf′ro͞ol′) *n.* Self-government.

self-sac·ri·fice (sĕlf′săk′rə-fīs′) *n.* Sacrifice of one's personal interests or well-being for the sake of others or for a cause. **—self-sac′ri·fic′ing** *adj.*

self·same (sĕlf′sām′) *adj.* Being the very same; identical. See Synonyms at **same.** **—self′same′ness** *n.*

self-sat·is·fac·tion (sĕlf′săt′ĭs-făk′shən) *n.* Satisfaction, especially complacent satisfaction, with oneself or with one's accomplishments. **—self′-sat′is·fied′** (-fīd′) *adj.*

self-scru·ti·ny (sĕlf′skro͞ot′n-ē) *n.* **1.** Examination of one's thoughts or emotions. **2.** Scrutiny of one's appearance.

self-seal·ing (sĕlf′sē′lĭng) *adj.* **1.** Capable of sealing itself, as after being pierced: *a self-sealing tire.* **2.** Sealable without the application of moisture: *a self-sealing envelope.*

self-search·ing (sĕlf′sûr′chĭng) *n.* Careful examination of one's feelings and actions and their motivation. **—self′-search·ing** *adj.*

self-seed·ed (sĕlf′sē′dĭd) *adj. Botany.* Self-sown.

self-seek·ing (sĕlf′sē′kĭng) *adj.* **1.** Pursuing only one's own ends or interests. **2.** Exhibiting concern only with promoting one's own ends or interests: *self-seeking maneuvers.* **—self-seeking** *n.* Determined pursuit of one's own ends or interests. **—self′-seek′er** *n.*

self-se·lec·tion (sĕlf′sĭ-lĕk′shən) *n.* **1.** Selection of or by oneself. **2.** Selection of merchandise by oneself from a display counter or rack in a store. **—self′-se·lect′ed** *adj.* **—self′-se·lec′tive** *adj.*

self-serv·ice (sĕlf′sûr′vĭs) *adj.* Being a retail commercial enterprise or a service in which the customers or users help themselves: *a self-service market; a self-service elevator.* **—self′-serv′ice** *n.*

self-serv·ing (sĕlf′sûr′vĭng) *adj.* **1.** Serving one's own interests, especially without concern for the needs or interests of others. **2.** Exhibiting concern solely for one's own interests: *a speech full of self-serving comments.* **—self′-serv′ing·ly** *adv.*

self-sown (sĕlf′sōn′) *adj. Botany.* Growing from seed dispersal effected by a natural agent, such as the wind or a bird, rather than by human agency.

self-start·er (sĕlf′stär′tər) *n.* **1.** See **starter** (sense 2). **2.** One who displays an unusual amount of initiative. **—self′-start′ing** *adj.*

self-stick (sĕlf′stĭk′) also **self-stick·ing** (-stĭk′ĭng) *adj.* Self-adhesive: *a self-stick envelope.*

self-stud·y (sĕlf′stŭd′ē) *n.* **1.** Study or examination of oneself. **2.** A form of study in which one is to a large extent responsible for one's own instruction.

self-styled (sĕlf′stīld′) *adj.* As characterized by oneself, often without right or justification: *"poets, real or self-styled"* (Constantine Fitzgibbon). See Usage Note at **so-called.**

self-suf·fi·cient (sĕlf′sə-fĭsh′ənt) *adj.* **1.** Able to provide for oneself without the help of others; independent. **2.** Having undue confidence; smug. **—self′-suf·fi′cien·cy** *n.*

self-sup·port (sĕlf′sə-pôrt′, -pōrt′) *n.* The act of or capacity for supporting oneself, especially financially, without the help of others. **—self′-sup·port′ed, self′-sup·port′ing** *adj.*

self-sus·tain·ing (sĕlf′sə-stā′nĭng) *adj.* Able to sustain oneself or itself independently. **—self′-sus·tain′ing·ly** *adv.*

self-taught (sĕlf′tôt′) *adj.* Having taught oneself without formal instruction or the help of others.

self-tol·er·ance (sĕlf′tŏl′ər-əns) *n.* Tolerance by the body's immune system to its own cells and tissues.

self-treat·ment (sĕlf′trēt′mənt) *n.* Treatment of oneself without professional supervision to alleviate an illness or condition.

self-trust (sĕlf′trŭst′) *n.* Self-confidence.

self-un·der·stand·ing (sĕlf′ŭn′dər-stăn′dĭng) *n.* Self-knowledge.

self-val·i·dat·ing (sĕlf′văl′ĭ-dā′tĭng) *adj.* Having validation within itself; not needing validation from the outside: *a self-validating classic.*

self-will (sĕlf′wĭl′) *n.* Willfulness, especially in satisfying one's own desires or adhering to one's own opinions. **—self′-willed′** *adj.*

self-wind·ing (sĕlf′wīn′dĭng) *adj.* Designed in such a way that manual winding is unnecessary. Used of clocks and watches.

self-worth (sĕlf′wûrth′) *n.* Self-esteem; self-respect.

Sel·juk (sĕl′jo͞ok′, sĕl-jo͞ok′). A Turkish dynasty ruling in central and western Asia from the 11th to the 13th century.

Sel·kirk (sĕl′kûrk′), **Alexander.** 1676–1721. Scottish sailor who was marooned (1704–1709) on an island off Chile and is thought to have inspired Daniel Defoe's *Robinson Crusoe* (published 1719).

sell (sĕl) *v.* **sold** (sōld), **sell·ing, sells.** —*tr.* **1.** To exchange or deliver for money or its equivalent. **2.** To offer for sale, as for one's business or livelihood: *The partners sell textiles.* **3.** To give up or surrender in exchange for a price or reward: *sell one's soul to the devil.* **4.** To be responsible for the sale of; promote successfully: *Publicity sold that product.* **5.** To persuade (another) to recognize the worth or desirability of: *They sold me on the idea.* —*intr.* **1.** To exchange ownership for money or its equivalent; engage in selling. **2.** To be sold or be on sale: *Grapes are selling high this season.* **3.** To attract prospective buyers; be popular on the market: *an item that sells well.* **4.** To be approved of; gain acceptance. **—sell** *n.* **1.** The activity of selling. **2.** An instance of selling: *"The political sell isn't ordinary marketing"* (Brad Edmondson). **3.** *Slang.* An item that sells in a particular way: *a book that turned out to be a difficult sell.* ***—phrasal verbs.*** **sell off.** To get rid of by selling, often at reduced prices. **sell out. 1.** To put all of one's goods or possessions up for sale. **2.** *Slang.* To betray one's cause or colleagues: *He sold out to the other side.* ***—idioms.*** **sell a bill of goods.** *Informal.* To take unfair advantage of. **sell down the river.** *Informal.* To betray the true trust or faith of. **sell short. 1.** To contract for the sale of securities or commodities one expects to own at a later date and at more advantageous terms. **2.** To underestimate the true value or worth of: *Don't sell your colleague short; she's a smart lawyer.* [Middle English *sellen,* from Old English *sellan,* to give, sell.] **—sell′a·ble** *adj.*

sell·back (sĕl′băk′) *n.* The act or an instance of selling something back that one had previously bought.

sell·er (sĕl′ər) *n.* **1.** One that sells; a vendor. **2.** An item that sells in a certain way: *This washing machine has been an excellent seller.*

sell·er's market also **sell·ers' market** (sĕl′ərz) *n., pl.* **sell·ers' markets.** A market condition characterized by high prices and a supply of commodities falling short of demand.

sell·ing climax (sĕl′ĭng) *n.* A sharp decline in stock prices on a heavy volume of trading followed by a rally.

selling point *n.* An aspect of a product or service that is stressed in advertising or marketing.

sell·off (sĕl′ôf′, -ŏf′) *n.* The sale or disposal of a relatively large number of stocks, bonds, or commodities that often causes a sharp decline in prices.

sell·out (sĕl′out′) *n.* **1.** The act of selling out. **2.** An event for which all the tickets are sold. **3.** *Slang.* One who has betrayed one's principles or an espoused cause.

Sel·ma (sĕl′mə). A city of south-central Alabama west of Montgomery. In 1965 it was the site of a voter registration drive led by Martin Luther King, Jr. Population, 26,684.

sel·syn (sĕl′sĭn) *n. Physics.* A device by which angular movement or position in a generator is transmitted to a motor. [SEL(F) + SYN(CHRONOUS).]

selt·zer (sĕlt′sər) *n.* **1.** A natural effervescent spring water of high mineral content. **2.** See **soda water** (sense 1a). [From German *Selterser (Wasser),* (water) of Selters, a village of central Germany.]

sel·va (sĕl′və) *n.* A dense tropical rain forest usually having a cloud cover, especially one in the Amazon Basin. [Spanish, forest, from Latin *silva.*]

sel·vage also **sel·vedge** (sĕl′vĭj) *n.* **1.a.** The edge of a fabric that is woven so that it will not fray or ravel. **b.** An ornamental fringe at either end of an oriental rug. **2.** The edge plate of a lock that has a slot for a bolt. [Middle English (influenced by Middle Low German *selfegge*) : *self,* self; see SELF + *egge,* edge; see EDGE.]

selves (sĕlvz) *n.* Plural of **self.**

Selz·nick (sĕlz′nĭk), **David Oliver.** 1902–1965. American film producer known especially for his adaptation of popular novels, including *Gone With the Wind* (1939) and *A Farewell to Arms* (1958).

David O. Selznick

SEM *abbr.* Scanning electron microscope.

sem. *abbr.* Seminary.

Sem. *abbr.* Semitic.

se·man·teme (sĭ-măn′tēm′) *n. Linguistics.* An irreducible unit of meaning. [SEMANT(IC) + –EME.]

se·man·tic (sĭ-măn′tĭk) also **se·man·ti·cal** (-tĭ-kəl) *adj.* **1.** Of or relating to meaning, especially meaning in language. **2.** Of, relating to, or according to the science of semantics. [French *sémantique,* from Greek *sēmantikos,* significant, from *sēmantos,* marked, from *sēmainein, sēman-,* to signify, from *sēma,* sign.] **—se·man′ti·cal·ly** *adv.*

se·man·ti·cist (sĭ-măn′tĭ-sĭst) *n.* A specialist in semantics.

se·man·tics (sĭ-măn′tĭks) *n. (used with a sing. or pl. verb).* **1.** *Linguistics.* The study or science of meaning in language forms. **2.** *Logic.* The study of relationships between signs and symbols and what they represent. In this sense, also called *semasiology.*

sem·a·phore (sĕm′ə-fôr′, -fōr′) *n.* **1.** A visual signaling apparatus with flags, lights, or mechanically moving arms, as one used on a railroad. **2.** A visual system for sending information by means of two flags that are held one in each hand, using an alphabetic code based on the position of the signaler's arms. **—semaphore** *tr. & intr.v.* **-phored, -phor·ing, -phores.** To send (a message) or to signal by semaphore. [Greek *sēma,* sign + –PHORE.] **—sem′a·phor′ic** *adj.* **—sem′a·phor′i·cal·ly** *adv.*

Se·ma·rang (sə-mär′äng). A city of northern Java, Indonesia, on the Java Sea east of Jakarta. It is a major port and industrial center. Population, 1,026,671.

se·ma·si·ol·o·gy (sĭ-mā′sē-ŏl′ə-jē, -zē-) *n. Logic.* See **semantics** (sense 2). [Greek *sēmasia,* meaning (from *sēmainein,* to signify; see SEMANTIC) + -LOGY.] **—se·ma′si·o·log′i·cal** (-ə-lŏj′ĭ-kəl) *adj.* **—se·ma′si·ol′o·gist** *n.*

se·mat·ic (sĭ-măt′ĭk) *adj.* Serving as a warning or signal of danger. Used especially of the coloring of some poisonous animals. [From Greek *sēma, sēmat-,* sign.]

sem·bla·ble (sĕm′blə-bəl) *adj.* **1.** Having a resemblance; resembling or like: *unfamiliar symbols semblable to religious icons.* **2.** Seeming; apparent: *a semblable hit-and-run accident.* **—semblable** *n. Archaic.* Something that closely resembles something else. [Middle English, from Old French, from *sembler,* to resemble, from Latin *simulāre,* to simulate. See SIMULATE.] **—sem′bla·bly** *adv.*

sem·blance (sĕm′bləns) *n.* **1.** An outward or token appearance: *"Foolish men mistake transitory semblance for eternal fact"* (Thomas Carlyle). **2.** A representation; a copy. **3.** The barest trace; a modicum: *not a semblance of truth to the story.* [Middle English, from Old French, from *sembler,* to resemble. See SEMBLABLE.]

se·mé (sə-mā′) *adj. Heraldry.* Having a design embellished with small, delicate figures, such as a lacing of stars or flowers. [French, from Old French, past participle of *semer,* to sow, scatter, from Latin *sēmināre,* from *sēmen, sēmin-,* seed. See **sē-** in Appendix.]

se·mei·ol·o·gy (sē′mē-ŏl′ə-jē, sĕm′ē-, sē′mī-) *n.* Variant of **semiology.**

se·mei·ot·ic (sē′mē-ŏt′ĭk, sĕm′ē-, sē′mī-) also **se·mei·ot·i·cal** (-ĭ-kəl) *adj.* Variants of **semiotic.**

se·mei·ot·ics (sē′mē-ŏt′ĭks, sĕm′ē-, sē′mī-) *n.* Variant of **semiotics.**

se·meme (sē′mēm′) *n. Linguistics.* The meaning expressed by a morpheme. [Greek *sēma,* sign + –EME.]

se·men (sē′mən) *n.* A viscous, whitish secretion of the male reproductive organs, containing spermatozoa and serving as their transporting medium. [Middle English, from Latin *sēmen,* seed, semen. See **sē-** in Appendix.]

Se·me·nov (sə-myô′nəf), **Nikolai Nikolayevich.** 1896–1986. Soviet chemist. He shared a 1956 Nobel Prize for research on the kinetics of chemical reactions.

se·mes·ter (sə-mĕs′tər) *n.* One of two divisions of 15 to 18 weeks each of an academic year. [German, from Latin *(cursus) sēmēstris,* (course) of six months, from **sex-mēnstris* : *sē-,* six (from *sex;* see **s(w)eks** in Appendix) + *mēnsis,* month; see **mē-**[2] in Appendix.]

sem·i (sĕm′ī, sĕm′ē) *n., pl.* **sem·is.** *Informal.* **1.a.** A semitrailer. **b.** A tractor-trailer. **2.** A semifinal.

semi– *pref.* **1.** Half: *semicircle.* **2.** Partial; partially: *semiconscious.* **3.** Resembling or having some of the characteristics of:

ă pat	oi boy
ā pay	ou out
âr care	o͝o took
ä father	o͞o boot
ĕ pet	ŭ cut
ē be	ûr urge
ĭ pit	th thin
ī pie	*th* this
îr pier	hw which
ŏ pot	zh vision
ō toe	ə about, item
ô paw	♦ regionalism

Stress marks: **′** (primary); ′ (secondary), as in **dictionary** (dĭk′shə-nĕr′ē)

semidome

semiofficial. **4.** Occurring twice during: *semimonthly.* See Usage Note at **bi–¹.** [Middle English, from Latin *sēmi-,* half. See **sēmi-** in Appendix.]

sem·i·ab·stract (sĕm′ē-ăb-străkt′, -ăb′străkt′, sĕm′ī-) *adj.* Of or relating to an art form characterized by stylized but recognizable subject matter. **—sem′i·ab·strac′tion** *n.*

sem·i·an·nu·al (sĕm′ē-ăn′yo͞o-əl, sĕm′ī-) *adj.* Occurring or issued twice a year. **—sem′i·an′nu·al·ly** *adv.*

sem·i·a·quat·ic (sĕm′ē-ə-kwŏt′ĭk, -kwăt′-, sĕm′ī-) *adj.* Adapted for living or growing in or near water; not entirely aquatic: *a semiaquatic plant or animal.*

Sem·i-Ar·i·an (sĕm′ē-âr′ē-ən, -âr′-, sĕm′ī-) *n.* One of the members of the Homoiousian party led by the fourth-century A.D. Arian bishop Basil of Ancyra. **—Sem′i-Ar′i·an** *adj.* **—Sem′i-Ar′i·an·ism** *n.*

sem·i·ar·id (sĕm′ē-ăr′ĭd) *adj.* Characterized by relatively low annual rainfall of 25 to 50 centimeters (10 to 20 inches) and having scrubby vegetation with short, coarse grasses; not completely arid. **—sem′i·a·rid′i·ty** (-ə-rĭd′ĭ-tē, -ă-rĭd′-) *n.*

sem·i·at·tached (sĕm′ē-ə-tăcht′, sĕm′ī-) *adj.* Partially attached or joined: *a semiattached two-family frame house.*

sem·i·au·to·bi·o·graph·i·cal (sĕm′ē-ô′tə-bī′ə-grăf′ĭ-kəl, sĕm′ī-) *adj.* Of, relating to, or being a work that falls between fiction and autobiography: *a semiautobiographical film; a semiautobiographical novel.*

sem·i·au·to·mat·ed (sĕm′ē-ô′tə-mā′tĭd, sĕm′ī-) *adj.* Partially automated.

sem·i·au·to·mat·ic (sĕm′ē-ô′tə-măt′ĭk, sĕm′ī-) *adj.* **1.** Partially automatic. **2.** Ejecting a shell and loading the next round of ammunition automatically after each shot has been fired; autoloading. Used of a firearm. **—semiautomatic** *n.* A semiautomatic firearm.

sem·i·au·ton·o·mous (sĕm′ē-ô-tŏn′ə-məs, sĕm′ī-) *adj.* **1.** Partially self-governing. **2.** Having the powers of self-government within a larger organization or structure. **—sem′i·au·ton′o·mous·ly** *adv.* **—sem′i·au·ton′o·my** *n.*

sem·i·breve (sĕm′ē-brĕv′, -brēv′, sĕm′ī-) *n.* *Chiefly British.* A whole note in music.

sem·i·cen·ten·ni·al (sĕm′ē-sĕn-tĕn′ē-əl, sĕm′ī-) *adj.* Marking the 50th anniversary of an event. **—semicentennial** *n.* A 50th anniversary or its celebration.

sem·i·cir·cle (sĕm′ĭ-sûr′kəl) *n.* **1.** A half of a circle as divided by a diameter. **2.** An object or arrangement of objects or people in the shape of half a circle. **—sem′i·cir′cu·lar** (-kyə-lər) *adj.*

semicircular canal *n.* Any of three tubular and looped structures of the inner ear, together functioning in maintenance of the sense of balance in the body.

sem·i·civ·i·lized (sĕm′ē-sĭv′ə-līzd′, sĕm′ī-) *adj.* Partly civilized.

sem·i·clas·si·cal (sĕm′ē-klăs′ĭ-kəl, sĕm′ī-) *adj.* *Music.* **1.** Of, relating to, or being a work that in style or form falls between the classical and popular genres. **2.** Of, relating to, or being a classical composition that enjoys popular appeal because of modern elements.

sem·i·co·lon (sĕm′ĭ-kō′lən) *n.* A mark of punctuation (;) used to connect independent clauses and indicating a closer relationship between the clauses than a period does.

sem·i·co·ma (sĕm′ē-kō′mə, sĕm′ī-) *n.* A partial or mild comatose state; a coma from which a person may be roused by various stimuli. **—sem′i·co′ma·tose′** (-kō′mə-tōs′, -kŏm′ə-) *adj.*

sem·i·con·duc·tor (sĕm′ē-kən-dŭk′tər, sĕm′ī-) *n.* Any of various solid crystalline substances, such as germanium or silicon, having electrical conductivity greater than insulators but less than good conductors. **—sem′i·con·duct′ing** *adj.*

sem·i·con·scious (sĕm′ē-kŏn′shəs, sĕm′ī-) *adj.* Partially conscious; not completely aware of sensations. **—sem′i·con′scious·ly** *adv.* **—sem′i·con′scious·ness** *n.*

sem·i·con·ser·va·tive (sĕm′ē-kən-sûr′və-tĭv, sĕm′ī-) *adj.* Of or designating the replication of a nucleic acid molecule, especially DNA, by separation of the two original strands of the molecule so that each acts as a template on which a new, complementary strand is laid down.

sem·i·dark·ness (sĕm′ē-därk′nĭs, sĕm′ī-) *n.* Partial darkness.

sem·i·des·ert (sĕm′ē-dĕz′ərt, sĕm′ī-) *n.* A semiarid area often located between a desert and a grassland or woodland.

sem·i·de·tached (sĕm′ē-dĭ-tăcht′, sĕm′ī-) *adj.* Attached to something on one side only: *a semidetached house.*

sem·i·di·am·e·ter (sĕm′ē-dī-ăm′ĭ-tər, sĕm′ī-) *n.* The apparent radius of a celestial body when viewed as a disk from Earth.

sem·i·di·ur·nal (sĕm′ē-dī-ûr′nəl, sĕm′ī-) *adj.* **1.** Of, relating to, occurring, or performed during half a day. **2.** Occurring or coming approximately once every 12 hours, as the tides. **3.** Of or relating to the arc described by a celestial body between its meridian passage and its points of rising or setting.

sem·i·di·vine (sĕm′ē-dĭ-vīn′, sĕm′ī-) *adj.* Not fully divine but more than mortal, as a demigod in Greek mythology.

sem·i·doc·u·men·ta·ry (sĕm′ē-dŏk′yə-mĕn′tə-rē, sĕm′ī-) *n., pl.* **-ries.** A book, movie, or television program presenting a fictional story that incorporates many factual details or actual events. **—sem′i·doc′u·men′ta·ry** *adj.*

sem·i·dome (sĕm′ē-dōm′, sĕm′ī-) *n.* A roof covering a semicircular space; half a dome.

sem·i·dry (sĕm′ēdrī′, sĕm′ī-) *adj.* **1.** Partially dry. **2.** Moderately dry. Used of wine.

sem·i·el·lip·ti·cal (sĕm′ē-ĭ-lĭp′tĭ-kəl, sĕm′ī-) *adj.* Having the form or shape of half of an ellipse, especially when divided along the major axis.

sem·i·feu·dal (sĕm′ē-fyo͞od′l, sĕm′ī-) *adj.* Partially feudal: *a semifeudal social and economic system; a landed, semifeudal class of people.*

sem·i·fi·nal (sĕm′ē-fī′nəl, sĕm′ī-) *n.* **1.** A match, a competition, or an examination that precedes the final one. **2.** One of the two competitions of the next to the last round in an elimination tournament. **—sem′i·fi′nal** *adj.* **—sem′i·fi′nal·ist** *n.*

sem·i·fin·ished (sĕm′ē-fĭn′ĭsht, sĕm′ī-) *adj.* **1.** Made, treated, or sold to be used in a finished product: *semifinished steel.* **2.** Partially finished: *a semifinished basement.*

sem·i·flex·i·ble (sĕm′ē-flĕk′sə-bəl, sĕm′ī-) *adj.* Partially or somewhat flexible: *semiflexible tubing.*

sem·i·flex·ion (sĕm′ē-flĕk′shən, sĕm′ī-) *n.* The position of a limb or muscle halfway between flexion and extension.

sem·i·flu·id (sĕm′ē-flo͞o′ĭd, sĕm′ī-) *adj.* Intermediate in flow properties between solids and liquids; highly viscous. **—sem′i·flu′id** *n.* **—sem′i·flu·id′i·ty** *n.*

sem·i·for·mal (sĕm′ē-fôr′məl, sĕm′ī-) *adj.* **1.** Moderately formal: *a semiformal dance.* **2.** Suitable or appropriate for a moderately formal occasion: *semiformal attire.*

sem·i·gloss (sĕm′ē-glŏs′, -glôs′, sĕm′ī-) *n.* A paint that dries with a finish that is between gloss and flat. **—sem′i·gloss′, sem′i·gloss′y** *adj.*

sem·i·gov·ern·men·tal (sĕm′ē-gŭv′ərn-mĕn′tl, sĕm′ī-) *adj.* Partially owned or managed by a government or government agency.

sem·i·group (sĕm′ē-gro͞op′, sĕm′ī-) *n.* *Mathematics.* A set for which there is a binary operation that is closed and associative.

sem·i·hard (sĕm′ē-härd′, sĕm′ī-) *adj.* Intermediate between hard and soft: *a semihard cheese.*

sem·i-in·de·pend·ent (sĕm′ē-ĭn′dĭ-pĕn′dənt, sĕm′ī-) *adj.* **1.** Partially independent. **2.** Semiautonomous.

sem·i-in·fi·nite (sĕm′ē-ĭn′fə-nĭt, sĕm′ī-) *adj.* *Mathematics.* Unbounded in one direction or dimension.

sem·i·liq·uid (sĕm′ē-lĭk′wĭd, sĕm′ī-) *adj.* Intermediate in properties, especially in flow properties, between liquids and solids. **—sem′i·liq′uid** *n.* **—sem′i·liq·uid′i·ty** *n.*

sem·i·lit·er·ate (sĕm′ē-lĭt′ər-ĭt, sĕm′ī-) *adj.* **1.** Having achieved an elementary level of ability in reading and writing. **2.** Having limited knowledge or understanding, especially of a technical subject. **—sem′i·lit′er·a·cy** (-ər-ə-sē) *n.*

Sé·mil·lon also **Se·mil·lon** (sā′mĕl-yôɴ) *n.* A variety of late-ripening grapes, often blended with sauvignon blanc grapes to produce a dry white wine with a crisp taste. [French, from obsolete *sémilion,* from dialectal *semilhoun,* from Old Provençal *semilhar,* to sow, from *seme,* seed, from Latin *sēmen.* See SEMEN.]

sem·i·log (sĕm′ē-lôg′, -lŏg′, sĕm′ī-) *adj.* *Mathematics.* Semilogarithmic.

sem·i·log·a·rith·mic (sĕm′ē-lô′gə-rĭth′mĭk, -lŏg′ə-, sĕm′ī-) *adj.* *Mathematics.* Having one logarithmic and one arithmetic scale: *semilogarithmic graph paper.*

sem·i·lu·nar (sĕm′ē-lo͞o′nər, sĕm′ī-) also **sem·i·lu·nate** (-lo͞o′nāt′) *adj.* Shaped like a half-moon; crescent-shaped.

semilunar bone *n.* See **lunate bone.**

semilunar cartilage *n.* Either of the crescent-shaped wedges of fibrocartilage found in the knee joint.

semilunar valve *n.* Either of two valves, one located at the opening of the aorta and the other at the opening of the pulmonary artery, each consisting of three crescent-shaped cusps and serving to prevent blood from flowing back into the ventricles.

sem·i·lu·nate (sĕm′ē-lo͞o′nāt′, sĕm′ī-) *adj.* Variant of **semilunar.**

sem·i·mem·bra·nous (sĕm′ē-mĕm′brə-nəs, sĕm′ī-) *adj.* Partly membranous, as one of the hamstring muscles.

sem·i·month·ly (sĕm′ē-mŭnth′lē, sĕm′ī-) *adj.* Occurring or issued twice a month. **—semimonthly** *n., pl.* **-lies.** A semimonthly publication. **—semimonthly** *adv.* At intervals twice monthly. See Usage Note at **bi–¹.**

sem·i·mys·ti·cal (sĕm′ē-mĭs′tĭ-kəl, sĕm′ī-) *adj.* Somewhat mystical: *a semimystical tradition.*

sem·i·nal (sĕm′ə-nəl) *adj.* **1.** Of, relating to, containing, or conveying semen or seed. **2.** Of, relating to, or having the power to originate; creative. **3.** Highly influential in an original way; constituting or providing a basis for further development. [Middle English, from Old French, from Latin *sēminālis,* from *sēmen, sēmin-,* seed. See SEMEN.] **—sem′i·nal·ly** *adv.*

seminal duct *n.* The duct of the testis that carries semen outward, especially the part of the duct that runs from the epididymis to the ejaculatory duct.

seminal fluid *n.* Semen, especially the fluid part of semen without the spermatozoa.

seminal vesicle *n.* Either of a pair of pouchlike glands situated on each side of the male urinary bladder that secrete seminal fluid and nourish and promote the movement of spermatozoa through the urethra.

sem·i·nar (sĕm′ə-när′) *n.* **1.a.** A small group of advanced students in a college or graduate school engaged in original research or intensive study under the guidance of a professor who meets regularly with them to discuss their reports and findings. **b.** A course of study so pursued. **c.** A scheduled meeting of such a group. **2.** A meeting for an exchange of ideas; a conference. [German, from Latin *sēminārium,* seed plot. See SEMINARY.]

sem·i·nar·i·an (sĕm′ə-nâr′ē-ən) also **sem·i·nar·ist** (-ĭst) *n.* A student at a seminary.

sem·i·nar·y (sĕm′ə-nĕr′ē) *n., pl.* **-ies.** *Abbr.* **sem. 1.a.** A school, especially a theological school for the training of priests, ministers, or rabbis. **b.** A school of higher education, especially a private school for girls. **2.** A place or environment in which something is developed or nurtured. [Middle English, seed plot, from Latin *sēminārium,* from *sēminārius,* of seed, from *sēmen, sēmin-,* seed. See **sē-** in Appendix.]

sem·i·nif·er·ous (sĕm′ə-nĭf′ər-əs) *adj. Biology.* **1.** Conveying, containing, or producing semen. **2.** Bearing seed. [Latin *sēmen, sēmin-,* seed, semen; see SEMEN + –FEROUS.]

sem·i·niv·o·rous (sĕm′ə-nĭv′ər-əs) *adj.* Feeding on seeds: *seminivorous birds.* [Latin *sēmen, sēmin-,* seed; see SEMEN + –VOROUS.]

Sem·i·nole (sĕm′ə-nōl′) *n., pl.* **Seminole** or **-noles. 1.a.** A Native American people made up of various primarily Creek groups who moved into northern Florida during the 18th and 19th centuries, later inhabiting the Everglades region as well, with present-day populations in Oklahoma and southern Florida. The Seminole Wars ended in the removal of the majority of the Seminoles to Indian Territory. **b.** A member of this people. **2.** Either of the Muskogean languages of the Seminole. [Alteration of *Seminolie,* from Creek *simalóoni, simanóoli,* runaway, from American Spanish *cimarrón.* See MAROON[1].] **—Sem′i·nole′** *adj.*

Seminole bread *n.* See **coontie.**

sem·i·no·ma (sĕm′ə-nō′mə) *n., pl.* **-mas** or **-ma·ta** (-mə-tə). A malignant tumor of the testis arising from sperm-forming tissue. [Latin *sēmen, sēmin-,* semen; see SEMEN + –OMA.]

sem·i·no·mad (sĕm′ē-nō′măd′, sĕm′ī-) *n.* One of a people whose living habits are largely nomadic but who plant some crops at a base point. **—sem′i·no·mad′ic** *adj.*

sem·i·nude (sĕm′ē-no͞od′, -nyo͞od′, sĕm′ī-) *adv. & adj.* Only partially clothed: *posed seminude for a painter; seminude statues.* **—sem′i·nu′di·ty** *n.*

sem·i·of·fi·cial (sĕm′ē-ə-fĭsh′əl, sĕm′ī-) *adj.* Having some official authority or sanction. **—sem′i·of·fi′cial·ly** *adv.*

se·mi·ol·o·gy also **se·mei·ol·o·gy** (sē′mē-ŏl′ə-jē, sĕm′ē-, sē′mī-) *n.* **1.a.** The science that deals with signs or sign language. **b.** The use of signs in signaling, as with a semaphore. **2.** *Medicine.* Symptomatology. [Greek *sēmeion,* sign; see SEMIOTIC + –LOGY.]

sem·i·o·paque (sĕm′ē-ō-pāk′, sĕm′ī-) *adj.* Partially opaque.

se·mi·ot·ic (sē′mē-ŏt′ĭk, sĕm′ē-, sē′mī-) also **se·mi·ot·i·cal** (-ĭ-kəl) or **se·mei·ot·ic** (sē′mē-, sĕm′ē-, sē′mī-), **se·mei·ot·i·cal** (-ĭ-kəl) *adj.* **1.** Of or relating to semantics. **2.** *Medicine.* Relating to symptomatology. [Greek *sēmeiōtikos,* observant of signs, significant, from *sēmeiōsis,* indication, from *sēmeioun,* to signal, to interpret as a sign, from *sēmeion,* sign, from *sēma.*]

se·mi·ot·ics also **se·mei·ot·ics** (sē′mē-ŏt′ĭks, sĕm′ē-, sē′mī-) *n.* (*used with a sing. verb*). Semantics. **—se′mi·o·ti′cian** (-ə-tĭsh′ən) *n.*

sem·i·o·vip·a·rous (sĕm′ē-ō-vĭp′ər-əs, sĕm′ī-) *adj.* Bearing living young that are incompletely developed, as a kangaroo or other marsupial.

Sem·i·pa·la·tinsk (sĕm′ē-pə-lä′tĭnsk, syĭ-myĭ-). A city of northeast Kazakhstan on the Irtysh River north-northeast of Alma-Ata. Founded as a fortress in 1718, it is a port and processing center. Population, 317,000.

sem·i·pal·mate (sĕm′ē-păl′māt′, -pä′-, -päl′māt′, sĕm′ī-) also **sem·i·pal·mat·ed** (-mā′tĭd) *adj.* Having partial or reduced webbing between the toes, as some wading birds do.

semipalmated plover *n.* A small plover *(Charadrius semipalmatus)* that breeds in the arctic New World and has a web between the middle and inner toes.

sem·i·par·a·site (sĕm′ē-păr′ə-sīt′, sĕm′ī-) *n.* See **hemiparasite** (sense 1). **—sem′i·par′a·sit′ic** (-sĭt′ĭk) *adj.* **—sem′i·par′a·sit·ism** (-sĭ-tĭz′əm) *n.*

sem·i·per·me·a·ble (sĕm′ē-pûr′mē-ə-bəl, sĕm′ī-) *adj.* **1.** Partially permeable. **2.** Allowing passage of certain, especially small, molecules or ions but acting as a barrier to others. Used of biological and synthetic membranes. **—sem′i·per′me·a·bil′i·ty** *n.*

sem·i·po·lit·i·cal (sĕm′ē-pə-lĭt′ĭ-kəl, sĕm′ī-) *adj.* Political in some aspects or activities.

sem·i·por·ce·lain (sĕm′ē-pôr′sə-lĭn, -pōr′-, sĕm′ī-) *n.* Any of several glazed ceramic wares resembling porcelain but having little or no translucency.

sem·i·pre·cious stone (sĕm′ē-prĕsh′əs, sĕm′ī-) *n.* A gem, such as an opal, that has commercial value but is not as rare or expensive as a precious stone.

sem·i·pri·vate (sĕm′ē-prī′vĭt, sĕm′ī-) *adj.* Shared with usually one to three other hospital patients: *a semiprivate room.*

sem·i·pro (sĕm′ē-prō′, sĕm′ī-) *adj. Informal.* Semiprofessional: *a semipro baseball player.* **—sem′i·pro′** *n.*

sem·i·pro·fes·sion·al (sĕm′ē-prə-fĕsh′ə-nəl, sĕm′ī-) *adj. Sports.* **1.** Taking part in a sport for pay but not on a full-time basis. **2.** Composed of or engaged in by semiprofessional players. **—semiprofessional** *n.* **1.** *Sports.* A semiprofessional player. **2.** One whose occupation or work has some of the characteristics of a profession or of a professional. **—sem′i·pro·fes′sion·al·ly** *adv.*

sem·i·pub·lic (sĕm′ē-pŭb′lĭk, sĕm′ī-) *adj.* **1.** Partially but not entirely open to the use of the public: *prohibited smoking in public and semipublic places.* **2.** Partially but not totally owned by the public: *purchases made by semipublic organizations such as universities, utilities, and the postal service.* **3.** Open to the knowledge and judgment of only a part of the public: *Any public or semipublic expression of racism is controversial.* **—sem′i·pub′lic·ly** *adv.*

sem·i·qua·ver (sĕm′ē-kwā′vər) *n. Chiefly British & Music.* A sixteenth note.

sem·i·re·tired (sĕm′ē-rĭ-tīrd′, sĕm′ī-) *adj.* Working only on a part-time basis, as for reasons of ill health or advanced age. **—sem′i·re·tire′ment** (-tīr′mənt) *n.*

sem·i·rig·id (sĕm′ē-rĭj′ĭd, sĕm′ī-) *adj.* Partly or moderately rigid.

sem·i·round (sĕm′ē-round′, sĕm′ī-) *adj.* Having a round side and a flat side. **—semiround** (sĕm′ē-round′, sĕm′ī-) *n.* Something that has a round side and a flat side.

sem·i·ru·ral (sĕm′ē-ro͝or′əl, sĕm′ī-) *adj.* Having both rural and urban characteristics: *a semirural town; a semirural environment; a semirural way of life.*

sem·i·skilled (sĕm′ē-skĭld′, sĕm′ī-) *adj.* **1.** Possessing some skills but not enough to do specialized work: *semiskilled dockworkers.* **2.** Requiring limited skills: *a semiskilled job.*

sem·i·soft (sĕm′ē-sôft′, -sŏft′, sĕm′ī-) *adj.* **1.** Of medium softness. **2.** Firm but easily sliced: *semisoft cheese.*

sem·i·sol·id (sĕm′ē-sŏl′ĭd, sĕm′ī-) *adj.* Intermediate in properties, especially in rigidity, between solids and liquids. **—semisolid** (sĕm′ē-sŏl′ĭd, sĕm′ī-) *n.* A semisolid substance, such as a stiff dough or firm gelatin.

sem·i·staged (sĕm′ē-stājd′, sĕm′ī-) *adj.* Performed and presented without all the usual stage effects, costumes, or participants: *a semistaged version of an opera.*

sem·i·ster·ile (sĕm′ē-stĕr′əl, -īl′, sĕm′ī-) *adj.* Not completely fertile; partly sterile: *semisterile pollen; semisterile male pupae.*

sem·i·sub·mers·i·ble (sĕm′ē-səb-mûr′sə-bəl, sĕm′ī-) *n.* A seagoing, self-propelled barge that rides at anchor, stands on partially submerged vertical legs on submerged pontoons, and serves as living quarters and a base of operations in offshore drilling. Also called *semisubmersible rig.* **—sem′i·sub·mer′si·ble** *adj.*

sem·i·sweet (sĕm′ē-swēt′, sĕm′ī-) *adj.* Having a small amount of sweetening: *semisweet chocolate.*

sem·i·syn·thet·ic (sĕm′ē-sĭn-thĕt′ĭk, sĕm′ī-) *adj.* **1.** Prepared by chemical synthesis from natural materials: *a semisynthetic antibiotic.* **2.** Consisting of a mixture of natural and synthetic substances: *a semisynthetic culture medium.*

Sem·ite (sĕm′īt′) *n.* **1.** A member of a group of Semitic-speaking peoples of the Near East and northern Africa, including the Arabs, Arameans, Babylonians, Carthaginians, Ethiopians, Hebrews, and Phoenicians. **2.** A Jew. **3.** *Bible.* A descendant of Shem. [Back-formation from SEMITIC.]

sem·i·ter·res·tri·al (sĕm′ē-tə-rĕs′trē-əl, sĕm′ī-) *adj.* Not growing or living entirely on land; partly terrestrial: *a semiterrestrial crustacean.*

Se·mit·ic (sə-mĭt′ĭk) *adj. Abbr.* **Sem. 1.** Of or relating to the Semites or their languages or cultures. **2.** Of, relating to, or constituting a subgroup of the Afro-Asiatic language group that includes Arabic, Hebrew, Amharic, and Aramaic. **—Semitic** *n. Abbr.* **Sem. 1.** The Semitic languages. **2.** Any one of the Semitic languages. [New Latin *Sēmiticus,* from *Sēmita,* Semite, from Late Latin *Sēm,* Shem, eponymous ancestor of the Semites, from Greek, from Hebrew *Šēm.*]

Se·mit·ics (sə-mĭt′ĭks) *n.* (*used with a sing. verb*). The study of the history, languages, and cultures of the Semitic peoples. **—Se·mit′i·cist** (-ĭ-sĭst) *n.*

Sem·i·tism (sĕm′ĭ-tĭz′əm) *n.* **1.** A Semitic word or idiom. **2.** Semitic traits, attributes, or customs. **3.** A policy or predisposition in favor of Jews.

sem·i·tone (sĕm′ē-tōn′, sĕm′ī-) *n. Music.* An interval equal to a half tone in the standard diatonic scale. Also called *half step, half tone.* **—sem′i·ton′ic** (-tŏn′ĭk) *adj.* **—sem′i·ton′i·cal·ly** *adv.*

sem·i·trail·er (sĕm′ē-trā′lər, sĕm′ī-) *n.* A trailer having a set or several sets of wheels at the rear only, with the forward portion being supported by the truck tractor or towing vehicle.

sem·i·trans·par·ent (sĕm′ē-trăns-pâr′ənt, -păr′-, sĕm′ī-) *adj.* Partially transparent.

sem·i·trop·i·cal (sĕm′ē-trŏp′ĭ-kəl, sĕm′ī-) *adj.* Partly tropical; subtropical.

ă pat	oi boy
ā pay	ou out
âr care	o͝o took
ä father	o͞o boot
ĕ pet	ŭ cut
ē be	ûr urge
ĭ pit	th thin
ī pie	*th* this
îr pier	hw which
ŏ pot	zh vision
ō toe	ə about, item
ô paw	♦ regionalism

Stress marks: ′ (primary); ′ (secondary), as in **dictionary** (dĭk′shə-nĕr′ē)

sem·i·vow·el (sĕm′ĭ-vou′əl) *n. Linguistics.* A sound that has the quality of one of the high vowels, as (ē) or (o͞o), and that functions as a consonant before vowels, as the initial sounds of *yell* and *well.* Also called *glide.*

sem·i·week·ly (sĕm′ē-wēk′lē, sĕm′ī-) *adj.* Issued or occurring twice a week. **—semiweekly** *n., pl.* **-lies.** A semiweekly event or publication. **—semiweekly** *adv.* Twice weekly. See Usage Note at **bi–¹.**

sem·i·year·ly (sĕm′ē-yîr′lē, sĕm′ī-) *adj.* Issued or occurring twice a year or once every half year. **—semiyearly** *n., pl.* **-lies.** A semiyearly event or publication. **—semiyearly** *adv.* Every half year.

sem·o·li·na (sĕm′ə-lē′nə) *n.* The gritty, coarse particles of wheat left after the finer flour has passed through a bolting machine, used for pasta. [Alteration of Italian *semolino,* diminutive of *semola,* bran, from Latin *simila,* fine flour, probably of Semitic origin.]

sem·pi·ter·nal (sĕm′pĭ-tûr′nəl) *adj.* Enduring forever; eternal. See Synonyms at **infinite.** [Middle English, from Old French *sempiternel,* from Late Latin *sempiternālis,* from Latin *sempiternus* : *semper,* always; see **sem-¹** in Appendix + *aeternus,* eternal; see **aiw-** in Appendix.] **—sem′pi·ter′ni·ty** (-nĭ-tē) *n.*

sem·pli·ce (sĕm′plĭ-chā′) *adv. & adj. Music.* In a simple or plain manner. Used chiefly as a direction. [Italian, from Latin *simplex, simplic-,* simple. See **sem-¹** in Appendix.]

sem·pre (sĕm′prā) *adv. Music.* In the same manner throughout. Used chiefly as a direction. [Italian, always, from Latin *semper.* See **sem-¹** in Appendix.]

sen¹ (sĕn) *n., pl.* **sen.** See table at **currency.** [Japanese, from Chinese (Mandarin) *qián,* money, coin.]

sen² (sĕn) *n., pl.* **sen.** See table at **currency.** [Indonesian *senti, sen,* ultimately from CENT.]

sen. or **Sen.** *abbr.* **1.** Senate; senator. **2.** Senior.

se·nar·i·us (sə-nâr′ē-əs) *n., pl.* **-i·i** (-ē-ī′, -ē-ē′). A Latin verse consisting of six iambic feet. [Latin *sēnārius,* consisting of six each, senarius. See SENARY.]

sen·a·ry (sĕn′ə-rē) *adj.* **1.** Of or relating to the number six. **2.** Having six things or parts. [Latin *sēnārius,* from *sēnī,* six each, from *sex,* six. See **s(w)eks** in Appendix.]

sen·ate (sĕn′ĭt) *n. Abbr.* **sen., Sen. 1.** An assembly or a council of citizens having the highest deliberative and legislative functions in a government, specifically: **a. Senate.** The upper house of the U.S. Congress, to which two members are elected from each state by popular vote for a six-year term. **b.** Often **Senate.** The upper house in the bicameral legislature of many states in the United States. **c. Senate.** The upper legislative house in Canada, France, and some other countries. **d.** The supreme council of state of the ancient Roman Republic and later of the Roman Empire. **2.** The building or hall in which such a council or assembly meets. **3.** A governing, advisory, or disciplinary body of some colleges and universities composed of faculty members and sometimes student representatives. [Middle English *senat,* from Old French, from Latin *senātus,* from *senex, sen-,* old, an elder. See **sen-** in Appendix.]

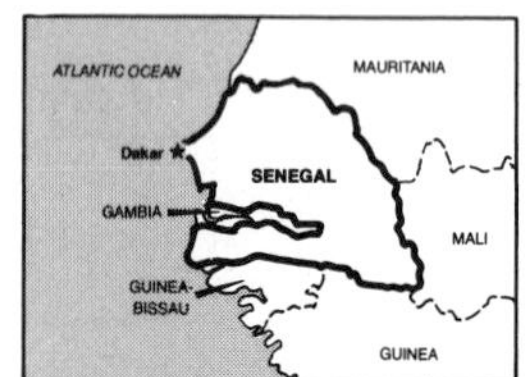

Senegal

sen·a·tor (sĕn′ə-tər) *n. Abbr.* **sen., Sen.** A member of a senate. **—sen′a·tor·ship′** *n.*

sen·a·to·ri·al (sĕn′ə-tôr′ē-əl, -tōr′-) *adj.* **1.** Of, concerning, or befitting a senator or senate. **2.** Composed of senators. **—sen′a·to′ri·al·ly** *adv.*

senatorial courtesy *n.* The custom in the U.S. Senate of refusing to confirm a presidential appointment to office opposed by both senators from the state of the appointee or by the senior senator of the President's party.

senatorial district *n.* A territorial district from which a senator is elected.

send¹ (sĕnd) *v.* **sent** (sĕnt), **send·ing, sends.** —*tr.* **1.** To cause to be conveyed by an intermediary to a destination: *send goods by plane.* **2.** To dispatch, as by a communications medium: *send a message by radio.* **3.a.** To direct to go on a mission: *sent troops into the Middle East.* **b.** To require or enable to go: *sent her children to college.* **c.** To direct (a person) to a source of information; refer: *sent the student to the reference section of the library.* **4.a.** To give off (heat, for example); emit or issue: *a stove that sends forth great warmth.* **b.** To utter or otherwise emit (sound): *sent forth a cry of pain.* **5.** To hit so as to direct or propel with force; drive: *The batter sent the ball to left field. The slap on my back sent me staggering.* **6.** To cause to take place or occur: *We will meet whatever vicissitudes fate may send.* **7.a.** To put or drive into a given state or condition: *horrifying news that sent them into a panic.* **b.** *Slang.* To transport with delight; carry away: *That music really sends me.* —*intr.* **1.** To dispatch someone to do an errand or convey a message: *Let's send out for hamburgers.* **2.** To dispatch a request or an order, especially by mail: *send away for a new catalogue.* **3.** To transmit a message or messages: *The radio operator was still sending when the ship went down.* **—*phrasal verbs.* send down.** *Chiefly British.* To suspend or dismiss from a university. **send for.** To request to come by means of a message or messenger; summon. **send in. 1.** To cause to arrive or to be delivered to the recipient: *Let's send in a letter of protest.* **2.** *Sports.* To put (a player) into or back into a game or contest: *The coach is sending in the kicker.* **3.** To cause (someone) to arrive in or become involved in a particular place or situation: *The commander sent in the sappers. It's time to send in the lawyers.* **send up.** *Informal.* **1.** To send to jail: *was sent up for 20 years.* **2.** To make a parody of: *"grandiloquently eccentric but witty verbiage . . . that would send up the nastiness of suburban London"* (New York). **—*idioms.* send flying.** *Informal.* To cause to be knocked or scattered about with force: *a blow to the table that sent the dishes flying.* **send packing.** To dismiss (someone) abruptly. [Middle English *senden,* from Old English *sendan.* See **sent-** in Appendix.] **—send′er** *n.*

SYNONYMS: *send, dispatch, forward, route, ship, transmit.* The central meaning shared by these verbs is "to cause to go or be taken to a destination": *sent the package by parcel post; dispatched a union representative to the factory; forwarding the mail to their new address; routed the soldiers through New York; shipping oil in tankers; transmitting money by cable.*

send² (sĕnd) *v. & n. Nautical.* Variant of **scend.**

Sen·dai (sĕn-dī′). A city of northeast Honshu, Japan, on an inlet of the Pacific Ocean north of Tokyo. It is an important cultural and educational center. Population, 700,248.

Sendai virus *n.* A paramyxovirus used in research laboratories for its tendency to induce genetically different cells or nuclei to fuse, the resulting hybrid cells having useful properties such as the ability to synthesize specific antibodies. [After SENDAI.]

sen·dal (sĕn′dl) *n.* A thin, light silk used in the Middle Ages for fine garments, church vestments, and banners. [Middle English *cendal,* from Old French, ultimately from Greek *sindōn,* fine linen.]

send·off (sĕnd′ôf′, -ŏf′) *n.* **1.** A demonstration of affection and good wishes for the beginning of a new undertaking. **2.** A farewell: *gave our guests a hearty sendoff at the airport.*

send-up or **send·up** (sĕnd′ŭp′) *n. Informal.* An amusing imitation or parody; a takeoff: *"The absurd trial is, of course, a send-up of the Dublin courts"* (New Yorker).

se·ne (sā′nā) *n., pl.* **sene.** See table at **currency.** [Samoan, from English CENT.]

Sen·e·ca (sĕn′ĭ-kə) *n., pl.* **Seneca** or **-cas. 1.a.** A Native American people formerly inhabiting western New York from Seneca Lake to Lake Erie, with present-day populations in this same area and in southeast Ontario. The Seneca are the westernmost member of the original Iroquois confederacy. **b.** A member of this people. **2.** The Iroquoian language of the Seneca. [From Dutch *Sennecaas,* probably of Mahican origin.]

Seneca, Lucius Annaeus. Known as "the Younger." 4 B.C.?–A.D. 65. Roman Stoic philosopher, writer, and tutor of Nero. His works include treatises on rhetoric and governance and numerous plays that influenced Renaissance and Elizabethan drama.

Seneca Falls. A village of west-central New York on the Seneca River east-southeast of Rochester. The first women's rights convention was held here in 1848. Population, 7,466.

Seneca Lake. A lake of west-central New York connected with Cayuga Lake by the **Seneca River,** about 105 km (65 mi) long. Seneca Lake is the largest of the Finger Lakes.

Seneca snakeroot *n.* An eastern North American plant *(Polygala senega)* having a terminal cluster of small white flowers and roots that are used medicinally.

se·nec·ti·tude (sĭ-nĕk′tĭ-to͞od′, -tyo͞od′) *n.* Old age; elderliness. [Medieval Latin *senectitūdō,* from Latin *senectūs,* from *senex, sen-,* old, an elder. See **sen-** in Appendix.]

sen·e·ga (sĕn′ĭ-gə) *n.* The dried roots of the Seneca snakeroot, used medicinally as an expectorant. [Alteration of SENECA (from its use by this people).]

Sen·e·gal (sĕn′ĭ-gôl′, -gäl′). A country of western Africa on the Atlantic Ocean. First settled in prehistoric times, it was colonized by Portuguese, Dutch, French, and British traders and became a French possession in the 19th century. Senegal achieved independence in 1960. Dakar is the capital and the largest city. Population, 6,038,000. **—Sen′e·ga·lese′** (-gô-lēz′, -lēs′, -gə-) *adj. & n.*

Senegal River. A river of western Africa rising in western Mali and flowing about 1,609 km (1,000 mi) generally northwest and west along the Mauritania-Senegal border to the Atlantic Ocean.

Sen·e·gam·bi·a (sĕn′ĭ-găm′bē-ə). A region of western Africa watered by the Senegal and Gambia rivers.

se·nes·cent (sĭ-nĕs′ənt) *adj.* Growing old; aging. [Latin *senēscēns, senēscent-,* present participle of *senēscere,* to grow old, inchoative of *senēre,* to be old, from *senex, sen-,* old. See **sen-** in Appendix.] **—se·nes′cence** *n.*

sen·e·schal (sĕn′ə-shəl) *n.* An official in a medieval noble household in charge of domestic arrangements and the administration of servants; a steward or major-domo. [Middle English, from Old French, of Germanic origin.]

se·nile (sē′nīl′, sĕn′īl′) *adj.* **1.** Relating to, characteristic of, or resulting from old age. **2.** Exhibiting the symptoms of senility, as impaired memory or the inability to perform certain mental tasks. **3.** *Geology.* Worn away nearly to the base level, as at the end of an erosion cycle. [Latin *senīlis,* from *senex, sen-,* old. See **sen-** in Appendix.] **—se′nile′ly** *adv.*

WORD HISTORY: In earlier writings one finds phrases such as "a *senile* maturity of judgment" and "green and vigorous *senility,*" demonstrating that these two words have not always been burdened with their current negative connotations. *Senile* and *senility* are examples of pejoration, the process by which a word's meaning changes for the worse over time. Even though *senile* (first recorded in 1661) and *senility* (first recorded in 1778) initially had neutral senses such as "pertaining to old age," it is probable that the weakness (in particular the mental weakness) that sometimes accompanies old age eventually caused negative senses to predominate. Certainly some pejorative associations were present in Latin *senīlis,* "relating to an old man, aged," the ultimate source of both words, and in related Latin words such as *senēscere,* which could mean "to deteriorate with age." But it seems that pejorative associations have taken over these words in English through general usage, perhaps because average life expectancy has risen steadily over the years.

---

senile dementia *n.* A progressive, abnormally accelerated deterioration of mental faculties and emotional stability in old age, occurring especially in Alzheimer's disease.

se•nil•i•ty (sĭ-nĭl′ĭ-tē) *n.* **1.** The state of being senile. **2.** The mental and physical deterioration characteristic of old age.

sen•ior (sēn′yər) *adj.* **1.** *Abbr.* **Sr., sr.** Of, relating to, or being the older of two, especially the older of two persons having the same name, as father and son. **2.** *Abbr.* **sen., Sen. a.** Being in a position, rank, or grade above others of the same set or class: *a senior officer; the senior ship in the battle group.* **b.** Having precedence in making certain decisions. **3.** *Abbr.* **sen., Sen., Sr., sr.** Of or relating to the fourth and last year of high school or college: *our senior class.* **—senior** *n.* **1.** *Abbr.* **sen., Sen. a.** A person who is older than another: *She is eight years my senior.* **b.** A senior citizen: *"The interests of seniors tend to be . . . varied . . . Their energy levels . . . can be every bit as intense as those expended by younger people"* (Elaine Sherman). **2.** *Abbr.* **sen., Sen., Sr., sr. a.** One that is of a higher position, rank, or grade than another in the same set or class. **b.** A student in the fourth year of high school or college. [Middle English, from Latin, comparative of *senex,* old. See **sen-** in Appendix.]

senior chief petty officer *n. Abbr.* **SCPO, CPOS 1.** A noncommissioned rank in the U.S. Navy that is above chief petty officer and below master chief petty officer. **2.** One who holds this rank.

senior citizen *n.* A person of or over the age of retirement. **—sen′ior-cit′i•zen** (sēn′yər-sĭt′ĭ-zən) *adj.* **—senior citizenry** *n.*

senior debt *n.* A class of corporate debt that has priority with respect to interest and principal over other classes of debt and over all classes of equity by the same issuer.

senior high school *n.* A high school usually constituting grades 10, 11, and 12.

sen•ior•i•ty (sēn-yôr′ĭ-tē, -yŏr′-) *n.* **1.** The state of being older than another or others or higher in rank than another or others. **2.** Precedence of position, especially precedence over others of the same rank by reason of a longer span of service.

senior lecturer *n. Chiefly British.* A university teacher, especially one ranking next below a reader.

senior master sergeant *n. Abbr.* **S.M.Sgt., SMSGT 1.** A noncommissioned rank in the U.S. Air Force that is above master sergeant and below chief master sergeant. **2.** One who holds this rank.

sen•i•ti (sĕn′ĭ-tē) *n., pl.* **seniti.** See table at **currency.** [Tongan, from English CENT.]

Sen•lac (sĕn′lăk′). A hill in southern England near Hastings. The battle fought here in 1066, in which William the Conqueror defeated Harold II, is known as the Battle of Hastings.

sen•na (sĕn′ə) *n.* **1.** Any of various plants of the genus *Cassia,* having pinnately compound leaves and showy, nearly regular, usually yellow flowers. **2.** The dried leaves of *C. angustifolia* or *C. acutifolia,* used medicinally as a cathartic. [New Latin, from Arabic *sanā'.*]

Sen•nach•er•ib (sĭ-năk′ər-ĭb). Died 681 B.C. King of Assyria (704–681) who invaded Judea, subjugated Babylon, and rebuilt Nineveh.

sen•net[1] (sĕn′ĭt) *n.* A call on a trumpet or cornet signaling the ceremonial exits and entrances of actors in Elizabethan drama. [Perhaps variant of SIGNET.]

sen•net[2] (sĕn′ĭt) *n.* Any of several barracudas, especially *Sphyraena borealis,* of the western Atlantic. [Origin unknown.]

Sen•nett (sĕn′ĭt), **Mack.** 1880?–1960. Canadian-born American filmmaker known for his slapstick motion pictures featuring the Keystone Kops.

sen•night (sĕn′īt′) *n. Archaic.* A week. [Middle English *senight,* contraction of *seveniht,* from Old English *seofon nihta,* seven nights : *seofon,* seven; see SEVEN + *nihta,* pl. of *niht,* night; see NIGHT.]

sen•nit (sĕn′ĭt) *n.* **1.** *Nautical.* Braided cordage formed by plaiting several strands of rope fiber or similar material. **2.** Plaited straw, grass, or palm leaves for making hats. [Origin unknown.]

se•no•pi•a (sĭ-nō′pē-ə) *n.* Improvement of near vision sometimes occurring in the aged because of swelling of the crystalline lens in incipient cataract. [Latin *senex, sen-,* old; see **sen-** in Appendix + –OPIA.]

se•ñor (sān-yôr′, sĕ-nyôr′) *n., pl.* **se•ño•res** (sān-yôr′ās, sĕ-nyô′rĕs). **1.** *Abbr.* **Sr. a.** Used as a courtesy title before the surname, full name, or professional title of a man in a Spanish-speaking area. **b.** Used as a form of polite address for a man in a Spanish-speaking area. **2.** A Spanish or Spanish-speaking man. [Spanish, from Old Spanish *sennor,* from Vulgar Latin *senior, lord, from Latin, senior. See SENIOR.]

se•ño•ra (sān-yôr′ə, sĕ-nyô′rä) *n.* **1.** *Abbr.* **Sra. a.** Used as a courtesy title before the surname or full name of a married woman in a Spanish-speaking area. **b.** Used as a form of polite address for a woman in a Spanish-speaking area. **2.** A Spanish or Spanish-speaking woman. [Spanish, feminine of *señor,* señor. See SEÑOR.]

se•ño•res (sān-yôr′ās, sĕ-nyô′rĕs) *n.* Plural of **señor.**

se•ño•ri•ta (sān′yə-rē′tə, sĕ′nyô-rē′tä) *n.* **1.** *Abbr.* **Srta. a.** Used as a courtesy title before the surname or full name of a girl or an unmarried woman in a Spanish-speaking area. **b.** Used as a form of address for a girl or young woman in a Spanish-speaking area. **2.** A Spanish or Spanish-speaking unmarried woman or girl. [Spanish, diminutive of *señora,* señora. See SEÑORA.]

sennit

sen•sate (sĕn′sāt′) also **sen•sat•ed** (-sā′tĭd) *adj.* **1.** Perceived by a sense or the senses. **2.** Having physical sensation. [Middle English *sensat,* from Late Latin *sēnsātus,* gifted with sense, from Latin *sēnsus,* sense. See SENSE.] **—sen′sate′ly** *adv.*

sen•sa•tion (sĕn-sā′shən) *n.* **1. a.** A perception associated with stimulation of a sense organ or with a specific body condition: *the sensation of heat; a visual sensation.* **b.** The faculty to feel or perceive; physical sensibility: *The patient has very little sensation left in the right leg.* **c.** An indefinite, generalized body feeling: *a sensation of lightness.* **2.** A state of heightened interest or emotion: *"The anticipation produced in me a sensation somewhat between bliss and fear"* (James Weldon Johnson). **3. a.** A state of intense public interest and excitement: *"The purser made a sensation as sailors like to do, by predicting a storm"* (Evelyn Waugh). **b.** A cause of such interest and excitement. See Synonyms at **wonder.** [French, from Old French, from Medieval Latin *sēnsātiō, sēnsātiōn-,* from Late Latin *sēnsātus,* gifted with sense. See SENSATE.]

sen•sa•tion•al (sĕn-sā′shə-nəl) *adj.* **1.** Of or relating to sensation. **2.** Arousing or intended to arouse strong curiosity, interest, or reaction, especially by exaggerated or lurid details: *sensational journalistic reportage of the scandal.* **3.** Outstanding; spectacular: *We attended a sensational concert—one never to be forgotten.* **—sen•sa′tion•al•ly** *adv.*

sen•sa•tion•al•ism (sĕn-sā′shə-nə-lĭz′əm) *n.* **1. a.** The use of sensational matter or methods, especially in writing, journalism, or politics. **b.** Sensational subject matter. **c.** Interest in or the effect of such subject matter. **2.** *Philosophy.* The theory that sensation is the only source of knowledge. **3.** The ethical doctrine that feeling is the only criterion of good. **—sen•sa′tion•al•ist** *n.* **—sen•sa′tion•al•is′tic** *adj.*

sen•sa•tion•al•ize (sĕn-sā′shə-nə-līz′) *tr.v.* **-ized, -iz•ing, -iz•es.** To cast and present in a manner intended to arouse strong interest, especially through inclusion of exaggerated or lurid details: *"doubted the ability of the liberal press to handle such information fairly, to refrain from sensationalizing it"* (Bob Woodward and Carl Bernstein). **—sen•sa′tion•al•i•za′tion** (-shə-nə-lĭ-zā′shən) *n.*

sense (sĕns) *n.* **1. a.** Any of the faculties by which stimuli from outside or inside the body are received and felt, as the faculties of hearing, sight, smell, touch, taste, and equilibrium. **b.** A perception or feeling produced by a stimulus; sensation: *a sense of fatigue and hunger.* **2. senses.** The faculties of sensation as means of providing physical gratification and pleasure. **3.** Intuitive or acquired perception or ability to estimate: *a sense of diplomatic timing.* **a.** A capacity to appreciate or understand: *a keen sense of humor.* **b.** A vague feeling or presentiment: *a sense of impending doom.* **c.** Recognition or perception either through the senses or through the intellect; consciousness: *has no sense of shame.* **4. a.** Often **senses.** Normal ability to think or reason soundly; correct judgment: *Come to your senses.* **b.** Something sound or reasonable: *There's no sense in waiting three hours.* **5. a.** A meaning that is conveyed, as in speech or writing; signification: *The sense of the novel is the inevitability of human tragedy.* **b.** One of the meanings of a word or phrase: *The word* set *has many senses.* See Synonyms at **meaning. 6. a.** Judgment; consensus: *sounding out the sense of the electorate on capital punishment.* **b.** Intellectual interpretation, as of the significance of an event or the conclusions reached by a group: *I came away from the meeting with the sense that we had resolved all outstanding issues.* **—sense** *tr.v.* **sensed, sens•ing, sens•es. 1.** To become aware of; perceive. **2.** To grasp; understand. **3.** To detect automatically: *sense radioactivity.* [Middle English, meaning, from Old French *sens,* from Latin *sēnsus,* the faculty of perceiving, from past participle of *sentīre,* to feel. See **sent-** in Appendix.]

sense datum *n.* A basic, unanalyzable sensation, such as color, sound, or smell, experienced upon stimulation of a sense organ or receptor.

sen•sei (sĕn′sā′, sĕn-sā′) *n., pl.* **-seis. 1.** A judo or karate teacher. **2.** A teacher or mentor. **3.** Used as a form of address for such a person. [Japanese, teacher, master.]

sense•less (sĕns′lĭs) *adj.* **1.** Lacking sense or meaning; meaningless. See Synonyms at **meaningless. 2.** Deficient in sense; foolish or stupid. **3.** Insensate; unconscious. **—sense′less•ly** *adv.* **—sense′less•ness** *n.*

sense organ *n.* A specialized organ or structure, such as the eye, ear, tongue, nose, or skin, where sensory neurons are concen-

ă pat	oi boy
ā pay	ou out
âr care	ŏŏ took
ä father	ōō boot
ĕ pet	ŭ cut
ē be	ûr urge
ĭ pit	th thin
ī pie	*th* this
îr pier	hw which
ŏ pot	zh vision
ō toe	ə about, item
ô paw	♦ regionalism

Stress marks: ′ (primary); ′ (secondary), as in **dictionary** (dĭk′shə-nĕr′ē)

trated and which functions as a receptor. Also called *sensor.*

sense perception *n.* Perception by or based on stimulation of the senses.

sen·si·bil·i·ty (sĕn′sə-bĭl′ĭ-tē) *n., pl.* **-ties. 1.** The ability to feel or perceive. **2.a.** Keen intellectual perception: *the sensibility of a painter to color.* **b.** Mental or emotional responsiveness toward something, such as the feelings of another. **3.** Receptiveness to impression, whether pleasant or unpleasant; acuteness of feeling. Often used in the plural: *"The sufferings of the Cuban people shocked our sensibilities"* (George F. Kennan). **4.** Refined awareness and appreciation in matters of feeling. **5.** The quality of being affected by changes in the environment.

sen·si·ble (sĕn′sə-bəl) *adj.* **1.** Perceptible by the senses or by the mind. **2.** Readily perceived; appreciable. **3.** Having the faculty of sensation; able to feel or perceive. **4.** Having a perception of something; cognizant: *"I am sensible that a good deal more is still to be done"* (Edmund Burke). See Synonyms at **aware. 5.** Acting with or exhibiting good sense: *a sensible person; a sensible choice.* [Middle English, from Old French, from Latin *sēnsibilis,* from *sēnsus,* sense. See SENSE.] **—sen′si·ble·ness** *n.* **—sen′si·bly** *adv.*

sensible horizon *n.* The plane intersecting an observer's position perpendicular to the line formed by the observer's nadir and zenith.

sen·sil·lum (sĕn-sĭl′əm) *n., pl.* **-sil·la** (-sĭl′ə). A simple sensory receptor consisting of one cell or a few cells, especially a hairlike epithelial cell projecting through the cuticle of arthropods. [New Latin *sēnsillum,* diminutive of Latin *sēnsus,* sense. See SENSE.]

sen·si·tive (sĕn′sĭ-tĭv) *adj.* **1.** Capable of perceiving with a sense or senses. **2.** Responsive to external conditions or stimulation. **3.** Susceptible to the attitudes, feelings, or circumstances of others. **4.** Quick to take offense; touchy. **5.** Easily irritated: *sensitive skin.* **6.** Readily altered by the action of an agent: *film that is sensitive to light.* **7.** Registering very slight differences or changes of condition. Used of an instrument. **8.** Fluctuating or tending to fluctuate, as in price: *sensitive stocks.* **9.** Of or relating to classified information: *sensitive defense data; holds a sensitive position in the State Department.* **—sensitive** *n.* **1.** A sensitive person. **2.** One held to be endowed with psychic or occult powers. [Middle English, from Old French *sensitif,* from Medieval Latin *sēnsitīvus,* from Latin *sēnsus,* sense. See SENSE.] **—sen′si·tive·ly** *adv.* **—sen′si·tive·ness** *n.*

sensitive plant *n.* **1.** A shrubby tropical American plant *(Mimosa pudica)* having mauve flower heads and bipinnately compound leaves with leaflets and leafstalks that fold and droop when touched. Also called *touch-me-not.* **2.** Any of various similar plants, such as *Cassia nictitans,* of eastern and central North America.

sen·si·tiv·i·ty (sĕn′sĭ-tĭv′ĭ-tē) *n., pl.* **-ties. 1.** The quality or condition of being sensitive. **2.** The capacity of an organ or organism to respond to stimulation. **3.** *Electronics.* The degree of response of a receiver or an instrument to an incoming signal or to a change in the incoming signal; the signal strength required by an FM tuner to reduce noise and distortion. **4.** The degree of response of a plate or film to light, especially to light of a specified wavelength.

sensitivity training *n.* Training in small groups in which people learn how to interact with each other by developing a sensitive awareness and understanding of themselves and of their relationships with others.

sen·si·tize (sĕn′sĭ-tīz′) *v.* **-tized, -tiz·ing, -tiz·es.** —*tr.* **1.** To make sensitive: *"The polarity principle . . . sensitizes the observer to the coexistence of seemingly contradictory phenomena"* (Heinz Eulau). **2.** To make (a film or plate) sensitive to light, especially to light of a specific wavelength. **3.** To make hypersensitive or reactive to an antigen, such as pollen, especially by a second or repeated exposure. —*intr.* To become sensitive or hypersensitive. **—sen′si·ti·za′tion** (-tĭ-zā′shən) *n.* **—sen′si·tiz′er** *n.*

sen·si·tom·e·ter (sĕn′sĭ-tŏm′ĭ-tər) *n.* **1.** A device used for measuring the sensitivity of photographic film to light. **2.** A similar device for measuring the sensitivity of eyes to light. [SENSIT(IVITY) + -METER.] **—sen′si·to·met′ric** (-tə-mĕt′rĭk) *adj.* **—sen′si·tom′e·try** *n.*

sen·sor (sĕn′sər, -sôr′) *n.* **1.** A device, such as a photoelectric cell, that receives and responds to a signal or stimulus. **2.** See **sense organ.**

sen·so·ri·a (sĕn-sôr′ē-ə, -sōr′-) *n.* A plural of **sensorium.**

sen·so·ri·al (sĕn-sôr′ē-əl, -sōr′-) *adj.* Of or relating to sensations or sensory impressions. **—sen·so′ri·al·ly** *adv.*

sen·so·ri·mo·tor (sĕn′sə-rē-mō′tər) *adj.* Of, relating to, or combining the functions of the sensory and motor activities: *sensorimotor nerve centers; sensorimotor pathways.*

sen·so·ri·neu·ral (sĕn′sə-rē-nŏŏr′əl, -nyŏŏr′-) *adj.* Of, relating to, or involving the sensory nerves, especially as they affect the hearing: *sensorineural deafness.*

sen·so·ri·um (sĕn-sôr′ē-əm, -sōr′-) *n., pl.* **-so·ri·ums** or **-so·ri·a** (-sôr′ē-ə, -sōr′-). **1.** The part of the brain that receives and coordinates all the stimuli conveyed to various sensory centers. **2.** The entire sensory system of the body. [Late Latin *sēnsōrium,* organ of sensation, from Latin *sēnsus,* sense. See SENSE.]

sen·so·ry (sĕn′sə-rē) *adj.* **1.** Of or relating to the senses or sensation. **2.** Transmitting impulses from sense organs to nerve centers; afferent.

sensory deprivation *n.* Deprivation of sensory stimulation, as by prolonged isolation inside a sealed, unlighted chamber or tank, in order to observe physical and especially psychological reactions.

sen·su·al (sĕn′shōō-əl) *adj.* **1.** Relating to or affecting any of the senses or a sense organ; sensory. **2.a.** Of, relating to, given to, or providing gratification of the physical and especially the sexual appetites. See Synonyms at **sensuous. b.** Suggesting sexuality; voluptuous. **c.** Physical rather than spiritual or intellectual. **d.** Lacking in moral or spiritual interests; worldly. **—sen′su·al·ly** *adv.* **—sen′su·al·ness** *n.*

sen·su·al·ism (sĕn′shōō-ə-lĭz′əm) *n.* **1.** Sensuality. **2.** The ethical doctrine that the pleasures of the senses are the highest good. **3.** *Philosophy.* Sensationalism. **—sen′su·al·ist** *n.* **—sen′su·al·is′tic** *adj.*

sen·su·al·i·ty (sĕn′shōō-ăl′ĭ-tē) *n.* **1.** The quality or state of being sensual or lascivious. **2.** Excessive devotion to sensual pleasures.

sen·su·al·ize (sĕn′shōō-ə-līz′) *tr.v.* **-ized, -iz·ing, -iz·es.** To make sensual. **—sen′su·al·i·za′tion** (-ə-lĭ-zā′shən) *n.*

sen·su·ous (sĕn′shōō-əs) *adj.* **1.** Of, relating to, or derived from the senses. **2.** Appealing to or gratifying the senses. **3.a.** Readily affected through the senses. **b.** Highly appreciative of the pleasures of sensation. **—sen′su·os′i·ty** (-ŏs′ĭ-tē), **sen′su·ous·ness** (-əs-nĭs) *n.* **—sen′su·ous·ly** *adv.*

SYNONYMS: *sensuous, sensual, luxurious, voluptuous, sybaritic, epicurean.* These adjectives mean of, given to, or furnishing satisfaction of the senses. *Sensuous* can refer to any of the senses but usually applies to those involved in aesthetic enjoyment, as of art or music: *"The sensuous joy from all things fair/His strenuous bent of soul repressed"* (John Greenleaf Whittier). *Sensual* more often applies to the physical senses or appetites, particularly those associated with sexual pleasure: *"Of music Dr. Johnson used to say that it was the only sensual pleasure without vice"* (William Seward). *Luxurious* in this comparison suggests a surrender to physical comfort, as that provided by a sumptuous lifestyle, leading to a delightful feeling of well-being: *stayed in a luxurious, flower-filled suite with a crystal chandelier and thick oriental rugs. Voluptuous* principally implies abandoning oneself to pleasures, especially sensual pleasures: *"Lucullus . . . returned to Rome to lounge away the remainder of his days in voluptuous magnificence"* (J.A. Froude). *Sybaritic* even more strongly suggests devotion to pleasure and luxury; the term implies excess and sometimes connotes effeteness or decadence: *A chinchilla robe of sybaritic lavishness was draped over the bed. Epicurean* stresses the pleasure of indulging a taste for fine food and drink: *an epicurean banquet of exquisitely prepared food accompanied throughout by vintage champagne.*

Sen·sur·round (sĕn′sə-round′). A trademark used for a motion-picture sound effect consisting of low-frequency sound signals felt by the audience as vibrations.

sent (sĕnt) *v.* Past tense and past participle of **send**[1].

sen·te (sĕn′tā) *n., pl.* **li·sen·te** (lē-sĕn′tā). See table at **currency.** [Sotho (Sesotho), from English CENT.]

sen·tence (sĕn′təns) *n.* **1.** A grammatical unit that is syntactically independent and has a subject that is expressed or, as in imperative sentences, understood and a predicate that contains at least one finite verb. **2.** *Law.* **a.** A court judgment, especially a judicial decision of the punishment to be inflicted on one adjudged guilty. **b.** The penalty meted out. **3.** *Archaic.* A maxim. **4.** *Obsolete.* An opinion, especially one given formally after deliberation. **—sentence** *tr.v.* **-tenced, -tenc·ing, -tenc·es.** *Law.* To pronounce sentence upon (one adjudged guilty). See Synonyms at **condemn.** [Middle English, opinion, from Old French, from Latin *sententia,* from *sentiēns, sentient-,* present participle of *sentīre,* to feel. See **sent-** in Appendix.] **—sen·ten′tial** (sĕn-tĕn′shəl) *adj.* **—sen·ten′tial·ly** *adv.*

sen·tenc·er (sĕn′tən-sər) *n.* *Law.* One, such as a court or judge, that pronounces sentence.

sentence stress *n.* *Linguistics.* The variation in emphasis or vocal stress on the syllables of words within a sentence.

sen·tenc·ing (sĕn′tən-sĭng) *Law. adj.* **1.** Relating to a judicial sentence: *sentencing guidelines for juvenile defendants.* **2.** Being or relating to the one who pronounces a judicial sentence: *"Prosecutors and sentencing judges alike try to deal with individuals on an individual basis, without regard to social status"* (Hiller B. Zobel). **—sentencing** *n.* **1.** The act of pronouncing a judicial sentence on a defendant. **2.** The sentence so pronounced.

sen·ten·tia (sĕn-tĕn′shə, -shē-ə) *n., pl.* **-ti·ae** (-shē-ē′). An adage or aphorism. [Latin. See SENTENCE.]

sen·ten·tious (sĕn-tĕn′shəs) *adj.* **1.** Terse and energetic in expression; pithy. **2.a.** Abounding in aphorisms. **b.** Given to aphoristic utterances. **3.a.** Abounding in pompous moralizing. **b.** Given to pompous moralizing. [Middle English, from Old French *sententieux,* from Latin *sententiōsus,* full of meaning, from *sententia,* opinion. See SENTENCE.] **—sen·ten′tious·ly** *adv.* **—sen·ten′tious·ness** *n.*

sen·tience (sĕn′shəns, -shē-əns) *n.* **1.** The quality or state of being sentient; consciousness. **2.** Feeling as distinguished from perception or thought.

sen•tient (sĕn′shənt, -shē-ənt) *adj.* **1.** Having sense perception; conscious: *"The living knew themselves just sentient puppets on God's stage"* (T.E. Lawrence). **2.** Experiencing sensation or feeling. [Latin *sentiēns, sentient-*, present participle of *sentīre*, to feel. See **sent-** in Appendix.] **—sen′tient•ly** *adv.*

sen•ti•ment (sĕn′tə-mənt) *n.* **1.a.** A cast of mind; general mental disposition: *Anti-American sentiment is running high in some countries.* **b.** An opinion about a specific matter; a view. See Synonyms at **opinion. 2.** A thought, a view, or an attitude based on feeling or emotion instead of reason. **3.** The emotional import of a passage. **4.a.** Susceptibility to tender, romantic, or nostalgic feeling. **b.** An expression of such susceptibility. **5.a.** Emotion that borders on mawkishness. **b.** Romantic, nostalgic feeling verging on sentimentality. **6.** The expression of delicate and sensitive feeling, especially in art and literature. See Synonyms at **feeling. 7.** A vague feeling or awareness; sensation: *"overpowered by an intense sentiment of horror"* (Edgar Allan Poe). [Middle English *sentement*, from Old French, from Medieval Latin *sentīmentum*, from Latin *sentīre*, to feel. See **sent-** in Appendix.]

sen•ti•men•tal (sĕn′tə-mĕn′tl) *adj.* **1.a.** Characterized or swayed by sentiment. **b.** Affectedly or extravagantly emotional. **2.** Resulting from or colored by emotion rather than reason or realism. **3.** Appealing to the sentiments, especially to romantic feelings: *sentimental music.* **—sen′ti•men′tal•ly** *adv.*

SYNONYMS: *sentimental, bathetic, maudlin, mawkish, mushy, romantic, schmaltzy, slushy, soppy.* The central meaning shared by these adjectives is "excessively or insincerely emotional": *a sentimental soap opera; a bathetic novel; maudlin expressions of sympathy; mawkish sentiment; mushy effusiveness; a romantic adolescent; a schmaltzy song; slushy poetry; a soppy letter.*

sen•ti•men•tal•ism (sĕn′tə-mĕn′tl-ĭz′əm) *n.* **1.** A predilection for the sentimental. **2.** An idea or expression marked by excessive sentiment. **—sen′ti•men′tal•ist** *n.*

sen•ti•men•tal•i•ty (sĕn′tə-mĕn-tăl′ĭ-tē) *n., pl.* **-ties. 1.** The quality or condition of being excessively or affectedly sentimental. **2.** A sentimental idea or an expression of it.

sen•ti•men•tal•ize (sĕn′tə-mĕn′tl-īz′) *v.* **-ized, -iz•ing, -iz•es.** *—tr.* To imbue or regard with sentiment; be sentimental about. *—intr.* To behave in a sentimental manner. **—sen′ti•men′tal•i•za′tion** (-mĕn′tl-ĭ-zā′shən) *n.*

sen•ti•nel (sĕn′tə-nəl) *n.* One that keeps guard; a sentry. **—sentinel** *tr.v.* **-neled, -nel•ing, -nels** or **-nelled, -nel•ling, -nels. 1.** To watch over as a guard. **2.** To provide with a guard. **3.** To post as a guard. [French *sentinelle*, from Italian *sentinella*, probably from Old Italian *sentina*, vigilance, from *sentire*, to watch, from Latin *sentīre*, to feel. See **sent-** in Appendix.]

sen•try (sĕn′trē) *n., pl.* **-tries. 1.** A guard, especially a soldier posted at a given spot to prevent the passage of unauthorized persons. **2.** The duty of a sentry; watch. [Perhaps alteration of obsolete *sentrinel*, variant of SENTINEL.]

sentry box *n.* A small shelter for a posted sentry.

Seoul (sōl). The capital and largest city of South Korea, in the northwest part of the country east of Inchon. Founded in the 14th century, it became the country's capital in 1948 and was twice occupied by Communist forces during the Korean War. Population, 9,646,000.

sep. *abbr.* Separate; separation.

se•pal (sē′pəl) *n.* One of the separate, usually green parts forming the calyx of a flower. [New Latin *sepalum*, perhaps blend of Greek *skepē*, covering, and Latin *petalum*, petal; see PETAL.] **—se′paled, sep′a•lous** (sĕp′ə-ləs) *adj.*

se•pal•oid (sē′pə-loid′, sĕp′ə-) also **se•pal•ine** (-līn′, -lĭn) *adj.* Resembling or characteristic of a sepal.

–sepalous *suff.* Having a specified kind or number of sepals: *gamosepalous.*

sep•a•ra•ble (sĕp′ər-ə-bəl, sĕp′rə-) *adj.* Possible to separate: *separable sheets of paper.* **—sep′a•ra•bil′i•ty** *n.* **—sep′a•ra•bly** *adv.*

sep•a•rate (sĕp′ə-rāt′) *v.* **-rat•ed, -rat•ing, -rates.** *—tr.* **1.a.** To set or keep apart; disunite. **b.** To space apart; scatter: *small farms that were separated one from another by miles of open land.* **c.** To sort: *separate mail by postal zones.* **2.** To differentiate or discriminate between; distinguish: *a researcher who separated the various ethnic components of the population sample.* **3.** To remove from a mixture or combination; isolate. **4.** To part (a couple), often by decree: *She was separated from her husband last year.* **5.** To terminate a contractual relationship, as military service, with; discharge. *—intr.* **1.** To come apart. **2.** To withdraw: *The state threatened to separate from the Union.* **3.** To part company; disperse. **4.** To stop living together as spouses. **5.** To become divided into components or parts: *Oil and water tend to separate.* **—separate** (sĕp′ər-ĭt, sĕp′rĭt) *adj. Abbr.* **sep. 1.** Set or kept apart; disunited. **2.a.** Existing as an independent entity. **b.** Often **Separate.** Having undergone schism or estrangement from a parent body: *Separate churches.* **3.** Dissimilar from all others; distinct: *"a policeman's way of being separate from you even when he was being nice"* (John le Carré). **4.** Not shared; individual: *two people who held separate views on the issue.* **5.** *Archaic.* Withdrawn from others; solitary. **—separate** (sĕp′ər-ĭt, sĕp′rĭt) *n. Abbr.* **sep.** A garment, such as a skirt, jacket, or pair of slacks, that may be purchased separately and worn in various combinations with other garments. [Middle English *separaten*, from Latin *sēparātus*, past participle of *sēparāre* : *sē-*, apart; see **s(w)e-** in Appendix + *parāre*, to prepare; see **perə-¹** in Appendix.] **—sep′a•rate•ly** *adv.* **—sep′a•rate•ness** *n.*

SYNONYMS: *separate, divide, part, sever, sunder, divorce.* These verbs are compared as they mean to become or cause to become parted, disconnected, or disunited. *Separate* applies both to putting apart and to keeping apart: *"In the darkness and confusion, the bands of these commanders became separated from each other"* (Washington Irving). *The Pyrenees separate France and Spain. The child's parents have separated. Divide* implies separation by or as if by cutting, splitting, or branching into parts, portions, or shares; the term is often used to refer to separation into opposing or hostile groups: *We divided the orange into segments.* "[The rich] *divide with the poor the produce of all their improvements"* (Adam Smith). *"'A house divided against itself cannot stand.' I believe this government cannot endure permanently half slave and half free"* (Abraham Lincoln). *Part* refers most often to the separation of closely associated persons or things: *"None shall part us from each other"* (W.S. Gilbert). *"I remember the way we parted"* (Algernon Swinburne). *Sever* usually implies abruptness and force in the cutting off of a part from the whole or the breaking up of an association or a relationship: *"His head was nearly severed from his body"* (H.G. Wells). *The United States severed diplomatic relations with Cuba in 1961. Sunder* stresses violent tearing or wrenching apart: *The country was sundered by civil war into two embattled states. Divorce* implies the separation of the elements of a relationship or union: *"a priest and a soldier, two classes of men circumstantially divorced from the kind and homely ties of life"* (Robert Louis Stevenson). See also Synonyms at **distinct, single.**

sep•a•ra•tion (sĕp′ə-rā′shən) *n. Abbr.* **sep. 1.a.** The act or process of separating. **b.** The condition of being separated. **2.** The place at which a division or parting occurs. **3.** An interval or a space that separates; a gap. **4.a.** *Law.* An agreement or a court decree terminating a spousal relationship. **b.** Discharge, as from employment or military service.

sep•a•ra•tion•ist (sĕp′ə-rā′shə-nĭst) *n.* A separatist.

sep•a•ra•tist (sĕp′ər-ə-tĭst, sĕp′rə-, sĕp′ə-rā′-) *n.* **1.** One who secedes or advocates separation, especially from an established church; a sectarian or separationist. **2.** One who advocates disjunction of a group from a larger group or political unit: *Basque separatists.* **3.** One who advocates cultural, ethnic, or racial separation. **—sep′a•ra•tism** *n.* **—sep′a•ra•tist** *adj.* **—sep′a•ra•tis′tic** *adj.*

sep•a•ra•tive (sĕp′ə-rā′tĭv, sĕp′ər-ə-, sĕp′rə-) *adj.* Tending to separate or to cause separation.

sep•a•ra•tor (sĕp′ə-rā′tər) *n.* One that separates, as a device for separating cream from milk.

sepd. *abbr.* Separated.

Se•phar•di (sə-făr′dē) *n., pl.* **-dim** (-dĭm). A descendant of the Jews who lived in Spain and Portugal during the Middle Ages until persecution culminating in expulsion in 1492 forced them to leave. [Modern Hebrew *Sĕpāraddi*, Spaniard, from *Sĕpārad*, Spain.] **—Se•phar′dic** (-dĭk) *adj.*

se•pi•a (sē′pē-ə) *n.* **1.a.** A dark brown ink or pigment originally prepared from the secretion of the cuttlefish. **b.** A drawing or picture done in this pigment. **c.** A photograph in a brown tint. **2.** *Color.* A dark grayish yellow brown to dark or moderate olive brown. **—sepia** *adj.* **1.** *Color.* Of the color sepia. **2.** Done or made in sepia. [Middle English, cuttlefish, from Latin *sēpia*, cuttlefish, ink, from Greek, cuttlefish; perhaps akin to *sēpein*, to make rotten.]

Se•pik (sā′pĭk). A river, about 1,126 km (700 mi) long, of northern Papua New Guinea.

se•pi•o•lite (sē′pē-ə-līt′) *n.* See **meerschaum** (sense 1). [Greek *sēpion*, cuttlebone (from *sēpia*, cuttlefish; see SEPIA) + -LITE.]

se•poy (sē′poi′) *n.* A regular soldier in some Middle Eastern countries, especially an Indian soldier formerly serving under British command. [Probably from Portuguese *sipae*, from Urdu *sipāhī*, from Persian, cavalryman, from *sipāh*, army.]

sep•pu•ku (sĕp′o͞o-ko͞o, sĕ-po͞o′-) *n.* Hara-kiri. [Japanese : *seppu*, to cut + *ku*, abdomen.]

sep•sis (sĕp′sĭs) *n., pl.* **-ses** (-sēz). **1.** The presence of pathogenic organisms or their toxins in the blood or tissues. **2.** The poisoned condition resulting from the presence of pathogens or their toxins, as in septicemia. [Greek *sēpsis*, putrefaction, from *sēpein*, to make rotten.]

sept (sĕpt) *n.* A division of a family, especially a division of a clan. [Probably alteration of SECT.]

Sept. or **Sept** *abbr.* September.

sep•ta (sĕp′tə) *n.* Plural of **septum.**

sep•tage (sĕp′tĭj) *n.* The waste content found in a septic tank.

sep•tal (sĕp′təl) *adj.* Of or relating to a septum or septa.

sep•tar•i•um (sĕp-târ′ē-əm) *n., pl.* **-i•a** (-ē-ə). An irregular polygonal system of calcite-filled cracks occurring in certain rock concretions. [Latin *saeptum*, partition; see SEPTUM + -ARIUM.] **—sep•tar′i•an** *adj.*

sep•tate (sĕp′tāt′) *adj.* Divided by a septum or septa.

sep•tec•to•my (sĕp-tĕk′tə-mē) *n., pl.* **-mies.** Surgical exci-

sentry box
At Saint James's Palace, London

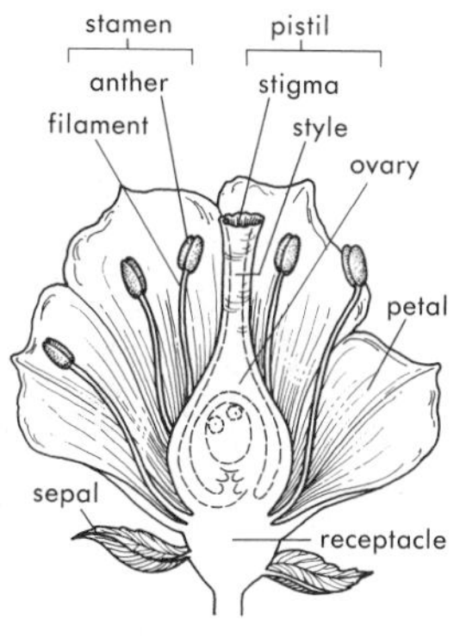

sepal

ă pat	oi boy
ā pay	ou out
âr care	o͝o took
ä father	o͞o boot
ĕ pet	ŭ cut
ē be	ûr urge
ĭ pit	th thin
ī pie	*th* this
îr pier	hw which
ŏ pot	zh vision
ō toe	ə about, item
ô paw	♦ regionalism

Stress marks: **′** (primary); ′ (secondary), as in **dictionary** (dĭk′shə-nĕr′ē)

sion of a septum or part of a septum, especially the nasal or atrial septum.

Sep·tem·ber (sĕp-tĕm′bər) *n. Abbr.* **Sept., Sept** The ninth month of the year in the Gregorian calendar. See table at **calendar.** [Middle English *Septembre,* from Old French, from Latin *September,* the seventh month, from *septem,* seven. See **septm̥** in Appendix.]

Sep·tem·brist (sĕp-tĕm′brĭst) *n.* **1.** A bloodthirsty revolutionist or terrorist. **2.** One of the mob that massacred the imprisoned royalists in Paris, France, in September 1792.

sep·te·nar·i·us (sĕp′tə-nâr′ē-əs) *n., pl.* **-i·i** (-ē-ī′). A Latin verse used only in comedy and consisting of seven iambic feet or a catalectic iambic tetrameter. [Latin *septēnārius,* of seven, from *septēnī,* seven each, from *septem,* seven. See SEPTENNIAL.]

sep·ten·ni·al (sĕp-tĕn′ē-əl) *adj.* **1.** Occurring every seven years. **2.** Consisting of or continuing for seven years. **—septennial** *n.* An event that occurs every seven years. [From Late Latin *septennium,* period of seven years, from Latin *septennis,* of seven years : *septem,* seven; see **septm̥** in Appendix + *annus,* year; see **at-** in Appendix.] **—sep·ten′ni·al·ly** *adv.*

sep·ten·tri·on (sĕp-tĕn′trē-ŏn′, -ən) *n. Obsolete.* Northern regions; the north. [Middle English, from Old French, from Latin *septentriōnēs,* seven plow oxen, the seven principal stars of Ursa Major : *septem,* seven; see **septm̥** in Appendix + *triōnēs* (pl. of *triō, triōn-,* plow ox; see **tere-**[1] in Appendix).] **—sep·ten′tri·o·nal** (-trē-ə-nəl) *adj.*

sep·tet also **sep·tette** (sĕp-tĕt′) *n.* **1.** A group of seven. **2.** *Music.* **a.** A composition for seven voices or instruments. **b.** The performers playing such a composition. [German *Septett,* from Latin *septem,* seven. See **septm̥** in Appendix.]

sep·tic (sĕp′tĭk) *adj.* **1.** Of, relating to, having the nature of, or affected by sepsis. **2.** Causing sepsis; putrefactive. [Latin *sēpticus,* putrefying, from Greek *sēptikos,* from *sēptos,* rotten, from *sēpein,* to make rotten.] **—sep·tic′i·ty** (-tĭs′ĭ-tē) *n.*

sep·ti·ce·mi·a (sĕp′tĭ-sē′mē-ə) *n.* A systemic disease caused by pathogenic organisms or their toxins in the bloodstream. Also called *blood poisoning.* [SEPTIC + -EMIA.] **—sep′ti·ce′mic** (-mĭk) *adj.*

sep·ti·ci·dal (sĕp′tĭ-sīd′l) *adj. Botany.* Dehiscing by splitting along or through the septa. Used of a seed capsule. [SEPT(UM) + Latin *-cidere,* to cut (from *caedere;* see CAESURA) + -AL[1].] **—sep′ti·ci′dal·ly** *adv.*

septic sore throat *n.* An infection of the throat, often epidemic, caused by hemolytic streptococci and characterized by fever and inflammation of the tonsils. Also called *strep throat.*

septic tank *n.* A sewage-disposal tank in which a continuous flow of waste material is decomposed by anaerobic bacteria.

sep·tif·ra·gal (sĕp-tĭf′rə-gəl) *adj. Botany.* Dehiscing by the breaking away of the valves from its partitions. Used of a seed capsule. [SEPT(UM) + Latin *frangere,* to break; see **bhreg-** in Appendix.] **—sep·tif′ra·gal·ly** *adv.*

sep·ti·lat·er·al (sĕp′tə-lăt′ər-əl) *adj.* Seven-sided. [Latin *septem,* seven; see SEPTET + LATERAL.]

Sept Îles or **Sept-Îles** (sĕt-ēl′) also **Sev·en Isles** (sĕv′ən). A city of eastern Quebec, Canada, on the St. Lawrence River near its mouth. Population, 29,262.

sep·til·lion (sĕp-tĭl′yən) *n.* **1.** The cardinal number equal to 10^{24}. **2.** *Chiefly British.* The cardinal number equal to 10^{42}. [French : Latin *septem,* seven; see SEPTET + French *-illion* (as in *million,* million, from Old French *milion;* see MILLION).] **—sep·til′lion** *adj.*

sep·til·lionth (sĕp-tĭl′yənth) *n.* **1.** The ordinal number matching the number septillion in a series. **2.** One of a septillion equal parts. **—sep·til′lionth** *adv. & adj.*

sep·tu·a·ge·nar·i·an (sĕp′to͞o-ə-jə-nâr′ē-ən, -tyo͞o-, -cho͞o-) *n.* A person who is 70 years old or between the ages of 70 and 80. **—septuagenarian** *adj.* **1.** Being 70 years old or between the ages of 70 and 80. **2.** Of or relating to a septuagenarian. [From Latin *septuāgēnārius,* of the number seventy, from *septuāgēnī,* seventy each, from *septuāgintā,* seventy. See SEPTUAGINT.]

Sep·tu·a·ges·i·ma (sĕp′to͞o-ə-jĕs′ə-mə, -jā′zə-, -cho͞o-) *n.* The third Sunday before Lent. [Middle English, from Old French, from Late Latin *septuāgēsima (diēs),* seventieth (day), feminine of Latin *septuāgēsimus,* from *septuāgintā,* seventy. See SEPTUAGINT.]

Sep·tu·a·gint (sĕp′to͞o-ə-jĭnt′, sĕp-to͞o′ə-jənt, -tyo͞o′-) *n.* A Greek translation of the Old Testament made in the third century B.C. [Latin *septuāgintā,* seventy (from the traditional number of its translators) : *septem,* seven; see **septm̥** in Appendix + *-gintā,* ten times; see **dekm̥** in Appendix.]

sep·tum (sĕp′təm) *n., pl.* **-ta** (-tə). A thin partition or membrane that divides two cavities or soft masses of tissue in an organism: *the nasal septum; the atrial septum of the heart.* [Latin *saeptum,* partition, from neuter past participle of *saepīre,* to enclose, from *saepēs,* fence.]

septum pel·lu·ci·dum (pə-lo͞o′sĭ-dəm) *n., pl.* **septa pel·lu·ci·da** (-də). *Anatomy.* A thin membrane of nervous tissue that forms the medial wall of the lateral ventricles in the brain. [New Latin *septum pellūcidum* : *septum,* septum + Latin *pellūcidus,* transparent.]

sep·tu·ple (sĕp-to͞o′pəl, -tyo͞o′-, -tŭp′əl) *adj.* **1.** Consisting of or containing seven. **2.** Multiplied by seven. **—septuple** *tr.v.* **-pled, -pling, -ples.** To multiply by seven. [Late Latin *septuplus,* sevenfold : Latin *septem,* seven; see **septm̥** in Appendix + *-plus,* -fold; see **pel-**[2] in Appendix.]

sep·tu·plet (sĕp-tŭp′lĭt, -to͞o′plĭt, -tyo͞o′-) *n.* **1.** One of seven offspring delivered at a single birth. **2. septuplets.** The seven offspring of one birth. **3.** A group of seven persons or things. [SEPTU(PLE) + (TRI)PLET.]

sep·ul·cher (sĕp′əl-kər) *n.* **1.** A burial vault. **2.** A receptacle for sacred relics, especially in an altar. **—sepulcher** *tr.v.* **-chered, -cher·ing, -chers.** To place into a sepulcher; inter. [Middle English *sepulcre,* from Old French, from Latin *sepulcrum,* from *sepultus,* past participle of *sepelīre,* to bury the dead.]

se·pul·chral (sə-pŭl′krəl, -po͝ol′-) *adj.* **1.** Of or relating to a burial vault or a receptacle for sacred relics. **2.** Suggestive of the grave; funereal. **—se·pul′chral·ly** *adv.*

sep·ul·chre (sĕp′əl-kər) *n. & v. Chiefly British.* Variant of **sepulcher.**

sep·ul·ture (sĕp′əl-cho͝or′, -chər) *n.* **1.** The act of interment; burial. **2.** A sepulcher. [Middle English, from Old French, from Latin *sepultūra,* from *sepultus,* past participle of *sepelīre,* to bury the dead.]

seq. *abbr.* **1.** Sequel. **2.** *Latin.* Sequens (the following).

seqq. *abbr. Latin.* Sequentia (the following [things]).

se·qua·cious (sĭ-kwā′shəs) *adj.* **1.** Persisting in a continuous intellectual or stylistic direction: *"I make these notes, but am tired of notes . . . I want something sequacious now & robust"* (Virginia Woolf). **2. a.** Disposed to follow another or others, as a leader. **b.** Slavishly unthinking and uncritical. [From Latin *sequāx, sequāc-,* pursuing, from *sequī,* to follow. See **sekʷ-**[1] in Appendix.] **—se·qua′cious·ly** *adv.* **—se·quac′i·ty** (-kwăs′ĭ-tē) *n.*

se·quel (sē′kwəl) *n. Abbr.* **seq. 1.** Something that follows; a continuation. **2.** A literary work complete in itself but continuing the narrative of an earlier work. **3.** A result or consequence. See Synonyms at **effect.** [Middle English *sequele,* from Old French *sequelle,* from Latin *sequēla,* from *sequī,* to follow. See **sekʷ-**[1] in Appendix.]

se·quel·a (sĭ-kwĕl′ə) *n., pl.* **-quel·ae** (-kwĕl′ē). **1.** A pathological condition resulting from a disease. **2.** A secondary consequence or result. [Latin *sequēla,* sequel. See SEQUEL.]

se·que·na·tor (sē′kwə-nā′tər) *n.* See **sequencer** (sense 2). [SEQUEN(CER) + -ATOR.]

se·quence (sē′kwəns, -kwĕns′) *n.* **1.** A following of one thing after another; succession. **2.** An order of succession; an arrangement. **3.** A related or continuous series. See Synonyms at **series. 4.** *Games.* Three or more playing cards in consecutive order; a run. **5.** A series of single film shots so edited as to constitute an aesthetic or dramatic unit; an episode. **6.** *Music.* A melodic or harmonic pattern successively repeated at different pitches with or without a key change. **7.** *Roman Catholic Church.* A hymn sung between the gradual and the Gospel. **8.** *Mathematics.* An ordered set of quantities, as x, $2x^2$, $3x^3$, $4x^4$. **9.** *Biochemistry.* The order of constituents in a polymer, especially the order of nucleotides in a nucleic acid or of the amino acids in a protein. **—sequence** *tr.v.* **-quenced, -quenc·ing, -quenc·es. 1.** To organize or arrange in a sequence. **2.** To determine the order of constituents in (a polymer, such as a nucleic acid or protein molecule). [Middle English, a type of hymn, from Old French, from Medieval Latin *sequentia,* hymn, that which follows, from Late Latin, from Latin *sequēns, sequent-,* present participle of *sequī,* to follow. See **sekʷ-**[1] in Appendix.]

se·quenc·er (sē′kwən-sər, -kwĕn′-) *n.* **1.** *Computer Science.* A device that sorts cards, data, or programs in a prearranged sequence. **2.** An apparatus for determining the order of constituents in a biological polymer. In this sense, also called *sequenator.*

se·quent (sē′kwənt) *adj.* **1.** Following in order or time; subsequent. **2.** Following as a result; consequent. **—sequent** *n.* A result; a consequence. [Latin *sequēns, sequent-,* present participle of *sequī,* to follow. See SEQUENCE.]

se·quen·tial (sĭ-kwĕn′shəl) *adj.* **1.** Forming or characterized by a sequence, as of units or musical notes. **2.** Sequent. **—se·quen′ti·al′i·ty** (-shē-ăl′ĭ-tē) *n.* **—se·quen′tial·ly** *adv.*

se·ques·ter (sĭ-kwĕs′tər) *v.* **-tered, -ter·ing, -ters.** *—tr.* **1.** To cause to withdraw into seclusion. **2.** To remove or set apart; segregate. See Synonyms at **isolate. 3.** *Law.* **a.** To take temporary possession of (property) as security against legal claims. **b.** To requisition and confiscate (enemy property). *—intr. Chemistry.* To undergo sequestration. [Middle English *sequestren,* from Old French, from Latin *sequestrāre,* to give up for safekeeping, from Latin *sequester,* depositary, trustee. See **sekʷ-**[1] in Appendix.]

se·ques·tra (sĭ-kwĕs′trə) *n.* Plural of **sequestrum.**

se·ques·trant (sĭ-kwĕs′trənt) *n.* A chemical that promotes sequestration.

se·ques·trate (sē′kwĭ-strāt′, sĕk′wĭ-, sĭ-kwĕs′trāt′) *tr.v.* **-trat·ed, -trat·ing, -trates. 1.** *Chiefly British.* To seize; confiscate: *"The sheriffs . . . will be able to seize stock and other assets, and to sequestrate bank accounts belonging to defaulters"* (Daily Telegraph). **2.** To seclude; sequester. [Middle English *sequestraten,* from Latin *sequestrāre, sequestrāt-,* to give up for safekeeping. See SEQUESTER.]

se·ques·tra·tion (sē′kwĭ-strā′shən, sĕk′wĭ-) *n.* **1.** The act of sequestering; segregation. **2.** *Law.* **a.** Seizure of property. **b.** A writ authorizing seizure of property. **3.** *Chemistry.* The inhibition or prevention of normal ion behavior by combination with added materials, especially the prevention of metallic ion precipitation from solution by formation of a coordination compound with a phosphate.

se·ques·trum (sĭ-kwĕs′trəm) *n., pl.* **-tra** (-trə). A fragment of dead bone separated from healthy bone as a result of injury or disease. [Latin, deposit, from neuter of *sequester,* depositary, trustee. See **sekʷ-¹** in Appendix.]

se·quin (sē′kwĭn) *n.* **1.** A small shiny ornamental disk, often sewn on cloth; a spangle. **2.** A gold coin of the Venetian Republic. In this sense, also called *zecchino.* **—sequin** *tr.v.* **-quined, -quin·ing, -quins.** To affix sequins to (a garment, for example). [French, from Old French, Venetian coin, from Italian *zecchino,* from *zecca,* mint, from Arabic *sikkah,* coin die.]

se·quoi·a (sĭ-kwoi′ə) *n.* **1.** See **redwood** (sense 1). **2.** Giant sequoia. [New Latin *Sequoia,* genus name, after SEQUOYA.]

Se·quoy·a or **Se·quoy·ah** (sĭ-kwoi′ə). Also called George Guess. 1770?–1843. Cherokee scholar who developed a system of transcribing the Cherokee language.

ser. *abbr.* **1.** Serial. **2.** Series. **3.** Sermon.

se·ra (sîr′ə) *n.* A plural of **serum.**

sé·rac (sə-răk′, sā-) *n.* A large pointed mass of ice in a glacier isolated by intersecting crevasses. [French, cottage cheese, sérac, perhaps from Vulgar Latin **serāceum,* whey, from Latin *serum.*]

se·ra·glio (sə-răl′yō, -räl′-) *n., pl.* **-glios. 1.** A large harem. **2.** A sultan's palace. [Italian *serraglio,* enclosure, seraglio, probably partly from Vulgar Latin **serraculum,* enclosure (from **serrāre,* to lace up, from Latin *serāre,* from *sera,* door-bar), and partly from Turkish *saray,* palace (from Persian *sarāī,* inn; see CARAVANSARY).]

ser·al (sîr′əl) *adj.* Of or relating to an ecological sere: *a seral stage; a seral community.*

se·ra·pe also **sa·ra·pe** (sə-rä′pē, -răp′ē) *n.* A long blanketlike shawl, often brightly colored and fringed at the ends, worn especially by Mexican men. [American Spanish *sarape.*]

ser·aph (sĕr′əf) *n., pl.* **-a·phim** (-ə-fĭm) or **-aphs. 1.** A celestial being having three pairs of wings. **2.** *Theology.* One of the first order of angels. [Back-formation from pl. *seraphim,* from Middle English *seraphin,* from Old English, from Late Latin *seraphīn,* from Greek *seraphim,* from Hebrew *śərāpîm,* pl. of *śārāp.*] **—se·raph′ic** (sə-răf′ĭk), **se·raph′i·cal** (-ĭ-kəl) *adj.* **—se·raph′i·cal·ly** *adv.*

Se·ra·pis (sə-rā′pĭs) *n. Mythology.* An ancient Egyptian god of the lower world, also worshiped in ancient Greece and Rome.

Serb (sûrb) *n.* A member of a southern Slavic people that is the principal ethnic group of Serbia and adjacent regions of Yugoslavia. [Serbian *Srb.*]

Ser·bi·a (sûr′bē-ə). A historical region and former kingdom of eastern Yugoslavia. Serbs settled in the region in the 6th to the 7th century and formed an independent kingdom in the 13th to the 14th century but then fell under Turkish domination, which ended finally in 1878. The new kingdom of Serbia was an important Balkan power until the onset of World War I, precipitated in part by the assassination of Archduke Francis Ferdinand by a Serbian nationalist. Serbia was later a major constituent of the Kingdom of the Serbs, Croats, and Slovenes, which formed the nucleus of modern-day Yugoslavia.

Ser·bi·an (sûr′bē-ən) *n.* **1.** A native or inhabitant of Serbia; a Serb. **2.** Serbo-Croatian as spoken in Serbia and adjacent regions of Yugoslavia, written in a Cyrillic alphabet. **—Serbian** *adj.* Of or relating to Serbia or its people, language, or culture.

Ser·bo-Cro·a·tian (sûr′bō-krō-ā′shən) *n.* **1.** The Slavic language of the Serbs and the Croats. **2.** A native speaker of Serbo-Croatian. **—Serbo-Croatian** *adj.* Of or relating to Serbo-Croatian or those who speak it.

sere¹ also **sear** (sîr) *adj.* Withered; dry: *sere vegetation at the edge of the desert.* [Middle English, from Old English *sēar.*]

sere² (sîr) *n.* The entire sequence of ecological communities successively occupying an area from the initial stage to the climax. [From SERIES.]

♦**ser·e·nade** (sĕr′ə-nād′, sĕr′ə-nād′) *n.* **1.** *Music.* A complimentary performance given to honor or express love for someone. **2.** *South Atlantic U.S.* See **shivaree.** See Regional Note at **shivaree. 3.** *Music.* An instrumental composition written for a small ensemble and having characteristics of the suite and the sonata. **—serenade** *v.* **-nad·ed, -nad·ing, -nades.** *Music.* —*tr.* To perform a serenade for. —*intr.* To perform a serenade. [French *sérénade,* from Italian *serenata,* from *sereno,* calm, clear, the open air, from Latin *serēnus.* See SERENE.] **—ser′e·nad′er** *n.*

ser·en·dip·i·ty (sĕr′ən-dĭp′ĭ-tē) *n.* The faculty of making fortunate discoveries by accident. [From the characters in the Persian fairy tale *The Three Princes of Serendip,* who made such discoveries, from Persian *Sarandīp,* Sri Lanka, from Arabic *Sarandīb.*] **—ser′en·dip′i·tous** *adj.* **—ser′en·dip′i·tous·ly** *adv.*

WORD HISTORY: We are indebted to the English author Horace Walpole for coining the word *serendipity.* In one of his 3,000 or more letters, on which his literary reputation primarily rests, and specifically in a letter of January 28, 1754, Walpole says that "this discovery, indeed, is almost of that kind which I call Serendipity, a very expressive word." Perhaps the word itself came to him by serendipity. Walpole formed the word on an old name for Sri Lanka, *Serendip.* He explained that this name was part of the title of "a silly fairy tale, called *The Three Princes of Serendip*: as their highnesses traveled, they were always making discoveries, by accidents and sagacity, of things which they were not in quest of . . . One of the most remarkable instances of this *accidental sagacity* (for you must observe that *no* discovery of a thing you *are* looking for, comes under this description) was of my Lord Shaftsbury [Anthony Ashley Cooper], who happening to dine at Lord Chancellor Clarendon's [Edward Hyde], found out the marriage of the Duke of York [later James II] and Mrs. Hyde [Anne Hyde, Clarendon's daughter], by the respect with which her mother [Frances Aylesbury Hyde] treated her at table."

se·rene (sə-rēn′) *adj.* **1.** Unaffected by disturbance; calm and unruffled. See Synonyms at **calm. 2.** Unclouded; fair: *serene skies and a bright blue sea.* **3.** Often **Serene.** Used as a title and form of address for certain members of royalty: *Her Serene Highness; His Serene Highness.* [Middle English, from Latin *serēnus,* serene, clear.] **—se·rene′ly** *adv.* **—se·rene′ness** *n.*

Ser·en·get·i Plain (sĕr′ən-gĕt′ē). An area of northern Tanzania bordering on Kenya and Lake Victoria. It is noted for its extensive wildlife preserve.

se·ren·i·ty (sə-rĕn′ĭ-tē) *n.* The state or quality of being serene; tranquillity. See Synonyms at **equanimity.**

serf (sûrf) *n.* **1.** A member of a servile, feudal class of people in Europe, bound to the land and owned by a lord. **2.** A person in servitude. [Middle English, from Old French, from Latin *servus,* slave.] **—serf′dom** *n.*

serge (sûrj) *n.* A twilled cloth of worsted or worsted and wool, often used for suits. [Middle English *sarge,* from Old French, from Vulgar Latin **sārica,* from Latin *sērica (vestis),* silken (clothing), feminine of *sēricus,* silken, from Greek *sērikos,* of the Seres, silken, from *Sēres,* a people of Eastern Asia.]

ser·geant (sär′jənt) *n. Abbr.* **Sgt. 1.a.** Any of several ranks of noncommissioned officers in the U.S. Army, Air Force, or Marine Corps. **b.** One who holds any of these ranks. **2.a.** The rank of police officer next below a captain, lieutenant, or inspector. **b.** A police officer holding this rank. **3.** See **sergeant at arms.** [Middle English *sergeaunte,* a common soldier, from Old French *sergent,* from Medieval Latin *serviēns, servient-,* servant, soldier, from Late Latin, public official, from Latin, present participle of *servīre,* to serve, from *servus,* slave.] **—ser′gean·cy, ser′geant·ship′** *n.*

sergeant at arms *n., pl.* **sergeants at arms.** An officer appointed to keep order within an organization, such as a legislative, judicial, or social body. Also called *sergeant.*

sergeant first class *n., pl.* **sergeants first class.** *Abbr.* **SFC 1.** A noncommissioned rank in the U.S. Army that is above staff sergeant and below master sergeant. **2.** One who holds this rank.

sergeant fish *n.* **1.** See **cobia. 2.** See **snook¹.**

sergeant major *n., pl.* **sergeants major** or **sergeant majors. 1.** *Abbr.* **Sgt. Maj., SM a.** Used as a title for a noncommissioned officer serving as chief administrative assistant of a headquarters unit of the U.S. Army, Air Force, or Marine Corps. **b.** One who holds this title. **2.** *Chiefly British.* A noncommissioned officer of the highest rank. **3.** A small damselfish *(Abudefduf saxatilis)* of warm seas, having a flattened body with dark vertical stripes. In this sense, also called *cow pilot.*

se·ri·al (sîr′ē-əl) *adj. Abbr.* **ser. 1.** Of, forming, or arranged in a series. **2.a.** Published or produced in installments, as a novel or television drama. **b.** Relating to such publication or production. **3.** *Music.* Relating to or based on a 12-tone row. **4.** *Computer Science.* **a.** Of or relating to the sequential transmission of all the bits of a byte over one wire: *a serial port; a serial printer.* **b.** Of or relating to the sequential performance of multiple operations: *serial processing.* **—serial** *n. Abbr.* **ser.** A literary or dramatic work published or produced in installments. **—se′ri·al·ly** *adv.*

se·ri·al·ism (sîr′ē-ə-lĭz′əm) *n. Music.* **1.** Serial compositions. **2.** The theory or composition of serial music. **—se′ri·al·ist** *n.*

se·ri·al·ize (sîr′ē-ə-līz′) *tr.v.* **-ized, -iz·ing, -iz·es.** To write or publish in serial form. **—se′ri·al·i·za′tion** (-ə-lĭ-zā′shən) *n.*

serial killer *n.* A person who attacks and slays more than three victims one by one during a relatively short period of time. Also called *serial murderer.* **—serial killing** *n.*

serial number *n.* A number that is one of a series and is used for identification, as of a machine, weapon, or motor vehicle.

se·ri·ate (sîr′ē-āt′, -ĭt) *adj.* Arranged or occurring in a series or in rows. **—se′ri·ate′ly** *adv.*

se·ri·a·tim (sîr′ē-ā′tĭm, -ăt′ĭm) *adv.* One after another; in a series. [Medieval Latin *seriātim,* from Latin *seriēs,* series. See SERIES.]

se·ri·ceous (sĭ-rĭsh′əs) *adj.* **1.** Silky. **2.** *Botany.* Covered with soft, silky hairs. [Latin *sēriceus,* silken, alteration of *sēricus.* See SERGE.]

ser·i·cin (sĕr′ĭ-sĭn) *n.* A viscous, gelatinous protein that forms on the surface of raw-silk fibers. [Latin *sēricus,* silken; see SERGE + -IN.]

ser·ic·te·ri·um (sĕr′ĭk-tîr′ē-əm) *n., pl.* **-te·ri·a** (-tîr′ē-ə). The silk-producing gland or glands of an insect, especially a silkworm. [New Latin *sērictērium,* from Greek *sērikon,* silk, from neuter of *sērikos,* silken, from *Sēres,* a people of East Asia.]

Sequoya

serape

ă pat	oi boy
ā pay	ou out
âr care	ŏŏ took
ä father	ōō boot
ĕ pet	ŭ cut
ē be	ûr urge
ĭ pit	th thin
ī pie	*th* this
îr pier	hw which
ŏ pot	zh vision
ō toe	ə about, item
ô paw	♦ regionalism

Stress marks: **′** (primary); ′ (secondary), as in **dictionary** (dĭk′shə-nĕr′ē)

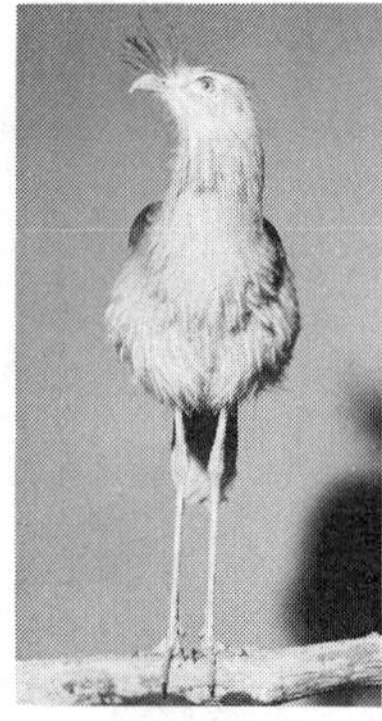

seriema
Crested seriema
Cariama cristata

ser·i·e·ma (sĕr′ē-ē′mə) *n.* Either of two cranelike birds *(Cariama cristata* or *Chunga burmeisteri)* of southern South America, having a tuftlike crest at the base of the bill and living mostly on land where they feed on snakes, worms, and insects. [Spanish, from Tupi *sariema.*]

se·ries (sîr′ēz) *n., pl.* **series.** *Abbr.* **ser. 1.** A number of objects or events arranged or coming one after the other in succession. **2.** *Physics & Chemistry.* A group of objects related by linearly varying successive differences in form or configuration: *a radioactive decay series; the paraffin alkane series.* **3.** *Mathematics.* The sum of a sequentially ordered finite or infinite set of terms. **4.** *Geology.* A group of rock formations closely related in time of origin and distinct as a group from other formations. **5.** *Grammar.* A succession of coordinate elements in a sentence. **6. a.** A succession of usually continuously numbered issues or volumes of a publication, published with related authors or subjects and similar formats. **b.** A succession of regularly aired television programs, each one of which is complete in and of itself. **7. a.** *Sports.* A number of games played one after the other by the same opposing teams. **b.** *Baseball.* The World Series. **8.** *Linguistics.* A set of vowels or dipthongs related by ablaut, as in *sing, sang, sung,* and *song.* **—*idiom.* in series.** In an arrangement that forms a series. [Latin *seriēs,* from *serere,* to join. See **ser-**[2] in Appendix.]

SYNONYMS: *series, succession, progression, sequence, chain, train, string.* These nouns denote a number of things placed or occurring one after the other. *Series* refers to like, related, or identical things arranged or occurring in order: *a series of days; a series of facts.* A *succession* is a series whose elements follow each other, generally in order of time and without interruption: *a succession of failures.* A *progression* is a series that reveals a definite pattern of advance: *a geometric progression.* In a *sequence* things follow one another in chronological or numerical order or in an order that indicates a causal or logical relationship or a recurrent pattern: *a natural sequence of ideas. Chain* suggests a series of things that are closely linked or connected: *the chain of command; a chain of proof. Train* can apply to a procession of people, animals, or vehicles or to a sequence of ideas or events: *a train of mourners; my train of thought.* A *string* is a continuous series or succession of similar or uniform elements likened to objects threaded on a long cord: *a string of islands; a string of questions.*
USAGE NOTE: *Series* is both a singular and a plural form. When it has the singular sense of "one set," it takes a singular verb, even when *series* is followed by *of* and a plural noun: *A series of lectures is scheduled.* When it has the plural sense of "one or more sets," it takes a plural verb: *Two series of lectures are scheduled: one for experts and one for laypeople.*

serif

series circuit *n.* An electric circuit connected so that current passes through each circuit element in turn without branching.

se·ries-wound (sîr′ēz-wound′) *adj. Electricity.* Of, relating to, or being a motor or dynamo in which the armature circuit and the field circuit are connected in series with the external circuit.

ser·if (sĕr′ĭf) *n. Printing.* A fine line finishing off the main strokes of a letter, as at the top and bottom of *M.* [Perhaps from Dutch *schreef,* line, from Middle Dutch *screve,* from *scriven,* to write, from Latin *scrībere.* See **skrībh-** in Appendix.]

ser·i·graph (sĕr′ĭ-grăf′) *n.* A print made by the silk-screen process. [Latin *sēricum,* silk, neuter of *sēricus,* silken; see SERGE + -GRAPH.] **—se·rig′ra·pher** (sə-rĭg′rə-fər) *n.* **—se·rig′ra·phy** (-fē) *n.*

ser·in (sĕr′ĭn) *n.* Any of several Old World finches of the genus *Serinus* having yellowish plumage, especially a European species *(S. serinus)* closely related to the canary. [French, from Old French, perhaps from Old Provençal *serena,* a kind of bird, from Late Latin *sīrēna,* from Latin *sīrēn,* from Greek *seirēn.*]

ser·ine (sĕr′ēn′) *n.* An amino acid, $CH_2OHCH(NH_2)COOH$, that is a common constituent of many proteins. [SER(ICIN) + -INE[2].]

se·ri·o·com·ic (sîr′ē-ō-kŏm′ĭk) *adj.* Both serious and comic. [SERIO(US) + COMIC.] **—se′ri·o·com′i·cal·ly** *adv.*

se·ri·ous (sîr′ē-əs) *adj.* **1.** Grave in quality or manner: *gave me a serious look.* **2. a.** Carried out in earnest: *engaged in serious drinking; made a serious attempt to learn how to ski backward; serious study of Italian.* **b.** Deeply interested or involved: *a serious card player.* **c.** Designed for and addressing grave and earnest tastes: *serious art; serious music.* **d.** Not trifling or jesting: *I'm serious: we expect you to complete the assignment on time. She has posed a serious question that deserves a thoughtful response.* **e.** Of such character or quality as to appeal to the expert, the connoisseur, or the sophisticate: *"They cost us serious money . . . but delivered a unique feature"* (Frederick C. Mish). *"Serious power requires presence in a political House"* (William Safire). *"Every serious kitchen needs at least one peppermill"* (Washington Post). **3.** Concerned with important rather than trivial matters: *a serious student of history.* **4. a.** Being of such import as to cause anxiety: *serious injuries; a serious turn of events.* **b.** Too complex to be easily answered or solved: *raised some serious objections to the proposal.* [Middle English, from Old French *serieux,* from Late Latin *sēriōsus,* from Latin *sērius.*] **—se′ri·ous·ly** *adv.* **—se′ri·ous·ness** *n.*

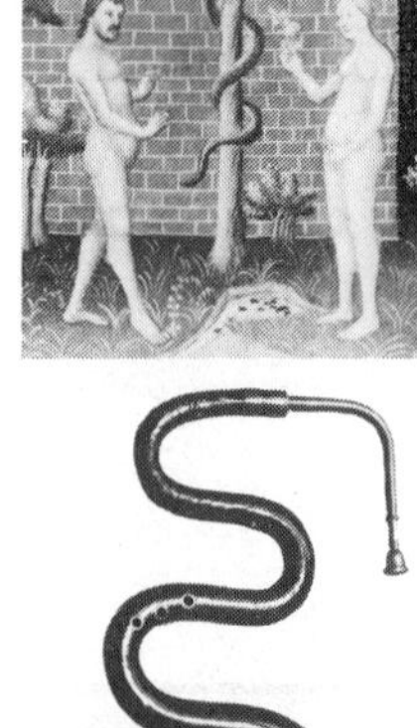

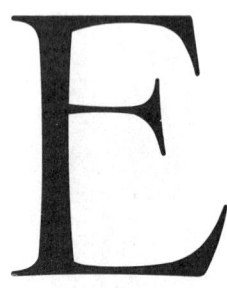

serpent
Top: Detail from a late 15th-century French manuscript, *De la Cité de Dieu,* translated from the Latin by Raoul de Presles
Bottom: 16th-century German or Italian

SYNONYMS: *serious, sober, grave, solemn, earnest, sedate, staid.* These adjectives are compared as they refer to the manner, appearance, disposition, or acts of persons and mean absorbed or marked by absorption in thought, pressing concerns, or significant work. *Serious* implies a concern with responsibility and work as opposed to play: *Serious students of music must familiarize themselves with the literature and idiom of all the important composers. Sober* emphasizes circumspection and self-restraint: *"a sober thoughtful man"* (Anthony Trollope). *"My sober mind was no longer intoxicated by the fumes of politics"* (Edward Gibbon). *Grave* suggests the dignity and somberness associated with weighty matters: *"The soldier . . . of today is . . . a quiet, grave man, busied in charts, exact in sums, master of the art of tactics"* (Walter Bagehot). *Solemn* often adds to *grave* the suggestion of impressiveness: *The judge's tone was solemn as he pronounced sentence on the convicted murderer. Earnest* implies sincerity and intensity of purpose: *Both sides in the dispute showed an earnest desire to reach an equitable solution. Sedate* implies a composed, dignified manner: *"One of those calm, quiet, sedate natures, to whom the temptations of turbulent nerves or vehement passions are things utterly incomprehensible"* (Harriet Beecher Stowe). *Staid* emphasizes dignity and an often strait-laced observance of propriety: *"a grave and staid God-fearing man"* (Tennyson).

ser·jeant (sär′jənt) *n. Chiefly British.* Variant of **sergeant** (sense 2).

Ser·kin (sûr′kĭn), **Rudolf.** 1903–1991. Czechoslovakian-born American pianist known for his interpretations of the works of Austrian and German composers.

ser·mon (sûr′mən) *n. Abbr.* **ser. 1.** A religious discourse delivered as part of a church service. **2.** An often lengthy and tedious speech of reproof or exhortation. [Middle English, from Old French, from Latin *sermō, sermōn-,* discourse. See **ser-**[2] in Appendix.] **—ser·mon′ic** (-mŏn′ĭk), **ser·mon′i·cal** (-ĭ-kəl) *adj.*

ser·mon·ette (sûr′mə-nĕt′) *n.* A short sermon.

ser·mon·ize (sûr′mə-nīz′) *v.* **-ized, -iz·ing, -iz·es.** *—tr.* To deliver a sermon to (someone). *—intr.* To deliver or speak as though delivering a sermon. **—ser′mon·iz′er** *n.*

Ser·mon on the Mount (sûr′mən) *n.* In the New Testament, a discourse of Jesus delivered on a Galilee mountainside.

sero– *pref.* Serum: *serotherapy.* [From SERUM.]

se·ro·con·ver·sion (sîr′ō-kən-vûr′zhən, -shən) *n.* Development of antibodies in blood serum as a result of infection or immunization.

se·ro·di·ag·no·sis (sîr′ō-dī′əg-nō′sĭs) *n., pl.* **-ses** (-sēz). Diagnosis of disease based on reactions in the blood serum of the body. **—se′ro·di′ag·nos′tic** (-nŏs′tĭk) *adj.*

se·rol·o·gy (sĭ-rŏl′ə-jē) *n., pl.* **-gies. 1.** The science that deals with the properties and reactions of serums, especially blood serum. **2.** The characteristics of a disease or an organism shown by study of blood serums: *the serology of acquired immune deficiency syndrome; the serology of mammals.* **—se′ro·log′ic** (sîr′ə-lŏj′ĭk), **se′ro·log′i·cal** (-ĭ-kəl) *adj.* **—se′ro·log′i·cal·ly** *adv.* **—se·rol′o·gist** *n.*

se·ro·neg·a·tive (sîr′ō-nĕg′ə-tĭv) *adj.* Showing a negative reaction to a test on blood serum for a disease, especially syphilis or AIDS.

se·ro·pos·i·tive (sîr′ō-pŏz′ĭ-tĭv) *adj.* Showing a positive reaction to a test on blood serum for a disease; exhibiting seroconversion. **—se′ro·pos′i·tiv′i·ty** *n.*

se·ro·pu·ru·lent (sîr′ō-pyŏŏr′ə-lənt, -pyŏŏr′yə-) *adj.* Consisting of serum and pus.

se·ro·sa (sĭ-rō′sə, -zə) *n., pl.* **-sas** or **-sae** (-sē, -zē). **1.** A serous membrane, especially one that lines the pericardial, pleural, and peritoneal cavities, enclosing their contents. **2.** The chorion of a bird or reptile embryo. [New Latin *serōsa,* feminine of *serōsus,* serous, from Latin *serum,* serum.] **—se·ro′sal** (-zəl) *adj.*

se·ro·si·tis (sîr′ō-sī′tĭs) *n.* Inflammation of a serous membrane.

se·ro·ther·a·py (sîr′ō-thĕr′ə-pē) *n., pl.* **-pies.** Treatment of disease by administration of a serum obtained from an immunized animal. **—se′ro·ther′a·pist** *n.*

se·rot·i·nal (sĭ-rŏt′n-əl, sĕr′ə-tī′nəl) *adj.* Serotinous.

ser·o·tine (sĕr′ə-tĭn, -tīn′) *n.* Any of a widely distributed genus *(Eptesicus)* of usually small brown bats, especially *E. serotinus,* of Europe and Asia. [From New Latin *sērōtinus,* species name, from Latin, coming late (from its habit of appearing late in the evening). See SEROTINOUS.]

se·rot·i·nous (sĭ-rŏt′n-əs, sĕr′ə-tī′nəs) *adj. Biology & Botany.* Late in developing or blooming. [Latin *sērōtinus,* coming late, from *sērō,* at a late hour, from *sērus,* late.]

se·ro·to·ner·gic (sĕr′ə-tn-ûr′jĭk) also **se·ro·to·ni·ner·gic** (-tō′nə-nûr′jĭk) *adj.* Activated by or capable of liberating serotonin, especially in transmitting nerve impulses: *serotonergic neurons; serotonergic drugs.* [SEROTON(IN) + *-ergic* (as in CHOLINERGIC).]

se·ro·to·nin (sĕr′ə-tō′nĭn, sîr′-) *n.* An organic compound, $C_{10}H_{12}N_2O$, formed from tryptophan and found in animal and human tissue, especially the brain, blood serum, and gastric mucous membranes, and active in vasoconstriction, stimulation of the smooth muscles, transmission of impulses between nerve cells, and regulation of cyclic body processes. [SERO- + TON(E) + -IN.]

se·ro·type (sîr′ə-tīp′, sĕr′-) *n.* A group of closely related microorganisms distinguished by a characteristic set of antigens.

—serotype *tr.v.* **-typed, -typ·ing, -types.** To classify according to serotype; assign to a particular serotype.

se·rous (sîr′əs) *adj.* Containing, secreting, or resembling serum.

serous fluid *n.* Any of various body fluids resembling serum, especially lymph.

serous membrane *n.* A thin membrane lining a closed body cavity and moistened with a serous fluid.

se·row (sə-rō′) *n.* Any of several goat antelopes of the genus *Capricornis,* of mountainous regions of eastern Asia, having short horns and a dark coat. [Origin unknown.]

Ser·pens (sûr′pənz, -pĕnz′) *n.* A constellation in the equatorial region of the northern sky, made up of two parts, *Serpens Cauda,* the "tail," and *Serpens Caput,* the "head," both near Hercules and Ophiuchus. [Latin *Serpēns,* from *serpēns,* serpent. See SERPENT.]

ser·pent (sûr′pənt) *n.* **1.** A reptile of the order Serpentes; a snake. **2.** Often **Serpent. a.** The creature that tempted Eve. **b.** Satan. **3.** A subtle, sly, or treacherous person. **4.** A firework that writhes while burning. **5.** *Music.* A deep-voiced wind instrument of serpentine shape, used principally in the 18th century, about 2.5 meters (8 feet) in length and made of brass or wood. **6. Serpent.** Serpens. [Middle English, from Old French, from Latin *serpēns, serpent-,* from present participle of *serpere,* to creep.]

ser·pen·tar·i·um (sûr′pən-târ′ē-əm) *n., pl.* **-i·ums** or **-i·a** (-ē-ə). A place where snakes are kept for study or display.

ser·pen·tine (sûr′pən-tēn′, -tīn′) *adj.* **1.** Of or resembling a serpent, as in form or movement; sinuous. **2.** Subtly sly and tempting. **—serpentine** (-tēn′) *n.* Any of a group of greenish, brownish, or spotted minerals, $Mg_3Si_2O_5(OH)_4$, used as a source of magnesium and asbestos, and in architecture as a decorative stone. [Middle English, from Old French *serpentin,* from Late Latin *serpentīnus,* from Latin *serpēns, serpent-,* serpent. See SERPENT.]

serpent star *n.* A brittle star.

ser·pi·go (sər-pī′gō) *n. Archaic.* A spreading skin eruption or disease, such as ringworm. [Middle English, from Medieval Latin *serpīgō,* from Latin *serpere,* to creep.] **—ser·pig′i·nous** (sər-pĭj′ə-nəs) *adj.*

Ser·ra (sĕr′ə), **Junípero.** Originally Miguel José Serra. Known as "the Apostle of California." 1713–1784. Spanish missionary who founded nine Franciscan missions in California (1769–1782).

ser·ran·id (sə-răn′ĭd, sĕr′ə-nĭd) *n.* Any of various fishes of the family Serranidae, such as the grouper. [From New Latin *Serranidae,* family name, from Latin *serra,* saw, sawfish.]

ser·rate (sĕr′āt′) *adj.* **1.** Having or forming a row of small, sharp, projections resembling the teeth of a saw: *serrate teeth; a serrate talon.* **2.** Having a saw-toothed edge or margin notched with toothlike projections: *serrate leaves.* **—serrate** *tr.v.* **-rat·ed, -rat·ing, -rates.** To make serrate or saw-toothed; jag the edge of. [Latin *serrātus,* saw-shaped, from *serra,* saw.]

ser·rat·ed (sĕr′ā′tĭd) *adj.* Notched like the edge of a saw; saw-toothed; serrate.

ser·ra·tion (sə-rā′shən, sĕ-) *n.* **1.** The state of being serrate. **2.** A series or set of teeth or notches. **3.** A single tooth or notch in a serrate edge.

ser·ried (sĕr′ēd) *adj.* Pressed or crowded together, especially in rows: *troops in serried ranks.* [Past participle of obsolete *serry,* to close ranks, from French *serré,* past participle of *serrer,* to crowd, fasten. See SEAR[2].] **—ser′ried·ly** *adv.*

ser·ru·late (sĕr′yə-lĭt, -lāt′, sĕr′ə-) also **ser·ru·lat·ed** (-lā′tĭd) *adj.* Having a minutely serrate margin, as in a leaflet of the rose. [New Latin *serrulātus,* from Latin *serrula,* diminutive of *serra,* saw.]

Ser·to·ri·us (sər-tôr′ē-əs, -tōr′-), **Quintus.** 123?–72 B.C. Roman general who ruled much of Spain in defiance of the Roman Senate.

ser·tu·lar·i·an (sûr′chə-lâr′ē-ən, sûr′tl-âr′-) *n.* Any of various colonial hydroids of the genus *Sertularia,* having stalkless polyps arranged in pairs along a long, branching stem. [From New Latin *Sertularia,* genus name, from Latin *sertula,* diminutive of *serta,* garland, from feminine past participle of *serere,* to join. See **ser-**[2] in Appendix.]

se·rum (sîr′əm) *n., pl.* **se·rums** or **se·ra** (sîr′ə). **1.** The clear yellowish fluid obtained upon separating whole blood into its solid and liquid components. Also called *blood serum.* **2.** Blood serum from the tissues of immunized animals, containing antibodies and used to transfer immunity to another individual. **3.** Watery fluid from animal tissue, such as that found in edema. **4.** Whey. [Latin, whey, serum.]

serum albumin *n.* A protein fraction of serum involved in maintaining osmotic pressure of the blood and used as a substitute for plasma in the treatment of shock.

serum globulin *n.* A protein fraction of serum composed chiefly of antibodies.

serum hepatitis *n.* See **hepatitis B.**

serum sickness *n.* A hypersensitive reaction to the administration of a foreign serum, characterized by fever, swelling, skin rash, and enlargement of the lymph nodes.

serv. *abbr.* **1.** Servant. **2.** Service.

ser·val (sûr′vəl, sər-văl′) *n.* A long-legged wildcat *(Felis serval)* of Africa, having a tawny coat with black spots and large erect ears without tufts. [French, from Portuguese *(lobo) cerval,* deerlike (wolf), lynx, from Late Latin *cervālis,* from Latin *cervus,* deer. See **ker-**[1] in Appendix.]

serval
Felis serval

ser·vant (sûr′vənt) *n. Abbr.* **serv. 1.** One who is privately employed to perform domestic services. **2.** One who is publicly employed to perform services, as for a government. **3.** One who expresses submission, recognizance, or debt to another: *your obedient servant.* [Middle English, from Old French, from present participle of *servir,* to serve. See SERVE.]

serve (sûrv) *v.* **served, serv·ing, serves.** *—tr.* **1.a.** To work for. **b.** To be a servant to. **2.a.** To prepare and offer (food, for example): *serve tea.* **b.** To place food before (someone); wait on: *served the guests a wonderful dinner.* **3.a.** To provide goods and services for (customers): *a hotel that has served tourists at the same location for 30 years.* **b.** To supply (goods or services) to customers. See Usage Note at **service. 4.** To assist (the celebrant) during Mass. **5.** To be of assistance to or promote the interests of; aid: *"Both major parties today seek to serve the national interest"* (John F. Kennedy). **6.** To spend or complete (time): *served four terms in Congress.* **7.** To fight or undergo military service for: *served her country for five years in the navy.* **8.** To give homage and obedience to: *served God.* **9.** To act toward (another) in a specified way; requite: *She has served me ill, and only that.* **10.** To copulate with. Used of male animals. **11.** To meet the needs or requirements of; satisfy: *serve the purpose.* **12.** *Law.* **a.** To deliver or present (a writ or summons). **b.** To present such a writ to. **13.** *Sports.* To put (a ball or shuttlecock) in play, as in tennis, badminton, or jai alai. **14.** To bind or whip (a rope) with fine cord or wire. *—intr.* **1.** To be employed as a servant. **2.** To do a term of duty: *serve in the U.S. Air Force; serve on a jury.* **3.** To act in a particular capacity: *serve as a clerk.* **4.** To be of service or use; function: *Let this incident serve as a reminder to future generations.* **5.** To meet requirements or needs; satisfy: *a device that will serve well.* **6.** To wait on tables: *serve at luncheon.* **7.** *Sports.* To put a ball or shuttlecock into play, as in court games. **8.** To assist the celebrant during Mass. **—serve** *n. Sports.* The right, manner, or act of serving in many court games. **—*idiom.* serve (someone) right.** To be deserved under the circumstances: *Punish him; it will serve him right for what he has done to you.* [Middle English *serven,* from Old French *servir,* from Latin *servīre,* from *servus,* slave.]

serve
Volleyball game

serv·er (sûr′vər) *n.* **1.a.** One who serves food and drink. **b.** Something, such as a tray, that is used in serving food and drink. **2.** An attendant to the celebrant at Mass. **3.** *Sports.* The player who serves, as in court games.

Ser·ve·tus (sər-vē′təs), **Michael.** Originally Miguel Serveto. 1511–1553. Spanish-born theologian and physician who described the circulation of blood. His denial of the doctrine of the Trinity led to his execution for heresy.

ser·vi·bar (sûr′vĭ-bär′) *n.* See **minibar.** [Probably SERVI(CE) + BAR[1].]

serv·ice (sûr′vĭs) *n. Abbr.* **serv., svc 1.a.** Employment in duties or work for another, especially for a government. **b.** A government branch or department and its employees: *the diplomatic service.* **2.a.** The armed forces of a nation. **b.** A branch of the armed forces of a nation. **3.a.** Work or duties performed for a superior. **b.** The occupation or duties of a servant. **4.a.** Work done for others as an occupation or a business: *provides full catering service.* **b.** A department or branch of a hospital staff that provides specified patient care: *the anesthesiology service; the chest service.* **5.** Installation, maintenance, or repairs provided or guaranteed by a dealer or manufacturer. **6.** A facility providing the public with the use of something, such as water or transportation. **7.a.** Acts of devotion to God; witness. **b.** A religious rite. **8.** An act of assistance or benefit to another or others; a favor. **9.a.** The serving of food or the manner in which it is served. **b.** A set of dishes or utensils: *a silver tea service.* **10.** *Sports.* The act, manner, or right of serving in many court games; a serve. **11.** Copulation with a female. **12.** *Law.* The serving of a writ or summons. **13.** The material, such as cord, used in binding or wrapping rope. **—service** *tr.v.* **-iced, -ic·ing, -ic·es.** *Abbr.* **serv. 1.** To make fit for use; adjust, repair, or maintain: *service a car.* **2.** To provide services to. **3.** To make interest payments on (a debt). **4.** To copulate with. **—service** *adj. Abbr.* **serv. 1.** Of or relating to the armed forces of a country. **2.** Intended for use in supplying or serving: *a service elevator; the service entrance.* **3.** Offering repairs or maintenance: *a service guarantee; a road service area.* **4.** Offering services to the public in response to need or demand: *a service industry.* [Middle English, from Old French, from Latin *servitium,* slavery, from *servus,* slave.]

service
Silver tea service

USAGE NOTE: Aside from specialized senses in finance (*service a debt*) and animal breeding (*service a mare*), *service* is used principally in the sense "to repair or maintain": *service the electric dishwasher.* In the sense "to supply goods or services to," *serve* is the most frequent or only choice: *One radio network serves three states.*

Ser·vice (sûr′vĭs), **Robert William.** 1874–1958. British-born Canadian writer of poetry and novels about life in the Yukon, including the ballad "The Shooting of Dan McGrew" (1907).

serv·ice·a·ble (sûr′vĭ-sə-bəl) *adj.* **1.** Ready for service; usable: *serviceable equipment.* **2.** Able to give long service; durable: *a heavy, serviceable fabric.* **—serv′ice·a·bil′i·ty, serv′ice·a·ble·ness** *n.* **—serv′ice·a·bly** *adv.*

ă **pat**	oi **boy**
ā **pay**	ou **out**
âr **care**	ŏŏ **took**
ä **father**	ōō **boot**
ĕ **pet**	ŭ **cut**
ē **be**	ûr **urge**
ĭ **pit**	th **thin**
ī **pie**	*th* **this**
îr **pier**	hw **which**
ŏ **pot**	zh **vision**
ō **toe**	ə **about, item**
ô **paw**	♦ **regionalism**

Stress marks: **′** (primary); ′ (secondary), as in **dictionary** (dĭk′shə-nĕr′ē)

serv•ice•ber•ry (sûr′vĭs-bĕr′ē) *n.* The shadbush or one of its fruit. [SERVICE (TREE) + BERRY.]

service break *n. Sports.* A game won on an opponent's serve, as in tennis.

service cap *n.* A flat-topped military cap with a visor.

service charge *n.* An additional charge for a service for which there is already a basic fee.

service line *n. Sports.* A boundary line, as in tennis or handball, that must not be overstepped in serving.

serv•ice•man (sûr′vĭs-măn′, -mən) *n.* **1.** A man who is a member of the armed forces. **2.** Also **service man.** A man whose work is the maintenance and repair of equipment.

service mark *n. Abbr.* **SM** A mark used in the sale or advertising of services to identify the services and distinguish them from the services of others.

serv•ice•per•son (sûr′vĭs-pûr′sən) *n., pl.* **-per•sons** or **-peo•ple** (-pē′pəl). **1.** A person who is a member of the armed forces. **2.** Also **service person.** A person whose work is the maintenance and repair of equipment.

service road *n.* A local road that runs parallel to an expressway or interstate highway and that provides access to the property bordering it. Also called *frontage road.*

service station *n.* **1.** A retail establishment at which motor vehicles are refueled, serviced, and sometimes repaired. Also called *filling station, gas station.* **2.** A business or branch of a business where services, especially repairs, can be obtained.

service stripe *n.* **1.** A stripe worn on an enlisted person's sleeve to indicate three years' service in the army or four years' service in the navy, for example. **2.** A stripe worn on the sleeve of the uniform of a bus driver, for example, to indicate years of seniority.

service tree *n.* Either of two Mediterranean trees *(Sorbus domestica* or *S. torminalis)* having clusters of white flowers, saw-toothed leaves, and edible brownish fruit. [From Middle English *serves,* pl. of *serve,* the service tree, from Old English *syrfe,* from Vulgar Latin **sorbea,* from Latin *sorbus.*]

serv•ice•wom•an (sûr′vĭs-wo͝om′ən) *n.* **1.** A woman who is a member of the armed forces. **2.** Also **service woman.** A woman whose work is the maintenance and repair of equipment.

ser•vi•ette (sûr′vē-ĕt′) *n. Chiefly British.* A table napkin. [French, from Old French *serviete,* perhaps from *servir,* to serve. See SERVE.]

ser•vile (sûr′vəl, -vīl′) *adj.* **1.** Abjectly submissive; slavish. **2. a.** Of or suitable to a slave or servant: *servile tasks such as floor scrubbing and barn work.* **b.** Of or relating to servitude or forced labor. [Middle English, from Latin *servīlis,* from *servus,* slave.] **—ser′vile•ly** *adv.* **—ser′vile•ness, ser•vil′i•ty** (sər-vĭl′ĭ-tē) *n.*

serv•ing (sûr′vĭng) *n.* **1.** The act of one that serves. **2.** An individual portion or helping of food or drink.

ser•vi•tor (sûr′vĭ-tər, -tôr′) *n.* One that performs the duties of a servant to another; an attendant. [Middle English *servitour,* from Anglo-Norman, from Latin *servītor,* from *servīre,* to serve. See SERVE.] **—ser′vi•tor•ship′** *n.*

ser•vi•tude (sûr′vĭ-to͞od′, -tyo͞od′) *n.* **1. a.** A state of subjection to an owner or a master. **b.** Lack of personal freedom, as to act as one chooses. **2.** Forced labor imposed as a punishment for crime: *penal servitude in labor camps.* **3.** *Law.* A right that grants use of another's property. [Middle English, from Old French, from Late Latin *servitūdō,* from Latin *servus,* slave.]

SYNONYMS: *servitude, bondage, slavery.* These nouns signify a state of subjugation to an owner or a master. *Servitude* sometimes refers broadly to the lack of freedom to act or live as one chooses, but it often implies the performance of involuntary labor or service for a master: *"The right of citizens of the United States to vote shall not be denied or abridged . . . on account of race, color, or previous condition of servitude"* (U.S. Constitution, 15th Amendment). *Bondage* emphasizes being bound to the service of another with virtually no hope of freedom: *"even compassionating those who hold in bondage their fellow men, not knowing what they do"* (John Quincy Adams). To be held in *slavery* is to be owned bodily by the person or persons one serves and to be treated as his or her property: *"I have borne thirteen children and seen them most all sold off into slavery"* (Sojourner Truth).

sesame
Top: Sesamum indicum
Bottom: Sesame seeds on a bagel

ser•vo (sûr′vō) *n., pl.* **-vos.** **1.** A servomechanism. **2.** A servomotor.

ser•vo•mech•a•nism (sûr′vō-mĕk′ə-nĭz′əm) *n.* **1.** A feedback system that consists of a sensing element, an amplifier, and a servomotor, used in the automatic control of a mechanical device. **2.** A self-regulating feedback system or mechanism: *"We do not need to know in detail how the minute chemical servomechanisms of the muscles operate in order to move our arms"* (Harper's). [SERVO(MOTOR) + MECHANISM.]

ser•vo•mo•tor (sûr′vō-mō′tər) *n.* A motor that controls the action of the mechanical device in a servomechanism. [French *servomoteur* : Latin *servus,* slave + French *moteur,* motor (from Old French, from Latin *mōtor,* that which sets in motion; see MOTOR).]

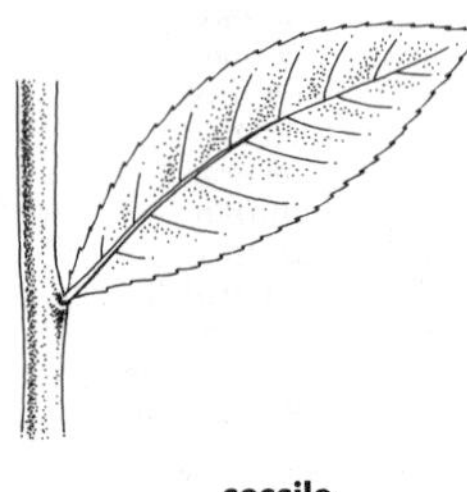

sessile

SES *abbr.* Socioeconomic status.

ses•a•me (sĕs′ə-mē) *n.* **1.** A tropical Asian plant *(Sesamum indicum)* bearing small, flat seeds used as food and as a source of oil. **2.** The seed of this plant. Also called *til.* [Middle English *sisamie,* from Latin *sēsamum,* from Greek *sēsamē, sēsamon,* of Semitic origin; akin to Akkadian *šamaššamu.*]

ses•a•moid (sĕs′ə-moid′) *adj.* Of or designating any of certain small modular bones or cartilages that develop in a tendon or in the capsule of a joint. **—sesamoid** *n.* A sesamoid bone or cartilage. [Greek *sēsamoeidēs,* shaped like a sesame seed : *sēsamon, sēsamē,* sesame; see SESAME + *-oeidēs,* -oid.] **—ses′a•moid′** *n.*

sesqui– *pref.* One and a half: *sesquicentennial.* [Latin *sēsqui-* : *sēmis,* a half; see **sēmi-** in Appendix + *-que,* and; see **k^{w}e** in Appendix.]

ses•qui•cen•ten•ni•al (sĕs′kwĭ-sĕn-tĕn′ē-əl) *adj.* Of or relating to a period of 150 years. **—sesquicentennial** *n.* A 150th anniversary or its celebration.

ses•quip•e•dal (sĕ-skwĭp′ĭ-dl) *adj.* Sesquipedalian. [Latin *sēsquipedālis,* of a foot and a half in length : *sēsqui-,* sesqui- + *pēs, ped-,* foot; see **ped-** in Appendix.]

ses•qui•pe•da•lian (sĕs′kwĭ-pĭ-dāl′yən) *n.* A long word. **—sesquipedalian** *adj.* **1.** Given to the use of long words. **2.** Long and ponderous; polysyllabic.

sess. *abbr.* Session.

ses•sile (sĕs′īl′, -əl) *adj.* **1.** *Botany.* Stalkless and attached directly at the base: *sessile leaves.* **2.** *Zoology.* Permanently attached or fixed; not free-moving: *a sessile barnacle.* [Latin *sessilis,* low, of sitting, from *sessus,* past participle of *sedēre,* to sit. See **sed-** in Appendix.] **—ses•sil′i•ty** (sĕ-sĭl′ĭ-tē) *n.*

ses•sion (sĕsh′ən) *n. Abbr.* **sess. 1. a.** A meeting of a legislative or judicial body for the purpose of transacting business. **b.** A series of such meetings. **c.** The term or duration of time that is taken by such a series of meetings. **2.** The part of a year or of a day during which a school holds classes. **3.** An assembly of people for a common purpose or because of a common interest: *a gossip session.* **4.** *Law.* A court of criminal jurisdiction in the United States: *the court of sessions.* **5.** A period of time devoted to a specific activity. [Middle English, from Old French, from Latin *sessiō, sessiōn-,* act of sitting, from *sessus,* past participle of *sedēre,* to sit. See **sed-** in Appendix.] **—ses′sion•al** *adj.* **—ses′sion•al•ly** *adv.*

Ses•sions (sĕsh′ənz), **Roger Huntington.** 1896–1985. American composer. An influential promoter of 20th-century music, he wrote polyphonic symphonies, instrumental works, and operas, such as *Montezuma* (1962).

ses•terce (sĕs′tûrs′) *n.* A silver or bronze coin of ancient Rome equivalent to one fourth of a denarius. [Latin *sēstertius,* a coin worth two and a half asses : *sēmis,* half; see **sēmi-** in Appendix + *tertius,* third; see **trei-** in Appendix.]

ses•ter•tium (sĕ-stûr′shəm, -shē-əm) *n., pl.* **-tia** (-shə, -shē-ə). A monetary unit of ancient Rome equivalent to 1,000 sesterces. [Latin *(mille) sēstertium,* (a thousand) sesterces, genitive pl. of *sēstertius,* sesterce. See SESTERCE.]

ses•tet (sĕ-stĕt′) *n.* **1.** A group of six lines of poetry, especially the last six lines of a Petrarchan sonnet. **2.** A poem or stanza containing six lines. [Italian *sestetto,* from *sesto,* sixth, from Latin *sextus.* See **s(w)eks** in Appendix.]

ses•ti•na (sĕ-stē′nə) *n.* A verse form first used by the Provençal troubadours, consisting of six six-line stanzas and a three-line envoy. The end words of the first stanza are repeated in varied order as end words in the other stanzas and also recur in the envoy. [Italian, from *sesto,* sixth, from Latin *sextus.* See **s(w)eks** in Appendix.]

Ses•tos (sĕs′təs, -tŏs). An ancient town of European Turkey at the narrowest point of the Dardanelles. In 481 B.C. Xerxes built a bridge of boats here to cross the Hellespont and invade Greece. Sestos is also the site of the legendary tale of Hero and Leander.

Ses•to San Gio•van•ni (sĕs′tō săn′ jô-vä′nē, sän′). A city of northern Italy, a suburb of Milan. Population, 94,738.

set[1] (sĕt) *v.* **set, set•ting, sets.** *—tr.* **1.** To put in a specified position; place: *set a book on a table.* **2.** To put into a specified state: *set the prisoner at liberty.* **3. a.** To put into a stable position: *set the fence post into a bed of concrete.* **b.** To fix firmly or in an immobile manner: *He set his jaw and concentrated on flying the plane through the storm.* **4.** To restore to a proper and normal state when dislocated or broken: *set a broken arm.* **5. a.** To adjust for proper functioning. **b.** To adjust (a saw) by deflecting the teeth. **c.** *Nautical.* To spread open to the wind: *set the sails.* **6.** To adjust according to a standard. **7.** To adjust (an instrument) to a specific point or calibration: *set an alarm clock.* **8.** To arrange properly for use: *set a place for a dinner guest; set a table.* **9.** To apply equipment, such as curlers and clips, to (hair) in order to style. **10.** *Printing.* **a.** To arrange (type) into words and sentences preparatory to printing; compose. **b.** To transpose into type. **11.** *Music.* **a.** To compose (music) to fit a given text. **b.** To write (words) to fit a given melodic line. **12.** To arrange scenery on (a theater stage). **13.** To prescribe the unfolding of (a scene) in a specific place: *a play that is set in Venice.* **14.** To prescribe or establish: *set a precedent.* **15.** To prescribe as a time for: *set June 6 as the day of the invasion.* **16.** To detail or assign (someone) to a particular duty, service, or station: *set the child to cleaning the closets; set guards around the perimeter.* **17.** To incite to hostile action: *a war that set families against one another.* **18. a.** To establish as the highest level of performance: *set a world aviation record.* **b.** To establish as a model: *A parent must set a good example for the children.* **19. a.** To put in a mounting;

mount: *set an emerald in a pendant.* **b.** To apply jewels to; stud: *a tiara that was set with diamonds.* **20.** To cause to sit. **21.a.** To put (a hen) on eggs for the purpose of hatching them. **b.** To put (eggs) beneath a hen or in an incubator. **22.** *Sports.* To position (oneself) in such a way as to be ready to start running a race. **23.a.** To value or regard something at the rate of: *She sets a great deal by good nutrition.* **b.** To fix at a given amount: *The judge set bail for the defendant at $50,000.* **c.** To make as an estimate of worth: *We set a high value on human life.* **24.** To point to the location of (game) by holding a fixed attitude. Used of a hunting dog. **25.** *Botany.* To produce, as after pollination: *set seed.* **26.a.** To prepare (a trap) for catching prey. **b.** To fix (a hook) firmly into a fish's jaw. —*intr.* **1.** To disappear below the horizon: *The sun set at seven that evening.* **2.** To diminish or decline; wane. **3.** To sit on eggs. Used of fowl. **4.a.** To become fixed; harden. See Synonyms at **coagulate. b.** To become permanent. Used of dye. **5.** To become whole; knit. Used of a broken bone. **6.** *Botany.* To mature or develop, as after pollination. **7.** *Nonstandard.* To sit: *"If Emmett drives, I could set up front"* (Bobbie Ann Mason). **8.** To position oneself preparatory to an action, such as running a race. —**set** *adj.* **1.** Fixed or established by agreement: *a set time for the launching.* **2.** Established by convention: *followed set procedures for filing a grievance.* **3.** Established deliberately; intentional: *Our set purpose is to win the conflict.* **4.** Fixed and rigid: *"His bearded face already has a set, hollow look"* (Conor Cruise O'Brien). **5.** Unwilling or very reluctant to change: *He is set in his ways.* **6.a.** Intent and determined: *"He is dead set against rushing abroad to build a plant"* (Fortune). **b.** Ready: *We are set to leave early tomorrow morning.* —**set** *n.* **1.a.** The act or process of setting. **b.** The condition resulting from setting. **2.** The manner in which something is positioned: *the set of her cap.* **3.** A permanent firming or hardening of a substance, as by cooling. **4.** The deflection of the teeth of a saw. **5.a.** The carriage or bearing of a part of the body. **b.** A particular psychological state, usually that of anticipation or preparedness: *"The mental set of an audience is crucial to his performance"* (Psychology Today). **6.** A descent below the horizon. **7.** The direction or course of wind or water. **8.** A seedling, slip, or cutting that is ready for planting. **9.** The act of arranging hair by waving and curling it. —***phrasal verbs.* set about.** To begin or start: *set about solving the problem.* **set apart. 1.** To reserve for a specific use. **2.** To make noticeable: *character traits that set her apart.* **set aside. 1.** To separate and reserve for a special purpose. **2.** To discard or reject. **3.** To declare invalid; annul or overrule: *The court has set aside the conviction.* **set at.** To attack or assail: *The dogs set at the fox.* **set back. 1.** To slow down the progress of; hinder. **2.** *Informal.* To cost: *That coat set me back $1,000.* **set by.** To reserve for future use: *It is wise to set food and money by in case of a future emergency.* **set down. 1.** To cause to sit; seat: *Set the baby down here.* **2.** To put in writing; record: *We set down the facts.* **3.a.** To regard; consider: *Just set him down as a sneak.* **b.** To assign to a cause; attribute: *Let's set the error down to inexperience.* **4.** To land (an aircraft): *The pilot set the plane down hard.* **set forth. 1.** To present for consideration; propose: *set forth a sound plan.* **2.** To express in words: *She has set forth her ideas.* **set forward.** To begin a journey. **set in. 1.** To insert: *set in the sleeve of a gown.* **2.** To begin to happen or be apparent: *"Evening was setting in as I took the road over Mountain Top"* (Charles Siebert). **3.** To move toward the shore. Used of wind or water. **set off. 1.a.** To give rise to; cause to occur: *set off a chemical reaction.* **b.** To cause to explode: *set off a bomb.* **2.** To indicate as being different; distinguish: *features setting him off from the crowd.* **3.** To direct attention to by contrast; accentuate: *set off a passage with italics.* **4.** To start on a journey: *set off for Europe.* **set out. 1.** To begin an earnest attempt; undertake: *He set out to understand why the plan had failed.* **2.** To lay out systematically and graphically: *set out a terrace.* **3.** To display for exhibition or sale. **4.** To plant: *set out seedlings.* **5.** To begin a journey: *She set out at dawn for town.* **set to. 1.** To begin working energetically; start in. **2.** To begin fighting. **set up. 1.** To place in an upright position. **2.a.** To elevate; raise. **b.** To raise in authority or power; invest with power: *They set the general up as a dictator.* **c.** To put (oneself) forward as; claim to be: *He has set himself up as an authority on the English language.* **d.** To assemble and erect: *set up a new machine.* **3.** To establish; found: *set up a charity.* **4.** To cause: *They set up howls of protest over new taxes.* **5.** To establish in business by providing capital, equipment, or other backing. **6.** *Informal.* **a.** To treat (someone) to drinks. **b.** To pay for (drinks). **7.** *Informal.* To stimulate or exhilarate: *a victory that really set the team up.* **8.** To lay plans for: *set up a kidnapping.* **9.** *Informal.* To put (someone else) into a compromising situation by deceit or trickery: *Swindlers have set me up.* **set upon.** To attack violently: *Guards set dogs upon the escaping prisoners.* —***idioms.* set fire to.** To cause to ignite and burn. **set foot in.** To enter. **set foot on.** To step on. **set in motion.** To give impetus to: *The indictment set the judicial process in motion.* **set (one's) heart on.** To be determined to do something. **set (one's) sights on.** To have as a goal: *She set her sights on medical school.* **set on fire. 1.** To cause to ignite and burn. **2.** To cause to become excited: *The music set the audience on fire.* **set sail.** *Nautical.* To begin a voyage on water. **set (someone) straight.** To correct (someone) by providing full and accurate information. **set store by.** To regard as valuable or worthwhile. **set the pace. 1.** To go at a speed that other competitors attempt to match or surpass. **2.** To behave or perform in a way that others try to emulate. **set the stage for.** To provide the underlying basis for: *saber rattling that set the stage for war.* **set up housekeeping.** To establish a household. **set up shop.** To establish one's business operations. [Middle English *setten,* from Old English *settan.* See **sed-** in Appendix.]

USAGE NOTE: Originally *set* meant "to cause (something) to sit," so that it is now in most cases a transitive verb: *She sets the book on the table. He sets the table. Sit* is generally an intransitive verb: *He sits at the table.* There are some exceptions: *The sun sets* (not *sits*). *A hen sets* (or *sits*) *on her eggs.*

set² (sĕt) *n.* **1.** A group of things of the same kind that belong together and are so used: *a chess set.* **2.** A group of persons sharing a common interest: *the high-school set.* See Synonyms at **circle. 3.** A group of books or periodicals published as a unit. **4.a.** A number of couples required for participation in a square dance. **b.** The movements constituting a square dance. **5.a.** The scenery constructed for a theatrical performance. **b.** The entire enclosure in which a movie is filmed; the sound stage. **6.** *Music.* **a.** A session of music, typically dance music, played before an intermission. **b.** The music so played. **7.** The collective receiving apparatus assembled to operate a radio or television. **8.** *Mathematics.* A collection of distinct elements having specific common properties: *a set of positive integers.* **9.a.** *Sports.* A group of tennis games constituting one division or unit of a match. **b.** *Football.* An offensive formation. [Middle English *sette,* from Old French, from Medieval Latin *secta,* retinue, from Latin, faction. See SECT.]

se·ta (sē′tə) *n., pl.* **-tae** (-tē). *Biology.* **1.** A stiff hair, bristle, or bristlelike process or part on an organism. **2.** *Botany.* The stalk of a moss capsule. [New Latin *sēta,* from Latin *saeta,* bristle.] —**se′tal** (sēt′l) *adj.*

se·ta·ceous (sĭ-tā′shəs) *adj.* **1.** Having or consisting of bristles; bristly: *a setaceous moth.* **2.** Resembling bristles or a bristle: *setaceous whiskers.* [SET(A) + -ACEOUS.] —**se·ta′ceous·ly** *adv.*

se·tae (sē′tē) *n.* Plural of **seta.**

set-a·side (sĕt′ə-sīd′) *n.* **1.** Something, such as land or a certain percentage of profits, that is set aside for a specific purpose. **2.** A federal program requiring that a certain percentage of government funds and contracts be reserved for businesses owned by women and members of minority groups.

set·back (sĕt′băk′) *n.* **1.** An unanticipated or sudden check in progress; a change from better to worse. **2.a.** A steplike recession in a wall. **b.** Any of a series of such recessions in the rise of a tall building. **3.** An automatically timed setting of a thermostat to a lower temperature, as in the home at night.

set back *n.* *Football.* An offensive back who lines up behind the quarterback.

set chisel *n.* A chisel with a cutting edge on a tapered shaft.

se-ten·ant or **se ten·ant** (sə-tĕn′ənt, sĕt′n-äN′, sə-tə-näN′) *n.* A block of commemorative stamps printed together on the same sheet but differing in design, color, value, or overprint. [French : *se,* reflexive pron. + *tenant,* present participle of *tenir,* to hold.] —**se-ten′ant** *adj.*

Seth (sĕth). In the Old Testament, the third son of Adam and Eve.

se·tif·er·ous (sĭ-tĭf′ər-əs) *adj.* Having setae or bristles; setaceous: *setiferous antennae.*

se·ti·form (sē′tə-fôrm′) *adj.* Shaped like a seta or bristle.

se·tig·er·ous (sĭ-tĭj′ər-əs) *adj.* Setiferous. [From Latin *sētiger* : *sēta,* bristle + *-ger* (from *gerere,* to bear).]

set-in (sĕt′ĭn′) *adj.* **1.** Made or placed as a part of another unit or structure: *a set-in stereo cabinet.* **2.** Made separately and stitched into the main part: *a dress with set-in sleeves.* —**set-in** *n.* Material, as for a book, that is inserted; an insert.

set·line (sĕt′līn′) *n.* A long fishing line towed by a boat and supporting many smaller lines bearing baited hooks. Also called *trawl, trawl line, trotline.*

set·off (sĕt′ôf′, -ŏf′) *n.* **1.** Something, such as a decoration, that sets off something else by contrast. **2.** Something that offsets or compensates for something else; a counterbalance. **3.a.** A counterclaim. **b.** Settlement of a debt by a debtor's establishing such a claim against a creditor. **4.** *Architecture.* A flat projection, as from a wall; a ledge. **5.** *Printing.* See **offset** (sense 10a).

Se·ton (sēt′n), Saint **Elizabeth Ann Bayley.** Known as "Mother Seton." 1774–1821. American religious leader. A widowed mother of five, she converted to Catholicism (1805), opened a parochial school in Maryland, and founded a religious order, the Sisters of Charity (1809). She was the first native-born American to be canonized (1975).

Elizabeth Seton

se·tose (sē′tōs′) *adj.* Bristly: setaceous.

set·out (sĕt′out′) *n.* **1.** A start or beginning; an outset. **2.a.** An arrangement or a display. **b.** An array of food, as on a buffet table; a spread. **3.** An entertaining event, such as a party.

set piece *n.* **1.** A realistic piece of stage scenery constructed to stand by itself. **2.** An often brilliantly executed artistic or literary work characterized by a formal pattern. **3.a.** A carefully planned and executed military operation. **b.** A situation, an activity, or a speech planned beforehand and carried out according to a prescribed pattern or formula.

set point *n.* *Sports.* **1.** A situation in which the set will be won by the player who scores the next point in a net game such as tennis. **2.** The point so scored.

ă pat	oi boy
ā pay	ou out
âr care	o͝o took
ä father	o͞o boot
ĕ pet	ŭ cut
ē be	ûr urge
ĭ pit	th thin
ī pie	*th* this
îr pier	hw which
ŏ pot	zh vision
ō toe	ə about, item
ô paw	♦ regionalism

Stress marks: ′ (primary); ′ (secondary), as in **dictionary** (dĭk′shə-nĕr′ē)

settee
c. 1805 American, attributed to John and Hugh Finlay

settle
Child's painted pine settle

set·screw (sĕt′skro͞o′) *n.* **1.** A screw, often without a head, used to hold two parts together. **2.** A screw used to regulate the tension of a spring.

Se·tswa·na (sĕt-swä′nə) also **Sech·ua·na** (sĕch-wä′-) *n.* See **Tswana** (sense 2).

set·tee (sĕ-tē′) *n.* **1.** A long wooden bench with a back. **2.** A small or medium-sized sofa. [Perhaps alteration of SETTLE, bench.]

set·ter (sĕt′ər) *n.* **1.** One that sets: *a setter of printing type; a setter of rabbit traps.* **2.** Any of several breeds of long-haired hunting dogs originally trained to indicate the presence of game by crouching in a set position.

set theory *n.* *Mathematics.* The study of the properties of sets.

set·ting (sĕt′ĭng) *n.* **1.** The position, direction, or way in which something, such as an automatic control, is set. **2. a.** The context and environment in which a situation is set; the background. **b.** The time, place, and circumstances in which a narrative, drama, or film takes place. **3.** The scenery constructed for a theatrical performance or movie production. **4.** *Music.* A composition written or arranged to fit a text, such as a poetical work. **5.** A mounting, as for a jewel. **6.** A place setting. **7.** A set of eggs in a hen's nest.

set·tle (sĕt′l) *v.* **-tled, -tling, -tles.** —*tr.* **1.** To put into order; arrange or fix definitely as desired. **2.** To put firmly into a desired position or place; establish. **3. a.** To establish as a resident or residents: *settled her family in Ohio.* **b.** To establish residence in; colonize: *Pioneers settled the West.* **c.** To establish in a residence, business, or profession. **4.** To restore calmness or comfort to. **5. a.** To cause to sink, become compact, or come to rest. **b.** To cause (a liquid) to become clear by forming a sediment. **6.** To subdue or make orderly. **7.** To establish on a permanent basis; stabilize. **8. a.** To make compensation for (a claim). **b.** To pay (a debt). **9.** To conclude (a dispute, for example) by a final decision. **10.** To decide (a lawsuit) by mutual agreement of the involved parties without court action. **11.** *Law.* To secure or assign (property or title) by legal action. —*intr.* **1.** To discontinue moving and come to rest in one place. **2.** To move downward; sink or descend, especially gradually: *Darkness settled over the fields. Dust settled in the road.* **3. a.** To become clear by the sinking of suspended particles. Used of liquids. **b.** To be separated from a solution or mixture as a sediment. **c.** To become compact by sinking, as sediment when stirred up. **4. a.** To establish one's residence: *settled in Canada.* **b.** To become established or localized: *The cold settled in my chest.* **5.** To reach a decision; determine: *We finally settled on a solution to the problem.* See Synonyms at **decide. 6. a.** To provide compensation for a claim. **b.** To pay a debt. —**settle** *n.* A long wooden bench with a high back, often including storage space beneath the seat. —***phrasal verbs.* settle down. 1.** To begin living a stable and orderly life: *He settled down as a farmer with a family.* **2.** To become less nervous or restless. **settle for.** To accept in spite of incomplete satisfaction: *had to settle for a lower wage than the one requested.* [Middle English *setlen,* to seat, from Old English *setlan,* from *setl,* seat. See **sed-** in Appendix.] —**set′tle·a·ble** *adj.*

set·tle·ment (sĕt′l-mənt) *n.* **1.** The act or process of settling. **2. a.** Establishment, as of a person in a business or of people in a new region. **b.** A newly colonized region. **3.** A small community. **4.** An arrangement, adjustment, or other understanding reached, as in financial or business proceedings: *a divorce settlement.* **5.** *Law.* **a.** Transfer of property to provide for the future needs of a person. **b.** Property thus transferred. **6.** A center providing community services in an underprivileged area. In this sense, also called *settlement house.*

set·tler (sĕt′lər) *n.* **1.** One who settles in a new region. **2.** One who settles or decides something.

set·tlings (sĕt′lĭngz) *pl.n.* Sediment; dregs.

set·tlor (sĕt′lər) *n.* *Law.* One that makes a business or financial settlement or a settlement of property.

set-to (sĕt′to͞o′) *n., pl.* **-tos.** A brief, usually heated conflict or argument.

Se·tú·bal (sə-to͞o′bəl). A city of southwest Portugal southeast of Lisbon on the **Bay of Setúbal,** an inlet of the Atlantic Ocean. Setúbal is a port and processing center with a shipbuilding industry. Population, 77,885.

set·up (sĕt′ŭp′) *n.* **1.** The way in which something is constituted, arranged, or planned. **2.** The gathering and organization of the equipment needed for an operation, a procedure, or a task. **3. a.** Physical makeup; physique. **b.** Body posture or carriage; militarily erect bearing. **4. a.** Often **setups.** *Informal.* The collective ingredients, such as ice, mixers, and glasses, necessary for serving various alcoholic drinks. **b.** A table setting, as in a restaurant. **5.** A camera position, as for a particular shot in a scene being filmed. **6.** *Slang.* **a.** A contest prearranged to result in an easy or faked victory. **b.** An endeavor intentionally made easy. **c.** A deceptive scheme, such as a fraud or hoax. **7.** A plan or strategy for a projected course of action.

Seu·rat (sə-rä′, sœ-), **Georges Pierre.** 1859–1891. French painter. A founder of neoimpressionism, he developed pointillism, the technique used in his masterpiece *Sunday Afternoon on the Island of La Grande Jatte* (1886).

Seuss (so͞os), Doctor. See Theodor Seuss **Geisel.**

Se·vas·to·pol (sə-văs′tə-pōl′, sĕv′ə-stō′pəl, syĭ-və-). Formerly **Se·bas·to·pol** (sə-băs′-tə-pōl′). A city of southern Ukraine in the Crimea on the Black Sea west of Yalta. Founded in the late 13th century on the site of an ancient Greek colony, it became Russia's principal Black Sea naval base after the 18th century. Population, 341,000.

sev·en (sĕv′ən) *n.* **1.** The cardinal number equal to 6 + 1. **2.** The seventh in a set or sequence. [Middle English, from Old English *seofon.* See **septm̥** in Appendix.] —**sev′en** *adj. & pron.*

Sev·en Hills of Rome (sĕv′ən; rōm). The hills upon which the ancient city of Rome was built, including the Palatine (traditional site of the founding of the city) and the Aventine, Caelian, Capitoline, Esquiline, Quirinal, and Viminal hills.

Seven Isles. See **Sept Îles.**

seven seas also **Seven Seas** *pl.n.* All the oceans of the world.

sev·en·teen (sĕv′ən-tēn′) *n.* **1.** The cardinal number equal to 16 + 1. **2.** The 17th in a set or sequence. [Middle English *seventene,* from Old English *seofontīne.* See **septm̥** in Appendix.] —**sev′en·teen′** *adj. & pron.*

sev·en·teenth (sĕv′ən-tēnth′) *n.* **1.** The ordinal number matching the number 17 in a series. **2.** One of 17 equal parts. —**sev′en·teenth′** *adv. & adj.*

sev·en·teen-year locust (sĕv′ən-tēn′yîr′) *n.* See **periodical cicada.**

sev·enth (sĕv′ənth) *n.* **1.** The ordinal number matching the number seven in a series. **2.** One of seven equal parts. **3.** *Music.* An interval encompassing seven diatonic degrees. [Middle English, alteration of *sefende,* from Old English *seofunda,* from *seofon,* seven. See SEVEN.] —**sev′enth** *adv. & adj.*

Sev·enth Avenue (sĕv′ənth). Known as "Fashion Avenue." A thoroughfare in New York City on Manhattan Island. It has long been considered the center of the garment and fashion industry in the United States.

Sev·enth-day Adventist (sĕv′ənth-dā′) *n.* A member of a sect of Adventism distinguished chiefly for its observance of the Sabbath on Saturday.

seventh heaven *n.* **1.** A state of great joy and satisfaction. **2.** The farthest of the concentric spheres containing the stars and constituting the dwelling place of God and the angels in the Moslem and cabalist systems.

sev·enth-inn·ing stretch (sĕv′ənth-ĭn′ĭng) *n.* *Baseball.* A juncture in a game, usually after six and one-half innings of play, when the fans get out of their seats to stretch their legs.

sev·en·ti·eth (sĕv′ən-tē-ĭth) *n.* **1.** The ordinal number matching the number 70 in a series. **2.** One of 70 equal parts. —**sev′en·ti·eth** *adv. & adj.*

sev·en·ty (sĕv′ən-tē) *n.* **1.** The cardinal number equal to 7 × 10. **2. seventies, Seventies. a.** The decade from 70 to 79 in a century. **b.** A decade or the numbers from 70 to 79: *They became grandparents in their seventies. The temperature hovered in the seventies.* [Middle English, from Old English *hundseofontig.* See **septm̥** in Appendix.] —**sev′en·ty** *adj. & pron.*

sev·en-up (sĕv′ən-ŭp′) *n.* *Games.* A card game requiring seven points to win. Also called *pitch.*

Seven Wonders of the World. In ancient times, the pyramids of Egypt; the Hanging Gardens of Babylon; Phidias's statue of Zeus at Olympia; the temple of Artemis at Ephesus; the tomb, or mausoleum, of King Mausolus at Halicarnassus; the Colossus of Rhodes; and either the Pharos, or lighthouse, at Alexandria or the walls of Babylon. The list of manmade wonders was first compiled by a Hellenistic traveler in the second century B.C.

sev·er (sĕv′ər) *v.* **-ered, -er·ing, -ers.** —*tr.* **1.** To set or keep apart; divide or separate. **2.** To cut off (a part) from a whole. **3.** To break up (a relationship, for example); dissolve. See Synonyms at **separate.** —*intr.* **1.** To become cut or broken apart. **2.** To become separated or divided from each other. [Middle English *severen,* from Anglo-Norman *severer,* from Vulgar Latin **sēperāre,* from Latin *sēparāre.* See SEPARATE.]

sev·er·a·ble (sĕv′ər-ə-bəl, sĕv′rə-) *adj.* Capable of being severed or separated; separable into legally distinct rights or obligations, as a contract. —**sev′er·a·bil′i·ty** *n.*

sev·er·al (sĕv′ər-əl, sĕv′rəl) *adj.* **1.** Being of a number more than two or three but not many: *several miles away.* **2.** Single; distinct: *"Pshaw! said I, with an air of carelessness, three several times"* (Laurence Sterne). **3.** Respectively different; various: *They parted and went their several ways.* See Synonyms at **distinct. 4.** *Law.* Relating separately to each party of a bond or note. —**several** *pron.* *(used with a pl. verb).* An indefinite but small number; some or a few: *Several of the workers went home sick.* [Middle English, separate, from Anglo-Norman, from Medieval Latin *sēparālis, sēperālis,* from Latin *sēpar,* from *sēparāre,* to separate. See SEPARATE.] —**sev′er·al·ly** *adv.*

sev·er·al·fold (sĕv′ər-əl-fōld′, sĕv′rəl-) *adj.* **1.** Having several parts or members. **2.** Being several times as much or as many. —**sev′er·al·fold′** *adv.*

sev·er·al·ty (sĕv′ər-əl-tē, sĕv′rəl-) *n., pl.* **-ties. 1.** The quality or condition of being separate and distinct. **2.** *Law.* **a.** A separate and individual right to possession or ownership that is not shared with any other person. **b.** Land, property, or an estate owned in severalty. **c.** The quality or condition of being held or owned in severalty.

sev·er·ance (sĕv′ər-əns, sĕv′rəns) *n.* **1. a.** The act or process of severing. **b.** The condition of being severed. **2.** Separation; partition.

severance pay *n.* A sum of money usually based on length of employment for which an employee is eligible upon termination.

severance tax *n.* A tax imposed by a state on the extraction of natural resources, such as oil, coal, or gas, that will be used in other states.

se•vere (sə-vîr′) *adj.* **-ver•er, -ver•est. 1.** Unsparing or harsh, as in treatment of others; strict. **2.** Marked by or requiring strict adherence to rigorous standards or high principles. **3.** Austere or dour; forbidding: *spoke in a severe voice.* **4.** Extremely plain in substance or style: *a severe black dress.* **5.** Causing sharp discomfort or distress; extremely violent or intense: *severe pain; a severe storm.* **6.** Very serious; grave or grievous: *severe mental illness.* **7.** Extremely difficult to perform or accomplish; trying: *a severe test of our loyalty.* [Latin *sevērus,* serious, strict. See **wēro-** in Appendix.] **—se•vere′ly** *adv.* **—se•vere′ness** *n.*

SYNONYMS: *severe, stern, austere, ascetic, strict.* These adjectives mean unsparing and exacting with respect to discipline or control. *Severe* implies adherence to rigorous standards or high principles; the term often suggests the imposition of harsh conditions: *"Praise or blame has but a momentary effect on the man whose love of beauty in the abstract makes him a severe critic on his own works"* (John Keats). *Stern* suggests unyielding disposition, uncompromising resolution, or forbidding appearance or nature: *"thought her husband a man fatally stern and implacable"* (George Meredith). *Austere* connotes sternness, qualities such as aloofness or lack of feeling or sympathy, and often rigid morality: *Austere officers demand meticulous conformity with military regulations.* *Ascetic* suggests self-discipline and self-denial and often renunciation of worldly pleasures for spiritual improvement: *"Be systematically ascetic . . . do . . . something for no other reason than that you would rather not do it"* (William James). *Strict* means requiring or showing stringent observance of obligations, rules, or standards: *"He could not be severe nor even passably strict"* (W.H. Hudson).

severe com•bined immunodeficiency (kəm-bīnd′) *n.* *Abbr.* **SCID** A usually fatal congenital disorder of the immune system in which the body is unable to produce enough B cells and T cells to resist infection.

se•ver•i•ty (sə-vĕr′ĭ-tē) *n., pl.* **-ties. 1.** The state or quality of being severe. **2.** The act or an instance of severe behavior, especially punishment.

Sev•ern (sĕv′ərn). A community of north-central Maryland, a suburb of Baltimore. Population, 20,147.

Se•ver•na•ya Zem•lya (sĕv′ər-nə-yä′ zĕm′lē-ä′, -lyä′, syĭ-vyĭr-). An archipelago of north-central Russia in the Arctic Ocean north of the Taimyr Peninsula.

Severn River. 1. A river of northwest Ontario, Canada, flowing about 676 km (420 mi) northeast to Hudson Bay. **2.** A river of southwest Great Britain rising in central Wales and flowing about 338 km (210 mi) in a curve through western England. It empties into Bristol Channel through a long estuary.

Se•ve•rod•vinsk (sĕv′ər-əd-vĭnsk′, syĭ-vyĭ-rəd-). A city of northwest Russia on an arm of the White Sea west of Arkhangelsk. It is a timber-shipping port. Population, 230,000.

Se•ve•rus (sə-vîr′əs), **Lucius Septimus.** A.D. 146–211. Emperor of Rome (193–211) who created a military monarchy and ruled as a despot.

se•vi•che (sə-vē′chā, sĕ-) *n.* Variant of **ceviche.**

Se•vier (sə-vîr′), **John.** 1745–1815. American Revolutionary soldier and politician. He led the settlers who defeated the Loyalists in the Battle of King's Mountain (1780) and later served as the first governor of Tennessee (1796–1801 and 1803–1809).

Sevier River. A river, about 451 km (280 mi) long, of west-central Utah flowing north then southwest through the **Sevier Desert.** It empties into **Sevier Lake,** a saline lake with no outlet.

Sé•vi•gné (sā-vēn-yā′), Marquise de. Title of Marie de Rabutin-Chantal. 1626–1696. French letter writer whose prolific correspondence depicts aristocratic life in the age of Louis XIV.

Se•ville (sə-vĭl′). A city of southwest Spain on the Guadalquivir River north-northeast of Cádiz. Settled in ancient times, it was an important settlement under the Romans, Vandals, and Visigoths and later under Ferdinand III of Castile, who made it his royal residence in 1248. The city especially prospered after the discovery of the New World and served as the chief port of colonial trade until the early 18th century. Population, 672,435.

Seville orange *n.* See **sour orange.** [After SEVILLE.]

Sè•vres (sĕv′rə) *n.* A fine French porcelain, often elaborately decorated. [After *Sèvres,* a city of north-central France.]

sev•ru•ga (sə-vro͞o′gə) *n.* **1.** A sturgeon *(Acipenser stellatus)* of the Caspian Sea, whose small gray roe is used for caviar. **2.** Caviar made from the roe of the sevruga. [Russian.]

sew (sō) *v.* **sewed, sewn** (sōn) or **sewed, sew•ing, sews.** *—tr.* **1.** To make, repair, or fasten by stitching, as with a needle and thread or a sewing machine: *sew a dress; sew on a button.* **2.** To furnish with stitches for the purpose of closing, fastening, or attaching: *sew an incision closed.* *—intr.* To work with a needle and thread or with a sewing machine. ***—phrasal verb.*** **sew up.** *Informal.* **1.** To complete successfully: *Our team has sewn up the championship.* **2.** To gain complete control of; monopolize. **3.** To make sure of: *campaign strategists who were trying to sew up the election results.* [Middle English *sewen,* from Old English *seowian.* See **syū-** in Appendix.] **—sew′a•ble** *adj.*

sew•age (so͞o′ĭj) *n.* Liquid and solid waste carried off in sewers or drains. [Perhaps *sew,* sewer (from Middle English, short for Anglo-Norman *sewere;* see SEWER¹) + -AGE.]

Sew•all (so͞o′əl), **Samuel.** 1652–1730. English-born American jurist who presided over the witchcraft trials at Salem, Massachusetts (1692).

Sew•ard (so͞o′ərd), **William Henry.** 1801–1872. American politician who as U.S. secretary of state (1861–1869) arranged the purchase of Alaska from Russia (1867), a transaction long known as "Seward's Folly."

Seward Peninsula. A peninsula of western Alaska projecting into the Bering Sea just below the Arctic Circle.

Sew•ell (so͞o′əl), **Anna.** 1820–1878. British writer of the children's classic *Black Beauty* (1877).

se•wel•lel (sə-wĕl′əl) *n.* A small, thick-bodied rodent *(Aplodontia rufa)* of the Pacific coast of North America, having tiny eyes and small ears and usually found in communal burrows dug in the banks of streams. Also called *mountain beaver.* [Chinook *šwalál,* robe of sewellel skins.]

sew•er¹ (so͞o′ər) *n.* An artificial, usually underground conduit for carrying off sewage or rainwater. [Middle English, from Anglo-Norman *sewere,* from Vulgar Latin **exaquāria* : Latin *ex-,* ex- + Latin *aquāria,* feminine of *aquārius,* pertaining to water (from *aqua,* water; see **akʷ-ā-** in Appendix).]

sew•er² (so͞o′ər) *n.* A medieval servant who supervised the serving of meals. [Middle English, from Anglo-Norman *asseour,* from *asseer,* to seat guests, from Latin *assidēre,* to sit down : *ad-,* ad- + *sedēre,* to sit; see **sed-** in Appendix.]

sew•er³ (sō′ər) *n.* One that sews: *a sewer of fine clothing.*

sew•er•age (so͞o′ər-ĭj) *n.* **1.** A system of sewers. **2.** Removal of waste materials by means of a sewer system. **3.** Sewage.

sew•ing (sō′ĭng) *n.* **1.** The act, occupation, or hobby of one who sews. **2.** The article on which one is working with needle and thread; needlework.

sewing circle *n.* A group of people, especially women, who meet regularly for the purpose of sewing, often for charitable causes.

sewing machine *n.* A machine for sewing, often having additional attachments for special stitching.

sewn (sōn) *v.* A past participle of **sew.**

sex (sĕks) *n.* **1.a.** The property or quality by which organisms are classified as female or male on the basis of their reproductive organs and functions. **b.** Either of the two divisions, designated female and male, of this classification. **2.** Females or males considered as a group. **3.** The condition or character of being female or male; the physiological, functional, and psychological differences that distinguish the female and the male. See Usage Note at **gender. 4.** The sexual urge or instinct as it manifests itself in behavior. **5.** Sexual intercourse. **6.** The genitalia. *—attributive.* Often used to modify another noun: *sex education; sex crimes.* **—sex** *tr.v.* **sexed, sex•ing, sex•es. 1.** To determine the sex of (an organism, especially a hatching chicken). **2.** *Slang.* **a.** To arouse sexually. Often used with *up.* **b.** To increase the appeal or attractiveness of. Often used with *up.* [Middle English, from Latin *sexus.*]

sex– *pref.* Six: *sexpartite.* [Latin, from *sex,* six. See **s(w)eks** in Appendix.]

sex•a•ge•nar•i•an (sĕk′sə-jə-nâr′ē-ən) *n.* A person who is 60 years old or between the ages of 60 and 70. **—sexagenarian** *adj.* **1.** Being 60 years old or between the ages of 60 and 70. **2.** Of or relating to a sexagenarian. [From Latin *sexāgēnārius,* sexagenary. See SEXAGENARY.]

sex•ag•e•nar•y (sĕk-săj′ə-nĕr′ē) *adj.* **1.** Relating to or proceeding by sixties. **2.** Sexagenarian. **—sexagenary** *n., pl.* **-ies.** A sexagenarian. [Latin *sexāgēnārius,* from *sexāgēnī,* sixty each, from *sexāgintā,* sixty : *sex,* six; see SEX– + *-gintā,* ten times; see **dekm̥** in Appendix.]

Sex•a•ges•i•ma (sĕk′sə-jĕs′ə-mə, -jā′zə-) *n.* The second Sunday before Lent. [Late Latin *sexāgēsima (diēs),* sixtieth (day), from feminine of Latin *sexāgēsimus,* sixtieth, from *sexāgintā,* sixty. See SEXAGENARY.]

sex•a•ges•i•mal (sĕk′sə-jĕs′ə-məl) *adj.* Of, relating to, or based on the number 60. [From Latin *sexāgēsimus,* sixtieth. See SEXAGESIMA.]

sex appeal *n.* **1.** Physical attractiveness or personal qualities that arouse others sexually. **2.** *Slang.* General appeal; power to interest or attract.

sex cell *n.* A germ cell or gamete.

sex•cen•te•nar•y (sĕk-sĕn′tə-nĕr′ē, sĕk′sĕn-tĕn′ə-rē) *adj.* Relating to 600 or to a 600-year period. **—sexcentenary** *n., pl.* **-ies.** A 600th anniversary or its commemoration. [From Latin *sexcentēnī,* six hundred each : *sex,* six; see SEX– + *centēnī,* a hundred each (from *centum,* hundred; see **dekm̥** in Appendix).]

sex change *n.* The modification of a person's biological sex characteristics, by surgery and hormone treatment, to approximate those of the opposite sex.

sex chromatin *n.* *Genetics.* See **Barr body.**

sex chromosome *n.* Either of a pair of chromosomes, usually designated X or Y, in the germ cells of most animals and some plants, that combine to determine the sex and sex-linked characteristics of an individual, with XX resulting in a female and XY in a male.

sex•duc•tion (sĕks-dŭk′shən) *n.* The process by which genet-

Sèvres

ă pat	oi boy
ā pay	ou out
âr care	o͝o took
ä father	o͞o boot
ĕ pet	ŭ cut
ē be	ûr urge
ĭ pit	th thin
ī pie	*th* this
îr pier	hw which
ŏ pot	zh vision
ō toe	ə about, item
ô paw	♦ regionalism

Stress marks: **′** (primary); ′ (secondary), as in **dictionary** (dĭk′shə-nĕr′ē)

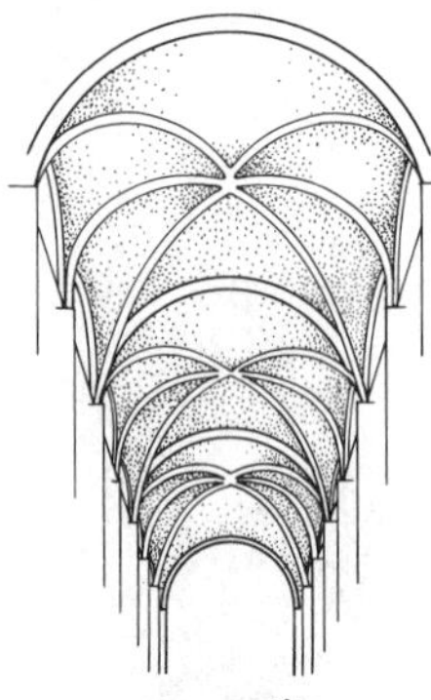
sexpartite
Series of sexpartite vaults

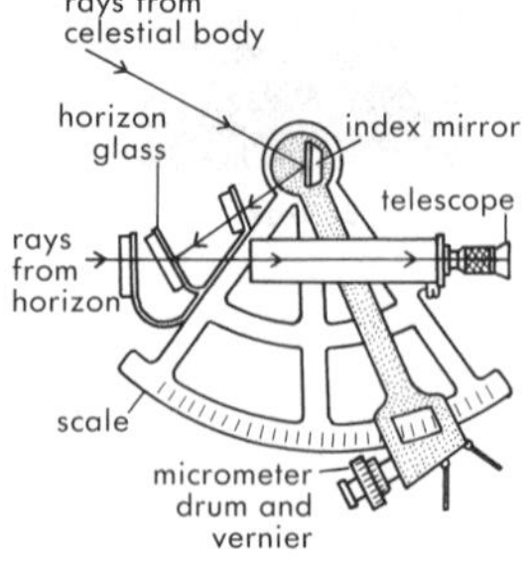

sextant

Anne Sexton

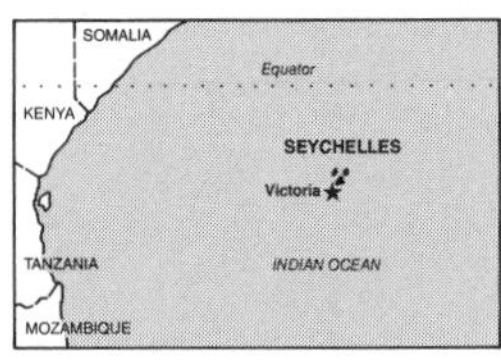

Seychelles

ă pat	oi boy
ā pay	ou out
âr care	ŏŏ took
ä father	ōō boot
ĕ pet	ŭ cut
ē be	ûr urge
ĭ pit	th thin
ī pie	*th* this
îr pier	hw which
ŏ pot	zh vision
ō toe	ə about, item
ô paw	♦ regionalism

Stress marks: **ʹ** (primary); ʹ (secondary), as in **dictionary** (dĭkʹshə-nĕrʹē)

ic material is transferred from one bacterium to another by a sex factor. [SEX + (TRANS)DUCTION.]

sex·en·ni·al (sĕk-sĕnʹē-əl) *adj.* **1.** Occurring every six years. **2.** Relating to or lasting six years. **—sexennial** *n.* An event that occurs every six years. [From Latin *sexennium,* of six years : *sex,* six; see SEX– + *annus,* year; see **at-** in Appendix.] **—sex·enʹni·al·ly** *adv.*

sex factor *n.* **1.** A bacterial plasmid that enables one bacterium to donate its genetic material to another bacterium by conjugation, resulting in genetic recombination. Also called *fertility factor, f factor.* **2.** A gene or chromosome that determines sex.

sex gland *n.* A testis or an ovary; a gonad.

sex hormone *n.* Any of various hormones, such as estrogen and androgen, affecting the growth or function of the reproductive organs, behavior, and development of secondary sex characteristics.

sex hygiene *n.* The branch of hygiene that is concerned with healthy sexual practices.

sex·ism (sĕkʹsĭzʹəm) *n.* **1.** Discrimination based on gender, especially discrimination against women. **2.** Attitudes, conditions, or behaviors that promote stereotyping of social roles based on gender. **—sexʹist** *adj. & n.*

sex kitten *n. Informal.* A young woman considered to have sex appeal.

sex·less (sĕksʹlĭs) *adj.* **1.** Lacking sexual characteristics; neuter. **2.** Lacking in sexual interest or activity: *a sexless marriage.* **—sexʹless·ly** *adv.* **—sexʹless·ness** *n.*

sex-lim·it·ed (sĕksʹlĭmʹĭ-tĭd) *adj.* **1.** Occurring or appearing only in one sex. Used of a genetic character or phenotype. **2.** Having a sex-limited character or phenotype.

sex linkage *n.* The condition in which a gene responsible for a specific trait is located on a sex chromosome, resulting in sexually dependent inheritance of the trait.

sex-linked (sĕksʹlĭngktʹ) *adj.* **1.** Carried by a sex chromosome, especially an X chromosome. Used of genes. **2.** Sexually determined. Used especially of inherited traits.

sex object *n.* A person regarded primarily as the focus of sexual attraction.

sex·ol·o·gy (sĕk-sŏlʹə-jē) *n.* The study of human sexual behavior. **—sexʹo·logʹic** (sĕkʹsə-lŏjʹĭk), **sexʹo·logʹi·cal** (-ĭ-kəl) *adj.* **—sex·olʹo·gist** *n.*

sex·par·tite (sĕks-pärʹtītʹ) *adj.* Composed of or divided into six parts, as a groined vault.

sex·ploi·ta·tion (sĕkʹsploi-tāʹshən) *n. Informal.* Exploitative use of explicit sexual material in the media and especially in movies. [SEX + (EX)PLOITATION.]

sex·pot (sĕksʹpŏtʹ) *n. Informal.* A woman considered to have sex appeal.

sex ratio *n.* The proportion of males to females in a given population, usually expressed as the number of males per 100 females.

sex symbol *n.* A person, especially an entertainer or a celebrity, who is widely acknowledged and appreciated for having sex appeal.

sext also **Sext** (sĕkst) *n. Ecclesiastical.* **1.** The fourth of the seven canonical hours. **2.** The time of day set aside for this service, usually the sixth hour, or noon. [Middle English *sexte,* from Late Latin *sexta,* from Latin *sexta (hōra),* sixth (hour), feminine of *sextus,* sixth. See **s(w)eks** in Appendix.]

Sex·tans (sĕksʹtənz) *n.* A constellation in the equatorial region of the sky near Leo and Hydra. Also called *Sextant.* [New Latin *sextāns,* sextant. See SEXTANT.]

sex·tant (sĕkʹstənt) *n.* **1.** A navigational instrument containing a graduated 60-degree arc, used for measuring the altitudes of celestial bodies. **2. Sextant.** See **Sextans.** [New Latin *sextāns, sextant-,* from Latin, sixth part (so called because the instrument's arc is a sixth of a circle), from *sextus,* sixth. See **s(w)eks** in Appendix.]

sex·tet (sĕk-stĕtʹ) *n.* **1.** *Music.* **a.** A group composed of six vocalists or musicians. **b.** A composition written for six performers. **2.** A group of six persons or things. [Alteration of SESTET.]

sex therapy *n.* The treatment of sexual dysfunction, such as impotence or frigidity, by methods involving counseling, psychotherapy, or behavior modification. **—sex therapist** *n.*

sex·tile (sĕkʹstĭlʹ, -stəl) *adj.* Of or relating to the position of two celestial bodies when they are 60° apart. [Latin *sextīlis,* one sixth, from *sextus,* sixth. See **s(w)eks** in Appendix.]

sex·til·lion (sĕk-stĭlʹyən) *n.* **1.** The cardinal number equal to 10^{21}. **2.** *Chiefly British.* The cardinal number written 10^{36}. [French : Latin *sextus,* sixth; see SEXTILE + French *-illion* (as in *million,* million, from Old French *milion;* see MILLION).] **—sex·tilʹlion** *adj. & pron.*

sex·til·lionth (sĕk-stĭlʹyənth) *n.* **1.** The ordinal number matching the number sextillion in a series. **2.** One of sextillion equal parts. **—sex·tilʹlionth** *adv. & adj.*

sex·to·dec·i·mo (sĕkʹstō-dĕsʹə-mōʹ) *n., pl.* **-mos.** *Printing.* **1.** The page size of a book composed of printer's sheets folded into 16 leaves or 32 pages. **2.** A book composed of sextodecimo pages. Also called *sixteenmo.* [Latin *sextōdecimō,* ablative of *sextusdecimus,* one sixteenth : *sextus,* sixth; see **s(w)eks** in Appendix + *decimus,* tenth (from *decem,* ten; see **dekm̥** in Appendix).]

sex·ton (sĕkʹstən) *n.* An employee or officer of a church who is responsible for the care and upkeep of church property and sometimes for ringing bells and digging graves. [Middle English *sextein,* from Anglo-Latin *sextānus,* probably from Medieval Latin *secristānus,* sacristan, variant of *sacristānus.* See SACRISTAN.]

Sex·ton (sĕkʹstən), **Anne.** 1928–1974. American poet whose works, including the collections *Live or Die* (1966) and *The Death Notebooks* (1974), document her struggle with mental illness and her search for faith.

sexton beetle *n.* See **burying beetle.**

sex·tu·ple (sĕk-stōōʹpəl, -styōōʹ-, -stŭpʹəl, sĕkʹstŭpʹəl) *tr. & intr.v.* **-pled, -pling, -ples.** To multiply or be multiplied by six. **—sextuple** *adj.* **1.** Containing or consisting of six parts. **2.** Larger or greater by six parts multiplied by six. **3.** *Music.* Having six beats to the measure. **—sextuple** *n.* A number six times larger than another. [Probably Latin *sextus;* see SEXTILE + *-uple* (as in QUINTUPLE).] **—sex·tuʹply** *adv.*

sex·tup·let (sĕk-stŭpʹlĭt, -stōōʹplĭt, -styōōʹ-, sĕkʹstŭp'lĭt) *n.* **1.** One of six offspring born in a single birth. **2.** A group of six similar persons or things; a sextet. [SEXTU(PLE) + (TRI)PLET.]

sex·tu·pli·cate (sĕk-stōōʹplĭ-kĭt, -styōōʹ-, -stŭpʹlĭ-) *adj.* Six times as many or as much. **—sextuplicate** (-kātʹ) *tr.v.* **-cat·ed, -cat·ing, -cates.** **1.** To make six times as great; multiply by six. **2.** To make six copies of. **—sextuplicate** *n.* **1.** One of six similar things. **2.** A set of six identical copies. [SEXTU(PLE) + (DU)PLICATE.] **—sex·tuʹpli·caʹtion** *n.*

sex·u·al (sĕkʹshōō-əl) *adj.* **1.** Of, relating to, involving, or characteristic of sex, sexuality, the sexes, or the sex organs and their functions. **2.** Implying or symbolizing erotic desires or activity. **3.** Of, relating to, or involving the union of male and female gametes: *sexual reproduction.* [Late Latin *sexuālis,* from Latin *sexus,* sex.] **—sexʹu·al·ly** *adv.*

sexual assault *n. Law.* Indecent conduct of a man toward another man, a woman, or a child or of a woman toward a child, accompanied by the threat or danger of physical suffering or injury or inducing fear, shame, humiliation, and mental anguish.

sexual harrassment *n.* Unwanted and offensive sexual advances or sexually derogatory or discriminatory remarks, as those made by an employer to an employee.

sexual intercourse *n.* **1.** Coitus between human beings. **2.** Sexual union between human beings involving genital contact other than vaginal penetration by the penis.

sex·u·al·i·ty (sĕkʹshōō-ălʹĭ-tē) *n.* **1.** The condition of being characterized and distinguished by sex. **2.** Concern with or interest in sexual activity. **3.** Sexual character or potency.

sex·u·al·ize (sĕkʹshōō-ə-līzʹ) *tr.v.* **-ized, -iz·ing, -iz·es.** To make sexual in character or quality: *"the thesis that one can sexualize life completely without ever bumping into responsibility"* (Stephen Koch). **—sexʹu·al·i·zaʹtion** (-ə-lĭ-zāʹshən) *n.*

sexually trans·mit·ted disease (trăns-mĭtʹĭd, trănz-) *n. Abbr.* **STD** Any of various diseases, including chancroid, chlamydia, gonorrhea, and syphilis, that are usually contracted through sexual intercourse or other intimate sexual contact.

sexual orientation *n.* The direction of one's sexual interest toward members of the same, opposite, or both sexes.

sexual relations *pl.n.* **1.** Sexual intercourse. **2.** Sexual activity between individuals.

sexual selection *n.* Selection driven by the competition for mates, considered an adjunct to natural selection.

sex·y (sĕkʹsē) *adj.* **-i·er, -i·est.** **1.** Arousing or tending to arouse sexual desire or interest. **2.** *Slang.* Highly appealing or interesting; attractive: *"The recruiting brochures are getting sexier"* (Jack R. Wentworth). **—sexʹi·ly** *adv.* **—sexʹi·ness** *n.*

Sey·chelles (sā-shĕlʹ, -shĕlzʹ). An island country in the western Indian Ocean north of Madagascar. Discovered by the Portuguese in the early 1500's, the islands were claimed by the French in the mid-1700's but were taken by the British in 1794. The Seychelles were a crown colony from 1903 until 1976, when the country gained its independence. Victoria, on Mahé Island, is the capital. Population, 64,718.

Sey·fert galaxy (sēʹfərt, sīʹ-) *n.* A spiral galaxy with a small, compact, bright nucleus that exhibits variable light intensity and radio-wave emission. [After Carl K. *Seyfert* (1911–1960), American astronomer.]

Sey·mour (sēʹmôr', -mōrʹ), **Jane.** 1509?–1537. Queen of England (1536–1537) as the third wife of Henry VIII. She died after giving birth to Henry's heir, Edward VI.

sf or **SF** *abbr.* Science fiction.

SF *abbr.* **1.** *Baseball.* Sacrifice fly. **2.** *Accounting.* Sinking fund.

sf. *abbr. Music.* Sforzando.

SFC *abbr.* Sergeant first class.

sfer·ics also **spher·ics** (sfîrʹĭks, sfĕrʹ-) *n. (used with a sing. verb).* **1.** The study of atmospherics, especially using electronic detectors. **2.** See **atmospherics** (sense 1). [Shortening and alteration of ATMOSPHERICS.]

Sfor·za (sfôrtʹsə, sfôrʹtsä). Family of Milanese political leaders, including **Francesco** (1401–1466), a captain of mercenaries who declared himself duke of Milan (1450). His son **Ludovico** (1451?–1508) was duke of Milan (1481–1499) and a patron of Leonardo da Vinci.

Sforza, Count **Carlo.** 1873–1952. Italian diplomat who was a severe critic of Mussolini's rise to power.

sfor·zan·do (sfôrt-sänʹdō) also **for·zan·do** (fôrt-sänʹdō) *Music —adv. & adj. Abbr.* **sf., sfz.** Suddenly and strongly accented. Used chiefly as a direction. —*n., pl.* **-dos** or **-di** (-dē). A sforzando tone or chord. [Italian, gerund of *sforzare,* to use force : *s-,* intensive pref. (from Latin *ex-;* see EX–) + *forzare,* to force (from Vulgar Latin **fortiāre,* from Latin *fortis,* strong; see FORTIS).] —**sfor·zan′do** *adv.*

S.F.S.R. *abbr.* Soviet Federated Socialist Republic.

sfu·ma·to (sfo͞o-mä′tō) *n.* The blurring or softening of sharp outlines in painting by subtle and gradual blending of one tone into another. [Italian, from past participle of *sfumare,* to evaporate, fade out : *s-,* from (from Latin *ex-;* see EX–) + *fumare,* to smoke (from Latin *fumāre*).]

sfz. *abbr. Music.* Sforzando.

sg *abbr.* Specific gravity.

Sg *abbr. Bible.* Song of Songs.

SG *abbr.* **1.** Senior grade. **2.** Surgeon General.

S.G. or **SG** *abbr.* Solicitor general.

sgd. *abbr.* Signed.

sgraf·fi·to (skră-fē′tō, zgrä-) *n., pl.* **-ti** (-tē). **1.** Decoration produced on pottery or ceramic by scratching through a surface of plaster or glazing to reveal a different color underneath. **2.** Ware decorated in this manner. [Italian, past participle of *sgraffire,* to scratch, from *sgraffio,* a scratch, from *sgraffiare,* to scratch, from Old Italian : *s-,* intensive pref.; see SFORZANDO + *graffiare,* to scratch; see GRAFFITO.]

's Gra·ven·ha·ge (skrä′vən-hä′gə, SKHrä′vən-hä′KHə). See The **Hague.**

Sgt. *abbr.* Sergeant.

Sgt. Maj. *abbr.* Sergeant major.

sh (sh) *interj.* Used to urge silence.

sh. *abbr.* **1.** Share. **2.** Sheet.

Shaan·xi (shän′shē′) also **Shen·si** (shĕn′sē′). A province of east-central China crossed by the Wei He. One of the earliest cultural and political centers of China, the province is densely populated and highly industrialized. Xi'an is the capital. Population, 30,020,000.

Sha·ba (shä′bə). Formerly **Ka·tan·ga** (kə-täng′gə, -tăng′-). A region of southeast Zaire bordering on Zambia. It proclaimed itself the republic of Katanga in 1960 and seceded from Congo (now Zaire). The insurrection was put down in 1963 with the aid of United Nations troops.

Sha'·ban also **Shaa·ban** (shə-bän′, shä-, shô-) *n.* The eighth month of the year in the Moslem calendar. See table at **calendar.** [Arabic *ša'bān.*]

Shab·bat (shə-bät′, shä′bəs) *n. Judaism.* The Sabbath. [Hebrew *šabbāt,* sabbath.]

shab·by (shăb′ē) *adj.* **-bi·er, -bi·est. 1.** Wearing threadbare clothing. **2.a.** Showing signs of wear and tear; threadbare or worn-out: *shabby furniture.* **b.** Dilapidated or deteriorated in condition, especially through neglect; seedy: *a shabby little park.* **3.a.** Despicable; mean: *a shabby trick.* **b.** Not generous or just; unfair: *shabby treatment.* **c.** Of mediocre or substandard quality: *a shabby performance.* [From obsolete *shab,* scab, from Middle English *shab,* from Old English *sceabb.*] —**shab′bi·ly** *adv.* —**shab′bi·ness** *n.*

Sha·bu·oth (shə-vo͞o′ōt′, -əs, shä′vo͞o-ōt′) *n.* Variant of **Shavuot.**

sha·bu-sha·bu (shä′bo͞o-shä′bo͞o) *n.* A Japanese dish consisting of a simmering pot of broth, vegetables, and noodles in which thin-sliced beef or sometimes chicken is quickly cooked at table and then dipped into a flavorful sauce. [Japanese, imitative of bubbling water.]

shack (shăk) *n.* A small, crudely built cabin; a shanty. —**shack** *intr.v.* **shack·ed, shack·ing, shacks.** To live or dwell: *farm hands shacking in bunkhouses.* —***idiom.*** **shack up.** *Slang.* **1.** To sleep together or live in sexual intimacy without being married. **2.** To live, room, or stay at a place: *I'm shacking up with my cousin till I find a place of my own.* [Possibly from American Spanish *jacal,* from Nahuatl *xacalli,* adobe hut : *xámitl,* adobe + *calli,* house, hut.]

shack·le (shăk′əl) *n.* **1.** A metal fastening, usually one of a pair, for encircling and confining the ankle or wrist of a prisoner or captive; a fetter or manacle. **2.** A hobble for an animal. **3.** Any of several devices, such as a clevis, used to fasten or couple. **4.** A restraint or check to action or progress. Often used in the plural: *economic shackles that precluded further investment.* —**shackle** *tr.v.* **-led, -ling, -les. 1.** To confine with shackles; fetter. **2.** To fasten or connect with a shackle. **3.** To restrict, confine, or hamper. See Synonyms at **hamper[1].** [Middle English *shakel,* from Old English *sceacel,* fetter.] —**shack′ler** *n.*

shack·o (shăk′ō, shä′kō, shä′-) *n.* Variant of **shako.**

shad (shăd) *n., pl.* **shad** or **shads.** Any of several food fishes of the genus *Alosa,* especially the North American species *A. sapidissima,* related to the herrings but atypical in swimming up streams from marine waters to spawn. [Middle English **shad,* from Old English *sceadd.*]

shad·ber·ry (shăd′bĕr′ē) *n.* The fruit of the shadbush.

shad·blow (shăd′blō′) *n.* See **shadbush.**

shad·bush (shăd′bo͝osh′) *n.* Any of various North American shrubs or trees of the genus *Amelanchier,* having white flowers, edible blue-black or purplish fruit, and smooth, gray, striped twigs. Also called *Juneberry, shadblow.*

shad·dock (shăd′ək) *n.* **1.** A tropical southeast Asian tree (*Citrus maxima*) closely related to the grapefruit and having very large fruit with thick rinds and coarse-grained pulp. **2.** The edible yellow, pear-shaped fruit of the shaddock. Also called *pomelo, pompelmous, pumelo.* [After Captain *Shaddock,* 17th-century English ship commander.]

shade (shād) *n.* **1.** Light diminished in intensity as a result of the interception of the rays; partial darkness. **2.** An area or a space of partial darkness. **3.** Cover or shelter provided by interception by an object of the sun or its rays. **4.** Any of various devices used to reduce or screen light or heat. **5. shades.** *Slang.* Sunglasses. **6.** Relative obscurity. **7. shades.** Dark shadows gathering at dusk: *"The shades of night are falling fast"* (Henry Wadsworth Longfellow). **8.** The part of a picture or photograph depicting darkness or shadow. **9.** The degree to which a color is mixed with black or is decreasingly illuminated; gradation of darkness. **10.** A slight difference or variation; a nuance: *shades of meaning.* **11.** A small amount; a trace: *detected a shade of bitterness in her remarks.* **12.** A disembodied spirit; a ghost. **13. shades.** A present reminder of a person or situation in the past: *shades of my high-school days.* —**shade** *v.* **shad·ed, shad·ing, shades.** —*tr.* **1.** To screen from light or heat. **2.** To obscure or darken. **3.** To cause shade in or on. **4.a.** To represent degrees of shade or shadow in: *shade a drawing.* **b.** To produce (gradations of light or color) in a drawing or picture. **5.** To change or vary by slight degrees: *shade the meaning.* **6.** To make a slight reduction in: *shade prices.* —*intr.* To pass from one quality, color, or thing to another by very slight changes or degrees. [Middle English, from Old English *sceadu.*] —**shad′er** *n.*

SYNONYMS: *shade, penumbra, shadow, umbra, umbrage.* The central meaning shared by these nouns is "an area of comparative darkness resulting from the blocking of light rays": *sitting in the shade; Earth's penumbra; in the shadow of the curtains; the umbra beyond the footlights; sheltered in the umbrage of a rain forest.* See also Synonyms at **nuance.**

shade tree *n.* A tree planted chiefly to provide shade from sunlight.

shad·fly (shăd′flī′) *n.* See **mayfly.**

shad·ing (shā′dĭng) *n.* **1.** A screening against light or heat. **2.** The lines or other marks used to fill in outlines of a sketch, an engraving, or a painting to represent gradations of color or darkness. **3.** A small variation, gradation, or difference.

sha·doof also **sha·duf** (shä-do͞of′) *n.* A device consisting of a long suspended pole weighted at one end and having a bucket at the other end, used in the Near East and especially Egypt for raising water, as for the irrigation of land. [Arabic *šādūf.*]

shad·ow (shăd′ō) *n.* **1.** An area that is not or is only partially irradiated or illuminated because of the interception of radiation by an opaque object between the area and the source of radiation. **2.** The rough image cast by an object blocking rays of illumination. See Synonyms at **shade. 3.** An imperfect imitation or copy. **4. shadows.** The darkness following sunset. **5.a.** A feeling of gloom or unhappiness. **b.** A cause of gloom or unhappiness. **6.** A shaded area in a picture or photograph. **7.** A mirrored image or reflection. **8.** A phantom; a ghost. **9.a.** One, such as a detective or spy, that follows or trails another. **b.** A constant companion. **10.** A faint indication; a premonition. **11.** A vestige or remnant. **12.** An insignificant portion or amount; a trace: *beyond a shadow of a doubt.* **13.** Shelter; protection. —**shadow** *v.* **-owed, -ow·ing, -ows.** —*tr.* **1.** To cast a shadow on; shade. **2.** To make gloomy or dark; cloud. **3.** To represent vaguely, mysteriously, or prophetically. **4.** To darken in a painting or drawing; shade in. **5.** To follow, especially in secret; trail. —*intr.* **1.** To change by gradual degrees. **2.** To become clouded over as if with shadows: *Her face shadowed with sorrow.* —**shadow** *adj.* Not having official status: *a shadow government of exiled leaders; a shadow cabinet.* [Middle English, from Old English *sceaduwe,* oblique case of *sceadu,* shade, shadow.] —**shad′ow·er** *n.*

shad·ow·box (shăd′ō-bŏks′) *intr.v.* **-boxed, -box·ing, -box·es.** To spar with an imaginary opponent, as for exercise or training purposes. —**shad′ow·box′ing** *n.*

shadow box *n.* A shallow, framed, rectangular box usually with a glass front that is used for holding and protecting items on display.

shadow dance *n.* A dance presented by casting shadows of dancers on a screen.

shad·ow·graph (shăd′ō-grăf′) *n.* **1.** An image produced by casting a shadow on a screen. **2.** See **shadow play. 3.** See **radiograph.**

shadow play *n.* A play presented by casting shadows of puppets or actors on a screen. Also called *shadowgraph, shadow show.*

shad·ow·y (shăd′ō-ē) *adj.* **-i·er, -i·est. 1.** Relating to or resembling a shadow. **2.** Full of or dark with shadow. See Synonyms at **dark. 3.** Lacking distinctness; faint. **4.** Lacking substance. —**shad′ow·i·ly** *adv.* —**shad′ow·i·ness** *n.*

Shad·rach (shăd′răk). In the Old Testament, a young man who with Abednego and Meshach emerged unharmed from the fiery furnace of Babylon.

sha·duf (shä-do͞of′) *n.* Variant of **shadoof.**

shad·y (shā′dē) *adj.* **-i·er, -i·est. 1.** Full of shade; shaded. **2.** Casting shade: *a shady grove.* **3.** Quiet, dark, or concealed; hidden. **4.** Of dubious character or honesty; questionable. See Synonyms at **dark.** —**shad′i·ly** *adv.* —**shad′i·ness** *n.*

Jane Seymour
1536 portrait by
Hans Holbein the Younger

shackle
Top: Spinnaker snap shackle
Bottom: Reverse key shackle

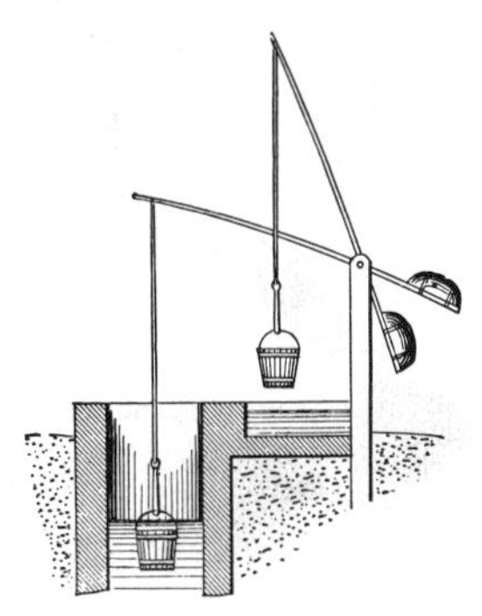

shadoof

shadowgraph

shagbark
Carya ovata

shaggymane
Coprinus comatus

ă pat oi boy
ā pay ou out
âr care o͝o took
ä father o͞o boot
ĕ pet ŭ cut
ē be ûr urge
ĭ pit th thin
ī pie *th* this
îr pier hw which
ŏ pot zh vision
ō toe ə about, item
ô paw ♦ regionalism

Stress marks: **′** (primary); ′ (secondary), as in **dictionary** (dĭk′shə-nĕr′ē)

shaft (shăft) *n.* **1.a.** The long, narrow stem or body of a spear or an arrow. **b.** A spear or an arrow. **2.a.** A projectile suggestive of a spear or an arrow in appearance or configuration. **b.** *Informal.* A scornfully satirical comment; a barb. **c.** *Slang.* Harsh, unfair treatment. Often used with *the*: *The president of the airline really gave the unions the shaft.* **3.** A ray or beam of light. **4.** The handle of any of various tools or implements. **5.** The main axis of a feather, especially its distal portion. **6.** *Anatomy.* **a.** The midsection of a long bone; diaphysis. **b.** The section of a hair projecting from the surface of the body. **7.** *Architecture.* **a.** A column or an obelisk. **b.** The section of a column between the capital and the base. **8.** One of two parallel poles between which an animal is harnessed to a vehicle. **9.** A long, generally cylindrical bar, especially one that rotates and transmits power, as the drive shaft of an engine. **10.** A long, narrow, often vertical passage sunk into the earth, as for mining ore; a tunnel. **11.** A vertical passage housing an elevator. **12.** A duct or conduit for the passage of air, as for ventilation or heating. **—shaft** *tr.v.* **shaft•ed, shaft•ing, shafts. 1.** To equip with a shaft. **2.** *Slang.* To treat in a harsh, unfair way: *"He had been shafted by the press quite a bit"* (Frank Deford). [Middle English, from Old English *sceaft.*]

Shaftes•bur•y (shăfts′bĕr′ē, -bə-rē), First Earl of. Title of Anthony Ashley Cooper. 1621–1683. English politician. Originally a Royalist, he later opposed Charles II in the English Civil War and is considered the founder of the Whig Party.

shaft•ing (shăf′tĭng) *n.* **1.** A system of shafts, as in a mechanical device, for transmitting motion or power. **2.** Material from which shafts are made. **3.** *Slang.* An instance of harsh or unfair treatment: *got a shafting when they bought that house.*

shag[1] (shăg) *n.* **1.** A tangle or mass, especially of rough, matted hair. **2.a.** A coarse long nap, as on a woolen cloth. **b.** Cloth having such a nap. **3.** A rug with a thick, rough pile. **4.** Coarse shredded tobacco. **—shag** *tr.v.* **shagged, shag•ging, shags. 1.** To make shaggy; roughen. **2.a.** To chase and bring back; fetch. **b.** *Baseball.* To chase and catch (fly balls) in practice. [Middle English **shagge*, from Old English *sceacga*, matted hair.]

shag[2] (shăg) *n.* A dance step of the 1930's consisting of a hop on each foot in turn. **—shag** *intr.v.* **shagged, shag•ging, shags.** To perform or execute this dance. [Origin unknown.]

shag[3] (shăg) *n.* Either of two marine birds *(Phalacrocorax aristotelis* or *P. punctatus)* of Europe and North Africa, related to the cormorant. [Perhaps from its shaggy crest.]

shag•bark (shăg′bärk′) *n.* An eastern North American hickory tree *(Carya ovata)* having shaggy bark, pinnately compound leaves, and hard-shelled nuts with edible seeds. Also called *shellbark.*

shag•gy (shăg′ē) *adj.* **-gi•er, -gi•est. 1.** Having, covered with, or resembling long rough hair or wool. **2.** Bushy and matted: *shaggy hair.* **3.** Having a rough nap or surface, as a textile. **4.** Poorly groomed; unkempt. **5.** Marked by a lack of order or clarity in thinking, planning, or performance. **—shag′gi•ly** *adv.* **—shag′gi•ness** *n.*

shaggy cap *n.* See **shaggymane.**

shag•gy-dog story (shăg′ē-dôg′, -dŏg′) *n. Informal.* A long, drawn-out anecdote ending with an absurd or anticlimactic punch line.

shag•gy•mane also **shag•gy mane** (shăg′ē-mān′) *n.* An edible inky cap mushroom *(Coprinus comatus)* having shaggy scales covering the cap. Also called *shaggy cap.*

sha•green (shə-grēn′) *n.* **1.** The rough hide of a shark or ray, covered with numerous bony denticles and used as an abrasive and as leather. **2.** An untanned leather with a granular surface that is often dyed green. [French *chagrin, sagrin,* from Turkish *sağri*, crupper, leather.] **—sha•green′** *adj.*

shah (shä) *n.* Used formerly as a title for the hereditary monarch of Iran. [Persian *shāh*, king, from Old Persian *khshāyathiya-*.] **—shah′dom** *n.*

Sha•hap•ti•an (shä-hăp′tē-ən) *n.* Variant of **Sahaptian.**

Sha•hap•tin (shä-hăp′tĭn) *n.* Variant of **Sahaptin.**

Shah Ja•han (shä′ jə-hän′). 1592–1666. Mogul emperor of India (1628–1658) whose reign ushered in the golden age of Mogul art and architecture. The Taj Mahal was built at his request as a memorial to his favorite wife.

Shahn (shän), **Benjamin.** Known as "Ben." 1898–1969. Lithuanian-born American artist whose works, such as *The Passion of Sacco and Vanzetti* (1931–1932), reflect social and political themes.

shai•tan (shī-tän′, shā-) *n.* **1.** Often **Shaitan.** *Islam.* The Devil; Satan. **2.** An evil spirit; a fiend. [Arabic *šayṭān*, from Hebrew *śāṭān*. See SATAN.]

shake (shāk) *v.* **shook** (sho͝ok), **shak•en** (shā′kən), **shak•ing, shakes.** *—tr.* **1.** To cause to move to and fro with jerky movements. **2.** To cause to quiver, tremble, vibrate, or rock. **3.** To cause to lose stability or waver: *a crisis that shook my deepest beliefs.* **4.** To remove or dislodge by jerky movements: *shook the dust from the cushions.* **5.a.** To bring to a specified condition by or as if by shaking: *"It is not easy to shake one's heart free of the impression"* (John Middleton Murry). **b.** *Slang.* To get rid of: *couldn't shake the man who was following us.* **6.** To disturb or agitate; unnerve: *She was shaken by the news of the disaster.* **7.** To brandish or wave, especially in anger: *shake one's fist.* **8.** To clasp (hands) in greeting or leave-taking or as a sign of agreement. **9.** *Music.* To trill (a note). **10.** *Games.* To rattle and mix (dice) before casting. *—intr.* **1.** To move to and fro in short, irregular, often jerky movements. **2.** To tremble, as from cold or in anger. **3.** To be unsteady; totter or waver. **4.** To move something vigorously up and down or from side to side, as in mixing. **5.** *Music.* To trill. **6.** To shake hands: *Let's shake on it.* **—shake** *n.* **1.** The act of shaking. **2.** A trembling or quivering movement. **3.** *Informal.* An earthquake. **4.a.** A fissure in rock. **b.** A crack in timber caused by wind or frost. **5.** *Informal.* A moment or an instant; a trice: *I'll do it in a shake.* **6.** *Music.* A trill. **7.a.** See **milk shake** (sense 1). **b.** A beverage in which the ingredients are mixed by shaking. **8.** A rough shingle used to cover rustic buildings, such as barns: *cedar shakes.* **9. shakes.** *Informal.* Uncontrollable trembling, as in a person who is cold, frightened, feverish, or ill. Often used with *the*: *was suffering from a bad case of the shakes.* **10.** *Slang.* A bargain or deal: *getting a fair shake.* ***—phrasal verbs.*** **shake down. 1.** *Slang.* To extort money from. **2.** *Slang.* To make a thorough search of: *shook down the prisoners' cells for hidden weapons.* **3.** To subject (a new ship or aircraft) to shakedown testing. **4.** To become acclimated or accustomed, as to a new environment or a new job. **shake off.** To free oneself of; get rid of: *We shook off our fears.* **shake up. 1.** To upset by or as if by a physical jolt or shock: *was badly shaken up by the accident.* **2.** To subject to a drastic rearrangement or reorganization: *new management bent on shaking up the company.* ***—idioms.*** **give (someone) the shake.** *Slang.* To escape from or get rid of: *We managed to give our pursuers the shake.* **no great shakes.** *Slang.* Unexceptional; ordinary: *"stepping in between the victim and the bully, even when the victim happens to be no great shakes"* (Louis Auchincloss). **shake a leg.** *Informal.* **1.** To dance. **2.** To move quickly; hurry up. **shake (another's) tree.** *Slang.* To arouse to action or reaction; disturb: "[He] *so shook Hollywood's tree that . . . all manner of . . . people called me unsolicited to itemize his mistakes or praise his courage"* (Tina Brown). **shake a stick at.** *Slang.* To point out, designate, or name: *"All of a sudden there came into being a vast conservative infrastructure: think-tanks . . . and more foundations than you could shake a stick at"* (National Review). [Middle English *shaken*, from Old English *sceacan.*] **—shak′a•ble, shake′a•ble** *adj.*

SYNONYMS: *shake, tremble, quake, quiver, shiver, shudder.* These verbs mean to manifest involuntary vibratory movement. *Shake* is the most general: *The child's small body shook with weeping. The floor shook when she walked across the room. Tremble* implies quick, rather slight movement, as from excitement, weakness, or anger: *I could feel the youngster's hand tremble in mine. The apple blossoms trembled in the wind. Quake* refers to more violent movement, as that caused by shock or upheaval: *I was so terrified that my legs began to quake. Quiver* suggests a slight, rapid, tremulous movement: *"Her lip quivered like that of a child about to cry"* (Booth Tarkington). *Shiver* involves rapid, rather slight trembling, as of a person experiencing chill: *"as I in hoary winter night stood shivering in the snow"* (Robert Southwell). *Shudder* applies chiefly to convulsive shaking caused by fear, horror, or revulsion: *"She starts like one that spies an adder / . . . The fear whereof doth make him shake and shudder"* (Shakespeare). See also Synonyms at **agitate, dismay.**

shake•down (shāk′doun′) *n.* **1.** *Slang.* Extortion of money, as by blackmail. **2.** *Slang.* A thorough search of a place or person. **3.** A period of appraisal followed by adjustments to improve efficiency or functioning. **—shakedown** *adj.* Serving to test the performance of a ship or an aircraft and to familiarize the crew with operation of the craft: *a shakedown cruise; a shakedown flight.*

WORD HISTORY: In 1969 a majority of the members of the *American Heritage Dictionary* Usage Panel felt that the noun *shakedown* in the sense "extortion" and the related phrasal verb *shake down* were acceptable in writing, though both are now labeled *slang.* It would seem that certain usages take a while to attain respectability because of the company they keep. *Shake* and the verb phrase *shake out of* already meant "to steal" in Middle English. This usage of *shake* is still found in the 19th and 20th centuries. Both *shake* and *shake out of* in the sense "to steal" are clearly related to *shake down,* which is first recorded in 1872, *shake down* being glossed "to extort money from individuals." This is a slang usage, probably occurring, as had the verb *shake,* largely in contexts having to do with criminal or corrupt behavior. As our Panel realized, the verb and the later noun *shakedown* (first recorded in 1902 in the United States) have now moved from the lingo of criminals, loan sharks, and politicians into wider currency.

shak•en (shā′kən) *v.* Past participle of **shake.**

shake•out (shāk′out′) *n.* **1.** The elimination of competing businesses or products in a particular field. **2.** A decline in the values of certain securities that usually results in a depressed stock market.

shak•er (shā′kər) *n.* **1.a.** One that shakes: *a shaker of long-held beliefs and traditions.* **b.** One that impels, encourages, or supervises action. **2.a.** A container used for shaking: *salt and pepper shakers.* **b.** A container used to mix or blend by shaking: *a cocktail shaker.* **3. Shaker.** A member of a Christian group originating in England in 1747, practicing communal living and observing celibacy. **—shaker** also **Shaker** *adj.* Relating to or constituting a style produced by Shakers that is distinctively simple, unornamented, functional, and finely crafted: *Shaker furniture.*

Shaker Heights. A city of northeast Ohio, a residential suburb of Cleveland. It is named after a Shaker community that existed here from 1822 to 1889. Population, 32,487.

Shake·speare (shāk′spîr), **William.** 1564–1616. English playwright and poet whose body of works is considered the greatest in English literature. His plays, many of which were performed at the Globe Theatre in London, include historical works, such as *Richard II,* comedies, including *Much Ado about Nothing* and *As You Like It,* and tragedies, such as *Hamlet, Othello,* and *King Lear.* He also composed 154 sonnets. The earliest collected edition of his plays, the First Folio, contained 36 plays and was published posthumously (1623). **—Shake·spear′e·an, Shake·spear′i·an** *adj. & n.*

Shake·spear·e·an·a or **Shake·spear·i·an·a** (shāk-spîr′ē-ăn′ə, -ä′nə) *n.* A collection of items by or relating to Shakespeare.

Shakespearean sonnet *n.* The sonnet form perfected by Shakespeare, composed of three quatrains and a terminal couplet in iambic pentameter with the rhyme pattern *abab cdcd efef gg.* Also called *Elizabethan sonnet, English sonnet.*

Shake·spear·i·an·a (shāk-spîr′ē-ăn′ə, -ä′nə) *n.* Variant of **Shakespeareana.**

shake·up (shāk′ŭp′) *n.* A thorough, often drastic reorganization, as of the personnel in a business or government.

shak·ing palsy (shā′kĭng) *n.* See **Parkinson's disease.**

shak·o also **shack·o** (shăk′ō, shā′kō, shä′-) *n., pl.* **-os** or **-oes.** A stiff, cylindrical military dress hat with a metal plate in front, a short visor, and a plume. [French *schako,* from Hungarian *csákó,* from *csákós (süveg),* pointed (cap), from *csák,* peak, perhaps from Middle High German *zacke,* tack, nail.]

Shak·ta (shäk′tə, säk′-) *n. Hinduism.* One who worships Shakti. [Sanskrit *śāktaḥ,* from *śaktiḥ,* Shakti. See SHAKTI.] **—Shak′tism** *n.* **—Shak′tist** *n.*

Shak·ti (shŭk′tē, shäk′-) *n.* **1.** The active, manifest power that creates the universe. **2.** The consort of the male expression of the divine, especially of the god Shiva. [Sanskrit *śaktiḥ,* from *śaknoti,* he is strong.]

shak·y (shā′kē) *adj.* **-i·er, -i·est. 1.** Trembling or quivering; tremulous: *a shaky voice.* **2.** Lacking soundness or sturdiness, as of construction: *a shaky table.* **3.a.** Not to be depended on; precarious: *a shaky alliance.* **b.** Wavering in firmness: *a shaky belief.* **c.** Open to question or doubt: *shaky evidence.* **—shak′i·ly** *adv.* **—shak′i·ness** *n.*

shale (shāl) *n.* A fissile rock composed of layers of claylike, fine-grained sediments. [Probably from Middle English, shell, from Old English *scealu.* See **skel-**[1] in Appendix.] **—shal′ey** *adj.*

shale oil *n.* A crude oil that is obtained from oil shale by heating and distillation.

shall (shăl) *aux.v.* past tense **should** (shŏŏd). **1.** Used before a verb in the infinitive to show: **a.** Something that will take place or exist in the future: *We shall arrive tomorrow.* **b.** Something, such as an order, a promise, a requirement, or an obligation: *You shall leave now. He shall answer for his misdeeds. The penalty shall not exceed two years in prison.* **c.** The will to do something or have something take place: *I shall go out if I feel like it.* **d.** Something that is inevitable: *That day shall come.* **2.** *Archaic.* **a.** To be able to. **b.** To have to; must. [Middle English *shal,* from Old English *sceal.* See **skel-**[2] in Appendix.]

USAGE NOTE: The traditional rules for using *shall* and *will* prescribe a highly complicated pattern of use in which the meanings of the forms change according to the person of the subject. In the first person, *shall* is used to indicate simple futurity: *I shall* (not *will*) *have to buy another ticket.* In the second and third persons, the same sense of futurity is expressed by *will: The comet will* (not *shall*) *return in 87 years. You will* (not *shall*) *probably encounter some heavy seas when you round the point.* The use of *will* in the first person and of *shall* in the second and third may express determination, promise, obligation, or permission, depending on the context. Thus *I will leave tomorrow* indicates that the speaker is determined to leave; *You and she shall leave tomorrow* is likely to be interpreted as a command. The sentence *You shall have your money* expresses a promise ("I will see that you get your money"), whereas *You will have your money* makes a simple prediction. • Such, at least, are the traditional rules. But the distinction has never taken firm root outside of what H.W. Fowler described as "the English of the English" (as opposed to that of the Scots and Irish), and even there it has always been subject to variation. Despite the efforts of generations of American schoolteachers, the distinction is largely alien to the modern American idiom. In America *will* is used to express most of the senses reserved for *shall* in English usage, and *shall* itself is restricted to first person interrogative proposals, as in *Shall we go?* and to certain fixed expressions, such as *We shall overcome. Shall* is also used in formal style to express an explicit obligation, as in *Applicants shall provide a proof of residence,* though this sense is also expressed by *must* or *should.* In speech the distinction that the English signal by the choice of *shall* or *will* may be rendered by stressing the auxiliary, as in *I* will *leave tomorrow* ("I intend to leave"); by choosing another auxiliary, such as *must* or *have to;* or by using an adverb such as *certainly.* • Many earlier American writers observed the traditional distinction between *shall* and *will,* and some continue to do so. The practice cannot be called incorrect, though it may strike American ears as somewhat mannered. But the distinction is difficult for those who do not come by it natively, and Americans who essay a *shall* in an unfamiliar context run considerable risk of getting it wrong, and so of being caught out in that most embarrassing of linguistic gaffes, the bungled Anglicism. See Usage Note at **should.**

shal·loon (shə-lo͞on′, shă-) *n.* A lightweight wool or worsted twill fabric, used chiefly for coat linings. [French *chalon,* after CHÂLONS-SUR-MARNE.]

shal·lop (shăl′əp) *n. Nautical.* A small open boat fitted with oars or sails, or both, and used primarily in shallow waters. [French *chaloupe,* from Dutch *sloep,* sloop; see SLOOP, or perhaps from obsolete French *chaloppe,* nutshell (from Old French *eschalope,* from *escale, eschale,* shell, husk; see SCALE[1]).]

shal·lot (shə-lŏt′, shăl′ət) *n.* **1.** A type of onion with long, pointed, pear-shaped, aggregated bulbs. **2.** The mild-flavored bulb of this plant, used in cookery. Also called *eschalot.* [Obsolete French *eschalotte,* from Old French *eschaloigne,* from Vulgar Latin **escalōnia.* See SCALLION.]

shal·low (shăl′ō) *adj.* **-er, -est. 1.** Measuring little from bottom to top or surface; lacking physical depth. **2.** Lacking depth of intellect, emotion, or knowledge: *"This is a shallow parody of America"* (Lloyd Rose). See Synonyms at **superficial. 3.** Marked by insufficient inhalation of air; weak: *shallow respirations.* **—shallow** *n.* A part of a body of water of little depth; a shoal. Often used in the plural: *abandoned the boat in the shallows.* **—shallow** *tr. & intr.v.* **-lowed, -low·ing, -lows.** To make or become shallow. [Middle English *shalowe.*] **—shal′low·ly** *adv.* **—shal′low·ness** *n.*

shal·lu (shăl′o͞o) *n.* A variety of sorghum native to and widely cultivated in India and Africa. [Marathi *śḷū.*]

sha·lom (shä-lōm′, shə-) *interj.* Used as a traditional Jewish greeting or farewell. [Hebrew *šālôm,* peace.]

sha·lom a·lei·chem (shô′ləm ə-lā′KHəm, -kəm, shä-lōm′ ä-lā-KHĕm′) *interj.* Used as a traditional Jewish greeting or farewell. [Hebrew *šālôm ʿalêkem,* peace be with you.]

shalt (shălt) *aux.v. Archaic.* A second person singular present tense of **shall.**

sham (shăm) *n.* **1.** Something false or empty that is purported to be genuine; a spurious imitation. **2.** The quality of deceitfulness; empty pretense. **3.** One who assumes a false character; an impostor: *"He a man! Hell! He was a hollow sham!"* (Joseph Conrad). **4.** A decorative cover made to simulate an article of household linen and used over or in place of it: *a pillow sham.* **—sham** *adj.* Not genuine; fake: *sham diamonds; sham modesty.* **—sham** *v.* **shammed, sham·ming, shams.** *—tr.* To put on the false appearance of; feign: *"shamming insanity to get his tormentors to leave him alone"* (John Wain). *—intr.* To assume a false appearance or character; dissemble. [Perhaps dialectal variant of SHAME.] **—sham′mer** *n.*

sha·man (shä′mən, shā′-) *n.* A member of certain tribal societies who acts as a medium between the visible world and an invisible spirit world and who practices magic or sorcery for purposes of healing, divination, and control over natural events. [Russian, from Tungus *šaman,* Buddhist monk, shaman, from Tocharian *samāne,* from Prakrit *samaṇa,* from Sanskrit *śramaṇaḥ,* from *śrámaḥ,* religious exercise.] **—sha·man′ic** (shə-măn′ĭk) *adj.*

sha·man·ism (shä′mə-nĭz′əm, shā′-) *n.* **1.** The animistic religion of certain peoples of northern Asia in which mediation between the visible and spirit worlds is effected by shamans. **2.** A similar religion or set of beliefs, especially among certain Native American peoples. **—sha′man·ist** *n.* **—sha′man·is′tic** *adj.*

Sha·mash (shä′măsh′) *n. Mythology.* The sun god of Assyro-Babylonian religion, worshiped as the author of justice and compassion. [Akkadian *šamaš,* sun.]

sham·ble (shăm′bəl) *intr.v.* **-bled, -bling, -bles.** To walk in an awkward, lazy, or unsteady manner, shuffling the feet. **—shamble** *n.* A shuffling gait. [Probably from obsolete *shamble,* awkward, ungainly, from Middle English *schamil,* butcher's table. See SHAMBLES.]

sham·bles (shăm′bəlz) *pl.n. (used with a sing. verb).* **1.a.** A scene or condition of complete disorder or ruin: *"The economy was in a shambles"* (W. Bruce Lincoln). **b.** Great clutter or jumble; a total mess: *made dinner and left the kitchen a shambles.* **2.a.** A place or scene of bloodshed or carnage. **b.** A scene or condition of great devastation. **3.** A slaughterhouse. **4.** *Archaic.* A meat market or butcher shop. [From Middle English *shamel, shambil,* place where meat is butchered and sold, from Old English *sceamol,* table, from Latin *scabillum, scamillum,* diminutive of *scamnum,* bench, stool.]

USAGE NOTE: The original sense of *shambles* to denote a meat market is by now so obscure in American usage that it must be counted the height of pedantry to insist, as a few critics continue to do, that the word should be used metaphorically only to refer to a scene of carnage.

WORD HISTORY: Leaving the place a shambles is not considered desirable, but it is better than it might once have been. The history of the word begins innocently enough with the Latin word *scam-*

William Shakespeare

shallop

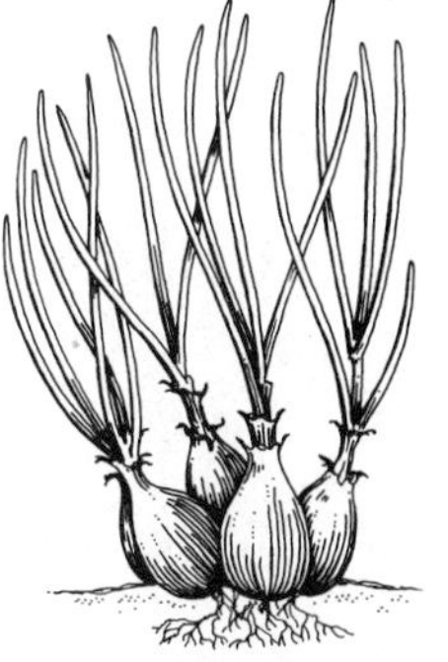

shallot
Allium ascalonicum

num, "a stool or bench serving as a seat, step, or support for the feet, for example." The diminutive *scamillum,* "low stool," was borrowed by speakers of Old English as *sceamol,* "stool, bench, table." Old English *sceamol* became Middle English *shamel,* which developed the specific sense in the singular and plural of "a place where meat is butchered and sold." The Middle English compound *shamelhouse* meant "slaughterhouse," a sense that the plural *shambles* developed (first recorded in 1548) along with the figurative sense "a place or scene of bloodshed" (first recorded in 1593). Our current, much more generalized meanings, such as "a scene or condition of disorder," are first recorded as of 1926. Although in the 1969 edition of the *American Heritage Dictionary* we recorded the fact that there was some objection to this sense, 85 percent of our Usage Panel found it acceptable in writing. It is indeed difficult to imagine most users of American English giving the word any other meaning.

---

sham·bol·ic (shăm-bŏl′ĭk) *adj. Chiefly British.* Disorderly, chaotic, or undisciplined in procedure, behavior, or manner: *"Its oil equipment industries are located in rebellious provinces, its transportation system is in a shambolic state, and its currency is virtually worthless"* (London Sunday Times). [Probably from alteration of SHAMBLES.] —**sham·bol′i·cal·ly** *adv.*

shame (shām) *n.* **1.a.** A painful emotion caused by a strong sense of guilt, embarrassment, unworthiness, or disgrace. **b.** Capacity for such a feeling: *Have you no shame?* **2.** One that brings dishonor, disgrace, or condemnation. **3.** A condition of disgrace or dishonor; ignominy. See Synonyms at **disgrace. 4.** A great disappointment. —**shame** *tr.v.* **shamed, sham·ing, shames. 1.** To cause to feel shame; put to shame. **2.** To bring dishonor or disgrace on. **3.** To disgrace by surpassing. **4.** To force by making ashamed: *He was shamed into making an apology.* —***idiom.* put to shame. 1.** To fill with shame; disgrace. **2.** To outdo thoroughly; surpass: *Your productivity has put the rest of us to shame.* [Middle English, from Old English *sceamu.*]

shame·faced (shām′fāst′) *adj.* **1.** Indicative of shame; ashamed: *a shamefaced explanation.* **2.** Extremely modest or shy; bashful. [Alteration of obsolete *shamefast,* bashful, ashamed, from Middle English, from Old English *sceamfæst : sceamu,* shame + *fæst,* fixed; see FAST[1].] —**shame′fac′ed·ly** (-fā′sĭd-lē) *adv.* —**shame′fac′ed·ness** *n.*

shame·ful (shām′fəl) *adj.* **1.a.** Causing shame; disgraceful. **b.** Giving offense; indecent. **2.** *Archaic.* Full of shame; ashamed. —**shame′ful·ly** *adv.* —**shame′ful·ness** *n.*

shame·less (shām′lĭs) *adj.* **1.** Feeling no shame; impervious to disgrace. **2.** Marked by a lack of shame: *a shameless lie.* —**shame′less·ly** *adv.* —**shame′less·ness** *n.*

SYNONYMS: *shameless, brazen, barefaced, brash, impudent, unblushing.* These adjectives apply to people and personal behavior that are in defiance of social or moral proprieties and are marked by a bold lack of shame. *Shameless* implies a lack of modesty, sense of decency, or regard for the rights or feelings of others: *a shameless liar; a shameless accusation. Brazen* suggests flagrant, insolent audacity: *a brazen impostor; brazen arrogance. Barefaced* specifies undisguised brazenness: *a barefaced hypocrite; a barefaced lie. Brash* stresses impetuousness, lack of tact, and often crass indifference to consequences or to considerations of decency: *A brash newcomer disputed the age-old rules for admission to the club. Impudent* suggests offensive boldness or effrontery: *an impudent student; an impudent misrepresentation. Unblushing* implies an inappropriate lack of shame or embarrassment: *an unblushing apologist for fascism; unblushing obsequiousness.*

---

sham·mes (shä′məs) *n., pl.* **sham·mo·sim** (shä-mô′sĭm). *Judaism.* **1.** A sexton in a synagogue. **2.** The candle used to light the other eight candles of a Hanukkah menorah. [Yiddish *shames,* from Hebrew *šammāš.*]

sham·my (shăm′ē) *n.* Variant of **chamois** (sense 2).

sham·poo (shăm-po͞o′) *n., pl.* **-poos. 1.** Any of various liquid or cream preparations of soap or detergent used to wash the hair and scalp. **2.** Any of various cleaning agents for rugs, upholstery, or cars. **3.** The act or process of washing or cleaning with shampoo. —**shampoo** *tr. & intr.v.* **-pooed, -poo·ing, -poos.** To wash or undergo washing with shampoo. [From Hindi *cāpō,* imperative of *cāpnā,* to press.] —**sham·poo′er** *n.*

sham·rock (shăm′rŏk′) *n.* Any of several plants, such as a clover or wood sorrel, having compound leaves with three small leaflets, considered the national emblem of Ireland. [Irish Gaelic *seamróg,* diminutive of *seamar,* clover, from Middle Irish *semar.*]

sha·mus (shä′məs, shā′-) *n. Slang.* **1.** A police officer. **2.** A private detective. [Perhaps alteration of SHAMMES.]

Shan (shän, shăn) *n., pl.* **Shan** or **Shans. 1.** A member of any of a group of tribes inhabiting the hills and plateaus of northeast Burma and adjacent parts of China, Laos, and Thailand. **2.** The Tai language of the Shan. —**Shan** *adj.* Of or relating to the Shan or their language or culture.

Shan·dong (shän′dông′) also **Shan·tung** (shăn′tŭng′, shän′to͝ong′). A province of eastern China bordered by the Gulf of Bo Hai and the Yellow Sea. The eastern part of the province forms the **Shandong Peninsula.** Settled since very early times, it became a province under the Ming dynasty. Jinan is the capital. Population, 76,950,000.

shan·dy (shăn′dē) *n., pl.* **-dies. 1.** Shandygaff. **2.** A drink made of beer and lemonade.

shan·dy·gaff (shăn′dē-găf′) *n.* A drink made of beer or ale mixed with ginger beer, ginger ale, or lemonade. [Origin unknown.]

Shang (shăng). A Chinese dynasty (traditionally dated 1766–1122 B.C.) whose capital was present-day Anyang. The dynasty's reign was marked by a highly developed social structure, advanced writing, and the use of bronze.

shang·hai (shăng-hī′, shăng′hī′) *tr.v.* **-haied, -hai·ing, -hais. 1.** To kidnap (a man) for compulsory service aboard a ship, especially after drugging him. **2.** To induce or compel (someone) to do something, especially by fraud or force: *We were shanghaied into buying worthless securities.* [After SHANGHAI[1], from the former custom of kidnapping sailors to man ships going to China.] —**shang·hai′er** *n.*

Shang·hai[1] (shăng-hī′, shăng′-). A city of eastern China at the mouth of the Yangtze River (Chang Jiang) southeast of Nanjing. The largest city in the country, Shanghai was opened to foreign trade by the Treaty of Nanking (1842) and quickly prospered. France, Great Britain, and the United States all held large concessions in the city until the early 20th century. Population, 6,980,000. The municipality of Shanghai is administered as a separate governmental unit. Population, 12,170,000.

Shang·hai[2] (shăng-hī′) *n.* See **Cochin China[2].** [After SHANGHAI[1].]

Shan·gri-la (shăng′grĭ-lä′) *n.* **1.** An imaginary, remote paradise on earth; utopia. **2.** A distant and secluded hideaway, usually of great beauty and peacefulness. [After *Shangri-La,* the imaginary land in the novel *Lost Horizon* by James Hilton.]

shank (shăngk) *n.* **1.a.** The part of the human leg between the knee and ankle. **b.** A corresponding part in other vertebrates. **2.a.** The whole leg of a human being. **b.** A leg or leglike part. **3.** A cut of meat from the leg of a steer, calf, sheep, or lamb. **4.** The long, narrow part of a nail or pin. **5.** A stem, stalk, or similar part. **6.** *Nautical.* The stem of an anchor. **7.** The long shaft of a fishhook. **8.** The part of a tobacco pipe between the bowl and stem. **9.** The shaft of a key. **10.** The narrow section of the handle of a spoon. **11.a.** The narrow part of the sole of a shoe under the instep. **b.** A piece of material, such as metal, that is used to reinforce or shape this part of a shoe. **12.** A projection, such as a ring, on the back of a button by which it is sewn to cloth. **13.a.** See **tang[1]** (sense 5). **b.** The part of a tool, such as a drill, that connects the functioning head to the handle. **14.a.** The latter or remaining part, especially of a period of time. **b.** The early or primary part of a period of time: *the shank of the evening.* —**shank** *tr.v.* **shanked, shank·ing, shanks.** *Sports.* To hit (a golf ball) with the heel of the club, causing the ball to veer in the wrong direction. [Middle English *shanke,* from Old English *sceanca.*] —**shanked** *adj.*

Shan·kar (shän′kär, shăng′-), **Ravi.** Born 1920. Indian-born musician and composer who popularized classical Indian music in the West.

shank·piece (shăngk′pēs′) *n.* An arch support inserted into the shank of a shoe.

Shan·non (shăn′ən). A river, about 386 km (240 mi) long, rising in north-central Ireland and flowing generally south and west to the Atlantic Ocean through a long, deep estuary.

Shan·si (shän′sē′). See **Shanxi.**

shan't (shănt, shänt). Shall not.

shan·tey (shăn′tē) *n. Music.* Variant of **chantey.**

Shan·tou (shän′tou′) also **Swa·tow** (swä′tou′). A city of southeast China on the South China Sea east-northeast of Hong Kong. It is a trade and industrial center with shipbuilding facilities. Population, 400,000.

shan·tung (shăn-tŭng′) *n.* **1.** A heavy fabric with a rough, nubby surface, made of spun wild silk. **2.** A rayon or cotton fabric that is imitative of this silk fabric. [After *Shantung* (Shandong), China.]

Shan·tung (shăn′tŭng′, shän′to͝ong′). See **Shandong.**

shan·ty[1] (shăn′tē) *n., pl.* **-ties.** A roughly built, often ramshackle cabin; a shack. [Probably from Canadian French *chantier,* hut in a lumber camp, from French, timberyard, from Old French, gantry, from Latin *canthērius,* rafter, nag, from Greek *kanthēlios,* pack ass.]

shan·ty[2] (shăn′tē) *n. Music.* Variant of **chantey.**

shan·ty·town (shăn′tē-toun′) *n.* A town or a section of a town consisting chiefly of shacks.

Shan·xi (shän′shē′) also **Shan·si** (-sē′). A province of northeast China bordered on the north by a section of the Great Wall. In the Chinese-Japanese War (1937–1945) it was a center of guerrilla warfare. Taiyuan is the capital. Population, 26,270,000.

shape (shāp) *n.* **1.a.** The characteristic surface configuration of a thing; an outline or a contour. See Synonyms at **form. b.** Something distinguished from its surroundings by its outline. **2.** The contour of a person's body; the figure. **3.a.** A definite, distinctive form: *"The bomb gave the shape of life, outer and inner, an irreversible charge; a sense of fatefulness would now lie on all things"* (Alfred Kazin). **b.** A desirable form: *a fabric that holds its shape.* **4.** A form or condition in which something may exist or appear; embodiment: *a god in the shape of a swan.* **5.** Assumed or false appearance; guise. **6.** A ghostly form; a phantom. **7.** Something, such as a mold or pattern, used to give or determine form. **8.** The proper condition of something necessary for action, effectiveness, or use: *an athlete in excellent shape.* **—shape** *v.* **shaped, shap·ing, shapes.** *—tr.* **1.** To give a particular form to; create. **2.** To cause to conform to a particular form or pattern; adapt to fit. **3.a.** To plan to bring about the realization or accomplishment of; devise. **b.** To embody in a definite form: *shaped a folk legend into a full-scale opera.* **4.a.** To adapt to a particular use or purpose; adjust. **b.** To direct the course of: *"He shaped history as well as being shaped by it"* (Robert J. Samuelson). *—intr.* **1.** To come to pass; happen. **2.** To take on a definite shape or form. Often used with *up* or *into.* ***—phrasal verb.*** **shape up. 1.** *Informal.* To turn out; develop. **2.** To improve so as to meet a standard: *Either shape up or ship out.* [Middle English, from Old English *gesceap,* a creation.] **—shap′a·ble, shape′a·ble** *adj.* **—shaped** *adj.* **—shap′er** *n.*

SHAPE *abbr.* Supreme Headquarters Allied Powers, Europe.

shape·less (shāp′lĭs) *adj.* **1.** Lacking a definite shape. **2.** Lacking symmetrical or attractive form. **—shape′less·ly** *adv.* **—shape′less·ness** *n.*

SYNONYMS: *shapeless, amorphous, formless, unformed, unshaped.* The central meaning shared by these adjectives is "having no distinct shape": *a mass of shapeless slag; an amorphous cloud of insects; an aggregate of formless particles; an unformed personality; unshaped dough.*
ANTONYM: *shapely.*

shape·ly (shāp′lē) *adj.* **-li·er, -li·est. 1.** Having a distinct shape. **2.** Having a pleasing shape. **—shape′li·ness** *n.*

shap·en (shā′pən) *v. Archaic.* A past participle of **shape. —shapen** *adj.* Having a definite, specified shape. Often used in combination: *an ill-shapen vase.*

shape·up or **shape-up** (shāp′ŭp′) *n.* An assembled group of dock workers from which the day's work crew is chosen by a representative of the union.

Sha·pir·o (shə-pîr′ō), **Karl Jay.** Born 1913. American poet and critic known for his early poems concerning World War II and his later works in free verse.

Shap·ley (shăp′lē), **Harlow.** 1885–1972. American astronomer noted for his work in cosmology and photometry.

shard (shärd) also **sherd** (shûrd) *n.* **1.** A piece of broken pottery, especially one found in an archaeological dig; a potsherd. **2.a.** A fragment of a brittle substance, as of glass or metal. **b.** A small piece or part: *"shards of intense emotional relationships that once existed"* (Maggie Scarf). **3.** *Zoology.* **a.** A tough sheath or covering, such as a shell, scale, or plate. **b.** The elytron or outer wing covering of a beetle. [Middle English *sherd,* from Old English *sceard,* cut, notch. See **sker-**[1] in Appendix.]

share[1] (shâr) *n.* **1.** A part or portion belonging to, distributed to, contributed by, or owed by a person or group. **2.** An equitable portion: *do one's share of the work.* **3.** *Abbr.* **sh., shr.** Any of the equal parts into which the capital stock of a corporation or company is divided. **—share** *v.* **shared, shar·ing, shares.** *—tr.* **1.** To divide and parcel out in shares; apportion. **2.** To participate in, use, enjoy, or experience jointly with another or others. **3.** To accord a share in (something) to another or others: *shared her chocolate bar with a friend.* *—intr.* To have a share or part: *shared in the profits.* ***—idiom.*** **go shares.** To be concerned or partake equally or jointly, as in a business venture. [Middle English, from Old English *scearu,* division. See **sker-**[1] in Appendix.] **—share′a·ble, shar′a·ble** *adj.* **—shar′er** *n.*

SYNONYMS: *share, participate, partake.* These verbs refer to acquiring, having, using, being involved in, or experiencing something jointly with another or others. *Share* applies both to giving and to receiving partial possession, use, or enjoyment: *"Share my harvest and my home"* (Thomas Hood). *"You English gentlefolk do not let us share your griefs; you keep them to yourselves"* (John Galsworthy). It can also refer to possession, use, or enjoyment in common by a group: *"Their wives and families shared their lot"* (George Bancroft). *The manufacturer and the dealer shared in the expense of advertising. Participate* implies taking part in something, such as an activity, together with another or others: *"if we had been allowed to participate in the vital processes of America's national growth"* (Richard Wright). *Partake* often refers to having or taking a portion of something, such as food; it can also mean to have part of the quality, nature, or character of something: *"partake of many gifts of fortune and power that I was never born to"* (Joseph Addison); *"an inarticulate noise partaking of a groan and a grunt"* (Joseph Conrad).

share[2] (shâr) *n.* A plowshare. [Middle English, from Old English *scēar.* See **sker-**[1] in Appendix.]

share·crop (shâr′krŏp′) *v.* **-cropped, -crop·ping, -crops.** *—intr.* To work as a sharecropper. *—tr.* To work (land) or grow (crops) as a sharecropper.

share·crop·per (shâr′krŏp′ər) *n.* A tenant farmer who gives a share of the crops raised to the landlord in lieu of rent.

share·hold·er (shâr′hōl′dər) *n.* One that owns or holds a share or shares of stock; a stockholder. Also called *shareowner.* **—share′hold′ing** *n.*

share·own·er (shâr′ō′nər) *n.* See **shareholder.**

Sha·ri (shä′rē) also **Cha·ri** (shä′rē, shä-rē′). A river of north-central Africa rising in the Central African Republic and flowing about 2,253 km (1,400 mi) northwest through southern Chad to Lake Chad.

sha·ri·'a or **sha·ri·a** also **sha·ri·'ah** (shä-rē′ä) *n. Islam.* The code of law based on the Koran. [Arabic *šarʿīya,* lawfulness, from *šarʿī,* lawful, from *aš-šarʿ,* Revelation, Islamic law.]

sha·rif (shə-rēf′) *n.* Variant of **sherif.**

shark (shärk) *n.* **1.** Any of numerous chiefly marine carnivorous fishes of the class Chondrichthyes (subclass Elasmobranchii), which are sometimes large and voracious and have a streamlined, torpedolike body, five to seven gill openings on each side of the head, a large oil-filled liver, a cartilaginous skeleton, and tough skin covered with small toothlike scales. **2.a.** A person regarded as ruthless, greedy, or dishonest. **b.** A vicious usurer. **3.** *Slang.* A person unusually skilled in a particular activity: *a card shark.* **—shark** *v.* **sharked, shark·ing, sharks.** *—tr. Archaic.* To obtain by deceitful means. *—intr.* To practice or live by fraud and trickery. [Origin unknown.]

shark·skin (shärk′skĭn′) *n.* **1.** The skin of a shark. **2.** Leather made from the skin of a shark. **3.** A rayon and acetate fabric having a smooth, somewhat shiny surface.

shark sucker *n.* See **remora.**

Shar·on (shăr′ən). A city of western Pennsylvania on the Ohio border north-northwest of Pittsburgh. It is an industrial center. Population, 19,057.

Sharon, Plain of. A fertile plain of western Israel extending along the Mediterranean coast south of Haifa.

sharp (shärp) *adj.* **sharp·er, sharp·est. 1.** Having a thin edge or a fine point suitable for or capable of cutting or piercing. **2.a.** Having clear form and detail: *a sharp photographic image.* **b.** Terminating in an edge or a point: *sharp, angular cliffs; a sharp nose.* **c.** Clearly and distinctly set forth: *sharp contrasts in behavior.* **3.** Abrupt or acute: *a sharp drop; a sharp turn.* **4.a.** Intellectually penetrating; astute. **b.** Marked by keenness and accuracy of perception: *sharp hearing.* **5.** Crafty or deceitful, as in business dealings: *sharp selling practices.* **6.** Vigilant; alert: *kept a sharp lookout for shoplifters.* **7.a.** Briskly or keenly cold and cutting: *a sharp wind.* **b.** Harsh or biting in tone or character: *sharp criticism.* **8.** Fierce or impetuous; violent: *a sharp temper; a sharp assault.* **9.** Intense; severe: *a sharp pain.* **10.a.** Sudden and shrill: *a sharp whistle.* **b.** Sudden and brilliant or dazzling: *a sharp flash of lightning.* **11.** Strongly affecting the senses of smell and taste: *a sharp, pungent odor; a sharp cheese.* **12.** Composed of hard, angular particles: *sharp sand.* **13.** *Music.* **a.** Raised in pitch by a semitone. **b.** Being above the proper pitch. **c.** Having the key signature in sharps. **14.** *Linguistics.* Voiceless. Used of a consonant. **15.** *Informal.* Attractive or stylish: *a sharp jacket.* **—sharp** *adv.* **1.** In a sharp manner: *hit me sharp on the brow.* **2.** Punctually; exactly: *at three o'clock sharp.* **3.** *Music.* Above the true or proper pitch. **—sharp** *n.* **1.** *Music.* **a.** A note or tone raised one semitone above its normal pitch. **b.** A sign (♯) indicating this. **2.** A slender sewing needle with a fine point. **3.** *Informal.* **a.** An expert. **b.** A shrewd cheater. **—sharp** *v.* **sharped, sharp·ing, sharps.** *Music.* *—tr.* To raise in pitch by a semitone. *—intr.* To play or sing above the proper pitch. [Middle English *sharp,* from Old English *scearp,* slope. See **sker-**[1] in Appendix.] **—sharp′ly** *adv.* **—sharp′ness** *n.*

SYNONYMS: *sharp, keen, acute.* These adjectives all apply literally to fine edges, points, or tips: *a sharp knife; a keen blade; a leaf with an acute end.* Figuratively they indicate mental alertness and clarity of comprehension. *Sharp* suggests quickness and astuteness: *"a young man of sharp and active intellect"* (John Henry Newman). *Keen* implies clear-headedness and acuity: *Women with keen intelligent minds are making inroads in formerly male-dominated occupations. Acute* suggests penetrating perception or discernment: *an acute observer of politics and politicians.* See also Synonyms at **fashionable.**

sharp·en (shär′pən) *tr. & intr.v.* **-ened, -en·ing, -ens.** To make or become sharp or sharper. **—sharp′en·er** *n.*

sharp·er (shär′pər) *n.* One that deals dishonestly with others, especially a cheating gambler.

sharp-eyed (shärp′īd′) *adj.* **1.** Having keen eyesight. **2.** Keenly perceptive or observant; alert.

sharp·ie (shär′pē) *n., pl.* **-ies. 1.** *Nautical.* A long, narrow, flat-bottomed fishing boat having a centerboard and one or two masts, each rigged with a triangular sail. **2.a.** An alert, quick-witted person. **b.** A sharper. [From SHARP.]

sharp-nosed (shärp′nōzd′) *adj.* **1.** Having a thin, pointed nose or snout. **2.** Having a keen sense of smell.

Sharps·burg (shärps′bûrg′). A town of northern Maryland west of Frederick. It is the site of the Civil War Battle of Antietam (September 16–17, 1862), in which Union forces repulsed Gen. Robert E. Lee's troops.

sharp-shinned hawk (shärp′shĭnd′) *n.* A small North American hawk *(Accipiter striatus)* that has short, rounded wings and a long tail, and preys on other birds.

sharp·shoot·er (shärp′sho͞o′tər) *n.* **1.** One who is highly proficient at shooting. **2.a.** The second military grade of proficiency in the use of rifles and other small arms. **b.** One who holds this grade of proficiency.

sharp·shoot·ing (shärp′sho͞o′tĭng) *n.* **1.** High proficiency in shooting firearms. **2.** Accurate, often unexpected verbal or written attack.

Harlow Shapley

sharpie
Detail from an oil painting of a two-masted sharpie by Albert S. Bigelow

sharp-shinned hawk
Accipiter striatus

ă pat	oi boy
ā pay	ou out
âr care	o͝o took
ä father	o͞o boot
ĕ pet	ŭ cut
ē be	ûr urge
ĭ pit	th thin
ī pie	*th* this
îr pier	hw which
ŏ pot	zh vision
ō toe	ə about, item
ô paw	♦ regionalism

Stress marks: ′ (primary); ′ (secondary), as in **dictionary** (dĭk′shə-nĕr′ē)

sharp-tailed grouse
Tympanuchus phasianellus

George Bernard Shaw

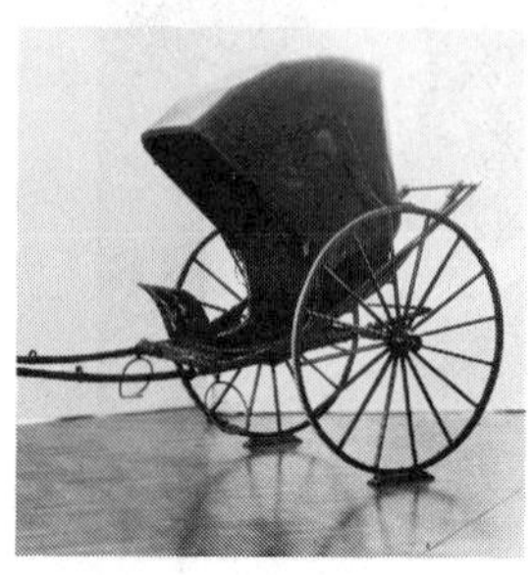
shay

sharp-sight·ed (shärp′sī′tĭd) *adj.* **1.** Having keen eyesight. **2.** Keenly perceptive or alert. **—sharp′-sight′ed·ly** *adv.* **—sharp′-sight′ed·ness** *n.*

sharp-tail (shärp′tāl′) *n.* The sharp-tailed grouse.

sharp-tailed grouse (shärp′tāld′) *n.* A grouse *(Tympanuchus phasianellus)* of the northwest United States and Canada, having a short pointed tail, a pale color, and dark V-shaped breast markings.

sharp-tailed sparrow *n.* A North American sparrow *(Ammospiza caudacuta)* with sharp-pointed tail feathers, often found about salt marshes.

sharp-tongued (shärp′tŭngd′) *adj.* Harsh, critical, or sarcastic in speech.

sharp-wit·ted (shärp′wĭt′ĭd) *adj.* Having or exhibiting keenly perceptive intellect. **—sharp′-wit′ted·ness** *n.*

shash·lik or **shash·lick** (shäsh-lĭk′, shäsh′lĭk) *n.* A dish consisting of marinated cubes of lamb or beef grilled or roasted on a spit, often with slices of eggplant, onion, and tomato; shish kebab. [Russian *shashlyk,* of Turkish origin.]

Shas·ta (shăs′tə), **Mount.** A volcanic peak, 4,319.4 m (14,162 ft) high, of the Cascade Range in northern California. Discovered in 1827, it has hot sulfurous springs near the summit.

Shasta daisy *n.* A hybrid daisy derived from *Chrysanthemum maximum* and *C. lacustre,* having large white daisylike flower heads. [After Mount SHASTA.]

shat (shăt) *v. Obscene.* A past tense and a past participle of **shit.**

Shatt al Ar·ab or **Shatt-al-Ar·ab** (shăt′ ăl ăr′əb, shät′). A river channel, about 193 km (120 mi) long, of southeast Iraq formed by the confluence of the Tigris and Euphrates rivers and flowing southeast to the Persian Gulf. The Shatt al Arab forms part of the Iraq-Iran border, and navigation rights to the channel have long been disputed by the two countries.

shat·ter (shăt′ər) *v.* **-tered, -ter·ing, -ters.** *—tr.* **1.** To cause to break or burst suddenly into pieces, as with a violent blow. **2.a.** To damage seriously; disable: *His health was shattered by the disease.* **b.** To cause the destruction or ruin of; destroy: *The outcome of the conflict shattered our dreams of peace and prosperity.* *—intr.* To break into pieces; smash or burst. See Synonyms at **break.** **—shatter** *n.* **1.a.** The act of shattering. **b.** The condition of being shattered. **2.** Often **shatters.** A splintered or fragmented condition: *a rare piece of porcelain now in shatters.* [Middle English *shateren,* from Old English **sceaterian,* to scatter.] **—shat′ter·ing·ly** *adv.*

shatter cone *n.* A conical fragment of rock that is formed from the high pressure in volcanism or meteorite impact and has striations radiating from the apex.

shat·ter·proof (shăt′ər-pro͞of′) *adj.* Resistant to shattering: *shatterproof goggles.*

shatterproof glass *n.* See **safety glass** (sense 1).

Shav·a·no Peak (shăv′ə-nō). A mountain, 4,339.8 m (14,229 ft) high, in the Sawatch Range of the Rocky Mountains in central Colorado.

shave (shāv) *v.* **shaved, shaved** or **shav·en** (shā′vən), **shav·ing, shaves.** *—tr.* **1.a.** To remove the beard or other body hair from, with a razor or shaver. **b.** To cut (the beard, for example) at the surface of the skin with a razor or shaver. **2.** To crop, trim, or mow closely: *shave a meadow.* **3.a.** To remove thin slices from: *shave a board.* **b.** To cut or scrape into thin slices; shred: *shave chocolate.* **4.** To come close to or graze in passing. See Synonyms at **brush**[1]. **5.a.** To purchase (a note) at a reduction greater than the legal or customary rate. **b.** To cut (a price) by a slight margin. *—intr.* To remove beard or hair with a razor or shaver. **—shave** *n.* **1.** The act, process, or result of shaving. **2.** A thin slice or scraping; a shaving. **3.** Any of various tools used for shaving. [Middle English *shaven,* to scrape, from Old English *sceafan.*]

shav·er (shā′vər) *n.* **1.a.** One who shaves. **b.** A device, especially an electric razor, that is used in shaving. **2.** *Informal.* A small child, especially a boy.

Sha·vi·an (shā′ve-ən) *adj.* Of, relating to, or characteristic of George Bernard Shaw or his works: *Shavian wit.* **—Shavian** *n.* An admirer or a disciple of George Bernard Shaw. [From *Shavius,* pseudo-Latin form of the name *Shaw.*]

shav·ing (shā′vĭng) *n.* **1.** A thin slice or sliver, as of wood or metal, that is shaved off. **2.** The act of one that shaves.

Sha·vu·ot also **Sha·bu·oth** (shə-vo͞o′ōt′, -əs, shä′vo͞ot-ôt′) *n. Judaism.* A feast held on the sixth and seventh days of Sivan in commemoration of the revelation of the Law on Mount Sinai and the celebration of the wheat festival in ancient times. Also called *Pentecost.* [Hebrew *šābūʿôt,* from *šābûaʿ,* week.]

Shaw (shô), **Anna Howard.** 1847–1919. British-born American physician and reformer who was president of the National American Woman Suffrage Association (1904–1915).

Shaw, George Bernard. 1856–1950. Irish-born British playwright. A founder of the Fabian Society, he wrote plays of iconoclastic social criticism, including *Arms and the Man* (1894), *Pygmalion* (1913), and *Saint Joan* (1923). He won the 1925 Nobel Prize for literature.

Shaw, Henry Wheeler. Pen name Josh Billings. 1818–1885. American humorist noted for his essays on rural life, characterized by intentional misspellings and published annually in the *Farmers' Allminax* (1869–1880).

Sha·win·i·gan (shə-wĭn′ĭ-gən). A city of southern Quebec, Canada, on the St. Maurice River northwest of Trois Rivières. Its hydroelectric station supplies power for the city's pulp and paper mills and other processing plants. Population, 23,011.

shawl (shôl) *n.* A square or oblong piece of cloth worn as a covering for the head, neck, and shoulders. **—shawl** *tr.v.* **shawled, shawl·ing, shawls.** To cover with or as if with such a piece of cloth. [Ultimately from Persian *shāl.*]

shawm (shôm) *n. Music.* Any of various early double-reed wind instruments, forerunners of the modern oboe. [Middle English *shalmie,* from Old French *chalemie,* alteration of *chalemel,* from Late Latin *calamellus,* diminutive of Latin *calamus,* reed, from Greek *kalamos.*]

Shawn (shôn), **Ted.** 1891–1972. American dancer and choreographer noted for his partnership with Ruth Saint Denis. Together they founded the Denishawn Dance School (1915), for which he choreographed works based on Native American themes.

Shaw·nee[1] (shô-nē′) *n., pl.* **Shawnee** or **-nees. 1.a.** A Native American people formerly inhabiting parts of the Cumberland and central Ohio valleys, with present-day populations in Oklahoma. The Shawnee figured prominently in the resistance to white settlement of the Ohio Valley in the late 18th and early 19th centuries. **b.** A member of this tribe. **2.** The Algonquian language of the Shawnee. [Back-formation from obsolete *Shawnese,* from Shawnee *shaawanooki,* those of the south, Shawnee.]

Shaw·nee[2] (shô-nē′, shô′nē). **1.** A city of northeast Kansas, a suburb of Kansas City. Population, 29,653. **2.** A city of central Oklahoma on the North Canadian River east-southeast of Oklahoma City. Population, 26,506.

♦ **Shawnee cake** *n. New England.* See **johnnycake.** See Regional Note at **johnnycake.**

Shaw·wal (shə-wäl′) *n.* The tenth month of the year in the Moslem calendar. See table at **calendar.** [Arabic *šawwāl.*]

shay (shā) *n. Informal.* A chaise. [Back-formation from CHAISE (taken as pl.).]

Shays (shāz), **Daniel.** 1747?–1825. American Revolutionary soldier and insurrectionist who with a band of armed men raided a government arsenal in Springfield, Massachusetts, to protest the state legislature's indifference to the plight of farmers (1787). The raid, known as Shays's Rebellion, was quashed by militia.

she (shē) *pron.* **1.a.** Used to refer to the woman or girl previously mentioned or implied. See Usage Note at **I**[1]. **b.** Used to refer to a female animal. **2.** Used in place of *it* to refer to certain inanimate things, such as ships and nations, traditionally perceived as female: *"The sea is mother-death and she is a mighty female"* (Anne Sexton). **—she** *n.* A female animal or person: *Is the cat a she?* [Middle English *she,* probably alteration of Old English *sēo,* feminine demonstrative pron. See **so-** in Appendix.]

s/he (shē′ər-hē′, shē′hē′) *pron.* Used as a gender-neutral alternative to *he* or *she.*

shea butter (shē, shā) *n.* A whitish or yellowish fat obtained from the seeds of the shea tree, used as food and for making soap and candles.

sheaf (shēf) *n., pl.* **sheaves** (shēvz). **1.** A bundle of cut stalks of grain or similar plants bound with straw or twine. **2.** A collection of items held or bound together: *a sheaf of printouts.* **3.** An archer's quiver. **—sheaf** *tr.v.* **sheafed, sheaf·ing, sheafs.** To gather and bind into a bundle. [Middle English *sheef,* from Old English *scēaf.*]

shear (shîr) *v.* **sheared, sheared** or **shorn** (shôrn, shōrn), **shear·ing, shears.** *—tr.* **1.** To remove (fleece or hair) by cutting or clipping. **2.** To remove the hair or fleece from. **3.** To cut with or as if with shears: *shearing a hedge.* **4.** To divest or deprive as if by cutting: *The prisoners were shorn of their dignity.* *—intr.* **1.** To use a cutting tool such as shears. **2.** To move or proceed by or as if by cutting: *shear through the wheat.* **3.** *Physics.* To become deformed by forces tending to produce a shearing strain. **—shear** *n.* **1.a.** A pair of scissors. Often used in the plural. **b.** Any of various implements or machines that cut with a scissorlike action. Often used in the plural. **2.** The act, process, or result of shearing. **3.** Something cut off by shearing. **4.** The act, process, or fact of shearing. Used to indicate a sheep's age: *a two-shear ram.* **5.** Also **sheers** (shîrz) *(used with a sing. or pl. verb).* An apparatus used to lift heavy weights, consisting of two or more spars joined at the top and spread at the base, the tackle being suspended from the top. **6.** *Physics.* **a.** An applied force or system of forces that tends to produce a shearing strain. Also called *shearing stress, shear stress.* **b.** A shearing strain. [Middle English *sheren,* from Old English *sceran.* N., from Middle English *shere,* from Old English *scēar.* See **sker-**[1] in Appendix.] **—shear′er** *n.*

sheared (shîrd) *adj.* Shaped or finished by shearing, especially cut or trimmed to a uniform length: *a sheared fur coat.*

shear·ing strain (shîr′ĭng) *n. Physics.* A condition in or deformation of an elastic body caused by forces that tend to produce an opposite but parallel sliding motion of the body's planes.

shearing stress *n. Physics.* See **shear** (sense 6a).

shear·ling (shîr′lĭng) *n.* **1.** A year-old sheep that has been sheared once. **2.** The skin of a shearling or of a newly sheared sheep or lamb, tanned and with the wool on.

shear stress *n. Physics.* See **shear** (sense 6a).

shear·wa·ter (shîr′wô′tər, -wŏt′ər) *n.* Any of various oceanic birds of the genus *Puffinus,* having a short, hooked bill with tube-shaped nostrils and long, slender wings that appear to shear the water as the bird flies along the surface.

sheat·fish (shēt′fĭsh′) *n., pl.* **sheatfish** or **-fish·es.** A very large freshwater catfish *(Silurus glanis)* of central and eastern Europe and western Asia. [Alteration of obsolete *sheathfish* : SHEATH (translation of German *Scheide,* sheathfish) + FISH.]

sheath (shēth) *n., pl.* **sheaths** (shēthz, shēths). **1.a.** A case for a blade, as of a sword. **b.** Any of various similar coverings. **2.** *Biology.* An enveloping tubular structure, such as the base of a grass leaf that surrounds the stem or the tissue that encloses a muscle or nerve fiber. **3.** A close-fitting dress. **—sheath** *tr.v.* **sheathed, sheath·ing, sheaths** (shēthz, shēths). To encase or cover with or as if with a sheath; sheathe. [Middle English *shethe,* from Old English *scēath.* See **skei-** in Appendix.]

sheath·bill (shēth′bĭl′) *n.* Either of two pigeonlike shore birds *(Chionia alba* or *C. minor)* of Antarctic regions, having white plumage and a horny covering on the base of the bill.

sheathe (shēth) *tr.v.* **sheathed, sheath·ing, sheathes. 1.** To insert into or provide with a sheath. **2.** To retract (a claw) into a sheath. **3.** To enclose with a protective covering; encase. [Middle English *shethen,* from *shethe,* sheath. See SHEATH.] **—sheath′er** *n.*

sheath·ing (shē′thĭng) *n.* **1.** A layer of boards or of other wood or fiber materials applied to the outer studs, joists, and rafters of a building to strengthen the structure and serve as a base for an exterior weatherproof cladding. **2.** *Nautical.* An exterior covering on the underwater part of a ship's hull that protects it against marine growths. **3.** The act of providing sheathing.

sheath knife *n.* A knife that has a fixed blade and fits into a sheath.

shea tree (shē, shā) *n.* A tropical African tree *(Butyrospermum parkii)* having oily seeds that yield shea butter. [Mandingo (Bambara) *si.*]

sheave¹ (shēv) *tr.v.* **sheaved, sheav·ing, sheaves.** To collect and bind into a sheaf. [From SHEAF.]

sheave² (shēv, shĭv) *n.* A wheel or disk with a grooved rim, especially one used as a pulley. [Middle English *sheve.* See **skei-** in Appendix.]

sheaves (shēvz) *n.* Plural of **sheaf.**

She·ba (shē′bə). An ancient country of southern Arabia comprising present-day Yemen. Its people colonized Ethiopia in the tenth century B.C. and were known for their wealth and commercial prosperity. In the Old Testament, the queen of Sheba made a celebrated visit to King Solomon.

she·bang (shə-băng′) *n. Slang.* A situation, an organization, a contrivance, or a set of facts or things: *organized and ran the whole shebang.* [Origin unknown.]

She·bat (shə-bät′, -vät′) *n.* Variant of **Shevat.**

she·been (shə-bēn′) *n.* An unlicensed drinking establishment, especially in Ireland, Scotland, and South Africa. [Irish Gaelic *séibín,* measure of grain, grain tax, bad ale, diminutive of *séibe,* mug, bottle.]

She·bel·le or **She·be·li** (shə-bā′lē). A river, about 1,609 km (1,000 mi) long, of northeast Africa rising in central Ethiopia and flowing southeast into Somalia then southwest in a course parallel to the Indian Ocean coastline.

She·boy·gan (shə-boi′gən). A city of eastern Wisconsin on Lake Michigan north of Milwaukee. Founded c. 1835 on the site of a fur-trading post established in 1795, it is a shipping and manufacturing center. Population, 48,085.

shed¹ (shĕd) *v.* **shed, shed·ding, sheds.** *—tr.* **1.** To cause to pour forth: *shed tears.* **2.** To diffuse or radiate; send forth or impart: *shed light.* **3.** To repel without allowing penetration: *A duck's feathers shed water.* **4.a.** To lose by natural process: *a snake shedding its skin.* **b.** To rid oneself of (something not wanted or needed): *I shed 25 pounds as a result of my new diet.* *—intr.* **1.** To lose a natural growth or covering by natural process. **2.** To pour forth, fall off, or drop out: *All the leaves have shed.* **—shed** *n.* **1.** Something that sheds, especially an elevation in the earth's surface from which water flows in two directions. **2.** Something that has been shed. **—*idiom.* shed blood.** To take life, especially with violence; kill. [Middle English *sheden,* to separate, shed, from Old English *scēadan,* to divide. See **skei-** in Appendix.]

shed² (shĕd) *n.* **1.** A small structure, either freestanding or attached to a larger structure, serving for storage or shelter. **2.** A large low structure often open on all sides. [Alteration of Middle English *shadde,* perhaps variant of *shade,* shade. See SHADE.]

she'd (shēd). **1.** She had. **2.** She would.

shed·der (shĕd′ər) *n.* One that sheds, as a long-haired animal or a molting snake.

shed dormer *n. Architecture.* A dormer having a roof that slopes in the same direction as the roof in which the dormer is located.

she-dev·il (shē′dĕv′əl) *n.* A woman regarded as cruel.

shed·row (shĕd′rō′) *n.* A row or double row of horse barns at a racetrack, having a separate stall for each horse and fronting a walkway.

sheen (shēn) *n.* **1.** Glistening brightness; luster: *the sheen of old satin in candlelight.* **2.** Splendid attire. **3.** A glossy surface given to textiles. [From Middle English *shene,* beautiful, from Old English *sciene.* See **keu-** in Appendix.]

Sheen (shēn), **Fulton John.** 1895–1979. American Roman Catholic prelate known for his radio and television broadcasts, his support of prayer in public schools, and his opposition to Communism and birth control.

shee·ny¹ (shē′nē) *adj.* Lustrous; glistening.

shee·ny² (shē′nē) *n., pl.* **-nies.** *Offensive Slang.* Used as a disparaging term for a Jew. [Origin unknown.]

sheep (shēp) *n., pl.* **sheep. 1.** Any of various usually horned ruminant mammals of the genus *Ovis* in the family Bovidae, especially the domesticated species *O. aries,* raised in many breeds for wool, edible flesh, or skin. **2.** Leather made from the skin of one of these animals. **3.a.** A person regarded as timid, weak, or submissive. **b.** One who is easily swayed or led. [Middle English, from Old English *scēap.*]

sheep·ber·ry (shēp′bĕr′ē) *n.* Either of two eastern North American shrubs or trees *(Viburnum lentago* or *V. prunifolium)* having clusters of white flowers and edible blue-black berries. Also called *nannyberry.*

sheep·cote (shēp′kōt′, -kŏt′) *n. Chiefly British.* A sheepfold.

sheep dip also **sheep-dip** (shēp′dĭp′) *n.* Any of various preparations of liquid disinfectant into which sheep are dipped to destroy parasites and to clean their wool, especially before shearing.

sheep·dog also **sheep dog** (shēp′dôg′, -dŏg′) *n.* A dog trained to guard and herd sheep. Also called *shepherd dog.*

sheep·fold (shēp′fōld′) *n.* A pen for sheep.

sheep·herd·er (shēp′hûr′dər) *n.* A person who herds sheep, especially on an open range; a shepherd. **—sheep′herd′ing** *n.*

sheep·ish (shē′pĭsh) *adj.* **1.** Embarrassed, as by consciousness of a fault: *a sheepish grin.* **2.** Meek or stupid. **—sheep′ish·ly** *adv.* **—sheep′ish·ness** *n.*

sheep ked (kĕd) *n.* See **sheep tick.** [Origin unknown.]

sheep laurel *n.* An eastern North American evergreen shrub *(Kalmia angustifolia)* having flowers with rose-pink or crimson bell-shaped corollas, and poisonous leaves. Also called *lambkill.*

sheep's eyes (shēps) *pl.n.* Shyly amorous glances.

sheep·shank (shēp′shăngk′) *n.* A knot used to shorten a line.

sheeps·head (shēps′hĕd′) *n.* **1.** A food fish *(Archosargus probatocephalus)* of the Atlantic and Gulf coasts of the United States, having dark, vertical markings. **2.** A freshwater drum *(Aplodinotus grunniens)* commonly found from the Great Lakes to Texas. **3.** A redfish *(Semicossyphus pulcher)* of the Gulf of California, caught commercially or as a game fish.

sheep·shear·ing (shēp′shîr′ĭng) *n.* **1.** The act of shearing sheep. **2.a.** The time or season when sheep are sheared. **b.** Festivities held at this time. **—sheep′shear′er** *n.*

sheep·skin (shēp′skĭn′) *n.* **1.** The skin of a sheep either tanned with the fleece left on or in the form of leather or parchment. **2.** *Informal.* A diploma. *—attributive.* Often used to modify another noun: *sheepskin rugs; sheepskin coats.*

sheep tick *n.* A wingless, louselike fly *(Melophagus ovinus)* that is parasitic to sheep, causing skin irritations that result in loss of wool. Also called *sheep ked.*

sheer¹ (shîr) *intr. & tr.v.* **sheered, sheer·ing, sheers.** To swerve or cause to swerve from a course. **—sheer** *n.* **1.** A swerving or deviating course. **2.** *Nautical.* **a.** The upward curve or amount of upward curve of the longitudinal lines of a ship's hull as viewed from the side. **b.** The position in which a ship is placed to enable it to keep clear of a single bow anchor. [Probably partly from Low German *scheren,* to move to and from: said of boats, and partly from Dutch *scheren,* to withdraw; see **sker-¹** in Appendix.]

sheer² (shîr) *adj.* **sheer·er, sheer·est. 1.** Thin, fine, and transparent: *sheer curtains; sheer chiffon.* See Synonyms at **airy. 2.a.** Completely such, without qualification or exception: *sheer stupidity; sheer happiness.* **b.** Free from admixture or adulterants; unmixed: *sheer alcohol.* See Synonyms at **pure. c.** Considered or operating apart from anything else: *got the job through sheer persistence.* **3.** Almost perpendicular; steep: *sheer rock cliffs.* See Synonyms at **steep¹. —sheer** *adv.* **1.** Almost perpendicularly. **2.** Completely; altogether. [Obsolete *shere,* thin, clear, partly from Middle English *shir,* bright, clear (from Old English *scīr*) and partly from Middle English *skir,* bright, clean (from Old Norse *skærr*).] **—sheer′ly** *adv.* **—sheer′ness** *n.*

sheers (shîrz) *n. (used with a sing. or pl. verb).* Variant of **shear** (sense 5).

sheet¹ (shēt) *n. Abbr.* **sh., sht. 1.** A broad rectangular piece of fabric serving as a basic article of bedding. **2.a.** A broad, thin, usually rectangular mass or piece of material, such as paper, metal, glass, or plywood. **b.** A flat or very shallow, usually rectangular pan used for baking. **3.** A broad, flat, continuous surface or expanse: *a sheet of ice.* **4.** A moving expanse: *a sheet of flames.* **5.** A newspaper, especially a tabloid. **6.** *Geology.* A broad, relatively thin deposit or layer of igneous or sedimentary rock. **7.** A large block of stamps printed by a single impression of a plate before the individual stamps have been separated. **—sheet** *v.* **sheet·ed, sheet·ing, sheets.** *—tr.* **1.** To cover with, wrap in, or provide with a sheet. **2.** To make into sheets. *—intr.* To flow or fall in a sheet: *rain sheeting against the windshield.* **—sheet** *adj.* Being in the form of a sheet: *sheet aluminum.* [Middle English *shete,* cloth, from Old English *scēte.* See **skeud-** in Appendix.]

sheet² (shēt) *Nautical. n.* **1.** A rope or chain attached to one or both of the lower corners of a sail, serving to move or extend it. **2. sheets.** The spaces at either end of an open boat in front of and behind the seats. **—sheet** *intr.v.* **sheet·ed, sheet·ing, sheets.**

shears
Top: Straight-cut metal shears
Center: Pinking shears
Bottom: Pruning shears

sheath
Late 19th-century Ojibwa beaded knife sheath

shed²

ă pat	oi boy
ā pay	ou out
âr care	ŏŏ took
ä father	ōō boot
ĕ pet	ŭ cut
ē be	ûr urge
ĭ pit	th thin
ī pie	*th* this
îr pier	hw which
ŏ pot	zh vision
ō toe	ə about, item
ô paw	♦ regionalism

Stress marks: ′ (primary); ′ (secondary), as in **dictionary** (dĭk′shə-nĕr′ē)

To extend in a certain direction. Used of the sheets of a sail. **—*idiom.* three sheets to** (or **in**) **the wind.** *Informal.* Drunk. [Middle English *shete,* from Old English *scēat(line),* sheet (line), from *scēata,* corner of a sail. See **skeud-** in Appendix.]

sheet anchor *n.* **1.** *Nautical.* A large extra anchor intended for use in an emergency. **2.** A source of aid in time of emergency or danger.

sheet bend

sheet bend *n.* *Nautical.* A knot in which one rope or piece of yarn is made fast to the bight of another.

sheet glass *n.* Glass drawn from a molten bath into a thin sheet of film, commonly used to make windows.

sheet•ing (shē′tĭng) *n.* **1.** Material, such as metal or cloth, used to make sheets or a sheet. **2.** The act or process of providing with or forming into sheets.

sheet lightning *n.* Lightning that appears as a broad, sheetlike illumination of parts of a thundercloud, caused by the reflection of a lightning flash.

sheet metal *n.* Metal that has been rolled into a sheet having a thickness between foil and plate. **—sheet′-met′al** (shēt′-mĕt′l) *adj.*

sheet music *n.* *Music.* Compositions printed on unbound sheets of paper.

Sheet•rock (shēt′rŏk′). A trademark used for plasterboard. This trademark often occurs in print in lowercase: *"The instrument has three scales of sensitivity calibrated for detection of moisture in most building materials such as . . . sheetrock"* (Mechanical Engineering). *"*[It]* is excellent for installing lights, installing ceiling tile, taping sheetrock . . . and other jobs"* (Engineering News-Record). It also occurs as a verb: *"We're going to sheetrock the ceiling"* (New York Times).

sheldrake
Tadorna tadorna

Shef•field (shĕf′ēld′). A borough of north-central England east of Manchester. The highly industrialized city has long specialized in the production of cutlery and steel. Population, 547,600.

she•getz (shā′gĭts) *n., pl.* **shkotz•im** (shkôt′sĭm). *Offensive.* A non-Jewish boy or young man. [Yiddish *sheygets,* from Hebrew *šeqeṣ,* blemish.]

sheik also **sheikh** (shēk, shāk) *n.* **1.** *Islam.* **a.** A religious official. **b.** A leader of an Arab family or village. **c.** Used as a form of address for such an official or leader. **2. sheik.** *Slang.* A romantically alluring man. [Arabic *šayḫ,* old man, chief, from *šāḫa,* to be old.]

shei•ka also **shei•kha** (shā′kä, -KHä) *n.* *Islam.* A sheik's wife. [Arabic *šayḫa,* old woman, matron, feminine of *šayḫ,* old man, sheik. See SHEIK.]

sheik•dom also **sheikh•dom** (shēk′dəm, shāk′-) *n.* The area ruled by a sheik.

sheikh (shēk, shāk) *n.* *Islam.* Variant of **sheik.**

shei•kha (shā′kä, -KHä) *n.* *Islam.* Variant of **sheika.**

shei•la (shē′lə) *n.* *Australian.* A girl or young woman. [From the personal name *Sheila.*]

shek•el (shĕk′əl) *n.* **1.** See table at **currency.** **2. a.** Any of several ancient units of weight, especially a Hebrew unit equal to about a half ounce. **b.** A gold or silver coin equal in weight to one of these units, especially the chief silver coin of the ancient Hebrews. **3.** *Slang.* **a.** A coin. **b. shekels.** Money. [Hebrew *šeqel,* from *šāqal,* to weigh, from Canaanite *ṯql.*]

Mary Wollstonecraft Shelley
Detail of a c. 1840 portrait by Richard Rothwell (1800–1868)

She•ki•nah (shĭ-kē′nə, -KHē′-, -kī′-) *n.* *Judaism.* A visible manifestation of the divine presence as described in Jewish theology. [Hebrew *šĕkīnâ,* from *šākan,* to dwell.]

shel•drake (shĕl′drāk′) *n.* **1.** Any of various large Old World ducks of the genus *Tadorna,* especially *T. tadorna,* having predominantly black and white plumage. Also called *shelduck.* **2.** See **merganser.** [Middle English *shelddrake* : *scheld,* variegated; see **skel-**[1] in Appendix + *drake,* drake.]

shel•duck (shĕl′dŭk′) *n.* See **sheldrake** (sense 1). [SHEL(DRAKE) + DUCK[1].]

shelf (shĕlf) *n., pl.* **shelves** (shĕlvz). **1. a.** A flat, usually rectangular structure composed of a rigid material, such as wood, glass, or metal, fixed at right angles to a wall or other vertical surface and used to hold or store objects. **b.** The contents or capacity of such a structure. **c.** Something, such as a projecting ledge of rock or a balcony, that resembles such a structure. **2.** A reef, sandbar, or shoal. **3.** Bedrock. **—*idioms.* off the shelf.** Available from merchandise in stock; not custom-made. **on the shelf. 1.** In a state of disuse. **2. a.** Unemployed. **b.** Out of circulation. **c.** Retired. [Middle English, probably from Middle Low German *schelf.* See **skel-**[1] in Appendix.] **—shelf′ful′** (-fo͝ol′) *n.*

Percy Bysshe Shelley
1819 portrait by Amelia Curran (1775–1847)

shelf fungus *n.* See **bracket fungus.**

shelf ice *n.* An extension of glacial ice into coastal waters that is in contact with the bottom near the shore but not toward the outer edge of the shelf.

shelf life *n.* The length of time a product may be stored, as on a supermarket shelf, without deteriorating.

Shel•i•kof Strait (shĕl′ĭ-kôf′). A strait of southern Alaska between the Alaska Peninsula and Kodiak and Afognak islands.

shell (shĕl) *n.* **1. a.** The usually hard outer covering that encases certain organisms, such as mollusks, insects, and turtles; the carapace. **b.** A similar outer covering on an egg, a fruit, or a nut. **c.** The material that constitutes such a covering. **2.** Something resembling or having the form of a shell, especially: **a.** An external, usually hard, protective or enclosing case or cover. **b.** A framework or an exterior, as of a building. **c.** A thin layer of pastry. **d.** The external part of the ear. **3.** *Nautical.* **a.** The hull of a ship. **b.** A long, narrow racing boat propelled by rowers. **4.** A small glass for beer. **5. a.** A projectile or piece of ammunition, especially the hollow tube containing explosives used to propel such a projectile. **b.** A metal or cardboard case containing the charge, primer, and shot fired from a shotgun. **6.** An attitude or a manner adopted to mask one's true feelings. **7.** *Physics.* **a.** Any of the set of hypothetical spherical surfaces centered on the nucleus of an atom that contain the orbitals of electrons having the same principal quantum number. **b.** An analogous pattern of protons and neutrons within a nucleus. **8. a.** A usually sleeveless and collarless, typically knit blouse. **b.** The outermost layer of a lined garment such as a coat or jacket: *a parka with a waterproof shell.* **9.** *Computer Science.* A program that works with the operating system as a command processor, used to enter commands and initiate their execution. **—shell** *v.* **shelled, shell•ing, shells.** *—tr.* **1. a.** To remove the shell of; shuck: *shell oysters.* **b.** To remove from a shell: *shell peas.* **2.** To separate the kernels of (corn) from the cob. **3.** To fire shells at; bombard. **4. a.** To defeat decisively. **b.** *Baseball.* To hit the pitches of (a pitcher) hard and with regularity: *shelled the pitcher for eight runs in the first inning.* *—intr.* **1.** To shed or become free of a shell. **2.** To look for or collect shells, as on a seashore. **—*phrasal verb.* shell out.** *Informal.* To hand over; pay: *had to shell out $500 in car repairs.* [Middle English, from Old English *scell.* See **skel-**[1] in Appendix.] **—shell** *adj.* **—shell′er** *n.*

she'll (shēl). **1.** She will. **2.** She shall.

shel•lac also **shel•lack** (shə-lăk′) *n.* **1.** A purified lac in the form of thin yellow or orange flakes, often bleached white and widely used in varnishes, paints, inks, sealants, and formerly in phonograph records. **2.** A thin varnish made by dissolving this substance in denatured alcohol, used to finish wood. **3.** An old phonograph record containing this substance, typically played at 78 rpm. **—shellac** *tr.v.* **-lacked, -lack•ing, -lacs. 1.** To coat or finish with shellac. **2.** *Slang.* **a.** To strike repeatedly and severely; batter. **b.** To defeat decisively. [SHEL(L) + LAC (translation of French *laque en écailles,* lac in thin plates).]

shell•back (shĕl′băk′) *n.* *Nautical.* **1.** A sailor who has crossed the equator. **2.** A veteran sailor.

shell•bark (shĕl′bärk′) *n.* **1.** See **shagbark. 2.** An eastern North American hickory *(Carya laciniosa)* having shaggy bark, pinnately compound leaves, and large, compressed, globose, reddish or yellow nuts.

shell bean *n.* Any of various beans cultivated for their edible seeds rather than their pods.

Shel•ley (shĕl′ē), **Mary Godwin Wollstonecraft.** 1797–1851. British writer best known for the Gothic novel *Frankenstein, or the Modern Prometheus* (1818). She married Percy Bysshe Shelley in 1816.

Shelley, Percy Bysshe. 1792–1822. British romantic poet whose works include "Ode to the West Wind" (1819), "To a Skylark" (1820), the lyric drama *Prometheus Unbound* (1820), and "Adonais" (1821), an elegy to John Keats.

shell•fire (shĕl′fīr′) *n.* The shooting or exploding of artillery shells.

shell•fish (shĕl′fĭsh′) *n., pl.* **shellfish** or **-fish•es.** An aquatic animal, such as a mollusk or crustacean, that has a shell or shell-like exoskeleton. **—shell′fish′ing** *n.*

shell•fish•er•y (shĕl′fĭsh′ə-rē) *n., pl.* **-ies. 1.** The industry or occupation of catching, processing, or selling shellfish. **2.** A fishing ground for shellfish.

shell•flow•er (shĕl′flou′ər) *n.* **1.** A tall eastern Mediterranean plant *(Molucella laevis)* having flowers with a tiny corolla and a large, green, bell-shaped calyx that enlarges considerably in the fruit. **2.** A tall tropical Asian plant *(Alpinia zerumbet)* having fragrant, showy, funnel-shaped, variously colored flowers.

shell game *n.* **1.** *Games.* A game, usually involving gambling, in which a person hides a small object underneath one of three nutshells, thimbles, or cups, then shuffles them about on a flat surface while spectators try to guess the final location of the object. Also called *thimblerig.* **2.** A fraud or deception perpetrated by shifting conspicuous things to hide something else.

shell jacket *n.* See **mess jacket.**

shell parakeet *n.* See **budgerigar.**

shell pink *n.* *Color.* A pinkish white to strong yellowish pink, including grayish and light yellowish pinks. **—shell′-pink′** (shĕl′pĭngk′) *adj.*

shell•proof (shĕl′pro͞of′) *adj.* Designed or constructed to withstand shellfire.

shell shock *n.* **1.** Any of various acute, often hysterical neuroses originating in trauma suffered under fire in modern warfare. **2.** Combat fatigue.

shell-shocked or **shell•shocked** (shĕl′shŏkt′) *adj.* **1.** Suffering from shell shock. **2.** Stunned, distressed, or exhausted from a prolonged trauma or an unexpected difficulty.

Shel•ta (shĕl′tə) *n.* A secret jargon used by Gypsies in Great Britain and Ireland, based on systematic inversion or alteration of the initial consonants of Gaelic words. [From Shelta *Sheldrū,* perhaps alteration of Irish Gaelic *béarla,* language, English, from Old Irish *bélrae,* language, from *bél,* mouth.]

shel•ter (shĕl′tər) *n.* **1. a.** Something that provides cover or protection, as from the weather. **b.** A refuge; a haven. **c.** An establishment that provides temporary housing for homeless people. **2.** The state of being covered or protected. **—shelter** *v.* **-tered, -ter·ing, -ters.** *—tr.* **1.** To provide cover or protection for. **2.** To invest (income) to protect it from taxation. *—intr.* To take cover; find refuge. [Perhaps from Middle English *sheltron,* tight battle formation, from Old English *scildtruma* : *scield,* shield; see SHIELD + *truma,* troop; see **deru-** in Appendix.] **—shel′ter·er** *n.* **—shel′ter·less** *adj.*

SYNONYMS: *shelter, cover, retreat, refuge, asylum, sanctuary.* These nouns refer to places affording protection, as from danger, or to the state of being protected. *Shelter* usually implies a covered or enclosed area that protects temporarily, as from injury or attack: *A cold frame provides shelter for the seedlings. "And the dead tree gives no shelter"* (T.S. Eliot). *Cover* suggests something, as bushes, that conceals: *The army mounted the invasion under cover of darkness. Retreat* applies chiefly to a secluded place to which one retires for meditation, peace, or privacy: *Their cabin in the woods served as a retreat from the pressures of business. Refuge* suggests a place of escape from pursuit or from difficulties that beset one: *"vagrants and criminals, who make this wild country a refuge from justice"* (Sir Walter Scott). *"The great advantage of a hotel is that it's a refuge from home life"* (George Bernard Shaw). *Asylum* adds to *refuge* the idea of legal protection against a pursuer or of immunity from arrest: *"O! receive the fugitive and prepare in time an asylum for mankind"* (Thomas Paine). *Sanctuary* denotes a sacred or inviolable place of refuge: *Some of the political refugees found sanctuary in a monastery.*

shel·ter·belt (shĕl′tər-bĕlt′) *n.* A barrier of trees and shrubs that protects against the wind and reduces erosion.

shel·tered workshop (shĕl′tərd) *n.* A workplace that provides a supportive environment where physically or mentally challenged persons can acquire job skills and vocational experience.

shelter tent *n.* A small tent usually pitched by securing together two or more pieces of waterproof material. Also called *pup tent.*

shel·tie also **shel·ty** (shĕl′tē) *n., pl.* **-ties.** *Informal.* **1.** A Shetland pony. **2.** A Shetland sheepdog. [Probably from Old Norse *Hjalti,* Shetlander, from *Hjaltland,* Shetland Islands.]

Shel·ton (shĕl′tən). A city of southwest Connecticut on the Housatonic River north-northeast of Bridgeport. Settled in 1697, it is a manufacturing center. Population, 31,314.

shelve (shĕlv) *v.* **shelved, shelv·ing, shelves.** *—tr.* **1.** To place or arrange on a shelf. **2.** To put away as though on a shelf; put aside: *"As usual, Dixon shelved this question"* (Kingsley Amis). See Synonyms at **defer**[1]. **3.** To cause to retire from service; dismiss. **4.** To furnish or outfit with shelves. *—intr.* To slope gradually; incline. [Back-formation from *shelves,* pl. of SHELF.] **—shelv′er** *n.*

shelves (shĕlvz) *n.* Plural of **shelf.**

shelv·ing (shĕl′vĭng) *n.* **1.** Shelves considered as a group. **2.** Material for shelves. **3.** An incline; a slope.

Shem (shĕm). In the Old Testament, the eldest son of Noah and the brother of Japheth and Ham.

Shen·an·do·ah Valley (shĕn′ən-dō′ə). A valley of northern Virginia between the Allegheny Mountains and the Blue Ridge. Drained by the **Shenandoah River,** about 241 km (150 mi) long, the valley was first explored in the early 1700's and was an important gateway to the frontier.

she·nan·i·gan (shə-năn′ĭ-gən) *n. Informal.* **1.a.** A deceitful trick; an underhanded act. **b.** Often **shenanigans.** Remarks intended to deceive; deceit. **2.a.** A playful or mischievous act; a prank. **b.** Often **shenanigans.** Mischief; prankishness. [Origin unknown.]

Shen·si (shĕn′sē′). See **Shaanxi.**

Shen·yang (shŭn′yäng′). Formerly **Muk·den** (mo͝ok′dən, -dĕn′, mo͝ok′-). A city of northeast China east-northeast of Beijing. The capital of Liaoning province, it was the site of the so-called Mukden, or Manchurian, Incident (1931), in which the Japanese army used an explosion on the railroad north of the city as a pretext to occupy Manchuria. Population, 3,250,000.

She·ol (shē′ōl′, shē-ōl′) *n. Bible.* The underworld of the Old Testament, where the dead dwelt in darkness. [Hebrew *šə'ôl.*]

Shep·ard (shĕp′ərd), **Alan Bartlett, Jr.** Born 1923. American astronaut who on a 15-minute flight on May 5, 1961, became the first American in space. He also commanded the Apollo 14 mission to the moon (1971).

shep·herd (shĕp′ərd) *n.* **1.** One who herds, guards, and tends sheep. **2.** One who cares for and guides a group of people, as a minister or teacher. **—shepherd** *tr.v.* **-herd·ed, -herd·ing, -herds.** To herd, guard, tend, or guide as or in the manner of a shepherd. See Synonyms at **guide.** [Middle English *shepherde,* from Old English *scēaphierde* : *scēap,* sheep + *hierde,* herdsman.]

shepherd dog *n.* See **sheepdog.**

shep·herd·ess (shĕp′ər-dĭs) *n.* A girl or woman who herds, guards, and tends sheep.

shep·herd's pie (shĕp′ərdz) *n.* A meat pie baked in a crust of mashed potatoes.

shepherd's purse *n.* A common Eurasian weed *(Capsella bursa-pastoris)* having small white flowers and flat, heart-shaped or triangular fruit. [From its pouchlike pods.]

Sher·a·ton (shĕr′ə-tn) *adj.* Of or relating to a style of English furniture that originated about 1800, characterized by simple designs, straight lines, thin legs, and classical ornamentation. [After Thomas SHERATON.]

Sheraton, Thomas. 1751–1806. British furniture designer known for his graceful neoclassical designs and his published manuals, including *The Cabinet-Maker and Upholsterer's Drawing Book* (1791–1794).

sher·bet (shûr′bĭt) *n.* **1.** Also **sher·bert** (-bûrt′). A frozen dessert made primarily of fruit juice, sugar, and water, and also containing milk, egg white, or gelatin. **2.** *Chiefly British.* A beverage made of sweetened diluted fruit juice. **3.** Also **sherbert.** *Australian.* An alcoholic beverage, especially beer. [Ottoman Turkish, sweet fruit drink, from Persian *sharbat,* from Arabic *šarbah,* drink, from *šariba,* to drink.]

WORD HISTORY: The word *sherbet* has been in the English language for several centuries (first recorded in 1603) but not as a name for what one normally thinks of as sherbet. The word came into English from Ottoman Turkish *sherbet* or Persian *sharbat,* both going back to Arabic *šarbah,* "drink." The Turkish and Persian words referred to a beverage of sweetened, diluted fruit juice that was popular in the Middle East and imitated in Europe. Eventually in Europe *sherbet* came to refer to a carbonated drink. Because the original Middle Eastern drink contained fruit and was often cooled with snow, *sherbet* was applied to the frozen dessert (first recorded in 1891). It is thus distinguished slightly from *sorbet,* which can also mean "a fruit-flavored ice served between courses of a meal." *Sorbet* (first recorded in English in 1585) goes back through French (*sorbet*) and then Italian (*sorbetto*) to the same Turkish *sherbet* that gave us *sherbet.*

Sher·brooke (shûr′bro͝ok′). A city of southern Quebec, Canada, on the St. François River east of Montreal. It is a trade and manufacturing center. Population, 74,075.

sherd (shûrd) *n.* Variant of **shard.**

Sher·i·dan (shĕr′ĭ-dn), **Philip Henry.** 1831–1888. American Union general who was active in the Chattanooga (1863) and Wilderness (1864) campaigns and routed Confederate forces at the Battle of Five Forks (1865).

Sheridan, Richard Brinsley. 1751–1816. British playwright and politician known for his satirical comedies of manners, including *The Rivals* (1775), which features the catachrestic character Mrs. Malaprop.

she·rif also **sha·rif** (shə-rēf′) *n.* **1.** A descendant of the prophet Mohammed through his daughter Fatima. **2.** The chief magistrate of Mecca in Ottoman times. **3.** A Moroccan prince or ruler. [Arabic *šarīf,* noble, from *šarafa,* to be highborn.]

sher·iff (shĕr′ĭf) *n.* **1.** The chief law enforcement officer for the courts in a U.S. county. **2.** An officer of a county or an administrative region in England, Northern Ireland, and Scotland, charged mainly with judicial duties. [Middle English, the representative of royal authority in a shire, from Old English *scīrgerēfa* : *scīr,* shire + *gerēfa,* reeve.]

Sher·man (shûr′mən). A city of northeast Texas near the Oklahoma border north of Dallas. Settled as a way station on a stagecoach route, it is now a highway and rail junction with varied industries. Population, 30,413.

Sherman, James Schoolcraft. 1855–1912. Vice President of the United States (1909–1912) under William Howard Taft. He died in office.

Sherman, John. 1823–1900. American politician. A U.S. senator from Ohio (1861–1877 and 1881–1897), he wrote and sponsored the Sherman Antitrust Act (1890).

Sherman, Mount. A peak, 4,281 m (14,036 ft) high, in the Park Range of the Rocky Mountains in central Colorado.

Sherman, Roger. 1721–1793. American Revolutionary patriot and politician who was a signer of the Declaration of Independence (1776), the Articles of Confederation (1781), and the U.S. Constitution (1787).

Sherman, William Tecumseh. 1820–1891. American Union general. Appointed commander of all Union troops in the West (1864), he captured Atlanta (1864) and led a destructive March to the Sea, which effectively cut the Confederacy in two.

she·root (shə-ro͞ot′) *n.* Variant of **cheroot.**

Sher·pa (shûr′pə) *n., pl.* **Sherpa** or **-pas.** A member of a people of Tibetan descent living on the southern side of the Himalaya Mountains in Nepal and Sikkim, noted for their ability at mountaineering.

sher·ry (shĕr′ē) *n., pl.* **-ries.** **1.** A fortified Spanish wine ranging from very dry to sweet and from amber to brown. **2.** A similar wine made elsewhere. [Alteration of *sherris* (taken as pl.), after *Xeres* (Jerez), Spain.]

's Her·to·gen·bosch (sĕr′tō-gən-bôs′, -KHən-). A city of south-central Netherlands north-northwest of Eindhoven. Chartered c. 1185, it was a fortress city until 1874. Population, 89,059.

Sher·wood (shûr′wo͝od′), **Robert Emmet.** 1896–1955. American playwright whose works include *Idiot's Delight* (1936), *Abe Lincoln in Illinois* (1938), and *There Shall Be No Night* (1940), each of which won a Pulitzer Prize.

Sherwood Forest. A former royal forest of central England famed as the site of the legendary exploits of Robin Hood and his followers.

Alan Shepard

Sheraton

William Tecumseh Sherman

ă pat	oi boy
ā pay	ou out
âr care	o͝o took
ä father	o͞o boot
ĕ pet	ŭ cut
ē be	ûr urge
ĭ pit	th thin
ī pie	*th* this
îr pier	hw which
ŏ pot	zh vision
ō toe	ə about, item
ô paw	♦ regionalism

Stress marks: **′** (primary); ′ (secondary), as in **dictionary** (dĭk′shə-nĕr′ē)

Shetland pony

Shetland sheepdog

shield
Detail from a c. 515 B.C. Greek krater

shillelagh

Sherwood Park. A city of central Alberta, Canada, a suburb of Edmonton. Population, 29,285.

Shet·land (shĕt′lənd) *n.* **1.** A fine yarn made from the wool of sheep raised in the Shetland Islands and used for knitting and weaving. **2.** A garment, especially a sweater, made of this yarn. [After the SHETLAND (ISLANDS).]

Shetland Islands. An archipelago of northern Scotland in the Atlantic Ocean northeast of the Orkney Islands. The islands were occupied by Norse invaders and colonists after the late ninth century and were annexed by Scotland in 1472.

Shetland pony *n.* A small, compactly built pony of a breed originating in the Shetland Islands, having a long thick mane and tail.

Shetland sheepdog *n.* A herding dog of a breed developed in the Shetland Islands, having a rough coat and resembling a small collie.

She·vat (shə-vät′, shvät) also **She·bat** (shə-bät′, -vät′) *n.* The fifth month of the year in the Jewish calendar. See table at **calendar.** [Hebrew *šĕbāṭ*.]

Shev·chen·ko (shĕf-chĕng′kō), **Taras Grigoryevich.** 1814–1861. Ukrainian poet who is considered the father of modern Ukrainian literature.

shew (shō) *v. Archaic.* Variant of **show.**

shew·bread (shō′brĕd′) *n. Archaic.* Variant of **showbread.**

Shey·enne (shī-ĕn′, -ăn′). A river, about 523 km (325 mi) long, rising in central North Dakota and flowing east, south, and northeast to the Red River of the North above Fargo.

shf or **SHF** *abbr.* Superhigh frequency.

Shi·ah or **Shi·a** also **Shi·'ah** or **Shi·'a** (shē′ə) *Islam.* —*n.* **1.** *(used with a pl. verb).* The Shiites. **2.** *(used with a sing. verb).* A Shiite. —*adj.* Shiite. [Arabic *šī'ah*, following, sect, from Syriac *sī'ā*, company, band.]

shi·at·su (shē-ät′so͞o) *n.* A form of therapeutic massage in which pressure is applied with the thumbs and palms to those areas of the body used in acupuncture. Also called *acupressure.* [Short for Japanese *shiatsuryōhō* : *shi*, finger + *atsu-*, pressure + *ryōhō*, treatment.]

shib·ah (shĭv′ə) *n. Judaism.* Variant of **shiva.**

shib·bo·leth (shĭb′ə-lĭth, -lĕth′) *n.* **1.** A word or pronunciation that distinguishes people of one group or class from those of another. **2.a.** A word or phrase identified with a particular group or cause; a catchword. **b.** A commonplace saying or idea. **3.** A custom or practice that betrays one as an outsider. [Ultimately from Hebrew *šibbōlet*, torrent of water, from the use of this word to distinguish one tribe from another, who pronounced it *sibbōleth* (Judges 12:4–6).]

shied[1] (shīd) *v.* Past tense and past participle of **shy**[1].

shied[2] (shīd) *v.* Past tense and past participle of **shy**[2].

shield (shēld) *n.* **1.** A broad piece of armor made of rigid material and strapped to the arm or carried in the hand for protection against hurled or thrusted weapons. **2.** A person or thing that provides protection. **3.** A protective device or structure, as: **a.** A steel sheet attached to an artillery piece to protect gunners from small-arms fire and shrapnel. **b.** *Physics.* A wall or housing of concrete or lead built around a nuclear reactor to prevent the escape of radiation. **c.** *Electronics.* A structure or arrangement of metal plates or mesh designed to protect a piece of electronic equipment from electrostatic or magnetic interference. **d.** A pad worn, as at the armpits, to protect a garment from perspiration. **4.** *Zoology.* A protective plate or similar hard outer covering; a scute or scutellum. **5.** Something that resembles a shield, as: **a.** An escutcheon. **b.** A decorative emblem that often serves to identify an organization or a government. **c.** A police officer's badge. **6.** *Geology.* A large lowland area, the geologic nucleus of a continent, whose bedrock consists of igneous and metamorphic rocks that are usually Precambrian in age: *the Canadian Shield.* —**shield** *v.* **shield·ed, shield·ing, shields.** —*tr.* **1.** To protect or defend with or as if with a shield; guard. See Synonyms at **defend. 2.** To cover up; conceal. —*intr.* To act or serve as a shield or safeguard. [Middle English *sheld*, from Old English *scield.* See **skel-**[1] in Appendix.] —**shield′er** *n.*

shield law *n.* A law that protects journalists from being compelled to reveal confidential sources of information.

Shield of David (shēld) *n.* See **Magen David.**

shiel·ing (shē′lĭng, -lĭn) *n. Chiefly British.* **1.** A shepherd's hut. **2.** A mountain pasture used in the summer. [From Scots *shiel*, hut, from Middle English *shele*, possibly from Old English **scēla*, probably of Scandinavian origin. See **(s)keu-** in Appendix.]

shi·er (shī′ər) *adj.* A comparative of **shy**[1].

shies[1] (shīz) *v.* Third person singular present tense of **shy**[1]. —**shies** *n.* Plural of **shy**[1].

shies[2] (shīz) *v.* Third person singular present tense of **shy**[2]. —**shies** *n.* Plural of **shy**[2].

shi·est (shī′ĭst) *adj.* A superlative of **shy**[1].

shift (shĭft) *v.* **shift·ed, shift·ing, shifts.** —*tr.* **1.** To exchange (one thing) for another of the same class: *shifted assignments among the students.* **2.** To move or transfer from one place or position to another. **3.** To alter (position or place). **4.** To change (gears), as in an automobile. **5.** *Linguistics.* To alter phonetically as part of a systematic historical change. —*intr.* **1.** To change position, direction, place, or form. **2.a.** To provide for one's own needs; get along: *"See me safe up: for my coming down, I can shift for myself"* (Thomas More). **b.** To get along by tricky or evasive means. **3.** To change gears, as when driving an automobile. **4.** *Linguistics.* To be altered as part of a systematic historical change. Used of speech sounds. **5.** To select uppercase characters by depressing a key on a typewriter or computer keyboard. —**shift** *n.* **1.** A change from one person or configuration to another; a substitution. **2.a.** A group of workers that relieve another on a regular schedule. **b.** The working period of such a group: *worked the night shift.* **3.a.** A means to an end; an expedient. **b.** A stratagem; a trick. **4.** A change in direction: *a shift in the wind.* **5.** A change in attitude, judgment, or emphasis. **6.** A change in position, as: **a.** *Music.* A change of the position of the hand in playing the violin or a similar instrument. **b.** *Football.* A rearrangement of players from one formation to another just prior to the snap of the ball. **c.** *Baseball.* A rearrangement of one or more fielders for improved defense against a particular hitter. **d.** *Geology.* See **fault** (sense 3). **e.** *Computer Science.* Movement of characters in a register to the left or right. **7.** *Physics.* A change in wavelength, causing a movement of a spectral band or line. **8.** *Linguistics.* **a.** A systematic change of the phonetic or phonemic structure of a language. **b.** Functional shift. **9.a.** A loosely fitting dress that hangs straight from the shoulder; a chemise. **b.** A woman's undergarment; a slip or chemise. [Middle English *shiften*, from Old English *sciftan*, to arrange, divide.] —**shift′er** *n.*

shift key *n.* A key on a typewriter or computer keyboard that, when depressed, changes letters from lowercase to uppercase.

shift·less (shĭft′lĭs) *adj.* **1.a.** Lacking ambition or purpose; lazy: *a shiftless student.* **b.** Characterized by a lack of ambition or energy: *studied in a shiftless way.* **2.** Lacking resourcefulness or efficiency; incompetent. [SHIFT, expedient + -LESS.] —**shift′less·ly** *adv.* —**shift′less·ness** *n.*

shift·y (shĭf′tē) *adj.* **-i·er, -i·est. 1.** Having, displaying, or suggestive of deceitful character; evasive or untrustworthy. **2.** Distinguished by frequent changes in direction: *shifty winds.* **3.** Able to accomplish what is needed; resourceful. —**shift′i·ly** *adv.* —**shift′i·ness** *n.*

shi·gel·la (shĭ-gĕl′ə) *n., pl.* **-gel·lae** (-gĕl′ē) also **-gel·las.** Any of various nonmotile, rod-shaped bacteria of the genus *Shigella,* which includes some species that cause dysentery. [New Latin *Shigella*, genus name, after Kiyoshi *Shiga* (1870–1957), Japanese bacteriologist.]

shig·el·lo·sis (shĭg′ə-lō′sĭs) *n., pl.* **-ses** (-sēz). Dysentery caused by any of various species of shigellae, occurring most frequently in areas where poor sanitation and malnutrition are prevalent and commonly affecting children and infants.

Shih·kia·chwang (shœ′kyä′chwäng′). See **Shijiazhuang.**

Shih Tzu (shē′ dzo͞o′) *n.* A small dog of a breed originally developed in Tibet, having a long thick coat, short legs, a broad head with a short square muzzle, and a tail that curls over the back. [Chinese (Mandarin) *shī zi (gǒu)*, lion (dog), Shih Tzu.]

Shi·ism also **Shi·'ism** (shē′ĭz′əm) *n. Islam.* The religion or doctrines of the Shiites.

shi·i·ta·ke (shē-tä′kē, shē′ē-tä′kĕ) *n., pl.* **shiitake.** An edible eastern Asian mushroom *(Lentinus edodes)* having an aromatic, fleshy, golden or dark brown to blackish cap and an inedible, tough stipe. Also called *Chinese black mushroom, golden oak mushroom, Oriental black mushroom.* [Japanese : *shi*, oak + *take*, mushroom.]

Shi·ite also **Shi·'ite** (shē′īt′) *Islam.* —*n.* A member of the branch of Islam that regards Ali and his descendants as the legitimate successors to Mohammed and rejects the first three caliphs. —*adj.* Of or relating to the Shiites or their branch of Islam. —**Shi·it′ic** (-ĭt′ĭk) *adj.*

Shi·jia·zhuang (shœ′jyä′jwäng′) also **Shih·kia·chwang** (-kyä′chwäng′). A city of northeast China southwest of Beijing. An industrial center, it is the capital of Hebei province. Population, 1,127,800.

shi·ka·ri (shĭ-kär′ē, -kăr′ē) *n., pl.* **-ris. 1.** A big-game hunter. **2.** A guide for big-game hunting. [Hindi *shikārī*, from Persian, from *shikār*, hunting, from Middle Persian *shkār*.]

Shi·ko·ku (shē-kô′ko͞o, shē′kô-ko͞o′). An island of southern Japan between southwest Honshu and eastern Kyushu. It was held by various feudal families from early times until c. 1600.

shik·sa also **shik·se** (shĭk′sə) *n. Offensive.* Used as a disparaging term for a non-Jewish girl or woman. [Yiddish *shikse*.]

shill (shĭl) *Slang. n.* One who poses as a satisfied customer or an enthusiastic gambler to dupe bystanders into participating in a swindle. —**shill** *v.* **shilled, shill·ing, shills.** —*intr.* To act as a shill. —*tr.* **1.** To act as a shill for (a deceitful enterprise). **2.** To lure (a person) into a swindle. [Perhaps short for *shillaber*.]

shil·le·lagh also **shil·la·lah** (shə-lā′lē, -lə) *n.* A cudgel of oak, blackthorn, or other hardwood. [After *Shillelagh*, a village of east-central Ireland.]

shil·ling (shĭl′ĭng) *n.* **1.** *Abbr.* **s.** A coin used in the United Kingdom, worth one twentieth of a pound, 5 new pence, or 12 old pence prior to 1971. **2.** See table at **currency. 3.** *Printing.* A virgule. [Middle English, from Old English *scilling*.]

Shil·luk (shĭ-lo͝ok′) *n., pl.* **Shilluk** or **-luks. 1.** A member of a people inhabiting the western bank of the Nile River in southern Sudan. **2.** The Nilotic language of the Shilluk.

shil·ly-shal·ly (shĭl′ē-shăl′ē) *intr.v.* **-lied** (-lēd), **-ly·ing, -lies** (-lēz). **1.** To procrastinate. **2.** To be unable to come to a decision; vacillate. **3.** To spend time on insignificant things; dawdle. **—shilly-shally** *adj.* Hesitant; vacillating. **—shilly-shally** *n., pl.* **-lies.** Procrastination; hesitation. **—shilly-shally** *adv.* In a hesitant manner; irresolutely. [Reduplication of the question *shall I?*] **—shil′ly-shal′li·er** *n.*

Shi·loh (shī′lō). **1.** An ancient village of central Palestine northwest of the Dead Sea. In the Old Testament, it was a meeting place and sanctuary for the Israelites and the site of a tabernacle where the Ark of the Covenant was kept until its capture by the Philistines. **2.** A locality in southwest Tennessee east of Memphis. The Civil War Battle of Shiloh (April 6–7, 1862) ended in the withdrawal of Confederate troops but claimed more than 10,000 casualties on both the Union and Confederate sides.

shim (shĭm) *n.* A thin, often tapered piece of material, such as wood, stone, or metal, used to fill gaps, make something level, or adjust something to fit properly. **—shim** *tr.v.* **shimmed, shim·ming, shims.** To fill in, level, or adjust by using shims or a shim. [Origin unknown.]

shim·mer (shĭm′ər) *intr.v.* **-mered, -mer·ing, -mers. 1.** To shine with a subdued, flickering light. See Synonyms at **flash. 2.** To appear as a wavering or flickering image, as in a reflection on water or through heat waves in air. **—shimmer** *n.* A flickering or tremulous light. [Middle English *shimeren,* from Old English *scimerian.*] **—shim′mer·ing·ly** *adv.* **—shim′mer·y** *adj.*

shim·my (shĭm′ē) *n., pl.* **-mies. 1.** Abnormal vibration or wobbling, as of the wheels of an automobile. **2.** A dance popular in the 1920's, characterized by rapid shaking of the body. **3.** A chemise. **—shimmy** *intr.v.* **-mied, -my·ing, -mies. 1.** To vibrate or wobble abnormally. **2.** To shake the body in or as if in dancing the shimmy. [Perhaps from alteration of CHEMISE.]

Shi·mo·no·se·ki (shĭm′ə-nō-sĕk′ē, shē′mô-nô-). A city of extreme southwest Honshu, Japan, on Korea Strait. The treaty ending the Sino-Japanese War was signed here on April 17, 1895. Population, 269,167.

shin[1] (shĭn) *n.* **1.a.** The front part of the leg below the knee and above the ankle. **b.** The shinbone. **2.** The lower foreleg in beef cattle. Used of cuts of meat. **—shin** *v.* **shinned, shin·ning, shins.** —*tr.* **1.** To climb (a rope or pole, for example) by gripping and pulling alternately with the hands and legs. **2.** To kick or hit in the shins. —*intr.* **1.** To climb something by shinning it. **2.** To move quickly on foot. [Middle English *shine,* from Old English *scinu.* See **skei-** in Appendix.]

shin[2] (shĕn, shĭn) *n.* The 22nd letter of the Hebrew alphabet. See table at **alphabet.** [Hebrew *šin,* variant of *šen,* tooth (from the shape of the letter).]

Shi·nar (shī′nər, -när′). An ancient country on the lower courses of the Tigris and Euphrates rivers.

shin·bone (shĭn′bōn′) *n.* See **tibia** (sense 1).

shin·dig (shĭn′dĭg′) *n.* **1.** A festive party, often with dancing. Also called *shindy.* **2.** See **shindy** (sense 1). [Probably alteration of SHINDY.]

shin·dy (shĭn′dē) *n., pl.* **-dies. 1.** A commotion; an uproar. Also called *shindig.* **2.** See **shindig** (sense 1). [Perhaps alteration of SHINNY[1].]

shine (shīn) *v.* **shone** (shōn) or **shined, shin·ing, shines.** —*intr.* **1.** To emit light. **2.** To reflect light; glint or glisten. **3.** To distinguish oneself in an activity or a field; excel. **4.** To be immediately apparent: *Delight shone in her eyes.* —*tr.* **1.** To aim or cast the beam or glow of (a light). **2.** *past tense and past participle* **shined.** To make glossy or bright by polishing. **—shine** *n.* **1.** Brightness from a source of light; radiance. **2.** Brightness from reflected light; luster. **3.** A shoeshine. **4.** Excellence in quality or appearance; splendor. **5.** Fair weather: *rain or shine.* **6. shines.** *Informal.* Pranks or tricks. **7.** *Slang.* Whiskey; moonshine. **8.** *Offensive Slang.* Used as a disparaging term for a Black person. ***—idiom.*** **take a shine to.** *Informal.* To like spontaneously. [Middle English *shinen,* from Old English *scīnan.*]

shin·er (shī′nər) *n.* **1.** One that shines, as a star, jewel, or coin. **2.** *Slang.* A black eye: *got a real shiner from stumbling into the door.* **3.a.** Any of numerous small, often silvery North American freshwater fishes of the family Cyprinidae, especially one of the genus *Notropis.* **b.** Any of various other small silvery fishes.

shin·gle[1] (shĭng′gəl) *n.* **1.** A thin oblong piece of material, such as wood or slate, that is laid in overlapping rows to cover the roof or sides of a house or other building. **2.** *Informal.* A small signboard, as one indicating a professional office: *She has to take the bar exam before she can hang out her shingle.* **3.** A woman's close-cropped haircut. **—shingle** *tr.v.* **-gled, -gling, -gles. 1.** To cover (a roof or building) with shingles. **2.** To cut (hair) short and close to the head. [Middle English, from Old English *scindel, scingal,* from Late Latin *scindula,* alteration of Latin *scandula* (influenced by *scindere,* to split).] **—shin′gler** *n.*

shin·gle[2] (shĭng′gəl) *n.* **1.** Beach gravel consisting of large smooth pebbles unmixed with finer material. **2.** A stretch of shore or beach covered with such gravel. [Middle English.] **—shin′gly** *adj.*

shin·gles (shĭng′gəlz) *pl.n.* *(used with a sing. or pl. verb).* An acute viral infection characterized by inflammation of the sensory ganglia of certain spinal or cranial nerves and the eruption of vesicles along the affected nerve path. It usually strikes only one side of the body and is often accompanied by severe neuralgia. Also called *herpes zoster.* [Middle English, alteration (influenced by Old French *cengles,* pl. of *cengle,* shingles, from Medieval Latin *cingulus,* and by Old French *sengle, single, chingle,* belt, from Latin *cingulum*) of Medieval Latin *cingulus* (translation of Greek *zōstēr,* girdle, shingles), variant of Latin *cingulum,* girdle (from the fact that the inflammation often extends around the middle of the body), from *cingere,* to gird. See **kenk-** in Appendix.]

shin·leaf (shĭn′lēf′) *n.* Any of various Eurasian and North American woodland perennial herbs of the genera *Moneses* and *Pyrola,* especially *P. elliptica,* having a basal cluster of elliptic to oblong leaves and white to pink flowers. [Probably from the use of its leaves in plasters for sore legs.]

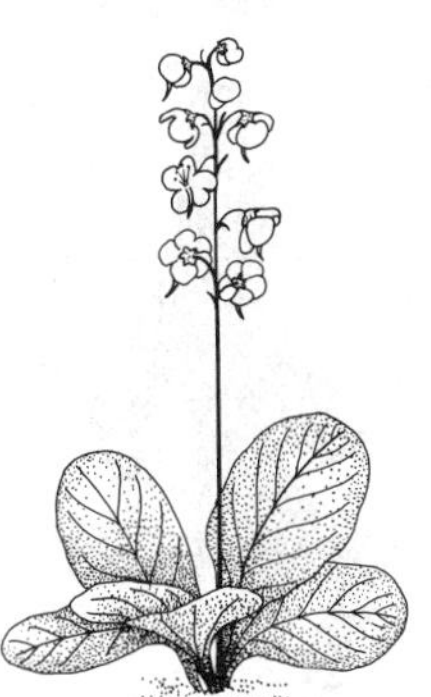

shinleaf
Pyrola elliptica

shin·ny[1] also **shin·ney** (shĭn′ē) *n., pl.* **-nies** also **-neys.** *Sports.* **1.** Field hockey that is played informally with curved sticks and a ball, can, or similar object. **2.** The curved stick used in this game. [Probably from the phrase *shin ye,* a cry used in the game.]

shin·ny[2] (shĭn′ē) *intr.v.* **-nied** (-nēd), **-ny·ing, -nies** (-nēz). To climb by shinning. [Alteration of SHIN[1].]

shin·plas·ter (shĭn′plăs′tər) *n.* **1.** A piece of paper money issued privately and devalued by inadequate security or by inflation. **2.** A piece of paper money of small denomination issued by the government, especially one issued by the U.S. government from 1862 to 1878. [From its resemblance to paper used in plasters for sore legs.]

shin splints also **shin·splints** (shĭn′splĭnts′) *pl.n.* *(used with a sing. or pl. verb).* Any of various painful conditions of the shins caused by inflammation of the surrounding muscles, frequently occurring among joggers and runners.

Shin·to (shĭn′tō) *n.* A religion native to Japan, characterized by veneration of nature spirits and ancestors and by a lack of formal dogma. [Japanese *shintō* : *shin,* gods (from Chinese *shén*) + *dō,* the Way of Taoism (from Chinese *dào*).] **—Shin′to** *adj.* **—Shin′to·ism** *n.* **—Shin′to·ist** *adj. & n.* **—Shin′to·is′tic** *adj.*

shin·y (shī′nē) *adj.* **-i·er, -i·est. 1.** Radiating light; bright. **2.** Bright from reflected light; glistening. **3.** Having a sheen from being rubbed or worn smooth. **—shin′i·ness** *n.*

ship (shĭp) *n.* **1.** *Nautical.* **a.** A vessel of considerable size for deep-water navigation. **b.** A sailing vessel having three or more square-rigged masts. **2.** An aircraft or a spacecraft. **3.** The crew of one of these vessels. **4.** One's fortune: *When my ship comes in, I'll move to a better apartment.* **—ship** *v.* **shipped, ship·ping, ships.** —*tr.* **1.** *Nautical.* To place or receive on board a ship. **2.** To cause to be transported by or as if by ship; send. See Synonyms at **send**[1]. **3.** To hire (a person) for work on a ship. **4.** *Nautical.* To take in (water) over the side of a ship. —*intr.* *Nautical.* **1.** To go aboard a ship; embark. **2.** To travel by ship. **3.** To hire oneself out or enlist for service on a ship. ***—phrasal verb.*** **ship out. 1.** *Nautical.* To accept a position on board a ship and serve as a crew member: *shipped out on a tanker.* **2.** To leave, as for a distant place: *troops shipping out to the Far East.* **3.** To send, as to a distant place. **4.** *Informal.* To quit, resign from, or otherwise vacate a position: *Shape up or ship out.* ***—idiom.*** **tight ship.** A well-managed and efficient business, household, or organization: *We run a tight ship.* [Middle English, from Old English *scip.*]

-ship *suff.* **1.a.** Quality, state, or condition: *scholarship.* **b.** Something that shows or possesses a quality, state, or condition: *courtship.* **2.** Rank, status, or office: *professorship.* **3.** Art, skill, or craft: *penmanship.* **4.** A collective body: *readership.* [Middle English, from Old English *-scipe.*]

ship biscuit *n.* See **hardtack.**

ship·board (shĭp′bôrd′, -bōrd′) *n.* **1.** *Nautical.* The condition of being aboard a ship: *on shipboard.* **2.** *Archaic.* The side of a ship. **—shipboard** *adj.* *Nautical.* Existing or occurring on board a ship: *a shipboard fire.*

ship·borne (shĭp′bôrn′, -bōrn′) *adj.* *Nautical.* Transported by ship.

ship·build·ing (shĭp′bĭl′dĭng) *n.* The art or business of designing and constructing ships. **—ship′build′er** *n.*

ship canal *n.* A canal wide and deep enough to serve ships. Also called *shipway.*

ship fever *n.* See **typhus.**

ship fitter *n.* **1.** One who positions the structural pieces of a ship for riveting and welding. **2.** A sailor in the U.S. Navy who does sheet-metal work and plumbing on board a ship.

ship·lap (shĭp′lăp′) *n.* Wooden siding rabbeted so that the edge of one board overlaps the one next to it in a flush joint. **—ship′lapped′** *adj.*

ship·load (shĭp′lōd′) *n.* The amount a ship can carry.

ship·man (shĭp′mən) *n.* *Nautical.* **1.** A sailor. **2.** A shipmaster.

ship·mas·ter (shĭp′măs′tər) *n.* *Nautical.* The officer in command of a merchant ship.

ship·mate (shĭp′māt′) *n.* *Nautical.* A sailor serving on the same ship as another; a fellow sailor.

ship·ment (shĭp′mənt) *n.* *Abbr.* **shpt. 1.** The act or an instance of shipping goods. **2.** A quantity of goods or cargo that are shipped together.

ship money *n.* A tax once levied on English maritime towns and shires to provide ships for war.

ship of the line *n., pl.* **ships of the line.** *Nautical.* A warship large enough to take a position in the line of battle.

ship·per (shĭp′ər) *n.* One that consigns or receives goods for transportation.

ship·ping (shĭp′ĭng) *n.* **1.** The act or business of transporting

ă **p**a**t**	oi **boy**
ā **pay**	ou **out**
âr **care**	o͝o **took**
ä **father**	o͞o **boot**
ĕ **pet**	ŭ **cut**
ē **be**	ûr **urge**
ĭ **pit**	th **thin**
ī **pie**	*th* **this**
îr **pier**	hw **which**
ŏ **pot**	zh **vision**
ō **toe**	ə **about, item**
ô **paw**	♦ **regionalism**

Stress marks: ′ (primary); ′ (secondary), as in **dictionary** (dĭk′shə-nĕr′ē)

Shiva
11th- to 12th-century Indian bronze

goods. **2.** The body of ships belonging to one port, industry, or country, often referred to in aggregate tonnage. **3.** Passage or transport on a ship.

shipping clerk *n.* One who is employed to prepare, pack, receive, or record shipments of goods.

shipping fever *n.* Any of various diseases contracted by cattle or other animals during shipping or similarly stressful events, especially one caused by bacteria of the genus *Pasteurella,* characterized by fever and coughing.

ship-rigged (shĭp′rĭgd′) *adj. Nautical.* Rigged with three or more masts and square sails.

ship·shape (shĭp′shāp′) *adj.* Marked by meticulous order and neatness; tidy. See Synonyms at **neat**[1]. [Short for obsolete *shipshapen,* arranged as a ship should be : SHIP + *shapen,* past participle of SHAPE.] **—ship′shape′** *adv.*

ship·side (shĭp′sīd′) *n. Nautical.* The area of a dock adjacent to a ship.

ship's papers (shĭps) *pl.n. Nautical.* The documents, such as the ship's license, logbook, or bills of lading, that a ship must carry under international law and that must be shown on inspection.

ship·way (shĭp′wā′) *n.* **1.** The structure supporting a ship during construction or in dry dock. **2.** See **ship canal.**

ship·worm (shĭp′wûrm′) *n.* Any of various wormlike marine mollusks of the genera *Teredo* and *Bankia,* having rudimentary bivalve shells with which they bore into wood, especially the submerged timbers of ships, often doing extensive damage.

ship·wreck (shĭp′rĕk′) *n.* **1.** *Nautical.* **a.** The destruction of a ship, as by storm or collision. **b.** The remains of a wrecked ship. **2.** A complete failure or ruin. **—shipwreck** *tr.v.* **-wrecked, -wreck·ing, -wrecks. 1.** *Nautical.* **a.** To cause (a ship) to be destroyed, as by storm or collision. **b.** To cause (a passenger or sailor on a ship) to suffer shipwreck. **2.** To ruin utterly.

ship·wright (shĭp′rīt′) *n.* One that builds or repairs ships.

ship·yard (shĭp′yärd′) *n.* A yard where ships are built or repaired.

Shi·ras (shī′rəs), **George.** 1832–1924. American jurist who served as an associate justice of the U.S. Supreme Court (1892–1903).

Shi·raz (shē-räz′). A city of southwest-central Iran south-southeast of Tehran. It has long been an important commercial center noted for its carpets and metalworks. The ruins of ancient Persepolis are nearby. Population, 800,000.

shire (shīr) *n.* **1.** A former administrative division of Great Britain, equivalent to a county. **2.** Often **Shire.** A Shire horse. [Middle English, from Old English *scīr,* official charge, administrative district.]

Shire horse *n.* A large, powerful draft horse of a breed originating in central England, having long hair that grows from the knee and hock.

Shir·er (shīr′ər), **William Lawrence.** Born 1904. American journalist and historian known for his vivid radio broadcasts from Berlin at the outset of World War II and for the popular history *The Rise and Fall of the Third Reich* (1960).

shire town *n. Chiefly British.* See **county town.**

shirk (shûrk) *v.* **shirked, shirk·ing, shirks.** *—tr.* To avoid or neglect (a duty or responsibility). *—intr.* To avoid work or duty. [Perhaps from German *Schurke,* scoundrel; akin to Old High German *fiurscurgo,* demon : *fiur,* fire + *scurigen,* to stir up.] **—shirk′er** *n.*

Shir·ley (shûr′lē), **James.** 1596–1666. English playwright known for his comedies of manners, such as *The Lady of Pleasure* (1635).

Shirley, William. 1694–1771. British colonial administrator who was governor of Massachusetts (1741–1749 and 1753–1756) and commanded British forces in the French and Indian War.

Shirley poppy *n.* A variety of the corn poppy having scarlet, pink, or salmon flowers. [After *Shirley,* district of Croydon in southeast England.]

shirr (shûr) *tr.v.* **shirred, shirr·ing, shirrs. 1.** To gather (cloth) into decorative rows by parallel stitching. **2.** To cook (unshelled eggs) by baking until set. [Origin unknown.]

shirt (shûrt) *n.* **1.** A garment for the upper part of the body, typically having a collar, sleeves, and a front opening. **2.** An undershirt. **3.** A nightshirt. ***—idioms.*** **keep (one's) shirt on.** *Slang.* To remain calm or patient: *The plane doesn't land for another hour, so keep your shirt on.* **lose (one's) shirt.** *Slang.* To lose everything one has or owns. **the shirt off (one's) back.** *Slang.* The maximum one is able to give or lose: *The only thing those swindlers didn't take was the shirt off my back.* [Middle English *shirte,* from Old English *scyrte,* skirt. See **sker-**[1] in Appendix.]

shirt·dress also **shirt-dress** (shûrt′drĕs′) *n.* A dress tailored like a shirt with a collar and buttons down the front. Also called *shirtwaist.*

shirt·ing (shûr′tĭng) *n.* Fabric suitable for making shirts.

shirt·sleeve (shûrt′slēv′) *n.* **1.** The sleeve of a shirt. **2. shirtsleeves.** The state of wearing no coat, jacket, or other outer garment over one's shirt: *dined in shirtsleeves; balmy weather that had them down to their shirtsleeves.* **—shirtsleeve** *adj.* **1.** Also **shirt·sleeved** (-slēvd′). Dressed without a coat: *shirtsleeve spectators; a shirtsleeved orchestra.* **2.** Also **shirtsleeves.** Calling for the removal of a coat or jacket; not requiring a coat or jacket for comfort: *shirtsleeve weather; a shirtsleeves picnic.* **3.** Also **shirtsleeves.** Marked by informality or straightforwardness: *shirtsleeve politics; a shirtsleeves conference.*

shirt·tail (shûrt′tāl′) *n.* **1.** The part of a shirt that extends below the waist, especially in the back. **2.** A brief addition at the end of a newspaper article. **—shirttail** *adj.* **1.** Very young: *shirttail kids.* **2.** Of little value; inadequate or small: *a shirttail cabin in the woods.*

shirt·waist (shûrt′wāst′) *n.* **1.** A woman's blouse or bodice styled like a tailored shirt. **2.** See **shirtdress.**

shirt·y (shûr′tē) *adj.* **-i·er, -i·est.** *Chiefly British.* Ill-tempered; angry: *"He saw how shirty she was about it"* (P.G. Wodehouse). [Probably from *to get someone's shirt out,* to annoy, or *to keep one's shirt on,* to keep from being annoyed.]

shish ke·bab also **shish ke·bob** or **shish ka·bob** (shĭsh′ kə-bŏb′) *n.* A dish consisting of pieces of seasoned meat and sometimes vegetables roasted on skewers and served with condiments. [Armenian *shish kabab,* from Turkish *şiş kebabiu* : *şiş,* skewer + *kebap,* roast meat.]

shit (shĭt) *Obscene. v.* **shit** also **shat** (shăt), **shit·ting, shits.** *—intr.* To defecate. *—tr.* **1.** To defecate in. **2.** To tease or try to deceive. **—shit** *n.* **1.** Excrement. **2.** The act or an instance of defecating. **3. shits.** Diarrhea. Used with *the.* **4.a.** Something considered disgusting, of poor quality, foolish, or otherwise totally unacceptable. **b.** A person regarded as mean or contemptible. **5.** A narcotic or an intoxicant, such as marijuana or heroin. **6.** Things; items. **7.** Foolishness; nonsense. **8.** Trouble or difficulty. **—shit** *interj.* Used to express surprise, anger, or extreme displeasure. ***—phrasal verb.*** **shit on.** To treat with malice or extreme disrespect. ***—idioms.*** **get (one's) shit together.** To get organized; put one's affairs or possessions in order. **give a shit.** To care the least bit. **no shit. 1.** Used to express disbelief. **2.** Used to express scornful acknowledgement of the obvious. **up shit creek (without a paddle).** In dire circumstances with no hope of help. **when the shit hits the fan.** When the situation goes awry; when trouble starts. [Middle English *shiten,* from Old English **scītan.* See **skei-** in Appendix.]

shit·faced (shĭt′fāst′) *adj. Obscene.* Intoxicated; drunk.

shit·head (shĭt′hĕd′) *n. Obscene.* **1.** A person regarded as inept or foolish. **2.** A person regarded as objectionable or contemptible.

shit·less (shĭt′lĭs) *adj. Obscene.* Extremely frightened. [From the reflex of involuntary defecation that can result from extreme terror.]

shit·list also **shit list** (shĭt′lĭst′) *n. Obscene.* A list of persons who are strongly disapproved of.

shit·tah (shĭt′ə) *n.* A tree, probably a species of acacia, that was a source of a wood mentioned frequently in the Bible. [Hebrew *šiṭṭâ.*]

shit·tim·wood (shĭt′ĭm-wo͝od′) *n.* **1.** The wood of the shittah, used to make the ark of the Hebrew tabernacle. **2.** Either of two deciduous eastern North American trees or shrubs *(Bumelia lanuginosa* or *B. lycioides)* having very hard wood and black, fleshy fruit. [Hebrew *šiṭṭîm,* pl. of *šiṭṭâ,* shittah + WOOD[1].]

shit·ty (shĭt′ē) *adj.* **-ti·er, -ti·est.** *Obscene.* **1.** Of very poor quality; highly inferior. **2.** Contemptible; despicable. **3.** Unfortunate; unpleasant. **4.** Being in a state of discomfort or unhappiness; miserable. **5.** Incompetent; inept. **6.** Trivial.

shiv (shĭv) *n. Slang.* A knife, razor, or other sharp or pointed implement, especially one used as a weapon. [Probably Romany *chiv,* blade.]

shiv·a also **shiv·ah** or **shib·ah** (shĭv′ə) *n. Judaism.* A seven-day period of formal mourning observed after the funeral of a close relative. [Yiddish *shive,* from Hebrew *šib'â,* seven.]

Shi·va (shē′və) also **Si·va** (shē′və, sē′-) *n. Hinduism.* One of the principal Hindu deities, worshiped as the destroyer and restorer of worlds and in numerous other complementary forms. Shiva is often conceived as a member of the triad also including Brahma and Vishnu. [Sanskrit *śivaḥ,* from *śiva-,* auspicious, dear. See **kei-**[1] in Appendix.] **—Shi′va·ism, Si′va·ism** *n.* **—Shi′va·ist, Si′va·ist** *n.*

shiv·ah (shĭv′ə) *n. Judaism.* Variant of **shiva.**

♦**shiv·a·ree** (shĭv′ə-rē′, shĭv′ə-rē′) *n. Midwestern & Western U.S.* A noisy mock serenade for newlyweds. Also called *charivari,* ♦*belling,* ♦*horning,* ♦*serenade.* [Alteration of CHARIVARI.]

♦ ***REGIONAL NOTE:*** *Shivaree* is the most common American regional form of *charivari,* a French word meaning "a noisy mock serenade for newlyweds" and probably deriving in turn from a Late Latin word meaning "headache." The term, most likely borrowed from French traders and settlers along the Mississippi River, was well established in the United States by 1805; an account dating from that year describes a shivaree in New Orleans: *"The house is mobbed by thousands of the people of the town, vociferating and shouting with loud acclaim . . . many* [are] *in disguises and masks; and all have some kind of discordant and noisy music, such as old kettles, and shovels, and tongs. . . . All civil authority and rule seems laid aside"* (John F. Watson). The word *shivaree* is especially common along and west of the Mississippi River, giving it an unusual north-south dialect boundary (most dialect boundaries run east-west in the United States). Alva L. Davis and Raven I. McDavid, Jr., call *shivaree* "one of the most widely distributed folk terms borrowed by American English from any European language." Some regional equivalents are *belling,* used in Pennsylvania, West Virginia, and Ohio; *horning,* from upstate New

York, Rhode Island, and western New England; and *serenade,* a term used chiefly in the South Atlantic states.

Shive·ly (shīv′lē). A city of northern Kentucky, a residential suburb of Louisville. Population, 16,819.

shiv·er¹ (shĭv′ər) *v.* **-ered, -er·ing, -ers.** —*intr.* **1.** To shake with or as if with cold; tremble. See Synonyms at **shake. 2.** To quiver or vibrate, as by the force of the wind. —*tr. Nautical.* To cause (a sail) to flutter by sailing too close to the wind. —**shiver** *n.* **1.** An instance of shivering. **2. shivers.** An attack of shivering. Used with *the.* [Middle English *chiveren, shiveren.*]

shiv·er² (shĭv′ər) *v.* **-ered, -er·ing, -ers.** —*intr.* To break into fragments or splinters; shatter. —*tr.* To cause to break suddenly into fragments or splinters. See Synonyms at **break.** —**shiver** *n.* A fragment or splinter. [Middle English *shiveren,* from *shivere,* splinter. See **skei-** in Appendix.]

shiv·er·y¹ (shĭv′ə-rē) *adj.* **1.** Trembling, as from cold or fear. **2.** Causing shivers; chilling.

shiv·er·y² (shĭv′ə-rē) *adj.* Easily broken; brittle.

Shi·zu·o·ka (shē′zo͞o-ô′kä). A city of east-central Honshu, Japan, on Suruga Bay southwest of Yokohama. It is a port and processing center. Population, 468,362.

shkotz·im (shkôt′sĭm) *n. Offensive.* Plural of **shegetz.**

shle·miel (shlə-mēl′) *n. Slang.* Variant of **schlemiel.**

shlep (shlĕp) *v. & n. Slang.* Variant of **schlep.**

shlock (shlŏk) *n. & adj.* Variant of **schlock.**

shmear (shmîr) *n. Slang.* Variant of **schmeer.**

shmuck (shmŭk) *n. Slang.* Variant of **schmuck.**

shoal¹ (shōl) *n.* **1.** A shallow place in a body of water. **2.** A sandy elevation of the bottom of a body of water, constituting a hazard to navigation; a sandbank or sandbar. —**shoal** *v.* **shoaled, shoal·ing, shoals.** —*intr.* To become shallow: *The river shoals suddenly here from eight to two fathoms.* —*tr.* **1.** To make shallow: *The approach to the harbor was shoaled in the storm.* **2.** To come or sail into a shallower part of. —**shoal** *adj.* Having little depth; shallow. [Middle English *shold,* shallow, shallows, from Old English *sceald,* shallow.]

shoal² (shōl) *n.* **1.** A large group; a crowd. **2.** A large school of fish or other marine animals. —**shoal** *intr.v.* **shoaled, shoal·ing, shoals.** To come together in large numbers; throng. [Probably Middle Low German or Middle Dutch *schōle;* see **skel-¹** in Appendix.]

shoat also **shote** (shōt) *n.* A young pig just after weaning. [Middle English *shote,* perhaps of Middle Low German origin.]

shock¹ (shŏk) *n.* **1.a.** A violent collision or impact; a heavy blow. See Synonyms at **collision. b.** The effect of such a collision or blow. **2.a.** Something that jars the mind or emotions as if with a violent, unexpected blow. **b.** The disturbance of function, equilibrium, or mental faculties caused by such a blow; violent agitation. **3.** A severe offense to one's sense of propriety or decency; an outrage. **4.** A generally temporary state of massive physiological reaction to severe physical or emotional trauma, usually characterized by marked loss of blood pressure and depression of vital processes. **5.** The sensation and muscular spasm caused by an electric current passing through the body or a body part. **6.** A sudden economic disturbance, such as a rise in the price of a commodity. **7.** A shock absorber. —**shock** *v.* **shocked, shock·ing, shocks.** —*tr.* **1.** To strike with great surprise and emotional disturbance. **2.** To strike with disgust; offend. **3.** To induce a state of physical shock in (a person). **4.** To subject (an animal or a person) to an electric shock. —*intr.* To come into contact violently, as in battle; collide. [French *choc,* from *choquer,* to collide with, from Old French *chuquier,* perhaps of Germanic origin.]

shock² (shŏk) *n.* **1.** A number of sheaves of grain stacked upright in a field for drying. **2.** A thick, heavy mass: *a shock of white hair.* —**shock** *tr.v.* **shocked, shock·ing, shocks.** To gather (grain) into shocks. [Middle English *shok.*]

shock absorber *n.* A device used to absorb mechanical shocks, as a hydraulic or pneumatic piston used to dampen the jarring sustained in a moving motor vehicle.

shock·er (shŏk′ər) *n.* One that startles, shocks, or horrifies, as a sensational story or novel.

shock·ing (shŏk′ĭng) *adj.* **1.** Highly disturbing emotionally. **2.** Highly offensive; indecent or distasteful. **3.** Very vivid or intense in tone: *shocking pink.* —**shock′ing·ly** *adv.*

Shock·ley (shŏk′lē), **William Bradford.** 1910–1989. British-born American physicist. He shared a 1956 Nobel Prize for the development of the electronic transistor.

shock·proof (shŏk′pro͞of′) *adj.* Constructed or designed to withstand blows or jarring.

shock therapy *n.* Any of various treatments for mental disorders, such as major depression or schizophrenia, in which a convulsion or brief coma is induced by administering a drug or passing an electric current through the brain. Also called *shock treatment.*

shock troops *pl.n.* Soldiers specially chosen, trained, and armed to lead an attack. [Translation of German *Stosstruppen* : *Stoss,* shock + *Truppen,* pl. of *Truppe,* troop.]

shock wave *n.* **1.** A large-amplitude compression wave, as that produced by an explosion or by supersonic motion of a body in a medium. **2.** A violent disruption, disturbance, or reaction: *Shock waves of revolution shattered the government.*

shod (shŏd) *v.* Past tense and a past participle of **shoe.**

shod·den (shŏd′n) *v.* A past participle of **shoe.**

shod·dy (shŏd′ē) *adj.* **-di·er, -di·est. 1.** Made of or containing inferior material. **2.a.** Of poor quality or craft. **b.** Rundown; shabby. **3.** Dishonest or reprehensible: *shoddy business practices.* **4.** Conspicuously and cheaply imitative. —**shoddy** *n., pl.* **-dies. 1.a.** Woolen yarn made from scraps or used clothing, with some new wool added. **b.** Cloth made from or containing such yarn. **2.** Something of inferior quality; a cheap imitation. [Origin unknown.] —**shod′di·ly** *adv.* —**shod′di·ness** *n.*

shoe (sho͞o) *n.* **1.** A durable covering for the human foot, made of leather or similar material with a rigid sole and heel, usually extending no higher than the ankle. **2.** A horseshoe. **3.** A part or device that is located at the base of something or that functions as a protective covering, as: **a.** A strip of metal fitted onto the bottom of a sled runner. **b.** The base for the supports of the superstructure of a bridge. **c.** The ferrule on the end of a cane. **d.** The casing of a pneumatic tire. **4.** A device that retards or stops the motion of an object, as the part of a brake that presses against the wheel or drum. **5.** The sliding contact plate on an electric train or streetcar that conducts electricity from the third rail. **6.** A chute, as for conveying grain from a hopper. **7.** *Games.* A case from which playing cards are dealt one at a time. **8. shoes.** *Informal.* **a.** Position; status: *You would understand my decision if you put yourself in my shoes.* **b.** Plight: *I wouldn't want to be in her shoes.* —*attributive.* Often used to modify another noun: *shoe polish; a shoe shop.* —**shoe** *tr.v.* **shod** (shŏd), **shod** or **shod·den** (shŏd′n), **shoe·ing, shoes. 1.** To furnish or fit with a shoe or shoes. **2.** To cover with a wooden or metal guard to protect against wear. —***idioms.* the shoe is on the other foot.** *Informal.* The circumstances have been reversed; an unequal relationship has been inverted. **wait for the other shoe to drop.** *Slang.* To defer action or decision until another matter is finished or resolved. [Middle English, from Old English *scōh.*]

shoe·bill (sho͞o′bĭl′) *n.* A tall wading bird *(Balaeniceps rex)* native to swampy regions of eastern tropical Africa, having slaty plumage, long black legs, a stubby neck, and a large shoelike bill with a hook on the upper mandible.

shoe boil *n.* A growth over the elbow of a horse, caused by repeated bruising by the hoof or the rough floor when lying down and leading to lameness.

shoe·box (sho͞o′bŏks′) *n.* **1.** An oblong box, usually made of cardboard, for holding a pair of shoes. **2.** Something resembling or suggestive of such a box, as a plain, rectangular building or a cramped room or dwelling.

shoe·horn (sho͞o′hôrn′) *n.* A smooth, curved implement, often of plastic or metal, inserted at the heel to help put on a shoe. —**shoehorn** *tr.v.* **-horned, -horn·ing, -horns.** To squeeze into or as if into an insufficient space: *The usher shoehorned us into the back of the crowded theater.*

shoe·lace (sho͞o′lās′) *n.* A string or cord used for lacing and fastening shoes. Also called *shoestring.*

shoe·mak·er (sho͞o′mā′kər) *n.* One that makes or repairs shoes. —**shoe′mak′ing** *n.*

shoe·pac also **shoe·pack** (sho͞o′păk′) *n.* A heavy, warm, waterproof laced boot. [Alteration (influenced by SHOE) of pidgin Delaware *seppock,* shoe, shoes, from Unami Delaware *chípahko,* shoes.]

shoe·shine (sho͞o′shīn′) *n.* **1.** A shiny finish put on a pair of shoes by brushing and buffing with polish. **2.** The act or an instance of putting a shiny finish on shoes.

shoe·string (sho͞o′strĭng′) *n.* **1.** See **shoelace. 2.** A small sum of money; capital that is barely adequate: *a company that started on a shoestring.* —**shoestring** *adj.* **1.** Long and slender: *shoestring potatoes.* **2.** Marked by or consisting of a small amount of money: *a shoestring budget.*

shoestring catch *n. Sports.* A running catch made near the ground.

shoe·tree (sho͞o′trē′) *n.* A form made of wood, metal, or other inflexible material inserted into a shoe to stretch it or preserve its shape.

sho·far (shō′fär′, -fər) *n., pl.* **sho·fars** or **sho·froth** (shō-frōt′, -frōs′). *Judaism.* A trumpet made of a ram's horn, blown by the ancient Hebrews during religious ceremonies and as a signal in battle, now sounded in the synagogue during Rosh Hashanah and at the end of Yom Kippur. [Hebrew *šôpār,* ram's horn, shofar.]

sho·gi (shō′gē) *n. Games.* A Japanese game similar to chess that is played on a board with 81 squares, each side having 20 pieces. [Japanese *shogi,* from Chinese (Mandarin) *jiàng qí* : *jiàng,* commander in chief, chief chess piece + *qí,* board game, such as chess.]

sho·gun (shō′gən) *n.* The hereditary commander of the Japanese army who until 1867 exercised absolute rule under the nominal leadership of the emperor. [Japanese *shōgun,* general.]

sho·gun·ate (shō′gə-nĭt, -nāt′) *n.* The government, rule, or office of a shogun.

sho·ji (shō′jē) *n., pl.* **shoji** or **-jis.** A translucent screen consisting of a wooden frame covered in rice paper, used as a sliding door or partition in a Japanese house. [Japanese *shōji.*]

Sho·la·pur (shō′lə-po͝or′). A city of west-central India on the Deccan Peninsula east-southeast of Bombay. It is a trade and textile-manufacturing center. Population, 511,103.

Sho·lo·khov (shô′lə-kôf′, -KHəf), **Mikhail Aleksandrovich.**

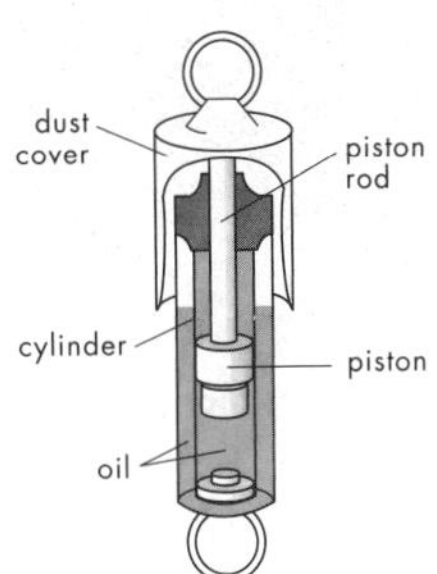

shock absorber
Hydraulic shock absorber

shoemaker

ă pat	oi boy
ā pay	ou out
âr care	o͝o took
ä father	o͞o boot
ĕ pet	ŭ cut
ē be	ûr urge
ĭ pit	th thin
ī pie	*th* this
îr pier	hw which
ŏ pot	zh vision
ō toe	ə about, item
ô paw	♦ regionalism

Stress marks: ′ (primary); ′ (secondary), as in **dictionary** (dĭk′shə-nĕr′ē)

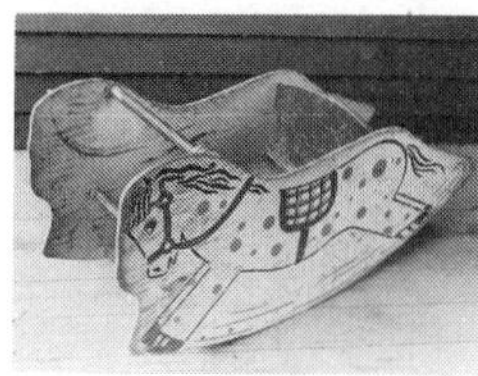

shoofly

shoot-the-chute

1905–1984. Russian writer whose four-part novel *And Quiet Flows the Don* (1928–1940) concerns the effect of World War I and the Russian Revolution on Cossack life. He won the 1965 Nobel Prize for literature.

shone (shōn) *v.* A past tense and a past participle of **shine.**

shoo (sho͞o) *interj.* Used to frighten away animals or birds. **—shoo** *tr.v.* **shooed, shoo·ing, shoos.** To drive or frighten away by or as if by crying "shoo."

shoo·fly (sho͞o′flī′) *n.* **1.** A child's rocker having the seat built between two flat sides cut in the shape of an animal. **2.** *Slang.* An undercover police officer who checks on the honesty and performance of other police officers.

shoofly pie *n.* A pie with a filling of molasses and brown sugar. [So called because one will supposedly have to shoo away the flies attracted to the sweet filling.]

shoo-fly plant (sho͞o′flī′) *n.* See **apple of Peru.**

shoo-in (sho͞o′ĭn′) *n. Informal.* **1.** A sure winner. **2.** One that has a sure chance of being chosen, as for a job or other position.

shook¹ (sho͝ok) *n.* A set of parts for assembling a barrel or packing box. [Probably from *shook cask,* variant of *shaken cask,* cask broken down for shipment, from *shaken,* dismantled and packed for transport, past participle of SHAKE, to scatter, shed.]

shook² (sho͝ok) *v.* Past tense of **shake.**

shook-up (sho͝ok-ŭp′) *adj. Slang.* Emotionally upset or excited; shaken.

shoon (sho͞on) *n. Archaic.* A plural of **shoe.**

shoot (sho͞ot) *v.* **shot** (shŏt), **shoot·ing, shoots.** *—tr.* **1.a.** To hit, wound, or kill with a missile fired from a weapon. **b.** To remove or destroy by firing or projecting a missile: *shot out the window.* **c.** To make (a hole, for example) by firing a weapon. **2.** To fire or let fly (a missile) from a weapon. **3.a.** To discharge (a weapon). **b.** To detonate or cause to explode: *shot off a firecracker.* **4.** To inject (a drug, for example) with a hypodermic syringe. **5.** To throw out or release (a fishing line, for example). **6.a.** To send forth suddenly, intensely, or swiftly: *The burning building shot sparks onto the adjacent roof. He shot an angry look at me.* **b.** To emit (a ray or rays of light or another form of energy). **c.** To utter (sounds or words) forcefully, rapidly, or suddenly: *She shot a retort to the insult.* **d.** *Slang.* To give, send, or hand quickly: *Shoot me that stapler.* **7.** *Informal.* To spend, use up, or waste: *They shot their savings on a new boat.* **8.** To pass over or through swiftly: *shooting the rapids.* **9.** To cover (country) in hunting for game. **10.** To record on film: *shot the scene in one take.* **11.** To cause to project or protrude; extend: *shot out her arm to prevent the bottle from falling.* **12.** To begin to grow or produce; put forth. **13.** To pour, empty out, or discharge down or as if down a chute: *shot gravel into the hole.* **14.** *Sports & Games.* **a.** To throw or propel (a ball, marble, or other projectile in a game) in a specific direction or toward the objective. **b.** To accomplish (the objective) of a game involving projectiles; score (a point, basket, stroke, or goal). **c.** To play (a game involving projectiles or dice, such as golf, craps, or pool). **d.** To attain (a given score) in golf. **e.** To throw (the dice or a given score) in craps. **15.** To slide (the bolt of a lock) into or out of its fastening. **16.** To plane (the edge of a board) straight. **17.** To variegate (colored cloth) by interweaving weft threads of a different color. **18.** To measure the altitude of with a sextant or other instrument: *shot the star.* *—intr.* **1.** To discharge a missile from a weapon. **2.** To discharge or fire; go off. **3.a.** To gush or spurt: *Water shot out of the geyser.* **b.** To appear suddenly: *The sun shot through a break in the clouds.* **4.** To move swiftly; dart. **5.** To be felt moving or as if moving in the body: *Pain shot through my lower leg.* **6.** To protrude; project: *The headland shoots far out into the sea.* **7.** To engage in hunting or the firing of weapons, especially for sport: *is shooting in Scotland during the fall.* **8.** To put forth new growth; germinate. **9.a.** To take pictures. **b.** To begin filming a scene in a movie. **10.** *Sports & Games.* To propel a ball or other object toward the goal or in a specific direction or manner. **11.** *Games.* To throw dice. **12.** *Slang.* To begin talking. Often used in the imperative: *I know you have something to tell me, so shoot!* **13.** To slide into or out of a fastening. Used of the bolt of a lock. **—shoot** *n.* **1.** The motion or movement of something that is propelled, driven, or discharged. **2.a.** The young growth arising from a germinating seed; a sprout. **b.** A bud, young leaf, or other new growth on a plant. **3.** A narrow, swift, or turbulent section of a stream. **4.a.** The act of discharging a weapon or letting fly a missile. **b.** *Informal.* The launching of a rocket or similar missile. **5.a.** An organized shooting activity, such as a skeet tournament or hunt. **b.** A round of shots in a contest with firearms. **6.a.** A photographic assignment or session. **b.** A cinematographic session. **7.** The distance a shot travels; the range. **8.** *Nautical.* The interval between strokes in rowing. **9.** A sharp twinge or spasm of pain. **10.** An inclined channel for moving something; a chute. **11.** A body of ore in a vein. **—shoot** *interj.* Used to express surprise, mild annoyance, or disappointment. ***—phrasal verbs.*** **shoot down. 1.** To bring down (an aircraft, for example) by hitting and damaging with gunfire or a missile. **2.** *Informal.* To ruin the aspirations of; disappoint. **3.** *Informal.* **a.** To put an end to; defeat: *shot down the proposal.* **b.** To expose as false; discredit: *shot down his theory.* **shoot for** (or **at**). *Informal.* To strive or aim for; have as a goal. **shoot up. 1.** *Informal.* To grow or get taller rapidly. **2.** To increase dramatically in amount. **3.** To riddle with bullets. **4.** To damage or terrorize (a town, for example) by intense or random gunfire. **5.** *Slang.* To inject a drug with a hypodermic syringe. ***—idioms.*** **shoot from the hip.** *Slang.* To act or speak on a matter without forethought. **shoot off (one's) mouth** (or **face**). *Slang.* **1.** To speak indiscreetly. **2.** To brag; boast. **shoot (one's) bolt.** *Slang.* To do all within one's power; exhaust all of one's resources or capabilities. **shoot straight.** To talk or deal honestly. **shoot the bull.** *Slang.* To spend time talking; talk idly. **shoot the works.** *Informal.* To expend all of one's efforts or capital. [Middle English *shoten,* from Old English *scēotan.* See **skeud-** in Appendix.] **—shoot′er** *n.*

shoot·down (sho͞ot′doun′) *n.* **1.** Destruction of a flying aircraft by a missile attack or gunfire. **2.** An instance of such destruction.

shoot-'em-up (sho͞ot′əm-ŭp′) *n. Informal.* An entertainment, such as a movie or television show, featuring gunfire and violence.

shoot·ing gallery (sho͞o′tĭng) *n.* **1.** An enclosed target range for practice or competition with firearms. **2.** *Slang.* A place where illegal drugs may be obtained, prepared, and taken by injection, often with equipment provided on the premises.

shooting iron *n. Slang.* A firearm, especially a handgun.

shooting script *n.* The final version of a movie or television script with the scenes arranged in sequence as they are to be filmed or taped.

shooting star *n.* **1.** See **meteor. 2.** Any of several North American perennial herbs of the genus *Dodecatheon,* having nodding flowers with reflexed petals.

shooting stick *n.* A stick resembling a cane, pointed at one end with a folding seat at the other, typically used by spectators at outdoor sporting events.

shoot·out also **shoot-out** (sho͞ot′out′) *n.* **1.a.** A gunfight. **b.** A battle between military forces. **c.** *Slang.* A dispute or conflict to settle a disagreement: *The marriage ended in a legal shootout.* **2.** *Sports.* **a.** A high-scoring period or game. **b.** A means of resolving a tie after overtime in a soccer game, in which five players from each side alternately take individual shots on goal.

shoot-the-chute also **chute-the-chute** (sho͞ot′*thə*-sho͞ot′) *n.* An amusement ride consisting of a steep slide often with a pool of water at the end.

shoot-up (sho͞ot′ŭp′) *n. Slang.* **1.** The act or an instance of shooting up a drug. **2.** A gunfight; a shootout.

shop (shŏp) *n.* **1.** Also **shoppe.** A small retail store or a specialty department in a large store. **2.** An atelier. **3.** A place for manufacturing or repairing goods or machinery. **4.** A commercial or industrial establishment. **5.** A business establishment; an office or a center of activity. **6.** A home workshop. **7.a.** A schoolroom fitted with machinery and tools for instruction in industrial arts. **b.** The industrial arts as a technical science or course of study. **—shop** *v.* **shopped, shop·ping, shops.** *—intr.* **1.** To visit stores in search of merchandise or bargains. **2.** To look for something with the intention of acquiring it. *—tr.* To visit or buy from (a store). ***—phrasal verb.*** **shop around. 1.** To go from store to store in search of merchandise or bargains. **2.** To look for something, such as a better job. **3.** To offer (a large block of common stock, for example) for sale to various parties: "[The company] *is now actively being shopped around, with a prospectus in circulation"* (Marianne Yen). ***—idiom.*** **talk shop.** To talk about one's work. [Middle English *shoppe,* from Old English *sceoppa,* treasure house.]

shop·keep·er (shŏp′kē′pər) *n.* One who owns or manages a shop.

shop·lift (shŏp′lĭft′) *v.* **-lift·ed, -lift·ing, -lifts.** *—intr.* To steal merchandise from a store that is open for business. *—tr.* To steal (articles or an article) from a store that is open for business. **—shop′lift′er** *n.* **—shop′lift′ing** *n.*

shoppe (shŏp) *n.* Variant of **shop** (sense 1).

shop·per (shŏp′ər) *n.* **1.** One who visits stores in search of merchandise or bargains. **2.** A commercial agent who compares the merchandise and prices of competing merchants. **3.** A commercial employee who fills mail or telephone orders. **4.** A newspaper containing advertisements and some local news, usually distributed free.

shop·ping bag (shŏp′ĭng) *n.* A strong bag with handles for carrying a shopper's purchases.

shop·ping-bag lady (shŏp′ĭng-băg′) *n. Slang.* A bag lady.

shopping center *n.* A group of stores and often restaurants and other businesses having a common parking lot.

shopping mall *n.* **1.** An urban shopping area limited to pedestrians. **2.** A shopping center with stores and businesses facing a system of enclosed walkways for pedestrians.

shop steward *n.* A union member elected to represent coworkers in dealings with management.

shop·talk (shŏp′tôk′) *n.* **1.** Talk or conversation concerning one's work or business. **2.** The jargon used in a specific business or field.

shop·worn (shŏp′wôrn′, -wōrn′) *adj.* **1.** Tarnished, frayed, faded, or otherwise defective from being on display in a store. **2.** Worn-out, as from overuse; trite: *shopworn anecdotes.* See Synonyms at **trite.**

sho·ran (shôr′ăn′, shōr′-) *n.* A relatively short-range navigation system by which a ship or an aircraft can determine its position with high precision by measuring the times required for a radar signal to reach and return from each of two ground stations of known position. [*sho(rt)-ra(nge) n(avigation).*]

shore[1] (shôr, shōr) *n.* **1.** The land along the edge of an ocean, a sea, a lake, or a river; a coast. **2.** Often **shores.** Land; country: *far from our native shores.* **3.** Land as opposed to water: *a sailor with an assignment on shore.* —*attributive.* Often used to modify another noun: *shore dwellings; shore erosion.* [Middle English *shore,* from Old English *scora.* See **sker-[1]** in Appendix.]

shore[2] (shôr, shōr) *tr.v.* **shored, shor·ing, shores.** To support by or as if by a prop: *shored up the sagging floors; shored up the peace initiative.* **—shore** *n.* A beam or timber propped against a structure to provide support. [Middle English *shoren,* from *shore,* prop, probably from Middle Low German *schōre,* barrier, or Middle Dutch *scōre,* prop.]

shore[3] (shôr, shōr) *v. Archaic.* A past tense of **shear.**

shore bird also **shore·bird** (shôr′bûrd′, shōr′-) *n.* Any of various birds, such as the sandpiper, plover, or snipe, that frequent the shores of coastal or inland waters.

shore bug *n.* Any of numerous small predatory insects of the family Saldidae, found along the shores of streams and other bodies of water where they sometimes dig burrows.

shore crab *n.* Any of numerous crabs, such as the spider crab of the United States or the common edible crab *Carcinus maenas,* usually found along seashores.

shore dinner *n.* A meal consisting of seafood.

shore fly *n.* Any of numerous minute black flies of the family Ephydridae, living in damp or marshy places.

shore·front (shôr′frŭnt′, shōr′-) *n.* Land situated on the edge of a body of water. —*attributive.* Often used to modify another noun: *shorefront erosion; shorefront cottages.*

shore leave *n.* Leave of absence granted to a sailor to go ashore.

shore·line (shôr′līn′, shōr′-) *n.* The edge of a body of water.

shore patrol *n. Abbr.* **SP** A detail of the U.S. Navy, Marine Corps, or Coast Guard serving as military police ashore.

Shore·view (shôr′vyo͞o′, shōr′-). A city of eastern Minnesota, a residential suburb of St. Paul. Population, 17,300.

shore·ward (shôr′wərd, shōr′-) *adv. & adj.* Toward, to, or on the shore. **—shore′wards** (-wərdz) *adv.*

shor·ing (shôr′ĭng, shōr′-) *n.* **1.** The act or operation of propping with shores. **2.** A system of supporting shores.

shorn (shôrn, shōrn) *v.* A past participle of **shear.**

short (shôrt) *adj.* **short·er, short·est. 1.** Having little length; not long. **2.** Having little height; not tall. **3.** Extending not far or not far enough: *a short toss.* **4.a.** Lasting a brief time: *a short holiday.* **b.** Appearing to pass quickly: *finished the job in a few short months.* **5.** Not lengthy; succinct: *short and to the point.* **6.a.** Rudely brief; abrupt. **b.** Easily provoked; irascible. **7.** Inadequate; insufficient: *oil in short supply; were short on experience.* **8.** Lacking in length or amount: *a board that is short two inches.* **9.** Lacking in breadth or scope: *a short view of the problem.* **10.** Deficient in retentiveness: *a short memory.* **11.a.** Not owning the stocks or commodities one is selling in anticipation of a fall in prices. **b.** Of or relating to a short sale. **12.a.** Containing a large amount of shortening; flaky: *a short pie crust.* **b.** Not ductile; brittle: *short iron.* **13.a.** *Linguistics.* Of, relating to, or being a speech sound of relatively brief duration, as the first vowel sound in the Latin word *mălus,* "evil," as compared with the same or a similar sound of relatively long duration, as the first vowel sound in the Latin word *mālus,* "apple tree." **b.** *Grammar.* Of, relating to, or being a pronunciation of vowel sounds, as the pronunciation (ă) in *pat,* (ĕ) in *pet,* (ĭ) in *pit,* (ŏ) in *pot,* (ŭ) in *putt,* and (o͝o) in *put.* **c.** Historically descended from a vowel of brief duration. **14.a.** Unstressed; unaccented. Used of a syllable in accentual prosody. **b.** Being of relatively brief duration. Used of a syllable in quantitative prosody. **15.** *Slang.* Close to the end of a tour of military duty. **—short** *adv.* **1.** Abruptly; quickly: *stop short.* **2.** In a rude or curt manner. **3.** At a point before a given limit or goal: *a missile that landed short of the target.* **4.** At a disadvantage: *We were caught short by the sudden storm.* **5.** Without owning what one is selling: *selling a commodity short.* **—short** *n.* **1.** Something short, as: **a.** *Linguistics.* A briefly articulated speech sound or syllable. **b.** A brief film; a short subject. **c.** A size of clothing less long than the average for that size. **d. shorts.** Short trousers extending to the knee or above. **e. shorts.** Men's undershorts. **2.a.** A short sale. **b.** One that sells short. **3. shorts.** A byproduct of wheat processing that consists of germ bran and coarse meal or flour. **4. shorts.** Clippings or trimmings that remain as byproducts in various manufacturing processes, often used to make an inferior variety of the product. **5.a.** A short circuit. **b.** A malfunction caused by a short circuit. **6.** *Baseball.* A shortstop. **—short** *v.* **short·ed, short·ing, shorts.** —*tr.* **1.** To cause a short circuit in. **2.** *Informal.* To give (one) less than one is entitled to; shortchange. **3.a.** To sell (a stock that one does not own) in anticipation of making a profit when its price falls; make a short sale. **b.** To sell unowned stock in (the stock market) in anticipation of making a profit when prices fall. —*intr.* To short-circuit. **—*idioms.* for short.** As an abbreviation: *He's called Ed for short.* **in short.** In summary; briefly. **short for.** An abbreviation of: *Ed is short for Edward.* **short of. 1.** Having an inadequate supply of: *We're short of cash.* **2.** Less than: *Nothing short of her best effort was required to make the team.* **3.** Other than; without resorting to: *Short of yelling at him, I had no other way to catch his attention.* **4.** Not quite willing to undertake or do; just this side of: *She stopped short of throwing out the old photo.* **the short end of the stick.** The worst side of an unequal deal. [Middle English, from Old English *sceort, scort.* See **sker-[1]** in Appendix.] **—short′ness** *n.*

short account *n.* **1.** The account of one that sells short. **2.** See **short interest.**

short·age (shôr′tĭj) *n.* A deficiency in amount.

short-billed marsh wren (shôrt′bĭld′) *n.* A small brownish wren *(Cistothorus platensis)* of eastern North America, living in shallow sedge marshes and damp grassy meadows.

short·bread (shôrt′brĕd′) *n.* A cookie made of flour, sugar, and much butter or other shortening.

short·cake (shôrt′kāk′) *n.* **1.** A dessert consisting of a crisp, light cake served with fruit and topped with cream. **2.** The cake made for this dessert.

short·change (shôrt′chānj′) *tr.v.* **-changed, -chang·ing, -chang·es. 1.** To give (someone) less change than is due in a transaction. **2.** *Informal.* To treat unfairly or deceitfully; cheat: *"a deceitful cook who skimps on ingredients and shortchanges guests"* (Jacques Pepin). **—short′chang′er** *n.*

short circuit *n.* A low-resistance connection accidentally established between two points in an electric circuit.

short-cir·cuit (shôrt′sûr′kĭt) *v.* **-cuit·ed, -cuit·ing, -cuits.** —*tr.* **1.** To cause to have a short circuit. **2.** *Informal.* To hamper the progress of; impede. **3.** To bypass. —*intr.* To become affected with a short circuit.

short·com·ing (shôrt′kŭm′ĭng) *n.* A deficiency; a flaw.

short covering *n.* The buying of securities, stocks, or commodities in order to close out a short sale.

short·cut (shôrt′kŭt′) *n.* **1.** A more direct route than the customary one. **2.** A means of saving time or effort. [From CUT, direct route.] **—short′cut′** *v.*

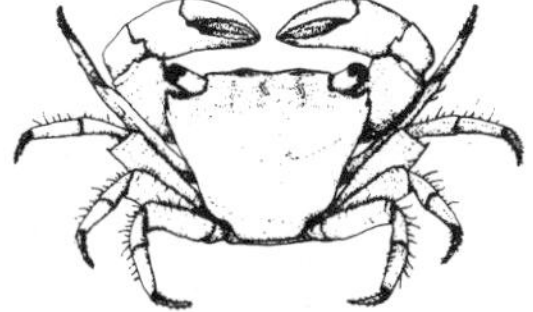

shore crab
Common shore crab
Pachygrapsus transversus

short-day (shôrt′dā′) *adj.* Of, relating to, or being a plant that flowers only after exposure to light periods shorter than a certain critical length, as in early spring or fall.

short division *n. Mathematics.* The process of dividing one number by another without writing down all the steps, especially when the divisor is a single digit.

short·en (shôr′tn) *v.* **-ened, -en·ing, -ens.** —*tr.* **1.** To make short or shorter. **2.** *Nautical.* To take in (a sail) so that less canvas is exposed to the wind. **3.** To reduce in force, efficacy, or intensity. **4.** To add shortening to (dough) so as to make flaky. —*intr.* To become short or shorter. **—short′en·er** *n.*

SYNONYMS: *shorten, abbreviate, abridge, curtail, truncate.* The central meaning shared by these verbs is "to diminish the length, duration, or extent of by or as if by cutting": *smoking that will shorten her life; abbreviated the speech; abridging the rights of citizens; curtailed their visit; truncated the conversation.*
ANTONYM: *lengthen.*

short·ened form (shôr′tnd) *n. Linguistics.* An abbreviated form of a polysyllabic word, as *auto* for *automobile.*

short·en·ing (shôr′tn-ĭng, shôrt′nĭng) *n.* **1.** A fat, such as butter or lard, used to make cake or pastry light or flaky. **2.** A shortened form of something, as a word. **3.** The act of one that shortens. **4.** The act or process of becoming shorter.

short·fall (shôrt′fôl′) *n.* **1.** A failure to attain a specified amount or level; a shortage. **2.** The amount by which a supply falls short of expectation, need, or demand.

short fuse *n. Slang.* A quick temper.

short·hair (shôrt′hâr′) *n.* Either of two breeds of shorthaired cats, characterized by a slender muscular body, large head, broad muzzle, and large round eyes.

short·haired (shôrt′hârd′) *adj.* Having a coat of short hair. Used of animals.

short·hand (shôrt′hănd′) *n.* **1.** A system of rapid handwriting employing symbols to represent words, phrases, and letters. **2.** A system, a form, or an instance of abbreviated or formulaic reference: *"The classical error is to regard a scientific law as only a shorthand for its instances"* (Jacob Bronowski).

short-hand·ed (shôrt′hăn′dĭd) *adj.* Lacking the usual or necessary number of workers, employees, players, or assistants.

short·horn (shôrt′hôrn′) *n.* Any of a breed of beef or dairy cattle that originated in northern England, having short, curved horns or no horns and usually red, white, or roan in color. Also called *Durham.*

short-horned grasshopper (shôrt′hôrnd′) *n.* A grasshopper of the family Locustidae (or Acrididae), including the locusts that swarm over large areas destroying vegetation.

short hundredweight *n.* See **hundredweight** (sense 1).

shor·ti·a (shôr′tē-ə) *n.* Any of various eastern North American and Asian evergreen stemless herbs of the genus *Shortia,* having glossy basal leaves and white, pink, or blue nodding flowers on long stalks. [New Latin, genus name, after Charles Wilkins *Short* (1794–1863), American physician and botanist.]

short·ie (shôr′tē) *n. & adj.* Variant of **shorty.**

short interest *n.* The total number of stocks, securities, or commodity shares in an account or in the market generally that have been sold short and not yet repurchased. Also called *short account, short position.*

short·leaf pine (shôrt′lēf′) *n.* A pine tree *(Pinus echinata)*

ă pat	oi boy
ā pay	ou out
âr care	o͝o took
ä father	o͞o boot
ĕ pet	ŭ cut
ē be	ûr urge
ĭ pit	th thin
ī pie	*th* this
îr pier	hw which
ŏ pot	zh vision
ō toe	ə about, item
ô paw	♦ regionalism

Stress marks: ′ (primary); ′ (secondary), as in **dictionary** (dĭk′shə-nĕr′ē)

common in the southeast United States, having dark bluish-green leaves grouped in fascicles of two. Also called *yellow pine.*

short·list also **short-list** (shôrt′lĭst′) *n.* A list of preferable items or candidates that have been selected for final consideration, as in making an award or filling a position.

short-list (shôrt′lĭst′) *tr.v.* **-list·ed, -list·ing, -lists.** To include (a candidate for a job, for example) on a shortlist.

short-lived (shôrt′lĭvd′, -līvd′) *adj.* Living or lasting only a short time; ephemeral.

USAGE NOTE: The pronunciation (-līvd) is etymologically correct since the compound is derived from the noun *life,* rather than from the verb *live.* But the pronunciation (-lĭvd) is by now so common that it cannot be considered an error. In the most recent survey 43 percent of the Usage Panel preferred (-lĭvd), 39 percent preferred (-līvd), and 18 percent found both pronunciations equally acceptable.

short·ly (shôrt′lē) *adv.* **1.** In a short time; soon. **2.** In a few words; concisely. **3.** In an abrupt manner; curtly.

short-nosed cattle louse (shôrt′nōzd′) *n.* A sucking louse *(Haematopinus eurysternus)* that is parasitic on cattle.

short order *n.* An order of food prepared and served quickly, as in a diner. **—short′-or′der** (shôrt′ôr′dər) *adj.*

short position *n.* **1.** A short sale that has not yet been covered. **2.** See **short interest.**

short-range (shôrt′rānj′) *adj.* **1.** Designed for or limited to short distances: *a short-range airliner.* **2.** Of or relating to the near future: *short-range goals.*

short ribs *pl.n.* The rib ends of beef between the rib roast and the plate.

short sale *n.* The sale of a security that one does not own but has borrowed in anticipation of making a profit by paying for it after its price has fallen.

short shrift *n.* **1.** Summary, careless treatment; scant attention: *These annoying memos will get short shrift from the boss.* **2.** Quick work. **3.a.** A short respite, as from death. **b.** The brief time before execution granted a condemned prisoner for confession and absolution.

short sight *n.* See **myopia** (sense 1).

short·sight·ed (shôrt′sī′tĭd) *adj.* **1.** Nearsighted; myopic. **2.** Lacking foresight. **—short′sight′ed·ly** *adv.* **—short′sight′ed·ness** *n.*

short-spo·ken (shôrt′spō′kən) *adj.* Given to shortness or abruptness in manner or speech; curt.

short·stop (shôrt′stŏp′) *n.* *Baseball.* **1.** The field position between second and third base. **2.** The infielder who occupies this position.

short story *n.* A short piece of prose fiction, having few characters and aiming at unity of effect.

short subject *n.* A brief film often shown before a feature-length film.

short-tailed shrew
Blarina brevicauda

short-tailed shrew (shôrt′tāld′) *n.* Any of various shrews of the genus *Blarina* and related genera, found in North America and eastern Asia, having much shorter tails and standing higher than the common shrew.

short-tem·pered (shôrt′tĕm′pərd) *adj.* Easily or quickly moved to anger; irascible.

short-term (shôrt′tûrm′) *adj.* **1.** Involving or lasting a relatively brief time. **2.a.** Payable or reaching maturity within a relatively brief time, such as a year: *a short-term loan.* **b.** Acquired over a relatively brief time: *short-term capital gains.*

short ton *n.* *Abbr.* **s.t.** See **ton** (sense 1).

short·wave (shôrt′wāv′) *adj.* **1.** Having a wavelength of approximately 20 to 200 meters. **2.** Capable of receiving or transmitting at wavelengths of approximately 20 to 200 meters: *a shortwave radio.*

short wave *n.* *Abbr.* **sw** An electromagnetic wave with a wavelength of approximately 200 meters or less, especially a radio wave in the 20 to 200 meter range.

short-wind·ed (shôrt′wĭn′dĭd) *adj.* **1.** Breathing with quick, labored breaths. **2.** Likely to have difficulty in breathing, especially from exertion. **3.** Brief and succinct. **4.** Choppy; disconnected.

short·y also **short·ie** (shôr′tē) *Informal.* —*n., pl.* **-ies. 1.** A person short in stature. **2.** A thing of less than average size, length, extension, or duration. —*adj.* Of less than average size or length: *shorty gloves; a shortie nightgown.*

Sho·sho·ne also **Sho·sho·ni** (shō-shō′nē) *n., pl.* **Shoshone** or **-nes** also **Shoshoni** or **-nis. 1.** A Native American people comprising three divisions, specifically: **a.** A group inhabiting parts of Idaho, northern Utah, eastern Oregon, and western Montana, now mostly in southeast Idaho. Also called *Northern Shoshone, Snake.* **b.** A group inhabiting the Great Basin area of Idaho, Utah, and Nevada south to Death Valley, California, now mostly in Nevada. Also called *Western Shoshone.* **c.** A group inhabiting the Wind River valley of western Wyoming. Also called *Eastern Shoshone, Wind River Shoshone.* **2.** A member of this people or any of its divisions. **3.** Any of the languages of the Shoshone people. [Probably from Eastern Shoshone band name.] **—Sho·sho′ne·an** *adj.*

Shoshone Falls. A waterfall, 64.7 m (212 ft) high, in the Snake River of southern Idaho.

Shoshone River. A river, about 193 km (120 mi) long, of northwest Wyoming flowing northeast to the Bighorn River.

Shos·ta·ko·vich (shŏs′tə-kō′vĭch, -kô′-, shə-stə-), **Dmitri.** 1906–1975. Russian composer. Considered among the greatest composers of the 20th century, he is particularly known for his 15 symphonies and also wrote chamber music, operas, and ballets.

shot[1] (shŏt) *n.* **1.** The firing or discharge of a weapon, such as a gun. **2.** The distance over which something is shot; the range. **3.a.** An attempt to hit a target with a projectile: *His shot at the bear missed by inches.* **b.** An attempt to reach a target with a rocket: *a moon shot.* **4.a.** *Sports.* An attempt to score in a game, as in soccer or hockey. **b.** *Baseball.* A home run. **5.** *Sports & Games.* **a.** The flight or path of a projectile in a game. **b.** A stroke in a game, as in golf or billiards. **6.** A pointed or critical remark. **7.** *Informal.* **a.** An attempt; a try: *took a shot at losing weight.* **b.** A guess. **c.** An opportunity: *gave him a fair shot at the part in the play.* **d.** A chance at odds; something to bet on: *The horse was a four-to-one shot.* **8.a.** A solid projectile designed to be discharged from a firearm or cannon. **b.** *pl.* **shot.** Such projectiles considered as a group. **c.** *pl.* **shot.** Tiny lead or steel pellets, especially ones used in a shotgun cartridge. **d.** One of these pellets. **9.** *Sports.* The heavy metal ball that is put for distance in the shot put. **10.** One who shoots in a particular way: *a good shot with the rifle and the bow.* **11.a.** A charge of explosives used in blasting mine shafts. **b.** A detonation of an explosive charge. **12.a.** A photographic view or exposure: *got a good shot of that last model.* **b.** A developed photographic image. **c.** A single cinematic view or take. **13.a.** A hypodermic injection. **b.** A small amount given or applied at one time: *a shot of oxygen.* **14.** A drink, especially a jigger of liquor. **15.** An amount to be paid, as for drinks; a bill. **16.** *Nautical.* A length of chain equal to 15 fathoms (90 feet) in the United States and 12½ fathoms (75 feet) in Great Britain. **—shot** *tr.v.* **shot·ted, shot·ting, shots.** To load or weight with shot. ***—idioms.*** **like a shot.** Very quickly. **shot in the arm.** *Informal.* Something that boosts one's spirits. **shot in the dark.** *Informal.* **1.** A wild, unsubstantiated guess. **2.** An attempt that has little chance of succeeding. [Middle English, from Old English *sceot, scot.* See **skeud-** in Appendix.]

shot[2] (shŏt) *v.* Past tense and past participle of **shoot. —shot** *adj.* **1.a.** Of changeable or variegated color; iridescent. **b.** Streaked or flecked with or as if with yarn of a different color: *a blue suit shot with purple; a forest glade that was shot with sunlight.* **c.** Interspersed or permeated with a distinctive quality: *Her apology was shot with irony.* **2.** *Informal.* Worn-out; ruined.

shot clock *n.* *Basketball.* A device that indicates how many seconds a team has to take a shot or else lose possession of the ball.

shote (shōt) *n.* Variant of **shoat.**

♦ **shot·gun** (shŏt′gŭn′) *n.* **1.** A smooth-bore gun that fires shot over short ranges. Also called *scattergun.* **2.** *Football.* An offensive formation, used especially for passing, in which the quarterback receives the snap several yards behind the line of scrimmage. **3.** *New Orleans.* A house whose architecture is characterized by several rooms joined in a straight line from the front to the back: *"Shotguns* [are] *so named because a shotgun fired through the front door of these long, narrow homes could pass straight through the house and out the back door without hitting any barriers"* (Melissa O. Fryauf). See Regional Note at **beignet.**

shotgun marriage *n.* A marriage that is forced or necessitated because of pregnancy. Also called *shotgun wedding.*

shot hole *n.* **1.** A drilled hole in which an explosive charge is placed before detonation. **2.** A hole made in wood by an insect.

shot put *n.* *Sports.* **1.** An athletic event in which contestants attempt to put a heavy metal ball as far as possible. **2.** The standard ball used in this competition. **—shot′-put′ter** (shŏt′-pŏŏt′ər) *n.* **—shot′-put′ting** *n.*

shott (shŏt) *n.* Variant of **chott.**

shot·ten (shŏt′n) *adj.* Having recently spawned and thus being less desirable as food. Used of fish, especially herring. [Middle English *shoten,* past participle of *shoten,* to shoot. See SHOOT.]

should (shŏŏd) *aux.v.* Past tense of **shall. 1.** Used to express obligation or duty: *You should send her a note.* **2.** Used to express probability or expectation: *They should arrive at noon.* **3.** Used to express conditionality or contingency: *If she should fall, then so would I.* **4.** Used to moderate the directness or bluntness of a statement: *I should think he would like to go.*

USAGE NOTE: Like the rules governing the use of *shall* and *will* on which they are based, the traditional rules governing the use of *should* and *would* are largely ignored in modern American practice. Either *should* or *would* can now be used in the first person to express conditional futurity: *If I had known that, I would* (or somewhat more formally, *should*) *have answered differently.* But in the second and third persons only *would* is used: *If he had known that, he would* (not *should*) *have answered differently. Would* cannot always be substituted for *should,* however. *Should* is used in all three persons in a conditional clause: *if I* (or *you* or *he*) *should decide to go. Should* is also used in all three persons to express duty or obligation (the equivalent of *ought to*): *I* (or *you* or *he*) *should go.* On the other hand, *would* is used to express volition or promise: *I agreed that I would do it.* Either *would* or *should* is possible as an auxiliary with *like, be inclined, be glad, prefer,* and related verbs: *I would* (or *should*) *like to call your attention to an oversight.* Here *would* was acceptable on all levels to a large majority of the Usage Panel in an earlier survey and is more common in American usage than *should.* • *Should have* is sometimes incorrectly written *should of* by writers who have mistaken the source of the spoken contraction *should've.* See Usage Notes at **if, rather, shall.**

shoul•der (shōl′dər) *n.* **1.a.** The joint connecting the arm with the torso. **b.** The part of the human body between the neck and upper arm. **2.a.** The joint of a vertebrate animal that connects the forelimb to the trunk. **b.** The part of an animal near this joint. **c.** The part of a bird's wing between the wrist and the trunk. **3.** Often **shoulders.** The area of the back from one shoulder to the other. **4.** A cut of meat including the joint of the foreleg and adjacent parts. **5.** The portion of a garment that covers the shoulder. **6.** An angled or sloping part, as: **a.** The angle between the face and flank of a bastion in a fortification. **b.** The area between the body and neck of a bottle or vase. **7.** The area of an item or object that serves as an abutment or surrounds a projection, as: **a.** The end surface of a board from which a tenon projects. **b.** *Printing.* The flat surface on the body of type that extends beyond the letter or character. **8.** The edge or border running on either side of a roadway. **—shoulder** *v.* **-dered, -der•ing, -ders.** *—tr.* **1.** To carry or place (a burden, for example) on the shoulders. **2.** To take on; assume: *shouldered the blame for his friends.* **3.** To push or apply force to, with or as if with the shoulder. **4.** To make (one's way) by or as if by shoving obstacles with one's shoulders. *—intr.* **1.** To push with the shoulders. **2.** To make one's way by or as if by shoving obstacles with one's shoulders. ***—idioms.*** **put (one's) shoulder to the wheel.** To apply oneself vigorously; make a concentrated effort. **shoulder to shoulder. 1.** In close proximity; side by side. **2.** In close cooperation. **straight from the shoulder. 1.** Delivered directly from the shoulder. Used of a punch. **2.** Honestly; candidly. [Middle English *shulder,* from Old English *sculdor.*]

shoulder bag *n.* An often large handbag carried by a strap that is looped over the shoulder.

shoulder belt *n.* See **shoulder harness.**

shoulder blade *n.* See **scapula.**

shoulder board *n.* One of a pair of oblong pieces of stiffened cloth worn on each shoulder of a military uniform and carrying insignia identifying the wearer's rank. Also called *shoulder mark.*

shoulder girdle *n.* The pectoral girdle, especially of a human being.

shoulder harness *n.* A safety belt used with a seat belt in a vehicle and worn diagonally across the chest and over the shoulder. Also called *shoulder belt.*

shoulder holster *n.* A leather holster hung from the shoulder and usually worn underneath the arm, allowing a handgun to be concealed underneath a coat.

shoulder knot *n.* **1.** Either of two detachable braided cords worn on each shoulder of the full-dress uniform of a commissioned officer. **2.** An ornamental knot of ribbon or lace formerly worn on the shoulder.

shoulder mark *n.* See **shoulder board.**

shoulder patch *n.* A cloth patch bearing identifying markings, worn on the upper portion of the sleeve of a uniform.

shoulder strap *n.* **1.** A strap, usually one of a pair, supporting a garment from the shoulder. **2.** A strap worn across the shoulder to support an item, such as a bag.

should•est (sho͝od′ĭst) or **shouldst** (sho͝odst) *aux.v. Archaic.* A second person singular past tense of **shall.**

should•n't (sho͝od′nt). Should not.

shouldst (sho͝odst) *aux.v.* Variant of **shouldest.**

shout (shout) *n.* A loud cry. **—shout** *tr. & intr.v.* **shout•ed, shout•ing, shouts.** To say with or utter a shout. ***—phrasal verb.*** **shout down.** To overwhelm or silence by shouting loudly. [Middle English *shoute,* perhaps from Old Norse *skūta,* a taunt.] **—shout′er** *n.*

SYNONYMS: *shout, bawl, bellow, holler, howl, roar, whoop, yell.* The central meaning shared by these verbs is "to say with or make a loud, strong cry": *fans shouting their approval; bawling out orders; bellowing with rage; hollered a warning; howling with pain; a crowd roaring its disapproval; children whooping at play; troops yelling as they attacked.*

shout•ing distance (shou′tĭng) *n.* A short distance: *lived within shouting distance of each other.*

shove (shŭv) *v.* **shoved, shov•ing, shoves.** *—tr.* **1.** To push forward or along. **2.** To push rudely or roughly. See Synonyms at **push.** *—intr.* To push someone or something with force. **—shove** *n.* The act of shoving; a push. ***—phrasal verb.*** **shove off. 1.** To push (a boat) away from shore in leaving. **2.** *Informal.* To leave. [Middle English *shoven,* from Old English *scūfan.*] **—shov′er** *n.*

shov•el (shŭv′əl) *n.* **1.** A tool with a handle and a broad scoop or blade for digging and moving material, such as dirt or snow. **2.** A large mechanical device or vehicle for heavy digging or excavation. **3.** The amount that a shovel can hold; a shovelful: *One shovel of dirt.* **—shovel** *v.* **-eled, -el•ing, -els** also **-elled, -el•ling, -els.** *—tr.* **1.** To move or remove with a shovel. **2.** To make with a shovel: *shoveled a path through the snow.* **3.** To convey or throw in a rough or hasty way, as if with a shovel: *He shoveled the food into his mouth.* **4.** To clear or excavate with or as if with a shovel: *shoveling off the driveway after the snowstorm; shovels out the hall closet once a year.* *—intr.* To dig or work with a shovel. [Middle English, from Old English *scofl.*]

shov•el•er also **shov•el•ler** (shŭv′ə-lər, shŭv′lər) *n.* **1.** One that shovels: *a shoveler of snow; a fast shoveler.* **2.** A widely distributed duck *(Anas clypeata)* that lives chiefly in marshes and has a long, broad bill fringed with bristles, which it uses to strain food from mud and water.

shov•el•ful (shŭv′əl-fo͝ol′) *n.* The amount that a shovel can hold.

shovel hat *n.* A stiff, broad-brimmed, low-crowned hat, turned up at the sides and projecting in front, worn by some English clergymen.

shov•el•head (shŭv′əl-hĕd′) *n.* A small hammerhead shark *(Sphyrna tiburo),* the head of which looks like a rounded spade, that is found in shallow waters of the Atlantic and Pacific.

shov•el•ler (shŭv′ə-lər, shŭv′lər) *n.* Variant of **shoveler.**

shov•el•nose (shŭv′əl-nōz′) *n.* A sturgeon *(Scaphirhynchus platorhynchus)* of the Mississippi River, having a broad flat snout. Also called *hackleback, shovel-nosed sturgeon.*

shov•el-nosed (shŭv′əl-nōzd′) *adj.* Having a broad, flattened snout, bill, or head.

shovel-nosed sturgeon *n.* See **shovelnose.**

show (shō) *v.* **showed, shown** (shōn) or **showed, show•ing, shows.** *—tr.* **1.a.** To cause or allow to be seen; display. **b.** To display for sale, in exhibition, or in competition: *showed her most recent paintings.* **2.** To conduct; guide: *showed them to the table.* **3.** To direct one's attention to; point out: *show them the biggest squash in the garden.* **4.** To manifest (an emotion or a condition, for example); reveal: *showed displeasure at his remark; a carpet that shows wear.* **5.** To permit access to (a house, for example) when offering for sale or rent. **6.** To reveal (oneself) as in one's behavior or condition: *The old boat showed itself to be seaworthy.* **7.** To indicate; register: *The altimeter showed that the plane was descending.* **8.a.** To demonstrate by reasoning or procedure: *showed that the hypothesis was wrong; a film that showed how to tune a piano.* **b.** To demonstrate to by reasoning or procedure; inform or prove to: *showed him how to fix the camera; showed her that it could really happen.* **9.** To grant; bestow: *showed no mercy to the traitors.* **10.** *Law.* To plead; allege: *show cause.* *—intr.* **1.** To be or become visible or evident. **2.** *Slang.* To make an appearance; show up: *didn't show for her appointment.* **3.a.** To be exhibited publicly: *What's showing at the movie theater tonight?* **b.** To give a performance or present an exhibition. **4.** *Sports.* To finish third or better in a horserace or dog race. **—show** *n.* **1.** A display; a manifestation: *made a show of strength.* **2.a.** A trace or an indication, as of oil in a well. **b.** The discharge of bloody mucus from the vagina indicating the start of labor. **c.** The first discharge of blood in menstruation. **3.** A false appearance; a pretense: *only a show of kindness.* **4.a.** A striking appearance or display; a spectacle. **b.** A pompous or ostentatious display. **5.** Display or outward appearance: *This antique tea service is just for show. His smile was for show.* **6.a.** A public exhibition or entertainment. **b.** A radio or television program. **c.** A movie. **d.** A theatrical troupe or company. **7.** *Informal.* An affair or undertaking: *ran the whole show.* **8.** *Sports.* Third place at the finish, as in a horserace. ***—phrasal verbs.*** **show off.** To display or behave in an ostentatious or conspicuous way. **show up. 1.** To be clearly visible. **2.** To put in an appearance; arrive. **3.** To expose or reveal the true character or nature of: *showed their efforts up as a waste of time.* **4.** *Informal.* To surpass, as in ability or intelligence. ***—idioms.*** **get the show on the road.** *Slang.* To get started. **show (one's) hand. 1.** *Games.* To display one's cards with faces up. **2.** To state one's intentions or reveal one's resources, especially when previously hidden. **show (one's) heels.** To depart from quickly; flee. **show (someone) a good time.** To occupy (someone) with amusing things; entertain. [Middle English *sheuen, shouen,* from Old English *scēawian,* to look at, display. See **keu-** in Appendix.]

SYNONYMS: *show, display, expose, parade, exhibit, flaunt.* These verbs mean to present something to view. *Show* is the most general: *The jeweler showed the necklace to the customer. "She hated to show her feelings"* (John Galsworthy). *Display* often suggests an attempt to present something to best advantage: *The dealer spread the rug out to display the pattern. "Few 'letters home' of successful men or women display the graces of modesty and self-forgetfulness"* (H.G. Wells). *Expose* usually involves uncovering something or bringing it out from concealment: *The excavation exposed a staggering number of Bronze Age artifacts.* The term can often imply revelation of something better left concealed: *His comment exposed his insensitivity. Parade* usually suggests a pretentious or boastful presentation: *"He early discovered that, by parading his unhappiness before the multitude, he produced an immense sensation"* (Macaulay). *Exhibit* implies open presentation that invites inspection: *"The works of art, by being publicly exhibited and offered for sale, are becoming articles of trade"* (Prince Albert). *Flaunt* implies an unabashed, often arrogant display: *"Every great hostelry flaunted the flag of some foreign potentate"* (John Dos Passos). See also Synonyms at **appear.**

show-and-tell or **show and tell** (shō′ən-tĕl′) *n.* **1.** An educational activity in which a child displays an object to the class and talks about it. **2.** A public presentation or display.

show bill *n.* An advertising poster.

shoulder holster

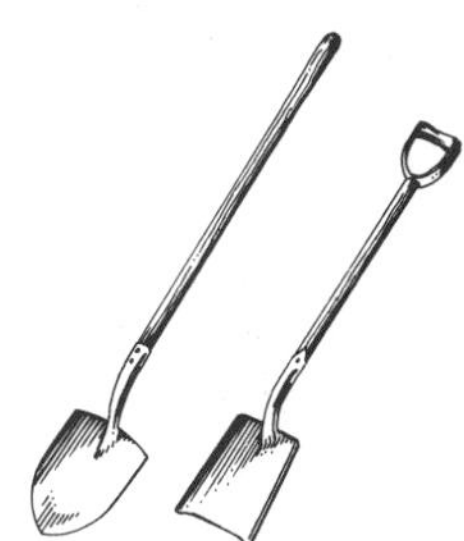

shovel
Left: Rounded mouth
Right: Tapered mouth

ă pat	oi boy
ā pay	ou out
âr care	o͝o took
ä father	o͞o boot
ĕ pet	ŭ cut
ē be	ûr urge
ĭ pit	th thin
ī pie	*th* this
îr pier	hw which
ŏ pot	zh vision
ō toe	ə about, item
ô paw	♦ regionalism

Stress marks: ′ (primary); ′ (secondary), as in **dictionary** (dĭk′shə-nĕr′ē)

shrike
Loggerhead shrike
Lanius ludovicianus

show biz *n. Slang.* Show business. **—show′-biz′, show′-biz′** (shō′bĭz′) *adj.*

show·boat (shō′bōt′) *n.* **1.** *Nautical.* A river steamboat having a troupe of performers and a theater aboard for performances on the river. **2.** One who seeks attention by ostentatious behavior; a showoff. **—showboat** *intr.v.* **-boat·ed, -boat·ing, -boats.** To show off.

show·bread (shō′brĕd′) *n.* The 12 loaves of blessed unleavened bread placed every Sabbath in the sanctuary of the Tabernacle as an offering by the Hebrew priests of ancient Israel. [Translation of German *Schaubrot* (*Schau,* sight, show + *Brot,* bread), translation of Greek *artoi enōpioi* (*artoi,* pl. of *artos,* loaf of bread + *enōpioi,* pl. of *enōpios,* facing), translation of Hebrew *leḥem pānîm* (*leḥem,* bread + *pānîm,* divine presence).]

show business *n.* The entertainment industry.

show·case (shō′kās′) *n.* **1.** A display case or cabinet, as in a store or museum. **2.** A setting in which someone or something may be displayed, especially to advantage. **—showcase** *tr.v.* **-cased, -cas·ing, -cas·es.** *Usage Problem.* To display prominently, especially to advantage.

USAGE NOTE: In theatrical language a *showcase* is a production designed to display usually unknown performers, and the verb *showcase* is used to refer to the act of exposure, whether of new talent — *"His productions showcased black singers but didn't cut them in on the lucrative action"* (James Wolcott) — or of established stars — "[The producer] *has crafted backgrounds which perfectly showcase* [the singer's] *vocals and driving rhythm guitar"* (Elijah Wald). Like other show business jargon, such as the verb use of *premiere,* this usage is properly exempt from criticism; we expect from P.T. Barnum a measure of exaggeration and grammatical license that we might not accept in other kinds of linguistic commerce. But since its inception in the 1940's, the verb has acquired a wider pattern of use. It is applied to the exposure of athletes and to the display of products: *"Recruiters promise a proud young man that he'll be a starter and a star, showcased for the pro scouts"* (Pete Axthelm). *"In the financial services section, stock-trading desks had been set up showcasing* [the company's] *computers"* (Boston Globe). *"Other recent first ladies also showcased American clothing"* (Paula Span). *"The South Koreans . . . hope the Olympics will . . . showcase their country's breathtaking economic progress"* (Nancy Cooper). These uses clearly preserve the metaphoric sense of a showcase in which a commodity is displayed to advantage. But other uses of the verb take it further from its original sense. It is used to mean simply "to hold up to admiration," even when the object is not something that can be hired or purchased: *"I feel great because Project Excellence is going to honor, to showcase, these youngsters who have risen above ridicule, hung in against myriad handicaps, and shown that they can be the best"* (Carl T. Rowan). Still more opaque is use of the verb to mean simply "to expose to public view," even when its object is neither admirable nor desirable: *"The Democrats were going to showcase all the wretchedness and decay and insolvency as a symbol of Republican not-so-benign neglect"* (Chicago Tribune). In this sense the verb is sometimes applied even to unintended exposure: *"But his news conference showcased once again his propensity for self-inflicted wounds"* (Newsweek). In these last two usages the verb no longer has any connection to the idea of a showcase, nor does it retain any hint of its theatrical character. The development of the verb nicely exemplifies the process whereby metaphors are eviscerated after death.

show·down (shō′doun′) *n.* **1.** An event, especially a confrontation, that forces an issue to a conclusion. **2.** *Games.* The laying down of the players' cards face up to determine the winner of the pot in poker.

show·er¹ (shou′ər) *n.* **1.** A brief fall of precipitation, such as rain, hail, or sleet. **2.** A fall of a group of objects, especially from the sky. *a meteor shower; a shower of leaves.* **3.** An abundant flow; an outpouring: *a shower of praise.* **4.** A party held to honor and present gifts to someone: *a bridal shower.* **5.a.** A bath in which the water is sprayed on the bather in fine streams from a showerhead, usually secured overhead: *take a shower.* **b.** The stall or tub in which such a bath is taken. **—shower** *v.* **-ered, -er·ing, -ers.** *—tr.* **1.** To pour down in a shower: *showered confetti on the parade.* **2.** To cover with or as if with a shower. **3.** To bestow abundantly or liberally. See Synonyms at **barrage².** *—intr.* **1.** To fall or pour down in or as if in a shower. **2.** To wash oneself in a shower. [Middle English *shour,* from Old English *scūr.*] **—show′er·y** *adj.*

show·er² (shō′ər) *n.* One that shows: *a shower of thoroughbred horses; a shower of great affection.*

show·er bath (shou′ər) *n.* A shower: *After a shower bath you will feel refreshed.*

show·er·head (shou′ər-hĕd′) *n.* A perforated nozzle for spraying water on a bather taking a shower.

show·girl (shō′gûrl′) *n.* A woman, typically attired in an elaborately decorated costume, who performs in a musical or theatrical production.

show·ing (shō′ĭng) *n.* **1.** The act of presenting or displaying. **2.** Performance, as in a competition or test of skill: *a poor showing.* **3.** A presentation of evidence, facts, or figures.

show·man (shō′mən) *n.* **1.** A theatrical producer. **2.** A man who has a flair for dramatic or ostentatious behavior. **—show′man·ship′** *n.*

shown (shōn) *v.* A past participle of **show.**

show·off (shō′ôf′, -ŏf′) *n.* **1.** The act of showing off. **2.** One who shows off.

show·piece (shō′pēs′) *n.* Something exhibited, especially as an outstanding example of its kind.

show place also **show·place** (shō′plās′) *n.* **1.** A place, such as a house or an estate, that is viewed and frequented for its beauty or historical noteworthiness. **2.** A beautiful or ornate place.

show room *n.* A large room in which merchandise is displayed.

show·stop·per (shō′stŏp′ər) *n. Informal.* **1.** A performance or performer that evokes so much applause from the audience that the show is interrupted. **2.** A particularly arresting person or thing, especially one that draws attention away from others or brings a course of action to a halt. **—show′stop′ping** *adj.*

show·time or **show time** (shō′tīm′) *n.* **1.** The time at which an entertainment, such as the showing of a movie, is scheduled to start. **2.** *Slang.* The time at which an activity is to begin.

show·y (shō′ē) *adj.* **-i·er, -i·est. 1.** Making an imposing or aesthetically pleasing display; striking: *showy flowers.* **2.** Displaying brilliance and virtuosity of ability or performance: *a showy violin solo.* **3.** Marked by or prone to ostentatious, often tasteless display; flashy. **—show′i·ly** *adv.* **—show′i·ness** *n.*

SYNONYMS: *showy, flamboyant, ostentatious, pretentious, splashy.* The central meaning shared by these adjectives is "marked by striking, often excessively conspicuous display": *a cheap, showy rhinestone bracelet; an entertainer's flamboyant personality; an ostentatious sable coat; a pretentious scholarly edition; a splashy advertising campaign.*

shp or **s.hp.** *abbr.* Shaft horsepower.

shpt. *n.* Shipment.

shr. *abbr.* Share.

shrank (shrăngk) *v.* A past tense of **shrink.**

shrap·nel (shrăp′nəl) *n., pl.* **shrapnel. 1.a.** An artillery shell containing metal balls fused to explode in the air above enemy troops. **b.** The metal balls in such a weapon. **2.** Shell fragments from a high-explosive shell. [After Henry *Shrapnel* (1761–1842), British army officer.]

WORD HISTORY: Henry Shrapnel received no compensation for the invention named after him other than having his name live on in connection with it. This deadly artillery shell, invented by Shrapnel, a British artillery officer, in his spare time and at his own expense, was given its first test in South America during the British seizure of part of Suriname (1799–1802), but shrapnel came into its own during the Peninsular War (1808–1814) between Great Britain, Spanish guerrillas, Portugal, and Napoleonic France. Shrapnel's shell was first officially called the *spherical case shot,* but it seems that early on it was called the *shrapnel shell* as well (first recorded in 1806), and this was the name eventually adopted by the British army. The word *shrapnel* came to be used by itself as a collective noun, and even though the shrapnel shell is no longer used, people have for some time (first recorded in 1940) called the fragments from a shell, mine, or bomb *shrapnel,* thus ensuring the continued existence, if not the immortality, of Henry Shrapnel's name.

shred (shrĕd) *n.* **1.** A long, irregular strip cut or torn off. **2.** A small amount; a particle: *not a shred of evidence.* **—shred** *tr.v.* **shred·ded** or **shred, shred·ding, shreds.** To cut or tear into shreds. [Middle English *shrede,* from Old English *scrēade.*] **—shred′der** *n.*

Shreve·port (shrēv′pôrt′, -pōrt′). A city of northwest Louisiana on the Red River near the Texas border. Founded in the 1830's, it grew rapidly after the discovery of oil in the region (1906). Population, 205,815.

shrew (shrōō) *n.* **1.** Any of various small, chiefly insectivorous mammals of the family Soricidae, resembling a mouse but having a long, pointed snout and small eyes and ears. Also called *shrewmouse.* **2.** A woman with a violent, scolding, or nagging temperament; a scold. [Middle English *shrewe,* villian, from Old English *scrēawa,* shrewmouse.]

shrewd (shrōōd) *adj.* **shrewd·er, shrewd·est. 1.** Characterized by keen awareness, sharp intelligence, and often a sense of the practical. **2.** Disposed to artful and cunning practices; tricky. **3.** Sharp; penetrating: *a shrewd wind.* [Middle English *shrewed,* wicked, from *shrew,* rascal. See SHREW.] **—shrewd′ly** *adv.*

SYNONYMS: *shrewd, sagacious, astute, perspicacious.* These adjectives mean having or showing keen awareness, sound judgment, and often resourcefulness, especially in practical matters. *Shrewd* suggests a sharp intelligence, hardheadness, and often an intuitive grasp of practical considerations: *"He was too shrewd to go along with them upon a road which could lead only to their overthrow"* (J.A. Froude). *Sagacious* connotes prudence, circumspection, discernment, and farsightedness: *"He was observant and thoughtful, and given to asking sagacious questions"* (John Galt). *Astute* suggests shrewdness, canniness, and an immunity to being misled: *An astute tenant always reads the small print in a lease. Perspicacious* implies penetration and clear-sightedness: *She is much too* *perspicacious to be taken in by such a spurious argument.* See also Synonyms at **clever.**

---

shrewd·ness (shro͞od′nĭs) *n.* **1.** The quality of being shrewd. **2.** An aggregation of apes. See Synonyms at **flock**[1].

shrew·ish (shro͞o′ĭsh) *adj.* Ill-tempered; nagging. **—shrew′ish·ly** *adv.* **—shrew′ish·ness** *n.*

shrew mole *n.* Any of several shrewlike moles of the family Talpidae, especially *Neurotrichus gibbsii* of western North America, *Uropsilus soricipes* of central Asia, and *Urotrichus talpoides* of Japan.

shrew·mouse (shro͞o′mous′) *n.* See **shrew** (sense 1).

Shrews·bur·y (shro͞oz′bĕr′ē, -bə-rē). **1.** A municipal borough of western England on the Severn River west-northwest of Birmingham. An ancient Saxon and Norman stronghold, it is now a transportation hub with varied industries. Population, 60,400. **2.** A town of central Massachusetts, a manufacturing suburb of Worcester. Population, 22,674.

shriek (shrēk) *n.* **1.** A shrill, often frantic cry. **2.** A sound suggestive of such a cry. **—shriek** *v.* **shrieked, shriek·ing, shrieks.** —*intr.* **1.** To utter a shriek. **2.** To make a sound similar to a shriek. —*tr.* To utter with a shriek. See Synonyms at **scream.** [Middle English *skriken, shriken,* of Scandinavian origin; akin to Old Norse *skrækja.*] **—shriek′er** *n.*

shrie·val (shrē′vəl) *adj.* Of or relating to a sheriff. [From obsolete *shrieve,* variant of SHERIFF.] **—shrie′val·ty** *n.*

shrift (shrĭft) *n. Archaic.* **1.** The act of shriving. **2.** Confession to a priest. **3.** Absolution given by a priest. [Middle English, from Old English *scrift,* from Latin *scrīptum,* something written, from neuter past participle of *scrībere,* to write. See SHRIVE.]

shrike (shrīk) *n.* Any of various carnivorous oscine birds of the family Laniidae, having a screeching call and a strong hooked bill with a toothlike projection and often impaling its prey on sharp-pointed thorns or barbs of wire fencing. [Probably from Middle English **shrik,* from Old English *scrīc,* thrush.]

shrill (shrĭl) *adj.* **shrill·er, shrill·est.** **1.** High-pitched and piercing in tone or sound: *the shrill wail of a siren.* **2.** Producing a sharp, high-pitched tone or sound: *a shrill fife.* **3.** Sharp or keen to the senses; harshly vivid: *shrill colors.* **—shrill** *v.* **shrilled, shrill·ing, shrills.** —*tr.* To utter in a shrill manner; scream. —*intr.* To produce a shrill cry or sound. [Middle English *shrille.*] **—shrill′ness** *n.* **—shril′ly** *adv.*

shrimp (shrĭmp) *n., pl.* **shrimp** or **shrimps.** **1.a.** Any of various small, chiefly marine decapod crustaceans of the suborder Natantia, many species of which are edible, having a compressed or elongated body with a well-developed abdomen, long legs and antennae, and a long spinelike projection of the carapace. **b.** Any of various similar crustaceans, such as certain isopods and amphipods. **2.** *Slang.* **a.** A person regarded as unimportant. **b.** A person who is small in stature. **—shrimp** *intr.v.* **shrimped, shrimp·ing, shrimps.** To fish for shrimp. [Middle English *shrimpe,* possibly of Low German origin.] **—shrimp′er** *n.*

shrimp·fish (shrĭmp′fĭsh′) *n., pl.* **shrimpfish** or **-fish·es.** Any of various small, slender tropical marine fishes of the family Centriscidae, related to the sea horses and pipefish.

shrine (shrīn) *n.* **1.** A container or receptacle for sacred relics; a reliquary. **2.a.** The tomb of a venerated person, such as a saint. **b.** A place at which devotion is paid to a venerated person. **3.** A site hallowed by a venerated object or its associations: *Independence Hall, shrine of American liberty.* **—shrine** *tr.v.* **shrined, shrin·ing, shrines.** To enshrine. [Middle English, from Old English *scrīn,* box, from Latin *scrīnium,* case for books or papers.]

Shrin·er (shrī′nər) *n.* A member of a U.S. secret fraternal order that is not Masonic but that admits only Knights Templars and 32nd-degree Masons as members. [After the Ancient Arabic Order of Nobles of the Mystic *Shrine,* their fraternal order.]

shrink (shrĭngk) *v.* **shrank** (shrăngk) or **shrunk** (shrŭngk), **shrunk** or **shrunk·en** (shrŭng′kən), **shrink·ing, shrinks.** —*intr.* **1.** To become constricted from heat, moisture, or cold. See Synonyms at **contract.** **2.** To become reduced in amount or value; dwindle: *His savings quickly shrank.* **3.** To draw back instinctively, as from something alarming; recoil. See Synonyms at **recoil.** **4.** To show reluctance; hesitate: *shrink from making such a sacrifice.* —*tr.* To cause to shrink. **—shrink** *n.* **1.a.** The act of shrinking. **b.** The degree to which something shrinks; shrinkage. **2.** *Slang.* A psychiatrist. [Middle English *shrinken,* to wither, shrivel up, from Old English *scrincan.* See **sker-**[2] in Appendix.] **—shrink′a·ble** *adj.* **—shrink′er** *n.*

shrink·age (shrĭng′kĭj) *n.* **1.** The process of shrinking. **2.** The amount or proportion by which something shrinks. **3.** A reduction in value; depreciation. **4.** The total weight loss sustained by livestock in shipment to a market. **5.** Loss of merchandise, especially through theft.

shrink·ing violet (shrĭng′kĭng) *n. Informal.* A shy or retiring person.

shrink-wrap (shrĭngk′răp′) *n.* A protective wrapping for articles of merchandise consisting of a clear plastic film that is wound about the articles and then shrunk by heat to form a sealed, tight-fitting package. Also called *shrink package.* **—shrink-wrap** *tr.v.* **-wrapped, -wrap·ping, -wraps.** To wrap (an article of merchandise) in protective clear plastic film.

shrive (shrīv) *v.* **shrove** (shrōv) or **shrived, shriv·en** (shrĭv′ən) or **shrived, shriv·ing, shrives.** —*tr.* **1.** To hear the confession of and give absolution to (a penitent). **2.** To obtain absolution for (oneself) by confessing and doing penance. —*intr. Archaic.* **1.** To make or go to confession. **2.** To hear confessions. [Middle English *schriven,* from Old English *scrīfan,* from Latin *scrībere,* to write. See **skrībh-** in Appendix.] **—shriv′er** *n.*

shriv·el (shrĭv′əl) *intr. & tr.v.* **-eled, -el·ing, -els** or **-elled, -el·ling, -els.** **1.** To become or make shrunken and wrinkled, often by drying: *Leaves die, fall, and shrivel. The heat shriveled the unwatered seedlings.* **2.** To lose or cause to lose vitality or intensity: *My enthusiasm shriveled as the project wore on. Inflation shriveled the buying power of the dollar.* **3.** To become or make much less or smaller; dwindle. [Origin unknown.]

shriv·en (shrĭv′ən) *v.* A past participle of **shrive.**

Shrop·shire[1] (shrŏp′shîr′, -shər). A historical region of western England on the Welsh border. It was part of the kingdom of Mercia during Anglo-Saxon times.

Shrop·shire[2] (shrŏp′shîr′, -shər, -shîr′) *n.* A large, hornless, black-faced sheep of a breed developed in Shropshire and raised for meat and wool.

shroud (shroud) *n.* **1.** A cloth used to wrap a body for burial; a winding sheet. **2.** Something that conceals, protects, or screens: *under a shroud of fog.* **3.a.** *Nautical.* One of a set of ropes or wire cables stretched from the masthead to the sides of a vessel to support the mast. **b.** A similar supporting line for a smokestack or comparable structure. **c.** One of the ropes connecting the harness and the canopy of a parachute. **—shroud** *v.* **shroud·ed, shroud·ing, shrouds.** —*tr.* **1.** To wrap (a corpse) in burial clothing. **2.** To shut off from sight; screen. See Synonyms at **block.** **3.** *Archaic.* To shelter; protect. —*intr. Archaic.* To take cover; find shelter. [Middle English, garment, from Old English *scrūd.*]

shrove (shrōv) *v.* A past tense of **shrive.**

Shrove Monday (shrōv) *n.* The Monday before Ash Wednesday.

Shrove Sunday *n.* The Sunday before Ash Wednesday.

Shrove·tide (shrōv′tīd′) *n.* The three days, Shrove Sunday, Shrove Monday, and Shrove Tuesday, preceding Ash Wednesday. [Middle English *shroftide* : *shrof-,* shriving (from *shriven,* to shrive; see SHRIVE) + *tid,* time; see TIDE[1].]

Shrove Tuesday *n.* The day before Ash Wednesday.

shrub[1] (shrŭb) *n.* A woody plant of relatively low height, having several stems arising from the base and lacking a single trunk; a bush. [Middle English *shrubbe,* from Old English *scrybb.* See **sker-**[1] in Appendix.]

shrub[2] (shrŭb) *n.* A beverage made from fruit juice, sugar, and a liquor such as rum or brandy. [From Arabic *šurb,* a drink, from *šariba,* to drink.]

shrub·ber·y (shrŭb′ə-rē) *n., pl.* **-ies.** A group or planting of shrubs.

shrub·by (shrŭb′ē) *adj.* **-bi·er, -bi·est.** **1.** Consisting of, planted with, or covered with shrubs. **2.** Of or resembling a shrub. **—shrub′bi·ness** *n.*

shrug (shrŭg) *v.* **shrugged, shrug·ging, shrugs.** —*tr.* To raise (the shoulders), especially as a gesture of doubt, disdain, or indifference. —*intr.* To raise the shoulders, especially as a gesture of doubt, disdain, or indifference. **—shrug** *n.* **1.** An expressive gesture of raising the shoulders. **2.** A woman's short jacket or sweater open down the front. **—*phrasal verb.* shrug off.** **1.** To minimize the importance of: *shrugged off the defeat and talked about tonight's game.* **2.** To get rid of: *shrug off a burden.* **3.** To wriggle out of (clothing). [Middle English *shruggen.*]

shrunk (shrŭngk) *v.* A past tense and a past participle of **shrink.**

shrunk·en (shrŭng′kən) *v.* A past participle of **shrink.**

sht. *abbr.* Sheet.

shtetl (shtĕt′l, shtāt′l) *n.* A small Eastern European Jewish community of former times. [Yiddish, from Middle High German *stetel,* diminutive of *stat,* town, from Old High German, place. See **stā-** in Appendix.]

shtick also **schtick** or **shtik** (shtĭk) *n. Slang.* **1.** A characteristic attribute, talent, or trait that is helpful in securing recognition or attention: *tried a new shtick in restaurant design.* **2.** An entertainment routine or gimmick. [Yiddish *shtik,* piece, routine, from Middle High German *stücke,* piece, from Old High German *stukki,* crust, fragment.]

Shu·bra al Khay·mah (sho͞o-brä′ äl kī-mä′, -mäкн′). A city of northeast Egypt, a suburb of Cairo. Population, 515,500.

shuck (shŭk) *n.* **1.a.** A husk, pod, or shell, as of an ear of corn, a pea, or a hickory nut. **b.** The shell of an oyster or a clam. **2.** *Informal.* Something worthless. Often used in the plural: *an issue that didn't amount to shucks.* **—shuck** *tr.v.* **shucked, shuck·ing, shucks.** **1.** To remove the husk or shell from. **2.** *Informal.* To cast off: *shucked their coats and cooled off; a city trying to shuck a sooty image.* **—shucks** (shŭks) *interj.* Used to express mild disappointment, disgust, or annoyance. [Origin unknown.] **—shuck′er** *n.*

shud·der (shŭd′ər) *intr.v.* **-dered, -der·ing, -ders.** **1.** To shiver convulsively, as from fear or revulsion. See Synonyms at **shake.** **2.** To vibrate; quiver: *The airplane shuddered in the turbulence.* **—shudder** *n.* A convulsive shiver, as from fear or revulsion; a tremor. [Middle English *shodderen,* perhaps of Middle Dutch or Middle Low German origin.] **—shud′der·ing·ly** *adv.*

shuf·fle (shŭf′əl) *v.* **-fled, -fling, -fles.** —*tr.* **1.** To slide (the feet) along the floor or ground while walking. **2.** To move (some-

shrimp

shrine
Offerings to Buddha

Shropshire[2]

ă pat	oi boy
ā pay	ou out
âr care	o͝o took
ä father	o͞o boot
ĕ pet	ŭ cut
ē be	ûr urge
ĭ pit	th thin
ī pie	*th* this
îr pier	hw which
ŏ pot	zh vision
ō toe	ə about, item
ô paw	♦ regionalism

Stress marks: ′ (primary); ′ (secondary), as in **dictionary** (dĭk′shə-nĕr′ē)

thing) from one place to another; transfer or shift. **3.** To put aside or under cover quickly; shunt: *shuffled the bill under a pile of junk mail.* **4.** To mix together; jumble. **5.** *Games.* To mix together (playing cards, tiles, or dominoes) so as to make a random order of arrangement. —*intr.* **1.** To move with short sliding steps, without or barely lifting the feet: *The crowd shuffled out of the theater.* **2.** To dance casually with sliding and tapping steps. **3.** To move about from place to place; shift: *shuffled around looking for work.* **4.** To act in a shifty or deceitful manner; equivocate. **5.** *Games.* To mix playing cards, tiles, or dominoes together so as to make their order random. **—shuffle** *n.* **1.** A short sliding step or movement, or a walk characterized by such steps. **2.** A dance in which the feet slide along or move close to the floor. **3.** An evasive or deceitful action; an equivocation. **4.** A confused mixture; a jumble. **5.** *Games.* **a.** An act of shuffling cards, dominoes, or tiles. **b.** A player's right or turn to do this. [Middle English *shovelen,* probably of Middle Dutch or Middle Low German origin.] **—shuf′fler** *n.*

shuffleboard

shuf·fle·board (shŭf′əl-bôrd′, -bōrd′) *n. Games.* **1.** A game in which disks are slid with a pronged cue along a smooth, level surface toward one of two usually triangular targets painted on the surface and divided into numbered scoring areas. **2.** A surface on which this game is played. [Alteration of obsolete *shove-board* : SHOVE + BOARD.]

shul (shōōl, shŏŏl) *n. Judaism.* A synagogue. [Yiddish, from Middle High German *schuol,* school, from Old High German *scuola,* from Latin *scola.* See SCHOOL[1].]

Shu·men (shōō′mĕn′). A city of northeast Bulgaria west of Varna. Founded in 927, the city was strategically important during the Russo-Turkish Wars of the 18th and 19th centuries. Population, 107,000.

shun (shŭn) *tr.v.* **shunned, shun·ning, shuns.** To avoid deliberately; keep away from. See Synonyms at **escape.** [Middle English *shunnen,* from Old English *scunian,* to abhor.] **—shun′ner** *n.*

shun·pike (shŭn′pīk′) *n.* A side road taken to avoid the tolls or traffic of a turnpike. **—shunpike** *intr.v.* **-piked, -pik·ing, -pikes.** To travel on side roads, avoiding turnpikes. **—shun′pik′er** *n.*

shunt (shŭnt) *n.* **1.** The act or process of turning aside or moving to an alternate course. **2.** A railroad switch. **3.** *Electricity.* A low-resistance connection between two points in an electric circuit that forms an alternative path for a portion of the current. Also called *bypass.* **4.** *Medicine.* A passage between two natural body channels, such as blood vessels, especially one created surgically to divert or permit flow from one pathway or region to another; a bypass. **—shunt** *v.* **shunt·ed, shunt·ing, shunts.** —*tr.* **1.** To turn or move aside or onto another course: *shunting traffic around an accident.* **2.** To evade by putting aside or ignoring: *urgent problems that society can no longer shunt aside.* **3.** To switch (a train or car) from one track to another. **4.** *Electricity.* To provide or divert (current) by means of a shunt. —*intr.* **1.** To move or turn aside. **2.** *Electricity.* To become diverted by means of a shunt. Used of a circuit. [Middle English *shunten,* to flinch.] **—shunt′er** *n.*

shutter
Open shutters

shush (shŭsh) *interj.* Used to express a demand for silence. **—shush** *tr.v.* **shushed, shush·ing, shush·es.** To demand silence from by saying "shush": *"Simon shushed him quickly as though he had spoken too loudly in church"* (William Golding).

shut (shŭt) *v.* **shut, shut·ting, shuts.** —*tr.* **1.** To move (a door or lid, for example) so as to block passage through an opening. **2.** To block entrance to or exit from; close: *shut a corridor.* **3.** To fasten with a lock, catch, or latch. **4.** To confine in or as if in a closed space: *shut them in a cage.* **5.** To exclude from or as if from a closed space: *shut the cats out of the house.* **6.** To cause to stop operating: *shut down a restaurant; a school that was shut for the vacation.* —*intr.* **1.** To move or become moved so as to block passage; close: *a door that shuts by itself.* **2.** To stop operating, especially automatically: *The electricity shuts off at midnight.* **—shut** *n.* **1.** The act or time of shutting. **2.** The line of connection between welded pieces of metal. **—*phrasal verbs.*** **shut off. 1.** To stop the flow or passage of; cut off: *shut off the hot water by closing a valve.* **2.** To close off; isolate: *loners who shut themselves off from the community.* **shut out.** *Sports.* To prevent (an opponent) from scoring any runs or points. **shut up. 1.** To cause (someone) to stop speaking; silence. **2.** To stop speaking. **—*idiom.* shut (one's) eyes to.** To refuse to consider or acknowledge: *administrators who shut their eyes to pervasive corruption.* [Middle English *shutten,* from Old English *scyttan.* See **skeud-** in Appendix.]

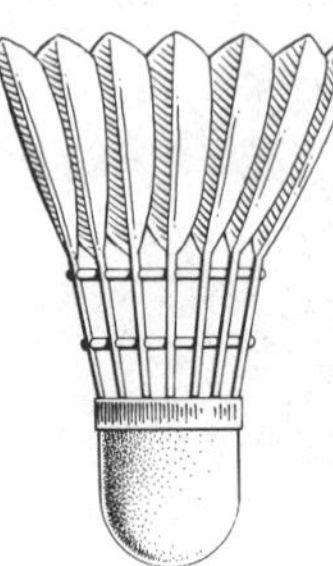

shuttlecock

shut·down (shŭt′doun′) *n.* A cessation of operations or activity, as at a factory.

Shute (shōōt), **Nevil.** Pen name of Nevil Shute Norway. 1899–1960. British writer whose novels include *A Town Like Alice* (1950) and *On the Beach* (1957), both set in Australia.

shut·eye (shŭt′ī′) *n. Slang.* Sleep.

shut-in (shŭt′ĭn′) *n.* A person confined indoors by illness or disability. **—shut-in** (shŭt-ĭn′) *adj.* **1.** Confined to a home or hospital, as by illness. **2.** Disposed to avoid social contact; excessively withdrawn or introverted.

shut·off (shŭt′ôf′, -ŏf′) *n.* **1.** A device that shuts something off. **2.** A stoppage; a cessation.

shut·out (shŭt′out′) *n.* **1.** See **lockout. 2.** *Sports.* A game in which one side does not score.

shut·ter (shŭt′ər) *n.* **1.** One that shuts, as: **a.** A hinged cover or screen for a window, usually fitted with louvers. **b.** A mechanical device of a camera that controls the duration of a photographic exposure, as by opening and closing to allow light coming through the lens to expose a plate or film. **2. shutters.** *Music.* The movable louvers on a pipe organ, controlled by pedals, that open and close the swell box. **—shutter** *tr.v.* **-tered, -ter·ing, -ters. 1.** To furnish or close with shutters: *locked the doors and shuttered the windows.* **2.** To cause to cease operations; close down: *shuttered the store for the holiday.*

shut·ter·bug (shŭt′ər-bŭg′) *n. Informal.* An enthusiastic amateur photographer.

shut·tle (shŭt′l) *n.* **1.** A device used in weaving to carry the woof thread back and forth between the warp threads. **2.** A device for holding the thread in tatting and netting and in a sewing machine. **3. a.** Regular travel back and forth over an established, often short route by a vehicle. **b.** A vehicle used in such travel: *took the shuttle across town.* **c.** A route used by a vehicle in such travel: *the Washington–New York air shuttle.* **4.** A space shuttle. **5.** Travel between disputing parties by a diplomatic intermediary. **—shuttle** *v.* **-tled, -tling, -tles.** —*intr.* To go, move, or travel back and forth by or as if by a shuttle: *business people who shuttle between European capitals.* —*tr.* **1.** To cause to move back and forth frequently. **2.** To transport by or as if by a shuttle: *shuttle a scientific payload to an orbiting space station.* [Middle English *shutille,* from Old English *scytel,* dart. See **skeud-** in Appendix.] **—shut′tler** *n.*

shut·tle·cock (shŭt′l-kŏk′) *n. Sports.* A small rounded piece of cork or rubber with a conical crown of feathers or plastic, used in badminton. Also called *bird, birdie.* **—shuttlecock** *tr.v.* **-cocked, -cock·ing, -cocks.** To throw or send back and forth like a shuttlecock.

shut·tle·craft (shŭt′l-krăft′) *n.* A reusable space vehicle for transporting astronauts or material back and forth; a space shuttle.

shuttle diplomacy *n.* Diplomatic negotiations conducted by an official intermediary who travels frequently between the nations involved. **—shuttle diplomat** *n.*

shy[1] (shī) *adj.* **shi·er, shi·est** or **shy·er, shy·est. 1.** Easily startled; timid. **2. a.** Drawing back from contact or familiarity with others; retiring or reserved. **b.** Marked by reserve or diffidence: *a shy glance.* **3.** Distrustful; wary: *shy of strangers.* **4.** Not having paid an amount due, as one's ante in poker. **5.** Short; lacking: *Eleven is one shy of a dozen.* **—shy** *intr.v.* **shied** (shīd), **shy·ing, shies** (shīz). **1.** To move suddenly, as if startled; start. **2.** To draw back, as from fear or caution; recoil. **—shy** *n., pl.* **shies** (shīz). A sudden movement, as from fright; a start. [Middle English *shei,* from Old English *scēoh.*] **—shy′er** *n.* **—shy′ly** *adv.* **—shy′ness** *n.*

SYNONYMS: *shy, bashful, diffident, modest, coy, demure.* These adjectives mean not forward but marked by a retiring nature, reticence, or a reserve of manner. One who is *shy* draws back from others, either because of a withdrawn nature or out of timidity: *"The poor man was shy and hated society"* (George Bernard Shaw). *Bashful* suggests self-consciousness or awkwardness in the presence of others: *"I never laughed, being bashful./Lowering my head, I looked at the wall"* (Ezra Pound). *Diffident* implies lack of self-confidence: *He was too diffident to express his opinion. Modest* is associated with an unassertive nature, absence of vanity, and freedom from pretension: *Despite her fame she remained the modest, unassuming person she had been as a student. Coy* usually implies feigned, often flirtatious shyness: *"yielded with coy submission"* (John Milton). *Demure* often denotes an affected shyness or modesty: *"I really don't know how to write a check," she said, with a demure sidelong glance.*

shy[2] (shī) *v.* **shied** (shīd), **shy·ing, shies** (shīz). —*tr.* To throw (something) with a swift motion; fling. —*intr.* To throw something with a swift motion. **—shy** *n., pl.* **shies** (shīz). **1.** A quick throw; a fling. **2.** *Informal.* A gibe; a sneer. **3.** *Informal.* An attempt; a try. [Perhaps from SHY[1].]

shy·lock (shī′lŏk′) *n.* **1.** A ruthless moneylender; a loan shark. **2. Shylock.** The ruthless usurer in Shakespeare's play *The Merchant of Venice.* **—shylock** *intr.v.* **-locked, -lock·ing, -locks.** To lend money at exorbitant interest rates.

shy·ster (shī′stər) *n. Slang.* An unethical, unscrupulous practitioner, especially of law. [Probably alteration of German *Scheisser,* son of a bitch, bastard, from *scheissen,* to defecate, from Middle High German *schīzen,* from Old High German *skīzzan.* See **skei-** in Appendix.] **—shy′ster·ism** *n.*

WORD HISTORY: The origin of *shyster* was not known for certain until recently. According to one etymology, *shyster* comes from the surname of one *Scheuster,* a disreputable and almost certainly nonexistent mid-19th-century attorney. In his book *Human Words,* a collection of words formed from the names of people, Robert Hendrickson says that Dr. Henry Bosley Woolf and others "list the New York advocate as a possible source." But the actual etymology, according to Gerald L. Cohen, a student of the word, is less flattering. According to this etymology, the word is derived from the German term *scheisser,* meaning literally "one who defecates," from the verb *scheissen,* "to defecate," with the English suffix *-ster,* "one who does," substituted for the German suffix *-er,* meaning the same thing. *Sheisser,* which is chiefly a

ă pat	oi boy
ā pay	ou out
âr care	ŏŏ took
ä father	ōō boot
ĕ pet	ŭ cut
ē be	ûr urge
ĭ pit	th thin
ī pie	*th* this
îr pier	hw which
ŏ pot	zh vision
ō toe	ə about, item
ô paw	♦ regionalism

Stress marks: **′** (primary); ′ (secondary), as in **dictionary** (dĭk′shə-nĕr′ē)

pejorative term, is the German equivalent of our English terms *bastard* and *son of a bitch. Sheisser* is generally thought to have been borrowed directly into English as the word *shicer,* which, among other things, is an Australian English term for an unproductive mine or claim, a sense also recorded for the word *shyster.*

si (sē) *n. Music.* Ti. [Italian, from Medieval Latin. See GAMUT.]

Si The symbol for the element **silicon.**

SI *abbr. French.* Système International [d'Unités] (International System [of Units]).

si·a·bon (sē′ə-bən) *n.* The hybrid offspring of a male gibbon and a female siamang. [SIA(MANG) + (GIB)BON.]

si·al (sī′ăl′) *n.* Rock rich in silicon and aluminum forming the upper layer of the earth's crust beneath all continental land masses. [SI(LICON) + AL(UMINUM).]

si·a·lad·en·i·tis (sī′ə-lăd′n-ī′tĭs) *n.* Inflammation of a salivary gland. [Greek *sialon,* saliva + ADENITIS.]

si·al·a·gogue (sī-ăl′ə-gôg′, -gŏg′) *n.* A drug or other agent that increases the flow of saliva. [Greek *sialon,* saliva + –AGOGUE.] **—si′al·a·gog′ic** (sī′ə-lə-gŏj′ĭk) *adj.*

si·al·ic acid (sī-ăl′ĭk) *n.* Any of a group of amino carbohydrates that are components of mucoproteins and glycoproteins, especially in animal tissue and blood cells. [Greek *sialon,* saliva + –IC.]

Si·al·kot (sē-äl′kōt′). A city of northeast Pakistan north of Lahore. It is a trade and processing center. Population, 252,000.

si·a·lo·mu·cin (sī′ə-lō-myo͞o′sĭn, sī-ăl′ō-) *n.* A mucin containing sialic acid. [Greek *sialon,* saliva + MUCIN.]

si·al·or·rhe·a also **si·al·or·rhoe·a** (sī-ăl′ə-rē′ə) *n.* An excessive secretion of saliva. [Greek *sialon,* saliva + –RRHEA.]

Si·am (sī-ăm′). See **Thailand.**

si·a·mang (sē′ə-măng′, sē-äm′əng) *n.* A large black gibbon *(Symphalangus syndactylus* or *Hylobates syndactylus)* of Sumatra and the Malay Peninsula, having an inflatable throat sac and a web of skin joining the second and third toes. [Malay.]

Si·a·mese (sī′ə-mēz′, -mēs′) *adj.* **1.** Of or relating to Siam; Thai. **2.** Closely connected or very similar; twin. **3. siamese.** Of or being a Y-shaped dual connection between two pipes or hoses and a larger pipe or hose. **—Siamese** *n., pl.* **Siamese. 1.** A native or inhabitant of Siam; a Thai. **2.** The Thai language. [After *Siam* (Thailand).]

Siamese cat *n.* A short-haired cat of a breed developed in the Far East, having blue eyes and a pale fawn or gray coat with darker ears, face, tail, and feet.

Siamese fighting fish *n.* A small, often brightly colored, aggressive freshwater fish *(Betta splendens)* native to Malaysia and Thailand that has large fins and tail and is popular in home aquariums.

Siamese twin *n.* Either of a pair of identical twins born with their bodies joined at some point, a result of the incomplete division of the ovum from which the twins developed. [After Chang and Eng (1811–1874), joined Chinese twins born in *Siam* (Thailand).]

Si·an (sē′än′, shē′-). See **Xi'an.**

Siang Kiang (syäng′ kyäng′, shyäng′). See **Xiang Jiang.**

Siang·tan (syäng′tän′, shyäng′-). See **Xiangtan.**

Šiau·liai (shyou′lyī′). A city of northern Lithuania northwest of Vilnius. Under the control of the Polish crown from 1589 until 1772, it passed to Russia in 1795. The city is now an industrial center. Population, 134,000.

sib (sĭb) *n.* **1.a.** A blood relation; a relative. **b.** A person's relatives considered as a group; kinfolk. **2.** A brother or sister; a sibling. **3.** *Anthropology.* A kinship group consisting of two or more lineages considered as being related, as by common descent from a mythic ancestor. **—sib** *adj.* Related by blood; kindred. [Middle English *sibbe,* from Old English *sibb.* See **s(w)e-** in Appendix.]

Sib. *abbr.* **1.** Siberia. **2.** Siberian.

Si·be·li·us (sĭ-bā′lē-əs, -bāl′yəs), **Jean.** 1865–1957. Finnish composer whose romantic, nationalistic works include the symphonic poems *Finlandia* (1899) and *Valse Triste* (1903).

Si·be·ri·a[1] (sī-bîr′ē-ə). *Abbr.* **Sib.** A region of central and eastern Russia stretching from the Ural Mountains to the Pacific Ocean. The extensive area was annexed by Russia in stages during the 16th and 17th centuries. Used as a place of exile for political prisoners since the early 17th century, it was settled by Russians after the construction of the Trans-Siberian Railroad (completed in 1905) and developed for its mineral resources after World War II. **—Si·be′ri·an** *adj. & n.*

Si·be·ri·a[2] (sī-bîr′ē-ə) *n.* A remote, undesirable locale: *"found herself not at the State House but exiled to the Registry of Motor Vehicles—the Siberia of state government"* (Howie Carr).

Siberian husky *n.* See **husky**[3] (sense 1).

sib·i·lant (sĭb′ə-lənt) *Linguistics. adj.* Of, characterized by, or producing a hissing sound like that of (s) or (sh): *the sibilant consonants; a sibilant bird call.* **—sibilant** *n.* A sibilant speech sound, such as English (s), (sh), (z), or (zh). [Latin *sībilāns, sībilant-,* present participle of *sībilāre,* to hiss.] **—sib′i·lance, sib′i·lan·cy** *n.* **—sib′i·lant·ly** *adv.*

sib·i·late (sĭb′ə-lāt′) *intr. & tr.v.* **-lat·ed, -lat·ing, -lates.** To utter or pronounce with a hissing sound. [Latin *sībilāre, sībilāt-,* to hiss.] **—sib′i·la′tion** *n.*

Si·biu (sē-byo͞o′). A city of central Romania northwest of Bucharest. Settled in the 12th century by German colonists from Saxony, it was destroyed by Tartars in 1241. The rebuilt city came under Austrian control in 1699. Population, 172,117.

sib·ling (sĭb′lĭng) *n.* One of two or more individuals having one or both parents in common; a brother or sister. [Middle English, from Old English, from *sibb,* kinsman. See SIB.]

sibling species *n.* Any of two or more related species that are morphologically nearly identical but are incapable of producing fertile hybrids.

Si·bu·yan Sea (sē′bo͞o-yän′). A sea in the central Philippines bordered by southern Luzon, Mindoro, and the Visayan Islands.

sib·yl (sĭb′əl) *n.* **1.** One of a number of women regarded as oracles or prophets by the ancient Greeks and Romans. **2.** A woman prophet. [Middle English *sibile,* from Old French, from Latin *Sibylla,* from Greek *Sibulla.*]

sib·yl·line (sĭb′ə-līn′, -lēn′) also **si·byl·ic** or **si·byl·lic** (sĭ-bĭl′ĭk) *adj.* **1.** Coming from, characteristic of, or relating to a sibyl. **2.** Prophetic; oracular.

sic[1] (sĭk) *adv.* Thus; so. Used in written texts to indicate that a surprising or paradoxical word, phrase, or fact is not a mistake and is to be read as it stands. [Latin *sīc.* See **so-** in Appendix.]

sic[2] also **sick** (sĭk) *tr.v.* **sicced, sic·cing, sics** also **sicked, sick·ing, sicks. 1.** To set upon; attack. **2.** To urge or incite to hostile action; set: *sicced the dogs on the intruders.* [Dialectal variant of SEEK.]

Sic. *abbr.* **1.** Sicilian. **2.** Sicily.

sic·ca·tive (sĭk′ə-tĭv) *n.* A substance added to paints and some medicines to promote drying; a drier. [Late Latin *siccātīvus,* drying, from Latin *siccātus,* past participle of *siccāre,* to dry, from *siccus,* dry.]

Si·chuan also **Sze·chwan** or **Sze·chuan** (sĕch′wän′). A province of south-central China. Settled by non-Chinese peoples, it was incorporated into the empire (c. third century A.D.) by the Qin dynasty. Chengdu is the capital. Population, 101,800,000.

Si·ci·ly (sĭs′ə-lē). *Abbr.* **Sic.** An island of southern Italy in the Mediterranean Sea west of the southern end of the Italian peninsula. It was colonized from the 8th century B.C. by Greeks, who displaced the earlier Phoenician settlers. The next conquerors were Carthaginians, who in turn were conquered by Romans in the 3rd century B.C. After a succession of other rulers the island came under the control of the Normans in the 11th century A.D. and formed the nucleus of the Kingdom of the Two Sicilies, consisting of Sicily and southern Italy. The island continued to change hands until a later kingdom was conquered by Giuseppe Garibaldi in 1860 and became part of unified Italy. **—Si·cil′ian** (sĭ-sĭl′yən) *adj. & n.*

sick[1] (sĭk) *adj.* **sick·er, sick·est. 1.a.** Suffering from or affected with a physical illness; ailing. **b.** Of or for sick persons: *sick wards.* **c.** Nauseated. **2.a.** Mentally ill or disturbed. **b.** Unwholesome; morbid: *a sick joke.* **3.** Defective; unsound: *a sick economy.* **4.a.** Deeply distressed; upset: *sick with worry.* **b.** Disgusted; revolted. **c.** Weary; tired: *sick of it all.* **d.** Pining; longing: *sick for his native land.* **5.a.** In need of repairs: *a sick ship.* **b.** Constituting an unhealthy environment for those working or residing within: *a sick office building.* **6.** Unable to produce a profitable yield of crops: *sick soil.* ***—idiom.* sick and tired.** Thoroughly weary, discouraged, or bored. [Middle English, from Old English *sēoc.*]

sick[2] (sĭk) *v.* Variant of **sic**[2]**.**

sick·bay (sĭk′bā′) *n.* **1.** The hospital and dispensary of a ship. **2.** A place where the sick or injured are treated.

sick·bed (sĭk′bĕd′) *n.* A sick person's bed.

sick call *n.* **1.** A daily lineup of military personnel requiring medical attention. **2.** A signal announcing the time for such a lineup.

sick·en (sĭk′ən) *tr. & intr.v.* **-ened, -en·ing, -ens.** To make or become sick. See Synonyms at **disgust. —sick′en·er** *n.*

sick·en·ing (sĭk′ə-nĭng) *adj.* **1.** Revolting or disgusting; loathsome: *a sickening stench.* **2.** Causing sickness. **—sick′en·ing·ly** *adv.*

sick headache *n.* **1.** A headache accompanied by nausea. **2.** A migraine.

sick·ie (sĭk′ē) *n. Slang.* One who is mentally or emotionally deranged or perverted.

sick·ish (sĭk′ĭsh) *adj.* **1.** Somewhat sick. **2.** Somewhat nauseated. **3.** Somewhat revolting or nauseating. **—sick′ish·ly** *adv.* **—sick′ish·ness** *n.*

sick·le (sĭk′əl) *n.* **1.** An implement having a semicircular blade attached to a short handle, used for cutting grain or tall grass. **2.** The cutting mechanism of a reaper or mower. **—sickle** *v.* **-led, -ling, -les.** *—tr.* **1.** To cut with a sickle. **2.** To deform (a red blood cell) into an abnormal crescent shape. *—intr.* To assume an abnormal crescent shape. Used of red blood cells. [Middle English *sikel,* from Old English *sicol,* from Vulgar Latin **sicila,* from Latin *sēcula.* See **sek-** in Appendix.]

sick leave *n.* Paid absence from work allowed an employee because of sickness.

sick·le·bill (sĭk′əl-bĭl′) *n.* Any of several birds having long sharply curved bills, as *Falculea palliata,* a passerine bird of Madagascar, and *Hemignathus procerus,* a Hawaiian honeycreeper.

sickle cell *n.* An abnormal, crescent-shaped red blood cell that results from a single change in the amino acid sequence of the

Siamese cat

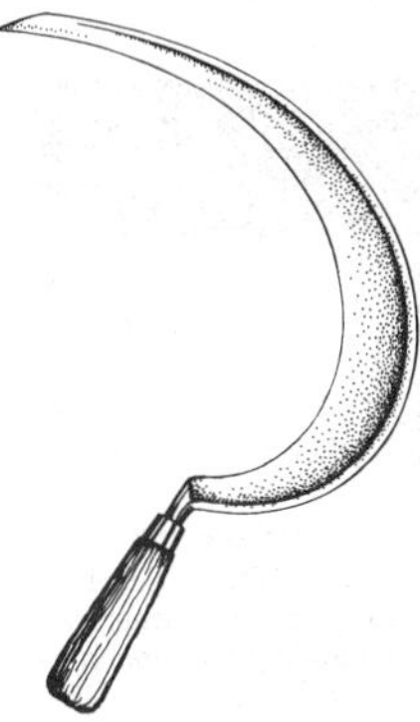

sickle

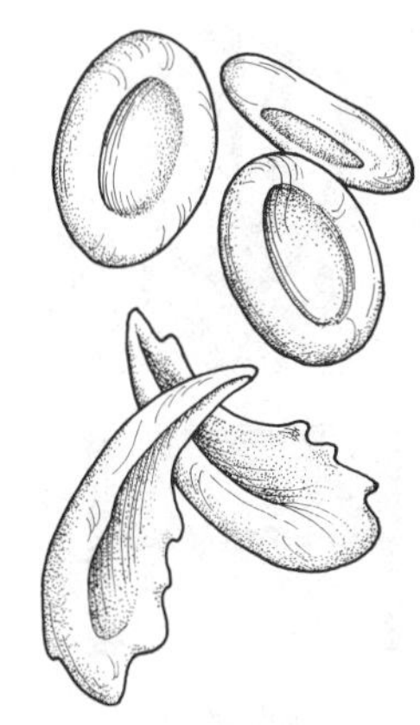

sickle cell
Top: Red blood cells
Bottom: Sickle cells

cell's hemoglobin, which causes the cell to contort, especially under low-oxygen conditions.

sickle cell anemia *n.* A chronic, usually fatal anemia marked by crescent-shaped red blood cells, occurring almost exclusively in Black people of Africa or of African descent, and characterized by episodic pain in the joints, fever, leg ulcers, and jaundice. The disease is caused by a recessive gene. Also called *sickle cell disease.*

sickle cell trait *n.* A hereditary condition, usually harmless and without symptoms, in which an individual carries only one gene for sickle cell anemia.

sickle feather *n.* Any of the long, curving feathers in the tail of a rooster.

sick·le·mi·a (sĭk′ə-lē′mē-ə) *n.* Sickle cell anemia or sickle cell trait.

sick list *n.* A list of sick personnel.

sick·ly (sĭk′lē) *adj.* **-li·er, -li·est. 1.** Prone to sickness. **2.** Of, caused by, or associated with sickness: *a sickly pallor.* **3.** Conducive to sickness: *a sickly climate.* **4.** Causing nausea; nauseating. **5.** Lacking vigor or strength; feeble or weak: *a sickly handshake.* **—sickly** *tr.v.* **-lied, -ly·ing, -lies.** To make sickly: *"Timidity . . . sicklies the whole cast of thought in action"* (Henry Adams). **—sick′li·ness** *n.* **—sick′ly, sick′li·ly** *adv.*

sick·ness (sĭk′nĭs) *n.* **1.** The condition of being sick; illness. **2.** A disease; a malady. **3.** Nausea. **4.** A defective or unsound condition.

sick·o (sĭk′ō) *n., pl.* **-os.** *Slang.* One who is mentally or emotionally deranged or perverted. [From SICK[1].]

sideboard
Late 18th- to early 19th-century American mahogany sideboard by Thomas Howard, Jr. (1774–1833)

sick·out (sĭk′out′) *n.* An organized job action in which employees absent themselves from work on the pretext of illness.

sick pay *n.* Wages paid to an employee who is absent because of illness.

sick·room (sĭk′ro͞om′, -ro͝om′) *n.* A room occupied by a sick person.

sic pas·sim (sĭk păs′ĭm) *adv.* Thus everywhere. Used to indicate that a term or an idea is to be found throughout a text. [Latin *sīc passim* : *sīc,* thus + *passim,* everywhere.]

Si·cy·on (sĭsh′ē-ŏn′, sĭs′-). An ancient city of southern Greece in the northeast Peloponnesus near the Gulf of Corinth. It reached the height of its power under the tyrant Cleisthenes in the sixth century B.C.

Sid·dons (sĭd′nz), **Sarah.** 1755–1831. British actress known for her Shakespearean roles, especially Lady Macbeth.

sid·dur (sĭd′ər, -o͝or′) *n., pl.* **sid·du·rim** (sĭ-do͝or′ĭm, sĭ′do͝o-rĭm′). *Judaism.* A prayer book containing prayers for the various days of the year. [Hebrew *siddûr,* arrangement, from *sidder,* to arrange.]

side (sīd) *n.* **1.** *Mathematics.* **a.** A line bounding a plane figure. **b.** A surface bounding a solid figure. **2.** A surface of an object, especially a surface joining a top and bottom: *the four sides of a box.* **3.** A surface of an object that extends more or less perpendicularly from an observer standing in front: *the side of the ship.* **4.** Either of the two surfaces of a flat object: *the front side of a piece of paper; the two sides of a record.* **5. a.** The part within an object or area to the left or right of the observer or of its vertical axis. **b.** The left or right half of the trunk of a human or animal body: *always sleeps on his side; a side of beef.* **6. a.** The space immediately next to someone: *stood at her father's side.* **b.** The space immediately next to something. Often used in combination: *courtside; dockside.* **7.** One of two or more contrasted parts or places within an area, identified by its location with respect to a center: *the north side of the park.* **8.** An area separated from another area by an intervening feature, such as a line or barrier: *on this side of the Atlantic; the district on the other side of the railroad tracks.* **9. a.** One of two or more opposing individuals, groups, teams, or sets of opinions. **b.** One of the positions maintained in a dispute or debate. **10.** A distinct aspect: *the shy side of his personality.* See Synonyms at **phase. 11.** Line of descent: *my aunt on my mother's side.* **12.** *Chiefly British.* Affected superiority; arrogance. **—side** *adj.* **1.** Located on a side: *a side door.* **2.** From or to one side; oblique: *a side view.* **3.** Minor; incidental: *a side interest.* **4.** In addition to the main part; supplementary: *a side benefit.* **—side** *v.* **sid·ed, sid·ing, sides.** *—tr.* **1.** To provide sides or siding for: *side a frame house with aluminum.* **2.** To be positioned next to: *a couch that is sided by low tables.* **3.** To be in agreement with; support. *—intr.* To align oneself in a disagreement: *sided with the conservatives in Congress; siding against the bill.* **—*idioms.* on the side. 1.** In addition to the main portion: *coleslaw on the side.* **2.** In addition to the main occupation or activity: *did some consulting work on the side.* **side by side.** Next to each other; close together. **this side of.** *Informal.* Verging on; short of: *shady deals that were just this side of criminal.* [Middle English, from Old English *sīde.*]

sidecar

side·arm (sīd′ärm′) *adj.* *Sports.* Thrown with or marked by a sideways motion of the arm between shoulder and hip height and relatively parallel to the ground: *a sidearm baseball pitch.* **—side′arm′** *adv.*

side arm *n.* A small weapon, such as a pistol, carried at the side or waist.

side·band also **side band** (sīd′bănd′) *n.* Either of the two bands of frequencies, one just above and one just below a carrier frequency, that result from modulation of a carrier wave.

side chair
1790–1800 American Classical Revival style

side·bar (sīd′bär′) *n.* **1.** A short, often boxed auxiliary news story that is printed alongside a longer article and that typically presents additional, contrasting, or late-breaking news. **2.** *Law.* A conference between a judge and the attorneys of a case being tried, held outside of the jury's range of hearing.

side·board (sīd′bôrd′, -bōrd′) *n.* **1.** A piece of dining room furniture having drawers and shelves for linens and tableware. **2.** A board that forms a side or part of a side: *the sideboards of a skating rink.*

side·burns (sīd′bûrnz′) *pl.n.* Growths of hair down the sides of a man's face in front of the ears, especially when worn with the rest of the beard shaved off. [Alteration of BURNSIDES.]

side·car (sīd′kär′) *n.* **1.** A one-wheeled car for a single passenger, attached to the side of a motorcycle. **2.** A cocktail combining brandy, an orange-flavored liqueur, and lemon juice.

side chair *n.* A straight-backed chair without arms, usually part of a dining room set.

sid·ed (sī′dĭd) *adj.* Having sides usually of a specified number or kind. Often used in combination: *many-sided; marble-sided.* **—sid′ed·ness** *n.*

side dish *n.* A dish served as an accompaniment to the main course.

side drum *n.* *Music.* See **snare drum.**

side effect *n.* A peripheral or secondary effect, especially an undesirable secondary effect of a drug or therapy.

side-glance (sīd′glăns′) *n.* **1.** A glance cast to the side. **2.** An indirect or brief reference; an allusion.

side·kick (sīd′kĭk′) *n.* *Slang.* A close companion or comrade.

side·light (sīd′līt′) *n.* **1.** A light coming from the side. **2.** *Nautical.* Either of two lights, red to port, green to starboard, shown by ships at night. **3.** A piece of incidental or contrasting information.

side·line (sīd′līn′) *n.* **1.** *Sports.* **a.** A line along either of the two sides of a playing court or field, marking its limits. **b. sidelines.** The space outside such limits, occupied by spectators and inactive players. **2. sidelines.** The position or point of view of those who observe rather than participate in an activity: *the political sidelines.* **3.** A subsidiary line of merchandise. **4.** An activity pursued in addition to one's regular occupation. **—sideline** *tr.v.* **-lined, -lin·ing, -lines.** *Informal.* To remove or keep from active participation.

side·lin·er (sīd′lī′nər) *n.* One that remains on the sidelines; a nonparticipant.

side·ling (sīd′lĭng) *adj.* **1.** Directed to one side; oblique. **2.** Sloping; inclined. **—sideling** *adv.* Obliquely; sideways.

side·long (sīd′lông′, -lŏng′) *adj.* **1.** Directed to one side; sideways: *a sidelong glance.* **2.** So as to slant; sloping. **—sidelong** *adv.* **1.** On or toward the side; sideways. **2.** In an oblique manner. [Alteration of SIDELING.]

side·man (sīd′măn′) *n.* *Music.* A member of a jazz band who is not the leader or a featured soloist.

side·piece (sīd′pēs′) *n.* A part forming the side of something else: *a chair with curved sidepieces.*

sider– *pref.* Variant of **sidero–.**

si·de·re·al (sī-dîr′ē-əl) *adj.* **1.** Of, relating to, or concerned with the stars or constellations; stellar. **2.** Measured or determined by means of the apparent daily motion of the stars: *sidereal time.* [From Latin *sīdereus,* from *sīdus, sīder-,* constellation, star.]

sidereal day *n.* The time required for a complete rotation of the earth in reference to any star or to the vernal equinox at the meridian, equal to 23 hours, 56 minutes, 4.09 seconds in units of mean solar time.

sidereal hour *n.* A 24th part of a sidereal day.

sidereal month *n.* The average period of revolution of the moon around the earth in reference to a fixed star, equal to 27 days, 7 hours, 43 minutes in units of mean solar time.

sidereal time *n.* Time based on the rotation of the earth with reference to the background of stars.

sidereal year *n.* The time required for one complete revolution of the earth about the sun, relative to the fixed stars, or 365 days, 6 hours, 9 minutes, 9.54 seconds in units of mean solar time.

sid·er·ite (sĭd′ə-rīt′) *n.* **1.** An ore of iron, $FeCO_3$. **2.** A meteorite consisting mainly of iron and nickel. **—sid′er·it′ic** (-ə-rĭt′ĭk) *adj.*

sidero– or **sider–** *pref.* Iron: *siderolite.* [Greek *sidēro-,* from *sidēros,* iron.]

sid·er·o·chrome (sĭd′ər-ə-krōm′) *n.* Any of various chemical compounds that transport iron across cell membranes, as in bacteria.

sid·er·o·cyte (sĭd′ər-ə-sīt′) *n.* A red blood cell containing granules of iron that are not part of the cell's hemoglobin.

sid·er·o·lite (sĭd′ər-ə-līt′) *n.* A meteorite composed of a mixed mass of iron and stone.

sid·er·o·sis (sĭd′ə-rō′sĭs) *n.* Chronic inflammation of the lungs caused by excessive inhalation of dust containing iron salts or particles.

side·sad·dle (sīd′săd′l) *n.* A saddle designed so that the rider sits with both legs on one side of the horse. **—sidesaddle** *adv.* On a sidesaddle.

side·show (sīd′shō′) *n.* **1.** A small show offered in addition to the main attraction, as at a circus. **2.** A diversion or spectacle that is incidental to a larger set of circumstances or a bigger issue:

"Administrations with little room to maneuver at home have historically looked for sideshows abroad" (Joan Didion).

side·slip (sīdʹslĭpʹ) *intr.v.* **-slipped, -slip·ping, -slips. 1.** To slip or skid to one side. **2.** *Sports.* To slide sideways and downward in skiing. **3.** To fly sideways and downward in an airplane along the lateral axis to reduce altitude without gaining speed or as the result of banking too deeply. **—sideʹslipʹ** *n.*

side·spin (sīdʹspĭnʹ) *n.* A rotary motion that spins a ball horizontally.

side·split·ting (sīdʹsplĭtʹĭng) *adj.* **1.** Convulsively hearty; uproarious. Used of laughter. **2.** Causing convulsive laughter: *a sidesplitting comedy.* **—sideʹsplitʹting·ly** *adv.*

side·step (sīdʹstĕpʹ) *v.* **-stepped, -step·ping, -steps.** *—intr.* **1.** To step aside: *sidestepped to make way for the runner.* **2.** To dodge an issue or a responsibility. *—tr.* **1.** To step out of the way of. **2.** To evade; skirt: *sidestep a difficult question.* **—sideʹstepʹper** *n.*

side step *n.* A step to one side, as in boxing or dancing.

side-strad·dle hop (sīdʹstrădʹl) *n. Sports.* A jumping jack.

side·stream smoke (sīdʹstrēmʹ) *n.* The stream of smoke from the burning end of a cigar, cigarette, or pipe.

side·stroke (sīdʹstrōkʹ) *Sports. n.* A swimming stroke in which a person swims on one side and thrusts the arms forward and downward alternately while performing a scissors kick. **—sidestroke** *intr.v.* **-stroked, -strok·ing, -strokes.** To swim with a sidestroke. **—sideʹstrokʹer** *n.*

side·swipe (sīdʹswīpʹ) *tr.v.* **-swiped, -swip·ing, -swipes.** To strike along the side in passing. **—sideswipe** *n.* **1.** A glancing blow on or along the side. **2.** An incidental critical remark; a gibe. **—sideʹswipʹer** *n.*

side·track (sīdʹtrăkʹ) *v.* **-tracked, -track·ing, -tracks.** *—tr.* **1.** To divert from a main issue or course: *I was sidetracked from my work by an unexpected visitor.* **2.** To delay or block the progress of deliberately: *"a bill that would sidetrack food irradiation in this country"* (Alexis Beck). **3.** To switch from a main railroad track to a siding. *—intr.* **1.** To deviate from a main issue or course. **2.** To run into a siding. **—sidetrack** *n.* A railroad siding.

side·walk (sīdʹwôkʹ) *n.* A paved walkway along the side of a street. *—attributive.* Often used to modify another noun: *a sidewalk fruit stand; sidewalk chalk artists.*

sidewalk superintendent *n. Slang.* A pedestrian who stops to watch construction or demolition work.

side·wall (sīdʹwôlʹ) *n.* **1.** A wall that forms the side of something. **2.** A side surface of an automobile tire, between the edge of the tread and the wheel rim.

side·ward (sīdʹwərd) *adv. & adj.* Toward or at one side. **—sideʹwards** (-wərdz) *adv.*

side·ways (sīdʹwāzʹ) also **side·way** (-wāʹ) *—adv. & adj.* **1.** Toward one side: *took a step sideways; a sideways glance.* **2.** From one side: *a painting lit sideways; sideways pressure.* **3.** With the side forward: *turned sideways to show the profile; a sideways view.*

side-wheel (sīdʹhwēlʹ, -wēlʹ) *adj. Nautical.* Of, relating to, or being a steamboat with a paddle wheel on each side.

side-wheel·er (sīdʹhwēʹlər, -wēʹ-) *n. Nautical.* A side-wheel steamboat.

side-whis·kers (sīdʹhwĭsʹkərz, -wĭsʹ-) *pl.n.* Whiskers worn usually long on the sides of a man's face.

side·wind·er (sīdʹwīnʹdər) *n.* **1.** A small rattlesnake *(Crotalus cerastes)* of the southwest United States and Mexico that moves by a distinctive lateral looping motion of its body and has two hornlike scaly projections above its eyes. **2.** A powerful swinging punch delivered from the side.

side·wise (sīdʹwīzʹ) *adv. & adj.* Sideways.

Si·di-bel-Ab·bès (sēʹdē-bĕl-ə-bĕsʹ). A city of northwest Algeria south of Oran. It was the headquarters of the French Foreign Legion until 1962. Population, 112,988.

sid·ing (sīʹdĭng) *n.* **1.** Material, such as boards or shingles, used for surfacing the outside walls of a frame building. **2.** A short section of railroad track connected by switches with a main track.

si·dle (sīdʹl) *v.* **-dled, -dling, -dles.** *—intr.* **1.** To move sideways: *sidled through the narrow doorway.* **2.** To advance in an unobtrusive, furtive, or coy way: *swindlers who sidle up to tourists.* *—tr.* To cause to move sideways: *We sidled the canoe to the riverbank.* **—sidle** *n.* **1.** An unobtrusive, furtive, or coy advance. **2.** A sideways movement. [Back-formation from SIDELING.] **—siʹdling·ly** *adv.*

Sid·ney (sĭdʹnē). A city of west-central Ohio west-northwest of Columbus. It is a manufacturing center. Population, 17,657.

Sidney, Sir **Philip.** 1554–1586. English poet, soldier, and politician. His most important works are the sonnet sequence *Astrophel and Stella* and the collection of pastoral idylls *Arcadia,* both published posthumously.

Si·don (sīdʹn). An ancient city of Phoenicia on the Mediterranean Sea in present-day southwest Lebanon. Founded in the third millennium B.C., it was an important trade center known for its glassware and purple dyes.

Sid·ra (sĭdʹrə), **Gulf of.** An inlet of the Mediterranean Sea off northern Libya west of Benghazi.

SIDS *abbr.* Sudden infant death syndrome.

siege (sēj) *n.* **1.** The surrounding and blockading of a city, town, or fortress by an army attempting to capture it. **2.** A prolonged period, as of illness: *a siege of asthma.* **3.** *Obsolete.* A seat, especially a throne. **—siege** *tr.v.* **sieged, sieg·ing, sieg·es.** To subject to a siege; besiege. See Synonyms at **besiege.** [Middle English *sege,* from Old French, seat, from Vulgar Latin **sedicum,* from **sedicāre,* to sit, from Latin *sedēre.* See **sed-** in Appendix.]

Sie·gen (zēʹgən). A city of west-central Germany east of Cologne. The birthplace of the painter Rubens, it is today heavily industrialized. Population, 107,774.

Siege Perilous (sēj) *n.* In Arthurian legend, a seat at King Arthur's Round Table kept for the knight destined to find the Holy Grail and fatal for any other occupant.

Sieg·fried (sēgʹfrēdʹ, sĭgʹ-) *n.* The warrior hero of the *Nibelungenlied* and other Germanic medieval epics, whose story is essentially that of his Norse prototype Sigurd. [German, from Middle High German *Sīfrit,* from Old High German *Sigifrith* : *sigu,* victory; see **segh-** in Appendix + *fridu,* peace; see **prī-** in Appendix.]

sie·mens (sēʹmənz) *n., pl.* **siemens.** *Abbr.* **S, s** A unit of electrical conductance in the International System, equal to one ampere per volt. [After Ernst Werner von SIEMENS.]

Sie·mens (sēʹmənz, zēʹ-), **Ernst Werner von.** 1816–1892. German engineer who made notable improvements to telegraphic and electrical apparatus. His brother **Karl Wilhelm,** later Sir **Charles William Siemens** (1823–1883), invented a regenerative steam engine and designed a steamship for laying long-distance cables.

Si·en·a (sē-ĕnʹə, syĕʹnä). A city of west-central Italy south of Florence. Founded by Etruscans, it became independent in the 12th century and gradually evolved into a wealthy city known especially for its leadership of the Sienese school of art (13th–14th centuries). Population, 61,888. **—Siʹe·neseʹ** (-nēzʹ, -nēsʹ) *adj. & n.*

Sien·kie·wicz (shĕn-kyāʹvĭch, -kyĕʹ-), **Henryk.** 1846–1916. Polish writer. Although he is most widely known for his historical novel *Quo Vadis?* (1896), his critical reputation rests on his works of Polish history, including *With Fire and Sword* (1883). Sienkiewicz won the 1905 Nobel Prize for literature.

si·en·na (sē-ĕnʹə) *n.* **1.** A special clay containing iron and manganese oxides, used as a pigment for oil and watercolor painting. **2.** *Color.* **a.** Raw sienna. **b.** Burnt sienna. [Short for *terra-sienna,* from Italian *terra di Sienna,* earth of Siena, after SIENA.]

si·er·o·zem (sī-ĕrʹə-zĕmʹ, sē-ĕrʹə-zhômʹ) *n.* Any of a group of soils found in cool to temperate arid regions that is brownish gray at the surface with a lighter layer below and is based in a carbonate or hardpan layer. [Russian *serozem* : *seryĭ,* gray + Old Russian *zemĭ,* earth; see **dhghem-** in Appendix.]

si·er·ra (sē-ĕrʹə) *n.* **1.** A rugged range of mountains having an irregular or jagged profile. See Usage Note at **redundancy. 2. a.** A Spanish mackerel *(Scomberomorus sierra)* of the Pacific coast of tropical America. **b.** See **cero.** [Spanish, saw, sierra, from Latin *serra,* saw.] **—si·erʹran** *adj.*

WORD HISTORY: Perhaps in formal contexts it is wise after mentioning a mountain range such as the Sierra Nevada to refer to it next as *the Sierras* rather than *the Sierra Mountains,* since *mountains* is inherent in *sierra.* Nonetheless, many Californians and Nevadans in particular will be very familiar with phrases such as *the Sierra Mountains.* Such phrases are used because to a non-Spanish speaker *sierra* does not necessarily have a meaning, unless one is familiar with the English word *sierra,* "a rugged range of mountains having an irregular profile," borrowed from Spanish. In Spanish *sierra* originally meant "saw" and so was aptly applied to a range of hills or mountains rising in peaks that suggested the teeth of a saw. It comes from Latin *serra,* "saw," to which can also be traced our word *serrated.*

Si·er·ra Le·one (sē-ĕrʹə lē-ōnʹ, -ōʹnē). A country of western Africa on the Atlantic coast. First visited by the Portuguese in the 1460's, the region became a British protectorate in 1896 and achieved independence in 1961. Freetown is the capital and the largest city. Population, 3,381,000.

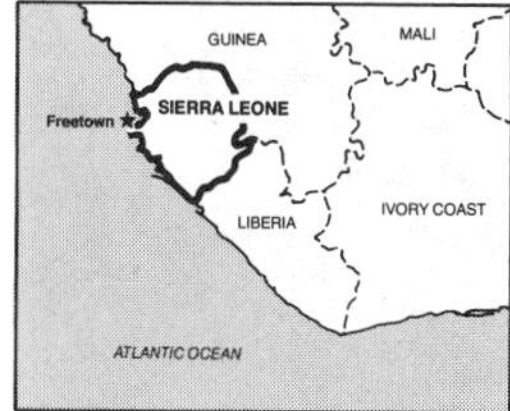

Sierra Leone

Si·er·ra Ma·dre del Sur (sē-ĕrʹə mäʹdrā dĕl so͝orʹ, syĕrʹä mäʹthrĕ). A mountain range of southern Mexico along the Pacific coast.

Sierra Madre Oc·ci·den·tal (ŏkʹsĭ-dĕnʹtəl, ôkʹsē-*th*ĕn-tälʹ). A mountain range of northwest Mexico running parallel to the Pacific coastline and adjoining the Mexican plateau. It extends for about 1,609 km (1,000 mi) southward from the border of Arizona.

Sierra Madre Or·ien·tal (ôrʹē-ĕn-tälʹ, ô-ryĕn-). A mountain range of northeast Mexico rising as barren hills south of the Rio Grande and paralleling the coast of the Gulf of Mexico.

Si·er·ra Ne·va·da (sē-ĕrʹə nə-vădʹə, -väʹdə). **1.** (*also* syĕrʹä nĕ-väʹ*th*ä). A mountain range of southern Spain along the Mediterranean coast east of Granada. It rises to 3,480.4 m (11,411 ft) at Mulhacén. **2.** A mountain range of eastern California extending about 644 km (400 mi) between the Sacramento and San Joaquin valleys and the Nevada border. Mount Whitney, 4,420.7 m (14,494 ft), is the highest elevation.

Sierra Vis·ta (vĭsʹtə). A city of southeast Arizona southeast of Tucson near the Mexican border. It is a cattle-raising and mining region. Population, 25,968.

si·es·ta (sē-ĕsʹtə) *n.* A rest or nap after the midday meal.

ă pat	oi boy
ā pay	ou out
âr care	o͝o took
ä father	o͞o boot
ĕ pet	ŭ cut
ē be	ûr urge
ĭ pit	th thin
ī pie	*th* this
îr pier	hw which
ŏ pot	zh vision
ō toe	ə about, item
ô paw	♦ regionalism

Stress marks: **ʹ** (primary); ʹ (secondary), as in **dictionary** (dĭkʹshə-nĕrʹē)

sieve
At an archaeological dig

[Spanish, from Latin *sexta (hōra),* sixth (hour), midday, feminine of *sextus,* sixth. See SEXT.]

sieve (sĭv) *n.* A utensil of wire mesh or closely perforated metal, used for straining, sifting, ricing, or purééing. **—sieve** *v.* **sieved, siev·ing, sieves.** *—tr.* To pass through a sieve. *—intr.* To use a sieve; sift. [Middle English *sive,* from Old English *sife.*]

sieve plate *n. Botany.* The perforated end wall of a sieve tube cell.

sieve tube *n. Botany.* A series of cells joined end to end, forming a tube through which nutrients are conducted in flowering plants and brown algae.

sift (sĭft) *v.* **sift·ed, sift·ing, sifts.** *—tr.* **1.** To put (flour, for example) through a sieve or other straining device in order to separate the fine from the coarse particles. **2.** To distinguish as if separating with a sieve: *sifted the candidates for the job.* **3.** To apply by scattering with or as if with a sieve: *sift sugar on a dessert.* **4.** To examine and sort carefully: *sift the evidence.* *—intr.* **1.** To make use of a sieve. **2.** To pass through or as if through a sieve: *a meal that sifts easily.* **3.** To make a careful examination: *sifted through back issues of the magazine.* [Middle English *siften,* from Old English *siftan.*] **—sift′er** *n.*

sig. *abbr.* **1.** Signal. **2.** Signature. **3.** Often **Sig.** Signor; signore.

Sig. *abbr.* **1.** *Latin.* Signa (mark or label it). **2.** *Medicine.* Signature. **3.** *Latin.* Signetur (let it be marked or labeled).

sigh (sī) *v.* **sighed, sigh·ing, sighs.** *—intr.* **1.a.** To exhale audibly in a long, deep breath, as in weariness or relief. **b.** To emit a similar sound: *willows sighing in the wind.* **2.** To feel longing or grief; yearn: *sighing for their lost youth.* *—tr.* **1.** To express with or as if with an audible exhalation. **2.** *Archaic.* To lament. **—sigh** *n.* The act or sound of sighing. [Middle English *sighen,* probably back-formation from *sighte,* past tense of *siken,* to sigh, from Old English *sīcan.*] **—sigh′er** *n.*

♦ **sight** (sīt) *n.* **1.** The ability to see. **2.** The act or fact of seeing: *hoping for a sight of land; caught sight of a rare bird.* **3.** Field of vision. **4.** The foreseeable future; prospect: *no solution in sight.* **5.** Something seen; a view. **6.** Something worth seeing; a spectacle: *the sights of London.* **7.** *Informal.* Something unsightly: *Your hair is a sight.* **8.a.** A device used to assist aim by guiding the eye, as on a firearm or surveying instrument. **b.** An aim or observation taken with such a device. **9.** An opportunity to observe or inspect. **10.** *Upper Southern U.S.* A large number or quantity: *A sight of people were there.* **—sight** *v.* **sight·ed, sight·ing, sights.** *—tr.* **1.** To perceive with the eyes; get sight of: *sighted land after 40 days at sea.* **2.** To observe through a sight or an optical instrument: *sight a target.* **3.** To adjust the sights of (a rifle, for example). **4.** To take aim with (a firearm). *—intr.* **1.** To direct one's gaze; look carefully. **2.** To take aim: *sighted along the barrel of the gun.* ***—idioms.*** **on sight.** Immediately upon being seen: *threatened to shoot looters on sight.* **out of sight.** *Slang.* Remarkable; incredible: *The graduation party was out of sight.* **sight for sore eyes.** *Informal.* One whom it is a relief or joy to see. **sight unseen.** Without seeing the object in question: *bought the horse sight unseen.* [Middle English, from Old English *sihth, gesiht,* something seen. See **sekʷ-²** in Appendix.]

sight draft *n. Abbr.* **SD.** A draft or bill that is payable on demand or upon presentation. Also called *demand draft.*

sight·ed (sī′tĭd) *adj.* **1.** Having the ability to see. **2.** Having eyesight of a specified kind. Often used in combination: *keen-sighted.* **—sight′ed·ness** *n.*

sight gag *n.* A comic bit or effect that depends on sight rather than words.

sight·ing (sī′tĭng) *n.* The act of catching sight of something, especially something unusual or searched for: *a sighting of a whale in the harbor; a reported sighting of a UFO.*

sight·less (sīt′lĭs) *adj.* **1.** Unable to see with the eyes; blind. **2.** Invisible. **—sight′less·ly** *adv.* **—sight′less·ness** *n.*

sight·line also **sight line** (sīt′līn′) *n.* A line of sight, especially one between a spectator and the spectacle in a theater or stadium.

sight·ly (sīt′lē) *adj.* **-li·er, -li·est.** **1.** Pleasing to see; visually appealing. **2.** Affording a fine view; scenic. **—sight′li·ness** *n.*

sight-read (sīt′rēd′) *v.* **-read** (-rĕd′), **-read·ing, -reads.** *—tr.* To read or perform (music, for example) without preparation or prior acquaintance. *—intr.* To read or perform something on sight without preparation or prior acquaintance. **—sight′-read′er** *n.*

sight rhyme *n.* See **eye rhyme.**

sight·see (sīt′sē′) *intr.v.* **-saw** (-sô′), **-seen** (-sēn′), **-see·ing, -sees.** To tour sights of interest. **—sight′se′er** *n.*

sight·see·ing (sīt′sē′ĭng) *n.* The act or pastime of visiting sights of interest. **—sightseeing** *adj.* Used or engaged in sightseeing: *a sightseeing bus; a sightseeing tour.*

sig·il (sĭj′əl, sĭg′ĭl) *n.* **1.** A seal; a signet. **2.** A sign or an image considered magical. [Latin *sigillum,* diminutive of *signum,* sign. See SIGN.]

Sig·is·mund (sĭg′ĭs-mənd). 1368–1437. Holy Roman emperor (1433–1437) and king of Hungary (1387–1437) and Bohemia (1419–1437). He helped end the Great Schism (1378–1417) by convening the Council of Constance (1414–1418).

sig·ma (sĭg′mə) *n.* **1.** The 18th letter of the Greek alphabet. See table at **alphabet. 2.** A sigma factor. **3.** A sigma hyperon. [Greek, of Phoenician origin; akin to Hebrew *sāmek,* samekh.] **—sig′mate′** (-māt′) *adj.*

sigma factor *n.* A protein component of RNA polymerase that determines the specific site on DNA where transcription begins.

sigma hyperon *n.* Any of three unstable subatomic particles in the baryon family, having a mass of 2,328 to 2,343 times that of the electron and a positive, neutral, or negative elecric charge. See table at **subatomic particle.**

sig·moid (sĭg′moid′) also **sig·moi·dal** (sĭg-moid′l) *adj.* **1.** Having the shape of the letter S. **2.** Of or relating to the sigmoid flexure of the colon. [Greek *sigmoeidēs* : *sigma,* sigma; see SIGMA + *-oeidēs,* -oid.]

sigmoid flexure *n.* An S-shaped section of the colon between the descending section and the rectum. Also called *sigmoid colon.*

sig·moid·o·scope (sĭg-moi′də-skōp′) *n.* A tubular instrument for visual examination of the sigmoid flexure. **—sig·moid′o·scop′ic** (-skŏp′ĭk) *adj.* **—sig′moid·os′co·py** (sĭg′-moi-dŏs′kə-pē) *n.*

sign (sīn) *n.* **1.** Something that suggests the presence or existence of a fact, condition, or quality. **2.a.** An act or a gesture used to convey an idea, a desire, information, or a command: *gave the go-ahead sign.* **b.** Sign language. **3.a.** A displayed structure bearing lettering or symbols, used to identify or advertise a place of business: *a motel with a flashing neon sign outside.* **b.** A posted notice bearing a designation, direction, or command: *an EXIT sign above a door; a traffic sign.* **4.** A conventional figure or device that stands for a word, a phrase, or an operation; a symbol, as in mathematics or in musical notation. **5.** *pl.* **sign.** An indicator, such as a dropping or footprint, of the trail of an animal: *looking for deer sign.* **6.** A trace or vestige: *no sign of life.* **7.** A portentous incident or event; a presage: *took the eclipse as a sign from God.* **8.** A body manifestation that serves to indicate the presence of malfunction or disease. **9.** One of the 12 divisions of the zodiac, each named for a constellation and represented by a symbol. **—sign** *v.* **signed, sign·ing, signs.** *—tr.* **1.** To affix one's signature to. **2.** To write (one's signature). **3.** To approve or ratify (a document) by affixing a signature, seal, or other mark: *sign a bill into law.* **4.** To hire or engage by obtaining a signature on a contract: *signed a rookie pitcher for next season; sign up actors for a tour.* **5.** To relinquish or transfer title to by signature: *signed away all her claims to the estate.* **6.** To provide with a sign or signs: *sign a new highway.* **7.** To communicate with a sign or by sign language: *signed his approval; sign instructions to a hearing-impaired teammate.* **8.** To consecrate with the sign of the cross. *—intr.* **1.** To make a sign or signs; signal. **2.** To use sign language. **3.** To write one's signature. ***—phrasal verbs.*** **sign in.** To record the arrival of (another or oneself) by signing a register. **sign off. 1.** To announce the end of a communication; conclude. **2.** To stop transmission after identifying the broadcasting station. **3.** *Informal.* To express approval formally or conclusively: *got the Congress to sign off on the tax proposal.* **sign on. 1.** *Informal.* To enlist oneself, especially as an employee: *"Retired politicians often sign on with top-dollar law firms"* (New York Times). **2.** To start transmission with an identification of the broadcasting station. **sign out.** To record the departure of (another or oneself) by signing a register. **sign up.** To agree to be a participant or recipient by signing one's name; enlist: *signed up for military service; signing up for a pottery course.* [Middle English *signe,* from Old French, from Latin *signum.* See **sekʷ-¹** in Appendix.] **—sign′er** *n.*

SYNONYMS: *sign, badge, mark, token, symptom, note.* These nouns are compared as they denote an outward indication of the existence or presence of something not immediately evident. *Sign* is the most general: *A high forehead is thought to be a sign of intelligence. "The exile of Gaveston was the sign of the barons' triumph"* (John R. Green). *"The V sign is the symbol of the unconquerable will of the occupied territories"* (Winston S. Churchill). *Badge* usually refers to something that is worn as an insignia of membership, is an emblem of achievement, or is a characteristic sign: *The sheriff's badge was shaped like a star. "Sweet mercy is nobility's true badge"* (Shakespeare). *Mark* can refer to a visible trace or impression (*a laundry mark*) or to an indication of a distinctive trait or characteristic: *Intolerance is the mark of a bigot.* The term can also denote a lasting effect, as of an experience: *Poverty had left its mark. Token* usually refers to evidence or proof of something intangible: *sent flowers as a token of her affection. Symptom* suggests outward evidence of a process or condition, especially an adverse condition: *"dying of a hundred good symptoms"* (Alexander Pope); *"the gale having rather increased than shown any symptoms of abating"* (Frederick Marryat). *Note* applies to the sign of a particular quality or feature: *"the eternal note of sadness"* (Matthew Arnold). See also Synonyms at **gesture.**

Si·gnac (sēn-yăk′), **Paul.** 1863–1935. French neoimpressionist painter. He painted mainly landscapes and marine views, such as *Port of St. Tropez* (1916).

sign·age (sī′nĭj) *n.* **1.** Signs considered as a group. **2.** The design or use of signs and symbols.

sig·nal (sĭg′nəl) *n. Abbr.* **sig. 1.a.** An indicator, such as a gesture or colored light, that serves as a means of communication. See Synonyms at **gesture. b.** A message communicated by such means. **2.** Something that incites action: *The peace treaty was the signal for mass celebrations.* **3.** *Electronics.* An impulse or a fluctuating electric quantity, such as voltage, current, or electric field strength, whose variations represent coded information. **4.**

The sound, image, or message transmitted or received in telegraphy, telephony, radio, television, or radar. **—signal** *adj.* Notably out of the ordinary: *a signal feat.* See Synonyms at **noticeable.** **—signal** *v.* **-naled, -nal·ing, -nals** or **-nalled, -nal·ling, -nals.** *—tr.* **1.** To make a signal to: *I signaled the driver to proceed.* **2.** To relate or make known by signals: *They have signaled their willingness to negotiate.* *—intr.* To make a signal or signals. [Middle English, from Old French, from Medieval Latin *signāle,* from neuter of Late Latin *signālis,* of a sign, from Latin *signum,* sign. See SIGN.] **—sig′nal·er, sig′nal·ler** *n.*

sig·nal·ize (sĭg′nə-līz′) *tr.v.* **-ized, -iz·ing, -iz·es. 1.** To make remarkable or conspicuous: *a life signalized by high accomplishments.* **2.** To point out particularly. **—sig′nal·i·za′tion** (-nə-lĭ-zā′shən) *n.*

sig·nal·ly (sĭg′nə-lē) *adv.* To a conspicuous degree; notably.

sig·nal·ment (sĭg′nəl-mənt) *n.* A detailed description of a person's appearance, as for police files. [French *signalement,* from *signaler,* to mark out, from *signal,* signal. See SIGNAL.]

sig·na·to·ry (sĭg′nə-tôr′ē, -tōr′ē) *adj.* Bound by signed agreement: *the signatory parties to a contract.* **—signatory** *n., pl.* **-ries.** One that has signed a treaty or other document. [Latin *signātōrius,* from *signātus,* past participle of *signāre,* to mark, from *signum,* sign. See SIGN.]

sig·na·ture (sĭg′nə-chər) *n.* **1.** *Abbr.* **sig.** One's name as written by oneself. **2.** The act of signing one's name. **3.** A distinctive mark, characteristic, or sound indicating identity: *A surprise ending is the signature of an O. Henry short story.* **4.** *Abbr.* **Sig., S.** *Medicine.* The part of a physician's prescription containing directions to the patient. **5.** *Music.* **a.** A sign used to indicate key. **b.** A sign used to indicate tempo. **6.** *Printing.* **a.** A letter, number, or symbol placed at the bottom of the first page on each sheet of printed pages of a book as a guide to the proper sequence of the sheets in binding. **b.** A large sheet printed with four or a multiple of four pages that when folded becomes a section of the book. [French, from Old French, from Medieval Latin *signātūra,* from Latin *signātus,* past participle of *signāre,* to mark, from *signum,* sign. See SIGN.]

sign·board (sīn′bôrd′, -bōrd′) *n.* A board bearing a sign.

sig·net (sĭg′nĭt) *n.* **1.** A seal, especially one used officially to mark documents. **2.** The impression made with such a seal. **—signet** *tr.v.* **-net·ed, -net·ing, -nets.** To mark or endorse with a signet. [Middle English, from Old French, diminutive of *signe,* sign. See SIGN.]

signet ring *n.* A finger ring bearing an engraved signet. Also called *seal ring.*

sig·nif·i·cance (sĭg-nĭf′ĭ-kəns) also **sig·nif·i·can·cy** (-kən-sē) *n.* **1.** The state or quality of being significant. See Synonyms at **importance. 2.** A meaning that is expressed. **3.** A covert or implied meaning. See Synonyms at **meaning.**

significance level *n. Statistics.* See **level of significance.**

sig·nif·i·cant (sĭg-nĭf′ĭ-kənt) *adj.* **1.** Having or expressing a meaning; meaningful. **2.** Having or expressing a covert meaning; suggestive: *a significant glance.* See Synonyms at **expressive. 3.** Having or likely to have a major effect; important: *a significant change in the tax laws.* **4.** Fairly large in amount or quantity: *significant casualties.* **5.** *Statistics.* Of or relating to observations or occurrences that are too closely correlated to be attributed to chance and therefore indicate a systematic relationship. [Latin *significāns, significant-,* present participle of *significāre,* to signify. See SIGNIFY.] **—sig·nif′i·cant·ly** *adv.*

significant digits *pl.n. Mathematics.* The digits of the decimal form of a number beginning with the leftmost nonzero digit and extending to the right to include all digits warranted by the accuracy of measuring devices used to obtain the numbers. Also called *significant figures.*

significant other *n.* **1.** A person, such as a spouse or lover, with whom one shares a long-term sexual relationship. **2.** A person, such as a family member or close friend, who is important or influential in one's life: *"The most important variable in successful smoking cessation is the support of significant others in the new nonsmoker's life"* (Carolyn Reuben).

sig·ni·fi·ca·tion (sĭg′nə-fĭ-kā′shən) *n.* **1.** The established meaning of a word. See Synonyms at **meaning. 2.** The act of signifying; indication.

sig·nif·i·ca·tive (sĭg-nĭf′ĭ-kā′tĭv) *adj.* **1.** Tending to signify or indicate; indicative. **2.** Having meaning; significant. **—sig·nif′i·ca′tive·ness** *n.*

sig·ni·fy (sĭg′nə-fī′) *v.* **-fied, -fy·ing, -fies.** *—tr.* **1.** To denote; mean. See Synonyms at **mean**[1]. **2.** To make known, as with a sign or word: *signify one's intent.* *—intr.* **1.** To have meaning or importance. See Synonyms at **count**[1]. **2.** *Slang.* To exchange humorous insults in a verbal game. [Middle English *signifien,* from Old French *signifier,* from Latin *significāre* : *signum,* sign; see SIGN + *-ficāre,* -fy.] **—sig′ni·fi′a·ble** *adj.* **—sig′ni·fi′er** *n.*

si·gnior (sēn-yôr′, -yōr′) *n.* Variant of **signor.**

si·gnio·ry (sēn′yə-rē) *n.* Variant of **signory.**

sign language *n.* **1.** A language that uses manual movements to convey grammatical structure and meaning. **2.** A method of communication, as between speakers of different languages, that uses hand movements and other gestures.

sign manual *n., pl.* **signs manual.** A signature, especially that of a monarch at the top of a royal decree.

sign of the cross *n.* A gesture describing the form of a cross, made in token of faith in Jesus or as an invocation of God's blessing.

si·gnor also **si·gnior** (sēn-yôr′, -yōr′) *n., pl.* **si·gno·ri** (sēn-yôr′ē, -yōr′ē) also **si·gniors** or **si·gnors.** *Abbr.* **S., Sig., sig.** Used as a courtesy title for a man in an Italian-speaking area, equivalent to *Mr.* [Italian, variant of *signore.* See SIGNORE.]

si·gno·ra (sēn-yôr′ə, -yōr′ə, -yô′rä) *n., pl.* **si·gno·re** (sēn-yôr′ā, -yōr′ā, -yô′rĕ) or **si·gno·ras.** Used as a courtesy title for a married woman in an Italian-speaking area, equivalent to *Mrs.* [Italian, feminine of *signore,* signore. See SIGNORE.]

si·gno·re (sēn-yôr′ā, -yōr′ā, -yô′rĕ) *n., pl.* **si·gno·ri** (sēn-yô′rē, -yōr′ē). *Abbr.* **S., Sig., sig.** Used as a form of polite address for a man in an Italian-speaking area. [Italian, from Medieval Latin *senior,* lord, from Latin, elder. See SENIOR.]

si·gno·ri (sēn-yô′rē, -yōr′ē) *n.* **1.** A plural of **signor. 2.** A plural of **signore.**

si·gno·ri·na (sēn′yə-rē′nə, -yô-rē′nä) *n., pl.* **-ne** (-nā, -nĕ) or **-nas.** Used as a courtesy title for an unmarried woman in an Italian-speaking area, equivalent to *Miss.* [Italian, diminutive of *signora,* signora. See SIGNORA.]

si·gno·ry or **si·gnio·ry** (sēn′yə-rē) *n., pl.* **-ries.** See **seigniory.** [Middle English *signorie,* from Old French *seigneurie,* from *seigneur,* seignior. See SEIGNIOR.]

sign·post (sīn′pōst′) *n.* **1.** A post supporting a sign that has information or directions. **2.** An indication, a sign, or a guide.

Sig·urd (sĭg′ərd) *n. Mythology.* A warrior hero in Norse myth who wins an accursed hoard of gold, awakens Brynhild from her enchanted sleep, marries a princess, and is slain through Brynhild's jealous contrivance.

Si·gurds·son (sĭg′ərd-sən, -œrth-sôn′), **Jón.** 1811–1879. Icelandic politician and scholar who secured a constitution for his country from Denmark (1874).

Si·ha·nouk (sē′ə-no͝ok′), Prince **Norodom.** Born 1922. Cambodian politician who served as prime minister (1955–1957) and became head of state in 1960. Sihanouk was deposed in 1970 and briefly returned to power (1975–1976) during the Pol Pot regime.

Si·ha·sa·pa (sə-hä′sə-pə) *n., pl.* **Sihasapa** or **-pas. 1.** A Native American people constituting a subdivision of the Teton Sioux. **2.** A member of this people. Also called *Blackfoot, Blackfoot Sioux.*

si·ka (sē′kə) *n.* A medium-sized deer *(Cervus nippon)* native to Japan and China but naturalized in Europe and other countries, having a small head, compact body, and mostly spotted reddish or chestnut coat. Several of its subspecies are endangered in the wild. [Japanese *shika,* deer.]

Sikes·ton (sīk′stən). A city of southeast Missouri west-southwest of Cairo, Illinois. It is a trade and processing center. Population, 17,431.

Sikh (sēk) *n.* An adherent of Sikhism. **—Sikh** *adj.* Of or relating to the Sikhs or to Sikhism. [Hindi, from Sanskrit *śiṣyaḥ,* disciple, from *śikṣati,* he wishes to learn, desiderative of *śaknoti,* is able.]

Sikh·ism (sēk′ĭz′əm) *n.* The doctrines and practices of a monotheistic religion founded in northern India in the 16th century and combining elements of Hinduism and Islam.

Si Kiang (sē′ kyäng′, shē′). See **Xi Jiang.**

Sik·kim (sĭk′ĭm). A region and former kingdom of northeast India in the eastern Himalaya Mountains between Nepal and Bhutan. Long isolated from the outside world, Sikkim was virtually a dependency of Tibet until the 19th century, when it came under British protection. The protectorate passed to India in 1949 and became an integral part of that country in 1975.

Si·kor·sky (sĭ-kôr′skē), **Igor Ivan.** 1889–1972. Russian-born American aviation pioneer. He designed (1939) the first successful American helicopter.

si·lage (sī′lĭj) *n.* Fodder prepared by storing and fermenting green forage plants in a silo. [Short for ENSILAGE.]

sil·ane (sĭl′ān′) *n.* Any of a group of silicon hydrides having the general formula SiH that are analogous to the paraffin hydrocarbons. [SIL(ICON) + (METH)ANE.]

sild (sĭld) *n., pl.* **sild** or **silds.** A young herring other than a sprat that is processed as a sardine in Norway. [Norwegian and Danish, from Old Norse *sīld,* herring.]

si·lence (sī′ləns) *n.* **1.** The condition or quality of being or keeping still and silent. **2.** The absence of sound; stillness. **3.** A period of time without speech or noise. **4.** Refusal or failure to speak out. **—silence** *tr.v.* **-lenced, -lenc·ing, -lenc·es. 1.** To make silent or bring to silence: *silenced the crowd with a gesture.* **2.** To curtail the expression of; suppress: *silencing all criticism; silenced their opponents.* [Middle English, from Old French, from Latin *silentium,* from *silēns, silent-,* present participle of *silēre,* to be silent.]

si·lenc·er (sī′lən-sər) *n.* One that silences, especially a device attached to the muzzle of a firearm to muffle the sound of firing.

si·le·ni (sī-lē′nī) *n. Greek Mythology.* Plural of **silenus.**

si·lent (sī′lənt) *adj.* **1.** Marked by absence of noise or sound; still. **2.** Not inclined to speak; not talkative. **3.** Unable to speak. **4.** Refraining from speech: *Do be silent.* **5.** Not voiced or expressed; unspoken: *a silent curse; silent consent.* **6.** Inactive; quiescent: *a silent volcano.* **7.** *Linguistics.* Having no phonetic value; unpronounced: *the silent* b *in subtle.* **8.** Having no spoken dialogue and usually no soundtrack. Used of a film. **—silent** *n.* A silent movie. [Latin *silēns, silent-,* present participle of *silēre,* to be silent.] **—si′lent·ly** *adv.* **—si′lent·ness** *n.*

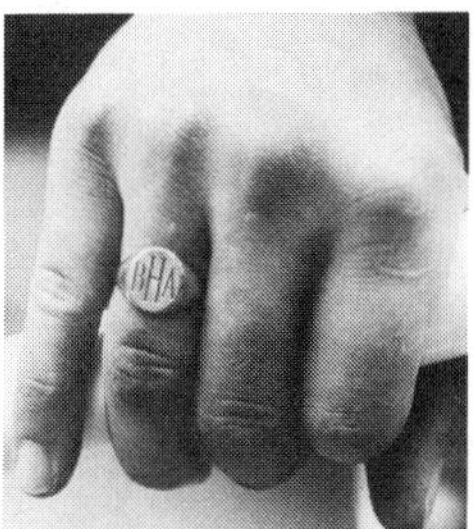

signet ring

signpost

sika
Cervus nippon

ă pat	oi boy
ā pay	ou out
âr care	o͝o took
ä father	o͞o boot
ĕ pet	ŭ cut
ē be	ûr urge
ĭ pit	th thin
ī pie	*th* this
îr pier	hw which
ŏ pot	zh vision
ō toe	ə about, item
ô paw	♦ regionalism

Stress marks: **′** (primary); ′ (secondary), as in **dictionary** (dĭk′shə-nĕr′ē)

silhouette
By an unidentified 18th-century artist

SYNONYMS: *silent, reticent, reserved, taciturn, secretive, uncommunicative, tightlipped.* These adjectives describe people who are sparing with speech. *Silent* often implies a habitual disinclination to speak or to speak out: *"the great silent majority"* (Richard M. Nixon). The term may also mean refraining from speech, as out of fear or confusion: *"He must be warned prior to any questioning that he has the right to remain silent"* (Earl Warren). *Reticent* suggests a tendency to keep one's thoughts, feelings, and personal affairs to oneself: *"She had been shy and reticent with me, and now . . . she was telling me aloud the secrets of her inmost heart"* (W.H. Hudson). *Reserved* suggests aloofness and reticence: *"a reserved man, whose inner life was intense and sufficient to him"* (Arnold Bennett). *Taciturn* implies unsociableness and a tendency to speak only when it is absolutely necessary: *"At the Council board he was taciturn; and in the House of Lords he never opened his lips"* (Macaulay). *Secretive* implies a lack of openness about or even concealment of matters that could in all conscience be discussed: *too secretive to disclose her vacation plans. Uncommunicative* suggests a disposition to withhold opinions, feelings, or knowledge from others: *Her uncle was a silent, uncommunicative Yankee farmer. Tightlipped* strongly implies a steadfast unwillingness to divulge information being sought: *The general remained tightlipped when reporters asked him about the rumored invasion.* See also Synonyms at **still**[1].

silent butler *n.* A small receptacle with a handle and hinged cover, used for collecting ashes and crumbs.

silent partner *n.* One that makes financial investments in a business enterprise but does not participate in its management.

silent treatment *n. Informal.* Maintenance of aloof silence toward another as an expression of one's anger or disapproval: *The rest of the class gave the tattletale the silent treatment.*

si·le·nus (sī-lē′nəs) *n., pl.* **-ni** (-nī). *Greek Mythology.* Any of the minor woodland deities and companions of Dionysus, depicted on Greek vases as men with the tails, ears, and hoofs of horses. [Latin *sīlēnus,* from Greek *silēnos,* from *Silēnos,* Silenus.]

Si·le·nus (sī-lē′nəs) *n. Greek Mythology.* A satyr, usually depicted as drunken and jolly, in the entourage of Dionysus. [Latin, from Greek *Silēnos.*]

si·le·sia (sī-lē′zhə, -shə, sī-) *n.* A sturdy twilled cotton fabric used for linings and pockets. [After SILESIA.]

Si·le·sia (sī-lē′zhə, -shə, sī-). A region of central Europe primarily in southwest Poland and northern Czechoslovakia. Settled by Slavic peoples c. A.D. 500, the region was long contested by various states and principalities. After World War I Silesia was partitioned among Germany, Poland, and Czechoslovakia. Much of the Czechoslovakian section passed to Germany and Poland after the signing of the Munich Pact in 1938. Germany occupied Polish Silesia from 1939 to 1945, and after World War II Poland annexed most of German Silesia. **Upper Silesia,** in southern Poland, is an important industrialized area. **—Si·le′sian** *adj. & n.*

silk-cotton tree
Ceiba pentandra

si·lex (sī′lĕks′) *n.* **1.** Silica. **2.** Finely ground tripoli used as an inert paint filler. [Latin, hard stone, flint.]

sil·hou·ette (sĭl′o͞o-ĕt′) *n.* **1.** A drawing consisting of the outline of something, especially a human profile, filled in with a solid color. **2.** An outline that appears dark against a light background. See Synonyms at **outline. —silhouette** *tr.v.* **-et·ted, -et·ting, -ettes.** To cause to be seen as a silhouette; outline: *Figures were silhouetted against the setting sun.* [French, after Étienne de *Silhouette* (1709–1767), French finance minister.]

silic– *pref.* Variant of **silici–.**

sil·i·ca (sĭl′ĭ-kə) *n.* A white or colorless crystalline compound, SiO_2, occurring abundantly as quartz, sand, flint, agate, and many other minerals and used to manufacture a wide variety of materials, especially glass and concrete. [New Latin, from Latin *silex, silic-,* hard stone, flint.]

silica gel *n.* Amorphous silica that resembles white sand and is used as a drying and dehumidifying agent, as a catalyst and catalyst carrier, as an anticaking agent in cosmetics, and in chromatography.

sil·i·cate (sĭl′ĭ-kāt′, -kĭt) *n.* **1.** Any of numerous compounds containing silicon, oxygen, and one or more metals; a salt of silicic acid. **2.** Any of a large group of minerals, forming over 90 percent of the earth's crust, that consist of SiO_2 or SiO_4 groupings combined with one or more metals and sometimes hydrogen.

silk-screen

si·li·ceous (sĭ-lĭsh′əs) *adj.* Containing, resembling, relating to, or consisting of silica. [Latin *siliceus,* of flint, from *silex, silic-,* flint.]

silici– or **silic–** *pref.* **1.** Silicon: *silicate.* **2.** Silica: *silicify.* [From SILICON and SILICA.]

si·lic·ic (sĭ-lĭs′ĭk) *adj.* Relating to, resembling, containing, or derived from silica or silicon.

silicic acid *n.* A jellylike substance, $SiO_2{\cdot}nH_2O$, produced when sodium silicate solution is acidified.

sil·i·cide (sĭl′ĭ-sīd′) *n.* A compound of silicon with another element or radical.

sil·i·cif·er·ous (sĭl′ĭ-sĭf′ər-əs) *adj.* Bearing, producing, or in partial combination with silica.

si·lic·i·fy (sĭ-lĭs′ə-fī′) *v.* **-fied, -fy·ing, -fies.** *—tr.* To convert into or impregnate with silica. *—intr.* To become converted into or impregnated with silica. **—si·lic′i·fi·ca′tion** (-fĭ-kā′shən) *n.*

sil·i·cle (sĭl′ĭ-kəl) *n. Botany.* A short silique usually having a length less than three times its width. [Latin *silicula,* diminutive of *siliqua,* seed pod.]

sil·i·con (sĭl′ĭ-kən, -kŏn′) *n. Symbol* **Si** A nonmetallic element occurring extensively in the earth's crust in silica and silicates, having both an amorphous and a crystalline allotrope, and used doped or in combination with other materials in glass, semiconducting devices, concrete, brick, refractories, pottery, and silicones. Atomic number 14; atomic weight 28.086; melting point 1,410°C; boiling point 2,355°C; specific gravity 2.33; valence 4. See table at **element.** [From SILICA.]

silicon carbide *n.* A bluish-black crystalline compound, SiC, one of the hardest known substances, used as an abrasive and heat-refractory material and in single crystals as semiconductors, especially in high-temperature applications.

silicon dioxide *n.* Silica.

sil·i·cone (sĭl′ĭ-kōn′) *n.* Any of a group of semi-inorganic polymers based on the structural unit R_2SiO, where R is an organic group, characterized by wide-range thermal stability, high lubricity, extreme water repellence, and physiological inertness and used in adhesives, lubricants, protective coatings, paints, electrical insulation, synthetic rubber, and prosthetic replacements for bodily parts.

Sil·i·con Valley (sĭl′ĭ-kən, -kŏn′). A region of western California southeast of San Francisco known for its high-technology design and manufacturing industries.

sil·i·co·sis (sĭl′ĭ-kō′sĭs) *n.* A disease of the lungs caused by continued inhalation of the dust of siliceous minerals and characterized by progressive fibrosis and a chronic shortness of breath. **—sil′i·cot′ic** (-kŏt′ĭk) *adj.*

si·lique (sĭ-lēk′) *n.* A dry, dehiscent, elongated fruit, characteristic of the mustard family, having two valves that fall away leaving a central partition. [French, from Old French, from Latin *siliqua,* seed pod.] **—sil′i·quous** (sĭl′ĭ-kwəs), **sil′i·quose′** (-kwōs′) *adj.*

silk (sĭlk) *n.* **1.a.** A fine, lustrous fiber composed mainly of fibroin and produced by certain insect larvae to form cocoons, especially the strong, elastic, fibrous secretion of silkworms used to make thread and fabric. **b.** Thread or fabric made from this fiber. **c.** A garment made from this fabric. **2. silks.** *Sports.* The brightly colored identifying garments of a jockey or harness driver. **3.** A silky, filamentous material, such as the webbing spun by certain spiders or the styles forming a tuft on an ear of corn. **—silk** *adj.* Composed of or similar to the fiber or the fabric silk. **—silk** *intr.v.* **silked, silk·ing, silks.** To develop silk. Used of corn. [Middle English, from Old English *sioloc,* probably of Slavic origin, ultimately from Chinese.]

silk cotton *n.* A silky fiber, such as kapok, attached to the seeds of certain trees.

silk-cot·ton tree (sĭlk′kŏt′n) *n.* **1.** A spiny, deciduous, North American tree *(Ceiba pentandra)* having palmately compound leaves and cultivated for its leathery fruit that contain the silklike fiber kapok. **2.** Either of two trees *(Bombax ceiba* or *Cochlospermum religiosum)* having seeds surrounded by silky hairs.

silk·en (sĭl′kən) *adj.* **1.** Made of silk. **2.** Resembling silk in texture or appearance; smooth and lustrous. See Synonyms at **sleek. 3.** Delicately pleasing or caressing in effect: *a silken voice.* **4.** Luxurious.

silk gland *n.* Any of the glands in silk-spinning insects and spiders that secrete a protein liquid that hardens into silk on exposure to air.

silk hat *n.* A man's silk-covered top hat.

silk oak *n.* An Australian evergreen tree *(Grevillea robusta)* having divided, fernlike leaves and showy, one-sided clusters of orange flowers.

Silk Road (sĭlk). An ancient trade route between China and the Mediterranean Sea extending some 6,440 km (4,000 mi) and linking China with the Roman Empire. Marco Polo followed the route on his journey to Cathay.

silk-screen also **silk·screen** (sĭlk′skrēn′) *n.* **1.** A stencil method of printmaking in which a design is imposed on a screen of silk or other fine mesh, with blank areas coated with an impermeable substance, and ink is forced through the mesh onto the printing surface. Also called *screen-printing, silk-screen process.* **2.** A print made by this method. **—silk′-screen′** *v.*

silk stocking *n.* A wealthy, aristocratic, or elegantly dressed person.

silk-stock·ing (sĭlk′stŏk′ĭng) *adj.* Wealthy; aristocratic: *a silk-stocking district; silk-stocking prep schools.*

silk tree *n.* An Asian tree *(Albizzia julibrissin)* having pinnately compound leaves and heads of pinkish flowers with many long filaments. Also called *mimosa.*

silk·weed (sĭlk′wēd′) *n.* See **milkweed.**

silk·worm (sĭlk′wûrm′) *n.* Any of various caterpillars that produce silk cocoons, especially the larva of a moth *(Bombyx mori)* native to Asia that spins a cocoon of fine, strong, lustrous fiber that is the source of commercial silk.

silkworm moth *n.* Any of the moths, chiefly of the family Bombycidae, whose larvae produce silk cocoons.

silk·y (sĭl′kē) *adj.* **-i·er, -i·est. 1.** Resembling silk; lustrous. See Synonyms at **sleek. 2.** Made of silk; silken. **3.** Covered with or characterized by fine, soft hairs or feathers: *a silky chick.* **4.**

Ingratiating; seductive: *spoke with silky plausibility.* **—silk′i·ly** *adv.* **—silk′i·ness** *n.*

silky terrier *n.* A toy terrier of a breed developed from a cross between the Australian terrier and the Yorkshire terrier, characterized by long, silky, bluish-gray hair, tan markings, and erect ears.

sill (sĭl) *n.* **1.** The horizontal member that bears the upright portion of a frame, especially the horizontal member that forms the base of a window. **2.** *Geology.* An approximately horizontal sheet of igneous rock intruded between older rock beds. [Middle English *sille,* from Old English *syll,* threshold.]

Sill (sĭl), **Mount.** A peak, 4,316.7 m (14,153 ft) high, in the Sierra Nevada of east-central California.

sil·la·bub (sĭl′ə-bŭb′) *n.* Variant of **syllabub.**

Sil·lan·pää (sĭl′ən-pă′), **Frans Eemil.** 1888–1964. Finnish writer whose novels include *Meek Heritage* (1919) and *The Maid Silja* (1931). He won the 1939 Nobel Prize for literature.

Sills (sĭlz), **Beverly.** Born 1929. American operatic soprano and manager who joined the New York City Opera in 1953 and was its general director from 1980 to 1989.

sil·ly (sĭl′ē) *adj.* **-li·er, -li·est. 1.** Exhibiting a lack of wisdom or good sense; foolish. See Synonyms at **foolish. 2.** Lacking seriousness or responsibleness; frivolous: *indulged in silly word play; silly pet names for each other.* **3.** Semiconscious; dazed: *knocked silly by the impact.* [Middle English *seli, silli,* blessed, innocent, hapless, from Old English *gesælig,* blessed.] **—sil′li·ly** (sĭl′ə-lē) *adv.* **—sil′li·ness** *n.*

si·lo (sī′lō) *n., pl.* **-los. 1.a.** A tall cylindrical structure, usually beside a barn, in which fodder is stored. **b.** A pit dug for the same purpose. **2.** An underground shelter for a missile, usually equipped to launch the missile or to raise it into a launching position. **—silo** *tr.v.* **-loed, -lo·ing, -los.** To store in a silo. [Spanish.]

Si·lo·ne (sĭ-lō′nē, sē-lô′nĕ), **Ignazio.** 1900–1978. Italian novelist whose best-known works, *Bread and Wine* (1937) and *The Seed Beneath the Snow* (1941), were written while he was in exile from the Fascist regime in Italy.

si·lox·ane (sĭ-lŏk′sān′, sī-) *n.* Any of a class of organic or inorganic chemical compounds of silicon, oxygen, and usually carbon and hydrogen, based on the structural unit R_2SiO, where R is an alkyl group, usually methyl. [SIL(ICON) + OX(YGEN) + (METH)ANE.]

silt (sĭlt) *n.* A sedimentary material consisting of very fine particles intermediate in size between sand and clay. **—silt** *v.* **silt·ed, silt·ing, silts.** —*intr.* To become filled with silt: *an old channel that silted up.* —*tr.* To fill, cover, or obstruct with silt: *River sediments gradually silted the harbor.* [Middle English *cylte,* probably of Scandinavian origin. See **sal-** in Appendix.] **—silt·a′tion** *n.* **—silt′y** *adj.*

silt·stone (sĭlt′stōn′) *n.* A fine-grained rock of consolidated silt.

Sil·u·res (sĭl′yə-rēz′) *pl.n.* A people described by Tacitus as occupying southeast Wales at the time of the Roman invasion. [Latin.]

Si·lu·ri·an (sĭ-lo͝or′ē-ən, sī-) *adj.* **1.** Of or relating to the Silures or their culture. **2.** *Geology.* Of, belonging to, or being the geologic time, system of rocks, or sedimentary deposits of the third period of the Paleozoic Era, characterized by the development of early invertebrate land animals and land plants. See table at **geologic time. —Silurian** *n. Geology.* The Silurian Period or its system of deposits. [From SILURES (so called because the Silures lived in the part of Wales where the rocks were first identified).]

si·lu·rid (sĭ-lo͝or′ĭd, sī-) *adj.* Of or belonging to the family Siluridae, which includes various freshwater catfishes of Europe and Asia, typically having a short dorsal fin and a long anal fin. **—silurid** *n.* A silurid fish. [From New Latin *Silūridae,* family name, from Latin *silūrus,* a large freshwater fish, from Greek *silouros,* sheatfish. See **ors-** in Appendix.]

sil·va also **syl·va** (sĭl′və) *n., pl.* **-vas** or **-vae** (-vē). **1.** The trees or forests of a region. **2.** A written work on the trees or forests of a region. [Latin, forest.]

sil·van (sĭl′vən) *adj. & n.* Variant of **sylvan.**

Sil·va·nus also **Syl·va·nus** (sĭl-vā′nəs) *n. Roman Mythology.* A god of forests, fields, and herding.

sil·ver (sĭl′vər) *n.* **1.** *Symbol* **Ag** A lustrous white, ductile, malleable metallic element, occurring both uncombined and in ores such as argentite, having the highest thermal and electrical conductivity of the metals. It is highly valued for jewelry, tableware, and other ornamental use and is widely used in coinage, photography, dental and soldering alloys, electrical contacts, and printed circuits. Atomic number 47; atomic weight 107.868; melting point 960.8°C; boiling point 2,212°C; specific gravity 10.50; valence 1, 2. See table at **element. 2.** This metallic element as a commodity or medium of exchange. **3.** Coins made of this metallic element. **4.a.** Domestic articles, such as tableware, made of or plated with silver. **b.** Tableware, especially eating and serving utensils, made of steel or another metal. **5.** *Color.* A lustrous medium gray. **6.** A silver salt, especially silver nitrate, used to sensitize paper. **—silver** *adj.* **1.** Made of or containing silver: *a silver bowl; silver ore.* **2.** Resembling silver, especially in having a lustrous shine; silvery. **3.** *Color.* Of a lustrous medium gray: *silver hair.* **4.** Having a soft, clear, resonant sound. **5.** Eloquent; persuasive: *a silver voice.* **6.** Favoring the adoption of silver as a standard of currency: *the silver plank of the 1896 Democratic platform.* **7.** Of or constituting a 25th anniversary. **—silver** *v.* **-vered, -ver·ing, -vers.** —*tr.* **1.** To cover, plate, or adorn with silver or a similar lustrous substance. **2.** To give a silver color to. **3.** To coat (photographic paper) with a film of silver nitrate or other silver salt. —*intr.* To become silvery. [Middle English, from Old English *siolfor, seolfor,* probably ultimately from Akkadian *ṣarpu,* refined silver, from *ṣarāpu,* to smelt, refine.]

silver age *n.* A period of history secondary in achievement to that of a golden age.

sil·ver·back (sĭl′vər-băk) *n.* A mature male gorilla having silvery white hair across the back.

sil·ver·bell tree (sĭl′vər-bĕl′) *n.* Any of several trees or shrubs of the genus *Halesia,* especially *H. carolina,* of the southeast United States, having drooping, bell-shaped white flowers and dry, oblong, four-winged fruit.

sil·ver·ber·ry (sĭl′vər-bĕr′ē) *n.* **1.** A northeast North American shrub *(Elaeagnus commutata)* having silvery flowers, leaves, and berries. **2.** See **oleaster.**

silver bromide *n.* A pale yellow crystalline compound, AgBr, that turns black on exposure to light and is used as the light-sensitive component on ordinary photographic film and plates.

silver certificate *n.* A bill formerly issued as legal tender by the U.S. government in representation of deposited silver bullion.

silver chloride *n.* A white granular powder, AgCl, that turns dark on exposure to light and is used in photographic emulsions, photometry, and silver plating.

silver cord *n.* The emotional bond between a mother and her offspring. [After *The Silver Cord,* a play by Sidney Coe Howard.]

silver dollar *n. Botany.* **1.** See **honesty** (sense 4). **2.** A spineless, hemispherical cactus *(Astrophytum asterias)* native to Texas and northern Mexico, having large yellow flowers.

sil·ver·eye (sĭl′vər-ī′) *n.* See **white-eye.**

sil·ver·fish (sĭl′vər-fĭsh′) *n., pl.* **silverfish** or **-fish·es. 1.** Any of various fishes having silvery scales, such as a tarpon or silverside. **2.** A small silvery or gray bristletail *(Lepisma saccharina)* that feeds on the starchy material in bookbindings, wallpaper, clothing, and food, often causing extensive damage.

silver fox *n.* **1.** A red fox of the melanistic form, having black fur tipped with white. **2.** The fur of a silver fox, especially as an article of clothing.

silver hake *n.* A marine food fish *(Merluccius bilinearis)* with silvery scales, common in American Atlantic coastal waters.

silver iodide *n.* A pale yellow, odorless powder, AgI, that darkens on exposure to light and is used in photographic emulsions, rainmaking, and medicine, especially as an antiseptic.

silver lining *n.* A hopeful or comforting prospect in the midst of difficulty. [From the proverb "Every cloud has a silver lining."]

silver maple *n.* **1.** A North American deciduous tree *(Acer saccharinum)* having palmately dissected leaves that are silvery below and light green above. **2.** The hard, brittle wood of this tree.

sil·vern (sĭl′vərn) *adj.* **1.** Composed of silver. **2.** Resembling silver; silvery. [Middle English, alteration (influenced by *silver,* silver) of Old English *silfren,* from *siolfor.* See SILVER.]

silver nitrate *n.* A poisonous colorless crystalline compound, $AgNO_3$, that becomes grayish black when exposed to light in the presence of organic matter and is used in manufacturing photographic film, silvering mirrors, dyeing hair, plating silver, and in medicine as a cautery and an antiseptic.

silver perch *n.* Any of various silvery fishes, such as the white crappie, resembling perch. Also called *mademoiselle.*

silver plate *n.* **1.** A coating or plating of silver. **2.** Tableware, such as flatware or hollowware, made of or coated with silver.

sil·ver-plate (sĭl′vər-plāt′) *tr.v.* **-plat·ed, -plat·ing, -plates.** To coat (an object) with a thin layer of silver, especially by electroplating.

sil·ver·point (sĭl′vər-point′) *n.* **1.** A technique of drawing on specially prepared paper with a silver-tipped instrument. **2.** A drawing made by use of this technique.

silver protein *n.* A colloidal preparation of silver oxide and protein, usually gelatin or albumin, used as an antibacterial agent.

sil·ver·rod (sĭl′vər-rŏd′) *n.* An eastern North American plant *(Solidago bicolor)* related to the goldenrods but having white rather than yellow flower heads.

silver salmon *n.* See **coho salmon.**

silver screen *n.* See **screen** (sense 6). [From a type of movie screen covered with silver-colored metallic paint.]

sil·ver·side (sĭl′vər-sīd′) also **sil·ver·sides** (-sīdz′) *n.* Any of various chiefly marine fishes of the family Atherinidae, characteristically having a broad silvery band along each side and including the grunion.

sil·ver·smith (sĭl′vər-smĭth′) *n.* One that makes, repairs, or replates articles of silver.

silver spoon *n.* Inherited wealth. [From the proverb "born with a silver spoon in one's mouth."]

silver standard *n.* A monetary standard under which a specified quantity of silver constitutes the basic unit of currency.

Silver Star *n.* A U.S. military decoration awarded for gallantry in action.

Beverly Sills

silo

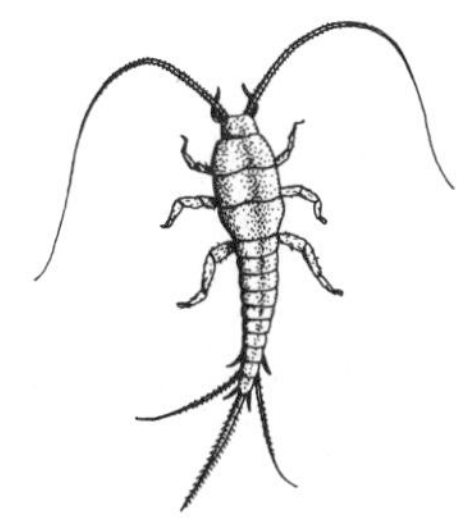
silverfish
Lepisma saccharina

ă pat	oi boy
ā pay	ou out
âr care	o͝o took
ä father	o͞o boot
ĕ pet	ŭ cut
ē be	ûr urge
ĭ pit	th thin
ī pie	*th* this
îr pier	hw which
ŏ pot	zh vision
ō toe	ə about, item
ô paw	♦ regionalism

Stress marks: ′ (primary); ′ (secondary), as in **dictionary** (dĭk′shə-nĕr′ē)

Neil Simon

sil·ver·tip (sĭl′vər-tĭp′) *n.* See **grizzly bear.**

sil·ver-tongued (sĭl′vər-tŭngd′) *adj.* Having or exhibiting the power of fluent and persuasive speech; eloquent.

sil·ver·ware (sĭl′vər-wâr′) *n.* **1.** Hollowware and flatware made of or plated with silver. **2.** Metal eating and serving utensils.

sil·ver·weed (sĭl′vər-wēd′) *n.* A low-growing, stoloniferous plant *(Potentilla anserina)* having yellow flowers and rosettes of pinnate leaves that are silvery beneath. Also called *goose grass.*

sil·ver·work (sĭl′vər-wûrk′) *n.* Decorative work done in silver.

sil·ver·y (sĭl′və-rē) *adj.* **1.** Containing or coated with silver. **2.** Resembling silver in color or luster: *"A fountain threw high its silvery water"* (Harriet Beecher Stowe). **3.** Having a clear, softly resonant sound: *a silvery laugh.* **—sil′ver·i·ness** *n.*

sil·vex (sĭl′vĕks′) *n.* A solid, toxic, selective herbicide, $C_9H_7O_3Cl_3$, used primarily against woody plants. [Probably Latin *silva,* forest + EX(TERMINATOR).]

sil·vi·chem·i·cal (sĭl′vĭ-kĕm′ĭ-kəl) *n.* Any of various chemicals derived from wood. [Latin *silva,* forest + CHEMICAL.]

sil·vic·o·lous (sĭl-vĭk′ə-ləs) *adj.* Growing in or inhabiting woodlands. [From Latin *silvicola,* inhabitant of the forest : *silva,* forest + *colere,* to dwell, till; see **kʷel-**[1] in Appendix.]

sil·vi·cul·ture (sĭl′vĭ-kŭl′chər) *n.* The care and cultivation of forest trees. [Latin *silva,* forest + CULTURE.] **—sil′vi·cul′tur·al** *adj.* **—sil′vi·cul′tur·al·ly** *adv.* **—sil′vi·cul′tur·ist** *n.*

si·ma (sī′mə) *n.* The lower layer of the earth's outer crust that underlies the sial and is rich in silica, iron, and magnesium. [SI(LICA) + MA(GNESIUM).]

Sim·chat To·rah (sĕm-KHät′ tô-rä′) also **Sim·chas To·rah** (sĭm′KHəs tôr′ə, tōr′ə) *n. Judaism.* A festival celebrating the Law of Moses and the completion of the year's cycle and subsequent new beginning, observed on the 23rd day of Tishri. [Hebrew *śimḥat tôrâ,* rejoicing over the Law, Simchas Torah : *śimḥat,* inflectional form of *śimḥâ,* joy, merriment (from *śāmaḥ,* to rejoice) + *tôrâ,* torah.]

Sim·coe (sĭm′kō), **Lake.** A lake of southeast Ontario, Canada, between Georgian Bay and Lake Ontario.

Si·me·non (sē-mə-nôN′), **Georges Joseph Christian.** 1903–1989. Belgian-born French writer known especially for his detective novels featuring Inspector Maigret, including *The Strange Case of Peter the Left* (1931) and *Maigret's Memoirs* (1950).

Sim·e·on[1] (sĭm′ē-ən). In the Old Testament, a son of Jacob and Leah and the forebear of one of the tribes of Israel.

Sim·e·on[2] (sĭm′ē-ən). In the New Testament, the devout Jew who proclaimed the Nunc Dimittis while holding the infant Jesus in his arms.

Simeon Sty·li·tes (stī-lī′tēz), Saint. A.D. 390?–459. Syrian Christian ascetic. The first of the "pillar-dwelling" ascetics, he spent 30 years atop a column.

Sim·fer·o·pol (sĭm′fə-rō′pəl, syĭm-fyə-rô′-). A city of southern Ukraine in the southern Crimea northeast of Sevastopol. Originally settled by Scythians, it was annexed by Russia in 1784. Population, 331,000.

sim·i·an (sĭm′ē-ən) *adj.* Relating to, characteristic of, or resembling an ape or a monkey. **—simian** *n.* An ape or a monkey. [From Latin *sīmia,* ape, probably from *sīmus,* snub-nosed, from Greek *simos.*]

sim·i·lar (sĭm′ə-lər) *adj.* **1.** Related in appearance or nature; alike though not identical. **2.** *Mathematics.* Having corresponding angles equal and corresponding line segments proportional. Used of geometric figures: *similar triangles.* [French *similaire,* from Latin *similis,* like. See **sem-**[1] in Appendix.] **—sim′i·lar·ly** *adv.*

sim·i·lar·i·ty (sĭm′ə-lăr′ĭ-tē) *n., pl.* **-ties. 1.** The quality or condition of being similar; resemblance. See Synonyms at **likeness. 2.** A corresponding aspect or feature; equivalence: *a similarity of writing styles.*

sim·i·le (sĭm′ə-lē) *n.* A figure of speech in which two essentially unlike things are compared, often in a phrase introduced by *like* or *as,* as in *"How like the winter hath my absence been"* or *"So are you to my thoughts as food to life"* (Shakespeare). [Middle English, from Latin, from neuter of *similis,* like. See SIMILAR.]

si·mil·i·tude (sĭ-mĭl′ĭ-to͞od′, -tyo͞od′) *n.* **1.** Similarity; resemblance. See Synonyms at **likeness. 2.a.** One closely resembling another; a counterpart. **b.** A perceptible likeness. **3.** *Archaic.* A simile, an allegory, or a parable. [Middle English, from Old French, from Latin *similitūdō,* from *similis,* like. See SIMILAR.]

Si·mi Valley (sē′mē, sĭm′ē). A city of southern California, a manufacturing suburb of Los Angeles. Population, 77,500.

Sim·men·tal also **Sim·men·thal** (zĭm′ən-täl′) *n.* Any of a Swiss breed of large, muscular cattle, having a reddish body and a white face and raised for meat and milk. [After *Simmental,* a valley of the Simme River in southwest-central Switzerland.]

sim·mer (sĭm′ər) *v.* **-mered, -mer·ing, -mers.** *—intr.* **1.** To be cooked gently or remain just at or below the boiling point. **2.a.** To be filled with pent-up emotion; seethe. **b.** To be in a state of gentle ferment: *thoughts simmering in the back of her mind.* *—tr.* **c.** To cook (food) gently in a liquid just at or below the boiling point. **d.** To keep (a liquid) near or just below the boiling point. See Synonyms at **boil**[1]. **—simmer** *n.* The state or process of simmering. ***—phrasal verb.* simmer down.** To become calm after excitement or anger. [Alteration of Middle English *simpire,* to simmer, probably of imitative origin.]

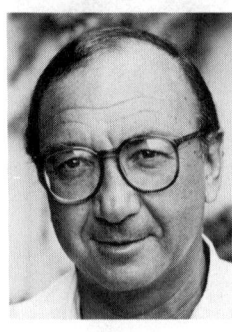

sim·nel (sĭm′nəl) *n. Chiefly British.* **1.** A crisp bread made of fine wheat flour. **2.** A rich fruitcake sometimes covered with almond paste and traditionally eaten at mid-Lent, Easter, and Christmas. [Middle English, from Old French *siminel,* from Medieval Latin *siminellus,* ultimately from Latin *simila,* fine flour, probably of Semitic origin.]

si·mo·le·on (sĭ-mō′lē-ən) *n. Slang.* A dollar. [Origin unknown.]

Si·mon (sē-mōN′), **Claude Eugene Henri.** Born 1913. French writer who was a proponent of the antinovel. He won the 1985 Nobel Prize for literature.

Si·mon (sī′mən), **Herbert Alexander.** Born 1916. American economist. He won a 1978 Nobel Prize for his research into the decision-making process within economic organizations.

Simon, Neil. Born 1927. American playwright whose lighthearted comedies of middle-class life include *The Odd Couple* (1965) and *Plaza Suite* (1968).

si·mo·ni·ac (sĭ-mō′nē-ăk′, sī-) *n.* One who practices simony. **—si·mo′ni·ac′, si′mo·ni′a·cal** (sī′mə-nī′ə-kəl, sĭm′ə-) *adj.* **—si′mo·ni′a·cal·ly** *adv.*

Si·mon·i·des of Ce·os (sī-mŏn′ĭ-dēz; sē′ŏs). 556?–468? B.C. Greek lyric poet who is known especially for his elegies in honor of the slain warriors at Marathon and Thermopylae.

Simon Le·gree (lə-grē′) *n.* A brutal taskmaster. [After *Simon Legree,* a cruel slave dealer in the novel *Uncle Tom's Cabin* by Harriet Beecher Stowe.]

si·mon-pure (sī′mən-pyo͝or′) *adj.* **1.** Genuinely and thoroughly pure. **2.** Superficially or hypocritically virtuous. [From the phrase *the real Simon Pure,* after *Simon Pure,* a character in *A Bold Stroke for a Wife,* a play by Susannah Centlivre (1669–1723).]

si·mo·ny (sī′mə-nē, sĭm′ə-) *n.* The buying or selling of ecclesiastical pardons, offices, or emoluments. [Middle English *simonie,* from Old French, from Late Latin *simōnia,* after *Simon* Magus, a sorcerer who tried to buy spiritual powers from the Apostle Peter (Acts 8:9–24).] **—si′mo·nist** *n.*

Simon Ze·lo·tes (zē-lō′tēz) or **Simon the Ca·naan·ite** (kā′nə-nīt′). First century A.D. In the Old Testament, one of the 12 Apostles. Although nothing certain is known of his life, he is thought to have been a member of the Zealots.

si·moom (sĭ-mo͞om′) also **si·moon** (-mo͞on′) *n.* A strong, hot, sand-laden wind of the Sahara and Arabian deserts: *"Stephen's heart had withered up like a flower of the desert that feels the simoom coming from afar"* (James Joyce). Also called *samiel.* [Arabic *samūm,* poisonous, simoom, from *samma,* to poison, from Aramaic *sammā,* drug, poison.]

simp (sĭmp) *n. Slang.* One who is regarded as simple or foolish.

sim·pa·ti·co (sĭm-pä′tĭ-kō′, -păt′ĭ-) *adj.* **1.** Of like mind or temperament; compatible. **2.** Having attractive qualities; pleasing. [Italian *simpatico* (from *simpatia,* sympathy) or Spanish *simpático* (from *simpatía,* sympathy), both from Latin *sympathīa.* See SYMPATHY.]

sim·per (sĭm′pər) *v.* **-pered, -per·ing, -pers.** *—intr.* To smile in a silly, self-conscious, often coy manner. *—tr.* To utter or express with a silly, self-conscious, often coy smile: *simpered a lame excuse.* **—simper** *n.* A silly, self-conscious, often coy smile. See Synonyms at **smile.** [Perhaps of Scandinavian origin.] **—sim′per·er** *n.* **—sim′per·ing·ly** *adv.*

sim·ple (sĭm′pəl) *adj.* **-pler, -plest. 1.** Having or composed of only one thing, element, or part. See Synonyms at **pure. 2.** Not involved or complicated; easy: *a simple task.* See Synonyms at **easy. 3.** Being without additions or modifications; mere: *a simple "yes" or "no."* **4.** Having little or no ornamentation; not embellished or adorned: *a simple dress.* **5.** Not elaborate, elegant, or luxurious. See Synonyms at **plain. 6.** Unassuming or unpretentious; not affected. **7.a.** Having or manifesting little sense or intelligence. **b.** Uneducated; ignorant. **c.** Unworldly or unsophisticated. See Synonyms at **naive. 8.** Not guileful or deceitful; sincere. **9.** Humble or lowly in condition or rank: *a simple woodcutter.* **10.** Ordinary or common: *a simple head cold.* **11.a.** Being a fundamental or rudimentary element; basic. **b.** Not important or significant; trivial. **12.** *Biology.* Having no divisions or branches; not compound: *a simple leaf; a simple eye or lens.* **13.** *Music.* Being without figuration or elaboration: *a simple tone.* **—simple** *n.* **1.** A single component of a complex, especially one that is unanalyzable. **2.** A fool; a simpleton. **3.** A person of humble birth or condition. **4.** A medicinal plant or the medicine obtained from it. [Middle English, from Old French, from Latin *simplus;* see **sem-**[1] in Appendix, and from *simplex;* see SIMPLEX.] **—sim′ple·ness** *n.*

simple closed curve *n. Mathematics.* A curve, such as a circle, that is closed and does not intersect itself. Also called *Jordan curve.*

simple equation *n. Mathematics.* A linear equation.

simple fraction *n. Mathematics.* A fraction in which both the numerator and the denominator are whole numbers.

simple fracture *n.* A bone fracture that causes little or no damage to the surrounding soft tissues.

simple fruit *n.* A fruit, such as a pea pod, an orange, or a tomato, that develops from a single pistil.

simple harmonic motion *n. Physics.* See **harmonic motion.**

simple interest *n.* Interest paid only on the original principal, not on the interest accrued.

simple machine *n.* A simple device, such as a lever, a pulley, or an inclined plane; a machine.

simple microscope *n.* A microscope having one lens or lens system, such as a magnifying glass or hand lens.

sim·ple-mind·ed or **sim·ple·mind·ed** (sĭm′pəl-mīn′dĭd) *adj.* **1.** Lacking in subtlety or sophistication; artless or naive: *a simple-minded horror movie; simpleminded generalizations.* **2.** Stupid or silly; foolish. **3.** Mentally impaired. **—sim′ple-mind′ed·ly** *adv.* **—sim′ple-mind′ed·ness** *n.*

simple pendulum *n.* See **pendulum** (sense 1).

simple protein *n.* A protein, such as a globulin or histone, that yields only amino acids upon hydrolysis.

simple sentence *n.* A sentence having no coordinate or subordinate clauses, as *The cat purred.*

Sim·ple Si·mon (sĭm′pəl sī′mən) *n.* A foolish fellow; a simpleton. [After *Simple Simon,* a character in a nursery rhyme.]

simple sugar *n.* See **monosaccharide.**

sim·ple·ton (sĭm′pəl-tən) *n.* A person who is felt to be deficient in judgment, good sense, or intelligence; a fool. [SIMPLE + *-ton,* as in surnames such as *Chesterton.*]

sim·plex (sĭm′plĕks′) *adj.* **1.** Consisting of or marked by only one part or element. **2.** Of or relating to a telecommunications system in which only one message can be sent in either direction at one time. **—simplex** *n., pl.* **-plex·es** or **-pli·ces** (-plĭ-sēz′). **1.** *Mathematics.* A Euclidean geometric spatial element having the minimum number of boundary points, such as a line segment in one-dimensional space, a triangle in two-dimensional space, or a tetrahedron in three-dimensional space. **2.** *Linguistics.* A word that has no affixes and is not part of a compound; a simple word. [Latin *simplex,* simple. See **sem-**[1] in Appendix.]

sim·plic·i·ty (sĭm-plĭs′ĭ-tē) *n., pl.* **-ties.** **1.** The property, condition, or quality of being simple or uncombined. **2.** Absence of luxury or showiness; plainness. **3.** Absence of affectation or pretense. **4.a.** Lack of sophistication or subtlety; naiveté. **b.** Lack of good sense or intelligence; foolishness. **5.a.** Clarity of expression. **b.** Austerity in embellishment. [Middle English *simplicite,* from Old French, from Latin *simplicitās,* from *simplex, simplic-,* simple. See **sem-**[1] in Appendix.]

sim·pli·fy (sĭm′plə-fī′) *tr.v.* **-fied, -fy·ing, -fies.** To make simple or simpler, as: **c.** To reduce in complexity or extent. **d.** To reduce to fundamental parts. **e.** To make easier to understand. [French *simplifier,* from Old French, from Medieval Latin *simplificāre* : Latin *simplus,* simple; see SIMPLE + Latin *-ficāre,* -fy.] **—sim′pli·fi·ca′tion** (-fĭ-kā′shən) *n.* **—sim′pli·fi′er** *n.*

sim·plism (sĭm′plĭz′əm) *n.* The tendency to oversimplify an issue or a problem by ignoring complexities or complications. [French *simplisme,* from *simple,* simple, from Old French. See SIMPLE.] **—sim·plis′tic** (sĭm-plĭs′tĭk) *adj.* **—sim·plis′ti·cal·ly** *adv.*

Sim·plon Pass (sĭm′plŏn′, săN-plôN′). A pass, 2,010 m (6,590 ft) high, between the Lepontine and Pennine Alps in southern Switzerland. A nearby railroad tunnel system, 19.8 km (12.3 mi) long, extends southeastward into Italy.

sim·ply (sĭm′plē) *adv.* **1.a.** In a plain and unadorned way: *dresses simply.* **b.** In an unambiguous way; clearly: *explained the concept simply.* **2.** Not wisely or sensibly; foolishly. **3.** Merely; only: *It is simply a matter of time.* **4.** Absolutely; altogether: *simply delicious.* **5.** Frankly; candidly: *You are, quite simply, the best candidate for the job.*

simply connected *adj. Mathematics.* Of, being, or characterized by a surface that is divided into two separate parts by every simple closed curve within it.

Simp·son (sĭmp′sən), Sir **James Young.** 1811–1870. Scottish physician who pioneered the use of ether and chloroform in obstetrics (1847).

Simpson, O(renthal) J(ames). Born 1947. American athlete who was the first professional football player to rush more than 2,000 yards in a season.

Simpson Desert. A desert region of central Australia. The barren, uninhabited area was first crossed in 1939.

Sims·bur·y (sĭmz′bĕr′ē, -bə-rē). A town of northern Connecticut northwest of Hartford. Incorporated in 1670, it is a manufacturing center. Population, 21,161.

sim·u·la·cra (sĭm′yə-lā′krə, -lăk′rə) *n.* Plural of **simulacrum.**

sim·u·la·cre (sĭm′yə-lā′kər, -lăk′ər) *n. Archaic.* A simulacrum. [Middle English, from Old French, from Latin *simulācrum.* See SIMULACRUM.]

sim·u·la·crum (sĭm′yə-lā′krəm, -lăk′rəm) *n., pl.* **-la·cra** (-lā′krə, -lăk′rə). **1.** An image or a representation. **2.** An unreal or vague semblance. [Latin *simulācrum* : *simulāre,* to simulate; see SIMULATE + *-crum,* n. suff.]

sim·u·lar (sĭm′yə-lər, -lär′) *Archaic. n.* One that simulates; a pretender. **—simular** *adj.* Simulated; sham. [From Latin *simulāre,* to simulate. See SIMULATE.]

sim·u·late (sĭm′yə-lāt′) *tr.v.* **-lat·ed, -lat·ing, -lates.** **1.a.** To have or take on the appearance, form, or sound of; imitate. **b.** To make in imitation of or as a substitute for. See Synonyms at **imitate.** **2.** To make a pretense of; feign: *simulate interest.* See Synonyms at **pretend.** **3.** To create a representation or model of (a physical system, for example). [Latin *simulāre, simulāt-,* from *similis,* like. See SIMILAR.] **—sim′u·la′tive** *adj.*

sim·u·lat·ed (sĭm′yə-lā′tĭd) *adj.* Made in resemblance of or as a substitute for another. See Synonyms at **artificial.**

sim·u·la·tion (sĭm′yə-lā′shən) *n.* **1.** The act or process of simulating. **2.** An imitation; a sham. **3.** Assumption of a false appearance. **4.a.** Imitation or representation, as of a potential situation or in experimental testing. **b.** Representation of the operation or features of one process or system through the use of another: *computer simulation of an in-flight emergency.*

sim·u·la·tor (sĭm′yə-lā′tər) *n.* One that simulates, especially an apparatus that generates test conditions approximating actual or operational conditions.

si·mul·cast (sī′məl-kăst′, sĭm′əl-) *v.* **-cast·ed, -cast·ing, -casts.** *—intr.* To broadcast simultaneously by FM and AM radio or by radio and television. *—tr.* To broadcast (a program) by simulcasting. **—simulcast** *n.* A broadcast so transmitted. [SIMUL(TANEOUS) + (BROAD)CAST.]

si·mu·li·um (sə-myo͞o′lē-əm) *n.* Any of a genus *(Simulium)* of black flies, several species of which transmit the parasitic filarial worms that cause onchocerciasis. [New Latin *Simulium,* type genus, from Latin *simulāre,* to simulate. See SIMULATE.]

si·mul·ta·ne·ous (sī′məl-tā′nē-əs, sĭm′əl-) *adj.* **1.** Happening, existing, or done at the same time. See Synonyms at **contemporary.** **2.** *Mathematics.* Containing variables for which there are values that can satisfy all the equations: *simultaneous equations.* [Latin *simul,* at the same time; see **sem-**[1] in Appendix + English *-taneous,* as in INSTANTANEOUS.] **—si′mul·ta′ne·ous·ly** *adv.* **—si′mul·ta′ne·ous·ness, si′mul·ta·ne′i·ty** (-tə-nē′ĭ-tē, -nā′-) *n.*

sin[1] (sĭn) *n.* **1.** A transgression of a religious or moral law, especially when deliberate. **2.** *Theology.* **a.** Deliberate disobedience to the known will of God. **b.** A condition of estrangement from God resulting from such disobedience. **3.** Something regarded as being shameful, deplorable, or utterly wrong. See Synonyms at **offense.** **—sin** *intr.v.* **sinned, sin·ning, sins.** **1.** To violate a religious or moral law. **2.** To commit an offense or a violation. [Middle English *sinne,* from Old English *synn.* See **es-** in Appendix.]

sin[2] (sēn, sĭn) *n.* The 21st letter of the Hebrew alphabet. See table at **alphabet.** [Hebrew *śin.*]

sin[3] *abbr. Mathematics.* Sine.

Si·nai (sī′nī′), **Mount.** A mountain, about 2,288 m (7,500 ft) high, of the south-central Sinai Peninsula. It is thought to be the peak on which Moses received the Ten Commandments.

Sinai Peninsula. A peninsula linking southwest Asia with northeast Africa at the northern end of the Red Sea between the Gulf of Suez and the Gulf of Aqaba. Israel occupied the peninsula in 1956 and from 1967 to 1982, when it was returned to Egyptian control under the terms of the Camp David Accords (1978) and an Egyptian-Israeli treaty (1979).

sin·an·thro·pus (sī-năn′thrə-pəs, sĭ-, sī′năn-thrō′pəs, sĭn′-ăn-) *n.* See **Peking man.** [New Latin *Sinanthropus,* former genus name : SINO– + Greek *anthrōpos,* human being.]

sin·a·pism (sĭn′ə-pĭz′əm) *n.* See **mustard plaster.** [French *sinapisme,* from Late Latin *sināpismus,* from Greek *sinapismos,* use of a mustard plaster, from *sinapizein,* to apply a mustard plaster, from *sinapi,* mustard.]

Si·na·tra (sə-nä′trə), **Francis Albert.** Known as "Frank." Born 1915. American singer and actor known for his mellifluous voice. His film credits include *From Here to Eternity* (1953), for which he won an Academy Award.

since (sĭns) *adv.* **1.** From then until now or between then and now: *They left town and haven't been here since.* **2.** Before now; ago: *a name long since forgotten.* **3.** After some point in the past; at a subsequent time: *My friend has since married and moved to California.* **—since** *prep.* **1.** Continuously from: *They have been friends since childhood.* **2.** Intermittently from: *She's been skiing since childhood.* **—since** *conj.* **1.** During the period subsequent to the time when: *He hasn't been home since he graduated.* **2.** Continuously from the time when: *They have been friends ever since they were in grade school.* **3.** Inasmuch as; because: *Since you're not interested, I won't tell you about it.* [Middle English *sinnes,* contraction of *sithenes* : *sithen,* since (from Old English *siththan* : *sīth,* after + *than,* variant of *thām,* dative of *thæt,* that; see THAT) + *-es,* adv. suff.; see –S[3].]

sin·cere (sĭn-sîr′) *adj.* **-cer·er, -cer·est.** **1.** Not feigned or affected; genuine: *sincere indignation.* **2.** Being without hypocrisy or pretense; true: *a sincere friend.* **3.** *Archaic.* Pure; unadulterated. [Latin *sincērus.* See **ker-**[2] in Appendix.] **—sin·cere′ly** *adv.* **—sin·cere′ness** *n.*

SYNONYMS: *sincere, unaffected, unfeigned, wholehearted, hearty, heartfelt.* These adjectives mean genuine, honest, and devoid of hypocrisy or pretense. *Sincere* implies freedom from sham, misrepresentation, dissimulation, or duplicity: *"A friend is a person with whom I may be sincere. Before him, I may think aloud"* (Ralph Waldo Emerson). *Unaffected* and *unfeigned* especially suggest freedom from dissembling: *Many Americans viewed the war in Vietnam with unaffected revulsion. Their hosts received them with unfeigned pleasure. Wholehearted* implies genuineness of

O.J. Simpson

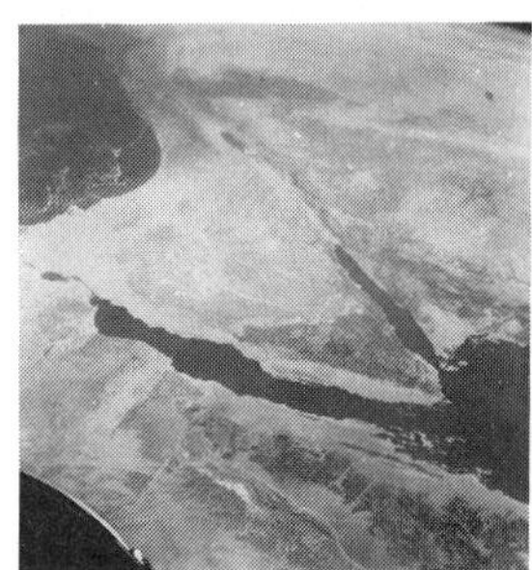

Sinai Peninsula
Aerial view from Gemini XI spacecraft, 1966

Frank Sinatra

ă pat	oi boy
ā pay	ou out
âr care	o͝o took
ä father	o͞o boot
ĕ pet	ŭ cut
ē be	ûr urge
ĭ pit	th thin
ī pie	*th* this
îr pier	hw which
ŏ pot	zh vision
ō toe	ə about, item
ô paw	♦ regionalism

Stress marks: ′ (primary); ′ (secondary), as in **dictionary** (dĭk′shə-nĕr′ē)

feeling and unconditional commitment or unstinting devotion: *The senator's party gave its wholehearted support to her presidential candidacy. Hearty* suggests exuberant, unrestrained warmth of feeling openly expressed: *sent hearty greetings; received hearty thanks. Heartfelt* stresses depth and earnestness of feeling: *heartfelt condolences; heartfelt joy.*

sin·cer·i·ty (sĭn-sĕr′ĭ-tē) *n.* The quality or condition of being sincere; genuineness, honesty, and freedom from duplicity.

sin·ci·put (sĭn′sə-pət) *n., pl.* **sin·ci·puts** or **sin·cip·i·ta** (sĭn-sĭp′ĭ-tə). **1.** The upper half of the cranium, especially the anterior portion above and including the forehead. **2.** The forehead. [Latin : *sēmi-,* semi- + *caput,* head; see **kaput-** in Appendix.] **—sin·cip′i·tal** (-sĭp′ĭ-tl) *adj.*

sine

sine $\phi = \frac{a}{Hyp}$

Sin·clair (sĭn-klâr′, sĭng-), **Harry Ford.** 1876–1956. American oil executive who served a nine-month prison sentence for his part in the Teapot Dome scandal (1923).

Sinclair, Upton Beall. 1878–1968. American writer and reformer. His concern with social justice is apparent in his novels, including *The Jungle* (1906) and *Boston* (1928).

Sind (sĭnd). A historical region of southern Pakistan along the lower Indus River. Inhabited since prehistoric times, it was held by Moslem dynasties from the 11th century until 1843, when it was annexed to British India. Sind became part of Pakistan in 1947.

Sin·dhi (sĭn′dē) *n., pl.* **Sindhi** or **-dhis. 1.** A member of a predominantly Moslem people of Sind. **2.** The Indic language of Sind. **—Sindhi** *adj.* Of or relating to Sind or its people, language, or culture. [Arabic *sindīy,* from SIND.]

sine (sīn) *n. Abbr.* **sin.** *Mathematics.* **1.** The ordinate of the endpoint of an arc of a unit circle centered at the origin of a Cartesian coordinate system, the arc being of length x and measured counterclockwise from the point (1, 0) if x is positive or clockwise if x is negative. **2.** In a right triangle, the ratio of the length of the side opposite an acute angle to the length of the hypotenuse. [Medieval Latin *sinus* (mistranslation of Arabic *jayb,* sine, as if *jayb,* fold in a garment), from Latin, curve, fold.]

sine curve

$y = \sin x$

si·ne·cure (sī′nĭ-kyo͝or′, sĭn′ĭ-) *n.* **1.** A position or an office that requires little or no work but provides a salary. **2.** *Archaic.* An ecclesiastical benefice not attached to the spiritual duties of a parish. [From Medieval Latin *(beneficium) sine cūrā,* (benefice) without cure (of souls) : Latin *sine,* without + Latin *cūrā,* ablative of *cūra,* care; see CURE.] **—si′ne·cur·ism** *n.* **—si′ne·cur′ist** *n.*

sine curve *n. Mathematics.* The graph of the equation $y = \sin x$. Also called *sinusoid.*

si·ne di·e (sī′nī dī′ē, sĭn′ā dē′ā′) *adv. Abbr.* **s.d.** Without a day specified for a future meeting; indefinitely: *Parliament was dismissed sine die.* [Medieval Latin : Latin *sine,* without + Latin *diē,* ablative of *diēs,* day.]

si·ne pro·le (sī′nī prō′lē, sĭn′ā) *adv. Abbr.* **s.p.** *Law.* Without offspring. [New Latin *sine prōlē* : Latin *sine,* without + Latin *prōlē,* ablative of *prōlēs,* offspring.]

si·ne qua non (sĭn′ĭ kwä nōn′, nōn′, sī′nī, kwā) *n.* An essential element or condition: *"The perfect cake is the sine qua non of the carefully planned modern wedding"* (J.M. Hilary). [Late Latin *sine quā (causā) nōn,* without which (cause) not : Latin *sine,* without + Latin *quā,* ablative of *quī,* which, what, who + Latin *causā,* ablative of *causa,* cause + Latin *nōn,* not.]

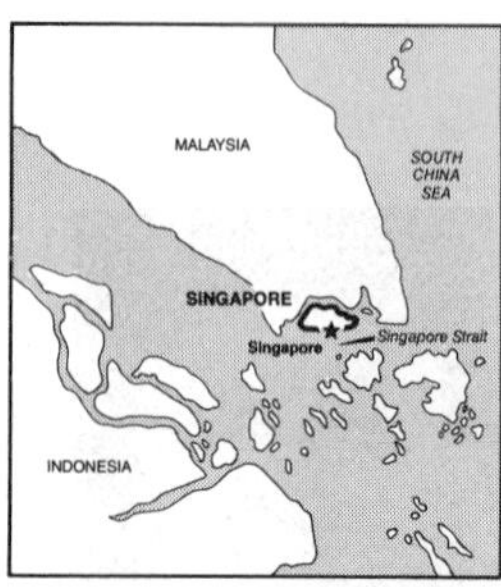

Singapore

sin·ew (sĭn′yo͞o) *n.* **1.** A tendon. **2.** Vigorous strength; muscular power. **3.** The source or mainstay of vitality and strength. Often used in the plural: *"Good company and good discourse are the very sinews of virtue"* (Izaak Walton). **—sinew** *tr.v.* **-ewed, -ew·ing, -ews.** To strengthen with or as if with sinews. [Middle English *sinewe,* from Old English, oblique form of *seonu, sinu.*]

sine wave *n. Physics.* A waveform with deviation that can be graphically expressed as the sine curve.

sin·ew·y (sĭn′yo͞o-ē) *adj.* **1. a.** Consisting of or resembling sinews. **b.** Having many sinews; stringy and tough: *a sinewy cut of beef.* **2.** Lean and muscular. See Synonyms at **muscular. 3.** Strong and vigorous: *sinewy prose.*

sin·fo·ni·a (sĭn-fō′nē-ə) *n. Music.* **1.** An instrumental composition serving as an overture, as to an opera or a cantata, especially in the 18th century. **2.** A symphonic composition. [Italian, from Latin *symphōnia,* group of musicians. See SYMPHONY.]

sin·fo·niet·ta (sĭn′fə-nyĕt′ə, -fō-) *n. Music.* **1.** A symphony that is shorter than usual or that calls for fewer than the usual number of instruments. **2.** A small symphony orchestra, especially one consisting of stringed instruments only. [Italian, diminutive of *sinfonia,* sinfonia. See SINFONIA.]

sin·ful (sĭn′fəl) *adj.* Marked by or full of sin; wicked. **—sin′ful·ly** *adv.* **—sin′ful·ness** *n.*

sing (sĭng) *v.* **sang** (săng) or **sung** (sŭng), **sung, sing·ing, sings.** *—intr.* **1.** *Music.* **a.** To utter a series of words or sounds in musical tones. **b.** To vocalize songs or selections. **c.** To perform songs or selections as a trained or professional singer. **d.** To produce sounds when played: *made the violin sing.* **2. a.** To make melodious sounds: *birds singing outside the window.* **b.** To give or have the effect of melody; lilt. **3.** To make a high whining, humming, or whistling sound. **4.** To be filled with a buzzing or ringing sound. **5. a.** To proclaim or extol something in verse. **b.** To write poetry. **6.** *Slang.* To give information or evidence against someone. *—tr.* **1.** *Music.* **a.** To produce the musical sound of: *sang a love song.* **b.** To utter with musical inflections: *She sang the message.* **c.** To bring to a specified state by singing: *sang the baby to sleep.* **2.** To intone or chant (parts of the Mass, for example). **3.** To proclaim or extol, especially in verse: *sang his praises.* **—sing** *n. Music.* A gathering of people for group singing. ***—phrasal verb.* sing out.** To call out loudly. [Middle English *singen,* from Old English *singan.* See **sengʷh-** in Appendix.] **—sing′a·ble** *adj.*

Isaac Bashevis Singer
Photographed in 1987

sing. *abbr. Grammar.* Singular.

sing-a·long (sĭng′ə-lông′, -lŏng′) *n. Music.* **1.** A casual gathering for group singing; a songfest. **2.** A spontaneous group singing, as by an audience at a performance.

Sin·ga·pore (sĭng′gə-pôr′, -pōr′, sĭng′ə-). A country of southeast Asia comprising **Singapore Island** and adjacent smaller islands. The sparsely populated island of Singapore was ceded to the British East India Company in 1819, and the city was founded the same year by Sir Thomas Raffles. The British took complete control in 1824 and added Singapore to the newly formed Straits Settlements in 1826. Held by the Japanese from 1942 to 1945, Singapore became a crown colony in 1946, a self-governing state in 1959, part of the Federation of Malaysia in 1963, and fully independent in 1965. The city of **Singapore** is the capital. Population, 2,529,100. **—Sin′ga·por′e·an** *adj. & n.*

Singapore Strait. A strait off the southern end of the Malay Peninsula between Singapore Island and the Riau Archipelago. It connects the Strait of Malacca with the South China Sea.

singe (sĭnj) *tr.v.* **singed, singe·ing, sing·es. 1.** To burn superficially; scorch. **2.** To burn off the feathers or bristles of (a carcass of a bird or an animal) by subjecting briefly to flame. See Synonyms at **burn**[1]. **3.** To burn the ends of (hair, for example). **4.** To burn the nap from (cloth) in manufacturing. **—singe** *n.* A slight or surface burn; a scorch. [Middle English *sengen,* from Old English *sengan.*]

sing·er[1] (sĭng′ər) *n.* **1.** *Music.* One who sings, especially a trained or professional vocalist. **2.** A poet. **3.** A songbird.

sing·er[2] (sĭn′jər) *n.* One that singes.

Sing·er (sĭng′ər), **Isaac Bashevis.** 1904–1991. Polish-born American Yiddish writer who has published such collections as *Gimpel the Fool* (1957) and *Passions* (1975). He won the 1978 Nobel Prize for literature.

Singer, Isaac Merritt. 1811–1875. American inventor and manufacturer who patented (1851) a sewing machine capable of making continuous stitches.

Sin·gha·lese (sĭng′gə-lēz′, -lēs′) or **Sin·ha·lese** (sĭn′hə-) *—n., pl.* **Singhalese** or **Sinhalese. 1.** A member of a people constituting the majority of the population of Sri Lanka. **2.** The Indic language of the Singhalese that is the chief language of Sri Lanka. *—adj.* Of or relating to Sri Lanka, the Singhalese, or their language or culture. [Sanskrit *Siṁhalam,* Sri Lanka + -ESE.]

sin·gle (sĭng′gəl) *adj.* **1.** Not accompanied by another or others; solitary. **2. a.** Consisting of one part, aspect, or section: *a single thickness; a single serving.* **b.** Having the same application for all; uniform: *a single moral code for all.* **c.** Consisting of one in number: *She had but a single thought, which was to escape.* **3.** Not divided; unbroken: *a single slab of ice.* **4. a.** Separate from others; individual and distinct: *Every single child will receive a gift.* **b.** Having individual opponents; involving two individuals only: *single combat.* **5. a.** Honest; undisguised: *a single adoration.* **b.** Wholly attentive: *You must judge the contest with a single eye.* **6.** Designed to accommodate one person: *a single bed.* **7. a.** Unmarried. **b.** Lacking a partner: *a single parent.* **c.** Relating to the unmarried state: *enjoys the single life.* **d.** Of or relating to celibacy. **8.** *Botany.* Having only one rank or row of petals: *a single flower.* **—single** *n.* **1.** One that is separate and individual. **2.** An accommodation for one person, as in a hotel. **3. a.** An unmarried person. **b. singles.** Unmarried persons considered as a group: *a bar for singles.* **4.** A one-dollar bill. **5.** A phonograph record, especially a forty-five, having one song on each side. **6.** *Baseball.* A hit by which a batter reaches first base safely; a one-base hit. **7.** *Sports.* **a.** A hit for one run in cricket. **b.** A golf match between two players. **c.** Often **singles.** A tennis or badminton match between two players. **—single** *v.* **-gled, -gling, -gles.** *—tr.* **1.** To choose or distinguish from others. Often used with *out: We singled her out from the list of applicants.* **2.** *Baseball.* **a.** To cause (a base runner) to score or advance by making a one-base hit: *singled him to second.* **b.** To cause the scoring of (a run) by a one-base hit. *—intr. Baseball.* To make a single. [Middle English *sengle,* from Old French, from Latin *singulus.* See **sem-**[1] in Appendix.] **—sin′gle·ness** *n.*

SYNONYMS: *single, sole, unique, solitary, lone, separate.* These adjectives are compared as they signify being one in number. What is *single* is not associated with, accompanied by, or combined with another or others: *"means of destruction . . . in the employment of which no single nation can in fact have a monopoly"* (Declaration on Atomic Energy). *Sole* implies being the only one in existence or the only one under consideration: *"The sole wall decoration of his studio was a Japanese print"* (Arnold Bennett). *Unique* in careful usage applies to what is the only one of its kind in existence: *"The greatness of art is not to find what is common but what is unique"* (Isaac Bashevis Singer). *Solitary* refers to what stands alone: *"A solitary precedent . . . which has never been reexamined, cannot be conclusive"* (Henry Clay). *Lone* applies to what stands apart from others: *"It is the lone worker who makes the first advance in a subject: the details may be worked out by a team"* (Alexander Fleming). *Separate* implies being single and disunited from all others under consideration: *"Each separate dying ember wrought its ghost upon the floor"* (Edgar Allan Poe).

---

single blind *n.* A testing procedure in which the administrators do not tell the subjects if they are being given a test treatment or a control treatment in order to avoid accidental bias in the results. **—sin′gle-blind′** (sĭng′gəl-blīnd′) *adj.*

single bond *n.* A covalent bond in which one electron pair is shared by two atoms.

sin·gle-breast·ed (sĭng′gəl-brĕs′tĭd) *adj.* Closing with a narrow overlap and fastened down the front with a single row of buttons: *a single-breasted suit.*

sin·gle-cell protein (sĭng′gəl-sĕl′) *n. Abbr.* **SCP** A protein extracted from bacterial or yeast cells grown in methanol or in various petroleum fractions and used as a substitute for fish and other protein-rich foods, especially in animal feeds, or as a food supplement where diets are deficient in protein.

single cross *n. Genetics.* The hybrid of two inbred lines. It can be represented as AB, the product of the cross A × B, where A and B represent inbred lines.

single entry *n. Accounting.* A system of bookkeeping in which a business keeps only a single account showing amounts due and amounts owed.

sin·gle-fam·i·ly (sĭng′gəl-făm′ə-lē, -făm′lē) *adj.* Relating to or being a dwelling designed for one family only: *a single-family home; single-family occupancy.*

single file *n.* A line of people, animals, or things standing or moving one behind the other. Also called *Indian file.* **—single file** *adv.*

sin·gle-foot (sĭng′gəl-fo͝ot′) *n.* A rapid gait of a horse in which each foot strikes the ground separately; the rack. No longer in technical use. **—single-foot** *intr.v.* **-foot·ed, -foot·ing, -foots.** To go at the single-foot. **—sin′gle-foot′er** *n.*

sin·gle-hand (sĭng′gəl-hănd′) *tr.v.* **-hand·ed, -hand·ing, -hands.** *Nautical.* To sail (a boat) without the help of others: *"a business executive who single-hands her own small cruising cutter"* (Tony Gibbs). **—sin′gle-hand′er** *n.*

sin·gle-hand·ed (sĭng′gəl-hăn′dĭd) *adj.* **1.** Working or done without help; unassisted. **2.** Intended for use with one hand. **3.** Having or using only one hand. **—single-handed** *adv.* In a single-handed manner. **—sin′gle-hand′ed·ly** *adv.* **—sin′gle-hand′ed·ness** *n.*

sin·gle-heart·ed (sĭng′gəl-här′tĭd) *adj.* Sincere and dedicated. **—sin′gle-heart′ed·ly** *adv.*

sin·gle·hood (sĭng′gəl-ho͝od′) *n.* The state of being unmarried.

sin·gle-is·sue (sĭng′gəl-ĭsh′o͞o) *adj.* Of, relating to, or concerned with only a single public, especially controversial, issue, to the exclusion of all other factors, concerns, facts, and issues: *single-issue groups; single-issue politics.*

single knot *n.* See **overhand knot.**

sin·gle-mind·ed (sĭng′gəl-mīn′dĭd) *adj.* **1.** Having one overriding purpose or goal: *the single-minded pursuit of money.* **2.** Steadfast; resolute: *He was single-minded in his determination to stop smoking.* **—sin′gle-mind′ed·ly** *adv.* **—sin′gle-mind′ed·ness** *n.*

sin·gle-phase (sĭng′gəl-fāz′) *adj.* Producing, carrying, or powered by a single alternating voltage.

sin·gles bar (sĭng′gəlz) *n.* A bar patronized especially by unmarried men and women. Also called *dating bar.*

sin·gle-space (sĭng′gəl-spās′) *v.* **-spaced, -spac·ing, -spac·es.** *Printing.* —*tr.* To type or print (copy) without leaving a blank line between lines. —*intr.* To type or print copy without line spaces.

single standard *n.* A set of principles applying the same standard to everyone, especially a moral code regarding the sexual behavior of both men and women.

sin·gle·stick (sĭng′gəl-stĭk′) *n.* **1.** A one-handed fencing stick fitted with a hand guard. **2.** The art, sport, or exercise of fencing with such a stick.

sin·gle·stick·er (sĭng′gəl-stĭk′ər) *n. Nautical.* A sailboat with one mast; a sloop.

sin·glet (sĭng′glĭt) *n.* **1.** *Chiefly British.* A man's jersey undershirt. **2.** *Physics.* A multiplet with a single member.

single tax *n.* A system by which all revenue is derived from a tax on one thing, especially land.

sin·gle·ton (sĭng′gəl-tən) *n.* **1.** *Games.* A playing card that is the only one of its suit in a player's hand. **2. a.** An individual separated or distinguished from two or more of its group. **b.** An offspring born alone. [From the name *Singleton* (influenced by SINGLE).]

sin·gle-track (sĭng′gəl-trăk′) *adj.* **1.** Having just one track. **2.** Lacking mental range or flexibility; one-track: *a single-track mind.*

sin·gle·tree (sĭng′gəl-trē′) *n.* See **whiffletree.** [Alteration (influenced by DOUBLETREE) of SWINGLETREE.]

sin·gle·wide (sĭng′gəl-wīd′) *n.* A mobile home 14 feet (4.3 meters) in width, used as a permanent residence. **—sin′gle·wide′** *adj.*

sin·gly (sĭng′glē) *adv.* **1.** Without the presence of others; alone. **2.** Without the help of others; single-handed. **3.** One by one; individually.

sing·song (sĭng′sông′, -sŏng′) *n.* **1.** Verse characterized by mechanical regularity of rhythm and rhyme. **2.** A monotonously rising and falling inflection of the voice. **—singsong** *adj.* Monotonous in vocal inflection or rhythm. **—sing′song′y** *adj.*

sing·spiel (sĭng′spēl′, zĭng′shpēl′) *n.* An 18th-century German musical comedy featuring folk songs interspersed with dialogue. [German : *singen,* to sing (from Middle High German, from Old High German *singan;* see **seng**ʷ**h-** in Appendix) + *Spiel,* play; see SPIEL.]

sin·gu·lar (sĭng′gyə-lər) *adj.* **1.** Being only one; individual. **2.** Being the only one of a kind; unique. **3.** Being beyond what is ordinary or usual; remarkable. **4.** Deviating from the usual or expected; odd. See Synonyms at **strange. 5.** *Abbr.* **s., sing.** *Grammar.* **a.** Of, relating to, or being a noun, pronoun, or adjective denoting a single person or thing or several entities considered as a single unit. **b.** Of, relating to, or being a verb expressing the action or state of a single subject. **6.** *Logic.* Of or relating to the specific as distinguished from the general; individual. **—singular** *n. Abbr.* **s., sing.** *Grammar.* **1.** The singular number or a form designating it. **2.** A word having a singular number. [Middle English *singuler,* from Old French, from Latin *singulāris,* from *singulus,* single. See SINGLE.] **—sin′gu·lar·ly** *adv.* **—sin′gu·lar·ness** *n.*

sin·gu·lar·i·ty (sĭng′gyə-lăr′ĭ-tē) *n., pl.* **-ties. 1.** The quality or condition of being singular. **2.** A trait marking one as distinct from others; a peculiarity. **3.** Something uncommon or unusual. **4.** *Astrophysics.* A point in space-time at which gravitational forces cause matter to have infinite density and infinitesimal volume, and space and time to become infinitely distorted. **5.** *Mathematics.* A point at which the derivative does not exist for a given function of a random variable but every neighborhood of which contains points for which the derivative exists. In this sense, also called *singular point.*

sin·gu·lar·ize (sĭng′gyə-lə-rīz′) *tr.v.* **-ized, -iz·ing, -iz·es.** To make conspicuous; distinguish.

singular point *n. Mathematics.* See **singularity** (sense 5).

Sin·ha·lese (sĭn′hə-lēz′, -lēs′) *n. & adj.* Variant of **Singhalese.**

Si·ni·cism (sī′nĭ-sĭz′əm, sĭn′ĭ-) *n.* A custom or trait peculiar to the Chinese. [From *Sinic,* Chinese, from Medieval Latin *Sīnicus,* Chinese, from Late Latin *Sīnae,* the Chinese. See SINO–.]

Si·ni·cize (sī′nĭ-sīz′, sĭn′ĭ-) *tr.v.* **-cized, -ciz·ing, -ciz·es.** To make Chinese in character or to change or modify by Chinese influence. **—Si′ni·ci·za′tion** (-sĭ-zā′shən) *n.*

Si·ni·fy (sī′nə-fī′, sĭn′ə-) *tr.v.* **-fied, -fy·ing, -fies.** To Sinicize. [Late Latin *Sīnae,* the Chinese; see SINO– + –FY.] **—Si′ni·fi·ca′tion** (-fĭ-kā′shən) *n.*

sin·is·ter (sĭn′ĭ-stər) *adj.* **1.** Suggesting or threatening evil: *a sinister smile.* **2.** Presaging trouble; ominous: *sinister storm clouds.* **3.** Attended by or causing disaster or inauspicious circumstances. **4.** On the left side; left. **5.** *Heraldry.* Situated on or being the side of a shield on the wearer's left and the observer's right. [Middle English *sinistre,* unfavorable, from Old French, from Latin *sinister,* on the left, unlucky.] **—sin′is·ter·ly** *adv.* **—sin′is·ter·ness** *n.*

SYNONYMS: *sinister, baleful, malign.* These adjectives apply to what is indicative of or threatens great harm, disaster, or evil. *Sinister* usually implies impending or lurking danger that makes its presence felt by ominous signs or portents: *"The Kremlin has sinister connotations . . . The aesthetic reality is otherwise"* (Henry A. Kissinger). *Baleful* intensifies the sense of menace; it suggests a deadly, virulent, or poisonous quality: *"The Florida eagles are slightly smaller than the others, but they have the same fierce, baleful look"* (John Corry). *Malign* applies to what manifests an evil disposition, nature, influence, or intent: *"The Devil . . . with jealous leer malign/Eyed them askance"* (John Milton).

---

sin·is·tral (sĭn′ĭ-strəl, sĭ-nĭs′trəl) *adj.* **1.** Of or facing the left side. **2.** Left-handed. **3.** *Zoology.* Relating to or being a gastropod shell that has its aperture to the left when facing the observer with the apex upward. **—sin′is·tral·ly** *adv.*

sin·is·trorse (sĭn′ĭ-strôrs′) *adj.* Growing upward in a spiral that turns from right to left: *a sinistrorse vine.* [Latin *sinistrōrsus,* turned toward the left, from **sinistrōversus* : *sinistrō,* toward the left, from ablative of *sinister,* left + *vorsus,* past participle of *vortere,* variant of *vertere,* to turn. See **wer-**[2] in Appendix.] **—sin′is·trorse′ly** *adv.*

sin·is·trous (sĭn′ĭ-strəs, sĭ-nĭs′trəs) *adj. Archaic.* Sinister; ill-omened. **—sin′is·trous·ly** *adv.*

Si·nit·ic (sī-nĭt′ĭk, sĭ-) *n.* The branch of Sino-Tibetan that comprises Chinese. [SIN(O)– + *-itic,* as in SEMITIC.] **—Si·nit′ic** *adj.*

sink (sĭngk) *v.* **sank** (săngk) or **sunk** (sŭngk), **sunk, sink·ing, sinks.** —*intr.* **1.** To descend to the bottom; submerge. **2. a.** To fall or drop to a lower level, especially to go down slowly or in stages: *The water in the lake sank several feet during the long, dry summer.* **b.** To subside or settle gradually, as a massive or weighty structure. **3.** To appear to move downward, as the sun or moon in setting. **4.** To slope downward; incline. **5.** To pass into a specified condition: *She sank into a deep sleep.* **6. a.** To deteriorate in quality or condition: *The patient is sinking fast. The family sank into a state of disgrace.* **b.** To diminish, as in value.

ă pat	oi boy
ā pay	ou out
âr care	o͝o took
ä father	o͞o boot
ĕ pet	ŭ cut
ē be	ûr urge
ĭ pit	th thin
ī pie	*th* this
îr pier	hw which
ŏ pot	zh vision
ō toe	ə about, item
ô paw	♦ regionalism

Stress marks: ′ (primary); ′ (secondary), as in **dictionary** (dĭk′shə-nĕr′ē)

7. To become weaker, quieter, or less forceful: *His voice sank to a whisper.* **8. a.** To drop or fall slowly, as from weakness or fatigue: *The exhausted runner sank to the ground.* **b.** To feel great disappointment or discouragement: *Her heart sank within her.* **9.** To seep or soak; penetrate: *The water is sinking into the ground.* **10.** To make an impression; become felt or understood: *The meaning finally sank in.* —*tr.* **1.** To cause to descend beneath a surface: *sink a ship.* **2.** To cause to drop or lower: *sank the bucket into the well.* **3.** To force into the ground: *sink a piling.* **4.** To dig or drill (a mine or well) in the earth. **5.** To occupy the full attention of; engross. **6. a.** To make weaker, quieter, or less forceful. **b.** To reduce in quantity or worth. **7.** To debase the nature of; degrade. **8.** To bring to a low or ruined state; defeat or destroy. **9.** To suppress or hide: *He sank his arrogance and apologized.* **10.** *Informal.* To defeat, as in a game. **11. a.** To invest: *sink money into a new housing project.* **b.** To invest without any prospect of return. **12.** To pay off (a debt). **13.** *Sports.* To get (a ball) into a hole or basket. **—sink** *n.* **1.** A water basin fixed to a wall or floor and having a drainpipe and generally a piped supply of water. **2.** A cesspool. **3.** A sinkhole. **4.** In thermodynamics, the part of a system from which heat, or more generally, energy is removed from the system. **5.** A place regarded as wicked and corrupt. **—*idiom.* sink or swim.** *Informal.* To succeed or fail without alternative. [Middle English *sinken,* from Old English *sincan.*] **—sink′a·ble** *adj.*

sink·age (sĭng′kĭj) *n.* **1.** The process, amount, or degree of sinking. **2.** A sunken area; a depression.

sink·er (sĭng′kər) *n.* **1.** One that sinks, as a weight used for sinking fishing lines or nets. **2.** *Slang.* A doughnut. **3.** *Baseball.* A sinkerball.

sink·er·ball (sĭng′kər-bôl′) *n.* *Baseball.* A pitched ball that sinks sharply as it reaches the plate; a sinker.

sink·hole (sĭngk′hōl′) *n.* A natural depression in a land surface communicating with a subterranean passage, generally occurring in limestone regions and formed by solution or by collapse of a cavern roof.

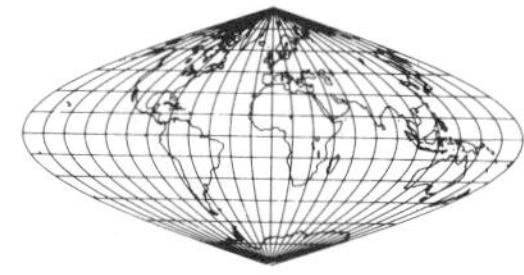
sinusoidal projection

Sin·kiang Ui·ghur or **Sin·kiang Ui·gur** (sĭn′kyăng′ wē′gər, shĭn′jyăng′). See **Xinjiang Uygur.**

sink·ing fund (sĭng′kĭng) *n.* *Abbr.* **SF** *Accounting.* A fund accumulated to pay off a corporate or public debt.

sin·ner (sĭn′ər) *n.* **1.** One that sins or does wrong; a transgressor. **2.** A scamp.

Sinn Fein (shĭn fān′, fē′ĭn) *n.* An Irish political and cultural society founded about 1905 to promote political and economic independence from England, unification of Ireland, and a renewal of Irish culture. It now constitutes the political branch of the Irish Republican Army. [Irish Gaelic *sinn féin* : *sinn,* we (from Middle Irish, from Old Irish) + *féin,* self (from Middle Irish, from Old Irish; see **s(w)e-** in Appendix).] **—Sinn Fein′er** *n.* **—Sinn′ Fein′ism** *n.*

Sino– *pref.* Chinese: *Sinology.* [From Late Latin *Sīnae,* the Chinese, from Greek *Sinai,* from Arabic *Sīn,* China, probably from Chinese *Qin,* the first dynasty (221–206 B.C.) under which China was united.]

si·no·a·tri·al (sī′nō-ā′trē-əl) *adj.* Of or relating to the sinoatrial node: *a sinoatrial heart block.* [SIN(US) + ATRIAL.]

sinoatrial node *n.* A small mass of specialized cardiac muscle fibers located in the posterior wall of the right atrium of the heart that acts as a pacemaker by generating at regular intervals the electric impulses of the heartbeat. Also called *sinoauricular node, sinus node.*

si·no·au·ric·u·lar (sī′nō-ô-rĭk′yə-lər) *adj.* Sinoatrial. [SIN(US) + AURICULAR.]

sinoauricular node *n.* See **sinoatrial node.**

Si·no·logue also **Sin·o·log** (sī′nə-lôg′, -lŏg′, sĭn′ə-) *n.* A student of or specialist in Sinology.

Si·nol·o·gy (sī-nŏl′ə-jē, sĭ-) *n.* The study of Chinese language, literature, or civilization. **—Si′no·log′i·cal** (sī′nə-lŏj′ĭ-kəl, sĭn′ə-) *adj.* **—Si·nol′o·gist** *n.*

Si·no·pe (sə-nō′pē) *n.* The satellite of Jupiter that is 17th in distance from the planet. [Latin *Sinōpē,* woman said to have been unsuccessfully courted by Zeus, from Greek.]

Si·no·phile (sī′nə-fīl′, sĭn′ə-) *n.* One who admires China, its people, or its culture. **—Si′no·phil′i·a** (-fĭl′ē-ə) *n.*

Si·no·phobe (sī′nə-fōb′, sĭn′-) *n.* One who fears or dislikes China, its people, or its culture. **—Si′no·pho′bi·a** (-fō′bē-ə) *n.* **—Si′no·pho′bic** (-fō′bĭk) *adj.*

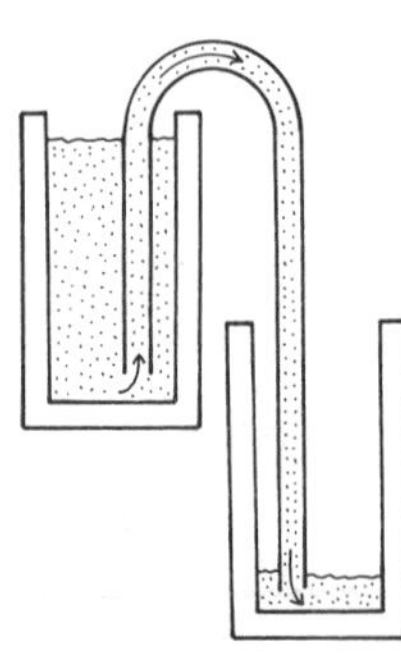
siphon

Si·no-Ti·bet·an (sī′nō-tĭ-bĕt′n, sĭn′ō-) *n.* A language family that includes the Sinitic and Tibeto-Burman branches. **—Si′-no-Ti·bet′an** *adj.*

sin·se·mil·la (sĭn′sə-mē′yə, -mĭl′ə) *n.* A highly potent form of marijuana obtained from unpollinated female plants. [Spanish : *sin,* without (from Latin *sine*) + *semilla,* seed (from Old Spanish dialectal *semilia,* alteration of Late Latin *sēminia,* neuter pl. of *sēminium,* from *sēmen;* see SEMEN).]

sin tax *n.* *Informal.* A tax on certain items, such as cigarettes and alcohol, that are regarded as neither necessities nor luxuries.

sin·ter (sĭn′tər) *n.* **1.** *Geology.* A chemical sediment or crust, as of porous silica, deposited by a mineral spring. **2.** A mass formed by sintering. **—sinter** *v.* **-tered, -ter·ing, -ters.** —*tr.* To cause (metallic powder, for example) to form a coherent mass by heating without melting. —*intr.* To form a coherent mass by heating without melting. [German, from Middle High German, dross, metal slag, from Old High German.] **—sin′ter·a·bil′i·ty** *n.*

sin·u·ate (sĭn′yo͞o-ĭt, -āt′) *intr.v.* **-at·ed, -at·ing, -ates.** To bend or curve; wind in and out: *a road that sinuates through the Alps.* **—sinuate** also **sin·u·at·ed** (-ā′tĭd) *adj.* Having a wavy indented margin, as a leaf. [Latin *sinuāre, sinuāt-,* to bend, from *sinus,* curve.] **—sin′u·ate·ly** *adv.* **—sin′u·a′tion** *n.*

Sin·ui·ju (shĭn′wē-jo͞o′). A city of western North Korea on Korea Bay at the mouth of the Yalu River. It is a port and railroad terminus connected by bridge with Dandong, China. Population, 300,000.

sin·u·os·i·ty (sĭn′yo͞o-ŏs′ĭ-tē) *n.,* *pl.* **-ties. 1.** The quality or condition of being sinuous. **2.** A bending or curving shape or movement.

sin·u·ous (sĭn′yo͞o-əs) *adj.* **1.** Characterized by many curves or turns; winding: *a sinuous stream.* **2.** Characterized by supple and lithe movements: *the sinuous grace of a dancer.* **3.** Not direct; devious. **4.** Sinuate: *a sinuous leaf.* [From Latin *sinuōsus,* from *sinus,* curve.] **—sin′u·ous·ly** *adv.* **—sin′u·ous·ness** *n.*

si·nus (sī′nəs) *n.* **1.** A depression or cavity formed by a bending or curving. **2.** *Anatomy.* **a.** A dilated channel or receptacle containing chiefly venous blood. **b.** Any of various air-filled cavities in the bones of the skull, especially one communicating with the nostrils. **3.** *Pathology.* A fistula leading from a pus-filled cavity. **4.** *Botany.* A recess or an indentation between lobes of a leaf or corolla. [Middle English, hollow in the body, from Medieval Latin *sinus,* from Latin, curve, hollow.]

si·nus·i·tis (sī′nə-sī′tĭs) *n.* Inflammation of the sinuses or a sinus, especially in the nasal region.

sinus node *n.* See **sinoatrial node.**

si·nu·soid (sī′nə-soid′, -nyə-) *n.* **1.** *Mathematics.* See **sine curve. 2.** *Anatomy.* Any of the venous cavities through which blood passes in various glands and organs, such as the adrenal gland and the liver. [Medieval Latin *sinus,* sine; see SINE + –OID.] **—si′nu·soi′dal** (-soid′l) *adj.* **—si′nu·soi′dal·ly** *adv.*

sinusoidal projection *n.* A map projection in which areas are equal to corresponding areas on a globe, the parallels and the prime meridian being straight lines and the other meridians being increasingly curved outward from the prime meridian.

sinus ve·no·sus (vē-nō′səs) *n.* The first chamber in the heart of fish, amphibians, and reptiles, which receives blood from the veins and contracts to force the blood into the atrium. [New Latin *sinus vēnōsus* : Medieval Latin *sinus,* sinus + Latin *vēnōsus,* venous.]

Si·on (sī′ən) *n.* Variant of **Zion**[2].

Siou·an (so͞o′ən) *n.* **1.** A large North American Indian language family spoken from Lake Michigan to the Rocky Mountains and southward to Arkansas. **2.** A member of a Siouan-speaking people. [SIOU(X) + –AN[1].] **—Siou′an** *adj.*

Sioux (so͞o) *n.,* *pl.* **Sioux** (so͞o, so͞oz). **1. a.** A group of Native American peoples, also known as the Dakota, inhabiting the northern Great Plains from Minnesota to eastern Montana and from southern Saskatchewan to Nebraska. Present-day Sioux populations are located mainly in North and South Dakota. **b.** A member of any of these peoples. **2.** Any of the Siouan languages of the Sioux peoples. [North American French, short for *nadoués-sioux,* from Ottowa *naadowesiwag.*] **—Sioux** *adj.*

Sioux City. A city of northwest Iowa on the Missouri River near the South Dakota–Nebraska border. It is a processing center for an agricultural and livestock area. Population, 82,003.

Sioux Falls. A city of southeast South Dakota near the Minnesota border. First settled c. 1856, it was abandoned in 1862 and reestablished as a military post in 1865. It is now the largest city in the state. Population, 81,343.

sip (sĭp) *v.* **sipped, sip·ping, sips.** —*tr.* **1.** To drink in small quantities. **2.** To drink from in sips. —*intr.* To drink something in sips. **—sip** *n.* **1.** The act of sipping. **2.** A small quantity of liquid sipped. [Middle English *sippen.* See **seuə-**[2] in Appendix.] **—sip′per** *n.*

si·phon also **sy·phon** (sī′fən) —*n.* **1.** A pipe or tube fashioned or deployed in an inverted U shape and filled until atmospheric pressure is sufficient to force a liquid from a reservoir in one end of the tube over a barrier higher than the reservoir and out the other end. **2.** *Zoology.* A tubular organ, especially of aquatic invertebrates such as squids or clams, by which water is taken in or expelled. —*v.* **-phoned, -phon·ing, -phons.** —*tr.* To draw off or convey through or as if through a siphon. —*intr.* To pass through a siphon. [Middle English, from Latin *siphō, sīphōn-,* from Greek *siphōn.*] **—si′phon·al, si·phon′ic** (sī-fŏn′ĭk) *adj.*

si·phon·o·phore (sī-fŏn′ə-fôr′, -fōr′, sī′fə-nə-) *n.* Any of various transparent, often subtly colored marine hydrozoans of the order Siphonophora, consisting of a floating or swimming colony of polyplike and medusalike individuals and including the Portuguese man-of-war. [From New Latin *Siphonophora,* order name : Greek *siphō, siphōn-,* tube + Greek *-phora,* neuter pl. of *-phoros,* -phore.]

si·phon·o·stele (sī-fŏn′ə-stēl′, sī′fə-nə-stē′lē) *n.* A type of stele in which the vascular cylinder surrounds a pith, as in the stem of the sunflower. [SIPHON + STELE.] **—si·phon′o·ste′lic** (-stē′lĭk) *adj.*

si·phun·cle (sī′fŭng′kəl) *n.* **1.** A tubelike structure in the body of a shelled cephalopod, such as a nautilus, extending through each chamber of the shell. **2.** A tubular organ on the abdomen of an aphid, from which a waxy fluid is secreted as a pheromone when the insect is attacked. In this sense, also called *cornicle.* [Latin *sīphunculus,* diminutive of *sīphō, sīphōn-,* siphon. See SIPHON.] **—si·phun′cu·lar** (-kyə-lər), **si·phun′cu·late** (-lĭt) *adj.*

Sip·par (sĭ-pär′). An ancient city of northern Babylonia on the Euphrates River south-southwest of present-day Baghdad. In early times it was a religious center devoted to the worship of the sun god Shamash.

sip·pet (sĭp′ĭt) *n.* A small piece of toast or bread soaked in gravy or other liquid or used as a garnish. [From *sip,* alteration of SOP.]

Si·quei·ros (sĭ-kā′rōs), **David Alfaro.** 1896?–1974. Mexican mural painter whose works depict political protest and revolution. His best-known painting is the mural *The March of Humanity* (1968) in Mexico City.

sir (sûr) *n.* **1. Sir.** Used as an honorific before the given name or the full name of baronets and knights. **2.** Used as a form of polite address for a man: *Don't forget your hat, sir.* **3.** Used as a salutation in a letter: *Dear Sir or Madam.* [Middle English, variant of *sire.* See SIRE.]

sir·dar (sûr′där′, sər-där′) *n.* A person of high rank, especially in India. [Hindi *sardār,* from Persian : *sar,* head; see **ker-**[1] in Appendix + *-dār,* holder; see **dher-** in Appendix.]

sire (sīr) *n.* **1.** A father. **2.** *Abbr.* **s.** The male parent of an animal, especially a domesticated mammal such as a horse. **3.** *Archaic.* A male ancestor; a forefather. **4.** *Archaic.* A gentleman of rank. **5.** *Archaic.* Used as a form of address for a superior, especially a king. **—sire** *tr.v.* **sired, sir·ing, sires.** To father; beget. [Middle English, from Old French, from Vulgar Latin **seior,* from Latin *senior,* older, comparative of *senex,* old. See **sen-** in Appendix.]

sir·ee (sə-rē′) *n. Informal.* Variant of **sirree.**

si·ren (sī′rən) *n.* **1.a.** A device in which compressed air or steam is driven against a rotating perforated disk to create a loud, often wailing sound as a signal or warning. **b.** An electronic device producing a similar sound as a signal or warning: *a police car siren.* **2.** Any of several salamanders of the family Sirenidae, such as the mud eel, having an eellike body, permanent external gills, small forelegs, and no hind limbs. [French *sirène,* from Old French *sereine,* Siren, from Late Latin *Sīrēna,* from Latin *Sīrēn,* from Greek *Seirēn.*]

Si·ren (sī′rən) *n.* **1.** *Greek Mythology.* One of a group of sea nymphs who by their sweet singing lured mariners to destruction on the rocks surrounding their island. **2. siren.** A woman regarded as seductive and beautiful. [Middle English *serein,* from Old French *sereine.* See SIREN.]

si·re·ni·an (sī-rē′nē-ən) *n.* See **sea cow. —sirenian** *adj.* Of or belonging to the order of sea cows. [From New Latin *Sīrēnia,* order name, from Latin *Sīrēn,* Siren. See SIREN.]

siren song *n.* An enticing plea or appeal, especially one that is deceptively alluring.

si·ri·a·sis (sĭ-rī′ə-sĭs) *n.* See **sunstroke.** [Latin *sīriāsis,* from Greek *seiriasis,* from *seirian,* to be hot, from *Seirios,* Sirius. See SIRIUS.]

Sir·i·us (sĭr′ē-əs) *n.* A star in the constellation Canis Major, the brightest star in the sky, approximately 8.6 light-years distant from Earth. Also called *Dog Star, Sothis.* [Latin *Sīrius,* from Greek *Seirios,* from *seirios,* burning.]

sir·loin (sûr′loin′) *n.* A cut of meat, especially of beef, from the upper part of the loin just in front of the round. [Middle English *surloine,* from Old French *surlonge,* **surloigne* : *sur,* above (from Latin *super;* see **uper** in Appendix) + *longe, loigne,* loin; see LOIN.]

si·roc·co (sə-rŏk′ō) also **sci·roc·co** (shə-, sə-) *n., pl.* **-cos. 1.** A hot, humid south or southeast wind of southern Italy, Sicily, and the Mediterranean islands, originating in the Sahara Desert as a dry, dusty wind but becoming moist as it passes over the Mediterranean. **2.** A hot or warm southerly wind, especially one moving toward a low barometric pressure center. [Italian *scirocco,* from Arabic *šarq,* east.]

Sí·ros (sē′rôs′). See **Syros.**

sir·rah (sĭr′ə) *n. Obsolete.* Mister; fellow. Used as a contemptuous form of address. [Alteration of SIR.]

sir·ree also **sir·ee** (sə-rē′) *n. Informal.* Sir. Used for emphasis after *yes* or *no.*

sir·up (sĭr′əp, sûr′-) *n.* Variant of **syrup.**

sir·up·y (sĭr′ə-pē, sûr-) *adj.* Variant of **syrupy.**

sir·vente (sîr-väɴt′, sər-vĕnt′) also **sir·ven·tes** (sər-vĕn′tĭs, -vĕnts′) *n., pl.* **-ventes** (-väɴt′, -vĕnts′) also **-vent·es** (-vĕn′təs). A form of lyric verse of the Provençal troubadours satirizing political figures, personal rivals, or social morals. [French, from Provençal *sirventes,* from Old Provençal, from *sirvent,* servant (the position of a lover towards his mistress), from Latin *serviēns, servient-,* present participle of *servīre,* to serve, from *servus,* servant.]

Sir Wil·fred Lau·ri·er (wĭl′frĭd lôr′ē-ā′, lŏr′-), **Mount.** A peak, 3,583.8 m (11,750 ft) high, in the Cariboo Mountains of southeast British Columbia, Canada.

sis (sĭs) *n. Informal.* Sister.

si·sal (sī′səl) *n.* **1.** A Mexican and Central American plant *(Agave sisalana)* widely cultivated for its large, sword-shaped leaves that yield stiff fibers used for cordage and rope. **2.** The fiber of this plant or of other members of the genus *Agave.* [American Spanish, after *Sisal,* a town of southeast Mexico in the Yucatán.]

sis·co·wet (sĭs′kə-wĕt′) *n.* A fat, thick-bodied variety of the lake trout, found in the upper part of Lake Superior. [Short for Ojibwa *pēmitēwiskawēt* : *pimitēw-,* oil + *iskawē,* to have flesh of a specified type.]

sis·kin (sĭs′kĭn) *n.* Any of several small finches, such as *Carduelis spinus,* a greenish-yellow finch of Eurasia related to the goldfinch, or the pine siskin of North America. [Obsolete Dutch *sīsken,* from Middle Dutch, diminutive of *sīs,* from Middle Low German *csītze,* of Slavic origin.]

Sis·ley (sĭs′lē, sĭz′-, sēs-lā′), **Alfred.** 1839–1899. British-born French impressionist painter noted for his outdoor scenes, including *Boat During the Flood* (1876).

Sis·mon·di (sĭs-mŏn′dē, sēs-môɴ-dē′), **Jean Charles Léonard Simon de.** 1773–1842. Swiss historian and economist. He was one of the first to attack the classical economics of Adam Smith and argue for the regulation of competition.

Sis·se·ton (sĭs′ĭ-tən) *n., pl.* **Sisseton** or **-tons. 1.** A Native American people of the Santee branch of the Sioux. **2.** A member of this people.

sis·si·fied (sĭs′ə-fīd′) *adj.* Of, relating to, or having the characteristics of a sissy; timid, cowardly, or effeminate.

sis·sy (sĭs′ē) *n., pl.* **-sies. 1.** A boy or man regarded as effeminate. **2.** A person regarded as timid or cowardly. **3.** *Informal.* Sister. [Diminutive of SIS.] **—sis′si·ness, sis′sy·ness** *n.* **—sis′sy** *adj.* **—sis′sy·ish** *adj.*

sissy bar *n. Informal.* A narrow bar shaped like an inverted U that is attached behind the seat of a motorcycle or bicycle and supports the operator or a passenger.

sis·ter (sĭs′tər) *n. Abbr.* **s. 1.a.** A girl or woman having the same mother and father as another. **b.** A girl or woman having one parent in common with another; a half sister. **c.** The daughter of a person's stepparent by a previous marriage; a stepsister. **2.** A girl or woman who shares a common ancestry, allegiance, character, or purpose with another or others, specifically: **a.** A kinswoman. **b.** A woman fellow member, as of a sorority. **c.** A fellow woman, friend, or companion. **d.** A soul sister. **e.** A woman who advocates, fosters, or takes part in the feminist movement. **3.** *Informal.* Used as a form of address for a woman or girl. **4. Sister.** *Abbr.* **Sr.** *Ecclesiastical.* **a.** A member of a religious order of women; a nun. **b.** Used as a form of address for such a woman, alone or followed by the woman's name. **5.** *Chiefly British.* A nurse, especially the head nurse in a ward. **6.** One identified as female and closely related to another: *"the sisters Death and Night"* (Walt Whitman). **—sister** *adj.* **1.** Related by or as if by sisterhood; closely related: *sister ships; sister cities.* **2.** *Genetics.* Of or being one of an identical pair: *sister chromatids.* [Middle English, partly from Old English *sweostor* and from Old Norse *systir;* see **swesor-** in Appendix.]

sis·ter·hood (sĭs′tər-hŏŏd′) *n.* **1.** The state or relationship of being a sister or sisters. **2.** The quality of being sisterly. **3.** A society, especially a religious society, of women. **4.** Association or unification of women in a common cause.

sis·ter-in-law (sĭs′tər-ĭn-lô′) *n., pl.* **sis·ters-in-law** (sĭs′tərz-). **1.** The sister of one's husband or wife. **2.** The wife of one's brother. **3.** The wife of the brother of one's spouse.

sis·ter·ly (sĭs′tər-lē) *adj.* Of, characteristic of, or befitting sisters or a sister. **—sisterly** *adv.* As a sister. **—sis′ter·li·ness** *n.*

Sis·tine (sĭs′tēn′, sĭ-stēn′) also **Six·tine** (sĭk′stēn′, -stīn′) *adj.* **1.** Of or relating to one of the popes named Sixtus, especially Sixtus IV (1414–1484; reigned 1471–1484). **2.** Of or relating to the Sistine Chapel in the Vatican. [Italian *sistino,* from New Latin *sixtīnus,* from Medieval Latin *Sixtus,* the name of several popes, from Latin *Sextus,* Roman praenomen, from *sextus,* sixth. See SEXT.]

sis·trum (sĭs′trəm) *n., pl.* **-trums** or **-tra** (-trə). *Music.* A percussion instrument of ancient Egypt consisting of metal rods or loops attached to a metal frame. [Middle English, from Latin *sīstrum,* from Greek *seistron,* from *seiein,* to shake.]

Sis·y·phe·an (sĭs′ə-fē′ən) *adj.* **1.** *Greek Mythology.* Of or relating to Sisyphus. **2.** Endlessly laborious or futile: *"Their patients' lack of education and the high cost of medicine make health care a Sisyphean task"* (Frank Gibney, Jr.). [From Latin *Sisyphēius,* from Greek *Sisupheios,* from *Sisuphos,* Sisyphus.]

Sis·y·phus (sĭs′ə-fəs) *n. Greek Mythology.* A cruel king of Corinth condemned forever to roll a huge stone up a hill in Hades only to have it roll down again on nearing the top. [Latin *Sisyphus,* from Greek *Sisuphos.*]

sit (sĭt) *v.* **sat** (săt), **sit·ting, sits.** *—intr.* **1.** To rest with the torso vertical and the body supported on the buttocks. **2.a.** To rest with the hindquarters lowered onto a supporting surface. Used of animals. **b.** To perch. Used of birds. **3.** To cover eggs for hatching; brood. **4.** To be situated or located: *a house that sits on a hill.* **5.** To lie or rest: *Dishes were sitting on a shelf.* See Usage Note at **set**[1]. **6.** To pose for an artist or a photographer. **7.a.** To occupy a seat as a member of a body of officials: *sit in Congress.* **b.** To be in session. **8.** To remain inactive or unused: *Her expensive skis sat gathering dust.* **9.** To affect one with or as if with a burden; weigh: *Official duties sat heavily upon the governor.* **10.** To fit, fall, or drape in a specified manner: *The jacket sits perfectly on you.* **11.** To be agreeable to one; please: *The idea didn't sit well with any of us.* **12.** *Chiefly British.* To take an examination, as for a degree. **13.** To blow from a particular di-

David Siqueiros

sisal
Agave sisalana

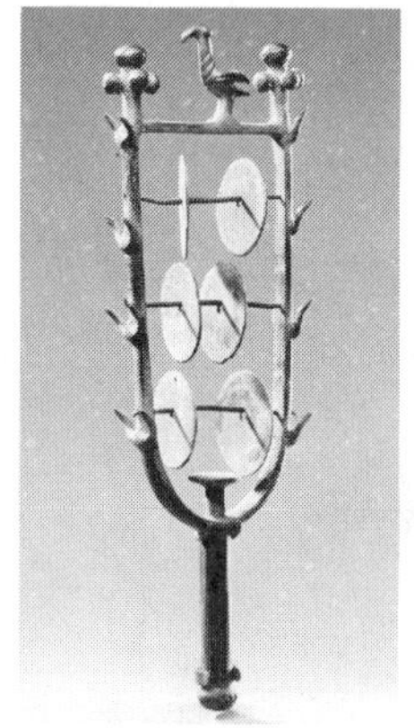
sistrum
c. 2300–2000 B.C. bronze Anatolian sistrum

ă pat	oi boy
ā pay	ou out
âr care	ŏŏ took
ä father	ōō boot
ĕ pet	ŭ cut
ē be	ûr urge
ĭ pit	th thin
ī pie	*th* this
îr pier	hw which
ŏ pot	zh vision
ō toe	ə about, item
ô paw	♦ regionalism

Stress marks: ′ (primary); ′ (secondary), as in **dictionary** (dĭk′shə-nĕr′ē)

rection. Used of the wind. **14.** To keep watch or take care of a child. —*tr.* **1.** To cause to sit; seat: *Sit yourself over there.* **2.** To keep one's seat on (an animal): *She sits her horse well.* **3.** To sit on (eggs) for the purpose of hatching. **4.** To provide seating accommodation for: *a theater that sits 1,000 people.* —**sit** *n.* **1.a.** The act of sitting. **b.** A period of time spent sitting. **2.** The way in which an article of clothing, such as a dress or jacket, fits. —***phrasal verbs.*** **sit down.** To take a seat. **sit in. 1.** To attend or participate in as a visitor: *sat in on the discussion.* **2.** To take part in a sit-in. **sit on** (or **upon**). **1.** To confer about. **2.** *Informal.* To suppress or repress: *sat on the evidence.* **3.** *Informal.* To postpone action or resolution regarding. **4.** *Slang.* To rebuke sharply; reprimand. **sit out. 1.** To stay until the end of. **2.** To refrain from taking part in: *sit out a dance.* **sit up. 1.** To rise from lying down to a sitting position. **2.** To sit with the spine erect. **3.** To stay up later than the customary bedtime. **4.** To become suddenly alert: *The students sat up when he mentioned the test.* —***idioms.*** **sit on (one's) hands.** To fail to act. **sit pretty.** *Informal.* To be in a very favorable position. **sit tight.** *Informal.* To be patient and await the next move. [Middle English *sitten,* from Old English *sittan.* See **sed-** in Appendix.]

sitar

si·tar (sĭ-tär′) *n. Music.* A stringed instrument of India made of seasoned gourds and teak and having a track of 20 metal frets with 6 or 7 main playing strings above and 13 sympathetic resonating strings below. [Hindi *sitār,* from Persian : *si,* three; see **trei-** in Appendix + *tār,* string; see **ten-** in Appendix.] —**si·tar′ist** *n.*

sit·a·tun·ga also **sit·u·tun·ga** (sĭt′ə-to͝ong′ə) *n.* A medium-sized antelope *(Tragelaphus spekei)* of central and eastern Africa, having splayed hooves adapted to swampy and aquatic habitats. [Of Bantu origin.]

sit·com also **sit-com** (sĭt′kŏm′) *n. Informal.* A situation comedy.

sit-down (sĭt′doun′) *n.* **1.** A work stoppage in which the workers refuse to leave their place of employment until their demands are considered or met. Also called *sit-down strike, sit-in.* **2.** An obstruction of normal activity by the act of a large group sitting down in public to express a grievance or protest. **3.** *Informal.* An act, instance, or period of sitting. **4.** *Informal.* A meal for people seated at a table. —**sit-down** *adj.* **1.** Performed or accomplished while sitting down: *a sit-down discussion; a sit-down protest.* **2.** Intended for people seated at a table: *a sit-down dinner for 12.*

site (sīt) *n.* **1.** The place where a structure or group of structures was, is, or is to be located: *a good site for the school.* **2.** The place or setting of something: *a historic site; a job site.* —**site** *tr.v.* **sit·ed, sit·ing, sites.** To situate or locate on a site: *sited the power plant by the river.* [Middle English, from Old French, from Latin *situs.* See SITUS.]

site-spe·ci·fic (sīt′spĭ-sĭf′ĭk) *adj.* Created, planned, or intended for a particular site: *a site-specific sculpture; site-specific theater in the park.*

sith (sĭth) *conj. Archaic.* Since. [Middle English *sithe,* from Old English *siththa,* variant of *siththan.* See SINCE.] —**sith** *adv. & prep.*

sit-in (sĭt′ĭn′) *n.* **1.** See **sit-down** (sense 1). **2.** An organized protest demonstration in which participants seat themselves in an appropriate place and refuse to move. **3.** The act of occupying the seats or an area of a segregated establishment to protest racial discrimination.

Sit·ka (sĭt′kə). A town of southeast Alaska on the western coast of Baranof Island. Founded by Aleksandr Baranov in 1799, it was the capital of Russian America and later the capital of Alaska from 1867 to 1906. Population, 7,803.

si·tol·o·gy (sī-tŏl′ə-jē) *n.* See **dietetics.** [Greek *sitos,* food, grain + –LOGY.]

si·to·ma·ni·a (sī′tə-mā′nē-ə, -mān′yə) *n.* An abnormal craving for food. [Greek *sitos,* food, grain + –MANIA.]

si·to·pho·bi·a (sī′tə-fō′bē-ə) *n.* An abnormal aversion to food. [Greek *sitos,* food, grain + –PHOBIA.]

si·tos·ter·ol (sī-tŏs′tə-rôl′, -rōl′, -rŏl′, sī-) *n.* Any of a group of sterols that occur in high concentrations in certain plants, such as yams, and are used in the synthesis of steroid hormones. [Greek *sitos,* food, grain + STEROL.]

sit·ter (sĭt′ər) *n.* **1.** One that sits, especially: **a.** A person who cares for young children when the parents are not home; a baby sitter. **b.** A person who poses or models, as for a portrait. **2.** A brooding hen.

Sit·ter (sĭt′ər), **Willem de.** 1872–1934. Dutch astronomer noted for his work on cosmology and relativity.

sit·ting (sĭt′ĭng) *n.* **1.** The act or position of one that sits. **2.** A period during which one is seated and occupied with a single activity, such as posing for a portrait or reading a book. **3.** A session, as of a legislature or court. **4.a.** An act, a condition, or a period of brooding on eggs by a bird; incubation. **b.** The number of eggs under a brooding bird; a clutch. —**sitting** *adj.* **1.** Incubating a nest of eggs: *a sitting hen.* **2.** Occupying an official position; incumbent. **3.a.** Of or for sitting: *a sitting posture; a sitting area in a bus station.* **b.** Done or executed while sitting.

Sitting Bull
Photographed in the 1880's

Sit·ting Bull (sĭt′ĭng bo͝ol′). 1834?–1890. Hunkpapa Sioux leader who guided his people to victory against Gen. George A. Custer's cavalry at the Battle of the Little Bighorn (1876).

sitting duck *n. Informal.* An easy target or victim.

sitting room *n.* A living room.

sit·u·ate (sĭch′o͞o-āt′) *tr.v.* **-at·ed, -at·ing, -ates. 1.** To place in a certain spot or position; locate. **2.** To place under particular circumstances or in a given condition. —**situate** (-ĭt, -āt′) *adj. Archaic.* Situated. [Middle English, from Medieval Latin *situāre, situāt-,* to place, from Latin *situs,* location. See **tkei-** in Appendix.]

sit·u·at·ed (sĭch′o͞o-ā′tĭd) *adj.* **1.** Having a place or location; located: *a cabin nicely situated on a quiet riverbank.* **2.** Supplied with money: *a family that has always been well situated.*

sit·u·a·tion (sĭch′o͞o-ā′shən) *n.* **1.a.** The way in which something is positioned vis-à-vis its surroundings. **b.** The place in which something is situated; a location. **2.** Position or status with regard to conditions and circumstances. **3.** The combination of circumstances at a given moment; a state of affairs. See Synonyms at **state. 4.** A critical, problematic, or striking set of circumstances. **5.** A position of employment; a post. —**sit′u·a′tion·al** *adj.* —**sit′u·a′tion·al·ly** *adv.*

situation comedy *n.* A humorous radio or television series featuring the reactions of a regular cast of characters to unusual situations, such as misunderstandings or embarrassing coincidences; a sitcom.

situation ethics *n. (used with a sing. or pl. verb).* A system of ethics that evaluates acts in light of their situational context rather than by the application of moral absolutes.

sit-up (sĭt′ŭp′) *n. Sports.* A physical exercise in which one uses the abdominal muscles to raise the torso from a supine to a sitting position and then lies down again without moving the legs.

si·tus (sī′təs) *n., pl.* **situs.** Position, especially normal or original position, as of a body organ or part. [Latin. See **tkei-** in Appendix.]

situs in·ver·sus (ĭn-vûr′səs) *n.* A congenital condition in which the organs of the viscera are transposed through the sagittal plane so that the heart, for example, is on the right side of the body. [New Latin : Latin *situs,* location + Latin *inversus,* past participle of *invertere,* to invert.]

sit·u·tun·ga (sĭt′ə-to͝ong′ə) *n.* Variant of **sitatunga.**

Sit·well (sĭt′wĕl′, -wəl). Family of British writers, including Dame **Edith Sitwell** (1887–1964), whose experimental poetry is collected in volumes such as *Clowns' Houses* (1918) and *Music and Ceremonies* (1963). Her brother Sir **Osbert** (1892–1969) is known especially for his five-volume autobiography (1944–1950). Their younger brother **Sacheverell** (1897–1988) wrote several volumes of poetry, including *Agamemnon's Tomb* (1972).

sitz bath (sĭts, zĭts) *n.* **1.** A bathtub shaped like a chair in which one bathes in a sitting position, immersing only the hips and buttocks. **2.** A bath taken in such a tub especially for therapeutic reasons. [Partial translation of German *Sitzbad* : *Sitz,* act of sitting (from *sitzen,* to sit, from Middle High German, from Old High German *sizzen;* see **sed-** in Appendix) + *Bad,* bath.]

sitz·krieg (sĭt′skrēg′, zĭt′-) *n.* Warfare marked by a lack of aggression or progress. [German *Sitz,* act of sitting (from *sitzen,* to sit, from Middle High German, from Old High German *sizzen;* see **sed-** in Appendix) + German *Krieg,* war (from Middle High German *krieg,* from Old High German *krēg,* stubbornness; see **g^werə-[1]** in Appendix).]

sitz·mark (sĭt′smärk′, zĭt′-) *n. Sports.* A hollow made in the snow by a skier who has fallen backward. [Partial translation of German *Sitzmarke* : *Sitz,* act of sitting (from *sitzen,* to sit, from Middle High German, from Old High German *sizzen;* see **sed-** in Appendix) + *Marke,* mark.]

Si·va (shē′və, sē′-) *n. Hinduism.* Variant of **Shiva.**

Si·van (sĭv′ən) *n.* The ninth month of the year in the Jewish calendar. See table at **calendar.** [Hebrew *siwān,* from Akkadian *Simānu,* the month Simanu.]

Si·vas (sĭ-väs′, sē-). A city of central Turkey east of Ankara. An important city of Asia Minor under the Romans, Byzantines, and Seljuk Turks, it was sacked by Tamerlane in 1400 and fell to the Ottoman Turks in the 15th century. Population, 172,864.

Si·wa·lik Hills (sĭ-wä′lĭk). A range of the southern Himalaya Mountains extending about 1,689 km (1,050 mi) from southwest Kashmir through northern India into southern Nepal.

six (sĭks) *n.* **1.** The cardinal number equal to 5 + 1. **2.** The sixth in a set or sequence. **3.** Something having six parts, units, or members, especially a motor vehicle having six cylinders. —***idiom.*** **at sixes and sevens.** In a state of confusion or disorder. [Middle English, from Old English. See **s(w)eks** in Appendix.] —**six** *adj. & pron.*

six-gun (sĭks′gŭn′) *n.* A six-chambered revolver.

Six Nations (sĭks) *pl.n.* The Iroquois confederacy after it was joined by the Tuscarora in 1722.

six-pack (sĭks′păk′) *n.* **1.** Six units of a commodity, especially six cans or bottles of a beverage, such as beer, sold in a pack. **2.** The contents of a six-pack.

six·pence (sĭks′pəns) *n. Chiefly British.* **1.** A coin formerly used in Britain and worth six pennies. **2.** The sum of six pennies.

six·pen·ny (sĭks′pĕn′ē, -pə-nē) *adj.* **1.** Valued at, selling for, or worth sixpence. **2.** Of little worth; paltry.

sixpenny nail *n.* A nail 2 inches (5.1 centimeters) long.

six-shoot·er (sĭks′sho͞o′tər) *n. Informal.* A six-chambered revolver; a six-gun.

six·teen (sĭk-stēn′) *n.* **1.** The cardinal number equal to the sum of 15 + 1. **2.** The 16th in a set or sequence. [Middle English *sixtene,* from Old English *sixtȳne.* See **s(w)eks** in Appendix.] **—six·teen′** *adj. & pron.*

six·teen·mo (sĭk-stēn′mō) *n., pl.* **-mos.** *Printing.* See **sextodecimo.**

six·teen·pen·ny nail (sĭk′stēn-pĕn′ē) *n.* A nail 3½ inches (9 centimeters) long.

six·teenth (sĭk-stēnth′) *n.* **1.** The ordinal number matching the number 16 in a series. **2.** One of 16 equal parts. **—six·teenth′** *adv. & adj.*

sixteenth note *n. Music.* A note having one sixteenth the time value of a whole note.

sixth (sĭksth) *n.* **1.** The ordinal number matching the number six in a series. **2.** One of six equal parts. **3.** *Music.* **a.** An interval of six degrees in a diatonic scale. **b.** A tone separated by this interval from a given tone. **c.** The harmonic combination of two tones separated by this interval. **d.** The sixth tone of a scale; the submediant. **—sixth** *adv. & adj.*

sixth sense *n.* A power of perception seemingly independent of the five senses; keen intuition.

six·ti·eth (sĭk′stē-ĭth) *n.* **1.** The ordinal number matching the number 60 in a series. **2.** One of 60 equal parts. **—six′ti·eth** *adv. & adj.*

Six·tine (sĭk′stēn′, -stīn′) *adj.* Variant of **Sistine.**

six·ty (sĭks′tē) *n., pl.* **-ties. 1.** The cardinal number equal to 6 × 10. **2. sixties. a.** Often **Sixties.** The decade from 60 to 69 in a century. **b.** A decade or the numbers from 60 to 69: *They planned to retire in their sixties. The breeze kept the temperature in the sixties.* [Middle English, from Old English *sixtig.* See **s(w)eks** in Appendix.] **—six′ty** *adj. & pron.*

six·ty-fourth note (sĭks′tē-fôrth′, -fōrth′) *n. Music.* A note having one sixty-fourth the time value of a whole note.

six·ty-nine (sĭks′tē-nīn′) *n. Vulgar Slang.* Oral-genital sex between two people at the same time.

siz·a·ble also **size·a·ble** (sī′zə-bəl) *adj.* Of considerable size; fairly large. **—siz′a·ble·ness** *n.* **—siz′a·bly** *adv.*

size¹ (sīz) *n.* **1.** The physical dimensions, proportions, magnitude, or extent of an object. **2.** Any of a series of graduated categories of dimension whereby manufactured articles, such as shoes and clothing, are classified. **3. a.** Considerable extent, amount, or dimensions: *a debt of enormous size.* **b.** Relative amount or number, as of population or contents: *What size is Cleveland?* **4.** Character, value, or status with reference to relative importance or the capacity to meet given requirements: *Try this proposal on for size.* **5.** The actual state of affairs: *That's about the size of the situation.* **—size** *tr.v.* **sized, siz·ing, siz·es. 1.** To arrange, classify, or distribute according to size. **2.** To make, cut, or shape to a required size. **—size** *adj.* Sized. Often used in combination: *bite-size appetizers; an economy-size package.* ***—phrasal verb.*** **size up.** To make an estimate, an opinion, a judgment of: *She sized up her opponent.* [Middle English *sise,* from Old French, court session, law, short for *assise.* See ASSIZE.] **—siz′er** *n.*

size² (sīz) *n.* Any of several gelatinous or glutinous substances usually made from glue, wax, or clay and used as a glaze or filler for porous materials such as paper, cloth, or wall surfaces. **—size** *tr.v.* **sized, siz·ing, siz·es.** To treat or coat with size or a similar substance. [Middle English *sise,* probably from Old French, a setting. See SIZE¹.]

size·a·ble (sī′zə-bəl) *adj.* Variant of **sizable.**

sized (sīzd) *adj.* Having a particular or specified size. Often used in combination: *a medium-sized car; an average-sized house.*

siz·ing (sī′zĭng) *n.* **1.** A glaze or filler; size. **2.** Treatment of a fabric or other surface with size.

siz·zle (sĭz′əl) *intr.v.* **-zled, -zling, -zles. 1.** To make the hissing sound characteristic of frying fat. **2.** To seethe with anger or indignation. **3.** To be very hot: *a summer day that sizzled.* **—sizzle** *n.* A hissing sound. [Perhaps frequentative of Middle English *sissen,* to hiss, of imitative origin.] **—siz′zling·ly** *adv.*

siz·zler (sĭz′lər) *n.* **1.** One that sizzles. **2.** *Informal.* A very hot day.

S.J. *abbr.* Society of Jesus.

Sjael·land (shĕl′ăn′) also **Zea·land** (zē′lənd). An island of eastern Denmark bounded by the Kattegat and the Baltic Sea. Separated from Sweden by the Oresund, it is the largest island of Denmark and the site of Copenhagen, the country's capital.

sjam·bok (shăm-bŏk′, -bŭk′) *South African. n.* A heavy whip, usually made of animal hide. **—sjambok** *tr.v.* **-boked, -bok·ing, -boks.** To hit or beat with a sjambok. [Afrikaans, from Malay *cambuk,* whip, from Hindi *cābuk,* from Persian *chābuk.*]

S.J.D. *abbr. Latin.* Scientiae Juridicae Doctor (Doctor of Juridical Science).

Sjö·gren's syndrome (shō′grənz, shœ′-) *n.* A chronic inflammation of the lachrymal and salivary glands, often accompanied by rheumatoid arthritis and the presence of autoantibodies in the blood, occurring chiefly among women. [After Henrik Samuel Conrad *Sjögren* (born 1899), Swedish ophthalmologist.]

SK *abbr.* Saskatchewan.

sk. *abbr.* Sack.

Skag·er·rak also **Skag·er·ak** (skăg′ə-răk′, skä′gə-räk′). A broad strait between Norway and Denmark linking the North Sea and the Kattegat.

Skag·way (skăg′wā′). A town of southeast Alaska at the head of the Lynn Canal north-northwest of Juneau. It was a boom town and the gateway to the Klondike during the Alaskan gold rush (1897–1898). Population, 768.

skald also **scald** (skôld, skäld) *n.* A medieval Scandinavian poet, especially one writing in the Viking age. [Old Norse *skāld.* See **sekʷ-³** in Appendix.] **—skald′ic** *adj.*

Skan·e·at·e·les Lake (skăn′ē-ăt′ləs, skĭn′-). A lake of central New York. It is one of the Finger Lakes.

skat (skăt) *n. Games.* **1.** A card game for three persons that is played with 32 cards, sevens through aces. **2.** One of the combinations of cards occurring in this game. [German, from Italian *scarto,* a discarded card, from *scartare,* to reject : *s-,* out; see SFUMATO + *carta,* card (from Latin *charta,* paper made of papyrus; see CARD¹).]

skate¹ (skāt) *n. Sports.* **1.** An ice skate. **2.** A roller skate. **3.** The act or a period of skating. **—skate** *intr.v.* **skat·ed, skat·ing, skates. 1.** To glide or move along on or as if on skates. **2.** *Informal.* To act in an irresponsible or superficial manner. [From Dutch *schaats,* stilt, skate (taken as pl.), from Middle Dutch *schaetse,* from Old North French *escache,* stilt, perhaps of Germanic origin.]

skate² (skāt) *n.* Any of various rays of the genus *Raja,* having a flattened body and greatly expanded pectoral fins that extend around the head. [Middle English *scate,* from Old Norse *skata.*]

skate³ (skāt) *n.* **1.** A fellow; a person. **2.** A decrepit horse; a nag. [Perhaps alteration of dialectal *skite,* contemptible person, probably from dialectal *skite,* to defecate, from Middle English *skiten,* from Old Norse *skīta.* See **skei-** in Appendix.]

skate·board (skāt′bôrd′, -bōrd′) *Sports. n.* A short, narrow board having a set of four roller skate wheels mounted under it and usually ridden in a standing or crouching position. **—skateboard** *intr.v.* **-board·ed, -board·ing, -boards.** To ride on a skateboard. **—skate′board′er** *n.*

skateboard

skat·er (skā′tər) *n.* **1.** One who skates, as on ice. **2.** See **water strider.**

skat·ole (skăt′ōl, -ôl) also **skat·ol** (-ôl, -ōl, -ŏl) *n.* A white crystalline organic compound, C_9H_9N, having a strong fecal odor, found naturally in feces, beets, and coal tar and used as a fixative in the manufacture of perfume. [Greek *skōr, skat-,* dung; see **sker-³** in Appendix + -OLE.]

Skaw (skô). A cape on the northern extremity of Jutland, Denmark, extending into the Skagerrak.

skean (skēn) *n.* A double-edged dagger formerly used in Ireland and Scotland. [Middle English *skene,* from Irish Gaelic *scian,* from Old Irish *scīan.* See **skei-** in Appendix.]

Skeat (skēt), **Walter William.** 1835–1912. English philologist who wrote *An Etymological Dictionary of the English Language* (1879–1882) and began the systematic study of English place names.

ske·dad·dle (skĭ-dăd′l) *intr.v.* **-dled, -dling, -dles.** *Informal.* To leave hastily; flee. [Origin unknown.]

Skee·na (skē′nə). A river rising in western British Columbia, Canada, and flowing about 579 km (360 mi) generally south and west to the Pacific Ocean near Prince Rupert.

skeet (skēt) *n.* A form of trapshooting in which clay targets are thrown from traps to simulate birds in flight and are shot at from different stations. [Alteration of SHOOT.]

♦ **skee·ter** (skē′tər) *n. Chiefly Southern U.S.* See **mosquito.** See Regional Note at **possum.** [Shortening and alteration of MOSQUITO.]

♦ **skeeter hawk** *n. South Atlantic U.S.* See **dragonfly.** See Regional Note at **dragonfly.**

skeg (skĕg) *n. Nautical.* **1.** A timber that connects the keel and the sternpost of a ship. **2.** An arm extending to the rear of the keel to support the rudder and protect the propeller. **3.** A series of timbers attached to the stern of a small boat, serving as a keel to keep the boat on course. [Dutch *scheg,* perhaps from Old Norse *skegg,* beard, beak of a ship.]

skein (skān) *n.* **1. a.** A length of thread or yarn wound in a loose, elongated coil. **b.** Something suggesting the coil of a skein; a complex tangle: *a twisted skein of lies.* **2.** A flock of geese or similar birds in flight. See Synonyms at **flock¹.** [Middle English *skeine,* from Old French *escaigne.*]

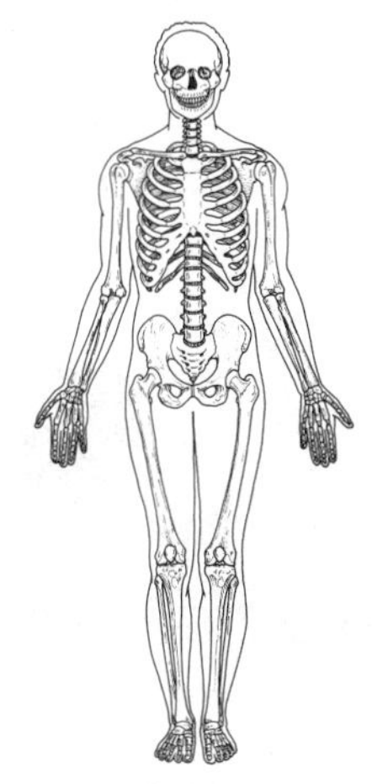

skeleton

skel·e·tal (skĕl′ĭ-tl) *adj.* **1.** Of, relating to, forming, or of the nature of a skeleton: *the skeletal system.* **2.** Attached to or formed by a skeleton: *skeletal muscles.* **—skel′e·tal·ly** *adv.*

skel·e·ton (skĕl′ĭ-tn) *n.* **1. a.** The internal structure composed of bone and cartilage that protects and supports the soft organs, tissues, and other parts of a vertebrate organism; endoskeleton. **b.** The hard external supporting and protecting structure in many invertebrates, such as mollusks and crustaceans, and certain vertebrates, such as turtles; exoskeleton. **2.** A supporting structure or framework, as of a building. **3.** An outline or a sketch. **4.** Something reduced to its basic or minimal parts. **5.** One that is very thin or emaciated. **—skeleton** *adj.* **1.** Of, relating to, or resembling a skeleton. **2.** Reduced to the basic or minimal parts or members: *a skeleton crew.* **3.** *Computer Science.* Of or relating to a set of incomplete instructions intended to be completed by a specialized program. ***—idiom.*** **skeleton in (one's) closet.** A source of shame or disgrace, as in a family, that is kept secret. [Greek *skeleton (sōma),* dried-up (body), neuter of *skeletos,* from *skellesthai,* to dry up.]

skel·e·ton·ize (skĕl′ĭ-tn-īz′) *tr.v.* **-ized, -iz·ing, -iz·es. 1.**

ă pat	oi boy
ā pay	ou out
âr care	ŏŏ took
ä father	ōō boot
ĕ pet	ŭ cut
ē be	ûr urge
ĭ pit	th thin
ī pie	*th* this
îr pier	hw which
ŏ pot	zh vision
ō toe	ə about, item
ô paw	♦ regionalism

Stress marks: **′** (primary); ′ (secondary), as in **dictionary** (dĭk′shə-nĕr′ē)

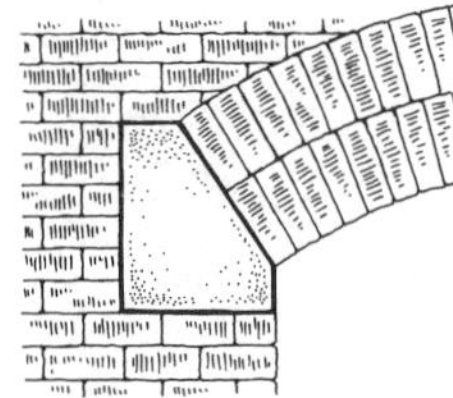

skewback

ski

ski boot

skiff
c. 1948 Seaford skiff by Paul A. Ketcham, after an 1880 boat by Samuel Gritman

skimmer
Black skimmer
Rynchops nigra

To reduce to skeleton form: *"Carnivorous beetles . . . can skeletonize a bat within hours"* (Scientific American). **2.** To outline or sketch briefly. **3.** To reduce in size or number: *skeletonize a hospital staff.*

skeleton key *n.* A key with a large portion of the bit filed away so that it can open different locks. Also called *passkey.*

skell (skĕl) *n. Slang.* A homeless person who lives as a derelict. [Origin unknown.]

skel·lum (skĕl′əm) *n. Scots.* A rascal; a rogue. [Dutch *schelm,* from Low German, from Middle Low German.]

Skel·ton (skĕl′tən), **John.** 1460?–1529. English poet and scholar noted for his satires, including *Speke Parrot* (1521) and *Colyn Cloute* (1522).

skep (skĕp) *n.* A beehive, especially one of straw. [Middle English, basket, from Old Norse *skeppa,* a dry measure, and from Old English *sceppe* (from Old Norse *skeppa*).]

skep·tic also **scep·tic** (skĕp′tĭk) *n.* **1.** One who instinctively or habitually doubts, questions, or disagrees with assertions or generally accepted conclusions. **2.** One inclined to skepticism in religious matters. **3.** *Philosophy.* **a.** Often **Skeptic.** An adherent of a school of skepticism. **b. Skeptic.** A member of an ancient Greek school of skepticism, especially that of Pyrrho of Elis (360?–272? B.C.). [Latin *Scepticus,* disciple of Pyrrho of Elis, from Greek *Skeptikos,* from *skeptesthai,* to examine. See **spek-** in Appendix.]

skep·ti·cal also **scep·ti·cal** (skĕp′tĭ-kəl) *adj.* **1.** Marked by or given to doubt; questioning: *a skeptical attitude; skeptical of political promises.* **2.** Relating to or characteristic of skeptics or skepticism. —**skep′ti·cal·ly** *adv.*

skep·ti·cism also **scep·ti·cism** (skĕp′tĭ-sĭz′əm) *n.* **1.** A doubting or questioning attitude or state of mind; dubiety. See Synonyms at **uncertainty. 2.** *Philosophy.* The doctrine that absolute knowledge is impossible and that inquiry must be a process of doubting in order to acquire approximate or relative certainty. **3.** Doubt or disbelief of religious tenets.

sker·ry (skĕr′ē) *n., pl.* **-ries.** A small rocky reef or island. [Scots, diminutive of Old Norse *sker.* See **sker-**[1] in Appendix.]

sketch (skĕch) *n.* **1.** A hasty or undetailed drawing or painting often made as a preliminary study. **2.** A brief, general account or presentation; an outline. **3. a.** A brief, light, or informal literary composition, such as an essay or a short story. **b.** *Music.* A brief composition, especially for the piano. **c.** A short, often satirical scene or play in a revue or variety show; a skit. **4.** *Informal.* An amusing person. —**sketch** *v.* **sketched, sketch·ing, sketch·es.** —*tr.* To make a sketch of; outline. —*intr.* To make a sketch. [Dutch *schets,* from Italian *schizzo,* from *schizzare,* to splash, of imitative origin.] —**sketch′er** *n.*

sketch·book (skĕch′bo͝ok′) *n.* **1.** A pad of paper used for sketching. Also called *sketchpad.* **2.** A book of literary sketches.

sketch·pad (skĕch′păd′) *n.* See **sketchbook** (sense 1).

sketch·y (skĕch′ē) *adj.* **-i·er, -i·est. 1.** Resembling a sketch; giving only major points or parts. **2. a.** Lacking in substance or completeness; incomplete. **b.** Slight; superficial. —**sketch′i·ly** *adv.* —**sketch′i·ness** *n.*

skew (skyo͞o) *v.* **skewed, skew·ing, skews.** —*intr.* **1.** To take an oblique course or direction. **2.** To look obliquely or sideways. —*tr.* **1.** To turn or place at an angle. **2.** To give a bias to; distort. —**skew** *adj.* **1.** Placed or turned to one side; asymmetrical. **2.** Distorted or biased in meaning or effect. **3.** Having a part that diverges, as in gearing. **4. a.** *Mathematics.* Neither parallel nor intersecting. Used of straight lines in space. **b.** *Statistics.* Not symmetrical about the mean. Used of distributions. —**skew** *n.* An oblique or slanting movement, position, or direction. [Middle English *skewen,* to escape, run sideways, from Old North French *eskiuer,* of Germanic origin.] —**skew′ness** *n.*

skew arch *n. Architecture.* An arch having sides not at right angles to the face of its abutments.

skew·back (skyo͞o′băk′) *n. Architecture.* Either of two inset abutments sloped to support a segmental arch.

skew·bald (skyo͞o′bôld′) *adj.* Having spots or patches of white on a coat of a color other than black: *a skewbald horse.* —**skewbald** *n.* A skewbald animal, especially a horse. [Middle English *skeued,* of mixed colors (probably from *skeu,* sky, cloud, of Scandinavian origin; see **(s)keu-** in Appendix) + BALD.]

skew·er (skyo͞o′ər) *n.* **1.** A long metal or wooden pin used to secure or suspend food during cooking; a spit. **2.** Any of various picks or rods having a function or shape similar to a skewer. —**skewer** *tr.v.* **-ered, -er·ing, -ers.** To hold together or pierce with or as if with a skewer. [Middle English *skuer,* perhaps of Scandinavian origin.]

skew lines *pl.n. Mathematics.* Straight lines that are not in the same plane and do not intersect.

ski (skē) *n., pl.* **skis. 1.** *Sports.* **a.** One of a pair of long flat runners of plastic, metal, or wood that curve upward in front and may be attached to a boot for gliding or traveling over snow. **b.** A waterski. **2.** Something that is used as a runner on a vehicle: *a helicopter with skis for landing on snow and ice.* —**ski** *v.* **skied, ski·ing, skis.** —*intr.* To travel or glide on skis, especially as a sport. —*tr.* To travel or glide over on skis: *ski a mountain slope.* [Norwegian, from Old Norse *skīdh,* stick, snowshoe. See **skei-** in Appendix.] —**ski′a·ble** *adj.* —**ski′er** *n.*

ski·a·gram (skī′ə-grăm′) *n.* **1.** A picture or photograph made up of shadows or outlines. **2.** See **radiograph.** [Greek *skia,* shadow + -GRAM.]

ski·a·graph (skī′ə-grăf′) *n.* See **radiograph.**

ski·ag·ra·phy (skī-ăg′rə-fē) *n.* **1.** The art or technique of making skiagrams. **2.** See **radiography.** [Greek *skiagraphia,* painting in light and shade : *skia,* shadow + *-graphia,* -graphy.]

ski·a·scope (skī′ə-skōp′) *n.* See **retinoscope.** [Greek *skia,* shadow + -SCOPE.]

ski·as·co·py (skī-ăs′kə-pē) *n., pl.* **-pies.** See **retinoscopy.**

ski·bob (skē′bŏb′) *n. Sports.* A vehicle for gliding downhill over snow, consisting of two skis one behind the other on a metal frame, steering handlebars connected to the forward ski, and a low seat attached to the longer rear ski for the rider who wears small skis for balance. —**ski′bob·ber** *n.* —**ski′bob′bing** *n.*

ski boot *n. Sports.* A stiff padded plastic or leather boot that is fastened to the foot with strong buckles or laces and locked into place in a ski binding.

skid (skĭd) *n.* **1.** The act of sliding or slipping over a surface, often sideways. **2. a.** A plank, log, or timber, usually one of a pair, used as a support or as a track for sliding or rolling heavy objects. **b.** A pallet for loading or handling goods, especially one having solid sideboards and no bottom. **c.** One of several logs or timbers forming a skid road. **3. skids.** *Nautical.* A wooden framework attached to the side of a ship to prevent damage, as when unloading. **4.** A shoe or drag applying pressure to a wheel to brake a vehicle. **5.** A runner in the landing gear of certain aircraft. **6. skids.** *Slang.* A path to ruin or failure: *His career hit the skids. Her life is now on the skids.* —**skid** *v.* **skid·ded, skid·ding, skids.** —*intr.* **1.** To slide sideways while moving because of loss of traction: *The truck skidded on a patch of ice.* See Synonyms at **slide. 2.** To slide without revolving: *wheels skidding on oily pavement.* **3.** To move sideways in a turn because of insufficient banking. Used of an airplane. —*tr.* **1.** To brake (a wheel) with a skid. **2.** To haul on a skid or skids. [Perhaps of Scandinavian origin.]

skid·der (skĭd′ər) *n.* **1. a.** One that skids: *a sports car that was a real skidder.* **b.** One that makes use of a skid. **2.** A heavy, four-wheel tractor used to haul logs over rugged terrain.

skid·dy (skĭd′ē) *adj.* **-di·er, -di·est.** Liable to skid or cause skidding: *a light, skiddy car; skiddy roads.*

skid fin *n.* An upright auxiliary airfoil formerly placed above the upper wing in biplanes to increase lateral stability.

skid road *n.* **1.** A track made of logs laid transversely about five feet apart that is used to haul logs to a loading platform or a mill. **2.** *Slang.* Skid row.

skid row (rō) *n. Slang.* A squalid district inhabited chiefly by derelicts and vagrants. [Alteration of SKID ROAD (from the fact that it once referred to a downtown area frequented by loggers).]

skied (skīd) *v.* Past tense and past participle of **sky.**

skies (skīz) *n.* Plural of **sky.** —**skies** *v.* Third person singular present tense of **sky.**

skiff (skĭf) *n. Nautical.* A flat-bottomed open boat of shallow draft, having a pointed bow and a square stern and propelled by oars, sail, or motor. [Middle English *skif,* from Old French *esquif,* from Old Italian *schifo,* of Germanic origin.]

skif·fle (skĭf′əl) *n. Music.* Jazz, folk, or country music played by performers who use unconventional instruments, such as kazoos, washboards, or jugs. [Origin unknown.]

ski·jor·ing (skē′jôr′ĭng, -jōr′-) *n. Sports.* A sport in which a skier is drawn over ice or snow by a horse or vehicle. [Norwegian *skikjøring* : *ski,* ski; see SKI + *kjøring,* driving (from *kjøre,* to drive, from Old Norse *keyra*).]

ski jump *Sports. n.* **1.** A jump or leap made by a skier. **2.** A course or chute prepared for a ski jump. —**ski jump** *intr.v.* **ski jumped, ski jump·ing, ski jumps.** To execute a ski jump. —**ski jumper** *n.*

ski jumping *n. Sports.* A competitive event in which a skier jumps from a ski jump and is judged on both form and the distance jumped.

skil·ful (skĭl′fəl) *adj.* Variant of **skillful.**

ski lift *n. Sports.* A power-driven conveyer, usually with attached tow bars, suspended chairs, or gondolas, used to carry skiers to the top of a trail or slope. Also called *ski tow.*

skill (skĭl) *n.* **1.** Proficiency, facility, or dexterity that is acquired or developed through training or experience. See Synonyms at **ability. 2. a.** An art, a trade, or a technique, particularly one requiring use of the hands or body. **b.** A developed talent or ability: *writing skills.* **3.** *Obsolete.* A reason. [Middle English *skil,* from Old Norse, discernment. See **skel-**[1] in Appendix.]

skilled (skĭld) *adj.* **1.** Having or showing skill; expert. See Synonyms at **proficient. 2.** Requiring specialized ability or training: *a skilled trade.*

♦ **skil·let** (skĭl′ĭt) *n.* **1.** See **frying pan.** See Regional Note at **frying pan. 2.** *Chiefly British.* A long-handled stewing pan or saucepan sometimes having legs. [Middle English *skelet,* from Old French *escuelete,* diminutive of *escuele,* plate, from Latin *scutella,* diminutive of *scutra,* platter.]

skill·ful also **skil·ful** (skĭl′fəl) *adj.* **1.** Possessing or exercising skill; expert. See Synonyms at **proficient. 2.** Characterized by or requiring skill. —**skill′ful·ly** *adv.* —**skill′ful·ness** *n.*

skim (skĭm) *v.* **skimmed, skim·ming, skims.** —*tr.* **1. a.** To remove floating matter from (a liquid). **b.** To remove (floating matter) from a liquid. **c.** To take away the choicest or most readily attainable contents or parts from. **2.** To coat or cover with or as if with a thin layer, as of scum. **3.a.** To throw so as to bounce or slide: *skimming stones on the pond.* **b.** To glide or pass quickly and lightly over. See Synonyms at **brush**[1]. **4.** To read or glance through (a book, for example) quickly or superficially. **5.** *Slang.* To fail to declare part of (certain income, such as winnings) to avoid tax payment. —*intr.* **1.** To move or pass swiftly and lightly over or near a surface; glide. **2.** To give a quick and superficial reading, scrutiny, or consideration; glance: *skimmed through the newspaper.* **3.** To become coated with a thin layer. **4.** *Slang.* To fail to declare certain income to avoid tax payment. **—skim** *n.* **1.** The act of skimming. **2.** Something that has been skimmed. **3.** A thin layer or film. **4.** *Slang.* The profit gained by skimming. [Middle English *skimmen,* perhaps from Old French *escumer,* to remove scum, from *escume,* scum, of Germanic origin. See **(s)keu-** in Appendix.]

ski mask *n.* A knitted covering for the head and face, worn especially by skiers for protection from the cold.

skim·mer (skĭm′ər) *n.* **1.** One that skims, such as a large perforated spoon used in skimming liquids. **2.** A light, usually straw hat with a stiff wide brim and a flat shallow crown. **3.a.** Any of several chiefly coastal birds of the genus *Rynchops,* having long narrow wings and a long bill with a longer lower mandible for skimming the water's surface for food. **b.** A black skimmer.

skim milk *n.* Milk from which the cream has been removed.

ski·mo·bile (skē′mō-bēl′, -mə-) *n.* See **snowmobile.**

skimp (skĭmp) *v.* **skimped, skimp·ing, skimps.** —*tr.* **1.** To deal with hastily, carelessly, or with poor material: *concentrated on reelection, skimping other matters.* **2.** To give inadequate funds to; be stingy with: *misers who skimp their own children.* —*intr.* To be stingy or very thrifty. **—skimp** *adj.* Scanty; skimpy. [Obsolete *skimp,* scanty, perhaps from alteration of SCRIMP.]

skimp·y (skĭm′pē) *adj.* **-i·er, -i·est. 1.** Inadequate, as in size or fullness, especially through economizing or stinting: *a skimpy meal.* See Synonyms at **meager. 2.** Unduly thrifty; niggardly. **—skimp′i·ly** *adv.* **—skimp′i·ness** *n.*

skin (skĭn) *n.* **1.** The membranous tissue forming the external covering or integument of an animal and consisting in vertebrates of the epidermis and dermis. **2.** An animal pelt, especially the comparatively pliable pelt of a small or young animal: *a tent made of goat skins.* **3.** A usually thin, closely adhering outer layer: *the skin of a peach; a sausage skin; the skin of an aircraft.* **4.** A container for liquids that is made of animal skin. **5.** *Informal.* One's life or physical survival: *They lied to save their skins.* **—skin** *v.* **skinned, skin·ning, skins.** —*tr.* **1.** To remove skin from: *skinned and gutted the rabbit.* **2.** To bruise, cut, or injure the skin or surface of: *She skinned her knee.* **3.** To remove (an outer covering); peel off: *skin off the thin bark.* **4.** To cover with or as if with skin: *skin the framework of a canoe.* **5.** *Slang.* To fleece; swindle. —*intr.* **1.** To become covered with or as if with skin: *In January the pond skins over with ice.* **2.** To pass with little room to spare: *We barely skinned by.* **—skin** *adj. Slang.* Of, relating to, or depicting pornography: *skin magazines.* **—*idioms.* by the skin of (one's) teeth.** By the smallest margin. **get under (one's) skin. 1.** To irritate or stimulate; provoke. **2.** To become an obsession. **under the skin.** Beneath the surface; fundamentally: *enemies who are really brothers under the skin.* [Middle English, from Old Norse *skinn.* See **sek-** in Appendix.] **—skin′less** *adj.*

skin-deep (skĭn′dēp′) *adj.* Superficial; shallow: *skin-deep civility.* **—skin-deep** *adv.* In a shallow manner; superficially.

skin-dive (skĭn′dīv′) *intr.v.* **-dived, -div·ing, -dives.** *Sports.* To engage in skin diving.

skin diving *n. Sports.* The sport of swimming under water with flippers and a face mask and usually with a snorkel rather than a portable air supply. **—skin diver** *n.*

skin effect *n.* The tendency of alternating current to flow near the surface of a conductor.

skin flick *n. Slang.* A pornographic film.

skin·flint (skĭn′flĭnt′) *n.* One who is very reluctant to spend money; a miser.

skin game *n. Slang.* **1.** A fraudulent gambling game. **2.** A swindle.

skin graft *n.* A surgical graft of healthy skin from one part of the body to another or from one individual to another in order to replace damaged or lost skin.

skin graft·ing (grăf′tĭng) *n.* The act or process of making a skin graft.

skin·head (skĭn′hĕd′) *n. Slang.* **1.** A person with a shaven head. **2.** A member of any of various groups of white British or American youths who shave their heads, gather at rock concerts and sports events, and sometimes participate in white-supremacist and anti-immigrant activities.

skink (skĭngk) *n.* Any of numerous smooth, shiny lizards of the family Scincidae, having a cylindrical body and small or rudimentary legs and living chiefly in temperate and tropical regions. [Latin *scincus,* from Greek *skinkos.*]

skinned (skĭnd) *adj.* Having skin of a specified kind. Often used in combination: *fair-skinned; dark-skinned.*

♦**skin·ner** (skĭn′ər) *n.* **1.** One that flays, dresses, or sells animal skins. **2.** *Western U.S.* A mule driver.

Skin·ner (skĭn′ər), **B(urrhus) F(rederick).** 1904–1990. American psychologist. A leading behaviorist, Skinner influenced the fields of psychology and education with his theories of stimulus-response behavior. His books include *Walden Two* (1961) and *Beyond Freedom and Dignity* (1971).

Skinner, Cornelia Otis. 1901–1979. American actress and writer known for her one-woman shows, which she wrote and produced.

Skinner, Otis. 1858–1942. American actor whose theater credits include *Kismet* (1911–1914), *Blood and Sand* (1921), and numerous Shakespearean productions.

Skinner box *n.* A soundproof, light-resistant box or cage used in laboratories to isolate an animal for experiments in operant conditioning and usually containing only a bar or lever to be pressed by the animal to gain a reward, such as food, or to avoid a painful stimulus, such as a shock. [After Burrhus Frederick SKINNER.]

Skin·ner·i·an (skĭ-nîr′ē-ən) *adj.* Of or relating to the behavioristic theories and methods of B.F. Skinner. **—Skinnerian** *n.* A follower of B.F. Skinner's theories or methods. **—Skin′ner·ism** (skĭn′ə-rĭz′əm) *n.*

skin·ny (skĭn′ē) *adj.* **-ni·er, -ni·est. 1.** Very thin. See Synonyms at **lean**[2]. **2.** Of, relating to, or resembling skin. **—skinny** *n. Slang.* Inside information; the real facts: *People listen to the show in order to get the straight skinny.* **—skin′ni·ness** *n.*

skin·ny-dip (skĭn′ē-dĭp′) *intr.v.* **-dipped, -dip·ping, -dips.** *Informal.* To swim in the nude. **—skin′ny-dip′per** *n.* **—skin·ny-dip·ping** *n.*

skin patch *n.* See **transdermal patch.**

skin-pop (skĭn′pŏp′) *tr.v.* **-popped, -pop·ping, -pops.** *Slang.* To inject (a drug) beneath the skin rather than into a vein. **—skin′-pop′ping** *n.*

skin search *n.* See **strip search.**

skin test *n.* A test for detecting an allergy or infectious disease, performed by means of a patch test, a scratch test, or an intracutaneous injection of an allergen or extract of the disease-causing organism.

skin·tight (skĭn′tīt′) *adj.* Fitting closely or clinging to the skin.

skip (skĭp) *v.* **skipped, skip·ping, skips.** —*intr.* **1.a.** To move by hopping on one foot and then the other. **b.** To leap lightly about. **2.** To bounce over or be deflected from a surface; skim or ricochet. **3.** To pass from point to point, omitting or disregarding what intervenes: *skipped through the list hurriedly; skipping over the dull passages in the novel.* **4.** To be promoted in school beyond the next regular class or grade. **5.** *Informal.* To leave hastily; abscond: *skipped out of town.* **6.** To misfire. Used of an engine. —*tr.* **1.** To leap or jump lightly over: *skip rope.* **2.** To pass over without mentioning; omit: *skipped the minor details of the story.* **3.** To cause to bounce lightly over a surface; skim. **4.** To be promoted beyond (the next grade or level). **5.** *Informal.* To leave hastily: *The fugitive skipped town.* **6.** *Informal.* To fail to attend: *We skipped science class again.* **—skip** *n.* **1.** A leaping or jumping movement, especially a gait in which hops and steps alternate. **2.** An act of passing over something; an omission. [Middle English *skippen,* perhaps of Scandinavian origin.] **—skip′pa·ble** *adj.*

skip distance *n.* The smallest separation between a transmitter and a receiver that permits radio signals of a specific frequency to travel from one to the other by reflection from the ionosphere.

skip·jack (skĭp′jăk′) *n., pl.* **skipjack** or **-jacks. 1.** Any of several marine food fishes of the genus *Euthynnus,* related to and resembling the tuna, especially an economically important striped species *(E. pelamis)* occurring in all tropical areas. **2.** Any of various fishes, such as the bluefish, that habitually leap out of the water. **3.** *pl.* **-jacks.** *Nautical.* A small sailboat having a bottom shaped like a flat V and vertical sides.

ski pole *n. Sports.* A lightweight pole with a handgrip, sometimes a wrist strap, and a sharp point encircled slightly above by a disk, used in pairs by snow skiers.

skip·per[1] (skĭp′ər) *n.* **1.** *Nautical.* The master of a ship. **2.** A coach, director, or other leader. **—skipper** *tr.v.* **-pered, -per·ing, -pers.** To act as the skipper of. [Middle English, from Middle Dutch, from *scip,* ship.]

skip·per[2] (skĭp′ər) *n.* **1.** One that skips: *a student who was a notorious skipper of Friday classes.* **2.** Any of numerous butterflies of the families Hesperiidae and Megathymidae, having a hairy mothlike body, hooked tips on the antennae, and a darting flight pattern. **3.** Any of several marine fishes that often leap above water, especially the saury *Cololabis saira* of Pacific waters.

skirl (skûrl) *v.* **skirled, skirl·ing, skirls.** *Music.* —*intr.* To produce a high, shrill, wailing tone. Used of bagpipes. —*tr.* To play (a piece) on bagpipes. **—skirl** *n.* **1.** *Music.* The shrill sound made by the chanter pipe of bagpipes. **2.** A shrill, wailing sound: *"The skirl of a police whistle split the stillness"* (Sax Rohmer). [Middle English *skrillen, skirlen,* probably of Scandinavian origin.]

skir·mish (skûr′mĭsh) *n.* **1.** A minor battle in war, as one between small forces or between large forces avoiding direct conflict. **2.** A minor or preliminary conflict or dispute: *a skirmish over the rules before the debate began.* **—skirmish** *intr.v.* **-mished, -mish·ing, -mish·es.** To engage in a minor battle or dispute. [Middle English *skirmisshe,* alteration (influenced by

skink
Five-lined skink
Eumeces fasciatus

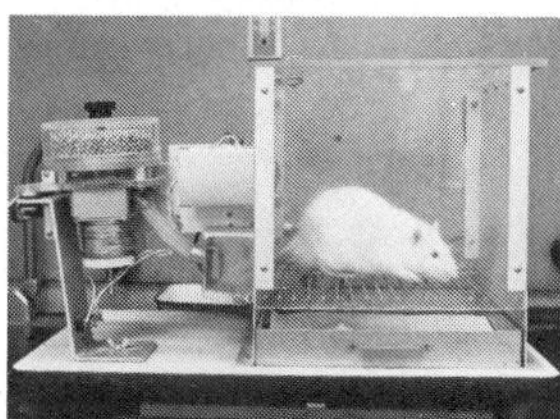

Skinner box
Food box at the left

ski pole
Downhill ski pole

ă pat	oi boy
ā pay	ou out
âr care	o͝o took
ä father	o͞o boot
ĕ pet	ŭ cut
ē be	ûr urge
ĭ pit	th thin
ī pie	*th* this
îr pier	hw which
ŏ pot	zh vision
ō toe	ə about, item
ô paw	♦ regionalism

Stress marks: **′** (primary); ′ (secondary), as in **dictionary** (dĭk′shə-nĕr′ē)

parietal bone
frontal bone
sphenoid bone
zygomatic bone
nasal
maxilla
mandible

skull

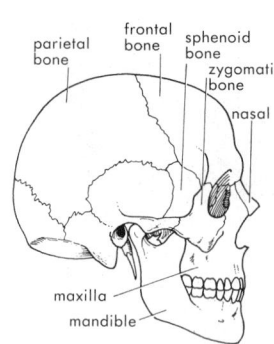

Middle English *skirmisshen,* to brandish a weapon, from Old French *eskermir, eskirmiss-,* to fight with a sword, fence) of *skarmush,* from Old French *eskarmouch,* from Old Italian *scaramuccia,* of Germanic origin. See **sker-**[1] in Appendix.] **—skir′mish·er** *n.*

Skí·ros also **Sky·ros** or **Scy·ros** (skī′rəs, skē′rôs). An island of eastern Greece in the Aegean Sea northeast of Euboea. Occupied by Athenians in the fifth century B.C., it is the largest of the Northern Sporades Islands.

skir·ret (skûr′ĭt) *n.* An eastern Asian plant *(Sium sisarum)* having a cluster of tuberous, sweetish, edible roots. [Middle English *skirwhit,* alteration (influenced by *skir,* pure, bright; see SHEER[2], and *white,* white; see WHITE) of Old French *eschervi,* probably from Arabic *karawyā,* caraway.]

skirt (skûrt) *n.* **1.** The part of a garment, such as a dress or coat, that hangs freely from the waist down. **2.** A garment hanging from the waist and worn by women and girls. **3.** One of the leather flaps hanging from the side of a saddle. **4.** The lower outer section of a rocket vehicle. **5.** An outer edge; a border or margin: *a base camp on the skirt of the mountain.* **6. skirts.** The edge, as of a town; the outskirts. **7.** *Offensive Slang.* Used as a disparaging term for a woman. **—skirt** *v.* **skirt·ed, skirt·ing, skirts.** *—tr.* **1.** To lie along or form the edge of; border: *the creek that skirts our property.* **2.** To pass around rather than across or through: *changed their course to skirt the storm.* **3.** To pass close to; miss narrowly: *The bullet skirted an artery.* **4.** To evade, as by circumlocution: *skirted the controversial issue.* *—intr.* To lie along, move along, or be an edge or a border. [Middle English, from Old Norse *skyrta,* shirt. See **sker-**[1] in Appendix.]

skull and crossbones

skirt steak *n.* A boneless cut of beef from the lower part of the brisket.

ski run *n.* *Sports.* A slope or trail for skiing.

skit (skĭt) *n.* **1.** A short, usually comic dramatic performance or work; a theatrical sketch. **2.** A short humorous or satirical piece of writing. [Origin unknown.]

ski touring *n.* *Sports.* Cross-country skiing for pleasure rather than competition. **—ski tourer** *n.*

ski tow *n.* *Sports.* **1.** A ski lift in which skiers cling to a continuous rope as they are pulled up a slope. **2.** See **ski lift.**

skit·ter (skĭt′ər) *v.* **-tered, -ter·ing, -ters.** *—intr.* **1.** To move rapidly along a surface, usually with frequent light contacts or changes of direction; skip or glide quickly: *lizards that skitter away when approached.* **2.** To fish by drawing a lure or baited hook over the surface of the water with a skipping movement. *—tr.* To cause to skitter. [Probably frequentative of dialectal *skite,* to run rapidly, perhaps of Scandinavian origin; akin to Old Norse *skjōta,* to shoot. See SHOOT.]

skit·ter·y (skĭt′ə-rē) *adj.* Moving quickly, restlessly, or irregularly; skittish.

skit·tish (skĭt′ĭsh) *adj.* **1.** Moving quickly and lightly; lively. **2.** Restlessly active or nervous; restive. **3.** Undependably variable; mercurial or fickle. **4.** Shy; bashful. [Middle English, perhaps of Scandinavian origin; akin to Old Norse *skjōta,* to shoot. See SHOOT.] **—skit′tish·ly** *adv.* **—skit′tish·ness** *n.*

skunk
Striped skunk
Mephitis mephitis

skit·tle (skĭt′l) *n.* *Games.* **1. skittles** *(used with a sing. verb).* A British form of ninepins, in which a wooden disk or ball is thrown to knock down the pins. **2.** One of the pins used in skittles. [Perhaps of Scandinavian origin.]

skive (skīv) *tr.v.* **skived, skiv·ing, skives.** To cut thin layers off (leather or rubber, for example); pare. [Of Scandinavian origin. See **skei-** in Appendix.]

skiv·er (skī′vər) *n.* **1.** One, such as a cutting tool, that skives. **2.** A soft, thin leather split off the outside of sheepskin and used for bookbinding.

Skiv·vies (skĭv′ēz). A trademark used for underwear. This trademark often occurs in lowercase in print: *"The venerable white-underwear company . . . had dabbled in socks, sweats, and fashion skivvies"* (Advertising Age). *"About 500 yards away, on three destroyers snubbed up to the dock, men were clambering on the deck in their skivvies"* (Smithsonian).

ski·wear (skē′wâr′) *n.* *Sports.* Clothing appropriate for various types of skiing.

skoal (skōl) *interj.* Used as a drinking toast. [Danish and Norwegian *skaal,* cup, skoal, from Old Norse *skāl,* bowl, drinking vessel. See **skel-**[1] in Appendix.]

skydive

Sko·kie (skō′kē). A village of northeast Illinois, an industrial suburb of Chicago. Population, 60,278.

Skop·je (skôp′yā′, -yĕ) or **Skop·lje** (-lā′, -lyĕ). A city of southeast Yugoslavia on the Vardar River south-southeast of Belgrade. Dating from Roman times, it was under Turkish control from 1392 until 1913. Population, 406,400.

skosh (skōsh) *n.* *Slang.* A small amount; a bit: *"This is a well-plotted, economical thriller. Although the beginning is a skosh slow,* [the author] *picks up the pace"* (T. Jefferson Parker). [Japanese *sukoshi.*]

Skr. *abbr.* Sanskrit.

Skt. *abbr.* Sanskrit.

sku·a (skyo͞o′ə) *n.* **1.** Any of several large predatory sea birds of the genus *Catharacta* related to the jaeger, especially the great skua. **2.** *Chiefly British.* See **jaeger** (sense 1). [New Latin, alteration of Faroese *skūvur, from Old Norse *skūfr,* tassel, sea gull.]

skul·dug·ger·y (skŭl-dŭg′ə-rē) *n.* Variant of **skullduggery.**

skulk (skŭlk) *intr.v.* **skulked, skulk·ing, skulks.** **1.** To lie in hiding, as out of cowardice or bad conscience; lurk. **2.** To move about stealthily. **3.** To evade work or obligation; shirk. **—skulk** *n.* **1.** One who hides, lurks, or practices evasion. **2.** A congregation of vermin, especially foxes, or of thieves. See Synonyms at **flock**[1]. [Middle English *skulken,* of Scandinavian origin.] **—skulk′er** *n.*

skull (skŭl) *n.* **1.** The bony or cartilaginous framework of the head of vertebrates, made up of the bones of the braincase and face; cranium. **2.** *Informal.* The head, regarded as the seat of thought or intelligence: *Use your skull and solve the problem.* **3.** A death's-head. [Middle English *skulle,* probably of Scandinavian origin.]

skull and crossbones *n., pl.* **skulls and crossbones.** A representation of a human skull above two long crossed bones, a symbol of death once used by pirates and now used as a warning label on poisons.

skull·cap (skŭl′kăp′) *n.* **1.a.** A light, close-fitting, brimless cap sometimes worn indoors. **b.** A yarmulke. **2.** Any of various plants of the genus *Scutellaria,* having clusters of two-lipped flowers.

skull·dug·ger·y or **skul·dug·ger·y** (skŭl-dŭg′ə-rē) *n., pl.* **-ger·ies.** Crafty deception or trickery or an instance of it. [Probably alteration of Scots *sculduddery,* obscenity, fornication.]

skulled (skŭld) *adj.* **1.** Having or provided with a skull: *skulled vertebrates.* **2.** Having a specified kind of skull. Often used in combination: *broad-skulled.*

skull session *n.* **1.** *Informal.* A meeting, as of executives or advisers, for discussing strategy or policy. **2.** *Sports.* A meeting of the members of an athletic team for instruction in plays or strategy.

skunk (skŭngk) *n.* **1.a.** Any of several small, mostly carnivorous New World mammals of the genus *Mephitis* and related genera, having a bushy tail and black fur with white markings and ejecting a foul-smelling oily liquid from glands near the anus when frightened or in danger. Also called *polecat.* **b.** The glossy black and white fur of this mammal. **2.** *Slang.* **a.** A person regarded as obnoxious or despicable. **b.** A person whose company is avoided. **—skunk** *tr.v.* **skunked, skunk·ing, skunks.** *Slang.* **1.** To defeat overwhelmingly, especially by keeping from scoring. **2.a.** To cheat (someone). **b.** To fail to pay (an amount due). [Of Massachusett origin.]

skunk bear *n.* See **wolverine** (sense 1).

skunk cabbage *n.* **1.** An ill-smelling, eastern North American swamp plant *(Symplocarpus foetidus)* having minute flowers enclosed in a mottled greenish or purplish spathe. **2.** A western North American plant *(Lysichitum americanum)* having a bright yellow spathe with an inflated upper part.

skunk grape *n.* See **fox grape.**

Skunk River (skŭngk). A river, about 425 km (264 mi) long, rising in central Iowa and flowing generally southeast to the Mississippi River.

skunk·weed (skŭngk′wēd′) *n.* A dioecious, ill-smelling, dichotomously branched annual plant *(Croton texensis)* of the central and southwest United States.

skunk·works (skŭngk′wûrks′) *pl.n.* *(used with a sing. verb). Slang.* A small, loosely structured corporate research and development unit or subsidiary formed to foster innovation. [After Big Barnsmell's *Skonk Works,* where the bootleg Kickapoo Joy Juice was brewed, in Al Capp's comic strip *Li'l Abner.*]

sky (skī) *n., pl.* **skies** (skīz). **1.** The expanse of air over any given point on Earth; the upper atmosphere as seen from Earth's surface. **2.** Often **skies.** The appearance of the upper atmosphere, especially with reference to weather: *Threatening skies portend a storm.* **3.** The celestial regions; the heavens: *stars in the southern sky.* **4.** The highest level or degree: *reaching for the sky.* **—sky** *tr.v.* **skied** (skīd), **sky·ing, skies** (skīz). **1.** To hit or throw (a ball, for example) high in the air. **2.** To hang (a painting, for example) high up on the wall, above the line of vision. [Middle English, from Old Norse *skȳ,* cloud. See **(s)keu-** in Appendix.]

sky blue *n.* *Color.* A light to pale blue, from a light greenish to light purplish blue.

sky·box (skī′bŏks′) *n.* An elevated, usually enclosed compartment or suite containing box seats and typically entertainment facilities for special guests or important attendees at events held in a sports stadium.

sky·cap (skī′kăp′) *n.* A porter who helps travelers with their luggage at an airport. [SKY + (RED)CAP.]

sky·dive (skī′dīv′) *intr.v.* **-dived, -div·ing, -dives.** *Sports.* To jump and fall freely from an airplane, performing various maneuvers before pulling the ripcord of a parachute. **—sky′div′er** *n.* **—sky′div′ing** *n.*

Skye (skī), **Isle of.** An island of northwest Scotland in the Inner Hebrides. It is known for its rugged mountainous scenery.

Skye terrier *n.* A small terrier of a breed native to the Isle of Skye, having a long low body, short legs, and shaggy hair.

sky·ey (skī′ē) *adj.* Of, from, or resembling the sky: *"a sheet of skyey water"* (John Updike).

sky-high (skī′hī′) *adv.* **1.** To a very high level: *The garbage was piled sky-high.* **2.** In a lavish or enthusiastic manner: *The critics praised the play sky-high.* **3.** In pieces or to pieces; apart: *Sappers blew the bridge sky-high.* **—sky-high** *adj.* **1.** High up in the air: *sky-high trees.* **2.** Exorbitantly high in cost or value: *sky-high prices; sky-high stocks.*

sky-hook or **sky·hook** (skī′ho͝ok′) *n.* A helicopter whose fuselage is configured so as to be mounted with a steel line and hook used to lift and transport heavy objects.

sky·jack (skī′jăk′) *tr.v.* **-jacked, -jack·ing, -jacks.** To subject (an aircraft) to air piracy. [SKY + (HI)JACK.] **—sky′jack′er** *n.* **—sky′jack′ing** *n.*

sky·lark (skī′lärk′) *n.* An Old World lark *(Alauda arvensis)* having brownish plumage and noted for its singing while in flight. **—skylark** *intr.v.* **-larked, -lark·ing, -larks.** To play actively and boisterously; frolic.

sky·light (skī′līt′) *n.* An overhead window, as in a roof, admitting daylight.

sky·line (skī′līn′) *n.* **1.** The line along which the surface of the earth and the sky appear to meet; the horizon. **2.** The outline of a group of buildings or a mountain range seen against the sky.

sky marshal *n.* An armed federal law-enforcement officer assigned to prevent and interdict air piracy and acts of terrorism involving commercial aircraft.

sky pilot *n. Slang.* A member of the clergy, especially a military chaplain.

sky·rock·et (skī′rŏk′ĭt) *n.* A firework that ascends high into the air where it explodes in a brilliant cascade of flares and starlike sparks. **—skyrocket** *intr. & tr.v.* **-et·ed, -et·ing, -ets.** To rise or cause to rise rapidly and suddenly: *Wheat prices skyrocketed. Discovery of oil here has skyrocketed land values.*

Sky·ros (skī′rəs, skē′rôs). See **Skíros.**

sky·sail (skī′səl, -sāl′) *n. Nautical.* A small square sail above the royal in a square-rigged vessel.

sky·scrap·er (skī′skrā′pər) *n.* A very tall building.

sky·walk (skī′wôk′) *n.* An elevated, usually enclosed walkway between two buildings.

sky·ward (skī′wərd) *adv. & adj.* At or toward the sky. **—sky′wards** *adv.*

sky wave *n.* A radio wave that travels upward.

sky·way (skī′wā′) *n.* **1.** A route regularly used by airplanes; an air lane. **2.** An elevated highway.

sky·writ·ing (skī′rī′tĭng) *n.* **1.** The process of writing in the sky by releasing a visible vapor from an airplane. **2.** The letters or words so formed. **—sky′writ′er** *n.*

SL *abbr.* **1.** Salvage loss. **2.** Sea level. **3.** Source language. **4.** South latitude.

sl. *abbr.* **1.** Slightly. **2.** Slow.

s.l. *abbr. Latin.* Sine loco (without place of publication).

Sla (slä). See **Salé.**

slab¹ (slăb) *n.* **1.** A broad, flat, thick piece, as of cake, stone, or cheese. **2.** An outside piece cut from a log when squaring it for lumber. **3.** *Baseball.* The pitcher's rubber. **—slab** *tr.v.* **slabbed, slab·bing, slabs. 1.** To make or shape into slabs or a slab. **2.** To cover or pave with slabs. **3.** To dress (a log) by cutting slabs. [Middle English.]

slab² (slăb) *adj. Archaic.* Viscid. [Probably of Scandinavian origin; akin to Danish *slab,* mud.]

slab-sid·ed (slăb′sī′dĭd) *adj.* **1.** Having flat sides. **2.** *Informal.* Tall and slim; lanky.

slack¹ (slăk) *adj.* **slack·er, slack·est. 1.** Moving slowly; sluggish: *a slack pace.* **2.** Lacking in activity; not busy: *a slack season for the travel business.* **3.** Not tense or taut; loose: *a slack rope; slack muscles.* See Synonyms at **loose. 4.** Lacking firmness; flaccid: *a slack grip.* **5.** Lacking in diligence or due care or concern; negligent: *a slack worker.* See Synonyms at **negligent. 6.** Flowing or blowing with little speed: *a slack current; slack winds.* **—slack** *v.* **slacked, slack·ing, slacks.** —*tr.* **1.** To make slower or looser; slacken. **2.** To be careless or remiss in doing: *slack one's duty.* **3.** To slake (lime). —*intr.* **1.** To be or become slack. **2.** To evade work; shirk. **—slack** *n.* **1.** A loose part, as of a rope or sail. **2.** A lack of tension; looseness. **3.** A period of little activity; a lull. **4.a.** A cessation of movement in a current of air or water. **b.** An area of still water. **5.** Unused capacity: *still some slack in the economy.* **6. slacks.** Casual trousers that are not part of a suit. **—slack** *adv.* In a slack manner: *a banner hanging slack.* ***—phrasal verb.* slack off.** To decrease in activity or intensity. [Middle English *slak,* from Old English *slæc.* See **slēg-** in Appendix.] **—slack′ly** *adv.* **—slack′ness** *n.*

slack² (slăk) *n.* A mixture of coal fragments, coal dust, and dirt that remains after screening coal. [Middle English *sleck.*]

slack³ (slăk) *n. Chiefly British.* **1.** A small dell or hollow. **2.** A bog; a morass. [Middle English *slak,* from Old Norse *slakki.*]

slack-baked (slăk′bākt′) *adj.* Not fully baked or done; half-baked: *slack-baked bread.*

slack·en (slăk′ən) *tr. & intr.v.* **-ened, -en·ing, -ens. 1.** To make or become slower; slow down: *The runners slackened their pace. Air speed slackened.* **2.** To make or become less tense, taut, or firm; loosen: *I slackened the line to let the fish swim. The tension in the board room finally slackened.* **3.** To make or become less vigorous, intense, or severe; ease: *slacken discipline; afraid that morale might slacken.*

slack·er (slăk′ər) *n.* One that shirks work or responsibility, especially one that tries to evade military service in wartime.

slack water *n.* **1.** The period at high or low tide when there is no visible flow of water. **2.** An area in a sea or river unaffected by currents; still water.

slag (slăg) *n.* **1.** The vitreous mass left as a residue by the smelting of metallic ore. **2.** See **scoria** (sense 1). **—slag** *tr. & intr.v.* **slagged, slag·ging, slags.** To change into slag or form slag. [Low German *slagge,* from Middle Low German.] **—slag′gy** *adj.*

slain (slān) *v.* Past participle of **slay.**

slake (slāk) *v.* **slaked, slak·ing, slakes.** —*tr.* **1.** To satisfy (a craving); quench: *slaked her thirst.* **2.** To lessen the force or activity of; moderate: *slaking his anger.* **3.** To cool or refresh by wetting or moistening. **4.** To combine (lime) chemically with water or moist air. —*intr.* To undergo a slaking process; crumble or disintegrate, as lime. [Middle English *slaken,* to abate, from Old English *slacian,* from *slæc,* slack, sluggish. See SLACK¹.]

slaked lime (slākt) *n.* See **calcium hydroxide.**

sla·lom (slä′ləm) *Sports. n.* **1.** The act or sport of skiing in a zigzag course. **2.** A race on skis or in vehicles along such a course, laid out with flag-marked poles. —*attributive.* Often used to modify another noun: *a slalom course; the slalom event.* **—slalom** *intr.v.* **-lomed, -lom·ing, -loms.** To race in or as if in a slalom. [Norwegian *slalåm* : *sla*d, sloping + *låm,* path.] **—sla′lom·er, sla′lom·ist** *n.*

slam¹ (slăm) *v.* **slammed, slam·ming, slams.** —*tr.* **1.** To shut with force and loud noise: *slammed the door.* **2.** To put, throw, or otherwise forcefully move so as to produce a loud noise: *slammed the book on the desk.* **3.** To hit or strike with great force. **4.** *Slang.* To criticize harshly; censure forcefully. —*intr.* **1.** To close or swing into place with force so as to produce a loud noise. **2.** To hit something with force; crash: *slammed into a truck.* **—slam** *n.* **1.a.** A forceful impact that makes a loud noise. **b.** A noise so produced. **2.** An act of shutting forcefully and loudly: *the slam of a door.* **3.** *Slang.* A harsh or devastating criticism. [Perhaps of Scandinavian origin; akin to Old Norse *slambra,* to strike at.]

slam² (slăm) *n. Games.* The winning of all the tricks or all but one during the play of one hand in bridge and other whist-derived card games. [Origin unknown.]

slam-bang (slăm′băng′) *adv. & adj. Slang.* **1.** With force and much noise: *drove slam-bang through the barricade; a slam-bang collision.* **2.** With heedless speed; slapdash. **3.** With vigorous, relentless action and pace: *a thriller that proceeds slam-bang to its conclusion; a slam-bang movie car chase.*

slam danc·ing (dăn′sĭng) *n.* A style of dancing, usually performed to punk rock, in which participants collide violently with one another. **—slam dance** *v.*

slam-dunk or **slam dunk** (slăm′dŭngk′) *n.* **1.** *Basketball.* A very dramatic, highly forceful dunk shot. **2.** *Slang.* A forceful, dramatic move: *"I ask* [him] *whether the slam dunk of the indictment was a spontaneous or planned bit of theater"* (Ron Rosenbaum). **—slam-dunk** *v.* **-dunked, -dunk·ing, -dunks.** —*intr. Basketball.* To make a very dramatic, highly forceful dunk shot. —*tr.* **1.** *Basketball.* To shoot (the ball) forcefully and dramatically into the basket. **2.** *Slang.* To make a forceful, dramatic move against (another): *"They've stopped slam-dunking each other and begun designing strategies with the . . . aim of moving those on welfare into decent jobs"* (David L. Kirp).

slam·mer (slăm′ər) *n. Slang.* A jail. [From SLAM¹.]

s.l.a.n. *abbr. Latin.* Sine loco, anno, vel nomine (without place, year, or name of publication).

slan·der (slăn′dər) *n.* **1.** *Law.* Oral communication of false statements injurious to a person's reputation. **2.** A false and malicious statement or report about someone. **—slander** *v.* **-dered, -der·ing, -ders.** —*tr.* To communicate a slander about. See Synonyms at **malign.** —*intr.* To utter or spread slander. [Middle English *slaundre,* from Old French *esclandre,* alteration of *escandle,* from Latin *scandalum,* cause of offense, stumbling block. See SCANDAL.] **—slan′der·er** *n.* **—slan′der·ous** *adj.* **—slan′der·ous·ly** *adv.*

slang (slăng) *n.* **1.** A kind of language occurring chiefly in casual and playful speech, made up typically of short-lived coinages and figures of speech that are deliberately used in place of standard terms for added raciness, humor, irreverence, or other effect. **2.** Language peculiar to a group; argot or jargon: *thieves' slang.* **—slang** *v.* **slanged, slang·ing, slangs.** —*intr.* **1.** To use slang. **2.** To use angry and abusive language: *persuaded the parties to quit slanging and come to the bargaining table.* —*tr.* To attack with abusive language; vituperate. [Origin unknown.] **—slang′i·ly** *adv.* **—slang′i·ness** *n.* **—slang′y** *adj.*

slant (slănt) *v.* **slant·ed, slant·ing, slants.** —*tr.* **1.** To give a direction other than perpendicular or horizontal to; make diagonal; cause to slope: *She slants her letters from upper right to lower left.* **2.** To present so as to conform to a particular bias or appeal to a certain audience: *The story was slanted in favor of the strikers.* —*intr.* To have or go in a direction other than perpendicular or horizontal; slope. **—slant** *n.* **1.a.** A line, plane, course, or direction that is other than perpendicular or horizontal; a slope. **b.** A sloping thing or piece of ground. **2.** *Printing.* A virgule. **3.a.** A personal point of view or opinion. **b.** A bias. **4.** *Offensive Slang.* Used as a disparaging term for an Asian person. [Alteration of obsolete *slent,* from Middle English *slenten,* to fall aslant, perhaps of Scandinavian origin.] **—slant′ing·ly** *adv.*

SYNONYMS: *slant, incline, lean, slope, tilt, tip.* The central meaning shared by these verbs is "to depart or cause to depart

skyline
Sydney, Australia

skyscraper
John Hancock Center, Chicago, Illinois

skywalk

slalom

ă pat	oi boy
ā pay	ou out
âr care	o͝o took
ä father	o͞o boot
ĕ pet	ŭ cut
ē be	ûr urge
ĭ pit	th thin
ī pie	*th* this
îr pier	hw which
ŏ pot	zh vision
ō toe	ə about, item
ô paw	♦ regionalism

Stress marks: **′** (primary); ′ (secondary), as in **dictionary** (dĭk′shə-nĕr′ē)

slash
A Young Lady, 1567, by Steven van der Meulen

from true vertical or horizontal": *rays of the setting sun slanting through the window; inclined her head toward the speaker; leaned against the railing; a sloping driveway; tilted her hat at a rakish angle; tipped his chair against the wall.*

slant rhyme *n.* See **off rhyme.**

slant·ways (slănt′wāz′) *adv.* Slantwise.

slant·wise (slănt′wīz′) *adv.* At a slant or slope; obliquely. **—slantwise** *adj.* Slanting; oblique.

slap (slăp) *n.* **1.a.** A sharp blow made with the open hand or with a flat object; a smack. **b.** The sound of such a blow. **2.** A sharp insult: *a slap to one's pride.* **—slap** *v.* **slapped, slap·ping, slaps.** *—tr.* **1.** To strike with a flat object, such as the palm of the hand. **2.** To cause to strike sharply and loudly: *slapping the sticks together.* **3.** To put or place with a loud sharp sound: *"He took a clipping from his wallet and slapped it on the bar"* (Nathanael West). **4.** To criticize or insult sharply. *—intr.* To strike or beat with the force and sound of a slap: *waves slapping against the raft.* **—slap** *adv. Informal.* Directly and with force. ***—phrasal verb.*** **slap down. 1.** To restrain or correct by means of a sharp blow or emphatic censure: *"thought* [he] *was getting a little uppity and needed to be slapped down"* (New York Times). **2.** To put a sudden end to; suppress: *slap down divisive criticism.* ***—idiom.*** **slap on the wrist.** A nominal or token punishment. [Middle English *slappe.*] **—slap′per** *n.*

slap·dash (slăp′dăsh′) *adj.* Hasty and careless, as in execution. *slapdash work.* **—slapdash** *adv.* In a reckless, haphazard manner.

slap·hap·py (slăp′hăp′ē) *adj.* **-pi·er, -pi·est.** *Slang.* **1.** Dazed, silly, or incoherent from or as if from blows to the head; punch-drunk. **2.** Happy-go-lucky.

slap·jack (slăp′jăk′) *n.* **1.** A pancake; a flapjack. **2.** *Games.* A simple game of cards. [SLAP + (FLAP)JACK.]

slap shot *n. Sports.* A fast-moving shot made in hockey with a full swinging stroke.

slap·stick (slăp′stĭk′) *n.* **1.** A boisterous form of comedy marked by chases, collisions, and crude practical jokes. **2.** A paddle designed to produce a loud whacking sound, formerly used by performers in farces.

WORD HISTORY: When we talk about slapstick, we probably do not think of two sticks slapping together, yet the word has its origin in a device that was made of two flat pieces of wood fastened at one end. This device made a loud sound if one struck someone with it, a much louder sound than a single piece would have made. Such a sound and such a blow were the stuff of comedy, albeit the comedy of farce and pantomine in which this device was originally used (the word is first recorded in 1896). Through its use with other nouns, such as *comedy, slapstick* developed an abstract sense that encompassed far more than its original literal meaning. *Slapstick* by itself (first recorded in 1926) could now refer to the whole genre of comedy in which the literal slapstick played a role.

slash (slăsh) *v.* **slashed, slash·ing, slash·es.** *—tr.* **1.** To cut or form by cutting with forceful sweeping strokes: *slash a path through the underbrush.* **2.** To lash with sweeping strokes. **3.** To make a gash or gashes in. **4.** To cut a slit or slits in, especially so as to reveal an underlying color: *slash a sleeve.* **5.** To criticize sharply: *The work of the composer has been slashed by the reviewers.* **6.** To reduce or curtail drastically: *slash prices for a clearance sale.* *—intr.* **1.** To make forceful sweeping strokes with or as if with a sharp instrument. **2.** To cut one's way with such strokes: *We slashed through the dense jungle.* **—slash** *n.* **1.** A forceful sweeping stroke made with a sharp instrument. **2.** A long cut or other opening made by such a stroke; a gash or slit. **3.** A decorative slit in a fabric or garment. **4.** Branches and other residue left on a forest floor after the cutting of timber. **5.** Often **slashes.** Wet or swampy ground overgrown with bushes and trees. **6.** *Printing.* A virgule. [Perhaps from obsolete French *esclachier,* to break, variant of *esclater,* from Old French, from *esclat,* splinter. See SLAT.] **—slash′er** *n.*

sled

slash·ing (slăsh′ĭng) *adj.* **1.** Bitingly critical or satiric: *slashing wit.* **2.** Dashing; pelting: *a slashing hailstorm.* **3.** Brilliant; intense: *slashing colors.* **—slash′ing·ly** *adv.*

slash pine *n.* A pine tree *(Pinus elliotti)* of swampy coastal areas of the southeast United States that yields pulp, rosin, timber, and turpentine.

slat (slăt) *n.* **1.** A narrow strip of metal or wood, as in a Venetian blind. **2.** A movable auxiliary airfoil running along the leading edge of the wing of an airplane. **3. slats.** *Slang.* The ribs. **—slat** *tr.v.* **slat·ted, slat·ting, slats.** To provide or make with slats: *slatting the back of a chair.* [Middle English *sclat,* from Old French *esclat,* splinter, probably of Germanic origin.]

♦**slatch** (slăch) *n. New England.* **1.** A momentary lull between breaking waves, favorable for launching a boat. **2.** A lull in a high windstorm. [Variant of SLACK¹.]

♦***REGIONAL NOTE:*** In New England a *slatch* can be a lull between breaking waves or a lull in a high windstorm. Its use is recorded as far back as the 17th century: *"When it hath beene a sett of foule weather and that there comes an Interim . . . of faire weather . . . they call it a little Slatch of faire weather"* (Nomenclator Navalis). Occurrence of the word in both its senses, formerly in Britain and now in New England, attests continuous use down through the centuries of the Old English word *slæc,* which is pronounced today as it was in Old English. *Slæc* is also the source of modern *slack,* the relationship of *slatch* and *slack* being evidenced in the use of *slatch* in 17th-century nautical parlance to denote the slack part of a rope or cable on a ship.

slate (slāt) *n.* **1.** A fine-grained metamorphic rock that splits into thin, smooth-surfaced layers. **2.a.** A piece of this rock cut for use as roofing or surfacing material or as a writing surface. **b.** A writing tablet made of a similar material. **3.** A record of past performance or activity: *starting with a clean slate.* **4.** A list of the candidates of a political party running for various offices. **5.** *Color.* A dark or bluish gray to dark bluish or dark purplish gray. **—slate** *adj.* **1.** Made of a fine-grained metamorphic rock: *a slate roof.* **2.** *Color.* Of the color slate. **—slate** *tr.v.* **slat·ed, slat·ing, slates. 1.** To cover (a roof, for example) with slate. **2.** To put on a list of candidates. **3.** To schedule or designate: *slated the art history lecture for Thursday afternoon.* [Middle English *sclate,* from Old French *esclate,* splinter, feminine of *esclat.* See SLAT.]

slate black *n. Color.* A purplish black. **—slate′-black′** (slāt′blăk′) *adj.*

slate blue *n. Color.* A grayish blue to dark bluish gray. **—slate′-blue′** (slāt′blo͞o′) *adj.*

slate-col·ored junco (slāt′kŭl′ərd) *n.* A junco *(Junco hyemalis)* of eastern North America, having dark gray upper parts and a white abdomen.

slat·er (slā′tər) *n.* **1.** One employed to lay slate surfaces, as on roofs. **2.** Any of several small isopod crustaceans, such as the sow bug.

Sla·ter (slā′tər), **Samuel.** 1768–1835. British-born textile pioneer in America. He oversaw construction of the nation's first successful water-powered cotton mill (1790–1793).

slath·er (slăth′ər) *tr.v.* **-ered, -er·ing, -ers.** *Informal.* **1.** To use or give great amounts of; lavish: *slathered gifts and attention on their only child.* **2.a.** To spread thickly: *slather onions on the steak.* **b.** To cover with something spread thickly: *bagels slathered with cream cheese.* **—slather** *n. Slang.* A great amount. Often used in the plural: *slathers of jewels.* [Origin unknown.]

slat·ing (slā′tĭng) *n.* Slates for covering roofs, walls, or other surfaces.

slat·tern (slăt′ərn) *n.* An untidy, dirty woman. [Perhaps from dialectal *slattering,* slovenly, present participle of dialectal *slatter,* to slop.]

slat·tern·ly (slăt′ərn-lē) *adj.* **1.** Characteristic of or befitting a slattern. **2.** Slovenly; untidy. **—slat′tern·li·ness** *n.*

slat·y (slā′tē) *adj.* **-i·er, -i·est. 1.** Composed of or resembling slate. **2.** Having the color of slate.

slaugh·ter (slô′tər) *n.* **1.** The killing of animals for food. **2.** The killing of a large number of people; a massacre: *"I could not give my name to aid the slaughter in this war, fought on both sides for grossly material ends"* (Sylvia Pankhurst). **—slaughter** *tr.v.* **-tered, -ter·ing, -ters. 1.** To kill (animals) for food; butcher. **2.a.** To kill (people) in large numbers; massacre. **b.** To kill in a violent or brutal manner. [Middle English, of Scandinavian origin; akin to Old Norse *slātr,* butchery.] **—slaugh′ter·er** *n.* **—slaugh′ter·ous** *adj.*

slaugh·ter·house (slô′tər-hous′) *n.* **1.** A place where animals are butchered. **2.** A scene of massacre or carnage.

Slav (släv) *n.* A member of one of the Slavic-speaking peoples of eastern Europe. [Middle English *Sclave,* from Medieval Latin *Sclāvus,* from Late Greek *Sklabos,* alteration of Old Slavic *Slovēninŭ.*]

Slav. *abbr.* Slavic.

slave (slāv) *n.* **1.** One bound in servitude as the property of a person or household. **2.** One who is abjectly subservient to a specified person or influence: *"I was still the slave of education and prejudice"* (Edward Gibbon). **3.** One who works extremely hard. **4.** A machine or component controlled by another machine or component. *—attributive.* Often used to modify another noun: *slave labor; a slave cylinder.* **—slave** *intr.v.* **slaved, slav·ing, slaves. 1.** To work very hard or doggedly; toil. **2.** To trade in or transport slaves. [Middle English *sclave,* from Old French *esclave,* from Medieval Latin *sclāvus,* from *Sclāvus,* Slav (from the widespread enslavement of captured Slavs in the early Middle Ages). See SLAV.]

slave ant *n.* An ant captured and raised as a worker by slave-making ants.

Slave Coast (slāv). A region of western Africa bordering the Bight of Benin on the Gulf of Guinea. It was notorious as the exportation base for slaves from the 16th century to the early 19th century.

slave driver *n.* **1.** An overseer of slaves at work. **2.** A severely exacting employer or supervisor.

slave·hold·er (slāv′hōl′dər) *n.* One who owns or holds slaves. **—slave′hold′ing** *adj. & n.*

slave-mak·ing ant (slāv′mā′kĭng) *n.* Any of various species of ant, such as *Formica sanguinea* of Europe, that raid the nests of other ants and carry off the pupae in order to provide workers for their own colony.

slav·er¹ (slăv′ər) *intr.v.* **-ered, -er·ing, -ers. 1.** To slobber; drool. **2.** To behave in an obsequious manner; fawn. See Synonyms at **fawn¹. —slaver** *n.* **1.** Saliva drooling from the mouth.

2. Senseless and effusive talk; drivel. [Middle English *slaveren,* probably from Old Norse *slafra.*]

slav•er² (slā′vər) *n.* One, such as a person or ship, that is engaged in the trafficking of slaves.

Slave River. A river, about 499 km (310 mi) long, of west-central Canada flowing between Lake Athabasca in northeast Alberta and Great Slave Lake in the southern Northwest Territories.

slav•er•y (slā′və-rē, slāv′rē) *n., pl.* **-ies. 1.** The state of one bound in servitude as the property of a slaveholder or household. See Synonyms at **servitude. 2.a.** The practice of owning slaves. **b.** A mode of production in which slaves constitute the principal work force. **3.** The condition of being subject or addicted to a specified influence. **4.** A condition of hard work and subjection: *wage slavery.*

slave state *n.* **1.** Any of the 15 states of the Union in which slavery was legal before the Civil War, including Alabama, Arkansas, Delaware, Florida, Georgia, Kentucky, Louisiana, Maryland, Mississippi, Missouri, North Carolina, South Carolina, Tennessee, Texas, and Virginia. **2.** A nation under totalitarian rule.

slave trade *n.* Traffic in slaves.

slav•ey (slā′vē) *n., pl.* **-eys.** A household servant, especially an overworked one.

Slav•ic (slä′vĭk) *adj. Abbr.* **Slav.** Of or relating to the Slavs or their languages. **—Slavic** *n. Abbr.* **Slav.** A branch of the Indo-European language family that includes Bulgarian, Belorussian, Czech, Macedonian, Polish, Russian, Serbo-Croatian, Slovak, Slovene, Ukrainian, and Wendish.

slav•ish (slā′vĭsh) *adj.* **1.** Of or characteristic of a slave or slavery; servile: *Her slavish devotion to her job ruled her life.* **2.** Showing no originality; blindly imitative: *a slavish copy of the original.* **—slav′ish•ly** *adv.* **—slav′ish•ness** *n.*

slav•oc•ra•cy (slā-vŏk′rə-sē) *n., pl.* **-cies.** A ruling group of slaveholders or advocates of slavery, as in the southern United States before 1865. **—slav′o•crat′** (slā′və-krăt′) *n.* **—slav′-o•crat′ic** *adj.*

Sla•vo•ni•a (slə-vō′nē-ə, -vōn′yə). A historical region of northern Yugoslavia between the Drava and Sava rivers. Originally part of the Roman province of Pannonia, it became a Slavic state in the seventh century and has long been allied with Croatia. Slavonia became part of Yugoslavia in 1918. **—Sla•vo′ni•an** *adj. & n.*

Sla•von•ic (slə-vŏn′ĭk) *n.* Slavic. [From Medieval Latin *Sclāvōnia,* Slavic lands, from *Sclāvus,* Slav. See SLAV.] **—Sla•von′ic** *adj.*

Slav•o•phile (slä′və-fīl′) also **Slav•o•phil** (-fĭl) *n.* **1.** An admirer of Slavic peoples or their culture. **2.** A person advocating the supremacy of Slavic culture, especially over western European influences, as in 19th-century Russia. **—Sla•voph′-i•lism** (slə-vŏf′ə-lĭz′əm) *n.*

slaw (slô) *n.* Coleslaw.

slay (slā) *tr.v.* **slew** (slo͞o), **slain** (slān), **slay•ing, slays. 1.** To kill violently. **2.** *Slang.* To overwhelm, as with laughter or love: *Those old jokes still slay me.* [Middle English *slen, slayen,* from Old English *slēan.*] **—slay′er** *n.*

SLBM *abbr.* Submarine-launched ballistic missile.

SLCM *abbr.* Submarine-launched cruise missile.

sld. *abbr.* **1.** Sailed. **2.** Sealed. **3.** Sold.

SLE *abbr.* Systemic lupus erythematosus.

sleave (slēv) *n. Archaic.* A fine thread or skein of thread. [From Middle English **sleven,* to disentangle, from Old English **slǣfan,* to cut, from *slāf,* past tense of *slīfan,* to split.]

sleaze (slēz) *n.* A sleazy condition, quality, or appearance: *"His record of public service is untouched by any stain of shadiness or sleaze"* (James J. Kilpatrick). [Back-formation from SLEAZY.]

slea•zy (slē′zē) *adj.* **-zi•er, -zi•est. 1.a.** Shabby, dirty, and vulgar; tawdry: *"sleazy storefronts with torn industrial carpeting and dirt on the walls"* (Seattle Weekly). **b.** Dishonest or corrupt; disreputable: *Some sleazy characters hang around casinos.* **2.** Made of low-quality materials; cheap or shoddy. **3.** Thin and loosely woven; flimsy: *The coat has a sleazy lining.* [Origin unknown.] **—slea′zi•ly** *adv.* **—slea′zi•ness** *n.*

sled (slĕd) *n.* **1.** A vehicle mounted on runners, used for carrying people or loads over ice and snow; a sledge. **2.** A light wooden frame on runners, used by children for coasting over snow or ice. **—sled** *v.* **sled•ded, sled•ding, sleds.** *—tr.* To carry on or convey by a sled. *—intr.* To ride or use a sled. [Middle English *sledde,* from Middle Dutch.] **—sled′der** *n.*

sled•ding (slĕd′ĭng) *n.* **1.** Use of a sled. **2.** Conditions conducive to the use of a sled. **3.** *Informal.* A specific kind of progress toward a goal; the going: *"The bill . . . faces tough sledding in Congressional conference"* (New York Times).

sled dog *n.* A dog, such as a husky, used to pull a dogsled, especially in Arctic regions.

sledge (slĕj) *n.* A vehicle mounted on low runners drawn by work animals, such as horses or dogs, and used for transporting loads across ice, snow, and rough ground. **—sledge** *tr. & intr.v.* **sledged, sledg•ing, sledg•es.** To convey or travel on a sledge. [Dutch dialectal *sleedse,* perhaps diminutive of Dutch *slede,* sled, from Middle Dutch *sledde.*]

sledge•ham•mer (slĕj′hăm′ər) *n.* A long heavy hammer, often wielded with both hands, used for driving wedges and posts and for other heavy work. **—sledgehammer** *tr.v.* **-mered, -mer•ing, -mers.** To strike with or as if with a sledgehammer. **—sledgehammer** *adj.* Ruthlessly severe; crushing: *sledgehammer prosecutorial tactics.* [Middle English *slegge,* sledgehammer (from Old English *slecg*) + HAMMER.]

sleek (slēk) *adj.* **sleek•er, sleek•est. 1.** Smooth and lustrous as if polished; glossy: *brushed her hair until it was sleek.* **2.** Well-groomed and neatly tailored. **3.** Healthy or well-fed; thriving. **4.** Polished or smooth in manner, especially in an unctuous way; slick. **—sleek** *tr.v.* **sleeked, sleek•ing, sleeks. 1.** To make sleek; slick: *sleeked his hair with pomade.* **2.** To gloss over; conceal. [Variant of SLICK.] **—sleek′ly** *adv.* **—sleek′ness** *n.*

SYNONYMS: *sleek, glossy, satiny, silken, silky, slick.* The central meaning shared by these adjectives is "having a smooth, gleaming surface": *sleek black fur; glossy auburn hair; satiny gardenia petals; silken butterfly wings; silky skin; slick seals and otters.*

sleep (slēp) *n.* **1.a.** A natural, periodic state of rest for the mind and body, in which the eyes usually close and consciousness is completely or partially lost, so that there is a decrease in bodily movement and responsiveness to external stimuli. During sleep the brain in human beings and other mammals undergoes a characteristic cycle of brain-wave activity that includes intervals of dreaming. **b.** A period of this form of rest. **c.** A state of inactivity resembling or suggesting sleep, unconsciousness, dormancy, hibernation, or death. **2.** *Botany.* The folding together of leaflets or petals at night or in the absence of light. **—sleep** *v.* **slept** (slĕpt), **sleep•ing, sleeps.** *—intr.* **1.** To be in the state of sleep or to fall asleep. **2.** To be in a condition resembling sleep. *—tr.* **1.** To pass or get rid of by sleeping: *slept away the day; went home to sleep off the headache.* **2.** To provide sleeping accommodations for: *This tent sleeps three comfortably.* ***—phrasal verbs.*** **sleep around.** *Informal.* To be sexually active with more than one partner. **sleep in. 1.** To sleep at one's place of employment: *a butler and a chauffeur who sleep in.* **2.a.** To oversleep: *I missed the morning train because I slept in.* **b.** To sleep late on purpose: *After this week's work, I will sleep in on Saturday.* **sleep out. 1.** To sleep at one's own home, not at one's place of employment. **2.** To sleep away from one's home. **sleep over.** To spend the night as a guest in another's home. **sleep with.** To have sexual relations with. ***—idiom.*** **sleep on it.** *Informal.* To consider something overnight before deciding. [Middle English *slepe,* from Old English *slǣp.* See **slēb-** in Appendix.]

sleep apnea *n.* A temporary suspension of breathing occurring repeatedly during sleep that often affects overweight people or those having an obstruction in the breathing tract, an abnormally small throat opening, or a neurological disorder.

sleep•er (slē′pər) *n.* **1.** One that sleeps: *a heavy sleeper who was not wakened by the cat burglar.* **2.** A sleeping car. **3.** Children's pajamas, usually with legs that cover the feet. Often used in the plural. **4.a.** One that achieves unexpected recognition or success, as a racehorse, a movie, or a marketed product. **b.** A spy or saboteur who is planted in an enemy country and who lives unobtrusively as a citizen of that country until activated into clandestine operations by a prearranged signal. **5.** A horizontal structural member on or near the ground that supports weight. **6.** *Chiefly British.* A railroad crosstie. **7.** Any of various usually small marine and freshwater fishes of the family Eleotridae, related to the gobies but lacking a sucking disk and noted for their habit of lying immobile.

sleep-in (slēp′ĭn′) *adj.* Living at one's place of employment: *a sleep-in housekeeper.*

sleep•ing bag (slē′pĭng) *n.* A large, warmly lined, usually zippered bag for sleeping, especially outdoors.

sleeping car *n.* A railroad car having accommodations for sleeping.

sleeping pill *n.* A sedative or hypnotic drug, especially a barbiturate, in the form of a pill or capsule used to relieve insomnia.

sleeping sickness *n.* **1.** An often fatal, endemic infectious disease of human beings and animals in tropical Africa, caused by either of two trypanosomes *(Trypanosoma rhodesiense* or *T. gambiense)* transmitted by the tsetse fly and characterized by fever, severe headache, and lymph node swelling in the early stages, followed by extreme weakness, sleepiness, and deep coma. Also called *African sleeping sickness.* **2.** See **encephalitis lethargica.**

sleep-learn•ing (slēp′lûr′nĭng) *n.* Instruction in a subject, such as a foreign language, during sleep, usually by means of recordings. Also called *hypnopedia.*

sleep•less (slēp′lĭs) *adj.* **1.a.** Marked by a lack of sleep: *a sleepless night.* **b.** Unable to sleep. **2.** Always alert or active; never resting: *a sleepless district of the city.* **—sleep′less•ly** *adv.* **—sleep′less•ness** *n.*

sleep•o•ver (slēp′ō′vər) *n.* **1.** An instance of spending the night as a guest at another's home. **2.** An overnight guest.

sleep•walk (slēp′wôk′) *intr.v.* **-walked, -walk•ing, -walks.** To walk or perform other motor acts while asleep; somnambulate. [Back-formation from SLEEPWALKING.] **—sleep′walk′er** *n.*

sleep•walk•ing (slēp′wô′kĭng) *n.* The act or an instance of walking or performing another activity associated with wakefulness while asleep or in a sleeplike state. Also called *noctambulism, somnambulism.*

sleep•wear (slēp′wâr′) *n.* Nightclothes.

sleep•y (slē′pē) *adj.* **-i•er, -i•est. 1.a.** Ready for or needing sleep. **b.** Sluggish from sleep. **2.** Inducing sleep. **3.** Inactive; quiet: *a sleepy rural town.* **—sleep′i•ly** *adv.* **—sleep′i•ness** *n.*

sledge

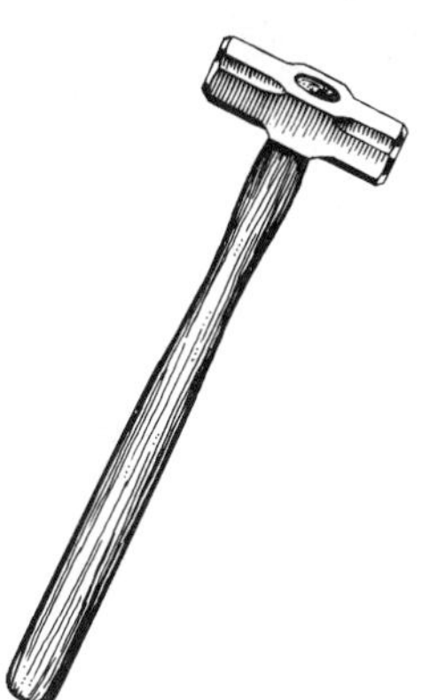

sledgehammer

sleeping bag

ă pat	oi boy
ā pay	ou out
âr care	o͝o took
ä father	o͞o boot
ĕ pet	ŭ cut
ē be	ûr urge
ĭ pit	th thin
ī pie	*th* this
îr pier	hw which
ŏ pot	zh vision
ō toe	ə about, item
ô paw	♦ regionalism

Stress marks: **′** (primary); ′ (secondary), as in **dictionary** (dĭk′shə-nĕr′ē)

sleigh

slide

sleep·y·head (slē′pē-hĕd′) *n. Informal.* A sleepy person.
sleepy sickness *n.* See **encephalitis lethargica.**
sleet (slēt) *n.* **1.** Precipitation consisting of generally transparent frozen or partially frozen raindrops. **2.** A mixture of rain and snow or hail. **3.** A thin icy coating that forms when rain or sleet freezes, as on trees or streets. **—sleet** *intr.v.* **sleet·ed, sleet·ing, sleets.** To shower sleet. [Middle English *slete,* from Old English **slēte.*] **—sleet′y** *adj.*
sleeve (slēv) *n.* **1.** A part of a garment that covers all or part of an arm. **2.** A case into which an object or a device fits: *a record sleeve.* **—sleeve** *tr.v.* **sleeved, sleev·ing, sleeves.** To furnish or fit with sleeves or a sleeve. ***—idiom.* up (one's) sleeve.** Hidden but ready to be used: *I still have a few tricks up my sleeve.* [Middle English *sleve,* from Old English *slēf.* See **sleubh-** in Appendix.] **—sleeve′less** *adj.*
sleeve coupling *n.* A thin steel cylinder joining the ends of two lengths of shafting or pipe.
sleeve dog *n.* A very small Pekingese, usually 15 centimeters (6 inches) or less in height.
sleigh (slā) *n.* A light vehicle mounted on runners and having one or more seats, usually drawn by a horse over snow or ice. **—sleigh** *intr.v.* **sleighed, sleigh·ing, sleighs.** To ride in or drive a sleigh. [Dutch *slee,* variant of *slede,* from Middle Dutch *slēde.*] **—sleigh′er** *n.*
sleight (slīt) *n.* **1.** Deftness; dexterity. **2.** A clever or skillful trick or deception; an artifice or a stratagem. [Middle English, alteration of *sleahthe,* from Old Norse *slœgdh,* from *slœgr,* sly.]
sleight of hand *n., pl.* **sleights of hand. 1.** A trick or set of tricks performed by a juggler or magician so quickly that the manner of execution cannot be observed; legerdemain. **2.** Performance of conjuring tricks. **3.** Skill in performing conjuring tricks.
slen·der (slĕn′dər) *adj.* **-er, -est. 1.a.** Having little width in proportion to height or length; long and thin: *a slender rod.* **b.** Thin and delicate in build; gracefully slim: *"She was slender as a willow shoot is slender—and equally graceful, equally erect"* (Frank Norris). **2.** Small in amount or extent; meager: *slender wages; a slender chance of survival.* [Middle English *sclendre, slendre.*] **—slen′der·ly** *adv.* **—slen′der·ness** *n.*
slen·der·ize (slĕn′də-rīz′) *tr. & intr.v.* **-ized, -iz·ing, -iz·es.** To make or become slender or more slender.
slender loris *n.* A very small, tailless loris *(Loris gracilis)* of southern India and Sri Lanka, having large eyes with dark circles around them and very short fingers and toes.
slept (slĕpt) *v.* Past tense and past participle of **sleep.**
sleuth (slo͞oth) *n.* **1.** A detective. **2.** See **sleuthhound** (sense 1). **—sleuth** *v.* **sleuthed, sleuth·ing, sleuths.** *—tr.* To track or follow. *—intr.* To act as a detective. [Short for SLEUTHHOUND.]

WORD HISTORY: To track down the history of the word *sleuth* requires a bit of etymological sleuthing in itself. The immediate ancestor of our word is the compound *sleuthhound,* "a dog, such as a bloodhound, used for tracking or pursuing." This term took on a figurative sense, "tracker, pursuer," which is closely related to the sense "detective." From *sleuthhound* came the shortened form *sleuth,* recorded in the sense "detective" as early as 1872. The first part of the term *sleuthhound* means "track, path, trail," and is first recorded in a Middle English work written probably around 1200. The Middle English word, which had the form *sloth,* with *eu* representing the Scots development of the Middle English (ō), was a borrowing of the Old Norse word *slōdh,* "a track or trail."

sleuth·hound (slo͞oth′hound′) *n.* **1.** A dog used for tracking or pursuing, such as a bloodhound. Also called *sleuth.* **2.** A detective. [Middle English *sleuth,* animal track (from Old Norse *slōdh*) + HOUND.]
slew¹ also **slue** (slo͞o) *n. Informal.* A large amount or number; a lot: *a slew of unpaid bills.* [Irish Gaelic *sluagh,* multitude, from Old Irish *slúag.*]
slew² (slo͞o) *v.* Past tense of **slay.**
slew³ (slo͞o) *n.* Variant of **slough¹.**
slew⁴ (slo͞o) *v. & n.* Variant of **slue¹.**
slice (slīs) *n.* **1.** A thin, broad piece cut from a larger amount. **2.** A portion or share: *a slice of the profits.* **3.a.** A knife with a broad, thin, flexible blade, used for cutting and serving food. **b.** A similar implement for spreading printing ink. **4.** *Sports.* **a.** A stroke that causes a ball to curve off course to the right or, if the player is left-handed, to the left. **b.** The course followed by such a ball. **—slice** *v.* **sliced, slic·ing, slic·es.** *—tr.* **1.** To cut or divide into slices: *slice a loaf of bread.* **2.** To cut from a larger piece: *slice off a piece of salami.* **3.** To cut through or across with or as if with a knife: *The harvester sliced the field.* **4.** To divide into portions or shares; parcel out. **5.** To spread, work at, or clear away with a bladed tool such as a slice bar. **6.** *Sports.* To hit (a ball) with a slice. *—intr.* **1.** To move like a knife: *The destroyer sliced through the water.* **2.** *Sports.* To hit a ball with a slice. [Middle English, splinter, from Old French *esclice,* from *esclicier,* to splinter, of Germanic origin.] **—slice′a·ble** *adj.* **—slic′er** *n.*
slice bar *n.* An iron tool with a broad flat end, used to loosen and clear out clinkers from furnace grates.
slice of life *n., pl.* **slices of life.** An episode of actual experience represented realistically and with little alteration in a dramatic, fictional, or reportorial work. **—slice′-of-life′** (slīs′əv-līf′) *adj.*
slick (slĭk) *adj.* **slick·er, slick·est. 1.** Smooth, glossy, and slippery: *sidewalks slick with ice.* See Synonyms at **sleek. 2.** Deftly executed; adroit: *"as slick as a sonnet, but as dull as ditch water"* (Tallulah Bankhead). **3.** Shrewd; wily. **4.** Superficially attractive or plausible but lacking depth or soundness; glib: *a slick writing style.* See Synonyms at **glib. —slick** *n.* **1.** A smooth or slippery surface or area. **2.a.** A floating film of oil. **b.** A trail of floating material: *a garbage slick.* **3.** An implement used to make a surface slick, especially a chisel used for smoothing and polishing. **4.** *Informal.* A magazine, usually of large popular readership, printed on high-quality glossy paper. **5.** A racing automobile tire with a smooth tread. **6.** *Slang.* An unarmed military aircraft, such as a spotter plane or helicopter. **—slick** *tr.v.* **slicked, slick·ing, slicks. 1.** To make smooth, glossy, or oily. **2.** *Informal.* To make neat, trim, or tidy: *slicked themselves up for the camera.* [Middle English *slike,* from Old English **slice.* See **lei-** in Appendix.] **—slick′ly** *adv.* **—slick′ness** *n.*
slick·en (slĭk′ən) *tr. & intr.v.* **-ened, -en·ing, -ens.** To make or become slick. **—slick′en·er** *n.*
slick·en·side (slĭk′ən-sīd′) *n.* A polished, striated rock surface caused by one rock mass sliding over another in a fault plane. [Dialectal *slicken,* glossy (alteration of SLICK) + SIDE.]
slick·er (slĭk′ər) *n.* **1.a.** A long water-repellant coat usually made of oilskin. **b.** A raincoat made of a glossy or shiny material, such as plastic or rubber. **2.** A tool for dressing hides. **3.** *Informal.* A cheat; a swindler. **4.** *Informal.* A person with stylish clothing and manners.
slid (slĭd) *v.* Past tense and past participle of **slide.**
slid·den (slĭd′n) *v. Archaic.* A past participle of **slide.**
slide (slīd) *v.* **slid** (slĭd), **slid·ing, slides.** *—intr.* **1.** To move over a surface while maintaining smooth, continuous contact. **2.** To coast on a slippery surface, such as ice or snow. **3.** To pass smoothly and quietly; glide: *slid past the door without anyone noticing.* **4.** To go unattended or unacted upon: *Let the matter slide.* **5.** To lose a secure footing or positioning; shift out of place; slip: *slid on the ice and fell.* **6.a.** To move downward: *Prices began to slide.* **b.** To return to a less favorable or less worthy condition. **7.** *Baseball.* To drop down and skid, usually feet first, into a base to avoid being put out. *—tr.* To cause to slide or slip. **—slide** *n.* **1.** A sliding movement or action. **2.** A smooth surface or track for sliding, usually inclined: *a water slide.* **3.** A playground apparatus for children to slide on, typically consisting of a smooth chute mounted by means of a ladder. **4.** A part that operates by sliding, as the U-shaped section of tube on a trombone that is moved to produce various tones. **5.** An image on a transparent base for projection on a screen. **6.** A small glass plate for mounting specimens to be examined under a microscope. **7.** A fall of a mass of rock, earth, or snow down a slope; an avalanche or a landslide. **8.** *Music.* **a.** A slight portamento used in violin playing, passing quickly from one note to another. **b.** An ornamentation consisting of two grace notes approaching the main note. [Middle English *sliden,* from Old English *slīdan.*]

SYNONYMS: *slide, slip, glide, coast, skid, slither.* These verbs mean to move smoothly and continuously over or as if over a slippery surface. *Slide* usually implies rapid, easy movement without loss of contact with the surface: *coal sliding down a chute; "the drops sliding from a lifted oar"* (Theodore Roethke). *Slip* can refer to smooth, easy, and quiet passage: *"the jackals . . . slipping back to the hills"* (Lord Dunsany). More often, however, the term is applied to accidental sliding resulting in loss of balance or foothold: *slipped on a patch of ice and sprained his ankle. Glide* refers to smooth, free-flowing, seemingly effortless movement: *"four snakes gliding up and down a hollow"* (Ralph Waldo Emerson). *A submarine glided silently through the water. Coast* applies especially to downward movement resulting from the effects of gravity or momentum: *The driver turned off the engine and let the truck coast down the incline. Skid* implies an uncontrolled, often sideways sliding caused by a lack of traction: *The bus skidded on wet pavement. Slither* can mean to slip and slide, as on an uneven surface, often with friction and noise: *"The detached crystals slithered down the rock face for a moment and then made no further sound"* (H.G. Wells). The word can also suggest the sinuous, gliding motion of a reptile: *An iguana slithered across the path.*

Sli·dell (slĭ-dĕl′). A city of southeast Louisiana northeast of New Orleans. It is primarily residential. Population, 26,718.
slid·er (slī′dər) *n.* **1.** One that slides: *The snowy hill was filled with young sliders.* **2.** *Baseball.* A fast pitch that breaks in the same direction as a curve ball at the last moment.
slide rule *n.* A device consisting of two logarithmically scaled rules mounted to slide along each other so that multiplication, division, and other more complex computations are reduced to the mechanical equivalent of addition or subtraction.
slide valve *n.* A valve that slides back and forth over ports, especially one in the cylinder wall of a steam engine that permits the intake and outflow of steam to move the piston.
slid·ing scale (slī′dĭng) *n.* A scale in which indicated prices, taxes, or wages vary in accordance with another factor, as wages with the cost-of-living index or medical charges with a patient's income.
sli·er (slī′ər) *adj.* A comparative of **sly.**

sli•est (slī′ĭst) *adj.* A superlative of **sly.**

slight (slīt) *adj.* **slight•er, slight•est. 1.** Small in size, degree, or amount: *a slight tilt; a slight surplus.* **2.** Lacking strength, substance, or solidity; frail: *a slight foundation; slight evidence.* **3.** Of small importance or consideration; trifling: *slight matters.* **4.** Small and slender in build or construction; delicate. **—slight** *tr.v.* **slight•ed, slight•ing, slights. 1.** To treat as of small importance; make light of. **2.** To treat with discourteous reserve or inattention. **3.** To do negligently or thoughtlessly; scant. **—slight** *n.* **1.** The act or an instance of slighting. **2.** A deliberate discourtesy; a snub: *"It is easier to recount grievances and slights than it is to set down a broad redress of such grievances and slights"* (Elizabeth Kenny). [Middle English, slender, smooth, possibly of Scandinavian origin. See **lei-** in Appendix.] **—slight′ness** *n.*

slight•ing (slī′tĭng) *adj.* Conveying or constituting a slight; belittling: *a slighting look.* **—slight′ing•ly** *adv.*

slight•ly (slīt′lē) *adv.* **1.** *Abbr.* **sl.** To a small degree or extent; somewhat. **2.** Slenderly; delicately: *slightly built.*

Sli•go (slī′gō). A municipal borough of northern Ireland on **Sligo Bay,** an inlet of the Atlantic Ocean. There are megalithic ruins nearby. Population, 17,232.

slim (slĭm) *adj.* **slim•mer, slim•mest. 1.** Small in girth or thickness in proportion to height or length; slender. **2.** Small in quantity or amount; meager: *slim chances of success.* **—slim** *intr. & tr.v.* **slimmed, slim•ming, slims. 1.** To become or make slim. **2.** To lose or cause to lose weight, as by dieting or exercise. [Dutch, bad, sly, from Middle Dutch *slimp, slim,* bad, crooked.] **—slim′ly** *adv.* **—slim′mer** *n.* **—slim′ness** *n.*

slime (slīm) *n.* **1.** A thick, sticky, slippery substance. **2.** A mucous substance secreted by certain animals, such as fish or slugs. **3.** Vile or disgusting matter. **—slime** *tr.v.* **slimed, slim•ing, slimes. 1.** To smear with slime. **2.** To remove slime from (fish to be canned, for example). [Middle English, from Old English *slīm.* See **lei-** in Appendix.]

slime mold *n.* **1.** Any of various primitive organisms of the phylum Acrasiomycota, especially of the genus *Dictyostelium,* that grow on dung and decaying vegetation and have a life cycle characterized by a slimelike amoeboid stage and a multicellular reproductive stage. Also called *cellular slime mold.* **2.** Any of various organisms of the phylum Myxomycota that grow on decaying vegetation and in moist soil and have a similar but more advanced life cycle. Also called *myxomycete, plasmodial slime mold.*

slim•nas•tics (slĭm-năs′tĭks) *n. (used with a sing. or pl. verb).* Physical exercises designed to facilitate weight loss. [SLIM + (GYM)NASTICS.]

slim•sy (slĭm′zē) also **slimp•sy** (slĭmp′sē) *adj.* **-si•er, -si•est.** *Informal.* Frail; flimsy. [Blend of SLIM and FLIMSY.]

slim•y (slī′mē) *adj.* **-i•er, -i•est. 1.** Consisting of or resembling slime; viscous. **2.** Covered with or exuding slime. **3.** Vile; foul. **—slim′i•ly** *adv.* **—slim′i•ness** *n.*

sling[1] (slĭng) *n.* **1. a.** A weapon consisting of a looped strap in which a stone is whirled and then let fly. **b.** A slingshot. **2.** A looped rope, strap, or chain for supporting, cradling, or hoisting something, especially: **a.** A strap of a shoe that fits over the heel. **b.** A strap used to carry a rifle over the shoulder. **c.** *Nautical.* A rope or chain for supporting a yard. **d.** A band suspended from the neck to support an injured arm or hand. **3.** The act of hurling a missile. **—sling** *tr.v.* **slung** (slŭng), **sling•ing, slings. 1.** To hurl with or as if with a sling. See Synonyms at **throw. 2.** To place or carry in a sling. **3.** To move by means of a sling; raise or lower in a sling: *sling cargo into a hold.* **4.** To hang loosely or freely; let swing. [Middle English *slinge.*] **—sling′er** *n.*

sling[2] (slĭng) *n.* A drink consisting of brandy, whiskey, or gin, sweetened and usually lemon-flavored. [Origin unknown.]

sling•shot (slĭng′shŏt′) *n.* A Y-shaped stick having an elastic strap attached to the prongs, used for flinging small stones.

slink (slĭngk) *v.* **slunk** (slŭngk) also **slinked, slink•ing, slinks.** *—intr.* To move in a quiet, furtive manner; sneak: *slunk away ashamed; a cat slinking through the grass toward its prey.* *—tr.* To give birth to prematurely: *The cow slinked its calf.* **—slink** *n.* An animal, especially a calf, born prematurely. **—slink** *adj.* Born prematurely. [Middle English *slinken,* from Old English *slincan.*] **—slink′ing•ly** *adv.*

slink•y (sling′kē) *adj.* **-i•er, -i•est. 1.** Stealthy, furtive, and sneaking. **2.** *Informal.* Graceful, sinuous, and sleek: *wore a slinky outfit to the party.* **—slink′i•ly** *adv.* **—slink′i•ness** *n.*

slip[1] (slĭp) *v.* **slipped, slip•ping, slips.** *—intr.* **1. a.** To move smoothly, easily, and quietly: *slipped into bed.* **b.** To move stealthily; steal. **2.** To pass gradually, easily, or imperceptibly: *"It is necessary to write, if the days are not to slip emptily by"* (Vita Sackville-West). **3. a.** To slide involuntarily and lose one's balance or foothold. See Synonyms at **slide. b.** To slide out of place; shift position: *The gear slipped.* **4.** To escape, as from a grasp, fastening, or restraint: *slipped away from his pursuers.* **5.** To decline from a former or standard level; fall off. **6.** To fall behind a scheduled production rate. **7.** To fall into fault or error. *—tr.* **1.** To cause to move in a smooth, easy, or sliding motion: *slipped the bolt into place.* **2.** To place or insert smoothly and quietly. **3.** To put on or remove (clothing) easily or quickly: *slip on a sweater; slipped off her shoes.* **4.** To get loose or free from; elude. **5.** To bring forth (young) prematurely. Used of animals. **6.** To unleash or free (a dog or hawk) to pursue game. **7.** To release, loose, or unfasten: *slip a knot.* **8.** To dislocate (a bone). **9.** To pass (a knitting stitch) from one needle to another without knitting it. **—slip** *n.* **1.** The act or an instance of slipping or sliding. **2.** An accident or a mishap, especially a falling down. **3. a.** An error in conduct or thinking; a mistake. **b.** A slight error or oversight, as in speech or writing: *a slip of the tongue.* **4.** *Nautical.* **a.** A docking place for a ship between two piers. **b.** A slipway. **5.** *Nautical.* The difference between a vessel's actual speed through water and the speed at which the vessel would move if the screw were propelling against a solid. **6. a.** A woman's undergarment of dress length, suspended from shoulder straps. **b.** A half-slip. **7.** A pillowcase. **8.** *Geology.* **a.** A smooth crack at which rock strata have moved on each other. **b.** A small fault. **c.** The relative displacement of formerly adjacent points on opposite sides of a fault. **9.** The difference between optimal and actual output in a mechanical device. **10.** Movement between two parts where none should exist, as between a pulley and a belt. **11.** A sideways movement of an airplane when banked too far. ***—idioms.* give (someone) the slip.** *Slang.* To escape the pursuit of. **let slip.** To say inadvertently. **slip one over on.** *Informal.* To hoodwink; trick. [Middle English *slippen,* probably of Middle Low German or Middle Dutch origin. See **lei-** in Appendix.]

slip[2] (slĭp) *n.* **1.** A part of a plant cut or broken off for grafting or planting; a scion or cutting. **2.** A long, narrow piece; a strip. **3.** A slender, youthful person: *a slip of a child.* **4.** A small piece of paper, especially a small form, document, or receipt: *a deposit slip; a sales slip.* **5.** A narrow pew in a church. **—slip** *tr.v.* **slipped, slip•ping, slips.** To make a slip from (a plant or plant part). [Probably from Middle Low German or Middle Dutch *slippe.*]

slip[3] (slĭp) *n.* Thinned potter's clay used for decorating or coating ceramics. [Middle English, slime, from Old English *slypa.* See **sleubh-** in Appendix.]

SLIP *abbr. Computer Science.* Symmetric list processor.

slip•case (slĭp′kās′) *n.* A protective box with one open end or more, used for storing a book. **—slip′cased′** *adj.*

slip•cov•er (slĭp′kŭv′ər) *n.* A fitted, removable cover of cloth or other material for a piece of upholstered furniture. **—slipcover** *tr.v.* **-ered, -er•ing, -ers.** To provide with a slipcover.

slip•knot (slĭp′nŏt′) *n.* **1.** A knot made with a loop so that it slips easily along the rope or cord around which it is tied. **2.** A knot made so that it can readily be untied by pulling one free end. Also called *running knot.*

slip-on (slĭp′ŏn′, -ôn′) *n.* A garment easily donned or removed. **—slip′-on′** *adj.*

slip•o•ver (slĭp′ō′vər) *n.* A garment, such as a sweater, designed to be put on or taken off over the head.

slip•page (slĭp′ĭj) *n.* **1.** The act or an instance of slipping, especially movement away from an original or secure place. **2.** The amount or extent of slipping. **3.** A decline in level, performance, or achievement. **4.** Loss of motion or power because of slipping.

slipped disk (slĭpt) *n.* Protrusion of a part of an intervertebral disk through the fibrocartilage, occurring usually in the lower lumbar region and often causing back pain or sciatica.

slip•per (slĭp′ər) *n.* A low shoe that can be slipped on and off easily and usually worn indoors. **—slip′pered** *adj.*

slipper flower *n.* See **calceolaria.**

slip•per•wort (slĭp′ər-wûrt′, -wôrt′) *n.* See **calceolaria.**

slip•per•y (slĭp′ə-rē) *adj.* **-i•er, -i•est. 1.** Causing or tending to cause sliding or slipping: *a slippery sidewalk.* **2.** Tending to slip, as from one's grasp: *a slippery bar of soap.* **3.** Not trustworthy; elusive or tricky: *"How extraordinarily slippery a liar the camera is"* (James Agee). [Alteration of obsolete *slipper,* from Middle English, from Old English *slipor.* See **lei-** in Appendix.] **—slip′per•i•ness** *n.*

slippery elm *n.* **1.** A deciduous eastern North American tree *(Ulmus rubra)* having hard wood and mucilaginous, aromatic inner bark formerly used medicinally. **2.** The wood of this tree.

slippery slope *n.* A tricky, precarious situation: *"On the slippery slope of modernity, helped along by Rousseau and Nietzsche, man slid irresistibly toward the twentieth-century crisis of the West"* (Gordon S. Wood).

slip ring *n.* A metal ring mounted on a rotating part of a machine to provide a continuous electrical connection through brushes on stationary contacts.

slip-sheet (slĭp′shēt′) *Printing. n.* A blank sheet of paper slipped between newly printed sheets to prevent offsetting. **—slip-sheet** *tr.v.* **-sheet•ed, -sheet•ing, -sheets.** To insert blank sheets between (printed sheets).

slip•shod (slĭp′shŏd′) *adj.* **1.** Marked by carelessness; sloppy or slovenly. See Synonyms at **sloppy. 2.** Slovenly in appearance; shabby or seedy. **—slip′shod′di•ness** *n.*

slip•slop (slĭp′slŏp′) *n.* **1.** Trivial conversation or writing; twaddle. **2.** *Archaic.* Unappetizing liquid or watery food; slops. [Reduplication of SLOP[1].]

slip•stitch (slĭp′stĭch′) *n.* A concealed stitch used for sewing together two layers of fabric, as with hems and facings, made by running the needle through the underside of the lesser piece and through a few threads of the main piece.

slip•stream (slĭp′strēm′) *n.* **1.** The turbulent flow of air driven backward by the propeller or propellers of an aircraft. Also

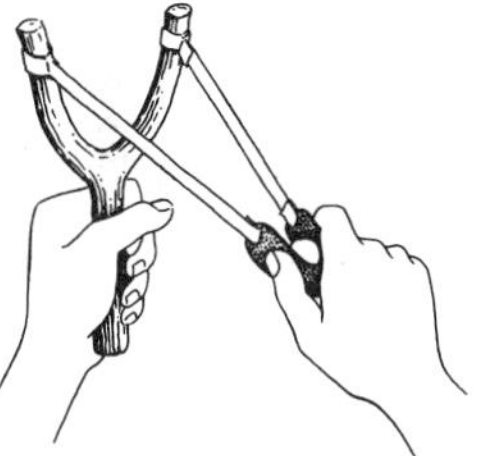

slingshot

slipknot

ă **pat**	oi **boy**
ā **pay**	ou **out**
âr **care**	o͝o **took**
ä **father**	o͞o **boot**
ĕ **pet**	ŭ **cut**
ē **be**	ûr **urge**
ĭ **pit**	th **thin**
ī **pie**	*th* **this**
îr **pier**	hw **which**
ŏ **pot**	zh **vision**
ō **toe**	ə **about, item**
ô **paw**	♦ **regionalism**

Stress marks: **′** (primary); ′ (secondary), as in **dictionary** (dĭk′shə-nĕr′ē)

called *race.* **2.** The region of reduced air pressure and forward suction produced by and immediately behind a fast-moving ground vehicle. **—slipstream** *intr.v.* **-streamed, -stream·ing, -streams.** To drive or cycle in the slipstream of a vehicle ahead.

slip-up (slĭp′ŭp′) *n.* An error; an oversight.

slip·ware (slĭp′wâr′) *n.* Pottery coated or decorated with slip.

slip·way (slĭp′wā′) *n. Nautical.* A sloping surface leading down to the water, on which ships are built or repaired.

slit (slĭt) *n.* A long, straight, narrow cut or opening. **—slit** *tr.v.* **slit, slit·ting, slits. 1.** To make a slit or slits in. **2.** To cut lengthwise into strips; split. [Middle English *slitte,* from *slitten,* to split, from Old English *slītan,* to cut up.] **—slit′ter** *n.* **—slit′ty** *adj.*

sloop

slith·er (slĭth′ər) *v.* **-ered, -er·ing, -ers.** *—intr.* **1.** To slip and slide, as on a loose or uneven surface, often with friction and noise. **2.** To glide or slide like a reptile. See Synonyms at **slide.** *—tr.* To cause to slither. **—slither** *n.* A slithering movement or gait. [Middle English *slethren,* variant of *sliddren,* from Old English *slidrian,* frequentative of *slīdan,* to slide.] **—slith′er·y** *adj.*

slit trench *n.* A narrow, shallow trench dug during combat for the protection of a single soldier or a small group of soldiers.

Sli·ven (slĭv′ən). A city of east-central Bulgaria east of Sofia. Contested by Bulgaria and the Byzantine Empire in medieval times and by Russia and Turkey in the 19th century, it is now a textile center with varied industries. Population, 104,000.

sliv·er (slĭv′ər) *n.* **1.** A slender piece cut, split, or broken off; a splinter: *slivers of broken glass.* **2.** A small narrow piece, portion, or plot: *a sliver of land.* **3.** (*also* slī′vər). A continuous strand of loose wool, flax, or cotton, ready for drawing and twisting. **—sliver** *tr. & intr.v.* **-ered, -er·ing, -ers.** To split or become split into slivers. [Middle English *slivere,* from *sliven,* to split, from Old English *slīfan.*]

sliv·o·vitz (slĭv′ə-vĭts) *n.* A dry colorless plum brandy. [Serbo-Croatian *šljivovica,* from *šljiva,* plum. See **slī-** in Appendix.]

Sloan (slōn), **John French.** 1871–1951. American painter whose scenes of urban life include *Sunday, Women Drying Their Hair* (1912) and *Backyards, Greenwich Village* (1914).

slob (slŏb) *n. Informal.* A person regarded as slovenly, crude, or obnoxious. [Irish Gaelic *slab,* mud, from Old Irish, probably of Scandinavian origin; akin to Swedish dialectal *slabb,* mud.] **—slob′bish** *adj.*

slob·ber (slŏb′ər) *v.* **-bered, -ber·ing, -bers.** *—intr.* **1.** To let saliva or liquid spill out from the mouth; drool. **2.** To express sentiment or enthusiasm effusively or incoherently; gush. *—tr.* To wet or smear with or as if with saliva or liquid dribbled from the mouth. **—slobber** *n.* **1.** Saliva or liquid running from the mouth; drool. **2.** Effusive or incoherent expression; drivel. [Middle English *sloberen,* perhaps of Low German origin.] **—slob′ber·er** *n.* **—slob′ber·y** *adj.*

sloe (slō) *n.* **1.** See **blackthorn. 2.** Either of two eastern North American plum trees or shrubs, *Prunus alleghaniensis,* having dark purple fruit, or *P. americana,* having yellow or red fruit. **3.** The tart, plumlike fruit of either of these plants. [Middle English *slo,* from Old English *slā.* See **slī-** in Appendix.]

sloe-eyed (slō′īd′) *adj.* Having slanted, dark eyes.

sloe gin *n.* A liqueur having a gin base, flavored with fresh sloes.

slog (slŏg) *v.* **slogged, slog·ging, slogs.** *—intr.* **1.** To walk or progress with a slow, heavy pace; plod: *slog across the swamp; slogged through both volumes.* **2.** To work diligently for long hours: *slogged away at Latin.* *—tr.* **1.** To make (one's way) with a slow, heavy pace against resistance. **2.** To strike with heavy blows. **—slog** *n.* **1.** A long, exhausting progress, march, or hike: *a student's weary slog through Cicero; a slog through miles of jungle.* **2.** Long, hard work: *an 18-hour slog in the hay fields.* [Perhaps alteration of SLUG[3].] **—slog′ger** *n.*

slo·gan (slō′gən) *n.* **1.** A phrase expressing the aims or nature of an enterprise, an organization, or a candidate; a motto. **2.** A phrase used repeatedly, as in advertising or promotion: *"all the slogans and shibboleths coined out of the ideals of the peoples for the uses of imperialism"* (Margaret Sanger). **3.** A battle cry of a Scottish clan. [Alteration of Scots *slogorne,* battle cry, from Gaelic *sluagh-ghairm* : *sluagh,* host; see SLEW[1] + *gairm,* shout.]

slo·gan·eer (slō′gə-nîr′) *n.* One that invents or uses slogans. **—sloganeer** *intr.v.* **-eered, -eer·ing, -eers.** To invent or use slogans.

slo·gan·ize (slō′gə-nīz′) *tr.v.* **-ized, -iz·ing, -iz·es.** To express as or in slogans or a slogan. **—slo′gan·iz·er** *n.*

sloop (slo͞op) *n. Nautical.* A single-masted, fore-and-aft-rigged sailing boat with a short standing bowsprit or none at all and a single headsail set from the forestay. [Dutch *sloep,* from Middle Dutch *slūpen,* to glide. See **sleubh-** in Appendix.]

sloop of war *n., pl.* **sloops of war.** *Nautical.* A small, armed vessel larger than a gunboat, carrying guns on one deck only.

sloth
Brown-throated three-toed sloth
Bradypus variegatus

slop[1] (slŏp) *n.* **1.** Spilled or splashed liquid. **2.** Soft mud or slush. **3.** Unappetizing watery food or soup. **4.** Often **slops.** Waste food used to feed pigs or other animals; swill. **5.** Often **slops.** Mash remaining after alcohol distillation. **6.** Often **slops.** Human excrement. **7.** Repulsively effusive writing or speech; drivel. **—slop** *v.* **slopped, slop·ping, slops.** *—intr.* **1.** To be spilled or splashed: *Suds slopped over the rim of the washtub.* **2.** To spill over; overflow. **3.** To walk heavily or messily in or as if in mud; plod: *"He slopped along in broken slippers, hands in pockets, whistling"* (Alan Sillitoe). **4.** To express oneself effusively; gush. *—tr.* **1.** To spill (liquid). **2.** To spill liquid on. **3.** To serve unappetizingly or clumsily; dish out. **4.** To feed slops to (animals). [Middle English *sloppe,* a muddy place, perhaps from Old English **sloppe,* dung, slime. See **sleubh-** in Appendix.]

slop[2] (slŏp) *n.* **1. slops.** Articles of clothing and bedding issued or sold to sailors. **2. slops.** Short, full trousers worn in the 16th century. **3.** A loose outer garment, such as a smock or overalls. **4. slops.** *Chiefly British.* Cheap, ready-made garments. [Middle English *sloppe,* a kind of garment, from Old English *-slop* (in *oferslop,* surplice. See **sleubh-** in Appendix.)]

slope (slōp) *v.* **sloped, slop·ing, slopes.** *—intr.* **1.** To diverge from the vertical or horizontal; incline: *a roof that slopes.* See Synonyms at **slant. 2.** To move on a slant; ascend or descend: *sloped down the trail.* *—tr.* To cause to slope: *sloped the path down the bank.* **—slope** *n.* **1.** An inclined line, surface, plane, position, or direction. **2.** A stretch of ground forming a natural or artificial incline: *ski slopes.* **3. a.** A deviation from the horizontal. **b.** The amount or degree of such deviation. **4.** *Mathematics.* **a.** The rate at which an ordinate of a point of a line on a coordinate plane changes with respect to a change in the abscissa. **b.** The tangent of the angle of inclination of a line, or the slope of the tangent line for a curve or surface. **5.** *Offensive Slang.* Used as a disparaging term for an Asian person. [Probably from Middle English *aslope,* sloping.] **—slop′er** *n.* **—slop′ing·ly** *adv.*

slo-pitch (slō′pĭch′) *n. Sports.* Variant of **slow-pitch.**

slop·py (slŏp′ē) *adj.* **-pi·er, -pi·est. 1.** Marked by a lack of neatness or order; untidy: *a sloppy room.* **2.** Marked by a lack of care or precision; slipshod: *sloppy use of language.* **3.** *Informal.* Oversentimental; gushy. **4.** Of, resembling, or covered with slop; muddy or slushy: *sloppy ground.* **5.** Watery and unappetizing: *a sloppy stew.* **6.** Spotted or splashed with liquid. **—slop′pi·ly** *adv.* **—slop′pi·ness** *n.*

SYNONYMS: *sloppy, slovenly, unkempt, slipshod.* These adjectives apply to people, their appearance, their way of thinking, or their work and mean marked by an absence of due or proper care or attention. *Sloppy* evokes the idea of careless spilling, spotting, or splashing; it suggests slackness, untidiness, or diffuseness: *a sloppy kitchen; sloppy dress. "I do not see how the sloppiest reasoner can evade that"* (H.G. Wells). *Slovenly* implies habitual negligence and a lack of system or thoroughness: *a slovenly appearance; a slovenly writer; slovenly inaccuracies. Unkempt* stresses dishevelment resulting from a neglectful lack of proper maintenance: *"an unwashed brow, an unkempt head of hair"* (Sir Walter Scott). *During the owners' absence the lawn became dreadfully unkempt. Slipshod* suggests a relaxed indulgence toward imperfection, a casual inattention to detail, and a general absence of meticulousness: *"the new owners' camp . . . a slipshod and slovenly affair, tent half stretched, dishes unwashed"* (Jack London); *"slipshod talk"* (George Eliot).

sloppy joe or **sloppy Joe** (jō) *n.* A bun filled or covered with ground beef cooked in a spicy tomato sauce.

slop·work (slŏp′wûrk′) *n.* **1. a.** The manufacture of inexpensive, low-quality, ready-to-wear clothes. **b.** Cheap ready-to-wear clothes. **2.** Careless or hasty work.

slosh (slŏsh) *v.* **sloshed, slosh·ing, slosh·es.** *—tr.* **1.** To spill or splash (a liquid) copiously or clumsily: *slosh paint on the floor.* **2.** To agitate in a liquid: *slosh clothes in a solution of bleach and detergent.* *—intr.* To splash, wade, or flounder in water or another liquid: *sloshed through the creek.* **—slosh** *n.* **1.** Slush. **2.** The sound of splashing liquid. [Perhaps blend of SLOP[1] and SLUSH.] **—slosh′y** *adj.*

sloshed (slŏsht) *adj. Slang.* Intoxicated; drunk. [From past participle of SLOSH.]

slot[1] (slŏt) *n.* **1.** A narrow opening; a groove or slit: *a slot for coins in a vending machine; a mail slot.* **2.** A gap between a main and an auxiliary airfoil to provide space for airflow and facilitate the smooth passage of air over the wing. **3. a.** An assigned place in a sequence or schedule: *a new time slot for a TV program.* **b.** A position of employment in an organization or a hierarchy. **4.** *Computer Science.* A socket in a microcomputer that will accept a plug-in circuit board: *expansion slots.* **—slot** *tr.v.* **slot·ted, slot·ting, slots. 1.** To cut or make a slot or slots in. **2.** To put into or assign to a slot. [Middle English, hollow of the breastbone, from Old French *esclot.*]

slot[2] (slŏt) *n.* The track or trail of an animal, especially a deer. [Obsolete French *esclot,* horse's hoofprint, from Old French, perhaps from Old Norse *slōdh,* track.]

slot car *n. Games.* An electric toy racing car that fits into a slotted track and is controlled by a rheostat held by the operator.

sloth (slôth, slōth, slŏth) *n.* **1.** Aversion to work or exertion; laziness; indolence. **2.** Any of various slow-moving, arboreal, edentate mammals of the family Bradypodidae of South and Central America, having long hooklike claws by which they hang upside down from tree branches and feeding on leaves, buds, and fruits, especially: **a.** A member of the genus *Bradypus,* having three long-clawed toes on each forefoot. Also called *ai, three-toed sloth.* **b.** A member of the genus *Choloepus,* having two toes on each forefoot. Also called *two-toed sloth, unau.* **3.** A company of bears. See Synonyms at **flock[1].** [Middle English *slowth,* from *slow,* slow. See SLOW.]

sloth bear *n.* A bear *(Melursus ursinus)* of India and Sri Lanka, having a long snout, long sticky tongue, and dark shaggy hair and feeding on plants and insects, especially termites and the larvae of bees.

sloth·ful (slôth′fəl, slōth′-, slŏth′-) *adj.* Disinclined to work or exertion; lazy. See Synonyms at **lazy.** —**sloth′ful·ly** *adv.* —**sloth′ful·ness** *n.*

slot machine *n.* A vending or gambling machine operated by the insertion of coins into a slot.

slot racing *n. Games.* The racing of slot cars. —**slot racer** *n.*

slouch (slouch) *v.* **slouched, slouch·ing, slouch·es.** —*intr.* **1.** To sit, stand, or walk with an awkward, drooping, excessively relaxed posture. **2.** To droop or hang carelessly, as a hat. —*tr.* To cause to droop; stoop. —**slouch** *n.* **1.** An awkward, drooping, excessively relaxed posture or gait. **2.** *Slang.* An awkward, lazy, or inept person: *good at chess and no slouch at bridge, either.* [Origin unknown.] —**slouch′i·ly** *adv.* —**slouch′i·ness** *n.* —**slouch′y** *adj.*

slouch hat *n.* A soft hat with a broad, flexible brim.

slough¹ (slo͞o, slou) also **slew** (slo͞o) *n.* **1.** A depression or hollow, usually filled with deep mud or mire. **2.** Also **slue.** A stagnant swamp, marsh, bog, or pond, especially as part of a bayou, an inlet, or a backwater. **3.** A state of deep despair or moral degradation. [Middle English, from Old English *slōh.*] —**slough′y** *adj.*

slough² (slŭf) *n.* **1.** The dead outer skin shed by a reptile or an amphibian. **2.** *Medicine.* A layer or mass of dead tissue separated from surrounding living tissue, as in a wound, a sore, or an inflammation. **3.** An outer layer or covering that is shed. —**slough** *v.* **sloughed, slough·ing, sloughs.** —*intr.* **1.** To be cast off or shed; come off: *The snake's skin sloughs off.* **2.** To shed a slough. **3.** *Medicine.* To separate from surrounding living tissue. Used of dead tissue. —*tr.* To discard as undesirable or unfavorable; get rid of: *slough off former associates.* [Middle English *slughe.*]

Slough (slou). A municipal borough of southeast England, a residential and industrial suburb of London. Population, 96,900.

Slo·vak (slō′väk′, -văk′) also **Slo·va·ki·an** (slō-vä′kē-ən, -văk′ē-ən) —*n.* **1.** A member of a Slavic people living in Slovakia. **2.** The Slavic language of the Slovaks. —*adj.* Of or relating to Slovakia or its people, language, or culture. [Slovak *Slovák.*]

Slo·vak·i·a (slō-vä′kē-ə, -văk′ē-ə). A historical region of southern Czechoslovakia. Settled by Slavic peoples c. sixth century A.D., it was generally under Hungarian rule from the tenth century until 1918, when it became part of Czechoslovakia.

slov·en (slŭv′ən) *n.* One who is habitually careless in personal appearance or work. [Middle English *slovein,* perhaps from Middle Flemish *sloovin,* a scold, gossip, from Middle Low German *slôven,* to dress carelessly; akin to Dutch *sloof,* untidy woman. See **sleubh-** in Appendix).]

Slo·vene (slō′vēn′) also **Slo·ve·ni·an** (slō-vē′nē-ən, -vēn′-yən) —*n.* **1.** A member of a Slavic people living in Slovenia. **2.** The Slavic language of the Slovenes. —*adj.* Of or relating to Slovenia or its people, language, or culture. [German *Slowene,* from Slovene *Slovênec,* ultimately from Old Slavic *Slověninŭ,* Slav.]

Slo·ve·ni·a (slō-vē′nē-ə, -vēn′yə). A historical region of northwest Yugoslavia. In ancient times Illyrian and Celtic peoples inhabited the area, which was ruled by Rome after the first century B.C. and settled by Slavs in the sixth century A.D. Slovenia came under Austrian control after 1335 and joined the Kingdom of Serbs, Croats, and Slovenes (later Yugoslavia) in 1918.

slov·en·ly (slŭv′ən-lē) *adj.* **1.** Untidy, as in dress or appearance. **2.** Marked by negligence; slipshod. See Synonyms at **sloppy.** —**slov′en·li·ness** *n.* —**slov′en·ly** *adv.*

slow (slō) *adj.* **slow·er, slow·est.** *Abbr.* **sl. 1.a.** Not moving or able to move quickly; proceeding at a low speed: *a slow train; slow walkers.* **b.** Marked by a retarded tempo: *a slow waltz.* **2.a.** Taking or requiring a long time: *the slow job of making bread.* **b.** Taking more time than is usual: *a slow worker; slow progress in the peace negotiations.* **3.** Registering a time or rate behind or below the correct one: *a slow clock.* **4.** Lacking in promptness or willingness; not precipitate: *They were slow to accept our invitation.* **5.** Characterized by a low volume of sales or transactions: *Business was slow today.* **6.** Lacking liveliness or interest; boring: *a slow party.* **7.** Not having or exhibiting intellectual or mental quickness: *a slow learner.* **8.** Only moderately warm; low: *a slow oven.* —**slow** *adv.* **slower, slowest. 1.** So as to fall behind the correct time or rate: *The watch runs slow.* **2.** At a low speed: *Go slow!* —**slow** *v.* **slowed, slow·ing, slows.** —*tr.* **1.** To make slow or slower. **2.** To delay; retard. —*intr.* To become slow or slower. [Middle English, from Old English *slāw.*] —**slow′ly** *adv.* —**slow′ness** *n.*

SYNONYMS: *slow, dilatory, leisurely, laggard, deliberate.* These adjectives mean taking more time than is usual or necessary. *Slow* is the least specific: *slow speech; slow growth; a slow bus; a slow heartbeat; a slow but meticulous worker; slow to anger. Dilatory* implies lack of promptness caused by delay, procrastination, or indifference: *His credit suffered because he was dilatory in paying his bills. Leisurely* suggests a relaxed lack of haste: *We took a leisurely trip around Europe. Laggard* implies hanging back or falling behind: *"the horses' laggard pace"* (Rudyard Kipling). *Deliberate* suggests a lack of hurry traceable especially to caution, need, self-restraint, or careful consideration, as of consequences: *She went about her work in a systematic and deliberate manner.* See also Synonyms at **delay, stupid.**

USAGE NOTE: *Slow* may sometimes be used instead of *slowly* when it comes after the verb: *We drove the car slow.* In formal writing *slowly* is generally preferred. *Slow* is often used in speech and informal writing, especially when brevity and forcefulness are sought: *Drive slow! Slow* is also the established idiomatic form with certain senses of common verbs: *The watch runs slow. Take it slow.*

slow burn *n. Slang.* A gradually increasing sense or show of anger: *did a slow burn while waiting three hours in the doctor's office.*

slow·down (slō′doun′) *n.* The act or process of slowing down; a slackening of pace: *a production slowdown.*

slow-foot·ed (slō′fo͝ot′ĭd) *adj.* Proceeding at a tediously slow pace: *a slow-footed story.* —**slow′-foot′ed·ness** *n.*

slow infection *n.* An infection having a long incubation period, as that caused by a slow virus or by a prion.

slow loris *n.* A large loris *(Nycticebus coucang)* of Indonesia, having a corpulent, almost tailless body and noted for its very slow, cautious movements.

slow match *n.* A match or fuse that burns slowly at a known rate and is used to set off explosives.

slow motion *n.* A filmmaking technique in which the action as projected is slower than the original action. —**slow′-mo′tion** (slō′mō′shən) *adj.*

slow neutron *n.* A neutron in thermal equilibrium with the surrounding medium, especially one produced by fission and slowed by a moderator. Also called *thermal neutron.*

slow-pitch also **slo-pitch** (slō′pĭch′) *n. Sports.* Softball in which there are ten players to a team and legal pitches must travel in an arc from three to ten feet high.

slow·poke (slō′pōk′) *n. Informal.* One that moves, works, or acts slowly.

slow virus *n.* Any of a group of animal viruses that cause diseases having an unusually long incubation period, as Creutzfeldt-Jakob disease. Also called *lentivirus.*

slow virus disease *n.* A disease caused by a slow virus.

slow-wit·ted or **slow·wit·ted** (slō′wĭt′ĭd) *adj.* Slow to comprehend; dull. —**slow′-wit′ted·ly** *adv.* —**slow′-wit′ted·ness** *n.*

slow·worm (slō′wûrm′) *n.* A limbless lizard *(Anguis fragilis)* of Europe, western Asia, and northern Africa, having a smooth snakelike body and feeding chiefly on slugs. Also called *blindworm.* [Alteration (influenced by *slow,* slow) of Middle English *slowurm,* from Old English *slāwyrm* : *slā-,* earthworm, slowworm + *wyrm,* worm; see WORM.]

sloyd (sloid) *n.* A system of manual training developed in Sweden, based on the use of tools in woodworking. [Swedish *slöjd,* skill, skilled labor; akin to Old Norse *slœgdh,* dexterity. See SLEIGHT.]

SLR *abbr.* Single-lens reflex camera.

slub (slŭb) *tr.v.* **slubbed, slub·bing, slubs.** To draw out and twist (a strand of silk or other textile fiber) in preparation for spinning. —**slub** *n.* **1.** A soft, thick nub in yarn that is either an imperfection or purposely set for a desired effect. **2.** A slightly twisted roll of fiber, as of silk or cotton. [Origin unknown.]

sludge (slŭj) *n.* **1.** Semisolid material such as the type precipitated by sewage treatment. **2.** Mud, mire, or ooze covering the ground or forming a deposit, as on a riverbed. **3.** Finely broken or half-formed ice on a body of water, especially the sea. **4.** An agglutination or aggregation of blood cells forming a semisolid mass that often impedes circulation. —**sludge** *intr.v.* **sludged, sludg·ing, sludg·es.** To agglutinate or aggregate into a semisolid mass; form a sludge. Used of blood cells. [Perhaps alteration of dialectal *slutch,* mire.] —**sludg′y** *adj.*

slue¹ also **slew** (slo͞o) —*v.* **slued, slu·ing, slues** also **slewed, slew·ing, slews.** —*tr.* **1.** To turn (something) on an axis; rotate: *slued the swivel chair around; sluing the boom of a crane.* **2.** To turn sharply; veer: *braked and slued the car around.* —*intr.* **1.** To turn about an axis; pivot. **2.** To turn or slide sideways or off course; skid. —*n.* **1.** The act of sluing. **2.** The position to which something has slued. [Origin unknown.]

slue² (slo͞o) *n.* Variant of **slew¹.**

slue³ (slo͞o) *n.* Variant of **slough¹** (sense 2).

slug¹ (slŭg) *n.* **1.** A round bullet larger than buckshot. **2.** *Informal.* A shot of liquor. **3.** A small metal disk for use in a vending or gambling machine, especially one used illegally. **4.** A lump of metal or glass prepared for further processing. **5.** *Printing.* **a.** A strip of type metal, less than type-high and thicker than a lead, used for spacing. **b.** A line of cast type in a single strip of metal. **c.** A compositor's type line of identifying marks or instructions, inserted temporarily in copy. **6.** *Physics.* The unit of mass that is accelerated at the rate of one foot per second per second when acted on by a force of one pound weight. —**slug** *tr.v.* **slugged, slug·ging, slugs.** *Printing.* To add slugs to. [Perhaps from SLUG² (from its shape).]

slug² (slŭg) *n.* **1.** Any of various small, snaillike, chiefly terrestrial gastropod mollusks of the genus *Limax* and related genera, having a slow-moving elongated body with no shell or only a flat rudimentary shell on or under the skin. **2.** The smooth, soft larva of certain insects, such as the sawfly. **3.** A slimy mass of aggre-

slug²
Limax maximus

ă pat	oi boy
ā pay	ou out
âr care	o͝o took
ä father	o͞o boot
ĕ pet	ŭ cut
ē be	ûr urge
ĭ pit	th thin
ī pie	*th* this
îr pier	hw which
ŏ pot	zh vision
ō toe	ə about, item
ô paw	♦ regionalism

Stress marks: **′** (primary); ′ (secondary), as in **dictionary** (dĭk′shə-nĕr′ē)

gated amoeboid cells from which the sporophore of a cellular slime mold develops. **4.** *Informal.* A sluggard. [Middle English *slugge,* sluggard, probably of Scandinavian origin.]

slug³ (slŭg) *tr.v.* **slugged, slug·ging, slugs.** To strike heavily, especially with the fist or a bat. **—slug** *n.* A hard, heavy blow, as with the fist or a baseball bat. [Possibly from SLUG¹.]

slug·a·bed (slŭg′ə-bĕd′) *n.* One inclined to stay in bed out of laziness.

slug·fest (slŭg′fĕst′) *n.* **1.** *Slang.* A fight marked by an extended exchange of heavy blows. **2.** *Baseball.* A game in which there are many hits and runs scored.

slug·gard (slŭg′ərd) *n.* A slothful person; an idler. **—sluggard** *adj.* Lazy. [Middle English *sluggart,* probably from *sluggi,* lazy, probably of Scandinavian origin.] **—slug′gard·ly** *adj.* **—slug′gard·ness** *n.*

slug·ger (slŭg′ər) *n.* **1.** One that slugs, as a fighter who delivers hard, swinging punches. **2.** *Baseball.* A batter who hits many extra-base hits.

slug·ging average (slŭg′ĭng) *n.* *Baseball.* A player's total number of bases reached on hits divided by official times at bat, expressed as a three-digit decimal and used as a measure of batting power. Also called *slugging percentage.*

slug·gish (slŭg′ĭsh) *adj.* **1.** Displaying little movement or activity; slow; inactive: *a sluggish stream; sluggish growth.* **2.** Lacking alertness, vigor, or energy; inert or indolent. **3.** Slow to perform or respond to stimulation. [Middle English, probably from *slugge,* lazy person. See SLUG².] **—slug′gish·ly** *adv.* **—slug′gish·ness** *n.*

sluice

sluice (slo͞os) *n.* **1.a.** An artificial channel for conducting water, with a valve or gate to regulate the flow: *sluices connecting a reservoir with irrigated fields.* **b.** A valve or gate used in such a channel; a floodgate: *open sluices to flood a dry dock.* Also called *sluice gate.* **2.** A body of water impounded behind a floodgate. **3.** A sluiceway. **4.** A long inclined trough, as for carrying logs or separating gold ore. **—sluice** *v.* **sluiced, sluic·ing, sluic·es.** *—tr.* **1.** To flood or drench with or as if with a flow of released water. **2.** To wash with water flowing in a sluice: *sluicing sediment for gold.* **3.** To draw off or let out by a sluice: *sluice floodwater.* **4.** To send (logs, for example) down a sluice. *—intr.* To flow out from or as if from a sluice. [Middle English *scluse,* from Old French *escluse,* from Late Latin *exclūsa,* from Latin, feminine past participle of *exclūdere,* to shut out. See EXCLUDE.]

sluice·way (slo͞os′wā′) *n.* An artificial channel, especially one for carrying off excess water.

slum (slŭm) *n.* A heavily populated urban area characterized by substandard housing and squalor. Often used in the plural. *—attributive.* Often used to modify another noun: *slum housing; slum districts.* **—slum** *intr.v.* **slummed, slum·ming, slums.** To visit impoverished areas or squalid locales, especially out of curiosity or for amusement. [Origin unknown.] **—slum′mer** *n.* **—slum′my** *adj.*

slum·ber (slŭm′bər) *v.* **-bered, -ber·ing, -bers.** *—intr.* **1.** To sleep. **2.** To be dormant or quiescent. *—tr.* To pass (time) in sleep. **—slumber** *n.* **1.** Sleep. **2.** A state of inactivity or dormancy. [Middle English *slumeren, slumberen,* frequentative of *slumen,* to doze, probably from *slume,* light sleep, from Old English *slūma.*] **—slum′ber·er** *n.* **—slum′ber·ing·ly** *adv.*

slum·ber·ous (slŭm′bər-əs) or **slum·brous** (-brəs) *adj.* **1.** Sleepy; drowsy. **2.a.** Suggestive of or resembling sleep: *a slumberous torpor.* **b.** Quiet; tranquil. **3.** Causing or inducing sleep; soporific. **—slum′ber·ous·ly** *adv.* **—slum′ber·ous·ness** *n.*

slumber party *n.* An overnight party in which teenage girls wear nightgowns or pajamas, socialize, and sleep over.

slum·ber·y (slŭm′bə-rē) *adj.* Slumberous.

slum·gul·lion (slŭm-gŭl′yən) *n.* A watery meat stew. [Perhaps *slum,* muddy deposit in a mining sluice + dialectal *gullion,* mud (perhaps from Irish Gaelic *goilín,* pit).]

slum·lord (slŭm′lôrd′) *n.* An owner of slum property, especially one that overcharges tenants and allows the property to deteriorate. [SLUM + (LAND)LORD.]

slump (slŭmp) *intr.v.* **slumped, slump·ing, slumps.** **1.** To fall or sink heavily; collapse: *She slumped, exhausted, onto the sofa.* **2.** To droop, as in sitting or standing; slouch. **3.** To decline suddenly; fall off: *Business slumped after the holidays.* **4.a.** To sink or settle, as into mud or slush. **b.** To slide down or spread out thickly, as mud or fresh concrete. **—slump** *n.* **1.** The act or an instance of slumping. **2.** A drooping or slouching posture: *read defeat in the slump of his shoulders.* **3.** A sudden falling off or decline, as in activity, prices, or business: *a stock market slump; a slump in farm prices.* **4.** An extended period of poor performance, especially in a sport or competitive activity: *a slump in a batting average.* [Probably of Scandinavian origin; akin to Norwegian *slumpa,* to slump.]

slung (slŭng) *v.* Past tense and past participle of **sling¹.**

slunk (slŭngk) *v.* A past tense and a past participle of **slink.**

slur (slûr) *tr.v.* **slurred, slur·ring, slurs.** **1.** To pronounce indistinctly. **2.** To speak slightingly of; disparage. **3.** To pass over lightly or carelessly; treat without due consideration. **4.** *Music.* **a.** To glide over (a series of notes) smoothly without a break. **b.** To mark with a slur. **5.** *Printing.* To blur or smear. **—slur** *n.* **1.** A disparaging remark; an aspersion. **2.** A slurred utterance or sound. **3.** *Music.* **a.** A curved line connecting notes on a score to indicate that they are to be played or sung legato. **b.** A passage played or sung in this manner. **4.** *Printing.* A smeared or blurred impression. [Probably from Middle English *sloor,* mud.]

slurb (slûrb) *n.* *Informal.* An unsightly suburban area marked by crowded or poorly built dwellings. [Perhaps SL(OVENLY) + (SUB)URB.]

slurp (slûrp) *v.* **slurped, slurp·ing, slurps.** *—tr.* To eat or drink noisily. *—intr.* To eat or drink something noisily. **—slurp** *n.* **1.** A loud sucking noise made in eating or drinking. **2.** *Slang.* A mouthful of a liquid: *took a slurp of grape juice.* [Dutch *slurpen.*]

slur·ry (slûr′ē) *n., pl.* **-ries.** A thin mixture of a liquid, especially water, and any of several finely divided substances, such as cement, plaster of Paris, or clay particles. [Middle English *slori,* perhaps from *sloor,* mud.]

slush (slŭsh) *n.* **1.** Partially melted snow or ice. **2.** Soft mud; slop; mire. **3.** *Nautical.* Grease or fat discarded from a ship's galley. **4.** A greasy compound used as a lubricant for machinery. **5.** Maudlin speech or writing; sentimental drivel. **6.** A drink made of flavored syrup poured over crushed ice. **7.** *Informal.* Unsolicited manuscripts submitted to a publisher. **—slush** *v.* **slushed, slush·ing, slush·es.** *—tr.* **1.** To daub (machinery) with slush. **2.** To fill (joints in masonry) with mortar. **3.** *Nautical.* To wash down (a deck) by splashing with water. **4.** To splash or soak with slush or mud. *—intr.* **1.** To walk or proceed through slush. **2.** To make a splashing or slushy sound. [Perhaps of Scandinavian origin; akin to Norwegian *slask,* sloppy weather.]

slush fund *n.* **1.** A fund raised for undesignated purposes, especially: **a.** A fund raised by a group for corrupt practices, such as bribery or graft. **b.** A fund used by a group, as for entertainment. **2.** Money formerly raised by the sale of garbage from a warship to buy small items of luxury for the crew.

slush·y (slŭsh′ē) *adj.* **-i·er, -i·est.** **1.** Consisting of, covered with, or full of slush. **2.** Resembling slush, as in consistency. **3.** Revoltingly sentimental; maudlin. See Synonyms at **sentimental.** **—slush′i·ly** *adv.* **—slush′i·ness** *n.*

slut (slŭt) *n.* **1.a.** A woman considered sexually promiscuous. **b.** A prostitute. **2.** A slovenly woman; a slattern. **3.** A female dog. [Middle English *slutte.*] **—slut′tish** *adj.* **—slut′tish·ly** *adv.* **—slut′tish·ness** *n.*

SLV *abbr.* Standard launch vehicle.

sly (slī) *adj.* **sli·er, sli·est** also **sly·er, sly·est.** **1.** Adept in craft or cunning. **2.** Lacking or marked by a lack of candor. **3.** Playfully mischievous; roguish. **—*idiom.* on the sly.** In a way intended to escape notice: *took extra payments on the sly.* [Middle English *sleigh,* from Old Norse *slœgr.*] **—sly′ly** *adv.* **—sly′ness** *n.*

SYNONYMS: *sly, cunning, tricky, crafty, wily, foxy, artful, guileful.* These adjectives mean disposed to or marked by indirection or deviousness in the gaining of an end. *Sly* usually implies surreptitiousness, secretiveness, and lack of candor: *"You think he's open and blunt—he's as sly as a mink"* (George W. Cable). *Cunning* stresses cleverness and ingenuity, often at the expense of moral principles: *"Cunning men pass for wise"* (Francis Bacon). *Tricky* emphasizes shiftiness, deception, and absence of scruples: *Under the façade of morality and patriotism can be perceived the false and tricky political opportunist that he is. Crafty* suggests mastery of devious and underhanded methods or schemes: *Crafty plotters make the best intelligence agents. Wily* suggests subterfuge or stratagem intended to entrap: *Her father was a wily old attorney. Foxy* implies cunning and craft and usually long experience in the use of trickery: *The parvenu was much too foxy to let slip even a hint of his working-class background. Artful* emphasizes adroitness in maneuvering to accomplish a purpose: *She won the case by her artful manipulation of the jury's emotions. Guileful* suggests an insidious, often treacherous nature: *"a guileful tournament organizer who manipulates and dehumanizes athletes"* (Jeremiah Tax).

sly·boots (slī′bo͞ots′) *pl.n.* *(used with a sing. verb). Informal.* A sly person.

slype (slīp) *n.* *Architecture.* A covered passage, especially one between the transept and chapter house of a cathedral. [Perhaps akin to Dutch dialectal *slijpe,* secret path.]

Sm The symbol for the element **samarium.**

SM *abbr.* **1.** Sergeant major. **2.** Service mark. **3.** Or **S.M.** Soldier's Medal. **4.** Stage manager. **5.** Stationmaster.

sm. *abbr.* Small.

S.M. *abbr.* *Latin.* Scientiae Magister (Master of Science).

S-M or **s-m** *abbr.* Sadomasochism.

SMA *abbr.* Sergeant major of the army.

smack¹ (smăk) *v.* **smacked, smack·ing, smacks.** *—tr.* **1.** To press together and open (the lips) quickly and noisily, as in eating or tasting. **2.** To kiss noisily. **3.** To strike sharply and with a loud noise. *—intr.* **1.** To make or give a smack. **2.** To collide sharply and noisily: *The ball smacked against the side of the house.* **—smack** *n.* **1.** The loud, sharp sound of smacking. **2.** A noisy kiss. **3.** A sharp blow or slap. **—smack** *adv.* **1.** With a smack: *fell smack on her head.* **2.** Directly: *"We were smack in the middle of another controversy about a public man's personal life"* (Ellen Goodman). [Perhaps of Middle Flemish origin, or perhaps of imitative origin.]

smack² (smăk) *n.* **1.a.** A distinctive flavor or taste. See Synonyms at **taste.** **b.** A suggestion or trace. **2.** A small amount; a smattering. **—smack** *intr.v.* **smacked, smack·ing, smacks. 1.** To have a distinctive flavor or taste. Used with *of.* **2.** To give an indication; be suggestive. Often used with *of: "an agenda that does not smack of compromise"* (Time). [Middle English, from Old English *smæc.*]

smack[3] (smăk) *n. Nautical.* A sloop-rigged boat used chiefly in fishing, especially to transport the catch to market. [Dutch or Low German *smak,* from *smakken,* to fling, dash.]

smack[4] (smăk) *n. Slang.* Heroin. [Probably variant of *smeck,* from Yiddish *shmek,* a sniff, smell, from *shmekn,* to sniff, smell, from Middle High German *smecken, smacken,* to smell, taste, from Old High German *smac,* smell, taste.]

smack-dab (smăk′dăb′) *adv. Slang.* Squarely; directly: *stood smack-dab in the middle of the freeway.* [SMACK[1] + DAB[1], with a sudden contact.]

smack·er (smăk′ər) *n.* **1.** A loud kiss. **2.** A resounding blow. **3.** *Slang.* A dollar.

smack·ing (smăk′ĭng) *adj.* Brisk; vigorous; spanking: *a smacking breeze.*

small (smôl) *adj.* **small·er, small·est.** *Abbr.* **s., sm. 1.** Being below the average in size or magnitude. **2.** Limited in importance or significance; trivial: *a small matter.* **3.** Limited in degree or scope: *small farm operations.* **4.** Lacking position, influence, or status; minor: *"A crowd of small writers had vainly attempted to rival Addison"* (Macaulay). **5.** Unpretentious; modest: *made a small living; helped the cause in my own small way.* **6.** Not fully grown; very young. **7.** Narrow in outlook; petty: *a small mind.* **8.** Having been belittled; humiliated: *Their comments made me feel small.* **9.** Diluted; weak. Used of alcoholic beverages. **10.** Lacking force or volume: *a small voice.* **—small** *adv.* **1.** In small pieces: *Cut the meat up small.* **2.** Without loudness or forcefulness; softly. **3.** In a small manner. **—small** *n.* **1.** Something smaller than the rest: *the small of the back.* **2. smalls. a.** Small things considered as a group. **b.** *Chiefly British.* Small items of clothing. [Middle English *smal,* from Old English *smæl.*] **—small′ish** *adj.* **—small′ness** *n.*

SYNONYMS: *small, diminutive, little, miniature, minuscule, minute, petite, tiny, wee.* The central meaning shared by these adjectives is "being notably below the average in size or magnitude": *a small house; diminutive in stature; little hands; a miniature camera; a minuscule amount of rain; minute errors; a petite figure; tiny feet; a wee bit better.*
ANTONYM: *large.*

small arm *n.* A firearm that can be carried in the hand.

small beer *n.* **1.** Weak or inferior beer. **2.** Unimportant things; trivia. **—small beer** *adj.* Trivial; unimportant.

small-bore (smôl′bôr′, -bōr′) *adj.* **1.** Of, relating to, or being a firearm of .22 caliber. **2.** Trivial or parochial in character: *"the petty talking points . . . and small-bore scandals that regularly intrude on campaigns"* (New Republic).

small calorie *n.* See **calorie** (sense 1).

small capital *n. Abbr.* **sc, s.c.** A letter having the form of a capital letter but smaller; for example: SMALL CAPITALS.

small change *n.* **1.** Coins of low denomination. **2.** Something of little value or significance.

small-claims court (smôl′klāmz′) *n. Law.* A special court established for simplified and efficient handling of small claims on debts.

small·clothes (smôl′klōthz′, -klōz′) *pl.n.* **1.** Men's close-fitting knee breeches worn in the 18th century. **2.** *Chiefly British.* Small items of clothing, such as underclothes or handkerchiefs.

small fry *n.* **1.** Small children. **2.** Young or small fish. **3.** Persons or things regarded as unimportant.

small hours *pl.n.* The early hours after midnight.

small intestine *n.* The narrow, winding, upper part of the intestine where digestion is completed and nutrients are absorbed by the blood. It extends from the pylorus to the cecum and consists of the duodenum, the jejunum, and the ileum.

small-mind·ed (smôl′mīn′dĭd) *adj.* **1.** Having a narrow or selfish attitude. **2.** Characterized by pettiness or selfishness. **—small′-mind′ed·ly** *adv.* **—small′-mind′ed·ness** *n.*

small·mouth bass (smôl′mouth′ băs) *n.* A North American freshwater food and game fish *(Micropterus dolomieui)* having a shorter upper jaw than the similar largemouth bass.

small potatoes *pl.n. Informal.* **1.** A person or thing regarded as unimportant. **2.** An insignificant amount or sum.

small·pox (smôl′pŏks′) *n.* An acute, highly infectious, often fatal disease caused by a poxvirus and characterized by high fever and aches with subsequent widespread eruption of pimples that blister, produce pus, and form pockmarks. Also called *variola.*

small print *n.* See **fine print.**

Smalls (smôlz), **Robert.** 1839–1915. American Union soldier and politician. After being forced to serve in the Confederate Navy, he took command of a ship and delivered it to Union forces. Smalls subsequently became a captain (1863–1866) and the highest-ranking Black officer in the Union Navy. He later served as a U.S. representative from South Carolina (1875–1879 and 1881–1887).

small-scale (smôl′skāl′) *adj.* **1.** Limited in scope or extent; modest: *a small-scale plan.* **2.** Created on a small scale: *a small-scale model of the new city hall.*

small talk *n.* Casual or trivial conversation.

small·time or **small-time** (smôl′tīm′) *adj. Informal.* Insignificant or unimportant; minor: *a smalltime actor.* **—small′-tim′er** *n.*

small time *n. Informal.* A modest or minor level of attainment in a competitive field: *a critical success that took her from the small time all the way to Hollywood.*

smalt (smôlt) *n.* A deep blue paint and ceramic pigment produced by pulverizing a glass made of silica, potash, and cobalt oxide. [French, from Italian *smalto,* enamel, glaze, of Germanic origin. See **mel-[1]** in Appendix.]

smalt·ite (smôl′tīt′) also **smalt·ine** (smôl′tĭn, -tēn′) *n.* A white to silver-gray mineral, $(Co,Ni)As_3$, that is an important ore of cobalt.

smarm·y (smär′mē) *adj.* **-i·er, -i·est. 1.** Hypocritically, complacently, or effusively earnest. See Synonyms at **unctuous. 2.** Sleek. [From *smarm,* to smear.] **—smarm·i·ness** *n.*

♦**smart** (smärt) *adj.* **smart·er, smart·est. 1.a.** Characterized by sharp, quick thought; bright. See Synonyms at **intelligent. b.** Amusingly clever; witty: *a smart quip; a lively, smart conversation.* **c.** Impertinent; insolent: *That's enough of your smart talk.* **2.** Energetic or quick in movement: *a smart pace.* **3.** Canny and shrewd in dealings with others: *a smart business person.* **4.** Fashionable; elegant: *a smart suit; a smart restaurant; the smart set.* See Synonyms at **fashionable. 5.a.** Of, relating to, or being a highly automated device, especially one that imitates human intelligence: *smart missiles.* **b.** *Computer Science.* Having the capacity to perform operations independently of the computer. Used of a computer terminal. **6.** *New England & Southern U.S.* Accomplished; talented: *He's a right smart ball player.* **—smart** *intr.v.* **smart·ed, smart·ing, smarts. 1.a.** To cause a sharp, usually superficial, stinging pain: *The slap delivered to my face smarted.* **b.** To be the location of such a pain: *The incision on my leg smarts.* **c.** To feel such a pain. **2.** To suffer acutely, as from mental distress, wounded feelings, or remorse: *"No creature smarts so little as a fool"* (Alexander Pope). **3.** To suffer or pay a heavy penalty. **—smart** *n.* **1.** Sharp mental or physical pain. See Synonyms at **pain. 2. smarts.** *Slang.* Intelligence; expertise: *"Like courting the prettiest girl in school, the chase requires smarts"* (Jackie MacMullan). ***—phrasal verb.*** **smart off.** *Informal.* To speak or act impertinently. ***—idiom.*** **right smart.** *New England & Southern U.S.* A lot; a considerable amount: *He did right smart of the work himself.* [Middle English, stinging, keen, alert, from Old English *smeart,* causing pain.] **—smart′ly** *adv.* **—smart′ness** *n.*

♦***REGIONAL NOTE:*** *Smart* is a word that has digressed considerably from its original meaning of "stinging, sharp," as in *a smart blow.* The standard meaning of "clever, intelligent," probably picks up on the original semantic element of vigor or quick movement. *Smart* has taken on other senses as a regionalism. In New England and in the South *smart* can mean "accomplished, talented." The phrase *right smart* can even be used as a noun meaning "a considerable number or amount": *"We have read right smart of that book"* (Catherine C. Hopley).

smart al·eck (ăl′ĭk) *n. Informal.* **1.** A person regarded as obnoxiously self-assertive. **2.** An impudent person. [Perhaps after *Aleck* Hoag, 19th-century American confidence man and thief.] **—smart′-al′eck** (smärt′ăl′ĭk), **smart′-al′eck·y** (-ĭ-kē) *adj.*

smart-ass (smärt′ăs′) *n. Slang.* A smart aleck. **—smart′-ass′** *adj.*

smart bomb *n.* A bomb that can be guided by radio waves or a laser beam to its target.

smart card *n.* A plastic card resembling a credit card that contains a computer chip, which enables the holder to perform various operations, such as mathematical calculations, paying of bills, and the purchasing of goods and services.

smart·en (smär′tn) *v.* **-ened, -en·ing, -ens.** *—tr.* **1.** To improve in appearance or stylishness; spruce up. **2.** To make quicker: *smarten the pace.* *—intr.* To make oneself smart or smarter.

smart money *n.* **1.** *Games.* Bets or a bet placed by experienced gamblers or those having privileged information. **2.** *Informal.* **a.** Experienced, well-informed investors: *Smart money is supporting the conservative presidential candidate.* **b.** Investments made by people experienced and well informed in matters of finance. **3.** *Law.* Compensation beyond the value of actual harm, awarded by a jury in cases of gross negligence or willful misconduct.

smart rock *n.* A ground-based projectile that can be launched to destroy warheads or missiles.

smart·weed (smärt′wēd′) *n.* Any of various marsh plants of the genus *Polygonum,* having sheathlike stipules and small, densely clustered pink, white, or green flowers.

smart·y (smär′tē) *n., pl.* **-ies.** *Informal.* **1.** A smart aleck. **2.** A quick-witted person.

smar·ty-pants (smär′tē-pănts′) *pl.n.* *(used with a sing. verb). Informal.* A smart aleck.

smash (smăsh) *v.* **smashed, smash·ing, smash·es.** *—tr.* **1.** To break (something) into pieces suddenly, noisily, and violently; shatter. See Synonyms at **break. 2.a.** To throw or dash (something) violently so as to shatter or crush. See Synonyms at **crush. b.** To strike with a heavy blow; batter. **3.** *Sports.* To hit (a ball

smack[3]
Watercolor of the *Emma C. Berry* by John F. Leavitt

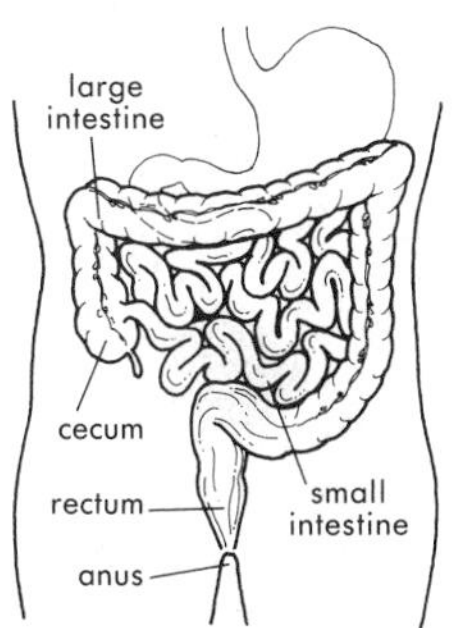

small intestine

ă **pat**	oi **boy**
ā **pay**	ou **out**
âr **care**	o͝o **took**
ä **father**	o͞o **boot**
ĕ **pet**	ŭ **cut**
ē **be**	ûr **urge**
ĭ **pit**	th **thin**
ī **pie**	*th* **this**
îr **pier**	hw **which**
ŏ **pot**	zh **vision**
ō **toe**	ə **about, item**
ô **paw**	♦ **regionalism**

Stress marks: ′ (primary); ′ (secondary), as in **dictionary** (dĭk′shə-nĕr′ē)

Joseph Smith

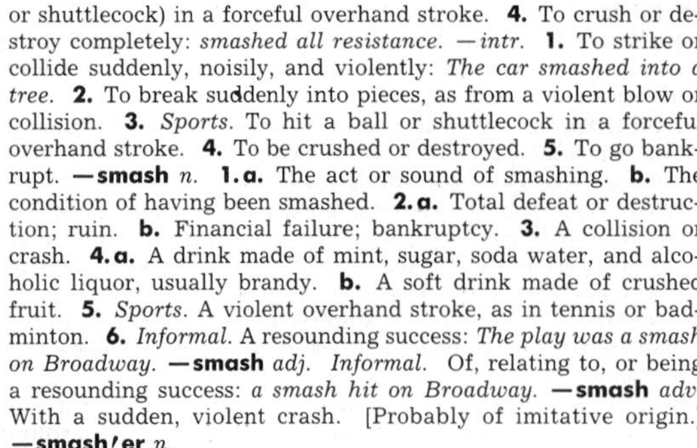

or shuttlecock) in a forceful overhand stroke. **4.** To crush or destroy completely: *smashed all resistance.* —*intr.* **1.** To strike or collide suddenly, noisily, and violently: *The car smashed into a tree.* **2.** To break suddenly into pieces, as from a violent blow or collision. **3.** *Sports.* To hit a ball or shuttlecock in a forceful overhand stroke. **4.** To be crushed or destroyed. **5.** To go bankrupt. **—smash** *n.* **1.a.** The act or sound of smashing. **b.** The condition of having been smashed. **2.a.** Total defeat or destruction; ruin. **b.** Financial failure; bankruptcy. **3.** A collision or crash. **4.a.** A drink made of mint, sugar, soda water, and alcoholic liquor, usually brandy. **b.** A soft drink made of crushed fruit. **5.** *Sports.* A violent overhand stroke, as in tennis or badminton. **6.** *Informal.* A resounding success: *The play was a smash on Broadway.* **—smash** *adj.* *Informal.* Of, relating to, or being a resounding success: *a smash hit on Broadway.* **—smash** *adv.* With a sudden, violent crash. [Probably of imitative origin.] **—smash′er** *n.*

smashed (smăsht) *adj.* *Slang.* Intoxicated; drunk.

smash·ing (smăsh′ĭng) *adj.* **1.** Serving to smash: *a smashing blow to the head.* **2.** *Informal.* Extraordinarily impressive or fine; wonderful: *a smashing success.* **—smash′ing·ly** *adv.*

smash·up (smăsh′ŭp′) *n.* **1.** A total collapse or defeat. **2.** A serious collision between vehicles; a wreck.

smat·ter (smăt′ər) *v.* **-tered, -ter·ing, -ters.** —*tr.* **1.** To speak (a language) without fluency: *smatters Russian.* **2.** To study or approach superficially; dabble in. —*intr.* To prattle: *smattered on about her vacation.* **—smatter** *n.* A smattering. [Middle English *smateren,* to make dirty, speak foolishly, chatter.] **—smat′ter·er** *n.*

smat·ter·ing (smăt′ər-ĭng) *n.* **1.** Superficial or piecemeal knowledge: *"a smattering of everything, and a knowledge of nothing"* (Charles Dickens). **2.** A small, scattered amount or number: *a smattering of raindrops.*

smaze (smāz) *n.* A relatively dry atmospheric mixture of smoke and haze. [SM(OKE) + (H)AZE [1].]

smear (smîr) *v.* **smeared, smear·ing, smears.** —*tr.* **1.a.** To spread or daub with a sticky, greasy, or dirty substance. **b.** To apply by spreading or daubing: *smeared suntan lotion on my face and arms.* **2.** To stain by or as if by spreading or daubing with a sticky, greasy, or dirty substance. **3.** To stain or attempt to destroy the reputation of; vilify: *political enemies who smeared his name.* **4.** *Slang.* To defeat utterly; smash. —*intr.* To be or become stained or dirtied. **—smear** *n.* **1.** A mark made by smearing; a spot or blot. **2.** A substance to be spread on a surface. **3.** *Biology.* A sample, as of blood or bacterial cells, spread on a slide for microscopic examination or on the surface of a culture medium. **4.** An attempt to destroy a reputation; vilification or slander. [Middle English *smeren,* to anoint, from Old English *smerian.*]

Kate Smith

♦**smear·case** (smîr′kās′) *n.* *Pennsylvania.* See **cottage cheese.** See Regional Note at **gum band.** [Pennsylvania Dutch *Schmierkees,* from German *Schmierkäse,* a kind of spreadable cheese : *schmieren,* to smear (from Middle High German *smirwen,* from Old High German) + *Käse,* cheese (from Middle High German *kaese,* from Old High German *kāsi,* from Latin *cāseus*).]

smear test *n.* See **Pap smear.**

smear word *n.* An abusive or disparaging word or phrase directed against a person or group.

smear·y (smîr′ē) *adj.* **-i·er, -i·est.** **1.** Having been smeared. **2.** Tending to smear or soil. **—smear′i·ness** *n.*

smeg·ma (smĕg′mə) *n.* A sebaceous secretion, especially the cheesy secretion that collects under the prepuce or around the clitoris. [Latin, detergent, from Greek *smēgma,* from *smēkhein,* to wash off.]

smell (smĕl) *v.* **smelled** or **smelt** (smĕlt), **smell·ing, smells.** —*tr.* **1.** To perceive the scent of (something) by means of the olfactory nerves. **2.** To sense the presence of by or as if by the olfactory nerves; detect or discover: *We smelled trouble ahead. The select committee was supposed to smell out corruption in law enforcement.* —*intr.* **1.** To use the sense of smell; perceive the scent of something. **2.** To have or emit an odor: *"The breeze smelled exactly like Vouvray—flowery, with a hint of mothballs underneath"* (Anne Tyler). **3.** To be suggestive; have a touch of something: *a cave that smells of terror.* **4.** To have or emit an unpleasant odor; stink: *This closet smells.* **5.** To appear to be dishonest; suggest evil or corruption. **—smell** *n.* **1.** The sense by which odors are perceived; the olfactory sense. **2.** That quality of something that may be perceived by the olfactory sense. **3.** The act or an instance of smelling. **4.** A distinctive enveloping or characterizing quality; an aura or a trace: *the smell of success.* ***—idiom.*** **smell a rat.** *Slang.* To suspect that something is wrong. [Middle English *smellen.*]

SYNONYMS: *smell, aroma, odor, scent.* The central meaning shared by these nouns is "a quality that can be perceived by the olfactory sense": *the smell of gas; the aroma of frying onions; hospital odors; the scent of pine needles.*

smell·ing salts (smĕl′ĭng) *pl.n.* *(used with a sing. or pl. verb).* Any of various preparations of ammonium carbonate and perfume, sniffed as a restorative or stimulant especially to relieve faintness and headache.

smell·y (smĕl′ē) *adj.* **-i·er, -i·est.** *Informal.* Having a noticeable, usually unpleasant or offensive odor.

smelt[1] (smĕlt) *v.* **smelt·ed, smelt·ing, smelts.** —*tr.* To melt or fuse (ores) in order to separate the metallic constituents. —*intr.* To melt or fuse. Used of ores. [Dutch or Low German *smelten,* from Middle Dutch or Middle Low German; see **mel-**[1] in Appendix.]

smelt[2] (smĕlt) *n., pl.* **smelts** or **smelt.** Any of various small silvery marine and freshwater food fishes of the family Osmeridae, found in cold waters of the Northern Hemisphere, especially *Osmerus mordax* of North America and *O. eperlanus* of Europe. [Middle English, from Old English. See **mel-**[1] in Appendix.]

smelt[3] (smĕlt) *v.* A past tense and a past participle of **smell.**

smelt·er (smĕl′tər) *n.* **1.a.** An apparatus for smelting. **b.** Also **smelt·er·y** (smĕl′tə-rē), *pl.* **-ies.** An establishment for smelting. **2.** One who is engaged in the smelting industry.

Sme·ta·na (smĕt′n-ə, smĕ′tä-nä), **Bedřich.** 1824–1884. Czechoslovakian composer whose works include the opera *The Bartered Bride* (1866) and the cycle of tone poems *My Country* (1879).

Smeth·wick (smĕth′ĭk). A borough of central England, an industrial suburb of Birmingham. Population, 309,900.

smew (smyo͞o) *n.* A small Old World merganser *(Mergus albellus),* the male of which has white and black plumage and a white crest. [Origin unknown.]

smid·gen also **smid·geon** or **smid·gin** (smĭj′ən) *n.* A very small quantity or portion; a bit or mite: *"a smidgen of genius, a sliver of cutting truth"* (John Simon). [Probably alteration of dialectal *smitch,* particle, perhaps ultimately from Middle English *smite,* perhaps from past participle of *smiten,* to smite. See SMITE.]

smi·lax (smī′lăks′) *n.* **1.** See **catbrier. 2.** A slender vine *(Asparagus asparagoides)* that has glossy foliage and is popular as a floral decoration. [Latin *smīlax,* bindweed, from Greek *smilax.*]

smile (smīl) *n.* **1.** A facial expression characterized by an upward curving of the corners of the mouth and indicating pleasure, amusement, or derision. **2.** A pleasant or favorable disposition or aspect. **—smile** *v.* **smiled, smil·ing, smiles.** —*intr.* **1.** To have or form a smile. **2.a.** To look with favor or approval: *Fortune smiled on our efforts.* **b.** To express cheerful acceptance or equanimity: *We smiled at the bad weather and kept going.* —*tr.* **1.** To express with a smile: *Grandmother smiled her consent.* **2.** To effect or accomplish with or as if with a smile. [From Middle English *smilen,* to smile, probably of Scandinavian origin. See **smei-** in Appendix.] **—smil′er** *n.* **—smil′ey, smil′y** *adj.* **—smil′ing·ly** *adv.* **—smil′ing·ness** *n.*

SYNONYMS: *smile, grin, simper, smirk.* These nouns denote facial expressions, as those indicating amusement, in which the mouth is curved upward slightly at the corners. *Smile* is the most general, since it can cover a wide range of feeling, from affection to malice: *"She met his eye with her sweet hospitable smile"* (Henry James). *"Tom saw a smile of contempt pass over the young curate's features"* (Henry Kingsley). A *grin* is a broad smile that exposes the teeth; often it is a spontaneous expression of mirth, good humor, approval, or triumph: *"And he owned with a grin,/ That his favorite sin/Is pride that apes humility"* (Robert Southey). A *simper* is a silly, self-conscious, often coy smile: *The model looked at her reflection in the mirror with an idiotic simper.* A *smirk* is an affected smile that often expresses an offensive smugness: *The old libertine looked with a knowing smirk at the beautiful young woman.*

smi·lo·don (smī′lə-dŏn′) *n.* Any of the large saber-toothed tigers of the genus *Smilodon,* widely distributed during the Pleistocene Epoch. [New Latin *smilodōn* : Greek *smilē,* knife + -ODON.]

smirch (smûrch) *tr.v.* **smirched, smirch·ing, smirch·es.** **1.** To soil, stain, or dirty with or as if with a smearing agent: *"their tough, hostile faces, smirched by the grime and rust"* (Henry Roth). **2.** To dishonor; defame. **—smirch** *n.* Something, such as a blot, smear, or stain, that smirches. [Middle English *smorchen.*]

smirk (smûrk) *intr.v.* **smirked, smirk·ing, smirks.** To smile in an affected, often offensively self-satisfied manner. **—smirk** *n.* An affected, often offensively self-satisfied smile. See Synonyms at **smile.** [Middle English *smirken,* from Old English *smercian,* to smile. See **smei-** in Appendix.] **—smirk′er** *n.* **—smirk′ing·ly, smirk′i·ly** *adv.* **—smirk′y** *adj.*

smite (smīt) *v.* **smote** (smōt), **smit·ten** (smĭt′n) or **smote, smit·ing, smites.** —*tr.* **1.a.** To inflict a heavy blow on, with or as if with the hand, a tool, or a weapon. **b.** To drive or strike (a weapon, for example) forcefully onto or into something else. **2.** To attack, damage, or destroy by or as if by blows. **3.a.** To afflict: *The population was smitten by the plague.* **b.** To afflict retributively; chasten or chastise. **4.** To affect sharply with great feeling: *He was smitten by deep remorse.* —*intr.* To deal a blow with or as if with the hand or a hand-held weapon. [Middle English *smiten,* from Old English *smītan,* to smear.] **—smit′er** *n.*

smith (smĭth) *n.* **1.** A metalworker, especially one who works metal when it is hot and malleable. Often used in combination: *a silversmith; a goldsmith.* **2.** A blacksmith. **3.** One who makes or works at something specified. Often used in combination: *a locksmith; a wordsmith.* [Middle English, from Old English.]

Smith (smĭth), **Adam.** 1723–1790. Scottish political economist and philosopher. His *Wealth of Nations* (1776) laid the foundations of classical free-market economic theory.

Smith, Alfred Emanuel. Known as "the Happy Warrior." 1873–1944. American politician. He served as governor of New York

(1919–1920 and 1923–1928) and was defeated in the 1928 presidential election by Herbert Hoover.

Smith, Bessie. 1894?–1937. American singer who became a leading jazz and blues singer in the 1920's and recorded with musicians such as Louis Armstrong and Benny Goodman.

Smith, Hannah Whitall. 1832–1911. American evangelist, writer, and reformer who was a founder of the Woman's Christian Temperance Union (1874).

Smith, Ian. Born 1919. Zimbabwean politician who unilaterally declared independence from Great Britain for the former colony of Rhodesia in 1965.

Smith, John. 1580?–1631. English colonist, explorer, and writer whose maps and accounts of his explorations in Virginia and New England were invaluable to later explorers and colonists.

Smith, Joseph. 1805–1844. American religious leader. He founded (1830) the Church of Jesus Christ of Latter-day Saints and led his congregation westward from New York State to western Illinois, where he was murdered by an anti-Mormon mob.

Smith, Julia Evelina. 1792–1886. American suffragist. With her sister **Abby Hadassah Smith** (1797–1878) she became famous for refusing to pay taxes until she could vote.

Smith, Kathryn Elizabeth. Known as "Kate." 1909–1986. American singer noted especially for her rendition of Irving Berlin's "God Bless America," first performed in 1938.

Smith, Margaret Chase. Born 1897. American politician who served as a U.S. representative (1940–1949) and senator (1949–1973) from Maine.

Smith, Sydney. 1771–1845. British religious leader and writer known for his witty polemics, especially his defense of the political emancipation of Catholics in England.

smith·er·eens (smĭth′ə-rēnz′) *pl.n. Informal.* Fragments or splintered pieces; bits: *The dish broke into smithereens.* [From Irish Gaelic *smidirīn*, diminutive of *smiodar*, small fragment.]

smith·er·y (smĭth′ə-rē) *n., pl.* **-ies. 1.** The occupation or craft of a smith. **2.** See **smithy.**

Smith·son (smĭth′sən), **James.** 1765–1829. British chemist, mineralogist, and philanthropist. His gift to the United States helped establish (1846) the Smithsonian Institution.

smith·son·ite (smĭth′sə-nīt′) *n.* A mineral, $ZnCO_3$, sometimes used as a source of zinc. [After James SMITHSON.]

Smith·town (smĭth′toun′). A community of southeast New York on northern Long Island north of Islip. It is mainly residential. Population, 23,000.

smith·y (smĭth′ē, smĭth′ē) *n., pl.* **-ies.** A blacksmith's shop; a forge. Also called *smithery.* [Middle English, from Old Norse *smidhja.*]

smit·ten (smĭt′n) *v.* A past participle of **smite.**

SMN *abbr.* Seaman.

smock (smŏk) *n.* A loose coatlike outer garment, often worn to protect the clothes while working. **—smock** *tr.v.* **smocked, smock·ing, smocks. 1.** To clothe in a smock. **2.** To decorate (fabric) with smocking. [Middle English, woman's undergarment, from Old English *smoc.*]

smock·ing (smŏk′ĭng) *n.* Needlework decoration of small, regularly spaced gathers stitched into a honeycomb pattern.

smog (smŏg, smôg) *n.* **1.** Fog that has become mixed and polluted with smoke. **2.** A form of air pollution produced when sunlight causes hydrocarbons and nitrogen oxides from automotive emissions to combine in a photochemical reaction. [SM(OKE) + (F)OG[1].] **—smog′gy** *adj.* **—smog′less** *adj.*

WORD HISTORY: Smog is so much a part of modern, industrialized life that it is difficult to realize that at one time neither smog nor the word for it existed. The word, of course, followed the phenomenon perhaps by half a century, for air pollution was noticed during the Industrial Revolution. The word *smog* is first recorded in 1905 in a newspaper report of a meeting of the Public Health Congress. Dr. H.A. des Vœux gave a paper entitled "Fog and Smoke," in which, in the words of the *Daily Graphic* of July 26, "he said it required no science to see that there was something produced in great cities which was not found in the country, and that was smoky fog, or what was known as 'smog.' " The next day the *Globe* remarked that "Dr. des Vœux did a public service in coining a new word for the London fog." Since Dr. des Vœux's creation of this blend, much more has been learned about the composition of smog; unfortunately, it is still with us.

smoke (smōk) *n.* **1.** The vaporous system made up of small particles of carbonaceous matter in the air, resulting mainly from the burning of organic material, such as wood or coal. **2.** A suspension of fine solid or liquid particles in a gaseous medium. **3.** A cloud of fine particles. **4.** Something insubstantial, unreal, or transitory. **5.a.** The act of smoking a form of tobacco: *went out for a smoke.* **b.** The duration of this act. **6.** *Informal.* Tobacco in a form that can be smoked, especially a cigarette: *money to buy smokes.* **7.** A substance used in warfare to produce a smoke screen. **8.** Something used to conceal or obscure. **9.** *Color.* A pale to grayish blue to bluish or dark gray. **—smoke** *v.* **smoked, smok·ing, smokes.** —*intr.* **1.a.** To draw in and exhale smoke from a cigarette, cigar, or pipe: *It's forbidden to smoke here.* **b.** To engage in smoking regularly or habitually: *He smoked for years before stopping.* **2.** To emit smoke or a smokelike substance: *chimneys smoking in the cold air.* **3.** To emit smoke excessively: *The station wagon smoked even after the tune-up.* **4.** *Slang.* **a.** To go or proceed at high speed. **b.** To play or perform energetically: *The band was really smoking in the second set.* —*tr.* **1.a.** To draw in and exhale the smoke of (tobacco, for example): *I've never smoked a panatela.* **b.** To do so regularly or habitually: *I used to smoke filtered cigarettes.* **2.** To preserve (meat or fish) by exposure to the aromatic smoke of burning hardwood, usually after pickling in salt or brine. **3.a.** To fumigate (a house, for example). **b.** To expose (animals, especially insects) to smoke in order to immobilize or drive away. **4.** To expose (glass) to smoke in order to darken or change its color. **5.** *Slang.* To kill; murder. ***—phrasal verb.* smoke out. 1.** To force out of a place of hiding or concealment by or as if by the use of smoke. **2.** To detect and bring to public view; expose or reveal: *smoke out a scandal.* [Middle English, from Old English *smoca.*] **—smok′a·ble, smoke′a·ble** *adj.*

smoke bomb *n.* A bomb designed to give out thick smoke upon exploding, used especially to mark a target or to create a smoke screen.

smoke detector *n.* An alarm device that automatically detects the presence of smoke.

smoke-filled room (smōk′fĭld′) *n.* **1.** A room filled with smoke, especially tobacco smoke. **2.** A place, especially a hotel room near a political or business convention, where a group of influential people gather to negotiate or make deals in private: *Many party members were tired of having nominations decided in smoke-filled rooms.*

smoke·house (smōk′hous′) *n.* A structure in which meat or fish is cured with smoke.

smoke·jump·er (smōk′jŭm′pər) *n.* A firefighter who drops by parachute into a forest fire.

smoke·less (smōk′lĭs) *adj.* **1.** Emitting or containing little or no smoke: *smokeless factory stacks.* **2.** Free from the use of smoking tobacco or from the smoke generated by such use: *a smokeless society; a smokeless office setting.*

smokeless powder *n.* A relatively smoke-free propellant charge composed mainly of nitrocellulose, used in projectiles and small artillery rockets.

smokeless tobacco *n.* **1.** Tobacco cut for chewing. **2.** See **snuff[3]** (sense 1a).

smok·er (smō′kər) *n.* **1.** One who smokes tobacco. **2.** A device, such as a stove, that emits smoke. **3.** A smoking car. **4.** An informal social gathering for men.

smok·er's cough (smō′kərz) *n.* A rough, dry cough caused by excessive smoking of tobacco.

smoke screen or **smoke·screen** (smōk′skrēn′) *n.* **1.** A mass of dense artificial smoke used to conceal military areas or operations from an enemy. **2.** An action or a statement used to conceal actual plans or intentions.

smoke·stack (smōk′stăk′) *n.* A large chimney or vertical pipe through which combustion vapors, gases, and smoke are discharged. **—smokestack** *adj.* Of, relating to, or being firms, industries, or places involved in heavy manufacturing or in the processing of materials: *smokestack industries such as steel and iron.*

smoke tree *n.* Either of two deciduous plants, *Cotinus obovatus,* a tree of the southern United States, or *C. coggygria,* a shrub of Eurasia, having plumelike clusters of small yellowish flowers. [From the resemblance of the flower clusters to puffs of smoke.]

Smok·ey (smō′kē) *n. Slang.* A law-enforcement officer on highway patrol. [From the resemblance of some state troopers' hats to that of *Smokey* the Bear, an animal who formerly warned against fires in U.S. Forest Service posters.]

smok·ing (smō′kĭng) *adj.* **1.** Engaging in the smoking of tobacco: *smoking passengers.* **2.** Designated or reserved for smokers: *the smoking section of a restaurant.* **3.** Of or relating to the use of tobacco: *corporate smoking policies.*

smoking car *n.* A railroad car in which smoking is allowed; a smoker.

smoking gun *n. Informal.* Something that serves as indisputable evidence or proof, especially of a crime: *"There is no smoking gun or paper trail to* [the CIA]*"* (Thomas Polgar).

smoking jacket *n.* A man's evening jacket, often made of a fine fabric, elaborately trimmed, and usually worn at home.

smoking room *n.* A room, as in a hotel or private club, set aside for smokers.

smok·ing-room (smō′kĭng-ro͞om′, -ro͝om′) *adj.* Marked by indecency; obscene: *smoking-room humor.*

smok·y (smō′kē) *adj.* **-i·er, -i·est. 1.** Emitting smoke in profuse volume: *a smoky stove.* **2.** Mixed or filled with smoke: *smoky corridors.* **3.** Resembling smoke: *a smoky haze.* **4.** Discolored or soiled with or as if with smoke: *"The smoky Sicilian afternoon sun tinged the green landscape with red"* (Mario Puzo). **5.** Tasting of smoke: *smoky sausages.* **—smok′i·ly** *adv.* **—smok′i·ness** *n.*

Smok·y Hill River (smō′kē). A river rising in eastern Colorado and flowing about 901 km (560 mi) eastward across central Kansas to join the Republican River and form the Kansas River.

smoky quartz *n.* A transparent or semitransparent brown or gray to nearly black variety of quartz, used as a gemstone. Also called *cairngorm.*

Smoky River. A river, about 402 km (250 mi) long, of west-central Alberta, Canada, flowing northward to the Peace River.

Margaret Chase Smith
Photographed in 1954

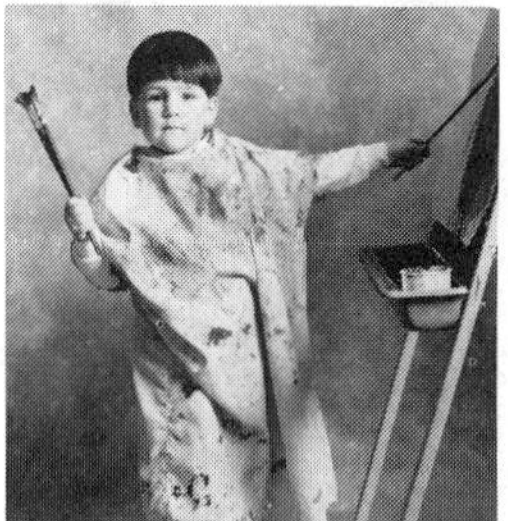

smock

smokestack

ă pat	oi boy
ā pay	ou out
âr care	o͝o took
ä father	o͞o boot
ĕ pet	ŭ cut
ē be	ûr urge
ĭ pit	th thin
ī pie	*th* this
îr pier	hw which
ŏ pot	zh vision
ō toe	ə about, item
ô paw	♦ regionalism

Stress marks: **′** (primary); ′ (secondary), as in **dictionary** (dĭk′shə-nĕr′ē)

snaffle

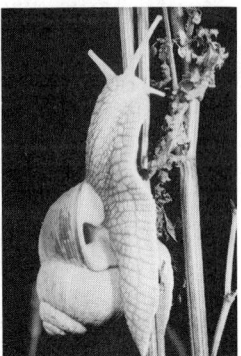

snail

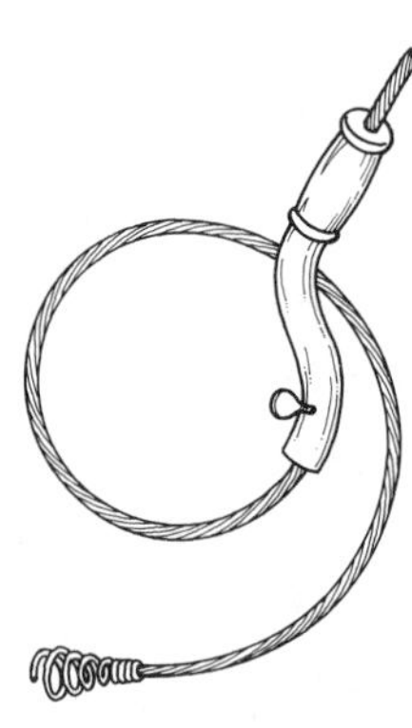

snake
Plumber's snake

smol·der also **smoul·der** (smōl′dər) —*intr.v.* **-dered, -der·ing, -ders. 1.** To burn with little smoke and no flame. **2.** To exist in a suppressed state: *Revolution smoldered in the masses.* **3.** To show signs of repressed anger or hatred. —*n.* Thick smoke resulting from a slow fire. [Middle English *smolderen,* to suffocate, from *smolder,* smoke, probably alteration of *smorther,* from Old English *smorian,* to smoke.]

Smo·lensk (smō-lĕnsk′, smə-). A city of western Russia on the Dnieper River west-southwest of Moscow. First mentioned in the ninth century, it was burned by Napoleon's troops in 1812. Population, 331,000.

Smol·lett (smŏl′ĭt), **Tobias George.** 1721–1771. British writer known for his adventure novels, such as *Roderick Random* (1748) and *Peregrine Pickle* (1751).

smolt (smōlt) *n.* A young salmon at the stage intermediate between the parr and the grilse, when it becomes covered with silvery scales and first migrates from fresh water to the sea. [Middle English, from Medieval Latin *smoltus,* probably of Old English origin.]

smooch (smo͞och) *Slang. n.* A kiss. —**smooch** *intr.v.* **smooched, smooch·ing, smooch·es.** To kiss. [Alteration of English dialectal *smouch,* perhaps imitative of the sound of a kiss.]

smooth (smo͞o*th*) *adj.* **smooth·er, smooth·est. 1.** Having a surface free from irregularities, roughness, or projections; even. See Synonyms at **level. 2.** Having a fine texture: *a smooth fabric.* **3.** Having an even consistency: *a smooth pudding.* **4.** Having an even or gentle motion or movement: *a smooth ride.* **5.** Having no obstructions or difficulties: *a smooth operation.* See Synonyms at **easy. 6.** Serene: *a smooth temperament.* **7.** Bland: *a smooth wine.* **8.** Ingratiatingly polite and agreeable. See Synonyms at **suave. 9.** Having no grossness or coarseness in dress or manner. —**smooth** *v.* **smoothed, smooth·ing, smoothes.** —*tr.* **1.** To make (something) even, level, or unwrinkled. **2.** To rid of obstructions, hindrances, or difficulties. **3.** To soothe or tranquilize; make calm. **4.** To make less harsh or crude; refine. —*intr.* To become smooth. —**smooth** *n.* **1.** The act of smoothing. **2.** A smooth surface. [Middle English *smothe,* from Old English *smōth.*] —**smooth′er** *n.* —**smooth′ly** *adv.* —**smooth′ness** *n.*

smooth·bore also **smooth bore** (smo͞o*th*′bôr′, -bōr′) —*adj.* Having no rifling within the barrel. Used of a firearm. —*n.* A firearm having no rifling.

smooth breathing *n.* **1.** The symbol (') written over some initial vowels and diphthongs in ancient Greek to indicate that a word does not begin with the sound (h). **2.** In ancient Greek, an initial vowel or diphthong not preceded by the sound (h).

smooth collie *n.* A collie similar to the rough collie but having a short, dense, flat coat.

smooth dogfish *n.* Any of several dogfishes lacking a spine in front of the dorsal fin, especially a species *(Mustelus canis)* found abundantly on the American Atlantic coast and often used in classrooms for dissection and study.

smooth·en (smo͞o′*th*ən) *tr. & intr.v.* **-ened, -en·ing, -ens.** To make or become smooth.

smooth fox terrier *n.* A small fox terrier of a breed developed in England, having a smooth white coat with patches of black or tan.

smooth hound *n.* Any dogfish of the genus *Mustelus,* especially a smooth dogfish *(M. mustelus)* of southern Europe, found occasionally in American Atlantic waters.

smooth·ie also **smooth·y** (smo͞o′*th*ē) *n., pl.* **-ies.** *Slang.* **1.** A person regarded as being assured and artfully ingratiating in manner. **2.** A smooth-tongued person.

smooth muscle *n.* Muscle tissue that contracts without conscious control, having the form of thin layers or sheets made up of spindle-shaped, unstriated cells with single nuclei and found in the walls of the internal organs, such as the stomach, intestine, bladder, and blood vessels, excluding the heart.

smooth-tongued (smo͞o*th*′tŭngd′) *adj.* Speaking or spoken in an artfully suave manner; ingratiating. See Synonyms at **glib.**

smooth·y (smo͞o′*th*ē) *n. Slang.* Variant of **smoothie.**

smor·gas·bord (smôr′gəs-bôrd′, -bōrd′) *n.* **1.** A buffet meal featuring a varied number of dishes. **2.** A varied collection: *"a smorgasbord of fashionable paranormal beliefs"* (Martin Gardner). [Swedish *smörgåsbord* : *smörgås,* bread and butter (*smör,* butter, from Old Norse + Swedish dialectal *gås,* lump of butter, from Old Norse *gās,* goose; see GOSLING) + *bord,* table (from Old Norse *bordh*).]

smote (smōt) *v.* Past tense and a past participle of **smite.**

smoth·er (smŭ*th*′ər) *v.* **-ered, -er·ing, -ers.** —*tr.* **1.a.** To suffocate (another). **b.** To deprive (a fire) of the oxygen necessary for combustion. **2.** To conceal, suppress, or hide: *Management smothered the true facts of the case. We smothered our indignation and pressed onward.* **3.** To cover (a foodstuff) thickly with another foodstuff: *smother chicken in sauce.* **4.** To lavish a surfeit of a given emotion on (someone): *The grandparents smothered the child with affection.* —*intr.* **1.a.** To suffocate. **b.** To be extinguished. **2.** To be concealed or suppressed. **3.** To be surfeited with an emotion. —**smother** *n.* Something, such as a dense cloud of smoke or dust, that smothers or tends to smother. [Middle English *smotheren,* from *smorther,* dense smoke. See SMOLDER.]

♦**smoth·er·y** (smŭ*th*′ə-rē) *adj. Upper Southern U.S.* Confined. Used of a place: *"Other places do seem so cramped up and smothery, but a raft don't"* (Mark Twain).

smoul·der (smōl′dər) *v. & n.* Variant of **smolder.**

SMSA *abbr.* Standard metropolitan statistical area.

S.M.Sgt. or **SMSGT** *abbr.* Senior master sergeant.

smudge (smŭj) *v.* **smudged, smudg·ing, smudg·es.** —*tr.* **1.** To make dirty, especially in one small area. **2.** To smear or blur (something). **3.** To fill (an orchard or another planted area) with dense smoke from a smudge pot in order to prevent damage from insects or frost. —*intr.* **1.** To smear something as with dirt, soot, or ink. **2.** To become smudged: *Photo negatives smudge easily.* —**smudge** *n.* **1.** A blotch or smear. **2.** A smoky fire used as a protection against insects or frost. [Middle English *smogen.*] —**smudg′i·ly** *adv.* —**smudg′i·ness** *n.* —**smudg′y** *adj.*

smudge pot *n.* A receptacle in which oil or another smoky fuel is burned to protect an orchard from insects or frost.

smug (smŭg) *adj.* **smug·ger, smug·gest.** Exhibiting or feeling great or offensive satisfaction with oneself or with one's situation; self-righteously complacent: *"the smug look of a toad breakfasting on fat marsh flies"* (William Pearson). [Perhaps akin to Low German *smuck,* neat, from Middle Low German, from *smucken,* to adorn.] —**smug′ly** *adv.* —**smug′ness** *n.*

smug·gle (smŭg′əl) *v.* **-gled, -gling, -gles.** —*tr.* **1.** To import or export without paying lawful customs charges or duties. **2.** To bring in or take out illicitly or by stealth. —*intr.* To engage in smuggling. [Probably Low German *smukkeln, smuggeln,* or Middle Dutch *smokkelen.*] —**smug′gler** *n.*

smut (smŭt) *n.* **1.a.** A particle of dirt. **b.** A smudge made by soot, smoke, or dirt. **2.a.** Obscenity in speech or writing. **b.** Pornography. **3.a.** Any of various plant diseases, especially of cereal grasses, caused by parasitic fungi of the order Ustilaginales that form black, powdery masses of spores on the affected parts. **b.** A fungus causing such a disease. —**smut** *v.* **smut·ted, smut·ting, smuts.** —*tr.* **1.** To blacken or smudge, as with smoke or grime. **2.** To affect (a plant) with smut. **3.** To free (grain, for example) from smut. **4.** To make obscene. —*intr.* **1.** To emit smut. **2.** To be or become blackened or smudged. **3.** To become affected with smut, as a plant. [From Middle English *smotten, smutten,* to defile.] —**smut′ti·ly** *adv.* —**smut′ti·ness** *n.* —**smut′ty** *adj.*

smutch (smŭch) *tr.v.* **smutched, smutch·ing, smutch·es.** To soil or stain. —**smutch** *n.* A stain or spot of dirt. [Perhaps alteration of SMUDGE.] —**smutch′y** *adj.*

Smuts (smŭts, smœts), **Jan Christiaan.** 1870–1950. South African soldier and politician. He was a Boer commander in the South African War (1899–1902) and prime minister of the Union of South Africa (1919–1924 and 1939–1948).

SMV *abbr.* Slow-moving vehicle.

Smyr·na (smûr′nə). **1.** A city of northwest Georgia, a residential suburb of Atlanta. Population, 20,312. **2.** See **Izmir.**

Sn The symbol for the element **tin** (sense 1). [From Late Latin *stannum,* tin. See STANNIC.]

s.n. *abbr. Latin.* Sine nomine (without name).

snack (snăk) *n.* **1.** A hurried or light meal. **2.** Food eaten between meals. —**snack** *intr.v.* **snacked, snack·ing, snacks.** To eat a snack. [Middle English *snak,* variant of *snacche,* trap, bite, from *snacchen,* to snap. See SNATCH.] —**snack′er** *n.*

snack bar *n.* A lunch counter or small restaurant where light meals are served.

snaf·fle (snăf′əl) *n.* A bit for a horse, consisting of two bars jointed at the center. —**snaffle** *tr.v.* **-fled, -fling, -fles.** To put on or control with a snaffle. [Origin unknown.]

sna·fu (snă-fo͞o′) *Slang. n., pl.* **-fus.** A chaotic or confused situation. —**snafu** *adj.* In a state of confusion or chaos. —**snafu** *tr.v.* **-fued, -fu·ing, -fus.** To make confused or chaotic. [*s(ituation) n(ormal), a(ll) f(ucked) u(p).*]

♦**snag** (snăg) *n.* **1.** A rough, sharp, or jagged protuberance, as: **a.** A tree or a part of a tree that protrudes above the surface in a body of water. Also called *sawyer.* See Regional Note at **preacher. b.** A snaggletooth. **2.** A break, pull, or tear in fabric. **3.** An unforeseen or hidden obstacle. See Synonyms at **obstacle. 4.** A short or imperfectly developed branch of a deer's antler. —**snag** *v.* **snagged, snag·ging, snags.** —*tr.* **1.** To tear, break, hinder, or destroy by or as if by a snag: *snagged a stocking on a splinter.* **2.** *Informal.* To catch unexpectedly and quickly: *snagged a bargain.* **3.** To free of snags: *snagged the river.* **4.** *Missouri.* To catch (fish): *"We violate all speed limits . . . to catch the opening of the annual paddlefish snagging season"* (John Hoey). —*intr.* To be damaged by a snag: *His sweater snagged on a tree branch.* [Of Scandinavian origin.] —**snag′gy** *adj.*

snag·gle·tooth (snăg′əl-to͞oth′) *n.* A tooth that is broken or not in alignment with the others. [From SNAG + TOOTH.] —**snag′gle·toothed′** *adj.*

snail (snāl) *n.* **1.** Any of numerous aquatic or terrestrial mollusks of the class Gastropoda, typically having a spirally coiled shell, broad retractile foot, and distinct head. **2.** A slow-moving, lazy, or sluggish person. [Middle English, from Old English *snægl.*]

snail bore *n.* A gastropod mollusk *(Urosalpinx cinerea)* that injures oysters by boring into their shells.

snail darter *n.* A small snail-eating darter *(Percina tanasi)* that formerly was found only in the Little Tennessee River. It was thought to have become extinct after construction of a dam, but later was discovered in several other Tennessee streams.

snail fever *n.* See **schistosomiasis.**

snail kite *n.* A kite *(Rostrhamus sociabilis)* of the warm parts of North and South America that usually travels in small flocks preying on snails.

snail-paced (snāl′pāst′) *adj.* Moving with extreme slowness.

snake (snāk) *n.* **1.** Any of numerous scaly, legless, sometimes venomous reptiles of the suborder Serpentes or Ophidia (order Squamata), having a long, tapering, cylindrical body and found in most tropical and temperate regions. **2.** A treacherous person. Also called *snake in the grass.* **3.** A long, highly flexible metal wire or coil used for cleaning drains. Also called *plumber's snake.* **4.** *Economics.* A fixing of the value of currencies to each other within defined parameters, which when graphed visually shows these currencies remaining parallel in value to each other as a unit despite fluctuations with other currencies. **—snake** *v.* **snaked, snak·ing, snakes.** *—tr.* **1.** To drag or pull lengthwise, especially to drag with a rope or chain. **2.** To pull with quick jerks. **3.** To move in a sinuous or gliding manner: *tried to snake the rope along the ledge.* *—intr.* To move with a sinuous motion: *The river snakes through the valley.* [Middle English, from Old English *snaca.*]

Snake¹ (snāk) *n., pl.* **Snake** or **Snakes.** See **Shoshone** (sense 1a).

Snake² (snāk) *n.* See **Hydra** (sense 2).

snake·bird (snāk′bûrd′) *n.* See **anhinga.**

snake·bite (snāk′bīt′) *n.* **1.** The bite of a snake. **2.** Poisoning resulting from the bite of a venomous snake.

snake charmer *n.* One who uses rhythmic music and body movements to control snakes.

snake dance *n.* **1.** A ceremonial dance of the Hopi in which the dancers traditionally carry live snakes in their mouths. **2.** A procession of people who join hands and move forward in a zigzag line.

♦ **snake doctor** *n.* **1.** *Chiefly Southern U.S.* See **dragonfly.** See Regional Note at **dragonfly.** **2.** See **hellgrammite.**

snake eggplant *n.* A variety of eggplant having long, slender fruits that are curled at one end.

snake eyes *pl.n. (used with a sing. verb). Games.* A throw of two dice that turns up one spot on each.

♦ **snake feeder** *n.* *Midland U.S.* See **dragonfly.** See Regional Note at **dragonfly.**

snake fence *n.* See **worm fence.**

snake·fish (snāk′fĭsh′) *n., pl.* **snakefish** or **-fish·es.** Any of several fishes having some resemblance to a snake, especially the lizardfish *Trachinocephalus myops* of the eastern Atlantic and western Pacific.

snake·head (snāk′hĕd′) *n.* *Botany.* See **turtlehead.**

snake in the grass *n., pl.* **snakes in the grass.** See **snake** (sense 2).

snake·mouth (snāk′mouth′) *n.* A North American orchid *(Pogonia ophioglossoides)* having a solitary rose-purple flower with a fringed lip.

snake oil *n.* **1.** A worthless preparation fraudulently peddled as a cure for many ills. **2.** Speech or writing intended to deceive; humbug.

snake pit *n.* *Slang.* **1.** A place of disorder and chaos. **2.** A mental health facility.

snake plant *n.* A stemless plant *(Sansevieria trifasciata)* having narrow, rigid, often mottled leaves and widely cultivated as a houseplant.

Snake River. A river of the northwest United States rising in northwest Wyoming and flowing about 1,670 km (1,038 mi) through southern Idaho, along the Oregon-Idaho and Idaho-Washington borders, and through southeast Washington to the Columbia River. Discovered in 1805 by the Lewis and Clark expedition, the river has spectacular deep gorges and is an important source of hydroelectric power.

snake·root (snāk′ro͞ot′, -ro͝ot′) *n.* Any of various plants, such as black cohosh, rattlesnake master, sanicle, or wild ginger, having roots reputed to cure snakebite.

snake·skin (snāk′skĭn′) *n.* The skin of a snake, especially when prepared as leather.

snake·stone (snāk′stōn′) *n.* **1.** A small stone or piece of porous substance reputed to cure snakebite. **2.** See **whetstone.**

snake·weed (snāk′wēd′) *n.* Any of various plants, such as bistort, reputed to have the power to cure snakebite.

snak·y (snā′kē) *adj.* **-i·er, -i·est.** **1.** Relating to or characteristic of snakes. **2.** Having the form or movement of a snake; serpentine. **3.** Overrun with snakes. **4.** Treacherous; sly. **—snak′i·ly** *adv.* **—snak′i·ness** *n.*

snap (snăp) *v.* **snapped, snap·ping, snaps.** *—intr.* **1.** To make a brisk, sharp cracking sound: *"Logs snapped in the grate"* (James Fox). **2.** To break suddenly with a brisk, sharp, cracking sound. **3.a.** To give way abruptly under pressure or tension: *With so many people crowding onto the platform, its supports snapped.* **b.** To suffer a physical or mental breakdown, especially while under stress: *feared that the troops would snap from constant fatigue.* **4.** To bring the jaws briskly together, often with a clicking sound; bite. **5.** To snatch or grasp suddenly and with eagerness: *snap at a chance to go to China.* **6.** To speak abruptly or sharply: *snapped at the child.* **7.** To move swiftly and smartly: *snap to attention.* See Synonyms at **jerk¹.** **8.** To flash or appear to flash light; sparkle: *eyes that snapped with anger.* **9.** To open, close, or fit together with a click: *The lock snapped shut. The jacket snaps in front.* *—tr.* **1.** To snatch at with or as if with the teeth; bite. **2.** To pull apart or break with a snapping sound. **3.** To utter abruptly or sharply: *The sergeant snapped out a command.* **4.a.** To cause to emit a snapping sound: *snap a whip.* **b.** To close or latch with a snapping sound: *snapped the purse shut.* **5.** To cause to move abruptly and smartly: *"His head was snapped back by a sudden scream from the bed"* (James Michener). **6.a.** To take (a photograph). **b.** To photograph: *snapped the governor as she was getting into her car.* **7.** *Football.* To center (a football); hike. **—snap** *n.* **1.** A sudden, sharp cracking sound or the action producing such a sound. **2.** A sudden breaking. **3.** A clasp, catch, or other fastening device that operates with a snapping sound. **4.** A sudden attempt to bite, snatch, or grasp. **5.a.** The sound produced by rapid movement of a finger from the thumb tip to the base of the thumb. **b.** The act of producing this sound. **6.** The sudden release of something held under pressure or tension. **7.** A thin, crisp, usually circular cookie: *a ginger snap.* **8.a.** Capacity to make a snapping sound; elasticity: *This waistband has lost its snap.* **b.** *Informal.* Briskness, liveliness, or energy. **9.** A brief spell of brisk, cold weather. **10.** Something accomplished without effort. See Synonyms at **breeze¹.** **11.a.** A snapshot. **b.** The taking of a snapshot. **12.** A snap bean. **13.** *Football.* The passing of a football from the center to a back that initiates each play. Also called *hike.* **—snap** *adj.* **1.** Made or done suddenly, with little or no preparation: *a snap decision.* **2.** Fastening with a snap: *snap pockets.* **3.** *Informal.* Simple; easy: *a snap assignment.* **—snap** *adv.* With a snap. ***—phrasal verbs.*** **snap back.** To recover quickly. **snap up.** To acquire quickly: *snapped up the introductory offer.* ***—idiom.*** **snap out of it.** *Informal.* To move quickly back to one's normal condition from an undesirable condition, such as depression, grief, or self-pity. [Probably from Middle English *snappe,* a quick bite, probably from Middle Low German or Middle Dutch *snappen,* to seize, snap.]

snake charmer

snapdragon

snap bean *n.* A string bean cultivated for its crisp, edible pods.

snap-brim (snăp′brĭm′) *n.* A hat having a flexible brim, usually turned down in front and up at the back.

snap·drag·on (snăp′drăg′ən) *n.* Any of several plants of the genus *Antirrhinum,* especially the widely cultivated Mediterranean herb *A. majus,* having showy racemes of two-lipped, variously colored flowers. [From the imagined resemblance of the flowers to the mouth of a dragon.]

snap·per (snăp′ər) *n.* **1.** One that snaps. **2.** *pl.* **snapper** or **-pers.** Any of numerous widely distributed marine fishes of the family Lutjanidae (or Lutianidae), many of which are prized as food fishes, that are found chiefly in warm coastal waters of the Pacific and Atlantic. **3.** A snapping turtle. **4.** See **schnapper.**

snap·ping beetle (snăp′ĭng) *n.* See **click beetle.**

snapping turtle *n.* Any of several large freshwater turtles of the family Chelydridae of North, Central, and northern South America, having a rough shell and powerful hooked jaws that close with a snap, especially the common North American species *Chelydra serpentina* and the alligator snapping turtle of the south-central United States.

snap·pish (snăp′ĭsh) *adj.* **1.** Likely to snap or bite: *a snappish mongrel.* **2.** Irritable and curt: *a snappish tone of voice.* **—snap′pish·ly** *adv.* **—snap′pish·ness** *n.*

snap·py (snăp′ē) *adj.* **-pi·er, -pi·est.** **1.** *Informal.* Lively or energetic; brisk. **2.** *Informal.* Smart or chic. **3.** Snappish: *a snappy retort.* **—snap′pi·ly** *adv.* **—snap′pi·ness** *n.*

snap roll *n.* An aerial maneuver in which an aircraft is put through a sharp roll of 360° about its longitudinal axis.

snap·shoot (snăp′sho͞ot′) *tr.v.* **-shot** (-shŏt′), **-shoot·ing, -shoots.** To take a snapshot of. **—snap′shoot′er** *n.*

snap·shot (snăp′shŏt′) *n.* **1.** A photograph taken with a small hand-held camera. **2.** An isolated observation: *a sociopolitical snapshot of the electorate.*

snare¹ (snâr) *n.* **1.** A trapping device, often consisting of a noose, used for capturing birds and small mammals. **2.** Something that serves to entangle the unwary. **3.** A surgical instrument with a wire loop controlled by a mechanism in the handle, used to remove growths, such as tumors and polyps. **—snare** *tr.v.* **snared, snar·ing, snares.** To trap with or as if with a snare. See Synonyms at **catch.** [Middle English, from Old English *snearu* and from Old Norse *snara.*] **—snar′er** *n.*

snare² (snâr) *n.* *Music.* **1.** Any of the wires or cords stretched across the lower skin of a snare drum to increase reverberation. **2.** A snare drum. [Probably from Dutch *snaar,* string, from Middle Dutch *snāre.*]

snare drum *n.* *Music.* A small double-headed drum having one or more wires or cords stretched across the bottom head to increase reverberation. Also called *side drum.*

snarl¹ (snärl) *v.* **snarled, snarl·ing, snarls.** *—intr.* **1.** To growl viciously while baring the teeth. **2.** To speak angrily or threateningly. *—tr.* To utter with anger or hostility: *snarled a retort.* **—snarl** *n.* **1.** A vicious growl. **2.** A vicious, hostile utterance. [Frequentative of obsolete *snar,* perhaps from Dutch or Low German *snarren,* to rattle, probably of imitative origin.] **—snarl′er** *n.* **—snarl′ing·ly** *adv.* **—snarl′y** *adj.*

snarl² (snärl) *n.* **1.** A tangled mass, as of hair or yarn. **2.** A confused, complicated, or tangled situation; a predicament.

ă pat	oi boy
ā pay	ou out
âr care	o͝o took
ä father	o͞o boot
ĕ pet	ŭ cut
ē be	ûr urge
ĭ pit	th thin
ī pie	*th* this
îr pier	hw which
ŏ pot	zh vision
ō toe	ə about, item
ô paw	♦ regionalism

Stress marks: ′ (primary); ′ (secondary), as in **dictionary** (dĭk′shə-nĕr′ē)

—snarl *v.* **snarled, snarl·ing, snarls.** *—intr.* To become tangled or confused. *—tr.* **1.** To tangle or knot (hair, for example). **2.** To confuse; complicate. [Middle English *snarle,* trap, probably diminutive of *snare.* See SNARE [1].] **—snarl′er** *n.* **—snarl′y** *adj.*

snatch (snăch) *v.* **snatched, snatch·ing, snatch·es.** *—tr.* **1.a.** To grasp or seize hastily, eagerly, or suddenly. **b.** *Sports.* To raise (a weight) in one quick, uninterrupted motion from the floor to a position over the lifter's head. **2.** To grasp or seize illicitly. *—intr.* To make grasping or seizing motions: *snatched at the lamp cord.* **—snatch** *n.* **1.** The act of snatching; a quick grasp or grab. **2.** A brief period of time: *"At the end we preferred to travel all night,/Sleeping in snatches"* (T.S. Eliot). **3.** A small amount; a bit or fragment: *a snatch of dialogue.* **4.** *Slang.* A kidnapping. **5.** *Sports.* A lift in weightlifting in which the weight is raised in one uninterrupted motion from the floor to a position over the lifter's head. [Middle English *snacchen.*] **—snatch′er** *n.*

snatch block *n.* *Nautical.* A block that can be opened on one side to receive the looped part of a rope.

snatch·y (snăch′ē) *adj.* **-i·er, -i·est.** Occurring in snatches; intermittent: *a snatchy conversation.*

snaz·zy (snăz′ē) *adj.* **-zi·er, -zi·est.** *Slang.* Fashionable or flashy. [Origin unknown.] **—snaz′zi·ness** *n.*

SNCC *abbr.* Student Nonviolent Coordinating Committee.

Snead (snēd), **Samuel Jackson.** Known as "Sam." Born 1912. American golfer who won three Professional Golfers' Association championships (1942, 1949, and 1951) and three Masters tournaments (1949, 1952, and 1954).

sneak (snēk) *v.* **sneaked** also **snuck** (snŭk), **sneak·ing, sneaks.** *—intr.* **1.** To go or move in a quiet, stealthy way. **2.** To behave in a cowardly or servile manner. *—tr.* To move, give, take, or put in a quiet, stealthy manner: *sneak candy into one's mouth; sneaked a look at the grade sheet.* **—sneak** *n.* **1.** A person regarded as stealthy, cowardly, or underhanded. **2.** An instance of sneaking; a quiet, stealthy movement. **3.** *Informal.* A sneaker. **—sneak** *adj.* **1.** Carried out in a clandestine manner: *sneak preparations for war.* **2.** Perpetrated without warning: *a sneak attack by terrorists.* [Probably akin to Middle English *sniken,* to creep, from Old English *snīcan.*]

USAGE NOTE: *Snuck* is an Americanism first introduced in the 19th century as a nonstandard regional variant of *sneaked.* But widespread use of *snuck* has become more common with every generation. It is now used by educated speakers in all regions, and there is some evidence to suggest that it is more frequent among younger speakers than *sneaked* is. Formal written English is naturally and properly more conservative than other varieties, of course, and here *snuck* still meets with much resistance. Many writers and editors have a lingering unease about the form, particularly if they recall its nonstandard origins. In fact, our consolidated citations, exhibiting almost 10,000 instances of *sneaked* and *snuck,* indicate that *sneaked* is preferred by a factor of 7 to 2. And 67 percent of the Usage Panel disapproves of *snuck.* Nevertheless, in recent years *snuck* has been quietly establishing itself in formal writing. An electronic search of a wide range of reputable publications turns up hundreds of citations for *snuck,* not just in sports writing but in news columns and commentary: *"He ran up huge hotel bills and then snuck out without paying"* (George Stade). *"In the dressing room beforehand, while the NBC technician was making me up, Jesse Jackson snuck up behind me and began playfully powdering my face"* (Bruce Babbitt). *"Raisa Gorbachev snuck away yesterday afternoon for a 65-minute helter-skelter tour of San Francisco"* (San Francisco Chronicle). *"The Reagan administration snuck in some illegal military assistance before that"* (New Republic). Our citation files also contain a number of occurrences of *snuck* in serious fiction: *"He had snuck away from camp with a cabinmate"* (Anne Tyler). *"I ducked down behind the paperbacks and snuck out"* (Garrison Keillor).

sneak·er (snē′kər) *n.* A sports shoe usually made of canvas and having soft rubber soles. Also called *tennis shoe.*

sneak·ing (snē′kĭng) *adj.* **1.** Acting in a stealthy, furtive way. **2.** Unavowed; secret. **3.** Gradually growing or persistent: *a sneaking hunch.* **—sneak′ing·ly** *adv.*

sneak preview *n.* A single public showing of a movie before its general release.

sneak thief *n.* One who steals without breaking into buildings or using violence.

sneak·y (snē′kē) *adj.* **-i·er, -i·est.** Furtive; surreptitious. **—sneak′i·ly** *adv.* **—sneak′i·ness** *n.*

sneer (snîr) *n.* **1.** A scornful facial expression characterized by a slight raising of one corner of the upper lip. **2.** A contemptuous facial expression, sound, or statement. **—sneer** *v.* **sneered, sneer·ing, sneers.** *—tr.* To utter with a sneer or in a sneering manner. *—intr.* **1.** To assume a scornful, contemptuous, or derisive facial expression. **2.** To speak in a scornful, contemptuous, or derisive manner. [From Middle English *sneren,* to mock, alteration of Old English *fnǣran,* to breathe heavily. See **pneu-** in Appendix.] **—sneer′er** *n.* **—sneer′ful, sneer′y** *adj.* **—sneer′ing·ly** *adv.*

sneeze (snēz) *intr.v.* **sneezed, sneez·ing, sneez·es.** To expel air forcibly from the mouth and nose in an explosive, spasmodic involuntary action resulting chiefly from irritation of the nasal mucous membrane. **—sneeze** *n.* An instance or the sound of sneezing. ***—phrasal verb.*** **sneeze at.** *Slang.* To treat as unimportant: *These deficits are nothing to sneeze at.* [Middle English *snesen,* probably alteration (perhaps influenced by *snorten,* to snort, and *snoren,* snore) of *nesen,* alteration of *fnesen,* from Old English *fnēosan.* See **pneu-** in Appendix.] **—sneez′er** *n.* **—sneez′y** *adj.*

sneeze·weed (snēz′wēd′) *n.* **1.** Any of several New World herbs of the genus *Helenium* of the composite family, having yellow to red-purple rayed flower heads. **2.** See **sneezewort.**

sneeze·wort (snēz′wûrt′, -wôrt′) *n.* A Eurasian herb *(Achillea ptarmica)* of the composite family, having aromatic, linear, finely serrate leaves and clusters of white flower heads grouped in corymbs. Also called *sneezeweed.*

Snef·fels (snĕf′əlz), **Mount.** A peak, 4,315.8 m (14,150 ft) high, in the San Juan Mountains of southwest Colorado.

snell (snĕl) *n.* A length of fine threadlike material, such as monofilament or gut, that connects a fishhook to a heavier line; a length of leader. [Origin unknown.]

Snel·len chart (snĕl′ən) *n.* A chart for testing visual acuity, usually consisting of letters, numbers, or pictures printed in lines of decreasing size which a patient is asked to read or identify at a fixed distance. [After Herman *Snellen* (1834–1908), Dutch ophthalmologist.]

Snellen test *n.* A test for visual acuity using a Snellen chart.

SNG *abbr.* **1.** Substitute natural gas. **2.** Synthetic natural gas.

snib (snĭb) *tr.v.* **snibbed, snib·bing, snibs.** *Chiefly British.* To latch (a door or window): "[The] *window is snibbed on the inner side"* (Arthur Conan Doyle). [Origin unknown.]

snick (snĭk) *v.* **snicked, snick·ing, snicks.** *—tr.* **1.** To cut with short strokes; snip: *snicked off a corner of the material.* **2.** To make a small cut (in); nick. **3.** To cause (something) to click: *I snicked the door shut.* *—intr.* **1.** To snip: *snicked with the shears.* **2.** To make a nick or nicks. **3.** To click: *The latch snicked open.* **—snick** *n.* **1.** A cut made by snicking. **2.** A clicking sound: *"I heard a little snick and a flashlight came on"* (Anthony Hyde). [Origin unknown.]

snick·er (snĭk′ər) *intr.v.* **-ered, -er·ing, -ers.** To utter a partly stifled laugh: *"I have seen the eternal Footman hold my coat, and snicker"* (T.S. Eliot). **—snicker** *n.* A snide, slightly stifled laugh. [Perhaps imitative.] **—snick′er·ing·ly** *adv.*

snick·er·snee (snĭk′ər-snē′) *n.* **1.** A knife resembling a sword. **2.** *Archaic.* The act of fighting with knives. [Alteration of obsolete *stick or snee,* to cut and thrust in fighting with a knife, from Dutch *steken of snijden* : *steken,* to stab (from Middle Dutch; see **steig-** in Appendix) + *of,* or (from Middle Dutch) + *snijden,* to cut (from Middle Dutch *sniden*).]

snide (snīd) *adj.* **snid·er, snid·est.** Derogatory in a malicious, superior way; sarcastic. [Origin unknown.] **—snide′ly** *adv.* **—snide′ness** *n.*

sniff (snĭf) *v.* **sniffed, sniff·ing, sniffs.** *—intr.* **1.a.** To inhale a short, audible breath through the nose, as in smelling something. **b.** To sniffle. **2.** To use the sense of smell, as in savoring or investigating: *sniffed at the jar to see what it held.* **3.** To regard something in a contemptuous or dismissive manner: *The critics sniffed at the adaptation of the novel to film.* **4.** *Informal.* To pry; snoop: *The reporters came sniffing around for more details.* *—tr.* **1.** To inhale forcibly through the nose: *sniffed the cool morning air.* **2.** To smell, as in savoring or investigating: *sniffed the lilacs; sniffed the breeze for traces of smoke.* **3.** To perceive or detect by or as if by sniffing: *dogs that sniffed out the trail through the snow; sniffed trouble ahead.* **4.** To utter in a contemptuous or haughty manner: *The countess sniffed her disapproval.* **—sniff** *n.* **1.** An instance or the sound of sniffing. **2.** Something sniffed or perceived by or as if by sniffing; a whiff: *a sniff of perfume; a sniff of scandal.* [Middle English *sniffen,* probably of Scandinavian origin.] **—sniff′a·ble** *adj.* **—sniff′er** *n.*

sniff dog *n.* A dog specially trained to locate illicit drugs or explosives by using its sense of smell.

snif·fle (snĭf′əl) *intr.v.* **-fled, -fling, -fles.** **1.** To breathe audibly through a runny or congested nose. **2.** To weep or whimper lightly with spasmodic congestion of the nose. **—sniffle** *n.* **1.** The act or sound of sniffling. **2. sniffles.** A condition, such as a head cold, accompanied by congestion of the nose. Used with *the.* [Frequentative of SNIFF.] **—snif′fler** *n.* **—snif′fly** (snĭf′ə-lē, snĭf′lē) *adj.*

sniff·y (snĭf′ē) *adj.* **-i·er, -i·est.** *Informal.* Disposed to showing arrogance or contempt; haughty. **—sniff′i·ly** *adv.* **—sniff′i·ness** *n.*

snifter

snif·ter (snĭf′tər) *n.* **1.** A pear-shaped goblet with a narrow top, used especially in serving brandy. **2.** *Slang.* A small portion of liquor. [From Middle English *snifteren,* to sniff, perhaps of Scandinavian origin.]

snig·ger (snĭg′ər) *n.* A snicker. **—snigger** *intr.v.* **-gered, -ger·ing, -gers.** To snicker. [Perhaps alteration of SNICKER.]

snip (snĭp) *v.* **snipped, snip·ping, snips.** *—tr.* To cut, clip, or separate (something) with short, quick strokes. *—intr.* To cut or clip with short, quick strokes. **—snip** *n.* **1.** An instance of snipping or the sound produced by snipping. **2.a.** A small cut made with scissors or shears. **b.** A small piece cut or clipped off. **c.** A bit or scrap: *snips of information about the upcoming merger.* **3.** *Informal.* **a.** One that is small or slight in size or stature. **b.** A person regarded as impertinent or mischievous. **4. snips** *(used with a sing. or pl. verb).* Hand shears used in cutting sheet metal.

5. *Slang.* Something easily accomplished. [Dutch or Low German *snippen.*]

snipe (snīp) *n.* **1.** *pl.* **snipe** or **snipes. a.** Any of various long-billed shore birds of the genus *Gallinago* or *Capella,* related to the woodcocks and sandpipers, especially the common, widely distributed species *G. gallinago* or *C. gallinago.* **b.** Any of various similar or related birds. **2.** A shot, especially a gunshot, from a concealed place. **—snipe** *intr.v.* **sniped, snip·ing, snipes. 1.** To shoot at individuals from a concealed place. **2.** To shoot snipe. **3.** To make malicious, underhand remarks or attacks. [Middle English, probably from Old Norse *-snīpa,* as in *mȳrisnīpa,* marsh snipe.]

snipe·fish (snīp′fĭsh′) *n., pl.* **snipefish** or **-fish·es.** Any of various small marine fishes of the family Macrorhamphosidae, found in tropical and temperate regions and characterized by a long snout and a very long spine extending from the dorsal fin backward toward the tail.

snip·er (snī′pər) *n.* **1.** A skilled military shooter detailed to spot and pick off enemy soldiers from a concealed place. **2.** One who shoots at other people from a concealed place.

snip·pet (snĭp′ĭt) *n.* **1.** A bit, scrap, or morsel: *"sparkling black bass . . . strewn with snippets of coriander and basil"* (Gael Greene). **2.** *Informal.* A small or mischievous person.

snip·pet·y (snĭp′ĭ-tē) *adj.* **-i·er, -i·est. 1.** Made up of snippets. **2.** *Informal.* Snippy; impertinent.

snip·py (snĭp′ē) *adj.* **-pi·er, -pi·est.** *Informal.* **1.** Sharp-tongued; impertinent. **2.** Occurring in pieces; fragmentary: *a snippy account of the incident.*

snit (snĭt) *n. Informal.* A state of agitation or irritation. [Origin unknown.]

snitch (snĭch) *Slang. v.* **snitched, snitch·ing, snitch·es.** *—tr.* To steal (something, usually something of little value); pilfer. See Synonyms at **steal.** *—intr.* To turn informer: *He snitched on his comrades.* **—snitch** *n.* **1.** A thief. **2.** An informer. [Origin unknown.] **—snitch′er** *n.*

sniv·el (snĭv′əl) *intr.v.* **-eled, -el·ing, -els** or **-elled, -el·ling, -els. 1.** To sniffle. **2.** To complain or whine tearfully. **3.** To run at the nose. **—snivel** *n.* **1.** The act of sniffling or sniveling. **2.** Nasal mucus. [Middle English *snivelen,* from Old English **snyflan.*] **—sniv′el·er** *n.*

snob (snŏb) *n.* **1.** One who overtly imitates, obsequiously admires, and offensively seeks to associate only with those one regards as one's superiors and who tends to rebuff or ignore altogether those one regards as one's inferiors: *"A snob is someone who judges all things, from shoes and dinner parties to love and beauty, according to their social rating"* (Tom Wolfe). **2.** One who affects an offensive air of self-satisfied superiority in matters of taste or intellect. [Earlier *snob,* cobbler, lower-class person, person who aspires to social prominence.] **—snob′by** *adj.*

WORD HISTORY: Snobs look down at their inferiors, but at one time snobs looked up at their betters. The word *snob,* the ultimate origins of which are uncertain, is first found in 1781 in the sense "shoemaker, cobbler," a regional and informal usage. The word is recorded around 1796 in a slang usage particular to Cambridge University, "a townsman as opposed to a gownsman." Both senses may have fed into the sense first found in 1831, "a member of the ordinary or lower classes." Along with this sense went another (1838), "a person without proper breeding or taste." From these two senses arose the sense first recorded in 1848, "a person who looks up to his or her social betters and tries to copy or associate with them." We can see how this sense could blend into the other familiar sense, "one who looks down on those considered inferior" (1911).

snob appeal *n.* Qualities that seem to substantiate social or intellectual pretensions.

snob·ber·y (snŏb′ə-rē) *n., pl.* **-ies.** Snobbish behavior or an instance of it.

snob·bish (snŏb′ĭsh) *adj.* Of, befitting, or resembling a snob; pretentious. **—snob′bish·ly** *adv.* **—snob′bish·ness** *n.*

snob·bism (snŏb′ĭz′əm) *n.* Snobbery.

Sno-Cat (snō′kăt′). A trademark used for an automotive vehicle with tractor treads for traveling over snow.

snoek (sno͝ok) *n., pl.* **snoek** or **snoeks.** A large, small-scaled marine food fish *(Thyristes atun)* of the family Gempylidae, widely distributed in the Southern Hemisphere. [Afrikaans, from Middle Dutch *snoec.*]

snol·ly·gos·ter (snŏl′ē-gŏs′tər) *n. Slang.* One, especially a politician, who is guided by personal advantage rather than by consistent, respectable principles. [Perhaps alteration of *snallygaster,* a mythical beast said to prey on poultry and children, perhaps from Pennsylvania Dutch *schnelle geeschter* : Middle High German *snēl,* quick (from Old High German) + Middle High German *geist,* spirit (from Old High German).]

snood (sno͞od) *n.* **1.** A small netlike cap worn by women to keep the hair in place. **2.** A headband or fillet. **—snood** *tr.v.* **snood·ed, snood·ing, snoods.** To hold (the hair) in place with a snood. [Middle English *snod,* headband, from Old English *snōd.* See **(s)nē-** in Appendix.]

snook¹ (sno͝ok, sno͞ok) *n., pl.* **snook** or **snooks.** Any of several chiefly marine percoid fishes of the family Centropomidae, especially *Centropomus undecimalis,* a food and game fish of warm Atlantic waters. Also called *sergeant fish.* [Dutch *snoek,* pike, from Middle Dutch *snoec.*]

snook² (sno͝ok, sno͞ok) *n.* A gesture of derision or defiance. ***—idiom.* cock a snook.** *Chiefly British.* To thumb one's nose: "[The clock] *is set wrong and hung crooked, as if to cock a snook at the importance of time"* (Kevin Crossley-Holland). [Origin unknown.]

snook·er (sno͝ok′ər) *n. Games.* Pocket billiards played with 15 red balls and 6 balls of other colors. **—snooker** *tr.v.* **-ered, -er·ing, -ers. 1.** *Slang.* **a.** To lead (another) into a situation in which all possible choices are undesirable; trap. **b.** To fool; dupe: *"Snookered by a lot of malarkey about drilling costs, a Texas jury . . . added $3 billion of punitive damages"* (New Republic). **2.** *Games.* To leave one's opponent in the game of snooker unable to take a direct shot without striking a ball out of the required order. [Origin unknown.]

snoop (sno͞op) *intr.v.* **snooped, snoop·ing, snoops.** To pry into the private affairs of others, especially by prowling about. **—snoop** *n.* One who snoops. [Dutch *snoepen,* to eat on the sly.] **—snoop′er** *n.*

snoop·y (sno͞o′pē) *adj.* **-i·er, -i·est.** *Informal.* Likely to snoop; nosy. See Synonyms at **curious. —snoop′i·ly** *adv.* **—snoop′i·ness** *n.*

snoot (sno͞ot) *Informal. n.* **1.** A snout or nose. **2.** A snob. **—snoot** *tr.v.* **snoot·ed, snoot·ing, snoots.** To treat haughtily: *a couple who were snooted by the headwaiter.* [Dialectal variant of SNOUT.]

snoot·y (sno͞o′tē) *adj.* **-i·er, -i·est.** *Informal.* **1.** Snobbishly aloof; haughty. **2.** High-class; exclusive. **—snoot′i·ly** *adv.* **—snoot′i·ness** *n.*

snooze (sno͞oz) *intr.v.* **snoozed, snooz·ing, snooz·es.** To take a light nap; doze. **—snooze** *n.* A brief light sleep. [Origin unknown.]

Sno·qual·mie Falls (snō-kwŏl′mē). A waterfall, 82.4 m (270 ft) high, in the **Snoqualmie River,** about 113 km (70 mi) long, of west-central Washington.

snore (snôr, snōr) *intr.v.* **snored, snor·ing, snores.** To breathe during sleep with harsh, snorting noises caused by vibration of the soft palate. **—snore** *n.* **1.** The act or an instance of snoring. **2.** The noise so produced. [Middle English *snoren,* to snort, from *fnoren,* from Old English *fnora,* sneezing. See **pneu-** in Appendix.] **—snor′er** *n.*

snor·kel (snôr′kəl) *n.* **1.** A breathing apparatus used by skin divers, consisting of a long tube held in the mouth. **2.** A retractable vertical tube in a submarine that contains air-intake and exhaust pipes for the engines and for ventilation, permitting extended periods of submergence at periscope depth. **—snorkel** *intr.v.* **-keled, -kel·ing, -kels.** To dive using a snorkel. [German *Schnorchel,* from dialectal, nose (from its resemblance in shape to a nose).] **—snor′kel·er** *n.*

snorkel

Snor·ri Stur·lu·son (snôr′ē stûr′lə-sən, snŏr′ē stœr′lə-sŏn). 1179–1241. Icelandic historian and chieftain whose works include *Heimskringla* and the *Prose,* or *Younger, Edda.*

snort (snôrt) *n.* **1.a.** A rough, noisy sound made by breathing forcefully through the nostrils, as a horse or pig does. **b.** A similar sound: *the snort of a steam engine.* **2.** *Slang.* **a.** A drink of liquor, especially when swallowed in one gulp. **b.** Cocaine or heroin, especially a small amount sniffed at one time. **c.** The liquor or drug so taken. **—snort** *v.* **snort·ed, snort·ing, snorts.** *—intr.* **1.a.** To breathe noisily and forcefully through the nostrils. **b.** To make a sound resembling noisy inhalation: *"The wind snorted across the Kansas plains"* (Gail Sheehy). **2.** To make an abrupt noise expressive of scorn, ridicule, or contempt. **3.** *Slang.* To ingest a drug, such as cocaine or heroin, by sniffing. *—tr.* **1.** To express by snorting: *He snorted his disapproval.* **2.** *Slang.* To ingest by sniffing: *snorted cocaine.* [From Middle English *snorten,* to snort, from *fnorten,* variant of *fnoren.* See SNORE.] **—snort′er** *n.*

snot (snŏt) *n. Vulgar Slang.* **1.** Nasal mucus; phlegm. **2.** A person regarded as annoying, arrogant, or impertinent. [Middle English, from Old English *gesnot.*]

snot·ty (snŏt′ē) *adj.* **-ti·er, -ti·est.** *Vulgar Slang.* **1.** Dirtied with nasal mucus. **2.** Impertinent; arrogant. **—snot′ti·ly** *adv.* **—snot′ti·ness** *n.*

snout (snout) *n.* **1.a.** The projecting nose, jaws, or anterior facial part of an animal's head. **b.** A similar prolongation of the anterior portion of the head in certain insects, such as weevils; a rostrum. **c.** A spout or nozzle shaped like such a projection. **2.** *Slang.* The human nose. [Middle English, probably of Old English origin.]

snout beetle *n.* A weevil of the family Curculionidae, having the front of the head elongated to form a snout. Also called *curculio.*

snow (snō) *n.* **1.** Frozen precipitation in the form of white or translucent hexagonal ice crystals that fall in soft, white flakes. **2.** A falling of snow; a snowstorm. **3.** Something resembling snow, as: **a.** The white specks on a television screen resulting from weak reception. **b.** *Slang.* Cocaine. **c.** *Slang.* Heroin. *—attributive.* Often used to modify another noun: *the snow season; snow removal.* **—snow** *v.* **snowed, snow·ing, snows.** *—intr.* To fall as or in snow. *—tr.* **1.** To cover, shut off, or close off with snow: *We were snowed in.* **2.** *Slang.* To overwhelm with insincere talk, especially with flattery. ***—phrasal verb.* snow under. 1.** To overwhelm: *I was snowed under with work.* **2.** To

ă pat	oi boy
ā pay	ou out
âr care	o͝o took
ä father	o͞o boot
ĕ pet	ŭ cut
ē be	ûr urge
ĭ pit	th thin
ī pie	*th* this
îr pier	hw which
ŏ pot	zh vision
ō toe	ə about, item
ô paw	♦ regionalism

Stress marks: ′ (primary); ′ (secondary), as in **dictionary** (dĭk′shə-nĕr′ē)

snowboard

snow goose

snowmobile

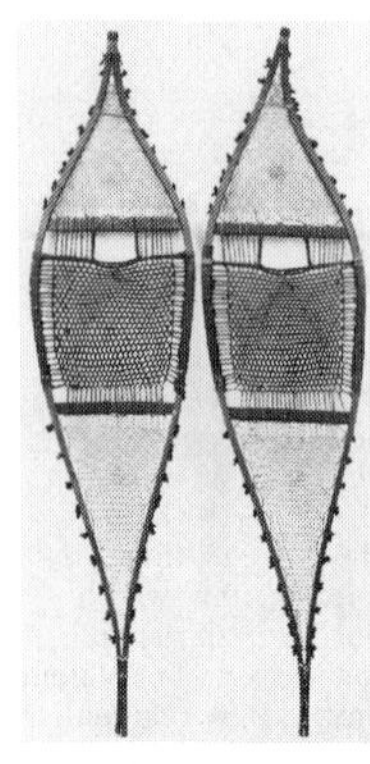
snowshoe
19th-century Eastern Plains Indians snowshoes

defeat by a very large margin. [Middle English, from Old English *snāw*.]

Snow (snō), **C(harles) P(ercy).** Baron Snow of Leicester. 1905–1980. British writer and scientist who is known especially for his 11-volume series *Strangers and Brothers* (1940–1970).

♦**snow·ball** (snō′bôl′) *n.* **1.a.** A mass of soft, wet snow packed into a ball that can be thrown, as in play. **b.** *Chiefly Southern U.S.* A cup of crushed or shaved ice flavored with colored syrup. **2.** Any of several plants having rounded clusters of white flowers, as the guelder rose and certain species of the arrowwood. **—snowball** *v.* **-balled, -ball·ing, -balls.** —*intr.* **1.** To grow rapidly in significance, importance, or size: *problems that snowballed by the hour.* **2.** To throw snowballs. —*tr.* **1.** To cause to grow or increase rapidly. **2.** To throw snowballs at.

snow·bell (snō′bĕl′) *n.* Any of various shrubs or trees of the genus *Styrax,* especially *S. japonicus* and *S. obassia* of eastern Asia, having bell-shaped white flowers. Also called *storax.*

Snow·belt also **Snow Belt** (snō′bĕlt′). The northern and northeast United States.

snow·ber·ry (snō′bĕr′ē) *n.* **1.** Any of various shrubs of the genus *Symphoricarpos,* especially *S. albus* of North America, having small pinkish flowers and white berries. **2.** Any of various tropical American shrubs or vines of the genus *Chiococca,* having white globular fruit and small yellow or white flowers clustered in lateral racemes.

snow·bird (snō′bûrd′) *n.* **1.** Any of several birds, such as the junco and the snow bunting, common in snowy regions. **2.** *Slang.* One who moves from a cold to a warm place in the winter.

snow blindness *n.* A usually temporary loss of vision and inflammation of the conjunctiva and cornea, caused by exposure of the eyes to bright sunlight and ultraviolet rays reflected from snow or ice. **—snow′-blind′** (snō′blīnd′), **snow′-blind′ed** (-blīn′dĭd) *adj.*

snow·blink (snō′blĭngk′) *n.* A white sky glow reflected from snowfields.

snow blower *n.* See **snow thrower.**

snow·board (snō′bôrd′, -bōrd′) *Sports. n.* A board resembling a small surfboard and equipped with bindings, used for descending snow-covered slopes on one's feet but without ski poles. **—snowboard** *intr.v.* **-board·ed, -board·ing, -boards.** To use a snowboard. **—snow′board′er** *n.*

snow·bound (snō′bound′) *adj.* Confined in one place by heavy snow.

snow bunting *n.* A finch *(Plectrophenax nivalis)* of northern regions, having predominantly white winter plumage. Also called *snowflake.*

snow·bush (snō′bo͝osh′) also **snow·brush** (-brŭsh′) *n.* A spiny shrub *(Ceanothus cordulatus)* of California and Oregon, having large clusters of small white flowers.

snow·cap (snō′kăp′) *n.* Snow covering a mountain peak, especially such snow existing year-round. **—snow′capped′** *adj.*

snow cone *n.* A confection made of crushed ice and flavored syrup inserted into a paper cone and mounded on top.

Snow·don (snōd′n). A massif of northwest Wales. Rising to 1,085.8 m (3,560 ft), it is the highest elevation in Wales.

snow·drift (snō′drĭft′) *n.* A mass or bank of snow piled up by the wind.

snow·drop (snō′drŏp′) *n.* Any of several bulbous Eurasian plants of the genus *Galanthus,* having solitary, nodding white flowers that bloom in early spring.

snowdrop tree *n.* The silverbell tree.

snow·fall (snō′fôl′) *n.* **1.** A fall of snow. **2.** The amount of snow that falls during a given period or in a specified area.

snow fence *n.* Temporary fencing composed of thin upright slats wired together, used to prevent snow from drifting onto walks or roads.

snow·flake (snō′flāk′) *n.* **1.** A single flake or crystal of snow. **2.** Any of several bulbous European herbs of the genus *Leucojum,* having white or whitish flowers and fleshy fruit. **3.** See **snow bunting.**

snow goose *n.* A North American wild goose *(Chen caerulescens* or *Anser caerulescens)* that breeds in Arctic regions, having a dusky gray color phase when young and a white plumage with black wingtips as an adult.

snow-in-sum·mer (snō′ĭn-sŭm′ər) *n.* A wooly, white, mat-forming perennial herb *(Cerastium tomentosum)* native to Italy and widely cultivated in rock gardens for its showy white flowers with notched petals.

snow job *n. Slang.* An effort to deceive, overwhelm, or persuade with insincere talk, especially flattery.

snow leopard *n.* A large feline mammal *(Panthera uncia)* of the highlands of central Asia, having long, thick, whitish-gray fur with dark markings like those of a leopard. Also called *ounce.*

snow line *n.* **1.** The lower altitudinal boundary of a snow-covered area, especially of one that is perennially covered, such as the snowcap of a mountain. **2.** The fluctuating latitudinal boundaries around the polar regions marking the extent of snow cover.

snow·mak·ing (snō′mā′kĭng) *n.* Production of artificial snow in the form of granular ice particles for use on ski slopes.

snow·man (snō′măn′) *n.* A figure of a person made from packed snow, usually formed by piling large snowballs on top of each other.

Snow·mass Mountain (snō′măs). A peak, 4,298.1 m (14,092 ft) high, in the Elk Mountains of west-central Colorado.

snow·melt (snō′mĕlt′) *n.* **1.** The runoff from melting snow. **2.** A period or season when such runoff occurs: *streams that flood during snowmelt.*

snow·mo·bile (snō′mō-bēl′, -mə-) *n.* A small vehicle with skilike runners in front and tanklike treads, used for driving in or traveling on snow. Also called *skimobile.* [SNOW + (AUTO)MOBILE.] **—snow′mo·bil′er** *n.* **—snow′mo·bil′ing** *n.*

snow mold *n.* **1.** A disease of grasses appearing as grayish-white or pinkish patches after heavy snow has melted and caused by fungi that thrive at low temperatures. **2.** A fungus that causes this disease.

snow-on-the-moun·tain (snō′ŏn-*thə*-moun′tən, -ôn-) *n.* A widely cultivated plant *(Euphorbia marginata)* of the central United States, having white-margined leaves and showy white bracts. Also called *ghostweed.*

snow pea *n.* **1.** A variety of the common pea *(Pisum sativum* var. *macrocarpon)* in the pea family, having a soft, thick pod that lacks the fibrous inner lining present in the common pea. **2.** The edible young pod of this plant. Also called *sugar pea.*

snow pellet *n.* A small white ice particle that falls as precipitation and breaks apart easily when it lands on a surface. Often used in the plural. Also called *graupel, soft hail.*

snow plant *n.* A fleshy saprophytic plant *(Sarcodes sanguinea)* of the mountains of western North America, having a scaly reddish stalk and scarlet flowers.

snow·plow (snō′plou′) *n.* **1.** A plowlike device or vehicle used to remove snow, especially from roads and railroad tracks. **2.** *Sports.* A maneuver in snow skiing in which the tips of the skis are brought together in order to slow or stop progress. **—snowplow** *intr.v.* **-plowed, -plow·ing, -plows.** *Sports.* To perform a snowplow maneuver in skiing.

snow·shoe (snō′sho͞o′) *n.* A racket-shaped frame containing interlaced leather strips that can be attached to the foot to facilitate walking on deep snow. **—snowshoe** *intr.v.* **-shoed, -shoe·ing, -shoes.** To travel on snowshoes. **—snow′sho′er** *n.*

snowshoe rabbit *n.* A medium-sized hare *(Lepus americanus)* of northern North America, having large, heavily furred feet and fur that is white in winter and brown in summer. Also called *snowshoe hare, varying hare.*

snow·storm (snō′stôrm′) *n.* A storm marked by heavy snowfall.

snow·suit (snō′so͞ot′) *n.* A child's zippered winter coverall.

snow thrower *n.* A machine that clears snow from a surface by scooping the snow and projecting it forcefully through a chute. Also called *snow blower.*

snow tire *n.* A tire with a deep tread or studs to give added traction on snow-covered surfaces.

snow-white (snō′hwīt′, -wīt′) *adj.* Pure white; white as snow.

snow·y (snō′ē) *adj.* **-i·er, -i·est. 1.a.** Abounding in or covered with snow: *a snowy day.* **b.** Subject to snow: *a snowy climate.* **2.** Resembling or suggesting snow, especially in whiteness: *snowy linens.* **—snow′i·ly** *adv.* **—snow′i·ness** *n.*

snowy egret *n.* A medium-sized egret *(Egretta thula)* with white plumage, black legs, and yellow feet, found in warm parts of the Western Hemisphere. It was once widely hunted for its white, lacelike aigrettes that grow during the breeding season.

snowy owl *n.* A large diurnal owl *(Nyctea scandiaca)* of Arctic and subarctic regions, having snow-white plumage with dark markings.

snowy plover *n.* A small plover *(Charadrius alexandrinus)* of the western United States and Mexico, generally yellowish gray above and snowy white below and on the sides of the head.

snub (snŭb) *tr.v.* **snubbed, snub·bing, snubs. 1.** To ignore or behave coldly toward; slight. **2.** To dismiss, turn down, or frustrate the expectations of. **3.** *Nautical.* **a.** To check the movement of (a rope or cable running out) by turning it quickly about a post. **b.** To secure (a vessel, for example) in this manner. **4.** To stub out (a cigarette, for example). **—snub** *n.* **1.** A deliberate slight or affront. **2.** *Nautical.* A sudden checking, as of a rope or cable running out. **—snub** *adj.* Unusually short: *a snub nose.* [Middle English *snubben,* to rebuke; akin to Old Norse *snubba.*] **—snub′ber** *n.*

snub-nosed (snŭb′nōzd′) *adj.* **1.** Having a short, turned-up nose. **2.** Having an extremely short barrel: *a snub-nosed pistol.*

snuck (snŭk) *v. Usage Problem.* A past tense and a past participle of **sneak.** See Usage Note at **sneak.**

snuff¹ (snŭf) *v.* **snuffed, snuff·ing, snuffs.** —*tr.* **1.** To inhale (something) audibly through the nose; sniff. **2.** To sense or examine by smelling; sniff at. —*intr.* To sniff; inhale. **—snuff** *n.* The act of snuffing or the sound produced by it; a snuffle. [Middle English *snoffen,* to snuff a candle, sniffle, probably from *snoffe,* snuff. See SNUFF².]

snuff² (snŭf) *n.* The charred portion of a candlewick. **—snuff** *tr.v.* **snuffed, snuff·ing, snuffs. 1.** To extinguish: *snuffed out the candles.* **2.** To put a sudden end to; destroy: *lives that were snuffed out by car accidents.* **3.** To cut off the charred portion of (a candlewick). [Middle English *snoffe,* possibly of Low German origin.]

snuff³ (snŭf) *n.* **1.a.** A preparation of finely pulverized tobacco that can be drawn up into the nostrils by inhaling. Also called *smokeless tobacco.* **b.** The quantity of this tobacco that is inhaled at a single time; a pinch. **2.** A powdery substance, such as a medicine, taken by inhaling. **—snuff** *intr.v.* **snuffed, snuff·ing, snuffs.** To use or inhale snuff. **—*idiom.* up to snuff.** *Informal.* **1.** Normal in health. **2.** Up to standard; adequate. [Dutch *snuf,* short for *snuftabak* : Dutch *snuffen,* to sniff; see SNUFFLE + *tabak,* tobacco.]

snuff·box (snŭf′bŏks′) *n.* A small, often decorated box with a hinged lid, used for carrying snuff.

snuff·er¹ (snŭf′ər) *n.* One who uses snuff.

snuff·er² (snŭf′ər) *n.* **1.a.** A candlesnuffer. **b.** One who snuffs out candles. **2. snuffers.** An instrument resembling a pair of shears that is used for cutting the snuff from or for extinguishing candles.

snuff film *n. Slang.* A movie involving explicit pornography and culminating in the violent death of a participant in a sex act.

snuf·fle (snŭf′əl) *v.* **-fled, -fling, -fles.** *—intr.* **1.** To breathe noisily, as through a blocked nose. **2.** To sniff. **3.** To talk or sing nasally; whine. *—tr.* To utter in a snuffling tone. **—snuffle** *n.* **1.** The act of snuffling or the sound produced by it. **2. snuffles.** The sniffles. Used with *the.* [Probably from Dutch *snuffelen,* to sniff about, probably frequentative of *snuffen,* to sniff, from Middle Dutch *snuiven.*] **—snuf′fler** *n.* **—snuf′fly** *adj.*

snug¹ (snŭg) *adj.* **snug·ger, snug·gest.** **1.** Comfortably sheltered; cozy. **2.** Small but well arranged: *a snug apartment.* See Synonyms at **comfortable. 3.a.** Closely secured and well built; compact: *a snug little sailboat.* **b.** Close-fitting: *a snug jacket.* **c.** *Nautical.* Seaworthy. **4.a.** Offering freedom from financial worry: *a snug living.* **b.** Safe; secure: *a snug hideout.* **—snug** *v.* **snugged, snug·ging, snugs.** *—tr.* To make snug or secure. *—intr.* To nestle; snuggle. **—*phrasal verb.* snug down.** *Nautical.* To prepare (a vessel) to weather a storm, as by securing movable gear. [Of Scandinavian origin; akin to Swedish *snygg,* neat, trim.] **—snug, snug′ly** *adv.* **—snug′ness** *n.*

snug² (snŭg) *n. Chiefly British.* A very small private room in a pub. [Short for SNUGGERY.]

snug·ger·y (snŭg′ə-rē) *n., pl.* **-ies.** *Chiefly British.* A snug position or place.

snug·gle (snŭg′əl) *v.* **-gled, -gling, -gles.** *—intr.* **1.** To lie or press close together; cuddle. **2.** To curl up closely or comfortably; nestle: *snuggled happily under the covers.* *—tr.* To draw close or hold closely, as for comfort or in affection; hug. [Frequentative of SNUG¹.]

so¹ (sō) *adv.* **1.** In the condition or manner expressed or indicated; thus: *Hold the brush so.* **2.** To the amount or degree expressed or understood; to such an extent: *She was so weary that she fell.* **3.** To a great extent; to such an evident degree: *But the idea is so obvious.* **4.** Because of the reason given; consequently: *She was weary and so fell.* **5.** Afterward; then: *to the gas station and so home.* **6.** In the same way; likewise: *You were on time and so was I.* **7.** Apparently; well, then. Used in expressing astonishment, disapproval, or sarcasm: *So you think you've got troubles?* **8.** In truth; indeed: *"You aren't right." "I am so!"* **—so** *adj.* **1.** True; factual: *I wouldn't have told you this if it weren't so.* **2.** In good order: *Everything on his desk must be exactly so.* **—so** *conj. Usage Problem.* **1.** With the result or consequence that: *He failed to appear, so we went on without him.* **2.** In order that: *I stayed so I could see you.* **—so** *pron.* Such as has already been suggested or specified; the same: *She became a loyal friend and remained so.* **—so** *interj.* Used to express surprise or comprehension: *So! You've finished your work at last.* **—*idioms.* and so on** (or **forth).** And similarly; and continuing in a like manner. **so as to.** In order to: *Mail your package early so as to ensure its timely arrival.* **so that. 1.** In order that: *I stopped so that you could catch up.* **2.** With the result or consequence that. [Middle English, from Old English *swā.* See **swo-** in Appendix.]

USAGE NOTE: Many critics and grammarians have insisted that *so* must be followed by *that* in formal writing when used to introduce a clause giving the reason for or purpose of an action: *He stayed so that he could see the second feature.* But this rule is best regarded as a stylistic preference; in such clauses *that* is frequently omitted even by reputable writers in formal contexts, as in *They will have to double up so* (or *so that*) *room can be found for the new arrivals.* • Both *so* and *so that* are acceptably used to introduce clauses that state a result or consequence: *The Bay Bridge was still closed, so* (or *so that*) *the drive from San Francisco to the Berkeley campus took an hour and a half.* • *So* is frequently used in informal speech to string together the elements of a narrative. This practice should not be carried over into formal writing, where the absence of contextual information generally requires that connections be made more explicit. • Critics have sometimes objected to the use of *so* as an intensive meaning "to a great degree or extent," as in *We were so relieved to learn that the deadline had been extended.* This usage is most common in informal contexts, perhaps because unlike the neutral *very,* it presumes that the listener or reader will be sympathetic with the speaker's evaluation of the situation. (Thus one would be more apt to say *It was so unfair of them not to invite you* than to say *It was so fortunate that I didn't have to put up with your company.*) For just this reason, the construction may occasionally be used to good effect in more formal contexts to invite the reader to take the point of view of the speaker or subject: *The request seemed to her to be quite reasonable; it was so unfair of the manager to refuse.* But in the absence of stylistic motive, this use of *so* should be reserved for familiar discourse. • New England speakers often use a negative form such as *so didn't* where other varieties would use the positive *so did,* as in *Sophie ate all her strawberries and so didn't Amelia.* Since this usage may confuse a speaker who has not previously encountered it, it is best avoided in writing. See Usage Note at **as¹.**

so² (sō) *n. Music.* Variant of **sol¹.**

so. or **So.** *abbr.* South; southern.

s.o. *abbr.* **1.** Seller's option. **2.** *Baseball.* Strikeout.

soak (sōk) *v.* **soaked, soak·ing, soaks.** *—tr.* **1.a.** To make thoroughly wet or saturated by or as if by placing in liquid. **b.** To immerse in liquid for a period of time. **2.** To absorb (liquid, for example) through or as if through pores or interstices. **3.** To remove (a stain, for example) by continued immersion: *soaked out the grease spots.* **4.** *Informal.* To take in or accept mentally, especially eagerly and easily: *soaked up the gossip.* **5.** *Informal.* **a.** To drink (alcoholic liquor), especially to excess. **b.** To make (a person) drunk. **6.** *Slang.* To overcharge (a person). *—intr.* **1.** To be immersed until thoroughly saturated. **2.** To penetrate or permeate; seep: *The speaker paused to let her words soak in.* **3.** *Slang.* To drink to excess. **—soak** *n.* **1.a.** The act or process of soaking. **b.** The condition of being soaked. **2.** Liquid in which something may be soaked. **3.** *Slang.* A drunkard. [Middle English *soken,* from Old English *socian.* See **seuə-²** in Appendix.] **—soak′er** *n.*

soak·age (sō′kĭj) *n.* **1.a.** The process of soaking. **b.** The condition of being soaked. **2.** The amount of liquid that soaks into, through, or out of an object.

so-and-so (sō′ən-sō′) *n., pl.* **-sos. 1.** An unnamed or unspecified person or thing. **2.** *Informal.* A son of a gun.

soap (sōp) *n.* **1.** A cleansing agent, manufactured in bars, granules, flakes, or liquid form, made from a mixture of the sodium salts of various fatty acids of natural oils and fats. **2.** A metallic salt of a fatty acid, as of aluminum or iron. **3.** *Slang.* Money, especially that which is used for bribery. **4.** *Slang.* A soap opera. **—soap** *tr.v.* **soaped, soap·ing, soaps. 1.** To treat or cover with or as if with soap. **2.a.** *Informal.* To softsoap; cajole. **b.** *Slang.* To bribe. **—*idiom.* no soap.** *Slang.* **1.** Not possible or permissible. **2.** Unsuccessful; futile. [Middle English *sope,* from Old English *sāpe.*]

soap·bark (sōp′bärk′) *n.* **1.** A Chilean evergreen tree *(Quillaja saponaria)* of the rose family, having bark used as soap and as a source of saponin. **2.** The bark of this tree.

soap·ber·ry (sōp′bĕr′ē) *n.* **1.a.** Any of various chiefly tropical trees of the genus *Sapindus,* having pulpy fruit that lathers like soap. **b.** The fruit of any of these trees. **2.** The buffalo berry.

soap·box (sōp′bŏks′) *n.* **1.** A carton in which soap is packed. **2.** A temporary platform used while making an impromptu or nonofficial public speech. **—soapbox** *intr.v.* **-boxed, -box·ing, -box·es.** *Informal.* To engage in impromptu or nonofficial public speaking, often flamboyantly. **—*idiom.* on (one's) soapbox.** Speaking one's views passionately or self-importantly.

soap bubble *n.* **1.** A bubble, especially a large one, formed from soapy water. **2.** Something beautiful but transient, insubstantial, or illusory.

soap opera *n.* A drama, typically performed as a serial on daytime television or radio, characterized by stock characters and situations, sentimentality, and melodrama. [From its originally having been sponsored by soap companies.]

soap plant *n.* **1.** Any of several bulbous plants of the genus *Chlorogalum,* especially *C. pomeridianum,* of western North America, having small white flowers and bulbs formerly used as soap. **2.** Any of various plants having parts used as soap.

soap·stone (sōp′stōn′) *n.* A soft metamorphic rock composed mostly of the mineral talc. Also called *steatite.* [From its smooth soapy feel.]

soap·suds (sōp′sŭdz′) *pl.n.* Suds from soapy water.

soap·wort (sōp′wûrt′, -wôrt′) *n.* See **bouncing Bet.** [From its yielding a soapy substance when the leaves are bruised.]

soap·y (sō′pē) *adj.* **-i·er, -i·est. 1.** Consisting of or containing soap: *soapy water.* **2.** Covered with soap: *soapy hands.* **3.** Resembling soap: *a soapy consistency.* **4.** *Slang.* Unctuous; oily: *soapy compliments.* **—soap′i·ly** *adv.* **—soap′i·ness** *n.*

soar (sôr, sōr) *intr.v.* **soared, soar·ing, soars. 1.** To rise, fly, or glide high and with little apparent effort. **2.** To climb swiftly or powerfully. **3.** To glide in an aircraft while maintaining altitude. **4.** To ascend suddenly above the normal or usual level: *Our spirits soared.* See Synonyms at **rise. —soar** *n.* **1.** The act of soaring. **2.** The altitude or scope attained in soaring. [Middle English *soren,* from Old French *essorer,* from Vulgar Latin **exaurāre* : Latin *ex-,* ex- + Latin *aura,* air (from Greek, breeze; see AURA).] **—soar′er** *n.* **—soar′ing·ly** *adv.*

soar·ing (sôr′ĭng, sōr′-) *n.* The act of gliding while maintaining altitude, especially the sport of flying a heavier-than-air craft by using ascending currents of air. **—soaring** *adj.* Ascending to a level markedly higher than the usual: *soaring fuel costs; the soaring spires of the cathedral.*

so·a·ve (sō-ä′vā) *n.* A dry white Italian table wine. [Italian, from Latin *suāvis,* sweet, delightful. See **swād-** in Appendix.]

So·ay (soi, sō′ā) *n.* A small, brownish, short-tailed sheep *(Ovis aries)* of a breed that originated on the island of Soay in the Outer Hebrides.

snuffers

ă pat	oi boy
ā pay	ou out
âr care	ŏŏ took
ä father	ōō boot
ĕ pet	ŭ cut
ē be	ûr urge
ĭ pit	th thin
ī pie	*th* this
îr pier	hw which
ŏ pot	zh vision
ō toe	ə about, item
ô paw	♦ regionalism

Stress marks: **′** (primary); ′ (secondary), as in **dictionary** (dĭk′shə-nĕr′ē)

sob (sŏb) *v.* **sobbed, sob·bing, sobs.** —*intr.* **1.** To weep aloud with convulsive gasping; cry uncontrollably. See Synonyms at **cry. 2.** To make a sound resembling that of loud weeping. —*tr.* **1.** To utter with sobs. **2.** To put or bring (oneself) into a specified condition by sobbing: *sob oneself to sleep.* —**sob** *n.* The act or sound of sobbing. [Middle English *sobben,* perhaps of Low German origin.] —**sob′bing·ly** *adv.*

SOB *abbr. Vulgar.* Son of a bitch.

so·ber (sō′bər) *adj.* **-er, -est. 1.** Habitually abstemious in the use of alcoholic liquors or drugs; temperate. **2.** Not intoxicated or affected by the use of drugs. **3.** Plain or subdued: *sober attire.* **4.** Devoid of frivolity, excess, exaggeration, or speculative imagination; straightforward: *gave a sober assessment of the situation.* **5.** Marked by seriousness, gravity, or solemnity of conduct or character. See Synonyms at **serious. 6.** Marked by circumspection and self-restraint. —**sober** *tr. & intr.v.* **-bered, -ber·ing, -bers.** To make or become sober. [Middle English, from Old French *sobre,* from Latin *sōbrius.* See **s(w)e-** in Appendix.] —**so′ber·ly** *adv.* —**so′ber·ness** *n.*

so·ber-sid·ed (sō′bər-sī′dĭd) *adj.* Devoid of extreme qualities, such as exaggeration; sober. —**so′ber-sid′ed·ness** *n.*

so·ber·sides (sō′bər-sīdz′) *pl.n. (used with a sing. verb).* A sober-sided person.

so·bri·e·ty (ə-brī′ĭ-tē, sō-) *n.* **1.** Gravity in bearing, manner, or treatment. **2.** Moderation in or abstinence from consumption of alcoholic liquor or use of drugs: *"three years of drug-free sobriety"* (Ron Rosenbaum). See Synonyms at **abstinence.** [Middle English *sobriete,* from Old French, from Latin *sōbrietās,* from *sōbrius,* sober. See SOBER.]

so·bri·quet (sō′brĭ-kā′, -kĕt′, sō′brĭ-kā′, kĕt′) also **sou·bri·quet** (so͞o′brĭ-kā′, -kĕt′, so͞o′brĭ-kā′, -kĕt′) *n.* **1.** An affectionate or humorous nickname. **2.** An assumed name. [French, from Old French *soubriquet,* chuck under the chin.]

sob sister *n.* **1.** A journalist, especially a woman, employed as a writer or an editor of sob stories. **2.** A sentimental, ineffective person who seeks to do good.

sob story *n.* **1.** A tale of personal hardship or misfortune intended to arouse pity. **2.** A maudlin plea given as an explanation or a rationalization.

soc. *abbr.* **1.** Social. **2.** Socialist. **3.** Society.

so·ca (sō′kə) *n. Music.* A style of music, originating in the West Indies, that is a blend of soul and calypso. [SO(UL) + CA(LYPSO).]

soc·age (sŏk′ĭj, sō′kĭj) *n. Law.* Feudal tenure of land by a tenant, in return for agricultural or other nonmilitary services or for payment of rent in money. [Middle English *sokage,* from *soke,* soke. See SOKE.] —**soc′ag·er** *n.*

so-called (sō′kôld′) *adj.* **1.** Commonly called: *"new buildings . . . in so-called modern style"* (Graham Greene). **2.** Incorrectly termed: *a so-called manager, unable to inspire a team effort.*

USAGE NOTE: Quotation marks are not used to set off descriptions that follow expressions such as *so-called* and *self-styled,* which themselves relieve the writer of responsibility for the attribution: *his so-called foolproof method* (not *"foolproof method"*).

soccer
1982 World Cup soccer competition in Madrid, Spain

soc·cer (sŏk′ər) *n. Sports.* A game played on a rectangular field with net goals at either end in which two teams of 11 players each maneuver a round ball mainly by kicking or butting or by using any part of the body except the arms and hands in attempts to score points. [Alteration of *assoc.,* abbreviation of *association football.*]

So·chi (sō′chē, sô′chĭ). A city of extreme southwest Russia on the northeast shore of the Black Sea. It is a popular health resort. Population, 310,000.

so·cia·bil·i·ty (sō′shə-bĭl′ĭ-tē) *n., pl.* **-ties. 1.** The disposition or quality of being sociable. **2.** An instance of being sociable.

so·cia·ble (sō′shə-bəl) *adj.* **1.** Fond of the company of others; gregarious. **2.** Marked by or affording occasion for agreeable conversation and conviviality. See Synonyms at **social. 3.** Pleasant, friendly, and affable. See Synonyms at **gracious.** —**sociable** *n.* A social. [French, from Latin *sociābilis,* from *sociāre,* to share, join, from *socius,* companion. See **sekʷ-¹** in Appendix.] —**so′cia·ble·ness** *n.* —**so′cia·bly** *adv.*

so·cial (sō′shəl) *adj. Abbr.* **soc. 1.a.** Living together in communities. **b.** Of or relating to communal living. **c.** Of or relating to society. **2.** Living together in organized groups or similar close aggregates: *Ants are social insects.* **3.** Involving allies or members of a confederacy. **4.** Of or relating to the upper classes. **5.a.** Inclined to seek out or enjoy the company of others; sociable. **b.** Spent in or marked by friendly relations or companionship. **c.** Intended for convivial activities. **6.** Of, relating to, or occupied with matters affecting human welfare: *social problems; a social policy.* —**social** *n.* An informal social gathering, as of the members of a church congregation. [Middle English *sociale,* domestic, from Old French *social,* from Latin *sociālis,* of companionship, from *socius,* companion. See **sekʷ-¹** in Appendix.]

SYNONYMS: *social, companionable, convivial, gregarious, sociable.* The central meaning shared by these adjectives is "inclined to, marked by, or passed in friendly companionship with others": *had a social cup of coffee; a companionable pet; a woman of convivial nature; a gregarious person who avoids solitude; a sociable conversation.*
ANTONYM: *antisocial.*

social climber *n.* One who strives for acceptance in fashionable society.

social contract *n.* An agreement among the members of an organized society or between the governed and the government defining and limiting the rights and duties of each.

social Darwinism *n.* The application of Darwinism to the study of human society, specifically a theory in sociology that individuals or groups achieve advantage over others as the result of genetic or biological superiority.

social democracy *n.* A political theory advocating the use of democratic means to achieve a gradual transition from capitalism to socialism. —**social democrat** *n.* —**social democratic** *adj.*

social disease *n.* **1.** A sexually transmitted disease; a venereal disease. **2.** A disease having its highest incidence among socioeconomic groups predisposed to it by a given set of adverse living or working conditions.

social engineering *n.* The application of sociological principles to particular social problems. —**social engineer** *n.*

social insurance *n.* An insurance program carried out or mandated by a government to provide economic assistance to the unemployed, the elderly, or the disabled.

so·cial·ism (sō′shə-lĭz′əm) *n.* **1.a.** A social system in which the means of producing and distributing goods are owned collectively and political power is exercised by the whole community. **b.** The theory or practice of those who support such a social system. **2.** The building of the material base for communism under the dictatorship of the proletariat in Marxist-Leninist theory.

so·cial·ist (sō′shə-lĭst) *n. Abbr.* **soc. 1.** An advocate of socialism. **2.** Often **Socialist.** A member of a political party or group that advocates socialism. —**socialist** *adj.* **1.** Of, promoting, or practicing socialism. **2. Socialist.** Of, belonging to, or constituting a socialist party or political group.

so·cial·is·tic (sō′shə-lĭs′tĭk) *adj.* Of, advocating, or tending toward socialism. —**so′cial·is′ti·cal·ly** *adv.*

socialist realism *n.* A Marxist aesthetic doctrine that seeks to promote the development of social consciousness through didactic use of literature, art, and music.

so·cial·ite (sō′shə-līt′) *n.* One prominent in fashionable society.

so·ci·al·i·ty (sō′shē-ăl′ĭ-tē) *n., pl.* **-ties. 1.a.** The state or quality of being sociable; sociability. **b.** An instance of sociableness. **2.** The tendency to form communities and societies.

so·cial·ize (sō′shə-līz′) *v.* **-ized, -iz·ing, -iz·es.** —*tr.* **1.** To place under government or group ownership or control. **2.** To make fit for companionship with others; make sociable. **3.** To convert or adapt to the needs of society. —*intr.* To take part in social activities. —**so′cial·i·za′tion** (-shə-lĭ-zā′shən) *n.* —**so′cial·iz′er** *n.*

so·cial·ized medicine (sō′shə-līzd′) *n.* A system for providing medical and hospital care for all at a nominal cost by means of government regulation of health services and subsidies derived from taxation.

so·cial·ly (sō′shə-lē) *adv.* **1.** In a social way. **2.** With regard to society: *socially important.* **3.** By society: *socially accepted behavior.*

soc·ial-mind·ed (sō′shəl-mīn′dĭd) *adj.* Interested in social service or the welfare of society in general.

social psychiatry *n.* The branch of psychiatry that deals with the relationship between social environment and mental illness. —**social psychiatrist** *n.*

social psychology *n.* The branch of human psychology that deals with the behavior of groups and the influence of social factors on the individual. —**social psychologist** *n.*

social register *n.* A directory listing persons of social prominence in a community.

social science *n.* **1.** The study of human society and of individual relationships in and to society. **2.** A scholarly or scientific discipline that deals with such study, generally regarded as including sociology, psychology, anthropology, economics, political science, and history. —**social scientist** *n.*

social secretary *n.* A personal secretary who handles social correspondence and appointments.

social security *n.* **1.** A government program that provides economic assistance to persons faced with unemployment, disability, or agedness, financed by assessment of employers and employees. **2.** The economic assistance provided by social security.

social service *n.* **1.** Organized efforts to advance human welfare; social work. **2.** Often **social services.** Services, such as free school lunches, provided by a government for its disadvantaged citizens.

social studies *pl.n. (used with a sing. or pl. verb).* A course of study including geography, history, government, and sociology, taught in secondary and elementary schools.

social work *n.* Organized work intended to advance the social conditions of a community, and especially of the disadvantaged, by providing psychological counseling, guidance, and assistance, especially in the form of social services. —**social worker** *n.*

so·ci·e·tal (sə-sī′ĭ-tl) *adj.* Of or relating to the structure, organization, or functioning of society. **—so·ci′e·tal·ly** *adv.*

so·ci·e·ty (sə-sī′ĭ-tē) *n., pl.* **-ties.** *Abbr.* **soc., s., S. 1.a.** The totality of social relationships among human beings. **b.** A group of human beings broadly distinguished from other groups by mutual interests, participation in characteristic relationships, shared institutions, and a common culture. **c.** The institutions and culture of a distinct self-perpetuating group. **2.** An organization or association of persons engaged in a common profession, activity, or interest: *a folklore society; a society of bird watchers.* **3.a.** The rich, privileged, and fashionable social class. **b.** The socially dominant members of a community. **4.** Companionship; company: *enjoys the society of friends and family members.* **5.** *Biology.* A colony or community of organisms, usually of the same species: *an insect society.* [French *société,* from Old French, from Latin *societās,* fellowship, from *socius,* companion. See **sekʷ-¹** in Appendix.]

So·ci·e·ty Islands (sə-sī′ĭ-tē). An island group of French Polynesia in the southern Pacific Ocean east of Samoa. First visited by a Portuguese navigator in the early 17th century, the islands were named by Capt. James Cook in the 18th century and became a French protectorate in 1843.

Society of Friends *n.* A Christian denomination, founded in the mid-17th century in England, that rejects formal sacraments, a formal creed, a priesthood, and violence; the Quakers.

Society of Jesus *n. Abbr.* **S.J.** The Jesuits.

So·cin·i·an (sō-sĭn′ē-ən) *n.* An adherent of a 16th-century Italian sect holding unitarian views, including denial of the divinity of Jesus. **—Socinian** *adj.* Of or relating to the Socinians or their doctrines. [New Latin *Sociniānus,* after Laelius SOCINUS and Faustus SOCINUS.] **—So·cin′i·an·ism** *n.*

So·ci·nus (sō-sī′nəs), **Faustus.** Originally Fausto Paolo Sozzini. 1539–1604. Italian theologian who based his anti-Trinitarian teachings on the doctrine formulated by his uncle **Laelius Socinus** (1525–1562), originally Lelio Francesco Maria Sozzini. Their system of Socinianism greatly influenced the development of Unitarian theology.

socio– *pref.* **1.** Society: *sociometry.* **2.** Social: *socioeconomic.* [French, from Latin *socius,* companion. See **sekʷ-¹** in Appendix.]

so·ci·o·bi·ol·o·gy (sō′sē-ō-bī-ŏl′ə-jē, -shē-) *n.* The study of the biological determinants of social behavior, based on the theory that such behavior is often genetically transmitted and subject to evolutionary processes. **—so′ci·o·bi′o·log′i·cal** (-bī′ə-lŏj′ĭ-kəl) *adj.* **—so′ci·o·bi·ol′o·gist** *n.*

so·ci·o·cul·tur·al (sō′sē-ō-kŭl′chər-əl, -shē-) *adj.* Of or involving both social and cultural factors. **—so′ci·o·cul′tur·al·ly** *adv.*

so·ci·o·ec·o·nom·ic (sō′sē-ō-ĕk′ə-nŏm′ĭk, -ē′kə-, -shē-) *adj.* Of or involving both social and economic factors.

so·ci·o·lin·guis·tics (sō′sē-ō-lĭng-gwĭs′tĭks, -shē-) *n. (used with a sing. verb).* The study of language and linguistic behavior as influenced by social and cultural factors. **—so′ci·o·lin′guist** *n.* **—so′ci·o·lin·guis′tic** *adj.*

so·ci·ol·o·gy (sō′sē-ŏl′ə-jē, -shē-) *n.* **1.** The study of human social behavior, especially the study of the origins, organization, institutions, and development of human society. **2.** Analysis of a social institution or societal segment as a self-contained entity or in relation to society as a whole. [French *sociologie* : *socio-,* socio- + *-logie,* study (from Greek *-logia;* see -LOGY).] **—so′ci·o·log′ic** (-ə-lŏj′ĭk), **so′ci·o·log′i·cal** (-ĭ-kəl) *adj.* **—so′ci·o·log′i·cal·ly** *adv.* **—so′ci·ol′o·gist** *n.*

so·ci·om·e·try (sō′sē-ŏm′ĭ-trē, -shē-) *n.* The quantitative study of interpersonal relationships in populations, especially the study and measurement of preferences.

so·ci·o·path (sō′sē-ə-păth′, -shē-) *n.* One who is affected with a personality disorder marked by aggressive, antisocial behavior. **—so′ci·o·path′ic** *adj.*

so·ci·o·po·li·ti·cal (sō′sē-ō-pə-lĭt′ĭ-kəl, -shē-) *adj.* Involving both social and political factors.

so·ci·o·psy·cho·log·i·cal (sō′sē-ō-sī′kə-lŏj′ĭ-kəl, -shē-) *adj.* **1.** Of or relating to social psychology. **2.** Of, relating to, or combining social and psychological factors.

so·ci·o·re·lig·ious (sō′sē-ō-rĭ-lĭj′əs, -shē-) *adj.* Involving social and religious factors.

sock¹ (sŏk) *n.* **1.** *pl.* **socks** or **sox** (sŏks). A short stocking reaching a point between the ankle and the knee. **2.** *Meteorology.* A windsock. **3.a.** A light shoe worn by comic actors in ancient Greek and Roman plays. **b.** Comic drama; comedy: *"He . . . knew all niceties of the sock and buskin"* (Byron). **—sock** *tr.v.* **socked, sock·ing, socks.** To provide with socks. ***—phrasal verbs.*** **sock away.** *Informal.* To put (money) away in a safe place for future use. **sock in.** To close to air traffic: *fog that socked in the airport.* [Middle English *socke,* from Old English *socc,* a kind of light shoe, from Latin *soccus,* possibly from Greek *sunkhis, sukkhos,* Phyrgian shoe.]

sock² (sŏk) *v.* **socked, sock·ing, socks.** —*tr.* To hit or strike forcefully; punch. —*intr.* To deliver a blow. **—sock** *n.* A hard blow or punch. ***—idiom.*** **sock it to (someone).** *Slang.* To deliver a forceful comment, reprimand, or physical blow to someone else. [Origin unknown.]

sock·dol·a·ger also **sock·dol·o·ger** (sŏk-dŏl′ə-jər) *n. Slang.* **1.** A conclusive blow or remark. **2.** Something outstanding. [Origin unknown.]

sock·et (sŏk′ĭt) *n.* **1.** An opening or a cavity into which an inserted part is designed to fit: *a light-bulb socket.* **2.** *Anatomy.* **a.** The concave part of a joint that receives the end of a bone. **b.** A hollow or concavity into which a part, such as the eye, fits. **—socket** *tr.v.* **-et·ed, -et·ing, -ets.** To furnish with or insert into a socket. [Middle English *soket,* from Anglo-Norman, spearhead, diminutive of *soc,* plowshare, probably of Celtic origin. See **sū-** in Appendix.]

socket wrench *n.* A wrench with a usually interchangeable socket to fit over a nut or bolt.

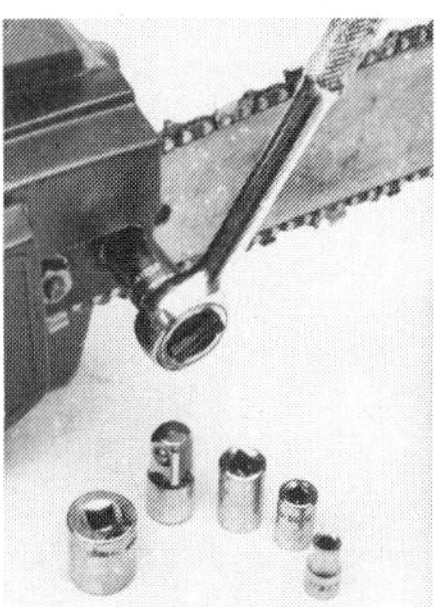

socket wrench

sock·eye salmon (sŏk′ī′) *n.* A salmon *(Oncorhynchus nerka)* of northern Pacific coastal waters that is a commercially valuable food fish. Also called *blueback salmon, red salmon.* [By folk etymology from Halkomelem (a Central Coast Salish language) *sthə́qə'y.*]

sock·o (sŏk′ō) *adj. Slang.* Impressive and effective; excellent. [From SOCK².]

so·cle (sō′kəl) *n. Architecture.* **1.** A plain square block higher than a plinth, serving as a pedestal for sculpture, a vase, or a column. **2.** A plain plinth supporting a wall. [French, from Italian *zoccolo,* wooden shoe, from Latin *socculus,* diminutive of *soccus,* a kind of light shoe. See SOCK¹.]

So·co·tra (sə-kō′trə). An island of Yemen in the Indian Ocean at the mouth of the Gulf of Aden. Known to the ancient Greeks, it came under British protection in 1886 and joined Southern Yemen (now Yemen) in 1967.

Soc·ra·tes (sŏk′rə-tēz′). 470?–399 B.C. Greek philosopher who initiated a question-and-answer method of teaching as a means of achieving self-knowledge. His theories of virtue and justice have survived through the writings of Plato, his most important pupil. Socrates was tried for corrupting the minds of Athenian youth and subsequently put to death (399).

Socrates
Copy of an early fourth-century B.C. herma

So·crat·ic (sə-krăt′ĭk, sō-) *adj.* Of or relating to Socrates or the Socratic method: *a Socratic approach to teaching.*

Socratic irony *n.* Profession of ignorance and of willingness to learn as one interrogates another on the meaning of a term.

Socratic method *n.* Employment of Socratic irony in a philosophical discussion resulting either in a mutual confession of ignorance with a promise of further investigation or in the elicitation of a truth assumed to be innate in all rational beings.

sod¹ (sŏd) *n.* **1.** A section of grass-covered surface soil held together by matted roots; turf. **2.** The ground, especially when covered with grass. **—sod** *tr.v.* **sod·ded, sod·ding, sods.** To cover with sod. [Middle English, from Middle Low German or Middle Dutch *sode.*]

sod² (sŏd) *Chiefly British. n.* **a.** A sodomite. **b.** A person regarded as obnoxious or contemptible. **c.** A fellow; a guy: *"Poor sod, he almost got lucky for once"* (Jack Higgins). **—sod** *tr.v.* **sod·ded, sod·ding, sods.** To damn. Often used in the imperative with *off.* [Short for SODOMITE.]

♦**so·da** (sō′də) *n.* **1.a.** Any of various forms of sodium carbonate. **b.** Chemically combined sodium. **2.a.** Carbonated water. **b.** *Northeastern U.S.* See **soft drink.** See Regional Note at **tonic. 3.** A refreshment made from carbonated water, ice cream, and usually a flavoring. **4.** *Games.* The card turned face up at the beginning of faro. [Middle English *sode, soda,* saltwort, soda, from Old Italian *soda,* perhaps from Arabic *suwwād,* saltwort.]

soda ash *n.* Sodium carbonate in powdery white form, used especially as an industrial chemical.

soda biscuit *n.* **1.** A breadlike biscuit leavened with baking soda. **2.** See **soda cracker.**

soda cracker *n.* A thin, usually square cracker leavened slightly with baking soda. Also called *soda biscuit.*

♦**soda fountain** *n.* **1.** An apparatus with faucets for dispensing soda water. **2.** A counter equipped for preparing and serving soft drinks, ice-cream dishes, or sandwiches. In this sense, also called ♦*spa.* See Regional Note at **spa.**

soda jerk *n. Informal.* One who works at a soda fountain. [Short for *soda jerker.*]

soda lime *n.* A mixture of calcium oxide and sodium or potassium hydroxide, used as a drying agent and carbon dioxide absorbent.

so·da·list (sōd′l-ĭst, sō-dăl′ĭst) *n.* A member of a sodality.

so·da·lite (sōd′l-īt′) *n.* A blue-white vitreous mineral, $Na_4Al_3Si_3O_{12}Cl$, found in igneous rocks.

so·dal·i·ty (sō-dăl′ĭ-tē) *n., pl.* **-ties. 1.** A society or an association, especially a devotional or charitable society for the laity in the Roman Catholic Church. **2.** Fellowship. [French *sodalité,* from Old French, from Latin *sodālitās,* fellowship, from *sodālis,* companion. See **s(w)e-** in Appendix.]

soda niter *n.* See **sodium nitrate.**

♦**soda pop** *n.* See **soft drink.**

soda water *n.* **1.a.** Effervescent water, usually containing salts, charged under pressure with purified carbon dioxide gas, used as a beverage or mixer. Also called *carbonated water, club soda, seltzer.* **b.** See **soft drink. 2.** A solution of water, sodium bicarbonate, and acid.

sod·bus·ter (sŏd′bŭs′tər) *n. Slang.* A farmer.

sod·den (sŏd′n) *adj.* **1.** Thoroughly soaked; saturated. **2.** Soggy and heavy from improper cooking; doughy. **3.** Expressionless, stupid, or dull, especially from drink. **4.** Unimaginative; torpid. **—sodden** *tr. & intr.v.* **-dened, -den·ing, -dens.** To make or become sodden. [Middle English *soden,* boiled, past participle

ă pat	oi boy
ā pay	ou out
âr care	ŏŏ took
ä father	ōō boot
ĕ pet	ŭ cut
ē be	ûr urge
ĭ pit	th thin
ī pie	*th* this
îr pier	hw which
ŏ pot	zh vision
ō toe	ə about, item
ô paw	♦ regionalism

Stress marks: **′** (primary); ′ (secondary), as in **dictionary** (dĭk′shə-nĕr′ē)

of *sethen,* to boil. See SEETHE.] **—sod′den·ly** *adv.* **—sod′den·ness** *n.*

Sod·dy (sŏd′ē), **Frederick.** 1877–1956. British chemist. He won a 1921 Nobel Prize for investigations into the origin and nature of isotopes.

Sö·der·blom (sœ′dər-blo͞om′), **Nathan.** 1866–1931. Swedish prelate and historian. He won the 1930 Nobel Peace Prize for his ecumenical activities.

Sö·der·täl·je (sœ′dər-tĕl′yə). A city of southeast Sweden, an industrial suburb of Stockholm. Population, 79,429.

so·di·um (sō′dē-əm) *n. Symbol* **Na** A soft, light, extremely malleable silver-white metallic element that reacts explosively with water, is naturally abundant in combined forms, especially in common salt, and is used in the production of a wide variety of industrially important compounds. Atomic number 11; atomic weight 22.99; melting point 97.8°C; boiling point 892°C; specific gravity 0.971; valence 1. See table at **element.** [SOD(A) + –IUM.]

sodium alginate *n.* A colorless or light yellow powdery or crystalline compound, $C_6H_7O_6Na$, used as a food thickener and stabilizer and in medicines, paint, and paper coating.

sodium ammonium phosphate *n.* A colorless, odorless crystalline compound, $NaNH_4HPO_4{\cdot}4H_2O$, used in the blowpipe analysis of minerals.

sodium barbital *n.* A white powder, $C_8H_{11}N_2NaO_3$, the soluble sodium salt of barbital, used as a hypnotic and sedative.

sodium benzoate *n.* The sodium salt of benzoic acid, $NaC_7H_5O_2$, used as a food preservative, an antiseptic, and an intermediate in dye manufacture and in the production of pharmaceuticals. Also called *benzoate of soda.*

sofa
Mid 19th-century American

sodium bicarbonate *n.* See **baking soda.**

sodium borate *n.* A crystalline compound, $Na_2B_4O_7{\cdot}10H_2O$, used in the manufacture of glass, detergents, and pharmaceuticals.

sodium carbonate *n.* A white powdery compound, Na_2CO_3, used in the manufacture of baking soda, sodium nitrate, glass, ceramics, detergents, and soap.

sodium chlorate *n.* A colorless crystalline compound, $NaClO_3$, used as a bleaching and oxidizing agent and in explosives.

sodium chloride *n.* A colorless or white crystalline compound, NaCl, used in the manufacture of chemicals and as a food preservative and seasoning.

sodium citrate *n.* A white crystalline or granular compound, $Na_3C_6H_5O_7{\cdot}2H_2O$, used in photography and in medicine especially as an anticoagulant of blood stored for transfusion.

sodium cyanide *n.* A poisonous white crystalline compound, NaCN, used in extracting gold and silver from ores and in dye manufacture.

sodium cyclamate *n.* An artificially prepared salt of cyclamic acid, $C_6H_{13}NO_3SNa$, formerly used as a low-calorie sweetener but now banned because of the possible carcinogenic effects of its metabolic products.

sodium dichromate *n.* A poisonous red-orange crystalline compound, $Na_2Cr_2O_7{\cdot}2H_2O$, used as an oxidizing agent.

sodium fluoride *n.* A colorless crystalline salt, NaF, used in fluoridation of water, in treatment of tooth decay, and as an insecticide and a disinfectant.

sodium glu·ta·mate (glo͞o′tə-māt′) *n.* Monosodium glutamate.

sodium hydrosulfite *n.* A yellowish powder, $Na_2S_2O_4$, used as a bleaching and reducing agent. Also called *hydrosulfite, sodium hyposulfite.*

sodium hydroxide *n.* A strongly alkaline compound, NaOH, used in the manufacture of chemicals and soaps and in petroleum refining. Also called *caustic soda, lye.*

sodium hypochlorite *n.* An unstable salt, NaOCl, usually stored in solution and used as a fungicide and an oxidizing bleach.

sodium hyposulfite *n.* **1.** See **sodium hydrosulfite. 2.** See **sodium thiosulfate.**

sodium nitrate *n.* A white crystalline compound, $NaNO_3$, used in solid rocket propellants, in the manufacture of explosives and glass and pottery enamel, and as fertilizer. Also called *caliche, Chile saltpeter, saltpeter, soda niter.*

sodium pentothal *n.* Thiopental sodium.

sodium perborate *n.* A white odorless crystalline compound, $NaBO_2{\cdot}H_2O_2{\cdot}3H_2O$, used as a mild alkaline oxidizing agent in dentifrices, as a topical antiseptic and deodorant, and as an industrial reagent.

sodium peroxide *n.* A yellowish-white powder, Na_2O_2, used industrially as an oxidizing and bleaching agent and medically as a germicide, an antiseptic, and a disinfectant.

sodium phosphate *n.* Any of various sodium salts of phosphoric acid, especially NaH_2PO_4, Na_2HPO_4, and Na_3PO_4, widely used in pharmaceutical manufacturing, medicine, and chemistry.

so·di·um-po·tas·si·um pump (sō′dē-əm-pə-tăs′ē-əm) *n.* A mechanism of active transport that moves potassium ions into and sodium ions out of a cell.

sodium propionate *n.* A clear crystalline compound, CH_3CH_2COONa, used as a fungicide and bactericide, especially to prevent food spoilage.

sodium silicate *n.* Any of various water-soluble silicate glass compounds used as a preservative for eggs, in plaster and cement, and in various purification and refining processes. Also called *soluble glass, water glass.*

sodium sulfate *n.* A white crystalline compound, Na_2SO_4, used to manufacture paper, glass, dyes, and pharmaceuticals.

sodium sulfide *n.* A hygroscopic yellow compound, Na_2S, used as a metal ore reagent and in photography, engraving, and printing.

sodium sulfite *n.* A white crystalline or powdered compound, Na_2SO_3, used in preserving foods, silvering mirrors, developing photographs, and making dyes.

sodium thiosulfate *n.* A white, translucent crystalline compound, $Na_2S_2O_3{\cdot}5H_2O$, used as a photographic fixing agent and as a bleach. Also called *hypo, hyposulfite, sodium hyposulfite.*

so·di·um-va·por lamp (sō′dē-əm-vā′pər) *n.* An electric lamp containing a small amount of sodium and neon gas, used in generating yellow light for lighting streets and highways.

Sod·om¹ (sŏd′əm). A city of ancient Palestine possibly located south of the Dead Sea. In the Old Testament, it was destroyed along with Gomorrah because of its wickedness and depravity.

Sod·om² or **sod·om** (sŏd′əm) *n.* A place well known for vice and corruption. [After SODOM¹.]

sod·om·ite (sŏd′ə-mīt′) *n.* One who engages in sodomy.

sod·om·ize (sŏd′ə-mīz′) *tr.v.* **-ized, -iz·ing, -iz·es.** To subject to an act of sodomy, especially forcibly.

sod·om·y (sŏd′ə-mē) *n.* **1.** Anal copulation of one male with another. **2.** Anal or oral copulation with a member of the opposite sex. **3.** Copulation with an animal. [Middle English *sodomie,* from Old French, from *Sodome,* Sodom, from Latin *Sodoma,* from Greek, from Hebrew *s'dōm.*]

so·ev·er (sō-ĕv′ər) *adv.* At all; in any way: *"Space to breathe, how short soever"* (Ben Jonson).

SOF *abbr.* Sound on film.

so·fa (sō′fə) *n.* A long upholstered seat usually with a back and arms. [Turkish, from Arabic *ṣuffah,* carpet, divan.]

sofa bed *n.* A sofa whose seat unfolds to form a bed.

so·far (sō′fär′) *n.* A system for determining the position of survivors lost at sea by which an explosion is set off underwater, the time needed for the waves to reach three different locations is calculated, and the position of the explosion is ascertained by triangulation. [*so(und) f(ixing) a(nd) r(anging).*]

so far as *conj.* Insofar as: *So far as I am concerned, the project is over.*

sof·fit (sŏf′ĭt) *n.* The underside of a structural component, such as a beam, an arch, a staircase, or a cornice. [French *soffite,* from Italian *soffitto,* from Vulgar Latin **suffictus,* past participle of *suffīgere,* to fasten beneath. See SUFFIX.]

S. of Sol. *abbr. Bible.* Song of Solomon.

So·fi·a (sō′fē-ə, sō-fē′ə). The capital and largest city of Bulgaria, in the west-central part of the country. Originally a Thracian settlement, it passed over the centuries to Rome, Byzantium, two Bulgarian kingdoms, Ottoman Turkey, and Russia. In 1879 it became the capital of Bulgaria. Population, 1,102,100.

soft (sôft, sŏft) *adj.* **soft·er, soft·est. 1.a.** Easily molded, cut, or worked. **b.** Yielding readily to pressure or weight. **2.** Out of condition; flabby. **3.** Smooth or fine to the touch: *a soft fabric.* **4.a.** Not loud, harsh, or irritating: *a soft voice.* **b.** Not brilliant or glaring; subdued: *soft colors.* **5.** Not sharply drawn or delineated: *soft charcoal shading; a scene filmed in soft focus.* **6.** Mild; balmy: *a soft breeze.* **7.a.** Of a gentle disposition; tender. **b.** Affectionate: *a soft glance.* **c.** Attracted or emotionally involved: *He has been soft on her for years.* **d.** Not stern; lenient. **e.** Lacking strength of character; weak. **f.** *Informal.* Simple; feeble. **g.** Gradually declining in trend; not firm: *a soft economy; a soft computer market.* **8.a.** *Informal.* Easy: *a soft job.* **b.** Based on conciliation or negotiation rather than on threats or power plays: *took a soft line toward their opponents.* **9.** Informal and entertaining without confronting difficult issues or hard facts: *a soft story about a senator's private life.* **10.** Using or based on data that is not readily quantifiable or amenable to experimental verification or refutation: *soft evidence; the soft sciences.* **11.** Of or relating to a paper currency as distinct from a hard currency backed by gold. **12.** Having low dissolved mineral content. **13.** *Linguistics.* **a.** Sibilant rather than guttural, as *c* in *certain* and *g* in *gem.* **b.** Voiced and weakly articulated: *a soft consonant.* **c.** Palatalized, as certain consonants in Slavic languages. **14.** Unprotected against nuclear attack: *soft missile launching sites; a soft target.* **—soft** *n.* A soft object or part. **—soft** *adv.* In a soft manner; gently. [Middle English, pleasant, calm, from Old English *sōfte.*] **—soft′ly** *adv.* **—soft′ness** *n.*

soft·ball (sôft′bôl′, sŏft′-) *n. Sports.* **1.** A variation of baseball played on a smaller diamond with a larger, softer ball that is pitched underhand. **2.** The ball used in this game.

soft-boiled (sôft′boild′, sŏft′-) *adj.* **1.** Boiled in the shell to a soft consistency. Used of an egg. **2.** *Informal.* **a.** Softhearted; lenient. **b.** Sentimental.

soft·bound (sôft′bound′, sŏft′-) *adj.* Not bound between hard covers: *softbound books.*

soft chancre *n.* See **chancroid.**

soft clam *n.* See **soft-shell clam.**

soft coal *n.* See **bituminous coal.**

soft-coat·ed wheaten terrier (sôft′kō′tĭd, sŏft′-) *n.* A medium-sized terrier of a breed that originated in Ireland, having a wheat-colored coat of soft, wavy hair.

soft-core (sôft′kôr′, -kōr′, sŏft′-) *adj.* **1.** Being less explicit than hard-core material in depicting or describing sexual activity: *soft-core pornography.* **2.** Moderate: *a soft-core sports fan.*

soft·cov·er (sôft′kŭv′ər, sŏft′-) *adj.* Not bound between hard covers: *softcover books; a softcover edition.*

♦ **soft drink** *n.* A nonalcoholic, flavored, carbonated beverage, usually commercially prepared and sold in bottles or cans. Also called ♦*cold drink,* ♦*pop,* ♦*soda,* ♦*soda pop,* ♦*soda water,* ♦*tonic.* See Regional Note at **tonic.**

soft drug *n.* A drug that is believed to be nonaddictive and less damaging to the health than a hard drug.

soft·en (sô′fən, sŏf′ən) *v.* **-ened, -en·ing, -ens.** —*tr.* **1.** To make soft or softer. **2.** To undermine or reduce the strength, morale, or resistance of. **3.** To make less harsh, strident, or critical: *softened the last paragraph of the letter.* —*intr.* To become soft or softer. —**soft′en·er** *n.*

soft-finned (sôft′fĭnd′, sŏft′-) *adj.* Having fins supported by flexible cartilaginous rays; not spiny-finned. Used of bony fishes.

soft goods *pl.n.* See **dry goods.**

soft hail *n.* See **snow pellet.**

soft·head (sôft′hĕd′, sŏft′-) *n.* A person regarded as foolish.

soft·head·ed (sôft′hĕd′ĭd, sŏft′-) *adj.* Lacking judgment, realism, or firmness. —**soft′head′ed·ly** *adv.* —**soft′head′ed·ness** *n.*

soft·heart·ed (sôft′här′tĭd, sŏft′-) *adj.* Easily moved; tender. —**soft′heart′ed·ly** *adv.* —**soft′heart′ed·ness** *n.*

soft·ie (sôf′tē, sŏf′-) *n.* Variant of **softy.**

soft-land (sôft′lănd′, sŏft′-) *intr. & tr.v.* **-land·ed, -land·ing, -lands.** To make or cause to make a soft landing.

soft landing *n.* The landing of a space vehicle on a celestial body or on Earth in such a way as to prevent damage or destruction of the vehicle.

soft-lin·er (sôft′lī′nər, sŏft′-) *n.* One that takes a moderate or flexible approach, especially on a political issue.

soft news *n.* News, as in a newspaper or television report, that does not deal with formal or serious topics and events. —**soft′-news′** (sôft′no͞oz′, -nyo͞oz′, sŏft′-) *adj.*

soft palate *n.* The movable fold, consisting of muscular fibers enclosed in mucous membrane, that is suspended from the rear of the hard palate and closes off the nasal cavity from the oral cavity during swallowing or sucking.

soft paste also **soft-paste** (sôft′pāst′, sŏft′-) *n.* Any of various ceramics containing frit and refined clay.

soft pedal *n. Music.* A pedal used to mute tone, as on a piano.

soft-ped·al (sôft′pĕd′l, sŏft′-) *tr.v.* **-aled, -al·ing, -als** or **-alled, -al·ling, -als. 1.** *Music.* To soften or mute the tone of by depressing the soft pedal. **2.** *Informal.* To make less emphatic or obvious; play down: *soft-pedal a potentially explosive issue.*

soft rock *n. Music.* A style of rock 'n' roll characterized by the predominance of melody and minimal use of electronic modulations.

soft roe *n.* The spermatozoa or testes of a fish; milt.

soft sculpture *n.* A sculpture made of pliant materials, such as cloth or foam rubber.

soft sell *n. Informal.* A subtly persuasive, low-pressure method of selling or advertising.

soft-shell (sôft′shĕl′, sŏft′-) also **soft-shelled** (-shĕld′) —*adj.* Having a soft, brittle, or unhardened shell. Used of an aquatic animal. —*n.* A soft-shelled aquatic animal.

soft-shell clam *n.* A common edible North American clam *(Mya arenaria)* having a thin, elongated shell, found especially along the Atlantic coast. Also called *soft clam, steamer.*

soft-shell crab *n.* A marine crab before its shell has hardened after molting, especially the edible species *(Callinectes sapidus)* of eastern North America in this stage.

soft-shelled (sôft′shĕld′, sŏft′-) *adj.* Variant of **soft-shell.**

soft-shelled turtle *n.* Any of various freshwater turtles of the family Trionychidae, having a flat carapace covered with leathery skin and fleshy, elongated snout.

soft-shoe (sôft′sho͞o′, sŏft′-) *n.* Tap dancing performed while wearing shoes without metal taps.

soft shoulder *n.* A border of soft earth running along the edge of a road.

soft soap *n.* **1.** A fluid or semifluid soap. **2.** *Informal.* Flattery; cajolery.

soft-soap (sôft′sōp′, sŏft′-) *tr.v.* **-soaped, -soap·ing, -soaps.** *Informal.* To flatter in order to gain something; cajole. —**soft′-soap′er** *n.*

soft-spo·ken (sôft′spō′kən, sŏft′-) *adj.* **1.** Speaking with a soft or gentle voice: *a soft-spoken instructor.* **2.** Smooth; ingratiating: *a soft-spoken attempt at bribery.*

soft spot *n.* **1.** A tender or sentimental feeling. **2.** A weak or vulnerable point: *a soft spot in his defenses.* **3.** See **fontanel.**

soft-top (sôft′tŏp′) *n.* A car having a top constructed of cloth or a combination of metal and cloth. —**soft′-top′** *adj.*

soft touch *n.* One easily persuaded or taken advantage of.

soft·ware (sôft′wâr′, sŏft′-) *n. Computer Science.* The programs, routines, and symbolic languages that control the functioning of the hardware and direct its operation. —*attributive.* Often used to modify another noun: *software manufacturers; software sales.*

soft water *n.* Water containing little or no dissolved salts of calcium or magnesium, especially water containing less than 85.5 parts per million of calcium carbonate.

soft·wood (sôft′wo͝od′, sŏft′-) *n.* **1.** The wood of a coniferous tree. **2.** A coniferous tree.

soft·y or **soft·ie** (sôf′tē, sŏf′-) *n., pl.* **-ies.** *Informal.* **1.** A person regarded as weak or sentimental. **2.** A person who finds it difficult to punish or be strict.

SOG *abbr.* Special Operations Group.

sog·gy (sŏg′ē, sô′gē) *adj.* **-gi·er, -gi·est. 1.** Saturated or sodden with moisture; soaked: *soggy clothes.* **2.** Lacking spirit; dull: *a soggy bit of dialogue.* **3.** Humid; sultry: *a soggy afternoon in August.* [From dialectal *sog,* to be soaked (from Middle English *soggon,* soaked, probably of Scandinavian origin) or from dialectal *sog,* swamp.] —**sog′gi·ly** *adv.* —**sog′gi·ness** *n.*

Sog·na·fjord or **Sog·ne Fjord** (sông′nə-fyôr′). An inlet of the Norwegian Sea in southwest Norway extending inland about 193 km (120 mi). It is the longest and deepest fjord in the country.

So·ho (sō′hō′). **1.** A district of central London, England. Inhabited in the 17th century mainly by immigrants, it is known today for its restaurants, theaters, and nightclubs. **2.** Also **So·Ho.** A district of New York City on southwest Manhattan Island noted for its galleries, shops, restaurants, and artists' lofts. The area is *so*uth of *Ho*uston Street, hence the name.

soi-di·sant (swä′dē-zäɴ′) *adj.* Self-styled; so-called. [French : *soi,* oneself + *disant,* saying.]

soi·gné also **soi·gnée** (swän-yā′) *adj.* **1.** Showing sophisticated elegance; fashionable: *a soigné little club.* **2.** Well-groomed; polished: *The soigné duchess received her guests in the drawing room.* [French, from Old French, past participle of *soigner,* to take care of, of Germanic origin.]

soil[1] (soil) *n.* **1.** The top layer of the earth's surface, consisting of rock and mineral particles mixed with organic matter. **2.** A particular kind of earth or ground: *sandy soil.* **3.** Country; land: *native soil.* **4.** The agricultural life: *a woman of the soil.* **5.** A place or condition favorable to growth; a breeding ground. [Middle English, from Anglo-Norman, a piece of ground, from Latin *solium,* seat. See **sed-** in Appendix.]

soil[2] (soil) *v.* **soiled, soil·ing, soils.** —*tr.* **1.** To make dirty, particularly on the surface. **2.** To disgrace; tarnish: *a reputation soiled by scandal.* **3.** To corrupt; defile. **4.** To dirty with excrement. —*intr.* To become dirty, stained, or tarnished. —**soil** *n.* **1.a.** The state of being soiled. **b.** A stain. **2.** Filth, sewage, or refuse matter. **3.** Manure, especially human excrement, used as fertilizer. [Middle English *soilen,* from Old French *souiller,* from Vulgar Latin **suculāre* (from Late Latin *suculus,* diminutive of Latin *sūs,* pig; see **sū-** in Appendix) or from *souil,* pigsty, wallow (from Latin *solium,* seat; see SOIL[1]).]

soil[3] (soil) *tr.v.* **soiled, soil·ing, soils. 1.** To feed (livestock) with soilage. **2.** To purge (livestock) by feeding with green food. [Origin unknown.]

soil·age (soi′lĭj) *n.* Green crops cut for feeding penned livestock.

soil pipe *n.* A drainpipe that carries off wastes from a plumbing fixture, especially from a toilet.

soil·ure (soil′yər) *n.* **1.** Soiling or the condition of being soiled. **2.** A blot, stain, or smudge.

soi·ree also **soi·rée** (swä-rā′) *n.* An evening party or reception. [French *soirée,* from Old French *seree,* from *seir,* evening, from Latin *sērō,* at a late hour, from *sērus,* late.]

so·journ (sō′jûrn′, sō-jûrn′) *intr.v.* **-journed, -journ·ing, -journs.** To reside temporarily. See Synonyms at **stay**[1]. —**sojourn** *n.* A temporary stay; a brief period of residence. [Middle English *sojournen,* from Old French *sojorner,* from Vulgar Latin **subdiurnāre* : Latin *sub-,* sub- + Late Latin *diurnum,* day (from Latin, daily ration, from neuter of *diurnus,* daily, from *diēs,* day; see **deiw-** in Appendix).] —**so′journ′er** *n.*

soke (sōk) *n.* **1.** In early English law, the right of local jurisdiction, generally one of the feudal rights of lordship. **2.** The district over which soke jurisdiction was exercised. [Middle English, from Medieval Latin *sōca,* from Old English *sōcn,* act of seeking. See **sāg-** in Appendix.]

sol[1] (sōl) also **so** (sō) *n. Music.* The fifth tone of the diatonic scale in solfeggio. [Middle English, from Medieval Latin. See GAMUT.]

sol[2] (sŏl) *n.* An old French coin worth 12 deniers. [French, from Old French, from Late Latin *solidus,* solidus. See SOLIDUS.]

sol[3] (sōl) *n., pl.* **so·les** (sō′lās). A monetary unit fomerly used in Peru, worth 1⁄1000 of an inti. [Spanish, sun (from the drawing on the coin), from Latin *sōl,* sun. See **sāwel-** in Appendix.]

sol[4] (sôl, sōl) *n.* A colloidal solution. [From SOLUTION.]

Sol (sŏl, sōl) *n.* The sun. [Middle English, from Latin *sōl.* See **sāwel-** in Appendix.]

sol. *abbr.* **1.** Solicitor. **2.** Soluble. **3.** Solution.

so·la[1] (sō′lə) *n.* A plural of **solum.**

so·la[2] (sō′lə) *adv.* By oneself; alone. Used as a stage direction to a female character. [Italian, feminine of *solo,* solo. See SOLO.]

sol·ace (sŏl′ĭs) *n.* **1.** Comfort in sorrow, misfortune, or distress; consolation. **2.** A source of comfort or consolation. —**solace** *tr.v.* **-aced, -ac·ing, -ac·es. 1.** To comfort, cheer, or console, as in

soft-shelled turtle
Eastern spiny soft-shelled turtle
Trionyx spiniferus spiniferus

ă **pat**	oi **boy**
ā **pay**	ou **out**
âr **care**	o͝o **took**
ä **father**	o͞o **boot**
ĕ **pet**	ŭ **cut**
ē **be**	ûr **urge**
ĭ **pit**	th **thin**
ī **pie**	*th* **this**
îr **pier**	hw **which**
ŏ **pot**	zh **vision**
ō **toe**	ə **about, item**
ô **paw**	♦ **regionalism**

Stress marks: ′ (primary); ′ (secondary), as in **dictionary** (dĭk′shə-nĕr′ē)

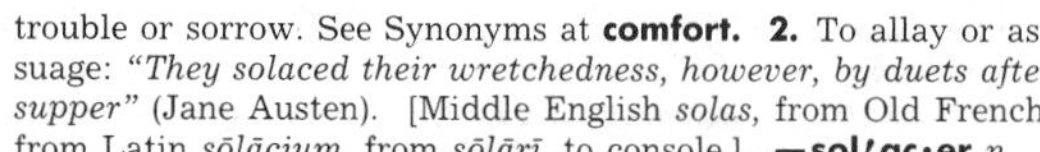

trouble or sorrow. See Synonyms at **comfort.** **2.** To allay or assuage: *"They solaced their wretchedness, however, by duets after supper"* (Jane Austen). [Middle English *solas,* from Old French, from Latin *sōlācium,* from *sōlārī,* to console.] **—sol′ac·er** *n.*

so·lan (sō′lən) *n.* See **gannet.** [Middle English *soland* : Old Norse *sūla,* pillar, gannet + Old Norse *önd,* duck.]

so·la·nine (sō′lə-nēn′, -nĭn) also **so·la·nin** (-nĭn) *n.* A bitter poisonous alkaloid, $C_{45}H_{73}NO_{15}$, derived from potato sprouts, tomatoes, and nightshade and having narcotic properties formerly used to treat epilepsy. [French, from Latin *sōlānum,* nightshade, from *sōl,* sun. See **sāwel-** in Appendix.]

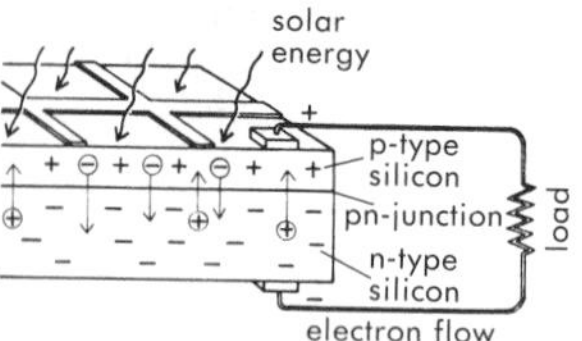

solar cell

so·lar (sō′lər) *adj.* **1.** Of, relating to, or proceeding from the sun: *solar rays.* **2.** Using or operated by energy derived from the sun: *a solar heating system.* **3.** Determined or measured in reference to the sun: *the solar year.* [Middle English, from Latin *sōlāris,* from *sōl,* sun. See **sāwel-** in Appendix.]

solar battery *n.* A system consisting of a large number of connected solar cells.

solar cell *n.* A semiconductor device that converts the energy of sunlight into electric energy. Also called *photovoltaic cell.*

solar constant *n.* The average density of solar radiation measured outside Earth's atmosphere and at Earth's mean distance from the sun, equal to 0.140 watt per square centimeter.

solar day *n.* A mean solar day.

solar flare *n.* A sudden eruption of hydrogen gas on the surface of the sun, usually associated with sunspots and accompanied by a burst of ultraviolet radiation that is often followed by a magnetic disturbance.

solar furnace *n.* A parabolic reflector that focuses solar radiation at a point to obtain temperatures as high as 4,000°C (7,200°F).

solar house *n.* A house having large quantities of heat-absorbing material behind large glass areas, designed to use solar radiation for heating.

so·lar·i·a (sō-lâr′ē-ə, sə-) *n.* A plural of **solarium.**

so·lar·im·e·ter (sō′lə-rĭm′ĭ-tər) *n.* An instrument used to measure the flux of solar radiation through a surface.

so·lar·i·um (sō-lâr′ē-əm, sə-) *n., pl.* **-i·a** (-ē-ə) or **-i·ums.** A room, gallery, or glassed-in porch exposed to the sun. [Latin *sōlārium,* terrace, flat housetop, from *sōl,* sun. See **sāwel-** in Appendix.]

so·lar·ize (sō′lə-rīz′) *v.* **-ized, -iz·ing, -iz·es.** *—tr.* To affect by exposing to the sun's rays. *—intr.* To be overexposed. Used of photographic film. **—so′lar·i·za′tion** (-lər-ĭ-zā′shən) *n.*

solar house

solar month *n.* One twelfth of a solar year, totaling 30 days 10 hours 29 minutes 3.8 seconds.

solar panel *n.* A group of connected solar cells.

solar plexus *n.* **1.** The large network of sympathetic nerves and ganglia located in the peritoneal cavity behind the stomach and having branching tracts that supply nerves to the abdominal viscera. **2.** The pit of the stomach. [From its radially branching ganglia.]

solar system *n.* The sun together with the nine planets and all other celestial bodies that orbit the sun.

solar wind (wĭnd) *n.* A stream of ionized particles ejected at high speeds from the surface of the sun.

solar year *n.* The period of time required for the earth to make one complete revolution around the sun, measured from one vernal equinox to the next and equal to 365 days, 5 hours, 48 minutes, 45.51 seconds. Also called *astronomical year, tropical year.*

so·la·ti·um (sō-lā′shē-əm) *n., pl.* **-ti·a** (-shē-ə). *Law.* Compensation for injured feelings as distinct from financial loss or physical suffering. [Late Latin *sōlācium, sōlātium,* compensation, solace, from Latin. See SOLACE.]

sold (sōld) *v.* Past tense and past participle of **sell.**

sol·dan (sŏl′dən, sōl′-) also **sou·dan** (sōōd′n) *n.* A sultan in Egypt. [Middle English, from Old French, from Arabic *sulṭān.*]

sol·der (sŏd′ər) *n.* **1.** Any of various fusible alloys, usually tin and lead, used to join metallic parts. **2.** Something that joins or cements. **—solder** *v.* **-dered, -der·ing, -ders.** *—tr.* To serve as a bond between; join. *—intr.* **1.** To unite or repair things with solder. **2.** To be joined by or as if by solder. [Middle English *soudur,* from Old French *soudure, soldure,* from *souder, soulder,* to solder, from Latin *solidāre,* to make solid, from *solidus,* solid. See SOLID.] **—sol′der·er** *n.*

solar panel
On the Skylab satellite

sol·dier (sōl′jər) *n.* **1.** One who serves in an army. **2.** An enlisted person or a noncommissioned officer. **3. a.** An active, loyal, and militant follower: *a soldier in the environmental coalition.* **b.** A trusted follower of an organized crime leader. **4.** A sexually undeveloped form of certain ants and termites, having large heads and powerful jaws specialized to serve as fighting weapons. **—soldier** *intr.v.* **-diered, -dier·ing, -diers.** **1.** To be or serve as a soldier. **2.** To make a show of working in order to escape punishment. [Middle English *soudier,* mercenary, from Anglo-Norman *soudeour, soldeier* and Old French *soudoior, soudier,* both from Old French *sol, soud,* sou, from Late Latin *solidum, soldum,* pay, from *solidus,* solidus. See SOLIDUS.]

WORD HISTORY: Why do soldiers fight? One answer is hidden away in the word *soldier* itself. Its first recorded occurrence is found in a work composed around 1300, the word having come into Middle English (as *soudier*) from Old French *soudoior* and Anglo-Norman *soudeour.* The Old French word, first recorded in the 12th century, is derived from *sol* or *soud,* Old French forms of Modern French *sou.* There is no longer a French coin named *sou,* but the meaning of the word *sou* alerts us to the fact that money is involved. Indeed, Old French *sol* referred to a coin and also meant "pay," and a *soudoior* was a man who fought for pay. This was a concept worth expressing in an era when many men were not paid for fighting but did it in service to a feudal superior. Thus *soldier* is parallel to the word *mercenary,* which goes back to Latin *mercēnnārius,* derived from *merces,* "pay," and meaning "working for pay." The word could also be used as a noun, one of whose senses was "a soldier of fortune."

sol·dier·ly (sōl′jər-lē) *adj.* Of, relating to, or befitting a soldier.

soldier of fortune *n., pl.* **soldiers of fortune.** One who will serve in any army for personal gain or love of adventure.

sol·diers' home (sōl′jərz) *n.* A government-funded institution for the care of armed forces veterans.

sol·dier·y (sōl′jə-rē) *n.* **1.** Soldiers considered as a group. **2.** The profession of soldiering.

sold-out (sōld′out′) *adj.* Having all tickets or accommodations completely sold, especially ahead of time.

sole¹ (sōl) *n.* **1.** The underside of the foot. **2.** The underside of a shoe or boot, often excluding the heel. **3.** The part on which something else rests while in a vertical position, especially: **a.** The bottom surface of a plow. **b.** *Sports.* The bottom surface of the head of a golf club. **—sole** *tr.v.* **soled, sol·ing, soles.** **1.** To furnish (a shoe or boot) with a sole. **2.** *Sports.* To put the sole of (a golf club) on the ground, as in preparing to make a stroke. [Middle English, from Old French, from Latin *solea,* sandal, from *solum,* bottom, sole of the foot.]

sole² (sōl) *adj.* **1.** Being the only one: *the sole survivor of the crash.* See Synonyms at **single.** **2.** Of or relating to only one individual or group; exclusive: *The court has the sole right to decide.* **3.** *Law.* Single; unmarried. [Middle English, alone, from Old French *sol,* from Latin *sōlus.* See **s(w)e-** in Appendix.]

sole³ (sōl) *n., pl.* **sole** or **soles.** **1.** Any of various chiefly marine flatfish of the family Soleidae, related to and resembling the flounders, especially any of several European species, such as *Solea solea,* valued as food fishes. **2.** Any of various other flatfish, especially certain coastal flounders. [Middle English, from Old French, from Latin *solea,* sandal, flatfish (from its shape). See SOLE¹.]

sol·e·cism (sŏl′ĭ-sĭz′əm, sō′lĭ-) *n.* **1.** A nonstandard usage or grammatical construction. **2.** A violation of etiquette. **3.** An impropriety, a mistake, or an incongruity. [Latin *soloecismus,* from Greek *soloikismos,* from *soloikizein,* to speak incorrectly, from *soloikos,* speaking incorrectly, after *Soloi* (Soli), an Athenian colony in Cilicia where a dialect regarded as substandard was spoken.] **—sol′e·cist** *n.* **—sol′e·cis′tic** *adj.*

So·le·dad (sō′lə-dăd′, sô′lĕ-*thäth*′). A city of northern Colombia, a suburb of Barranquilla. Population, 156,846.

sole·ly (sōl′lē, sō′lē) *adv.* **1.** Alone; singly: *solely responsible.* **2.** Entirely; exclusively: *did it solely for love.*

sol·emn (sŏl′əm) *adj.* **1.** Deeply earnest, serious, and sober. **2.** Somberly or gravely impressive. See Synonyms at **serious.** **3.** Performed with full ceremony: *a solemn High Mass.* **4.** Invoking the force of religion; sacred: *a solemn vow.* **5.** Gloomy; somber. [Middle English *solemne,* from Old French, from Latin *sollemnis,* established, customary. See **sol-** in Appendix.] **—sol′emn·ly** *adv.* **—sol′emn·ness** *n.*

so·lem·ni·ty (sə-lĕm′nĭ-tē) *n., pl.* **-ties.** **1.** The quality or condition of being solemn. **2.** A solemn observance or proceeding.

sol·em·nize (sŏl′əm-nīz′) *tr.v.* **-nized, -niz·ing, -niz·es.** **1.** To celebrate or observe with dignity and gravity. See Synonyms at **observe.** **2.** To perform with formal ceremony. **3.** To make serious or grave. **—sol′em·ni·za′tion** (-nĭ-zā′shən) *n.*

so·le·no·don (sə-lē′nə-dŏn′, -lĕn′ə-) *n.* A large ratlike insectivorous mammal of the family Solenodontidae, especially *Solenodon paradoxus* of Hispaniola and *S. cubanus* of Cuba, characterized by a long tubular snout and a long, stiff, scaly tail. [New Latin *Sōlēnodōn,* type genus : Greek *sōlēn,* pipe, channel + *-odōn,* -odon.]

so·le·noid (sō′lə-noid′) *n.* **1.** A current-carrying coil of wire that acts like a magnet when a current passes through it. **2.** An assembly used as a switch, consisting of a coil and a metal core free to slide along the coil axis under the influence of the magnetic field. [French *solénoïde,* from Greek *sōlēnoeidēs,* pipe-shaped : *sōlēn,* pipe + *-oeidēs,* -oid.] **—so′le·noi′dal** (-noid′l) *adj.* **—so′le·noi′dal·ly** *adv.*

So·lent (sō′lənt). A narrow channel between the Isle of Wight and the southern mainland of England. The Solent provides access to the port of Southampton.

sole·plate (sōl′plāt′) *n.* The underside of a clothes iron.

sole·print (sōl′prĭnt′) *n.* **1.** A print of the sole of the foot. **2.** A print of the sole of the foot made for identification, as of a newborn infant.

so·les (sō′lās) *n.* Plural of **sol³.**

so·le·us (sō′lē-əs) *n., pl.* **-le·i** (-lē-ī′). A broad, flat muscle of the calf of the leg, situated under the gastrocnemius. [New Latin, from Latin *solea,* sandal. See SOLE¹.]

sol-fa (sōl-fä′) *Music. n.* **1.** The set of syllables *do, re, mi, fa, sol, la,* and *ti,* used to represent the tones of the scale. **2.** Use of these syllables. **—sol-fa** *intr. & tr.v.* **-faed, -fa·ing, -fas.** To use the sol-fa syllables or sing using these syllables. [Italian *solfa,* from Medieval Latin : *sol,* note of the scale; see GAMUT + *fa,* note of the scale; see GAMUT.]

sol·fa·ta·ra (sōl′fə-tär′ə) *n.* A volcanic area that gives off sulfurous gases and steam. [Italian, from *solfo,* sulfur, from Latin *sulfur.*] **—sol′fa·ta′ric** *adj.*

sol·fège (sŏl-fĕzh′, sōl-) *n. Music.* Solfeggio. [French, from Italian *solfeggio.* See SOLFEGGIO.]

sol·feg·gio (sŏl-fĕj′ē-ō′, -fĕj′ō) *n., pl.* **-feg·gi** (-fĕj′ē) or **-gios.** *Music.* **1.** Use of the sol-fa syllables to note the tones of the scale; solmization. **2.** A singing exercise in which the sol-fa syllables are used. [Italian, from *solfa,* sol-fa. See SOL-FA.]

sol·fe·ri·no (sŏl′fə-rē′nō) *n. Color.* A moderate purplish red. [After *Solferino,* a village of northern Italy, from the discovery of a dye of this color in the same year that a battle was fought there (1859).]

so·lic·it (sə-lĭs′ĭt) *v.* **-it·ed, -it·ing, -its.** *—tr.* **1.** To seek to obtain by persuasion, entreaty, or formal application: *a candidate who solicited votes among the factory workers.* **2.** To petition persistently; importune: *solicited the neighbors for donations.* **3.** To entice or incite to evil or illegal action. **4.** To approach or accost (a person) with an offer of sexual services. *—intr.* **1.** To make solicitation or petition for something desired. **2.** To approach or accost someone with an offer of sexual services in return for payment. [Middle English *soliciten,* to disturb, from Old French *solliciter,* from Latin *sollicitāre,* from *sollicitus,* troubled. See SOLICITOUS.] **—so·lic′i·ta′tion** *n.*

so·lic·i·tor (sə-lĭs′ĭ-tər) *n. Abbr.* **sol. 1.** One that solicits, especially one that seeks trade or contributions. **2.** The chief law officer of a city, town, or government department. **3.** *Chiefly British.* An attorney who is not a member of the bar and who may be heard only in the lower courts. See Synonyms at **lawyer.**

solicitor general *n., pl.* **solicitors general.** *Abbr.* **S.G., SG 1.** A law officer assisting an attorney general. **2.** The chief law officer in a state not having an attorney general.

so·lic·i·tous (sə-lĭs′ĭ-təs) *adj.* **1.a.** Anxious or concerned: *a solicitous parent.* **b.** Expressing care or concern: *made solicitous inquiries about our family.* See Synonyms at **thoughtful. 2.** Full of desire; eager. **3.** Marked by or given to anxious care and often hovering attentiveness. **4.** Extremely careful; meticulous: *solicitous in matters of behavior.* [Latin *sollicitus* : *sollus,* entire; see **sol-** in Appendix + *citus,* past participle of *ciēre,* to set in motion; see **kei-**[2] in Appendix.] **—so·lic′i·tous·ly** *adv.* **—so·lic′i·tous·ness** *n.*

so·lic·i·tude (sə-lĭs′ĭ-to͞od′, -tyo͞od′) *n.* **1.** The state of being solicitous; care or concern, as for the well-being of another. See Synonyms at **anxiety. 2.** Often **solicitudes.** A cause of anxiety or concern.

sol·id (sŏl′ĭd) *adj.* **-er, -est. 1.a.** Of definite shape and volume; not liquid or gaseous. **b.** Firm or compact in substance. See Synonyms at **firm**[1]**. 2.** Not hollowed out: *a solid block of wood.* **3.** Being the same substance or color throughout: *solid gold.* **4.** *Mathematics.* Of or relating to three-dimensional geometric figures or bodies. **5.** Having no gaps or breaks; continuous: *a solid line of people.* **6.** Of good quality and substance: *a solid foundation.* **7.** Substantial; hearty: *a solid meal.* **8.** Sound; reliable: *solid facts.* **9.** Financially sound. **10.** Upstanding and dependable: *a solid citizen.* **11.** Written without a hyphen or space. For example, the word *software* is a solid compound. **12.** *Printing.* Having no leads between the lines. **13.** Acting together; unanimous: *a solid voting bloc.* **—solid** *n.* **1.** A substance having a definite shape and volume; one that is neither liquid nor gaseous. **2.** *Mathematics.* A geometric figure having three dimensions. [Middle English *solide,* from Old French, from Latin *solidus.* See **sol-** in Appendix.] **—sol′id·ly** *adv.* **—sol′id·ness** *n.*

solid angle *n. Mathematics.* An angle formed by three or more planes intersecting at a common point.

sol·i·dar·i·ty (sŏl′ĭ-dăr′ĭ-tē) *n.* A union of interests, purposes, or sympathies among members of a group; fellowship of responsibilities and interests: *"The perennial conflict between national egoism and international solidarity becomes more and more visible"* (Isaac Deutscher). See Synonyms at **unity.** [French *solidarité,* from *solidaire,* interdependent, from Old French, in common, from Latin *solidus,* solid, whole. See SOLID.]

solid geometry *n. Mathematics.* The branch of mathematics that deals with three-dimensional figures and surfaces.

sol·i·di (sŏl′ĭ-dī′) *n.* Plural of **solidus.**

so·lid·i·fy (sə-lĭd′ə-fī′) *v.* **-fied, -fy·ing, -fies.** *—tr.* **1.** To make solid, compact, or hard. **2.** To make strong or united. *—intr.* To become solid or united. **—so·lid′i·fi·ca′tion** (-fĭ-kā′shən) *n.*

so·lid·i·ty (sə-lĭd′ĭ-tē) *n.* **1.** The condition or property of being solid. **2.** Soundness of mind, moral character, or finances.

solid of revolution *n. Mathematics.* A volume generated by the rotation of a plane figure about an axis in its plane.

solid propellant *n.* A rocket propellant in solid form, combining both fuel and oxidizer in the form of a compact, cohesive grain.

solid solution *n.* A homogeneous crystalline structure in which one or more types of atoms or molecules may be partly substituted for the original atoms and molecules without changing the structure.

sol·id-state (sŏl′ĭd-stāt′) *adj.* **1.** Characteristic of or relating to the physical properties of solid materials, especially to the electromagnetic, thermodynamic, and structural properties of crystalline solids. **2.** Based on or consisting chiefly or exclusively of semiconducting materials, components, and related devices.

sol·i·dus (sŏl′ĭ-dəs) *n., pl.* **-di** (-dī′). **1.** A gold coin of the Roman Empire used in Europe until the 15th century. Also called *bezant.* **2.** *Printing.* A virgule; a slash. [Middle English, from Late Latin *(nummus) solidus,* a solid (sesterce), from Latin *solidus,* solid. See SOLID.]

So·li·hull (sō′lĭ-hŭl′). A borough of central England, a residential suburb of Birmingham. Population, 198,500.

so·lil·o·quize (sə-lĭl′ə-kwīz′) *intr. & tr.v.* **-quized, -quiz·ing, -quiz·es.** To utter or put into the form of a soliloquy. **—so·lil′o·quist** (-kwĭst), **so·lil′o·quiz′er** (-kwī′zər) *n.*

so·lil·o·quy (sə-lĭl′ə-kwē) *n., pl.* **-quies. 1.a.** A dramatic or literary form of discourse in which a character reveals his or her thoughts when alone or unaware of the presence of other characters. **b.** A specific speech or piece of writing in this form of discourse. **2.** The act of speaking to oneself. [Late Latin *sōliloquium* : Latin *sōlus,* alone; see **s(w)e-** in Appendix + Latin *loquī,* to speak; see **tolkʷ-** in Appendix.]

So·ling·en (zō′lĭng-ən). A city of west-central Germany east-southeast of Düsseldorf. Chartered in 1374, it is noted for its cutlery. Population, 158,418.

sol·ip·sism (sŏl′ĭp-sĭz′əm, sō′lĭp-) *n. Philosophy.* **1.** The theory that the self is the only thing that can be known and verified. **2.** The theory or view that the self is the only reality. [Latin *sōlus,* alone; see **s(w)e-** in Appendix + Latin *ipse,* self + —ISM.] **—sol′ip·sist** *n.* **—sol′ip·sis′tic** *adj.*

sol·i·taire (sŏl′ĭ-târ′) *n.* **1.** A gem, such as a diamond, that is set alone. **2.** *Games.* Any of a number of card games played by one person. **3.** Any of several thrushes of the genus *Myadestes,* found in North and Central America and noted for their beautiful song. [French, solitary, from Old French. See SOLITARY.]

sol·i·tar·y (sŏl′ĭ-tĕr′ē) *adj.* **1.** Existing, living, or going without others; alone: *a solitary traveler.* See Synonyms at **alone. 2.** Happening, done, or made alone: *a solitary evening; solitary pursuits such as reading and sewing.* **3.** Remote from civilization; secluded: *a solitary retreat.* **4.** Having no companions; lonesome or lonely. **5.** *Zoology.* Living alone or in pairs only: *solitary wasps; solitary sparrows.* **6.** Single and set apart from others: *a solitary instance of cowardice.* See Synonyms at **single. —solitary** *n., pl.* **-ies. 1.** A person who lives alone; a recluse. **2.** Solitary confinement. [Middle English, from Old French *solitaire,* from Latin *sōlitārius,* from *sōlitās,* solitude, from *sōlus,* alone. See **s(w)e-** in Appendix.] **—sol′i·tar′i·ly** (-târ′ə-lē) *adv.* **—sol′i·tar′i·ness** *n.*

solitary confinement *n.* The confinement of a prisoner in isolation from all other prisoners.

sol·i·tude (sŏl′ĭ-to͞od′, -tyo͞od′) *n.* **1.** The state or quality of being alone or remote from others. **2.** A lonely or secluded place. [Middle English, from Old French, from Latin *sōlitūdō,* from *sōlus,* alone. See **s(w)e-** in Appendix.]

SYNONYMS: *solitude, isolation, seclusion, retirement.* These nouns denote the state of being alone. *Solitude* implies the absence of all others: *"The worst solitude is to be destitute of sincere friendship"* (Francis Bacon). *"I love tranquil solitude"* (Percy Bysshe Shelley). *Isolation* emphasizes total separation or detachment from others: *"the isolation of Crusoe, depicted by Defoe's genius"* (Winston Churchill). *"The beast and the monk, robbed of the isolation that is life to either, will die"* (E.M. Forster). *Seclusion* suggests removal or a setting apart from others, though not necessarily complete inaccessibility; the term often connotes a withdrawal from social contact: *After the funeral the widow and family spent several days in seclusion. Retirement* suggests a withdrawal from active life or to a retreat, as for serenity or privacy: *"an elegant sufficiency, content,/Retirement, rural quiet, friendship, books"* (James Thomson).

sol·i·tud·i·nar·i·an (sŏl′ĭ-to͞od′n-âr′ē-ən, -tyo͞od′-) *n.* One leading a solitary or secluded life. [Latin *sōlitūdō, sōlitūdin-,* solitude; see SOLITUDE + —ARIAN.]

sol·ler·et (sŏl′ə-rĕt′) *n.* A steel shoe made of overlapping plates, forming a part of a medieval suit of armor. [French, from Old French, diminutive of *soller,* shoe, from Late Latin *subtēlāris (calceus),* (shoegear) for the sole of the foot, from *subtēl,* the hollow of the foot : Latin *sub-,* sub- + Latin *talus,* ankle; see TALUS[1].]

solleret
Pair of 1460 Italian sollerets

sol·mi·za·tion (sŏl′mĭ-zā′shən) *n. Music.* The act or a system of using syllables, such as *do, re,* and *mi,* to represent the tones of the scale. [French *solmisation,* from *solmiser,* to sol-fa : *sol,* note of the scale (from Medieval Latin; see GAMUT) + *mi,* note of the scale (from Medieval Latin; see GAMUT).]

soln. *abbr.* Solution.

so·lo (sō′lō) *n., pl.* **-los. 1.** *Abbr.* **s.** *Music.* A composition or passage for an individual voice or instrument, with or without accompaniment. **2.** A performance by or intended for a single individual. **3.** *Games.* Any of various card games in which one player singly opposes others. **—solo** *adj.* **1.** *Music.* Composed, arranged for, or performed by a single voice or instrument. **2.** Made or done by a single individual. **—solo** *adv.* Unaccompa-

ă pat	oi boy
ā pay	ou out
âr care	o͝o took
ä father	o͞o boot
ĕ pet	ŭ cut
ē be	ûr urge
ĭ pit	th thin
ī pie	*th* this
îr pier	hw which
ŏ pot	zh vision
ō toe	ə about, item
ô paw	♦ regionalism

Stress marks: ′ (primary); ′ (secondary), as in **dictionary** (dĭk′shə-nĕr′ē)

nied; alone: *flew solo from Anchorage to Miami.* **—solo** *intr.v.* **-loed, -lo•ing, -los. 1.** To perform a solo. **2.** To fly an airplane without a companion or an instructor, especially for the first time. [Italian, from Latin *sōlus,* alone. See **s(w)e-** in Appendix.]

so•lo•ist (sō′lō-ĭst) *n.* One who performs a solo.

so•lo•is•tic (sō′lō-ĭs′tĭk) *adj. Music.* **1.** Of, relating to, or containing a solo or soloist. **2.** Having elements or qualities of or appropriate to a solo or a soloist: *a passage requiring soloistic virtuosity; a balanced ensemble with no soloistic egos.*

So•lo man (sō′lō) *n.* An extinct hominid primate *(Homo soloensis)* known from fossil remains of the late Pleistocene Epoch. [After the *Solo* River of central Java.]

Sol•o•mon (sŏl′ə-mən). fl. tenth century B.C. King of Israel famous for his wisdom and his architectural projects, including the Temple in Jerusalem.

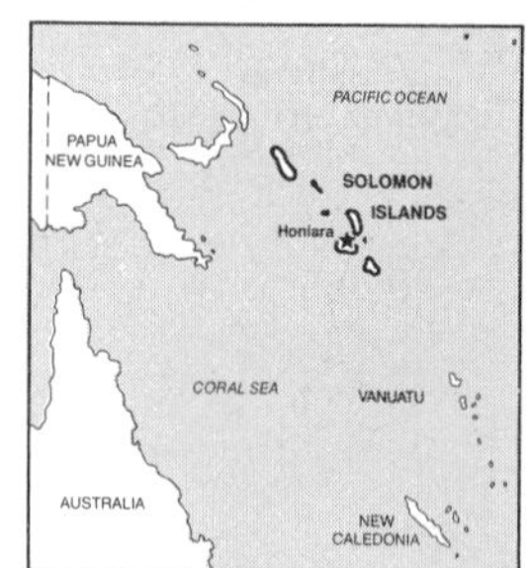

Solomon Islands[2]

Sol•o•mon•ic (sŏl′ə-mŏn′ĭk) *adj.* Exhibiting or requiring the exercise of great wisdom, especially in making difficult decisions: *"The court also will have to make the Solomonic determination whether any age limit applies"* (Tom Wicker).

Solomon Islands[1]**.** An island group of the western Pacific Ocean east of New Guinea. The volcanic islands, first visited by European explorers in the 1560's, were divided between Germany and Great Britain in the late 19th century. Australia assumed control of the northern islands in 1920. Today the northern Solomons are part of Papua New Guinea. The southern islands are an independent country.

Solomon Islands[2]**.** A country comprising the Solomon Islands southeast of Bougainville. A British protectorate after 1893, the islands achieved independence in 1978. Honiara, on Guadalcanal Island, is the capital. Population, 212,868.

Sol•o•mon's feather (sŏl′ə-mənz) *n.* See **false Solomon's seal.**

Solomon's plume *n.* See **false Solomon's seal.**

Solomon's seal *n.* **1.** A six-pointed star or hexagram supposed to possess mystical powers. **2.** Any of several plants of the genus *Polygonatum,* having paired, drooping, greenish or yellowish flowers.

Solomon's zigzag *n.* See **false spikenard.**

so•lon (sō′lən, -lŏn′) *n.* **1.** A wise lawgiver. **2.** A legislator. [After SOLON.]

So•lon (sō′lən, -lŏn′). 638?–559? B.C. Athenian lawgiver and poet. His reforms preserved a class system based on wealth but ended privilege by birth.

so long *interj. Informal.* Used to express good-bye.

so long as *conj.* **1.** During the time that; while. **2.** Provided that.

Solomon's seal

sol•stice (sŏl′stĭs, sōl′-, sôl′-) *n.* **1.** *Astronomy.* Either of two times of the year when the sun is at its greatest distance from the celestial equator. The summer solstice in the Northern Hemisphere occurs about June 21, when the sun is in the zenith at the tropic of Cancer; the winter solstice occurs about December 21, when the sun is over the tropic of Capricorn. The summer solstice is the longest day of the year and the winter solstice is the shortest. **2.** A highest point or culmination. [Middle English, from Old French, from Latin *sōlstitium* : *sōl,* sun; see **sāwel-** in Appendix + *-stitium,* a stoppage; see **stā-** in Appendix.] **—sol•sti′tial** (-stĭsh′əl) *adj.*

sol•u•bil•i•ty (sŏl′yə-bĭl′ĭ-tē) *n., pl.* **-ties. 1.** The quality or condition of being soluble. **2.** The amount of a substance that can be dissolved in a given amount of solvent.

sol•u•bi•lize (sŏl′yə-bə-līz′) *tr.v.* **-lized, -liz•ing, -liz•es.** To make (substances such as fats and lipids) soluble in water by the action of a detergent or similar agent.

sol•u•ble (sŏl′yə-bəl) *adj. Abbr.* **sol. 1.** That can be dissolved, especially easily dissolved: *soluble fats.* **2.** Possible to solve or explain: *soluble mysteries.* [Middle English, from Old French, from Late Latin *solūbilis,* from Latin *solvere,* to loosen. See **leu-** in Appendix.] **—sol′u•ble•ness** *n.* **—sol′u•bly** *adv.*

soluble glass *n.* See **sodium silicate.**

soluble RNA *n. Abbr.* **sRNA** Transfer RNA.

so•lum (sō′ləm) *n., pl.* **-la** (-lə) or **-lums.** The upper layers of a soil profile in which topsoil formation occurs. [Latin, base, ground.]

so•lus (sō′ləs) *adv. & adj.* By oneself; alone. Used as a stage direction to a male character. [Latin *sōlus,* alone. See SOLO.]

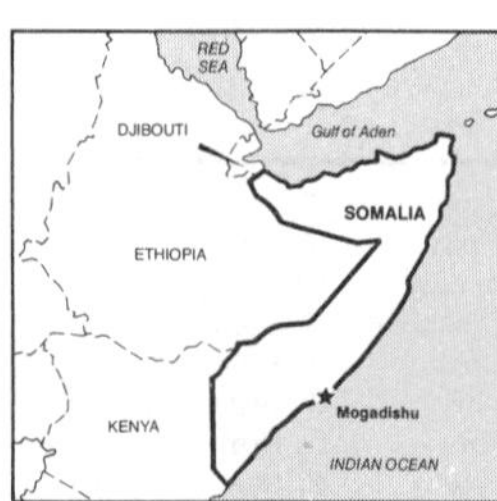

Somalia

sol•ute (sŏl′yo͞ot, sō′lo͞ot) *n.* A substance dissolved in another substance, usually the component of a solution present in the lesser amount. **—solute** *adj.* Being in solution; dissolved. [From Middle English, loose, porous, from Latin *solūtus,* past participle of *solvere,* to loosen. See **leu-** in Appendix.]

so•lu•tion (sə-lo͞o′shən) *n. Abbr.* **sol., soln. 1.a.** A homogeneous mixture of two or more substances, which may be solids, liquids, gases, or a combination of these. **b.** The process of forming such a mixture. **2.** The state of being dissolved. **3.a.** The method or process of solving a problem. **b.** The answer to or disposition of a problem. **4.** *Law.* Payment or satisfaction of a claim or debt. **5.** The act of separating or breaking up; dissolution. [Middle English, from Old French, from Latin *solūtiō, solūtiōn-,* from *solūtus,* past participle of *solvere,* to loosen. See SOLUTE.]

So•lu•tre•an also **So•lu•tri•an** (sə-lo͞o′trē-ən) *adj.* Of or relating to the Old World Upper Paleolithic culture that succeeded the Aurignacian and was characterized by improved flint implements and stylized symbolic forms of art. [French *solutréen,* after *Solutré-Pouilly,* a village of east-central France.]

solv•a•ble (sŏl′və-bəl, sôl′-) *adj.* Possible to solve: *solvable problems; a solvable riddle.* **—solv′a•bil′i•ty, solv′a•ble•ness** *n.*

sol•va•tion (sŏl-vā′shən, sôl-) *n.* Any of a class of chemical reactions, such as the formation of hydrated copper sulfate in aqueous solution, in which solute and solvent molecules combine with relatively weak covalent bonds. [SOLV(ENT) + -ATION.]

Sol•vay (sŏl′vā, sôl-vā′), **Ernest.** 1838–1922. Belgian chemist and industrialist who developed the Solvay process and established a number of factories for producing sodium carbonate.

Solvay process *n.* A process used to produce large quantities of sodium carbonate from sodium chloride, ammonia, and carbon dioxide. [After Ernest SOLVAY.]

solve (sŏlv, sôlv) *tr.v.* **solved, solv•ing, solves. 1.** To find a solution to. **2.** To work out a correct solution to (a problem). [Middle English *solven,* to loosen, from Latin *solvere.* See **leu-** in Appendix.] **—solv′er** *n.*

SYNONYMS: *solve, decipher, resolve, unravel.* The central meaning shared by these verbs is "to clear up or explain something puzzling or unintelligible": *solve a riddle; can't decipher his handwriting; resolve a problem; unravel a mystery.*

sol•vent (sŏl′vənt, sôl′-) *adj.* **1.** Capable of meeting financial obligations. **2.** *Chemistry.* Capable of dissolving another substance. **—solvent** *n.* **1.** *Chemistry.* **a.** A substance in which another substance is dissolved, forming a solution. **b.** A substance, usually a liquid, capable of dissolving another substance. **2.** Something that solves or explains. [French, from Latin *solvēns, solvent-,* present participle of *solvere,* to loosen. See SOLVE.] **—sol′ven•cy** *n.*

sol•vol•y•sis (sŏl-vŏl′ĭ-sĭs, sôl-) *n.* A chemical reaction in which the solute and solvent react to form a new compound. [SOLV(ENT) + -LYSIS.] **—sol′vo•lyt′ic** (-və-lĭt′ĭk) *adj.*

Sol•way Firth (sŏl′wā′). An arm of the Irish Sea separating northwest England from southwest Scotland.

Sol•zhe•ni•tsyn (sōl′zhə-nēt′sĭn, səl-zhə-nyē′tsĭn), **Aleksandr Isayevich.** Born 1918. Soviet writer and dissident whose works, including *One Day in the Life of Ivan Denisovich* (1962) and *The Gulag Archipelago* (1973–1975), exposed the brutality of the Soviet labor camp system. He was awarded the Nobel Prize for literature in 1970.

Som. *abbr.* Somalia.

so•ma (sō′mə) *n., pl.* **-ma•ta** (-mə-tə) or **-mas. 1.** The entire body of an organism, exclusive of the germ cells. **2.** See **cell body. 3.** The body of an individual as contrasted with the mind or psyche. [New Latin *sōma,* from Greek, body. See **teuə-** in Appendix.]

So•ma•li (sō-mä′lē) *n., pl.* **Somali** or **-lis. 1.** A member of a Moslem people of Somalia and adjacent parts of Ethiopia, Kenya, and Djibouti. **2.** The Cushitic language of the Somali and an official language of Somalia.

So•ma•li•a (sō-mä′lē-ə, -mäl′yə). *Abbr.* **Som.** A country of extreme eastern Africa on the Gulf of Aden and the Indian Ocean. Arab and Persian traders first established outposts in the region between the seventh and tenth centuries. The present state was formed in 1960 from colonies previously held by Italy and Great Britain. Mogadishu is the capital and the largest city. Population, 3,645,000. **—So•ma′li•an** *adj. & n.*

So•ma•li•land (sō-mä′lē-lănd′, sə-). A region of eastern Africa comprising present-day Somalia, Djibouti, and southeast Ethiopia. The area was a target of European colonization after the opening of the Suez Canal in 1869.

so many *adj.* **1.** Forming an unspecified number: *issued so many memos each week.* **2.** Forming a group: *The troops fought like so many tigers.*

so•ma•ta (sō′mə-tə) *n.* A plural of **soma.**

so•mat•ic (sō-măt′ĭk) *adj.* **1.** Of, relating to, or affecting the body, especially as distinguished from a body part, the mind, or the environment; corporeal or physical. See Synonyms at **bodily. 2.** Of or relating to the wall of the body cavity, especially as distinguished from the head, limbs, or viscera. **3.** Of or relating to a somatic cell or the somatoplasm. [French *somatique,* from Greek *sōmatikos,* from *sōma, sōmat-,* body. See SOMA.] **—so•mat′i•cal•ly** *adv.*

somatic cell *n.* Any cell of a plant or an animal other than a germ cell. Also called *body cell.*

somato– *pref.* **1.** Body: *somatology.* **2.** Soma: *somatoplasm.* [Greek *sōmato-,* from *sōma, sōmat-,* body. See **teuə-** in Appendix.]

so•mat•o•gen•ic (sō-măt′ə-jĕn′ĭk, sō′mə-tə-) also **so•mat•o•ge•net•ic** (-jə-nĕt′ĭk) *adj.* Of somatic origin; developing from the somatic cells.

so•ma•tol•o•gy (sō′mə-tŏl′ə-jē) *n.* **1.** The physiological and anatomical study of the body. **2.** See **physical anthropology. —so′ma•to•log′ic** (sō′mə-tl-ŏj′ĭk, sō-măt′l-), **so′ma•to•log′i•cal** (-ĭ-kəl) *adj.* **—so′ma•tol′o•gist** *n.*

so•mat•o•me•din (sō-măt′ə-mēd′n, sō′mə-tə-) *n.* Any of a group of peptides produced by the liver upon stimulation by somatotropin that act directly on cartilage cells to stimulate skeletal growth. [Perhaps SOMATO(TROPIN) + (INTER)MED(IARY) + -IN.]

so•mat•o•plasm (sō-măt′ə-plăz′əm, sō′mə-tə-) *n.* **1.** The entirety of specialized protoplasm, other than germ plasm, constituting the body. **2.** The protoplasm of a somatic cell. **—so′ma·to·plas′tic** (sō′mə-tə-plăs′tĭk) *adj.*

so·mat·o·pleure (sō-măt′ə-plo͝or′, sō′mə-tə-) *n.* A complex sheet of embryonic cells in craniate vertebrates, formed by association of part of the mesoderm with the ectoderm and developing as the internal body wall. [New Latin *somatopleura* : SOMATO– + Greek *pleura,* side.] **—so·mat′o·pleu′ral** (-plo͝or′əl), **so·mat′o·pleu′ric** (-plo͝or′ĭk) *adj.*

so·mat·o·sen·so·ry (sə-măt′ə-sĕn′sə-rē, sō′mə-tə-) *adj.* Of or relating to the perception of sensory stimuli from the skin and internal organs: *the somatosensory area of the cerebral cortex.*

so·mat·o·stat·in (sō-măt′ə-stăt′n, sō′mə-tə-) *n.* A polypeptide hormone produced by the hypothalamus and the pancreas that inhibits the secretion of various other hormones, such as somatotropin, glucagon, insulin, thyrotropin, and gastrin. [SOMATO(TROPIN) + –STAT + –IN.]

so·mat·o·ther·a·py (sō-măt′ə-thĕr′ə-pē, sō′mə-tə-) *n., pl.* **-pies.** Treatment of mental illness by physical means, such as drugs, shock therapy, or lobotomy.

so·mat·o·troph·in (sə-măt′ə-trō′fĭn, sō′mə-tə-) *n.* Variant of **somatotropin.**

so·mat·o·trop·ic hormone (sə-măt′ə-trŏp′ĭk, -trō′pĭk, sō′mə-tə-) *n.* See **somatotropin.**

so·mat·o·tro·pin (sə-măt′ə-trō′pĭn, sō′mə-tə-) also **so·mat·o·tro·phin** (-trō′fĭn) *n.* A polypeptide hormone secreted by the anterior lobe of the pituitary gland that promotes growth of the body, especially by stimulating the release of somatomedin, and that influences the metabolism of proteins, carbohydrates, and lipids. Also called *growth hormone, somatotropic hormone.* [SOMATO– + –TROP(IC) + –IN.]

so·mat·o·type (sō-măt′ə-tīp′, sō′mə-tə-) *n.* The structure or build of a person, especially to the extent to which it exhibits the characteristics of an ectomorph, an endomorph, or a mesomorph. **—so·mat′o·typ′ic** (-tĭp′ĭk) *adj.*

som·ber (sŏm′bər) *adj.* **1.a.** Dark; gloomy. **b.** Dull or dark in color. **2.a.** Melancholy; dismal: *a somber mood.* **b.** Serious; grave. [French *sombre,* from Old French, from *sombrer, to cast a shadow, from Late Latin *subumbrāre,* from Latin *sub umbrā,* in shadow : *sub,* sub- + *umbrā,* ablative of *umbra,* shadow.] **—som′ber·ly** *adv.* **—som′ber·ness** *n.*

som·bre (sŏm′bər) *adj. Chiefly British.* Variant of **somber.**

som·bre·ro (sŏm-brâr′ō, səm-) *n., pl.* **-ros.** A large straw or felt hat with a broad brim and tall crown, worn especially in Mexico and the American southwest. [Spanish, perhaps from *sombra,* shade, probably from *sombrar,* to shade, from Late Latin *subumbrāre,* to cast a shadow. See SOMBER.]

Som·bre·ro (sŏm-brâr′ō, səm-). An island of St. Christopher-Nevis in the Leeward Islands of the West Indies.

som·brous (sŏm′brəs) *adj. Archaic.* Somber in aspect or in character: *"where . . . the sombrous pine/And yew-tree o'er the silver rocks decline"* (William Wordsworth).

some (sŭm) *adj.* **1.** Being an unspecified number or quantity: *some people; some sugar.* **2.** Unknown or unspecified by name: *Some man called.* **3.** *Logic.* Being part and perhaps all of a class. **4.** *Informal.* Remarkable: *She is some skier.* **—some** *pron.* **1.** An indefinite or unspecified number or portion: *We took some of the books to the auction.* See Usage Note at **every. 2.** An indefinite additional quantity: *did the assigned work and then some.* **—some** *adv.* **1.** Approximately; about: *Some 40 people attended the rally.* **2.** *Informal.* Somewhat: *some tired.* [Middle English, from Old English *sum,* a certain one. See **sem-**[1] in Appendix.]

–some[1] *suff.* Characterized by a specified quality, condition, or action: *bothersome.* [Middle English *-som,* from Old English *-sum,* -like. See **sem-**[1] in Appendix.]

–some[2] *suff.* A group of a specified number of members: *threesome.* [Middle English *-sum,* from Old English *sum,* some. See SOME.]

–some[3] *suff.* **1.** Body: *centrosome.* **2.** Chromosome: *monosome.* [From Greek *sōma,* body. See **teuə-** in Appendix.]

some·bod·y (sŭm′bŏd′ē, -bŭd′ē, -bə-dē) *pron.* An unspecified or unknown person; someone. See Usage Note at **he**[1]. **—somebody** *n., pl.* **-ies.** *Informal.* A person of importance: *"Obviously she was somebody—a real presence in the room"* (Oleg Cassini).

some·day (sŭm′dā′) *adv.* At an indefinite time in the future.

USAGE NOTE: *Someday* (adverb) and *sometime* express future time indefinitely. For example, *We'll succeed someday. Come sometime. Let's meet sometime when your schedule permits.* This sense can also be conveyed by *some day* and *some time.* The two-word forms are always used when *some* is an adjective modifying and specifying a more particular *day* or *time* (used as nouns): *Come some day* (not someday) *soon.* Choose *some day* (not *someday*) *that is not so busy.* See Usage Note at **sometime.**

some·how (sŭm′hou′) *adv.* In a way not specified, understood, or known.

some·one (sŭm′wŭn′, -wən) *pron.* An unspecified or unknown person; somebody. **—someone** *n. Informal.* A somebody.

some·place (sŭm′plās′) *adv. & n.* Somewhere: *"I didn't care where I was from so long as it was someplace else"* (Garrison Keillor). See Usage Note at **everyplace.**

♦**som·er·sault** also **sum·mer·sault** (sŭm′ər-sôlt′) *—n.* **1.** An acrobatic stunt in which the body rolls in a complete circle, heels over head. Also called *somerset,* ♦*tumbleset.* **2.** A complete reversal, as of sympathies or opinions. *—intr.v.* **-sault·ed, -sault·ing, -saults.** To execute a somersault. [Obsolete French *sombresault,* variant of *sobresault,* from Old Provençal *sobresaut* : *sobre-,* above (from Latin *suprā;* see **uper** in Appendix) + *saut,* leap (from Latin *saltus,* from past participle of *salīre,* to leap; see **sel-** in Appendix).]

som·er·set also **sum·mer·set** (sŭm′ər-sĕt′) *—n.* See **somersault** (sense 1). *—intr.v.* **-set·ted, -set·ting, -sets.** To perform a somersault. [Alteration of SOMERSAULT.]

Som·er·set (sŭm′ər-sĕt′, -sĭt). **1.** A town of southeast Massachusetts, a residential suburb of Fall River. Population, 18,813. **2.** A community of central New Jersey, a suburb of New Brunswick. Population, 21,731.

Somerset Island. An island of Northwest Territories, Canada, separated from Boothia Peninsula by a narrow strait.

Som·er·ville (sŭm′ər-vĭl′). A city of eastern Massachusetts, a residential and industrial suburb of Boston. Population, 77,372.

Somerville, Mary Fairfax Greig. 1780–1872. British mathematician and astronomer whose *Physical Geography* (1848) won her international acclaim. The first women's college at Oxford University was funded by and named after her.

so·mes·thet·ic (sō′mĕs-thĕt′ĭk) *adj.* Somatosensory. [*som(a)* + Greek *aisthētikos,* of sense perception; see AESTHETIC.]

some·thing (sŭm′thĭng) *pron.* **1.** An undetermined or unspecified thing: *"We're all recalling something, furtively seeking something"* (Virginia Woolf). **2.** One having essentially the same attributes, character, or essence as another: *"Something of the Crusades* [survives] *in the modern traveler"* (Anatole Broyard). **—something** *n. Informal.* A remarkable or important thing or person: *He thinks he is something in that uniform.* **—something** *adv.* **1.** A little; somewhat: *She looks something like her mother.* **2.** *Informal.* To an extreme degree: *He drinks something fierce.* ***—idioms.*** **something else.** *Informal.* One that is very special or quite remarkable: *Her new film is something else.* **something of.** To some extent: *Our professor is something of an eccentric.*

some·time (sŭm′tīm′) *adv.* **1.** At an indefinite or unstated time: *I'll meet you sometime this afternoon.* **2.** At an indefinite time in the future: *Let's get together sometime.* **3.** *Obsolete.* Sometimes. **4.** *Archaic.* Formerly. **—sometime** *adj.* **1.** Having been at some prior time; former: *a sometime secretary.* **2.** *Usage Problem.* Occasional.

USAGE NOTE: *Sometime* as an adjective has been employed to mean "former" since the 15th century. It has come to be used in the 20th century with the meaning "occasional": *the team's sometime star and sometime problem child.* This latter use, however, is unacceptable to a majority of the Usage Panel. See Usage Note at **someday.**

some·times (sŭm′tīmz′) *adv.* **1.** At times; now and then. **2.** *Obsolete.* At some previous time; formerly.

some·way (sŭm′wā′) also **some·ways** (-wāz′) *adv.* In some way or another; somehow.

some·what (sŭm′hwŏt′, -wŏt′, -hwŭt′, -wŭt′, -hwət, -wət) *adv.* To some extent or degree; rather. **—somewhat** *pron.* Something.

some·where (sŭm′hwâr′, -wâr′) *adv.* **1.** At, in, or to a place not specified or known: *found it somewhere in the woods.* **2.** To a place or state of further development or progress: *finally getting somewhere.* **3.** Approximately; roughly: *somewhere about halfway through.* **—somewhere** *n.* An unknown or unspecified place: *"A big dog, a hound with a strain of mastiff from somewhere"* (William Faulkner).

some·wheres (sŭm′hwârz′, -wârz′) *adv. Informal.* Somewhere.

so·mite (sō′mīt′) *n.* **1.** *Zoology.* See **metamere. 2.** A segmental mass of mesoderm in the vertebrate embryo, occurring in pairs along the notochord and developing into muscles and vertebrae. [Greek *sōma,* body; see SOMA + –ITE[1].] **—so·mit′ic** (sō-mĭt′ĭk) *adj.*

Somme (sŏm, sôm). A river, about 241 km (150 mi) long, of northern France flowing west and northwest to the English Channel. Tanks were first used in warfare during the devastating Battle of the Somme (1916).

som·me·lier (sŭm′əl-yā′, sô′mə-lyā′) *n.* A wine steward in a restaurant. [French, from Old French, officer in charge of provisions, pack-animal driver, alteration of *sommerier, from *sommier,* beast of burden, from Vulgar Latin **saumārius.* See SUMMER[2].]

somn– *pref.* Variant of **somni–.**

som·nam·bu·late (sŏm-năm′byə-lāt′) *intr.v.* **-lat·ed, -lat·ing, -lates.** To walk or perform another act while asleep or in a sleeplike condition. **—som·nam′bu·lar** (-lər) *adj.* **—som′nam·bu·la′tion** *n.*

som·nam·bu·lism (sŏm-năm′byə-lĭz′əm) *n.* See **sleepwalking. —som·nam′bu·list** *n.* **—som·nam′bu·lis′tic** *adj.*

somni– or **somn–** *pref.* Sleep: *somnambulate.* [From Latin *somnus,* sleep. See **swep-** in Appendix.]

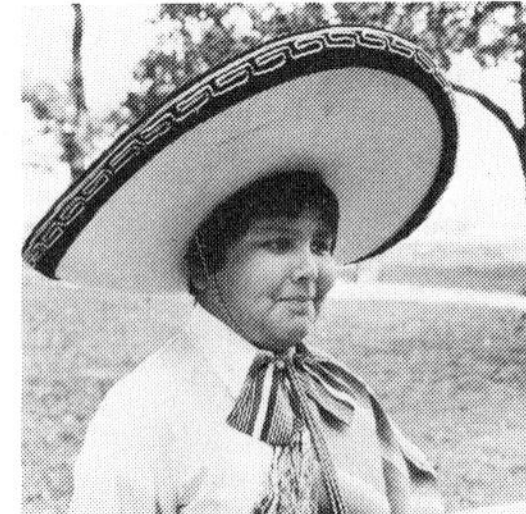

sombrero

ă pat	oi boy
ā pay	ou out
âr care	o͝o took
ä father	o͞o boot
ĕ pet	ŭ cut
ē be	ûr urge
ĭ pit	th thin
ī pie	*th* this
îr pier	hw which
ŏ pot	zh vision
ō toe	ə about, item
ô paw	♦ regionalism

Stress marks: ′ (primary); ′ (secondary), as in **dictionary** (dĭk′shə-nĕr′ē)

som·ni·fa·cient (sŏm′nə-fā′shənt) *adj.* Tending to produce sleep; hypnotic. —**som′ni·fa′cient** *n.*

som·nif·er·ous (sŏm-nĭf′ər-əs) also **som·nif·ic** (-nĭf′ĭk) *adj.* Inducing sleep; soporific. —**som·nif′er·ous·ly** *adv.*

som·nil·o·quy (sŏm-nĭl′ə-kwē) *n., pl.* **-quies.** The act or habit of talking in one's sleep. [SOMNI– + Latin *loquī,* to speak; see SOLILOQUY.] —**som·nil′o·quist** *n.*

som·no·lence (sŏm′nə-ləns) *n.* A state of drowsiness; sleepiness.

som·no·lent (sŏm′nə-lənt) *adj.* **1.** Drowsy; sleepy. **2.** Inducing or tending to induce sleep; soporific. [Middle English *sompnolent,* from Old French, from Latin *somnolentus* : *somnus,* sleep; see **swep-** in Appendix + *-olentus,* abounding in.] —**som′no·lent·ly** *adv.*

So·mo·za De·bay·le (sə-mō′zə də-bī′lā, sô-mô′sä *thĕ*-vī′lĕ), **Anastasio.** 1925–1980. Nicaraguan politician who headed Nicaragua's army and took over the presidency in 1963. In 1979 Somoza was overthrown by the Sandinista National Liberation Front, and he was later assassinated in Paraguay.

so much *adv.* **1.** In that degree; to that extent. Used with the comparative form of adjectives: *If she wins the award, so much the better for the team.* **2.** In such a degree; to such an extent: *The ideas of the candidates are so much alike that he could see no difference between them.* —**so much** *adj.* **1.** So great in quantity, degree, or extent: *There's been so much rain the crops are rotting in the fields.* **2.** Equivalent or equal in quantity, degree, or extent: *The report sounded like so much baloney.* —**so much** *pron.* **1.** An unspecified amount or degree: *charged so much a yard.* **2.** Everything that can be said or done. Used to summarize or dismiss something: *So much for the real story behind this sensational trial.*

so much as *adv.* Used as an intensive to indicate something unexpected; even: *He wouldn't so much as look at me.*

son (sŭn) *n. Abbr.* **s. 1.** One's male child. **2.** A male descendant. **3.** A man considered as if in a relationship of child to parent: *a son of the soil.* **4.** One personified or regarded as a male descendant. **5.** Used as a familiar form of address for a young man. **6. Son.** The second person of the Trinity. [Middle English, from Old English *sunu.* See **seuə-**[1] in Appendix.] —**son′ly** *adj.*

so·nance (sō′nəns) *n.* Sound.

so·nant (sō′nənt) *Linguistics. adj.* Voiced, as a speech sound. —**sonant** *n.* **1.** A voiced speech sound. **2.** A syllabic consonant in Indo-European. [Latin *sonāns, sonant-,* present participle of *sonāre,* to sound. See **swen-** in Appendix.]

so·nar (sō′när′) *n.* **1.** A system using transmitted and reflected underwater sound waves to detect and locate submerged objects or measure the distance to the floor of a body of water. **2.** An apparatus, as one in a submarine, using sonar. **3.** Echolocation. [*so(und) na(vigation and) r(anging).*]

so·na·ta (sə-nä′tə) *n. Music.* A composition for one to four instruments, one of which is usually a keyboard instrument, usually consisting of three or four independent movements varying in key, mood, and tempo. [Italian, from feminine past participle of *sonare,* to sound, from Latin *sonāre.* See **swen-** in Appendix.]

sonata form *n. Music.* A form consisting of three sections, the exposition, development, and recapitulation, often followed by a coda.

son·a·ti·na (sŏn′ə-tē′nə) *n. Music.* A sonata having shorter movements than the typical sonata. [Italian, diminutive of *sonata,* sonata. See SONATA.]

Sond·heim (sŏnd′hīm′), **Stephen.** Born 1930. American composer and lyricist whose musicals include *Gypsy* (1959) and *Sweeney Todd* (1979).

sone (sōn) *n.* A subjective unit of loudness, as perceived by a person with normal hearing, equal to the loudness of a pure tone having a frequency of 1,000 hertz at 40 decibels. [Latin *sonus,* a sound. See **swen-** in Appendix.]

son et lu·mière (sôn′ ā lüm-yâr′) *n.* A theatrical entertainment presented at night in a historic, usually outdoor setting, using recorded sound, lighting, and other effects to relate the history of the place. [French : *son,* sound + *et,* and + *lumière,* light.]

song (sông, sŏng) *n.* **1.** *Music.* **a.** A brief composition written or adapted for singing. **b.** The act or art of singing: *broke into song.* **2.** A distinctive or characteristic sound made by an animal, such as a bird or an insect. **3. a.** Poetry; verse. **b.** A lyric poem or ballad. —***idiom.* for a song.** *Informal.* At a low price: *bought the antique tray for a song.* [Middle English, from Old English *sang.* See **sengʷh-** in Appendix.]

Song also **Sung** (so͝ong). A Chinese dynasty (960–1279). Under its rule China achieved one of its highest levels of culture and prosperity.

song and dance *n., pl.* **song and dances** or **songs and dances. 1.** A theatrical performance that combines singing and dancing. **2.** *Slang.* **a.** An excessively elaborate effort to explain or justify. **b.** An elaborate story or explanation intended to deceive or mislead.

song·bird (sông′bûrd′, sŏng′-) *n.* A bird, especially one of the suborder Oscines of passerine birds, having a melodious song or call.

Song Da (sông′ dä′). See **Black River** (sense 1).

song·fest (sông′fĕst′, sŏng′-) *n.* A casual gathering for group singing.

song·ful (sông′fəl, sŏng′-) *adj.* Melodious; tuneful. —**song′ful·ly** *adv.* —**song′ful·ness** *n.*

Song·hai also **Song·hay** (sông′hī′, sŏng-gī′). An ancient empire of western Africa in present-day Mali. It was founded c. 700 by Berbers and reached the height of its power around 1500.

Song Hong (sông′ hông′). See **Red River** (sense 1).

Song·hua (so͝ong′hwä′) also **Sun·ga·ri** (so͝ong′gə-rē′). A river of northeast China rising near the North Korean border and flowing about 1,850 km (1,150 mi) northwest, east, and northeast to the Amur River.

Song of Solomon (sông, sŏng) *n. Abbr.* **S. of Sol.** *Bible.* See table at **Bible.**

Song of Songs (sôngz, sŏngz) *n. Abbr.* **Sg** *Bible.* See table at **Bible.**

song·smith (sông′smĭth′, sŏng′-) *n. Music.* See **songwriter.**

song sparrow *n.* A common North American sparrow *(Melospiza melodia)* having streaked brownish plumage and noted for its melodious song.

song·ster (sông′stər, sŏng′-) *n.* **1.** *Music.* **a.** One who sings. **b.** See **songwriter. 2.** A songbird.

song·stress (sông′strĭs, sŏng′-) *n. Music.* **1.** A woman who performs songs, especially ballads or popular songs. **2.** A woman who writes songs.

song thrush *n.* An Old World songbird *(Turdus philomelos)* having brown upper plumage and a spotted breast. Also called *mavis.*

song·writ·er (sông′rī′tər, sŏng′-) *n. Music.* One who writes lyrics or tunes, or both, for songs. Also called *songsmith, songster.*

son·ic (sŏn′ĭk) *adj.* **1.** Of or relating to audible sound: *a sonic wave.* **2.** Having a speed approaching or being that of sound in air, about 1,220 kilometers (760 miles) per hour at sea level. **3.** *Slang.* Extremely exciting and fast-paced: *a sonic lifestyle.* [From Latin *sonus,* a sound. See **swen-** in Appendix.] —**son′ic·al·ly** *adv.*

sonic barrier *n.* The sudden sharp increase in aerodynamic drag experienced by aircraft approaching the speed of sound. Also called *sound barrier.*

sonic boom *n.* An explosive sound caused by the shock wave preceding an aircraft traveling at or above the speed of sound.

son-in-law (sŭn′ĭn-lô′) *n., pl.* **sons-in-law** (sŭnz′-). The husband of one's daughter.

son·net (sŏn′ĭt) *n.* **1.** A 14-line verse form usually having one of several conventional rhyme schemes. **2.** A poem in this form. [French or Italian *sonetto* (French, from Italian), from Old Provençal *sonet,* diminutive of *son,* song, from Latin *sonus,* a sound. See **swen-** in Appendix.]

sonnet cycle *n.* See **sonnet sequence.**

son·net·eer (sŏn′ĭ-tîr′) *n.* **1.** A composer of sonnets. **2.** An inferior poet.

sonnet sequence *n.* A group of sonnets having a single subject or controlling idea. Also called *sonnet cycle.*

son·ny (sŭn′ē) *n., pl.* **-nies.** Used as a familiar form of address for a boy or young man. [Diminutive of SON.]

sono– *pref.* Sound: *sonobuoy.* [From Latin *sonus,* sound. See SONIC.]

so·no·buoy (sŏn′ə-bo͞o′ē, -boi′) *n.* A buoy equipped with an acoustic receiver and a radio transmitter that emits radio signals when it detects underwater sounds.

son of a bitch *Vulgar. n., pl.* **sons of bitches.** *Abbr.* **SOB** A person regarded as thoroughly mean or disagreeable. —**son of a bitch** *interj.* Used to express annoyance, disgust, disappointment, or amazement.

son of a gun *Informal. n., pl.* **sons of guns.** A person; a fellow: *That son of a gun knows how to sell cars and sell them well.* —**son of a gun** *interj.* Used to express annoyance, disappointment, or surprise.

Son of God *n.* Jesus.

Son of Man *n.* Jesus.

son·o·gram (sŏn′ə-grăm′, sō′nə-) *n.* An image, as of an unborn fetus or an internal body organ, produced by ultrasonography. Also called *echogram, sonograph, ultrasonogram.*

son·o·graph (sŏn′ə-grăf′, sō′nə-) *n.* See **sonogram.** —**so·nog′ra·pher** (sə-nŏg′rə-fər) *n.* —**son′o·graph′ic** *adj.*

so·nog·ra·phy (sə-nŏg′rə-fē) *n.* Ultrasonography.

so·nom·e·ter (sə-nŏm′ĭ-tər) *n.* See **audiometer.**

so·no·rant (sə-nôr′ənt, -nōr′-, sŏn′ər-) *n. Linguistics.* A voiced consonant regarded as a syllabic sound, as the last sound in the word *sudden.* [SONOR(OUS) + –ANT.]

so·nor·i·ty (sə-nôr′ĭ-tē, -nŏr′-) *n., pl.* **-ties. 1.** The quality or state of being sonorous; resonance. **2.** A sound.

so·no·rous (sə-nôr′əs, -nōr′-, sŏn′ər-) *adj.* **1.** Having or producing sound. **2.** Having or producing a full, deep, or rich sound. **3.** Impressive in style of speech: *a sonorous oration.* [From Latin *sonōrus,* from *sonor,* sound, from *sonāre,* to sound. See **swen-** in Appendix.] —**so·no′rous·ly** *adv.* —**so·no′rous·ness** *n.*

sons-in-law (sŭnz′ĭn-lô′) *n.* Plural of **son-in-law.**

Son·tag (sŏn′tăg′), **Susan.** Born 1933. American writer noted for her essays on contemporary culture, especially those contained in *Against Interpretation* (1966).

Soo Canals (so͞o). See **Sault Sainte Marie Canals.**

soo·chong (so͞o′chŏng′, -shŏng′) *n.* Variant of **souchong.**

Soo·chow (so͞o′chou′, -jō′). See **Suzhou.**

soon (so͞on) *adv.* **soon·er, soon·est. 1.** In the near future;

shortly. **2.** Without hesitation; promptly: *came as soon as possible.* **3.** Before the usual or appointed time; early. **4.** With willingness; readily: *I'd as soon leave right now.* **5.** *Obsolete.* Immediately. —***idioms.*** **no sooner than.** As soon as: *No sooner was the frost off the ground than the work began.* **sooner or later.** At some time; eventually: *Sooner or later you will have to face the facts.* [Middle English *sone,* from Old English *sōna,* immediately.]

USAGE NOTE: *No sooner,* as a comparative adverb, should be followed by *than* not *when,* as in these typical examples: *No sooner had she come than the maid knocked. I had no sooner left than she called.*

soon·er (so͞o′nər) *n. Slang.* **1.** A person who settled homestead land in the western United States before it was officially made available, in order to have first choice of location. **2. Sooner.** A native or resident of Oklahoma. [From SOON.]

Soong (so͝ong). Chinese family including **Charles Jones Soong** (died 1927), a Methodist missionary, and his son **T.V. Soong** (1894–1971), who was premier of the Nationalist government (1944–1947). His sister **Soong Ch'ing-ling** (1892–1981) married Sun Yat-Sen, and their younger sister **Soong Mei-ling** (born c. 1897) married Chiang Kai-Shek.

soot (so͝ot, so͞ot) *n.* The fine black particles, chiefly composed of carbon, produced by incomplete combustion of coal, oil, wood, or other fuels. [Middle English, from Old English *sōt.* See **sed-** in Appendix.] —**soot** *v.*

sooth (so͞oth) *Archaic. adj.* **1.** Real; true. **2.** Soft; smooth. —**sooth** *n.* Truth; reality. [Middle English, from Old English *sōth.* See **es-** in Appendix.] —**sooth′ly** *adv.*

soothe (so͞oth) *v.* **soothed, sooth·ing, soothes.** —*tr.* **1.** To calm or placate. **2.** To ease or relieve (pain, for example). —*intr.* To bring comfort, composure, or relief. [Middle English *sothen,* to verify, from Old English *sōthian,* from *sōth,* true. See **es-** in Appendix.] —**sooth′er** *n.*

sooth·fast (so͞oth′făst′) *adj. Archaic.* **1.** Truthful; honest. **2.** True; real. [Middle English *sothfast,* from Old English *sōthfæst* : *sōth,* truth; see SOOTH + *fæst,* fixed, fast; see FAST[1].]

sooth·ing (so͞o′thĭng) *adj.* Tending to soothe. —**sooth′ing·ly** *adv.* —**sooth′ing·ness** *n.*

sooth·say (so͞oth′sā′) *intr.v.* **-said** (-sĕd′), **-say·ing, -says** (-sĕz′). To foretell future events; predict. [Back-formation from SOOTHSAYER.]

sooth·say·er (so͞oth′sā′ər) *n.* One who claims to be able to foretell events or predict the future; a seer.

sooth·say·ing (so͞oth′sā′ĭng) *n.* **1.** The art or practice of foretelling events. **2.** A prediction; a prophecy.

soot·y (so͝ot′ē, so͞o′tē) *adj.* **-i·er, -i·est. 1.** Covered with or as if with soot. **2.** Of or producing soot. —**soot′i·ness** *n.*

sooty grouse *n.* See **blue grouse.**

sooty mold *n.* **1.** A blackish growth produced by fungi of the genus *Capnodium,* which grows in the droppings of aphids on plants. **2.** Any of the fungi that produce such growth.

sooty shearwater *n.* A shearwater *(Puffinus griseus)* of the Pacific and Atlantic oceans, having sooty gray or brown plumage and dark bill and feet. Also called *mutton-bird.*

sooty tern *n.* A tern *(Sterna fuscata)* found along most tropical coasts, having black plumage above and white below. Also called *wide-awake.*

sop (sŏp) *v.* **sopped, sop·ping, sops.** —*tr.* **1.** To dip, soak, or drench in a liquid; saturate. **2.** To take up by absorption: *sop up water with a paper towel.* —*intr.* To be or become thoroughly soaked or saturated. —**sop** *n.* **1.** A piece of food soaked or dipped in a liquid. **2. a.** Something yielded to placate or soothe. **b.** A bribe. [From Middle English *soppe,* bread dipped in liquid, from Old English *sopp-,* in *soppcuppe,* cup for dipping bread in. See **seuə-**[2] in Appendix.]

SOP *abbr.* Standard operating procedure.

sop. *abbr. Music.* Soprano.

soph. *abbr.* Sophomore.

soph·ism (sŏf′ĭz′əm) *n.* **1.** A plausible but fallacious argument. **2.** Deceptive or fallacious argumentation. [Middle English *sophime, sophisme,* from Old French *sophime,* from Latin *sophisma,* from Greek, from *sophizesthai,* to be subtle, from *sophos,* clever, wise.]

soph·ist (sŏf′ĭst) *n.* **1. a.** One skilled in elaborate and devious argumentation. **b.** A scholar or thinker. **2. Sophist. a.** A Greek philosopher of pre-Socratic times who inquired about and speculated on theology, metaphysics, mathematics, and the natural and biological sciences. **b.** A professional philosopher and teacher, especially one belonging to a group of fifth-century B.C. Greek philosophers who specialized in dialectic, argumentation, and rhetoric and who were often known for their elaborate and specious arguments. [Middle English *sophiste,* from Latin *sophista,* from Greek *sophistēs,* from *sophizesthai,* to become wise, from *sophos,* clever.]

so·phis·tic (sə-fĭs′tĭk) or **so·phis·ti·cal** (-tĭ-kəl) *adj.* **1.** Of, relating to, or characteristic of sophists. **2.** Apparently sound but really fallacious; specious: *sophistic refutations.* —**so·phis′ti·cal·ly** *adv.*

so·phis·ti·cate (sə-fĭs′tĭ-kāt′) *v.* **-cat·ed, -cat·ing, -cates.** —*tr.* **1.** To cause to become less natural, especially to make less naive and more worldly. **2.** To make impure; adulterate. See Synonyms at **adulterate. 3.** To make more complex or inclusive; refine. —*intr.* To use sophistry. —**sophisticate** (-kĭt) *n.* A sophisticated person. [Middle English *sophisticaten,* to adulterate, from Medieval Latin *sophisticāre, sophisticāt-,* from Latin *sophisticus,* sophistic, from Greek *sophistikos,* from *sophistēs,* sophist. See SOPHIST.] —**so·phis′ti·ca′tion** *n.* —**so·phis′ti·ca′tor** *n.*

so·phis·ti·cat·ed (sə-fĭs′tĭ-kā′tĭd) *adj.* **1.** Having acquired worldly knowledge or refinement; lacking natural simplicity or naiveté. **2.** Very complex or complicated: *the latest and most sophisticated technology.* **3.** Suitable for or appealing to the tastes of sophisticates: *a sophisticated drama.* —**so·phis′ti·cat′ed·ly** *adv.*

soph·is·try (sŏf′ĭ-strē) *n., pl.* **-tries. 1.** Plausible but fallacious argumentation. **2.** A plausible but misleading or fallacious argument.

Soph·o·cles (sŏf′ə-klēz′). 496?–406 B.C. Greek dramatist. Together with Euripides and Aeschylus, he is considered one of the greatest dramatists of ancient Greece. His surviving plays include *Ajax, Oedipus Rex, Antigone,* and *Oedipus at Colonus.* —**Soph′o·cle′an** *adj.*

Sophocles

soph·o·more (sŏf′ə-môr′, -mōr′, sŏf′môr′, -mōr′) *n. Abbr.* **soph. 1. a.** A second-year student in a U.S. college. **b.** A tenth-grade student in a U.S. high school. **2.** A person in the second year of carrying out an endeavor. —*attributive.* Often used to modify another noun: *her sophomore year; a sophomore class.* [Alteration (probably influenced by Greek *sophos,* wise, and *mōros,* dull) of *sophumer,* from obsolete *sophom,* sophism, dialectic exercise, variant of SOPHISM.]

soph·o·mor·ic (sŏf′ə-môr′ĭk, -mōr′-, -mŏr′-) *adj.* **1.** Of or characteristic of a sophomore. **2.** Exhibiting great immaturity and lack of judgment: *sophomoric behavior such as driving too fast in an attempt to show off.* —**soph′o·mor′i·cal·ly** *adv.*

so·por (sō′pər, -pôr′) *n.* A deep, lethargic, or unnatural sleep. [Latin. See **swep-** in Appendix.]

sop·o·rif·er·ous (sŏp′ə-rĭf′ər-əs, sō′pə-) *adj.* Inducing or tending to induce sleep; soporific. —**sop′o·rif′er·ous·ly** *adv.* —**sop′o·rif′er·ous·ness** *n.*

sop·o·rif·ic (sŏp′ə-rĭf′ĭk, sō′pə-) *adj.* **1.** Inducing or tending to induce sleep. **2.** Drowsy. —**soporific** *n.* A drug or other substance that induces sleep; a hypnotic.

sop·ping (sŏp′ĭng) *adj.* Thoroughly soaked; drenched. —**sopping** *adv.* Extremely; very: *sopping wet.*

sop·py (sŏp′ē) *adj.* **-pi·er, -pi·est. 1.** Soaked; sopping. **2.** Rainy. **3.** Sentimental; maudlin. See Synonyms at **sentimental.**

so·pra·ni·no (sō′prə-nē′nō, sŏp′rə-) *n., pl.* **-nos.** *Music.* An instrument, such as a recorder, that is higher in pitch than the soprano of its family. [Italian, diminutive of *soprano,* soprano. See SOPRANO.]

so·pran·o (sə-prăn′ō, -prä′nō) *n., pl.* **-os.** *Abbr.* **s., S., sop.** *Music.* **1.** The highest singing voice of a woman or young boy. **2.** A singer having such a voice. **3.** A part written in the range of such a voice. **4.** The tonal range characteristic of a soprano. **5.** An instrument with this range. —*attributive.* Often used to modify another noun: *a soprano balalaika; a soprano aria.* [Italian, from *sopra,* above, from Latin *suprā.* See **uper** in Appendix.]

soprano clef *n. Music.* The C clef positioned to indicate that the bottom line of a staff represents the pitch of middle C.

so·ra (sôr′ə, sōr′ə) *n.* A North American rail *(Porzana carolina)* having grayish-brown plumage and a short stout bill, commonly found in freshwater bogs or swamps. [Origin unknown.]

sorb[1] (sôrb) *tr.v.* **sorbed, sorb·ing, sorbs.** To take up and hold, as by absorption or adsorption. [Back-formation from ADSORB and ABSORB.] —**sorb′a·bil′i·ty** *n.* —**sorb′a·ble** *adj.* —**sorb′ent** *adj. & n.*

sorb[2] (sôrb) *n.* **1.** Any of several Old World trees of the genus *Sorbus* in the rose family, as the service tree or the rowan. **2.** The fruit of any of these plants. [French *sorbe,* sorb fruit, from Old French *sourbe,* from Vulgar Latin **sorba,* from Latin *sorbum.*]

Sorb (sôrb) *n.* See **Wend.** [German *Sorbe,* perhaps variant of *Serbe,* Serb, from Serbian *Serb.*]

sor·be·fa·cient (sôr′bə-fā′shənt) *adj.* Promoting absorption. Used of a medicine or an agent. —**sor′be·fa′cient** *n.*

sor·bet (sôr′bĭt, sôr-bā′) *n.* A frozen dessert similar to a frappé, usually made from fruit juice and having a mushy consistency. [French, from Ottoman Turkish *sherbet,* sweet fruit drink. See SHERBET.]

Sor·bi·an (sôr′bē-ən) *n.* **1.** See **Wend. 2.** See **Wendish.** —**Sor′bi·an** *adj.*

sor·bic acid (sôr′bĭk) *n.* A white crystalline solid, $C_6H_8O_2$, found in the berries of the mountain ash and also synthesized, used as a food preservative and fungicide. [From SORB[2].]

sor·bi·tol (sôr′bĭ-tôl′, -tōl′, -tŏl′) *n.* A white, sweetish, crystalline alcohol, $C_6H_8(OH)_6$, found in various berries and fruits or prepared synthetically, used as a flavoring agent, a sugar substitute for people with diabetes, and a moisturizer in cosmetics and other products. [SORB[2] + -IT(E)[2] + -OL[1].]

sor·bose (sôr′bōs′) *n.* A white, sweetish crystalline sugar, $C_6H_{12}O_6$, used in the manufacture of ascorbic acid. [SORB(ITOL) + -OSE[2].]

sor·cer·er (sôr′sər-ər) *n.* One who practices sorcery; a wizard. [Middle English *sorser, sorcerer,* from Old French *sorcier,* from Vulgar Latin **sortiārius,* from Latin *sors, sort-,* lot, fortune. See **ser-**[2] in Appendix.]

ă pat	oi boy
ā pay	ou out
âr care	o͝o took
ä father	o͞o boot
ĕ pet	ŭ cut
ē be	ûr urge
ĭ pit	th thin
ī pie	*th* this
îr pier	hw which
ŏ pot	zh vision
ō toe	ə about, item
ô paw	♦ regionalism

Stress marks: **′** (primary); ′ (secondary), as in **dictionary** (dĭk′shə-nĕr′ē)

sor·cer·ess (sôr′sər-ĭs) *n.* A woman who practices sorcery.

sor·cer·y (sôr′sə-rē) *n.* Use of supernatural power over others through the assistance of spirits; witchcraft. [Middle English *sorcerie,* from Old French, from *sorcier,* sorcerer. See SORCERER.] **—sor′cer·ous** *adj.* **—sor′cer·ous·ly** *adv.*

sord (sôrd) *n.* A flight of mallards. See Synonyms at **flock**[1]. [Middle English *sorde,* from *sorden,* to rise up in flight, from Old French *sordre,* from Latin *surgere,* to rise.]

sor·did (sôr′dĭd) *adj.* **1.** Filthy or dirty; foul. **2.** Depressingly squalid; wretched: *sordid shantytowns.* **3.** Morally degraded: *"The sordid details of his orgies stank under his very nostrils"* (James Joyce). See Synonyms at **mean**[2]. **4.** Exceedingly mercenary; grasping. [Middle English *sordide,* festering, purulent, from Latin *sordidus,* dirty, from *sordēre,* to be dirty.] **—sor′did·ly** *adv.* **—sor′did·ness** *n.*

sor·di·no (sôr-dē′nō) *n., pl.* **-ni** (-nē). *Music.* A mute for an instrument. [Italian, from *sordo,* deaf, mute, from Latin *surdus.*]

sore (sôr, sōr) *adj.* **sor·er, sor·est. 1.** Painful to the touch; tender. **2.** Feeling physical pain; hurting: *sore all over.* **3.** Causing misery, sorrow, or distress; grievous: *in sore need.* **4.** Causing embarrassment or irritation: *a sore subject.* **5.** Full of distress; sorrowful. **6.** *Informal.* Angry; offended. **—sore** *n.* **1.** An open skin lesion, wound, or ulcer. **2.** A source of pain, distress, or irritation. **—sore** *tr.v.* **sored, sor·ing, sores.** To mutilate the legs or feet of (a horse) in order to induce a particular gait in the animal. **—sore** *adv. Archaic.* Sorely. [Middle English, from Old English *sār.*] **—sore′ness** *n.*

so·re·di·um (sə-rē′dē-əm) *n., pl.* **-di·a** (-dē-ə). A specialized asexual reproductive unit of lichens consisting of a mass of algal cells surrounded by fungal hyphae. [New Latin, diminutive of Greek *sōros,* heap. See SORUS.] **—so·re′di·al** (-dē-əl) *adj.*

sore·head (sôr′hĕd′, sōr′-) *n. Slang.* One who is easily offended, annoyed, or angered.

So·rel (sə-rĕl′, sô-). A city of southern Quebec, Canada, at the confluence of the St. Lawrence and Richelieu rivers. It was founded in 1672 on the site of Fort Richelieu, established in 1665. Population, 20,347.

So·rel (sô-rĕl′), **Georges.** 1847–1922. French political philosopher whose works advanced the revolutionary syndicalist movement. His most important book is *Reflections on Violence* (1908).

sore·ly (sôr′lē, sōr′-) *adv.* **1.** Painfully; grievously. **2.** Extremely; greatly: *Their skills were sorely needed.*

Sor·en·sen (sûr′ən-sən), **Soren Peter Lauritz.** 1868–1939. Danish chemist who devised the pH scale for measuring the acidity or alkalinity of solutions.

sore throat *n.* Any of various inflammations of the tonsils, pharynx, or larynx characterized by pain in swallowing.

sor·gho (sôr′gō) *n.* Variant of **sorgo.**

sor·ghum (sôr′gəm) *n.* **1.** An Old World grass *(Sorghum bicolor),* several varieties of which are widely cultivated as grain and forage or as a source of syrup. **2.** Syrup made from the juice of this plant. [New Latin *Sorghum,* genus name, from Italian *sorgo,* a tall cereal grass, probably from Medieval Latin *surgum,* perhaps variant of Vulgar Latin **syricum,* from neuter of Latin *Syricus,* Syrian, from SYRIA.]

sor·go also **sor·gho** (sôr′gō) *n., pl.* **-gos** also **-ghos.** Any of various sorghums that are cultivated as a source of syrup. Also called *sweet sorghum.* [Italian. See SORGHUM.]

so·ri (sôr′ī, sōr′ī) *n.* Plural of **sorus.**

sor·i·cine (sôr′ĭ-sīn′, sŏr′-) *adj.* Of, belonging to, or resembling the shrews. [Latin *sōricīnus,* from *sōrex, sōric-,* shrew.]

so·ri·tes (sə-rī′tēz, sô-) *n., pl.* **sorites.** *Logic.* A form of argument in which a series of incomplete syllogisms is so arranged that the predicate of each premise forms the subject of the next until the subject of the first is joined with the predicate of the last in the conclusion. [Latin *sōrītēs,* from Greek *sōreitēs,* from *sōros,* heap. See **teuə-** in Appendix.]

So·ro·ca·ba (sôr′o͝o-kä′bä). A city of southern Brazil west of São Paulo. It is a commercial center. Population, 254,672.

so·ro·ral (sə-rôr′əl, -rōr′-) *adj.* Of, relating to, or resembling a sister; sisterly. [From Latin *soror,* sister. See **swesor-** in Appendix.]

so·ror·ate (sə-rôr′ĭt, -rōr′-) *n.* The custom of marriage of a man to his wife's sister or sisters, usually after the wife has died or proved sterile. [From Latin *soror,* sister. See SORORAL.]

so·ror·i·cide (sə-rôr′ĭ-sīd′, -rŏr′-) *n.* **1.** The killing of one's sister. **2.** One who kills one's own sister. [Latin *soror,* sister + -CIDE.] **—so·ror′i·cid′al** (-sīd′l) *adj.*

so·ror·i·ty (sə-rôr′ĭ-tē, -rŏr′-) *n., pl.* **-ties. 1.** A chiefly social organization of women students at a college or university, usually designated by Greek letters. **2.** An association or a society of women. [Medieval Latin *sorōritās,* from Latin *soror, sorōr-,* sister. See **swesor-** in Appendix.]

sorp·tion (sôrp′shən) *n.* **1.** The process of sorbing. **2.** The state of being sorbed. [Back-formation from ABSORPTION and ADSORPTION.] **—sorp′tive** *adj.*

sor·rel[1] (sôr′əl, sŏr′-) *n.* **1.** Any of several plants of the genus *Rumex,* having acid-flavored leaves sometimes used as salad greens, especially *R. acetosella,* a widely naturalized Eurasian species. Also called *dock.* **2.** Any of various plants of the genus *Oxalis,* having usually compound leaves with three leaflets. [Middle English *sorel,* from Old French *surele,* from *sur,* sour, of Germanic origin.]

sorrel[1]
Yellow oxalis
Oxalis europaea

sor·rel[2] (sôr′əl, sŏr′-) *n.* **1.** *Color.* A brownish orange to light brown. **2.** A sorrel-colored horse or other animal. [From Middle English *sorel,* sorrel-colored, from Old French, from *sor,* red-brown, of Germanic origin.]

sorrel tree *n.* See **sourwood.**

Sor·ren·to (sə-rĕn′tō, sôr-rĕn′tô). A town of southern Italy on the **Sorrento Peninsula** separating the Bay of Naples from the Gulf of Salerno. The city is a popular tourist center and summer resort. Population, 17,301.

sor·row (sŏr′ō, sôr′ō) *n.* **1.** Mental suffering or pain caused by injury, loss, or despair. See Synonyms at **regret. 2.** A source or cause of sorrow; a misfortune. **3.** Expression of sorrow; grieving. **—sorrow** *intr.v.* **-rowed, -row·ing, -rows.** To feel or express sorrow; grieve. See Synonyms at **grieve.** [Middle English *sorwe,* from Old English *sorg.*] **—sor′row·er** *n.*

sor·row·ful (sŏr′ō-fəl, -ə-fəl, sôr′-) *adj.* Affected with, marked by, causing, or expressing sorrow. See Synonyms at **sad. —sor′row·ful·ly** *adv.* **—sor′row·ful·ness** *n.*

sor·ry (sŏr′ē, sôr′ē) *adj.* **-ri·er, -ri·est. 1.** Feeling or expressing sympathy, pity, or regret: *I'm sorry I'm late.* **2.** Worthless or inferior; paltry: *a sorry excuse.* **3.** Causing sorrow, grief, or misfortune; grievous: *a sorry development.* [Middle English *sori,* from Old English *sārig,* sad, from *sār,* sore.] **—sor′ri·ly** *adv.* **—sor′ri·ness** *n.*

sort (sôrt) *n.* **1.** A group of persons or things of the same general character; a kind. See Usage Note at **kind**[2]. **2.** Character or nature: *books of all sorts.* See Synonyms at **type. 3.** One that typifies a group or exemplifies a characteristic: *The clerk is a decent sort.* **4.** A way of acting or behaving. **5. sorts.** *Printing.* One of the characters in a font of type. **—sort** *tr.v.* **sort·ed, sort·ing, sorts. 1.** To arrange according to class, kind, or size; classify. See Synonyms at **arrange. 2.** To separate from others: *sort out the wheat from the chaff.* **3.** To clarify by going over mentally: *She tried to sort out her problems.* **—*idioms.* after a sort.** In a haphazard or imperfect way: *managed to paint the chair after a sort.* **of sorts** (or **of a sort**). **1.** Of a mediocre or inferior kind: *a constitutional government of a sort.* **2.** Of one kind or another: *knew many folktales of sorts.* **out of sorts. 1.** Slightly ill. **2.** Irritable; cross: *The teacher is out of sorts this morning.* **sort of.** *Informal.* Somewhat; rather: *"Gambling and prostitution . . . have been prohibited, but only sort of"* (George F. Will). [Middle English, from Old French, from Latin *sors, sort-,* lot. See **ser-**[2] in Appendix.] **—sort′a·ble** *adj.* **—sort′er** *n.*

sor·ta·tion (sôr-tā′shən) *n.* Sorting, especially when mechanized or automated: *the sortation of baggage; sortation of parcels.*

sor·tie (sôr′tē, sôr-tē′) *n.* **1.a.** An armed attack made from a place surrounded by enemy forces. **b.** The troops making such an attack. **2.** A flight of a combat aircraft on a mission. **—sortie** *intr.v.* **-tied, -tie·ing, -ties.** To go on a sortie. [French, from feminine past participle of *sortir,* to go out, from Old French.]

sor·ti·lege (sôr′tl-ĭj) *n.* **1.** The act or practice of foretelling the future by drawing lots. **2.** Sorcery; witchcraft. [Middle English, from Old French, from Medieval Latin *sortilegium,* from *sortilegus,* diviner : Latin *sors, sort-,* lot; see **ser-**[2] in Appendix + Latin *legere,* to read; see **leg-** in Appendix.]

so·rus (sôr′əs, sōr′-) *n., pl.* **so·ri** (sôr′ī, sōr′ī). **1.** A cluster of sporangia borne on the underside of a fern frond. **2.** A reproductive structure in certain fungi and lichens. [New Latin *sōrus,* from Greek *sōros,* heap. See **teuə-** in Appendix.]

S O S (ĕs′ō-ĕs′) *n.* **1.** The letters represented by the Morse signal • • • — — — • • •, used as an international distress signal, especially by ships and aircraft. **2.** A call or signal for help.

So·sno·wiec (sŏs-nô′vyĕts). A city of southern Poland, an industrial suburb of Katowice. Population, 255,000.

so-so (sō′sō′) *adj.* Neither very good nor very bad; passable: *a so-so performance; feeling so-so.* **—so-so** *adv.* Neither very well nor very poorly; passably: *I swam so-so, but better than yesterday.*

so·ste·nu·to (sō′stə-no͞o′tō, sô′-) *Music. adv. & adj.* Beyond or being sustained beyond a note's full value. Used chiefly as a direction. **—sostenuto** *n., pl.* **-tos** or **-ti** (-tē). A sostenuto passage or movement. [Italian, past participle of *sostenere,* to sustain, from Latin *sustinēre.* See SUSTAIN.]

sot (sŏt) *n.* A drunkard. [Middle English, fool, from Old English *sott,* from Old French *sot.*]

so·te·ri·ol·o·gy (sō-tîr′ē-ŏl′ə-jē) *n.* The theological doctrine of salvation as effected by Jesus. [Greek *sōtērion,* deliverance (from *sōtēr,* savior, from *saos, sōs,* safe; see **teuə-** in Appendix) + -LOGY.] **—so·te′ri·o·log′ic** (-ə-lŏj′ĭk), **so·te′ri·o·log′i·cal** (-ĭ-kəl) *adj.*

So·thic (sō′thĭk, sŏth′ĭk) *adj.* **1.** Of, relating to, or deriving from the name of Sothis. **2.** Being the ancient Egyptian calendar year, consisting of 365¼ days. **3.** Being a cycle consisting of 1,460 years of 365 days in the ancient Egyptian calendar. [From Greek *Sōthis,* the star Sirius. See SOTHIS.]

So·this (sō′thĭs) *n.* See **Sirius.** [Greek *Sōthis,* from Egyptian *spdt.*]

So·tho (sō′tō) *n.* **1.** A group of closely related Bantu languages, including Tswana, spoken in southern Africa. **2.** Any of these languages.

so·tol (sō′tōl′) *n.* **1.** Any of several tall woody plants of the genus *Dasylirion* of the southwest United States and adjacent Mexico, having prickly-margined leaves and a large panicle of whitish unisexual flowers. **2.** An alcoholic beverage produced from the trunks of these plants. [Perhaps from Spanish *soto,* thicket, woods, from Latin *saltus,* narrow pass, woodland.]

sot·ted (sŏt′ĭd) *adj.* Muddled or stupefied, especially with liquor; besotted. **—sot′ted·ly** *adv.* **—sot′ted·ness** *n.*

sot·tish (sŏt′ĭsh) *adj.* **1.** Stupefied from or as if from drink. **2.** Tending to drink excessively; drunken. **—sot′tish·ly** *adv.* **—sot′tish·ness** *n.*

sot·to vo·ce (sŏt′ō vō′chē, sôt′tô vô′chĕ) *adv. & adj.* **1.** In soft tones, as not to be overheard; in an undertone: *"There were aspersions cast, sotto voce, but knees quickly folded into curtsies when introductions were in order"* (Barbara Lazear Ascher). **2.** *Music.* In very soft tones. Used chiefly as a direction. [Italian : *sotto,* under + *voce,* voice.]

sou (so͞o) *n. Abbr.* **s.** One of several coins formerly used in France, worth a small amount. [French, from Old French *sol,* from Late Latin *solidus,* solidus. See SOLIDUS.]

sou. or **Sou.** *abbr.* South; southern.

sou·a·ri nut (so͞o-är′ē) *n.* **1.** A South American evergreen tree *(Caryocar nuciferum)* having opposite, trifoliate leaves and drupes with nutlike stones containing seeds used as food and a source of cooking oil. **2.** The nut of this tree. Also called *butternut.* [French *saouari,* from Galibi *sawarra.*]

sou·bise (so͞o-bēz′) *n.* A sauce made with onions or onion purée. [French, after Charles de Rohan, Prince de *Soubise* (1715–1787), French soldier.]

sou·brette (so͞o-brĕt′) *n.* **1.a.** A saucy, coquettish, intriguing maidservant in comedies or comic opera. **b.** An actress or a singer taking such a part. **2.** A young woman regarded as flirtatious or frivolous. [French, from Provençal *soubreto,* feminine of *soubret,* conceited, from *soubra,* to leave aside, from Old Provençal *sobrar,* to be excessive, from Latin *superāre,* from *super,* above. See **uper** in Appendix.]

sou·bri·quet (so͞o′brĭ-kā′, -kĕt′, so͞o′brĭ-kā′, -kĕt′) *n.* Variant of **sobriquet.**

sou·chong also **soo·chong** (so͞o′chŏng′, -shŏng′) *n.* Any of several varieties of black tea native to China and adjacent regions. [Chinese (Mandarin) *xiǎo zhǒng* : *xiǎo,* small + *zhǒng,* kind.]

sou·dan (so͞od′n) *n.* Variant of **soldan.**

souf·flé (so͞o-flā′) *n.* A light, fluffy baked dish made with egg yolks and beaten egg whites combined with various other ingredients and served as a main dish or sweetened as a dessert. [French, from past participle of *souffler,* to puff up, from Old French *soffler,* from Latin *sufflāre* : *sub–,* sub- + *flāre,* to blow; see **bhlē-** in Appendix.] **—souf·flé′** *adj.* **—souf·fléd′** *adj.*

Sou·fri·ère (so͞o′frē-ĕr′). A volcano, 1,234.6 m (4,048 ft) high, on St. Vincent Island in the Windward Islands of the West Indies. A violent eruption in 1902 killed more than 1,000 people.

sough (sŭf, sou) *intr.v.* **soughed, sough·ing, soughs.** To make a soft murmuring or rustling sound. **—sough** *n.* A soft murmuring or rustling sound, as of the wind or a gentle surf. [Middle English *swowen, soughen,* from Old English *swōgan.*]

sought (sôt) *v.* Past tense and past participle of **seek.**

souk (so͞ok, sho͞ok) *n.* An open-air market, or a part of such a market, in an Arab city. [Arabic *sūq.*]

soul (sōl) *n.* **1.** The animating and vital principle in human beings, credited with the faculties of thought, action, and emotion and often conceived as an immaterial entity. **2.** The spiritual nature of human beings, regarded as immortal, separable from the body at death, and susceptible to happiness or misery in a future state. **3.** The disembodied spirit of a dead human being; a shade. **4. Soul.** *Christian Science.* God. **5.** A human being: *"the homes of some nine hundred souls"* (Garrison Keillor). **6.** The central or integral part; the vital core: *"It saddens me that this network . . . may lose its soul, which is after all the quest for news"* (Marvin Kalb). **7.** A person considered as the perfect embodiment of an intangible quality; a personification: *I am the very soul of discretion.* **8.** A person's emotional or moral nature: *"An actor is . . . often a soul which wishes to reveal itself to the world but dare not"* (Alec Guinness). **9.** A sense of ethnic pride among Black people and especially African-Americans, expressed in areas such as language, social customs, religion, and music. **10.** A strong, deeply felt emotion conveyed by a speaker or an artist. **11.** Soul music. [Middle English, from Old English *sāwol.*]

soul brother *n. Slang.* A fellow Black man.

soul food *n.* Food, such as ham hocks and collard greens, traditionally eaten by southern American Black people.

soul·ful (sōl′fəl) *adj.* Full of or expressing deep feeling; profoundly emotional. **—soul′ful·ly** *adv.* **—soul′ful·ness** *n.*

soul kiss *n.* A kiss in which the tongue enters the partner's mouth; a French kiss.

soul·less (sōl′lĭs) *adj.* Lacking sensitivity or the capacity for deep feeling. **—soul′less·ly** *adv.* **—soul′less·ness** *n.*

soul mate *n.* One of two persons compatible with each other in disposition, point of view, or sensitivity.

soul music *n. Music.* Popular music developed by American Black people, combining elements of gospel music and rhythm and blues.

soul-search·ing (sōl′sûr′chĭng) *n.* A penetrating examination of one's motives, convictions, and attitudes.

soul sister *n. Slang.* A fellow Black woman.

sound¹ (sound) *n.* **1.a.** Vibrations transmitted through an elastic material or a solid, liquid, or gas, with frequencies in the approximate range of 20 to 20,000 hertz, capable of being detected by human organs of hearing. **b.** Transmitted vibrations of any frequency. **c.** The sensation stimulated in the organs of hearing by such vibrations in the air or other medium. **d.** Such sensations considered as a group. **2.** A distinctive noise: *a hollow sound.* **3.** The distance over which something can be heard: *within sound of my voice.* **4.** *Linguistics.* **a.** An articulation made by the vocal apparatus: *a vowel sound; a speech sound.* **b.** The distinctive character of such an articulation: *The words* bear *and* bare *have the same sound.* **5.** A mental impression; an implication: *didn't like the sound of the invitation.* **6.** Auditory material that is recorded, as for a movie. **7.** Meaningless noise. **8.** *Music.* A distinctive style, as of an orchestra or a singer. **9.** *Archaic.* Rumor; report. **—sound** *v.* **sound·ed, sound·ing, sounds.** *—intr.* **1.a.** To make or give forth a sound: *The siren sounded.* **b.** To be given forth as a sound: *The fanfare sounded.* **2.** To present a particular impression: *That argument sounds reasonable. —tr.* **1.** To cause to give forth or produce a sound: *sounded the gong.* **2.** To summon, announce, or signal by a sound: *sound a warning.* **3.** *Linguistics.* To articulate; pronounce: *sound a vowel.* **4.** To make known; celebrate: *"Nations unborn your mighty names shall sound"* (Alexander Pope). **5.** To examine (a body organ or part) by causing to emit sound; auscultate. ***—phrasal verb.* sound off. 1.** To express one's views vigorously: *was always sounding off about higher taxes.* **2.** To count cadence when marching in military formation. [Middle English *soun,* from Old French *son,* from Latin *sonus.* See **swen-** in Appendix.]

sound² (sound) *adj.* **sound·er, sound·est. 1.** Free from defect, decay, or damage; in good condition. **2.** Free from disease or injury. See Synonyms at **healthy. 3.** Having a firm basis; unshakable: *a sound foundation.* **4.** Financially secure or safe: *a sound economy.* **5.a.** Based on valid reasoning: *a sound observation.* See Synonyms at **valid. b.** Free from logical flaws: *sound reasoning.* **c.** *Logic.* Of or relating to an argument in which all the premises are true and the conclusion follows from the premises. **6.** Thorough; complete: *a sound flogging.* **7.** Deep and unbroken; undisturbed: *a sound sleep.* **8.** Free from moral defect; upright. **9.** Worthy of confidence; trustworthy. **10.** Marked by or showing common sense and good judgment; levelheaded: *a sound approach to the problem.* **11.** Compatible with an accepted point of view; conservative. **12.** *Law.* Legally valid. **—sound** *adv.* Thoroughly; deeply: *sound asleep.* [Middle English, from Old English *gesund.*] **—sound′ly** *adv.* **—sound′ness** *n.*

sound³ (sound) *n.* **1.** *Abbr.* **sd.** A long, relatively wide body of water, larger than a strait or a channel, connecting larger bodies of water. **2.** A long, wide ocean inlet. **3.** The air bladder of a fish. [Middle English, from Old English *sund,* swimming, sea.]

sound⁴ (sound) *v.* **sound·ed, sound·ing, sounds.** *—tr.* **1.** To measure the depth of (water), especially by means of a weighted line; fathom. **2.** To try to learn the attitudes or opinions of: *sounded out her feelings.* **3.** To probe (a body cavity) with a sound. *—intr.* **1.** To measure depth. **2.** To dive swiftly downward. Used of a whale or fish. **3.** To look into a possibility; investigate. **—sound** *n.* An instrument used to examine or explore body cavities, as for foreign bodies or other abnormalities, or to dilate strictures in them. [Middle English *sounden,* from Old French *sonder,* from *sonde,* sounding line, probably of Germanic origin.] **—sound′a·ble** *adj.*

sound-a·like (sound′ə-līk′) *n.* One that closely resembles another in sound, especially by imitation of voice or of musical style: *an Enrico Caruso sound-alike.*

sound barrier *n.* **1.** See **sonic barrier. 2.** A set of tall wooden, plastic, or concrete barriers placed along a road or highway to muffle the sound of traffic.

sound bite *n. Slang.* A very brief broadcast statement, as by a politician during a news report: *"The box has been spitting forth maddening nine-second sound bites"* (Mary McGrory).

sound·board (sound′bôrd′, -bōrd′) *n. Music.* See **sounding board** (sense 1).

sound box *n. Music.* A hollow chamber in the body of an instrument, such as a violin or a cello, that intensifies the resonance of the tone.

sound camera *n.* A movie camera equipped to record sound and visual image synchronously.

sound effects *pl.n.* Imitative sounds, as of thunder or an explosion, produced artificially for theatrical purposes, as for a film, play, or radio program.

sound·er¹ (soun′dər) *n.* One that makes a sound: *a sounder of alarms.*

sound·er² (soun′dər) *n.* One that sounds, especially a device for making soundings of the sea.

sound·er³ (soun′dər) *n.* A herd of wild boar. See Synonyms at **flock¹.** [Middle English, from Old French *sondre,* of Germanic origin.]

sound·ing¹ (soun′dĭng) *n.* **1.** The act of one that sounds. **2.** A probe of the environment for scientific observation. **3.a.** A measured depth of water. **b.** Often **soundings.** Water shallow enough for depth measurements to be taken by a hand line.

sound·ing² (soun′dĭng) *adj.* **1.** Emitting a full sound; resonant. **2.** Noisy but with little significance.

sounding board *n.* **1.** *Music.* **a.** A thin board forming the upper portion of the resonant chamber in an instrument, such as a violin or piano, and serving to increase resonance. **b.** A structure placed behind or over a podium or platform to reflect music

souk

ă pat	oi boy
ā pay	ou out
âr care	o͝o took
ä father	o͞o boot
ĕ pet	ŭ cut
ē be	ûr urge
ĭ pit	th thin
ī pie	*th* this
îr pier	hw which
ŏ pot	zh vision
ō toe	ə about, item
ô paw	♦ regionalism

Stress marks: ′ (primary); ′ (secondary), as in **dictionary** (dĭk′shə-nĕr′ē)

or a speaker's voice to an audience. Also called *soundboard.* **2.** A person or group whose reactions to an idea, opinion, or point of view will serve as a measure of its effectiveness or acceptability. **3.** A device or means serving to spread or popularize an idea or a point of view.

sounding lead (lĕd) *n. Nautical.* The metal weight at the end of a sounding line.

sounding line *n. Nautical.* A line marked at intervals of fathoms and weighted at one end, used to determine the depth of water. Also called *lead line.*

sounding rocket *n.* A rocket used to make observations anywhere within Earth's atmosphere.

sound•less (sound′lĭs) *adj.* Making no sound. See Synonyms at **still**[1]. **—sound′less•ly** *adv.* **—sound′less•ness** *n.*

sound•man (sound′măn′) *n.* One in charge of recording, transmitting, or amplifying sound or of producing sound effects, as for a television or radio broadcast.

sound pollution *n.* See **noise pollution.**

sound•proof (sound′pro͞of′) *adj.* Not penetrable by audible sound. **—sound′proof′** *v.*

sound rang•ing (rān′jĭng) *n.* A method for locating a source of sound, such as an enemy gun, by measuring the travel time of the sound wave to microphones at known positions.

sound stage also **sound•stage** (sound′stāj′) *n.* A usually soundproof room or studio used for the production of movies.

sound•track also **sound track** (sound′trăk′) *n.* **1.** The narrow strip at one side of a movie film that carries the sound recording. **2. a.** The music that accompanies a movie. **b.** A commercial phonograph record or tape of such music.

sound truck *n.* A truck or other vehicle having one or more loudspeakers, usually situated on top, typically used for broadcasting political or commercial messages.

sound wave *n.* A longitudinal pressure wave of audible or inaudible sound.

soup (so͞op) *n.* **1.** A liquid food prepared from meat, fish, or vegetable stock combined with various other ingredients and often containing solid pieces. **2.** *Slang.* Something having the appearance or a consistency suggestive of soup, especially: **a.** Dense fog. **b.** Nitroglycerine. **3.** A chaotic or unfortunate situation. ***—phrasal verb.*** **soup up.** *Slang.* To modify (something) so as to increase its capacity to perform or satisfy, especially to add horsepower or greater speed potential to (an engine or a vehicle): *souped up the 1959 Ford; souping up old sound systems.* ***—idiom.*** **in the soup.** *Slang.* Having difficulties; in trouble. [Middle English *soupe,* from Old French, of Germanic origin; see **seuə-**[2] in Appendix. *Soup up,* from SOUP, material injected into a horse to make it run faster (influenced by SUPERCHARGE).]

sousaphone

soup•çon (so͞op-sôɴ′, so͞op′sŏn′) *n.* A very small amount; a trace: *not a soupçon of mercy.* [French, from Old French *sospeçon,* suspicion, from Latin *suspectiō, suspectiōn-,* fear, from *suspectus,* past participle of *suspicere,* to suspect. See SUSPECT.]

soup du jour (so͞op′ də zho͝or′) *n., pl.* **soups du jour.** A soup featured by a restaurant on a given day. [French *soupe du jour* : *soupe,* soup + *du,* of the + *jour,* day.]

soup kitchen *n.* A place where food is offered free or at very low cost to the needy.

soup•spoon (so͞op′spo͞on′) *n.* A spoon somewhat larger than a teaspoon, used for eating soup.

soup•y (so͞o′pē) *adj.* **-i•er, -i•est. 1.** Having the appearance or consistency of soup. **2.** *Slang.* Foggy: *soupy weather.* **3.** *Informal.* Sentimental.

sour (sour) *adj.* **sour•er, sour•est. 1.** Having a taste characteristic of that produced by acids; sharp, tart, or tangy. **2.** Made acid or rancid by fermentation. **3.** Having the characteristics of fermentation or rancidity; tasting or smelling of decay. **4. a.** Bad-tempered and morose; peevish: *a sour temper.* **b.** Displeased with something one formerly admired or liked; disenchanted: *sour on ballet.* **5.** Not measuring up to the expected or usual ability or quality; bad. **6.** Of or relating to excessively acid soil that is damaging to crops. **7.** Containing excessive sulfur compounds. Used of gasoline. **—sour** *n.* **1.** The sensation of sour taste, one of the four primary tastes. **2.** Something sour. **3.** A mixed drink made especially with whiskey, lemon or lime juice, sugar, and sometimes soda water. **—sour** *tr. & intr.v.* **soured, sour•ing, sours. 1.** To make or become sour. **2.** To make or become disagreeable or disenchanted. [Middle English, from Old English *sūr.*] **—sour′ish** *adj.* **—sour′ly** *adv.* **—sour′ness** *n.*

SYNONYMS: *sour, acid, acidulous, dry, tart.* The central meaning shared by these adjectives is "having a taste like that produced by an acid": *sour cider; acid, unripe grapes; an acidulous tomato; dry white wine; tart cherries.*

sour•ball (sour′bôl′) *n.* A round piece of hard, tart candy.

source (sôrs, sōrs) *n.* **1.** The point at which something springs into being or from which it derives or is obtained. **2.** The point of origin, such as a spring, of a stream or river. See Synonyms at **origin. 3.** One that causes, creates, or initiates; a maker. **4.** One, such as a person or document, that supplies information: *A reporter is only as reliable as his or her sources.* **5.** *Physics.* The point or part of a system where energy or mass is added to the system. **—source** *v.* **sourced, sourc•ing, sourc•es.** *—tr.* **1.** To specify the origin of (a communication); document: *The report is thoroughly sourced.* **2.** To obtain (parts or materials) from another business, country, or locale for manufacture: *They sourced the spoke nuts from our company.* *—intr.* To obtain parts or materials from another business, country, or locale: *They are sourcing from abroad in order to save money.* [Middle English, from Old French *sourse,* from feminine past participle of *sourdre,* to rise, from Latin *surgere.* See SURGE.]

source book *n.* **1.** A primary document, as of history, literature, or religion, on which secondary writings are based. **2.** A collection of such documents.

source language *n. Abbr.* **SL** The language from which a translation is to be made.

sour cherry *n.* **1.** A deciduous shrub or small tree *(Prunus cerasus)* having white flowers and tart red fruit. **2.** The edible fruit of this plant.

sour cream *n.* **1.** Cream that has soured naturally by the action of lactic-acid bacteria, used in baking certain breads and cakes. **2.** A smooth, thick, artificially soured cream, widely used as an ingredient in soups, salads, and various meat dishes.

sour•dine (so͝or-dēn′) *n. Music.* **1.** An obsolete double-reed instrument with a soft tone. **2.** A mute, especially one for a violin. **3.** A stop on an organ producing a low, soft, muted tone. [French, from Italian *sordina,* feminine of *sordino,* a mute, diminutive of *sordo,* deaf, mute, from Latin *surdus.*]

sour•dough (sour′dō′) *n.* **1.** Sour fermented dough used as leaven in making bread. **2.** An early settler or prospector, especially in Alaska and northwest Canada.

sour grapes *pl.n.* Denial of the desirability of something after one has found out that it cannot be reached or acquired: *The losers' scorn for the award is pure sour grapes.*

sour gum *n.* A deciduous tree *(Nyssa sylvatica)* of the eastern United States and Mexico, having glossy, somewhat leathery leaves and soft wood. Also called *black gum, pepperidge.*

Sou•ris (so͝or′ĭs). A river, about 724 km (450 mi) long, rising in southern Saskatchewan, Canada, and flowing southeast in a great loop into northern North Dakota then north and northeast to the Assiniboine River in southwest Manitoba.

sour mash *n.* **1.** A mixture of new mash and mash from a preceding run used to distill certain malt whiskeys. **2.** Whiskey so distilled.

sour orange *n.* A spiny evergreen tree *(Citrus aurantium)* native to southern Vietnam and widely cultivated in warmer regions, having globose, reddish-orange, highly acidic fruit. Also called *bigarade, bitter orange, Seville orange.*

sour•puss (sour′po͝os′) *n. Slang.* A habitually gloomy or sullen person. [SOUR + PUSS[2].]

sour salt *n.* Crystals of citric acid used in cooking.

sour•sop (sour′sŏp′) *n.* **1.** A tropical American evergreen tree *(Annona muricata)* bearing spiny fruit with tart edible pulp. **2.** The fruit of this tree.

sour•wood (sour′wo͝od′) *n.* A deciduous tree *(Oxydendrum arboreum)* of the eastern United States, having drooping terminal panicles of small, white, urn-shaped flowers. Also called *sorrel tree.* [So called from its sour-tasting leaves.]

Sou•sa (so͞o′zə, -sə), **John Philip.** Known as "the March King." 1854–1932. American bandmaster and composer who wrote marches such as *Stars and Stripes Forever* (1897).

sou•sa•phone (so͞o′zə-fōn′, -sə-) *n. Music.* A large brass wind instrument, similar in range to the tuba, having a flaring bell and a shape adapted to being carried in marching bands. [After John Philip SOUSA.]

souse[1] (sous) *v.* **soused, sous•ing, sous•es.** *—tr.* **1.** To plunge into a liquid. **2.** To make soaking wet; drench. See Synonyms at **dip. 3.** To steep in a mixture, as in pickling. **4.** *Slang.* To make intoxicated. *—intr.* To become immersed or soaking wet. **—souse** *n.* **1.** The act or process of sousing. **2. a.** Food steeped in pickle, especially pork trimmings. **b.** The liquid used in pickling; brine. **3.** *Slang.* **a.** A drunkard. **b.** A period of heavy drinking; a binge. [Middle English *sousen,* probably from Old French **souser,* to pickle, from *souz, sous,* pickled meat, of Germanic origin. See **sal-** in Appendix.]

souse[2] (sous) *v.* **soused, sous•ing, sous•es.** *Archaic. —tr.* To pounce on; attack. *—intr.* To swoop down, as an attacking hawk does. **—souse** *n. Obsolete.* A swooping motion of attack. [From Middle English *souse,* swooping motion, alteration of *sours,* source, a rising. See SOURCE.]

sous•lik (sŭs′lĭk) *n.* Variant of **suslik.**

Sousse (so͞os) also **Su•sah** or **Su•sa** (so͞o′sə, -zə). A city of northeast Tunisia on an inlet of the Mediterranean Sea. Founded in ancient times by the Phoenicians, it was an important city under the Romans and Carthaginians and later under the Arabs (9th–11th centuries) and the French (19th–20th centuries). Population, 69,530.

sous vide (so͞o vēd′) *n.* The cooking of various ingredients in a plastic pouch. [French, in a vacuum, vacuum-packed : *sous,* under + *vide,* vacuum.] **—sous-vide′** (so͞o-vēd′) *adj.*

sou•tache (so͞o-tăsh′) *n.* A narrow flat braid in a herringbone pattern, used for trimming and embroidery. [French, from Hungarian *sujtás.*]

sou•tane (so͞o-tän′ -tăn′) *n.* A cassock, especially one that buttons up and down the front. [French, alteration (influenced by French *sous,* under) of obsolete *sottane,* from Italian *sottana,* from *sotto,* under, from Latin *subtus,* from *sub.* See **upo** in Appendix.]

Sou•ter (so͞o′tər), **David Hackett.** Born 1939. American jurist who was appointed an associate justice of the U.S. Supreme Court in 1990.

south (south) *n. Abbr.* **S, S., s, s., so., So., sou., Sou. 1.a.** The direction along a meridian 90° clockwise from east; the direction to the right of sunrise. **b.** The cardinal point on the mariner's compass 180° clockwise from due north and directly opposite north. **2.** An area or a region lying in the south. **3.** Often **South. a.** The southern part of the earth. **b.** The southern part of a region or country. **4. South.** The southern part of the United States, especially the states that fought for the Confederacy in the Civil War. **—south** *adj. Abbr.* **S, S., s, s., so., So., sou., Sou. 1.** To, toward, of, facing, or in the south. **2.** Originating in or coming from the south: *a hot south wind.* **—south** *adv. Abbr.* **S, S., s, s., so., So., sou., Sou.** In, from, or toward the south. [Middle English, from Old English *sūth.* See **sāwel-** in Appendix.]

South Af•ri•ca (ăf′rĭ-kə). *Abbr.* **S.Afr., S.A.** A country of southern Africa on the Atlantic and Indian oceans. First settled by the Dutch in the 17th century, the region passed to Great Britain in 1814 but was contested by descendants of the Dutch settlers in the Boer War (1899–1902). The British and Boer colonies formed a union in 1910 and became a republic in 1961. Pretoria is the administrative capital; Cape Town, the legislative capital; and Bloemfontein, the judicial capital. Johannesburg is the largest city. Population, 24,208,140. **—South Af′ri•can** *adj. & n.*

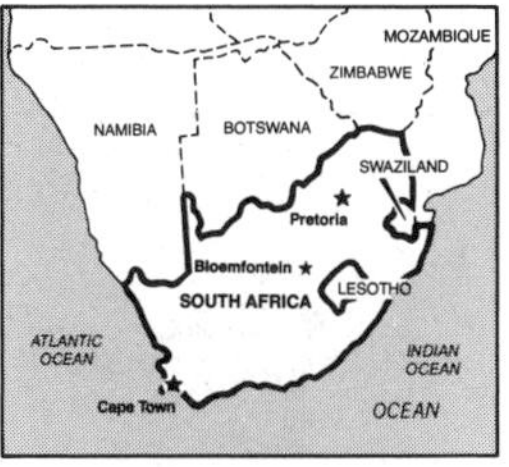

South Africa

South A•mer•i•ca (ə-mĕr′ĭ-kə). *Abbr.* **S.A.** A continent of the southern Western Hemisphere southeast of North America between the Atlantic and Pacific oceans. It extends from the Caribbean Sea to Cape Horn. **—South A•mer′i•can** *adj. & n.*

South•amp•ton (south-hămp′tən, sou-thămp′-). **1.** A borough of south-central England on an inlet of the English Channel opposite the Isle of Wight. Founded on the site of Roman and Saxon settlements, it has long been a major port, especially for passenger ships. Population, 208,800. **2.** A village of southeast New York on the southeast coast of Long Island. It is primarily a summer resort. Population, 4,000.

Southampton, Third Earl of. Title of Henry Wriothesley. 1573–1624. English politician, soldier, and patron of Shakespeare as well as a number of other Elizabethan poets. Shakespeare's *Venus and Adonis* and *Rape of Lucrece* are dedicated to him.

Southampton Island. An island of eastern Northwest Territories, Canada, at the entrance to Hudson Bay.

South At•lan•tic Ocean (ăt-lăn′tĭk). The southern part of the Atlantic Ocean, extending from the equator to Antarctica.

South•a•ven (south′ā′vən). A community of extreme northwest Mississippi, a suburb of Memphis, Tennessee. Population, 16,071.

South Bend. A city of northern Indiana near the Michigan border northwest of Fort Wayne. A fur-trading post was established here in 1820. Population, 109,727.

south•bound (south′bound′) *adj.* Going toward the south.

South•bridge (south′brĭj′). A town of south-central Massachusetts southwest of Worcester. Incorporated in 1816, it is a manufacturing center. Population, 16,665.

south by east *n. Abbr.* **SbE** The direction or point on the mariner's compass halfway between due south and south-southeast, or 168°45′ east of due north. **—south by east** *adv. & adj. Abbr.* **SbE** Toward or from south by east.

south by west *n. Abbr.* **SbW** The direction or point on the mariner's compass halfway between due south and south-southwest, or 168°45′ west of due north. **—south by west** *adv. & adj. Abbr.* **SbW** Toward or from south by west.

South Car•o•li•na (kăr′ə-lī′nə). *Abbr.* **SC, S.C.** A state of the southeast United States bordering on the Atlantic Ocean. It was admitted as one of the original Thirteen Colonies in 1788. First visited by Spanish explorers in the early 1500's, the region was granted by Charles II of England to eight of his principal supporters in 1663. The territory was divided into the colonies of North Carolina and South Carolina in 1729. South Carolina was a leader in the movement for independence from Great Britain and was the first state to secede from the Union (1860), thus precipitating the Civil War. Columbia is the capital and the largest city. Population, 3,122,184. **—South Car′o•lin′i•an** (-lĭn′ē-ən) *adj. & n.*

South Central Niger-Congo *n.* A branch of the Niger-Congo language family.

South Chi•na Sea (chī′nə). An arm of the western Pacific Ocean bounded by southeast China, Taiwan, the Philippines, Borneo, and Vietnam.

South Da•ko•ta (də-kō′tə). *Abbr.* **SD, S.D., S.Dak.** A state of the north-central United States. It was admitted as the 40th state in 1889. Acquired in the Louisiana Purchase, the region became part of the Dakota Territory in 1861 and was split off from North Dakota at the time it achieved statehood. Pierre is the capital and Sioux Falls the largest city. Population, 690,768. **—South Da•ko′tan** *adj. & n.*

South De•ca•tur (dĭ-kā′tər). A community of northwest Georgia, a suburb of Atlanta. Population, 28,100.

South•down (south′doun′) *n.* Any of a breed of small, hornless sheep of English origin, having short, dense, fine-textured wool. [After the SOUTH DOWNS.]

South Downs (dounz). See **Downs.**

south•east (south-ēst′, sou-ēst′) *n. Abbr.* **SE 1.** The direction or point on the mariner's compass halfway between due south and due east, or 135° east of due north. **2.** An area or a region lying in the southeast. **3. Southeast.** A region of the southeast United States generally including Alabama, Georgia, South Carolina, and Florida. **—southeast** *adj. Abbr.* **SE 1.** To, toward, of, facing, or in the southeast. **2.** Originating in or coming from the southeast: *a southeast wind.* **—southeast** *adv. Abbr.* **SE** In, from, or toward the southeast. **—south•east′ern** *adj.*

Southeast A•sia (ā′zhə, ā′shə). A region of Asia bounded roughly by the Indian subcontinent on the west, China on the north, and the Pacific Ocean on the east. It includes Indochina, the Malay Peninsula, and the Malay Archipelago. **—Southeast A′sian** *adj. & n.*

southeast by east *n. Abbr.* **SEbE** The direction or point on the mariner's compass halfway between southeast and east-southeast, or 123°45′ east of due north. **—southeast by east** *adv. & adj. Abbr.* **SEbE** Toward or from southeast by east.

southeast by south *n. Abbr.* **SEbS** The direction or point on the mariner's compass halfway between southeast and south-southeast, or 146°15′ east of due north. **—southeast by south** *adv. & adj. Abbr.* **SEbS** Toward or from southeast by south.

south•east•er (south-ē′stər, sou-ē′-) *n.* A storm or gale blowing from the southeast.

south•east•er•ly (south-ē′stər-lē, sou-ē′-) *adj.* **1.** Situated toward the southeast. **2.** Coming or being from the southeast. **—south•east′er•ly** *adv.*

south•east•ward (south-ēst′wərd, sou-ēst′-) *adv. & adj.* Toward, to, or in the southeast. **—southeastward** *n.* A southeastward direction, point, or region. **—south•east′ward•ly** *adv. & adj.* **—south•east′wards** *adv.*

South El Mon•te (ĕl mŏn′tē). A city of southern California, a suburb of Los Angeles. Population, 16,623.

South•end-on-Sea (sou′thĕnd-ŏn-sē′, -ôn-). A borough of southeast England at the mouth of the Thames River estuary. It is a manufacturing center and seaside resort. Population, 157,100.

south•er (sou′*th*ər) *n.* A strong wind coming from the south.

south•er•ly (sŭ*th*′ər-lē) *adj.* **1.** Situated toward the south. **2.** Coming or being from the south: *southerly winds.* **—southerly** *n., pl.* **-lies.** A storm or wind coming from the south. **—south′er•ly** *adv.*

south•ern (sŭ*th*′ərn) *adj. Abbr.* **S, S., s, s., so., So., sou., Sou. 1.** Situated in, toward, or facing the south. **2.** Coming from the south: *southern breezes.* **3.** Native to or growing in the south. **4.** Often **Southern.** Of, relating to, or characteristic of southern regions or the South. **5.** Being south of the equator. [Middle English *southerne,* from Old English *sūtherne.* See **sāwel-** in Appendix.] **—south′ern•ness′** *n.*

Southern Alps (ălps). A mountain range of South Island, New Zealand, paralleling the western coast and rising to 3,766.4 m (12,349 ft).

Southern Bug (bo͝og, bo͞ok). See **Bug** (sense 2).

Southern Cross *n.* A constellation in the Southern Hemisphere near Centaurus and Musca. Also called *Crux.*

Southern Crown *n.* See **Corona Australis.**

Southern Educated Standard *n.* See **Received Pronunciation.**

south•ern•er also **South•ern•er** (sŭ*th*′ər-nər) *n.* A native or inhabitant of the south, especially the southern United States.

Southern Hemisphere *n.* **1.** The half of the earth south of the equator. **2.** *Astronomy.* The half of the celestial sphere south of the celestial equator.

South•ern•ism (sŭ*th*′ər-nĭz′əm) *n.* **1.** An expression or a pronunciation characteristic of the southern United States or southern England. **2.** A trait, an attitude, or a practice characteristic of the South or southerners, especially in the United States.

southern lights *pl.n.* See **aurora australis.**

south•ern•most (sŭ*th*′ərn-mōst′) *adj.* Farthest south.

Southern Paiute *n.* **1.** See **Paiute** (sense 1b). **2.** The Uto-Aztecan language of the Southern Paiute.

Southern prickly ash *n.* See **Hercules' club** (sense 2).

Southern Spor•a•des (spôr′ə-dēz′, spô-rä′*th*ĕs). See **Sporades.**

south•ern•wood (sŭ*th*′ərn-wo͝od′) *n.* An aromatic southern European shrubby woody plant *(Artemisia abrotanum)* having finely divided grayish foliage and globose, nodding, creamy-white flower heads. Also called *old man.*

Southern Yem•en (yĕm′ən, yā′mən). A former country of southwest Asia on the Arabian Peninsula. A British protectorate from 1882 to 1914, it became fully independent in 1967 and united with North Yemen in 1990 to form the new country of Yemen.

South Eu•clid (yo͞o′klĭd). A city of northeast Ohio, a residential suburb of Cleveland. Population, 25,713.

Sou•they (sou′*th*ē, sŭ*th*′ē), **Robert.** 1774–1843. British writer noted for his romantic poetry, criticism, and biographical works.

South•field (south′fēld′). A city of southeast Michigan, an industrial suburb of Detroit on the Rouge River. Population, 75,568.

South Frig•id Zone (frĭj′ĭd). See **Frigid Zone.**

South•gate (south′gāt′). A city of southeast Michigan, a residential suburb of Detroit. Population, 32,058.

ă pat	oi boy
ā pay	ou out
âr care	o͝o took
ä father	o͞o boot
ĕ pet	ŭ cut
ē be	ûr urge
ĭ pit	th thin
ī pie	*th* this
îr pier	hw which
ŏ pot	zh vision
ō toe	ə about, item
ô paw	♦ regionalism

Stress marks: ′ (primary); ′ (secondary), as in **dictionary** (dĭk′shə-nĕr′ē)

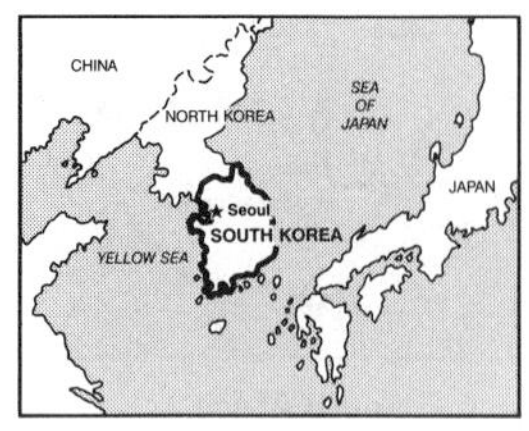

South Korea

South Gate. A city of southern California, an industrial suburb of Los Angeles. Population, 66,784.

South Geor·gia (jôr′jə). A British-administered island in the southern Atlantic Ocean east of Cape Horn. A dependency of the Falkland Islands, it was claimed by Capt. James Cook in 1775.

South Hol·land (hŏl′ənd). A village of northeast Illinois, an industrial suburb of Chicago. Population, 24,977.

south·ing (sou′thĭng) *n.* **1.** The difference in latitude between two positions as a result of a movement to the south. **2.** Progress toward the south.

South·ing·ton (sŭth′ĭng-tən). A town of central Connecticut northeast of Waterbury. It has been a manufacturing center since the 1770's. Population, 36,879.

South Island. An island of New Zealand southwest of North Island, from which it is separated by Cook Strait. It is the larger but less populous of the country's two principal islands.

South Kings·town (kĭngz′toun′). A town of southern Rhode Island south-southwest of Providence. It was a stronghold of the Narragansett during King Philip's War (1675–1676). Population, 20,414.

South Ko·re·a (kə-rē′ə, kô-, kō-). A country of eastern Asia at the southern end of the Korean peninsula. Part of the ancient country of Korea, it has been divided from North Korea since the end of the Korean War (1950–1953). Seoul is the capital and the largest city. Population, 39,951,000. **—South Ko·re′an** *adj. & n.*

South Lake Ta·hoe (tä′hō). A city of eastern California on Lake Tahoe near the Nevada border. Population, 20,681.

south·land or **South·land** (south′lănd′, -lənd) *n.* A region in the south of a country or an area. **—south′land·er** *n.*

South Loup (lo͞op). A river, about 245 km (152 mi) long, of central Nebraska flowing east and southeast to unite with the North Loup and Middle Loup rivers and form the Loup River.

South Mi·am·i Heights (mī-ăm′ē, -ăm′ə). A city of southeast Florida, a suburb of Miami. Population, 18,000.

South Mil·wau·kee (mĭl-wô′kē). A city of southeast Wisconsin, a manufacturing suburb of Milwaukee. Population, 21,069.

South Na·han·ni (nə-hăn′ē). A river, about 563 km (350 mi) long, of southwest Northwest Territories, Canada, flowing to the Liard River.

South Or·ange (ôr′ĭnj, ŏr′-). A village of northeast New Jersey west of Newark. Mainly residential, it is the site of Seton Hall University (established 1856). Population, 16,971.

South Ork·ney Islands (ôrk′nē). A group of British-administered islands in the southern Atlantic Ocean southeast of Cape Horn. A dependency of the Falkland Islands, the island group was first visited by sealers in 1821.

South Pa·cif·ic Ocean (pə-sĭf′ĭk). The southern part of the Pacific Ocean, extending from the equator to Antarctica.

South Pas·a·de·na (păs′ə-dē′nə). A city of southern California, a suburb of Los Angeles. Population, 22,681.

South Pass. A broad valley in southwest Wyoming at the southern end of the Wind River Range. It was a gateway for immigration to the Far West along the Oregon Trail.

south·paw (south′pô′) *n. Slang.* A left-handed person, especially a left-handed baseball pitcher. [From the practice in baseball of arranging the diamond with the batter facing east to avoid the afternoon sun. A left-handed pitcher facing west would therefore have his pitching arm toward the south of the diamond.]

South Plain·field (plān′fēld′). A borough of northeast-central New Jersey southwest of Elizabeth. It is an industrial center. Population, 20,521.

South Platte River (plăt). A river of central and northeast Colorado and west-central Nebraska flowing about 724 km (450 mi) eastward to the North Platte River to form the Platte River.

South Po·lar Region (pō′lər). See **Polar Regions.**

South Pole *n.* **1.a.** The southern end of Earth's axis of rotation, a point in Antarctica. **b.** The celestial zenith of this terrestrial point. **c. south pole.** The southern end of the axis of rotation of a planet or other celestial body. **2. south pole.** The south-seeking magnetic pole of a straight magnet.

South·port (south′pôrt′, -pōrt′). A borough of northwest England on Liverpool Bay north of Liverpool. It is a seaside resort with varied light industries. Population, 90,000.

South Port·land (pôrt′lənd, pōrt′-). A city of southwest Maine, a residential suburb of Portland. Population, 22,712.

South River. The Delaware River. It was so named by Dutch explorers to distinguish it from the North River, an estuary of the Hudson River.

south·ron (sŭth′rən) *n.* **1.** Often **Southron.** A person who lives in the south, especially an Englishman as called by a Scotsman. **2.** A native or inhabitant of the American South. Used by the Confederates in the Civil War. **—southron** *adj. Scots.* Southern. [Middle English, variant of *southerne,* southern. See SOUTHERN.]

South Saint Paul (sānt pôl′). A city of southeast Minnesota, an industrial suburb of St. Paul on the Mississippi River. Population, 21,235.

South Sand·wich Islands (sănd′wĭch′, săn′-). A group of British-administered volcanic islands in the southern Atlantic Ocean east-southeast of Cape Horn. Formerly part of the Falkland Islands Dependency, the islands were discovered in 1775 and are now included in the British Antarctic Territory.

South San Fran·cis·co (săn′ frən-sĭs′kō). A city of western California, an industrial suburb of San Francisco on San Francisco Bay. Population, 49,393.

South Sas·katch·e·wan River (să-skăch′ə-wän′, -wən). A river of Canada flowing about 885 km (550 mi) from southern Alberta to central Saskatchewan to join the North Saskatchewan River and form the Saskatchewan River.

South Sea Islands. The islands of the southern Pacific Ocean, roughly coextensive with Oceania. **—South Sea Is′land·er** *n.*

South Seas. The oceans south of the equator, especially the southern Pacific Ocean. The name **South Sea,** or *El Mar del Sur,* was originally used by Balboa for the entire Pacific Ocean (discovered in 1513).

South Shet·land Islands (shĕt′lənd). An archipelago in the southern Atlantic Ocean off Antarctica. Formerly used as land bases by sealers and whalers, the islands are part of the British Antarctic Territory although they have also been claimed by Argentina and Chile.

South Shields (shēldz). A borough of northeast England at the mouth of the Tyne River east of Newcastle. Founded in the 13th century, it is a shipbuilding center. Population, 162,500.

south-south·east (south′south-ēst′, sou′sou-ēst′) *n. Abbr.* **SSE** The direction or point on the mariner's compass halfway between south and southeast, or 157°30′ east of due north. **—south-southeast** *adj. Abbr.* **SSE** To, toward, of, facing, or in the south-southeast. **—south-southeast** *adv. Abbr.* **SSE** In, from, or toward the south-southeast.

south-south·west (south′south-wĕst′, sou′sou-wĕst′) *n. Abbr.* **SSW** The direction or point on the mariner's compass halfway between due south and southwest, or 157°30′ west of due north. **—south-southwest** *adj. Abbr.* **SSW** To, toward, of, facing, or in the south-southwest. **—south-southwest** *adv. Abbr.* **SSW** In, from, or toward the south-southwest.

South Tem·per·ate Zone (tĕm′pər-ĭt, tĕm′prĭt). See **Temperate Zone.**

South Vi·et·nam (vē-ĕt′näm′, -năm′, vē′ĭt-, vyĕt′-). A former country of southeast Asia. It existed from 1954, after the fall of the French at Dien Bien Phu, to 1975, when the South Vietnamese government collapsed at the end of the Vietnam War. It is now part of the country of Vietnam. **—South Vi·et′nam·ese′** (-nə-mēz′, -mēs′) *adj. & n.*

south·ward (south′wərd, sŭth′ərd) *adv. & adj.* Toward, to, or in the south. **—southward** *n.* A southward direction, point, or region. **—south′ward·ly** *adv. & adj.* **—south′wards** *adv.*

South Wa·zir·i·stan (wə-zîr′ĭ-stăn′, -stän′). See **Waziristan.**

south·west (south-wĕst′, sou-wĕst′) *n. Abbr.* **SW** **1.** The direction or point on the mariner's compass halfway between due south and due west, or 135° west of due north. **2.** An area or a region lying in the southwest. **3. Southwest.** A region of the southwest United States generally including New Mexico, Arizona, Texas, California, and Nevada and sometimes Utah and Colorado. **—southwest** *adj. Abbr.* **SW** **1.** To, toward, of, facing, or in the southwest. **2.** Originating in or coming from the southwest: *a southwest wind.* **—southwest** *adv. Abbr.* **SW** In, from, or toward the southwest. **—south·west′ern** *adj.*

South-West Af·ri·ca (south′wĕst ăf′rĭ-kə). See **Namibia.**

southwest by south *n. Abbr.* **SWbS** The direction or point on the mariner's compass halfway between southwest and south-southwest, or 146°15′ west of due north. **—southwest by south** *adv. & adj. Abbr.* **SWbS** Toward or from southwest by south.

southwest by west *n. Abbr.* **SWbW** The direction or point on the mariner's compass halfway between southwest and west-southwest, or 123°45′ west of due north. **—southwest by west** *adv. & adj. Abbr.* **SWbW** Toward or from southwest by west.

south·west·er (south-wĕs′tər, sou-wĕs′-) also **sou′·west·er** (sou-wĕs′-) *n.* **1.** A storm or gale blowing from the southwest. **2.** A waterproof hat of material such as plastic, oilskin, or canvas, with a broad brim behind to protect the neck.

south·west·er·ly (south-wĕs′tər-lē, sou-wĕs′-) *adj.* **1.** Situated toward the southwest. **2.** Coming or being from the southwest. **—south·west′er·ly** *adv.*

south·west·ward (south-wĕst′wərd, sou-wĕst′-) *adv. & adj.* Toward, to, or in the southwest. **—southwestward** *n.* A southwestward direction, point, or region. **—south·west′ward·ly** *adv. & adj.* **—south·west′wards** *adv.*

South Whit·ti·er (hwĭt′ē-ər, wĭt′-). A community of southern California, a suburb of Los Angeles. Population, 43,815.

South Wind·sor (wĭn′zər). A town of north-central Connecticut north-northeast of Hartford. It was set off from Windsor in 1845. Population, 17,198.

Sou·tine (so͞o-tēn′), **Chaim.** 1893–1943. Lithuanian-born French expressionist painter whose works are often disturbing presentations of distorted figures and gruesome subjects. Among his paintings are *Side of Beef* (1925) and *The Head Valet* (1928).

sou·ve·nir (so͞o′və-nîr′, so͞o′və-nîr′) *n.* A token of remembrance; a memento. [French, from Old French, to recall, memory, from Latin *subvenīre,* to come to mind : *sub-,* sub- + *venīre,* to come; see **gʷā-** in Appendix.]

sou′·west·er (sou-wĕs′tər) *n.* Variant of **southwester.**

sov·er·eign (sŏv′ər-ĭn, sŏv′rĭn) *n. Abbr.* **sov. 1.** One that exercises supreme, permanent authority, especially in a nation or other governmental unit, as: **a.** A king, queen, or other noble person who serves as chief of state; a ruler or monarch. **b.** A national governing council or committee. **2.** A nation that governs territory outside its borders. **3.** A gold coin formerly used in Great Britain. **—sovereign** *adj. Abbr.* **sov. 1.** Self-governing; independent: *a sovereign state.* **2.** Having supreme rank or power: *a sovereign prince.* **3.** Paramount; supreme: *her sovereign virtue is compassion.* **4.a.** Of superlative strength or efficacy: *a sovereign remedy.* **b.** Unmitigated: *sovereign contempt.* [Middle English *soverain,* from Old French, from Vulgar Latin **superānus,* from Latin *super,* above. See **uper** in Appendix.] **—sov′er·eign·ly** *adv.*

sov·er·eign·ty (sŏv′ər-ĭn-tē, sŏv′rĭn-) *n., pl.* **-ties. 1.** Supremacy of authority or rule as exercised by a sovereign or sovereign state. **2.** Royal rank, authority, or power. **3.** Complete independence and self-government. **4.** A territory existing as an independent state.

so·vi·et (sō′vē-ĕt′, -ĭt, sŏv′ē-, sō′vē-ĕt′) *n.* **1.** One of the popularly elected legislative assemblies that exist at local, regional, and national levels in the Soviet Union. **2. a. Soviet.** A native or inhabitant of the Soviet Union. **b. Soviets.** The government of the Soviet Union. Used with *the.* **—soviet** *adj.* **1.** Often **Soviet.** Of or relating to the Union of Soviet Socialist Republics. **2.** Of or relating to a soviet. [Russian *sovét,* council, soviet, from Old Russian *sŭvětŭ.* See **ksun-** in Appendix.]

so·vi·et·ize also **So·vi·et·ize** (sō′vē-ĭ-tīz′, sŏv′ē-) *tr.v.* **-ized, -iz·ing, -iz·es. 1.** To cause to come under Soviet control. **2.** To cause to conform to Soviet political, social, and cultural policy. **—so′vi·et·i·za′tion** (-ĭ-tĭ-zā′shən) *n.*

So·vi·et·ol·o·gy (sō′vē-ĭ-tŏl′ə-jē, sŏv′ē-) *n.* Study of the Soviet Union, especially of its government. **—So′vi·et·ol′o·gist** *n.*

Soviet Union. The Union of Soviet Socialist Republics.

sov·khoz (sŏf-kôz′, sôv-KHôz′) *n.* A state-owned farm in the Soviet Union that pays wages to its workers. [Russian, short for *sovetskoe khozyaĭstvo,* soviet farm.]

sow¹ (sō) *v.* **sowed, sown** (sōn) or **sowed, sow·ing, sows.** *—tr.* **1.** To scatter (seed) over the ground for growing. **2.** To impregnate (a growing medium) with seed. **3.** To propagate; disseminate: *sow rumors and dissension.* **4.** To strew or cover with something; spread thickly. *—intr.* To scatter seed for growing. [Middle English *sowen,* from Old English *sāwan.* See **sē-** in Appendix.] **—sow′er** *n.*

sow² (sou) *n.* **1.a.** An adult female hog. **b.** The adult female of several other animals, such as the bear. **2.a.** A channel that conducts molten iron to the molds in a pig bed. **b.** The mass of metal solidified in such a channel or mold. [Middle English, from Old English *sugu, sū.* See **sū-** in Appendix.]

sow·bel·ly (sou′bĕl′ē) *n. Informal.* Salt pork.

sow·bread (sou′brĕd′) *n.* The cyclamen.

sow bug (sou) *n.* Any of various small terrestrial isopod crustaceans, chiefly of the genera *Oniscus* and *Porcellio,* commonly found under logs or stones and having an oval, segmented body. Also called *wood louse.* [From its piglike shape.]

So·we·to (sə-wē′tō, -wā′-). A city of northeast South Africa southwest of Johannesburg. Comprised of a number of townships inhabited by Black South Africans, it has been a center of racial strife since the late 1970's. Population, 868,580.

sown (sōn) *v.* A past participle of **sow¹.**

sow thistle (sou) *n.* Any of various plants of the genus *Sonchus,* especially *S. oleraceus* of Eurasia, having prickly leaves and rayed, yellow flower heads.

sox (sŏks) *n.* A plural of **sock¹** (sense 1).

soy (soi) *n.* **1.** The soybean. **2.** A salty brown liquid condiment made by fermenting soybeans in brine. [Dutch *soja, soya,* from Japanese *shō-yu,* from Chinese (Mandarin) *jiàng yóu,* soy sauce : *jiàng,* soy paste + *yóu,* sauce.]

soy·a (soi′ə) *n.* The soybean. [Dutch. See SOY.]

soy·bean (soi′bēn′) *n.* **1.** A southeast Asian annual leguminous plant *(Glycine max),* widely cultivated for forage and soil improvement and for its nutritious seeds. **2.** The seed of this plant.

So·yin·ka (shô-yĭng′kə), **Wole.** Born 1934. Nigerian writer known for his important contributions to the development of Nigerian theater and literature. His plays include *A Dance of the Forests* (1960) and *A Play of Giants* (1984). Soyinka won the 1986 Nobel Prize for literature.

soy·milk (soi′mĭlk′) *n.* A milk substitute made from soybeans, often supplemented with vitamins.

SP *abbr.* **1.** Self-propelled. **2.** Shore patrol. **3.** Single pole. **4.** Specialist. **5.** Submarine patrol.

sp. *abbr.* **1.** Special. **2.** Species. **3.** Specific. **4.** Specimen. **5.** Spelling.

Sp. *abbr.* Spanish.

s.p. *abbr. Law.* Sine prole.

♦ **spa** (spä) *n.* **1.** A resort providing therapeutic baths. **2.** A resort area having mineral springs. **3.** A fashionable hotel or resort. **4.** A health spa. **5.** A tub for relaxation or invigoration, usually including a device for raising whirlpools in the water. **6.** *Eastern New England.* See **soda fountain** (sense 2). [After *Spa,* a resort town of eastern Belgium.]

♦ ***REGIONAL NOTE:*** The word *spa,* taken from the name of the famous mineral springs in Spa, Belgium, has become a common noun denoting any place with a medicinal or mineral spring. Less well known is its regional sense, "soda fountain," probably an allusion to the carbonated or "mineral" water that is a staple ingredient of many soda fountain concoctions.

Spaak (späk), **Paul Henri Charles.** 1889–1972. Belgian politician who was the first president of the United Nations General Assembly (1946) and later served as the secretary-general of NATO (1957–1961).

space (spās) *n.* **1.a.** *Mathematics.* A set of elements or points satisfying specified geometric postulates: *non-Euclidean space.* **b.** The infinite extension of the three-dimensional field in which all matter exists. **2.a.** The expanse in which the solar system, stars, and galaxies exist; the universe. **b.** The region of this expanse beyond Earth's atmosphere. **3.** A blank or empty area: *the spaces between words.* **4.** An area provided for a particular purpose: *a parking space.* **5.** Reserved or available accommodation on a public transportation vehicle. **6.a.** A period or interval of time. **b.** A little while: *Let's rest for a space.* **7.** Sufficient freedom from external pressure to develop or explore one's needs, interests, and individuality: *"The need for personal space inevitably asserts itself"* (Maggie Scarf). **8.** *Music.* One of the intervals between the lines of a staff. **9.** *Printing.* One of the blank pieces of type or other means used for separating words or characters. **10.** One of the intervals during the telegraphic transmission of a message when the key is open or not in contact. **11.** Blank sections in printed material or broadcast time available for use by advertisers. **—space** *v.* **spaced, spac·ing, spac·es.** *—tr.* **1.** To organize or arrange with spaces between. **2.** To separate or keep apart. **3.** *Slang.* To stupefy or disorient from or as if from a drug. Often used with *out: The antihistamine spaces me out so I can't think clearly.* *—intr. Slang.* To be or become stupefied or disoriented. Often used with *out: I was supposed to meet her, but I spaced out and forgot.* [Middle English, area, from Old French *espace,* from Latin *spatium.*] **—spac′er** *n.*

space age also **Space Age** (spās) *n.* The period from 1957 through the present, in which spacecraft have been placed in orbit around Earth and sent to explore celestial bodies. **—space′-age′** (spās′āj′) *adj.*

space bar *n.* **1.** A bar at the bottom of the keyboard of a typewriter that when pressed down introduces a blank horizontal space into the typewritten matter, as between words. **2.** *Computer Science.* A bar with a similar position on the keyboard of a terminal, used to move the cursor or execute a function in a program.

space biology *n.* See **exobiology.**

space·borne (spās′bôrn′, -bōrn′) *adj.* Operating in or involving equipment operating in outer space.

space·bridge (spās′brĭj′) *n.* An international communication by television, transmitted by artificial satellite.

space cadet *n. Slang.* One who shows difficulty in grasping reality or in responding appropriately to it; a spacy person: *"the screwups and the space cadets—in other words, the fringe element"* (Linda Ellerbee).

space capsule *n.* A vehicle or compartment of a vehicle designed to transport, protect, and support human beings or animals in outer space or at very high altitudes in Earth's atmosphere.

space charge *n.* The excess of electrons or ions in a given volume.

space·craft (spās′krăft′) *n., pl.* **spacecraft.** A vehicle intended to be launched into space. Also called *spaceship.*

spaced (spāst) *adj. Slang.* Spaced-out.

spaced-out (spāst′out′) *adj. Slang.* Stupefied or disoriented from or as if from a drug.

space·far·ing (spās′fâr′ĭng) *n.* The launching of vehicles into outer space. **—spacefaring** *adj.* Engaged in the launching of vehicles into outer space: *"efforts in planetary exploration . . . achieved in cooperation with other spacefaring nations"* (Chet Raymo). **—space′far′er** *n.*

space flight *n.* Flight beyond the atmosphere of Earth.

space heater *n.* An appliance that warms a small area, such as one room, typically by radiant electric heat.

space lattice *n.* See **crystal lattice.**

space·less (spās′lĭs) *adj.* Having no limits or boundaries.

space medicine *n.* The medical science that is concerned with the biological, physiological, and psychological effects of space flight on human beings.

space·port (spās′pôrt′, -pōrt′) *n.* An installation for sheltering, testing, maintaining, and launching spacecraft.

space probe *n.* A spacecraft carrying instruments intended for use in exploration of the physical properties of outer space or celestial bodies other than Earth.

space science *n.* **1.** Any of several scientific disciplines, such as exobiology, that study phenomena occurring in the upper atmosphere, in space, or on celestial bodies other than Earth. **2.** A discipline related to or dealing with the problems of space flight. **—space scientist** *n.*

space·ship or **space ship** (spās′shĭp′) *n.* See **spacecraft.**

space shuttle *n.* A reusable spacecraft with wings for controlled descent in the atmosphere, designed to transport astronauts between Earth and an orbiting space station and also used to deploy and retrieve satellites.

space sickness *n.* Motion sickness caused by sustained

soybean
Glycine max

Wole Soyinka

space shuttle
Atlantis landing at Edwards Air Force Base, California, March 1990

ă pat	oi boy
ā pay	ou out
âr care	ŏŏ took
ä father	ōō boot
ĕ pet	ŭ cut
ē be	ûr urge
ĭ pit	th thin
ī pie	*th* this
îr pier	hw which
ŏ pot	zh vision
ō toe	ə about, item
ô paw	♦ regionalism

Stress marks: ′ (primary); ′ (secondary), as in **dictionary** (dĭk′shə-nĕr′ē)

spadix
Calla lily
Zantedeschia aethiopica

weightlessness during space flight, usually accompanied by disturbance of the inner ear. —**space′sick′** (spās′sĭk′) *adj.*

space station *n.* A large satellite equipped to support a human crew and designed to remain in orbit around Earth for an extended period and serve as a base for launching exploratory expeditions, conducting scientific research, repairing satellites, and performing other space-related activities.

space suit *n.* A protective pressure suit designed to permit the wearer relatively free movement in space.

space-time (spās′tīm′) *n. Physics.* The four-dimensional continuum of one temporal and three spatial coordinates in which any event or physical object is located.

space walk *n.* An excursion by an astronaut outside a spacecraft in space; extravehicular activity. —**space walk** *v.* —**space walker** *n.*

space•ward (spās′wərd) *adv. & adj.* Toward, to, or in outer space.

space writer *n.* A writer, such as a journalist, who is paid according to the amount of space his or her material occupies in print.

spac•ey (spā′sē) *adj. Slang.* Variant of **spacy.**

spa•cial (spā′shəl) *adj.* Variant of **spatial.**

spac•ing (spā′sĭng) *n.* **1.a.** The act of arranging with intervening spaces. **b.** The result of so arranging. **c.** A system of or allowance for intervals: *the close spacing of the theater seats.* **2.** Spaces or a space, as in printed matter.

spa•cious (spā′shəs) *adj.* **1.** Generous or large in area or extent; roomy. **2.** Vast in range or scope: *a spacious view.* —**spa′cious•ly** *adv.* —**spa′cious•ness** *n.*

SYNONYMS: *spacious, ample, capacious, commodious, roomy.* The central meaning shared by these adjectives is "having or affording a generous amount of space": *a spacious apartment; an ample kitchen; a capacious purse; a commodious harbor; roomy pockets.*

Spack•le (spăk′əl). A trademark used for a powder to be mixed with water or a ready-to-use plastic paste designed to fill cracks and holes in plaster before painting or papering. This trademark often occurs in lowercase in print: *"In the Sierra . . . the snow generally is the consistency of spackle"* (San Francisco Chronicle). It also occurs as a verb in various contexts: *"Two young men quietly spackled and whitewashed the walls . . . for an exhibition"* (New York Times). *"Support compensates, underpins, retrofits, translates, spackles, patches and reinforces"* (Computerworld). The trademark has also generated a derivative noun: *"Some professional spacklers can do this with a 5-inch knife"* (Newsday).

spac•y or **spac•ey** (spā′sē) *adj.* **-i•er, -i•est.** *Slang.* **1.** Stupefied or disoriented from or as if from drug use. **2.** Eccentric; offbeat.

spade[1] (spād) *n.* **1.** A sturdy digging tool having a thick handle and a heavy, flat blade that can be pressed into the ground with the foot. **2.** Any of various similar digging or cutting tools. —**spade** *tr.v.* **spad•ed, spad•ing, spades.** To dig or cut with a spade. [Middle English, from Old English *spadu.*]

spade[2] (spād) *n.* **1.** *Games.* **a.** A black, leaf-shaped figure on certain playing cards. **b.** A playing card with this figure. **c.** Also **spades** *(used with a sing. or pl. verb).* The suit of cards represented by this figure. **2.** *Offensive Slang.* Used as a disparaging term for a Black person. —***idiom.* in spades.** To a considerable degree: *They had financial trouble in spades.* [Italian *spade,* pl. of *spada,* card suit, from Latin *spatha,* sword, broad-bladed stirrer, from Greek *spathē,* broad blade.]

spade•fish (spād′fĭsh′) *n., pl.* **spadefish** or **-fish•es.** Any of several marine food fishes of the family Ephippidae, especially *Chaetodipterus faber,* of the American Atlantic coastal waters, noted for its craving for shellfish. [From its shape.]

spade•foot toad (spād′fo͝ot′) *n.* Any of several toads of the family Pelobatidae, widely distributed over Europe, southern Asia, northern Africa, and North America, some of which are able to dig deep burrows easily by means of a horny projection on the side of the hind foot.

spade•work (spād′wûrk′) *n.* **1.** Work requiring a spade. **2.** Preparatory work necessary for a project or an activity.

spa•dix (spā′dĭks) *n., pl.* **-di•ces** (-dĭ-sēz′). *Botany.* A fleshy clublike spike bearing minute flowers, usually enclosed within a sheathlike spathe, characteristic of aroid plants, such as the calla and the jack-in-the-pulpit. [Latin *spādīx,* broken-off palm branch, from Greek, from *span,* to stretch.]

spa•ghet•ti (spə-gĕt′ē) *n.* **1.** A pasta made into long solid strings and cooked by boiling. **2.** *Electricity.* A slender tube of insulating material that covers bare wire. [Italian, pl. diminutive of *spago,* cord.]

spa•ghet•ti•ni (spăg′ĭ-tē′nē) *n.* A form of pasta that is thinner than spaghetti but not as thin as vermicelli. [Italian, diminutive of *spaghetti,* spaghetti. See SPAGHETTI.]

spaghetti Western *n.* A low-budget Western film made by a European, especially an Italian, film company.

spa•gyr•ic (spə-gĭr′ĭk) also **spa•gyr•i•cal** (-ĭ-kəl) *adj.* Relating to or resembling alchemy. [New Latin *spagiricus.*]

Spain

Spain (spān). A country of southwest Europe comprising most of the Iberian Peninsula and the Balearic and Canary Islands. Inhabited since the Stone Age, the region was colonized by Phoenicians and Greeks and later ruled by Carthage and Rome (after 201 B.C.). Barbarians first invaded Spain in A.D. 409 but were supplanted by Moors from North Africa (711–719), who organized a kingdom known for its learning and splendor. The Moors were gradually displaced by small Christian states and were ousted from their last stronghold, Granada, in 1492. Ferdinand of Aragon and Isabella of Castile then became rulers of a united Spain, which became a world power through exploration and conquest. After the empire was lost in the 18th and 19th centuries, Spain experienced social and economic unrest that culminated in the Spanish Civil War (1936–1939) and the rise of Francisco Franco. Madrid is the capital and the largest city. Population, 38,872,389.

spake (spāk) *v. Archaic.* A past tense of **speak.**

spall (spôl) *n.* A chip, fragment, or flake from a piece of stone or ore. —**spall** *v.* **spalled, spall•ing, spalls.** —*tr.* To break up into chips or fragments. —*intr.* To chip or crumble. [Middle English *spalle.*]

spal•la•tion (spô-lā′shən) *n.* A nuclear reaction in which many particles are ejected from an atomic nucleus by incident particles of sufficiently high energy.

Spam (spăm). A trademark used for a canned meat product consisting primarily of chopped pork pressed into a loaf.

span[1] (spăn) *n.* **1.** The extent or measure of space between two points or extremities, as of a bridge or roof; the breadth. **2.** The distance between the tips of the wings of an airplane. **3.** The section between two intermediate supports of a bridge. **4.** Something, such as a railroad trestle or bridge, that extends from one point to another. **5.** The distance from the tip of the thumb to the tip of the little finger when the hand is fully extended, formerly used as a unit of measure equal to about nine inches (23 centimeters). **6.** A period of time: *a span of life.* —**span** *tr.v.* **spanned, span•ning, spans. 1.** To measure by or as if by the fully extended hand. **2.** To encircle with the hand or hands in or as if in measuring. **3.** To extend across in space or time: *a bridge that spans the gorge; a career that spanned 40 years.* [Middle English, unit of measurement, from Old English *spann.* See **(s)pen-** in Appendix.]

span[2] (spăn) *tr.v.* **spanned, span•ning, spans.** To bind or fetter. —**span** *n.* **1.** *Nautical.* A stretch of rope made fast at either end. **2.** A pair of animals, such as oxen, matched in size, strength, or color and driven as a team. [Dutch *spannen,* to harness, from Middle Dutch. See **(s)pen-** in Appendix.]

span[3] (spăn) *v. Archaic.* A past tense of **spin.**

Span. *abbr.* Spanish.

spa•na•ko•pi•ta (spä′nä-kō′pē-tä) *n.* A Greek spinach pie, typically served as an appetizer and made with layers of buttered filo pastry and a filling of sautéed chopped spinach, onions and scallions, feta cheese, spices, and sometimes eggs. [Modern Greek *spanakopita : spanaki,* spinach (from Medieval Greek *spanakin, spanakion,* ultimately from Persian *aspanākh*) + *pita,* pie; see PITA[1].]

Span•dau (spän′dou′, shpän′-). A district of Berlin, Germany. Chartered in 1232, it is the site of a fortress used for Nazi war criminals after the Nuremberg trials of 1945 to 1946.

span•dex (spăn′dĕks) *n.* A synthetic fiber or fabric made from a polymer containing polyurethane, used in the manufacture of elastic clothing. —**spandex** *adj.* Of or relating to spandex or its elastic qualities. [By alteration of *expands,* third person sing. present tense of EXPAND.]

span•drel also **span•dril** (spăn′drəl) *n. Architecture.* **1.** The triangular space between the left or right exterior curve of an arch and the rectangular framework surrounding it. **2.** The space between two arches and a horizontal molding or cornice above them. [Middle English *spaundrell,* probably from *spandre,* space between supporting timbers, from Anglo-Norman *spaundre,* from *spandre,* to spread out, from Latin *expandere.* See EXPAND.]

spang (spăng) *adv. Informal.* Precisely; squarely: *fell spang into the middle of the puddle.* [Probably from dialectal *spang,* to leap, jerk, bang, probably of imitative origin.]

span•gle (spăng′gəl) *n.* **1.** A small, often circular piece of sparkling metal or plastic sewn especially on garments for decoration. **2.** A small sparkling object, drop, or spot: *spangles of sunlight.* —**spangle** *v.* **-gled, -gling, -gles.** —*tr.* To adorn or cause to sparkle by covering with or as if with spangles: *Lights spangled the night skyline.* —*intr.* To sparkle in the manner of spangles. [Middle English *spangel,* diminutive of *spange,* from Middle Dutch, clasp. See **(s)pen-** in Appendix.] —**span′gly** *adj.*

Spang•lish (spăng′glĭsh) *n.* Spanish characterized by numerous borrowings from English.

Span•iard (spăn′yərd) *n.* A native or inhabitant of Spain. [Middle English, from Old French *Espaniard,* from *Espaigne,* Spain, from Latin *Hispānia.*]

span•iel (spăn′yəl) *n.* **1.** Any of several breeds of small-sized to medium-sized dogs, usually having drooping ears, short legs, and a wavy, silky coat. **2.** A docile or servile person. [Middle English *spainol,* from Old French *espaignol,* Spaniard, Spanish dog, from Vulgar Latin **Hispāniōlus,* Spanish, from *Hispānia,* Spain.]

Span•ish (spăn′ĭsh) *adj. Abbr.* **Sp., Span. 1.** Of or relating to Spain or its people or culture. **2.** Of or relating to the Spanish language. —**Spanish** *n. Abbr.* **Sp., Span. 1.** The Romance language of the largest part of Spain and most of Central and South America. **2.** The people of Spain. [Alteration (influenced by Latin *Hispānia,* Spain) of Middle English *Spainish,* from *Spaine,* Spain, from Old French *Espaigne.* See SPANIARD.]

Spanish A·mer·i·ca (ə-mĕr′ĭ-kə). The former Spanish possessions in the New World, including most of South and Central America, Mexico, Cuba, Puerto Rico, the Dominican Republic, and other small islands in the Caribbean Sea.

Spanish American *n.* **1.** A native or inhabitant of Spanish America. **2.** A U.S. citizen or resident of Hispanic descent. **—Span·ish-A·mer·i·can** (spăn′ĭsh-ə-mĕr′ĭ-kən) *adj.* **1.** Of or relating to Spanish America or its peoples or cultures. **2.** Of or relating to Spain and America, especially the United States. See Usage Note at **Hispanic.**

Spanish bayonet *n.* Any of several New World plants of the genus *Yucca,* especially *Y. aloifolia* or *Y. baccata,* having a tall woody stem, stiff swordlike pointed leaves, and a large cluster of white flowers.

Spanish cedar *n.* **1.** Any of several tropical American trees of the genus *Cedrela,* especially *C. odorata,* having reddish aromatic wood used for cabinetwork and cigar boxes. **2.** The wood of this tree. Also called *cigar-box cedar.*

Spanish chestnut *n.* **1.** A deciduous Mediterranean tree *(Castanea sativa)* bearing edible nuts enclosed in a spiny bur. **2.** The nut of this tree. Also called *marron.*

Spanish fly *n.* See **cantharis.**

Spanish Lake. A community of east-central Missouri, a suburb of St. Louis. Population, 20,632.

Spanish lime *n.* See **genip** (sense 2).

Spanish mackerel *n.* Any of various marine food fishes of the genus *Scomberomorus,* especially a commercially important species, *S. maculatus,* of American Atlantic coastal waters.

Spanish Main (mān). **1.** The coastal region of mainland Spanish America in the 16th and 17th centuries, extending from the Isthmus of Panama to the mouth of the Orinoco River. **2.** The section of the Caribbean Sea crossed by Spanish ships in colonial times. The treasure-laden ships were often raided by English buccaneers.

Spanish moss *n.* An epiphytic bromeliad plant *(Tillandsia usneoides)* of the southeast United States and tropical America, having gray threadlike stems drooping in densely matted clusters.

Spanish needles *pl.n. (used with a sing. or pl. verb).* See **beggar ticks** (sense 1a).

Spanish omelet *n.* An omelet served with an often spicy sauce of tomatoes, onions, and peppers.

Spanish onion *n.* A mild-flavored, yellow-skinned onion *(Allium fistulosum)* having yellowish-white flowers.

Spanish paprika *n.* A mild seasoning made from pimientos.

Spanish rice *n.* A dish consisting of rice cooked with tomatoes, spices, chopped onions, and green peppers.

Spanish Sa·ha·ra (sə-hâr′ə, -hăr′ə, -hä′rə). See **Western Sahara.**

spank (spăngk) *v.* **spanked, spank·ing, spanks.** *—tr.* To slap on the buttocks with a flat object or with the open hand, as for punishment. *—intr.* To move briskly or spiritedly. **—spank** *n.* A slap on the buttocks. [Perhaps of imitative origin.]

spank·er (spăng′kər) *n. Nautical.* A usually gaff-headed sail set from the aftermost lower mast of a sailing ship.

spank·ing (spăng′kĭng) *adj.* **1.** *Informal.* Exceptional of its kind; remarkable. **2.** Swift and vigorous: *a spanking pace.* **3.** Brisk and fresh: *a spanking breeze.* **—spanking** *adv.* Used as an intensive: *a spanking clean shirt.* **—spanking** *n.* A number of slaps on the buttocks delivered in rapid succession, as for punishment. [Perhaps of Scandinavian origin.] **—spank′ing·ly** *adv.*

span·ner (spăn′ər) *n.* **1.** A wrench having a hook, hole, or pin at the end for meshing with a related device on another object. **2.** *Chiefly British.* A wrench. [German, winding tool, from *spannen,* to stretch, from Middle High German, from Old High German *spannan.* See **(s)pen-** in Appendix.]

span-new (spăn′no͞o′, -nyo͞o′) *adj.* Entirely new. [Middle English *spannewe,* partial translation of Old Norse *spānnȳr* : *spānn,* shingle, chip + *nȳr,* new; see **newo-** in Appendix.]

span·worm (spăn′wûrm′) *n.* See **measuring worm.** [From SPAN[1].]

spar[1] (spär) *n.* **1.** *Nautical.* A wooden or metal pole, such as a mast, boom, yard, or bowsprit, used to support sails and rigging. **2.** A usually metal pole used as part of a crane or derrick. **3.** A principal structural member in an airplane wing or a tail assembly that runs from tip to tip or from root to tip. **—spar** *tr.v.* **sparred, spar·ring, spars. 1.** To supply with spars. **2.** *Archaic.* To fasten with a bolt. [Middle English *sparre,* rafter.]

spar[2] (spär) *intr.v.* **sparred, spar·ring, spars. 1.a.** To box, especially to make boxing motions without hitting one's opponent. **b.** To participate in a practice or exhibition boxing match. **2.** To bandy words about in argument; dispute. **3.** To fight by striking with the feet and spurs. Used of gamecocks. **—spar** *n.* **1.** A motion of attack or defense in boxing. **2.** A sparring match. [Middle English *sparren,* to thrust or strike rapidly, perhaps from Old French *esparer,* to kick, from Old Italian *sparare,* to fling : *s-,* intensive pref. (from Latin *ex-,* ex-) + *parare,* to ward off; see PARRY.]

spar[3] (spär) *n.* A nonmetallic, readily cleavable, translucent or transparent light-colored mineral with a shiny luster, such as feldspar. [Low German, from Middle Low German.]

SPAR also **Spar** (spär) *n.* A member of the women's reserve of the U.S. Coast Guard, disbanded as a separate unit in 1946. [Contraction of Latin *semper parātus,* always prepared, the motto of the U.S. Coast Guard : *semper,* always + *parātus,* prepared.]

spare (spâr) *v.* **spared, spar·ing, spares.** *—tr.* **1.** To refrain from treating harshly; treat mercifully or leniently. **2.** To refrain from harming or destroying. **3.** To save or relieve from experiencing or doing (something): *spared herself the trouble of going.* **4.** To hold back from; withhold or avoid: *spared no expense for the celebration.* **5.** To use with restraint: *Don't spare the mustard.* **6.** To give or grant out of one's resources; afford: *Can you spare ten minutes?* *—intr.* **1.** To be frugal. **2.** To refrain from inflicting harm; be merciful or lenient. **—spare** *adj.* **spar·er, spar·est. 1.a.** Kept in reserve: *a spare part; a spare pair of sneakers.* **b.** Being in excess of what is needed; extra. See Synonyms at **superfluous. c.** Free for other use; unoccupied: *spare time.* **2.a.** Not lavish, abundant, or excessive: *a spare diet.* See Synonyms at **meager. b.** Lean and trim. See Synonyms at **lean[2]. 3.** Not profuse or copious. **—spare** *n.* **1.** A replacement, especially a tire, reserved for future need. **2.** *Sports.* **a.** The act of knocking down all ten pins with two successive rolls of a bowling ball. **b.** The score so made. ***—idiom.* to spare.** In addition to what is needed: *We paid our bills and had money to spare.* [Middle English *sparen,* from Old English *sparian.*] **—spare′ly** *adv.* **—spare′ness** *n.* **—spar′er** *n.*

spare·ribs (spâr′rĭbz′) *pl.n.* Pork ribs with most of the meat trimmed off. [Alteration of obsolete *ribspare,* from Low German *ribbesper,* pickled pork ribs roasted on a spit, from Middle Low German *ribbespēr* : *ribbe,* rib + *spēr,* spear, spit.]

sparge (spärj) *tr.v.* **sparged, sparg·ing, sparg·es. 1.** To spray or sprinkle. **2.** To introduce air or gas into (a liquid). **—sparge** *n.* A sprinkle. [Obsolete French *espargier,* from Old French, from Latin *spargere.*] **—sparg′er** *n.*

spar·id (spăr′ĭd, spâr′-) *adj.* Of or belonging to the family Sparidae, which includes the porgies and sea breams. **—sparid** *n.* A member of the Sparidae. [From New Latin *Sparidae,* family name, from *Sparus,* type genus, from Latin, a kind of fish, from Greek *sparos.*]

spar·ing (spâr′ĭng) *adj.* **1.** Given to or marked by prudence and restraint in the use of material resources. **2.** Deficient or limited in quantity, fullness, or extent. **3.** Forbearing; lenient. **—spar′ing·ly** *adv.* **—spar′ing·ness** *n.*

SYNONYMS: *sparing, frugal, thrifty, economical.* These adjectives mean exercising or reflecting care in the use of resources, such as money. *Sparing* stresses restraint, as in expenditure: *sparing in bestowing gifts; neither profligate nor sparing of her time. Frugal* implies self-denial and abstention from luxury: *a frugal diet; a frugal farmer. Thrifty* suggests industry, care, and diligence in conserving means: *is excessively thrifty because he remembers the Depression. Economical* emphasizes prudence, skillful management, and the avoidance of waste: *an economical shopper; the most economical use of energy.*

spark[1] (spärk) *n.* **1.** An incandescent particle, especially: **a.** One thrown off from a burning substance. **b.** One resulting from friction. **c.** One remaining in an otherwise extinguished fire; an ember. **2.** A glistening particle, as of metal. **3.a.** A flash of light, especially a flash produced by electric discharge. **b.** A short pulse or flow of electric current. **4.** A trace or suggestion, as: **a.** A quality or feeling with latent potential; a seed or germ: *the spark of genius.* **b.** A vital, animating, or activating factor: *the spark of revolution.* **5. sparks** *(used with a sing. verb). Informal.* A radio operator aboard a ship. **6.** *Electricity.* **a.** The luminous phenomenon resulting from a disruptive discharge through an insulating material. **b.** The discharge itself. **—spark** *v.* **sparked, spark·ing, sparks.** *—intr.* **1.** To give off sparks. **2.** To give an enthusiastic response. **3.** To operate correctly. Used of the ignition system of an internal-combustion engine. *—tr.* **1.** To set in motion; activate: *The incident sparked a controversy.* **2.** To rouse to action; spur: *A cheering crowd sparked the runner to triumph.* [Middle English *sparke,* from Old English *spearca.* V., from Middle English *sparken,* from Old English *spearcian.*] **—spark′er** *n.*

spark[2] (spärk) *n.* **1.** An elegantly dressed, highly self-conscious young man. **2.** A male suitor; a beau. **—spark** *v.* **sparked, spark·ing, sparks.** *—tr.* To court or woo. *—intr.* To play the suitor. [Perhaps of Scandinavian origin, or from SPARK[1].] **—spark′er** *n.*

Spark (spärk), **Muriel Sarah.** Born 1918. Scottish writer known for her satirical novels, including *Memento Mori* (1958) and *The Prime of Miss Jean Brodie* (1961).

spark arrester *n.* **1.** A device designed to keep sparks from escaping, as at a chimney opening. **2.** A device used to control electric sparking at a point where a circuit is made or broken.

spark chamber *n.* A device consisting of electrically charged parallel metal plates in a chamber filled with inert gas, used to detect and measure a charged subatomic particle as it passes through the chamber, leaving a trail of sparks.

spark coil *n.* An induction coil used to produce a spark, as in an internal-combustion engine.

spark gap *n.* A gap in an otherwise complete electric circuit across which a discharge occurs at a prescribed voltage.

Spanish moss
Tillandsia usneoides, on trees in Cypress Gardens, Florida

spanker

ă **pat**	oi **boy**
ā **pay**	ou **out**
âr **care**	o͝o **took**
ä **father**	o͞o **boot**
ĕ **pet**	ŭ **cut**
ē **be**	ûr **urge**
ĭ **pit**	th **thin**
ī **pie**	*th* **this**
îr **pier**	hw **which**
ŏ **pot**	zh **vision**
ō **toe**	ə **about, item**
ô **paw**	♦ **regionalism**

Stress marks: **′** (primary); ′ (secondary), as in **dictionary** (dĭk′shə-nĕr′ē)

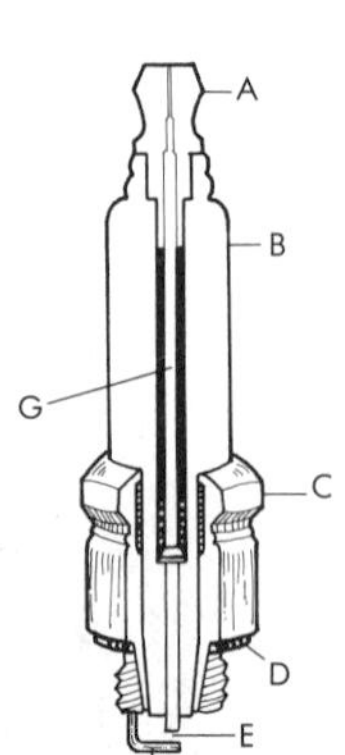

spark plug
Cross section of a spark plug
A. Terminal
B. Insulator
C. Body
D. Gasket
E. Gap
F. Ground electrode
G. Center electrode

spark generator *n.* See **spark transmitter.**

spark·ing plug (spär′kĭng) *n. Chiefly British.* A spark plug.

spar·kle (spär′kəl) *v.* **-kled, -kling, -kles.** —*intr.* **1.** To give off sparks. **2.** To give off or reflect flashes of light; glitter. See Synonyms at **flash. 3.** To be brilliant in performance. **4.a.** To shine with animation: *He has eyes that sparkle.* **b.** To flash with wit: *Her conversation sparkled throughout the evening.* **5.** To release gas bubbles; effervesce: *Champagne sparkles.* —*tr.* To cause to flash and glitter: *Sunlight was sparkling the waves.* **—sparkle** *n.* **1.** A small spark or gleaming particle. **2.** A glittering quality. **3.** Brilliant animation; vivacity. **4.** Emission of gas bubbles; effervescence. [Middle English *sparklen,* frequentative of *sparken,* to spark. See SPARK[1].]

spar·kle·ber·ry (spär′kəl-bĕr′ē) *n.* See **farkleberry.**

spar·kler (spär′klər) *n.* **1.** One, such as a highly polished metallic surface or a virtuoso performer, that sparkles. **2.** *Informal.* A diamond. **3.** A firework that burns slowly and gives off a shower of sparks.

spar·kling water (spär′klĭng) *n.* Water charged with carbon dioxide.

sparkling wine *n.* Any of various effervescent wines, such as champagne, produced by a process involving fermentation in the bottle.

spark·ly (spär′klē) *adj.* **-li·er, -li·est. 1.a.** Giving off tiny flashes of light; glittery: *a dress with sparkly sequins.* **b.** Lively; vivacious: *a sparkly personality.* **2.** Effervescent.

spark·plug (spärk′plŭg′) *tr.v.* **-plugged, -plug·ging, -plugs.** *Informal.* To inspire or energize (an endeavor, for example).

spark plug *n.* **1.** A device inserted in the head of an internal-combustion engine cylinder that ignites the fuel mixture by means of an electric spark. **2.** *Informal.* One who gives life or energy to an endeavor.

Sparks (spärks). A city of western Nevada east of Reno. It is a tourist center with varied light industries. Population, 40,780.

spark transmitter *n.* A source of alternating current, especially a now obsolete radio transmitter, that derives its output from the oscillating discharge of a capacitor to an inductor and across a spark gap. Also called *spark generator.*

spark·y (spär′kē) *adj.* **-i·er, -i·est.** Animated; lively.

spar·ling (spär′lĭng) *n.* **1.** The common European smelt *(Osperus eperlanus).* **2.** A young or immature herring. [Middle English *sperlinge,* from Old French *esperlinge,* of Germanic origin; akin to Middle Dutch *spierlinc.*]

spar·row (spăr′ō) *n.* **1.** Any of various small New World finches of the family Emberizidae, having brownish or grayish plumage and including the song sparrow, white-throated sparrow, chipping sparrow, vesper sparrow, and other closely related species. **2.** Any of several similar or related birds, such as the house sparrow or the Java sparrow. [Middle English *sparowe,* from Old English *spearwa.*]

♦ **spar·row·grass** (spăr′ə-grăs′, spăr′ō-) *n. Eastern U.S.* Asparagus. [By folk etymology from ASPARAGUS.]

sparrow hawk
Falco sparverius

sparrow hawk *n.* **1.** A small hawk *(Accipter nisus)* of Europe, Africa, and central Asia that has short, broad wings and preys on sparrows and other small birds. **2.** A small North American falcon *(Falco sparverius)* that hovers over fields and pastures, feeding chiefly on insects and mice. In this sense, also called *American kestrel.*

sparse (spärs) *adj.* **spars·er, spars·est.** Occurring, growing, or settled at widely spaced intervals; not thick or dense. See Synonyms at **meager.** [Latin *sparsus,* past participle of *spargere,* to scatter.] **—sparse′ly** *adv.* **—sparse′ness, spar′si·ty** (spär′sĭ-tē) *n.*

Spar·ta (spär′tə) also **Lac·e·dae·mon** (lăs′ĭ-dē′mən). A city-state of ancient Greece in the southeast Peloponnesus. Settled by Dorian Greeks, it was noted for its militarism and reached the height of its power in the sixth century B.C. A protracted rivalry with Athens led to the Peloponnesian Wars (460–404) and Sparta's hegemony over all of Greece. Its ascendancy was broken by Thebans in 371.

Spar·ta·cus (spär′tə-kəs). Died 71 B.C. Thracian gladiator who led a slave revolt in Italy (73–71). He defeated Roman armies in southern Italy, but his forces were crushed at Lucania (71), where Spartacus was killed and many of his troops were crucified.

Spar·tan (spär′tn) *adj.* **1.** Of or relating to Sparta or its people. **2.a.** Rigorously self-disciplined or self-restrained. **b.** Simple, frugal, or austere: *a Spartan diet; a Spartan lifestyle.* **c.** Marked by brevity of speech; laconic. **d.** Courageous in the face of pain, danger, or adversity. **—Spartan** *n.* **1.** A citizen of Sparta. **2.** One of Spartan character. **—Spar′tan·ism** *n.* **—Spar′tan·ly** *adv.*

Spar·tan·burg (spär′tn-bûrg′). A city of northwest South Carolina northwest of Columbia at the foot of the Blue Ridge. It is a processing and manufacturing center. Population, 43,968.

spar·te·ine (spär′tē-ēn′, -ĭn) *n.* A bitter, poisonous, liquid alkaloid, $C_{15}H_{26}N_2$, obtained from the broom *Cytisus scoparius* or the lupin *Lupinus luteus,* whose sulfate has been used in medicine as a heart stimulant and as a way of inducing contraction of the uterus during labor. [New Latin *Spartium,* broom genus (from Latin *spartum,* a kind of broom, from Greek *sparton*) + -INE[2].]

spar varnish *n.* A waterproof varnish.

spasm (spăz′əm) *n.* **1.** A sudden, involuntary contraction of a muscle or group of muscles. **2.** A sudden burst of energy, activity, or emotion. [Middle English *spasme,* from Old French, from Latin *spasmus,* from Greek *spasmos,* from *span,* to pull.]

spas·mod·ic (spăz-mŏd′ĭk) *adj.* **1.** Relating to, affected by, or having the character of a spasm; convulsive. **2.** Happening intermittently; fitful: *spasmodic rifle fire.* **3.** Given to sudden outbursts of energy or feeling; excitable. [New Latin *spasmōdicus,* from Greek *spasmōdēs,* from *spasmos,* spasm. See SPASM.] **—spas·mod′i·cal·ly** *adv.*

spas·mo·lyt·ic (spăz′mə-lĭt′ĭk) *n.* See **antispasmodic. —spas′mo·lyt′ic** *adj.*

spas·tic (spăs′tĭk) *adj.* **1.** Of, relating to, or characterized by spasms: *a spastic colon; a spastic form of cerebral palsy.* **2.** Affected by spastic paralysis. **—spastic** *n.* A person affected with spastic paralysis. [Latin *spasticus,* from Greek *spastikos,* from *span,* to pull.] **—spas′ti·cal·ly** *adv.* **—spas·tic′i·ty** (spă-stĭs′ĭ-tē) *n.*

spastic paralysis *n.* A chronic pathological condition in which the muscles are affected by persistent spasms and exaggerated tendon reflexes because of damage to motor nerves of the central nervous system.

spat[1] (spăt) *v.* A past tense and a past participle of **spit**[1].

spat[2] (spăt) *n., pl.* **spat** or **spats. 1.** An oyster or similar bivalve mollusk in the larval stage, especially when it settles to the bottom and begins to develop a shell. **2.** The spawn of an oyster or a similar mollusk. **—spat** *intr.v.* **spat·ted, spat·ting, spats.** To spawn. Used of oysters and similar mollusks. [Middle English.]

spat[3] (spăt) *n.* A cloth or leather gaiter covering the shoe upper and the ankle and fastening under the shoe with a strap. Often used in the plural. [Short for *spatterdash* : SPATTER + DASH[1].]

spat[4] (spăt) *n.* **1.** A brief quarrel. **2.** *Informal.* A slap or smack. **3.** A spattering sound, as of raindrops. **—spat** *v.* **spat·ted, spat·ting, spats.** —*intr.* **1.** To engage in a brief quarrel. **2.** To strike with a light spattering sound; slap. —*tr. Informal.* To slap. [Origin unknown.]

spatch·cock (spăch′kŏk) *n.* A dressed and split chicken for roasting or broiling on a spit. **—spatchcock** *tr.v.* **-cocked, -cock·ing, -cocks. 1.** To prepare (a dressed chicken) for grilling by splitting open. **2.** To introduce or interpose, especially in a labored or unsuitable manner: *"Some excerpts from a Renaissance mass are spatchcocked into Gluck's pallid Don Juan music"* (Alan Rich). [Perhaps alteration of *spitchcock,* a way of cooking an eel.]

spate (spāt) *n.* **1.** A sudden flood, rush, or outpouring: *"It issues a spate of words from the loudspeakers and the politicians"* (Virginia Woolf). **2.** *Chiefly British.* **a.** A flash flood. **b.** A freshet resulting from a downpour of rain or melting of snow. **c.** A sudden heavy fall of rain. [Middle English.]

spathe (spāth) *n. Botany.* A leaflike bract that encloses or subtends a flower cluster or spadix, as in the jack-in-the-pulpit and the calla. [Latin *spatha,* broadsword, from Greek *spathē,* broad blade.]

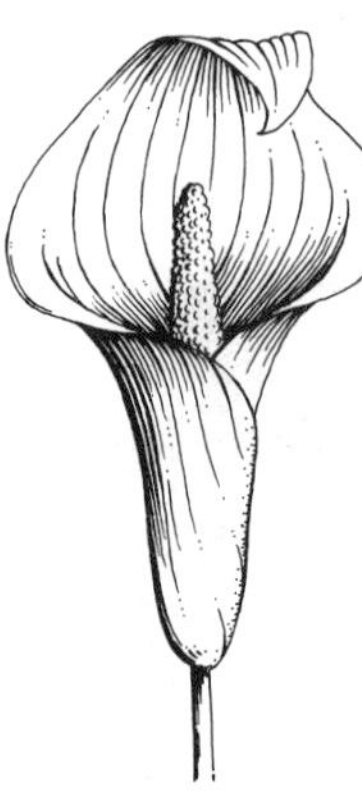
spathe
Calla lily
Zantedeschia aethiopica

spath·ic (spăth′ĭk) *adj.* Having good cleavage. Used of minerals. [German *Spath, Spat,* spar (from Middle High German *spāt*) + -IC.]

spa·tial also **spa·cial** (spā′shəl) *adj.* Of, relating to, involving, or having the nature of space. [From Latin *spatium,* space.] **—spa′ti·al′i·ty** (spā′shē-ăl′ĭ-tē) *n.* **—spa′tial·ly** *adv.*

spa·ti·o·tem·po·ral (spā′shē-ō-tĕm′pər-əl) *adj.* **1.** Of, relating to, or existing in both space and time. **2.** Of or relating to space-time. [Latin *spatium,* space + TEMPORAL[1].] **—spa′ti·o·tem′po·ral·ly** *adv.*

spat·ter (spăt′ər) *v.* **-tered, -ter·ing, -ters.** —*tr.* **1.** To scatter (a liquid) in drops or small splashes. **2.** To spot, splash, or soil. **3.** To sully the reputation of; defame. —*intr.* **1.** To come forth in drops or small splashes: *Hot grease spattered in all directions.* **2.** To fall in or as if in a shower, as rain or bullets. **—spatter** *n.* **1.a.** The act of spattering. **b.** The condition of being spattered. **2.** A spattering sound. **3.a.** A drop or splash of something spattered. **b.** A small amount; a smattering: *just a spatter of praise.* [Perhaps of Low German origin.]

spat·ter·dock (spăt′ər-dŏk′) *n.* An aquatic plant *(Nuphar advena)* of eastern Mexico and the eastern and central United States, having emergent broad leaves and globe-shaped yellow flowers. [SPATTER + DOCK[4].]

spat·u·la (spăch′ə-lə) *n.* **1.** A small implement having a broad, flat, flexible blade that is used especially to mix, spread, or lift material. **2.** A device, such as a small wooden paddle, used to press down the tongue during an examination of the mouth or throat. [Latin, flat piece of wood, splint, diminutive of *spatha,* broadsword. See SPATHE.] **—spat′u·lar** *adj.*

spat·u·late (spăch′ə-lĭt) *adj.* Shaped like a spatula.

spav·in (spăv′ĭn) *n.* **1.** Bog spavin. **2.** Bone spavin. [Middle English *spaven,* from Old French *espavain,* swelling, perhaps of Germanic origin.]

spav·ined (spăv′ĭnd) *adj.* **1.** Afflicted with spavin: *a spavined horse.* **2.** Marked by damage, deterioration, or ruin: *a junkyard full of spavined vehicles.*

spawn (spôn) *n.* **1.** The eggs of aquatic animals such as bivalve mollusks, fishes, and amphibians. **2.** Offspring occurring in numbers; brood. **3.** A person who is the issue of a parent or family. **4.** The source of something; a germ or seed. **5.** A product or an outcome. **6.** Mycelia of mushrooms or other fungi grown in specially prepared organic matter for planting in beds. **—spawn** *v.* **spawned, spawn·ing, spawns.** *—intr.* **1.** To deposit eggs; produce spawn. **2.** To produce offspring in large numbers. *—tr.* **1.** To produce or deposit (spawn). **2.** To produce in large numbers. **3.** To give rise to; engender: *tyranny that spawned revolt.* **4.** To cause to spawn; bring forth; produce: *a family that had spawned a monster.* **5.** To plant with mycelia grown in specially prepared organic matter. [Middle English *spawne,* from *spawnen,* to spawn, from Anglo-Norman *espaundre,* from Latin *expandere.* See EXPAND.] **—spawn′er** *n.*

spay (spā) *tr.v.* **spayed, spay·ing, spays.** To remove surgically the ovaries of (an animal). [Middle English *spaien,* from Anglo-Norman *espeier,* to cut with a sword, from *espee,* sword, from Latin *spatha.* See SPATHE.]

SPCA *abbr.* Society for the Prevention of Cruelty to Animals.

SPCC *abbr.* Society for the Prevention of Cruelty to Children.

speak (spēk) *v.* **spoke** (spōk), **spo·ken** (spō′kən), **speak·ing, speaks.** *—intr.* **1.** To utter words or articulate sounds with ordinary speech modulation; talk. **2.a.** To convey thoughts, opinions, or emotions orally. **b.** To express oneself. **c.** To be on speaking terms: *They are no longer speaking.* **3.** To deliver an address or a lecture: *The president of NOW was to speak at the rally.* **4.a.** To make a statement in writing: *The biography speaks of great loneliness.* **b.** To act as spokesperson: *spoke for the entire staff.* **5.a.** To convey a message by nonverbal means: *Actions speak louder than words.* **b.** To be expressive: *spoke with her eyes.* **c.** To be appealing: *His poetry speaks to one's heart.* **6.** To make a reservation or request. Often used with *for*: *Is this dance spoken for? I spoke for the last slice of pizza.* **7.a.** To produce a characteristic sound: *The drums spoke.* **b.** To give off a sound on firing. Used of guns or cannon. **8.** To make communicative sounds. **9.** To give an indication or a suggestion: *His manners spoke of good upbringing.* *—tr.* **1.** To articulate in a speaking voice: *spoke words of wisdom.* **2.** To converse in or be able to converse in (a language): *speaks German.* **3.a.** To express aloud; tell: *speak the truth.* **b.** To express in writing. **4.** *Nautical.* To hail and communicate with (another vessel) at sea. **5.** To convey by nonverbal means: *His eyes spoke volumes.* ***—phrasal verbs.*** **speak out.** To talk freely and fearlessly, as about a public issue. **speak up.** **1.** To speak loud enough to be audible. **2.** To speak without fear or hesitation. ***—idioms.*** **so to speak.** In a manner of speaking: *can't see the forest for the trees, so to speak.* **speak down to.** To speak condescendingly to: *She never spoke down to her audience.* **to speak of.** Worthy of mention: *There's nothing new to speak of.* [Middle English *speken,* from Old English *sprecan, specan.*] **—speak′a·ble** *adj.*

SYNONYMS: *speak, talk, converse, discourse.* These verbs mean to express one's thoughts by uttering words. *Speak* and *talk,* often interchangeable, are the most general: *He ate his meal without once speaking to his dinner companion. "Why don't you speak for yourself, John?"* (Henry Wadsworth Longfellow). *"On an occasion of this kind it becomes more than a moral duty to speak one's mind. It becomes a pleasure"* (Oscar Wilde). *I want to talk with you about vacation plans. "We must know . . . what we are talking about"* (Henry James). *"Let's talk sense to the American people"* (Adlai E. Stevenson). *Converse* stresses interchange of thoughts and ideas: *"With thee conversing I forget all time"* (John Milton). *Discourse* usually refers to formal, extended speech: *"striding through the city, stick in hand, discoursing spontaneously on the writings of Hazlitt"* (Manchester Guardian Weekly).

speak·eas·y (spēk′ē′zē) *n., pl.* **-ies.** A place for the illegal sale and consumption of alcoholic drinks, as during Prohibition in the United States.

speak·er (spē′kər) *n.* **1.a.** One who speaks. **b.** A spokesperson. **2.** One who delivers a public speech. **3.** Often **Speaker.** The presiding officer of a legislative assembly. **4.** A loudspeaker. **—speak′er·ship′** *n.*

speak·er·phone (spē′kər-fōn′) *n.* A telephone or telephone attachment that contains both a loudspeaker and a microphone, allowing several persons to participate in a call at the same time without the telephone receiver being held.

speak·ing (spē′kĭng) *adj.* **1.a.** Capable of speech. **b.** Involving speaking or talking: *has a speaking part in the play.* **2.** Expressive or telling; eloquent. **3.** True to life; lifelike: *a speaking likeness.* ***—idiom.*** **on speaking terms.** **1.** Friendly enough to exchange superficial remarks: *We're on speaking terms with the new neighbors.* **2.** Ready and willing to communicate; not alienated or estranged: *on speaking terms again after their quarrel.*

speaking in tongues *n.* See **gift of tongues.**

speaking tube *n.* A tube used for speaking from one room of a building or ship to another.

spear¹ (spîr) *n.* **1.** A weapon consisting of a long shaft with a sharply pointed end. **2.** A shaft with a sharp point and barbs for spearing fish. **3.** A soldier armed with a spear. **—spear** *v.* **speared, spear·ing, spears.** *—tr.* **1.** To pierce with or as if with a spear. **2.** To catch with a thrust of the arm: *spear a football.* *—intr.* To stab at something with or as if with a spear. [Middle English *spere,* from Old English.] **—spear′er** *n.* **—spear′like′** *adj.*

spear² (spîr) *n.* A slender stalk, as of asparagus. **—spear** *intr.v.* **speared, spear·ing, spears.** To sprout like a spear. [Alteration of SPIRE².]

spear-car·ri·er (spîr′kăr′ē-ər) *n.* **1.** A minor member of an operatic or dramatic cast, usually having no speaking part. **2.** One whose presence or performance has little effect on an occurrence, a group, or an organization.

spear·fish¹ (spîr′fĭsh′) *n., pl.* **spearfish** or **-fish·es.** Either of two large marine game fishes *(Tetrapturus angustirostris* or *T. belone)* related to the sailfish and marlin, having the upper jaw elongated into a spearlike projection.

spear·fish² (spîr′fĭsh′) *intr.v.* **-fished, -fish·ing, -fish·es.** To fish with a spear, spearlike implement, or spear gun. **—spear′fish′er** *n.* **—spear′fish′ing** *n.*

spear grass *n.* See **feather grass.**

spear gun *n.* A device for mechanically shooting a spearlike missile under water, as in spearfishing.

spear·head (spîr′hĕd′) *n.* **1.** The sharpened head of a spear. **2.a.** The leading forces in a military thrust. **b.** The driving force in a given action, endeavor, or movement. **—spearhead** *tr.v.* **-head·ed, -head·ing, -heads.** To be the leader of: *"spearheaded the effort to offer classes in settlement houses* [and] *provide lecturers to women's clubs"* (Catherine Clinton).

spear·man (spîr′mən) *n.* A man, especially a soldier, armed with a spear.

spear·mint (spîr′mĭnt′) *n.* An aromatic Eurasian plant *(Mentha spicata)* having clusters of small purplish flowers and yielding an oil used widely as a flavoring.

spear·wort (spîr′wûrt′, -wôrt′) *n.* Any of several plants related to the buttercups, especially *Ranunculus flammula,* native to Eurasia, having lance-shaped leaves and yellow flowers.

spear¹

spec (spĕk) *Informal. n.* **1. specs.** The specifications, as for a building to be constructed. **2.** Speculation. **—spec** *tr.v.* **spec'd, spec'ing, specs** or **specced, spec·cing, specs.** To write or supply specifications for. **—spec** *adj.* **1.** Of or relating to specifications: *a manufacturer's spec sheet.* **2.** Done, constructed, produced, or purchased as a speculation: *a spec job; a spec house.* ***—idiom.*** **on spec.** On a speculation basis; with no assurance of profit: *houses built on spec; writes TV commercials on spec.* **—spec′'er** *n.*

spec. *abbr.* **1.** Special. **2.** Specifically. **3.** Specification. **4.** Speculation.

spe·cial (spĕsh′əl) *adj. Abbr.* **sp., spec.** **1.** Surpassing what is common or usual; exceptional: *a special occasion; a special treat.* **2.a.** Distinct among others of a kind: *a special type of paint; a special medication for arthritis.* **b.** Primary: *His special satisfaction comes from volunteer work.* **3.** Peculiar to a specific person or thing; particular: *my own special chair; the special features of a computer.* **4.a.** Having a limited or specific function, application, or scope: *a special role in the mission.* **b.** Arranged for a particular occasion or purpose: *a special visit from her daughter.* **5.** Regarded with particular affection and admiration: *a special friend.* **6.** Additional; extra: *a special holiday flight.* **—special** *n.* **1.** Something arranged, issued, or appropriated to a particular service or occasion: *rode to work on the commuter special.* **2.** A featured attraction, such as a reduced price: *a special on salmon.* **3.** A single television production that features a specific work, a given topic, or a particular performer. [Middle English, from Old French *especial,* from Latin *speciālis,* from *speciēs,* kind. See SPECIES.] **—spe′cial·ly** *adv.* **—spe′cial·ness** *n.*

spearmint
Mentha spicata

special act *n.* A legislative act that applies only to a particular person or area.

special court-martial *n.* A court-martial consisting of at least three officers for trying intermediate offenses.

special delivery *n. Abbr.* **SD, S.D.** The delivery of a piece of mail, for an additional charge, by a special messenger rather than by scheduled delivery.

special education *n.* Classroom or private instruction involving techniques, exercises, and subject matter designed for students whose learning needs cannot be met by a standard school curriculum.

special effect *n.* A visual or sound effect added to a movie or a taped television show during processing. Often used in the plural.

Spe·cial Forces (spĕsh′əl) *pl.n.* A division of the U.S. Army composed of soldiers specially trained in guerrilla fighting.

special handling *n.* The handling of fourth-class or parcel-post mail as first-class mail for an extra charge.

special interest *n.* A person, a group, or an organization attempting to influence legislators in favor of one particular interest or issue. **—spe′cial-in′ter·est** (spĕsh′əl-ĭn′trĭst, -tər-ĭst, -trĕst′) *adj.*

spe·cial·ism (spĕsh′ə-lĭz′əm) *n.* **1.** Concentration of one's efforts in a given occupation or field of study. **2.** A field of specialization.

spe·cial·ist (spĕsh′ə-lĭst) *n.* **1.** One who is devoted to a particular occupation or branch of study or research: *"Specialists . . . tend to think in grooves"* (Elaine Morgan). **2.** A physician whose practice is limited to a particular branch of medicine or surgery, especially one who is certified by a board of physicians: *a specialist in oncology.* **3.** *Abbr.* **SP** Any of several noncommissioned ranks in the U.S. Army that correspond to that of corporal through sergeant first class. **—spe′cial·ist, spe′cial·is′tic** *adj.*

spe·ci·al·i·ty (spĕsh′ē-ăl′ĭ-tē) *n., pl.* **-ties.** **1.** A distinguishing mark or feature. **2. specialities.** Special points of consideration; particulars. **3.** *Chiefly British.* A specialty.

ă pat	oi boy
ā pay	ou out
âr care	o͝o took
ä father	o͞o boot
ĕ pet	ŭ cut
ē be	ûr urge
ĭ pit	th thin
ī pie	*th* this
îr pier	hw which
ŏ pot	zh vision
ō toe	ə about, item
ô paw	♦ regionalism

Stress marks: ′ (primary); ′ (secondary), as in **dictionary** (dĭk′shə-nĕr′ē)

spe·cial·i·za·tion (spĕsh′ə-lĭ-zā′shən) *n.* **1.** The act of specializing or the process of becoming specialized. **2.** *Biology.* **a.** Adaptation, as of an organ or organism, to a specific function or environment. **b.** A character, a feature, or an organism resulting from such adaptation.

spe·cial·ize (spĕsh′ə-līz′) *v.* **-ized, -iz·ing, -iz·es.** —*intr.* **1.** To pursue a special activity, occupation, or field of study. **2.** *Biology.* To develop so as to become adapted to a specific function or environment; undergo specialization. **3.** To concentrate on a particular activity or product: *The shop specializes in mountain-climbing gear.* —*tr.* **1.** To make specific mention of; particularize. **2.** To give a particular character or function to: *specialized her field of research.* **3.** *Biology.* To adapt to a particular function or environment; cause to undergo specialization. **4.** To specify the payee in endorsing (a check).

special jury *n. Law.* See **blue-ribbon jury.**

Special Olympics *pl.n.* A program of competitive sports events fashioned after the Olympic games and intended for physically or mentally challenged athletes.

special pleading *n.* **1.** *Law.* Assertion of new or special matter to offset the opposing party's allegations, as an alternative to direct denial. **2.** A presentation of an argument that emphasizes only a favorable or single aspect of the question at issue.

special relativity *n.* The physical theory of space and time developed by Albert Einstein, based on the postulates that all the laws of physics are equally valid in all frames of reference moving at a uniform velocity and that the speed of light from a uniformly moving source is always the same, regardless of how fast or slow the source or its observer is moving. The theory has as consequences the relativistic mass increase of rapidly moving objects, the Lorentz-Fitzgerald contraction, time dilatation, and the principle of mass-energy equivalence. Also called *special theory of relativity.*

special session *n.* A session of a court or legislative body held in addition to the regular sessions.

special theory of relativity *n.* See **special relativity.**

spe·cial·ty (spĕsh′əl-tē) *n., pl.* **-ties.** **1.** A special pursuit, occupation, aptitude, or skill. See Synonyms at **forte**[1]. **2.** A branch of medicine or surgery, such as cardiology or neurosurgery, in which a physician specializes; the field or practice of a specialist. **3.** A special feature or characteristic; a peculiarity. **4.** The state or quality of being special or distinctive. **5.** An item or a product of a distinctive kind or of particular superiority: *French pastry is the chef's specialty.* **6.** *Law.* A special contract or agreement, especially a deed kept under seal.

spe·ci·a·tion (spē′shē-ā′shən, -sē-) *n.* The evolutionary formation of new biological species, usually by the division of a single species into two or more genetically distinct ones. [SPECI(ES) + -ATION.] **—spe′ci·a′tion·al** *adj.*

spe·cie (spē′shē, -sē) *n.* Coined money; coin. **—*idiom.* in specie. 1.** In coin. **2.** In a similar manner; in kind: *repaid the offense in specie.* **3.** *Law.* In the same kind or shape; as specified. [From *(in) specie,* (in) the actual form, from Latin *(in) speciē,* (in) kind, ablative of *speciēs.* See SPECIES.]

spe·cies (spē′shēz, -sēz) *n., pl.* **species.** *Abbr.* **sp. 1.** *Biology.* **a.** A fundamental category of taxonomic classification, ranking below a genus or subgenus and consisting of related organisms capable of interbreeding. See table at **taxonomy. b.** An organism belonging to such a category, represented in binomial nomenclature by an uncapitalized Latin adjective or noun following a capitalized genus name, as in *Ananas comosus,* the pineapple, and *Equus caballus,* the horse. **2.** *Logic.* A class of individuals or objects grouped by virtue of their common attributes and assigned a common name; a division subordinate to a genus. **3. a.** A kind, variety, or type: *"No species of performing artist is as self-critical as a dancer"* (Susan Sontag). **b.** The human race; humankind. **4.** *Roman Catholic Church.* **a.** The outward appearance or form of the Eucharistic elements that is retained after their consecration. **b.** Either of the consecrated elements of the Eucharist. **5.** *Obsolete.* **a.** An outward form or appearance. **b.** Specie. [Middle English, logical classification, from Latin *speciēs,* a seeing, kind, form. See **spek-** in Appendix.]

spectacled
Spectacled bear
Tremarctos ornatus

spe·cies·ism (spē′shē-zĭz′əm, -sē-) *n.* Human intolerance or discrimination on the basis of species, especially as manifested by cruelty to or exploitation of animals. **—spe′cies·ist′** *adj. & n.*

spe·cies-spe·cif·ic (spē′shēz-spĭ-sĭf′ĭk, -sēz-) *adj.* Limited to or found only in one species: *a species-specific antibody; a species-specific virus.* **—spe′cies-spec′i·fic′i·ty** (-spĕs′ə-fĭs′ĭ-tē) *n.*

specif. *abbr.* **1.** Specific. **2.** Specifically.

spec·i·fi·a·ble (spĕs′ə-fī′ə-bəl) *adj.* Possible to specify: *specifiable complaints.*

spe·cif·ic (spĭ-sĭf′ĭk) *adj. Abbr.* **specif., sp. 1.** Explicitly set forth; definite. See Synonyms at **explicit. 2.** Relating to, characterizing, or distinguishing a species. **3.** Special, distinctive, or unique: *specific qualities and attributes.* **4. a.** Intended for, applying to, or acting on a particular thing: *a specific remedy for warts.* **b.** Concerned particularly with the subject specified. Often used in combination: *"age-specific voting patterns"* (A. Dianne Schmidley). **5. a.** Designating a disease produced by a particular microorganism or condition. **b.** Having a remedial influence or effect on a particular disease. **6.** *Immunology.* Having an affinity limited to a particular antibody or antigen. **7. a.** Designating a customs charge levied on merchandise by unit or weight rather than according to value. **b.** Designating a commodity rate applicable to the transportation of a single commodity between named points. **—specific** *n.* **1. a.** Something particularly fitted to a use or purpose. **b.** A remedy intended for a particular ailment or disorder. **2. a.** A distinguishing quality or attribute. **b. specifics.** Distinct items or details; particulars. [Late Latin *specificus* : Latin *speciēs,* kind, species; see SPECIES + Latin *-ficus,* -fic.] **—spe·cif′i·cal·ly** *adv.* **—spec′i·fic′i·ty** (spĕs′ə-fĭs′ĭ-tē) *n.*

spec·i·fi·ca·tion (spĕs′ə-fĭ-kā′shən) *n. Abbr.* **spec. 1.** The act of specifying. **2. a. specifications.** A detailed, exact statement of particulars, especially a statement prescribing materials, dimensions, and quality of work for something to be built, installed, or manufactured. **b.** A single item or article that has been specified. **3.** An exact written description of an invention by an applicant for a patent.

specific epithet *n.* The uncapitalized Latin adjective or noun that follows a capitalized genus name in binomial nomenclature and serves to distinguish a species from others in the same genus, as *saccharum* in *Acer saccharum* (sugar maple). Also called *trivial name.*

specific gravity *n. Abbr.* **sg, sp gr** The ratio of the mass of a solid or liquid to the mass of an equal volume of distilled water at 4°C (39°F) or of a gas to an equal volume of air or hydrogen under prescribed conditions of temperature and pressure.

specific heat *n. Abbr.* **sp ht 1.** The ratio of the amount of heat required to raise the temperature of a unit mass of a substance by one unit of temperature to the amount of heat required to raise the temperature of a similar mass of a reference material, usually water, by the same amount. **2.** The amount of heat, measured in calories, required to raise the temperature of one gram of a substance by one Celsius degree.

specific impulse *n.* A performance measure for rocket propellants that is equal to units of thrust per unit weight of propellant consumed per unit time. Also called *specific thrust.*

specific performance *n. Law.* The performance of a contract as specified in its terms.

specific resistance *n. Electricity.* Electrical resistivity.

specific thrust *n.* See **specific impulse.**

spec·i·fy (spĕs′ə-fī′) *tr.v.* **-fied, -fy·ing, -fies. 1.** To state explicitly or in detail: *specified the amount needed.* **2.** To include in a specification. **3.** To state as a condition: *specified that they be included in the will.* [Middle English *specifien,* from Old French *specifier,* from Late Latin *specificāre,* from *specificus,* specific. See SPECIFIC.] **—spec′i·fi′er** *n.*

spec·i·men (spĕs′ə-mən) *n. Abbr.* **sp. 1.** An individual, an item, or a part representative of a class, genus, or whole. See Synonyms at **example. 2.** A sample, as of tissue, blood, or urine, used for analysis and diagnosis. **3.** *Informal.* An individual; a person: *a disagreeable specimen.* [Latin, example, from *specere,* to look at. See **spek-** in Appendix.]

spe·cious (spē′shəs) *adj.* **1.** Having the ring of truth or plausibility but actually fallacious: *a specious argument.* **2.** Deceptively attractive. [Middle English, attractive, from Latin *speciōsus,* from *speciēs,* appearance, from *specere,* to look at. See **spek-** in Appendix.] **—spe′cious·ly** *adv.* **—spe′ci·os′i·ty** (-shē-ŏs′ĭ-tē), **spe′cious·ness** (-shəs-nĭs) *n.*

USAGE NOTE: A *specious* argument is not simply a false one but one that has the ring of truth. Those aware of the specialized use of the word may therefore sense a certain contradiction in hearing an argument described as *obviously specious* or *specious on the face of things;* if the fallaciousness is apparent, the argument was probably not plausible-sounding to begin with.

speck (spĕk) *n.* **1.** A small spot, mark, or discoloration. **2.** A tiny amount; a bit: *not a speck of truth in her story.* **—speck** *tr.v.* **specked, speck·ing, specks.** To mark with specks. [Middle English *specke,* from Old English *specca.*]

speck·le (spĕk′əl) *n.* A speck or small spot, especially a natural dot of color on skin, plumage, or foliage. [Middle English *spakle.*] **—speck′le** *v.*

speck·led (spĕk′əld) *adj.* **1.** Dotted or covered with speckles, especially flecked with small spots of contrasting color. **2.** Of a mixed character; motley.

speckled trout *n.* See **brook trout.**

specs also **specks** (spĕks) *pl.n. Informal.* Eyeglasses; spectacles.

spec·ta·cle (spĕk′tə-kəl) *n.* **1. a.** Something that can be seen or viewed, especially something of a remarkable or impressive nature. **b.** A public performance or display, especially one on a large or lavish scale. **c.** A regrettable public display, as of bad behavior: *drank too much and made a spectacle of himself.* **2. spectacles. a.** A pair of eyeglasses. **b.** Something resembling eyeglasses in shape or function. [Middle English, from Old French, from Latin *spectāculum,* from *spectāre,* to watch, frequentative of *specere,* to look at. See **spek-** in Appendix.]

spec·ta·cled (spĕk′tə-kəld) *adj.* **1.** Wearing spectacles. **2.** Having markings suggesting spectacles. Used of animals.

spec·tac·u·lar (spĕk-tăk′yə-lər) *adj.* Of the nature of a spectacle; impressive or sensational. **—spectacular** *n.* Something that is spectacular, as: **a.** A single dramatic production of unusual length or lavishness. **b.** An elaborate display. **—spec·tac′u·lar′i·ty** (-lăr′ĭ-tē) *n.* **—spec·tac′u·lar·ly** *adv.*

spec·tate (spĕk′tāt) *intr.v.* **-tat·ed, -tat·ing, -tates.** *Sports.* To attend (a horserace or other sporting event, for example) as a spectator. [Back-formation from SPECTATOR.]

spec·ta·tor (spĕk′tā′tər) *n.* An observer of an event. [Latin *spectātor,* from *spectāre,* to watch. See SPECTACLE.] **—spec′ta·to′ri·al** (-tə-tôr′ē-əl, -tōr′-) *adj.* **—spec′ta·tor·ship′** *n.*

spec·ter (spĕk′tər) *n.* **1.** A ghostly apparition; a phantom. **2.** A haunting or disturbing image or prospect: *the terrible specter of nuclear war.* [French *spectre,* from Latin *spectrum,* appearance, apparition. See SPECTRUM.]

spec·ti·no·my·cin (spĕk′tə-nō-mī′sĭn) *n.* A broad-spectrum antibiotic, $C_{14}H_{24}N_2O_7$, obtained from a species of gram-negative bacteria *(Streptomyces spectabilis)* or produced synthetically, used especially in the treatment of penicillin-resistant gonorrhea. [New Latin : *spect(abilis),* species name (from Latin, visible, from *spectāre,* to watch; see SPECTACLE) + (ACT)INOMYCIN.]

spec·tra (spĕk′trə) *n.* A plural of **spectrum.**

spec·tral (spĕk′trəl) *adj.* **1.** Of or resembling a specter; ghostly. **2.** Of, relating to, or produced by a spectrum. **—spec·tral′i·ty** (-trăl′ĭ-tē), **spec′tral·ness** (-trəl-nĭs) *n.* **—spec′tral·ly** *adv.*

spectral line *n.* An isolated bright or dark line in a spectrum produced by emission or absorption of light of a single wavelength.

spec·tre (spĕk′tər) *n. Chiefly British.* Variant of **specter.**

spec·trin (spĕk′trĭn) *n.* A protein of high molecular weight that is a major component of the membrane of red blood cells. [SPECT(E)R (so called because a red blood cell without hemoglobin is called a *ghost*) + –IN.]

spectro– *pref.* Spectrum: *spectrograph.* [From SPECTRUM.]

spec·tro·gram (spĕk′trə-grăm′) *n.* A graphic or photographic representation of a spectrum.

spec·tro·graph (spĕk′trə-grăf′) *n.* **1.** A spectroscope equipped to photograph or otherwise record spectra. **2.** A spectrogram. **—spec′tro·graph′ic** *adj.* **—spec′tro·graph′i·cal·ly** *adv.* **—spec·trog′ra·phy** (-trŏg′rə-fē) *n.*

spec·tro·he·li·o·gram (spĕk′trō-hē′lē-ə-grăm′) *n.* A photograph of the sun taken in a narrow wavelength band centered on a selected wavelength.

spec·tro·he·li·o·graph (spĕk′trō-hē′lē-ə-grăf′) *n.* An instrument used to make spectroheliograms. **—spec′tro·he′li·o·graph′ic** *adj.* **—spec′tro·he′li·og′ra·phy** (-ŏg′rə-fē) *n.*

spec·tro·he·li·o·scope (spĕk′trō-hē′lē-ə-skōp′) *n.* An instrument used to observe solar radiation directly. **—spec′tro·he′li·o·scop′ic** (-skŏp′ĭk) *adj.*

spec·trom·e·ter (spĕk-trŏm′ĭ-tər) *n.* A spectroscope equipped with scales for measuring wavelengths or indexes of refraction. **—spec′tro·met′ric** (-trə-mĕt′rĭk) *adj.* **—spec·trom′e·try** *n.*

spec·tro·pho·tom·e·ter (spĕk′trō-fō-tŏm′ĭ-tər) *n. Physics.* An instrument used to determine the intensity of various wavelengths in a spectrum of light. **—spec′tro·pho′to·met′ric** (-fō′tə-mĕt′rĭk) *adj.* **—spec′tro·pho·tom′e·try** *n.*

spec·tro·scope (spĕk′trə-skōp′) *n.* An instrument for producing and observing spectra. **—spec′tro·scop′ic** (-skŏp′ĭk), **spec′tro·scop′i·cal** (-ĭ-kəl) *adj.* **—spec′tro·scop′i·cal·ly** *adv.*

spectroscopic analysis *n.* Analysis of a spectrum to determine characteristics of its source; for example, analysis of the optical spectrum of an incandescent body to determine its composition or motion.

spectroscopic binary *n.* A binary star system that is identified by periodically shifting lines in its spectrum.

spec·tros·co·py (spĕk-trŏs′kə-pē) *n., pl.* **-pies.** Study of spectra, especially experimental observation of optical spectra. **—spec·tros′co·pist** *n.*

spec·trum (spĕk′trəm) *n., pl.* **-tra** (-trə) or **-trums. 1.** *Physics.* The distribution of a characteristic of a physical system or phenomenon, especially: **a.** The distribution of energy emitted by a radiant source, as by an incandescent body, arranged in order of wavelengths. **b.** The distribution of atomic or subatomic particles in a system, as in a magnetically resolved molecular beam, arranged in order of masses. **2.** A graphic or photographic representation of such a distribution. **3. a.** A range of values of a quantity or set of related quantities. **b.** A broad sequence or range of related qualities, ideas, or activities: *the whole spectrum of 20th-century thought.* [Latin, appearance, from *specere,* to look at. See **spek-** in Appendix.]

spec·u·la (spĕk′yə-lə) *n.* A plural of **speculum.**

spec·u·lar (spĕk′yə-lər) *adj.* Of, resembling, or produced by a mirror or speculum. **—spec′u·lar·ly** *adv.*

spec·u·late (spĕk′yə-lāt′) *v.* **-lat·ed, -lat·ing, -lates.** —*intr.* **1.** To meditate on a subject; reflect. **2.** To engage in a course of reasoning often based on inconclusive evidence. See Synonyms at **conjecture, think. 3.** To engage in the buying or selling of a commodity with an element of risk on the chance of profit. —*tr.* To assume to be true without conclusive evidence: *speculated that high cholesterol was a contributing factor to the patient's health problems.* [Latin *speculārī, speculāt-,* to observe, from *specula,* watchtower, from *specere,* to look at. See **spek-** in Appendix.]

spec·u·la·tion (spĕk′yə-lā′shən) *n. Abbr.* **spec. 1. a.** Contemplation or consideration of a subject; meditation. **b.** A conclusion, an opinion, or a theory reached by conjecture. **c.** Reasoning based on inconclusive evidence; conjecture or supposition. **2. a.** Engagement in risky business transactions on the chance of quick or considerable profit. **b.** A commercial or financial transaction involving speculation.

spec·u·la·tive (spĕk′yə-lə-tĭv, -lā′-) *adj.* **1.** Of, characterized by, or based upon contemplative speculation. See Synonyms at **theoretical. 2. a.** Given to conjecture or speculation. **b.** Marked by inquisitive interest: *raised a speculative eyebrow.* **3. a.** Engaging in, given to, or involving financial speculation: *speculative brokers; speculative stocks.* **b.** Spent in speculation: *speculative funds.* **c.** Involving chance; risky: *speculative business enterprises.* **—spec′u·la·tive·ly** *adv.* **—spec′u·la·tive·ness** *n.*

spec·u·la·tor (spĕk′yə-lā′tər) *n.* One that speculates: *a commodities speculator; a speculator regarding the future turn of events.*

spec·u·lum (spĕk′yə-ləm) *n., pl.* **-la** (-lə) or **-lums. 1.** A mirror or polished metal plate used as a reflector in optical instruments. **2.** An instrument for dilating the opening of a body cavity for medical examination. **3.** *Zoology.* **a.** A bright, often iridescent patch of color on the wings of certain birds, especially ducks. **b.** A transparent spot in the wings of some butterflies or moths. [Middle English, surgical speculum, from Latin, mirror, from *specere,* to look at. See **spek-** in Appendix.]

sped (spĕd) *v.* A past tense and a past participle of **speed.**

speech (spēch) *n.* **1. a.** The faculty or act of speaking. **b.** The faculty or act of expressing or describing thoughts, feelings, or perceptions by the articulation of words. **2.** Something spoken; an utterance. **3.** Vocal communication; conversation. **4. a.** A talk or public address: *"The best impromptu speeches are the ones written well in advance"* (Ruth Gordon). **b.** A printed copy of such an address. **5.** One's habitual manner or style of speaking. **6.** The language or dialect of a nation or region: *American speech.* **7.** The sounding of a musical instrument. **8.** The study of oral communication, speech sounds, and vocal physiology. **9.** *Archaic.* Rumor. [Middle English *speche,* from Old English *sprǣc, spǣc.*]

speech community *n.* A group of speakers, whether located in one area or scattered, who recognize the same language or dialect of a language as a standard.

speech·i·fy (spē′chə-fī′) *intr.v.* **-fied, -fy·ing, -fies.** To give a speech: *"In Washington, cabinet secretaries pose and speechify"* (Jonathan Alter). **—speech′i·fi′er** *n.*

speech·less (spēch′lĭs) *adj.* **1.** Lacking the faculty of speech. **2.** Temporarily unable to speak, as through astonishment. See Synonyms at **dumb. 3.** Refraining from speech; silent. **4.** Unexpressed or inexpressible in words: *speechless admiration.* **—speech′less·ly** *adv.* **—speech′less·ness** *n.*

speech·mak·er (spēch′mā′kər) *n.* One who makes a speech. **—speech′mak′ing** *n.*

speech pathology *n.* The study of speech disorders such as stuttering and dysphasia. **—speech pathologist** *n.*

speech therapy *n.* Treatment of speech defects and disorders, especially through use of exercises and audio-visual aids that develop new speech habits. **—speech therapist** *n.*

speech·writ·er (spēch′rī′tər) *n.* One who writes speeches for others, especially as a profession. **—speech′writ′ing** *n.*

speed (spēd) *n.* **1.** *Physics.* The rate or a measure of the rate of motion, especially: **a.** Distance traveled divided by the time of travel. **b.** The limit of this quotient as the time of travel becomes vanishingly small; the first derivative of distance with respect to time. **c.** The magnitude of a velocity. **2.** Swiftness of action. **3. a.** The act of moving rapidly. **b.** The state of being in rapid motion; rapidity. **4.** A transmission gear or set of gears in a motor vehicle. **5. a.** A numerical expression of the sensitivity of a photographic film, plate, or paper to light. **b.** The capacity of a lens to accumulate light at an appropriate aperture. **c.** The length of time required or permitted for a camera shutter to open and admit light. **6.** *Slang.* Amphetamine. **7.** *Slang.* One that suits or appeals to a person's inclinations, skills, or character: *Living in a large city is not my speed.* **8.** *Archaic.* Prosperity; luck. **—speed** *v.* **sped** (spĕd) or **speed·ed, speed·ing, speeds.** —*tr.* **1.** To cause to go, move, or proceed quickly; hasten. **2.** To increase the speed or rate of; accelerate: *speed up a car; sped production.* **3.** To wish Godspeed to. **4.** To further, promote, or expedite (a legal action, for example). **5.** *Archaic.* To help to succeed or prosper; aid. —*intr.* **1. a.** To go, move, or proceed quickly: *sped to the rescue.* **b.** To drive at a speed exceeding a legal limit: *was speeding on the freeway.* **2.** To pass quickly: *The days sped by. The months have sped along.* **3.** To move, work, or happen at a faster rate; accelerate: *His pulse speeded up.* **4.** *Archaic.* **a.** To prove successful; prosper. **b.** To get along in a specified manner; fare. ***—idiom.* up to speed. 1. a.** Operating at maximum speed. **b.** Producing something or performing at an acceptable rate or level. **2.** *Informal.* Fully informed of or conversant with: *I'm not up to speed on these issues yet.* [Middle English *spede,* from Old English *spēd,* success, swiftness. See **spē-** in Appendix.]

SYNONYMS: *speed, hurry, hasten, quicken, accelerate, precipitate.* These verbs mean to proceed or cause to proceed rapidly or more rapidly. *Speed* refers to swift motion or action: *The train sped through the countryside. Postal workers labored overtime to speed delivery of the Christmas mail. Hurry* implies a markedly faster rate than usual, often with concomitant confusion or com-

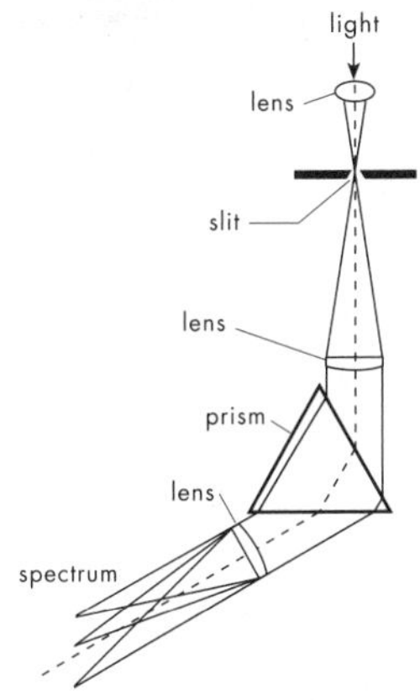

spectroscope

ă pat	oi boy
ā pay	ou out
âr care	ŏŏ took
ä father	ōō boot
ĕ pet	ŭ cut
ē be	ûr urge
ĭ pit	th thin
ī pie	*th* this
îr pier	hw which
ŏ pot	zh vision
ō toe	ə about, item
ô paw	♦ regionalism

Stress marks: ′ (primary); ′ (secondary), as in **dictionary** (dĭk′shə-nĕr′ē)

motion: *If you don't hurry, you'll miss the plane. Don't let anyone hurry you into making a decision you'll regret later. Hasten* suggests urgency and often eager or rash swiftness: *I hasten to respond to your invitation. Put the hot broth in the refrigerator for an hour to hasten cooling. Quicken* and especially *accelerate* refer to increase in rate of activity, growth, or progress: *The dancer's breathing quickened as she approached the end of her solo. The runner quickened his pace as he drew near to the finish line. Despite efforts to eradicate it, corruption persists, though it doesn't accelerate. Heat greatly accelerates the deterioration of perishable foods. Precipitate* implies suddenness or impetuousness that often causes something to happen abruptly or prematurely: *The mere mention of the issue precipitated an outburst of indignation during the meeting.* See also Synonyms at **haste.**

WORD HISTORY: The fable of the tortoise and the hare teaches us that speed does not always spell success. Historically in English, however, it does: the Old English word *spēd,* from which our word *speed* is descended, originally meant "prosperity, successful outcome, ability, or quickness." A corresponding verb, *spēdan,* in Modern English the verb *speed,* meant "to succeed, prosper, or achieve a goal"; and an adjective, *spēdig,* the ancestor of our word *speedy,* meant "wealthy, powerful." Except for archaic uses the words today relate only to the general sense of "velocity." The meaning "success" is retained chiefly in the compound *Godspeed,* a noun formed from the phrase meaning "God prosper you."

speed•ball (spēd′bôl′) *n. Sports.* **1.** A game resembling soccer but differing mainly in that a ball caught on the fly may be passed with the hands and points may be scored by a forward pass over the goal line. **2.** *Slang.* An intravenous dose of cocaine mixed with heroin or an amphetamine.

speed bump

speed•boat (spēd′bōt′) *n. Nautical.* A fast motorboat.

speed•boat•ing (spēd′bō′tĭng) *n. Nautical.* The act or sport of operating a speedboat. **—speed′boat′er** *n.*

speed brake *n.* A flap on an aircraft for decreasing speed while in flight in preparation for landing.

speed bump *n.* An artificial ridge set crosswise into the surface of a street, parking lot, or driveway to make the operators of vehicles decrease speed.

speed•er (spē′dər) *n.* One that speeds, especially a driver who exceeds a legal or safe speed.

speed freak *n. Slang.* A habitual user of stimulant drugs, especially amphetamines or methamphetamine.

speed•ing (spē′dĭng) *adj.* Moving with speed. **—speeding** *n.* The act or an instance of driving especially a motor vehicle faster than is allowed by law.

speed limit *n.* The maximum speed legally permitted on a given stretch of road.

speed•om•e•ter (spĭ-dŏm′ĭ-tər, spē-) *n.* **1.** An instrument for indicating speed. **2.a.** An instrument for indicating distance traveled as well as rate of speed. **b.** An odometer.

speed-read (spēd′rēd′) *v.* **-read** (-rĕd′), **-read•ing, -reads.** *—tr.* To read (a book, newspaper, or magazine, for example) by means of speed-reading. *—intr.* To practice or engage in speed-reading. **—speed′-read′er** *n.*

speed-read•ing (spēd′rē′dĭng) *n.* A method of reading rapidly by assimilating several words or phrases at a glance or by skimming.

speed shop *n. Slang.* An automotive shop that caters to hot rodders.

speed skate *n. Sports.* An ice skate for racing, fitted with a long blade that extends beyond the heel and toe of the sole of the boot. Also called *racing skate.*

speed skat•ing (skā′tĭng) *n. Sports.* Competitive racing on speed skates, usually around an oval course. **—speed skater** *n.*

speed•ster (spēd′stər) *n.* **1.** One who drives very fast. **2.** A fast car.

speed trap *n.* Police officers or electronic devices concealed and deployed on a stretch of road to catch speeding drivers.

speed•up (spēd′ŭp′) *n.* **1.** An increase in speed; acceleration. **2.** A required acceleration of work or production without an increase in pay.

speed walking *n. Sports.* See **race walking.**

speed•way (spēd′wā′) *n.* **1.** *Sports.* A course for automobile or motorcycle racing. **2.** A road designed for fast-moving traffic; an expressway.

Speed•way (spēd′wā′). A town of central Indiana west of Indianapolis. It is the site of the annual Indianapolis 500 auto race. Population, 12,641.

speed•well (spēd′wĕl′) *n.* Any of various plants of the genus *Veronica,* having opposite leaves and clusters of small, usually blue flowers.

speed•writ•ing (spēd′rī′tĭng) *n.* Shorthand that uses letters of the alphabet instead of symbols. **—speed′writ′er** *n.*

speed•y (spē′dē) *adj.* **-i•er, -i•est. 1.** Characterized by rapid motion; swift. **2.** Accomplished or arrived at without delay; prompt. See Synonyms at **fast[1]**. **—speed′i•ly** *adv.* **—speed′i•ness** *n.*

Speer (spîr, shpâr), **Albert.** 1905–1981. German architect and Nazi politician. He was Hitler's architect (1934–1945) and minister of armaments (1942–1945).

speiss (spīs) *n.* An arsenic compound or a mixture of arsenic compounds resulting from the smelting of iron, cobalt, nickel, and copper ores. [German *Speise,* food, speiss, from Middle High German *spīse,* food, from Old High German *spīsa,* probably from Medieval Latin *spēnsa,* storehouse, or *spēsa,* provisions, both from Latin *expēnsa (pecūnia),* (money) paid out. See EXPENSE.]

Speke (spēk), **John Hanning.** 1827–1864. British explorer in Africa. He and Sir Richard Burton were the first Europeans to explore Lake Tanganyika (1858).

spe•le•ol•o•gy (spē′lē-ŏl′ə-jē) *n.* **1.** The scientific study of caves. **2.** Exploration of caves. [French *spéléologie* : Latin *spēlēum,* cave (from Greek *spēlaion*) + *-logie,* -logy.] **—spe′le•o•log′i•cal** (-ə-lŏj′ĭ-kəl) *adj.* **—spe′le•ol′o•gist** *n.*

spell[1] (spĕl) *v.* **spelled** or **spelt** (spĕlt), **spell•ing, spells.** *—tr.* **1.** To name or write in order the letters constituting (a word or part of a word). **2.** To constitute the letters of (a word): *These letters spell* animal. **3.** To add up to; signify: *Their unwise investment could spell financial ruin. —intr.* To form words by means of letters. ***—phrasal verbs.* spell down.** To defeat in a spelling bee. **spell out. 1.** To make perfectly clear and understandable: *asked him to spell out his objectives.* **2.** To read slowly and laboriously. **3.** To puzzle out; comprehend by study. [Middle English *spellen,* to read letter by letter, from Old French *espeller* (of Germanic origin) and from Old English *spellian,* to tell (from *spell,* discourse).]

spell[2] (spĕl) *n.* **1.a.** A word or formula believed to have magic power. **b.** A bewitched state; a trance. **2.** A compelling attraction; charm or fascination: *the spell of the theater.* **—spell** *tr.v.* **spelled, spell•ing, spells.** To put (someone) under a spell; bewitch. [Middle English, discourse, from Old English.]

spell[3] (spĕl) *n.* **1.** A short, indefinite period of time. **2.** *Informal.* A period of weather of a particular kind: *a dry spell.* **3.a.** One's turn at work. **b.** A period of work; a shift. **4.** *Australian.* A period of rest. **5.** *Informal.* A period of physical or mental disorder or distress: *a dizzy spell.* **6.** *Informal.* A short distance. **—spell** *v.* **spelled, spell•ing, spells.** *—tr.* **1.** To relieve (someone) from work temporarily by taking a turn. **2.** To allow to rest a while. *—intr.* **1.** To take turns working. **2.** *Australian.* To rest for a time from an activity. [From Middle English *spelen,* to spare, from Old English *spelian,* to represent, substitute for.]

spell•bind (spĕl′bīnd′) *tr.v.* **-bound** (-bound′), **-bind•ing, -binds.** To hold under or as if under a spell; enchant or fascinate. [Back-formation from SPELLBOUND.] **—spell′bind′ing•ly** *adv.*

spell•bind•er (spĕl′bīn′dər) *n.* One that holds others spellbound, especially an enthralling speaker or a particularly interesting book.

spell•bound (spĕl′bound′) *v.* Past tense of **spellbind. —spellbound** *adj.* Entranced by or as if by a spell; fascinated.

spell•down (spĕl′doun′) *n.* See **spelling bee.**

spell•er (spĕl′ər) *n.* **1.** One who spells words: *students who are good spellers.* **2.** An elementary textbook containing exercises that teach spelling.

spell•ing (spĕl′ĭng) *n. Abbr.* **sp. 1.a.** The forming of words with letters in an accepted order; orthography. **b.** The art or study of orthography. **2.** The way in which a word is spelled.

spelling bee *n.* A contest in which competitors are eliminated as they fail to spell a given word correctly. Also called *spelldown.*

spelt[1] (spĕlt) *n.* A hardy wheat grown mostly in Europe. [Middle English, from Old English, from Late Latin *spelta,* probably of Germanic origin; akin to Middle Dutch *spelte,* wheat.]

spelt[2] (spĕlt) *v.* A past tense and a past participle of **spell[1]**.

spel•ter (spĕl′tər) *n.* Zinc, especially in the form of ingots, slabs, or plates. [Probably of Dutch or Low German origin.]

spe•lunk•er (spĭ-lŭng′kər, spē′lŭng′-) *n.* One who explores and studies caves chiefly as a hobby. [From obsolete *spelunk,* cave, from Middle English, from Old French *spelunque,* from Latin *spēlunca,* from Greek *spēlunx.*] **—spe′lunk′ing** *n.*

spen•cer[1] (spĕn′sər) *n. Nautical.* A trysail. [Perhaps from the name *Spencer.*]

spen•cer[2] (spĕn′sər) *n.* **1.** A short double-breasted overcoat worn by men in the early 19th century. **2.** A close-fitting, waist-length jacket worn by women. [After George John *Spencer,* Second Earl Spencer (1758–1834).]

Spen•cer (spĕn′sər), **Herbert.** 1820–1903. British philosopher who attempted to apply the theory of evolution to philosophy and ethics in his series *Synthetic Philosophy* (1855–1893).

Spencer Gulf. An inlet of the Indian Ocean off south-central Australia between the Eyre and Yorke peninsulas.

Spen•ce•ri•an[1] (spĕn-sîr′ē-ən) *adj.* Of or relating to Herbert Spencer or his philosophy. **—Spencerian** *n.* A follower of Herbert Spencer.

Spen•ce•ri•an[2] (spĕn-sîr′ē-ən) *adj.* Of or relating to an ornate style of writing employing rounded letters slanted to the right. [After Platt Rogers *Spencer* (1800–1864), American handwriting expert.]

Spen•cer•ism (spĕn′sə-rĭz′əm) also **Spen•ce•ri•an•ism** (spĕn-sîr′ē-ə-nĭz′əm) *n.* The system of logical positivism developed by Herbert Spencer, setting forth the idea that evolution is the passage from the simple, indefinite, and incoherent to the complex, definite, and coherent.

spend (spĕnd) *v.* **spent** (spĕnt), **spend•ing, spends.** *—tr.* **1.** To use up or put out; expend: *spent an hour each day exercising.* **2.** To pay out (money). **3.** To wear out; exhaust: *The storm finally spent itself.* **4.** To pass (time) in a specified manner or place: *spent their vacation in Paris.* **5.a.** To throw away; squander:

spent all their creative resources on futile projects. **b.** To give up (one's time or efforts, for example) to a cause; sacrifice. —*intr.* **1.** To pay out or expend money. **2.** To be exhausted or consumed. [Middle English *spenden,* partly from Old English *-spendan* (from Latin *expendere,* to expend; see EXPEND) and partly from Old French *despendre,* to weigh out; see DISPENSE.] **—spend′a·ble** *adj.* **—spend′er** *n.*

SYNONYMS: *spend, disburse, expend.* The central meaning shared by these verbs is "to pay or give out money or an equivalent in return for something": *spent five dollars for a movie ticket; disbursing funds from the corporate account; expending energy on a project.*
ANTONYM: *save.*

Spen·der (spĕn′dər), Sir **Stephen Harold.** Born 1909. British writer whose poetry reflects personal emotional responses to social and political injustices. His works include the collection *The Still Center* (1939) and *Generous Days* (1971).

spend·ing money (spĕn′dĭng) *n.* Cash for small personal needs.

spend·thrift (spĕnd′thrĭft′) *n.* One who spends money recklessly or wastefully. **—spendthrift** *adj.* Wasteful or extravagant: *spendthrift bureaucrats.* [SPEND + THRIFT, accumulated wealth (obsolete).]

Speng·ler (spĕng′lər, -glər, shpĕng′-), **Oswald.** 1880–1936. German philosopher who argued that civilizations and cultures are subject to the same cycle of growth and decay as human beings. His major work is *The Decline of the West* (1918–1922).

Spen·ser (spĕn′sər), **Edmund.** 1552?–1599. English poet known chiefly for his allegorical epic romance *The Faerie Queene* (1590–1596). His other works include the pastoral *Shepeardes Calendar* (1579) and the lyrical marriage poem Epithalamion (1595). **—Spen·se′ri·an** (spĕn-sîr′ē-ən) *adj.*

Spenserian sonnet *n.* A sonnet form composed of three quatrains and a couplet in iambic pentameter with the rhyme scheme *abab bcbc cdcd ee.*

Spenserian stanza *n.* A stanza consisting of eight lines of iambic pentameter and a final alexandrine, rhymed *ababbcbcc,* first used by Edmund Spenser in *The Faerie Queene.*

spent (spĕnt) *v.* Past tense and past participle of **spend.** **—spent** *adj.* **1.** Used up; consumed: *a spent youth.* **2.** Having come to an end; passed: *a spent era of opulence.* **3.** Depleted of energy, force, or strength; exhausted: *At the end of the hot day the spent workers slept under a shady tree.* **4.** *Nautical.* Of or relating to a vessel at the end of a voyage, with fuel, stores, and water consumed and cargo discharged.

sperm[1] (spûrm) *n., pl.* **sperm** or **sperms. 1.** A male gamete or reproductive cell; a spermatozoon. **2.** Semen. [Middle English *sperme,* semen, from Old French *esperme,* from Late Latin *sperma,* from Greek. See **sper-** in Appendix.] **—sperm′ous** *adj.*

sperm[2] (spûrm) *n.* A substance, such as spermaceti, associated with the sperm whale. [Short for SPERMACETI.]

sperm– *pref.* Variant of **spermi–.**

–sperm *suff.* Seed: *endosperm.* [Greek *-spermos,* from *sperma,* seed. See SPERM[1].]

sperma– *pref.* Variant of **spermi–.**

sper·ma·ce·ti (spûr′mə-sē′tē, -sĕt′ē) *n., pl.* **-tis.** A white, waxy substance consisting of various esters of fatty acids, obtained from the head of the sperm whale or another cetacean and used for making candles, ointments, and cosmetics. [Middle English, from Medieval Latin *spermacētī* : Late Latin *sperma,* semen; see SPERM[1] + Latin *cētī,* genitive of *cētus,* whale; see CETUS.]

sper·ma·go·ni·um also **sper·mo·go·ni·um** (spûr′mə-gō′nē-əm) *n., pl.* **-ni·a** (-nē-ə). *Botany.* A cup-shaped cavity or receptacle in which the spermatia of certain lichens and fungi are produced. [New Latin : *sperma,* sperm; see SPERM[1] + *-gonium,* seed, cell (from Greek *gonos,* seed; see GONO–).]

sper·ma·ry (spûr′mə-rē) *n., pl.* **-ries.** An organ or a gland in which male gametes are formed, especially in invertebrate animals. [New Latin *spermārium,* from Late Latin *sperma,* semen. See SPERM[1].]

spermat– *pref.* Variant of **spermato–.**

sper·ma·tan·gi·um (spûr′mə-tăn′jē-əm) *n., pl.* **-gi·a** (-jē-ə). A structure that produces spermatia in red algae. [New Latin : SPERMAT(IUM) + *-angium,* vessel (from Greek *angeion*).]

sper·ma·the·ca (spûr′mə-thē′kə) *n.* A receptacle in the reproductive tracts of certain female invertebrates, especially insects, in which spermatozoa are received and stored until needed to fertilize the ova. [Late Latin *sperma,* semen; see SPERM[1] + THECA.] **—sper′ma·the′cal** *adj.*

sper·ma·ti·a (spər-mā′shē-ə, -shə) *n.* Plural of **spermatium.**

sper·mat·ic (spər-măt′ĭk) *adj.* **1.** Of, relating to, or resembling sperm: *a spermatic substance; a spermatic filament.* **2.** Containing, conveying, or producing sperm: *the spermatic duct.* **3.** Of or relating to a spermary.

spermatic cord *n.* A cordlike structure, consisting of the vas deferens and its accompanying arteries, veins, nerves, and lymphatic vessels, that passes from the abdominal cavity through the inguinal canal down into the scrotum to the back of the testicle.

sper·ma·tid (spûr′mə-tĭd) *n.* Any of the four haploid cells formed by meiosis in a male organism that develop into spermatozoa without further division.

sper·ma·ti·um (spər-mā′shē-əm, -shəm) *n., pl.* **-ti·a** (-shē-ə, -shə). A nonmotile cell in red algae and certain lichens and fungi that functions as a male gamete. [New Latin, from Greek *spermation,* diminutive of *sperma, spermat-,* semen. See SPERM[1].] **—sper·ma′tial** (-shəl) *adj.*

spermato– or **spermat–** *pref.* **1.** Seed: *spermatophyte.* **2. a.** Sperm: *spermatic.* **b.** Spermatozoon: *spermatophore.* [Greek, from *sperma, spermat-,* seed. See SPERM[1].]

sper·mat·o·cide (spər-măt′ə-sīd′, spûr′mə-tə-) *n.* See **spermicide. —sper·mat′o·cid′al** (-sīd′l) *adj.*

sper·mat·o·cyte (spər-măt′ə-sīt′, spûr′mə-tə-) *n.* A diploid cell that undergoes meiosis to form four spermatids. A primary spermatocyte divides into two secondary spermatocytes, which in turn divide to form the spermatids.

sper·mat·o·gen·e·sis (spər-măt′ə-jĕn′ĭ-sĭs, spûr′mə-tə-) *n.* Formation and development of spermatozoa by meiosis and spermiogenesis. **—sper·mat′o·ge·net′ic** (-jə-nĕt′ĭk), **sper·mat′o·gen′ic** (-jĕn′ĭk) *adj.*

sper·mat·o·go·ni·um (spər-măt′ə-gō′nē-əm, spûr′mə-tə-) *n., pl.* **-ni·a** (-nē-ə). Any of the cells of the gonads in male organisms that are the progenitors of spermatocytes. [New Latin : SPERMATO– + *-gonium,* seed; see SPERMAGONIUM.] **—sper·mat′o·go′ni·al** (-nē-əl) *adj.*

sper·mat·o·phore (spər-măt′ə-fôr′, -fōr′, spûr′mə-tə-) *n.* A capsule or compact mass of spermatozoa extruded by the males of certain invertebrates and primitive vertebrates and directly transferred to the reproductive parts of the female. **—sper′ma·toph′o·ral** (spûr′mə-tŏf′ər-əl) *adj.*

sper·mat·o·phyte (spər-măt′ə-fīt′, spûr′mə-tə-) *n.* A seed-bearing plant, such as a conifer or a flowering plant. **—sper·mat′o·phyt′ic** (-fĭt′ĭk) *adj.*

sper·mat·or·rhe·a also **sper·mat·or·rhoe·a** (spər-măt′ə-rē′ə, spûr′mə-tə-) *n.* Involuntary discharge of semen without orgasm.

sper·mat·o·zo·a (spər-măt′ə-zō′ə, spûr′mə-tə-) *n.* Plural of **spermatozoon.**

sper·mat·o·zo·id (spər-măt′ə-zō′ĭd, spûr′mə-tə-) *n.* A ciliated male gamete produced in an antheridium. [SPERMATOZO(ON) + –ID.]

sper·mat·o·zo·on (spər-măt′ə-zō′ŏn′, -ən, spûr′mə-tə-) *n., pl.* **-zo·a** (-zō′ə). The mature fertilizing gamete of a male organism, usually consisting of a round or cylindrical nucleated cell, a short neck, and a thin, motile tail. Also called *sperm cell, zoosperm.* **—sper·mat′o·zo′al** (-zō′əl), **sper·mat′o·zo′an** (-zō′ən), **sper·mat′o·zo′ic** (-zō′ĭk) *adj.*

spermi– or **sperma–** or **spermo–** or **sperm–** *pref.* **1.** Seed: *spermophile.* **2.** Sperm: *spermine.* [Greek *spermo-, sperm-,* from *sperma,* seed. See SPERM[1].]

sper·mi·cide (spûr′mĭ-sīd′) *n.* An agent that kills spermatozoa, especially one used as a contraceptive. Also called *spermatocide.* **—sper′mi·cid′al** (-sīd′l) *adj.*

sper·mi·dine (spûr′mĭ-dēn′) *n.* A polyamine compound, $C_7H_{19}N_3$, found in ribosomes and living tissues and having various metabolic functions. It was originally isolated from semen. [SPERM(I)– + –ID(E) + –INE[2].]

sper·mine (spûr′mēn′) *n.* A crystalline polyamine compound, $C_{10}H_{26}N_4$, present in ribosomes and found widely in living tissues along with spermidine. It was originally isolated from semen.

sper·mi·o·gen·e·sis (spûr′mē-ō-jĕn′ĭ-sĭs) *n.* Transformation of a spermatid into a spermatozoon. [New Latin *spermium,* spermatozoon (probably from Late Latin *sperma,* semen; see SPERM[1]) + –GENESIS.] **—sper′mi·o·ge·net′ic** (-jə-nĕt′ĭk) *adj.*

spermo– *pref.* Variant of **spermi–.**

sper·mo·go·ni·um (spûr′mə-gō′nē-əm) *n. Botany.* Variant of **spermagonium.**

sperm oil *n.* A yellow, waxy oil obtained from the head of the sperm whale and used as an industrial lubricant.

sperm·o·phile (spûr′mə-fīl′) *n.* The ground squirrel.

sperm whale *n.* Any of several large, toothed whales of the family *Physeteridae,* especially *Physeter catadon* or *P. macrocephalus,* of tropical and temperate oceans, whose massive head has a cavity containing sperm oil and spermaceti and whose long intestines often contain ambergris. Also called *cachalot.*

Sper·ry (spĕr′ē), **Elmer Ambrose.** 1860–1930. American engineer and inventor of numerous electrical devices, including the gyrocompass, a nonmagnetic navigational aid (1910).

sper·ry·lite (spĕr′ĭ-līt′) *n.* A white crystalline platinum mineral, essentially $PtAs_2$. [After Francis L. *Sperry,* 19th-century Canadian chemist.]

spes·sar·tite (spĕs′ər-tīt′) also **spes·sar·tine** (-tēn′) *n.* A red to brownish-red mineral of the garnet group, $Mn_3Al_2(SiO_4)_3$. [French, after *Spessart,* a hilly area of central Germany.]

spew (spyo͞o) *v.* **spewed, spew·ing, spews.** —*tr.* **1.** To send or force out in or as if in a stream; eject forcefully or in large amounts: *a volcano that spewed molten lava; spewed invective at his opponent.* **2.** To vomit or otherwise cast out through the mouth. —*intr.* **1.** To flow or gush forth: *Water was spewing from the hydrant.* **2.** To vomit. **—spew** *n.* Something spewed. [Middle English *spewen,* from Old English *spīwan.*] **—spew′er** *n.*

Spey·er (spīr, spī′ər, shpī′ər) also **Spires** (spīrz). A city of

ă pat	oi boy
ā pay	ou out
âr care	o͝o took
ä father	o͞o boot
ĕ pet	ŭ cut
ē be	ûr urge
ĭ pit	th thin
ī pie	*th* this
îr pier	hw which
ŏ pot	zh vision
ō toe	ə about, item
ô paw	♦ regionalism

Stress marks: ′ (primary); ′ (secondary), as in **dictionary** (dĭk′shə-nĕr′ē)

southwest West Germany on the Rhine River. It became a free imperial city in 1111. Population, 43,748.

SPF also **spf** *abbr.* Sun protection factor.

sp gr *abbr.* Specific gravity.

sphag·num (sfăg′nəm) *n.* Any of various pale or ashy mosses of the genus *Sphagnum,* the decomposed remains of which form peat. [New Latin, from Latin *sphagnos,* a kind of moss, from Greek, a kind of shrub.] **—sphag′nous** *adj.*

sphal·er·ite (sfăl′ə-rīt′) *n.* The primary ore of zinc, occurring in usually yellow-brown or brownish-black crystals or cleavage masses, essentially ZnS with some cadmium, iron, and manganese. Also called *blende, zinc blende.* [Greek *sphaleros,* slippery, deceitful (from *sphallein,* to trip, from its being easily mistaken for galena) + -ITE[1].]

sphen– *pref.* Variant of **spheno–.**

sphene (sfēn) *n.* A titanium accessory mineral in some granite and metamorphic rocks, $CaTiSiO_5$, occurring in usually small brown or yellow crystals and sometimes used as a gemstone. Also called *titanite.* [French *sphène,* from Greek *sphēn,* wedge.]

sphe·nic (sfē′nĭk) *adj.* Shaped like a wedge.

spheno– or **sphen–** *pref.* Wedge; wedge-shaped: *sphenodon.* [Greek *sphēno-,* from *sphēn,* wedge.]

sphe·no·don (sfē′nə-dŏn′, sfĕn′ə-) *n.* See **tuatara.**

sphe·no·gram (sfē′nə-grăm′, sfĕn′ə-) *n.* A cuneiform character.

sphe·noid (sfē′noid′) *n.* The sphenoid bone. **—sphenoid** *adj.* **1.** Wedge-shaped. **2.** Of or relating to the sphenoid bone. **—sphe·noi′dal** (-noid′l) *adj.*

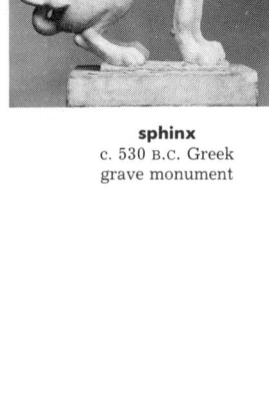

sphinx
c. 530 B.C. Greek grave monument

sphenoid bone *n.* A compound bone with winglike processes, situated at the base of the skull.

spher– *pref.* Variant of **sphero–.**

spher·al (sfîr′əl) *adj.* **1.** Of, relating to, or having the shape of a sphere; spherical. **2.** Symmetrical.

sphere (sfîr) *n.* **1.** *Mathematics.* A three-dimensional surface, all points of which are equidistant from a fixed point. **2.** A spherical object or figure. **3.** A celestial body, such as a planet or star. **4.** The sky, appearing as a hemisphere to an observer: *the sphere of the heavens.* **5.** Any of a series of concentric, transparent, revolving globes that together were once thought to contain the moon, sun, planets, and stars. **6.** The extent of a person's knowledge, interests, or social position. **7.** An area of power, control, or influence; domain. See Synonyms at **field. —sphere** *tr.v.* **sphered, spher·ing, spheres. 1.** To form into a sphere. **2.** To put in or within a sphere. **3.** To surround or encompass. [Middle English *spere,* from Old French *espere,* from Latin *sphaera,* from Greek *sphaira.*] **—sphe·ric′i·ty** (sfĭ-rĭs′ĭ-tē) *n.*

sphere of influence *n., pl.* **spheres of influence.** A territorial area over which political or economic influence is wielded by one nation.

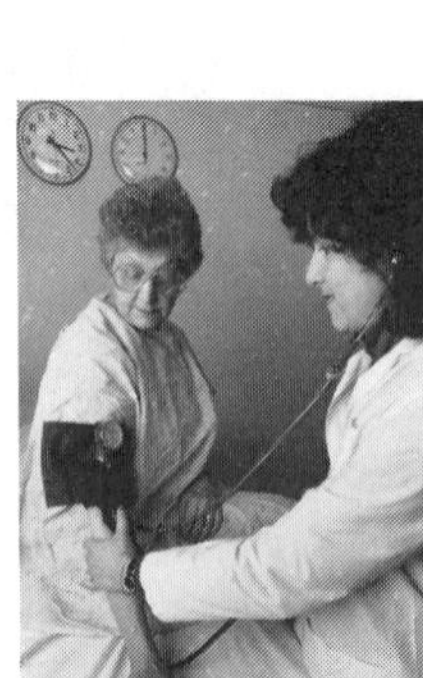

sphygmomanometer

spher·i·cal (sfîr′ĭ-kəl, sfĕr′-) also **spher·ic** (-ĭk) *adj.* **1.a.** Having the shape of a sphere; globular. **b.** Having a shape approximating that of a sphere. **2.** Of or relating to a sphere. **3.** Of or relating to celestial bodies. **—spher′i·cal·ly** *adv.* **—spher′i·cal·ness** *n.*

spherical aberration *n.* A blurred image that occurs when light from the margin of a lens or mirror with a spherical surface comes to a shorter focus than light from the central portion.

spherical angle *n.* *Mathematics.* The angle formed at the intersection of the arcs of two great circles.

spher·i·cal-co·or·di·nate system (sfîr′ĭ-kəl-kō-ôr′dn-ĭt, -āt′, sfĕr′-) *n.* *Mathematics.* A three-dimensional system for locating points in space by means of a radius vector and two angles measured from the center of a sphere with respect to two arbitrary, fixed, perpendicular directions.

spherical excess *n.* *Mathematics.* The difference between the sum of the angles of a spherical triangle and the sum of the angles of a plane triangle.

spherical geometry *n.* *Mathematics.* The geometry of circles, angles, and figures on the surface of a sphere.

spherical polygon *n.* A part of a spherical surface that is bounded by arcs of three or more great circles.

spherical triangle *n.* A triangle the three sides of which are arcs of great circles.

spherical trigonometry *n.* *Mathematics.* The modified form of trigonometry applied to spherical triangles.

spher·ics[1] (sfîr′ĭks, sfĕr′-) *n.* *(used with a sing. verb). Mathematics.* **1.** Spherical geometry. **2.** Spherical trigonometry.

spher·ics[2] (sfîr′ĭks, sfĕr′-) *n.* Variant of **sferics.**

sphero– or **spher–** *pref.* Sphere: *spherometer.* [Latin *sphaero-,* from Greek *sphairo-,* from *sphaira,* sphere.]

sphe·roid (sfîr′oid′, sfĕr′-) *n.* A body that is shaped like a sphere but is not perfectly round, especially an ellipsoid that is generated by revolving an ellipse around one of its axes. **—sphe·roi′dal** (-oid′l), **sphe·roi′dic** (-oi′dĭk) *adj.* **—sphe·roi′dal·ly** *adv.* **—sphe′roi·dic′i·ty** (-dĭs′ĭ-tē) *n.*

sphe·rom·e·ter (sfĭ-rŏm′ĭ-tər) *n.* An instrument for measuring the curvature of a surface, as of a sphere or cylinder.

spher·o·plast (sfîr′ə-plăst′, sfĕr′-) *n.* A bacterial cell whose cell wall is absent or deficient, causing it to have a spherical form.

spher·ule (sfîr′o͞ol, -yo͞ol, sfĕr′-) *n.* A miniature sphere; a globule. [Late Latin *sphaerula,* diminutive of Latin *sphaera,* ball. See SPHERE.] **—spher′u·lar** (sfîr′yə-lər, sfĕr′-) *adj.*

spher·u·lite (sfîr′yə-līt′, -ə-līt′, sfĕr′-) *n.* A small, usually spheroid body consisting of radiating crystals, found in obsidian and other glassy lava rocks. **—spher′u·lit′ic** (-lĭt′ĭk) *adj.*

spher·y (sfîr′ē) *adj.* **-i·er, -i·est. 1.** Of or relating to the celestial spheres. **2.** Resembling a celestial body.

sphinc·ter (sfĭngk′tər) *n.* A ringlike muscle that normally maintains constriction of a body passage or orifice and that relaxes as required by normal physiological functioning. [Late Latin *sphinctēr,* from Greek *sphinktēr,* from *sphingein,* to bind tight.] **—sphinc′ter·al** *adj.*

sphin·ges (sfĭn′jēz′) *n.* A plural of **sphinx.**

sphin·gid (sfĭn′jĭd) *n.* A moth of the family Sphingidae; a hawk moth. **—sphingid** *adj.* Of or belonging to the family Sphingidae. [From New Latin *Sphingidae,* family name, from *Sphinx,* type genus, from Latin, sphinx. See SPHINX.]

sphin·go·sine (sfĭng′gə-sēn′) *n.* A basic, long-chain, unsaturated amino alcohol, $C_{18}H_{37}NO_2$, found combined with lipids in the brain and in nerve tissue. [Greek *sphingos,* genitive of *sphinx,* sphinx + -INE[2].]

sphinx (sfĭngks) *n., pl.* **sphinx·es** or **sphin·ges** (sfĭn′jēz′). **1.** *Mythology.* A figure in Egyptian myth having the body of a lion and the head of a man, ram, or hawk. **2.** *Greek Mythology.* A winged creature having the head of a woman and the body of a lion, noted for killing those who could not answer its riddle. **3.** A puzzling or mysterious person. [Middle English *Spynx,* from Latin *Sphinx,* from Greek.]

sphinx moth *n.* See **hawk moth.**

sphra·gis·tics (sfrə-jĭs′tĭks) *n.* *(used with a sing. verb).* The study of seals and signets. [French *sphragistique,* from Late Greek *sphragistikos,* of seals, from Greek *sphragistos,* stamped, sealed, from *sphragis,* seal.]

sp ht *abbr.* Specific heat.

sphygm– *pref.* Variant of **sphygmo–.**

sphyg·mic (sfĭg′mĭk) *adj.* *Physiology.* Of or relating to the pulse.

sphygmo– or **sphygm–** *pref.* Pulse: *sphygmograph.* [Greek *sphugmo-,* from *sphugmos,* pulsation, from *sphuzein, sphug-,* to throb.]

sphyg·mo·gram (sfĭg′mə-grăm′) *n.* The record or tracing produced by a sphygmograph.

sphyg·mo·graph (sfĭg′mə-grăf′) *n.* An instrument for graphically recording the form, strength, and variations of the arterial pulse. **—sphyg′mo·graph′ic** *adj.* **—sphyg·mog′ra·phy** (-mŏg′rə-fē) *n.*

sphyg·moid (sfĭg′moid′) *adj.* *Physiology.* Resembling a pulse.

sphyg·mo·ma·nom·e·ter (sfĭg′mō-mə-nŏm′ĭ-tər) also **sphyg·mom·e·ter** (sfĭg-mŏm′ĭ-tər) *n.* An instrument for measuring blood pressure in the arteries, especially one consisting of a pressure gauge and a rubber cuff that wraps around the upper arm and inflates to constrict the arteries. **—sphyg′mo·man′o·met′ric** (-măn′ə-mĕt′rĭk) *adj.* **—sphyg′mo·man′o·met′ri·cal·ly** *adv.* **—sphyg′mo·ma·nom′e·try** *n.*

spic also **spick** (spĭk) *n.* *Offensive Slang.* Used as a disparaging term for a Hispanic person. [Alteration of obsolete *spig,* a Mexican, short for *spiggoty,* perhaps from an accented pronunciation of *(No) speak the (English).*]

spi·ca (spī′kə) *n., pl.* **-cae** (-kē, -sē) or **-cas.** A bandage applied in overlapping opposite spirals to immobilize a digit or limb. [Latin *spīca,* ear of grain (from its shape).]

Spi·ca (spī′kə) *n.* A spectroscopic binary star, 245 light-years from Earth, one of the brightest stars in the sky and the brightest star in the constellation Virgo. [Latin *Spīca;* from *spīca,* ear of grain.]

spi·cae (spī′kē, -sē) *n.* A plural of **spica.**

spic-and-span (spĭk′ən-spăn′) *adj.* Variant of **spick-and-span.**

spi·cate (spī′kāt′) *adj.* Borne in or forming a spike. [Latin *spīcātus,* from *spīca,* ear of grain.]

spic·ca·to (spĭ-kä′tō) *Music. n., pl.* **-tos.** A technique of bowing in which the bow is made to bounce slightly from the string. **—spiccato** *adj.* Of or employing spiccato. [Italian, past participle of *spiccare,* to separate : *s-,* from (from Latin *ex-;* see EX–) + *piccare,* to pierce, impale (from Vulgar Latin **piccāre;* see PICK[1]).]

spice (spīs) *n.* **1.a.** Any of various pungent, aromatic plant substances, such as cinnamon or nutmeg, used to flavor foods or beverages. **b.** These substances considered as a group. **2.** Something that adds zest or flavor. **3.** A pungent aroma; a perfume. **—spice** *tr.v.* **spiced, spic·ing, spic·es. 1.** To season with spices. **2.** To add zest or flavor to. [Middle English, from Old French *espice,* from Late Latin *speciēs,* wares, spices, from Latin, kind. See SPECIES.]

spice·ber·ry (spīs′bĕr′ē) *n.* **1.** An eastern Asian shrub *(Ardisia crenata)* having numerous, long-lasting, coral-red fleshy fruit. **2.** Coralberry.

spice·bush (spīs′bo͝osh′) *n.* An aromatic deciduous shrub *(Lindera benzoin)* of eastern North America, having clusters of early-blooming small yellow flowers.

spicebush swallowtail *n.* A large swallowtail *(Papilio troilus)* of eastern North America that feeds on spicebushes, having dark forewings with yellow marginal spots and bluish-green hindwings.

Spice Islands (spīs). See **Moluccas.**

spic·er·y (spī′sə-rē) *n., pl.* **-ies. 1.** Spices considered as a group. **2.** The aromatic or pungent quality of spices. **3.** *Archaic.* A place where spices are stored.

spick (spĭk) *n. Offensive Slang.* Variant of **spic.**

spick-and-span also **spic-and-span** (spĭk′ən-spăn′) *adj.* **1.** Immaculately clean; spotless. See Synonyms at **neat**[1]. **2.** Brand-new; fresh. [Short for obsolete *spick and span-new* : *spick,* spike (variant of SPIKE[1]) + SPAN-NEW.]

spic·u·la[1] (spĭk′yə-lə) *n.* Plural of **spiculum.**

spic·u·la[2] (spĭk′yə-lə) *n.* Variant of **spicule.**

spic·u·lae (spĭk′yə-lē) *n.* A plural of **spicule.**

spic·u·la·tion (spĭk′yə-lā′shən) *n.* Formation into a spicule or spicules.

spic·ule (spĭk′yo͞ol) also **spic·u·la** (-yə-lə) *n., pl.* **-ules** also **-u·lae** (-yə-lē). A small needlelike structure or part, such as one of the silicate or calcium carbonate processes supporting the soft tissue of certain invertebrates, especially sponges. [Latin *spīculum.* See SPICULUM.] **—spic′u·lar** (-yə-lər), **spic′u·late** (-yə-lĭt, -lāt′) *adj.*

spic·u·lum (spĭk′yə-ləm) *n., pl.* **-la** (-lə). A spicule or similar needlelike structure, such as a spine of an echinoderm or a copulatory organ in a nematode. [Latin *spīculum,* diminutive of *spīca,* point, ear of grain.]

spic·y (spī′sē) *adj.* **-i·er, -i·est. 1.** Having the flavor, aroma, or quality of spice. **2.** Piquant; zesty: *a spicy tomato sauce.* **3.** High-spirited; lively. **4.** Slightly scandalous; risqué: *a spicy Hollywood romance.* **—spic′i·ly** *adv.* **—spic′i·ness** *n.*

♦ **spi·der** (spī′dər) *n.* **1.** Any of numerous arachnids of the order Araneae, having a body divided into a cephalothorax bearing eight legs, two poison fangs, and two feelers and an unsegmented abdomen bearing several spinnerets that produce the silk used to make nests, cocoons, or webs for trapping insects. **2.** One that resembles a spider, as in appearance, character, or movement. **3.** *New England, Upper Northern & South Atlantic U.S.* See **frying pan.** See Regional Note at **frying pan. 4.** A trivet. [Middle English *spither,* from Old English *spīthra.* See **(s)pen-** in Appendix.]

spider crab *n.* Any of various crabs, such as those of the genera *Libinia* and *Macrocheira,* having long legs and a relatively small triangular body.

spider flower *n.* See **cleome.**

spider lily *n.* **1.** Any of various bulbous, lilylike tropical American plants of the genus *Hymenocallis,* having narrow leaves and umbels of white flowers. **2.** See **crinum.**

spider mite *n.* See **red spider.**

spider monkey *n.* Any of several tropical American monkeys of the genus *Ateles,* having long legs and a long prehensile tail and lacking a thumb.

spi·der·wort (spī′dər-wûrt′, -wôrt′) *n.* Any of various New World herbs of the genus *Tradescantia,* especially *T. virginiana,* having three-petaled blue or purple flowers with six hairy stamens. [Probably from its thin, hairy stamens.]

spi·der·y (spī′də-rē) *adj.* **1.a.** Resembling a spider in form, characteristics, or behavior. **b.** Resembling a spider's web; very fine: *spidery handwriting.* **2.** Infested with spiders.

spied (spīd) *v.* Past tense and past participle of **spy.**

spie·gel (spē′gəl) *n.* Spiegeleisen. [Short for SPIEGELEISEN.]

spie·gel·ei·sen (spē′gə-lī′zən) *n.* An alloy of iron containing approximately 15 percent manganese and small quantities of carbon and silicon, used in the Bessemer process. [German : *Spiegel,* mirror (from Middle High German *spiegel,* from Old High German *spiagal,* from Latin *speculum;* see SPECULUM) + *Eisen,* iron (from Middle High German *īsen,* from Old High German *īsan;* see **eis-** in Appendix).]

spiel (spēl, shpēl) *Informal. n.* A lengthy, usually extravagant speech or argument intended to persuade: *"I made my spiel about how I could add to this company"* (Carl Icahn). **—spiel** *v.* **spieled, spiel·ing, spiels. —spiel** *intr. & tr.v.* To talk or say (something) at length or extravagantly. [German, play, or Yiddish *shpil,* both from Middle High German *spil,* from Old High German.] **—spiel′er** *n.*

Spiel·berg (spēl′bûrg′), **Steven.** Born 1947. American film director whose works include *Raiders of the Lost Ark* (1981) and *E.T.* (1982).

spies (spīz) *n.* Plural of **spy. —spies** *v.* Third person singular present tense of **spy.**

spiff (spĭf) *Informal. tr.v.* **spiffed, spiff·ing, spiffs.** To make attractive, stylish, or up-to-date: *spiffed up the the old storefront.* **—spiff** *n.* Attractiveness or charm in appearance, dress, or manners: *"He may need more than spiff to get him through the bad patches ahead"* (James Wolcott). [Possibly from dialectal *spiff,* well-dressed.]

spiff·y (spĭf′ē) *Informal. adj.* **-i·er, -i·est.** Smart in appearance or dress; stylish. **—spiffy** *tr.v.* **-ied, -y·ing, -ies.** To make attractive, stylish, or up-to-date: *spiffying up my wardrobe.* [Possibly from dialectal *spiff,* dandified.] **—spiff′i·ly** *adv.* **—spiff′i·ness** *n.*

spig·ot (spĭg′ət) *n.* **1.** A faucet. **2.** A wooden faucet placed in the bunghole of a cask. **3.** The vent plug of a cask. [Middle English, perhaps from Old French **espigot,* diminutive of Old Provençal *espiga,* ear of grain, from Latin *spīca.*]

spike[1] (spīk) *n.* **1.a.** A long, thick, sharp-pointed piece of wood or metal. **b.** A heavy nail. **2.** A sharp-pointed projection along the top of a fence or wall. **3.a.** One of several sharp metal projections set in the sole or in the sole and heel of an athletic shoe for grip. **b.** A pair of athletic shoes having such projections. **4. spikes.** A pair of spike heels. **5.** An unbranched antler of a young deer. **6.** A young mackerel of small size, usually 15 centimeters (6 inches) or less in length. **7.** A sharp rise followed by a sharp decline in a graph or in the tracing of a scientific instrument. **8.a.** *Sports.* The act of driving a volleyball at a sharp angle into the opponent's court by jumping near the net and hitting the ball down hard from above. **b.** *Football.* The act of slamming the ball to the ground after succeeding in an important play, as after scoring a touchdown. **—spike** *tr.v.* **spiked, spik·ing, spikes. 1.** To secure or provide with a spike. **2.** To impale, pierce, or injure with a spike. **3.** *Informal.* To put an end to; block: *spike a rumor.* **4.** *Informal.* To add alcoholic liquor to: *The punch was spiked with rum.* **5.** *Sports.* To drive (a ball) in a spike. **6.** To render (a muzzleloading gun) useless by driving a spike into the vent. [Middle English, from Old Norse *spīk.*] **—spiked** *adj.*

spike[2] (spīk) *n.* **1.** An ear of grain, as of wheat. **2.** *Botany.* A usually elongated, unbranched inflorescence with stalkless flowers arranged along an axis. [Middle English, from Latin *spīca.*]

spike heel *n.* **1.** A very thin high heel used on a woman's shoe. **2.** A woman's shoe with a very thin high heel.

spike lavender *n.* An aromatic Mediterranean plant *(Lavandula latifolia)* of the mint family, yielding an oil similar to that of true lavender.

spike·let (spīk′lĭt) *n.* A small or secondary spike, characteristic of grasses and sedges, having a varying number of reduced flowers each subtended by one or two scalelike bracts.

spike·nard (spīk′närd′) *n.* **1.** An aromatic perennial herb *(Nardostachys jatamansi)* of the Himalaya Mountains, having rose-purple flowers. Also called *nard.* **2.** An ointment of antiquity, probably prepared from this aromatic plant of India. **3.** A North American plant *(Aralia racemosa)* having small greenish flowers, aromatic roots, and bipinnately compound leaves. [Middle English, from Anglo-Norman, from Medieval Latin *spīca nardī* : Latin *spīca,* spike, ear + Latin *nardī,* genitive of *nardus,* nard.]

spik·y (spī′kē) *adj.* **-i·er, -i·est. 1.** Having one or more projecting sharp points. **2.** Grouchy or cross in temperament. **—spik′i·ly** *adv.* **—spik′i·ness** *n.*

spile (spīl) *n.* **1.** A post used as a foundation; a pile. **2.** A wooden plug; a bung. **3.** A spigot used in taking sap from a tree. **—spile** *tr.v.* **spiled, spil·ing, spiles.** To support, plug, or tap with a spile. [Dutch *spijl,* wooden pin, from Middle Dutch *spīle.*]

spill[1] (spĭl) *v.* **spilled** or **spilt** (spĭlt), **spill·ing, spills.** *—tr.* **1.** To cause or allow (a substance) to run or fall out of a container. **2.** To scatter (objects) from containment: *spilled the armload of books on the desk.* **3.** To shed (blood). **4.** *Nautical.* **a.** To relieve the pressure of wind on (a sail). **b.** To cause or allow (wind) to be lost from a sail. **5.** To cause to fall: *The rider was spilled by his horse.* **6.** *Informal.* To disclose (something previously unknown); divulge: *The witness spilled all the details about the suspect.* *—intr.* **1.** To run or fall out of a container or containment. **2.** To come to the ground suddenly and involuntarily. **3.** To pour out or spread beyond limits: *Fans spilled onto the playing field.* **—spill** *n.* **1.** The act of spilling. **2.** An amount spilled. **3.** A fall, as from a horse. **4.** A spillway. [Middle English *spillen,* to shed blood, to spill, from Old English *spillan,* to kill.] **—spill′er** *n.*

WORD HISTORY: One is not supposed to cry over spilled milk, but at one time the word *spill* was associated with many tears. Old English *spillan,* the ancestor of Modern English *spill,* had meanings such as "to destroy, mutilate, kill." The hints of its future life in connection with substances falling out of containers, often wastefully, were contained in the senses "to waste" and "to shed blood." But many people, castles, and fortunes were "spilled" before people started spilling milk, at least judging from the recorded evidence. *Spill* is first recorded in the sense "to cause a substance to fall out of a container" in a work composed in the 14th century. Since then, much water, milk, and gravy have been spilled, while most of the senses having to do with destruction and bloodshed have become obsolete or archaic.

spill[2] (spĭl) *n.* **1.** A piece of wood or rolled paper used to light a fire. **2.** A small peg or rod, especially one used as a plug; a spile. [Middle English *spille.*]

spill·age (spĭl′ĭj) *n.* **1.** The act of spilling. **2.** An amount spilled.

Spil·lane (spə-lān′), **Mickey.** Born 1918. American writer known for his violent detective novels that feature the hard-boiled detective Mike Hammer.

spill·back (spĭl′băk′) *n.* Arrested traffic flow in which vehicles that are stopped partway through an intersection because of a blockage ahead prevent crossing traffic from moving.

spil·li·kin (spĭl′ĭ-kĭn) *n. Games.* **1. spillikins** *(used with a sing. verb).* The game of jackstraws. **2.** One of the straws used in playing jackstraws. [Probably alteration of Flemish *spelleken,* diminutive of *spelle,* pin, from Middle Flemish, ultimately from Medieval Latin *spīnula,* diminutive of Latin *spīna,* thorn.]

spill·o·ver (spĭl′ō′vər) *n.* **1.** The act or an instance of spilling

Steven Spielberg

ă pat	oi boy
ā pay	ou out
âr care	o͝o took
ä father	o͞o boot
ĕ pet	ŭ cut
ē be	ûr urge
ĭ pit	th thin
ī pie	*th* this
îr pier	hw which
ŏ pot	zh vision
ō toe	ə about, item
ô paw	♦ regionalism

Stress marks: ′ (primary); ′ (secondary), as in **dictionary** (dĭk′shə-nĕr′ē)

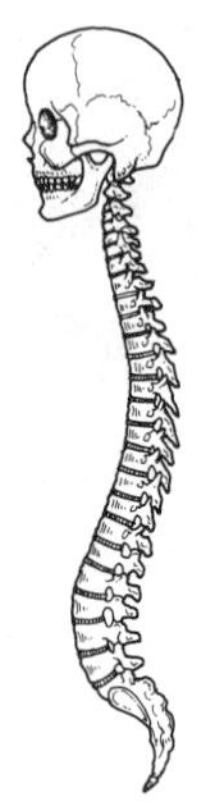
spinal column

spinet

spinnaker
Parachute spinnaker on a catamaran

spinning wheel
Foot-operated spinning wheel

over. **2.** An amount or a quantity spilled over. **3.** A side effect arising from or as if from an unpredicted source: *The income from their garage sale was a spillover from their habit of not throwing anything away.*

spill·way (spĭl′wā′) *n.* A channel for an overflow of water, as from a reservoir.

spilt (spĭlt) *v.* A past tense and a past participle of **spill**[1].

spilth (spĭlth) *n.* **1.** The act of spilling. **2.** An amount spilled. [From SPILL[1].]

spin (spĭn) *v.* **spun** (spŭn), **spin·ning, spins.** —*tr.* **1.a.** To draw out and twist (fibers) into thread. **b.** To form (thread or yarn) in this manner. **2.** To form (a web or cocoon, for example) by extruding viscous filaments. **3.** To make or produce by or as if by drawing out and twisting. **4.a.** To tell, especially imaginatively: *spun tales for the children.* **b.** To prolong or extend: *spin out a visit with an old friend.* **5.** To cause to rotate swiftly; twirl. **6.** To shape or manufacture by a twirling or rotating process. **7.** *Slang.* To play (a phonograph record or records), especially as a disc jockey. —*intr.* **1.** To make thread or yarn by drawing out and twisting fibers. **2.** To extrude viscous filaments, forming a web or cocoon. **3.** To rotate rapidly; whirl. See Synonyms at **turn. 4.** To seem to be whirling, as from dizziness; reel: *My head spun after doing a cartwheel.* **5.** To ride or drive rapidly. **6.** To fish with a light rod, lure, and line and a reel with a stationary spool. —**spin** *n.* **1.** The act of spinning. **2.** A swift whirling motion. **3.** A state of mental confusion. **4.** *Informal.* A short drive in a vehicle: *took a spin in the new car.* **5.** The flight condition of an aircraft in a nose-down, spiraling, stalled descent. **6.a.** The distinctive complex of connotations or implications inherent in a point of view: *"Dryden . . . was adept at putting spin on an apparently neutral recital of facts"* (Robert M. Adams). **b.** Distinctive character; style: *an innovative chef who puts a new spin on traditional fare.* **c.** *Slang.* Interpretation, especially of a politician's words, promulgated to sway public opinion. **7.** *Physics.* **a.** The intrinsic angular momentum of a subatomic particle. Also called *spin angular momentum.* **b.** The total angular momentum of an atomic nucleus. **c.** A quantum number expressing spin angular momentum. —***phrasal verbs.* spin off.** To derive (a company or product, for example) from something larger. **spin out.** To rotate out of control, as a skidding car leaving a roadway. —***idiom.* spin (one's) wheels.** *Informal.* To expend effort with no result. [Middle English *spinnen,* from Old English *spinnan.* See **(s)pen-** in Appendix.]

spi·na bif·i·da (spī′nə bĭf′ĭ-də) *n.* A congenital defect in which the spinal column is imperfectly closed so that part of the meninges or spinal cord protrudes, often resulting in hydrocephalus and other neurological disorders. Also called *schistorrhachis.* [New Latin *spīna bifida* : Latin *spīna,* spine + Latin *bifida,* feminine of *bifidus,* split in two.]

spin·ach (spĭn′ĭch) *n.* **1.** A widely cultivated southwest Asian plant *(Spinacia oleracea)* having succulent, edible leaves. **2.** The leaves of this plant, eaten as a vegetable. [Middle English, from Old French *espinache,* from Medieval Latin *spinachium,* from Arabic *'isfānāḫ,* from Persian *aspanākh.*]

spi·nal (spī′nəl) *adj.* **1.** Of, relating to, or situated near the spine or spinal cord; vertebral: *spinal injury.* **2.** Resembling a spine or spinous part. —**spinal** *n.* An anesthetic injected into the spinal cord to induce partial or complete anesthesia. —**spi′nal·ly** *adv.*

spinal anesthesia *n.* Partial or complete anesthesia produced by injecting an anesthetic into the spinal canal.

spinal canal *n.* The passage formed by successive openings in the articulated vertebrae through which the spinal cord and its membranes pass. Also called *vertebral canal.*

spinal column *n.* The series of articulated vertebrae, separated by intervertebral disks and held together by muscles and tendons, that extends from the cranium to the coccyx or the end of the tail, encasing the spinal cord and forming the supporting axis of the body; the spine. Also called *vertebral column.*

spinal cord *n.* The thick, whitish cord of nerve tissue that extends from the medulla oblongata down through the spinal column and from which the spinal nerves branch off to various parts of the body.

spinal ganglion *n.* Any of the sensory ganglia situated on the dorsal root of each spinal nerve.

spinal meningitis *n.* Inflammation of the membranes enclosing the spinal cord, especially a usually fatal form that affects infants and young children and is caused by a strain of gram-negative bacteria *(Hemophilus influenzae)* formerly thought to cause influenza.

spinal nerve *n.* Any of the nerves that arise in pairs from the spinal cord. There are 31 pairs of spinal nerves in the human body.

spin angular momentum *n.* *Physics.* See **spin** (sense 7a).

spin control *n.* *Slang.* Efforts made especially by politicians to ensure a favorable interpretation of their words and actions: *"Frequently events matter less than . . . spin control—who in which campaign can explain why something doesn't mean what it seems"* (Edward M. Kennedy).

♦ **spin·dle** (spĭn′dl) *n.* **1.a.** A rod or pin, tapered at the ends, on which fibers are spun by hand into thread and then wound. **b.** A similar rod or pin used for spinning on a spinning wheel. **c.** A pin or rod holding a bobbin or spool on which thread is wound on an automated spinning machine. **2.** Any of various mechanical parts that revolve or serve as axes for larger revolving parts, as in a lock, an axle, a phonograph turntable, or a lathe. **3.** Any of various long, thin, stationary rods, as: **a.** A spike on which papers may be impaled. **b.** A baluster. **4.** *Biology.* The spindle-shaped achromatic structure, composed of microtubules, along which the chromosomes are distributed in mitosis and meiosis. **5.** *Coastal New Jersey.* See **dragonfly.** See Regional Note at **dragonfly.** —**spindle** *v.* **-dled, -dling, -dles.** —*tr.* To impale or perforate on a spindle: *Do not fold, spindle, or mutilate this card.* —*intr.* To grow into a thin, elongated, or weak form. [Middle English *spindel,* from Old English *spinel.* See **(s)pen-** in Appendix.]

spindle cell *n.* A spindle-shaped cell characteristic of certain tumors.

spindle fiber *n.* One of a network of achromatic filaments that extend inward from the poles of a dividing cell, forming a spindle-shaped figure.

spindle tree *n.* Any of various shrubs or trees of the genus *Euonymus,* having brightly colored, arillate seeds and small, greenish or purplish axillary flowers. [So called because the wood is often used to make spindles.]

spin·dling (spĭnd′lĭng) *adj.* Spindly.

spin·dly (spĭnd′lē) *adj.* **-dli·er, -dli·est.** Slender and elongated, especially in a way that suggests weakness.

spin-doc·tor (spĭn′dŏk′tər) *n.* *Slang.* A representative for a person, especially a politician, who publicizes favorable interpretations of that person's words or actions: *"Some inconspicuous remark . . . could come back to haunt either candidate; the pundits' and spin-doctors' remarks could change public perceptions of the debate"* (Newsweek).

spin·drift (spĭn′drĭft′) *n.* Windblown sea spray. Also called *spoondrift.* [Variant of Scots *spenedrift* : *spene* (variant of obsolete *spoon,* to run before the wind) + DRIFT.]

spine (spīn) *n.* **1.** The spinal column of a vertebrate. **2.** *Zoology.* Any of various pointed projections, processes, or appendages of animals. **3.** *Botany.* A strong, sharp-pointed, usually woody outgrowth from a stem or leaf; a thorn. **4.** Something that resembles or suggests a backbone, as: **a.** The hinged back of a book. **b.** The crest of a ridge. **5.** Strength of character; courage or willpower. [Middle English, from Old French *espine,* from Latin *spīna.*]

spi·nel also **spi·nelle** (spĭ-nĕl′) *n.* A hard, variously colored mineral with composition $MgAl_2O_4$, with iron, zinc, or manganese sometimes partly or wholly replacing magnesium. The red variety is valued as a gem and is sometimes confused with ruby. [Italian *spinella,* diminutive of *spina,* thorn (from its sharply pointed crystals), from Latin *spīna.*]

spine·less (spīn′lĭs) *adj.* **1.** Lacking courage or willpower. **2.** *Biology.* **a.** Having no spiny processes. **b.** Lacking a spinal column; invertebrate. —**spine′less·ly** *adv.* —**spine′less·ness** *n.*

spi·nelle (spĭ-nĕl′) *n.* Variant of **spinel.**

spi·nes·cent (spī-nĕs′ənt) *adj.* *Biology.* **1.** Having a spine or spines. **2.** Terminating in a spine. [Late Latin *spīnēscēns, spīnēscent-,* present participle of *spīnēscere,* to become thorny, from Latin *spīna,* thorn.] —**spi·nes′cence** *n.*

spin·et (spĭn′ĭt) *n.* *Music.* **1.a.** A small, compact upright piano. **b.** A small, compact upright electronic organ. **2.** A small harpsichord with a single keyboard. [Obsolete French *espinette,* from Italian *spinetta,* perhaps diminutive of *spīna,* thorn (presumably so called because the strings of the original instrument were plucked with quills). See SPINEL.]

Spin·garn (spĭn′gärn′), **Joel Elias.** 1875–1939. American poet and critic. He was a founder (1909) and president (1930–1939) of the National Association for the Advancement of Colored People.

spi·nif·er·ous (spī-nĭf′ər-əs) *adj.* *Biology.* Spine-bearing. [From Late Latin *spīnifer* : Latin *spīna,* thorn + Latin *-fer,* -fer.]

spi·ni·fex (spī′nə-fĕks′) *n.* Any of various clump-forming, perennial Australian grasses, chiefly of the genus *Triodia,* growing in arid regions and having awl-shaped, pointed leaves. [New Latin *Spīnifex,* former genus name : Latin *spīna,* thorn + Latin *-fex;* see **dhē-** in Appendix.]

spin·na·ker (spĭn′ə-kər) *n.* *Nautical.* A large triangular sail set on a spar that swings out opposite the mainsail, used on racing yachts when running before the wind. [Origin unknown.]

spin·ner (spĭn′ər) *n.* **1.** One that spins: *a spinner of flax; a spinner of tall tales.* **2.** A fishing lure that rotates rapidly. **3.** A fairing fitted over the hub of the propeller in some aircraft. **4.** *Games.* A device consisting of a dial and an arrow that is spun to indicate the next move in some board games.

spin·ner·et (spĭn′ə-rĕt′) *n.* **1.** Any of various tubular structures from which spiders and certain insect larvae, such as silkworms, secrete the silk threads from which they form webs or cocoons. **2.** A device for making rayon, nylon, and other synthetic fibers, consisting of a plate pierced with holes through which plastic material is extruded in filaments.

spin·ney (spĭn′ē) *n., pl.* **-neys.** *Chiefly British.* A small grove; a copse. [Obsolete French *espinoi,* from Old French *espinei,* thorny place, from Vulgar Latin **spīnēta,* pl. of Latin *spīnētum,* thorn hedge, from *spīna,* thorn.]

spin·ning (spĭn′ĭng) *n.* **1.** The process of making fibrous material into yarn or thread. **2.** The act of fishing with a light rod, lure, and line and a reel with a stationary spool.

spinning frame *n.* A machine that draws and twists fibers into yarn and winds it on spindles.

spinning jenny *n.* An early form of spinning machine having several spindles.

spinning wheel *n.* An apparatus for making yarn or thread, consisting of a foot-driven or hand-driven wheel and a single spindle.

spi·no·cer·e·bel·lar (spī′nō-sĕr′ə-bĕl′ər) *adj.* Of, relating to, or involving both the spinal cord and the cerebellum: *spinocerebellar degeneration.*

spin·off or **spin-off** (spĭn′ôf′, -ŏf′) *n.* **1.a.** A divestiture by a corporation of a division or subsidiary by issuing to stockholders shares in a new company set up to continue the operations of the division or subsidiary. **b.** The new company formed by such a divestiture. **2.** Something, such as a product, that is derived from something larger and more or less unrelated; a byproduct. **3.** Something derived from an earlier work, such as a television show starring a character who had a popular minor role in another show.

spi·nose (spī′nōs′) *adj.* Bearing spines; spiny: *a spinose plant.* [Latin *spīnōsus,* from *spīna,* thorn.] **—spi′nose′ly** *adv.* **—spi·nos′i·ty** (-nŏs′ĭ-tē) *n.*

spi·nous (spī′nəs) *adj.* **1.** Resembling a spine or thorn. **2.** Having spines or similar projections; spiny.

spinous process *n.* The long rearward projection from the arch of a vertebra that provides a point of attachment for muscles and ligaments.

spin·out (spĭn′out′) *n.* An instance of spinning out: *a motorist who was injured in a spinout.*

Spi·no·za (spĭ-nō′zə), **Baruch** or **Benedict.** 1632–1677. Dutch philosopher and theologian whose controversial pantheistic doctrine advocated an intellectual love of God. His best-known work is *Ethics* (1677).

Spi·no·zism (spĭ-nō′zĭz′əm) *n. Philosophy.* A monistic approach to philosophy in which all reality is held to consist of one substance, usually termed God or Nature, of which minds and bodies are both attributes. [After Baruch SPINOZA.] **—Spi·no′zist** *adj. & n.* **—Spi·no·zis′tic** *adj.*

spin·ster (spĭn′stər) *n.* **1.** A woman who has remained single beyond the conventional age for marrying. **2.** A single woman. **3.** A person whose occupation is spinning. [Middle English *spinnestere,* female spinner of thread : *spinnen,* to spin; see SPIN + *-estere, -ster,* -ster.] **—spin′ster·hood′** *n.* **—spin′ster·ish, spin′ster·ly** *adj.*

spin·thar·i·scope (spĭn-thăr′ĭ-skōp′) *n.* A device for observing individual scintillations produced by ionizing radiation, as one consisting of a tube with a magnifying lens at one end and a phosphorescent screen and speck of radioactive salt at the other. [Greek *spintharis,* spark + -SCOPE.] **—spin·thar′i·scop′ic** (-skŏp′ĭk) *adj.*

spin-the-bot·tle (spĭn′thə-bŏt′l) *n. Games.* A game in which players take turns spinning a bottle and kissing the person it points toward when it comes to rest.

spin·to (spĭn′tō) *adj. Music.* Of, relating to, or being a lyric operatic voice with some attributes of the dramatic voice: *a spinto soprano.* [Italian, past participle of *spingere,* to push, from Vulgar Latin **expingere* : Latin *ex-,* ex- + Latin *pangere,* to fasten; see IMPINGE.] **—spin′to** *n.*

spi·nule (spĭn′yo͞ol) *n.* A small spine or thorn. [Latin *spīnula,* diminutive of *spīna,* thorn.]

spi·nu·lose (spĭn′yə-lōs′) also **spi·nu·lous** (spī′nyə-ləs) *adj.* **1.** Having spinules. **2.** Shaped like a spinule.

spin wave *n. Physics.* A wave propagated through a crystal lattice as a result of shifts in atomic magnetic fields associated with the spin angular momentum of electrons in the lattice.

spin·y (spī′nē) *adj.* **-i·er, -i·est. 1.** Bearing or covered with spines, thorns, or similar stiff projections. **2.** Shaped like a spine. **3.** Difficult; troublesome. **—spin′i·ness** *n.*

spiny anteater *n.* See **echidna.**

spin·y-finned (spī′nē-fĭnd′) *adj.* Having fins supported by sharp, spiny, inflexible rays. Used of a fish.

spin·y-head·ed worm (spī′nē-hĕd′ĭd) *n.* Any of various worms of the phylum Acanthocephala that live parasitically in the intestines of vertebrates and are characterized by a cylindrical, retractile proboscis that bears many rows of hooked spines. Also called *acanthocephalan.*

spiny lobster *n.* Any of various edible marine decapod crustaceans of the family Palinuridae, having a spiny carapace and lacking the large pincers characteristic of true lobsters. Also called *crayfish, langouste, rock lobster, sea crayfish.*

spin·y-rayed (spī′nē-rād′) *adj.* Spiny-finned.

spir·a·cle (spĭr′ə-kəl, spī′rə-) *n.* **1.** *Zoology.* A respiratory aperture, especially: **a.** Any of several tracheal openings in the exoskeleton of an insect or a spider. **b.** A small respiratory opening behind the eye of certain fishes, such as sharks, rays, and skates. **c.** The blowhole of a cetacean. **2.** An aperture or opening through which air is admitted and expelled. [Middle English, from Latin *spīrāculum,* from *spīrāre,* to breathe.] **—spi·rac′u·lar** (spĭ-răk′yə-lər, spī-) *adj.*

spi·rae·a (spī-rē′ə) *n.* Variant of **spirea.**

spi·ral (spī′rəl) *n.* **1.a.** A curve on a plane that winds around a fixed center point at a continuously increasing or decreasing distance from the point. **b.** A three-dimensional curve that turns around an axis at a constant or continuously varying distance while moving parallel to the axis; a helix. **c.** Something having the form of such a curve: *a spiral of black smoke.* **2.** *Printing.* A spiral binding. **3.** The course or flight path of an object rotating on its longitudinal axis. **4.** A continuously accelerating increase or decrease: *the wage-price spiral.* **—spiral** *adj.* **1.** Of or resembling a spiral. **2.** Circling around a center at a continuously increasing or decreasing distance. **3.** Coiling around an axis in a constantly changing series of planes; helical. **4.** *Printing.* Relating to or having a spiral binding: *a spiral notebook.* **—spiral** *v.* **-raled, -ral·ing, -rals** also **-ralled, -ral·ling, -rals.** —*intr.* **1.** To take a spiral form or course. **2.** To rise or fall with steady acceleration. —*tr.* To cause to take a spiral form or course. [Medieval Latin *spīrālis,* of a spiral, from Latin *spīra,* coil. See SPIRE[2].] **—spi·ral′i·ty** (spī-răl′ĭ-tē) *n.* **—spi′ral·ly** *adv.*

spiral binding *n. Printing.* A binding for notebooks and booklets in which a cylindrical spiral of wire or plastic is passed through a row of punched holes at the edge of a tablet. **—spi′ral-bound′** (spī′rəl-bound′) *adj.*

spiral galaxy *n.* A galaxy having a spiral structure.

spi·rant (spī′rənt) *Linguistics. n.* See **fricative. —spirant** *adj.* Fricative. [Latin *spīrāns, spīrant-,* present participle of *spīrāre,* to breathe.]

spire[1] (spīr) *n.* **1.** A top part or point that tapers upward; a pinnacle. **2.** A structure or formation, such as a steeple, that tapers to a point at the top. **3.** A slender, tapering part, such as a newly sprouting blade of grass. **—spire** *v.* **spired, spir·ing, spires.** —*tr.* To furnish with a spire. —*intr.* To rise and taper steeply. [Middle English, from Old English *spīr.*]

spire[2] (spīr) *n.* **1.a.** A spiral. **b.** A single turn of a spiral; a whorl. **2.** The area farthest from the aperture and nearest the apex on a coiled gastropod shell. [Latin *spīra,* coil, from Greek *speira.*]

spi·re·a also **spi·rae·a** (spī-rē′ə) *n.* **1.** Any of various shrubs of the genus *Spiraea* of the rose family, having clusters of small white or pink flowers and including the bridal wreath, hardhack, and meadowsweet. **2.** See **astilbe.** [Latin *spiraea,* meadowsweet, from Greek *speiraia,* privet, from *speira,* coil.]

spi·reme (spī′rēm′) also **spi·rem** (-rĕm′) *n. Biology.* **1.** The tangle of filaments that appears at the beginning of the prophase portion of meiosis or mitosis. **2.** Any of these filaments. [German *Spirem,* from Greek *speirēma,* coil, from *speirasthai,* to be coiled around, from *speira,* coil.]

Spires (spīrz). See **Speyer.**

spi·rif·er·ous (spī-rĭf′ər-əs) *adj.* Having a spiral structure or spiral parts. [Probably from New Latin *spīrifer* : Latin *spīra,* coil; see SPIRE[2] + Latin *-fer,* -fer.]

spi·ril·lum (spī-rĭl′əm) *n., pl.* **-ril·la** (-rĭl′ə). **1.** Any of various aerobic bacteria of the genus *Spirillum,* having an elongated spiral form and bearing a tuft of flagella. **2.** Any of various other spiral-shaped microorganisms. [New Latin *Spīrillum,* genus name, diminutive of Latin *spīra,* coil. See SPIRE[2].]

spir·it (spĭr′ĭt) *n.* **1.a.** The vital principle or animating force within living beings. **b.** Incorporeal consciousness. **2.** The soul, considered as departing from the body of a person at death. **3. Spirit.** The Holy Spirit. **4. Spirit.** *Christian Science.* God. **5.** A supernatural being, as: **a.** An angel or a demon. **b.** A being inhabiting or embodying a particular place, object, or natural phenomenon. **c.** A fairy or sprite. **6.a.** The part of a human being associated with the mind, will, and feelings: *Though unable to join us today, they are with us in spirit.* **b.** The essential nature of a person or group. **7.** A person as characterized by a stated quality: *He is a proud spirit.* **8.a.** An inclination or a tendency of a specified kind: *Her actions show a generous spirit.* **b.** A causative, activating, or essential principle: *The couple's engagement was announced in a joyous spirit.* **9. spirits.** A mood or an emotional state: *The guests were in high spirits. His sour spirits put a damper on the gathering.* **10.** A particular mood or an emotional state characterized by vigor and animation: *sang with spirit.* **11.** Strong loyalty or dedication: *team spirit.* **12.** The predominant mood of an occasion or a period: *"The spirit of 1776 is not dead"* (Thomas Jefferson). **13.** The actual though unstated sense or significance of something: *the spirit of the law.* **14.** Often **spirits** *(used with a sing. verb).* An alcohol solution of an essential or volatile substance. **15. spirits.** An alcoholic beverage, especially distilled liquor. **—spirit** *tr.v.* **-it·ed, -it·ing, -its. 1.** To carry off mysteriously or secretly: *The documents had been spirited away.* **2.** To impart courage, animation, or determination to; inspirit. [Middle English, from Old French *espirit,* from Latin *spīritus,* breath, from *spīrāre,* to breathe.]

spir·it·ed (spĭr′ĭ-tĭd) *adj.* **1.** Full of or characterized by animation, vigor, or courage: *a spirited debate.* **2.** Having a specified mood or nature. Often used in combination: *high-spirited; low-spirited.* **—spir′it·ed·ly** *adv.* **—spir′it·ed·ness** *n.*

spir·it·ism (spĭr′ĭ-tĭz′əm) *n.* **1.** The belief that the dead communicate with the living; spiritualism. **2.** The practices or doctrines of those holding such a belief. **—spir′it·ist** *n.* **—spir′it·is′tic** *adj.*

spirit lamp *n.* A lamp that burns alcohol or other liquid fuel.

spir·it·less (spĭr′ĭt-lĭs) *adj.* Lacking energy or enthusiasm; listless. **—spir′it·less·ly** *adv.* **—spir′it·less·ness** *n.*

spirit level *n.* See **level** (sense 7a).

spirit of turpentine *n.* See **turpentine** (sense 1).

spirit of wine *n.* Rectified ethyl alcohol.

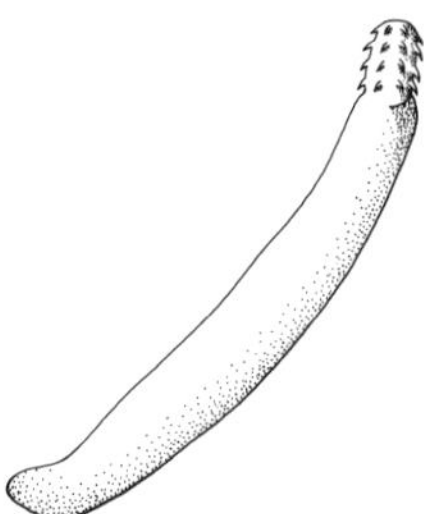

spiny-headed worm

spiral
Staircase

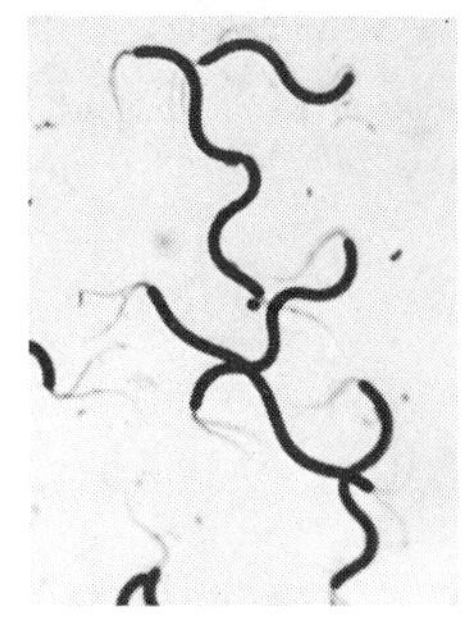

spirillum
Magnified image of spirilla

ă pat	oi boy
ā pay	ou out
âr care	o͝o took
ä father	o͞o boot
ĕ pet	ŭ cut
ē be	ûr urge
ĭ pit	th thin
ī pie	*th* this
îr pier	hw which
ŏ pot	zh vision
ō toe	ə about, item
ô paw	♦ regionalism

Stress marks: ′ (primary); ′ (secondary), as in **dictionary** (dĭk′shə-nĕr′ē)

spir·it·ous (spĭr′ĭ-təs) *adj.* **1.** Spirituous. **2.** *Archaic.* Highly refined; pure.

spirit rap·ping (răp′ĭng) *n.* Communication by knocking or rapping, believed to be produced by spirits of the dead, as at a séance.

spir·i·tu·al (spĭr′ĭ-cho͞o-əl) *adj.* **1.** Of, relating to, consisting of, or having the nature of spirit; not tangible or material. See Synonyms at **immaterial. 2.** Of, concerned with, or affecting the soul. **3.** Of, from, or relating to God; deific. **4.** Of or belonging to a church or religion; sacred. **5.** Relating to or having the nature of spirits or a spirit; supernatural. **—spiritual** *n.* **1.** *Music.* **a.** A religious folk song of American Black origin. **b.** A work composed in imitation of such a song. **2.** Often **spirituals.** Religious, spiritual, or ecclesiastical matters. [Middle English, from Old French *spirituel,* from Latin *spīrituālis,* of breathing, spiritual, from *spīritus,* breath. See SPIRIT.] **—spir′i·tu·al·ly** *adv.* **—spir′i·tu·al·ness** *n.*

spiritual bouquet *n.* *Roman Catholic Church.* A card sent by a person indicating that certain devotional acts will be undertaken on behalf of another person, as in honor of a special occasion or in memoriam.

spir·i·tu·al·ism (spĭr′ĭ-cho͞o-ə-lĭz′əm) *n.* **1.a.** The belief that the dead communicate with the living, as through a medium. **b.** The practices or doctrines of those holding such a belief. **2.** A philosophy, doctrine, or religion emphasizing the spiritual aspect of being. **—spir′i·tu·al·ist** *n.* **—spir′i·tu·al·is′tic** *adj.*

spir·i·tu·al·i·ty (spĭr′ĭ-cho͞o-ăl′ĭ-tē) *n., pl.* **-ties. 1.** The state, quality, manner, or fact of being spiritual. **2.** The clergy. **3.** Often **spiritualities.** Something, such as property or revenue, that belongs to the church or to a cleric.

spir·i·tu·al·ize (spĭr′ĭ-cho͞o-ə-līz′) *tr.v.* **-ized, -iz·ing, -iz·es. 1.** To impart a spiritual nature to. **2.** To invest with or treat as having a spiritual sense or meaning. **—spir′i·tu·al·i·za′tion** (-ə-lĭ-zā′shən) *n.* **—spir′i·tu·al·iz′er** *n.*

spir·i·tu·al·ty (spĭr′ĭ-cho͞o-əl-tē) *n., pl.* **-ties.** Property or revenue belonging to the church or to a cleric; spirituality.

spir·i·tu·el also **spir·i·tu·elle** (spĭr′ĭ-cho͞o-ĕl′, spē′rē-to͞o-ĕl′, -tü-) *adj.* Having or evidencing a refined mind and wit. [French, from Old French, spiritual. See SPIRITUAL.]

spir·i·tu·ous (spĭr′ĭ-cho͞o-əs) *adj.* **1.** Having the nature of or containing alcohol; alcoholic. **2.** Distilled. Used of an alcoholic beverage. **—spir′i·tu·os′i·ty** (-ŏs′ĭ-tē), **spir′i·tu·ous·ness** (-əs-nĭs) *n.*

spiro– *pref.* Respiration: *spirometer.* [From Latin *spīrāre,* to breathe.]

spi·ro·chete (spī′rə-kēt′) *n.* Any of various slender, spiral, motile bacteria of the order Spirochaetales, many of which are pathogenic, causing syphilis, relapsing fever, yaws, and other diseases. [New Latin *Spīrochaeta,* genus name : Latin *spīra,* coil; see SPIRE[2] + New Latin *chaeta,* bristle, hair; see CHAETA.] **—spi′ro·chet′al** (-kēt′l) *adj.*

spi·ro·che·to·sis (spī′rə-kē-tō′sĭs) *n., pl.* **-ses** (-sēz). Any of various diseases, such as syphilis, caused by infection with spirochetes.

spi·ro·graph (spī′rə-grăf′) *n.* An instrument for registering the depth and rapidity of respiratory movements. **—spi′ro·graph′ic** *adj.* **—spi′ro·graph′i·cal·ly** *adv.* **—spi·rog′ra·phy** (spī-rŏg′rə-fē) *n.*

spi·ro·gy·ra (spī′rə-jī′rə) *n.* Any of various filamentous freshwater green algae of the genus *Spirogyra,* having chloroplasts in spirally twisted bands. [New Latin *Spīrogyra,* genus name : Latin *spīra,* coil; see SPIRE[2] + Greek *guros,* ring.]

spi·roid (spī′roid′) *adj.* Resembling a spiral.

spi·rom·e·ter (spī-rŏm′ĭ-tər) *n.* An instrument for measuring the volume of air entering and leaving the lungs. **—spi′ro·met′ric** (-rə-mĕt′rĭk) *adj.* **—spi·rom′e·try** *n.*

spi·ro·no·lac·tone (spī′rə-nō-lăk′tōn, spī-rō′-, spī-rŏn′ə-) *n.* A steroid derivative, $C_{24}H_{32}O_4S$, that blocks the action of aldosterone, used as a diuretic in the treatment of hypertension. [Alteration of *spirolactone* : Latin *spīra,* coil; see SPIRAL + LACTONE.]

spi·ro·plas·ma (spī′rə-plăz′mə) *n.* Any of numerous bacteria of the genus *Spiroplasma* that vary in form, lack flagella, and are associated with various plant diseases. These bacteria and the related mycoplasma are the only bacteria without cell walls. [New Latin *Spīroplasma,* genus name : Latin *spīra,* coil; see SPIRE[2] + PLASMA.]

spirt (spûrt) *n. & v.* *Chiefly British.* Variant of **spurt.**

spir·u·la (spĭr′yə-lə, spīr′ə-) *n., pl.* **-lae** (-lē′). A small cephalopod mollusk of the genus *Spirula,* having a spirally coiled, partitioned internal shell. [Late Latin *spīrula,* twisted cake, diminutive of Latin *spīra,* coil. See SPIRE[2].]

spit[1] (spĭt) *n.* **1.** Saliva, especially when expectorated; spittle. **2.** The act of expectorating. **3.** Something, such as the frothy secretion of spittle bugs, that resembles expectorated saliva. **4.** A brief, scattered fall of rain or snow. **5.** *Informal.* The perfect likeness: *He's the spit and image of his father.* **—spit** *v.* **spat** (spăt) or **spit, spit·ting, spits.** *—tr.* **1.** To eject from the mouth: *spat out the watermelon seeds.* **2.** To eject as if from the mouth: *a fire spitting sparks.* **3.** To emit suddenly and forcefully: *spat out an insult.* *—intr.* **1.** To eject matter from the mouth; expectorate. **2.** To express contempt or animosity by or as if by ejecting matter from the mouth. **3.** To make a hissing or sputtering noise. **4.** To rain or snow in light, scattered drops or flakes. **—*phrasal verb.*** **spit up.** To vomit. [Middle English, from *spitten,* to spit, from Old English *spittan,* ultimately of imitative origin.]

spit[2] (spĭt) *n.* **1.** A slender, pointed rod on which meat is impaled for broiling. **2.** A narrow point of land extending into a body of water. **—spit** *tr.v.* **spit·ted, spit·ting, spits.** To impale on or as if on a spit. [Middle English, from Old English *spitu.*]

spit·al (spĭt′l) *n.* *Archaic.* A hospital, especially one for patients with contagious diseases. [Middle English *spitel,* short for *hospital.* See HOSPITAL.]

spit and polish *n.* Attention to appearance and order, as in a military unit. **—spit′-and-pol′ish** (spĭt′n-pŏl′ĭsh) *adj.*

spit·ball (spĭt′bôl′) *n.* **1.** A piece of paper chewed and shaped into a lump for use as a projectile. **2.** *Baseball.* An illegal pitch in which a foreign substance, such as saliva, is applied to the ball before it is thrown. In this sense, also called *spitter.*

spit curl *n.* A spiral curl of hair pressed flat against the cheek, temple, or forehead. [From the use of saliva to fix the curl.]

spite (spīt) *n.* **1.** Malicious ill will prompting an urge to hurt or humiliate. **2.** An instance of malicious feeling. **—spite** *tr.v.* **spit·ed, spit·ing, spites. 1.a.** To show spite toward. **b.** To vent spite on. **2.a.** To fill with spite. **b.** To annoy: *He did it just to spite her.* **—*idiom.* in spite of.** Not stopped by; regardless of: *They kept going in spite of their fears.* [Middle English, short for *despit.* See DESPITE.]

spite·ful (spīt′fəl) *adj.* Filled with, prompted by, or showing spite; malicious. **—spite′ful·ly** *adv.* **—spite′ful·ness** *n.*

spit·fire (spĭt′fīr′) *n.* A quick-tempered or highly excitable person.

Spit·head (spĭt′hĕd′). A channel off southern England between Portsmouth and the Isle of Wight. It connects with the Solent on the west and was formerly used as a rendezvous for the British fleet.

Spits·ber·gen (spĭts′bûr′gən). An island of Norway in Svalbard in the Arctic Ocean east of northern Greenland. Discovered by Willem Barents in 1596, the island became part of Norway in 1925.

Spit·te·ler (shpĭt′l-ər, shpĭt′lər, spĭt′-), **Carl.** 1845–1924. Swiss writer known especially for his epic *Olympian Spring* (1910). He won the 1919 Nobel Prize for literature.

spit·ter (spĭt′ər) *n.* **1.** One that spits: *a spitter of invective.* **2.** *Baseball.* See **spitball** (sense 2).

spit·ting cobra (spĭt′ĭng) *n.* See **ringhals.**

spitting image *n.* A perfect likeness or counterpart. [Alteration of *spit and image,* from *spit,* an exact likeness, as in *the very spit of.* See SPIT[1].]

spit·tle (spĭt′l) *n.* **1.** Spit; saliva. **2.** The frothy liquid secreted by spittlebugs. [Middle English *spitel,* alteration (influenced by *spit,* spit) of *spatel,* from Old English *spātl.*]

spit·tle·bug (spĭt′l-bŭg′) *n.* Any of various leaping, homopterous insects of the family Cercopidae, the nymphs of which form frothy masses of liquid on plant stems. Also called *froghopper, spittle insect.*

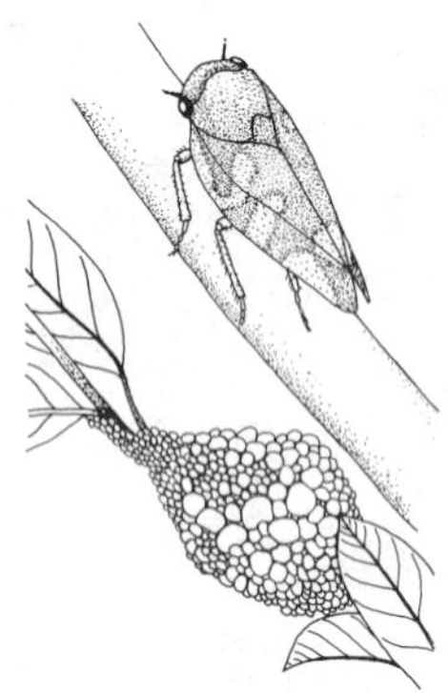

spittlebug
Top: Adult European spittlebug *Aphrophora alvi*
Bottom: Nymph enclosed in mass of spittle

spit·toon (spĭ-to͞on′) *n.* A bowl-shaped, usually metal vessel, often with a funnel-shaped cover, into which tobacco chewers periodically spit. [SPIT[1] + *-oon,* as in BALLOON.]

spitz (spĭts) *n.* A dog belonging to any of several northern breeds, such as the Pomeranian or Samoyed, characterized by a long, thick, usually white coat, pointed muzzle and ears, and a tail curled over the back. [German *Spitz,* from *spitz,* pointed, from Middle High German *spiz,* from Old High German *spizzi.*]

spiv (spĭv) *n.* *Chiefly British.* **1.** One, usually unemployed, who lives by one's wits. **2.** One who shirks work or responsibility; a slacker. [Dialectal *spif,* dandified, dandy.]

splanch·nic (splăngk′nĭk) *adj.* Of or relating to the viscera; visceral: *a splanchnic nerve.* [New Latin *splanchnicus,* from Greek *splankhnikos,* from *splankhna,* inward parts.]

splanch·nol·o·gy (splăngk-nŏl′ə-jē) *n.* **1.** The scientific study of the viscera and its organs. **2.** The characteristics and structure of the visceral system of an animal. [New Latin *splanchno-,* of viscera (from Greek *splankhna,* viscera) + –LOGY.]

splanch·no·pleure (splăngk′nə-plo͝or′) *n.* A layer of embryonic cells formed in vertebrates by association of part of the mesoderm with the endoderm and developing into the wall of the viscera. [New Latin *splanchnopleura* : *splanchno-,* of viscera; see SPLANCHNOLOGY + Greek *pleura,* side.] **—splanch′no·pleur′ic** *adj.*

splash (splăsh) *v.* **splashed, splash·ing, splash·es.** *—tr.* **1.** To propel or scatter (a fluid) about in flying masses. **2.** To scatter fluid onto in flying masses; wet, stain, or soil with flying fluid. **3.** To cause (something) to scatter fluid in flying masses: *splashed their hands in the water.* **4.** To make (one's way) with or by scattering of fluid. **5.** To apply patches or spots of a contrasting, usually bright, color to: *a floral pattern that was splashed with pink; moonlight splashing the deserted courtyard.* **6.** To display or publicize very noticeably: *Their engagement was splashed all over the tabloids.* *—intr.* **1.a.** To cause a fluid to scatter in flying masses: *splashed about in the swimming pool.* **b.** To fall into or move through fluid with this effect: *We splashed through the waves.* **2.a.** To move, spill, or fly about in scattered masses: *Whipped cream splashed onto the counter.* **b.** To produce a sound or sight associated with this effect. **—splash** *n.* **1.** The act or sound of splashing: *went for a splash in the lake; heard the splash* *of the fish being thrown back.* **2.a.** A flying mass of fluid. **b.** A small amount, especially of a fluid: *a splash of liqueur on the cake.* **3.** A marking produced by or as if by scattered fluid: *a splash of light.* **4.** A great though often short-lived impression; a stir: *a publicity splash.* **—*phrasal verb.* splash down.** To land in water. Used of a spacecraft or missile. [Probably alteration of PLASH.] **—splash′er** *n.*

splash·board (splăsh′bôrd′, -bōrd′) *n.* **1.** A structure that protects the upper part of a vehicle from splashes of mud. **2.** *Nautical.* A screen on a boat to keep water from splashing onto the deck. **3.** A board for closing a spillway or sluice.

splash·down (splăsh′doun′) *n.* The landing of a spacecraft or missile in water.

splash·guard (splăsh′gärd′) *n.* See **mudguard.**

splash·y (splăsh′ē) *adj.* **-i·er, -i·est. 1.** Making or likely to make splashes. **2.** Covered with splashes of color. **3.** Showy; ostentatious. See Synonyms at **showy. —splash′i·ly** *adv.* **—splash′i·ness** *n.*

splat¹ (splăt) *n.* A slat of wood, as one in the middle of a chair back. [Perhaps from Middle English *splatten,* to split open, perhaps from Medieval Latin *splattāre,* of Low German origin.]

splat² (splăt) *n.* A smacking or splashing noise. **—splat** *adv.* With a smacking or splashing noise: *landed splat on the floor.* [Imitative.]

splat·ter (splăt′ər) *v.* **-tered, -ter·ing, -ters.** *—tr.* To spatter (something), especially to soil with splashes of liquid. *—intr.* To spatter, especially to move or fall so as to cause splashes. **—splatter** *n.* A splash of liquid. [Perhaps blend of SPLASH and SPATTER.]

splay (splā) *adj.* **1.** Spread or turned out. **2.** Clumsy or clumsily formed; awkward. **—splay** *n. Architecture.* An oblique angle or bevel given to the sides of an opening in a wall so that the opening is wider on one side of the wall than on the other. **—splay** *v.* **splayed, splay·ing, splays.** *—tr.* **1.** To spread (the limbs, for example) out or apart, especially clumsily. **2.** To make slanting or sloping; bevel. **3.** To dislocate (a bone). Used of an animal. *—intr.* **1.** To be spread out or apart. **2.** To slant or slope. [From Middle English *splayen,* to spread out, short for *displayen.* See DISPLAY.]

splay·foot (splā′fo͝ot′) *n.* **1.** A physical deformity characterized by abnormally flat and turned-out feet. **2.** A foot so affected. **—splay′foot′ed** *adj.*

spleen (splēn) *n.* **1.a.** A large, highly vascular lymphoid organ, lying in the human body to the left of the stomach below the diaphragm, serving to store blood, disintegrate old blood cells, filter foreign substances from the blood, and produce lymphocytes. **b.** A homologous organ or tissue in other vertebrates. **2.** *Obsolete.* This organ conceived as the seat of emotions or passions. **3.** Ill temper: *vent one's spleen.* **4.** *Archaic.* Melancholy. **5.** *Obsolete.* A whim; a caprice. [Middle English *splen,* from Old French *esplen,* from Latin *splēn,* from Greek.] **—spleen′y** *adj.*

spleen·ful (splēn′fəl) *adj.* Affected by or filled with spleen; irritable.

spleen·wort (splēn′wûrt′, -wôrt′) *n.* Any of numerous widely distributed evergreen ferns of the genus *Asplenium,* having undivided to featherlike fronds and oblong to linear sori located on the small veins. [So called because it was thought to cure spleen disorders.]

splen– *pref.* Variant of **spleno–.**

splen·dent (splĕn′dənt) *adj.* **1.** Shining or lustrous; brilliant. **2.** Admired by many; illustrious. [Middle English, from Old French *esplendent,* from Latin *splendēns, splendent-,* present participle of *splendēre,* to shine.]

splen·did (splĕn′dĭd) *adj.* **1.** Brilliant with light or color; radiant: *a splendid field of poppies.* **2.** Imposing by reason of showiness or grandeur; magnificent: *splendid costumes.* **3.** Admired by many; illustrious: *splendid achievements.* **4.** Admirable for boldness or purity; surpassing: *splendid character.* **5.** Very good or satisfying; praiseworthy: *a splendid performance in the examinations.* [Latin *splendidus,* from *splendēre,* to shine.] **—splen′did·ly** *adv.* **—splen′did·ness** *n.*

splen·dif·er·ous (splĕn-dĭf′ər-əs) *adj.* Splendid: *"The working genius of American design has been . . . a refining of utilitarian purity into a kind of splendiferous native simplicity"* (Jay Cocks). [Middle English, from Medieval Latin *splendiferus,* from Late Latin *splendōrifer* : Latin *splendor,* splendor; see SPLENDOR + Latin *-fer,* -fer.]

splen·dor (splĕn′dər) *n.* **1.** Great light or luster; brilliance. **2.a.** Magnificent appearance or display; grandeur. **b.** Something grand or magnificent. **3.** Great fame; glory. [Middle English *splendoure,* from Old French *splendour,* from Latin *splendor,* from *splendēre,* to shine.] **—splen′dor·ous, splen′drous** (splĕn′drəs) *adj.*

splen·dour (splĕn′dər) *n. Chiefly British.* Variant of **splendor.**

sple·nec·to·my (splĭ-nĕk′tə-mē) *n., pl.* **-mies.** Surgical removal of the spleen. **—sple·nec′to·mize′** (-mīz′) *v.*

sple·net·ic (splĭ-nĕt′ĭk) also **sple·net·i·cal** (-ĭ-kəl) *—adj.* **1.** Of or relating to the spleen. **2.** Affected or marked by ill humor or irritability. *—n.* A person regarded as irritable. [Late Latin *splēnēticus,* from Latin *splēn,* spleen. See SPLEEN.] **—sple·net′i·cal·ly** *adv.*

splen·ic (splĕn′ĭk) *adj.* Of, in, near, or relating to the spleen.

sple·ni·us (splē′nē-əs) *n., pl.* **-ni·i** (-nē-ī′). Either of two muscles of the back of the neck, extending from the upper vertebrae to the base of the skull, that rotate and extend the head and neck. [New Latin *splēnius,* from Latin *splēnium,* patch, plaster (from its shape), from Greek *splēnion,* from *splēn,* spleen.] **—sple′ni·al** (-nē-əl) *adj.*

spleno– or **splen–** *pref.* Spleen: *splenomegaly.* [Greek *splēno-,* from *splēn,* spleen.]

sple·no·meg·a·ly (splē′nō-mĕg′ə-lē, splĕn′ō-) *n., pl.* **-lies.** Enlargement of the spleen.

splice (splīs) *tr.v.* **spliced, splic·ing, splic·es. 1.a.** To join (film, for example) at the ends. **b.** To join (ropes, for example) by interweaving strands. **2.** To join (pieces of wood) by overlapping and binding at the ends. **3.** To join together or insert (segments of DNA or RNA) so as to form new genetic combinations or alter a genetic structure. **4.** *Slang.* To join in marriage: *They went to Las Vegas to get spliced.* **—splice** *n.* **1.** A joining by splicing. **2.** A place where parts have been spliced. [Obsolete Dutch *splissen,* from Middle Dutch.] **—splic′er** *n.*

spline (splīn) *n.* **1.a.** Any of a series of projections on a shaft that fit into slots on a corresponding shaft, enabling both to rotate together. **b.** The groove or slot for such a projection. **2.** A flexible piece of wood, hard rubber, or metal used in drawing curves. **3.** A wooden or metal strip; a slat. [Origin unknown.]

splint (splĭnt) *n.* **1.** A thin piece split off from a larger piece; a splinter. **2.a.** A rigid device used to prevent motion of a joint or of the ends of a fractured bone. **b.** A dental appliance put on the teeth to protect them from grinding or from moving out of place. **3.** A thin, flexible wooden strip, such as one used in the making of baskets or chair bottoms. **4.** A plate or strip of metal. **5.** A bony enlargement of the cannon bone or splint bone of a horse. **—splint** *tr.v.* **splint·ed, splint·ing, splints.** To support or restrict with or as if with a splint. [Middle English, from Middle Dutch or Middle Low German *splinte.*]

splint bone *n.* Either of two small metacarpal or metatarsal bones in horses or related animals.

splin·ter (splĭn′tər) *n.* **1.** A sharp, slender piece, as of wood, bone, glass, or metal, split or broken off from a main body. **2.** A splinter group. **—splinter** *v.* **-tered, -ter·ing, -ters.** *—intr.* To split or break into sharp, slender pieces; form splinters. See Synonyms at **break.** *—tr.* To cause to splinter. [Middle English, from Middle Dutch.] **—splin′ter·y** *adj.*

splinter group *n.* A group, such as a religious sect or political faction, that has broken away from a parent group.

split (splĭt) *v.* **split, split·ting, splits.** *—tr.* **1.** To divide from end to end or along the grain by or as if by a sharp blow. See Synonyms at **tear¹. 2.a.** To break, burst, or rip apart with force; rend. See Synonyms at **break. b.** To affect with force in a way that suggests tearing apart: *A lightning bolt split the night sky.* **3.** To separate (people or groups, for example); disunite. **4.** To divide and share: *split a dessert.* **5.** To divide, as for convenience or proper ordering: *split the project up into stages.* **6.** To separate (leather, for example) into layers. **7.** To mark (a vote or ballot) in favor of candidates from different parties. **8.** To divide (stock) by issuing multiples of the existing stock with a corresponding reduction in the price of each share, so that the total value of the stock is unchanged. **9.** *Sports.* To win half the games of (a series or double-header). **10.** *Slang.* To depart from; leave: *They split Miami when the hurricane was forecast.* *—intr.* **1.** To become separated into parts, especially to undergo lengthwise division. **2.** To become broken or ripped apart, especially from internal pressure. **3.** To become or admit of being divided: *Let's split up into teams. This poem doesn't split up into stanzas very well.* **4.** *Informal.* To become divided or part company as a result of discord or disagreement: *She split with the regular party organization. They split up after a year of marriage.* **5.** To divide or share something with others. **6.** *Slang.* To depart; leave: *All the older kids have split to go dancing.* **—split** *n.* **1.** The act of splitting or the result of it. **2.** A breach or rupture in a group. **3.** A splinter. **4.** Something divided and portioned out; a share. **5.** A strip of flexible wood used for making baskets. **6.a.** A bottle of an alcoholic or carbonated beverage half the usual size. **b.** A drink of half the usual quantity. **c.** A half pint. **7.** A dessert of sliced fruit, ice cream, and toppings. **8.** Often **splits.** *Sports.* An acrobatic feat in which the legs are stretched out straight in opposite directions at right angles to the trunk. **9.** *Sports.* An arrangement of bowling pins left standing after a bowl, in which two or more pins remain standing with one or more pins between them knocked down. **10.** A single thickness of a split hide. **—split** *adj.* **1.** Having been divided or separated. **2.** Fissured longitudinally; cleft. **3.a.** Quoted in 16ths rather than in 8ths. Used of stocks. **b.** Having been split. Used of stocks. **—*idiom.* split hairs.** To see or make trivial distinctions; quibble. [Dutch *splitten,* from Middle Dutch.] **—split′ter** *n.*

Split (splĭt). A city of western Yugoslavia on the Dalmatian coast of the Adriatic Sea. Founded as a Roman colony, it later grew around a palace built by Diocletian in the early fourth century A.D. Population, 193,600.

split-brain (splĭt′brān′) *adj.* Of, relating to, or subjected to surgical separation of the hemispheres of the brain by severing the corpus callosum: *split-brain operation to prevent epileptic seizures.*

split infinitive *n. Grammar.* An infinitive verb form with an

splat¹

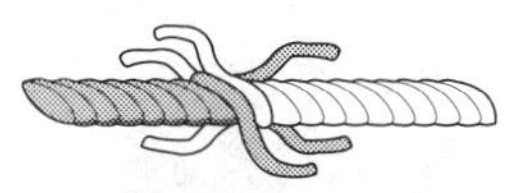

splice

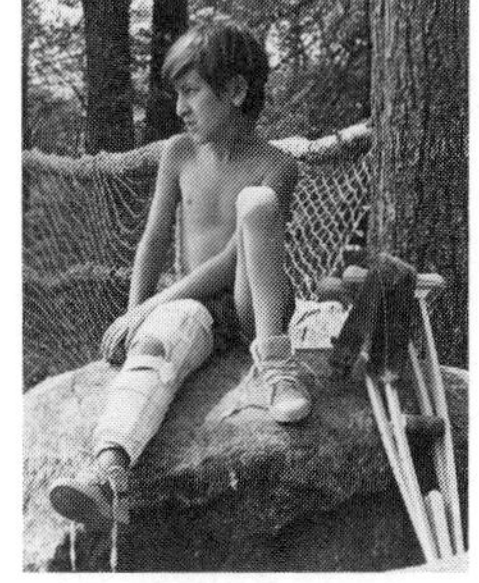

splint

ă pat	oi boy
ā pay	ou out
âr care	o͝o took
ä father	o͞o boot
ĕ pet	ŭ cut
ē be	ûr urge
ĭ pit	th thin
ī pie	*th* this
îr pier	hw which
ŏ pot	zh vision
ō toe	ə about, item
ô paw	♦ regionalism

Stress marks: **′** (primary); ′ (secondary), as in **dictionary** (dĭk′shə-nĕr′ē)

split rail
Split-rail fence

Benjamin Spock
Photographed in 1982

sponge

element, usually an adverb, interposed between *to* and the verb form, as in *to boldly go.*

USAGE NOTE: The split infinitive has been present in English ever since the 14th century, but it was not until the 19th century that grammarians first labeled and condemned the usage. In the 20th century many linguists and writers have rallied to its defense. H.W. Fowler chided that class of people "who would as soon be caught putting their knives in their mouths as splitting an infinitive," but whose aversion springs only "from tame acceptance of the misinterpreted opinion of others." No plausible rationale has ever been advanced for the rule, though it may arise from a hazy notion that because the Latin infinitive is a single word, the equivalent English construction must be treated as if it were indivisible. Still, many people who dislike the construction avoid it without difficulty. The sense of the sentence *To better understand the miners' plight, he went to live in their district* is just as easily expressed by *To understand the miners' plight better, he went to live in their district.* In some cases avoidance of the split infinitive may result in a stylistic improvement. The sentence *We are seeking a plan to gradually, systematically, and economically relieve the burden* becomes clearer if the adverbs are placed at the end: *We are seeking a plan to relieve the burden on our employees gradually, systematically, and economically.* (In an earlier survey the example having the split infinitive was accepted by only 23 percent of the Usage Panel.) But in other cases the effort to avoid a split infinitive may have unfortunate consequences. In *The tenant coalition is planning to aggressively seek cooperative ownership of the apartments the city acquired,* any attempt to reposition the adverb *aggressively* would create an ambiguity. In *We intend to use every political favor we are owed to soundly defeat this bill and its riders,* any other position will create an unnatural rhythm. In *We expect our output to more than double in a year,* the phrase *more than* is intrinsic to the sense of the infinitive phrase, though the split infinitive could be avoided by use of another phrase, such as *to increase by more than 100 percent.* In this example the split infinitive is accepted by 87 percent of the Usage Panel. • Excessive zeal in avoiding the split infinitive may result in an unnecessarily awkward placement of adverbs in constructions involving the auxiliary verbs *be* and *have.* When we read sentences like *I want this clearly to be understood,* we may suspect that the placement of *clearly* is the result of an effort to avoid the construction *to be clearly understood,* under the misapprehension that the latter involves a split infinitive. By the same token, there are no grounds for objecting to the position of the adverb in the sentence *He is committed to laboriously assembling all of the facts of the case.* What is "split" here is not an infinitive but a prepositional phrase.

split-lev·el (splĭt′lĕv′əl) *adj.* Having the floor levels of adjoining rooms separated by about half a story: *a split-level ranch house.* **—split′-lev′el** *n.*

split personality *n.* See **multiple personality.**

split rail *n.* A fence rail split lengthwise from a log. **—split′-rail′** (splĭt′rāl′) *adj.*

split second *n.* An instant; a flash. [Short for *split second hands,* a stopwatch with two second hands, one beneath the other, one of which may be stopped independently of the other.]

split shift *n.* A working shift divided into two or more periods of time, such as morning and evening, with a break of several hours between them.

split ticket *n.* **1.** A ballot cast for candidates of two or more political parties. **2.** A ticket that includes the names of candidates from more than one party.

split·ting (splĭt′ĭng) *adj.* Very severe: *a splitting headache.*

splotch (splŏch) *n.* An irregularly shaped spot, stain, or colored or discolored area: *"spectacular splotches of color and beauty in the blossoms"* (Wendy Lyon Moonan). **—splotch** *tr.v.* **splotched, splotch·ing, splotch·es.** To mark with splotches or a splotch. [Perhaps blend of SPOT, BLOT[1] and BOTCH.] **—splotch′i·ness** *n.* **—splotch′y** *adj.*

splurge (splûrj) *v.* **splurged, splurg·ing, splurg·es.** *—intr.* **1.** To indulge in an extravagant expense or luxury. **2.** To be showy or ostentatious. *—tr.* To spend extravagantly or wastefully. **—splurge** *n.* **1.** An extravagant display. **2.** An expensive indulgence; a spree. [Perhaps blend of SPLASH and SURGE.] **—splurg′y** *adj.*

splut·ter (splŭt′ər) *v.* **-tered, -ter·ing, -ters.** *—intr.* **1.** To make a spitting sound. **2.** To speak incoherently, as when confused or angry. *—tr.* To utter or express hastily and incoherently. **—splutter** *n.* A spluttering noise. [Perhaps alteration of SPUTTER.] **—splut′ter·er** *n.* **—splut′ter·y** *adj.*

Spock (spŏk), **Benjamin McLane.** Born 1903. American pediatrician, educator, and writer. His book *Baby and Child Care,* originally published in 1946, had a great influence on child-rearing.

Spode (spōd). A trademark used for a brand of fine china and earthenware.

Spode, Josiah. 1754–1827. British potter. In 1800 he founded a pottery that became famous for its bone china.

spod·u·mene (spŏj′ə-mēn′) *n.* A greenish to pinkish or lilac mineral, $LiAlSi_2O_6$, used as a source of lithium and in transparent varieties as a gemstone. [French *spodumène,* from German *Spodumen,* from Greek *spodoumenos,* present participle of *spodousthai,* to be burned to ashes, from *spodos,* wood ashes (because the mineral becomes ash gray when exposed to air).]

spoil (spoil) *v.* **spoiled** or **spoilt** (spoilt), **spoil·ing, spoils.** *—tr.* **1.a.** To impair the value or quality of. See Synonyms at **injure. b.** To damage irreparably; ruin. **2.** To impair the completeness, perfection, or unity of; flaw grievously: *spoiled the party.* **3.** To do harm to the character, nature, or attitude of by oversolicitude, overindulgence, or excessive praise. See Synonyms at **pamper. 4.** *Archaic.* **a.** To plunder; despoil. **b.** To take by force. *—intr.* **1.** To become unfit for use or consumption, as from decay. Used especially of perishables, such as food. See Synonyms at **decay. 2.** To pillage. **—spoil** *n.* **1. spoils. a.** Goods or property seized from a victim after a conflict, especially after a military victory. **b.** Incidental benefits reaped by a winner, especially political patronage enjoyed by a successful party or candidate. **2.** An object of plunder; prey. **3.** Refuse material removed from an excavation. **4.** *Archaic.* The act of plundering; spoliation. ***—phrasal verb.* spoil for.** To be eager for: *spoiling for a fight.* [Middle English *spoilen,* to plunder, from Old French *espoillier,* from Latin *spoliāre,* from *spolium,* booty.]

spoil·age (spoi′lĭj) *n.* **1.a.** The process of becoming spoiled. **b.** The condition of being spoiled. **2.a.** Something that has been spoiled. **b.** The degree to which something has been spoiled.

spoil·er (spoi′lər) *n.* **1.** One who seizes spoils or booty. **2.** Something that causes spoilage. **3.a.** A long, narrow hinged plate on the upper surface of an airplane wing that reduces lift and increases drag when raised. **b.** An air deflector mounted usually at the rear of an automobile to reduce lift at high speeds. **4.** A candidate for office whose chances of winning are slight but who may get enough votes to prevent one of the leading candidates from winning.

spoil·sport (spoil′spôrt′, -spōrt′) *n.* One who mars the pleasure of others.

spoils system (spoilz) *n.* The postelection practice of rewarding loyal supporters of the winning candidates and party with appointive public offices.

spoilt (spoilt) *v.* A past tense and a past participle of **spoil.**

Spo·kane (spō-kăn′). A city of eastern Washington near the Idaho border on the falls of the **Spokane River,** about 193 km (120 mi) long. Settled on the site of a trading fort established in 1810, Spokane is a trade and processing center in an agricultural, lumbering, and mining region. Population, 171,300.

spoke[1] (spōk) *n.* **1.** One of the rods or braces connecting the hub and rim of a wheel. **2.** *Nautical.* One of the handles projecting from the rim of a ship's steering wheel. **3.** A rod or stick that may be inserted into a wheel to prevent it from turning. **4.** A rung of a ladder. **—spoke** *tr.v.* **spoked, spok·ing, spokes. 1.** To equip with spokes. **2.** To impede (a wheel) by inserting a rod. [Middle English, from Old English *spāca.*]

spoke[2] (spōk) *v.* **1.** Past tense of **speak. 2.** *Archaic.* A past participle of **speak.**

spo·ken (spō′kən) *v.* Past participle of **speak. —spoken** *adj.* **1.** Expressed orally; uttered: *spoken words.* **2.** Speaking or using speech in a specified manner or voice. Often used in combination: *soft-spoken; plainspoken.*

spoke·shave (spōk′shāv′) *n.* A drawknife of a design originally used for shaping spokes, now used for making a variety of rounded edges.

spokes·man (spōks′mən) *n.* A man who speaks on behalf of another or others. See Usage Note at **man.** [Probably *spoke,* past participle of SPEAK + MAN.]

spokes·per·son (spōks′pûr′sən) *n.* A spokesman or a spokeswoman. See Usage Note at **man.**

spokes·wom·an (spōks′wo͝om′ən) *n.* A woman who speaks on behalf of another or others. See Usage Note at **man.**

spo·li·a·tion (spō′lē-ā′shən) *n.* **1.** The act of despoiling or plundering. **2.** Seizure of neutral vessels at sea by a belligerent power in time of war. **3.** *Law.* Intentional alteration or destruction of a document. [Middle English *spoliacioun,* from Anglo-Norman *spoliacioun,* from Latin *spoliātiō, spoliātiōn-,* from *spoliātus,* past participle of *spoliāre,* to despoil. See SPOIL.] **—spo′li·a′tor** *n.*

spon·da·ic (spŏn-dā′ĭk) *adj.* Of, relating to, or consisting of spondees. [French *spondaïque,* from Late Latin *spondaicus,* alteration of *spondīacus,* from Greek *spondeiakos,* from *spondeios,* spondee. See SPONDEE.]

spon·dee (spŏn′dē′) *n.* A metrical foot consisting of two long or stressed syllables. [Middle English *sponde,* from Old French *spondee,* from Latin *spondēum,* from neuter of *spondēus,* of libations, spondaic, from Greek *spondeios,* from *spondē,* libation (from its use in songs performed at libations). See **spend-** in Appendix.]

spon·dy·li·tis (spŏn′dl-ī′tĭs) *n.* Inflammation of the vertebrae. [Greek *spondulos,* vertebra + –ITIS.]

spon·dy·lo·sis (spŏn′dl-ō′sĭs) *n.* Degeneration of the spinal column, especially a fusion and immobilization of the vertebral bones. [Greek *spondulos,* vertebra + –OSIS.]

sponge (spŭnj) *n.* **1.a.** Any of numerous aquatic, chiefly marine invertebrate animals of the phylum Porifera, characteristically having a porous skeleton composed of fibrous material or siliceous or calcareous spicules and often forming irregularly shaped colonies attached to an underwater surface. **b.** The light, fibrous, flexible, absorbent skeleton of certain of these organisms, used for bathing, cleaning, and other purposes. **2.** Porous plastics, rubber, cellulose, or other material, similar in absorbency to this skeleton and used for the same purposes. **3.** A gauze pad used to absorb blood and other fluids, as in surgery or the dressing of a wound. **4.** A small absorbent contraceptive pad that contains a spermicide and is placed against the cervix of the uterus before sexual intercourse. **5.** Dough that has been or is being leavened. **6.** A light cake, such as sponge cake. **7.** A sponge bath. **8.** One who habitually depends on others for one's own maintenance. **9.a.** *Informal.* A glutton. **b.** *Slang.* A drunkard. **—sponge** *v.* **sponged, spong·ing, spong·es.** *—tr.* **1.** To moisten, wipe, or clean with or as if with a sponge: *sponge off the table.* **2.** To wipe out; erase. **3.** To absorb with or as if with a sponge: *sponge up the mess.* **4.** *Informal.* To obtain free: *sponge a meal.* *—intr.* **1.** To fish for sponges. **2.** *Informal.* To live by relying on the generosity of others: *sponged off her parents.* [Middle English, from Old English, from Latin *spongia,* from Greek, from *spongos.*]

sponge bath *n.* A bath in which the bather is washed with a wet sponge or washcloth without being immersed.

sponge cake *n.* A very light, porous cake made of flour, sugar, beaten eggs, and flavoring and containing no shortening.

sponge mushroom *n.* The morel.

spong·er (spŭn′jər) *n.* **1.** One that gathers sponges. **2.** *Informal.* A person who sponges on others; a parasite.

sponge rubber *n.* A soft, porous rubber used in toys, cushions, gaskets, and weather stripping and as a vibration dampener.

spon·gin (spŭn′jĭn) *n.* A horny, sulfur-containing protein related to keratin that forms the skeletal structure of certain classes of sponges.

spon·gi·o·blast (spŭn′jī-ə-blăst′) *n.* Any of the embryonic epithelial cells that give rise to the neuroglia. [Latin *spongia,* sponge; see SPONGE + –BLAST.]

spon·gi·o·cyte (spŭn′jē-ə-sīt′) *n.* Any of the cells of the neuroglia. [Latin *spongia,* sponge; see SPONGE + –CYTE.]

spon·go·coel (spŏng′gə-sēl′) *n. Zoology.* The central cavity of a sponge, which opens to the outside by way of the osculum. [Greek *spongo-,* sponge (from *spongos*) + –COEL.]

spong·y (spŭn′jē) *adj.* **-i·er, -i·est.** Resembling a sponge in elasticity, absorbency, or porousness. **—spong′i·ness** *n.*

spongy mesophyll *n.* A leaf tissue consisting of loosely arranged, chloroplast-bearing, usually lobed cells. Also called *spongy parenchyma.*

spon·son (spŏn′sən) *n.* **1.** *Nautical.* Any of several structures that project from the side of a boat or ship, especially a gun platform. **2.** A short, curved, air-filled projection on the hull of a seaplane, imparting stability in the water. [Perhaps alteration of EXPANSION.]

spon·sor (spŏn′sər) *n.* **1.** One who assumes responsibility for another person or a group during a period of instruction, apprenticeship, or probation. **2.** One who vouches for the suitability of a candidate for admission. **3.** A legislator who proposes and urges adoption of a bill. **4.** One who presents a candidate for baptism or confirmation; a godparent. **5.** One that finances a project or an event carried out by another person or group, especially a business enterprise that pays for radio or television programming in return for advertising time. **—sponsor** *tr.v.* **-sored, -sor·ing, -sors.** To act as a sponsor for. [Late Latin *spōnsor,* sponsor in baptism, from Latin, surety, from *spōnsus,* past participle of *spondēre,* to pledge. See **spend-** in Appendix.] **—spon·so′ri·al** (-sôr′ē-əl, -sōr′-) *adj.* **—spon′sor·ship′** *n.*

spon·ta·ne·i·ty (spŏn′tə-nē′ĭ-tē, -nā′-) *n., pl.* **-ties. 1.** The quality or condition of being spontaneous. **2.** Spontaneous behavior, impulse, or movement.

spon·ta·ne·ous (spŏn-tā′nē-əs) *adj.* **1.** Happening or arising without apparent external cause; self-generated. **2.** Arising from a natural inclination or impulse and not from external incitement or constraint. **3.** Unconstrained and unstudied in manner or behavior. **4.** Growing without cultivation or human labor; indigenous. [From Late Latin *spontāneus,* of one's own accord, from Latin *sponte.* See **(s)pen-** in Appendix.] **—spon·ta′ne·ous·ly** *adv.* **—spon·ta′ne·ous·ness** *n.*

SYNONYMS: *spontaneous, impulsive, instinctive, involuntary, automatic.* These adjectives mean acting, reacting, or happening without apparent forethought, prompting, or planning. *Spontaneous* applies to what arises naturally rather than resulting from external constraint or stimulus: *The two suddenly embraced in a spontaneous gesture of affection. "The highest and best form of efficiency is the spontaneous cooperation of a free people"* (Woodrow Wilson). *Impulsive* refers to the operation of a sudden urge or feeling not governed by reason: *Letting her friend borrow her car was an impulsive act that she immediately regretted. Instinctive* implies behavior prompted by instinct as a natural consequence of membership in a species: *"Nor is head-hunting, body-snatching, or killing for food instinctive or natural"* (Bronislaw Malinowski). The term also applies to what reflects or comes about as a result of a natural inclination or innate impulse: *Offering to help the accident victims seems as instinctive as breathing. Involuntary* refers to what is not subject to the control of the will: *"It* [becoming a hero] *was involuntary. They sank my boat"* (John F. Kennedy). *Automatic* suggests the unthinking, unfeeling functioning of a machine; it implies an unvarying mechanical response or reaction: *She accepted the subpoena with an automatic "thank you."*

spontaneous abortion *n.* See **miscarriage** (sense 1).

spontaneous combustion *n.* Ignition of a substance, such as oily rags or hay, caused by a localized heat-increasing reaction between the oxidant and the fuel and not involving addition of heat from an outside source.

spontaneous generation *n.* See **abiogenesis.**

spon·toon (spŏn-to͞on′) *n.* A short pike carried by infantry officers in the 18th century. [French *sponton,* from Italian *spuntone : s-,* intensive pref.; see SFORZANDO + *puntone,* kind of weapon, augmentative of *punto,* point (from Latin *pūnctum,* from neuter past participle of *pungere,* to pierce, prick; see **peuk-** in Appendix).]

spoof (spo͞of) *n.* **1.** Nonsense; tomfoolery. **2.** A hoax. **3.** A gentle satirical imitation; a light parody. **—spoof** *tr.v.* **spoofed, spoof·ing, spoofs. 1.** To deceive. **2.** To do a spoof of; satirize gently. [Origin unknown.]

spool

WORD HISTORY: When a comedian spoofs a television show or someone watches such a spoof, one is indebted to Arthur Roberts (1852–1933), a British comedian who invented a game called *Spoof,* which involved trickery and nonsense. The first recorded reference to the game in 1884 refers to its revival. It was not long before the word *spoof* took on the general sense "nonsense, trickery," first recorded in 1889. The verb *spoof* is first recorded in 1889 as well, in the sense "to deceive." These senses are less widely used now than the noun sense "a light parody or satirical imitation," first recorded in 1958, and the verb sense "to satirize gently," first recorded in 1927. In the 1969 *American Heritage Dictionary* the Usage Panel found both usages acceptable in writing at all levels, which seems the obvious finding since these senses had come to be so important to the use of the term.

spook (spo͝ok) *n.* **1.** *Informal.* A ghost; a specter. **2.** *Slang.* A secret agent; a spy. **—spook** *v.* **spooked, spook·ing, spooks.** *Informal. —tr.* **1.** To haunt. **2.** To frighten, especially to startle and cause nervous activity in (an animal or animals). *—intr.* To become frightened and nervous. Used especially of animals. [Dutch, from Middle Dutch *spooc.*]

spook·y (spo͞o′kē) *adj.* **-i·er, -i·est.** *Informal.* **1.** Suggestive of ghosts or a ghost; eerie. **2.** Easily startled; skittish. **—spook′i·ly** *adv.* **—spook′i·ness** *n.*

spool (spo͞ol) *n.* **1.a.** A cylinder of wood, plastic, cardboard, or other material on which wire, thread, or string is wound. **b.** The amount of wire, thread, or string wound on such a cylinder. **c.** Something similar to such a cylinder in shape or function. **2.** A reel for magnetic tape. **—spool** *tr. & intr.v.* **spooled, spool·ing, spools.** To wind or be wound on or off a spool. [Middle English *spole,* from Old North French *espole* and from Middle Dutch and Middle Low German *spoele* (Old North French, from Middle Dutch).]

spool·ing (spo͞o′lĭng) *n. Computer Science.* The temporary storage of information that occurs while that information awaits further processing. [From the acronym *spool* or *simultaneous peripheral operations on line.*]

spoon (spo͞on) *n.* **1.** A utensil consisting of a small, shallow bowl on a handle, used in preparing, serving, or eating food. **2.** Something similar to this utensil or its bowl, as: **a.** A shiny, curved, metallic fishing lure. **b.** A paddle or an oar with a curved blade. **3.** *Sports.* The three wood golf club. **—spoon** *v.* **spooned, spoon·ing, spoons.** *—tr.* **1.** To lift, scoop up, or carry with or as if with a spoon. **2.** *Sports & Games.* To shove or scoop (a ball) into the air. *—intr.* **1.** To fish with a spoon lure. **2.** *Sports & Games.* To give a ball an upward scoop. **3.** *Informal.* To engage in amorous behavior, such as kissing or caressing. [Middle English, from Old English *spōn,* chip of wood.] **—spoon′a·ble** *adj.*

spoonbill
Roseate spoonbill
Ajaia ajaja

spoon·bill (spo͞on′bĭl′) *n.* **1.a.** Any of several long-legged wading birds similar to the ibis but having a long, flat bill with a broadly spatulate tip. **b.** Any of various broad-billed ducks, such as the shoveler. **2.** See **paddlefish.**

♦ **spoon bread** *n. Chiefly Southern U.S.* A soft, light bread made with cornmeal, eggs, butter, and milk, baked in a bowl.

spoon·drift (spo͞on′drĭft′) *n.* See **spindrift.** [Obsolete *spoon,* to run before the wind + DRIFT.]

spoon·er·ism (spo͞o′nə-rĭz′əm) *n.* A transposition of sounds of two or more words, especially a ludicrous one, such as *Let me sew you to your sheet* for *Let me show you to your seat.* [After William Archibald *Spooner* (1844–1930), British cleric and scholar.]

spoon·ey (spo͞o′nē) *adj.* Variant of **spoony.**

spoon-feed (spo͞on′fēd′) *tr.v.* **-fed** (-fĕd′), **-feed·ing, -feeds. 1.** To feed (another) with a spoon. **2.** To treat (another) in a way that discourages independent thought or action, as by overindulgence. **3.a.** To provide (another) with knowledge or information in an oversimplified way. **b.** To provide (knowledge or information) in an oversimplified way.

spoon·ful (spo͞on′fo͝ol′) *n., pl.* **-fuls.** The amount that a spoon holds.

spoon·y also **spoon·ey** (spo͞o′nē) *adj.* **-i·er, -i·est. 1.** Enamored in a silly or sentimental way. **2.** Feebly sentimental; gushy.

ă pat	oi boy
ā pay	ou out
âr care	o͝o took
ä father	o͞o boot
ĕ pet	ŭ cut
ē be	ûr urge
ĭ pit	th thin
ī pie	*th* this
îr pier	hw which
ŏ pot	zh vision
ō toe	ə about, item
ô paw	♦ regionalism

Stress marks: ′ (primary); ′ (secondary), as in **dictionary** (dĭk′shə-nĕr′ē)

sporran
Edward VII wearing a leather sporran, c. 1880

spoor (spo͝or) *n.* The track or trail of an animal, especially a wild animal. **—spoor** *tr. & intr.v.* **spoored, spoor·ing, spoors.** To track (an animal) by following its spoor or to engage in such tracking. [Afrikaans, from Middle Dutch. See **spere-** in Appendix.]

spor– *pref.* Variant of **sporo–.**

Spor·a·des (spôr′ə-dēz′, spô-rä′thēs). Two island groups of Greece in the Aegean Sea, consisting of the **Northern Sporades** off the central mainland and the **Southern Sporades** off the coast of Turkey.

spo·rad·ic (spə-răd′ĭk, spô-) also **spo·rad·i·cal** (-ĭ-kəl) *adj.* **1.** Occurring at irregular intervals; having no pattern or order in time. See Synonyms at **periodic. 2.** Appearing singly or at widely scattered localities, as a plant or disease. **3.** Isolated; unique: *a sporadic example.* [Medieval Latin *sporadicus,* scattered, from Greek *sporadikos,* from *sporas, sporad-.* See **sper-** in Appendix.] **—spo·rad′i·cal·ly** *adv.* **—spo·rad′i·cal·ness** *n.*

spo·ran·gi·a (spə-răn′jē-ə) *n.* Plural of **sporangium.**

spo·ran·gi·o·phore (spə-răn′jē-ə-fôr′, -fōr′) *n.* **1.** A specialized branch bearing one or more sporangia. **2.** A stalk of a sporangium. [SPORANGI(UM) + –PHORE.]

spo·ran·gi·um (spə-răn′jē-əm) *n., pl.* **-gi·a** (-jē-ə). A single-celled or many-celled structure in which spores are produced, as in fungi, algae, mosses, and ferns. Also called *spore case.* [New Latin : SPOR(O)– + Greek *angeion,* vessel; see ANGIO–.] **—spo·ran′gi·al** (-jē-əl) *adj.*

spore (spôr, spōr) *n.* **1.** A small, usually single-celled reproductive body that is highly resistant to desiccation and heat and is capable of growing into a new organism, produced especially by certain bacteria, fungi, algae, and nonflowering plants. **2.** A dormant, nonreproductive body formed by certain bacteria in response to adverse environmental conditions. **—spore** *intr.v.* **spored, spor·ing, spores.** To produce spores. [Greek *spora,* seed. See **sper-** in Appendix.] **—spo·ra′ceous** (spə-rā′shəs, spô-, spō-) *adj.*

spore case *n.* See **sporangium.**

spore·ling (spôr′lĭng, spōr′-) *n.* A young plant produced by a germinated spore.

spore mother cell *n.* A cell that undergoes meiosis and usually produces four spores.

spo·ri·cide (spôr′ĭ-sīd′, spōr′-) *n.* An agent used to kill spores. **—spo′ri·cid′al** (-sīd′l) *adj.*

spo·rif·er·ous (spə-rĭf′ər-əs, spô-, spō-) *adj.* Producing spores.

Spork (spôrk). A trademark used for a plastic eating utensil having a spoonlike bowl and tines.

sporo– or **spor–** *pref.* Spore: *sporocyte.* [Greek, from *spora,* seed. See **sper-** in Appendix.]

spo·ro·carp (spôr′ə-kärp′, spōr′-) *n.* **1.** A multicellular structure in which spores are formed, especially in red algae and certain fungi and slime molds. **2.** A receptacle containing sporangia, as in the pepperwort.

spo·ro·cyst (spôr′ə-sĭst′, spōr′-) *n.* **1.** A resting cell that produces asexual plant spores. **2. a.** A protective case or cyst in which sporozoites develop and from which they are transferred to different hosts. **b.** A sporozoite enclosed in such a case; an encysted sporozoan. **3.** A saclike larval stage in many trematode worms.

spo·ro·cyte (spôr′ə-sīt′, spōr′-) *n.* A cell that produces haploid spores during meiosis.

spo·ro·gen·e·sis (spôr′ə-jĕn′ĭ-sĭs, spōr′-) *n.* **1.** Production or formation of spores. **2.** Reproduction by means of spores. **—spo′ro·gen′ic** (-jĕn′ĭk), **spo·rog′e·nous** (spə-rŏj′ə-nəs, spô-, spō-) *adj.*

spo·rog·o·ny (spə-rŏg′ə-nē, spô-, spō-) *n.* Reproduction by multiple fission of a spore or zygote, characteristic of many sporozoans. Sporogony results in the production of sporozoites. **—spo′ro·gon′ic** (spôr′ə-gŏn′ĭk, spōr′-), **spo·rog′o·nous** (spə-rŏg′ə-nəs, spô-, spō-) *adj.*

spo·ront (spôr′ŏnt, spōr′-) *n.* An organism or a cell produced by sporogony, especially in the life cycle of various parasitic microorganisms.

spo·ro·phore (spôr′ə-fôr′, spōr′ə-fōr′) *n.* A spore-bearing structure, especially in fungi.

spo·ro·phyll (spôr′ə-fĭl′, spōr′-) *n.* A leaf or leaflike organ that bears spores.

spo·ro·phyte (spôr′ə-fīt′, spōr′-) *n.* The spore-producing phase in the life cycle of a plant that exhibits alternation of generations. **—spo′ro·phyt′ic** (-fĭt′ĭk) *adj.*

spo·ro·plasm (spôr′ə-plăz′əm, spōr′-) *n.* An infective mass of protoplasm within a spore that is injected into a host cell by various parasitic microorganisms.

spo·ro·pol·len·in (spôr′ə-pŏl′ə-nĭn, spōr′-) *n.* A polymer that constitutes the outer wall of spores and pollen grains.

spo·ro·tri·cho·sis (spôr′ə-trĭ-kō′sĭs, spōr′-) *n.* A chronic infectious disease of domestic mammals and human beings, characterized by nodules or ulcers in the lymph nodes and skin and caused by a saprophytic or parasitic fungus of the genus *Sporothrix,* especially *S. schenckii,* commonly found in soil and wood.

–sporous *suff.* Having a specified number or kind of spores: *heterosporous.*

spo·ro·zo·an (spôr′ə-zō′ən, spōr′-) *n.* Any of numerous parasitic protozoans of the class Sporozoa, most of which reproduce sexually and asexually in alternate generations by means of spores. They are frequently transmitted by bloodsucking insects to different hosts, where they cause many serious diseases, such as malaria and coccidiosis. [From New Latin *Sporozoa,* class name : SPORO– + *-zoa,* pl. of *-zoon,* -zoon.] **—spo′ro·zo′an** *adj.*

spo·ro·zo·ite (spôr′ə-zō′īt′, spōr′-) *n.* Any of the minute undeveloped sporozoans produced by multiple fission of a zygote or spore, especially at the stage just before it infects a new host cell. [SPOROZO(AN) + –ITE[1].]

spor·ran (spôr′ən, spŏr′-) *n.* A leather or fur pouch worn at the front of the kilt in the traditional dress of men of the Scottish Highlands. [Scottish Gaelic *sporan,* from Middle Irish *sparán,* possibly from Late Latin *bursa,* bag. See BURSA.]

♦ **sport** (spôrt, spōrt) *n.* **1.** An activity involving physical exertion and skill that is governed by a set of rules or customs and often undertaken competitively. **2.** An active pastime; recreation. **3. a.** Mockery; jest: *He made sport of his own looks.* **b.** An object of mockery, jest, or play: *treated our interests as sport.* **c.** A joking mood or attitude: *She made the remark in sport.* **4. a.** One known for the manner of one's acceptance of rules, especially of a game, or of a difficult situation: *a poor sport.* **b.** *Informal.* One who accepts rules or difficult situations well. **c.** *Informal.* A pleasant companion: *was a real sport during the trip.* **5.** *Informal.* **a.** A person who lives a jolly, extravagant life. **b.** A gambler at sporting events. **6.** *Biology.* An organism that shows a marked change from the normal type or parent stock, typically as a result of mutation. **7.** *Maine.* See **summercater.** See Regional Note at **summercater. 8.** *Obsolete.* Amorous dalliance; lovemaking. **—sport** *v.* **sport·ed, sport·ing, sports.** *—intr.* **1.** To play or frolic. **2.** To joke or trifle. **3.** *Biology.* To mutate. *—tr.* To display or show off: *"His shoes sported elevated heels"* (Truman Capote). **—sport** or **sports** *adj.* **1.** Of, relating to, or appropriate for sports: *sport fishing; sports equipment.* **2.** Designed or appropriate for outdoor or informal wear: *a sport shirt.* [Middle English *sporte,* short for *disporte,* from Old French *desport,* pleasure, from *desporter,* to divert. See DISPORT.] **—sport′ful** *adj.* **—sport′ful·ly** *adv.* **—sport′ful·ness** *n.*

sport·ing (spôr′tĭng, spōr′-) *adj.* **1.** Used in or appropriate for sports: *sporting goods.* **2.** Characterized by sportsmanship. **3.** Of or associated with gambling. **—sport′ing·ly** *adv.*

sporting chance *n. Informal.* A fair chance for success.

spor·tive (spôr′tĭv, spōr′-) *adj.* **1.** Playful; frolicsome. **2.** Relating to or interested in sports. **3.** *Archaic.* Amorous or wanton. **—spor′tive·ly** *adv.* **—spor′tive·ness** *n.*

sports car (spôrts, spōrts) *n.* An automobile equipped for racing, especially an aerodynamically shaped one-passenger or two-passenger vehicle having a low center of gravity and steering and suspension designed for precise control at high speeds.

sports·cast (spôrts′kăst′, spōrts′-) *n.* A radio or television broadcast of a sports event or of sports news. [SPORTS + (BROAD)CAST.] **—sports′cast′er** *n.*

sports·man (spôrts′mən, spōrts′-) *n.* **1.** A man who is active in sports. **2.** A person whose conduct and attitude exhibit sportsmanship. **—sports′man·like′, sports′man·ly** *adj.*

sports·man·ship (spôrts′mən-shĭp′, spōrts′-) *n.* **1.** The fact or practice of participating in sports or a sport. **2.** Conduct and attitude considered as befitting participants in sports, especially fair play, courtesy, striving spirit, and grace in losing.

sports massage *n.* A system of massage, originally designed for athletes, that focuses on specific areas of the body, such as a knee or shoulder, that have been stressed or injured.

sports medicine *n.* The branch of medicine that deals with injuries or illnesses resulting from participation in sports and athletic activities.

sports·wear (spôrts′wâr′, spōrts′-) *n.* Clothes designed for comfort and casual wear.

sports·wom·an (spôrts′wo͝om′ən, spōrts′-) *n.* **1.** A woman who is active in sports. **2.** A woman whose conduct and attitude exhibit sportsmanship.

sports·writ·er (spôrts′rī′tər, spōrts′-) *n.* A person who writes about sports, especially for a newspaper or magazine.

sport·y (spôr′tē, spōr′-) *adj.* **-i·er, -i·est. 1.** Appropriate for sport or participation in sports. **2.** Exhibiting sportsmanship; sporting. **3.** Flashy; jazzy. **—sport′i·ly** *adv.* **—sport′i·ness** *n.*

spor·u·late (spôr′yə-lāt′, spōr′-) *intr.v.* **-lat·ed, -lat·ing, -lates.** To produce or release spores. [From New Latin *sporula,* small spore, diminutive of *spora,* spore, from Greek, seed. See SPORE.] **—spor′u·la′tion** *n.*

spot (spŏt) *n.* **1.** A place of relatively small and definite limits. **2. a.** A mark on a surface differing sharply in color from its surroundings. **b.** A stain or blot. **3.** *Games.* **a.** A mark or pip on a playing card; a spade, club, diamond, or heart. **b.** A playing card with a specified number of such marks on it indicating its value. **4.** *Informal.* A piece of paper money worth a specified number of dollars. **5. a.** A location; a locale. **b.** A point of interest: *There are a lot of spots to visit in the old city.* **c.** A position or an item in an ordered arrangement. **6.** *Informal.* A situation, especially a troublesome one. **7.** A flaw in one's reputation or character. **8.** A short presentation or commercial on television or radio between major programs: *a news spot.* **9.** *Informal.* A spotlight. **10.** *pl.* **spot** or **spots.** A small croaker *(Leiostomus xan-*

thurus) of North American Atlantic waters, having a dark mark above each pectoral fin and valued as a food and sport fish. **11.** *Chiefly British.* A small amount; a bit. **—spot** *v.* **spot·ted, spot·ting, spots.** *—tr.* **1.** To cause a spot or spots to appear on, especially: **a.** To soil with spots. **b.** To decorate with spots; dot. **2.** To harm; besmirch. **3.** To place in a particular location; situate precisely. **4.** To detect or discern, especially visually; spy. **5.** To remove spots from, as in a laundry. **6.** *Sports.* To yield a favorable scoring margin to: *spotted their opponents 11 points.* *—intr.* **1.** To become marked with spots. **2.** To cause a discoloration or make a stain. **3.** To locate targets from the air during combat or training missions. **—spot** *adj.* **1.** Made, paid, or delivered immediately: *a spot sale.* **2.** Of, relating to, or being a market in which payment or delivery is immediate: *the spot market in oil.* **3.** Involving random or selective instances or actions: *a spot investigation.* **4.** Presented between major radio or television programs: *a spot announcement.* **—*idioms.* in spots.** Now and then; here and there; occasionally. **on the spot. 1.** Without delay; at once. **2.** At the scene of action. **3.** Under pressure or attention; in a pressed position. [Middle English, from Old English.] **—spot′ta·ble** *adj.*

spot check *n.* An inspection or investigation that is carried out at random or limited to a few instances.

spot-check (spŏt′chĕk′) *tr. & intr.v.* **-checked, -check·ing, -checks.** To subject to or make a spot check.

spot·less (spŏt′lĭs) *adj.* **1.** Perfectly clean. See Synonyms at **clean. 2.** Free from blemish; impeccable. **—spot′less·ly** *adv.* **—spot′less·ness** *n.*

spot·light (spŏt′līt′) *n.* **1.a.** A strong beam of light that illuminates only a small area, used especially to center attention on a stage performer. **b.** A lamp that produces such a light. **2.** Public notoriety or prominence: *She was in the spotlight after she won the marathon.* **3.** An artificial source of light with a strongly focused beam, as on an automobile. **—spotlight** *tr.v.* **-light·ed** or **-lit** (-lĭt), **-light·ing, -lights. 1.** To illuminate with a spotlight. **2.** To focus attention on.

spot price *n.* The market price of a commodity.

Spot·syl·va·nia (spŏt′səl-vān′yə). A village of northeast Virginia southwest of Fredericksburg. It was the site of a major but inconclusive Civil War battle (May 8–21, 1864).

spot·ted (spŏt′ĭd) *adj.* Marked or stained with or as if with spots: *a spotted fabric, our spotted honor.*

spotted cranesbill *n.* See **wild geranium.**

spotted fever *n.* **1.** Any of various often fatal infectious diseases, such as typhus and Rocky Mountain spotted fever, characterized by skin eruptions and caused by rickettsia that are transmitted by ticks and mites. **2.** An epidemic form of cerebrospinal meningitis.

spotted salamander *n.* A common salamander *(Ambystoma maculatum)* of North America, having a black and yellow body with two rows of yellow spots along the back.

spotted sandpiper *n.* A small brownish-gray North American shore bird *(Actitis macularia)* that in summer acquires white underparts with many small black spots. Also called *peetweet.*

spot·ter (spŏt′ər) *n.* **1.** One that applies spots. **2.** One that looks for, locates, and reports something, as: **a.** A military or civil defense lookout. **b.** *Informal.* A person hired to detect dishonest acts by employees, as in a bank. **3.** *Sports.* **a.** One who identifies players on the field, as for a radio or television announcer. **b.** One who is responsible for watching and guarding a performer during practice to prevent injury, as in gymnastics or water-skiing. **4.** One employed by a dry cleaner to remove spots.

spot·ty (spŏt′ē) *adj.* **-ti·er, -ti·est. 1.** Lacking consistency; uneven. **2.** Having or marked with spots; spotted. **—spot′ti·ly** *adv.* **—spot′ti·ness** *n.*

spot weld·ing (wĕl′dĭng) *n.* Welding of overlapping pieces of metal at small points by application of great pressure and electric current. **—spot′-weld′** (spŏt′wĕld′) *v.* **—spot′-weld′er** *n.*

spou·sal (spou′zəl, -səl) *adj.* **1.** Of or relating to marriage; nuptial. **2.** Of or relating to a spouse. **—spousal** *n.* Marriage; nuptials. Often used in the plural. [From Middle English *spousaille,* marriage, from Old French *espousaille,* from Latin *spōnsālia,* betrothal, from neuter pl. of *spōnsālis,* of marriage, from *spōnsus,* past participle of *spondēre,* to pledge. See SPOUSE.]

spouse (spous, spouz) *n.* A marriage partner; a husband or wife. **—spouse** (spouz, spous) *tr.v.* **spoused, spous·ing, spous·es.** *Archaic.* To marry; wed. [Middle English, from Old French *spous,* from Latin *spōnsus,* from past participle of *spondēre,* to pledge. See **spend-** in Appendix.]

spout (spout) *v.* **spout·ed, spout·ing, spouts.** *—intr.* **1.** To gush forth in a rapid stream or in spurts. **2.** To discharge a liquid or other substance continuously or in spurts. **3.** *Informal.* To speak volubly and tediously. *—tr.* **1.** To cause to flow or spurt out. **2.** To utter volubly and tediously. **3.** *Chiefly British.* To pawn. **—spout** *n.* **1.** A tube, mouth, or pipe through which liquid is released or discharged. **2.** A continuous stream of liquid. **3.** The burst of spray from the blowhole of a whale. **4.** *Chiefly British.* A pawnshop. [Middle English *spouten,* ultimately of imitative origin.] **—spout′er** *n.*

♦**spout·ing** (spou′tĭng) *n.* *Chiefly Pennsylvania & New Jersey.* See **gutter** (sense 2). See Regional Note at **gutter.**

spp. *abbr.* Species (plural).

S.P.Q.R. or **SPQR** *abbr.* *Latin.* Senatus Populusque Romanus (the Senate and the people of Rome).

spr. *abbr.* Spring.

sprach·ge·fühl (shpräкн′gə-fül′) *n.* A feeling for language; an ear for the idiomatically correct or appropriate. [German : *Sprache,* language (from Middle High German *sprāche,* from Old High German *sprāhha*) + *Gefühl,* feeling (from *fühlen,* to feel, from Middle High German *vuelen,* from Old High German *vuolen;* see **pōl-** in Appendix).]

sprag (sprăg) *n.* **1.a.** A piece of wood or metal wedged beneath a wheel or between spokes to keep a vehicle from rolling. **b.** A pointed stake lowered at an angle into the ground from a vehicle to prevent movement. **2.** A prop to support a mine roof. [Perhaps of Scandinavian origin.]

sprain (sprān) *n.* **1.** A painful wrenching or laceration of the ligaments of a joint. **2.** The condition resulting from a sprain. **—sprain** *tr.v.* **sprained, sprain·ing, sprains.** To cause a sprain to (a joint or ligament). [Origin unknown.]

sprang (sprăng) *v.* A past tense of **spring.**

sprat (sprăt) *n.* **1.** A small marine food fish *(Clupea sprattus)* of northeast Atlantic waters that is eaten fresh or smoked and is often canned in oil as a sardine. Also called *brisling.* **2.** Any of various other similar fishes, such as a young herring. [Middle English *sprot, spratte,* from Old English *sprot.*]

sprawl (sprôl) *v.* **sprawled, sprawl·ing, sprawls.** *—intr.* **1.** To sit or lie with the body and limbs spread out awkwardly. **2.** To spread out in a straggling or disordered fashion: *untidy tenements sprawling toward the river.* *—tr.* To cause to spread out in a straggling or disordered fashion. **—sprawl** *n.* **1.** A sprawling position or posture. **2.** Haphazard growth or extension outward, especially that resulting from real estate development on the outskirts of a city: *urban sprawl.* [Middle English *sprawlen,* from Old English *sprēawlian,* to writhe. See **sper-** in Appendix.] **—sprawl′er** *n.*

spray¹ (sprā) *n.* **1.** Water or other liquid moving in a mass of dispersed droplets, as from a wave. **2.a.** A fine jet of liquid discharged from a pressurized container. **b.** A pressurized container; an atomizer. **c.** Any of numerous commercial products, including paints, cosmetics, and insecticides, that are dispensed from containers in this manner. *—attributive.* Often used to modify another noun: *spray paint; a spray can.* **—spray** *v.* **sprayed, spray·ing, sprays.** *—tr.* **1.** To disperse (a liquid) in a mass or jet of droplets. **2.** To apply a spray to (a surface). *—intr.* **1.** To discharge sprays of liquid. **2.** To move in the form of a spray. [From obsolete *spray,* to sprinkle, from Middle Dutch *sprayen.*] **—spray′er** *n.*

spray² (sprā) *n.* **1.** A small branch bearing buds, flowers, or berries. **2.** Something, such as a decorative motif, that resembles such a branch. [Middle English, from Old English **spræg.*]

spread (sprĕd) *v.* **spread, spread·ing, spreads.** *—tr.* **1.** To open to a fuller extent or width; stretch: *spread out the tablecloth; a bird spreading its wings.* **2.** To make wider the gap between; move farther apart: *spread her fingers.* **3.a.** To distribute over a surface in a layer: *spread varnish on the steps.* **b.** To cover with a layer: *spread a cracker with butter.* **4.a.** To distribute widely: *The tornado spread destruction.* **b.** To make a wide or extensive arrangement of: *We spread the bicycle parts out on the floor.* **c.** To exhibit or display the full extent of: *the scene that was spread before us.* **5.** To cause to become widely seen or known; scatter or disseminate: *spread the news; spread the beam of the flashlight.* **6.a.** To prepare (a table) for eating; set. **b.** To arrange (food or a meal) on a table. **7.** To flatten (a rivet end, for example) by pounding. *—intr.* **1.** To be extended or enlarged. **2.** To become distributed or widely dispersed. **3.** To increase in range of occurrence; become known or prevalent over a wide area: *The word spread fast.* **4.** To be exhibited, displayed, or visible in broad or full extent: *the vista spread seemingly to infinity.* **5.** To become or admit of being distributed in a layer. **6.** To become separated; be forced farther apart. **—spread** *n.* **1.a.** The act of spreading. **b.** Dissemination, as of news; diffusion. **2.a.** An open area of land; an expanse. **b.** A ranch, a farm, or an estate. **3.** The extent or limit to which something is or can be spread; range. **4.** A cloth covering for a bed, table, or other piece of furniture. **5.** *Informal.* An abundant meal laid out on a table. **6.** A food to be spread on bread or crackers. **7.a.** Two facing pages of a magazine or newspaper, often with related matter extending across the fold. **b.** A story or advertisement running across two or more columns of a magazine or newspaper. **8.** A difference, as between two figures or totals. **9.a.** A position taken in two or more options or futures contracts in order to profit from a change in their relative prices. **b.** The difference between the price asked and bid for a particular security. [Middle English *spreden,* from Old English *-sprǣdan,* as in *tōsprǣden,* to spread out. See **sper-** in Appendix.] **—spread′a·bil′i·ty** *n.* **—spread′a·ble** *adj.* **—spread′a·bly** *adv.*

spread eagle *n.* **1.a.** The figure of an eagle with wings and legs spread. **b.** The emblem on the obverse of the Great Seal of the United States. **2.** A posture or design resembling such an emblem or figure.

spread-ea·gle (sprĕd′ē′gəl) *adj.* **1.** Positioned with the arms and legs stretched out. **2.** *Informal.* Full of patriotic or jingoistic rhetoric. **—spread-eagle** *v.* **-gled, -gling, -gles.** *—tr.* To place in a spread-eagle position, especially as a means of punishment.

spotlight

spotter
Spotter at a weightlifting workout

spread eagle
Detail from a mid 19th-century American quilt

ă pat	oi boy
ā pay	ou out
âr care	o͝o took
ä father	o͞o boot
ĕ pet	ŭ cut
ē be	ûr urge
ĭ pit	th thin
ī pie	*th* this
îr pier	hw which
ŏ pot	zh vision
ō toe	ə about, item
ô paw	♦ regionalism

Stress marks: ′ (primary); ′ (secondary), as in **dictionary** (dĭk′shə-nĕr′ē)

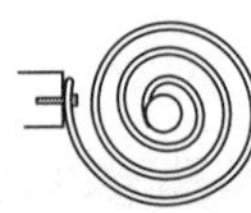

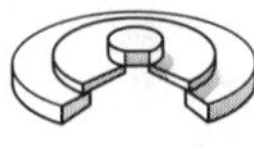

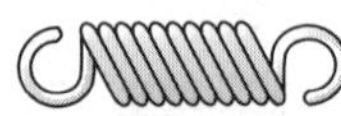

spring
Top: Spiral
Center: Disk
Bottom: Helical

springbok
Female springbok
Antidorcas marsupialis

springer spaniel

ă pat — oi boy
ā pay — ou out
âr care — o͝o took
ä father — o͞o boot
ĕ pet — ŭ cut
ē be — ûr urge
ĭ pit — th thin
ī pie — *th* this
îr pier — hw which
ŏ pot — zh vision
ō toe — ə about, item
ô paw — ♦ regionalism

Stress marks: **′** (primary); ′ (secondary), as in **dictionary** (dĭk′shə-nĕr′ē)

—*intr.* **1.** To assume a spread-eagle position. **2.** To make a grandiloquent, patriotic speech.

spread·er (sprĕd′ər) *n.* One that spreads, as: **a.** A butter knife. **b.** A farm or garden implement for scattering fertilizer or seed. **c.** A device, such as a bar, for keeping wires or stays apart.

spread·ing factor (sprĕd′ĭng) *n.* See **hyaluronidase.**

spread·sheet (sprĕd′shēt′) *n. Computer Science.* **1.** An accounting or bookkeeping program for a computer. **2.** The display, with multiple columns and rows, that such a program allows to be printed.

sprech·stim·me (shprĕkн′shtĭm′ə) *n.* A form of dramatic declamation between singing and speaking, in which the speaker uses lilt and rhythm but not precise pitches. [German : *sprechen,* to speak (from Middle High German *sprēchen,* from Old High German *sprehhan*) + *Stimme,* voice (from Middle High German *stimme,* from Old High German *stimma*).]

spree (sprē) *n.* **1.** A carefree, lively outing. **2.** A drinking bout. **3.** Overindulgence in an activity. See Synonyms at **binge.** [Perhaps alteration of Scots *spreath,* cattle raid, from Irish and Scottish Gaelic *spréidh, spré,* cattle, wealth, from Middle Irish *preit, preid,* booty, ultimately from Latin *praeda.* See **ghend-** in Appendix.]

WORD HISTORY: A spending spree seems a far cry from a cattle raid, yet etymologists have suggested that the word *spree* comes from the Scots word *spreath,* "cattle raid." The word *spree* is first recorded in a poem in Scots dialect in 1804 in the sense of "a lively outing." This sense is closely connected with a sense recorded soon afterward (in 1811), "a drinking bout," while the familiar sense "an overindulgence in an activity," as in a *spending spree,* is recorded in 1849. Scots and Irish dialect also have a sense "a fight," which may help connect the word and the sense "lively outing" with the Scots word *spreath,* meaning variously, "booty," "cattle taken as spoils," "a herd of cattle taken in a raid," and "cattle raid." The Scots word comes from Irish and Scottish Gaelic *spréidh,* "cattle," which in turn ultimately comes from Latin *praeda,* "booty." This last link reveals both the importance of the Latin language to Gaelic and a connection between cattle and plunder in earlier Irish and Scottish societies.

Spree (sprā, shprā). A river, about 402 km (250 mi) long, of eastern Germany rising near the Czechoslovakian border and flowing generally north to the Havel River at Berlin.

spri·er (sprī′ər) *adj.* A comparative of **spry.**

spri·est (sprī′ĭst) *adj.* A superlative of **spry.**

sprig (sprĭg) *n.* **1.a.** A small shoot or twig of a plant. **b.** An ornament in this shape. **2.** A small brad without a head. **3.** A young, immature person. **—sprig** *tr.v.* **sprigged, sprig·ging, sprigs.** **1.** To decorate with a design of sprigs. **2.** To remove a sprig or sprigs from (a bush or tree). **3.** To fasten with a small headless brad. [Middle English *sprigge,* alteration of *spring,* from Old English, source of water.] **—sprig′ger** *n.*

spright (sprīt) *n.* Variant of **sprite.**

spright·ful (sprīt′fəl) *adj.* Full of life; sprightly.

spright·ly (sprīt′lē) *adj.* **-li·er, -li·est.** Full of spirit and vitality; lively; brisk. **—sprightly** *adv.* In a lively, animated manner. **—spright′li·ness** *n.*

sprig·tail (sprĭg′tāl′) *n.* **1.** See **pintail.** **2.** See **ruddy duck.**

spring (sprĭng) *v.* **sprang** (sprăng) or **sprung** (sprŭng), **sprung, spring·ing, springs.** —*intr.* **1.** To move upward or forward in a single quick motion or a series of such motions; leap. **2.** To move suddenly on or as if on a spring: *The door sprang shut. The emergency room team sprang into action.* **3.** To appear or come into being quickly: *New businesses were springing up rapidly.* **4.** To issue or emerge suddenly: *A cry sprang from her lips. A thought springs to mind.* **5.** To extend or curve upward, as an arch. **6.** To arise from a source; develop. See Synonyms at **stem**[1]. **7.** To become warped, split, or cracked. Used of wood. **8.** To move out of place; come loose, as parts of a mechanism. **9.** *Slang.* To pay another's expenses: *He said he would spring for the dinner.* —*tr.* **1.** To cause to leap, dart, or come forth suddenly. **2.** To jump over; vault. **3.** To release from a checked or inoperative position; actuate: *spring a trap.* **4.a.** To cause to warp, split, or crack, as a mast. **b.** To bend by force. **5.** To present or disclose unexpectedly or suddenly: *"He sprung on the world this novel approach to political journalism"* (Curtis Wilkie). **6.** *Slang.* To cause to be released from prison or other confinement. **—spring** *n. Abbr.* **spr.** **1.** An elastic device, such as a coil of wire, that regains its original shape after being compressed or extended. **2.** An actuating force or factor; a motive. **3.a.** Elasticity; resilience. **b.** Energetic bounce: *a spring to one's step.* **4.** The act or an instance of jumping or leaping. **5.** A usually rapid return to normal shape after removal of stress; recoil. **6.** A small stream of water flowing naturally from the earth. **7.** A source, an origin, or a beginning. **8.a.** The season of the year, occurring between winter and summer, during which the weather becomes warmer and plants revive, extending in the Northern Hemisphere from the vernal equinox to the summer solstice and popularly considered to comprise March, April, and May. **b.** A time of growth and renewal. **9.** A warping, bending, or cracking, as that caused by excessive force. **10.** *Architecture.* The point at which an arch or a vault rises from its support. **—spring** *adj.* **1.** Of or acting like a spring; resilient. **2.** Having or supported by springs: *a spring mattress.* **3.a.** Of, having to do with, occurring in, or appropriate to the season of spring: *spring showers; spring planting.* **b.** Grown during the season of spring: *spring crops.* [Middle English *springen,* from Old English *springan.* N., Middle English *springe,* from Old English *spring,* wellspring.]

spring beauty *n.* Any of various succulent, spring-flowering plants of the genus *Claytonia,* especially *C. virginica,* of eastern North America, having narrow leaves and racemes of white or pinkish flowers.

spring·board (sprĭng′bôrd′, -bōrd′) *n.* **1.** *Sports.* **a.** A flexible board mounted on a fulcrum with one end secured, used by gymnasts to gain momentum, as in vaulting. **b.** See **diving board.** **2.** Something that helps to launch a career or an activity.

spring·bok (sprĭng′bŏk′) also **spring·buck** (-bŭk′) *n., pl.* **springbok** or **-boks** also **springbuck** or **-bucks.** A small brown and white gazelle *(Antidorcas marsupialis)* of southern Africa, noted for its habit of repeatedly leaping high into the air when startled. [Afrikaans : *spring,* to leap up (from Middle Dutch *springhen*) + *bok,* male deer (from Middle Dutch *boc*).]

spring break *n.* A period of recess, usually lasting one week, during the spring term at school.

spring·buck (sprĭng′bŭk′) *n.* Variant of **springbok.**

spring chicken *n.* **1.** A young chicken, especially one from two to ten months old, having tender meat. **2.** *Slang.* A young person.

spring-clean·ing (sprĭng′-klē′nĭng) *n.* A thorough cleaning, especially of a residence when winter is over.

Spring·dale (sprĭng′dāl′). A city of northwest Arkansas north of Fayetteville. It is a trade, processing, and shipping center. Population, 23,185.

springe (sprĭnj) *n.* **1.** A device for snaring small game, made by attaching a noose to a branch under tension. **2.** A trap or snare. [Middle English, branch, spring. See SPRING.]

♦ **spring·er** (sprĭng′ər) *n.* **1.** A springer spaniel. **2.** *Western U.S.* A cow about to give birth. **3.** *Architecture.* The bottom stone of an arch resting on the impost.

springer spaniel *n.* A dog of either of two breeds of spaniels, the English springer spaniel or the Welsh springer spaniel.

spring fever *n.* A feeling of languor or yearning brought on by the coming of spring.

Spring·field (sprĭng′fēld′). **1.** The capital of Illinois, in the central part of the state. It became the state capital in 1837 and is the site of Abraham Lincoln's grave. Population, 99,637. **2.** A city of southwest Massachusetts on the Connecticut River near the Connecticut border. Settled in 1636, it is an important manufacturing center. Population, 152,319. **3.** A city of southwest Missouri south-southwest of Kansas City. In a resort area of the Ozark Plateau, it is a trade, shipping, and manufacturing hub. Population, 133,116. **4.** A city of west-central Ohio west of Columbus. It grew as a trade and manufacturing center after the completion of the National Road (1838) and the coming of the railroad (mid-1800's). Population, 72,563. **5.** A city of west-central Oregon east of Eugene. Near the foothills of the Cascade Range, it is a processing center. Population, 41,621. **6.** A community of southeast Pennsylvania, a suburb of Philadelphia. Population, 25,326.

Springfield rifle *n.* A magazine-fed breechloading bolt-action .30-caliber rifle used by the U.S. Army especially in World War I. [After SPRINGFIELD, Massachusetts.]

spring·form pan (sprĭng′fôrm′) *n.* A cake pan having an upright rim that can be unclamped and detached from the bottom of the pan.

spring·halt (sprĭng′hôlt′) *n.* See **stringhalt.** [Alteration of STRINGHALT.]

spring·hare (sprĭng′hâr′) *n.* A burrowing nocturnal rodent *(Pedetes capensis)* of southern Africa, having long powerful hind legs with which it leaps like a kangaroo. [Partial translation of Afrikaans *springhaas* : *spring,* to leap up; see SPRINGBOK + *haas,* hare.]

spring·head (sprĭng′hĕd′) *n.* A fountainhead; a source: *a society that was the springhead of Western legal thought.*

spring·house (sprĭng′hous′) *n.* A small storehouse constructed over a spring and used to keep food cool.

spring·let (sprĭng′lĭt) *n.* A small spring of water; a rill.

spring-load·ed (sprĭng′lō′dĭd) *adj.* Secured or loaded by means of a spring.

spring lock *n.* A lock in which the bolt shoots automatically by means of a spring.

spring peeper *n.* A small, brownish tree frog *(Hyla crucifer)* of eastern North America, having a characteristic shrill, high-pitched call.

spring roll *n.* See **egg roll.** [Translation of Chinese (Mandarin) *chūn juǎn.*]

spring·tail (sprĭng′tāl′) *n.* Any of various small wingless insects of the order Collembola, having abdominal appendages that act as springs to catapult them through the air. Also called *collembolan.*

spring·tide (sprĭng′tīd′) *n.* Springtime.

spring tide *n.* **1.** The exceptionally high and low tides that occur at the time of the new moon or the full moon when the sun, moon, and earth are approximately aligned. **2.** A great flood or rush, as of emotion.

spring·time (sprĭngʹtīmʹ) *n.* The season of spring.

Spring Valley (sprĭng). A village of southeast New York near the New Jersey border west-northwest of White Plains. Mainly residential, it is also a summer resort. Population, 20,537.

spring·wood (sprĭngʹwo͝odʹ) *n.* Young, usually soft wood that lies directly beneath the bark and develops in early spring.

spring·y (sprĭngʹē) *adj.* **-i·er, -i·est. 1.** Marked by resilience; elastic. See Synonyms at **flexible. 2.** Abounding in freshwater springs. **—springʹi·ly** *adv.* **—springʹi·ness** *n.*

sprin·kle (sprĭngʹkəl) *v.* **-kled, -kling, -kles.** *—tr.* **1.** To scatter in drops or particles: *sprinkled sugar on the cereal.* **2.** To scatter drops or particles on. **3.** To intersperse with something as if by scattering: *sprinkled his speech with quotations.* **4.** To distribute or intersperse at random. *—intr.* **1.** To scatter something in drops or particles. **2.** To fall or rain in small or infrequent drops. **—sprinkle** *n.* **1.** The act of sprinkling. **2.** A light rainfall. **3.** A small amount. **4. sprinkles.** Small particles of candy sprinkled on ice cream as a topping. [Middle English *sprenklen,* perhaps of Middle Dutch or Middle Low German origin.]

sprin·kler (sprĭngʹklər) *n.* **1.** One that sprinkles, especially: **a.** An outlet on a sprinkler system. **b.** A device with perforations through which water issues from a hose to sprinkle a lawn. **2.** A sprinkler system. **—sprinkler** *tr.v.* **-klered, -kler·ing, -klers.** To equip with a sprinkler system.

sprinkler system *n.* A fire-extinguishing system consisting of a network of overhead pipes that release water automatically when a predetermined temperature has been reached.

sprin·kling (sprĭngʹklĭng) *n.* **1.** A small amount or quantity; a modicum. **2.** A small quantity scattered or sparsely distributed.

sprint (sprĭnt) *n.* **1.** *Sports.* A short race at top speed. **2.** A burst of speed or activity. **—sprint** *intr.v.* **sprint·ed, sprint·ing, sprints.** To run or move at top speed for a brief period. [Possibly alteration of Middle English *sprenten,* to spring up, of Scandinavian origin; akin to Swedish dialectal *sprinta* and Old Norse *spretta,* to jump.] **—sprintʹer** *n.*

sprit (sprĭt) *n.* *Nautical.* **1.** A pole that extends diagonally across a fore-and-aft sail from the lower part of the mast to the peak of the sail. **2.** A bowsprit. [Middle English, from Old English *sprēot,* pole. See **sper-** in Appendix.]

sprite also **spright** (sprīt) *n.* **1.** A small or elusive supernatural being; an elf or a pixy. **2.** An elflike person. **3.** A specter or ghost. **4.** *Archaic.* A soul. [Middle English *spreit,* from Old French *espirit,* from Latin *spīritus.* See SPIRIT.]

sprit·sail (sprĭtʹsəl, -sālʹ) *n.* *Nautical.* A sail extended by a sprit.

spritz (sprĭts, shprĭts) *tr.v.* **spritzed, spritz·ing, spritz·es.** To squirt or spray (something) quickly. **—spritz** *n.* A quick squirt or spray, as of carbonated water. [Pennsylvania Dutch *schpritze,* from Middle High German *sprützen,* to spray. See **sper-** in Appendix.]

spritz·er (sprĭtʹsər, shprĭtʹ-) *n.* A drink made of wine and carbonated water. [German, from *spritzen,* to spray, from Middle High German *sprützen.* See **sper-** in Appendix.]

sprock·et (sprŏkʹĭt) *n.* **1.** Any of various toothlike projections arranged on a wheel rim to engage the links of a chain. **2.** A cylinder with a toothed rim that engages in the perforations of photographic or movie film to pull it through a camera or projector. [Origin unknown.]

sprocket wheel *n.* A wheel rimmed with toothlike projections, used to engage the links of a chain in a pulley or drive system.

sprout (sprout) *v.* **sprout·ed, sprout·ing, sprouts.** *—intr.* **1.** To begin to grow; give off shoots or buds. **2.** To emerge and develop rapidly. *—tr.* To cause to come forth and grow. **—sprout** *n.* **1.** Young plant growth, such as a bud or shoot. **2.** Something resembling or suggestive of a sprout, as in rapid growth: *"a tall blond sprout of a boy"* (Anne Tyler). **3. sprouts.** Brussels sprouts. [Middle English *spruten,* from Old English *sprūtan.* See **sper-** in Appendix.]

spruce¹ (spro͞os) *n.* **1.a.** Any of various coniferous evergreen trees of the genus *Picea,* having needlelike foliage, drooping cones, and soft wood often used for paper pulp. **b.** Any of various similar or related trees. **c.** The wood of any of these trees. **2.** *Color.* A grayish green to dark greenish black. [Short for obsolete *Spruce fir,* Prussian fir, from Middle English *spruce,* Prussia, alteration of *Pruce,* from Anglo-Norman *Pruz,* from Medieval Latin *Prussia.*]

spruce² (spro͞os) *adj.* **spruc·er, spruc·est.** Neat, trim, and smart in appearance. See Synonyms at **neat¹. —spruce** *v.* **spruced, spruc·ing, spruc·es.** *—tr.* To make neat and trim: *spruced up the chairs with new slipcovers.* *—intr.* To make oneself neat and smart in appearance: *He was sprucing for the school dance.* [Perhaps from obsolete *spruce leather,* Prussian leather, from Middle English *spruce,* Prussia. See SPRUCE¹.] **—spruceʹly** *adv.* **—spruceʹness** *n.*

spruce budworm *n.* The highly destructive larva of a tortricid moth *(Choristoneura fumiferana)* of the northern United States and southern Canada that feeds on the needles, buds, and branch tips of spruce, fir, and other forest conifers.

spruce grouse *n.* A grouse *(Canachites canadensis)* that is dark gray barred with black, found in swampy forests of northern North America, and popular as a game bird.

spruce pine *n.* See **scrub pine** (sense 1).

sprue (spro͞o) *n.* A chronic, chiefly tropical disease characterized by diarrhea, emaciation, and anemia, caused by defective absorption of nutrients from the intestinal tract. [Dutch *spruw,* from Middle Dutch *sprouwe.*]

sprung (sprŭng) *v.* A past tense and the past participle of **spring.**

sprung rhythm *n.* A poetic rhythm designed to imitate the rhythm of speech, in which each foot has one stressed syllable, either standing alone or followed by a varying number of unstressed syllables. [Coined by Gerard Manley HOPKINS.]

spry (sprī) *adj.* **spri·er, spri·est** or **spry·er, spry·est.** Lively, active, and brisk; vigorous. See Synonyms at **nimble.** [Perhaps of Scandinavian origin; akin to Swedish dialectal *sprygg,* brisk.] **—spryʹly** *adv.* **—spryʹness** *n.*

s.p.s. *abbr.* *Latin.* Sine prole superstite (without surviving issue).

spt. *abbr.* Seaport.

spud (spŭd) *n.* **1.** *Slang.* A potato. **2.** A sharp spadelike tool used for rooting or digging out weeds. *—tr.* **spud·ded, spud·ding, spuds. 1.** To remove with a sharp spadelike tool. **2.** To begin drilling operations on: *spud an oil well.* [Middle English *spudde,* short knife.]

spue (spyo͞o) *v. & n.* *Obsolete.* Variant of **spew.**

spume (spyo͞om) *n.* Foam or froth on a liquid, as on the sea. **—spume** *intr.v.* **spumed, spum·ing, spumes.** To froth or foam. [Middle English, from Old French *espume,* from Latin *spūma.*] **—spuʹmous, spumʹy** *adj.*

spu·mo·ni or **spu·mo·ne** (spo͞o-mōʹnē) *n.* An Italian ice cream having layers of different colors or flavors and often containing fruits and nuts. [Italian, augmentative of *spuma,* foam, from Latin *spūma.*]

spun (spŭn) *v.* Past tense and past participle of **spin.**

spun glass *n.* **1.** See **fiberglass. 2.** Fine blown glass having delicate threading or filigree.

spunk (spŭngk) *n.* **1.** *Informal.* Spirit; pluck. **2.** Punk, touchwood, or other tinder. [Scottish Gaelic *spong,* tinder, from Latin *spongia,* sponge. See SPONGE.]

spunk·y (spŭngʹkē) *adj.* **-i·er, -i·est.** *Informal.* Spirited; plucky. **—spunkʹi·ly** *adv.* **—spunkʹi·ness** *n.*

spun silk *n.* A yarn made from short-fibered silk and silk waste.

spun sugar *n.* See **cotton candy.**

spun yarn *n.* *Nautical.* A lightweight line made of several rope yarns loosely wound together, used for seizings on board ship.

spur (spûr) *n.* **1.** A short spike or spiked wheel that attaches to the heel of a rider's boot and is used to urge a horse forward. **2.** Something that serves as a goad or an incentive. **3.** A spurlike attachment or projection, as: **a.** A spinelike process on the leg of some birds. **b.** A climbing iron; a crampon. **c.** A gaff attached to the leg of a gamecock. **d.** A short or stunted branch of a tree. **e.** A bony outgrowth or protuberance. **4.** A lateral ridge projecting from a mountain or mountain range. **5.** An oblique reinforcing prop or stay of timber or masonry. **6.** *Botany.* A tubular or saclike extension of the corolla or calyx of a flower, as in a columbine or larkspur. **7.** An ergot growing on rye. **8.** A spur track. **—spur** *v.* **spurred, spur·ring, spurs.** *—tr.* **1.** To urge (a horse) on by the use of spurs. **2.** To incite or stimulate: *"A business tax cut is needed to spur industrial investment"* (New York Times). *—intr.* **1.** To ride quickly by spurring a horse. **2.** To proceed in haste. [Middle English *spure,* from Old English *spura.* See **sperə-** in Appendix.]

spurge (spûrj) *n.* Any of various plants of the genus *Euphorbia,* characteristically having milky juice and small unisexual flowers that are surrounded by a cuplike structure composed of fused bracts. [Middle English, from Old French *espurge,* from *espurgier,* to purge (from its use as a purgative), from Latin *expūrgāre.* See EXPURGATE.]

spur gear *n.* A gear with teeth radially arrayed on the rim parallel to its axis.

spurge laurel *n.* A low-growing, evergreen Eurasian shrub *(Daphne laureola)* having glossy leaves and small yellowish-green flowers.

spu·ri·ous (spyo͝orʹē-əs) *adj.* **1.** Lacking authenticity or validity in essence or origin; not genuine; false. **2.** Of illegitimate birth. **3.** *Botany.* Similar in appearance but unlike in structure or function. Used of plant parts. [From Late Latin *spurius,* from Latin, illegitimate, probably of Etruscan origin.] **—spuʹri·ous·ly** *adv.* **—spuʹri·ous·ness** *n.*

spurious wing *n.* See table at **alula.**

spurn (spûrn) *v.* **spurned, spurn·ing, spurns.** *—tr.* **1.** To reject disdainfully or contemptuously; scorn. See Synonyms at **refuse¹. 2.** To kick at or tread on disdainfully. *—intr.* To reject something contemptuously. **—spurn** *n.* **1.** A contemptuous rejection. **2.** *Archaic.* A kick. [Middle English *spurnen,* from Old English *spurnan.* See **sperə-** in Appendix.] **—spurnʹer** *n.*

spur-of-the-mo·ment (spûrʹəv-thə-mōʹmənt) *adj.* Occurring or made hastily on impulse: *a spur-of-the moment choice.*

spurred (spûrd) *adj.* **1.** Wearing spurs: *Spurred riders sat astride sleek mares.* **2.** Having spurs or a spur: *spurred flowers; spurred boots.*

spur·ry also **spur·rey** (spûrʹē, spŭrʹē) *n., pl.* **-ries** also

sprinkler

spruce¹
Norway spruce
Picea abies

spur
c. 1730 American
silver spur

-reys. Any of several weedy, low-growing herbs of the genera *Spergula* or *Spergularia,* especially *Spergula arvensis* native to Europe, having linear whorled leaves and small white flowers. [Dutch *spurrie,* from Middle Dutch *speurie,* probably from Medieval Latin *spergula,* probably from Latin *spargere,* to scatter.]

spur shoot *n.* A slow-growing, much reduced, short shoot, as in the ginkgo, larch, and cedar.

spurt (spûrt) *n.* **1.** A sudden forcible gush or jet. **2.** A sudden short burst, as of energy or activity. **—spurt** *v.* **spurt·ed, spurt·ing, spurts.** *—intr.* **1.** To gush forth suddenly in a jet. **2.** To make a brief intense effort. *—tr.* To force out in a sudden jet. [Origin unknown.]

spur track *n.* A short side track that connects with the main track of a railroad system.

spu·ta (spyo͞o′tə) *n.* Plural of **sputum.**

sput·nik (spo͝ot′nĭk, spŭt′-, spo͞ot′nyĭk) *n.* Any of a series of Soviet satellites sent into Earth orbit, especially the first, launched October 4, 1957. [Russian *sputnik (zemlyi),* fellow traveler (of Earth) : *so-, s-,* together; see **ksun** in Appendix + *put′,* path, way; see **pent-** in Appendix + *-nik,* n. suff.]

sput·ter (spŭt′ər) *v.* **-tered, -ter·ing, -ters.** *—intr.* **1.** To spit out or spray particles of saliva or food from the mouth in noisy bursts. **2.** To spit out words or sounds in an excited or confused manner. **3.** To make sporadic spitting or popping sounds: *The fire sputtered and died.* **4.** *Physics.* To cause the atoms of a solid to be removed from the surface by bombardment with atoms in a discharge tube. *—tr.* **1.** To eject in short bursts with spitting or popping sounds. **2.** To utter in an excited or confused manner. **3.** *Physics.* To coat (a solid surface) with metal atoms by sputtering. **—sputter** *n.* **1.** The act or sound of sputtering. **2.** Matter emitted in sputtering. **3.** Excited or confused utterance. [Probably of Low German origin; akin to Dutch *sputteren.*] **—sput′ter·er** *n.* **—sput′ter·y** *adj.*

spu·tum (spyo͞o′təm) *n., pl.* **-ta** (-tə). Matter coughed up and usually ejected from the mouth, including saliva, foreign material, and substances such as mucus or phlegm, from the respiratory tract. [Latin *spūtum,* from neuter past participle of *spuere,* to spit.]

Spuy·ten Duy·vil Creek (spīt′n dī′vəl). A narrow channel in southeast New York separating northern Manhattan Island from the mainland and linking the Harlem and Hudson rivers.

spy (spī) *n., pl.* **spies** (spīz). **1.** An agent employed by a state to obtain secret information, especially of a military nature, concerning its potential or actual enemies. **2.** One employed by a company to obtain confidential information about its competitors. **3.** One who secretly keeps watch on another or others. **4.** An act of spying. **—spy** *v.* **spied** (spīd), **spy·ing, spies** (spīz). *—tr.* **1.** To observe secretly with hostile intent. **2.** To discover by close observation. **3.** To catch sight of: *spied the ship on the horizon.* **4.** To investigate intensively. *—intr.* **1.** To engage in espionage. **2.** To seek or observe something secretly and closely. **3.** To make a careful investigation: *spying into other people's activities.* [Middle English *spie,* from Old French *espie,* from *espier,* to watch, of Germanic origin. See **spek-** in Appendix.]

spy·glass (spī′glăs′) *n.* **1.** A small telescope. **2.** A pair of binoculars. Often used in the plural.

spy·mas·ter (spī′măs′tər) *n.* One who directs clandestine intelligence activities.

Spy·ri (spîr′ē, shpîr′ē), **Johanna.** 1827?–1901. Swiss writer whose best-known children's story is *Heidi* (1880).

sq. *abbr.* **1.** Squadron. **2.** Square.

squab (skwŏb) *n.* **1.** A young, newly hatched, or unfledged pigeon. **2.a.** A soft, thick cushion, as for a couch. **b.** A couch. **—squab** *adj.* Young and undeveloped; newly hatched or unfledged: *a squab chick.* [Probably of Scandinavian origin.]

squab·ble (skwŏb′əl) *intr.v.* **-bled, -bling, -bles.** To engage in a disagreeable argument, usually over a trivial matter; wrangle. See Synonyms at **argue. —squabble** *n.* A noisy quarrel, usually about a trivial matter. [Probably of Scandinavian origin; akin to Swedish dialectal *squabb,* fat flesh.] **—squab′bler** *n.*

squad (skwŏd) *n.* **1.** A small group of people organized in a common endeavor or activity. **2.** The smallest tactical unit of military personnel. **3.** A small unit of police officers. **4.** *Sports.* An athletic team. [Obsolete French *esquade,* from Old French *escadre,* from Old Spanish *escuadra* and Old Italian *squadra,* both from Vulgar Latin **exquadra,* square. See SQUARE.]

squad car *n.* A police automobile connected by radio with headquarters. Also called *cruiser, patrol car, prowl car.*

squad·ron (skwŏd′rən) *n. Abbr.* **sq. 1.** A naval unit consisting of two or more divisions of a fleet. **2.** An armored cavalry unit subordinate to a regiment and consisting of two or more troops. **3.** A basic tactical air force unit, subordinate to a group and consisting of two or more flights. **4.** An organized multitude: *"Squadrons of flies like particles of dust danced up and down"* (T.E. Lawrence). [Italian *squadrone,* augmentative of *squadra,* squad. See SQUAD.]

squad room *n.* **1.** A room in a police station where officers assemble, as for assignment or briefing. **2.** A room in a barracks in which a number of troops are lodged.

squa·lene (skwā′lēn′) *n.* A colorless unsaturated aliphatic hydrocarbon, $C_{30}H_{50}$, found especially in human sebum and in the liver oil of sharks, that is an intermediate in the biosynthesis of cholesterol and is used in biochemical research. [New Latin *Squalus,* shark genus (from its occurrence in the liver oil of sharks) (from Latin *squalus,* a sea fish) + -ENE.]

squal·id (skwŏl′ĭd) *adj.* **1.** Dirty and wretched, as from poverty or lack of care. See Synonyms at **dirty. 2.** Morally repulsive; sordid: *"the squalid atmosphere of intrigue, betrayal, and counterbetrayal"* (W. Bruce Lincoln). [Latin *squālidus,* from *squālēre,* to be filthy, from *squālus,* filthy.] **—squal′id·ly** *adv.* **—squal′id·ness, squa·lid′i·ty** (skwŏ-lĭd′ĭ-tē) *n.*

squall¹ (skwôl) *n.* A loud, harsh cry. **—squall** *intr.v.* **squalled, squall·ing, squalls.** To scream or cry loudly and harshly. [Probably of Scandinavian origin; akin to Old Norse *skvala,* to squeal.] **—squall′er** *n.*

squall² (skwôl) *n.* **1.** A brief, sudden, violent windstorm, often accompanied by rain or snow. **2.** *Informal.* A brief commotion. **—squall** *intr.v.* **squalled, squall·ing, squalls.** To blow strongly for a brief period. [Probably of Scandinavian origin.]

squall line *n.* A line of thunderstorms preceding a cold front.

squall·y (skwô′lē) *adj.* **-i·er, -i·est. 1.** Characterized by gusts of wind. **2.** *Informal.* Marked by commotion or disturbance.

squal·or (skwŏl′ər) *n.* A filthy and wretched condition or quality. [Latin *squālor,* from *squālēre,* to be filthy. See SQUALID.]

squa·ma (skwā′mə, skwä′-) *n., pl.* **-mae** (-mē′). **1.** A scale or scalelike structure. **2.** A thin platelike mass, as of bone. [Latin *squāma.*] **—squa′mate′** (-māt′) *adj.*

squa·ma·tion (skwə-mā′shən) *n.* **1.** The condition of being scaly. **2.** An arrangement of scales, as on a fish.

squa·mi·form (skwā′mə-fôrm′) *adj.* Having the shape of scales or a scale.

squa·mo·sal (skwə-mō′səl) *adj.* Of or relating to the thin, platelike part of the human temporal bone or to a corresponding part in other vertebrates. **—squamosal** *n.* A squamosal bone. [From Latin *squāmōsus,* squamous. See SQUAMOUS.]

squa·mous (skwā′məs, skwä′-) also **squa·mose** (-mōs′) *adj.* **1.** Covered with or formed of scales; scaly. **2.** Resembling a scale or scales; thin and flat like a scale: *the squamous cells of the cervix.* **3.** Of or relating to the thin, platelike part of the temporal bone. [Latin *squāmōsus,* from *squāma,* scale.] **—squa′mous·ly** *adv.* **—squa′mous·ness** *n.*

squamous cell carcinoma *n.* A carcinoma that arises from squamous epithelium and is the most common form of skin cancer. Also called *cancroid.*

squamous epithelium *n.* Epithelium consisting of one or more cell layers, the most superficial of which is composed of flat, scalelike or platelike cells.

squa·mule (skwā′myo͞ol, skwä′-) *n.* A small, loosely attached thallus lobe of certain lichens. [Latin *squāmula,* diminutive of *squāma,* scale.]

squa·mu·lose (skwā′myə-lōs′, skwä′-) *adj.* **1.** Having or consisting of minute scales. **2.** Having a thallus consisting of numerous squamules. Used of certain lichens. [Latin *squāmula,* diminutive of *squāma,* scale + -OSE¹.]

squan·der (skwŏn′dər) *tr.v.* **-dered, -der·ing, -ders. 1.** To spend wastefully or extravagantly; dissipate. See Synonyms at **waste. 2.** *Obsolete.* To scatter. **—squander** *n.* Extravagant expenditure; prodigality. [Origin unknown.] **—squan′der·er** *n.* **—squan′der·ing·ly** *adv.*

Squan·to (skwŏn′tō). Died 1622. Native American who helped the English colonists in Massachusetts develop agricultural techniques and served as an interpreter between the colonists and the Wampanoag.

square (skwâr) *n. Abbr.* **sq. 1.** A plane figure having four equal sides. **2.** Something having an equal-sided rectangular form: *a square of cloth.* **3.** A T-shaped or L-shaped instrument for drawing or testing right angles. **4.** *Mathematics.* The product obtained when a number or quantity is multiplied by itself. **5.** *Games.* Any of the quadrilateral spaces on a board, as in chess. **6.a.** An open, usually four-sided area at the intersection of two or more streets, often planted with grass and trees for use as a park. **b.** A rectangular space enclosed by streets and occupied by buildings; a block. **7.** *Slang.* A person who is regarded as dull, rigidly conventional, and out of touch with current trends. **—square** *adj.* **squar·er, squar·est. 1.** Having four equal sides and four right angles. **2.** Forming a right angle. **3.a.** Expressed in units measuring area: *square feet.* **b.** Having a specified length in each of two equal dimensions. **4.** *Nautical.* Set at right angles to the mast and keel. Used of the yards of a square-rigged ship. **5.** Approximately rectangular and equilateral in cross section: *a square house.* **6.** Characterized by blocklike solidity or sturdiness. **7.** Honest; direct: *a square answer.* **8.** Just; equitable: *a square deal.* **9.** Having been paid up; settled. **10.** *Sports.* Even; tied. **11.** *Slang.* Rigidly conventional; dull. **—square** *v.* **squared, squar·ing, squares.** *—tr.* **1.** To cut to a square or rectangular shape. **2.** To test for conformity to a desired plane, straight line, or right angle. **3.** To mark into squares. Often used with *off.* **4.a.** To bring into conformity or agreement: *She could not square the request with her principles.* **b.** To bring (oneself) into a better position or relation: *He tried to square himself with his parents.* **5.** To set straight or at approximate right angles: *square one's cap.* **6.** To bring into balance; settle: *square a debt.* **7.** *Sports.* To even the score of: *to square a game.* **8.** *Mathematics.* **a.** To raise (a number or quantity) to the second power. **b.** To find a square equal in area to (the area of a given figure). **9.** *Informal.* To bribe or fix: *a party in litigation that tried to square the judge.* *—intr.* **1.** *Mathematics.* To be at right angles. **2.** To agree or conform: *a* *story that doesn't square with the facts.* —**square** *adv.* **1.** *Mathematics.* At right angles. **2.** In a square shape. **3.** In a solid manner; firmly. **4.** Directly; straight: *ran square into each other.* **5.** In an honest, straightforward manner. —***phrasal verbs.*** **square away. 1.** *Nautical.* To square the yards of a sailing vessel. **2.** To put away or in order. **square off.** To assume a fighting stance; prepare to fight. **square up.** To settle a bill or debt. —***idioms.*** **on the square. 1.** *Mathematics.* At right angles. **2.** Honestly and openly: *has always dealt on the square.* **out of square. 1.** *Mathematics.* Not at exact right angles. **2.** Not in agreement. **square peg in a round hole.** *Informal.* A misfit. [Middle English, from Old French *esquarre,* from Vulgar Latin **exquadra,* from **exquadrāre,* to square : Latin *ex-,* ex- + *quadrāre,* to square (from *quadrum,* a square; see **k^wetwer-** in Appendix).] —**square′ly** *adv.* —**square′ness** *n.* —**squar′er** *n.*

square bracket *n.* See **bracket** (sense 4a).

square dance *n.* **1.** A dance in which sets of four couples form squares. **2.** Any of various similar group dances of rural origin. —**square′-dance′** (skwâr′dăns′) *v.* —**square dancer** *n.* —**square danc′ing** *n.*

square knot *n.* A common double knot in which the loose ends are parallel to the standing parts, most often used to join the ends of two cords or lines.

square matrix *n. Mathematics.* A matrix with equal numbers of rows and columns.

square meal *n.* A substantial, nourishing meal.

square measure *n.* A system of units used in measuring area.

square one *n. Informal.* The starting point. [Alluding to board games with numbered squares in which a penalized player may have to return to the starting point.]

square-rigged (skwâr′rĭgd′) *adj. Nautical.* Fitted with square sails as the principal sails.

square-rig·ger (skwâr′rĭg′ər) *n. Nautical.* A square-rigged vessel.

square root *n. Mathematics.* A divisor of a quantity that when squared gives the quantity.

square sail *n. Nautical.* A four-sided sail extended by a yard suspended horizontally across the mast.

square shooter *n. Informal.* One who is honest, forthright, and fair.

square·tail (skwâr′tāl′) *n.* See **brook trout.**

squar·ish (skwâr′ĭsh) *adj.* Somewhat or almost square. —**squar′ish·ly** *adv. & n.* —**squar′ish·ness** *n.*

squar·rose (skwăr′ōs′, skwär′-) *adj.* **1.** *Biology.* Having rough or spreading scalelike processes. **2.** *Botany.* Spreading or recurved at the tip: *squarrose bracts.* [Latin *squarrōsus,* scabby.]

squash¹ (skwŏsh, skwôsh) *n.* **1.** Any of various tendril-bearing plants of the genus *Cucurbita,* having fleshy edible fruit with a leathery rind and unisexual flowers. **2.** The fruit of any of these plants, eaten as a vegetable. [From alteration of Narragansett *askútasquash.*]

squash² (skwŏsh, skwôsh) *v.* **squashed, squash·ing, squash·es.** —*tr.* **1.** To beat, squeeze, or press into a pulp or a flattened mass; crush. See Synonyms at **crush. 2.** To put down or suppress; quash: *squash a revolt.* **3.** To silence or fluster, as with crushing words: *squash a heckler.* —*intr.* **1.** To become crushed, flattened, or pulpy, as by pressure or impact. **2.** To move with a splashing or sucking sound, as when walking through boggy ground. —**squash** *n.* **1.a.** The act or sound of squashing. **b.** The fact or condition of being squashed. **2.** A crushed or crowded mass: *a squash of people.* **3.** *Sports.* A racket game played in a closed walled court with a rubber ball. **4.** *Chiefly British.* A citrus-based soft drink. —**squash** *adv.* With a squashing sound. [Middle English *squachen,* from Old French *esquasser,* from Vulgar Latin **exquassāre* : Latin *ex-,* intensive pref.; see EX– + Latin *quassāre,* to shatter, frequentative of *quatere,* to shake; see **kwēt-** in Appendix.] —**squash′er** *n.*

squash bug *n.* A blackish North American insect *(Anasa tristis)* that is destructive to squash, pumpkins, and other crops.

squash·y (skwŏsh′ē, skwô′shē) *adj.* **-i·er, -i·est. 1.** Easily squashed. **2.** Overripe and soft; pulpy. **3.** Boggy; marshy: *squashy ground.* —**squash′i·ly** *adv.* —**squash′i·ness** *n.*

squat (skwŏt) *v.* **squat·ted, squat·ting, squats.** —*intr.* **1.** To sit in a crouching position with knees bent and the hams resting on or near the heels. **2.** To crouch down, as an animal does. **3.** To settle on unoccupied land without legal claim. **4.** To occupy a given piece of public land in order to acquire title to it. —*tr.* **1.** To put (oneself) into a crouching posture. **2.** To occupy as a squatter. —**squat** *adj.* **squat·ter, squat·test. 1.** Short and thick. **2.** Crouched in a squatting position. —**squat** *n.* **1.** The act of squatting. **2.** A squatting or crouching posture. **3.** A lift or a weightlifting exercise in which one squats and stands while holding a weighted barbell supported by the back of the shoulders. **4.** The place occupied by a squatter. **5.** The lair of an animal such as a hare. [Middle English *squatten,* from Old French *esquatir,* to crush : *es-,* intensive pref. (from Latin *ex-*; see EX–) + *quatir,* to press flat (from Vulgar Latin **coāctīre,* from Latin *coāctus,* past participle of *cōgere,* to compress : *co-,* co- + *agere,* to drive; see **ag-** in Appendix).] —**squat′ter** *n.*

squaw (skwô) *n. Offensive.* **1.** A Native American woman, especially a wife. **2.** A woman or wife. [Massachusett *squa,* younger woman.]

squaw·fish (skwô′fĭsh′) *n., pl.* **squawfish** or **-fish·es.** Any of several large cyprinid freshwater fishes of the genus *Ptychocheilus,* of western North America.

squawk (skwôk) *v.* **squawked, squawk·ing, squawks.** —*intr.* **1.** To utter a harsh scream; screech. **2.** *Informal.* To complain or protest noisily or peevishly. —*tr.* To utter with or as if with a squawk. —**squawk** *n.* **1.** A loud screech. **2.** A noisy complaint. [Imitative.] —**squawk′er** *n.*

squawk box *n. Informal.* The speaker on an intercom or a public-address system.

squaw man *n. Offensive.* A white or other non-Native American man having a Native American wife and usually living with her people.

squaw·root (skwô′ro͞ot′, -ro͝ot′) *n.* **1.** An eastern North American plant *(Conopholis americana)* parasitic on the roots of oaks and other trees and having tubular yellowish flowers and a stem covered with brownish scales. **2.** An eastern North American plant *(Trillium erectum)* having ill-smelling, purple to yellow flowers with three petals and dark red, six-angled fruit.

Squaw Valley (skwô). A valley of northeast California in the Sierra Nevada west of Lake Tahoe. A popular ski resort, it was the site of the 1960 Winter Olympics.

square knot

squeak (skwēk) *v.* **squeaked, squeak·ing, squeaks.** —*intr.* **1.** To give forth a short, shrill cry or sound. **2.** *Slang.* To turn informer. —*tr.* To utter in a thin, shrill voice. —**squeak** *n.* **1.** A short shrill cry or sound, such as that made by a mouse or a rusty hinge. **2.** An escape: *a close squeak.* —***phrasal verb.*** **squeak through** (or **by**). To manage barely to pass, win, or survive: *squeaked through the test; squeaks by on a limited income.* [Middle English *squeken,* perhaps of Scandinavian origin; akin to Old Norse *skvakka,* to croak.]

squeak·er (skwē′kər) *n.* **1.** One that squeaks. **2.** *Informal.* Something, such as an election, that is won, passed, or achieved by the narrowest of margins or at the very last moment.

squeak·y (skwē′kē) *adj.* **-i·er, -i·est. 1.** Characterized by squeaking tones: *a squeaky voice.* **2.** Tending to squeak: *squeaky shoes.* —**squeak′i·ly** *adv.* —**squeak′i·ness** *n.*

squeak·y-clean (skwē′kē-klēn′) *adj. Informal.* **1.** Perfectly clean: *squeaky-clean hair.* **2.** Free from moral fault or taint; untarnished and virtuous: *"Despite its squeaky-clean image,* [the agency] *suffered waste and inefficiency"* (William D. Marbach).

squeal (skwēl) *v.* **squealed, squeal·ing, squeals.** —*intr.* **1.** To give forth a loud, shrill cry or sound. **2.** *Slang.* To turn informer; betray an accomplice or a secret. —*tr.* To utter or produce with a squeal. —**squeal** *n.* A loud, shrill cry or sound: *a squeal of surprise; the squeal of tires.* [Middle English *squelen,* probably of imitative origin.] —**squeal′er** *n.*

squash¹

squea·mish (skwē′mĭsh) *adj.* **1.a.** Easily nauseated or sickened. **b.** Nauseated. **2.** Easily shocked or disgusted. **3.** Excessively fastidious or scrupulous. [Middle English *squeimous,* alteration of Anglo-Norman *escoymous.*] —**squea′mish·ly** *adv.* —**squea′mish·ness** *n.*

squee·gee (skwē′jē) *n.* **1.** A T-shaped implement having a crosspiece edged with rubber or leather that is drawn across a surface to remove water, as in washing windows. **2.** *Printing.* A similar implement or a rubber roller used in printing and photography. —**squeegee** *tr.v.* **-geed, -gee·ing, -gees.** To wipe or smooth with a squeegee. [Perhaps from obsolete *squeege,* to press, alteration of SQUEEZE.]

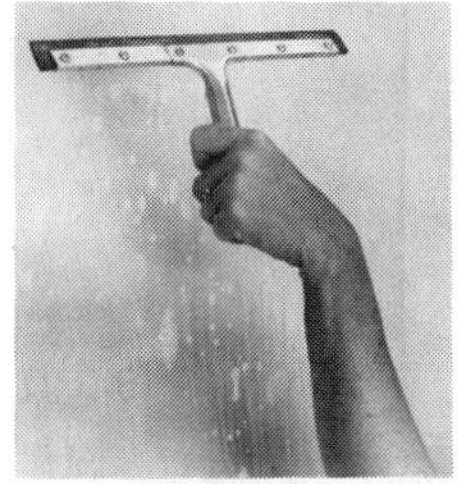
squeegee

squeeze (skwēz) *v.* **squeezed, squeez·ing, squeez·es.** —*tr.* **1.** To press hard on or together; compress. **2.** To press gently, as in affection: *squeezed her hand.* **3.** To exert pressure on, as by way of extracting liquid: *squeeze an orange.* **4.** To extract by or as if by applying pressure: *squeeze juice from a lemon; squeezed a confession out of a suspect.* **5.** To extract by dishonest means; extort. **6.** To oppress with burdensome demands. **7.** To obtain room for by pressure; cram: *squeezed her books into the briefcase.* **8.** To manage to find time or space for. **9.** *Games.* To force (an opponent) to use a potentially winning card in a trick he or she cannot take in bridge. —*intr.* **1.** To give way under pressure. **2.** To exert pressure. **3.** To force one's way: *squeeze through a crowd; squeeze into a tight space.* —**squeeze** *n.* **1.** The act or an instance of squeezing. **2.** An amount squeezed out: *a squeeze of lemon.* **3.** A handclasp or brief embrace. **4.** A group crowded together; a crush. **5.** *Informal.* A squeeze play. **6.** Financial pressure caused by shortages or narrowing economic margins. **7.** *Games.* A forced discard of a potentially winning card in bridge. —***phrasal verbs.*** **squeeze off.** To fire (a round of bullets) by squeezing the trigger. **squeeze through** (or **by**). To manage narrowly to pass, win, or survive. [Probably alteration of obsolete *quease,* to press, from Middle English *queisen,* from Old English *cwȳsan.*] —**squeez′a·ble** *adj.* —**squeez′er** *n.*

squeeze·box (skwēz′bŏks′) *n. Music.* An accordion.

squeeze play *n.* **1.** *Baseball.* A play in which the batter attempts to bunt so that a runner on third base may score. **2.** *Informal.* Pressure exerted to obtain a concession or achieve a goal.

squelch (skwĕlch) *v.* **squelched, squelch·ing, squelch·es.** —*tr.* **1.** To crush by or as if by trampling; squash. **2.** To put down or silence, as with a crushing retort: *squelch a rumor.* —*intr.* To produce a splashing, squishing, or sucking sound; as when walking through ooze. —**squelch** *n.* **1.** A squishing sound. **2.** A crushing reply. **3.** An electric circuit that cuts off a radio receiver when the signal is too weak for reception of anything but noise. [Probably imitative.] —**squelch′er** *n.*

sque·teague (skwĭ-tēg′) *n., pl.* **squeteague. 1.** See **weak-**

ă pat	oi boy
ā pay	ou out
âr care	o͝o took
ä father	o͞o boot
ĕ pet	ŭ cut
ē be	ûr urge
ĭ pit	th thin
ī pie	*th* this
îr pier	hw which
ŏ pot	zh vision
ō toe	ə about, item
ô paw	♦ regionalism

Stress marks: **′** (primary); ′ (secondary), as in **dictionary** (dĭk′shə-nĕr′ē)

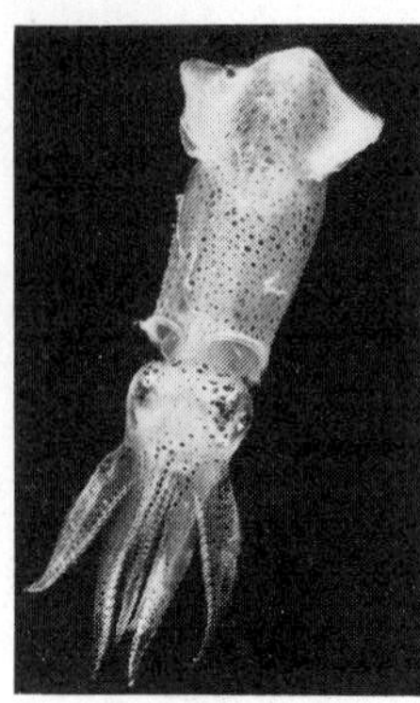
squid

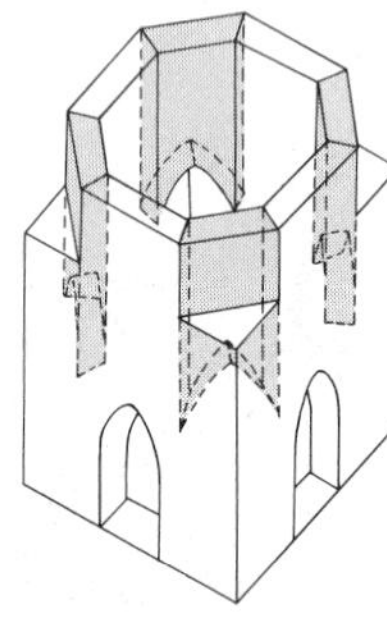
squinch ¹

squirrel

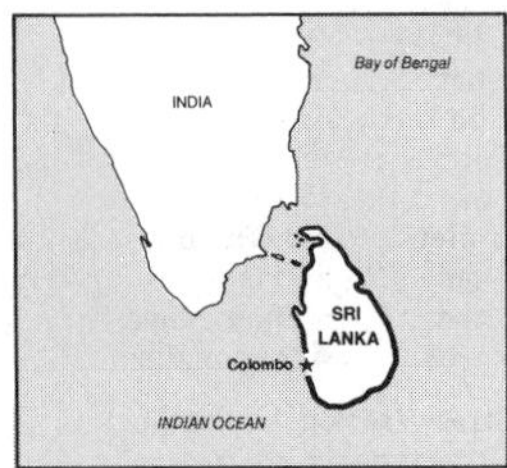

Sri Lanka

fish. **2.** Any of several fishes related to the weakfish. [Of Algonquian origin.]

squib (skwĭb) *n.* **1.a.** A small firecracker. **b.** A broken firecracker that burns but does not explode. **2.a.** A brief satirical or witty writing or speech, such as a lampoon. **b.** A short, sometimes humorous piece in a newspaper or magazine, usually used as a filler. **—squib** *v.* **squibbed, squib•bing, squibs.** *—intr.* To write or utter squibs. *—tr.* **1.** To write or utter squibs against; lampoon. **2.** *Football.* To kick (the ball) low on a kickoff so that it bounces along the ground. [Probably imitative.]

squib kick *n. Football.* A kickoff in which the ball is kicked low so that it will bounce along the ground, making it difficult to field and return.

squid (skwĭd) *n., pl.* **squids** or **squid.** Any of various marine cephalopod mollusks of the genus *Loligo* and related genera, having a usually elongated body, ten arms surrounding the mouth, a vestigial internal shell, and a pair of triangular or rounded fins. [Origin unknown.]

squig•gle (skwĭg′əl) *n.* A small wiggly mark or scrawl. **—squiggle** *intr.v.* **-gled, -gling, -gles. 1.** To squirm and wriggle. **2.** To make squiggles. [Perhaps blend of SQUIRM and WIGGLE.] **—squig′gly** *adj.*

squill (skwĭl) *n.* **1.** Any of several bulbous Eurasian and African plants of the genus *Scilla,* having narrow leaves and bell-shaped blue, white, or pink flowers. **2.** See **sea onion** (sense 1). **3.** The dried inner scales of the bulbs of any of these plants, used as rat poison and formerly as a cardiac stimulant, expectorant, and diuretic. [Middle English, from Latin *scilla, squilla,* shrimp, squill, from Greek *skilla.*]

squil•la (skwĭl′ə) *n., pl.* **squil•las** or **squil•lae** (skwĭl′ē′). Any of various burrowing predatory marine crustaceans of the order Stomatopoda, having movable stalked eyes and a pair of jointed grasping appendages. Also called *mantis crab, mantis shrimp.* [New Latin *Squilla,* genus name, from Latin *squilla,* shrimp. See SQUILL.]

squinch¹ (skwĭnch) *n.* A quarter-spherical segment of masonry vaulting or corbeling carried across an interior angle of a square tower to support a circular or octagonal superstructure. [Alteration of *scuncheon,* from Middle English *sconchon,* from Old French *escoinson* : *es-,* out of (from Latin *ex-;* see EX–) + *coin,* angle, wedge; see COIN.]

squinch² (skwĭnch) *tr.v.* **squinched, squinch•ing, squinch•es.** To squeeze, twist, or draw together: *squinched her eyes shut.* [Alteration of SQUINT.]

squint (skwĭnt) *v.* **squint•ed, squint•ing, squints.** *—intr.* **1.** To look with the eyes partly closed, as in bright sunlight. **2.a.** To look or glance sideways. **b.** To look askance, as in disapproval. **3.** To have an indirect reference or inclination. **4.** To be affected with strabismus. *—tr.* **1.** To cause to squint. **2.** To close (the eyes) partly while looking. **—squint** *n.* **1.** The act or an instance of squinting. **2.a.** A sideways glance. **b.** A quick look or glance: *Take a squint at this view.* **3.** An oblique reference or inclination. **4.** See **strabismus. 5.** A hagioscope. **—squint** *adj.* **1.** Looking obliquely or askance. **2.** Squint-eyed. [Short for ASQUINT.] **—squint′er** *n.* **—squint′y** *adj.*

squint-eyed (skwĭnt′īd′) *adj.* **1.** Affected with strabismus. **2.** Looking with narrowed or squinting eyes. **3.** Looking askance, as in envy.

squir•ar•chy (skwīr′är′kē) *n.* Variant of **squirearchy.**

squire (skwīr) *n.* **1.** A man who attends or escorts a woman; a gallant. **2.** An English country gentleman, especially the chief landowner in a district. **3.** A judge or another local dignitary. **4.** A young nobleman attendant upon a knight and ranked next below a knight in feudal hierarchy. **—squire** *tr.v.* **squired, squir•ing, squires.** To attend as a squire; escort. [Middle English *squier,* from Old French *esquier.* See ESQUIRE.]

squire•ar•chy or **squir•ar•chy** (skwīr′är′kē) *n., pl.* **-chies.** The landed gentry considered as a group or class.

squirm (skwûrm) *intr.v.* **squirmed, squirm•ing, squirms. 1.** To twist about in a wriggling, snakelike motion; writhe. **2.** To feel or exhibit signs of humiliation or embarrassment. See Synonyms at **writhe. —squirm** *n.* **1.** The act of squirming. **2.** A squirming movement. [Origin unknown.] **—squirm′er** *n.* **—squirm′y** *adj.*

squir•rel (skwûr′əl, skwŭr′-) *n.* **1.** Any of various arboreal rodents of the genus *Sciurus* and related genera of the family Sciuridae, having a long flexible bushy tail and including the fox squirrel, gray squirrel, and red squirrel. Also called *tree squirrel.* **2.** Any of various other rodents of the family Sciuridae, as the ground squirrel or the flying squirrel. **3.** The fur of one of these rodents. **—squirrel** *tr.v.* **-reled, -rel•ing, -rels** or **-relled, -rel•ling, -rels.** To hide or store: *squirreled away her money.* [Middle English *squirel,* from Anglo-Norman *esquirel,* from Vulgar Latin **scūriolus,* diminutive of **scūrius,* alteration of Latin *sciūrus,* from Greek *skiouros* : *skia,* shadow + *oura,* tail; see **ors-** in Appendix.]

squirrel corn *n.* A low-growing North American plant *(Dicentra canadensis)* having finely divided basal leaves, fragrant whitish flowers tinged with purple, and small yellow tubers resembling grains of corn.

squir•rel•fish (skwûr′əl-fĭsh′, skwŭr′-) *n., pl.* **squirrelfish** or **-fish•es.** Any of various nocturnal fishes of the genus *Holocentrus* and related genera, of warm marine waters, having large eyes like those of squirrels and a usually brightly colored body.

squir•rel•ly (skwûr′ə-lē, skwŭr′-) *adj. Slang.* **1.** Eccentric. **2.** Cunningly unforthcoming or reticent.

squirrel monkey *n.* Any of several small, brightly colored arboreal monkeys of the genus *Saimiri,* widely distributed in South and Central American tropical forest regions, having a white face with black nose and mouth, short fur, and a long nonprehensile tail.

squirt (skwûrt) *v.* **squirt•ed, squirt•ing, squirts.** *—intr.* **1.** To issue forth in a thin forceful stream or jet; spurt. **2.** To eject liquid in a jet. *—tr.* **1.** To eject (liquid) forcibly in a thin stream from a narrow opening. **2.** To wet with a spurt of liquid. **—squirt** *n.* **1.** The act of squirting. **2.** An instrument, such as a syringe, used for squirting. **3.** A squirted jet of liquid. [Middle English *squirten,* possibly of Middle Dutch or Middle Low German origin; akin to Low German *swirtjen.*] **—squirt′er** *n.*

squirt gun *n.* A toy gun designed to squirt a stream of water. Also called *water gun, water pistol.*

squirt•ing cucumber (skwûr′tĭng) *n.* A hairy Mediterranean vine *(Ecballium elaterium)* having fruit that when ripe discharges its seeds and juice explosively.

squish (skwĭsh) *v.* **squished, squish•ing, squish•es.** *—tr.* To squeeze or crush together or into a flat mass; squash. *—intr.* To emit the gurgling or sucking sound of soft mud being walked on. **—squish** *n.* **1.** A squishing sound. **2.** *Slang.* A person regarded as weak and ineffective. [Probably alteration of SQUASH².]

squish•y (skwĭsh′ē) *adj.* **squish•i•er, squish•i•est. 1.** Soft and wet; spongy. **2.** Sloppily sentimental.

sr *abbr.* Steradian.

Sr The symbol for the element **strontium.**

Sr. *abbr.* **1.** Or **sr.** Senior. **2.** Señor. **3.** *Ecclesiastical.* Sister (religious).

Sra. *abbr.* Señora.

Sra•nan (srä′nən) *n.* See **Sranantongo.**

Sra•nan•ton•go (srä′nən-tŏng′gō) *n.* A creole based on English, spoken in coastal Suriname and widely used as a lingua franca. Also called *Sranan, taki-taki.* [Sranantongo : *Sranan,* Suriname + *tongo,* tongue (from English TONGUE).]

Sri Lan•ka (srē läng′kə). Formerly **Cey•lon** (sĭ-lŏn′, sā-). An island country in the Indian Ocean off southeast India. Inhabited from ancient times, the island attracted Arab, Portuguese, Dutch, and British traders for its wealth of spices. It became a British colony in 1798 and achieved independence in 1948. Colombo is the capital and the largest city. Population, 14,848,364. **—Sri Lan′kan** *adj. & n.*

Sri•na•gar (srē-nŭg′ər). A city of northern India on the Jhelum River north of Amritsar. Founded in the sixth century A.D., it has long been a noted resort. Population, 594,775.

sRNA *n.* Soluble RNA.

SRO *abbr.* **1.** Single room occupancy. **2.** Standing room only.

Srta. *abbr.* Señorita.

SS¹ (ĕs′ĕs′) *n.* An elite quasi-military unit of the Nazi party that served as Hitler's personal guard and as a special security force in Germany and the occupied countries. [German, abbr. for *Schutzstaffel* : *Schutz,* defense + *Staffel,* echelon.]

SS² *abbr.* Saints.

ss. *abbr.* **1.** Or **ss.** Scilicet. **2.** Semis (one half).

S.S. *abbr.* **1.** Social Security. **2.** Or **SS.** Steamship. **3.** Sunday school. **4.** Sworn statement.

s/s *abbr.* Same size.

SSA *abbr.* Social Security Administration.

SSE *abbr.* South-southeast.

S.Sgt. or **SSGT** *abbr.* Staff sergeant.

SSI *abbr.* Supplemental Security Income.

ssp. *abbr.* Subspecies.

S.S.R. or **SSR** *abbr.* Soviet Socialist Republic.

SST *abbr.* Supersonic transport.

SSW *abbr.* South-southwest.

ST *abbr.* Standard time.

st. *abbr.* **1.** Stanza. **2.** Start. **3.** State. **4.** Or **St.** Statute. **5.** *Printing.* Stet. **6.** Stitch. **7.** Stone (weight). **8.** Or **St.** Strait. **9.** Or **St.** Street. **10.** Strophe.

St. *abbr.* Saint.

s.t. *abbr.* Short ton.

–st *suff.* Variant of **–est².**

sta. *abbr.* **1.** Station. **2.** Stationary.

stab (stăb) *v.* **stabbed, stab•bing, stabs.** *—tr.* **1.** To pierce or wound with or as if with a pointed weapon. **2.** To plunge (a pointed weapon or instrument) into something. **3.** To make a thrusting or poking motion at or into: *stabbed the air with his fingers.* *—intr.* **1.** To thrust with or as if with a pointed weapon: *stabbed at the food with her fork.* **2.** To inflict a wound with or as if with a pointed weapon. **—stab** *n.* **1.** A thrust with a pointed weapon or instrument. **2.** A wound inflicted with or as if with a pointed weapon. **3.** A sudden piercing pain. **4.** An attempt; a try: *made a stab at the answer.* **—*idiom.* stab (someone) in the back.** To harm (someone) by treachery or betrayal of trust. [Middle English *stabben.*] **—stab′ber** *n.*

sta•bile (stā′bīl, -bəl, -bīl′, -bēl′) *adj.* Immobile; unchangeable; stable. **—stabile** *n.* An abstract sculpture, usually of sheet metal, resembling a mobile but having no moving parts. [Latin *stabilis,* stable. See STABLE¹.]

sta·bil·i·ty (stə-bĭl′ĭ-tē) *n., pl.* **-ties. 1.** The state or quality of being stable, especially: **a.** Resistance to change, deterioration, or displacement. **b.** Constancy of character or purpose; steadfastness. **c.** Reliability; dependability. **2.** The ability of an object, such as a ship or an aircraft, to maintain equilibrium or resume its original position after displacement, as by the sea or strong winds. **3.** *Roman Catholic Church.* A vow committing a Benedictine monk to one monastery for life.

sta·bi·lize (stā′bə-līz′) *v.* **-lized, -liz·ing, -liz·es.** —*tr.* **1.** To make stable or steadfast. **2.** To maintain the stability of (an airplane or ship, for example) by means of a stabilizer. **3.** To keep from fluctuating; fix the level of: *stabilize prices.* —*intr.* To become stable, steadfast, or fixed. —**sta′bi·li·za′tion** (-lĭ-zā′shən) *n.*

sta·bi·liz·er (stā′bə-lī′zər) *n.* **1.** One that makes or keeps something stable: *"The New Deal equipped the economy with built-in stabilizers"* (Arthur M. Schlesinger, Jr.). **2.** *Nautical.* A device, such as a gyroscopically controlled fin, that prevents excessive rolling of a ship in heavy seas. **3.** An airfoil that stabilizes an aircraft or a missile in flight. **4.** *Chemistry.* A substance that renders or maintains a solution, mixture, suspension, or state resistant to chemical change.

stabilizer bar *n.* See **anti-sway bar.**

sta·ble¹ (stā′bəl) *adj.* **-bler, -blest. 1.a.** Resistant to change of position or condition; steadfast. **b.** Maintaining equilibrium; self-restoring. **2.** Immutable; permanent; enduring. **3.a.** Consistently dependable. **b.** Not subject to mental illness or irrationality. **4.** *Physics.* Having no known mode of decay; indefinitely long-lived. Used of atomic particles. **5.** *Chemistry.* Not easily decomposed or otherwise modified chemically. [Middle English, from Old French *estable,* from Latin *stabilis.* See **stā-** in Appendix.] —**sta′ble·ness** *n.* —**sta′bly** *adv.*

sta·ble² (stā′bəl) *n.* **1.a.** A building for the shelter and feeding of domestic animals, especially horses and cattle. **b.** A group of animals lodged in such a building. **2.a.** All the racehorses belonging to a single owner or racing establishment. See Synonyms at **flock¹. b.** The personnel employed to keep and train such a group of racehorses. **3.** A group, as of athletes, under common management, authority, or ownership: *a stable of prizefighters.* —**stable** *v.* **-bled, -bling, -bles.** —*tr.* To put or keep in or as if in a stable. —*intr.* To live in or as if in a stable. [Middle English, from Old French *estable,* from Latin *stabulum,* stable, standing place. See **stā-** in Appendix.]

stab·lish (stăb′lĭsh) *tr.v.* **-lish, -lished, -lish·ing.** *Archaic.* To establish.

stac·ca·to (stə-kä′tō) *adj.* **1.** *Abbr.* **stacc.** *Music.* Cut short crisply; disconnected: *staccato octaves.* **2.** Marked by or composed of abrupt, disconnected parts or sounds: *staccato applause.* —**staccato** *n., pl.* **-tos** or **-ti** (-tē). A staccato manner or sound. [Italian, past participle of *staccare,* to detach, short for *distaccare,* from obsolete French *destacher,* from Old French *destachier.* See DETACH.] —**stac·ca′to** *adv.*

stack (stăk) *n.* **1.** A large, usually conical pile of straw or fodder arranged for outdoor storage. **2.** An orderly pile, especially one arranged in layers. See Synonyms at **heap. 3.** *Computer Science.* A section of memory and its associated registers used for temporary storage of information in which the item most recently stored is the first to be retrieved. **4.** A group of three rifles supporting each other, butt downward and forming a cone. **5.a.** A chimney or flue. **b.** A group of chimneys arranged together. **6.** A vertical exhaust pipe, as on a ship or locomotive. **7.** Often **stacks. a.** An extensive arrangement of bookshelves. **b.** The area of a library in which most of the books are shelved. **8.** A stackup. **9.** An English measure of coal or cut wood, equal to 108 cubic feet (3.06 cubic meters). **10.** *Informal.* A large quantity: *a stack of work to do.* —**stack** *v.* **stacked, stack·ing, stacks.** —*tr.* **1.** To arrange in a stack; pile. **2.** To load or cover with stacks or piles: *stacked the dishwasher.* **3.a.** *Games.* To prearrange the order of (a deck of cards) so as to increase the chance of winning. **b.** To prearrange or fix unfairly so as to favor a particular outcome: *tried to stack the jury.* **4.** To direct (aircraft) to circle at different altitudes while waiting to land. —*intr.* To form a stack. —***phrasal verb.* stack up.** *Informal.* **1.** To measure up or equal: *Their gift doesn't stack up against his.* **2.** To make sense; add up: *Her report just doesn't stack up.* [Middle English *stac,* from Old Norse *stakkr.*] —**stack′a·ble** *adj.* —**stack′er** *n.*

stacked (stăkt) *adj. Slang.* Attractively formed and large-breasted.

stacked heel *n.* A shoe heel made of several layers of material.

stack·up (stăk′ŭp′) *n.* A deployment of aircraft circling an airport at designated altitudes while awaiting instructions to land.

stac·te (stăk′tē) *n.* A sweet spice used by the ancient Jews in making incense. [Middle English *stacten,* myrrh resin, from Latin *stactē,* from Greek *staktē,* from feminine of *staktos,* oozing, from *stazein, stag-,* to ooze.]

stad·dle (stăd′l) *n.* A base or support, especially a platform on which hay or straw is stacked. [Middle English *stathel,* from Old English *stathol.* See **stā-** in Appendix.]

stad·hold·er (stăd′hōl′dər) also **stadt·hold·er** (stăt′-) *n.* **1.** A governor or viceroy formerly stationed in a province of the Netherlands. **2.** The chief magistrate of the former Netherlands republic. [Partial translation of Dutch *stadhouder* : *stad,* place; see **stā-** in Appendix + *houder,* holder.]

sta·di·a¹ (stā′dē-ə) *n.* **1.a.** A telescopic instrument having two parallel lines through which intervals on a calibrated rod are observed, used to measure distances. **b.** The parallel lines in this instrument. **c.** The calibrated rod so used. **2.** The technique of measuring distances with this instrument. [Italian, probably from Latin, pl. of *stadium,* a unit of length. See STADIUM.]

sta·di·a² (stā′dē-ə) *n.* A plural of **stadium.**

sta·di·um (stā′dē-əm) *n., pl.* **-di·ums** or **-di·a** (-dē-ə). **1.** A large, usually open structure for sports events with tiered seating for spectators. **2.** A course on which foot races were held in ancient Greece, usually semicircular and having tiers of seats for spectators. **3.** An ancient Greek measure of distance, based on the length of such a course and equal to about 185 meters (607 feet). **4.** *Medicine.* A stage or period in the course of a disease. **5.** *Biology.* A stage in the development or life history of an organism. [Middle English, unit of length, from Latin, from Greek *stadion,* perhaps alteration (influenced by *stadios,* firm) of *spadion,* racetrack, from *span,* to pull.]

stadium

stadt·hold·er (stăt′hōl′dər) *n.* Variant of **stadholder.**

Staël (stäl), Madame de. In full Baronne Anne Louise Germaine Necker de Staël-Holstein. 1766–1817. French writer, literary patron, and critic who introduced romanticism to French literature in *On Germany* (1810).

Madame de Staël
1810 portrait by Jean Baptiste Isabey (1767–1855)

staff¹ (stăf) *n., pl.* **staffs** or **staves** (stāvz). **1.a.** A stick or cane carried as an aid in walking or climbing. **b.** A stout stick used as a weapon; a cudgel. **c.** A pole on which a flag is displayed; a flagstaff. **d.** A rod or baton carried as a symbol of authority. **2.** *pl.* **staffs.** A rule or similar graduated stick used for testing or measuring, as in surveying. **3.** *pl.* **staffs. a.** A group of assistants to a manager, an executive, or another person in authority. **b.** A group of military officers assigned to assist a commanding officer in an executive or advisory capacity. **c.** The personnel who carry out a specific enterprise: *the nursing staff of a hospital.* **4.** Something that serves as a staple or support. **5.** *Music.* A set of five horizontal lines and four intermediate spaces used in notation to represent a sequence of pitches. In this sense, also called *stave.* —**staff** *tr.v.* **staffed, staff·ing, staffs. 1.** To provide with a staff of workers or assistants. **2.** To serve on the staff of. [Middle English *staf,* from Old English *stæf.*]

staff² (stăf) *n.* A building material of plaster and fiber used as an exterior wall covering of temporary buildings, as at expositions. [Perhaps from German *stoff,* stuff.]

Staf·fa (stăf′ə). An island of western Scotland in the Inner Hebrides west of Mull.

staff·er (stăf′ər) *n. Informal.* A member of a staff: *White House staffers.*

staff of life *n., pl.* **staves of life** or **staffs of life.** A staple or necessary food, especially bread.

Staf·ford (stăf′ərd). A municipal borough of west-central England north-northwest of Birmingham. The birthplace of Izaak Walton, it is a manufacturing center. Population, 55,100.

Staf·ford·shire bull terrier (stăf′ərd-shîr′, -shər) *n.* A small, stocky, powerful dog of a breed developed in England by crossing bulldogs and terriers, having a short, smooth, variously colored coat, a broad head with dropped ears, a short muscular neck, and widely set forelegs. [After *Staffordshire,* a county of west-central England.]

Staffordshire terrier *n.* See **American Staffordshire terrier.** [After *Staffordshire,* a county of west-central England.]

staff sergeant *n. Abbr.* **S. Sgt., SSGT 1.a.** A noncommissioned rank in the U.S. Army that is above sergeant and below sergeant first class. **b.** A noncommissioned rank in the U.S. Air Force that is above sergeant and below technical sergeant. **c.** A noncommissioned rank in the U.S. Marine Corps that is above sergeant and below gunnery sergeant. **2.** One who holds the rank of staff sergeant.

staff¹

staff tree *n.* See **bittersweet** (sense 1).

stag (stăg) *n.* **1.** The adult male of various deer, especially the red deer. **2.** An animal, especially a pig, castrated after reaching sexual maturity. **3.a.** A man who attends a social gathering unaccompanied by a woman. **b.** A woman who attends a social gathering unaccompanied by a man. **4.** A social gathering for men only. —**stag** *adj.* **1.** Of or for men only: *a stag party.* **2.** Pornographic: *stag films.* —**stag** *adv.* Unaccompanied: *went to the dance stag.* —**stag** *intr.v.* **stagged, stag·ging, stags. 1.** To attend a social gathering unaccompanied by a woman. **2.** To attend a social gathering unaccompanied by a man. [Middle English *stagge,* from Old English *stagga.* See **stegh-** in Appendix.]

stag beetle *n.* Any of numerous large beetles of the family Lucanidae, the males of which have large, elaborately branched and toothed mandibles resembling the antlers of a stag.

stage (stāj) *n.* **1.** A raised and level floor or platform. **2.a.** A raised platform on which theatrical performances are presented. **b.** An area in which actors perform. **c.** The acting profession, or the world of theater. Used with *the: The stage is her life.* **3.** The scene of an event or a series of events. **4.** A platform on a microscope that supports a slide for viewing. **5.** A scaffold for workers. **6.** A resting place on a journey, especially one providing overnight accommodations. **7.** The distance between stopping places on a journey; a leg: *proceeded in easy stages.* **8.** A stagecoach. **9.** A level or story of a building. **10.** The height of the surface of a river or other fluctuating body of water above a set point: *at flood stage.* **11.a.** A level, degree, or period of time in the course of a process, especially a step in development: *the tod-*

ă pat	oi boy
ā pay	ou out
âr care	o͝o took
ä father	o͞o boot
ĕ pet	ŭ cut
ē be	ûr urge
ĭ pit	th thin
ī pie	*th* this
îr pier	hw which
ŏ pot	zh vision
ō toe	ə about, item
ô paw	♦ regionalism

Stress marks: ′ (primary); ′ (secondary), as in **dictionary** (dĭk′shə-nĕr′ē)

stagecoach
c. 1890 Concord stagecoach

stained glass
Tiffany stained glass window

ă pat	oi boy
ā pay	ou out
âr care	o͝o took
ä father	o͞o boot
ĕ pet	ŭ cut
ē be	ûr urge
ĭ pit	th thin
ī pie	*th* this
îr pier	hw which
ŏ pot	zh vision
ō toe	ə about, item
ô paw	♦ regionalism

Stress marks: **ʹ** (primary); ʹ (secondary), as in **dictionary** (dĭkʹshə-nĕrʹē)

dler stage. **b.** A point in the course of an action or series of events: *too early to predict a winner at this stage.* **12.** One of two or more successive propulsion units of a rocket vehicle that fires after the preceding one has been jettisoned. **13.** *Geology.* A subdivision in the classification of stratified rocks, ranking just below a series and representing rock formed during a chronological age. **14.** *Electronics.* An element or a group of elements in a complex arrangement of parts, especially a single tube or transistor and its accessory components in an amplifier. **—stage** *v.* **staged, stag·ing, stag·es.** —*tr.* **1.** To exhibit or present on or as if on a stage: *stage a boxing match.* **2.** To produce or direct (a theatrical performance). **3.** To arrange and carry out: *stage an invasion.* —*intr.* **1.** To be adaptable to or suitable for theatrical presentation. **2.** To stop at a designated place in the course of a journey: *"tourists from London who had staged through Warsaw"* (Frederick Forsyth). [Middle English, from Old French *estage,* from Vulgar Latin **staticum,* from Latin *status,* past participle of *stāre,* to stand. See **stā-** in Appendix.] **—stageʹfulʹ** *n.*

stage·coach (stājʹkōchʹ) *n.* A four-wheeled horse-drawn vehicle formerly used to transport mail, parcels, and passengers over a regular route.

stage·craft (stājʹkrăftʹ) *n.* Skill in the techniques and devices of the theater.

stage fright *n.* Acute nervousness associated with performing or speaking before an audience.

stage·hand (stājʹhăndʹ) *n.* A worker who shifts scenery, adjusts lighting, and performs other tasks required in a theatrical production.

stage left *n.* The area of the stage to one's left when facing the audience.

stage-man·age (stājʹmănʹĭj) *tr.v.* **-aged, -ag·ing, -ag·es. 1.** To serve as overall supervisor of the stage and actors for (a theatrical production). **2.** To direct or manipulate from behind the scenes, as to achieve a desired effect; orchestrate: *"felt certain that* [the] *demonstrations had . . . been carefully stage-managed"* (Time). **—stage management** *n.* **—stage manager** *n.*

stag·er (stāʹjər) *n.* One who possesses the wisdom of long experience.

stage right *n.* The area of the stage to one's right when facing the audience.

stage-struck (stājʹstrŭkʹ) *adj.* Enthralled by the theater or intensely eager for a career in acting.

stage whisper *n.* **1.** The conventional whisper of an actor, intended to be heard by the audience but supposedly inaudible to others on stage. **2.** A whisper intended to be overheard.

stag·ey (stāʹjē) *adj.* Variant of **stagy.**

stag·fla·tion (stăg-flāʹshən) *n.* Sluggish economic growth coupled with a high rate of inflation and unemployment. [STAG(NATION) + (IN)FLATION.] **—stag·flaʹtion·arʹy** (-shə-nĕrʹē) *adj.*

stag·gard (stăgʹərd) *n.* A male red deer in its fourth year. [Middle English, from *stagge,* stag. See STAG.]

stag·ger (stăgʹər) *v.* **-gered, -ger·ing, -gers.** —*intr.* **1.** To move or stand unsteadily, as if under a great weight; totter. **2.** To begin to lose confidence or strength of purpose; waver. —*tr.* **1.** To cause to totter, sway, or reel: *The blow staggered him.* **2. a.** To overwhelm with emotion or astonishment. **b.** To cause to waver or lose confidence. **3.** To place on or as if on alternating sides of a center line; set in a zigzag row or rows: *theater seats that were staggered for clear viewing.* **4.** To arrange in alternating or overlapping time periods: *staggered the nurses' shifts.* **5.** To arrange (the wings of a biplane) so that the leading edge of one wing is either ahead of or behind the leading edge of the other wing. **—stagger** *n.* **1.** A tottering, swaying, or reeling motion. **2.** A staggered pattern, arrangement, or order. **3. staggers.** *(used with a sing. verb).* Any of various diseases of the nervous system in animals, especially horses, cattle, or other domestic animals, characterized by a lack of coordination in moving, a staggering gait, and frequent falling. In this sense, also called *blind staggers.* [Alteration of Middle English *stakeren,* from Old Norse *stakra,* frequentative of *staka,* to push.] **—stagʹger·er** *n.* **—stagʹger·y** *adj.*

stag·ger·bush (stăgʹər-bo͝oshʹ) *n.* A deciduous shrub *(Lyonia mariana)* of the eastern United States, having poisonous foliage and white or pink flowers clustered in racemes.

stag·ger·ing (stăgʹər-ĭng) *adj.* Causing great astonishment, amazement, or dismay; overwhelming: *a staggering achievement; a staggering defeat.* **—stagʹger·ing·ly** *adv.*

stag·horn fern (stăgʹhôrnʹ) *n.* Any of several tropical epiphytic ferns of the genus *Platycerium,* having large, dichotemously divided fertile fronds that resemble antlers.

staghorn sumac *n.* An eastern North American deciduous shrub or tree *(Rhus typhina)* having pinnately compound leaves, a dense terminal panicle of small greenish flowers, and hairy crimson fruit.

stag·hound (stăgʹhoundʹ) *n.* Any of several dogs, such as a deerhound, formerly used in hunting stags and other large game.

stag·ing (stāʹjĭng) *n.* **1.** A temporary platform or system of platforms used for support; scaffolding. **2.** The process or manner of putting on a play on the stage. **3.** The act of jettisoning a stage of a multistage rocket. **4. a.** The operation of stagecoaches as an enterprise. **b.** Travel by stagecoach.

staging area *n.* A place where troops or equipment in transit are assembled and processed, as before a military operation.

Sta·gi·ra (stə-jīʹrə) or **Sta·gi·rus** (-rəs). An ancient city of Macedonia in northeast Greece, the birthplace of Aristotle.

stag·nant (stăgʹnənt) *adj.* **1.** Not moving or flowing; motionless. **2.** Foul or stale from standing: *stagnant ponds.* **3. a.** Showing little or no sign of activity or advancement; not developing or progressing; inactive: *a stagnant economy.* **b.** Lacking vitality or briskness; sluggish or dull: *a stagnant mind.* [Latin *stagnāns, stagnant-,* present participle of *stagnāre,* to be stagnant. See STAGNATE.] **—stagʹnan·cy** *n.* **—stagʹnant·ly** *adv.*

stag·nate (stăgʹnātʹ) *intr.v.* **-nat·ed, -nat·ing, -nates.** To be or become stagnant. [Latin *stagnāre, stagnāt-,* from *stagnum,* swamp.] **—stag·naʹtion** *n.*

stag·y also **stag·ey** (stāʹjē) *adj.* **-i·er, -i·est.** Having a theatrical character or quality; artificial and affected. See Synonyms at **dramatic.** **—stagʹi·ly** *adv.* **—stagʹi·ness** *n.*

staid (stād) *adj.* **1.** Characterized by sedate dignity and often a strait-laced sense of propriety; sober. See Synonyms at **serious. 2.** Fixed; permanent: *"There is nothing settled, nothing staid in this universe"* (Virginia Woolf). [From obsolete *staid,* past participle of STAY[1].] **—staidʹly** *adv.* **—staidʹness** *n.*

stain (stān) *v.* **stained, stain·ing, stains.** —*tr.* **1.** To discolor, soil, or spot. **2.** To bring into disrepute; taint or tarnish. **3.** To color (glass, for example) with a coat of penetrating liquid dye or tint. **4.** To treat (specimens for the microscope) with a reagent or dye that makes visible certain structures without affecting others. —*intr.* To produce or receive discolorations. **—stain** *n.* **1.** A discolored or soiled spot or smudge. **2.** A blemish on one's moral character or reputation. **3.** A liquid substance applied especially to wood that penetrates the surface and imparts a rich color. **4.** A reagent or dye used for staining microscopic specimens. [Middle English *steinen,* partly from Old French *desteindre, desteign-,* to deprive of color (*des-,* dis- + Latin *tingere, tīnct-,* to dye) and partly from Old Norse *steina,* to paint.] **—stainʹa·ble** *adj.* **—stainʹer** *n.*

SYNONYMS: *stain, blot, brand, stigma, taint.* The central meaning shared by these nouns is "a mark of discredit or disgrace, as on one's good name": *a stain on his honor; the blot of treason; the brand of cowardice; the stigma of ignominious defeat; the taint of vice.*

stained glass (stānd) *n.* Glass colored by mixing pigments inherently in the glass, by fusing colored metallic oxides onto the glass, or by painting and baking transparent colors on the glass surface.

Staines (stānz). An urban district of southeast England on the Thames River west-southwest of London. It is mainly residential with some varied industries. Population, 92,800.

stain·less (stānʹlĭs) *adj.* **1.** Without stain or blemish: *a stainless reputation.* **2.** Resistant to stain or corrosion: *stainless metal.* **—stainʹless·ly** *adv.*

stainless steel *n.* Any of various steels alloyed with at least 10 percent chromium and sometimes containing other elements and that are resistant to corrosion or rusting associated with exposure to water and moist air.

stair (stâr) *n.* **1.** Often **stairs.** A series or flight of steps; a staircase. **2.** One of a flight of steps. [Middle English, from Old English *stǣger.* See **steigh-** in Appendix.]

stair·case (stârʹkāsʹ) *n.* A flight or series of flights of steps and a supporting structure connecting separate levels. Also called *stairway.*

stair·way (stârʹwāʹ) *n.* See **staircase.**

stair·well (stârʹwĕlʹ) *n.* A vertical shaft around which a staircase has been built.

stake (stāk) *n.* **1.** A piece of wood or metal pointed at one end for driving into the ground as a marker, fence pole, or tent peg. **2. a.** A vertical post to which an offender is bound for execution by burning. **b.** Execution by burning. Used with *the: condemned to the stake.* **3.** A vertical post secured in a socket at the edge of a platform, as on a truck bed, to help retain the load. **4.** *Mormon Church.* A territorial division consisting of a group of wards under the jurisdiction of a president. **5.** Often **stakes.** *Sports & Games.* **a.** Money or property risked in a wager or gambling game. See Synonyms at **bet. b.** The prize awarded the winner of a contest or race. **c.** A race offering a prize to the winner, especially a horserace in which the prize consists of money contributed equally by the horse owners. **6. a.** A share or an interest in an enterprise, especially a financial share. **b.** Personal interest or involvement: *a stake in her children's future.* **7.** A grubstake. **—stake** *tr.v.* **staked, stak·ing, stakes. 1. a.** To mark the location or limits of with or as if with stakes: *stake out a claim.* **b.** To claim as one's own: *staked out a place for herself in industry.* **2.** To fasten, secure, or support with a stake or stakes. **3.** To tether or tie to a stake. **4.** To gamble or risk; hazard. **5.** To provide working capital for; finance. ***—phrasal verb.*** **stake out. 1.** To assign (a police officer, for example) to an area to conduct surveillance. **2.** To keep under surveillance. ***—idiom.*** **at stake.** At risk; in question. [Middle English, from Old English *staca.*]

stake·hold·er (stākʹhōlʹdər) *n.* **1.** *Games.* One who holds the bets in a game or contest. **2.** One who has a share or an interest, as in an enterprise.

stake·out (stāk′out′) *n.* Surveillance of an area, a building, or a person, especially by the police.

Sta·kha·nov·ite (stə-kä′nə-vīt′) *n.* A Soviet worker honored and rewarded for exceptional diligence in increasing production. [After Aleksei Grigorievich *Stakhanov* (1906–1977), Soviet miner.]

sta·lac·tite (stə-lăk′tīt′, stăl′ək-) *n.* An icicle-shaped mineral deposit, usually calcite or aragonite, hanging from the roof of a cavern, formed from the dripping of mineral-rich water. [New Latin *stalactītēs,* from Greek *stalaktos,* dripping, from *stalassein, stalak-,* to drip.] **—sta·lac′ti·form′** *adj.* **—stal′ac·tit′ic** (stăl′ăk-tĭt′ĭk, stə-lăk′-) *adj.*

WORD HISTORY: The words *stalagmite* and *stalactite* have confused many a person. A look into the history of the Greek sources of these two words may help. Both words can be traced back to the word *stalassein,* "to drip," which is appropriate since both words denote deposits in caves formed by the dripping of mineral-rich water. The Greek base from which *stalassein* was formed was *stalak–* and to this base were added several endings that concern us, specifically *–ma,* a noun suffix most frequently denoting the result of an action, *–mo–,* a suffix denoting the action of a verb as well as a result, and *–to–,* an adjective suffix forming verbal adjectives. With these suffixes and the addition of the inflectional endings, as well as a sound change from (k) to (g) before (m), we get *stalagma,* "that which drops, a drop," *stalagmos,* "dropping, dripping of stalactites," and *stalaktos,* "dropping, dripping." Using these Greek words, Olaus Wormius formed the Modern Latin word *stalactītēs,* the *stalac–* part meaning "dripping" and the *–ītēs* part being commonly used to name fossils and minerals when preceded by a form expressing a physical characteristic, in this case "dripping." Wormius also used the term *stalagmītēs,* the *stalag–* portion expressing the notion of what drops, taken either from *stalagma,* "that which drops, a drop," or *stalagmos,* "dropping of stalactites." *Stalactītēs* and *stalagmītēs,* of course, are the sources of our English words *stalactite* (first recorded in 1677), the formation on the tops of caves, and *stalagmite* (first recorded in 1681), the formation on the bottoms of caves. They have been causing trouble ever since.

sta·lag (stä′läg′, stăl′ăg′) *n.* A German prisoner of war camp for officers and enlisted personnel. [German, short for *Stammlager,* base camp : *Stamm,* base, stem (from Middle High German *stam,* from Old High German) + *Lager,* camp, bed (from Middle High German *leger,* from Old High German *legar,* bed, lair; see LAGER).]

sta·lag·mite (stə-lăg′mīt′, stăl′əg-) *n.* A conical mineral deposit, usually calcite or aragonite, built up on the floor of a cavern, formed from the dripping of mineral-rich water. [New Latin *stalagmītēs,* a drop, from Greek *stalagma,* a drop, or *stalagmos,* dropping, both from *stalassein, stalak-,* to drip.] **—stal′ag·mit′ic** (stăl′əg-mĭt′ĭk, stə-lăg′-) *adj.*

stale[1] (stāl) *adj.* **stal·er, stal·est. 1.** Having lost freshness, effervescence, or palatability: *stale bread; stale air.* **2.** Lacking originality or spontaneity: *a stale joke.* See Synonyms at **trite. 3.** Impaired in efficacy, vigor, or spirit, as from inactivity or boredom. **4.** *Law.* Having lost effectiveness or force through lack of exercise or action. [Middle English, settled, clear: used of beer or wine, probably from Old French *estale,* slack, settled, clear, from *estaler,* to come to a standstill, halt, from *estal,* standing place, stand, of Germanic origin. See **stel-** in Appendix.] **—stale** *v.* **—stale′ly** *adv.* **—stale′ness** *n.*

stale[2] (stāl) *intr.v.* **staled, stal·ing, stales.** To urinate. Used especially of horses and camels. **—stale** *n.* The urine of certain animals, especially horses and camels. [Middle English *stalen,* possibly of Low German origin; akin to Middle Low German *stallen.*]

stale·mate (stāl′māt′) *n.* **1.** A situation in which further action is blocked; a deadlock. **2.** *Games.* A drawing position in chess in which the king, although not in check, can move only into check and no other piece can move. **—stalemate** *tr.v.* **-mat·ed, -mat·ing, -mates.** To bring into a stalemate. [Obsolete *stale* (from Middle English, probably from Anglo-Norman *estale,* fixed position, from Old French *estal*; see STALE[1]) + MATE[2].]

Sta·lin (stä′lĭn, stăl′ĭn), **Joseph.** Originally Iosif Vissarionovich Dzhugashvili. 1879–1953. Soviet politician. The successor of Lenin, he was general secretary of the Communist Party (1922–1953) and premier (1941–1953) of the U.S.S.R. His rule was marked by the exile of Trotsky (1929), a purge of the government and military, the forced collectivization of agriculture, a policy of industrialization, and a victorious but devastating role for the Soviets in World War II.

Sta·lin·grad (stä′lĭn-grăd′, stə-lyĭn-grät′). See **Volgograd.**

Sta·lin·ism (stä′lə-nĭz′əm) *n.* The bureaucratic, authoritarian exercise of state power and mechanistic application of Marxist-Leninist principles associated with Stalin. **—Sta′lin·ist** *adj. & n.* **—Sta′lin·ize′** *v.*

stalk[1] (stôk) *n.* **1.a.** A stem or main axis of a herbaceous plant. **b.** A stem or similar structure that supports a plant part such as a flower, flower cluster, or leaf. **2.** A slender or elongated support or structure, as one that holds up an organ or another body part. [Middle English, probably diminutive of *stale,* upright of a ladder, post, handle, from Old English *stalu.* See **stel-** in Appendix.] **—stalk′y** *adj.*

stalk[2] (stôk) *v.* **stalked, stalk·ing, stalks.** *—intr.* **1.** To walk with a stiff, haughty, or angry gait: *stalked off in a huff.* **2.** To move threateningly or menacingly. **3.** To track prey or quarry. *—tr.* **1.** To pursue by tracking stealthily. **2.** To go through (an area) in pursuit of prey or quarry. [Middle English *stalken,* from Old English *-stealcian,* to move stealthily (in *bestealcian*).] **—stalk′er** *n.*

stalked (stôkt) *adj.* Having a stalk or stem. Often used in combination: *long-stalked; short-stalked.*

stalk-eyed (stôk′īd′) *adj.* Having the eye at the end of a stalk, as various crustaceans.

stalk·ing-horse (stô′kĭng-hôrs′) *n.* **1.** Something used to cover one's true purpose; a decoy. **2.** A sham candidate put forward to conceal the candidacy of another or to divide the opposition. **3.a.** A horse trained to conceal the hunter while stalking. **b.** A canvas screen made in the figure of a horse, used for similar concealment.

stall[1] (stôl) *n.* **1.** A compartment for one domestic animal in a barn or shed. **2.a.** A booth, cubicle, or stand used by a vendor, as at a market. **b.** A small compartment: *a shower stall.* **3.a.** An enclosed seat in the chancel of a church. **b.** A pew in a church. **4.** *Chiefly British.* A seat in the front part of a theater. **5.** A space marked off, as in a garage, for parking a motor vehicle. **6.** A protective sheath for a finger or toe. **7.** The sudden, unintended loss of power or effectiveness in an engine. **8.** A condition in which an aircraft or airfoil experiences an interruption of airflow resulting in loss of lift and a tendency to drop. **—stall** *v.* **stalled, stall·ing, stalls.** *—tr.* **1.** To put or lodge in a stall. **2.** To maintain in a stall for fattening: *to stall cattle.* **3.** To check the motion or progress of; bring to a standstill. **4.** To cause (an engine) accidentally to stop running. **5.** To cause (an aircraft) to go into a stall. *—intr.* **1.** To live or be lodged in a stall. Used of an animal. **2.** To stick fast in mud or snow. **3.** To come to a standstill: *Negotiations stalled.* **4.** To stop running as a result of mechanical failure: *The car stalled on the freeway.* **5.** To lose forward flying speed, causing a stall. Used of an aircraft. [Middle English *stalle,* from Old English *steall,* standing place, stable. See **stel-** in Appendix.]

stall[2] (stôl) *n.* A ruse or tactic used to mislead or delay. **—stall** *v.* **stalled, stall·ing, stalls.** *—tr.* To employ delaying tactics against: *stall off creditors.* *—intr.* To employ delaying tactics: *stalling for time.* [Alteration (influenced by STALL[1]) of obsolete *stale,* pickpocket's accomplice, from Middle English, decoy, from Anglo-Norman *estale,* of Germanic origin; possibly akin to Old English *stǣl, stathol,* place, position. See STADDLE.]

stall-feed (stôl′fēd′) *tr.v.* **-fed** (-fĕd′), **-feed·ing, -feeds.** To lodge and feed (an animal) in a stall for the purpose of fattening.

stal·lion (stăl′yən) *n.* An adult male horse that has not been castrated, especially one kept for breeding. [Middle English *stalione,* alteration of *staloun,* from Anglo-Norman *estaloun,* of Germanic origin. See **stel-** in Appendix.]

stal·wart (stôl′wərt) *adj.* **1.** Having or marked by imposing physical strength. **2.** Firm and resolute; stout. See Synonyms at **strong. —stalwart** *n.* **1.** One who is physically and morally strong. **2.** One who steadfastly supports an organization or a cause: *party stalwarts.* [Middle English, alteration of *stalworth,* from Old English *stǣlwierthe,* serviceable, probably alteration of **statholwierthe,* steadfast : *stathol,* foundation; see STADDLE + *weorth,* valuable; see **wer-**[2] in Appendix.] **—stal′wart·ly** *adv.* **—stal′wart·ness** *n.*

sta·men (stā′mən) *n., pl.* **sta·mens** or **sta·mi·na** (stā′mə-nə, stăm′ə-). The pollen-producing reproductive organ of a flower, usually consisting of a filament and an anther. [Latin *stāmen,* thread. See **stā-** in Appendix.]

Stam·ford (stăm′fərd). A city of southwest Connecticut on Long Island Sound and the New York border. Settled in 1641, it is primarily residential. Population, 102,453.

stamin– *pref.* Stamen: *staminate.* [Latin *stāmen, stāmin-,* thread, warp. See STAMEN.]

stam·i·na[1] (stăm′ə-nə) *n.* Physical or moral strength to resist or withstand illness, fatigue, or hardship; endurance. [Latin *stāmina,* pl. of *stāmen,* thread. See STAMEN.]

sta·mi·na[2] (stā′mə-nə, stăm′ə-) *n.* A plural of **stamen.**

stam·i·nal[1] (stăm′ə-nəl) *adj.* Of or relating to stamina or endurance.

sta·mi·nal[2] (stā′mə-nəl, stăm′ə-) *adj.* Of or relating to stamens or a stamen.

sta·mi·nate (stā′mə-nĭt, -nāt′, stăm′ə-) *adj.* Having stamens but lacking pistils: *staminate flowers.*

stam·i·node (stā′mə-nōd′, stăm′ə-) also **stam·i·no·di·um** (stā′mə-nō′dē-əm, stăm′ə-) *n., pl.* **-nodes -no·di·a** (-nō′dē-ə). A sterile stamen, sometimes resembling a petal, as in the canna. [New Latin *staminōdium,* from Latin *stāmen, stāmin-,* thread. See STAMEN.]

sta·mi·no·dy (stā′mə-nō′dē, stăm′ə-) *n.* Transformation of a floral organ into a stamen. [STAMINODE + -Y[2].]

stam·mel (stăm′əl) *n.* **1.** *Archaic.* The red color of a coarse woolen cloth sometimes used for undergarments. **2.** *Obsolete.* A coarse woolen cloth for undergarments. [Probably alteration of *stamin,* from Middle English *stamyn,* from Old French *estamine,* from Vulgar Latin **stāminea,* from Latin, feminine of *stāmineus,*

stalactite and stalagmite

Joseph Stalin

stall[1]
In a barn

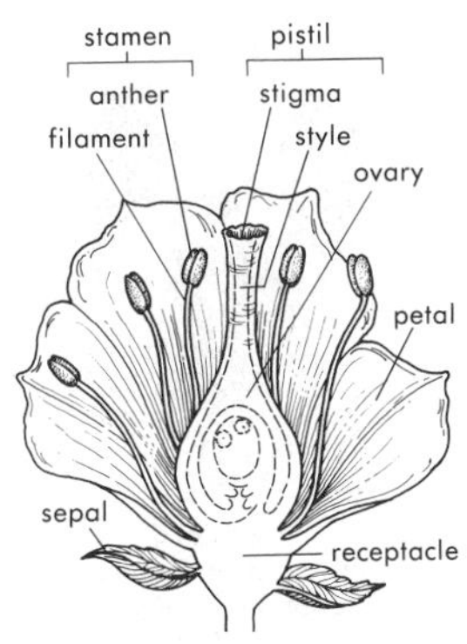

stamen

consisting of threads, from *stāmen, stāmin-,* thread. See **stā-** in Appendix.]

stam·mer (stăm′ər) *v.* **-mered, -mer·ing, -mers.** —*intr.* To speak with involuntary pauses or repetitions. —*tr.* To utter with involuntary pauses or repetitions. —**stammer** *n.* A way of speaking characterized by involuntary pauses or repetitions. [Middle English *stameren,* from Old English *stamerian.*] —**stam′mer·er** *n.* —**stam′mer·ing·ly** *adv.*

SYNONYMS: *stammer, stutter.* These verbs apply to hesitant, stumbling, or halting speech. To *stammer* is generally to speak with involuntary pauses or repetitions, as from nervousness or confusion: *The witness stammered and then fell silent. "He commanded himself sufficiently to stammer out his regrets"* (Frederick Marryat). *Stutter* usually refers to spasmodic repetition or prolongation of sounds, especially consonants, often as a result of a speech impediment: *Those who stutter often receive speech therapy. Caught shoplifting, the culprit stuttered a few transparent lies.*

stamp (stămp) *v.* **stamped, stamp·ing, stamps.** —*tr.* **1.** To bring down (the foot) forcibly. **2.** To bring the foot down onto (an object or a surface) forcibly. **3.** To extinguish or destroy by or as if by trampling underfoot: *stamped the rebellion; stamp out a fire.* **4.** To crush or grind with a heavy instrument: *stamp ore.* **5.** To form or cut out by application of a mold, form, or die. **6.** To imprint or impress with a mark, design, or seal. **7.** To impress forcibly or permanently. **8.** To affix an adhesive stamp to. **9.** To identify, characterize, or reveal: *stamped her a traitor to the cause.* —*intr.* **1.** To thrust the foot forcibly downward. **2.** To walk with forcible, heavy steps. See Usage Note at **stomp.** —**stamp** *n.* **1.** The act of stamping. **2.a.** An implement or a device used to impress, cut out, or shape something to which it is applied. **b.** An impression or a shape formed by such an implement or device. See Synonyms at **impression. 3.** An official mark, design, or seal that indicates ownership, approval, completion, or the payment of a tax. **4.a.** A small piece of gummed paper sold by a government for attachment to an article that is to be mailed; a postage stamp. **b.** A similar piece of gummed paper issued for a specific purpose: *trading stamps.* **5.** An identifying or characterizing mark or impression: *His work bears the stamp of genius.* **6.** Characteristic nature or quality: *a person of her stamp.* [Middle English *stampen,* possibly alteration of Old English *stempan,* to pound in a mortar.]

stam·pede (stăm-pēd′) *n.* **1.** A sudden frenzied rush of panic-stricken animals. **2.** A sudden headlong rush or flight of a crowd of people. **3.** A mass impulsive action: *a stampede of support for the candidate.* —**stampede** *v.* **-ped·ed, -ped·ing, -pedes.** —*tr.* **1.** To cause (a herd of animals) to flee in panic. **2.** To cause (a crowd of people) to act on mass impulse. —*intr.* **1.** To flee in a headlong rush. **2.** To act on mass impulse. [Spanish *estampida,* uproar, stampede, from Provençal, from *estampir,* to stamp, of Germanic origin.] —**stam·ped′er** *n.*

WORD HISTORY: The Spanish word *estampida,* meaning "explosion, bang, crash, uproar," seems very fitting to describe a rush of animals, such as buffaloes, horses, or cattle, and was so used first in American Spanish. From this use came our word *stampede* (actually from the Spanish *estampido,* a masculine noun corresponding to the feminine *estampida,* first recorded in 1828). Thus *stampede,* now a general English word, is an Americanism, that is, a word or expression that originated in the United States. Later the United States was to see stampedes of miners who rushed westward to find gold. Not surprisingly, an early instance of this word to describe a stampede of human beings is found in the *San Francisco Herald* in 1851.

stamp·er (stăm′pər) *n.* One, such as a worker or a machine, that stamps: *a metal stamper.*

stamp·ing ground (stăm′pĭng) *n.* A customary territory or favorite gathering place.

stamp mill *n.* **1.** A machine that crushes ore. **2.** A building in which ore is crushed.

stance (stăns) *n.* **1.** The attitude or position of a standing person or animal, especially the position assumed by an athlete preparatory to action. See Synonyms at **posture. 2.** Mental posture; point of view: *"Peru . . . has also toughened its stance toward foreign investors"* (Abraham F. Lowenthal). [French, position, from Italian *stanza,* from Vulgar Latin **stantia,* from Latin *stāns, stant-,* present participle of *stāre,* to stand. See **stā-** in Appendix.]

standard
1812 American standard of the New England Guards by Jesse Churchill (1773–1819)

stanch[1] (stônch, stänch, stănch) also **staunch** (stônch, stänch) *tr.v.* **stanched, stanch·ing, stanch·es** also **staunched, staunch·ing, staunch·es. 1.** To stop or check the flow of (blood or tears, for example). **2.** To stop the flow of blood from (a wound). **3.** To check or allay: *"My anxiety is stanched; I am at peace"* (Scott Turow). See Usage Note at **staunch**[1]. [Middle English *stanchen,* from Old French *estanchier,* from Vulgar Latin **stanticāre,* to stop, probably from Latin *stāns, stant-,* present participle of *stāre,* to stand. See **stā-** in Appendix.] —**stanch′er** *n.*

stanch[2] (stônch, stänch, stănch) *adj.* Variant of **staunch**[1]. See Usage Note at **staunch**[1].

stan·chion (stăn′chən, -shən) *n.* **1.** An upright pole, post, or support. **2.** A framework consisting usually of two vertical bars, used to secure cattle in a stall. —**stanchion** *tr.v.* **-chioned, -chion·ing, -chions. 1.** To equip with stanchions. **2.** To confine (cattle) by means of stanchions. [Middle English *stanchon,* from Old French *estanchon,* probably from *estance,* act of standing upright, prop, from *estans,* present participle of *ester,* to stand, from Latin *stāre.* See **stā-** in Appendix.]

stand (stănd) *v.* **stood** (sto͝od), **stand·ing, stands.** —*intr.* **1.a.** To rise to an upright position on the feet. **b.** To assume or maintain an upright position as specified: *stand straight; stand to one side.* **2.a.** To maintain an upright position on the feet. **b.** To maintain an upright or vertical position on a base or support: *The urn stands on a pedestal.* **c.** To be placed or situated: *The building stands at the corner.* **3.a.** To remain stable, upright, or intact: *The old school still stands.* **b.** To remain valid, effective, or unaltered: *The agreement stands.* **4.** To be or show a specified figure or amount: *The balance stands at $500.* **5.** To measure a specified height when in an upright position: *stands six feet tall.* **6.** To take up or maintain a specified position, altitude, or course: *He stands on his earlier offer. We will stand firm.* **7.** To be in a position of possible gain or loss: *She stands to make a fortune.* **8.a.** To be in a specified state or condition: *I stand corrected. We stand in awe of the view.* **b.** To exist in a particular form: *Send the message as it now stands.* **9.** To be at a specified level on or as if on a scale: *stands third in her class; stands high in reputation.* **10.a.** To come to a stop; remain motionless. **b.** To remain stationary or inactive: *The car stood in the garage all winter.* **11.** To remain without flowing or being disturbed; be or become stagnant. **12.** *Nautical.* To take or hold a particular course or direction: *a ship standing to windward.* **13.** To be available as a sire. Used of horses. **14.** *Chiefly British.* To be a candidate for public office. —*tr.* **1.** To cause to stand; place upright. **2.** To engage in or encounter: *stand battle.* **3.a.** To resist successfully; withstand: *stand the test of time; will not stand close examination.* **b.** To put up with patiently or resolutely; bear: *can't stand the heat.* See Synonyms at **bear**[1]. **4.** To submit to or undergo: *stand trial.* **5.** To tolerate and benefit from: *I could stand a good night's sleep.* **6.** To perform the duty of: *stand guard.* **7.** *Informal.* To treat (someone) or pay the cost of (food or drink): *She stood him to a drink. We'll stand dinner.* —**stand** *n.* **1.** The act of standing. **2.** A ceasing of work or activity; a standstill or halt. **3.** A stop on a performance tour. **4.** The place or station where a person stands. **5.** A booth, stall, or counter for the display of goods for sale. **6.** A parking space reserved for taxis. **7.** A desperate or decisive effort at defense or resistance, as in a battle: *made their stand at the river.* **8.** A position or an opinion one is prepared to uphold: *must take a stand on environmental issues.* **9. stands.** The bleachers at a playing field or stadium. **10.** *Law.* A witness stand. **11.** A small rack, prop, or table for holding any of various articles: *a music stand; a bedside stand.* **12.** A group or growth of tall plants or trees: *a stand of pine.* —***phrasal verbs.* stand by. 1.** To be ready or available to act. **2.** To wait for something, such as a broadcast, to resume. **3.** To remain uninvolved; refrain from acting: *stood by and let him get away.* **4.** To remain loyal to; aid or support: *stands by her friends.* **5.** To keep or maintain: *stood by her decision.* **stand down. 1.** *Law.* To leave a witness stand. **2.** To withdraw, as from a political contest. **3.** To go off duty. **stand for. 1.** To represent; symbolize. **2.** To advocate or support: *stands for freedom of the press.* **3.** To put up with; tolerate: *We will not stand for impertinent behavior.* **stand in.** To act as a stand-in. **stand off. 1.** To stay at a distance; remain apart or aloof. **2.** To put off; evade. **3.** *Nautical.* To maintain a course away from shore. **stand on. 1.** To be based on; depend on: *The success of the project stands on management's support of it.* **2.** To insist on observance of: *stand on ceremony; stand on one's rights.* **stand out. 1.** To protrude; project. **2.** To be conspicuous, distinctive, or prominent. **3.** To refuse compliance or maintain opposition; hold out: *stand out against a verdict.* **4.** *Nautical.* To maintain a course away from shore. **stand over. 1.** To watch or supervise closely. **2.** To hold over; postpone. **stand to.** To take up positions for action. **stand up. 1.** To remain valid, sound, or durable: *His claim will not stand up in court. Our old car has stood up well over time.* **2.** *Informal.* To fail to keep a date with. —***idioms.* stand a chance.** To have a chance, as of gaining or accomplishing something. **stand on (one's) own** (or **two) feet.** To be independent and responsible for oneself. **stand pat. 1.** To refuse to change one's position or opinion. **2.** *Games.* To play one's poker hand without drawing. **stand to reason.** To be consistent with reason: *It stands to reason that if we leave late, we will arrive late.* **stand up for.** To side with; defend. **stand up to.** To confront fearlessly; face up to. **stand up with.** To act as best man or maid of honor for (the groom or bride) at a wedding. [Middle English *standen,* from Old English *standan.* See **stā-** in Appendix.] —**stand′er** *n.*

stand-a·lone (stănd′ə-lōn′) *adj. Computer Science.* Of, relating to, or being a self-contained, usually independently operating, computer system or device: *a stand-alone terminal.*

stan·dard (stăn′dərd) *n. Abbr.* **std. 1.** A flag, banner, or ensign, especially: **a.** The ensign of a chief of state, nation, or city. **b.** A long, tapering flag bearing heraldic devices distinctive of a person or corporation. **c.** An emblem or flag of an army, raised on a pole to indicate the rallying point in battle. **d.** The colors of a mounted or motorized military unit. **2.a.** An acknowledged measure of comparison for quantitative or qualitative value; a criterion. **b.** An object that under specified conditions defines, represents, or records the magnitude of a unit. **3.** The set proportion by weight of gold or silver to alloy metal prescribed for use in coinage. **4.** The commodity or commodities used to back a monetary system. **5.a.** A degree or level of requirement, excellence, or attainment. **b.** *Often* **standards.** A requirement of moral conduct. **6.** *Chiefly British.* A grade level in elementary schools. **7.** A pedestal, stand, or base. **8.** *Botany.* **a.** The large upper petal of the flower of a pea or related plant. **b.** One of the narrow, upright petals of an iris. Also called *banner, vexillum.* **9.** A shrub or small tree that through grafting or training has a single stem of limited height with a crown of leaves and flowers at its apex. **10.** *Music.* A composition that is continually used in repertoires. **—standard** *adj.* **1.** Serving as or conforming to a standard of measurement or value. **2.** Widely recognized as a model of authority or excellence: *a standard reference work.* **3.** Acceptable but of less than top quality: *a standard grade of beef.* **4.** Normal, familiar, or usual: *the standard excuse.* **5.** Commonly used or supplied: *standard car equipment.* **6.** *Linguistics.* Conforming to established educated usage in speech or writing. [Middle English, from Old French *estandard,* rallying place, probably from Frankish **standhard* : **standan,* to stand; see **stā-** in Appendix + **hard,* fast, hard; see **kar-** in Appendix.] **—stan′dard·ly** *adv.*

SYNONYMS: *standard, benchmark, criterion, gauge, measure, touchstone, yardstick.* The central meaning shared by these nouns is "a point of reference against which individuals are compared and evaluated": *a book that is a standard of literary excellence; a painting that is a benchmark of quality; educational criteria; behavior that is a gauge of self-control; government funding, a measure of the importance of the arts; success, a touchstone of opportunity, ambition, and ability; farm failures, a yardstick of federal banking policy.* See also Synonyms at **ideal.**

stan·dard-bear·er (stăn′dərd-bâr′ər) *n.* **1.** One who carries a standard or banner, especially of a military unit. **2.** An outstanding leader or representative of a movement, an organization, or a political party.

stan·dard·bred (stăn′dərd-brĕd′) *n.* Any of an American breed of trotting and pacing horses developed especially for harness racing by crossing Thoroughbreds with Morgans and other breeds.

standard candle *n.* A candela.

standard deviation *n. Abbr.* **SD, S.D.** *Statistics.* A statistic used as a measure of the dispersion or variation in a distribution, equal to the square root of the arithmetic mean of the squares of the deviations from the arithmetic mean.

Stan·dard English (stăn′dərd) *n.* The variety of English that is most widely accepted as the spoken and written language of educated speakers in formal and informal contexts and is characterized by generally accepted conventions of spelling, grammar, and vocabulary while admitting some regional differences, especially in pronunciation and vocabulary.

standard error *n. Statistics.* The standard deviations of the sample in a frequency distribution, obtained by dividing the standard deviation by the total number of cases in the frequency distribution.

standard gauge *n.* **1.** A railroad track having a width of 56½ inches (143.5 centimeters). **2.** A railroad or railroad car built to standard gauge specification.

stan·dard·ize (stăn′dər-dīz′) *tr.v.* **-ized, -iz·ing, -iz·es. 1.** To cause to conform to a standard. **2.** To evaluate by comparing with a standard. **—stan′dard·i·za′tion** (-dər-dĭ-zā′shən) *n.*

standard of living *n., pl.* **standards of living.** A level of material comfort as measured by the goods, services, and luxuries available to an individual, a group, or a nation.

standard operating procedure *n. Abbr.* **SOP** Established procedure to be followed in carrying out a given operation or in a given situation.

standard time *n. Abbr.* **ST** The time in any of 24 time zones, usually the mean solar time at the central meridian of each zone. In the continental United States, there are four standard time zones: Eastern, using the 75th meridian; Central, using the 90th meridian; Mountain, using the 105th meridian; and Pacific, using the 120th meridian.

stand·by (stănd′bī′) *n., pl.* **-bys. 1.** One that can always be relied on, as in an emergency. **2.** A favorite or frequent choice. **3.** One kept in readiness to serve as a substitute. **—standby** *adj.* **1.** Kept in reserve for use when needed: *a standby generator.* **2.** Of, relating to, or waiting for unreserved travel space that is made available by an airline only shortly before departure: *standby passengers.* **—standby** *adv.* On a standby basis: *flew standby to New York.* **—*idiom.* on standby.** Ready and waiting.

stand-down or **stand·down** (stănd′doun′) *n.* A withdrawal, as of a military presence.

stand·ee (stăn-dē′) *n.* One using standing room. See Usage Note at **-ee[1].**

stand-in (stănd′ĭn′) *n.* **1.** One who substitutes for an actor while lights and camera are adjusted or during hazardous action. **2.** A substitute.

stand·ing (stăn′dĭng) *n.* **1.a.** Status with respect to rank, reputation, or position in society or a profession. **b.** High reputation; esteem: *a person of standing in the community.* **2.** Continuance in time; duration: *a friendship of long standing.* **3.** *Law.* The right or capacity to initiate a suit. **4.** The act of one that stands. **5.** A place where a person or thing stands. **—standing** *adj.* **1.a.** Remaining upright; erect. **b.** Not cut down: *standing timber.* **2.** Performed or done from a standing position: *a standing jump; a standing ovation.* **3.** Permanent and unchanging; fixed. **4.** Remaining in force or use indefinitely: *a standing invitation.* **5.** Not movable; stationary. **6.** Not flowing or circulating; stagnant.

standing army *n.* A permanent army maintained in time of peace and war.

standing crop *n.* The total amount of living organisms, as of plankton, in a specific area at a given time.

standing order *n.* An order or rule held to be in force until specifically changed or withdrawn, especially a regulation relating to military or parliamentary procedure.

standing room *n.* Space in which to stand, as in a public place where all seats are filled. **—stand′ing-room′** (stăn′dĭng-ro͞om′, -ro͝om′) *adj.*

standing wave *n.* A wave characterized by lack of vibration at certain points, between which areas of maximum vibration occur periodically. Standing waves are produced whenever a wave is confined within boundaries, as in the vibrating string of a musical instrument. Also called *stationary wave.*

Stan·dish (stăn′dĭsh′), **Miles** or **Myles.** 1584?–1656. English colonist in America. Hired by the English Pilgrims to accompany them on their voyage to the New World (1620), he emerged as a military and political leader in the early years of the colony.

stand·off (stănd′ôf′, -ŏf′) *n.* **1.** A tie or draw, as in a contest. **2.** A situation in which one force neutralizes or counterbalances the other. **3.** A standoff insulator. **—standoff** *adj.* Standoffish.

standoff insulator *n.* An insulator used to support a conductor a specified distance from a surface.

stand·off·ish (stănd-ô′fĭsh, -ŏf′ĭsh) *adj.* Aloof or reserved. **—stand·off′ish·ness** *n.*

stand·out (stănd′out′) *n. Informal.* One that is conspicuous by virtue of excellence or superiority: *"In the hard-working . . . supporting cast, there are two standouts"* (New York).

stand·pat·ter (stănd′păt′ər) *n.* One who maintains opposition to change, as in politics. **—stand′pat′tism** *n.*

stand·pipe (stănd′pīp′) *n.* A large vertical pipe into which water is pumped in order to produce a desired pressure.

stand·point (stănd′point′) *n.* A position from which things are considered or judged; a point of view. [Translation of German *Standpunkt.*]

stand·still (stănd′stĭl′) *n.* Complete cessation of activity or progress: *Work came to a standstill.*

stand·up or **stand-up** (stănd′ŭp′) *adj.* **1.** Standing erect; upright: *a standup collar.* **2.** Taken, done, or used while standing: *a standup supper; a standup bar.* **3.** Of or designating a performer who stands alone on a stage, as in a nightclub, and delivers a comic monologue. **4.** *Slang.* Courageous and steadfast: *a standup guy.*

Stan·ford (stăn′fərd), **Leland.** 1824–1893. American financier of the Central Pacific Railroad (built 1863–1869) and founder of Stanford University (1885).

Stan·ford-Bi·net test (stăn′fərd-bĭ-nā′) *n.* A standard intelligence test adapted from the Binet-Simon scale for use in the United States, especially in the assessment of children. [After *Stanford* University in western California near Palo Alto.]

stang (stăng) *v. Obsolete.* A past tense of **sting.**

stan·hope (stăn′hōp′, stăn′əp) *n.* A light, open, horse-drawn carriage with one seat and two or four wheels. [After the Reverend Fitzroy *Stanhope* (1787–1864), British clergyman.]

Stan·is·las I Lesz·czyń·ski (stăn′ĭ-slôs lĕsh-chĭn′skē). 1677–1766. King of Poland (1704–1709 and 1733–1736) whose second reign was marked by the War of the Polish Succession (1733–1735).

Stan·i·slav·sky (stăn′ĭ-släv′skē, -släf′-, stə-nyĭ-), **Konstantin.** 1863–1938. Russian actor and director. A founder of the Moscow Art Theater, he produced many of Chekhov's plays and developed an innovative method of acting that emphasizes the psychological motivation of the actor.

stank (stăngk) *v.* A past tense of **stink.**

Stan·ley or **Port Stan·ley** (stăn′lē). A town of the eastern Falkland Islands on the Atlantic Ocean. It is the administrative capital of the British dependency. Population, 1,050.

Stanley, Edward George Geoffrey Smith. 14th Earl of Derby. 1799–1869. British politician who served as prime minister (1852, 1858–1859, and 1866–1868).

Stanley, Francis Edgar. 1849–1918. American inventor who with his twin brother **Freelan** (1849–1940) developed a steam-powered automobile, the Stanley Steamer (1897).

Stanley, Sir **Henry Morton.** 1841–1904. British journalist and explorer known for his expedition into Africa in search of David Livingstone, whom he greeted with the words "Doctor Livingstone, I presume?" (1871).

Stanley, Wendell Meredith. 1904–1971. American biochemist. He shared a 1946 Nobel Prize for discovering methods of producing pure enzymes and virus proteins.

Stanley Pool. A lakelike expansion of the Congo River in west-central Africa on the Congo-Zaire border between Kinshasa and Brazzaville.

Stan·ley·ville (stăn′lē-vĭl′). See **Kisangani.**

stan·nic (stăn′ĭk) *adj.* Of, relating to, or containing tin, especially with valence 4. [Late Latin *stannum,* tin (from Latin, an alloy of silver and lead, alteration of *stagnum,* probably of Celtic origin) + -IC.]

ă pat	oi boy
ā pay	ou out
âr care	o͝o took
ä father	o͞o boot
ĕ pet	ŭ cut
ē be	ûr urge
ĭ pit	th thin
ī pie	*th* this
îr pier	hw which
ŏ pot	zh vision
ō toe	ə about, item
ô paw	♦ regionalism

Stress marks: **′** (primary); ′ (secondary), as in **dictionary** (dĭk′shə-nĕr′ē)

Elizabeth Cady Stanton
Photographed in the 1890's

starfish
Astropecten articulatus

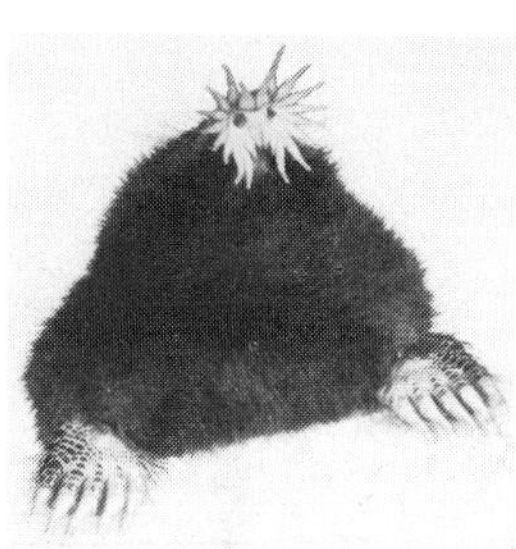
star-nosed mole
Condylura cristata

stannic chloride *n.* A colorless caustic liquid, $SnCl_4$, made from tin treated with chlorine and used as a conductive coating and in ceramics.

stan·nite (stăn′īt′) *n.* A gray to black mineral, Cu_2FeSnS_4, having a metallic luster. Also called *tin pyrites.* [Late Latin *stannum,* tin; see STANNIC + –ITE [1].]

stan·nous (stăn′əs) *adj.* Of, relating to, or containing tin, especially with valence 2. [Late Latin *stannum,* tin; see STANNIC + –OUS.]

stannous fluoride *n.* A white powder, SnF_2, used to fluoridate toothpaste.

Stan·o·voy Range or **Stan·o·voi Range** (stăn′ə-voi′, stə-nə-voi′). A mountain range, about 724 km (450 mi) long, of southeast Russia north of the Amur River.

Stan·ton (stăn′tən). A city of southern California, a residential suburb in the Los Angeles–Long Beach metropolitan area. Population, 23,723.

Stanton, Edwin McMasters. 1814–1869. American public official who served as U.S. secretary of war (1862–1868). His dismissal by President Andrew Johnson and his subsequent refusal to leave office precipitated the impeachment of Johnson.

Stanton, Elizabeth Cady. 1815–1902. American feminist and social reformer. She helped organize the first women's rights convention, held in Seneca Falls, New York (1848), for which she wrote a Declaration of Sentiments calling for the reform of discriminatory practices that perpetuated sexual inequality.

stan·za (stăn′zə) *n. Abbr.* **st.** One of the divisions of a poem, composed of two or more lines usually characterized by a common pattern of meter, rhyme, and number of lines. [Italian. See STANCE.] **—stan·za′ic** (-zā′ĭk) *adj.*

sta·pe·dec·to·my (stā′pĭ-dĕk′tə-mē, -pē-) *n., pl.* **-mies.** Surgical removal of the stapes. [New Latin *stapēs, stapēd-,* stapes; see STAPES + –ECTOMY.]

sta·pe·des (stā′pĭ-dēz′) *n.* A plural of **stapes.**

sta·pe·li·a (stə-pē′lē-ə) *n.* Any of various plants of the genus *Stapelia,* including the starfish flower. [New Latin *Stapelia,* genus name, after Jan Bode van *Stapel* (died 1636), Dutch botanist.]

sta·pes (stā′pēz) *n., pl.* **stapes** or **sta·pe·des** (stā′pĭ-dēz′). The innermost of the three small bones of the middle ear, shaped somewhat like a stirrup. Also called *stirrup bone.* [New Latin *stapēs, stapēd-,* from Medieval Latin, stirrup.] **—sta·pe′di·al** (stā-pē′dē-əl) *adj.*

staph (stăf) *n. Informal.* Staphylococcus. **—staph** *adj.*

staph·y·lin·id (stăf′ə-lĭn′ĭd, -lī′nĭd) *n.* See **rove beetle.** [From New Latin *Staphylinidae,* family name, from *Staphylinus,* type genus, from Greek *staphulinos,* kind of insect, probably from *staphulē,* bunch of grapes.]

staphylo– *pref.* **1.** Cluster; resembling a cluster: *staphylococcus.* **2.** The uvula: *staphyloplasty.* [New Latin, from Greek *staphulē,* bunch of grapes.]

staph·y·lo·coc·cus (stăf′ə-lō-kŏk′əs) *n., pl.* **-coc·ci** (-kŏk′sī, -kŏk′ī). A spherical gram-positive parasitic bacterium of the genus *Staphylococcus,* usually occurring in grapelike clusters and causing boils, septicemia, and other infections. **—staph′y·lo·coc′cal** (-kŏk′əl), **staph′y·lo·coc·′cic** (-kŏk′sĭk, -kŏk′ĭk) *adj.*

staph·y·lo·plas·ty (stăf′ə-lō-plăs′tē) *n., pl.* **-ties.** Plastic surgery of the uvula and the soft palate. **—staph′y·lo·plas′tic** *adj.*

staph·y·lor·rha·phy also **staph·y·lor·a·phy** (stăf′ə-lôr′ə-fē) *n., pl.* **-phies.** Repair of a cleft palate by plastic surgery. [STAPHYLO– + Greek *rhaphē,* suture (from *rhaptein,* to sew; see **wer-** [2] in Appendix).]

sta·ple[1] (stā′pəl) *n.* **1.** A principal raw material or commodity grown or produced in a region. **2.** A major item of trade in steady demand. **3.** A basic dietary item, such as flour, rice, or corn. **4.** A basic or principal element or feature. **5.** The fiber of cotton, wool, or flax, graded as to length and fineness. **—staple** *adj.* **1.** Produced or stocked in large quantities to meet steady demand: *Wheat is a staple crop.* **2.** Principal; main: *a staple topic of conversation.* **—staple** *tr.v.* **-pled, -pling, -ples.** To grade (fibers) according to length and fineness. [Middle English, official market for purchase of export goods, from Anglo-Norman *estaple,* perhaps from Middle Dutch *stāpel,* heap, emporium.]

sta·ple[2] (stā′pəl) *n.* **1.** A U-shaped metal loop with pointed ends, driven into a surface to hold a bolt, hook, or hasp or to hold wiring in place. **2.** A thin piece of wire in the shape of a square bracket that is driven by a device through sheets of paper or similar material and flattened to serve as a fastening. **—staple** *tr.v.* **-pled, -pling, -ples.** To secure or fasten by means of a staple or staples. [Middle English, from Old English *stapol,* post, pillar.]

sta·pler[1] (stā′plər) *n.* One who deals in staple goods or staple fibers.

sta·pler[2] (stā′plər) *n.* A device used to bind material together by means of staples.

star (stär) *n.* **1.** *Astronomy.* **a.** A self-luminous celestial body consisting of a mass of gas held together by its own gravity in which the energy generated by nuclear reactions in the interior is balanced by the outflow of energy to the surface, and the inward-directed gravitational forces are balanced by the outward-directed gas and radiation pressures. **b.** Any of the celestial bodies visible at night from Earth as relatively stationary, usually twinkling points of light. **c.** Something regarded as resembling such a celestial body. **2.** A graphic design having five or more radiating points, often used as a symbol of rank or merit. **3.** An artistic performer or athlete whose leading role or superior performance is acknowledged. **4.** An asterisk (*). **5.** A white spot on the forehead of a horse. **6.** A planet or constellation of the zodiac believed in astrology to influence personal destiny. **7. stars.** The future; destiny. Often used with *the.* **—star** *adj.* Of, relating to, or being an outstanding, famous perfomer: *a star figure skater.* **—star** *v.* **starred, star·ring, stars.** *—tr.* **1. a.** To ornament with stars. **b.** To award or mark with a star for excellence. **2.** To mark with an asterisk. **3.** To present or feature (a performer) in a leading role. *—intr.* **1.** To play the leading role in a theatrical or film production. **2.** To do an outstanding job; perform excellently. ***—idioms.*** **have stars in (one's) eyes.** To be dazzled or enraptured, as with romantic love. **see stars.** To experience bright, flashing sensations, as from a blow to the head. [Middle English *sterre,* from Old English *steorra.* See **ster-** [3] in Appendix.]

star anise *n.* **1.** An aromatic eastern Asian evergreen tree *(Illicium verum)* having purple-red flowers and starlike clusters of anise-scented fruit. **2.** The fruit of this plant, used in Oriental cooking and medicine.

star apple *n.* **1.** A tropical American evergreen tree *(Chrysophyllum cainito)* having smooth-skinned, green or purple fruit and purplish flowers. **2.** The edible fruit of this tree.

Sta·ra Za·go·ra (stä′rə zə-gôr′ə, stä′rä zä-gô′rä). A city of central Bulgaria east-northeast of Plovdiv. It is an industrial center and railroad hub. Population, 152,000.

star·board (stär′bərd) *n. Abbr.* **stbd.** The right-hand side of a ship or an aircraft as one faces forward. **—starboard** *adj.* On the right-hand side as one faces forward. **—starboard** *adv.* To or toward the right-hand side as one faces forward. [Middle English *sterbord,* from Old English *stēorbord* : *stēor-,* a steering; see **stā-** in Appendix + *bord,* side of a ship.]

star·burst (stär′bûrst′) *n.* A shape or design with emanating rays that resembles the flash of light produced by an exploding star.

star cactus *n.* **1.** Any of various Mexican cacti of the genus *Astrophytum,* having yellow flowers with usually red centers. **2.** See **haworthia.** [From its starlike spine clusters.]

starch (stärch) *n.* **1.** A naturally abundant nutrient carbohydrate, $(C_6H_{10}O_5)_n$, found chiefly in the seeds, fruits, tubers, roots, and stem pith of plants, notably in corn, potatoes, wheat, and rice, and varying widely in appearance according to source but commonly prepared as a white, amorphous, tasteless powder. **2.** Any of various substances, such as natural starch, used to stiffen cloth, as in laundering. **3. starches.** Foods having a high content of starch, as rice, breads, and potatoes. **4. a.** Stiff behavior. **b.** Vigor; mettle. **—starch** *tr.v.* **starched, starch·ing, starch·es.** To stiffen with starch. [Middle English *starche,* substance used to stiffen cloth (sense uncertain), from *sterchen,* to stiffen, from Old English **stercan.* See **ster-** [1] in Appendix.]

Star Chamber (stär) *n.* **1.** A 15th-century to 17th-century English court consisting of judges who were appointed by the Crown and sat in closed session on cases involving state security. **2. star chamber.** A court or group that engages in secret, harsh, or arbitrary procedures. [So called because the ceiling of the original courtroom was decorated with stars.]

star-cham·ber (stär′chām′bər) *adj.* Secret, harsh, or arbitrary, as in procedures. [From STAR CHAMBER.]

starch syrup *n.* See **glucose** (sense 2).

starch wheat *n.* See **emmer.**

starch·y (stär′chē) *adj.* **-i·er, -i·est. 1. a.** Containing starch. **b.** Stiffened with starch. **2.** Of or resembling starch. **3.** Stiff; formal: *"this starchy, old-fashioned hotel room"* (Anne Tyler). **—starch′i·ly** *adv.* **—starch′i·ness** *n.*

star-crossed (stär′krôst′, -krŏst′) *adj.* Opposed by fate; ill-fated: *star-crossed lovers.*

star·dom (stär′dəm) *n.* **1.** The status of a performer or an entertainer acknowledged as a star. **2.** Star performers considered as a group.

star·dust (stär′dŭst′) *n.* **1.** A dreamlike, romantic, or uncritical sense of well-being. **2.** A cluster of stars too distant to be seen individually, resembling a dimly luminous cloud of dust. Not in scientific use. **3.** Minute particles of matter that fall to Earth from the stars. Not in scientific use. ***—idiom.*** **have stardust in (one's) eyes.** To be uncritically or unrealistically optimistic.

stare (stâr) *v.* **stared, star·ing, stares.** *—intr.* **1.** To look directly and fixedly, often with a wide-eyed gaze. See Synonyms at **gaze. 2.** To be conspicuous; stand out. **3.** To stand on end; bristle, as hair or feathers. *—tr.* To look at directly and fixedly: *stared him in the eyes.* **—stare** *n.* An intent gaze. ***—phrasal verb.*** **stare down.** To cause to waver or give in by or as if by staring. ***—idiom.*** **stare (one) in the face. 1.** To be plainly visible or obvious; force itself on (one's) attention: *The money on the table was staring her in the face.* **2.** To be obvious though initially overlooked: *The explanation had been staring him in the face all along.* **3.** To be imminent or unavoidable: *Bankruptcy now stares us in the face.* [Middle English *staren,* from Old English *starian.* See **ster-** [1] in Appendix.] **—star′er** *n.*

sta·rets (stär′yĭts) *n., pl.* **star·tsy** (stärt′sē). A spiritual adviser, often a monk or religious hermit, in the Eastern Orthodox Church. [Russian, elder, starets, from Old Church Slavonic *staritsĭ,* elder, from *starŭ,* old. See **stā-** in Appendix.]

star facet *n.* One of the eight small triangular facets in the crown of a brilliant-cut gem.

star·fish (stär′fĭsh′) *n., pl.* **starfish** or **-fish·es.** Any of various marine echinoderms of the class Asteroidea, characteristically having a thick, often spiny body with five arms extending from a central disk. Also called *asteroid, sea star.*

starfish flower *n.* Any of numerous tropical and southern African succulent plants of the genus *Stapelia,* having mottled, star-shaped, ill-smelling flowers. Also called *carrion flower.*

star·flow·er (stär′flou′ər) *n.* **1.** Any of several small plants of the genus *Trientalis,* especially *T. borealis,* of northeast North America, having white starlike flowers. **2.** Any of several plants having starlike flowers.

star fruit *n.* See **carambola** (sense 2). [From the shape of its cross section.]

star·gaze (stär′gāz′) *intr.v.* **-gazed, -gaz·ing, -gaz·es. 1.** To gaze at the stars. **2.** To daydream.

star·gaz·er (stär′gā′zər) *n.* **1.a.** *Informal.* An astronomer. **b.** An astrologer. **2.** A daydreamer. **3.** Any of various bottom-dwelling marine percoid fishes of the families Uranoscopidae and Dactyloscopidae, having eyes on the top of the head.

star grass *n.* **1.** Any of various plants of the genus *Hypoxis,* having grasslike leaves and star-shaped, white or yellow flowers. **2.** See **colicroot.**

stark (stärk) *adj.* **stark·er, stark·est. 1.** Bare; blunt: *"His language has become increasingly stark, to the point of sounding strident"* (Robert Pear). **2.** Complete or utter; extreme: *stark poverty; a stark contrast.* **3.** Harsh; grim: *"faced with that stark future"* (Robert C. McFarlane). "[They] *found it hard to accept such a stark portrait of unrelieved failure"* (W. Bruce Lincoln). **—stark** *adv.* Utterly; entirely: *stark raving mad.* [Middle English, stiff, severe, strong, from Old English *stearc.* See **ster-**[1] in Appendix.] **—stark′ly** *adv.* **—stark′ness** *n.*

stark·ers (stär′kərz) *adj. Chiefly British.* Stark naked. [Alteration of *stark naked.*]

star·let (stär′lĭt) *n.* **1.** A small star. **2.** A young film actress publicized as a future star.

star·light (stär′līt′) *n.* The light from the stars.

star·ling[1] (stär′lĭng) *n.* Any of various Old World passerine birds of the family Sturnidae, characteristically having a short tail, pointed wings, and dark, often iridescent plumage, especially *Sturnus vulgaris,* widely naturalized in North America. [Middle English, from Old English *stærlinc* : *stær,* starling + *-linc,* noun suff.; see −LING[1].]

star·ling[2] (stär′lĭng) *n.* A protective structure of pilings surrounding a pier of a bridge. [Perhaps alteration of Middle English *stadelinge,* from *stathel,* foundation, from Old English *stathol.* See **stā-** in Appendix.]

star·lit (stär′lĭt′) *adj.* Illuminated by starlight.

star-nosed mole (stär′nōzd′) *n.* A mole *(Condylura cristata)* of North America, having 22 small fleshy tentacles encircling the end of its nose in a starlike pattern.

star-of-Beth·le·hem (stär′əv-bĕth′lĭ-hĕm′) *n., pl.* **star-of-Bethlehem** or **stars-of-Bethlehem** (stärz′-). **1.** Any of numerous bulbous perennial herbs of the genus *Ornithogalum* in the lily family, especially *O. arabicum* or *O. umbellatum,* native to the Mediterranean region and having narrow leaves and a cluster of star-shaped white flowers. **2.** Any of several similar or related plants. [After the star that guided the Magi to Bethlehem.]

Star of David *n., pl.* **Stars of David** or **Star of Davids.** See **Magen David.**

Starr (stär), **Belle.** Originally Myra Belle Shirley. 1848–1889. American outlaw whose Oklahoma cabin became a hideout for fugitives from justice. Her criminal exploits are largely unsubstantiated.

Starr, Ringo. Originally Richard Starkey. Born 1940. British musician who was the colorful drummer of The Beatles (1962–1970).

star·ry (stär′ē) *adj.* **-ri·er, -ri·est. 1.** Marked or set with stars or starlike objects. **2.** Shining or glittering like stars. **3.** Shaped like a star. **4.** Illuminated by stars; starlit. **5.** Of, relating to, or coming from the stars; stellar. **—star′ri·ness** *n.*

star·ry-eyed (stär′ē-īd′) *adj.* Having a naively enthusiastic, overoptimistic, or romantic view; unrealistic: *a starry-eyed reformer; starry-eyed idealism.*

Stars and Bars (stärz) *n. (used with a sing. or pl. verb).* The first Confederate flag.

Stars and Stripes *n. (used with a sing. or pl. verb).* The flag of the United States.

star sapphire *n.* A sapphire with a polished convex surface exhibiting asterism.

star shell *n.* An artillery shell that explodes in midair with a shower of lights, used for illumination and signaling.

star·ship (stär′shĭp′) *n.* A crewed spacecraft designed for interstellar travel.

stars-of-Beth·le·hem (stärz′əv-bĕth′lĭ-hĕm′) *n.* A plural of **star-of-Bethlehem.**

Star-Span·gled Banner (stär′spăng′gəld) *n.* The flag of the United States.

star·struck or **star-struck** (stär′strŭk′) *adj.* Fascinated by or exhibiting a fascination with fame or famous people: *"The star-struck tone of the text suggests that the author is giving us an exclusive peek into the secret lives of the justices"* (Richard A. Epstein).

start (stärt) *v.* **start·ed, start·ing, starts.** *—intr.* **1.** To begin an activity or a movement; set out. **2.** To have a beginning; commence. See Synonyms at **begin. 3.** To move suddenly or involuntarily: *started at the loud noise.* **4.** To come quickly into view, life, or activity; spring forth. **5.** *Sports.* To be in the initial lineup of a game or race. **6.** To protrude or bulge. **7.** To become loosened or disengaged. *—tr.* **1.** To commence; begin. **2.** To set into motion, operation, or activity. **3.** To introduce; originate. **4.** *Sports.* **a.** To play in the initial lineup of (a game). **b.** To put (a player) into the initial lineup of a game. **c.** To enter (a participant) into a race or game. **5.** To found; establish: *start a business.* **6.** To tend in an early stage of development: *start seedlings.* **7.** To rouse (game) from its hiding place or lair; flush. **8.** To cause to become displaced or loosened. **—start** *n. Abbr.* **st. 1.a.** A beginning; a commencement. **b.** The beginning of a new construction project: *a large number of new housing starts this year.* **2.** A place or time of beginning. **3.** *Sports.* **a.** A starting line for a race. **b.** A signal to begin a race. **c.** An instance of beginning a game or race: *a pitcher who won his first five starts.* **4.** A startled reaction or movement. **5.** A part that has become dislocated or loosened. **6.** A position of advantage over others, as in a race or an endeavor; a lead. **7.** An opportunity granted to pursue a career or course of action. ***—idioms.*** **start something.** *Informal.* To cause trouble. **to start with. 1.** At the beginning; initially. **2.** In any case. [Middle English *sterten,* to move or leap suddenly, from Old English **styrtan.* See **ster-**[1] in Appendix.]

start·er (stär′tər) *n.* **1.** One that starts. **2.** An attachment for starting an internal-combustion engine without hand cranking. Also called *self-starter.* **3.** A device that initiates a flow of high voltage across the electrodes of a fluorescent lamp. **4.** *Sports.* **a.** One who signals the start of a race. **b.** A participant that starts in a game or race. **5.** *Baseball.* **a.** The first pitcher for a team in a game. **b.** A pitcher who regularly begins games for a team. **6.** The first in a series, especially the first course of a meal; an appetizer. ***—idiom.*** **for starters.** *Informal.* To begin with; initially: *"Deborah believes him, indicating, for starters, that she isn't the brightest"* (Judith Crist).

star thistle *n.* Any of several plants of the genus *Centaurea,* especially *C. calcitrapa,* native to Eurasia, having spiny purplish flower heads.

start·ing block (stär′tĭng) *n.* **1.** *Sports.* An apparatus that braces a runner's feet at the start of a race, consisting of two angled supports adjustably mounted on a rigid frame that is usually anchored to the track. **2.** The beginning of a period of time or an endeavor.

starting gate *n. Sports.* **1.** A series of stalls with interconnected doors that open simultaneously at the beginning of a race. **2.** A movable barrier that starts an automatic timer when pushed aside by a competitor, such as a skier.

starting line *n. Sports.* The point or line at which a race begins.

star·tle (stär′tl) *v.* **-tled, -tling, -tles.** *—tr.* **1.** To cause to make a quick involuntary movement or start. **2.** To alarm, frighten, or surprise suddenly. See Synonyms at **frighten.** *—intr.* To become alarmed, frightened, or surprised. **—startle** *n.* A sudden mild shock; a start. [Middle English *stertlen,* to run about, from Old English *steartlian,* to kick. See **ster-**[1] in Appendix.] **—star′tling·ly** *adv.* **—star′tling·ness** *n.*

star·tsy (stärt′sē) *n.* Plural of **starets.**

start-up or **start·up** (stärt′ŭp′) *—n.* **1.** The act or process of setting into operation or motion. **2.** A business or an undertaking that has recently begun operation: *grew from a tiny start-up to a multimillion-dollar corporation.* *—attributive.* Often used to modify another noun: *start-up costs; plagued by startup problems.*

star·va·tion (stär-vā′shən) *n.* **1.** The act or process of starving. **2.** The condition of being starved.

starve (stärv) *v.* **starved, starv·ing, starves.** *—intr.* **1.** To suffer or die from extreme or prolonged lack of food. **2.** *Informal.* To be hungry. **3.** To suffer from deprivation. **4.** *Archaic.* To suffer or die from cold. *—tr.* **1.** To cause to starve. **2.** To force to a specified state by starving. [Middle English *sterven,* to die, from Old English *steorfan.* See **ster-**[1] in Appendix.]

starve·ling (stärv′lĭng) *n.* One that is starving or being starved. **—starveling** *adj.* **1.** Starving. **2.** Poor in quality; inadequate.

star·wort (stär′wûrt′, -wôrt′) *n.* Any of various plants having star-shaped flowers or flower heads, as the aster or the stitchwort.

stash (stăsh) *Slang. tr.v.* **stashed, stash·ing, stash·es.** To hide or store away in a secret place. **—stash** *n.* **1.** A store or cache of money or valuables. **2.** Something hidden away. [Origin unknown.]

sta·sis (stā′sĭs, stăs′ĭs) *n., pl.* **sta·ses** (stā′sēz, stăs′ēz). **1.** A condition of balance among various forces; motionlessness: *"Language is a primary element of culture, and stasis in the arts is tantamount to death"* (Charles Marsh). **2.** *Pathology.* Stoppage of the normal flow of a body substance, as of blood through an artery or of intestinal contents through the bowels. [Greek, stationariness. See **stā-** in Appendix.]

–stasis *suff.* **1.** Slowing; stoppage: *bacteriostasis.* **2.** Stable state: *homeostasis.* [From Greek *stasis,* standstill. See STASIS.]

Stas·sen (stăs′ən), **Harold Edward.** Born 1907. American politician who served as governor of Minnesota (1938–1943) and

Belle Starr

Ringo Starr

starting block

ă pat	oi boy
ā pay	ou out
âr care	ŏŏ took
ä father	ōō boot
ĕ pet	ŭ cut
ē be	ûr urge
ĭ pit	th thin
ī pie	*th* this
îr pier	hw which
ŏ pot	zh vision
ō toe	ə about, item
ô paw	♦ regionalism

Stress marks: **′** (primary); ′ (secondary), as in **dictionary** (dĭk′shə-nĕr′ē)

made numerous unsuccessful bids for the Republican presidential nomination.

stat¹ (stăt) *n.* A statistic.

stat² (stăt) *adv.* With no delay; at once. **—stat** *adj.* Immediate: *"Next I want a stat EKG and a chest film"* (David Shobin). [Short for Latin *statim.* See **stā-** in Appendix.]

stat. *abbr.* **1.** Stationary. **2.** Statistic; statistics. **3.** Statuary. **4.** Statute.

-stat *suff.* **1.** Something that stabilizes: *rheostat.* **2.** A device for reflecting something specified in a constant direction: *heliostat.* **3.** Something that inhibits: *fungistat.* [New Latin *-stata,* from Greek *-statēs,* one that causes to stand, or from *statos,* standing; see **stā-** in Appendix.]

state (stāt) *n. Abbr.* **st. 1.** A condition or mode of being, as with regard to circumstances: *a state of confusion.* **2.** A condition of being in a stage or form, as of structure, growth, or development: *the fetal state.* **3.** A mental or emotional condition: *in a manic state.* **4.** *Informal.* A condition of excitement or distress. **5.** *Physics.* The condition of a physical system with regard to phase, form, composition, or structure: *Ice is the solid state of water.* **6.** Social position or rank. **7.** Ceremony; pomp: *foreign leaders dining in state at the White House.* **8. a.** The supreme public power within a sovereign political entity. **b.** The sphere of supreme civil power within a given polity: *matters of state.* **9.** A specific mode of government: *the socialist state.* **10.** A body politic, especially one constituting a nation: *the states of Eastern Europe.* **11.** One of the more or less internally autonomous territorial and political units composing a federation under a sovereign government: *the 48 contiguous states of the Union.* **—state** *adj.* **1.** Of or relating to a body politic or to an internally autonomous territorial or political unit constituting a federation under one government: *a monarch dealing with state matters; the department that handles state security.* **2.** Owned and operated by a state: *state universities.* **—state** *tr.v.* **stat·ed, stat·ing, states.** To set forth in words; declare. [Middle English, from Old French *estat,* from Latin *status.* See **stā-** in Appendix.]

SYNONYMS: *state, condition, situation, status.* These nouns denote the mode of being or form of existence of a person or thing. *State* and *condition,* the most general, are largely interchangeable: *a state* (or *condition*) *of disrepair; a healthy state* (or *condition*). *"Every body continues in its state of rest . . . unless it is compelled to change that state by forces impressed upon it"* (Isaac Newton). *"The condition of man . . . is a condition of war of everyone against everyone"* (Thomas Hobbes). *Situation* more narrowly refers to a state or condition at a particular time as determined by a combination of circumstances: *"Eternal truths will be neither true nor eternal unless they have fresh meaning for every new social situation"* (Franklin D. Roosevelt). *Status* usually applies to a person or thing considered in relation to others of the same class. With reference to persons it implies relative standing; with respect to things it is roughly equivalent to *state* or *situation*: *"Mr. Polly's status was that of a guest pure and simple"* (H.G. Wells). *What is the current status of the arms-reduction negotiations?*

state attorney *n. Law.* A prosecuting attorney for a state.

State Col·lege (stāt kŏl′ĭj). A borough of central Pennsylvania northwest of Harrisburg. Mainly residential, it is the seat of Pennsylvania State University (established 1855). Population, 36,130.

state·craft (stāt′krăft′) *n.* The art of leading a country: *"They placed free access to scientific knowledge far above the exigencies of statecraft"* (Anthony Burgess).

state·hood (stāt′ho͝od′) *n.* The status of being a state, especially of the United States, rather than being a territory or dependency.

state·hood·er (stāt′ho͝od′ər) *n.* One who is in favor of granting statehood to a particular territory or region.

state·house also **state house** (stāt′hous′) *n.* A building in which a state legislature holds sessions; a state capitol.

state·less (stāt′lĭs) *adj.* **1.** Having no state. **2.** Not having any recognized citizenship in a state or nation. **—state′less·ness** *n.*

state·let (stāt′lĭt) *n.* A small state: *"Most of the islands have become independent statelets with freely elected governments"* (Economist).

state·ly (stāt′lē) *adj.* **-li·er, -li·est. 1.** Dignified and impressive, as in size or proportions. See Synonyms at **grand. 2.** Majestic; lofty. **—stately** *adv.* In a ceremonious or imposing manner. [Middle English *statly,* from *state,* state, rank. See STATE.] **—state′li·ness** *n.*

state·ment (stāt′mənt) *n.* **1.** The act of stating or declaring. **2.** Something stated; a declaration. **3.** *Law.* A formal pleading. **4.** An abstract of a commercial or financial account showing an amount due; a bill. **5.** A monthly report sent to a debtor or bank depositor. **6.** *Computer Science.* An elementary instruction in a source language. **—*idiom.* make a statement.** To create a certain impression: *Glass, exposed beams, and antiques all combine to make a strong decorative statement.*

Stat·en Island (stăt′n). Formerly **Rich·mond** (rĭch′mənd). A borough of New York City coextensive with **Staten Island** in New York Bay in southeast New York southwest of Manhattan Island. First visited by Henry Hudson in 1609, the island was permanently settled in the mid-1600's and became part of New York City in 1898. The borough name was officially changed in April 1975, although the island still constitutes the county of Richmond. Population, 352,121.

state of the art *n.* The highest level of development, as of a device, technique, or scientific field, achieved at a particular time: *"Forty or fifty years ago the state of the art in radio was represented by crackling noises coming from a console of . . . Aztec-temple shape"* (New Yorker). **—state′-of-the-art′** (stāt′əv-thē-ärt′) *adj.*

state prison *n.* A prison maintained by a state for the confinement of people convicted of felonies.

stat·er¹ (stā′tər) *n.* A resident of a particular state or type of state. Often used in combination: *Lone Star staters; farm staters; the struggle between slave staters and free staters.*

sta·ter² (stā′tər) *n.* Any of various gold, silver, or electrum coins of ancient Greece. [Middle English, from Late Latin *statēr,* from Greek, from *histanai, sta-,* to set on a scale, weigh. See SYSTEM.]

state·room (stāt′ro͞om′, -ro͝om′) *n.* A private cabin or compartment with sleeping accommodations on a ship or train.

state's evidence (stāts) *n. Law.* **1.** Evidence for the prosecution in U.S. state or federal trials. **2.** One that gives evidence for the state in criminal proceedings.

States-Gen·er·al (stāts′jĕn′ər-əl) *pl.n.* **1.** A legislative assembly of representatives from the estates of the nation, as opposed to a provincial assembly. **2.** The legislative assembly in France before the Revolution. Also called *Estates-General.* [Translation of French *états généreaux* and Dutch *Staten-Generaal.*]

♦ **state·side** (stāt′sīd′) *adj.* **1.** Of or in the continental United States. **2.** *Alaska.* Of or in the 48 contiguous states of the United States. **—stateside** *adv. Informal.* **1.** To, toward, or in the continental United States. **2.** *Alaska.* To, toward, or in the 48 contiguous states of the United States.

♦ ***REGIONAL NOTE:*** Especially since World War II, the adverb *stateside* has commonly been used by Americans traveling abroad to mean "to, toward, or in the United States." During the postwar period the term gained currency among Alaskans, familiar with the feeling of being far removed from the rest of the continental United States. They adopted *stateside* into their vocabularies as a way of referring to their fellow Americans to the south. Russell Tabbert of the University of Alaska observes that *stateside* "has some currency primarily as a noun modifier, but also as an adverbial," as in this instance: *"Most of the owners live in Anchorage; some 14% live stateside"* (Alaska Magazine). It may or may not be capitalized. *Stateside, the lower states, the South,* and *(the) Outside* are all used in Alaska to denote "the 48 contiguous states." All these terms, however, are losing out to *the Lower 48,* which, as Tabbert points out, is always spelled in Alaska with a capital L and with Arabic numerals.

states·man (stāts′mən) *n.* **1.** A man who is a leader in national or international affairs. **2.** A male political leader regarded as a disinterested promoter of the public good. **3.** A man who is a respected leader in a given field: *"a mature statesman of American letters"* (Toby Thompson). **—states′man·like′, states′man·ly** *adj.* **—states′man·ship′** *n.*

states' rights also **States' rights** (stāts) *pl.n.* **1.** All rights not delegated to the federal government by the Constitution nor denied by it to the states. **2.** The political position advocating strict interpretation of the Constitution with regard to the limitation of federal powers and the extension of the autonomy of the individual state to the greatest possible degree. **—states' righter** *n.*

States' Rights Party *n.* A former political party founded in 1948 by Southern Democrats to consolidate opposition to civil rights policies of the regular Democratic Party.

States·ville (stāts′vĭl′, -vəl). A city of west-central North Carolina north of Charlotte. Founded in 1789, it is a trade and processing center. Population, 18,622.

states·wom·an (stāts′wo͝om′ən) *n.* **1.** A woman who is a leader in national or international affairs: *"In foreign policy,* [she] *relishes her role as a senior stateswoman of the West"* (Boston Globe). **2.** A woman political leader regarded as a disinterested promoter of the public good. **3.** A woman who is a respected leader in a given field.

state·wide (stāt′wīd′) *adj.* Occurring or extending throughout a state: *a statewide recycling program.* **—statewide** *adv.* Throughout a state: *a candidate who was popular statewide.*

stat·ic (stăt′ĭk) *adj.* **1. a.** Having no motion; being at rest; quiescent. **b.** Fixed; stationary. **2.** *Physics.* Of or relating to bodies at rest or forces that balance each other. **3.** *Electricity.* Of, relating to, or producing stationary charges; electrostatic. **4.** Of, relating to, or produced by random radio noise. **—static** *n.* **1.** Random noise, such as crackling in a receiver or specks on a television screen, produced by atmospheric disturbance of the signal. **2.** *Informal.* **a.** Back talk. **b.** Interference; obstruction. **c.** Angry or heated criticism. [New Latin *staticus,* relating to weight, from Greek *statikos,* causing to stand, from *statos,* standing. See **stā-** in Appendix.] **—stat′i·cal** *adj.* **—stat′i·cal·ly** *adv.*

static dump *n. Computer Science.* A printed or stored copy of the contents of a computer memory that is made at an inactive point in a program, usually at the end of a routine.

stat·i·ce (stăt′ĭ-sē′, stăt′ĭs) *n.* See **sea lavender.** [Latin *staticē*, an astringent plant, from Greek *statikē*, from feminine of *statikos*, causing to stand, astringent, from *statos*, standing. See **stā-** in Appendix.]

static electricity *n.* **1.** An accumulation of electric charge on an insulated body. **2.** Electric discharge resulting from the accumulation of electric charge on an insulated body.

static memory *n. Computer Science.* A memory that contains fixed information and retains its programmed state as long as the power is on.

static pressure *n.* The pressure exerted by a still liquid or gas, especially water or air.

static routine *n. Computer Science.* A subroutine with the addresses of the operands being the only parameters.

stat·ics (stăt′ĭks) *n. (used with a sing. or pl. verb).* The equilibrium mechanics of stationary bodies.

static tube *n.* A specialized tube used to measure the static pressure in a stream of fluid.

sta·tion (stā′shən) *n. Abbr.* **sta.** **1.** The place or position where a person or thing stands or is assigned to stand; a post: *a sentry station.* **2.** The place, building, or establishment from which a service is provided or operations are directed: *a police station.* **3.** A stopping place along a route, especially a stop for refueling or for taking on passengers; a depot. **4.** Social position; rank. **5.** An establishment equipped for observation and study: *a radar station.* **6.** An establishment equipped for radio or television transmission. **7.** An input or output point along a communications system. **8.** *Ecology.* **a.** The normal habitat of a particular plant or animal community. **b.** The exact place of occurrence of a species or individual within a given habitat. **—station** *tr.v.* **-tioned, -tion·ing, -tions.** To assign to a position; post. [Middle English *stacioun*, from Old French *station*, from Latin *statiō, statiōn-*. See **stā-** in Appendix.]

sta·tion·ar·y (stā′shə-nĕr′ē) *adj. Abbr.* **sta., stat.** **1.a.** Not moving. **b.** Not capable of being moved; fixed. **2.** Unchanging: *a stationary sound.* **—stationary** *n., pl.* **-ar·ies.** One that is stationary. [Middle English *stacionarie*, from Old French *stationnaire*, from Medieval Latin *statiōnārius*, from Latin, belonging to a military station, from *statiō, statiōn-*, station. See STATION.]

stationary bicycle *n.* See **exercise bicycle.**

stationary front *n.* A transition zone between two nearly stationary air masses of different density.

stationary orbit *n.* A geostationary orbit.

stationary satellite *n.* An artificial satellite in a synchronous orbit.

stationary wave *n.* See **standing wave.**

station break *n.* An intermission in a radio or television program for identification of the network or station.

sta·tion·er (stā′shə-nər) *n.* **1.** One that sells stationery. **2.** *Archaic.* **a.** A publisher. **b.** A bookseller. [Middle English *staciouner*, a bookseller, from Medieval Latin *statiōnārius*, shopkeeper (as against a peddler), probably from Latin *statiō, statiōn-*, place of business. See STATION.]

sta·tion·er·y (stā′shə-nĕr′ē) *n.* **1.** Writing paper and envelopes. **2.** Writing materials and office supplies.

station house also **sta·tion·house** (stā′shən-hous′) *n.* **1.** A police station. **2.** A fire station.

sta·tion·mas·ter (stā′shən-măs′tər) *n. Abbr.* **SM** An official in charge of a railroad or bus station.

Sta·tions of the Cross (stā′shənz) *pl.n. Roman Catholic Church.* **1.** A devotion consisting of prayers and meditations before each of 14 crosses or images set up in a church or along a path commemorating the events of the Passion of Jesus. **2.** The 14 crosses of this devotion, often accompanied by images or pictures representing the events of the Passion of Jesus.

sta·tion-to-sta·tion (stā′shən-tə-stā′shən) *adj.* Of, relating to, or designating a long-distance telephone call in which the caller is charged upon reaching anyone at the receiving number. **—station-to-station** *adv.* By station-to-station long-distance telephone.

station wagon *n.* An automobile having an extended interior with a third seat or luggage platform and a tailgate. [Originally a covered wagon used to convey passengers from a train station to their hotel.]

stat·ism (stā′tĭz′əm) *n.* The practice or doctrine of giving a centralized government control over economic planning and policy. **—stat′ist** *adj. & n.*

sta·tis·tic (stə-tĭs′tĭk) *n. Abbr.* **stat.** **1.** A numerical datum. **2.** A numerical value, such as standard deviation or mean, that characterizes the sample or population from which it was derived. [Ultimately from New Latin *statisticus*, of statecraft. See STATISTICS.]

sta·tis·ti·cal (stə-tĭs′tĭ-kəl) *adj.* Of, relating to, or employing statistics or the principles of statistics. **—sta·tis′ti·cal·ly** *adv.*

stat·is·ti·cian (stăt′ĭ-stĭsh′ən) *n.* **1.** A mathematician specializing in statistics. **2.** A compiler of statistical data.

sta·tis·tics (stə-tĭs′tĭks) *n. Abbr.* **stat.** **1.** *(used with a sing. verb).* The mathematics of the collection, organization, and interpretation of numerical data, especially the analysis of population characteristics by inference from sampling. **2.** *(used with a pl. verb).* Numerical data. [From German *Statistik*, political science, from New Latin *statisticus*, of state affairs, from Italian *statista*, person skilled in statecraft, from *stato*, state, from Old Italian, from Latin *status*, position, form of government. See **stā-** in Appendix.]

Sta·tius (stā′shəs, -shē-əs), **Publius Papinus.** A.D. 45?–96? Roman poet known for his epics *Thebaid* and *Achilleid.*

sta·tive (stā′tĭv) *Grammar. adj.* Belonging to or designating a class of verbs that express a state or condition. **—stative** *n.* A verb of the stative class.

stato– *pref.* **1.** Resting; remaining: *statoblast.* **2.** Equilibrium; balance: *statocyst.* [From Greek *statos*, standing, placed. See **stā-** in Appendix.]

stat·o·blast (stăt′ə-blăst′) *n.* An asexually produced encapsulated bud of a freshwater bryozoan that is released upon disintegration of the parent colony in autumn, remains inactive through winter, and develops into a new organism in spring.

stat·o·cyst (stăt′ə-sĭst′) *n.* A small organ of balance in many invertebrates, consisting of a fluid-filled sac containing statoliths that stimulate sensory cells and help indicate position when the animal moves. Also called *otocyst.*

stat·o·lith (stăt′l-ĭth′) *n.* A small, movable concretion of calcium carbonate found in statocysts; an otolith.

sta·tor (stā′tər) *n.* The stationary part of a motor, dynamo, turbine, or other working machine about which a rotor turns. [Latin, one that stands, from *stāre*, to stand. See **stā-** in Appendix.]

stat·o·scope (stăt′ə-skōp′) *n.* **1.** A barometer for recording small variations in atmospheric pressure. **2.** A device for indicating small changes in the altitude of an airplane.

stat·u·ar·y (stăch′o͞o-ĕr′ē) *n., pl.* **-ies.** *Abbr.* **stat.** **1.** Statues collectively. **2.** The art of making statues. **3.** A sculptor. **—statuary** *adj.* Of, relating to, or suitable for a statue. [From Latin *statuārius*, of a statue, from *statua*, statue. See STATUE.]

stat·ue (stăch′o͞o) *n.* A three-dimensional form or likeness sculpted, modeled, carved, or cast in material such as stone, clay, wood, or bronze. [Middle English, from Old French, from Latin *statua*, from *statuere*, to set up. See STATUTE.]

stat·u·esque (stăch′o͞o-ĕsk′) *adj.* Suggestive of a statue, as in proportion, grace, or dignity; stately. **—stat′u·esque′ly** *adv.*

stat·u·ette (stăch′o͞o-ĕt′) *n.* A small statue.

stat·ure (stăch′ər) *n.* **1.** The natural height of a human being or an animal in an upright position. **2.** An achieved level; status. [Middle English, from Old French, from Latin *statūra*, from *status*, past participle of *stāre*, to stand. See **stā-** in Appendix.]

sta·tus (stā′təs, stăt′əs) *n.* **1.** Position relative to that of others; standing: *Her status is that of a guest.* **2.** High standing; prestige: *a position of status in the community.* **3.** *Law.* The legal character or condition of a person or thing: *the status of a minor.* **4.** A state of affairs; situation. See Synonyms at **state.** [Latin. See **stā-** in Appendix.]

status quo *n.* The existing condition or state of affairs. [Latin, state in which : *status*, state + *quō*, in which, ablative of *quī*, which.]

status symbol *n.* Something, such as a possession or an activity, by which one's social or economic prestige is measured.

stat·u·ta·ble (stăch′ə-tə-bəl) *adj.* **1.** Enacted, regulated, or authorized by statute; statutory. **2.** *Law.* Legally punishable; recognized by statute: *a statutable offense.*

stat·ute (stăch′o͞ot) *n. Abbr.* **st., St., stat.** **1.** *Law.* A law enacted by a legislature. **2.** A decree or an edict, as of a ruler. **3.** An established law or rule, as of a corporation. [Middle English, from Old French *estatut*, from Late Latin *statūtum*, from neuter of Latin *statūtus*, past participle of *statuere*, to set up, from *status*, position. See **stā-** in Appendix.]

statute law *n.* A law established by legislative enactment.

statute mile *n.* See **mile** (sense 1).

statute of limitations *n., pl.* **statutes of limitations.** *Law.* A statute setting a time limit on legal action in certain cases.

stat·u·to·ry (stăch′ə-tôr′ē, -tōr′ē) *adj.* **1.** Of or relating to a statute. **2.** Enacted, regulated, or authorized by statute. **—stat′u·to′ri·ly** *adv.*

statutory offense *n. Law.* A legal offense declared by statute.

statutory rape *n.* Sexual relations with a person who has not reached the statutory age of consent.

staunch[1] (stônch, stänch) also **stanch** (stônch, stänch, stănch) *adj.* **staunch·er, staunch·est** also **stanch·er, stanch·est.** **1.** Firm and steadfast; true. See Synonyms at **faithful.** **2.** Having a strong or substantial construction or constitution. [Middle English *staunche*, from Anglo-Norman *estaunche*, from *estaunchier*, to stanch, variant of Old French *estanchier*. See STANCH[1].] **—staunch′ly** *adv.* **—staunch′ness** *n.*

USAGE NOTE: *Staunch* is more common than *stanch* as the spelling of the adjective. *Stanch* is more common than *staunch* as the spelling of the verb.

staunch[2] (stônch, stänch) *v.* Variant of **stanch**[1]. See Usage Note at **staunch**[1].

Staun·ton (stăn′tən). An independent city of north-central Virginia west-northwest of Charlottesville. The birthplace of Woodrow Wilson, it is a trade and processing center. Population, 21,857.

stau·ro·lite (stôr′ə-līt′) *n.* A brownish to black mineral, chiefly $(FeMg)_2Al_9Si_4O_{23}(OH)$, often having crossed intergrown

ă pat	oi boy
ā pay	ou out
âr care	o͝o took
ä father	o͞o boot
ĕ pet	ŭ cut
ē be	ûr urge
ĭ pit	th thin
ī pie	*th* this
îr pier	hw which
ŏ pot	zh vision
ō toe	ə about, item
ô paw	♦ regionalism

Stress marks: **′** (primary); ′ (secondary), as in **dictionary** (dĭk′shə-nĕr′ē)

crystals and sometimes used as a gem. [Greek *stauros,* cross; see **stā-** in Appendix + -LITE.] **—stau'ro·lit'ic** (-lĭt'ĭk) *adj.*

Sta·vang·er (stə-văng'ər). A city of southwest Norway south of Bergen on an inlet of the North Sea. Probably founded in the eighth century, it is a processing center with a shipbuilding industry. Population, 92,012.

stave (stāv) *n.* **1.** A narrow strip of wood forming part of the sides of a barrel, tub, or similar structure. **2.** A rung of a ladder or chair. **3.** A staff or cudgel. **4.** *Music.* See **staff**[1] (sense 5). **5.** A set of verses; a stanza. **—stave** *v.* **staved** or **stove** (stōv), **stav·ing, staves.** *—tr.* **1.** To break in or puncture the staves of. **2.** To break or smash a hole in. **3.** To crush or smash inward. **4.** To furnish with staves. *—intr.* To be or become crushed in. ***—phrasal verb.* stave off.** To keep or hold off; repel: *"For 12 years, we've sought to stave off this ultimate threat of disaster"* (New York Times). [Back-formation from *staves,* pl. of STAFF[1].]

steamboat

staves (stāvz) *n.* A plural of **staff**[1].

staves·a·cre (stāvz'ā'kər) *n.* **1.** A larkspur, *Delphinium staphisagria,* of southern Europe, with greenish-white flowers. **2.** The poisonous seeds of this plant, formerly used medicinally as an emetic, a cathartic, and an external parasiticide. [By folk etymology from Middle English *staphisagre,* from Latin *staphis agria,* from Greek : *staphis,* stavesacre + *agria,* feminine of *agrios,* wild; see **agro-** in Appendix.]

Stav·ro·pol (stăv-rō'pəl, stäv'rə-pəl). A city of southwest Russia southeast of Rostov. It was founded as a fortress town in 1777. Population, 293,000.

stay[1] (stā) *v.* **stayed, stay·ing, stays.** *—intr.* **1.** To continue to be in a place or condition: *stay home; stay calm.* **2.** To remain or sojourn as a guest or lodger: *stayed at a motel.* **3.** To stop moving; halt. **4.** To wait; pause. **5.** To endure or persist: *stayed with the original plan.* **6.** To keep up in a race or contest: *tried to stay with the lead runner.* **7.** *Games.* To meet a bet in poker without raising it. **8.** To stand one's ground; remain firm. **9.** *Archaic.* To cease from a specified activity. *—tr.* **1.** To stop or halt; check. **2.** To postpone; delay. **3.** To delay or stop the effect of (an order, for example) by legal action or mandate: *stay a prisoner's execution.* **4.** To satisfy or appease temporarily: *stayed his anger.* **5.** To remain during: *stayed the week with my parents; stayed the duration of the game.* **6.** To wait for; await: *"I will not stay thy questions. Let me go;/Or if thou follow me, do not believe/ But I shall do thee mischief in the wood"* (Shakespeare). **—stay** *n.* **1.** The act of halting; check. **2.** The act of coming to a halt. **3.** A brief period of residence or visiting. **4.** A suspension or postponement of a legal action or an execution: *granted a stay to the prisoner's execution.* ***—idioms.* stay put.** To remain in a fixed or established position. **stay the course.** To hold out or persevere to the end of a race or challenge. [Middle English *steien,* from Old French *ester, esteir,* from Latin *stāre.* See **stā-** in Appendix.]

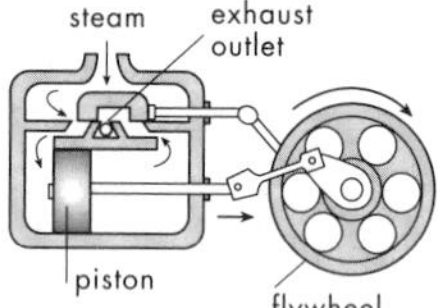

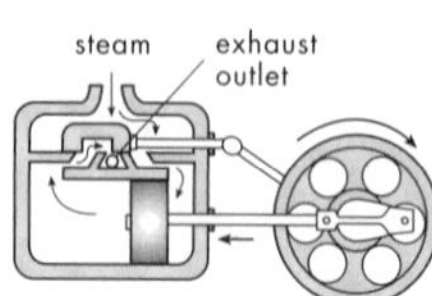

steam engine
Rightward (*top*) and leftward (*bottom*) movements of a slide valve steam engine

SYNONYMS: *stay, remain, wait, abide, tarry, linger, sojourn.* These verbs mean to continue to be in a given place. *Stay* is the least specific, though it can also suggest that the person involved is a guest or visitor: *We stayed at home all evening. "Must you go? Can't you stay?"* (Charles J. Vaughan). *Remain* is sometimes synonymous with *stay* but more often implies continuing or being left after others have gone: *A few people came to boo but remained to applaud. Please remain for a minute at the end of the meeting; I want a word with you in private. Wait* suggests remaining in readiness, anticipation, or expectation: *"Your father is waiting for me to take a walk with him"* (Booth Tarkington). *Abide* implies continuing for a lengthy period: *"Abide with me"* (Henry Francis Lyte). *Tarry* and *linger* both imply a delayed departure, but *linger* more strongly suggests reluctance to leave: *"She was not anxious but puzzled that her husband tarried"* (Eden Phillpotts). *"I alone sit lingering here"* (Henry Vaughan). To *sojourn* is to reside temporarily in a place: *"He was sojourning at* [a] *hotel in Bond Street"* (Anthony Trollope). See also Synonyms at **defer**[1].

stay[2] (stā) *tr.v.* **stayed, stay·ing, stays.** **1.** To brace, support, or prop up. **2.** To strengthen or sustain mentally or spiritually. **3.** To rest or fix on for support. **—stay** *n.* **1.** A support or brace. **2.** A strip of bone, plastic, or metal, used to stiffen a garment or part, such as a corset or shirt collar. **3. stays.** A corset. [Middle English *staien,* from Old French *estaiier,* from *estaie,* a support, of Germanic origin.]

stay[3] (stā) *n.* **1.** *Nautical.* A heavy rope or cable, usually of wire, used as a brace or support for a mast or spar. **2.** A rope used to steady, guide, or brace. **—stay** *tr. & intr.v.* **stayed, stay·ing, stays.** *Nautical.* To put (a ship) on the opposite tack or to come about. [Middle English, from Old English *stæg.*]

stay·ing power (stā'ĭng) *n.* The ability to endure or last.

stay-in strike (stā'ĭn') *n.* A job action that consists of a slowdown or work stoppage by employees who remain at their workplace.

stay·sail (stā'səl, -sāl') *n.* *Nautical.* A triangular sail hoisted on a stay.

stbd. *abbr.* Starboard.

STD *abbr.* Sexually transmitted disease.

std. *abbr.* Standard.

Ste. *abbr.* *French.* Sainte (feminine form of saint).

stead (stĕd) *n.* **1.** The place, position, or function properly or customarily occupied by another. **2.** Advantage; service; purpose: *"His personal relationship with the electorate stands in good stead"* (John Sears). **—stead** *tr.v.* **stead·ed, stead·ing, steads.** To be of advantage or service to; benefit. [Middle English *stede,* from Old English. See **stā-** in Appendix.]

stead·fast also **sted·fast** (stĕd'făst', -fəst) *adj.* **1.** Fixed or unchanging; steady. **2.** Firmly loyal or constant; unswerving. See Synonyms at **faithful.** [Middle English *stedefast,* from Old English *stedefæst* : *stede,* place; see STEAD + *fæst,* fixed, fast; see **past-** in Appendix.] **—stead'fast'ly** *adv.* **—stead'fast'ness** *n.*

stead·y (stĕd'ē) *adj.* **-i·er, -i·est.** **1.** Firm in position or place; fixed. **2.** Direct and unfaltering; sure. **3.** Free or almost free from change, variation, or fluctuation; uniform: *a steady increase in value; a steady breeze.* **4.** Not easily excited or upset: *steady nerves.* **5.** Unwavering, as in purpose; steadfast. **6.** Reliable; dependable. **7.** Temperate; sober. **—steady** *tr. & intr.v.* **stead·ied, stead·y·ing, stead·ies.** To make or become steady. **—steady** *interj.* *Nautical.* Used to direct a helmsman to keep a ship's head in the same direction: *Steady as she goes!* **—steady** *n., pl.* **-ies.** The person whom one dates regularly, usually exclusively. **—stead'i·er** *n.* **—stead'i·ly** *adv.* **—stead'i·ness** *n.*

SYNONYMS: *steady, even, equable, uniform, constant.* These adjectives mean marked by lack of variation or change. *Steady,* the most general, can imply continuity, regularity, firmness, or steadfastness: *Steady progress; the steady tick of the clock; a steady hand on the tiller; a steady, hard-working woman. Even* suggests the absence of irregularity or fluctuation: *maintaining an even tempo; has an even disposition. Equable* usually implies an intrinsic or innate characteristic leading to a lack of variation, especially extreme variation: *"The West Indian climate is . . . the most equable in the world"* (Alec Waugh). *Her father, an equable and genial man, is tolerant of her spirited stubbornness. Uniform* emphasizes sameness, as in character or degree, in all aspects, parts, or elements: *"Language was not uniform throughout the country but fell into dialects"* (Kemp Malone). *"Over all this the clouds shed a uniform and purplish shadow"* (Robert Louis Stevenson). *Constant* implies invariability, as in nature or form: *"Terror is the feeling which arrests the mind in the presence of whatsoever is grave and constant in human sufferings and unites it with the secret cause"* (James Joyce).

steady state *n.* *Physics.* A stable condition that does not change over time or in which change in one direction is continually balanced by change in another.

stead·y-state theory (stĕd'ē-stāt') *n.* A cosmological theory that assumes that the average density of matter in the universe is constant in space and time and that the expansion of the universe, required on other grounds, is compensated for by the continuous creation of matter. Also called *continuous creation theory.*

steak (stāk) *n.* **1.** A slice of meat, typically beef, usually cut thick and across the muscle grain and served broiled or fried. **2.** A thick slice of a large fish cut across the body. **3.** A patty of ground meat broiled or fried. [Middle English *steike,* from Old Norse *steik.* See **steig-** in Appendix.]

steak au poiv·re (ō pwäv'rə) *n., pl.* **steaks au poivre.** Steak studded with coarsely ground pepper before cooking and often flambéed with cognac. [STEAK + French *au poivre,* with pepper (*au,* with the + *poivre,* pepper).]

steak house or **steak·house** (stāk'hous') *n.* A restaurant that specializes in beefsteak dishes.

steak knife *n.* A table knife with a sharp, usually serrated steel blade.

steak tartare *n.* Raw ground beef mixed with onion, seasoning, and raw egg, eaten as an appetizer. Also called *tartare steak.* [STEAK + French *tartare,* Tartar.]

steal (stēl) *v.* **stole** (stōl), **sto·len** (stō'lən), **steal·ing, steals.** *—tr.* **1.** To take (the property of another) without right or permission. **2.** To get or effect surreptitiously or artfully: *steal a kiss; stole the ball from an opponent.* **3.** To move, carry, or place surreptitiously. **4.** To draw attention unexpectedly in (an entertainment), especially by being the outstanding performer: *The magician's assistant stole the show with her comic antics.* **5.** *Baseball.* To advance safely to (another base) during the delivery of a pitch, without the aid of a base hit, walk, passed ball, or wild pitch. *—intr.* **1.** To commit theft. **2.** To move, happen, or elapse stealthily or unobtrusively. **3.** *Baseball.* To steal a base. **—steal** *n.* **1.** The act of stealing. **2.** *Slang.* A bargain. ***—idiom.* steal (someone's) thunder.** To use, appropriate, or preempt the use of another's idea, especially to one's own advantage and without consent by the originator. [Middle English *stelen,* from Old English *stelan.*] **—steal'er** *n.*

SYNONYMS: *steal, purloin, filch, snitch, pilfer, cop, hook, swipe, lift, pinch.* These verbs mean to take another's property wrongfully, often surreptitiously. *Steal* is the most general: *stole a car; stealing a few moments for relaxation; research that was stolen by a colleague.* To *purloin* is to make off with something, often in a breach of trust: *purloined the key to his safe-deposit box. Filch* and *snitch* often suggest that what is stolen is of little value, while *pilfer* sometimes connotes theft of or in small quantities: *filched an ashtray from the restaurant; snitch a handkerchief; strawberries pilfered from the farmer. Cop, hook,* and *swipe* frequently connote quick, furtive snatching or seizing: *copped a necklace from the counter; planning to hook a fur coat; swiped a magazine from the doctor's waiting room.* To *lift* is to pick or take something up surreptitiously and keep it for oneself: *The pickpocket lifted* *my wallet. Pinch* suggests stealing something by or as if by squeezing it between the thumb and the fingers: *went into the study and pinched a dollar bill.*

stealth (stĕlth) *n.* **1.** The act of moving, proceeding, or acting in a covert way. **2.** The quality or characteristic of being furtive or covert. **3.** *Archaic.* The act of stealing. [Middle English *stelth,* probably from Old English **stǣlth.*]

stealth·y (stĕlʹthē) *adj.* **-i·er, -i·est.** Marked by or acting with quiet, caution, and secrecy intended to avoid notice. See Synonyms at **secret.** **—stealthʹi·ly** *adv.* **—stealthʹi·ness** *n.*

steam (stēm) *n.* **1.a.** The vapor phase of water. **b.** A mist of cooling water vapor. **2.a.** Pressurized water vapor used for heating, cooking, or to provide mechanical power. **b.** The power produced by a machine using pressurized water vapor. **c.** Steam heating. **3.** Power; energy. **—steam** *v.* **steamed, steam·ing, steams.** *—intr.* **1.** To produce or emit steam. **2.** To become or rise up as steam. **3.** To become misted or covered with steam. **4.** To move by means of steam power. **5.** *Informal.* To become very angry; fume. *—tr.* To expose to steam, as in cooking. [Middle English *steme,* from Old English *stēam.*]

steam bath *n.* **1.** The act of bathing through exposure to steam, which induces perspiration. **2.** A room or building equipped to provide bathing with steam.

steam beer *n.* A highly effervescent beer originally brewed in the western United States.

steam·boat (stēmʹbōtʹ) *n. Nautical.* A steamship, especially one used on rivers and other inland waterways.

steam boiler *n.* A closed tank in which water is converted into steam under pressure.

steam chest *n.* A compartment in a steam engine through which steam is delivered from the boiler to a cylinder.

steam engine *n.* An engine that converts the heat energy of pressurized steam into mechanical energy, especially one in which steam drives a piston in a closed cylinder.

steam·er (stēʹmər) *n. Abbr.* **str. 1.** *Nautical.* A steamship. **2.** A vehicle, a machine, or an engine driven by steam. **3.** A container in which something is steamed. **4.** See **soft-shell clam.**

steamer rug *n.* A warm blanket used especially by shipboard passengers while sitting in deck chairs.

steamer trunk *n.* A small trunk originally designed to fit under the bunk of a steamship cabin.

steam·fit·ter (stēmʹfĭtʹər) *n.* One who installs and repairs heating, ventilating, refrigerating, and air-conditioning systems. **—steamʹfitʹting** *n.*

steam heat·ing (hēʹtĭng) *n.* A heating system in which steam is generated in a boiler and piped to radiators.

steam iron *n.* A pressing iron that holds and heats water to be emitted as steam on the cloth being pressed.

steam·rol·ler (stēmʹrōʹlər) *n.* **1.a.** A steam-driven machine equipped with a heavy roller for smoothing road surfaces. **b.** A similar machine with an internal-combustion engine. **2.** A ruthless or irresistible force or power. **—steamroller** also **steam·roll** (-rōlʹ) *v.* **-rol·lered, -rol·ler·ing, -rol·lers** also **-rolled, -roll·ing, -rolls.** *—tr.* **1.** To smooth or level (a road) with a steamroller. **2.** To overwhelm or suppress ruthlessly; crush. *—intr.* To move or proceed with overwhelming or crushing force.

steam·ship (stēmʹshĭpʹ) *n. Abbr.* **S.S., SS** *Nautical.* A large vessel propelled by one or more steam-driven screws, propellers, or paddles.

steam shovel *n.* **1.** A large, steam-driven machine for digging. **2.** See **power shovel.**

steam table *n.* A table in which containers of cooked food are kept warm by hot water or steam circulating below.

steam turbine *n.* A turbine operated by highly pressurized steam directed against vanes on a rotor.

steam·y (stēʹmē) *adj.* **-i·er, -i·est. 1.** Filled with or emitting steam. **2.** Erotic. **—steamʹi·ly** *adv.* **—steamʹi·ness** *n.*

ste·ap·sin (stē-ăpʹsĭn) *n.* A digestive enzyme of pancreatic juice that catalyzes the hydrolysis of fats to fatty acids and glycerol. [Greek *stear,* tallow; see **stei-** in Appendix + (PE)PSIN.]

ste·a·rate (stēʹə-rātʹ, stîrʹātʹ) *n.* A salt or an ester of stearic acid. [STEAR(IC) + -ATE[2].]

ste·ar·ic (stē-ărʹĭk, stîrʹĭk) *adj.* **1.** Of, relating to, or similar to stearin or fat. **2.** Of or relating to stearic acid. [French *stéarique,* from Greek *stear,* tallow. See **stei-** in Appendix.]

stearic acid *n.* A colorless, odorless, waxlike fatty acid, $CH_3(CH_2)_{16}COOH$, occurring in natural animal and vegetable fats, used in making soaps, candles, lubricants, and other products.

ste·a·rin (stēʹər-ĭn, stîrʹĭn) also **ste·a·rine** (stēʹər-ĭn, -ə-rēnʹ, stîrʹĭn) *n.* **1.** A colorless, odorless, tasteless ester of glycerol and stearic acid, $C_3H_5(C_{18}H_{35}O_2)_3$, found in most animal and vegetable fats and used in the manufacture of soaps, candles, and adhesives and for textile sizing. Also called *tristearin.* **2.** The solid form of fat. [French *stéarine* : Greek *stear,* tallow; see **stei-** in Appendix + French *-ine,* -in.]

ste·a·rop·tene (stēʹə-rŏpʹtēnʹ) *n.* The portion of a natural essential oil that separates out as a white, crystalline solid on cooling or standing. [STEAR(IC) + Greek *ptēnos,* flying; see **pet-** in Appendix.]

steat- *pref.* Variant of **steato-.**

ste·a·tite (stēʹə-tītʹ) *n.* See **soapstone.** [Latin *steatītis,* a precious stone, from Greek, from *stear, steat-,* tallow. See **stei-** in Appendix.] **—steʹa·titʹic** (-tĭtʹĭk) *adj.*

steato- or **steat-** *pref.* Fat: *steatolysis.* [Greek, from *stear, steat-,* tallow. See **stei-** in Appendix.]

ste·a·tol·y·sis (stēʹə-tŏlʹĭ-sĭs) *n.* Digestive emulsification of fats before absorption and assimilation.

ste·at·o·pyg·i·a (stē-ătʹə-pĭjʹē-ə, -pīʹjē-ə) *n.* An extreme accumulation of fat on the buttocks. [STEATO- + Greek *pugē,* rump + -IA[1].] **—ste'at·o·pyg'ic** (-pĭjʹĭk, -pīʹjĭk), **ste'a·to·py'gous** (-pīʹgəs) *adj.*

ste·at·or·rhe·a also **ste·at·or·rhoe·a** (stēʹə-tə-rēʹə, stē-ătʹə-) *n.* **1.** Overaction of the sebaceous glands. **2.** Excessive discharge of fat in the feces.

ste·a·to·sis (stēʹə-tōʹsĭs) *n.* Accumulation of fat in the interstitial tissue of an organ.

Steb·bins (stĕbʹĭnz), **Emma.** 1815–1882. American sculptor known especially for her *Angel of the Waters (Bethesda Fountain)* (1873) in New York's Central Park.

sted·fast (stĕdʹfăstʹ, -fəst) *adj.* Variant of **steadfast.**

steed (stēd) *n.* A horse, especially a spirited one. [Middle English *stede,* from Old English *stēda,* stallion. See **stā-** in Appendix.]

steel (stēl) *n.* **1.** A generally hard, strong, durable, malleable alloy of iron and carbon, usually containing between 0.2 and 1.5 percent carbon, often with other constituents such as manganese, chromium, nickel, molybdenum, copper, tungsten, cobalt, or silicon, depending on the desired alloy properties, and widely used as a structural material. **2.** Something, such as a sword, that is made of steel. **3.** A quality suggestive of this alloy, especially a hard, unflinching character. **4.** *Color.* Steel gray. **—steel** *adj.* **1.a.** Made with, relating to, or consisting of steel: *steel beams; the steel industry; a bicycle with a steel frame.* **b.** Very firm or strong: *a steel grip.* **2.** *Color.* Of a steel gray. **—steel** *tr.v.* **steeled, steel·ing, steels. 1.** To cover, plate, edge, or point with steel. **2.** To make hard, strong, or obdurate; strengthen: *He steeled himself for disappointment.* [Middle English *stel,* from Old English *stȳle, stēl.*]

steel band *n. Music.* A band of Trinidadian origin, composed chiefly of tuned percussion instruments fashioned from oil drums.

steel blue *n.* **1.** *Color.* A medium grayish blue. **2.** One of several blue colors taken on by steel while being tempered.

steel drum *n. Music.* A metal percussion instrument of Trinidadian origin, fashioned from an oil barrel and having a concave array of flattened areas that produce different tones when struck. **—steel drummer** *n.*

Steele (stēl), **Mount.** A mountain, 5,076.4 m (16,644 ft) high, in the St. Elias Mountains of southwest Yukon Territory, Canada.

Steele, Sir **Richard.** 1672–1729. English writer of plays and essays who founded and edited *The Tatler* (1709–1711) and, with Joseph Addison, *The Spectator* (1711–1712).

steel engraving *n.* **1.** The art or process of engraving on a steel plate. **2.** An impression produced with an engraved steel plate.

steel gray *n. Color.* A dark to purplish gray.

steel guitar *n. Music.* **1.** An acoustic guitar with a metal resonator built into the body, often played with a slide and producing a twangy, variable tone. **2.** See **Hawaiian guitar.**

steel·head (stēlʹhĕdʹ) *n.* The anadromous variety of rainbow trout, being larger and having darker spots than the freshwater variety.

steel-trap (stēlʹtrăpʹ) *adj.* Very quick and keen; trenchant: *a steel-trap intellect.*

steel wool *n.* Fine fibers of steel matted or woven together to form an abrasive for cleaning, smoothing, or polishing.

steel·work (stēlʹwûrkʹ) *n.* **1.** Something made of steel. **2.** **steelworks.** *(used with a sing. verb).* A plant where steel is made; a foundry. **—steelʹworkʹer** *n.*

steel·y (stēʹlē) *adj.* **-i·er, -i·est. 1.** Made of steel. **2.** Resembling steel, as in color or hardness: *steely eyes.* **—steelʹi·ness** *n.*

steel·yard (stēlʹyärdʹ) *n.* A balance consisting of a scaled arm suspended off center, a hook at the shorter end on which to hang the object being weighed, and a counterbalance at the longer end that can be moved to find the weight. [STEEL + YARD[1], rod.]

Steen (stān), **Jan.** 1626?–1679. Dutch genre painter known for his humorous and moralistic depictions of domestic life and revelry, including *Flemish Feast in an Inn* (1674).

steen·bok (stēnʹbŏkʹ, stānʹ-) also **stein·bok** (stīnʹ-) *n.* A small antelope *(Raphicerus campestris)* of southern and eastern Africa, having a brownish coat and short, pointed horns in the male and living chiefly in dry grasslands. [Afrikaans, from Middle Dutch *steenboc,* ibex : *steen,* stone; see **stei-** in Appendix + *boc,* buck.]

steep¹ (stēp) *adj.* **steep·er, steep·est. 1.** Having a sharp inclination; precipitous. **2.** At a rapid or precipitous rate: *a steep rise in salaries.* **3.a.** Excessive; stiff: *a steep price.* **b.** Ambitious; difficult: *a steep undertaking.* **—steep** *n.* A precipitous slope. [Middle English *stepe,* from Old English *stēap.*] **—steepʹly** *adv.* **—steepʹness** *n.*

SYNONYMS: *steep, abrupt, precipitous, sheer.* The central meaning shared by these adjectives is "so sharply inclined as to be

steamroller

steel band

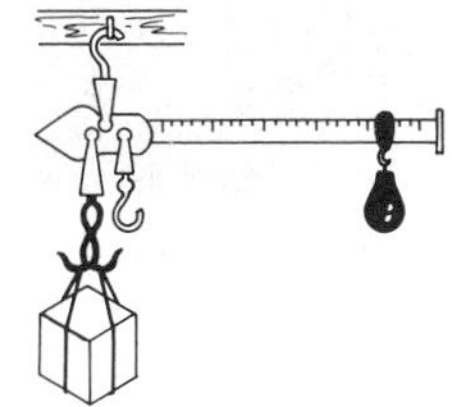
steelyard

ă pat	oi boy
ā pay	ou out
âr care	ŏŏ took
ä father	ōō boot
ĕ pet	ŭ cut
ē be	ûr urge
ĭ pit	th thin
ī pie	*th* this
îr pier	hw which
ŏ pot	zh vision
ō toe	ə about, item
ô paw	♦ regionalism

Stress marks: **ʹ** (primary); ʹ (secondary), as in **dictionary** (dĭkʹshə-nĕrʹē)

steeple
Place of Meditation, Eisenhower Center, Abilene, Kansas

stein

John Steinbeck

Gloria Steinem

almost perpendicular": *steep cliffs; an abrupt canyon; precipitous hills; a sheer descent of rock.*

steep² (stēp) *v.* **steeped, steep·ing, steeps.** —*tr.* **1.** To soak in liquid in order to cleanse, soften, or extract a given property from. **2.** To infuse or subject thoroughly to. **3.** To make thoroughly wet; saturate. —*intr.* To undergo a soaking in liquid. —**steep** *n.* **1.a.** The act or process of steeping. **b.** The state of being steeped. **2.** A liquid, bath, or solution in which something is steeped. [Middle English *stepen,* perhaps of Old English origin.] —**steep′er** *n.*

steep·en (stē′pən) *tr. & intr.v.* **-ened, -en·ing, -ens.** To make or become steep or steeper.

stee·ple (stē′pəl) *n.* **1.** A tall tower forming the superstructure of a building, such as a church or temple, and usually surmounted by a spire. **2.** A spire. [Middle English *stepel,* from Old English *stēpel.*]

stee·ple·bush (stē′pəl-bo͝osh′) *n.* See **hardhack.**

stee·ple·chase (stē′pəl-chās′) *n.* **1.** *Sports.* **a.** A horserace across open country or over an obstacle course. **b.** A footrace of usually 3,000 meters over a closed track with four hurdles and a water obstacle. **2.** A course of action containing many obstacles. [From the use of church steeples as landmarks.] —**stee′ple·chas′er** *n.*

stee·pled (stē′pəld) *adj.* **1.** Having steeples or a steeple: *picturesque, steepled villages; a tiny, steepled church.* **2.** Steeply inclined: *steepled roofs.*

stee·ple·jack (stē′pəl-jăk′) *n.* One who builds or maintains very high structures, such as steeples.

steer¹ (stîr) *v.* **steered, steer·ing, steers.** —*tr.* **1.** To guide by means of a device such as a rudder, paddle, or wheel. **2.a.** To direct the course of. **b.** To maneuver (a person) into a place or course of action. See Synonyms at **guide.** —*intr.* **1.** To guide a vessel or vehicle. **2.** To follow or move in a set course. **3.** To admit of being steered or guided: *a craft that steers easily.* —**steer** *n.* A piece of advice. [Middle English *steren,* from Old English *stēran.* See **stā-** in Appendix.] —**steer′a·ble** *adj.* —**steer′er** *n.*

steer² (stîr) *n.* A young ox, especially one castrated before sexual maturity and raised for beef. [Middle English, from Old English *stēor.* See **stā-** in Appendix.]

steer·age (stîr′ĭj) *n.* **1.** The act or practice of steering. **2.** *Nautical.* **a.** The effect of the helm on a ship. **b.** The steering apparatus of a ship. **c.** The section of a passenger ship, originally near the rudder, providing the cheapest passenger accommodations.

steer·age·way (stîr′ĭj-wā′) *n. Nautical.* The minimum rate of motion required for a ship or boat to be maneuvered by the helm.

steer·ing committee (stîr′ĭng) *n.* A committee that sets agendas and schedules of business, as for a legislative body or another assemblage.

steering gear *n.* The mechanism by which dispositions of the steering controls of a vehicle are transferred to the part that interacts with the external medium.

steering wheel *n.* A wheel that controls steering, as on a boat or in an automotive vehicle.

steers·man (stîrz′mən) *n. Nautical.* One who steers a ship.

steeve¹ (stēv) *Nautical. n.* A spar or derrick with a block at one end, used for stowing cargo. —**steeve** *tr.v.* **steeved, steev·ing, steeves.** To stow or pack (cargo) in the hold of a ship. [From Middle English *steven,* to stow, probably from Old Spanish *estibar,* to steeve, or from Old Catalan *stivar,* both from Latin *stīpāre.*]

steeve² (stēv) *Nautical. n.* The angle formed by the bowsprit and the horizon or the keel. —**steeve** *v.* **steeved, steev·ing, steeves.** —*tr.* To incline (a bowsprit) upward at an angle with the horizon or the keel. —*intr.* To have an upward inclination. Used of a bowsprit. [Origin unknown.]

Ste·fáns·son (stĕf′ən-sən), **Vilhjálmur.** 1879–1962. Canadian-born explorer and ethnologist who studied the language and culture of the Eskimo.

Stef·fens (stĕf′ənz), **(Joseph) Lincoln.** 1866–1936. American journalist. As managing editor of *McClure's Magazine* (1902–1906), he exposed governmental corruption in a series of articles, thereby inaugurating the era of muckraking journalism.

steg·o·don (stĕg′ə-dŏn′) *n.* Any of various extinct elephantlike mammals of the genus *Stegodon* and related genera, of the Pliocene to the Pleistocene. [New Latin *Stegodon,* genus name : Greek *stegos,* roof (from *stegein,* to cover; see **(s)teg-** in Appendix) + -ODON (so called because of the distinctive ridges on its molars).]

steg·o·saur (stĕg′ə-sôr′) also **steg·o·sau·rus** (stĕg′ə-sôr′əs) *n.* Any of several herbivorous dinosaurs of the suborder *Stegosauria* of the Jurassic to the Cretaceous, having a double row of upright bony plates along the back, long hind legs, a short neck, and a relatively small head. [New Latin *Stegosaurus,* genus name : Greek *stegos,* roof; see STEGODON + New Latin *saurus,* lizard; see SAURY.]

Stei·chen (stī′kən), **Edward Jean.** 1879–1973. American photographer who was a pioneer of photography as a fine art.

stein (stīn) *n.* A mug, especially one for beer, usually holding about a pint. [German, probably short for *Steinkrug,* stone jug : *Stein,* stone (from Middle High German, from Old High German; see **stei-** in Appendix) + *Krug,* jug.]

Stein (stīn), **Gertrude.** 1874–1946. American writer of experimental novels, essays, and plays. In Paris during the 1920's she was a central member of a group of American expatriates, including Ernest Hemingway. Her works include *Three Lives* (1908) and *The Autobiography of Alice B. Toklas* (1933).

Stein·beck (stīn′bĕk′), **John Ernst.** 1902–1968. American writer of short stories and novels, most notably *The Grapes of Wrath* (1939), which concerns the social and economic plight of migrant farm workers in California. He won the 1962 Nobel Prize for literature.

Stein·berg (stīn′bûrg′, -bərg), **Saul.** Born 1914. Romanian-born American graphic artist and cartoonist whose witty, satirical works have appeared in the *New Yorker.*

stein·bok (stīn′bŏk′) *n.* Variant of **steenbok.**

Stein·em (stī′nəm), **Gloria.** Born 1934. American feminist, writer, and a founding editor (1972) of *Ms.* magazine.

Stein·er (stī′nər, shtī′-), **Rudolf.** 1861–1925. Austrian social philosopher who founded a Christianized school of theosophy, called anthroposophy, which recognizes the existence of pure thought that is independent of the senses.

Stein·heim man (stīn′hīm′, shtīn′-) *n.* An extinct hominid *(Homo steinheimensis)* known from skull fragments of the middle Pleistocene and thought to be an ancestor of Neanderthal man. [After *Steinheim,* a village of south-central Germany.]

Stein·man (stīn′mən), **David Barnard.** 1886–1960. American civil engineer who designed numerous suspension bridges, including the George Washington Bridge in New York City (1931).

Stein·metz (stīn′mĕts′, shtīn′-), **Charles Proteus.** 1865–1923. German-born American electrical engineer and inventor known for his theoretical studies of alternating current, which made possible advancements in electrical generators and motors.

Stein·way (stīn′wā′), **Henry Engelhard.** 1797–1871. German-born American piano maker who founded the Steinway & Sons piano company in New York City (1853).

ste·le (stē′lē) *n., pl.* **-les** or **-lae** (-lē). **1.** An upright stone or slab with an inscribed or sculptured surface, used as a monument or as a commemorative tablet in the face of a building. **2.** *Botany.* The central core of vascular tissue in a plant stem or root. [Greek *stēlē,* pillar. See **stel-** in Appendix.] —**ste′lar** (-lər) *adj.*

Stel·la (stĕl′ə), **Frank Philip.** Born 1936. American painter whose abstract works are characterized by geometric forms, brilliant colors, and often irregularly shaped canvases.

stel·lar (stĕl′ər) *adj.* **1.** Of, relating to, or consisting of stars. **2.a.** Of or relating to a star performer. **b.** Outstanding; principal. [Late Latin *stellāris,* from Latin *stēlla,* star. See **ster-³** in Appendix.]

stellar wind (wĭnd) *n.* The varying flow of plasma ejected from the surface of a star into interstellar space.

stel·late (stĕl′āt′) also **stel·lat·ed** (-ā′tĭd) *adj.* Arranged or shaped like a star; radiating from a center. [Latin *stēllātus,* from *stēlla,* star. See **ster-³** in Appendix.] —**stel′late·ly** *adv.*

Stel·ler's eider (stĕl′ərz) *n.* A small black-and-white eider *(Polysticta stelleri)* of Alaska, Canada, and Siberia. [After Georg Wilhelm *Steller* (1709–1746), German naturalist.]

Steller's jay *n.* A bird *(Cyanocitta stelleri)* of western North America, having a black crested head, sooty-brown back and shoulders, and blue wings and tail and related to the blue jay. [After Georg Wilhelm *Steller* (1709–1746), German naturalist.]

Steller's sea lion *n.* A large sea lion *(Eumetopias jubata)* with a prominent mane, found from the Bering Sea to the California coast. [After Georg Wilhelm *Steller* (1709–1746), German naturalist.]

stel·li·form (stĕl′ə-fôrm′) *adj.* Shaped like a star. [New Latin *stēllifōrmis* : Latin *stēlla,* star; see STELLAR + Latin *-formis,* form (from *fōrma*).]

stel·lu·lar (stĕl′yə-lər) *adj.* **1.** Having the form of a small star. **2.** Bespangled with small stars. [From Late Latin *stēllula,* diminutive of Latin *stēlla,* star. See STELLAR.]

stem¹ (stĕm) *n.* **1.a.** The main ascending axis of a plant; a stalk or trunk. **b.** A slender stalk supporting or connecting another plant part, such as a leaf or flower. **2.** A banana stalk bearing several bunches of bananas. **3.** A connecting or supporting part, especially: **a.** The tube of a tobacco pipe. **b.** The slender upright support of a wineglass or goblet. **c.** The small projecting shaft with an expanded crown by which a watch is wound. **d.** The rounded rod in the center of certain locks about which the key fits and is turned. **e.** The shaft of a feather or hair. **f.** The upright stroke of a typeface or letter. **g.** *Music.* The vertical line extending from the head of a note. **4.** The main line of descent of a family. **5.** *Linguistics.* The main part of a word to which affixes are added. **6.** *Nautical.* The curved upright beam at the fore of a vessel into which the hull timbers are scarfed to form the prow. **7.** The tubular glass structure mounting the filament or electrodes in an incandescent bulb or vacuum tube. —**stem** *v.* **stemmed, stem·ming, stems.** —*intr.* To have or take origin or descent. —*tr.* **1.** To remove the stem of. **2.** To provide with a stem. **3.** To make headway against: *managed to stem the rebellion.* —*idiom.* **from stem to stern.** From one end to another. [Middle English, from Old English *stefn, stemn.* See **stā-** in Appendix.]

SYNONYMS: stem, arise, derive, emanate, flow, issue, originate, proceed, rise, spring. The central meaning shared by these verbs is "to come forth or come into being": *customs stemming from the past; misery arising from war; rights deriving from citizenship; disapproval emanating from the teacher; happiness that flows from their friendship; prejudice that issues from fear; a proposal originating in the Congress; a mistake that proceeded from carelessness; rebellion rising in the provinces; new industries springing up.*

stem² (stĕm) *v.* **stemmed, stem·ming, stems.** —*tr.* **1.** To stop or hold back by or as if by damming; stanch. **2.** To plug or tamp (a blast hole, for example). **3.** *Sports.* To point (skis) inward. —*intr. Sports.* To point skis inward in order to slow down or turn. [Middle English *stemmen,* from Old Norse *stemma.*]

stem cell *n.* An unspecialized cell that gives rise to a specific specialized cell, such as a blood cell.

stem chris·tie (krĭs′tē) *n. Sports.* A turn in skiing made by stemming the uphill ski, transferring weight to its inside edge, and bringing the other ski into a parallel position midway through the turn.

stem·ma (stĕm′ə) *n., pl.* **stem·ma·ta** (stĕm′ə-tə) or **stem·mas. 1.** A scroll recording the genealogy of an ancient Roman family; a family tree. **2.** The genealogy of the manuscripts of a literary work. **3.** A small, circular, simple eye present in various insect larvae. [Latin *stemma, stemmat-,* from Greek, garland, from *stephein,* to encircle.]

stemmed (stĕmd) *adj.* **1.** Having the stems removed. **2.** Provided with a stem or a specific type of stem. Often used in combination: *stemmed goblets; long-stemmed roses.*

stem rust *n.* A rust disease affecting the stem of a plant.

stem·son (stĕm′sən) *n. Nautical.* A piece of supporting timber bolted to the stem and keelson at their junction near the bow of a wooden vessel. [STEM[1] + (KEEL)SON.]

stem turn *n. Sports.* A turn in skiing made by stemming the uphill ski, transferring weight to its inside edge, and bringing the other ski into a parallel position after the turn is completed.

stem·ware (stĕm′wâr′) *n.* Glassware mounted on a stem with a broad base.

stem-wind·er (stĕm′wīn′dər) *n.* **1.** A stem-winding watch. **2.** A rousing oration, especially a political one.

stem-wind·ing (stĕm′wīn′dĭng) *adj.* **1.** Wound by turning an expanded crown on the stem. **2.** Of, relating to, or characterized by rousing oration: *"a stem-winding style that one associates with the Senate of a hundred years ago"* (New Yorker).

sten. *abbr.* Stenographer; stenography.

stench (stĕnch) *n.* A strong, foul odor; a stink. [Middle English, from Old English *stenc,* odor.]

SYNONYMS: stench, fetor, malodor, reek, stink. The central meaning shared by these nouns is "a penetrating, objectionable odor": *the stench of burning rubber; the fetor of polluted waters; the malodor of diesel fumes; the reek of stale sweat; a stink of decayed flesh.*

sten·cil (stĕn′səl) *n.* **1.** A sheet, as of plastic or cardboard, in which a desired lettering or design has been cut so that ink or paint applied to the sheet will reproduce the pattern on the surface beneath. **2.** The lettering or design produced with such a sheet. **3.** The process of printing with such a sheet. —**stencil** *tr.v.* **-ciled, -cil·ing, -cils** or **-cilled, -cil·ling, -cils. 1.** To mark with a stencil. **2.** To produce by stencil. [From Middle English *stencelled,* adorned brightly, from Old French *estenceler,* to adorn brightly, from *estencele,* spark, from Vulgar Latin **stincilla,* alteration of Latin *scintilla,* spark.] —**sten′cil·er** *n.*

Sten·dhal (stĕn-däl′, stăn-, stäN-). Pen name of Marie Henri Beyle. 1783–1842. French writer who influenced the development of the modern novel with his psychologically penentrating romances, such as *The Red and the Black* (1830).

Sten·gel (stĕng′gəl), **Charles Dillon.** Known as "Casey." 1890?–1975. American baseball player and manager, most notably of the New York Yankees (1948–1960).

sten·o (stĕn′ō) *n., pl.* **-os. 1.** A stenographer. **2.** Stenography.

steno– *pref.* Narrow; small: *stenotopic.* [Greek, from *stenos.*]

sten·o·bath·ic (stĕn′ə-băth′ĭk) *adj.* Limited to or able to live only within a narrow range of water depths. Used of aquatic organisms. [STENO– + Greek *bathos,* depth + –IC.] —**sten′o·bath′** *n.*

stenog. *abbr.* Stenographer; stenography.

sten·o·graph (stĕn′ə-grăf′) *n.* **1.** A keyboard machine for reproducing letters in a shorthand system. **2.** A character in shorthand.

ste·nog·ra·pher (stə-nŏg′rə-fər) *n. Abbr.* **sten., stenog.** One who is skilled in stenography, especially one employed to take and transcribe dictation or testimony.

ste·nog·ra·phy (stə-nŏg′rə-fē) *n. Abbr.* **sten., stenog. 1.** The art or process of writing in shorthand. **2.** The art or practice of transcribing speech with a stenograph machine. **3.** Material transcribed in shorthand. —**sten′o·graph′ic** (stĕn′ə-grăf′ĭk), **sten′o·graph′i·cal** (-ĭ-kəl) *adj.* —**sten′o·graph′i·cal·ly** *adv.*

sten·o·ha·line (stĕn′ə-hā′līn, -hăl′īn) *adj.* Limited to or able to live only within a narrow range of saltwater concentrations. Used of aquatic organisms. [STENO– + Greek *halinos,* of salt (from *hals, hal-,* salt; see HALO–).]

ste·noph·a·gous (stə-nŏf′ə-gəs) *adj.* Feeding on a single kind or limited variety of food.

ste·nosed (stə-nōzd′, -nōst′) *adj.* Characterized by stenosis. [STENOS(IS) + –ED[3].]

ste·no·sis (stə-nō′sĭs) *n., pl.* **-ses** (-sēz). A constriction or narrowing of a duct or passage; a stricture. [New Latin, from Greek *stenōsis,* a narrowing, from *stenoun,* to narrow, from *stenos,* narrow.] —**ste·not′ic** (-nŏt′ĭk) *adj.*

sten·o·ther·mal (stĕn′ə-thûr′məl) also **sten·o·ther·mic** (-mĭk) or **sten·o·ther·mous** (-məs) *adj.* Capable of living or growing only within a limited range of temperature. —**sten′o·therm′** *n.*

sten·o·top·ic (stĕn′ə-tŏp′ĭk) *adj.* Able to adapt only to a narrow range of environmental conditions. Used of a plant or an animal. [STENO– + Greek *topos,* place + –IC.]

sten·o·type (stĕn′ə-tīp′) *n.* **1.** A keyboard machine used to record dictation in shorthand by a series of phonetic symbols. **2.** A phonetic symbol or combination of symbols produced by such a machine. —**stenotype** *tr.v.* **-typed, -typ·ing, -types.** To record or transcribe (matter) with a stenotype machine. [STENO(GRAPHY) + TYPE.] —**sten′o·typ′ist** *n.*

sten·o·typ·y (stĕn′ə-tī′pē) *n., pl.* **-ies.** The art or process of transcribing with a stenotype machine.

sten·tor (stĕn′tôr′) *n.* Any of several trumpet-shaped, ciliate protozoans of the genus *Stentor,* living in dark freshwater pools and feeding chiefly on smaller microorganisms. [After *Stentor,* a Greek herald. See STENTORIAN.]

sten·to·ri·an (stĕn-tôr′ē-ən, -tōr′-) *adj.* Extremely loud: *a stentorian voice.* See Synonyms at **loud.** [After *Stentor,* a loud-voiced Greek herald in the *Iliad.*]

step (stĕp) *n.* **1.a.** The single complete movement of raising one foot and putting it down in another spot, as in walking. **b.** A manner of walking; a particular gait. **c.** A fixed rhythm or pace, as in marching: *keep step.* **d.** The sound of a footstep. **e.** A footprint: *steps in the mud.* **2.a.** The distance traversed by moving one foot ahead of the other. **b.** A very short distance: *just a step away.* **c. steps.** Course; path: *turned her steps toward home.* **3.a.** A rest for the foot in ascending or descending. **b. steps.** Stairs. **c.** Something, such as a ledge or an offset, that resembles a step of a stairway. **4.a.** One of a series of actions, processes, or measures taken to achieve a goal. **b.** A stage in a process: *followed every step in the instructions.* **5.** A degree in progress or a grade or rank in a scale: *a step up in the corporate hierarchy.* **6.** *Music.* The interval that separates two successive tones of a scale. **7.** *Nautical.* The block in which the heel of a mast is fixed. —**step** *v.* **stepped, step·ping, steps.** —*intr.* **1.** To put or press the foot: *step on the gas.* **2.** To shift or move slightly by taking a step or two: *step back.* **3.** To walk a short distance to a specified place or in a specified direction: *step over to the corner.* **4.** To move with the feet in a particular manner: *step lively.* **5.** To move into a new situation by or as if by taking a single step: *stepping into a life of ease.* **6.** To treat with arrogant indifference: *He is always stepping on other people.* —*tr.* **1.** To put or set (the foot) down: *step foot on land.* **2.** To measure by pacing: *step off ten yards.* **3.** To furnish with steps; make steps in: *terraces that are stepped along the hillside.* **4.** *Computer Science.* To cause (a computer) to execute a single instruction. **5.** *Nautical.* To place (a mast) in its step. —***phrasal verbs.* step down. 1.** To resign from a high post. **2.** To reduce, especially in stages: *stepping down the electric power.* **step in. 1.** To enter into an activity or a situation. **2.** To intervene. **step out. 1.** To walk briskly. **2.** To go outside for a short time. **3.** *Informal.* To go out for a special evening of entertainment. **4.** To withdraw; quit. **step up. 1.** To increase, especially in stages: *step up production.* **2.** To come forward: *step up and be counted.* —***idioms.* in step. 1.** Moving in rhythm. **2.** In conformity with one's environment: *in step with the times.* **out of step. 1.** Not moving in rhythm: *recruits marching out of step.* **2.** Not in conformity with one's environment: *out of step with the times.* **step by step.** By degrees. **step on it.** *Informal.* To go faster; hurry. [Middle English, from Old English *stæpe, stepe.*]

step– *pref.* Related by means of a remarriage rather than by blood: *stepparent.* [Middle English, from Old English *stēop-.*]

step·broth·er (stĕp′brŭth′ər) *n.* A son of one's stepparent.

step·child (stĕp′chīld′) *n.* **1.** A spouse's child by a previous marriage. **2.** Something that does not receive appropriate care, respect, or attention: *"Demography has a reputation for being the stepchild of . . . economics"* (Louis Pol).

step dance *n.* A dance in which emphasis is placed on certain steps, such as clogging or tapping, rather than body position or gesture.

step·daugh·ter (stĕp′dô′tər) *n.* A spouse's daughter by a previous marriage.

step-down (stĕp′doun′) *adj.* **1.** Decreasing in stages: *a step-down gear.* **2.** *Electricity.* Serving to reduce voltage: *a step-down transformer.* —**step-down** *n.* A reduction in amount or size.

step·fam·i·ly (stĕp′făm′ə-lē, -făm′lē) *n., pl.* **-lies.** A family with one or more stepchildren.

step·fa·ther (stĕp′fä′thər) *n.* The husband of one's mother and not one's natural father.

steph·a·no·tis (stĕf′ə-nō′tĭs) *n., pl.* **-tis·es.** Any of various

stele
Mid second-century A.D.
Roman niche stele

stencil

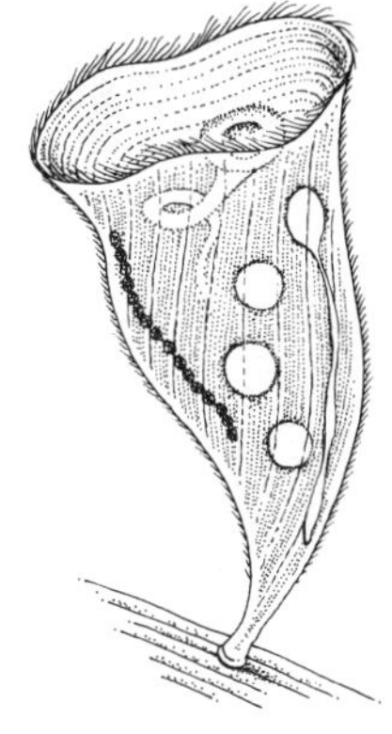

stentor

ă pat	oi boy
ā pay	ou out
âr care	ŏŏ took
ä father	ōō boot
ĕ pet	ŭ cut
ē be	ûr urge
ĭ pit	th thin
ī pie	*th* this
îr pier	hw which
ŏ pot	zh vision
ō toe	ə about, item
ô paw	♦ regionalism

Stress marks: ′ (primary); ′ (secondary), as in **dictionary** (dĭk′shə-nĕr′ē)

woody climbing plants of the genus *Stephanotis,* especially *S. floribunda* of Madagascar, cultivated for its showy, fragrant, white flowers. [Greek *stephanōtis,* deserving a crown, from *stephanos,* crown, wreath, from *stephein,* to crown.]

Ste·phen (stē′vən), Saint. Died c. A.D. 36. Christian protomartyr who, according to tradition, was stoned to death after his defense of Christianity before the Sanhedrin.

Stephen I. Often called Saint Stephen. 975?–1038. King of Hungary (997?–1038). Considered the founder of the Hungarian state, he maintained strong ties with the Roman Catholic Church, advocated the building of churches and abbeys, and organized a standing army.

Stephen, Sir **Leslie.** 1832–1904. British writer and editor whose works include *The History of English Thought in the Eighteenth Century* (1876) and biographies of Samuel Johnson, Alexander Pope, and others.

Stephen of Blois (blwä). 1097?–1154. King of England (1135–1154). The grandson of William the Conquerer, he was the last Norman king of England.

Ste·phens (stē′vənz), **Alexander Hamilton.** 1812–1883. American politician who was vice president of the Confederacy (1861–1865) under Jefferson Davis.

Stephens, James. 1882–1950. Irish writer of poems and novels, such as *The Crock of Gold* (1912).

Ste·phen·son (stē′vən-sən), **George.** 1781–1848. British railway pioneer who built a practical steam locomotive (1814) and the first passenger railway (1825). His son **Robert** (1803–1859) built railroads, locomotives, and bridges.

step-in (stĕp′ĭn′) *adj.* Put on by stepping into: *a step-in robe.* —**step-in** *n.* **1. step-ins.** Panties with wide legs. **2.** A step-in garment.

step·lad·der (stĕp′lăd′ər) *n.* A portable ladder with a hinged supporting frame and usually topped with a small platform.

step·moth·er (stĕp′mŭth′ər) *n.* The wife of one's father and not one's natural mother.

step·par·ent (stĕp′pâr′ənt, -păr′-) *n.* A stepfather or stepmother.

steppe (stĕp) *n.* A vast semiarid grass-covered plain, as found in southeast Europe, Siberia, and central North America. [German, from Russian *step′*.]

stepped-up (stĕpt′ŭp′) *adj.* Increased in pace or intensity; heightened: *a stepped-up political campaign.*

step·per (stĕp′ər) *n.* **1.** One that steps, especially in a fast or spirited manner. **2.** *Informal.* A dancer.

step·ping-off place (stĕp′ĭng-ôf′, -ŏf′) *n.* **1.** The last stop on an outbound line, as of a train. **2.** A place or point from which one leaves for unfamiliar regions.

step·ping·stone (stĕp′ĭng-stōn′) *n.* **1.** A stone that provides a place to step, as in crossing a stream. **2.** An advantageous position for advancement toward a goal.

step rocket *n.* See **multistage rocket.**

step·sib·ling (stĕp′sĭb′lĭng) *n.* A stepbrother or a stepsister.

step·sis·ter (stĕp′sĭs′tər) *n.* A daughter of one's stepparent.

step·son (stĕp′sŭn′) *n.* A spouse's son by a previous marriage.

step stool *n.* A stool, often with folding steps attached, on which one stands to reach high objects.

step turn *n. Sports.* A turn in skiing made by lifting one ski, putting it down again pointed in the direction of the turn, and transferring one's weight to it while bringing the other ski into a parallel position.

step-up (stĕp′ŭp′) *adj.* **1.** Increasing in steps or by stages. **2.** *Electricity.* Serving to increase voltage: *a step-up transformer.* —**step-up** *n.* An increase in size, amount, or activity.

step·wise (stĕp′wīz′) *adj.* **1.** Marked by a gradual progression as if step by step: *"The* [people's] *height has increased sharply, stepwise by generation"* (James Fallows). **2.** *Music.* Moving from one tone to an adjacent one. —**step′wise′** *adv.*

ster. *abbr.* Sterling.

–ster *suff.* **1.** One that is associated with, participates in, makes, or does: *songster.* **2.** One that is: *youngster.* [Middle English, from Old English *-estre,* female agent suff.]

ste·ra·di·an (stĭ-rā′dē-ən) *n. Abbr.* **sr** A unit of measure equal to the solid angle subtended at the center of a sphere by an area on the surface of the sphere that is equal to the radius squared: *The total solid angle of a sphere is 4π steradians.* See table at **measurement.** [STE(REO)– + RADIAN.]

ster·co·ra·ceous (stûr′kə-rā′shəs) also **ster·co·rous** (stûr′kər-əs) *adj.* Consisting of or relating to excrement. [Latin *stercus, stercor-,* dung; see **sker-**[3] in Appendix + –ACEOUS.]

stere (stîr) *n. Abbr.* **s** A unit of volume equal to one cubic meter. [French *stère,* from Greek *stereos,* solid, hard. See **ster-**[1] in Appendix.]

ster·e·o (stĕr′ē-ō′, stîr′-) *n., pl.* **-os. 1.a.** A stereophonic sound-reproduction system. **b.** Stereophonic sound. **2.** A stereotype. **3.** A stereoscopic system or photograph. —**stereo** *adj.* **1.** Stereophonic. **2.** Stereoscopic.

stereo– *pref.* **1.** Solid; solid body: *stereotropism.* **2.** Three-dimensional: *stereoscope.* [Greek, from *stereos,* solid. See **ster-**[1] in Appendix.]

ster·e·o·bate (stĕr′ē-ō-bāt′, stîr′-) *n. Architecture.* **1.** See **stylobate. 2.** The foundation of a stone building, its top course sometimes being a stylobate. [Latin *stereobatēs,* from Greek **stereobatēs* : *stereos,* solid; see STEREO– + *-batēs,* walker (from *bainein,* to go; see **gʷā-** in Appendix).]

ster·e·o·chem·is·try (stĕr′ē-ō-kĕm′ĭ-strē, stîr′-) *n.* The branch of chemistry that deals with spatial arrangements of atoms in molecules and the effects of these arrangements on the chemical and physical properties of substances. —**ster′e·o·chem′i·cal** (-ĭ-kəl) *adj.*

ster·e·o·chro·my (stĕr′ēə-krō′mē, stîr′-) *n., pl.* **-mies.** The art or process of mural painting with pigments mixed with water glass. —**ster′e·o·chrome′** *n.* —**ster′e·o·chro′mic** *adj.* —**ster′e·o·chro′mi·cal·ly** *adv.*

ster·e·o·gram (stĕr′ē-ə-grăm′, stîr′-) *n.* **1.** A picture or diagram designed to give the impression of solidity. **2.** A stereograph.

ster·e·o·graph (stĕr′ēə-grăf′, stîr′-) *n.* Two stereoscopic pictures or one picture with two superposed stereoscopic images, designed to give a three-dimensional effect when viewed through a stereoscope or special glasses. —**stereograph** *tr.v.* **-graphed, -graph·ing, -graphs.** To make a stereographic picture of.

ster·e·og·ra·phy (stĕr′ē-ŏg′rə-fē, stîr′-) *n.* **1.** The art or technique of depicting solid bodies on a plane surface. **2.** Photography that involves the use of stereoscopic equipment. —**ster′e·o·graph′ic** (-ə-grăf′ĭk), **ster′e·o·graph′i·cal** (-ĭ-kəl) *adj.* —**ster′e·o·graph′i·cal·ly** *adv.*

ster·e·o·i·so·mer (stĕr′ē-ō-ī′sə-mər, stîr′-) *n.* One of a set of isomers whose molecules have the same atoms bonded to each other but differ in the way these atoms are arranged in space.

ster·e·o·i·som·er·ism (stĕr′ē-ō-ī-sŏm′ə-rĭz′əm, stîr′-) *n.* Isomerism created by differences in the spatial arrangement of atoms in a molecule. —**ster′e·o·i′so·mer′ic** (-ī′-sə-mĕr′ĭk) *adj.*

ster·e·ol·o·gy (stĕr′ē-ŏl′ə-jē, stîr′-) *n.* The study of three-dimensional properties of objects or matter usually observed two-dimensionally. —**ster′e·o·log′ic** (-ə-lŏj′ĭk), **ster′e·o·log′i·cal** (-ĭ-kəl) *adj.* —**ster′e·o·log′i·cal·ly** *adv.* —**ster′e·ol′o·gist** *n.*

ster·e·o·mi·cro·scope (stĕr′ē-ō-mī′krə-skōp′, stîr′-) *n.* A microscope optically equipped for stereoscopic viewing. —**ster′e·o·mi′cro·scop′ic** (-skŏp′ĭk) *adj.* —**ster′e·o·mi·cros′co·py** (-mī-krŏs′kə-pē) *n.*

ster·e·o·phon·ic (stĕr′ēə-fŏn′ĭk, stîr′-) *adj.* Of or used in a sound-reproduction system that uses two or more separate channels to give a more natural distribution of sound. —**ster′e·o·phon′i·cal·ly** *adv.* —**ster′e·oph′on·y** (-ē-ŏf′ə-nē) *n.*

ster·e·op·sis (stĕr′ē-ŏp′sĭs, stîr′-) *n.* Stereoscopic vision.

ster·e·op·ti·con (stĕr′ē-ŏp′tĭ-kŏn′, stîr′-) *n.* A magic lantern, especially one with two projectors arranged so as to produce dissolving views. [New Latin : STEREO– + Greek *optikon,* neuter of *optikos,* optic; see OPTIC.]

ster·e·o·scope (stĕr′ē-ə-skōp′, stîr′-) *n.* An optical instrument with two eyepieces used to impart a three-dimensional effect to two photographs of the same scene taken at slightly different angles.

ster·e·o·scop·ic (stĕr′ē-ə-skŏp′ĭk, stîr′-) *adj.* **1.** Of or relating to stereoscopy. **2.** Of or relating to a stereoscope. —**ster′e·o·scop′i·cal·ly** *adv.*

ster·e·os·co·py (stĕr′ē-ŏs′kə-pē, stîr′-) *n.* **1.** The viewing of objects as three-dimensional. **2.** The technique of making or using stereoscopes and stereoscopic slides. —**ster′e·os′co·pist** *n.*

ster·e·o·tax·is (stĕr′ē-ə-tăk′sĭs, stîr′-) also **ster·e·o·tax·y** (stĕr′ē-ə-tăk′sē, stîr′-) *n.* **1.** A method in neurosurgery and neurological research for locating points within the brain using an external, three-dimensional frame of reference usually based on the Cartesian coordinate system. **2.** Movement of an organism in response to contact with a solid body. In this sense, also called *thigmotaxis.* —**ster′e·o·tac′tic** (-tăk′tĭk), **ster′e·o·tax′ic** (-tăk′sĭk), **ster′e·o·tac′ti·cal** (-tăk′tĭ-kəl), **ster′e·o·tax′i·cal** (-tăk′sĭ-kəl) *adj.* —**ster′e·o·tac′ti·cal·ly, ster′e·o·tax′i·cal·ly** *adv.*

ster·e·ot·ro·pism (stĕr′ē-ŏt′rə-pĭz′əm, stîr′-) *n.* See **thigmotropism.** —**ster′e·o·trop′ic** (-ē-ə-trŏp′ĭk) *adj.*

ster·e·o·type (stĕr′ē-ə-tīp′, stîr′-) *n.* **1.** A conventional, formulaic, and oversimplified conception, opinion, or image: *"Regional stereotypes have been part of America since its founding. . . . Westerners are trendy, Midwesterners are dull, Northeasterners are brainy, and Southerners are lazy"* (Brad Edmondson). **2.** One that is regarded as embodying or conforming to a set image or type. **3.** *Printing.* A metal printing plate cast from a matrix molded from a raised surface, such as type. —**stereotype** *tr.v.* **-typed, -typ·ing, -types. 1.** To make a stereotype of. **2.** To characterize by a stereotype: *"Elderly Americans are the neglected sector of the fashion industry, stereotyped by blue hair and polyester pantsuits"* (American Demographics). **3.** To give a fixed, unvarying form to. **4.** To print from a stereotype. [French *stéréotype,* stereotype printing : *stéréo–,* solid (from Greek *stereo-;* see STEREO–) + *type,* printing type (from Old French, symbol, from Late Latin *typus;* see TYPE).] —**ster′e·o·typ′er** *n.* —**ster′e·o·typ′ic** (-tĭp′ĭk), **ster′e·o·typ′i·cal** (-ĭ-kəl) *adj.* —**ster′e·o·typ′i·cal·ly** *adv.*

ster·e·o·typed (stĕr′ē-ə-tīpt′, stîr′-) *adj.* **1.** Lacking originality or creative force. See Synonyms at **trite. 2.** *Printing.* Printed or reproduced from stereotype plates.

ster•e•o•ty•py (stĕr′ē-ə-tī′pē, stîr′-) *n., pl.* **-pies. 1.** Excessive repetition or lack of variation in movements, ideas, or patterns of speech. **2.** *Printing.* The process or art of making stereotype plates.

ster•e•o•vi•sion (stĕr′ē-ō-vĭzh′ən, stîr′-) *n.* Visual perception of or exhibition in three dimensions.

ster•ic (stĕr′ĭk, stîr′-) also **ster•i•cal** (-ĭ-kəl) *adj. Physics & Chemistry.* Of or relating to the spatial arrangement of atoms in a molecule. [STER(EO)– + –IC.] **—ster′i•cal•ly** *adv.*

ste•rig•ma (stə-rĭg′mə) *n., pl.* **-ma•ta** (-mə-tə). A slender projection of the basidium of some fungi that bears a basidiospore. [New Latin, from Greek *stērigma,* support, from *stērizein, stērig-,* to support. See **ster-**[1] in Appendix.] **—ster′ig•mat′ic** (stĕr′ĭg-măt′ĭk, stîr′-) *adj.*

ster•il•ant (stĕr′ə-lənt) *n.* A sterilizing agent.

ster•ile (stĕr′əl, -īl′) *adj.* **1.** Not producing or incapable of producing offspring. **2. a.** Not producing or incapable of producing seed, fruit spores, or other reproductive structures. Used of plants or their parts. **b.** Producing little or no vegetation; unfruitful: *sterile land.* **3.** Free from live bacteria or other microorganisms: *a sterile operating area; sterile instruments.* **4.** Lacking imagination, creativity, or vitality. **5.** Lacking the power to function; not productive or effective; fruitless: *a sterile discussion.* [Middle English, from Old French, from Latin *sterilis.*] **—ster′ile•ly** *adv.* **—ster′ile•ness, ste•ril′i•ty** (stə-rĭl′ĭ-tē) *n.*

SYNONYMS: *sterile, infertile, barren, unfruitful, impotent.* These adjectives in literal usage mean not producing or unable to produce offspring; figuratively they suggest a lack of productiveness. To be *sterile* is to be incapable of reproducing; by extension the term implies a lack of vitality, creativity, or effectiveness: *a sterile conclusion; sterile pleasures. Infertile* is synonymous with *sterile*: *an infertile imagination. Barren* especially describes one who has tried and failed to have children; it can also apply to what is devoid of profit, interest, or enjoyment: *barren efforts; barren praise. Unfruitful* literally means not bearing fruit or offspring and figuratively means not having a useful result: *an unfruitful discussion. Impotent* specifies the inability of a male to engage in sexual intercourse; in a general sense it implies powerlessness: *impotent rage.*

ster•il•i•za•tion (stĕr′ə-lĭ-zā′shən) *n.* **1.** The act or procedure of sterilizing. **2.** The condition of being sterile or sterilized.

ster•il•ize (stĕr′ə-līz′) *tr.v.* **-ized, -iz•ing, -iz•es. 1.** To make free from live bacteria or other microorganisms. **2.** To deprive (a person or an animal) of the ability to produce offspring, as by removing the reproductive organs. **3. a.** To make incapable of bearing fruit or germinating. **b.** To render (land) unfruitful. **4.** *Economics.* To place (gold) in safekeeping so as not to affect the supply of money or credit. **5.** To make inoffensive or innocuous: *sterilized the terminology with euphemisms.* **—ster′il•iz′er** *n.*

ster•let (stûr′lĭt) *n.* A sturgeon *(Acipenser ruthenus)* of the Black and Caspian seas, used as a source of caviar. [Russian *sterlyad′,* from Old Russian *sterlyagi,* of Germanic origin.]

ster•ling (stûr′lĭng) *n. Abbr.* **ster., stg. 1.** British money, especially the pound as the basic monetary unit of the United Kingdom. **2.** British coinage of silver or gold, having as a standard of fineness 0.500 for silver and 0.91666 for gold. **3. a.** Sterling silver. **b.** Articles, such as tableware, made of sterling silver. **—sterling** *adj. Abbr.* **ster., stg. 1.** Consisting of or relating to sterling or British money. **2.** Made of sterling silver: *a sterling teaspoon.* **3.** Of the highest quality: *a person of sterling character.* [Middle English, silver penny : possibly *sterre,* star; see STAR + *-ling,* diminutive suff. (from the small star stamped on the coin); see –LING[1].]

Ster•ling (stûr′lĭng). A city of northwest Illinois southwest of Rockford. It is an industrial center. Population, 16,273.

Sterling Heights. A city of southeast Michigan, a suburb of Detroit. Population, 108,999.

sterling silver *n.* **1.** An alloy of 92.5 percent silver with copper or another metal. **2.** Objects made of this alloy.

Ster•li•ta•mak (stĕr′lĭ-tə-măk′, stĭr′lyĭ-tə-mäk′). A city of western Russia on the Belaya River west of Magnitogorsk. Center of a chemical complex, it has varied heavy industries. Population, 240,000.

stern[1] (stûrn) *adj.* **stern•er, stern•est. 1.** Hard, harsh, or severe in manner or character: *a stern disciplinarian.* See Synonyms at **severe. 2.** Grim, gloomy, or forbidding in appearance or outlook. **3.** Firm or unyielding; uncompromising. **4.** Inexorable; relentless: *stern necessity.* [Middle English *sterne,* from Old English *styrne.* See **ster-**[1] in Appendix.] **—stern′ly** *adv.* **—stern′ness** *n.*

stern[2] (stûrn) *n.* **1.** *Nautical.* The rear part of a ship or boat. **2.** A rear part or section. [Middle English *sterne,* perhaps of Scandinavian origin; akin to Old Norse *stjōrn,* rudder. See **stā-** in Appendix.]

Stern (stûrn), **Isaac.** Born 1920. Russian-born American violinist who is considered among the great 20th-century virtuosos.

Stern, Otto. 1888–1969. German-born American physicist. He won a 1943 Nobel Prize for detecting the magnetic movements of atomic particles.

ster•na (stûr′nə) *n.* A plural of **sternum.**

ster•nal (stûr′nəl) *adj.* Of, relating to, or near the sternum.

stern chaser *n.* A gun or cannon mounted on the stern of a ship for firing at a pursuing vessel.

Sterne (stûrn), **Laurence.** 1713–1768. British writer whose masterpiece, *Tristram Shandy* (1761–1767), was a precursor to modern stream-of-consciousness novels.

stern•fore•most (stûrn′fôr′mōst′, -fōr′-) *adv. Nautical.* With the stern foremost; backward.

ster•nite (stûr′nīt) *n.* The ventral shield or plate of each segment of the body of an insect or other arthropod. [STERN(UM) + –ITE[1].]

stern knee *n. Nautical.* See **sternson.**

stern•most (stûrn′mōst′) *adj. Nautical.* Closest to the stern.

ster•no•cla•vic•u•lar (stûr′nō-klə-vĭk′yə-lər) *adj.* Of, relating to, or connecting the sternum and the clavicle.

ster•no•clei•do•mas•toid (stûr′nō-klī′də-măs′toid) *n.* Either of two muscles of the neck that serve to flex and rotate the head. [STERN(UM) + Greek *kleis, kleid-,* collarbone + MASTOID.]

ster•no•cos•tal (stûr′nō-kŏs′təl) *adj.* Of or relating to both the sternum and the ribs. [STERN(UM) + Latin *costa,* rib; see **kost-** in Appendix + –AL[1].]

stern•post (stûrn′pōst′) *n. Nautical.* The principal upright post at the stern of a vessel, usually serving to support the rudder.

stern sheets *pl.n. Nautical.* The stern area of an open boat.

stern•son (stûrn′sən) *n. Nautical.* A bar of metal or wood set between the keelson and the sternpost to fortify the joint. Also called *stern knee.* [STERN[2] + (KEEL)SON.]

ster•num (stûr′nəm) *n., pl.* **-nums** or **-na** (-nə). A long flat bone in most vertebrates that is situated along the ventral midline of the thorax and articulates with the ribs. The manubrium of the sternum articulates with the clavicles in human beings and certain other vertebrates. Also called *breastbone.* [New Latin, from Greek *sternon,* breast, breastbone. See **ster-**[2] in Appendix.]

ster•nu•ta•tion (stûr′nyə-tā′shən) *n.* **1.** The act of sneezing. **2.** A sneeze. [Middle English *sternutacioun,* from Latin *sternūtātiō, sternūtātiōn-,* from *sternūtātus,* past participle of *sternūtāre,* frequentative of *sternuere,* to sneeze.]

ster•nu•ta•tor (stûr′nyə-tā′tər) *n.* A substance that irritates the nasal and respiratory passages and causes coughing, sneezing, lacrimation, and sometimes vomiting.

ster•nu•ta•to•ry (stûr-nyo͞o′tə-tôr′ē, -tōr′ē, -no͞o′-) *adj.* Causing or tending to cause sneezing. **—sternutatory** *n., pl.* **-ries.** A sternutatory substance, such as pepper.

stern•ward (stûrn′wərd) *adv. & adj. Nautical.* Toward, to, or in the stern. **—stern′wards** *adv.*

stern•way (stûrn′wā′) *n. Nautical.* The backward movement of a vessel.

stern-wheel•er (stûrn′hwē′lər, -wē′lər) *n. Nautical.* A steamboat propelled by a paddle wheel at the stern.

ster•oid (stîr′oid′, stĕr′-) *n.* Any of numerous naturally occurring or synthetic fat-soluble organic compounds having as a basis 17 carbon atoms arranged in four rings and including the sterols and bile acids, adrenal and sex hormones, certain natural drugs such as digitalis compounds, and the precursors of certain vitamins. [STER(OL) + –OID.] **—ster′oid′, ste•roid′al** (stĭ-roid′l, stĕ-) *adj.*

ste•roid•o•gen•e•sis (stĭ-roi′də-jĕn′ĭ-sĭs, stîr′oi-, stĕr′-) *n.* Production of steroids by living organisms. **—ste•roid′o•gen′ic** (-jĕn′ĭk) *adj.*

ster•ol (stîr′ôl′, -ōl′, -ŏl′, stĕr′-) *n.* Any of a group of predominantly unsaturated solid alcohols of the steroid group, such as cholesterol and ergosterol, present in the fatty tissues of plants and animals. [Short for CHOLESTEROL.]

Ster•o•pe (stĕr′ə-pē′) also **As•ter•o•pe** (ă-stĕr′-) *n.* **1.** *Greek Mythology.* One of the seven Pleiades. **2.** One of the stars in the constellation Pleiades.

ster•tor (stûr′tər) *n.* A heavy snoring sound in respiration. [New Latin, from Latin *stertere,* to snore.] **—ster′to•rous** *adj.* **—ster′to•rous•ly** *adv.*

stet (stĕt) *v.* **stet•ted, stet•ting, stets.** *Abbr.* **st.** *Printing.* *—intr.* To direct that a letter, word, or other matter marked for omission or correction is to be retained. Used in the imperative. *—tr.* To nullify (a correction or deletion) in printed matter. [Latin, third person sing. present subjunctive of *stāre,* to stand. See **stā-** in Appendix.]

steth•o•scope (stĕth′ə-skōp′) *n.* Any of various instruments used for listening to sounds produced within the body. [French *stéthoscope* : Greek *stēthos,* chest + French *-scope,* an instrument for viewing (from Latin *-scopium;* see –SCOPE).] **—steth′o•scop′ic** (-skŏp′ĭk), **steth′o•scop′i•cal** (-ĭ-kəl) *adj.* **—steth′o•scop′i•cal•ly** *adv.* **—ste•thos′co•py** (stĕ-thŏs′kə-pē) *n.*

Stet•son (stĕt′sən). A trademark used for a hat having a high crown and wide brim.

Stet•tin (stə-tēn′, shtĕ-). See **Szczecin.**

Steu•ben (sto͞o′bən, styo͞o′-, sto͞o-bĕn′, styo͞o-, shtoi′bən), Baron **Friedrich Wilhelm Ludolf Gerhard Augustin von.** 1730–1794. Prussian-born American Revolutionary military leader who trained the previously undisciplined troops under Gen. George Washington.

Steu•ben•ville (sto͞o′bĭn-vĭl′, styo͞o′-). A city of eastern Ohio on the Ohio River south of Youngstown. Permanent settlement began here in 1797 on the site of Fort Steuben (1786–1790). Population, 26,400.

Isaac Stern
Photographed in 1990

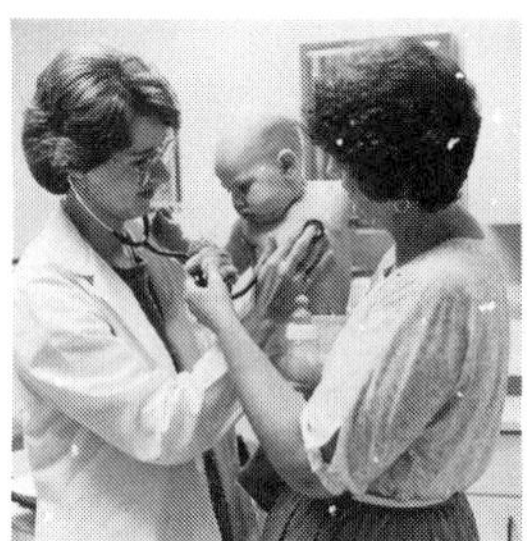

stethoscope

ă pat	oi boy
ā pay	ou out
âr care	o͝o took
ä father	o͞o boot
ĕ pet	ŭ cut
ē be	ûr urge
ĭ pit	th thin
ī pie	*th* this
îr pier	hw which
ŏ pot	zh vision
ō toe	ə about, item
ô paw	♦ regionalism

Stress marks: **′** (primary); ′ (secondary), as in **dictionary** (dĭk′shə-nĕr′ē)

stevedore

ste•ve•dore (stē′vĭ-dôr′, -dōr′) *n.* One who is employed in the loading or unloading of ships. —**stevedore** *v.* **-dored, -dor•ing, -dores.** —**stevedore** *tr. & intr.v.* To load or unload the cargo of (a ship) or to engage in the process of loading or unloading such a vessel. [Spanish *estibador,* from *estibar,* to stow, from Latin *stīpāre,* to pack.]

ste•ve•dore's knot (stē′vĭ-dôrz′, -dōrz′) also **stevedore knot** *n. Nautical.* A knot tied in the end of a line to prevent it from unreeving.

Ste•ven•age (stē′və-nĭj). An urban district of southeast England north of London. It was the first new town to be designated under a parliamentary act of 1946 to decentralize population and industry. Population, 74,500.

Ste•vens (stē′vənz), **George.** 1905–1975. American filmmaker who directed *A Place in the Sun* (1951), *Giant* (1956), and numerous other motion pictures.

Stevens, John Paul. Born 1920. American jurist who was appointed an associate justice of the U.S. Supreme Court in 1975.

Stevens, Nettie Marie. 1861–1912. American cytogeneticist whose studies on the chromosomes of the common mealworm led to the discovery of the chromosomal determination of sex.

Stevens, Thaddeus. 1792–1868. American politician. A U.S. representative from Pennsylvania (1849–1853 and 1859–1868), he led the impeachment proceedings against President Andrew Johnson (1868).

Stevens, Wallace. 1879–1955. American poet whose artful and innovative works, including "Peter Quince at the Clavier" and "Sunday Morning" (both 1923), concern the role of imagination in bringing order to a chaotic world.

Ste•vens-John•son syndrome (stē′vənz-jŏn′sən) *n.* A severe inflammatory eruption of the skin and mucous membranes, usually occurring in children and young adults following a respiratory infection or as an allergic reaction to drugs or other substances. [After Albert Mason *Stevens* (1884–1945) and Frank Chambliss *Johnson* (1894–1934), American pediatricians.]

Ste•ven•son (stē′vən-sən), **Adlai Ewing.** 1835–1914. Vice President of the United States (1893–1897) under Grover Cleveland. His grandson **Adlai Ewing** (1900–1965) was the Democratic nominee for President in 1952 and 1956.

Stevenson, Robert Louis Balfour. 1850–1894. British writer of essays, poetry, and novels, most notably *Treasure Island* (1883), *The Strange Case of Dr. Jekyll and Mr. Hyde* (1886), and *Kidnapped* (1886).

Stevens Point. A city of central Wisconsin south of Wausau. Paper and furniture are among its manufactures. Population, 22,970.

stew[1] (sto͞o, styo͞o) *v.* **stewed, stew•ing, stews.** —*tr.* To cook (food) by simmering or boiling slowly. —*intr.* **1.** To undergo cooking by boiling slowly or simmering. See Synonyms at **boil**[1]. **2.** *Informal.* To suffer with oppressive heat or stuffy confinement; swelter. **3.** *Informal.* To be in a state of anxiety or agitation. See Synonyms at **brood.** —**stew** *n.* **1.a.** A dish cooked by stewing, especially a mixture of meat or fish and vegetables with stock. **b.** A mixture likened to this dish. **2.** *Informal.* Mental agitation: *in a stew over the lost keys.* **3.** Often **stews.** *Archaic.* A brothel. [Middle English *stewen,* to bathe in a steam bath, stew, from Old French *estuver,* possibly from Vulgar Latin **extūpāre,* **extūfāre,* to bathe, evaporate : Latin *ex-,* ex- + Vulgar Latin **tūfus,* hot vapor (from Greek *tuphos,* fever; see TYPHUS).] —**stew′y** *adj.*

stew[2] (sto͞o, styo͞o) *n. Informal.* A flight attendant. [Short for STEWARDESS.]

stew•ard (sto͞o′ərd, styo͞o′-) *n.* **1.** One who manages another's property, finances, or other affairs. **2.** One who is in charge of the household affairs of a large estate, club, hotel, or resort. **3.** A ship's officer who is in charge of provisions and dining arrangements. **4.** An attendant on a ship or an airplane. **5.** An official who supervises or helps to manage an event. **6.** A shop steward. —**steward** *v.* **-ard•ed, -ard•ing, -ards.** —**steward** *intr. & tr.v.* To serve as a steward or as the steward of. [Middle English, from Old English *stigweard, stīward* : *stig, stī,* hall + *weard,* keeper; see **wer-**[3] in Appendix.] —**stew′ard•ship′** *n.*

stew•ard•ess (sto͞o′ər-dĭs, styo͞o′-) *n.* A woman flight attendant. See Usage Note at **-ess.**

Stew•art (sto͞o′ərt, styo͞o′-), **Dugald.** 1753–1828. British philosopher who was an exponent of the school of common sense.

Stewart, Henry. See Lord **Darnley.**

Stewart, James. Born 1908. American actor known for his portrayals of incorruptible and modest heroes in motion pictures such as *It's a Wonderful Life* (1946).

Stewart, Potter. 1915–1985. American jurist who served as an associate justice of the U.S. Supreme Court (1958–1981).

Stewart, Robert. Second Marquis of Londonderry. See Viscount **Castlereagh.**

stew•ar•tia (sto͞o-är′shə, -shē-ə, -tē-ə, styo͞o-) *n.* Any of various deciduous trees or shrubs of the genus *Stewartia,* native to eastern North America and tropical eastern Asia, having fragrant, showy, white flowers and smooth brown bark that peels into thin flakes. [New Latin *Stewartia,* genus name, after John *Stuart,* Third Earl of Bute (1713–1792), British politician.]

Stewart Island. A volcanic island of southern New Zealand off the southern coast of South Island. It was discovered in 1808 by the British, who bought it from the Maori in 1864.

Stewart River. A river, about 533 km (331 mi) long, of central Yukon Territory, Canada, flowing west to the Yukon River.

stewed (sto͞od, styo͞od) *adj.* **1.** Cooked by stewing: *stewed prunes.* **2.** *Informal.* Intoxicated; drunk.

St. Ex. *abbr.* Stock Exchange.

stg. *abbr.* Sterling.

stge. *abbr.* Storage.

sthe•ni•a (sthə-nī′ə, sthē′nē-ə) *n.* A condition of bodily strength, vigor, or vitality. [New Latin, from Greek *sthenos,* strength.]

sthen•ic (sthĕn′ĭk) *adj.* Relating to or marked by sthenia; strong, vigorous, or active.

Sthe•no (sthē′nō) *n. Greek Mythology.* One of the three Gorgons.

stib•ine (stĭb′ēn) *n.* A colorless, flammable poisonous gas, SbH_3, often used as a fumigant. [From Middle English *stibium,* antimony, from Latin, variant of *stimi,* from Greek *stibi, stimmi,* of Coptic origin; akin to Egyptian *sṭm.*]

stib•nite (stĭb′nīt′) *n.* A lead-gray mineral, Sb_2S_3, that is the chief source of antimony. [French *stibine,* stibnite (from Latin *stibium,* antimony; see STIBINE) + –ITE[1].]

stich (stĭk) *n.* A line of verse. [Greek *stikhos.* See **steigh-** in Appendix.]

stich•ic (stĭk′ĭk) *adj.* Composed of verses having the same metrical form.

sti•chom•e•try (stĭ-kŏm′ĭ-trē) *n.* The division of a prose piece into lines of fixed length or into lines whose lengths correspond to the natural divisions of sense, as in manuscripts written before the adoption of punctuation. [Greek *stikhos,* stich; see **steigh-** in Appendix + –METRY.] —**stich′o•met′ric** (stĭk′ə-mĕt′rĭk) *adj.*

stich•o•myth•i•a (stĭk′ə-mĭth′ē-ə) also **sti•chom•y•thy** (stĭ-kŏm′ə-thē) *n.* An ancient Greek arrangement of dialogue in drama, poetry, and disputation in which single lines of verse or parts of lines are spoken by alternate speakers. [Greek *stikhomuthia,* from *stikhomuthein,* to speak in alternating lines : *stikhos,* stich; see **steigh-** in Appendix + *muthos,* speech.] —**stich′o•myth′ic** *adj.*

stick (stĭk) *n.* **1.** A long, slender piece of wood, especially: **a.** A branch or stem cut from a tree or shrub. **b.** A piece of wood, such as a tree branch, that is used for fuel, cut for lumber, or shaped for a specific purpose. **c.** A wand, staff, baton, or rod. **d.** *Sports & Games.* Any of various implements shaped like a rod and used in play: *a hockey stick.* **2.** A walking stick; a cane. **3.** Something slender and often cylindrical in form: *a stick of dynamite.* **4.** *Slang.* A marijuana cigarette. **5.a.** The control device of an aircraft that operates the elevators and ailerons. **b.** *Informal.* A stick shift. **6.** *Nautical.* A mast or a part of a mast. **7.** *Printing.* **a.** A composing stick. **b.** A stickful. **8.a.** A group of bombs released to fall across an enemy target in a straight row. **b.** *Slang.* A group of paratroopers exiting an aircraft in succession. **9.** A timber tree. **10.** *Informal.* A piece of furniture. **11.** A poke, thrust, or stab with a stick or similar object: *a stick in the ribs.* **12.** A threatened penalty: *using both a carrot and a stick to keep allies in line.* **13.** The condition or power of adhering: *a glue with plenty of stick.* **14. sticks.** *Informal.* **a.** A remote area; backwoods: *moved to the sticks.* **b.** A city or town regarded as dull or unsophisticated. **15.** *Informal.* A person regarded as stiff, boring, or spiritless. **16.** *Archaic.* A difficulty or an obstacle; a delay. —**stick** *v.* **stuck** (stŭk), **stick•ing, sticks.** —*tr.* **1.** To pierce, puncture, or penetrate with a pointed instrument. **2.** To kill by piercing. **3.** To thrust or push (a pointed instrument) into or through another object. **4.** To fasten into place by forcing an end or point into something: *stick a hook on the wall.* **5.** To fasten or attach with or as if with pins, nails, or similar devices. **6.** To fasten or attach with an adhesive material, such as glue or tape. **7.** To cover or decorate with objects piercing the surface. **8.** To fix, impale, or transfix on a pointed object: *stick an olive on a toothpick.* **9.** To put, thrust, or push: *stuck a flower in his buttonhole; sticking her head out the window.* **10.** To detain or delay. **11.** *past tense and past participle* **sticked** (stĭkt) To prop (a plant) with sticks or brush on which to grow. **12.** *past tense and past participle* **sticked.** *Printing.* To set (type) in a composing stick. **13.** *Informal.* To confuse, baffle, or puzzle: *Sometimes even simple questions stick me.* **14.** To cover or smear with something sticky. **15.** *Informal.* To put blame or responsibility on; burden: *stuck me with the bill.* **16.** *Slang.* To defraud or cheat: *The dealer stuck me with shoddy merchandise.* —*intr.* **1.** To be or become fixed or embedded in place by having the point thrust in. **2.** To become or remain attached or in close association by or as if by adhesion; cling: *stick together in a crowd; stuck with me on the unfamiliar trail.* **3.a.** To remain firm, determined, or resolute: *stuck to basic principles.* **b.** To remain loyal or faithful: *stick by a friend through difficult times.* **c.** To persist or endure: *a bad name that has stuck.* **4.** To scruple or hesitate: *She sticks at nothing—no matter how difficult.* **5.** To be at or come to a standstill; become fixed, blocked, checked, or obstructed: *stuck in traffic for an hour.* **6.** To project or protrude: *hair sticking out on his head; an antenna sticking up on the roof.* —***phrasal verbs.*** **stick around.** *Informal.* To remain; linger. **stick out. 1.** To be prominent. **2.** *Informal.* To put up with: *had to stick out a bad situation in the office.* **stick up.** To rob, especially at gunpoint. —***idioms.*** **be stuck on.** *Informal.* To be very fond of. **stick it to.** *Slang.* To treat severely or wrongfully. **stick (one's) neck out.** *Informal.* To make oneself vulnerable; take a risk. **stick to** (or **by**)

one's guns. To hold fast to an opinion or a set course of action. **stick to (one's) knitting.** *Informal.* To mind one's own business. **stick to (one's) ribs.** *Informal.* To be substantial or filling. Used of food. **stick up for.** To defend or support. [Middle English *stikke,* from Old English *sticca.* See **steig-** in Appendix.]

stick·ball (stĭk′bôl′) *n. Sports.* A form of baseball played with a rubber ball and a stick, such as one made from the handle of a broom, for a bat. **—stick′ball′er** *n.*

sticked (stĭkt) *v.* **1.** Past tense and past participle of **stick** (sense 11). **2.** *Printing.* Past tense and past participle of **stick** (sense 12).

stick·er (stĭk′ər) *n.* **1.** One that sticks, as a gummed or adhesive label or patch. **2.** A tenacious, diligent, or persistent person. **3.** A thorn, prickle, or barb.

sticker price *n.* See **list price.**

stick figure *n.* A picture of a human or animal figure showing the head as a circle and the rest of the body as a combination of straight lines.

stick·ful (stĭk′fo͝ol′) *n. Printing.* The amount of type a composing stick will hold.

stick·han·dle (stĭk′hăn′dl) *intr.v.* **-dled, -dling, -dles.** *Sports.* To move, maneuver, and have control over the puck in ice hockey or the ball in lacrosse and field hockey. **—stick′han′dler** *n.*

stick·ing plaster (stĭk′ĭng) *n.* See **plaster** (sense 3).

sticking point *n.* A point, an issue, or a situation that causes or is likely to cause an impasse.

stick insect *n.* Any of several insects of the family Phasmidae, as the walking stick, that resemble sticks or twigs.

stick-in-the-mud (stĭk′ĭn-*thə*-mŭd′) *n., pl.* **stick-in-the-muds.** *Informal.* One who lacks initiative, imagination, or enthusiasm.

stick·le (stĭk′əl) *intr.v.* **-led, -ling, -les. 1.** To argue or contend stubbornly, especially about trivial or petty points. **2.** To have or raise objections; scruple. [Variant of Middle English *stightlen,* to contend, frequentative of *stighten,* to arrange, from Old English *stihtian, stihtan.* See **steigh-** in Appendix.]

stick·le·back (stĭk′əl-băk′) *n.* Any of various small freshwater and marine fishes of the family Gasterosteidae, having erectile spines along the back. [Middle English *stikelbak* : Old English *sticel,* prick; see **steig-** in Appendix + Middle English *bak,* back; see BACK[1].]

stick·ler (stĭk′lər) *n.* **1.** One who insists on something unyieldingly: *a stickler for neatness.* **2.** Something puzzling or difficult.

stick·pin (stĭk′pĭn′) *n.* A decorative pin worn on a necktie.

stick·seed (stĭk′sēd′) *n.* Any of various plants of the genera *Hackelia* or *Lappula,* having small barbed fruits that cling to clothing or fur.

stick shift *n.* An automotive transmission with a shift lever operated by hand.

stick·tail (stĭk′tāl′) *n.* See **suricate.**

stick·tight (stĭk′tīt′) *n.* See **beggar ticks** (sense 1a).

stick-to-it·ive·ness (stĭk-to͞o′ĭ-tĭv-nĭs) *n. Informal.* Unwavering pertinacity; perseverance: *"You've got to have reasonable goals and the stick-to-itiveness to get there"* (J. Robert Buchanan).

stick·um (stĭk′əm) *n.* An adhesive substance. [STICK + *-um* (variant of 'EM).]

stick·up (stĭk′ŭp′) *n. Slang.* A robbery, especially at gunpoint. [From the expression *"Stick up your hands!"*]

stick·weed (stĭk′wēd′) *n.* Any of various plants having clinging seeds or fruit, especially ragweed.

stick·y (stĭk′ē) *adj.* **-i·er, -i·est. 1.** Having the property of adhering or sticking to a surface; adhesive. **2.** Covered with an adhesive agent. **3.** Warm and humid; muggy: *a sticky day.* **4.** *Informal.* Painful or difficult: *a sticky situation.* **5.** *Economics.* Tending to remain the same despite changes in the economy. Used of prices or wages. **—stick′i·ly** *adv.* **—stick′i·ness** *n.*

sticky wicket *n. Informal.* A difficult or embarrassing problem or situation.

stied (stīd) *v.* Past tense and past participle of **sty[1].**

Stieg·litz (stēg′lĭts), **Alfred.** 1864–1946. American photographer whose works include a series of photographs of his wife, Georgia O'Keeffe.

sties[1] (stīz) *n.* Plural of **sty[1]. —sties** *v.* Third person singular present tense of **sty[1].**

sties[2] (stīz) *n.* Plural of **sty[2].**

stiff (stĭf) *adj.* **stiff·er, stiff·est. 1.** Difficult to bend; rigid. **2. a.** Not moving or operating easily or freely; resistant: *a stiff hinge.* **b.** Lacking ease or comfort of movement; not limber: *a stiff neck.* **3.** Drawn tightly; taut. **4. a.** Rigidly formal. **b.** Lacking ease or grace. **5.** Not liquid, loose, or fluid; thick: *stiff dough.* **6.** Firm, as in purpose; resolute. **7.** Having a strong, swift, steady force or movement: *a stiff current; a stiff breeze.* **8.** Potent or strong: *a stiff drink.* **9.** Difficult, laborious, or arduous: *a stiff hike; a stiff examination.* **10.** Difficult to comprehend or accept; harsh or severe: *a stiff penalty.* **11.** Excessively high: *a stiff price.* **12.** *Nautical.* Not heeling over much in spite of great wind or the press of the sail. **—stiff** *adv.* **1.** In a stiff manner: *frozen stiff.* **2.** To a complete extent; totally: *bored stiff.* **—stiff** *n. Slang.* **1.** A corpse. **2.** A person regarded as constrained, priggish, or overly formal. **3.** A drunk. **4.** A person: *a lucky stiff; just an ordinary working stiff.* **5.** A hobo; a tramp. **6.** A person who tips poorly. **—stiff** *tr.v.* **stiffed, stiff·ing, stiffs.** *Slang.* **1.** To tip (someone) inadequately or not at all, as for a service rendered: *paid the dinner check but stiffed the waiter.* **2. a.** To cheat (someone) of something owed: *My roommate stiffed me out of last month's rent.* **b.** To fail to give or supply (something expected or promised). [Middle English, from Old English *stīf.*] **—stiff′ish** *adj.* **—stiff′ly** *adv.* **—stiff′ness** *n.*

SYNONYMS: *stiff, rigid, inflexible, inelastic, tense.* These adjectives are compared as they describe what is very firm and does not easily bend or give way. *Stiff,* the least specific, refers to what can be flexed only with difficulty (*a brush with stiff bristles; a stiff collar*); with reference to persons it often suggests a lack of ease, cold formality, or fixity, as of purpose: *"stiff in opinions"* (John Dryden). *Rigid* and *inflexible* apply to what cannot be bent without damage or deformation (*a table made of rigid plastic; an inflexible knife blade*); figuratively they describe what does not relent or yield: *"under the dictates of a rigid disciplinarian"* (Thomas B. Aldrich). *"In religion the law is written, and inflexible, never to do evil"* (Oliver Goldsmith). *Inelastic* refers largely to what lacks elasticity and so will not stretch and spring back without marked physical change: *an inelastic substance. Tense* means stretched tight; it is applied literally to body structures such as muscles and figuratively to what is marked by tautness or strain: *"that tense moment of expectation"* (Arnold Bennett).

stickleback
Three-spine stickleback
Gasterosteus aculeatus

stiff-arm (stĭf′ärm′) *Football. tr.v.* **-armed, -arm·ing, -arms.** To straight-arm. **—stiff-arm** *n.* A straight-arm.

stiff·en (stĭf′ən) *tr. & intr.v.* **-ened, -en·ing, -ens.** To make or become stiff or stiffer. **—stiff′en·er** *n.*

stiff-necked (stĭf′nĕkt′) *adj.* Stubborn and arrogant or aloof. See Synonyms at **obstinate.**

stiff upper lip *n.* Concealment of emotions or feelings, especially of grief or fear; great restraint or composure.

sti·fle[1] (stī′fəl) *v.* **-fled, -fling, -fles.** *—tr.* **1.** To interrupt or cut off (the voice, for example). **2.** To keep in or hold back; repress: *stifled my indignation.* See Synonyms at **suppress. 3.** To kill by preventing respiration; smother or suffocate. *—intr.* **1.** To feel smothered or suffocated by or as if by close confinement in a stuffy room. **2.** To die of suffocation. [Middle English *stifilen,* alteration (influenced by Old Norse *stīfla,* to stop up) of *stuffen, stuflen,* to stifle, choke, drown, from Old French *estoufer,* of Germanic origin.] **—sti′fler** *n.*

sti·fle[2] (stī′fəl) *n.* The joint of the hind leg analogous to the human knee in certain quadrupeds, such as the horse. [Middle English, possibly from Old French *estivel,* pipe, leg, tibia, from Latin *stīpes,* stick.]

sti·fling (stī′flĭng) *adj.* **1.** Very hot or stuffy almost to the point of being suffocating. **2.** Being of such a character or nature as to engender a feeling of stultification, repression, or suffocation: *"The scholarly correctness of our age can be stifling"* (Annalyn Swan). **—sti′fling·ly** *adv.*

stig·ma (stĭg′mə) *n., pl.* **stig·ma·ta** (stĭg-mä′tə, -măt′ə, stĭg′mə-) or **stig·mas. 1.** A mark or token of infamy, disgrace, or reproach: *"Party affiliation has never been more casual . . . The stigmata of decay are everywhere"* (Arthur M. Schlesinger, Jr.). See Synonyms at **stain. 2.** A small mark; a scar or birthmark. **3.** *Medicine.* **a.** A mark or spot on the skin that bleeds as a symptom of hysteria. **b.** A mark or characteristic indicative of a history of a disease or abnormality. **4. stigmata.** Marks or sores corresponding to and resembling the crucifixion wounds of Jesus, sometimes occurring during religious ecstasy or hysteria. **5.** *Biology.* A small mark, spot, or pore, such as the respiratory spiracle of an insect or an eyespot in certain algae. **6.** *Botany.* The receptive apex of the pistil of a flower, on which pollen is deposited at pollination. **7.** *Archaic.* A mark burned into the skin of a criminal or slave; a brand. [Middle English *stigme,* brand, from Latin *stigma, stigmat-,* from Greek, tattoo mark, from *stizein, stig-,* to prick. See **steig-** in Appendix.] **—stig′mal** *adj.*

stig·mas·ter·ol (stĭg-măs′tə-rôl′, -rōl′) *n.* A sterol, $C_{29}H_{48}O$, obtained from soybeans or Calabar beans. [New Latin *(Physo)stigma,* Calabar bean genus; see PHYSOSTIGMINE + STEROL.]

stig·ma·ta (stĭg-mä′tə, -măt′ə, stĭg′mə-) *n.* A plural of **stigma.**

stig·mat·ic (stĭg-măt′ĭk) *adj.* **1.** Relating to, resembling, or having stigmata or a stigma. **2.** Anastigmatic. **—stigmatic** *n.* A person marked with religious stigmata. **—stig·mat′i·cal·ly** *adv.*

stig·ma·tism (stĭg′mə-tĭz′əm) *n.* **1.** The condition of being affected by stigmata. **2.** The state of a refracting or reflecting system in which light rays from a single point are accurately focused at another point. **3.** Normal eyesight.

stig·ma·tist (stĭg′mə-tĭst) *n.* A stigmatic.

stig·ma·tize (stĭg′mə-tīz′) *tr.v.* **-tized, -tiz·ing, -tiz·es. 1.** To characterize or brand as disgraceful or ignominious. **2.** To mark with stigmata or a stigma. **3.** To cause stigmata to appear on. [Medieval Latin *stigmatizāre,* to brand, from Greek *stigmatizein,* to mark, from *stigma, stigmat-,* tattoo mark. See STIGMA.] **—stig′ma·ti·za′tion** (-tĭ-zā′shən) *n.* **—stig′ma·tiz′er** *n.*

Sti·kine (stĭ-kēn′). A river rising in the **Stikine Mountains** of northwest British Columbia, Canada, and flowing about 539 km (335 mi) generally west and southwest through southeast Alaska to the Pacific Ocean.

stil·bene (stĭl′bēn′) *n.* A colorless or yellowish crystalline compound, $C_{14}H_{12}$, used in the manufacture of dyes and optical

ă pat	oi boy
ā pay	ou out
âr care	o͝o took
ä father	o͞o boot
ĕ pet	ŭ cut
ē be	ûr urge
ĭ pit	th thin
ī pie	*th* this
îr pier	hw which
ŏ pot	zh vision
ō toe	ə about, item
ô paw	♦ regionalism

Stress marks: ′ (primary); ′ (secondary), as in **dictionary** (dĭk′shə-nĕr′ē)

bleaches and as a phosphor. [Greek *stilbos,* shining (from *stilbein,* to shimmer) + -ENE.]

stil·bes·trol (stĭl-bĕs′trôl′, -trōl′, -trŏl′) *n.* DES. [STILB(ENE) + ESTR(US) + -OL [1].]

stil·bite (stĭl′bīt′) *n.* A white or yellow lustrous zeolite mineral, essentially $(Ca,Na)_2Al_2Si_7O_{18}·7H_2O$. [French, from Greek *stilbos,* shining. See STILBENE.]

stile[1] (stīl) *n.* **1.** A set or series of steps for crossing a fence or wall. **2.** A turnstile. [Middle English, from Old English *stigel.* See **steigh-** in Appendix.]

stile[2] (stīl) *n.* A vertical member of a panel or frame, as in a door or window sash. [Probably from Dutch *stijl,* doorpost, from Middle Dutch, possibly from Latin *stilus,* pole, post.]

sti·let·to (stĭ-lĕt′ō) *n., pl.* **-tos** or **-toes. 1.a.** A small dagger with a slender, tapering blade. **b.** Something shaped like such a dagger. **2.** A small, sharp-pointed instrument used for making eyelet holes in needlework. [Italian, diminutive of *stilo,* dagger, from Latin *stilus,* stylus, spike.]

stiletto heel *n.* A high heel on women's shoes that is thinner than a spike heel.

still life
Fruit, 1868, by Paul Lacroix (active in America 1858–1869)

Stil·i·cho (stĭl′ĭ-kō′), **Flavius.** 365?–408 A.D. Roman general who defended the Western Empire from the invading Goths and Vandals.

still[1] (stĭl) *adj.* **still·er, still·est. 1.** Free of sound. **2.** Low in sound; hushed or subdued. **3.** Not moving or in motion. **4.** Free from disturbance, agitation, or commotion. **5.** Free from a noticeable current: *a still pond; still waters.* **6.** Not carbonated; lacking effervescence: *a still wine.* **7.** Of or relating to a single or static photograph as opposed to a movie. **—still** *n.* **1.** Silence; quiet: *the still of the night.* **2.** A still photograph, especially one taken from a scene of a movie and used for promotional purposes. **3.** A still-life picture. **—still** *adv.* **1.** Without movement; motionlessly: *stand still.* **2.** Up to or at the time indicated; yet: *still unfinished; will still be here tomorrow.* **3.** In increasing amount or degree: *and still further complaints.* **4.** All the same; nevertheless. **—still** *v.* **stilled, still·ing, stills.** *—tr.* **1.** To make still or tranquil. **2.** To make quiet; silence. **3.** To make motionless. **4.** To allay; calm: *The parents stilled their child's fears of the dark.* *—intr.* To become still. [Middle English, from Old English *stille.* See **stel-** in Appendix.]

SYNONYMS: *still, quiet, silent, noiseless, soundless.* These adjectives mean marked by or making no sound, noise, or movement. *Still* implies lack of motion or disturbance; the term often connotes rest or tranquillity: *"But after tempest . . . /There came a day as still as heaven"* (Tennyson). *Quiet* suggests the absence of noise, bustle, tumult, or agitation: *"life being very short, and the quiet hours of it few"* (John Ruskin). *Silent* refers to absence of sound or noise and may suggest a profound hush: *"I like the silent church before the service begins"* (Ralph Waldo Emerson). *Noiseless* and *soundless* mean without sound but usually imply freedom from disturbing sound: *"th' inaudible and noiseless foot of time"* (Shakespeare); *"the soundless footsteps on the grass"* (John Galsworthy).

stilt
A pair of stilts

still[2] (stĭl) *n.* **1.** An apparatus for distilling liquids, such as alcohols, consisting of a vessel in which the substance is vaporized by heat and a cooling device in which the vapor is condensed. **2.** A distillery. [From Middle English *stillen,* to distill, from *distillen.* See DISTILL.]

Still (stĭl), **Andrew Taylor.** 1828–1917. American physician who founded osteopathy (1874).

still alarm *n.* A fire alarm transmitted silently, as by telephone, rather than by sounding the conventional signal apparatus.

still and all *adv. Informal.* After taking everything into consideration; nevertheless; however: *Still and all, our objective can be achieved.*

still·birth (stĭl′bûrth′) *n.* **1.** The birth of a dead child or fetus. **2.** A child or fetus dead at birth.

still·born (stĭl′bôrn′) *adj.* **1.** Dead at birth. **2.** Failing before or at the very beginning or inception; abortive: *a stillborn plot to assassinate the President.*

still hunt *n.* The hunting of game by stalking or ambushing. **—still′-hunt′** (stĭl′hŭnt′) *v.* **—still′-hunt′er** *n.*

stil·li·form (stĭl′ə-fôrm′) *adj.* Shaped like a drop; globular. [Latin *stilla,* drop + -FORM.]

still life *n., pl.* **still lifes. 1.** Representation of inanimate objects, such as flowers or fruit, in painting or photography. **2.** A painting, picture, or photograph of inanimate objects. **—still′-life′** (stĭl′līf′) *adj.*

still·ness (stĭl′nĭs) *n.* The state or an instance of being quiet or calm: *"The stillness that permeates the valleys is visual as well as acoustical"* (Barry Lopez).

Still·son (stĭl′sən). A trademark used for a monkey wrench having serrated jaws that tighten as pressure is applied to the handle.

still water *n.* A flat or level section of a stream where no flow or motion of the current is discernible and the water is still. **—still′-wa′ter** (stĭl′wô′tər, -wŏt′ər) *adj.*

Still·wa·ter (stĭl′wô′tər, -wŏt′ər). A city of north-central Oklahoma north-northeast of Oklahoma City. Founded in 1889, it is the seat of Oklahoma State University (established 1890). Population, 38,268.

still·y (stĭl′ē) *adj.* **-i·er, -i·est.** Quiet; calm. **—stil′ly** *adv.*

stilt (stĭlt) *n.* **1.** Either of a pair of long, slender poles each equipped with a raised footrest to enable the user to walk elevated above the ground. **2.** Any of various tall posts or pillars used as support, as for a dock or building: *a beach house on stilts.* **3.** *pl.* **stilt** or **stilts a.** An American wading bird *(Himantopus mexicanus)* that has long pink legs, black and white plumage, and a long slender bill, and that ranges from the United States to Peru and Brazil and is related to the avocet. **b.** A related bird *(Cladorhyncus leucocephala)* of Australia. **—stilt** *tr.v.* **stilt·ed, stilt·ing, stilts.** To place or raise on stilts. [Middle English *stilte.* See **stel-** in Appendix.]

stilt·ed (stĭl′tĭd) *adj.* **1.** Stiffly or artificially formal; stiff. **2.** *Architecture.* Having some vertical length between the impost and the beginning of the curve. Used of an arch. **—stilt′ed·ly** *adv.* **—stilt′ed·ness** *n.*

Stil·ton (stĭl′tən) *n.* A rich, waxy cheese with a blue-green mold and a wrinkled rind. [After *Stilton,* a village of east-central England.]

stilt root *n. Botany.* An aerial root.

Stil·well (stĭl′wĕl′, -wəl), **Joseph Warren.** Known as "Vinegar Joe" or **"Uncle Joe."** 1883–1946. American army officer who commanded Allied forces in China, Burma, and India during World War II.

Stim·son (stĭm′sən), **Henry Lewis.** 1867–1950. American public official who served as U.S. secretary of state (1929–1933) and secretary of war (1940–1945) during World War II. He was the chief adviser on atomic weaponry to Presidents Franklin D. Roosevelt and Harry S. Truman.

stim·u·lant (stĭm′yə-lənt) *n.* **1.** An agent, especially a chemical agent such as caffeine, that temporarily arouses or accelerates physiological or organic activity. **2.** A stimulus or an incentive: *"An age of political excitement is usually a stimulant to literature"* (Will Durant). **3.** A food or drink, especially an alcoholic drink, believed to have a stimulating effect. **—stimulant** *adj.* Serving as or being a stimulus; stimulating.

stim·u·late (stĭm′yə-lāt′) *v.* **-lat·ed, -lat·ing, -lates.** *—tr.* **1.** To rouse to activity or heightened action, as by spurring or goading; excite. See Synonyms at **provoke. 2.** To increase temporarily the activity of (a body organ or part). **3.** To excite or invigorate (a person, for example) with a stimulant. *—intr.* To act or serve as a stimulant or stimulus. [Latin *stimulāre, stimulāt-,* to goad on, from *stimulus,* goad.] **—stim′u·lat′er, stim′u·la′tor** *n.* **—stim′u·lat′ing·ly** *adv.* **—stim′u·la′tion** *n.* **—stim′u·la′tive, stim′u·la·to′ry** (-lə-tôr′ē, -tōr′ē) *adj.*

stim·u·lus (stĭm′yə-ləs) *n., pl.* **-li** (-lī′). **1.** Something causing or regarded as causing a response. **2.** An agent, an action, or a condition that elicits or accelerates a physiological or psychological activity or response. **3.** Something that incites or rouses to action; an incentive: *"Works which were in themselves poor have often proved a stimulus to the imagination"* (W.H. Auden). [Latin, goad.]

sting (stĭng) *v.* **stung** (stŭng), **sting·ing, stings.** *—tr.* **1.** To pierce or wound painfully with or as if with a sharp-pointed structure or organ, as that of certain insects. **2.** To cause to feel a sharp, smarting pain by or as if by pricking with a sharp point: *smoke stinging our eyes.* **3.** To cause to suffer keenly in the mind or feelings: *Those harsh words stung me bitterly.* **4.** To spur on by or as if by sharp irritation. **5.** *Slang.* To cheat or overcharge. *—intr.* **1.** To have, use, or wound with or as if with a sharp-pointed structure or organ, as that of certain insects. **2.** To cause or feel a sharp, smarting pain. **—sting** *n.* **1.** The act of stinging. **2.** The wound or pain caused by or as if by stinging. **3.** A sharp, piercing organ or part, often ejecting a venomous secretion, as the modified ovipositor of a bee or wasp or the spine of certain fishes. **4.** A stinging power, quality, or capacity. **5.** A keen stimulus or incitement; a goad or spur: *the sting of curiosity.* **6.** *Slang.* A complicated confidence game planned and executed with great care, especially an operation organized and implemented by undercover agents to apprehend criminals. [Middle English *stingen,* from Old English *stingan.* See **stegh-** in Appendix.] **—sting′ing·ly** *adv.*

sting·a·ree (stĭng′ə-rē′) *n.* See **stingray.** [Alteration of STINGRAY.]

sting·er (stĭng′ər) *n.* **1.** One that stings, especially something such as an insult, that stings or wounds mentally. **2.** A stinging organ or part. **3.** A sharp blow. **4.** *Slang.* One who participates in or organizes the operation of a sting. **5.** A cocktail of crème de menthe and brandy.

sting·ing cell (stĭng′ĭng) *n.* See **nematocyst.**

stinging hair *n.* A glandular plant hair that expels an irritating fluid.

stinging nettle *n.* **1.** A dioecious perennial Eurasian herb *(Urtica dioica)* having stinging hairs, inconspicuous greenish flowers, and coarsely toothed leaves. **2.** A perennial herb *(Cnidoscolus stimulosus)* of the southeast United States, having stinging hairs and fragrant white flowers.

sting·ray (stĭng′rā′) *n.* Any of various rays of the family Dasyatidae, having a whiplike tail armed with one or more venomous spines capable of inflicting severe injury. Also called *stingaree.*

stin·gy (stĭn′jē) *adj.* **-gi·er, -gi·est. 1.** Giving or spending reluctantly. **2.** Scanty or meager: *a stingy meal; stingy with details about the past.* [Perhaps alteration of dialectal *stingy,* stinging, from STING.] **—stin′gi·ly** *adv.* **—stin′gi·ness** *n.*

SYNONYMS: *stingy, close, close-fisted, niggardly, penny-pinching, miserly, parsimonious, penurious, tight, tightfisted.* These adjectives mean reluctant or marked by reluctance to spend money or part with possessions. *Stingy,* the most general, implies absence of generosity and often an inclination toward meanness of spirit: *She practices economy without being stingy. Close* and *close-fisted* imply both stinginess and exceeding caution: *Poverty has taught them to be close with their money. The old peasant was an avaricious and close-fisted fellow. Niggardly* implies a tendency to be grudging and petty: *Don't be niggardly; you can afford to share your good fortune. Penny-pinching* heightens the implications of *niggardly* and sometimes suggests foolish economy: *Penny-pinching landlords stinted their tenants on heat and hot water. Miserly* implies greed and the hoarding of wealth for its own sake: *"He was a miserly wretch who grudged us food to eat, and clothes to wear"* (Charles Dickens). *Parsimonious* emphasizes excessive frugality: *The appropriations committee, suddenly and ill-advisedly parsimonious, cut funds for assistance to the disadvantaged. Penurious* implies ungenerous or petty unwillingness to spend money, usually to an extreme degree: *"He lived in the most penurious manner, and denied himself every indulgence"* (William Godwin). *Tight* and *tightfisted* suggest not only niggardliness but also a close and vigilant control over one's funds and possessions: *tight with the family, generous to others; "too tightfisted to spend a few dollars"* (Sinclair Lewis).

stink (stĭngk) *v.* **stank** (stăngk) or **stunk** (stŭngk), **stunk, stink·ing, stinks.** —*intr.* **1.** To emit a strong foul odor. **2.a.** To be highly offensive or abhorrent. **b.** To be in extremely bad repute. **3.** *Slang.* To have something to an extreme or offensive degree: *a family that stinks with money; a deed that stinks of treachery.* **4.** *Slang.* To be of an extremely low or bad quality: *This job stinks.* —*tr.* To cause to stink: *garbage that stinks up the yard.* —**stink** *n.* A strong offensive odor; a stench. See Synonyms at **stench.** —***idiom.*** **make** (or **raise**) **a stink.** *Slang.* To make a great fuss. [Middle English *stinken,* from Old English *stincan,* to emit a smell.] —**stink'y** *adj.*

stink·a·roo (stĭng'kə-ro͞o', stĭng'kə-ro͞o') *n. Slang.* Variant of **stinkeroo.**

stink·ball (stĭngk'bôl') *n.* See **stinkpot** (sense 4).

stink bomb *n.* A small bomb, often in the form of a capsule, that emits a foul odor on detonation.

stink·bug (stĭngk'bŭg') *n.* Any of numerous hemipterous insects of the family Pentatomidae, having a broad, flattened body and emitting a foul odor.

stink·er (stĭng'kər) *n. Slang.* **1.** A person regarded as irritating, disgusting, or contemptible. **2.** *Slang.* Something very difficult: *The interview was a real stinker.*

stink·er·oo also **stink·a·roo** (stĭng'kə-ro͞o', stĭng'kə-ro͞o') *n., pl.* **-er·oos** also **-a·roos.** *Slang.* One that is contemptible, disgusting, irritating, or very bad. [From STINKER.]

stink·horn (stĭngk'hôrn') *n.* Any of several foul-smelling fungi of the order Phallales, such as *Phallus impudicus* or *P. ravenelii,* having a thick, cylindrical stalk and a narrow cap.

stink·ing (stĭng'kĭng) *adj.* **1.** Having a foul smell; fetid. **2.** *Slang.* Very drunk. —**stinking** *adv. Slang.* Used as an intensive: *stinking rich.* —**stink'ing·ly** *adv.* —**stink'ing·ness** *n.*

stinking ash *n.* An eastern North American deciduous ornamental tree or shrub *(Ptelea trifoliata)* having trifoliolate leaves and oblong to heart-shaped samara with reticulate wings. Also called *water ash.*

stinking chamomile *n.* See **mayweed.**

stink·o (stĭng'kō) *adj. Slang.* **1.** Very drunk. **2.** Of poor or inferior quality. [From STINK.]

stink·pot (stĭngk'pŏt') *n.* **1.** *Slang.* A person who is despised. **2.** A small musk turtle *(Sternotherus odoratus)* of the eastern and southern United States, usually found on the bottom of ponds and small streams. **3.** *Slang.* A motorboat. **4.** An earthenware jar containing combustibles emitting a suffocating smoke, formerly used in naval warfare. In this sense, also called *stinkball.*

stink stone also **stink·stone** (stĭngk'stōn') *n.* A variety of limestone that emits a disagreeable odor when struck or rubbed.

stink·weed (stĭngk'wēd') *n.* Any of various plants that have flowers or foliage with an unpleasant odor.

stink·wood (stĭngk'wo͝od') *n.* **1.a.** A southern African deciduous tree *(Ocotea bullata)* having wood with an unpleasant odor. **b.** The hard, heavy wood of this tree, used in cabinetwork. **2.** Any of several trees having wood with an unpleasant odor.

stint¹ (stĭnt) *v.* **stint·ed, stint·ing, stints.** —*tr.* **1.** To restrict or limit, as in amount or number; be sparing with. **2.** *Archaic.* To cause to stop. —*intr.* **1.** To subsist on a meager allowance; be frugal. **2.** *Archaic.* To stop or desist. —**stint** *n.* **1.** A fixed amount or share of work allotted. See Synonyms at **task. 2.** A limitation or restriction: *working without stint.* [Middle English *stinten,* to cease, from Old English *styntan,* to blunt.] —**stint'er** *n.* —**stint'ing·ly** *adv.*

stint² (stĭnt) *n.* Any of several small sandpipers of the genera *Erolia* or *Calidris,* of northern regions. [Middle English *stint,* from Old English.]

stip. *abbr.* **1.** Stipend. **2.** Stipulation.

stipe (stīp) *n. Botany.* A supporting stalk or stemlike structure, especially the stalk of a pistil, the petiole of a fern frond, or the stalk that supports the cap of a mushroom. [French, from Latin *stīpes,* post.]

sti·pel (stī'pəl, stī-pĕl') *n. Botany.* A minute stipule at the base of a leaflet. [New Latin *stipella,* diminutive of *stipula,* stipule. See STIPULE.] —**sti·pel'late** (stī-pĕl'ĭt, stī'pə-lāt') *adj.*

sti·pend (stī'pĕnd', -pənd) *n. Abbr.* **stip.** A fixed and regular payment, such as a salary for services rendered or an allowance. [Middle English *stipendie,* from Old French, from Latin *stīpendium,* soldier's pay, from **stipipendium* : *stips, stip-,* a small payment + *pendere,* to weigh, pay; see SUSPEND.]

sti·pen·di·ar·y (stī-pĕn'dē-ĕr'ē) *adj.* **1.** Receiving a stipend. **2.** Compensated by stipend: *stipendiary services.* —**stipendiary** *n., pl.* **-ies.** A recipient of a stipend.

sti·pes (stī'pēz) *n., pl.* **stip·i·tes** (stĭp'ĭ-tēz'). **1.** The basal segment of the maxilla of an insect or a crustacean. **2.** *Botany.* A stalklike support or structure; a stipe. [New Latin *stīpes, stīpit-,* from Latin, post.] —**sti'pi·form'** (stī'pə-fôrm'), **stip'i·ti·form'** (stĭp'ĭ-tə-) *adj.*

stip·i·tate (stĭp'ĭ-tāt') *Botany. adj.* Supported on or having a stipe.

stip·i·tes (stĭp'ĭ-tēz') *n.* Plural of **stipes.**

stip·ple (stĭp'əl) *tr.v.* **-pled, -pling, -ples. 1.** To draw, engrave, or paint in dots or short strokes. **2.** To apply (paint, for example) in dots or short strokes. **3.** To dot, fleck, or speckle: *"They crossed a field stippled with purple weeds"* (Flannery O'Connor). —**stipple** *n.* **1.** A method of drawing, engraving, or painting using dots or short strokes. **2.** The effect produced by stippling. [Dutch *stippelen,* frequentative of *stippen,* to speckle, from *stip,* dot, from Middle Dutch.] —**stip'pler** *n.*

stip·u·lar (stĭp'yə-lər) *adj.* Of, relating to, or resembling a stipule.

stip·u·late¹ (stĭp'yə-lāt') *v.* **-lat·ed, -lat·ing, -lates.** —*tr.* **1.a.** To lay down as a condition of an agreement; require by contract. **b.** To specify or arrange in an agreement: *stipulate a date of payment and a price.* **2.** To guarantee or promise (something) in an agreement. —*intr.* **1.** To make an express demand or provision in an agreement. **2.** To form an agreement. [Latin *stipulārī, stipulāt-,* to bargain.] —**stip'u·la'tor** *n.*

stip·u·late² (stĭp'yə-lĭt) *adj. Botany.* Having stipules.

stip·u·la·tion (stĭp'yə-lā'shən) *n. Abbr.* **stip. 1.** The act of stipulating. **2.** Something stipulated, especially a term or condition in an agreement. —**stip'u·la·to'ry** (-lə-tôr'ē, -tōr'ē) *adj.*

stip·ule (stĭp'yo͞ol) *n. Botany.* One of the usually small, paired appendages at the base of a leafstalk in certain plants, such as roses and beans. [New Latin *stipula,* from Latin, stalk. See STUBBLE.] —**stip'uled'** *adj.*

stir¹ (stûr) *v.* **stirred, stir·ring, stirs.** —*tr.* **1.a.** To pass an implement through (a liquid, for example) in circular motions so as to mix or cool the contents: *stirred the soup before tasting it.* **b.** To introduce (an ingredient, for example) into a liquid or mixture: *stirred a cup of sugar into the cake batter.* **c.** To mix together the ingredients of before cooking or use: *stirred up some popover batter; stirred the paint.* **2.** To alter the placement of slightly; disarrange: *had not stirred out of line.* **3.** To cause to move briskly or vigorously; bestir. **4.a.** To rouse, as from indifference, and prompt to action. See Synonyms at **provoke. b.** To provoke deliberately: *stirred by trouble.* **5.** To excite strong feelings in. —*intr.* **1.** To change position slightly: *The dog stirred in its sleep.* **2.a.** To move about actively; bestir oneself. **b.** To move away from a customary or usual place or position: *instructed the guards not to stir from their posts.* **3.** To take place; happen. **4.** To be capable of being stirred: *a mixture that stirs easily.* **5.** To be roused or affected by strong feelings: *"His wrath so stirred within him, that he could have struck him dead"* (Charles Dickens). —**stir** *n.* **1.** A stirring, mixing, or poking movement. **2.** A slight movement. **3.** A disturbance or commotion. **4.** An excited reaction; a ferment. [Middle English *stiren,* from Old English *styrian,* to excite, agitate.] —**stir'rer** *n.*

stir² (stûr) *n. Slang.* Prison. [Origin unknown.]

stir-cra·zy (stûr'krā'zē) *adj. Informal.* Distraught or restless from long confinement in or as if in prison.

stir-fry (stûr'frī') *tr.v.* **-fried** (-frīd'), **-fry·ing, -fries** (-frīz'). To fry quickly in a small amount of oil over high heat while stirring continuously. —**stir-fry** *n.* Food fried quickly in this manner: *a chicken and vegetable stir-fry.*

stirk (stûrk) *n. Chiefly British.* A heifer or bullock, especially between one and two years old. [Middle English, from Old English *stīrc.* See **stā-** in Appendix.]

Stir·ling (stûr'lĭng). A borough of central Scotland on the Forth River west-northwest of Edinburgh. Its medieval castle was the birthplace of James II of Scotland. Population, 38,400.

stirps (stûrps) *n., pl.* **stir·pes** (stûr'pēz). **1.** A line of descendants of common ancestry; stock. **2.** *Law.* A person from whom a family is descended. [Latin, stem, lineage.]

stir·ring (stûr'ĭng) *adj.* **1.** Exciting strong feelings, as of inspiration; rousing. See Synonyms at **moving. 2.** Active; lively. —**stirring** *n.* A slight motion or moving about: *restless stirrings in the audience.* —**stir'ring·ly** *adv.*

stir·rup (stûr'əp, stĭr'-) *n.* **1.** A flat-based loop or ring hung from either side of a horse's saddle to support the rider's foot in mounting and riding; a stirrup iron. **2.** A part or device shaped like an inverted U in which something is supported, held, or fixed. **3.** *Nautical.* A rope on a ship that hangs from a yard and has an

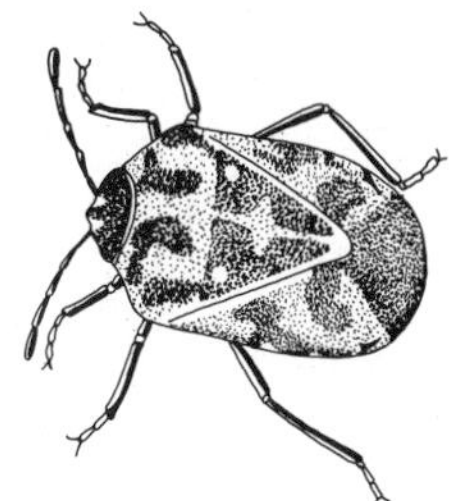

stinkbug
Harlequin stinkbug
Murgantia histrionica

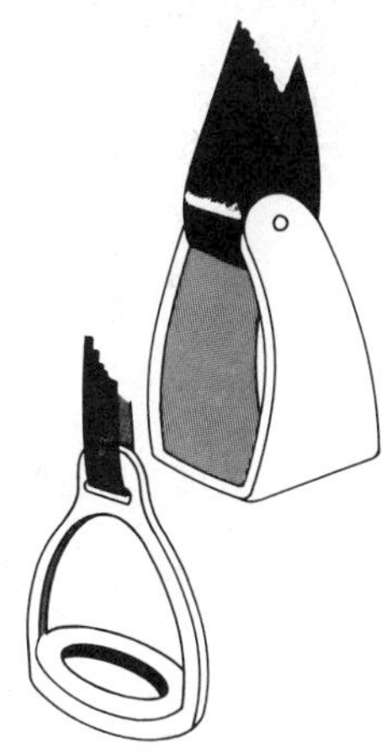

stirrup
Top: Western
Bottom: English

ă pat	oi boy
ā pay	ou out
âr care	o͝o took
ä father	o͞o boot
ĕ pet	ŭ cut
ē be	ûr urge
ĭ pit	th thin
ī pie	*th* this
îr pier	hw which
ŏ pot	zh vision
ō toe	ə about, item
ô paw	♦ regionalism

Stress marks: **'** (primary); ' (secondary), as in **dictionary** (dĭk'shə-nĕr'ē)

eye at the end through which a footrope is passed for support. [Middle English *stirope,* from Old English *stīgrāp* : *stīgan,* to mount; see **steigh-** in Appendix + *rāp,* rope.]

stirrup bone *n.* See **stapes.**

stir·rup-cup (stûr′əp-kŭp′, stĭr′-) *n.* A farewell drink, especially for a rider who is mounted to depart.

stirrup iron *n.* A stirrup.

stirrup leather *n.* The strap used to fasten a stirrup to a saddle. Also called *stirrup strap.*

stish·ov·ite (stĭsh′ə-vīt′) *n.* A dense tetragonal polymorph of quartz that is formed under great pressure and is often associated with meteoroid impact. [After S.M. *Stishov,* 20th-century Russian mineralogist.]

stitch (stĭch) *n. Abbr.* **st. 1.** A single complete movement of a threaded needle in sewing or surgical suturing. **2.a.** A single loop of yarn around an implement such as a knitting needle. **b.** The link, loop, or knot made in this way. **3.** A mode of arranging the threads in sewing, knitting, or crocheting: *a purl stitch.* **4.** A sudden sharp pain, especially in the side. See Synonyms at **pain. 5.** *Informal.* An article of clothing: *wore not a stitch.* **6.** *Informal.* The least part; a bit: *didn't do a stitch of work.* **7.** A ridge between two furrows. **—stitch** *v.* **stitched, stitch·ing, stitch·es.** *—tr.* **1.a.** To fasten or join with or as if with stitches. **b.** To mend or repair with stitches: *stitched up the tear.* **2.** To decorate or ornament with or as if with stitches: *"The sky was stitched with stars"* (Mario Puzo). **3.** To fasten together with staples or thread. *—intr.* To make stitches; sew. ***—idiom.*** **in stitches.** *Informal.* Laughing uncontrollably. [Middle English *stiche,* from Old English *stice,* sting. See **steig-** in Appendix.] **—stitch′er** *n.*

stitch·er·y (stĭch′ə-rē) *n.* Needlework; sewing.

stitch·wort (stĭch′wûrt′, -wôrt′) *n.* Any of several low-growing plants of the genus *Stellaria,* having opposite leaves and small, white, star-shaped flowers. [Middle English, from Old English *sticwyrt,* agrimony : *stice,* stich (from its alleged ability to cure sharp pains in the side); see STITCH + *wyrt,* plant; see WORT [1].]

stith·y (stĭth′ē, stĭth′ē) *n., pl.* **-ies. 1.** An anvil. **2.** A forge or smithy. [Middle English *stethi,* from Old Norse *stedhi.* See **stā-** in Appendix.]

sti·ver (stī′vər) *n.* **1.** A nickel coin used in the Netherlands and worth 1/20 of a guilder. **2.** Something of small value. [Dutch *stuiver,* from Middle Dutch *stuyver.*]

stk. *abbr.* Stock.

S.T.M *abbr. Latin.* Sacrae Theologiae Magister (Master of Sacred Theology).

sto·a (stō′ə) *n., pl.* **sto·as** or **sto·ae** (stō′ē′). An ancient Greek covered walk or colonnade, usually having columns on one side and a wall on the other. [Greek, porch. See **stā-** in Appendix.]

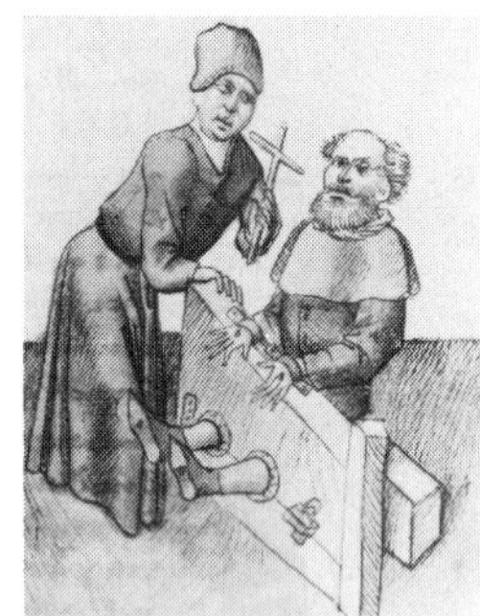

stocks

♦ **stoat** (stōt) *n., pl.* **stoat** or **stoats.** *Chiefly British.* The ermine, especially when in its brown color phase. [Middle English *stote.*]

♦ **stob** (stŏb) *n. Chiefly Southern U.S.* A short, straight piece of wood, such as a stake. [Middle English, stump, variant of *stubbe, stub.* See STUB.]

♦ ***REGIONAL NOTE:*** The Southern word *stob* means a short, straight stick of wood: *"Jim Rozier's skill with a piece of iron and a hardwood stob sets up a vibration in the earth that Sopchoppy worms find extremely disagreeable"* (Charles Kuralt). Related to *stub* and *stubby, stob* is one of numerous Indo-European cognates, for example, Greek *stupos,* meaning "stump (of a tree or branch)." In Middle English *stob* seems to have been a variant spelling of *stub,* with one of its meanings being "the amputated stump of a human limb." However, the word has chiefly denoted a short piece of wood, such as "a small post or stake or stump of a shrub, [and is] commonly so used in many, if not all, parts of the [American] South" (Charles F. Smith).

sto·chas·tic (stō-kăs′tĭk) *adj.* **1.** Of, relating to, or characterized by conjecture; conjectural. **2.** *Statistics.* **a.** Involving or containing a random variable or variables: *stochastic calculus.* **b.** Involving chance or probability: *a stochastic simulation.* [Greek *stokhastikos,* from *stokhastēs,* diviner, from *stokhazesthai,* to guess at, from *stokhos,* aim, goal. See **stegh-** in Appendix.] **—sto·chas′ti·cal·ly** *adv.*

stock (stŏk) *n. Abbr.* **s., stk. 1.** A supply accumulated for future use; a store. **2.** The total merchandise kept on hand by a merchant, commercial establishment, warehouse, or manufacturer. **3.** All the animals kept or raised on a farm; livestock. **4.a.** The capital or fund that a corporation raises through the sale of shares entitling the stockholder to dividends and to other rights of ownership, such as voting rights. **b.** The number of shares that each stockholder possesses. **c.** The part of a tally or record of account formerly given to a creditor. **d.** A debt symbolized by a tally. **5.** The trunk or main stem of a tree or another plant. **6.a.** A plant or stem onto which a graft is made. **b.** A plant or tree from which cuttings and slips are taken. **7.a.** The original progenitor of a family line. **b.** The descendants of a common ancestor; a family line, especially of a specified character: *comes from farming stock.* **c.** Ancestry or lineage; antecedents. **d.** The type from which a group of animals or plants has descended. **e.** A race, family, or other related group of animals or plants. **f.** An ethnic group or other major division of the human race. **g.** A group of related languages. **h.** A group of related families of languages. **8.** The raw material out of which something is made. **9.** The broth in which meat, fish, bones, or vegetables are simmered for a relatively long period, used as a base in preparing soup, gravy, or sauces. **10.a.** A main upright part, especially a supporting structure or block. **b. stocks.** *Nautical.* The timber frame that supports a ship during construction. **c.** A frame in which a horse or other animal is held for shoeing or for veterinary treatment. Often used in the plural. **11. stocks.** A device consisting of a heavy timber frame with holes for confining the ankles and sometimes the wrists, formerly used for punishment. **12.** *Nautical.* A crosspiece at the end of the shank of an anchor. **13.** The wooden block from which a bell is suspended. **14.a.** The rear wooden, metal, or plastic handle or support of a rifle, a pistol, or an automatic weapon, to which the barrel and mechanism are attached. **b.** The long supporting structure and mooring beam of field-gun carriages that trails along the ground to provide stability and support. **15.** A handle, such as that of a whip, a fishing rod, or various carpentry tools. **16.** The frame of a plow, to which the share, handles, coulter, and other parts are fastened. **17.a.** A theatrical stock company. **b.** The repertoire of such a company. **c.** A theater or theatrical activity, especially outside of a main theatrical center: *a small role in summer stock.* **18.** *Botany.* Any of several Eurasian and Mediterranean plants of the genus *Matthiola* in the mustard family, especially *M. incana,* widely cultivated for its clusters of showy, variously colored flowers. **19.** *Games.* The portion of a pack of cards or of a group of dominoes that is not dealt out but is drawn from during a game. **20.** *Geology.* A body of intrusive igneous rock of which less than 100 square kilometers (40 square miles) is exposed. **21.** *Zoology.* A compound organism, such as a colony of zooids. **22.a.** Personal reputation or status: *a teacher whose stock with the students is rising.* **b.** Confidence or credence: *I put no stock in that statement.* **23.a.** A long white neckcloth worn as part of a formal riding habit. **b.** A broad scarf worn around the neck, especially by certain clerics. **24.** Rolling stock. **—stock** *v.* **stocked, stock·ing, stocks.** *—tr.* **1.** To provide or furnish with a stock of something, especially: **a.** To supply (a shop) with merchandise. **b.** To supply (a farm) with livestock. **c.** To fill (a stream, for example) with fish. **2.** To keep for future sale or use. **3.** To provide (a rifle, for example) with a stock. **4.** *Obsolete.* To put (someone) in the stocks as a punishment. *—intr.* **1.** To gather and lay in a supply of something: *stock up on canned goods.* **2.** To put forth or sprout new shoots. Used of a plant. **—stock** *adj.* **1.** Kept regularly in stock: *a stock item.* **2.** Repeated regularly without any thought or originality; routine: *a stock answer.* **3.** Employed in dealing with or caring for stock or merchandise: *a stock clerk.* **4.a.** Of or relating to the raising of livestock: *stock farming.* **b.** Used for breeding: *a stock mare.* **5.a.** Of or relating to a stock company or its repertoire. **b.** Of or being a conventional character or situation that recurs in many literary or cinematic works. ***—idioms.*** **in stock.** Available for sale or use; on hand. **out of stock.** Not available for sale or use. [Middle English *stok,* from Old English *stocc,* tree trunk.] **—stock′age** *n.* **—stock′er** *n.*

stock·ade (stŏ-kād′) *n.* **1.** A defensive barrier made of strong posts or timbers driven upright side by side into the ground. **2.a.** A similar fenced or enclosed area, especially one used for protection. **b.** A jail on a military base. **—stockade** *tr.v.* **-ad·ed, -ad·ing, -ades.** To fortify, protect, or surround with a stockade. [Obsolete French *estacade, estocade,* from Spanish *estacada,* from *estaca,* stake, of Germanic origin.]

stock·breed·ing (stŏk′brē′dĭng) *n.* The breeding and raising of livestock. **—stock′breed′er** *n.*

Stock·bridge (stŏk′brĭj′) *n.* A subtribe of the Mahican confederacy formerly inhabiting southwest Massachusetts, with a present-day population in central Wisconsin.

stock·bro·ker (stŏk′brō′kər) *n.* One that acts as an agent in the buying and selling of stocks or other securities; a broker. **—stock′bro′ker·age** *n.* **—stock′brok′ing** *n.*

stock car *n.* **1.** *Sports.* An automobile of a standard make modified for racing. **2.** A railroad car for carrying livestock.

stock certificate *n.* A certificate establishing ownership of a stated number of shares in a corporation's stock.

stock company *n.* **1.** A company or corporation whose capital is divided into shares. **2.** A permanent company that performs a repertoire of plays, usually at a single theater.

stock dove (dŭv) *n.* A common Old World bird *(Columba oenas)* having grayish plumage. [Probably from its living in hollow tree trunks.]

stock exchange *n. Abbr.* **SE 1.** A place where stocks, bonds, or other securities are bought and sold. **2.** An association of stockbrokers who meet to buy and sell stocks and bonds according to fixed regulations. Also called *stock market.*

stock·fish (stŏk′fĭsh′) *n., pl.* **stockfish** or **-fish·es.** A fish, such as a cod or haddock, cured by being split and air-dried without salt. [Middle English *stokfish,* translation of Middle Dutch *stocvisch* : *stoc,* tree limb (perhaps from its being dried on wooden racks) + *vische,* fish.]

stock·hold·er (stŏk′hōl′dər) *n.* One who owns a share or shares of stock in a company. Also called *stockowner.* **—stock′hold′ing** *n.*

Stock·holm (stŏk′hōlm′, -hōm′). The capital and largest city of Sweden, in the eastern part of the country on the Baltic Sea. Founded in the mid-13th century, it grew as a trade center allied with the Hanseatic League. Stockholm was the leading city of the

ă pat	oi boy
ā pay	ou out
âr care	ŏŏ took
ä father	ōō boot
ĕ pet	ŭ cut
ē be	ûr urge
ĭ pit	th thin
ī pie	*th* this
îr pier	hw which
ŏ pot	zh vision
ō toe	ə about, item
ô paw	♦ regionalism

Stress marks: ′ (primary); ′ (secondary), as in **dictionary** (dĭk′shə-nĕr′ē)

kingdom of Sweden after 1523 but did not become the official capital until 1634. Population, 653,455.

Stockholm syndrome *n.* A phenomenon in which a hostage begins to identify with and grow sympathetic to his or her captor. [After STOCKHOLM, where a hostage in a 1973 bank robbery became romantically attached to one of her captors.]

stock·i·nette also **stock·i·net** (stŏk′ə-nĕt′) *n.* An elastic knitted fabric used especially in making undergarments, bandages, and babies' clothes. [Alteration of *stocking net.*]

stockinette stitch *n.* A knitting pattern made by alternating rows of plain stitches and purl stitches.

stock·ing (stŏk′ĭng) *n.* **1.** A close-fitting, usually knitted covering for the foot and leg made from nylon, silk, cotton, wool, and similar yarns. **2.** An item resembling this covering. [From dialectal *stock,* from Middle English *stokke,* leg covering, probably from *stok,* stock. See STOCK.] **—stock′inged** *adj.*

stocking cap *n.* A close-fitting knitted cap that resembles a stocking and often has a long tapering tail with a tassel attached.

stocking mask *n.* A stocking, usually of nylon, that is worn over the head to distort and disguise facial features, often used as a mask by a criminal in the commission of a crime.

stock-in-trade also **stock in trade** (stŏk′ĭn-trād′, stŏk′ĭn-trād′) *n.* **1.** All the merchandise and equipment kept on hand and used in carrying on a business. **2.** The resources available to and habitually called on by a person in a given situation: *A ready wit is her stock-in-trade.*

stock·job·ber (stŏk′jŏb′ər) *n. Chiefly British.* A stock-exchange operator who deals only with brokers. **—stock′job′ber·y** *n.*

stock·man (stŏk′mən) *n.* **1.** A man who owns or raises livestock. **2.** A man who is in charge of livestock or works on a stock farm. **3.** A man who is employed in a stockroom or warehouse.

stock market *n.* **1.** See **stock exchange. 2.** The business transacted at a stock exchange. **3.** The prices offered for stocks and bonds in general: *a rising stock market.* **—stock′-mar′ket** (stŏk′mär′kĭt) *adj.*

stock·own·er (stŏk′ō′nər) *n.* See **stockholder. —stock′own′er·ship′** *n.*

stock·pile (stŏk′pīl′) *n.* A supply stored for future use, usually carefully accrued and maintained. **—stockpile** *tr.v.* **-piled, -pil·ing, -piles.** To accumulate and maintain a supply of for future use. **—stock′pil′er** *n.*

Stock·port (stŏk′pôrt′, -pōrt′). A borough of northwest England on the Mersey River south of Manchester. Chartered in 1220, it produces textiles and machinery. Population, 291,000.

stock·pot (stŏk′pŏt′) *n.* **1.** A pot used for preparing soup stock. **2.** A rich supply or resource.

stock·room also **stock room** (stŏk′ro͞om′, -ro͝om′) *n.* A room in which a store of goods or materials is kept.

stock saddle *n.* A large, heavy, often ornamented saddle with a raised curved pommel originally used on cattle ranches in the West and Southwest. Also called *western saddle.*

stock-still (stŏk′stĭl′) *adj.* Completely still; motionless.

stock·tak·ing (stŏk′tā′kĭng) *n.* **1.** A reappraisal of a situation, a person, or one's own position or prospects. **2.** The act or process of inventorying merchandise or the supplies on hand.

Stock·ton (stŏk′tən). A city of central California on the San Joaquin River south of Sacramento. Settled in 1848 just prior to the gold rush, it is an inland port and a trade and processing center. Population, 149,779.

Stockton, Francis Richard. Called "Frank." 1834–1902. American writer known for his short story "The Lady or the Tiger?" (1882).

Stock·ton-on-Tees (stŏk′tən-ŏn-tēz′, -ôn-). A borough of northeast England west-northwest of Middlesbrough. It is a shipbuilding center. Population, 172,600.

stock·y (stŏk′ē) *adj.* **-i·er, -i·est. 1.** Solidly built; sturdy. **2.** Chubby; plump. **—stock′i·ly** *adv.* **—stock′i·ness** *n.*

stock·yard (stŏk′yärd′) *n.* A large enclosed yard, usually with pens or stables, in which livestock, such as cattle or pigs, are temporarily kept until slaughtered, sold, or shipped elsewhere.

stodg·y (stŏj′ē) *adj.* **-i·er, -i·est. 1.a.** Dull, unimaginative, and commonplace. **b.** Prim or pompous; stuffy: *"Why is the middle-class so stodgy—so utterly without a sense of humor!"* (Katherine Mansfield). See Synonyms at **dull. 2.** Indigestible and starchy; heavy: *stodgy food.* **3.** Solidly built; stocky. [From *stodge,* thick filling food, from *stodge,* to cram.] **—stodg′i·ly** *adv.* **—stodg′i·ness** *n.*

sto·gy or **sto·gie** (stō′gē) *n., pl.* **-gies. 1.** A cheap cigar. **2.** A roughly made heavy shoe or boot. [After *Conestoga,* a village of southeast Pennsylvania.]

sto·ic (stō′ĭk) *n.* **1.** One who is seemingly indifferent to or unaffected by joy, grief, pleasure, or pain. **2. Stoic.** *Philosophy.* A member of a Greek school of philosophy, founded by Zeno about 308 B.C., believing that human beings should be free from passion and should calmly accept all occurrences as the unavoidable result of divine will or of the natural order. **—stoic** also **sto·i·cal** (-ĭ-kəl) *adj.* Seemingly indifferent to or unaffected by pleasure or pain; impassive: *"stoic resignation in the face of hunger"* (John F. Kennedy). [Middle English *Stoic,* a Stoic, from Latin *Stōicus,* from Greek *Stōikos,* from *stoa (poikilē),* (Painted) Porch, where Zeno taught. See **stā-** in Appendix.] **—sto′i·cal·ly** *adv.* **—sto′i·cal·ness** *n.*

stoi·chi·om·e·try (stoi′kē-ŏm′ĭ-trē) *n.* **1.** Calculation of the quantities of reactants and products in a chemical reaction. **2.** The quantitative relationship between reactants and products in a chemical reaction. [Greek *stoikheion,* element; see **steigh-** in Appendix + –METRY.] **—stoi′chi·o·met′ric** (-ə-mĕt′rĭk) *adj.* **—stoi′chi·o·met′ri·cal·ly** *adv.*

sto·i·cism (stō′ĭ-sĭz′əm) *n.* **1.** Indifference to pleasure or pain; impassiveness. **2. Stoicism.** *Philosophy.* The doctrines or philosophy of the Stoics.

stoke (stōk) *v.* **stoked, stok·ing, stokes.** *—tr.* **1.** To stir up and feed (a fire or furnace). **2.** To feed fuel to and tend the fire of (a furnace). *—intr.* **1.** To feed or tend a furnace or fire. **2.** *Informal.* To eat steadily and in large quantities. [Back-formation from STOKER.]

stoked (stōkt) *adj. Slang.* **1.** Exhilarated or excited. **2.** Being or feeling high or intoxicated, especially from a drug.

stoke·hold (stōk′hōld′) *n. Nautical.* The area or compartment into which a ship's furnaces or boilers open.

stoke·hole (stōk′hōl′) *n.* **1.** The space about the opening in a furnace or boiler. **2.** *Nautical.* A stokehold. [Translation of Dutch *stookgat.*]

Stoke-on-Trent (stōk′ŏn-trĕnt′, -ôn-). A borough of west-central England south of Manchester. Center of an important pottery-making industry, it also has iron and steel mills. Josiah Wedgwood and Josiah Spode lived here. Population, 250,700.

Stoke Po·ges (stōk pō′jĭs). A village of southeast-central England west of London. It is generally considered to be the setting for Thomas Gray's *Elegy Written in a Country Churchyard* (published 1751).

stok·er (stō′kər) *n.* **1.** One who is employed to feed fuel to and tend a furnace, as on a steam locomotive or a steamship. **2.** A mechanical device for feeding coal to a furnace. [Dutch, from *stoken,* to stoke, from Middle Dutch *stōken,* to poke.]

Sto·ker (stō′kər), **Abraham.** Known as "Bram." 1847–1912. British writer of the gothic horror novel *Dracula* (1897).

Stokes-Ad·ams syndrome (stōks′ăd′əmz) *n.* An occasional temporary stoppage or extreme slowing of the pulse as a result of heart block, causing dizziness, fainting, and sometimes convulsions. [After William *Stokes* (1804–1878) and Robert *Adams* (1791–1875), Irish physicians.]

Sto·kow·ski (stə-kôv′skē, -kôf′-, -kou′-), **Leopold Antoni Stanislaw.** 1882–1977. British-born American conductor of the Philadelphia Orchestra (1914–1936) and other major symphonies. He founded the American Symphony Orchestra in 1962.

STOL *abbr.* Short takeoff and landing.

stole¹ (stōl) *n.* **1.** *Ecclesiastical.* A long scarf, usually of embroidered silk or linen, worn over the left shoulder by deacons and over both shoulders by priests and bishops while officiating. **2.** A woman's long scarf of cloth or fur worn about the shoulders. **3.** A long robe or outer garment worn by matrons in ancient Rome. [Middle English, from Old English, from Latin *stola,* garment, robe, from Greek *stolē.* See **stel-** in Appendix.]

stole² (stōl) *v.* Past tense of **steal.**

sto·len (stō′lən) *v.* Past participle of **steal.**

stol·id (stŏl′ĭd) *adj.* **-er, -est.** Having or revealing little emotion or sensibility; impassive: *"the incredibly massive and stolid bureaucracy of the Soviet system"* (John Kenneth Galbraith). [Latin *stolidus,* unmoving, stupid. See **stel-** in Appendix.] **—sto·lid′i·ty** (stŏ-lĭd′ĭ-tē, stə-), **stol′id·ness** (stŏl′ĭd-nĭs) *n.* **—stol′id·ly** *adv.*

stol·len (stō′lən) *n., pl.* **stollen** or **-lens.** A rich yeast bread containing raisins, citron, and chopped nutmeats. [German, prop, support, stollen. See STULL.]

sto·lon (stō′lŏn′, -lən) *n.* **1.** *Botany.* A shoot that bends to the ground or that grows horizontally above the ground and produces roots and shoots at the nodes. **2.** *Zoology.* A stemlike structure of certain colonial organisms from which new individuals arise by budding. [Latin *stolō, stolōn-,* shoot. See **stel-** in Appendix.] **—sto′lon·ate′** (-lə-nāt′) *adj.*

sto·lon·if·er·ous (stō′lə-nĭf′ər-əs) *adj.* Bearing or forming stolons. **—sto′lon·if′er·ous·ly** *adv.*

sto·ma (stō′mə) *n., pl.* **-ma·ta** (-mə-tə) or **-mas. 1.** *Botany.* One of the minute pores in the epidermis of a leaf or stem through which gases and water vapor pass. Also called *stomate.* **2.** *Anatomy.* A small aperture in the surface of a membrane. **3.** A surgically constructed opening, especially one in the abdominal wall that permits the passage of waste after a colostomy or an ileostomy. **4.** *Zoology.* A mouthlike opening, such as the oral cavity of a nematode. [New Latin, from Greek *stoma,* mouth.]

stom·ach (stŭm′ək) *n.* **1.a.** The enlarged, saclike portion of the alimentary canal, one of the principal organs of digestion, located in vertebrates between the esophagus and the small intestine. **b.** A similar digestive structure of many invertebrates. **c.** Any of the four compartments into which the stomach of a ruminant is divided. **2.** The abdomen or belly. **3.** An appetite for food. **4.** A desire or inclination, especially for something difficult or unpleasant: *had no stomach for quarrels.* **5.** Courage; spirit. **6.** *Obsolete.* Pride. **—stomach** *tr.v.* **-ached, -ach·ing, -achs. 1.** To bear; tolerate. **2.** *Obsolete.* To resent. [Middle English, from Old French *stomaque, estomac,* from Latin *stomachus,* from Greek *stomakhos,* from *stoma,* mouth.]

stom·ach·ache (stŭm′ək-āk′) *n.* Pain in the stomach or abdomen.

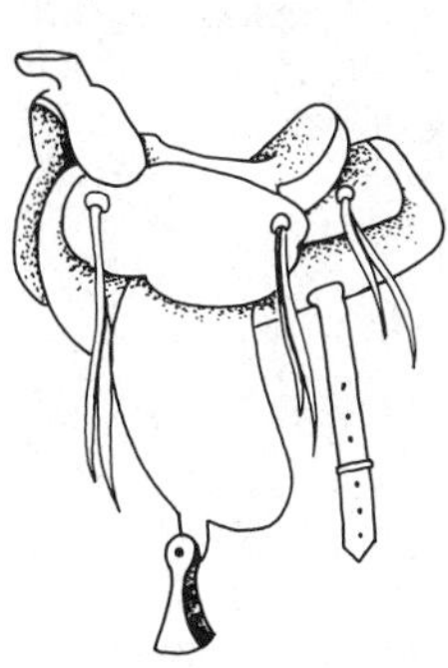
stock saddle

stole¹
Ecclesiastical stole

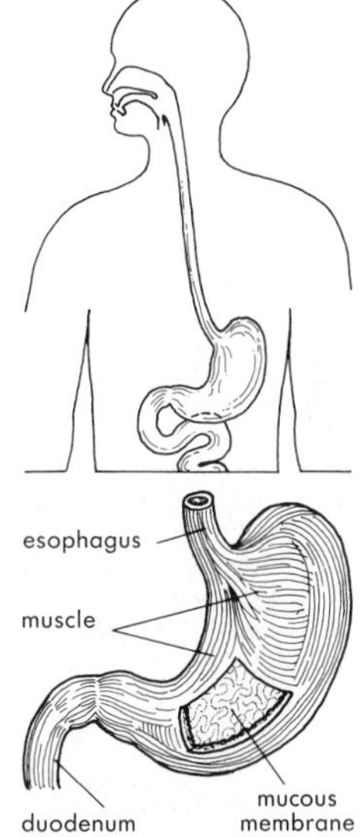

stomach

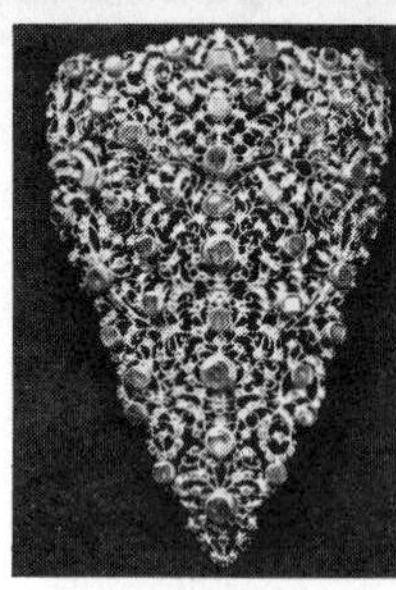

stomacher
Top: Portrait of a Woman, c. 1625–1630, attributed to Pieter Claesz Soutman (1580?–1657)
Bottom: Early 18th-century Flemish

stom·ach·er (stŭm′ə-kər) *n.* A heavily embroidered or jeweled garment formerly worn over the chest and stomach, especially by women.

sto·mach·ic (stə-măk′ĭk) *adj.* **1.** Of or relating to the stomach; gastric. **2.** Beneficial to or stimulating digestion in the stomach. —**stomachic** *n.* An agent, such as a medicine, that strengthens or stimulates the stomach. —**sto·mach′i·cal·ly** *adv.*

stomach pump *n.* A suction pump with a flexible tube inserted into the stomach through the mouth and esophagus to empty the stomach in an emergency, as in a case of poisoning.

stomach tooth *n.* A canine tooth of the lower jaw. [From the gastric disturbances that often accompany its emergence.]

stomach worm *n.* Any of various parasitic nematode worms that infest the stomachs of animals, especially *Haemonchus contortus,* a parasite of sheep and other ruminants.

stomat– *pref.* Variant of **stomato–.**

sto·ma·ta (stō′mə-tə) *n.* A plural of **stoma.**

sto·ma·tal (stō′mə-təl) *adj.* Of, relating to, resembling, or having a stoma.

sto·mate (stō′māt′) *n. Botany.* See **stoma** (sense 1). [Perhaps back-formation from STOMATA.]

sto·mat·ic (stō-măt′ĭk) *adj.* **1.** Of or relating to the mouth. **2.** Of, having, or resembling a stoma.

sto·ma·ti·tis (stō′mə-tī′tĭs) *n.* Inflammation of the mucous tissue of the mouth.

stomato– or **stomat–** *pref.* Mouth; stoma: *stomatitis.* [From Greek *stoma, stomat-,* mouth.]

sto·ma·tol·o·gy (stō′mə-tŏl′ə-jē) *n.* The medical study of the mouth and its diseases. —**sto′ma·to·log′i·cal** (-tə-lŏj′ĭ-kəl), **sto′ma·to·log′ic** (-lŏj′ĭk) *adj.* —**sto′ma·tol′o·gist** *n.*

sto·mat·o·pod (stō-măt′ə-pŏd′) *n.* Any of various marine crustaceans of the order Stomatopoda, which includes the squilla. [From New Latin *Stomatopoda,* order name : STOMATO– + –POD.]

sto·ma·tous (stō′mə-təs) *adj.* Of, having, or resembling a stoma.

–stome *suff.* Mouth; stoma: *peristome.* [From Greek *stoma,* mouth.]

sto·mo·de·um also **sto·mo·dae·um** (stō′mə-dē′əm) *n., pl.* **-de·a** also **-dae·a** (-dē′ə). The anterior or oral portion of the alimentary canal of an embryo. [New Latin : Greek *stoma,* mouth + Greek *hodaios,* on the way (from *hodos,* road).] —**sto′mo·de′al** (-dē′əl) *adj.*

stomp (stŏmp, stômp) *v.* **stomped, stomp·ing, stomps.** —*tr.* To tread or trample heavily or violently on. —*intr.* To tread or trample heavily or violently. —**stomp** *n.* **1.** A dance involving a rhythmical, heavy step. **2.** The jazz music for this dance. [Variant of STAMP.] —**stomp′er** *n.* —**stomp′ing·ly** *adv.*

USAGE NOTE: *Stomp* and *stamp* are interchangeable in the sense "to trample" or "to tread on violently": *stomped* (or *stamped*) *to death; stomping* (or *stamping*) *horses.* Only *stamp* is used in the sense "to eliminate": *stamp out a fire; stamp out poverty. Stamp* is also standard in the sense "to strike the ground with the foot, as in anger or frustration," as in *He stamped his foot and began to cry.* In an earlier survey the use of *stomp* in this example was rejected by a large majority of the Usage Panel.

–stomy *suff.* A surgical operation in which an artificial opening is made into a specified organ or part: *colostomy.* [Greek *stoma,* opening, mouth + –Y^2.]

stone (stōn) *n.* **1.a.** Concreted earthy or mineral matter; rock. **b.** Such concreted matter of a particular type. Often used in combination: *sandstone; soapstone.* **2.** A small piece of rock. **3.** Rock or a piece of rock shaped or finished for a particular purpose, especially: **a.** A piece of rock that is used in construction: *a coping stone; a paving stone.* **b.** A gravestone or tombstone. **c.** A grindstone, millstone, or whetstone. **d.** A milestone or boundary. **4.** A gem or precious stone. **5.** Something, such as a hailstone, resembling a stone in shape or hardness. **6.** *Botany.* The hard covering enclosing the seed in certain fruits, such as the cherry, plum, or peach. **7.** *Pathology.* A mineral concretion in an organ, such as the kidney or gallbladder, or other body part; a calculus. **8.** *pl.* **stone.** *Abbr.* **st.** A unit of weight in Great Britain, 14 pounds (6.4 kilograms). **9.** *Printing.* A table with a smooth surface on which page forms are composed. —**stone** *adj.* **1.** Relating to or made of stone: *a stone wall.* **2.** Made of stoneware or earthenware. —**stone** *adv.* Used as an intensive. Often used in combination: *stone cold; standing stone still.* —**stone** *tr.v.* **stoned, ston·ing, stones. 1.** To hurl or throw stones at, especially to kill with stones. **2.** To remove the stones or pits from. **3.** To furnish, fit, pave, or line with stones. **4.** To rub on or with a stone in order to polish or sharpen. **5.** *Obsolete.* To make hard or indifferent. [Middle English, from Old English *stān.* See **stei-** in Appendix.] —**ston′er** *n.*

Stone (stōn), **Edward Durell.** 1902–1978. American architect who was an exponent of the International Style. Among his notable designs is the Kennedy Center for the Performing Arts in Washington, D.C. (1964).

Stone, Harlan Fiske. 1872–1946. American jurist who served as an associate justice (1925–1941) and the chief justice (1941–1946) of the U.S. Supreme Court.

Stone, I(sidor) F(einstein). 1907–1989. American journalist who championed liberal causes in *I.F. Stone's Weekly* (1953–1971).

Stone, Lucy. 1818–1893. American feminist and social reformer who organized the first national women's rights convention, held in Worcester, Massachusetts (1850), and was a founder of the American Woman Suffrage Association (1869).

Stone Age *n.* The earliest known period of human culture, characterized by the use of stone tools.

stone-blind (stōn′blīnd′) *adj.* Completely blind. —**stone′-blind′ness** *n.*

stone-broke (stōn′brōk′) *adj. Informal.* Completely broke; having no money.

stone canal *n.* A calcareous duct in echinoderms that leads from the madreporite to a ring-shaped canal around the mouth.

stone·cat (stōn′kăt′) *n.* A yellowish-brown freshwater catfish *(Noturus flavus)* of the Mississippi Valley and Great Lakes region, having poisonous pectoral spines.

stone cell *n.* A nearly isodiametric sclereid that is found in certain fruits, such as the quince and pear.

stone·chat (stōn′chăt′) *n.* A small Old World thrush *(Saxicola torquata)* of open, grassy regions, the male of which has a black head, dark wings and tail, and chestnut underparts. [From the resemblance of its call to the sound of falling pebbles.]

stone crab *n.* A large edible crab *(Menippe mercenaria)* found along the Atlantic coast of the southern United States.

stone·crop (stōn′krŏp′) *n.* **1.** Any of various plants of the genus *Sedum,* having fleshy leaves and variously colored flowers. **2.** Any of various related plants. [Middle English, from Old English *stāncropp* : *stān,* stone; see STONE + *cropp,* cluster, sprout.]

stone·cut·ter (stōn′kŭt′ər) *n.* **1.** One that cuts or carves stone. **2.** A machine that is used to dress stone. —**stone′cut′ting** *n.*

stoned (stōnd) *adj. Slang.* **1.** Intoxicated; drunk. **2.** Under the influence of a mind-altering drug.

stone-deaf (stōn′dĕf′) *adj.* Completely deaf.

stone-faced (stōn′fāst′) *adj.* Variant of **stony-faced.**

stone·fish (stōn′fĭsh′) *n., pl.* **stonefish** or **-fish·es.** Any of several tropical scorpion fishes of the genus *Synanceja,* especially *S. Verrucosa,* which resembles a small rock and ejects a deadly venom from spines on its dorsal fin. [From its resemblance to an encrusted stone.]

stone·fly (stōn′flī′) *n.* Any of numerous weak-flying insects of the order Plecoptera, whose flat, elongated nymphs live under stones along the banks of streams. Adult and larval stoneflies are used as fishing bait. Also called *plecopteran.*

stone fruit *n.* See **drupe.**

stone-ground (stōn′ground′) *adj.* Ground between millstones, especially buhrstones: *stone-ground flour.*

Stone·ham (stō′nəm). A town of northeast Massachusetts, a residential suburb of Boston. Population, 21,424.

stone·heart·ed (stōn′här′tĭd) *adj.* Variant of **stonyhearted.**

Stone·henge (stōn′hĕnj′). A group of standing stones on Salisbury Plain in southern England. Dating to c. 2000–1800 B.C., the megaliths are enclosed by a circular ditch and embankment that may date to c. 2800. The arrangement of the stones suggests that Stonehenge was used as a religious center and also as an astronomical observatory.

stone lily *n.* A fossil crinoid.

stone marten *n.* **1.** A Eurasian marten *(Martes foina)* having brown fur with lighter underfur and often inhabiting rocky inlets and crevices. **2.** The fur of this animal.

stone·ma·son (stōn′mā′sən) *n.* One that prepares and lays stones in building. —**stone′ma′son·ry** *n.*

stone mint *n.* An aromatic eastern North American plant *(Cunila origanoides)* of the mint family, having clusters of small purplish or white flowers. Also called *dittany.* [So called because it grows in rocky places.]

Stone Mountain. A massive granite monadnock, 514.2 m (1,686 ft) high, in northwest-central Georgia east of Atlanta. Its northeast wall contains a huge Confederate memorial (carved 1917–1967).

stone·roll·er (stōn′rō′lər) *n.* **1.** A minnow *(Campostoma anomalum)* of the central and southern United States, having a horny ridge near the edge of the lower lip used for scraping food from the bottom of a body of water. **2.** A sucker *(Hypentelium nigricans)* of the central and southern United States, common in swift or rocky streams.

stone's throw (stōnz) *n.* A short distance.

stone·wall (stōn′wôl′) *v.* **-walled, -wall·ing, -walls.** —*intr.* **1.** *Informal.* **a.** To engage in delaying tactics; stall: *"stonewalling for time in order to close the missile gap"* (James Reston). **b.** To refuse to answer or cooperate. **2.** *Sports.* To play defensively rather than trying to score in cricket. —*tr. Informal.* To refuse to answer or cooperate with; resist or rebuff: *"I want you to stonewall it, let them plead the Fifth Amendment"* (Richard M. Nixon). —**stone′wall′er** *n.*

stone·ware (stōn′wâr′) *n.* A heavy, nonporous, nontranslucent pottery, such as jasper ware, that is fired at a high temperature.

stone·wash·ing (stōn′wôsh′ĭng) *n.* A process of washing garments or material, usually denim, in large industrial machines

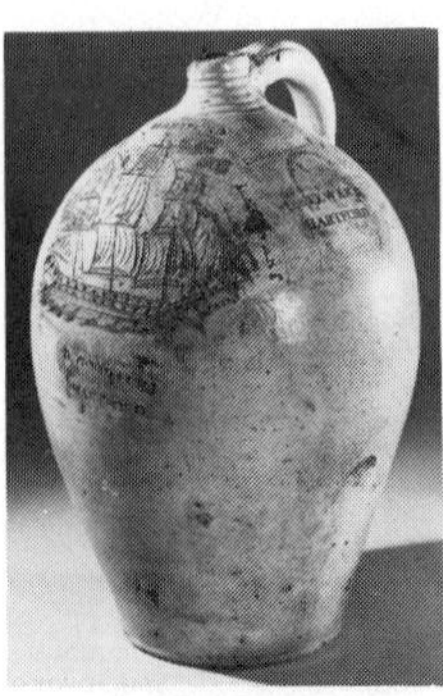

stoneware
c. 1830 American

with pumice pebbles to soften and abrade the material by friction. **—stone′wash′** *v.*

stone·work (stōn′wûrk′) *n.* **1.** The technique or process of working in stone. **2.** Work made of stone; stone masonry. **—stone′work′er** *n.*

stone·wort (stōn′wûrt′, -wôrt′) *n.* Any of various submerged aquatic algae of the genus *Chara* that are frequently encrusted with calcium carbonate deposits and have nodes with whorled, filamentlike branches.

ston·ey (stō′nē) *adj.* Variant of **stony.**

Ston·ey Creek (stō′nē). A town of southeast Ontario, Canada, at the west end of Lake Ontario south of Hamilton. The British defeated the Americans here on June 6, 1813, during the War of 1812. Population, 36,762.

Ston·ing·ton (stō′nĭng-tən). A town of southeast Connecticut on Long Island Sound east of New London. Settled in 1649, it was once a major shipbuilding and whaling center. Population, 16,220.

ston·y also **ston·ey** (stō′nē) *adj.* **-i·er, -i·est. 1.** Covered with or full of stones: *a stony beach.* **2.** Resembling stone, as in hardness. **3. a.** Hardhearted and unfeeling; unemotional. **b.** Exhibiting no feeling or warmth; impassive: *a stony expression.* **4.** Emotionally numbing or paralyzing: *a stony feeling of fear.* **—ston′i·ly** *adv.* **—ston′i·ness** *n.*

stony coral *n.* A coral with a hard calcareous skeleton, especially of the order Scleractinia.

ston·y-faced (stō′nē-fāst′) also **stone-faced** (stōn′-) *adj.* Exhibiting no emotion or feeling; expressionless.

ston·y·heart·ed (stō′nē-här′tĭd) also **stone·heart·ed** (stōn′-) *adj.* Devoid of kindness or sympathy; hardhearted. **—ston′y·heart′ed·ly** *adv.* **—ston′y·heart′ed·ness** *n.*

Ston·y Point (stō′nē). A village of southeast New York on the Hudson River north of New City. Its blockhouse, captured by British troops in May 1779, was retaken in July by Gen. Anthony Wayne's forces. Population, 8,270.

Stony Tun·gus·ka (to͝ong-go͞o′skə, to͞on-). See **Tunguska.**

stood (sto͝od) *v.* Past tense and past participle of **stand.**

stooge (sto͞oj) *n.* **1.** The straight man to a comedian. **2.** One who allows oneself to be used for another's profit or advantage; a puppet. **3.** *Slang.* A stool pigeon. **—stooge** *intr.v.* **stooged, stoog·ing, stoog·es.** To be a stooge or behave like one. [Origin unknown.]

stool (sto͞ol) *n.* **1.** A backless and armless single seat supported on legs or a pedestal. **2.** A low bench or support for the feet or knees in sitting or kneeling, as a footrest. **3.** A toilet seat; a commode. **4. a.** A bowel movement; an evacuation. **b.** Evacuated fecal matter. **5.** *Botany.* **a.** A stump or rootstock that produces shoots or suckers. **b.** A shoot or growth from such a stump or rootstock. **—stool** *intr.v.* **stooled, stool·ing, stools. 1.** *Botany.* To send up shoots or suckers. **2.** To evacuate the bowels; defecate. **3.** *Slang.* To act as a stool pigeon. [Middle English, from Old English *stōl.* See **stā-** in Appendix.]

stool·ie (sto͞o′lē) *n.* *Slang.* A stool pigeon.

stool pigeon *n.* **1.** *Slang.* A person acting as a decoy or as an informer, especially one who is a spy for the police. **2.** A pigeon used as a decoy. [From the practice of tying decoy pigeons to a stool to attract other pigeons.]

stoop¹ (sto͞op) *v.* **stooped, stoop·ing, stoops.** —*intr.* **1.** To bend forward and down from the waist or the middle of the back: *had to stoop in order to fit into the cave.* **2.** To walk or stand, especially habitually, with the head and upper back bent forward. **3.** To bend or sag downward. **4. a.** To lower or debase oneself. **b.** To descend from a superior position; condescend. **5.** To yield; submit. **6.** To swoop down, as a bird in pursuing its prey. —*tr.* **1.** To bend (the head or body) forward and down. **2.** To debase; humble. **—stoop** *n.* **1.** The act of stooping. **2.** A forward bending of the head and upper back, especially when habitual. **3.** An act of self-abasement or condescension. **4.** A descent, as of a bird of prey. [Middle English *stoupen,* from Old English *stūpian.*]

SYNONYMS: *stoop, condescend, deign.* The central meaning shared by these verbs is "to descend to a level considered inappropriate to one's dignity": *stooping to contemptible methods to realize their ambitions; won't condescend to acknowledge his rival's greeting; didn't even deign to reply.*

♦ **stoop²** (sto͞op) *n.* *Northeastern U.S.* A small porch, platform, or staircase leading to the entrance of a house or building. [Dutch *stoep,* front verandah, from Middle Dutch.]

stoop³ (sto͞op) *n.* Variant of **stoup.**

stoop·ball (sto͞op′bôl′) *n.* *Sports.* A game patterned on baseball in which a player throws a ball against a stoop or wall and the number of bounces indicates the bases reached.

stoop·er (sto͞o′pər) *n.* **1.** One that stoops. **2.** *Slang.* One who looks for winning pari-mutuel tickets carelessly discarded by others at a racetrack.

stop (stŏp) *v.* **stopped, stop·ping, stops.** —*tr.* **1.** To close (an opening) by covering, filling in, or plugging up. **2.** To constrict (an opening or orifice). **3.** To obstruct or block passage on (a road, for example). **4.** To prevent the flow or passage of: *tried to stop the bleeding.* **5.** To cause to halt, cease, or desist: *stopped me and asked directions.* **6.** To desist from; cease: *stop running.* **7.** To order a bank to withhold payment of: *stopped the check.* **8.** To cause (a motor, for example) to cease operation or function; halt. **9.** *Music.* **a.** To press down (a string on a stringed instrument) on the fingerboard to produce a desired pitch. **b.** To close (a hole on a wind instrument) with the finger in sounding a desired pitch. —*intr.* **1.** To cease moving, progressing, acting, or operating; come to a halt: *The clock stopped at some point during the night.* **2.** To put an end to what one is doing; cease: *had to stop at an exciting place in the book.* **3.** To interrupt one's course or journey for a brief visit or stay: *stop at the store; stopped at a friend's for a few nights.* **—stop** *n.* **1.** The act of stopping or the condition of being stopped; cessation. **2.** A finish; an end. **3.** A stay or visit, as one taken during a trip. **4.** A place at which someone or something stops: *a regular stop on my paper route; a bus stop.* **5.** A device or means that obstructs, blocks, or plugs up. **6.** An order given to a bank to withhold payment on a check. **7.** A part in a machine that stops or regulates movement. **8.** The effective aperture of a lens, controlled by a diaphragm. **9.** A mark of punctuation, especially a period. **10.** *Music.* **a.** The act of stopping a string or hole on an instrument. **b.** A fret on a stringed instrument. **c.** A hole on a wind instrument. **d.** A device such as a key for closing the hole on a wind instrument. **e.** A tuned set of pipes, as in an organ. **f.** A knob, key, or pull that regulates such a set of pipes. **11.** *Nautical.* A line used for securing something temporarily: *a sail stop.* **12.** *Linguistics.* **13.** See **plosive. 14.** The depression between the muzzle and top of the skull of an animal, especially a dog. **15.** *Games.* A stopper. **16.** *Architecture.* A projecting stone, often carved, at the end of a molding. **—stop** *adj.* Of, relating to, or being of use at the end of an operation or activity: *a stop code.* ***—phrasal verb.* stop down.** To reduce (the aperture) of a lens. [Middle English *stoppen,* from Old English *-stoppian,* probably from Vulgar Latin **stuppāre,* to caulk, from Latin *stuppa,* tow, broken flax, from Greek *stuppē.*] **—stop′pa·ble** *adj.*

SYNONYMS: *stop, cease, desist, discontinue, halt, quit.* The central meaning shared by these verbs is "to bring or come to a cessation": *stop arguing; ceased crying; desist from complaining; discontinued the treatment; halting the convoy; quit laughing.*
ANTONYM: *start.*

stop·cock (stŏp′kŏk′) *n.* A valve that regulates the flow of fluid through a pipe; a faucet.

stope (stōp) *n.* An excavation in the form of steps made by the mining of ore from steeply inclined or vertical veins. **—stope** *tr.v.* **stoped, stop·ing, stopes.** To remove (ore) from or mine by means of a stope. [Perhaps from Low German, step, from Middle Low German *stōpe.*] **—stop′er** *n.*

Stopes (stōps), **Marie Carmichael.** 1880–1958. British paleontologist and social reformer who opened England's first birth control clinic (1924) in London and later promoted family planning in the Far East.

stop·gap (stŏp′găp′) *n.* An improvised substitute for something lacking; a temporary expedient. See Synonyms at **makeshift.** —*attributive.* Often used to modify another noun: *stopgap measures; a stopgap leader.*

stop·light (stŏp′līt′) *n.* **1.** A light on the rear of a vehicle that is activated when the brakes are applied. Also called *brake light.* **2.** See **traffic light.**

stop order *n.* An order to a broker to buy or sell a stock when it reaches a specified level of decline or gain in price.

stop·o·ver (stŏp′ō′vər) *n.* **1.** An interruption in the course of a journey for stopping or visiting at a certain place. **2.** A place visited briefly in the course of a journey.

stop·page (stŏp′ĭj) *n.* The act of stopping or the condition of being stopped; a halt: *called for a work stoppage.*

stop payment *n.* An order to one's bank not to honor a check one has drawn.

stop·per (stŏp′ər) *n.* **1.** A device, such as a cork or plug, that is inserted to close an opening. **2.** One that causes something to stop: *a conversation stopper.* **3.** *Computer Science.* The topmost memory location in a device or system. **4.** *Games.* A card or cards enabling one to prevent one's opponents from winning all the tricks in a hand of bridge. **—stopper** *tr.v.* **-pered, -per·ing, -pers.** To close with or as if with a stopper.

stop·ple (stŏp′əl) *n.* A stopper; a plug. **—stopple** *tr.v.* **-pled, -pling, -ples.** To close with a stopper or plug. [Middle English *stoppell,* from Middle English *stoppen,* to stop. See STOP.]

stop sign *n.* A traffic sign that indicates that traffic is required to come to a complete stop before proceeding.

stop street *n.* A street intersection at which a vehicle must come to a complete stop before entering a through street.

stop·watch (stŏp′wŏch′) *n.* A watch that can be instantly started and stopped by pushing a button and used to measure an exact duration of time.

stor·age (stôr′ĭj, stōr′-) *n.* *Abbr.* **stge., stor. 1. a.** The act of storing goods or the state of being stored. **b.** A space for storing goods. **c.** The price charged for keeping goods stored. **2.** The charging or regenerating of a storage battery. **3.** *Computer Science.* The part of a computer that stores information for subsequent use or retrieval. —*attributive.* Often used to modify another noun: *a storage closet; storage facilities.*

storage battery *n.* *Electricity.* A group of reversible or rechargeable secondary cells acting as a unit. Also called *secondary battery.*

stonework
Whitfield House Museum, the oldest stone house in the United States, in Guilford, Connecticut

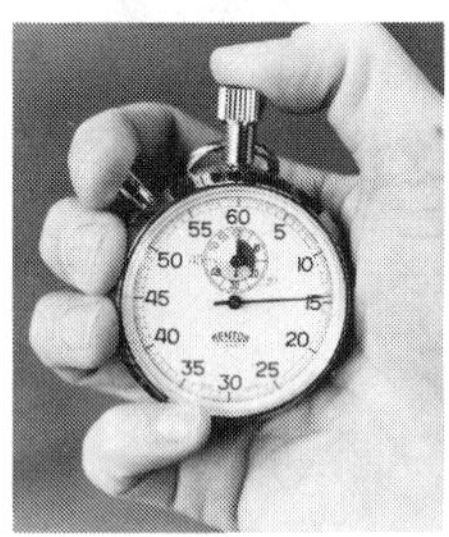

stopwatch

ă **pat**	oi **boy**
ā **pay**	ou **out**
âr **care**	o͝o **took**
ä **father**	o͞o **boot**
ĕ **pet**	ŭ **cut**
ē **be**	ûr **urge**
ĭ **pit**	th **thin**
ī **pie**	*th* **this**
îr **pier**	hw **which**
ŏ **pot**	zh **vision**
ō **toe**	ə **a**bout, it**e**m
ô **paw**	♦ regionalism

Stress marks: ′ (primary); ′ (secondary), as in **dictionary** (dĭk′shə-nĕr′ē)

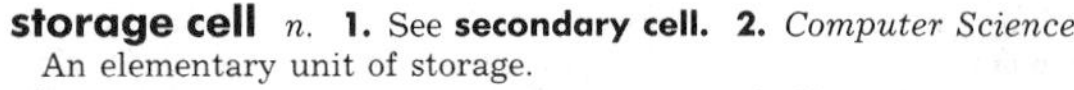

storage cell *n.* **1.** See **secondary cell. 2.** *Computer Science.* An elementary unit of storage.

sto·rax (stôr′ăks′, stōr′-) *n.* **1.** See **snowbell. 2.** *Botany.* An aromatic resin obtained from the snowbell. Also called *styrax.* **3.** *Botany.* A brownish, aromatic resin used in perfume and medicine and obtained from any of several trees of the genus *Liquidambar,* especially *L. orientalis,* of Turkey. Also called *styrax.* [Middle English, from Latin, alteration of *styrax,* from Greek *sturax,* perhaps of Semitic origin.]

store (stôr, stōr) *n.* **1.** A place where merchandise is offered for sale; a shop. **2.** A stock or supply reserved for future use: *a squirrel's store of acorns.* **3. stores.** Supplies, especially of food, clothing, or arms. **4.** A place where commodities are kept; a warehouse or storehouse. **5.** A great quantity or number; an abundance. **—store** *tr.v.* **stored, stor·ing, stores. 1.** To reserve or put away for future use. **2.** To fill, supply, or stock. **3.** To deposit or receive in a storehouse or warehouse for safekeeping. ***—idiom.* in store.** Forthcoming: *great trouble in store for her.* [Middle English *stor,* supply, from Old French *estor,* from *estorer,* to build, from Latin *īnstaurāre,* to restore. See **stā-** in Appendix.] **—stor′a·ble** *adj.* **—stor′er** *n.*

stork
Yellow-billed stork
Ibis ibis

store-bought (stôr′bôt′, stōr′-) *adj. Informal.* Manufactured and purchased at retail; not homemade: *store-bought clothes; store-bought cookies.*

store cheese *n.* Cheddar.

store·front (stôr′frŭnt′, stōr′-) *n.* **1.** The side of a store or shop facing a street. **2.** A room or suite of rooms in a commercial building at street level: *a political office in a storefront.* **—storefront** *adj.* **1.** Of, relating to, or being that side of a store facing a street: *storefront window boxes.* **2.** Operating in a room or suite of rooms in a commercial building at street level: *a storefront lawyer.* —*attributive.* Often used to modify another noun: *storefront legal aid offices; a storefront bookstall.*

store·house (stôr′hous′, stōr′-) *n.* **1.** A place or building in which goods are stored; a warehouse. **2.** An abundant source or supply: *a storehouse of knowledge.*

store·keep·er (stôr′kē′pər, stōr′-) *n.* **1.** One who keeps a retail store or shop; a shopkeeper. **2.** One who is in charge of receiving or distributing stores or supplies, such as military or naval supplies. **—store′keep′ing** *n.*

store·own·er (stôr′ō′nər) *n.* One who owns or operates a store or shop.

store·room (stôr′ro͞om′, -ro͝om′, stōr′-) *n.* A room in which things are stored.

store·wide (stôr′wīd′, stōr′-) *adj.* Involving, applying to, or occurring throughout a whole store: *a storewide sale; storewide renovations.*

sto·rey (stôr′ē, stōr′ē) *n. Chiefly British.* Variant of **story[2].**

sto·reyed (stôr′ēd, stōr′-) *adj. Chiefly British.* Variant of **storied[2].**

sto·ried[1] (stôr′ēd, stōr′-) *adj.* **1.** Celebrated or famous in history or story: *a storied chieftain of guerrillas.* **2.** Ornamented with designs representing scenes from history, legend, or story: *storied tapestry.*

sto·ried[2] (stôr′ēd, stōr′-) *adj.* Having or consisting of a specified number of stories. Often used in combination: *a three-storied house; a multistoried office building.*

stork (stôrk) *n.* Any of various large wading birds of the family Ciconiidae, chiefly of the Eastern Hemisphere, having long legs and a long straight bill. [Middle English, from Old English *storc.* See **ster-[1]** in Appendix.]

storks·bill (stôrks′bĭl′) *n.* **1.** Any of various plants of the genus *Erodium,* having fruit with a narrow beaklike tip. **2.** See **geranium** (sense 2).

storksbill
Erodium cicutarium

storm (stôrm) *n.* **1.** An atmospheric disturbance manifested in strong winds accompanied by rain, snow, or other precipitation and often by thunder and lightning. **2.** *Meteorology.* A wind with a speed from 64 to 73 miles (from 103 to 117 kilometers) per hour, according to the Beaufort scale. Also called *violent storm.* **3.** A heavy shower of objects, such as bullets or missiles. **4.** A strong or violent outburst, as of emotion or excitement: *a storm of tears.* **5.** A violent disturbance or upheaval, as in political, social, or domestic affairs: *a storm of protest.* **6.** A violent, sudden attack on a fortified place. **—storm** *v.* **stormed, storm·ing, storms.** —*intr.* **1.a.** To blow forcefully. **b.** To precipitate rain, snow, hail, or sleet. **2.** To be extremely angry; rant and rage. **3.** To move or rush tumultuously, violently, or angrily: *stormed into the room.* —*tr.* To assault, capture, or captivate by storm. See Synonyms at **attack. *—idiom.* take by storm.** To captivate completely: *a new play that took New York City by storm.* [Middle English, from Old English.]

storm·bound (stôrm′bound′) *adj.* Delayed, confined, or cut off from communication by a storm.

storm cellar *n.* See **cyclone cellar.**

storm center *n.* **1.** The central area of a storm, especially the point of lowest barometric pressure within a storm. **2.** A center of trouble, disturbance, or argument.

storm door *n.* An outer or additional door added for protection against inclement weather.

storm petrel *n.* Any of various small sea birds of the family Hydrobatidae, especially *Hydrobates pelagicus,* of the North Atlantic and the Mediterranean, having sooty plumage and a white rump. Also called *stormy petrel.*

storm trooper *n.* **1.a.** A member of the Nazi militia noted for brutality and violence. **b.** One who resembles or behaves like a member of the Nazi militia. **2.** A member of a force of shock troops.

storm window *n.* A secondary window attached over the usual window to protect against the wind and cold.

storm·y (stôr′mē) *adj.* **-i·er, -i·est. 1.** Subject to, characterized by, or affected by storms; tempestuous. **2.** Characterized by violent emotions, passions, speech, or actions: *a stormy argument.* **—storm′i·ly** *adv.* **—storm′i·ness** *n.*

stormy petrel *n.* **1.** See **storm petrel. 2.** One who brings discord or appears at the onset of trouble; a rebel.

sto·ry[1] (stôr′ē, stōr′ē) *n., pl.* **-ries. 1.** An account or recital of an event or a series of events, either true or fictitious. **2.** A usually fictional prose or verse narrative intended to interest or amuse the hearer or reader; a tale. **3.** A short story. **4.** An incident, experience, or subject that furnishes or would be interesting material for a narrative: *"He was colorful, he was charismatic, he was controversial, he was a good story"* (Terry Ann Knopf). **5.** The plot of a narrative or dramatic work. **6.** A report, a statement, or an allegation of facts. **7.a.** A news article or broadcast. **b.** The event, situation, or other material for such an article or broadcast. **8.** An anecdote. **9.** A lie. **10.** Romantic legend or tradition. **—story** *tr.v.* **-ried, -ry·ing, -ries. 1.** To decorate with scenes representing historical or legendary events. **2.** *Archaic.* To tell as a story. [Middle English *storie,* from Old French *estorie, estoire,* from Latin *historia.* See HISTORY.]

sto·ry[2] (stôr′ē, stōr′ē) *n., pl.* **-ries. 1.** A complete horizontal division of a building, constituting the area between two adjacent levels. **2.** The set of rooms on the same level of a building. [Middle English *storie, story,* from Medieval Latin *historia,* picture, story (probably from painted windows or sculpture on the front of buildings), from Latin, history. See HISTORY.]

Sto·ry (stôr′ē, stōr′ē), **Joseph.** 1779–1845. American jurist who served as an associate justice of the U.S. Supreme Court (1811–1845).

sto·ry·board (stôr′ē-bôrd′, stōr′ē-bōrd′) *n.* A hanging panel of rough sketches depicting the plot, action, and characters in the sequential scenes of a film, an animated cartoon, a television show, or a filmed advertisement that is being proposed or made. **—sto′ry·board′** *v.*

sto·ry·book (stôr′ē-bo͝ok′, stōr′-) *n.* A book containing a collection of stories, usually for children. **—storybook** *adj.* Occurring in or resembling the style or content of a storybook: *storybook characters; a storybook romance.*

story line *n.* The plot of a story or dramatic work.

sto·ry·tell·er (stôr′ē-tĕl′ər, stōr′-) *n.* **1.a.** One who tells or writes stories. **b.** One who relates anecdotes. **2.** *Informal.* One who tells lies. **—sto′ry·tell′ing** *n.*

sto·ry·writ·er (stôr′ē-rī′tər, stōr′-) *n.* **1.** One who writes stories. **2.** One who writes news stories, as for the electronic or print media.

stoss (stŏs, stôs, shtōs) *adj.* Facing the direction from which a glacier moves. Used of a rock or slope in its path. [From German *Stoss,* push, blow, from *stossen,* to push, from Middle High German *stōzen,* from Old High German *stōzan.*]

sto·tin·ka (stō-tĭng′kə) *n., pl.* **-ki** (-kē). See table at **currency.** [Bulgarian, from *sto,* hundred, from Old Church Slavonic *sŭto.* See **dekm̥** in Appendix.]

Stough·ton (stōt′n). A town of eastern Massachusetts northwest of Brockton. It is a manufacturing center. Population, 26,710.

stound (stound) *n. Archaic.* A short time; a while. [Middle English, from Old English *stund.* See **stā-** in Appendix.]

stoup also **stoop** (sto͞op) *n.* **1.** *Ecclesiastical.* A basin or font for holy water at the entrance of a church. **2.** A drinking vessel, such as a cup or tankard. **3.** *Scots.* A bucket or pail. [Middle English *stoup,* bucket, jar, from Old Norse *staup,* cup.]

Stour (stour, sto͝or, stōr). A river, about 64 km (40 mi) long, of southeast England emptying into the North Sea in two channels enclosing the Isle of Thanet.

stout (stout) *adj.* **stout·er, stout·est. 1.** Having or marked by boldness, bravery, or determination; firm and resolute. **2.** Strong in body; sturdy. **3.** Strong in structure or substance; solid or substantial. See Synonyms at **strong. 4.** Bulky in figure; thickset or corpulent. See Synonyms at **fat. 5.** Powerful; forceful. **6.** Stubborn or uncompromising: *put up stout resistance to the proposal.* **—stout** *n.* **1.a.** A thickset or corpulent person. **b.** A garment size for a large or heavy figure. **2.** A strong, very dark beer or ale. [Middle English, from Old French *estout,* of Germanic origin. See **stel-** in Appendix.] **—stout′ish** *adj.* **—stout′ly** *adv.* **—stout′ness** *n.*

stout·en (stout′n) *tr. & intr.v.* **-ened, -en·ing, -ens.** To make or become stout or stouter.

stout·heart·ed (stout′här′tĭd) *adj.* Brave; courageous. **—stout′heart′ed·ly** *adv.* **—stout′heart′ed·ness** *n.*

stove[1] (stōv) *n.* **1.** An apparatus in which electricity or a fuel is used to furnish heat, as for cooking or warmth. **2.** A device that produces heat for specialized, especially industrial, purposes. **3.** A kiln. **4.** *Chiefly British.* A hothouse. [Middle English, heated room, probably from Middle Low German or Middle Dutch, both probably from Vulgar Latin *$ext\bar{u}fa$, from *$ext\bar{u}f\bar{a}re$, to heat with steam. See STEW[1].]

WORD HISTORY: A stove to us is something we expect to find in a room, but at one time a stove was a room, specifically, a room for taking a hot-air or steam bath (first recorded in 1456). Around 1545 the word is recorded with reference to another room, such as a bedroom, heated with a furnace. The devices used to heat these rooms came to be called *stoves* as well, a use first found sometime between 1550 and 1625. Of course, heating devices that we would call *stoves* had long been in existence, going back to Roman times. However, the stove as the chief cooking device, taking the place of the fireplace, dates only to around the mid-19th century with the widespread use of wood-burning or coal-burning cooking stoves.

stove² (stōv) *v.* A past tense and a past participle of **stave.**

stove·pipe (stōv′pīp′) *n.* **1.** A pipe, usually of thin sheet iron, used to conduct smoke or fumes from a stove into a chimney flue. **2.** A man's tall silk hat.

sto·ver (stō′vər) *n.* The dried stalks and leaves of a cereal crop, used as fodder after the grain has been harvested. [Middle English, provisions, from Norman French *estovers,* from Old French *estovier,* to be necessary, from Latin *est opus,* it is necessary : *est,* third person sing. present tense of *esse,* to be; see ESSENCE + *opus,* need, work; see OPUS.]

stove·top (stōv′tŏp′) *n.* The top surface of a stove, especially when used for cooking. **—stovetop** *adj.* Used or prepared on the top of a cooking stove: *a stovetop casserole; stovetop cooking.*

stow (stō) *tr.v.* **stowed, stow·ing, stows. 1. a.** To place or arrange, especially in a neat, compact way: *stowed his gear in the footlocker.* **b.** To fill (a place or container) by packing tightly. **2.** To store for future use: *stowed carrots and potatoes in the root cellar.* **3.** *Slang.* To refrain from; stop. **4.** To provide lodging for; quarter. ***—phrasal verb.*** **stow away. 1.** To hide oneself aboard a conveyance in order to obtain free transportation. **2.** *Informal.* To consume (food or drink) greedily. [Middle English *stowen,* from *stowe,* place, from Old English *stōw.* See **stā-** in Appendix.]

Stow (stō). A city of northeast Ohio, a chiefly residential suburb of Akron. Population, 25,303.

stow·age (stō′ĭj) *n.* **1. a.** The act, manner, or process of stowing. **b.** The state of being stored. **2. a.** Space or room for storage. **b.** A place or container for storage. **3.** Goods in storage or to be stowed. **4.** A charge for storing goods.

stow·a·way (stō′ə-wā′) *n.* A person who hides aboard a ship or other conveyance in order to obtain free passage.

Stowe (stō), **Harriet (Elizabeth) Beecher.** 1811–1896. American writer whose antislavery novel *Uncle Tom's Cabin* (1852) had great political influence and advanced the cause of abolition.

STP *abbr.* Standard temperature and pressure.

STR *abbr.* Synchronous transmitter receiver.

str. *abbr.* **1.** Steamer. **2.** Or **Str.** Strait. **3.** *Music.* Stringed. **4.** Strophe.

stra·bis·mus (strə-bĭz′məs) *n.* A visual defect in which one eye cannot focus with the other on an objective because of imbalance of the eye muscles. Also called *squint.* [New Latin, from Greek *strabismos,* condition of squinting, from *strabizein,* to squint, from *strabos,* squinting. See **streb(h)-** in Appendix.] **—stra·bis′mal** (-məl), **stra·bis′mic** (-mĭk) *adj.*

Stra·bo (strā′bō′). 63? B.C.–A.D. 24? Greek geographer and historian whose great work, *Geography,* is the only extant text that describes the people and countries known to the Greeks and Romans during the reign of Augustus.

stra·bot·o·my (strə-bŏt′ə-mē) *n., pl.* **-mies.** The surgical cutting of a muscle or tendon of the eye to correct strabismus. [Greek *strabos,* squinting; see **streb(h)-** in Appendix + –TOMY.]

Stra·chey (strā′kē), **(Giles) Lytton.** 1880–1932. British historian and biographer noted for his urbane, witty, and critical biographical works, including *Eminent Victorians* (1918).

strad·dle (străd′l) *v.* **-dled, -dling, -dles.** *—tr.* **1. a.** To stand or sit with a leg on each side of; bestride: *straddle a horse.* **b.** To be on both sides of; extend over or across: *a car straddling the centerline.* **2.** To appear to favor both sides of (an issue). **3.** To fire shots behind and in front of (a target) in order to determine the range. *—intr.* **1.** To walk, stand, or sit with the legs wide apart, especially to sit astride. **2.** To spread out in a disorderly way; sprawl. **3.** To appear to favor both sides of an issue. **—straddle** *n.* **1.** The act or posture of sitting astride. **2.** An equivocal or a noncommittal position. **3.** The option to buy or sell a specific asset, such as a block of stock, at a predetermined price before a certain date. ***—idiom.*** **straddle the fence.** *Informal.* To be undecided or uncommitted. [Akin to STRIDE.] **—strad′dler** *n.*

Stra·di·va·ri (străd′ə-vâr′ē, -vär′ē), **Antonio.** Often called **Antonius Stradivarius.** 1644?–1737. Italian violinmaker who developed the proportions of the modern violin and created instruments of unsurpassed beauty and tone. His sons **Francesco** (1671–1743) and **Omobono** (1679–1742) carried on the family tradition of fine artistry.

strafe (strāf) *tr.v.* **strafed, straf·ing, strafes.** To attack (ground troops, for example) with a machine gun or cannon from a low-flying aircraft. **—strafe** *n.* An attack of machine-gun or cannon fire from a low-flying aircraft. [From German *(Gott) strafe (England),* (God) punish (England), a common World War I slogan, from *strafen,* to punish, from Middle High German *strāfen,* to contest, admonish.] **—straf′er** *n.*

Straf·ford (străf′ərd), First Earl of. Title of Thomas Wentworth. 1593–1641. English politician who was the principal minister to Charles I. He was convicted of treason and was executed.

strag·gle (străg′əl) *intr.v.* **-gled, -gling, -gles. 1.** To stray or fall behind. **2.** To proceed or spread out in a scattered or irregular group. **—straggle** *n.* A scattered or disorderly group, as of people or things. [Middle English *straglen,* to wander.] **—strag′gler** *n.*

strag·gly (străg′lē) *adj.* **-gli·er, -gli·est.** Growing or spread out in a disorderly or aimless way: *straggly ivy.*

straight (strāt) *adj.* **straight·er, straight·est. 1.** Extending continuously in the same direction without curving: *a straight line.* **2.** Having no waves or bends: *straight hair.* **3.** Erect; upright: *has a straight, strong back.* **4.** Perfectly horizontal or vertical; level or even: *The mirror isn't straight.* **5. a.** Direct and candid: *a straight answer.* **b.** Following a direct or correct method or approach; systematic: *straight reasoning.* **c.** Coming from a reliable source; factual: *a straight tip; straight information.* **6. a.** Showing or marked by honesty or fair-mindedness: *straight business dealings.* **b.** Right; correct: *made sure the facts were straight in the report.* **7.** Neatly arranged; orderly: *The room is straight again.* **8. a.** Uninterrupted; consecutive: *sick for five straight days; their fourth straight victory.* **b.** Having the parts or details in correct sequence. **c.** *Games.* Made up of five cards constituting a sequence in poker. **9.** Characterized by undeviating support, as of a principle or a political party: *always votes a straight party line; a straight Democrat.* **10. a.** Not deviating from what is considered socially normal, usual, or acceptable; conventional. **b.** Conventional to an extreme degree. **c.** Heterosexual. **11.** *Slang.* Not being under the influence of alcohol or drugs. **12. a.** Not deviating from the normal or strict form: *straight Freudian analysis.* **b.** Not altered, embellished, or modified: *does straight comedy.* **13. a.** Concerned with serious or important matters: *a straight drama without comedy or music.* **b.** Of or relating to a straight man. **14.** Not mixed with anything else; undiluted: *straight bourbon.* **15.** Sold without discount regardless of the amount purchased. **—straight** *adv.* **1.** In a straight line; directly. **2.** In an erect posture; upright. **3.** Without detour or delay: *went straight home.* **4.** Without circumlocution; candidly: *I'll say it to you straight: you're wrong.* **5.** In a neat and orderly condition: *put the living room straight.* **6.** In an honest, law-abiding, or virtuous manner: *lives straight.* **7.** Without stopping; continuously: *walked six hours straight.* **8.** Without embellishment or modification: *tell the joke straight; play the role straight.* **9.** Without ice, water, or a mixer: *drinks her whiskey straight.* **—straight** *n.* **1. a.** The straight part, as of a road: *"The car darted forward on to the straight"* (Kingsley Amis). **b.** *Sports & Games.* The straight part of a racecourse between the winning post and the last turn. **2.** A straight line. **3.** A straight form or position. **4.** *Games.* A poker hand containing five cards of various suits in numerical sequence, ranked above three of a kind and below a flush. **5. a.** A conventional person, especially one considered a member of established society. **b.** A heterosexual person. **6.** *Slang.* A person who does not use illegal drugs. ***—idiom.*** **straight up.** Served without ice: *a martini straight up.* [Middle English, from past participle of *strecchen,* to stretch. See STRETCH.] **—straight′ly** *adv.* **—straight′ness** *n.*

straight-a·head (strāt′ə-hĕd′) *adj.* Conforming to a conventional style or mode; standard: *straight-ahead rock music; a straight-ahead whodunit.*

straight and narrow *n.* The way of proper conduct and moral integrity. Often used with *the*: *kept strictly to the straight and narrow.* [Probably alteration of *"Strait is the gate, and narrow is the way, which leadeth unto life"* (Matthew 7:14).]

straight angle *n.* *Mathematics.* An angle of 180°.

straight-arm (strāt′ärm′) *tr.v.* **-armed, -arm·ing, -arms. 1.** *Football.* To ward off (a tackler) by holding the arm out straight with the elbow locked and the palm of the hand placed against the opponent's body; stiff-arm. **2.** To force or ward off by or as if by holding the arm out straight. **—straight-arm** *n.* *Football.* The act or an instance of straight-arming.

straight arrow *n.* *Informal.* **1.** A morally upright person. **2.** A person regarded as being extremely conventional. [From the phrase *straight as an arrow.*] **—straight′ar′row** (strāt′ăr′ō) *adj.*

straight·a·way (strāt′ə-wā′) *adj.* **1.** Extending in a straight line or course without a curve or turn. **2.** Unhesitating; immediate: *a straightaway denial.* **—straightaway** *n.* A straight course, stretch, or track. **—straightaway** (strāt′ə-wā′) *adv.* At once; immediately.

straight-backed (strāt′băkt′) *adj.* Having a straight back: *a slim, straight-backed dancer; a straight-backed wooden chair.*

straight chain *n.* An organic molecular structure in the form of an unbranched open chain.

straight·edge (strāt′ĕj′) *n.* A rigid flat rectangular bar, as of wood or metal, with a straight edge for testing or drawing straight lines. **—straight′edged′** *adj.*

straight·en (strāt′n) *tr. & intr.v.* **-ened, -en·ing, -ens.** To make or become straight or straighter. **—straight′en·er** *n.*

straight face *n.* A face that betrays no sign of emotion. **—straight′-faced′** (strāt′fāst′) *adj.* **—straight′-faced′ly** (-fāst′lē, -fā′sĭd-lē) *adv.*

straight flush *n.* *Games.* A hand in which all five cards are

stovepipe

Harriet Beecher Stowe
Photographed c. 1880

ă pat	oi boy
ā pay	ou out
âr care	ŏŏ took
ä father	ōō boot
ĕ pet	ŭ cut
ē be	ûr urge
ĭ pit	th thin
ī pie	*th* this
îr pier	hw which
ŏ pot	zh vision
ō toe	ə about, item
ô paw	♦ regionalism

Stress marks: ′ (primary); ′ (secondary), as in **dictionary** (dĭk′shə-nĕr′ē)

straight razor

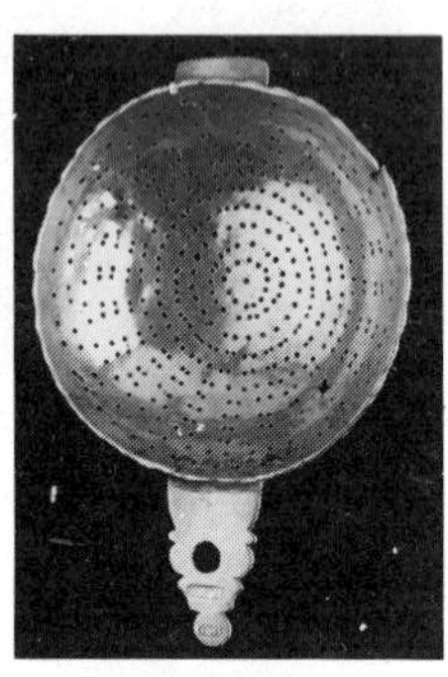
strainer
c. 1740 silver punch strainer, 3⅛″ diameter, by Peter David (1707–1755)

of the same suit and in numerical sequence, ranked above four of a kind in poker.

straight·for·ward (strāt-fôr′wərd) *adj.* **1.** Proceeding in a straight course; direct. **2.a.** Not circuitous or evasive; honest and frank. See Synonyms at **frank**[1]. **b.** Free from ambiguity or pretense; plain and open. **—straightforward** *adv.* In a direct course or an honest manner. **—straight·for′ward·ly** *adv.* **—straight·for′ward·ness** *n.* **—straight·for′wards** *adv.*

straight-from-the-shoul·der (strāt′frəm-*thə*-shōl′dər) *adj. Informal.* Frank and forthright: *straight-from-the-shoulder reporting.*

straight·jack·et (strāt′jăk′ĭt) *n. & v.* Variant of **straitjacket.**

straight-laced (strāt′lāst′) *adj.* Variant of **strait-laced.**

straight-line (strāt′līn′) *adj.* **1.** Lying in a straight line. **2.** Relating to a device whose linkage produces or copies motion in straight lines. **3.** *Accounting.* Of or being a mode of amortization by equal payments at stated intervals over a given period of time.

straight man *n.* The partner in a comedy team who feeds lines to the other comedian, who then makes witty replies.

straight off *adv.* At once; immediately: *discovered straight off that the furnace wasn't working.*

straight-out (strāt′out′) *adj.* **1.** Straightforward; blunt: *gave them a straight-out "no."* **2.** Complete; unmitigated: *a straight-out error.*

straight poker *n. Games.* Poker in which each player is dealt five cards face down, bets are made, and the showdown takes place without any new cards being drawn.

straight razor *n.* A razor consisting of a blade hinged to a handle into which it slips when not in use.

straight shooter *n. Informal.* One who is honest and forthright. **—straight′-shoot′ing** (strāt′sho͞o′tĭng) *adj.*

straight ticket *n.* A ballot cast for all the candidates of one party.

straight·way (strāt′wā′, -wā′) *adv.* **1.** In a direct course: *plunged straightway to the rocks below.* **2.** Without delay; at once: *Straightway a storm began to brew.*

strain[1] (strān) *v.* **strained, strain·ing, strains.** *—tr.* **1.** To pull, draw, or stretch tight: *strained the sheets over the bed.* **2.** To exert or tax to the utmost: *straining our ears to hear.* **3.** To injure or impair by overuse or overexertion; wrench: *strain a muscle.* **4.** To stretch or force beyond the proper or legitimate limit: *strain a point.* **5.** To alter (the relations between the parts of a structure or shape) by applying an external force; deform. **6.a.** To pass (gravy, for example) through a filtering agent such as a strainer. **b.** To draw off or remove by filtration: *strained the pulp from the juice.* **7.** To embrace or clasp tightly; hug. *—intr.* **1.** To make violent or steady efforts; strive hard: *straining to reach the finish line.* **2.** To be or become wrenched or twisted. **3.** To be subjected to great stress. **4.** To pull forcibly or violently: *The dog strained at its leash.* **5.** To stretch or exert one's muscles or nerves to the utmost. **6.** To filter, trickle, or ooze. **7.** To be extremely hesitant; balk: *a mule that strained at the lead.* **—strain** *n.* **1.a.** The act of straining. **b.** The state of being strained. **2.a.** Extreme or laborious effort, exertion, or work. **b.** A great or excessive pressure, demand, or stress on one's body, mind, or resources: *the strain of managing both a family and a career.* **3.** A wrench, twist, or other physical injury resulting from excessive tension, effort, or use. **4.** *Physics.* A deformation produced by stress. **5.** An exceptional degree or pitch: *a strain of zealous idealism.* [Middle English *streinen,* from Old French *estreindre, estrein-,* to bind tightly, from Latin *stringere.* See **streig-** in Appendix.]

strain[2] (strān) *n.* **1.** The collective descendants of a common ancestor; a race, stock, line, or breed. **2.** Any of the various lines of ancestry united in an individual or a family; ancestry or lineage. **3.** *Biology.* A group of organisms of the same species, having distinctive characteristics but not usually considered a separate breed or variety: *a superior strain of wheat; a smooth strain of bacteria.* **4.** An artificial variety of a domestic animal or cultivated plant. **5.** A kind or sort: *imaginings of a morbid strain.* **6.a.** An inborn or inherited tendency or character. **b.** A streak; a trace. See Synonyms at **streak. 7.a.** The tone, tenor, or substance of a verbal utterance or of a particular action or behavior: *spoke in a passionate strain.* **b.** A prevailing quality, as of attitude or behavior. **8.** Often **strains.** *Music.* A passage of expression; a tune or an air: *melodic strains of the violin.* **9.a.** A passage of poetic and especially lyrical expression. **b.** An outburst or a flow of eloquent or impassioned language. [Middle English *strene,* from Old English *strēon,* something gained, offspring. See **ster-**[2] in Appendix.]

strained (strānd) *adj.* **1.** Having been passed through a strainer: *a bowl of strained peaches.* **2.** Done with or marked by excessive effort; forced: *strained humor.* **3.** Extended beyond proper limits: *a strained meaning.* **4.** Antagonized to the verge of open conflict: *strained relations.*

strain·er (strā′nər) *n.* **1.** One that strains, as a device used to separate liquids from solids. **2.** An apparatus for tightening, stretching, or strengthening.

strain gauge *n.* An extensometer.

strain·ing beam (strā′nĭng) *n. Architecture.* A horizontal tie beam connecting two queen posts in a roof truss. Also called *straining piece.*

strain·om·e·ter (strā-nŏm′ĭ-tər) *n.* An extensometer.

strait (strāt) *n. Abbr.* **str., Str., st., St. 1.** Also **straits.** A narrow channel joining two larger bodies of water. **2.** A position of difficulty, perplexity, distress, or need. Often used in the plural: *in desperate straits.* **—strait** *adj.* **1.a.** Difficult; stressful. **b.** Having or marked by limited funds or resources. **2.** *Archaic.* **a.** Narrow. **b.** Affording little space or room; confined. **c.** Fitting tightly. **3.** *Archaic.* Strict, rigid, or righteous. [Middle English *streit,* narrow, a strait, from Old French *estreit,* tight, narrow, from Latin *strictus,* past participle of *stringere,* to draw tight. See **streig-** in Appendix.] **—strait′ly** *adv.* **—strait′ness** *n.*

strait·en (strāt′n) *tr.v.* **-ened, -en·ing, -ens. 1.a.** To make narrow. **b.** To enclose in a limited area; confine. **2.** To put or bring into difficulties or distress, especially financial hardship. **3.** *Archaic.* To restrict in latitude or scope.

strait·jack·et also **straight·jack·et** (strāt′jăk′ĭt) *—n.* **1.** A long-sleeved jacketlike garment used to bind the arms tightly against the body as a means of restraining a violent patient or prisoner. **2.** Something that restricts, hinders, or confines: *the straitjacket of bureaucratic paperwork.* *—tr.v.* **-et·ed, -et·ing, -ets.** To restrain, restrict, or hinder by or as if by confining in a straitjacket.

strait-laced also **straight-laced** (strāt′lāst′) *adj.* **1.** Excessively strict in behavior, morality, or opinions. **2.** Having or wearing a tightly laced garment. **—strait′-lac′ed·ly** (-lā′sĭd-lē, -lāst′lē) *adv.* **—strait′-lac′ed·ness** *n.*

Straits Settlements (strāts). A former British crown colony comprising parts of the southern and western Malay Peninsula and adjacent islands, including Singapore. Formed in 1826, it was under Indian control until 1867, when the British assumed direct authority. Singapore became a separate colony in 1946; the remaining portions of the Straits Settlements were granted to Australia and the Federation of Malaya (later Malaysia) in the 1950's.

strake (strāk) *n. Nautical.* A single continuous line of planking or metal plating extending on a vessel's hull from stem to stern. [Middle English, probably from Old English **straca.*]

Stral·sund (sträl′so͝ont′, shträl′zo͝ont′). A city of northeast Germany on an inlet of the Baltic Sea opposite Rügen Island. Chartered in 1234, it was a leading member of the Hanseatic League and changed hands many times before it passed to Prussia in 1815. Population, 75,335.

stra·mo·ni·um (strə-mō′nē-əm) *n.* **1.** See **jimsonweed. 2.** The dried poisonous leaves of the jimsonweed, used in the treatment of asthma. [New Latin.]

strand[1] (strănd) *n.* The land bordering a body of water; a beach. **—strand** *v.* **strand·ed, strand·ing, strands.** *—tr.* **1.** To drive or run ashore or aground. **2.** To bring into or leave in a difficult or helpless position: *The convoy was stranded in the desert.* **3.** *Baseball.* To leave (a base runner) on base at the end of an inning. *—intr.* **1.** To be driven or run ashore or aground. **2.** To be brought into or left in a difficult or helpless position. [Middle English, from Old English.]

strand[2] (strănd) *n.* **1.** A complex of fibers or filaments that have been twisted together to form a cable, rope, thread, or yarn. **2.a.** A single filament, such as a fiber or thread, of a woven or braided material. **b.** A wisp or tress of hair. **3.** Something, such as a string of pearls, that is plaited or twisted into a ropelike length. **4.** One of the elements woven together to make an intricate whole, such as the plot of a novel. **—strand** *tr.v.* **strand·ed, strand·ing, strands. 1.** To make or form (a rope, for example) by twisting strands together. **2.** To break a strand of (a rope, for example). [Middle English *strond.*]

Strand (strănd). A thoroughfare in west-central London, England, running parallel to the northern bank of the Thames River and eastward from Trafalgar Square in the West End to the City of London. Among its well-known fixtures is the Savoy Hotel.

strand line also **strand·line** (strănd′līn′) *n.* A shoreline, especially one marking an earlier and higher water level.

strange (strānj) *adj.* **strang·er, strang·est. 1.** Not previously known; unfamiliar. **2.a.** Out of the ordinary; unusual or striking. **b.** Differing from the normal. **3.** Not of one's own or a particular locality, environment, or kind; exotic. **4.a.** Reserved in manner; distant. **b.** Not comfortable or at ease; constrained. **5.** Not accustomed or conditioned: *She was strange to her new duties.* **6.** *Archaic.* Of, relating to, or characteristic of another place or part of the world; foreign. **—strange** *adv.* In a strange manner. [Middle English, from Old French *estrange,* extraordinary, foreign, from Latin *extrāneus,* adventitious, foreign, from *extrā,* outside, from feminine ablative of *exter,* outward. See **eghs** in Appendix.] **—strange′ly** *adv.*

SYNONYMS: *strange, peculiar, odd, queer, quaint, outlandish, singular, eccentric, curious.* These adjectives describe what deviates from the usual or customary. *Strange* refers especially to what is unfamiliar, unknown, or inexplicable: *"I do hate to be chucked in the dark aboard a strange ship. I wonder where they keep their fresh water"* (Joseph Conrad). *Peculiar* particularly describes what is distinct from all others: *The kitchen was redolent with the peculiar aromatic odor of cloves.* Something that is *odd* fails to accord with what is ordinary, usual, or expected, while something *queer* deviates markedly from the norm; both terms can suggest strangeness or peculiarity: *I find it odd that his name is never mentioned. "Now, my suspicion is that the universe is not only queerer than we suppose, but queerer than we can suppose"*

(J.B.S. Haldane). *Quaint* refers to pleasing or old-fashioned peculiarity: *"the quaint streets of New Orleans, that most foreign of American cities"* (Winston Churchill). *Outlandish* suggests alien or bizarre strangeness: *"They were dressed in a quaint, outlandish fashion"* (Washington Irving). *Singular* describes what is unique or unparalleled; the term often suggests an unusual or peculiar quality that arouses curiosity or wonder: *Such poise is singular in one so young. Eccentric* refers particularly to what departs strikingly from the recognized or conventional: *Many consider Berlioz's compositions to be innovative but eccentric. Curious* suggests strangeness or novelty that excites interest: *Americans living abroad often acquire a curious hybrid accent.* See also Synonyms at **foreign.**

---

strange·ness (strānj′nĭs) *n.* **1.** The quality or condition of being strange. **2.** *Physics.* A quantum number equal to hypercharge minus baryon number, indicating the possible transformations of an elementary particle upon strong interaction with another elementary particle.

strange particle *n. Physics.* An unstable elementary particle created in high-energy particle collisions having a short life and a strangeness quantum number other than zero.

strange quark *n. Abbr.* **s** *Physics.* A quark with a charge of −⅓, a mass about 988 times that of the electron, and a strangeness of −1. See table at **subatomic particle.**

strang·er (strān′jər) *n.* **1.** One who is neither a friend nor an acquaintance. **2.** A foreigner, a newcomer, or an outsider. **3.** One who is unaccustomed to or unacquainted with something specified; a novice: *a stranger to our language; no stranger to hardship.* **4.** A visitor or guest. **5.** *Law.* One that is neither privy nor party to a title, an act, or a contract. [Middle English, from Old French *estrangier,* from *estrange,* strange. See STRANGE.]

stran·gle (străng′gəl) *v.* **-gled, -gling, -gles.** —*tr.* **1.a.** To kill by squeezing the throat so as to choke or suffocate; throttle. **b.** To cut off the oxygen supply of; smother. **2.** To suppress, repress, or stifle: *strangle a scream.* **3.** To inhibit the growth or action of; restrict: *"That artist is strangled who is forced to deal with human beings solely in social terms"* (James Baldwin). —*intr.* **1.** To become strangled. **2.** To die from suffocation or strangulation; choke. [Middle English *stranglen,* from Old French *estrangler,* from Latin *strangulāre,* from Greek *strangalan,* from *strangalē,* halter.] **—stran′gler** *n.*

stran·gle·hold (străng′gəl-hōld′) *n.* **1.** *Sports.* An illegal wrestling hold used to choke an opponent. **2.** A force, an influence, or an action that restricts or suppresses freedom or progress. In this sense, also called *throttlehold.*

strangler fig *n.* An evergreen tree *(Ficus aurea)* of southern Florida and the West Indies, having elliptic leaves and yellow fruit. [From the fact that it strangles its host.]

stran·gles (străng′gəlz) *pl.n. (used with a sing. verb).* An infectious disease of horses and related animals, caused by the bacterium *Streptococcus equi* and characterized by inflammation of the nasal mucous membrane and abscesses under the jaw and around the throat that cause a strangling or choking sensation. [From Middle English *strangle,* strangulation, from *stranglen,* to strangle. See STRANGLE.]

stran·gu·late (străng′gyə-lāt′) *v.* **-lat·ed, -lat·ing, -lates.** —*tr.* **1.** To strangle. **2.** *Pathology.* To compress, constrict, or obstruct (an organ, a duct, or other body part) so as to cut off the flow of blood or other fluid: *strangulate an intestinal hernia.* —*intr.* To be or become strangled, compressed, constricted, or obstructed. [Latin *strangulāre, strangulāt-.* See STRANGLE.]

stran·gu·la·tion (străng′gyə-lā′shən) *n.* **1.a.** The act of strangling or strangulating. **b.** The state of being strangled or strangulated. **2.** *Pathology.* Constriction of a body part so as to cut off the flow of blood or another fluid: *strangulation of the intestine.*

stran·gu·ry (străng′gyə-rē) *n.* Slow, painful urination, caused by muscular spasms of the urethra and bladder. [Middle English, from Latin *strangūria,* from Greek *strangouria* : *stranx, strang-,* drop, trickle + *-ouria,* -uria.]

strap (străp) *n.* **1.a.** A long, narrow strip of pliant material such as leather. **b.** Such a strip equipped with a buckle or similar fastener for binding or securing objects. **2.** A thin, flat metal or plastic band used for fastening or clamping objects together or into position. **3.** A narrow band formed into a loop for grasping with the hand. **4.** A razor strop. **5.** A strip of leather used in flogging. **—strap** *tr.v.* **strapped, strap·ping, straps. 1.** To fasten or secure with a strap. **2.** To beat with a strap. **3.** To sharpen (a razor, for example). [Alteration of STROP.]

strap·hang (străp′hăng′) *intr.v.* **-hung** (-hŭng′), **-hang·ing, -hangs.** To travel as a straphanger, as on a subway or bus.

strap·hang·er (străp′hăng′ər) *n.* **1.** One who grips a hanging strap or similar device for support while riding as a passenger on a bus or subway. **2.** One who uses public transportation.

strap·hung (străp′hŭng′) *v.* Past tense and past participle of **straphang.**

strap·less (străp′lĭs) *adj.* Having no strap or straps, as a dress or an undergarment. **—strapless** *n.* A garment having no strap or straps.

strap·pa·do (stră-pā′dō, -pä′-) *n., pl.* **-does. 1.** A form of torture in which the victim is lifted off the ground by a rope attached to the wrists, which have been tied behind the back, and then is dropped partway to the ground with a jerk. **2.** The apparatus employed in this method of torture. [Alteration of French *strapade,* from Old French, from Old Italian *strappata,* from *strappare,* to stretch tight, of Germanic origin.]

strapped (străpt) *adj. Informal.* In financial need: *We are strapped for cash right now.*

strap·per (străp′ər) *n.* A powerfully built, robust person.

strap·ping (străp′ĭng) *adj.* Having a sturdy, muscular physique; robust. **—strapping** *n.* **1.** Straps considered as a group. **2.** Material for making straps.

Stras·bourg (sträs′bo͝org′, sträz′-, sträz-bo͝or′). A city of northeast France near the German border east of Nancy. Strategically important since ancient times, it became a free imperial city in 1262, was occupied by France in 1681, and passed to Germany in 1871. The city was recovered by France in 1919. Population, 248,712.

strass (străs) *n.* See **paste**[1] (sense 4). [German *Strass* or French *stras,* both perhaps after Josef *Strasser,* 18th-century German jeweler.]

stra·ta (strā′tə, străt′ə) *n.* A plural of **stratum.**

strat·a·gem (străt′ə-jəm) *n.* **1.** A military maneuver designed to deceive or surprise an enemy. **2.** A clever, often underhanded scheme for achieving an objective. See Synonyms at **artifice.** [Middle English, from Old French *stratageme,* from Old Italian *stratagemma,* from Latin *stratēgēma,* from Greek, from *stratēgein,* to be a general, from *stratēgos,* general : *stratos,* army; see **ster-**[2] in Appendix + *agein,* to lead; see **ag-** in Appendix.]

stra·te·gic (strə-tē′jĭk) also **stra·te·gi·cal** (-jĭ-kəl) *adj.* **1.** Of or relating to strategy. **2.a.** Important or essential in relation to a plan of action: *a strategic withdrawal.* **b.** Essential to the effective conduct of war: *strategic materials.* **c.** Highly important to an intended objective: *The committee discussed strategic marketing factors.* **3.** Intended to destroy the military potential of an enemy: *strategic bombing.* **—stra·te′gi·cal·ly** *adv.*

stra·te·gics (strə-tē′jĭks) *n. (used with a sing. verb).* The art of strategy.

strat·e·gist (străt′ə-jĭst) *n.* One who is skilled in strategy.

strat·e·gize (străt′ə-jīz′) *v.* **-gized, -giz·ing, -giz·es.** —*tr.* To plan a strategy for (a business or financial venture, for example). —*intr.* To determine strategies; plan: *"a lot to think about and strategize about and anticipate"* (New Yorker).

strat·e·gy (străt′ə-jē) *n., pl.* **-gies. 1.a.** The science and art of using all the forces of a nation to execute approved plans as effectively as possible during peace or war. **b.** The science and art of military command as applied to the overall planning and conduct of large-scale combat operations. **2.** A plan of action resulting from strategy or intended to accomplish a specific goal. See Synonyms at **plan. 3.** The art or skill of using stratagems in endeavors such as politics and business. [French *stratégie,* from Greek *stratēgia,* office of a general, from *stratēgos,* general. See STRATAGEM.]

Strat·ford (străt′fərd). **1.** A city of southeast Ontario, Canada, west-southwest of Toronto. It is an industrial center and the home of the Stratford Shakespearean Festival (founded 1953). Population, 26,262. **2.** A town of southwest Connecticut on Long Island Sound northeast of Bridgeport. Settled in 1639, it is a manufacturing center and site of the annual American Shakespeare Festival (established 1955). Population, 50,541.

Strat·ford-up·on-Av·on (străt′fərd-ə-pŏn-ā′vən, -pôn-) also **Strat·ford-on-Av·on** (-ŏn-, -ôn-). A municipal borough of central England south-southeast of Birmingham. William Shakespeare was born and died in the borough, which has long been a popular tourist center. An annual festival includes performances by the Royal Shakespeare Company. Population, 20,800.

strath (străth) *n. Scots.* A wide, flat river valley. [Scottish Gaelic *srath,* from Old Irish. See **ster-**[2] in Appendix.]

stra·ti (strā′tī, străt′ī) *n.* Plural of **stratus.**

strati– *pref.* Stratum: *stratiform.* [From STRATUM.]

stra·tic·u·late (stră-tĭk′yə-lĭt) *adj. Geology.* Having thin layers. [From STRATUM.] **—stra·tic′u·la′tion** (-lā′shən) *n.*

strat·i·fi·ca·tion (străt′ə-fĭ-kā′shən) *n.* **1.a.** Formation or deposition of layers, as of rock or sediments. **b.** The condition of being stratified. **2.** A layered configuration.

strat·i·fi·ca·tion·al grammar (străt′ə-fĭ-kā′shə-nəl) *n.* A grammar based on the theory that language is made up of a hierarchical series of layers linked by rules.

strat·i·fied charge engine (străt′ə-fīd′) *n.* An internal-combustion engine with a divided ignition cylinder that uses the ignition of rich fuel in a small chamber near the spark plug to improve the combination of a very lean mixture throughout the rest of the cylinder.

strat·i·form (străt′ə-fôrm′) *adj.* Forming a layer or arranged in layers.

strat·i·fy (străt′ə-fī′) *v.* **-fied, -fy·ing, -fies.** —*tr.* **1.** To form, arrange, or deposit in layers. **2.** To preserve (seeds) by placing them between layers of moist sand or similar material. **3.a.** To arrange or separate into castes, classes, or social levels. **b.** To separate into a sequence of graded status levels. —*intr.* **1.** To become layered; form strata. **2.** To develop different levels of caste, class, privilege, or status.

stra·tig·ra·phy (strə-tĭg′rə-fē) *n.* The study of rock strata, especially the distribution, deposition, and age of sedimentary rocks. **—strat′i·graph′ic** (străt′ĭ-grăf′ĭk), **strat′i·graph′i·cal** (-ĭ-kəl) *adj.* **—strat′i·graph′i·cal·ly** *adv.*

ă pat	oi boy
ā pay	ou out
âr care	o͝o took
ä father	o͞o boot
ĕ pet	ŭ cut
ē be	ûr urge
ĭ pit	th thin
ī pie	*th* this
îr pier	hw which
ŏ pot	zh vision
ō toe	ə about, item
ô paw	♦ regionalism

Stress marks: ′ (primary); ′ (secondary), as in **dictionary** (dĭk′shə-nĕr′ē)

exosphere
400 km (250 mi)
ionosphere 50 – 400 km (30 – 250 mi)
thermosphere
80 km (50 mi)
mesosphere
30 km (19 mi)
stratosphere
10 km (6 mi)
troposphere
0 km (0 mi)

stratosphere

stra·toc·ra·cy (strə-tŏk′rə-sē) *n., pl.* **-cies.** Government by the armed forces. [Greek *stratos,* army; see **ster-²** in Appendix + -CRACY.] **—strat′o·crat′ic** (străt′ə-krăt′ĭk) *adj.*

stra·to·cu·mu·lus (strā′tō-kyo͞om′yə-ləs, străt′ō-) *n., pl.* **-li** (-lī′). A low-lying cloud formation occurring in extensive horizontal layers with rounded summits. [STRAT(US) + CUMULUS.]

strat·o·pause (străt′ə-pôz′) *n.* The boundary between the stratosphere and the mesosphere located at an altitude of about 55 kilometers (35 miles) above the earth's surface. [STRATO(SPHERE) + PAUSE.]

strat·o·sphere (străt′ə-sfîr′) *n.* **1.** The region of the atmosphere above the troposphere and below the mesosphere. **2.** An extremely high or the highest point or degree on a ranked scale: *the governmental stratosphere; business expenses in the stratosphere.* [French *stratosphère* : Latin *strātus,* a spreading out; see STRATUS + *-sphère,* sphere (from Old French *espere;* see SPHERE).]

strat·o·spher·ic (străt′ə-sfîr′ĭk, -sfĕr′-) *adj.* **1.** Of, relating to, or characteristic of the stratosphere. **2.** Extremely or unreasonably high: *"money borrowed at today's stratospheric rates of interest"* (New York Times). **—strat′o·spher′i·cal·ly** *adv.*

strat·o·vol·ca·no (străt′ō-vŏl-kā′nō, strā′tō-) *n., pl.* **-nos.** A volcano composed of alternating layers of lava and ash. [STRAT(UM) + VOLCANO.]

stra·tum (strā′təm, străt′əm) *n., pl.* **-ta** (-tə) or **-tums. 1.** A horizontal layer of material, especially one of several parallel layers arranged one on top of another. **2.** *Geology.* A bed or layer of sedimentary rock having approximately the same composition throughout. **3.** A level of society composed of people with similar social, cultural, or economic status. **4.** One of a number of layers, levels, or divisions in an organized system: *a complex poem with many strata of meaning.* [Latin *strātum,* a covering, from neuter past participle of *sternere,* to spread. See STRATUS.] **—stra′tal** (-təl) *adj.*

USAGE NOTE: The standard singular form is *stratum;* the standard plural is *strata* (or sometimes *stratums*) but not *stratas.*

stratum cor·ne·um (kôr′nē-əm) *n., pl.* **strata cornea.** The horny outer layer of the epidermis, consisting mainly of dead or peeling cells. [New Latin : STRATUM + Latin *corneum,* neuter of *corneus,* horny; see CORNEA.]

stra·tus (strā′təs, străt′əs) *n., pl.* **stra·ti** (-tī). A low-altitude cloud formation consisting of a horizontal layer of gray clouds. [From Latin *strātus,* past participle of *sternere,* to stretch, extend. See **ster-²** in Appendix.]

Straus (strous, shtrous), **Oscar.** 1870–1954. Austrian-born French composer noted for his operettas, including *The Chocolate Soldier* (1908).

Johann Strauss the Younger
Photographed in the 1890's

Strauss (strous, shtrous), **Johann.** Known as "the Elder." 1804–1849. Austrian violinist and composer of waltzes and other works, notably *Redetzky March* (1848). His son **Johann** (1825–1899), known as "the Younger," is sometimes called "the Waltz King" and is best remembered for his numerous waltzes, such as "The Blue Danube" (1867).

Strauss (strous), **Levi.** 1829?–1902. American clothing manufacturer who developed heavy denim trousers and founded Levi Strauss and Company (1850).

Strauss (strous, shtrous), **Richard.** 1864–1949. German composer known chiefly for his symphonic poems, such as *Don Quixote* (1897), and his operas, including *Salome* (1905).

Stra·vin·sky (strə-vĭn′skē), **Igor Fyodorovich.** 1882–1971. Russian-born composer of ballets, including *The Rite of Spring* (1913), symphonies, operas, such as *The Rake's Progress* (1951), and other works.

straw (strô) *n.* **1.a.** Stalks of threshed grain, used as bedding and food for animals, for thatching, and for weaving or braiding, as into baskets. **b.** A single stalk of threshed grain. **2.** Something, such as a hat or basket, made of straw. **3.** A slender tube used for sucking up a liquid. **4.a.** Something of minimal value or importance. **b.** Something with too little substance to provide support in a crisis: *Near the end we were grasping at straws.* **—straw** *adj.* **1.** Of, relating to, or made of straw: *a straw mat.* **2.** Containing or used for straw, as a barn or feeding trough. **3.** *Color.* Of the color of straw; yellowish. **4.** Having little or no value or substance; unimportant. **5.** Of, relating to, or constituting a straw man. ***—idiom.*** **straw in the wind.** A slight hint of something to come. [Middle English, from Old English *strēaw.* See **ster-²** in Appendix.] **—straw′y** *adj.*

strawberry

straw·ber·ry (strô′bĕr′ē) *n.* **1.** Any of various low-growing plants of the genus *Fragaria,* having white flowers and an aggregate fruit that consists of a red, fleshy, edible receptacle and numerous seedlike fruitlets. **2.** The aggregate fruit of this plant. [Middle English, from Old English *strēawberige* : *strēaw,* straw; see STRAW + *berige, berie,* berry; see BERRY.]

WORD HISTORY: Izaak Walton's 1655 comment, "We may say of Angling as Dr. Boteler said of Strawberries; Doubtless God could have made a better berry, but doubtless God never did," is perhaps the nicest use of the word *strawberry* in its history. This history goes back much further in English to the Old English period when the word is first recorded. We know that *strawberry* was formed during that period from the Old English ancestors of our words *straw* and *berry.* What is not known is why the word *straw* is the first part of this compound. One possibility is that the small, one-seeded fruits on the surface of a strawberry resemble fragments of straw.

strawberry bass (băs) *n.* See **black crappie.**

strawberry blite (blīt) *n.* A weedy European plant *(Chenopodium capitatum)* having minute petalless flowers and red, berrylike fruit.

strawberry bush *n.* An erect to straggly shrub *(Euonymus americanus)* of the eastern United States having inconspicuous flowers and showy pinkish fruit.

strawberry mark *n.* A raised, shiny, red nevus or birthmark, occurring usually on the face or scalp and resembling a strawberry.

strawberry roan *n.* A horse having reddish hair mixed with white.

strawberry shrub *n.* See **Carolina allspice.**

strawberry tomato *n.* **1.** Any of several plants of the genus *Physalis,* as *P. pubescens* and *P. pruinosa,* of eastern North America, having yellow flowers and edible yellowish fruit enclosed in a persistent husklike calyx. **2.** The fruit of this plant.

strawberry tree *n.* Any of several evergreen shrubs of the genus *Arbutus,* especially *A. unedo,* native to southern Europe, having shiny leaves, drooping clusters of white or pinkish flowers, and scarlet strawberrylike fruit.

straw·board (strô′bôrd′, -bōrd′) *n.* A coarse yellow cardboard made of straw pulp.

straw boss *n. Informal.* A worker who acts as a boss or crew leader in addition to performing regular duties.

straw·flow·er (strô′flou′ər) *n.* A stout Australian plant *(Helichrysum bracteatum)* having flower heads with showy, variously colored bracts that retain their color when dried.

straw-hat (strô′hăt′) *adj.* Of or relating to summer theater that operates in suburban or resort areas. [From the fashion of wearing straw hats during the summer.]

straw man *n.* **1.** A person who is set up as cover or a front for a questionable enterprise. **2.** An argument or opponent set up so as to be easily refuted or defeated. **3.** A bundle of straw made into the likeness of a man and often used as a scarecrow.

straw mushroom *n.* A tropical and subtropical edible mushroom *(Volvariella volvacea)* having a white cap and a long stipe with a swollen base.

straw vote *n.* An unofficial vote or poll indicating the trend of opinion on a candidate or an issue.

straw wine *n.* A sweet dessert wine made from grapes that have been dried on straw.

straw·worm (strô′wûrm′) *n.* The destructive larva of a wasp *(Harmolita grandis),* of western North America, that infests stalks of grain.

straw yellow *n. Color.* A pale yellow.

stray (strā) *intr.v.* **strayed, stray·ing, strays. 1.a.** To move away from a group, deviate from the correct course, or go beyond established limits. **b.** To become lost. **2.** To wander about without a destination or purpose; roam. See Synonyms at **wander. 3.** To follow a winding course; meander. **4.** To deviate from a moral, proper, or right course; err. **5.** To become diverted from a subject or train of thought; digress. See Synonyms at **swerve. —stray** *n.* One that has strayed, especially a domestic animal wandering about. **—stray** *adj.* **1.** Straying or having strayed; wandering or lost: *stray cats and dogs.* **2.** Scattered or separate: *a few stray crumbs.* [Middle English *straien,* from Old French *estraier,* from *estree,* highway, from Latin *strāta.* See STREET.] **—stray′er** *n.*

streak (strēk) *n.* **1.** A line, mark, smear, or band differentiated by color or texture from its surroundings. **2.** A slight contrasting element; a trace: *"There was a streak of wildness in him"* (Olga Carlisle). **3.** *Informal.* **a.** A brief run or stretch, as of luck. **b.** An unbroken series, as of wins or losses. **4.** *Mineralogy.* The color of the fine powder produced when a mineral is rubbed against a hard surface. Used as a distinguishing characteristic. **5.** *Botany.* Any of various viral diseases of plants characterized by the appearance of discolored stripes on the leaves or stems. **6.** *Microbiology.* A bacterial culture inoculated by drawing a bacteria-laden needle across the surface of a solid culture medium. **—streak** *v.* **streaked, streak·ing, streaks.** *—tr.* **1.** To mark with streaks: *rain streaking the pavement.* **2.** To lighten (strands of hair) with a chemical preparation. **3.** *Microbiology.* To inoculate in order to produce a streak. *—intr.* **1.** To form streaks. **2.** To be or become streaked. **3.** To move at high speed; rush. [Middle English *streke,* line, from Old English *strica.* See **streig-** in Appendix.] **—streak′er** *n.*

SYNONYMS: *streak, strain, vein.* The central meaning shared by these nouns is "an intermixture of an unexpected quality, as in a person's character": *a streak of humor; a strain of melancholy; a vein of stubbornness.*

streak·y (strē′kē) *adj.* **-i·er, -i·est. 1.** Marked with, characterized by, or occurring in streaks. **2.** Variable or uneven in character or quality. **—streak′i·ly** *adv.* **—streak′i·ness** *n.*

stream (strēm) *n.* **1.a.** A flow of water in a channel or bed, as a brook, rivulet, or small river. **b.** A steady current in such a flow of water. **2.** A steady current of a fluid. **3.** A steady flow or succession: *a stream of insults.* See Synonyms at **flow. 4.** A trend, course, or drift, as of opinion, thought, or history. **5.** A beam or ray of light. **6.** *Chiefly British.* A course of study to which students are tracked. **—stream** *v.* **streamed, stream•ing, streams.** —*intr.* **1.** To flow in or as if in a stream. **2.** To pour forth or give off a stream; flow: *My eyes were streaming with tears.* **3.** To come or go in large numbers; pour: *Traffic was streaming by. Fan mail streamed in.* **4.** To extend, wave, or float outward: *The banner streamed in the breeze.* **5.a.** To leave a continuous trail of light. **b.** To give forth a continuous stream of light rays or beams; shine. —*tr.* To emit, discharge, or exude (a body fluid, for example). **—*idiom.* on stream.** In or into operation or production: *a new power plant soon to go on stream.* [Middle English *streme,* from Old English *strēam.* See **sreu-** in Appendix.] **—stream′y** *adj.*

stream•bed (strēm′bĕd′) *n.* The channel through which a natural stream of water runs or used to run.

stream•er (strē′mər) *n.* **1.a.** A long narrow flag, banner, or pennant. **b.** A long narrow strip of material used for ornament or decoration. **2.** A column of light shooting across the sky in the aurora borealis. **3.** An extension of rays from the sun's corona. **4.** A newspaper headline that runs across a full page.

stream•let (strēm′lĭt) *n.* A small stream.

stream•line (strēm′līn′) *tr.v.* **-lined, -lin•ing, -lines. 1.** To construct or design in a form that offers the least resistance to fluid flow. **2.** To improve the appearance or efficiency of; modernize. **3.a.** To organize. **b.** To simplify. **—streamline** *n.* **1.** A line that is parallel to the direction of flow of a fluid at a given instant. **2.** The path of one particle in a flowing fluid. **3.** A contour of a body constructed so as to offer minimum resistance to a fluid flow.

stream•lined (strēm′līnd′) *adj.* **1.a.** Designed or arranged to offer the least resistance to fluid flow. **b.** Reduced to essentials; lacking anything extra. **c.** Effectively organized or simplified: *a streamlined method of production.* **2.** Having flowing, graceful lines; sleek: *a streamlined convertible.* **3.** Improved in appearance or efficiency; modernized.

stream of consciousness *n., pl.* **streams of consciousness. 1.** A literary technique that presents the thoughts and feelings of a character as they develop. **2.** *Psychology.* The conscious experience of an individual regarded as a continuous, flowing series of images and ideas running through the mind. **—stream′-of-con′scious•ness** (strēm′əv-kŏn′shəs-nĭs) *adj.*

stream•side (strēm′sīd′) *n.* The land adjacent to a stream.

Stream•wood (strēm′wo͝od′). A village of northeast Illinois, a suburb of Chicago. Population, 23,456.

street (strēt) *n.* **1.** *Abbr.* **st., St. a.** A public way or thoroughfare in a city or town, usually with a sidewalk or sidewalks. **b.** Such a public way considered apart from the sidewalks: *Don't play in the street.* **c.** A public way or road along with the houses or buildings abutting it: *lives on a quiet street.* **2.** The people living, working, or habitually gathering in or along a street: *The whole street protested the new parking regulations.* **3. Street.** A district, such as Wall Street in New York City, that is identified with a specific profession. Often used with *the.* **4.** The streets of a city viewed as the scene of crime, poverty, or dereliction. **—street** *adj.* **1.** Near or giving passage to a street: *a street door.* **2.a.** Taking place in the street: *a street brawl; street crime.* **b.** Living or making a living on the streets: *street people; a street vendor.* **c.** Performing on the street: *street musicians; a street juggler.* **d.** Crude; vulgar: *street language; street humor.* **3.** Appropriate for wear or use in public: *street clothes.* **—*idiom.* on (or in) the street. 1.** Without a job; idle. **2.** Without a home; homeless. **3.** Out of prison; at liberty. [Middle English *strete,* from Old English *strǣt, strēt,* from Late Latin *strāta,* paved road, from Latin, feminine past participle of *sternere,* to stretch, extend, pave. See **ster-**[2] in Appendix.]

street•car (strēt′kär′) *n.* A public vehicle operated on rails along a regular route, usually through the streets of a city.

street fighter *n.* **1.** One who has learned fighting skills in the streets as opposed to being formally trained in the art of boxing. **2.** An extremely aggressive person who often employs underhand tactics in interpersonal relationships.

street•light (strēt′līt′) *n.* One of a series of lights that are usually attached to tall poles, are spaced at intervals along a public street or roadway, and are illuminated from dusk to dawn.

street•scape (strēt′skāp′) *n.* **1.** An artistic representation of a street. **2.** Surroundings composed of streets: *the urban streetscape.*

street-smart (strēt′smärt′) *adj. Informal.* Having or displaying street smarts: *"a street-smart young hairdresser in Liverpool"* (New Yorker).

street smarts *pl.n. Informal.* Shrewd awareness of how to survive in an often hostile urban environment.

street theater *n.* Dramatization of social and political issues, usually enacted outside, as on the street or in a park. Also called *guerrilla theater.*

street•walk•er (strēt′wô′kər) *n.* A prostitute, especially one who solicits in the streets. **—street′walk′ing** *n.*

street•wise (strēt′wīz′) *adj. Informal.* Having the shrewd awareness, experience, and resourcefulness needed for survival in a difficult, often dangerous urban environment.

strength (strĕngkth, strĕngth, strĕnth) *n.* **1.** The state, property, or quality of being strong. **2.** The power to resist attack; impregnability. **3.** The power to resist strain or stress; durability. **4.** The ability to maintain a moral or intellectual position firmly. **5.** Capacity or potential for effective action: *a show of strength.* **6.a.** The number of people constituting a normal or ideal organization: *The police force has been at half strength since the budget cuts.* **b.** Military capability in terms of personnel and materiel: *an army of fearsome strength.* **7.a.** A source of power or force. **b.** One that is regarded as the embodiment of protective or supportive power; a support or mainstay. **c.** An attribute or a quality of particular worth or utility; an asset. **8.** Degree of intensity, force, effectiveness, or potency in terms of a particular property, as: **a.** Degree of concentration, distillation, or saturation; potency. **b.** Operative effectiveness or potency. **c.** Intensity, as of sound or light. **d.** Intensity or vehemence, as of emotion or language. **9.** Effective or binding force; efficacy: *the strength of an argument.* **10.** Firmness of or a continuous rising tendency in prices, as on the stock market. **11.** *Games.* Power derived from the value of playing cards held. **—*idiom.* on the strength of.** On the basis of: *She was hired on the strength of her computer skills.* [Middle English, from Old English *strengthu.*]

SYNONYMS: *strength, power, might, energy, force.* These nouns are compared as they denote the capacity to act or work effectively. *Strength* refers especially to physical, mental, or moral robustness or vigor: *"enough work to do, and strength enough to do the work"* (Rudyard Kipling). *"We are of course a nation of differences. Those differences don't make us weak. They're the source of our strength"* (Jimmy Carter). *Power* is the ability to do something and especially to produce an effect: *"I do not think the United States would come to an end if we lost our power to declare an Act of Congress void"* (Oliver Wendell Holmes, Jr.). *Might* often implies abundant or extraordinary power: *"With twenty-five squadrons of fighters he could defend the island against the whole might of the German Air Force"* (Winston S. Churchill). *Energy* in this comparison refers especially to a latent source of power: *"The same energy of character which renders a man a daring villain would have rendered him useful to society, had that society been well organized"* (Mary Wollstonecraft). *Force* is the application of power or strength: *"the overthrow of our institutions by force and violence"* (Charles Evans Hughes).

strength•en (strĕngk′thən, strĕng′-, strĕn′-) *v.* **-ened, -en•ing, -ens.** —*tr.* To make strong or increase the strength of. —*intr.* To become strong or stronger. **—strength′en•er** *n.*

stren•u•ous (strĕn′yo͞o-əs) *adj.* **1.** Requiring great effort, energy, or exertion: *a strenuous task.* **2.** Vigorously active; energetic or zealous. [From Latin *strēnuus.*] **—stren′u•os′i•ty** (-ŏs′ĭ-tē), **stren′u•ous•ness** (-əs-nĭs) *n.* **—stren′u•ous•ly** *adv.*

strep (strĕp) *adj.* Streptococcal. **—strep** *n.* Streptococcus.

strep throat *n.* See **septic sore throat.**

strepto– *pref.* **1.** Twisted; twisted chain: *streptococcus.* **2.** Streptococcus: *streptolysin.* **3.** Streptomyces: *streptonigrin.* [From Greek *streptos,* from *strephein,* to turn. See **streb(h)-** in Appendix.]

strep•to•ba•cil•lus (strĕp′tō-bə-sĭl′əs) *n., pl.* **-cil•li** (-sĭl′ī). Any of various gram-negative, rod-shaped, often pathogenic bacteria of the genus *Streptobacillus,* occurring in chains, especially *S. moniliformis,* which causes a type of rat-bite fever.

strep•to•car•pus (strĕp′tə-kär′pəs) *n., pl.* **-pus•es.** See **Cape primrose.** [New Latin, genus name : STREPTO– + *-carpus,* -carpous.]

strep•to•coc•cal (strĕp′tə-kŏk′əl) also **strep•to•coc•cic** (-kŏk′sĭk, -kŏk′ĭk) *adj.* Of, relating to, or caused by a streptococcus.

strep•to•coc•cus (strĕp′tə-kŏk′əs) *n., pl.* **-coc•ci** (-kŏk′sī, -kŏk′ī). A round to ovoid, gram-positive, often pathogenic bacterium of the genus *Streptococcus* that occurs in pairs or chains, many species of which destroy red blood cells and cause various diseases in human beings, including erysipelas, scarlet fever, and septic sore throat.

strep•to•dor•nase (strĕp′tō-dôr′nās, -nāz) *n.* An enzyme produced by hemolytic streptococci that is used medicinally, often in combination with streptokinase, to dissolve purulent or fibrinous secretions from infections. [STREPTO– + D(E)O(XY)– + R(IBO)N(UCLE)ASE.]

strep•to•kin•ase (strĕp′tō-kĭn′ās, -āz, -kī′nās, -nāz) *n.* A proteolytic enzyme produced by hemolytic streptococci, capable of dissolving fibrin and used medically to dissolve blood clots.

strep•to•ly•sin (strĕp′tə-lī′sĭn) *n.* Any of several hemolysins derived from some strains of streptococci.

strep•to•my•ces (strĕp′tə-mī′sēz) *n., pl.* **streptomyces.** Any of various actinomycetes of the genus *Streptomyces,* including several strains that produce antibiotics. [New Latin *Streptomyces,* genus name : STREPTO– + Greek *mukēs,* fungus.]

strep•to•my•cin (strĕp′tə-mī′sĭn) *n.* An antibiotic, $C_{21}H_{39}O_{12}N_7$, produced by the actinomycete *Streptomyces griseus,* used to treat tuberculosis and other bacterial infections. [STREPTOMYC(ES) + –IN.]

strep•to•ni•grin (strĕp′tə-nī′grĭn) *n.* A highly toxic antibiotic, $C_{25}H_{22}N_4O_8$, produced by an actinomycete *(Streptomyces flocculus)* and active against various types of tumors. [STREPTO– + Latin *niger, nigr-,* black + –IN.]

streetcar

ă pat	oi boy
ā pay	ou out
âr care	o͝o took
ä father	o͞o boot
ĕ pet	ŭ cut
ē be	ûr urge
ĭ pit	th thin
ī pie	*th* this
îr pier	hw which
ŏ pot	zh vision
ō toe	ə about, item
ô paw	♦ regionalism

Stress marks: ′ (primary); ′ (secondary), as in **dictionary** (dĭk′shə-nĕr′ē)

strep·to·thri·cin (strĕp′tə-thrī′sĭn, -thrĭs′ĭn) *n.* Any of a group of antibiotics produced by an actinomycete *(Streptomyces lavendulae)* and active against both gram-positive and gram-negative bacteria and some fungi. [New Latin *Streptothrix, Streptothric-*, genus of bacteria (STREPTO– + Greek *thrix, trikh-*, hair) + –IN.]

strep·to·var·i·cin (strĕp′tō-vâr′ĭ-sĭn) *n.* Any of a group of antibiotics produced by an actinomycete *(Streptomyces spectabilis)* and active against various bacteria and viruses. [STREPTO(MYCES) + VARI(OUS) + –(MY)CIN.]

strep·to·zot·o·cin (strĕp′tə-zŏt′ə-sĭn) *n.* An antibiotic, $C_8H_{15}N_3O_7$, produced by an actinomycete *(Streptomyces achromogenes)* and active against tumors but damaging to insulin-producing cells and now also regarded as a carcinogen. [STREPTO– + ZO(O)– + *-tocin* (alteration of TOXIN).]

Stre·se·mann (strā′zə-män′, shtrā′-), **Gustav.** 1878–1929. German politician who served as foreign minister (1923–1929) and was largely responsible for Germany's conciliatory and cooperative policies after World War I. He shared the 1929 Nobel Peace Prize.

stress (strĕs) *n.* **1.** Importance, significance, or emphasis placed on something. See Synonyms at **emphasis. 2.** *Linguistics.* **a.** The relative force with which a sound or syllable is spoken. **b.** The emphasis placed on the sound or syllable spoken most forcefully in a word or phrase. **3. a.** The relative force of sound or emphasis given a syllable or word in accordance with a metrical pattern. **b.** A syllable having strong relative emphasis in a metrical pattern. **4.** *Music.* Accent or a mark representing it. **5.** *Physics.* **a.** An applied force or system of forces that tends to strain or deform a body. **b.** The internal resistance of a body to such an applied force or system of forces. **6. a.** A mentally or emotionally disruptive or upsetting condition occurring in response to adverse external influences and capable of affecting physical health, usually characterized by increased heart rate, a rise in blood pressure, muscular tension, irritability, and depression. **b.** A stimulus or circumstance causing such a condition. **7.** A state of extreme difficulty, pressure, or strain: *"He presided over the economy during the period of its greatest stress and danger"* (Robert J. Samuelson). **—stress** *tr.v.* **stressed, stress·ing, stress·es. 1.** To place emphasis on: *stressed basic fire safety.* **2.** To give prominence to (a syllable or word) in pronouncing or in accordance with a metrical pattern. **3.** To subject to physical or mental pressure, tension, or strain. **4.** To subject to mechanical pressure or force. **5.** To construct so as to withstand a specified stress. ***—phrasal verb.* stress out.** *Slang.* To subject to or undergo extreme stress, as from working. [Middle English *stresse*, hardship, partly from *destresse* (from Old French; see DISTRESS) and partly from Old French *estrece*, narrowness, oppression (from Vulgar Latin **strictia*, from Latin *strictus*, past participle of *stringere*, to draw tight; see STRAIT).]

STRESS (strĕs) *n. Computer Science.* A language designed for use in solving structural analysis problems in civil engineering. [*str(uctural) e(ngineering) s(ystems) s(olver).*]

stressed-out (strĕsd′out′) *adj. Slang.* Undergoing or suffering the effects of extreme stress: *"frequent asides that are often exasperating to today's more stressed-out public"* (James Wilcox).

stress fracture *n.* A fracture of bone caused by repeated application of a heavy load, such as the constant pounding on a surface by runners, gymnasts, and dancers.

stress·ful (strĕs′fəl) *adj.* Full of or tending to cause stress. **—stress′ful·ly** *adv.* **—stress′ful·ness** *n.*

stress·less (strĕs′lĭs) *adj.* **1.** *Linguistics.* Having no phonetic stress: *a stressless syllable.* **2.** Having no metrical stress. **3.** Causing no stress: *enjoyed a stressless hour of peace and quiet.*

stres·sor (strĕs′ər) *n.* An agent, a condition, or another stimulus that causes stress to an organism.

stress test *n.* A graded test to measure an individual's heart rate and oxygen intake while undergoing strenuous physical exercise, as on a treadmill.

stretch (strĕch) *v.* **stretched, stretch·ing, stretch·es.** *—tr.* **1.** To lengthen, widen, or distend: *stretched the sweater out of shape.* **2.** To cause to extend from one place to another or across a given space: *stretched the banner between two poles.* **3.** To make taut; tighten: *stretched the tarpaulin until it ripped.* **4.** To reach or put forth; extend: *stretched out his hand.* **5. a.** To extend (oneself or one's limbs, for example) to full length: *stretches herself after waking up; stretched his calves before running.* **b.** To extend (oneself) when lying down: *she stretched herself out on the couch and fell asleep.* **c.** To put to torture on the rack. **6.** To wrench or strain (a muscle, for example). **7. a.** To extend or enlarge beyond the usual or proper limits: *stretch the meaning of a word; stretch one's imagination.* **b.** To subject to undue strain: *This situation really stretches my patience.* **8. a.** To expand in order to fulfill a larger function: *stretch a budget; stretch a paycheck.* **b.** To increase the quantity of by admixture or dilution: *stretch a meal by thinning the stew.* **9.** To prolong: *stretch out an argument; stretch the payments.* **10.** *Informal.* To fell by a blow: *stretched his opponent in the first round.* *—intr.* **1.** To become lengthened, widened, or distended. **2.** To extend or reach over a distance or an area or in a given direction: *"On both sides of us stretched the wet plain"* (Ernest Hemingway). **3.** To lie down at full length: *stretched out on the bed for a nap.* **4.** To extend one's muscles or limbs, as after prolonged sitting or on awakening. **5.** To extend over a given period of time: *"This story stretches over a whole generation"* (William Golding). **—stretch** *n.* **1.** The act of stretching or the state of being stretched. **2.** The extent or scope to which something can be stretched; elasticity. **3.** A continuous or unbroken length, area, or expanse: *an empty stretch of highway.* **4.** A straight section of a racecourse or track, especially the section leading to the finish line. **5. a.** A continuous period of time. **b.** *Slang.* A term of imprisonment: *served a two-year stretch.* **c.** *Informal.* The last stage of an event, a period, or a process. **6.** *Baseball.* The movement in which a pitcher raises both hands to the height of the head and then lowers them to the waist for a short pause before pitching the ball. It is used as an alternative to a wind-up, especially when runners are on base. **—stretch** *adj.* **1.** Made of an elastic material that stretches easily: *stretch pants.* **2.** Of, relating to, or being a vehicle, such as a limousine or passenger jet, having an extended seating area that provides extra space for more passengers, leg room, or amenities. ***—idiom.* stretch (one's) legs.** To go for a walk, especially after a lengthy period of sitting. [Middle English *strecchen*, from Old English *streccan*.] **—stretch′a·bil′i·ty** *n.* **—stretch′a·ble** *adj.*

stretch·er (strĕch′ər) *n.* **1.** A litter, usually of canvas stretched over a frame, used to transport the sick, wounded, or dead. **2.** One that stretches, such as the wooden framework on which canvas is stretched for an oil painting. **3.** A usually horizontal tie beam or brace serving to support or extend a framework. **4.** A brick or stone laid parallel to the face of a wall.

stretch·er-bear·er (strĕch′ər-bâr′ər) *n.* One who helps carry a stretcher or litter.

stretch mark *n.* A white, shiny line on the skin of the abdomen, breasts, thighs, or buttocks caused by the stretching and weakening of elastic tissues as a result of pregnancy or obesity, for example.

stretch-out (strĕch′out′) *n.* **1. a.** The act of stretching out. **b.** The condition of being stretched out. **c.** An extension or a prolongation, such as the time required for paying a debt. **2.** An increase in the work required of industrial workers without a commensurate pay increase.

stretch receptor *n.* A sensory receptor in a muscle that responds to the stretching of tissue.

stretch reflex *n.* A reflex contraction of a muscle in response to stretching of an attached tendon or of the muscle itself.

stretch runner *n. Sports.* A runner or racehorse that makes a strong effort in the last stretch of a race.

stretch·y (strĕch′ē) *adj.* **-i·er, -i·est. 1.** Capable of being stretched: *a stretchy fabric.* **2.** Tending to stretch excessively.

Stret·ford (strĕt′fərd). A municipal borough of northwest England, an industrial suburb of Manchester. Population, 222,200.

stret·ta (strĕt′ə) *n., pl.* **stret·te** (strĕt′ā) or **stret·tas.** *Music.* See **stretto** (sense 2). [Italian, feminine of *stretto*, stretto. See STRETTO.]

stret·to (strĕt′ō) *n., pl.* **stret·ti** (strĕt′ē) or **stret·tos.** *Music.* **1.** A close succession or overlapping of voices in a fugue, especially in the final section. **2.** A final section, as of an oratorio, performed with an acceleration in tempo to produce a climax. In this sense, also called *stretta.* [Italian, narrow, stretto, from Latin *strictus*, strict. See STRICT.]

streu·sel (stro͞o′zəl, stroi′-) *n.* A crumblike topping for coffee cakes and rich breads, consisting of flour, sugar, butter, cinnamon, and sometimes chopped nutmeats. [German, streusel, from Middle High German *ströusel*, something strewn, from *ströuwen*, to sprinkle, from Old High German *strowwen*. See **ster-**[2] in Appendix.]

strew (stro͞o) *tr.v.* **strewed, strewn** (stro͞on) or **strewed, strew·ing, strews. 1.** To spread here and there; scatter: *strewing flowers down the aisle.* **2.** To cover (an area or a surface) with things scattered or sprinkled: *"Italy . . . was strewn thick with the remains of Roman buildings"* (Bernard Berenson). **3.** To be or become dispersed over (a surface). **4.** To spread (something) over a wide area; disseminate. [Middle English *strewen*, from Old English *strēowian*. See **ster-**[2] in Appendix.]

stri·a (strī′ə) *n., pl.* **stri·ae** (strī′ē). **1.** A thin, narrow groove or channel. **2.** A thin line or band, especially one of several that are parallel or close together: *a characteristic stria of contractile tissue.* [Latin. See **streig-** in Appendix.]

stri·ate (strī′āt′) *tr.v.* **-at·ed, -at·ing, -ates.** To mark with striae or striations. **—striate** also **stri·at·ed** (-ā′tĭd) *adj.* **1.** Marked with striae; striped, grooved, or ridged. **2.** Consisting of a stria or striae. [From Latin *striātus*, furrowed, from *stria*, furrow. See STRIA.]

striated muscle *n.* Skeletal, voluntary, and cardiac muscle, distinguished from smooth muscle by transverse striations of the fibers.

stri·a·tion (strī-ā′shən) *n.* **1.** The state of being striated or having striae. **2.** One of a number of parallel lines or scratches on the surface of a rock that were inscribed by rock fragments embedded in the base of a glacier as it moved across the rock. **3.** The form taken by striae. **4.** A stria.

strick·en (strĭk′ən) *v.* A past participle of **strike. —stricken** *adj.* **1.** Struck or wounded, as by a projectile. **2. a.** Affected by something overwhelming, such as disease, trouble, or painful emotion. **b.** Incapacitated; disabled. **3.** Having the contents made even with the top of a measuring device or container; level: *a stricken measure of flour.*

strick·le (strĭk′əl) *n.* **1.** An instrument used to level off grain or other material in a measure. **2.** A foundry tool used to shape a mold in sand or loam. **3.** A tool for sharpening scythes. [Middle English *strikelle,* perhaps from Old English *stricel,* teat, strickle. See **streig-** in Appendix.] **—strick′le** *v.*

strict (strĭkt) *adj.* **strict·er, strict·est. 1.** Precise; exact: *a strict definition.* **2.** Complete; absolute: *strict loyalty.* **3.** Kept within narrowly specific limits: *a strict application of a law.* **4.** Rigorous in the imposition of discipline: *a strict parent.* **5.** Exacting in enforcement, observance, or requirement; stringent: *strict standards.* See Synonyms at **severe. 6.** Conforming completely to established rule, principle, or condition: *a strict vegetarian.* **7.** *Botany.* Stiff, narrow, and upright. [Middle English *stricte,* narrow, small, from Latin *strictus,* tight, strict, past participle of *stringere,* to draw tight. See **streig-** in Appendix.] **—strict′ly** *adv.* **—strict′ness** *n.*

stric·ture (strĭk′chər) *n.* **1.** A restraint, limit, or restriction. **2.** An adverse remark or criticism; censure. **3.** *Pathology.* An abnormal narrowing of a duct or passage. [Middle English, an abnormal narrowing of a bodily part, from Late Latin *strictūra,* contraction, from Latin *strictus,* past participle of *stringere,* to draw tight. See STRICT.]

stride (strīd) *v.* **strode** (strōd), **strid·den** (strĭd′n), **strid·ing, strides.** *—intr.* **1.** To walk with long steps, especially in a hasty or vigorous way. **2.** To take a single long step, as in passing over an obstruction. **3.** To stand or sit astride; straddle. *—tr.* **1.** To walk with long steps on, along, or over: *striding the stage.* **2.** To step over or across: *stride a brook.* **3.** To be astride of; straddle. **—stride** *n.* **1.** The act of striding. **2.a.** A single long step. **b.** The distance traveled in such a step. **3.a.** A single coordinated movement of the four legs of a horse or other animal, completed when the legs return to their initial relative position. **b.** The distance traveled in such a movement. **4.** A step of progress; an advance. Often used in the plural: *making great strides in their studies.* ***—idioms.*** **hit (one's) stride. 1.** To achieve a steady, effective pace. **2.** To attain a maximum level of competence. **take in (one's) stride.** To cope with calmly, without interrupting one's normal routine: *taking their newfound wealth in stride.* [Middle English *striden,* from Old English *strīdan.*] **—strid′er** *n.*

stri·dent (strīd′nt) *adj.* Loud, harsh, grating, or shrill; discordant. See Synonyms at **loud, vociferous.** [Latin *strīdēns, strīdent-,* present participle of *strīdere,* to make harsh sounds, ultimately of imitative origin.] **—stri′dence, stri′den·cy** *n.* **—stri′dent·ly** *adv.*

stride piano *n. Music.* A style of jazz piano playing in which the melody is played by the right hand while a single note is played by the left hand in alternation with a chord that is an octave or more higher. [From *stride bass* (from the motions of the left hand).] **—stride pianist** *n.*

stri·dor (strī′dər, -dôrʹ) *n.* **1.** A harsh, shrill, grating, or creaking sound. **2.** *Pathology.* A harsh, high-pitched sound in inhalation or exhalation. [Latin *strīdor,* from *strīdere,* to make harsh sounds, ultimately of imitative origin.]

strid·u·late (strĭj′ə-lātʹ) *v.* **-lat·ed, -lat·ing, -lates.** *—intr.* To produce a shrill grating, chirping, or hissing sound by rubbing body parts together, as certain insects do. *—tr.* To produce by rubbing body parts together: *"The crickets stridulated their everlasting monotonous meaningful note"* (John Updike). [From Latin *strīdulus,* stridulous. See STRIDULOUS.] **—stridʹu·la′tion** *n.* **—strid′u·la·toʹry** (-lə-tôrʹē, -tōrʹē) *adj.*

strid·u·lous (strĭj′ə-ləs) *adj.* **1.** Characterized by or making a shrill grating sound or noise. **2.** Relating to or characterized by stridor. [From Latin *strīdulus,* from *strīdere,* to make harsh sounds, ultimately of imitative origin.] **—strid′u·lous·ly** *adv.*

strife (strīf) *n.* **1.** Heated, often violent dissension; bitter conflict. See Synonyms at **discord. 2.** A struggle, fight, or quarrel. **3.** Contention or competition between rivals. **4.** *Archaic.* Earnest endeavor or striving. [Middle English *strif,* from Old French *estrit, estrif,* from Frankish **strīd.*]

strig·il (strĭj′əl) *n.* An instrument used in ancient Greece and Rome for scraping the skin after a bath. [Latin *strigilis.* See **streig-** in Appendix.]

stri·gose (strī′gōsʹ) *adj.* **1.** *Zoology.* Marked with fine, close-set grooves, ridges, or streaks. **2.** *Botany.* Having stiff, straight, closely appressed hair: *strigose leaves.* [New Latin *strigōsus,* from *striga,* bristle, from Latin, windrow, furrow. See **streig-** in Appendix.]

strike (strīk) *v.* **struck** (strŭk), **struck** or **strick·en** (strĭk′ən), **strik·ing, strikes.** *—tr.* **1.a.** To hit sharply, as with the hand, the fist, or a weapon. **b.** To inflict (a blow). **2.** To penetrate or pierce: *was struck in the leg by a bullet.* **3.a.** To collide with or crash into: *She struck the desk with her knee.* **b.** To cause to come into violent or forceful contact: *She struck her knee against the desk.* **c.** To thrust (a weapon, for example) in or into someone or something: *struck the sword into the dragon.* **d.** To damage or destroy, as by forceful contact: *Lightning struck the tree.* **4.** To make a military attack on; assault. **5.** To afflict suddenly, as with a disease or an impairment: *was stricken with cancer.* **6.** To cause to become by or as if by a blow: *struck him dead.* **7.a.** To snap at or seize (a bait). **b.** To hook (a fish that has taken the bait) by a pull on the line. **8.** To wound by biting. Used especially of a snake. **9.** To form by stamping, printing, or punching: *strike a medallion.* **10.** To produce or play by manipulating strings or keys: *strike a B flat; strike* w, t, *and* y *on the typewriter.* **11.** To indicate by a percussive or chiming sound: *The clock struck nine.* **12.** To produce as if by playing a musical instrument: *The report struck a positive note in the final paragraph.* **13.a.** To produce by friction or a blow: *struck fire from the flints.* **b.** To produce flame, light, or a spark from by friction: *strike a match.* **14.** To remove or separate with or as if with a blow: *struck the wasp from his shoulder; struck off the diseased branch with a machete.* **15.** To eliminate or expunge: *strike a statement from the court records.* **16.a.** To come upon; discover: *struck gold.* **b.** To come to; attain: *finally struck the main trail.* **17.a.** To fall upon; shine on: *A bright light struck her face.* **b.** To become audible to: *An odd sound struck his ear.* **18.** To affect keenly or forcibly; impress. See Synonyms at **affect[1]. 19.** To enter one's mind; occur to: *The thought struck me from out of the blue.* **20.a.** To cause (a strong emotion) to penetrate deeply: *struck terror into their hearts.* **b.** To affect or overcome with strong emotion: *She was struck with alarm at the news.* **21.a.** To make and confirm the terms of (a bargain). **b.** To achieve (a balance, for example) by careful weighing or reckoning. **22.** To take on or assume (a pose, for example). **23.** *Nautical.* **a.** To haul down (a mast or sail). **b.** To lower (a flag or sail) in salute or surrender. **c.** To lower (cargo) into a hold. **24.** To remove (theatrical properties) from the stage. **25.** To dismantle and pack up for departure: *strike camp.* **26.** To undertake a strike against (an employer). **27.a.** To level or even (a measure, as of grain). **b.** To smooth or shape with a strickle. **28.a.** To send (plant roots) out or down. **b.** To cause (a plant cutting) to take root. *—intr.* **1.** To deal a blow or blows with or as if with the fist or a weapon; hit. **2.** To aim a stroke or blow. **3.** To make contact suddenly or violently; collide: *A car and a bus struck at the intersection.* **4.** To begin a military attack: *The enemy struck unexpectedly.* **5.** To penetrate or pierce: *The cold struck right through our jackets.* **6.** To take bait: *The fish are striking.* **7.** To dart or shoot suddenly forward in an attempt to inflict a bite or wound. Used of snakes and wild animals. **8.** To set out or proceed, especially in a new direction: *struck off into the forest.* **9.** To begin to move: *The horse struck into a gallop.* **10.a.** To send out roots. **b.** To sprout. **11.a.** To indicate the time by making a percussive or chiming sound: *The clock struck just as we left.* **b.** To become indicated by percussive or chiming sounds: *The hour has struck.* **12.** To become ignited. **13.** To discover something suddenly or unexpectedly: *struck on a new approach.* **14.** To fall, as light or sound: *sunlight striking on the cliffs; a din struck upon their ears.* **15.** To have an effect; make an impression. **16.** To engage in a strike against an employer. **17.** To interrupt by pushing oneself forward: *struck rudely into the conversation.* **18.** To strive diligently for a specific technical rating in the U.S. Navy. **—strike** *n.* **1.** An act or a gesture of striking. **2.** An attack, especially a military air attack on a single group of targets. **3.a.** A cessation of work by employees in support of demands made on their employer, as for higher pay or improved conditions. **b.** A temporary stoppage of normal activity undertaken as a protest. **4.** A sudden achievement or valuable discovery, as of a precious mineral. **5.a.** The taking of bait by a fish. **b.** A pull on a fishing line indicating this. **6.** A quantity of coins or medals struck at the same time. **7.** *Baseball.* **a.** A pitched ball that is counted against the batter, typically one that is swung at and missed, fouled off, or judged to have passed through the strike zone. **b.** A perfectly thrown ball. **8.** An unfavorable condition, circumstance, or characteristic; a disadvantage. **9.** *Sports.* The knocking down of all the pins in bowling with the first bowl of a frame. **10.** The taking root and growing of a plant cutting. **11.** *Geology.* The course or bearing of the outcrop of an inclined bed or structure on a level surface. **12.** A strickle. ***—phrasal verbs.*** **strike down. 1.** To cause to fall by a blow. **2.** To incapacitate or kill: *He was struck down by tuberculosis while in his twenties.* **3.** To render ineffective; cancel: *The court struck down the law as unconstitutional.* **strike out. 1.** To begin a course of action. **2.** To set out energetically. **3.** *Baseball.* **a.** To pitch three strikes to (a batter), putting the batter out. **b.** To be struck out. **4.** To fail in an endeavor. **strike up. 1.a.** To start to play music or sing: *The band suddenly struck up.* **b.** To start to play or sing (something): *The orchestra struck up a waltz.* **c.** To cause to start to play or sing: *Strike up the band!* **2.** To initiate or begin: *strike up a conversation; struck up a friendship.* ***—idioms.*** **on strike.** Engaged in a work stoppage: *Most of the employees were on strike.* **strike hands.** To conclude a bargain or reach an agreement. **strike it rich.** *Informal.* To have sudden financial success. [Middle English *striken,* from Old English *strīcan,* to stroke. See **streig-** in Appendix.]

strike·bound (strīk′boundʹ) *adj.* Closed, immobilized, or slowed down by a strike: *a strikebound airline.*

strike·break·er (strīk′brāʹkər) *n.* One who works or provides an employer with workers during a strike. **—strike′·breakʹing** *n.*

strike·out (strīk′outʹ) *n. Abbr.* **s.o.** *Baseball.* An out made by a batter charged with three strikes and credited to the pitcher who threw the strikes.

strike·o·ver (strīk′ōʹvər) *n.* The act or an instance of typing a character over one already typed.

strik·er (strī′kər) *n.* **1.** One who strikes, as an employee on strike against an employer. **2.** One that strikes, as the clapper in a bell or the firing pin in a gun. **3.a.** A harpoon. **b.** One who uses a harpoon; a harpooner. **4.** An enlisted person in usually intensive training for a naval technical rating. **5.** *Sports.* A forward on a soccer team.

strike zone *n. Baseball.* The area over home plate through

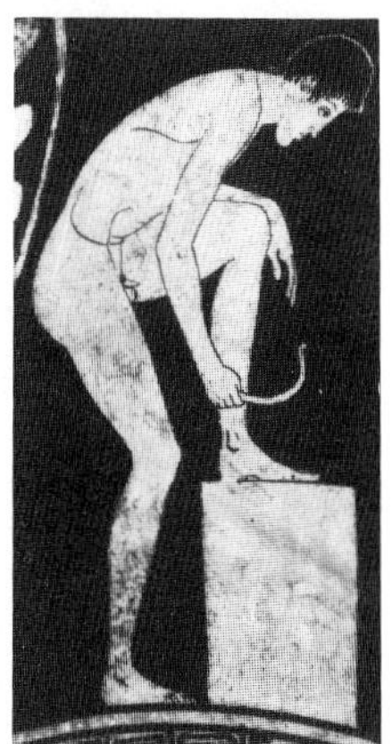

strigil

ă pat	oi boy
ā pay	ou out
âr care	o͝o took
ä father	o͞o boot
ĕ pet	ŭ cut
ē be	ûr urge
ĭ pit	th thin
ī pie	*th* this
îr pier	hw which
ŏ pot	zh vision
ō toe	ə about, item
ô paw	♦ regionalism

Stress marks: ′ (primary); ʹ (secondary), as in **dictionary** (dĭk′shə-nĕrʹē) which a pitch must pass to be called a strike, roughly between the batter's armpits and knees.

strik·ing (strī′kĭng) *adj.* Arresting the attention and producing a vivid impression on the sight or the mind. See Synonyms at **noticeable.** —**strik′ing·ly** *adv.* —**strik′ing·ness** *n.*

striking price *n.* The price at which a put or call option may be exercised.

Strind·berg (strĭnd′bûrg, strĭn′-, strĭn′bĕr′ē), **(Johan) August.** 1849–1912. Swedish writer of novels and plays, including *Miss Julie* (1888) and *The Dance of Death* (1901), which are noted for their psychological realism. —**Strind·berg′i·an** *adj.*

string (strĭng) *n.* **1.** A cord usually made of fiber, used for fastening, tying, or lacing. **2.** Something configured as a long, thin line: *limp strings of hair.* **3.** A plant fiber. **4.** A set of objects threaded together: *a string of beads.* **5.** A series of similar or related acts, events, or items arranged or falling in or as if in a line. See Synonyms at **series. 6.** *Computer Science.* A set of consecutive characters treated by a computer as a single item. **7.** *Informal.* **a.** A set of animals, especially racehorses, belonging to a single owner; a stable. **b.** A scattered group of businesses under a single ownership or management: *a string of boutiques.* **8.** *Sports.* A group of players ranked according to ability within a team: *He made the second string.* **9.** *Music.* **a.** A cord stretched on an instrument and struck, plucked, or bowed to produce tones. **b.** *Also* **strings.** The section of a band or an orchestra composed of stringed instruments. **c.** *Also* **strings.** Stringed instruments or their players considered as a group. **10.** *Architecture.* **a.** A stringboard. **b.** A stringcourse. **11.** *Games.* The balk line in billiards. **12.** *Sports.* A complete game consisting of ten frames in bowling. **13.** Also **strings.** *Informal.* A limiting or hidden condition: *a gift with no strings attached.* —**string** *v.* **strung** (strŭng), **string·ing, strings.** —*tr.* **1.** To fit or furnish with strings or a string: *string a guitar.* **2.** To thread on a string. **3.** To arrange in a string or series. **4.** To fasten, tie, or hang with a string or strings. **5.** To stretch out or extend: *string a wire across a room.* **6.** To strip (vegetables) of fibers. —*intr.* **1.** To form strings or become stringlike. **2.** To extend or progress in a string, line, or succession. —***phrasal verbs.*** **string along.** *Informal.* **1.** To go along with something; agree. **2.** To keep (someone) waiting or in a state of uncertainty. **3.** To fool, cheat, or deceive. **string up.** *Informal.* To kill (someone) by hanging. —***idiom.*** **on the string.** Under one's complete control or influence. [Middle English, from Old English *streng.*]

string bass (bās) *n.* *Music.* See **double bass.**

string bean *n.* **1.a.** A bushy or climbing tropical American plant *(Phaseolus vulgaris)* widely cultivated for its narrow, green, edible pods. **b.** The green pod of this plant, eaten as a vegetable. Also called *green bean.* **2.** *Slang.* A tall, thin person.

string·board (strĭng′bôrd′, -bōrd′) *n.* A board that runs along the side of a staircase to support or cover the ends of the steps.

string·course (strĭng′kôrs′, -kōrs′) *n.* *Architecture.* A horizontal band or molding set in the face of a building as a design element.

stringed (strĭngd) *adj.* *Abbr.* **str.** *Music.* **1.** Having strings. Often used in combination: *a six-stringed lute.* **2.** Produced by stringed instruments: *stringed chamber music.*

stringed instrument *n.* *Music.* An instrument, such as a violin, viola, cello, or double bass, in which sound is produced by plucking, striking, or bowing taut strings.

strin·gen·do (strĭn-jĕn′dō) *adj.* *Music.* Played with an accelerating tempo. Used chiefly as a direction. [Italian, gerund of *stringere,* to draw tight, from Latin. See **streig-** in Appendix.] —**strin·gen′do** *adv.*

strin·gent (strĭn′jənt) *adj.* **1.** Imposing rigorous standards of performance; severe: *stringent safety measures.* **2.** Constricted; tight: *operating under a stringent time limit.* **3.** Characterized by scarcity of money, credit restrictions, or other financial strain: *stringent economic policies.* [Latin *stringēns, stringent-,* present participle of *stringere,* to draw tight. See **streig-** in Appendix.] —**strin′gen·cy** *n.* —**strin′gent·ly** *adv.*

string·er (strĭng′ər) *n.* **1.** One that strings: *a stringer of beads.* **2.** *Architecture.* **a.** A long, heavy horizontal timber used as a support or connector. **b.** A stringboard. **3.** A horizontal timber used to support upright posts. **4.** *Sports.* A member of a specified string or squad on a team. Often used in combination: *a first-stringer; a second-stringer.* **5.** A part-time or freelance correspondent for the news media.

string·halt (strĭng′hôlt′) *n.* A nervous disorder in horses characterized by spasmodic movements in the hind legs that cause the feet to rise abnormally high. Also called *springhalt.* [STRING, tendon + HALT[2].] —**string′halt′ed** *adj.*

string line *n.* *Games.* The balk line in billiards.

string quartet *n.* *Music.* **1.** Four people playing stringed instruments, traditionally including a first and second violinist, a violist, and a cellist. **2.** A composition for such a group.

string tie *n.* A narrow necktie, usually tied in a bow.

string·y (strĭng′ē) *adj.* **-i·er, -i·est. 1.** Consisting of, resembling, or containing strings or a string. **2.** Slender and sinewy; wiry. **3.** Forming strings, as a viscous liquid; ropy. —**string′i·ly** *adv.* —**string′i·ness** *n.*

strip[1] (strĭp) *v.* **stripped, strip·ping, strips.** —*tr.* **1.a.** To remove clothing or covering from. **b.** To deprive of (clothing or covering). **2.** To deprive of honors, rank, office, privileges, or possessions; divest. **3.a.** To remove all excess detail from; reduce to essentials. **b.** To remove equipment, furnishings, or supplementary parts or attachments from. **4.** To clear of a natural covering or growth; make bare: *strip a field.* **5.** To remove an exterior coating, as of paint or varnish, from: *stripped and refinished the old chest of drawers.* **6.** To remove the leaves from the stalks of. Used especially of tobacco. **7.** To dismantle (a firearm, for example) piece by piece. **8.** To damage or break the threads of (a screw, for example) or the teeth of (a gear). **9.** To press the last drops of milk from (a cow or goat, for example) at the end of milking. **10.** To rob of wealth or property; plunder or despoil. **11.** To mount (a photographic positive or negative) on paper to be used in making a printing plate. —*intr.* **1.a.** To undress completely. **b.** To perform a striptease. **2.** To fall away or be removed; peel. —**strip** *n.* A striptease. [Middle English *stripen,* from Old English *-strȳpan,* to plunder, in *bestrȳpan.*]

SYNONYMS: *strip, divest, denude, bare.* These verbs signify to remove clothing, coverings, possessions, or attributes from someone or something. *Strip* often suggests forceful or abrupt peeling or tearing off: *"a party of fifteen or twenty . . . stripped to their shirts"* (Frederick Marryat). *"He stripped the skin from the banana"* (John Galsworthy). *Divest* usually specifies deprivation, as of rank or its symbols: *"That all men . . . have certain inherent rights, of which . . . they cannot by any compact . . . divest their posterity"* (George Mason). To *denude* is to remove a usual or natural covering: *Construction began only after the tract had been denuded of trees. Bare* implies uncovering and exposing, as to view: *Bystanders bared their heads as the funeral procession passed.*

strip[2] (strĭp) *n.* **1.a.** A long narrow piece, usually of uniform width: *a strip of paper; strips of beef.* **b.** A long narrow region of land or body of water. **2.** A comic strip. **3.** An airstrip. **4.** An area, as along a busy street or highway, that is lined with a great number and variety of commercial establishments. —**strip** *tr.v.* **stripped, strip·ping, strips.** To cut or tear into strips. [Middle English, perhaps from Middle Low German *strippe,* strap, thong.]

strip-crop·ping (strĭp′krŏp′ĭng) *n.* The growing of a cultivated crop, such as cotton, and a sod-forming crop, such as alfalfa, in alternating strips following the contour of the land, in order to minimize erosion.

stripe[1] (strīp) *n.* **1.a.** A long narrow band distinguished, as by color or texture, from the surrounding material or surface. **b.** A textile pattern of parallel bands or lines on a contrasting background. **c.** A fabric having such a pattern. **2.** A strip of cloth or braid worn on a uniform to indicate rank, awards received, or length of service; a chevron. **3.** Sort; kind: *"All Fascists are not of one mind, one stripe"* (Lillian Hellman). —**stripe** *tr.v.* **striped, strip·ing, stripes.** To mark with stripes or a stripe. [Middle English, possibly from Middle Dutch or Middle Low German *strīpe.*]

stripe[2] (strīp) *n.* A stroke or blow, as with a whip. [Middle English.]

striped (strīpt, strī′pĭd) *adj.* Having lines or bands of different color or texture.

striped bass (băs) *n.* A North American food and game fish *(Morone saxatilis)* chiefly of coastal waters, having dark longitudinal stripes along its sides. Striped bass, which swim up rivers to spawn, are occasionally found in landlocked bodies of water. Also called *rockfish, striper.*

striped gopher *n.* A ground squirrel *(Citellus decemlineatus)* of western North America, marked with white lines over the back and flanks.

striped maple *n.* An eastern North American deciduous tree *(Acer pensylvanicum)* having smooth bark striped with vertical white lines and roundish, three-lobed leaves. Also called *moosewood.*

striped marlin *n.* A small marlin *(Tetrapturus audex* or *Makaira audex)* of the Pacific and Indian oceans, marked with vertical stripes along the sides.

striped skunk *n.* A North American skunk *(Mephitis mephitis)* commonly found from southern Canada to northern Mexico, having a pair of white stripes running from the top of the head to the tail.

striped squirrel *n.* Any of several small rodents with striped markings on the back, especially the chipmunk of North America.

strip·er (strī′pər) *n.* **1.** *Slang.* A member of the armed forces, a cadet corps, or a commercial flight crew who wears stripes designating rank or length of service. Often used in combination: *a three-striper; a four-striper.* **2.** See **striped bass.**

strip·film (strĭp′fĭlm′) *n.* See **filmstrip.**

strip·ing (strī′pĭng) *n.* **1.** The act or process of marking or decorating with stripes. **2.a.** The stripes placed on something. **b.** A pattern of stripes.

strip·ling (strĭp′lĭng) *n.* An adolescent youth. [Middle English, possibly from *strip,* strip. See STRIP[2].]

strip mine *n.* An open mine, especially a coal mine, whose seams or outcrops run close to ground level and are exposed by the removal of topsoil and overburden.

strip-mine (strĭp′mīn′) *v.* **strip-mined, strip-min·ing, strip-mines.** —*tr.* **1.** To mine (ore) from a strip mine. **2.** To subject to strip mining: *strip-mined the land.* —*intr.* To engage in strip mining. —**strip miner** *n.*

stripped-down (strĭpt′doun′) *adj.* Having only essential or minimal features; lacking anything extra: *a stripped-down stage setting; a stripped-down budget.*

strip·per (strĭp′ər) *n.* **1.** One that strips, as one that strips photographic negatives or positives. **2.** A chemical product for removing a surface covering, such as paint or varnish, from furniture or floors. **3.** *Slang.* One who performs a striptease. **4.** An oil well that produces ten barrels or fewer per day.

strip poker *n. Games.* Poker in which the losing players in each hand must remove an article of clothing.

strip search *n.* The act or an instance of subjecting a person to strip-searching. Also called *skin search.*

strip-search (strĭp′sûrch′) *tr.v.* **-searched, -search·ing, -search·es.** To search (a person) for illegal articles, such as drugs or weapons, by first requiring the removal of all clothing.

strip·tease also **strip tease** (strĭp′tēz′) *n.* A performance, as in a burlesque act, in which a person slowly removes clothing, usually to musical accompaniment. —**strip′teas′er** *n.*

strip·y (strī′pē) *adj.* **-i·er, -i·est.** Marked with or suggestive of stripes; striped.

strive (strīv) *intr.v.* **strove** (strōv), **striv·en** (strĭv′ən), or **strived, striv·ing, strives. 1.** To exert much effort or energy; endeavor. **2.** To struggle or fight forcefully; contend: *strive against injustice.* [Middle English *striven,* from Old French *estriver,* from *estrit, estrif,* quarrel. See STRIFE.] —**striv′er** *n.* —**striv′ing·ly** *adv.*

strobe (strōb) *n.* **1.** A strobe light. **2.** Stroboscope. **3.** A spot of higher than normal intensity in the sweep of an indicator, as on a radar screen, used as a reference mark for determining distance.

strobe light *n.* A flash lamp that produces high-intensity short-duration light pulses by electric discharge in a gas.

stro·bi·la (strō-bī′lə) *n., pl.* **-lae** (-lē). A part or structure that buds to form a series of segments, as the main body part of a tapeworm or the polyp stage in certain jellyfish. [New Latin, from Greek *strobilē,* twisted plug of lint, from *strobilos,* pine cone. See STROBILUS.] —**stro·bi′lar** *adj.*

stro·bi·la·ceous (strō′bə-lā′shəs) *adj.* Of or resembling a strobile; conelike.

stro·bi·la·tion (strō′bə-lā′shən) *n.* Asexual reproduction by division into body segments, as in tapeworms and jellyfish.

stro·bi·lus (strō-bī′ləs) also **stro·bile** (strō′bīl′, -bəl) *n., pl.* **-bi·li** (-bī′lī) or **-biles.** A conelike structure, such as a pine cone, the fruit of the hop, or a cone of a club moss, that consists of overlapping sporophylls spirally arranged along a central axis. [Late Latin, pine cone, from Greek *strobilos,* twisted object, pine cone, from *strobos,* a whirling. See **streb(h)-** in Appendix.]

strob·o·scope (strō′bə-skōp′) *n.* Any of various instruments used to observe moving objects by making them appear stationary, especially with pulsed illumination or mechanical devices that intermittently interrupt observation. [Greek *strobos,* a whirling; see **streb(h)-** in Appendix + –SCOPE.] —**stro′bo·scop′ic** (-skŏp′ĭk) *adj.* —**stro′bo·scop′i·cal·ly** *adv.*

stro·bo·tron (strō′bə-trŏn′) *n.* A gas-filled cathode tube that produces bright flashes of light for a stroboscope. [STROBO(SCOPE) + –TRON.]

strode (strōd) *v.* Past tense of **stride.**

Stro·heim (strō′hīm′), **Erich von.** 1885–1957. Austrian-born American actor and director who is best known for his roles in *La Grande Illusion* (1937) and *Sunset Boulevard* (1950).

stroke[1] (strōk) *n.* **1.** The act or an instance of striking, as with the hand, a weapon, or a tool; a blow or an impact. **2.a.** The striking of a bell or gong. **b.** The sound so produced. **c.** The time so indicated: *at the stroke of midnight.* **3.** A sudden action or process having a strong impact or effect: *a stroke of lightning.* **4.** A sudden occurrence or result: *a stroke of luck; a stroke of misfortune.* **5.** A sudden severe attack, as of paralysis or sunstroke. **6.** A sudden loss of brain function caused by a blockage or rupture of a blood vessel to the brain, characterized by loss of muscular control, diminution or loss of sensation or consciousness, dizziness, slurred speech, or other symptoms that vary with the extent and severity of the damage to the brain. Also called *cerebral accident, cerebrovascular accident.* **7.** An inspired or effective idea or act: *a stroke of genius.* **8.a.** A single uninterrupted movement, especially when repeated or in a back-and-forth motion: *the stroke of a pendulum.* **b.** Any of a series of movements of a piston from one end of the limit of its motion to another. **9.a.** A single completed movement of the limbs and body, as in swimming or rowing. **b.** The manner or rate of executing such a movement: *My favorite stroke is butterfly. She had a very rapid stroke.* **10.** *Nautical.* **a.** The rower who sits nearest the coxswain or the stern and sets the tempo for the other rowers. **b.** The position occupied by this person. **11.** *Sports.* **a.** A movement of the upper torso and arms for the purpose of striking a ball, as in golf or tennis. **b.** The manner of executing such a movement. **12.a.** A single mark made by a writing or marking implement, such as a pen. **b.** The act of making such a mark. **c.** A printed line in a graphic character that resembles such a mark. **13.** A distinctive effect or deft touch, as in literary composition. —**stroke** *v.* **stroked, strok·ing, strokes.** —*tr.* **1.a.** To mark with a single short line. **b.** To draw a line through; cancel: *stroked out the last sentence.* **2.** *Nautical.* To set the pace for (a rowing crew). **3.** To hit or propel (a ball, for example) with a smoothly regulated swing. —*intr.* **1.** To make or perform a stroke. **2.** *Nautical.* To row at a particular rate per minute. [Middle English, probably from Old English **strāc.* See **streig-** in Appendix.]

stroke[2] (strōk) *tr.v.* **stroked, strok·ing, strokes. 1.** To rub lightly, with or as if with the hand or something held in the hand; caress. **2.** *Informal.* To behave attentively or flatteringly toward, especially in order to restore to confidence or win over. —**stroke** *n.* A light caressing movement, as of the hand. [Middle English *stroken,* from Old English *strācian,* from **strāc,* stroke. See STROKE[1].] —**strok′er** *n.*

stroll (strōl) *v.* **strolled, stroll·ing, strolls.** —*intr.* **1.** To go for a leisurely walk: *stroll in the park.* **2.** To travel from place to place seeking work or gain. —*tr.* To walk along or through at a leisurely pace: *stroll the beach.* —**stroll** *n.* A leisurely walk. [Probably German dialectal *strollen,* variant of *strolchen,* from *Strolch,* fortuneteller, vagabond, perhaps from Italian dialectal *strolegh,* from Italian *astròlogo,* astrologer, fortuneteller, from Latin *astrologus,* astronomer, astrologer, from Greek *astrologos.* See ASTROLOGY.]

stroll·er (strō′lər) *n.* **1.** One who strolls: *elderly strollers in the park.* **2.** A light four-wheeled chairlike carriage for transporting small children. **3.** An itinerant actor or performer. **4.** A vagabond.

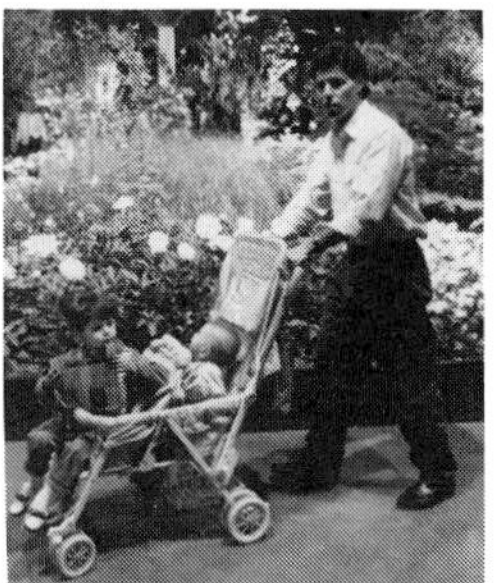

stroller
Baby stroller

stro·ma (strō′mə) *n., pl.* **-ma·ta** (-mə-tə). **1.** The connective tissue framework of an organ, a gland, or other structure, as distinguished from the tissues performing the special function of the organ or part. **2.** The spongy, colorless framework of a red blood cell or other cell. [Late Latin *strōma,* mattress, covering, from Greek, bed. See **ster-**[2] in Appendix.] —**stro′mal** *adj.* —**stro·mat′ic** (-măt′ĭk) *adj.*

stro·mat·o·lite (strō-măt′l-īt′) *n.* A widely distributed sedimentary structure consisting of laminated carbonate or silicate rocks, produced over geologic time by the trapping, binding, or precipitating of sediment by groups of microorganisms, primarily cyanobacteria. [Late Latin *strōma, strōmat-,* covering; see STROMA + –LITE.] —**stro·mat′o·lit′ic** (-măt′l-ĭt′ĭk) *adj.*

Strom·bo·li (strŏm′bə-lē, strôm′bô-). An island of southern Italy in the Lipari Islands off northeast Sicily in the Tyrrhenian Sea. Its active volcano, 926.6 m (3,038 ft) high, erupted violently in 1930 and 1966.

strong (strông) *adj.* **strong·er, strong·est. 1.a.** Physically powerful; capable of exerting great physical force. **b.** Marked by great physical power: *a strong blow to the head.* **2.** In good or sound health; robust: *a strong constitution; a strong heart.* **3.** Economically or financially sound or thriving: *a strong economy.* **4.** Having force of character, will, morality, or intelligence: *a strong personality.* **5.** Having or showing ability or achievement in a specified field: *students who are strong in chemistry.* **6.** Capable of the effective exercise of authority: *a strong leader.* **7.a.** Capable of withstanding force or wear; solid, tough, or firm: *a strong building; a strong fabric.* **b.** Having great binding strength: *a strong adhesive.* **8.** Not easily captured or defeated: *a strong flank; a strong defense.* **9.** Not easily upset; resistant to harmful or unpleasant influences: *strong nerves; a strong stomach.* **10.** Having force or rapidity of motion: *a strong current.* **11.a.** Persuasive, effective, and cogent: *a strong argument.* **b.** Forceful and pointed; emphatic: *a strong statement.* **c.** Forthright and explicit, often offensively so: *strong language.* **12.** Extreme; drastic: *had to resort to strong measures.* **13.** Having force of conviction or feeling; uncompromising: *strong faith; a strong supporter.* **14.** Intense in degree or quality: *a strong emotion; strong motivation.* **15.a.** Having an intense or offensive effect on the senses: *strong light; strong vinegar; strong cologne.* **b.** Clear and loud: *a strong voice.* **c.** Readily noticeable; remarkable: *a strong resemblance; a strong contrast.* **d.** Readily detected or received: *a strong radio signal.* **16.a.** Having a high concentration of an essential or active ingredient: *mixed a strong solution of bleach and water.* **b.** Containing a considerable percentage of alcohol: *strong punch.* **c.** Powerfully effective: *a strong painkiller.* **17.** *Color.* Characterized by a high degree of saturation. **18.** Having a specified number of units or members: *a military force 100,000 strong.* **19.** Marked by steady or rising prices: *a strong market.* **20.** *Linguistics.* **a.** Of or relating to those verbs in Germanic languages that form their past tense by a change in stem vowel, and their past participles by a change in stem vowel and sometimes by adding the suffix *-(e)n,* as *sing, sang, sung* or *tear, tore, torn.* **b.** Of or relating to the inflection of nouns or adjectives in Germanic languages with endings that historically did not contain a suffix with an *-n-.* **21.** Stressed or accented in pronunciation or poetic meter. Used of a word or syllable. —**strong** *adv.* In a strong, powerful, or vigorous manner; forcefully: *a salesperson who comes on too strong.* [Middle English, from Old English *strang.*] —**strong′ish** *adj.* —**strong′ly** *adv.*

SYNONYMS: *strong, stout, sturdy, tough, stalwart, tenacious.* These adjectives are compared as they mean having or showing vigor, durability, or power of body or spirit. *Strong* is the most general: *strong arms; a strong grip; a strong rope; strong resistance. "I am as strong as a bull moose"* (Theodore Roosevelt). *Stout* stresses the ability to endure, as by virtue of physical strength, solidity of construction, or resoluteness: *a stout branch; stout walls; a stout advocate. "It was enough to place horror upon the stoutest heart in the world"* (Daniel Defoe). *Sturdy,* like *stout,* implies ruggedness of body or construction or firmness of spirit or

ă pat	oi boy
ā pay	ou out
âr care	ŏŏ took
ä father	ōō boot
ĕ pet	ŭ cut
ē be	ûr urge
ĭ pit	th thin
ī pie	*th* this
îr pier	hw which
ŏ pot	zh vision
ō toe	ə about, item
ô paw	♦ regionalism

Stress marks: **′** (primary); ′ (secondary), as in **dictionary** (dĭk′shə-nĕr′ē)

purpose: *sturdy limbs; sturdy opposition; "sturdy russet boots"* (George W. Cable). *Tough* suggests physical or moral strength to resist opposition, strain, or hardship: *tough little burros hauling carts; "a tough but nervous, tenacious but restless race"* (Samuel Eliot Morison). *Stalwart* implies imposing strength or determination: *a stalwart proponent of tax reform; "proud of her stalwart, good-looking son"* (Booth Tarkington). *Tenacious* stresses persistence, as in holding fast to a position or goal: *"tenacious in upholding strict discipline"* (Sir Walter Scott).

Strong (strông), **William.** 1808–1895. American jurist who served as an associate justice of the U.S. Supreme Court (1870–1880).

strong-arm (strông′ärm′) *Informal. adj.* Using physical force or coercion: *strong-arm tactics.* **—strong-arm** *tr.v.* **-armed, -arm·ing, -arms. 1.** To use physical force or coercion against. **2.** To rob by force.

strong·box (strông′bŏks′) *n.* A stoutly made box or safe in which valuables are deposited.

strong breeze *n. Meteorology.* A wind having a speed ranging from 25 to 31 miles (39 to 50 kilometers) per hour, according to the Beaufort scale.

strong force *n. Physics.* See **strong interaction.**

strong gale *n. Meteorology.* A wind having a speed ranging from 47 to 54 miles (75 to 86 kilometers) per hour, according to the Beaufort scale.

strong·hold (strông′hōld′) *n.* **1.** A fortified place or a fortress. **2. a.** A place of survival or refuge: *one of the last strongholds of an age-old tradition.* **b.** An area dominated or occupied by a special group or distinguished by a special quality: *a feminist stronghold; a stronghold of democracy.*

strong interaction *n.* A fundamental interaction between elementary particles that causes protons and neutrons to bind together in the atomic nucleus. Also called *strong force.*

strong·man (strông′măn′) *n.* **1.** A powerful, influential political figure who exercises leadership and control by force. **2.** One who performs feats of strength, as at a circus.

strong-mind·ed (strông′mīn′dĭd) *adj.* **1.** Having a determined will. **2.** Having a vigorous, independent mind. **—strong′-mind′ed·ly** *adv.* **—strong′-mind′ed·ness** *n.*

strong·point (strông′point′) *n.* A military stronghold.

strong room *n.* A strongly built fireproof room designed for the safekeeping of money or valuables.

strong side *n. Football.* The side of a formation having more players; the side on which the tight end is positioned.

strong suit *n.* **1.** A quality, an activity, or a skill in which a person excels: *Foreign policy was the President's strong suit.* **2.** *Games.* A long suit in a card game such as bridge that contains high cards.

Strongs·ville (strôngz′vĭl′). A city of northeast Ohio, a residential suburb of Cleveland. Population, 28,577.

stron·gyle also **stron·gyl** (strŏn′jīl′, -jəl) *n.* Any of various nematode worms of the family Strongylidae, often parasitic in the gastrointestinal tract of mammals, especially horses. [New Latin *Strongylus,* type genus, from Greek *strongulos,* compact.]

stron·gy·lo·sis (strŏn′jə-lō′sĭs) *n.* Infestation with strongyles.

stron·ti·an·ite (strŏn′chē-ə-nīt′, -shə-nīt′) *n.* A gray to yellowish-green ore of strontium, $SrCO_3$. [*strontian,* strontianite (short for *Strontian earth,* after *Strontian,* a village of west-central Scotland) + -ITE [1].]

stron·ti·um (strŏn′chē-əm, -tē-əm, -shəm) *n. Symbol* **Sr** A soft, silvery, easily oxidized metallic element that ignites spontaneously in air when finely divided. Strontium is used in pyrotechnic compounds and various alloys. Atomic number 38; atomic weight 87.62; melting point 769°C; boiling point 1,384°C; specific gravity 2.54; valence 2. See table at **element.** [From New Latin *strontia,* strontium oxide, from *strontian.* See STRONTIANITE.] **—stron′tic** (-tĭk) *adj.*

strontium 90 *n.* The strontium isotope with mass 90, having a half-life of 28 years, used for its high-energy beta emission in certain nuclear electric power sources and constituting a radiation hazard in fallout.

strop (strŏp) *n.* **1.** A strap, especially a short rope whose ends are spliced together to make a ring. **2.** A flexible strip of leather or canvas used for sharpening a razor. **—strop** *tr.v.* **stropped, strop·ping, strops.** To sharpen (a razor) on a strop. [Middle English *strope,* band of leather, probably from Old English, thong for an oar, from Latin *stroppus,* twisted cord, from Greek *strophos,* from *strephein,* to turn. See **streb(h)-** in Appendix.]

stro·phan·thin (strō-făn′thĭn) *n.* A toxic glycoside or mixture of glycosides obtained from the seeds of certain plants of the genus *Strophanthus,* especially *S. kombé,* used medicinally as a cardiac stimulant. [New Latin *Strophanthus,* genus name (Greek *strophos,* twisted cord; see STROP + Greek *anthos,* flower) + -IN.]

stro·phe (strō′fē) *n. Abbr.* **str., st. 1. a.** The first of a pair of stanzas of alternating form on which the structure of a given poem is based. **b.** A stanza containing irregular lines. **2.** The first division of the triad constituting a section of a Pindaric ode. **3. a.** The first movement of the chorus in classical Greek drama while turning from one side of the orchestra to the other. **b.** The part of a choral ode sung while this movement is executed. [Greek *strophē,* a turning, stanza, from *strephein,* to turn. See **streb(h)-** in Appendix.] **—stro′phic** (strō′fĭk, strŏf′ĭk) *adj.*

stro·phoid (strō′foid′) *n.* A plane curve generated by a point that maintains a distance from the y-axis along a straight line equal to the y-intercept. [Greek *strophos,* twisted cord (from *strephein,* to turn; see **streb(h)-** in Appendix) + -OID.]

stroph·u·lus (strŏf′yə-ləs) *n., pl.* **-li** (-lē). A disease, especially common among children, sometimes associated with intestinal disturbances and characterized by a papular eruption of the skin. Also called *red gum.* [New Latin, from Greek *strophos,* twisted cord, from *strephein,* to turn. See **streb(h)-** in Appendix.]

strop·py (strŏp′ē) *adj.* **-pi·er, -pi·est.** *Chiefly British.* Easily offended or annoyed; ill-tempered or belligerent. [Perhaps alteration of OBSTREPEROUS.]

stroud (stroud) *n.* A coarse woolen cloth or blanket. [After *Stroud,* an urban district of southwest-central England.]

strove (strōv) *v.* Past tense of **strive.**

struck (strŭk) *v.* Past tense and a past participle of **strike.** **—struck** *adj.* Affected or shut down by a labor strike.

struck jury *n. Law.* A jury, especially a special jury, selected from an original panel of 48 members from which each party strikes off names until the list is reduced to the required number.

struc·tur·al (strŭk′chər-əl) *adj.* **1. a.** Of, relating to, having, or characterized by structure: *structural simplicity.* **b.** Affecting structure: *structural damage.* **2.** Used in or necessary to building: *structural beams.* **3.** Concerned with or resulting from political or especially economic structure. **4.** *Geology.* Of or relating to the structure of rocks and other aspects of the earth's crust. **5.** *Biology.* Of or relating to organic structure; morphological. **6.** Relating to or concerned with systematic structure in a particular field of study, such as linguistics or the behavioral sciences. **—structural** *n.* A part of a structure that bears a weight, or the structural piece used for such a part. **—struc′tur·al·ly** *adv.*

structural formula *n.* A chemical formula that shows how the atoms and bonds in a molecule are arranged.

structural gene *n.* A gene that determines the amino acid sequence of a protein.

struc·tur·al·ism (strŭk′chər-ə-lĭz′əm) *n.* **1.** A method of analyzing phenomena, as in anthropology, linguistics, psychology, or literature, chiefly characterized by contrasting the elemental structures of the phenomena in a system of binary opposition. **2.** A school that advocates and employs such a method. **—struc′tur·al·ist** *adj. & n.*

struc·tur·al·ize (strŭk′chər-ə-līz′) *tr.v.* **-ized, -iz·ing, -iz·es.** To form, organize, or incorporate into a structure. **—struc′tur·al·i·za′tion** (-ə-lĭ-zā′shən) *n.*

structural linguistics *n. (used with a sing. verb).* **1.** A method of synchronic linguistic analysis employing structuralism, especially in contrasting those formal structures, such as phonemes or sentences, that make up systems, such as phonology or syntax. **2.** A school of linguistics developed in the United States from the 1930's to the 1950's that advocated and employed such a method.

structural steel *n.* Steel shaped for use in construction.

struc·ture (strŭk′chər) *n.* **1.** Something made up of a number of parts that are held or put together in a particular way: *hierarchical social structure.* **2.** The way in which parts are arranged or put together to form a whole; makeup: *triangular in structure.* **3.** The interrelation or arrangement of parts in a complex entity: *political structure; plot structure.* **4.** Something constructed. See Synonyms at **building. 5.** *Biology.* **a.** The arrangement or formation of the tissues, organs, or other parts of an organism. **b.** An organ or other part of an organism. **—structure** *tr.v.* **-tured, -tur·ing, -tures.** To give form or arrangement to: *structure a curriculum; structure one's day.* [Middle English, the process of building, from Latin *strūctūra,* from *strūctus,* past participle of *struere,* to construct. See **ster-** [2] in Appendix.]

struc·tured (strŭk′chərd) *adj.* **1.** Highly organized: *a structured environment.* **2.** *Psychology.* Having a limited number of correct or nearly correct answers. Used of a test.

structured programming *n. Computer Science.* A method of designing and writing programs in which the statements are organized in a specific manner to minimalize error or misinterpretation.

stru·del (strōōd′l, shtrōōd′l) *n.* A pastry made with fruit or cheese rolled up in a thin sheet of dough and then baked. [German, strudel, from Middle High German, whirlpool.]

strug·gle (strŭg′əl) *v.* **-gled, -gling, -gles.** *—intr.* **1.** To exert muscular energy, as against a material force or mass: *struggled with the heavy load.* **2.** To be strenuously engaged with a problem, a task, or an undertaking. **3.** To make a strenuous effort; strive: *struggled to be polite.* **4.** To contend or compete: *"The human being struggles with his environment"* (Karl A. Menninger). **5.** To progress with difficulty: *struggled through calculus.* *—tr.* To move or place (something) with an effort: *struggled the heavy desk into the elevator.* **—struggle** *n.* **1.** The act of struggling. **2.** Strenuous effort; striving. **3.** Combat; strife: *armed struggle.* [Middle English *struglen.*] **—strug′gler** *n.* **—strug′gling·ly** *adv.*

strum (strŭm) *v.* **strummed, strum·ming, strums.** *—tr.* **1.** To play (a stringed musical instrument) by stroking or brushing the strings: *strum a banjo.* **2.** To play (music) on a stringed instrument in this way: *strum chords on a guitar.* *—intr.* To play a stringed instrument by strumming. **—strum** *n.* The act or sound of strumming. [Perhaps imitative.] **—strum′mer** *n.*

stru·ma (stro͞o′mə) *n., pl.* **-mae** (-mē) or **-mas. 1.a.** See **scrofula. b.** See **goiter. 2.** *Botany.* A cushionlike swelling at the base of a moss capsule. [Latin *strūma,* scrofulous tumor.] **—stru·mat′ic** (-măt′ĭk), **stru′mose′** (-mōs′), **stru′mous** (-məs) *adj.*

Stru·ma (stro͞o′mə). A river, about 348 km (216 mi) long, of western Bulgaria and northeast Greece flowing southward to an inlet of the Aegean Sea.

strum·pet (strŭm′pĭt) *n.* A prostitute. [Middle English.]

strung (strŭng) *v.* Past tense and past participle of **string. —strung** *adj.* Tense or exhausted: *His strung nerves made it difficult for him to relax.*

strung-out (strŭng′out′) *adj. Slang.* **1.a.** Stupefied from ingestion of a drug. **b.** Addicted to a drug. **2.a.** Severely debilitated from long-term drug use. **b.** Physically or emotionally exhausted.

strut (strŭt) *v.* **strut·ted, strut·ting, struts.** *—intr.* To walk with pompous bearing; swagger. *—tr.* **1.** To display in order to impress others: *She strutted all her new clothes before the guests.* **2.** To brace with a supporting bar or rod. **—strut** *n.* **1.** A pompous, self-important gait. **2.** A bar or rod used to brace a structure against forces applied from the side. ***—idiom.* strut (one's) stuff.** *Slang.* To behave or perform in an ostentatious manner; show off. [Middle English *strouten,* to stand out, from Old English *strūtian,* to stand out stiffly. See **ster-**[1] in Appendix.] **—strut′ter** *n.* **—strut′ting·ly** *adv.*

SYNONYMS: *strut, swagger, swank.* The central meaning shared by these verbs is "to walk or conduct oneself with exaggerated self-importance or affected superiority": *a pompous lecturer strutting back and forth across the stage; a parvenu swaggering around at a party; a newly elected senator's wife swanking around town.*

stru·thi·ous (stro͞o′thē-əs, -thē-) *adj.* Of, relating to, or resembling an ostrich or a related bird; ratite. [From Late Latin *strūthiō,* ostrich, from Late Greek *strouthiōn,* from Greek *strouthos.*]

strych·nine (strĭk′nīn′, -nĭn, -nēn′) *n.* An extremely poisonous white crystalline alkaloid, $C_{21}H_{22}O_2N_2$, derived from nux vomica and related plants, used as a poison for rodents and other pests and topically in medicine as a stimulant for the central nervous system. [French, from New Latin *Strychnos,* genus name, from Latin *strychnon,* a kind of nightshade, from Greek *strukhnon.*]

strych·nin·ism (strĭk′nĭ-nĭz′əm, -nī-, -nē-) *n.* A pathological condition induced by strychnine poisoning.

Stu·art (sto͞o′ərt, styo͞o′-). Ruling house of Scotland (1371–1603) and of England and Scotland (1603–1649 and 1660–1714).

Stuart, Charles Edward. Known as "the Young Pretender." 1720–1788. Pretender to the British throne. The grandson of James II, he led the last Jacobite rising (1745–1746), claiming the throne for his father, James Edward Stuart, but was defeated in battle and fled to France.

Stuart, Gilbert Charles. 1755–1828. American painter particularly known for his portraits of George Washington.

Stuart, Henry. See Lord **Darnley.**

Stuart, James Ewell Brown. Known as "Jeb." 1833–1864. American Confederate general who commanded brilliantly at the battles of Bull Run (1861 and 1862), Antietam (1862), and Fredericksburg (1862). His tactical error at Gettysburg (1863) contributed to the Confederate defeat there. Stuart was mortally wounded during the Wilderness Campaign (1864).

Stuart, James (Francis) Edward. Known as "the Old Pretender." 1688–1766. Pretender to the British throne. The son of James II, he made two unsuccessful attempts to take the throne (1708–1715). The final Jacobite rising (1745–1746), also a failure, was conducted on his behalf by his son Charles Edward Stuart.

♦**stub** (stŭb) *n.* **1.** The usually short end remaining after something bigger has been used up: *a pencil stub; a cigarette stub.* See Regional Note at **stob. 2.** Something cut short or arrested in development: *a stub of a tail.* **3.a.** The part of a check or receipt retained as a record. **b.** The part of a ticket returned as a voucher of payment. **—stub** *tr.v.* **stubbed, stub·bing, stubs. 1.a.** To pull up (weeds) by the roots. **b.** To clear (a field) of weeds. **2.** To strike (one's toe or foot) against something accidentally. **3.** To snuff out (a cigarette butt) by crushing. [Middle English *stubbe,* tree stump, from Old English *stybb.*]

stub·ble (stŭb′əl) *n.* **1.** The short, stiff stalks of grain or hay remaining on a field after harvesting. **2.** Something resembling this material, especially the short bristly hairs on a man's unshaven face. [Middle English *stuble,* from Old French *estuble,* from Latin *stupula, stupla,* variant of *stipula,* straw, diminutive of *stīpes,* stalk.] **—stub′bled** *adj.* **—stub′bly** *adj.*

stub·born (stŭb′ərn) *adj.* **-er, -est. 1.a.** Unreasonably, often perversely unyielding; bullheaded. **b.** Firmly resolved or determined; resolute. See Synonyms at **obstinate. 2.** Characterized by perseverance; persistent. **3.** Difficult to treat or deal with; resistant to treatment or effort: *stubborn soil; stubborn stains.* [Middle English *stuborn.*] **—stub′born·ly** *adv.* **—stub′born·ness** *n.*

Stubbs (stŭbz), **William.** 1825–1901. British historian and prelate known for his study of the constitutional history of medieval England.

♦**stub·by** (stŭb′ē) *adj.* **-bi·er, -bi·est. 1.a.** Having the nature of or suggesting a stub, as in shortness, broadness, or thickness: *stubby fingers.* **b.** Having a short, stocky build. **2.** Short and blunt, as from much use: *a stubby pencil.* See Regional Note at **stob. 3.** Covered with or made of stubs. **4.** Short and bristly: *a stubby beard.* **—stub′bi·ly** *adv.* **—stub′bi·ness** *n.*

stub nail *n.* A short, thick nail.

stuc·co (stŭk′ō) *n., pl.* **-coes** or **-cos. 1.** A durable finish for exterior walls, usually composed of cement, sand, and lime, and applied while wet. **2.** A fine plaster for interior wall ornamentation, such as moldings. **3.** A plaster or cement finish for interior walls. **4.** Stuccowork. **—stucco** *tr.v.* **-coed, -co·ing, -coes** or **-cos.** To finish or decorate with stucco. [Italian, of Germanic origin.]

stuc·co·work (stŭk′ō-wûrk′) *n.* Ornamental work or moldings or a finish done in stucco. **—stuc′co·work′er** *n.*

stuck (stŭk) *v.* Past tense and past participle of **stick.**

stuck-up (stŭk′ŭp′) *adj. Informal.* Snobbish; conceited.

stud[1] (stŭd) *n.* **1.** An upright post in the framework of a wall for supporting sheets of lath, wallboard, or similar material. **2.** A small knob, nail head, or rivet fixed in and slightly projecting from a surface. **3.a.** A small ornamental button mounted on a short post for insertion through an eyelet, as on a dress shirt. **b.** A buttonlike earring mounted on a slender post, as of gold or steel, for wearing in a pierced earlobe. **4.a.** Any of various protruding pins or pegs in machinery, used mainly as a support or pivot. **b.** One of a number of small metal cleats embedded in a snow tire to increase traction on slippery or snowy roads. **5.** A metal crosspiece used as a brace in a link, as in a chain cable. **—stud** *tr.v.* **stud·ded, stud·ding, studs. 1.** To provide with or construct with studs or a stud. **2.** To set with studs or a stud: *stud a bracelet with rubies.* **3.** To be scattered over: *Daisies studded the meadow.* [Middle English *stode,* from Old English *studu.* See **stā-** in Appendix.]

stud[2] (stŭd) *n.* **1.a.** A group of animals, especially horses, kept for breeding. **b.** A male animal, such as a stallion, that is kept for breeding. **c.** A stable or farm where these animals are kept. **2.** *Slang.* A man regarded as virile and sexually active. **3.** *Games.* Stud poker. ***—idiom.* at stud.** Available or offered for breeding. Used of animals. [Middle English *stod,* establishment for breeding horses, from Old English *stōd.* See **stā-** in Appendix.]

stud. *abbr.* Student.

stud·book (stŭd′bo͝ok′) *n.* A book registering the pedigrees of thoroughbred animals, especially horses.

stud·ding (stŭd′ĭng) *n.* **1.a.** The wood framework of a wall or partition. **b.** Lumber cut for studs. **2.** Something with which a surface is studded.

stud·ding·sail (stŭn′səl, stŭd′ĭng-sāl′) *n. Nautical.* A narrow rectangular sail set from extensions of the yards of square-rigged ships. [Origin unknown.]

stu·dent (sto͞od′nt, styo͞od′-) *n. Abbr.* **stud. 1.** One who attends a school, college, or university. **2.a.** One who makes a study of something. **b.** An attentive observer: *a student of world affairs. —attributive.* Often used to modify another noun: *student government; student issues.* [Middle English, alteration (influenced by Latin *studēre,* to study) of *studient, studiant,* from Old French *estudiant,* one who studies, from present participle of *estudier,* to study, from Medieval Latin *studiāre,* from Latin *studium,* study. See STUDY.]

student lamp *n.* A reading lamp having a flexible, adjustable neck and intended for use on a desk.

student teacher *n.* A college student pursuing a degree in education who, as an intern in teaching methodology, teaches in a classroom under the supervision and guidance of an experienced, certified teacher. Also called *practice teacher.* **—student teaching** *n.*

student union *n.* A building on a college campus with facilities for social and organizational activities.

stud·fish (stŭd′fĭsh′) *n., pl.* **studfish** or **-fish·es.** Either of two small, brightly colored topminnows *(Fundulus catenatus* or *F. stellifer)* of the southeast United States.

stud·horse also **stud horse** (stŭd′hôrs′) *n.* A stallion kept for breeding.

stud·ied (stŭd′ēd) *adj.* **1.** Resulting from deliberation and careful thought: *a studied decision.* **2.** Lacking spontaneity; contrived: *a studied smile.* **3.** Learned; knowledgeable. **—stud′ied·ly** *adv.* **—stud′ied·ness** *n.*

stu·di·o (sto͞o′dē-ō, styo͞o′-) *n., pl.* **-os. 1.** An artist's workroom. **2.** A photographer's establishment. **3.** An establishment where an art is taught or studied: *a dance studio.* **4.a.** A room or building for movie, television, or radio productions. **b.** A room or building where tapes and records are produced. [Italian, from Latin *studium,* eagerness, application. See STUDY.]

studio apartment *n.* A small apartment usually consisting of one main living space, a small kitchen, and a bathroom.

studio couch *n.* A couch that can be made to serve as a double bed by sliding the frame of a cot from beneath it.

stu·di·ous (sto͞o′dē-əs, styo͞o′-) *adj.* **1.a.** Given to diligent study: *a quiet, studious child.* **b.** Conducive to study. **2.** Marked by steady attention and effort; assiduous: *made a studious attempt to fix the television set.* **3.** Giving or evincing careful re-

strut

Gilbert Stuart
Self-portrait

J.E.B. Stuart
Photographed in the early 1860's

ă pat	oi boy
ā pay	ou out
âr care	o͝o took
ä father	o͞o boot
ĕ pet	ŭ cut
ē be	ûr urge
ĭ pit	th thin
ī pie	*th* this
îr pier	hw which
ŏ pot	zh vision
ō toe	ə about, item
ô paw	♦ regionalism

Stress marks: ′ (primary); ′ (secondary), as in **dictionary** (dĭk′shə-nĕr′ē)

gard; heedful: *"The major . . . was very studious of his appearance"* (H.E. Bates). **4.** Deliberate; contrived. [Middle English, from Latin *studiōsus,* from *studium,* eagerness. See STUDY.] **—stu′di·ous·ly** *adv.* **—stu′di·ous·ness** *n.*

stud poker *n. Games.* Poker in which the first round of cards, and often the last, is dealt face down and the others face up. [Probably short for *studhorse poker.*]

stud·work (stŭd′wûrk′) *n.* **1.** Work ornamented or covered with studs. **2.** The supportive framework of a wall or partition.

stud·y (stŭd′ē) *n., pl.* **-ies. 1.a.** The act or process of studying. **b.** The pursuit of knowledge, as by reading, observation, or research. **2.** Attentive scrutiny. **3.** A branch of knowledge. **4. studies.** A branch or department of learning: *graduate studies.* **5.a.** A work, such as a thesis, that results from studious endeavor. **b.** A literary work on a particular subject. **c.** A preliminary sketch, as for a work of art or literature. **6.** *Music.* A composition intended as a technical exercise. **7.** A state of mental absorption: *She is in a deep study.* **8.** A room intended or equipped for studying or writing. **9.a.** One who memorizes something, especially a performer with reference to his or her ability to memorize a part: *He is a quick study.* **b.** Memorization of a part in a play. **—study** *v.* **-ied, -y·ing, -ies.** *—tr.* **1.** To apply one's mind purposefully to the acquisition of knowledge or understanding of (a subject). **2.** To read carefully. **3.** To memorize. **4.** To take (a course) at a school. **5.** To inquire into; investigate. **6.** To examine closely; scrutinize. **7.** To give careful thought to; contemplate: *study the next move.* *—intr.* **1.** To apply oneself to learning, especially by reading. **2.** To pursue a course of study. **3.** To ponder; reflect. [Middle English *studie,* from Old French *estudie,* from Latin *studium,* from *studēre,* to study.]

study hall *n.* **1.** A schoolroom reserved for study. **2.** A period set aside for study.

stuff (stŭf) *n.* **1.** The material out of which something is made or formed; substance. **2.** The essential substance or elements; essence: *"We are such stuff/As dreams are made on"* (Shakespeare). **3.** *Informal.* **a.** Unspecified material: *Put that stuff over there.* **b.** Household or personal articles considered as a group. **c.** Worthless objects. **4.** *Slang.* Specific talk or actions: *Don't give me that stuff about being tired.* **5.** *Sports.* **a.** The control a player has over a ball, especially to give it spin, english, curve, or speed. **b.** The spin, english, curve, or speed imparted to a ball: *"where we could watch the stuff, mainly curves, that the pitchers were putting on the ball"* (James Henry Gray). **6.** Special capability: *The team really showed its stuff and won the championship.* **7.** *Chiefly British.* Woven material, especially woolens. **8.** *Slang.* Money; cash. **9.** *Slang.* A habit-forming drug, especially heroin. **—stuff** *v.* **stuffed, stuff·ing, stuffs.** *—tr.* **1.a.** To pack tightly; cram: *stuff a Christmas stocking.* **b.** To block (a passage); plug: *stuff a crack with caulking.* **2.a.** To fill with an appropriate stuffing: *stuff a pillow.* **b.** To fill (an animal skin) to restore its natural form for mounting or display. **3.** To cram with food. **4.** To fill (the mind): *His head is stuffed with silly notions.* **5.** To put fraudulent votes into (a ballot box). **6.** To apply a preservative and softening agent to (leather). *—intr.* To overeat; gorge. ***—idioms.*** **stuff it.** *Vulgar Slang.* Used as an intensive to express extreme anger, frustration, or disgust. **stuff (one's) face.** *Slang.* To eat greedily. [Middle English, from Old French *estoffe,* from *estoffer,* to equip, of Germanic origin.] **—stuff′er** *n.*

stuffed derma (stŭft) *n.* See **derma**[2].

stuffed shirt *n. Informal.* A person regarded as pompous or stiff.

stuff·ing (stŭf′ĭng) *n.* **a.** Padding put in cushions and upholstered furniture. **b.** Food put into the cavity of a piece of meat or a hollowed-out vegetable.

stuffing box *n.* An enclosure containing packing to prevent leakage around a moving machine part.

stuff shot *n. Basketball.* See **dunk shot.**

stuff·y (stŭf′ē) *adj.* **-i·er, -i·est. 1.** Lacking sufficient ventilation; close. **2.** Having the respiratory passages blocked: *a stuffy nose.* **3.a.** Dull and boring: *a stuffy lecture.* **b.** Rigidly adhering to standards of conduct; strait-laced: *"I went to one stuffy upper class dinner party on my first night & I go to another tonight"* (Evelyn Waugh). **—stuff′i·ly** *adv.* **—stuff′i·ness** *n.*

stull (stŭl) *n.* **1.** A supporting timber or other prop in a mine. **2.** A platform braced against the sides of a working area in a mine. [Probably from German *Stollen,* from Middle High German *stolle,* prop, support, from Old High German *stollo.* See **stel-** in Appendix.]

stul·ti·fy (stŭl′tə-fī′) *tr.v.* **-fied, -fy·ing, -fies. 1.** To render useless or ineffectual; cripple. **2.** To cause to appear stupid, inconsistent, or ridiculous. **3.** *Law.* To allege or prove insane and so not legally responsible. [Late Latin *stultificāre,* to make foolish : Latin *stultus,* foolish; see **stel-** in Appendix + Latin *-ficāre,* -fy.] **—stul′ti·fi·ca′tion** (-fĭ-kā′shən) *n.* **—stul′ti·fi′er** *n.*

stum (stŭm) *n.* **1.** Unfermented or partly fermented grape juice; must. **2.** Vapid wine renewed by an admixture of stum. **—stum** *tr.v.* **stummed, stum·ming, stums.** To ferment (vapid wine) by adding stum. [Dutch *stom,* dumb, stum, from Middle Dutch.]

stum·ble (stŭm′bəl) *v.* **-bled, -bling, -bles.** *—intr.* **1.a.** To miss one's step in walking or running; trip and almost fall. **b.** To proceed unsteadily or falteringly; flounder. See Synonyms at **blunder. c.** To act or speak falteringly or clumsily. **2.** To make a mistake; blunder. **3.** To fall into evil ways; err. **4.** To come upon accidentally or unexpectedly: *"The urge to wider voyages . . . caused men to stumble upon New America"* (Kenneth Cragg). *—tr.* To cause to stumble. **—stumble** *n.* **1.** The act of stumbling. **2.** A mistake or blunder. [Middle English *stumblen,* probably of Scandinavian origin; akin to Old Norse *stumra.*] **—stum′bler** *n.* **—stum′bling·ly** *adv.*

stum·ble·bum (stŭm′bəl-bŭm′) *n. Slang.* **1.** A person regarded as blundering or inept. **2.** *Sports.* A punch-drunk or second-rate prizefighter.

stum·bling block (stŭm′blĭng) *n.* An obstacle or impediment.

stump (stŭmp) *n.* **1.** The part of a tree trunk left protruding from the ground after the tree has fallen or has been felled. **2.** A part, as of a branch, limb, or tooth, remaining after the main part has been cut away, broken off, or worn down. **3.a. stumps.** *Informal.* The legs. **b.** An artificial leg. **4.** A short, thickset person. **5.** A heavy footfall. **6.** A place or an occasion used for political or campaign oratory: *candidates out on the stump.* **7.** A short, pointed roll of leather or paper or wad of rubber for rubbing on a charcoal or pencil drawing to shade or soften it. **8.** *Sports.* Any one of the three upright sticks in a cricket wicket. **—stump** *tr.v.* **stumped, stump·ing, stumps. 1.** To reduce to a stump. **2.** To clear stumps from: *stump a field.* **3.** To stub (a toe or foot). **4.** To traverse (a district) making political speeches: *a candidate stumping the state.* **5.** To shade (a drawing) with a stump. **6.** *Informal.* To challenge (someone); defy. **7.** *Informal.* To bring to a halt; baffle. [Middle English *stumpe,* possibly from Middle Low German *stump.*] **—stump′er** *n.* **—stump′i·ness** *n.* **—stump′y** *adj.*

stump·age (stŭm′pĭj) *n.* **1.** Standing timber regarded as a commodity. **2.** The value of standing timber. **3.** The right to cut standing timber.

stun (stŭn) *tr.v.* **stunned, stun·ning, stuns. 1.** To daze or render senseless, by or as if by a blow. **2.** To overwhelm or daze with a loud noise. **3.** To stupefy, as with the emotional impact of an experience; astound. See Synonyms at **daze. —stun** *n.* A blow or shock that stupefies. [Middle English *stonen,* Old French *estoner,* from Vulgar Latin **extonāre* : Latin *ex-,* ex- + Latin *tonāre,* to thunder; see **(s)tenə-** in Appendix.]

stung (stŭng) *v.* Past tense and past participle of **sting.**

stun gun *n.* A weapon designed to stun or temporarily immobilize a victim by firing pellets or bags of shot or sand or by delivering a high-voltage electric shock.

stunk (stŭngk) *v.* A past tense and the past participle of **stink.**

stun·ner (stŭn′ər) *n.* One that stuns, as: **a.** An astounding, unexpected event. **b.** An exceptionally good-looking person.

stun·ning (stŭn′ĭng) *adj.* **1.** Causing or capable of causing emotional shock or loss of consciousness. **2.** Of a strikingly attractive appearance. **3.a.** Impressive: *gave a stunning performance.* **b.** Surprising: *The President's final decision came with stunning suddenness.* **—stun′ning·ly** *adv.*

stunt[1] (stŭnt) *tr.v.* **stunt·ed, stunt·ing, stunts.** To check the growth or development of. **—stunt** *n.* **1.** One that stunts. **2.** One that is stunted. **3.** A plant disease that causes dwarfing. [From Middle English *stunnt,* foolish, short-witted, short (influenced by Old Norse *stuttr,* short, dwarfish) from Old English *stunt.*] **—stunt′ed·ness** *n.*

stunt[2] (stŭnt) *n.* **1.** A feat displaying unusual strength, skill, or daring. **2.** Something of an unusual nature done for publicity. **—stunt** *intr.v.* **stunt·ed, stunt·ing, stunts.** To perform stunts or a stunt. [Origin unknown.]

stunt box *n. Computer Science.* An electronic device designed to control the nonprinting functions of a teleprinter.

stunt·man (stŭnt′măn′) *n.* A man who substitutes for a performer in scenes requiring physical daring or involving physical risk.

stunt·wom·an (stŭnt′wo͝om′ən) *n.* A woman who substitutes for a performer in scenes requiring physical daring or involving physical risk.

stu·pa (sto͞o′pə) *n.* See **tope**[3]. [Sanskrit *stūpaḥ,* summit, stupa.]

stupe (sto͞op, styo͞op) *n.* A hot, wet, often medicated cloth used as a compress. [Middle English, from Latin *stuppa, stūpa,* tow, from Greek *stuppē.*]

stu·pe·fa·cient (sto͞o′pə-fā′shənt, styo͞o′-) *adj.* Inducing stupor; stupefying or narcotic. **—stupefacient** *n.* A drug, such as a narcotic, that induces stupor. [Latin *stupefaciēns, stupefacient-,* present participle of *stupefacere,* to stupefy. See STUPEFY.]

stu·pe·fac·tion (sto͞o′pə-făk′shən, styo͞o′-) *n.* **1.a.** The act or an instance of stupefying. **b.** The state of being stupefied. **2.** Great astonishment or consternation.

stu·pe·fac·tive (sto͞o′pə-făk′tĭv, styo͞o′-) *adj.* Stupefacient. **—stu′pe·fac′tive** *n.*

stu·pe·fy (sto͞o′pə-fī′, styo͞o′-) *tr.v.* **-fied, -fy·ing, -fies. 1.** To dull the senses or faculties of. See Synonyms at **daze. 2.** To amaze; astonish. [Middle English *stupefien,* from Old French *stupefier,* from Latin *stupefacere* : *stupēre,* to be stunned + *facere,* to make; see FACT.] **—stu′pe·fi′er** *n.* **—stu′pe·fy′ing·ly** *adv.*

stu·pen·dous (sto͞o-pĕn′dəs, styo͞o-) *adj.* **1.** Of astounding force, volume, degree, or excellence; marvelous. **2.** Amazingly large or great; huge. See Synonyms at **enormous.** [From Late Latin *stupendus,* stunning, gerundive of Latin *stupēre,* to be stunned.] **—stu·pen′dous·ly** *adv.* **—stu·pen′dous·ness** *n.*

stu·pid (sto͞o′pĭd, styo͞o′-) *adj.* **-er, -est. 1.** Slow to learn or understand; obtuse. **2.** Lacking or marked by a lack of intelligence. **3.** In a stupor; stupefied. **4.** In a dazed or stunned state. **5.** Pointless; worthless: *a stupid job.* **—stupid** *n.* A person regarded as stupid. [Latin *stupidus,* from *stupēre,* to be stunned.] **—stu′pid·ly** *adv.* **—stu′pid·ness** *n.*

SYNONYMS: *stupid, slow, dumb, dull, obtuse, dense.* These adjectives mean lacking or marked by a lack of intellectual acuity. *Stupid,* the most inclusive, means wanting in intelligence: *Despite a lack of formal education, she was far from stupid. Slow* and *dumb* imply chronic sluggishness of perception, reaction, or understanding: *The school offers special tutorials for slow learners. It was dumb of him to say yes. Dull* suggests a lack of keenness of intellect: *"It is the dull man who is always sure"* (H.L. Mencken). *Obtuse* implies a lack of quickness, sensitivity, or perceptiveness: *At the time, I was too obtuse to grasp the true implications of her behavior. Dense* suggests impenetrability of mind: *The woman kept signaling that it was time to leave, but her escort was so dense that he just kept sitting there.*

stu·pid·i·ty (sto͞o-pĭd′ĭ-tē, styo͞o-) *n., pl.* **-ties. 1.** The quality or condition of being stupid. **2.** A stupid act, remark, or idea.

stu·por (sto͞o′pər, styo͞o′-) *n.* **1.** A state of reduced or suspended sensibility. **2.** A state of mental numbness, as that resulting from shock; a daze. See Synonyms at **lethargy.** [Middle English, from Latin, from *stupēre,* to be stunned.] **—stu′por·ous** *adj.*

stur·dy (stûr′dē) *adj.* **-di·er, -di·est. 1.** Having or showing rugged physical strength. **2.** Substantially made or built; stout: *sturdy canvas.* **3.** Marked by resoluteness or determination; firm: *sturdy resistance.* **4.** Vigorous or robust. See Synonyms at **strong.** **—sturdy** *n.* See **gid.** [Middle English, stubborn, reckless, sturdy, from Old French *estourdi,* past participle of *estourdir,* to stun, perhaps from Vulgar Latin **exturdīre,* to be giddy as a thrush : Latin *ex-,* intensive pref.; see EX– + Latin *turdus,* thrush.] **—stur′di·ly** *adv.* **—stur′di·ness** *n.*

stur·geon (stûr′jən) *n.* Any of various large, ganoid freshwater and marine fishes of the family Acipenseridae of the Northern Hemisphere, having edible flesh and valued as a source of caviar and isinglass. [Middle English, from Anglo-Norman, from Old French *estourgeon,* of Germanic origin.]

Sturm und Drang (shto͝orm′ o͝ont dräng′) *n.* **1.** Turmoil; ferment: *"A book's historical roots represent another barrier; so does the personal Sturm und Drang of the author"* (Robert Kanigel). **2.** A late-18th-century German romantic literary movement whose works typically depicted the struggles of a highly emotional individual against conventional society. [German, storm and stress, after *Sturm und Drang,* a drama by Friedrich Maximilian von Klinger (1752–1831).]

stut·ter (stŭt′ər) *v.* **-tered, -ter·ing, -ters.** *—intr.* To speak with a spasmodic repetition or prolongation of sounds. *—tr.* To utter with spasmodic repetition or prolongation of sounds. See Synonyms at **stammer.** **—stutter** *n.* The act or habit of stuttering. [Frequentative of dialectal *stut,* from Middle English *stutten.*] **—stut′ter·er** *n.* **—stut′ter·ing·ly** *adv.*

Stutt·gart (stŭt′gärt′, sto͝ot′-, shto͝ot′-). A city of southwest Germany on the Neckar River south-southeast of Heidelberg. Chartered in the 13th century, it developed as an industrial center in the 19th and early 20th centuries and was heavily bombed during World War II. Population, 561,567.

Stuy·ve·sant (stī′vĭ-sənt), **Peter** or **Petrus.** 1592?–1672. Dutch colonial administrator. The last Dutch governor (1646–1664) of New Netherland, he was unpopular for his harsh leadership and in 1664 was forced to surrender the colony to England.

sty[1] (stī) *n., pl.* **sties** (stīz). **1.** An enclosure for swine. **2.** A filthy place. **—sty** *tr. & intr.v.* **stied** (stīd), **sty·ing, sties** (stīz). To shut up in or live in a sty. [Middle English, from Old English *stī-, stig.*]

sty[2] also **stye** (stī) *n., pl.* **sties** also **styes** (stīz). Inflammation of one or more sebaceous glands of an eyelid. [Alteration of Middle English *styanye* : *styan,* sty (from Old English *stīgend,* from present participle of *stīgan,* to rise; see **steigh-** in Appendix) + *eye, ye,* eye; see EYE.]

styg·i·an also **Styg·i·an** (stĭj′ē-ən) *adj.* **1.a.** Gloomy and dark. **b.** Infernal; hellish. **2.** Of or relating to the river Styx. [From Latin *Stygius,* from Greek *Stugios,* from *Stux, Stug-,* Styx.]

styl– *pref.* Variant of **stylo–.**

sty·lar (stī′lər, -lär′) *adj.* **1.** Of, relating to, or resembling a stylus. **2.** *Botany & Zoology.* Of or relating to a style.

sty·late (stī′lāt′) *adj.* Having a style or styles.

style (stīl) *n.* **1.** The way in which something is said, done, expressed, or performed: *a style of speech and writing.* **2.** The combination of distinctive features of literary or artistic expression, execution, or performance characterizing a particular person, group, school, or era. **3.** Sort; type: *a style of furniture.* **4.** A quality of imagination and individuality expressed in one's actions and tastes: *does things with style.* **5.a.** A comfortable and elegant mode of existence: *living in style.* **b.** A mode of living: *the style of the very rich.* **6.a.** The fashion of the moment, especially of dress; vogue. **b.** A particular fashion: *the style of the 1920's.* See Synonyms at **fashion.** **7.** A customary manner of presenting printed material, including usage, punctuation, spelling, typography, and arrangement. **8.** A form of address; a title. **9.a.** An implement used for etching or engraving. **b.** A slender, pointed, writing instrument used by the ancients on wax tablets. **10.** The needle of a phonograph. **11.** The gnomon of a sundial. **12.** *Botany.* The usually slender part of a pistil, situated between the ovary and the stigma. **13.** *Zoology.* A slender, tubular, or bristlelike process: *a cartilaginous style.* **14.** *Medicine.* A surgical probing instrument; a stylet. **15.** *Obsolete.* A pen. **—style** *tr.v.* **styled, styl·ing, styles. 1.** To call or name; designate: *George VI styled his brother Duke of Windsor.* **2.** To make consistent with rules of style: *style a manuscript.* **3.** To give style to: *style hair.* [Middle English, from Old French, from Latin *stylus, stilus,* spike, pointed instrument used for writing, style. See STYLUS.] **—styl′er** *n.* **—styl′ing** *n.*

style·book (stīl′bo͝ok′) *n.* A book giving rules and examples of usage, punctuation, and typography, used in preparation of copy for publication.

sty·let (stī-lĕt′, stī′lĭt) *n.* **1.** A slender, pointed instrument or weapon, such as a stiletto. **2.a.** A surgical probe. **b.** A fine wire that is run through a catheter, cannula, or hollow needle to keep it stiff or clear of debris. **3.** *Zoology.* A small, stiff, needlelike organ or appendage, such as the feeding organ of a tardigrade. [French, from Italian *stiletto,* stiletto. See STILETTO.]

sty·li (stī′lī) *n.* A plural of **stylus.**

styli– *pref.* Variant of **stylo–.**

sty·li·form (stī′lə-fôrm′) *adj.* Having the shape of a style; slender and pointed: *a styliform bone or appendage.*

styl·ish (stī′lĭsh) *adj.* Conforming to the current fashion; modish. See Synonyms at **fashionable.** **—styl′ish·ly** *adv.* **—styl′ish·ness** *n.*

styl·ist (stī′lĭst) *n.* **1.** A writer or speaker who cultivates an artful literary style. **2.** A designer of or consultant on styles in decorating, dress, or beauty.

sty·lis·tic (stī-lĭs′tĭk) *adj.* Of or relating to style, especially literary style. **—sty·lis′ti·cal·ly** *adv.*

sty·lis·tics (stī-lĭs′tĭks) *n. (used with a sing. verb).* The study of the use of elements of language style, such as metaphor, in particular contexts.

sty·lite (stī′līt′) *n.* One of a number of early Christian ascetics who lived unsheltered on the tops of high pillars. [Late Greek *stulitēs,* from Greek *stulos,* pillar. See **stā-** in Appendix.] **—sty·lit′ic** (-lĭt′ĭk) *adj.* **—sty′lit·ism** (stī′lī′tĭz-əm) *n.*

styl·ize (stī′līz′) *tr.v.* **-ized, -iz·ing, -iz·es. 1.** To restrict or make conform to a particular style. **2.** To represent conventionally; conventionalize. **—styl′i·za′tion** (stī′lĭ-zā′shən) *n.* **—styl′iz′er** *n.*

stylo– or **styli–** or **styl–** *pref.* Style: *stylopodium.* [From Latin *stilus, stylus,* stake, stem, style. See STYLUS.]

sty·lo·bate (stī′lə-bāt′) *n. Architecture.* The immediate foundation of a row of classical columns. Also called *stereobate.* [Latin *stylobata,* from Greek *stulobatēs* : *stulos,* pillar; see **stā-** in Appendix + *bainein,* to walk; see **g^wā-** in Appendix.]

sty·loid (stī′loid′) *adj.* **1.** Resembling a style in shape; slender and pointed: *the styloid muscles in carnivores.* **2.** *Anatomy.* Of, relating to, or designating any of several slender, pointed bone processes, especially the spine that projects from the base of the temporal bone.

sty·lo·lite (stī′lə-līt′) *n.* A secondary structure found along contacting surfaces of adjacent calcareous rock layers, the contact zone appearing in cross section as a series of jagged interlocking up-and-down projections that resemble a suture or the tracing of a stylus. [Greek *stulos,* pillar; see STYLITE + –LITE.]

sty·lo·po·di·um (stī′lə-pō′dē-əm) *n., pl.* **-di·a** (-dē-ə). An enlargement at the base of the style of flowers in certain plants of the parsley family.

sty·lus (stī′ləs) *n., pl.* **-lus·es** or **-li** (-lī). **1.** A sharp, pointed instrument used for writing, marking, or engraving. **2.** A phonograph needle. **3.** A sharp, pointed tool used for cutting record grooves. [Latin, alteration (influenced by Greek *stulos,* pillar; see STYLITE) of *stilus.*]

sty·mie also **sty·my** (stī′mē) *—tr.v.* **-mied** (-mēd), **-mie·ing** also **-my·ing** (-mē-ĭng), **-mies** (-mēz). To thwart; stump: *a problem in thermodynamics that stymied half the class.* *—n.* **1.** An obstacle or obstruction. **2.** *Sports.* A situation in golf in which an opponent's ball obstructs the line of play of one's own ball on the putting green. [Origin unknown.]

styp·sis (stĭp′sĭs) *n.* The action or application of a styptic. [Late Latin *stȳpsis,* from Greek *stupsis,* from *stuphein,* to contract.]

styp·tic (stĭp′tĭk) *adj.* **1.** Contracting the tissues or blood vessels; astringent. **2.** Tending to check bleeding by contracting the tissues or blood vessels; hemostatic. **—styptic** *n.* A styptic drug or substance. [Middle English *stiptik,* from Old French *stiptique,* from Latin *stȳpticus,* from Greek *stuptikos,* from *stuphein,* to contract.] **—styp·tic′i·ty** (-tĭs′ĭ-tē) *n.*

styptic pencil *n.* A short medicated stick, often of alum, applied to a cut to check bleeding.

Styr (stîr). A river, about 436 km (271 mi) long, of northwest Ukraine flowing northward to the Pripet River.

sty·rax (stī′răks) *n. Botany.* See **storax** (sense 1). [Latin. See STORAX.]

sty·rene (stī′rēn′) *n.* A colorless oily liquid, $C_6H_5CH{:}CH_2$, the monomer for polystyrene. [Latin *styrax,* storax; see STORAX + –ENE.]

Sty·ro·foam (stī′rə-fōm′). A trademark used for a light, re

sturgeon

Peter Stuyvesant
c. 1660 portrait attributed to Henri Couturrier

ă pat	oi boy
ā pay	ou out
âr care	o͝o took
ä father	o͞o boot
ĕ pet	ŭ cut
ē be	ûr urge
ĭ pit	th thin
ī pie	*th* this
îr pier	hw which
ŏ pot	zh vision
ō toe	ə about, item
ô paw	♦ regionalism

Stress marks: **′** (primary); ′ (secondary), as in **dictionary** (dĭk′shə-nĕr′ē)

SUBATOMIC PARTICLES

Subatomic particles fall into two major groups: the elementary particles and the hadrons. An **elementary particle** is not composed of any smaller particles and therefore represents the most fundamental form of matter. A **hadron** is composed of elementary particles called **quarks**. This table contains the most common subatomic particles, including the major constituents of the **atom**—the **electron** (an elementary particle), and the **proton** and the **neutron** (hadrons).

Explanation of Column Headings:
PARTICLE SYMBOL A superscript indicates charge.
ANTIPARTICLE SYMBOL Typically the same as the particle symbol but with a bar above or parentheses around it.

COMPOSITION The combination of quarks that make up the hadron. Some hadrons are members of **multiplets** that differ in **isospin** and their compositions are best described by using mathematical expressions.
MASS Expressed as a multiple of an electron's mass, 9.1066 x 10^{-28}g or 0.511 MeV.
ELECTRIC CHARGE Expressed as a multiple of an electron's charge, 1.602 x 10^{-19} coulomb. The antiparticle has a charge opposite that of its corresponding particle, except when both are neutral.
LIFETIME The average time in seconds that the particle exists. "Stable" means that the particle has no known mode of decay.

ELEMENTARY PARTICLES

FAMILY NAME	PARTICLE NAME	PARTICLE SYMBOL	ANTI-PARTICLE SYMBOL	MASS	ELECTRIC CHARGE	LIFETIME IN SECONDS
classon	photon	γ	(γ)	0	0	stable
	graviton	g	(g)	0	0	stable
weakon	W particle	W^-	W^+	160,000	−1	?
	Z particle	Z	Z	180,000	0	?
lepton	electron	e or e^-	e^+	1	−1	stable
	electron neutrino	ν_e	$\bar{\nu}_e$	about 0	0	stable
	muon	μ or μ^-	μ^+	209	−1	2.2 x 10^{-6}
	muon neutrino	ν_μ	$\bar{\nu}_\mu$	<0.49	0	stable
	tau	τ or τ^-	τ^+	3,490	−1	3.0 x 10^{-13}
	tau neutrino	ν_τ	$\bar{\nu}_\tau$	<69	0	stable (?)
quark	up	u	$\bar{u}$	607	+⅔	stable
	down	d	$\bar{d}$	607	−⅓	stable
	charm	c	$\bar{c}$	2,900	+⅔	?
	strange	s	$\bar{s}$	988	−⅓	?
	top	t	$\bar{t}$	> 100,000	+⅔	?
	bottom	b	$\bar{b}$	10,000	−⅓	?

HADRONS

FAMILY NAME	PARTICLE NAME	PARTICLE SYMBOL	ANTI-PARTICLE SYMBOL	COMPOSITION	MASS	ELECTRIC CHARGE	LIFETIME IN SECONDS
baryon							
nucleon	proton	p	$\bar{p}$	uud	1,836	+1	stable
	neutron	n	$\bar{n}$	udd	1,839	0	8.98 x 10^{2}*
hyperon	lambda	Λ^0	$\bar{\Lambda}^0$	uds	2,183	0	2.6 x 10^{-10}
	sigma	Σ^+	$\bar{\Sigma}^+$	uus	2,328	+1	0.8 x 10^{-10}
		Σ^0	$\bar{\Sigma}^0$	$\frac{(ud \pm du)s}{\sqrt{2}}$	2,334	0	6.0 x 10^{-20}
		Σ^-	$\bar{\Sigma}^-$	dds	2,343	−1	1.5 x 10^{-10}
	xi	Ξ^0	$\bar{\Xi}^0$	uss	2,573	0	2.9 x 10^{-10}
		Ξ^-	$\bar{\Xi}^-$	dss	2,585	−1	1.6 x 10^{-10}
	omega	Ω^-	$\bar{\Omega}^-$	sss	3,272	−1	0.8 x 10^{-10}
meson	pion	π^+	π^-	$u\bar{d}$	273	+1	2.6 x 10^{-8}
		π^0	π^0	$\frac{(u\bar{u} - d\bar{d})}{\sqrt{2}}$	264	0	8.4 x 10^{-17}
	kaon**	K^+	$\bar{K}^-$	$u\bar{s}$	966	+1	1.2 x 10^{-8}
		K^0	$\bar{K}^0$	$d\bar{s}$	974	0	8.9 x 10^{-11} or 5.2 x 10^{-8}
	J particle	J or Ψ	J or Ψ	$c\bar{c}$	6,060	0	1.0 x 10^{-20}
	omega	ω	ω	$\frac{(u\bar{u} + d\bar{d})}{\sqrt{2}}$	1,532	0	6.6 x 10^{-23}

* Neutrons are stable when bound within the nucleus.
** The neutral kaon is composed of two particles; the average lifetime of each particle is given.

silient polystyrene plastic. This trademark often occurs in print in lowercase: *"throw-away plates, utensils and styrofoam trays"* (Washington Post). *"selfpropelled boats from styrofoam"* (New York Times).

Sty·ron (stī′rən), **William.** Born 1925. American writer primarily known for his novels, including *Lie Down in Darkness* (1951) and *The Confessions of Nat Turner* (1967).

Styx (stĭks) *n. Greek Mythology.* The river across which the souls of the dead are ferried, one of the five rivers in Hades. [Latin, from Greek *Stux.*]

su·a·ble (so͞o′ə-bəl) *adj. Law.* Subject to suit in a court of law. **—su′a·bil′i·ty** *n.*

sua·sion (swā′zhən) *n.* Persuasion: *moral suasion.* [Middle English, from Old French, from Latin *suāsiō, suāsiōn-,* from *suāsus,* past participle of *suādēre,* to advise. See **swād-** in Appendix.]

sua·sive (swā′sĭv) *adj.* Having the power to persuade or convince; persuasive. [Latin *suāsus,* past participle of *suādēre,* to advise; see SUASION + –IVE.] **—sua′sive·ly** *adv.* **—sua′sive·ness** *n.*

suave (swäv) *adj.* **suav·er, suav·est.** Smoothly agreeable and courteous. [French, agreeable, from Old French, from Latin *suāvis,* delightful, sweet. See **swād-** in Appendix.] **—suave′ly** *adv.* **—suave′ness, suav′i·ty** (swä′vĭ-tē) *n.*

SYNONYMS: *suave, smooth, urbane, diplomatic, politic.* These adjectives mean effortlessly gracious, tactful, and polite. *Suave* suggests courtesy, social polish, and often a degree of sophistication: *"That same year he made his Broadway debut, playing a suave radio journalist"* (Edward Hudson). *Smooth* stresses a deliberate, usually ingratiating agreeableness: *The manager pacified the irate customer with a smooth apology for the error. Urbane* implies a high degree of refinement together with the assurance that comes from wide social experience: *"Urbane and pliant . . . he was at ease even in the drawing rooms of Paris"* (R.R. Palmer). *Diplomatic* suggests skill, tact, and sensitivity in dealing with others: *The hostess averted a confrontation between the two guests with an adroit and diplomatic change of subject. Politic* implies artful management, prudence, or expedience: *"He was too politic to quarrel with so important a personage"* (John Lothrop Motley).

♦**sub¹** (sŭb) *n. Informal.* **1.** See **submarine** (sense 1). **2.** See **submarine** (sense 2). See Regional Note at **submarine.**

sub² (sŭb) *Informal. n.* A substitute. **—sub** *intr.v.* **subbed, sub·bing, subs.** To act as a substitute.

sub. *abbr.* **1.** Subaltern. **2.** Suburb; suburban.

sub– *pref.* **1.** Below; under; beneath: *subsoil.* **2.a.** Subordinate; secondary: *subplot.* **b.** Subdivision: *subregion.* **3.** Less than completely or normally; nearly; almost: *subhuman.* [Middle English, from Latin, from *sub,* under. See **upo** in Appendix.]

sub·ab·dom·i·nal (sŭb′ăb-dŏm′ə-nəl) *adj.* Located or occurring below the abdomen.

sub·ac·id (sŭb-ăs′ĭd) *adj.* Somewhat sharp or acid in character: *subacid remarks.*

sub·a·cute (sŭb′ə-kyo͞ot′) *adj.* **1.** Somewhat or moderately acute: *subacute petals and sepals.* **2.** Between acute and chronic: *subacute fever symptoms; subacute endocarditis.* **—sub′a·cute′ly** *adv.*

subacute scle·ros·ing panencephalitis (sklə-rō′sĭng) *n.* An often fatal degenerative disease of the central nervous system occurring chiefly in young people, caused by slow infection with a measles virus and characterized by progressive loss of mental and motor functions ending in dementia and paralysis.

sub·ad·dress (sŭb′ə-drĕs′) *n. Computer Science.* A section of a computer device for input and output accessible through an operation code.

sub·aer·i·al (sŭb-âr′ē-əl) *adj.* Located or occurring on or near the surface of the earth.

sub·al·pine (sŭb-ăl′pīn′) *adj.* **1.** Of or relating to regions at or near the foot of the Alps. **2.** Of, relating to, inhabiting, or growing in mountainous regions just below the timberline.

sub·al·tern (sŭb-ôl′tərn, sŭb′əl-tûrn′) *adj. Abbr.* **sub. 1.** Lower in position or rank; secondary. **2.** *Chiefly British.* Holding a military rank just below that of captain. **3.** *Logic.* In the relation of a particular proposition to a universal with the same subject, predicate, and quality. **—subaltern** *n. Abbr.* **sub. 1.** A subordinate. **2.** *Chiefly British.* A subaltern officer. **3.** *Logic.* A subaltern proposition. [French *subalterne,* from Old French, from Late Latin *subalternus* : Latin *sub-,* sub- + Latin *alternus,* alternate (from *alter,* other; see **al-¹** in Appendix).]

sub·al·ter·nate (sŭb-ôl′tər-nĭt) *adj.* **1.** Subordinate. **2.** *Botany.* Arranged in an alternating pattern but tending to become opposite. Used of leaves. **—sub·al′ter·na′tion** (-nā′shən) *n.*

sub·ant·arc·tic (sŭb′ănt-ärk′tĭk, -är′tĭk) *adj.* Of or resembling regions just north of the Antarctic Circle.

sub·ap·i·cal (sŭb-ăp′ĭ-kəl, -ā′pĭ-) *adj.* Located below or near an apex. **—sub·ap′i·cal·ly** *adv.*

sub·a·que·ous (sŭb-ā′kwē-əs, -ăk′wē-) *adj.* **1.** Formed or adapted for underwater use or operation; submarine. **2.** Found or occurring underwater: *subaqueous organisms; subaqueous rocks.*

sub·a·rach·noid (sŭb′ə-răk′noid) *adj.* Situated or occurring beneath the arachnoid membrane, or between the arachnoid and the pia mater: *subarachnoid space; subarachnoid anesthesia.*

sub·arc·tic (sŭb-ärk′tĭk, -är′tĭk) *adj.* Of or resembling regions just south of the Arctic Circle.

sub·ar·id (sŭb-ăr′ĭd) *adj.* Somewhat arid; moderately dry.

sub·as·sem·bly (sŭb′ə-sĕm′blē) *n., pl.* **-blies.** An assembled unit forming a component to be incorporated into a larger assembly.

sub·a·tom·ic (sŭb′ə-tŏm′ĭk) *adj.* **1.** Of or relating to the constituents of the atom. **2.** Having dimensions or participating in reactions characteristic of the constituents of the atom.

subatomic particle *n.* Any of various units of matter below the size of an atom, including the elementary particles.

sub·au·di·tion (sŭb′ô-dĭsh′ən) *n.* **1.** The act of understanding and mentally supplying a word or thought that has been implied but not expressed. **2.** A word or thought supplied by subaudition. [Late Latin *subaudītiō, subaudītiōn-,* from *subaudītus,* past participle of *subaudīre,* to supply an omitted word : Latin *sub-,* sub- + Latin *audīre,* to hear; see **au-** in Appendix.]

sub·ax·il·lar·y (sŭb-ăk′sə-lĕr′ē) *adj.* Situated beneath the axilla or armpit: *subaxillary glands; subaxillary feathers.*

sub·base (sŭb′bās′) *n.* The lowermost front strip or molding of a baseboard.

sub·base·ment (sŭb′bās′mənt) *n.* A floor beneath a main basement of a building.

sub·bass (sŭb′bās′) *n. Music.* A pedal stop on an organ that produces the lowest tones, having 16 or 32 feet.

sub·cab·i·net (sŭb′kăb′ə-nĭt) *adj.* Of, relating to, or being an administrative position below cabinet level: *initially held talks at the subcabinet level.*

sub·cal·i·ber (sŭb-kăl′ə-bər) *adj.* **1.** Smaller in caliber than the barrel of the gun from which it was fired. Used of projectiles. **2.** Of or relating to such projectiles.

sub·car·ri·er (sŭb′kăr′ē-ər) *n. Physics.* A section of a transmitted wave used to modify the information-carrying section of the wave.

sub·car·ti·lag·i·nous (sŭb′kär-tl-ăj′ə-nəs) *adj.* **1.** Located beneath a cartilage. **2.** Partly cartilaginous.

sub·cat·e·go·ry (sŭb-kăt′ĭ-gôr′ē, -gōr′ē, sŭb′kăt′-) *n., pl.* **-ries.** A subdivision that has common differentiating characteristics within a larger category.

sub·ceil·ing (sŭb′sē′lĭng) *n.* See **sublimit.**

sub·ce·les·tial (sŭb′sĭ-lĕs′chəl) *adj.* **1.** Lower than celestial; terrestrial. **2.** Mundane.

sub·cel·lu·lar (sŭb-sĕl′yə-lər) *adj.* **1.** Situated or occurring within a cell: *subcellular organelles.* **2.** Smaller in size than ordinary cells: *subcellular organisms.* **3.** Below the cellular level: *subcellular research.*

sub·cen·ter (sŭb′sĕn′tər) *n.* A secondary center, especially a commercial or shopping area located away from the main business sector of a city. **—sub·cen′tral** (-trəl) *adj.*

sub·chas·er (sŭb′chā′sər) *n. Informal.* A submarine chaser.

sub·class (sŭb′klăs′) *n.* **1.** A subdivision of a set or class. **2.** *Biology.* A taxonomic category of related organisms ranking between a class and an order.

sub·cla·vi·an (sŭb-klā′vē-ən) *adj. Anatomy.* **1.** Situated beneath the clavicle. **2.** Of or relating to a subclavian part. **3.** Of or relating to the subclavian artery or vein. **—subclavian** *n.* A subclavian structure, such as a nerve or muscle. [From New Latin *subclāvius* : SUB– + Latin *clāvis,* key; see CLAVICLE.]

subclavian artery *n.* A part of a major artery of the upper extremities or forelimbs that passes beneath the clavicle and is continuous with the axillary artery.

subclavian vein *n.* A part of a major vein of the upper extremities or forelimbs that passes beneath the clavicle and is continuous with the axillary vein.

sub·cli·max (sŭb-klī′măks′) *n. Ecology.* A stage in the ecological succession of a plant or animal community immediately preceding a climax, and often persisting because of the effects of fire, flood, or other conditions. **—sub′cli·mac′tic** (-măk′tĭk) *adj.*

sub·clin·i·cal (sŭb-klĭn′ĭ-kəl) *adj.* Not manifesting characteristic clinical symptoms. Used of a disease or condition. **—sub·clin′i·cal·ly** *adv.*

sub·com·mit·tee (sŭb′kə-mĭt′ē) *n.* A subordinate committee composed of members appointed from a main committee.

sub·com·pact (sŭb-kŏm′păkt′) *n.* An automobile smaller than a compact.

sub·com·po·nent (sŭb′kəm-pō′nənt) *n.* A portion of a component, especially a piece of electronic equipment that can be incorporated into a component of a larger unit; a subassembly: *testing the subcomponents of the new weapons system.*

sub·con·fer·ence (sŭb′kŏn′fər-əns, -frəns) *n.* A subcommittee of a congressional conference.

sub·con·scious (sŭb-kŏn′shəs) *adj.* Not wholly conscious; partially or imperfectly conscious: *subconscious perceptions.* **—subconscious** *n.* The part of the mind below the level of conscious perception. Often used with *the.* **—sub·con′scious·ly** *adv.* **—sub·con′scious·ness** *n.*

sub·con·ti·nent (sŭb′kŏn′tə-nənt, sŭb-kŏn′-) *n.* **1.** A large landmass, such as India, that is part of a continent but is considered either geographically or politically as an independent entity. **2.** A large landmass, such as Greenland, that is smaller than a continent. **—sub′con·ti·nen′tal** (-nĕn′tl) *adj.*

sub·con·tract (sŭb-kŏn′trăkt′, sŭb′kŏn′trăkt) *n.* A contract that assigns some of the obligations of a prior contract to another party. **—subcontract** (sŭb-kŏn′trăkt′, sŭb′kən-trăkt′) *intr. & tr.v.* **-tract·ed, -tract·ing, -tracts.** To make a subcontract or a subcontract for.

sub·con·trac·tor (sŭb-kŏn′trăk′tər, sŭb′kən-trăk′tər) *n.* One that enters into a subcontract and assumes some of the obligations of the primary contractor.

sub·con·trar·y (sŭb-kŏn′trĕr′ē) *n., pl.* **-ries.** *Logic.* A proposition related to another in such a way that both may be true, but both cannot be false.

sub·cor·tex (sŭb-kôr′tĕks) *n., pl.* **-ti·ces** (-tĭ-sēz′). The portion of the brain immediately below the cerebral cortex. **—sub·cor′ti·cal** (-tĭ-kəl) *adj.* **—sub·cor′ti·cal·ly** *adv.*

sub·crit·i·cal (sŭb-krĭt′ĭ-kəl) *adj.* **1.** Having a mass of fissionable material that is less than that needed for a chain reaction. **2.** Of less than critical importance.

sub·cul·ture (sŭb′kŭl′chər) *n.* **1.** A cultural subgroup differentiated by status, ethnic background, residence, religion, or other factors that functionally unify the group and act collectively on each member. **2.** One culture of microorganisms derived from another. **—sub·cul′tur·al** *adj.*

sub·cu·ta·ne·ous (sŭb′kyo͞o-tā′nē-əs) *adj.* Located, found, or placed just beneath the skin: *subcutaneous tissue; a subcutaneous implant.* **—sub′cu·ta′ne·ous·ly** *adv.*

sub·cu·tis (sŭb-kyo͞o′tĭs) *n.* A layer of connective tissue beneath the dermis.

sub·dea·con (sŭb-dē′kən) *n.* **1.** A cleric ranking just below a deacon. **2.** A cleric who acts as assistant to the deacon at High Mass.

sub·deb (sŭb′dĕb′) *n. Informal.* A subdebutante.

sub·deb·u·tante (sŭb-dĕb′yə-tänt′) *n.* **1.** A teenage girl approaching her debut. **2.** A girl in her middle teens.

sub·di·ac·o·nate (sŭb′dī-ăk′ə-nĭt) *n.* The office, order, or

William Styron
Photographed in 1990

ă pat	oi boy
ā pay	ou out
âr care	o͝o took
ä father	o͞o boot
ĕ pet	ŭ cut
ē be	ûr urge
ĭ pit	th thin
ī pie	*th* this
îr pier	hw which
ŏ pot	zh vision
ō toe	ə about, item
ô paw	♦ regionalism

Stress marks: ′ (primary); ′ (secondary), as in **dictionary** (dĭk′shə-nĕr′ē)

rank of subdeacon. [Late Latin *subdiāconātus,* from *subdiāconus,* subdeacon (partial translation of Late Greek *hupodiakonos*) : Latin *sub-,* sub- + Greek *diakonos,* attendant.] **—sub′di·ac′o·nal** *adj.*

sub·di·rec·to·ry (sŭb′dĭ-rĕk′tə-rē, -dī-) *n., pl.* **-ries.** *Computer Science.* A subdivision of a computer directory.

sub·dis·ci·pline (sŭb′dĭs′ə-plĭn) *n.* A field of specialized study within a broader discipline; a subfield.

sub·di·vide (sŭb′dĭ-vīd′, sŭb′dĭ-vīd′) *v.* **-vid·ed, -vid·ing, -vides.** *—tr.* **1.** To divide a part or parts of into smaller parts. **2.** To divide into a number of parts, especially to divide (land) into lots. *—intr.* To form into subdivisions. **—sub′di·vid′er** *n.*

sub·di·vi·sion (sŭb′dĭ-vĭzh′ən, sŭb′dĭ-vĭzh′ən) *n.* **1.a.** The act or process of subdividing. **b.** A subdivided part. **2.** An area composed of subdivided lots. **—sub′di·vi′sion·al** *adj.*

sub·dom·i·nant (sŭb-dŏm′ə-nənt) *n. Music.* The fourth tone of a diatonic scale, next below the dominant. **—sub·dominant** *adj.* **1.** *Zoology.* Less than dominant; ranking below one that is dominant: *the subdominant male in a pride of lions.* **2.** *Ecology.* Prevalent in a community but below the dominant in importance. Used of a species.

sub·duc·tion (səb-dŭk′shən) *n.* A geologic process in which one edge of one crustal plate is forced below the edge of another. [French, from Latin *subductus,* past participle of *subdūcere,* to draw away from below : *sub-,* sub- + *dūcere,* to lead; see **deuk-** in Appendix.]

sub·due (səb-do͞o′, -dyo͞o′) *tr.v.* **-dued, -du·ing, -dues. 1.** To conquer and subjugate; vanquish. See Synonyms at **defeat. 2.** To quiet or bring under control by physical force or persuasion; make tractable. **3.** To make less intense or prominent; tone down: *Subdued my excitement about the upcoming holiday.* **4.** To bring (land) under cultivation: *Farmers subdued the arid lands of Australia.* [Middle English *subduen,* alteration (influenced by Latin *subdere,* to subject) of Old French *suduire,* to seduce, from Latin *subdūcere,* to withdraw (probably influenced by Latin *sēdūcere,* to seduce; see SEDUCE) : *sub-,* away; see SUB– + *dūcere,* to lead; see **deuk-** in Appendix.] **—sub·du′a·ble** *adj.* **—sub·du′er** *n.*

sub·dur·al (səb-do͝or′əl, -dyo͝or′-) *adj.* Located or occurring beneath the dura mater: *subdural space; a subdural hematoma.*

sub·em·ployed (sŭb′em-ploid′) *adj.* Of or relating to workers or segments of the paid labor force that are unemployed, underemployed, or underpaid. **—sub′em·ploy′ment** *n.*

sub·en·try (sŭb′ĕn′trē) *n., pl.* **-tries.** An entry, such as one in an account, a catalog, or a reference work, that is included within a main entry.

sub·e·qua·to·ri·al (sŭb′ē-kwə-tôr′ē-əl, -tōr′-, -ĕk-wə-) *adj.* Belonging to a region adjacent to an equatorial area.

su·ber·ic acid (so͞o-bĕr′ĭk) *n.* A colorless crystalline dibasic acid, $HOOC(CH_2)_6COOH$, used in the manufacture of plastics. [French *subérique,* from Latin *sūber,* cork.]

su·ber·in (so͞o′bər-ĭn) *n.* A waxy waterproof substance present in the cell walls of cork tissue in plants. [French *subérine* : Latin *sūber,* cork + French *-ine,* adj. suff.; see –INE[2].]

su·ber·i·za·tion (so͞o′bər-ĭ-zā′shən) *n.* Deposition of suberin on the walls of plant cells and their subsequent conversion into cork tissue.

su·ber·ize (so͞o′bə-rīz′) *tr.v.* **-ized, -iz·ing, -iz·es.** To cause to undergo suberization. [From Latin *sūber,* cork.]

su·ber·ose (so͞o′bə-rōs′) also **su·ber·ous** (-bər-əs) *adj.* Of, relating to, or resembling cork or cork tissue. [Latin *sūber,* cork + –OSE[1].]

sub·fam·i·ly (sŭb′făm′ə-lē) *n., pl.* **-lies. 1.** *Biology.* A taxonomic category of related organisms ranking between a family and a genus. **2.** *Linguistics.* A division of languages below a family and above a branch.

sub·field (sŭb′fēld′) *n.* **1.** A subdivision of a field of study; a subdiscipline. **2.** *Mathematics.* A field that is a subset of another field.

sub·floor·ing (sŭb′flôr′ĭng, -flōr′-) or **sub·floor** (-flôr′, -flōr′) *n.* A rough floor over which a finished floor, flooring material, or carpet is laid.

sub·fos·sil (sŭb′fŏs′əl) *adj.* Partly fossilized: *subfossil animals and plants.* **—subfossil** *n.* A subfossil organism.

sub·freez·ing (sŭb-frē′zĭng) *adj.* Below freezing.

sub·fusc (sŭb-fŭsk′) *adj.* Of a dark, dull, or somber color. **—subfusc** *n.* Dark, dull clothing. [Latin *subfuscus,* brownish : *sub-,* sub- + *fuscus,* dark.]

sub·gen·e·ra (sŭb′jĕn′ər-ə) *n.* Plural of **subgenus.**

sub·gen·re (sŭb′zhän′rə) *n.* A subcategory within a particular genre: *The academic mystery is a subgenre of the mystery novel.*

sub·ge·nus (sŭb′jē′nəs) *n., pl.* **-gen·e·ra** (-jĕn′ər-ə). *Biology.* An occasionally used taxonomic category ranking between a genus and a species. **—sub′ge·ner′ic** (-jə-nĕr′ĭk) *adj.*

sub·gla·cial (sŭb-glā′shəl) *adj.* Formed or deposited beneath a glacier. **—sub′gla′cial·ly** *adv.*

sub·grade (sŭb′grād′) *n.* The level layer of rock or earth upon which the foundation of a road or railway is laid.

sub·group (sŭb′gro͞op′) *n.* **1.** A distinct group within a group; a subdivision of a group. **2.** A subordinate group. **3.** *Mathematics.* A nonempty subset of a group.

sub·gum (sŭb′gŭm′) *n.* A dish of Chinese origin made with mixed vegetables. [Chinese (Cantonese) *shap kam,* mixture.]

sub·har·mon·ic (sŭb′här-mŏn′ĭk) *adj.* Of, relating to, or being a wave with a frequency that is a fraction of a fundamental frequency.

sub·head (sŭb′hĕd′) *n.* **1.** The heading or title of a subdivision of a printed subject. **2.** A subordinate heading or title.

sub·hu·man (sŭb-hyo͞o′mən) *adj.* **1.** Below the human race in evolutionary development. **2.** Regarded as not being fully human. **—sub·hu′man** *n.*

Su·bic Bay (so͞o′bĭk). An inlet of the South China Sea off west-central Luzon, Philippines, west of Manila Bay.

sub·in·dex (sŭb-ĭn′dĕks) *n., pl.* **-di·ces** (-dĭ-sēz′). **1.** *Mathematics.* A subscript. **2.** *pl.* **-dic·es** or **-dex·es** An index of measurement based on relatively few variables, especially a trade index based on the performance of a particular group or type of stocks.

sub·in·dus·try (sŭb′ĭn′də-strē) *n., pl.* **-tries. 1.** A subgroup within an industry. **2.** A business or an industry that arises from or provides materials and services to a larger industry: *a subindustry supplying accessories for home computers.*

sub·in·feu·date (sŭb′ĭn-fyo͞o′dāt′) also **sub·in·feud** (-fyo͞od′) *tr.v.* **-dat·ed, -dat·ing, -dates** also **-feud·ed, -feud·ing, -feuds.** To lease (lands) by subinfeudation.

sub·in·feu·da·tion (sŭb′ĭn-fyo͞o-dā′shən) *n.* **1.** The sublease of a portion of a feudal estate by a vassal to a subtenant who pays fealty to the vassal. **2.** The lands so leased. **—sub′in·feu′da·to′ry** (-fyo͞o′də-tôr′ē, -tōr′ē) *adj.*

sub·ir·ri·gate (sŭb-ĭr′ĭ-gāt′) *tr.v.* **-gat·ed, -gat·ing, -gates.** To irrigate from beneath, as by underground pipes. **—sub′ir·ri·ga′tion** *n.*

su·bi·to (so͞o′bē-tō′) *adv. Music.* Quickly; suddenly. Used chiefly as a direction. [Italian, from Latin *subitō,* from neuter ablative sing. of *subitus,* sudden, from past participle of *subīre,* to come secretly. See SUDDEN.]

subj. *abbr.* **1.** Subject. **2.** Subjective. **3.** Subjunctive.

sub·ja·cent (sŭb-jā′sənt) *adj.* **1.** Located beneath or below; underlying. **2.** Lying at a lower level but not directly beneath. [Latin *subiacēns, subiacent-,* present participle of *subiacēre,* to lie beneath : *sub-,* sub- + *iacēre,* to lie; see **yē-** in Appendix.] **—sub·ja′cen·cy** *n.*

sub·ject (sŭb′jĭkt) *adj.* **1.** Being in a position or in circumstances that place one under the power or authority of another or others: *All citizens in this nation are subject to the law.* **2.** Prone; disposed: *a child who is subject to colds.* **3.** Likely to incur or receive; exposed: *a directive that could be subject to misinterpretation.* **4.** Contingent or dependent: *Your vacation is subject to the changing weather patterns.* **—subject** *n. Abbr.* **subj. 1.** One who is under the rule of another or others, especially one who owes allegiance to a government or ruler. **2.a.** One concerning which something is said or done: *She is a subject of gossip in the office.* **b.** Something that is treated or indicated in a work of art. **c.** *Music.* A theme of a composition, especially a fugue. **3.** A course or area of study: *Math is her best subject.* **4.** A basis for action; a cause. **5.a.** One that experiences or is subjected to something: *They made him the subject of ridicule.* **b.** One that is the object of clinical study: *The experiment involved 12 subjects.* **c.** One who is under surveillance: *The subject was observed leaving the scene of the murder.* **d.** A corpse intended for study and dissection. **6.** *Grammar.* The noun, noun phrase, or pronoun in a sentence or clause that denotes the doer of the action or what is described by the predicate and that in some languages, such as English, can be identified by its characteristic position in simple sentences and in other languages, such as Latin, by inflectional endings. **7.** *Logic.* The term of a proposition about which something is affirmed or denied. **8.** *Philosophy.* **a.** The essential nature or substance of something as distinguished from its attributes. **b.** The mind or thinking part as distinguished from the object of thought. **—subject** (səb-jĕkt′) *tr.v.* **-ject·ed, -ject·ing, -jects. 1.** To submit for consideration. **2.** To submit to the authority of. **3.** To expose to something: *The patients on that ward were subjected to infection.* **4.** To cause to experience: *The campers were subjected to extreme weather.* **5.** To subjugate; subdue. [Middle English, from Old French, from Latin *subiectus,* from past participle of *subicere,* to subject : *sub-,* sub- + *iacere,* to throw; see **yē-** in Appendix.] **—sub·jec′tion** (səb-jĕk′shən) *n.*

SYNONYMS: *subject, matter, topic, theme.* These nouns denote the principal idea or point of a speech, a piece of writing, or an artistic work. *Subject* is the most general: *"Well, honor is the subject of my story"* (Shakespeare). *Matter* refers to the material that is the object of thought or discourse: *"This distinction seems to me to go to the root of the matter"* (William James). A *topic* is a subject of discussion, argument, or conversation: *"They would talk of nothing but high life . . . with other fashionable topics, such as pictures, taste, Shakespeare"* (Oliver Goldsmith). *Theme* refers especially to a subject, an idea, a point of view, or a perception that is developed and expanded on in a work of art: *"To produce a mighty book, you must choose a mighty theme"* (Herman Melville). See also Synonyms at **citizen, dependent.**

sub·jec·tive (səb-jĕk′tĭv) *adj. Abbr.* **subj. 1.a.** Proceeding from or taking place within a person's mind such as to be unaffected by the external world. **b.** Particular to a given person;

personal: *subjective experience.* **2.** Moodily introspective. **3.** Existing only in the mind; illusory. **4.** *Psychology.* Existing only within the experiencer's mind. **5.** *Medicine.* Of, relating to, or designating a symptom or condition perceived by the patient and not by the examiner. **6.** Expressing or bringing into prominence the individuality of the artist or author. **7.** *Grammar.* Relating to or being the nominative case. **8.** Relating to the real nature of something; essential. **—sub·jec′tive·ly** *adv.* **—sub·jec′tive·ness, sub′jec·tiv′i·ty** (sŭb′jĕk-tĭv′ĭ-tē) *n.*

subjective idealism *n. Philosophy.* The theory that nature has no objective existence independent of the minds that perceive it.

sub·jec·tiv·ism (səb-jĕk′tə-vĭz′əm) *n.* **1.** The quality of being subjective. **2.a.** The doctrine that all knowledge is restricted to the conscious self and its sensory states. **b.** A theory or doctrine that emphasizes the subjective elements in experience. **3.** The theory that individual conscience is the only valid standard of moral judgment. **—sub·jec′tiv·ist** *n.* **—sub·jec′tiv·is′tic** *adj.*

subject matter *n.* Matter under consideration in a written work or speech; a theme.

subject quote *n. Business.* See **nominal quote.**

sub·join (səb-join′) *tr.v.* **-joined, -join·ing, -joins.** To add at the end; append. [Obsolete French *subjoindre,* from Latin *subiungere* : *sub-,* sub- + *iungere,* to join; see **yeug-** in Appendix.]

sub·join·der (səb-join′dər) *n.* Something subjoined. [From SUBJOIN (on the model of REJOINDER).]

sub ju·di·ce (sŭb jo͞o′dĭ-sē′, so͝ob yo͞o′dĭ-kā′) *adv. Law.* Under judicial deliberation; before a judge or court of law. [Latin *sub iūdice* : *sub,* beneath, before + *iūdice,* ablative of *iūdex, iūdic-,* judge.]

sub·ju·gate (sŭb′jə-gāt′) *tr.v.* **-gat·ed, -gat·ing, -gates. 1.** To bring under control; conquer. See Synonyms at **defeat. 2.** To make subservient; enslave. [Middle English *subjugaten,* from Latin *subiugāre, subiugāt-* : *sub-,* sub- + *iugum,* yoke; see **yeug-** in Appendix.] **—sub′ju·ga′tion** *n.* **—sub′ju·ga′tor** *n.*

sub·junc·tion (səb-jŭngk′shən) *n.* **1.** The act of subjoining or the condition of being subjoined. **2.** Something subjoined. [Late Latin *subiūnctiō, subiūnctiōn-,* from Latin *subiūnctus,* past participle of *subiungere,* to subjoin. See SUBJOIN.]

sub·junc·tive (səb-jŭngk′tĭv) *Grammar. adj. Abbr.* **subj.** Of, relating to, or being a mood of a verb used in some languages for contingent or hypothetical action, action viewed subjectively, or grammatically subordinate statements. **—subjunctive** *n. Abbr.* **subj. 1.** The subjunctive mood. **2.** A subjunctive construction. See Usage Note at **if.** [Late Latin *subiūnctīvus,* from Latin *subiūnctus,* past participle of *subiungere,* to subjoin, subordinate. See SUBJOIN.]

sub·king·dom (sŭb′kĭng′dəm) *n. Biology.* A taxonomic category of related organisms constituting a major division of a kingdom.

sub·late (sŭb′lāt′) *tr.v.* **-lat·ed, -lat·ing, -lates.** *Logic.* To negate, deny, or contradict. [From Latin *sublātus,* past participle of *tollere,* to take away : *sub-,* sub- + *lātus,* taken; see **telə-** in Appendix.]

sub·lease (sŭb′lēs′) *tr.v.* **-leased, -leas·ing, -leas·es. 1.** To sublet (property). **2.** To rent (property) under a sublease. **—sublease** (sŭb′lēs′) *n.* A lease of property granted by a lessee.

sub·let (sŭb′lĕt′) *tr.v.* **-let, -let·ting, -lets. 1.** To rent (property one holds by lease) to another. **2.** To subcontract (work). **—sublet** (sŭb′lĕt′) *n.* Property, especially an apartment, rented by a tenant to another party.

sub·le·thal (sŭb-lē′thəl) *adj.* Less than lethal: *sublethal dosages.* **—sub·le′thal·ly** *adv.*

sub·li·cense (sŭb-lī′səns) *n.* A license giving rights of production or marketing of products or services to a person or company that is not the primary holder of such rights. **—sublicense** *tr.v.* **-censed, -cens·ing, -cens·es.** To grant a sublicense to or for. **—sub′li·cen·see′** *n.*

sub·li·mate (sŭb′lə-māt′) *v.* **-mat·ed, -mat·ing, -mates.** —*tr.* **1.** *Chemistry.* To cause (a solid or gas) to change state without becoming a liquid. **2.** *Psychology.* To modify the natural expression of (an instinctual impulse, especially a sexual one) in a socially acceptable manner. —*intr. Chemistry.* To transform directly from the solid to the gaseous state or from the gaseous to the solid state without becoming a liquid. [Latin *sublīmāre, sublīmāt-,* to elevate, from *sublīmis,* uplifted.]

sub·li·ma·tion (sŭb′lə-mā′shən) *n.* **1.** The act or process of sublimating. **2.** Something that has been sublimated.

sub·lime (sə-blīm′) *adj.* **1.** Characterized by nobility; majestic. **2.a.** Of high spiritual, moral, or intellectual worth. **b.** Not to be excelled; supreme. **3.** Inspiring awe; impressive. **4.** *Archaic.* Raised aloft; set high. **5.** *Obsolete.* Of lofty appearance or bearing; haughty: *"not terrible,/That I should fear . . . /But solemn and sublime"* (John Milton). **—sublime** *n.* **1.** Something sublime. **2.** An ultimate example. **—sublime** *v.* **-limed, -lim·ing, -limes.** —*tr.* **1.** To render sublime. **2.** *Chemistry.* To cause to sublimate. —*intr. Chemistry.* To sublimate. [French, from Old French, sublimated, from Latin *sublīmis,* uplifted.] **—sub·lime′ly** *adv.* **—sub·lime′ness, sub·lim′i·ty** (sə-blĭm′ĭ-tē) *n.*

sub·lim·i·nal (sŭb-lĭm′ə-nəl) *adj. Psychology.* **1.** Below the threshold of conscious perception. Used of stimuli. **2.** Inadequate to produce conscious awareness but able to evoke a response: *subliminal propaganda.* [SUB– + Latin *līmen, līmin-,* threshold.] **—sub·lim′i·nal·ly** *adv.*

sub·lim·it (sŭb-lĭm′ĭt) *n.* A limit or ceiling placed on a subdivision of a larger category, especially of nuclear weapons: *negotiating sublimits on the number of land-based, intermediate-range missiles.* Also called *subceiling.*

sub·lin·gual (sŭb-lĭng′gwəl) *adj.* Situated beneath or on the underside of the tongue. **—sublingual** *n.* A sublingual part, such as a gland, an artery, or a duct. **—sub·lin′gual·ly** *adv.*

sub·lit·er·ar·y (sŭb-lĭt′ə-rĕr′-ē) *adj.* **1.** Of, relating to, having the qualities of, or producing subliterature. **2.** Not written as or intended to be literature: *subliterary works such as letters and diaries.*

sub·lit·er·ate (sŭb-lĭt′ər-ĭt) *adj.* **1.** Not interested in or able to read artistic literature. **2.** Of, relating to, or being language that is dialectal, slangy, or full of jargon.

sub·lit·er·a·ture (sŭb′lĭt′ər-ə-cho͝or′, -chər) *n.* Writings, such as romance novels and mysteries, that appeal to popular tastes and are considered inferior in style and content to more artistic literature.

sub·lit·to·ral (sŭb-lĭt′ər-əl) *adj.* **1.** Of or situated near the seashore. **2.** Lying between the low tide line and the edge of the continental shelf or ranging in depth to about 100 fathoms or 200 meters (660 feet).

sub·lu·na·ry (sŭb-lo͞o′nə-rē, sŭb′lo͞o-nĕr′ē) also **sub·lu·nar** (-lo͞o′nər) *adj.* **1.** Situated beneath the moon. **2.** Of this world; earthly. [Late Latin *sublūnāris* : Latin *sub-,* sub- + Latin *lūna,* moon; see **leuk-** in Appendix.]

sub·lux·a·tion (sŭb′lŭk-sā′shən) *n.* Incomplete or partial dislocation of a bone in a joint.

sub·ma·chine gun (sŭb′mə-shēn′) *n.* A lightweight automatic or semiautomatic gun fired from the shoulder or hip.

sub·man·dib·u·lar (sŭb′măn-dĭb′yə-lər) *adj.* Submaxillary.

sub·mar·gin·al (sŭb-mär′jə-nəl) *adj.* **1.** Near the margin of a body, an organ, or a part: *submarginal tentacles.* **2.** Of low productivity; infertile.

♦**sub·ma·rine** (sŭb′mə-rēn′, sŭb′mə-rēn′) *n.* **1.** A ship capable of operating submerged. Also called *sub.* **2.** A large sandwich consisting of a long roll split lengthwise and filled with layers of meat, cheese, tomatoes, lettuce, and condiments. In this sense, also called ♦*bomber,* ♦*Cuban sandwich,* ♦*grinder,* ♦*hero,* ♦*hoagie,* ♦*Italian,* ♦*Italian sandwich,* ♦*poor boy,* ♦*sub,* ♦*torpedo,* ♦*wedge,* ♦*zep.* **—submarine** *adj.* Beneath the surface of the water; undersea. **—submarine** *v.* **-rined, -rin·ing, -rines.** —*tr.* **1.** To attack by submarine, especially with torpedoes. **2.** *Sports.* To knock down with a blow to the legs. **3.** *Baseball.* To pitch (a ball) with an underhand motion. —*intr.* **1.** To operate a submarine. **2.** To slide, drive, or throw under something.

♦***REGIONAL NOTE:*** The long sandwich featuring layers of meat and cheese on a crusty Italian roll goes by a variety of names. *Submarine, sub,* and *hero* are widespread terms, not assignable to any particular region. Most of the localized terms are clustered in the northeast United States, where the greatest numbers of Italian Americans live. Jane Stern, having studied the great variety of American names for this sandwich, finds that upstate New Yorkers call it a *bomber,* while speakers downstate refer to a *wedge.* In the Delaware Valley, including Philadelphia and southern New Jersey, the sandwich is called a *hoagie.* In Italian restaurants in New England the menu is likely to include a *grinder.* Speakers in Miami use the name *Cuban sandwich* and in Maine, *Italian sandwich,* but in the southern Midwest, according to Stern, the name *Italian* is common, with both *Italian* and *Italian sandwich* recapturing the authentic nationality of the sandwich. In New Orleans the same sandwich is called a *poor boy* and is likely to be offered in a most un-Italian version featuring fried oysters.

submarine chaser *n.* A small, fast ship equipped to pursue and attack submarines.

sub·ma·rin·er (sŭb-mə-rē′nər, sŭb′măr′ə-nər) *n.* A member of the crew of a submarine.

sub·mar·ket (sŭb′mär′kĭt) *n.* A geographic, economic, or specialized subdivision of a market. **—submarket** *adj.* Being below what is usual in a particular market: *submarket wages; submarket interest rates.*

sub·max·il·la (sŭb′măk-sĭl′ə) *n., pl.* **-max·il·lae** (-măk-sĭl′ē). The lower jaw or mandible, especially in human beings.

sub·max·il·lar·y (sŭb-măk′sə-lĕr′ē) *adj.* **1.** Of or relating to the lower jaw: *a submaxillary fracture.* **2.** Situated beneath the maxilla: *the submaxillary salivary glands.* **—submaxillary** *n., pl.* **-ies.** An anatomical part, such as a gland or nerve, that is situated beneath the maxilla.

sub·me·di·ant (sŭb-mē′dē-ənt) *n. Music.* The sixth tone of a diatonic scale. Also called *superdominant.*

sub·merge (səb-mûrj′) *v.* **-merged, -merg·ing, -merg·es.** —*tr.* **1.** To place under water. See Synonyms at **dip. 2.** To cover with water; inundate. **3.** To hide from view; obscure. —*intr.* To go under or as if under water. [Latin *submergere* : *sub-,* sub- + *mergere,* to plunge.] **—sub·mer′gence** *n.*

sub·merged (səb-mûrjd′) *adj.* **1.** *Botany.* Growing or remaining under water: *submerged leaves.* **2.** Living in poverty or misery. **3.** Having been hidden.

ă pat	oi boy
ā pay	ou out
âr care	o͝o took
ä father	o͞o boot
ĕ pet	ŭ cut
ē be	ûr urge
ĭ pit	th thin
ī pie	*th* this
îr pier	hw which
ŏ pot	zh vision
ō toe	ə about, item
ô paw	♦ regionalism

Stress marks: ′ (primary); ′ (secondary), as in **dictionary** (dĭk′shə-nĕr′ē)

submersible
Underwater submersible *Alvin,* Woods Hole Oceanographic Institution

sub·mer·gi·ble (səb-mûr′jə-bəl) *adj.* That can be immersed in or can remain under water: *a submergible electric frying pan; a submergible research vehicle.* **—sub·mer′gi·bil′i·ty** *n.*

sub·merse (səb-mûrs′) *tr.v.* **-mersed, -mers·ing, -mers·es.** To submerge. [Probably back-formation from *submersion,* act of submerging, from Late Latin *submersiō, submersiōn-,* from Latin *submersus,* past participle of *submergere,* to submerge. See SUBMERGE.] **—sub·mer′sion** (-mûr′zhən, -shən) *n.*

sub·mersed (səb-mûrst′) *adj. Botany.* Growing or remaining under water.

sub·mers·i·ble (səb-mûr′sə-bəl) *adj.* Submergible. **—submersible** *n.* A vessel capable of operating or remaining under water.

sub·mi·cro·scop·ic (sŭb′mī-krə-skŏp′ĭk) *adj.* Too small to be resolved by an optical microscope. **—sub′mi·cro·scop′i·cal·ly** *adv.*

sub·min·i·a·ture (sŭb-mĭn′ē-ə-cho͝or′, -chər) *adj.* Smaller than miniature; exceedingly small.

sub·min·i·a·tur·ize (sŭb′mĭn′ē-ə-chə-rīz′) *tr.v.* **-ized, -iz·ing, -iz·es.** To make subminiature, especially to manufacture or design (electronic equipment) in subminiature size. **—sub·min′i·a·tur·i·za′tion** (-chər-ĭ-zā′shən) *n.*

sub·min·i·mum wage (sŭb′mĭn′ə-məm, sŭb-mĭn′-) *n.* A wage paid under certain conditions to certain categories of workers, such as trainees, that is less than the established minimum wage.

sub·miss (səb-mĭs′) *adj. Archaic.* Submissive. [Latin *submissus,* past participle of *submittere,* to set under. See SUBMIT.]

sub·mis·sion (səb-mĭsh′ən) *n.* **1. a.** The act of submitting to the power of another: *"Oppression that cannot be overcome does not give rise to revolt but to submission"* (Simone Weil). **b.** The state of having submitted. See Synonyms at **surrender. 2.** The state of being submissive or compliant; meekness. **3. a.** The act of submitting something for consideration. **b.** Something so submitted: *read three fiction manuscripts and other such submissions.* [Middle English *submissioun,* from Old French *submission,* from Latin *submissiō, submissiōn-,* a lowering, from *submissus,* past participle of *submittere,* to set under. See SUBMIT.]

sub·mis·sive (səb-mĭs′ĭv) *adj.* Inclined or willing to submit. See Synonyms at **obedient. —sub·mis′sive·ly** *adv.* **—sub·mis′sive·ness** *n.*

sub·mit (səb-mĭt′) *v.* **-mit·ted, -mit·ting, -mits.** *—tr.* **1.** To yield or surrender (oneself) to the will or authority of another: *"Nothing but contempt is due to those people who ask us to submit to unmerited oppression"* (Christabel Pankhurst). **2.** To subject to a condition or process. **3.** To commit (something) to the consideration or judgment of another. See Synonyms at **propose. 4.** To offer as a proposition or contention: *I submit that the terms are entirely unreasonable. —intr.* **1.** To give in to the authority, power, or desires of another. See Synonyms at **yield. 2.** To allow oneself to be subjected to something. [Middle English *submitten,* from Latin *submittere,* to set under : *sub-,* sub- + *mittere,* to cause to go.] **—sub·mit′tal** (-mĭt′l) *n.* **—sub·mit′ter** *n.*

sub·mon·tane (sŭb′mŏn′tān′, -mŏn-tān′) *adj.* Located under or at the base of a mountain or mountain range.

sub·mu·co·sa (sŭb′myo͞o-kō′sə) *n.* A layer of loose connective tissue beneath a mucous membrane. **—sub′mu·co′sal** *adj.* **—sub′mu·co′sal·ly** *adv.*

sub·mul·ti·ple (sŭb-mŭl′tə-pəl) *n. Mathematics.* A number that is an exact divisor of another number.

sub·net (sŭb′nĕt′) *n.* A system of interconnections within a communications system that allows the components to communicate directly with each other.

sub·nor·mal (sŭb-nôr′məl) *adj.* Less than normal; below the average. **—subnormal** *n.* One who is regarded as subnormal in some respect, such as in intelligence or coordination. **—sub′nor·mal′i·ty** (-nôr-măl′ĭ-tē) *n.*

sub·nu·cle·ar (sŭb-no͞o′klē-ər, -nyo͞o′-) *adj.* Of or located within the nucleus of an atom; smaller than the nucleus.

sub·o·ce·an·ic (sŭb′ō-shē-ăn′ĭk) *adj.* Formed, situated, or occurring beneath the ocean or the ocean bed.

sub·or·bi·tal (sŭb-ôr′bĭ-tl) *adj.* **1.** Having or following a trajectory of less than one orbit. Used of a rocket or spacecraft. **2.** *Anatomy.* Situated on or below the floor of the orbit of the eye. **—suborbital** *n.* A suborbital part, such as a bone, nerve, or cartilage.

sub·or·der (sŭb′ôr′dər) *n.* **1.** *Biology.* A taxonomic category of related organisms ranking between an order and a family. **2.** A subdivision of a category termed an order.

sub·or·di·nate (sə-bôr′dn-ĭt) *adj.* **1.** Belonging to a lower or inferior class or rank; secondary. **2.** Subject to the authority or control of another. **—subordinate** *n.* One that is subordinate. **—subordinate** (sə-bôr′dn-āt′) *tr.v.* **-nat·ed, -nat·ing, -nates. 1.** To put in a lower or inferior rank or class. **2.** To make subservient; subdue. [Middle English *subordinat,* from Medieval Latin *subōrdinātus,* past participle of *subōrdināre,* to put in a lower rank : Latin *sub-,* sub- + Latin *ōrdināre,* to set in order (from *ōrdō, ōrdin-,* order; see **ar-** in Appendix).] **—sub·or′di·nate·ly** *adv.* **—sub·or′di·nate·ness, sub·or′di·na′tion** (-nā′shən) *n.* **—sub·or′di·na′tive** (-nə′tĭv) *adj.*

subordinate clause *n. Grammar.* See **dependent clause.**

subordinate conjunction *n. Grammar.* A conjunction, such as *that, who, which,* and *where,* that introduces a dependent clause.

sub·orn (sə-bôrn′) *tr.v.* **-orned, -orn·ing, -orns. 1.** To induce (a person) to commit an unlawful or evil act. **2.** *Law.* **a.** To induce (a person) to commit perjury. **b.** To procure (perjured testimony). [Latin *subōrnāre : sub-,* secretly; see SUB– + *ōrnāre,* to equip; see **ar-** in Appendix.] **—sub′or·na′tion** (sŭb′ôr-nā′shən) *n.* **—sub·orn′er** *n.*

Su·bo·ti·ca also **Su·bo·ti·tsa** (so͞o′bə-tē′tsə, -bô-). A city of northeast Yugoslavia near the Hungarian border. It is a railroad junction and an industrial center. Population, 93,500.

sub·ox·ide (sŭb-ŏk′sīd′) *n.* An oxide containing a relatively small amount of oxygen.

sub·par (sŭb-pär′) *adj.* **1.** Not measuring up to traditional standards of performance, value, or production. **2.** *Sports.* Below par in a hole, round, or game of golf.

sub·per·i·os·te·al (sŭb′pĕr-ē-ŏs′tē-əl) *adj.* Beneath the periosteum: *subperiosteal tooth implants.*

sub·phy·lum (sŭb′fī′ləm) *n., pl.* **-la** (-lə). *Biology.* A taxonomic category of related organisms ranking between a phylum and a class.

sub·plot (sŭb′plŏt′) *n.* **1.** A plot subordinate to the main plot of a literary work or film. Also called *counterplot, underplot.* **2.** A subdivision of a plot of land, especially a plot used for experimental purposes.

sub·poe·na (sə-pē′nə) *Law. n.* A writ requiring appearance in court to give testimony. **—subpoena** *tr.v.* **-naed, -na·ing, -nas.** To serve or summon with such a writ. [Middle English *suppena,* from Medieval Latin *sub poenā,* under a penalty (from the opening words of the writ) : Latin *sub,* under; see SUB– + Latin *poenā,* ablative of *poena,* penalty, from Greek *poinē*; see **k^wei-**[1] in Appendix.]

sub·pop·u·la·tion (sŭb′pŏp-yə-lā′shən) *n.* A part or subdivision of a population, especially one originating from some other population: *microbial subpopulations.*

sub·po·ten·cy (sŭb-pōt′n-sē) *n.* **1.** Reduction in potency, as of a drug. **2.** Reduction in the power to transmit hereditary characteristics. **—sub·po′tent** *adj.*

sub·prin·ci·pal (sŭb-prĭn′sə-pəl) *n.* **1.** An assistant school principal. **2.** An auxiliary or bracing rafter in a frame. **3.** *Music.* An open diapason subbass in an organ.

sub·pro·fes·sion·al (sŭb′prə-fĕsh′ə-nəl) *n.* A paraprofessional. **—sub′pro·fes′sion·al** *adj.*

sub·pro·gram (sŭb′prō′grăm, -grəm) *n. Computer Science.* A program contained within another program that operates semi-independently of the encasing program.

sub·re·gion (sŭb′rē′jən) *n.* A subdivision of a region, especially an ecological region. **—sub′re′gion·al** *adj.*

sub·rep·tion (sŭb-rĕp′shən) *n.* **1.** A calculated misrepresentation through concealment of the facts. **2.** An inference drawn from such a misrepresentation. [Late Latin *subreptiō, subreptiōn-,* from Latin, theft, from *subreptus,* past participle of *surripere, subripere,* to take away secretly. See SURREPTITIOUS.] **—sub′rep·ti′tious** (-tĭsh′əs) *adj.*

sub·ring (sŭb′rĭng′) *n. Mathematics.* A subset of a ring that is itself a ring.

sub·ro·gate (sŭb′rō-gāt′) *tr.v.* **-gat·ed, -gat·ing, -gates.** To substitute (one person) for another. [Middle English **subrogaten,* from Latin *subrogāre, subrogāt- : sub-,* instead of; see SUB– + *rogāre,* to ask; see **reg-** in Appendix.]

sub·ro·ga·tion (sŭb′rō-gā′shən) *n.* The substitution of one person for another, especially the legal doctrine of substituting one creditor for another.

sub ro·sa (sŭb rō′zə) *adv.* In secret; privately or confidentially: *held the meeting sub rosa.* [Latin *sub rosā,* under the rose (from the practice of hanging a rose over a meeting as a symbol of confidentiality) : *sub,* under + *rosā,* ablative of *rosa,* rose.]

sub-ro·sa (səb-rō′zə) *adj.* Secret, private, or confidential: *a sub-rosa agreement.*

sub·rou·tine (sŭb′ro͞o-tēn′) *n. Computer Science.* A set of instructions that performs a specific task for a main routine, requiring direction back to the proper place in the main routine on completion of the task.

subs. *abbr.* Subscription.

sub-Sa·har·an (sŭb′sə-hâr′ən, -hăr′-, -här′-) *adj.* Of, relating to, or situated in the region of Africa south of the Sahara.

sub·sam·ple (sŭb′săm′pəl) *n.* A sample drawn from a larger sample. **—subsample** (sŭb-săm′pəl) *tr.v.* **-pled, -pling, -ples.** To take a subsample from (a larger sample).

sub·scap·u·lar (sŭb-skăp′yə-lər) *Anatomy. adj.* Situated below or on the underside of the scapula. **—subscapular** *n.* A subscapular part, such as an artery or a nerve.

sub·scribe (səb-scrīb′) *v.* **-scribed, -scrib·ing, -scribes.** *—tr.* **1.** To pledge or contribute (a sum of money). **2.** To sign (one's name) at the end of a document. **3.** To sign one's name to in attestation, testimony, or consent: *subscribe a will. —intr.* **1.** To contract to receive and pay for a certain number of issues of a publication, for tickets to a series of events or performances, or for a utility service, for example. **2.** To promise to pay or contribute money: *subscribe to a charity.* **3.** To feel or express hearty approval: *I subscribe to your opinion.* See Synonyms at **assent. 4.** To sign one's name. **5.** To affix one's signature to a document as a witness or to show consent. [Middle English *subscriben,* from

Latin *subscrībere* : *sub-*, sub- + *scrībere,* to write; see **skrībh-** in Appendix.] **—sub·scrib′er** *n.*

sub·script (sŭb′skrĭpt′) *n.* A distinguishing character or symbol written directly beneath or next to and slightly below a letter or number. **—subscript** *adj.* Written beneath. [From Latin *subscrīptus,* past participle of *subscrībere,* to subscribe. See SUBSCRIBE.]

sub·scrip·tion (səb-skrĭp′shən) *n. Abbr.* **subs. 1.** A purchase made by signed order, as for a periodical for a specified period of time or for a series of performances. **2.** Acceptance, as of articles of faith, demonstrated by the signing of one's name. **3.a.** The raising of money from subscribers. **b.** A sum of money so raised. **4.** The signing of one's name, as to a document. **5.** Something subscribed. [Middle English *subscripcion,* from Old French *subscription,* from Latin *subscrīptiō, subscrīptiōn-,* something written underneath, from *subscrīptus,* past participle of *subscrībere,* to subscribe. See SUBSCRIBE.] **—sub·scrip′tive** *adj.* **—sub·scrip′tive·ly** *adv.*

sub·se·quence (sŭb′sĭ-kwĕns′, -kwəns) *n.* **1.** Something that is subsequent; a sequel. **2.** The fact or quality of being subsequent. **3.** (-sē′kwəns). *Mathematics.* A sequence that is contained in another sequence.

sub·se·quent (sŭb′sĭ-kwĕnt′, -kwənt) *adj.* Following in time or order; succeeding. [Middle English, from Old French, from Latin *subsequēns, subsequent-,* present participle of *subsequī,* to follow close after : *sub-,* close after; see SUB– + *sequī,* to follow; see **sek^{w}-**[1] in Appendix.] **—sub′se·quent′ly** *adv.*

sub·sere (sŭb′sîr′) *n. Ecology.* A secondary series of ecological communities beginning after succession has been interrupted by fire, grazing, agriculture, or another destructive agent.

sub·serve (səb-sûrv′) *tr.v.* **-served, -serv·ing, -serves.** To serve to promote (an end); be useful to. [Latin *subservīre* : *sub-,* sub- + *servīre,* to serve; see SERVE.]

sub·ser·vi·ent (səb-sûr′vē-ənt) *adj.* **1.** Subordinate in capacity or function. **2.** Obsequious; servile. **3.** Useful as a means or an instrument; serving to promote an end. [Latin *subserviēns, subservient-,* present participle of *subservīre,* to subserve. See SUBSERVE.] **—sub·ser′vi·ence, sub·ser′vi·en·cy** *n.* **—sub·ser′vi·ent·ly** *adv.*

sub·set (sŭb′sĕt′) *n.* A set contained within a set.

sub·shell (sŭb′shĕl′) *n.* One or more orbitals in the electron shell of an atom.

sub·shrub (sŭb′shrŭb′) *n.* **1.** An herb having a woody lower stem. **2.** A low shrub; an undershrub.

sub·side (səb-sīd′) *intr.v.* **-sid·ed, -sid·ing, -sides. 1.** To sink to a lower or normal level. **2.** To sink or settle down, as into a sofa. **3.** To sink to the bottom, as a sediment. **4.** To become less agitated or active; abate. See Synonyms at **decrease.** [Latin *subsīdere* : *sub-,* sub- + *sīdere,* to settle; see **sed-** in Appendix.] **—sub·si′dence** (səb-sīd′ns, sŭb′sĭ-dns) *n.*

sub·sid·i·ar·y (səb-sĭd′ē-ĕr′ē) *adj.* **1.** Serving to assist or supplement; auxiliary. **2.** Secondary in importance; subordinate. **3.** Of, relating to, or of the nature of a subsidy. **—subsidiary** *n., pl.* **-ar·ies. 1.** One that is subsidiary to another. **2.** A subsidiary company. **3.** *Music.* A theme subordinate to a main theme or subject. [Latin *subsidiārius,* from *subsidium,* support. See SUBSIDY.] **—sub·sid′i·ar′i·ly** (-âr′ə-lē) *adv.*

subsidiary cell *n.* A plant epidermal cell that is associated with guard cells and differs morphologically from other epidermal cells. Also called *accessory cell.*

subsidiary company *n.* A company having more than half of its stock owned by another company.

sub·si·dize (sŭb′sĭ-dīz′) *tr.v.* **-dized, -diz·ing, -diz·es. 1.** To assist or support with a subsidy. **2.** To secure the assistance of by granting a subsidy. **—sub′si·di·za′tion** (-dĭ-zā′shən) *n.* **—sub′si·diz′er** *n.*

sub·si·dy (sŭb′sĭ-dē) *n., pl.* **-dies. 1.** Monetary assistance granted by a government to a person or group in support of an enterprise regarded as being in the public interest. See Synonyms at **bonus. 2.** Financial assistance given by one person or government to another. **3.** Money formerly granted to the British Crown by Parliament. [Middle English *subsidie,* from Anglo-Norman, from Latin *subsidium,* support : *sub-,* behind, beneath; see SUB– + *sedēre,* to sit; see **sed-** in Appendix.]

sub·sist (səb-sĭst′) *v.* **-sist·ed, -sist·ing, -sists.** —*intr.* **1.a.** To exist; be. **b.** To remain or continue in existence. See Synonyms at **be. 2.** To maintain life; live: *subsisted on one meal a day.* **3.** To be logically conceivable. —*tr.* To maintain or support with provisions. [Latin *subsistere,* to support : *sub-,* sub- + *sistere,* to stand; see **stā-** in Appendix.] **—sub·sist′er** *n.*

sub·sis·tence (səb-sĭs′təns) *n.* **1.** The act or state of subsisting. **2.** A means of subsisting, especially means barely sufficient to maintain life. See Synonyms at **livelihood. 3.** Something that has real or substantial existence. **4.** *Theology.* Hypostasis. **—sub·sis′tent** *adj.*

sub·soil (sŭb′soil′) *n.* The layer or bed of earth beneath the topsoil. **—subsoil** *tr.v.* **-soiled, -soil·ing, -soils.** To plow or turn up the subsoil of. **—sub′soil′er** *n.*

sub·so·lar (sŭb-sō′lər) *adj.* **1.** Situated directly beneath the sun. **2.** Located between the tropics; equatorial.

sub·son·ic (sŭb-sŏn′ĭk) *adj.* **1.** Of less than audible frequency. **2.** Having a speed less than that of sound in a designated medium.

subsp. *abbr.* Subspecies.

sub·spe·cial·ize (sŭb-spĕsh′ə-līz′) *intr.v.* **-ized, -iz·ing, -iz·es.** To have or pursue a subspecialty: *subspecialize in cosmetic surgery.* **—sub·spe′cial·ist** (-spĕsh′ə-lĭst) *n.* **—sub·spe′cial·i·za′tion** (-spĕsh′ə-lĭ-zā′shən) *n.*

sub·spe·cial·ty (sŭb′spĕsh′əl-tē) *n., pl.* **-ties.** A narrow field of study or work within a specialty, as pediatric dermatology or geriatric psychiatry.

sub·spe·cies (sŭb′spē′shēz, -sēz) *n., pl.* **subspecies.** *Abbr.* **ssp., subsp.** *Biology.* A subdivision of a taxonomic species, usually based on geographic distribution. **—sub′spe·cif′ic** (-spĭ-sĭf′ĭk) *adj.*

subst. *abbr.* **1.** Substantive. **2.** Substitute.

sub·stage (sŭb′stāj′) *n.* The part of a microscope located below the stage on which attachments are held in place.

sub·stance (sŭb′stəns) *n.* **1.a.** That which has mass and occupies space; matter. **b.** A material of a particular kind or constitution. **2.a.** Essential nature; essence. **b.** Gist; heart. **3.** That which is solid and practical in character, quality, or importance: *a plan without substance.* **4.** Density; body: *Air has little substance.* **5.** Material possessions; goods; wealth: *a person of substance.* [Middle English, from Old French, from Latin *substantia,* from *substāns, substant-,* present participle of *substāre,* to be present : *sub-,* sub- + *stāre,* to stand; see **stā-** in Appendix.]

SYNONYMS: *substance, burden, core, gist, pith, purport.* The central meaning shared by these nouns is "the essential import or significance of something spoken or written": *the substance of her complaint; the burden of the President's speech; the core of an article; the gist of the prosecutor's argument; the pith and marrow of an essay; the purport of a document.*

substance abuse *n.* Excessive use of addictive substances, especially alcohol and narcotic drugs. Also called *chemical abuse.* **—substance abuser** *n.*

substance P *n.* A short-chain polypeptide that functions as a neurotransmitter especially in the transmission of pain impulses from peripheral receptors to the central nervous system.

sub·stan·dard (sŭb-stăn′dərd) *adj.* **1.** Failing to meet a standard; below standard. **2.** *Linguistics.* **a.** Of, relating to, or indicating a pattern of linguistic usage that does not conform to that of the prestige group in a speech community or to that of the standard language. **b.** Not in accord with notions of good English; nonstandard. See Usage Note at **nonstandard.**

sub·stan·ti·a ge·lat·i·no·sa (səb-stăn′shē-ə jə-lăt′n-ō′sə) *n.* A narrow, dense, vertical band of gelatinous gray matter forming the dorsal part of the posterior column of the spinal cord and serving to integrate the sensory stimuli that give rise to the sensations of heat and pain. [New Latin *substantia gelatinōsa* : Latin *substantia,* substance + New Latin *gelatinōsus,* gelatinous.]

sub·stan·tial (səb-stăn′shəl) *adj.* **1.** Of, relating to, or having substance; material. **2.** True or real; not imaginary. **3.** Solidly built; strong. **4.** Ample; sustaining: *a substantial breakfast.* **5.** Considerable in importance, value, degree, amount, or extent: *won by a substantial margin.* **6.** Possessing wealth or property; well-to-do. **—substantial** *n.* **1.** An essential. Often used in the plural. **2.** A solid thing. Often used in the plural. [Middle English *substancial,* from Old French *substantiel,* from Latin *substantiālis,* from *substantia,* substance. See SUBSTANCE.] **—sub·stan′ti·al′i·ty** (-shē-ăl′ĭ-tē), **sub·stan′tial·ness** (-shəl-nĭs) *n.* **—sub·stan′tial·ly** *adv.*

substantia ni·gra (nī′grə, nĭg′rə) *n.* A layer of large, pigmented nerve cells in the mesencephalon that produce dopamine and whose destruction is associated with Parkinson's disease. [New Latin : Latin *substantia,* substance + Latin *nigra,* feminine of *niger,* black.]

sub·stan·ti·ate (səb-stăn′shē-āt′) *tr.v.* **-at·ed, -at·ing, -ates. 1.** To support with proof or evidence; verify: *substantiate an accusation.* See Synonyms at **confirm. 2.a.** To give material form to; embody. **b.** To make firm or solid. **3.** To give substance to; make real or actual. [New Latin *substantiāre, substantiāt-,* from Latin *substantia,* substance. See SUBSTANCE.] **—sub·stan′ti·a′tion** *n.*

sub·stan·ti·val (sŭb′stən-tī′vəl) *adj. Grammar.* Of or relating to the nature of a substantive. **—sub′stan·ti′val·ly** *adv.*

sub·stan·tive (sŭb′stən-tĭv) *adj. Abbr.* **s., sb., subst. 1.** Substantial; considerable. **2.** Independent in existence or function; not subordinate. **3.** Not imaginary; actual; real. **4.** Of or relating to the essence or substance; essential: *substantive information.* **5.** Having a solid basis; firm. **6.** *Grammar.* Expressing or designating existence; for example, the verb *to be.* **7.** *Grammar.* Designating a noun or noun equivalent. **—substantive** *n. Abbr.* **s., sb., subst.** *Grammar.* A word or group of words functioning as a noun. [Middle English *substantif,* self-sufficient, independent, from Old French, substantive, from Late Latin *substantīvus,* from Latin *substantia,* substance. See SUBSTANCE.] **—sub′stan·tive·ly** *adv.* **—sub′stan·tive·ness** *n.*

substantive right *n.* A basic right, such as life or liberty, seen as constituting part of the order of society and considered independent of and not subordinate to the body of human law.

sub·sta·tion (sŭb′stā′shən) *n.* A subsidiary or branch station, as of a post office or an electric utility.

sub·stit·u·ent (səb-stĭch′ōō-ənt) *n.* An atom, a radical, or a group substituted for another in a chemical compound.

ă pat	oi boy
ā pay	ou out
âr care	ŏŏ took
ä father	ōō boot
ĕ pet	ŭ cut
ē be	ûr urge
ĭ pit	th thin
ī pie	*th* this
îr pier	hw which
ŏ pot	zh vision
ō toe	ə about, item
ô paw	♦ regionalism

Stress marks: ′ (primary); ′ (secondary), as in **dictionary** (dĭk′shə-nĕr′ē)

—substituent *adj.* Of or relating to such an atom or group. [Latin *substituēns, substituent-,* present participle of *substituere,* to substitute. See SUBSTITUTE.]

sub·sti·tute (sŭb′stĭ-to͞ot′, -tyo͞ot′) *n. Abbr.* **subst. 1.** One that takes the place of another; a replacement: *"Fantasies are more than substitutes for unpleasant reality"* (Barbara Grizzuti Harrison). **2.** *Grammar.* A word or construction used in place of another word, phrase, or clause. **—substitute** *v.* **-tut·ed, -tut·ing, -tutes.** *—tr.* To put or use (a person or thing) in place of another: *"substituting moral power for physical force"* (Elizabeth Cady Stanton). *—intr.* To take the place of another: *"Only art can substitute for nature"* (Leonard Bernstein). [Middle English, from Old French *substitut,* from Latin *substitūtus,* past participle of *substituere,* to substitute : *sub-,* in place of; see SUB– + *statuere,* to cause to stand; see **stā-** in Appendix.] **—sub′sti·tut′a·bil′it·y** *n.* **—sub′sti·tut′a·ble** *adj.*

sub·sti·tu·tion (sŭb′stĭ-to͞o′shən, -tyo͞o′-) *n.* **1. a.** The act or an instance of substituting. **b.** The state of being substituted. **2.** One that is substituted; a replacement. **—sub′sti·tu′tion·al, sub′sti·tu′tion·ar′y** *adj.* **—sub′sti·tu′tion·al·ly** *adv.*

sub·sti·tu·tive (sŭb′stĭ-to͞o′tĭv, -tyo͞o′-) *adj.* Serving or capable of serving as a substitute.

sub·stra·ta (sŭb′strā′tə, -străt′ə) *n.* A plural of **substratum.**

sub·strate (sŭb′strāt′) *n.* **1.** The material or substance on which an enzyme acts. **2.** *Biology.* A surface on which an organism grows or is attached. **3.** An underlying layer; a substratum. [From SUBSTRATUM.]

sub·strat·o·sphere (sŭb-străt′ə-sfîr′) *n.* The upper portion of the troposphere. **—sub′strat·o·spher′ic** (-sfîr′ĭk, -sfĕr′-) *adj.*

sub·stra·tum (sŭb′strā′təm, -străt′əm) *n., pl.* **-stra·ta** (-strā′tə, -străt′ə) or **-stra·tums. 1. a.** An underlying layer. **b.** A layer of earth beneath the surface soil; subsoil. **2.** A foundation or groundwork. **3.** The material on which another material is coated or fabricated. **4.** *Philosophy.* The characterless substance that supports attributes of reality. **5.** *Biology.* A substrate. [New Latin, from neuter of Latin *substrātus,* past participle of *substernere,* to lay under : *sub-,* sub- + *sternere,* to stretch, spread; see **ster-**[2] in Appendix.] **—sub·stra′tive** *adj.*

sub·struc·tion (sŭb-strŭk′shən) *n.* A foundation; a substructure. [Latin *substrūctiō, substrūctiōn-,* from *substrūctus,* past participle of *substruere,* to build beneath : *sub-,* sub- + *struere,* to build, pile up; see **ster-**[2] in Appendix.] **—sub·struc′tion·al** *adj.*

sub·struc·ture (sŭb′strŭk′chər) *n.* **1.** The supporting part of a structure; the foundation. **2.** The earth bank or bed supporting railroad tracks. **—sub·struc′tur·al** *adj.*

sub·sume (səb-so͞om′) *tr.v.* **-sumed, -sum·ing, -sumes.** To classify, include, or incorporate in a more comprehensive category or under a general principle: *"The evolutionarily later always subsumes and includes the evolutionarily earlier"* (Frederick Turner). [Medieval Latin *subsūmere* : Latin *sub-,* sub- + Latin *sūmere,* to take; see **em-** in Appendix.] **—sub·sum′a·ble** *adj.*

sub·sump·tion (səb-sŭmp′shən) *n.* **1. a.** The act of subsuming. **b.** Something subsumed. **2.** *Logic.* The minor premise of a syllogism. [Latin *subsūmptiō, subsūmptiōn-,* a subsuming, from *subsūmptus,* past participle of *subsūmere,* to subsume. See SUBSUME.] **—sub·sump′tive** *adj.*

sub·sur·face (sŭb′sûr′fəs, sŭb-sûr′-) *adj.* Of, relating to, or situated in an area beneath a surface, especially the surface of the earth or of a body of water.

sub·teen (sŭb′tēn′) *adj.* Relating to, intended for, or being a preadolescent child or children; preteen: *a subteen dance.* **—subteen** *n.* **1.** See **preteen. 2. subteens.** The preadolescent years.

sub·tem·per·ate (sŭb-tĕm′pər-ĭt, -tĕm′prĭt) *adj.* Of, relating to, or occurring within the colder regions of the Temperate Zones.

sub·ten·ant (sŭb-tĕn′ənt) *n.* One that rents property, such as land or a house, from a tenant. **—sub·ten′an·cy** *n.*

sub·tend (səb-tĕnd′) *tr.v.* **-tend·ed, -tend·ing, -tends. 1.** *Mathematics.* To be opposite to and delimit: *The side of a triangle subtends the opposite angle.* **2.** To underlie so as to enclose or surround: *flowers subtended by leafy bracts.* [Latin *subtendere,* to extend underneath : *sub-,* sub- + *tendere,* to extend; see **ten-** in Appendix.]

sub·ter·fuge (sŭb′tər-fyo͞oj′) *n.* A deceptive stratagem or device: *"the paltry subterfuge of an anonymous signature"* (Robert Smith Surtees). [French, from Old French *suterfuge,* from Late Latin *subterfugium,* from Latin *subterfugere,* to escape : *subter,* secretly, beneath; see **upo** in Appendix + *fugere,* to flee.]

sub·ter·mi·nal (sŭb-tûr′mə-nəl) *adj.* Located or occurring near an end.

sub·ter·ra·ne·an (sŭb′tə-rā′nē-ən) *adj.* **1.** Situated or operating beneath the earth's surface; underground. **2.** Hidden; secret: *subterranean motives for murder.* [Latin *subterrāneus* : *sub-,* sub- + *terra,* earth; see **ters-** in Appendix.] **—sub′ter·ra′ne·an·ly** *adv.*

sub·ter·res·tri·al (sŭb′tə-rĕs′trē-əl) *adj.* Subterranean; underground.

sub·text (sŭb′tĕkst′) *n.* **1.** The implicit meaning or theme of a literary text. **2.** The underlying personality of a dramatic character as implied or indicated by a script or text and interpreted by an actor in performance. **—sub·tex·tu·al** (-tĕks′cho͞o-əl) *adj.*

sub·ther·a·peu·tic (sŭb′thĕr-ə-pyo͞o′tĭk) *adj.* Below the dosage levels used to treat diseases: *subtherapeutic feeding of penicillin to livestock.* **—sub′ther·a·peu′ti·cal·ly** *adv.*

sub·thresh·old (sŭb-thrĕsh′ōld′, -hōld′) *adj. Psychology.* Not strong enough to be perceived or to produce a response. Used of a stimulus.

sub·tile (sŭt′l, sŭb′təl) *adj.* Subtle. [Middle English, from Old French *subtil,* from Latin *subtīlis,* fine, delicate. See SUBTLE.] **—sub′tile·ly** *adv.* **—sub·til′i·ty** (səb-tĭl′ĭ-tē), **sub′tile·ness** (sŭt′l-nĭs, sŭb′təl-), **sub′til·ty** (sŭt′l-tē, sŭb′təl-) *n.*

sub·ti·lin (sŭb′tə-lĭn) *n.* An antibiotic peptide obtained from the bacterium *Bacillus subtilis* that is active against gram-positive bacteria and various pathogenic fungi. [New Latin *subtīlis,* species name (from Latin, delicate; see SUBTLE) + –IN.]

sub·til·i·sin (sŭb-tĭl′ə-sĭn) *n.* An extracellular enzyme produced by certain strains of a soil bacterium *(Bacillus amyloliquefaciens)* that breaks down proteins into polypeptides and resembles trypsin in its action. [New Latin *(Bacillus) subtīlis,* bacteria species; see SUBTILIN + –IN.]

sub·til·ize (sŭt′l-īz′, sŭb′tə-līz′) *v.* **-ized, -iz·ing, -iz·es.** *—tr.* To render subtle: *"I need to tell stories. I find new friends, new listeners, subtilize my lies"* (Helen Yglesias). *—intr.* To argue or discuss with subtlety; make fine distinctions. **—sub′til·i·za′tion** (-ĭ-zā′shən) *n.*

sub·ti·tle (sŭb′tīt′l) *n.* **1.** A secondary, usually explanatory title, as of a literary work. **2. a.** A printed translation of the dialogue of a foreign-language film shown at the bottom of the screen. **b.** A printed narration or portion of dialogue flashed on the screen between the scenes of a silent film. **—subtitle** *tr.v.* **-tled, -tling, -tles. 1.** To give a subtitle to. **2.** To provide with subtitles: *a film that was subtitled for English-speaking audiences.*

sub·tle (sŭt′l) *adj.* **sub·tler, sub·tlest. 1. a.** So slight as to be difficult to detect or analyze; elusive. **b.** Not immediately obvious; abstruse: *"subtle smiles resulting from subjectively humorous experiences unguessed by the world at large"* (Josephine Dodge Bacon). **2.** Able to make fine distinctions: *a subtle mind.* **3. a.** Characterized by skill or ingenuity; clever: *"a journalist whose subtle views on the hard issues of our time are rooted in a tough mind and a demanding ethical sensibility"* (New Republic). **b.** Crafty or sly; devious. **c.** Operating in a hidden, usually injurious way; insidious. [Middle English *sotil,* from Old French, from Latin *subtīlis.* See **teks-** in Appendix.] **—sub′tle·ness** *n.* **—sub′tly** *adv.*

sub·tle·ty (sŭt′l-tē) *n., pl.* **-ties. 1.** The quality or state of being subtle. **2.** Something subtle, especially a nicety of thought or a fine distinction.

sub·ton·ic (sŭb-tŏn′ĭk) *n. Music.* The seventh tone of a diatonic scale, immediately below the tonic.

sub·top·ic (sŭb′tŏp′ĭk) *n.* One of the divisions into which a main topic may be divided.

sub·tor·rid (sŭb-tôr′ĭd, -tŏr′-) *adj.* Subtropical.

sub·to·tal (sŭb-tōt′l) *adj.* Less than total; incomplete. **—subtotal** (sŭb′tōt′l) *n.* The total of part of a series of numbers. **—subtotal** (sŭb′tōt′l) *v.* **-taled, -tal·ing, -tals** also **-talled, -tal·ling, -tals.** *—tr.* To total part of (a series of numbers). *—intr.* To arrive at a subtotal.

sub·tract (səb-trăkt′) *v.* **-tract·ed, -tract·ing, -tracts.** *—tr.* To take away; deduct. *—intr. Mathematics.* To perform the arithmetic operation of subtraction. [Latin *subtrahere, subtrāct-* : *sub-,* sub- + *trahere,* to draw.] **—sub·tract′er** *n.*

sub·trac·tion (səb-trăk′shən) *n.* **1.** The act or process of subtracting; deduction. **2.** *Mathematics.* The arithmetic operation of finding the difference between two quantities or numbers.

sub·trac·tive (səb-trăk′tĭv) *adj.* **1.** Producing or involving subtraction. **2.** *Color.* Of or being a color produced by light passing through more than one colorant, each of which inhibits certain wavelengths, as in mixtures of pigments. **3.** Of, relating to, or being a photographic process that produces a positive image by superposing or mixing substances that selectively absorb colored light.

sub·tra·hend (sŭb′trə-hĕnd′) *n. Mathematics.* A quantity or number to be subtracted from another. [From Latin *subtrahendum,* neuter gerundive of *subtrahere,* to subtract. See SUBTRACT.]

sub·tribe (sŭb′trīb′) *n.* A subdivision of a tribe.

sub·trop·i·cal (sŭb-trŏp′ĭ-kəl) *adj.* Of, relating to, or being the geographic areas adjacent to the Tropics.

sub·trop·ics (sŭb-trŏp′ĭks) *pl.n.* Subtropical regions.

su·bu·late (so͞o′byə-lĭt, -lāt′, sŭb′yə-) *adj. Biology.* Tapering to a point; awl-shaped: *a subulate leaf.* [New Latin *sūbulātus,* from Latin *sūbula,* awl. See **syū-** in Appendix.]

sub·um·brel·la (sŭb′ŭm-brĕl′ə) *n.* The concave underside of the body of a jellyfish.

sub·u·nit (sŭb′yo͞o′nĭt) *n.* A subdivision of a larger unit.

sub·urb (sŭb′ûrb′) *n. Abbr.* **sub. 1.** A usually residential area or community outlying a city. **2. suburbs.** The usually residential region around a major city; the environs. [Middle English *suburbe,* from Old French, from Latin *suburbium* : *sub-,* sub- + *urbs, urb-,* city.]

sub·ur·ban (sə-bûr′bən) *adj. Abbr.* **sub. 1.** Of, relating to, or characteristic of a suburb. **2.** Located or residing in a suburb. **3.** Of, relating to, or characteristic of the culture, customs, and manners typical of life in the suburbs. —**suburban** *n.* A suburbanite.

sub·ur·ban·ite (sə-bûr′bə-nīt′) *n.* One who lives in a suburb.

sub·ur·ban·ize (sə-bûr′bə-nīz′) *tr.v.* **-ized, -iz·ing, -izes.** To render suburban; impart a suburban character to. —**sub·ur′ban·i·za′tion** (-bə-nĭ-zā′shən) *n.*

sub·ur·bi·a (sə-bûr′bē-ə) *n.* **1.** The suburbs. **2.a.** Suburbanites considered as a group. **b.** Suburbanites considered as a cultural class.

sub·ven·tion (səb-vĕn′shən) *n.* **1.** Provision of help, aid, or support. **2.** An endowment or a subsidy, as that given by a government to an institution for research; a grant of financial aid. [Middle English *subvencioun,* a subsidy by the state, from Old French *subvention,* monetary assistance, from Late Latin *subventiō, subventiōn-,* assistance, from Latin *subventus,* past participle of *subvenīre,* to come to help : *sub-,* beneath, behind; see SUB– + *venīre,* to come; see **gʷā-** in Appendix.] —**sub·ven′tion·ar′y** *adj.*

sub·ver·sion (səb-vûr′zhən, -shən) *n.* **1.a.** The act or an instance of subverting. **b.** The condition of being subverted. **2.** *Obsolete.* A cause of overthrow or ruin. [Middle English *subversioun,* from Old French *subversion,* from Late Latin *subversiō, subversiōn-,* from Latin *subversus,* past participle of *subvertere,* to subvert. See SUBVERT.] —**sub·ver′sion·ar′y** *adj.*

sub·ver·sive (səb-vûr′sĭv, -zĭv) *adj.* Intended or serving to subvert, especially intended to overthrow or undermine an established government: *"Sex and creativity are often seen by dictators as subversive activities"* (Erica Jong). —**subversive** *n.* One who advocates or is regarded as advocating subversion. —**sub·ver′sive·ly** *adv.* —**sub·ver′sive·ness** *n.*

sub·vert (səb-vûrt′) *tr.v.* **-vert·ed, -vert·ing, -verts. 1.** To destroy completely; ruin: *"schemes to subvert the liberties of a great community"* (Alexander Hamilton). **2.** To undermine the character, morals, or allegiance of; corrupt. **3.** To overthrow completely: *"Economic assistance . . . must subvert the existing . . . feudal or tribal order"* (Henry A. Kissinger). See Synonyms at **overthrow.** [Middle English *subverten,* from Old French *subvertir,* from Latin *subvertere* : *sub-,* sub- + *vertere,* to turn; see **wer-**[2] in Appendix.] —**sub·vert′er** *n.*

sub·vi·rus (sŭb-vī′rəs) *n., pl.* **-rus·es.** A viral protein or other substance smaller than a virus and having some of the properties of a virus. —**sub·vi′ral** (-rəl) *adj.*

sub·vo·cal (sŭb-vō′kəl) *adj.* Characterized by movement of the lips or other speech organs without making audible sounds: *subvocal speech.* —**sub·vo′cal·ly** *adv.*

sub·vo·cal·ize (sŭb-vō′kə-līz′) *tr. & intr.v.* **-ized, -iz·ing, -iz·es.** To articulate or engage in articulation by moving the lips or other speech organs without making audible sounds, as in reading to oneself. —**sub·vo′cal·i·za′tion** (-kə-lĭ-zā′shən) *n.* —**sub·vo′cal·iz′er** *n.*

sub·way (sŭb′wā′) *n.* **1.a.** An underground urban railroad, usually operated by electricity. **b.** A passage for such a railroad. **2.** An underground tunnel or passage, as for a water main or for pedestrians.

suc·ce·da·ne·um (sŭk′sĭ-dā′nē-əm) *n., pl.* **-ne·a** (-nē-ə). A substitute. [New Latin *succēdāneum,* from Latin, neuter sing. of *succēdāneus,* substituted, from *succēdere,* to succeed. See SUCCEED.]

suc·ceed (sək-sēd′) *v.* **-ceed·ed, -ceed·ing, -ceeds.** —*intr.* **1.** To come next in time or succession; follow after another, replace another in an office or a position: *She succeeded to the throne.* **2.** To accomplish something desired or intended: *"Success is counted sweetest/By those who ne'er succeed"* (Emily Dickinson). **3.** *Obsolete.* To devolve upon a person by way of inheritance. —*tr.* **1.** To come after in time or order; follow. **2.** To come after and take the place of. See Synonyms at **follow.** [Middle English *succeden,* from Old French *succeder,* from Latin *succēdere* : *sub-,* near; see SUB– + *cēdere,* to go; see **ked-** in Appendix.] —**suc·ce′dent** (sək-sēd′nt) *adj.* —**suc·ceed′er** *n.*

suc·cès d'es·time (sük-sĕ′ dĕs-tēm′) *n.* An important but unpopular success or achievement. [French : *succès,* success + *de,* of + *estime,* esteem.]

suc·cès fou (sük-sĕ′ fo͞o′) *n.* A wild success. [French : *succès,* success + *fou,* mad.]

suc·cess (sək-sĕs′) *n.* **1.** The achievement of something desired, planned, or attempted: *attributed their success in business to hard work.* **2.a.** The gaining of fame or prosperity: *an artist spoiled by success.* **b.** The extent of such gain. **3.** One that is successful: *The plan was a success.* **4.** *Obsolete.* A result or an outcome. [Latin *successus,* from past participle of *succēdere,* to succeed. See SUCCEED.]

suc·cess·ful (sək-sĕs′fəl) *adj.* **1.** Having a favorable outcome: *a successful heart transplant.* **2.** Having obtained something desired or intended: *was successful in stopping the leak of oil.* **3.** Having achieved wealth or eminence: *a successful architect.* —**suc·cess′ful·ly** *adv.* —**suc·cess′ful·ness** *n.*

suc·ces·sion (sək-sĕsh′ən) *n.* **1.** The act or process of following in order or sequence. **2.** A group of people or things arranged or following in order; a sequence: *"A succession of one-man stalls offered soft drinks"* (Alec Waugh). See Synonyms at **series. 3.a.** The sequence in which one person after another succeeds to a title, throne, dignity, or estate. **b.** The right of a person or line of persons to so succeed. **c.** The person or line having such a right. **4.a.** The act or process of succeeding to the rights or duties of another. **b.** The act or process of becoming entitled as a legal beneficiary to the property of a deceased person. **5.** *Ecology.* The gradual and orderly process of ecosystem development brought about by changes in community composition and the production of a climax characteristic of a particular geographic region. [Middle English, from Old French, from Latin *successiō, successiōn-,* from *successus,* past participle of *succēdere,* to succeed. See SUCCEED.] —**suc·ces′sion·al** *adj.* —**suc·ces′sion·al·ly** *adv.*

suc·ces·sive (sək-sĕs′ĭv) *adj.* **1.** Following in uninterrupted order; consecutive: *on three successive days.* **2.** Of, characterized by, or involving succession: *the government successive to the fallen monarchy.* —**suc·ces′sive·ly** *adv.* —**suc·ces′sive·ness** *n.*

successive approximation *n. Mathematics.* A method for estimating the value of an unknown quantity by repeated comparison to a sequence of known quantities.

suc·ces·sor (sək-sĕs′ər) *n.* One that succeeds another.

suc·ci·nate (sŭk′sə-nāt′) *n.* A salt or an ester of succinic acid.

suc·cinct (sək-sĭngkt′) *adj.* **-er, -est. 1.** Characterized by clear, precise expression in few words; concise and terse: *a succinct reply; a succinct style.* **2.** *Archaic.* Encircled as if by a girdle; girded. [Middle English *succincte,* girt, from Old French, from Latin *succīnctus,* past participle of *succingere,* to gird from below : *sub-,* sub- + *cingere,* to gird; see **kenk-** in Appendix.] —**suc·cinct′ly** *adv.* —**suc·cinct′ness** *n.*

suc·cin·ic acid (sək-sĭn′ĭk) *n.* A colorless crystalline dicarboxylic acid, $C_4H_6O_4$, occurring naturally in amber and important in the Krebs cycle. It is also synthesized for use in pharmaceuticals and perfumes. [French *succinique,* from Latin *succinum,* amber.]

suc·cin·yl·cho·line (sŭk′sə-nĭl-kō′lēn) *n.* A crystalline compound, $C_{14}H_{30}N_2O_4$, formed by esterification of succinic acid with choline and used medically to produce brief but complete muscular relaxation. [SUCCIN(IC ACID) + –YL + CHOLINE.]

suc·cin·yl·sul·fa·thi·a·zole (sŭk′sə-nĭl-sŭl′fə-thī′ə-zōl′) *n.* An antibacterial drug, $C_{13}H_{13}N_3O_5S_2$, derived from sulfonamide and used in the prevention and treatment of gastrointestinal infections. [SUCCIN(IC ACID) + –YL + SULFA(NILAMIDE) + THIAZOLE.]

suc·cor (sŭk′ər) *n.* **1.** Assistance in time of distress; relief. **2.** One that affords assistance or relief. —**succor** *tr.v.* **-cored, -cor·ing, -cors.** To give assistance to in time of want, difficulty, or distress. See Synonyms at **help.** [Middle English *sucur,* back-formation from *sucurs* (taken as pl.), from Old French *secors,* from Medieval Latin *succursus,* from past participle of Latin *succurrere,* to run to the aid of, succor : *sub-,* sub- + *currere,* to run; see **kers-** in Appendix.] —**suc′cor·a·ble** *adj.* —**suc′cor·er** *n.*

suc·co·ry (sŭk′ə-rē) *n., pl.* **-ries.** See **chicory** (sense 1). [Perhaps alteration (influenced by Middle Low German *suckerie,* or Middle Dutch *suckereie*) of Middle English *cicoree.* See CHICORY.]

suc·co·tash (sŭk′ə-tăsh′) *n.* A stew consisting of kernels of corn, lima beans, and tomatoes. [Narragansett *msíckquatash,* boiled whole-kernel corn.]

Suc·coth also **Suk·koth** (so͝ok′əs, so͞o-kōs′, so͞o-kôt′) *n. Judaism.* A harvest festival commemorating the booths in which the Israelites resided during their 40 years in the wilderness, lasting for either 8 or 9 days and beginning on the eve of the 15th of Tishri. [Hebrew *sukkôt,* (feast of) booths, pl. of *sukkâ,* booth.]

suc·cour (sŭk′ər) *n. & v. Chiefly British.* Variant of **succor.**

suc·cu·bus (sŭk′yə-bəs) also **suc·cu·ba** (-bə) *n., pl.* **-bus·es** or **-bi** (-bī′, -bē′) also **-bae** (-bē′, -bī′). **1.** A female demon supposed to descend upon and have sexual intercourse with a man while he sleeps. **2.** An evil spirit; a demon. [Middle English, from Medieval Latin, alteration (influenced by Late Latin *incubus,* incubus; see INCUBUS) of Latin *succuba,* paramour, from *succubāre,* to lie under : *sub-,* sub- + *cubāre,* to lie down.]

suc·cu·lent (sŭk′yə-lənt) *adj.* **1.** Full of juice or sap; juicy. **2.** *Botany.* Having thick, fleshy, water-storing leaves or stems. **3.** Highly interesting or enjoyable; delectable: *a succulent bit of gossip.* —**succulent** *n. Botany.* A succulent plant, such as a sedum or cactus. [Latin *succulentus,* from *succus,* juice. See **seue-**[2] in Appendix.] —**suc′cu·lence, suc′cu·len·cy** *n.* —**suc′cu·lent·ly** *adv.*

suc·cumb (sə-kŭm′) *intr.v.* **-cumbed, -cumb·ing, -cumbs. 1.** To submit to an overpowering force or yield to an overwhelming desire; give up or give in. See Synonyms at **yield. 2.** To die. [Middle English *succomben,* to bring down, from Old French *succomber,* from Latin *succumbere,* to lie under, yield : *sub-,* sub- + *-cumbere,* to lie down, as in *accumbere,* to lie down.]

suc·cus (sŭk′əs) *n., pl.* **suc·ci** (sŭk′ī, -sī). A fluid, such as gastric juice or vegetable juice, contained in or secreted by living tissue.

suc·cus·sion (sə-kŭsh′ən) *n.* **1.** The act or process of shaking violently, especially as a method of diagnosis to detect the presence of fluid and air in a body cavity. **2.** The condition of being shaken violently. [Latin *succussiō, succussiōn-,* from *succussus,* past participle of *succutere,* to toss up : *sub-,* up from below; see SUB– + *quatere,* to shake; see **kwēt-** in Appendix.] —**suc·cus′sa·to′ry** (sə-kŭs′ə-tôr′ē, -tōr′ē) *adj.*

such (sŭch) *adj.* **1.a.** Of this kind: *a single parent, one of many such people in the neighborhood.* **b.** Of a kind specified or implied: *a boy such as yourself.* **2.a.** Of a degree or quality indi-

subway
Prague, Czechoslovakia, subway system

ă pat	oi boy
ā pay	ou out
âr care	o͝o took
ä father	o͞o boot
ĕ pet	ŭ cut
ē be	ûr urge
ĭ pit	th thin
ī pie	*th* this
îr pier	hw which
ŏ pot	zh vision
ō toe	ə about, item
ô paw	♦ regionalism

Stress marks: ′ (primary); ′ (secondary), as in **dictionary** (dĭk′shə-nĕr′ē)

cated: *Their anxiety was such that they could not sleep.* **b.** Of so extreme a degree or quality: *never dreamed of such wealth.* **—such** *adv.* **1.** To so extreme a degree; so: *such beautiful flowers; such a funny character.* **2.** Very; especially: *She has been in such poor health lately.* **—such** *pron.* **1.a.** Such a person or persons or thing or things: *was the mayor and as such presided over the council; expected difficulties, and such occurred.* **b.** Itself alone or within itself: *Money as such will seldom bring total happiness.* **2.** Someone or something implied or indicated: *Such are the fortunes of war.* **3.** Similar things or people; the like: *pins, needles, and such.* ***—idiom.*** **such as.** For example. [Middle English, from Old English *swylc.* See **swo-** in Appendix.]

such and such *adj.* Not specified; unnamed or undetermined: *They agreed to meet at such and such an hour.*

such·like (sŭch′līk′) *adj.* Of the same kind; similar. **—suchlike** *pron.* Persons or things of such a kind.

Sü·chow (so͞o′chou′, sü′jō′). See **Xuzhou.**

suck (sŭk) *v.* **sucked, suck·ing, sucks.** *—tr.* **1.** To draw (liquid) into the mouth by movements of the tongue and lips that create suction. **2.a.** To draw in by establishing a partial vacuum: *a cleaning device that sucks up dirt.* **b.** To draw in by or as if by a current in a fluid. **c.** To draw or pull as if by suction: *teenagers who are sucked into a life of crime.* **3.** To draw nourishment through or from: *suck a baby bottle.* **4.** To hold, moisten, or maneuver (a sweet, for example) in the mouth. **5.** *Vulgar Slang.* To perform fellatio on. *—intr.* **1.** To draw something in by or as if by suction: *felt the drain starting to suck.* **2.** To draw nourishment; suckle. **3.** To make a sound caused by suction. **4.** *Slang.* To behave obsequiously; fawn. Often used with *up.* **5.** *Vulgar Slang.* To be disgustingly disagreeable or offensive. **—suck** *n.* **1.** The act or sound of sucking. **2.** Suction. **3.** Something drawn in by sucking. ***—phrasal verb.*** **suck in.** To take advantage of; cheat; swindle. [Middle English *suken,* from Old English *sūcan.* See **seuə-²** in Appendix.]

Sudan

suck·er (sŭk′ər) *n.* **1.** One that sucks, especially an unweaned domestic animal. **2.** *Informal.* **a.** One who is easily deceived; a dupe. **b.** One that is indiscriminately attracted to something specified: *"The nation's capital is a sucker for a symbolic gesture"* (Jonathan Alter). **3.** *Slang.* **a.** An unspecified thing. Used as a generalized term of reference, often as an intensive: *"our goal of getting that sucker on the air before old age took the both of us"* (Linda Ellerbee). **b.** A person. Used as a generalized term of reference, often as an intensive: *He's a mean sucker.* **4.** A lollipop. **5.a.** A piston or piston valve, as in a suction pump or syringe. **b.** A tube or pipe, such as a siphon, through which something is sucked. **6.** Any of numerous chiefly North American freshwater fishes of the family Catostomidae, having a toothless jaw and a thick-lipped mouth adapted for feeding by suction. **7.** *Zoology.* An organ or other structure adapted for sucking nourishment or for clinging to objects by suction. **8.** *Botany.* A secondary shoot produced from the base or roots of a woody plant that gives rise to a new plant. **—sucker** *v.* **-ered, -er·ing, -ers.** *—tr.* **1.** To strip suckers or shoots from (plants). **2.** *Informal.* To trick; dupe: *sucker a tourist into a confidence game.* *—intr.* *Botany.* To send out suckers or shoots.

suck·er·fish (sŭk′ər-fĭsh′) *n., pl.* **suckerfish** or **-fish·es.** See **remora.**

sucker punch *n.* *Slang.* An unexpected punch or blow.

suck·fish (sŭk′fĭsh′) *n., pl.* **suckfish** or **-fish·es. 1.** See **remora. 2.** A clingfish *(Caularchus maendricus)* of the Pacific coast of the United States.

suck·ing (sŭk′ĭng) *adj.* Not yet weaned.

sucking louse *n.* Any of various small wingless insects of the order Anoplura that have mouthparts adapted for piercing and sucking.

suck·le (sŭk′əl) *v.* **-led, -ling, -les.** *—tr.* **1.a.** To cause or allow to take milk at the breast or udder; nurse. **b.** To take milk at the breast or udder of. **2.** To take in as sustenance; have as nourishment. **3.** To nourish as if with the milk of the breast; nurture: *"a pagan suckled in a creed outworn"* (William Wordsworth). *—intr.* To suck at the breast or udder. [Middle English *suclen,* perhaps from *suklinge,* suckling. See SUCKLING.]

suck·ler (sŭk′lər) *n.* **1.** An unweaned mammal, especially a suckling calf. **2.** An animal that suckles its young; a mammal.

suck·ling (sŭk′lĭng) *n.* A young mammal that has not been weaned. **—suckling** *adj.* Unweaned. [Middle English *suklinge* : *souken, suken,* to suck; see SUCK + *-ling,* one that is young; see -LING¹.]

Suck·ling (sŭk′lĭng), Sir **John.** 1609–1642. English poet and courtier whose witty, unaffected works include *Session of the Poets* and *Aglaura* (both 1637).

su·crase (so͞o′krās′, -krāz′) *n.* See **invertase.** [French *sucre,* sugar (from Old French *sukere;* see SUGAR) + -ASE.]

su·cre (so͞o′krā) *n.* See table at **currency.** [American Spanish, after Antonio José de SUCRE.]

Su·cre (so͞o′krā, -krĕ). The constitutional capital of Bolivia, in the south-central part of the country southeast of La Paz. Founded in 1538 as Chuquisaca, it was renamed in 1840 to honor the first president of the country. Population, 86,609.

Su·cre (so͞o′krā), **Antonio José de.** 1795–1830. South American military leader who helped secure independence from Spain and served as the first president of Bolivia (1826–1828).

su·crose (so͞o′krōs′) *n.* A crystalline disaccharide carbohydrate, $C_{12}H_{22}O_{11}$, found in many plants but extracted as ordinary sugar mainly from sugar cane and sugar beets, widely used as a sweetener or preservative and in the manufacture of plastics and cellulose. Also called *saccharose.* [French *sucre,* sugar; see SUCRASE + -OSE².]

sucrose polyester *n.* A complex synthetic compound of sucrose and fatty acids that the body is unable to digest or absorb, produced commerically as a partial substitute for fats in cooking oils, shortening, butter, and other high-calorie or high-cholesterol foods.

suc·tion (sŭk′shən) *n.* **1.** The act or process of sucking. **2.** A force that causes a fluid or solid to be drawn into an interior space or to adhere to a surface because of the difference between the external and internal pressures. **—suction** *tr.v.* **-tioned, -tion·ing, -tions. 1.** To draw away or remove by the force of suction: *suction fluid from the lungs.* **2.** To clean or evacuate (a body cavity, for example) by the force of suction. **—suction** *adj.* **1.** Creating suction. **2.** Operating or operated by suction. [Late Latin *sūctiō, sūctiōn-,* from Latin *sūctus,* past participle of *sūgere,* to suck. See **seuə-²** in Appendix.]

suction lipectomy *n.* See **liposuction.**

suction pump *n.* A pump for drawing up a liquid by means of suction produced by a piston drawn through a cylinder.

suction stop *n.* *Linguistics.* See **click** (sense 3).

suc·to·ri·al (sŭk-tôr′ē-əl, -tōr′-) *adj.* **1.** Adapted for sucking or clinging by suction: *a suctorial organ.* **2.** Having organs or parts adapted for sucking or clinging. [From New Latin *sūctōrius,* from Latin *sūctus,* past participle of *sūgere,* to suck. See **seuə-²** in Appendix.]

suc·to·ri·an (sŭk-tôr′ē-ən, -tōr′-) *n.* A protozoan of the class Suctoria, having in its immature form a small, round, ciliated body but in its adult form being stalked and sessile, lacking cilia, and feeding by means of suctorial tentacles. [From New Latin *Suctoria,* class name, from neuter pl. of *suctorius,* suctorial. See SUCTORIAL.]

Su·dan (so͞o-dăn′). **1.** A region of northern Africa south of the Sahara and north of the equator. It extends across the continent from the Atlantic coast to the mountains of Ethiopia. **2.** A country of northeast Africa south of Egypt. Inhabited since prehistoric times, the region was conquered by Egypt in 1820–1822 and jointly administered by Great Britain and Egypt after 1899. Sudan achieved its independence in 1956. Khartoum is the capital and the largest city. Population, 20,564,364. **—Su′da·nese′** (so͞od′n-ēz′, -ēs′) *adj. & n.*

su·da·to·ri·um (so͞o′də-tôr′ē-əm, -tōr′-) *n., pl.* **-to·ri·a** (-tôr′ē-ə, -tōr′ē-ə). A hot-air room used for sweat baths. Also called *sudatory.* [Latin *sūdātōrium,* from neuter of *sūdātōrius,* for sweating, from *sūdātus,* past participle of *sūdāre,* to sweat. See **sweid-** in Appendix.]

su·da·to·ry (so͞o′də-tôr′ē, -tōr′ē) *adj.* Sudorific. **—sudatory** *n., pl.* **-ries. 1.** See **sudatorium. 2.** See **sudorific.**

Sud·bur·y (sŭd′bĕr′ē, -bə-rē). A city of southeast Ontario, Canada, north of Georgian Bay. It is the center of a rich mining region. Population, 91,829.

sudd (sŭd) *n.* A floating mass of vegetation that often obstructs navigation in tropical rivers. [Arabic, obstruction, sudd, from *sadda,* to obstruct.]

sud·den (sŭd′n) *adj.* **1.** Happening without warning; unforeseen: *a sudden storm.* **2.** Characterized by hastiness; abrupt or rash: *a sudden decision.* See Synonyms at **impetuous. 3.** Characterized by rapidity; quick and swift. ***—idiom.*** **all of a sudden.** Very quickly and unexpectedly; suddenly. [Middle English *sodain,* from Old French, from Vulgar Latin **subitānus,* from Latin *subitāneus,* from *subitus,* from past participle of *subīre,* to approach stealthily : *sub-,* secretly; see SUB- + *īre,* to go; see **ei-** in Appendix.] **—sud′den·ly** *adv.* **—sud′den·ness** *n.*

sudden death *n.* *Sports.* Extra play added to a tied game, the winner being the first to score. **—sud′den-death′** (sŭd′n-dĕth′) *adj.*

sudden infant death syndrome *n.* *Abbr.* **SIDS** A fatal syndrome that affects sleeping infants under a year old, characterized by a sudden cessation of breathing and thought to be caused by a defect in the central nervous system. Also called *crib death.*

Su·de·ten (so͞o-dā′tn, zo͞o-) also **Su·de·tes** (so͞o-dē′tēz). A series of mountain ranges along the Czechoslovakian-Polish border between the Elbe and Oder rivers. The mountains extend for about 298 km (185 mi) and rise to 1,603 m (5,256 ft).

Su·de·ten·land (so͞o-dāt′n-lănd′, -länt′, zo͞o-). A historical region of northwest Czechoslovakia along the Polish border. Seized by the Germans in September 1938, it was restored to Czechoslovakia in 1945.

Su·de·tes (so͞o-dē′tēz). See **Sudeten.**

su·dor·if·er·ous (so͞o′də-rĭf′ər-əs) *adj.* Producing or secreting sweat: *sudoriferous glands.* [From Late Latin *sūdōrifer* : Latin *sūdor,* sweat; see **sweid-** in Appendix + Latin *-fer,* -fer.]

su·dor·if·ic (so͞o′də-rĭf′ĭk) *adj.* Causing or increasing sweat. **—sudorific** *n.* A sudorific medicine. Also called *sudatory.* [New Latin *sūdōrificus* : Latin *sūdor,* sweat; see **sweid-** in Appendix + Latin *-ficus,* -fic.]

Su·dra (so͞o′drə) *n.* **1.** The fourth of the four Hindu classes, comprising artisans, laborers, and menials. **2.** A member of this caste. [Sanskrit *śūdraḥ.*]

suds (sŭdz) *pl.n.* **1.** Soapy water. **2.** Foam; lather. **3.** *Slang.*

Beer. [Perhaps from obsolete Dutch *zudse,* marsh, from Middle Dutch *sudse.*]

suds•y (sŭd′zē) *adj.* **-i•er, -i•est.** Full of or resembling suds.

sue (so͞o) *v.* **sued, su•ing, sues.** —*tr.* **1.** *Law.* **a.** To petition (a court) for redress of grievances or recovery of a right. **b.** To institute proceedings against (a person) for redress of grievances. **c.** To carry (an action) through to a final decision. **2.** To court; woo. **3.** *Obsolete.* To make a petition to; appeal to; beseech. —*intr.* **1.** *Law.* To institute legal proceedings; bring suit. **2.** To make an appeal or entreaty: *"I sue for grace, and thou deny'st me"* (Francis Quarles). **3.** To pay court; woo. [Middle English *sewen,* from Anglo-Norman *suer,* from Vulgar Latin **sequere,* to follow, from Latin *sequī.* See **sekʷ-¹** in Appendix.] —**su′er** *n.*

Sue (so͞o), **Eugène.** 1804–1857. French writer known for his sensational novels that depict the sordid side of city life, including *The Mysteries of Paris* (1842–1843).

suede also **suède** (swād) *n.* **1.** Leather with a soft napped surface. **2.** Fabric made to resemble suede. [Short for *Suède gloves,* from French *gants de Suède,* gloves of Sweden, from *Suède,* Sweden.]

su•et (so͞o′ĭt) *n.* The hard fatty tissues around the kidneys of cattle and sheep, used in cooking and for making tallow. [Middle English, from Anglo-Norman **suet,* accusative of *sue,* tallow, variant of Old French *sieu,* from Latin *sēbum.*]

Sue•to•ni•us (swē-tō′nē-əs). Originally Gaius Suetonius Tranquillus. fl. second century A.D. Roman historian whose major work, *Lives of the Caesars,* is an account of the lives of the first 12 Roman emperors.

Su•ez (so͞o-ĕz′, so͞o′ĕz′). A city of northeast Egypt at the head of the Gulf of Suez and the southern terminus of the Suez Canal. It became a major port after the opening of the canal. Population, 254,000.

Suez, Gulf of. An arm of the Red Sea off northeast Egypt west of the Sinai Peninsula.

Suez, Isthmus of. An isthmus of northeast Egypt connecting Africa and Asia. It is bordered by the Mediterranean Sea on the north and the Gulf of Suez on the south.

Suez Canal. A ship canal, about 166 km (103 mi) long, traversing the Isthmus of Suez and linking the Red Sea and the Gulf of Suez with the Mediterranean Sea. Built under the supervision of Ferdinand de Lesseps, it was opened in November 1869 and after 1875 came under British control. The British withdrew in June 1956, and in July President Gamal Abdel Nasser of Egypt nationalized the canal, precipitating a crisis in which Israel invaded Egypt and Great Britain and France sent armed forces to retake the canal. United Nations intervention forced an armistice, and the canal was reopened in April 1957. The canal was again closed in July 1967 during the Arab-Israeli War and remained closed until June 1975.

suf. *abbr.* **1.** Sufficient. **2.** *Grammar.* Suffix.

suff. *abbr.* **1.** Sufficient. **2.** *Grammar.* Suffix.

Suff. *abbr.* Suffragan.

suf•fer (sŭf′ər) *v.* **-fered, -fer•ing, -fers.** —*intr.* **1.** To feel pain or distress; sustain loss, injury, harm, or punishment. **2.** To tolerate or endure evil, injury, pain, or death. See Synonyms at **bear¹. 3.** To appear at a disadvantage: *"He suffers by comparison with his greater contemporary"* (Albert C. Baugh). —*tr.* **1.** To undergo or sustain (something painful, injurious, or unpleasant): *"Ordinary men have always had to suffer the history their leaders were making"* (Herbert J. Muller). **2.** To experience; undergo: *suffer a change in staff.* See Synonyms at **experience. 3.** To endure or bear; stand: *would not suffer fools.* **4.** To permit; allow: *"They were not suffered to aspire to so exalted a position as that of streetcar conductor"* (Edmund S. Morgan). [Middle English *suffren,* from Old French *sufrir,* from Vulgar Latin **sufferīre,* from Latin *sufferre* : *sub-,* sub- + *ferre,* to carry; see **bher-¹** in Appendix.] —**suf′fer•er** *n.* —**suf′fer•ing•ly** *adv.*

USAGE NOTE: In general usage *suffer* is preferably used with *from,* rather than *with,* in constructions such as *He suffered from hypertension.* According to 94 percent of the Usage Panel, *suffered with* would be unacceptable in the preceding example. In medical usage *suffer with* is sometimes employed with reference to the actual pain or discomfort caused by a condition, while *suffer from* is used more broadly in reference to a condition, such as anemia, that is detrimental but not necessarily painful.

suf•fer•a•ble (sŭf′ər-ə-bəl, sŭf′rə-) *adj.* Possible to suffer, endure, or permit; tolerable: *sufferable punishment; sufferable difficulties.* —**suf′fer•a•ble•ness** *n.* —**suf′fer•a•bly** *adv.*

suf•fer•ance (sŭf′ər-əns, sŭf′rəns) *n.* **1.** Patient endurance, especially of pain or distress. **2.** Suffering; misery. **3.** Sanction or permission implied or given by failure to prohibit; tacit consent; tolerance. [Middle English *suffrance,* from Old French *sufrance,* from Latin *sufferentia,* from *sufferēns, sufferent-,* present participle of *sufferre,* to suffer. See SUFFER.]

suf•fer•ing (sŭf′ər-ĭng, sŭf′rĭng) *n.* **1.** The condition of one who suffers; pain or distress. **2.** A source of pain or distress.

suf•fice (sə-fīs′) *v.* **-ficed, -fic•ing, -fic•es.** —*intr.* **1.** To meet present needs or requirements; be sufficient: *These rations will suffice until next week.* **2.** To be equal to a specified task; be capable: *No words will suffice to convey my grief.* —*tr.* To satisfy the needs or requirements of; be enough for. [Middle English *suffisen,* from Old French *suffire, suffis-,* from Latin *sufficere* : *sub-,* sub- + *facere,* to make; see **dhē-** in Appendix.] —**suf•fic′er** *n.*

suf•fi•cien•cy (sə-fĭsh′ən-sē) *n., pl.* **-cies. 1.** The condition or quality of being sufficient. **2.** An adequate amount or quantity. **3.** Adequate means to live in modest comfort.

suf•fi•cient (sə-fĭsh′ənt) *adj.* **1.** *Abbr.* **suf., suff.** Being as much as is needed. **2.** *Archaic.* Competent; qualified. [Middle English, from Old French, from Latin *sufficiēns, sufficient-,* present participle of *sufficere,* to suffice. See SUFFICE.] —**suf•fi′cient•ly** *adv.*

***SYNONYMS:** sufficient, adequate, enough.* The central meaning shared by these adjectives is "being what is needed without being in excess": *has sufficient income for a comfortable retirement; bought an adequate supply of food; drew enough water to fill the tub.*
***ANTONYM:** insufficient.*

suf•fix (sŭf′ĭks) *Grammar. n. Abbr.* **suff., suf.** An affix added to the end of a word or stem, serving to form a new word or functioning as an inflectional ending, such as *-ness* in *gentleness, -ing* in *walking,* or *-s* in *sits.* —**suffix** *tr.v.* **-fixed, -fix•ing, -fix•es.** To add as a suffix. [New Latin *suffīxum,* from Latin, neuter of *suffīxus,* past participle of *suffīgere,* to fasten underneath, affix : *sub-,* sub- + *fīgere,* to fix, fasten; see **dhīgʷ-** in Appendix.] —**suf′fix•al** *adj.* —**suf•fix′ion** (sə-fĭk′shən) *n.*

suf•fo•cate (sŭf′ə-kāt′) *v.* **-cat•ed, -cat•ing, -cates.** —*tr.* **1.** To kill or destroy by preventing access of air or oxygen. **2.** To impair the respiration of; asphyxiate. **3.** To cause discomfort to by or as if by cutting off the supply of fresh air. **4.** To suppress the development, imagination, or creativity of; stifle: *"The rigid formality of the place suffocated her"* (Thackeray). —*intr.* **1.** To die from lack of air or oxygen; be asphyxiated. **2.** To feel discomfort from lack of fresh air. **3.** To become or feel suppressed; be stifled. [Latin *suffōcāre, suffōcāt-* : *sub-,* sub- + *faucēs,* throat.] —**suf′fo•ca′ting•ly** *adv.* —**suf′fo•ca′tion** *n.* —**suf′fo•ca′tive** *adj.*

Suf•folk¹ (sŭf′ək). **1.** A historical region of eastern England bordering on the North Sea. Settled in prehistoric times, it was part of the Anglo-Saxon kingdom of East Anglia. Its name means the "southern people," as opposed to the "northern people" of Norfolk. **2.** (*also* -ôk′). An independent city of southeast Virginia southeast of Portsmouth, it was burned by the British in 1779 and occupied by Union forces in 1862. Population, 47,621.

Suf•folk² (sŭf′ək) *n.* **1.** Any of an English breed of hornless sheep with black face and black legs, raised for high-quality mutton. **2.** Any of a breed of English draft horses of a chestnut color, having short legs and a thickset heavy body. [After *Suffolk,* a county of eastern England.]

suf•fra•gan (sŭf′rə-gən) *n. Abbr.* **Suff., Suffr. 1.** A bishop elected or appointed as an assistant to the bishop or ordinary of a diocese, having administrative and episcopal responsibilities but no jurisdictional functions. **2.** A bishop regarded in position as subordinate to an archbishop or a metropolitan. —**suffragan** *adj.* Of, being, or relating to a suffragan. [Middle English, from Old French, from Medieval Latin *suffrāgāneus,* voting, supporting, from Latin *suffrāgium,* support, right to vote, from *suffrāgārī,* to express support. See **bhreg-** in Appendix.] —**suf′fra•gan•ship′** *n.*

suf•frage (sŭf′rĭj) *n.* **1.a.** The right or privilege of voting; the franchise. **b.** The exercise of such a right. **2.** A vote cast in deciding a disputed question or in electing a person to office. **3.** A short intercessory prayer. [Middle English, intercessory prayer, from Old French, from Medieval Latin *suffrāgium,* from Latin, the right to vote, from *suffrāgārī,* to express support. See **bhreg-** in Appendix.]

suf•fra•gette (sŭf′rə-jĕt′) *n.* An advocate of woman suffrage, especially in the United Kingdom. See Usage Note at **-ette.** —**suf′fra•get′tism** *n.*

suf•fra•gist (sŭf′rə-jĭst) *n.* An advocate of the extension of political voting rights, especially to women. —**suf′fra•gism** *n.*

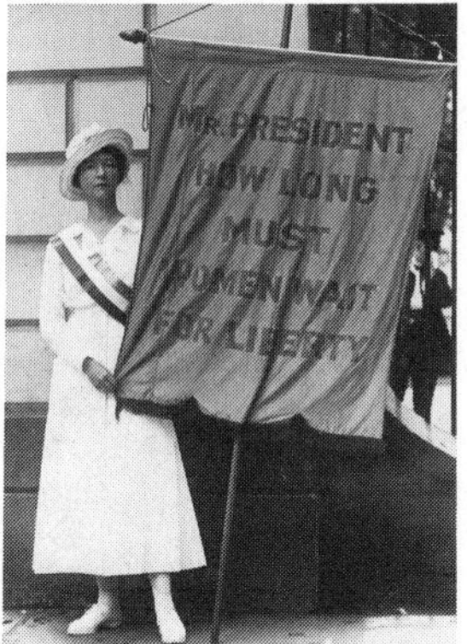

suffragist
Demonstrating outside the White House, 1917

suf•fru•tes•cent (sŭf′ro͞o-tĕs′ənt) also **suf•fru•ti•cose** (sŭf-ro͞o′tĭ-kōs′) *adj. Botany.* Having a stem that is woody only at the base; somewhat shrubby. [New Latin *suffrutēscēns, suffrutēscent-* : Latin *sub-,* sub- + New Latin *frutēscēns,* frutescent (from Latin *frutex,* shrub).]

suf•fuse (sə-fyo͞oz′) *tr.v.* **-fused, -fus•ing, -fus•es.** To spread through or over, as with liquid, color, or light: *"The sky above the roof is suffused with deep colors"* (Eugene O'Neill). See Synonyms at **charge.** [Latin *suffundere, suffūs-* : *sub-,* sub- + *fundere,* to pour; see **gheu-** in Appendix.] —**suf•fu′sion** *n.* —**suf•fu′sive** (-fyo͞o′sĭv, -zĭv) *adj.*

Su•fi (so͞o′fē) *Islam. n.* A Moslem mystic. —**Sufi** *adj.* Of or relating to the Sufis. [Arabic *Ṣūfīy,* (man) of wool, Sufi, from *ṣūf,* wool (probably from their woolen garments).] —**Su′fic** (-fĭk), **Su•fis′tic** (-fĭs′tĭk) *adj.*

Su•fism (so͞o′fĭz′əm) *n.* Islamic mysticism.

sug•ar (sho͝og′ər) *n.* **1.** A sweet crystalline or powdered substance, white when pure, consisting of sucrose obtained mainly from sugar cane and sugar beets and used in many foods, drinks, and medicines to improve their taste. Also called *table sugar.* **2.** Any of a class of water-soluble crystalline carbohydrates, including sucrose and lactose, having a characteristically sweet taste and classified as monosaccharides, disaccharides, and trisaccharides. **3.** A unit, such as a lump or cube, in which sugar is dis-

ă pat	oi boy
ā pay	ou out
âr care	o͝o took
ä father	o͞o boot
ĕ pet	ŭ cut
ē be	ûr urge
ĭ pit	th thin
ī pie	*th* this
îr pier	hw which
ŏ pot	zh vision
ō toe	ə about, item
ô paw	♦ regionalism

Stress marks: ′ (primary); ′ (secondary), as in **dictionary** (dĭk′shə-nĕr′ē)

pensed or taken. **4.** *Slang.* Sweetheart. Used as a term of endearment. **—sugar** *v.* **-ared, -ar·ing, -ars.** *—tr.* **1.** To coat, cover, or sweeten with sugar. **2.** To make less distasteful or more appealing. *—intr.* **1.** To form sugar. **2.** To form granules; granulate. **3.** To make sugar or syrup from sugar maple sap. Often used with *off.* [Middle English *sugre,* from Old French *sukere,* from Medieval Latin *succārum,* from Old Italian *zucchero,* from Arabic *sukkar,* from Persian *shakar,* from Sanskrit *śarkarā,* grit, ground sugar.] **—sug′ar·er** *n.*

sugar apple *n.* See **sweetsop.**

sugar beet *n.* A form of the common beet *(Beta vulgaris)* having fleshy white roots from which sugar is obtained.

sug·ar·ber·ry (shŏŏg′ər-bĕr′ē) *n.* See **hackberry.**

sug·ar·bird (shŏŏg′ər-bûrd′) *n.* Any of various honeyeaters, especially a South African bird *(Promerops cafer)* with a long, curved bill that feeds mainly on the nectar of trees of the genus *Protea.*

Sugarloaf Mountain

sugar bush *n.* A grove of sugar maples used as a source of maple syrup or maple sugar. Also called *sugar orchard.*

sugar cane *n.* A tall tropical southeast Asian grass *(Saccharum officinarum)* having thick, solid, tough stems that are a chief commercial source of sugar.

sug·ar·coat (shŏŏg′ər-kōt′) *tr.v.* **-coat·ed, -coat·ing, -coats. 1.** To cause to seem more appealing or pleasant: *a sentimental treatment that sugercoats a harsh reality.* **2.** To coat with sugar: *sugarcoat a pill.*

sugar corn *n.* See **sweet corn.**

sug·ar-cured (shŏŏg′ər-kyŏŏrd′) *adj.* Cured with a preparation of sugar, salt, and nitrate: *a sugar-cured ham.*

sugar daddy *n. Slang.* A wealthy, usually older man who gives expensive gifts to a young person in return for sexual favors or companionship.

sugar diabetes *n.* Insulin-dependent diabetes mellitus.

sug·ared (shŏŏg′ərd) *adj.* **1.** Sweetened with sugar. **2.** Made more appealing or pleasant.

sug·ar·house (shŏŏg′ər-hous′) *n.* A sugar refinery or processing plant, especially a building in which maple sap is boiled down to yield maple syrup and maple sugar.

sug·ar·ing off (shŏŏg′ər-ĭng) *n.* **1.** The process or an instance of boiling down maple sap to yield maple syrup and maple sugar. **2.** An informal social gathering in which the guests help make maple sugar.

sug·ar·less (shŏŏg′ər-lĭs) *adj.* **1.** Containing no sugar. **2.** Sweetened with a substance other than sucrose: *sugarless gum; sugarless candy.*

sugar loaf *n.* **1.** A large conical loaf of pure concentrated sugar. **2.** Something, such as a mountain, that resembles a loaf of sugar in shape. **—sug′ar-loaf′** (shŏŏg′ər-lōf′) *adj.*

Sug·ar·loaf Mountain (shŏŏg′ər-lōf′). A rocky peak in Rio de Janeiro, Brazil, at the entrance to Guanabara Bay. An aerial railroad leads to the summit, 395.3 m (1,296 ft) high.

sugar maple
Acer saccharum

sugar maple *n.* **1.** An eastern North American maple tree *(Acer saccharum)* having sap that is the source of maple syrup and maple sugar and variously grained hard wood used in cabinetmaking. **2.** The wood of this tree Also called *hard maple, rock maple.*

sugar of lead (lĕd) *n.* See **lead acetate.**

sugar of milk *n.* Lactose.

sugar orchard *n.* See **sugar bush.**

sugar pea *n.* See **snow pea.**

sugar pine *n.* A tall evergreen timber tree *(Pinus lambertiana)* of the Pacific coast of North America, having needles with white lines on the back that are grouped in fascicles of five.

sug·ar·plum (shŏŏg′ər-plŭm′) *n.* A small round piece of sugary candy.

sug·ar·y (shŏŏg′ə-rē) *adj.* **-i·er, -i·est. 1.** Characterized by or containing sugar: *sugary foods.* **2.** Tasting or looking like sugar. **3.** Excessively or cloyingly sweet: *sugary compliments; a sugary smile.* **—sug′ar·i·ness** *n.*

sug·gest (səg-jĕst′, sə-jĕst′) *tr.v.* **-gest·ed, -gest·ing, -gests. 1.** To offer for consideration or action; propose: *suggest things for children to do; suggested that we take a walk.* **2.** To bring or call to mind by logic or association; evoke: *a cloud that suggests a mushroom; a ringlike symbol suggesting unity.* **3.** To make evident indirectly; intimate or imply: *a silence that suggested disapproval.* **4.** To serve as or provide a motive for; prompt or demand: *Such a crime suggests apt punishment.* [Latin *suggerere, suggest-* : *sub-,* up; see SUB– + *gerere,* to carry.] **—sug·gest′er** *n.*

SYNONYMS: *suggest, imply, hint, intimate, insinuate.* These verbs mean to convey thoughts or ideas by indirection. *Suggest* refers to the calling of something to mind as the result of an association of ideas or train of thought: *"his erect and careless attitude suggesting assurance and power"* (Joseph Conrad). To *imply* is to suggest a thought or an idea that is unexpressed but that can be inferred from something else, such as a statement, that is more explicit: *The effusive praise the professor heaped on one of the students seemed to imply indifference toward or disapproval of the rest. Hint* refers to an oblique or covert suggestion that often contains clues: *He hinted that he would accept an invitation if it were extended. My imagination supplied the explanation you only hinted at. Intimate* applies to indirect, subtle expression that often reflects discretion, tact, or reserve: *She intimated that she and her husband were having marital problems.* To *insinuate* is to suggest something, usually something unpleasant, in a covert, sly, and underhanded manner: *The columnist insinuated—but never actually asserted—that the candidate had underworld ties.*

sug·gest·i·bil·i·ty (səg-jĕs′tə-bĭl′ĭ-tē, sə-jĕs′-) *n.* Responsiveness or susceptibility to suggestion.

sug·gest·i·ble (səg-jĕs′tə-bəl, sə-jĕs′-) *adj.* Readily influenced by suggestion: *suggestible young minds.*

sug·ges·tion (səg-jĕs′chən, sə-jĕs′-) *n.* **1.** The act of suggesting. **2.** Something suggested: *We ordered the shrimp, a suggestion of the waiter.* **3.** The sequential process by which one thought or mental image leads to another. **4. a.** A psychological process by which an idea is induced in or adopted by another without argument, command, or coercion. **b.** An idea or response so induced. **5.** A hint or trace: *just a suggestion of makeup; the first suggestion of trouble ahead.*

sug·ges·tive (səg-jĕs′tĭv, sə-jĕs′-) *adj.* **1. a.** Tending to suggest; evocative: *artifacts suggestive of an ancient society.* **b.** Stimulating further thought: *"Suggestive here is the Southern, often Western and rural locus of these tales"* (Mark Muro). **c.** Conveying a hint or suggestion: *conveyed the message with a few suggestive words.* **2.** Tending to suggest something improper or indecent: *a controversial song with highly suggestive lyrics.* **—sug·ges′tive·ly** *adv.* **—sug·ges′tive·ness** *n.*

Su·har·to (sə-här′tō, sŏŏ-). Born 1921. Indonesian military and political leader who seized power from Sukarno (1967) and was elected president in 1968.

Sui (swā). A Chinese dynasty (581–618) that reunified China after a period of declining centralized government.

su·i·cid·al (sŏŏ′ĭ-sīd′l) *adj.* **1.** Causing, intending, or relating to suicide: *a suicidal act; suicidal impulses.* **2.** Dangerous to oneself or to one's interests; self-destructive or ruinous: *a suicidal corporate takeover strategy.* **—su′i·cid′al·ly** *adv.*

su·i·cide (sŏŏ′ĭ-sīd′) *n.* **1.** The act or an instance of intentionally killing oneself. **2.** The destruction or ruin of one's own interests: *It is professional suicide to involve oneself in illegal practices.* **3.** One who commits suicide. [Latin *suī,* of oneself; see **s(w)e-** in Appendix + –CIDE.]

suicide watch *n.* A procedural tour of duty in a prison in which guards frequently check the cells of inmates suspected of suicidal tendencies.

su·i·cid·ol·o·gy (sŏŏ′ĭ-sī-dŏl′ə-jē) *n.* The study of suicide, suicidal behavior, and suicide prevention. **—su′i·cid·ol′o·gist** *n.*

su·i ge·ne·ris (sŏŏ′ī′ jĕn′ər-ĭs, sŏŏ′ē) *adj.* Being the only example of its kind; unique: *"sui generis works like Mary Chesnut's Civil War diary"* (Linda Orr). [Latin *suī generis* : *suī,* of its own + *generis,* genitive of *genus,* kind.]

sui ju·ris (jŏŏr′ĭs) *adj. Law.* Capable of managing one's own affairs. [Latin *suī iūris* : *suī,* of one's own + *iūris,* genitive of *iūs,* right, law.]

su·int (sŏŏ′ĭnt, swĭnt) *n.* A natural grease formed from dried perspiration found in the fleece of sheep, used as a source of potash. [French, from Old French, from *suer,* to sweat, from Latin *sūdāre.* See **sweid-** in Appendix.]

suit (sŏŏt) *n.* **1. a.** A set of matching outer garments, especially one consisting of a coat with trousers or a skirt. **b.** A costume for a special activity: *a diving suit; a running suit.* **2.** A group of things used together; a set or collection: *a suit of sails; a suit of tools.* **3.** *Games.* Any of the four sets of 13 playing cards (clubs, diamonds, hearts, and spades) in a standard deck, the members of which bear the same marks. **4.** Attendance required of a vassal at his feudal lord's court or manor. **5.** *Law.* A court proceeding to recover a right or claim. **6.** The act or an instance of courting a woman; courtship: *She was inclined to accept his suit.* **—suit** *v.* **suit·ed, suit·ing, suits.** *—tr.* **1.** To meet the requirements of; fit: *This candidate does not suit our qualifications.* **2.** To make appropriate or suitable; adapt: *builders who suit the house to the owner's specifications.* **3.** To be appropriate for; befit: *a color that suits you.* **4.** To please; satisfy: *a choice that suits us all.* **5.** To provide with clothing; dress: *The NCOs suited the recruits in green uniforms.* *—intr.* **1.** To be suitable or acceptable. **2.** To be in accord; agree or match. ***—phrasal verb.* suit up.** To put on clothing designed for a special activity: *suits up in shorts for a jog.* [Middle English *sute,* from Anglo-Norman, from Vulgar Latin **sequita,* act of following, feminine of **sequitus,* past participle of **sequere,* to follow, from Latin *sequī.* See SUITOR.]

Su·i·ta (sŏŏ-ē′tə, -tä). A city of southern Honshu, Japan, an industrial suburb of Osaka. Population, 348,946.

suit·a·ble (sŏŏ′tə-bəl) *adj.* Appropriate to a purpose or an occasion. See Synonyms at **fit**[1]. **—suit′a·bil′i·ty, suit′a·ble·ness** *n.* **—suit′a·bly** *adv.*

suit·case (sŏŏt′kās′) *n.* A usually rectangular piece of luggage for carrying clothing.

suite (swēt) *n.* **1.** A staff of attendants or followers; a retinue. **2. a.** A group of related things intended to be used together; a set. **b.** (*also* sŏŏt). A set of matching furniture: *a dining room suite.* **3.** A series of connected rooms used as a living unit. **4.** *Music.* An instrumental composition consisting of a succession of dances in the same or related keys. [French, from Old French. See SUIT.]

suit·ing (sŏŏ′tĭng) *n.* Fabric from which suits are made.

suit·or (so͞o′tər) *n.* **1.** A man who is courting a woman. **2.** A person who makes a petition or request. **3.** *Law.* A person who sues in court; a plaintiff; a petitioner. **4.** A person or group seeking to purchase controlling interest in a company. [Middle English, plaintiff, from Anglo-Norman, from Latin *secūtor,* follower, from *secūtus,* past participle of *sequī,* to follow. See **sekʷ-¹** in Appendix.]

Su·kar·no (so͞o-kär′nō). 1901–1970. Indonesian politician who obtained his country's independence from the Netherlands (1949), served as Indonesia's first president (1949–1967), and was ousted from office by a coup d'état.

su·ki·ya·ki (so͞o′kē-yä′kē, skē-yä′kē) *n.* A Japanese dish of sliced meat, bean curd, and vegetables seasoned and fried together. [Japanese.]

Suk·koth (so͝ok′əs, so͞o-kōs′, so͞o-kôt′) *n.* *Judaism.* Variant of **Succoth.**

Su·la·we·si (so͞o′lä-wā′sē). See **Celebes.**

sul·cate (sŭl′kāt′) *adj.* *Biology.* Having narrow, deep furrows or grooves, as a stem or tissue. [Latin *sulcātus,* past participle of *sulcāre,* to furrow, from *sulcus,* furrow.]

sul·cus (sŭl′kəs) *n., pl.* **-ci** (-kī, -sī). **1.** A deep, narrow furrow or groove, as in an organ or a tissue. **2.** *Anatomy.* Any of the narrow fissures separating adjacent convolutions of the brain. [Latin.] **—sul′cal** *adj.*

Su·lei·man I (so͞o′lā-män′, -lə-). Known as "Suleiman the Magnificent." 1494?–1566. Sultan of Turkey (1520–1566) under whose governance the Ottoman Empire reached the height of its power.

sulf– *pref.* Variant of **sulfo–.**

sul·fa (sŭl′fə) *adj.* Of, relating to, or containing sulfanilamide or any sulfa drug: *sulfa pills; a sulfa powder.* [Short for SULFA(NILAMIDE).]

sul·fa·di·u·zine (sŭl′fə-dī′ə-zēn′) *n.* A sulfa drug, $C_{10}H_{10}N_4O_2S$, used in the treatment of meningitis and other infections.

sulfa drug *n.* Any of a group of synthetic organic compounds, derived chiefly from sulfanilamide, chemically similar to PABA and capable of inhibiting bacterial growth and activity by interfering with the metabolic processes in bacteria that require PABA. Also called *sulfonamide.*

sul·fa·nil·a·mide (sŭl′fə-nĭl′ə-mīd′, -mĭd) *n.* A white, odorless crystalline sulfonamide, $C_6H_8N_2SO_2$, used in the treatment of various bacterial infections. [SULF(O)– + ANIL(INE) + AMIDE.]

sul·fa·tase (sŭl′fə-tās′) *n.* Any of a group of enzymes that catalyze the hydrolysis of sulfuric acid esters and are found in animal tissues and bacteria. [SULFAT(E) + –ASE.]

sul·fate (sŭl′fāt′) *n.* A chemical compound containing the bivalent group SO_4. **—sulfate** *v.* **-fat·ed, -fat·ing, -fates.** *—tr.* **1.** To treat or react with sulfuric acid or a sulfate. **2.** *Electricity.* To cause lead sulfate to accumulate on (the plates of a lead-acid storage battery). *—intr.* To become sulfated. [French, from Latin *sulfur,* sulfur.]

sul·fa·thi·a·zole (sŭl′fə-thī′ə-zōl′) *n.* A sulfa drug, $C_9H_9N_3O_2S_2$, once widely used in the treatment of gonorrhea, bacterial pneumonia, and other bacterial infections. It has been replaced by less toxic sulfonamides.

sul·fide (sŭl′fīd′) *n.* A compound of bivalent sulfur with an electropositive element or group, especially a binary compound of sulfur with a metal.

sul·fin·pyr·a·zone (sŭl′fĭn-pīr′ə-zōn′) *n.* A drug, $C_{23}H_{20}N_2O_3S$, related to phenylbutazone, that promotes urinary excretion of uric acid and is used in the treatment of gout. [SULFIN(YL) + PYR(O)– + AZ(OLE) + –ONE.]

sul·fi·nyl (sŭl′fə-nĭl′) *n.* The bivalent group SO. Also called *thionyl.* [SULF(O)– + –IN + –YL.]

sul·fite (sŭl′fīt′) *n.* A salt or an ester of sulfurous acid. **—sul·fit′ic** (-fĭt′ĭk) *adj.*

sulfo– or **sulf–** *pref.* Sulfur: *sulfate.* [From SULFUR.]

sulfon– *pref.* **1.** Sulfonic: *sulfonamide.* **2.** Sulfonyl: *sulfonmethane.* [From SULFONE.]

sul·fon·a·mide (sŭl-fŏn′ə-mīd′, -mĭd) *n.* **1.** Any of a group of organic sulfur compounds containing the radical O_2NH_2 and including the sulfa drugs. **2.** See **sulfa drug.**

sul·fo·nate (sŭl′fə-nāt′) *n.* A salt or an ester of sulfonic acid. **—sulfonate** *tr.v.* **-nat·ed, -nat·ing, -nates. 1.** To introduce into (an organic compound) one or more sulfonic acid groups. **2.** To treat with sulfonic acid. **—sul′fo·na′tion** *n.*

sul·fone (sŭl′fōn′) *n.* Any of various organic sulfur compounds having a sulfonyl group attached to two carbon atoms, especially such a compound formerly used as a drug to treat leprosy or tuberculosis.

sul·fon·ic (sŭl-fŏn′ĭk) *adj.* Of or relating to the chemical group SO_2OH.

sulfonic acid *n.* Any of several organic acids containing one or more sulfonic groups.

sul·fo·ni·um (sŭl-fō′nē-əm) *n.* A positive ion or univalent radical containing trivalent sulfur, such as H_3S. [SULF(O)– + (AMM)ONIUM.]

sul·fon·meth·ane (sŭl′fŏn-mĕth′ān′, -fŏn-) *n.* A colorless crystalline or powdered compound, $C_7H_{16}O_4S_2$, used medicinally as a hypnotic.

sul·fo·nyl (sŭl′fə-nĭl′) *n.* The bivalent radical SO_2. Also called *sulfuryl.*

sul·fo·nyl·u·re·a (sŭl′fə-nĭl-yo͞o-rē′ə) *n.* Any of a group of hypoglycemic drugs, such as tolbutamide, that act on the beta cells of the pancreas to increase the secretion of insulin.

sulf·ox·ide (sŭl-fŏk′sīd′) *n.* Any of various organic compounds that contain a sulfinyl group.

sul·fur also **sul·phur** (sŭl′fər) *—n.* *Symbol* **S** A pale yellow nonmetallic element occurring widely in nature in several free and combined allotropic forms. It is used in black gunpowder, rubber vulcanization, the manufacture of insecticides and pharmaceuticals, and in the preparation of sulfur compounds such as hydrogen sulfide and sulfuric acid. Atomic number 16; atomic weight 32.064; melting point (rhombic) 112.8°C; (monoclinic) 119.0°C; boiling point 444.6°C; specific gravity (rhombic) 2.07; (monoclinic) 1.957; valence 2, 4, 6. See table at **element.** *—tr.v.* **-fured, -fur·ing, -furs** also **-phured, -phur·ing, -phurs.** To treat with sulfur or a compound of sulfur. [Middle English, from Anglo-Norman *sulfre,* from Latin *sulfur.*]

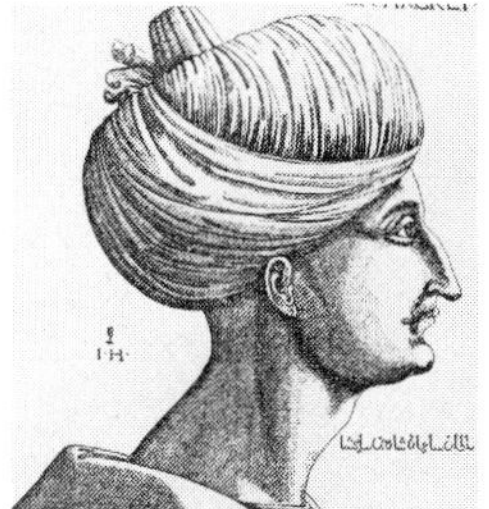

Suleiman I

sul·fu·rate (sŭl′fə-rāt′, -fyə-) *tr.v.* **-rat·ed, -rat·ing, -rates.** To treat or combine with sulfur. **—sul′fu·ra′tion** *n.*

sulfur bacterium *n.* Any of several bacteria that oxidize inorganic sulfur compounds, especially a rod-shaped, gram-negative bacterium of the genus *Thiobacillus.*

sulfur dioxide *n.* A colorless, extremely irritating gas or liquid, SO_2, used in many industrial processes, especially the manufacture of sulfuric acid.

sul·fu·re·ous (sŭl-fyo͝or′ē-əs) *adj.* Of or relating to sulfur; sulfurous.

sul·fu·ret (sŭl′fə-rĕt′, -fyə-) *tr.v.* **-ret·ed, -ret·ing, -rets** or **-ret·ted, -ret·ting, -rets.** To sulfurize. **—sulfuret** *n.* A sulfide. [From New Latin *sulfurētum,* sulfide : *sulf-,* sulfur (from Latin *sulfur*) + *-urētum,* obsolete chemical suff.]

sul·fu·ric (sŭl-fyo͝or′ĭk) *adj.* Of, relating to, or containing sulfur, especially with valence 6.

sulfuric acid *n.* A highly corrosive, dense, oily liquid, H_2SO_4, colorless to dark brown depending on its purity and used to manufacture a wide variety of chemicals and materials including fertilizers, paints, detergents, and explosives. Also called *oil of vitriol, vitriol.*

sul·fur·ize (sŭl′fə-rīz′, -fyə-) *tr.v.* **-ized, -iz·ing, -iz·es. 1.** To treat or impregnate with sulfur; sulfuret. **2.** To bleach or fumigate with sulfur or sulfur dioxide. **—sul′fur·i·za′tion** (-fər-ĭ-zā′shən, -fyər-) *n.*

sul·fur·ous (sŭl′fər-əs, -fyər-, sŭl-fyo͝or′əs) *adj.* **1.** Of, relating to, derived from, or containing sulfur, especially with valence 4. **2.** Characteristic of or emanating from burning sulfur. **3.** Also **sul·phur·ous.** Fiery; hellish.

sulfurous acid *n.* A colorless solution of sulfur dioxide in water, H_2SO_3, characterized by a suffocating sulfurous odor, used as a bleaching agent, preservative, and disinfectant.

sulfur trioxide *n.* A corrosive compound, SO_3, having three solid forms that may coexist in a given sample, used in the sulfonation of organic compounds.

sul·fur·yl (sŭl′fə-rĭl′, -fyə-) *n.* See **sulfonyl.**

sulfuryl chloride *n.* A colorless liquid, SO_2Cl_2, having a pungent odor, used as a chlorinating and dehydrating agent and in the manufacture of pharmaceuticals, dyestuffs, and poison gases.

sulk (sŭlk) *intr.v.* **sulked, sulk·ing, sulks.** To be sullenly aloof or withdrawn, as in silent resentment or protest. **—sulk** *n.* A mood or display of sullen aloofness or withdrawal: *stayed home in a sulk; a case of the sulks.* [Back-formation from SULKY¹.]

sulk·y¹ (sŭl′kē) *adj.* **-i·er, -i·est. 1.** Sullenly aloof or withdrawn. **2.** Gloomy; dismal: *sulky weather.* [Perhaps alteration of obsolete *sulke,* sluggish, perhaps ultimately from Old English *āsolcen,* from past participle of *āseolcan,* to become sluggish.] **—sulk′i·ly** *adv.* **—sulk′i·ness** *n.*

sulky²
Harness racing

sulk·y² (sŭl′kē) *n., pl.* **-ies.** A light, open two-wheeled vehicle accommodating only the driver and drawn by one horse, used especially in harness racing. [From SULKY¹ (from its having only one seat).]

Sul·la (sŭl′ə), **Lucius Cornelius.** 138–78 B.C. Roman general and dictator (82–79) who marched on Rome and seized power from his political rival Marius (88).

sul·lage (sŭl′ĭj) *n.* **1.** Silt deposited by a current of water. **2.** Waste materials or sewage; refuse. [Perhaps from French *souiller,* to soil. See SULLY.]

sul·len (sŭl′ən) *adj.* **-er, -est. 1.** Showing a brooding ill humor or silent resentment; morose or sulky. **2.** Gloomy or somber in tone, color, or portent: *sullen, gray skies.* **3.** Sluggish; slow: *the sullen current of a canal.* [Middle English *solein,* from Anglo-Norman *solein,* alone, from *sol,* single, from Latin *sōlus,* by oneself alone. See **s(w)e-** in Appendix.] **—sul′len·ly** *adv.* **—sul′len·ness** *n.*

Sul·li·van (sŭl′ə-vən), **Anne Mansfield.** 1866–1936. American educator. Visually impaired herself, she was the teacher and lifelong companion of Helen Keller.

Sullivan, Sir **Arthur Seymour.** 1842–1900. British composer known for a series of comic operas, including *H.M.S. Pinafore* (1878) and *The Gondoliers* (1889), written with the lyricist W.S. Gilbert.

Sullivan, Edward Vincent. Known as "Ed." 1902–1974. Amer-

ă pat	oi boy
ā pay	ou out
âr care	o͝o took
ä father	o͞o boot
ĕ pet	ŭ cut
ē be	ûr urge
ĭ pit	th thin
ī pie	*th* this
îr pier	hw which
ŏ pot	zh vision
ō toe	ə about, item
ô paw	♦ regionalism

Stress marks: **′** (primary); ′ (secondary), as in **dictionary** (dĭk′shə-nĕr′ē)

ican columnist and host of *The Ed Sullivan Show* (1948–1971), a television variety show.

Sullivan, Harry Stack. 1892–1949. American psychiatrist who theorized that personality is largely determined by one's interpersonal relations and the assimilation of societal values.

Sullivan, John Lawrence. 1858–1918. American prizefighter who was the heavyweight champion from 1882 to 1892. In 1889 he fought the last bare-knuckles title bout.

Sullivan, Louis Henry or **Henri.** 1856–1924. American architect known for his early steel-frame designs for skyscrapers and for his influential dictum "Form follows function."

sul·ly (sŭl′ē) *tr.v.* **-lied, -ly·ing, -lies. 1.** To mar the cleanness or luster of; soil or stain. **2.** To defile; taint. **—sully** *n., pl.* **-lies.** *Archaic.* Something that stains or spots. [Probably from French *souiller,* from Old French. See SOIL[2].]

Sul·ly (sŭl′ē, so͞o-lē′, sü-), Duc de. Title of Maximilien de Béthune. 1560–1641. French politician. As chief minister to Henry IV, he replenished the treasury and encouraged industry.

Sul·ly (sŭl′ē), **Thomas.** 1783–1872. British-born American painter of portraits and historical scenes, such as *Washington's Passage of the Delaware* (c. 1818).

Sul·ly-Prud·homme (sŭl′ē-pro͞o′dəm, sü-lē′prü-dôm′), **René François Armand.** 1839–1907. French poet whose early works are melancholic, while his later poems are concerned with scientific and philosophical theories. He won the 1901 Nobel Prize for literature.

sul·phur[1] (sŭl′fər) *n.* Any of various butterflies of the genus *Colias* and related genera of the family Pieridae, having yellow or orange wings marked with black.

sul·phur[2] (sŭl′fər) *n. & v.* Variant of **sulfur.**

Sul·phur (sŭl′fər). A city of southwest Louisiana west of Lake Charles. Population, 19,709.

sul·phur-bot·tom (sŭl′fər-bŏt′əm) *n.* See **blue whale.**

sul·phur·ous (sŭl′fər-əs, -fyər-, sŭl-fyo͝or′əs) *adj.* Variant of **sulfurous** (sense 3).

sul·tan (sŭl′tən) *n.* **1.** A ruler of a Moslem country, especially of the former Ottoman Empire. **2.** A powerful person: *a sultan of vice and corruption.* [French, from Old French, ruler of Turkey, from Turkish, from Arabic *sulṭān,* from Aramaic *šulṭānā,* from *šəlēṭ,* to rule.]

sul·tan·a (sŭl-tăn′ə, -tä′nə) *n.* **1.a.** The wife, mother, sister, or daughter of a sultan. **b.** The mistress of a sultan, king, or prince. **2.** A small yellow seedless raisin of a kind originally produced in Asia Minor. [Italian, feminine of *sultano,* sultan, from Arabic *sulṭān.* See SULTAN.]

sul·tan·ate (sŭl′tə-nāt′) *n.* **1.** The office, power, or reign of a sultan. **2.** A country ruled by a sultan.

sul·try (sŭl′trē) *adj.* **-tri·er, -tri·est. 1.a.** Very humid and hot: *sultry July weather.* **b.** Extremely hot; torrid: *the sultry sands of the desert.* **2.** Sensual; voluptuous: *a sultry look; a sultry dance.* [From obsolete *sulter,* to swelter, possibly alteration of SWELTER.] **—sul′tri·ly** *adv.* **—sul′tri·ness** *n.*

sumac
Staghorn sumac
Rhus typhina

Su·lu (so͞o′lo͞o) *n., pl.* **Su·lu** or **-lus.** A member of a Moslem people inhabiting the Sulu Archipelago. [Sama *sulu,* current.]

Sulu Sea. An arm of the western Pacific Ocean between the Philippines and northern Borneo. The **Sulu Archipelago,** a chain of small islands belonging to the Philippines, separates the Sulu Sea from the Celebes Sea southwest of Mindanao.

sum (sŭm) *n. Mathematics.* **1.a.** An amount obtained as a result of adding numbers. **b.** An arithmetic problem: *a child good at sums.* **2.** The whole amount, quantity, or number; an aggregate: *the sum of the team's combined experience.* **3.** An amount of money: *paid an enormous sum.* **4.** A summary: *my view of the world, in sum.* **5.** The central idea or point; the gist. **—sum** *tr.v.* **summed, sum·ming, sums. 1.** *Mathematics.* To add. **2.** To give a summary of; summarize. ***—phrasal verb.* sum up. 1.** To present the substance of (material) in a condensed form; summarize: *sum up the day's news; concluded the lecture by summing up.* **2.** To describe or assess concisely: *an epithet that sums up my feelings.* [Middle English *summe,* from Old French, from Latin *summa,* from feminine of *summus,* highest. See **uper** in Appendix.]

su·mac also **su·mach** (so͞o′măk, sho͞o′-) *n.* Any of various shrubs or small trees of the genus *Rhus,* having compound leaves, clusters of small greenish flowers, and usually red, hairy fruit. Some species, such as the poison ivy and poison oak, cause an acute itching rash on contact. [Middle English, preparation made from sumac, from Old French (possibly via Medieval Latin *sumach*), from Arabic *summāq,* sumac tree, probably from Aramaic *sĕmēq,* to be red.]

Su·ma·tra (so͞o-mä′trə). An island of western Indonesia in the Indian Ocean south of the Malay Peninsula. Visited by Marco Polo c. 1292, it came under Dutch control in the 17th century. Sumatra joined independent Indonesia in 1949. **—Su·ma′tran** *adj. & n.*

Sum·ba (so͞om′bə, -bä). An island of south-central Indonesia in the Lesser Sunda Islands south of Flores. First visited by Europeans in 1522, it passed to the Dutch in 1866.

Sum·ba·wa (so͞om-bä′wə, -wä). A volcanic island of south-central Indonesia in the Lesser Sunda Islands west of Flores. The Dutch gained control in 1905 after signing treaties with the local chieftains.

Su·mer (so͞o′mər). An ancient country of southern Mesopotamia in present-day southern Iraq. Archaeological evidence dates the beginnings of Sumer to the fifth millennium B.C. By 3000 a flourishing civilization existed, which gradually exerted power over the surrounding area and culminated in the Akkadian dynasty founded (c. 2340) by Sargon I. Sumer declined after 2000 and was later absorbed by Babylonia and Assyria. The Sumerians are believed to have invented the cuneiform system of writing.

Su·me·ri·an (so͞o-mîr′ē-ən, -mĕr′-) *adj.* Of or relating to ancient Sumer or its people, language, or culture. **—Sumerian** *n.* **1.** A member of an ancient people, probably of non-Semitic origin, who established a nation of city-states in Sumer in the fourth millennium B.C. that is one of the earliest known historic civilizations. **2.** The language of the Sumerians, of no known linguistic affiliation.

sum·ma cum lau·de (so͞om′ə ko͝om lou′də, -dā, -dē) *adv. & adj.* With the greatest honor. Used to express the highest academic distinction: *graduated summa cum laude; a summa cum laude graduate.* [Latin *summā cum laude,* with highest praise : *summā,* feminine ablative of *summus,* highest + *cum,* with + *laude,* ablative of *laus,* praise.]

sum·ma·rize (sŭm′ə-rīz′) *intr. & tr.v.* **-rized, -riz·ing, -riz·es.** To make a summary or make a summary of. **—sum′ma·ri·za′tion** (sŭm′ər-ĭ-zā′shən) *n.* **—sum′ma·ri′zer** *n.*

sum·ma·ry (sŭm′ə-rē) *adj.* **1.** Presenting the substance in a condensed form; concise: *a summary review.* **2.** Performed speedily and without ceremony: *summary justice; a summary rejection.* **—summary** *n., pl.* **-ries.** A presentation of the substance of a body of material in a condensed form or by reducing it to its main points; an abstract. [Middle English, from Medieval Latin *summārius,* of or concerning the sum, from Latin *summa,* sum. See SUM.] **—sum·mar′i·ly** (sə-mĕr′ə-lē) *adv.* **—sum′ma·ri·ness** *n.*

summary court-martial *n.* A court-martial consisting of one officer, convened and held to try relatively minor offenses.

sum·mate (sə-māt′) *v.* **-ma·ted, -ma·ting, -mates.** *—tr.* To sum up: *summate a legal argument.* *—intr.* To form or constitute a cumulative effect.

sum·ma·tion (sə-mā′shən) *n.* **1.** The act or process of adding; addition. **2.** A sum or an aggregate. **3.** A concluding part of a speech or an argument containing a summary of principal points, especially of a case before a court of law. **4.** *Physiology.* The process by which multiple or repeated stimuli can produce a response in a nerve, muscle, or other part that one stimulus alone cannot produce. [New Latin *summātiō, summātiōn-,* from Late Latin *summātus,* past participle of *summāre,* to sum up, from Latin *summa,* sum. See SUM.]

sum·mer[1] (sŭm′ər) *n.* **1.** The usually warmest season of the year, occurring between spring and autumn and constituting June, July, and August in the Northern Hemisphere, or, as calculated astronomically, extending from the summer solstice to the autumnal equinox. **2.** A period of fruition, fulfillment, happiness, or beauty. **3.** A year: *a girl of 13 summers.* **—summer** *v.* **-mered, -mer·ing, -mers.** *—tr.* To lodge or keep during the summer: *summered the herd in the south meadow.* *—intr.* To pass the summer: *They summered at a beach resort.* **—summer** *adj.* **1.** Of, having to do with, occurring in, or appropriate to the season of summer: *summer heat; summer attire.* **2.** Grown during the season of summer: *summer crops.* [Middle English *sumer,* from Old English *sumor.* See **sem-[2]** in Appendix.] **—sum′mer·ly** *adv. & adj.*

sum·mer[2] (sŭm′ər) *n. Architecture.* **1.** A heavy horizontal timber that serves as a supporting beam, especially for the floor above. **2.** A lintel. **3.** A large, heavy stone usually set on the top of a column or pilaster to support an arch or a lintel. [Middle English, beam, pack animal, from Anglo-Norman *sumer,* from Vulgar Latin **saumārius,* from Late Latin *sagmārius,* pertaining to a packsaddle, packhorse, from *sagma,* packsaddle. See SUMPTER.]

♦ **sum·mer·ca·ter** (sŭm′ər-kā′tər) *n. Maine.* A summer resident of Maine. Also called ♦*sport.* [Probably SUMMER[1] + (VA)CAT(ION) + -ER[1].]

♦ ***REGIONAL NOTE:*** Since the Civil War Maine has been a favorite vacation spot for New Englanders and tourists from further away. Predictably, certain words in the lexicon of Maine betray a wry Yankee impatience with these outsiders and city folks who come up to Maine only for summer relaxation. Along the coast the summer resident is called a *summercater;* inland, the word for a nonresident is *sport.* Or the Maine native may merely refer collectively to folks *from away.* Much Maine real estate is designated *nonresident*—that is, it is set aside for these summer residents on whom Maine's economy is so dependent.

summer cypress *n.* A Eurasian annual plant *(Kochia scoparia)* having narrow, dense foliage that turns bright red.

summer flounder *n.* A fluke *(Paralichthys dentatus)* of the Atlantic coast of the United States, valued as a food and game fish.

sum·mer·house (sŭm′ər-hous′) *n.* A small, roofed structure in a park or garden affording shade and rest; a gazebo.

sum·mer·sault (sŭm′ər-sôlt′) *n. & v.* Variant of **somersault.**

summer savory *n.* See **savory[2]** (sense 1).

summer school *n.* An academic session held during the summer, chiefly for supplementary and remedial study.

sum·mer·set (sŭm′ər-sĕt′) *n. & v.* Variant of **somerset.**

summer solstice *n.* In the Northern Hemisphere, the solstice that occurs on about June 21.

summer squash *n.* Any of several varieties of squash, such as the crookneck or the cymling, that are eaten shortly after being picked rather than kept in storage.

summer stock *n.* Theatrical productions of stock companies presented during the summer.

summer tanager *n.* A New World bird *(Piranga rubra)* that catches insects in flight and whose plumage is rose-red in the adult male and, in the female, yellowish olive-green above and light brownish-orange below.

sum·mer·time (sŭm′ər-tīm′) *n.* The summer season.

sum·mer·wood (sŭm′ər-wo͝od′) *n.* Wood that is produced during the latter part of the growing season and is harder and less porous than springwood.

sum·mer·y (sŭm′ə-rē) *adj.* Of, intended for, or suggesting summer.

sum·ming-up (sŭm′ĭng-ŭp′) *n., pl.* **sum·mings-up** (sŭm′ĭngz-). A summary, often including an assessment.

sum·mit (sŭm′ĭt) *n.* **1.** The highest point or part; the top. **2.** The highest level or degree that can be attained. **3.a.** The highest level, as of government officials. **b.** A summit conference. [Middle English *somet,* from Old French *sommette,* diminutive of *som,* top, from Latin *summum,* from neuter of *summus,* highest. See **uper** in Appendix.]

SYNONYMS: *summit, peak, pinnacle, acme, apex, zenith, climax.* These nouns all mean the highest point. *Summit* denotes the highest level attainable: *"This* [appointment] *had been the summit of Mr. Bertram's ambition"* (Sir Walter Scott). *Peak* usually refers to the uppermost point: *"It was the peak of summer in the Berkshires"* (Saul Bellow). *Pinnacle* denotes a towering height, as of achievement: *The articulation of the theory of relativity catapulted Albert Einstein to the pinnacle of fame. Acme* refers to an ultimate point, as of perfection: *The artist's gifts are at their acme. Apex* is the culminating point: *The Nazi regime represents the apex of oppression and intimidation. Zenith* is the point of highest achievement, most complete development, or greatest power: *"Chivalry was then in its zenith"* (Henry Hallam). *Climax* refers to the point of greatest strength, effect, or intensity that marks the end point of an ascending process: *The collapse of the government was merely the climax of a series of constitutional crises.*

Sum·mit (sŭm′ĭt). A city of northeast New Jersey west of Newark. It is mainly residential. Population, 21,071.

summit conference *n.* A conference of leaders, especially a conference of the highest-ranking officials of two or more governments.

sum·mit·eer (sŭm′ĭ-tîr′) *n.* An official who takes part in a summit conference.

sum·mit·ry (sŭm′ĭ-trē) *n.* **1.** The holding of a summit conference: *"Modern summitry began at Versailles in 1919"* (George F. Will). **2.** Participation in summit conferences.

sum·mon (sŭm′ən) *tr.v.* **-moned, -mon·ing, -mons. 1.** To call together; convene. **2.** To request to appear; send for. See Synonyms at **call. 3.** *Law.* To order to appear in court by the issuance of a summons. **4.** To order to take a specified action; bid: *summon the captain to surrender.* **5.** To call forth; evoke: *"He summoned up a smile, though it seemed to take all his strength"* (Colin Turnbull). [Middle English *somonen,* from Old French *somondre,* from Vulgar Latin **summonere,* from Latin *summonēre,* to remind privately, hint to : *sub-,* secretly; see SUB– + *monēre,* to warn; see **men-**[1] in Appendix.] **—sum′mon·er** *n.*

sum·mons (sŭm′ənz) *n., pl.* **-mons·es. 1.** A call by an authority to appear, come, or do something. **2.** *Law.* **a.** A notice summoning a defendant to appear in court. **b.** A notice summoning a person to report to court as a juror or witness. **—summons** *tr.v.* **-monsed, -mons·ing, -mons·es.** *Law.* To serve a court summons to. [Middle English *somons,* from Old French *somonse,* from feminine past participle of *somondre,* to summon. See SUMMON.]

sum·mum bo·num (so͝om′əm bō′nəm) *n.* The greatest or supreme good. [Latin : *summum,* neuter of *summus,* highest + *bonum,* good.]

Sum·ner (sŭm′nər), **Charles.** 1811–1874. American politician. A U.S. senator from Massachusetts (1851–1874), he was a brilliant orator with an uncompromising opposition to slavery.

Sumner, William Graham. 1840–1910. American sociologist who developed the concepts of folkways and mores and is noted for his social Darwinist theories.

su·mo (so͞o′mō) *n. Sports.* A Japanese form of wrestling in which a fighter loses if forced from the ring or if any part of his body except the soles of his feet touches the ground. [Japanese *sumō.*]

sump (sŭmp) *n.* **1.a.** A low-lying place, such as a pit, that receives drainage. **b.** A cesspool. **2.** A hole at the lowest point of a mine shaft into which water is drained in order to be pumped out. **3.** The crankcase or oil reservoir of an internal-combustion engine. [Middle English *sompe,* marsh, from Middle Low German *sump* or from Middle Dutch *somp.* Sense 2, from German *Sumpf,* swamp, sump, from Middle High German *sumpf,* swamp.]

sump·ter (sŭmp′tər) *n.* A pack animal, such as a horse or mule. [Middle English, driver of a packhorse, from Old French *sometier,* from Vulgar Latin **saumatārius,* from Late Latin *sagma, sagmat-,* packsaddle, from Greek, from *sattein,* to pack.]

sump·tu·ar·y (sŭmp′cho͞o-ĕr′ē) *adj.* **1.** Regulating or limiting personal expenditures. **2.a.** Regulating commercial or real-estate activities: *sumptuary laws discouraging construction of large houses on small plots of land.* **b.** Regulating personal behavior on moral or religious grounds: *sumptuary laws forbidding gambling.* [Latin *sūmptuārius,* from *sūmptus,* expense, from past participle of *sūmere,* to take, buy. See **em-** in Appendix.]

sump·tu·ous (sŭmp′cho͞o-əs) *adj.* Of a size or splendor suggesting great expense; lavish: *"He likes big meals, so I cook sumptuous ones"* (Anaïs Nin). [Middle English, from Old French *sumptueux,* from Latin *sūmptuōsus,* from *sūmptus,* expense. See SUMPTUARY.] **—sump′tu·ous·ly** *adv.* **—sump′tu·ous·ness** *n.*

Sum·ter (sŭm′tər). A city of central South Carolina east of Columbia. Founded in 1799, it is a trade and processing center. Population, 24,890.

Su·my (so͞o′mē). A city of northern Ukraine northwest of Kharkov. Its manufactures include mining equipment and heavy machinery. Population, 256,000.

sun (sŭn) *n.* **1.** A star that is the basis of the solar system and that sustains life on Earth, being the source of heat and light. It has a mean distance from Earth of about 150 million kilometers (93 million miles), a diameter of approximately 1,390,000 kilometers (864,000 miles), and a mass about 330,000 times that of Earth. **2.** A star that is the center of a planetary system. **3.** The radiant energy, especially heat and visible light, emitted by the sun; sunshine. **—sun** *v.* **sunned, sun·ning, suns.** *—tr.* To expose to the sun's rays, as for warming, drying, or tanning. *—intr.* To expose oneself or itself to the sun. ***—idioms.*** **in the sun.** In the public eye. **under the sun.** On earth; in the world. [Middle English, from Old English *sunne.* See **sāwel-** in Appendix.]

Sun. *abbr.* Sunday.

sun·baked (sŭn′bākt′) *adj.* Baked, dried, or hardened by exposure to sunlight: *sunbaked bricks; the sunbaked salt flats.*

sun·bath (sŭn′băth′, -bäth′) *n.* An exposure of the body to sun.

sun·bathe (sŭn′bāth′) *intr.v.* **-bathed, -bath·ing, -bathes.** To expose the body to the sun. **—sun′bath′er** (-bā′thər) *n.*

sun·beam (sŭn′bēm′) *n.* A ray of sunlight. [Middle English *sunnebem,* from Old English *sunnebēam* (translation of Late Latin *columna lūcis,* pillar of light) : *sunne,* sun; see SUN + *bēam,* tree, building post; see BEAM.]

WORD HISTORY: The period of European history from the 5th to the 11th century, although often called the Dark Ages, in fact did much to preserve and extend the light of civilization. One of the relatively minor contributions of the time, albeit a fortunate one for us, is the addition of the word *sunbeam* to the English language. The word is believed to have entered English in the 9th century through the work of the English king Alfred the Great. A scholar as well as a king, Alfred undertook a number of translations of great Latin writings, rendering them into the English of his time, now known as Old English. Among the works translated during Alfred's reign was a store of narratives and information about England's earliest connections with the Church, called the *Historia Ecclesiastica Gentis Anglorum,* or *The Ecclesiastical History of the English People,* a work composed by the Venerable Bede. Several times in his book Bede uses the Latin phrase *columna lucis,* which we would today translate as "a column of light." Since the Old English translator did not have the word *column* in his vocabulary, he substituted the word *beam,* which meant "a tree" or "a building post made from a tree." *Columna lucis* thus became *sunnebeām,* or "sun post," which survives as our *sunbeam.* If *sunbeam* is perhaps a less stately expression than "column of light," it has nevertheless served us well. From it the word *beam* alone came to mean "a ray or rays of light"; it subsequently became a verb meaning "to radiate." It now allows us not only to beam with pride or happiness but also to beam our broadcasts to other countries and ourselves, as some would have it, through space. *Column* would never do.

Sun·belt also **Sun Belt** (sŭn′bĕlt′). The southern and southwest United States.

sun·bird (sŭn′bûrd′) *n.* Any of various small, tropical Old World passerine birds of the family Nectariniidae, having a slender, downward-curving bill and often brightly colored plumage in the male.

sun bittern *n.* A cranelike tropical American bird *(Eurypyga helias),* having mottled brownish plumage and often spreading its wings and tail in a showy display.

sun block also **sun blocker** *n.* A preparation, as of PABA, that prevents sunburn by filtering out the sun's ultraviolet rays, usually offering more protection than a sunscreen.

sun·bon·net (sŭn′bŏn′ĭt) *n.* A woman's wide-brimmed bonnet with a flap at the back to protect the neck from the sun.

sun·bow (sŭn′bō′) *n.* A rainbowlike display of colors resulting from refraction of sunlight through a spray of water.

sun·burn (sŭn′bûrn′) *n.* Inflammation or blistering of the skin caused by overexposure to direct sunlight. **—sunburn** *v.* **-burned** or **-burnt** (-bûrnt′), **-burn·ing, -burns. —sunburn** *tr. & intr.v.* To affect or be affected with sunburn.

sun·burst (sŭn′bûrst′) *n.* **1.** A sudden burst of sunlight, as through broken clouds. **2.a.** A pattern or design consisting of a

sumo

sunburst

ă pat	oi boy
ā pay	ou out
âr care	o͝o took
ä father	o͞o boot
ĕ pet	ŭ cut
ē be	ûr urge
ĭ pit	th thin
ī pie	*th* this
îr pier	hw which
ŏ pot	zh vision
ō toe	ə about, item
ô paw	♦ regionalism

Stress marks: **′** (primary); ′ (secondary), as in **dictionary** (dĭk′shə-nĕr′ē)

central disk with radiating spires projecting in the manner of sunbeams. **b.** A jeweled brooch with such a design.

Sun City. A community of south-central Arizona, a residential suburb of Phoenix. Population, 40,505.

sun·dae (sŭn′dē, -dā′) *n.* A dish of ice cream with a topping such as syrup, fruits, nuts, or whipped cream. [Origin unknown.]

Sun·da Islands (sŭn′də, sōōn′-). A group of islands of the western Malay Archipelago between the South China Sea and the Indian Ocean. The **Greater Sunda Islands** include Sumatra, Borneo, Java, and Celebes; the **Lesser Sunda Islands** lie east of Java and extend from Bali to Timor. Sumatra and Java are separated by the **Sunda Strait,** a narrow channel linking the Indian Ocean with the Java Sea.

sun dance *n.* A religious ceremony widely practiced among Native American peoples of the Great Plains, typically marked by several days of fasting and group dancing and sometimes including ritual self-torture, as in penance or to induce a trance or vision.

Sun·day (sŭn′dē, -dā′) *n. Abbr.* **S., Sun. 1.** The first day of the week. **2.** The Sabbath for many Christians. [Middle English, from Old English *sunnandæg.* See **sāwel-** in Appendix.]

Sunday, William Ashley. Known as "Billy." 1862–1935. American evangelist. Originally a professional baseball player (1883–1891), he began preaching in 1896 and became a Presbyterian minister in 1903.

Sunday punch *n. Slang.* **1.** A knockout blow. **2.** Something that is capable of delivering a destructive blow to an opponent or opposing force.

sundial

Sunday school *n. Abbr.* **S.S. 1.** A school, generally affiliated with a church or synagogue, that offers religious instruction for children on Sundays. **2.** The teachers and pupils of such a school.

sun deck *n.* A roof, balcony, or terrace used for sunbathing.

sun·der (sŭn′dər) *v.* **-dered, -der·ing, -ders.** —*tr.* To break or wrench apart; sever. See Synonyms at **separate.** —*intr.* To break into parts. —**sunder** *n.* A division or separation. [Middle English *sundren,* from Old English *sundrian.*] —**sun′der·ance** *n.*

Sun·der·land (sŭn′dər-lənd). A borough of northeast England on the North Sea east-southeast of Newcastle. It was established as a shipbuilding center in the 14th century on the site of a Saxon community. Population, 299,100.

sun·dew (sŭn′dōō′, -dyōō′) *n.* Any of several insectivorous plants of the genus *Drosera,* growing in wet ground and having leaves covered with sticky hairs. Also called *drosera.* [Obsolete Dutch *sondauw* (translation of Latin *rōs sōlis,* dew of the sun) : *son,* sun (from Middle Dutch *sonne;* see **sāwel-** in Appendix) + *dauw,* dew (from Middle Dutch *dau;* see **dheu-**[1] in Appendix).]

sun·di·al (sŭn′dī′əl) *n.* An instrument that indicates local apparent solar time by the shadow cast by a central projecting pointer on a surrounding calibrated dial.

sun disk *n.* An ancient Middle Eastern symbol consisting of a disk set between outspread wings, representing the sun god.

sun·dog (sŭn′dôg′, -dŏg′) *n.* **1.** A parhelion. **2.** A small halo or rainbow near the horizon just off the parhelic circle.

sun·down (sŭn′doun′) *n.* The time of sunset.

sun·down·er (sŭn′dou′nər) *n.* **1.** *Australian.* A vagrant; a tramp. **2.** *Chiefly British.* A drink taken at sundown.

sun·dress (sŭn′drĕs′) *n.* A light summer dress with a bodice that exposes the arms and shoulders.

sun·dries (sŭn′drēz) *pl.n.* Articles too small or numerous to be specified; miscellaneous items. [From SUNDRY.]

sun·drops (sŭn′drŏps′) *pl.n. (used with a sing. or pl. verb).* See **evening primrose.**

sun·dry (sŭn′drē) *adj.* Various; miscellaneous: *a purse containing keys, wallet, and sundry items.* [Middle English *sundri,* from Old English *syndrig,* separate.]

sun·fish (sŭn′fĭsh′) *n., pl.* **sunfish** or **-fish·es. 1.** Any of various small North American percoid freshwater fishes of the family Centrarchidae, having laterally compressed, often brightly colored bodies and including the crappies, black bass, bluegill, and pumpkinseed. **2.** Any of several large marine fishes of the family Molidae, especially the ocean sunfish. [From its roundish body and bright colors.]

sun·flow·er (sŭn′flou′ər) *n.* **1.a.** Any of several plants of the genus *Helianthus,* especially *H. annuus,* having tall coarse stems and large, yellow-rayed flower heads that produce edible seeds rich in oil. **b.** The seedlike fruit or the seeds of this plant. **2.** *Color.* A brilliant yellow to strong or vivid orange yellow.

sunflower
Helianthus annuus

sung (sŭng) *v.* A past tense and the past participle of **sing.**

Sung (sōōng). See **Song.**

Sun·ga·ri (sōōng′gə-rē). See **Songhua.**

sun·glass (sŭn′glăs′) *n.* **1.** A convex lens used to focus the sun's rays and produce heat, especially for ignition. **2. sunglasses.** Eyeglasses with tinted or polarizing lenses to protect the eyes from the sun's glare.

sun·glow (sŭn′glō′) *n.* A rose or yellow glow in the sky preceding sunrise or following sunset.

sun god *n. Mythology.* A god that personifies the sun.

sunk (sŭngk) *v.* A past tense and the past participle of **sink.**

sunk·en (sŭng′kən) *v. Obsolete.* A past participle of **sink.** —**sunken** *adj.* **1.** Depressed, fallen in, or hollowed: *sunken cheeks.* **2.** Situated beneath the surface of the water or ground; submerged: *a sunken reef.* **3.** Below a surrounding level: *a sunken meadow.*

sunk fence *n.* A ditch with a retaining wall set into it to divide lands without marring the landscape.

sun lamp *n.* **1.** A lamp that radiates ultraviolet rays used in therapeutic and cosmetic treatments. **2.** A high-intensity lamp with parabolic mirrors, used in photography.

sun·less (sŭn′lĭs) *adj.* **1.** Being without sunlight; dark or overcast: *a sunless moor.* **2.** Gloomy; cheerless: *a sunless life.* —**sun′less·ness** *n.*

sun·light (sŭn′līt′) *n.* The light of the sun; sunshine.

Sun·light Peak (sŭn′līt′). A mountain, 4,288 m (14,059 ft) high, in the San Juan Mountains of southwest Colorado.

sun·lit (sŭn′lĭt′) *adj.* Illuminated by the sun.

sunn (sŭn) *n.* **1.** A tropical Asian plant *(Crotalaria juncea)* having clusters of yellow flowers. **2.** A tough fiber obtained from the stems of this plant, used for cordage. [Hindi *san,* from Sanskrit *śāṇa-,* hempen.]

Sun·na also **Sun·nah** (sōōn′ə) *n. Islam.* **1.** The way of life prescribed as normative in Islam, based on the teachings and practices of Mohammed and on exegesis of the Koran. **2.** Mohammed's way of life viewed as a model for Moslems. [Arabic *sunnah,* custom, rule, Sunna.]

Sun·ni (sōōn′ē) *n. Islam.* **1.** The branch of Islam that accepts the first four caliphs as rightful successors of Mohammed. **2.** *pl.* **Sunni** or **-nis** A Moslem belonging to this branch; a Sunnite. [Arabic *sunnīy,* adherent of the Sunna, from *sunnah,* Sunna.] —**Sun′ni** *adj.*

Sun·nite (sōōn′īt′) *n. Islam.* A Sunni Moslem. [From SUNNI.]

sun·ny (sŭn′ē) *adj.* **-ni·er, -ni·est. 1.** Exposed to or abounding in sunshine: *a sunny room.* **2.** Cheerful; genial: *a sunny smile.* —**sun′ni·ly** *adv.* —**sun′ni·ness** *n.*

sun·ny-side up (sŭn′ē-sīd′) *adj.* Fried only on one side. Used of eggs.

Sun·ny·vale (sŭn′ē-vāl′). A city of western California west-northwest of San Jose. Its manufactures include electronic equipment and pharmaceuticals. Population, 106,618.

sun protection factor *n. Abbr.* **SPF, spf** The degree to which a sun block, a sunscreen, suntan lotion, or a similar preparation protects the skin from ultraviolet rays.

sun·rise (sŭn′rīz′) *n.* **1.** The event or time of the daily first appearance of the sun above the eastern horizon. **2.** An outset or emergence: *the sunrise of classical art and sculpture.*

Sun·rise (sŭn′rīz′). A city of southeast Florida east of Fort Lauderdale. Population, 39,681.

Sunrise Manor. A community of southeast Nevada, a suburb of Las Vegas. Population, 44,155.

sun·roof (sŭn′rōōf′, -rŏŏf′) *n.* A roof on a motor vehicle, such as an automobile, having a panel that can be slid back or raised.

sun·room (sŭn′rōōm′, -rŏŏm′) *n.* A room or an enclosed porch with glass or transparent plastic walls or numerous windows, oriented and designed to admit much sunlight. Also called *sunspace.*

sun·scald (sŭn′skôld′) *n.* Localized injury or death of the tissues of a woody plant caused by excessive sun in summer and by the combined effects of sun and low temperatures in winter.

sun·screen (sŭn′skrēn′) *n.* A preparation, often in the form of a cream or lotion, used to protect the skin from the damaging ultraviolet rays of the sun. —**sun′screen′ing** *adj.*

sun·set (sŭn′sĕt′) *n.* **1.** The event or time of the daily disappearance of the sun below the western horizon. **2.** A decline or final phase: *the sunset of an empire.* —**sunset** *adj.* Providing for the automatic termination of a government program or agency unless deliberately reauthorized by law: *a state-funded program with a sunset provision.*

sun·shade (sŭn′shād′) *n.* Something, such as an awning or a billed cap, that is used or worn as a protection from the sun's rays.

sun·shine (sŭn′shīn′) *n.* **1.** The light or the direct rays from the sun. **2.a.** Radiant cheerfulness; geniality. **b.** A source of cheerfulness. —**sunshine** *adj.* Requiring governmental bodies to hold open meetings and sometimes to permit public access to records: *a sunshine law.* —**sun′shin′y** *adj.*

sun·space (sŭn′spās′) *n.* See **sunroom.**

sun·spot (sŭn′spŏt′) *n.* Any of the relatively cool dark spots appearing periodically in groups on the surface of the sun that are associated with strong magnetic fields.

sun·stone (sŭn′stōn′) *n.* See **aventurine** (sense 2).

sun·stroke (sŭn′strōk′) *n.* Heat stroke caused by exposure to the sun and characterized by a rise in temperature, convulsions, and coma. Also called *insolation, siriasis.*

sun·tan (sŭn′tăn′) *n.* A tan color on the skin resulting from exposure to the sun. —**sun′tanned′** *adj.*

sun·up (sŭn′ŭp′) *n.* The time of sunrise.

Sun Valley. A resort town of south-central Idaho east of Boise. Its lodge, opened in 1936, was built by the Union Pacific Railroad to attract passenger traffic to the West. Population, 545.

sun·ward (sŭn′wərd) *adv. & adj.* Toward or at the sun: *a comet's sunward plunge; bathers facing sunward.* —**sun′wards** *adv.*

Sun Yat-sen (sōōn′ yät′sĕn′). 1866–1925. Chinese politician who served as provisional president of the republic after the fall of the Manchu (1911–1912).

sup¹ (sŭp) *tr. & intr.v.* **supped, sup·ping, sups.** To eat or drink (something) or engage in eating or drinking by taking small swallows or mouthfuls: *supped the hot soup; supped away daintily.* **—sup** *n.* A small swallow or mouthful of liquid food; a sip. [Middle English *soupen,* from Old English *sūpan.* See **seuə-²** in Appendix.]

sup² (sŭp) *intr.v.* **supped, sup·ping, sups.** To eat an evening meal; have supper. [Middle English *soupen,* from Old French *souper,* from *soupe,* soup. See SOUP.]

sup. *abbr.* **1.** Superior. **2.** *Grammar.* **a.** Superlative. **b.** Supine. **3.a.** Supplement. **b.** Supplementary. **4.** Supply. **5.** *Latin.* Supra (above).

Sup.Ct. *abbr. Law.* **1.** Superior court. **2.** Supreme court.

su·per (so͞o′pər) *n.* **1.** *Informal.* An article or a product of superior size, quality, or grade. **2.** *Informal.* **a.** A superintendent in an apartment or office building. **b.** A supernumerary. **3.** *Printing.* A thin starched cotton mesh used to reinforce the spines and covers of books. **—super** *adj. Informal.* **1.** Very large, great, or extreme: *"yet another super Skyscraper"* (Dylan Thomas). **2.** Excellent; first-rate: *a super party.* **—super** *adv. Informal.* Especially; extremely: *a super accurate missile; was super careful.* **—super** *tr.v.* **-pered, -per·ing, -pers.** *Printing.* To reinforce (a book spine or cover) with super.

super. *abbr.* Superior.

super– *pref.* **1.** Above; over; upon: *superimpose.* **2.** Superior in size, quality, number, or degree: *superfine.* **3.a.** Exceeding a norm: *supersaturate.* **b.** Excessive in degree or intensity: *supersubtle.* **c.** Containing a specified ingredient in an unusually high proportion: *superphosphate.* **4.** More inclusive than a specified category: *superorder.* [Latin, from *super,* over, above. See **uper** in Appendix.]

su·per·a·ble (so͞o′pər-ə-bəl) *adj.* Possible to overcome; surmountable: *superable problems.* [Latin *superābilis,* from *superāre,* to overcome, from *super,* over. See **uper** in Appendix.] **—su′per·a·ble·ness** *n.* **—su′per·a·bly** *adv.*

su·per·a·bound (so͞o′pər-ə-bound′) *intr.v.* **-bound·ed, -bound·ing, -bounds.** To be unusually or excessively abundant.

su·per·a·bun·dant (so͞o′pər-ə-bŭn′dənt) *adj.* Abundant to excess. **—su′per·a·bun′dance** *n.* **—su′per·a·bun′dant·ly** *adv.*

su·per·a·gen·cy (so͞o′pər-ā′jən-sē) *n., pl.* **-cies.** A large government agency composed of or coordinating a number of smaller agencies.

su·per·al·loy (so͞o′pər-ăl′oi) *n.* Any of several complex temperature-resistant alloys.

su·per·an·nu·ate (so͞o′pər-ăn′yo͞o-āt′) *tr.v.* **-at·ed, -at·ing, -ates. 1.** To allow to retire on a pension because of age or infirmity. **2.** To set aside or discard as old-fashioned or obsolete. [Back-formation from SUPERANNUATED.]

su·per·an·nu·at·ed (so͞o′pər-ăn′yo͞o-ā′tĭd) *adj.* **1.** Retired or ineffective because of advanced age: *"Nothing is more tiresome than a superannuated pedagogue"* (Henry Adams). See Synonyms at **elderly. 2.** Outmoded; obsolete: *superannuated laws.* [From Medieval Latin *superannuātus,* over one year old : Latin *super-,* super- + Latin *annus,* year; see **at-** in Appendix.]

su·perb (so͞o-pûrb′) *adj.* **1.** Of unusually high quality; excellent: *a superb wine; superb skill.* **2.** Majestic; imposing: *The cheetah is a superb animal.* **3.** Rich; luxurious. [Latin *superbus,* arrogant, superior. See **uper** in Appendix.] **—su·perb′ly** *adv.* **—su·perb′ness** *n.*

super band *n.* The range of radio frequencies from 216 to 600 megahertz, used primarily for citizens band and cable television transmission.

su·per·cal·en·der (so͞o′pər-kăl′ən-dər) *n.* A calender with a number of rollers for giving a high finish or gloss to paper. **—supercalender** *tr.v.* **-dered, -der·ing, -ders.** To process (paper) in a supercalender.

su·per·car·go (so͞o′pər-kär′gō) *n., pl.* **-goes** or **-gos.** An officer on a merchant ship who has charge of the cargo and its sale and purchase. [Alteration (influenced by SUPER–) of *supracargo,* alteration (influenced by SUPRA–) of Spanish *sobrecargo* : *sobre-,* over (from Latin *super-;* see SUPER–) + *cargo,* cargo; see CARGO.]

su·per·charge (so͞o′pər-chärj′) *tr.v.* **-charged, -charg·ing, -charg·es. 1.** To increase the power of (an engine, for example), as by fitting with a supercharger. **2.** To charge heavily or excessively: *an atmosphere that was supercharged with tension.*

su·per·charg·er (so͞o′pər-chär′jər) *n.* A blower or compressor, usually driven by the engine, for supplying air under high pressure to the cylinders of an internal-combustion engine.

su·per·cil·i·ar·y (so͞o′pər-sĭl′ē-ĕr′ē) *adj.* **1.** Of, relating to, or being in the area of the eyebrow: *the superciliary arch of the frontal bone.* **2.** Located over the eyebrow or the eye: *a superciliary patch of color.* [New Latin *superciliāris,* from Latin *supercilium,* eyebrow. See SUPERCILIOUS.]

su·per·cil·i·ous (so͞o′pər-sĭl′ē-əs) *adj.* Feeling or showing haughty disdain. See Synonyms at **proud.** [Latin *superciliōsus,* from *supercilium,* eyebrow, pride : *super-,* super- + *cilium,* lower eyelid; see **kel-¹** in Appendix.] **—su′per·cil′i·ous·ly** *adv.* **—su′per·cil′i·ous·ness** *n.*

su·per·class (so͞o′pər-klăs′) *n. Biology.* A taxonomic category of related organisms ranking below a phylum and above a class.

su·per·clus·ter (so͞o′pər-klŭs′tər) *n.* A group of neighboring clusters of galaxies.

su·per·col·lid·er (so͞o′pər-kə-līd′ər) *n. Physics.* A high-energy particle accelerator.

su·per·co·lum·nar (so͞o′pər-kə-lŭm′nər) *adj. Architecture.* **1.** Having one order of columns above another. **2.** Situated above a colonnade or column.

su·per·com·put·er (so͞o′pər-kəm-pyo͞o′tər) *n. Computer Science.* A mainframe computer that is among the largest, fastest, or most powerful of those available at a given time.

su·per·con·duc·tiv·i·ty (so͞o′pər-kŏn′dŭk-tĭv′ĭtē) *n.* The flow of electric current without resistance in certain metals, alloys, and ceramics at temperatures near absolute zero, and in some cases at temperatures hundreds of degrees above absolute zero. **—su′per·con·duc′tive** (-kən-dŭk′tĭv) *adj.* **—su′per·con·duc′tor** (-dŭk′tər) *n.*

su·per·con·ti·nent (so͞o′pər-kŏn′tə-nənt) *n.* A large hypothetical continent, especially Pangaea, that is thought to have split into smaller ones in the geologic past. Also called *protocontinent.*

su·per·cool (so͞o′pər-ko͞ol′) *v.* **-cooled, -cool·ing, -cools.** *—tr.* To cool (a liquid) below a transition temperature without the transition occurring, especially to cool below the freezing point without solidification. *—intr.* To become supercooled.

su·per·cur·rent (so͞o′pər-kûr′ənt, -kŭr′-) *n.* An electrical current flowing through a superconductor.

su·per·del·e·gate (so͞o′pər-dĕl′ĭ-gāt′, -gĭt) *n.* An elected official or political party leader who attends a presidential nominating convention and who may or may not have made a commitment to vote for a candidate.

su·per·dom·i·nant (so͞o′pər-dŏm′ə-nənt) *n. Music.* See **submediant.**

su·per·du·per (so͞o′pər-do͞o′pər) *adj. Slang.* Great; marvelous. [Reduplication of SUPER.]

su·per·e·go (so͞o′pər-ē′gō, -ĕg′ō) *n., pl.* **-gos.** In Freudian theory, the division of the psyche that is formed through the internalization of moral standards of parents and society, and censors and restrains the ego. Mostly unconscious, it is composed of the ego ideal and the conscience.

su·per·em·i·nent (so͞o′pər-ĕm′ə-nənt) *adj.* Preeminent. **—su′per·em′i·nence** *n.* **—su′per·em′i·nent·ly** *adv.*

su·per·er·o·gate (so͞o′pər-ĕr′ə-gāt′) *intr.v.* **-gat·ed, -gat·ing, -gates.** To do more than is required, ordered, or expected. [Late Latin *superērogāre, superērogāt-,* to spend over and above : Latin *super-,* super- + Latin *ērogāre,* to spend (*ē-, ex-,* ex- + *rogāre,* to ask; see **reg-** in Appendix).] **—su′per·er′o·ga′tion** (-gā′shən).

su·per·e·rog·a·to·ry (so͞o′pər-ĭ-rŏg′ə-tôr′ē, -tōr′ē) also **su·per·e·rog·a·tive** (-tĭv) *adj.* **1.** Performed or observed beyond the required or expected degree. **2.** Superfluous; unnecessary: *"It was supererogatory for her to gloat"* (Mary McCarthy).

su·per·fam·i·ly (so͞o′pər-făm′ə-lē) *n., pl.* **-lies.** *Biology.* A taxonomic category of related organisms ranking below an order or its subdivisions and above a family.

su·per·fec·ta (so͞o′pər-fĕk′tə) *n. Sports & Games.* A method of betting in which the bettor, in order to win, must pick the first four finishers of a race in the correct sequence. [SUPER– + (PER)FECTA.]

su·per·fe·cun·da·tion (so͞o′pər-fē′kən-dā′shən, -fĕk′ən-) *n.* Fertilization of more than one ovum within a single menstrual cycle by separate acts of coitus, especially by different males.

su·per·fe·tate (so͞o′pər-fē′tāt′) *intr.v.* **-tat·ed, -tat·ing, -tates.** To conceive when a fetus is already present in the uterus. [Latin *superfētāre, superfētāt-* : *super-,* super- + *fētāre,* to breed (from *fētus,* offspring; see **dhē(i)-** in Appendix).]

su·per·fe·ta·tion (so͞o′pər-fē-tā′shən) *n.* Formation or development of a second fetus when one is already present in the uterus, occurring normally in some animal species.

su·per·fi·cial (so͞o′pər-fĭsh′əl) *adj.* **1.** Of, affecting, or being on or near the surface: *a superficial wound.* **2.** Concerned with or comprehending only what is apparent or obvious; shallow. **3.** Apparent rather than actual or substantial: *a superficial resemblance.* **4.** Trivial; insignificant: *made only a few superficial changes in the manuscript.* [Middle English, from Old French *superficiel,* from Latin *superficiālis,* from *superficiēs,* surface. See SUPERFICIES.] **—su′per·fi′ci·al′i·ty** (-fĭsh′ē-ăl′ĭ-tē), **su′per·fi′cial·ness** (-fĭsh′əl-nĭs) *n.* **—su′per·fi′cial·ly** *adv.*

***SYNONYMS:** superficial, shallow, cursory.* These adjectives mean lacking in depth or thoroughness. *Superficial* applies to people or their thoughts or actions and means concerned largely with what is obvious or on the surface: *"Only the most superficial mind would assert nowadays that man is a reasonable creature"* (H.G. Wells). *Shallow* emphasizes lack of intellectual or emotional profundity: *"I do not take a great interest in many people . . . for I find most of them shallow"* (Booth Tarkington). *Cursory* implies haste and lack of meticulous attention to detail: *A cursory inspection of the house failed to reveal its structural flaws.*

su·per·fi·cies (so͞o′pər-fĭsh′ēz, -fĭsh′ē-ēz′) *n., pl.* **superficies. 1.** The outer surface of an area or a body. **2.** External appearance or aspect. [Latin *superficiēs* : *super-,* super- + *faciēs,* face; see FACE.]

su·per·fine (so͞o′pər-fīn′) *adj.* **1.** Of exceptional quality or

Sun Yat-sen
Photographed in the 1920's

ă pat	oi boy
ā pay	ou out
âr care	o͝o took
ä father	o͞o boot
ĕ pet	ŭ cut
ē be	ûr urge
ĭ pit	th thin
ī pie	*th* this
îr pier	hw which
ŏ pot	zh vision
ō toe	ə about, item
ô paw	♦ regionalism

Stress marks: **′** (primary); ′ (secondary), as in **dictionary** (dĭk′shə-nĕr′ē)

refinement. **2.** Excessively delicate or refined. **3.** Of extra fine texture: *superfine sandpaper.* **—su′per·fine′ness** *n.*

su·per·flu·id (so͞o′pər-flo͞o′ĭd) *n.* A fluid, such as a liquid form of helium, exhibiting a frictionless flow at temperatures close to absolute zero. **—su′per·flu·id′i·ty** (-flo͞o-ĭd′ĭ-tē) *n.*

su·per·flu·i·ty (so͞o′pər-flo͞o′ĭ-tē) *n., pl.* **-ties. 1.** The quality or condition of being superfluous. **2.** Something superfluous: *could do without such superfluities as a second car.* **3.** Overabundance; excess.

su·per·flu·ous (so͞o-pûr′flo͞o-əs) *adj.* Being beyond what is required or sufficient. [Middle English, from Old French *superflueux,* from Latin *superfluus,* from *superfluere,* to overflow : *super-,* super- + *fluere,* to flow; see **bhleu-** in Appendix.] **—su·per′flu·ous·ly** *adv.* **—su·per′flu·ous·ness** *n.*

SYNONYMS: *superfluous, excess, extra, spare, supernumerary, surplus.* The central meaning shared by these adjectives is "being more than is needed, desired, required, or appropriate": *delete superfluous words; trying to lose excess weight; found some extra change on the dresser; sleeping in the spare room; supernumerary ornamentation; surplus cheese distributed to the needy.*

su·per·gal·ax·y (so͞o′pər-găl′ək-sē) *n., pl.* **-ies.** A very large group of galaxies.

su·per·gene (so͞o′pər-jēn′) *n.* A group of closely linked genes occupying a large chromosomal segment and frequently functioning as a genetic unit.

su·per·gi·ant (so͞o′pər-jī′ənt) *n.* Any of various very large bright stars, such as Betelgeuse or Rigel, having a luminosity that is thousands of times greater than that of the sun.

super giant slalom *n. Sports.* A downhill skiing race that has fewer gates set farther apart than those used in a giant slalom.

su·per·graph·ics (so͞o′pər-grăf′ĭks) *n. (used with a sing. or pl. verb).* Brightly colored and simply designed graphic shapes of billboard proportions.

su·per·heat (so͞o′pər-hēt′) *tr.v.* **-heat·ed, -heat·ing, -heats. 1.** To heat excessively; overheat. **2.** To heat (steam or other vapor not in contact with its own liquid) beyond its saturation point at a given pressure. **3.** To heat (a liquid) above its boiling point without causing vaporization. **—superheat** (so͞o′pər-hēt′) *n.* **1.** The amount by which a vapor is superheated. **2.** The heat imparted during the process of superheating. **—su′per·heat′er** *n.*

su·per·he·lix (so͞o′pər-hē′lĭks) *n., pl.* **-he·lix·es** or **-hel·i·ces** (hĕl′ĭ-sēz′, hē′lĭ-). A molecular structure, as of a protein or DNA, in which a helix is itself coiled into a helix. **—su′per·hel′i·cal** (-hĕl′ĭ-kəl, -hē′lĭ-) *adj.* **—su′per·hel′i·cal·ly** *adv.*

su·per·he·ro (so͞o′pər-hîr′ō) *n., pl.* **-roes.** A figure, especially in a comic strip or cartoon, endowed with superhuman powers and usually portrayed as fighting evil or crime.

su·per·het·er·o·dyne (so͞o′pər-hĕt′ər-ə-dīn′) *adj.* Of, relating to, or being a form of radio reception in which the frequency of an incoming radio signal is mixed with a locally generated signal and converted to an intermediate frequency in order to facilitate amplification and the rejection of unwanted signals. **—superheterodyne** *n.* A superheterodyne radio receiver. [SUPER(SONIC) + HETERODYNE.]

su·per·high frequency (so͞o′pər-hī′) *n. Abbr.* **shf, SHF** A radio frequency between 3,000 and 30,000 megahertz.

su·per·high·way (so͞o′pər-hī′wā′) *n.* **1.** A broad highway, often with six or more lanes, used for high-speed traffic. **2.** See **expressway.**

su·per·hu·man (so͞o′pər-hyo͞o′mən) *adj.* **1.** Above or beyond the human; preternatural or supernatural. **2.** Beyond ordinary or normal human ability, power, or experience: *"soldiers driven mad by superhuman misery"* (John Reed). **—su′per·hu·man′i·ty** (-măn′ĭ-tē) *n.* **—su′per·hu′man·ly** *adv.*

su·per·im·pose (so͞o′pər-ĭm-pōz′) *tr.v.* **-posed, -pos·ing, -pos·es. 1.** To lay or place (something) on or over something else. **2.** To add as a distinct feature, element, or quality: *superimposed her own interpretation when she retold the story.* **—su′per·im·pos′a·ble** *adj.* **—su′per·im′po·si′tion** (-ĭm′pə-zĭsh′ən) *n.*

su·per·in·cum·bent (so͞o′pər-ĭn-kŭm′bənt) *adj.* Lying or resting on or above something. [Latin *superincumbēns, superincumbent-,* present participle of *superincumbere,* to lie on top of : *super-,* super- + *incumbere,* to lie down; see INCUMBENT.] **—su′per·in·cum′bence, su′per·in·cum′ben·cy** *n.*

su·per·in·duce (so͞o′pər-ĭn-do͞os′, -dyo͞os′) *tr.v.* **-duced, -duc·ing, -duc·es.** To introduce as an addition. [Latin *superindūcere* : *super-,* super- + *indūcere,* to lead in; see INDUCE.] **—su′per·in·duc′tion** (-dŭk′shən) *n.*

su·per·in·fect (so͞o′pər-ĭn-fĕkt′) *tr.v.* **-fect·ed, -fect·ing, -fects.** To cause (a cell, for example) to be further infected with a microorganism; infect a second time or more.

su·per·in·fec·tion (so͞o′pər-ĭn-fĕk′shən) *n.* **1.** The act or process of superinfecting a cell or an organism. **2.** An infection following a previous infection, especially when caused by microorganisms that have become resistant to the antibiotics used earlier.

su·per·in·tend (so͞o′pər-ĭn-tĕnd′, so͞o′prĭn-) *tr.v.* **-tend·ed, -tend·ing, -tends.** To oversee and direct; supervise. See Synonyms at **supervise.** [Late Latin *superintendere* : Latin *super-,* super- + Latin *intendere,* to direct one's attention to; see INTEND.] **—su′per·in·ten′dence** *n.*

su·per·in·ten·dent (so͞o′pər-ĭn-tĕn′dənt, so͞o′prĭn-) *n. Abbr.* **supt., Supt. 1.** A person who has the authority to supervise or direct. **2.** A janitor or custodian in a building, especially in an apartment house. **—su′per·in·ten′dent** *adj.*

su·pe·ri·or (so͞o-pîr′ē-ər) *adj. Abbr.* **sup., super. 1.** Higher than another in rank, station, or authority: *a superior officer.* **2.** Of a higher nature or kind. **3.** Of great value or excellence; extraordinary. **4.** Greater in number or amount than another: *an army defeated by superior numbers of enemy troops.* **5.** Affecting an attitude of disdain or conceit; haughty and supercilious. **6.** Above being affected or influenced; indifferent or immune: *"Trust magnates were superior to law"* (Gustavus Myers). **7.** Located higher than another; upper. **8.** *Botany.* Inserted or situated above the perianth. Used of an ovary. **9.** *Printing.* Set above the main line of type. **10.** *Logic.* Of wider or more comprehensive application; generic. Used of a term or proposition. **—superior** *n.* **1.** One who surpasses another in rank or quality. **2.** *Ecclesiastical.* The head of a religious community, such as a monastery, an abbey, or a convent. **3.** *Printing.* A superior character, as the number 2 in x^2. [Middle English, from Old French, from Latin, comparative of *superus,* upper, from *super,* over. See **uper** in Appendix.] **—su·pe′ri·or′i·ty** (-ôr′ĭ-tē, -ŏr′-) *n.* **—su·pe′ri·or·ly** *adv.*

Su·pe·ri·or (so͞o-pîr′ē-ər). A city of northwest Wisconsin on Lake Superior opposite Duluth, Minnesota. The city grew after the discovery of iron ore nearby in the 1880's. Population, 29,571.

Superior, Lake. The largest and westernmost of the Great Lakes, between the north-central United States and southern Ontario, Canada. Probably first sighted by French explorers in the early 1600's, it is an important link in the Great Lakes–St. Lawrence Seaway system.

superior conjunction *n.* The position of a celestial body when it is on the opposite side of the sun from Earth.

superior court *n. Abbr.* **Sup.Ct.** *Law.* A court of general jurisdiction, above the inferior courts and below the higher courts of appeal.

superiority complex *n.* **1.** An exaggerated feeling of being superior to others. **2.** A psychological defense mechanism in which feelings of superiority counter or conceal feelings of inferiority.

superior planet *n.* A planet whose mean distance from the sun is greater than that of Earth.

su·per·ja·cent (so͞o′pər-jā′sənt) *adj.* Resting or lying immediately above or on something else. [Latin *superiacēns, superiacent-,* present participle of *superiacēre,* to lie over : *super-,* super- + *iacēre,* to lie down; see **yē-** in Appendix.]

su·per·jet (so͞o′pər-jĕt′) *n.* A supersonic jet airplane.

su·per·la·tive (so͞o-pûr′lə-tĭv) *adj.* **1.** Of the highest order, quality, or degree; surpassing or superior to all others. **2.** Excessive or exaggerated. **3.** *Abbr.* **sup.** *Grammar.* Of, relating to, or being the extreme degree of comparison of an adjective or adverb, as in *best* or *brightest.* **—superlative** *n.* **1.** Something of the highest possible excellence. **2.** The highest degree; the acme. **3.** *Abbr.* **sup.** *Grammar.* **a.** The superlative degree. **b.** An adjective or adverb expressing the superlative degree, as in *brightest,* the superlative of the adjective *bright,* or *most brightly,* the superlative of the adverb *brightly.* [Middle English *superlatif,* from Old French, from Late Latin *superlātīvus,* from Latin *superlātus,* past participle of *superferre,* to carry over a person or thing, exaggerate : *super-,* super- + *lātus,* past participle of *ferre,* to carry; see **tele-** in Appendix.] **—su·per′la·tive·ly** *adv.*

su·per·li·ner (so͞o′pər-lī′nər) *n.* **1.** *Nautical.* A very large, luxurious oceangoing passenger ship. **2. a.** A railway car that is fitted with more capacious, comfortable, or luxurious accommodations than usual. **b.** A railway train composed of such cars.

su·per·lu·na·ry (so͞o′pər-lo͞o′nə-rē) also **su·per·lu·nar** (-nər) *adj.* Situated beyond the moon. [SUPER– + (SUB)LUNARY.]

su·per·lux·u·ry (so͞o′pər-lŭg′zhə-rē, -lŭk′shə-) *adj.* Exhibiting great opulence: *superluxury cars; superluxury hotels; a superluxury apartment.*

su·per·ma·jor·i·ty (so͞o′pər-mə-jôr′ĭ-tē, -jŏr′-) *n., pl.* **-ties.** A percentage higher than 50 percent required for approval of a motion or an action determined by vote, as among the shareholders of a company.

su·per·man (so͞o′pər-măn′) *n.* **1.** A man with more than human powers. **2.** An ideal superior man who, according to Nietzsche, forgoes transient pleasure, exercises creative power, lives at a level of experience beyond standards of good and evil, and is the goal of human evolution. In this sense, also called *overman.* [Translation of German *Übermensch* : *über-,* super- + *Mensch,* man.]

WORD HISTORY: *Overman* and *Beyondman* hardly seem likely names for a superhero, but perhaps *Overman* might be "leaping tall buildings at a single bound" had the German word *Übermensch* been translated differently than it was. However, Nietzsche's term for the ideal superior man was translated into English as *superman,* first recorded in a work by George Bernard Shaw published in 1903. Such a term comes to us through a process called loan translation, or calque formation, whereby the semantic components of a word or phrase in one language are literally translated into their equivalents in another language, German *Übermensch,* made up of *über,* "super–," and *Mensch,* "man," thus becoming *superman.* Because *über–* can also be translated "beyond" and "over," we also find *overman* and *beyondman* as calques for the word *Übermensch,* but they did not take root. Shaw, in a letter written before 1917, noted that "some of our most felicitous writers . . . had been using such desperate and unspeakable forms as Beyondman, when the glib Superman was staring them in the face all the time." Hence, when it came to naming a new comic strip hero, *Superman* was the logical choice, a name first recorded in 1938.

su·per·mar·ket (so͞o′pər-mär′kĭt) *n.* A large self-service retail market that sells food and household goods.

su·per·mar·ket·er (so͞o′pər-mär′kĭ-tər) *n.* One who owns or operates a supermarket.

su·per·mol·e·cule (so͞o′pər-mŏl′ĭ-kyo͞ol′) *n.* See **macromolecule.**

su·per·mom (so͞o′pər-mŏm′) *n. Informal.* A mother who performs the traditional duties of housework and childcare while also holding full-time employment.

su·per·nal (so͞o-pûr′nəl) *adj.* **1.** Celestial; heavenly. **2.** Of, coming from, or being in the sky or high above. [Middle English, from Old French, from Latin *supernus.* See **uper** in Appendix.] **—su·per′nal·ly** *adv.*

su·per·na·tant (so͞o′pər-nāt′nt) *adj.* Floating on the surface. **—supernatant** also **su·per·nate** (so͞o′pər-nāt′) *n.* The clear fluid above a sediment or precipitate. [Latin *supernatāns, supernatant-,* present participle of *supernatāre,* to float : *super-,* super- + *natāre,* to swim; see **snā-** in Appendix.]

su·per·nat·u·ral (so͞o′pər-năch′ər-əl) *adj.* **1.** Of or relating to existence outside the natural world. **2.** Attributed to a power that seems to violate or go beyond natural forces. **3.** Of or relating to a deity. **4.** Of or relating to the immediate exercise of divine power; miraculous. **5.** Of or relating to the miraculous. **—supernatural** *n.* That which is supernatural. **—su′per·nat′u·ral·ly** *adv.* **—su′per·nat′u·ral·ness** *n.*

su·per·nat·u·ral·ism (so͞o′pər-năch′ər-ə-lĭz′əm) *n.* **1.** The quality of being supernatural. **2.** Belief in a supernatural agency that intervenes in the course of natural laws. **—su′per·nat′u·ral·ist** *n.* **—su′per·nat′u·ral·is′tic** *adj.*

su·per·nor·mal (so͞o′pər-nôr′məl) *adj.* **1.** Greatly exceeding the normal or average but still obeying natural laws. **2.** Paranormal.

su·per·no·va (so͞o′pər-nō′və) *n., pl.* **-vae** (-vē) or **-vas.** A rare celestial phenomenon involving the explosion of most of the material in a star, resulting in an extremely bright, short-lived object that emits vast amounts of energy.

su·per·nu·mer·ar·y (so͞o′pər-no͞o′mə-rĕr′ē, -nyo͞o′-) *adj.* **1.** Exceeding a fixed, prescribed, or standard number; extra. **2.** Exceeding the required or desired number or amount; superfluous. See Synonyms at **superfluous. —supernumerary** *n., pl.* **-ies. 1.** One that is in excess of the regular, necessary, or usual number. **2.** An actor without a speaking part, as one who appears in a crowd scene. [Latin *supernumerārius* : *super,* above; see SUPER– + *numerum,* accusative of *numerus,* number; see **nem-** in Appendix.]

su·per·or·der (so͞o′pər-ôr′dər) *n. Biology.* A taxonomic category of related organisms ranking below a class or subclass and above an order.

su·per·or·di·nate (so͞o′pər-ôr′dn-ĭt) *adj.* **1.** Of higher rank, status, or value. **2.** *Logic.* Of or being the relation of a universal proposition to a particular proposition in which the terms are the same and occur in the same order. [SUPER– + (SUB)ORDINATE.] **—su′per·or′di·nate** *n.* **—su′per·or′di·nate′** (-ôr′dn-āt′) *v.* **—su′per·or′di·na′tion** (-ôr′dn-ā′shən) *n.*

su·per·or·gan·ism (so͞o′pər-ôr′gə-nĭz′əm) *n.* A group of organisms, such as an insect colony, that functions as a social unit.

su·per·o·vu·late (so͞o′pər-ō′vyə-lāt′, -ŏv′yə-) *v.* **-lat·ed, -lat·ing, -lates.** —*intr.* To produce mature ova at an accelerated rate or in a large number at one time. —*tr.* To cause (an animal) to superovulate. **—su′per·o·vu·la′tion** *n.*

su·per·par·a·sit·ism (so͞o′pər-păr′ə-sĭ-tĭz′əm, -sī-) *n.* Infestation of parasites by other parasites. **—su′per·par′a·sit′ic** (-sĭt′ĭk) *adj.*

su·per·phos·phate (so͞o′pər-fŏs′fāt′) *n.* **1.** An acid phosphate. **2.** A mixture of gypsum and monobasic calcium phosphate resulting from the action of sulfuric acid on phosphate rock, used as a fertilizer.

su·per·phys·i·cal (so͞o′pər-fĭz′ĭ-kəl) *adj.* **1.** Exceeding or going beyond the purely physical. **2.** Not explained by known physical laws; preternatural or supernatural.

su·per·pose (so͞o′pər-pōz′) *tr.v.* **-posed, -pos·ing, -pos·es. 1.** To set or place (one thing) over or above something else. **2.** *Mathematics.* To place (one geometric figure) over another so that all like parts coincide. [Probably French *superposer,* back-formation from *superposition,* superposition, from Late Latin *superpositiō, superpositiōn-,* from Latin *superpositus,* past participle of *superpōnere,* to place over : *super-,* super- + *pōnere,* to place; see POSITION.]

su·per·po·si·tion (so͞o′pər-pə-zĭsh′ən) *n.* **1.** The act of superposing or the state of being superposed: *"Yet another technique in the forensic specialist's repertoire is photo superposition"* (Patrick Nuyghe). **2.** *Geology.* The principle that in a group of stratified sedimentary rocks the lowest were the earliest to be deposited.

su·per·pow·er (so͞o′pər-pou′ər) *n.* A powerful and influential nation, especially a nuclear power that dominates its allies or client states in an international power bloc.

su·per·re·al·ism (so͞o′pər-rē′ə-lĭz′əm) *n.* An artistic and literary movement characterized by extreme realism. **—su′per·re′al, su′per·re′al·is′tic** *adj.* **—su′per·re′al·ist** *n.*

su·per·rich (so͞o′pər-rĭch′) *adj.* **1.** Of, relating to, or being the wealthiest. **2.** Containing the richest ingredients: *superrich chocolate ice cream.* **—superrich** *n. (used with a pl. verb).* The most wealthy people considered as a group or class. Often used with *the: Only the superrich were able to afford trips to that resort.*

su·per·sat·u·rate (so͞o′pər-săch′ə-rāt′) *tr.v.* **-rat·ed, -rat·ing, -rates. 1.** To cause (a chemical solution) to be more highly concentrated than is normally possible under given conditions of temperature and pressure. **2.** To cause (a vapor) to exceed the normal saturation vapor pressure at a given temperature. **—su′per·sat′u·ra′tion** *n.*

su·per·sav·er (so͞o′pər-sā′vər) *n.* An airline ticket, purchased typically well ahead of the departure date, that affords the purchaser considerable savings over regular fare. —*attributive.* Often used to modify another noun: *supersaver fares; supersaver tickets.*

su·per·scribe (so͞o′pər-skrīb′) *tr.v.* **-scribed, -scrib·ing, -scribes. 1.** To write on the outside or upper part of (a letter, for example). **2.** To write (a name or an address, for example) on the top or outside. [Latin *superscrībere,* to write over : *super-,* super- + *scrībere,* to write; see **skrībh-** in Appendix.]

su·per·script (so͞o′pər-skrĭpt′) *n.* A character set, printed, or written above and immediately to one side of another: *In* x^2 *the superscript is 2.* [Latin *superscrīptus,* past participle of *superscrībere,* to write over. See SUPERSCRIBE.] **—su′per·script** *adj.*

su·per·scrip·tion (so͞o′pər-skrĭp′shən) *n.* **1.** Something written above or outside something else. **2.** The act of superscribing. **3.** The part of a prescription that bears the Latin word *recipe* represented by the symbol ℞.

su·per·sede (so͞o′pər-sēd′) *tr.v.* **-sed·ed, -sed·ing, -sedes. 1.** To take the place of; replace. **2.** To cause to be set aside, especially to displace as inferior or antiquated. See Synonyms at **replace.** [Middle English *superceden,* to postpone, from Old French *superceder,* from Latin *supersedēre,* to refrain from : *super-,* super- + *sedēre,* to sit; see **sed-** in Appendix.] **—su′per·sed′er** *n.* **—su′per·ses′sion** (-sĕsh′ən) *n.*

su·per·se·de·as (so͞o′pər-sē′dē-əs) *n. Law.* A writ containing a command to stay legal proceedings, as in the halting or delaying of the execution of a sentence. [Middle English, from Medieval Latin, from Latin *supersedeās,* you must desist (from the writ), second person sing. present subjunctive of *supersedēre,* to desist from. See SUPERSEDE.]

su·per·se·dure (so͞o′pər-sē′jər) *n.* **1.** The act or process of superseding. **2.** Replacement of a queen bee that has grown old or weak by one that is younger or more vigorous.

su·per·sen·si·ble (so͞o′pər-sĕn′sə-bəl) *adj.* Beyond or above perception by the senses. **—su′per·sen′si·bly** *adv.*

su·per·son·ic (so͞o′pər-sŏn′ĭk) *adj.* **1.** Having, caused by, or relating to a speed greater than the speed of sound in a given medium, especially air. **2.** Of or relating to sound waves beyond human audibility. **—su′per·son′i·cal·ly** *adv.*

su·per·son·ics (so͞o′pər-sŏn′ĭks) *n. (used with a sing. verb).* The study of phenomena produced by the motion of a body through a medium at velocities greater than that of sound.

supersonic transport *n. Abbr.* **SST** A large transport airplane engineered to operate at supersonic speeds.

su·per·star (so͞o′pər-stär′) *n.* **1.** A widely acclaimed star, as in movies or sports, who has great popular appeal. **2.** One that is extremely popular or prominent or that is a major attraction. **—su′per·star′dom** (so͞o′pər-stär′dəm) *n.*

su·per·sta·tion (so͞o′pər-stā′shən) *n.* A television or radio station that broadcasts to a nationwide audience by satellite, cable, or both.

su·per·sti·tion (so͞o′pər-stĭsh′ən) *n.* **1.** An irrational belief that an object, an action, or a circumstance not logically related to a course of events influences its outcome. **2. a.** A belief, practice, or rite irrationally maintained by ignorance of the laws of nature or by faith in magic or chance. **b.** A fearful or abject state of mind resulting from such ignorance or irrationality. **c.** Idolatry. [Middle English *superesticion,* from Old French *superstition,* from Latin *superstitiō, superstitiōn-,* from *superstes, superstit-,* standing over. See **stā-** in Appendix.]

su·per·sti·tious (so͞o′pər-stĭsh′əs) *adj.* **1.** Inclined to believe in superstition. **2.** Of, characterized by, or proceeding from superstition. **—su′per·sti′tious·ly** *adv.* **—su′per·sti′tious·ness** *n.*

su·per·store (so͞o′pər-stôr′, -stōr′) *n.* A very large supermarket that stocks extremely diversified merchandise, such as food and automotive parts, together and in quantity.

su·per·stra·tum (so͞o′pər-strā′təm, -străt′əm) *n., pl.* **-stra·ta** (-strā′tə, -străt′ə). **1.** One layer or stratum superimposed on another. **2.** *Linguistics.* The language of a later, invading people imposed on and leaving features in an indigenous language.

su·per·string (so͞o′pər-strĭng′) *n. Physics.* A hypothetical particle consisting of a very short one-dimensional string existing

ă pat	oi boy
ā pay	ou out
âr care	o͝o took
ä father	o͞o boot
ĕ pet	ŭ cut
ē be	ûr urge
ĭ pit	th thin
ī pie	*th* this
îr pier	hw which
ŏ pot	zh vision
ō toe	ə about, item
ô paw	♦ regionalism

Stress marks: **′** (primary); ′ (secondary), as in **dictionary** (dĭk′shə-nĕr′ē)

in ten dimensions. It is the elementary particle in a theory of space-time incorporating supersymmetry. [SUPER(SYMMETRY) + STRING.]

su·per·struc·ture (so͞o′pər-strŭk′chər) *n.* **1.** A physical or conceptual structure extended or developed from a basic form. **2.** The part of a building or other structure above the foundation. **3.** *Nautical.* The parts of a ship's structure above the main deck. **4.** The rails, sleepers, and other parts of a railway. **5.** In Marxist theory, the ideologies or institutions of a society as distinct from the basic processes and direct social relations of material production and economics.

su·per·sym·me·try (so͞o′pər-sĭm′ĭ-trē) *n. Physics.* A hypothetical symmetry that relates fermions to bosons and gravitational force to forces that operate on the subatomic level.

su·per·tank·er (so͞o′pər-tăng′kər) *n. Nautical.* A very large ship, usually between 100,000 and 400,000 displacement tons, used for transporting oil and other liquids in large quantities.

su·per·ti·tle (so͞o′pər-tīt′l) *n.* A written translation of the dialogue or lyrics of a foreign-language performance of an opera or a choral work, for example, shown on a screen above the performers. Also called *surtitle.* **—su′per·ti′tled** *adj.*

su·per·ton·ic (so͞o′pər-tŏn′ĭk) *n. Music.* The second tone of a diatonic scale.

Su·per Tuesday (so͞o′pər) *n.* The day on which, in a presidential election year, a number of states hold their primary presidential elections.

su·per·vene (so͞o′pər-vēn′) *intr.v.* **-vened, -ven·ing, -venes. 1.** To come or occur as something extraneous, additional, or unexpected. See Synonyms at **follow. 2.** To follow immediately after; ensue. [Latin *supervenīre* : *super-*, super- + *venīre,* to come; see **gʷā-** in Appendix.] **—su′per·ven′ient** (-vēn′yənt) *adj.* **—su′per·ven′tion** (-vĕn′shən) *n.*

su·per·vise (so͞o′pər-vīz′) *tr.v.* **-vised, -vis·ing, -vis·es.** To have the charge and direction of; superintend. [Middle English **supervisen,* from Medieval Latin *supervidēre, supervīs-* : Latin *super-*, super- + Latin *vidēre,* to see; see **weid-** in Appendix.]

SYNONYMS: *supervise, boss, overlook, oversee, superintend.* The central meaning shared by these verbs is "to have the direction and oversight of the performance of others": *supervised a team of investigators; bossed a construction crew; overlooking farm hands; overseeing plumbers and electricians; superintend a household staff.*

su·per·vi·sion (so͞o′pər-vĭzh′ən) *n.* The act, process, or function of supervising. See Synonyms at **care.**

su·per·vi·sor (so͞o′pər-vī′zər) *n. Abbr.* **supvr. 1.** One who supervises. **2.** One who is in charge of a particular department or unit, as in a governmental agency or school system. **3.** One who is an elected administrative officer in certain U.S. counties and townships. **—su′per·vi′so·ry** (-vī′zə-rē) *adj.*

su·per·wom·an (so͞o′pər-wo͝om′ən) *n.* **1.** A woman who performs all the duties typically associated with several different full-time roles, such as wage earner, graduate student, mother, and wife. **2.** A woman with more than human powers.

su·pi·nate (so͞o′pə-nāt′) *v.* **-nat·ed, -nat·ing, -nates.** *—tr.* **1.** To turn (the hand and forearm) so that the palm is upward or forward. **2.** To turn (the foot or leg) so that the sole is outward. *—intr.* To be supinated. [Latin *supīnāre, supīnāt-*, from *supīnus,* backward. See SUPINE.] **—su′pi·na′tion** *n.*

su·pi·na·tor (so͞o′pə-nā′tər) *n.* A muscle, especially in the forearm, that effects or assists supination.

su·pine (so͞o-pīn′, so͞o′pīn′) *adj.* **1.** Lying on the back or having the face upward. See Synonyms at **prone. 2.** Having the palm upward. Used of the hand. **3.** Marked by or showing lethargy, passivity, or blameworthy indifference. See Synonyms at **inactive. 4.** Inclined; sloping. **—supine** *n. Abbr.* **sup.** *Grammar.* A defective Latin verbal noun of the fourth declension, having very limited syntax and only two cases, an accusative in *-tum* or *-sum* and an ablative in *-tū* or *-sū.* The accusative form is sometimes considered to be the fourth principal part of the Latin verb. [Middle English *supin,* Latin verbal noun, from Late Latin *supīnum,* from neuter of Latin *supīnus,* lying on the back, going back. See **upo** in Appendix.] **—su·pine′ly** *adv.* **—su·pine′ness** *n.*

supp. *abbr.* **1.** Supplement. **2.** Supplementary.

sup·per (sŭp′ər) *n.* **1. a.** A light evening meal when dinner is taken at midday. **b.** A light meal eaten before going to bed. **2.** A dance or social affair where supper is served. [Middle English, from Old French *souper,* to sup, supper. See SUP[2].]

sup·per·time (sŭp′ər-tīm′) *n.* The time of day during which supper is usually eaten.

suppl. *abbr.* **1.** Supplement. **2.** Supplementary.

sup·plant (sə-plănt′) *tr.v.* **-plant·ed, -plant·ing, -plants. 1.** To usurp the place of, especially through intrigue or underhanded tactics. **2.** To displace and substitute for (another): *The word processor has largely supplanted electric typewriters.* See Synonyms at **replace.** [Middle English *supplanten,* from Old French *supplanter,* from Latin *supplantāre,* to trip up : *sub-*, sub- + *planta,* sole of the foot; see **plat-** in Appendix.]

sup·ple (sŭp′əl) *adj.* **-pler, -plest. 1.** Readily bent; pliant. **2.** Moving and bending with agility; limber. **3.** Yielding or changing readily; compliant or adaptable. See Synonyms at **flexible.** **—supple** *tr. & intr.v.* **-pled, -pling, -ples.** To make or become supple. [Middle English *souple,* from Old French, from Latin *supplex,* suppliant. See **plāk-**[1] in Appendix.] **—sup′ple·ness** *n.* **—sup′ply, sup′ple·ly** *adv.*

sup·ple·ment (sŭp′lə-mənt) *n. Abbr.* **sup., supp., suppl. 1.** Something added to complete a thing, make up for a deficiency, or extend or strengthen the whole. **2.** A section added to a book or document to give further information or to correct errors. **3.** A separate section devoted to a special subject inserted into a periodical, such as a newspaper. **4.** *Mathematics.* The angle or arc that when added to a given angle or arc makes 180° or a semicircle. In this sense, also called *supplementary angle.* **—supplement** (-mĕnt′) *tr.v.* **-ment·ed, -ment·ing, -ments.** To provide or form a supplement to. [Middle English, from Old French, from Latin *supplēmentum,* from *supplēre,* to complete. See SUPPLY.] **—sup′ple·men·tar′i·ty** (-târ′ĭ-tē) *n.* **—sup′ple·men′ta·ry** (-mĕn′tə-rē, -trē), **sup′ple·men′tal** (-mĕn′tl) *adj.* **—sup′ple·men·ta′tion** (-mĕn-tā′shən) *n.*

supplementary angle *n. Mathematics.* See **supplement** (sense 4).

sup·ple·tion (sə-plē′shən) *n. Linguistics.* The use of an unrelated form to complete a paradigm, as the past tense *went* of the verb *go, goes, going, gone.* [From Latin *supplētus,* past participle of *supplēre,* to supply. See SUPPLY.]

sup·pli·ant (sŭp′lē-ənt) *adj.* Asking humbly and earnestly; beseeching. **—suppliant** *n.* A supplicant. [From Middle English, one who supplicates, from Old French, present participle of *supplier,* to entreat, from Latin *supplicāre.* See SUPPLICATE.] **—sup′pli·ance** *n.* **—sup′pli·ant·ly** *adv.*

sup·pli·cant (sŭp′lĭ-kənt) *n.* One who supplicates; a suppliant. **—supplicant** *adj.* Supplicating. [From Latin *supplicāns, supplicant-*, present participle of *supplicāre,* to kneel down. See SUPPLICATE.]

sup·pli·cate (sŭp′lĭ-kāt′) *v.* **-cat·ed, -cat·ing, -cates.** *—tr.* **1.** To ask for humbly or earnestly, as by praying. **2.** To make a humble entreaty to; beseech. *—intr.* To make a humble, earnest petition; beg. [Middle English *supplicaten,* from Latin *supplicāre, supplicāt-*, from *supplex, supplic-*, suppliant. See SUPPLE.] **—sup′pli·ca′tion** *n.* **—sup′pli·ca·to′ry** (-kə-tôr′ē, -tōr′ē) *adj.*

sup·ply (sə-plī′) *v.* **-plied, -ply·ing, -plies.** *—tr.* **1.** To make available for use; provide. **2.** To furnish or equip with: *supplied sheets for every bed.* **3.** To fill sufficiently; satisfy: *supply a need.* **4.** To make up for (a deficiency, for example); compensate for. **5.** To serve temporarily as a substitute in (a church, for example). *—intr.* To fill a position as a substitute. **—supply** *n., pl.* **-plies.** *Abbr.* **sup. 1.** The act of supplying. **2.** Something that is or can be supplied. **3.** An amount available or sufficient for a given use; stock. **4.** Often **supplies.** Materials or provisions stored and dispensed when needed. **5.** *Economics.* The amount of a commodity available for meeting a demand or for purchase at a given price. **6.** A cleric serving as a substitute or temporary pastor. [Middle English *supplien,* to help, complete, furnish with additional troops, from Old French *soupleer,* to fill up, from Latin *supplēre* : *sub-*, from below; see SUB– + *plēre,* to fill; see **pele-**[1] in Appendix.] **—sup·pli′er** *n.*

sup·ply-side (sə-plī′sīd′) *adj.* Of, relating to, or being an economic theory that increased availability of money for investment, achieved through reduction of taxes especially in the higher tax brackets, will increase productivity, economic activity, and income throughout the economic system. **—supply side** *n.* **—sup·ply′-sid′er** *n.*

sup·port (sə-pôrt′, -pōrt′) *tr.v.* **-port·ed, -port·ing, -ports. 1.** To bear the weight of, especially from below. **2.** To hold in position so as to keep from falling, sinking, or slipping. **3.** To be capable of bearing; withstand. **4.** To keep from weakening or failing; strengthen. **5.** To provide for or maintain, by supplying with money or necessities. **6.** To furnish corroborating evidence for. **7.** To aid the cause, policy, or interests of. **8.** To endure; tolerate. **9. a.** To act (a part or role). **b.** To act in a secondary or subordinate role to (a leading performer). **—support** *n.* **1. a.** The act of supporting. **b.** The state of being supported. **2.** One that supports. **3.** Maintenance, as of a family, with the necessities of life. [Middle English *supporten,* from Old French *supporter,* from Latin *supportāre,* to carry : *sub-*, from below; see SUB– + *portāre,* to carry; see **per-**[2] in Appendix.]

SYNONYMS: *support, uphold, back, advocate, champion.* These verbs are compared as they mean to give aid or encouragement to a person or cause. *Support* is the most general: *is being supported by friends in her effort to surmount the tragedy; "the policy of Cromwell, who supported the growing power of France against the declining power of Spain"* (William E.H. Lecky). To *uphold* is to maintain or affirm in the face of a challenge or strong opposition: *"The Declaration of Right upheld the principle of hereditary monarchy"* (Edmund Burke). *Back* suggests material or moral support intended to contribute to or assure success: *"There is only one proved method of assisting the advancement of pure science—that of picking men of genius, backing them heavily, and leaving them to direct themselves"* (James B. Conant). *Advocate* implies verbal support, often in the form of pleading or arguing: *Scientists advocate a reduction in saturated fats in the human diet.* To *champion* is to fight for one that is under attack or lacks the strength or ability to act in its own behalf: *"championed the government* *and defended the system of taxation"* (Samuel Chew). See also Synonyms at **livelihood.**

sup·port·a·ble (sə-pôr′tə-bəl, -pōr′-) *adj.* Bearable; endurable: *supportable burdens.* **—sup·port′a·bil′i·ty** *n.* **—sup·port′a·bly** *adv.*

sup·port·er (sə-pôr′tər, -pōr′-) *n.* **1.** One that supports, as a structural member of a building. **2.** One who promotes or advocates; an adherent: *a supporter of capitalism.* **3.** An athletic supporter. **4.** *Heraldry.* An animal or a figure that supports a shield in a coat of arms.

support hose *pl.n.* Elasticized stockings designed to reduce stress on the blood vessels in the legs, as for people with varicose veins. Also called *support stockings.*

sup·por·tive (sə-pôr′tĭv, -pōr′-) *adj.* Furnishing support or assistance. **—sup·por′tive·ly** *adv.* **—sup·por′tive·ness** *n.*

support level *n.* A price at which a security or the market becomes attractive to investors.

support stockings *pl.n.* See **support hose.**

support system *n.* A network of personal or professional contacts available to a person or an organization for practical or moral support when needed.

sup·pos·a·ble (sə-pō′zə-bəl) *adj.* That can be supposed or conjectured: *a supposable outcome.* **—sup·pos′a·bly** *adv.*

sup·pose (sə-pōz′) *v.* **-posed, -pos·ing, -pos·es.** *—tr.* **1.** To assume to be true or real for the sake of argument or explanation: *Suppose we win the lottery.* **2.a.** To believe, especially on uncertain or tentative grounds: *Scientists supposed that large dinosaurs lived in swamps.* **b.** To consider to be probable or likely: *I suppose it will rain.* **3.** To imply as an antecedent condition; presuppose: *"Patience must suppose pain"* (Samuel Johnson). **4.** To consider as a suggestion: *Suppose we dine together.* *—intr.* To imagine; conjecture. [Middle English *supposen,* from Old French *supposer,* alteration (influenced by *poser,* to place; see POSE[1]) of Medieval Latin *suppōnere,* from Latin, to put under : *sub-,* sub- + *pōnere,* to place; see **apo-** in Appendix.]

sup·posed (sə-pōzd′, -pō′zĭd) *adj.* **1.** Presumed to be true or real without conclusive evidence. **2.** Intended: *medication that is supposed to relieve pain.* **3.a.** Required: *He is supposed to go to the store.* **b.** Permitted: *We are not supposed to smoke here.* **c.** Firmly believed; expected: *You're supposed to be my friend.* **—sup·pos′ed·ly** (-pō′zĭd-lē) *adv.*

SYNONYMS: *supposed, conjectural, hypothetical, putative, reputed, suppositious, supposititious.* The central meaning shared by these adjectives is "put forth or accepted as being true on inconclusive grounds": *the supposed cause of inflation; conjectural criticism; the site of a hypothetical colony; a foundling's putative father; the reputed author of the article; suppositious reconstructions of dead languages; supposititious hypotheses.*
ANTONYM: *certain.*

sup·pos·ing (sə-pō′zĭng) *conj.* Assuming that: *Supposing we're right, what should we do?*

sup·po·si·tion (sŭp′ə-zĭsh′ən) *n.* **1.** The act of supposing. **2.** Something supposed; an assumption. **—sup′po·si′tion·al** *adj.* **—sup′po·si′tion·al·ly** *adv.*

sup·po·si·tious (sŭp′ə-zĭsh′əs) *adj.* Supposititious. See Synonyms at **supposed.**

sup·pos·i·ti·tious (sə-pŏz′ĭ-tĭsh′əs) *adj.* **1.** Substituted with fraudulent intent; spurious. **2.** Hypothetical; supposed. See Synonyms at **supposed.** [From Latin *suppositīcius,* from *suppositus,* past participle of *suppōnere,* to substitute. See SUPPOSE.] **—sup·pos′i·ti′tious·ly** *adv.* **—sup·pos′i·ti′tious·ness** *n.*

sup·pos·i·tive (sə-pŏz′ĭ-tĭv) *adj.* Of the nature of, including, or involving supposition. **—suppositive** *n. Grammar.* A conjunction, such as *if* or *providing,* that introduces a supposition. **—sup·pos′i·tive·ly** *adv.*

sup·pos·i·to·ry (sə-pŏz′ĭ-tôr′ē, -tōr′ē) *n., pl.* **-ries.** *Medicine.* A small plug of medication designed to melt at body temperature within a body cavity other than the mouth, especially the rectum or vagina. Also called *bougie.* [Middle English, from Old French *suppositorie,* from Medieval Latin *suppositōrium,* from Late Latin, neuter of *suppositōrius,* placed under, from Latin *suppositus,* past participle of *suppōnere,* to put under. See SUPPOSE.]

sup·press (sə-prĕs′) *tr.v.* **-pressed, -press·ing, -press·es.** **1.** To put an end to forcibly; subdue. **2.** To curtail or prohibit the activities of. **3.** To keep from being revealed, published, or circulated. **4.** To deliberately exclude unacceptable desires or thoughts from the mind. **5.** To inhibit the expression of (an impulse, for example); check: *suppress a smile.* **6.** To reduce the incidence or severity of (a hemorrhage or a cough, for example); arrest. [Middle English *suppressen,* from Latin *supprimere, suppress-* : *sub-,* sub- + *premere,* to press; see **per-**[4] in Appendix.] **—sup·press′ant** *n.* **—sup·press′i·ble** *adj.*

SYNONYMS: *suppress, stifle, repress.* These verbs mean to hold in check something requiring or struggling to find an outlet. *Suppress* suggests the exercise of force that drastically inhibits or crushes: *"There is the world of ideas and the world of practice; the French are often for suppressing the one and the English the other; but neither is to be suppressed"* (Matthew Arnold). To *stifle* is to keep back something, such as an impulse or an emotion, as if by smothering it: *"This was a sinful curiosity, and I stifled it to the best of my ability"* (John Galt). *Repress* often implies keeping something under control by an act of volition: *"To save his life he could not repress a chuckle"* (Booth Tarkington).

sup·press·er (sə-prĕs′ər) *n.* Variant of **suppressor** (sense 1).

sup·pres·sion (sə-prĕsh′ən) *n.* **1.** The act of suppressing. **2.** The state of being suppressed. **3.** *Psychiatry.* Conscious exclusion of unacceptable desires, thoughts, or memories from the mind. **4.** *Botany.* The failure of an organ or part to develop.

sup·pres·sive (sə-prĕs′ĭv) *adj.* Tending or serving to suppress.

sup·pres·sor (sə-prĕs′ər) *n.* **1.** Or **sup·press·er.** One that suppresses: *a suppressor of free speech.* **2.** A gene that suppresses the phenotypic expression of another gene, especially of a mutant gene. **3.** A device, such as a resistor or grid, that is used in an electrical or electronic system to reduce unwanted currents.

suppressor T cell *n.* A T cell that reduces or suppresses the immune response of B cells or of other T cells to an antigen.

sup·pu·rate (sŭp′yə-rāt′) *intr.v.* **-rat·ed, -rat·ing, -rates.** To form or discharge pus. [Middle English *suppuraten,* from Latin *suppūrāre, suppūrāt-* : *sub-,* sub- + *pūs, pūr-,* pus; see **pū-** in Appendix.]

sup·pu·ra·tion (sŭp′yə-rā′shən) *n.* **1.** The formation or discharge of pus. **2.** Pus. **—sup′pu·ra′tive** *adj.*

supr. *abbr.* Supreme.

supra– *pref.* **1.** Above; over; on top of: *suprarenal.* **2.** Greater than; transcending: *supramolecular.* [Latin, from *suprā,* above, beyond. See **uper** in Appendix.]

su·pra·cel·lu·lar (so͞o′prə-sĕl′yə-lər) *adj.* Above the level of a cell or cells: *supracellular biology.*

su·pra·gen·ic (so͞o′prə-jĕn′ĭk) *adj.* Above the level of the gene or genes: *supragenic functions of a chromosome.*

su·pra·glot·tal (so͞o′prə-glŏt′l) *adj.* **1.** Above or anterior to the glottis. **2.** *Linguistics.* Designating a phone or phoneme produced by the speech organs anterior to the glottis.

su·pra·lim·i·nal (so͞o′prə-lĭm′ə-nəl) *adj.* Being above the threshold of consciousness or of sensation. Used of stimuli.

su·pra·max·il·la (so͞o′prə-măk-sĭl′ə) *n., pl.* **-max·il·lae** (-măk-sĭl′ē). The upper jaw or jawbone. **—su′pra·max′il·lar′y** (-măk′sə-lĕr′ē) *adj. & n.*

su·pra·mo·lec·u·lar (so͞o′prə-mə-lĕk′yə-lər) *adj.* **1.** Consisting of more than one molecule. **2.** Of greater complexity than a molecule.

su·pra·na·tion·al (so͞o′prə-năsh′ə-nəl, -năsh′nəl) *adj.* Extending beyond or transcending established borders or spheres of influence held by separate nations: *a supranational economy; supranational federations.*

su·pra·or·bi·tal (so͞o′prə-ôr′bĭ-tl) *adj.* Located above the orbit of the eye: *the supraorbital ridge.*

su·pra·re·nal (so͞o′prə-rē′nəl) *adj.* Located on or above the kidney. **—suprarenal** *n.* A suprarenal part, especially an adrenal gland.

suprarenal gland *n.* See **adrenal gland.**

su·pra·scap·u·lar (so͞o′prə-skăp′yə-lər) *adj.* Located above the scapula, as an artery or a nerve.

su·pra·vi·tal (so͞o′prə-vīt′l) *adj.* Relating to or capable of staining living cells after their removal from a living or recently dead organism: *a supravital stain.*

su·prem·a·cist (so͝o-prĕm′ə-sĭst) *n.* One who believes that a certain group is or should be supreme.

su·prem·a·cy (so͝o-prĕm′ə-sē) *n., pl.* **-cies.** **1.** The quality or condition of being supreme. **2.** Supreme power or authority.

su·prem·a·tism (so͝o-prĕm′ə-tĭz′ən) *n.* A school and theory of geometric abstract art that originated in Russia in the early 20th century and influenced constructivists. [Russian *suprematizm,* from French *suprématie,* supremacy, from SUPREMACY.] **—su·prem′a·tist** *adj. & n.*

su·preme (so͝o-prēm′) *adj.* **-er, -est.** *Abbr.* **supr.** **1.** Greatest in power, authority, or rank; paramount or dominant. **2.** Greatest in importance, degree, significance, character, or achievement. **3.** Ultimate; final: *the supreme sacrifice.* [Latin *suprēmus,* superlative of *superus,* upper, from *super,* over. See **uper** in Appendix.] **—su·preme′ly** *adv.* **—su·preme′ness** *n.*

su·prême (so͝o-prēm′, -prĕm′) *n.* **1.** A rich velouté made with chicken stock, cream, and egg yolks. Also called *sauce suprême.* **2.** A dish made or served with this sauce, especially the breast and wing of chicken or other fowl. Also called *suprême de volaille.* **3.a.** A sherbet glass with a large bowl. **b.** A dessert served in such a glass. **4.a.** A container, such as a glass bowl, used for serving cold food in an inner container that nestles on crushed or cracked ice. **b.** Food served in such a vessel. [French, supreme, suprême, from Latin *suprēmus,* supreme. See SUPREME.]

Su·preme Being (so͝o-prēm′) *n.* God.

Supreme Court *n. Abbr.* **S.C., Sup.Ct.** *Law.* **1.** The highest federal court in the United States, consisting of nine justices and having jurisdiction over all other courts in the nation. **2. supreme court.** The highest court in most states within the United States. In this sense, also called *high court.*

suprême de vo·laille (vô-lī′) *n.* See **suprême** (sense 2). [French : *suprême,* suprême + *de,* of + *volaille,* fowl.]

Supreme Soviet *n.* The legislature of the Soviet Union, consisting of two houses, one whose members are elected on the basis

ă pat	oi boy
ā pay	ou out
âr care	o͝o took
ä father	o͞o boot
ĕ pet	ŭ cut
ē be	ûr urge
ĭ pit	th thin
ī pie	*th* this
îr pier	hw which
ŏ pot	zh vision
ō toe	ə about, item
ô paw	♦ regionalism

Stress marks: ′ (primary); ′ (secondary), as in **dictionary** (dĭk′shə-nĕr′ē)

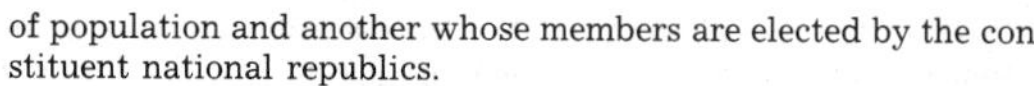

of population and another whose members are elected by the constituent national republics.

su·pre·mo (so͞o-prē′mō′, sə-) *n., pl.* **-mos.** *Chiefly British.* One who is highest in authority or command, as of an organization. [Spanish and Italian, supreme, supremo, from Latin *suprēmus.* See SUPREME.]

supt. or **Supt.** *abbr.* Superintendent.

supvr. *abbr.* Supervisor.

Su·qua·mish (sə-kwä′mĭsh) *n., pl.* **Suquamish** or **-mish·es. 1.a.** A Native American people formerly inhabiting an area of the eastern shore of Puget Sound. The Suquamish became extinct as a people in the 20th century. **b.** A member of this people. **2.** The Salish language of the Suquamish.

sur. *abbr.* **1.** Surface. **2.** Surplus.

Sur. *abbr.* Suriname.

sur– *pref.* **1.** Over; above; upon: *surprint.* **2.** Additional: *surtax.* [Middle English, from Old French, from Latin *super-.* See **uper** in Appendix.]

su·ra (so͝or′ə) *n. Islam.* Any of the 114 chapters or sections of the Koran. [Arabic *sūrah,* from Hebrew *šûrâ,* row, line.]

Su·ra·ba·ya also **Su·ra·ba·ja** (so͝or′ə-bä′yə). A city of northeast Java, Indonesia, on the Java Sea. It is an important naval base. Population, 2,027,913.

su·rah (so͝or′ə) *n.* A soft twilled fabric of silk or of a blend of silk and rayon. [French *surat,* after SURAT.]

Su·ra·kar·ta (so͝or′ə-kär′tə). A city of south-central Java, Indonesia, east of Bandung. It is a market and processing center noted for its vast, walled palace built by the former sultans of the region. Population, 469,888.

su·ral (so͝or′əl) *adj.* Of or relating to the calf of the leg. [New Latin *sūrālis,* from Latin *sūra,* calf of the leg.]

Su·rat (so͝or′ət, sə-răt′). A city of west-central India on the Gulf of Cambay north of Bombay. Once the chief port of India, it is now a railroad junction and manufacturing center. Population, 776,583.

sur·base (sûr′bās′) *n. Architecture.* A molding or border above the base of a structure such as a baseboard.

sur·based[1] (sûr′bāst′) *adj. Architecture.* Having a surbase.

sur·based[2] (sûr′bāst′) *adj. Architecture.* Of or relating to an arch with a rise less than half its span. [From French *surbaissé,* past participle of *surbaisser,* to flatten : *sur-,* intensive pref. (from Old French; see SUR–) + *baisser,* to lower (from Old French *baissier,* from Vulgar Latin **bassiāre;* see ABASE).]

sur·cease (sûr′sēs′, sər-sēs′) *tr. & intr.v.* **-ceased, -ceas·ing, -ceas·es.** To bring or come to an end; stop. **—surcease** *n.* Cessation. [Middle English *surcesen,* variant (influenced by *cesen,* to cease; see CEASE) of *sursesen,* from Anglo-Norman *surseser,* from Old French *surseoir, sursis-,* to refrain, from Latin *supersedēre.* See SUPERSEDE.]

sur·charge (sûr′chärj′) *n.* **1.** An additional sum added to the usual amount or cost. **2.** An overcharge, especially when unlawful. **3.** An additional or excessive burden; an overload. **4.a.** A new value or denomination overprinted on a postage or revenue stamp. **b.** The stamp to which a new value has been applied. **5.** *Law.* The act of surcharging. **—surcharge** *tr.v.* **-charged, -charg·ing, -charg·es. 1.** To charge (a person) an additional sum. **2.** To overcharge (a person). **3.** To place an excessive burden on; overload. **4.** To fill beyond usual capacity; overfill. **5.** To print a surcharge on (a postage or revenue stamp). **6.** *Law.* To show an omission of a credit in (an account). **7.** To require (a person) to reimburse funds spent without authorization. [Middle English, from *surchargen,* to overtax, from Old French *surcharger* : *sur-,* sur- + *chargier,* to charge; see CHARGE.]

sur·cin·gle (sûr′sĭng′gəl) *n.* **1.** A girth that binds a saddle, pack, or blanket to the body of a horse. **2.** *Archaic.* The fastening belt on a clerical cassock; a cincture. [Middle English *sursengle,* from Old French *surcengle* : *sur-,* sur- + *cengle,* belt (from Latin *cingula,* from *cingere,* to gird; see CINGULUM).] **—sur′cin′gle** *v.*

sur·coat (sûr′kōt′) *n.* **1.** A loose outer coat or gown. **2.** A tunic worn in the Middle Ages by a knight over his armor. [Middle English *surcote,* from Old French : *sur-,* sur- + *cote,* coat; see COAT.]

surcoat
Detail from an early 16th-century breviary of Queen Eleanor of Portugal, showing Saint Barbara wearing a sleeveless surcoat

sur·cu·lose (sûr′kyə-lōs′) *adj. Botany.* Producing suckers: *a surculose shrub.* [Latin *surculōsus,* woody, from *surculus,* diminutive of *surus,* branch, post.]

surd (sûrd) *n.* **1.** *Mathematics.* An irrational number, such as $\sqrt{2}$. **2.** *Linguistics.* A voiceless sound in speech. **—surd** *adj. Linguistics.* Voiceless, as a sound. [Medieval Latin *surdus* (from Latin, speechless), translation of Arabic *(jaḏr) 'aṣamm,* deaf (root), surd, translation of Greek *alogos,* speechless, surd.]

sure (sho͝or) *adj.* **sur·er, sur·est. 1.** Impossible to doubt or dispute; certain. **2.** Not hesitating or wavering; firm: *sure convictions.* **3.** Confident, as of something awaited or expected: *sure of ultimate victory.* **4.a.** Bound to come about or happen; inevitable: *sure defeat.* **b.** Having one's course directed; destined or bound: *sure to succeed.* **5.** Certain not to miss or err; steady: *a sure hand on the throttle.* **6.a.** Worthy of being trusted or depended on; reliable. **b.** Free from or marked by freedom from doubt: *sure of her friends.* **7.** Careful to do something: *asked me to be sure to turn off the stove.* **8.** *Obsolete.* Free from harm or danger; safe. **—sure** *adv. Informal.* Surely; certainly. **—*idioms.* for sure.** *Informal.* Certainly; unquestionably: *We'll win for sure.* **make sure.** To establish something without doubt; make certain: *Make sure he writes it down.* **to be sure.** Indeed; certainly. [Middle English, from Old French, safe, from Latin *sēcūrus.* See SECURE.] **—sure′ness** *n.*

SYNONYMS: *sure, certain, confident, positive.* These adjectives are compared as they mean feeling or showing no doubt. *Sure* and *certain* are frequently used interchangeably; *sure,* however, is the more subjective term, whereas *certain* may imply belief based on experience or evidence: *"Never teach a child anything of which you are not yourself sure"* (John Ruskin). *"In this world nothing is certain but death and taxes"* (Benjamin Franklin). *Confident* suggests assurance founded on faith or reliance in oneself or in others: *The senator is confident of reelection. Positive* suggests full, emphatic certainty: *The prosecutor had positive proof of the defendant's guilt.* See also Synonyms at **certain.**

sure-fire (sho͝or′fīr′) *adj. Informal.* Bound to be successful or perform as expected: *a sure-fire solution to the problem.*

sure-foot·ed or **sure·foot·ed** (sho͝or′fo͝ot′ĭd) *adj.* **1.a.** Not liable to stumble or fall. **b.** Designed so as to hold well to the road: *an automobile that is sure-footed on curves.* **2.** Confident and capable: *"demonstrates a sure-footed storytelling talent"* (Michiko Kakutani). **—sure′-foot′ed·ly** *adv.* **—sure′-foot′ed·ness** *n.*

sure·ly (sho͝or′lē) *adv.* **1.** With confidence; unhesitatingly. **2.** Undoubtedly; certainly: *You surely can't be serious.* **3.** Without fail: *Slowly but surely spring returns.*

sur·e·ty (sho͝or′ĭ-tē) *n., pl.* **-ties. 1.** The condition of being sure, especially of oneself; self-assurance. **2.** Something beyond doubt; a certainty. **3.** A pledge or formal promise made to secure against loss, damage, or default; a guarantee or security. **4.** One who has contracted to be responsible for another, especially one who assumes responsibilities or debts in the event of default. [Middle English *surte,* from Old French, from Latin *sēcūritās,* from *sēcūrus,* sure. See SECURE.] **—sur′e·ty·ship′** *n.*

surf (sûrf) *n.* The waves of the sea as they break upon a shore or reef. **—surf** *intr.v.* **surfed, surf·ing, surfs.** *Sports.* To engage in surfing. [Origin unknown.] **—surf′y** *adj.*

sur·face (sûr′fəs) *n. Abbr.* **sur. 1.a.** The outer or the topmost boundary of an object. **b.** A material layer constituting such a boundary. **2.** *Mathematics.* **a.** The boundary of a three-dimensional figure. **b.** The two-dimensional locus of points located in three-dimensional space. **c.** A portion of space having length and breadth but no thickness. **3.** The superficial or external aspect: *"a flamboyant, powerful confidence man who lives entirely on the surface of experience"* (Frank Conroy). **4.** An airfoil. **—surface** *adj.* **1.** Relating to, on, or at a surface: *surface algae in the water.* **2.a.** Superficial. **b.** Apparent as opposed to real. **—surface** *v.* **-faced, -fac·ing, -fac·es.** —*tr.* **1.** To form the surface of: *We used asphalt to surface over the driveway.* **2.** To apply a surface to: *surface a road.* **3.** To provide with a surface. —*intr.* **1.** To rise to the surface. **2.** To emerge after concealment. **3.** To work or dig a mine at or near the surface of the ground. **—*idiom.* on the surface.** To all intents and purposes; to all outward appearances: *a soldier who, on the surface, appeared brave and patriotic.* [French : *sur-,* above (from Old French; see SUR–) + *face,* face (from Old French; see FACE).]

sur·face-ac·tive (sûr′fəs-ăk′tĭv) *adj.* Of, relating to, or being a substance capable of reducing the surface tension of a liquid in which it is dissolved. Used especially of detergents.

sur·face-ef·fect ship (sûr′fəs-ĭ-fĕkt′) *n.* A ground-effect vehicle that operates over water.

surface lift *n. Sports.* A ski lift, such as a T-bar, that conveys skiers up a slope without raising them off the ground.

surface of revolution *n., pl.* **surfaces of revolution.** *Mathematics.* A surface generated by revolving a plane curve about an axis in its plane.

surface plate *n.* See **planometer.**

surface tension *n.* **1.** A property of liquids arising from unbalanced molecular cohesive forces at or near the surface, as a result of which the surface tends to contract and has properties resembling those of a stretched elastic membrane. **2.** A measure of this property.

sur·face-to-air missile (sûr′fəs-to͞o-âr′) *n. Abbr.* **SAM** A guided missile launched from the ground against an airborne target.

sur·fac·tant (sər-făk′tənt, sûr′făk′-) *n.* **1.** A surface-active substance. **2.** A substance composed of lipoprotein that is secreted by the alveolar cells of the lung and serves to maintain the stability of pulmonary tissue by reducing the surface tension of fluids that coat the lung. [SURF(ACE)-ACT(IVE) + A(GE)NT.]

surf and turf *n.* Seafood and beefsteak served as the main course of a meal, as in a restaurant.

surf·bird (sûrf′bûrd′) *n.* A shore bird *(Aphriza virgata)* of the Pacific coast of North and South America, having dark, spotted plumage and a black tail with a broad white base.

surf·board (sûrf′bôrd′, -bōrd′) *n. Sports.* A long, narrow, somewhat rounded board, used for surfing.

surfboard

surf·board·er (sûrf′bôr′dər, -bōr′-) *n. Sports.* See **surfer.**

surf·board·ing (sûrf′bôr′dĭng, -bōr′-) *n. Sports.* See **surfing.**

surf·boat (sûrf′bōt′) *n. Nautical.* A strong, seaworthy boat that can be launched or landed in heavy surf.

surf·cast·ing (sûrf′kăs′tĭng) *n.* The activity of fishing from shore, especially by casting one's line into the surf. —**surf′cast′er** *n.*

surf clam *n.* Any of various usually large edible clams of the family Mactridae, commonly living in the surf of coastal waters.

surf duck *n.* A scoter, especially the surf scoter.

sur·feit (sûr′fĭt) *v.* **-feit·ed, -feit·ing, -feits.** —*tr.* To feed or supply to excess, satiety, or disgust. See Synonyms at **satiate.** —*intr. Archaic.* To overindulge. —**surfeit** *n.* **1. a.** Overindulgence in food or drink. **b.** The result of such overindulgence; satiety or disgust. **2.** An excessive amount. [Middle English *surfeten,* from *surfait,* excess, from Old French, from past participle of *surfaire,* to overdo : *sur-,* sur- + *faire,* to do (from Latin *facere;* see **dhē-** in Appendix).] —**sur′feit·er** *n.*

surf·er (sûr′fər) *n. Sports.* One who engages in surfing. Also called *surfboarder.*

surf·er's knobs (sûr′fərz) *pl.n.* Tumorlike skin nodules just below the knees, on the tops of the feet, and often on the toes, common among surfers who paddle in a kneeling position. Also called *surfer's knee, surfer's knots.*

surf fish *n.* See **surfperch.**

sur·fi·cial (sər-fĭsh′əl) *adj.* Of, relating to, or occurring on or near the surface of the earth. [SURF(ACE) + (SUPERF)ICIAL.]

surf·ing (sûr′fĭng) *n. Sports.* The sport of riding on the crest or along the tunnel of a wave, especially while standing or lying on a surfboard. Also called *surfboarding.*

surf·perch (sûrf′pûrch′) *n., pl.* **surfperch** or **-perch·es.** Any of various viviparous marine fishes of the family Embiotocidae, found in shallow waters along the North American Pacific coast. Also called *surf fish.*

surf scoter *n.* A North American sea duck *(Melanitta perspicillata),* the male of which is black with a white forehead and nape.

surf·side (sûrf′sīd′) *adj.* Situated or sited at or near the seashore: *surfside parties; a surfside road.*

surg. *abbr.* Surgeon; surgery; surgical.

surge (sûrj) *v.* **surged, surg·ing, surg·es.** —*intr.* **1.** To move in a billowing or swelling manner in or as if in waves. See Synonyms at **rise. 2.** To roll or be tossed about on waves, as a boat. **3.** To move like advancing waves: *The fans surged forward to see the movie star.* **4.** To increase suddenly. Used of electric current or voltage. **5.** *Nautical.* To slip around a windlass. Used of a rope. —*tr. Nautical.* To loosen or slacken (a cable) gradually. —**surge** *n.* **1.** A heavy, billowing, or swelling motion like that of great waves. **2. a.** Wave motion with low height and a shorter period than a swell. **b.** A coastal rise in water level caused by wind. **3.** A sudden onrush: *a surge of joy.* **4.** A sudden, transient increase or oscillation in electric current or voltage. **5.** An instability in the power output of an engine. **6.** *Astronomy.* A brief, violent disturbance occurring during the eruption of a solar flare. **7.** *Nautical.* **a.** The part of a windlass into which the cable surges. **b.** A temporary release or slackening of a cable. [Probably French *sourdre, sourge-* (from Old French) and French *surgir,* to rise (from Old French, to cast anchor, from Old Catalan), both from Latin *surgere,* to rise : *sub-,* from below; see SUB– + *regere,* to lead straight; see **reg-** in Appendix.]

sur·geon (sûr′jən) *n. Abbr.* **surg.** A physician specializing in surgery. [Middle English *surgien,* from Anglo-Norman, short for Old French *cirurgien,* from *cirurgie,* surgery. See SURGERY.]

sur·geon·fish (sûr′jən-fĭsh′) *n., pl.* **surgeonfish** or **-fish·es.** Any of various bright-colored tropical marine fishes of the family Acanthuridae, having one or more sharp, erectile spines near the base of the tail. [From its lancetlike spines, which resemble surgeons' instruments.]

Sur·geon General (sûr′jən) *n., pl.* **Surgeons General.** *Abbr.* **SG 1.** The chief general officer in the medical departments of the U.S. Army, Navy, or Air Force. **2.** The chief medical officer in the U.S. Public Health Service or in a state public health service.

sur·geon's knot (sûr′jənz) *n., pl.* **surgeons' knots.** Any of several knots, especially one similar to a square knot, used in surgery for tying ligatures or stitching incisions.

sur·ger·y (sûr′jə-rē) *n., pl.* **-ies.** *Abbr.* **surg. 1.** The branch of medicine that deals with the diagnosis and treatment of injury, deformity, and disease by manual and instrumental means. **2.** A surgical operation or procedure, especially one involving the removal or replacement of a diseased organ or tissue. **3.** An operating room or a laboratory of a surgeon or of a hospital's surgical staff. **4.** The skill or work of a surgeon. **5.** *Chiefly British.* **a.** A physician's, dentist's, or veterinarian's office. **b.** The period during which a physician, dentist, or veterinarian consults with or treats patients in the office. [Middle English *surgerie,* from Old French, short for *cirurgerie,* from *cirurgie,* from Latin *chīrūrgia,* from Greek *kheirourgia,* from *kheirourgos,* working by hand : *kheir,* hand; see **ghesor-** in Appendix + *ergon,* work; see **werg-** in Appendix.]

sur·gi·cal (sûr′jĭ-kəl) *adj. Abbr.* **surg. 1.** Of, relating to, or characteristic of surgeons or surgery. **2.** Used in surgery. **3.** Resulting from or occurring after surgery. [From SURGEON.] —**sur′gi·cal·ly** *adv.*

sur·gi·cen·ter (sûr′jĭ-sĕn′tər) *n.* A surgical facility for operations that do not require hospitalization. [SURGI(CAL) + CENTER.]

Su·ri·ba·chi (so͝or′ə-bä′chē), **Mount.** A volcanic hill on Iwo Jima in the western Pacific Ocean. It is famous for the dramatic photograph of U.S. Marines raising the American flag on its summit on February 23, 1945, after the island was captured from the Japanese.

su·ri·cate (so͝or′ĭ-kāt′) *n.* A small, burrowing, carnivorous mammal *(Suricata suricatta)* of southern Africa, related to the mongoose and having grayish fur and a long tail, which it uses for balance when it stands on its hind legs. Also called *sticktail.* [French, from obsolete Dutch *surikat,* macaque, probably of South African origin.]

su·ri·mi (sə-rē′mē, so͞o-) *n.* Minced, processed fish used in the preparation of imitation seafood, especially imitation crabmeat, lobster, and scallops. [Japanese, from *suru,* to process, mash.]

Su·ri·na·me (sü′rē-nä′mə) also **Su·ri·nam** (so͝or′ə-năm′, -näm′). Formerly **Dutch Gui·a·na** (dŭch gē-ăn′ə, -ä′nə, gī-). *Abbr.* **Sur.** A country of northeast South America on the Atlantic Ocean. First colonized by the British, the region was ceded to the Dutch in 1667 and became an autonomous territory of the Netherlands in 1954. Full independence was achieved in 1975. Paramaribo is the capital and the largest city. Population, 354,860. —**Su′ri·na·mese′** (-nä-mēz′, -mēs′) *adj. & n.*

Suriname River also **Surinam River.** A river of Suriname flowing about 644 km (400 mi) northward to the Atlantic Ocean.

sur·ly (sûr′lē) *adj.* **-li·er, -li·est. 1.** Sullenly ill-humored; gruff. **2.** *Obsolete.* Arrogant; domineering. [Middle English *sirly,* masterful, lordly, from *sir,* lord. See SIR.] —**sur′li·ly** *adv.* —**sur′li·ness** *n.*

WORD HISTORY: The fact that the word *surly* means "churlish" nicely indicates its fall in status. *Churlish* derives from the word *churl,* which in its Old English form *ceorl* meant "a man without rank, a member of the lowest rank of freemen," as well as "peasant" in general. In Old English *ceorl* may have been a term of contempt; it certainly became one in Middle English, where *cherl* meant "base fellow, boor," with *churlish* descending in meaning accordingly. *Surly,* on the other hand, started its life at the top of the scale but fell just as far. Looking at instances of this word in Middle English and Early Modern English, we see that *surly* was only one spelling for this word, another spelling being *sirly,* which makes it clear that it came from the word *sir,* the term of honor for a knight or for a person of rank or importance in general. Thus *sirly,* the form under which the early spellings of the word are entered in the *Oxford English Dictionary,* first meant "lordly." *Surly,* entered as a separate word in the *OED* and first recorded in 1566, meant perhaps "lordly, majestic," in its earliest use, subsequently being used in the sense "masterful, imperious, arrogant." As the gloss "arrogant" makes clear, the word *sirly* could have a negative sense, and it is this area of meaning that is responsible for the current "churlish" sense of the word.

sur·mise (sər-mīz′) *v.* **-mised, -mis·ing, -mis·es.** —*tr.* To infer (something) without sufficiently conclusive evidence. —*intr.* To make a guess or conjecture. See Synonyms at **conjecture.** —**surmise** *n.* An idea or opinion based on insufficiently conclusive evidence; a conjecture. [Middle English *surmisen,* to accuse, from Old French *surmise,* feminine past participle of *surmettre* : *sur-,* sur- + *mettre,* to put (from Latin *mittere*).]

sur·mount (sər-mount′) *tr.v.* **-mount·ed, -mount·ing, -mounts. 1.** To overcome (an obstacle, for example); conquer. **2.** To ascend to the top of; climb. **3. a.** To place something above; top. **b.** To be above or on top of: *The church steeple surmounts the square.* **4.** *Obsolete.* To surpass or exceed in amount. [Middle English *surmonten,* from Old French *surmonter* : *sur-,* sur- + *monter,* to mount; see MOUNT[1].] —**sur·mount′a·ble** *adj.* —**sur·mount′er** *n.*

sur·mul·let (sər-mŭl′ĭt, sûr′mŭl′-) *n., pl.* **surmullet** or **-lets.** See **goatfish.** [French *surmulet,* from Old French *sormulet* : probably *sor,* reddish brown (of Germanic origin) + *mulet,* mullet; see MULLET.]

sur·name (sûr′nām′) *n.* **1.** A name shared in common to identify the members of a family, as distinguished from each member's given name. Also called *family name.* **2.** A nickname or an epithet added to a person's name. —**surname** *tr.v.* **-named, -nam·ing, -names.** To give a surname to. [Middle English, partial translation of Old French *surnom* : *sur-,* sur- + *nom,* name.]

sur·pass (sər-păs′) *tr.v.* **-passed, -pass·ing, -pass·es. 1.** To be beyond the limit, powers, or capacity of; transcend: *misery that surpasses comprehension.* **2.** To be or go beyond, as in degree or quality; exceed. See Synonyms at **excel.** [French *surpasser,* from Old French, to transgress : *sur-,* sur- + *passer,* pass; see PASS.]

sur·pass·ing (sər-păs′ĭng) *adj.* Exceptional; exceeding: *monuments of surpassing splendor.* —**sur·pass′ing·ly** *adv.*

sur·plice (sûr′plĭs) *n.* A loose-fitting, white ecclesiastical gown with wide sleeves, worn over a cassock. [Middle English *surplis,* from Anglo-Norman *surpliz,* variant of Old French *sourpeliz,* from Medieval Latin *superpellīcium* : Latin *super-,* super- + Medieval Latin *pellīcium,* fur coat (from Latin, neuter of *pellīcius,* made of skin, from *pellis,* skin; see **pel-**[3] in Appendix).]

sur·plus (sûr′pləs, -plŭs′) *adj. Abbr.* **s., sur.** Being more than or in excess of what is needed or required: *surplus grain.* See Synonyms at **superfluous.** —**surplus** *n.* **1.** An amount or a quantity in excess of what is needed. **2.** *Accounting.* **a.** Total

surfcasting

Suriname

surplice

ă pat	oi boy
ā pay	ou out
âr care	o͝o took
ä father	o͞o boot
ĕ pet	ŭ cut
ē be	ûr urge
ĭ pit	th thin
ī pie	*th* this
îr pier	hw which
ŏ pot	zh vision
ō toe	ə about, item
ô paw	♦ regionalism

Stress marks: ′ (primary); ′ (secondary), as in **dictionary** (dĭk′shə-nĕr′ē)

Mary Surratt
19th-century mezzotint

surrealism
The False Mirror,
1928, by René Magritte
The Museum of Modern Art, New York. Purchase. Oil on canvas, 21¼" × 31⅞"

assets minus the sum of all liabilities. **b.** Excess of a corporation's net assets over the face value of its capital stock. **c.** Excess of receipts over expenditures. [Middle English, an excess, surplus, from Old French, an excess, from Medieval Latin *superplūs* : Latin *super-*, super- + Latin *plūs*, more; see **pelə-**[1] in Appendix.]

sur·plus·age (sûr′plə-sĭj) *n.* **1.** Surplus; excess. **2.** An excess of words; verbiage. **3.** *Law.* Irrelevant matter in a pleading.

surplus value *n.* The difference between the value of the product produced by labor and the actual price of labor as paid out in wages in Marxian analysis of capitalism.

sur·print (sûr′prĭnt′) *tr.v.* **-print·ed, -print·ing, -prints. 1.** To overprint. **2.** To superimpose (a second negative) on a previously printed image of the first negative. **—sur′print′** *n.*

sur·pris·al (sər-prī′zəl) *n.* The act of surprising or the state of being surprised.

sur·prise also **sur·prize** (sər-prīz′) *—tr.v.* **-prised, -pris·ing, -pris·es** also **-prized, -priz·ing, -priz·es. 1.** To encounter suddenly or unexpectedly; take or catch unawares. **2.** To attack or capture suddenly and without warning. **3.** To cause to feel wonder, astonishment, or amazement, as at something unanticipated. **4.a.** To cause (someone) to do or say something unintended. **b.** To elicit or detect through surprise. *—n.* **1.** The act of surprising or the condition of being surprised. **2.** Something, such as an unexpected encounter, event, or gift, that surprises. [Middle English *surprisen*, to overcome, from Old French *surprise*, feminine past participle of *surprendre*, to surprise : *sur-*, sur- + *prendre*, to take (from Latin *prehendere, prendere*, to seize; see **ghend-** in Appendix).] **—sur·pris′er** *n.* **—sur·pris′ing** *adj.* **—sur·pris′ing·ly** *adv.*

SYNONYMS: *surprise, astonish, amaze, astound, dumbfound, flabbergast.* These verbs mean to affect a person strongly as being unexpected or unusual. To *surprise* is to fill with often sudden wonder or disbelief as being unanticipated or out of the ordinary: *"Never tell people* how *to do things. Tell them* what *to do and they will surprise you with their ingenuity"* (George S. Patton). *Astonish* suggests overwhelming surprise: *The sight of such an enormous crowd astonished us. Amaze* implies astonishment and often bewilderment: *The violinist's virtuosity has amazed audiences all over the world. Astound* connotes shock, as from something unprecedented in one's experience: *We were astounded at the high cost of traveling in Japan. Dumbfound* adds to *astound* the suggestion of perplexity and often wordlessness: *His denial that he had witnessed the accident dumbfounded me. Flabbergast* is used as a more colorful equivalent of *astound, astonish,* or *amaze*: *"The aldermen . . . were . . . flabbergasted; they were speechless from bewilderment"* (Benjamin Disraeli).

surr. *abbr.* Surrender.

Sur·ratt (sə-răt′), **Mary Eugenia Jenkins.** 1820?–1865. American alleged conspirator in Abraham Lincoln's assassination. She was convicted as a conspirator and executed along with three others, although it now appears that she knew nothing about the plot to kill the President.

sur·re·al (sə-rē′əl) *adj.* **1.** Having qualities attributed to or associated with surrealism: *"grim, surreal political critiques"* (Lloyd Rose). **2.** Having an oddly dreamlike quality. [Back-formation from SURREALISM.] **—sur·re′al·ly** *adv.*

sur·re·al·ism (sə-rē′ə-lĭz′əm) *n.* **1.** A 20th-century literary and artistic movement that attempts to express the workings of the subconscious and is characterized by fantastic imagery and incongruous juxtaposition of subject matter. **2.** Literature or art produced in this style. [French *surréalisme* : *sur-*, beyond (from Old French; see SUR–) + *réalisme*, realism (from *réalité*, reality, from Medieval Latin *reālitās*, from *reālis*, real; see REAL[1]).] **—sur·re′al·ist** *n.*

sur·re·al·is·tic (sə-rē′ə-lĭs′tĭk) *adj.* **1.** Of or relating to surrealism. **2.** Having an oddly dreamlike or unreal quality. **—sur·re′al·is′ti·cal·ly** *adv.*

sur·re·but·ter (sûr′rĭ-bŭt′ər) also **sur·re·but·tal** (-bŭt′l) *n. Law.* A plaintiff's reply to a defendant's rebuttal.

sur·re·join·der (sûr′rĭ-join′dər) *n. Law.* A plaintiff's reply to a defendant's rejoinder.

sur·ren·der (sə-rĕn′dər) *v.* **-dered, -der·ing, -ders.** *—tr.* **1.** To relinquish possession or control of to another because of demand or compulsion. **2.** To give up in favor of another. **3.** To give up or give back (something that has been granted): *surrender a contractual right.* **4.** To give up or abandon: *surrender all hope.* **5.** To give over or resign (oneself) to something, as to an emotion: *surrendered himself to grief.* **6.** *Law.* To restore (an estate, for example), especially to give up (a lease) before expiration of the term. *—intr.* To give oneself up, as to an enemy. **—surrender** *n. Abbr.* **surr. 1.** The act or an instance of surrendering. **2.** *Law.* **a.** The delivery of a prisoner, fugitive from justice, or other principal in a suit into legal custody. **b.** The act of surrendering or of being surrendered to bail. **c.** Restoration of an estate. [Middle English *surrenderen*, from Old French *surrendre* : *sur-*, sur- + *rendre*, to deliver; see RENDER.]

SYNONYMS: *surrender, submission, capitulation.* These nouns denote the act of giving up one's person, one's possessions, or people under one's command to the authority, power, or control of another. *Surrender* is the most general: *"No terms except unconditional and immediate surrender can be accepted"* (Ulysses S. Grant). *Submission* stresses the subordination of the side that has yielded: *"Our cruel and unrelenting enemy leaves us only the choice of brave resistance, or the most abject submission"* (George Washington). *Capitulation* implies surrender under specific prearranged conditions: *Lack of food and ammunition forced the commander of the rebels to consider a capitulation.* See also Synonyms at **relinquish.**

sur·rep·ti·tious (sûr′əp-tĭsh′əs) *adj.* **1.** Obtained, done, or made by clandestine or stealthy means. **2.** Acting with or marked by stealth. See Synonyms at **secret.** [Middle English, from Latin *surreptīcius*, from *surreptus*, past participle of *surripere*, to take away secretly : *sub-*, secretly; see SUB– + *rapere*, to seize; see **rep-** in Appendix.] **—sur′rep·ti′tious·ly** *adv.* **—sur′rep·ti′tious·ness** *n.*

sur·rey (sûr′ē, sŭr′ē) *n., pl.* **-reys.** A four-wheeled horse-drawn pleasure carriage having two or four seats. [Short for *Surrey cart*, after *Surrey*, a county of southeast England.]

Sur·rey (sûr′ē, sŭr′ē). A historical region of southeast England. Dominated by Mercia and Wessex in Anglo-Saxon times, it was overrun by the Danes in the ninth century.

Surrey, Earl of. See Henry **Howard.**

sur·ro·ga·cy (sûr′ə-gə-sē, sŭr′-) *n., pl.* **-cies. 1.** The condition of being a surrogate, especially a surrogate mother. **2.** *Law.* The office of a surrogate.

sur·ro·gate (sûr′ə-gĭt, -gāt′, sŭr′-) *n.* **1.** One that takes the place of another; a substitute. **2.a.** A person or an animal that functions as a substitute for another, as in a social or family role. **b.** A surrogate mother. **3.** *Psychology.* A figure of authority who takes the place of the father or mother in a person's unconscious or emotional life. **4.** *Law.* A judge in New York and some other states having jurisdiction over the probate of wills and the settlement of estates. **—surrogate** *adj.* Substitute. **—surrogate** (-gāt′) *tr.v.* **-gat·ed, -gat·ing, -gates. 1.** To put in the place of another, especially as a successor; replace. **2.** To appoint (another) as a replacement for oneself. [Middle English, from Latin *surrogātus*, past participle of *surrogāre*, to substitute, variant of *subrogāre*. See SUBROGATE.]

surrogate mother *n.* **1.** A woman who is paid to bear a child for another woman, either through artificial insemination by the other woman's husband, or by carrying until birth the other woman's surgically implanted fertilized egg. **2.** One that acts as, serves as, or is a mother substitute. **—surrogate motherhood** *n.*

sur·round (sə-round′) *tr.v.* **-round·ed, -round·ing, -rounds. 1.** To extend on all sides of simultaneously; encircle. **2.** To enclose or confine on all sides so as to bar escape or outside communication. **—surround** *n.* **1.** Something, such as fencing or a border, that surrounds: *a fireplace surround.* **2.a.** The area around a thing or place: *inflammation extending to the surround of the eye.* **b.** Surroundings; environment: *"It was the country, the flat agricultural surround, that so ravished me"* (Listener). **3.** A method of hunting wild animals by surrounding them and driving them to a place from which they cannot escape. [Middle English *surrounden*, to inundate, from Old French *suronder*, from Late Latin *superundāre* : Latin *super-*, super- + Latin *undāre*, to rise in waves (from *unda*, wave; see **wed-**[1] in Appendix).]

SYNONYMS: *surround, circle, compass, encircle, encompass, environ, gird, girdle, ring.* The central meaning shared by these verbs is "to lie around and bound on all sides": *a city surrounded by suburbs; a crown circling a king's head; a mountain peak compassed by fog; a belt encircling her waist; a lake that encompasses an island; oases environed by the desert; a castle girded by a moat; gardens girdling a bird bath; a dinner table ringed with guests.*

sur·round·ings (sə-roun′dĭngz) *pl.n.* The external circumstances, conditions, and objects that affect existence and development; the environment.

sur·tax (sûr′tăks′) *n.* **1.** An additional tax. **2.** A tax levied on corporations or individuals after net income has exceeded a certain level. **—surtax** *tr.v.* **-taxed, -tax·ing, -tax·es.** To levy a surtax on.

sur·ti·tle (sûr′tīt′l) *n.* See **supertitle.**

sur·veil (sər-vāl′) *tr.v.* **-veilled, -veil·ling, -veils.** *Usage Problem.* To keep under surveillance. [Back-formation from SURVEILLANCE.]

USAGE NOTE: *Surveil* has encountered the same kind of critical resistance that was once accorded to other back-formations such as *diagnose* and *donate.* It remains to be seen whether it too will eventually come to be regarded as useful and unexceptionable.

sur·veil·lance (sər-vā′ləns) *n.* **1.** Close observation of a person or group, especially one under suspicion. **2.** The act of observing or the condition of being observed.

sur·veil·lant (sər-vā′lənt) *adj.* Exercising surveillance. **—surveillant** *n.* One that exercises surveillance. [French, present participle of *surveiller*, to watch over : *sur-*, over (from Old French; see SUR–) + *veiller*, to watch (from Old French *veillier*, from Latin *vigilāre*, from *vigil*, watchful; see **weg-** in Appendix).]

sur·vey (sər-vā′, sûr′vā′) *v.* **-veyed, -vey·ing, -veys.** *—tr.* **1.** To examine or look at in a comprehensive way. **2.** To inspect carefully; scrutinize: *"Two women were surveying the other peo-*

ă pat	oi boy
ā pay	ou out
âr care	ŏŏ took
ä father	ōō boot
ĕ pet	ŭ cut
ē be	ûr urge
ĭ pit	th thin
ī pie	*th* this
îr pier	hw which
ŏ pot	zh vision
ō toe	ə about, item
ô paw	♦ regionalism

Stress marks: ′ (primary); ′ (secondary), as in **dictionary** (dĭk′shə-nĕr′ē)

ple on the platform" (Thomas Wolfe). See Synonyms at **see[1]**. **3.** To determine the boundaries, area, or elevations of (land or structures on the earth's surface) by means of measuring angles and distances, using the techniques of geometry and trigonometry. **4.** *Chiefly British.* To inspect and determine the structural condition of (a building). **5.** To conduct a statistical survey on. **6.** To range one's gaze leisurely over. —*intr.* To make a survey. **—survey** (sûr′vā′) *n., pl.* **-veys. 1.** A detailed inspection or investigation. **2.** A general or comprehensive view. **3.a.** The process of surveying. **b.** A report on or map of what has been surveyed. [Middle English *surveien,* from Old French *surveeir,* from Medieval Latin *supervidēre* : Latin *super-,* super- + Latin *vidēre,* to look; see **weid-** in Appendix.] **—sur·vey′or** *n.*

survey course *n.* An academic course consisting of an overview of a broad topic or field of knowledge.

sur·vey·ing (sər-vā′ĭng) *n.* The measurement of dimensional relationships, as of horizontal distances, elevations, directions, and angles, on the earth's surface especially for use in locating property boundaries, construction layout, and mapmaking.

sur·vey·or's level (sər-vā′ərz) *n., pl.* **surveyors' levels.** An instrument having a telescope and attached spirit level mounted on a tripod and rotating around a vertical axis.

sur·viv·a·ble (sər-vī′və-bəl) *adj.* **1.** Capable of surviving: *survivable organisms in a hostile environment.* **2.** That can be survived: *a survivable, but very serious, illness.* **—sur·viv′a·bil′i·ty** *n.*

sur·viv·al (sər-vī′vəl) *n.* **1.a.** The act or process of surviving. **b.** The fact of having survived. **2.** Something, such as an ancient custom or belief, that has survived. —*attributive.* Often used to modify another noun: *survival techniques; survival equipment.*

sur·vi·val·ist (sər-vī′və-lĭst) *n.* One who has personal or group survival as a primary goal in the face of difficulty, opposition, and especially the threat of natural catastrophe, nuclear war, or societal collapse.

survival of the fittest *n.* Natural selection conceived of as a struggle for life in which only those organisms best adapted to existing conditions are able to survive and reproduce.

sur·vive (sər-vīv′) *v.* **-vived, -viv·ing, -vives.** —*intr.* To remain alive or in existence. —*tr.* **1.** To live longer than; outlive: *She survived her husband by five years.* **2.** To live or persist through: *plants that can survive frosts.* See Synonyms at **outlive.** [Middle English *surviven,* from Old French *sourvivre,* from Latin *supervīvere* : *super-,* super- + *vīvere,* to live; see **g^{w}ei-** in Appendix.] **—sur·vi′vor** *n.*

sur·vi·vor·ship (sər-vī′vər-shĭp′) *n.* **1.** *Law.* The right of a person who survives a partner or joint owner to the entire ownership of something that was previously owned jointly. **2.** The condition of being a survivor.

Su·sa (so͞o′sə, -zə). A ruined city of southwest Iran south of Hamaden. It was the capital of the kingdom of Elam and a capital of the Persian Empire under Cyrus the Great.

Su·sah or **Su·sa** (so͞o′sə, -zə). See **Sousse.**

Su·san B. An·tho·ny Day (so͞o′zən bē′ ăn′thə-nē) *n.* February 15, observed in the United States in commemoration of the birth in 1820 of the women's suffrage leader and feminist Susan B. Anthony.

Su·san·na (so͞o-zăn′ə). In the Apocrypha, a captive in Babylon who was falsely accused of adultery and was rescued by Daniel.

sus·cep·tance (sə-sĕp′təns) *n.* *Electronics.* The imaginary part of the complex representation of admittance. [*(electric) suscept(ibility),* a measure of the ease of polarization of a dielectric + -ANCE.]

sus·cep·ti·bil·i·ty (sə-sĕp′tə-bĭl′ĭ-tē) *n., pl.* **-ties. 1.** The quality or condition of being susceptible. **2.** The capacity to be affected by deep emotions or strong feelings; sensitivity. **3. susceptibilities.** Sensibilities; feelings.

sus·cep·ti·ble (sə-sĕp′tə-bəl) *adj.* **1.** Easily influenced or affected: *"She suddenly was too susceptible to her past"* (Jimmy Breslin). **2.** Likely to be affected with: *susceptible to colds.* **3.** Especially sensitive; highly impressionable. **4.** Capable of accepting or permitting: *susceptible of proof.* [Late Latin *susceptibilis,* from Latin *susceptus,* past participle of *suscipere,* to receive : *sub-,* from below; see SUB- + *capere,* to take; see **kap-** in Appendix.] **—sus·cep′ti·ble·ness** *n.* **—sus·cep′ti·bly** *adv.*

sus·cep·tive (sə-sĕp′tĭv) *adj.* **1.** Receptive. **2.** Susceptible. **—sus·cep′tive·ness, sus·cep·tiv′i·ty** *n.*

su·shi (so͞o′shē) *n.* Small cakes of cold cooked rice wrapped in seaweed, dressed with vinegar, and topped or wrapped with slices of raw or cooked fish, egg, or vegetables. [Japanese.]

Su·si·a·na (so͞o′zē-ä′nə, -ăn′ə). See **Elam.**

sus·lik (sŭs′lĭk) also **sous·lik** (so͞os′-) *n.* **1.** Any of several ground squirrels of Europe and Asia, especially the small grayish European species *Citellus citellus.* **2.** The pelt or fur of this animal. [Russian, from Old Russian *susolu.*]

sus·pect (sə-spĕkt′) *v.* **-pect·ed, -pect·ing, -pects.** —*tr.* **1.** To surmise to be true or probable; imagine: *I suspect they are very disappointed.* **2.** To have doubts about; distrust: *I suspect his motives.* **3.** To think (a person) guilty without proof: *The police suspect her of murder.* —*intr.* To have suspicion. **—suspect** (sŭs′pĕkt′) *n.* One who is suspected, especially of having committed a crime. **—suspect** (sŭs′pĕkt′, sə-spĕkt′) *adj.* Open to or viewed with suspicion: *a suspect policy; suspect motives.* [Middle English *suspecten,* from Old French *suspecter,* from Latin *suspectāre,* frequentative of *suspicere,* to look up at, suspect : *su-, sub-,* from below; see SUB- + *specere,* to look at; see **spek-** in Appendix.]

sus·pend (sə-spĕnd′) *v.* **-pend·ed, -pend·ing, -pends.** —*tr.* **1.** To bar for a period from a privilege, office, or position, usually as a punishment: *suspend a student from school.* **2.** To cause to stop for a period; interrupt: *suspended the trial.* **3.a.** To hold in abeyance; defer: *suspend judgment.* See Synonyms at **defer[1]**. **b.** To render temporarily ineffective: *suspend a jail sentence; suspend all parking regulations.* **4.** To hang so as to allow free movement: *suspended the mobile from the ceiling.* **5.** To support or keep from falling without apparent attachment, as by buoyancy: *suspend oneself in the water.* —*intr.* **1.** To cease for a period; delay. **2.** To fail to make payments or meet obligations. [Middle English *suspenden,* from Old French *suspendre,* from Latin *suspendere* : *sub-,* from below; see SUB- + *pendere,* to hang; see **(s)pen-** in Appendix.]

surveyor's level

sus·pend·ed animation (sə-spĕn′dĭd) *n.* A temporary state of interrupted breathing and loss of consciousness resembling death, caused especially by asphyxia.

sus·pend·er (sə-spĕn′dər) *n.* **1.** One, such as a hook, that suspends something else. **2.** An often elastic strap worn over the shoulders to support trousers. Often used in the plural. **3.** *Chiefly British.* A garter.

sus·pense (sə-spĕns′) *n.* **1.** The condition of being physically suspended. **2.a.** The state or quality of being undecided, uncertain, or doubtful. **b.** Pleasurable excitement and anticipation regarding an outcome, such as the ending of a mystery novel. **3.** Anxiety or apprehension resulting from an uncertain, undecided, or mysterious situation. [Middle English, from Old French *suspens,* from Latin *suspēnsus,* past participle of *suspendere,* to suspend. See SUSPEND.] **—sus·pense′ful** *adj.*

suspender
A pair of suspenders

suspense account *n.* A temporary account in which entries of credits or charges are made until their proper disposition can be determined.

sus·pen·sion (sə-spĕn′shən) *n.* **1.** The act of suspending or the condition of being suspended, especially: **a.** A temporary abrogation or deferment. **b.** A debarment, as from office or privilege. **c.** A postponement of judgment, opinion, or decision. See Synonyms at **pause. 2.** *Music.* **a.** The prolongation of one or more tones of a chord into a following chord to create a temporary dissonance. **b.** The tone so prolonged. **3.** A device from which a mechanical part is suspended. **4.** The system of springs and other devices that insulates the chassis of a vehicle from shocks transmitted through the wheels. **5.** *Chemistry.* A relatively coarse, noncolloidal dispersion of solid particles in a liquid.

suspension bridge *n.* A bridge having the roadway suspended from cables that are anchored at either end and usually supported at intervals by towers.

suspension point *n.* One of a series of dots, usually three, used to indicate an incomplete statement or the omission of a word or words from a written text. Often used in the plural.

sus·pen·sive (sə-spĕn′sĭv) *adj.* **1.** Serving or tending to suspend or temporarily stop something. **2.** Characterized by or causing suspense. **—sus·pen′sive·ly** *adv.* **—sus·pen′sive·ness** *n.*

suspension
From Bach's Fourth Fugue

sus·pen·sor (sə-spĕn′sər) *n.* **1.** *Botany.* A multicellular filamentous structure developed from a zygote in seed-bearing plants and connecting the embryo to the endosperm. **2.** An athletic supporter. [New Latin *suspēnsor,* one that suspends, from Latin *suspēnsus,* past participle of *suspendere,* to suspend. See SUSPEND.]

sus·pen·so·ry (sə-spĕn′sə-rē) *adj.* **1.** Supporting or suspending: *a suspensory bandage.* **2.** Delaying completion. **—suspensory** *n., pl.* **-ries. 1.** A support or truss. **2.** An athletic supporter.

suspensory ligament *n.* A ligament that supports an organ or a body part, especially a fibrous membrane that holds the lens of the eye in place.

sus·pi·cion (sə-spĭsh′ən) *n.* **1.** The act of suspecting something, especially something wrong, on little evidence or without proof. **2.** The condition of being suspected, especially of wrongdoing. **3.** A state of uncertainty; doubt. See Synonyms at **uncertainty. 4.** A minute amount; trace. **—suspicion** *tr.v.* **-cioned, -cion·ing, -cions.** *Non-Standard.* To suspect. [Middle English, alteration (influenced by Old French *suspicion,* from Latin *suspīciō, suspīciōn-,* from *suspicere,* to watch) of *suspecioun,* from Anglo-Norman, variant of Old French *sospeçon,* from Latin *suspectiō, suspectiōn-,* from *suspectus,* past participle of *suspicere,* to watch. See SUSPECT.] **—sus·pi′cion·al** *adj.*

sus·pi·cious (sə-spĭsh′əs) *adj.* **1.** Arousing or apt to arouse suspicion: *suspicious behavior.* **2.** Tending to suspect; distrustful: *a suspicious nature.* **3.** Expressing suspicion: *a suspicious look.* **—sus·pi′cious·ly** *adv.* **—sus·pi′cious·ness** *n.*

sus·pire (sə-spīr′) *intr.v.* **-pired, -pir·ing, -pires. 1.** To breathe: *"And from that one intake of fire/All creatures still warmly suspire"* (Robert Frost). **2.** To sigh. [Middle English *suspiren,* to sigh, from Old French, from Latin *suspīrāre* : *sub-,* from below; see SUB- + *spīrāre,* to breathe.] **—sus′pi·ra′tion** (sŭs′pə-rā′shən) *n.*

suspension bridge
San Francisco–Oakland Bay Bridge

Sus·que·han·na (sŭs′kwə-hăn′ə) *n., pl.* **Susquehanna** or **-nas.** See **Susquehannock** (sense 1).

Susquehanna River. A river of the northeast United States rising in central New York and flowing about 714 km (444 mi)

Joan Sutherland

swage
Early 19th-century American swage (*top*) used to form relief design of a bird on the bowl of a spoon (*bottom*)

south through eastern Pennsylvania and northeast Maryland to Chesapeake Bay.

Sus·que·han·nock (sŭs′kwə-hăn′ək) *n., pl.* **Susquehannock** or **-nocks. 1.a.** A Native American people formerly located along the Susquehanna River in New York, Pennsylvania, and Maryland. The Susquehanna were extinct by 1763. **b.** A member of this people. Also called *Conestoga, Susquehanna.* **2.** The Iroquoian language of the Susquehannock.

suss (sŭs) *tr.v.* **sussed, suss·ing, suss·es.** *Slang.* **1.** To infer or discover; figure out: *"I think I'm good at sussing out what's going on"* (Ry Cooder). **2.** To size up; study: *"Suss out the designers in whom you are interested"* (Lucia van der Post). [Probably short for SUSPECT.]

Sus·sex (sŭs′ĭks). An Anglo-Saxon kingdom of southern England bordering on the English Channel. Founded in the fifth century A.D., it was captured by the kingdom of Wessex in 825.

Sussex spaniel *n.* A strong, stocky dog of a breed developed in Sussex, a county of southeast England, having long ears, short legs, and a silky golden-brown coat.

sus·tain (sə-stān′) *tr.v.* **-tained, -tain·ing, -tains. 1.** To keep in existence; maintain. **2.** To supply with necessities or nourishment; provide for. **3.** To support from below; keep from falling or sinking; prop. **4.** To support the spirits, vitality, or resolution of; encourage. **5.** To bear up under; withstand: *can't sustain the blistering heat.* **6.** To experience or suffer: *sustained a fatal injury.* See Synonyms at **experience. 7.** To affirm the validity of: *The judge has sustained the prosecutor's objection.* **8.** To prove or corroborate; confirm. **9.** To keep up (a joke or an assumed role, for example) competently. [Middle English *sustenen,* from Old French *sustenir,* from Latin *sustinēre* : *sub-,* from below; see SUB– + *tenēre,* to hold; see **ten-** in Appendix.] **—sus·tain′a·bil′i·ty** *n.* **—sus·tain′a·ble** *adj.* **—sus·tain′er** *n.* **—sus·tain′ment** *n.*

sus·tained yield (sə-stānd′) *n.* **1.** The continuing yield of a biological resource, such as timber from a forest, by controlled periodic harvesting. **2.** The quantity of a resource harvested in this manner.

sus·tain·ing pedal (sə-stā′nĭng) *n.* The right pedal of a piano, which stops the action of the dampers and allows the strings to vibrate freely. Also called *loud pedal, reverberation pedal.*

sustaining program *n.* A radio or television program that is supported by the station or network on which it appears and that has no commercial announcements.

sus·te·nance (sŭs′tə-nəns) *n.* **1.a.** The act of sustaining. **b.** The condition of being sustained. **2.** The supporting of life or health; maintenance: *"to deliver in every morning six beeves, forty sheep, and other victuals for my sustenance"* (Jonathan Swift). **3.** Something, especially food, that sustains life or health. **4.** Means of livelihood. See Synonyms at **livelihood.** [Middle English, from Old French, from *sustenir,* to sustain. See SUSTAIN.]

sus·ten·tac·u·lar (sŭs′tən-tăk′yə-lər, -tĕn-) *adj. Anatomy.* Serving to support: *sustentacular muscle fibers.* [From Late Latin *sustentāculum,* support, from Latin *sustentāre,* to support, frequentative of *sustinēre,* to sustain. See SUSTAIN.]

sustentacular cell *n.* One of the supporting cells of an epithelial membrane or tissue.

sus·ten·ta·tion (sŭs′tən-tā′shən, -tĕn-) *n.* **1.** Something that sustains; a support. **2.** Sustenance. [Middle English, from Old French, from Latin *sustentātiō, sustentātiōn-,* from *sustentātus,* past participle of *sustentāre,* to support. See SUSTENTACULAR.] **—sus′ten·ta′tive** (-tā′tĭv) *adj.*

Su·su (so͞o′so͞o) *n., pl.* **Susu** or **Su·sus. 1.** A member of a West African people inhabiting parts of Guinea and Sierra Leone. **2.** The Mande language of the Susu.

su·sur·ra·tion (so͞o′sə-rā′shən) also **su·sur·rus** (so͞o-sûr′əs, -sŭr′-) *n.* A soft, whispering or rustling sound; a murmur. [Middle English *susurracioun,* from Late Latin *susurrātiō, susurrātiōn-,* from Latin *susurrātus,* past participle of *susurrāre,* to whisper, from *susurrus,* whisper, ultimately of imitative origin.] **—su·sur′rant** (so͞o-sûr′ənt, -sŭr′-), **su·sur′rous** (-sûr′əs, -sŭr′-) *adj.*

Suth·er·land (sŭth′ər-lənd), **Earl Wilbur, Jr.** 1915–1974. American physiologist. He won a 1971 Nobel Prize for research on the function of hormones.

Sutherland, George. 1862–1942. British-born American jurist and politician. He served as a U.S. representative (1901–1903) and senator (1905–1917) from Utah and was an associate justice of the U.S. Supreme Court (1922–1938).

Sutherland, Joan. Born 1926. Australian operatic soprano noted especially for her interpretations of Gaetano Donizetti's *Lucia di Lammermoor* and Vincenzo Bellini's *Norma.*

Sutherland Falls. A waterfall, 581 m (1,904 ft) high, of southwest South Island, New Zealand.

Sut·lej (sŭt′lĕj′). A river, about 1,448 km (900 mi) long, flowing from southwest Xizang (Tibet) through northern India and eastern Pakistan, where it is joined by the Chenab River. It is one of the five rivers of the Punjab.

sut·ler (sŭt′lər) *n.* An army camp follower who peddled provisions to the soldiers. [Obsolete Dutch *soeteler,* from Low German *sudeler, suteler,* from German *sudeln,* to dirty, from Middle High German *sudelen.*]

su·tra (so͞o′trə) *n.* **1.** *Hinduism.* Any of various aphoristic doctrinal summaries produced for memorization generally between 500 and 200 B.C. and later incorporated into Hindu literature. **2.** Also **sut·ta** (so͝ot′ə). *Buddhism.* A scriptural narrative, especially a text traditionally regarded as a discourse of the Buddha. [Sanskrit *sūtram,* thread, sutra. See **syū-** in Appendix.]

sut·tee also **sa·ti** (sŭ-tē′, sŭt′ē′) *n.* **1.** The now illegal act or practice of a Hindu widow's cremating herself on her husband's funeral pyre in order to fulfill her true role as wife. **2.** *pl.* **-tees** also **-tis** A widow who commits such an act. [Sanskrit *satī,* virtuous woman, suttee, feminine of *sant-, sat-,* true, virtuous. See **es-** in Appendix.]

Sut·ter (sŭt′ər), **John Augustus.** 1803–1880. American pioneer, raised in Switzerland. The discovery of gold on his land led to the California gold rush (1848–1849).

Sutt·ner (zo͝ot′nər, so͝ot′-), **Bertha von.** 1843–1914. Austrian pacifist who wrote the novel *Lay Down Your Arms* (1889). She was the first woman to receive the Nobel Peace Prize (1905).

su·ture (so͞o′chər) *n.* **1.a.** The process of joining two surfaces or edges together along a line by or as if by sewing. **b.** The material, such as thread, gut, or wire, that is used in this procedure. **c.** The line so formed. **2.** *Medicine.* **a.** The fine thread or other material used surgically to close a wound or join tissues. **b.** The surgical method used to close a wound or join tissues. **3.** *Anatomy.* The line of junction or an immovable joint between two bones, especially of the skull. **4.** *Biology.* A seamlike joint or line of articulation, such as the line of dehiscence in a dry fruit or the spiral seam marking the junction of whorls of a gastropod shell. **—suture** *tr.v.* **-tured, -tur·ing, -tures.** To join by means of sutures or a suture. [Middle English, from Latin *sūtūra,* from *sūtus,* past participle of *suere,* to sew. See **syū-** in Appendix.] **—su′tur·al** *adj.* **—su′tur·al·ly** *adv.*

Su·va (so͞o′və, -vä). The capital of Fiji, on the southeast coast of Viti Levu. It is a commercial center. Population, 74,000.

Su·vo·rov (so͞o-vôr′əf), Count **Aleksandr Vasilevich.** 1729–1800. Russian field marshal who became famous for his successful campaigns in the Russo-Turkish War (1787–1792).

Su·wan·nee (sə-wä′nē). A river, about 386 km (240 mi) long, flowing from southeast Georgia across northern Florida to the Gulf of Mexico.

Su·won (so͞o′wŭn′). A city of northwest South Korea south of Seoul. It is a textile-manufacturing center. Population, 374,000.

su·ze·rain (so͞o′zər-ən, -zə-rān′) *n.* **1.** A nation that controls another nation in international affairs but allows it domestic sovereignty. **2.** A feudal lord to whom fealty was due. [French, from Old French *suserain* : probably *sus,* up (from Latin *sūrsum, sūsum,* upward, from **subsvorsum,* turned upward : *subs-, sub-,* from under; see SUB– + *vorsum,* neuter of *vorsus,* variant of *versus,* past participle of *vertere,* to turn; see VERSUS) + *souverein,* sovereign; see SOVEREIGN.] **—su′ze·rain** *adj.*

su·ze·rain·ty (so͞o′zər-ən-tē, -zə-rān′tē) *n., pl.* **su·ze·rain·ties.** The power or domain of a suzerain.

Su·zhou (so͞o′jō′) also **Soo·chow** (-chou′, -jō′). A city of eastern China west-northwest of Shanghai. Probably founded before the fifth century B.C., the old walled city was noted for its pagodas and silk manufacturing. Population, 695,500.

SV40 (ĕs′vē-fôr′tē) *n.* A virus that causes cancers in monkeys and that is used widely in genetic and medical research. [*s(imian) v(irus) 40.*]

Sval·bard (sväl′bär′). A Norwegian archipelago comprising Spitsbergen and other islands in the Arctic Ocean north of the mainland. The islands are rich in mineral resources.

svc *abbr.* Service.

Sved·berg (svĕd′bərg, -bĕr′ē), **The.** In full Theodor Svedberg. 1884–1971. Swedish chemist. He won a 1926 Nobel Prize for his work on disperse systems.

svelte (svĕlt) *adj.* **svelt·er, svelt·est.** Slender or graceful in figure or outline; slim. [French, from Italian *svelto,* from past participle of *svellere,* to stretch out, from Vulgar Latin **exvellere,* from Latin *ēvellere* : *ē, ex-,* ex- + *vellere,* to pull.] **—svelte′ly** *adv.* **—svelte′ness** *n.*

Sven·ga·li (svĕn-gä′lē, sfĕn-) *n., pl.* **-lis.** A person who, with evil intent, tries to persuade another to do what is desired: *"a crafty Svengali who lures talented people with grand promises yet gives them little lasting operational authority"* (Chris Welles). [After *Svengali,* the hypnotist villain in the novel *Trilby* by George du Maurier.]

Sverd·lovsk (sfĕrd-lôfsk′, svyĭrd-). A city of west-central Russia in the eastern foothills of the Ural Mountains. Nicholas II and his family may have been executed here (1918) after the Russian Revolution. Population, 1,300,000.

Sver·drup (sfĕr′drəp, svĕr′-, svăr′dro͝op), **Otto Neumann.** 1855–1930. Norwegian explorer who led many expeditions to the Arctic and observed a number of previously unknown islands.

Sver·drup Islands (sfĕr′drəp, svĕr′-). A group of islands of the northern Northwest Territories, Canada, in the Arctic Ocean west of Ellesmere Island.

svgs. *abbr.* Savings.

sw *abbr.* Short wave.

SW *abbr.* **1.** Southwest. **2.** Southwestern.

sw. *abbr.* Switch.

Sw. *abbr.* Swedish.

swab also **swob** (swŏb) *—n.* **1.a.** A small piece of absorbent material attached to the end of a stick or wire and used for cleansing or applying medicine. **b.** A specimen of mucus or other material removed with a swab. **2.** A sponge or patch of absorbent material used to clean the bore of a firearm or cannon. **3.** A mop used for cleaning floors or decks. **4.a.** One who uses such a mop, especially on a ship. **b.** *Slang.* A sailor. Also called *swabbie.* **5.** A lout. —*tr.v.* **swabbed, swab·bing, swabs** also **swobbed, swob·bing, swobs. 1.** To use a swab on. **2.** To clean with a swab. [Back-formation from *swabber,* mop for a ship's deck (from obsolete Dutch **zwabber,* from *zwabben,* to mop) or from obsolete Dutch *swabbe,* mop (from Middle Dutch).]

swab·bie also **swab·by** (swŏb′ē) *n., pl.* **-bies.** *Slang.* See **swab** (sense 4).

Swa·bi·a (swā′bē-ə). A historical region of southwest Germany that originally included parts of present-day France and Switzerland. It was divided into small principalities and fiefdoms after 1268, but its prosperous towns often banded together in defensive leagues, most notably the **Swabian League** of 1488 to 1534. —**Swa′bi·an** *adj. & n.*

swad·dle (swŏd′l) *tr.v.* **-dled, -dling, -dles. 1.** To wrap or bind in bandages; swathe. **2.** To wrap (a baby) in swaddling clothes. **3.** To restrain or restrict. —**swaddle** *n.* A band or cloth used for swaddling. [Middle English *swadlen,* probably back-formation from *swadling (band),* swaddling (cloth), or *swathelbonde,* both from *swathel-,* probably frequentative of Old English *swathian,* to swathe.]

swad·dling clothes (swŏd′lĭng) *pl.n.* **1.** Strips of cloth wrapped around a newborn infant to hold its legs and arms still. **2.** Restrictions imposed on the immature.

swag (swăg) *n.* **1.a.** An ornamental drapery or curtain draped in a curve between two points. **b.** An ornamental festoon of flowers or fruit. **c.** A carving or plaster molding of such an ornament. **2.** *Slang.* Stolen property; loot. **3.** *Australian.* The pack or bundle containing the personal belongings of a swagman. **4.** *Slang.* Herbal tea in a plastic sandwich bag sold as marijuana to an unsuspecting customer. —**swag** *intr.v.* **swagged, swag·ging, swags. 1.** *Chiefly British.* To lurch or sway. **2.** *Australian.* To travel about with a pack or swag. [Probably of Scandinavian origin.]

swage (swāj) *n.* **1.** A tool used in bending or shaping cold metal. **2.** A stamp or die for marking or shaping metal with a hammer. **3.** A swage block. —**swage** *tr.v.* **swaged, swag·ing, swag·es.** To bend or shape by or as if by using a swage. [Middle English, ornamental border, from Old French *souage.*]

swage block *n.* A metal block with holes or grooves for shaping metal objects.

swag·ger (swăg′ər) *v.* **-gered, -ger·ing, -gers.** —*intr.* **1.** To walk or conduct oneself with an insolent or arrogant air; strut. See Synonyms at **strut. 2.** To brag; boast. —*tr.* To browbeat or bully (someone). —**swagger** *n.* **1.** A swaggering movement or gait. **2.** Boastful or conceited expression; braggadocio. [Probably frequentative of SWAG.] —**swag′ger·er** *n.* —**swag′ger·ing·ly** *adv.*

swagger stick *n.* A short metal-tipped cane carried especially by officers in the armed forces.

swag·man (swăg′măn′) *n. Australian.* A man who seeks casual work while traveling about carrying his swag.

Swa·hi·li (swä-hē′lē) *n., pl.* **Swahili** or **-lis. 1.** A member of a predominantly Moslem people inhabiting the coast and islands of eastern Africa from Somalia to Mozambique. **2.** The Bantu language of the Swahili that is the official language of Tanzania and is widely used as a lingua franca in eastern and east-central Africa. In this sense, also called *Kiswahili.* [Swahili, from Arabic *sawāḥilīy,* belonging to the coasts : *sawāḥil,* pl. of *sāḥil,* coast + *-īy,* belonging to.] —**Swa·hi′li·an** *adj.*

swain (swān) *n.* **1.** A country lad, especially a young shepherd. **2.** A beau. [Middle English, young man, servant, from Old Norse *sveinn.* See **s(w)e-** in Appendix.]

Swain·son's hawk (swān′sənz) *n.* A slender hawk *(Buteo swainsoni)* having long, pointed wings, found in the grasslands of the western United States. [After William *Swainson* (1789–1855), British naturalist.]

Swainson's thrush *n.* See **olive-backed thrush.** [After William *Swainson* (1789–1855), British naturalist.]

swale (swāl) *n.* A low tract of land, especially when moist or marshy. [Perhaps from Middle English, shade, perhaps of Scandinavian origin; akin to Old Norse *svalr,* cool.]

swal·low[1] (swŏl′ō) *v.* **-lowed, -low·ing, -lows.** —*tr.* **1.** To cause (food or drink, for example) to pass through the mouth and throat into the stomach. **2.** To put up with (something unpleasant): *swallowed the insults and kept on working.* **3.** To refrain from expressing; suppress: *swallow one's feelings.* **4.** To consume or destroy as if by ingestion; devour: *a building that was swallowed up by fire.* **5.** *Slang.* To believe without question: *swallowed the alibi.* **6.** To take back; retract: *swallow one's words.* —*intr.* To perform the act of swallowing. —**swallow** *n.* **1.** The act of swallowing. **2.** An amount swallowed. **3.** *Nautical.* The channel through which a rope runs in a block or a mooring chock. [Middle English *swalowen,* from Old English *swelgan.* See **swel-** in Appendix.] —**swal′low·er** *n.*

swal·low[2] (swŏl′ō) *n.* **1.** Any of various small, graceful, swift-flying passerine birds of the family Hirundinidae, having long, pointed wings, a usually notched or forked tail, and a large mouth for catching flying insects and noted for their regular migrations in large numbers, often over long distances. **2.** Any of various similar birds, such as a swift. [Middle English *swalowe,* from Old English *swealwe.*]

swal·low·tail (swŏl′ō-tāl′) *n.* **1.a.** The deeply forked tail of a swallow. **b.** Something similar to the tail of a swallow. **2.** *Informal.* A swallow-tailed coat. **3.** Any of various colorful, widely distributed butterflies of the family Papilionidae, usually having an extension at the end of each hind wing that resembles the tails of certain swallows.

swal·low-tailed (swŏl′ō-tāld′) *adj.* **1.** Having a deeply forked tail. Used of various birds. **2.** Resembling the tail of a swallow.

swallow-tailed coat *n.* A man's black coat worn for formal daytime occasions and having a long rounded and split tail. Also called *tailcoat.*

swallow-tailed kite *n.* A raptor *(Elanoides forficatus)* with bold black and white plumage and a deeply forked tail, found along the southeast and Gulf coasts of the United States and common in Florida.

swal·low·wort (swŏl′ō-wûrt′, -wôrt′) *n.* **1.** See **celandine** (sense 1). **2.** Any of several vines of the genus *Cynanchum,* especially *C. nigrum,* native to Europe, having clusters of small brownish-purple flowers. [From the shape of its pod.]

swam (swăm) *v.* Past tense of **swim.**

swa·mi (swä′mē) *n., pl.* **swa·mis. 1.** *Hinduism.* A religious teacher. **2.** A mystic; a yogi. **3.** Used as a form of address for such a person. [Hindi *svāmī,* master, swami, from Sanskrit *svāmī,* nominative sing. of *svāmin-,* being one's own master, possessing proprietary rights. See **s(w)e-** in Appendix.]

Swam·mer·dam (svä′mər-däm′), **Jan.** 1637–1680. Dutch naturalist known for his pioneering microscopic research. He was the first to describe red blood cells (1658).

swamp (swŏmp, swômp) *n.* **1.a.** A seasonally flooded bottomland with more woody plants than a marsh and better drainage than a bog. **b.** A lowland region saturated with water. **2.** A situation or place fraught with difficulties and imponderables: *a corporate swamp; a financial swamp.* —**swamp** *v.* **swamped, swamp·ing, swamps.** —*tr.* **1.** To drench in or cover with or as if with water. **2.** To inundate or burden; overwhelm: *She was swamped with work.* **3.** *Nautical.* To fill (a ship or boat) with water to the point of sinking it. —*intr.* To become full of water or sink. [Perhaps of Low German origin.] —**swamp′i·ness** *n.* —**swamp′y** *adj.*

swamp boat *n. Nautical.* A flat-bottomed boat powered by an airplane propeller projecting above the stern and used in swamps or shallow waters. Also called *airboat.*

swamp·er (swŏm′pər, swôm′-) *n.* **1.** One who lives in or close to a swamp. **2.** One who clears a swamp or forest. **3.a.** A helper, as in a restaurant. **b.** A truck driver's assistant.

swamp fever *n.* **1.** See **malaria** (sense 1). **2.** A viral disease in horses marked by progressive anemia, a staggering gait, and fever. **3.** See **leptospirosis.**

swamp·land (swŏmp′lănd′, swômp′-) *n.* Land of swampy consistency or having many swamps on it.

swamp pink *n.* An orchid *(Arethusa bulbosa)* of northeast North America having a solitary, usually rose-colored flower with a purple-spotted, yellow-crested lip. Also called *arethusa, dragon's mouth.*

swamp potato *n. Botany.* Arrowhead.

swan (swŏn) *n.* **1.** Any of various large aquatic birds of the family Anatidae chiefly of the genera *Cygnus* and *Olor,* having webbed feet, a long slender neck, and usually white plumage. **2. Swan.** See **Cygnus.** —**swan** *intr.v.* **swanned, swan·ning, swans.** *Chiefly British.* To travel around from place to place: *"Swanning around Europe nowadays, are we?"* (Jeffrey Archer). [Middle English, from Old English. See **swen-** in Appendix.]

swan dive *n. Sports.* A dive performed with the legs straight together, the back arched, and the arms stretched out from the sides.

swank (swăngk) *adj.* **swank·er, swank·est. 1.** Imposingly fashionable or elegant; grand. See Synonyms at **fashionable. 2.** Ostentatious; pretentious. —**swank** *n.* **1.** Smartness in style or bearing; elegance. **2.** Swagger. —**swank** *intr.v.* **swanked, swank·ing, swanks.** To act in an ostentatious or pretentious way; swagger. See Synonyms at **strut.** [Perhaps akin to Middle High German *swanken,* to swing.]

swank·y (swăng′kē) *adj.* **-i·er, -i·est.** Swank. —**swank′i·ly** *adv.* —**swank′i·ness** *n.*

♦ **swan·ny** (swŏn′ē) *interj. Chiefly Southern U.S.* Used to express surprise: *Well, I swanny!* [Probably alteration of dialectal *Is' wan ye,* I shall warrant ye.]

Swan River daisy *n.* An Australian plant *(Brachycome iberidifolia)* of the composite family, cultivated for its showy blue, rose, or white flower heads. [After the *Swan,* a river of southwest Australia.]

swan's-down also **swans·down** (swŏnz′doun′) *n.* **1.** The soft down of a swan. **2.** A soft woolen fabric used especially for baby clothes. **3.** Flannelette.

Swan·sea (swän′zē, -sē). A borough of southern Wales west-northwest of Cardiff. It is an industrial port on **Swansea Bay,** an inlet of the Bristol Channel. Population, 188,500.

swan·skin (swŏn′skĭn′) *n.* **1.** The skin of a swan with the feathers attached. **2.** Any of several flannel or cotton fabrics with a soft nap.

Swan·son (swŏn′sən), **Gloria.** 1899–1983. American actress

swallowtail
Black swallowtail butterfly
Papilio polyxenes asterius

swan
Mute swan
Cygnus olor

ă pat	oi boy
ā pay	ou out
âr care	ŏŏ took
ä father	ōō boot
ĕ pet	ŭ cut
ē be	ûr urge
ĭ pit	th thin
ī pie	*th* this
îr pier	hw which
ŏ pot	zh vision
ō toe	ə about, item
ô paw	♦ regionalism

Stress marks: ′ (primary); **′** (secondary), as in **dictionary** (dĭk′shə-nĕr′ē)

who appeared in numerous silent films and later made a heralded comeback in *Sunset Boulevard* (1950).

swan song *n.* **1.** A farewell or final appearance, action, or work. **2.** The beautiful legendary song sung only once by a swan in its lifetime, as it is dying. [From the belief that the swan sings as it dies.]

swap also **swop** (swŏp) *Informal.* —*v.* **swapped, swap·ping, swaps** also **swopped, swop·ping, swops.** —*intr.* To trade one thing for another. —*tr.* To exchange (one thing) for another. —*n.* An exchange of one thing for another. [Middle English *swappen,* to strike, strike the hands together in closing a bargain.] —**swap′per** *n.*

swap meet *n.* An informal gathering for the barter or sale of used articles or handicrafts.

sward (swôrd) also **swarth** (swôrth) *n.* **1.** Land covered with grassy turf. **2.** A lawn or meadow. [Middle English, from Old English *sweard,* skin.]

sware (swâr) *v. Archaic.* A past tense of **swear.**

swarf (swôrf) *n.* Fine metallic filings or shavings removed by a cutting tool. [Of Scandinavian origin; akin to Old Norse *svarf.*]

swarm[1] (swôrm) *n.* **1.** A large number of insects or other small organisms, especially when in motion. **2.** A group of bees with a queen bee in migration to establish a new colony. See Synonyms at **flock[1].** **3.** An aggregation of persons or animals, especially when in turmoil or moving in mass: *A swarm of friends congratulated him.* —**swarm** *v.* **swarmed, swarm·ing, swarms.** —*intr.* **1.a.** To move or emerge in a swarm. **b.** To leave a hive as a swarm. Used of bees. **2.** To move or gather in large numbers. **3.** To be overrun; teem: *a riverbank swarming with insects.* See Synonyms at **teem[1].** —*tr.* To fill with a crowd: *sailors swarming the ship's deck.* [Middle English, group of bees, from Old English *swearm.*] —**swarm′er** *n.*

swastika

swarm[2] (swôrm) *tr. & intr.v.* **swarmed, swarm·ing, swarms.** —*intr.* To climb by gripping with the arms and legs. —*tr.* To climb (something) in this manner. [Origin unknown.]

swarm spore *n.* See **zoospore.**

swart (swôrt) *adj. Archaic.* Swarthy. [Middle English *swarte,* from Old English *sweart.*]

swarth (swôth) *n.* Variant of **sward.**

swarth·y (swôr′thē) *adj.* **-i·er, -i·est.** Having a dark complexion. [Alteration of *swarty,* from SWART.] —**swarth′i·ly** *adv.* —**swarth′i·ness** *n.*

swash (swŏsh, swôsh) *n.* **1.a.** A splash of water or other liquid hitting a solid surface. **b.** The sound of such a splash. **2.a.** A narrow channel through which tides flow. **b.** A bar over which waves wash freely. **3.a.** Swagger or bluster. **b.** A swaggering or blustering person. —**swash** *v.* **swashed, swash·ing, swash·es.** —*intr.* **1.** To strike, move, or wash with a splashing sound. **2.** To swagger. —*tr.* **1.** To splash (a liquid). **2.** To splash a liquid against. [Probably imitative.]

swash·buck·ler (swŏsh′bŭk′lər, swôsh′-) *n.* **1.** A flamboyant swordsman or adventurer. **2.** A sword-wielding ruffian or bully. **3.** A dramatic or literary work dealing with a swashbuckler. [Probably from the striking of bucklers in fighting.] —**swash′buck′ling** *adj.*

Swaziland

swash letter *n. Printing.* An ornamental italic letter with elaborate, flowing flourishes and tails. [Origin unknown.]

swas·ti·ka (swŏs′tĭ-kə) *n.* **1.** The emblem of Nazi Germany, officially adopted in 1935. **2.** An ancient cosmic or religious symbol formed by a Greek cross with the ends of the arms bent at right angles in either a clockwise or a counterclockwise direction. [Sanskrit *svastikaḥ,* sign of good luck, swastika, from *svasti,* well-being. See **su-** in Appendix.]

swat (swŏt) *tr.v.* **swat·ted, swat·ting, swats.** To deal a sharp blow to; slap. —**swat** *n.* A sharp blow; a slap. [Alteration of SQUAT, to squash (obsolete and dialectal).]

swatch (swŏch) *n.* A sample strip cut from a piece of material. [Origin unknown.]

swath (swŏth, swôth) also **swathe** (swŏ*th,* swô*th,* swā*th*) *n.* **1.a.** The width of a scythe stroke or a mowing-machine blade. **b.** A path of this width made in mowing. **c.** The mown grass or grain lying on such a path. **2.** Something likened to a swath; a strip. —***idiom.* cut a swath. 1.** To create a great stir, impression, or display: *"He cut a bold and even sacrificial swath across American politics"* (Gail Sheehy). **2.** To extend in distinctive physical length and width: *"the surprising 17th Arrondissement, which cuts a generous swath across northwest Paris"* (Jean Rafferty). [Middle English *swathe,* from Old English *swæth,* track.]

swathe[1] (swŏ*th,* swô*th,* swā*th*) *tr.v.* **swathed, swath·ing, swathes. 1.** To wrap or bind with or as if with bandages. **2.** To enfold or constrict. —**swathe** *n.* A wrapping, binding, or bandage. [Middle English *swathen,* from Old English *swathian.*] —**swath′er** *n.*

swathe[2] (swŏ*th,* swô*th,* swā*th*) *n.* Variant of **swath.**

Swa·tow (swä′tou′). See **Shantou.**

swat·ter (swŏt′ər) *n.* **1.** A fly swatter. **2.** *Baseball.* A hard-hitting batter.

S wave *n.* A secondary wave.

sway (swā) *v.* **swayed, sway·ing, sways.** —*intr.* **1.** To swing back and forth or to and fro. See Synonyms at **swing. 2.** To incline or bend to one side; veer: *She swayed and put out a hand to steady herself.* **3.a.** To incline toward change, as in opinion or feeling. **b.** To fluctuate, as in outlook. —*tr.* **1.** To cause to swing back and forth or to and fro. **2.** To cause to incline or bend to one side. **3.** *Nautical.* To hoist (a mast or yard) into position. **4.a.** To divert; deflect. **b.** To exert influence on or control over: *His speech swayed the voters.* **5.** *Archaic.* **a.** To rule or govern. **b.** To wield, as a weapon or scepter. —**sway** *n.* **1.** The act of moving from side to side with a swinging motion. **2.** Power; influence. **3.** Dominion or control. [Middle English *sweien,* probably of Scandinavian origin.] —**sway′er** *n.* —**sway′ing·ly** *adv.*

sway·back (swā′băk′) *n.* Excessive inward or downward curvature of the spine, especially in a horse. —**sway′backed′** *adj.*

sway bar *n.* See **anti-sway bar.**

Swayne (swān), **Noah Haynes.** 1804–1884. American jurist who served as an associate justice of the U.S. Supreme Court (1862–1881).

Swaz. *abbr.* Swaziland.

Swa·zi (swä′zē) *n., pl.* **Swazi** or **-zis. 1.** A member of a southeast African people of Swaziland and adjacent parts of South Africa. **2.** The Nguni language of this people, closely related to Xhosa and Zulu.

Swa·zi·land (swä′zē-lănd′). *Abbr.* **Swaz.** A country of southeast Africa between South Africa and Mozambique. A British protectorate after 1903, it became independent in 1968. Mbabane is the capital and the largest city. Population, 585,000.

swbd or **swbd.** *abbr.* Switchboard.

SWbS *abbr.* Southwest by south.

SWbW *abbr.* Southwest by west.

Swe. *abbr.* Sweden; Swedish.

swear (swâr) *v.* **swore** (swôr, swōr), **sworn** (swôrn, swōrn), **swear·ing, swears.** —*intr.* **1.** To make a solemn declaration, invoking a deity or a sacred person or thing, in confirmation of and witness to the honesty or truth of such a declaration. **2.** To make a solemn promise; vow. **3.** To use profane oaths; curse. **4.** *Law.* To give evidence or testimony under oath. —*tr.* **1.** To declare or affirm solemnly by invoking a deity or a sacred person or thing. **2.** To promise or pledge with a solemn oath; vow: *He swore his oath of allegiance to the queen.* See Synonyms at **promise. 3.** To utter or bind oneself to (an oath). **4.** *Law.* To administer a legal oath to: *All the witnesses have been sworn.* **5.** To say or affirm earnestly and with great conviction. —***phrasal verbs.* swear at.** To use abusive, violent, or blasphemous language against; curse. **swear by. 1.** To have great reliance on or confidence in: *He swears by his personal physician.* **2.** To have reliable knowledge of; be sure of: *I think she said she was going to the library, but I couldn't swear by it.* **3.** To take an oath by: *He swore by all the angels and saints of heaven.* **swear in.** To administer a legal or official oath to: *swear in a mayor.* **swear off.** *Informal.* To pledge to renounce or give up: *She has sworn off cigarettes.* **swear out.** *Law.* To swear out (a warrant for arrest) by making a charge under oath. [Middle English *sweren,* from Old English *swerian.* See **swer-** in Appendix.] —**swear′er** *n.*

swear·word (swâr′wûrd′) *n.* An obscene or blasphemous word.

sweat (swĕt) *v.* **sweat·ed** or **sweat, sweat·ing, sweats.** —*intr.* **1.** To excrete perspiration through the pores in the skin; perspire. **2.** To exude in droplets, as moisture from certain cheeses or sap from a tree. **3.** To condense atmospheric moisture. **4.a.** To release moisture, as hay in the swath. **b.** To ferment, as tobacco during curing. **5.** *Informal.* **a.** To work long and hard. **b.** To suffer much, as for a misdeed. **6.** *Informal.* To fret or worry. —*tr.* **1.** To excrete (moisture) through a porous surface, such as the skin. **2.** To gather and condense (moisture) on a surface. **3.** To cause to perspire, as by drugs, heat, or strenuous exercise. **4.** To make damp or wet with perspiration. **5.** To cause to work excessively; overwork. **6.** To overwork and underpay (employees). **7.** *Slang.* **a.** To interrogate (someone) under duress: *The secret police sweated the suspected spy for hours.* **b.** To extract (information) from someone under duress: *The police sweated the information out of the suspect.* **8.** *Metallurgy.* To join (metal parts) by interposing cold solder and then heating. **9.** To steam (vegetables or other food). —**sweat** *n.* **1.** The colorless saline moisture excreted by the sweat glands; perspiration. **2.** Condensation of moisture in the form of droplets on a surface. **3.a.** The process of sweating. **b.** *Slang.* The condition of being sweated. **4.** Strenuous, exhaustive labor; drudgery. **5.** A run given to a horse as exercise before a race. **6.** *Informal.* An anxious, fretful condition. **7. sweats.** *Informal.* A sweat suit. —***phrasal verb.* sweat out.** *Slang.* **1.** To endure anxiously: *sweat out an examination.* **2.** To await (something) anxiously: *sweat out one's final grades.* —***idioms.* no sweat.** *Slang.* Easily done or handled. **sweat blood.** *Informal.* **1.** To work diligently or strenuously. **2.** To worry intensely. **sweat bullets.** *Slang.* To sweat profusely. **sweat of (one's) brow.** Hard work: *"keep what they produced by the sweat of their brow"* (Mario Puzo). [Middle English *sweten,* from Old English *swǣtan.* See **sweid-** in Appendix.]

sweat·band (swĕt′bănd′) *n.* **1.** A band of fabric or leather sewn inside the crown of a hat as protection against sweat. **2.** A band of material tied around the forehead or wrist to absorb sweat.

sweat·box (swĕt′bŏks′) *n.* **1.** A box in which something, such as hides or fruit, is fermented by sweating. **2.** *Slang.* A confined place where a person sweats, especially: **a.** An interrogation room. **b.** A prison cell used for special punishment.

sweat·er (swĕt′ər) *n.* **1.** One that sweats, especially profusely.

2. A jacket or pullover made especially of knit, crocheted, or woven wool, cotton, or synthetic yarn. **3.** Something, especially a sudorific, that induces sweating.

sweat gland *n.* Any of the numerous small, tubular glands that are found nearly everywhere in the skin of human beings and that secrete perspiration externally through pores to help regulate body temperature.

sweat·house (swĕt′hous′) *n.* Any of various permanent or portable structures typically heated by fire or by pouring water over hot stones and used by certain Native American peoples to induce sweating, as for medicinal, spiritual, or social purposes. Also called *sweat lodge.*

sweat·pants (swĕt′pănts′) *pl.n.* Cotton jersey pants usually having a drawstring or elasticized waist and elasticized cuffs worn especially for exercising.

sweat·shirt (swĕt′shûrt′) *n.* A usually long-sleeved, collarless, oversize pullover made traditionally of heavy cotton jersey that has a fleeced backing.

sweat·shop (swĕt′shŏp′) *n.* A shop or factory in which employees work long hours at low wages under poor conditions.

sweat suit *n.* A two-piece outfit consisting of a sweatshirt and sweat pants, usually worn for exercise.

sweat·y (swĕt′ē) *adj.* **-i·er, -i·est. 1.** Covered with or smelling of sweat. **2.** Causing sweat: *a sweaty job.* **—sweat′i·ly** *adv.* **—sweat′i·ness** *n.*

Swed. *abbr.* Sweden.

swede (swēd) *n.* See **rutabaga.** [From its introduction from Sweden.]

Swede (swēd) *n.* A native or inhabitant of Sweden. [Low German (from Middle Low German *Swēde*) or Dutch *Zweed* (from Middle Dutch *Swēde*).]

Swe·den (swēd′n). *Abbr.* **Swe., Swed.** A country of northern Europe on the eastern Scandinavian Peninsula. By the 17th century it was a major European power, controlling most of the Baltic coast. Sweden lost much of its territory in the Great Northern War (1700–1721) and acknowledged Norway's independence in 1905. Stockholm is the capital and the largest city. Population, 8,342,621.

Swe·den·borg (swēd′n-bôrg′, svād′n-bôr′ē), **Emanuel.** 1688–1772. Swedish scientist and theologian whose visions and writings inspired his followers to establish the Church of the New Jerusalem after his death. **—Swe′den·bor′gi·an** *adj. & n.*

Swed·ish (swē′dĭsh) *adj. Abbr.* **Sw.** Of or relating to Sweden, the Swedes, or their culture or language. **—Swedish** *n. Abbr.* **Sw., Swe.** The North Germanic language of Sweden and Finland.

Swedish massage *n.* A system of therapeutic massage and exercise for the muscles and joints, developed in Sweden in the 19th century.

Swedish turnip *n.* See **rutabaga.**

sweep (swēp) *v.* **swept** (swĕpt), **sweep·ing, sweeps.** —*tr.* **1.** To clean or clear, as of dirt, with or as if with a broom or brush: *sweep a chimney.* **2.** To clear away with or as if with a broom or brush: *swept snow from the steps.* **3.** To clear (a path or space) with or as if with a broom. **4.a.** To search thoroughly: *The counselors swept the dormitory during the fire drill.* **b.** *Electronics.* To search for and remove (eavesdropping devices) from a place: *swept the room for bugs.* **5.** To touch or brush lightly, as with a trailing garment: *willow branches sweeping the ground.* **6.** To pass over or through a surface or medium with a continuous movement: *He swept the sponge over the tile. The conductor swept her baton through the air.* **7.** To clear, drive, or convey with relentless force: *The flood waters swept away everything in their path.* **8.** To wipe out at a single stroke. Often used with *away*: *The incident in effect swept away all her dreams.* **9.** To remove or carry off with a swift brushing motion: *swept the cards off the table; swept the child into his arms.* **10.** To move across or through swiftly or with great intensity: *News of the lunar landing swept the country.* **11.** To pass quickly across, as when searching: *His gaze swept the horizon.* **12.** To drag the bottom of (a body of water). **13.a.** To win all the stages of (a game or contest): *swept the World Series.* **b.** To win overwhelmingly in: *The opposition party swept the election.* —*intr.* **1.** To clean or clear a surface with or as if with a broom or brush. **2.** *Electronics.* To search for and remove eavesdropping devices. **3.** To move swiftly with strong, steady force: *The wind swept over the plain.* **4.** To move swiftly in a lofty manner, as if in a trailing robe: *She swept by in silence.* **5.** To trail, as a long garment. **6.** To extend gracefully, especially in a long curve: *The hills sweep down to the sea.* **7.** To extend in a wide range: *Searchlights swept across the sky.* **—sweep** *n.* **1.** A clearing out or removal with or as if with a broom or brush. **2.** *Electronics.* The act or an instance of searching for and removing eavesdropping devices, as in a room. **3.a.** A wide curving motion: *a sweep of the arm.* **b.** The range or scope encompassed by sweeping: *the sweep of a lantern beam.* See Synonyms at **range. 4.** A broad reach or extent: *a sweep of green lawn.* **5.** A curve or contour: *the sweep of her hair.* **6.** One who sweeps, especially a chimney sweep. **7.** Often **sweeps.** Sweepings. **8.a.** The winning of all stages of a game or contest. **b.** An overwhelming victory or success. **9.** *Nautical.* A long oar used to propel a boat. **10.** A long pole attached to a pivot and used to raise or lower a bucket in a well. **11. sweeps.** *(used with a sing. or pl. verb). Informal.* Sweepstakes. **12.a. sweeps.** The period each fall, winter, and spring when television ratings are accrued and studied and advertising rates are reset. **b.** The national survey of local stations that is conducted to determine these ratings. **13.** *Electronics.* The steady motion of an electron beam across a cathode-ray tube. **—*idiom.* sweep (one) off (one's) feet.** To cause an immediate and strongly positive response in (a person); overwhelm. [Middle English *swepen,* perhaps from *swepe,* past tense of *swopen,* to sweep along. See SWOOP.] **—sweep′er** *n.*

sweep·back (swēp′băk′) *n.* The backward slant of the leading edge of an airfoil.

sweep·ing (swē′pĭng) *adj.* **1.** Having wide-ranging influence or effect: *sweeping changes.* **2.** Moving in or as if in a wide curve: *a sweeping gesture; a sweeping glance.* **3.** Indiscriminate; wholesale: *sweeping generalizations.* **4.** Overwhelming; complete: *a sweeping victory.* **—sweeping** *n.* **1.** The action of one that sweeps. **2. sweepings.** Things swept up; refuse. **—sweep′ing·ly** *adv.*

sweep·stakes (swēp′stāks′) *pl.n. (used with a sing. or pl. verb).* **1.** A lottery in which the participants' contributions form a fund that is awarded as a prize to one or several winners. **2.** An event or a contest, especially a horserace, the result of which determines the winner of such a lottery. **3.** The prize won in such a lottery.

sweet (swēt) *adj.* **sweet·er, sweet·est. 1.** Having the taste of sugar or a substance containing or resembling sugar, as honey or saccharin. **2.a.** Containing or derived from sugar. **b.** Retaining some natural sugar; not dry: *a sweet wine.* **3.a.** Pleasing to the senses; agreeable: *the sweet song of the lark; a sweet face.* **b.** Pleasing to the mind or feelings; gratifying: *sweet revenge.* **4.** Having a pleasing disposition; lovable: *a sweet child.* **5.** Kind; gracious: *It was sweet of him to help out.* **6.** Fragrant; perfumed: *a sweet scent.* **7.** Not saline or salted: *sweet water; sweet butter.* **8.** Not spoiled, sour, or decaying; fresh: *sweet milk.* **9.** Free of acid or acidity: *sweet soil.* **10.** Low in sulfur content: sweet fuel oil. **11.** *Music.* Of, relating to, or being a form of jazz characterized by adherence to a melodic line and to a time signature. **—sweet** *adv.* In a sweet manner; sweetly. **—sweet** *n.* **1.** Sweet taste or quality; sweetness. **2.** Something sweet to the taste. **3. sweets. a.** Foods, such as candy, pastries, puddings, or preserves, that are high in sugar content. **b.** *Informal.* Sweet potatoes: *candied sweets.* **4.** *Chiefly British.* **a.** A sweet dish, such as pudding, served as dessert. **b.** A sweetmeat or confection. **5.** A dear or beloved person. **6.** Something pleasing to the mind or feelings. **—*idiom.* sweet on.** *Informal.* Enamored of; in love with. [Middle English *swete,* from Old English *swēte.* See **swād-** in Appendix.] **—sweet′ly** *adv.* **—sweet′ness** *n.*

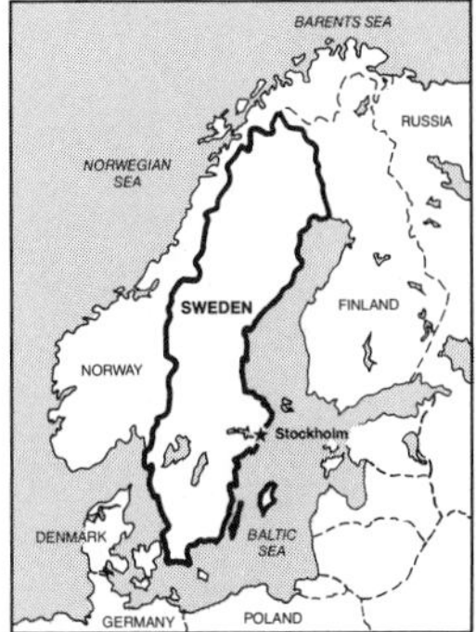

Sweden

Sweet (swēt), **Henry.** 1845–1912. British phonetician and philologist. A founder of modern phonetics, he is known especially for his *History of English Sounds* (1874).

sweet acacia *n.* A thorny shrub *(Acacia farnesiana)* of the pea family, native to tropical and subtropical America, having bipinnately compound leaves, small flower heads, and fragrant flowers that yield an essential oil used in perfumery.

sweet alyssum *n.* A widely cultivated annual or perennial herb *(Lobularia maritima)* of the mustard family, native to the Mediterranean region, having racemes of long-lasting flowers varying in size and color. Also called *alyssum.*

sweet-and-sour (swēt′n-sour′) *adj.* Flavored with a sauce containing sugar and vinegar: *sweet-and-sour pork.*

sweet basil *n.* See **basil** (sense 1).

sweet bay *n.* **1.** A shrub or small tree *(Magnolia virginiana)* of the southeast United States and eastern coastal areas north to Massachusetts, having large fragrant white flowers and red fruit. **2.** See **laurel** (sense 1).

sweet birch *n.* **1.** An eastern North American birch *(Betula lenta)* having aromatic stems with brownish bark that does not peel into papery flakes. **2.** The wood of this tree. Also called *black birch, cherry birch.*

sweet·bread (swēt′brĕd′) *n.* The thymus gland or pancreas of a young animal, especially a calf or lamb, used for food.

sweet·bri·er also **sweet·bri·ar** (swēt′brī′ər) *n.* A Eurasian rose *(Rosa eglanteria)* having prickly stems, fragrant leaves, bright pink flowers, and scarlet hips. Also called *eglantine.*

sweet cherry *n.* **1.** A large, widely cultivated deciduous tree *(Prunus avium)* of the rose family, native to Eurasia, having red-brown birchlike bark, white flowers, and sweet edible fruit. **2.** The fruit of the sweet cherry.

sweet cicely *n.* **1.** Any of various perennial New World herbs of the genus *Osmorhiza* of the parsley family, having fleshy aromatic roots, compound leaves, and clusters of small white flowers. **2.** An aromatic European perennial herb *(Myrrhis odorata)* having compound leaves and compound umbels of small white flowers. In this sense, also called *myrrh.* [Middle English *seseli,* from Latin *seselis,* from Greek.]

sweet cider *n.* Unfermented cider.

sweet clover *n.* See **melilot.**

sweet corn *n.* A variety of corn *(Zea mays* var. *rugosa),* the common table and canning corn, having kernels that are sweet when young. Also called *sugar corn.*

sweet·en (swēt′n) *v.* **-ened, -en·ing, -ens.** —*tr.* **1.** To make sweet or sweeter by adding sugar, honey, saccharin, or another sweet substance. **2.** To make more pleasant or more agreeable. **3.** To soften or soothe: *sweetened her mood.* **4.** To make bearable; alleviate. **5.** *Informal.* **a.** To increase the value of (collateral for a loan) by adding more securities. **b.** To enhance the attractiveness

ă **pat**	oi **boy**
ā **pay**	ou **out**
âr **care**	o͝o **took**
ä **father**	o͞o **boot**
ĕ **pet**	ŭ **cut**
ē **be**	ûr **urge**
ĭ **pit**	th **thin**
ī **pie**	*th* **this**
îr **pier**	hw **which**
ŏ **pot**	zh **vision**
ō **toe**	ə **about, item**
ô **paw**	♦ **regionalism**

Stress marks: ′ (primary); ′ (secondary), as in **dictionary** (dĭk′shə-nĕr′ē)

or financial desirability of (an offer, for example). **6.** *Games.* To increase the value of (an unwon poker pot) by adding stakes before reopening. **7.** To make less acidic: *sweeten the stomach with antacids.* **8.** To remove sulfur compounds from (fuel oil or gas). —*intr.* To become sweet.

sweet·en·er (swēt′n-ər) *n.* **1.** Something that sweetens. **2.** *Informal.* Something added as a further inducement or incentive.

sweet·en·ing (swēt′n-ĭng) *n.* **1.** The act or process of making sweet. **2.** Something that sweetens; a sweetener.

sweet fennel *n.* See **finocchio.**

sweet fern *n.* An aromatic deciduous shrub *(Comptonia peregrina)* of eastern North America, having narrow, deeply lobed, fernlike leaves and minute flowers grouped in catkinlike heads.

sweet flag *n.* A hardy perennial herb *(Acorus calamus)* of the Northern Hemisphere, growing in marshy places and having grasslike leaves, minute greenish flowers borne on a thick spadix, and aromatic rhizomes. Also called *calamus.*

sweet gale *n.* A deciduous swamp shrub *(Myrica gale)* of northern Eurasia and North America, having aromatic resinous leaves used in medicine and tiny yellowish fruits clustered in catkins. Also called *meadow fern.*

sweet gum *n.* **1.** Any of several trees of the genus *Liquidambar,* especially *L. styraciflua* of North America and Central America, having palmately lobed leaves, prickly, ball-like, woody fruit clusters, and wood used to make furniture. **2.** The aromatic resin obtained from this tree.

sweet·heart (swēt′härt′) *n.* **1.** One who is loved. **2.** Used as a familiar term of endearment. **3.** *Informal.* **a.** A person regarded as generous or lovable. **b.** Something cherished for its excellent qualities. —**sweetheart** *adj.* Involving privileged treatment of a favored party; illegally or unethically favorable: *"another land grab, another sweetheart deal based on political influence"* (Village Voice).

sweet·ie (swē′tē) *n.* *Informal.* Sweetheart; dear.

sweet·ing (swē′tĭng) *n.* **1.** A sweet apple. **2.** *Archaic.* Sweetheart.

sweet marjoram *n.* See **marjoram.**

sweet·meat (swēt′mēt′) *n.* A sweet delicacy, such as a piece of candy or crystallized fruit.

sweet pea *n.* An annual climbing herb *(Lathyrus odoratus)* of the pea family, native to Italy, cultivated for its variously colored, fragrant flowers.

sweet pepper *n.* The bell pepper.

sweet pepperbush *n.* A deciduous shrub *(Clethra alnifolia)* growing in moist ground from Maine to Florida and having long racemes of small, fragrant white flowers.

♦**sweet potato** *n.* **1.a.** A tropical American vine *(Ipomoea batatas)* having rose-violet or pale pink, funnel-shaped flowers, and cultivated for its fleshy, tuberous orange-colored root. **b.** The root of this vine, eaten cooked as a vegetable. Also called ♦*yam.* **2.** *Informal.* An ocarina.

sweet·shop (swēt′shŏp′) *n.* *Chiefly British.* A candy store.

sweet shrub *n.* Any of several North American deciduous shrubs of the genus *Calycanthus,* having opposite leaves, fragrant reddish-brown flowers with numerous petals and sepals, and many dry fruits enclosed in a cup.

sweet·sop (swēt′sŏp′) *n.* **1.** A tropical American evergreen tree *(Annona squamosa)* widely cultivated in the lowlands for its yellowish-green fruit with sweet, edible pulp. **2.** The fruit of this tree. Also called *sugar apple.*

sweet sorghum *n.* See **sorgo.**

sweet spot *n.* *Sports.* The place on a racket, club, bat, paddle, or ball where hits are most effective.

sweet sultan *n.* An Old World annual herb, *(Centaurea moschata)* in the composite family, widely cultivated for its showy, fragrant, varicolored flower heads.

sweet talk *n.* *Informal.* Flattery; cajolery.

sweet-talk (swēt′tôk′) *v.* **-talked, -talk·ing, -talks.** *Informal.* —*tr.* To coax or cajole with flattery. —*intr.* To use flattery.

sweet tooth *n.* *Informal.* A fondness or craving for sweets.

sweet William *n.* An annual, biennial, or perennial herb *(Dianthus barbatus),* native to Eurasia, widely cultivated as an ornamental for its flat-topped dense clusters of varicolored flowers.

sweet woodruff *n.* See **woodruff** (sense 1).

swell (swĕl) *v.* **swelled, swelled** or **swol·len** (swō′lən), **swell·ing, swells.** —*intr.* **1.** To increase in size or volume as a result of internal pressure; expand. **2.a.** To increase in force, size, number, or degree: *Membership in the club swelled.* **b.** To grow in loudness or intensity: *"The din in front swelled to a tremendous chorus"* (Stephen Crane). **3.** To bulge out, as a sail. **4.a.** To rise or extend above the surrounding level, as clouds. **b.** To rise in swells, as the sea. **5.a.** To be or become filled or puffed up, as with pride, arrogance, or anger. **b.** To rise from within: *Rage swelled within me.* —*tr.* **1.** To cause to increase in volume, size, number, degree, or intensity: *The governor's full public disclosure only swelled the chorus of protests.* **2.** To fill with emotion. —**swell** *n.* **1.a.** The act or process of swelling. **b.** The condition of being swollen. **2.** A swollen part; a bulge or protuberance. **3.** A long wave on water that moves continuously without breaking. **4.** A rise in the land; a rounded elevation. **5.** *Informal.* One who is fashionably dressed or socially prominent: *society swells.* **6.** *Music.* **a.** A crescendo followed by a gradual diminuendo. **b.** The sign indicating such a crescendo. **c.** A device on an instrument, such as an organ or a harpsichord, for regulating volume. —**swell** *adj.* **swell·er, swell·est.** *Informal.* **1.** Fashionably elegant; stylish. **2.** Excellent; wonderful: *had a swell time.* [Middle English *swellen,* from Old English *swellan.*]

swift
Top: Collapsible boxwood swift for yarn
Bottom: Chimney swift
Chaetura pelagica

swell box *n.* *Music.* A chamber housing one or more sets of organ pipes and having shutters that can be opened or shut to regulate the volume.

swelled head (swĕld) *n.* *Informal.* An unduly high opinion of oneself.

swell·fish (swĕl′fĭsh′) *n., pl.* **swellfish** or **-fish·es.** See **puffer.**

swell·head (swĕl′hĕd′) *n.* *Informal.* A person regarded as arrogant or conceited. —**swell′head′ed** *adj.* —**swell′head′ed·ness** *n.*

swell·ing (swĕl′ĭng) *n.* **1.** The state of being swollen. **2.** Something swollen, especially an abnormally swollen body part or area.

swel·ter (swĕl′tər) *v.* **-tered, -ter·ing, -ters.** —*intr.* To suffer from oppressive heat. —*tr.* **1.** To affect with oppressive heat. **2.** *Archaic.* To exude (venom, for example). —**swelter** *n.* A condition of oppressive heat. [Middle English *swelteren,* frequentative of *swelten,* to faint from heat, from Old English *sweltan,* to perish.]

swel·ter·ing (swĕl′tər-ĭng) *adj.* **1.** Oppressively hot and humid; sultry. **2.** Suffering from oppressive heat. —**swel′ter·ing·ly** *adv.*

swel·try (swĕl′trē) *adj.* **-tri·er, -tri·est.** Sweltering.

swept (swĕpt) *v.* Past tense and past participle of **sweep.**

swept·back (swĕpt′băk′) *adj.* **1.** Angled rearward from the points of attachment. Used especially of aircraft wings. **2.** Having wings of this type. Used of an aircraft.

swept·wing (swĕpt′wĭng′) *adj.* Having sweptback wings. Used of an aircraft. —**sweptwing** *n.* A sweptback wing.

swerve (swûrv) *tr. & intr.v.* **swerved, swerv·ing, swerves.** To turn aside or be turned aside from a straight course. —**swerve** *n.* The act of swerving. [Middle English *swerven,* from Old English *sweorfan,* to rub, scour.]

SYNONYMS: *swerve, depart, deviate, digress, diverge, stray, veer.* The central meaning shared by these verbs is "to turn away from a straight or prescribed course": *eyes that never once swerved from her face; won't depart from family traditions; deviated from their original plan; digressing from the principal topic; opinions that diverged; straying from the truth; veered the conversation away from politics.*

SWG *abbr.* Standard wire gauge.

swift (swĭft) *adj.* **swift·er, swift·est.** **1.** Moving or capable of moving with great speed; fast. See Synonyms at **fast**[1]. **2.** Coming, occurring, or accomplished quickly; instant: *a swift retort.* **3.** Quick to act or react; prompt: *swift to take steps.* —**swift** *adv.* Swiftly. Often used in combination: *swift-running.* —**swift** *n.* **1.a.** A cylinder on a carding machine. **b.** A reel used to hold yarn as it is being wound off. **2.** Any of various small, dark, insect-eating birds of the family Apodidae, related to the hummingbirds and noted for their long, strong wings and swift flight. **3.** Any of various small, fast-moving North American lizards of the genera *Sceloporus* and *Uta.* [Middle English, from Old English.] —**swift′ly** *adv.* —**swift′ness** *n.*

Swift (swĭft), **Gustavus Franklin.** 1839–1903. American meatpacker who was the first to use refrigerated railroad cars (1877).

Swift, Jonathan. 1667–1745. Irish-born English writer known for his satirical works, including *Gulliver's Travels* (1726) and *A Modest Proposal* (1729).

swig (swĭg) *Informal. n.* A deep draft, especially of liquor; a gulp. —**swig** *tr. & intr.v.* **swigged, swig·ging, swigs.** To drink (liquid) or engage in drinking liquid in great gulps. [Origin unknown.] —**swig′ger** *n.*

swill (swĭl) *v.* **swilled, swill·ing, swills.** —*tr.* **1.** To drink greedily or grossly: *"Unshaven horsemen swill the great wines of the Chateaux"* (W.H. Auden). **2.** To flood with water, as for washing. **3.** To feed (animals) with swill. —*intr.* To drink or eat greedily or to excess. —**swill** *n.* **1.** A mixture of liquid and solid food, such as table scraps, fed to animals, especially pigs; slop. **2.** Kitchen waste; garbage. **3.** A deep draft of liquor. **4.** Nonsense; rubbish. [Middle English *swilen,* to wash out, from Old English *swilian.* See **swel-** in Appendix.] —**swill′er** *n.*

swim (swĭm) *v.* **swam** (swăm), **swum** (swŭm), **swim·ming, swims.** —*intr.* **1.** To move through water by means of the limbs, fins, or tail. **2.** To move as though gliding through water. **3.** To float on water or another liquid. **4.a.** To be covered or flooded with or as if with a liquid: *chicken swimming in gravy.* **b.** To possess a superfluity; abound: *After winning the lottery, she was swimming in money.* **5.** To experience a floating or giddy sensation; be dizzy: *"his brain still swimming with the effects of the last night's champagne"* (Robert Smith Surtees). **6.** To appear to spin or reel lazily: *The room swam before my eyes.* —*tr.* **1.** To move through or across (a body of water) by swimming: *She swam the channel.* **2.** To execute (a particular stroke) in swimming. **3.** To cause to swim or float. —**swim** *n.* **1.a.** The act of swimming. **b.** A period of time spent swimming. **2.** A gliding motion. **3.** A state of dizziness. **4.** An area, as of a river, abounding in fish. —**swim** *adj.* Of, relating to, or used for swimming: *a swim mask.*

—*idioms.* **in the swim.** Active in the general current of affairs. **swim against the stream.** To move counter to a prevailing trend. [Middle English *swimmen,* from Old English *swimman.*] —**swim′ma·ble** *adj.* —**swim′mer** *n.*

swim bladder *n.* See **air bladder** (sense 1).

swim·mer·et (swĭm′ə-rĕt′, swĭm′ə-rĕt′) *n.* One of the paired abdominal appendages of certain aquatic crustaceans, such as shrimp, lobsters, and isopods, that function primarily for carrying the eggs in females and are usually adapted for swimming. Also called *pleopod.*

swim·mer's itch (swĭm′ərz) *n.* An itching inflammation of the skin caused by parasitic larval forms of certain schistosomes that penetrate into the skin, occurring after bathing in infested fresh or salt water.

swim·ming (swĭm′ĭng) *n.* The act, sport, or technique of one that swims. —**swimming** *adj.* **1.** Relating to or used in swimming. **2.** That swims: *swimming insects.*

swim·ming·ly (swĭm′ĭng-lē) *adv.* With great ease and success: *Things are going swimmingly.*

swimming pool *n.* A structure, often a concrete-lined excavation of rectangular shape, that is filled with water and used for swimming.

swim·suit (swĭm′so͞ot′) *n.* A garment worn while swimming. Also called *bathing suit.*

swim·wear (swĭm′wâr′) *n.* Clothing designed to be worn for swimming or with swimsuits.

Swin·burne (swĭn′bûrn′), **Algernon Charles.** 1837–1909. British poet and critic who wrote musical, often erotic verse in which he attacked the conventions of Victorian morality.

swin·dle (swĭn′dl) *v.* **-dled, -dling, -dles.** —*tr.* **1.** To cheat or defraud of money or property. **2.** To obtain by fraudulent means: *swindled money from the company.* —*intr.* To practice fraud as a means of obtaining money or property. —**swindle** *n.* The act or an instance of swindling. [Back-formation from *swindler,* one who swindles, from German *Schwindler,* giddy person, cheat, from *schwindeln,* to be dizzy, swindle, from Middle High German, from Old High German *swintilōn,* frequentative of *swintan,* to languish.] —**swin′dler** *n.*

Swin·don (swĭn′dən). A municipal borough of south-central England east-northeast of Bristol. It has an important locomotive industry. Population, 151,600.

swine (swīn) *n., pl.* **swine. 1.** Any of various omnivorous, even-toed ungulates of the family Suidae, including pigs, hogs, and boars, having a stout body with thick skin, a short neck, and a movable snout. **2.** A person regarded as brutish or contemptible. [Middle English, from Old English *swīn.* See **sū-** in Appendix.]

swine flu *n.* A highly contagious form of human influenza caused by a filterable virus identical or related to a virus formerly isolated from infected swine.

swine·herd (swīn′hûrd′) *n.* One who tends swine.

swine·pox (swīn′pŏks′) *n.* An acute infectious disease of domesticated swine caused by a virus and characterized by skin lesions.

swing (swĭng) *v.* **swung** (swŭng), **swing·ing, swings.** —*intr.* **1.** To move back and forth suspended or as if suspended from above. **2.** To hit at something with a sweeping motion of the arm: *swung at the ball.* **3.** To move laterally or in a curve: *The car swung over to the curb.* **4.** To turn in place on or as if on a hinge or pivot. **5.** To move along with an easy, swaying gait: *swinging down the road.* **6.** To propel oneself from one place or position to another by grasping a fixed support: *swinging through the trees.* **7.** To ride on a swing. **8.** To shift from one attitude, interest, condition, or emotion to another; vacillate. **9.** *Slang.* To be put to death by hanging. **10.** *Music.* **a.** To have a subtle, intuitively felt rhythm or sense of rhythm. **b.** To play with a subtle, intuitively felt sense of rhythm. **11.** *Slang.* **a.** To be lively, trendy, and exciting. **b.** To engage freely in promiscuous sex. **c.** To exchange sex partners. Used especially of married couples. —*tr.* **1.** To cause to move back and forth, as on a swing. **2.** To cause to move in a broad arc or curve: *swing a bat; swung the car over.* **3. a.** To cause to move with a sweeping motion: *swinging his arms.* **b.** To lift and convey with a sweeping motion: *swung the cargo onto the deck.* **4.** To suspend so as to sway or turn freely: *swung a hammock between two trees.* **5. a.** To suspend on hinges: *swing a shutter.* **b.** To cause to turn on hinges: *swung the door shut.* **6.** To cause to shift from one attitude, position, opinion, or condition to another. **7.** *Informal.* **a.** To manage or arrange successfully: *swing a deal.* **b.** To bring around to the desired result: *swing an election.* **8.** *Music.* To play (music) with a subtle, intuitively felt sense of rhythm. —**swing** *n.* **1.** The act or an instance of swinging; movement back and forth or in one particular direction. **2.** The sweep or scope of something that swings: *The pendulum's swing is 12 inches.* **3.** A blow or stroke executed with a sweeping motion of the arm. **4.** The manner in which one swings something, such as a bat or golf club. **5.** A shift from one attitude, position, or condition to another: *a swing to conservatism.* **6.** Freedom of action: *The children have free swing in deciding what color to paint their room.* **7. a.** A swaying, graceful motion: *has a swing to her walk.* **b.** A sweep back and forth: *the swing of a bird across the sky.* **8.** A course or tour that returns to the starting point: *a swing across the state while campaigning.* **9.** A seat suspended from above, as by ropes, on which one can ride back and forth for recreation. **10.** The normal rhythm of life or pace of activities: *back in the swing.* **11.** A steady, vigorous rhythm or movement, as in verse. **12.** A regular movement up or down, as in stock prices. **13.** *Music.* **a.** A type of popular dance music developed about 1935 and based on jazz but employing a larger band and simpler harmonic and rhythmic patterns. **b.** A ballroom dance performed to this music. **c.** A subtle, intuitively felt rhythmic quality or sense of rhythm. —**swing** *adj.* **1.** *Music.* Relating to or performing swing: *a swing band.* **2.** Determining an outcome; decisive: *the swing vote.* —*idiom.* **in full swing.** At the highest level of activity or operation. [Middle English *swingen,* to beat, brandish, from Old English *swingan,* to flog, strike, swing.] —**swing′y** *adj.*

SYNONYMS: *swing, oscillate, sway, rock, vibrate, fluctuate, undulate, waver.* These verbs mean to move in a back-and-forth, up-and-down, or to-and-fro pattern. *Swing* usually applies to arclike movement of something attached at one extremity and free at the other: *The ship's lanterns swung violently in the raging storm. The shutter swung open. Her purse swings from her shoulder on a long strap. Oscillate* refers to steady, uninterrupted back-and-forth motion, as that of a pendulum; in an extended sense it denotes vacillation, as between conflicting purposes: *"a king . . . oscillating between fear of Rome and desire of independence"* (Walter Besant). *Sway* suggests the movement of something unsteady, light, or flexible: *"thousands of the little yellow blossoms all swaying to the light wind"* (W.H. Hudson). To *rock* is to swing gently or rhythmically or sway or tilt violently: *"The ruins of the ancient church seemed actually to rock and threaten to fall"* (Sir Walter Scott). *Vibrate* usually implies quick periodic oscillations; it often suggests trembling, pulsating, or quivering: *"Music, when soft voices die,/Vibrates in the memory"* (Percy Bysshe Shelley). *Fluctuate* is most often used figuratively to imply fairly constant alternating change: *"Prices fluctuated violently from the irregularity of the crops"* (Lesley B. Simpson). *Undulate* implies smooth wavelike movement: *The ripe wheat undulated in the breeze like the incoming tide. Waver* suggests unsteady, uncertain movement: *"He stood with wavering hands, unable for a moment to begin"* (H.G. Wells).

swing-by (swĭng′bī′) *n., pl.* **-bys.** An interplanetary mission in which a space vehicle uses planetary gravitation for changes in course.

swinge (swĭnj) *tr.v.* **swinged, swinge·ing** also **swing·ing, swing·es.** *Archaic.* To punish with blows; thrash; beat. [Middle English *swengen,* to shake, dash, from Old English *swengan.*] —**swing′er** (swĭn′jər) *n.*

swing·er (swĭng′ər) *n.* **1.** One that swings: *a good swinger of baseball bats.* **2.** *Slang.* **a.** A person who actively seeks excitement and moves with the latest trends. **b.** A person who engages freely in promiscuous sex. **c.** A member of a couple, especially a married couple, who exchanges sexual partners.

swing·ing (swĭng′ĭng) *Slang. adj.* **1.** Spirited; up-to-date. **2.** Attracting a lively, trendy crowd: *a swinging nightclub.* **3.** *Slang.* **a.** Sexually promiscuous. **b.** Practicing exchange of partners, especially spouses, for sex.

swin·gle·tree (swĭng′gəl-trē) *n.* See **whiffletree.** [From English *swingle,* wooden instrument used for beating flax, from Middle English, from Middle Dutch *swinghel.*]

swing·man (swĭng′mən) *n. Basketball.* A team member who can play effectively in two different positions, especially forward and guard.

swing shift *n.* The work shift between the day and the night shifts, usually 4 P.M. to midnight.

swing-wing (swĭng′wĭng′) *adj.* Of, relating to, or being an airplane with wings constructed to allow the outer portion to fold back along the fuselage to produce streamlining at high speeds.

swin·ish (swī′nĭsh) *adj.* **1.** Resembling or befitting swine. **2.** Bestial or brutish.

swipe (swīp) *n.* **1.** A sweeping blow or stroke. **2.** *Informal.* A critical remark. **3.** A lever, especially one that raises the bucket in a well. —**swipe** *v.* **swiped, swip·ing, swipes.** —*tr.* **1.** To hit with a sweeping motion. **2.** *Informal.* To steal; filch. See Synonyms at **steal.** —*intr.* To make a sweeping stroke. [Perhaps variant of SWEEP.]

swirl (swûrl) *v.* **swirled, swirl·ing, swirls.** —*intr.* **1.** To move with a twisting or whirling motion; eddy. **2.** To be dizzy; swim. **3.** To be arranged in a spiral, whorl, or twist. —*tr.* **1.** To cause to move with a twisting or whirling motion. See Synonyms at **turn. 2.** To form into or arrange in a spiral, whorl, or twist. —**swirl** *n.* **1.** A whirling or eddying motion or mass: *a swirl of white water.* **2.** Something, such as a curl of hair, that coils, twists, or whirls. **3.** Whirling confusion or disorder: *"high-pressure farce built around the swirl of mistaken identities"* (Jay Carr). [Middle English *swyrl,* eddy, probably of Low German or Scandinavian origin.] —**swirl′y** *adj.*

swish (swĭsh) *v.* **swished, swish·ing, swish·es.** —*intr.* **1.** To move with a hissing or whistling sound, as a whip. **2.** To rustle, as silk. —*tr.* **1.** To cause to make a swishing sound. **2.** To strike or cut with a swishing sound. **3.** To whip with a rod. —**swish** *n.* **1. a.** A sharp whistling or rustling sound: *the swish of scythes.* **b.** A movement making such a sound. **2. a.** A rod used for flogging. **b.** A stroke made with such a rod. **3.** *Offensive Slang.* Used as a disparaging term for a gay or homosexual man. —**swish** *adj.* **1.**

Jonathan Swift
Detail of a c. 1718 portrait by Charles Jervas (1675–1739)

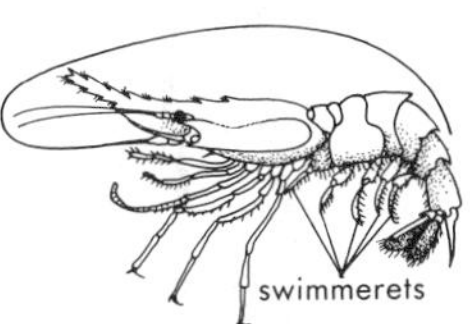

swimmeret
Of a shrimp

ă **pat**	oi **boy**
ā **pay**	ou **out**
âr **care**	o͝o **took**
ä **father**	o͞o **boot**
ĕ **pet**	ŭ **cut**
ē **be**	ûr **urge**
ĭ **pit**	th **thin**
ī **pie**	*th* **this**
îr **pier**	hw **which**
ŏ **pot**	zh **vision**
ō **toe**	ə **about, item**
ô **paw**	♦ **regionalism**

Stress marks: **′** (primary); ′ (secondary), as in **dictionary** (dĭk′shə-nĕr′ē)

Informal. Fashionable; posh: *"a swish pastry shop on the Rue du Bac"* (Julia Child). **2.** *Slang.* Effeminate. [Imitative.]

swish·y (swĭsh′ē) *adj.* **-i·er, -i·est. 1.** Producing a swishing sound. **2.** *Slang.* Effeminate.

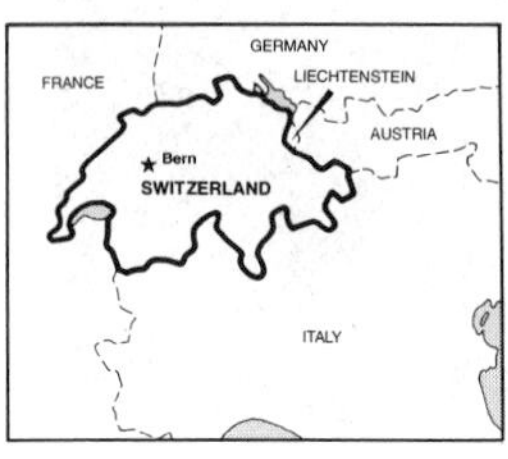

Switzerland

Swiss (swĭs) *adj.* Of or relating to Switzerland or its people or culture. **—Swiss** *n.* **1.** *pl.* **Swiss.** A native or inhabitant of Switzerland. **2.** Also **swiss.** A crisp, sheer cotton fabric used for curtains or light garments. **3.** A firm white or pale yellow cheese with a nutlike flavor and many holes, originally produced in Switzerland. [French *Suisse,* from Middle High German *Swīzer,* from *Swīz,* Switzerland.]

Swiss chard *n.* A variety of beet *(Beta vulgaris* var. *cicla)* having large succulent leaves used as a vegetable.

Swiss Guard *n.* A member of a corps of soldiers of Swiss birth employed at the Vatican as bodyguards to the pope.

Swiss steak *n.* A round steak pounded with flour and braised in stock with vegetables.

♦**switch** (swĭch) *n.* **1.** A slender flexible rod, stick, or twig, especially one used for whipping. **2.** The bushy tip of the tail of certain animals: *a cow's switch.* **3.** A thick strand of real or synthetic hair used as part of a coiffure. **4.** A flailing or lashing, as with a slender rod. **5.** *Abbr.* **sw.** A device used to break or open an electric circuit or to divert current from one conductor to another. **6.** *Abbr.* **sw.** A device consisting of two sections of railroad track and accompanying apparatus used to transfer rolling stock from one track to another. **7. a.** The act or process of operating a switching device. **b.** The result achieved by such an act. **8.** An exchange or a swap, especially one done secretly. **9.** A transference or shift, as of opinion or attention. **—switch** *v.* **switched, switch·ing, switch·es.** *—tr.* **1.** *Chiefly Southern U.S.* To whip with or as if with a switch, especially in punishing a child. **2.** To jerk or swish abruptly or sharply: *a cat switching its tail.* **3.** To shift, transfer, or divert: *switched the conversation to a lighter subject.* **4.** To exchange: *asked her brother to switch seats with her.* **5.** To connect, disconnect, or divert (an electric current) by operating a switch. **6.** To cause (an electric current or appliance) to begin or cease operation: *switched the lights on and off.* **7.** *Informal.* To produce as if by operating a control. Often used with *on: switched on the charm.* **8.** To move (rolling stock) from one track to another; shunt. *—intr.* **1.** To make or undergo a shift or an exchange: *The office has switched from typewriters to word processors.* **2.** To swish sharply from side to side. ***—phrasal verb.*** **switch off.** *Informal.* To stop paying attention; lose interest. [Probably of Low German or Flemish origin.] **—switch′a·ble** *adj.* **—switch′er** *n.*

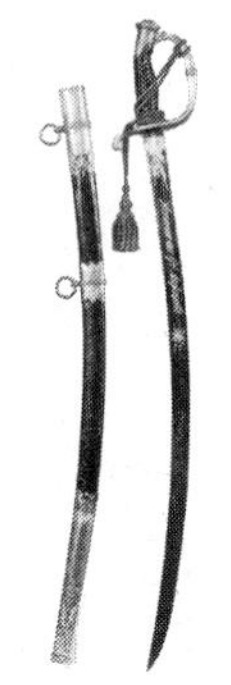

sword
Dress sword used by Lafayette

switch·back (swĭch′băk′) *n.* **1.** A road, trail, or railroad track that ascends a steep incline in a zigzag course. **2.** A sharp bend in a road or trail ascending a steep incline. **3.** *Chiefly British.* A roller coaster.

switch·blade (swĭch′blād′) *n.* A pocketknife having a spring-operated blade that opens instantly when a release on the handle is pressed. Also called *switchblade knife, switch knife.*

switch·board (swĭch′bôrd′, -bōrd′) *n.* *Abbr.* **swbd, swbd. 1.** One or more panels accommodating control switches, indicators, and other apparatus for operating electric circuits. **2.** See **telephone exchange.**

switch·er·oo (swĭch′ə-ro͞o′) *n., pl.* **-oos.** *Slang.* An unexpected variation or reversal. [Alteration of SWITCH.]

switch hitter *n.* *Baseball.* A player who can bat either right-handed or left-handed. **—switch′-hit′** (swĭch′hĭt′) *v.*

switch knife *n.* See **switchblade.**

switch·man (swĭch′mən) *n.* A man who operates railroad switches.

switch·o·ver (swĭch′ō′vər) *n.* A complete shift, as from one system to another.

switch·yard (swĭch′yärd′) *n.* An area where railroad cars are switched and trains assembled.

Switz. *abbr.* Switzerland.

Swit·zer (swĭt′sər) *n.* **1.** A Swiss. **2.** A Swiss Guard. [Ultimately from Middle High German *Swīzer.* See SWISS.]

Swit·zer·land (swĭt′sər-lənd). *Abbr.* **Switz.** A country of west-central Europe. It became part of the Holy Roman Empire in the 10th century but by 1499 had achieved independence as a confederation of cantons. Switzerland later adopted a federal constitution (1848) and maintained a policy of neutrality through both World Wars. Bern is the capital and Zurich the largest city. Population, 6,455,900.

swiv·el (swĭv′əl) *n.* **1.** A link, pivot, or another fastening so designed that it permits the free turning of attached parts. **2.** A pivoted support that allows an attached object, such as a chair or gun, to turn in a horizontal plane. **3.** A gun that turns on a pivot. **—swivel** *v.* **-eled, -el·ing, -els** or **-elled, -el·ling, -els.** *—tr.* **1.** To turn or rotate on or as if on a swivel. **2.** To secure, fit, or support with a swivel. *—intr.* To turn on or as if on a swivel. [Middle English *swyvel.*]

swivel chair *n.* A chair that swivels on its base.

swiv·el-hipped (swĭv′əl-hĭpt′) *adj.* Characterized by an exaggerated swinging movement of the hips.

swiv·et (swĭv′ĭt) *n.* *Informal.* Extreme distress or discomposure. [Origin unknown.]

swiz·zle (swĭz′əl) *n.* Any of various tall mixed drinks usually made with rum. [Origin unknown.]

swizzle stick *n.* A small, thin rod for stirring mixed drinks.

sycamore
American sycamore
Platanus occidentalis

swob (swŏb) *n. & v.* Variant of **swab.**

swol·len (swō′lən) *v.* A past participle of **swell. —swollen** *adj.* **1.** Expanded by or as if by internal pressure; distended: *a swollen toe.* **2.** Overblown; bombastic: *swollen rhetoric.*

swoon (swo͞on) *intr.v.* **swooned, swoon·ing, swoons. 1.** To faint. **2.** To be overwhelmed by ecstatic joy. **—swoon** *n.* **1.** A fainting spell; syncope. See Synonyms at **blackout. 2.** A state of ecstasy or rapture. [Middle English *swounen,* probably from *iswowen,* in a swoon, from Old English *geswōgen,* past participle of **swōgan,* to suffocate.]

swoop (swo͞op) *v.* **swooped, swoop·ing, swoops.** *—intr.* **1.** To move in a sudden sweep: *The bird swooped down on its prey.* **2.** To make a rush or an attack with or as if with a sudden sweeping movement. Often used with *down: The children swooped down on the pile of presents.* *—tr.* To seize or snatch in or as if in a sudden sweeping movement. **—swoop** *n.* The act or an instance of swooping. [Middle English *swopen,* to sweep along, from Old English *swāpan,* to sweep, swing.]

swoosh (swo͝osh, swo͞osh) *v.* **swooshed, swoosh·ing, swoosh·es.** *—intr.* **1.** To move with or make a rushing sound. **2.** To flow or swirl copiously. *—tr.* To cause to move with or make a rushing or swirling sound. [Imitative.]

swop (swŏp) *v. & n.* Variant of **swap.**

sword (sôrd) *n.* **1.** A weapon consisting typically of a long, straight or slightly curved, pointed blade having one or two cutting edges and set into a hilt. **2.** An instrument of death or destruction. **3. a.** The use of force, as in war. **b.** Military power or jurisdiction. ***—idioms.*** **at swords' points.** Ready for a fight. **put to the sword.** To kill; slay. [Middle English, from Old English *sweord.*]

sword bayonet *n.* A short sword that can be attached to the muzzle of a rifle for use as a bayonet.

sword·bill (sôrd′bĭl′) *n.* A hummingbird *(Ensifera ensifera)* of South America, having a slender bill that is longer than the head and body combined.

sword cane *n.* A cane with a hollow shaft in which a sword can be concealed.

sword dance *n.* A dance performed with swords, especially one performed around swords laid on the ground.

sword fern *n.* Any of various ferns of the genus *Nephrolepis,* including the Boston fern, having bipinnately compound fronds and sori at the vein tips.

sword·fish (sôrd′fĭsh′) *n., pl.* **swordfish** or **-fish·es.** A large marine food and game fish *(Xiphias gladius)* having a long swordlike extension of the upper jaw that is used chiefly as a means of defense and attack.

sword grass *n.* Any of various grasses or grasslike plants having pointed, swordlike leaves.

sword knot *n.* A decorative loop or tassel attached to the hilt of a sword.

sword lily *n.* *Botany.* See **gladiolus** (sense 1).

sword of Damocles *n.* Constant threat; imminent peril: *"the Latin American debt, overhanging American banks like the sword of Damocles"* (Arthur M. Schlesinger, Jr.). [After DAMOCLES.]

sword·play (sôrd′plā′) *n.* The act or art of using a sword, as in fencing.

swords·man (sôrdz′mən) *n.* **1.** A man who is skilled in the use of swords. **2.** A fencer. **—swords′man·ship′** *n.*

sword·tail (sôrd′tāl′) *n.* A small, brightly colored, livebearing freshwater fish *(Xiphophorus helleri)* of Central America, having a long, tapering extension of the caudal fin in the male and popular in home aquariums.

swore (swôr, swōr) *v.* Past tense of **swear.**

sworn (swôrn, swōrn) *v.* Past participle of **swear. —sworn** *adj.* **1.** Having been asserted as true under oath: *sworn statements by witnesses.* **2.** Bound or empowered by an oath: *a sworn official.* **3.** Avowed: *a sworn friend.*

swum (swŭm) *v.* Past participle of **swim.**

swung (swŭng) *v.* Past tense and past participle of **swing.**

swung dash *n.* *Printing.* A character (~) used to stand for all or part of a word that has previously been spelled out.

Syb·a·ris (sĭb′ər-ĭs). An ancient Greek city of southern Italy on the Gulf of Taranto. Noted for its wealth and luxury, it was destroyed in warfare with Crotona in 510 B.C.

Syb·a·rite (sĭb′ə-rīt) *n.* **1.** Often **sybarite.** A person devoted to pleasure and luxury; a voluptuary. **2.** A native or inhabitant of Sybaris. [Latin *Sybarīta,* native of Sybaris, from Greek *Subaritēs,* from *Subaris,* Sybaris.] **—syb′a·rit·ism** (-rĭ-tĭz′əm) *n.*

syb·a·rit·ic (sĭb′ə-rĭt′ĭk) *adj.* **1.** Devoted to or marked by often excessive or effete luxury. See Synonyms at **sensuous. 2. Sybaritic.** Of or relating to Sybaris or its people. **—syb′a·rit′i·cal·ly** *adv.*

syc·a·mine (sĭk′ə-mīn′, -mĭn) *n.* A tree mentioned in the New Testament, thought to be a species of mulberry. [Latin *sȳcamīnus,* from Greek *sukaminos,* of Semitic origin.]

syc·a·more (sĭk′ə-môr′, -mōr′) *n.* **1.** Any of various deciduous trees of the genus *Platanus,* especially *P. occidentalis* of eastern North America, having palmately lobed leaves, ball-like, nodding, hairy fruit clusters, and bark that flakes off in large colorful patches. Also called *buttonball, buttonwood.* **2.** A Eurasian deciduous maple tree *(Acer pseudoplatanus)* having palmately lobed leaves, winged fruits, and greenish flowers. **3.** A fig tree *(Ficus* *sycomorus)* of Africa and adjacent southwest Asia, mentioned in the Bible, having clusters of figs borne on short leafless twigs. [Middle English *sicamour,* a kind of fig tree, from Old French *sicamor,* from Latin *sȳcomorus,* from Greek *sukomoros* : *sukon,* fruit of the fig + *moron,* black mulberry.]

syce (sīs) *n.* A stableman or groom, especially in India. [Hindi *sā'is,* from Arabic, from *sāsa,* to administer.]

sy·cee (sī-sē′) *n.* Lumps of pure silver bearing the stamp of a banker or an assayer and formerly used in China as money. [Chinese (Cantonese) *sai sz,* fine silk (so called because the pure silver can be spun into fine threads), corresponding to Mandarin *xì sī* : *xì,* thin, fine + *sī,* silk, thread.]

sy·co·ni·um (sī-kō′nē-əm) *n., pl.* **-ni·a** (-nē-ə). The fleshy multiple fruit of the fig, consisting primarily of the enlarged, hollow, globose floral receptacle open at the apex and containing numerous fruitlets. [New Latin, from Greek *sukon,* fig.]

syc·o·phan·cy (sĭk′ə-fən-sē, sī′kə-) *n., pl.* **-cies.** The fawning behavior of a sycophant; servile flattery.

syc·o·phant (sĭk′ə-fənt, sī′kə-) *n.* A servile self-seeker who attempts to win favor by flattering influential people. [Latin *sȳcophanta,* informer, slanderer, from Greek *sukophantēs,* informer : *sukon,* fig + *-phantēs,* one who shows (from *phainein,* to show; see **bhā-**[1] in Appendix).] **—syc′o·phan′tic** (-făn′tĭk), **syc′o·phan′ti·cal** (-tĭ-kəl) *adj.* **—syc′o·phan′ti·cal·ly** *adv.*

syc·o·phan·tism (sĭk′ə-fən-tĭz′əm, sī′kə-) *n.* Sycophancy.

sy·co·sis (sī-kō′sĭs) *n.* A chronic inflammation of the hair follicles, especially of the beard, characterized by eruption of pimples and nodules. [Greek *sukōsis,* ulcer resembling a fig, from *sukon,* fig.]

Syd·en·ham's chorea (sĭd′n-əmz) *n.* A nervous disorder occurring chiefly in childhood or during pregnancy, closely associated with rheumatic fever, and characterized by rapid, jerky, involuntary movements of the body. Also called *Saint Vitus' dance.* [After Thomas *Sydenham* (1624–1689), English physician.]

Syd·ney (sĭd′nē). **1.** A city of southeast Australia on an inlet of the Tasman Sea. The largest city in Australia, it is the country's chief port and main cultural and financial center. Metropolitan area population, 3,358,550. **2.** A city of Nova Scotia, Canada, on eastern Cape Breton Island. It is a commercial and industrial center. Population, 29,444.

sy·e·nite (sī′ə-nīt′) *n.* An igneous rock composed primarily of alkali feldspar together with other minerals, such as hornblende. [Latin *Syēnītēs (lapis),* (stone) of Syene, from *Syēnē,* Syene, an ancient city of southern Egypt, from Greek *Suēnē.*] **—sy′e·nit′ic** (-nĭt′ĭk) *adj.*

syl. *abbr.* Syllable.

syll. *abbr.* Syllable.

syl·la·bar·y (sĭl′ə-bĕr′ē) *n., pl.* **-ies.** **1.** A list of syllables. **2.** A list or set of written characters for a language, each character representing a syllable. [New Latin *syllabārium,* from Latin *syllaba,* syllable. See SYLLABLE.]

syl·la·bi (sĭl′ə-bī′) *n.* A plural of **syllabus.**

syl·lab·ic (sĭ-lăb′ĭk) *adj.* **1.** *Linguistics.* **a.** Of, relating to, or consisting of a syllable or syllables. **b.** Designating a consonant that forms a syllable without a vowel, such as the (l) in *riddle* (rĭd′l). **c.** Pronounced with every syllable distinct. **2.** Of or being a form of verse based on the number of syllables in a line rather than on the arrangement of accents or quantities. **—syllabic** *n. Linguistics.* A syllabic sound. [Medieval Latin *syllabicus,* from Greek *sullabikos,* from *sullabē,* syllable. See SYLLABLE.] **—syl·lab′i·cal·ly** *adv.*

syl·lab·i·fy (sĭ-lăb′ĭ-fī′) or **syl·lab·i·cate** (-kāt′) *tr.v.* **-fied, -fy·ing, -fies** or **-cat·ed, -cat·ing, -cates.** To form or divide into syllables. **—syl·lab′i·fi·ca′tion** (-fĭ-kā′shən), **syl·lab′i·ca′tion** (-kā′shən) *n.*

syl·la·bism (sĭl′ə-bĭz′əm) *n.* **1.** Division of a word or phrase into syllables. **2.** Use of syllabic characters in writing. [Latin *syllaba,* syllable; see SYLLABLE + –ISM.]

syl·la·bize (sĭl′ə-bīz′) *tr.v.* **-bized, -biz·ing, -biz·es.** To syllabify. [Medieval Latin *syllabizāre,* to quibble, from Greek *sullabizein,* to syllabify, from *sullabē,* syllable. See SYLLABLE.]

syl·la·ble (sĭl′ə-bəl) *n. Abbr.* **syl., syll.** **1.** *Linguistics.* **a.** A unit of spoken language consisting of a single uninterrupted sound formed by a vowel, diphthong, or syllabic consonant alone, or by any of these sounds preceded, followed, or surrounded by one or more consonants. **b.** One or more letters or phonetic symbols written or printed to approximate a spoken syllable. **2.** The slightest bit of spoken or written expression: *Do not alter a syllable of this message.* **—syllable** *tr.v.* **-bled, -bling, -bles.** *Linguistics.* To pronounce in syllables. [Middle English *sillable,* from Anglo-Norman, alteration of Old French *sillabe,* from Latin *syllaba,* from Greek *sullabē,* from *sullabein,* second aorist of *sullambanein,* to combine in pronunciation : *sun-,* syn- + *lambanein,* to take.]

syl·la·bub also **sil·la·bub** (sĭl′ə-bŭb′) *n.* **1.** A drink made of sweetened milk or cream curdled with wine or spirits. **2.** A cold dessert made with sweetened cream thickened with gelatin and beaten with wine, spirits, or fruit juice. [Origin unknown.]

syl·la·bus (sĭl′ə-bəs) *n., pl.* **-bus·es** or **-bi** (-bī′). **1.** An outline or a summary of the main points of a text, lecture, or course of study. **2.** *Law.* A short statement preceding a report on an adjudged case and containing a summary of the court's rulings on each point involved. [Medieval Latin, probably alteration (influenced by Greek *sullambanein,* to put together; see SYLLABLE) of Latin *sillybus,* parchment label, from Greek *sillubos.*]

syl·lep·sis (sĭ-lĕp′sĭs) *n., pl.* **-ses** (-sēz). A construction in which a word governs two or more other words but agrees in number, gender, or case with only one, or has a different meaning when applied to each of the words, as in *He lost his coat and his temper.* [Late Latin *syllēpsis,* from Greek *sullēpsis* : *sun-,* syn- + *lēpsis,* a taking (from *lambanein,* to take).] **—syl·lep′tic** (-lĕp′tĭk) *adj.*

syl·lo·gism (sĭl′ə-jĭz′əm) *n.* **1.** *Logic.* A form of deductive reasoning consisting of a major premise, a minor premise, and a conclusion; for example, *All human beings are mortal,* the major premise, *I am a human being,* the minor premise, *therefore, I am mortal,* the conclusion. **2.** Reasoning from the general to the specific; deduction. **3.** A subtle or specious piece of reasoning. [Middle English *silogisme,* from Old French, from Latin *syllogismus,* from Greek *sullogismos,* from *sullogizesthai,* to infer : *sun-,* syn- + *logizesthai,* to count, reckon (from *logos,* reason; see **leg-** in Appendix).]

syl·lo·gist (sĭl′ə-jĭst) *n.* One who uses or is skilled in syllogistic reasoning.

syl·lo·gis·tic (sĭl′ə-jĭs′tĭk) also **syl·lo·gis·ti·cal** (-tĭ-kəl) *adj.* Of, relating to, resembling, or consisting of a syllogism or syllogisms. **—syl′lo·gis′ti·cal·ly** *adv.*

syl·lo·gize (sĭl′ə-jīz′) *v.* **-gized, -giz·ing, -giz·es.** *—intr.* To reason or argue by means of syllogisms. *—tr.* To deduce by syllogism. **—syl′lo·gi·za′tion** (-jĭ-zā′shən) *n.* **—syl′lo·giz′er** *n.*

sylph (sĭlf) *n.* **1.** A slim, graceful woman or girl. **2.** Any of a class of elemental, soulless beings that in the theories of Paracelsus were believed to inhabit the air. [New Latin *sylpha,* perhaps blend of Latin *sylvestris,* of the forest (from *silva, sylva,* forest) and Latin *nympha,* nymph; see NYMPH.]

sylph·id (sĭl′fĭd) *n.* A young or diminutive sylph. **—sylphid** *adj.* Relating to or resembling a sylph. [French *sylphide,* from *sylphe,* sylph, from New Latin *sylpha.* See SYLPH.]

syl·va (sĭl′və) *n.* Variant of **silva.**

syl·van also **sil·van** (sĭl′vən) *—adj.* **1.** Relating to or characteristic of woods or forest regions. **2.** Located in or inhabiting a wood or forest. **3.** Abounding in trees; wooded. *—n.* One that lives in or frequents the woods. [Medieval Latin *sylvānus,* from Latin *Silvānus,* god of the woods, from *silva,* forest.]

syl·van·ite (sĭl′və-nīt′) *n.* A pale brass-yellow to silver-white ore of gold and silver, chiefly $(Au,Ag)Te_2$. [French, after TRANSYLVANIA.]

Syl·va·nus (sĭl-vā′nəs) *n. Roman Mythology.* Variant of **Silvanus.**

syl·vat·ic (sĭl-văt′ĭk) *adj.* **1.** Affecting only wild animals: *sylvatic rabies; sylvatic and domestic bacterial strains.* **2.** Sylvan. [Latin *sylvāticus,* of the forest, wild, from *silva, sylva,* forest.]

syl·vite (sĭl′vīt′) also **syl·vine** (-vēn′) or **syl·vin·ite** (-vĭ-nīt′) *n.* A colorless vitreous potassium chloride mineral, the major ore of potassium. [Alteration of *sylvine,* from French, from New Latin *(sal digestivus) Sylvii,* (digestive salt) of Sylvius, probably after Franz de la Boë, or Franciscus *Sylvius* (1614–1672), German-born Dutch physician.]

sym. *abbr.* **1.** Symbol. **2.** Symmetrical. **3.** *Music.* Symphony.

sym– *pref.* Variant of **syn–.**

sym·bi·ont (sĭm′bē-ŏnt′, -bī-) *n.* An organism in a symbiotic relationship. Also called *symbiote.* [Greek *sumbiōn, sumbiount-,* present participle of *sumbioun,* to live together. See SYMBIOSIS.] **—sym′bi·on′tic** *adj.*

sym·bi·o·sis (sĭm′bē-ō′sĭs, -bī-) *n., pl.* **-ses** (-sēz). **1.** *Biology.* A close, prolonged association between two or more different organisms of different species that may, but does not necessarily, benefit each member. **2.** A relationship of mutual benefit or dependence. [Greek *sumbiōsis,* companionship, from *sumbioun,* to live together, from *sumbios,* living together : *sun-,* syn- + *bios,* life; see **gʷei-** in Appendix.] **—sym′bi·ot′ic** (-ŏt′ĭk), **sym′bi·ot′i·cal** (-ĭ-kəl) *adj.* **—sym′bi·ot′i·cal·ly** *adv.*

sym·bi·ote (sĭm′bē-ōt′, -bī-) *n.* See **symbiont.** [French, from Greek *sumbiōtēs,* companion, from *sumbioun,* to live together. See SYMBIOSIS.]

sym·bol (sĭm′bəl) *n. Abbr.* **sym.** **1.** Something that represents something else by association, resemblance, or convention, especially a material object used to represent something invisible. **2.** A printed or written sign used to represent an operation, an element, a quantity, a quality, or a relation, as in mathematics or music. **—symbol** *tr.v.* **-boled, -bol·ing, -bols.** To symbolize. [Middle English *symbole,* creed, from Old French, from Latin *symbolum,* token, mark, from Greek *sumbolon,* token for identification (by comparison with a counterpart) : *sun-,* syn- + *ballein,* to throw; see **gʷelə-** in Appendix.]

SYNONYMS: *symbol, attribute, emblem.* The central meaning shared by these nouns is "something associated with and standing for, representing, or identifying something else": *scales, the symbol of justice; the scepter, an attribute of royal power; the thistle, the emblem of Scotland.*

sym·bol·ic (sĭm-bŏl′ĭk) also **sym·bol·i·cal** (-ĭ-kəl) *adj.* **1.** Of, relating to, or expressed by means of symbols or a symbol. **2.**

symbiosis
Egret and hippopotamus

ă pat — oi boy
ā pay — ou out
âr care — ŏŏ took
ä father — ōō boot
ĕ pet — ŭ cut
ē be — ûr urge
ĭ pit — th thin
ī pie — *th* this
îr pier — hw which
ŏ pot — zh vision
ō toe — ə about, item
ô paw — ♦ regionalism

Stress marks: ′ (primary); ′ (secondary), as in **dictionary** (dĭk′shə-nĕr′ē)

SYMBOLS AND SIGNS

The following symbols and signs and their designations are among those most commonly used. The designations do not exhaust the meanings that may be attached to the symbols. Symbols consisting of letters of the alphabet are entered in the regular alphabetical sequence of entries. See also symbols in tables at **element, measurement, subatomic particle,** and **proofread,** and foreign letters at **alphabet.**

ASTRONOMY

☉ or ☼	sun
● or ◍	new moon
☽	first quarter
○ or ☺	full moon
☾	last quarter
☿	Mercury
♀	Venus
⊖ or ⊕	Earth
♂	Mars
♃	Jupiter
♄	Saturn
♅	Uranus
♆	Neptune
♇	Pluto
♈	Aries
♉	Taurus
♊	Gemini
♋	Cancer
♌	Leo
♍	Virgo
♎	Libra
♏	Scorpio
♐	Sagittarius
♑	Capricorn
♒	Aquarius
♓	Pisces
☌	conjunction
☍	opposition
△	trine
□	quadrature
✶	sextile
☊	ascending node
☋	descending node

BIOLOGY

☉ or ①	annual
⊙ or ②	biennial
♃	perennial
♂ or ♂	male
♀	female
□	male (in charts)
○	female (in charts)

CHEMISTRY

⌬	benzene ring
→	reaction direction
⇄	reversible reaction
↓	precipitate
↑	gas

DIACRITICS

´	acute
`	grave
˜	tilde
ˆ	circumflex
¯	macron
˘	breve
¨	dieresis
¸	cedilla

MATHEMATICS

+	plus
−	minus
±	plus or minus
∓	minus or plus
×	multiplied by
÷	divided by
=	equal to
≠	not equal to
≈	approximately equal to
≡	identical with
≢	not identical with
≍	equivalent
≅	congruent to
>	greater than
≯	not greater than
<	less than
≮	not less than
≧ or ≥	greater than or equal to
≦ or ≤	less than or equal to
| |	absolute value
≐	approaches
→	approaches
∝	proportional to, varies as
∥	parallel
⊥	perpendicular
∠	angle
∟	right angle
△	triangle
□	square
▭	rectangle
▱	parallelogram
○	circle
⌒	arc of circle
⊥̲	equilateral
≙	equiangular
√	radical; root; square root
∛	cube root
∜	fourth root
Σ	sum
! or ⌊	factorial product
∞	infinity
∫	integral
ƒ	function
∂ or δ	differential; variation
π	pi
∪	logical sum or union
∩	logical product or intersection
⊂	is contained in
⊃	implication
∈	is a member of; mean error
:	is to; ratio
::	as; proportion
∴	therefore
∵	because

METEOROLOGY

◍	rain
✱	snow
⊠	snow on ground
←	ice crystals
◬	hail
△	sleet
∨	frostwork
⊔	hoarfrost
≡	fog
∞	haze; dust haze
T	thunder
⚡	lightning
⦶	solar corona
⊕	solar halo
ꓘ	thunderstorm

PHARMACOLOGY

℞	take
ĀĀ, Ā, or āā	of each
℔	pound
℥	ounce
ʒ	dram
℈	scruple
f℥	fluid ounce
fʒ	fluid dram
♏	minim

PHYSICS

°	degree
′	minute
″	second
△	increment, change
ω	angular frequency; solid angle
Ω	ohm
μΩ	microhm
MΩ	megohm
Φ	magnetic flux
Ψ	dielectric flux; electrostatic flux
Λ	equivalent conductivity
→	direction of flow
⇄	electric current

TYPOGRAPHY

[ ]	brackets
{ }	braces
‾	vinculum (above letter)
( )	parentheses
& or &	and; ampersand
#	number
/	virgule; slash
©	copyright
%	per cent
℅	care of
℀	account of
@	at
*	asterisk
†	dagger
‡	double dagger
§	section
☞	index
‸	caret

Serving as a symbol. **3.** Using symbolism: *symbolic art.* **—sym·bol′i·cal·ly** *adv.* **—sym·bol′i·cal·ness** *n.*

symbolic address *n. Computer Science.* An address expressed in symbolic form as a convenience to the programmer.

sym·bol·i·cal (sĭm-bŏl′ĭ-kəl) *adj.* Variant of **symbolic.**

symbolic language *n. Computer Science.* A high-level programming language.

symbolic logic *n.* A treatment of formal logic in which a system of symbols is used to represent quantities and relationships. Also called *mathematical logic.*

sym·bol·ism (sĭm′bə-lĭz′əm) *n.* **1.** The practice of representing things by means of symbols or of attributing symbolic meanings or significance to objects, events, or relationships. **2.** A system of symbols or representations. **3.** A symbolic meaning or representation. **4.** Revelation or suggestion of intangible conditions or truths by artistic invention. **5. Symbolism.** The movement, theory, or practice of the late 19th-century Symbolists.

sym·bol·ist (sĭm′bə-lĭst) *n.* **1.** One who uses symbols or symbolism. **2.a.** One who interprets or represents conditions or truths by the use of symbols or symbolism. **b.** *Often* **Symbolist.** Any of a group of chiefly French writers and artists of the late 19th century who expressed their ideas and emotions indirectly through symbols. **—symbolist** *adj.* **1.** Of or relating to symbolism. **2.** Often **Symbolist.** Of or relating to the Symbolists. **—sym′bol·is′tic** *adj.* **—sym′bol·is′ti·cal·ly** *adv.*

sym·bol·ize (sĭm′bə-līz′) *v.* **-ized, -iz·ing, -iz·es.** *—tr.* **1.** To serve as a symbol of: *"Munich, the 1938 Hitler-Chamberlain meeting that now symbolizes the idea of appeasement"* (Jonathan Alter). **2.** To represent or identify by a symbol. *—intr.* To use symbols. **—sym′bol·i·za′tion** (-bə-lĭ-zā′shən) *n.* **—sym′bol·iz′er** *n.*

sym·bol·o·gy (sĭm-bŏl′ə-jē) *n.* **1.** The study or interpretation of symbols or symbolism. **2.** The use of symbols.

sym·met·all·ism (sĭm-mĕt′l-ĭz′əm) *n.* A system of coinage in which a unit of currency is pegged to a combination of two or more metals in fixed proportions.

sym·met·ri·cal (sĭ-mĕt′rĭ-kəl) also **sym·met·ric** (-rĭk) *adj. Abbr.* **sym.** Of or exhibiting symmetry. **—sym·met′ri·cal·ly** *adv.*

symmetric group *n. Mathematics.* A group consisting of all possible permutations of a given number of items.

symmetric matrix *n. Mathematics.* A matrix that is its own transpose.

sym·me·trize (sĭm′ĭ-trīz′) *tr.v.* **-trized, -triz·ing, -triz·es.** To give symmetry to; make symmetrical or proportional. **—sym′me·tri·za′tion** (-trĭ-zā′shən) *n.*

sym·me·try (sĭm′ĭ-trē) *n., pl.* **-tries. 1.** Exact correspondence of form and constituent configuration on opposite sides of a dividing line or plane or about a center or an axis. See Synonyms at **proportion. 2.** A relationship of characteristic correspondence, equivalence, or identity among constituents of an entity or between different entities: *the narrative symmetry of the novel.* **3.** Beauty as a result of balance or harmonious arrangement. [Latin *symmetria,* from Greek *summetria,* from *summetros,* of like measure : *sun-,* syn- + *metron,* measure; see **mē-**[2] in Appendix.]

Sym·onds (sĭm′əndz, sĭ′məndz), **John Addington.** 1840–1893. British writer noted for his seven-volume series *The Renaissance in Italy* (1875–1886).

Sy·mons (sī′mənz), **Arthur.** 1865–1945. British poet and literary critic who translated many French symbolist works into English and wrote *The Symbolist Movement in Literature* (1899).

sym·pa·thec·to·my (sĭm′pə-thĕk′tə-mē) *n., pl.* **-mies.** Surgical removal of a part of the sympathetic nervous system. [SYMPATH(ETIC) + -ECTOMY.]

sym·pa·thet·ic (sĭm′pə-thĕt′ĭk) *adj.* **1.** Of, expressing, feeling, or resulting from sympathy: *a sympathetic glance.* **2.** Favorably inclined: *not at all sympathetic to her proposal.* **3.** Agreeably suited to one's disposition or mood; congenial: *sympathetic surroundings.* **4.** Of, relating to, or acting on the sympathetic nervous system: *a sympathetic neuron; sympathetic stimulation.* **5. a.** Relating to or being vibrations, especially musical tones, produced in one body by energy from a nearby vibrating body and having the same frequency as the vibration of the nearby body. **b.** Emitting such vibrations: *sympathetic strings.* [Greek *sumpathētikos,* from *sumpatheia,* sympathy. See SYMPATHY.] **—sym′pa·thet′i·cal·ly** *adv.*

sympathetic ink *n.* See **invisible ink.**

sympathetic nervous system *n. Anatomy.* The part of the autonomic nervous system originating in the thoracic and lumbar regions of the spinal cord that in general inhibits or opposes the physiological effects of the parasympathetic nervous system, as in tending to reduce digestive secretions, speeding up the heart, and contracting blood vessels.

sym·pa·thize (sĭm′pə-thīz′) *intr.v.* **-thized, -thiz·ing, -thiz·es. 1.** To feel or express compassion, as for another's suffering; commiserate. **2.** To share or understand the feelings or ideas of another: *sympathized with the goals of the committee.* **3.** To be in accord; correspond. **—sym′pa·thiz′er** *n.* **—sym′pa·thiz′ing·ly** *adv.*

sym·pa·tho·lyt·ic (sĭm′pə-thō-lĭt′ĭk) *adj.* Opposing the physiological effects caused by stimulation of the sympathetic nervous system: *a sympatholytic treatment.* [SYMPATH(ETIC) + –LYTIC.]

sym·pa·tho·mi·met·ic (sĭm′pə-thō-mĭ-mĕt′ĭk, -mī-) *adj.* Producing physiological effects resembling those caused by the activity or stimulation of the sympathetic nervous system: *a sympathomimetic hormone.* **—sympathomimetic** *n.* A sympathomimetic drug or agent. [SYMPATH(ETIC) + MIMETIC.]

sym·pa·thy (sĭm′pə-thē) *n., pl.* **-thies. 1. a.** A relationship or an affinity between people or things in which whatever affects one correspondingly affects the other. **b.** Mutual understanding or affection arising from this relationship or affinity. **2. a.** The act or power of sharing the feelings of another. **b.** *Often* **sympathies.** A feeling or an expression of pity or sorrow for the distress of another; compassion or commiseration. See Synonyms at **pity. 3.** Harmonious agreement; accord: *He is in sympathy with their beliefs.* **4.** A feeling of loyalty; allegiance. Often used in the plural: *His sympathies lie with his family.* **5.** *Physiology.* A relation between parts or organs by which a disease or disorder in one induces an effect in the other. [Latin *sympathīa,* from Greek *sumpatheia,* from *sumpathēs,* affected by like feelings : *sun-,* syn- + *pathos,* emotion; see **k^{w}ent(h)-** in Appendix.]

sympathy strike *n.* A strike by a body of workers for the purpose of supporting a cause or another group of strikers.

sym·pat·ric (sĭm-păt′rĭk) *adj. Ecology.* Occupying the same or overlapping geographic areas without interbreeding. Used of populations of closely related species. [SYN– + Greek *patra,* fatherland (from *patēr,* father; see **pəter-** in Appendix) + –IC.] **—sym·pat′ri·cal·ly** *adv.*

sym·pat·ry (sĭm′păt′rē, -pə-trē) *n., pl.* **-ries.** The occurrence of sympatric species or forms.

sym·pet·al·ous (sĭm-pĕt′l-əs) *adj.* Having united petals; gamopetalous.

sym·phon·ic (sĭm-fŏn′ĭk) *adj.* **1.** *Music.* Relating to or having the character or form of a symphony. **2.** Harmonious in sound.

symphonic poem *n. Music.* A piece of music, most popular in the late 19th century, that is based on an extramusical theme, such as a story or nationalistic ideal, and consists of a single extended movement for a symphony orchestra. Also called *tone poem.*

sym·pho·ni·ous (sĭm-fō′nē-əs) *adj.* Being in a state of accord; harmonious. **—sym·pho′ni·ous·ly** *adv.*

sym·pho·nist (sĭm′fə-nĭst) *n. Music.* One who composes symphonies.

sym·pho·ny (sĭm′fə-nē) *n., pl.* **-nies. 1.** *Abbr.* **sym.** *Music.* **a.** An extended piece in three or more movements for symphony orchestra, essentially a large-scale, complex sonata. **b.** An instrumental passage in a vocal or choral composition. **c.** An instrumental overture or interlude, as in early opera. **2.** *Music.* **a.** A symphony orchestra. **b.** An orchestral concert. **3.** Harmony, especially of sound or color. **4.** Something characterized by a harmonious combination of elements. [Middle English *symphonye,* harmony, from Old French *symphonie,* from Latin *symphōnia,* from Greek *sumphōnia,* from *sumphōnos,* harmonious : *sun-,* syn- + *phōnē,* sound; see **bhā-**^{2} in Appendix.]

symphony orchestra *n. Music.* A large orchestra composed of string, wind, and percussion sections.

sym·phy·sis (sĭm′fĭ-sĭs) *n., pl.* **-ses** (-sēz′). **1. a.** A growing together of bones originally separate, as of the two pubic bones or the two halves of the lower jawbone. **b.** A line or junction thus formed. **c.** An articulation in which bones are united by cartilage without a synovial membrane. **2.** The coalescence of similar parts or organs. [Greek *sumphusis,* from *sumphuein,* to cause to grow together : *sun-,* syn- + *phuein,* to cause to grow; see **bheuə-** in Appendix.] **—sym′phy·se′al** (sĭm′-fĭ-sē′əl), **sym·phys′i·al** (sĭm-fĭz′ē-əl) *adj.*

sym·po·di·um (sĭm-pō′dē-əm) *n., pl.* **-di·a** (-dē-ə). *Botany.* A primary axis that develops from a series of short lateral branches and often has a zigzag or irregular form, as in orchids of the genus *Cattleya.* Also called *pseudaxis.* [New Latin : SYN– + Greek *podion,* base (from *pous, pod-,* foot; see **ped-** in Appendix).] **—sym·po′di·al** (-dē-əl) *adj.* **—sym·po′di·al·ly** *adv.*

sym·po·si·a (sĭm-pō′zē-ə) *n.* A plural of **symposium.**

sym·po·si·ac (sĭm-pō′zē-ăk′) *adj.* Of, relating to, or appropriate to a symposium. **—symposiac** *n. Archaic.* A symposium.

sym·po·si·arch (sĭm-pō′zē-ärk′) *n.* **1.** The master or director of a symposium, especially one in ancient Greece. **2.** A toastmaster. [Greek *sumposiarkhos* : *sumposion,* symposium; see SYMPOSIUM + *arkhos,* ruler; see –ARCH.]

sym·po·si·ast (sĭm-pō′zē-ăst′, -əst) *n.* A participant in a symposium.

sym·po·si·um (sĭm-pō′zē-əm) *n., pl.* **-si·ums** or **-si·a** (-zē-ə). **1.** A meeting or conference for discussion of a topic, especially one in which the participants form an audience and make presentations. **2.** A collection of writings on a particular topic, as in a magazine. **3.** A convivial meeting for drinking, music, and intellectual discussion among the ancient Greeks. [Latin, drinking party, from Greek *sumposion* : *sun-,* syn- + *posis,* drinking; see **pō(i)-** in Appendix.]

symp·tom (sĭm′təm, sĭmp′-) *n.* **1.** A characteristic sign or indication of the existence of something else: *"The affair is a symptom of a global marital disturbance; it is not the disturbance itself"* (Maggie Scarf). See Synonyms at **sign. 2.** A sign or an indication of disorder or disease, especially when experienced by an individual as a change from normal function, sensation, or appearance. [Alteration (influenced by Late Latin *symptōma*) of Middle English *sinthoma,* symptom of a disease, from Medieval Latin *sinthōma,* from Late Latin *symptōma,* from Greek *sumptōma, sumptōmat-,* a happening, symptom of a disease, from *sumpiptein,* to coincide : *sun-,* syn- + *piptein,* to fall; see **pet-** in Appendix.] **—symp′tom·less** *adj.*

symp·to·mat·ic (sĭm′tə-măt′ĭk, sĭmp′-) *adj.* **1.** Of, relating to, or based on symptoms: *symptomatic relief.* **2.** Constituting a symptom, as of a disease: *the rash symptomatic of scarlet fever; a rise in unemployment symptomatic of a weakening economy.* **—symp′to·mat′i·cal·ly** *adv.*

symp·tom·a·tize (sĭm′tə-mə-tīz′, sĭmp′-) *v.* Variant of **symptomize.**

symp·to·ma·tol·o·gy (sĭm′tə-mə-tŏl′ə-jē, sĭmp′-) *n.* **1.** The medical science of symptoms. **2.** The combined symptoms of a disease. [New Latin *symptōmatologia* : Greek *sumptōma, sumptōmat-,* symptom; see SYMPTOM + Latin *-logia,* -logy.] **—symp′to·mat′o·log′i·cal** (-măt′l-ŏj′ĭ-kəl) *adj.* **—symp′to·mat′o·log′i·cal·ly** *adv.*

symp·tom·ize (sĭm′tə-mīz′, sĭmp′-) or **symp·tom·a·tize** (-tə-mə-tīz′) *tr.v.* **-ized, -iz·ing, -iz·es** or **-tized, -tiz·ing, -tiz·es.** To be a symptom of: *The infection is symptomized by chronic fatigue. High absenteeism often symptomizes job dissatisfaction.*

syn. *abbr.* Synonym; synonymous; synonymy.

syn– or **sym–** *pref.* **1. a.** Together; with: *synecology.* **b.** United: *syncarp.* **2. a.** Same; similar: *sympatric.* **b.** At the same time: *synesthesia.* [Greek *sun-,* from *sun.* See **ksun** in Appendix.]

syn·aer·e·sis (sĭ-nĕr′ĭ-sĭs) *n.* Variant of **syneresis.**

syn·aes·the·sia (sĭn′ĭs-thē′zhə) *n.* Variant of **synesthesia.**

syn·a·gogue also **syn·a·gog** (sĭn′ə-gŏg′, -gôg′) *n.* **1.** A building or place of meeting for worship and religious instruction in the Jewish faith. **2.** A congregation of Jews for the purpose of worship or religious study. **3.** The Jewish religion as organized or typified in local congregations. [Middle English, from Old French *sinagoge,* from Late Latin *synagōga,* from Greek *sunagōgē,* assembly, synagogue, from *sunagein,* to bring together : *sun-,* syn- + *agein,* to lead; see **ag-** in Appendix.] **—syn′a·gog′i·cal** (-gŏj′ĭ-kəl), **syn′a·gog′al** (-gŏg′əl, -gôg′-) *adj.*

syn·a·le·pha also **syn·a·loe·pha** (sĭn′ə-lē′fə) *n.* The blending into one syllable of two successive vowels of adjacent syllables, especially to fit a poetic meter; for example, *th' elite* for *the elite.* [New Latin, from Greek *sunaloiphē,* from *sunaleiphein,* to coalesce, unite two syllables : *sun-,* syn- + *aleiphein,* to smear; see **leip-** in Appendix.]

syn·apse (sĭn′ăps′, sĭ-năps′) *n.* The junction across which a nerve impulse passes from an axon terminal to a neuron, a muscle cell, or a gland cell. **—synapse** *intr.v.* **-apsed, -aps·ing, -aps·es. 1.** To form a synapse. **2.** To undergo synapsis. [Greek *sunapsis,* point of contact, from *sunaptein,* to join together : *sun-,* syn- + *haptein,* to fasten.]

syn·ap·sis (sĭ-năp′sĭs) *n., pl.* **-ses** (-sēz). The side-by-side association of homologous paternal and maternal chromosomes during the early prophase of meiosis. [New Latin, from Greek *sunapsis,* point of contact. See SYNAPSE.]

syn·ap·tic (sĭ-năp′tĭk) *adj.* Of or relating to synapsis or a synapse: *synaptic nerve endings; the synaptic phase in meiosis.* [From Greek *sunaptos,* joined together, from *sunaptein,* to join together. See SYNAPSE.] **—syn·ap′ti·cal·ly** *adv.*

synaptic gap *n.* The minute space between the cell membrane of an axon terminal and that of the target cell with which it synapses.

syn·ap·ti·ne·mal complex also **syn·ap·to·ne·mal complex** (sĭ-năp′tə-nĕm′əl) *n.* A ribbonlike structure consisting of three protein components and extending across the region of synapsed chromosomes during the prophase of meiosis. [SYNAPTI(C)

synagogue
Temple Ohabei Shalom, Brookline, Massachusetts

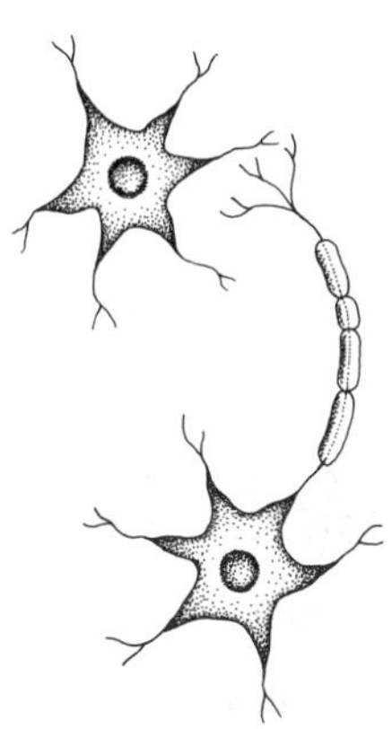

synapse

ă pat	oi boy
ā pay	ou out
âr care	ŏŏ took
ä father	ōō boot
ĕ pet	ŭ cut
ē be	ûr urge
ĭ pit	th thin
ī pie	*th* this
îr pier	hw which
ŏ pot	zh vision
ō toe	ə about, item
ô paw	♦ regionalism

Stress marks: **′** (primary); ′ (secondary), as in **dictionary** (dĭk′shə-nĕr′ē)

+ Greek *nēma,* thread; see **(s)nē-** in Appendix + –AL[1].]

syn·ap·to·some (sĭ-năp′tə-sōm′) *n.* A saclike structure formed by nerve endings at a synapse that remains intact after homogenization of nerve tissue. **—syn·ap′to·so′mal** *adj.*

syn·ar·thro·di·a (sĭn′är-thrō′dē-ə) *n., pl.* **-di·ae** (-dē-ē′). *Anatomy.* See **synarthrosis.** [SYN– + Greek *arthrōdia,* a kind of articulation (from *arthrōdēs,* well-jointed, from *arthron,* joint; see SYNARTHROSIS).] **—syn′ar·thro′di·al** *adj.* **—syn′ar·thro′di·al·ly** *adv.*

syn·ar·thro·sis (sĭn′är-thrō′sĭs) *n., pl.* **-ses** (-sēz). *Anatomy.* A form of articulation in which the bones are rigidly joined by fibrous tissue. Also called *synarthrodia.* [Greek *sunarthrōsis,* from *sunarthrousthai,* to be joined by articulation : *sun-,* syn- + *arthron,* a joint; see **ar-** in Appendix.]

sync or **synch** (sĭngk) *Informal.* —*n.* **1.** Synchronization: *"an effect like that of stereo speakers slightly out of sync"* (Time). **2.** Harmony; accord: *in sync with today's fashions.* —*intr. & tr.v.* **synced, sync·ing, syncs** or **synched, synch·ing, synchs.** To synchronize.

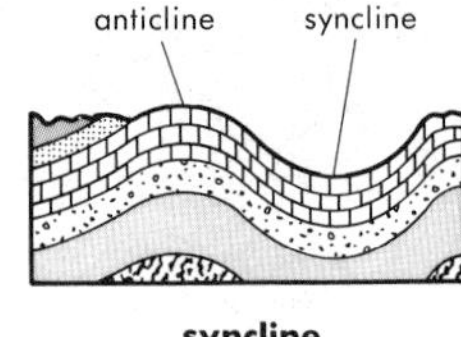

syncline

syn·carp (sĭn′kärp′) *n.* A fleshy compound fruit composed either of the fruits of several flowers, as in the pineapple and mulberry, or of several carpels of a single flower, as in the magnolia and raspberry.

syn·car·pous (sĭn-kär′pəs) *adj.* Having or consisting of united carpels. Used of a pistil. **—syn′car·py** *n.*

synch (sĭngk) *n. & v. Informal.* Variant of **sync.**

syn·chon·dro·sis (sĭng′kŏn-drō′sĭs, sĭn′-) *n., pl.* **-ses** (-sēz). A form of articulation in which the bones are rigidly fused by cartilage. [New Latin *synchondrōsis,* from Greek *sunkhondrōsis* : *sun-,* syn- + *khondros,* cartilage + *-ōsis,* -osis.]

syn·chro (sĭng′krō, sĭn′-) *n., pl.* **-chros.** A selsyn. [Short for SYNCHRONOUS.]

synchro– *pref.* Synchronized; synchronous: *synchrotron.*

syn·chro·cy·clo·tron (sĭng′krō-sī′klə-trŏn′, sĭn′-) *n.* A cyclotron that accelerates protons and positive ions by using frequency modulation to synchronize the phase of the accelerating potential with the frequency of the accelerated particles to compensate for relativistic increases in particle mass at high speeds.

syn·chro·flash (sĭng′krō-flăsh′, sĭn′-) *n.* A device used in photography to synchronize the peak of a flash created by a flash lamp with the opening of the camera shutter. **—syn′chro·flash′** *adj.*

syn·chro·mesh (sĭng′krə-mĕsh′, sĭn′-) *n.* **1.** An automotive gear-shifting system in which the gears are synchronized at the same speeds before engaging to effect a smooth shift. **2.** A gear in such a system. **—syn′chro·mesh′** *adj.*

syn·chro·nal (sĭng′krə-nəl, sĭn′-) *adj.* Synchronous.

syn·chron·ic (sĭn-krŏn′ĭk, sĭng-) *adj.* **1.** Synchronous. **2.a.** Descriptive. **b.** Relating to or being the study of events of a particular time or era without reference to historical context. **—syn·chron′i·cal·ly** *adv.*

syn·chro·nic·i·ty (sĭng′krə-nĭs′ĭ-tē, sĭn′-) *n., pl.* **-ties. 1.** The state or fact of being synchronous or simultaneous; synchronism. **2.** Coincidence of events that seem to be meaningfully related, conceived in the theory of Carl Jung as an explanatory principle on the same order as causality.

syncopation
From Mozart's Symphony no. 25

synchronic linguistics *n. (used with a sing. verb).* Descriptive linguistics.

syn·chro·nism (sĭng′krə-nĭz′əm, sĭn′-) *n.* **1.** Coincidence in time; simultaneousness. **2.** A chronological listing of historical personages or events so as to indicate parallel existence or occurrence. **3.** Representation in the same artwork of events that occurred at different times. **—syn′chro·nis′tic, syn′chro·nis′ti·cal** (-tĭ-kəl) *adj.* **—syn′chro·nis′ti·cal·ly** *adv.*

syn·chro·nize (sĭng′krə-nīz′, sĭn′-) *v.* **-nized, -niz·ing, -niz·es.** —*intr.* **1.** To occur at the same time; be simultaneous. **2.** To operate in unison. —*tr.* **1.a.** To cause to occur or operate with exact coincidence in time or rate: *We synchronized our watches.* **b.** To cause to occur or operate at the same time as something else: *They synchronized their trip with the annual tulip festival.* **2.** To arrange (historical events) in a synchronism so as to indicate parallel occurrence. **3.** To cause (soundtrack and action) to match exactly in a film. [Greek *sunkhronizein,* to be contemporary, from *sunkhronos,* contemporaneous. See SYNCHRONOUS.] **—syn′chro·ni·za′tion** (-nĭ-zā′shən) *n.*

syn·chro·nized swimming (sĭng′krə-nīzd′, sĭn′-) *n. Sports.* A sport or an exhibition in which swimmers, singly or in groups, perform dancelike movements often in time with music.

syn·chro·niz·er (sĭng′krə-nī′zər, sĭn′-) *n.* **1.** One that synchronizes: *a synchronizer of a multitude of dramatic events.* **2.** *Computer Science.* A storage device that compensates for a difference between the rates at which information is processed in two or more devices.

syn·chro·nous (sĭng′krə-nəs, sĭn′-) *adj.* **1.** Occurring or existing at the same time. See Synonyms at **contemporary. 2.** Moving or operating at the same rate. **3.a.** Having identical periods. **b.** Having identical period and phase. [From Late Latin *synchronus,* from Greek *sunkhronos* : *sun-,* syn- + *khronos,* time.] **—syn′chro·nous·ly** *adv.* **—syn′chro·nous·ness** *n.*

synchronous motor *n.* A motor having a speed directly proportional to the frequency of the alternating-current power that operates it.

synchronous orbit *n.* A geostationary orbit.

syn·chro·ny (sĭng′krə-nē, sĭn′-) *n., pl.* **-nies.** Simultaneous occurrence; synchronism. [From SYNCHRONOUS.]

syn·chro·tron (sĭng′krə-trŏn′, sĭn′-) *n.* An accelerator in which charged particles are accelerated around a fixed circular path by an electric field and held to the path by an increasing magnetic field.

synchrotron radiation *n.* Electromagnetic radiation emitted by high-energy particles when accelerated to relativistic speeds in a magnetic field.

syn·cli·nal (sĭn-klī′nəl) *adj.* **1.** Sloping downward from opposite directions to meet in a common point or line. **2.** *Geology.* Relating to, formed by, or forming a syncline.

syn·cline (sĭn′klīn′) *n. Geology.* A fold in rocks in which the rock layers dip inward from both sides toward the axis. [Back-formation from SYNCLINAL.]

syn·co·pate (sĭng′kə-pāt′, sĭn′-) *tr.v.* **-pat·ed, -pat·ing, -pates. 1.** *Grammar.* To shorten (a word) by syncope. **2.** *Music.* To modify (rhythm) by syncopation. [Late Latin *syncopāre, syncopāt-,* from *syncopē,* syncope. See SYNCOPE.] **—syn′co·pa′tor** *n.*

syn·co·pa·tion (sĭng′kə-pā′shən, sĭn′-) *n.* **1.** *Music.* A shift of accent in a passage or composition that occurs when a normally weak beat is stressed. **2.** Something, such as rhythm, that is syncopated. **3.** *Grammar.* Syncope.

syn·co·pe (sĭng′kə-pē, sĭn′-) *n.* **1.** *Grammar.* The shortening of a word by omission of a sound, letter, or syllable from the middle of the word; for example, *bos'n* for *boatswain.* **2.** *Pathology.* A brief loss of consciousness caused by a temporary deficiency of oxygen in the brain; a swoon. See Synonyms at **blackout.** [Middle English *sincopis,* from *sincopene,* from Late Latin *syncopēn,* accusative of *syncopē,* from Greek *sunkopē,* from *sunkoptein,* to cut short : *sun-,* syn- + *koptein,* to strike.] **—syn′co·pal** (sĭng′kə-pəl, sĭn′-), **syn·cop′ic** (sĭn-kŏp′ĭk) *adj.*

syn·cre·tism (sĭng′krĭ-tĭz′əm, sĭn′-) *n.* **1.** Reconciliation or fusion of differing systems of belief, as in philosophy or religion, especially when success is partial or the result is heterogeneous. **2.** *Linguistics.* The merging of two or more originally different inflectional forms. [Greek *sunkrētismos,* union, from *sunkrētizein,* to unite (in the manner of the Cretan cities) : *sun-,* syn- + *Krēs, Krēt-,* Cretan.] **—syn·cret′ic** (-krĕt′ĭk), **syn′cre·tis′tic** (-krĭ-tĭs′tĭk) *adj.* **—syn′cre·tist** *n.*

syn·cre·tize (sĭng′krĭ-tīz′, sĭn′-) *v.* **-tized, -tiz·ing, -tiz·es.** —*tr.* To reconcile and unite (differing religious beliefs, for example), especially with partial success or a heterogeneous result. —*intr.* To combine differing elements or beliefs, especially with partial success or a heterogeneous result. [Greek *sunkrētizein,* to unite against a common enemy. See SYNCRETISM.]

syn·cy·ti·um (sĭn-sĭsh′ē-əm) *n., pl.* **-cy·ti·a** (-sĭsh′ē-ə). A mass of cytoplasm with many nuclei but no internal cell boundaries. [New Latin : SYN– + CYT(O)– + –IUM.] **—syn·cy′ti·al** (-sĭsh′ē-əl) *adj.*

synd. *abbr.* Syndicate.

syn·dac·tyl (sĭn-dăk′təl) *Biology. n.* An animal, especially a bird or mammal, that has two or more fused digits. **—syndactyl** also **syn·dac·ty·lous** (-tə-ləs) *adj.* Of, relating to, or characterized by syndactyly. [French *syndactyle* : Greek *sun-,* syn- + Greek *daktulos,* finger.]

syn·dac·ty·ly (sĭn-dăk′tə-lē) or **syn·dac·tyl·ism** (-tə-lĭz′əm) *n. Biology.* **1.** The condition of having two or more fused digits, as occurs normally in certain mammals and birds. **2.** A congenital anomaly in human beings characterized by two or more fused fingers or toes.

syn·des·mo·sis (sĭn′dĕz-mō′sĭs, -dĕs-) *n., pl.* **-ses** (-sēz). An articulation in which the bones are joined by a ligament. [New Latin, from Greek *sundesmos,* bond, ligament, from *sundein,* to bind together. See SYNDETIC.] **—syn′des·mot′ic** (-mŏt′ĭk) *adj.*

syn·det·ic (sĭn-dĕt′ĭk) *adj.* **1.** Serving to connect, as a conjunction; copulative or conjunctive. **2.** Connected by a conjunction. [Greek *sundetikos,* from *sundetos,* bound together, from *sundein,* to bind together : *sun-,* syn- + *dein,* to bind.] **—syn·det′i·cal·ly** *adv.*

syn·dic (sĭn′dĭk) *n.* **1.** One appointed to represent a corporation, a university, or another organization in business transactions; a business agent. **2.** A civil magistrate or similar government official in some European countries. [French, from Old French *sindiz,* from Late Latin *syndicus,* from Greek *sundikos,* public advocate : *sun-,* syn- + *dikē,* justice; see **deik-** in Appendix.] **—syn′di·cal** *adj.*

syn·di·cal·ism (sĭn′dĭ-kə-lĭz′əm) *n.* A radical political movement that advocates bringing industry and government under the control of federations of labor unions by the use of direct action, such as general strikes and sabotage. [French *syndicalisme,* from *(chambre) syndicale,* trade union, feminine of *syndical,* of a labor union, from *syndic,* delegate. See SYNDIC.] **—syn′di·cal·ist** *adj. & n.* **—syn′di·cal·is′tic** *adj.*

syn·di·cate (sĭn′dĭ-kĭt) *n. Abbr.* **synd. 1.** An association of people or firms authorized to undertake a duty or transact specific business. **2.** An association of people or firms formed to engage in an enterprise or promote a common interest. **3.** A loose affiliation of gangsters in control of organized criminal activities. **4.** An agency that sells articles, features, or photographs for publication in a number of newspapers or periodicals simultaneously.

5. A company consisting of a number of separate newspapers; a newspaper chain. **6.** The office, position, or jurisdiction of a syndic or body of syndics. **—syndicate** (-kāt′) *v.* **-cat·ed, -cat·ing, -cates.** *—tr.* **1. a.** To organize into or manage as a syndicate. **b.** To sell shares in. **2.** To sell (a comic strip or column, for example) through a syndicate for simultaneous publication in newspapers or periodicals. **3.** To sell (a television series, for example) directly to independent stations. *—intr.* To join together in a syndicate. [French *syndicat,* from Old French, office of syndic, from Medieval Latin *syndicātus,* from Late Latin *syndicus,* syndic. See SYNDIC.] **—syn′di·ca′tion** *n.* **—syn′di·ca′tor** *n.*

syn·drome (sĭn′drōm′) *n.* **1.** A group of symptoms that collectively indicate or characterize a disease, a psychological disorder, or another abnormal condition. **2. a.** A complex of symptoms indicating the existence of an undesirable condition or quality. **b.** A distinctive or characteristic pattern of behavior: *Skipping breakfast and buying a cup of coffee on the way to work became a syndrome as the months wore on.* [Greek *sundromē,* concurrence of symptoms, from *sundromos,* running together : *sun-,* syn- + *dromos,* a running.] **—syn·drom′ic** (-drō′mĭk, -drŏm′ĭk) *adj.*

syne (sĭn) *Scots. adv.* **1.** Before now; ago. **2.** Afterwards; since then; since. **3.** Thereupon; next. **—syne** *conj.* Since. **—syne** *prep.* Since. [Scots, from Middle English *sitthen,* from Old English *siththan.*]

syn·ec·do·che (sĭ-nĕk′də-kē) *n.* A figure of speech in which a part is used for the whole (as *hand* for *sailor*), the whole for a part (as *the law* for *police officer*), the specific for the general (as *cutthroat* for *assassin*), the general for the specific (as *thief* for *pickpocket*), or the material for the thing from which it is made (as *steel* for *sword*). [Middle English, alteration (influenced by Latin *synecdochē*) of Middle English *synodoches,* from Medieval Latin *synodoche,* alteration of Latin *synecdochē,* from Greek *sunekdokhē,* from *sunekdekhesthai,* to take on a share of : *sun-,* syn- + *ekdekhesthai,* to understand (*ek-,* out of; see **eghs** in Appendix + *dekhesthai,* to take; see **dek-** in Appendix).] **—syn′ec·doch′ic** (sĭn′ĕk-dŏk′ĭk), **syn′ec·doch′i·cal** (-ĭ-kəl) *adj.*

syn·e·col·o·gy (sĭn′ĭ-kŏl′ə-jē) *n.* The study of the ecological interrelationships among communities of organisms. **—syn′e·co·log′ic** (-kə-lŏj′ĭk), **syn′e·co·log′i·cal** (-ĭ-kəl) *adj.*

syn·er·e·sis also **syn·aer·e·sis** (sĭ-nĕr′ĭ-sĭs) *n., pl.* **-ses** (-sēz′). **1.** *Linguistics.* The drawing together into one syllable of two consecutive vowels or syllables, as in the formation of a diphthong. **2.** *Chemistry.* Exudation of the liquid component of a gel. [Late Latin *synaeresis,* from Greek *sunairesis,* from *sunairein,* to contract : *sun-,* syn- + *hairein,* to take, grasp.]

syn·er·get·ic (sĭn′ər-jĕt′ĭk) also **syn·er·gic** (sĭ-nûr′jĭk) *adj.* Synergistic.

syn·er·gid (sĭ-nûr′jĭd, sĭn′ər-) *n.* One of two small cells lying near the egg in the mature embryo sac of a flowering plant. [New Latin *synergida,* from Greek *sunergos,* working together. See SYNERGISM.]

syn·er·gism (sĭn′ər-jĭz′əm) *n.* **1.** Synergy. **2.** *Theology.* The doctrine that individual salvation is achieved through a combination of human will and divine grace. [New Latin *synergismus,* from Greek *sunergos,* working together : *sun-,* syn- + *ergon,* work; see **werg-** in Appendix.]

syn·er·gist (sĭn′ər-jĭst) *n.* **1.** A synergistic organ, drug, or agent. **2.** *Theology.* An adherent of synergism.

syn·er·gis·tic (sĭn′ər-jĭs′tĭk) *adj.* **1.** Of or relating to synergy: *a synergistic effect.* **2.** Producing or capable of producing synergy: *synergistic drugs.* **3.** *Theology.* Of or relating to synergism. **—syn′er·gis′ti·cal·ly** *adv.*

syn·er·gy (sĭn′ər-jē) *n., pl.* **-gies. 1.** The interaction of two or more agents or forces so that their combined effect is greater than the sum of their individual effects. **2.** Cooperative interaction among groups, especially among the acquired subsidiaries or merged parts of a corporation, that creates an enhanced combined effect. [From Greek *sunergia,* cooperation, from *sunergos,* working together. See SYNERGISM.]

syn·e·sis (sĭn′ĭ-sĭs) *n.* A construction in which a form, such as a pronoun, differs in number but agrees in meaning with the word governing it, as in *If the group becomes too large, we can split them in two.* [Greek *sunesis,* union, understanding, from *sunienai,* to understand, bring together : *sun-,* syn- + *hienai,* to send, hurl; see **yē-** in Appendix.]

syn·es·the·sia also **syn·aes·the·sia** (sĭn′ĭs-thē′zhə) *n.* **1.** A condition in which one type of stimulation evokes the sensation of another, as when the hearing of a sound produces the visualization of a color. **2.** A sensation felt in one part of the body as a result of stimulus applied to another, as in referred pain. **3.** The description of one kind of sense impression by using words that normally describe another. **—syn′es·thet′ic** (-thĕt′ĭk) *adj.*

syn·es·thete (sĭn′ĭs-thēt′) *n.* A person who experiences synesthesia, as by having a secondary sensation of sound as color or of color as sound.

syn·fu·el (sĭn′fyo͞o′əl) *n.* A liquid or gaseous fuel derived from coal, shale, or tar sand, or obtained by fermentation of certain substances, such as grain. [SYN(THETIC) + FUEL.]

syn·ga·my (sĭng′gə-mē) *n.* The fusion of two gametes in fertilization. **—syn·gam′ic** (sĭn-găm′ĭk), **syn′ga·mous** (sĭng′gə-məs) *adj.*

Synge (sĭng), **John Millington.** 1871–1909. Irish playwright whose works, based on rural Irish life, include *The Playboy of the Western World* (1907).

Synge, Richard Laurence Millington. Born 1914. British biochemist. He shared a 1952 Nobel Prize for the development of partition chromatography.

syn·ge·ne·ic (sĭn′jə-nē′ĭk) *adj.* Genetically identical or closely related, so as to allow tissue transplant; immunologically compatible: *syngeneic grafts; syngeneic animals.* [From Greek *sungeneia,* kinship : *syn-,* syn- + *genos,* family; see **genə-** in Appendix.] **—syn·ge·ne′i·cal·ly** *adv.*

syn·gen·e·sis (sĭn-jĕn′ĭ-sĭs) *n.* Sexual reproduction. **—syn′ge·net′ic** (-jə-nĕt′ĭk) *adj.*

syn·i·ze·sis (sĭn′ĭ-zē′sĭs) *n., pl.* **-ses** (-sēz). **1.** *Linguistics.* The union in pronunciation of two adjacent vowels into one syllable without forming a diphthong. **2.** *Biology.* The phase of meiosis in some species in which the chromatin contracts into a mass at one side of the nucleus. [Late Latin *synizēsis,* from Greek *sunizēsis,* from *sunizein,* to collapse : *sun-,* syn- + *hizein,* to settle down; see **sed-** in Appendix.]

syn·kar·y·on (sĭn-kăr′ē-ŏn′, -ē-ən) *n.* The nucleus of a fertilized egg immediately after the male and female nuclei have fused. [SYN– + Greek *karuon,* nut, seed; see **kar-** in Appendix.] **—syn·kar′y·on′ic** (-ŏn′ĭk) *adj.*

syn·ki·ne·sis (sĭn′kə-nē′sĭs, -kī-, sĭng′-) *n.* Involuntary movement of muscles or limbs accompanying a voluntary movement. **—syn′ki·net′ic** (-nĕt′ĭk) *adj.*

syn·od (sĭn′əd) *n.* **1.** A council or an assembly of church officials or churches; an ecclesiastical council. **2.** A council or an assembly. [Middle English, from Latin *synodus,* from Greek *sunodos,* meeting, assembly : *sun-,* syn- + *hodos,* way, course.] **—syn′od·al** (sĭn′ə-dl) *adj.*

syn·od·ic (sĭ-nŏd′ĭk) or **syn·od·i·cal** (-nŏd′ĭ-kəl) *adj.* **1.** Of or relating to a synod; synodal. **2.** Relating to the conjunction of celestial bodies, especially the interval between two successive conjunctions of a planet or the moon with the sun. **—syn·od′i·cal·ly** *adv.*

synodic month *n.* See **lunar month.**

syn·o·nym (sĭn′ə-nĭm′) *n. Abbr.* **syn. 1.** A word having the same or nearly the same meaning as another word or other words in a language. **2.** A word or an expression that serves as a figurative or symbolic substitute for another. **3.** *Biology.* A scientific name of an organism or of a taxonomic group that has been superseded by another name at the same rank. [Middle English *sinonyme,* from Old French *synonyme,* from Latin *synōnymum,* from Greek *sunōnumon,* from neuter of *sunōnumos,* synonymous. See SYNONYMOUS.] **—syn′o·nym′ic, syn′o·nym′i·cal** *adj.* **—syn′o·nym′i·ty** *n.*

syn·on·y·mist (sĭ-nŏn′ə-mĭst) *n.* One who studies or discriminates synonyms.

syn·on·y·mize (sĭ-nŏn′ə-mīz′) *tr.v.* **-mized, -miz·ing, -miz·es.** To analyze or provide the synonyms of (words or a word).

syn·on·y·mous (sĭ-nŏn′ə-məs) *adj. Abbr.* **syn. 1.** Having the same or a similar meaning: *synonymous words.* **2.** Equivalent in connotation: *"a widespread impression that . . . Hollywood was synonymous with immorality"* (Doris Kearns Goodwin). [Medieval Latin *synōnymus,* from Greek *sunōnumos* : *sun-,* syn- + *onoma, onuma,* name; see **nō-men-** in Appendix.] **—syn·on′y·mous·ly** *adv.*

syn·on·y·my (sĭ-nŏn′ə-mē) *n., pl.* **-mies.** *Abbr.* **syn. 1.** The quality of being synonymous; equivalence of meaning. **2.** Study and classification of synonyms. **3.** A list, book, or system of synonyms. **4.** *Biology.* A chronological list or record of the scientific names that have been applied to a species and its subdivisions.

syn·op·sis (sĭ-nŏp′sĭs) *n., pl.* **-ses** (-sēz). A brief outline or general view, as of a subject or written work; an abstract or a summary. [Late Latin, from Greek *sunopsis,* general view : *sun-,* syn- + *opsis,* view; see **okʷ-** in Appendix.]

syn·op·size (sĭ-nŏp′sīz′) *tr.v.* **-sized, -siz·ing, -siz·es.** To make a synopsis of; summarize. [Greek *sunopsizein,* to sum up, from *sunopsis,* general view. See SYNOPSIS.]

syn·op·tic (sĭ-nŏp′tĭk) also **syn·op·ti·cal** (-tĭ-kəl) *adj.* **1.** Of or constituting a synopsis; presenting a summary of the principal parts or a general view of the whole. **2. a.** Taking the same point of view. **b.** *Often* **Synoptic.** Relating to or being the first three gospels of the New Testament, which correspond closely. [Greek *sunoptikos,* from *sunopsis,* general view. See SYNOPSIS.] **—syn·op′ti·cal·ly** *adv.*

syn·os·to·sis (sĭn′ŏs-tō′sĭs) *n., pl.* **-ses** (-sēz). The fusion of normally separate skeletal bones. [SYN– + Greek *osteon,* bone; see **ost-** in Appendix + –OSIS.] **—syn′os·tot′ic** (-tŏt′ĭk) *adj.*

syn·o·vi·a (sĭ-nō′vē-ə) *n.* A clear, viscid lubricating fluid secreted by membranes in joint cavities, sheaths of tendons, and bursae. [New Latin.] **—syn·o′vi·al** *adj.*

sy·no·vi·tis (sĭ′nə-vī′tĭs) *n.* Inflammation of a synovial membrane. [New Latin *synovium,* synovia-secreting membrane (from SYNOVIA) + –ITIS.]

syn·sep·al·ous (sĭn-sĕp′ə-ləs) *adj. Botany.* Having united sepals; gamosepalous.

syn·tac·tic (sĭn-tăk′tĭk) or **syn·tac·ti·cal** (-tĭ-kəl) *adj.* **1.** Of or relating to the rules of syntax. **2.** Conforming to accepted patterns of syntax. [Greek *suntaktikos,* putting together, from

John Millington Synge
1905 portrait by
John Butler Yeats
(1839–1922)

ă pat	oi boy
ā pay	ou out
âr care	o͝o took
ä father	o͞o boot
ĕ pet	ŭ cut
ē be	ûr urge
ĭ pit	th thin
ī pie	*th* this
îr pier	hw which
ŏ pot	zh vision
ō toe	ə about, item
ô paw	♦ regionalism

Stress marks: ′ (primary); ′ (secondary), as in **dictionary** (dĭk′shə-nĕr′ē)

suntaktos, constructed, from *suntassein,* to construct. See SYNTAX.] **—syn·tac′ti·cal·ly** *adv.*

syn·tac·tics (sĭn-tăk′tĭks) *n.* *(used with a sing. verb).* The branch of semiotics that deals with the formal properties of signs and symbols. [From SYNTACTIC.]

syn·tax (sĭn′tăks′) *n.* **1. a.** The study of the rules whereby words or other elements of sentence structure are combined to form grammatical sentences. **b.** A publication, such as a book, that presents such rules. **c.** The pattern of formation of sentences or phrases in a language. **d.** Such a pattern in a particular sentence or discourse. **2.** *Computer Science.* The rules governing construction of a machine language. **3.** A systematic, orderly arrangement. [French *syntaxe,* from Late Latin *syntaxis,* from Greek *suntaxis,* from *suntassein,* put in order : *sun-,* syn- + *tassein, tag-,* to arrange.]

synthesizer

syn·te·ny (sĭn′tə-nē) *n.* The condition of two or more genes being located on the same chromosome whether or not there is demonstrable linkage between them. [SYN– + Greek *tainia,* band; see TAENIA.] **—syn·ten′ic** (-tĕn′ĭk) *adj.*

synth (sĭnth) *Informal. n.* A synthesizer.

syn·the·sis (sĭn′thĭ-sĭs) *n., pl.* **-ses** (-sēz′). **1. a.** The combining of separate elements or substances to form a coherent whole. **b.** The complex whole so formed. **2.** *Chemistry.* Formation of a compound from simpler compounds or elements. **3.** *Philosophy.* **a.** Reasoning from the general to the particular; logical deduction. **b.** The combination of thesis and antithesis in the Hegelian dialectical process whereby a new and higher level of truth is produced. [Latin, collection, from Greek *sunthesis,* from *suntithenai,* to put together : *sun-,* syn- + *tithenai,* to put; see **dhē-** in Appendix.] **—syn′the·sist** *n.*

synthesis gas *n.* A mixture of gases made as feedstock, especially a fuel produced by controlled combustion of coal in the presence of water vapor.

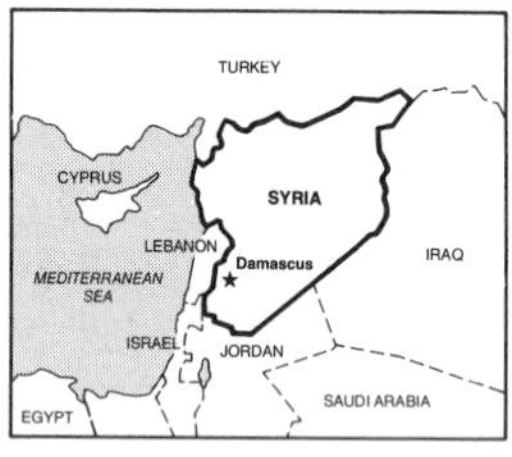

Syria

syn·the·size (sĭn′thĭ-sīz′) *v.* **-sized, -siz·ing, -siz·es.** *—tr.* **1.** To combine so as to form a new, complex product: *"His works synthesize photography, painting and linguistic devices"* (Paul Taylor). **2.** To form or produce by chemical synthesis. *—intr.* To form a synthesis.

syn·the·sized (sĭn′thĭ-sīzd′) *adj. Music.* **1.** Relating to or being an instrument whose sound is modified or augmented by a synthesizer. **2.** Relating to or being compositions or a composition performed on synthesizers or synthesized instruments.

syn·the·siz·er (sĭn′thĭ-sī′zər) *n.* **1.** One that synthesizes: *a synthesizer of varied ideas conceived by others.* **2.** *Music.* An electronic instrument, often played with a keyboard, that combines simple waveforms to produce more complex sounds, such as those of various other instruments.

syn·the·tase (sĭn′thĭ-tās′, -tāz′) *n.* See **ligase.** [SYNTHET(IC) + –ASE.]

syn·thet·ic (sĭn-thĕt′ĭk) *adj.* **1.** Relating to, involving, or of the nature of synthesis. **2.** *Chemistry.* Produced by synthesis, especially not of natural origin. **3. a.** Not natural or genuine; artificial or contrived: *"counterfeit rhetoric that flourishes when passions are synthetic"* (George F. Will). **b.** Prepared or made artificially: *synthetic leather.* See Synonyms at **artificial. 4.** *Linguistics.* Relating to or being a language, such as Latin or Russian, that uses inflectional affixes to express syntactic relationships. **5.** *Logic & Philosophy.* Relating to or being a proposition that attributes to a subject a predicate not inherent in the subject and that does not result in a contradiction if negated. **—synthetic** *n.* A synthetic chemical compound or material. [Greek *sunthetikos,* skilled in putting together, component, from *sunthetos,* combined, from *suntithenai,* to put together. See SYNTHESIS.] **—syn·thet′i·cal·ly** *adv.*

syringe

synthetic division *n. Mathematics.* A method of dividing polynomials when the divisor is a polynomial of the first degree, by using only the coefficients of the terms.

syn·ton·ic (sĭn-tŏn′ĭk) *adj. Psychology.* Characterized by a high emotional responsiveness to the environment. [From Greek *suntonos,* high-strung, intense, attuned, from *sunteinein,* to draw tight : *sun-,* syn- + *teinein,* to stretch; see **ten-** in Appendix.]

syn·tro·phism (sĭn-trō′fĭz′əm) also **syn·tro·phy** (sĭn′trə-fē) *n.* A biological relationship in which microorganisms of two different species or strains are mutually dependent on one another for nutritional requirements.

sy·pher (sī′fər) *tr.v.* **-phered, -pher·ing, -phers.** To overlap and even (chamfered or beveled plank edges) so that they form a flush surface. [Alteration of CIPHER, to chamfer away.]

syph·i·lis (sĭf′ə-lĭs) *n.* A chronic infectious disease caused by a spirochete *(Treponema pallidum),* either transmitted by direct contact, usually in sexual intercourse, or passed from mother to child in utero, and progressing through three stages characterized respectively by local formation of chancres, ulcerous skin eruptions, and systemic infection leading to general paresis. [New Latin, from *Syphilis, sive Morbus Gallicus,* "Syphilis, or the French Disease," title of a poem by Girolamo Fracastoro (1478?–1553), from *Syphilus,* the poem's protagonist.]

WORD HISTORY: In 1530 Girolamo Fracastoro, a physician, astronomer, and poet of Verona, published a poem entitled "Syphilis, sive Morbus Gallicus," translated as "Syphilis, or the French Disease." In Fracastoro's poem the name of this dreaded venereal disease is an altered form of the hero's name, *Syphilus.* The hero, a shepherd, is supposed to have been the first victim of the disease. Where the name *Syphilus* itself came from is not known for certain, but it has been suggested that Fracastoro borrowed the name from Ovid's *Metamorphoses.* In Ovid's work Sipylus (spelled *Siphylus* in some manuscripts) is the oldest son of Niobe, who lived not far from Mount Sipylon in Asia Minor. Fracastoro's poem about Syphilus was modeled on the story of Niobe. Although the etymology involving Sipylus was known to the editors of the *Oxford English Dictionary,* it was not accepted as their last word on the subject. C.T. Onions, one of the dictionary's editors, writing in the *Oxford Dictionary of English Etymology,* says that "*Syphilus* [the shepherd's name] is of unkn[own] origin." Fracastoro went on to use the term *syphilis* again in his medical treatise *De Contagione,* published in 1546. The word that Fracastoro used in Latin was eventually borrowed into English, being first recorded in 1718.

syph·i·lit·ic (sĭf′ə-lĭt′ĭk) *adj.* Of, relating to, or affected with syphilis. **—syphilitic** *n.* A person affected with syphilis. [New Latin *syphiliticus,* from *syphilis,* syphilis. See SYPHILIS.]

syph·i·loid (sĭf′ə-loid′) *adj.* Characteristic of or resembling syphilis.

sy·phon (sī′fən) *n. & v.* Variant of **siphon.**

Syr. *abbr.* Syria.

Syr·a·cuse (sîr′ə-kyo͞os′, -kyo͞oz′). **1.** A city of southeast Sicily, Italy, on the Ionian Sea south-southeast of Catania. Founded by colonists from Corinth in the eighth century B.C., it reached the height of its power in the fifth century but fell to the Romans in 212. Population, 117,689. **2.** A city of central New York east-southeast of Rochester. Originally a trading post and saltworks, it is now a manufacturing center. Population, 170,105.

Syr Dar·ya (sîr där′yə, dər-yä′). A river of southern Kirghiz, eastern Uzbekistan, northern Tadzhikistan, and southern Kazakhstan rising in the Tien Shan and flowing about 2,220 km (1,380 mi) northwest to the Aral Sea.

Syr·ette (sĭ-rĕt′). A trademark used for a collapsible tube having an attached hypodermic needle containing a single dose of medicine.

Sy·ri·a (sîr′ē-ə). *Abbr.* **Syr.** A country of southwest Asia on the eastern Mediterranean coast. Conquered by various powers in ancient times, it was a province of the Ottoman Empire (1516–1918) and became a French territory in 1920. Syria officially gained its independence in 1944. Damascus is the capital and the largest city. Population, 9,052,628. **—Syr′i·an** *adj. & n.*

Syr·i·ac (sîr′ē-ăk′) *n.* An ancient Aramaic language spoken in Syria from the 3rd to the 13th century that survives as the liturgical language of several Eastern Christian churches.

Syrian Desert. A desert region of northern Arabia occupying northern Saudi Arabia, western Iraq, southeast Syria, and eastern Jordan. It is crossed by a number of oil pipelines.

sy·rin·ga (sə-rĭng′gə) *n.* The mock orange. [New Latin, from Greek *surinx, suring-,* shepherd's pipe (from the use of its hollow stems to make pipes).]

sy·ringe (sə-rĭnj′, sîr′ĭnj) *n.* **1.** A medical instrument used to inject fluids into the body or draw them from it. **2.** A hypodermic syringe. [Middle English, alteration (influenced by Late Latin *sȳringēs,* pl. of *sȳrinx,* syrinx; see SYRINX) of *syryng,* from Medieval Latin *sȳringa,* from Late Latin, injection, from Greek *surinx, suring-,* shepherd's pipe.]

sy·rin·ges (sə-rĭn′jēz, -rĭng′gēz) *n.* A plural of **syrinx.**

sy·rin·go·my·e·li·a (sə-rĭng′gō-mī-ē′lē-ə) *n.* A chronic disease of the spinal cord characterized by the presence of fluid-filled cavities and leading to spasticity and sensory disturbances. [New Latin : Greek *surinx,* spinal cavity + Greek *muelos,* marrow (from *mus,* mouse, muscle; see **mūs-** in Appendix).] **—sy·rin′go·my·el′ic** (-ĕl′ĭk) *adj.*

syr·inx (sîr′ĭngks) *n., pl.* **sy·rin·ges** (sə-rĭn′jēz, -rĭng′gēz) or **syr·inx·es. 1.** *Music.* See **panpipe. 2.** *Zoology.* The vocal organ of a bird, consisting of thin vibrating muscles at or close to the division of the trachea into the bronchi. [Latin *sȳrinx,* from Greek *surinx.*] **—sy·rin′ge·al** (sə-rĭn′jē-əl) *adj.*

Sy·ros (sī′rŏs′) also **Sí·ros** (sē′rôs′). An island of Greece in the north-central Cyclades.

syr·phid (sûr′fĭd) *n.* Any of numerous flies of the family Syrphidae, many of which have a form or coloration mimicking that of bees or wasps. Adult syrphids feed on the nectar and pollen of flowers while the larvae of various species feed on plants and aphids. Also called *syrphus fly.* **—syrphid** *adj.* Of or belonging to the syrphids. [From New Latin *Syrphidae,* family name, from *Syrphus,* type genus, from Greek *surphos,* gnat.]

syr·phus fly (sûr′fəs) *n.* See **syrphid.** [New Latin *Syrphus,* fly genus. See SYRPHID.]

syr·up also **sir·up** (sĭr′əp, sûr′-) *n.* **1.** A thick, sweet, sticky liquid, consisting of a sugar base, natural or artificial flavorings, and water. **2.** The juice of a fruit or plant boiled with sugar until thick and sticky. **3.** A concentrated solution of sugar in water, often used as a vehicle for medicine. [Middle English *sirup,* from Old French *sirop,* from Medieval Latin *siropus,* from Arabic *šarāb,* from *šariba,* to drink.]

syr·up·y also **sir·up·y** (sĭr′ə-pē, sûr′-) *adj.* **1.** Resembling syrup in taste or consistency. **2.** Cloyingly sweet or sentimental.

sys·sar·co·sis (sĭs′är-kō′sĭs) *n., pl.* **-ses** (-sēz). The union or attachment of bones, such as the hyoid bone and lower jaw, by means of muscle. [Greek *sussarkōsis,* state of being overgrown with flesh, from *sussarkousthai,* to be overgrown with flesh : *sun-,* syn- + *sarkousthai,* passive of *sarkoun,* to make fleshy (from *sarx, sark-,* flesh).]

syst. *abbr.* System.

sys·tal·tic (sĭ-stôl′tĭk, -stăl′-) *adj.* Alternately contracting and dilating, as the heart; pulsating. [Late Latin *systalticus,* from Greek *sustaltikos,* from *sustellein,* to contract : *sun-,* syn- + *stellein,* to send; see **stel-** in Appendix.]

sys·tem (sĭs′təm) *n. Abbr.* **syst. 1.** A group of interacting, interrelated, or interdependent elements forming a complex whole. **2.** A functionally related group of elements, especially: **a.** The human body regarded as a functional physiological unit. **b.** An organism as a whole, especially with regard to its vital processes or functions. **c.** A group of physiologically or anatomically complementary organs or parts: *the nervous system; the skeletal system.* **d.** A group of interacting mechanical or electrical components. **e.** A network of structures and channels, as for communication, travel, or distribution. **3.** An organized set of interrelated ideas or principles. **4.** A social, economic, or political organizational form. **5.** A naturally occurring group of objects or phenomena: *the solar system.* **6.** A set of objects or phenomena grouped together for classification or analysis. **7.** A condition of harmonious, orderly interaction. **8.** An organized and coordinated method; a procedure. See Synonyms at **method. 9.** The prevailing social order; the establishment. Used with *the: You can't beat the system.* [Late Latin *systēma, systēmat-,* from Greek *sustēma,* from *sunistanai,* to combine : *sun-,* syn- + *histanai,* set up, establish; see **stā-** in Appendix.]

sys·tem·at·ic (sĭs′tə-măt′ĭk) also **sys·tem·at·i·cal** (-ĭ-kəl) *adj.* **1.** Of, characterized by, based on, or constituting a system. **2.** Carried on using step-by-step procedures. **3.** Purposefully regular; methodical. See Synonyms at **orderly. 4.** Of or relating to classification or taxonomy. **—sys′tem·at′i·cal·ly** *adv.*

sys·tem·at·ics (sĭs′tə-măt′ĭks) *n. (used with a sing. verb).* **1.** The science of systematic classification. **2.** A system of classification, as biosystematics. **3.** *Biology.* The systematic classification of organisms and the evolutionary relationships among them; taxonomy.

sys·tem·a·tism (sĭs′tə-mə-tĭz′əm, sĭ-stĕm′ə-) *n.* **1.** The practice of classifying or systematizing. **2.** Adherence to a system or systems.

sys·tem·a·tist (sĭs′tə-mə-tĭst, sĭ-stĕm′ə-) *n.* **1.** One who adheres to or formulates a system or systems. **2.** A taxonomist.

sys·tem·a·tize (sĭs′tə-mə-tīz′) *tr.v.* **-tized, -tiz·ing, -tiz·es.** To formulate into or reduce to a system: *"The aim of science is surely to amass and systematize knowledge"* (V. Gordon Childe). See Synonyms at **arrange. —sys′tem·a·ti·za′tion** (-tĭ-zā′shən) *n.* **—sys′tem·a·tiz′er** *n.*

sys·tem·ic (sĭ-stĕm′ĭk) *adj.* **1.** Of or relating to systems or a system. **2.a.** Of, relating to, or affecting the entire body or an entire organism: *systemic symptoms; a systemic poison.* **b.** Relating to or affecting a particular body system, especially the nervous system: *a systemic lesion.* **c.** *Physiology.* Of or relating to systemic circulation. **—sys·tem′i·cal·ly** *adv.*

systemic circulation *n. Physiology.* The general circulation of the blood through the body, as opposed to the circulation of the blood from the heart to the lungs and back to the heart.

systemic lupus er·y·the·ma·to·sus (ĕr′ə-thē′mə-tō′sĭs) *n. Abbr.* **SLE** A chronic disease of the connective tissue, characterized by fever, skin eruptions, pain in the muscles and joints, and anemia, and often affecting the kidneys, spleen, and various other organs.

sys·tem·ize (sĭs′tə-mīz′) *tr.v.* **-ized, -iz·ing, -iz·es.** To systematize. **—sys′tem·i·za′tion** (-tə-mĭ-zā′shən) *n.* **—sys′tem·iz′er** *n.*

sys·tems analysis (sĭs′təmz) *n.* **1.** The study of an activity or a procedure to determine the desired end and the most efficient method of obtaining this end. **2.** The act, process, or profession of systems analysis.

systems analyst *n.* One who performs systems analysis.

sys·to·le (sĭs′tə-lē) *n.* The rhythmic contraction of the heart, especially of the ventricles, by which blood is driven through the aorta and pulmonary artery after each dilation or diastole. [Greek *sustolē,* contraction, from *sustellein,* to contract. See SYSTALTIC.] **—sys·tol′ic** (sĭ-stŏl′ĭk) *adj.*

systolic pressure *n.* Blood pressure within the arteries when the heart muscle is contracting.

Syz·ran (sĭz′rən). A city of western Russia on the Volga River west of Kuibyshev. It is a major river port and rail center. Population, 173,000.

syz·y·gy (sĭz′ə-jē) *n., pl.* **-gies. 1.** *Astronomy.* **a.** Either of two points in the orbit of a celestial body where the body is in opposition to or in conjunction with the sun. **b.** Either of two points in the orbit of the moon when the moon lies in a straight line with the sun and Earth. **c.** The configuration of the sun, the moon, and Earth lying in a straight line. **2.** The combining of two feet into a single metrical unit in classical prosody. [Late Latin *sȳzygia,* from Greek *suzugia,* union, from *suzugos,* paired : *sun-,* syn- + *zugon,* yoke; see **yeug-** in Appendix.] **—sy·zyg′i·al** (sĭ-zĭj′ē-əl) *adj.*

Szcze·cin (shchĕt′sēn′) also **Stet·tin** (stə-tēn′, shtĕ-). A city of northwest Poland near the mouth of the Oder River. It was ruled by Sweden from 1648 to 1720, when it was ceded to Prussia. After World War II the city became part of Poland. Population, 390,800.

Sze·chuan (sĕch′wän′). See **Sichuan.**

Szechuan pepper or **Szechwan pepper** *n.* A Chinese tree or shrub *(Zanthoxylum simulans)* having aromatic bark, pinnately compound leaves, and spicy, two-valved, reddish, dry fruits.

Sze·chwan (sĕch′wän′). See **Sichuan.**

Sze·ged (sĕg′ĕd′). A city of southern Hungary on the Tisza River near the Yugoslavian border. It is a major river port and an agricultural center. Population, 178,591.

Szé·kes·fe·hér·vár (sā′kĕsh-fĕ′hâr-vär′). A city of central Hungary on the Danube River south-southwest of Budapest. It was the coronation and burial place of Hungary's kings from 1027 to 1527. Population, 110,203.

Szell (sĕl, zĕl), **George.** 1897–1970. Hungarian-born American conductor who was best known as the musical director of the Cleveland Orchestra (1946–1970).

Szent-Györ·gyi (sānt-jôr′jē, sĕnt-dyœr′dyĭ), **Albert.** 1893–1986. Hungarian-born American biochemist. He was the first to isolate vitamin C and won the 1937 Nobel Prize for discoveries relating to biological combustion.

Szi·lard (zĭl′ərd, zə-lärd′), **Leo.** 1898–1964. Hungarian-born American physicist and biologist. A member of the Manhattan Engineering Project, he helped develop the first atomic bomb. Szilard was later opposed to the construction and use of all nuclear weapons and devoted himself to studying molecular biology.

Szold (zōld), **Henrietta.** 1860–1945. American Zionist leader who was a founder of Hadassah (1912), the Women's Zionist Organization of America.

Szol·nok (sōl′nōk′). A city of central Hungary east-southeast of Budapest. It is an industrial center. Population, 79,619.

Szom·bat·hely (sŏm′bôt-hā′). A city of western Hungary near the Austrian border. Founded in Roman times, it is an industrial center. Population, 85,830.

Henrietta Szold

ă pat	oi boy
ā pay	ou out
âr care	o͝o took
ä father	o͞o boot
ĕ pet	ŭ cut
ē be	ûr urge
ĭ pit	th thin
ī pie	*th* this
îr pier	hw which
ŏ pot	zh vision
ō toe	ə about, item
ô paw	♦ regionalism

Stress marks: ′ (primary); ′ (secondary), as in **dictionary** (dĭk′shə-nĕr′ē)

Tt

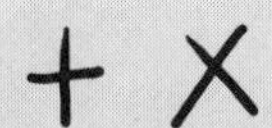

Phoenician
As the Phoenicians developed the notion of alphabetic writing, they began to use a cross or X-shaped mark to stand for the first sound of *tāw,* "mark, tally."

Early Greek
The Greeks wrote their version, *tau,* as a vertical stroke topped by a crossbar.

Roman
This form was well suited to the chiseled Roman inscriptional capitals that have come down to us.

t[1] or **T** (tē) *n., pl.* **t's** or **T's. 1.** The 20th letter of the modern English alphabet. **2.** Any of the speech sounds represented by the letter *t.* **3.** The 20th in a series. **4.** Something shaped like the letter T. ***—idiom.*** **to a T.** Perfectly; precisely: *This performer fits the role to a T.*

t[2] *abbr.* **1.** Troy (system of weights). **2.** *Physics.* Top quark.

T[1] The symbol for the isotope tritium.

T[2] *abbr.* **1.** Temperature. **2.** Tesla. **3.** *Mathematics.* Time reversal.

t. *abbr.* **1.** Tare. **2.** Teaspoon; teaspoonful. **3.** *Music.* Tempo. **4.** *Latin.* Tempore (in the time of). **5.** Or **T.** *Music.* Tenor. **6.** *Grammar.* Tense. **7.** Terminal. **8.** Or **T.** Territory. **9.** Or **T.** Time. **10.** Ton. **11.** Or **T.** Town; township. **12.** Transit. **13.** *Grammar.* Transitive.

T. *abbr.* **1.** Tablespoon; tablespoonful. **2.** *Bible.* Testament. **3.** Tuesday.

ta (tä) *interj. Chiefly British.* Used to express thanks. [Baby-talk alteration of *thank you.*]

Ta The symbol for the element **tantalum.**

TA *abbr.* Teaching assistant.

Taal[1] (tä-älʹ). A lake of southwest Luzon, Philippines, south of Manila. It contains Volcano Island, the site of the active volcano **Mount Taal.**

Taal[2] (täl) *n.* See **Afrikaans.** [Afrikaans, from Middle Dutch *tāle,* speech. See **del-**[2] in Appendix.]

tab[1] (tăb) *n.* **1.** A projection, flap, or short strip attached to an object to facilitate opening, handling, or identification. **2.** A small, usually decorative flap or tongue on a garment. **3.** A small auxiliary airfoil that is attached to a larger one and that helps stabilize an aircraft. **4.** A pull-tab. **—tab** *tr.v.* **tabbed, tab·bing, tabs.** To supply with a tab or tabs. [Origin unknown.]

tab[2] (tăb) *n.* **1.** *Informal.* A bill or check, such as one for a meal in a restaurant. **2.** A tabulator on a typewriter. ***—idiom.*** **keep tabs on.** *Informal.* To observe carefully: *Let's keep tabs on expenditures.* [Short for TABLET or TABULATION. Sense 2, short for TABULATOR.]

tab. *abbr.* Table.

ta·ba·nid (tə-bāʹnĭd, -bănʹĭd) *n.* Any of various bloodsucking dipterous flies of the family Tabanidae, which includes the horseflies. [New Latin *Tabānidae,* family name, from Latin *tabānus,* horsefly.] **—ta·baʹnid** *adj.*

tab·ard (tăbʹərd) *n.* **1.** A short, heavy cape of coarse cloth formerly worn outdoors. **2. a.** A tunic or capelike garment worn by a knight over his armor and emblazoned with his coat of arms. **b.** A similar garment worn by a herald and bearing his lord's coat of arms. **3.** An embroidered pennant attached to a trumpet. [Middle English, from Old French *tabart* or Old Spanish *tabardo.*]

tab·a·ret (tăbʹə-rĕtʹ) *n.* A strong upholstery fabric having alternating stripes of satin and moiré. [Probably from TABBY.]

Ta·bas·co (tə-băsʹkō). A trademark used for a very spicy sauce made from a strong-flavored red pepper. This trademark occurs in print in figurative contexts: *"It will likely be some time before normalcy is restored to classrooms after the Tabasco-tempered 11-day walkout"* (Christian Science Monitor).

ta·bas·co pepper (tə-băsʹkō) *n.* A very pungent pepper *(Capsicum frutescens)* grown principally in the Gulf Coast states for commercial production of hot sauces.

tab·bou·leh also **ta·boo·li** (tə-bo͞oʹlē) *n.* A finely chopped Lebanese salad made with bulgur wheat, scallions, tomatoes, mint, and parsley. [Arabic *tabbūlah.*]

♦**tab·by** (tăbʹē) *n., pl.* **-bies. 1.** A rich watered silk. **2.** A fabric of plain weave. **3. a.** A domestic cat with a striped or brindled coat of a gray or tawny color. **b.** A domestic cat, especially a female. **4.** A spinster. **5.** A prying woman; a gossip. **6.** *South Atlantic U.S.* A mixture of oyster shells, lime, sand, and water used as a building material. **—tabby** *adj.* **1.** Having light and dark striped markings: *a tabby cat.* **2.** Made of or resembling watered silk. [French *tabis,* from Old French *atabis,* from Medieval Latin *attabī,* from Arabic *ʻattābī,* after *al-ʻAttābīya,* a suburb of Baghdad, Iraq.]

tabard
Worn by armored warrior

tab·er·na·cle (tăbʹər-năkʹəl) *n.* **1.** Often **Tabernacle. a.** The portable sanctuary in which the Jews carried the Ark of the Covenant through the desert. **b.** The Jewish temple. **2.** Often **Tabernacle.** A case or box on a church altar containing the consecrated host and wine of the Eucharist. **3. a.** A place of worship. **b.** The Mormon temple. **4.** A niche for a statue or relic. **5.** *Nautical.* A boxlike support in which the heel of a mast is stepped. [Middle English, from Old French, from Late Latin *tabernāculum,* from Latin, tent, diminutive of *taberna,* hut. See TAVERN.] **—tabʹer·nacʹu·lar** (-năkʹyə-lər) *adj.*

ta·bes (tāʹbēz) *n., pl.* **tabes. 1.** Progressive bodily wasting or emaciation. **2.** Tabes dorsalis. [Latin *tābēs.*] **—ta·betʹic** (tə-bĕtʹĭk) *adj.*

ta·bes·cent (tə-bĕsʹənt) *adj.* Progressively wasting away. [Latin *tābēscēns, tābēscent-,* present participle of *tābēscere,* to waste away, inchoative of *tābēre,* from *tābēs,* a wasting away.] **—ta·besʹcence** *n.*

tabes dor·sa·lis (dôr-sāʹlĭs, -sălʹĭs) *n.* A late form of syphilis resulting in a hardening of the dorsal columns of the spinal cord and characterized by shooting pains, emaciation, loss of muscular coordination, and disturbances of sensation and digestion. Also called *locomotor ataxia.* [New Latin *tābēs dorsālis* : Latin *tābēs,* tabes + Late Latin *dorsālis,* dorsal.]

ta·bi (täʹbē) *n., pl.* **tabi** or **-bis.** A socklike cotton, silk, or nylon foot covering with a separate section for the big toe and a thick padded sole, worn in Japan with thong sandals, clogs, or zoris. [Japanese.]

tab·la (täʹblə, tŭbʹlə) *n. Music.* A small hand drum of India. [Hindi *tablā,* from Arabic *ṭabla,* from *ṭabl,* drum.]

tab·la·ture (tăbʹlə-cho͝orʹ, -chər) *n.* **1.** An engraved tablet or surface. **2.** *Music.* An early system of notation that used letters and symbols to indicate playing directions rather than tones. [French, alteration (influenced by Latin *tabula,* table) of Italian *intavolatura,* from *intavolare,* to put on a board : Latin *in-,* in- + *tavola,* table, board (from Latin *tabula*).]

ta·ble (tāʹbəl) *n. Abbr.* **tab. 1. a.** An article of furniture supported by one or more vertical legs and having a flat horizontal surface. **b.** The objects laid out for a meal on this article of furniture. **2.** The food and drink served at meals; fare: *kept an excellent table.* **3.** The company of people assembled around a table, as for a meal. **4.** *Games.* A piece of furniture serving as a playing surface, as for faro, roulette, or dice. Often used in the plural. **5.** *Games.* **a.** Either of the leaves of a backgammon board. **b. tables.** *Obsolete.* The game of backgammon. **6.** A plateau or tableland. **7. a.** A flat facet cut across the top of a precious stone. **b.** A stone or gem cut in this fashion. **8.** *Music.* The front part of the body of a stringed instrument. **9.** *Architecture.* **a.** A raised or sunken rectangular panel on a wall. **b.** A raised horizontal surface or continuous band on an exterior wall; a stringcourse. **10.** A part of the human palm framed by four lines, analyzed in palmistry. **11.** An orderly arrangement of data, especially one in which the data are arranged in columns and rows in an essentially rectangular form. **12.** An abbreviated list, as of contents; a synopsis. **13.** An engraved slab or tablet bearing an inscription or a device. **14.** *Anatomy.* The inner or outer flat layer of bones of the skull separated by the diploe. **15. tables.** A system of laws or decrees; a code: *the tables of Moses.* **—table** *tr.v.* **-bled, -bling, -bles. 1.** To put or place on a table. **2.** To postpone consideration of (a piece of legislation, for example); shelve. **3.** To enter in a list or table; tabulate. ***—idioms.*** **on the table. 1.** Up for discussion: *Two new proposals are on the table.* **2.** Postponed or put aside for consideration at a later date. **under the table. 1.** In secret. **2.** Into a completely intoxicated state: *drank themselves under the table.* [Middle English, from Old French, from Latin *tabula,* board.]

tab·leau (tăbʹlō, tă-blōʹ) *n., pl.* **tab·leaux** or **tab·leaus** (tăbʹlōzʹ, tă-blōzʹ). **1.** A vivid or graphic description: *The movie was a tableau of a soldier's life.* **2.** A striking incidental scene, as of a picturesque group of people: *"New public figures suddenly abound in the hitherto faceless totalitarian tableaux"* (John McLaughlin). **3.** An interlude during a scene when all the performers on stage freeze in position and then resume action as be fore. **4.** A tableau vivant. [French, from Old French *tablel,* diminutive of *table,* surface prepared for painting. See TABLE.]

tableau vi•vant (vē-väɴ′) *n., pl.* **tab•leaux vi•vants** (tă-blō′ vē-väɴ′). A scene presented on stage by costumed actors who remain silent and motionless as if in a picture. [French : *tableau,* picture + *vivant,* living.]

Ta•ble Bay (tā′bəl). An inlet of the Atlantic Ocean off southwest South Africa that forms the harbor of Cape Town.

ta•ble•cloth (tā′bəl-klôth′, -klŏth′) *n.* A cloth to cover a table, especially during a meal.

ta•ble d'hôte (tä′bəl dōt′, tă′blə) *n., pl.* **ta•bles d'hôte** (tä′bəl dōt′, tă′blə). **1.** A communal table for all the guests at a hotel or restaurant. **2.** A full-course meal offering a limited number of choices and served at a fixed price in a restaurant or hotel. In this sense, also called *prix fixe.* [French : *table,* table + *de,* of + *hôte,* host.]

ta•ble-hop (tā′bəl-hŏp′) *intr.v.* **-hopped, -hop•ping, -hops.** *Informal.* To move around from table to table greeting friends, as in a restaurant or nightclub. **—ta′ble-hop′per** *n.*

ta•ble•land (tā′bəl-lănd′) *n.* A flat, elevated region; a plateau or mesa.

ta•ble linen (tā′bəl) *n.* Tablecloths and napkins.

ta•ble•mate (tā′bəl-māt′) *n.* A person with whom one shares a table, as while dining.

table money *n. Chiefly British.* An allowance given especially to senior officers in the armed services for the official entertaining of visitors.

table salt *n.* See **salt** (sense 1).

ta•ble•side (tā′bəl-sīd′) *n.* The area beside or around a table, especially in a restaurant. **—tableside** *adv. & adj.* Made or prepared alongside a table: *lamb that was carved tableside; a tableside recitation of the menu.*

ta•ble•spoon (tā′bəl-spo͞on′) *n.* **1.** A large spoon used for serving food. **2.** *Abbr.* **T., tbs., tbsp.** A household cooking measure equal to 3 teaspoons, or ½ fluid ounce (15 milliliters). See table at **measurement.**

ta•ble•spoon•ful (tā′bəl-spo͞on-fo͝ol′) *n., pl.* **-fuls.** *Abbr.* **T., tbs., tbsp.** The amount that a tablespoon can hold.

table sugar *n.* See **sugar** (sense 1).

tab•let (tăb′lĭt) *n.* **1.** A slab or plaque, as of stone or ivory, with a surface that is intended for or bears an inscription. **2.a.** A thin sheet or leaf, used as a writing surface. **b.** A set of such leaves fastened together, as in a book. **c.** A pad of writing paper glued together along one edge. **3.** A small flat pellet of medication to be taken orally. **4.** A small flat cake of a prepared substance, such as soap. **—tablet** *tr.v.* **-let•ed, -let•ing, -lets. 1.** To inscribe on a tablet. **2.** To form into a tablet. [Middle English *tablette,* from Old French *tablete,* diminutive of *table,* table. See TABLE.]

table talk *n.* Casual mealtime conversation.

table tennis *n. Sports & Games.* A game similar to lawn tennis, played on a table with wooden paddles and a small hollow plastic ball.

ta•ble•top (tā′bəl-tŏp′) *n.* The flat surface of a table. **—tabletop** *adj.* Made or designed for use on the top of a table: *a tabletop copier; tabletop sculpture.*

ta•ble•ware (tā′bəl-wâr′) *n.* The dishes, glassware, and silverware used in setting a table for a meal.

table wine *n.* An unfortified wine considered suitable to be served with a meal.

tab•loid (tăb′loid′) *n.* A newspaper of small format giving the news in condensed form, usually with illustrated, often sensational material. [From *tabloid journalism,* from *Tabloid,* trademark for a drug or chemical in condensed form.]

ta•boo also **ta•bu** (tə-bo͞o′, tă-) *—n., pl.* **-boos** also **-bus. 1.** A ban or an inhibition resulting from social custom or emotional aversion. **2.a.** A prohibition, especially in Polynesia and other South Pacific islands, excluding something from use, approach, or mention because of its sacred and inviolable nature. **b.** An object, a word, or an act protected by such a prohibition. *—adj.* Excluded or forbidden from use, approach, or mention: *a taboo subject. —tr.v.* **-booed, -boo•ing, -boos** also **-bued, -bu•ing, -bus.** To exclude from use, approach, or mention; place under taboo. [Tongan *tabu,* under prohibition.]

WORD HISTORY: Among the many discoveries of Capt. James Cook was a linguistic one, the term *taboo.* Cook used this word in his journal of 1777 while he was in the Friendly Islands (now Tonga). Hence, even though similar words occur in other Polynesian languages, the form *taboo* from Tongan *tabu* is the form we have borrowed. The Tongans used *tabu* as an adjective; they spoke of persons or things that were *tabu,* that is, "under prohibition, forbidden, or set apart." Cook, besides borrowing the word into English, also made it into a noun referring to the prohibition itself and a verb meaning "to make someone or something taboo." From its origins in Polynesian society the word *taboo* has spread throughout the English-speaking world and has been applied in ways that never occurred to the people from whom Cook originally borrowed it.

ta•boo•li (tə-bo͞o′lē) *n.* Variant of **tabbouleh.**

ta•bor also **ta•bour** (tā′bər) *n. Music.* A small drum played by a fifer to accompany the fife. [Middle English *tabur,* from Old French, alteration of *tambur.* See TAMBOUR.]

tab•o•ret also **tab•ou•ret** (tăb′ə-rĕt′, -rā′) *n.* **1.** A low stool without a back or arms. **2.** A low stand or cabinet. **3.** An embroidery frame. [French *tabouret,* from Old French *taburet,* diminutive of *tabur,* tabor. See TABOR.]

ta•bour (tā′bər) *n. Music.* Variant of **tabor.**

tab•ou•ret (tăb′ə-rĕt′, -rā′) *n.* Variant of **taboret.**

Ta•briz¹ (tə-brēz′, tä-). A city of northwest Iran in Azerbaijan east of Lake Urmia. A commercial and industrial center, Tabriz has been subject to numerous devastating earthquakes since 858. Population, 852,000.

Ta•briz² (tä-brēz′) *n.* A cotton and wool Persian rug with designs of stylized animals, hunting scenes, and floral motifs.

ta•bu (tə-bo͞o′, tă-) *n., adj., & v.* Variant of **taboo.**

tab•u•lar (tăb′yə-lər) *adj.* **1.** Having a plane surface; flat. **2.** *Geology.* Tending to split into thin flat pieces. **3.** Organized as a table or list. **4.** Calculated by means of a table. [Latin *tabulāris,* of boards, from *tabula,* board.] **—tab′u•lar•ly** *adv.*

tab•u•la ra•sa (tăb′yə-lə rä′sə, -zə) *n., pl.* **tab•u•lae ra•sae** (tăb′yə-lē′ rä′sē, -zē). **1.a.** The mind before it receives the impressions gained from experience. **b.** The unformed, featureless mind in the philosophy of John Locke. **2.** A need or an opportunity to start from the beginning. [Medieval Latin *tabula rāsa* : Latin *tabula,* tablet + Latin *rāsa,* feminine of *rāsus,* erased.]

tab•u•lar•ize (tăb′yə-lə-rīz′) *tr.v.* **-ized, -iz•ing, -iz•es.** To put into tabular form; tabulate. **—tab′u•lar•i•za′tion** (-lər-ĭ-zā′shən) *n.*

tab•u•late (tăb′yə-lāt′) *tr.v.* **-lat•ed, -lat•ing, -lates. 1.** To arrange in tabular form; condense and list. **2.** To cut or form with a plane surface. **—tabulate** (tăb′yə-lĭt, -lāt′) *adj.* Having a plane surface. [Latin *tabula,* writing + –ATE¹.] **—tab′u•la′tion** *n.*

tab•u•la•tor (tăb′yə-lā′tər) *n.* **1.** One who tabulates: *a tabulator of racing scores.* **2.** A machine that reads, sorts, and prints out information from punched cards. **3.** A mechanism on a typewriter for setting automatic stops or margins for columns. **4.** *Computer Science.* A device for reading data from punched cards and producing printed lists or totals of the result.

TAC *abbr.* Tactical Air Command.

tac•a•ma•hac (tăk′ə-mə-hăk′) *n.* **1.** Any of several aromatic resinous substances used in ointments and incense. **2.** See **balsam poplar.** [Spanish *tacamaca, tacamahaca,* from Nahuatl *tecamaca.*]

ta•cet (tā′sĭt, tăs′ĭt, tä′kĕt′) *v. Music.* Be silent. Used chiefly as a direction. [Latin, third person sing. present tense of *tacēre,* to be silent.]

tach (tăk) *n. Informal.* A tachometer.

tache (tăch) *n. Archaic.* A clasp or buckle. [Middle English, from Old French, of Germanic origin.]

tach•i•na fly (tăk′ə-nə) *n.* Any of several bristly, usually grayish dipterous flies of the family Tachinidae, the larvae of which are parasitic on caterpillars and other insects. Also called *tachinid.* [New Latin *Tachina,* type genus, from Greek *takhinē,* feminine of *takhinos,* swift, from *takhos,* speed.]

tach•i•nid (tăk′ə-nĭd′) *n.* See **tachina fly. —tachinid** *adj.* Of or belonging to the family Tachinidae. [New Latin *Tachinidae,* family name, from *Tachina,* type genus. See TACHINA FLY.]

tach•isme or **tach•ism** (tăsh′ĭz′əm) *n.* A French school of art originating in the 1950's and characterized by irregular dabs and splotches of color applied haphazardly to the canvas. [French *tachisme,* from *tache,* stain, from Old French *teche,* mark, of Germanic origin. See **deik-** in Appendix.] **—tach′iste, tach′ist** *n.*

ta•chis•to•scope (tă-kĭs′tə-skōp′, tə-) *n.* An apparatus that projects a series of images onto a screen at rapid speed to test visual perception, memory, and learning. [Greek *takhistos,* superlative of *takhus,* swift + –SCOPE.] **—ta•chis′to•scop′ic** (-skŏp′ĭk) *adj.* **—ta•chis′to•scop′i•cal•ly** *adv.*

tach•o•graph (tăk′ə-grăf′) *n.* A machine that records the measurements of a tachometer, especially one in a vehicle recording its speed and the times at which it was driven. [Greek *takhos,* speed + –GRAPH.]

ta•chom•e•ter (tă-kŏm′ĭ-tər, tə-) *n.* An instrument used to measure the rotations per minute of a rotating shaft. [Greek *takhos,* speed + –METER.] **—tach′o•met′ric** (tăk′ə-mĕt′rĭk) *adj.* **—ta•chom′e•try** *n.*

tachy– *pref.* Rapid; accelerated: *tachymeter.* [Greek *takhu-,* from *takhus,* swift.]

tach•y•ar•rhyth•mi•a (tăk′ē-ə-rĭ*th*′mē-ə) *n.* An excessively rapid heartbeat accompanied by arrhythmia.

tach•y•car•di•a (tăk′ĭ-kär′dē-ə) *n.* A rapid heart rate, especially one above 100 beats per minute in an adult. [TACHY– + Greek *kardia,* heart; see CARDIA.] **—tach′y•car′di•ac** (-dē-ăk) *adj. & n.*

ta•chyg•ra•phy (tă-kĭg′rə-fē, tə-) *n.* The art or practice of rapid writing or shorthand, especially the stenography of the ancient Greeks and Romans.

tach•y•lyte also **tach•y•lite** (tăk′ə-līt′) *n.* A black, glassy basalt of volcanic origin. [German *Tachylyt* : Greek *takhu-,* tachy- + Greek *lutos,* soluble (from *luein,* to loosen; see **leu-** in Appendix).] **—tach′y•lyt′ic** (-lĭt′ĭk) *adj.*

ta•chym•e•ter (tă-kĭm′ĭ-tər, tə-) *n.* A surveying instrument

table tennis

taboret

tachina fly

ă pat	oi boy
ā pay	ou out
âr care	o͝o took
ä father	o͞o boot
ĕ pet	ŭ cut
ē be	ûr urge
ĭ pit	th thin
ī pie	*th* this
îr pier	hw which
ŏ pot	zh vision
ō toe	ə about, item
ô paw	♦ regionalism

Stress marks: ′ (primary); ′ (secondary), as in **dictionary** (dĭk′shə-nĕr′ē)

tackle
Football players

taco

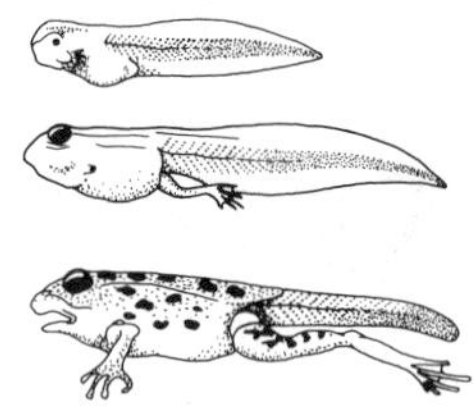
tadpole
Development of a northern leopard frog
Rana pipiens

used for the rapid determination of distances, elevations, and bearings. **—ta·chym′e·try** *n.*

tach·y·on (tăk′ē-ŏn′) *n.* A hypothetical subatomic particle that travels faster than the speed of light. **—tach′y·on′ic** *adj.*

tach·y·phy·lax·is (tak′ə-fĭ-lăk′sĭs) *n., pl.* **-lax·es** (-fĭ-lăk′sēz). **1.** Rapid desensitization to a toxic substance produced by inoculation with a series of small doses. **2.** A rapidly decreasing response to a drug following the initial doses.

tach·yp·ne·a (tăk′ĭp-nē′ə, tăk′ĭ-nē′ə) *n.* Rapid breathing. [New Latin : TACHY– + Greek *pnoiē,* breathing (from *pnein,* to breathe; see **pneu-** in Appendix).]

ta·chys·ter·ol (tə-kĭs′tə-rôl′, -rōl′, -rŏl′) *n.* An isomer of ergosterol that forms vitamin D_2 when irradiated with ultraviolet light.

tac·it (tăs′ĭt) *adj.* **1.** Not spoken: *indicated tacit approval by smiling and winking.* **2. a.** Implied by or inferred from actions or statements: *Management has given its tacit approval to the plan.* **b.** *Law.* Arising by operation of the law rather than through direct expression. **3.** *Archaic.* Not speaking; silent. [Latin *tacitus,* silent, past participle of *tacēre,* to be silent.] **—tac′it·ly** *adv.* **—tac′it·ness** *n.*

tac·i·turn (tăs′ĭ-tûrn′) *adj.* Habitually untalkative. See Synonyms at **silent.** [French *taciturne,* from Old French, from Latin *taciturnus,* from *tacitus,* silent. See TACIT.] **—tac′i·tur′ni·ty** (-tûr′nĭ-tē) *n.* **—tac′i·turn·ly** *adv.*

Tac·i·tus (tăs′ĭ-təs), **Publius Cornelius.** A.D. 55?–120? Roman public official and historian whose two greatest works, *Histories* and *Annals,* concern the period from the death of Augustus (A.D. 14) to the death of Domitian (96).

tack¹ (tăk) *n.* **1.** A short, light nail with a sharp point and a flat head. **2.** *Nautical.* **a.** A rope for holding down the weather clew of a course. **b.** A rope for hauling the outer lower corner of a studdingsail to the boom. **c.** The part of a sail, such as the weather clew of a course, to which this rope is fastened. **d.** The lower forward corner of a fore-and-aft sail. **3.** *Nautical.* **a.** The position of a vessel relative to the trim of its sails. **b.** The act of changing from one position or direction to another. **c.** The distance or leg sailed between changes of position or direction. **4. a.** A course of action meant to minimize opposition to the attainment of a goal. **b.** An approach, especially one of a series of changing approaches. **5.** A large, loose stitch made as a temporary binding or as a marker. **6.** Stickiness, as that of a newly painted surface. **—tack** *v.* **tacked, tack·ing, tacks.** *—tr.* **1.** To fasten or attach with or as if with a tack: *tacked the carpet down.* **2.** To fasten or mark (cloth or a seam, for example) with a loose basting stitch. **3.** To put together loosely and arbitrarily: *tacked some stories together in an attempt to write a novel.* **4.** To add as an extra item; append: *tacked two dollars onto the bill.* **5.** *Nautical.* To bring (a vessel) into the wind in order to change course or direction. *—intr.* **1.** *Nautical.* **a.** To change the direction or course of a vessel: *ready to tack on the captain's signal.* **b.** To change tack: *The ship tacked to starboard.* **2.** To change one's course of action. [Middle English *tak,* fastener, from Old North French *taque,* probably of Germanic origin.] **—tack′er** *n.* **—tack′less** *adj.*

tack² (tăk) *n.* Food, especially coarse or inferior foodstuffs. [Origin unknown.]

tack³ (tăk) *n.* The harness for a horse, including the bridle and saddle. *—attributive.* Often used to modify another noun: *a tack room; tack accessories.* [Short for TACKLE.]

tack hammer *n.* A light hammer used to drive tacks.

tack·ie (tăk′ē) *n.* *South African.* One of a pair of sneakers. [Origin unknown.]

tack·le (tăk′əl) *n.* **1.** The equipment used in a sport or an occupation, especially in fishing; gear. See Synonyms at **equipment.** **2.** (tăk′əl, tā′kəl). **3.** *Nautical.* **a.** A system of ropes and blocks for raising and lowering weights of rigging and pulleys for applying tension. **b.** A rope and its pulley. **4.** *Football.* **a.** Either of the two line players on a team positioned between the guard and the end. **b.** This position. **c.** The act of stopping an opposing player by seizing and throwing the player down. **—tackle** *v.* **-led, -ling, -les.** *—tr.* **1.** To take on and wrestle with (an opponent or a problem, for example). **2.** *Football.* To seize and throw down (an opposing player). **3.** To harness (a horse). *—intr.* *Football.* To seize and throw down an opponent. [Middle English *takel,* from Middle Dutch or Middle Low German; perhaps akin to Middle Dutch *taken,* to seize, grasp.] **—tack′ler** *n.*

tack·ling (tăk′lĭng) *n.* Gear; tackle.

tack·y¹ (tăk′ē) *adj.* **-i·er, -i·est.** Slightly adhesive or gummy to the touch; sticky. [From TACK¹.] **—tack′i·ness** *n.*

tack·y² (tăk′ē) *adj.* **-i·er, -i·est.** *Informal.* **1.** Neglected and in a state of disrepair: *a tacky old cabin in the woods.* **2. a.** Lacking style or good taste; tawdry: *tacky clothes.* **b.** Distasteful or offensive; tasteless: *a tacky remark.* [From *tackey,* an inferior horse.] **—tack′i·ly** *adv.* **—tack′i·ness** *n.*

Tac·na (tăk′nə, tăk′nä). A town of southern Peru north of Arica, Chile. The object of a long-standing dispute between Peru and Chile, it became part of Peru in 1929. Population, 97,173.

ta·co (tä′kō) *n., pl.* **-cos.** A corn tortilla folded around a filling such as ground meat or cheese. [American Spanish, from Spanish, plug, wad of bank notes.]

Ta·co·ma (tə-kō′mə). A city of west-central Washington on an arm of Puget Sound south of Seattle. A major seaport and railroad center, it is one of the chief industrial cities in the Northwest. Population, 158,501.

Ta·con·ic Mountains (tə-kŏn′ĭk). A range of the Appalachian Mountains in southeast New York, western Massachusetts, and southwest Vermont rising to 1,163.9 m (3,816 ft).

tac·o·nite (tăk′ə-nīt′) *n.* A variety of chert containing magnetite and hematite, mined as an iron ore. [After the TACONIC (MOUNTAINS).]

tact (tăkt) *n.* **1.** Acute sensitivity to what is proper and appropriate in dealing with others, including the ability to speak or act without offending. **2.** *Archaic.* The sense of touch. [French, from Old French, sense of touch, from Latin *tāctus,* from past participle of *tangere,* to touch. See **tag-** in Appendix.]

SYNONYMS: *tact, address, diplomacy, savoir-faire.* These nouns denote the ability to deal with others with skill, sensitivity, and finesse. *Tact* implies fine discernment of what is appropriate and the ability to speak or act without giving offense: *"He had . . . a tact that would preserve him from flagrant error in any society"* (Francis Parkman). *Address* suggests deftness and grace in social situations: *"With the charms of beauty she combined the address of an accomplished intriguer"* (Charles Merivale). *Diplomacy* implies adroit, tactful management of difficult situations: *Diplomacy secured the cooperation that confrontation had failed to elicit.* *Savoir-faire* involves knowing the right or graceful thing to say or do, either instinctively or as a result of social experience: *Living abroad taught him the savoir-faire that his rural upbringing had been unable to provide.*

tact·ful (tăkt′fəl) *adj.* Possessing or exhibiting tact; considerate and discreet: *a tactful person; a tactful remark.* **—tact′ful·ly** *adv.* **—tact′ful·ness** *n.*

tac·tic (tăk′tĭk) *n.* An expedient for achieving a goal; a maneuver. [French *tactique,* tactics, from Greek *taktika.* See TACTICS.]

tac·ti·cal (tăk′tĭ-kəl) *adj.* **1.** Of, relating to, or using tactics. **2. a.** Of, relating to, used in, or involving military or naval operations that are smaller, closer to base, and of less long-term significance than strategic operations. **b.** Carried out in support of military or naval operations: *tactical bombing.* **3.** Characterized by adroitness, ingenuity, or skill. **—tac′ti·cal·ly** *adv.*

tac·ti·cian (tăk-tĭsh′ən) *n.* **1.** One who is skilled in the planning and execution of military tactics. **2.** A clever maneuverer.

tac·tics (tăk′tĭks) *n.* **1. a.** *(used with a sing. verb).* The military science that deals with securing objectives set by strategy, especially the technique of deploying and directing troops, ships, and aircraft in efficient maneuvers against an enemy: *Tactics is a required course at all military academies.* **b.** *(used with a pl. verb).* Maneuvers used against an enemy: *Guerrilla tactics were employed during most of the war.* **2.** *(used with a sing. or pl. verb).* A procedure or set of maneuvers engaged in to achieve an end, an aim, or a goal. [New Latin *tactica,* from Greek *taktika,* from neuter pl. of *taktikos,* of order, from *taktos,* arranged, from *tassein, tag-,* to arrange.]

tac·tile (tăk′təl, -tīl′) *adj.* **1. a.** Perceptible to the sense of touch; tangible. **b.** Characterized by or conveying an illusion of tangibility: *"Heaney must thus continue to be a poet rich in tactile language"* (Helen Vendler). **2.** Used for feeling: *a tactile organ.* **3.** Of, relating to, or proceeding from the sense of touch; tactual: *a tactile reflex.* [From Latin *tāctilis,* from *tāctus,* past participle of *tangere,* to touch. See TACT.] **—tac′tile·ly** *adv.* **—tac·til′i·ty** (-tĭl′ĭ-tē) *n.*

tactile corpuscle *n.* Any of numerous minute oval end organs of touch in sensitive skin, as in the palms, fingertips, and soles of the feet. Also called *tactile bud.*

tactile hair *n.* Sensory hair, such as that of an insect, that responds to pressure or touch.

tac·tion (tăk′shən) *n.* The act of touching; contact. [Latin *tāctiō, tāctiōn-,* from *tāctus,* past participle of *tangere,* to touch. See TACT.]

tact·less (tăkt′lĭs) *adj.* Lacking or exhibiting a lack of tact; bluntly inconsiderate or indiscreet. **—tact′less·ly** *adv.* **—tact′less·ness** *n.*

tac·to·re·cep·tor (tăk′tō-rĭ-sĕp′tər) *n.* A receptor that responds to touch. [Latin *tāctus,* touch (from past participle of *tangere,* to touch; see **tag-** in Appendix) + RECEPTOR.]

tac·tu·al (tăk′cho͞o-əl) *adj.* Tactile. [Latin *tāctus,* touch; see TACT + –AL¹.] **—tac′tu·al·ly** *adv.*

tad (tăd) *n.* *Informal.* **1.** A small boy. **2.** A small amount or degree; a bit. [Perhaps short for TADPOLE.]

tad·pole (tăd′pōl′) *n.* The limbless aquatic larva of a frog or toad, having gills and a long flat tail. As the tadpole approaches the adult stage, legs and lungs develop, and the tail gradually disappears. Also called *polliwog.* [Middle English *taddepol* : *tadde, tode,* toad; see TOAD + *pol,* head; see POLL.]

Ta·dzhik (tä-jĭk′, tə-) *n. & adj.* Variant of **Tajik.**

Ta·dzhik·i (tä-jĭk′ē, tə-) *n. & adj.* Variant of **Tajiki.**

Ta·dzhik·i·stan (tä-jĭk′ĭ-stăn′, -stän′, tə-jĭ-kyĭ-stän′). A region of west-central Asia bordering on Afghanistan and China. It was settled by the Tajik by the 10th century and conquered by the Mongols in the 13th century. The region was acquired by Russia in 1895 and became a constituent republic in 1929. Dushanbe is the capital. Population, 4,499,000.

Tae·gu (tī-go͞o′). A city of southeast South Korea north-northwest of Pusan. It is an industrial and commercial center. Population, 2,031,000.

Tae·jon (tī-jôn′, -jŏn′). A city of central South Korea south-southeast of Seoul. It is an agricultural center and a railroad hub. Population, 800,000.

tae kwon do (tī′ kwŏn′ dō′) *n.* A Korean art of self-defense; a style of karate. [Korean *t'aekwŏndo* : *tae-*, to trample + *kwŏn*, fist + *-do*, way.]

tael (tāl) *n.* **1.** Any of various units of weight used in eastern Asia, roughly equivalent to 38 grams (1⅓ ounces). **2.** A monetary unit formerly used in China, equivalent in value to this weight of standard silver. [Portuguese, from Malay *tahil, tael*.]

tae·ni·a also **te·ni·a** (tē′nē-ə) *n., pl.* **-ni·ae** (-nē-ē′) or **-ni·as. 1.** A narrow band or ribbon for the hair that was worn in ancient Greece. **2.** *Architecture.* A band in the Doric order that separates the frieze from the architrave. **3.** *Anatomy.* A ribbonlike band of tissue or muscle. **4.** A flatworm of the genus *Taenia*, which includes many tapeworms. [Latin, ribbon, tapeworm, from Greek *tainia*. See **ten-** in Appendix.]

tae·ni·a·cide also **te·ni·a·cide** (tē′nē-ə-sīd′) *n.* An agent that kills tapeworms.

tae·ni·a·fuge also **te·ni·a·fuge** (tē′nē-ə-fyo͞oj′) *n.* An agent that expels tapeworms from the body.

tae·ni·a·sis also **te·ni·a·sis** (tē-nī′ə-sĭs) *n.* Infestation with tapeworms.

taf·fe·ta (tăf′ĭ-tə) *n.* A crisp, smooth, plain-woven fabric with a slight sheen, made of various fibers, such as silk, rayon, or nylon, and used especially for women's garments. **—taffeta** *adj.* Made of or resembling this fabric. [Middle English, from Old French *taffetas*, from Old Italian *taffetà*, from Turkish *tafta*, from Persian *tāftah*, silk or linen cloth, from past participle of *tāftan*, to twist, spin.]

taffeta weave *n.* See **plain weave.**

taf·fi·a (tăf′ē-ə) *n.* Variant of **tafia.**

taff·rail (tăf′rāl′, -rəl) *n.* *Nautical.* **1.** The rail around the stern of a vessel. **2.** The flat upper part of the stern of a vessel, made of wood and often richly carved. [Alteration of *tafferel*, carved panel, from Dutch *tafereel*, panel for carving or painting, from Middle Dutch *tafeleel, tafereel*, from Old French *tablel*. See TABLEAU.]

taffrail log *n.* *Nautical.* See patent log.

taf·fy (tăf′ē) *n., pl.* **-fies.** A sweet, chewy candy of molasses or brown sugar boiled until very thick and then pulled with the hands or by machine until the candy is glossy and holds its shape. [Origin unknown.]

taf·i·a also **taf·fi·a** (tăf′ē-ə) *n.* A cheap rum distilled from molasses and refuse sugar in the West Indies. [French, perhaps of West Indian Creole origin.]

Taft (tăft), **Helen.** 1861–1943. First Lady of the United States (1909–1913) as the wife of President William Howard Taft. She arranged for the planting of several thousand cherry trees around Washington, D.C.

Taft, Lorado. 1860–1936. American sculptor and writer whose allegorical sculptures include *The Fountain of Time* in Chicago (1922). He wrote *The History of American Sculpture* (1903).

Taft, William Howard. 1857–1930. The 27th President of the United States (1909–1913), whose term was marked by passage of the Payne-Aldrich Tariff Act (1909). He later served as the chief justice of the U.S. Supreme Court (1921–1930).

tag¹ (tăg) *n.* **1.** A strip of leather, paper, metal, or plastic attached to something or hung from a wearer's neck to identify, classify, or label: *sale tags on all coats and dresses.* **2.** The plastic or metal tip at the end of a shoelace. **3.** The contrastingly colored tip of an animal's tail. **4.** *Sports.* A bright piece of feather, floss, or tinsel surrounding the shank of the hook on a fishing fly. **5. a.** A dirty, matted lock of wool. **b.** A loose lock of hair. **6.** A rag; a tatter. **7.** A small, loose fragment: *I heard only tags and snippets of what was being said.* **8.** An ornamental flourish, especially at the end of a signature. **9.** A designation or an epithet, especially an unwelcome one: *He did not take kindly to the tag of pauper.* **10. a.** A brief quotation used in a discourse to give it an air of erudition or authority: *Shakespearean tags.* **b.** A cliché, saw, or similar short, conventional idea used to embellish a discourse: *These tags of wit and wisdom bore me.* **c.** The refrain or last lines of a song or poem. **d.** The closing lines of a speech in a play; a cue. **11.** *Computer Science.* A label assigned to identify data in memory. **12.** *Slang.* A graffito featuring a word or words, especially the author's name, rather than a picture: *"Instead of a cursive linear tag, Super Kool painted his name along the exterior of a subway car in huge block pink and yellow letters"* (Eric Scigliano). **—tag** *v.* **tagged, tag·ging, tags.** *—tr.* **1.** To label, identify, or recognize with or as if with a tag: *I tagged him as a loser.* See Synonyms at **mark¹. 2.** To put a ticket on (a motor vehicle) for a traffic or parking violation. **3.** To charge with a crime: *The suspect was tagged for arson.* **4.** To add as an appendage to: *tagged an extra paragraph on the letter.* **5.** To follow closely: *Excited children tagged the circus parade to the end of its route.* **6.** To cut the tags from (sheep). *—intr.* To follow after; accompany: *tagged after me everywhere; insisted on tagging along.* [Middle English *tagge*, dangling piece of cloth on a garment, possibly of Scandinavian origin.]

tag² (tăg) *n.* **1.** *Games.* A children's game in which one player pursues the others until he or she is able to touch one of them, who then in turn becomes the pursuer. **2.** *Baseball.* The act of putting another player out by touching the player with the ball when he or she is not on base. **3.** *Sports.* The act of touching a player as a substitute for tackling in touch football. **—tag** *tr.v.* **tagged, tag·ging, tags. 1.** To touch (another player) in the game of tag. **2.** *Baseball.* To touch (a runner) with the ball in order to put that player out. **3.** *Sports.* To touch (the runner) as a substitute for tackling in touch football. ***—phrasal verb.* tag up.** *Baseball.* To return to and touch a base with one foot before running to the next base after a fielder has caught a fly ball. [Perhaps variant of Scots *tig*, touch, tap, probably alteration of Middle English *tek*.]

TAG *abbr.* The Adjutant General.

Ta·ga·log (tə-gä′lôg, -ləg) *n., pl.* **Tagalog** or **-logs. 1.** A member of a people native to the Philippines and inhabiting Manila and its adjacent provinces. **2.** The Austronesian language of the Tagalog on which Filipino is based. [Tagalog : *taga*, native of + *ilog*, river.]

tag·a·long also **tag-a·long** (tăg′ə-lông′, -lŏng′) *n.* One that persistently follows another: *"Technological change separates the innovators from the tag-alongs"* (Thomas G. Exter).

Tag·an·rog (tăg′ən-rŏg′, tə-gən-rôk′). A city of southwest Russia on the **Gulf of Taganrog,** an arm of the Sea of Azov. Originally a colony of Pisa, it was annexed by Russia in 1769. Population, 289,000.

tag day *n.* A day on which collectors for a charitable fund solicit contributions, giving each contributor a tag.

tag end *n.* **1.** The very end. **2.** Something left over; a remnant.

tag·ger (tăg′ər) *n.* **1.** One that tags, especially the pursuer in the game of tag. **2. taggers.** Very thin sheet iron, usually plated with tin.

tag line also **tag·line** (tăg′līn′) *n.* **1.** An ending line, as in a play or joke, that makes a point. **2.** An often repeated phrase associated with an individual, an organization, or a commercial product; a slogan.

tag·ma (tăg′mə) *n., pl.* **-ma·ta** (-mə-tə). A distinct section of an anthropod, consisting of two or more adjoining segments, such as the cephalothorax of a spider. [Greek, arrangement, from *tassein, tag-*, to arrange.]

Ta·gore (tə-gôr′, -gōr′, tä-), Sir **Rabindranath.** 1861–1941. Bengali writer known especially for his collection of poetry *Gitanjali* (1912), based on traditional Hindu themes. He won the 1913 Nobel Prize for literature.

tag sale *n.* See **garage sale.**

Ta·gus (tā′gəs) also **Ta·jo** (tä′hō). A river of the Iberian Peninsula rising in east-central Spain and flowing generally westward about 941 km (585 mi) through central Portugal to the Atlantic Ocean.

ta·hi·ni (tə-hē′nē) *n.* A thick paste made from ground sesame seeds. [Turkish *tāhin*, sesame flour or oil, from Arabic dialectal *ṭaḥīne*, from *ṭaḥan*, to grind.]

Ta·hi·ti (tə-hē′tē). An island of the southern Pacific Ocean in the Windward group of the Society Islands in French Polynesia. It was first settled by Polynesians in the 14th century and became a French colony in 1880.

Ta·hi·tian (tə-hē′shən) *adj.* Of or relating to Tahiti or its people, language, or culture. **—Tahitian** *n.* **1.** A native or inhabitant of Tahiti. **2.** The Polynesian language of Tahiti.

Ta·hoe (tä′hō), **Lake.** A lake on the California-Nevada border west of Carson City, Nevada, at an elevation of 1,899.8 m (6,229 ft). It is a popular resort area.

tahr (tär) *n.* Any of several goatlike mammals of the genus *Hemitragus* of mountainous regions of Asia, having curved horns and a shaggy coat. [Nepalese *thār*.]

tah·sil·dar also **tah·seel·dar** (tə-sēl′där′) *n.* A district official in India in charge of revenues and taxation. [Urdu *taḥsīldār*, from Persian : *taḥṣīl*, collection, revenue (from Arabic, from *ḥaṣala*, to collect, from *ḥaṣala*, to acquire) + *-dār*, having; see **dher-** in Appendix.]

Tai (tī) also **Dai** (dī) *—n., pl.* **Tai** or **Tais** also **Dai** or **Dais. 1.** A family of languages spoken in southeast Asia and southern China that includes Thai, Lao, and Shan. **2.** A member of any of the Tai-speaking peoples of Thailand, Burma, Laos, China, and Vietnam. **3.** Thai. *—adj.* **1.** Of or relating to Tai, its speakers, or their culture. **2.** Thai.

tai chi or **Tai Chi** (tī′ chē′, jē′) also **tai chi chuan** or **Tai Chi Chuan** (chwän′) *n.* A Chinese system of physical exercises designed for self-defense and meditation. [Short for Chinese (Mandarin) *taì jí quán* : *taì*, highest + *jí*, reach + *quán*, boxing.]

Tai·chung (tī′cho͝ong′, -jo͝ong′) also **Tai·zhong** (-jông′). A city of west-central Taiwan southwest of Taipei. It is a food-processing and distribution center. Population, 621,566.

tai·ga (tī′gə) *n.* A subarctic, evergreen coniferous forest of northern Eurasia located just south of the tundra and dominated by firs and spruces. [Russian *taĭga*, of Altaic origin.]

tail¹ (tāl) *n.* **1.** The posterior part of an animal, especially when elongated and extending beyond the trunk or main part of the body. **2.** The bottom, rear, or hindmost part: *the tail of a shirt.* **3.** The rear end of a wagon or other vehicle. **4. a.** The rear portion of the fuselage of an aircraft. **b.** An assembly of stabilizing planes and control surfaces in this rear portion. **5.** The vaned rear portion of a bomb or missile. **6.** An appendage to the rear or

Helen Taft

William Howard Taft

ă pat	oi boy
ā pay	ou out
âr care	o͝o took
ä father	o͞o boot
ĕ pet	ŭ cut
ē be	ûr urge
ĭ pit	th thin
ī pie	*th* this
îr pier	hw which
ŏ pot	zh vision
ō toe	ə about, item
ô paw	♦ regionalism

Stress marks: ′ (primary); ′ (secondary), as in **dictionary** (dĭk′shə-nĕr′ē)

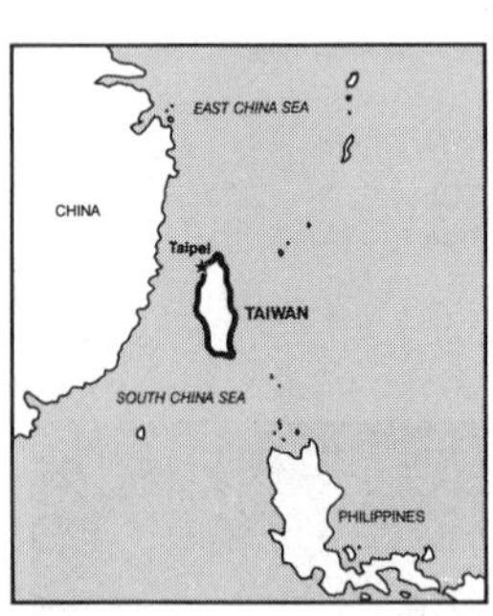

Taiwan

bottom of a thing: *the tail of a kite.* **7.** The long luminous stream of gas and dust forced from the head of a comet when it is close to the sun. **8.** A braid of hair; a pigtail. **9.** Something that follows or takes the last place: *the tail of a journey.* **10.** A train of followers; a retinue. **11.** The end of a line of persons or things. **12.** The short closing line of certain stanzas of verse. **13.** The refuse or dross remaining from processes such as distilling or milling. **14.** *Printing.* The bottom of a page; the bottom margin. **15.** Often **tails** *(used with a sing. verb).* The side of a coin not having the principal design and the date. **16.** *Informal.* The trail of a person or an animal in flight. **17.** *Informal.* A person assigned or employed to follow and report on someone else's movements and actions: *The police put a tail on the suspected drug dealer.* **18.** **tails. a.** A formal evening costume typically worn by men. **b.** A swallow-tailed coat. **19. a.** *Slang.* The buttocks. **b.** *Vulgar Slang.* A sexual partner, especially a woman or girl. **—tail** *adj.* **1.** Of or relating to a tail or tails: *tail feathers.* **2.** Situated in the tail, as of an airplane: *a tail gunner.* **—tail** *v.* **tailed, tail·ing, tails.** *—tr.* **1.** To provide with a tail: *tail a kite.* **2.** To deprive of a tail; dock. **3.** To serve as the tail of: *The Santa Claus float tailed the parade.* **4.** To connect (often dissimilar or incongruous objects) by or as if by the tail or end: *tail two ideas together.* **5.** *Architecture.* To set one end of (a beam, board, or brick) into a wall. **6.** *Informal.* To follow and keep under surveillance. *—intr.* **1.** To become lengthened or spaced when moving in a line: *The patrol tailed out in pairs.* **2.** *Architecture.* To be inserted at one end into a wall, as a floor timber or beam. **3.** *Informal.* To follow: *tailed after the leader.* **4.** *Nautical.* **a.** To go aground with the stern foremost. **b.** To lie or swing with the stern in a named direction, as when riding at anchor or on a mooring. ***—phrasal verbs.*** **tail down.** To ease a heavy load down a steep slope. **tail off** (or **away**). To diminish gradually; dwindle or subside: *The fireworks tailed off into darkness.* [Middle English, from Old English *tægel.*] **—tail′less** *adj.*

tail² (tāl) *Law. n.* Limitation of the inheritance of an estate to a particular party. **—tail** *adj. Law.* Being in tail: *a tail estate.* [Middle English *taille,* from Old French, division, from *taillier,* to cut. See TAILOR.]

tail·back (tāl′băk′) *n. Football.* The back on an offensive team who lines up farthest from the line of scrimmage.

tail beam *n. Architecture.* See **tailpiece** (sense 3).

tail·board (tāl′bôrd′, -bōrd′) *n.* See **tailgate** (sense 1).

tail·bone (tāl′bōn′) *n.* See **coccyx.**

tail·coat (tāl′kōt′) *n.* See **swallow-tailed coat.**

tailed frog (tāld) *n.* A frog *(Ascaphus turei)* of the Pacific Northwest, having in the male an external cloaca that resembles a tail and serves as a copulatory organ at breeding time.

tail end *n.* **1.** The rear or hindmost part. **2.** The very end; the conclusion.

tail fan *n.* The fanlike posterior structure of a lobster, shrimp, or other crustacean, formed from the telson and the last pair of uropods and used for backward locomotion.

tail fin also **tail·fin** (tāl′fĭn′) *n.* **1.** A fin at the posterior part of the body of a fish, crustacean, whale, or other aquatic animal. **2.** An ornamental projection shaped like a fin on the rear fender of an automobile. Also called *fin.*

tail·gate (tāl′gāt′) *n.* **1.** A hinged board or closure at the rear of a vehicle, such as a station wagon, that can be lowered during loading and unloading. Also called *tailboard.* **2.** One of the pair of gates downstream in a canal lock. **—tailgate** *v.* **-gat·ed, -gat·ing, -gates.** *—tr.* **1.** To drive so closely behind (another vehicle) that one cannot stop or swerve with ease in an emergency. **2.** *Slang.* To follow closely behind (another person), as in gaining access to an area requiring the use of an electronic identification card. *—intr.* **1.** To follow another vehicle too closely. **2.** To participate in a picnic that is served from the tailgate of a vehicle, as before a sports event. **—tail′gat′er** *n.*

tail-heav·y (tāl′hĕv′ē) *adj.* **-i·er, -i·est.** Having too much weight at the rear, either from overloading or from poor design and construction: *a tail-heavy cargo plane.*

tail·ing (tā′lĭng) *n.* **1. tailings.** Refuse or dross remaining after ore has been processed. **2.** *Architecture.* The portion of a tailed beam, brick, or board inside a wall.

tail lamp *n.* See **taillight.**

taille (tāl, tä′yə) *n.* A form of direct royal taxation that was levied in France before 1789 on nonprivileged subjects and lands and tended to weigh most heavily on the peasants. [French, from Old French, division. See TAIL².]

tail·light (tāl′līt′) *n.* A red light or one of a pair mounted on the rear end of a vehicle. Also called *tail lamp.*

tai·lor (tā′lər) *n. Abbr.* **tlr.** One that makes, repairs, and alters garments such as suits, coats, and dresses. **—tailor** *v.* **-lored, -lor·ing, -lors.** *—tr.* **1.** To make (a garment), especially to specific requirements or measurements. **2.** To fit or provide (a person) with clothes made to that person's measurements. **3.** To make, alter, or adapt for a particular end or purpose: *a speech that was tailored to an audience of business leaders.* *—intr.* To pursue the trade of a tailor. [Middle English, from Anglo-Norman *taillour,* from Old French *tailleor,* from *taillier,* to cut, from Late Latin *tāliāre,* from Latin *tālea,* a cutting.]

tai·lor·bird (tā′lər-bûrd′) *n.* Any of several Old World tropical passerine birds of the genus *Orthotomus,* that characteristically stitch leaves together with plant fibers to make nests.

tai·lored (tā′lərd) *adj.* **1.** Made by a tailor; custom-made. **2.** Simple, trim, or severe in line or design: *a neat, tailored dress; tailored curtains.*

tai·lor-made (tā′lər-mād′) *adj.* **1.** Made by a tailor. **2.** Perfectly fitted to a condition, preference, or purpose; made or as if made to order: *tailor-made renovations.* **—tailor-made** *n.* A garment made by a tailor.

tai·lor's chalk (tā′lərz) *n.* A thin piece of hard chalk used in tailoring for making temporary alteration marks on clothing.

tail·piece (tāl′pēs′) *n.* **1.** A piece forming an end; an appendage. **2.** *Printing.* An engraving or a design placed as an ornament at the end of a chapter or at the bottom of a page. **3.** *Architecture.* A beam tailed into a wall. Also called *tail beam.* **4.** *Music.* A triangular piece of ebony to which the lower ends of the strings of a violin or cello are attached.

tail·pipe also **tail pipe** (tāl′pīp′) *n.* The pipe through which exhaust gases from an engine are discharged. Also called *exhaust pipe.*

tail·race (tāl′rās′) *n.* **1.** The part of a millrace below the water wheel through which the spent water flows. **2.** A channel for floating away mine tailings and refuse.

tail·skid (tāl′skĭd′) *n.* A skid attached to the rear underside of certain airplanes to act as a runner.

tail·spin (tāl′spĭn′) *n.* **1.** The rapid descent of an aircraft in a steep, spiral spin. **2.** *Informal.* A loss of emotional control sometimes resulting in emotional collapse.

tail·stock (tāl′stŏk′) *n.* The movable part of a lathe that supports the dead center.

tail wind or **tail·wind** (tāl′wĭnd′) *n.* A wind blowing in the same direction as that of the course of an aircraft, a ship, or another vehicle.

Tai·myr Peninsula also **Tai·mir Peninsula** or **Tay·myr Peninsula** (tī-mîr′). A peninsula of north-central Russia extending northward between the Laptev and Kara seas.

tain (tān) *n.* **1.** A type of paper-thin tin plate. **2.** Tinfoil used as a backing for mirrors. [French, alteration of *étain,* tin, from Late Latin *stannum.* See STANNIC.]

Tai·nan (tī′nän′). A city of southwest Taiwan on the South China Sea. Settled in 1590, it is Taiwan's oldest city. Population, 609,934.

Taí·na·ron (tā′nə-rôn′, tĕ′nä-), **Cape.** Formerly **Cape Mat·a·pan** (măt′ə-păn′). A cape at the southernmost point of mainland Greece. The British won an important naval battle against the Italians off Cape Taínaron in 1941.

Taine (tān, tĕn), **Hippolyte Adolphe.** 1828–1893. French philosopher and historian who was a leading exponent of positivism and wrote *Origins of Contemporary France* (1875–1893).

Tai·no (tī′nō) *n., pl.* **Taino** or **-nos. 1.** A member of an Arawak people of the Greater Antilles and the Bahamas who became extinct under Spanish colonization during the 16th century. **2.** The language of this people. [Spanish, of American Indian origin.]

taint (tānt) *v.* **taint·ed, taint·ing, taints.** *—tr.* **1.** To affect with or as if with a disease. **2.** To affect with decay or putrefaction; spoil. See Synonyms at **contaminate. 3.** To corrupt morally. **4.** To affect with a tinge of something reprehensible. *—intr.* To become affected with decay or putrefaction; spoil. **—taint** *n.* **1.** A moral defect considered as a stain or spot. See Synonyms at **stain. 2.** An infecting touch, influence, or tinge. [Partly from obsolete *taynt,* to color, dye (from Anglo-Norman *teint,* from past participle of *teindre,* from Latin *tingere*) and partly from Middle English *tainten,* to convict (from Old French *ataint,* past participle of *ataindre,* to attain, touch upon; see ATTAIN).] **—taint′less** *adj.* **—taint′less·ly** *adv.* **—taint′less·ness** *n.*

tai·pan¹ (tī′păn′) *n.* **1.** A foreign businessman or a trader in China. **2.** A foreigner who is a chief executive of a business or company operating in China or Hong Kong; a tycoon. [Chinese *tài pān* : *tài,* big + *pān,* company.]

tai·pan² (tī′păn) *n.* A large, extremely venomous elapid snake *(Oxyuranus scutellatus)* of Australia and New Guinea, having long fangs and large venom glands. [Wik Munkan (Aboriginal language of northeast Australia) *dhayban.*]

Tai·pei also **Tai·peh** (tī′pā′, -bā′). The capital and largest city of Taiwan, in the northern part of the country. Founded in the 18th century, it was ruled by the Japanese from 1895 to 1945 and later became the headquarters of Chiang Kai-shek and the Chinese Nationalists when they fled mainland China (1949). Population, 2,327,641.

Tai·wan (tī′wän′). Officially **Republic of Chi·na** (chī′nə). Formerly **For·mo·sa** (fôr-mō′sə). A country off the southeast coast of China comprising the island of **Taiwan,** the Pescadores, and other smaller islands. An important trade center in the 19th century, Taiwan was ceded to Japan in 1895 and regained by China after World War II (1945). Taiwan broke off from mainland China in 1949. Taipei is the capital and the largest city. Population, 18,457,923.

Tai·wan·ese (tī′wä-nēz′, -nēs′) *adj.* Of or relating to Taiwan or its peoples, languages, or cultures. **—Taiwanese** *n., pl.* **Taiwanese. 1.** A native or inhabitant of Taiwan. **2.** The Minnan dialect of Chinese spoken on Taiwan.

Taiwan Strait. See **Formosa Strait.**

Tai·yu·an also **Tai·yü·an** (tī′yo͞o-än′, -yüän′). A city of northeast China southwest of Beijing. It is a coal-mining and steel-manufacturing center. Population, 1,390,000.

Tai·zhong (tī′jông′). See **Taichung.**

taj (täzh, täj) *n.* A tall conical cap worn by Moslems as a headdress of distinction. [Arabic *tāj,* from Persian, crown. See **(s)teg-** in Appendix.]

Ta·jik also **Ta·dzhik** (tä-jĭk′, tə-) *—n., pl.* **Tajik** or **-jiks** also **Tadzhik** or **-dzhiks. 1.** A member of a people inhabiting the Tadzhik S.S.R. and neighboring areas in the U.S.S.R., Afghanistan, and China. **2.** Tajiki. *—adj.* Tajiki.

Ta·jik·i also **Ta·dzhik·i** (tä-jĭk′ē, tə-) *—n.* The Iranian language of the Tajik people, closely related to Persian. *—adj.* Of or relating to the Tajik people or their language or culture.

Ta·jo (tä′hō). See **Tagus.**

ta·ka (tä′kə) *n.* See table at **currency.** [Bengali *ṭākā,* from Sanskrit *ṭaṅkaḥ,* stamped coin.]

ta·ka·he (tə-kä′ē, tə-kī′) *n.* An almost extinct flightless bird *(Notornis mantelli)* of New Zealand, having a large bill and brightly colored plumage. [Maori *takahē.*]

Ta·ka·mat·su (tä′kä-mät′so͞o). A city of northeast Shikoku, Japan, on the Inland Sea. It is a major seaport. Population, 327,001.

Ta·ka·tsu·ki (tə-kät′so͞o-kē, tä′kä-tso͞o′kē). A city of southwest Honshu, Japan, a commercial center between Osaka and Kyoto. Population, 348,743.

♦**take** (tāk) *v.* **took** (to͝ok), **tak·en** (tā′kən), **tak·ing, takes.** *—tr.* **1.** To get into one's possession by force, skill, or artifice, especially: **a.** To capture physically; seize: *take an enemy fortress.* **b.** To seize with authority; confiscate. **c.** To kill, snare, or trap (fish or game, for example). **d.** *Sports & Games.* To acquire in a game or competition; win: *took the crown in horseracing.* **e.** *Sports & Games.* To defeat: *Our team took the visitors three to one.* **f.** *Sports.* To catch (a ball in play), especially in baseball: *The player took it on the fly.* **g.** *Baseball.* To refrain from swinging at (a pitched ball). **2.** To grasp with the hands; grip: *Take your partner's hand.* **3.** To be affected with; come down with; contract: *The child has taken the flu.* **4.** To encounter or catch in a particular situation; come upon; discover: *Your actions took me by surprise.* **5.** To deal a blow to; strike or hit: *The boxer took his opponent a sharp jab to the ribs.* **6.** To affect favorably or winsomely; charm or captivate: *She was taken by the puppy.* **7. a.** To put (food or drink, for example) into the body; eat or drink: *took a little soup for dinner.* **b.** To draw in; inhale: *took a deep breath.* **8.** To expose one's body to (healthful or pleasurable treatment, for example): *take the sun; take the waters at a spa.* **9.** To bring or receive into a particular relation, association, or other connection: *take a new partner into the firm; take a company national.* **10.** To engage in sex with. **11.** To accept and place under one's care or keeping. **12.** To appropriate for one's own or another's use or benefit; obtain by purchase; secure or buy: *We always take season tickets.* **13.** To assume for oneself: *take all the credit.* **a.** To charge or oblige oneself with the fulfillment of (a task or duty, for example); commit oneself to: *She took the position of chair of the committee.* **b.** To pledge one's obedience to; impose (a vow or promise) upon oneself. **c.** To subject oneself to: *We took extra time to do the job properly.* **d.** To accept or adopt for one's own. **e.** To put forth or adopt as a point of argument, defense, or discussion. **f.** To require or have as a fitting or proper accompaniment: *Intransitive verbs take no direct object.* **14.** To pick out; select or choose: *take any card.* **a.** To choose for one's own use; avail oneself of the use of: *We took a rented car.* **b.** To use (something) as when in operation: *This camera takes 35mm film.* **c.** To use (something) as a means of conveyance or transportation: *take a train to Pittsburgh.* **d.** To use (something) as a means of safety or refuge: *take shelter from the storm.* **e.** To choose and then adopt (a particular route or direction) while on foot or while operating a vehicle: *Take a right at the next corner. The driver downshifted to take the corner.* **15.** To assume occupancy of: *take a seat.* **16.** To require (something) as a basic necessity: *It takes money to live in that town.* **17.** To obtain from a source; derive or draw: *The book takes its title from the Bible.* **18.** To obtain, as through measurement or a specified procedure: *took the patient's temperature.* **19.** To put down in shorthand or cursive writing: *take a letter.* **20.** To put down an image, a likeness, or a representation of by or as by drawing, painting, or photography: *took a picture of us.* **21. a.** To accept (something owed, offered, or given) either reluctantly or willingly: *take criticism.* **b.** To submit to (something inflicted); endure: *didn't take his punishment very well.* **c.** To withstand: *The dam took the heavy flood waters.* **22. a.** To accept or believe (something put forth) as true: *I'll take your word.* **b.** To follow (advice, a suggestion, or a lead, for example). **c.** To accept, handle, or deal with in a particular way: *He takes things in stride.* **d.** To consider in a particular relation or from a particular viewpoint: *take the bitter with the sweet.* **23.** To make or perform: *Many crucial decisions were taken as the path of the hurricane was plotted.* **24. a.** To allow to come in; give access or admission to; admit: *The boat took a lot of water but remained afloat.* **b.** To provide room for; accommodate: *We can't take more than 100 guests.* **c.** To become saturated or impregnated with (dye, for example). **25. a.** To understand or interpret: *May I take your smile as an indication of approval?* **b.** To consider; assume: *Take the matter as settled.* **c.** To consider to be equal to; reckon: *We take their number at 1,000.* **d.** To perceive or feel; experience: *I take pleasure in informing you that you have won the prize.* **26.** To carry, convey, lead, or cause to go along to another place: *Don't forget to take your umbrella. This bus takes you to New York.* See Usage Note at **bring. 27.** To remove from a place: *take the dishes from the sink.* **28.** To secure by removing: *The dentist took two molars.* **29.** To cause to die; kill or destroy: *The blight took these tomatoes.* **30.** To subtract: *take 15 from 30.* **31. a.** To commit and apply oneself to the study of: *take art lessons; take Spanish.* **b.** To study for with success: *took a degree in law.* **32.** *Informal.* To swindle, defraud, or cheat: *You've really been taken.* *—intr.* **1.** To acquire possession. **2.** To engage or mesh; catch, as gears or other mechanical parts. **3.** To start growing; root or germinate: *Have the seeds taken?* **4.** To have the intended effect; operate or work: *The transfusion apparently took.* **5.** To gain popularity or favor: *The television series, which didn't take, was later canceled.* **6.** To become: *He took sick.* **—take** *n.* **1. a.** The act or process of taking. **b.** That which is taken. **2. a.** A quantity collected at one time, especially the amount of profit or receipts taken on a business arrangement or venture. **b.** The number of fish, game birds, or other animals killed or captured at one time. **3.** *Sports.* The amount of money collected as admission to a sporting event; the gate. **4.** The uninterrupted running of a movie or television camera or a set of recording equipment in filming a movie or television program or cutting a record. **5. a.** A scene filmed or televised without interrupting the run of the camera. **b.** A recording made in a single session. **6. a.** A physical reaction, such as a rash, indicating a successful vaccination. **b.** A successful graft. **7.** *Slang.* An attempt or a try: *He got the answer on the third take.* ***—phrasal verbs.*** **take after. 1.** To follow as an example. **2.** To resemble in appearance, temperament, or character. **take apart. 1.** To divide into parts after disassembling. **2.** To dissect or analyze (a theory, for example), usually in an effort to discover hidden or innate flaws or weaknesses. **3.** *Slang.* To beat up; thrash. **take back.** To retract (something stated or written). **take down. 1.** To bring to a lower position from a higher one. **2.** To take apart; dismantle: *take down the Christmas tree.* **3.** To lower the arrogance or the self-esteem of (a person): *really took him down during the debate.* **4.** To put down in writing. **take for. 1.** To regard as: *Do you take me for a fool?* **2.** To consider mistakenly: *Don't take silence for approval.* **take in. 1.** To grant admittance to; receive as a guest or an employee. **2.** To reduce in size; make smaller or shorter: *took in the waist on the pair of pants.* **3.** To include or constitute. **4.** To understand: *couldn't take in the meaning of the word.* **5.** To deceive or swindle: *was taken in by a confidence artist.* **6.** To look at thoroughly; view: *took in the sights.* **7.** To accept (work) to be done in one's house for pay: *took in typing.* **8.** To convey (a prisoner) to a police station. **take off. 1.** To remove, as clothing: *take one's coat off; take off one's galoshes.* **2.** To release: *took the brake off.* **3.** To deduct as a discount: *took 20 percent off.* **4.** To carry off or away. **5.** *Slang.* **a.** To go off; leave: *took off in a hurry.* **b.** To achieve wide use or popularity: *a new movie that really took off.* **6.** To rise in flight: *The plane took off on time.* **7.** To discontinue: *took off the commuter special.* **8.** To withhold service due, as from one's work: *I'm taking off three days during May.* **take on. 1.** To undertake or begin to handle: *took on extra responsibilities.* **2.** To hire; engage: *took on more workers during the harvest.* **3.** To oppose in competition: *a wrestler who took on all comers.* **4.** *Informal.* To display violent or passionate emotion: *Don't take on so!* **5.** To acquire (an appearance, for example) as or as if one's own: *Over the years he has taken on the look of a banker.* **take out. 1.** To extract; remove: *took the splinter out.* **2.** To secure (a license, for example) by application to an authority. **3.** *Informal.* To escort, as a date. **4.** To give vent to: *Don't take your frustration out in such an aggressive manner.* **5.** To obtain as an equivalent in a different form: *took out the money owed in services.* **6.** *Informal.* To begin a course; set out: *The police took out after the thieves.* **7.** *Slang.* **a.** To kill; murder: *Two snipers took out an enemy platoon.* **b.** To search for and destroy in an armed attack or other such encounter: *Combat pilots, flying low to avoid radar, took out the guerrilla leader's bunker in a single mission.* **take over.** To assume the control or management of. **take to. 1.** To have recourse to; go to, as for safety: *took to the woods.* **2.** To develop as a habit or a steady practice: *take to drink.* **3.** To become fond of or attached to: *"Two keen minds that they are, they took to each other"* (Jack Kerouac). **take up. 1.** To raise; lift. **2.** To reduce in size; shorten or tighten: *take up a gown.* **3.** To pay off an outstanding debt, mortgage, or note. **4.** To accept (an option, a bet, or a challenge) as offered. **5.** To begin again; resume: *Let's take up where we left off.* **6.** To use up, consume, or occupy: *The extra duties took up most of my time.* **7.** To develop an interest in or devotion to. *take up mountain climbing.* **8.** To deal with: *Let's take up each problem one at a time.* **9.** To assume: *took up a friendly attitude.* **10.** To absorb or adsorb: *crops taking up nutrients.* **11.** To enter into (a profession or business): *took up engineering.* ***—idioms.*** **on the take.** *Informal.* Taking or seeking to take bribes or illegal income: *"There were policemen on the take"* (Scott Turow). **take a bath.** *Informal.* To experience serious financial loss: *"Small investors who latched on to hot new issues took a bath in Wall Street"* (Paul A. Samuelson). **take account of.** To take into consideration. **take away from.** To detract: *Her stringy hair takes away from her lovely face.* **take care.** To be careful: *Take care or you will slip on the ice.* **take care of.** To assume responsibility for the maintenance, support, or treatment of. **take charge.** To assume control or command. **take effect. 1.** To become operative, as under law or regulation: *The curfew takes effect at midnight.* **2.** To produce the desired reaction: *The an-*

ă pat	oi boy
ā pay	ou out
âr care	o͝o took
ä father	o͞o boot
ĕ pet	ŭ cut
ē be	ûr urge
ĭ pit	th thin
ī pie	*th* this
îr pier	hw which
ŏ pot	zh vision
ō toe	ə about, item
ô paw	♦ regionalism

Stress marks: ′ (primary); ′ (secondary), as in **dictionary** (dĭk′shə-nĕr′ē)

Takkakaw

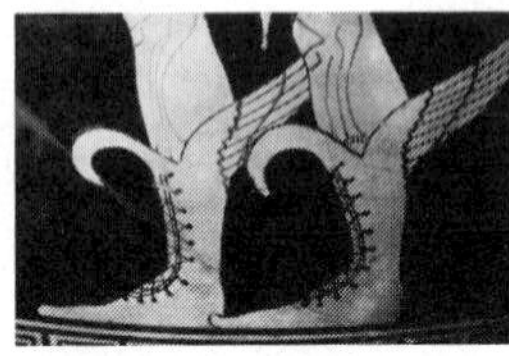
talaria
Detail from a Greek amphora

tibiotics at last began to take effect. **take exception.** To express opposition by argument; object to: *took exception to the prosecutor's line of questioning.* **take five** (or **ten**). *Slang.* To take a short rest or break, as of five or ten minutes. **take for granted. 1.** To consider as true, real, or forthcoming; anticipate correctly. **2.** To underestimate the value of: *a publisher who took the editors for granted.* **take heart.** To be confident or courageous. **take hold. 1.** To seize, as by grasping. **2.** To become established: *The newly planted vines quickly took hold.* **take it. 1.** To understand; assume: *As I take it, they won't accept the proposal.* **2.** *Informal.* To endure abuse, criticism, or other harsh treatment: *If you can dish it out, you've got to learn to take it.* **take it on the chin.** *Slang.* To endure punishment, suffering, or defeat. **take it or leave it.** To accept or reject unconditionally. **take it out on.** *Informal.* To abuse (someone) in venting one's own anger. **take kindly to. 1.** To be receptive to: *take kindly to constructive criticism.* **2.** To be naturally attracted or fitted to; thrive on. **take lying down.** *Informal.* To submit to harsh treatment with no resistance: *refused to take the snub lying down.* **take notice of.** To pay attention to. **take (one's) breath away.** To put into a state of awe or shock. **take (one's) time.** To act slowly or at one's leisure. **take place.** To happen; occur. **take root. 1.** To become established or fixed. **2.** To become rooted. **take shape.** To take on a distinctive form. **take sick.** *Chiefly Southern U.S.* To become ill. **take sides.** To associate with and support a particular faction, group, cause, or person. **take stock. 1.** To take an inventory. **2.** To make an estimate or appraisal, as of resources or of oneself. **take stock in.** To trust, believe in, or attach importance to. **take the bench.** *Law.* To assume a judicial position. **take the cake. 1.** To be the most outrageous or disappointing. **2.** To win the prize; be outstanding. **take the count. 1.** To be defeated. **2.** *Sports.* To be counted out in boxing. **take the fall** (or **hit**). *Slang.* To incur blame or censure, either willingly or unwillingly: *a senior official who took the fall for the failed intelligence operation.* **take the floor.** To rise to deliver a formal speech, as to an assembly. **take the heat.** *Slang.* To incur and endure heavy censure or criticism: *had a reputation for being able to take the heat in a crisis.* **take to the cleaners.** *Slang.* **1.** To rob or swindle. **2.** To take all the money or possessions of, as in a divorce action. **3.** To subject to withering criticism. **take up for.** To support (a person or group, for example) in an argument. **take up the cudgels.** To join in a dispute, especially in defense of a participant. **take up with.** *Informal.* To begin to associate with; consort with: *took up with a fast crowd.* [Middle English *taken,* from Old English *tacan,* from Old Norse *taka.*] **—tak′a·ble** *adj.*

take·a·way (tāk′ə-wā′) *n.* **1.** A concession, as in a lower level of health benefits, made by a labor union to a company in negotiating a new contract. **2.** *Sports.* The act or an instance of taking away the ball or puck from the team on the offensive, as by recovery of a fumbled football or by interception of a passed puck.

take-a·way (tāk′ə-wā′) *adj. Chiefly British.* Take-out.

take-charge (tāk′chärj′) *adj. Informal.* Possessing or exhibiting strong qualities of initiative, leadership, and management: *"take-charge people who are the center of all the action"* (George F. Will).

take·down (tāk′doun′) *adj.* Having the capability of being taken down or apart: *a takedown rifle; a takedown scaffold.* **—takedown** *n.* **1.a.** An article or apparatus that can be taken down or apart. **b.** The mechanism that allows an article or apparatus to be easily taken down. **2.** *Sports.* A move or maneuver in wrestling or the martial arts in which a standing opponent is forced to the floor. **3.** *Informal.* **a.** The act of humiliating a person. **b.** An instance of such humiliation: *She gave you quite a takedown.*

take-home pay (tāk′hōm′) *n.* The amount of one's salary remaining after federal, state, and often city income taxes and various other deductions have been withheld.

take-in (tāk′ĭn′) *n. Informal.* The act or an instance of swindling or cheating; a deception.

tak·en (tā′kən) *v.* Past participle of **take.**

take·off (tāk′ôf′, -ŏf′) *n.* **1.** The act of rising in flight. Used of an aircraft or a rocket. **2.** The point or place from which one takes off. **3.** *Informal.* An amusing imitative caricature or burlesque.

take·out also **take-out** (tāk′out′) *adj.* **1.** Intended to be eaten off the premises: *takeout pizza.* **2.** Selling or intended for the sale of food products to be consumed off the premises: *a takeout counter; takeout containers.* **—take′-out′** *n.*

take·o·ver also **take-o·ver** (tāk′ō′vər) *n.* The act or an instance of assuming control or management of or responsibility for something, especially the seizure of power, as in a nation, political organization, or corporation. **—take′o′ver** *adj.*

tak·er (tā′kər) *n.* One that takes or takes up something, such as a wager or purchase: *There were no takers on the bets.*

take-up (tāk′ŭp′) *n.* **1.** The act of taking or tightening up. **2.** A device for reducing slack or taking up lost motion, as one in a loom.

ta·kin (tä′kēn′) *n.* A large ruminant mammal *(Budorcas taxicolor)* of the mountains of China, Burma, and the Himalayas, having backward-pointing horns and a shaggy coat. [Possibly of Tibeto-Burman origin.]

tak·ing (tā′kĭng) *adj.* **1.** Capturing interest; fetching: *a taking smile.* **2.** Contagious; catching. Used of an infectious disease. **—taking** *n.* **1.** The act of one that takes. **2.** Something taken, as a catch of fish. **3. takings.** *Informal.* Receipts, especially of money.

ta·ki-ta·ki (tä′kē-tä′kē) *n.* See **Sranantongo.** [Probably alteration and reduplication of TALK.]

Tak·ka·kaw (tăk′ə-kô′). A waterfall, 503.3 m (1,650 ft) high, in southeast British Columbia, Canada. It is the highest waterfall in Canada.

Ta·kli·ma·kan also **Ta·kla·ma·kan** (tä′klə-mə-kän′). A desert of western China between the Tien Shan and the Kunlun Mountains.

Ta·ko·ma Park (tə-kō′mə). A city of central Maryland, a residential suburb of Washington, D.C. Population, 16,231.

ta·la (tä′lə) *n.* See table at **currency.** [Samoan, from English DOLLAR.]

tal·a·poin (tăl′ə-poin′) *n.* A small African monkey *(Cercopithecus talapoin),* the smallest of the guenons, having a long tail and greenish fur. [French, from Portuguese *talapões,* pl. of *talapão,* monk.]

ta·lar·i·a (tə-lâr′ē-ə) *pl.n.* Winged sandals such as those worn by Hermes and Iris as represented in Greco-Roman painting and sculpture. [Latin *tālāria,* from neuter pl. of *tālāris,* of the ankles, from *tālus,* ankle.]

Ta·la·ud Islands (tə-lout′, tä-lä′o͞od) or **Ta·laur Islands** (-lour′, -lä′o͝or). A group of islands of northeast Indonesia northeast of Sulawesi.

Tal·bot (tôl′bət, tăl′-) *n.* A large white or light-colored hound of an English variety, having long hanging ears and heavy jaws, formerly used for tracking and hunting. [Middle English, personal name, from Old French.]

Talbot, William Henry Fox. 1800–1877. British inventor and pioneer in photography who produced the first book illustrated with photographs (1844–1846).

talc (tălk) *n.* A fine-grained white, greenish, or gray mineral, $Mg_3Si_4O_{10}(OH)_2$, having a soft soapy feel and used in talcum and face powder, as a paper coating, and as a filler for paint and plastics. **—talc** *tr.v.* **talcked, talck·ing, talcs** or **talced, talc·ing, talcs.** To apply this substance to (a photographic plate, for example). [French, from Medieval Latin *talcum* and Old Spanish *talco,* both from Arabic *ṭalq,* from Persian *talk.*]

Tal·ca (täl′kä). A city of central Chile between Santiago and Concepción. Chile's independence was proclaimed here in 1818. Population, 128,544.

Tal·ca·hua·no (täl′kə-wä′nō, -hwä′-, täl′kä-). A city of central Chile on the Pacific Ocean near Concepción. It is an important naval base. Population, 202,368.

talc·ose (tăl′kōs′) also **talc·ous** (-kəs) or **talck·y** (-kē) *adj.* Made of or containing talc.

tal·cum (tăl′kəm) *n.* **1.** Talc. **2.** Talcum powder. [Medieval Latin. See TALC.]

talcum powder *n.* A fine, often perfumed powder made from purified talc for use on the skin.

tale (tāl) *n.* **1.** A recital of events or happenings; a report or revelation: *told us a long tale of woe.* **2.** A malicious story, piece of gossip, or petty complaint. **3.** A deliberate lie; a falsehood. **4.** A narrative of real or imaginary events; a story. **5.** *Archaic.* A tally or reckoning; a total. [Middle English, from Old English *talu.* See **del-**[2] in Appendix.]

tale·bear·er (tāl′bâr′ər) *n.* One who spreads malicious stories or gossip. **—tale′bear′ing** *adj. n.*

tal·ent (tăl′ənt) *n.* **1.** A marked innate ability, as for artistic accomplishment. See Synonyms at **ability. 2.a.** Natural endowment or ability of a superior quality. **b.** A person or group of people having such ability: *The company makes good use of its talent.* **3.** A variable unit of weight and money used in ancient Greece, Rome, and the Middle East. [Middle English, inclination, disposition, from Old French, from Medieval Latin, from Latin, balance, sum of money, from Greek *talanton.* See **tela-** in Appendix. Sense 3, Middle English, from Old English *talente,* from Latin *talenta,* pl. of *talentum,* from Greek *talanton.*] **—tal′ent·ed** *adj.* **—tal′ent·less** *adj.* **—tal′ent·less·ness** *n.*

talent scout *n.* An agent who goes in search of talented people for acting, sports, or business.

talent show *n.* A show that features amateur performers whose talents may win them recognition or awards.

ta·ler also **tha·ler** (tä′lər) *n., pl.* **taler** or **-lers** also **thaler** or **-lers.** Any of numerous silver coins that served as a unit of currency in certain Germanic countries between the 15th and 19th centuries. [German. See DOLLAR.]

tales (tālz, tā′lēz) *n., pl.* **tales.** *Law.* **1.** A group of people summoned to fill vacancies on a jury that has become deficient in number. **2.** The writ allowing for a summons of jurors. [Middle English, from Medieval Latin *tālēs dē circumstantibus,* such (persons) from those standing about (a phrase used in the writ), from Latin, pl. of *tālis,* such. See **to-** in Appendix.]

tales·man (tālz′mən, tā′lēz-) *n. Law.* One who is summoned under a writ of tales.

tale·tell·er (tāl′tĕl′ər) *n.* **1.** One who tells stories; a storyteller. **2.** A talebearer; a tattletale. **—tale′tell′ing** *adj. & n.*

ta·li (tā′lī′) *n.* Plural of **talus**[1]**.**

Ta·lien (tä′lyĕn′). See **Dalian.**

tal·i·on (tăl′ē-ən) *n.* A punishment identical to the offense, as the death penalty for murder. [Middle English *talioun,* from

Anglo-Norman, from Latin *tāliō, tāliōn-*. See **tela-** in Appendix.]

tal·i·ped (tăl′ə-pĕd′) *adj.* Having a clubfoot; clubfooted. **—taliped** *n.* A person with a clubfoot. [From New Latin *tālipēs, tāliped-*, clubfoot. See TALIPES.]

tal·i·pes (tăl′ə-pēz′) *n.* See **clubfoot** (sense 1). [New Latin *tālipēs, tāliped-* : Latin *tālus*, ankle + Latin *pēs, ped-*, foot; see -PED.]

tal·i·pot (tăl′ə-pŏt′) *n.* A tall palm tree *(Corypha umbraculifera)* of India and Sri Lanka, having a spreading crown of very large fanlike leaves and a giant inflorescence that is the largest among the flowering plants. [Ultimately from Sanskrit *tālapattram*, palm leaf used for writing : *tālaḥ*, fan palm; see TODDY + *pattram*, leaf; see **pet-** in Appendix.]

tal·is·man (tăl′ĭs-mən, -ĭz-) *n., pl.* **-mans. 1.** An object marked with magic signs and believed to confer on its bearer supernatural powers or protection. **2.** Something that apparently has magic power: *Beauty is sometimes a most powerful talisman.* [French *talisman* or Spanish *talismán* or Italian *talismano*, all from Arabic *ṭilasm*, from Late Greek *telesma*, from Greek, consecration ceremony, from *telein*, to consecrate, fulfill, from *telos*, result. See **kʷel-¹** in Appendix.]

tal·is·man·ic (tăl′ĭs-măn′ĭk, -ĭz-) also **tal·is·man·i·cal** (-ĭ-kəl) *adj.* **1.** Of or relating to talismans. **2.** Possessing or believed to possess magic power: *a talismanic amulet.*

talk (tôk) *v.* **talked, talk·ing, talks.** *—tr.* **1.** To articulate (words): *The baby is talking sentences now.* **2.** To give expression to in words: *talk treason.* **3.** To speak of or discuss (something): *talk music; talk business.* **4.** To speak or know how to speak in (an idiom or a language): *talked French with the flight crew.* **5.** To gain, influence, or bring into a specified state by talking: *talked me into coming; talked their way out of trouble.* **6.** To spend (a period of time) by or as if by talking: *talked the evening away.* *—intr.* **1.** To converse by means of spoken language: *We talked for hours.* See Synonyms at **speak. 2.** To articulate words: *The baby can talk.* **3.** To imitate the sounds of human speech: *The parrot talks.* **4.** To express one's thoughts or emotions by means of spoken language: *talked about the pros and cons of the issue.* **5.** To convey one's thoughts in a way other than by spoken words: *talk with one's hands.* **6.** To express one's thoughts in writing: *Voltaire talks about London in this book.* **7.** To parley or negotiate with someone: *Let's talk before continuing to fight.* **8.** To spread rumors; gossip: *If you do that, people will talk.* **9.** To allude to something: *Are you talking about last week?* **10.** To consult or confer with someone: *I talked with the doctor.* **11.** To reveal information concerning oneself or others, especially under pressure: *Has the prisoner talked?* **12.** *Informal.* To be efficacious: *Money talks.* **—talk** *n.* **1.** An exchange of ideas or opinions; a conversation. **2.** A speech or lecture. **3.** Hearsay, rumor, or speculation: *There is talk of bankruptcy.* **4.** A subject of conversation: *a musical that is the talk of the town.* **5.** Often **talks.** A conference or negotiation: *peace talks.* **6.** Jargon; slang: *prison talk.* **7.** Empty speech or unnecessary discussion: *much talk and no action.* **8.** A particular manner of speech: *baby talk; honeyed talk.* **9.** Something, such as the sounds of animals, felt to resemble human talk: *whale talk.* ***—phrasal verbs.*** **talk around. 1.** To persuade: *I talked them around to my point of view.* **2.** To speak indirectly about something: *talked around the subject but never got to the point.* **talk at.** To address someone orally with no regard for or interest in the person's reaction or response. **talk back. 1.** To make an impertinent reply: *a saucy child who talked back.* **2.** To make a belligerent response: *heavy guns talking back.* **talk down. 1.** To depreciate: *talked down the importance of the move.* **2.** To address someone with insulting condescension: *talked down to her subordinates.* **3.** To silence (a person), especially by speaking in a loud and domineering manner. **4.** To direct and control (the flight of an aircraft during an approach for landing) by radioed instructions either from the ground or a nearby aircraft. **talk out. 1.** To discuss (a matter) exhaustively: *I talked out the problem with a therapist.* **2.** To resolve or settle by discussion. **3.** *Chiefly British.* To block (proposed legislation) by filibustering. **talk over. 1.** To consider thoroughly in conversation; discuss: *talked the matter over.* **2.** To win someone over by persuasion: *talked them over to our side.* **talk up. 1.** To speak in favor of; promote: *talked the candidate up; talked up the new product.* **2.** To speak up in a frank, often insolent manner. ***—idioms.*** **talk big.** *Informal.* To brag. **talk sense.** To speak rationally and coherently. [Middle English *talken*. See **del-²** in Appendix.]

talk·a·thon (tôk′ə-thŏn′) *n.* A lengthy session of discussions, speeches, or debate. [TALK + (MAR)ATHON.]

talk·a·tive (tô′kə-tĭv) *adj.* Marked by or having a disposition to talk. **—talk′a·tive·ly** *adv.* **—talk′a·tive·ness** *n.*

SYNONYMS: *talkative, loquacious, garrulous, voluble, verbose, glib.* These adjectives mean having or marked by an inclination to talk. *Talkative* is the most neutral and often merely suggests sociability: *Rather quiet at first, she grew very talkative over her second glass of sherry. Loquacious* stresses fluency or readiness of speech: *"Jack became loquacious on his favorite topic"* (Frederick Marryat). *Garrulous* implies excessive talkativeness and often suggests rambling, tiresome speech: *"Old men are garrulous by nature"* (Cicero). *Voluble* connotes a ready, sometimes unending flow of words: *Her niece, an extremely voluble young woman, engages in soliloquies, not conversations. Verbose* implies a great, usually excessive number of words: *"a natural reserve accentuated by the verbose frankness of her husband"* (W. Somerset Maugham). *Glib* refers to fluent, easy, and smooth speech that often suggests shallowness, lack of sincerity, or questionable motives: *"Was I too glib about eternal things?"* (Theodore Roethke).

talk·back (tôk′băk′) *n.* A system of communications links in a television or radio studio that enables directions to be given while a program is being produced.

talk·er (tô′kər) *n.* One who talks, especially a loquacious or garrulous person.

talk·fest (tôk′fĕst′) *n. Informal.* A lengthy, often enjoyable conversation or discussion.

talk·ie (tô′kē) *n. Informal.* A movie with a sound track.

talk·ing book (tô′kĭng) *n.* A phonograph record of a reading of a book, designed for use by the visually impaired.

talking head *n. Slang.* **1.** The image of a person, as on a television documentary or news show, who talks at length directly to the camera and usually appears on the screen with only the head and upper part of the body visible. **2.** The person thus televised.

talking point *n.* Something, such as an especially persuasive point, that helps to support an argument or a discussion.

talk·ing-to (tô′kĭng-to͞o′) *n., pl.* **-tos.** *Informal.* A scolding; a dressing-down.

talk show *n.* A television or radio show in which noted people, such as authorities in a particular field, participate in discussions or are interviewed and often answer questions from viewers or listeners.

talk·y (tô′kē) *adj.* **-i·er, -i·est. 1.** Talkative; loquacious. **2.** Containing or given to too much talk: *a talky, boring play.* **—talk′i·ness** *n.*

tall (tôl) *adj.* **tall·er, tall·est. 1.a.** Having greater than ordinary height: *a tall woman.* **b.** Having considerable height, especially in relation to width; lofty: *tall trees.* See Synonyms at **high. 2.** Having a specified height: *a plant three feet tall.* **3.** *Informal.* Fanciful or exaggerated; boastful: *tall tales of heroic exploits.* **4.** Impressively great or difficult: *a tall order to fill.* **5.** *Archaic.* Excellent; fine. **—tall** *adv.* With proud bearing; straight: *stand tall.* [Middle English, brave, quick, from Old English *getæl*, swift. See **del-²** in Appendix.] **—tall′ish** *adj.* **—tall′ness** *n.*

Tal·la·de·ga (tăl′ə-dē′gə). A city of east-central Alabama east of Birmingham. Incorporated in 1835, it is an agricultural, quarrying, and mining center. Population, 19,128.

tal·lage (tăl′ĭj) *n.* An occasional tax levied by the Anglo-Norman kings on crown lands and royal towns. **—tallage** *tr.v.* **-laged, -lag·ing, -lag·es.** To levy a tax on. [Middle English *taillage*, from Old French, from *taillier*, to cut, tax. See TAILOR.]

Tal·la·has·see (tăl′ə-hăs′ē). The capital of Florida, in the northwest part of the state. Originally a Native American village, it was settled by the Spanish after 1539 and founded as the capital of the Florida Territory in 1824. Population, 81,548.

Tal·la·hatch·ie (tăl′ə-hăch′ē). A river, about 371 km (230 mi) long, rising in northern Mississippi and flowing generally southwest to the Yazoo River.

Tal·la·poo·sa (tăl′ə-po͞o′sə). A river rising in northwest Georgia and flowing about 431 km (268 mi) generally southwest to central Alabama, where it joins the Coosa River to form the Alabama River.

tall·boy (tôl′boi′) *n. Chiefly British.* A highboy.

tall drink *n.* A drink served in a tall glass and consisting typically of a liquor base with any of various mixes and flavorings.

Tal·ley·rand-Pé·ri·gord (tăl′ē-rănd′pĕr′ĭ-gôr′, tä-lĕ-räɴ-pā-rē-gôr′), **Charles Maurice de.** 1754–1838. French politician and diplomat known for his capacity to survive political change. He held a variety of public offices during the French Revolution, Napoleon's reign, the Bourbon restoration, and the reign of Louis Philippe.

Tal·linn also **Tal·lin** (tăl′ĭn, tä′lĭn). The capital of Estonia, in the northwest part of the country on the Gulf of Finland opposite Helsinki. Tallinn was a possession of the Livonian Knights (1346–1561) and Sweden (1561–1710) before being formally ceded to Russia (1721). Population, 464,000.

tal·lith also **tal·lis** (tä′lĭs, tä-lēt′) *n., pl.* **tal·lith·im** (tä-lē′sĭm, -lā′-, tä′lē-tēm′) or **tal·liths** also **tal·li·sim** (tä-lē′sĭm, -lā′-). *Judaism.* A shawl with ritually knotted fringe at each of four corners worn by Jews, especially at morning prayer. Also called *prayer shawl.* [Mishnaic Hebrew *ṭallît*, cover, from Hebrew *ṭillēl*, to cover.]

tall oil (täl, tôl) *n.* A resinous oily liquid composed of a mixture of rosin acids and fatty acids obtained as a byproduct in the treatment of pine pulp and used in soaps, emulsions, and lubricants. [Partial translation of German *Tallöl*, from partial translation of Swedish *tallolja* : *tall*, pine (from Old Norse *thöll*, young pine tree) + *olja*, oil.]

tal·low (tăl′ō) *n.* **1.** Hard fat obtained from parts of the bodies of cattle, sheep, or horses, and used in foodstuffs or to make candles, leather dressing, soap, and lubricants. **2.** Any of various similar fats, such as those obtained from plants. **—tallow** *tr.v.* **-lowed, -low·ing, -lows. 1.** To smear or cover with tallow. **2.** To fatten (animals) in order to obtain tallow. [Middle English *talow*.] **—tal′low·y** *adj.*

tal·ly (tăl′ē) *n., pl.* **-lies. 1.** A reckoning or score. **2.a.** A stick on which notches are made to keep a count or score. **b.** A stick

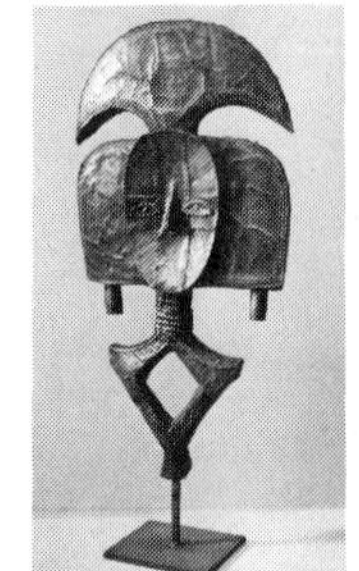

talisman
Late 19th-century reliquary figure from central Africa

tallith

ă pat	oi boy
ā pay	ou out
âr care	o͝o took
ä father	o͞o boot
ĕ pet	ŭ cut
ē be	ûr urge
ĭ pit	th thin
ī pie	*th* this
îr pier	hw which
ŏ pot	zh vision
ō toe	ə about, item
ô paw	♦ regionalism

Stress marks: ′ (primary); ′ (secondary), as in **dictionary** (dĭk′shə-nĕr′ē)

talon
Of a bald eagle

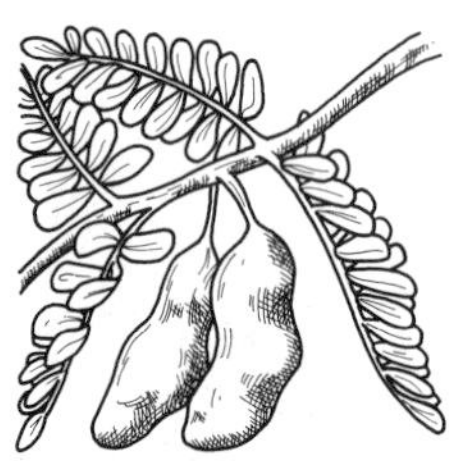
tamarind
Tamarindus indica

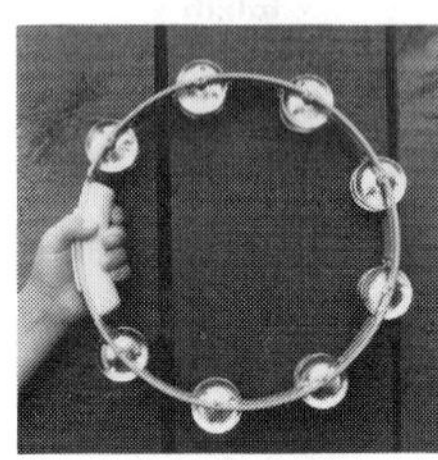
tambourine

tam-o'-shanter

on which notches were formerly made to keep a record of amounts paid or owed. **3.** A mark used in recording a number of acts or objects, most often in series of five, consisting of four vertical lines canceled diagonally or horizontally by a fifth line. **4.** A label, ticket, or piece of metal or wood used for identification or classification, especially in gardens and greenhouses. **5.** Something that is very similar or corresponds to something else; a double or counterpart. **6.** *Nautical.* A metal plate attached to a ship's machinery and bearing instructions for its use. **—tally** *v.* **-lied, -ly·ing, -lies.** *—tr.* **1.** To reckon or count. **2.** To record by making a mark. **3.** To label, as with a ticket, for identification or classification. **4.** To cause to correspond or agree. *—intr.* **1.** To be alike; correspond or agree: *The report tallies with your description of the accident.* **2.** To keep score. [Middle English *taly,* from Anglo-Norman *tallie,* from Medieval Latin *tallia,* from Latin *tālea,* stick.]

tal·ly·ho (tăl′ē-hō′) *interj.* Used to urge hounds on during a fox hunt. **—tallyho** *v.* **-hoed, -ho·ing, -hos.** *—tr.* To urge (hounds) on during a fox hunt by shouting "tallyho" when the fox is sighted. *—intr.* To shout "tallyho" as a hunting cry. **—tallyho** *n., pl.* **-hos. 1.** The cry of "tallyho." **2.** A fast coach drawn by four horses. [Probably alteration of French *taïaut,* from Old French *thialau, taho.*]

Tal·mi gold (täl′mē) *n.* A composite metal made of gold and brass, used in making jewelry. [German *Talmigold,* partial translation of French *Tal. mi-or,* contraction of *Tallois demi-or,* Tallois half-gold : Tallois (after *Tallois,* 19th-century Parisian inventor) + *demi-,* demi- + *or,* gold.]

Tal·mud (täl′mo͝od, tăl′məd) *n. Judaism.* The collection of ancient Rabbinic writings consisting of the Mishnah and the Gemara, constituting the basis of religious authority in Orthodox Judaism. [Mishnaic Hebrew *talmûd,* learning, instruction, from *lāmad,* to learn.] **—Tal·mu′dic** (tăl-mo͞o′dĭk, -myo͞o′-, tăl-), **Tal·mu′di·cal** (-dĭ-kəl) *adj.* **—Tal′mud·ist** (täl′mo͝o-dĭst, tăl′mə-) *n.*

tal·on (tăl′ən) *n.* **1.a.** The claw of a bird of prey. **b.** The similar claw of a predatory animal. **2.** Something similar to or suggestive of an animal's claw. **3.** The part of a lock that the key presses in order to shoot the bolt. **4.** *Games.* The part of the deck of cards in certain card games left on the table after the deal. **5.** *Architecture.* An ogee molding. [Middle English *taloun,* from Old French *talon,* heel, from Vulgar Latin **tālō, tālōn-,* from Latin *tālus,* ankle.]

ta·lus¹ (tā′ləs) *n., pl.* **-li** (-lī′). **1.** The bone of the ankle that articulates with the tibia and fibula to form the ankle joint. Also called *anklebone, astragalus.* **2.** The ankle. [Latin *tālus,* ankle.]

ta·lus² (tā′ləs) *n., pl.* **-lus·es.** A sloping mass of rock debris at the base of a cliff. [French *talus,* from Old French *talu,* sloping side of an earthwork, from Latin *talūtium,* gold-bearing outcrop, perhaps of Celtic origin.]

tam (tăm) *n.* A tam-o'-shanter.

ta·ma·le (tə-mä′lē) *n.* A Mexican dish made of fried chopped meat and crushed peppers, highly seasoned, rolled in cornmeal dough, wrapped in cornhusks, and steamed. [From American Spanish *tamales,* pl. of *tamal,* tamale, from Nahuatl *tamalli.*]

Ta·man (tə-män′). A peninsula of southwest Russia projecting westward between the Sea of Azov and the Black Sea.

ta·man·du·a (tə-măn′do͞o-ə) *n.* Either of two small nocturnal anteaters *(Tamandua tetradactyla* or *T. mexicana)* of Central and South America, having thick, bristly fur and dwelling in trees during the day. [Portuguese *tamanduá,* from Tupi *ta-monduá,* from *monduar,* to catch.]

Tam·a·rac (tăm′ə-răk′). A city of southeast Florida northwest of Fort Lauderdale. Population, 29,376.

tam·a·rack (tăm′ə-răk′) *n.* A deciduous North American larch tree *(Larix laricina)* having short needles borne on spur shoots. [Canadian French *tamarac,* Probably of Algonquian origin.]

tam·a·rau also **tam·a·rao** (tăm′ə-rou′) *n., pl.* **-raus** also **-raos.** A small, grayish black, short-horned buffalo *(Bubalus mindorensis)* of the island of Mindoro in the Philippines, closely related to the anoa. [Tagalog *tamaráw.*]

ta·ma·ril·lo (tăm′ə-rĭl′ō, -rē′yō) *n., pl.* **-los. 1.** A tree *(Cyphomandra betacea)* native to the Peruvian Andes and cultivated especially in New Zealand for its edible dark red or yellow plumlike fruit. **2.** The fruit of this tree. [Alteration of TOMATILLO.]

tam·a·rin (tăm′ə-rĭn, -răn′) *n.* Any of various small, long-tailed, arboreal monkeys of the genera *Leontideus* and *Saguinus* of Central and South America, resembling the marmosets but having a larger body, longer limbs, and lower canines that extend well beyond the incisors. [French, from Galibi.]

tam·a·rind (tăm′ə-rĭnd′) *n.* **1.** A tropical Asian evergreen tree *(Tamarindus indica)* having pinnately compound leaves, pale yellow flowers, and thick, cinnamon-brown pods containing an edible acid pulp. **2.** The fruit of this tree, eaten fresh or used in the preparation of chutney, curry, or soft drinks. [Middle English, from Old French *tamarinde,* from Arabic *tamr hindī* : *tamr,* date + *hindī,* of India.]

tam·a·risk (tăm′ə-rĭsk′) *n.* Any of numerous African and Eurasian shrubs or small trees of the genus *Tamarix,* having small scalelike leaves and racemes of white, pink, or red flowers. [Middle English *tamarisc,* from Late Latin *tamariscus,* variant of Latin *tamarīx, tamarīc-.*]

Ta·ma·yo (tä-mä′yō), **Rufino.** 1899–1991. Mexican artist whose bold, textured works were influenced by pre-Columbian symbols as well as cubism and expressionism.

tam·bac (tŏm′băk) *n.* Variant of **tombac.**

tam·ba·la (täm-bä′lə) *n.* See table at **currency.** [Perhaps from Chewa or Nyanja, cockerels.]

tam·bour (tăm′bo͝or′, tăm-bo͝or′) *n.* **1.** *Music.* A drum or drummer. **2.a.** A small wooden embroidery frame consisting of two concentric hoops between which fabric is stretched. **b.** Embroidery made on such a frame. **3.** A rolling front or top for a desk or table, consisting of narrow strips of wood glued to canvas. **4.** *Architecture.* **a.** The wall of a circular building surrounded with columns. **b.** The vertical part of a cupola. **—tambour** *v.* **-boured, -bour·ing, -bours.** *—tr.* To do (embroidery) on a frame consisting of two concentric hoops. *—intr.* To embroider at or on such a frame. [Middle English, from Old French, ultimately from Arabic *ṭanbūr,* lute.]

tam·bou·ra or **tam·bu·ra** (tŭm-bo͝or′ə) also **tan·bur** (tän-bo͝or′) *n. Music.* An unfretted lute of India and Turkey, used as a harmonic drone. [Urdu *ṭambūra,* from Persian *ṭanbūra,* from Arabic *ṭanbūr.*]

tam·bou·rin (tăm′bo͞o-rĭn, tän-bo͞o-rän′) *n.* **1.** *Music.* **a.** A long, narrow drum used in Provence. **b.** One who plays this drum. **2.** A style of dance in lively two-beat rhythm, accompanied by this drum. [Provençal *tambourin,* from Old French, diminutive of *tambour,* tambour. See TAMBOUR.]

tam·bou·rine (tăm′bə-rēn′) *n. Music.* An instrument consisting of a small drumhead with jingling disks fitted into the rim. It is shaken with one hand and struck with the other. [French *tambourin,* small drum, from Old French. See TAMBOURIN.]

Tam·bov (täm-bôf′, -bôv′). A city of western Russia southeast of Moscow. Founded as a fortress in 1636, it is a manufacturing center and railroad junction. Population 296,000.

tam·bu·ra (tŭm-bo͝or′ə) *n. Music.* Variant of **tamboura.**

tam·bu·rit·za (tăm-bo͝or′ĭt-sə, tăm′bə-rĭt′sə) *n. Music.* A Serbo-Croatian stringed instrument similar to a mandolin in shape and sound. [Serbo-Croatian *tàmburica,* diminutive of *tàmbura,* stringed instrument, from Ottoman Turkish *tambūra,* from Persian *ṭanbūra.* See TAMBOURA.]

Tam·bur·laine (tăm′bər-lān′). See **Tamerlane.**

tame (tām) *adj.* **tam·er, tam·est. 1.** Brought from wildness into a domesticated or tractable state. **2.** Naturally unafraid; not timid: *"The sea otter is gentle and relatively tame"* (Peter Matthiessen). **3.** Submissive; docile; fawning: *tame obedience.* **4.** Insipid; flat: *a tame Christmas party.* **5.** Sluggish; languid; inactive: *a tame river.* **—tame** *tr.v.* **tamed, tam·ing, tames. 1.** To make tractable; domesticate. **2.** To subdue or curb. **3.** To tone down; soften. [Middle English, from Old English *tam.* See **demə-** in Appendix.] **—tam′a·ble, tame′a·ble** *adj.* **—tame′ly** *adv.* **—tame′ness** *n.* **—tam′er** *n.*

Tam·er·lane (tăm′ər-lān′) or **Tam·bur·laine** (-bər-). 1336–1405. Mongolian conqueror who led his nomadic hordes from their capital at Samarkand in central Asia to overrun vast areas of Persia, Turkey, Russia, and India.

Tam·il (tăm′əl, tŭm′-, tä′məl) *n., pl.* **Tamil** or **-mils. 1.** A member of a Dravidian people of southern India and northern Sri Lanka. **2.** The Dravidian language of the Tamil. **—Tamil** *adj.* Of or relating to the Tamil or their language or culture. [Tamil.]

Tamm (täm), **Igor Yevgeneevich.** 1895–1971. Russian physicist. He shared a 1958 Nobel Prize for work leading to the development of a cosmic-ray counter.

Tam·muz also **Tham·muz** (tä′mo͝oz) *n.* The tenth month of the year in the Jewish calendar. See table at **calendar.** [Hebrew *Tammūz,* from Babylonian *Du'uzu,* the name of a god.]

tam-o'-shan·ter (tăm′ə-shăn′tər) *n.* A tight-fitting Scottish cap or braided bonnet, sometimes having a pompon, tassel, or feather in the center. [After the hero of "*Tam o' Shanter,*" a poem by Robert Burns.]

tamp (tămp) *tr.v.* **tamped, tamp·ing, tamps. 1.** To pack down tightly by a succession of blows or taps. **2.** To pack clay, sand, or dirt into (a drill hole) above an explosive. [Perhaps back-formation from *tampin,* variant of TAMPION.]

Tam·pa (tăm′pə). A city of west-central Florida on **Tampa Bay,** an inlet of the Gulf of Mexico. First visited by Spanish explorers in 1528, Tampa is a port of entry, a processing and shipping hub, and a tourist center. Population, 271,523.

tam·per¹ (tăm′pər) *v.* **-pered, -per·ing, -pers.** *—intr.* **1.** To interfere in a harmful manner: *tried to tamper with the decedent's will; tampering with the timing mechanism of the safe.* **2.** To tinker with rashly or foolishly: *Don't tamper with my feelings.* **3.** To engage in improper or secret dealings, as in an effort to influence: *tamper with a jury.* See Synonyms at **interfere.** *—tr.* To alter improperly. [Probably alteration of TEMPER.]

tamp·er² (tăm′pər) *n.* A neutron reflector in an atomic bomb that also delays the expansion of the exploding material, making possible a longer-lasting, more energetic, and more efficient explosion.

Tam·pe·re (tăm′pə-rā′, täm′-). A city of southwest Finland north-northwest of Helsinki. An important trade center since the 11th century, it is noted for its textile industry. Population, 168,150.

Tam·pi·co (tăm-pē′kō, täm-). A city of east-central Mexico near the Gulf of Mexico north-northeast of Mexico City. Settled by the Spanish in the 1530's, it is a major port, manufacturing center, and tourist resort. Population, 267,957.

tam·pi·on (tăm′pē-ən) also **tom·pi·on** (tŏm′-) *n.* A plug or cover for the muzzle of a cannon or gun to keep out dust and moisture. [Middle English, from Old French *tampon,* variant of *tapon,* rag for stopping a hole, of Germanic origin.]

tam·pon (tăm′pŏn′) *n.* A plug of absorbent material inserted into a body cavity or wound to check a flow of blood or to absorb secretions, especially one designed for insertion into the vagina during menstruation. **—tampon** *tr.v.* **-poned, -pon·ing, -pons.** To plug or stop with a tampon. [French, from Old French. See TAMPION.]

tam-tam[1] (tŭm′tŭm′, tăm′tăm′) *n. Music.* A gong having a metal disk struck with a felt-covered hammer or stick used in a gamelan orchestra. [Ultimately of imitative origin.]

tam-tam[2] (tŭm′tŭm′, tăm′tăm′) *n.* Variant of **tom-tom.**

tan[1] (tăn) *v.* **tanned, tan·ning, tans.** *—tr.* **1.** To convert (hide) into leather, as by treating with tannin. **2.** To make brown by exposure to the sun. **3.** *Informal.* To thrash; beat. *—intr.* To become brown or tawny from exposure to sun. **—tan** *n.* **1.** *Color.* A light or moderate yellowish brown to brownish orange. **2.** The brown color that sun rays impart to the skin. **3.** Tanbark. **4.a.** Tannin. **b.** A solution derived from tannin. **—tan** *adj.* **tan·ner, tan·nest. 1.** *Color.* Light or moderate yellowish-brown to brownish-orange. **2.** Having a suntan. **3.** Used in or relating to tanning. [Middle English *tannen,* from Old English **tannian,* from Medieval Latin *tannāre,* from *tannum,* tanbark, probably of Celtic origin.] **—tan′nish** *adj.*

tan[2] *abbr. Mathematics.* Tangent.

Tan (tăn) *n., pl.* **Tan** or **Tans.** See **Tanka.**

Ta·na (tä′nə, -nä), **Lake.** Also **Lake Tsa·na** (tsä′-). A lake of northwest Ethiopia. It is the largest lake in the country and the source of the Blue Nile.

tan·a·ger (tăn′ĭ-jər) *n.* Any of various small New World passerine birds of the family Thraupidae, often having brightly colored plumage in the males and usually living in forests. [New Latin *tanagra,* alteration of Portuguese *tangará,* from Tupi *tanagorá.*]

Tan·a·gra (tăn′ə-grə, tə-năg′rə). An ancient city of east-central Greece in eastern Boeotia. The Spartans defeated Athenian forces here in 457 B.C.

tan·a·grine (tăn′ə-grĭn) *adj.* Of, relating to, or belonging to the tanagers. [New Latin *tanagra,* tanager; see TANAGER + -INE[1].]

Tan·a·na (tăn′ə-nô′). A river of eastern and southern Alaska flowing about 764 km (475 mi) from the Wrangell Mountains northwest to the Yukon River.

Ta·nan·a·rive (tə-năn′ə-rēv′, tä-nä-nä-rēv′). See **Antananarivo.**

Tana River. 1. A river, about 805 km (500 mi) long, of central Kenya flowing in an arc northeast and south to the Indian Ocean. **2.** A river, about 322 km (200 mi) long, of northeast Norway forming part of the Norway-Finland border and emptying into an inlet of the Arctic Ocean.

tan·bark (tăn′bärk′) *n.* **1.** The bark of various trees used as a source of tannin. **2.** Shredded bark from which the tannin has been extracted, used to cover circus arenas, racetracks, and other surfaces. **3.** See **tan oak.**

tan·bur (tän-bo͝or′) *n. Music.* Variant of **tamboura.**

Tan·cred (tăng′krĭd). 1078?–1112. Norman soldier. A leader in the First Crusade (1096–1099), he served as regent of the principality of Antioch (1101–1112).

tan·dem (tăn′dəm) *n.* **1.** A two-wheeled carriage drawn by horses harnessed one before the other. **2.** A team of carriage horses harnessed in single file. **3.** A tandem bicycle. **4.** An arrangement of two or more persons or objects placed one behind the other. **—tandem** *adv.* One behind the other: *driving horses in tandem.* [Latin, at last, at length. See **to-** in Appendix.] **—tan′dem** *adj.*

tandem bicycle *n.* A bicycle built for two or more people sitting one behind the other.

tandem trailer *n.* A trucking rig consisting of a tractor pulling two trailers, one behind the other.

tan·door (tän-do͝or′) *n., pl.* **-doors** or **-door·i** (-do͝or′ē). A cylindrical oven made of clay, heated to a high heat over charcoal or wood, and used in India for baking bread and roasting meat. [Hindi and Urdu *tandūr,* from Persian, variant of *tannūr,* from Middle Persian, from Arabic, from *nūr,* light, fire.]

tan·door·i (tän-do͝or′ē) *adj.* Cooked in a tandoor. [Hindi *tandūri,* from *tandūr,* tandoor. See TANDOOR.]

Ta·ney (tô′nē), **Roger Brooke.** 1777–1864. American jurist who served as the chief justice of the U.S. Supreme Court (1836–1864). In the Dred Scott decision (1857) he ruled that slaves and their descendants had no rights as citizens.

tang[1] (tăng) *n.* **1.** A distinctively sharp taste, flavor, or odor, as that of orange juice. See Synonyms at **taste. 2.** A distinctive quality that adds piquancy. **3.** A trace, hint, or smattering. **4.** A sharp point, tongue, or prong. **5.** A projection by which a tool, such as a chisel or knife, is attached to its handle or stock. Also called *shank.* **6.** A surgeonfish. **—tang** *tr.v.* **tanged, tang·ing, tangs. 1.** To furnish with a tang. **2.** To give a tang to. [Middle English *tange,* of Scandinavian origin; akin to Old Norse *tangi,* point, sting.] **—tang′i·ness** *n.* **—tang′y** *adj.*

tang[2] (tăng) *n.* A loud ringing sound; a twang. **—tang** *intr. & tr.v.* **tanged, tang·ing, tangs.** To twang or cause to twang; ring. [Imitative.]

Tang (täng). A Chinese dynasty (618–907) that was known for its wealth and its encouragement of the arts and literature.

Tan·gan·yi·ka (tăn′gən-yē′kə, tăng′-). A former country of east-central Africa. A British mandate after 1920, it became independent in 1961 and joined with Zanzibar to form Tanzania in 1964. **—Tan′gan·yi′kan** *adj. & n.*

Tanganyika, Lake. A lake of east-central Africa between Zaire and Tanzania. The British explorers John Speke and Sir Richard Burton first sighted the lake in 1858.

tan·ge·lo (tăn′jə-lō′) *n., pl.* **-los. 1.** A hybrid citrus tree derived from grapefruit and tangerine, having aromatic fruit with a thin, smooth, moderately loose rind. **2.** The fruit of this tree. [Blend of TANGERINE and POMELO.]

tan·gen·cy (tăn′jən-sē) also **tan·gence** (-jəns) *n.* The condition of being tangent.

tan·gent (tăn′jənt) *adj.* **1.** Making contact at a single point or along a line; touching but not intersecting. **2.** Irrelevant. **—tangent** *n.* **1.** A line, curve, or surface touching but not intersecting another line, curve, or surface. **2.** *Abbr.* **tan** *Mathematics.* The trigonometric function of an acute angle in a right triangle that is the ratio of the length of the side opposite the angle to the length of the side adjacent to the angle. **3.** A sudden digression or change of course: *went off on a tangent during the courtroom argument.* **4.** *Music.* An upright pin in a keyboard instrument, especially in a clavichord, that rises to sound a string when a key is depressed and stops the string at a preset length to set the pitch. [Latin *(līnea) tangēns, tangent-,* touching (line), present participle of *tangere,* to touch. See **tag-** in Appendix.]

tan·gen·tial (tăn-jĕn′shəl) also **tan·gen·tal** (-jĕn′tl) *adj.* **1.** Of, relating to, or moving along or in the direction of a tangent. **2.** Merely touching or slightly connected. **3.** Only superficially relevant; divergent: *a tangential remark.* **—tan·gen′ti·al′i·ty** (-shē-ăl′ĭ-tē) *n.* **—tan·gen′tial·ly** *adv.*

tangent plane *n. Mathematics.* The plane containing all the lines tangent to a specified point on a surface.

tan·ger·ine (tăn′jə-rēn′, tăn′jə-rēn′) *n.* **1.** A small southeast Asian spiny evergreen tree *(Citrus reticulata)* having sweet edible fruit. **2.** The small, loose-skinned fruit of this tree. Also called *mandarin orange.* **3.** *Color.* A strong reddish orange to strong or vivid orange. [Short for *tangerine orange,* after *Tanger* (Tangier), Morocco.] **—tan′ger·ine′** *adj.*

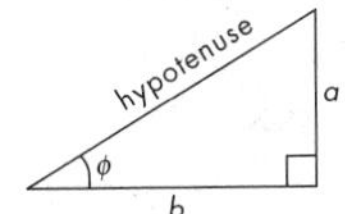

tangent
tangent $\phi = \frac{a}{b}$

WORD HISTORY: The name *tangerine* is like the skin of an orange, which when peeled off reveals something of interest. The name reflects the geographic source of the fruit, Tangier, Morocco, from which port the first tangerines were shipped to Europe in 1841. The word *tangerine,* from *Tangier* or *Tanger,* was already an English word (first recorded in 1710), meaning "of or pertaining to Tangier." This word had been formed with the suffix *-ine,* as in *Florentine.* The fruit was first called a *tangerine orange,* later reduced simply to *tangerine.* Confusion exists between the name *tangerine* and the name *mandarin,* and with good reason. The tangerine is a type of mandarin orange, so in fact the oranges shipped from Tangier could have been called *mandarins.* However, although both names can be used interchangeably in a general sense, there does now exist a particular type of orange called *tangerine* as distinguished from another type called specifically *mandarin.* The mandarin orange, which is native to China, is thought probably to have received its name because of its resemblance in color to the robes of a mandarin.

tan·gi·ble (tăn′jə-bəl) *adj.* **1.a.** Discernible by the touch; palpable: *a tangible roughness of the skin.* **b.** Possible to touch. **c.** Possible to be treated as fact; real or concrete: *tangible evidence.* **2.** Possible to understand or realize: *the tangible benefits of the plan.* **3.** *Law.* That can be valued monetarily: *tangible property.* **—tangible** *n.* **1.** Something palpable or concrete. **2. tangibles.** Material assets. [Late Latin *tangibilis,* from Latin *tangere,* to touch. See **tag-** in Appendix.] **—tan′gi·bil′i·ty, tan′gi·ble·ness** *n.* **—tan′gi·bly** *adv.*

Tan·gier (tăn-jîr′) also **Tan·giers** (-jîrz′). A city of northern Morocco at the west end of the Strait of Gibraltar. Founded in Roman times and later controlled by a variety of powers, including Portugal and Great Britain, it was administered as part of an international zone from 1923–1924 until 1956. Population, 266,346.

tan·gle[1] (tăng′gəl) *v.* **-gled, -gling, -gles.** *—tr.* **1.** To mix together or intertwine in a confused mass; snarl. **2.** To involve in hampering or awkward complications; entangle. **3.** To catch and hold in or as if in a net; entrap. See Synonyms at **catch.** *—intr.* **1.** To be or become entangled. **2.** *Informal.* To enter into argument, dispute, or conflict: *tangled with the law.* **—tangle** *n.* **1.** A confused, intertwined mass. **2.** A jumbled or confused state or condition. **3.** A state of bewilderment. **4.** *Informal.* An argument or altercation. [Middle English *tangilen,* to involve in an embarrassing situation, variant of *tagilen,* probably of Scandinavian origin; akin to Swedish dialectal *taggla,* to entangle.] **—tan′gly** *adj.*

tan·gle[2] (tăng′gəl) *n.* A large seaweed of the genus *Laminaria.* [Of Scandinavian origin; akin to Old Norse *thöngull,* seaweed.]

tan·gled (tăng′gəld) *adj.* Complicated and difficult to unravel. See Synonyms at **complex.**

ă pat	oi boy
ā pay	ou out
âr care	o͝o took
ä father	o͞o boot
ĕ pet	ŭ cut
ē be	ûr urge
ĭ pit	th thin
ī pie	*th* this
îr pier	hw which
ŏ pot	zh vision
ō toe	ə about, item
ô paw	♦ regionalism

Stress marks: **′** (primary); ′ (secondary), as in **dictionary** (dĭk′shə-nĕr′ē)

tank
Top: Fuel storage tanks
Bottom: M-1 army tank

tankard
Late 18th-century American pewter tankard by Frederick Bassett (1740–1800)

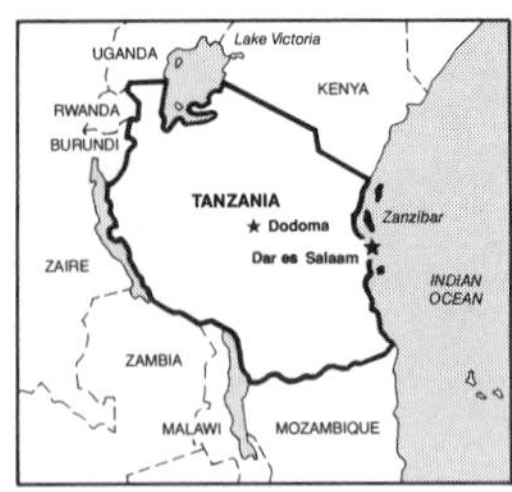

Tanzania

tan·go (tăng′gō) *n., pl.* **-gos. 1.** A Latin American ballroom dance in 2/4 or 4/4 time. **2.** The music for this dance. **—tango** *intr.v.* **-goed, -go·ing, -gos.** To perform this dance. [American Spanish, possibly of Niger-Congo origin; akin to Ibibio *tamgu,* to dance.] **—tan′go·like′** *adj.*

tan·go·re·cep·tor (tăng′gō-rĭ-sĕp′tər) *n.* A cutaneous receptor that responds to touch and pressure. [Latin *tangere,* to touch; see **tag-** in Appendix + RECEPTOR.]

tan·gram (tăng′grəm) *n. Games.* A Chinese puzzle consisting of a square cut into five triangles, a square, and a rhomboid, to be reassembled into different figures. [Perhaps partial translation of Chinese *táng tú* : *táng,* Tang, a Chinese dynasty + *tú,* picture, diagram.]

Tang·shan (täng′shän′, däng′-). A city of northeast China east-southeast of Beijing. It was devastated in 1976 by a massive earthquake in which an estimated 242,000 people were killed. Population, 921,100.

Tan·guy (täN-gē′), **Yves.** 1900–1955. French-born American surrealist painter whose works include *Indefinite Divisibility* (1942) and *Chess Set* (1950).

Ta·nis (tā′nĭs). An ancient city of Egypt in the eastern delta of the Nile River. Important during the XIX and XXI Dynasties, it was abandoned after the sixth century A.D.

tan·ist (tăn′ĭst, thô′nĭst) *n.* The heir apparent to an ancient Celtic chief, elected during the chief's lifetime. [Irish Gaelic *tánaiste,* second, tanist, from Old Irish *tānaise.* See **sed-** in Appendix.] **—tan′ist·ry** *n.*

tank (tăngk) *n.* **1.a.** A large, often metallic container for holding or storing liquids or gases. **b.** The amount that this container can hold: *buy a tank of gas.* **2.** A usually artificial pool, pond, reservoir, or cistern, especially one used to hold water for drinking or for irrigation. **3.** An enclosed, heavily armored combat vehicle that is mounted with cannon and guns and moves on caterpillar treads. **4.** *Slang.* A jail or jail cell. **—tank** *tr.v.* **tanked, tank·ing, tanks.** To place, store, or process in a tank. ***—phrasal verb.* tank up. 1.** *Slang.* To drink to the point of intoxication. **2.** To fill the tank of a motor vehicle with gasoline. [Partly from Gujarati *tānkh,* cistern (from Sanskrit *taḍāgaḥ,* pond, perhaps of Dravidian origin) and partly from Portuguese *tanque,* reservoir (variant of *estanque,* from *estancar,* to dam up, from Vulgar Latin **stanticāre;* see STANCH[1]).] **—tank′ful′** (-fo͝ol′) *n.* **—tank′less** *adj.*

tan·ka[1] (täng′kə) *n.* A Japanese verse form in five lines, the first and third composed of five syllables and the rest of seven. [Japanese.]

tan·ka[2] *n.* A Tibetan religious painting on fabric, usually portraying the Buddha or lamas in stereotyped aspects. [Tibetan *thaṅka,* something rolled up.]

Tan·ka (täng′kä) *n., pl.* **Tanka** or **-kas.** A member of a people in southern China and Hong Kong who live on small boats clustered in colonies. Also called *Tan.* [Cantonese *tan ka* : *tan,* tribal name (represented by the character for "egg") + *ka,* family, people, variant of Chinese (Mandarin) *jiā.*]

tank·age (tăng′kĭj) *n.* **1.a.** The act or process of putting or storing in a tank. **b.** The amount that a tank can hold. **c.** A fee for tank storage. **2.** Animal residues that remain after rendering fat in a slaughterhouse, used for fertilizer or feed.

tank·ard (tăng′kərd) *n.* A large drinking cup having a single handle and often a hinged cover, especially a tall pewter or silver mug. [Middle English, of unknown origin.]

tank destroyer *n. Abbr.* **TD** A high-speed armored vehicle equipped with antitank guns.

tanked (tăngkt) *adj. Slang.* Intoxicated; drunk.

tank·er (tăng′kər) *n.* **1.** A ship, plane, or truck constructed to transport liquids, such as oil, in bulk. **2.** A member of a military tank crew.

tank farm *n.* A group of tanks, as for the commercial storage of oil, sited together.

tank suit *n.* A simply designed one-piece swimsuit with shoulder straps.

tank top *n.* A sleeveless, tight-fitting, usually knit shirt with wide shoulder straps and no front opening. [From its resemblance to a TANK SUIT.]

tank town *n.* A small town. [So called because trains would stop there only to replenish water.]

tank trailer *n.* A truck trailer equipped as a tanker, used to carry liquids such as oil, milk, or chemicals.

tan·nate (tăn′āt′) *n.* A salt or an ester of tannic acid. [TANN(IN) + -ATE[2].]

tan·ner[1] (tăn′ər) *n.* One that tans hides.

tan·ner[2] (tăn′ər) *n. Chiefly British.* A sixpenny coin formerly used in Britain; a sixpence. [Origin unknown.]

tan·ner·y (tăn′ə-rē) *n., pl.* **-ies.** An establishment where hides are tanned.

tan·nic (tăn′ĭk) *adj.* Of, relating to, or obtained from tannin. [TANN(IN) + -IC.]

tannic acid *n.* **1.** A white or yellowish astringent powder, $C_{14}H_{10}O_9$, derived from nutgalls and used as a denaturant and in tanning and textiles. **2.** A lustrous yellowish to light brown amorphous, powdered, flaked, or spongy mass having the approximate composition $C_{76}H_{52}O_{46}$, derived from the bark and fruit of many plants and used in photography, as a mordant, and to clarify wine and beer.

tan·nif·er·ous (tă-nĭf′ər-əs) *adj.* Containing or yielding tannin.

tan·nin (tăn′ĭn) *n.* **1.** Tannic acid. **2.** Any of various chemically different substances capable of promoting tanning. [French, from *tan,* crushed oak bark, from Old French, from Medieval Latin *tannum.* See TAN[1].]

tan·ning (tăn′ĭng) *n.* **1.** The art or process of making leather from rawhides. **2.** Browning of the skin by exposure to sun and weather. **3.** *Informal.* A beating; a whipping.

tan oak or **tan·oak** (tăn′ōk′) *n.* An evergreen tree *(Lithocarpus densiflorus)* native to California and Oregon, having leathery leaves, erect male catkins, and tannin-yielding bark. Also called *tanbark.*

Ta·no·an (tä′nō-ən) *n.* An American Indian language family of New Mexico and northeast Arizona. [From Spanish *Tano,* name for the Southern Tewas of New Mexico, from Tewa.] **—Ta′no·an** *adj.*

tan·rec (tän′rĕk′) *n.* Variant of **tenrec.**

tan rot *n.* A disease of the strawberry plant caused by the fungus *Pezizella lythri* and marked by the formation of tan indentations on the surface of the fruit.

tan·sy (tăn′zē) *n., pl.* **-sies.** Any of several plants of the genus *Tanacetum,* especially *T. vulgare,* native to Eurasia, having corymbs of buttonlike yellow flower heads and aromatic, pinnately dissected leaves that are sometimes used medicinally. [Middle English, from Old French *tanesie,* from Vulgar Latin **tanacēta,* from Late Latin *tanacētum,* wormwood.]

Tan·ta (tän′tä). A city of northern Egypt in the Nile River delta north of Cairo. Population, 364,700.

tan·tal·ic (tăn-tăl′ĭk) *adj.* Of, relating to, or containing tantalum.

tan·ta·lite (tăn′tə-līt′) *n.* A black to red-brown mineral, $(Fe,Mn)(Ta,Nb)_2O_6$, distinguished from columbite by the predominance of tantalum over niobium and used as an ore of both elements. [TANTAL(UM) + -ITE[1].]

tan·ta·lize (tăn′tə-līz′) *tr.v.* **-lized, -liz·ing, -liz·es.** To excite (another) by exposing something desirable while keeping it out of reach. [From Latin *Tantalus,* Tantalus. See TANTALUS.] **—tan′ta·li·za′tion** (-lĭ-zā′shən) *n.* **—tan′ta·liz′er** *n.* **—tan′ta·liz′ing·ly** *adv.*

tan·ta·lum (tăn′tə-ləm) *n. Symbol* **Ta** A very hard, heavy, gray metallic element that is exceptionally resistant to chemical attack below 150°C. It is used to make light-bulb filaments, electrolytic capacitors, lightning arresters, nuclear reactor parts, and some surgical instruments. Atomic number 73; atomic weight 180.948; melting point 2,996°C; boiling point 5,425°C; specific gravity 16.6; valence 2, 3, 4, 5. See table at **element.** [New Latin, from Latin *Tantalus,* Tantalus (from its high resistance to acids). See TANTALUS.]

Tan·ta·lus (tăn′tə-ləs) *n. Greek Mythology.* A king who for his crimes was condemned in Hades to stand in water that receded when he tried to drink, and with fruit hanging above him that receded when he reached for it. [Latin, from Greek *Tantalos.* See **telə-** in Appendix.]

tan·ta·mount (tăn′tə-mount′) *adj.* Equivalent in effect or value: *a request tantamount to a demand.* [From obsolete *tantamount,* an equivalent, from Anglo-Norman *tant amunter,* to amount to as much : *tant,* so much, so great (from Latin *tantum,* neuter of *tantus,* from *tam,* so; see **to-** in Appendix) + *amunter,* to amount to, variant of Old French *amonter.* See AMOUNT.]

tan·ta·ra (tăn-tăr′ə, -tär′ə) *n.* **1.a.** *Music.* A trumpet or horn fanfare. **b.** A sound resembling such a fanfare. **2.** A hunting cry. [Imitative.]

tan·tiv·y (tăn-tĭv′ē) *adv.* At full gallop; at top speed. **—tantivy** *n., pl.* **-ies. 1.** A hunting cry. **2.** A fast, furious gallop; top speed. [Origin unknown.]

tan·tra (tŭn′trə, tăn′-) *n.* Any of a comparatively recent class of Hindu or Buddhist religious literature written in Sanskrit and concerned with mysticism and magic. [Sanskrit *tantram,* doctrine, loom. See **ten-** in Appendix.] **—tan′tric** (-trĭk) *adj.*

♦**tan·trum** (tăn′trəm) *n.* **1.** A fit of bad temper. **2.** Also called ♦*hissy fit.* [Origin unknown.]

Tan·tung (tän′to͝ong′). See **Dandong.**

Tan·za·ni·a (tăn′zə-nē′ə). *Abbr.* **Tanz.** A country of east-central Africa on the Indian Ocean. Inhabited since prehistoric times, most of the region became a German protectorate in 1891 and passed to the British in 1920 as Tanganyika. Zanzibar, a narrow strip along the coast, was a British protectorate after 1890. Tanganyika achieved independence in 1961 and joined with Zanzibar in 1964 to form Tanzania. Dar es Salaam is the de facto capital and the largest city; Dodoma is the official capital. Population, 17,557,000. **—Tan′za·ni′an** *adj. & n.*

tan·zan·ite (tăn′zə-nīt′) *n.* A transparent variety of zoisite, used as a gem. [After TANZANIA.]

Tao·ism (tou′ĭz′əm, dou′-) *n.* A principal philosophy and system of religion of China based on the teachings of Lao-tzu in the 6th century B.C. [From Chinese (Mandarin) *dào,* way.] **—Tao′ist** *n.* **—Tao·is′tic** *adj.*

Ta·or·mi·na (tä′ôr-mē′nä). A town of eastern Sicily, Italy, at the foot of Mount Etna overlooking the Ionian Sea. First founded in the eighth century B.C., it is a winter resort. Population, 10,085.

Taos¹ (tous, tä′ōs) *n., pl.* **Taos.** **1.a.** A Pueblo people located north-northeast of Santa Fe, New Mexico. **b.** A member of this people. **2.** The Tanoan language of the Taos people.

Taos² (tous, tä′ōs). **1.** A town of northern New Mexico north-northeast of Santa Fe. It developed as an art colony after 1898 and has attracted many artists and writers, including John Marin and D.H. Lawrence. Population, 3,369. **2.** A pueblo of northern New Mexico northeast of the town of Taos. Population, 1,030.

tap¹ (tăp) *v.* **tapped, tap·ping, taps.** —*tr.* **1.** To strike gently with a light blow or blows: *I tapped you on the shoulder to get your attention.* **2.** To give a light rap with: *tap a pencil.* **3.** To produce with a succession of light blows: *tap out a rhythm.* **4.** To select, as for membership in an organization; designate. See Synonyms at **appoint. 5.a.** To repair (shoe heels or toes) by applying a thin layer of leather or a substitute material. **b.** To attach metal plates to (shoe toes or heels). —*intr.* **1.** To deliver a gentle, light blow or blows. **2.** To walk making light clicks. —**tap** *n.* **1.a.** A gentle blow. **b.** The sound made by such a blow. **2.a.** A thin layer of leather or a substitute applied to a worn-down shoe heel or toe. **b.** A metal plate attached to the toe or heel of a shoe, as for tap-dancing. [Middle English *tappen,* possibly from Old French *taper.*]

tap² (tăp) *n.* **1.** A valve and spout used to regulate delivery of a fluid at the end of a pipe. **2.** A plug for a bunghole; a spigot. **3.a.** Liquor drawn from a spigot. **b.** Liquor of a particular brew, cask, or quality. **4.** *Medicine.* The removal of fluid from a body cavity: *a spinal tap.* **5.** A tool for cutting an internal screw thread. **6.** A makeshift terminal in an electric circuit. —**tap** *tr.v.* **tapped, tap·ping, taps. 1.** To furnish with a spigot or tap. **2.** To pierce in order to draw off liquid: *tap a maple tree.* **3.** To draw (liquid) from a vessel or container: *tap a new keg of beer.* **4.** *Medicine.* To withdraw fluid from (a body cavity). **5.** To make a connection with or open outlets from: *tap a water main.* **6.a.** To wiretap (a telephone). **b.** To establish an electric connection in (a power line), as to divert current secretly. **7.** To cut screw threads in (a collar, socket, or other fitting). **8.** *Informal.* To ask (a person) for money. —***idiom.*** **on tap. 1.** Ready to be drawn; in a tapped cask: *beer on tap.* **2.** Available for immediate use; ready: *extra personnel on tap.* [Middle English *tappe,* from Old English *tæppa.*]

ta·pa (tä′pə, tăp′ə) *n.* **1.** The inner bark of the paper mulberry. **2.** A paperlike cloth made in the South Pacific islands by pounding this bark or similar bark. [Marquesan and Tahitian.]

Ta·pa·jós also **Ta·pa·joz** (tăp′ə-zhôs′, tä′pä-). A river, about 965 km (600 mi) long, of northern Brazil flowing northeast to the Amazon River.

tap dance *n.* A dance in which the rhythm is sounded out by the clicking taps on the heels and toes of a dancer's shoes. —**tap dancer** *n.*

tap-dance (tăp′dăns′) *intr.v.* **-danced, -danc·ing, -danc·es.** To perform a tap dance.

tape (tāp) *n.* **1.** A narrow strip of strong woven fabric, as that used in sewing or bookbinding. **2.** A continuous narrow, flexible strip of cloth, metal, paper, or plastic, such as adhesive tape, magnetic tape, or ticker tape. **3.** A string stretched across the finish line of a racetrack to be broken by the winner. **4.** A tape recording. —**tape** *v.* **taped, tap·ing, tapes.** —*tr.* **1.a.** To fasten, secure, strengthen, or wrap with a tape. **b.** To bind together (the sections of a book) by applying strips of tape to. **2.** To measure with a tape measure. **3.** To record sounds or pictures on magnetic tape. —*intr.* To make a recording on magnetic tape. [Middle English, from Old English *tæppe.*] —**tape′a·ble** *adj.* —**tape′less** *adj.*

tape cartridge *n.* A cartridge containing an endless loop of magnetic tape and designed for automatic use on insertion into a compatible sound or video recorder or computer system.

tape deck *n.* A tape recorder and player having no built-in amplifiers or speakers, used as a component in an audio system.

tape grass *n.* See **eelgrass.**

tape·line (tāp′līn′) *n.* See **tape measure.**

tape measure *n.* A tape of cloth, paper, or steel marked off in a linear scale, as of inches or centimeters, for taking measurements. Also called *tapeline.*

ta·pé·nade (tä′pə-näd′) *n.* A spread of Provençal origin consisting of capers, black olives, and anchovies puréed with olive oil. [French, from Provençal *tapéno,* capers, perhaps ultimately of Arabic origin.]

tape player *n.* A self-contained machine for playing back recorded magnetic tapes.

ta·per (tā′pər) *n.* **1.** A small or very slender candle. **2.** A long wax-coated wick used to light candles or gas lamps. **3.** A source of feeble light. **4.a.** A gradual decrease in thickness or width of an elongated object. **b.** A gradual decrease, as in action or force. —**taper** *v.* **-pered, -per·ing, -pers.** —*intr.* **1.** To become gradually narrower or thinner toward one end. **2.** To diminish or lessen gradually. Often used with *off: The storm finally tapered off.* —*tr.* **1.** To make thinner or narrower at one end. **2.** To make smaller gradually. —**taper** *adj.* Gradually decreasing in size toward a point. [Middle English, from Old English *tapor,* possibly ultimately from Latin *papyrus,* papyrus (sometimes used for candle-wicks). See PAPER.] —**ta′per·ing·ly** *adv.*

tape-re·cord (tāp′rĭ-kôrd′) *tr.v.* **-cord·ed, -cord·ing, -cords.** To record on magnetic tape.

tape recorder *n.* A mechanical device for recording on magnetic tape and usually for playing back the recorded material.

tape recording *n.* **1.a.** A magnetic tape on which sound or visual images have been recorded. **b.** The material recorded on a magnetic tape. **2.** The act of recording on magnetic tape.

tap·es·try (tăp′ĭ-strē) *n., pl.* **-tries. 1.** A heavy cloth woven with rich, often varicolored designs or scenes, usually hung on walls for decoration and sometimes used to cover furniture. **2.** Something felt to resemble a richly and complexly designed cloth: *the tapestry of world history.* —**tapestry** *tr.v.* **-es·tried** (-ĭ-strēd), **-es·try·ing, -es·tries** (-ĭ-strēz). **1.** To hang or decorate with tapestry. **2.** To make, weave, or depict in a tapestry. [Middle English *tapiceri, tapstri,* from Old French *tapisserie,* from *tapisser,* to cover with carpet, from *tapis,* carpet, from Greek *tapētion,* diminutive of *tapēs,* perhaps of Iranian origin.]

ta·pe·tum (tə-pē′təm) *n., pl.* **-ta** (-tə). **1.** *Botany.* A nutritive tissue within the sporangium, particularly within an anther. **2.** *Anatomy.* **a.** A membranous layer or region, especially the iridescent membrane of the choroid of certain mammals. **b.** A layer of fibers of the corpus callosum forming the roof of part of the lateral ventricle of the brain. [Medieval Latin *tapētum,* coverlet, from Latin *tapēte,* **tapētum,* from Greek *tapēs, tapēt-.* See TAPESTRY.] —**ta·pe′tal** (-pēt′l) *adj.*

tape·worm (tāp′wûrm′) *n.* Any of various ribbonlike, often very long flatworms of the class Cestoda, that lack an alimentary canal and are parasitic in the intestines of vertebrates, including human beings.

ta·phon·o·my (tə-fŏn′ə-mē) *n.* **1.** The study of the conditions and processes by which organisms become fossilized. **2.** The conditions and processes of fossilization. [Greek *taphē,* grave + -NOMY.] —**taph′o·nom′ic** (tăf′ə-nŏm′ĭk) *adj.* —**ta·phon′o·mist** *n.*

tap house *n.* A tavern or bar.

tap·i·o·ca (tăp′ē-ō′kə) *n.* A beady starch obtained from the root of the cassava, used for puddings and as a thickening agent in cooking. [Portuguese, from Tupi *typióca* : *ty,* juice + *pyá,* heart + *oca,* to remove.]

ta·pir (tā′pər, tə-pîr′) *n.* Any of several large, chiefly nocturnal, odd-toed ungulates of the genus *Tapirus* of tropical America, the Malay Peninsula, and Sumatra, related to the horse and the rhinoceros, and having a heavy body, short legs, and a long, fleshy, flexible upper lip. [Perhaps French, ultimately from Tupi *tapiira,* tapir.]

tap·is (tăp′ē, tăp′ĭs, tă-pē′) *n. Obsolete.* Tapestry or comparable material used for draperies, carpeting, and furniture covering. —***idiom.*** **on the tapis.** Under consideration. [Middle English, from Old French. See TAPESTRY.]

tap-off (tăp′ôf′, -ŏf′) *n. Basketball.* See **tip-off².**

Tap·pan (tăp′ən), **Arthur.** 1786–1865. American merchant and abolitionist. With his brother **Lewis** (1788–1873) he founded the American Anti-Slavery Society (1833).

Tappan Zee (zē). A widening of the Hudson River in southeast New York. Maj. John André was hanged for treason in 1780 at the nearby village of **Tappan.**

tap·per (tăp′ər) *n.* One that taps.

tap·pet (tăp′ĭt) *n.* A lever or projecting arm that moves or is moved by contact with another part, usually to communicate a certain motion, as between a driving mechanism and a valve. [Probably from TAP¹.]

tap·ping (tăp′ĭng) *n.* **1.a.** The act of one that taps. **b.** The process or means by which something is tapped. **2.** Something that is taken or drawn by tapping.

tap·pit-hen (tăp′ĭt-hĕn′) *n. Scots.* **1.** A crested hen. **2.** A large mug with a knobbed lid. [Scots *tappit,* crested (variant of *topped,* past participle of TOP¹) + HEN.]

tap·room (tăp′ro͞om′, -ro͝om′) *n.* A bar or barroom.

tap·root (tăp′ro͞ot′, -ro͝ot′) *n.* The main root of a plant, usually stouter than the lateral roots and growing straight downward from the stem.

taps (tăps) *pl.n. (used with a sing. or pl. verb).* A bugle call or drum signal sounded at night, as at a military camp, as an order to put out lights and also sounded at military funerals and memorial services. [Perhaps alteration of *taptoo,* tattoo, variant of TATTOO¹.]

tap·ster (tăp′stər) *n.* One who draws and serves liquor for customers; a bartender.

tap water *n.* Water drawn directly from a tap or faucet.

tar¹ (tär) *n.* **1.** A dark, oily, viscous material, consisting mainly of hydrocarbons, produced by the destructive distillation of organic substances such as wood, coal, or peat. **2.** Coal tar. **3.** A solid residue of tobacco smoke containing byproducts of combustion. —**tar** *tr.v.* **tarred, tar·ring, tars.** To coat with or as if with tar. —***idiom.*** **tar and feather. 1.** To punish (a person) by covering with tar and feathers. **2.** To criticize severely and devastatingly; excoriate. [Middle English, from Old English *teru.* See **deru-** in Appendix.]

tar² (tär) *n. Informal.* A sailor. [Possibly short for TARPAULIN.]

Tar·a (tăr′ə). A village of eastern Ireland northwest of Dublin. It was the seat of Irish kings until the sixth century A.D.

tar·a·did·dle (tăr′ə-dĭd′l) *n.* Variant of **tarradiddle.**

Ta·ra·hu·ma·ra (tär′ə-ho͞o-mär′ə, tăr′-) *n., pl.* **Tarahumara** or **-ras. 1.** A member of a Native American people of

tapa

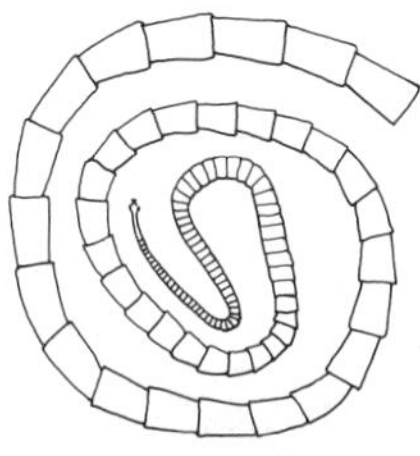
tapeworm

tapir
Baird's tapir
Tapirus bairdii

ă pat	oi boy
ā pay	ou out
âr care	o͝o took
ä father	o͞o boot
ĕ pet	ŭ cut
ē be	ûr urge
ĭ pit	th thin
ī pie	*th* this
îr pier	hw which
ŏ pot	zh vision
ō toe	ə about, item
ô paw	♦ regionalism

Stress marks: **′** (primary); ′ (secondary), as in **dictionary** (dĭk′shə-nĕr′ē)

north-central Mexico. **2.** The Uto-Aztecan language of the Tarahumara.

tarantula

ta·ra·ma·sa·la·ta (tä′rä-mä-sä-lä′tä) or **ta·ra·mo·sa·la·ta** (-mō-) *n.* A Greek appetizer consisting of a light paste of fish roe, olive oil, lemon juice, and moistened bread crumbs or mashed potatoes. [Modern Greek : *taramas,* preserved roe (from Turkish *tarama,* soft roe) + *salata,* salad (from Italian *insalata,* from feminine past participle of *insalare,* to salt : Latin *in-,* in, on; see IN–² + Vulgar Latin **salāre,* to salt, from Latin *sāl,* salt; see SAL).]

tar·an·tel·la (tăr′ən-tĕl′ə) *n.* **1.** A lively, whirling southern Italian dance once thought to be a remedy for tarantism. **2.** The music for this dance, in 6/8 time. [Italian, after TARANTO.]

tar·an·tism (tăr′ən-tĭz′əm) *n.* A disorder characterized by an uncontrollable urge to dance, especially prevalent in southern Italy from the 15th to the 17th century and popularly attributed to the bite of a tarantula. [New Latin *tarantismus,* after TARANTO.]

Ta·ran·to (tär′ən-tō′, tə-răn′tō, tä′rän-tô′). A city of southeast Italy east-southeast of Naples on the **Gulf of Taranto,** an arm of the Ionian Sea. Founded by Greeks from Sparta in the eighth century B.C., it was known as Tarentum in Roman times. Ruled by varied powers over the centuries, it became part of Italy in 1860. Population, 242,774.

ta·ran·tu·la (tə-răn′chə-lə) *n., pl.* **-las** or **-lae** (-lē′). **1.** Any of various large, hairy, chiefly tropical spiders of the family Theraphosidae, capable of inflicting a painful but not seriously poisonous bite. **2.** A large wolf spider *(Lycosa tarentula)* of southern Europe, once thought to cause tarantism. [Medieval Latin, from Old Italian *tarantola,* after TARANTO.]

Ta·ra·wa (tə-rä′wə, tăr′ə-wä′, tä′rä-). An atoll of Kiribati in the northern Gilbert Islands of the western Pacific Ocean. It was occupied by the Japanese in 1942 and retaken by U.S. Marines after a hard-fought battle in November 1943.

tar baby *n.* A situation or problem from which it is virtually impossible to disentangle oneself. [After "Bre'r Rabbit and the *Tar Baby,*" an Uncle Remus story by Joel Chandler Harris.]

Tar·bell (tär′bəl), **Ida Minerva.** 1857–1944. American muckraking writer and editor remembered for her investigations of industry, including *History of the Standard Oil Company* (1904).

tar·boosh also **tar·bush** (tär-bo͞osh′) *n.* A brimless, usually red felt cap with a silk tassel, worn by Moslem men, either by itself or as the base of a turban. [Arabic (Egyptian) *ṭarbūs,* from Turkish *terposh,* probably from Persian *sarposh,* headdress : *sar,* head + *pūsh,* covering.]

tar camphor *n.* See **naphthalene.**

tar·di·grade (tär′dĭ-grād′) *n.* Any of various slow-moving, microscopic invertebrates of the phylum Tardigrada, related to the arthropods and having four body segments and eight legs and living in water or damp moss. Also called *water bear.* **—tardigrade** *adj.* **1.** Of or belonging to the Tardigrada. **2.** Slow in action; slow-moving. [Latin *tardigradus,* slow-moving : *tardus,* slow + *-gradus,* walking, moving (from *gradī,* to go; see TRANSGRESS).]

targe
16th-century Italian

tar·dive (tär′dĭv) *adj.* Having symptoms that develop slowly or appear long after inception. Used of a disease. [French, feminine of *tardif,* from Old French, slow. See TARDY.]

tardive dyskinesia *n.* A chronic disorder of the nervous system characterized by involuntary jerky movements of the face, tongue, jaws, trunk, and limbs, usually developing as a late side effect of prolonged treatment with antipsychotic drugs.

tar·dy (tär′dē) *adj.* **-di·er, -di·est. 1.** Occurring, arriving, acting, or done after the scheduled, expected, or usual time; late. **2.** Moving slowly; sluggish. [Alteration of Middle English *tardive,* slow, from Old French *tardif,* from Vulgar Latin **tardīvus,* from Latin *tardus.*] **—tar′di·ly** *adv.* **—tar′di·ness** *n.*

SYNONYMS: *tardy, behindhand, late, overdue.* The central meaning shared by these adjectives is "not arriving, occurring, acting, or done at the scheduled, expected, or usual time": *tardy in making a dental appointment; behindhand with her car payments; late for the plane; an overdue bus.*
ANTONYM: *prompt.*

tare¹ (târ) *n.* **1.** Any of various weedy plants of the genus *Vicia,* especially the common vetch. **2.** Any of several weedy plants that grow in grain fields. **3. tares.** An unwelcome or objectional element. [Middle English.]

tare² (târ) *n.* **1.** *Abbr.* **t.** The weight of a container or wrapper that is deducted from the gross weight to obtain net weight. **2.** A deduction from gross weight made to allow for the weight of a container. **3.** *Chemistry.* A counterbalance, especially an empty vessel used to counterbalance the weight of a similar container. **—tare** *tr.v.* **tared, tar·ing, tares.** To determine or indicate the tare of, especially to weigh in order to find out the tare. [Middle English, from Old French, ultimately from Arabic *ṭarḥah,* that which is thrown away, from *ṭaraḥa,* to reject.]

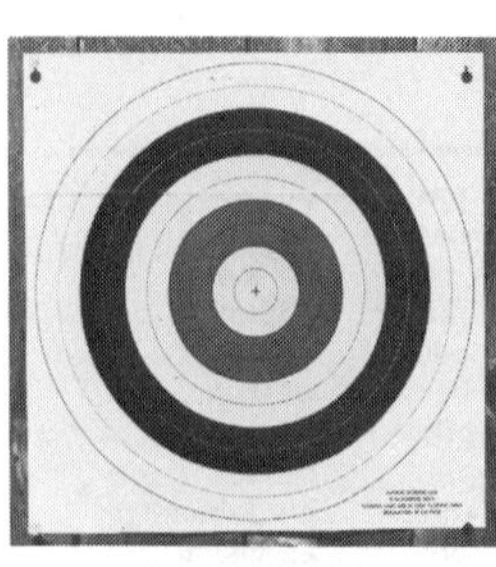
target

targe (tärj) *n. Archaic.* A light shield or buckler. [Middle English, from Old French. See TARGET.]

tar·get (tär′gĭt) *n. Abbr.* **tgt. 1. a.** An object, such as a padded disk with a marked surface, that is shot at to test accuracy in rifle or archery practice. **b.** Something aimed or fired at. **2.** An object of criticism or attack. **3.** One to be influenced or changed by an action or event. **4.** A desired goal. **5.** A railroad signal that indicates the position of a switch by its color, position, and shape. **6.** The sliding sight on a surveyor's leveling rod. **7.** A small, round shield. **8. a.** A structure in a television camera tube with a storage surface that is scanned by an electron beam to generate a signal output current similar to the charge-density pattern stored on the surface. **b.** A usually metal part in an x-ray tube on which a beam of electrons is focused and from which x-rays are emitted. *—attributive.* Often used to modify another noun: *a target group; a target market.* **—target** *tr.v.* **-get·ed, -get·ing, -gets. 1.** To make a target of. **2.** To aim at or for. **3.** To establish as a target or goal. ***—idiom.*** **on target.** Completely accurate, precise, or valid: *observations that were right on target.* [Middle English, small targe, from Old French *targuete,* variant of *targete,* diminutive of *targe,* light shield, of Germanic origin.]

tar·get·a·ble (tär′gĭ-tə-bəl) *adj.* That can be directed at a target: *independently targetable nuclear warheads.*

target date *n.* A date established as a target or goal, as for the completion of a project.

target language *n.* **1.** The language into which a text written in another language is to be translated. **2.** A language that a nonnative speaker is in the process of learning. **3.** *Computer Science.* The computer language, often a machine language, into which a document written in another computer language is to be translated. Also called *object language.*

Tar·gum (tär′go͞om′, -go͞om′) *n.* Any of several Aramaic translations or paraphrasings of the Old Testament. [Mishnaic Hebrew *targûm,* translation, interpretation, Targum, from Hebrew *tirgēm,* to interpret.]

Tar Heel or **Tar·heel** (tär′hēl′) *n.* A native or resident of North Carolina. [Perhaps from the tar that was once a major product of the state.]

tar·iff (tăr′ĭf) *n.* **1. a.** A list or system of duties imposed by a government on imported or exported goods. **b.** Duties or a duty imposed by a government on imported or exported goods. **2.** A schedule of prices or fees. **—tariff** *tr.v.* **-iffed, -iff·ing, -iffs.** To fix a duty or price on. [Italian *tariffa,* from Old Italian, from Arabic *ta'rīf,* notification, from *'arafa,* to know.]

Ta·rim He (tä′rēm′ hə′). A river of western China flowing about 2,092 km (1,300 mi) eastward to Lop Nur.

Tarim Pen·di (pŭn′dē′). An arid basin of western China south of the Tien Shan and traversed by the Tarim He. The ancient Silk Road passed through the region.

Tar·king·ton (tär′kĭng′tən), **(Newton) Booth.** 1869–1946. American writer whose novels include *The Magnificent Ambersons* (1918) and *Alice Adams* (1921), both of which won a Pulitzer Prize.

tar·la·tan also **tar·le·tan** (tär′lə-tən, -lə-tn) *n.* A thin, stiffly starched muslin in open plain weave. [French *tarlatane,* alteration of earlier *tarnatane.*]

tar·mac (tär′măk′) *n.* A tarmacadam road or surface, especially an airport runway. **—tarmac** *v.* **-macked, -mack·ing, -macs.** *—tr.* To cause (an aircraft) to sit on a taxiway. *—intr.* To sit on a taxiway. Used of an aircraft. [Originally a trademark.]

tar·mac·ad·am (tär′mə-kăd′əm) *n.* A pavement consisting of layers of crushed stone with a tar binder pressed to a smooth surface.

tarn (tärn) *n.* A small mountain lake, especially one formed by glaciers. [Middle English *terne,* of Scandinavian origin.]

Tarn (tärn). A river, about 378 km (235 mi) long, of southern France flowing west and southwest to the Garonne River.

♦ **tar·nal** (tär′nəl) *adj. & adv. Chiefly New England & Upper Southern U.S.* Damned. See Regional Note at **tarnation.** [Alteration of ETERNAL.] **—tar′nal·ly** *adv.*

♦ **tar·na·tion** (tär-nā′shən) *New England & Southern U.S. n.* The act of damning or the condition of being damned. **—tarnation** *interj.* Used to express anger or annoyance. [TARN(AL) + (DAMN)ATION.]

♦ ***REGIONAL NOTE:*** The noun and interjection *tarnation* illustrate suffixation, the addition of a suffix to a word. *Tarnation* and *darnation* (the latter probably having come first) are both euphemistic forms of *damnation. Tarnation* seems to have been influenced by *tarnal,* another mild oath derived from *(e)ternal!* The *Oxford English Dictionary* cites late-18th-century examples of *tarnation* from New England, indicating that it has been part of American speech since colonial days.

tar·nish (tär′nĭsh) *v.* **-nished, -nish·ing, -nish·es.** *—tr.* **1.** To dull the luster of; discolor, especially by exposure to air or dirt. **2. a.** To detract from or spoil; taint: *a tragedy that tarnished our hopes.* **b.** To cast aspersions on; sully: *slander that tarnished the senator's image.* *—intr.* **1.** To lose luster; become discolored. **2.** To diminish or become tainted. **—tarnish** *n.* **1.** The condition of being tarnished. **2.** Discoloration of a metal surface caused by corrosion or oxidation. **3.** The condition of being sullied. [Middle English *ternisshen,* from Old French *ternir, terniss-,* to dull, from *terne,* dull, of Germanic origin.] **—tar′nish·a·ble** *adj.*

Tar·nów (tär′no͞of′). A city of southeast Poland east of Cracow. It was a religious and cultural center in the 15th and 16th centuries. Population, 113,200.

ta·ro (tär′ō, tăr′ō) *n., pl.* **-ros. 1.** A widely cultivated tropical Asian plant *(Colocasia esculenta)* having broad, peltate leaves and a large, starchy, edible tuber. **2.** The tuber of this plant. Also called *cocoyam, dasheen, eddo.* [Of Polynesian origin.]

tar·ok also **tar·oc** (tăr′ək) *n. Games.* A card game developed in Italy in the 14th century, played with a 78-card pack consisting of four suits plus the 22 tarot cards as trumps. [Italian *tarocchi,* pl. of *tarocco,* tarot.]

tar·ot (tăr′ō, tə-rō′) *n. Games.* **1.** Any of a set of 22 playing cards consisting of a joker plus 21 cards depicting vices, virtues, and elemental forces, used in fortunetelling and as trump in tarok. **2. tarots.** Tarok. [French, from Italian *tarocco.*]

tarp (tärp) *n. Informal.* A tarpaulin.

tar·pa·per (tär′pā′pər) *n.* Heavy paper impregnated or coated with tar, used as a waterproof protective material in building.

tar·pau·lin (tär-pô′lĭn, tär′pə-) *n.* **1.** Material, such as waterproofed canvas, used to cover and protect things from moisture. **2.** A sheet of this material. [Probably alteration of TAR[1] + PALL[1] + –ING[2].]

tar pit *n.* An accumulation of natural tar or asphalt at the earth's surface, especially one that acts as a trap for animals and preserves their bones.

tar·pon (tär′pən) *n., pl.* **tarpon** or **-pons.** Any of several fishes of the family Elopidae or Megalopidae, especially a large silvery game fish *(Megalops atlanticus)* of Atlantic coastal waters. [Origin unknown.]

Tar·quin·i·i (tär-kwĭn′ē-ī′). An ancient city of central Italy northwest of Rome. Head of the Etruscan League, it was defeated by Roman forces in the fourth century B.C. and lost its independence in the third century. The modern village of Tarquinia has a museum displaying notable Etruscan antiquities.

tar·ra·did·dle also **tar·a·did·dle** (tăr′ə-dĭd′l) *n.* **1.** A petty falsehood; a fib. **2.** Silly pretentious speech or writing; twaddle. [Origin unknown.]

tar·ra·gon (tăr′ə-gŏn′, -gən) *n.* **1.** An aromatic Eurasian herb *(Artemisia dracunculus)* having linear to lance-shaped leaves and small, whitish-green flower heads arranged in loose, spreading panicles. **2.** The leaves of this plant used as seasoning. [New Latin *tarchon,* from Medieval Greek *tarkhōn,* from Arabic *ṭarḫūn,* perhaps from Greek *drakōn,* dragon, tarragon.]

Tar·ra·go·na (tăr′ə-gō′nə, tä′rä-gô′nä). A city of northeast Spain on the Mediterranean Sea west-southwest of Barcelona. A leading town of Roman Spain after the third century B.C., it fell to the Moors in A.D. 714. Population, 113,075.

Tar·ra·sa (tə-rä′sə, tä-rä′sä). A city of northeast Spain north-northwest of Barcelona. Founded in Roman times, it is an industrial center noted for its textiles. Population, 165,233.

tar·ri·ance (tăr′ē-əns) *n. Archaic.* **1.** The act of tarrying. **2.** A temporary stay; a sojourn.

Tar River. A river, about 346 km (215 mi) long, of northeast North Carolina flowing southeast to Pamlico Sound.

tar·ry[1] (tăr′ē) *v.* **-ried, -ry·ing, -ries.** —*intr.* **1.** To delay or be late in going, coming, or doing. See Synonyms at **stay**[1]. **2.** To wait. **3.** To remain or stay temporarily, as in a place; sojourn. —*tr. Archaic.* To wait for; await. —**tarry** *n.* A temporary stay; a sojourn. [Middle English *tarien.*] —**tar′ri·er** *n.*

tar·ry[2] (tär′ē) *adj.* **-ri·er, -ri·est.** Of, resembling, or covered with tar.

Tar·ry·town (tăr′ē-toun′). A village of southeast New York on the Hudson River north of New York City. Founded by the Dutch in the 17th century, it was the home of Washington Irving and the setting for many of his short stories. Population, 10,648.

tar·sal (tär′səl) *adj.* **1.** Of, relating to, or situated near the tarsus of the foot: *the tarsal bones.* **2.** Of or relating to the tarsus of the eyelid: *the tarsal ligaments.* [New Latin *tarsālis,* from *tarsus,* tarsus. See TARSUS.]

tarsal gland *n.* Any of the branched sebaceous glands located in the tarsus of the eyelid.

tarsal plate *n.* See **tarsus** (sense 2).

tar·si (tär′sī, -sē) *n.* Plural of **tarsus.**

tar·si·er (tär′sē-ər, -sē-ā′) *n.* Any of several small nocturnal arboreal primates of the genus *Tarsius,* of the East Indies and the Philippines, having large round eyes, a long tail, and long fingers and toes tipped with soft disklike pads. [French, from *tarse,* tarsus (from its elongated ankles), from New Latin *tarsus.* See TARSUS.]

tar·so·met·a·tar·sus (tär′sō-mĕt′ə-tär′səs) *n., pl.* **-si** (-sī, -sē). A compound bone between the tibia and the toes of a bird's leg, formed by fusion of the tarsal and metatarsal bones. —**tar′so·met′a·tar′sal** (-tär′səl) *adj.*

tar·sus (tär′səs) *n., pl.* **-si** (-sī, -sē). **1.a.** The section of the vertebrate foot between the leg and the metatarsus. **b.** The bones making up this section, especially the seven small bones of the human ankle. **2.** A fibrous plate that supports and shapes the edge of the eyelid. Also called *tarsal plate.* **3.** *Zoology.* **a.** The tarsometatarsus. **b.** The distal part of the leg of an arthropod, usually divided into segments. [New Latin, from Greek *tarsos,* ankle. See **ters-** in Appendix.]

Tar·sus (tär′səs). A city of southern Turkey near the Mediterranean Sea west of Adana. Settled in the Neolithic Period, it was one of the most important cities of Asia Minor under Roman rule (after 67 B.C.). Saint Paul was born in Tarsus. Population, 121,074.

tart[1] (tärt) *adj.* **tart·er, tart·est.** **1.** Having a sharp, pungent taste; sour. See Synonyms at **sour.** **2.** Sharp or bitter in tone or meaning; cutting. [Middle English, from Old English *teart,* severe. See **der-** in Appendix.] —**tart′ly** *adv.* —**tart′ness** *n.*

tart[2] (tärt) *n.* **1.a.** A small open pie with a sweet filling, as of custard or cooked fruit. **b.** *Chiefly British.* A pie. **2.a.** A prostitute. **b.** A woman considered to be sexually promiscuous. —**tart** *tr.v.* **tart·ed, tart·ing, tarts.** *Chiefly British.* To dress up or make fancy in a tawdry, garish way. [Middle English *tarte,* from Old French, perhaps alteration of *tartane,* from Late Latin *torta,* a kind of bread.]

tar·tan[1] (tär′tn) *n.* **1.a.** Any of numerous textile patterns consisting of stripes of varying widths and colors crossed at right angles against a solid background, each forming a distinctive design worn by the members of a Scottish clan. **b.** A twilled wool fabric or garment having such a pattern. **2.** A plaid fabric. [Middle English *tartane,* possibly from Old French *tiretaine,* linsey-woolsey, probably from *tiret,* a kind of cloth, from *tire,* silk cloth, from Latin *Tyrius,* Tyrian (cloth), from *Tyrus,* Tyre.] —**tar′tan** *adj.*

tar·tan[2] (tär′tn, tär-tăn′) *n. Nautical.* A small, single-masted Mediterranean ship with a large lateen sail. [French *tartane,* from Provençal *tartano,* from Old Provençal *tartana,* buzzard, of imitative origin.]

tar·tar (tär′tər) *n.* **1.** *Dentistry.* A hard, yellowish deposit on the teeth, consisting of organic secretions and food particles deposited in various salts, such as calcium carbonate. **2.** A reddish acid compound, chiefly potassium bitartrate, found in the juice of grapes and deposited on the sides of casks during winemaking. [Middle English *tartre,* potassium bitartrate, from Old French, from Medieval Latin *tartarum,* from Medieval Greek *tartaron.*]

Tar·tar (tär′tər) *n.* **1.** Also **Ta·tar** (tä′tər). A member of any of the Turkic and Mongolian peoples of central Asia who invaded western Asia and eastern Europe in the Middle Ages. **2.** Variant of **Tatar** (senses 1, 2). **3.** Often **tartar.** A person regarded as ferocious or violent. —***idiom.*** **catch a Tartar.** To grapple with an unexpectedly formidable opponent. [Middle English *Tartre,* from Old French *Tartare,* from Medieval Latin *Tartarus,* alteration (influenced by Latin *Tartarus,* Tartarus) of Persian *Tātār,* of Turkic origin.]

tartar emetic *n.* A poisonous crystalline compound, $K(SbO)C_4H_4O_6 \cdot \frac{1}{2}H_2O$, used in medicine as an expectorant and in the treatment of parasitic infections, such as schistosomiasis.

tar·tar·e·ous (tär-târ′ē-əs) *adj.* Consisting of or resembling tartar.

tar·tare steak (tär-tär′, tär′tər) *n.* See **steak tartare.**

tar·tar·ic (tär-tăr′ĭk) *adj.* Of, relating to, or derived from tartar or tartaric acid.

tartaric acid *n.* Any of four isomeric crystalline organic compounds, $C_4H_6O_6$, used to make cream of tartar and baking powder, as a sequestrant, in tanning, and in effervescent beverages and photographic chemicals.

tar·tar·ize (tär′tə-rīz′) *tr.v.* **-ized, -iz·ing, -iz·es.** To treat, impregnate, or combine with tartar. —**tar′tar·i·za′tion** (-tər-ĭ-zā′shən) *n.*

tar·tar·ous (tär′tər-əs) *adj.* Consisting of, derived from, or containing tartar.

tartar sauce *n.* Mayonnaise mixed with chopped onion, olives, pickles, and capers and served as a sauce with fish. [Translation of French *sauce tartare* : *sauce,* sauce + *tartare,* Tartar.]

Tar·ta·rus (tär′tər-əs) *n.* **1.** *Greek Mythology.* The abysmal regions below Hades where the Titans were confined. **2.** An infernal region; hell. [Latin, from Greek *Tartaros.*] —**Tar·tar′e·an** (-târ′ē-ən) *adj.*

Tar·ta·ry (tär′tə-rē) or **Ta·ta·ry** (tä′-). A vast region of eastern Europe and northern Asia controlled by the Mongols in the 13th and 14th centuries. It extended as far east as the Pacific Ocean under the rule of Genghis Khan.

tar·tine (tär-tēn′) *n.* A French open-faced sandwich, especially one with a rich or fancy spread. [French, from Old French, diminutive of *tarte,* tart. See TART[2].]

tart·ish[1] (tär′tĭsh) *adj.* Somewhat tart: *a tartish apple.*

tart·ish[2] (tär′tĭsh) *adj.* Resembling or suggesting a prostitute: *tartish attire.*

tart·let (tärt′lĭt) *n.* A small pastry tart.

tar·trate (tär′trāt′) *n.* A salt or an ester of tartaric acid.

tar·trat·ed (tär′trā′tĭd) *adj.* Containing, combined with, or derived from tartaric acid.

Tar·tu (tär′to͞o). A city of southeast Estonia southeast of Tallinn. Founded in 1030, it was a member of the Hanseatic League and became part of Russia in 1704. Tartu suffered extensive damage during World War II. Population, 111,000.

tar·tuffe also **tar·tufe** (tär-to͝of′, -to͞of′) *n.* A hypocrite, especially one who affects religious piety. [After the protagonist of *Tartuffe,* a play by Molière.] —**tar·tuf′fe·ry** *n.*

tart·y (tär′tē) *adj.* **-i·er, -i·est.** Of, relating to, or suggestive of a prostitute. —**tart′i·ly** *adv.* —**tart′i·ness** *n.*

Tar·vi·a (tär′vē-ə). A trademark used for a brand of asphalt pitch.

tar·weed (tär′wēd′) *n.* **1.** Any of several strong-smelling, resinous western American and Chilean plants of the genus *Madia,* having yellow, rayed flower heads. **2.** Any of several similar or related plants.

Tar·zan (tär′zən, -zăn′) *n.* A powerfully built man of great agility and valor. [After *Tarzan,* the hero of a series of jungle tales by Edgar Rice Burroughs.]

tarot

tarragon
Artemisia dracunculus

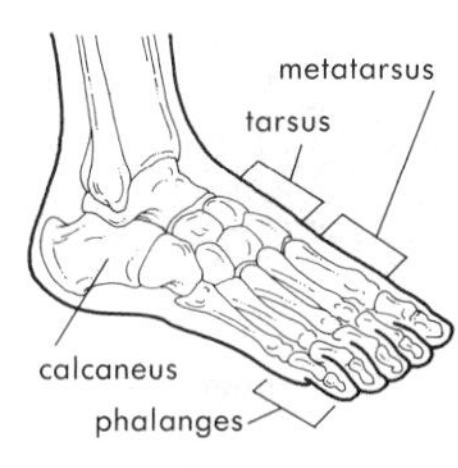

tarsus

tartan[1]

ă pat	oi boy
ā pay	ou out
âr care	o͝o took
ä father	o͞o boot
ĕ pet	ŭ cut
ē be	ûr urge
ĭ pit	th thin
ī pie	*th* this
îr pier	hw which
ŏ pot	zh vision
ō toe	ə about, item
ô paw	♦ regionalism

Stress marks: ′ (primary); ′ (secondary), as in **dictionary** (dĭk′shə-nĕr′ē)

TAS *abbr.* **1.** Telephone answering system. **2.** True airspeed.

Tas. *abbr.* Tasmania.

Tash·kent (tăsh-kĕnt′, täsh-). A city of eastern Uzbekistan west-southwest of Alma-Ata. One of the oldest cities of central Asia, it was ruled by Arabs and then Turks until 1865, when it was annexed by Russia. Population, 2,030,000.

task (tăsk) *n.* **1.** A piece of work assigned or done as part of one's duties. **2.** A difficult or tedious undertaking. **3.** A function to be performed; an objective. **—task** *tr.v.* **tasked, task·ing, tasks. 1.** To assign a task to or impose a task on. **2.** To overburden with labor; tax. ***—idiom.* take** (or **call** or **bring**) **to task.** To reprimand or censure. [Middle English *taske,* imposed work, tax, from Old North French *tasque,* from Vulgar Latin **tasca,* alteration of **taxa,* from Latin *taxāre,* to feel, reproach, reckon. See TAX.]

tassel
On a mortarboard

SYNONYMS: *task, job, chore, stint, assignment.* These nouns denote a piece of work that one must do. A *task* is a well-defined responsibility that is usually imposed by another and that may be burdensome: *"A man ought to read just as inclination leads him; for what he reads as a task will do him little good"* (Samuel Johnson). *Job* often suggests a specific short-term undertaking: *"did little jobs about the house with skill"* (W.H. Auden). *Chore* generally denotes a minor, routine, or odd job: *The farmer's morning chores included cleaning the stables and milking the cows. Stint* refers to a person's prescribed share of work: *Her stint as a lifeguard usually consumes three hours a day. Assignment* generally denotes a task allotted by a person in authority: *The reporter's assignment was to attend the trial and interview the principals at its conclusion.*

task force *n.* **1.** A temporary grouping of military units or forces under one commander for the performance of a specific operation or assignment. **2.** A temporary grouping of individuals and resources for the accomplishment of a specific objective: *a presidential task force to fight drug trafficking.*

task·mas·ter (tăsk′măs′tər) *n.* **1.** A man who imposes tasks, especially burdensome or laborious ones. **2.** A source of burden or responsibility: *The profession of medicine is a stern taskmaster.*

task·mis·tress (tăsk′mĭs′trĭs) *n.* A woman who imposes tasks, especially burdensome or laborious ones.

tatami

Tas·man (tăz′mən, täs′män), **Abel Janszoon.** 1603?–1659. Dutch navigator and explorer who was the first European to discover Tasmania and New Zealand (1642).

Tas·ma·ni·a (tăz-mā′nē-ə, -mān′yə). Formerly **Van Die·men's Land** (văn dē′mənz, vän). *Abbr.* **Tas.** An island of southeast Australia separated from the mainland by Bass Strait. Tasmania joined Australia in 1901. **—Tas·ma′ni·an** *adj. & n.*

Tasmanian devil *n.* A burrowing nocturnal carnivorous marsupial *(Sarcophilus harrisii)* of Tasmania, having a predominantly blackish coat and a long, almost hairless tail.

Tasmanian wolf *n.* A large wolflike carnivorous marsupial *(Thylacinus cynocephalus)* of Tasmania, having a pointed head and dark transverse stripes across its back. It is believed to be extinct. Also called *Tasmanian tiger, thylacine.*

Tas·man Sea (tăz′mən). An arm of the southern Pacific Ocean between southwest Australia and western New Zealand.

tasse (tăs) also **tas·set** (tăs′ĭt) *n.* One of a series of jointed overlapping metal splints hanging from a corselet, used as armor for the lower trunk and thighs. [Possibly French, pouch, from Old French, perhaps ultimately from Vulgar Latin **tasca,* task, money pouch. See TASK.]

tas·sel (tăs′əl) *n.* **1.** A bunch of loose threads or cords bound at one end and hanging free at the other, used as an ornament on curtains or clothing, for example. **2.** Something that resembles such an ornament, especially the pollen-bearing inflorescence of a corn plant. **—tassel** *v.* **-seled, -sel·ing, -sels** or **-selled, -sel·ling, -sels.** *—tr.* To fringe or decorate with tassels. *—intr.* To put forth a tassellike inflorescence. Used especially of corn. [Middle English, from Old French, fastening, clasp, from Vulgar Latin **tassellus,* blend of Latin *tessella,* small die; see TESSELLATE, and *taxillus,* diminutive of *tālus,* knucklebone, ankle.]

tas·set (tăs′ĭt) *n.* Variant of **tasse.**

Tas·so (tăs′ō, tä′sō), **Torquato.** 1544–1595. Italian poet who wrote the epic *Jerusalem Delivered* (1581), an account of the capture of the city during the First Crusade.

taste (tāst) *v.* **tast·ed, tast·ing, tastes.** *—tr.* **1.** To distinguish the flavor of by taking into the mouth. **2.** To eat or drink a small quantity of. **3.** To partake of, especially for the first time; experience. **4.** To perceive as if by the sense of taste. **5.** *Archaic.* To appreciate or enjoy. *—intr.* **1.** To distinguish flavors in the mouth. **2.** To have a distinct flavor: *The stew tastes salty.* **3.** To eat or drink a small amount. **4.** To have experience or enjoyment; partake: *tasted of the life of the very rich.* **—taste** *n.* **1.a.** The sense that distinguishes the sweet, sour, salty, and bitter qualities of dissolved substances in contact with the taste buds on the tongue. **b.** This sense in combination with the senses of smell and touch, which together receive a sensation of a substance in the mouth. **2.a.** The sensation of sweet, sour, salty, or bitter qualities produced by or as if by a substance placed in the mouth. **b.** The unified sensation produced by any of these qualities plus a distinct smell and texture; flavor. **c.** A distinctive perception as if by the sense of taste: *an experience that left a bad taste in my mouth.* **3.** The act of tasting. **4.** A small quantity eaten or tasted. **5.** A limited or first experience; a sample: *"Thousands entered the war, got just a taste of it, and then stepped out"* (Mark Twain). **6.** A personal preference or liking: *a taste for adventure.* **7.a.** The faculty of discerning what is aesthetically excellent or appropriate. **b.** A manner indicative of the quality of such discernment: *a room furnished with superb taste.* **8.a.** The sense of what is proper, seemly, or least likely to give offense in a given social situation. **b.** A manner indicative of the quality of this sense. **9.** *Obsolete.* The act of testing; trial. [Middle English *tasten,* to touch, taste, from Old French *taster,* from Vulgar Latin **tastāre,* probably alteration of Latin **taxāre,* probably frequentative of *tangere,* to touch. See **tag-** in Appendix.] **—tast′a·ble** *adj.*

SYNONYMS: *taste, flavor, relish, savor, smack, tang.* The central meaning shared by these nouns is "a quality that can be perceived by the gustatory sense": *the salty taste of anchovies; the pungent flavor of garlic; the aromatic relish of freshly brewed coffee; the savor of rich chocolate; the spicy smack of curry sauce; the fresh tang of lemonade.* See also Synonyms at **experience.**

taste bud *n.* Any of numerous spherical or ovoid clusters of receptor cells found mainly in the epithelium of the tongue and constituting the end organs of the sense of taste.

taste·ful (tāst′fəl) *adj.* **1.** Having, showing, or being in keeping with good taste. **2.** Pleasing in flavor; tasty. **—taste′ful·ly** *adv.* **—taste′ful·ness** *n.*

taste·less (tāst′lĭs) *adj.* **1.** Lacking flavor; insipid. **2.** Not having or showing good taste. **—taste′less·ly** *adv.* **—taste′less·ness** *n.*

taste·mak·er (tāst′mā′kər) *n.* One that determines or strongly influences current trends or styles, as in fashion or the arts.

tast·er (tā′stər) *n.* **1.** One that tastes, especially one who samples a food or beverage for quality. **2.** Any of several devices or implements used in tasting.

tast·y (tā′stē) *adj.* **-i·er, -i·est. 1.** Having a pleasing flavor; savory. **2.** Having or showing good taste; tasteful. **—tast′i·ly** *adv.* **—tast′i·ness** *n.*

tat¹ (tăt) *intr. & tr.v.* **tat·ted, tat·ting, tats.** To do tatting or produce (something) by tatting. [Probably back-formation from TATTING.]

tat² also **TAT** (tăt) *n.* A gene in the AIDS virus that stimulates the host cell to replicate genetic components of the virus. [*t(rans)-a(c)t(ivator) (gene).*]

TAT *abbr.* Thematic Apperception Test.

Ta·ta·bán·ya (tŏ′tŏ-bän′yə). A city of northwest Hungary west of Budapest. It is an industrial center. Population, 76,823.

ta·ta·mi (tä-tä′mē, tə-) *n., pl.* **tatami** or **-mis.** Straw matting used as a floor covering especially in a Japanese house. [Japanese.]

Ta·tar (tä′tər) *n.* **1.** Also **Tar·tar** (tär′tər). A member of a group of Turkic peoples inhabiting southeast European U.S.S.R., the Crimea, and parts of Central Asian and Siberian U.S.S.R. **2. Tartar.** Any of the Turkic languages of the Tatars. **3.** Variant of **Tartar** (sense 1). **4. tatar.** A ferocious or violent person; a tartar.

Tatar Strait. A channel of southeast Russia between Sakhalin Island and the mainland. It connects the Sea of Japan on the south with the Sea of Okhotsk on the north.

Ta·ta·ry (tä′tə-rē). See **Tartary.**

Tate (tāt), **Allen.** 1899–1979. American writer and editor. A leading exponent of New Criticism, he edited the *Sewanee Review* (1944–1946) and is known especially for his poetry, including "Ode to the Confederate Dead" (1926).

Tate, Nahum. 1652–1715. English poet and playwright who wrote a popular adaptation of Shakespeare's *King Lear* (1687) and was appointed poet laureate in 1692.

♦**ta·ter** (tā′tər) *n. Upper Southern U.S.* Variant of **potato.** See Regional Notes at **holler², possum.** [Shortening and alteration of POTATO.]

Ta·tra Mountains (tä′trə). A range of the Carpathian Mountains in east-central Europe along the Czechoslovakia-Poland border. The Tatras are a popular resort area.

tat·ter¹ (tăt′ər) *n.* **1.** A torn and hanging piece of cloth; a shred. **2. tatters.** Torn and ragged clothing; rags. **—tatter** *tr. & intr.v.* **-tered, -ter·ing, -ters.** To make or become ragged. [Middle English *tater,* of Scandinavian origin.]

tat·ter² (tăt′ər) *n.* One that makes tatting, especially as a livelihood.

tat·ter·de·mal·ion (tăt′ər-dĭ-māl′yən, -mā′lē-ən) *n.* A person wearing ragged or tattered clothing; a ragamuffin. **—tatterdemalion** *adj.* Ragged; tattered. [Probably TATTERED + *-demalion,* of unknown meaning.]

tat·tered (tăt′ərd) *adj.* **1.** Torn into shreds; ragged. **2.** Having ragged clothes; dressed in tatters. **3.a.** Shabby or dilapidated. **b.** Disordered or disrupted.

tat·ter·sall also **Tat·ter·sall** (tăt′ər-sôl′, -səl) *—n.* **1.** A pattern of dark lines forming squares on a light background. **2.** Cloth woven or printed with this pattern. *—adj.* Having a pattern of dark lines forming squares on a light background. [After *Tattersall's* horse market, London, England, after Richard *Tattersall* (1724–1795), British auctioneer.]

tat·ting (tăt′ĭng) *n.* **1.** Handmade lace fashioned by looping and knotting a single strand of heavy-duty thread on a small hand shuttle. **2.** The act or art of making such lace. [Origin unknown.]

tat·tle (tăt′l) *v.* **-tled, -tling, -tles.** —*intr.* **1.** To reveal the plans or activities of another; gossip. See Synonyms at **gossip. 2.** To chatter aimlessly; prate. —*tr.* To reveal through gossiping. **—tattle** *n.* **1.** Aimless chatter; prattle. **2.** Gossip; talebearing. **3.** A tattletale. [Middle English *tatelen,* to stammer, probably from Middle Dutch, of imitative origin.] **—tat′tling·ly** *adv.*

tat·tler (tăt′lər) *n.* **1.** One who tattles. **2.** Any of several shore birds related to and resembling the sandpipers, especially one of the genus *Heteroscelus* that is noted for its loud cry.

tat·tle·tale (tăt′l-tāl′) *n.* One who tattles on others; an informer or a talebearer. **—tattletale** *adj.* Revealing; telltale.

tattletale gray *n. Color.* White tinged with gray; grayish white.

tat·too[1] (tă-to͞o′) *n., pl.* **-toos. 1.** A signal sounded on a drum or bugle to summon soldiers or sailors to their quarters at night. **2.** A display of military exercises offered as evening entertainment. **3.** A continuous, even drumming or rapping. **—tattoo** *v.* **-tooed, -too·ing, -toos.** —*intr.* To beat out an even rhythm, as with the fingers. —*tr.* To beat or tap rhythmically on; rap or drum on. [Alteration of Dutch *taptoe,* tap-shut (closing time for taverns), tattoo : *tap,* spigot, tap (from Middle Dutch *tappe*) + *toe,* shut (from Middle Dutch; see **de-** in Appendix).]

tat·too[2] (tă-to͞o′) *n., pl.* **-toos.** A permanent mark or design made on the skin by a process of pricking and ingraining an indelible pigment or by raising scars. **—tattoo** *tr.v.* **-tooed, -too·ing, -toos. 1.** To mark (the skin) with a tattoo. **2.** To form (a tattoo) on the skin. [Of Polynesian origin.] **—tat·too′er** *n.* **—tat·too′ist** *n.*

WORD HISTORY: The practice of tattooing the body is prehistoric, but the English word *tattoo* was introduced fairly recently. Our word came from Polynesian languages such as Tahitian and Samoan and was introduced to English speakers by the explorer Capt. James Cook (who also gave us the word *taboo*). The earliest use of the verb *tattoo* in English is found in 1769 in his account of a voyage around the world from 1768 to 1771. Cook also used a noun in his writings of 1769 but treated it as a native word so he is not given credit for the first use of the noun in English (recorded in 1777). In any event, sailors introduced the custom into Europe from the Pacific societies in which it was practiced, and it has remained associated with sailors, although many other people have tattoos as well.

tat·ty (tăt′ē) *adj.* **-ti·er, -ti·est.** Somewhat worn, shabby, or dilapidated. [Probably from *tat,* a rag, shabby person.]

Ta·tum (tā′təm), **Arthur.** Known as "Art." 1910–1956. American jazz pianist whose harmonic and rhythmic innovations influenced many other jazz musicians.

Tatum, Edward Lawrie. 1909–1975. American biochemist. He shared a 1958 Nobel Prize for discovering how genes transmit hereditary characteristics.

Ta·tung (tä′to͝ong′). See **Datong.**

tau (tou, tô) *n.* **1.** The 19th letter of the Greek alphabet. See table at **alphabet. 2.** An elementary particle of the lepton family, having a mass about 3,490 times that of the electron, a negative electric charge, and a mean lifetime of 3×10^{-13} seconds. See table at **subatomic particle.** [Greek, of Phoenician origin; akin to Hebrew *tāw,* tav.]

Tau·ba·té (tou′bä-tĕ′). A city of southeast Brazil northeast of São Paulo. Founded in 1645, it is a commercial center with an important textile industry. Population, 155,376.

tau cross *n.* A cross in the form of a T. Also called *Saint Anthony's cross.*

taught (tôt) *v.* Past tense and past participle of **teach.**

tau neutrino *n.* A probably stable elementary particle in the lepton family having a mass less than 69 times that of the electron and no charge. See table at **subatomic particle.**

taunt[1] (tônt) *tr.v.* **taunt·ed, taunt·ing, taunts. 1.** To reproach in a mocking, insulting, or contemptuous manner. See Synonyms at **ridicule. 2.** To drive or incite (a person) by taunting. **—taunt** *n.* A scornful remark or tirade; a jeer. [Origin unknown.] **—taunt′er** *n.* **—taunt′ing·ly** *adv.*

taunt[2] (tônt) *adj. Nautical.* Unusually tall. Used of masts. [Origin unknown.]

Taun·ton (tôn′tən, tŏn′-). A city of southeast Massachusetts on the **Taunton River** north of Fall River. Settled in the 1630's, it is a metalworking and manufacturing center. Population, 45,001.

Tau·nus Mountains (tou′nəs, -no͝os′). A range of western Germany extending northeast from the Rhine River.

taupe (tōp) *n. Color.* A brownish gray. [French, from Old French, mole, from Latin *talpa.*] **—taupe** *adj.*

Tau·re·an (tôr′ē-ən) *n.* One born under sign of Taurus. **—Tau′re·an** *adj.*

tau·rine[1] (tôr′īn′) *adj.* Of, relating to, or resembling a bull. [Latin *taurīnus,* from *taurus,* bull. See **tauro-** in Appendix.]

tau·rine[2] (tôr′ēn′) *n.* A colorless crystalline substance, $C_2H_7NO_3S$, formed by the hydrolysis of taurocholic acid and found in the fluids of the muscles and lungs of many animals. [Greek *tauros,* bull (from its having been obtained first from ox bile); see **tauro-** in Appendix + -INE[2].]

tau·ro·cho·lic acid (tôr′ō-kō′lĭk, -kŏl′ĭk) *n.* A crystalline acid, $C_{26}H_{45}NO_7S$, involved in the emulsification of fats and occurring as a sodium salt in the bile of human beings, oxen, and other mammals. [Greek *tauros,* bull (from its having been obtained first from ox bile); see **tauro-** in Appendix + CHOLIC ACID.]

Tau·rus (tôr′əs) *n.* **1.** A constellation in the Northern Hemisphere near Orion and Aries. **2. a.** The second sign of the zodiac. **b.** One who is born under this sign. Also called *Bull.* [Middle English, from Latin, bull, the constellation Taurus. See **tauro-** in Appendix.]

Taurus Mountains. A range of southern Turkey extending about 563 km (350 mi) parallel to the Mediterranean coast. It rises to 3,736.6 m (12,251 ft) and has important mineral deposits.

Tau·sug (tô′so͞og′) *n.* An Austronesian language spoken in the Sulu Archipelago. [Tausug : *ta'u,* people + *su:g,* current.]

taut (tôt) *adj.* **taut·er, taut·est. 1.** Pulled or drawn tight; not slack. See Synonyms at **tight. 2.** Strained; tense: *nerves taut with anxiety.* **3. a.** Kept in trim shape; neat and tidy. **b.** Marked by the efficient, sparing, and concise use of something, such as language or detail: *a taut movie script.* [Middle English *tohte,* distended, perhaps ultimately from Old English *togian,* to drag. See TOW[1].] **—taut′ly** *adv.* **—taut′ness** *n.*

taut– *pref.* Variant of **tauto–.**

tau·taug (tô′tôg′, -tŏg′, tô-tôg′, -tŏg′) *n.* Variant of **tautog.**

taut·en (tôt′n) *tr. & intr.v.* **-ened, -en·ing, -ens.** To make or become taut.

tauto– or **taut–** *pref.* Same; identical: *tautomerism.* [Greek, from *tauto,* the same, contraction of *to auto* : *to,* the; see **to-** in Appendix + *auto,* neuter of *autos,* same, self.]

tau·tog also **tau·taug** (tô′tôg′, -tŏg′, tô-tôg′, -tŏg′) *n.* A dark-colored, edible marine fish *(Tautoga onitis)* found along the North American Atlantic coast. Also called *blackfish.* [Narragansett *tautaûg.*]

tau·tol·o·gize (tô-tŏl′ə-jīz′) *intr.v.* **-gized, -giz·ing, -giz·es.** To use tautology. **—tau·tol′o·gist** (-jĭst) *n.*

tau·tol·o·gy (tô-tŏl′ə-jē) *n., pl.* **-gies. 1. a.** Needless repetition of the same sense in different words; redundancy. **b.** An instance of such repetition. **2.** *Logic.* An empty or vacuous statement composed of simpler statements in a fashion that makes it logically true whether the simpler statements are factually true or false; for example, the statement *Either it will rain tomorrow or it will not rain tomorrow.* [Late Latin *tautologia,* from Greek, from *tautologos,* redundant : *tauto-,* tauto- + *logos,* saying; see -LOGY.] **—tau′to·log′i·cal** (tôt′l-ŏj′ĭ-kəl), **tau′to·log′ic** (-ĭk) *adj.* **—tau′to·log′i·cal·ly** *adv.*

tau·tom·er·ism (tô-tŏm′ə-rĭz′əm) *n.* Chemical isomerism characterized by relatively easy interconversion of isomeric forms in equilibrium. [TAUTO– + (ISO)MERISM.] **—tau′to·mer** (tô′tə-mər) *n.* **—tau′to·mer′ic** (tô′tə-mĕr′ĭk) *adj.*

tau·to·nym (tô′tə-nĭm′) *n.* A taxonomic designation, such as *Gorilla gorilla,* in which the genus and species names are the same, commonly used in zoology but no longer in botany. **—tau′to·nym′ic, tau·ton′y·mous** (tô-tŏn′ə-məs) *adj.* **—tau·ton′y·my** *n.*

tav also **taw** (täf, tôf) *n.* The 23rd letter of the Hebrew alphabet. See table at **alphabet.** [Hebrew *tāw,* mark, cross (sense uncertain).]

tav·ern (tăv′ərn) *n.* **1.** An establishment licensed to sell alcoholic beverages to be consumed on the premises. **2.** An inn for travelers. [Middle English *taverne,* from Old French, from Latin *taberna,* hut, tavern, probably from **traberna,* from *trabs, trab-,* beam. See TRAVE.]

ta·ver·na (tə-vûr′nə, tä-vĕr′nä) *n.* A café or small restaurant in Greece. [Modern Greek *taberna,* from Medieval Greek, from Late Greek, from Latin. See TAVERN.]

taw[1] (tô) *tr.v.* **tawed, taw·ing, taws.** To convert (skin) into white leather by mineral tanning, as with alum and salt. [Middle English *tawen,* from Old English *tawian,* to prepare.]

♦**taw[2]** (tô) *n.* **1.** *Chiefly Southern U.S.* A large, fancy marble used for shooting. **2.** The line from which a player shoots in marbles. **3.** A game of marbles. **—taw** *intr.v.* **tawed, taw·ing, taws.** To shoot a marble. [Origin unknown.]

taw[3] (täf, tôf) *n.* Variant of **tav.**

taw·dry (tô′drē) *adj.* **-dri·er, -dri·est.** Gaudy and cheap in nature or appearance. See Synonyms at **gaudy[1]. —tawdry** *n.* Cheap and gaudy finery. [From *tawdry lace,* lace necktie, alteration of *Saint Audrey's lace* (sold at the annual Saint Audrey's fair, Ely, England), after *Saint Audrey* (Saint Etheldreda), queen of Northumbria, who died in 679 of a throat tumor, supposedly because she delighted in fancy necklaces as a young woman.] **—taw′dri·ly** *adv.* **—taw′dri·ness** *n.*

Taw·ney (tô′nē), **Richard Henry.** 1880–1962. British economic historian noted for his studies of the development of capitalism, including *Religion and the Rise of Capitalism* (1926).

taw·ny (tô′nē) *n. Color.* A light brown to brownish orange. [Middle English, from Anglo-Norman *taune,* variant of Old French *tane,* from past participle of *taner,* to tan. See TAN[1].] **—taw′ni·ness** *n.* **—taw′ny** *adj.*

tawny owl *n.* A common owl *(Strix aluco)* of Eurasia and northern Africa, having tawny wormlike markings.

tax (tăks) *n.* **1.** A contribution for the support of a government required of persons, groups, or businesses within the domain of that government. **2.** A fee or due levied on the members of an organization to meet its expenses. **3.** A burdensome or excessive demand; a strain. **—tax** *tr.v.* **taxed, tax·ing, tax·es. 1.** To

tattoo[2]

tau cross

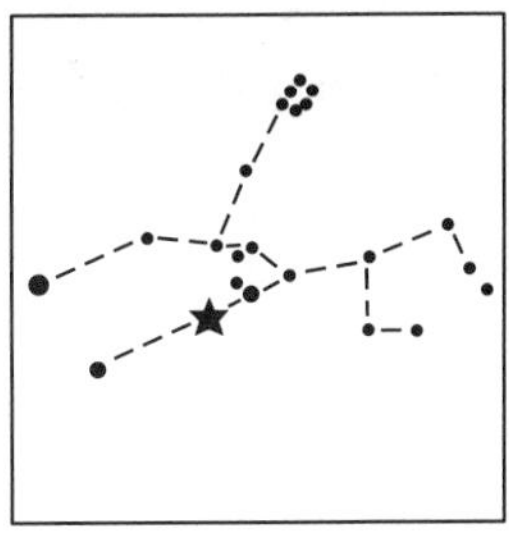

Taurus

ă pat	oi boy
ā pay	ou out
âr care	o͝o took
ä father	o͞o boot
ĕ pet	ŭ cut
ē be	ûr urge
ĭ pit	th thin
ī pie	*th* this
îr pier	hw which
ŏ pot	zh vision
ō toe	ə about, item
ô paw	♦ regionalism

Stress marks: ′ (primary); ′ (secondary), as in **dictionary** (dĭk′shə-nĕr′ē)

place a tax on (income, property, or goods). **2.** To exact a tax from. **3.** *Law.* To assess (court costs, for example). **4.** To make difficult or excessive demands upon: *a boss who taxed everyone's patience.* **5.** To make a charge against; accuse: *He was taxed with failure to appear on the day appointed.* [Middle English, from *taxen,* to tax, from Old French *taxer,* from Medieval Latin *taxāre,* from Latin, to touch, reproach, reckon, frequentative of *tangere,* to touch. See **tag-** in Appendix.] **—tax′er** *n.*

tax– *pref.* Variant of **taxo–.**

ta·xa (tăk′sə) *n.* Plural of **taxon.**

tax·a·ble (tăk′sə-bəl) *adj.* Subject to taxation: *taxable income.* **—taxable** *n.* One that is subject to taxation: *taxables such as cigarettes and liquor.* **—tax′a·bil′i·ty, tax′a·ble·ness** *n.* **—tax′a·bly** *adv.*

tax·a·tion (tăk-sā′shən) *n.* **1.a.** The act or practice of imposing taxes. **b.** The fact of being taxed. **2.** An assessed amount of tax. **3.** Revenue gained from taxes.

Tax·co (täs′kō). A town of southern Mexico south-southwest of Mexico City. An important mining town founded in 1529, it is a popular resort center. Population, 36,315.

tax-de·duct·i·ble (tăks′dĭ-dŭk′tə-bəl) *adj.* Exempt from inclusion in one's taxable income.

tax·eme (tăk′sēm′) *n. Linguistics.* A minimal linguistic feature, such as the order or stress of words in a compound or phonemes in a word. **—tax·e′mic** *adj.*

tax·es (tăk′sēz) *n. Biology & Medicine.* A plural of **taxis.**

tax evasion *n.* Intentional avoidance of tax payment usually by inaccurately declaring taxable income.

tax-ex·empt (tăks′ĭg-zĕmpt′) *adj.* **1.** Not subject to taxation, as the capital or income of a philanthropic organization. **2.** Producing interest that is exempt from income tax: *tax-exempt bonds.* **—tax-exempt** *n.* A tax-exempt security.

tax-free (tăks′frē′) *adj.* Not subject to taxation; tax-exempt.

tax·i (tăk′sē) *n., pl.* **tax·is** or **tax·ies.** A taxicab. **—taxi** *v.* **tax·ied** (tăk′sēd), **tax·i·ing** or **tax·y·ing, tax·ies** or **tax·is** (tăk′sēz). *—intr.* **1.** To be transported by taxi. **2.** To move slowly on the ground or on the surface of the water before takeoff or after landing: *an airplane taxiing down the runway.* *—tr.* **1.** To transport (someone or something) by or as if by taxi: *taxied the children to dance class; taxi documents to a law office.* **2.** To cause (an aircraft) to taxi. [Short for TAXIMETER, or TAXICAB.]

Zachary Taylor

WORD HISTORY: "Taxi" is much easier to yell into the traffic than *taximeter cabriolet,* the form from which *taxi* has ultimately been shortened. *Taximeter* comes from the French word *taximètre,* ultimately derived from Medieval Latin *taxāre,* "to tax," and the French combining form *-metre. Taximètre* originally meant, as did its English companion, "a device for measuring distance traveled," but this device was soon adapted to measure waiting time and compute and indicate the fare as well. *Taximeter,* first recorded in English in 1898 (an earlier form, *taxameter,* borrowed through French from German, was recorded in 1894), joined forces with *cab,* a shortening (1827) of *cabriolet,* "a two-wheeled, one-horse carriage." This word, first found in English in 1766, came from French *cabriolet,* of the same meaning, which in turn was derived from *cabriole,* "caper," because the vehicle moves along with a springing motion. *Cab,* the shortened form, was applied to other vehicles as well, including eventually public conveyances. Fitted with a taximeter, such a vehicle, first horse-drawn and then motorized, was known as a *taxameter cab* (1899), a *taximeter cab* (1907), and a *taxicab* (1907), among other names, including *taxi* (1907), a shortening of either *taximeter* or *taxicab.* Interestingly enough, the fullest form possible, *taximeter cabriolet,* is not recorded until 1959.

taxi– *pref.* Variant of **taxo–.**

tax·i·cab (tăk′sē-kăb′) *n.* An automobile that carries passengers for a fare, usually calculated by a taximeter. [TAXI(METER) + CAB [1].]

taxi dancer *n.* A woman employed, as by a dance hall or nightclub, to dance with the patrons for a fee. [From the fact that the dancers are hired, like taxis, for a short period of time.]

tax·i·der·my (tăk′sĭ-dûr′mē) *n.* The art or operation of preparing, stuffing, and mounting the skins of dead animals for exhibition in a lifelike state. **—tax′i·der′mal, tax′i·der′mic** *adj.* **—tax′i·der′mist** *n.*

tax·i·me·ter (tăk′sē-mē′tər) *n.* An instrument installed in a taxicab to measure distance traveled and waiting time and to compute and indicate the fare. [French *taximètre,* alteration of *taxamètre,* from German *Taxameter* : Medieval Latin *taxa,* tax (from *taxāre,* to tax; see TAX) + *-meter,* meter (from Greek *metron,* measure; see –METER).]

tax·i·met·rics (tăk′sə-mĕt′rĭks) *n. (used with a sing. verb).* See **numerical taxonomy.**

tax·ing (tăk′sĭng) *adj.* Burdensome; wearing: *a taxing business schedule.* **—tax′ing·ly** *adv.*

tax·is (tăk′sĭs) *n., pl.* **tax·es** (tăk′sēz). **1.** *Biology.* The responsive movement of a free-moving organism or cell toward or away from an external stimulus, such as light. **2.** *Medicine.* The moving of a body part by manipulation into normal position, as after a dislocation, fracture, or hernia. [Greek, arrangement, from *tassein, tattein, tag-,* to arrange.]

–taxis *suff.* **1.** Order; arrangement: *homotaxis.* **2.** Responsive movement; taxis: *chemotaxis.* [Greek, from *taxis.* See TAXIS.]

taxi squad *n. Football.* **1.** A group of professional players who are under contract to and practice with a team but are ineligible to play in official games. **2.** The four extra players on the roster of a professional team who are prepared to join the team on short notice, as to substitute for injured players.

taxi stand *n.* A reserved area where waiting taxicabs are parked.

tax·i·way (tăk′sē-wā′) *n.* A usually paved strip at an airport for use by aircraft in taxiing to and from a runway.

tax·man (tăks′măn′) *n.* One that is responsible for the collection of federal, state, or local taxes.

taxo– or **taxi–** or **tax–** *pref.* Order; arrangement: *taxidermy.* [From Greek *taxis.* See TAXIS.]

tax·on (tăk′sŏn′) *n., pl.* **ta·xa** (tăk′sə). *Biology.* A taxonomic category or group, such as a phylum, order, family, genus, or species. [New Latin, back-formation from TAXONOMY.]

tax·o·nom·ic (tăk′sə-nŏm′ĭk) also **tax·o·nom·i·cal** (-ĭ-kəl) *adj.* Of or relating to taxonomy: *a taxonomic designation.* **—tax′o·nom′i·cal·ly** *adv.*

tax·on·o·my (tăk-sŏn′ə-mē) *n., pl.* **-mies. 1.** The classification of organisms in an ordered system that indicates natural relationships. **2.** The science, laws, or principles of classification; systematics. **3.** Division into ordered groups or categories: *"Scholars have been laboring to develop a taxonomy of young killers"* (Aric Press). [French *taxonomie* : Greek *taxis,* arrangement; see TAXIS + *-nomie,* method (from Greek *-nomia;* see –NOMY).] **—tax·on′o·mist** *n.*

tax·pay·er (tăks′pā′ər) *n.* One that pays taxes or is subject to taxation. **—tax′pay′ing** *adj.*

tax return *n.* See **return** (sense 16).

tax shelter *n.* A financial operation, such as the use of special depletion allowances, that reduces taxes on current earnings. **—tax′-shel′tered** (tăks′shĕl′tərd) *adj.*

–taxy *suff.* Order; arrangement: *phyllotaxy.* [Greek *-taxia,* from *taktos,* arranged. See TAXIS.]

Tay (tā). A river of central Scotland rising in the Grampian Mountains and flowing about 190 km (118 mi) through **Loch Tay** to the **Firth of Tay,** an inlet of the North Sea.

Ta·yg·e·ta (tā-ĭj′ĭ-tə) *n.* **1.** *Greek Mythology.* One of the Pleiades. **2.** One of the six visible stars in the Pleiades cluster. [Latin *Tāygetē,* from Greek *Taugetē.*]

Tay·lor (tā′lər). A city of southeast Michigan, a suburb of Detroit. Population, 77,568.

Taylor, Edward. 1645?–1729. English-born American Puritan cleric and poet. Although his works were unpublished until 1939, he is now recognized as one of colonial America's finest poets.

Taylor, Elizabeth. Born 1932. British-born American actress. A childhood star after her appearance in *National Velvet* (1944), she later won an Academy Award for *Butterfield 8* (1960) and for *Who's Afraid of Virginia Woolf?* (1966).

Taylor, (James) Bayard. 1825–1878. American writer known especially for his travel books and his translation (1870–1871) of Goethe's *Faust.*

Taylor, Jeremy. 1613–1667. English bishop and writer whose most important works are *The Rule and Exercises of Holy Living* (1650) and *The Rule and Exercises of Holy Dying* (1651).

Taylor, (Joseph) Deems. 1885–1966. American composer and critic. He composed the suite for *Through the Looking Glass* (1918) and wrote *The Well-Tempered Listener* (1940).

Taylor, Laurette. 1884–1946. American actress best known for her portrayal of Amanda Wingfield in Tennessee Williams's *The Glass Menagerie.*

Taylor, Paul. Born 1930. American choreographer whose avant-garde work includes *Three Epitaphs* (1956) and *Orbs* (1966).

Taylor, Tom. 1817–1880. British playwright whose works include *Our American Cousin* (1858).

Taylor, Zachary. Known as "Old Rough and Ready." 1784–1850. The 12th President of the United States (1849–1850). An army officer in the Black Hawk War (1832) and the Second Seminole War (1835–1837), he became a national hero during the Mexican War (1846–1848) and was elected President in 1848. He died after less than two years in office.

Tay·lors·ville (tā′lərz-vĭl′). A community of north-central Utah, a suburb of Salt Lake City. Population, 17,448.

Tay·myr Peninsula (tī-mîr′). See **Taimyr Peninsula.**

tay·ra (tī′rə) *n.* A small South American carnivore *(Eira barbata)* closely related to the marten, having a broad head, slender body, and short dense fur. [Portuguese or Spanish *taira.*]

Tay-Sachs disease (tā′săks′) *n.* A hereditary disease that affects young children almost exclusively of eastern European Jewish descent, in which an enzyme deficiency leads to the accumulation of gangliosides in the brain and nerve tissue, resulting in mental retardation, convulsions, blindness, and, ultimately, death. [After Warren *Tay* (1843–1927), British physician, and Bernard *Sachs* (1858–1944), American neurologist.]

taz·za (tät′sə, -tsä) *n.* A shallow ornamental vessel usually on a pedestal. [Italian, cup, tazza, from Arabic *ṭast,* basin.]

Tb[1] The symbol for the element **terbium.**

Tb[2] *abbr. Bible.* Tobit.

TB also **T.B.** *abbr.* Tuberculosis.

t.b. *abbr.* **1.** Trial balance. **2.** Also **T.B.** Tubercle bacillus.

ă pat	oi boy
ā pay	ou out
âr care	ŏŏ took
ä father	ōō boot
ĕ pet	ŭ cut
ē be	ûr urge
ĭ pit	th thin
ī pie	*th* this
îr pier	hw which
ŏ pot	zh vision
ō toe	ə about, item
ô paw	♦ regionalism

Stress marks: **′** (primary); ′ (secondary), as in **dictionary** (dĭk′shə-nĕr′ē)

TAXONOMY OF LIFE

The taxonomic organization of species is hierarchical. Each species belongs to a genus, each genus belongs to a family, and so on through order, class, phylum, and kingdom. Associations within the hierarchy reflect evolutionary relationships, which are deduced typically from morphological and physiological similarities between species. So, for example, species in the same genus are more closely related and more alike than species in the same family.

Carolus Linnaeus, an eighteenth-century Swedish botanist, devised the system of **binomial nomenclature** used for naming species. In this system, each species is given a two-part Latin name, formed by appending a **specific epithet** to the genus name. By convention, the genus name is capitalized, and both the genus name and specific epithet are italicized, for example, *Canis familiaris* or simply *C. familiaris*.

Modern taxonomy recognizes five kingdoms, into which the estimated five million species of the world are divided. This table presents a familiar organism from each kingdom and the names of the taxonomic groups to which it belongs.

	DOG	SUGAR MAPLE	BREAD MOLD	INTESTINAL BACTERIUM	POND ALGA
KINGDOM	Animalia (animals)	Plantae (plants)	Fungi (fungi)	Prokaryotae (bacteria)	Protoctista (algae, protozoans, slime molds)
PHYLUM*	Chordata	Magnoliophyta	Zygomycota	Omnibacteria	Chlorophyta
CLASS	Mammalia	Rosidae	Zygomycetes	Enterobacteria	Euconjugatae
ORDER	Carnivora	Sapindales	Mucorales	Eubacteriales	Zygnematales
FAMILY	Canidae	Aceraceae	Mucoraceae	**	Zygnemataceae
GENUS	*Canis*	*Acer*	*Rhizopus*	*Escherichia*	*Spirogyra*
SPECIES	*C. familiaris*	*A. saccharum*	*R. stolonifer*	*E. coli*	*S. crassa*

* In botanical nomenclature, "division" is used instead of "phylum."
** *Escherichia coli* does not have a family classification.

TBA or **tba** *abbr.* To be announced.

T-bar (tē′bär′) *n. Sports.* A ski lift consisting of a bar suspended like an inverted T against which skiers lean while being towed uphill.

Tbi·li·si (tə-bə-lē′sē, -byĭ-lē′syĭ) also **Tif·lis** (tĭf′lĭs, tyə-flēs′). The capital of Georgia, in the southeast part of the region on the Kura River. An ancient city astride trade and migration routes between Europe and Asia Minor, it came under Russian control in 1801 and was a center of revolutionary activity in 1905. Population, 1,158,000.

T-bill (tē′bĭl′) *n.* A U.S. Treasury note.

T-bone (tē′bōn′) *n.* A thick porterhouse steak taken from the small end of the loin and containing a T-shaped bone. Also called *T-bone steak.*

tbs. *abbr.* **1.** Tablespoon. **2.** Tablespoonful.

tbsp. *abbr.* **1.** Tablespoon. **2.** Tablespoonful.

Tc The symbol for the element **technetium.**

T cell *n.* A principal type of white blood cell that completes maturation in the thymus and that has various roles in the immune system, including the identification of specific foreign antigens in the body and the activation and deactivation of other immune cells. Also called *T lymphocyte.* [*t(hymus-derived) cell.*]

Tchai·kov·sky (chī-kôf′skē), **Peter Ilich.** 1840–1893. Russian composer of often dramatic, richly expressive works, including the ballets *Swan Lake* (1877) and *The Nutcracker* (1892) and the opera *Eugene Onegin* (1879). **—Tchai·kov′sky·an, Tchai·kov′ski·an** *adj.*

tchotch·ke (chŏch′kə) *n.* Variant of **chachka.**

tchr. *abbr.* Teacher.

TD *abbr.* **1.** Tank destroyer. **2.** Also **td.** *Football.* Touchdown. **3.** Also **T.D.** Treasury Department.

TDD *abbr.* Telecommunications device for the deaf.

TDN also **T.D.N.** *abbr.* Total digestible nutrients.

TDY *abbr.* Temporary duty.

Te The symbol for the element **tellurium.**

tea (tē) *n.* **1.a.** An eastern Asian evergreen shrub or small tree *(Camellia sinensis)* having fragrant, nodding, cup-shaped white flowers and glossy leaves. **b.** The young, dried leaves of this plant, prepared by various processes and used to make a hot beverage. **2.** An aromatic, slightly bitter beverage made by steeping tea leaves in boiling water. **3.** Any of various beverages, made as by steeping the leaves of certain plants or by extracting an infusion especially from beef. **4.** Any of various plants having leaves used to make a tealike beverage. **5.** *Chiefly British.* **a.** An afternoon refreshment consisting usually of sandwiches and cakes served with tea. **b.** High tea. **6.** An afternoon reception or social gathering at which tea is served. **7.** *Slang.* Marijuana. [Probably Dutch *thee,* from Malay *teh,* from Chinese (Amoy) *te.*]

tea bag *n.* A small porous sack holding enough tea leaves to make an individual serving of tea.

tea ball *n.* A small perforated metal ball for holding tea leaves that are to be steeped in hot water.

tea·ber·ry (tē′bĕr′ē) *n.* **1.** See **wintergreen** (sense 1a). **2.** See **withe rod.** [From the use of its leaves as a tea substitute.]

tea biscuit *n.* Any of various plain cookies or biscuits often served with tea. Also called *teacake.*

tea caddy *n.* A small box or container for holding loose tea.

tea·cake (tē′kāk′) *n.* See **tea biscuit.**

tea·cart (tē′kärt′) *n.* See **tea wagon.**

tea ceremony *n.* The Japanese ceremonial ritual for the preparation, serving, and drinking of tea; chanoyu.

teach (tēch) *v.* **taught** (tôt), **teach·ing, teach·es.** *—tr.* **1.** To impart knowledge or skill to: *teaches children.* **2.** To provide knowledge of; instruct in: *teaches French.* **3.** To condition to a certain action or frame of mind: *teaching youngsters to be self-reliant.* **4.** To cause to learn by example or experience: *an accident that taught me a valuable lesson.* **5.** To advocate or preach: *teaches racial and religious tolerance.* **6.** To carry on instruction on a regular basis in: *taught high school for many years.* *—intr.* To give instruction, especially as an occupation. [Middle English *techen,* from Old English *tǣcan.* See **deik-** in Appendix.]

SYNONYMS: *teach, instruct, educate, train, school, discipline, drill.* These verbs mean to impart knowledge or skill. *Teach* is the most widely applicable: *teaching a child the alphabet; teaches political science. "We shouldn't teach great books; we should teach a love of reading"* (B.F. Skinner). *Instruct* usually suggests methodical teaching: *A graduate student instructed the freshmen in the rudiments of music theory. Educate* often implies formal instruction but especially stresses the development of innate capacities that leads to wide cultivation: *"All educated Americans, first or last, go to Europe"* (Ralph Waldo Emerson). *Train* suggests concentration on particular skills intended to fit a person for a desired role: *The young woman attends vocational school, where she is being trained as a computer technician. School* often implies an arduous learning process: *The violinist had been schooled to practice slowly to assure accurate intonation. Discipline* usually refers to the teaching of control, especially self-control: *The writer has disciplined himself to work between breakfast and lunch every day. Drill* implies rigorous instruction or training, often by repetition of a routine: *The French instructor drilled the students in irregular verbs.*

USAGE NOTE: Some grammarians have objected to the use of *teach* as a transitive verb when its object denotes an institution of learning, as in *Kim teaches grade school.* This usage has wide currency at all levels, however, and is supported by the analogy to phrases such as *grade-school teacher.* It should be regarded as entirely correct.

Teach (tēch) also **Thatch** (thăch), **Edward.** Known as "Blackbeard." Died 1718. English pirate who established a base on the North Carolina coast after 1713 and conducted acts of piracy off the coast of the American colonies and in the Caribbean.

teach·a·ble (tē′chə-bəl) *adj.* **1.** That can be taught: *teachable skills.* **2.** Able and willing to learn: *teachable youngsters.* **—teach′a·bil′i·ty, teach′a·ble·ness** *n.* **—teach′a·bly** *adv.*

teach·er (tē′chər) *n. Abbr.* **tchr.** One who teaches, especially one hired to teach.

teacher bird *n.* See **ovenbird** (sense 1). [Imitative of the bird's song.]

teach·er·ly (tē′chər-lē) *adj.* Of, relating to, or suggestive of a teacher: *"The tone is teacherly, unflappable, optimistic"* (Benjamin DeMott).

teach·ers college also **teach·ers' college** (tē′chərz) *n.* A college with a special curriculum for training teachers.

teach·er's pet (tē′chərz) *n., pl.* **teacher's pets** or **teachers' pets.** **1.** A student in special favor with a teacher. **2.** One who has gained favor with an authority.

Peter Ilich Tchaikovsky
Photographed in 1888

tea caddy
1737 English silver tea caddy by John Swift

teach-in (tēch′ĭn′) *n.* An extended session, as on a college or university campus, for lectures and discussions on an important, usually controversial issue.

teach•ing (tē′chĭng) *n.* **1.** The act, practice, occupation, or profession of a teacher. **2.a.** Something taught. **b.** A precept or doctrine. Often used in the plural: *the teachings of Buddha.* **—teaching** *adj.* **1.** Of, involving, or used for teaching: *teaching materials; teaching methods.* **2.** Working as a teacher or in teaching: *teaching assistants.*

teaching fellow *n.* A graduate student in a university or college who is awarded a fellowship that provides him or her with financial aid in exchange for teaching duties. **—teaching fellowship** *n.*

teaching hospital *n.* A hospital closely associated with a medical school and serving as a practical educational site for medical students, interns, and residents.

teaching machine *n.* Any of various devices designed to teach by presenting the student with a planned sequence of statements and questions and providing an immediate response to his or her answers.

tea•cup (tē′kŭp′) *n.* A small cup used with a saucer for serving tea.

tea•cup•ful (tē′kŭp-fo͝ol′) *n., pl.* **-fuls.** The amount that a teacup can hold.

tea dance *n.* A late-afternoon dance.

tea garden *n.* **1.** A garden open to the public where tea and light refreshments are served. **2.** A tea plantation.

tea•house (tē′hous′) *n.* A public establishment serving tea and light refreshments.

teak (tēk) *n.* **1.a.** A tall evergreen tree *(Tectona grandis)* of southeast Asia, having hard, heavy, durable yellowish-brown wood. **b.** The wood of this tree, used especially for furniture and in shipbuilding. **2.** *Color.* A grayish yellowish brown or grayish to moderate brown. [Portuguese *teca,* from Malayalam *tēkka.*] **—teak** *adj.*

tea•ket•tle (tē′kĕt′l) *n.* A covered kettle with a spout and handle, used for boiling water, as for tea.

teak•wood (tēk′wo͝od′) *n.* Teak.

teal (tēl) *n., pl.* **teal** or **teals. 1.** Any of several small, short-necked freshwater ducks, especially of the genus *Anas,* that feed on the surface of the water and often have brightly marked plumage. **2.** *Color.* A moderate or dark bluish green to greenish blue. [Middle English *tele.*] **—teal** *adj.*

team (tēm) *n.* **1.** *Sports & Games.* A group on the same side, as in a game. **2.** A group organized to work together: *a team of engineers.* **3.a.** Two or more draft animals used to pull a vehicle or farm implement. **b.** A vehicle along with the animal or animals harnessed to it. **4.** A group of animals exhibited or performing together, as horses at an equestrian show. **5.** A brood or flock. **6.** *Obsolete.* Offspring; lineage. *—attributive.* Often used to modify another noun: *team sports; a team effort.* See Usage Note at **collective noun. —team** *v.* **teamed, team•ing, teams.** *—tr.* **1.** To harness or join together so as to form a team. **2.** To transport or haul with a draft team. *—intr.* **1.** To form a team or an association. Often used with *up.* **2.** To drive a team or truck. [Middle English, team of draft animals, from Old English *tēam.* See **deuk-** in Appendix.]

team•mate (tēm′māt′) *n.* A fellow member of a team.

team play *n.* **1.** Collective play participated in by team members. **2.** Collective effort and mutual cooperation. **—team player** *n.*

team•ster (tēm′stər) *n.* **1.** One who drives a truck for hauling loads, especially as an occupation. **2.** One who drives a team.

team-teach (tēm′tēch′) *tr. & intr.v.* **-taught** (-tôt′), **-teach•ing, -teach•es.** To teach cooperatively with other teachers or to engage in such teaching.

team teaching *n.* A method of classroom instruction in which several teachers combine their individual subjects into one course which they teach as a team to a single group of students.

team•work (tēm′wûrk′) *n.* Cooperative effort by the members of a group or team to achieve a common goal.

Tea•neck (tē′nĕk′). A township of northeast New Jersey east-southeast of Paterson. It is mainly residential. Population, 42,355.

tea party *n.* An afternoon social gathering at which tea and light refreshments are served.

tea•pot (tē′pŏt′) *n.* A covered pot with a spout in which tea is steeped and from which it is served.

tea•poy (tē′poi′) *n.* **1.** A small table for holding a tea service. **2.** A small, decorative three-legged table. [Hindi *tipāī,* alteration (influenced by Hindi *tir,* three) of Persian *si-pāya,* three : *si,* three + Middle Persian *pāī,* foot; see **ped-** in Appendix.]

tear¹ (târ) *v.* **tore** (tôr, tōr), **torn** (tôrn, tōrn), **tear•ing, tears.** *—tr.* **1.** To pull apart or into pieces by force; rend. **2.** To make (an opening) by ripping: *tore a hole in my stocking.* **3.** To lacerate (the skin, for example). **4.** To separate forcefully; wrench: *tore the wrappings off the present.* **5.** To divide or disrupt: *was torn between opposing choices; a country that was torn by strife.* *—intr.* **1.** To become torn. **2.** To move with heedless speed; rush headlong. **—tear** *n.* **1.** The act of tearing. **2.** The result of tearing; a rip or rent. **3.** A great rush; a hurry. **4.** *Slang.* A carousal; a spree. ***—phrasal verbs.*** **tear around.** *Informal.* **1.** To move about in excited, often angry haste. **2.** To lead a wild life. **tear at. 1.** To pull at or attack violently: *The dog tore at the meat.* **2.** To distress greatly: *Their plight tore at his heart.* **tear away.** To remove (oneself, for example) unwillingly or reluctantly. **tear down. 1.** To demolish: *tear down old tenements.* **2.** To take apart; disassemble: *tear down an engine.* **3.** To vilify or denigrate. **tear into.** To attack with great vigor or violence: *tore into the food; tore into his opponent.* **tear off.** *Informal.* To produce hurriedly and casually: *tearing off article after news article.* **tear up. 1.** To tear to pieces. **2.** To make an opening in: *tore up the sidewalk to add a drain.* ***—idiom.*** **tear (one's) hair.** To be greatly upset or distressed. [Middle English *teren,* from Old English *teran.* See **der-** in Appendix.] **—tear′er** *n.*

SYNONYMS: *tear, rip, rend, split, cleave.* These verbs mean to separate or pull apart by force. *Tear* involves pulling something apart or into pieces: *"She tore the letter in shreds"* (Edith Wharton). *Rip* implies rough or forcible tearing apart or away, often along a dividing line such as a seam or joint: *Carpenters ripped up the old floorboards. Rend* usually refers to violent tearing or wrenching apart: *"Come as the winds come, when/Forests are rended"* (Sir Walter Scott). To *split* is to cut or break something into parts or layers, especially along its entire length or along a natural line of division: *"They* [wood stumps] *warmed me twice—once while I was splitting them, and again when they were on the fire"* (Henry David Thoreau). *Cleave* most often refers to splitting with or as if with a sharp instrument: *"The apple's cleft right through the core"* (J.C.F. von Schiller).

tear² (tîr) *n.* **1.a.** A drop of the clear salty liquid that is secreted by the lachrymal gland of the eye to lubricate the surface between the eyeball and eyelid and to wash away irritants. **b. tears.** A profusion of this liquid spilling from the eyes and wetting the cheeks, especially as an expression of emotion. **c. tears.** The act of weeping: *criticism that left me in tears.* **2.** A drop of a liquid or hardened fluid. **—tear** *intr.v.* **teared, tear•ing, tears.** To fill with tears. [Middle English, from Old English *tēar.* See **dakru-** in Appendix.]

tear•down (târ′down′) *n.* The act or process of taking apart or demolishing.

tear•drop (tîr′drŏp′) *n.* **1.** A single tear. **2.** An object shaped like a tear.

tear•ful (tîr′fəl) *adj.* **1.** Filled with or accompanied by tears: *tearful eyes; a tearful farewell.* **2.** So piteous as to excite tears: *a tearful melodrama.* **—tear′ful•ly** *adv.* **—tear′ful•ness** *n.*

tear gas (tîr) *n.* Any of various agents that on dispersal, usually from grenades or projectiles, irritate the eyes and cause blinding tears.

tear-gas (tîr′găs′) *tr.v.* **-gassed, -gas•sing, -gas•es.** To subject to tear gas: *"tear-gassed and arrested antiwar demonstrators"* (Pete Hamill).

tear•ing (târ′ĭng) *adj.* Marked by great or violent haste: *in a tearing hurry.*

tear•jerk•er (tîr′jûr′kər) *n.* *Slang.* A grossly sentimental story, drama, or performance. **—tear′-jerk′ing** *adj.*

tea•room (tē′ro͞om′, -ro͝om′) *n.* A restaurant or shop serving tea and other refreshments. Also called *teashop.*

tea rose *n.* **1.** Any of several cultivated roses derived from *Rosa odorata,* native to China, having fragrant yellowish or pink flowers. **2.** *Color.* A pale to strong yellowish pink.

tear sheet (târ) *n.* *Printing.* A page taken from a periodical and used chiefly to provide evidence to an advertiser of the publication of an advertisement.

tear•stain (tîr′stān′) *n.* A track or mark left by tears. **—tear′-stained′** *adj.*

tear•y (tîr′ē) *adj.* **-i•er, -i•est. 1.a.** Filled or wet with tears: *teary eyes.* **b.** Of or resembling tears. **2.** Causing weeping: *a teary movie; a teary good-bye.* **3.** Inclined to weep: *He becomes teary when he reminisces.* **—tear′i•ly** *adv.* **—tear′i•ness** *n.*

tear•y-eyed (tîr′ē-īd′) *adj.* **1.** Having tears in the eyes, as from emotion: *teary-eyed wedding guests.* **2.** Marked by tears or weeping: *a teary-eyed confession.*

Teas•dale (tēz′dāl′), **Sara.** 1884–1933. American poet whose classically styled lyrical works appeared in *Love Songs* (1917) and other collections.

tease (tēz) *v.* **teased, teas•ing, teas•es.** *—tr.* **1.** To annoy or pester; vex. **2.** To make fun of; mock playfully. **3.** To arouse hope, desire, or curiosity in without affording satisfaction. **4.a.** To urge persistently; coax: *teasing their mother for more candy.* **b.** To gain by persistent coaxing: *"the New York editor who could tease great books from the unpromising woolly jumble of an author's first draft"* (Ian Jack). **c.** To deal with or have an effect on as if by teasing. **5.** To cut (tissue, for example) into pieces for examination. **6.** To disentangle and dress the fibers of (wool, for example). **7.** To raise the nap of (cloth) by dressing, as with a fuller's teasel. **8.** To ruffle (the hair) by combing from the ends toward the scalp for an airy, full effect. *—intr.* To annoy or make fun of someone persistently. **—tease** *n.* **1.a.** The act of teasing. **b.** The state of being teased. **2.** One that teases, as: **a.** One given to playful mocking. **b.** A woman who behaves like a coquette. **c.** A preliminary remark or act intended to whet the curiosity. ***—phrasal verb.*** **tease out.** To get by or as if by untangling or releasing with a pointed tool or device: *"It takes a carefully trained expert to tease out the truth"* (Arthur Green). [Middle English *tesen,* to comb apart, from Old English *tǣsan.*] **—teas′ing•ly** *adv.*

tea·sel (tē′zəl) *n.* **1.** Any of several plants of the genus *Dipsacus,* native to the Old World, having flower heads surrounded by spiny bracts. **2.a.** The bristly flower head of *D. sativus,* used to produce a napped surface on wool and other fabrics. **b.** A wire device used to produce a napped surface. **—teasel** *tr.v.* **-seled, -sel·ing, -sels** or **-selled, -sel·ling, -sels.** To produce a napped surface on (a fabric). [Middle English *tesel,* from Old English *tǣsel.*]

teas·er (tē′zər) *n.* **1.a.** One that teases, as a device for teasing wool. **b.** One who engages in teasing; a tease. **2.** A puzzling problem. **3.** An advertisement that attracts customers by offering something extra or free. **4.** *Slang.* An attention-getting vignette or highlight presented before the start of a television show.

tea service *n.* A set of articles, such as matching cups and a teapot, used in serving tea. Also called *tea set.*

tea·shop (tē′shŏp′) *n.* **1.** See **tearoom. 2.** *Chiefly British.* A luncheonette or small restaurant.

tea·spoon (tē′spo͞on′) *n.* **1.** The common small spoon used especially in serving and consuming tea, coffee, and desserts. **2.** *Abbr.* **t., tsp., tsp** A household cooking measure equal to ⅓ tablespoon (about 5 milliliters). See table at **measurement.**

tea·spoon·ful (tē′spo͞on-fo͝ol′) *n., pl.* **-fuls.** *Abbr.* **t., tsp., tsp** The amount that a teaspoon can hold.

teat (tēt, tĭt) *n.* A nipple of the mammary gland; a mamilla. [Middle English *tete,* from Old French, of Germanic origin.] **—teat′ed** *adj.*

tea table *n.* A small table used for serving tea.

tea·time (tē′tīm′) *n.* The usual or traditional time for serving tea, as late afternoon.

tea towel *n.* A cloth for drying dishes; a dishtowel.

tea tray *n.* A tray for holding a tea service.

tea wagon *n.* A small table on wheels for serving tea or holding dishes. Also called *teacart.*

Te·bal·di (tə-bäl′dē, tĕ-), **Renata.** Born 1922. Italian-born operatic soprano known for her dramatic portrayal of heroines in works such as *Tosca* and *Madame Butterfly.*

Te·bet or **Te·beth** (tā′vās, tĕ-vĕt′) *n.* Variants of **Tevet.**

tec. *abbr.* **1.** Technical. **2.** Technician.

tech. *abbr.* **1.** Technical. **2.** Technician.

teched (tĕcht) *adj.* Variant of **tetched.**

tech·ie also **tek·kie** (tĕk′ē) *n. Informal.* One who studies or is highly interested or proficient in a technical field, especially electronics.

tech·ne·ti·um (tĕk-nē′shē-əm, -shəm) *n. Symbol* **Tc** A silvery-gray radioactive metal, the first synthetically produced element, having 14 isotopes with masses ranging from 92 to 105 and half-lives up to 2.6×10^6 years. It is used as a tracer and to eliminate corrosion in steel. Atomic number 43; melting point 2,200°C; specific gravity 11.50; valence 0, 2, 4, 5, 6, 7. See table at **element.** [From Greek *tekhnētos,* artificial, from *teknasthai,* to make by art, from *tekhnē,* art. See TECHNICAL.]

tech·ne·tron·ic (tĕk′nĭ-trŏn′ĭk) *adj.* Relating to or characterized by the changes effected by modern advances in technology and electronics: *the technetronic era; our technetronic society.* [TECHN(OLOGY) + E(LEC)TRONIC.]

tech·nic (tĕk′nĭk) *n.* **1. technics** *(used with a sing. or pl. verb).* The theory, principles, or study of an art or a process. **2. technics** *(used with a pl. verb).* Technical details, rules, or methods. **3.** Variant of **technique** (sense 2). **—technic** *adj.* Technical. [From Greek *tekhnikos,* of art, from *tekhnē,* art. See TECHNICAL.]

tech·ni·cal (tĕk′nĭ-kəl) *adj. Abbr.* **tec., tech. 1.** Of, relating to, or derived from technique. **2.a.** Having special skill or practical knowledge especially in a mechanical or scientific field: *a technical adviser.* **b.** Used in or peculiar to a specific field or profession; specialized: *technical terminology.* **3.a.** Belonging or relating to a particular subject: *technical expertise.* **b.** Of, relating to, or involving the practical, mechanical, or industrial arts or the applied sciences: *a technical school.* **4.a.** Abstract or theoretical: *a technical analysis.* **b.** Of, relating to, or employing the methodology of science; scientific. **5.** According to principle; formal rather than practical: *a technical advantage.* **6.** Industrial and mechanical; technological. **7.** Indicating a stock market in which prices are determined or affected by internal manipulation and speculation. **—technical** *n. Sports.* A technical foul. [From Greek *tekhnikos,* of art, from *tekhnē,* art. See **teks-** in Appendix.] **—tech′ni·cal·ly** *adv.*

technical foul *n. Sports.* A foul, especially in basketball, that is called on a player, coach, or team for unsportsmanlike conduct or infringement of a rule and does not usually involve physical contact with an opponent during play.

tech·ni·cal·i·ty (tĕk′nĭ-kăl′ĭ-tē) *n., pl.* **-ties. 1.** The quality or condition of being technical. **2.** Something meaningful or relevant only to a specialist: *a legal technicality.*

technical knockout *n. Abbr.* **TKO** *Sports.* A victory in boxing, with immediate termination of the match, awarded by the referee when it appears that one fighter is too badly injured to continue.

technical sergeant *n. Abbr.* **T. Sgt. 1.** A noncommissioned rank in the U.S. Air Force that is above staff sergeant and below master sergeant. **2.** One who holds this rank.

tech·ni·cian (tĕk-nĭsh′ən) *n. Abbr.* **tec., tech.** An expert in a technique, as: **a.** One whose occupation requires training in a specific technical process: *an electronics technician; an automotive technician.* **b.** One who is known for skill in an intellectual or artistic technique.

Tech·ni·col·or (tĕk′nĭ-kŭl′ər). A trademark used for a method of making color motion pictures in which films sensitive to different primary colors are exposed simultaneously and are later superimposed to produce the full-color print. This trademark, capitalized and lowercased, often occurs in figurative contexts in print: *"Trees in autumnal technicolor of crimson and gold turned suddenly white after a storm"* (Washington Post). *"In these garish, Technicolor vistas, in which the underlying rootlessness of Sargent's art is undiluted, he seems more neophyte tourist than lifelong traveler"* (Newsweek).

tech·nique (tĕk-nēk′) *n.* **1.** The systematic procedure by which a complex or scientific task is accomplished. **2.** Also **tech·nic** (tĕk′nĭk). **a.** The way in which the fundamentals, as of an artistic work, are handled. **b.** Skill or command in handling such fundamentals. See Synonyms at **art**[1]. [French, technical, technique, from Greek *tekhnikos,* technical. See TECHNICAL.]

tech·noc·ra·cy (tĕk-nŏk′rə-sē) *n., pl.* **-cies.** A government or social system controlled by technicians, especially scientists and technical experts. [Greek *tekhnē,* skill; see TECHNICAL + -CRACY.]

tech·no·crat (tĕk′nə-krăt′) *n.* **1.** An adherent or a proponent of technocracy. **2.** A technical expert, especially one in a managerial or administrative position. **—tech′no·crat′ic** *adj.*

technol. *abbr.* Technology.

tech·no·log·i·cal (tĕk′nə-lŏj′ĭ-kəl) also **tech·no·log·ic** (-lŏj′ĭk) *adj.* **1.** Relating to or involving technology, especially scientific technology. **2.** Affected by or resulting from scientific and industrial progress. **—tech′no·log′i·cal·ly** *adv.*

tech·nol·o·gist (tĕk-nŏl′ə-jĭst) *n.* A specialist in technology.

tech·nol·o·gize (tĕk-nŏl′ə-jīz′) *tr.v.* **-gized, -giz·ing, -giz·es.** To modify or affect by technology; make technological.

tech·nol·o·gy (tĕk-nŏl′ə-jē) *n., pl.* **-gies.** *Abbr.* **technol. 1.a.** The application of science, especially to industrial or commercial objectives. **b.** The scientific method and material used to achieve a commercial or industrial objective. **2.** *Anthropology.* The body of knowledge available to a civilization that is of use in fashioning implements, practicing manual arts and skills, and extracting or collecting materials. [Greek *tekhnologia,* systematic treatment of an art or craft : *tekhnē,* skill; see **teks-** in Appendix + *-logia,* -logy.]

tech·no·struc·ture (tĕk′nō-strŭk′chər) *n.* **1.** A large-scale corporate system. **2.** A network of skilled professionals who control such a corporate system. [TECHNO(LOGY) + STRUCTURE.]

tech·y (tĕch′ē) *adj.* Variant of **tetchy.**

tec·ta (tĕk′tə) *n.* Plural of **tectum.**

tec·ton·ic (tĕk-tŏn′ĭk) *adj.* **1.** *Geology.* Relating to, causing, or resulting from structural deformation of the earth's crust. **2.a.** Relating to construction or building. **b.** Architectural. [Late Latin *tectonicus,* from Greek *tektonikos,* from *tektōn,* builder. See **teks-** in Appendix.] **—tec·ton′i·cal·ly** *adv.*

tec·ton·ics (tĕk-tŏn′ĭks) *n. (used with a sing. verb).* **1.** The study of the earth's structural features. **2.** The art or science of construction, especially of large buildings.

tec·ton·ism (tĕk′tə-nĭz′əm) *n. Geology.* **1.** The structural behavior of an element of the earth's crust. **2.** Crustal instability. [TECTON(IC) + -ISM.]

tec·trix (tĕk′trĭks) *n., pl.* **-tri·ces** (-trĭ-sēz′). One of the coverts of a bird's wing. Often used in the plural. [Latin *tēctrix,* feminine of *tēctor,* plasterer, from *tēctus,* past participle of *tegere,* to cover. See **(s)teg-** in Appendix.]

tec·tum (tĕk′təm) *n., pl.* **-ta** (-tə). A rooflike structure of the body, especially the dorsal part of the mesencephalon. [Latin *tēctum,* roof, from neuter past participle of *tegere,* to cover. See **(s)teg-** in Appendix.] **—tec′tal** (-təl) *adj.*

Te·cum·seh (tĭ-kŭm′sə) or **Te·cum·tha** (-thə). 1768–1813. Shawnee leader who attempted to establish a confederacy to unify Native Americans against white encroachment. He sided with the British in the War of 1812 and was killed in the Battle of the Thames.

♦**ted** (tĕd) *tr.v.* **ted·ded, ted·ding, teds.** *Chiefly New England.* To strew or spread (newly mown grass, for example) for drying. [Middle English *tedden.*]

♦ ***REGIONAL NOTE:*** In 15th-century England the verb *ted* meant to spread newly cut hay to facilitate its drying. In the mid-19th century an American inventor produced a machine to ted the hay automatically and called it a *tedder.* Since modern English is inclined to make verbs out of nouns meaning implements or machines, the noun *tedder* became a verb with the same meaning as the original word *ted. Tedder,* a New England verb, also turns up in those parts of the Midwest that received settlers from New England.

♦**ted·der** (tĕd′ər) *Chiefly New England. n.* A machine that spreads newly mown hay for drying. See Regional Note at **ted. —tedder** *tr.v.* **-dered, -der·ing, -ders.** To ted.

ted·dy (tĕd′ē) *n., pl.* **-dies. 1.** A woman's undergarment combining a camisole top and panties. **2.** A teddy bear.

teddy bear also **Teddy bear** *n.* A child's toy bear, usually stuffed with soft material and covered with furlike plush. [After

teasel
Dipsacus sylvestris

ă pat	oi boy
ā pay	ou out
âr care	o͝o took
ä father	o͞o boot
ĕ pet	ŭ cut
ē be	ûr urge
ĭ pit	th thin
ī pie	*th* this
îr pier	hw which
ŏ pot	zh vision
ō toe	ə about, item
ô paw	♦ regionalism

Stress marks: ′ (primary); ′ (secondary), as in **dictionary** (dĭk′shə-nĕr′ē)

Teddy, nickname of Theodore Roosevelt, who was depicted in a cartoon sparing the life of a bear cub.]

Teddy boy *n.* A tough British youth wearing a modified style of Edwardian clothes. [From the name *Teddy,* nickname for *Edward,* after EDWARD VII.]

Te De·um (tā′ dā′əm, -o͞om, tē′ dē′əm) *n.* A hymn of praise to God sung as part of a liturgy. [From Late Latin *Tē Deum (laudāmus),* You, God, (we praise), the opening words of the hymn : Latin *tē,* you + Latin *deum,* accusative of *deus,* god.]

te·di·ous (tē′dē-əs) *adj.* **1.** Tiresome by reason of length, slowness, or dullness; boring. See Synonyms at **boring. 2.** *Obsolete.* Moving or progressing very slowly. [Middle English, from Late Latin *taediōsus,* from Latin *taedium,* tedium.] **—te′di·ous·ly** *adv.* **—te′di·ous·ness** *n.*

te·di·um (tē′dē-əm) *n.* The quality or condition of being tedious; tediousness or boredom. See Synonyms at **boredom.** [Latin *taedium,* from *taedēre,* to weary.]

tee[1] (tē) *n.* **1.** The letter *t.* **2.** Something shaped like a T. **3.** *Sports & Games.* A mark aimed at in certain games, such as curling or quoits. ***—idiom.* to a tee.** Perfectly; exactly: *a plan that suits me to a tee.*

tee[2] (tē) *n. Sports.* **1.** A small peg with a concave top for holding a golf ball for an initial drive. **2.** The designated area of each golf hole from which a player makes his or her first stroke. **—tee** *tr.v.* **teed, tee·ing, tees.** *Sports.* To place (a golf ball) on a tee. Often used with *up.* ***—phrasal verb.* tee off. 1.** *Sports.* To drive a golf ball from the tee. **2.** *Slang.* To start or begin: *They teed off the fundraising campaign with a dinner.* **3.** *Slang.* To make or become angry or disgusted: *The impertinent remarks teed the speaker off. He was teed off because it rained all weekend.* [Back-formation from obsolete Scots *teaz* (taken as a pl.).]

♦**tee·dle board** (tēd′l) *n. Northeastern Massachusetts.* See **seesaw** (sense 1). See Regional Note at **teeter-totter.** [Probably alteration of TEETERBOARD.]

teem[1] (tēm) *v.* **teemed, teem·ing, teems.** *—intr.* **1.** To be full of things; abound or swarm: *A drop of water teems with microorganisms.* **2.** *Obsolete.* To be or become pregnant; bear or produce young. *—tr. Archaic.* To give birth to. [Middle English *temen,* to beget, bear, from Old English *tīeman, tēman.* See **deuk-** in Appendix.] **—teem′er** *n.* **—teem′ing·ly** *adv.*

SYNONYMS: *teem, abound, bristle, crawl, overflow, swarm.* The central meaning shared by these verbs is "to be abundantly filled or richly supplied": *a street teeming with pedestrians; a garden abounding with flowers; roofs bristling with television antennas; a highway crawling with cars; a house overflowing with guests; a parade route swarming with spectators.*

teem[2]

teem[2] (tēm) *tr.v.* **teemed, teem·ing, teems.** To pour out or empty: *teemed the molten ore into a huge mold.* [Middle English *temen,* from Old Norse *tōma.*]

teen[1] (tēn) *n.* **1. teens. a.** The numbers 13 through 19. **b.** The 13th through 19th items in a series or scale, as years of a century or degrees of temperature. **2.** A teenager. **—teen** *adj.* Teenage.

teen[2] (tēn) *n. Archaic.* Misery; grief. [Middle English *tene,* from Old English *tēona.*]

teen·age or **teen-age** (tēn′āj′) also **teen·aged** or **teen-aged** (-ājd′) *adj.* Of, relating to, or applicable to those aged 13 through 19.

teen·ag·er also **teen-ag·er** (tēn′ā′jər) *n.* A person between the ages of 13 and 19; an adolescent.

teen·er (tē′nər) *n.* **1.** *Informal.* A teenager. **2.** *Slang.* An entertainment, especially a movie, aimed at a teenage audience.

teen·sy (tēn′sē) *adj.* **-si·er, -si·est.** *Informal.* Variant of **teeny.**

teen·sy-ween·sy (tēn′sē-wēn′sē) or **teen·y-ween·y** (tē′nē-wē′nē) *adj. Informal.* Tiny. [Alteration of *teeny-weeny,* reduplication and alteration of TEENY.]

tee·ny (tē′nē) also **teen·sy** (tēn′sē) *adj.* **-ni·er, -ni·est** also **-si·er, -si·est.** *Informal.* Tiny. [Alteration of TINY.]

teen·y·bop·per (tē′nē-bŏp′ər) *n. Slang.* **1.** A young teenage girl. **2.** A teenager who follows the latest fad or craze, as in dress or music. [TEEN[1] + –Y[1] + BOP[2] + –ER[1].]

tee·off (tē′ôf′, -ŏf′) *n. Sports.* The act or an instance of teeing off in golf.

tee·pee (tē′pē) *n.* Variant of **tepee.**

Tees (tēz). A river, about 113 km (70 mi) long, of northeast England flowing generally east to the North Sea.

tee shirt *n.* Variant of **T-shirt.**

♦**tee·ter** (tē′tər) *v.* **-tered, -ter·ing, -ters.** *—intr.* **1.** To walk or move unsteadily or unsurely; totter. **2.** To alternate, as between opposing attitudes or positions; vacillate. **3.** To seesaw. *—tr.* To cause to teeter or seesaw. **—teeter** *n. Northeastern U.S.* **1.** See **seesaw** (sense 1). See Regional Note at **teeter-totter. 2.** A teetering motion. [Middle English *titeren,* probably from Old Norse *titra,* to shake.]

♦**tee·ter·board** (tē′tər-bôrd′, -bōrd′) *n. Northeastern U.S.* **1.** See **seesaw** (sense 1). See Regional Note at **teeter-totter. 2.** *Sports.* A board with one end raised so that when an acrobat or a tumbler jumps onto it, another performer standing on the opposite end is tossed into the air.

♦**tee·ter-tot·ter** (tē′tər-tŏt′ər) *n. Inland Northern & Western U.S.* See **seesaw** (sense 1).

♦ ***REGIONAL NOTE:*** The outdoor toy usually called a *seesaw* has a number of regional names, New England having the greatest variety in the smallest area. In southeast New England it is called a *tilt* or a *tilting board.* Speakers in northeast Massachusetts call it a *teedle board;* in the Narragansett Bay area the term changes to *dandle* or *dandle board. Teeter* or *teeterboard* is used more generally in the northeast United States, while *teeter-totter,* probably the most common term after *seesaw,* is used across the inland northern states and westward to the West Coast. Both *seesaw* (from the verb *saw*) and *teeter-totter* (from *teeter,* as in *to teeter on the edge*) demonstrate the linguistic process called reduplication, where a word or syllable is doubled, often with a different vowel. Reduplication is typical of words that indicate repeated activity, such as riding up and down on a seesaw.

teeth (tēth) *n.* Plural of **tooth.**

teethe (tēth) *intr.v.* **teethed, teeth·ing, teethes.** To grow teeth; cut one's teeth. [Middle English *tethen,* from *teth,* pl. of *tooth,* tooth. See TOOTH.]

teeth·er (tē′thər) *n.* An object or a device, such as a teething ring, for a baby to bite on during teething.

teeth·ing (tē′thĭng) *n.* The eruption and cutting of teeth, especially the milk teeth; dentition.

teething ring *n.* A ring of hard plastic or rubber upon which a teething baby can bite.

teeth·ridge (tēth′rĭj′) *n.* The ridge of gum behind the upper front teeth.

tee·to·tal (tē′tōt′l) *adj.* **1.** Of, relating to, or practicing complete abstinence from alcoholic beverages. **2.** Total; absolute. [Probably partly TEE[1] (pronunciation of the first letter in *total*) + *total (abstinence),* and partly reduplication of TOTAL.] **—tee·to′tal·ly** *adv.*

tee·to·tal·er or **tee·to·tal·ler** (tē′tōt′l-ər) also **tee·to·tal·ist** (-ĭst) *n.* One who abstains completely from alcoholic beverages. **—tee·to′tal·ism** *n.*

tee·to·tum (tē-tō′təm) *n. Games.* A top, usually having four lettered sides, that is used to play various games of chance. [From earlier *T totum* (from the letter tee that appeared on one side of the toy), from *totum,* teetotum, from Latin *tōtum,* neuter sing. of *tōtus,* all. See **teutā-** in Appendix.]

te·fil·lin (tə-fĭl′ĭn, -fē-lēn′) *pl.n.* The phylacteries worn by Jewish men. [Hebrew *təpīlīn,* from Aramaic, attachments.]

TEFL *abbr.* Teaching English as a foreign language.

Tef·lon (tĕf′lŏn′). A trademark used for a waxy, opaque material, polytetrafluoroethylene, employed as a coating on cooking utensils and in industrial applications to prevent sticking. This trademark often occurs in figurative contexts in print: *"It would make of Gorbachev's stewardship a truly Teflon chairmanship, demonstrating that no Soviet actions, regardless of how egregious, will cling to him"* (New Republic). *"It's clear that because* [he] *doesn't aspire to saving the entire human race, he's not going to get what the other leaders get—a coating of moral and political Teflon"* (Wall Street Journal).

teg also **tegg** (tĕg) *n.* A sheep in its second year or before its first shearing. [Origin unknown.]

teg·men (tĕg′mən) *n., pl.* **-mi·na** (-mə-nə). A covering or an integument, such as the tough, leathery forewing of certain insects or the inner coat of a seed. Also called *tegmentum.* [Latin, covering, from *tegere,* to cover. See **(s)teg-** in Appendix.]

teg·men·tum (tĕg-mĕn′təm) *n.* **1.** See **tegmen. 2.** A part of the mesencephalon consisting of white fibers running lengthwise through gray matter. [Latin, covering, from *tegere,* to cover. See **(s)teg-** in Appendix.] **—teg·men′tal** (-təl) *adj.*

teg·mi·na (tĕg′mə-nə) *n.* Plural of **tegmen.**

te·gu (tĭ-go͞o′) *n.* A large, swift teiid lizard *(Tupinambis nigropunctatus)* of Colombia and Brazil, having yellow spots and stripes over a bluish-black body. [Portuguese *tejú,* from Tupi *teyú.*]

te·gua (tā′gwä, tā′wä) *n.* An ankle-high moccasin worn in parts of Mexico and the Southwest. [Origin unknown.]

Te·gu·ci·gal·pa (tə-go͞o′sə-găl′pə, tĕ-go͞o′sē-gäl′pä). The capital and largest city of Honduras, in the south-central part of the country. Founded in the late 16th century as a mining center, it became capital of the country in 1880. Population, 532,500.

teg·u·lar (tĕg′yə-lər) also **teg·u·lat·ed** (-lā′tĭd) *adj.* Relating to or resembling a tile. [From Latin *tēgula,* tile, from *tegere,* to cover. See **(s)teg-** in Appendix.] **—teg′u·lar·ly** *adv.*

teg·u·ment (tĕg′yə-mənt) *n.* A natural outer covering; an integument. [Middle English, from Latin *tegumentum,* from *tegere,* to cover. See **(s)teg-** in Appendix.] **—teg′u·men′ta·ry** (-mĕn′tə-rē, -mĕn′trē), **teg′u·men′tal** (-mĕn′tl) *adj.*

Teh·ran or **Te·he·ran** (tĕ′ə-răn′, -rän′, tĕ-răn′, -rän′). The capital and largest city of Iran, in the north-central part of the country south of the Caspian Sea. A commercial and industrial center, it became capital in the late 1700's. Population, 5,734,199.

Te·huan·te·pec (tə-wän′tə-pĕk′, tĕ-wän′tĕ-), **Isthmus of.** An isthmus of southern Mexico between the Bay of Campeche and the **Gulf of Tehuantepec,** a wide inlet of the Pacific Ocean.

Te·huel·che (tə-wĕl′chē, tā-wĕl′chā) *n., pl.* **Tehuelche** or **-ches. 1.** A member of a South American Indian people of Patagonia, virtually exterminated by the European settlers. **2.** The language of the Tehuelche. **—Te·huel′che·an** (-chē-ən) *adj.*

teig·lach (tāg′läkh′, tĭg′-) *pl.n. (used with a sing. or pl. verb).* A confection consisting of bits of dough cooked briefly in a mixture of honey, brown sugar, and nuts, then cooled and rolled into balls. [Yiddish *teyglekh,* from *teygl,* diminutive of *teyg,* dough, from Middle High German *teig,* from Old High German *teic.* See **dheigh-** in Appendix.]

tei·id (tē′ĭd) *adj.* Of or belonging to the Teiidae, a large family of mainly tropical American lizards characterized by a long forked tongue and the absence of bony plates beneath the scales. **—teiid** *n.* A lizard of the family Teiidae. [From New Latin *Teiidae,* family name, from *Teius,* type genus, from Portuguese *tejú,* tegu. See TEGU.]

Teil·hard de Char·din (tā-yär′ də shär-dăn′), **Pierre.** 1881–1955. French priest, paleontologist, and philosopher who maintained that the universe and humankind are evolving toward a perfect state.

Te Ka·na·wa (tĭ kä′nə-wə), Dame **Kiri.** Born 1944. New Zealand operatic soprano noted for her rich, lyric voice and her leading roles, such as Desdemona in Verdi's *Otello.*

tek·kie (tĕk′ē) *n. Informal.* Variant of **techie.**

tek·tite (tĕk′tīt′) *n.* Any of numerous generally small, rounded, dark brown to green glassy objects that are composed of silicate glass and are thought to have been formed by the impact of a meteorite with the earth's surface. [Greek *tēktos,* molten (from *tēkein,* to melt) + –ITE[1].] **—tek·tit′ic** (-tĭt′ĭk) *adj.*

tel. *abbr.* **1.** Telegram. **2.** Telegraph. **3.** Telegraphic. **4.** Telephone.

tel–[1] *pref.* Variant of **tele–.**

tel–[2] *pref.* Variant of **telo–.**

tel·aes·the·sia (tĕl′ĭs-thē′zhə) *n.* Variant of **telesthesia.**

tel·a·mon (tĕl′ə-mŏn′) *n., pl.* **-mon·es** (-mō′nēz). *Architecture.* A figure of a man used as a supporting pillar. [Latin *telamōn,* from Greek, bearer. See **tela-** in Appendix.]

Tel·a·mon (tĕl′ə-mən, -mŏn′) *n. Greek Mythology.* One of the Argonauts and the father of Ajax.

tel·a·mon·es (tĕl′ə-mō′nēz) *n. Architecture.* Plural of **telamon.**

tel·an·gi·ec·ta·sia (tĕl-ăn′jē-ĕk-tā′zhə) also **tel·an·gi·ec·ta·sis** (-ĕk′tə-sĭs) *n.* Chronic dilation of groups of capillaries causing elevated dark red blotches on the skin. [New Latin : TEL(O)– + Greek *angeion,* vessel; see ANGIO– + Greek *ektasis,* expansion (from *ekteinein,* to stretch out : *ek-, ex,* ex- + *teinein,* to stretch; see **ten-** in Appendix).] **—tel·an′gi·ec·tat′ic** (-tăt′ĭk) *adj.*

Tel A·viv–Jaf·fa (tĕl′ ə-vēv′-jăf′ə, -yäf′ə, ä-vēv′-). A city of west-central Israel on the Mediterranean Sea west-northwest of Jerusalem. Tel Aviv was founded in 1909 by settlers from the ancient city of Jaffa. The communities merged in 1950, forming what is now the largest city in Israel. Population, 323,400.

tele– or **tel–** *pref.* **1.** Distance; distant: *telesthesia.* **2.a.** Telegraph; telephone: *telegram.* **b.** Television: *telecast.* [Greek *tēle-,* from *tēle,* far off. See **kʷel-[2]** in Appendix.]

tel·e·cam·er·a (tĕl′ĭ-kăm′ər-ə, -kăm′rə) *n.* A television camera.

tel·e·cast (tĕl′ĭ-kăst′) *v.* **-cast** or **-cast·ed, -cast·ing, -casts.** *—intr.* To broadcast a television program. *—tr.* To broadcast (a program) by television. **—telecast** *n.* A television broadcast. **—tel′e·cast′er** *n.*

tel·e·com (tĕl′ĭ-kŏm′) *n. Informal.* Telecommunication.

tel·e·com·mu·ni·cate (tĕl′ĭ-kə-myo͞o′nĭ-kāt′) *v.* **-cat·ed, -cat·ing, -cates.** *—tr.* To transmit (data, for example) by telecommunication. *—intr.* To communicate by means of telecommunication: *telecommunicating with an overseas firm.* **—tel′e·com·mu′ni·ca′tor** *n.*

tel·e·com·mu·ni·ca·tion (tĕl′ĭ-kə-myo͞o′nĭ-kā′shən) *n.* **1.** Often **telecommunications.** *(used with a sing. verb).* The science and technology of communication at a distance by electronic transmission of impulses, as by telegraph, cable, telephone, radio, or television: *Telecommunications is an important area of professional growth.* **2.** Often **telecommunications.** *(used with a pl. verb).* The electronic systems used in transmitting messages, as by telegraph, cable, telephone, radio, or television: *Telecommunications were disrupted by the brownout.* **3.** A message so transmitted.

tel·e·com·mute (tĕl′ĭ-kə-myo͞ot′) *intr.v.* **-mut·ed, -mut·ing, -mutes.** *Computer Science.* To engage in telecommuting. **—tel′e·com·mut′er** *n.*

tel·e·com·mut·ing (tĕl′ĭ-kə-myo͞o′tĭng) *n. Computer Science.* The practice of working at home by using a modem and a computer terminal connected with one's business office.

tel·e·con·fer·ence (tĕl′ĭ-kŏn′fər-əns, -frəns) *n.* A conference held among people in different locations by means of telecommunications equipment, such as closed-circuit television. **—teleconference** *intr.v.* **-enced, -enc·ing, -enc·es.** To hold or participate in a teleconference. **—tel′e·con′fer·enc·ing** *n.*

Tel·e·cop·ier (tĕl′ə-kŏp′ē-ər). A trademark used for a transmitting and receiving telecommunication device for producing facsimile copies of documents.

tel·e·course (tĕl′ĭ-kôrs′, -kōrs′) *n.* A course of televised lectures, as one offered by a university.

tel·e·dra·ma (tĕl′ĭ-drä′mə, -drăm′ə) *n.* A drama intended especially for television presentation.

tel·e·du (tĕl′ĭ-do͞o′) *n.* A small carnivorous mammal *(Mydaus javanensis)* of Sumatra, Borneo, and Java, having a blackish coat and white forehead and characteristically emitting an offensive odor when disturbed. [Malay *tĕledu.*]

tel·e·fac·sim·i·le (tĕl′ə-făk-sĭm′ə-lē) *n.* A method for the electronic transmission and reproduction of graphic images or printed matter via signals sent over telephone lines.

tel·e·film (tĕl′ə-fĭlm′) *n.* A film produced for television broadcasting.

teleg. *abbr.* **1.** Telegram. **2.** Telegraph. **3.** Telegraphic. **4.** Telegraphy.

tel·e·gen·ic (tĕl′ə-jĕn′ĭk) *adj.* Having a physical appearance and exhibiting personal qualities that are deemed highly appealing to television viewers: *"Do we insist on a telegenic President?"* (William F. Buckley, Jr.). **—tel′e·gen′i·cal·ly** *adv.*

te·leg·o·ny (tə-lĕg′ə-nē) *n.* The supposed genetic influence of a previous sire on offspring of a subsequent sire from the same mother. **—tel′e·gon′ic** (tĕl′ə-gŏn′ĭk), **te·leg′o·nous** (tə-lĕg′ə-nəs) *adj.*

tel·e·gram (tĕl′ĭ-grăm′) *n. Abbr.* **tel., teleg.** A message transmitted by telegraph. **—telegram** *tr. & intr.v.* **-grammed, -gram·ming, -grams.** To telegraph (something) or be telegraphed.

tel·e·graph (tĕl′ĭ-grăf′) *n. Abbr.* **tel., teleg. 1.** A communications system that transmits and receives simple unmodulated electric impulses, especially one in which the transmission and reception stations are directly connected by wires. **2.** A message transmitted by telegraph; a telegram. **—telegraph** *v.* **-graphed, -graph·ing, -graphs.** *—tr.* **1.** To transmit (a message) by telegraph. **2.** To send or convey a message to (a recipient) by telegraph. **3.a.** To make known (a feeling or an attitude, for example) by nonverbal means: *telegraphed her derision with a smirk.* **b.** To make known (an intended action, for example) in advance or unintentionally: *By massing troops on the border, the enemy telegraphed its intended invasion to the target country.* *—intr.* To send or transmit a telegram. **—te·leg′ra·pher** (tə-lĕg′rə-fər), **te·leg′ra·phist** (-fĭst) *n.*

tel·e·graph·ic (tĕl′ĭ-grăf′ĭk) also **tel·e·graph·i·cal** (-ĭ-kəl) *adj.* **1.** *Abbr.* **tel., teleg.** Of, relating to, or transmitted by telegraph. **2.** Brief or concise: *a telegraphic style of writing.* **—tel′e·graph′i·cal·ly** *adv.*

telegraph plant *n.* A tropical Asian plant *(Desmodium motorium)* having trifoliolate compound leaves, whose lateral leaflets are very small and move by jerks under the influence of sunshine.

te·leg·ra·phy (tə-lĕg′rə-fē) *n. Abbr.* **teleg.** Communication by means of the telegraph.

Tel·e·gu (tĕl′ə-go͞o′) *n. & adj.* Variant of **Telugu.**

tel·e·ki·ne·sis (tĕl′ĭ-kĭ-nē′sĭs, -kī-) *n.* The movement of objects by scientifically inexplicable means, as by the exercise of an occult power. **—tel′e·ki·net′ic** (-nĕt′ĭk) *adj.* **—tel′e·ki·net′i·cal·ly** *adv.*

Te·lem·a·chus (tə-lĕm′ə-kəs) *n. Greek Mythology.* The son of Odysseus and Penelope, who helped his father kill Penelope's suitors.

Te·le·mann (tā′lə-män′), **Georg Philipp.** 1681–1767. German composer of the late baroque period. He wrote orchestral suites, chamber works, and operas.

tel·e·mark (tĕl′ə-märk′) *Sports. n.* A downhill turn performed on cross-country skis in which the knees are bent, the inside heel is lifted, and the weight is on the outside ski, which is advanced ahead of the other and angled inward until the turn is complete. **—telemark** *intr.v.* **-marked, -mark·ing, -marks.** To execute a telemark turn or to ski using this turn. [Norwegian, after *Telemark,* a region of southern Norway.]

tel·e·mar·ket·ing (tĕl′ə-mär′kĭ-tĭng) *n.* Use of the telephone in marketing goods or services. **—tel′e·mar′ket·er** *n.*

tel·e·me·ter (tĕl′ə-mē′tər, tə-lĕm′ĭ-tər) *n.* A measuring, transmitting, and receiving device used in telemetry. **—telemeter** (tĕl′ə-mē′tər) *tr.v.* **-tered, -ter·ing, -ters.** To measure, transmit, and receive (data) automatically from a distant source, as from a spacecraft or an electric power grid.

te·lem·e·try (tə-lĕm′ĭ-trē) *n.* The science and technology of automatic measurement and transmission of data by wire, radio, or other means from remote sources, as from space vehicles, to receiving stations for recording and analysis. **—tel′e·met′ric** (tĕl′ə-mĕt′rĭk), **tel′e·met′ri·cal** (-rĭ-kəl) *adj.* **—tel′e·met′ri·cal·ly** *adv.*

tel·en·ceph·a·lon (tĕl′ĕn-sĕf′ə-lŏn′, -lən) *n.* The anterior portion of the forebrain, constituting the cerebral hemispheres and related parts. Also called *endbrain.* **—tel′en·ce·phal′ic** (-sə-făl′ĭk) *adj.*

tel·e·ol·o·gy (tĕl′ē-ŏl′ə-jē, tē′lē-) *n., pl.* **-gies. 1.** *Philosophy.* The study of design or purpose in natural phenomena. **2.** The use of ultimate purpose or design as a means of explaining natural phenomena. **3.** Purposeful development, as in nature or history, toward a final end. [Greek *teleios, teleos,* perfect, complete (from *telos,* end, result; see **kʷel-[1]** in Appendix) + –LOGY.] **—tel′e·o·log′i·cal** (-ə-lŏj′ĭ-kəl), **tel′e·o·log′ic** (-ĭk) *adj.* **—tel′e·o·log′i·cal·ly** *adv.* **—tel′e·ol′o·gist** *n.*

tel·e·ost (tĕl′ē-ŏst′, tē′lē-) also **tel·e·os·te·an** (-ŏs′tē-ən) *—adj.* Of or belonging to the Teleostei or Teleostomi, a large group of fishes with bony skeletons, including most common fishes. The teleosts are distinct from the cartilaginous fishes such as

telecamera

ă pat	oi boy
ā pay	ou out
âr care	o͝o took
ä father	o͞o boot
ĕ pet	ŭ cut
ē be	ûr urge
ĭ pit	th thin
ī pie	*th* this
îr pier	hw which
ŏ pot	zh vision
ō toe	ə about, item
ô paw	♦ regionalism

Stress marks: ′ (primary); ′ (secondary), as in **dictionary** (dĭk′shə-nĕr′ē)

sharks, rays, and skates. —*n.* A teleost fish. [From New Latin *Teleostei,* group name (Greek *teleos,* complete; see TELEOLOGY + *ostęon,* bone; see **ost-** in Appendix) and from New Latin *Teleostomi,* group name (Greek *teleos,* complete + Greek *stoma,* mouth).]

te·lep·a·thy (tə-lĕp′ə-thē) *n.* Communication through means other than the senses. See Usage Notes at **mental telepathy, redundancy.** —**tel′e·path′ic** (tĕl′ə-păth′ĭk) *adj.* —**tel′e·path′i·cal·ly** *adv.* —**te·lep′a·thist** *n.*

tel·e·phone (tĕl′ə-fōn′) *n. Abbr.* **tel.** An instrument that converts voice and other sound signals into a form that can be transmitted to remote locations and that receives and reconverts waves into sound signals. —*attributive.* Often used to modify another noun: *telephone connections; a telephone call.* —**telephone** *v.* **-phoned, -phon·ing, -phones.** —*tr.* **1.** To speak with (a person) by telephone. **2.** To initiate or make a telephone connection with; place a call to. **3.** To transmit (a message, for example) by telephone. —*intr.* To engage in communication by telephone. —**tel′e·phon′er** *n.*

telephone booth

WORD HISTORY: When one telephones someone else, one never gives a second thought to the linguistic and etymological processes illustrated by the word *telephone.* To begin with, the noun *telephone* is one of a class of technological and scientific words that are made up of combining forms, in this case *tele–* and *–phone.* These forms are derived from classical languages: *tele–* is from the Greek combining form *tēle–* or *tēl–,* a form of *tēle,* meaning "afar, far off," while *–phone* is from Greek *phōnē,* "sound, voice." Such words derived from classical languages can be put together in French or German, for example, as well as in English. Which language actually gave birth to them cannot always be determined. In this case French *telephone* (about 1830) seems to have priority. The word was used for an acoustic apparatus, as it originally was in English (1844). Alexander Graham Bell appropriated the word for his invention in 1876, and in 1877 we have the first instance of the verb *telephone* meaning "to speak to by telephone." The verb is an example of a linguistic process called functional shift. This occurs when we use a noun as a verb, an adjective as a noun, or a noun as an adjective. Thus, we are changing the syntactic function of the word, just as we do when we *telephone* a friend.

telephone book *n.* A directory of the names of telephone subscribers with their numbers and often their addresses.

telephone booth *n.* A small enclosure containing a public telephone.

telephone exchange *n.* A central system of switches and other equipment that establishes connections between individual telephones. Also called *switchboard.*

telephone receiver *n.* The part of a telephone in which incoming electrical impulses are converted into sound.

tel·e·phon·ic (tĕl′ə-fŏn′ĭk) *adj.* **1.** Of or relating to telephones. **2.** Transmitted or conveyed by telephone. —**tel′e·phon′i·cal·ly** *adv.*

te·leph·o·ny (tə-lĕf′ə-nē) *n.* **1.** The transmission of sound between distant stations, especially by radio or telephone. **2.** The technology and manufacture of telephone equipment. —**te·leph′o·nist** *n.*

tel·e·pho·to (tĕl′ə-fō′tō) *adj.* **1.** Of or relating to a photographic lens or lens system used to produce a large image of a distant object. **2.** Of or relating to an instrument that electrically transmits photographs. —**telephoto** *n., pl.* **-tos. 1.** A telephoto lens. **2.** A photograph made with a telephoto lens; a telephotograph.

tel·e·pho·to·graph (tĕl′ə-fō′tə-grăf′) *n.* **1.** A telephoto. **2.** A photograph transmitted and reproduced by telephotography. —**telephotograph** *tr.v.* **-graphed, -graph·ing, -graphs. 1.** To photograph with a telephoto lens. **2.** To transmit by telephotography.

tel·e·pho·tog·ra·phy (tĕl′ə-fə-tŏg′rə-fē) *n.* **1.** The process or technique of photographing distant objects, using a telephoto lens on a camera. **2.** The technique or process of transmitting charts, pictures, and photographs over a distance. —**tel′e·pho′to·graph′ic** (-fō′tə-grăf′ĭk) *adj.*

tel·e·play (tĕl′ə-plā′) *n.* A play written or adapted for television.

tel·e·print·er (tĕl′ə-prĭn′tər) *n.* A teletypewriter.

tel·e·proc·ess·ing (tĕl′ə-prŏs′ĕs′ing, -prō′sĕs′-) *n. Computer Science.* Computer service by means of terminals remote from the central computer.

Tel·e·Promp·Ter (tĕl′ə-prŏmp′tər). A trademark used for a device employed in television to show an actor or a speaker an enlarged line-by-line reproduction of a script, unseen by the audience. This trademark often occurs in print in lowercase: *"With* [the President], *an old hand at reading from the teleprompter, the gestures nearly always matched the rhetoric"* (Boston Globe). *"Although he was cheered loudly by most delegates, leftist hecklers and a faulty teleprompter gave him some anxious moments"* (Chicago Tribune).

tel·e·ran (tĕl′ə-răn′) *n.* An air-traffic control system in which the image of a ground-based radar unit is televised to aircraft in the vicinity so that pilots may see their positions in relation to other aircraft. [Originally a trademark, short for *tele(vision) r(adar) a(ir) n(avigation).*]

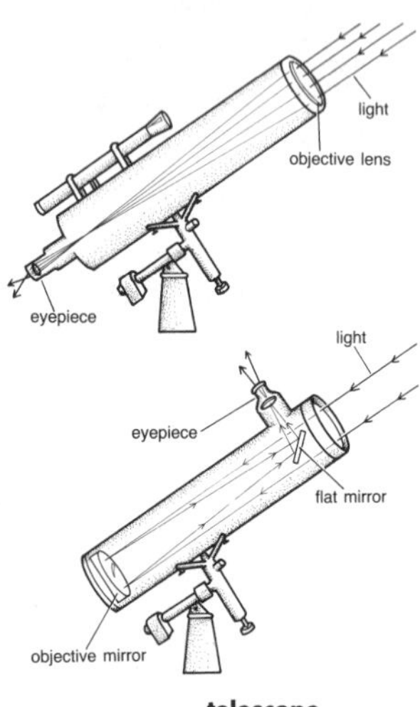

telescope
Top: Refracting telescope
Bottom: Reflecting telescope

tel·e·scope (tĕl′ĭ-skōp′) *n.* **1.** An arrangement of lenses or mirrors or both that gathers visible light, permitting direct observation or photographic recording of distant objects. **2.** Any of various devices, such as a radio telescope, used to detect and observe distant objects by their emission, transmission, reflection, or other interaction with invisible radiation. —**telescope** *v.* **-scoped, -scop·ing, -scopes.** —*tr.* **1.** To cause to slide inward or outward in overlapping sections, as the cylindrical sections of a small hand telescope do. **2.** To make more compact or concise; condense. —*intr.* To slide inward or outward in or as if in overlapping cylindrical sections: *a camp bucket that telescopes into a disk.* [New Latin *telescopium* or Italian *telescopio,* both from Greek *tēleskopos,* far-seeing : *tēle-,* tele- + *skopos,* watcher; see **spek-** in Appendix.]

Tel·e·scope Peak (tĕl′ĭ-skōp′). A mountain, 3,370 m (11,049 ft) high, in the Panamint Range of the Sierra Nevada in southeast California near the Nevada border.

tel·e·scop·ic (tĕl′ĭ-skŏp′ĭk) *adj.* **1.** Of or relating to a telescope. **2.** Seen or obtained by means of a telescope: *telescopic data.* **3.** Visible only by means of a telescope: *a bright star with a telescopic companion.* **4.** Capable of discerning distant objects: *telescopic vision.* **5.** Extensible or compressible by or as if by the sliding of overlapping sections. —**tel′e·scop′i·cal·ly** *adv.*

Tel·e·sco·pi·um (tĕl′ĭ-skō′pē-əm) *n.* A constellation in the Southern Hemisphere between Pavo and Sagittarius. [New Latin, from *telescopium,* telescope. See TELESCOPE.]

te·les·co·py (tə-lĕs′kə-pē) *n.* The art or study of making and operating telescopes. —**te·les′co·pist** *n.*

tel·e·shop·ping (tĕl′ə-shŏp′ĭng) *n.* The buying and selling of consumer products by way of television and telephone.

Te·les Pi·res (tĕl′ĭs pîr′ĭs). A river, about 965 km (600 mi) long, of central Brazil flowing northwest as a tributary of the Tapajós River.

tel·e·ster·e·o·scope (tĕl′ĭ-stĕr′ē-ə-skōp′, -stîr′-) *n.* A binocular telescope for stereoscopic viewing of distant objects.

tel·es·the·sia also **tel·aes·the·sia** (tĕl′ĭs-thē′zhə) *n.* Response to or perception of distant stimuli by extrasensory means. —**tel′es·thet′ic** (-thĕt′ĭk) *adj.*

Te·les·to (tə-lĕs′tō) *n.* The satellite of Saturn that is ninth in distance from the planet. [Greek *Telestō,* a daughter of Oceanus and Tethys.]

tel·e·text (tĕl′ĭ-tĕkst′) *n.* An electronic communications system in which printed information is broadcast by television signal to sets equipped with decoders.

tel·e·the·a·ter (tĕl′ə-thē′ə-tər) *n. Sports & Games.* A building in which horseraces are televised and off-track bets are placed.

tel·e·ther·mo·scope (tĕl′ə-thûr′mə-skōp′) *n.* An apparatus for indicating or recording the temperatures of distant or inaccessible locations.

tel·e·thon (tĕl′ə-thŏn′) *n.* A lengthy television program to raise funds for a charity. [TELE– + (MARA)THON.]

tel·e·tran·scrip·tion (tĕl′ə-trăn-skrĭp′shən) *n.* The transcription of television programs by means of a kinescope or videotape.

Tel·e·type (tĕl′ĭ-tīp′). A trademark used for a teletypewriter.

tel·e·type·writ·er (tĕl′ĭ-tīp′rī′tər) *n. Abbr.* **TT, TTY** An electromechanical typewriter that either transmits or receives messages coded in electrical signals carried by telegraph or telephone wires.

te·leu·to·spore (tə-lo͞o′tə-spôr′, -spōr′) *n.* See **teliospore.** [Greek *teleutē,* termination (from *telos,* end; see **kʷel-¹** in Appendix) + SPORE.] —**te·leu′to·spor′ic** (-spôr′ĭk, -spŏr′ĭk) *adj.*

tel·e·van·gel·ist (tĕl′ĭ-văn′jə-lĭst) *n.* An evangelist who conducts religious telecasts. [Blend of TELEVISION and EVANGELIST.] —**tel′e·van′gel·ism** *n.*

tel·e·vise (tĕl′ə-vīz′) *tr. & intr v.* **-vised, -vis·ing, -vis·es.** To broadcast or be broadcast by television. [Back-formation from TELEVISION.]

tel·e·vi·sion (tĕl′ə-vĭzh′ən) *n.* **1.** The transmission of visual images of moving and stationary objects, generally with accompanying sound, as electromagnetic waves and the reconversion of received waves into visual images. **2. a.** An electronic apparatus that receives electromagnetic waves and displays the reconverted images on a screen. **b.** The integrated audible and visible content of the electromagnetic waves received and converted by such an apparatus. **3.** The industry of producing and broadcasting television programs. —*attributive.* Often used to modify another noun: *television programs; television newscasters.* [French *télévision* : *télé-,* far (from Greek *tēle-,* tele–) + *vision,* vision; see VISION.]

tel·e·vi·sor (tĕl′ə-vī′zər) *n.* **1.** A television transmitter. **2.** A broadcaster of television programs; a telecaster.

tel·ex (tĕl′ĕks′) *n.* **1.** A communications system consisting of teletypewriters connected to a telephonic network to send and receive signals. **2.** A message sent or received by such a system. —**telex** *tr.v.* **-exed, -ex·ing, -ex·es.** To send (a message) by telex. [TEL(ETYPEWRITER) + EX(CHANGE).]

Tel·ford (tĕl′fərd). A borough of west-central England west-northwest of Birmingham. It is an industrial center in a coal-mining region. Population, 123,525.

te·li·a (tē′lē-ə) *n.* Plural of **telium.**

tel·ic (tĕl′ĭk, tē′lĭk) *adj.* Directed or tending toward a goal or purpose; purposeful. [Greek *telikos,* from *telos,* end. See **k^{w}el-**[1] in Appendix.]

te·li·o·spore (tē′lē-ə-spôr′, -spōr′) *n.* A thick-walled, usually blackish resting spore of some rusts and smuts, from which the basidium arises. Also called *teleutospore.* [TELI(UM) + SPORE.] **—te′li·o·spor′ic** (-spôr′ĭk, -spŏr′-) *adj.*

te·li·um (tē′lē-əm) *n., pl.* **-li·a** (-lē-ə). A pustulelike sorus formed on the tissue of a plant infected by a rust fungus and producing teliospores. [New Latin, from Greek *teleios,* complete. See TELEOLOGY.] **—te′li·al** (-lē-əl) *adj.*

tell (tĕl) *v.* **told** (tōld), **tell·ing, tells.** *—tr.* **1.** To give a detailed account of; narrate: *tell what happened; told us a story.* **2.** To communicate by speech or writing; express with words: *tell the truth; tell one's love.* **3.** To make known; reveal: *tell a secret; tell fortunes.* **4.** To notify; inform. **5.** To inform positively; assure: *I tell you, the plan will work.* **6.** To give instructions to; direct: *told the customers to wait in line.* **7.** To discover by observation; discern: *could easily tell that she was a newcomer.* **8.** To name or number one by one; count: *telling one's blessings; 16 windows, all told.* *—intr.* **1.** To give an account or a revelation: *was now prepared to break silence and tell.* **2.** To give evidence; inform: *He promised not to tell on his friend.* **3.** To have an effect or impact: *In this game every move tells.* ***—phrasal verb.*** **tell off.** *Informal.* To rebuke severely; reprimand. [Middle English *tellen,* from Old English *tellan.* See **del-**[2] in Appendix.] **—tell′a·ble** *adj.*

tell·er (tĕl′ər) *n.* **1.** One who tells: *a teller of tall tales.* **2.a.** A bank employee who receives and pays out money. **b.** A machine as in a bank, that automatically conducts personal financial transactions in response to a client's use of a coded card. **3.** A person appointed to count votes in a legislative assembly.

Tel·ler (tĕl′ər), **Edward.** Born 1908. Hungarian-born American physicist who helped develop the atomic bomb and provided the theoretical framework for the hydrogen bomb.

tell·ing (tĕl′ĭng) *adj.* Having force and producing a striking effect. See Synonyms at **valid.** **—tell′ing·ly** *adv.*

tell·tale (tĕl′tāl′) *n.* **1.** One who informs on another; a talebearer. **2.** Something that indicates or reveals information; a sign. **3.** Any of various devices that indicate or register information, especially: **a.** A time clock. **b.** *Nautical.* One of the brightly colored lengths of yarn or string attached to the shrouds and stays of a sailboat, serving to indicate wind direction relative to the boat's motion. **c.** A row of strips hung above a railroad track to warn a passing train of low clearance ahead. **4.** *Sports.* A resonant metal strip, 24 or 30 inches (61 or 76 centimeters) high, across the bottom of the front wall of a racquets or squash court above which the ball must be hit.

tellur– *pref.* Variant of **telluro–.**

tel·lu·ri·an (tĕ-lo͝or′ē-ən) *adj.* Of, relating to, or inhabiting Earth. **—tellurian** *n.* **1.** An inhabitant of Earth. **2.** Variant of **tellurion.**

tel·lu·ric (tĕ-lo͝or′ĭk) *adj.* **1.** Relating to Earth; terrestrial. **2.** Derived from or containing tellurium, especially with valence 6.

telluric acid *n.* A white, crystalline inorganic acid, H_6TeO_6, used as a chemical reagent.

tel·lu·ride (tĕl′yə-rīd′) *n.* A binary compound of tellurium.

tel·lu·ri·on (tĕ-lo͝or′ē-ŏn′) also **tel·lu·ri·an** (-ən) *n.* An apparatus that shows how the movement of Earth on its axis and around the sun causes day and night and the seasons. [New Latin : TELLURO– + Greek *-ion,* diminutive suff.]

tel·lu·ri·um (tĕ-lo͝or′ē-əm) *n. Symbol* **Te** A brittle, silvery-white metallic element usually found in combination with gold and other metals, produced commercially as a byproduct of the electrolytic refining of copper and used to alloy stainless steel and lead, in ceramics, and, in the form of bismuth telluride, in thermoelectric devices. Atomic number 52; atomic weight 127.60; melting point 449.5°C; boiling point 989.8°C; specific gravity 6.24; valence 2, 4, 6. See table at **element.**

telluro– or **tellur–** *pref.* **1.** Earth: *tellurian.* **2.** Tellurium: *tellurous.* [From Latin *tellūs, tellūr-,* earth.]

tel·lu·rom·e·ter (tĕl′yə-rŏm′ĭ-tər) *n.* A surveying instrument that measures distance by measuring the round-trip travel time of reflected microwaves.

tel·lu·rous (tĕl′yər-əs, tĕ-lo͝or′əs) *adj.* Of, relating to, or derived from tellurium, especially with valence 4.

tel·ly (tĕl′ē) *n., pl.* **-lies.** *Chiefly British.* A television set.

telo– or **tel–** *pref.* End: *telophase.* [From Greek *telos,* end. See **k^{w}el-**[1] in Appendix.]

tel·o·cen·tric (tĕl′ə-sĕn′trĭk, tē′lə-) *adj.* Having the centromere in a terminal position. Used of a chromosome.

tel·o·lec·i·thal (tĕl′ə-lĕs′ə-thəl, tē′lə-) *adj.* Having a yolk that is concentrated at one end: *a telolecithal egg.* [TELO– + Greek *lekithos,* egg yolk + –AL[1].]

tel·o·mere (tĕl′ə-mîr′, tē′lə-) *n.* Either end of a chromosome; a terminal chromosome.

tel·o·phase (tĕl′ə-fāz′, tē′lə-) *n.* The final stage of mitosis or meiosis during which the chromosomes of daughter cells are grouped in new nuclei. **—tel′o·phas′ic** *adj.*

tel·o·tax·is (tĕl′ə-tăk′sĭs) *n.* Movement or orientation of an organism toward or away from a particular stimulus.

tel·pher (tĕl′fər) *n.* **1.** A small traveling car, usually driven by electricity, suspended from or moving on an overhead rail or cable. **2.** A transportation system using telphers. **—telpher** *tr.v.* **-phered, -pher·ing, -phers.** To transport by telpher. [Alteration of *telepher* : TELE– + Greek *pherein,* to carry; see **bher-**[1] in Appendix.]

tel·son (tĕl′sən) *n.* **1.** The rearmost segment of the body of certain arthropods. **2.** An extension of this segment, such as the middle lobe of the tail fan of a lobster or the stinger of a scorpion. [Greek, limit.]

Tel·u·gu also **Tel·e·gu** (tĕl′ə-go͞o′) *—n., pl.* **Telugu** or **-gus** also **Telegu** or **-gus.** **1.** A Dravidian language spoken in central India. **2.** A member of the Dravidian people who speak Telugu. *—adj.* Of or relating to Telugu, its speakers, or their culture.

tem·blor (tĕm′blər, -blôr′) *n.* See **earthquake.** [Spanish, a trembling, earthquake, from *temblar,* to shake, from Vulgar Latin **tremulāre,* from Latin *tremulus,* shaking. See TREMULOUS.]

tem·er·ar·i·ous (tĕm′ə-râr′ē-əs) *adj.* Presumptuously or recklessly daring: *"I would never have been temerarious enough to make use of such a title on my own"* (Brendan Gill). See Synonyms at **reckless.** [From Latin *temerārius,* from *temere,* rashly.] **—tem′er·ar′i·ous·ly** *adv.* **—tem′er·ar′i·ous·ness** *n.*

te·mer·i·ty (tə-mĕr′ĭ-tē) *n.* Foolhardy disregard of danger; recklessness. [Middle English *temerite,* from Old French, from Latin *temeritās,* from *temere,* rashly.]

SYNONYMS: *temerity, audacity, effrontery, nerve, cheek, gall.* These nouns refer to striking, often aggressive boldness. *Temerity* implies a foolhardy flouting of danger: *Conducting the premiere of a symphony without a rehearsal requires temerity. Audacity* suggests heedlessness of the restraints imposed by prudence, propriety, or convention: *"In war nothing is impossible, provided you use audacity"* (George S. Patton). *Effrontery* and *nerve* denote impudent, arrogant, or shameless boldness: *He had the effrontery to suggest that she enjoyed being unhappy. A raise? When your work is so slipshod? You do have a nerve! Cheek* connotes cool impertinence and brashness: *Do you really have the cheek to insult your hosts? Gall* suggests brazenness and insolence: *With unmitigated gall he crashed the party and then criticized the food.*

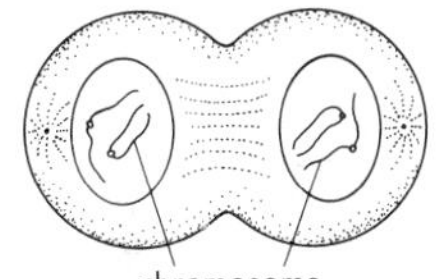

telophase

Tem·ne (tĕm′nē) *n., pl.* **Temne** or **-nes.** **1.** A member of a people living in Sierra Leone. **2.** The West Atlantic language of this people.

temp (tĕmp) *n. Informal.* A temporary worker, as in an office. [Short for *temporary worker.*]

temp. *abbr.* **1.** Temperance. **2.** Temperature. **3.** Template. **4.** Temporal. **5.** Temporary. **6.** *Latin.* Tempore (in the time of).

Tem·pe (tĕm′pē′). A city of south-central Arizona east of Phoenix. It is a resort and the seat of Arizona State University (established 1885). Population, 106,743.

Tempe, Vale of. A valley of northeast Greece between Mount Olympus and Mount Ossa. Strategically important in ancient times, it is noted for its rugged scenery.

tem·peh (tĕm′pā′) *n.* A high-protein food of Indonesian origin made from partially cooked, fermented soybeans. [Indonesian *tempe,* from Javanese, soybean cakes.]

tem·per (tĕm′pər) *v.* **-pered, -per·ing, -pers.** *—tr.* **1.** To modify by the addition of a moderating element; moderate: *"temper its doctrinaire logic with a little practical wisdom"* (Robert H. Jackson). See Synonyms at **moderate.** **2.** To bring to a desired consistency, texture, hardness, or other physical condition by or as if by blending, admixing, or kneading: *temper clay; paints that had been tempered with oil.* **3.** To harden or strengthen (metal or glass) by application of heat or by heating and cooling. **4.** To strengthen through experience or hardship; toughen: *soldiers who had been tempered by combat.* **5.** To adjust finely; attune: *a portfolio that is tempered to the investor's needs.* **6.** *Music.* To adjust (the pitch of an instrument) to a temperament. *—intr.* To be or become tempered. **—temper** *n.* **1.** A state of mind or emotions; disposition: *an even temper.* See Synonyms at **mood**[1]. **2.** Calmness of mind or emotions; composure: *lose one's temper.* **3.a.** A tendency to become easily angry or irritable: *a quick temper.* **b.** An outburst of rage: *a fit of temper.* **4.** A characteristic general quality; tone: *heroes who exemplified the medieval temper; the politicized temper of the 1930's.* **5.a.** The condition of being tempered. **b.** The degree of hardness and elasticity of a metal, chiefly steel, achieved by tempering. **6.** A modifying substance or agent added to something else. **7.** *Archaic.* A middle course between extremes; a mean. [Middle English *temperen,* from Old English *temprian,* from Latin *temperāre,* probably from *temper-,* variant of *tempor-,* stem of *tempus,* time, season.] **—tem′per·a·bil′i·ty** *n.* **—tem′per·a·ble** *adj.* **—tem′per·er** *n.*

tem·per·a (tĕm′pər-ə) *n.* **1.** A painting medium in which pigment is mixed with water-soluble glutinous materials such as size or egg yolk. Also called *poster color, poster paint.* **2.** Painting done in this medium. [Italian, from *temperare,* to mingle, from Latin *temperāre.* See TEMPER.]

tem·per·a·ment (tĕm′prə-mənt, tĕm′pər-ə-) *n.* **1.a.** The manner of thinking, behaving, or reacting characteristic of a specific person: *a nervous temperament.* See Synonyms at **disposition.** **b.** The distinguishing mental and physical characteristics of a human being according to medieval physiology, resulting from dominance of one of the four humors. **2.** Excessive irritability or sensitiveness: *an actor with too much temperament.* **3.** *Music.* Equal temperament. [Middle English, from Latin *temperāmentum,* from *temperāre,* to temper. See TEMPER.]

tem·per·a·men·tal (tĕm′prə-mĕn′tl, tĕm′pər-ə-) *adj.* **1.** Relating to or caused by temperament: *our temperamental differ-*

ă pat	oi boy
ā pay	ou out
âr care	o͝o took
ä father	o͞o boot
ĕ pet	ŭ cut
ē be	ûr urge
ĭ pit	th thin
ī pie	*th* this
îr pier	hw which
ŏ pot	zh vision
ō toe	ə about, item
ô paw	♦ regionalism

Stress marks: **′** (primary); ′ (secondary), as in **dictionary** (dĭk′shə-nĕr′ē)

ences. **2.** Excessively sensitive or irritable; moody. **3.** Likely to perform unpredictably; undependable: *a temperamental motor.* **—tem′per·a·men′tal·ly** *adv.*

tem·per·ance (tĕm′pər-əns, tĕm′prəns) *n. Abbr.* **temp. 1.** Moderation and self-restraint, as in behavior or expression. **2.** Restraint in the use of or abstinence from alcoholic liquors. See Synonyms at **abstinence.**

tem·per·ate (tĕm′pər-ĭt, tĕm′prĭt) *adj.* **1.** Exercising moderation and self-restraint: *learned to be temperate in eating and drinking.* **2.** Moderate in degree or quality; restrained: *temperate criticism.* **3.** Characterized by moderate temperatures, weather, or climate; neither hot nor cold. [Middle English *temperat,* from Latin *temperātus,* from past participle of *temperāre,* to temper. See TEMPER.] **—tem′per·ate·ly** *adv.* **—tem′per·ate·ness** *n.*

Tem·per·ate Zone (tĕm′pər-ĭt, tĕm′prĭt). Either of two intermediate latitude zones of the earth, the **North Temperate Zone,** between the Arctic Circle and the Tropic of Cancer, or the **South Temperate Zone,** between the Antarctic Circle and the Tropic of Capricorn.

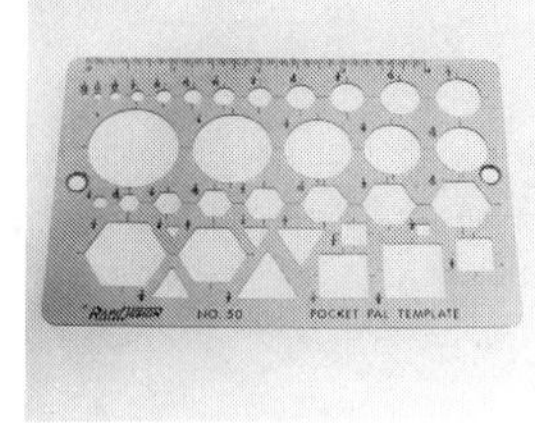

template

tem·per·a·ture (tĕm′pər-ə-cho͝or′, -chər, tĕm′prə-) *n. Abbr.* **T, temp. 1.a.** The degree of hotness or coldness of a body or an environment. **b.** A specific degree of hotness or coldness as indicated on or referred to a standard scale. **2.a.** The degree of heat in the body of a living organism, usually about 37.0°C (98.6°F) in human beings. **b.** An abnormally high condition of body heat caused by illness; a fever. [Middle English, temperate weather, from Latin *temperātūra,* due measure, from *temperātus,* past participle of *temperāre,* to mix. See TEMPER.]

temperature gradient *n.* The rate of change of temperature with displacement in a given direction from a given reference point.

tem·pered (tĕm′pərd) *adj.* **1.** Having a specified temper or disposition. Often used in combination: *sweet-tempered; ill-tempered.* **2.** Adjusted or attuned by the addition of a counterbalancing element; moderated or measured: *"prepare the country to expect hard choices and to appreciate tempered values and moderation in private and public life"* (Haynes Johnson). **3.** Made appropriately hard or flexible by tempering: *a sword of tempered steel.* **4.** Having the requisite degree of hardness or elasticity. Used of glass or a metal. **5.** *Music.* Tuned to temperament. Used of a scale, an interval, a semitone, or intonation.

tem·pest (tĕm′pĭst) *n.* **1.** A violent windstorm, frequently accompanied by rain, snow, or hail. **2.** Furious agitation, commotion, or tumult; an uproar: *"The tempest in my mind/Doth from my senses take all feeling"* (Shakespeare). **—tempest** *tr.v.* **-pest·ed, -pest·ing, -pests.** To cause a tempest around or in. **—*idiom.* tempest in a teacup** (or **teapot**). A great disturbance or uproar over a matter of little or no importance. [Middle English, from Old French *tempeste,* from Vulgar Latin **tempesta,* variant of Latin *tempestās,* from *tempus,* time.]

temple[1]
In Mysore, India

tem·pes·tu·ous (tĕm-pĕs′cho͞o-əs) *adj.* **1.** Of, relating to, or resembling a tempest: *tempestuous gales.* **2.** Tumultuous; stormy: *a tempestuous relationship.* [Middle English, from Late Latin *tempestuōsus,* from *tempestūs,* tempest, variant of *tempestās.* See TEMPEST.] **—tem·pes′tu·ous·ly** *adv.* **—tem·pes′tu·ous·ness** *n.*

tem·pi (tĕm′pē) *n.* A plural of **tempo.**

Tem·plar (tĕm′plər) *n.* **1.** A Knight Templar. **2. templar.** A lawyer or student of law having chambers in the Temple in London. [Middle English *templer,* from Anglo-Norman, from Medieval Latin *templārius,* from Latin *templum,* temple. See TEMPLE[1].]

tem·plate also **tem·plet** (tĕm′plĭt) *n. Abbr.* **temp. 1.** A pattern or gauge, such as a thin metal plate with a cut pattern, used as a guide in making something accurately, as in woodworking. **2.** A horizontal piece of stone or timber used to distribute weight or pressure, as over a door frame. **3.** *Biochemistry.* A molecule of a nucleic acid, such as DNA, that serves as a pattern or mold for the synthesis of a macromolecule, as of RNA. [Probably from French *templet,* diminutive of *temple,* temple of a loom. See TEMPLE[3].]

tem·ple[1] (tĕm′pəl) *n.* **1.a.** A building dedicated to religious ceremonies or worship. **b. Temple.** Either of two successive buildings in ancient Jerusalem serving as the primary center for Jewish worship. **c.** *Judaism.* A synagogue, especially of a Reform or Conservative congregation. **d.** *Mormon Church.* A building in which the sacred ordinances are administered. **2.** Something regarded as having within it a divine presence. **3.** A building used for meetings by any of several fraternal orders, especially the Knights Templars. **4.** A building reserved for a highly valued function: *the library, a temple of learning.* **5. Temple.** Either of two groups of buildings in London, the Inner Temple and the Middle Temple, that house two of the four Inns of Court and that occupy the site of the medieval Knights Templars establishment. [Middle English, from Old English *tempel,* from Latin *templum.* See **tem-** in Appendix.]

tem·ple[2] (tĕm′pəl) *n.* **1.** The flat region on either side of the forehead. **2.** Either of the sidepieces of a frame for eyeglasses that extends along the temple and over the ear. [Middle English, from Old French, from Vulgar Latin **tempula,* from Latin *tempora,* pl. of *tempus,* temple of the head.]

tem·ple[3] (tĕm′pəl) *n.* A device in a loom that keeps the cloth stretched to the correct width during weaving. [Middle English *tempille,* from Old French *temple,* possibly from Latin *templum,* small piece of timber. See **tem-** in Appendix.]

Temple. A city of central Texas south of Fort Worth. It is a processing and manufacturing center. Population, 42,483.

Temple, Shirley. See Shirley Temple **Black.**

Temple, Sir **William.** 1628–1699. English politician and writer whose prose style influenced Jonathan Swift and others.

Temple City. A city of southern California, a residential suburb of Los Angeles. Population, 28,972.

tem·plet (tĕm′plĭt) *n.* Variant of **template.**

temple tree *n.* See **frangipani** (sense 1).

tem·po (tĕm′pō) *n., pl.* **-pos** or **-pi** (-pē). **1.** *Abbr.* **t.** *Music.* The relative speed at which music is or ought to be played, often indicated on written compositions by a descriptive or metronomic direction to the performer. **2.** A characteristic rate or rhythm of activity; a pace: *"the tempo and the feeling of modern life"* (Robert L. Heilbroner). [Italian, from Latin *tempus,* time.]

tem·po·ral[1] (tĕm′pər-əl, tĕm′prəl) *adj.* **1.** Of, relating to, or limited by time: *a temporal dimension; temporal and spatial boundaries.* **2.** Of or relating to the material world; worldly: *the temporal possessions of the Church.* **3.** Lasting only for a time; not eternal; passing: *our temporal existence.* **4.** Secular or lay; civil: *lords temporal and spiritual.* **5.** *Grammar.* Expressing time: *a temporal adverb.* [Middle English, from Old French, from Latin *temporālis,* from *tempus, tempor-,* time.] **—tem′po·ral·ly** *adv.*

tem·po·ral[2] (tĕm′pər-əl, tĕm′prəl) *adj. Abbr.* **temp.** Of, relating to, or near the temples of the skull. [Late Latin *temporālis,* from Latin *tempora,* pl. of *tempus,* temple.]

temporal bone *n.* Either of a pair of compound bones forming the sides and base of the skull.

temporal lobe *n.* The lower lateral lobe of either cerebral hemisphere, located in front of the occipital lobe and containing the sensory center of hearing in the brain.

tem·po·ral·i·ty (tĕm′pə-răl′ĭ-tē) *n., pl.* **-ties. 1.** The condition of being temporal or bounded in time. **2. temporalities.** Temporal possessions, especially of the Church or clergy.

tem·po·rar·y (tĕm′pə-rĕr′ē) *adj. Abbr.* **temp.** Lasting, used, serving, or enjoyed for a limited time. **—temporary** *n., pl.* **-ies.** *Informal.* One that serves for a limited time: *staffed by temporaries.* [Latin *temporārius,* from *tempus, tempor-,* time.] **—tem′po·rar′i·ly** *adv.* **—tem′po·rar′i·ness** *n.*

SYNONYMS: *temporary, acting, ad interim, interim, provisional.* The central meaning shared by these adjectives is "assuming the duties of another for the time being": *a temporary chairperson; the acting dean; an ad interim admissions committee; an interim administration; a provisional mayor.*
ANTONYM: *permanent.*

tem·po·rize (tĕm′pə-rīz′) *intr.v.* **-rized, -riz·ing, -riz·es. 1.** To act evasively in order to gain time, avoid argument, or postpone a decision: *"Colonial officials . . . ordered to enforce unpopular enactments, tended to temporize, to find excuses for evasion"* (J.H. Parry). **2.** To engage in discussions or negotiations, especially so as to achieve a compromise or gain time. **3.** To yield to current circumstances or necessities; act to suit the time. [French *temporiser,* from Old French, from Medieval Latin *temporizāre,* to pass one's time, from Latin *tempus, tempor-,* time.] **—tem′po·ri·za′tion** (-pər-ĭ-zā′shən) *n.* **—tem′po·riz′er** *n.*

tem·po·ro·man·dib·u·lar (tĕm′pə-rō-măn-dĭb′yə-lər) *adj.* Of, relating to, or formed by the temporal bone and the mandible.

temporomandibular joint syndrome *n. Abbr.* **TMJ** A disorder caused by faulty articulation of the temporomandibular joint and characterized by facial pain, headache, ringing ears, dizziness, and stiffness of the neck.

tempt (tĕmpt) *v.* **tempt·ed, tempt·ing, tempts.** *—tr.* **1.** To try to get (someone) to do wrong, especially by a promise of reward. **2.** To be inviting or attractive to: *A second helping tempted me. We refused the offer even though it tempted us.* See Synonyms at **lure. 3.** To provoke or to risk provoking: *Don't tempt fate.* **4.** To cause to be strongly disposed: *He was tempted to walk out.* *—intr.* To be attractive or inviting: *a meal that tempts.* [Middle English *tempten,* from Old French *tempter,* from Latin *temptāre,* to feel, try.] **—tempt′a·ble** *adj.* **—tempt′er** *n.*

temp·ta·tion (tĕmp-tā′shən) *n.* **1.** The act of tempting or the condition of being tempted. **2.** Something tempting or enticing.

tempt·ing (tĕmp′tĭng) *adj.* Having strong appeal; enticing: *a tempting repast.* **—tempt′ing·ly** *adv.* **—tempt′ing·ness** *n.*

tempt·ress (tĕmp′trĭs) *n.* An alluring, bewitching woman. See Usage Note at **-ess.**

tem·pu·ra (tĕm′po͞o-rə, tĕm-po͝or′ə) *n.* A Japanese dish of vegetables and shrimp or other seafood dipped in batter and fried in deep fat. [Japanese.]

Te·mu·co (tĕ-mo͞o′kō). A city of central Chile south-southwest of Concepción. Founded in 1881, it is a trade center. Population, 157,297.

ten (tĕn) *n.* **1.** The cardinal number equal to 9 + 1. **2.** The tenth in a set or sequence. **3.** Something having ten parts, units, or members. **4.** *Games.* A playing card marked with ten spots. **5.** A ten-dollar bill. [Middle English, from Old English *tīen.* See **dekm̥** in Appendix.] **—ten** *adj. & pron.*

ten. *abbr.* **1.** Tenor. **2.** *Music.* Tenuto.

ten·a·ble (tĕn′ə-bəl) *adj.* **1.** Capable of being maintained in argument; rationally defensible: *a tenable theory.* **2.** Capable of being held against assault; defensible: *a tenable outpost.* [French, from Old French, from *tenir,* to hold, from Latin *tenēre.* See **ten-** in Appendix.] **—ten′a·bil′i·ty, ten′a·ble·ness** *n.* **—ten′a·bly** *adv.*

ten·ace (tĕn′ās′, tĕ-nās′, tĕn′ĭs) *n. Games.* A combination of two nonsequential high cards of the same suit, such as the king and jack of hearts, especially in a bridge or whist hand. [French, from Spanish *tenaza,* tongs, tenace, from *tenaces,* pl. of *tenaz,* tenacious, from Latin *tenāx, tenāc-.* See TENACIOUS.]

te·na·cious (tə-nā′shəs) *adj.* **1.** Holding or tending to hold persistently to something, such as a point of view. See Synonyms at **strong. 2.** Holding together firmly; cohesive: *a tenacious material.* **3.** Clinging to another object or surface; adhesive: *tenacious lint on my jacket.* **4.** Tending to retain; retentive: *a tenacious memory.* [From Latin *tenāx, tenāc-,* holding fast, from *tenēre,* to hold. See **ten-** in Appendix.] **—te·na′cious·ly** *adv.* **—te·na′cious·ness** *n.*

te·nac·i·ty (tə-năs′ĭ-tē) *n.* The state or quality of being tenacious. See Synonyms at **perseverance.**

te·nac·u·lum (tə-năk′yə-ləm) *n., pl.* **-la** (-lə). A long-handled, slender, hooked instrument for lifting and holding parts, such as blood vessels, during surgery. [Late Latin *tenāculum,* holder, from Latin *tenēre,* to hold. See **ten-** in Appendix.]

ten·an·cy (tĕn′ən-sē) *n., pl.* **-cies. 1.** Possession or occupancy of lands, buildings, or other property by title, under a lease, or on payment of rent. **2.** The period of a tenant's occupancy or possession. **3.** A habitation held or occupied by a tenant.

ten·ant (tĕn′ənt) *n.* **1.** One that pays rent to use or occupy land, a building, or other property owned by another. **2.** A dweller in a place; an occupant. **3.** *Law.* One who holds or possesses lands, tenements, or sometimes personal property by any kind of title. **—tenant** *tr. & intr.v.* **-ant·ed, -ant·ing, -ants.** To hold as a tenant or be a tenant. [Middle English, from Old French, from present participle of *tenir,* to hold, from Latin *tenēre.* See **ten-** in Appendix.]

tenant farmer *n.* One who farms land owned by another and pays rent in cash or in kind.

ten·ant·ry (tĕn′ən-trē) *n.* **1.** Tenants considered as a group. **2.** The condition of being a tenant; tenancy.

ten-cent store (tĕn′sĕnt′) *n.* See **five-and-ten.**

tench (tĕnch) *n., pl.* **tench** or **tench·es.** An edible Eurasian freshwater fish *(Tinca tinca)* having small scales and two barbels near the mouth. [Middle English *tenche,* from Old French, from Late Latin *tinca,* probably of Celtic origin.]

Ten Commandments (tĕn) *pl.n. Bible.* The ten injunctions given by God to Moses on Mount Sinai, serving as the basis of Mosaic Law.

tend[1] (tĕnd) *intr.v.* **tend·ed, tend·ing, tends. 1.** To have a tendency: *paint that tends toward bubbling and peeling over time.* **2.** To be disposed or inclined: *tends toward exaggeration.* **3.** To move or extend in a certain direction: *Our ship tended northward.* [Middle English *tenden,* from Old French *tendre,* from Latin *tendere.* See **ten-** in Appendix.]

tend[2] (tĕnd) *v.* **tend·ed, tend·ing, tends.** *—tr.* **1.** To have the care of; watch over; look after: *tend a child.* **2.** To manage the activities and transactions of; run: *tend bar; tend a store in the owner's absence.* *—intr.* **1.** To be an attendant or a servant. **2.** To apply one's attention; attend: *no time to tend to my diary.* [Middle English *tenden,* short for *attenden,* to wait on. See ATTEND.]

SYNONYMS: *tend, attend, mind, minister, watch.* The central meaning shared by these verbs is "to have the care or supervision of": *tended her plants; attending the sick; minded the furnace; ministering to flood victims; watched the house while the owners were away.*

ten·den·cious (tĕn-dĕn′shəs) *adj.* Variant of **tendentious.**

ten·den·cy (tĕn′dən-sē) *n., pl.* **-cies. 1.** Movement or prevailing movement in a given direction: *observed the tendency of the wind; the shoreward tendency of the current.* **2.** A characteristic likelihood: *fabric that has a tendency to wrinkle.* **3.** A predisposition to think, act, behave, or proceed in a particular way. **4.a.** An implicit direction or purpose: *not openly liberal, but that is the tendency of the book.* **b.** An implicit point of view in written or spoken matter; a bias. [Medieval Latin *tendentia,* from Latin *tendēns, tendent-,* present participle of *tendere,* to tend. See TEND[1].]

SYNONYMS: *tendency, trend, current, drift, tenor, inclination.* These nouns are compared as they refer to the direction or course of an action or a thought. *Tendency* implies a predisposition to proceed in a particular way: *"The tendency of our own day is . . . towards firm, solid, verifiable knowledge"* (William H. Mallock). *Trend* often applies to a general or prevailing direction, especially within a particular sphere: *"the trend of religious thought in recent times"* (James Harvey Robinson). *Current* suggests a course or flow, as of opinion, especially one representative of a given time or place: "[These] *words . . . express the whole current of modern feeling"* (James Bryce). A *drift* is a tendency that depends for its direction or course on the impetus of something likened to a shifting current of air or water: *Political conservatives fear a drift toward communism in Latin America. Tenor* implies a continuous, unwavering course: *"His conduct was . . . uniform and unvarying in its tenor"* (Frederick Marryat). *Inclination* usually refers to an individual's propensity for or disposition toward one thing rather than another: *"Man's capacity for justice makes democracy possible, but man's inclination to injustice makes democracy necessary"* (Reinhold Niebuhr).

ten·den·tious also **ten·den·cious** (tĕn-dĕn′shəs) *adj.* Marked by a strong implicit point of view; partisan: *a tendentious account of the recent elections.* [From Medieval Latin *tendentia,* a cause. See TENDENCY.] **—ten·den′tious·ly** *adv.* **—ten·den′tious·ness** *n.*

ten·der[1] (tĕn′dər) *adj.* **-er, -est. 1.a.** Easily crushed or bruised; fragile: *a tender petal.* **b.** Easily chewed or cut: *tender beef.* **2.** Young and vulnerable: *of tender age.* **3.** Frail; delicate. **4.** Sensitive to frost or severe cold; not hardy: *tender green shoots.* **5.a.** Easily hurt; sensitive: *tender skin.* **b.** Painful; sore: *a tender tooth.* **6.a.** Considerate and protective; solicitous: *a tender mother; his tender concern.* **b.** Characterized by or expressing gentle emotions; loving: *a tender glance; a tender ballad.* **c.** Given to sympathy or sentimentality; soft: *a tender heart.* **7.** *Nautical.* Likely to heel easily under sail; crank. **—tender** *tr.v.* **-dered, -der·ing, -ders. 1.** To make tender. **2.** *Archaic.* To treat with tender regard. [Middle English, from Old French *tendre,* from Latin *tener.* See **ten-** in Appendix.] **—ten′der·ly** *adv.* **—ten′der·ness** *n.*

ten·der[2] (tĕn′dər) *n.* **1.** A formal offer, as: **a.** *Law.* An offer of money or service in payment of an obligation. **b.** A written offer to contract goods or services at a specified cost or rate; a bid. **2.** Something, especially money, offered in payment. **—tender** *tr.v.* **-dered, -der·ing, -ders.** To offer formally: *tender a letter of resignation.* See Synonyms at **offer.** [From French *tendre,* to offer, from Old French, from Latin *tendere,* to hold forth, extend. See **ten-** in Appendix.] **—ten′der·er** *n.*

tend·er[3] (tĕn′dər) *n.* **1.** One who tends something: *a lathe tender.* **2.** *Nautical.* A vessel attendant on other vessels, especially one that ferries supplies between ship and shore. **3.** A railroad car attached to the rear of a locomotive and designed to carry fuel and water.

ten·der·foot (tĕn′dər-fo͝ot′) *n., pl.* **-foots** or **-feet** (-fēt′). **1.** A newcomer not yet hardened to rough outdoor life; a greenhorn. **2.** An inexperienced person; a novice. **3.** Often **Tenderfoot.** A Boy Scout of the lowest rank.

ten·der·heart·ed (tĕn′dər-här′tĭd) *adj.* Easily moved by another's distress; compassionate. **—ten′der·heart′ed·ly** *adv.* **—ten′der·heart′ed·ness** *n.*

ten·der·ize (tĕn′də-rīz′) *tr.v.* **-ized, -iz·ing, -iz·es.** To make (meat) tender, as by marinating, pounding, or applying a tenderizer. **—ten′der·i·za′tion** (-dər-ĭ-zā′shən) *n.*

ten·der·iz·er (tĕn′də-rī′zər) *n.* A substance, such as a plant enzyme, applied to meat to make it tender.

ten·der·loin (tĕn′dər-loin′) *n.* **1.** The tenderest part, as of a loin of beef. **2.** A city district notorious for vice and graft. [Sense 2, after the *Tenderloin,* an area of New York City (from the easy income it once afforded corrupt policemen).]

ten·di·ni·tis also **ten·do·ni·tis** (tĕn′də-nī′tĭs) *n.* Inflammation of a tendon. [New Latin *tendō, tendin-,* tendon; see TENDINOUS + –ITIS.]

ten·di·nous (tĕn′də-nəs) *adj.* **1.** Of, having, or resembling a tendon. **2.** Sinewy. [Latin *tendō, tendin-,* tendon (from Medieval Latin *tendō;* see TENDON) + –OUS.]

ten·don (tĕn′dən) *n.* A band of tough, inelastic fibrous tissue that connects a muscle with its bony attachment. [Medieval Latin *tendō, tendōn-,* alteration (influenced by Latin *tendere,* to stretch) of Greek *tenōn.* See **ten-** in Appendix.]

ten·do·ni·tis (tĕn′də-nī′tĭs) *n.* Variant of **tendinitis.**

tendon of Achilles *n., pl.* **tendons of Achilles.** Achilles tendon.

ten·dril (tĕn′drəl) *n.* **1.** A twisting, threadlike structure by which a twining plant, such as a grape or cucumber, grasps an object or a plant for support. **2.** Something, such as a ringlet of hair, that is long, slender, and curling. [French *tendrillon,* from Old French, diminutive of *tendron,* young shoot, from *tendre,* tender. See TENDER[1].]

Ten·e·brae (tĕn′ə-brā′, -brē′) *pl.n. (used with a sing. or pl. verb). Roman Catholic Church.* The office of matins and lauds sung on the last three days of Holy Week, with a ceremony of candles. [Medieval Latin, from Latin *tenebrae,* darkness.]

ten·e·brif·ic (tĕn′ə-brĭf′ĭk) *adj.* **1.** Serving to obscure or darken. **2.** Gloomy; dark. [Latin *tenebrae,* darkness + –FIC.]

te·neb·ri·o·nid (tə-nĕb′rē-ə-nĭd′, tĕn′ə-brī′-) *n.* See **darkling beetle.** [From New Latin *Tenebriōnidae,* family name, from *Tenebriō,* type genus, from Latin *tenebriō,* one who avoids light, from *tenebrae,* darkness.] **—te·neb′ri·o·nid′** *adj.*

ten·e·brous (tĕn′ə-brəs) also **te·neb·ri·ous** (tə-nĕb′rē-əs) *adj.* Dark and gloomy. [Middle English, from Old French *tenebreus,* from Latin *tenebrōsus,* from *tenebrae,* darkness.] **—ten′e·bros′i·ty** (-brŏs′ĭ-tē) *n.*

ten·e·ment (tĕn′ə-mənt) *n.* **1.** A building for human habitation, especially one that is rented to tenants. **2.** A rundown, low-rental apartment building whose facilities and maintenance barely meet minimum standards. **3.** *Chiefly British.* An apartment or a room leased to a tenant. **4.** *Law.* Property, such as land, rents, or franchises, held by one person leasing it from another. [Middle

Ten Commandments
Moses holding the Ten Commandments

ă pat	oi boy
ā pay	ou out
âr care	o͝o took
ä father	o͞o boot
ĕ pet	ŭ cut
ē be	ûr urge
ĭ pit	th thin
ī pie	*th* this
îr pier	hw which
ŏ pot	zh vision
ō toe	ə about, item
ô paw	♦ regionalism

Stress marks: ′ (primary); ′ (secondary), as in **dictionary** (dĭk′shə-nĕr′ē)

English, house, from Old French, from Medieval Latin *tenēmentum,* from Latin *tenēre,* to hold. See **ten-** in Appendix.] **—ten′e·men′tal** (-mĕn′tl), **ten′e·men′ta·ry** (-mĕn′tə-rē) *adj.*

Ten·er·ife (tĕn′ə-rĭf′, -rēf′, tĕ′nĕ-rē′fĕ). An island in the Canary Islands of Spain in the Atlantic Ocean.

te·nes·mus (tə-nĕz′məs) *n.* A painfully urgent but ineffectual attempt to urinate or defecate. [Medieval Latin *tēnesmus,* variant of Latin *tēnesmos,* from Greek *teinesmos,* from *teinein,* to strain, stretch. See **ten-** in Appendix.]

ten·et (tĕn′ĭt) *n.* An opinion, doctrine, or principle held as being true by a person or especially by an organization. See Synonyms at **doctrine.** [Probably from Medieval Latin, from Latin, third person sing. present indicative of *tenēre,* to hold. See **ten-** in Appendix.]

ten-gal·lon hat (tĕn′găl′ən) *n.* See **cowboy hat.** [Perhaps from Spanish *galón,* braid, galloon (wrapped in rows above the brim), from French *galon.* See GALLOON.]

Teng Hsiao-ping (tŭng′ shyou′pĭng′). See **Deng Xiaoping.**

te·ni·a (tē′nē-ə) *n.* Variant of **taenia.**

te·ni·a·cide (tē′nē-ə-sīd′) *n.* Variant of **taeniacide.**

te·ni·a·fuge (tē′nē-ə-fyo͞oj′) *n.* Variant of **taeniafuge.**

te·ni·a·sis (tē-nī′ə-sĭs) *n.* Variant of **taeniasis.**

Te·niers (tə-nîrz′, -nîrs′, tĕ-nyā′), **David.** Known as "the Elder." 1582–1649. Flemish painter of religious subjects. His son **David** (1610–1690), known as "the Younger," painted landscapes, religious subjects, and genre scenes.

Tennessee walking horse

Ten·nes·see (tĕn′ĭ-sē′, tĕn′ĭ-sē′). *Abbr.* **TN, Tenn.** A state of the southeast United States. It was admitted as the 16th state in 1796. First visited by the Spanish in 1540, the region was explored by Daniel Boone in 1769 and became part of the United States in 1783. The short-lived state of Franklin (1784–1788) formed the basis for the Territory of the United States South of the River Ohio (1790) and the later state of Tennessee. Nashville is the capital and Memphis the largest city. Population, 4,591,120. **—Ten′nes·se′an** *adj. & n.*

Tennessee River. A river of the southeast United States rising in eastern Tennessee and flowing about 1,049 km (652 mi) through northern Alabama, western Tennessee, and western Kentucky to the Ohio River.

Tennessee walking horse *n.* Any of a breed of lightly built saddle horse developed in Tennessee from Morgan and standard bred stock and having an easy gait. Also called *Tennessee walker.*

Tennessee warbler *n.* A small wood warbler *(Vermivora peregrina)* of North America, having greenish upper parts and a white underside.

Ten·niel (tĕn′yəl), Sir **John.** 1820–1914. British cartoonist and illustrator of *Alice's Adventures in Wonderland* (1865).

ten·nis (tĕn′ĭs) *n. Sports.* **1.** A game played with rackets and a light ball by two players or two pairs of players on a rectangular court, as of grass, clay, or asphalt, divided by a net. Also called *lawn tennis.* **2.** Court tennis. [Middle English *tenetz, tenyes,* court tennis, from Anglo-Norman *tenetz* and Old French *tenez,* pl. imperative of *tenir,* to hold, from Latin *tenēre.* See DETAIN.]

tennis
Serving at a pro tennis competition

WORD HISTORY: Surprisingly, the origin of the word *tennis* is not precisely known, even though much is known about the history of this sport. The word in the form *tenetz* is first recorded in a work written around 1400. The game referred to is what is now called *court tennis,* or *real tennis,* which is played on a large indoor court with a specially marked-out floor and high cement walls off which the ball may be played. It seems likely that the Middle English form *tenetz* is from *tenetz,* an Anglo-Norman variant of the Old French word *tenez,* the imperative of *tenir,* "to hold," and meaning "receive," said by the server to his opponent. As this evidence indicates, tennis originated in medieval France, but the French called the game, then as now, *la paume.* By *tennis* we do not mean what *tenetz* or *la paume* meant but rather *lawn tennis,* a term first recorded around 1874, shortly after an early form of lawn tennis, descended from court tennis, was introduced. Unlike court tennis, which is traditionally associated with the rich and the royal, tennis is open to players from a wide spectrum of society, although it certainly is not unconnected with the rich and the royal.

tennis bracelet *n.* A bracelet containing many small gemstones, such as diamonds, that are set and linked one after the other into a narrow chain.

tennis elbow *n.* A painful inflammation of the tissue surrounding the elbow, caused by strain from playing tennis and other sports.

tennis shoe *n.* See **sneaker.**

Ten·ny·son (tĕn′ĭ-sən), **Alfred.** First Baron Tennyson. Known as **Alfred, Lord Tennyson.** 1809–1892. British poet whose works, including *In Memoriam* (1850) and "The Charge of the Light Brigade" (1854), reflect Victorian sentiments and aesthetics. **—Ten′ny·so′ni·an** (-sō′nē-ən) *adj.*

teno– *pref.* Tendon: *tenotomy.* [From Greek *tenōn,* tendon. See **ten-** in Appendix.]

Te·noch·ti·tlán (tĕ-nôch′tē-tlän′). An ancient Aztec capital on the site of present-day Mexico City. Founded c. 1325, it was destroyed by the Spanish in 1521.

ten·on (tĕn′ən) *n.* A projection on the end of a piece of wood shaped for insertion into a mortise to make a joint. **—tenon** *tr.v.* **-oned, -on·ing, -ons. 1.** To provide with a tenon. **2.** To join with a tenon. [Middle English, from Old French, from *tenir,* to hold, from Latin *tenēre.* See **ten-** in Appendix.]

ten·o·ni·tis (tĕn′ə-nī′tĭs) *n.* Tendinitis.

ten·or (tĕn′ər) *n.* **1.** A continuous, unwavering course. See Synonyms at **tendency. 2.** The word, phrase, or subject with which the vehicle of a metaphor is identified, as *life* in *"Life's but a walking shadow"* (Shakespeare). **3. a.** The course of thought or argument running through something written or spoken. **b.** General sense; purport. **4.** *Law.* **a.** The exact meaning or actual wording of a document as distinct from its effect. **b.** An exact copy of a document. **5.** *Abbr.* **ten., t., T.** *Music.* **a.** The highest natural adult male voice. **b.** A part for this voice. **c.** One who sings this part. *—attributive.* Often used to modify another noun: *a tenor solo; a tenor part.* [Middle English, from Anglo-Norman, from Latin, uninterrupted course, from *tenēre,* to hold, continue. See **ten-** in Appendix.]

tenor clef *n. Music.* The C clef positioned to indicate that the fourth line from the bottom of a staff represents the pitch of middle C.

te·nor·rha·phy (tĕ-nôr′ə-fē) *n., pl.* **-phies.** The surgical uniting of divided tendons with sutures. [TENO– + Greek *rhaphē,* suture (from *rhaptein,* to sew; see **wer-**[2] in Appendix) + –Y[2].]

Te·nos (tē′nŏs′, -nôs′). See **Tínos.**

ten·o·syn·o·vi·tis (tĕn′ō-sĭn′ə-vī′tĭs) *n.* Inflammation of a tendon sheath.

te·not·o·my (tĕ-nŏt′ə-mē) *n., pl.* **-mies.** Surgical cutting or division of a tendon.

ten·pen·ny nail (tĕn′pĕn′ē, -pə-nē) *n.* A nail 3.0 inches (7.6 centimeters) long. [From its original price per hundred.]

ten·pin (tĕn′pĭn′) *n. Sports & Games.* **1.** One of the bottle-shaped pins used in bowling. **2. tenpins** *(used with a sing. verb).* See **bowling** (sense 1a).

ten·pound·er (tĕn′poun′dər) *n.* See **ladyfish.**

ten·rec (tĕn′rĕk′) also **tan·rec** (tän′-) *n.* Any of various insectivorous mammals of the family Tenrecidae, of Madagascar and adjacent islands, similar to the hedgehog but having a long pointed snout and often no tail. [French, from Malagasy *tandraka.*]

TENS (tĕnz) *n.* A technique used to relieve pain in an injured or diseased part of the body in which electrodes applied to the skin deliver intermittent stimulation to surface nerves, blocking the transmission of pain signals. [*t(ranscutaneous) e(lectrical) n(erve) s(timulation).*]

Ten·sas (tĕn′sô′). A river, about 402 km (250 mi) long, of northeast Louisiana flowing south to the Ouachita River.

tense[1] (tĕns) *adj.* **tens·er, tens·est. 1.** Tightly stretched; taut. See Synonyms at **stiff, tight. 2.** In a state of mental or nervous tension. **3.** Characterized by nervous tension or suspense. **4.** *Linguistics.* Enunciated with taut muscles, as the sound (t). **—tense** *tr. & intr.v.* **tensed, tens·ing, tens·es.** To make or become tense. [Latin *tēnsus,* past participle of *tendere,* to stretch. See **ten-** in Appendix.] **—tense′ly** *adv.* **—tense′ness** *n.*

tense[2] (tĕns) *n. Abbr.* **t.** *Grammar.* **1.** Any one of the inflected forms in the conjugation of a verb that indicates the time, such as past, present, or future, as well as the continuance or completion of the action or state. **2.** A set of tense forms indicating a particular time: *the future tense.* [Middle English *tens,* from Old French, time, from Latin *tempus.*]

ten·sile (tĕn′səl, -sīl′) *adj.* **1.** Of or relating to tension. **2.** Capable of being stretched or extended; ductile. [New Latin *tēnsilis,* from Latin *tēnsus,* stretched out. See TENSE[1].] **—ten·sil′i·ty** (tĕn-sĭl′ĭ-tē) *n.*

tensile strength *n. Abbr.* **T.S., t.s.** The resistance of a material to a force tending to tear it apart, measured as the maximum tension the material can withstand without tearing.

ten·sim·e·ter (tĕn-sĭm′ĭ-tər) *n.* An apparatus for measuring differences in vapor pressure. [TENSI(ON) + –METER.]

ten·si·om·e·ter (tĕn′sē-ŏm′ĭ-tər) *n.* **1.** An instrument for measuring tensile strength. **2.** An instrument used to measure the surface tension of a liquid. [TENSIO(N) + –METER.] **—ten′si·o·met′ric** (-ə-mĕt′rĭk) *adj.* **—ten′si·om′e·try** *n.*

ten·sion (tĕn′shən) *n.* **1. a.** The act or process of stretching something tight. **b.** The condition of so being stretched; tautness. **2. a.** A force tending to stretch or elongate something. **b.** A measure of such a force: *a tension on the cable of 50 pounds.* **3.** The interplay of conflicting elements in a piece of literature, especially a poem. **4. a.** Mental, emotional, or nervous strain: *working under great tension to make a deadline.* **b.** Barely controlled hostility or a strained relationship between people or groups: *the dangerous tension between opposing military powers.* **c.** Uneasy suspense: *a comic scene that relieved the tension of the drama.* **5.** A balanced relation between strongly opposing elements: *"the continuing, and essential, tension between two of the three branches of government, judicial and legislative"* (Haynes Johnson). **6.** A device for regulating tautness, especially a device that controls the tautness of thread on a sewing machine or loom. **7.** *Electricity.* Voltage or potential; electromotive force. **—tension** *tr.v.* **-sioned, -sion·ing, -sions.** To subject to tension; tighten. [Latin *tēnsiō, tēnsiōn-,* a stretching out, from *tēnsus,* past participle of *tendere,* to stretch. See TENSE[1].] **—ten′sion·al** *adj.*

ten·si·ty (tĕn′sĭ-tē) *n., pl.* **-ties.** The state of being tense; tenseness.

ten·sive (tĕn′sĭv) *adj.* **1.** Of or causing tension. **2.** *Physiology.* Giving or causing the sensation of stretching or tension.

ten·sor (tĕn′sər, -sôr′) *n.* **1.** *Anatomy.* A muscle that stretches or tightens a body part. **2.** *Mathematics.* A set of quantities that obey certain transformation laws relating the bases in one generalized coordinate system to those of another and involving partial derivative sums. Vectors are simple tensors. [New Latin *tēnsor,* from Latin *tēnsus,* past participle of *tendere,* to stretch. See TENSE[1].] **—ten·so′ri·al** (-sôr′ē-əl, -sōr′-) *adj.*

ten-speed (tĕn′spēd′) *n.* A bicycle that can be pedaled in ten different gears.

ten-strike (tĕn′strīk′) *n.* **1.** *Sports & Games.* A strike in bowling. **2.** *Informal.* A remarkably successful stroke or act.

tent[1] (tĕnt) *n.* **1.** A portable shelter, as of canvas, stretched over a supporting framework of poles with ropes and pegs. **2.** Something resembling such a portable shelter in construction or outline: *"her hair a dark tent, her face a thin triangle"* (Anne Tyler). **—tent** *v.* **tent·ed, tent·ing, tents.** *—intr.* To camp in a tent. *—tr.* **1.** To form a tent over. **2.** To supply with or put up in tents. [Middle English, from Old French *tente,* from Vulgar Latin **tendita,* from feminine past participle of Latin *tendere,* to stretch out. See **ten-** in Appendix.]

tent[2] (tĕnt) *n.* A small, cylindrical plug of lint or gauze used to keep open or probe a wound or an orifice. **—tent** *tr.v.* **tent·ed, tent·ing, tents.** To keep (a wound or an orifice) open with such a plug. [Middle English *tente,* from Old French, from *tenter,* to probe, from Latin *temptāre,* to feel, try. See TENTATIVE.]

tent[3] (tĕnt) *tr.v.* **tent·ed, tent·ing, tents.** *Scots.* **1.** To pay heed to. **2.** To attend; wait on. [Middle English *tenten,* from *tent,* attention, short for *attent,* from Old French *attente,* from Vulgar Latin **attendita,* from feminine past participle of Latin *attendere,* to wait on. See ATTEND.]

ten·ta·cle (tĕn′tə-kəl) *n.* **1.** *Zoology.* An elongated, flexible, unsegmented extension, as one of those surrounding the mouth or oral cavity of the squid, used for feeling, grasping, or locomotion. **2.** *Botany.* One of the sensitive hairs on the leaves of insectivorous plants, such as the sundew. **3.** A similar part or extension, especially with respect to the ability to grasp or stretch: *an espionage network with far-reaching tentacles.* [New Latin *tentaculum,* from Latin *tentāre,* to feel, try. See TENTATIVE.] **—ten·tac′u·lar** (-tăk′yə-lər) *adj.*

ten·ta·cled (tĕn′tə-kəld) *adj.* Provided with tentacles.

tent·age (tĕn′tĭj) *n.* A group or supply of tents.

ten·ta·tive (tĕn′tə-tĭv) *adj.* **1.** Not fully worked out, concluded, or agreed on; provisional: *just a tentative schedule.* **2.** Uncertain; hesitant. [Medieval Latin *tentātīvus,* from Latin *tentātus,* past participle of *tentāre,* to try, variant of *temptāre.*] **—ten′ta·tive·ly** *adv.* **—ten′ta·tive·ness** *n.*

tent caterpillar *n.* Any of several destructive caterpillars of the family Lasiocampidae, especially of the genus *Malacosoma,* whose colonies construct silken, tentlike webs in the branches of trees.

tent·ed (tĕn′tĭd) *adj.* **1.** Covered with tents. **2.** Sheltered in tents. **3.** Resembling a tent.

ten·ter (tĕn′tər) *n.* **1.** A framework on which milled cloth is stretched for drying without shrinkage. **2.** *Archaic.* A tenterhook. **—tenter** *tr.v.* **-tered, -ter·ing, -ters.** To stretch (cloth) on a tenter. [Middle English *teyntur, tentour,* probably ultimately from Latin *tentōrium,* shelter made of stretched skins, from *tendere,* to stretch. See TENT[1].]

ten·ter·hook (tĕn′tər-ho͝ok′) *n.* A hooked nail for securing cloth on a tenter. **—*idiom.* on tenterhooks.** In a state of uneasiness, suspense, or anxiety.

tenth (tĕnth) *n.* **1.** The ordinal number matching the number ten in a series. **2.** One of ten equal parts. [Middle English *tenthe,* alteration of *tethe,* from Old English *tēotha.* See **dekm̥** in Appendix.] **—tenth** *adv. & adj.*

tent stitch *n.* A short diagonal embroidery stitch that forms close, even, parallel rows to fill in a pattern or background.

ten·u·is (tĕn′yo͞o-ĭs) *n., pl.* **-u·es** (-yo͞o-ēz′). *Linguistics.* **1.** A voiceless stop. **2.** A voiceless, unaspirated stop in ancient Greek. [New Latin (translation of Greek *psilos*), from Latin, thin. See TENUOUS.]

te·nu·i·ty (tĕ-no͞o′ĭ-tē, -nyo͞o′-) *n.* The quality or condition of being tenuous; lack of thickness, density, or substance. [Middle English *tenuite,* from Old French, from Latin *tenuitās,* thinness, from *tenuis,* thin. See TENUOUS.]

ten·u·ous (tĕn′yo͞o-əs) *adj.* **1.** Long and thin; slender: *tenuous strands.* **2.** Having a thin consistency; dilute. **3.** Having little substance; flimsy: *a tenuous argument.* [Latin *tenuis.* See **ten-** in Appendix.] **—ten′u·ous·ly** *adv.* **—ten′u·ous·ness** *n.*

ten·ure (tĕn′yər, -yo͝or′) *n.* **1.a.** The act, fact, or condition of holding something in one's possession, as real estate or an office; occupation. **b.** A period during which something is held. **2.** The status of holding one's position on a permanent basis without periodic contract renewals: *a teacher granted tenure on a faculty.* [Middle English, from Old French *teneure,* from *tenir,* to hold, from Latin *tenēre,* to hold. See **ten-** in Appendix.] **—ten·u′ri·al** (-yo͝or′ē-əl) *adj.* **—ten·u′ri·al·ly** *adv.*

ten·ured (tĕn′yərd, -yo͝ord′) *adj.* Having tenure: *tenured civil servants; tenured faculty.*

te·nu·to (tā-no͞o′tō) *adv. & adj. Abbr.* **ten.** *Music.* So as to be held for the full time value; sustained. Used chiefly as a direction. [Italian, from past participle of *tenere,* to hold, from Latin *tenēre.* See **ten-** in Appendix.]

te·o·cal·li (tē′ə-kăl′ē, tē′ô-kä′lē) *n., pl.* **-lis. 1.** A temple of ancient Mexico and Central America, usually built on a pyramidal mound. **2.** The mound on which such a temple was built. [Nahuatl : *teōtl,* god + *calli,* house.]

te·o·sin·te (tē′ə-sĭn′tē, tā′ō-) *n.* A tall Mexican and Central American annual plant *(Zea mexicana)* related to corn and cultivated for fodder. [American Spanish, from Nahuatl *teocintli* : *teōtl,* sacred + *cintli,* dried ear of corn.]

Te·o·ti·hua·cán (tā′ə-tē′wä-kän′, tē′ô-). An ancient city of central Mexico northeast of present-day Mexico City. Its ruins include the Pyramid of the Sun and the Temple of Quetzalcoatl.

te·pa (tē′pə) *n.* A crystalline organophosphorus compound, $C_6H_{12}N_3OP$, used as an insect sterilant and in the treatment of certain forms of cancer. [*t(ri-)e(thylene) p(hosphorus) a(mide).*]

te·pal (tē′pəl, tĕp′əl) *n. Botany.* A division of the perianth of a flower having a virtually indistinguishable calyx and corolla, as in tulips and lilies. [French *tépale,* alteration (influenced by *sépale,* sepal, from New Latin *sepalum;* see SEPAL) of *pétale,* petal, from New Latin *petalum.* See PETAL.]

tep·a·ry bean (tĕp′ə-rē) *n.* **1.** An annual twining plant *(Phaseolus acutifolius* var. *latifolius)* of the southwest United States and adjacent Mexico, bearing edible beans. **2.** The bean of this plant. [Origin unknown.]

te·pee also **tee·pee** or **ti·pi** (tē′pē) *n.* A portable dwelling of certain Native American peoples, especially on the Great Plains, consisting of a conical framework of poles covered with skins or bark. [Sioux *tʰipi,* dwelling.]

Te·pic (tĕ-pēk′). A city of western Mexico northwest of Guadalajara. It is a commercial center. Population, 145,741.

tep·id (tĕp′ĭd) *adj.* **1.** Moderately warm; lukewarm. **2.** Lacking in emotional warmth or enthusiasm; halfhearted: *"the tepid conservatism of the fifties"* (Irving Howe). [Middle English, from Latin *tepidus,* from *tepēre,* to be lukewarm.] **—te·pid′i·ty, tep′id·ness** *n.* **—tep′id·ly** *adv.*

TEPP (tĕp) *n.* A crystalline organophosphorus compound, $C_8H_{20}O_7P_2$, that inhibits the action of acetylcholinesterase and is used as an insecticide and in medicine as a stimulant of the parasympathetic nervous system. [*t(etra)e(thyl)p(yro)p(hosphate).*]

te·qui·la (tə-kē′lə) *n.* An alcoholic liquor distilled from the fermented juice of the Central American century plant *Agave tequilana.* [American Spanish, after *Tequila,* a town of west-central Mexico.]

ter. *abbr.* **1.** Terrace. **2.** Territorial; territory.

tera– *pref.* One trillion (10^{12}): *terahertz.* [From Greek *teras,* monster. See **kʷer-** in Appendix.]

ter·a·hertz (tĕr′ə-hûrts′) *n. Abbr.* **THz** One trillion (10^{12}) hertz.

ter·a·ohm (tĕr′ə-ōm′) *n.* One trillion (10^{12}) ohms.

ter·aph (tĕr′əf) *n., pl.* **ter·a·phim** (-ə-fĭm). A small image or idol representing an ancient Semitic household god. [Back-formation from *teraphim,* teraphim, from Hebrew *tĕrāpîm,* household gods.]

ter·a·tism (tĕr′ə-tĭz′əm) *n.* A congenital malformation or monster. [Greek *teras, terat-,* monster; see TERATOID + –ISM.]

ter·a·to·car·ci·no·ma (tĕr′ə-tō-kär′sə-nō′mə) *n., pl.* **-mas** or **-ma·ta** (-mə-tə). A malignant teratoma, most often of the testes.

te·rat·o·gen (tə-răt′ə-jən, tĕr′ə-tə-) *n.* An agent, such as a virus, a drug, or radiation, that causes malformation of an embryo or a fetus. [Greek *teras, terat-,* monster; see **kʷer-** in Appendix + –GEN.]

ter·a·to·gen·e·sis (tĕr′ə-tə-jĕn′ĭ-sĭs) *n.* Development of malformed organisms or growths. [Greek *teras, terat-,* monster; see TERATOID + GENESIS.]

ter·a·to·gen·ic (tĕr′ə-tə-jĕn′ĭk) *adj.* Of, relating to, or causing malformations of an embryo or a fetus. **—ter′a·to·ge·nic′i·ty** (-jə-nĭs′ĭ-tē) *n.*

ter·a·toid (tĕr′ə-toid′) *adj. Biology.* Resembling a monster; grotesquely deformed. [Greek *teras, terat-,* monster; see **kʷer-** in Appendix + –OID.]

ter·a·tol·o·gy (tĕr′ə-tŏl′ə-jē) *n.* The biological study of malformations and monstrosities. [Greek *teras, terat-,* monster; see TERATOID + –LOGY.] **—ter′a·to·log′i·cal** (-ə-tl-ŏj′ĭ-kəl) *adj.* **—ter′a·tol′o·gist** *n.*

ter·a·to·ma (tĕr′ə-tō′mə) *n., pl.* **-mas** or **-ma·ta** (-mə-tə). A tumor consisting of different types of tissue, as of skin, hair, and muscle, caused by the development of independent germ cells. [Greek *teras, terat-,* monster; see **kʷer-** in Appendix + –OMA.] **—ter′a·to′ma·tous** (-tō′mə-təs) *adj.*

ter·bi·um (tûr′bē-əm) *n. Symbol* **Tb** A soft, silvery-gray metallic rare-earth element, used in x-ray and color television tubes. Atomic number 65; atomic weight 158.924; melting point 1,356°C; boiling point 3,123°C; specific gravity 8.229; valence 3, 4. See table at **element.** [After *Ytterby,* a town in Sweden.]

terbium metal *n.* Any of several rare-earth metals separable from other metals as a group and including europium, terbium, and gadolinium.

Ter·borch or **Ter Borch** (tər-bôrk′, -bôrKH′), **Gerard.** 1617–

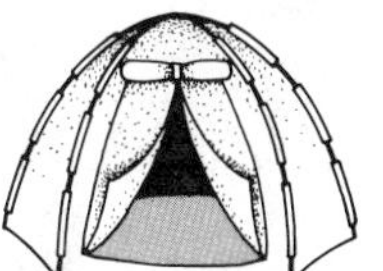

tent[1]
Top: Baker tent
Bottom: Pop tent

tepee
Modern Cheyenne tepee

ă pat	oi boy
ā pay	ou out
âr care	o͝o took
ä father	o͞o boot
ĕ pet	ŭ cut
ē be	ûr urge
ĭ pit	th thin
ī pie	*th* this
îr pier	hw which
ŏ pot	zh vision
ō toe	ə about, item
ô paw	♦ regionalism

Stress marks: **′** (primary); ′ (secondary), as in **dictionary** (dĭk′shə-nĕr′ē)

Mother Teresa

Valentina Tereshkova

termitarium

1681. Dutch painter of portraits and genre scenes noted for their subtle light and color, including *The Concert (c. 1675).*

terce (tûrs) *n.* Variant of **tierce** (sense 1).

Ter·cei·ra (tər-sîr′ə, tĕr-sā′rə). A Portuguese island of the central Azores in the northern Atlantic Ocean.

ter·cel (tûr′səl) also **tier·cel** (tîr′səl) *n.* A male hawk used in falconry. [Middle English, from Old French *terçuel,* from Vulgar Latin **tertiōlus,* diminutive of Latin *tertius,* third. See **trei-** in Appendix.]

ter·cen·ten·a·ry (tûr′sĕn-tĕn′ə-rē, tər-sĕn′tə-nĕr′ē) *n., pl.* **-ries.** A 300th anniversary or its celebration. **—tercentenary** *adj.* Of or relating to a span of 300 years or to a 300th anniversary. [Latin *ter,* thrice; see TERN[2] + CENTENARY.]

ter·cen·ten·ni·al (tûr′sĕn-tĕn′ē-əl) *n.* A tercentenary. **—tercentennial** *adj.* Tercentenary.

ter·cet (tûr′sĭt) *n.* **1.** A group of three lines of verse, often rhyming together or with another triplet. **2.** *Music.* See **triplet** (sense 4). [French, from Italian *terzetto,* from diminutive of *terzo,* third, from Latin *tertius.* See **trei-** in Appendix.]

ter·e·bene (tĕr′ə-bēn′) *n.* A mixture of terpenes prepared from oil of turpentine, used as an expectorant and antiseptic. [French *térébène,* from *térébinthe,* terebinth, from Old French *terebinte.* See TEREBINTH.]

te·reb·ic acid (tə-rĕb′ĭk, -rē′bĭk) *n.* A white crystalline compound, $C_7H_{10}O_4$, resulting from the action of nitric acid on oil of turpentine. [TEREB(INTH) + -IC.]

ter·e·binth (tĕr′ə-bĭnth′) *n.* A small Mediterranean tree *(Pistacia terebinthus)* that is a source of tanning material and turpentine. [Middle English *terebinthe,* from Old French *terebinte,* from Latin *terebinthus,* from Greek *terebinthos.*]

ter·e·bin·thine (tĕr′ə-bĭn′thĭn, -thīn′) also **ter·e·bin·thic** (-thĭk) *adj.* **1.** Of or relating to the terebinth. **2.** Relating to, consisting of, or resembling turpentine.

te·re·do (tə-rē′dō, -rā′dō) *n., pl.* **-dos.** A shipworm of the genus *Teredo.* [New Latin *Terēdō,* mollusk genus, from Latin *terēdō,* a kind of worm, from Greek *terēdōn.* See **terə-**[1] in Appendix.]

Ter·ence (tĕr′əns). 185?–159? B.C. Greek-born Roman playwright. Taken to Rome as the young slave of a senator, he was educated and then freed by his master. His comedies, such as *Phormio* and *Adelphi,* feature subtle humor and refined dialogue.

Te·re·sa (tə-rē′sə, -zə, -rā′-), Mother. Born 1910. Albanian-born Indian nun. Dedicated to relieving the suffering of India's desperately poor and dying people, she founded a Roman Catholic congregation of sisters, the Missionaries of Charity, in 1950. She won the 1979 Nobel Peace Prize.

Teresa, Saint. See Saint **Theresa.**

Te·resh·ko·va (tə-rĕsh-kō′və, tyĭ-ryĭ-shkô′və), **Valentina Vladmirovna.** Born 1937. Soviet cosmonaut who orbited the earth 48 times aboard *Vostok 6* in June 1963, thereby becoming the first woman in space.

Te·re·si·na (tĕr′ĭ-zē′nə). A city of northeast Brazil on the Parnaíba River east-southeast of Belém. Founded in 1852, it is a trade and distribution center. Population, 339,042.

te·rete (tĕ-rēt′) *adj.* Cylindrical but usually slightly tapering at both ends, circular in cross section, and smooth-surfaced. [From Latin *teres, teret-,* rounded. See **terə-**[1] in Appendix.]

Te·reus (tîr′ē-əs, tîr′yo͞os′) *n. Greek Mythology.* A king of Thrace who raped Philomela and who was changed into a hoopoe.

ter·ga (tûr′gə) *n.* Plural of **tergum.**

ter·gite (tûr′gīt′, -jīt′) *n.* A sclerite forming one of the constituents of a tergum.

ter·giv·er·sate (tər-jĭv′ər-sāt′, tûr′jĭ-vər-) *intr.v.* **-sat·ed, -sat·ing, -sates. 1.** To use evasions or ambiguities; equivocate. **2.** To change sides; apostatize. [Latin *tergiversārī, tergiversāt-* : *tergum,* the back + *versāre,* to turn; see **wer-**[2] in Appendix.] **—ter′gi·ver·sa′tion** *n.* **—ter′gi·ver·sa′tor** (-sā′tər) *n.*

ter·gum (tûr′gəm) *n., pl.* **-ga** (-gə). The upper or dorsal surface, especially of a body segment of an insect or other arthropod. [Latin, back.] **—ter′gal** (-gəl) *adj.*

ter·i·ya·ki (tĕr′ē-yä′kē) *n.* A Japanese dish consisting of grilled or broiled slices of marinated meat or shellfish. [Japanese : *teri,* glaze + *yaki,* to broil.]

term (tûrm) *n.* **1.a.** A limited period of time. **b.** A period of time that is assigned to a person to serve: *a six-year term as senator.* See Synonyms at **period. c.** A period when a school or court is in session. **2.a.** A point in time at which something ends; termination: *an apprenticeship nearing its term.* **b.** The end of a normal gestation period: *carried the fetus to term.* **c.** A deadline, as for making a payment. **3.** *Law.* **a.** A fixed period of time for which an estate is granted. **b.** An estate granted for a fixed period. **4.a.** A word or group of words having a particular meaning: *had to explain the term* gridlock. **b. terms.** Language of a certain kind; chosen words: *spoke in rather vague terms; praised him in glowing terms.* **5.** Often **terms.** One of the elements of a proposed or concluded agreement; a condition: *offered favorable peace terms; one of the terms of the lease; the terms of a divorce settlement.* **6. terms.** The relationship between two people or groups; personal footing: *on good terms with her in-laws.* **7.** *Mathematics.* **a.** One of the quantities composing a ratio or fraction or forming a series. **b.** One of the quantities connected by addition or subtraction signs in an equation; a member. **8.** *Logic.* Each of the two concepts being compared or related in a proposition. **9.** A stone or post marking a boundary, especially a squared and downward-tapering pillar adorned with a head and upper torso. **—term** *tr.v.* **termed, term·ing, terms.** To designate; call. **—*idiom.* in terms of. 1.** As measured or indicated by; in units of: *distances expressed in terms of kilometers as well as miles; cheap entertainment, but costly in terms of time wasted.* **2.** In relation to; with reference to: *"facilities planned and programmed in terms of their interrelationships, instead of evolving haphazardly"* (Wharton Magazine). [Middle English *terme,* from Old French, from Latin *terminus,* boundary. N., senses 4-8, from Middle English, from Medieval Latin *terminus,* from Late Latin, mathematical or logical term, from Latin, boundary, limit.]

term. *abbr.* **1.** Terminal. **2.** Termination.

ter·ma·gant (tûr′mə-gənt) *n.* A quarrelsome, scolding woman; a shrew. **—termagant** *adj.* Shrewish; scolding. [From Middle English *Termagaunt,* imaginary Moslem deity portrayed as a violent and overbearing character in medieval mystery plays, alteration of *Tervagant,* from Old French.]

term·er (tûr′mər) *n.* One that serves a specified term: *a second termer in the House of Representatives.*

ter·mi·na·ble (tûr′mə-nə-bəl) *adj.* **1.** Possible to terminate: *terminable activities; terminable employees.* **2.** Terminating after a designated date: *a terminable annuity.* **—ter′mi·na·bil′i·ty, ter′mi·na·ble·ness** *n.* **—ter′mi·na·bly** *adv.*

ter·mi·nal (tûr′mə-nəl) *adj. Abbr.* **term., t. 1.** Of, relating to, situated at, or forming a limit, a boundary, an extremity, or an end. **2.** *Botany.* Growing or appearing at the end of a stem, branch, stalk, or similar part. **3.** Of, relating to, occurring at, or being the end of a section or series; final. See Synonyms at **last**[1]. **4.** Relating to or occurring in a term or each term: *terminal inventories.* **5.** Causing, ending in, or approaching death; fatal: *terminal cancer; terminal heart disease; a terminal patient.* **—terminal** *n. Abbr.* **term., t. 1.** A point or part that forms the end. **2.** An ornamental figure or object placed at the end of a larger structure; a finial. **3.** *Electricity.* **a.** A position in a circuit or device at which a connection is normally established or broken. **b.** A passive conductor at such a position used to facilitate the connection. **4.a.** Either end of a railroad or other transportation line; a terminus. **b.** A station at the end of a transportation line or at a major junction on a transportation line. **c.** A town at the end of a transportation line. **5.** *Computer Science.* A device, often equipped with a keyboard and a video display, through which data or information can enter or leave a computer system. [Middle English, from Latin *termināIis,* from *terminus,* boundary.] **—ter′mi·nal·ly** *adv.*

ter·mi·nate (tûr′mə-nāt′) *v.* **-nat·ed, -nat·ing, -nates.** —*tr.* **1.** To bring to an end or a halt: *"His action terminated the most hopeful period of reform in Prussian history"* (Gordon A. Craig). **2.** To occur at or form the end of; conclude or finish: *a display of fireworks that terminated the festivities.* **3.** To discontinue the employment of; dismiss: *a company that terminated 300 workers.* —*intr.* **1.** To come to an end: *The oil pipeline terminates at a shipping port. Negotiations terminated yesterday.* See Synonyms at **complete. 2.** To have as an end or a result: *"The Peloponnesian war . . . terminated in the ruin of the Athenian commonwealth"* (Alexander Hamilton). [Latin *termināre, termināt-,* from *terminus,* end.]

ter·mi·na·tion (tûr′mə-nā′shən) *n. Abbr.* **term. 1.** The act of terminating or the condition of being terminated. **2.a.** The end of something in time; the conclusion. **b.** An end of something in space; a limit or an edge. **3.** A result; an outcome. **4.** *Linguistics.* The end of a word, as an inflectional ending, a suffix, or a final morpheme. **—ter′mi·na′tion·al** *adj.*

ter·mi·na·tive (tûr′mə-nā′tĭv) *adj.* Serving, designed, or tending to terminate; conclusive. **—ter′mi·na′tive·ly** *adv.*

ter·mi·na·tor (tûr′mə-nā′tər) *n.* **1.** One that terminates: *a terminator of unpopular policies.* **2.** The dividing line between the bright and shaded regions of the disk of the moon or an inner planet. **3.** A sequence of nucleotides that signals the end of transcription and the completion of the synthesis of a nucleic acid molecule from a template.

ter·mi·ni (tûr′mə-nī′) *n.* A plural of **terminus.**

ter·mi·nol·o·gy (tûr′mə-nŏl′ə-jē) *n., pl.* **-gies. 1.** The vocabulary of technical terms used in a particular field, subject, science, or art; nomenclature. **2.** The study of nomenclature. [German *Terminologie,* from Medieval Latin *terminus,* expression. See TERM.] **—ter′mi·no·log′i·cal** (-nə-lŏj′ĭ-kəl) *adj.* **—ter′mi·no·log′i·cal·ly** *adv.* **—ter′mi·nol′o·gist** *n.*

term insurance *n.* Insurance providing coverage for losses to the insured during a stated period but becoming void upon its expiration.

ter·mi·nus (tûr′mə-nəs) *n., pl.* **-nus·es** or **-ni** (-nī′). **1.** The final point; the end. **2.** An end point on a transportation line or the town in which it is located. **3.a.** A boundary or border. **b.** A stone or post marking a border. [Latin.]

ter·mi·tar·i·um (tûr′mĭ-târ′ē-əm) *n., pl.* **-i·a** (-ē-ə). A nest built by a colony of termites. Also called *termitary.*

ter·mi·tar·y (tûr′mĭ-tĕr′ē) *n., pl.* **-ies.** See **termitarium.**

ter·mite (tûr′mīt′) *n.* Any of numerous pale-colored, usually soft-bodied social insects of the order Isoptera that live mostly in warm regions and many species of which feed on wood, often destroying trees and wooden structures. Also called *white ant.* [New Latin *Termes,* genus name, from Late Latin *termes, termit-,* woodworm, alteration of Latin *tarmes.*]

ter·mit·ic (tər-mĭt′ĭk) *adj.* Of, relating to, or formed by termites.

term·less (tûrm′lĭs) *adj.* **1.** Having no bounds or limits; unending: *termless suffering.* **2.** Unconditional: *termless surrender.*

term paper *n.* A lengthy piece of written work required of a student on a topic drawn from the subject matter of a course of study.

tern[1] (tûrn) *n.* Any of various sea birds of the genus *Sterna* and related genera, related to and resembling the gulls but generally smaller and having a forked tail. [Of Scandinavian origin.]

tern[2] (tûrn) *n.* **1.** *Games.* A set of three, especially a combination of three numbers that wins a lottery prize. **2.** *Nautical.* A three-masted schooner. [Middle English *terne,* from Old French, from *ternes,* from Latin *ternās,* accusative pl. of *ternī,* three each, from *ter,* thrice. See **trei-** in Appendix.]

ter·na·ry (tûr′nə-rē) *adj.* **1.** Composed of three or arranged in threes. **2.** *Mathematics.* **a.** Having the base three. **b.** Involving three variables. **—ternary** *n., pl.* **-ries.** A group of three. [Middle English, from Latin *ternārius,* from *ternī,* three each. See TERN[2].]

ter·nate (tûr′nāt′, -nĭt) *adj.* Arranged in sets or groups of three, as a compound leaf with three leaflets. [New Latin *ternātus,* from Medieval Latin, past participle of *ternāre,* to treble, from Latin *ternī,* three each. See TERN[2].] **—ter′nate′ly** *adv.*

Ter·na·te (tər-nä′tā, tĕr-nä′tĕ). An island of eastern Indonesia in the northern Moluccas west of northeast Celebes. Settled by the Portuguese (1521–1574), it was subjugated by the Dutch in 1683.

terne (tûrn) *n.* Terneplate.

terne·plate (tûrn′plāt′) *n.* Sheet iron or steel plated with an alloy of three or four parts of lead to one part of tin, used as a roofing material. [Probably French *terne,* dull (from Old French; see TARNISH) + PLATE.]

Ter·ni (tĕr′nē). A city of central Italy north of Rome. It was part of the Papal States in the 14th century. Population, 111,401.

Ter·no·pol (tĕr-nō′pəl, tĭr-nô′-). A city of western Ukraine west-southwest of Kiev. Founded in 1540, it passed to Austria in 1772 and was held by Poland until its annexation by the U.S.S.R. in 1939. Population, 182,000.

ter·pene (tûr′pēn′) *n.* Any of various unsaturated hydrocarbons, $C_{10}H_{16}$, found in essential oils and oleoresins of plants such as conifers and used in organic syntheses. [Obsolete *terp(entine),* variant of TURPENTINE + –ENE.] **—ter·pe′nic** *adj.* **—ter′pe·noid′** *adj. & n.*

ter·pin·e·ol (tər-pĭn′ē-ôl′, -ōl′, -ŏl′) *n.* Any of three isomeric alcohols, $C_{10}H_{17}OH$, occurring naturally in the essential oils of certain plants and used as solvents in perfumes, soaps, and medicine. [TERP(ENE) + –INE[2] + –OL[1].]

ter·pin hydrate (tûr′pĭn) *n.* A crystalline powder, $C_{10}H_{20}O_2{}^*H_2O$, used in cough syrups as an expectorant or elixir. [TERP(ENE) + –IN.]

ter·pol·y·mer (tər-pŏl′ə-mər) *n.* A polymer that consists of three distinct monomers. [Latin *ter,* thrice; see **trei-** in Appendix + POLYMER.]

Terp·sich·o·re (tûrp-sĭk′ə-rē) *n.* **1.** *Greek Mythology.* The Muse of dancing and choral singing. **2. terpsichore.** The art of dancing. [Latin *Terpsichorē,* from Greek *Terpsikhorē,* from feminine of *terpsikhoros,* dance-loving : *terpein,* to delight + *khoros,* dance; see **gher-**[1] in Appendix.]

terp·si·cho·re·an (tûrp′sĭ-kə-rē′ən, tûrp′sĭ-kôr′ē-ən, -kōr′-) *adj.* Of or relating to dancing. **—terpsichorean** *n.* A dancer. [From TERPSICHORE.]

terr (tĕr) *n. Slang.* A terrorist.

terr. *abbr.* **1.** Terrace. **2.** Territorial; territory.

ter·ra (tĕr′ə) *n., pl.* **ter·rae** (tĕr′ē). A rough upland or mountainous region of the moon with a relatively high albedo. [Latin, earth, land. See TERRACE.]

terra al·ba (ăl′bə, ôl′bə) *n.* **1.** Finely pulverized gypsum used in making paper, paints, and as a nutrient for growing yeast. **2.** Kaolin. [New Latin : Latin *terra,* earth + Latin *albus,* white.]

ter·race (tĕr′ĭs) *n. Abbr.* **ter., terr. 1.a.** A porch or walkway bordered by colonnades. **b.** A platform extending outdoors from a floor of a house or an apartment building. **2.** An open, often paved area adjacent to a house serving as an outdoor living space; a patio. **3.** A raised bank of earth having vertical or sloping sides and a flat top: *turning a hillside into a series of ascending terraces for farming.* **4.** A flat, narrow stretch of ground, often having a steep slope facing a river, lake, or sea. **5.a.** A row of buildings erected on raised ground or on a sloping site. **b.** A section of row houses. **c.** A residential street on top of or climbing a slope. **6.** A narrow strip of landscaped earth in the middle of a street. **—terrace** *tr.v.* **-raced, -rac·ing, -rac·es. 1.** To provide (a house, for example) with a terrace or terraces. **2.** To form (a hillside or sloping lawn, for example) into terraces. [French, from Old French, from Old Provençal *terrassa,* from Vulgar Latin **terrācea,* feminine of **terrāceus,* earthen, from Latin *terra,* earth. See **ters-** in Appendix.]

terra cot·ta (kŏt′ə) *n.* **1.a.** A hard, semifired, waterproof ceramic clay used in pottery and building construction. **b.** Ceramic wares made of this material. **2.** A brownish orange. [Italian : *terra,* earth (from Latin; see TERRACE) + *cotta,* baked, cooked (from Latin *cōcta,* feminine past participle of *coquere,* to cook; see **pekʷ-** in Appendix).] **—ter′ra-cot′ta** (tĕr′ə-kŏt′ə) *adj.*

ter·rae (tĕr′ē) *n.* Plural of **terra.**

terra fir·ma (fûr′mə) *n.* Solid ground; dry land. [New Latin : Latin *terra,* earth + Latin *firmus,* solid.]

ter·rain (tə-rān′) *n.* **1.a.** An area of land; ground: *climbed a tree to view the surrounding terrain.* **b.** A particular geographic area; a region: *a guide who knows this terrain well.* **2.** The surface features of an area of land; topography: *boots designed for rugged terrain.* **3.** (*also* tĕr′ān). Variant of **terrane.** [French, from Old French, from Vulgar Latin **terrānum,* alteration of Latin *terrēnum,* from neuter of *terrēnus,* of the earth. See TERRENE.]

terra in·cog·ni·ta (ĭn′kŏg-nē′tə, -kŏg′nĭ-tə) *n., pl.* **terrae in·cog·ni·tae** (ĭn′kŏg-nē′tē, -kŏg′nĭ-tē′). **1.** An unknown land; an unexplored region: *"a vast and virtually final terra incognita left to terrestrial explorers"* (David F. Salisbury). **2.** A new or unexplored field of knowledge. [New Latin : Latin *terra,* land + *incognitus,* unknown.]

Ter·ra·my·cin (tĕr′ə-mī′sĭn). A trademark used for oxytetracycline.

ter·rane also **ter·rain** (tə-rān′, tĕr′ān) *n.* **1.** A series of related rock formations. **2.** An area having a preponderance of a particular rock or rock groups. [Alteration of TERRAIN.]

ter·ra·pin (tĕr′ə-pĭn) *n.* Any of various North American aquatic turtles of the family Emydiolae, especially the genus *Malaclemys,* which includes the diamondback terrapin. [Alteration of *torope,* from Virginia Algonquian.]

ter·ra·que·ous (tĕr-ā′kwē-əs, -ăk′wē-) *adj.* Composed of land and water. [Latin *terra,* earth; see **ters-** in Appendix + AQUEOUS.]

ter·rar·i·um (tə-râr′ē-əm) *n., pl.* **-i·ums** or **-i·a** (-ē-ə). A small enclosure or closed container in which selected living plants and sometimes small land animals, such as turtles and lizards, are kept and observed. [New Latin : Latin *terra,* earth; see TERRENE + –ARIUM.]

ter·raz·zo (tə-răz′ō, tĕ-rät′sō) *n.* A flooring material of marble or stone chips set in mortar and polished when dry. [Italian, perhaps from Old Provençal *terrassa,* terrace. See TERRACE.]

Ter·re Haute (tĕr′ə hōt′, hŭt′, hôt′). A city of western Indiana on the Wabash River west-southwest of Indianapolis. Founded as Fort Harrison in 1811, it is a commercial and industrial center and the seat of Indiana State University (established 1865). Population, 61,125.

ter·rene (tĕ-rēn′, tĕr′ēn′) *adj.* Of or relating to Earth; earthly. [Middle English, from Latin *terrēnus,* from *terra,* earth. See **ters-** in Appendix.]

ter·re·plein (tĕr′ə-plān′) *n.* A platform or level ground surface on which heavy guns are mounted. [French *terreplein,* from Italian *terrapieno,* from *terrapienare,* to fill with earth : *terra,* earth (from Latin; see **ters-** in Appendix) + *pieno,* full (from Latin *plēnus;* see **pelə-**[1] in Appendix).]

ter·res·tri·al (tə-rĕs′trē-əl) *adj.* **1.** Of or relating to Earth or its inhabitants. **2.** Having a worldly, mundane character or quality. **3.** Of, relating to, or composed of land. **4.** *Biology.* Living or growing on land; not aquatic: *a terrestrial plant or animal.* **—terrestrial** *n.* An inhabitant of Earth. [Middle English, from Latin *terrestris,* from *terra,* earth. See **ters-** in Appendix.] **—ter·res′tri·al·ly** *adv.* **—ter·res′tri·al·ness** *n.*

terrestrial planet *n.* Any of the four planets, Mercury, Venus, Earth, or Mars, that are nearest the sun and have similar size and density.

terrestrial radiation *n.* Electromagnetic radiation originating from Earth and its atmosphere.

ter·ret (tĕr′ĭt) *n.* **1.** One of the metal rings on a harness through which the reins pass. **2.** A ring on an animal's collar, used for attaching a leash. [Middle English *teret,* variant of *toret,* from Old French, diminutive of *tour, tor,* a round. See TOUR.]

terre-verte (tĕr′vĕrt′) *n.* An olive-green pigment commonly made from glauconite, used by artists. [French : *terre,* earth (from Latin *terra;* see **ters-** in Appendix) + *verte,* feminine of *vert,* green (from Old French *verd;* see VERDANT).]

ter·ri·ble (tĕr′ə-bəl) *adj.* **1.** Causing great fear or alarm; dreadful: *a terrible bolt of lightning; a terrible curse.* **2.** Extremely formidable: *terrible responsibilities.* **3.** Extreme in extent or degree: *"the life for which he had paid so terrible a price"* (Leslie Fiedler). **4.a.** Unpleasant; disagreeable: *had a terrible time at the party.* **b.** Markedly objectionable: *terrible hypocrisy.* [Middle English, from Old French, from Latin *terribilis,* from *terrēre,* to frighten.] **—ter′ri·ble·ness** *n.* **—ter′ri·bly** *adv.*

ter·ric·o·lous (tĕ-rĭk′ə-ləs) *adj. Biology.* Living on or in the ground: *terricolous worms.* [From Latin *terricola,* earth-dweller : *terra,* earth; see **ters-** in Appendix + *-cola,* -colous.]

ter·ri·er (tĕr′ē-ər) *n.* Any of several typically small, active breeds of hunting dog originally developed for driving game from burrows. [Middle English, from Old French *(chien) terrier,* ground (dog), terrier, from Medieval Latin *terrārius,* of the earth, from Latin *terra.* See **ters-** in Appendix.]

ter·rif·ic (tə-rĭf′ĭk) *adj.* **1.** Causing terror or great fear; terrifying: *a terrific wail.* **2.** Very bad or unpleasant; frightful: *a terrific headache.* **3.** Very good or fine; splendid: *a terrific tennis player.* **4.** Awesome; astounding: *terrific speed.* [Latin *terrificus* : *terrēre,* to frighten + *-ficus,* -fic.] **—ter·rif′i·cal·ly** *adv.*

ter·ri·fy (tĕr′ə-fī′) *tr.v.* **-fied, -fy·ing, -fies. 1.** To fill with terror; make deeply afraid; alarm. See Synonyms at **frighten. 2.**

terrace
Terraced rice fields in China

terrapin
Diamondback terrapin

ă pat	oi boy
ā pay	ou out
âr care	o͝o took
ä father	o͞o boot
ĕ pet	ŭ cut
ē be	ûr urge
ĭ pit	th thin
ī pie	*th* this
îr pier	hw which
ŏ pot	zh vision
ō toe	ə about, item
ô paw	♦ regionalism

Stress marks: ′ (primary); ′ (secondary), as in **dictionary** (dĭk′shə-nĕr′ē)

To menace or threaten; intimidate. [Latin *terrificāre,* from *terrificus,* terrific. See TERRIFIC.]

ter·rig·e·nous (tĕ-rĭj′ə-nəs) *adj. Geology.* Derived from the land, especially by erosive action. Used primarily of sediments. [From Latin *terrigena,* earth-born : *terra,* earth; see **ters-** in Appendix + −GENOUS.]

ter·rine (tə-rēn′) *n.* **1.** An earthenware dish for cooking and serving food. **2.** A food, especially a pâté or a mixture of chopped meat or fish and vegetables, that is cooked or served in such a dish. [French. See TUREEN.]

ter·ri·to·ri·al (tĕr′ĭ-tôr′ē-əl, -tōr′-) *adj. Abbr.* **ter., terr. 1.** Of or relating to the geographic area under a given jurisdiction: *the territorial limits of a country.* **2.** Relating or restricted to a particular territory; regional: *a territorial court.* **3.** Often **Territorial.** Of or relating to an administrative territory: *the territorial government of the U.S. Virgin Islands; Whitehorse, the territorial capital of the Yukon.* **4.** Often **Territorial.** Organized for national or home defense: *the British Territorial Army.* **5.** *Biology.* Displaying territoriality; defending a territory from intruders: *territorial behavior; a territorial species.* **—territorial** also **Territorial** *n.* A member of a territorial army. **—ter′ri·to′ri·al·ly** *adv.*

ter·ri·to·ri·al·ism (tĕr′ĭ-tôr′ē-ə-lĭz′əm, -tōr′-) *n.* **1.** A social system that gives authority and influence in a state to the landowners. **2.** A system of church government based on primacy of civil power. **—ter′ri·to′ri·al·ist** *n.*

ter·ri·to·ri·al·i·ty (tĕr′ĭ-tôr′ē-ăl′ĭ-tē, -tōr′-) *n., pl.* **-ties. 1.** The status of a territory. **2.** A behavior pattern in animals consisting of the occupation and defense of a territory.

ter·ri·to·ri·al·ize (tĕr′ĭ-tôr′ē-ə-līz′, -tōr′-) *tr.v.* **-ized, -iz·ing, -iz·es. 1.** To make a territory of; organize as a territory. **2.** To extend by adding territory. **—ter′ri·to′ri·al·i·za′tion** (-ə-lĭ-zā′shən) *n.*

territorial waters *pl.n.* Inland and coastal waters under the jurisdiction of a nation or state, especially the ocean waters within 3 or 12 miles (4.8 or 19.3 kilometers) of the shoreline.

ter·ri·to·ry (tĕr′ĭ-tôr′ē, -tōr′ē) *n., pl.* **-ries.** *Abbr.* **ter., terr., t., T. 1.** An area of land; a region. **2.** The land and waters under the jurisdiction of a government. **3. a.** A political subdivision of a country. **b.** A geographic region, such as a colonial possession, that is dependent on an external government: *the territories of the Holy Roman Empire.* **4.** Often **Territory. a.** A subdivision of the United States that is not a state and is administered by an appointed or elected governor and elected legislature. **b.** A similarly organized political subdivision of Canada or Australia. **5.** An area for which a person is responsible as a representative or an agent: *a salesperson's territory.* **6.** *Sports.* The area of a field defended by a specified team: *punted the ball deep into the opponent's territory.* **7.** *Biology.* An area occupied by a single animal, mating pair, or group and often vigorously defended against intruders, especially those of the same species. **8.** A sphere of action or interest; a province. See Synonyms at **field.** [Middle English, from Latin *territōrium,* from *terra,* earth. See **ters-** in Appendix.]

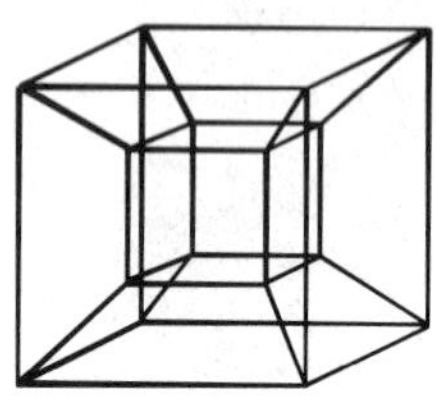
tesseract

ter·ror (tĕr′ər) *n.* **1.** Intense, overpowering fear. See Synonyms at **fear. 2.** One that instills intense fear: *a rabid dog that became the terror of the neighborhood.* **3.** The ability to instill intense fear: *the terror of jackboots pounding down the street.* **4.** Violence committed or threatened by a group to intimidate or coerce a population, as for military or political purposes. **5.** *Informal.* An annoying or intolerable pest: *that little terror of a child.* [Middle English *terrour,* from Old French *terreur,* from Latin *terror,* from *terrēre,* to frighten.]

ter·ror·ism (tĕr′ə-rĭz′əm) *n.* The unlawful use or threatened use of force or violence by a person or an organized group against people or property with the intention of intimidating or coercing societies or governments, often for ideological or political reasons.

ter·ror·ist (tĕr′ər-ĭst) *n.* One that engages in acts or an act of terrorism. **—terrorist** *adj.* Of, relating to, or constituting terrorism. **—ter′ror·is′tic** *adj.*

ter·ror·ize (tĕr′ə-rīz′) *tr.v.* **-ized, -iz·ing, -iz·es. 1.** To fill or overpower with terror; terrify. **2.** To coerce by intimidation or fear. See Synonyms at **frighten. —ter′ror·i·za′tion** (-ər-ĭ-zā′shən) *n.* **—ter′ror·iz′er** *n.*

ter·ry (tĕr′ē) *n., pl.* **-ries. 1.** One of the uncut loops that form the pile of a fabric. **2.** A pile fabric, usually woven of cotton, with uncut loops on both sides, used for bath towels and robes. In this sense, also called *terry cloth.* [Origin unknown.]

Ter·ry (tĕr′ē), Dame **Ellen Alice** or **Alicia.** 1847–1928. British actress. The preeminent English-speaking actress of her day, she was known for her Shakespearean roles and her correspondence with George Bernard Shaw.

terse (tûrs) *adj.* **ters·er, ters·est.** Brief and to the point; effectively concise. [Latin *tersus,* past participle of *tergēre,* to cleanse.] **—terse′ly** *adv.* **—terse′ness** *n.*

ter·tial (tûr′shəl) *adj.* Of, relating to, or designating the third row of flight feathers on the basal section of a bird's wing. **—tertial** *n.* A tertial feather. [Latin *tertius,* third; see TERTIARY + −AL[1].]

ter·tian (tûr′shən) *adj.* Recurring every other day or, when considered inclusively, every third day: *a tertian fever.* **—tertian** *n. Pathology.* A tertian fever, such as vivax malaria. [Middle English *terciane,* tertian fever, from Latin *(febris) tertiāna,* (fever) of the third (day), from *tertius,* third. See **trei-** in Appendix.]

ter·ti·ar·y (tûr′shē-ĕr′ē) *adj.* **1.** Third in place, order, degree, or rank. **2.** Of, relating to, or designating the short flight feathers nearest the body on the rear edge of a bird's wing. **3.** *Chemistry.* **a.** Of or relating to salts of acids containing three replaceable hydrogen atoms. **b.** Of or relating to organic compounds in which a group, such as an alcohol or amine, is bound to three nonelementary radicals. **4. Tertiary.** *Geology.* Of, belonging to, or being the geologic time, system of rocks, and sedimentary deposits of the first period of the Cenozoic Era, extending from the Cretaceous Period of the Mesozoic Era to the Quaternary Period of the Cenozoic Era, characterized by the appearance of modern flora and of apes and other large mammals. See table at **geologic time. —tertiary** *n., pl.* **-ies. 1.** A tertiary feather. **2. Tertiary.** *Geology.* The Tertiary Period or its system of deposits. **3.** *Roman Catholic Church.* A member of a religious Third Order. [Latin *tertiārius,* from *tertius,* third. See **trei-** in Appendix.]

tertiary color *n.* A color resulting from the mixture of two secondary colors.

tertiary consumer *n. Ecology.* An animal that feeds on secondary consumers in a food chain.

tertiary syphilis *n.* The final stage of syphilis, following a latent period that may last years, characterized by spread of the disease to many organs and tissues, including the skin, bones, joints, heart, brain, and spinal cord.

ter·ti·um quid (tûr′shē-əm kwĭd′, tĕr′tē-o͝om′) *n.* Something that cannot be classified into either of two groups considered exhaustive; an intermediate thing or factor. [Late Latin : Latin *tertium,* neuter of *tertius,* third + *quid,* something.]

Ter·tul·lian (tər-tŭl′yən, -tŭl′ē-ən). A.D. 160?–230? Carthaginian theologian who converted to Christianity (c. 193), broke with the Catholic Church (c. 207), and formed his own schismatic sect. His writings greatly influenced Western theology.

ter·va·lent (tər-vā′lənt, tûr′vā′-) *adj.* Trivalent.

ter·za ri·ma (tĕr′tsə rē′mə) *n., pl.* **ter·ze ri·me** (tĕr′tsĕ rē′mĕ). A verse form of Italian origin consisting of tercets of 10 or 11 syllables with the middle line rhyming with the first and third lines of the following tercet. [Italian : *terza,* third + *rima,* rhyme.]

TESL *abbr.* Teaching English as a second language.

tes·la (tĕs′lə) *n. Abbr.* **T** The unit of magnetic flux density in the International System, equal to one weber per square meter. See table at **measurement.** [After Nikola TESLA.]

Tes·la (tĕs′lə), **Nikola.** 1856–1943. Serbian-born American electrical engineer and physicist who discovered the principles of alternating current (1881) and invented numerous devices and procedures that were seminal to the development of radio and the harnessing of electricity.

tesla coil *n.* An air-core transformer that is used as a source of high-frequency power, as for x-ray tubes. [After Nikola TESLA.]

TESOL *abbr.* Teachers of English to speakers of other languages.

tes·sel·late (tĕs′ə-lāt′) *tr.v.* **-lat·ed, -lat·ing, -lates.** To form into a mosaic pattern, as by using small squares of stone or glass. [From Latin *tessellātus,* of small square stones, from *tessella,* small cube, diminutive of *tessera,* a square. See TESSERA.] **—tes′sel·la′tion** *n.*

tes·ser·a (tĕs′ər-ə) *n., pl.* **tes·ser·ae** (tĕs′ə-rē′). One of the small squares of stone or glass used in making mosaic patterns. [Latin, from Greek, neuter of *tesseres,* variant of *tessares,* four. See **k**[w]**etwer-** in Appendix.]

tes·ser·act (tĕs′ə-răkt′) *n.* The four-dimensional equivalent of a cube. [Greek *tessera,* neuter pl. of *tesseres,* four; see TESSERA + *aktis,* ray of light; see ACTINO−.]

tes·si·tu·ra (tĕs′ĭ-to͝or′ə) *n. Music.* The prevailing range of a vocal or instrumental part, within which most of the tones lie. [Italian, from Latin *textūra,* web, structure. See TEXTURE.]

test[1] (tĕst) *n.* **1.** A procedure for critical evaluation; a means of determining the presence, quality, or truth of something; a trial: *a test of one's eyesight; subjecting a hypothesis to a test; a test of an athlete's endurance.* **2.** A series of questions, problems, or physical responses designed to determine knowledge, intelligence, or ability. **3.** A basis for evaluation or judgment: *"A test of democratic government is how Congress and the president work together"* (Haynes Johnson). **4.** *Chemistry.* **a.** A physical or chemical change by which a substance may be detected or its properties ascertained. **b.** A reagent used to cause or promote such a change. **c.** A positive result obtained. **5.** A cupel. **—test** *v.* **test·ed, test·ing, tests.** *—tr.* **1.** To subject to a test; try: *tested the pen by scribbling on scrap paper; testing each mango for ripeness by pressing and smelling it; testing job applicants.* **2. a.** To determine the presence or properties of (a substance). **b.** To assay (metal) in a cupel. *—intr.* **1.** To undergo a test. **2.** To administer a test: *test for acid content; test for the presence of an antibody.* **3.** To achieve a score or rating on tests: *took the entrance examinations and tested high.* **4.** To exhibit a given characteristic when subjected to a test: *test positive for the tubercle bacillus.* [Middle English, cupel, from Old French, pot, from Latin *testū, testum.*] **—test′a·bil′i·ty** *n.* **—test′a·ble** *adj.*

test[2] (tĕst) *n.* A hard external covering, as that of certain amoebas, dinoflagellates, and sea urchins. [Latin *testa,* shell.]

test. *abbr.* **1.** *Law.* **a.** Testator. **b.** Testatrix. **2.** Testimony.

Test. *abbr. Bible.* Testament.

tes·ta (tĕs′tə) *n., pl.* **-tae** (-tē′). The often thick or hard outer coat of a seed. [Latin, shell.]

tes·ta·cean (tĕ-stā′shən) *n.* Any of various rhizopods of the order Testacea, characterized by the presence of a shell. [From

New Latin *Testācea,* order name, from Latin, neuter pl. of *testāceus,* covered with a shell, from *testa,* shell.] **—tes·ta′cean** *adj.*

tes·ta·ceous (tĕ-stā′shəs) *adj.* **1.** *Biology.* **a.** Having a hard shell or shell-like outer covering: *testaceous echinoderms.* **b.** Composed of a shell or shell-like material: *a testaceous operculum.* **2.** *Color.* Having the reddish-brown or brownish-yellow hue of bricks. [From Latin *testāceus,* from *testa,* shell.]

tes·ta·cy (tĕs′tə-sē) *n. Law.* The condition of being testate.

tes·tae (tĕs′tē′) *n.* Plural of **testa.**

tes·ta·ment (tĕs′tə-mənt) *n.* **1.** Something that serves as tangible proof or evidence: *The spacious plan of the city is a testament to the foresight of its founders.* **2.** A statement of belief; a credo: *my political testament.* **3.** *Law.* A written document providing for the disposition of a person's property after death; a will. **4. Testament.** *Abbr.* **T., Test.** *Bible.* Either of the two main divisions of the Bible. **5.** *Archaic.* A covenant between human beings and God. [Middle English, a will, from Latin *testāmentum,* from *testārī,* to make a will, from *testis,* witness. See **trei-** in Appendix.] **—tes′ta·men′tar·y** (-mĕn′tə-rē, -mĕn′trē) *adj.*

tes·tate (tĕs′tāt′) *adj. Law.* Having made a legally valid will before death. [Middle English, from Latin *testātus,* past participle of *testārī,* to make one's will. See TESTAMENT.]

tes·ta·tor (tĕs′tā′tər, tĕ-stā′tər) *n. Abbr.* **test.** *Law.* One who has made a legally valid will before death. [Middle English *testatour,* from Anglo-Norman, from Latin *testātor,* from *testārī,* to make one's will. See TESTAMENT.]

tes·ta·trix (tĕ-stā′trĭks) *n., pl.* **-tri·ces** (-trī-sēz′). *Abbr.* **test.** *Law.* A woman who has made a legally valid will before death. [Latin, feminine of *testātor,* testator. See TESTATOR.]

test case *n. Law.* A legal action whose outcome is likely to set a precedent or test the constitutionality of a statute.

test·cross (tĕst′krôs′, -krŏs′) *Genetics. n.* A cross between an individual exhibiting the dominant phenotype of a trait and an individual that is homozygous recessive for that trait in order to determine the genotype of the dominant individual. **—testcross** *tr.v.* **-crossed, -cross·ing, -cross·es.** To subject to a testcross.

test-drive (tĕst′drīv′) *tr.v.* **-drove** (-drōv), **-driv·en** (-drĭv′ən), **-driv·ing, -drives.** To drive (a motor vehicle) to evaluate performance and condition.

test·er¹ (tĕs′tər) *n.* One that tests: *a battery tester.*

tes·ter² (tĕs′tər, tē′stər) *n.* A canopy, as over a bed or pulpit. [Middle English, from Medieval Latin *testrum,* from Late Latin *testa,* skull, from Latin, shell.]

tes·ter³ (tĕs′tər) *n.* See **teston** (sense 2). [Alteration of TESTON.]

tes·tes (tĕs′tēz) *n.* Plural of **testis.**

tes·ti·cle (tĕs′tĭ-kəl) *n.* A testis, especially one contained within a scrotum. [Middle English *testicule,* from Latin *testiculus,* diminutive of *testis,* testis. See TESTIS.]

tes·tic·u·lar (tĕ-stĭk′yə-lər) *adj.* Of or relating to a testicle or testis.

tes·tic·u·late (tĕ-stĭk′yə-lĭt) *adj.* **1.** Having the shape of a testicle; ovoid. **2.** *Botany.* Having two oblong tubes, as some orchids. **3.** Testicular.

tes·ti·fy (tĕs′tə-fī′) *v.* **-fied, -fy·ing, -fies.** —*intr.* **1.** To make a declaration of truth or fact under oath; submit testimony: *witnesses testifying before a grand jury.* **2.** To express or declare a strong belief, especially to make a declaration of faith. **3.** To make a statement based on personal knowledge in support of an asserted fact; bear witness: *the exhilaration of weightlessness, to which many astronauts have testified.* **4.** To serve as evidence: *wreckage that testifies to the ferocity of the storm.* —*tr.* **1.** To declare publicly; make known: *testifying their faith.* **2.** To state or affirm under oath: *testified in court that he saw the defendant.* **3.** To bear witness to; provide evidence for. See Synonyms at **indicate.** [Middle English *testifien,* from Latin *testificārī* : *testis,* witness; see **trei-** in Appendix + *-ficārī,* -fy.] **—tes′ti·fi·ca′tion** (-fĭ-kā′shən) *n.* **—tes′ti·fi′er** *n.*

tes·ti·mo·ni·al (tĕs′tə-mō′nē-əl) *n.* **1.** A statement in support of a particular truth, fact, or claim. **2.** A written affirmation of another's character or worth; a personal recommendation. **3.** Something given in appreciation of a person's service or achievement; a tribute. **—testimonial** *adj.* Relating to or constituting a testimony or testimonial: *testimonial statements; a testimonial dinner.* [Middle English, from Old French, of evidence, from Late Latin *testimōniālis,* of evidence, from Latin *testimōnium,* testimony. See TESTIMONY.]

tes·ti·mo·ny (tĕs′tə-mō′nē) *n., pl.* **-nies.** *Abbr.* **test. 1.a.** A declaration by a witness under oath, as that given before a court or deliberative body. **b.** All such declarations, spoken or written, offered in a legal case or deliberative hearing. **2.** Evidence in support of a fact or an assertion; proof. **3.** A public declaration regarding a religious experience. **4.a.** The stone tablets inscribed with the Law of Moses. **b.** The ark containing these tablets. [Middle English, from Old French *testimonie,* from Latin *testimōnium,* from *testis,* witness. See TESTIFY.]

tes·tis (tĕs′tĭs) *n., pl.* **-tes** (-tēz). **1.** The reproductive gland in a male vertebrate, the source of spermatozoa and the androgens, normally occurring paired in an external scrotum in human beings and certain other mammals. **2.** An analogous gland in an invertebrate animal, such as a hydra or a mollusk. [Latin, witness, testis. See TESTIFY.]

test match *n. Sports.* A match in cricket or Rugby played by all-star teams from different countries.

tes·ton (tĕs′tŏn′) also **tes·toon** (tĕ-stōōn′) *n.* **1.** A 16th-century French silver coin. **2.** An English coin stamped with the image of Henry VIII's head. In this sense, also called *tester.* [French, from Italian *testone,* augmentative of *testa,* head, from Late Latin, skull, from Latin, shell.]

tes·tos·ter·one (tĕs-tŏs′tə-rōn′) *n.* A white crystalline steroid hormone, $C_{19}H_{28}O_2$, produced primarily in the testes and responsible for the development and maintenance of male secondary sex characteristics. It is also produced synthetically for use in medical treatment. [TEST(IS) + STER(OL) + –ONE.]

test paper *n.* **1.** A paper bearing a student's work for an examination. **2.** Paper saturated with a reagent, such as litmus, used in making chemical tests.

test pattern *n.* A geometric chart transmitted by a television station to assist viewers in adjusting reception.

test pilot *n.* A pilot who flies aircraft of new or experimental design to test them.

test stand *n.* A platform for static firing of rocket engines to test and determine performance characteristics.

test tube *n.* A clear, cylindrical glass tube usually open at one end and rounded at the other, used in laboratory experimentation.

test-tube (tĕst′tōōb′, -tyōōb′) *adj.* **1.** Produced or cultivated in a test tube. **2.** Conceived by or developed from artificial insemination.

test-tube baby *n.* A baby developed from an egg that was fertilized outside the body and then implanted in the uterus of the biological or surrogate mother.

tes·tu·di·nal (tĕs-tōōd′n-əl, -tyōōd′-) *adj.* Testudinate.

tes·tu·di·nate (tĕs-tōōd′n-ĭt, -āt′, -tyōōd′-) *adj.* Of, relating to, or resembling a turtle or tortoise. **—testudinate** *n.* A turtle or tortoise. [From New Latin *Testūdināta,* order name, from *Testūdō, Testūdin-,* type genus, from Latin, tortoise. See TESTUDO.]

tes·tu·do (tĕ-stōō′dō, -styōō′-) *n., pl.* **-dos. 1.** A Roman siege device consisting of a movable screen protecting the besiegers' approach to a wall. **2.** A cover formed by the overlapping shields of besiegers and held over their heads. [Latin *testūdō,* from *testa,* shell.]

tes·ty (tĕs′tē) *adj.* **-ti·er, -ti·est.** Irritated, impatient, or exasperated; peevish: *a testy cab driver; a testy refusal to help.* [Alteration of Middle English *testif,* headstrong, from Old French *testu,* from *teste,* head, from Late Latin *testa,* skull. See TESTON.] **—tes′ti·ly** *adv.* **—tes′ti·ness** *n.*

WORD HISTORY: To the casual eye *testy* and *heady* seem to have no connection until one becomes less casual and notes that both words refer to the head. The *head* in *heady* is easy to see both in the form of the word and in the meanings of the word The earliest sense, first recorded in a work composed before 1382, is "headlong, headstrong," which is clearly a "head" sense but so is the better known current sense "apt to go to the head, intoxicating." To see the *head* in *testy,* we must look back to the Old French word *testu,* the source of our word. *Testu* is derived from the Old French word *teste,* "head" (Modern French *tête*). In English *testy* developed another sense, "aggressive, contentious," which passed into the sense we are familiar with, "irritable."

Tet (tĕt) *n.* The lunar New Year as celebrated in Vietnam. [Vietnamese *têt.*]

te·tan·ic (tĕ-tăn′ĭk) *adj.* **1.** Of, relating to, or causing tetanus. **2.** Of, relating to, or causing tetany. **—te·tan′i·cal·ly** *adv.*

tet·a·nize (tĕt′-n-īz′) *tr.v.* **-nized, -niz·ing, -niz·es.** To affect with tetanic convulsions; produce or induce tetanus in. **—tet′a·ni·za′tion** (-nĭ-zā′shən) *n.*

tet·a·nus (tĕt′n-əs) *n.* **1.** An acute, often fatal disease characterized by spasmodic contraction of voluntary muscles, especially those of the neck and jaw, and caused by the toxin of the bacillus *Clostridium tetani,* which typically infects the body through a deep wound. Also called *lockjaw.* **2.** *Physiology.* A state of continuous muscular contraction, especially when induced artificially by rapidly repeated stimuli. [Middle English, from Latin, from Greek *tetanos,* rigid, tetanus. See **ten-** in Appendix.] **—tet′a·nal** (tĕt′n-əl) *adj.*

tet·a·ny (tĕt′n-ē) *n., pl.* **-nies.** An abnormal condition characterized by periodic painful muscular spasms and tremors, caused by faulty calcium metabolism and associated with diminished function of the parathyroid glands. [From TETANUS.]

tetched also **teched** (tĕcht) *adj. Informal.* Somewhat unbalanced mentally; touched. [Alteration (influenced by obsolete *tached,* of a given disposition) of TOUCHED.]

tetch·y also **tech·y** (tĕch′ē) *adj.* **-i·er, -i·est.** Peevish; testy: *"As a critic gets older, he or she usually grows more tetchy and limited in responses"* (James Wolcott). [Probably from Middle English *tache, teche,* blemish, from Old French *tache, teche,* from Vulgar Latin **tacca,* from Gothic *taikns,* sign. See **deik-** in Appendix.] **—tetch′i·ly** *adv.* **—tetch′i·ness** *n.*

tête-à-tête (tāt′ə-tāt′, tĕt′ə-tĕt′) *adv. & adj.* Without the intrusion of a third person; in intimate privacy: *talk tête-à-tête; a tête-à-tête supper.* **—tête-à-tête** *n.* **1.** A private conversation between two persons. **2.** A sofa for two, especially an S-shaped one allowing the occupants to face each other. [French : *tête,* head + *à,* to + *tête,* head.]

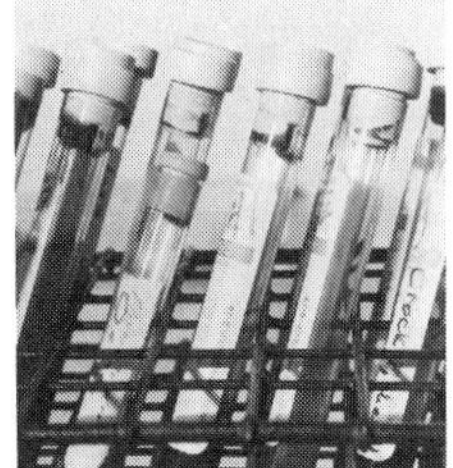

test tube
Test tubes in a laboratory

testudo

ă pat	oi boy
ā pay	ou out
âr care	ŏŏ took
ä father	ōō boot
ĕ pet	ŭ cut
ē be	ûr urge
ĭ pit	th thin
ī pie	*th* this
îr pier	hw which
ŏ pot	zh vision
ō toe	ə about, item
ô paw	♦ regionalism

Stress marks: ′ (primary); ′ (secondary), as in **dictionary** (dĭk′shə-nĕr′ē)

tête-bêche (tĕt′bĕsh′) *adj.* Of, relating to, or being a pair of postage stamps printed with one upside-down in relation to the other, either deliberately or accidentally. [French : *tête,* head (from Old French *teste,* from Late Latin *testa,* skull; see TESTER [2]) + *bêche* (short for obsolete *béchevet,* double head of a bed, from Old French : *bes-,* twice, from Latin *bis;* see BIS + *chevet,* from Late Latin *capitium,* opening for the head in a tunic, from Latin, head covering, from *caput, capit-,* head; see TRICEPS).]

teth (tĕt, tĕs) *n.* The ninth letter of the Hebrew alphabet. See table at **alphabet.** [Hebrew *ṭêt.*]

teth·er (tĕth′ər) *n.* **1.** A rope or chain for holding an animal in place, allowing it a short radius in which to move about. **2.** The extent or limit of one's resources, abilities, or endurance: *drought-stricken farmers at the end of their tether.* —**tether** *tr.v.* **-ered, -er·ing, -ers.** To fasten or restrict with or as if with a tether. [Middle English *tedir, tethir,* from Old Norse *tjōdhr.*]

teth·er·ball (tĕth′ər-bôl′) *n. Games.* A game played by two people using the hands or paddles and a ball hung by a cord from an upright post, the objective being to wind the cord around the post.

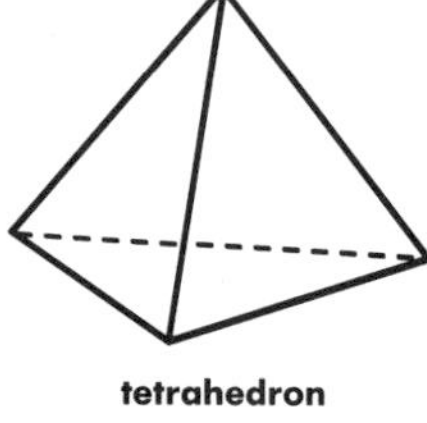

tetrahedron

Te·thys (tē′thĭs) *n.* **1.** *Greek Mythology.* A Titaness and sea goddess who was both sister and wife of Oceanus. **2.** *Astronomy.* The satellite of Saturn that is eighth in distance from the planet. [Greek *Tēthus.*]

Te·ton (tē′tŏn′) *n., pl.* **Teton** or **-tons. 1.** The largest and westernmost of the Sioux peoples, made up of seven groups including the Oglala, Hunkpapa, Brulé, and Miniconjou. The Teton became nomadic buffalo hunters after migrating westward in the 18th century and figured prominently in the resistance to white encroachment on the northern Great Plains. **2.** A member of this people. Also called *Lakota, Teton Dakota, Teton Sioux.*

Teton Range. A range of the Rocky Mountains in northwest Wyoming and southeast Idaho. The Tetons rise to 4,198.6 m (13,766 ft) at Grand Teton.

Teton Sioux *n.* See **Teton.**

tetr– *pref.* Variant of **tetra–.**

tet·ra (tĕt′rə) *n.* Any of numerous small, colorful tropical freshwater fish of the family Characidae, such as the neon tetra, found in South America and Africa, and often kept in home aquariums. Also called *characin.* [Short for New Latin *Tetragonopterini,* group name : Late Latin *tetragōnum,* tetragon; see TETRAGON + Greek *pteron,* wing.]

tetra– or **tetr–** *pref.* **1.** Four: *tetrode.* **2.** Containing four of a specified kind of atom, radical, or group: *tetrachloride.* [Greek. See **kʷetwer-** in Appendix.]

tet·ra·ba·sic (tĕt′rə-bā′sĭk) *adj.* **1.** Containing four replaceable hydrogen atoms in a molecule. Used of acids. **2.** Containing four univalent basic atoms or radicals. Used of bases or salts. —**tet′ra·ba·sic′i·ty** (-sĭs′ĭ-tē) *n.*

tet·ra·bran·chi·ate (tĕt′rə-brăng′kē-ĭt, -āt′) *adj.* Of, relating to, or being a cephalopod of the order Tetrabranchiata, characterized by two pairs of gills and including the chambered nautilus and many fossil species. —**tetrabranchiate** *n.* A tetrabranchiate cephalopod. [From New Latin *Tetrabranchiāta,* order name : TETRA– + Greek *brankhia.*]

tet·ra·caine (tĕt′rə-kān′) *n.* A crystalline compound, $C_{15}H_{24}N_2O_2$, related to procaine and used as a local anesthetic.

tet·ra·chlo·ride (tĕt′rə-klôr′īd′, -klōr′-) *n.* A chemical compound containing four chlorine atoms per molecule.

tet·ra·chord (tĕt′rə-kôrd′) *n. Music.* A series of four diatonic tones encompassing the interval of a perfect fourth. [Greek *tetrakhordon,* from neuter of *tetrakhordos,* four-stringed : *tetra-,* tetra- + *khordē,* string; see **gherə-** in Appendix.] —**tet′ra·chor′dal** (-kôr′dl) *adj.*

te·trac·id (tĕ-trăs′ĭd) *adj.* **1.** Capable of reacting with four molecules of a monobasic acid. Used of a base. **2.** Containing four replaceable hydrogen atoms. Used of an acid or acid salt. —**tetracid** *n.* An acid with four replaceable hydrogen atoms.

tet·ra·cy·cline (tĕt′rə-sī′klēn′, -klĭn) *n.* **1.** A yellow crystalline compound, $C_{22}H_{24}N_2O_8$, synthesized or derived from certain microorganisms of the genus *Streptomyces* and used as a broad-spectrum antibiotic. **2.** An antibiotic, such as chlortetracycline and oxytetracycline, having the same basic structure. [TETRA– + CYCL(IC) + –INE [2].]

tet·rad (tĕt′răd′) *n.* **1.** A group or set of four. **2.** A tetravalent atom, radical, or element. **3.** *Biology.* **a.** A group of four chromatids formed from each of a pair of homologous chromosomes that split longitudinally during the prophase of meiosis. **b.** *Botany.* A group of four cells, as of spores or pollen grains formed by division of one mother cell. [Greek *tetras, tetrad-.* See **kʷetwer-** in Appendix.]

tet·ra·dac·ty·lous (tĕt′rə-dăk′tə-ləs) *adj. Zoology.* Having four digits or claws on each extremity.

te·trad·y·mite (tĕ-trăd′ə-mīt′) *n.* A steel-gray mineral, chiefly Bi_2Te_2S. [German *Tetradymit,* from Late Greek *tetradumos,* fourfold (from the quadruple twin crystals in which it usually is found) : Greek *tetra-,* tetra- + *didumos,* double; see **dwo-** in Appendix.]

tet·ra·dy·na·mous (tĕt′rə-dī′nə-məs) *adj. Botany.* Having six stamens, two of which are shorter than the others, as in most plants of the mustard family. [TETRA– + Greek *dynamis,* strength; see DYNAMIC + –OUS.]

tet·ra·eth·yl lead also **tet·ra·eth·yl·lead** (tĕt′rə-ĕth′əl-lĕd′) *n.* A colorless, poisonous, oily liquid, $Pb(C_2H_5)_4$, used in gasoline for internal-combustion engines as an antiknock agent.

tetraethyl pyrophosphate *n.* TEPP.

tet·ra·gon (tĕt′rə-gŏn′) *n.* A four-sided polygon; a quadrilateral. [Late Latin *tetragōnum,* from Greek *tetragōnon* : *tetra-,* tetra- + *-gonon,* -gon.] —**te·trag′o·nal** (tĕ-trăg′ə-nəl) *adj.* —**te·trag′o·nal·ly** *adv.*

Tet·ra·gram·ma·ton (tĕt′rə-grăm′ə-tŏn′) *n.* The four Hebrew letters usually transliterated as YHWH or JHVH (Yahweh or Jehovah), used as a biblical proper name for God. [Middle English *Tetragramaton,* from Greek *tetragrammaton,* four-letter word, from neuter of *tetragrammatos,* four-lettered : *tetra-,* tetra- + *gramma, grammat-,* letter; see **gerbh-** in Appendix.]

tet·ra·he·dra (tĕt′rə-hē′drə) *n.* A plural of **tetrahedron.**

tet·ra·he·dral (tĕt′rə-hē′drəl) *adj.* **1.** Of or relating to a tetrahedron. **2.** Having four faces. —**tet′ra·he′dral·ly** *adv.*

tet·ra·he·drite (tĕt′rə-hē′drīt′) *n.* A grayish-black mineral, essentially $(CuFe)_{12}Sb_4S_{13}$, often containing other elements, and used as an ore of copper. [German *Tetraëdrit,* from Greek *tetraedros,* four-faced (from its four-faced crystals). See TETRAHEDRON.]

tet·ra·he·dron (tĕt′rə-hē′drən) *n., pl.* **-drons** or **-dra** (-drə). A polyhedron with four faces. [Late Greek *tetraedron,* from Greek, neuter of *tetraedros,* four-faced : *tetra-,* tetra- + *hedra,* face of a geometric solid; see **sed-** in Appendix.]

tet·ra·hy·dro·can·nab·i·nol (tĕt′rə-hī′drə-kə-năb′ə-nôl′, -nōl′, -nŏl′) *n.* THC.

tet·ra·hy·drox·y (tĕt′rə-hī-drŏk′sē) *adj.* Having four hydroxyl groups in a molecule.

te·tral·o·gy (tĕ-trăl′ə-jē, -trŏl′-) *n., pl.* **-gies. 1.** A series of four related dramatic, operatic, or literary works. **2.** *Medicine.* A complex of four symptoms. [Greek *tetralogia* : *tetra-,* tetra- + *-logia,* -logy.]

tetralogy of Fal·lot (fă-lō′) *n.* A congenital malformation of the heart characterized by a defect in the ventricular septum, misplacement of the origin of the aorta, narrowing of the pulmonary artery, and enlargement of the right ventricle. [After Étienne *Fallot* (1850–1911), French physician.]

tet·ra·mer (tĕt′rə-mər) *n.* A polymer consisting of four identical monomers. —**tet′ra·mer′ic** (-mĕr′ĭk) *adj.*

te·tram·er·ous (tĕ-trăm′ər-əs) *adj.* **1.** Having or consisting of four similar parts. **2.** *Botany.* Having flower parts, such as sepals, petals, and stamens, in sets of four, as in the evening primrose. —**te·tram′er·ism** *n.*

te·tram·e·ter (tĕ-trăm′ĭ-tər) *n.* **1.** A line of verse consisting of four metrical feet. **2.** A unit consisting of two pairs of feet in classical prosody. [Late Latin *tetrametrus,* from Greek *tetrametron,* from neuter of *tetrametros,* having four measures : *tetra-,* tetra- + *-metron,* measure; see –METER.] —**te·tram′e·ter** *adj.*

tet·ra·ploid (tĕt′rə-ploid′) *Genetics. adj.* Having four times the haploid number of chromosomes in the cell nucleus: *a tetraploid species.* —**tetraploid** *n.* A tetraploid individual. —**tet′ra·ploi′dy** *n.*

tet·ra·pod (tĕt′rə-pŏd′) *adj.* Having four feet, legs, or leglike appendages. —**tetrapod** *n.* A vertebrate animal with four feet, legs, or leglike appendages. —**tet′ra·pod′** *n.*

te·trap·ter·ous (tĕ-trăp′tər-əs) *adj.* Having four wings, as certain insects.

tet·rarch (tĕt′rärk′, tē′trärk′) *n.* **1.a.** A subordinate ruler. **b.** One of four joint rulers. **2.** A governor of one of four divisions of a country or province, especially in the ancient Roman Empire. **3.** The commander of a subdivision of a phalanx in ancient Greece. [Middle English *tetrarche,* a Roman tetrarch, from Old French, from Late Latin *tetrarcha,* from Latin *tetrarchēs,* from Greek *tetrarkhēs* : *tetra-,* tetra- + *-arkhēs,* -arch.] —**te·trar′chic** (tĕ-trär′kĭk, tē-) *adj.*

tet·rar·chy (tĕt′rär′kē, tē′trär′-) also **tet·rar·chate** (-kāt′, -kĭt) *n., pl.* **-chies** also **-chates. 1.** The area ruled by a tetrarch. **2.a.** Joint rule by four governors. **b.** The four governors so ruling.

tet·ra·spo·ran·gi·um (tĕt′rə-spə-răn′jē-əm) *n., pl.* **-gi·a** (-jē-ə). A unicellular sporangium found in certain red algae in which four tetraspores are produced from meiosis.

tet·ra·spore (tĕt′rə-spôr′, -spōr′) *n.* One of four spores produced from a tetrasporangium. —**tet′ra·spor′ic** (-spôr′ĭk, -spŏr′-) *adj.*

tet·ra·tom·ic (tĕt′rə-tŏm′ĭk) *adj.* **1.** Having four atoms per molecule. **2.** Having four replaceable univalent atoms or radicals.

tet·ra·va·lent (tĕt′rə-vā′lənt) *adj. Chemistry.* Having valence 4.

tet·raz·zi·ni also **Tetrazzini** (tĕt′rə-zē′nē) *adj.* Made with noodles, mushrooms, and almonds in a cream sauce topped with cheese: *turkey tetrazzini.* [After Luisa *Tetrazzini* (1871–1940), Italian operatic soprano.]

tet·rode (tĕt′rōd′) *n.* A four-element electron tube containing an anode, a cathode, a control grid, and an additional electrode.

te·tro·do·tox·in (tĕ-trō′də-tŏk′sĭn) *n.* A potent neurotoxin, $C_{11}H_{17}N_3O_3$, found in many puffers and certain newts. [New Latin *Tetrodon,* genus name (Greek *tetra-,* tetra- + New Latin *-odon,* -odon) + TOXIN.]

te·trox·ide (tĕ-trŏk′sīd′) *n.* A chemical compound containing four oxygen atoms per molecule.

tet·ryl (tĕt′rəl) *n.* A yellow crystalline compound, $C_7H_5N_5O_8$, used as a detonator.

♦**tet·ter** (tĕt′ər) *n. Chiefly Southern U.S.* Any of various skin diseases, such as eczema, psoriasis, or herpes, characterized by eruptions and itching. [Middle English *teter,* from Old English. See **der-** in Appendix.]

Tet·zel or **Te·zel** (tĕt′səl), **Johann.** 1465?–1519. German monk who was appointed to sell indulgences to raise funds for the Catholic Church. His simplistic and unorthodox sermons, regarded by many as symptomatic of the abuses within the Church, provoked Martin Luther to write his 95 theses (1517).

tet·ter·bush (tĕt′ər-bo͝osh′) *n.* An evergreen shrub *(Lyonia lucida)* of the southeast United States, having sharply angled branches, leathery, dark green leaves, and white to pink flowers.

Teut. *abbr.* Teuton; Teutonic.

Teu·to·bur·ger Wald (to͞o′tə-bûr′gər wôld′, toi′tō-bo͝or′-gər vält′). A range of hills in northwest Germany between the upper Ems and the Weser rivers. A monument near Detmold commemorates the victory of Arminius over Roman legions in A.D. 9.

Teu·ton (to͞ot′n, tyo͞ot′n) *n. Abbr.* **Teut. 1.** A member of an ancient people, probably of Germanic or Celtic origin, who lived in Jutland until about 100 B.C. **2.** A member of any of the peoples speaking a Germanic language, especially a German. [Latin *Teutōnī,* Teutons. See **teutā-** in Appendix.]

Teu·ton·ic (to͞o-tŏn′ĭk, tyo͞o-) *adj. Abbr.* **Teut. 1.** Of or relating to the ancient Teutons. **2.** Of or relating to the Germanic languages or their speakers. **—Teutonic** *n. Abbr.* **Teut.** Germanic. [Latin *Teutōnicus,* from *Teutōnī,* Teutons. See TEUTON.]

Teu·ton·ism (to͞ot′n-ĭz′əm, tyo͞ot′-) also **Teu·ton·i·cism** (to͞o-tŏn′ĭ-sĭz′əm, tyo͞o-) *n.* **1.** A German practice or idiom. **2.** German character or civilization. **—Teu′ton·ist** *n.*

Teu·ton·ize (to͞ot′n-īz′, tyo͞ot′-) *tr.v.* **-ized, -iz·ing, -iz·es.** To make German. **—Teu′ton·i·za′tion** (-ĭ-zā′shən) *n.*

Te·vet also **Te·bet** or **Te·beth** (tā′vās, tĕ-vĕt′) *n.* The fourth month of the year in the Jewish calendar. See table at **calendar.** [Hebrew *ṭēbēt,* from Akkadian *tebētu,* the month Tebetu (December/January).]

Te·wa (tā′wə, tē′wə) *n., pl.* **Tewa** or **-was. 1.a.** A group of Pueblo peoples of northern New Mexico. **b.** A member of any of these peoples. **2.** The group of Tanoan languages spoken by the Tewa.

Tewkes·bur·y (to͞oks′bĕr′ē, -bə-rē, -brē, tyo͞oks′-). A municipal borough of west-central England on the Severn River north-northeast of Gloucester. Edward IV's Yorkist forces defeated the Lancastrians here (1471) in the final battle of the Wars of the Roses. Population, 9,554.

Tewks·bur·y (to͞oks′bĕr′ē, -bə-rē, tyo͞oks′-). A town of northeast Massachusetts south of Lowell. Population, 24,635.

Tex. *abbr.* Texas.

Tex·ar·kan·a (tĕk′sär-kăn′ə). A city of southwest Arkansas on the Texas border southwest of Little Rock. Population, 21,338. It is adjacent to **Texarkana,** Texas, in the northeast part of that state. Population, 31,271. The twin cities form a trade and transportation center for the surrounding region.

tex·as (tĕk′səs) *n.* A structure on a river steamboat containing the pilothouse and the officers' quarters. [After TEXAS.]

Tex·as (tĕk′səs). *Abbr.* **TX, Tex.** A state of the south-central United States. It was admitted as the 28th state in 1845. Explored by the Spanish in the 16th and 17th centuries, the region became a province of Mexico in the early 19th century. Texans won their independence in 1836 after a gallant but losing stand at the Alamo in February and a defeat of Santa Ana's forces at the Battle of San Jacinto (April 21). Denied admission as a state by antislavery forces in the U.S. Congress, the leaders of Texas formed an independent republic that lasted until 1845. Austin is the capital and Houston the largest city. Population, 14,227,574. **—Tex′an** *adj. & n.*

Texas bluebonnet *n.* See **bluebonnet** (sense 1).

Texas City. A city of southeast Texas, an industrial suburb of Galveston on Galveston Bay. Population, 41,403.

Texas fever *n.* An infectious disease of cattle first identified in Texas, characterized by high fever, anemia, and emaciation and caused by a parasitic protozoan *(Babesia bigemina)* that is transmitted by cattle ticks.

Texas leagu·er (lē′gər) *n. Baseball.* A fly ball that drops between an infielder and an outfielder for a hit. [After the *Texas League,* a baseball minor league.]

Texas Ranger *n.* **1.** A member of a division of the Texas state highway patrol. **2.** A member of a mounted force of Texans organized in 1835 and active in maintaining order on the frontier.

Texas tower *n.* An offshore radar tower. [After TEXAS (from its resemblance to an offshore oil rig along the coast of Texas).]

Tex-Mex (tĕks′mĕks′) *adj. Informal.* Of or characterized by a blend of Mexican and southwest U.S. cultural elements: *Tex-Mex music; Tex-Mex food.*

text (tĕkst) *n.* **1.a.** The original words of something written or printed, as opposed to a paraphrase, translation, revision, or condensation. **b.** The words of a speech appearing in print. **2.** The body of a printed work as distinct from headings and illustrative matter on a page or from front and back matter in a book. **3.** One of the editions or forms of a written work: *After examining all three manuscripts, he published a new text of the poem.* **4.** A passage from the Scriptures or another authoritative source chosen for the subject of a discourse or cited for support in argument. **5.** A passage from a written work used as the starting point of a discussion. **6.** A subject; a topic. **7.** A textbook. [Middle English *texte,* from Old French, from Late Latin, written account, from Latin, structure, context, body of a passage, from past participle of *texere,* to weave, fabricate. See **teks-** in Appendix.]

text·book (tĕkst′bo͝ok′) *n.* A book used in schools or colleges for the formal study of a subject. **—textbook** *adj.* Being a characteristic example of its kind; classic: *a textbook case of schizophrenia.* **—text′book′ish** *adj.*

text edition *n.* An edition of a book designed especially for use in schools or colleges.

tex·tile (tĕks′tīl′, -təl) *n.* **1.** A cloth, especially one manufactured by weaving or knitting; a fabric. **2.** Fiber or yarn for weaving or knitting into cloth. *—attributive.* Often used to modify another noun: *a textile weave; textile mills.* [Latin, from neuter of *textilis,* woven, from *textus,* past participle of *texere,* to weave. See TEXT.]

tex·tu·al (tĕks′cho͞o-əl) *adj.* Of, relating to, or conforming to a text. **—tex′tu·al·ly** *adv.*

textual criticism *n.* **1.** The study of manuscripts or printings to determine the original or most authoritative form of a text, especially of a piece of literature. **2.** Literary criticism stressing close reading and detailed analysis of a particular text.

tex·tu·al·ism (tĕks′cho͞o-ə-lĭz′əm) *n.* **1.** Strict adherence to a text, especially of the Scriptures. **2.** Textual criticism, especially of the Scriptures. **—tex′tu·al·ist** *n.*

tex·tu·ar·y (tĕks′cho͞o-ĕr′ē) *adj.* Of, relating to, or contained in a text; textual. **—textuary** *n., pl.* **-ies.** A specialist in the study of the Scriptures.

tex·ture (tĕks′chər) *n.* **1.** A structure of interwoven fibers or other elements. **2.** The basic structure or composition, especially of something complex or fine: *the orderly texture of matter as seen through an electron microscope.* **3.a.** The appearance and feel of a surface: *the smooth texture of soap; the rough texture of plowed fields.* **b.** A rough or grainy surface quality: *Brick walls give a room texture.* **4.** Distinctive or identifying character or characteristics: *"the haunting contours and textures of the physical world"* (Joyce Carol Oates). **—texture** *tr.v.* **-tured, -tur·ing, -tures.** To give texture to, especially to impart desirable surface characteristics to: *texture a printing plate by lining and stippling it.* [Middle English, from Old French, from Latin *textūra,* from *textus,* past participle of *texere,* to weave. See TEXT.] **—tex′tur·al** *adj.* **—tex′tur·al·ly** *adv.* **—tex′tured** *adj.*

tex·tur·ize (tĕks′chə-rīz′) *tr.v.* **-ized, -iz·ing, -iz·es.** To give a desired texture to by a special process: *texturize polyester yarn.* **—tex′tur·iz′er** *n.*

Te·zel (tĕt′səl), **Johann.** See Johann **Tetzel.**

T.F. *abbr.* Territorial Force.

tfr. *abbr.* Transfer.

TG *abbr.* Transformational grammar.

t.g. *abbr.* Type genus.

TGIF *abbr.* Thank God it's Friday.

T-group (tē′gro͞op′) *n.* A group engaged in sensitivity training in sessions with a trained leader. [*t(raining) group.*]

tgt. *abbr.* Target.

Th[1] The symbol for the element **thorium.**

Th[2] *abbr. Bible.* Thessalonians.

Th. *abbr.* Thursday.

-th[1] *suff.* Variant of **-eth**[1].

-th[2] *suff.* **1.** Act; process: *spilth.* **2.** State; quality: *dearth.* [Middle English, from Old English *-thu,* n. suff.]

-th[3] also **-eth** *suff.* Used to form ordinal numbers: *millionth.* [Middle English *-the,* from Old English *-tha, -the.*]

Thack·er·ay (thăk′ə-rē, thăk′rē), **William Makepeace.** 1811–1863. British writer whose novels, including *Vanity Fair* (1847–1848), explore the ethical and social pretensions of largely amoral Victorian characters. **—Thack′er·ay·an** *adj.*

Thai (tī) *n., pl.* **Thai** or **Thais. 1.a.** A native or inhabitant of Thailand. **b.** A member of a Tai-speaking people who constitute the predominant ethnic group of Thailand. **2.** The language of the Tai family that is the official language of Thailand. **3.** Tai. **—Thai** *adj.* **1.** Of or relating to Thailand or its peoples, languages, or cultures. **2.** Tai.

Thai·land (tī′lănd′, -lənd). Formerly **Si·am** (sī-ăm′). *Abbr.* **Thai.** A country of southeast Asia on the **Gulf of Thailand** (formerly the Gulf of Siam), an arm of the South China Sea. A Thai state was first established in the region in the mid-14th century but was often dominated by other powers during the succeeding centuries. It became a constitutional monarchy in 1932. Thailand was occupied by the Japanese in World War II and was a strong supporter of the United States in the Vietnam War. Bangkok is the capital and the largest city. Population, 49,515,074.

thal·a·men·ceph·a·lon (thăl′ə-mĕn-sĕf′ə-lŏn′) *n. Anatomy.* See **diencephalon.** [THALAM(US) + ENCEPHALON.] **—thal′a·men′ce·phal′ic** (-sə-făl′ĭk) *adj.*

thal·a·mus (thăl′ə-məs) *n., pl.* **-mi** (-mī′). **1.** *Anatomy.* A large ovoid mass of gray matter situated in the posterior part of the forebrain that relays sensory impulses to the cerebral cortex. **2.** *Botany.* The receptacle of a flower. [Latin, inner chamber, from Greek *thalamos.*] **—tha·lam′ic** (thə-lăm′ĭk) *adj.* **—tha·lam′i·cal·ly** *adv.*

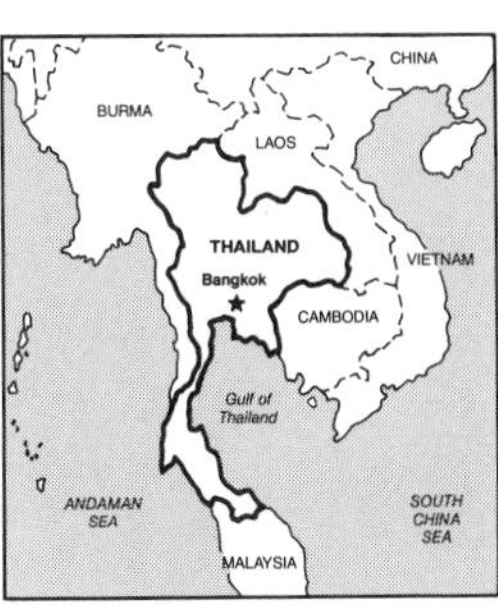

Thailand

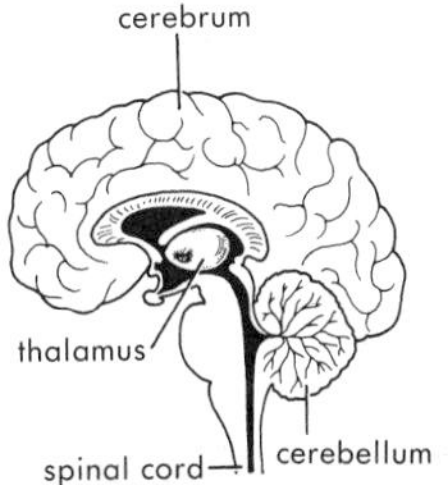

thalamus

ă pat	oi boy
ā pay	ou out
âr care	o͝o took
ä father	o͞o boot
ĕ pet	ŭ cut
ē be	ûr urge
ĭ pit	th thin
ī pie	*th* this
îr pier	hw which
ŏ pot	zh vision
ō toe	ə about, item
ô paw	♦ regionalism

Stress marks: ′ (primary); ′ (secondary), as in **dictionary** (dĭk′shə-nĕr′ē)

thal·as·se·mi·a (thăl′ə-sē′mē-ə) *n.* An inherited form of anemia occurring chiefly among people of Mediterranean descent, caused by faulty synthesis of part of the hemoglobin molecule. [Greek *thalassa,* sea + -EMIA.] **—thal′as·se′mic** *adj.*

tha·las·sic (thə-lăs′ĭk) *adj.* Of or relating to seas or oceans, especially smaller or inland seas. [French *thalassique,* from Greek *thalassa,* sea.]

thal·as·soc·ra·cy (thăl′ə-sŏk′rə-sē) *n., pl.* **-cies.** Naval or commercial supremacy on the seas. [Greek *thalassokratia* : *thalassa,* sea + *-kratia,* -cracy.] **—tha·las′so·crat′** (thə-lăs′-ə-krăt′) *n.*

tha·ler (tä′lər) *n.* Variant of **taler.**

Tha·les (thā′lēz). 624?–546? B.C. Greek philosopher who is traditionally considered the first Western philosopher and a founder of geometry and abstract astronomy. He maintained that matter is composed of water. **—Tha·le′sian** (thā-lē′zhən) *adj.*

Tha·li·a (thə-lī′ə, thā′lē-ə, thāl′yə) *n. Greek Mythology.* **1.** The Muse of comedy and pastoral poetry. **2.** One of the three Graces.

tha·lid·o·mide (thə-lĭd′ə-mīd′) *n.* A sedative and hypnotic drug, $C_{13}H_{10}N_2O_4$, withdrawn from sale after it was found to cause severe birth defects, especially of the limbs, when taken during pregnancy. [(PH)THAL(IC ACID) + (IM)ID(E) + (I)MIDE.]

thall– *pref.* Variant of **thallo–.**

thal·li (thăl′ī) *n.* A plural of **thallus.**

thal·lic (thăl′ĭk) *adj.* Of, relating to, or containing thallium, especially with valence 3.

thal·li·um (thăl′ē-əm) *n. Symbol* **Tl** A soft, malleable, highly toxic metallic element, used in photocells, infrared detectors, low-melting glass, and formerly in rodent and ant poisons. Atomic number 81; atomic weight 204.37; melting point 303.5°C; boiling point 1,457°C; specific gravity 11.85; valence 1, 3. See table at **element.** [THALL(O)– (from its green spectral line) + –IUM.]

thallo– or **thall–** *pref.* **1.a.** Young, green shoot: *thallium.* **b.** Thallus: *thalloid.* **2.** Thallium: *thallous.* [Greek, from *thallos.* See THALLUS.]

Thanksgiving cactus
Schlumbergera truncata

thal·loid (thăl′oid′) also **thal·loi·dal** (thə-loid′l) *adj.* Of, resembling, or constituting a thallus.

thal·lo·phyte (thăl′ə-fīt′) *n.* Any of a group of plantlike organisms showing no differentiation into stem, root, or leaf, including the algae, fungi, and lichens, formerly regarded as constituting a major division of the plant kingdom. **—thal′lo·phyt′ic** (-fĭt′ĭk) *adj.*

thal·lous (thăl′əs) *adj.* Of, relating to, or containing thallium, especially with valence 1.

thal·lus (thăl′əs) *n., pl.* **thal·li** (thăl′ī) or **-lus·es.** A plant body undifferentiated into stem, root, or leaf. [Latin, green stalk, from Greek *thallos,* from *thallein,* to sprout.]

Thames (tĕmz). **1.** A river, about 257 km (160 mi) long, of southeast Ontario, Canada, flowing southwest to Lake St. Clair. In the War of 1812 Gen. William Henry Harrison defeated British and Native American forces in the Battle of the Thames (October 5, 1813). **2.** A river of southern England flowing about 338 km (210 mi) eastward to a wide estuary on the North Sea. Navigable for large ships as far as London, it is the principal commercial waterway of the country. In its upper course above Oxford it is often called Isis. **3.** (thāmz, tămz). A tidal estuary of southeastern Connecticut flowing about 24 km (15 mi) to Long Island Sound.

U Thant
Photographed in the early 1960's

Tham·muz (tä′mo͝oz′) *n.* Variant of **Tammuz.**

than (thăn, thən) *conj.* Used to introduce the second element or clause of an unequal comparison: *She is a better athlete than I.* **—than** *prep. Usage Problem.* In comparison with: *disliked no one more than her.* [Middle English, from Old English *thanne, than.* See **to-** in Appendix.]

USAGE NOTE: Since the 18th century grammarians have insisted that *than* should be regarded as a conjunction in all its uses, so that a sentence such as *Bill is taller than Tom* should be construed as an elliptical version of the sentence *Bill is taller than Tom is.* According to this view, the case of a pronoun following *than* is determined by whether the pronoun serves as the subject or object of the verb that is "understood." Thus, the standard rule requires *Pat is taller than I* (not *me*) on the assumption that this sentence is elliptical for *Pat is taller than I am* but allows *The news surprised Pat more than me,* since this sentence is taken as elliptical for *The news surprised Pat more than it surprised me.* However, *than* is quite commonly treated as a preposition when followed by an isolated noun phrase, and as such occurs with a pronoun in the objective case: *John is taller than me.* Though this usage is still widely regarded as incorrect, it is predominant in speech and has reputable literary precedent. It is also consistent with the fact that *than* is clearly treated as a preposition in the *than whom* construction, as in *a poet than whom* (not *than who*) *no one has a dearer place in the hearts of his countrymen.* Still, the writer who risks a sentence such as *Mary is taller than him* in formal writing must be prepared to defend the usage against objections of critics who are unlikely to be dissuaded from their conviction that the usage is incorrect. • Comparatives using *as . . . as* can be analyzed in a parallel way to those using *than.* Traditional grammarians insist that *I am not as tall as he* is the only correct form, and though both literary precedent and syntactic arguments can be marshaled in support of the analysis of the second *as* as a preposition (which would license *I am not as tall as him*), one should treat this use of *as* as a conjunction in formal writing. See Usage Note at **as**[1].

Tha·na (tä′nə). A city of west-central India, a manufacturing suburb of Bombay. Population, 309,897.

than·age (thā′nĭj) *n.* **1.** The rank, jurisdiction, or office of a thane. **2.** The land held by a thane.

than·a·tol·o·gy (thăn′ə-tŏl′ə-jē) *n.* The study of death and dying, especially in their psychological and social aspects. [Greek *thanatos,* death + –LOGY.] **—than′a·to·log′i·cal** (-tl-ŏj′-ĭ-kəl) *adj.* **—than′a·tol′o·gist** *n.*

than·a·top·sis (thăn′ə-tŏp′sĭs) *n.* A meditation upon death. [Greek *thanatos,* death + –OPSIS.]

Than·a·tos (thăn′ə-tŏs′) *n.* **1.** Death as a personification or as a philosophical notion. **2.** *Psychiatry.* See **death instinct** (sense 1). [Greek.] **—than′a·tot′ic** (-tŏt′ĭk) *adj.*

thane (thān) *n.* **1.a.** A freeman granted land by the king in return for military service in Anglo-Saxon England. **b.** A man ranking above an ordinary freeman and below a nobleman in Anglo-Saxon England. **2.** A feudal lord or baron in Scotland. [Middle English, from Old English *thegn.* See **tek-** in Appendix.] **—thane′ship′** *n.*

Than·et (thăn′ĭt), **Isle of.** A peninsula of southeast England on the North Sea separated from the mainland by arms of the Stour River.

thank (thăngk) *tr.v.* **thanked, thank·ing, thanks. 1.** To express gratitude to; give thanks to: *He thanked her for the gift.* **2.** To hold responsible; credit: *We can thank the parade for this traffic jam.* [Middle English *thanken,* from Old English *thancian.* See **tong-** in Appendix.]

thank·ful (thăngk′fəl) *adj.* **1.** Aware and appreciative of a benefit; grateful. **2.** Expressive of gratitude: *a thankful smile.* **—thank′ful·ly** *adv.* **—thank′ful·ness** *n.*

thank·less (thăngk′lĭs) *adj.* **1.** Not feeling or showing gratitude; ungrateful. **2.** Not likely to be appreciated: *a thankless job.* **—thank′less·ly** *adv.* **—thank′less·ness** *n.*

thanks (thăngks) *pl.n.* **1.** Grateful feelings or thoughts; gratitude: *a heart full of thanks for our escape.* **2.** An expression of gratitude: *gave thanks to God; a note of thanks to a contributor.* **—thanks** *interj.* Used to express thanks. **—*idioms.* no thanks to.** Without the benefit of help from: *finally found the house, no thanks to these confusing directions.* **thanks to.** On account of; because of: *"our national good fortune in having avoided, thanks to the religion clauses of the First Amendment, the dismal possibilities of religious censorship"* (Benno C. Schmidt, Jr.).

thanks·giv·ing (thăngks-gĭv′ĭng) *n.* **1.** An act of giving thanks; an expression of gratitude, especially to God: *a hymn of thanksgiving.* **2. Thanksgiving.** Thanksgiving Day.

Thanksgiving cactus *n.* A Brazilian epiphytic cactus *(Schlumbergera truncata)* having irregular flowers and jointed flat stems with sharply serrate margins. Also called *crab cactus.* [From the time of year at which it blooms.]

Thanksgiving Day *n.* **1.** The fourth Thursday of November, observed as a legal holiday in the United States to commemorate the feast held at Plymouth in 1621 by the Pilgrim colonists and members of the Wampanoag people and marked by the giving of thanks to God for harvest and health. **2.** The second Monday of October, celebrated in Canada by the giving of thanks to God for harvest and health.

thank·wor·thy (thăngk′wûr′thē) *adj.* **-thi·er, -thi·est.** Worthy of or deserving thanks.

thank-you (thăngk′yo͞o′) *n.* An expression of gratitude: *said their thank-yous and departed.*

thank-you-ma'am (thăngk′yo͞o-măm′) *n.* A bump or depression in a road.

Thant (thänt, thănt), **U** 1909–1974. Burmese diplomat who served as the secretary-general of the United Nations (1961–1971).

Thap·sus (thăp′səs). An ancient city of northern Africa on the Mediterranean Sea in present-day Tunisia. Julius Caesar defeated Pompey's forces here in 46 B.C.

Thar Desert (tär) also **Great In·di·an Desert** (ĭn′dē-ən). A sandy region of northwest India and southeast Pakistan between the Indus and Sutlej river valleys.

Tharp (thärp), **Twyla.** Born 1941. American dancer and choreographer whose works, such as *Deuce Coupe* (1973), are drawn from several dance traditions.

Thá·sos (thā′sŏs′, thä′sôs). An island of northeast Greece in the northern Aegean Sea. It was colonized by Phoenicians and later ruled by Athens, Rome, Byzantium, and Turkey. The island was ceded to Greece in 1913.

that (thăt, thət) *pron., pl.* **those** (thōz). **1.a.** Used to refer to the one designated, implied, mentioned, or understood: *What kind of soup is that?* **b.** Used to refer to the one, thing, or type specified as follows: *The relics found were those of an earlier time.* **c.** Used to refer to the event, action, or time just mentioned: *After that, he became a recluse.* **2.** Used to indicate the farther or less immediate one: *That is for sale; this is not.* **3.** Used to emphasize the idea of a previously expressed word or phrase: *He was fed up, and that to a great degree.* **4.** The one, kind, or thing; something: *She followed the calling of that she loved.* **5. those.** Used to indicate an unspecified number of people: *those who refused to join.* **6.** Used as a relative pronoun to introduce a clause, especially a restrictive clause: *the car that has the flat tire.* **7.a.** In, on, by, or with which: *each summer that the concerts are performed.* **b.** According to what; insofar as: *He never knew her, that I know of.* **—that** *adj., pl.* **those. 1.** Being the one singled out, implied, or understood: *that place; those mountains.* **2.** Being the one further removed or less obvious: *That route is shorter than this one.* **—that** *adv.* **1.** To such an extent or degree: *Is your problem that complicated?* **2.** To a high degree; very: *didn't take what he said that seriously.* **—that** *conj.* **1.** Used to introduce a noun clause that is usually the subject or object of a verb or a predicate nominative: *"That contemporary American English is exuberantly vigorous is undeniable"* (William Arrowsmith). **2.** Used to introduce a subordinate clause stating a result, wish, purpose, reason, or cause: *She hoped that he would arrive on time. He was saddened that she felt so little for him.* **3.a.** Used to introduce an anticipated subordinate clause following the expletive *it* occurring as subject of the verb: *It is true that dental work is expensive.* **b.** Used to introduce a subordinate clause modifying an adverb or adverbial expression: *will go anywhere that they are welcome.* **c.** Used to introduce a subordinate clause that is joined to an adjective or noun as a complement: *was sure that she was right; the belief that rates will rise soon.* **4.** Used to introduce an elliptical exclamation of desire: *Oh, that I were rich!* ***—idioms.*** **at that. 1.** In addition; besides: *lived in one room, and a small room at that.* **2.** Regardless of what has been said or implied: *a long shot, but she just might win at that.* **that is.** To explain more clearly; in other words: *on the first floor, that is, the floor at street level.* [Middle English, from Old English *thæt.* See **to-** in Appendix.]

USAGE NOTE: The standard rule is that *that* should be used only to introduce a restrictive (or "defining") relative clause, which serves to identify the entity being talked about; in this use it should never be preceded by a comma. Thus, we say *The house that Jack built has been torn down,* where the clause *that Jack built* tells which house was torn down, or *I am looking for a book that is easy to read,* where *that is easy to read* tells what kind of book is desired. Only *which* is to be used with nonrestrictive (or "nondefining") clauses, which give additional information about an entity that has already been identified in the context; in this use, *which* is always preceded by a comma. Thus, we say *The students in Chemistry 10 have been complaining about the textbook, which* (not *that*) *is hard to follow.* The clause *which is hard to follow* does not indicate which text is being complained about; even if it were omitted, we would know that the phrase *the textbook* refers to the text in Chemistry 10. The use of *that* in nonrestrictive clauses like this, though once common in writing and still frequent in speech, is best avoided in formal style. • Some grammarians have argued that symmetry requires that *which* should be used only in nonrestrictive clauses, as *that* is to be used only in restrictive clauses. Thus, they suggest that we should avoid sentences such as *I need a book which will tell me all about city gardening,* where the clause *which will tell me all about city gardening* indicates which sort of book is needed. Such use of *which* is useful where two or more relative clauses are joined by *and* or *or,* as in *It is a philosophy in which the common man may find solace and which many have found reason to praise. Which* is also preferred to introduce a restrictive relative clause when the preceding phrase itself contains a *that,* as in *I can only give you that which I don't need* (not *that that I don't need*) or *We want to assign only that book which will be most helpful* (preferred to *that book that will be most helpful*). • *That* may be omitted in a relative clause when the subject of the clause is different from the referent of the phrase preceding the clause. Thus, we may say either *the book that I was reading* or *the book I was reading,* where the subject of the clause (*I*) is not the referent of the phrase *the book.* Omission of *that* in these cases has sometimes been described as incorrect, but the practice is extremely common and has ample precedent in reputable writing. • There have also been occasional objections to the omission of *that* in its use to introduce a subordinate clause, as in *I think we should try again.* But this usage is entirely idiomatic and is in fact favored with some of the verb phrases that can introduce such clauses: thus, one would more normally write *I take it she has passed the test* than *I take it that she has passed the test. That* should not be omitted, however, when the subordinate clause begins with an adverbial phrase or any element other than the subject: *She said that under no circumstances would she allow us to skip the meeting. The book argues that eventually the housing supply will increase.* This last sentence would be ambiguous if *that* were omitted, since the adverb *eventually* could then be construed as modifying either *argues* or *will increase.* See Usage Notes at **doubt, this, whatever, which, who.**

♦that·a·way (*thăt′ə-wā′*) *adv. Southern & Midland U.S.* That way. [Alteration of *that way.*]

♦ REGIONAL NOTE: The history of the English language is full of examples of epenthesis, the addition to a word of a vowel or consonant not part of the original word. This process is still active in regional dialects. Two examples now used chiefly in Southern and Midland dialects are *thisaway* and *thataway,* which show epenthetic vowels intruding between *this way* and *that way.* Another highly excoriated instance of vowel epenthesis, not regional, is the pronunciation of *athlete* as (ăth′ə-lēt′).

thatch (thăch) *n.* **1.** Plant stalks or foliage, such as reeds or palm fronds, used for roofing. **2.** Something, such as a thick growth of hair on the head, that resembles thatch. **3.** Dead turf, as on a lawn. **—thatch** *tr.v.* **thatched, thatch·ing, thatch·es.** To cover with or as if with thatch. [Middle English *thacche,* alteration (influenced by *thecchen, thacchen,* to thatch, from Old English *theccan,* to cover) of *thak,* from Old English *thæc.* See **(s)teg-** in Appendix.] **—thatch′er** *n.* **—thatch′y** *adj.*

Thatch (thăch), **Edward.** See Edward **Teach.**

Thatch·er (thăch′ər), **Margaret Hilda.** Born 1925. British Conservative politician who served as prime minister (1979–1990). Her administration was marked by anti-inflationary measures, a brief war in the Falkland Islands (1982), and the passage of a poll tax.

thau·ma·tol·o·gy (thô′mə-tŏl′ə-jē) *n., pl.* **-gies. 1.** The study of miracles. **2.** A discourse on miracles. [Greek *thauma, thaumat-,* wonder + -LOGY.]

thau·ma·turge (thô′mə-tûrj′) also **thau·ma·tur·gist** (-tûr′jĭst) *n.* A performer of miracles or magic feats. [Greek *thaumatourgos* : *thauma, thaumat-,* wonder + *ergon,* work; see **werg-** in Appendix.]

thau·ma·tur·gy (thô′mə-tûr′jē) *n.* The working of miracles or magic feats. **—thau′ma·tur′gic, thau′ma·tur′gi·cal** *adj.*

thaw (thô) *v.* **thawed, thaw·ing, thaws.** *—intr.* **1.** To change from a frozen solid to a liquid by gradual warming. See Synonyms at **melt. 2.** To lose stiffness, numbness, or impermeability by being warmed: *left the frozen turkey out until it thawed; thawed out by sitting next to the stove.* **3.** To become warm enough for snow and ice to melt. **4.** To become less formal, aloof, or reserved. *—tr.* To cause to thaw. **—thaw** *n.* **1.** The process of thawing. **2.** A period of warm weather during which ice and snow melt. **3.** A relaxation of reserve, restraints, or tensions. [Middle English *thawen,* from Old English *thawian.*]

Thay·er (thā′ər, thâr), **Sylvanus.** 1785–1872. American soldier and educator who was superintendent (1817–1833) of the United States Military Academy at West Point, New York.

Th.B. *abbr. Latin.* Theologiae Baccalaureus (Bachelor of Theology).

THC (tē′āch-sē′) *n.* A compound, $C_{21}H_{30}O_2$, obtained from cannabis or made synthetically, that is the primary intoxicant in marijuana and hashish. [T(ETRA)H(YDRO)C(ANNABINOL).]

Th.D. *abbr. Latin.* Theologiae Doctor (Doctor of Theology).

the[1] (*thē before a vowel; thə before a consonant*) *def.art.* **1.a.** Used before singular or plural nouns and noun phrases that denote particular, specified persons or things: *the baby; the dress I wore.* **b.** Used before a noun, and generally stressed, to emphasize one of a group or type as the most outstanding or prominent: *considered Lake Shore Drive to be* the *neighborhood to live in these days.* **c.** Used to indicate uniqueness: *the Prince of Wales; the moon.* **d.** Used before nouns that designate natural phenomena or points of the compass: *the weather; a wind from the south.* **e.** Used as the equivalent of a possessive adjective before names of some parts of the body: *grab him by the neck; an infection of the hand.* **f.** Used before a noun specifying a field of endeavor: *the law; the film industry; the stage.* **g.** Used before a proper name, as of a monument or ship: *the Alamo; the* Titanic. **h.** Used before the plural form of a numeral denoting a specific decade of a century or of a life span: *rural life in the Thirties.* **2.** Used before a singular noun indicating that the noun is generic: *The wolf is an endangered species.* **3.a.** Used before an adjective extending it to signify a class and giving it the function of a noun: *the rich; the dead; the homeless.* **b.** Used before an absolute adjective: *the best we can offer.* **4.** Used before a present participle, signifying the action in the abstract: *the weaving of rugs.* **5.** Used before a noun with the force of *per*: *cherries at $1.50 the box.* [Middle English, from Old English *the,* alteration (influenced by *thæt,* neuter demonstrative pron., *thæs,* genitive demonstrative pron., etc.) of *se,* masculine demonstrative pron. See **so-** in Appendix.]

the[2] (*thē before a vowel; thə before a consonant*) *adv.* **1.** Because of that. Used before a comparative: *thinks the worse of you after this mistake.* **2.** To that extent; by that much: *the sooner the better.* **3.** Beyond any other: *enjoyed reading the most.* [Middle English, from Old English *thȳ, thē.* See **to-** in Appendix.]

the- *pref.* Variant of **theo-.**

the·an·throp·ic (thē′ăn-thrŏp′ĭk) also **the·an·throp·i·cal** (-ĭ-kəl) *adj.* Both divine and human in nature or quality. [From Late Greek *theanthrōpos,* god-man : Greek *theo-,* theo- + Greek *anthrōpos,* man.]

the·an·thro·pism (thē-ăn′thrə-pĭz′əm) *n.* **1.** Attribution of human traits to God; anthropomorphism. **2.** *Theology.* The doctrine of the union of human and divine natures in Jesus. **—the·an′thro·pist** *n.*

the·ar·chy (thē′är′kē) *n., pl.* **-chies. 1.** Government or rule by a god or by priests; theocracy. **2.** A hierarchy of gods.

theat. *abbr.* Theater; theatrical.

the·a·ter or **the·a·tre** (thē′ə-tər) *n. Abbr.* **theat. 1.** A building, room, or outdoor structure for the presentation of plays, films, or other dramatic performances. **2.** A room with tiers of seats used for lectures or demonstrations: *an operating theater at a medical school.* **3.a.** Dramatic literature or its performance; drama: *the theater of Shakespeare and Marlowe.* **b.** The milieu of actors and playwrights. **4.a.** The quality or effectiveness of a theatrical production: *good theater; awful theater.* **b.** Dramatic material or the use of such material: *"His summation was a great piece of courtroom theater"* (Ron Rosenbaum). **5.** The audience

thatch
Thatched roof on a cottage in Hungary

Margaret Thatcher

ă pat	oi boy
ā pay	ou out
âr care	ŏŏ took
ä father	ōō boot
ĕ pet	ŭ cut
ē be	ûr urge
ĭ pit	th thin
ī pie	*th* this
îr pier	hw which
ŏ pot	zh vision
ō toe	ə about, item
ô paw	♦ regionalism

Stress marks: ′ (primary); ′ (secondary), as in **dictionary** (dĭk′shə-nĕr′ē)

assembled for a dramatic performance. **6.** A place that is the setting for dramatic events. **7.** A large geographic area in which military operations are coordinated: *the European theater during World War II.* [Middle English *theatre,* from Old French, from Latin *theātrum,* from Greek *theatron,* from *theasthai,* to watch, from *thea,* a viewing.]

WORD HISTORY: Those who have theories about the theater are no doubt quite observant, at least the etymology of the word leads one to think so. The words *theory* and *theater* are related in ancestry if we look back to the Greek sources of our words. The Greek ancestor of *theater* is *theatron,* "a place for seeing, especially for dramatic representation, theater." *Theatron* is derived quite logically from the verb *theasthai,* "to gaze at, contemplate, view as spectators, especially in the theater," from *thea,* "a viewing." The Greek ancestor of *theory* is *theōria,* which meant among other things "the sending of *theōroi* (state ambassadors sent to consult oracles or attend games)," "the act of being a spectator at the theater or games," "viewing," "contemplation by the mind," and "theory or speculation." The source of *theōria, theōros,* "an envoy sent to consult an oracle, spectator," is a compound of *thea,* "viewing," and *-oros,* "seeing." Thus, viewing is at the root of a theory and the theater.

the·a·ter·go·er (thē′ə-tər-gō′ər) *n.* One who often attends the theater. **—the′a·ter·go′ing** *adj. & n.*

the·a·ter-in-the-round (thē′ə-tər-ĭn-*thə*-round′) *n., pl.* **the·a·ters-in-the-round** (thē′ə-tərz-). See **arena theater.**

theater of the absurd *n.* A form of drama that emphasizes the absurdity of human existence by employing disjointed, repetitious, and meaningless dialogue, purposeless and confusing situations, and plots that lack realistic or logical development.

the·a·tre (thē′ə-tər) *n.* Variant of **theater.**

the·at·ri·cal (thē-ăt′rĭ-kəl) also **the·at·ric** (-rĭk) *—adj.* **1.** *Abbr.* **theat.** Of, relating to, or suitable for dramatic performance or the theater. **2.** Marked by exaggerated self-display and unnatural behavior; affectedly dramatic. See Synonyms at **dramatic.** *—n.* **1.** Often **theatricals.** Stage performances or a stage performance, especially by amateurs. **2. theatricals.** Affectedly dramatic gestures or behavior. **—the·at′ri·cal′i·ty** (-kăl′ĭ-tē), **the·at′ri·cal·ness** (-kəl-nĭs) *n.* **—the·at′ri·cal·ly** *adv.*

the·at·ri·cal·ism (thē-ăt′rĭ-kə-lĭz′əm) *n.* Theatrical manner or style; showiness.

the·at·ri·cal·ize (thē-ăt′rĭ-kə-līz′) *tr.v.* **-ized, -iz·ing, -iz·es. 1.** To adapt to performance on the stage; dramatize: *"All ethnic dance troupes theatricalize the dance of the folk"* (Robert J. Pierce). **2.** To make a spectacle of; display showily. **—the·at′ri·cal·i·za′tion** (-kə-lĭ-zā′shən) *n.* **—the·at′ri·cal·iz′er** *n.*

the·at·rics (thē-ăt′rĭks) *n.* **1.** *(used with a sing. verb).* The art of the theater. **2.** *(used with a pl. verb).* Theatrical effects or mannerisms; histrionics.

the·ba·ine (thē′bə-ēn′, thĭ-bā′ĭn) *n.* A poisonous alkaloid, $C_{19}H_{21}NO_3$, obtained from opium. Also called *paramorphine.* [New Latin *(herba) thēbaia,* (herb of) Thebes, Egyptian opium (from Latin *Thēbaea,* feminine of *Thēbaeus,* Theban, from *Thēbae,* Thebes, from Greek *Thēbai*) + -INE[2].]

the·be (tĕ′bĕ) *n.* See table at **currency.**

The·be (thē′bē) *n.* The satellite of Jupiter that is fifth in distance from the planet. [Latin *Thēbē,* a nymph, daughter of the river god Asopus, from Greek.]

Thebes (thēbz). **1.** An ancient city of Upper Egypt on the Nile River in present-day central Egypt. It flourished from the mid-22nd to the 18th century B.C. as a royal residence and a religious center for the worship of Amen. Its archaeological remains include many splendid temples and the tomb of Tutankhamen in the nearby Valley of the Kings. **2.** An ancient city of Boeotia in east-central Greece northwest of Athens. Originally a Mycenaen city, it reached the height of its power in the fourth century B.C. **—The′ban** (thē′bən) *adj. & n.*

the·ca (thē′kə) *n., pl.* **-cae** (-sē′, -kē′). A case, covering, or sheath, such as the pollen sac of an anther, the spore case of a moss, or the outer covering of the pupa of certain insects. [Latin, case, receptacle, from Greek *thēkē.* See **dhē-** in Appendix.] **—the′cal** (-kəl) *adj.*

the·cate (thē′kāt′) *adj.* Having a theca; encased or sheathed.

The Dalles (dălz). See The **Dalles.**

thee (*thē*) *pron.* The objective case of **thou**[1]. **1.a.** Used as the direct object of a verb. **b.** Used as the indirect object of a verb. **2.** Used as the object of a preposition. **3.** Used in the nominative as well as the objective case, especially by members of the Society of Friends.

thee·lin (thē′lĭn) *n.* See **estrone.** [Greek *thēlus,* female; see **dhē(i)-** in Appendix + -IN.]

thee·lol (thē′lôl′, -lōl′, -lŏl′) *n.* See **estriol.** [THEEL(IN) + -OL[2].]

theft (thĕft) *n.* **1.** The act or an instance of stealing; larceny. **2.** *Obsolete.* Something stolen. [Middle English, from Old English *thīefth.*]

their (*thâr*) *adj.* The possessive form of **they. 1.** Used as a modifier before a noun: *their accomplishments; their home town.* **2.** *Usage Problem.* His, her, or its: *"It is fatal for anyone who writes to think of their sex"* (Virginia Woolf). See Usage Note at **he**[1]. [Middle English, from Old Norse *theira,* theirs. See **to-** in Appendix.]

theirs (thârz) *pron. (used with a sing. or pl. verb).* **1.** Used to indicate the one or ones belonging to them: *The red house is theirs. If your car doesn't start, take theirs.* **2.** *Usage Problem.* His or hers: *brought his own lunch and expected everybody else to bring theirs.* See Usage Notes at **he**[1]. [Middle English, from *their,* their. See THEIR.]

the·ism (thē′ĭz′əm) *n.* Belief in the existence of a god or gods, especially belief in a personal God as creator and ruler of the world. **—the′ist** *n.* **—the·is′tic, the·is′ti·cal** *adj.* **—the·is′ti·cal·ly** *adv.*

The·lon (thē′lŏn′). A river, about 885 km (550 mi) long, of south-central Northwest Territories, Canada, east of Great Slave Lake.

them (*thĕm, thəm*) *pron.* The objective case of **they. 1.a.** Used as the direct object of a verb: *We saw them at the conference.* **b.** Used as the indirect object of a verb: *We gave them a round of applause.* **2.** Used as the object of a preposition: *This letter is addressed to them.* **3.** *Informal.* Used as a predicate nominative: *It's them.* See Usage Notes at **be, I**[1]. [Middle English, from Old Norse *theim* and Old English *thǣm;* see **to-** in Appendix.]

the·mat·ic (thĭ-măt′ĭk) *adj.* **1.** Of, relating to, or being a theme: *a scene of thematic importance.* **2.** *Linguistics.* Of, constituting, or relating to the theme of a word: *a thematic vowel.* [Greek *thematikos,* from *thema, themat-,* theme. See THEME.] **—the·mat′i·cal·ly** *adv.*

The·mat·ic Apperception Test (thĭ-măt′ĭk) *n. Abbr.* **TAT** A projective test in which the subject tells a story suggested by each of a standard set of pictures showing everyday situations.

theme (thēm) *n.* **1.** A topic of discourse or discussion. See Synonyms at **subject. 2.** A subject of artistic representation. **3.** An implicit or recurrent idea; a motif: *a theme of powerlessness that runs through the diary; a party with a tropical island theme.* **4.** A short composition assigned to a student as a writing exercise. **5.** *Music.* The principal melodic phrase in a composition, especially a melody forming the basis of a set of variations. **6.** *Linguistics.* A stem. [Middle English *teme, theme,* from Old French *tesme,* from Latin *thema,* from Greek. See **dhē-** in Appendix.] **—theme′less** *adj.*

theme park *n.* An amusement park in which all the settings and attractions have a central theme, such as the world of the future.

theme song *n. Music.* **1.** An often repeated song in a musical play that is identified with the work or one of its characters. **2.** A song that is identified with a performer, group, or radio or television program.

The·mis·to·cles (thə-mĭs′tə-klēz′). 527?–460? B.C. Athenian military and political leader. After persuading the Athenians to build a navy, he led the new fleet to victory over Persia in the Battle of Salamis (480).

them·selves (*thĕm*-sĕlvz′, *thəm*-) *pron.* **1.** Those ones identical with them: **a.** Used reflexively as the direct or indirect object of a verb or as the object of a preposition: *prepared themselves for the trip; gave themselves plenty of time; were left to themselves.* **b.** Used for emphasis: *The cooks themselves eat after all the guests have finished.* **c.** Used in an absolute construction: *Newcomers themselves, they knew few people at the party.* **2.** Their normal or healthy condition: *The members of the crew were themselves again after the crisis passed.*

then (*thĕn*) *adv.* **1.** At that time: *I was still in school then. Come at noon; I'll be ready then.* **2.** Next in time, space, or order; immediately afterward: *watched the late movie and then went to bed.* **3.** In addition; moreover; besides: *It costs $20, and then there's the sales tax to pay.* **4.** Used after *but* to qualify or balance a preceding statement: *The star was nervous, but then who isn't on the first night of a new play.* **5.** In that case; accordingly: *If traffic is heavy, then allow extra time.* **6.** As a consequence; therefore: *The case, then, is closed.* **—then** *n.* That time or moment: *The bus leaves at four; until then let's walk.* **—then** *adj.* Being so at that time: *the then chairman of the board.* ***—idiom.*** **and then some.** *Informal.* With considerably more in addition: *This project will take all our skill and then some.* [Middle English, from Old English *thenne.* See **to-** in Appendix.]

then and there *adv.* At that precise time and place; on the spot: *resigned then and there.*

the·nar (thē′när′) *n.* The fleshy mass on the palm of the hand at the base of the thumb. **—thenar** *adj.* Of or relating to the thenar. [Greek, palm of the hand.]

thence (*thĕns,* thĕns) *adv.* **1.** From that place; from there: *flew to Helsinki and thence to Moscow.* **2.** From that circumstance or source; therefrom. **3.** *Archaic.* From that time; thenceforth. See Usage Note at **whence.** [Middle English *thennes* : *thenne,* from there (from Old English *thanon;* see **to-** in Appendix) + *-es,* genitive sing. suff.; see -S[3].]

thence·forth (*thĕns*-fôrth′, -fōrth′, thĕns-) *adv.* From that time forward; thereafter.

thence·for·ward (*thĕns*-fôr′wərd, thĕns-) also **thence·for·wards** (-wərdz) *adv.* **1.** Thenceforth. **2.** From that time or place onward.

theo– or **the–** *pref.* God: *theomorphism.* [Greek, from *theos.* See **dhēs-** in Appendix.]

the·o·bro·mine (thē′ō-brō′mēn′) *n.* A bitter, colorless alkaloid, $C_7H_8N_4O_2$, derived from the cacao bean, found in chocolate products and used in medicine as a diuretic, vasodilator, and myocardial stimulant. [New Latin *Theobroma,* genus of trees (Greek *theo-,* theo- + *brōma,* food) + –INE[2].]

the·o·cen·tric (thē′ō-sĕn′trĭk) *adj.* Centering on God as the prime concern: *a theocentric cosmology.*

the·oc·ra·cy (thē-ŏk′rə-sē) *n., pl.* **-cies. 1.** A government ruled by or subject to religious authority. **2.** A state so governed.

the·o·crat (thē′ə-krăt′) *n.* **1.** A ruler of a theocracy. **2.** A believer in theocracy. **—the′o·crat′ic, the′o·crat′i·cal** *adj.* **—the′o·crat′i·cal·ly** *adv.*

The·oc·ri·tus (thē-ŏk′rĭ-təs). Third century B.C. Greek poet who composed the earliest known pastoral poems.

the·od·i·cy (thē-ŏd′ĭ-sē) *n., pl.* **-cies.** A vindication of God's goodness and justice in the face of the existence of evil. [After *Théodicée,* a work by Baron Gottfried Wilhelm von Leibnitz : Greek *theo-,* theo- + Greek *dikē,* order, right; see **deik-** in Appendix.]

the·od·o·lite (thē-ŏd′l-īt′) *n.* An optical instrument consisting of a small mounted telescope rotatable in horizontal and vertical planes, used to measure angles in surveying, meteorology, and navigation. [New Latin *theodolitus, theodelitus.*] **—the·od′o·lit′ic** (-lĭt′ĭk) *adj.*

The·o·do·ra (thē′ə-dôr′ə, -dōr′-). 508?–548. Byzantine empress (525–548) as the wife and adviser of Justinian I.

The·od·o·ric (thē-ŏd′ər-ĭk). Known as "the Great." A.D. 454?–526. King of the Ostrogoths (474–526) who founded the Ostrogoth kingdom in Italy (493).

The·o·do·sius I (thē′ə-dō′shəs, -shē-əs). Known as "Theodosius the Great." A.D. 346?–395. Emperor of Rome who ruled jointly (379–392) with Gratian and Valentinian II and independently (392–395). He prohibited pagan practices and in his will divided the empire between his two sons.

the·og·o·ny (thē-ŏg′ə-nē) *n., pl.* **-nies.** An account of the origin and genealogy of the gods. **—the′o·gon′ic** (-ə-gŏn′ĭk) *adj.*

theol. *abbr.* Theologian; theological; theology.

the·o·lo·gi·an (thē′ə-lō′jən) *n. Abbr.* **theol.** One who is learned in theology.

the·o·log·i·cal (thē′ə-lŏj′ĭ-kəl) also **the·o·log·ic** (-lŏj′ĭk) *adj. Abbr.* **theol.** Of or relating to theology or to specialized religious study. **—the′o·log′i·cal·ly** *adv.*

the·ol·o·gize (thē-ŏl′ə-jīz′) *v.* **-gized, -giz·ing, -giz·es.** —*tr.* To make theological in form or significance. —*intr.* To speculate about theology. **—the·ol′o·giz′er** *n.*

the·ol·o·gy (thē-ŏl′ə-jē) *n., pl.* **-gies.** *Abbr.* **theol. 1.** The study of the nature of God and religious truth; rational inquiry into religious questions. **2.** A system or school of opinions concerning God and religious questions. *Protestant theology; Jewish theology.* **3.** A course of specialized religious study usually at a college or seminary. [Middle English *theologie,* from Old French, from Latin *theologia,* from Greek : *theo-,* theo- + *-logia,* -logy.]

the·om·a·chy (thē-ŏm′ə-kē) *n., pl.* **-chies.** Strife or battle among gods, as in the Homeric poems. [Greek *theomakhia* : *theo-,* theo- + *makhia,* fighting (from *makhē,* battle).]

the·o·mor·phism (thē′ō-môr′fĭz′əm) *n.* Depiction or conception of human beings as having the form of a god. **—the′o·mor′phic** *adj.*

the·oph·a·ny (thē-ŏf′ə-nē) *n., pl.* **-nies.** An appearance of a god to a human being; a divine manifestation. [Medieval Latin *theophania,* from Late Greek *theophaneia* : Greek *theo-,* theo- + Greek *phainein, phan-,* to show; see **bhā-**[1] in Appendix.]

The·o·phras·tus (thē′ə-frăs′təs). 371?–287? B.C. Greek philosopher who succeeded Aristotle as leader of the Peripatetics and refined the work of Aristotle in botany and natural history.

the·oph·yl·line (thē-ŏf′ə-lĭn, thē′ō-fĭl′ēn′) *n.* A colorless crystalline alkaloid, $C_7H_8N_4O_2H_2O$, derived from tea leaves or made synthetically, used as a cardiac stimulant and diuretic. [THEO(BROMINE) + PHYLL(O)– + –INE[2].]

the·or·bo (thē-ôr′bō) *n., pl.* **-bos.** *Music.* A 17th-century lute having two sets of strings and an S-shaped neck with two sets of pegs, one set above and somewhat to the side of the other. [Italian *tiorba,* probably from Italian dialectal, traveling bag, from Slovenian *torba,* from Turkish, bag (from the bag in which mendicants carried it).]

the·o·rem (thē′ər-əm, thîr′əm) *n.* **1.** An idea that is demonstrably true or is assumed to be so. **2.** *Mathematics.* A proposition that has been or is to be proved on the basis of explicit assumptions. [Late Latin *theōrēma,* from Greek, from *theōrein,* to look at, from *theōros,* spectator. See THEORY.]

the·o·ret·i·cal (thē′ə-rĕt′ĭ-kəl) also **the·o·ret·ic** (-rĕt′ĭk) *adj.* **1.** Of, relating to, or based on theory. **2.** Restricted to theory; not practical: *theoretical physics.* **3.** Given to theorizing; speculative. [Late Latin *theōrēticus,* from Greek *theōrētikos,* from *theōrētos,* observable, from *theōrein,* to look at. See THEOREM.] **—the′o·ret′i·cal·ly** *adv.*

SYNONYMS: *theoretical, abstract, academic, hypothetical, speculative.* The central meaning shared by these adjectives is "concerned primarily with theories or hypotheses rather than practical considerations": *theoretical linguistics; abstract reasoning; a purely academic discussion; a hypothetical statement; speculative knowledge.*

the·o·re·ti·cian (thē′ər-ĭ-tĭsh′ən, thîr′ĭ-) *n.* One who formulates, studies, or is expert in the theory of a science or an art.

the·o·ret·ics (thē′ə-rĕt′ĭks) *n. (used with a sing. verb).* The theoretical part of a science or an art.

the·o·rist (thē′ər-ĭst, thîr′ĭst) *n.* One who theorizes; a theoretician.

the·o·rize (thē′ə-rīz′, thîr′īz) *v.* **-rized, -riz·ing, -riz·es.** —*intr.* To formulate theories or a theory; speculate. —*tr.* To propose a theory about. **—the′o·ri·za′tion** (-ər-ĭ-zā′shən) *n.* **—the′o·riz′er** *n.*

the·o·ry (thē′ə-rē, thîr′ē) *n., pl.* **-ries. 1.a.** Systematically organized knowledge applicable in a relatively wide variety of circumstances, especially a system of assumptions, accepted principles, and rules of procedure devised to analyze, predict, or otherwise explain the nature or behavior of a specified set of phenomena. **b.** Such knowledge or such a system. **2.** Abstract reasoning; speculation. **3.** A belief that guides action or assists comprehension or judgment: *rose early, on the theory that morning efforts are best; the modern architectural theory that less is more.* **4.** An assumption based on limited information or knowledge; a conjecture. [Late Latin *theōria,* from Greek, from *theōros,* spectator : probably *thea,* a viewing + *-oros,* seeing.]

theory of games *n.* See **game theory.**

the·os·o·phy (thē-ŏs′ə-fē) *n., pl.* **-phies. 1.** Religious philosophy or speculation about the nature of the soul based on mystical insight into the nature of God. **2.** Often **Theosophy.** The beliefs of a religious sect, the Theosophical Society, founded in New York City in 1875, incorporating aspects of Buddhism and Brahmanism. [Medieval Latin *theosophia,* from Late Greek : Greek *theo-,* theo- + Greek *sophia,* wisdom.] **—the′o·soph′ic** (-ə-sŏf′ĭk), **the′o·soph′i·cal** (-ĭ-kəl) *adj.* **—the′o·soph′i·cal·ly** *adv.* **—the·os′o·phist** *n.*

therap. *abbr.* Therapeutic; therapeutics.

ther·a·peu·tic (thĕr′ə-pyo͞o′tĭk) also **ther·a·peu·ti·cal** (-tĭ-kəl) *adj. Abbr.* **therap. 1.** Having or exhibiting healing powers: *a therapeutic agent; therapeutic exercises.* **2.** Of or relating to therapeutics. [New Latin *therapeuticus,* from Greek *therapeutikos,* from *therapeutēs,* one who administers, from *therapeuein,* from *theraps, therap-,* attendant. See THERAPY.] **—ther′a·peu′ti·cal·ly** *adv.*

therapeutic abortion *n.* An abortion induced for medical reasons, as when pregnancy poses a danger to the woman's health.

therapeutic index *n.* The ratio between the toxic dose and the therapeutic dose of a drug, used as a measure of the relative safety of the drug for a particular treatment.

ther·a·peu·tics (thĕr′ə-pyo͞o′tĭks) *n. (used with a sing. verb). Abbr.* **therap.** Medical treatment of disease; the art or science of healing. **—ther′a·peu′tist** *n.*

ther·a·pist (thĕr′ə-pĭst) *n.* One who specializes in the provision of a particular therapy.

the·rap·sid (thə-răp′sĭd) *n.* Any of various reptiles of the order Therapsida of the Permian and Triassic periods, many of which are considered to be direct ancestors of mammals. [From New Latin *Thērapsida,* order name : Greek *thēr,* wild animal; see THEROPOD + Greek *hapsis, hapsid-,* arch, vault (from the enlarged lower temporal opening characteristic of the order); see APSIS.] **—the·rap′sid** *adj.*

ther·a·py (thĕr′ə-pē) *n., pl.* **-pies. 1.** Treatment of illness or disability. **2.** Psychotherapy. **3.** Healing power or quality: *the therapy of fresh air and sun.* [New Latin *therapia,* from Greek *therapeia,* from *therapeuein,* to treat medically. See THERAPEUTIC.]

Ther·a·va·da (thĕr′ə-vä′də) *n. Buddhism.* See **Hinayana.** [Pali *theravāda* : *thera,* an elder (from Sanskrit *sthavira-,* old, venerable; see **stā-** in Appendix) + *vāda,* doctrine (from Sanskrit *vādaḥ,* statement, doctrine; see **wed-**[2] in Appendix).]

there (thâr) *adv.* **1.** At or in that place: *sit over there.* **2.** To, into, or toward that place: *wouldn't go there again.* **3.** At that stage, moment, or point: *Stop there before you make any more mistakes.* **4.** In that matter: *I can't agree with him there.* **—there** *pron.* **1.** Used to introduce a clause or sentence: *There are numerous items. There must be another exit.* **2.** Used to indicate an unspecified person in direct address: *Hello there.* **—there** *adj.* Used as an intensive: *That person there ought to know the directions to town.* **—there** *n.* That place or point: *stopped and went on from there.* **—there** *interj.* Used to express feelings such as relief, satisfaction, sympathy, or anger: *There, now I can have some peace!* [Middle English, from Old English *thǣr, thēr.* See **to-** in Appendix.]

USAGE NOTE: The standard rule states that when the pronoun *there* precedes a verb such as *be, seem,* or *appear,* the verb agrees in number with the following grammatical subject: *There is a great Italian deli across the street. There are fabulous wildflowers in the hills. There seems to be a blueberry pie cooking in the kitchen. There seem to be a few trees between me and the green.* Nonetheless, it is common in speech for the contraction *there's* to be used when technically a plural verb is called for, as in *There's a couple of good reasons for going.* There is also a tendency to use a singular verb when the phrase with which the verb must agree is a conjunction in which the subject closest to the verb is singular: *To the left, there is a beautiful entry hall, a sitting room, and*

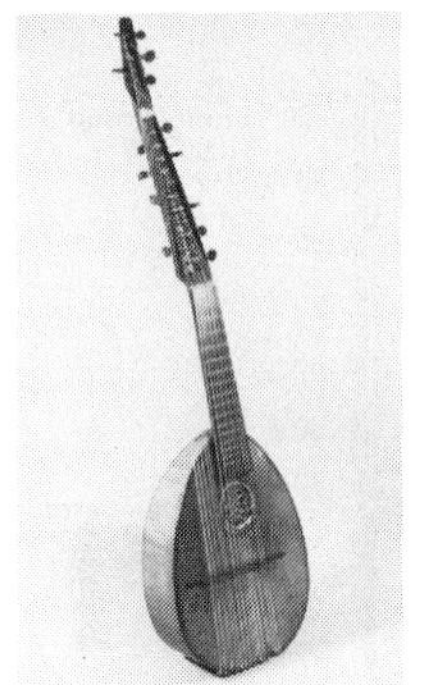

theorbo

ă pat	oi boy
ā pay	ou out
âr care	o͝o took
ä father	o͞o boot
ĕ pet	ŭ cut
ē be	ûr urge
ĭ pit	th thin
ī pie	*th* this
îr pier	hw which
ŏ pot	zh vision
ō toe	ə about, item
ô paw	♦ regionalism

Stress marks: ′ (primary); ′ (secondary), as in **dictionary** (dĭk′shə-nĕr′ē)

a sun porch. Although this usage is strictly incorrect, the attraction of the verb to the singular noun phrase following it is so strong that few writers manage to avoid the construction entirely. • The demonstrative forms *that there* and *this here* are nonstandard.

---

there·a·bouts (*thâr′ə-bouts′*) also **there·a·bout** (-bout′) *adv.* **1.** Near that place, about there: *somewhere in Kansas or thereabouts.* **2.** About that number, amount, or time.

there·af·ter (*thâr-ăf′tər*) *adv.* From a specified time onward; from then on.

there·a·gainst (*thâr′ə-gĕnst′*) *adv.* Against or in opposition to that.

there·at (*thâr-ăt′*) *adv.* **1.** At that place; there. **2.** At that event; on account of that.

there·by (*thâr-bī′*) *adv.* **1.** By that means; because of that. **2.** In connection with that: *"And thereby hangs a tale"* (Shakespeare).

thermograph

there·for (*thâr-fôr′*) *adv.* For that: *ordering goods and enclosing payment therefor.*

there·fore (*thâr′fôr′*, -fōr′) *adv.* For that reason or cause; consequently or hence. [Middle English : *there,* there; see THERE + *for, fore,* fore; see FOR.]

there·from (*thâr-frŭm′*, -frŏm′) *adv.* From that place, time, or thing.

there·in (*thâr-ĭn′*) *adv.* **1.** In that place, time, or thing. **2.** In that circumstance or respect.

there·in·af·ter (*thâr′ĭn-ăf′tər*) *adv.* In a later part, as of a speech or book.

ther·e·min (thĕr′ə-mĭn) *n. Music.* An electronic instrument played by moving the hands near its two antennas, often used for high tremolo effects. [After Leo *Theremin* (born 1896), Russian engineer and inventor.]

there·of (*thâr-ŭv′*, -ŏv′) *adv.* **1.** Of or concerning this, that, or it. **2.** From that cause or origin; therefrom.

there·on (*thâr-ŏn′*, -ôn′) *adv.* **1.** On or upon this, that, or it. **2.** *Archaic.* Following that immediately; thereupon.

The·re·sa or **Te·re·sa** (tə-rē′sə, -zə, -rā′-), Saint. Known as "Theresa of Ávila." 1515–1582. Spanish nun and mystical writer who founded the reformed order of Carmelites (1562). Her works include *The Way of Perfection,* published posthumously.

Thé·rèse de Li·sieux (tā-rĕz′ də lē-zyœ′), Saint. Known as "the Little Flower." 1873–1897. French nun whose autobiography, *Story of a Soul* (1898), recounts her search for spiritual innocence. She was canonized in 1925.

there·to (*thâr-to͞o′*) *adv.* **1.** To that, this, or it. **2.** *Archaic.* In addition to that; furthermore.

there·to·fore (*thâr′tə-fôr′*, -fōr′) *adv.* Until that time; before that.

there·un·der (*thâr-ŭn′dər*) *adv.* Under this, that, or it.

there·un·to (*thâr′ŭn-to͞o′*) *adv. Archaic.* To that, this, or it; thereto.

there·up·on (*thâr′ə-pŏn′*, -pôn′) *adv.* **1.** Concerning that matter; upon that. **2.** Directly following that; forthwith. **3.** In consequence of that; therefore.

there·with (*thâr-wĭth′*, -wĭth′) *adv.* **1.** With that, this, or it. **2.** In addition to that. **3.** *Archaic.* Immediately thereafter.

there·with·al (*thâr′wĭth-ôl′*, -wĭth-) *adv.* With all that, this, or it; besides.

the·ri·o·mor·phic (thîr′ē-ə-môr′fĭk) also **the·ri·o·mor·phous** (-fəs) *adj.* Thought of as having the form of a beast. Used of a deity. [Greek *thērion,* diminutive of *thēr,* wild beast; see THEROPOD + -MORPHIC.]

°F °C
220 100—boiling point (100°C) (212°F)
200 90
180 80
160 70
140 60
120 50
100 40 —body temperature (37°C) (98.6°F)
80 30
60 20
40 10
20 0—freezing point (0°C) (32°F)
0 -10
-20 -20
-40 -30
-40

thermometer

therm (thûrm) *n.* **1.a.** A unit of heat equal to 100,000 British thermal units. **b.** A unit of heat equal to 1,000 large calories. **2.a.** A unit of heat equal to the large calorie. **b.** A unit of heat equal to the small calorie. [Greek *thermē,* heat, from *thermos,* warm, hot. See **gʷher-** in Appendix.]

therm. *abbr.* Thermometer.

therm– *pref.* Variant of **thermo–.**

–therm *suff.* An animal having a specified kind of body temperature: *poikilotherm.* [From Greek *thermē,* heat, from *thermos,* warm, hot. See **gʷher-** in Appendix.]

ther·mal (thûr′məl) *adj.* **1.** Of, relating to, using, producing, or caused by heat. **2.** Intended or designed in such a way as to help retain body heat: *thermal underwear.* —**thermal** *n.* A rising current of warm air. —**ther′mal·ly** *adv.*

thermal neutron *n.* See **slow neutron.**

thermal noise *n.* Unwanted currents or voltages in an electronic component resulting from the agitation of electrons by heat. Also called *Johnson noise.*

thermal pollution *n.* Industrial discharge of heated water into a river, lake, or other body of water, causing a rise in temperature that endangers aquatic life.

therm·an·es·the·sia (thûrm′ăn-ĭs-thē′zhə) *n.* Inability to feel hot or cold; insensitivity to variations in temperature.

therm·es·the·sia (thûrm′ĭs-thē′zhə) *n.* Ability to feel hot or cold; sensitivity to variations in temperature.

ther·mic (thûr′mĭk) *adj.* Thermal.

therm·i·on (thûr′mī′ən) *n.* An electrically charged particle, especially an electron, emitted by a conducting material at high temperatures. —**therm′i·on′ic** (-mī-ŏn′ĭk) *adj.*

thermionic current *n.* A flow of thermions.

thermionic emission *n.* Emission of thermions, especially electrons, from a conducting material at high temperatures.

therm·i·on·ics (thûr′mī-ŏn′ĭks) *n.* (*used with a sing. or pl. verb*). The physics of thermionic phenomena.

thermionic tube *n.* An electron tube in which the source of electrons is a heated electrode.

therm·is·tor (thûr′mĭs′tər) *n.* A resistor made of semiconductors having resistance that varies rapidly and predictably with temperature. [THERM(AL) + (RES)ISTOR.]

Ther·mit (thûr′mĭt, -mĭt′). A trademark used for a welding and incendiary mixture of fine aluminum powder with a metallic oxide, usually iron, that when ignited yields an intense heat.

thermo– or **therm–** *pref.* **1.** Heat: *thermochemistry.* **2.** Thermoelectric: *thermojunction.* [From Greek *thermē,* heat, from *thermos,* warm, hot. See **gʷher-** in Appendix.]

ther·mo·cau·ter·y (thûr′mō-kô′tə-rē) *n., pl.* **-ies.** Cauterization using heat, as with a heated wire.

ther·mo·chem·is·try (thûr′mō-kĕm′ĭ-strē) *n.* The chemistry of heat and heat-associated chemical phenomena. —**ther′mo·chem′i·cal** (-ĭ-kəl) *adj.* —**ther′mo·chem′ist** *n.*

ther·mo·cline (thûr′mə-klīn′) *n.* A layer in a large body of water, such as a lake, that sharply separates regions differing in temperature, so that the temperature gradient across the layer is abrupt.

ther·mo·co·ag·u·la·tion (thûr′mō-kō-ăg′yə-lā′shən) *n.* The use of heat produced by high-frequency electric current to bring about localized destruction of tissues.

ther·mo·cou·ple (thûr′mə-kŭp′əl) *n.* A thermoelectric device used to measure temperatures accurately, especially one consisting of two dissimilar metals joined so that a potential difference generated between the points of contact is a measure of the temperature difference between the points.

ther·mo·dur·ic (thûr′mō-do͝or′ĭk, -dyo͝or′-) *adj.* Capable of surviving high temperatures, especially those of pasteurization. Used of a microorganism. [THERMO– + Latin *dūrāre,* to last; see **deuə-** in Appendix + –IC.]

ther·mo·dy·nam·ic (thûr′mō-dī-năm′ĭk) *adj.* **1.** Characteristic of or resulting from the conversion of heat into other forms of energy. **2.** Of or relating to thermodynamics. —**ther′mo·dy·nam′i·cal·ly** *adv.*

ther·mo·dy·nam·ics (thûr′mō-dī-năm′ĭks) *n.* **1.** (*used with a sing. verb*). Physics that deals with the relationships between heat and other forms of energy. **2.** (*used with a pl. verb*). Thermodynamic phenomena and processes.

ther·mo·e·lec·tric (thûr′mō-ĭ-lĕk′trĭk) also **ther·mo·e·lec·tri·cal** (-trĭ-kəl) *adj.* Characteristic of, resulting from, or using electrical phenomena occurring in conjunction with a flow of heat. —**ther′mo·e·lec′tri·cal·ly** *adv.*

ther·mo·e·lec·tric·i·ty (thûr′mō-ĭ-lĕk-trĭs′ĭ-tē, -ē′lĕk-) *n.* Electricity generated by a flow of heat, as in a thermocouple.

ther·mo·e·lec·tron (thûr′mō-ĭ-lĕk′trŏn′) *n.* An electron emitted by a material at high temperatures.

ther·mo·gen·e·sis (thûr′mō-jĕn′ĭ-sĭs, -mə-) *n.* Generation of heat, especially by physiological processes. —**ther′mo·ge·net′ic** (-jə-nĕt′ĭk), **ther′mo·gen′ic** (-jĕn′ĭk) *adj.*

ther·mo·gram (thûr′mə-grăm′) *n.* A record made by a thermograph.

ther·mo·graph (thûr′mə-grăf′) *n.* **1.** A thermometer that records the temperature it indicates. **2.** The apparatus used in diagnostic thermography.

ther·mog·ra·phy (thər-mŏg′rə-fē) *n., pl.* **-phies. 1.** A process for producing raised lettering, as on stationery or calling cards, by application of a powder that is fused by heat to the fresh ink. **2.** A diagnostic technique in which an infrared camera is used to measure temperature variations on the surface of the body, producing images that reveal sites of abnormal tissue growth. —**ther′mo·graph′ic** (-mə-grăf′ĭk) *adj.* —**ther′mo·graph′i·cal·ly** *adv.*

ther·mo·junc·tion (thûr′mō-jŭngk′shən) *n.* The point of contact between two dissimilar metals in a thermocouple at which a thermoelectric current is produced.

ther·mo·la·bile (thûr′mō-lā′bĭl, -bīl′) *adj.* Subject to destruction, decomposition, or great change by moderate heating. Used especially of biochemical substances. —**ther′mo·la·bil′i·ty** (-bĭl′ĭ-tē) *n.*

ther·mo·lu·mi·nes·cence (thûr′mō-lo͞o′mə-nĕs′əns) *n.* A phenomenon in which certain minerals release previously absorbed radiation upon being moderately heated. —**ther′mo·lu′mi·nes′cent** *adj.*

ther·mol·y·sis (thər-mŏl′ĭ-sĭs) *n., pl.* **-ses** (-sēz′). **1.** *Physiology.* Dissipation of heat from the body, as by evaporation. **2.** *Chemistry.* Dissociation or decomposition of compounds by heat. —**ther′mo·lyt′ic** (thûr′mə-lĭt′ĭk) *adj.*

ther·mom·e·ter (thər-mŏm′ĭ-tər) *n. Abbr.* **therm.** An instrument for measuring temperature, especially one having a graduated glass tube with a bulb containing a liquid, typically mercury or colored alcohol, that expands and rises in the tube as the temperature increases.

ther·mom·e·try (thər-mŏm′ĭ-trē) *n.* **1.** Measurement of temperature. **2.** The technology of temperature measurement. **—ther′mo·met′ric** (thûr′mō-mĕt′rĭk) *adj.*

ther·mo·mo·tor (thûr′mō-mō′tər) *n.* An engine operated by heat, especially by the expansion of heated air.

ther·mo·nu·cle·ar (thûr′mō-no͞o′klē-ər, -nyo͞o′-) *adj.* **1.** Of, relating to, or derived from the fusion of atomic nuclei at high temperatures: *thermonuclear reactions.* **2.** Of or relating to the use of atomic weapons based on fusion, especially as distinguished from those based on fission: *thermonuclear war.*

ther·mo·pe·ri·od·ism (thûr′mō-pîr′ē-ə-dĭz′əm) also **ther·mo·pe·ri·o·dic·i·ty** (-dĭs′ĭ-tē) *n.* The effect on an organism of the rhythmic fluctuation of temperature, including responses associated with thermal changes accompanying the alternation of day and night.

ther·mo·phil·ic (thûr′mə-fĭl′ĭk) *adj.* Requiring high temperatures for normal development, as certain bacteria. **—ther′mo·phile′** (-fīl′) *n.*

ther·mo·pile (thûr′mə-pīl′) *n.* A device consisting of a number of thermocouples connected in series or parallel, used for measuring temperature or generating current. [THERMO– + PILE[1].]

ther·mo·plas·tic (thûr′mə-plăs′tĭk) *adj.* Becoming soft when heated and hard when cooled. **—thermoplastic** *n.* A thermoplastic resin, such as polystyrene or polyethylene. **—ther′mo·plas·tic′i·ty** (-plă-stĭs′ĭ-tē) *n.*

Ther·mop·y·lae (thər-mŏp′ə-lē). A narrow pass of east-central Greece. It was the site of an unsuccessful Spartan stand against the Persians in 480 B.C.

ther·mo·re·cep·tor (thûr′mō-rĭ-sĕp′tər) *n. Biology.* A sensory receptor that responds to heat and cold.

ther·mo·reg·u·late (thûr′mō-rĕg′yə-lāt′) *intr.v.* **-lat·ed, -lat·ing, -lates. 1.** To regulate body temperature. **2.** To undergo thermoregulation.

ther·mo·reg·u·la·tion (thûr′mō-rĕg′yə-lā′shən) *n.* Maintenance of a constant internal body temperature that is independent from the environmental temperature: *mammalian thermoregulation.* **—ther′mo·reg′u·la·to′ry** (-rĕg′yə-lə-tôr′ē, -tōr′ē) *adj.*

Ther·mos (thûr′məs). A trademark used for a brand of vacuum bottles and other insulated containers.

ther·mo·set·ting (thûr′mō-sĕt′ĭng) *adj.* Permanently hardening or solidifying on being heated. Used of certain synthetic resins.

ther·mo·sphere (thûr′mə-sfîr′) *n.* The outermost shell of the atmosphere, between the mesosphere and outer space, where temperatures increase steadily with altitude. **—ther′mo·spher′ic** (-sfîr′ĭk, -sfĕr′ĭk) *adj.*

ther·mo·sta·ble (thûr′mō-stā′bəl) also **ther·mo·sta·bile** (-bəl, -bīl′) *adj.* Unaffected by relatively high temperatures, as certain ferments or toxins. **—ther′mo·sta·bil′i·ty** (-stə-bĭl′ĭ-tē) *n.*

ther·mo·stat (thûr′mə-stăt′) *n.* A device, as in a home heating system, a refrigerator, or an air conditioner, that automatically responds to temperature changes and activates switches controlling the equipment. **—ther′mo·stat′ic** *adj.* **—ther′mo·stat′i·cal·ly** *adv.*

ther·mo·tax·is (thûr′mə-tăk′sĭs) *n., pl.* **-tax·es** (-tăk′sēz). **1.** Movement of a living organism in response to changes in temperature. **2.** Normal regulation or adjustment of body temperature. **—ther′mo·tac′tic** (-tăk′tĭk), **ther′mo·tax′ic** (-tăk′sĭk) *adj.*

ther·mo·ther·a·py (thûr′mō-thĕr′ə-pē) *n., pl.* **-pies.** Medical therapy involving the application of heat.

ther·mot·ro·pism (thər-mŏt′rə-pĭz′əm) *n. Biology.* The tendency of plants or other organisms to bend toward or away from heat. **—ther′mo·trop′ic** (thûr′mə-trŏp′ĭk) *adj.*

-thermy *suff.* Heat: *diathermy.* [New Latin *-thermia,* from Greek *thermē,* heat, from *thermos,* warm, hot. See **gʷher-** in Appendix.]

the·ro·pod (thîr′ə-pŏd′) *n.* Any of various carnivorous dinosaurs of the suborder Theropoda, of the Jurassic and Cretaceous periods, characterized by short forelimbs. [From New Latin *Theropoda,* suborder name : Greek *thēr,* wild beast; see **ghwer-** in Appendix + New Latin *-poda,* -pod.] **—the·rop′o·dan** (thĭ-rŏp′ə-dən) *adj. & n.*

the·sau·rus (thĭ-sôr′əs) *n., pl.* **-sau·ri** (-sôr′ī′) or **-sau·rus·es. 1.** A book of synonyms, often including related and contrasting words and antonyms. **2.** A book of selected words or concepts, such as a specialized vocabulary of a particular field, as of medicine or music. [Latin *thēsaurus,* treasury, from Greek *thēsauros.*]

these (thēz) *pron. & adj.* Plural of **this.** [Middle English, from Old English *thæs,* variant of *thās,* pl. of *thes, this,* this. See **to-** in Appendix.]

the·ses (thē′sēz) *n.* Plural of **thesis.**

The·se·us (thē′sē-əs, -syo͞os′) *n. Greek Mythology.* A hero and king of Athens who slew the Minotaur and united Attica. **—The·se′an** (thĭ-sē′ən) *adj.*

the·sis (thē′sĭs) *n., pl.* **-ses** (-sēz). **1.** A proposition that is maintained by argument. **2.** A dissertation advancing an original point of view as a result of research, especially as a requirement for an academic degree. **3.** A hypothetical proposition, especially one put forth without proof. **4.** The first stage of the Hegelian dialectic process. **5.a.** The long or accented part of a metrical foot, especially in quantitative verse. **b.** The unaccented or short part of a metrical foot, especially in accentual verse. **6.** *Music.* The accented section of a measure. [Latin, from Greek, from *tithenai,* to put. See **dhē-** in Appendix. Sense 5 and 6, Middle English, from Late Latin, lowering of the voice, from Greek, downbeat, from *tithenai,* to put.]

thes·pi·an (thĕs′pē-ən) *adj.* **1.** Of or relating to drama; dramatic: *thespian talents.* **2. Thespian.** Of or relating to Thespis. **—thespian** *n.* An actor or actress.

Thes·pis (thĕs′pĭs). Sixth century B.C. Greek poet who reputedly originated Greek tragedy.

Thes·sa·lo·ni·ans (thĕs′ə-lō′nē-ənz) *pl.n. (used with a sing. verb). Abbr.* **Th, Thess.** *Bible.* See table at **Bible.**

Thes·sa·lo·ní·ki (thĕ′sä-lô-nē′kē) also **Thes·sa·lo·ni·ca** (-lô-nī′kə, -lŏn′ĭ-kə) or **Sa·lo·ni·ka** (sə-lŏn′ĭ-kə, săl′ə-nē′kə). A city of northeast Greece on an inlet of the Aegean Sea. Founded c. 315 B.C., it flourished after c. 146 as the capital of the Roman province of Macedon. Today it is a major port and the second-largest city in Greece. Population, 406,413.

Thes·sa·ly (thĕs′ə-lē). A region of east-central Greece between the Pindus Mountains and the Aegean Sea. Settled before 1000 B.C., it reached the height of its power in the sixth century B.C. but soon declined because of internal conflicts. **—Thes·sa′lian** (thĕ-sā′lē-ən, -sāl′yən), **Thes′sa·lo′ni·an** (-lō′nē-ən) *adj. & n.*

the·ta (thā′tə, thē′-) *n.* The eighth letter of the Greek alphabet. See table at **alphabet.** [Greek *thēta,* of Phoenician origin; akin to Hebrew *ṭēt,* teth.]

theta rhythm *n.* A waveform on an electroencephalogram having a frequency of 4 to 8 hertz, recorded chiefly in the hippocampus of carnivorous mammals when they are alert or aroused. Also called *theta wave.*

Thet·ford Mines (thĕt′fərd). A city of southern Quebec, Canada, south of Quebec City. It developed as a mining center after the discovery of asbestos deposits in 1876. Population, 19,965.

thet·ic (thĕt′ĭk, thē′tĭk) also **thet·i·cal** (thĕt′ĭ-kəl, thē′tĭ-) *adj.* **1.** Beginning with, constituting, or relating to the thesis in prosody. **2.** Presented dogmatically; arbitrarily prescribed. [Greek *thetikos,* from *thetos,* placed, from *tithenai,* to put. See **dhē-** in Appendix.] **—thet′i·cal·ly** *adv.*

The·tis (thē′tĭs) *n. Greek Mythology.* One of the Nereids, the wife of Peleus and mother of Achilles.

the·ur·gy (thē′ûr-jē) *n., pl.* **-gies. 1.** Divine or supernatural intervention in human affairs. **2.** The performance of miracles with supernatural assistance. **3.** Magic performed with the aid of beneficent spirits, as formerly practiced by the Neo-Platonists. [Late Latin *theurgia,* from Greek *theourgia,* sacramental rite, mystery : *theo-,* theo- + *-ourgia,* -urgy.] **—the·ur′gic, the·ur′gi·cal** *adj.* **—the·ur′gi·cal·ly** *adv.* **—the′ur·gist** *n.*

thew (thyo͞o) *n.* **1.** A well-developed sinew or muscle. **2.** Muscular power or strength. Often used in the plural. [Middle English, a virtue, from Old English *thēaw,* a custom, habit.] **—thew′y** *adj.*

they (*th*ā) *pron.* **1.** Used to refer to the ones previously mentioned or implied. **2.** *Usage Problem.* Used to refer to the one previously mentioned or implied, especially as a substitute for generic *he*: *Every person has rights under the law, but they don't always know them.* See Usage Note at **he**[1]. **3.a.** Used to refer to people in general. **b.** Used to refer to people in general as seen in a position of authority. [Middle English, from Old Norse *their,* masculine pl. demonstrative and personal pron. See **to-** in Appendix.]

they'd (*th*ād). **1.** They had. **2.** They would.

they'll (*th*āl). **1.** They will. **2.** They shall.

they're (*th*âr). They are.

they've (*th*āv). They have.

thi– *pref.* Variant of **thio–.**

thi·a·ben·da·zole (thī′ə-bĕn′də-zōl′) *n.* A white compound, $C_{10}H_7N_3S$, used medically as an antifungal agent and as an anthelmintic. [THIA(ZOLE) + BEN(ZO)– + (IMI)D(E) + AZOLE.]

thi·a·mine (thī′ə-mĭn, -mēn′) also **thi·a·min** (-mĭn) *n.* A vitamin, $C_{12}H_{17}ClN_4OS$, of the vitamin B complex, found in meat, yeast, and the bran coat of grains, and necessary for carbohydrate metabolism and normal neural activity. Also called *vitamin B_1.* [Alteration of *thiamin* : THI(O)– + (VIT)AMIN.]

thi·a·zide (thī′ə-zīd′, -zĭd) *n.* Any of a group of drugs that block reabsorption of sodium in the distal tubules of the kidneys, used as diuretics in the treatment of hypertension. [THI(O)– + AZ(O)– + –IDE.]

thi·a·zine (thī′ə-zēn′) *n.* Any of a class of organic chemical compounds containing a ring composed of one sulfur atom, one nitrogen atom, and four carbon atoms, used in making dyes.

thi·a·zole (thī′ə-zōl′) *n.* **1.** A colorless or pale yellow liquid, C_3H_3NS, containing a five-member ring composed of a nitrogen atom, a sulfur atom, and three carbon atoms, used in making dyes and fungicides. **2.** Any of various derivatives of this compound.

Thi·bo·daux (tĭb′ə-dō). A city of southeast Louisiana west-southwest of New Orleans. It is a commercial, industrial, and processing center. Population, 15,810.

thick (thĭk) *adj.* **thick·er, thick·est. 1.a.** Relatively great in extent from one surface to the opposite, usually in the smallest solid dimension; not thin: *a thick board.* **b.** Measuring a specified number of units in this dimension: *two inches thick.* **2.** Heavy in

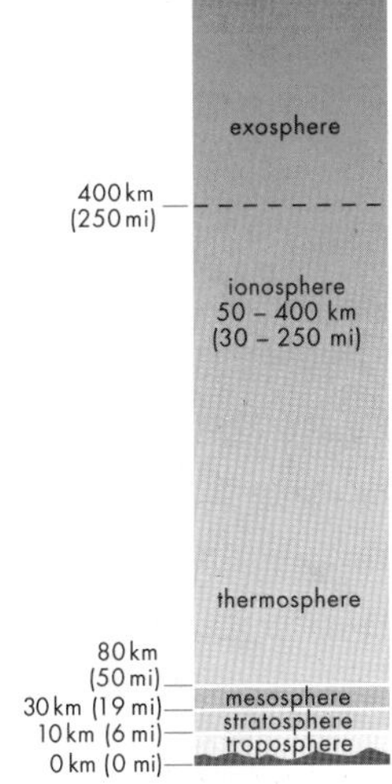

thermosphere

Theseus
Theseus and the Minotaur
by Antoine Louis Barye
(1796–1875)

ă pat	oi boy
ā pay	ou out
âr care	o͝o took
ä father	o͞o boot
ĕ pet	ŭ cut
ē be	ûr urge
ĭ pit	th thin
ī pie	*th* this
îr pier	hw which
ŏ pot	zh vision
ō toe	ə about, item
ô paw	♦ regionalism

Stress marks: **′** (primary); ′ (secondary), as in **dictionary** (dĭk′shə-nĕr′ē)

form, build, or stature; thickset: *a thick neck.* **3.** Having component parts in a close, crowded state or arrangement; dense: *a thick forest.* **4.** Having or suggesting a heavy or viscous consistency: *thick tomato sauce.* **5.** Having a great number; abounding: *a room thick with flies.* **6.** Impenetrable by the eyes: *a thick fog.* **7. a.** Not easy to hear or understand; indistinctly articulated: *the thick speech of a drunkard.* **b.** Producing indistinctly articulated sounds: *the thick tongues of barbarians.* **8.** Noticeably affecting sound; conspicuous: *a thick brogue.* **9.** *Informal.* Lacking mental agility; stupid. **10.** *Informal.* Very friendly; intimate: *thick friends.* **11.** *Informal.* Going beyond what is tolerable; excessive. **—thick** *adv.* **1.** In a thick manner; deeply or heavily: *Seashells lay thick on the beach.* **2.** In a close, compact state or arrangement; densely: *Dozens of braids hung thick from the back of her head.* **3.** So as to be thick; thickly: *Slice the bread thick for the best French toast.* **—thick** *n.* **1.** The thickest part. **2.** The most active or intense part: *in the thick of the fighting.* ***—idiom.* thick and thin.** Good and bad times: *They remained friends through thick and thin.* [Middle English *thicke,* from Old English *thicce.* See **tegu-** in Appendix.] **—thick′ish** *adj.* **—thick′ly** *adv.*

thick·en (thĭk′ən) *tr. & intr.v.* **-ened, -en·ing, -ens. 1.** To make or become thick or thicker: *Thicken the sauce with cornstarch. The crowd thickened near the doorway.* **2.** To make or become more intense, intricate, or complex: *The leader's hasty departure thickens the problems. Our apprehension thickened.* **—thick′en·er** *n.*

thick·en·ing (thĭk′ə-nĭng) *n.* **1.** The act or process of making or becoming thick. **2.** Material used to thicken: *stir in a thickening of flour and water.* **3.** A thickened part.

thick·et (thĭk′ĭt) *n.* **1.** A dense growth of shrubs or underbrush; a copse. **2.** Something suggestive of a dense growth of plants, as in impenetrability or thickness: *"the thicket of unreality which stands between us and the facts of life"* (Daniel J. Boorstin). [Old English *thiccet,* from *thicce,* thick. See THICK.]

thick·head (thĭk′hĕd′) *n.* A person regarded as stupid; a blockhead. **—thick′head′ed** *adj.*

thick-knee (thĭk′nē′) *n.* Any of various widely distributed, chiefly nocturnal, curlewlike shore birds of the family Burhinidae, having large heads, large yellow eyes, and knobby leg joints.

♦**thick milk** *n. Pennsylvania.* See **clabber.**

thick·ness (thĭk′nĭs) *n.* **1.** The quality or condition of being thick. **2.** The dimension between two surfaces of an object, usually the dimension of smallest measure. **3.** A layer, sheet, stratum, or ply: *Each floor is a single thickness of concrete.*

thick·set (thĭk′sĕt′) *adj.* **1.** Having a solid, stocky form or body; stout. **2.** Positioned or placed closely together.

thick-skinned (thĭk′skĭnd′) *adj.* **1.** Having a thick skin or rind. **2.** Not easily offended. **3.** Largely unaffected by the needs and feelings of other people; insensitive.

thick-wit·ted (thĭk′wĭt′ĭd) *adj.* Stupid; dull.

thief (thēf) *n., pl.* **thieves** (thēvz). One who steals, especially one who steals movable property by stealth rather than force. [Middle English, from Old English *thēof.*]

Thiers (tē-ĕr′), **Louis Adolphe.** 1797–1877. French politician and historian who was the first president (1871–1873) of the republic formed after the fall of Napoleon III.

thieve (thēv) *tr. & intr.v.* **thieved, thiev·ing, thieves.** To take (something) by theft or commit theft. [Perhaps from Old English *thēofian,* from *thēof,* thief.]

thiev·er·y (thē′və-rē) *n., pl.* **-ies.** The act or practice of thieving.

thieves (thēvz) *n.* Plural of **thief.**

thiev·ish (thē′vĭsh) *adj.* **1.** Given to thieving. **2.** Of, similar to, or characteristic of a thief; furtive.

thigh (thī) *n.* **1. a.** The portion of the human leg between the hip and the knee. **b.** The corresponding part of the hind leg of a quadruped or other vertebrate animal. **2.** The second segment of a bird's leg, containing the tibia and fibula. **3.** The femur of an insect's leg. [Middle English, from Old English *thēoh.* See **teuə-** in Appendix.]

thigh·bone (thī′bōn′) *n.* See **femur** (sense 1).

thig·mo·tax·is (thĭg′mə-tăk′sĭs) *n.* See **stereotaxis** (sense 2). [Greek *thigma,* touch (from *thinganein,* to touch; see **dheigh-** in Appendix) + -TAXIS.] **—thig′mo·tac′tic** (-tăk′tĭk) *adj.* **—thig′mo·tac′ti·cal·ly** *adv.*

thig·mot·ro·pism (thĭg-mŏt′rə-pĭz′əm) *n.* The turning or bending response of an organism upon direct contact with a solid surface or object. Also called *stereotropism.* [Greek *thigma,* touch; see THIGMOTAXIS + -TROPISM.] **—thig′mo·trop′ic** (thĭg′mə-trŏp′ĭk, -trō′pĭk).

thill (thĭl) *n.* Either of the two long shafts between which an animal is fastened when pulling a wagon. [Middle English *thille,* perhaps from Old English *thille,* plank.]

thim·ble (thĭm′bəl) *n.* **1.** A small cup made of metal, ceramic, plastic, leather, or other hard material, worn for protection on the finger that pushes the needle in sewing. **2.** Any of various tubular sockets or sleeves in machinery. **3.** *Nautical.* **a.** A metal ring fitted in an eye of a sail to prevent chafing. **b.** A metal ring around which a rope splice is passed. [Middle English *thimbil,* alteration of Old English *thȳmel,* leather finger covering, from *thūma,* thumb. See **teuə-** in Appendix.]

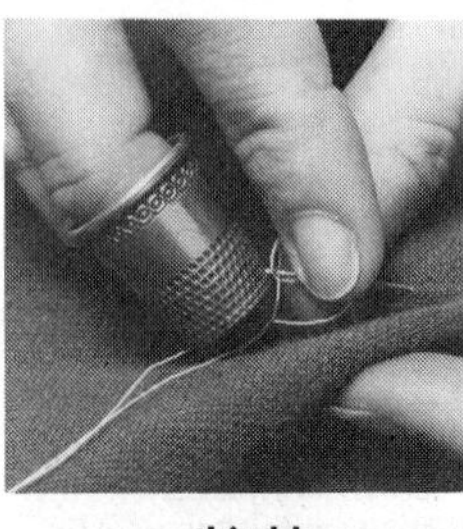

thimble

thim·ble·ber·ry (thĭm′bəl-bĕr′ē) *n.* **1.** Any of several North American raspberries, especially *Rubus parviflorus, R. occidentalis,* or *R. odoratus* of the rose family, having thimble-shaped aggregate fruit. **2.** The fruit of any of these plants.

thim·ble·ful (thĭm′bəl-fo͝ol′) *n.* **1.** A very small quantity. **2.** The amount that a thimble can hold.

thim·ble·rig (thĭm′bəl-rĭg′) *Games. n.* **1.** See **shell game** (sense 1). **2.** One who operates a thimblerig. **—thimblerig** *tr.v.* **-rigged, -rig·ging, -rigs.** To swindle with or as if with a thimblerig. **—thim′ble·rig′ger** *n.*

thim·ble·weed (thĭm′bəl-wēd′) *n.* Any of several North American plants of the genus *Anemone,* having cylindrical, thimblelike fruit clusters.

Thim·bu (thĭm′bo͞o′, tĭm′-) also **Thim·phu** (-po͞o′). The capital of Bhutan, in the western part of the country in the eastern Himalaya Mountains. Population, 8,982.

thi·mer·o·sal (thī-mĕr′ə-săl′) *n.* A cream-colored crystalline powder, $C_9H_9HgNaO_2S$, used as a local antiseptic for abrasions and minor cuts. [THI(O)- + MER(CURY) + -O- + SAL(ICYLATE).]

Thim·phu (thĭm′po͞o′, tĭm′-). See **Thimbu.**

thin (thĭn) *adj.* **thin·ner, thin·nest. 1. a.** Relatively small in extent from one surface to the opposite, usually in the smallest solid dimension: *a thin book.* **b.** Not great in diameter or cross section; fine: *thin wire.* **2.** Lean or slender in form, build, or stature. **3. a.** Not dense or concentrated; sparse: *the thin vegetation of the plateau.* **b.** More rarefied than normal: *thin air.* **4. a.** Flowing with relative ease; not viscous: *a thin oil.* **b.** Watery: *thin soup.* **5.** Sparsely supplied or provided; scanty: *a thin menu; thin trading.* **6.** Lacking force or substance; flimsy: *a thin attempt.* **7.** Lacking resonance or fullness; tinny: *The piano had a thin sound.* **8.** Lacking radiance or intensity: *thin light.* **9.** Not having enough photographic density or contrast to make satisfactory prints. Used of a negative. **—thin** *adv.* **1.** In a thin manner: *Spread the varnish thin if you don't want it to wrinkle.* **2.** So as to be thin: *Cut the cheese thin.* **—thin** *tr. & intr.v.* **thinned, thin·ning, thins.** To make or become thin or thinner. [Middle English, from Old English *thynne.* See **ten-** in Appendix.] **—thin′ly** *adv.* **—thin′ness** *n.* **—thin′nish** *adj.*

thine (thīn) *pron. (used with a sing. or pl. verb).* Used to indicate the one or ones belonging to thee. **—thine** *adj.* A possessive form of **thou**[1]. Used instead of *thy* before an initial vowel or *h*: *"The presidential candidates are practicing the first rule of warfare: know thine enemy"* (Eleanor Clift). [Middle English, from Old English *thīn.* See **tu-** in Appendix.]

thing (thĭng) *n.* **1.** An entity, an idea, or a quality perceived, known, or thought to have its own existence. **2. a.** The real or concrete substance of an entity. **b.** An entity existing in space and time. **c.** An inanimate object. **3.** Something referred to by a word, a symbol, a sign, or an idea; a referent. **4.** A creature: *the poor little thing.* **5.** An individual object: *There wasn't a thing in sight.* **6. a.** *Law.* That which can be possessed or owned. Often used in the plural: *things personal; things real.* **b. things.** Possessions; belongings: *packed her things and left.* **c.** An article of clothing: *Put on your things and let's go.* **7. things.** The equipment needed for an activity or a special purpose: *Where are my cleaning things?* **8.** An object or entity that is not or cannot be named specifically: *What is this thing for?* **9. a.** An act, deed, or work: *promised to do great things.* **b.** The result of work or activity: *is always building things.* **10.** A thought, a notion, or an utterance: *What a rotten thing to say!* **11.** A piece of information: *wouldn't tell me a thing about the project.* **12.** A means to an end: *just the thing to increase sales.* **13.** An end or objective: *In blackjack, the thing is to get nearest to 21 without going over.* **14.** A matter of concern: *many things on my mind.* **15.** A turn of events; a circumstance: *The accident was a terrible thing.* **16. a. things.** The general state of affairs; conditions: *"Beneath the smooth surface of things, something was wrong"* (Tom Wicker). **b.** A particular state of affairs; a situation: *Let's deal with this thing promptly.* **17.** *Informal.* A persistent illogical feeling, as a desire or an aversion; an obsession: *has a thing about seafood.* **18.** *Informal.* The latest fad or fashion; the rage: *Drag racing was the thing then.* **19.** *Slang.* An activity uniquely suitable and satisfying to one: *Let him do his own thing.* See Synonyms at **forte**[1]. ***—idioms.* first thing.** *Informal.* Right away; before anything else: *Do your assignments first thing in the morning.* **see** (or **hear**) **things.** To have hallucinations. **sure thing.** *Informal.* **1.** A certainty: *His election is a sure thing.* **2.** Of course; certainly: *Sure thing, I'll be there!* [Middle English, from Old English *thing.*]

thing·a·ma·bob or **thing·u·ma·bob** (thĭng′ə-mə-bŏb′) also **thing·um·bob** (thĭng′əm-bŏb′) *n. Informal.* A thingamajig. [Alteration of *thingumbob* : *thingum* (from THING) + BOB[2].]

thing·a·ma·jig also **thing·um·a·jig** (thĭng′ə-mə-jĭg′) *n. Informal.* Something difficult to classify or whose name has been forgotten or is not known. [Alteration of obsolete *thingum* (from THING) + JIG.]

thing-in-it·self (thĭng′ĭn-ĭt-sĕlf′) *n., pl.* **things-in-them·selves** (thĭngz′ĭn-*th*ĕm-sĕlvz′). *Philosophy.* See **noumenon** (sense 2). [Translation of German *Ding an sich.*]

thing·u·ma·bob (thĭng′ə-mə-bŏb′) *n.* Variant of **thingamabob.**

thing·um·a·jig (thĭng′ə-mə-jĭg′) *n.* Variant of **thingamajig.**

thing·um·bob (thĭng′əm-bŏb′) *n.* Variant of **thingamabob.**

think (thĭngk) *v.* **thought** (thôt), **think·ing, thinks.** *—tr.* **1.** To have or formulate in the mind. **2. a.** To reason about or reflect on; ponder: *Think how complex language is. Think the matter through.* **b.** To decide by reasoning, reflection, or pondering:

thinking what to do. **3.** To judge or regard; look upon: *I think it only fair.* **4.** To believe; suppose: *always thought he was right.* **5.a.** To expect; hope: *They thought she'd arrive early.* **b.** To intend: *They thought they'd take their time.* **6.** To call to mind; remember: *I can't think what her name was.* **7.** To visualize; imagine: *Think what a scene it will be at the reunion.* **8.** To devise or evolve; invent: *thought up a plan to get rich quick.* **9.** To bring into a given condition by mental preoccupation: *He thought himself into a panic over the impending examination.* **10.** To concentrate one's thoughts on: *"Think languor"* (Diana Vreeland). —*intr.* **1.** To exercise the power of reason, as by conceiving ideas, drawing inferences, and using judgment. **2.** To weigh or consider an idea: *They are thinking about moving.* **3.a.** To bring a thought to mind by imagination or invention: *No one before had thought of bifocal glasses.* **b.** To recall a thought or an image to mind: *She thought of her childhood when she saw the movie.* **4.** To believe; suppose: *He thinks of himself as a wit. It's later than you think.* **5.** To have care or consideration: *Think first of the ones you love.* **6.** To dispose the mind in a given way: *Do you think so?* **—think** *adj. Informal.* Requiring much thought to create or assimilate: *a think book.* **—think** *n.* The act or an instance of deliberate or extended thinking; a meditation. **—*idioms.* come to think of it.** *Informal.* When one considers the matter; on reflection: *Come to think of it, that road back there was the one we were supposed to take.* **think aloud** (or **out loud**). To speak one's thoughts audibly. **think nothing of.** To give little consideration to; regard as routine or usual: *thought nothing of a 50-mile trip every day.* **think twice.** To weigh something carefully: *I'd think twice before spending all that money.* [Middle English *thenken,* from Old English *thencan.* See **tong-** in Appendix.]

SYNONYMS: *think, cerebrate, cogitate, reason, reflect, speculate.* The central meaning shared by these verbs is "to use the powers of the mind, as in conceiving ideas or drawing inferences": *thought before answering; sat in front of the fire cerebrating; cogitating about business problems; reasons clearly; took time to reflect before deciding; speculating on what has happened.*

think·a·ble (thĭng′kə-bəl) *adj.* Possible to consider or be considered; conceivable: *plans that were not even thinkable.* **—think′a·bly** *adv.*

think·er (thĭng′kər) *n.* **1.** One who devotes much time to thought or meditation. **2.** One who thinks or reasons in a certain way: *a careful thinker.*

think·ing (thĭng′kĭng) *n.* **1.** The act or practice of one that thinks; thought. **2.** A way of reasoning; judgment: *To my thinking, this is not a good idea.* **—thinking** *adj.* Characterized by thought or thoughtfulness; rational: *We are thinking animals.*

thinking cap *n.* A state in which one thinks, especially carefully: *put on one's thinking cap.*

think piece *n.* A newspaper article consisting of news analysis, background material, and personal opinions.

think tank also **think-tank** (thĭngk′tăngk′) *n.* A group or an institution organized for intensive research and solving of problems, especially in the areas of technology, social or political strategy, or armament.

thin·ner (thĭn′ər) *n.* A liquid, such as turpentine, mixed with paint or varnish to reduce its viscosity and make it easier to apply.

thin-skinned (thĭn′skĭnd′) *adj.* **1.** Having a thin rind or skin. **2.** Oversensitive, especially to criticism or insult.

thio– or **thi–** *pref.* Containing sulfur, used especially of a compound in which oxygen has been replaced by a divalent sulfur: *thiourea.* [Greek *theio-,* from *theion,* sulfur.]

thi·o·car·ba·mide (thī′ō-kär′bə-mīd′) *n.* See **thiourea.**

thi·o·cy·a·nate (thī′ō-sī′ə-nāt′) *n.* A salt or an ester of thiocyanic acid.

thi·o·cy·an·ic acid (thī′ō-sī-ăn′ĭk) *n.* An unstable colorless liquid, HSCN, used in the form of esters as an insecticide.

Thi·o·kol (thī′ə-kôl′, -kōl′, -kŏl′). A trademark used for any of various polysulfide polymers in the form of liquids, water dispersions, and rubbers used in seals and sealants.

thi·ol (thī′ôl′, -ōl′, -ŏl′) *n.* See **mercaptan.**

thion– *pref.* Sulfur: *thionic.* [From Greek *theion,* sulfur.]

thi·on·ic (thī-ŏn′ĭk) *adj.* Of, relating to, containing, or derived from sulfur.

thi·o·nyl (thī′ə-nĭl′) *n.* See **sulfinyl.**

thi·o·pen·tal sodium (thī′ō-pĕn′tăl′, -tôl′) *n.* A yellowish-white hygroscopic powder, $C_{11}H_{17}N_2O_2SNa$, injected intravenously as a general anesthetic and used in psychotherapy to induce a relaxed state. [THIO– + PENT(OBARBIT)AL SODIUM.]

thi·o·phene (thī′ə-fēn′) *n.* A colorless liquid, C_4H_4S, used as a solvent. [THIO– + *-phene* (variant of PHENO–).]

thi·o·rid·a·zine (thī′ə-rĭd′ə-zēn′) *n.* A white or yellow powder, $C_{21}H_{26}N_2S_2$, a derivative of phenothiazine, that is used orally as a tranquilizer to treat various psychotic conditions. [THIO– + (PIPE)RID(INE) + AZINE.]

thi·o·sul·fate (thī′ō-sŭl′fāt′) *n.* A salt or an ester of thiosulfuric acid.

thi·o·sul·fu·ric acid (thī′ō-sŭl-fyo͝or′ĭk) *n.* An acid, $H_2S_2O_3$, formed by replacement of an oxygen atom by a sulfur atom in sulfuric acid, known only in solution or by its salts and esters.

thi·o·te·pa (thī′ō-tē′pə, -tĕp′ə) *n.* A crystalline compound, $C_6H_{12}N_3PS$, a sulfur-containing analogue of tepa, used to treat certain malignant tumors.

thi·o·ur·a·cil (thī′ō-yo͝or′ə-sĭl′) *n.* A white crystalline compound, $C_4H_4N_2OS$, that interferes with the synthesis of thyroxine, used to reduce the action of the thyroid gland, especially in the treatment of hyperthyroidism.

thi·o·u·re·a (thī′ō-yo͝o-rē′ə) *n.* A lustrous white crystalline compound, $(NH_2)_2CS$, used as a developer in photography and photocopying and in various organic syntheses. Also called *thiocarbamide.*

Thí·ra (thîr′ə, thē′rä). Formerly **San·to·rin** (săn′tə-rēn′). An island of southeast Greece in the southern Cyclades Islands north of Crete.

third (thûrd) *n.* **1.** The ordinal number matching the number three in a series. **2.** One of three equal parts. **3.** *Music.* **a.** An interval of three degrees in a diatonic scale. **b.** A tone separated by three degrees from a given tone, especially the third tone of a scale. **4.** The transmission gear or gear ratio used to produce forward speeds next higher to those of second in a motor vehicle. **5.** *Baseball.* Third base. **6. thirds.** Merchandise whose quality is below the standard set for seconds. [Middle English *thridde, therdde,* third, from Old English *thridda.* See **trei-** in Appendix.] **—third** *adv. & adj.*

third base *n. Baseball.* **1.** The third of the bases on the diamond counterclockwise from home plate; the last base to be reached by a runner before home plate. **2.** The position played by the third baseman.

third baseman *n. Baseball.* The infielder stationed near third base.

third class *n.* **1.** A class of mail in the U.S. postal system including all printed matter, except newspapers and magazines, that weighs less than 16 ounces and is unsealed. **2.** Accommodations, as on a ship or train, of the third and usually lowest order of luxury and price. **—third′-class′** (thûrd′klăs′) *adv. & adj.*

third degree *n.* Mental or physical torture used to obtain information or a confession from a prisoner.

third-de·gree burn (thûrd′dĭ-grē′) *n.* A severe burn in which the skin and underlying tissues are destroyed and sensitive nerve endings are exposed.

third dimension *n.* **1.** The quality of depth or thickness in an object or a space. **2.** The quality of seeming real or lifelike. **—third′-di·men′sion·al** (thûrd′dĭ-mĕn′shə-nəl) *adj.*

third eye *n.* A sensory structure capable of light reception, located on the dorsal side of the diencephalon in various reptiles. Also called *pineal eye.*

third eyelid *n.* See **nictitating membrane.**

third force *n.* A group of people or nations that mediates between two opposed groups, such as hostile nations.

third·hand (thûrd′hănd′) *adj.* **1.** Acquired from or through two intermediate sources: *a thirdhand report.* **2.a.** Previously used by two other owners. **b.** Dealing in merchandise previously used by two other owners. **—third′hand′** *adv.*

third house *n.* A legislative lobby. [From its role with respect to the two houses of which many legislatures consist.]

third·ly (thûrd′lē) *adv.* In the third place, rank, or order.

Third Order (thûrd) *n. Roman Catholic Church.* A confraternity of laypersons associated with a religious order.

third party *n.* **1.** A political party organized as opposition to the existing parties in a two-party system. **2.** One other than the principals involved in a transaction: *I pay rent to a third party, not directly to the landlord.*

third person *n. Grammar.* **1.a.** A set of grammatical forms used in referring to a person or thing other than the speaker or the one spoken to. **b.** A grammatical form belonging to such a set. **2.** Reference of a grammatical form to a person or thing other than the speaker or the one spoken to.

third rail *n.* The rail that supplies the high voltage to power a train on an electric railway.

third-rate (thûrd′rāt′) *adj.* Of third quality or value, especially of less quality or value than second-rate.

third-stream (thûrd′strēm′) *adj. Music.* Of, relating to, or being music that blends classical music with jazz improvisation. **—third stream** *n.*

Third World also **third world** *n.* **1.** Underdeveloped or developing countries, especially those not allied with Communist countries. **2.** Minority groups as a whole within a larger prevailing culture. **—Third World′er** (wûrl′dər) *n.*

thirst (thûrst) *n.* **1.a.** A sensation of dryness in the mouth and throat related to a need or desire to drink. **b.** The desire to drink. **2.** An insistent desire; a craving: *a thirst for knowledge.* **—thirst** *intr.v.* **thirst·ed, thirst·ing, thirsts. 1.** To feel a need to drink. **2.** To have a strong craving; yearn. See Synonyms at **yearn.** [Middle English, from Old English *thurst.* See **ters-** in Appendix.] **—thirst′er** *n.*

thirst·y (thûr′stē) *adj.* **-i·er, -i·est. 1.** Desiring to drink. **2.** Arid; parched: *thirsty fields.* **3.** Craving something: *thirsty for news.* **4.** Very absorbent: *a thirsty sponge.* **—thirst′i·ly** *adv.* **—thirst′i·ness** *n.*

thir·teen (thûr-tēn′) *n.* **1.** The cardinal number that is equal to the sum of 12 + 1. **2.** The 13th in a set or sequence. **3.** Something having 13 parts, units, or members. [Middle English *thyrtene,* alteration of *thrittene,* from Old English *thrēotīne.* See **trei-** in Appendix.] **—thir·teen′** *adj. & pron.*

ă pat	oi boy
ā pay	ou out
âr care	o͝o took
ä father	o͞o boot
ĕ pet	ŭ cut
ē be	ûr urge
ĭ pit	th thin
ī pie	*th* this
îr pier	hw which
ŏ pot	zh vision
ō toe	ə about, item
ô paw	♦ regionalism

Stress marks: ′ (primary); ′ (secondary), as in **dictionary** (dĭk′shə-nĕr′ē)

thistle
Scotch thistle
Onopordum acanthium

Thomson's gazelle
Gazella thomsoni

Thor

thir·teenth (thûr-tēnth′) *n.* **1.** The ordinal number matching the number 13 in a series. **2.** One of 13 equal parts. **—thir·teenth′** *adv. & adj.*

thir·ti·eth (thûr′tē-ĭth) *n.* **1.** The ordinal number matching the number 30 in a series. **2.** One of 30 equal parts. **—thir′ti·eth** *adv. & adj.*

thir·ty (thûr′tē) *n., pl.* **-ties. 1.** The cardinal number equal to 3 × 10. **2. thirties. a.** Often **Thirties.** The decade from 30 to 39 in a century. **b.** A decade or the numbers from 30 to 39: *They settled down in their thirties. The temperature fell into the thirties.* **3.** An indication of the end of a news story, usually written 30. **4.** *Sports.* The second point that is scored by one side in tennis. [Middle English *thritty, thirty,* from Old English *thrītig.* See **trei-** in Appendix.] **—thir′ty** *adj. & pron.*

thir·ty-sec·ond note (thûr′tē-sĕk′ənd) *n. Music.* A musical note with a time value equivalent to 1⁄32 of a whole note.

thir·ty-two·mo (thûr′tē-to͞o′mō) *n., pl.* **-mos.** *Printing.* **1.** The page size (3½ by 5½ inches) that results when a printer's sheet is folded into 32 equal sections. **2.** A book composed of pages of this size.

this (*th*ĭs) *pron., pl.* **these** (*th*ēz). **1. a.** Used to refer to the person or thing present, nearby, or just mentioned: *This is my cat. These are my tools.* **b.** Used to refer to what is about to be said: *Now don't laugh when you hear this.* **c.** Used to refer to the present event, action, or time: *said he'd be back before this.* **2.** Used to indicate the nearer or the more immediate one: *This is mine and that is yours.* **—this** *adj., pl.* **these. 1.** Being just mentioned or present in space, time, or thought: *She left early this morning.* **2.** Being nearer or more immediate: *this side and that side.* **3.** Being about to be stated or described: *Just wait till you hear this story.* **4.** *Informal.* Used as an emphatic substitute for the indefinite article: *looking for this book of recipes.* **—this** *adv.* To this extent; so: *never stayed out this late.* [Middle English, from Old English. See **to-** in Appendix.]

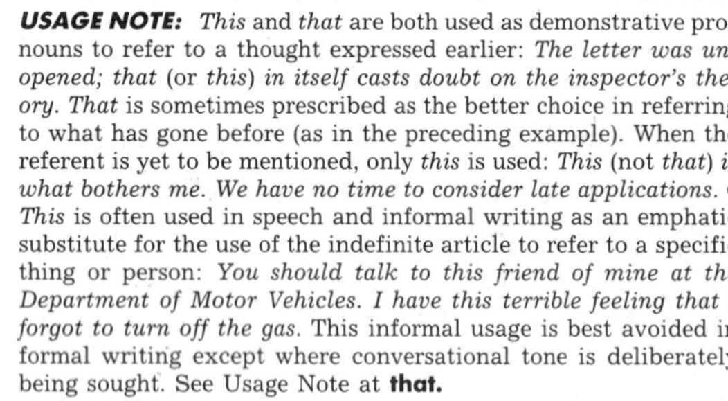

USAGE NOTE: *This* and *that* are both used as demonstrative pronouns to refer to a thought expressed earlier: *The letter was unopened; that* (or *this*) *in itself casts doubt on the inspector's theory. That* is sometimes prescribed as the better choice in referring to what has gone before (as in the preceding example). When the referent is yet to be mentioned, only *this* is used: *This* (not *that*) *is what bothers me. We have no time to consider late applications.* • *This* is often used in speech and informal writing as an emphatic substitute for the use of the indefinite article to refer to a specific thing or person: *You should talk to this friend of mine at the Department of Motor Vehicles. I have this terrible feeling that I forgot to turn off the gas.* This informal usage is best avoided in formal writing except where conversational tone is deliberately being sought. See Usage Note at **that.**

♦ **this·a·way** (*th*ĭs′ə-wā′) *adv. Southern & Midland U.S.* This way. See Regional Note at **thataway.**

This·be (thĭz′bē) *n. Greek & Roman Mythology.* The young woman of Babylon who killed herself after the suicide of her lover, Pyramus.

this·tle (thĭs′əl) *n.* **1.** Any of numerous weedy plants, chiefly of the genera *Cirsium, Carduus,* or *Onopordum* of the composite family, having prickly leaves and variously colored flower heads surrounded by prickly bracts. **2.** Any of various similar or related plants. [Middle English, from Old English *thistel.*]

thistle butterfly *n.* See **painted lady.** [So called because its larvae eat thistles.]

this·tle·down (thĭs′əl-doun′) *n.* The silky down attached to the seedlike fruit of a thistle; pappus.

thith·er (thĭ*th*′ər, *th*ĭ*th*′-) *adv.* To or toward that place; in that direction; there: *running hither and thither.* **—thither** *adj.* Located or being on the more distant side; farther: *the thither side of the pond.* [Middle English, from Old English *thider.* See **to-** in Appendix.]

thith·er·to (thĭ*th*′ər-to͞o′, *th*ĭ*th*′-) *adv.* Up to that time; until then.

thith·er·ward (thĭ*th*′ər-wərd, *th*ĭ*th*′-) *adv.* In that direction; thither.

thix·ot·ro·py (thĭk-sŏt′rə-pē) *n.* The property exhibited by certain gels of becoming fluid when stirred or shaken and returning to the semisolid state upon standing. [Greek *thixis,* touch (from *thinganein, thig-,* to touch; see **dheigh-** in Appendix) + -TROPY.] **—thix′o·trop′ic** (thĭk′sə-trŏp′ĭk) *adj.*

Th.M. *abbr. Latin.* Theologiae Magister (Master of Theology).

tho also **tho′** (*th*ō) *conj. & adv. Informal.* Though.

thole (thōl) *n. Nautical.* A thole pin.

thole pin *n. Nautical.* A wooden peg set in pairs in the gunwales of a boat to serve as an oarlock. [Middle English *tholle,* from Old English *thol.* See **teuə-** in Appendix.]

Thom·as (tŏm′əs), Saint. One of the 12 Apostles. According to the New Testament, he doubted that Jesus had risen from the dead until he saw the wounds.

Thomas, Clarence. Born 1948. American jurist who was appointed an associate justice of the U.S. Supreme Court in 1991.

Thomas, Dylan Marlais. 1914–1953. Welsh poet known for his bardic voice experiments with syllabic verse. He wrote highly personal poems, such as "Fern Hill" (1946), as well as essays, short fiction, and works for radio, including *Under Milk Wood* (1954).

Thomas, George Henry. 1816–1870. American Union general who fought at the Battle of Shiloh (1862) and was renowned for his stalwart defense during the Union defeat at Chickamauga (1863).

Thomas, Isaiah. 1749–1831. American publisher who founded the *Massachusetts Spy,* an anti-British newspaper (1770), and produced the first English Bible printed in the colonies.

Thomas, Lowell Jackson. 1892–1981. American radio commentator who was a correspondent during both World Wars, broadcast a nightly news program (1930–1976), and wrote and lectured widely on his travel adventures.

Thomas, Norman Mattoon. 1884–1968. American socialist leader. A founder of the American Civil Liberties Union (1920), he was the Socialist Party candidate for President six times between 1928 and 1948.

Thomas, Seth. 1785–1859. American clockmaker and a pioneer in the mass production of clocks.

Thomas à Kem·pis (ə kĕm′pĭs, ä). 1380?–1471. German ecclesiastic and writer of devotional literature, most probably including *The Imitation of Christ* (1426).

Thomas A·qui·nas (ə-kwī′nəs), Saint. See Saint Thomas **Aquinas.**

Thomas of Er·cel·doune (ûr′səl-do͞on′). Known as "Thomas the Rhymer." fl. 1220–1297. Scottish poet and seer. The reputed author of the romance *Sir Tristram,* he is associated with Merlin and other legendary soothsayers.

Thom·as·ville (tŏm′əs-vĭl′). A city of southern Georgia west of Valdosta. It is a farm trade center and winter resort. Population, 18,463.

Tho·mism (tō′mĭz′əm) *n.* The theological and philosophical system of Saint Thomas Aquinas, a system that dominated scholasticism. **—Tho′mist** *n.* **—Tho·mis′tic** *adj.*

Thomp·son (tŏmp′sən, tŏm′-), **Benjamin.** Count Rumford. 1753–1814. American-born British public official and physicist who conducted numerous experiments on heat and friction, concluding that heat is produced by moving particles.

Thompson, David. 1770–1857. Canadian explorer who followed the Columbia River to its mouth (1811) and mapped much of western Canada.

Thompson, Dorothy. 1894–1961. American journalist whose radio broadcasts and widely syndicated column "On the Record" (1936–1941) informed Americans of the impending threat of Nazi Germany.

Thompson, Francis. 1859–1907. British poet whose works, influenced by Keats and Shelley, include "The Hound of Heaven" (1893).

Thompson, Sir **John Sparrow David.** 1844–1894. Canadian politician who served as prime minister (1892–1894).

Thompson, Smith. 1768–1843. American jurist who served as an associate justice of the U.S. Supreme Court (1823–1843).

Thompson River. A river, about 489 km (304 mi) long, of southern British Columbia, Canada, flowing west and southwest to the Fraser River.

Thompson submachine gun *n.* A .45-caliber submachine gun. [After John Taliaferro *Thompson* (1860–1940), American army officer.]

Thom·son (tŏm′sən), **Elihu.** 1853–1937. British-born American electrical engineer and inventor who with Thomas Edison formed the General Electric Company (1892).

Thomson, Sir **George Paget.** 1892–1975. British physicist. He shared a 1937 Nobel Prize for the discovery of the diffraction of electrons by crystals.

Thomson, James[1]. 1700–1748. Scottish-born British poet whose works, most notably *The Seasons* (1726–1730) and *The Castle of Indolence* (1748), presaged romanticism.

Thomson, James[2]. Pen name "Bysshe Vanolis" or "B.V." Known as "the Poet of Despair." 1834–1882. Scottish-born British poet whose pessimistic works include *The City of Dreadful Night* (1874).

Thomson, Sir **Joseph John.** 1856–1940. British physicist. He won a 1906 Nobel Prize for investigating the electrical conductivity of gases.

Thomson, Virgil Garnett. 1896–1989. American composer and music critic known for the opera *Four Saints in Three Acts* (1927), with a libretto by Gertrude Stein.

Thom·son's gazelle (tŏm′sənz) *n.* A small gazelle *(Gazella thomsoni)* of eastern Africa, having a broad black stripe on each side of the body. [After Joseph *Thomson* (1858–1895), Scottish geologist and explorer.]

thong (thông, thŏng) *n.* **1.** A narrow strip, as of leather, used for binding or lashing. **2.** A whip of plaited leather or cord. **3.** A sandal held on the foot by a strip that fits between the first and second toes and is connected to a strap usually passing over the top or around the sides of the foot. [Middle English, from Old English *thwong.*]

Thor (thôr) *n. Mythology.* The Norse god of thunder. [Old Norse *Thōrr.* See **(s)tenə-** in Appendix.]

tho·ra·ces (thôr′ə-sēz′, thōr′-) *n.* A plural of **thorax.**

tho·rac·ic (thə-răs′ĭk) *adj.* Of, relating to, or situated in or near the thorax: *the thoracic vertebrae; the thoracic cavity.* **—tho·rac′i·cal·ly** *adv.*

thoracic duct *n.* The main duct of the lymphatic system, ascending through the thoracic cavity in front of the spinal column and discharging lymph and chyle into the blood through the left subclavian vein.

tho·ra·co·lum·bar (thôr′ə-kō-lŭm′bər, -bär, thōr′-) *adj.* **1.** Of or relating to the thoracic and lumbar parts of the spinal column. **2.** Of or relating to the thoracic and lumbar nerves.

tho·ra·co·plas·ty (thôr′ə-kō-plăs′tē, thōr′-) *n., pl.* **-ties.** Surgical removal of part of the ribs to cause the collapse of a diseased lung. [Latin *thōrāx, thōrāc-,* thorax; see THORAX + –PLASTY.]

tho·ra·cot·o·my (thôr′ə-kŏt′ə-mē, thōr′-) *n., pl.* **-mies.** Surgical incision of the chest wall. [Latin *thōrāx, thōrāc-,* thorax + –TOMY.]

tho·rax (thôr′ăks′, thōr′-) *n., pl.* **tho·rax·es** or **tho·ra·ces** (thôr′ə-sēz′, thōr′-). **1.** The part of the human body between the neck and the diaphragm, partially encased by the ribs and containing the heart and lungs; the chest. **2.** A part in other vertebrates that corresponds to the human thorax. **3.** The middle region of the body of an arthropod, between the head and the abdomen, in insects bearing the true legs and wings. [Middle English, from Latin *thōrāx,* breastplate, chest, from Greek *thōrax.*]

Tho·ra·zine (thôr′ə-zēn′, thōr′-). A trademark used for chlorpromazine.

Tho·reau (thə-rō′, thôr′ō), **Henry David.** 1817–1862. American writer. A seminal figure in the history of American thought, he spent much of his life in Concord, Massachusetts, where he became associated with the New England transcendentalists and lived for two years on the shore of Walden Pond (1845–1847). His works include "Civil Disobedience" (1849) and *Walden* (1854). **—Tho·reau′vi·an** (-vē-ən) *adj.*

Thor·finn Karl·sef·ni (thôr′fĭn kärl′sĕv-nē). fl. c. 1000. Icelandic explorer of the northeast coast of North America.

tho·ri·a (thôr′ē-ə, thōr′-) *n.* See **thorium dioxide.** [From THORIUM.]

tho·ric (thôr′ĭk, thŏr′-, thōr′-) *adj.* Of, relating to, or containing thorium. [THOR(IUM) + –IC.]

tho·rite (thôr′īt′, thōr′-) *n.* A vitreous brownish-yellow to black radioactive mineral, essentially $ThSiO_4$, an ore of thorium. [THOR(IUM) + –ITE[1].]

tho·ri·um (thôr′ē-əm, thōr′-) *n. Symbol* **Th** A radioactive silvery-white metallic element that is recovered commercially from monazite. Its longest-lived isotope, the only one that occurs naturally, is Th 232 with a half-life of 1.41×10^{10} years. It is used in magnesium alloys, and isotope 232 is a source of nuclear energy. Atomic number 90; atomic weight 232.038; approximate melting point 1,750°C; approximate boiling point 4,500°C; approximate specific gravity 11.7; valence 4. See table at **element.** [After THOR.]

thorium dioxide *n.* A heavy white powder, ThO_2, obtained from monazite and used mainly in ceramics, glass, and gas mantles and as a catalyst. Also called *thoria.*

thorn (thôrn) *n.* **1.** *Botany.* **a.** A modified branch in the form of a sharp, woody spine. **b.** Any of various shrubs, trees, or woody plants bearing sharp, woody spines. **2.** Any of various sharp, spiny protuberances; a prickle. **3.** One that causes sharp pain, irritation, or discomfort: *He is a thorn in my side.* **4.** The runic letter þ originally representing either sound of the Modern English *th,* as in *the* and *thin,* used in Old English and Middle English manuscripts. [Middle English, from Old English.] **—thorn′less** *adj.*

thorn apple *n.* See **datura.**

thorn·back (thôrn′băk′) *n.* **1.** A European ray *(Raja clavata)* having spines along the back. **2.** A fish *(Platyrhinoidis triseriata)* of Pacific waters, related to the guitarfish.

Thorn·dike (thôrn′dīk′), **Edward Lee.** 1874–1949. American educational psychologist noted for his study of animal intelligence and his methods of measuring intelligence.

Thorndike, Dame **Sybil.** 1882–1976. British actress who created the title role in George Bernard Shaw's *Saint Joan* (1924) and was known for her great versatility.

Thorn·ton (thôrn′tən). A city of north-central Colorado, a suburb of Denver. Population, 40,343.

Thornton, William. 1759–1828. American architect of the original design of the U.S. Capitol (1792). He was also the first superintendent of the U.S. Patent Office (1802–1828).

thorn·y (thôr′nē) *adj.* **-i·er, -i·est. 1.** Full of or covered with thorns. **2.** Spiny. **3.** Painfully controversial; vexatious: *a thorny situation; thorny issues.* **—thorn′i·ly** *adv.* **—thorn′i·ness** *n.*

tho·ron (thôr′ŏn′, thōr′-) *n.* A radioactive isotope of radon, Rn 220, having a half-life of 54.5 seconds and produced by the disintegration of thorium. [THOR(IUM) + –ON[2].]

thor·ough (thûr′ō, thŭr′ō) *adj.* **1.** Exhaustively complete: *a thorough search.* **2.** Painstakingly accurate or careful: *thorough research.* **3.** Absolute; utter: *a thorough pleasure.* **—thorough** *prep. & adv. Archaic.* Variant of **through.** [Middle English *thorow,* through, thorough, from Old English *thuruh,* from end to end, through. See **tere-**[2] in Appendix.] **—thor′ough·ly** *adv.* **—thor′ough·ness** *n.*

thor·ough·bass (thûr′ō-bās′, thûr′ə-, thŭr′-) or **thor·ough bass** *n. Music.* See **continuo.**

thorough brace *n.* One of several leather bands passed from front to back of a carriage, supporting it and serving as a spring. **—thor′ough-braced′** (thûr′ō-brāst′, thŭr′-) *adj.*

thor·ough·bred (thûr′ō-brĕd′, thûr′ə-, thŭr′-) *n.* **1.** A purebred or pedigreed animal, especially a horse. **2. Thoroughbred.** Any of a breed of horses, bred chiefly for racing, originating from a cross between Arabian stallions and English mares. **3.** A well-bred person. **—thoroughbred** *adj.* **1.** Bred of pure stock; purebred. **2. Thoroughbred.** Relating or belonging to horses of the Thoroughbred. **3.** Thoroughly trained or educated; well bred.

thor·ough·fare (thûr′ō-fâr′, thûr′ə-, thŭr′-) *n.* **1.** A main road or public highway. **2. a.** A place of passage from one location to another. **b.** Right to such passage. **3.** A heavily traveled passage, such as a waterway, strait, or channel. [Middle English *thurghfare* : *thurgh, thorow,* through; see THOROUGH + *fare,* road (from Old English *faru, fær,* from *faran,* to go; see FARE).]

thor·ough·go·ing (thûr′ō-gō′ĭng, thûr′ə-, thŭr′-) *adj.* **1.** Very thorough; complete: *thoroughgoing research.* **2.** Unmitigated; unqualified: *a thoroughgoing villain.*

thor·ough·paced (thûr′ō-pāst′, thûr′ə-, thŭr′-) *adj.* **1.** Trained in all paces or gaits, as a horse. **2.** Thoroughgoing; complete.

thor·ough·pin (thûr′ō-pĭn′, thûr′ə-, thŭr′-) *n.* An abnormal swelling on either side of the hock joint of horses and related animals.

thor·ough·wort (thûr′ō-wûrt′, -wôrt′, thûr′ə-, thŭr′-) *n.* See **boneset.** [THOROUGH, through (from the fact that its branches appear to grow through the leaves) + WORT[1].]

thorp (thôrp) *n. Archaic.* A hamlet. [Middle English, from Old English *thorp.* See **treb-** in Appendix.]

Thorpe (thôrp), **James Francis.** Known as "Jim." 1888–1953. American athlete. An outstanding collegiate football player, he later played professional football and baseball. He won the decathlon and pentathlon in the 1912 Olympics but was later disqualified because of his professional status.

Thor·vald·sen or **Thor·wald·sen** (tôr′wôl′sən, thôr′-, tŏŏr′väl′-), **(Albert) Bertel.** 1768?–1844. Danish sculptor. A leading neoclassicist, he executed sculptures of mythological characters, including Hebe (1806), and monuments, such as the *Lion of Lucerne* (1819).

those (thōz) *pron. & adj.* Plural of **that.** [Middle English *thos,* from Old English *thās,* these. See THESE.]

Thoth (thōth, tōt) *n. Mythology.* The Egyptian god of the moon and of wisdom and learning.

thou[1] (thou) *pron.* Used to indicate the one being addressed, especially in a literary, liturgical, or devotional context. [Middle English, from Old English *thū,* second person nominative sing. personal pron. See **tu-** in Appendix.]

thou[2] (thou) *n. Slang.* A thousand, especially of dollars.

though (thō) *conj.* **1.** Despite the fact that; although: *He still argues, though he knows he's wrong. Even though it was raining, she walked to work.* **2.** Conceding or supposing that; even if: *Though they may not succeed, they will still try.* See Usage Note at **although. —though** *adv.* **1.** However; nevertheless: *Snow is not predicted; we can expect some rain, though.* **2.** *Informal.* Used as an intensive: *Wouldn't that beat all, though?* [Middle English, of Scandinavian origin. See **to-** in Appendix.]

thought (thôt) *v.* Past tense and past participle of **think. —thought** *n.* **1.** The act or process of thinking; cogitation. **2.** A product of thinking. See Synonyms at **idea. 3.** The faculty of thinking or reasoning. **4.** The intellectual activity or production of a particular time or group: *ancient Greek thought; deconstructionist thought.* **5.** Consideration; attention: *didn't give much thought to what she said.* **6. a.** Intention; purpose. *There was no thought of coming home early.* **b.** Expectation or conception: *She had no thought that anything was wrong.* **7.** A trifle; a bit: *You could be a thought more considerate.* [Middle English, from Old English *gethōht, thōht.* See **tong-** in Appendix.]

thought·ful (thôt′fəl) *adj.* **1.** Engrossed in thought; contemplative. **2.** Exhibiting or characterized by careful thought: *a thoughtful essay.* **3.** Having or showing heed for the well-being or happiness of others and a propensity for anticipating their needs or wishes. **—thought′ful·ly** *adv.* **—thought′ful·ness** *n.*

SYNONYMS: *thoughtful, considerate, attentive, solicitous.* These adjectives mean having or showing concern for the well-being of others. Although *thoughtful* and *considerate* are often used interchangeably, *thoughtful* implies a tendency to anticipate needs or wishes, whereas *considerate* stresses sensitivity to another's feelings: *It was thoughtful of you to bring flowers. Apartment dwellers who have considerate neighbors are fortunate. Attentive* suggests devoted, assiduous attention: *The nurse was attentive to his patient, constantly checking to be sure she was comfortable. Solicitous* implies deep concern that often verges on anxiety or expresses itself in exaggerated and sometimes cloying attentiveness: *For heaven's sake, Mother, I am an adult! Stop being so solicitous.* See also Synonyms at **pensive.**

thought·less (thôt′lĭs) *adj.* **1.** Marked by or showing lack of due thought or care; careless. See Synonyms at **careless. 2.** Inconsiderate; inattentive: *a thoughtless remark.* **3.** Lacking thought: *The debate turned into thoughtless bickering.* **—thought′less·ly** *adv.* **—thought′less·ness** *n.*

thought reading *n.* Mind reading.

thou·sand (thou′zənd) *n.* The cardinal number equal to 10 × 100 or 10^3. [Middle English, from Old English *thūsend.* See **teuə-** in Appendix.] **—thou′sand** *adj. & pron.*

thoroughbred
Secretariat, winner of the Triple Crown in 1973

Jim Thorpe

Thoth
Detail of a XIX Dynasty relief of Pharaoh Seti I presenting an offering to Thoth

ă pat	oi boy
ā pay	ou out
âr care	ŏŏ took
ä father	ōō boot
ĕ pet	ŭ cut
ē be	ûr urge
ĭ pit	th thin
ī pie	*th* this
îr pier	hw which
ŏ pot	zh vision
ō toe	ə about, item
ô paw	♦ regionalism

Stress marks: ′ (primary); ′ (secondary), as in **dictionary** (dĭk′shə-nĕr′ē)

Thou·sand Island dressing (thou′zənd) *n.* A salad dressing made with mayonnaise, chili sauce, and seasonings. [Perhaps after the THOUSAND ISLANDS.]

Thousand Islands. A group of more than 1,800 islands of northern New York and southeast Ontario, Canada, in the St. Lawrence River at the outlet of Lake Ontario. The islands, some of which are privately owned, are a popular resort area.

Thousand Oaks. A city of southern California west of Los Angeles. Mainly residential, it has some light industry. Population, 77,797.

thou·sandth (thou′zəndth, -zənth) *n.* **1.** The ordinal number matching the number 1,000 in a series. **2.** One of 1,000 equal parts. **—thou′sandth** *adv. & adj.*

thp also **t.hp.** *abbr.* Thrust horsepower.

Thrace (thrās). A region and ancient country of the southeast Balkan Peninsula north of the Aegean Sea. In ancient times it extended as far north as the Danube River. The region was colonized by Greeks in the seventh century B.C. and later passed under the control of Rome, Byzantium, and Ottoman Turkey. Northern Thrace was annexed by Bulgaria in 1885, and eastern Thrace passed to Turkey in 1923.

Thra·cian (thrā′shən) *adj.* Of or relating to Thrace or its people. **—Thracian** *n.* **1.** A native or inhabitant of Thrace. **2.** The Indo-European language of the ancient Thracians.

Thrale (thrāl), Mrs. See Hester Lynch **Piozzi.**

thrall (thrôl) *n.* **1.a.** One, such as a slave or serf, who is held in bondage. **b.** One who is intellectually or morally enslaved. **2.** Servitude; bondage: *"a people in thrall to the miracles of commerce"* (Lewis H. Lapham). **—thrall** *tr.v.* **thralled, thrall·ing, thralls.** *Archaic.* To enslave. [Middle English, from Old English *thrǣl,* from Old Norse *thrǣll.*] **—thrall′dom, thral′dom** *n.*

thrash (thrăsh) *v.* **thrashed, thrash·ing, thrash·es.** *—tr.* **1.** To beat with or as if with a flail, especially as a punishment. See Synonyms at **beat.** **2.** To swing or strike in a manner suggesting the action of a flail: *The alligator thrashed its tail.* **3.** To defeat utterly; vanquish. **4.** To thresh. **5.** *Nautical.* To sail (a boat) against opposing winds or tides. *—intr.* **1.** To move wildly or violently: *thrashed about all night.* **2.** To strike or flail. **3.** To thresh. **4.** *Nautical.* To sail against opposing tides or winds. **—thrash** *n.* The act or an instance of thrashing. ***—phrasal verb.* thrash out.** To discuss fully. [Variant of THRESH.] **—thrash′er** *n.*

three-decker
H.M.S. *Victory,*
commanded by
Admiral Nelson

thrash·er (thrăsh′ər) *n.* Any of various New World songbirds of the genus *Toxostoma,* related to the mockingbird and having a long tail, a long curved beak, and usually a brown head and back. [Perhaps alteration of THRUSH [1].]

thrash·ing (thrăsh′ĭng) *n.* A severe beating.

thra·son·i·cal (thrā-sŏn′ĭ-kəl, thrə-) *adj.* Boastful. [After *Thrasō,* a character in *Eunuchus,* a play by Terence.] **—thra·son′i·cal·ly** *adv.*

Thras·y·bu·lus (thrăs′ə-byo͞o′ləs). Died c. 389 B.C. Athenian military and political leader who led the overthrow (403) of the tyrannical oligarchy established by Sparta in Athens.

thread (thrĕd) *n.* **1.a.** Fine cord of a fibrous material, such as cotton or flax, made of two or more filaments twisted together and used in needlework and the weaving of cloth. **b.** A piece of such cord. **2.a.** A thin strand, cord, or filament of natural or manufactured material. **b.** Something that suggests the fineness or thinness of such a strand, cord, or filament: *a thread of smoke.* **c.** Something that suggests the continuousness of such a strand, cord, or filament: *lost the thread of his argument.* **3.** A helical or spiral ridge on a screw, nut, or bolt. **4. threads.** *Slang.* Clothes. **—thread** *v.* **thread·ed, thread·ing, threads.** *—tr.* **1.a.** To pass one end of a thread through the eye of (a needle, for example). **b.** To pass (something) through in the manner of a thread: *thread the wire through the opening.* **c.** To pass a tape or film into or through (a device): *thread a film projector.* **d.** To pass (a tape or film) into or through a device. **2.** To connect by running a thread through; string: *thread beads.* **3.a.** To make one's way cautiously through: *threading dark alleys.* **b.** To make (one's way) cautiously through something. **4.** To occur here and there throughout; pervade: *"More than 90 geologic faults thread the Los Angeles area"* (Science News). **5.** To machine a thread on (a screw, nut, or bolt). *—intr.* **1.** To make one's way cautiously: *threaded through the shoals and sandbars.* **2.** To proceed by a winding course. **3.** To form a thread when dropped from a spoon, as boiling sugar syrup. [Middle English, from Old English *thrǣd.* See **tera-** [1] in Appendix.] **—thread′er** *n.*

thread·bare (thrĕd′bâr′) *adj.* **1.** Having the nap worn down so that the filling or warp threads show through; frayed or shabby: *threadbare rugs.* **2.** Wearing old, shabby clothing. **3.** Overused to the point of being worn out; hackneyed: *threadbare excuses.* See Synonyms at **trite.**

thread·fin (thrĕd′fĭn′) *n., pl.* **threadfin** or **-fins.** Any of various chiefly tropical marine fishes of the family Polynemidae, having threadlike rays extending from the lower part of the pectoral fin.

thread·worm (thrĕd′wûrm′) *n.* See **pinworm.**

thread·y (thrĕd′ē) *adj.* **-i·er, -i·est.** **1.** Consisting of or resembling thread; filamentous. **2.** Capable of forming or tending to form threads; viscid. **3.** *Medicine.* Weak and shallow. Used of a pulse. **4.** Lacking fullness of tone; thin: *a thready voice.* **—thread′i·ness** *n.*

threat (thrĕt) *n.* **1.** An expression of an intention to inflict pain, injury, evil, or punishment. **2.** An indication of impending danger or harm. **3.** One that is regarded as a possible danger; a menace. **—threat** *tr.v.* **threat·ed, threat·ing, threats.** *Archaic.* To threaten. [Middle English, from Old English *thrēat,* oppression. See **treud-** in Appendix.]

threat·en (thrĕt′n) *v.* **-ened, -en·ing, -ens.** *—tr.* **1.** To express a threat against. **2.** To be a source of danger to; menace. **3.** To give signs or warning of; portend. **4.** To announce the possibility of in a threat. *—intr.* **1.** To express or use threats. **2.** To indicate danger or harm. **—threat′en·er** *n.* **—threat′en·ing·ly** *adv.*

SYNONYMS: *threaten, menace, intimidate.* These verbs mean to foretell or give signs of impending peril, evil, or injury. *Threaten* most often refers to an indication of something disquieting or ominous, to appearance or action calculated or serving to deter, or to something that is a source of danger: *"a crack that threatened to become a split"* (Booth Tarkington). *"No future peace can be maintained if . . . armaments continue to be employed by nations which threaten, or may threaten, aggression outside of their frontiers"* (Atlantic Charter). *"The heretics were persecuted . . . because their beliefs threatened the vested interest of that day"* (James Harvey Robinson). *Menace* frequently stresses a frightening or hostile intention, effect, or result: *"A new and formidable danger menaced the western frontier"* (Macaulay). To *intimidate* is to threaten and fill with fear: *"an overall strategy by* [the country's] *leaders to reaffirm their revolutionary credentials in the eyes of the . . . world, to intimidate smaller countries in the region"* (Elaine Sciolino).

threat·ened (thrĕt′nd) *adj.* *Ecology.* At risk of becoming endangered. Used of a plant or an animal.

three (thrē) *n.* **1.** The cardinal number equal to the sum of 2 + 1. **2.** The third in a set or sequence. **3.** Something having three parts, units, or members. [Middle English, from Old English *thrī.* See **trei-** in Appendix.] **—three** *adj. & pron.*

three-bag·ger (thrē′băg′ər) *n.* *Baseball.* See **three-base hit.**

three-base hit (thrē′bās′) *n.* *Baseball.* A base hit that allows the batter to reach third base without being put out. Also called *three-bagger, triple.*

three-card monte (thrē′kärd) *n.* *Games.* A gambling game in which the dealer shows a player three cards, then turns them face down and moves them around, and the player must guess the position of a particular card.

three-col·or (thrē′kŭl′ər) *adj.* Of, relating to, or being a color printing or photographic process in which three primary colors are transferred by three different plates or filters to a surface, reproducing all the colors of the subject matter.

3-D or **3D** also **three-D** (thrē′dē′) *—adj.* Three-dimensional. *—n.* A three-dimensional medium, display, or performance, especially a cinematic or graphic medium in three dimensions: *They shot the movie in 3-D.*

three-deck·er (thrē′dĕk′ər) *n.* **1.** *Nautical.* A ship having three decks, especially one of a class of sail-powered warships with guns on three decks. **2.** Something with three levels or layers, as: **a.** A three-story apartment building. **b.** A sandwich having three slices of bread.

three-di·men·sion·al (thrē′dĭ-mĕn′shə-nəl, -dī-) *adj.* **1.** Of, relating to, having, or existing in three dimensions. **2.** Having or appearing to have extension in depth. **3.** Treating many aspects of a subject; lifelike: *a three-dimensional account of conditions under the new government.*

three-gait·ed (thrē′gā′tĭd) *adj.* Trained in the walk, trot, and canter. Used of a horse.

three-leg·ged race (thrē′lĕg′ĭd, -lĕgd′) *n.* *Games.* A race in which the contestants run in pairs with their near legs tied together.

Three Mile Island (thrē). An island in the Susquehanna River in southeast Pennsylvania southeast of Harrisburg. It was the site of a major nuclear accident on March 28, 1979, when a partial meltdown released radioactive material and forced the evacuation of thousands of nearby residents.

three-mile limit (thrē′mīl′) *n.* *Law.* The outer limit of the area extending three miles out to sea from the coast of a country, sometimes considered to constitute the country's territorial waters.

three·pence (thrĕp′əns, thrĭp′-, thrŭp′-) *n., pl.* **threepence** or **-penc·es.** **1.** A coin worth three pennies, formerly used in Great Britain. **2.** The sum of three pennies.

three·pen·ny (thrĕp′ə-nē, thrĭp′-, thrŭp′-) *adj.* **1.** Worth or priced at threepence. **2.** Very small; trifling.

three-piece (thrē′pēs′) *adj.* Made in or consisting of three parts or pieces, as a suit consisting of a jacket, trousers, and a vest.

three-ply (thrē′plī′) *adj.* Consisting of three layers or strands.

three-point landing (thrē′point′) *n.* An airplane landing in which the two main wheels and the nose wheel, tail wheel, or tailskid all touch the ground simultaneously.

three-quar·ter (thrē′kwôr′tər) *adj.* **1.** Relating to, consisting of, or extending to three fourths of the usual full length: *a skirt of three-quarter length.* **2.** Depicting the subject turned slightly from a full frontal view: *a three-quarter portrait.*

three-quarter binding *n. Printing.* A bookbinding in which the leather or fabric covering the spine extends onto the covers for one third of their width.

three-ring circus (thrē′rĭng′) *n.* **1.** A circus having simultaneous performances in three separate rings. **2.** *Informal.* A situation characterized by confusing, engrossing, or amusing activity.

three R's *pl.n.* Reading, writing, and arithmetic, considered as the fundamentals of elementary education. [From the phrase *reading, 'riting, and 'rithmetic,* alteration of *reading, writing, and arithmetic.*]

three·score (thrē′skôr′, -skōr′) *adj.* Being three times twenty; sixty. **—three′score′** *n. & pron.*

three·some (thrē′səm) *n.* **1.** A group of three persons or things. **2.** An activity involving three people, especially a golf match in which one player competes against two others who alternate their play. **—threesome** *adj.* Consisting of or performed by three.

three-spine stickleback (thrē′spīn′) also **three-spined stickleback** (-spīnd′) *n.* A stickleback *(Gasterosteus aculeatus)* having three separate dorsal spines, found throughout most of the Northern Hemisphere in both salt water and fresh water.

three-square (thrē′skwâr′) *adj.* Having an equilateral triangular cross section: *a three-square file.*

three-toed sloth (thrē′tōd′) *n.* See **sloth** (sense 2a).

three-toed woodpecker *n.* Either of two woodpeckers *(Picoides arcticus* or *P. tridactylus)* of northern North America, lacking the inner hind toe on each foot.

three-wheel·er (thrē′hwē′lər, -wē′-) *n.* A vehicle having three wheels, as a small, all-terrain motor vehicle.

threm·ma·tol·o·gy (thrĕm′ə-tŏl′ə-jē) *n.* The scientific breeding of domestic plants and animals. [Greek *thremma, thremmat-,* nursling + –LOGY.]

thren·o·dy (thrĕn′ə-dē) *n., pl.* **-dies.** A poem or song of mourning or lamentation. [Greek *thrēnōidia* : *thrēnos,* lament + *ōidē,* song; see ODE.] **—thre·no′di·al** (thrə-nō′dē-əl), **thre·nod′ic** (-nŏd′ĭk) *adj.* **—thren′o·dist** *n.*

thre·o·nine (thrē′ə-nēn′, -nĭn) *n.* A colorless crystalline amino acid, $C_4H_9NO_3$, that is derived from the hydrolysis of protein and is an essential component of human nutrition. [Probably from *threose,* a kind of sugar (alteration of *erythrose* : ERYTHRO– + –OSE[2]) + –INE[2].]

thresh (thrĕsh) *v.* **threshed, thresh·ing, thresh·es.** *—tr.* **1.a.** To beat the stems and husks of (grain or cereal plants) with a machine or flail to separate the grains or seeds from the straw. **b.** To separate (grains or seeds) in this manner. **2.** To discuss or examine (an issue, for example) repeatedly. **3.** To beat severely; thrash. *—intr.* **1.** To use a machine or flail to separate grain or seeds from straw. **2.** To thrash about; toss. [Middle English *thresshen,* from Old English *therscan.* See **terə-**[1] in Appendix.]

thresh·er (thrĕsh′ər) *n.* **1.** One that threshes: *a thresher of grain.* **2.** A threshing machine. **3.** Any of various large sharks of the genus *Alopias,* especially *A. vulpinus* of the Atlantic and eastern Pacific oceans, having a tail with a long whiplike upper lobe with which it strikes the surface of the water.

thresh·ing machine (thrĕsh′ĭng) *n.* A farm machine used in threshing grain or seed plants.

thresh·old (thrĕsh′ōld′, -hōld′) *n.* **1.** A piece of wood or stone placed beneath a door; a doorsill. **2.** An entrance or a doorway. **3.** The place or point of beginning; the outset. **4.** A point separating conditions that will produce a given effect from conditions of a higher or lower degree that will not produce the effect, as the intensity below which a stimulus is of sufficient strength to produce sensation or elicit a response: *a low threshold of pain.* [Middle English *thresshold,* from Old English *therscold, threscold.* See **terə-**[1] in Appendix.]

WORD HISTORY: Perhaps the tradition of carrying the bride over the threshold is dying out, but knowledge of the custom persists, leading one to wonder about the *–hold* or the *thresh–* in the word *threshold.* Scholars are still wondering about the last part of the word, but the *thresh–* can be explained. It is related to the word *thresh,* which refers to an agricultural process. This process of beating the stems and husks of grain or cereal plants to separate the grain or seeds from the straw was at one time done with the feet of oxen or human beings. Thus, the Germanic word **therskan,* or by the switching of sounds called metathesis, **threskan,* meant "thresh" and "tread." This association with the feet is probably retained in Old English *therscold* or *threscold* (Modern English *threshold*), "sill of a door (over which one treads)."

threw (thro͞o) *v.* Past tense of **throw.**

thrice (thrīs) *adv.* **1.** Three times. **2.** In a threefold quantity or degree. **3.** *Archaic.* Extremely; greatly. [Middle English *thries,* adverbial genitive of *thrie,* from Old English *thrīga.* See **trei-** in Appendix.]

thrift (thrĭft) *n.* **1.** Wise economy in the management of money and other resources; frugality. **2.** Vigorous growth of living things, such as plants. **3.** Any of several densely tufted plants of the genus *Armeria,* especially *A. maritima,* having white to pink flower heads with a funnel-shaped scarious calyx. **4.** A savings and loan association, credit union, or savings bank. Also called *thrift institution.* [Middle English, prosperity, perhaps from Old Norse, from *thrīfask,* to thrive. See THRIVE.]

thrift·less (thrĭft′lĭs) *adj.* **1.** Careless in handling money; wasteful. **2.** *Archaic.* Lacking usefulness or value. **—thrift′less·ly** *adv.* **—thrift′less·ness** *n.*

thrift shop *n.* A shop that sells used articles, especially clothing, as to benefit a charitable organization.

thrift·y (thrĭf′tē) *adj.* **-i·er, -i·est. 1.** Practicing or marked by thrift; wisely economical. See Synonyms at **sparing. 2.** Industrious and thriving; prosperous. **3.** Growing vigorously; thriving, as a plant. **—thrift′i·ly** *adv.* **—thrift′i·ness** *n.*

thrill (thrĭl) *v.* **thrilled, thrill·ing, thrills.** *—tr.* **1.** To cause to feel a sudden intense sensation; excite greatly. **2.** To give great pleasure to; delight. See Synonyms at **enrapture. 3.** To cause to quiver, tremble, or vibrate. *—intr.* **1.** To feel a sudden quiver of excitement or emotion. **2.** To quiver, tremble, or vibrate. **—thrill** *n.* **1.** A quivering or trembling caused by sudden excitement or emotion. **2.** A source or cause of excitement or emotion. **3.** *Pathology.* A slight palpable vibration that often accompanies certain cardiac and circulatory abnormalities. [Middle English *thrillen,* alteration of *thirlen,* to pierce, from Old English *thȳrlian,* from *thȳrel,* hole. See **terə-**[2] in Appendix.] **—thrill′ing·ly** *adv.*

thrill·er (thrĭl′ər) *n.* One that thrills, especially a sensational or suspenseful book, story, play, or movie.

thrips (thrĭps) *n., pl.* **thrips.** Any of various minute insects of the order Thysanoptera, having usually four narrow wings fringed with hairs, and many of which are major pests of cereals and fruit trees. [Latin, woodworm, from Greek.]

thrive (thrīv) *intr.v.* **thrived** or **throve** (thrōv), **thrived** or **thriv·en** (thrĭv′ən), **thriv·ing, thrives. 1.** To make steady progress; prosper. **2.** To grow vigorously; flourish: *"the wild deer that throve here"* (Tom Clancy). [Middle English *thriven,* from Old Norse *thrīfask,* reflexive of *thrīfa,* to seize.] **—thriv′er** *n.*

throat (thrōt) *n.* **1.** The anterior portion of the neck. **2.** *Anatomy.* The portion of the digestive tract that lies between the rear of the mouth and the esophagus and includes the fauces and the pharynx. **3.** A narrow passage or part suggestive of the human throat: *the throat of a horn.* **4.** *Botany.* The opening of a tubular corolla or calyx where the tube joins the limb. **—throat** *tr.v.* **throat·ed, throat·ing, throats.** To pronounce with a harsh or guttural voice. ***—idiom.* ram** (or **shove) down (someone's) throat.** *Informal.* To compel to accept or consider: *always ramming his political opinions down my throat.* [Middle English *throte,* from Old English.]

throat·latch (thrōt′lăch′) *n.* A strap passing under the neck of a horse for holding a bridle or halter in place.

throat·y (thrō′tē) *adj.* **-i·er, -i·est.** Uttered or sounding as if uttered deep in the throat; guttural, hoarse, or husky. **—throat′i·ly** *adv.* **—throat′i·ness** *n.*

throb (thrŏb) *intr.v.* **throbbed, throb·bing, throbs. 1.** To beat rapidly or violently, as the heart; pound. **2.** To vibrate, pulsate, or sound with a steady pronounced rhythm: *boat engines throbbing.* See Synonyms at **pulsate. —throb** *n.* The act of throbbing; a beating, palpitation, or vibration. [Middle English *throbben,* of imitative origin.] **—throb′bing·ly** *adv.*

throe (thrō) *n.* **1.** A severe pang or spasm of pain, as in childbirth. See Synonyms at **pain. 2. throes.** A condition of agonizing struggle or trouble: *a country in the throes of economic collapse.* [Middle English *throwe,* perhaps alteration of *thrawe,* from Old English *thrawu,* genitive of *thrēah,* pain, affliction.]

thromb– *pref.* Variant of **thrombo–.**

throm·bi (thrŏm′bī) *n.* Plural of **thrombus.**

throm·bin (thrŏm′bĭn) *n.* An enzyme in blood that facilitates blood clotting by reacting with fibrinogen to form fibrin.

thrombo– or **thromb–** *pref.* Blood clot; blood clotting: *thromboplastic.* [Greek, from *thrombos,* clot.]

throm·bo·cyte (thrŏm′bə-sīt′) *n.* See **platelet. —throm′bo·cyt′ic** (-sĭt′ĭk) *adj.*

throm·bo·cy·to·pe·ni·a (thrŏm′bə-sī′tə-pē′nē-ə) *n.* An abnormal decrease in the number of platelets in circulatory blood. **—throm′bo·cy′to·pe′nic** *adj.*

throm·bo·em·bo·lism (thrŏm′bō-ĕm′bə-lĭz′əm) *n.* The blocking of a blood vessel by a blood clot dislodged from its site of origin. **—throm′bo·em·bol′ic** (-ĕm-bŏl′ĭk) *adj.*

throm·bo·ki·nase (thrŏm′bō-kī′nās, -nāz) *n.* See **thromboplastin.**

throm·bol·y·sis (thrŏm-bŏl′ĭ-sĭs) *n., pl.* **-ses** (-sēz). Dissolution or destruction of a thrombus. **—throm′bo·lyt′ic** (-bə-lĭt′ĭk) *adj.*

throm·bo·phle·bi·tis (thrŏm′bō-flĭ-bī′tĭs) *n.* Inflammation of a vein caused by or associated with the formation of a blood clot.

throm·bo·plas·tic (thrŏm′bō-plăs′tĭk) *adj.* **1.** Causing or promoting blood clotting: *a thromboplastic protein.* **2.** Of or relating to thromboplastin. **—throm′bo·plas′ti·cal·ly** *adv.*

throm·bo·plas·tin (thrŏm′bō-plăs′tĭn) *n.* An enzyme that converts prothrombin to thrombin in the early stages of blood clotting. Also called *thrombokinase.*

throm·bo·sis (thrŏm-bō′sĭs) *n., pl.* **-ses** (-sēz). The formation, presence, or development of a thrombus. [New Latin *thrombōsis,* from Greek, a clotting, from *thrombousthai,* to clot, from *thrombos,* clot.]

throm·bo·sthe·nin (thrŏm′bō-sthē′nĭn) *n.* A contractile

ă pat	oi boy
ā pay	ou out
âr care	o͝o took
ä father	o͞o boot
ĕ pet	ŭ cut
ē be	ûr urge
ĭ pit	th thin
ī pie	*th* this
îr pier	hw which
ŏ pot	zh vision
ō toe	ə about, item
ô paw	♦ regionalism

Stress marks: **′** (primary); ′ (secondary), as in **dictionary** (dĭk′shə-nĕr′ē)

throne
Coronation throne of Edward the Confessor

protein in platelets that is active in the formation of blood clots. [THROMBO– + Greek *sthenos,* strength + –IN.]

throm·box·ane (thrŏm-bŏk′sān) *n.* Any of several compounds, originally derived from prostaglandin precursors in platelets, that stimulate aggregation of platelets and constriction of blood vessels. [THROMB(O)– + OX(O)– + –ANE.]

throm·bus (thrŏm′bəs) *n., pl.* **-bi** (-bī). A fibrinous clot formed in a blood vessel or in a chamber of the heart. [New Latin, from Greek *thrombos,* clot.]

throne (thrōn) *n.* **1.** A chair occupied by an exalted personage, such as a sovereign or bishop, on state or ceremonial occasions, often situated on a dais and sometimes having a canopy and ornate decoration. **2.a.** A personage who occupies a throne. **b.** The power, dignity, or rank of such a personage; sovereignty. **3. thrones.** *Theology.* The third of the nine orders of angels. **—throne** *tr. & intr.v.* **throned, thron·ing, thrones.** To install in or occupy a throne. [Middle English, alteration of *trone,* from Old French, from Latin *thronus,* from Greek *thronos.* See **dher-** in Appendix.]

throng (thrông, thrŏng) *n.* **1.** A large group of people gathered or crowded closely together; a multitude. See Synonyms at **crowd**[1]. **2.** A large group of things; a host. **—throng** *v.* **thronged, throng·ing, throngs.** *—tr.* **1.** To crowd into; fill: *commuters thronging the subway platform.* **2.** To press in on. *—intr.* To gather, press, or move in a throng. [Middle English, from Old English *gethrang.*]

thros·tle (thrŏs′əl) *n.* **1.** Any of various Old World thrushes, especially a song thrush. **2.** A machine formerly used for spinning fibers such as cotton or wool. [Middle English, from Old English.]

throt·tle (thrŏt′l) *n.* **1.** A valve that regulates the flow of a fluid, such as the valve in an internal-combustion engine that controls the amount of vaporized fuel entering the cylinders. **2.** A lever or pedal controlling such a valve. **—throttle** *tr.v.* **-tled, -tling, -tles. 1.a.** To regulate the flow of (fuel) in an engine. **b.** To regulate the speed of (an engine) with a throttle. **2.** To suppress: *tried to throttle the press.* **3.** To strangle; choke. [Short for *throttle valve,* from *throttle,* to strangle, choke, from Middle English *throtelen,* probably from *throte,* throat. See THROAT.] **—throt′tler** *n.*

throt·tle·hold (thrŏt′l-hōld′) *n.* See **stranglehold** (sense 2).

through (thro͞o) *prep.* **1.** In one side and out the opposite or another side of: *went through the tunnel.* **2.** Among or between; in the midst of: *a walk through the flowers.* **3.** By way of: *climbed in through the window.* **4.a.** By the means or agency of: *bought the antique vase through a dealer.* **b.** Into and out of the handling, care, processing, modification, or consideration of: *Her application went through our office. Run the figures through the computer.* **5.** Here and there in; around: *a tour through France.* **6.** From the beginning to the end of: *stayed up through the night.* **7.** At or to the end of; done or finished with, especially successfully: *We are through the initial testing period.* **8.** Up to and including: *a play that runs through December; a volume that covers A through D.* **9.** Past and without stopping for: *drove through a red light.* **10.** Because of; on account of: *She succeeded through hard work. He declined the honor through modesty.* **—through** *adv.* **1.** From one end or side to another or an opposite end or side: *opened the door and went through.* **2.** From beginning to end; completely: *I read the article once through.* **3.** Throughout the whole extent or thickness; thoroughly: *warmed the leftovers clear through; got soaked through in the rain; a letter that was shot through with the writer's personality.* **4.** Over the total distance; all the way: *drove through to their final destination.* **5.** To a conclusion or an accomplishment: *see a matter through.* **—through** *adj.* **1.** Allowing continuous passage; unobstructed: *a through street.* **2.a.** Affording transportation to a destination with few or no stops and no transfers: *a through bus; a through ticket.* **b.** Continuing on a highway without exiting: *through traffic; through lanes.* **3.** Passing or extending from one end, side, or surface to another: *a through beam.* **4.** Having finished; at completion: *She was through with the project.* **5.** Having no further concern, dealings, or connection: *I'm through with him.* **6.** Having no more use, value, or potential; washed up: *That swimmer is through as an athlete.* **—*idiom.*** **through and through. 1.** In every part; throughout: *wet through and through.* **2.** In every aspect: *a success through and through.* [Middle English *thurh, through,* from Old English *thurh.* See **terə-**[2] in Appendix.]

through·ly (thro͞o′lē) *adv. Archaic.* Thoroughly.

through·out (thro͞o-out′) *prep.* In, to, through, or during every part of; all through: *The road is kept open throughout the year.* **—throughout** *adv.* **1.** In or through all parts; everywhere: *The material is flawed throughout.* **2.** During the entire time or extent: *Though unsure how her speech would be received, she remained calm and professional throughout.*

through·put (thro͞o′po͝ot′) *n.* Output or production, as of a computer program, over a period of time.

through·way (thro͞o′wā′) *n.* Variant of **thruway.**

throve (thrōv) *v.* A past tense of **thrive.**

throw (thrō) *v.* **threw** (thro͞o), **thrown** (thrōn), **throw·ing, throws.** *—tr.* **1.** To propel through the air with a motion of the hand or arm. **2.** To discharge into the air by any means: *a machine that throws tennis balls; ash that was thrown by an erupting volcano.* **3.** To hurl or fling with great force or speed: *threw themselves on the food; jetsam that had been thrown up onto the shore.* **4.a.** To hurl to the ground or floor, as in a wrestling contest. **b.** To cause to fall off: *The horse threw its rider.* **5.** *Informal.* To cause confusion or perplexity in; disconcert or nonplus: *We didn't let our worries throw us.* **6.** To put on or off hastily or carelessly: *throw on a jacket.* **7.a.** To put (suddenly or forcefully) into a given condition, position, or activity: *threw him into a fit of laughter; threw some supper together; threw her leg over the arm of the chair.* **b.** To devote, apply, or direct: *threw all their resources into the new endeavor; threw the blame onto the others.* **8.** To form on a potter's wheel: *throw a vase.* **9.** To twist (fibers) into thread. **10.** *Games.* **a.** To roll (dice). **b.** To roll (a particular combination) with dice. **c.** To discard or play (a card). **11.** To send forth; project: *She threw me a look of encouragement.* **12.** To cause to fall on or over something; cast: *The rising sun threw shadows across the lawn. We threw sheets over the furniture before we painted the ceiling.* **13.** To bear (young). Used of cows or horses, for example. **14.** To arrange or give (a party, for example). **15.** To move (a lever or switch) in order to activate, deactivate, or control a device. **16.** *Informal.* To lose or give up (a contest, for example) purposely. **17.** To abandon oneself to; have: *heard the news and threw a fit.* **18.** To commit (oneself), especially for leniency or support: *threw himself on the mercy of the court.* **19.** To deliver (a punch), as in boxing: *threw a left hook.* *—intr.* To cast, fling, or hurl something. **—throw** *n.* **1.** The act or an instance of throwing. **2.** The distance to which something is or can be thrown: *a stone's throw away.* **3.** *Games.* **a.** A roll or cast of dice. **b.** The combination of numbers so obtained. **4.** *Informal.* A single chance, venture, or instance: *"could afford up to forty-five bucks a throw to wax sentimental over their heritage"* (John Simon). **5.** *Sports.* The act of throwing or a technique used to throw an opponent in wrestling. **6.a.** A light coverlet, such as an afghan. **b.** A scarf or shawl. **7.a.** The radius of a circle described by a crank, cam, or similar machine part. **b.** The maximum displacement of a machine part moved by another part, such as a crank or cam. **8.** *Geology.* The amount of vertical displacement of a fault. **—*phrasal verbs.*** **throw away. 1.a.** To get rid of as useless: *threw away yesterday's newspaper.* **b.** *Games.* To discard: *threw away two aces.* **2.a.** To fail to take advantage of: *threw away a chance to make a fortune.* **b.** To waste or use in a foolish way: *threw away her inheritance.* **3.** To utter or perform in an offhand, seemingly careless way: *The play's villain throws away the news that the house has burned down.* **throw back. 1.** To hinder the progress of; check: *The troops were thrown back.* **2.** To revert to an earlier type or stage in one's past. **3.** To cause to depend; make reliant. **throw in. 1.** To insert or introduce into the course of something: *threw in a few snide comments while they conversed.* **2.** To add (an extra thing or amount) with no additional charge. **3.** To engage (a clutch, for example). **throw off. 1.** To cast out; rid oneself of: *threw off all unpleasant memories.* **2.** To give off; emit: *exhaust pipes throwing off fumes.* **3.** To distract, divert, or mislead: *Crossing the stream, he threw the tracking dogs off. A wrong measurement threw her estimate off.* **4.** To do, finish, or accomplish in a casual or offhand way; toss off: *threw off a quick response to the letter.* **throw open.** To make more accessible, especially suddenly or dramatically: *threw open the nomination.* **throw out. 1.** To give off; emit: *searchlights throwing out powerful beams.* **2.** To reject or discard: *The committee threw out her proposal.* **3.** To get rid of as useless: *threw out the garbage.* **4.** *Informal.* To offer, as a suggestion or plan: *They sat around throwing out names of people they might want to invite to the party.* **5.** To force to leave a place or position, especially in an abrupt or unexpected manner: *The convicted judge was thrown out of office. The headwaiter threw the disorderly guest out.* **6.a.** To disengage (a clutch, for example). **b.** To put out of alignment: *threw my back out.* **7.** *Baseball.* To put out (a base runner) by throwing the ball to the player guarding the base to which the base runner is moving. **throw over. 1.** To overturn: *threw the cart over.* **2.** To abandon: *threw over her boyfriend of four years; threw over the company they themselves had founded.* **3.** To reject. **throw up. 1.** To vomit. **2.** To abandon; relinquish. *She threw up her campaign for mayor.* **3.** To construct hurriedly: *shoddy houses that were thrown up in a few months.* **4.** To refer to something repeatedly: *She threw up his past to him whenever they argued.* **5.** To project, play, or otherwise display (a slide, videotape, or other recorded image): *threw the tape of vacation highlights up on the screen.* **—*idioms.*** **throw (one's) weight around.** *Slang.* To use power or authority, especially in an excessive or heavy-handed way. **throw the baby out with the bath water.** *Slang.* To discard something valuable along with something not desired, usually unintentionally. **throw up (one's) hands.** To indicate or express utter hopelessness: *He threw up his hands and abandoned the argument.* [Middle English *throwen,* to turn, twist, hurl, from Old English *thrāwan.* See **terə-**[1] in Appendix.] **—throw′er** *n.*

SYNONYMS: *throw, cast, hurl, fling, pitch, toss, sling.* These verbs mean to propel something through the air with a motion of the hand or arm. *Throw* is the least specific: *throw a ball; threw the life preserver to the struggling swimmer; threw the book on the table. Cast* usually refers to throwing something light: *The angler cast her line into the stream. Hurl* and *fling* mean to throw with great force: *"Him the Almighty Power/Hurl'd headlong flaming from th' Ethereal Sky"* (John Milton). *The wedding guests were given confetti to fling at the bride and groom. Pitch* often means to throw with careful aim: *"a special basket in my study . . . into which I pitch letters, circulars, pamphlets and so forth"*

(H.G. Wells). *Toss,* in contrast, usually means to throw lightly or casually: *"Campton tossed the card away"* (Edith Wharton). *Sling* stresses force of propulsion: *The cook's helper slung the peeled potatoes into a huge enamel pot.* See also Synonyms at **confuse.**

throw·a·way (thrō′ə-wā′) *n., pl.* **-ways. 1.** Something designed or likely to be discarded after use, as a free handbill distributed on the street. **2.** A child or teenager who has been rejected, ejected, or abandoned by parents or guardians and lives on the streets. **—throwaway** *adj.* **1.a.** Designed or intended to be discarded after use: *throwaway packaging.* **b.** Readily discarding things: *a throwaway society.* **c.** Having been rejected, ejected, or abandoned by parents or guardians: *throwaway children living on the streets.* **2.** Written or delivered in a low-key or offhand manner: *"a sentence fragment or quirky throwaway metaphor"* (Joyce Carol Oates).

throw·back (thrō′băk′) *n.* **1.** A reversion to a former type or ancestral characteristic. **2.** See **atavism** (sense 2).

thrown (thrōn) *v.* Past participle of **throw.**

throw pillow *n.* A small pillow used chiefly for decoration, as on a couch.

throw rug *n.* See **scatter rug.**

throw·ster (thrō′stər) *n.* One that twists fibers into thread.

throw-weight or **throw weight** (thrō′wāt′) *n.* The total weight of the warhead or warheads, guidance systems, and other payload of a missile, not including the weight of the rocket.

thru (thro͞o) *prep., adv., & adj. Informal.* Through.

thrum[1] (thrŭm) *v.* **thrummed, thrum·ming, thrums.** *—tr.* **1.** *Music.* To play (a stringed instrument) idly or monotonously: *thrummed a guitar.* **2.** To speak, repeat, or recite in a monotonous tone of voice; drone. *—intr.* **1.** *Music.* To strum idly on a stringed instrument. **2.** To speak in a monotonous tone of voice; drone. **—thrum** *n.* A thrumming sound. [Imitative.]

thrum[2] (thrŭm) *n.* **1.a.** The fringe of warp threads left on a loom after the cloth has been cut off. **b.** One of these threads. **2.** A loose end, fringe, or tuft of thread. **3. thrums.** *Nautical.* Short bits of rope yarn inserted into canvas to roughen the surface. **—thrum** *tr.v.* **thrummed, thrum·ming, thrums. 1.** To cover or trim with thrums; fringe. **2.** *Nautical.* To sew thrums in (canvas). [Middle English, from Old English *(tunge)thrum,* ligament (of the tongue).]

thrush[1] (thrŭsh) *n.* **1.** Any of numerous migratory songbirds of the family Turdidae, usually having brownish upper plumage and a spotted breast and noted for a clear melodious song. **2.** Any of various similar or related birds, as a water thrush or thrasher. **3.** *Slang.* A woman who sings popular songs. [Middle English *thrushe,* from Old English *thrysce.*]

thrush[2] (thrŭsh) *n.* **1.** A contagious disease caused by a fungus, *Candida albicans,* that occurs most often in infants and children, characterized by small whitish eruptions on the mouth, throat, and tongue, and usually accompanied by fever, colic, and diarrhea. **2.** An infection of the frog of a horse's foot, characterized by a foul-smelling discharge and often resulting from unhygienic stall conditions. [Probably of Scandinavian origin.]

thrust (thrŭst) *v.* **thrust, thrust·ing, thrusts.** *—tr.* **1.** To push or drive quickly and forcibly. See Synonyms at **push. 2.** To issue or extend: *poplars thrusting their branches upward; thrust out his finger.* **3.** To force into a specified condition or situation: *She thrust herself through the crowd. He was thrust into a position of awesome responsibility.* **4.** To include or interpolate improperly. **5.** To force on an unwilling or improper recipient: *"Some have greatness thrust upon them"* (Shakespeare). **6.** *Archaic.* To stab; pierce. *—intr.* **1.** To shove something into or at something else; push. **2.** To pierce or stab with or as if with a pointed weapon. **3.** To force one's way. **—thrust** *n.* **1.** A forceful shove or push. **2.a.** A driving force or pressure. **b.** The forward-directed force developed in a jet or rocket engine as a reaction to the high-velocity rearward ejection of exhaust gases. **3.** A piercing movement made with or as if with a pointed weapon; a stab. **4.** The essence; the point: *The whole thrust of the project was to make money.* **5.** *Architecture.* Outward or lateral stress in a structure, such as an arch. **6.** An attack or assault, especially by an armed force. [Middle English *thrusten,* from Old Norse *thrȳsta.* See **treud-** in Appendix.] **—thrust′er** *n.* **—thrust′ful** *adj.*

thrust stage *n.* A stage that extends into the audience's portion of a theater beyond the usual location of the proscenium and often has seats facing it on three sides.

thru·way also **through·way** (thro͞o′wā′) *n.* See **expressway.**

Thu or **Thu.** *abbr.* Thursday.

Thu·cyd·i·des (tho͞o-sĭd′ĭ-dēz′). 460?–400? B.C. Greek historian. Considered the greatest historian of antiquity, he wrote a critical history of the Peloponnesian War that contains the funeral oration of Pericles.

thud (thŭd) *n.* **1.** A dull sound, as that of a heavy object striking a solid surface. **2.** A blow or fall causing such a sound. **—thud** *intr.v.* **thud·ded, thud·ding, thuds.** To make a heavy, dull sound. [Perhaps from Middle English *thudden,* to strike with a weapon, from Old English *thyddan,* of imitative origin.]

thug (thŭg) *n.* **1.** A cutthroat or ruffian; a hoodlum. **2.** One of a band of professional assassins formerly active in northern India. [Hindi *ṭhag,* perhaps from Sanskrit *sthagaḥ,* a cheat, from *sthagati, sthagayati,* he conceals. See **(s)teg-** in Appendix.] **—thug′ger·y** *n.* **—thug′gish** *adj.*

thu·ja (tho͞o′jə, thyo͞o′-) *n.* See **arborvitae** (sense 1). [New Latin *Thuja,* arborvitae genus, from Medieval Latin *thuia,* cedar, from Greek.]

Thu·le[1] (tho͞o′lē). The most northerly region of the habitable world to ancient Greek geographers. Posited as an island north of Britain, it has been variously identified with Iceland, Norway, and the Shetland Islands.

Thu·le[2] (to͞o′lē). A town of northwest Greenland northwest of Cape York. A U.S. naval base was built here during World War II. Population, 449.

thu·li·um (tho͞o′lē-əm, thyo͞o′-) *n. Symbol* **Tm** A bright, silvery rare-earth element obtained commercially from monazite, having an x-ray emitting isotope that is used in small portable medical x-ray units. Atomic number 69; atomic weight 168.934; melting point 1,545°C; boiling point 1,727°C; specific gravity 9.3; valence 2, 3. See table at **element.** [After THULE[1].]

thumb (thŭm) *n.* **1.a.** The short thick digit of the human hand, next to the index finger and opposable to each of the other four digits. **b.** A corresponding digit in other animals, especially primates. Also called *pollex.* **2.** The part of a glove or mitten that covers the thumb. **3.** *Architecture.* An ovolo. **—thumb** *v.* **thumbed, thumb·ing, thumbs.** *—tr.* **1.** To scan (written matter) by turning over pages with or as if with the thumb. **2.** To disarrange, soil, or wear by careless or frequent handling. **3.** *Informal.* To solicit (a ride) from a passing vehicle by signaling with the thumb. *—intr.* **1.** To scan written matter by turning over pages with or as if with the thumb: *thumbed through the latest issue of the magazine.* **2.** *Informal.* To hitchhike. ***—idioms.*** **all thumbs.** Lacking physical coordination, skill, or grace; clumsy. **thumb (one's) nose.** To express scorn or ridicule by or as if by placing the thumb on the nose and wiggling the fingers. **thumbs down.** An expression of rejection, refusal, or disapproval. **thumbs up.** An expression of approval, success, or hope. **under (one's) thumb.** Under the control of someone; subordinate to. [Middle English, from Old English *thūma.* See **teuə-** in Appendix.]

thumb·hole (thŭm′hōl′) *n.* **1.** An opening made to fit a thumb, as in a bowling ball. **2.** *Music.* The hole on a wind instrument that is opened or closed with the thumb.

thumb index *n. Printing.* A series of rounded indentations cut into the front edge of a book, each labeled, as with a letter, to indicate a section of the book. **—thumb′-in′dex** (thŭm′ĭn′dĕks) *v.*

thumb·nail (thŭm′nāl′) *n.* The nail of the thumb. **—thumbnail** *adj.* **1.** Of, relating to, or of the size of a thumbnail. **2.** Brief; cursory: *a thumbnail biography.*

thumb·nut (thŭm′nŭt′) *n.* See **wing nut.**

thumb piano *n. Music.* An African musical instrument, such as the kalimba or mbira, that has a small sound box fitted with a row of tuned tabs that are plucked with the thumbs.

thumb·print (thŭm′prĭnt′) *n.* A print made by the thumb, especially by the pad of the thumb.

thumb·screw (thŭm′skro͞o′) *n.* **1.** A screw designed so that it can be turned with the thumb and fingers. **2.** An instrument of torture formerly used to compress the thumb.

thumb·tack (thŭm′tăk′) *n.* A tack with a smooth, rounded head that can be pressed into place with the thumb. **—thumbtack** *tr.v.* **-tacked, -tack·ing, -tacks.** To affix with a thumbtack.

thump (thŭmp) *n.* **1.** A blow with a blunt object. **2.** The muffled sound produced by or as if by a blow with a blunt object; a thud. **—thump** *v.* **thumped, thump·ing, thumps.** *—tr.* **1.** To beat with or as if with a blunt object so as to produce a muffled sound or thud. **2.** *Informal.* To beat soundly or thoroughly; drub. *—intr.* **1.** To hit or fall in such a way as to produce a thump; pound. **2.** To walk with heavy steps; stump. **3.** To throb audibly. [Probably of imitative origin.] **—thump′er** *n.*

thump·ing (thŭm′pĭng) *adj. Informal.* Outstanding in size, degree, or quality: *a thumping success; a thumping party.* **—thump′ing·ly** *adv.*

Thun (to͞on), **Lake of.** A lake of central Switzerland southeast of Bern at the foot of the Bernese Alps.

thun·der (thŭn′dər) *n.* **1.** The crashing or booming sound produced by rapidly expanding air along the path of the electrical discharge of lightning. **2.** A sound that resembles or suggests thunder. **—thunder** *v.* **-dered, -der·ing, -ders.** *—intr.* **1.** To produce thunder. **2.** To produce sounds like thunder. **3.** To utter loud, vociferous remarks or threats. *—tr.* To express violently, commandingly, or angrily; roar. [Middle English, from Old English *thunor.* See **(s)tenə-** in Appendix.] **—thun′der·er** *n.*

Thun·der Bay (thŭn′dər). A city of southwest Ontario, Canada, on **Thunder Bay,** an inlet on the northwest shore of Lake Superior. A major port and industrial center, it was created in 1970 by the amalgamation of the twin cities of Port Arthur and Fort William. Population, 112,486.

thun·der·bird (thŭn′dər-bûrd′) *n.* A spirit of thunder, lightning, and rain in the form of a huge bird in the mythology of certain Native American peoples.

thun·der·bolt (thŭn′dər-bōlt′) *n.* **1.** A discharge of lightning accompanied by thunder. **2.** A flash of lightning conceived as a bolt or dart hurled from the heavens. **3.a.** One that acts with sudden and destructive fury. **b.** A startling, forceful action: *"Every political campaign manager saves a thunderbolt for the last week before Election Day"* (Art Buchwald).

thun·der·clap (thŭn′dər-klăp′) *n.* **1.** A single sharp crash of

thunderbird
Pueblo sand painting

ă pat	oi boy
ā pay	ou out
âr care	o͝o took
ä father	o͞o boot
ĕ pet	ŭ cut
ē be	ûr urge
ĭ pit	th thin
ī pie	*th* this
îr pier	hw which
ŏ pot	zh vision
ō toe	ə about, item
ô paw	♦ regionalism

Stress marks: ′ (primary); ′ (secondary), as in **dictionary** (dĭk′shə-nĕr′ē)

thyme

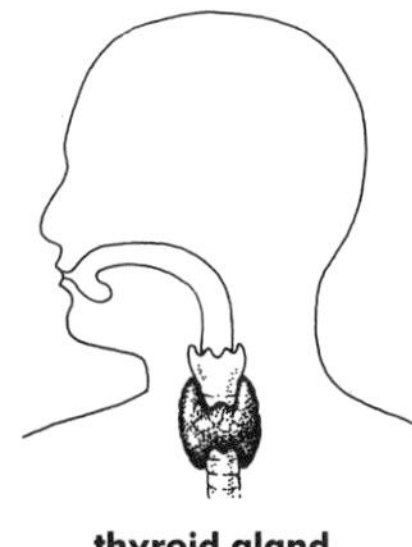
thyroid gland

thyrsus

ă pat oi boy
ā pay ou out
âr care o͝o took
ä father o͞o boot
ĕ pet ŭ cut
ē be ûr urge
ĭ pit th thin
ī pie *th* this
îr pier hw which
ŏ pot zh vision
ō toe ə about, item
ô paw ♦ regionalism

Stress marks: ′ (primary); ′ (secondary), as in **dictionary** (dĭk′shə-nĕr′ē)

thunder. **2.** Something, such as a startling or shocking piece of news, that is similar to thunder in suddenness or violence.

thun·der·cloud (thŭn′dər-kloud′) *n.* **1.** A large dark cloud charged with electricity and producing thunder and lightning; a cumulonimbus cloud. **2.** Something menacing or dreadful: *thunderclouds of impending war.*

thun·der·head (thŭn′dər-hĕd′) *n.* The swollen upper portion of a thundercloud, usually associated with the development of a thunderstorm.

thun·der·ous (thŭn′dər-əs) *adj.* **1.** Producing thunder or a similar sound. **2.** Loud and unrestrained in a way that suggests thunder: *thunderous applause.* **—thun′der·ous·ly** *adv.*

thun·der·show·er (thŭn′dər-shou′ər) *n.* A brief rainstorm accompanied by thunder and lightning.

thun·der·stone (thŭn′dər-stōn′) *n.* **1.** Any of various mineral concretions, such as a belemnite, formerly supposed to be thunderbolts. **2.** *Archaic.* A flash of lightning conceived as a stone; a thunderbolt.

thun·der·storm (thŭn′dər-stôrm′) *n.* A transient, sometimes violent storm of thunder and lightning, often accompanied by rain and sometimes hail.

thun·der·struck (thŭn′dər-strŭk′) *adj.* Affected with sudden astonishment or amazement.

thunk¹ (thŭngk) *n.* A dull, hollow sound: *the thunk of a metal pipe striking a tree.* **—thunk** *intr.v.* **thunked, thunk·ing, thunks.** To make a dull, hollow sound: *"Her hard shoes thunk on the stairs"* (Carolyn Chute). [Imitative.]

thunk² (thŭngk) *v. Non-Standard.* A past tense and a past participle of **think.**

Thur. *abbr.* Thursday.

Thur·ber (thûr′bər), **James Grover.** 1894–1961. American writer and cartoonist who was long associated with the *New Yorker* magazine. His essays, short stories, such as "The Secret Life of Walter Mitty" (1939), and drawings humorously depict the preoccupations of modern men and women.

thu·ri·ble (tho͝or′ə-bəl) *n.* A censer used in certain ecclesiastical ceremonies or liturgies. [Middle English *thorible,* from Old French *thurible,* from Latin *thūribulum,* from *thūs, thūr-,* incense, from Greek *thuos,* from *thuein,* to sacrifice.]

thu·ri·fer (tho͝or′ə-fər) *n.* An acolyte who carries a thurible. [Latin *thūrifer,* incense-bearing : *thūs, thūr-,* incense; see THURIBLE + *-fer,* -fer.]

Thu·rin·gi·a (tho͞o-rĭn′jē-ə, -jə). A historical region of central Germany south of the Harz Mountains and crossed by the **Thuringian Forest,** a range of low, wooded mountains. The region fell to the Franks in the 6th century A.D. and became a principality of the Holy Roman Empire in the 11th century.

Thu·rin·gi·an (tho͞o-rĭn′jē-ən, -jən) *adj.* Of or relating to Thuringia or its people or culture. **—Thuringian** *n.* **1.** A member of an ancient tribe inhabiting central Germany until the sixth century A.D. **2.** A native or inhabitant of Thuringia.

Thur·rock (thûr′ək, thŭr′-). An urban district of southeast England on the Thames River east of London. It is a port and an industrial center. Population, 126,800.

Thurs·day (thûrz′dē, -dā′) *n. Abbr.* **Thur., Thurs., Thu, Thu., Th.** The fifth day of the week. [Middle English, from Old English *thūres dæg,* alteration (influenced by Old Norse *thōrsdagr,* Thor's day) of *thunres dæg,* Thor's day (translation of Late Latin *Iovis diēs,* Jupiter's day) : *thunres,* genitive of *thunor,* thunder; see **(s)tene-** in Appendix + *dæg,* day; see DAY.]

Thursday Island. An island of northeast Australia in Torres Strait northwest of Cape York.

Thurs·ton Island (thûr′stən). An island off Antarctica between the Bellinghausen and Amundsen seas.

thus (*th*ŭs) *adv.* **1.** In this manner: *Lay the pieces out thus.* See Usage Note at **thusly. 2.** To a stated degree or extent; so. **3.** Therefore; consequently: *Thus it was necessary for me to resign.* **4.** For example: *Few of the nation's largest cities are state capitals; thus neither New York nor Chicago is the seat of its state's government.* [Middle English, from Old English. See **to-** in Appendix.]

thus·ly (*th*ŭs′lē) *adv. Usage Problem.* Thus.

USAGE NOTE: *Thusly* was introduced in the 19th century as an alternative for *thus* in sentences such as *Hold it thus* or *He put it thus.* The increasingly literary character of such uses of *thus* may have facilitated coinage of the new adverb *thusly,* particularly by poorly educated speakers who were straining for a stylish effect. Early citations for the word indicate clear association with rustic or illiterate speech, and though the word has subsequently gained some currency in educated usage, it is still widely regarded as incorrect. In an earlier survey the use of the word was judged unacceptable by a large majority of the Usage Panel. In formal writing *thus* can still be used as in the examples above; in other styles, expressions such as *this way* and *like this* are more natural.

Thut·mo·se III (tho͞ot-mō′sə). Died 1450 B.C. King of Egypt (1504?–1450) who conquered Syria and much of the Euphrates Valley and brought great wealth to Egypt.

thwack (thwăk) *tr.v.* **thwacked, thwack·ing, thwacks.** To strike or hit with a flat object; whack. **—thwack** *n.* A hard blow with a flat object; a whack. [Imitative.]

thwart (thwôrt) *tr.v.* **thwart·ed, thwart·ing, thwarts. 1.** To prevent the occurrence, realization, or attainment of: *They thwarted her plans.* **2.** To oppose and defeat the efforts, plans, or ambitions of. See Synonyms at **frustrate. —thwart** *n. Nautical.* A seat across a boat on which a rower may sit. **—thwart** *adj.* **1.** Extending, lying, or passing across; transverse. **2.** Eager to oppose, especially wrongly; perverse. **—thwart** *adv. & prep. Archaic.* Athwart; across. [Middle English *thwerten,* from *thwert,* across, from Old Norse *thvert,* neuter of *thverr,* transverse. See **terkʷ-** in Appendix.] **—thwart′er** *n.* **—thwart′ly** *adv.*

thy (*th*ī) *adj.* The possessive form of **thou.** Used as a modifier before a noun. [Middle English, variant of *thin,* thine, from Old English *thīn.* See **tu-** in Appendix.]

Thy·es·te·an (thī-ĕs′tē-ən, thī′ĭ-stē′ən) *adj.* Involving the eating of human flesh; cannibalistic: *a Thyestean feast.* [From THYESTES.]

Thy·es·tes (thī-ĕs′tēz) *n. Greek Mythology.* A king of Mycenae who unknowingly ate the flesh of his own sons, served to him by his brother Atreus, as revenge for seducing his wife and usurping the throne. [Greek *Thuestēs.*]

thy·la·cine (thī′lə-sīn′) *n.* See **Tasmanian wolf.** [From New Latin *Thylacinus,* genus name, from Greek *thulakos,* sack.]

thyme (tīm) *n.* **1.** Any of several aromatic Eurasian herbs or low shrubs of the genus *Thymus,* especially *T. vulgaris,* of southern Europe, having small, white to lilac flowers grouped in headlike clusters. **2.** The leaves of this plant, used as a seasoning. [Middle English, from Old French *thym,* from Latin *thymum,* from Greek *thumon.*]

thy·mec·to·my (thī-mĕk′tə-mē) *n., pl.* **-mies.** Surgical removal of the thymus.

–thymia *suff.* State or condition of mind: *schizothymia.* [New Latin, from Greek, from *thumos,* mind, soul.]

thy·mic¹ (tī′mĭk, thī′-) *adj.* Of or relating to thyme.

thy·mic² (thī′mĭk) *adj.* Of or relating to the thymus: *thymic nucleic acid.*

thy·mi·dine (thī′mĭ-dēn′) *n.* A nucleoside, $C_{10}H_{14}N_2O_5$, composed of thymine and deoxyribose. [THYM(INE) + –ID(E) + –INE².]

thy·mine (thī′mēn′) *n.* A pyrimidine base, $C_5H_6N_2O_2$, that is an essential constituent of DNA. [THYM(US) + –INE².]

thy·mo·cyte (thī′mə-sīt′) *n.* A lymphocyte that derives from the thymus and is the precursor of a T cell. [THYM(US) + –CYTE.]

thy·mol (thī′môl′, -mōl′) *n.* A white, crystalline, aromatic compound, $C_{10}H_{14}O$, derived from thyme oil and other oils or made synthetically and used as an antiseptic, a fungicide, and a preservative.

thy·mo·ma (thī-mō′mə) *n.* A usually benign tumor of the thymus, composed of epithelial and lymphoid cells.

thy·mo·sin (thī′mə-sĭn) *n.* A hormone secreted by the thymus that stimulates development of T cells.

thy·mus (thī′məs) *n., pl.* **-mus·es.** A small glandular organ that is situated behind the top of the breastbone, consisting mainly of lymphatic tissue and serving as the site of T cell differentiation. The thymus increases gradually in size and activity until puberty, undergoing involution thereafter. [New Latin, from Greek *thumos,* warty excrescence, thymus.]

thyro– or **thyr–** *pref.* Thyroid: *thyroxine.* [From THYROID.]

thy·ro·ac·tive (thī′rō-ăk′tĭv) *adj.* Stimulating activity of the thyroid gland: *a thyroactive agent.*

thy·ro·cal·ci·to·nin (thī′rō-kăl′sĭ-tō′nĭn) *n.* See **calcitonin.**

thy·ro·glob·u·lin (thī′rō-glŏb′yə-lĭn) *n.* A thyroid protein that stores iodine-containing hormones and is typically present in the colloid of thyroid gland follicles.

thy·roid (thī′roid′) *n.* **1.** The thyroid gland. **2.** The thyroid cartilage. **3.** A dried, powdered preparation of the thyroid gland of certain domestic animals, used in treatment of hypothyroid conditions. **4.** An artery, a vein, a nerve, or another part associated with the thyroid gland or thyroid cartilage. [Greek *thureoeidēs* : *thureos,* oblong shield (from *thura,* door; see **dhwer-** in Appendix) + *-oeidēs,* -oid.] **—thy·roi′dal** *adj.*

thyroid cartilage *n.* The largest cartilage of the larynx, having two broad processes that join anteriorly to form the Adam's apple.

thy·roid·ec·to·my (thī′roi-dĕk′tə-mē) *n., pl.* **-mies.** Surgical removal of the thyroid gland. **—thy′roid·ec′to·mize′** *v.*

thyroid gland *n.* A two-lobed endocrine gland found in all vertebrates, located in front of and on either side of the trachea in human beings, and producing various hormones, such as triiodothyronine and calcitonin.

thyroid hormone *n.* A hormone, especially thyroxine or triiodothyronine, produced by the thyroid gland.

thy·roid·i·tis (thī′roi-dī′tĭs) *n.* Inflammation of the thyroid gland.

thy·roid-stim·u·lat·ing hormone (thī′roid-stĭm′yə-lā′tĭng) *n. Abbr.* **TSH** See **thyrotropin.**

thy·ro·tox·i·co·sis (thī′rō-tŏk′sĭ-kō′sĭs) *n.* A toxic condition resulting from excessive amounts of thyroid hormones in the body, as occurs in hyperthyroidism, for example.

thy·ro·tro·pin (thī′rə-trō′pĭn, thī-rŏt′rə-) also **thy·ro·tro·phin** (-fĭn) *n.* A hormone secreted by the anterior lobe of the pituitary gland that stimulates and regulates the activity of the thyroid gland. Also called *thyroid-stimulating hormone, thyrotro-*

pic hormone. [THYRO– + –TROP(HIC) + –IN.] **—thy′ro·tro′pic** (-trō′pĭk, -trŏp′ĭk), **thy′ro·tro′phic** (-trō′fĭk, -trŏf′ĭk) *adj.*

thy·ro·tro·pin-re·leas·ing hormone (thī′rə-trō′pĭn-rĭ-lē′sĭng, thī-rŏt′rə-) *n.* A hormone secreted by the hypothalamus that stimulates release of thyrotropin.

thy·rox·ine (thī-rŏk′sēn′, -sĭn) also **thy·rox·in** (-rŏk′sĭn) *n.* An iodine-containing hormone, $C_{15}H_{11}I_4NO_4$, produced by the thyroid gland, that increases the rate of cell metabolism and regulates growth and that is made synthetically for treatment of thyroid disorders. [THYR(O)– + OX(Y)– + IN(DOLE).]

thyrse (thûrs) *n.* A dense, paniclelike flower cluster, as of the lilac, in which the lateral branches terminate in cymes. [Latin, thyrsus. See THYRSUS.]

thyr·si (thûr′sī) *n.* Plural of **thyrsus.**

thyr·soid (thûr′soid′) also **thyr·soid·al** (thûr-soid′l) *adj.* Shaped like or similar to a thyrse.

thyr·sus (thûr′səs) *n., pl.* **-si** (-sī). **1.** *Mythology.* A staff tipped with a pine cone and twined with ivy, carried by Dionysus, Dionysian revelers, and satyrs. **2.** *Botany.* A thyrse. [Latin, from Greek *thursos.*]

thy·sa·nu·ran (thĭ′sə-nŏŏr′ən, -nyŏŏr′-) *n.* A wingless insect of the order Thysanura, constituting the bristletails. **—thysanuran** *adj.* Of, relating to, or belonging to the order Thysanura. [From New Latin *Thysanura,* order name : Greek *thusanos,* tassel + Greek *-oura,* neuter pl. of *-ouros,* tailed (from *oura,* tail; see –UROUS).]

thy·self (*thī*-sĕlf′) *pron. Archaic.* Yourself. Used as the reflexive or emphatic form of *thee* or *thou.*

THz *abbr.* Terahertz.

ti[1] (tē) *n. Music.* The seventh tone in the diatonic scale in solfeggio. [Alteration of SI.]

ti[2] (tē) *n., pl.* **tis.** An eastern Asian tropical shrub *(Cordyline terminalis)* having tufts of long narrow leaves and panicles of white, yellowish, or reddish flowers. [Tahitian and Maori.]

Ti The symbol for the element **titanium.**

Ti·a·hua·na·co (tē′ə-wə-nä′kō). A site of pre-Incan ruins in western Bolivia near the southern end of Lake Titicaca. The ruins, including statues, monoliths, and a temple of the sun, are evidence of a civilization that flourished here from c. 1000 to 1300.

Tian·an·men Square (tyän′än′mĕn′). An extensive open area in central Beijing, China, adjacent to the Forbidden City. It has long been the site of festivals, government rallies, parades, and demonstrations, particularly in 1989.

Tian·jin (tyän′jĭn′) also **Tien·tsin** (tyĕn′tsĭn′). A city of northeast China near the Gulf of Bo Hai southeast of Beijing. It developed rapidly after becoming a treaty port in 1860 but was badly damaged (1900) during the Boxer Rebellion. Today it is a major industrial center. Population, 5,380,000.

Tian Shan (tyän′ shän′). See **Tien Shan.**

ti·ar·a (tē-ăr′ə, -âr′ə, -är′ə) *n.* **1.** An ornamental, often jeweled, crownlike semicircle worn on the head by women on formal occasions. **2.** The triple crown worn by the pope. [Latin *tiāra,* turban, headband, from Greek *tiara.*]

Ti·ber (tī′bər). A river of central Italy flowing about 406 km (252 mi) south and southwest through Rome to the Tyrrhenian Sea at Ostia.

Ti·be·ri·as (tī-bîr′ē-əs), **Lake.** See Sea of **Galilee.**

Ti·be·ri·us (tī-bîr′ē-əs). 42 B.C.–A.D. 37. Emperor of Rome (A.D. 14–37). Chosen by Augustus to be heir to the throne, he was a suspicious, tyrannical ruler. **—Ti·be′ri·an** (-ən) *adj.*

Ti·bet (tə-bĕt′). **1.** A historical region of central Asia between the Himalaya and Kunlun mountains. A center of Lamist Buddhism, Tibet first flourished as an independent kingdom in the seventh century. It fell under Mongol influence from the 13th to the 18th century and later came under Chinese control (1720). **2.** See **Xizang.**

Ti·bet·an (tĭ-bĕt′n) *adj.* Of or relating to Tibet, the Tibetans, or their language or culture. **—Tibetan** *n.* **a.** A native or inhabitant of Tibet. **b.** A member of a Buddhist people constituting the predominant ethnic population of Tibet and neighboring regions in China, Bhutan, and Nepal, with large displaced populations in India.

Tibetan Buddhism *n.* A form of Mahayana Buddhism with an admixture of indigenous animism that is practiced in Tibet, Mongolia, Bhutan, and neighboring areas.

Tibetan spaniel *n.* Any of a breed of small dog that originated in Tibet, having a thick silky coat and a plumed tail that curls over the back.

Tibetan terrier *n.* Any of a breed of medium-sized dog that originated in Tibet, having thick, long hair over the eyes and a fluffy tail that curls over the back.

Ti·bet·o-Bur·man (tĭ-bĕt′ō-bûr′mən) *n.* A branch of the Sino-Tibetan language family that includes Tibetan and Burmese. **—Ti·bet′o-Bur′man** *adj.*

tib·i·a (tĭb′ē-ə) *n., pl.* **-i·ae** (-ē-ē′) or **-i·as. 1.a.** The inner and larger of the two bones of the lower human leg, extending from the knee to the ankle. **b.** A corresponding bone in other vertebrates. Also called *shinbone.* **2.** The fourth division of an insect's leg, between the femur and the tarsi. **3.** *Music.* An ancient flute originally made from an animal's leg bone. [Latin *tībia,* pipe, shinbone.] **—tib′i·al** *adj.*

tib·i·o·fib·u·lar (tĭb′ē-ō-fĭb′yə-lər) *adj.* Of, relating to, or involving both the tibia and the fibula: *tibiofibular articulation.*

tib·i·o·tar·sus (tĭb′ē-ō-tär′səs) *n.* A long bone in the leg of a bird between the femur and the tarsometatarsus, consisting of the tibia fused with the proximal bones of the tarsus.

Ti·bur (tī′bər). See **Tivoli.**

tic (tĭk) *n.* A habitual spasmodic muscular movement or contraction, usually of the face or extremities. **—tic** *intr.v.* **ticced, tic·cing, tics.** To have a tic; produce tics. [French.]

tic dou·lou·reux (do͞o′lə-ro͞o′) *n.* See **trigeminal neuralgia.** [French : *tic,* tic + *douloureux,* painful.]

Ti·ci·no (tĭ-chē′nō). A river, about 248 km (154 mi) long, of southern Switzerland and northern Italy flowing generally southward to the Po River.

tick[1] (tĭk) *n.* **1.** A light, sharp, clicking sound made repeatedly by a machine, such as a clock. **2.** *Chiefly British.* A moment. **3.** A light mark used to check off or call attention to an item. **4.** *Informal.* A unit on a scale; a degree: *when interest rates move up a tick.* **—tick** *v.* **ticked, tick·ing, ticks.** —*intr.* **1.** To emit recurring clicking sounds: *as the clock ticked.* **2.** To function characteristically or well: *machines ticking away; curious about what makes people tick.* —*tr.* **1.** To count or record with or as if with the sound of ticks: *a clock ticking the hours; a taxi meter ticking the fare.* **2.** To mark or check off (a listed item) with a tick: *ticked off each name as the roll was called.* **—*phrasal verb.* tick off.** *Informal.* To make angry or annoyed: *Constant delays ticked me off.* [Middle English *tek,* light tap.]

tick[2] (tĭk) *n.* **1.** Any of numerous small bloodsucking parasitic arachnids of the family Ixodidae, many of which transmit febrile diseases, such as Rocky Mountain spotted fever and Lyme disease. **2.** Any of various usually wingless, louselike insects of the family Hippoboscidae that are parasitic on sheep, goats, and other animals. [Middle English *teke, tik,* perhaps from Old English **ticca.*]

tick[3] (tĭk) *n.* **1.a.** A cloth case for a mattress or pillow. **b.** A light mattress without inner springs. **2.** Ticking. [Middle English *tikke,* probably from Middle Dutch *tīke,* ultimately from Latin *thēca,* receptacle, from Greek *thēkē.* See **dhē-** in Appendix.]

tick[4] (tĭk) *n. Chiefly British.* Credit or an amount of credit. [Short for TICKET.]

tick·bird (tĭk′bûrd′) *n.* See **oxpecker.**

tick-borne (tĭk′bôrn′, -bōrn′) *adj.* Carried or transmitted by ticks: *a tick-borne disease.*

tick·er (tĭk′ər) *n.* **1.a.** A telegraphic instrument that receives news reports and prints them on paper tape. **b.** Any of various devices that receive and display similar information, such as stock market quotations, electronically. **2.** *Slang.* A watch. **3.** *Slang.* The heart.

ticker tape *n.* The paper strip on which a telegraphic ticker prints.

tick·et (tĭk′ĭt) *n.* **1.** *Abbr.* **tkt.** A paper slip or card indicating that its holder has paid for or is entitled to a specified service, right, or consideration: *a theater ticket; an airline ticket.* **2.** A certifying document, especially a captain's or pilot's license. **3.** An identifying or descriptive tag attached to merchandise; a label. **4.** A list of candidates proposed or endorsed by a political party; a slate. **5.** A legal summons, especially for a traffic violation. **6.** The proper or desirable thing: *A change of scene would be just the ticket for us.* **7.** *Informal.* A means to an end: *"He went to Washington . . . to become press secretary . . . it was his ticket out of the Delta"* (Nicholas Lamann). **—ticket** *tr.v.* **-et·ed, -et·ing, -ets. 1.** To provide with a ticket for passage or admission: *ticket all passengers through to Amsterdam.* **2.** To attach a ticket to; tag. See Synonyms at **mark**[1]. **3.** To designate for a specified use or end; destine: *funds that have been ticketed for research.* **4.** To serve (an offender) with a legal summons: *ticket a speeding motorist.* [Obsolete French *etiquet,* label, note, from Old French *estiquet,* notice, label, from Old Spanish *etiqueta,* from Old French *estiquet,* post serving as a target in certain sports, from *estiquier,* to stick, of Germanic origin. See **steig-** in Appendix.]

WORD HISTORY: The resemblance in form between the words *ticket* and *etiquette* is not accidental. Both words have the same ultimate source, Old French *estiquet,* but each was borrowed into English at a different time and with a different meaning. Old French *estiquet* meant "a note, label." Having been changed in form to *etiquet* in French, the word was adopted into English in the 16th century (first recorded in 1528) in a form, *tiket,* without the initial *e.* The earliest uses of the word in English were in the senses "a short written notice," "a notice posted in a public place," and "a written certification." The word is first recorded with reference to something like a ticket of admission in 1673. In French, meanwhile, the word (in the form *etiquette* in the 18th century) came to mean "ceremonial"; court ceremonies were noted down or labeled in a book known as *l'étiquette.* The French word was borrowed again into English, this time in its French form, which is first recorded in 1750.

ticket puncher *n. Slang.* A career military officer or businessperson whose primary concern is personal advancement.

tick fever *n.* Any of various febrile diseases transmitted by ticks, such as Rocky Mountain spotted fever and Texas fever.

tick·ing (tĭk′ĭng) *n.* A strong, tightly woven fabric of cotton or linen used to make pillow and mattress coverings.

tick·le (tĭk′əl) *v.* **-led, -ling, -les.** —*tr.* **1.** To touch (the body)

Tiananmen Square
Gate of Heavenly Peace
in the late 1980's

tiara
Jeweled tiara
worn by Nancy Astor

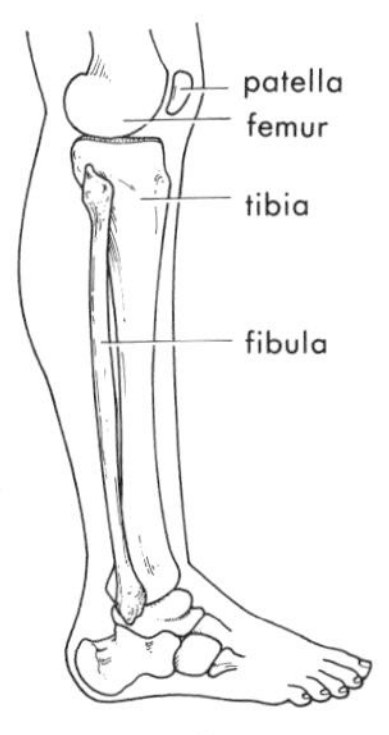

tibia

lightly so as to cause laughter or twitching movements. **2.a.** To tease or excite pleasurably; titillate: *suspense that tickles the reader's curiosity.* **b.** To fill with mirth or pleasure; delight. See Synonyms at **please.** —*intr.* To feel or cause a tingling sensation. —**tickle** *n.* **1.** The act of tickling. **2.** A tickling sensation. —***idiom.*** **tickle (one) pink.** *Informal.* To please; delight: *I was tickled pink by the compliment.* [Middle English *tikelen,* perhaps frequentative of *ticken,* to touch lightly.]

tick·ler (tĭk′lər) *n.* A memorandum, book, or file to aid the memory.

tick·lish (tĭk′lĭsh) *adj.* **1.** Sensitive to tickling. **2.** Easily offended or upset; touchy. **3.** Requiring skillful or tactful handling: *a ticklish matter.* —**tick′lish·ly** *adv.* —**tick′lish·ness** *n.*

tick·seed (tĭk′sēd′) *n.* **1.** See **coreopsis. 2.** See **beggar ticks** (sense 1a). [From TICK[2] (from its seed's shape).]

tick·tack also **tic-tac** (tĭk′tăk′) *n.* **1.** A steady ticking sound, as of a clock. **2.** A prankster's device for tapping on a door or window from a distance. [Imitative.]

tick·tack·toe also **tick-tack-toe** (tĭk′tăk′tō′) *n. Games.* A game played by two people, each trying to make a line of three X's or three O's in a boxlike figure with nine spaces. [Probably imitative of the sounds of the original children's game, in which players brought pencils down on a numbered slate with their eyes shut.]

tick·tock (tĭk′tŏk′) *n.* The ticking sound made by a clock. [Imitative.]

tick trefoil *n.* Any of various plants of the genus *Desmodium,* usually having trifoliolate compound leaves, racemes of small purplish or white flowers, and jointed seedpods with easily separable, one-seeded segments. [From TICK[2] (from the way its pods adhere to animals).]

tick·y-tack·y (tĭk′ē-tăk′ē) *n.* Shoddy material, as for the construction of standardized housing. —**ticky-tacky** *adj.* **1.** Made of shoddy material; cheaply built. **2.a.** Marked by a mediocre uniformity of appearance or style: *ticky-tacky rows of look-alike houses.* **b.** Tawdry; tacky. [Reduplication of TACKY[2].]

Ti·con·der·o·ga (tī′-kŏn-də-rō′gə). A resort village of northeast New York between Lake George and Lake Champlain. Fort Carillon, built by the French in 1755, was taken in 1759 by the British, who renamed it Fort Ticonderoga. American Revolutionary troops captured the fort in May 1775, but it was later abandoned without a struggle to British forces in July 1777 during the Saratoga Campaign.

tic·queur (tĭ-kûr′) *n.* A person affected with a tic. [French *tiqueur,* from *tic,* tic.]

tic-tac (tĭk′tăk′) *n.* Variant of **ticktack.**

t.i.d. *abbr. Latin.* Ter in die (three times a day).

tid·al (tīd′l) *adj.* **1.** Relating to or affected by tides: *the tidal maximum; tidal pools; tidal waters.* **2.** Dependent on or scheduled by the time of high tide: *a tidal ferry.* —**tid′al·ly** *adv.*

tidal air *n.* Tidal volume.

tidal volume *n.* The volume of air inhaled and exhaled at each breath.

tidal wave *n.* **1.** An unusual rise or incursion of water along the seashore, as from a storm or a combination of wind and spring tide. **2.** A tsunami. **3.** An overwhelming manifestation; a flood: *a tidal wave of illicit drugs; an emotional tidal wave.*

tid·bit (tĭd′bĭt′) also **tit·bit** (tĭt′-) *n.* A choice morsel, as of gossip or food: *"The book is chock-full of colorful tidbits about theater and theater people"* (Alec Guinness). [Perhaps obsolete and dialectal *tid,* tender + BIT[1].]

tid·dly·winks (tĭd′lē-wĭngks′) also **tid·dle·dy·winks** (tĭd′l-dē-) *pl.n. (used with a sing. verb). Games.* A game in which players try to snap small disks into a cup by pressing them on the edge with a larger disk. [Possibly dialectal *tiddly,* little + WINK.]

tide[1]
Top: High tide in the Bay of Fundy
Bottom: Low tide from the same perspective

tide[1] (tīd) *n.* **1.a.** The periodic variation in the surface level of the oceans and of bays, gulfs, inlets, and estuaries, caused by gravitational attraction of the moon and sun. **b.** A specific occurrence of such a variation: *awaiting the next high tide.* **c.** Flood tide. **2.** Stress exerted on a body or part of a body by gravitational attraction of another: *atmospheric tide; the tides that wrack Saturn's moons.* **3.** Something that fluctuates like the waters of the tide: *a rising tide of discontent.* See Synonyms at **flow. 4.** A time or season. Often used in combination: *eventide; Christmastide; Shrovetide.* **5.** A favorable occasion; an opportunity. —**tide** *v.* **tid·ed, tid·ing, tides.** —*intr.* **1.** To rise and fall like the tide. **2.** *Nautical.* To drift or ride with the tide: *tided off the reef; tiding up the Hudson.* —*tr.* To carry along with or as if with the tide. —***phrasal verb.*** **tide over.** To support through a difficult period: *I asked for $100 to tide me over till payday.* [Middle English, from Old English *tīd,* division of time. See **dā-** in Appendix.]

tide[2] (tīd) *intr.v.* **tid·ed, tid·ing, tides.** *Archaic.* To betide; befall. [Middle English *tiden,* from Old English *tīdan.* See **dā-** in Appendix.]

tide·land (tīd′lănd′) *n.* Coastal land submerged during high tide.

tide·mark (tīd′märk′) *n.* **1.** A line or an artificial indicator marking the high-water or low-water limit of the tides. **2.** A trace or an indication of past activity: *"Just along the highway into town is the last tidemark of the Nazi advance, a brutal tangle of brown sculpture"* (Regina Nadelson).

tide·rip (tīd′rĭp′) *n.* See **rip current.**

tide·wait·er (tīd′wā′tər) *n.* A customs officer who boards incoming ships at a harbor.

tide·wa·ter (tīd′wô′tər, -wŏt′ər) *n.* **1.** Water that inundates land at flood tide. **2.** Water affected by the tides, especially tidal streams. **3.** Low coastal land drained by tidal streams.

tide·way (tīd′wā′) *n.* A channel in which a tidal current runs.

tid·ing (tī′dĭng) *n.* A piece of information or news. Often used in the plural: *tidings of great joy; sad tidings.* See Synonyms at **news.** [Middle English *tiding,* perhaps from Old Norse *tīdhendi,* events, from *tīdhr,* occurring. See **dā-** in Appendix.]

ti·dy (tī′dē) *adj.* **-di·er, -di·est. 1.** Orderly and neat in appearance or procedure. See Synonyms at **neat[1]. 2.** *Informal.* Adequate; satisfactory: *a tidy arrangement.* **3.** *Informal.* Substantial; considerable: *a tidy sum.* —**tidy** *v.* **-died, -dy·ing, -dies.** —*tr.* To put in order: *tidied up the house.* —*intr.* To make things tidy: *tidied up after dinner.* —**tidy** *n., pl.* **-dies.** A decorative protective covering for the arms or headrest of a chair. [Middle English *tidi,* in season, healthy, from *tide,* time. See TIDE[1].] —**ti′di·ly** *adv.* —**ti′di·ness** *n.*

ti·dy·tips (tī′dē-tĭps′) *pl.n. (used with a sing. or pl. verb).* A Californian herb *(Layia platyglossa)* having daisylike flower heads.

tie (tī) *v.* **tied, ty·ing** (tī′ĭng), **ties.** —*tr.* **1.** To fasten or secure with or as if with a cord, rope, or strap: *tied the kite to a post; tie up a bundle.* **2.** To fasten by drawing together the parts or sides and knotting with strings or laces: *tied her shoes.* **3.a.** To make by fastening ends or parts: *tie a knot.* **b.** To put a knot or bow in: *tie a neck scarf.* **4.** To confine or restrict as if with cord: *duties that tied him to the office.* **5.** To bring together in relationship; connect or unite: *friends who were tied by common interests; people who are tied by blood or marriage.* **6.a.** To equal (an opponent or an opponent's score) in a contest. **b.** To equal an opponent's score in (a contest): *tied the game with minutes remaining.* **7.** *Music.* To join (notes) by a tie. —*intr.* **1.** To be fastened or attached: *The apron ties at the back.* **2.** To achieve equal scores in a contest. —**tie** *n.* **1.** A cord, string, or other means by which something is tied. **2.** Something that connects or unites; a link: *a blood tie; marital ties.* **3.** A necktie. **4.** A beam or rod that joins parts and gives support. **5.** One of the beams, usually made of wood, that are laid across a railroad bed to secure the rails. **6.a.** An equality of scores, votes, or performance in a contest: *The election ended in a tie.* **b.** A contest so resulting; a draw. **7.** *Music.* A curved line above or below two notes of the same pitch, indicating that the tone is to be sustained for their combined duration. —***phrasal verbs.*** **tie in.** To bring into or have a close or effective relation; connect or coordinate: *two events that do not tie in; tying the movie promotion in with the book sales.* **tie into.** To attack energetically. **tie up. 1.** *Nautical.* To secure or be secured to a shore or pier; dock. **2.** To impede the progress of; block: *The accident tied up traffic.* **3.** To keep occupied; engage: *She was tied up in a meeting all morning. The phone was tied up for an hour.* **4.** To place (funds) so as to make inaccessible for other uses: *tied up her cash in long-term investments.* —***idioms.*** **tie one on.** *Slang.* To become intoxicated; go on a drinking spree. **tie the knot.** *Slang.* **1.** To get married. **2.** To perform a marriage ceremony. [Middle English *tien,* from Old English *tīgan.* See **deuk-** in Appendix.]

Tiffany glass

tie·back (tī′băk′) *n.* **1.** A decorative loop of fabric, cord, or metal for parting and draping a curtain to the side. **2. tiebacks.** A pair of curtains intended to be tied back.

tie beam *n.* A horizontal beam that connects the rafters in a roof.

tie·break·er (tī′brā′kər) *n. Sports & Games.* An additional contest or period of play designed to establish a winner among tied contestants. —**tie′break′ing** *adj.*

tie clasp *n.* An ornamental clasp that holds the ends of a necktie to the shirt front. Also called *tie clip.*

tie-dye (tī′dī′) *tr.v.* **-dyed, -dye·ing, -dyes.** To dye (fabric) after tying parts of the fabric so that they will not absorb dye, giving the fabric a streaked or mottled look. —**tie-dye** *n.* **1.** The process of tie-dyeing. **2.** A tie-dyed fabric or garment.

tie-in (tī′ĭn′) *n.* One thing that is related to or connected with another.

tie line *n.* **1.** A communications link between extensions of a private telephone system. **2.** A connection between systems, such as electrical power or communications systems.

Tien Shan (tyĕn′ shän′) also **Tian Shan** (tyän′). A mountain range of central Asia extending about 2,414 km (1,500 mi) east-northeast through western Kirghiz, southwest Kazakhstan, and northwest China. It rises to 7,443.8 m (24,406 ft).

Tien·tsin (tyĕn′tsĭn′). See **Tianjin.**

Tie·po·lo (tē-ĕp′ə-lō′, tyĕ′pô-lô′), **Giovanni Battista.** 1696–1770. Italian painter. With his command of perspective, light, color, and composition, he produced a large body of secular and ecclesiastical works, including *The Banquet of Cleopatra* and *The Martyrdom of Saint Agatha* (both 1750).

tier[1] (tîr) *n.* **1.** One of a series of rows placed one above another: *a stadium with four tiers of seats.* **2.** A rank or class. —**tier** *tr. & intr.v.* **tiered, tier·ing, tiers.** To arrange (something) into or rise in tiers: *tier a wedding cake; balconies that tier upward.* [Middle English *tire,* row, rank, from Old French, from *tirer,* to draw out. See TIRADE.]

ti•er² (tī′ər) *n.* One that ties: *a tier of knots.*

tierce (tîrs) *n.* **1.** Also **terce** (tûrs). **a.** The third of the seven canonical hours. No longer in liturgical use. **b.** The time of day appointed for this service, usually the third hour after sunrise. **2.** A measure of liquid capacity, equal to a third of a pipe, or 42 gallons (159 liters). **3.** *Games.* A sequence of three cards of the same suit. **4.** *Sports.* The third position from which a parry or thrust can be made in fencing. **5.** *Music.* An interval of a third. [Middle English, from Old French, from feminine of *tiers,* third, from Latin *tertius.* See **trei-** in Appendix.]

tier•cel (tîr′səl) *n.* Variant of **tercel.**

Ti•er•ra del Fue•go (tē-ĕr′ə dĕl fwā′gō, tyĕr′rä *th*ĕl fwĕ′-gô). An archipelago off southern South America separated from the mainland by the Strait of Magellan. The main island, also called **Tierra del Fuego,** is divided between Chile and Argentina. Smaller islands of the archipelago are administered individually by the two countries. Ferdinand Magellan first sighted Tierra del Fuego in 1520.

tier table (tîr) *n.* A table having several shelflike tops, one above the other.

tie tack *n.* A short pin with a decorative head, used to attach a tie to a shirt front by means of a snap or chain.

Tie•tê (tyə-tā′, tyĭ-tĕ′). A river, about 805 km (500 mi) long, of southeast Brazil flowing generally northwest to the Paraná River.

Tie•tze's syndrome (tē′tsēz) *n.* Inflammation of the cartilage of the rib cage, causing pain in the chest similar to angina pectoris. [After Alexander *Tietze* (1864–1927), German surgeon.]

tie-up (tī′ŭp′) *n.* A temporary immobilization, as of traffic, work, or mechanical operation.

♦**tie vine** *n. Lower Southern U.S.* The wild morning glory.

tiff (tĭf) *n.* **1.** A fit of irritation. **2.** A petty quarrel. —**tiff** *intr.v.* **tiffed, tiff•ing, tiffs.** To quarrel. [Origin unknown.]

tif•fa•ny (tĭf′ə-nē) *n., pl.* **-nies.** A thin, transparent gauze of silk or cotton muslin. [Probably from obsolete French *tiphanie,* Epiphany, from Old French, from Late Latin *theophania.* See THEOPHANY.]

Tif•fa•ny (tĭf′ə-nē), **Louis Comfort.** 1848–1933. American artist who developed an opalescent colored glass that he used in stained-glass windows, lamps, and other decorations.

Tiffany glass *n.* Stained or iridescent glass of a kind popular in the early 1900's for vases and lampshades. [After Louis Comfort TIFFANY.]

tif•fin (tĭf′ĭn) *n. Chiefly British.* A meal at midday; a luncheon. [Short for *tiffing,* gerund of *tiff,* to sip.]

Tif•fin (tĭf′ĭn). A city of north-central Ohio south-southwest of Toledo. It is an industrial center. Population, 19,549.

Tif•lis (tĭf′lĭs, tyə-flēs′). See **Tbilisi.**

ti•ger (tī′gər) *n.* **1.a.** A large carnivorous feline mammal *(Panthera tigris)* of Asia, having a tawny coat with transverse black stripes. **b.** Any of various similar wild felines, such as the jaguar, mountain lion, or lynx. **2.** A person regarded as aggressive, audacious, or fierce. [Middle English *tigre,* from Old English *tigras,* tigers, and from Old French *tigre,* both from Latin *tigris,* from Greek. See **steig-** in Appendix.] —**ti′ger•ish** *adj.*

tiger beetle *n.* Any of numerous active, brightly colored, predatory beetles of the family Cicindelidae, chiefly of warm, sandy regions, having large jaws and sluggish larvae that live in vertical burrows.

tiger cat *n.* **1.** Any of various small wild felines, such as the ocelot, margay, or jaguarundi, that resemble the tiger in appearance or behavior. **2.** A domestic cat, especially a tabby, having markings like those of a tiger. **3.** A spotted dasyure *(Dasyurus maculatus),* the largest carnivorous marsupial in Australia.

ti•ger-eye (tī′gər-ī′) also **ti•ger's-eye** (tī′gərz-) *n.* A yellow-brown, semiprecious chatoyant gemstone consisting of quartz with parallel veins of silicified altered crocidolite.

tiger lily *n.* An eastern Asian perennial *(Lilium lancifolium)* having large black-spotted reddish-orange flowers with reflexed petals and purplish bulbils in the leaf axils.

tiger moth *n.* Any of numerous, often brightly colored moths of the family Arctiidae, characteristically having wings marked with spots or stripes.

tiger salamander *n.* A large terrestrial salamander *(Ambystoma tigrinum)* found in most parts of North America and having distinctive light olive bars or spots.

ti•ger's-eye (tī′gərz-ī′) *n.* Variant of **tiger-eye.**

tiger shark *n.* A large voracious shark *(Galeocerdo cuvieri)* of tropical waters, having a grayish-brown color with vertical bars along the sides.

tiger swallowtail *n.* A large swallowtail butterfly *(Papilio glaucus)* of eastern North America, mostly yellow with narrow black bands across the wings.

tight (tīt) *adj.* **tight•er, tight•est.** **1.** Fixed or fastened firmly in place: *a tight lid; tight screws; a tight knot.* **2.** Stretched or drawn out fully: *a tight wire; a tight drumhead.* **3.** Of such close construction as to be impermeable: *cloth tight enough to hold water; warm in our tight little cabin.* **4.a.** Leaving little empty space through compression; compact: *a tight suitcase; a tight weave.* **b.** Affording little spare time; full: *a tight schedule.* **5.** Closely reasoned or concise: *a tight argument; a tight style of writing.* **6.** Fitting close or too close to the skin; snug: *a tight collar; a fit that was much too tight.* **7.** *Slang.* Personally close; intimate: *"me and the D.A., who happen to be very tight with one another"* (Tom Wolfe). **8.** Experiencing a feeling of constriction: *a tight feeling in the chest.* **9.** Reluctant to spend or give; stingy. **10.a.** Obtainable with difficulty or only at a high price: *tight money.* **b.** Affected by scarcity: *a tight market.* **11.** Difficult to deal with or get out of: *a tight spot.* **12.** Barely profitable: *a tight bargain.* **13.** Closely contested; close: *a tight match.* **14.** *Chiefly British.* Neat and trim in appearance or arrangement. **15.** Marked by full control over elements or subordinates; firm: *tight management; a tight orchestral performance.* **16.** *Slang.* Intoxicated; drunk. **17.** *Baseball.* Inside. —**tight** *adv.* **tighter, tightest.** **1.** Firmly; securely. **2.** Soundly: *sleep tight.* **3.** Snugly or with constriction: *My shoes are laced too tight.* [Middle English, dense, of Scandinavian origin.] —**tight′ly** *adv.* —**tight′ness** *n.*

SYNONYMS: *tight, taut, tense.* The central meeaning shared by these adjectives is "not slack or loose on account of being pulled or drawn out fully": *a tight skirt; taut sails; tense piano strings.* See also Synonyms at **stingy.**

USAGE NOTE: *Tight* is used as an adverb following verbs that denote a process of closure or constriction, as *squeeze, shut, close, tie,* and *hold.* In this use it is subtly distinct from the adverb *tightly. Tight* denotes the state resulting from the process, whereas *tightly* denotes the manner of its application. As such, *tight* is more appropriate when the focus is on a state that endures for some time after the activity has ended. The sentence *She closed up the house tight* suggests preparation for an impending blizzard. By the same token, it is more natural to say *The windows were frozen tight* than *The windows were frozen tightly,* since in this case the tightness of the seal is not likely to be the result of the manner in which the windows were frozen. With a few verbs *tight* is used idiomatically as an intensive and is the only possible form: *sleep tight; sit tight. Tight* can be used only following the verb: *The house was tightly* (not *tight*) *shut.*

tight•en (tīt′n) *tr. & intr.v.* **-ened, -en•ing, -ens.** To make or become tight or tighter. —**tight′en•er** *n.*

tight end *n. Football.* An offensive end who lines up close to a tackle.

tight•fist•ed (tīt′fĭs′tĭd) *adj.* Close-fisted; stingy. See Synonyms at **stingy.** —**tight′fist′ed•ness** *n.*

tight•lipped also **tight-lipped** (tīt′lĭpt′) *adj.* **1.** Having the lips pressed together. **2.** Loath to speak; close-mouthed. See Synonyms at **silent.** —**tight′lipped′ness** *n.*

tight•rope (tīt′rōp′) *n.* **1.** A tightly stretched rope, usually of wire, on which acrobats perform high above the ground. **2.** An extremely precarious course or situation.

tights (tīts) *pl.n.* **1.** A snug stretchable garment covering the body from the waist or neck down, designed for general wear by women and girls. **2.** A similar garment designed for athletic use, worn especially by acrobats and dancers.

tight•wad (tīt′wŏd′) *n. Slang.* A miser.

Tig•lath-pi•le•ser III (tĭg′lăth-pə-lē′zər, -pī-). Died 727 B.C. King of Assyria (745–727) whose conquests greatly strengthened the empire.

tig•lic acid (tĭg′lĭk) *n.* A thick, syrupy poisonous liquid, $C_5H_8O_2$, derived from croton oil, having a spicy odor and used in making perfumes and flavoring agents. [From New Latin *tiglium,* specific epithet of *Croton tiglium,* perhaps from Greek *tilos,* liquid feces (from the use of croton oil as a purgative).]

ti•glon (tī′glən) also **ti•gon** (gən) *n.* The hybrid offspring of a male tiger and a female lion. [TIG(ER) + L(I)ON.]

Ti•gre (tē′grā, -grĕ). A city of eastern Argentina, a suburb of Buenos Aires in a fruit-growing area. Population, 199,366.

Ti•gré (tē-grā′) *n.* A Semitic language of northern Ethiopia.

ti•gress (tī′grĭs) *n.* **1.** A female tiger. **2.** A woman regarded as daring or fierce.

Ti•gri•nya (tə-grēn′yə) *n.* A Semitic language of northern Ethiopia.

Ti•gris (tī′grĭs). A river of southwest Asia rising in eastern Turkey and flowing about 1,850 km (1,150 mi) southeast through Iraq to the Euphrates River.

Ti•jua•na (tē′ə-wä′nə, tē-hwä′nä). A city of extreme northwest Mexico on the U.S. border south of San Diego. It is a popular tourist center. Population, 429,500.

Ti•kal (tē-käl′). A ruined Mayan city of northern Guatemala. It was the largest of the Mayan cities and may also be the oldest. Excavation and restoration of the ruins began in 1956.

tike (tīk) *n.* Variant of **tyke.**

ti•ki (tē′kē) *n., pl.* **-kis.** **1. Tiki.** *Mythology.* A male figure in Polynesian myth, sometimes identified as the first man. **2.** A wooden or stone image of a Polynesian god. **3.** A Maori figurine representing an ancestor, often intricately carved from greenstone and worn about the neck as a talisman. [Maori.]

til¹ (tĭl) *n.* See **sesame.** [Hindi, from Sanskrit *tilaḥ.*]

til² (tĭl) *prep.* Until. —**til** *conj.* Until. See Usage Note at **till².**

ti•la•pi•a (tə-lä′pē-ə, -lā′-) *n.* Any of various cichlid fishes of the genus *Tilapia,* native to Africa but introduced elsewhere as a valuable food fish. [New Latin *Tilapia,* genus name.]

Til•burg (tĭl′bûrg′, -bœrKH′). A city of southern Netherlands near the Belgian border southeast of Rotterdam. It has a major textile industry. Population, 154,094.

til•bur•y (tĭl′bĕr′ē, -bə-rē) *n., pl.* **-ies.** A light, two-wheeled,

tiger
Panthera tigris

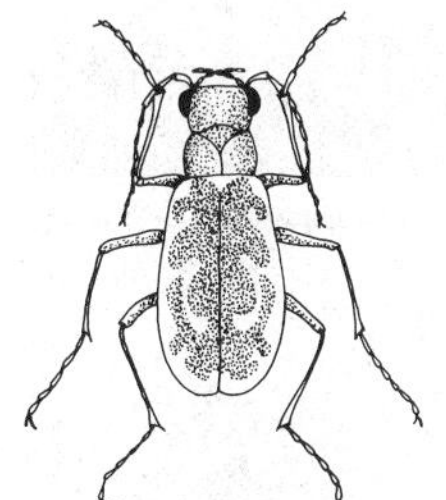

tiger beetle

tightrope
Philippe Petit at the Jerusalem Festival in 1987

ă pat	oi boy
ā pay	ou out
âr care	o͝o took
ä father	o͞o boot
ĕ pet	ŭ cut
ē be	ûr urge
ĭ pit	th thin
ī pie	*th* this
îr pier	hw which
ŏ pot	zh vision
ō toe	ə about, item
ô paw	♦ regionalism

Stress marks: ′ (primary); ′ (secondary), as in **dictionary** (dĭk′shə-nĕr′ē)

open carriage with two seats, used in the 19th century. [After *Tilbury*, a 19th-century London coach builder.]

til·de (tĭl′də) *n.* A diacritical mark (˜) placed over the letter *n* in Spanish to indicate the palatal nasal sound (ny), as in *cañon*, or over a vowel in Portuguese to indicate nasalization, as in *lã, pão*. [Spanish, alteration of obsolete Catalan *title*, from Latin *titulus*, superscription.]

Til·den (tĭl′dən), **Samuel Jones.** 1814–1886. American politician. The Democratic presidential nominee in 1876, he won the popular election but lost the presidency in an electoral college controversy that was settled by a Senate committee in favor of Rutherford B. Hayes.

Tilden, William Tatem, Jr. Known as "Big Bill." 1893–1953. American tennis player who dominated the sport in the 1920's, winning the U.S. men's singles championship seven times (1920–1925 and 1929) and the Wimbledon championship three times (1920, 1921 and 1930).

tile (tīl) *n.* **1.** A thin, flat or convex slab of hard material such as baked clay or plastic, laid in rows to cover walls, floors, and roofs. **2.** A short length of pipe made of clay or concrete, used in sewers and drains. **3.** A hollow fired clay or concrete block used for building walls. **4.** Tiles considered as a group. **5.** *Games.* A marked playing piece, as in mahjong. —*attributive.* Often used to modify another noun: *tile floors; a tile roof.* **—tile** *tr.v.* **tiled, til·ing, tiles.** To cover or provide with tiles. [Middle English, from Old English *tigele*, from Latin *tēgula*, from *tegere*, to cover. See **(s)teg-** in Appendix.]

tile
Top: Roofing tiles arranged in the mission pattern
Bottom: 18th-century Spanish tiles representing Asia (*above*) and Europe (*below*)

tile·fish (tīl′fĭsh′) *n., pl.* **tilefish** or **-fish·es.** A reddish-blue percoid marine food fish *(Lopholatilus chamaeleonticeps)* of deep Atlantic waters, having a fleshy flap on the nape and small yellow spots on the upper sides and fins. [*Tile-* (short for New Latin *Lopholatilus*, genus name : Greek *lophos*, crest, fin + *-latilus*, Latinized diminutive of Greek *latos*, a kind of perch) + FISH.]

til·er (tī′lər) *n.* **1.** One who lays tiles. **2.** The doorkeeper of a Masonic or other fraternal society's lodge.

til·ing (tī′lĭng) *n.* **1.** The laying of tiles. **2.** Tiles considered as a group. **3.** A tiled surface.

till¹ (tĭl) *tr.v.* **tilled, till·ing, tills.** To prepare (land) for the raising of crops, as by plowing and harrowing; cultivate. [Middle English *tilen*, from Old English *tilian*.] **—till′a·ble** *adj.*

till² (tĭl) *prep.* Until. **—till** *conj.* Until. [Middle English, from Old English *til*, from Old Norse.]

USAGE NOTE: *Till* and *until* are generally interchangeable in both writing and speech, though as the first word in a sentence *until* is usually preferred: *Until you get that paper written don't even think about going to the movies.* • *Till* is actually the older word, with *until* having been formed by the addition to it of the prefix *un–*, meaning "up to." In the 18th century the spelling *'till* became fashionable, as if *till* were a shortened form of *until*. Although *'till* is now nonstandard, *'til* is sometimes used in this way and is considered acceptable, though it is etymologically incorrect.

till³ (tĭl) *n.* **1.** A drawer, small chest, or compartment for money, as in a store. **2.** A supply of money; a purse. [Middle English *tille*.]

till⁴ (tĭl) *n.* Glacial drift composed of an unconsolidated, heterogeneous mixture of clay, sand, pebbles, cobbles, and boulders. [Origin unknown.]

till·age (tĭl′ĭj) *n.* **1.** Cultivation of land. **2.** Land that has been tilled.

Til·la·mook Bay (tĭl′ə-mo͝ok′). An inlet of the Pacific Ocean in northwest Oregon. The surrounding area is noted for its cheese.

til·land·si·a (tĭ-lănd′zē-ə) *n.* Any of various usually epiphytic bromeliad plants of the genus *Tillandsia*, such as Spanish moss, of tropical and subtropical America. [New Latin *Tillandsia*, genus name, after Elias *Tillands* (1640–1693), Finno-Swedish botanist.]

till·er¹ (tĭl′ər) *n.* One that tills land: *a tiller of soil.*

til·ler² (tĭl′ər) *n. Nautical.* A lever used to turn a rudder and steer a boat. [Middle English *tiler*, stock of a crossbow, from Old French *telier*, from Medieval Latin *tēlārium*, weaver's beam, from Latin *tēla*. See **teks-** in Appendix.]

til·ler³ (tĭl′ər) *n.* A shoot, especially one that sprouts from the base of a grass. **—tiller** *intr.v.* **-lered, -ler·ing, -lers.** To send forth shoots from the base. Used of a grass. [Middle English **tiller*, from Old English *telgor*.]

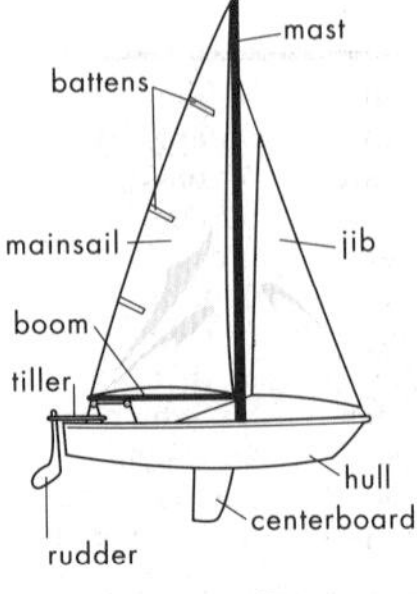

tiller²
Bermuda-rigged sloop

Til·lich (tĭl′ĭk, -ĭKH), **Paul Johannes.** 1886–1965. German-born American theologian and philosopher whose works, including *Systematic Theology* (1951–1963), bind Christianity to an understanding of modern culture.

Til·ly (tĭl′ē), Count of. Title of Johann Tserclaas. 1559–1632. Flemish field marshal during the Thirty Years' War.

♦ **tilt¹** (tĭlt) *v.* **tilt·ed, tilt·ing, tilts.** —*tr.* **1.** To cause to slope, as by raising one end; incline: *tilt a soup bowl; tilt a chair backward.* **2.a.** To aim or thrust (a lance) in a joust. **b.** To charge (an opponent); attack. **3.** To forge with a tilt hammer. —*intr.* **1.** To slope; incline. See Synonyms at **slant.** **2.** To favor one side over another in a dispute; lean: *"His views tilt unmistakably to the Arab position"* (William Safire). **3.a.** To fight with lances; joust. **b.** To engage in a combat or struggle; fight: *tilting at injustices.* **—tilt** *n.* **1.** The act of tilting or the condition of being tilted. **2.a.** An inclination from the horizontal or vertical; a slant: *adjusting the tilt of a writing table.* **b.** A sloping surface, as of the ground. **3.a.** A tendency to favor one side in a dispute: *the court's tilt toward conservative rulings.* **b.** An implicit preference; a bias: *"pitilessly illuminates the inaccuracies and tilts of the press"* (Nat Hentoff). **4.a.** A medieval sport in which two mounted knights with lances charged together and attempted to unhorse one another. **b.** A thrust or blow with a lance. **5.** A combat, especially a verbal one; a debate. **6.** A tilt hammer. **7.** *New England.* See **seesaw** (sense 1). See Regional Note at **teeter-totter.** ***—idiom.* at full tilt.** *Informal.* At full speed: *a tank moving at full tilt.* [Middle English *tilten*, to cause to fall, perhaps of Scandinavian origin.] **—tilt′er** *n.*

tilt² (tĭlt) *n.* A canopy or an awning for a boat, wagon, or cart. **—tilt** *tr.v.* **tilt·ed, tilt·ing, tilts.** To cover (a vehicle) with a canopy or an awning. [Middle English *telte*, tent, from Old English *teld*.]

tilth (tĭlth) *n.* **1.** Cultivation of land; tillage. **2.** Tilled earth. [Middle English, from Old English *tilth*, from *tilian*, to labor.]

tilt hammer *n.* A heavy forge hammer having a pivoted lever by which it is tilted up and then allowed to drop.

♦ **tilt·ing board** (tĭl′tĭng) *n. New England.* See **seesaw** (sense 1). See Regional Note at **teeter-totter.**

tilt·yard (tĭlt′yärd′) *n.* An enclosed yard for tilting contests.

Tim. *abbr. Bible.* Timothy.

tim·bal also **tym·bal** (tĭm′bəl) *n.* A kettledrum. [French *timbale*, from Old French, alteration (influenced by *cymbale*, cymbals) of *tamballe*, alteration (influenced by *tambour*, drum) of Old Spanish *atabal*, small drum, from Arabic *aṭ-ṭabl*, the drum.]

tim·bale (tĭm′bəl, tĭm-bäl′, tăm-) *n.* **1.** A custardlike dish of cheese, chicken, fish, or vegetables baked in a drum-shaped pastry mold. **2.** The pastry mold in which this food is baked. [French, timbal, mold. See TIMBAL.]

tim·ber (tĭm′bər) *n.* **1.a.** Trees or wooded land considered as a source of wood. **b.** Wood used as a building material; lumber. **2.a.** A dressed piece of wood, especially a beam in a structure. **b.** *Nautical.* A rib in a ship's frame. **3.** A person considered to have qualities suited for a particular activity: *That trainee is executive timber.* **—timber** *tr.v.* **-bered, -ber·ing, -bers.** To support or frame with timbers: *timber a mine shaft.* [Middle English, from Old English, building, trees for building. See **dem-** in Appendix.]

tim·bered (tĭm′bərd) *adj.* **1.** Covered with trees; wooded. **2.** Made of or framed by timbers, especially exposed timbers.

tim·ber·head (tĭm′bər-hĕd′) *n. Nautical.* An upper end of a timber that projects above a deck and is used as a bollard.

timber hitch *n.* A knot used for fastening a rope around a spar or log to be hoisted or towed.

tim·ber·ing (tĭm′bər-ĭng) *n.* Timber or objects and structures made of it.

tim·ber·land (tĭm′bər-lănd′) *n.* Forested land, especially land containing timber of commercial value.

tim·ber·line (tĭm′bər-līn′) *n.* **1.** The elevation in a mountainous region above which trees do not grow. **2.** The northern or southern latitude beyond which trees do not grow. Also called *tree line.*

timber rattlesnake *n.* A venomous snake *(Crotalus horridus* subsp. *horridus)* of the United States, typically having a yellowish-brown color and wide transverse bands on the back.

timber right *n.* A claim to the trees on property belonging to another. Often used in the plural.

timber wolf *n.* See **gray wolf.**

tim·ber·work (tĭm′bər-wûrk′) *n.* A structure made with timbers, as the framework of a boat or house.

tim·bre (tăm′bər, tĭm′-) *n.* **1.** The quality of a sound that distinguishes it from other sounds of the same pitch and volume. **2.** *Music.* The distinctive tone of an instrument or a singing voice. [French, from Old French, drum, clapperless bell, probably from Medieval Greek **timbanon*, drum, from Greek *tumpanon*, kettledrum.]

tim·brel (tĭm′brəl) *n. Music.* An ancient percussion instrument similar to a tambourine. [Diminutive of Middle English *timbre*, drum, from Old French. See TIMBRE.]

Tim·buk·tu (tĭm′bŭk-to͞o′, tĭm-bŭk′to͞o). A city of central Mali near the Niger River northeast of Bamako. Founded in the 11th century, it became a major trading center (primarily for gold and salt) by the 14th century. Timbuktu was sacked in 1593 by invaders and never recovered its glory. Population, 19,166.

time (tīm) *n.* **1.** *Abbr.* **t., T. a.** A nonspatial continuum in which events occur in apparently irreversible succession from the past through the present to the future. **b.** An interval separating two points on this continuum; a duration: *a long time since the last war; passed the time reading.* **c.** A number, as of years, days, or minutes, representing such an interval: *ran the course in a time just under four minutes.* **d.** A similar number representing a specific point on this continuum, reckoned in hours and minutes: *checked her watch and recorded the time, 6:17* A.M. **e.** A system by which such intervals are measured or such numbers are reckoned: *solar time.* **2.a.** Often **times.** An interval, especially a span of years, marked by similar events, conditions, or phenomena; an era: *hard times; a time of troubles.* **b. times.** The present with respect to prevailing conditions and trends: *You must change with the times.* **3.** A suitable or opportune moment or season: *a time for taking stock of one's life.* **4.a.** Periods or a period designated for a given activity: *harvest time; time for bed.* **b.** Periods or a period necessary or available for a given activity: *I have no time for golf.* **c.** A period at one's disposal: *Do you have time for a chat?* **5.** An appointed or fated moment, especially of death or giving birth: *He died before his time. Her time is near.* **6. a.** One of several instances: *knocked three times; addressed Congress for the last time before retirement.* **b. times.** Used to indicate the number of instances by which something is multiplied or divided: *This tree is three times taller than that one. My library is many times smaller than hers.* **7. a.** One's lifetime. **b.** One's period of greatest activity or engagement. **c.** A person's experience during a specific period or on a certain occasion: *had a good time at the party.* **8. a.** A period of military service. **b.** A period of apprenticeship. **c.** *Informal.* A prison sentence. **9. a.** The customary period of work: *hired for full time.* **b.** The period spent working. **c.** The hourly pay rate: *earned double time on Sundays.* **10.** The period during which a radio or television program or commercial is broadcast: *"There's television time to buy"* (Brad Goldstein). **11.** The rate of speed of a measured activity: *marching in double time.* **12.** *Music.* **a.** The characteristic beat of musical rhythm: *three-quarter time.* **b.** The rate of speed at which a piece of music is played; the tempo. **13.** *Chiefly British.* The hour at which a pub closes. **14.** *Sports.* A time-out. **—time** *adj.* **1.** Of, relating to, or measuring time. **2.** Constructed so as to operate at a particular moment: *a time release.* **3.** Payable on a future date or dates. **4.** Of or relating to installment buying: *time payments.* **—time** *tr.v.* **timed, tim·ing, times. 1.** To set the time for (an event or occasion). **2.** To adjust to keep accurate time. **3.** To adjust so that a force is applied or an action occurs at the desired time: *timed his swing so as to hit the ball squarely.* **4.** To record the speed or duration of: *time a runner.* **5.** To set or maintain the tempo, speed, or duration of: *time a manufacturing process.* ***—idioms.*** **against time.** With a quickly approaching time limit: *worked against time to deliver the manuscript before the deadline.* **at one time. 1.** Simultaneously. **2.** At a period or moment in the past. **at the same time.** However; nonetheless. **at times.** On occasion; sometimes. **behind the times.** Out-of-date; old-fashioned. **for the time being.** Temporarily. **from time to time.** Once in a while; at intervals. **high time.** Long overdue: *It's high time that you started working.* **in good time. 1.** In a reasonable length of time. **2.** When or before due. **3.** Quickly. **in no time.** Almost instantly; immediately. **in time. 1.** Before a time limit expires. **2.** Within an indefinite time; eventually: *In time they came to accept the harsh facts.* **3.** *Music.* In the proper tempo. **on time. 1.** According to schedule; punctual or punctually. **2.** By paying in installments. **time after time.** Again and again; repeatedly. **time and again.** Again and again; repeatedly. **time of (one's) life.** A highly pleasurable experience: *We had the time of our lives at the beach.* **time on (one's) hands.** An interval with nothing to do. **time was.** There was once a time: *"Time was when* [urban gangs] *were part of a . . . subculture that inner-city adolescence outgrew"* (George F. Will). [Middle English, from Old English *tīma.* See **dā-** in Appendix.]

time and a half *n.* A rate of pay that is one and a half times the regular rate, as for overtime work.

time and motion study *n.* An analysis of the efficiency with which an industrial operation is performed. Also called *motion study, time study.*

time bill *n.* A bill of exchange payable at an indicated future time.

time bomb *n.* **1.** A bomb with a detonating mechanism that can be set for a particular time. **2.** Something that threatens to have an abruptly disastrous outcome in the future.

time capsule *n.* A sealed container preserving articles and records of contemporary culture for perusal by scientists and scholars of the distant future.

time·card (tīm′kärd′) *n.* A card, either filled out by an employee or stamped by a time clock, recording the employee's starting and quitting times each work day.

time clock *n.* A clock that records the starting and quitting times of employees, usually by punching timecards.

time-con·sum·ing (tīm′kən-so͞o′mĭng) *adj.* Taking up much time.

time deposit *n.* A bank deposit that cannot be withdrawn before a date specified at the time of deposit.

time dilatation *n.* The relativistic slowing of a clock that moves with respect to a stationary observer. Also called *time dilation.*

timed-re·lease (tīmd′rĭ-lēs′) or **time-re·lease** (tīm′-) *adj.* Releasing ingredients gradually to produce a sustained effect: *a timed-release allergy medication; timed-release fertilizers.*

time exposure *n.* **1.** A photographic exposure made by leaving the shutter open a relatively long time, generally a second or more. **2.** An image so made.

time frame *n.* A period during which something takes place or is projected to occur: *"a start of deployment in the 1993 time frame"* (Harold Brown).

time-hon·ored (tīm′ŏn′ərd) *adj.* Respected or adhered to because of age or age-old observance.

time immemorial *n., pl.* **times immemorial. 1.** Time long past, beyond memory or record. Also called *time out of mind.* **2.** *Law.* Time antedating legal records.

time·keep·er (tīm′kē′pər) *n.* **1.** One who records time, as: **a.** *Sports.* One who keeps track of elapsed time in a sporting event. **b.** One who keeps records of the hours worked by employees. **2.** A device for keeping time; a timepiece. **—time′keep′ing** *adj.*

time-lapse (tīm′lăps′) *adj.* Of, using, or being a technique that photographs a naturally slow process, such as plant growth, on movie film at intervals, so that continuous projection of the frames gives an accelerated view of the process.

time·less (tīm′lĭs) *adj.* **1.** Independent of time; eternal. **2.** Unaffected by time; ageless. See Synonyms at **ageless. 3.** *Archaic.* Untimely or premature. **—time′less·ly** *adv.* **—time′less·ness** *n.*

time loan *n.* A loan to be paid within or by a specified time.

time lock *n.* A lock, as for a bank vault, containing a mechanism that prevents its being opened before a fixed time.

time·ly (tīm′lē) *adj.* **-li·er, -li·est. 1.** Occurring at a suitable or opportune time; well-timed. See Synonyms at **opportune. 2.** *Archaic.* Coming too early; premature. **—timely** *adv.* **1.** In time; opportunely. **2.** *Archaic.* Early; soon. **—time′li·ness** *n.*

time machine *n.* A fictional or hypothetical device by means of which one may travel into the future and the past.

time note *n.* An instrument, such as a promissory note, that specifies dates or a date of payment.

time·ous (tī′məs) *adj.* Timely. **—time′ous·ly** *adv.*

time-out also **time out** (tīm′out′) *n.* **1.** *Sports.* A brief cessation of play at the request of a sports team or an official for rest, consultation, or making substitutions. **2.** A short break from work or play.

time out of mind *n., pl.* **times out of mind.** See **time immemorial** (sense 1).

time·piece (tīm′pēs′) *n.* An instrument, such as a clock or watch, that measures, registers, or records time.

tim·er (tī′mər) *n.* **1.** One who keeps track of time; a timekeeper. **2.** A timepiece, especially one used for measuring and signaling the end of time intervals, as on a stove. **3.** A switch or regulator that controls or activates and deactivates another mechanism at set times. **4.** A device that controls the timing of the sparks that ignite the fuel in an internal-combustion engine.

time-re·lease (tīm′rĭ-lēs′) *adj.* Variant of **timed-release.**

time reversal *n.* *Abbr.* **T.** *Mathematics.* An operation representing a transformation from a given physical system undergoing a given sequence of events to a system in which the exact reverse sequence of events takes place.

times (tīmz) *prep.* *Mathematics.* Multiplied by: *Five times two is ten.*

time·sav·ing (tīm′sā′vĭng) *adj.* Serving to save time through an efficient method or a shorter route; expeditious. **—time′sav′er** *n.*

time·serv·er also **time-serv·er** (tīm′sûr′vər) *n.* One who conforms to the prevailing ways and opinions of one's time or condition for personal advantage; an opportunist. **—time′serv′ing** *adj. & n.*

time-share (tīm′shâr′) *v.* **-shared, -shar·ing, -shares.** *—tr.* **1.** *Computer Science.* To use (a computer) by time-sharing. **2.** To occupy (a vacation property) by time-sharing. *—intr.* To engage in time-sharing. **—time-share** *n.* **1.** Variant of **time-sharing** (sense 2). **2.** A property jointly owned or leased by time-sharing. **—time′-shar′er** *n.*

time-shar·ing (tīm′shâr′ĭng) *n.* **1.** *Computer Science.* A technique permitting many users simultaneous access to a central computer through remote terminals. **2.** Also **time-share** (-shâr′). Joint ownership or lease of vacation property by several people who take turns occupying the premises for fixed periods.

time sheet *n.* A sheet that records the number of hours worked by employees during a pay period.

time signature *n.* *Music.* A sign placed on a staff to indicate the meter, commonly a numerical fraction of which the numerator is the number of beats per measure and the denominator represents the kind of note getting one beat.

times sign *n.* *Mathematics.* The symbol × used to indicate multiplication.

Times Square (tīmz). An intersection in New York City formed by the juncture of Broadway, Seventh Avenue, and 42nd Street in midtown Manhattan. Long noted as a center of the city's entertainment district, it is the site of annual New Year's Eve celebrations.

time study *n.* See **time and motion study.**

time·ta·ble (tīm′tā′bəl) *n.* A schedule listing the times at which certain events, such as arrivals and departures at a transportation station, are expected to take place.

time-test·ed (tīm′tĕs′tĭd) *adj.* Proved effective over a long period of time: *a time-tested recipe.*

time warp *n.* A hypothetical discontinuity or distortion occurring in the flow of time that would move events from one time period to another or suspend the passage of time.

time·work (tīm′wûrk′) *n.* Work paid for at a rate per unit of time, as by the hour. **—time′work′er** *n.*

time·worn (tīm′wôrn′, -wōrn′) *adj.* **1.** Showing the effects of long use or wear: *timeworn lanes.* **2.** Used too often; trite: *timeworn expressions.*

time zone *n.* Any of the 24 longitudinal divisions of Earth's surface in which a standard time is kept, the primary division being that bisected by the Greenwich meridian. Each zone is 15°

ă pat	oi boy
ā pay	ou out
âr care	o͝o took
ä father	o͞o boot
ĕ pet	ŭ cut
ē be	ûr urge
ĭ pit	th thin
ī pie	*th* this
îr pier	hw which
ŏ pot	zh vision
ō toe	ə about, item
ô paw	♦ regionalism

Stress marks: ′ (primary); ′ (secondary), as in **dictionary** (dĭk′shə-nĕr′ē)

of longitude in width, with local variations, and observes a clock time one hour earlier than the zone immediately to the east.

Tim·gad (tĭm′găd′). An ancient Roman city in northeast Algeria. Founded by Trajan in A.D. 100, it is sometimes called "the Pompeii of North Africa" because of its extensive, well-preserved ruins.

tim·id (tĭm′ĭd) *adj.* **-er, -est. 1.** Lacking self-confidence; shy. **2.** Fearful and hesitant: *problems that call for bold, not timid, responses.* [Latin *timidus,* from *timēre,* to fear.] **—ti·mid′i·ty, tim′id·ness** *n.* **—tim′id·ly** *adv.*

SYNONYMS: *timid, timorous.* The central meaning shared by these adjectives is "hesitating to take action or assert oneself out of fear, apprehensiveness, or lack of self-confidence": *too timid to protest; timorous of venturing an opinion.*

tim·ing (tī′mĭng) *n.* The art or operation of regulating occurrence, pace, or coordination to achieve the most desirable effects, as in music, the theater, athletics, or mechanics.

timing chain *n.* The chain that drives the camshaft in an internal combustion engine.

Ti·mi·şoa·ra (tē′mē-shwär′ə). A city of western Romania near the Yugoslavian border west-northwest of Bucharest. First mentioned in 1247, it is a railroad hub and an industrial center. Population, 303,499.

Tim·mins (tĭm′ĭnz). A city of central Ontario, Canada, northeast of Sault Sainte Marie. Population, 46,114.

ti·moc·ra·cy (tī-mŏk′rə-sē) *n., pl.* **-cies. 1.** A state described by Plato as being governed on principles of honor and military glory. **2.** An Aristotelian state in which civic honor or political power is proportional to the property one owns. [Obsolete French *tymocracie,* from Medieval Latin *timocratia,* from Greek *timokratia* : *timē,* honor, value + *-kratia,* -cracy.] **—ti′mo·crat′ic** (tī′mə-krăt′ĭk) *adj.*

Ti·mor (tē′môr, tē-môr′). An island of southeast Indonesia, the easternmost of the Lesser Sundas. The western half of the island, formerly Netherlands Timor, became part of Indonesia in 1949. The eastern half was an overseas province of Portugal from 1914 until 1975.

tim·or·ous (tĭm′ər-əs) *adj.* Full of apprehensiveness; timid. See Synonyms at **timid.** [Middle English, from Old French *timoureus,* from Medieval Latin *timōrōsus,* from Latin *timor, timōr-,* fear, from *timēre,* to fear.] **—tim′or·ous·ly** *adv.* **—tim′or·ous·ness** *n.*

tinamou

Timor Sea. An arm of the Indian Ocean between Timor and Australia.

tim·o·thy (tĭm′ə-thē) *n., pl.* **-thies.** Any of several grasses of the genus *Phleum,* especially *P. pratense,* native to Eurasia, and *P. alpinum,* of North America, having a dense cylindrical inflorescence of compressed, one-flowered spikelets and widely cultivated for hay. [Probably after *Timothy* Hanson, an 18th-century American farmer.]

Tim·o·thy (tĭm′ə-thē) *n. Abbr.* **Tim., Tm.** *Bible.* See table at **Bible.**

Timothy, Saint. First century A.D. Christian leader and companion of Saint Paul. Two epistles of the New Testament, ascribed to Paul, are addressed to him.

tim·pa·ni also **tym·pa·ni** (tĭm′pə-nē) *pl.n. Music.* A set of kettledrums. [Italian, pl. of *timpano,* kettledrum, from Latin *tympanum,* drum. See TYMPANUM.]

tim·pa·nist also **tym·pa·nist** (tim′pə-nĭst) *n. Music.* One who plays the kettledrums and other percussion instruments in an orchestra.

tim·pa·num (tĭm′pə-nəm) *n.* Variant of **tympanum.**

Tim·u·cu·a (tĭm′ə-ko͞o′ə) *n., pl.* **Timucua** or **-cu·as. 1.a.** A Native American people formerly inhabiting much of northern Florida, extinct since the early 18th century. **b.** A member of this people. **2.** The extinct language of the Timucua.

tin (tĭn) *n.* **1.** *Symbol* **Sn** A malleable, silvery metallic element obtained chiefly from cassiterite. It is used to coat other metals to prevent corrosion and is a part of numerous alloys, such as soft solder, pewter, type metal, and bronze. Atomic number 50; atomic weight 118.69; melting point 231.89°C; boiling point 2,270°C; specific gravity 7.31; valence 2, 4. See table at **element. 2.** Tin plate. **3.** A container or box made of tin plate. **4.** *Chiefly British.* **a.** A container for preserved foodstuffs; a can. **b.** The contents of such a container. **—tin** *tr.v.* **tinned, tin·ning, tins. 1.** To plate or coat with tin. **2.** *Chiefly British.* To preserve or pack in tins; can. **—tin** *adj.* **1.** Of, relating to, or made of tin. **2.a.** Constructed of inferior material. **b.** Spurious. [Middle English, from Old English.]

WORD HISTORY: The history of the word *tin* may take us back to a time before Europe had been settled by speakers of Indo-European languages, such as the Germanic and Celtic languages. Related words for this metal are found in almost all Germanic languages, such as German *Zinn,* Swedish *tenn,* and Old English *tin* (as in Modern English), but no other Indo-European language family has such a word. The word may have been borrowed into the Germanic languages from a pre-Indo-European language of Western Europe. Such borrowing is supported by the fact that during the Bronze Age the Near East imported most of its tin and copper from Europe, where the metals were produced and metal objects were manufactured. Lest we be too amazed by this accomplishment, we might remember another remarkable achievement of pre-Indo-European society, the construction of huge megalithic monuments such as Stonehenge.

tin·a·mou (tĭn′ə-mo͞o′) *n.* Any of various chickenlike or quaillike birds of the family Tinamidae, living in grasslands and jungles of Central and South America. [French, perhaps of Galibi origin.]

Tin·ber·gen (tĭn′bər-gən, -bĕr′KHən), **Jan.** Born 1903. Dutch economist. He shared a 1969 Nobel Prize for the application of mathematics and statistical methods to economics. His brother **Nikolaas** (born 1907), a Dutch-born British ethologist, shared a 1973 Nobel Prize for studies of individual and social behavior patterns.

tin·cal (tĭng′kəl) *n.* Crude borax. [Malay *tingkal.*]

tin can *n.* **1.** A container of tin-coated sheet metal used especially for preserving food. **2.** *Informal.* A naval destroyer.

tinct (tĭngkt) *n.* A color or tint. **—tinct** *adj.* Colored lightly or faintly; tinged. [Middle English, a transforming elixir, from Latin *tīnctus,* a dyeing, from past participle of *tingere,* to dye.]

tinct. *abbr.* Tincture.

tinc·to·ri·al (tĭngk-tôr′ē-əl, -tōr′-) *adj.* Relating to the processes of dyeing or coloring. [From Latin *tīnctōrius,* from *tīnctus,* past participle of *tingere,* to dye.] **—tinc·to′ri·al·ly** *adv.*

tinc·ture (tĭngk′chər) *n.* **1.** A coloring or dyeing substance; a pigment. **2.** An imparted color; a tint. **3.** A quality that colors, pervades, or distinguishes. **4.** A trace or vestige: *"a faint tincture of condescension"* (Robert Craft). **5.** *Abbr.* **tinct.** An alcohol solution of a nonvolatile medicine: *tincture of iodine.* **6.** *Heraldry.* A metal, color, or fur. **—tincture** *tr.v.* **-tured, -tur·ing, -tures. 1.** To stain or tint with a color. **2.** To infuse, as with a quality; impregnate. [Middle English, from Latin *tīnctūra,* a dyeing, from *tīnctus,* past participle of *tingere,* to dye.]

Tin·dal or **Tin·dale** (tĭn′dl), **William.** See William **Tyndale.**

tin·der (tĭn′dər) *n.* Readily combustible material, such as dry twigs, used to kindle fires. [Middle English, from Old English *tynder.*]

tin·der·box (tĭn′dər-bŏks′) *n.* **1.** A metal box for holding tinder. **2.** A potentially explosive place or situation: *referred to the crowded prison as a tinderbox of suppressed violence.*

tine (tīn) *n.* **1.** A branch of a deer's antlers. **2.** A prong on an implement such as a fork or pitchfork. [Middle English, from Old English *tind.*] **—tined** (tīnd) *adj.*

tin·e·a (tĭn′ē-ə) *n.* Any of several infections of the skin, such as ringworm, caused by fungi. [Middle English, from Medieval Latin, from Latin, a gnawing worm.] **—tin′e·al** *adj.*

tinea bar·bae (bär′bē) *n.* See **barber's itch.** [New Latin : Medieval Latin *tinea,* tinea + Latin *barbae,* genitive of *barba,* beard.]

tinea cap·i·tis (kăp′ĭ-tĭs) *n.* A fungal infection of the scalp. [New Latin : Medieval Latin *tinea,* tinea + Latin *capitis,* genitive of *caput,* head.]

tinea cru·ris (kro͝or′ĭs) *n.* A fungal infection of the skin of the groin, occurring especially in males. Also called *jock itch.* [New Latin : Medieval Latin *tinea,* tinea + Latin *crūris,* genitive of *crūs,* leg.]

tin ear *n. Informal.* An insensitivity to music or to sounds of a given kind: *a writer with a tin ear for dialogue.*

tin·foil also **tin foil** (tĭn′foil′) *n.* A thin, pliable sheet of aluminum or of tin-lead alloy, used as a protective wrapping.

ting (tĭng) *n.* A single light metallic sound, as of a small bell. **—ting** *intr.v.* **tinged** (tĭngd), **ting·ing, tings.** To give forth a light metallic sound. [From Middle English *tingen,* to cause to ring, of imitative origin.]

tinge (tĭnj) *tr.v.* **tinged** (tĭnjd), **tinge·ing** or **ting·ing** (tĭn′jĭng), **ting·es. 1.** To apply a trace of color to; tint. **2.** To affect slightly, as with a contrasting quality: *"The air was blowy and tinged with rain"* (Joyce Carol Oates). **—tinge** *n.* **1.** A small amount of a color incorporated or added. **2.** A slight added element, property, or influence: *a tinge of regret.* [Middle English *tingen,* from Latin *tingere.*]

tin·gle (tĭng′gəl) *v.* **-gled, -gling, -gles.** *—intr.* **1.** To have a prickling, stinging sensation, as from cold, a sharp slap, or excitement: *tingled all over with joy.* **2.** To cause a prickling, stinging sensation or feeling: *The straw tingled.* *—tr.* To cause to tingle. **—tingle** *n.* A prickly or stinging sensation. [Middle English *tinglen,* alteration of *tinklen.* See TINKLE.] **—tin′gler** *n.* **—tin′gly** *adj.*

tin·horn (tĭn′hôrn′) *n. Slang.* A petty braggart who pretends to be rich and important. [From the horn-shaped metal can used by chuck-a-luck operators for shaking the dice.] **—tin′horn′** *adj.*

Ti·ni·an (tĭn′ē-ăn′, tē′nē-än′). An island of the western Pacific Ocean in the southern Mariana Islands. The planes that dropped atomic bombs on Hiroshima (August 6, 1945) and Nagasaki (August 9, 1945) were flown from Tinian.

tin·ker (tĭng′kər) *n.* **1.** A traveling mender of metal household utensils. **2.** One who enjoys experimenting with and repairing machine parts. **3.** A clumsy repairer or worker; a meddler. **—tinker** *v.* **-kered, -ker·ing, -kers.** *—intr.* **1.** To work as a tinker. **2.** To make unskilled or experimental efforts at repair; fiddle: *tinkered with the engine, hoping to discover the trouble; tinkering with the economy by trying various fiscal policies.* *—tr.*

1. To mend as a tinker. 2. To manipulate unskillfully or experimentally. [Middle English *tinkere.*]

tin·ker's damn also **tin·ker's dam** (tĭngʹkərz) *n. Slang.* The smallest degree or amount: *property that is not worth a tinker's damn.* [Probably from the reputation of tinkers for cursing.]

Tin·ker·toy (tĭngʹkər-toiʹ). A trademark used for a construction toy consisting of pieces that fit together.

tin·kle (tĭngʹkəl) *v.* **-kled, -kling, -kles.** —*intr.* To make light metallic sounds, as those of a small bell. —*tr.* **1.** To cause to tinkle. **2.** To signal or call by tinkling. **—tinkle** *n.* **1.** A light, clear metallic sound or a sound suggestive of it. **2.** The act of tinkling. [Middle English *tinklen,* frequentative of *tinken,* to emit a brief metallic sound, perhaps of imitative origin.] **—tinʹkly** *adj.*

Tin·ley Park (tĭnʹlē). A city of northeast Illinois, a residential suburb of Chicago. Population, 26,171.

tin liz·zie (lĭzʹē) *n. Slang.* A dilapidated or cheap car. [From the name *Lizzie,* a nickname for Elizabeth.]

tin·ner (tĭnʹər) *n.* **1.** A tin miner. **2.** One that makes or deals in tinware; a tinsmith.

tin·ni·tus (tĭ-nīʹtəs, tĭnʹĭ-) *n., pl.* **-tus·es.** A sound in one ear or both ears, such as buzzing, ringing, or whistling, occurring without an external stimulus and usually caused by a specific condition, such as an ear infection, the use of certain drugs, a blocked auditory tube or canal, or a head injury. [Latin *tinnītus,* from past participle of *tinnīre,* to ring, of imitative origin.]

tin·ny (tĭnʹē) *adj.* **-ni·er, -ni·est. 1.** Of, containing, or yielding tin. **2.** Tasting or smelling of tin: *tinny canned food.* **3.** Having a thin metallic sound: *a high tinny voice.* **4.** Weak or thin; flimsy. **—tinʹni·ly** *adv.* **—tinʹni·ness** *n.*

Tí·nos (tēʹnôsʹ) also **Te·nos** (tēʹnŏsʹ, -nôsʹ). An island of southeast Greece in the Cyclades Islands east-southeast of Athens.

Tin Pan Alley (tĭn) *n. Music.* **1.** A district associated with musicians, composers, and publishers of popular music. **2.** The publishers and composers of popular music considered as a group. [Probably from *tin pan,* tinny piano + ALLEY[1] (from the cheap pianos associated with music publishers' offices).]

tin plate *n.* Thin sheet iron or steel coated with tin to prevent rusting, used especially to make cans and pots.

tin-plate (tĭnʹplātʹ) *tr.v.* **-plat·ed, -plat·ing, -plates.** To coat with tin, as by dipping or electroplating. **—tinʹ-platʹer** *n.*

tin pyrites *n.* See **stannite.**

tin·sel (tĭnʹsəl) *n.* **1.** Very thin sheets, strips, or threads of a glittering material used as a decoration. **2.** Something sparkling or showy but basically valueless: *the tinsel of parties and promotional events.* **—tinsel** *adj.* **1.** Made of or decorated with tinsel. **2.** Gaudy, showy, and basically valueless. **—tinsel** *tr.v.* **-seled, -sel·ing, -sels** or **-selled, -sel·ling, -sels. 1.** To decorate with or as if with tinsel: *tinsel a Christmas tree.* **2.** To give a false sparkle to. [Middle English *tineseile,* from Old French *estincelle,* spangle, spark. See STENCIL.]

tin·smith (tĭnʹsmĭthʹ) *n.* One that makes and repairs things made of light metal.

tin·stone (tĭnʹstōnʹ) *n.* See **cassiterite.**

tint (tĭnt) *n.* **1.** A shade of a color, especially a pale or delicate variation. **2.** A gradation of a color made by adding white to it to lessen its saturation. **3.** A slight coloration; a tinge. **4.** A barely detectable amount or degree; a trace. **5.** A shaded effect in engraving produced by fine, close, parallel lines. **6.** *Printing.* A panel of light color on which matter in another color is to be printed, as in an illustration. **7.** A dye for the hair. **—tint** *tr. & intr.v.* **tint·ed, tint·ing, tints.** To give a tint to or take on a tint. [Alteration of TINCT.] **—tintʹer** *n.*

Tin·tag·el Head (tĭn-tăjʹəl). A promontory in southwest England northwest of Plymouth. The site of the ruins of a 12th century castle, it is said to be the birthplace of King Arthur.

tin·tin·nab·u·la (tĭnʹtĭ-năbʹyə-lə) *n.* Plural of **tintinnabulum.**

tin·tin·nab·u·lar (tĭnʹtĭ-năbʹyə-lər) also **tin·tin·nab·u·lar·y** (-lĕrʹē) or **tin·tin·nab·u·lous** (-ləs) *adj.* Of or relating to bells or the ringing of bells. [From TINTINNABULUM.]

tin·tin·nab·u·la·tion (tĭnʹtĭ-năbʹyə-lāʹshən) *n.* The ringing or sounding of bells. [From TINTINNABULUM.]

tin·tin·nab·u·lous (tĭnʹtĭ-năbʹyə-ləs) *adj.* Variant of **tintinnabular.**

tin·tin·nab·u·lum (tĭnʹtĭ-năbʹyə-ləm) *n., pl.* **-la** (-lə). A small, tinkling bell. [Middle English, from Latin *tintinnābulum,* from *tintinnāre,* to jingle, reduplication of *tinnīre,* to ring, of imitative origin.]

WORD HISTORY: We may have little occasion to use the word *tintinnabulum,* "a small, tinkling bell," but it nonetheless teaches us something important about the formation of words. The English word, first used in 1597, was adopted from Latin, in which *tintinnābulum,* meaning "a bell," was derived from the verb *tintinnāre,* "to make a sound such as a ringing or jangling." *Tintinnāre* was in turn derived from *tinnīre,* "to ring or clang." *Tinnīre* is formed by a process called onomatopeia, or the formation of words that imitate what they denote. In the case of *tinnīre* we can hear the resemblance between *tinn–* and a jingle or a ring. The verb *tintinnāre* was created from *tinnīre* by a process known as reduplication, in this case meaning that *tin–* duplicates *tinn–*. *Tintinn–* does indeed suggest a jingling, ringing sound. And a tintinnabulum makes such a sound.

Tin·to·ret·to (tĭnʹtə-rĕtʹō, tēnʹtô-rĕtʹtô). Originally Jacopo Robusti. 1518–1594. Italian painter of religious, mythological, and historical subjects as well as portraits. His works include *Saint George and the Dragon* (c. 1550).

tin·type (tĭnʹtīpʹ) *n.* See **ferrotype** (sense 1).

tin·work (tĭnʹwûrkʹ) *n.* **1.** Articles made of tin or tin plate. **2. tinworks** *(used with a sing. verb).* A place where tin is smelted and rolled.

ti·ny (tīʹnē) *adj.* **-ni·er, -ni·est.** Extremely small; minute. See Synonyms at **small.** [Alteration of Middle English *tine.*] **—tiʹni·ness** *n.*

tip[1] (tĭp) *n.* **1.** The end of a pointed or projecting object. **2.** A piece or an attachment, such as a cap or ferrule, meant to be fitted to the end of something else: *the barbed tip of a harpoon.* **—tip** *tr.v.* **tipped, tip·ping, tips. 1.** To furnish with a tip. **2.** To cover or decorate the tip of: *tip strawberries with chocolate.* **3.** To remove the tip of: *tip artichokes.* **4.** To dye the ends of (hair or fur) in order to blend or improve appearance. ***—phrasal verb.*** **tip in.** *Printing.* To attach (an insert) in a book by gluing along the binding edge: *tip in a color plate.* [Middle English.]

tip[2] (tĭp) *v.* **tipped, tip·ping, tips.** —*tr.* **1.** To push or knock over; overturn or topple: *bumped the table and tipped a vase.* **2.** To move to a slanting position; tilt: *tipped the sideview mirror slightly downward; a weight that tipped the balance.* **3.** To touch or raise (one's hat) in greeting. **4.** *Chiefly British.* **a.** To empty (something) by overturning; dump. **b.** To dump (rubbish, for example). —*intr.* **1.** To topple over; overturn. **2.** To become tilted; slant. See Synonyms at **slant. —tip** *n.* **1.** The act of tipping. **2.** A tilt or slant; an incline. **3.** *Chiefly British.* An area or a place for dumping something, such as rubbish or refuse, as from a mine. ***—idiom.*** **tip the scales. 1.** To register weight (at a certain amount). **2.** To offset the balance of a situation. [Middle English *tipen.*]

♦**tip[3]** (tĭp) *v.* **tipped, tip·ping, tips.** —*tr.* **1.** To strike gently; tap. **2. a.** *Baseball.* To hit (a pitched ball) with the side of the bat so that it glances off. **b.** *Sports.* To tap or deflect (a ball or puck, for example), especially in scoring. —*intr.* **1.** *Sports.* To deflect or glance off. Used of a ball or puck. **2.** *Lower Southern U.S.* To tiptoe. **—tip** *n.* **1.** A light blow; a tap. **2.** *Baseball.* A pitched ball that is tipped: *a foul tip.* [From Middle English *tippe,* a tap, perhaps of Low German origin.]

tip[4] (tĭp) *n.* **1.** A small sum of money given to someone for performing a service; a gratuity. **2. a.** A piece of confidential, advance, or inside information: *got a tip on the next race.* **b.** A helpful hint: *a column of tips on gardening.* **—tip** *v.* **tipped, tip·ping, tips.** —*tr.* **1. a.** To give a tip to: *tipped the waiter generously.* **b.** To give as a tip: *He tipped a dollar and felt that it was enough.* **2.** To provide with a piece of confidential, advance, or inside information: *a disgruntled gang member who tipped the police to the planned robbery.* —*intr.* To give tips or a tip: *one who tips lavishly.* ***—idiom.*** **tip (one's) hand.** To reveal one's resources or intentions. [Origin unknown.] **—tipʹper** *n.*

tip·cart (tĭpʹkärtʹ) *n.* A cart having a body that can be tilted to dump the contents.

ti·pi (tēʹpē) *n.* Variant of **tepee.**

tip-in (tĭpʹĭnʹ) *n.* **1.** *Basketball.* A field goal scored by tapping the ball into the basket with the fingertips. **2.** *Sports.* A goal in hockey scored at close range by a short stroke of a stick.

tip-off[1] (tĭpʹôfʹ, -ŏfʹ) *n. Informal.* **1.** A piece of confidential, advance, or inside information. **2.** An indication of an otherwise unknown fact or probability: *The judge called for a pitcher of water, a tip-off that the session would be long.*

tip-off[2] (tĭpʹôfʹ, -ŏfʹ) *n. Basketball.* An act of starting play at the beginning of a period with a jump ball. Also called *tap-off.* [TIP[3] + (KICK)OFF.]

tip of the iceberg *n., pl.* **tips of the iceberg.** A small evident part or aspect of something largely hidden: *afraid that these few cases of the disease might only be the tip of the iceberg.*

Tip·pe·ca·noe (tĭpʹē-kə-nōōʹ). A river, about 274 km (170 mi) long, rising in northeast Indiana and flowing generally southwest to the Wabash River. Gen. William Henry Harrison defeated the Shawnee in the Battle of Tippecanoe (1811).

Tip·per·ar·y (tĭpʹə-râr'ē). A town of south-central Ireland southwest of Dublin. The song "It's a Long Way to Tipperary" was used as marching music by the British Expeditionary Force in World War I. Population, 4,984.

tip·pet (tĭpʹĭt) *n.* **1.** A covering for the shoulders, as of fur, with long ends that hang in front. **2.** A long stole worn by members of the Anglican clergy. **3.** A long hanging part, as of a sleeve, hood, or cape. [Middle English *tipet,* perhaps from *tip,* tip of an object.]

tip·ple[1] (tĭpʹəl) *tr. & intr.v.* **-pled, -pling, -ples.** To drink (alcoholic liquor) or engage in such drinking, especially habitually or to excess. **—tipple** *n.* Alcoholic liquor. [Perhaps back-formation from Middle English *tipeler,* bartender.] **—tipʹpler** *n.*

tip·ple[2] (tĭpʹəl) *n.* **1. a.** An apparatus for unloading freight cars by tipping them. **b.** The place where this is done. **2.** A place for screening coal and loading it into trucks or railroad cars. [From dialectal *tipple,* to overturn, frequentative of TIP[2].]

Tip·poo Sa·hib (tĭpʹōō säʹĭb, -ēb, -hĭb). See **Tipu Sahib.**

tippet

ă pat	oi boy
ā pay	ou out
âr care	ŏŏ took
ä father	ōō boot
ĕ pet	ŭ cut
ē be	ûr urge
ĭ pit	th thin
ī pie	*th* this
îr pier	hw which
ŏ pot	zh vision
ō toe	ə about, item
ô paw	♦ regionalism

Stress marks: ʹ (primary); ʹ (secondary), as in **dictionary** (dĭkʹshə-nĕrʹē)

tip·py (tĭp′ē) *adj.* **-pi·er, -pi·est.** Likely to tip or tilt: *a tippy racing shell; a tippy card table.*

tip·staff (tĭp′stăf′) *n., pl.* **-staves** (-stāvz′, -stăvz′) or **-staffs. 1.** A staff with a metal tip, carried as a sign of office. **2.** An officer, such as a bailiff or constable, who carries a tipstaff. [Alteration of *tipped staff.*]

tip·ster (tĭp′stər) *n. Informal.* One who sells tips or information, as to bettors or speculators.

tip·sy (tĭp′sē) *adj.* **-si·er, -si·est. 1.** Slightly intoxicated. **2.** Unsteady or crooked. [From TIP[2].] **—tip′si·ly** *adv.* **—tip′si·ness** *n.*

tip·toe (tĭp′tō′) *intr.v.* **-toed, -toe·ing, -toes.** To walk or move quietly on one's toes. **—tiptoe** *n.* The tip of a toe. **—tiptoe** *adj.* **1.** Standing or walking on one's toes. **2.** Stealthy; wary. **—tiptoe** *adv.* **1.** On one's toes. **2.** Stealthily; warily. ***—idiom.*** **on tiptoe.** Full of anticipation; eager: *The children were on tiptoe before the birthday party.*

tip·top (tĭp′tŏp′) *n.* **1.** The highest point; the summit. **2.** The highest degree of quality or excellence. **—tiptop** *adj.* Excellent; first-rate: *an athlete in tiptop condition.* **—tiptop** *adv.* Very well; excellently.

Ti·pu Sa·hib (tē′po͞o sä′ĭb, -ēb, -hĭb) or **Tip·poo Sahib** (tĭp′o͞o). 1750?–1799. Sultan of Mysore (1782–1799) who resisted the increasing British military influence in his domain.

ti·rade (tī′răd′, tī-răd′) *n.* A long angry or violent speech, usually of a censorious or denunciatory nature; a diatribe. [French, from Old French, act of firing, from *tirer,* to draw out, endure, probably back-formation from *martirant,* present participle of *martirer,* to torture (influenced by *mar,* to one's misfortune, and *tiranz,* executioner, tyrant), from *martir,* martyr, from Late Latin *martyr.* See MARTYR.]

Ti·ran (tə-rän′). A strait off the southern tip of the Sinai Peninsula in northeast Egypt connecting the Red Sea with the Gulf of Aqaba.

Ti·ra·në also **Ti·ra·na** (tə-rä′nə, tē-). The capital of Albania, in the west-central part of the country. An industrial center and the country's largest city, Tiranë became capital of Albania in 1920. Population, 206,100.

Ti·ras·pol (tə-räs′pəl). A city of southwest Moldavia on the Dniester River east of Kishinev. Founded c. 1792 as a Russian fortress on the site of a Moldavian settlement, it is an agricultural processing center. Population, 162,000.

tire¹ (tīr) *v.* **tired, tir·ing, tires.** *—intr.* **1.** To grow weary. **2.** To grow bored or impatient. *—tr.* **1.** To diminish the strength or energy of; fatigue. **2.** To exhaust the interest or patience of; bore. [Middle English *tiren,* from Old English *tēorian, tyrian.* See **deu-¹** in Appendix.]

SYNONYMS: *tire, weary, fatigue, exhaust, jade.* These verbs mean to cause or undergo depletion of strength, energy, spirit, interest, or patience. *Tire* is the general, nonspecific term; it often suggests a state resulting from exertion, excess, dullness, or ennui: *Long hours of arduous hiking tired the scouts. "When a man is tired of London, he is tired of life"* (Samuel Johnson). *Weary,* like *tire,* is applicable to diminution of strength or endurance but often carries a stronger implication of dissatisfaction, as that resulting from what is irksome or boring: *found the journey wearying; soon wearied of their constant bickering. Fatigue* implies great weariness, as that caused by stress: *fatigued by the day's labors; "nothing so fatiguing as the eternal hanging on of an uncompleted task"* (William James). To *exhaust* is to wear out completely; the term connotes total draining of physical or emotional strength: *"Like all people who try to exhaust a subject, he exhausted his listeners"* (Oscar Wilde). *Jade* refers principally to dullness that most often results from overindulgence: *Even an exquisitely prepared dinner couldn't revive her jaded palate.*

tit¹
Blue tit
Parus caeruleus

tire² (tīr) *n.* **1.** A covering for a wheel, usually made of rubber reinforced with cords of nylon, fiberglass, or other material and filled with compressed air. **2.** A hoop of metal or rubber fitted around a wheel. [Middle English, iron rim of a wheel, probably from *tir,* attire, short for *atire,* from *attiren,* to attire. See ATTIRE.]

tire³ (tīr) *Archaic. tr.v.* **tired, tir·ing, tires.** To adorn or attire. **—tire** *n.* **1.** Attire. **2.** A headband or headdress. [Middle English *tiren,* short for *attiren,* to attire. See ATTIRE.]

tired (tīrd) *adj.* **1.a.** Exhausted of strength or energy; fatigued. **b.** Impatient; bored: *tired of the same old sandwiches.* **2.** Overused; hackneyed: *a tired joke.* **—tired′ly** *adv.* **—tired′ness** *n.*

tire·less (tīr′lĭs) *adj.* Not yielding to fatigue; untiring or indefatigable. **—tire′less·ly** *adv.* **—tire′less·ness** *n.*

SYNONYMS: *tireless, indefatigable, unflagging, untiring, unwearied, weariless.* The central meaning shared by these adjectives is "having or showing a capacity for prolonged and laborious effort": *a tireless worker; an indefatigable advocate of equal rights; unflagging pursuit of excellence; untiring energy; an unwearied researcher; a weariless defender of freedom of the press.*

tire·some (tīr′səm) *adj.* Causing fatigue or boredom; wearisome. See Synonyms at **boring. —tire′some·ly** *adv.* **—tire′some·ness** *n.*

Tîr·gu-Mu·reş (tîr′go͞o-mo͝or′ĕsh). A city of north-central Romania east-southeast of Cluj. It was ceded to Romania by Hungary in 1918. Population, 154,506.

Ti·rich Mir (tîr′ĭch mîr′). A mountain, 7,695.2 m (25,230 ft) high, of the Hindu Kush in northern Pakistan. It is the highest elevation in the range.

ti·ro (tī′rō) *n.* Variant of **tyro.**

Ti·rol (tə-rōl′, tī-, tī′rōl′). See **Tyrol.**

Tir·pitz (tûr′pĭts, tîr′-), **Alfred von.** 1849–1930. German admiral who organized the German navy of World War I.

Tir·so de Mo·li·na (tîr′sō dā mə-lē′nə, thĕ mô-lē′nä). Pen name of Gabriel Téllez. 1584?–1648. Spanish playwright whose popular works include *The Seducer of Seville* (1630), which introduced the character Don Juan.

Ti·ruch·chi·rap·pal·li (tîr′ə-chə-rä′pə-lē). A city of southeast India south-southwest of the Madras River. It is the site of a famous shrine to the Hindu god Shiva. Population, 362,045.

Tir·yns (tîr′ĭnz, tī′rĭnz). An ancient city of southern Greece in the eastern Peloponnesus. It contains the ruins of pre-Homeric palaces as well as prehistoric structures.

'tis (tĭz). It is.

Ti·sa (tē′sə). See **Tisza.**

ti·sane (tĭ-zăn′, -zän′) *n.* A herbal infusion or similar preparation drunk as a beverage or for its mildly medicinal effect. [*tisan,* barley water, from Old French *tisane,* from Latin *ptisana.* See PTISAN.]

Tish·ri (tĭsh′rē, -rā) *n.* The first month of the year in the Jewish calendar. See table at **calendar.** [Hebrew *tišri,* from Akkadian *tašrītu,* the month Tashritu (September/October).]

Ti·siph·o·ne (tĭ-sĭf′ə-nē) *n. Greek & Roman Mythology.* One of the three Furies.

tis·sue (tĭsh′o͞o) *n.* **1.** A fine, very thin fabric, such as gauze. **2.** Tissue paper. **3.** A soft, absorbent piece of paper used as toilet paper, a handkerchief, or a towel. **4.** An interwoven or interrelated number of things; a web; a network: *"The text is a tissue of mocking echoes"* (Richard M. Kain). **5.** *Biology.* An aggregation of morphologically similar cells and associated intercellular matter acting together to perform one or more specific functions in the body. There are four basic types of tissue: muscle, nerve, epidermal, and connective. [Middle English *tissu,* a rich kind of cloth, from Old French, from past participle of *tistre,* to weave, from Latin *texere.* See **teks-** in Appendix.] **—tis′su·ey** *adj.* **—tis′su·lar** *adj.*

tissue culture *n.* **1.** The technique or process of keeping tissue alive and growing in a culture medium. **2.** A culture of tissue grown by this technique or process.

tissue paper *n.* Thin, translucent paper used for packing, wrapping, or protecting delicate articles.

tissue plasminogen activator *n. Abbr.* **TPA, tPA** An enzyme that converts plasminogen to plasmin, used to dissolve blood clots rapidly and selectively, especially in the treatment of heart attacks.

Ti·sza (tĭs′ô) also **Ti·sa** (tē′sə). A river of central Europe rising in the Carpathian Mountains in the western Ukraine and flowing about 965 km (600 mi) generally southward across eastern Hungary and northern Yugoslavia to the Danube River.

♦tit¹ (tĭt) *n.* **1.** A titmouse. **2.** Any of various small, similar or related birds. **—tit** *adj. New England & Upstate New York.* Small; undersized. [Short for TITMOUSE. Adj., Middle English *tit-,* as in *titmose,* titmouse. See TITMOUSE.]

♦REGIONAL NOTE: *Tit* is an old Germanic word for "small" and is used in various northern European languages to refer to small objects, animals, or people, especially girls—for example, *titta* is a Norwegian dialect word for "little girl." The word is most common in American English in combinations that denote various small birds, such as the *titmouse* or *tomtit.* A *titman* in the 19th century could mean a small or stunted person, as Henry David Thoreau indicates when he calls his generation "a race of titmen." *Tit* and *titman* are still used in New England, mostly by farmers to refer to the runt of a litter of pigs.

tit² (tĭt) *n.* **1.** *Vulgar Slang.* A woman's breast. **2.** A teat. [Middle English, from Old English *titt.*]

tit. *abbr.* Title.

Tit. *abbr. Bible.* Titus.

Ti·tan (tīt′n) *n.* **1.** *Greek Mythology.* One of a family of giants, the children of Uranus and Gaea, who sought to rule heaven and were overthrown and supplanted by the family of Zeus. **2. titan.** A person of colossal size, strength, or achievement: *a titan of American industry.* **3.** The largest satellite of Saturn and the 14th in distance from the planet. It is the second largest satellite in the solar system. [Middle English, Helios, from Latin *Tītān,* from Greek *Titan.*]

ti·tan·ate (tīt′n-āt′) *n.* A salt or an ester of titanic acid.

Ti·tan·ess (tīt′n-ĭs) *n. Greek Mythology.* One of the daughters of Gaea and Uranus who sought to rule heaven and were overthrown and supplanted by Zeus.

Ti·ta·ni·a (tĭ-tā′nē-ə, -tān′yə, tī-) *n.* **1.** The queen of the fairies and wife of Oberon in medieval folklore. **2.** The satellite of Uranus that is fourth in distance from the planet. [From Latin *Tītānia,* the goddess Diana, sister to the sun, from feminine of *Tītānius,* of the Titans, from *Tītān,* Titan. See TITAN.]

ti·tan·ic¹ (tī-tăn′ĭk) *adj.* **1. Titanic.** Of or relating to the Titans. **2.a.** Having great stature or enormous strength; huge or colossal: *titanic creatures of the deep.* **b.** Of enormous scope, power, or influence: *"a deepening sense that some titanic event lay just beyond the horizon"* (W. Bruce Lincoln). **—ti·tan′i·cal·ly** *adv.*

ti·tan·ic[2] (tī-tăn′ĭk, -tā′nĭk, tĭ-) *adj.* Relating to or containing titanium, especially with valence 4.

titanic acid (tī-tăn′ĭk, -tā′nĭk, tĭ-) *n.* A powdered white inorganic acid, H_2TiO_3, derived from an acid solution of titanates and used as a mordant.

ti·tan·if·er·ous (tīt′n-ĭf′ər-əs) *adj.* Containing or yielding titanium.

Ti·tan·ism (tīt′n-ĭz′əm) *n.* The spirit of revolt against an established order; rebelliousness.

ti·tan·ite (tīt′n-īt′) *n.* See **sphene.**

ti·ta·ni·um (tī-tā′nē-əm, tĭ-) *n. Symbol* **Ti** A strong, low-density, highly corrosion-resistant, lustrous white metallic element that occurs widely in igneous rocks and is used to alloy aircraft metals for low weight, strength, and high-temperature stability. Atomic number 22; atomic weight 47.90; melting point 1,660°C; boiling point 3,287°C; specific gravity 4.54; valence 2, 3, 4. See table at **element.** [From Latin *Tītān,* Titan. See TITAN.]

titanium dioxide *n.* A white powder, TiO_2, used as an exceptionally opaque white pigment.

titanium white *n.* A durable white paint pigment consisting of titanium dioxide.

ti·tan·o·saur (tī-tăn′ə-sôr′, tīt′n-) *n.* Any of various plant-eating, amphibious sauropod dinosaurs of the genus *Titanosaurus,* common during the Cretaceous Period especially in South America. [New Latin *Titanosaurus,* genus name : Greek *Titan,* Titan + *saurus,* lizard; see SAURIAN.]

ti·tan·o·there (tī-tăn′ə-thîr′) *n.* Any of various extinct herbivorous hoofed mammals of the genus *Brontotherium* and related genera, of the Eocene and Oligocene epochs, resembling the rhinoceros. [New Latin *Titanotherium,* genus name : Greek *Titan,* Titan + Greek *thērion,* diminutive of *thēr,* wild beast; see THEROPOD.]

ti·tan·ous (tī-tăn′əs, -tā′nəs, tĭ-) *adj.* Relating to or containing titanium, especially with valence 3.

tit·bit (tĭt′bĭt′) *n.* Variant of **tidbit.**

ti·ter also **ti·tre** (tī′tər) *n.* **1.** Concentration of a substance in solution or the strength of such a substance determined by titration. **2.** The minimum volume needed to cause a particular result in titration. [French *titre,* from Old French *title,* title. See TITLE.]

tit for tat *n.* Repayment in kind, as for an injury; retaliation. [Probably alteration of *tip for tap.*]

tithe (tīth) *n.* **1.a.** A tenth part of one's annual income contributed voluntarily or due as a tax, especially for the support of the clergy or church. **b.** The institution or obligation of paying tithes. **2.** A tax or an assessment of one tenth. **3.a.** A tenth part. **b.** A very small part. **—tithe** *v.* **tithed, tith·ing, tithes.** *—tr.* **1.** To contribute or pay a tenth part of (one's annual income). **2.** To levy a tithe on. *—intr.* To pay a tithe. [Middle English, from Old English *tēotha.* See TENTH.] **—tith′a·ble** (tī′thə-bəl) *adj.* **—tith′er** *n.*

tith·ing (tī′thĭng) *n.* An administrative division consisting of ten householders in the old English system of frankpledge.

ti·ti[1] (tī′tī′, tē′tē′) *n., pl.* **-tis. 1.** A New World shrub or small tree *(Cyrilla racemiflora)* of warm swampy areas, having leathery leaves, yellow fruit, and white flowers in clustered racemes that are borne at the tip of the preceding season's growth. Also called *leatherwood.* **2.** An evergreen shrub or small tree *(Cliftonia monophylla)* of the southeast United States, having glossy leathery leaves, white to pinkish flowers clustered in racemes, and winged fruit. [Origin unknown.]

ti·ti[2] (tē-tē′) *n., pl.* **-tis.** Any of various small, long-tailed, arboreal monkeys of the genus *Callicebus,* living in tropical regions of South America. [Spanish *tití,* from Aymara *titi.*]

ti·tian (tĭsh′ən) *n. Color.* A brownish orange. [After TITIAN (from his frequent use of the color in his paintings).] **—ti′tian** *adj.*

Ti·tian (tĭsh′ən). Originally Tiziano Vecellio. 1488?–1576. Italian painter who introduced vigorous colors and the compositional use of backgrounds to the Venetian school. His works include the altarpiece *The Assumption of the Virgin* (1518). **—Ti′tian·esque′** *adj.*

Ti·ti·ca·ca (tĭt′ĭ-kä′kə, tē′tē-kä′kä), **Lake.** A freshwater lake of South America in the Andes on the Bolivia-Peru border.

tit·il·late (tĭt′l-āt′) *v.* **-lat·ed, -lat·ing, -lates.** *—tr.* **1.** To stimulate by touching lightly; tickle. **2.** To excite (another) pleasurably, superficially or erotically. *—intr.* To excite another, especially in a superficial, pleasurable manner: *"Once you decide to titillate instead of illuminate . . . you create a climate of expectation that requires a higher and higher level of intensity"* (Bill Moyers). [Latin *tītillāre, tītillāt-,* to tickle.] **—tit′il·lat′er** *n.* **—tit′il·lat′ing·ly** *adv.* **—tit′il·la′tion** *n.* **—tit′il·la′tive** *adj.*

tit·i·vate (tĭt′ə-vāt′) *tr.v.* **-vat·ed, -vat·ing, -vates.** To make decorative additions to; spruce up. [Alteration of earlier *tidivate* : perhaps TIDY + (ELE)VATE.] **—tit′i·va′tion** *n.*

tit·lark (tĭt′lärk′) *n.* See **pipit.** [*tit-,* as in TIT(MOUSE) + LARK[1].]

ti·tle (tīt′l) *n. Abbr.* **tit. 1.** An identifying name given to a book, play, film, musical composition, or other work. See Synonyms at **name. 2.** A general or descriptive heading, as of a book chapter. **3.a.** Often **titles.** Written material to be read by viewers that is included in a film or television show, typically presenting credits, narration, or dialogue. **b.** A written piece of translated dialogue superimposed at the bottom of the frame during a film; a subtitle. **4.** *Law.* A heading that names a document, statute, or proceeding. **5.** A division of a law book, declaration, or bill, generally larger than a section or article. **6.** A written work that is published or about to be published: *the titles in a press's fall catalog.* **7.** *Law.* **a.** The coincidence of all the elements that constitute the fullest legal right to control and dispose of property or a claim. **b.** The aggregate evidence that gives rise to a legal right of possession or control. **c.** The instrument, such as a deed, that constitutes this evidence. **8.a.** Something that provides a basis for or justifies a claim. **b.** A legitimate or alleged right. See Synonyms at **claim. 9.** A formal appellation attached to the name of a person or family by virtue of office, rank, hereditary privilege, noble birth, or attainment or used as a mark of respect. **10.** A descriptive name; an epithet. **11.** *Sports.* A championship. **12.** *Ecclesiastical.* **a.** A source of income or area of work required of a candidate for ordination in the Church of England. **b.** A Roman Catholic church in or near Rome having a cardinal for its nominal head. **—title** *tr.v.* **-tled, -tling, -tles. 1.** To give a title to; entitle. **2.** To call by a name; style. [Middle English, from Old English *titul,* superscription, and from Old French *title,* title, both from Latin *titulus.*]

Titian
c. 1550 self-portrait

ti·tled (tīt′ld) *adj.* Having a title, especially a noble title.

ti·tle·hold·er (tīt′l-hōl′dər) *n.* **1.** One, especially a champion, who holds a title. **2.** One that holds legal title to something, such as a motor vehicle.

title page *n. Abbr.* **t.p.** *Printing.* A page at the front of a book giving the complete title, the names of the author and publisher, and the place of publication.

ti·tlist (tīt′lĭst, -l-ĭst) *n.* The holder of a competitive title; a champion: *a chess titlist.*

♦ **tit·man** (tĭt′mən) *n. New England & Upstate New York.* **1.** A runt, especially one of a litter of pigs. **2.** A small person. See Regional Note at **tit**[1]. [TIT[1] + MAN.]

♦ **tit·mouse** (tĭt′mous′) *n., pl.* **-mice** (-mīs′). Any of numerous small insect-eating passerine birds of the family Paridae, found in woodland areas throughout the world and including especially members of the genus *Parus,* such as the chickadee. See Regional Note at **tit**[1]. [Alteration (influenced by *mous,* mouse) of Middle English *titmose* : *tit- (probably from Old Norse *tittr,* titmouse) + *mose,* titmouse (from Old English *māse,* titmouse).]

Ti·to (tē′tō), Marshal. Originally Josip Broz. 1892–1980. Yugoslavian politician who led the resistance to Nazi occupation during World War II, established independence from the U.S.S.R. (1948), and as president (1953–1980) pursued a national Communism that stressed neutrality in foreign affairs.

Ti·to·grad (tē′tō-grăd′, -gräd′). A city of southern Yugoslavia south-southwest of Belgrade near the Albanian border. It is a commercial center. Population, 73,000.

Ti·to·ism (tē′tō-ĭz′əm) *n.* The post-World War II Communist policies and practices associated with Marshal Tito, especially the assertion by a Communist nation of its interests independently of or in opposition to the Soviet Union.

Tito
Photographed in 1962

ti·trant (tī′trənt) *n.* A substance, such as a solution, of known concentration used in titration.

ti·trate (tī′trāt′) *tr. & intr.v.* **-trat·ed, -trat·ing, -trates.** To determine the concentration of (a solution) by titration or perform the operation of titration. [From French *titrer,* from *titre,* titer. See TITER.] **—ti′trat′a·ble** *adj.* **—ti′tra′tor** *n.*

ti·tra·tion (tī-trā′shən) *n.* The process, operation, or method of determining the concentration of a substance in solution by adding to it a standard reagent of known concentration in carefully measured amounts until a reaction of definite and known proportion is completed, as shown by a color change or by electrical measurement, and then calculating the unknown concentration.

ti·tre (tī′tər) *n.* Variant of **titer.**

ti·tri·met·ric (tī′trə-mĕt′rĭk) *adj.* Of or relating to measurement by titration. [TITR(ATION) + -METRIC.] **—ti′tri·met′ri·cal·ly** *adv.*

tit·ter (tĭt′ər) *intr.v.* **-tered, -ter·ing, -ters.** To laugh in a restrained, nervous way; giggle. **—titter** *n.* A nervous giggle. [Probably imitative.] **—tit′ter·er** *n.* **—tit′ter·ing·ly** *adv.*

tit·tle (tĭt′l) *n.* **1.** *Linguistics.* A small diacritic mark, such as an accent, a vowel mark, or a dot over an *i.* **2.** The tiniest bit; an iota. [Middle English *titil,* from Medieval Latin *titulus,* diacritical mark, from Latin, title, superscription.]

tit·tle-tat·tle (tĭt′l-tăt′l) *n.* Petty gossip; trivial talk. **—tittle-tattle** *intr.v.* **-tled, -tling, -tles.** To talk idly or foolishly; gossip. [Reduplication of TATTLE.]

tit·tup (tĭt′əp) *intr.v.* **-tuped, -tup·ing, -tups** or **-tupped, -tup·ping, -tups.** To move in a lively, capering manner; prance. **—tittup** *n.* A lively, capering manner of moving or walking; a prance. [Perhaps imitative of the sound of a horse's hoofs.]

tit·u·ba·tion (tĭch′ə-bā′shən) *n.* The staggering or stumbling gait characteristic of certain nervous disorders. [Latin *titubātiō, titubātiōn-,* a staggering, from *titubātus,* past participle of *titubāre,* to stagger.]

tit·u·lar (tĭch′ə-lər) *adj.* **1.** Relating to, having the nature of, or constituting a title. **2.a.** Existing in name only; nominal: *the titular head of the family.* **b.** Bearing the title of a church or

ă pat	oi boy
ā pay	ou out
âr care	ŏŏ took
ä father	ōō boot
ĕ pet	ŭ cut
ē be	ûr urge
ĭ pit	th thin
ī pie	*th* this
îr pier	hw which
ŏ pot	zh vision
ō toe	ə about, item
ô paw	♦ regionalism

Stress marks: **′** (primary); ′ (secondary), as in **dictionary** (dĭk′shə-nĕr′ē)

monastery that is no longer active. **1.** Bearing a title: *titular dignitaries.* **2.** Derived from a title: *the titular role in a play.* **—titular** *n.* One who holds a title. [From Latin *titulus,* title.]

tit·u·lar·y (tĭch′ə-lĕr′ē) *n., pl.* **-ies.** A titleholder; a titular.

Ti·tus[1] (tī′təs). A.D. 39–81. Emperor of Rome (79–81) whose reign was marked by the capture of Jerusalem (70) and by the construction of the Roman Colosseum.

Ti·tus[2] (tī′təs) *n. Abbr.* **Tit., Tt** *Bible.* See table at **Bible.**

Titus, Saint. First century A.D. Christian leader and companion of Saint Paul. An epistle of the New Testament, ascribed to Paul, is addressed to him.

toad
Woodhouse's toad
Bufo woodhousei

Ti·tus·ville (tī′təs-vĭl′). **1.** A city of eastern Florida east of Orlando. Incorporated in 1886, it is a commercial and residential center. Population, 31,910. **2.** A city of northwest Pennsylvania north-northeast of Pittsburgh. The first oil well in the United States was drilled here in April 1859. Population, 6,884.

Ti·u (tē′o͞o) *n. Mythology.* The Germanic god of war and the sky. [Old English *Tīw.* See **deiw-** in Appendix.]

Ti·vo·li (tĭv′ə-lē, tē′vô-lē) also **Ti·bur** (tī′bər). A city of central Italy east-northeast of Rome. Tivoli contains the ruins of several ancient Roman villas and is also noted for its waterfalls. Population, 50,969.

Ti·wa (tē′wə) *n., pl.* **Tiwa** or **-was. 1.a.** A group of Pueblo peoples of northern New Mexico. **b.** A member of any of these peoples. **2.** The group of Tanoan languages spoken by the Tiwa.

tiz·zy (tĭz′ē) *n., pl.* **-zies.** *Slang.* A state of nervous excitement or confusion; a dither. [Origin unknown.]

tk. *abbr.* Truck.

TKO (tē′kā-ō′) *abbr. Sports.* A technical knockout.

tkt. *abbr.* Ticket.

Tl The symbol for the element **thallium.**

t.l. or **t/l** *abbr.* Total loss.

Tlal·ne·pan·tla (tläl′nə-pänt′lä, -nĕ-). A city of south-central Mexico north of Mexico City. It is a communications and industrial center. Population, 778,173.

TLC *abbr.* Tender loving care.

Tlin·git (tlĭng′gĭt, tlĭng′ĭt) *n., pl.* **Tlingit** or **-gits. 1.a.** A Native American people inhabiting the coastal and island areas of southeast Alaska. **b.** A member of this people. **2.** The language of the Tlingit.

t.l.o. *abbr.* Total loss only.

tlr. *abbr.* Tailor.

T lymphocyte *n.* See **T cell.**

Tm[1] The symbol for the element **thulium.**

Tm[2] *abbr. Bible.* Timothy.

TM *abbr.* Trademark.

t.m. *abbr. Mathematics.* True mean.

T.M. *abbr.* Transcendental meditation.

T-maze (tē′māz′) *n. Psychology.* An experimental maze in the shape of a T, one arm of which leads to the correct path, while the other is without an exit.

tme·sis (tmē′sĭs, mē′-) *n., pl.* **-ses** (-sēz). Separation of the parts of a compound word by one or more intervening words; for example, *where I go ever* instead of *wherever I go.* [Late Latin *tmēsis,* from Greek, a cutting, from *temnein,* to cut. See **tem-** in Appendix.]

TMJ *abbr.* Temporomandibular joint.

TMJ syndrome *n.* Temporomandibular joint syndrome.

TN *abbr.* Tennessee.

tn. *abbr.* **1.** Ton. **2.** Town. **3.** Train.

tng. *abbr.* Training.

tnpk. *abbr.* Turnpike.

TNT (tē′ĕn-tē′) *n.* A yellow crystalline compound, $CH_3C_6H_2(NO_2)_3$, used mainly as a high explosive. [*t(ri)n(itro)t(oluene).*]

to (to͞o; tə *when unstressed*) *prep.* **1.a.** In a direction toward so as to reach: *went to the city.* **b.** Towards: *turned to me.* **2.a.** Reaching as far as: *The ocean water was clear all the way to the bottom.* **b.** To the extent or degree of: *loved him to distraction.* **c.** With the resultant condition of: *nursed her back to health.* **3.** Toward a given state: *helping minority women to economic equality.* **4.** In contact with; against: *their faces pressed to the windows.* **5.** In front of: *stood face to face.* **6.** Used to indicate appropriation or possession: *looked for the top to the jar.* **7.** Concerning; regarding: *waiting for an answer to my letter.* **8.** In a particular relationship with: *The brook runs parallel to the road.* **9.** As an accompaniment or a complement of: *danced to the tune.* **10.** Composing; constituting: *two cups to a pint.* **11.** In accord with: *job responsibilities suited to her abilities.* **12.** As compared with: *a book superior to his others.* **13.a.** Before: *The time is ten to five.* **b.** Up till; until: *worked from nine to five.* **14.a.** For the purpose of: *went out to lunch.* **b.** In honor of: *a toast to the queen.* **15.a.** Used before a verb to indicate the infinitive: *I'd like to go.* **b.** Used alone when the infinitive is understood: *Go if you want to.* **16.a.** Used to indicate the relationship of a verb with its complement: *refer to a dictionary; refer me to a dictionary.* **b.** Used with a reflexive pronoun to indicate exclusivity or separateness: *had the plane to ourselves.* **—to** *adv.* **1.** In one direction; toward a person or thing: *owls with feathers wrong end to.* **2.** Into a shut or closed position: *pushed the door to.* **3.** Into a state of consciousness: *The patient came to.* **4.** Into a state of action or attentiveness: *sat down for lunch and fell to.* **5.** *Nautical.* Into the wind. [Middle English, from Old English *tō.* See **de-** in Appendix.]

t.o. *abbr.* Turnover.

toad (tōd) *n.* **1.** Any of numerous tailless amphibians chiefly of the family Bufonidae, related to and resembling the frogs but characteristically more terrestrial and having a broader body and rougher, drier skin. **2.** The horned toad. **3.** A person regarded as repulsive. [Middle English *tadde, tode,* from Old English *tādige.*]

toad·eat·er (tōd′ē′tər) *n.* A toady. [Originally referring to a charlatan's helper who ate (or pretended to eat) poisonous toads so that his employer could display his prowess in expelling the poison.]

toad·fish (tōd′fĭsh′) *n., pl.* **toadfish** or **-fish·es.** Any of various slow-moving, scaleless, sharp-toothed fishes of the family Batrachoididae, having a broad, flattened head and a wide mouth, found in tropical and temperate waters.

toad·flax (tōd′flăks′) *n.* **1.** Any of various plants of the genus *Linaria,* having narrow leaves and spurred, two-lipped flowers. **2.** See **butter-and-eggs.**

toad·stone (tōd′stōn′) *n.* A stone once worn as a charm and believed to have been formed in the body of a toad.

toad·stool (tōd′sto͞ol′) *n.* An inedible or poisonous fungus with an umbrella-shaped fruiting body.

toad·y (tō′dē) *n., pl.* **-ies.** A person who flatters or defers to others for self-serving reasons; a sycophant. **—toady** *tr. & intr.v.* **-ied** (tō′dēd), **-y·ing, -ies** (tō′dēz). To be a toady to or behave like a toady. See Synonyms at **fawn**[1]. [From TOAD.]

WORD HISTORY: A toady is not a pleasant individual, and the origin of the word makes being a toady even less pleasant. *Toady* is obviously derived from the word *toad.* The *–y* suffix can have diminutive force, and the earliest recorded sense (around 1690) of *toady* (now obsolete), "a little or young toad," illustrates this force. The sense we know has nothing to do with baby toads but rather with the practice of certain quacks or charlatans who claimed that they could cast out poison. Toads were thought to be poisonous, so these charlatans would have an attendant eat a toad or pretend to eat one and then remove the poison from the attendant. Such an attendant is obviously a type of person who would do anything, and thus *toadeater* (first recorded 1629) was the perfect name for a flattering, fawning parasite. *Toadeater* and the verb derived from it, *toadeat,* influenced the sense of the noun and verb *toad* and the noun *toady,* so that both nouns could mean "sycophant" and the verb *toady* could mean "to act like a toady to someone."

to and fro *adv.* Back and forth.

to-and-fro (to͞o′ən-frō′) *n.* **1.** Movement back and forth; reciprocating movement. **2.** Debate over an issue; vacillation. **—to′-and-fro′** *adj.*

toast[1] (tōst) *v.* **toast·ed, toast·ing, toasts.** —*tr.* **1.** To heat and brown (bread, for example) by placing in a toaster or an oven or close to a fire. **2.** To warm thoroughly, as before a fire: *toast one's feet.* —*intr.* To become toasted: *This bread toasts well.* **—toast** *n.* Sliced bread heated and browned. [Middle English *tosten,* from Old French *toster,* from Vulgar Latin **tostāre,* frequentative of Latin *torrēre,* to parch, burn. See **ters-** in Appendix.]

toast[2] (tōst) *n.* **1.a.** The act of raising a glass and drinking in honor of or to the health of a person or thing. **b.** A proposal to drink to someone or something or a speech given before the taking of such a drink. **c.** The one honored by a toast. **2.** A person receiving much attention or acclaim: *the toast of Broadway.* **—toast** *v.* **toast·ed, toast·ing, toasts.** —*tr.* To drink to the health or honor of. —*intr.* To propose or drink a toast. [Perhaps from TOAST[1], from the use of spiced toast to flavor drinks.]

toast·er (tō′stər) *n.* A mechanical device used to toast bread, especially by exposure to electrically heated wire coils.

toast·mas·ter (tōst′măs′tər) *n.* A man who proposes the toasts and introduces the speakers at a banquet.

toast·mis·tress (tōst′mĭs′trĭs) *n.* A woman who proposes the toasts and introduces the speakers at a banquet.

toast·y (tō′stē) *adj.* **-i·er, -i·est.** Pleasantly warm.

to·bac·co (tə-băk′ō) *n., pl.* **-cos** or **-coes. 1.** Any of various plants of the genus *Nicotiana,* especially *N. tabacum,* native to tropical America and widely cultivated for its leaves, which are used primarily for smoking. **2.** The leaves of this plant, dried and processed chiefly for use in cigarettes, cigars, or snuff or for smoking in pipes. **3.** Products made from these plants. **4.** The habit of smoking tobacco: *I gave up tobacco.* **5.** A crop of tobacco. —*attributive.* Often used to modify another noun: *tobacco products; tobacco fields.* [Spanish *tabaco,* possibly of Caribbean origin or perhaps from Arabic *ṭabbāq,* name of various medicinal herbs.]

tobacco budworm *n.* The destructive larva of a noctuid moth *(Heliothis virescens)* that feeds on tobacco plants in the southern United States and cotton plants in Peru.

tobacco heart *n.* A rapid, irregular heart rate resulting from excessive use of tobacco.

tobacco hornworm *n.* The destructive larva of a hawk moth *(Manduca sexta)* of the southern United States and the West Indies that feeds on the leaves of tobacco plants. Also called *tobacco worm.*

tobacco mosaic *n.* Any of several diseases of tobacco and nightshade caused by the tobacco mosaic virus and characterized by mottled leaves.

tobacco mosaic virus *n.* A retrovirus that causes mosaic in tobacco and some other plants, widely used in the study of viruses and viral diseases.

to·bac·co·nist (tə-băk′ə-nĭst) *n.* A dealer in tobacco and smoking supplies.

tobacco road *n.* A poverty-stricken rural community. [After *Tobacco Road,* a novel by Erskine Caldwell.]

tobacco worm *n.* See **tobacco hornworm.**

To·ba·go (tə-bā′gō). An island of Trinidad and Tobago in the southeast West Indies northeast of Trinidad. First visited by Columbus in 1498, it became a British colony in 1899 and gained independence with Trinidad in 1962.

to-be (to͝o-bē′) *adj.* That is to be; future. Often used postpositively and in combination: *a graduate-to-be.*

To·bey (tō′bē), **Mark.** 1890–1976. American painter whose distinctive abstract style was inspired by Oriental calligraphy.

To·bit (tō′bĭt) *n. Bible.* **1.** In the Old Testament, a Hebrew captive in Nineveh. **2.** *Abbr.* **Tb** See table at **Bible.** [Greek *Tōbit,* from Hebrew *Ṭôbîyāh : ṭôb,* good + *yāh,* God.]

to·bog·gan (tə-bŏg′ən) *n.* A long, narrow, runnerless sled constructed of thin boards curled upward at the front end. **—toboggan** *intr.v.* **-ganed, -gan·ing, -gans. 1.** To coast, ride, or travel on a toboggan. **2.** *Slang.* To decline or fall rapidly: *His good fortune has tobogganed.* [Canadian French *tobagan,* from Micmac *topaghan.*] **—to·bog′gan·er, to·bog′gan·ist** *n.*

To·bol (tə-bôl′). A river of north-central Kazakhstan and west-central Russia rising in the southeast foothills of the Ural Mountains and flowing about 1,690 km (1,050 mi) northeastward to the Irtysh River.

to·by also **To·by** (tō′bē) *n., pl.* **-bies.** A drinking mug, usually in the shape of a stout man wearing a large three-cornered hat. [After *Toby,* a nickname for *Tobias.*]

To·can·tins (tō′kän-tēns′). A river, about 2,639 km (1,640 mi) long, flowing from central Brazil near Brasília northward to the Pará River southwest of Belém.

toc·ca·ta (tə-kä′tə) *n. Music.* A composition, usually for the organ or another keyboard instrument, in free style with full chords and elaborate runs. [Italian, from feminine past participle of *toccare,* to touch, from Vulgar Latin **toccāre.*]

To·char·i·an also **To·khar·i·an** (tō-kâr′ē-ən, -kär′-, -kăr′-) *n.* **1.** A member of a people of possible European origin, living in Chinese Turkistan until about the tenth century. **2.** The language of this people, recorded in two dialects dating from the seventh century and forming its own branch within Indo-European. [From Latin *Tocharī,* the Tocharians, from Greek *Tokharoi.*]

to·col·o·gy also **to·kol·o·gy** (tō-kŏl′ə-jē) *n.* The science of childbirth; midwifery or obstetrics. [Greek *tokos,* childbirth; see **tek-** in Appendix + -LOGY.]

to·coph·er·ol (tō-kŏf′ə-rôl′, -rōl′, -rŏl′) *n.* Any of a group of closely related, fat-soluble alcohols that behave similar to vitamin E and are present in milk, lettuce, and wheat germ oil and certain other vegetable oils. [Greek *tokos,* offspring; see TOCOLOGY + Greek *pherein,* to carry; see **bher-**[1] in Appendix + -OL[1].]

Tocque·ville (tōk′vĭl, tŏk′-, tôk-vēl′), **Alexis Charles Henri Clérel de.** 1805–1859. French politician, traveler, and historian. After touring the United States (1831–1832), he wrote *Democracy in America* (1835), a study of American institutions.

toc·sin (tŏk′sĭn) *n.* **1.a.** An alarm sounded on a bell. See Synonyms at **alarm. b.** A bell used to sound an alarm. **2.** A warning; an omen. [French, alteration of *toquassen,* from Old French *touque-sain,* from Old Provençal *tocasenh : tocar,* to strike (from Vulgar Latin **toccāre*) + *senh,* bell (from Late Latin *signum,* from Latin, signal; see SIGN).]

tod (tŏd) *n. Chiefly British.* **1.** A unit of weight for wool, especially one equivalent to about 28 pounds (12.7 kilograms). **2.** A bushy clump, as of ivy. [Middle English *todde.*]

to·day (tə-dā′) *n.* The present day, time, or age: *"Today's shocks are tomorrow's conventions"* (Carolyn Heilbrun). **—today** *adv.* **1.** During or on the present day. **2.** During or at the present time. **—today** *adj.* Concerned with or relating to the present time: *today issues; the today generation.* [Middle English *to dai,* from Old English *tō dæge : tō,* to; see TO + *dæge,* dative of *dæg,* day; see **agh-** in Appendix.]

Todd (tŏd), Sir **Alexander Robertus.** Born 1907. British chemist. He won a 1957 Nobel Prize for his study of nucleic acids and nucleotide structures.

Todd, Thomas. 1765–1826. American jurist who served as an associate justice of the U.S. Supreme Court (1807–1826).

tod·dle (tŏd′l) *intr.v.* **-dled, -dling, -dles. 1.** To walk with short, unsteady steps. **2.** To walk leisurely; stroll. **—toddle** *n.* An unsteady gait. [Origin unknown.]

tod·dler (tŏd′lər) *n.* **1.** One who toddles, especially a young child learning to walk. **2.** A size of clothing for children between the ages of about one and three years.

tod·dy (tŏd′ē) *n., pl.* **-dies. 1.** A hot toddy. **2.a.** The sweet sap of several tropical Asian palm trees, especially palmyra and *Caryota urens,* used as a beverage. **b.** A liquor fermented from this sap. [Hindi *tāṛī,* sap of palm, from *tāṛ,* palm, from Sanskrit *tālaḥ,* perhaps of Dravidian origin.]

to-do (tə-do͞o′) *n., pl.* **-dos** (-do͞oz′). *Informal.* A commotion or stir.

to·dy (tō′dē) *n., pl.* **-dies.** Any of various small birds of the family Todidae, of the West Indies, related to the kingfisher and the motmot and having colorful, predominantly green plumage and a bright red throat. [Probably from French *todier,* from New Latin *Todus,* genus name, from Latin *todus,* a kind of small bird.]

toe (tō) *n.* **1.a.** One of the digits of a vertebrate. **b.** The forepart of a foot or hoof. **c.** The terminal segment of an invertebrate's limb. **2.** The part of a sock, shoe, or boot that covers the digits of the foot. **3.** *Sports.* The end of the head on a golf club. **4.** The part of a vertical shaft that turns in a bearing. **5.** The lowest part, as of an embankment or a dam. **—toe** *v.* **toed, toe·ing, toes.** *—tr.* **1.** To touch, kick, or reach with the toe. **2.** *Sports.* To drive (a golf ball) with the toe of the club. **3.a.** To drive (a nail or spike) at an oblique angle. **b.** To fasten or secure with obliquely driven nails or spikes. *—intr.* To stand, walk, move, or be formed with the toes pointed in a specified direction: *He toes out.* **—*idioms.* on (one's) toes.** Ready to act; alert. **step** (or **tread**) **on (someone's) toes.** To hurt, offend, or encroach on the feelings, actions, or province of. **toe the line** (or **mark**). **1.** To adhere to doctrines or rules conscientiously; conform. **2.** *Sports & Games.* To touch a mark or line with the toe or hands in readiness for the start of a race or competition. [Middle English, from Old English *tā.* See **deik-** in Appendix.]

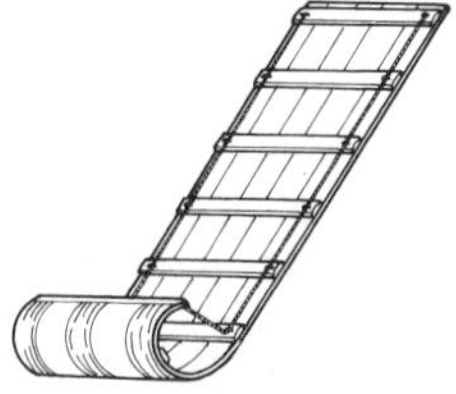

toboggan

toe·a (toi′ə) *n., pl.* **toea.** See table at **currency.** [Perhaps Pidgin English, from English DOLLAR.]

toe·cap (tō′kăp′) *n.* A reinforced covering of leather or metal for the toe of a shoe or boot.

toe crack *n.* A sand crack in the front part of a horse's hoof.

toed (tōd) *adj.* **1.** Having a toe, especially of a specified number or kind. Often used in combination: *an even-toed ungulate.* **2.a.** Driven obliquely: *a toed nail.* **b.** Secured by obliquely driven nails: *a toed beam.*

toe dance *n.* A dance that is performed on the toes, especially in ballet. **—toe dancer** *n.*

toe·hold (tō′hōld′) *n.* **1.** A small indentation or ledge on which the toe of a shoe can find support in climbing. **2.** A slight or initial yet significant advantage useful for future progress: *Family connections gave her a toehold in politics.* **3.** *Sports.* A wrestling hold in which one competitor wrenches the other's foot.

toe loop *n. Sports.* A jump in figure skating in which the skater, moving backwards, takes off from the back outer edge of one skate, makes a full spin in the air, and lands on the back outer edge of the same skate.

toe·nail (tō′nāl′) *n.* **1.** The thin, horny, transparent plate covering the upper surface of the end of a toe. **2.** A nail driven obliquely, as to join vertical and horizontal beams. **—toenail** *tr.v.* **-nailed, -nail·ing, -nails.** To secure (beams) with obliquely driven nails.

toby
c. 1780 Leeds creamware toby

toff (tŏf) *n. Chiefly British.* An elegantly dressed young man, often having exaggerated or affected manners: *"champagne, once a raffish drink suitable for toffs and weddings"* (Ian Jack). [Probably variant of TUFT, a gold tassel worn by titled students at Oxford and Cambridge.]

tof·fee (tô′fē, tŏf′ē) *n.* A hard, chewy candy made of brown sugar or molasses and butter. [Alteration of TAFFY.]

toft (tôft, tŏft) *n. Chiefly British.* **1.** A homestead. **2.** A hillock. [Middle English, from Old English, from Old Norse *topt.* See **dem-** in Appendix.]

to·fu (tō′fo͞o) *n.* A protein-rich food coagulated from an extract of soybeans and used in salads and cooked foods. [Japanese *tōfu,* from Chinese *dòufu : dòu,* bean + *fŭ,* fermented, curdled.]

tog (tŏg, tôg) *Informal. n.* **1. togs.** Clothes: *gardening togs.* **2.** A coat or cloak. **—tog** *tr.v.* **togged, tog·ging, togs.** To dress or clothe. [Short for obsolete *togeman,* from obsolete French *togue,* cloak, from Latin *toga,* garment. See TOGA.]

to·ga (tō′gə) *n.* **1.** A loose one-piece outer garment worn in public by male citizens in ancient Rome. **2.** A robe of office; a professional or ceremonial gown. [Latin. See **(s)teg-** in Appendix.] **—to′gaed** (tō′gəd) *adj.*

to·ga vi·ri·lis (tō′gə və-rē′lĭs, -rĭl′ĭs) *n.* **to·gae vi·ri·les** (tō′jē vĭ-rē′lēz, -rĭl′ēz, tō′gē, -gī). A white toga symbolizing manhood that boys of ancient Rome were allowed to wear at age 15. [Latin *toga virīlis : toga,* toga + *virīlis,* of a man.]

to·geth·er (tə-gĕth′ər) *adv.* **1.** In or into a single group, mass, or place: *We gather together.* **2.** In or into contact: *The cars crashed together. She mixed the chemicals together.* **3.a.** In association with or in relationship to one another; mutually or reciprocally: *getting along together.* **b.** By joint or cooperative effort: *We ironed the entire load of clothes together.* **4.** Regarded collectively; in total: *She is worth more than all of us together. Considered together, the proposals made little sense.* **5.** In or into a unified structure or arrangement: *put the food processor together.* **6.** Simultaneously: *The bells rang out together.* **7.** In harmony or accord: *We stand together on this issue.* **8.** *Informal.* Into an effective, coherent condition: *Get yourself together.* **—together** *adj. Slang.* **1.** Emotionally stable and effective in performance: *She's really together.* **2.** In tune with what is going on; hip. **—*idiom.* get** (or **put**) **it all together.** *Slang.* To unify and harmonize one's resources so as to perform with maximal

ă pat	oi boy
ā pay	ou out
âr care	o͝o took
ä father	o͞o boot
ĕ pet	ŭ cut
ē be	ûr urge
ĭ pit	th thin
ī pie	*th* this
îr pier	hw which
ŏ pot	zh vision
ō toe	ə about, item
ô paw	♦ regionalism

Stress marks: ′ (primary); ′ (secondary), as in **dictionary** (dĭk′shə-nĕr′ē)

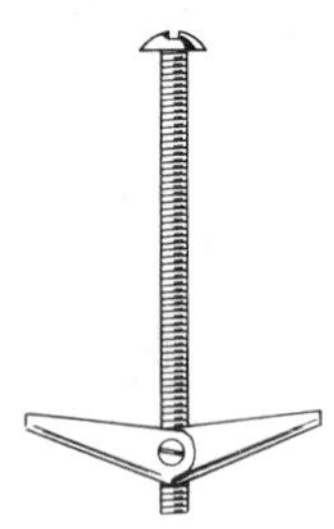

toggle bolt

Togo

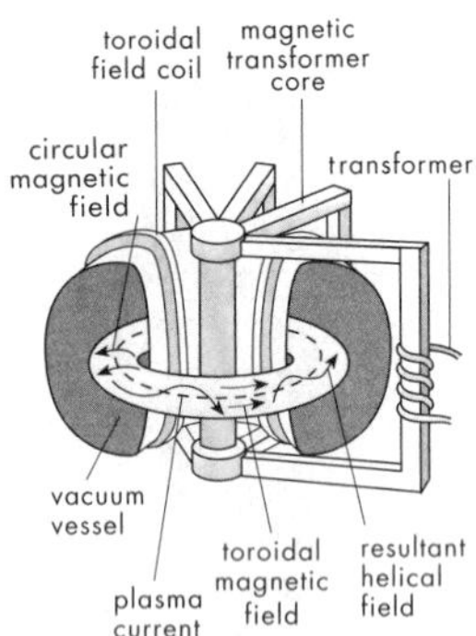

tokamak

tokonoma

effectiveness. [Middle English, from Old English *tōgædere.* See **ghedh-** in Appendix.] **—to·geth′er·ness** *n.*

USAGE NOTE: *Together with,* like *in addition to,* is often employed following the subject of a sentence or clause to introduce an addition. The addition, however, does not alter the number of the verb, which is governed by the subject: *The king* (singular), *together with two aides, is expected in an hour.* The same is true of *along with, besides,* and *in addition to.* See Usage Notes at **besides, like²**.

tog·ger·y (tŏg′ə-rē, tô′gə-) *n., pl.* **-ies. 1.** Clothing; togs. **2.** A clothing store.

tog·gle (tŏg′əl) *n.* **1.** A pin, rod, or crosspiece fitted or inserted into a loop in a rope, chain, or strap to prevent slipping, to tighten, or to hold an attached object. **2.** A device or an apparatus with a toggle joint. **—toggle** *v.* **-gled, -gling, -gles.** *—tr.* To furnish or fasten with a toggle. *—intr.* To alternate between two or more circuit configurations, usually by the operation of a single switch: *This printer lets you toggle between one font and another.* [Origin unknown.]

toggle bolt *n.* A fastener consisting of a threaded bolt and a spring-loaded toggle, used to secure objects to thin or hollow walls.

toggle joint *n.* A joint made of two arms attached by a pivot shaped like an elbow, allowing force to be exerted at the ends of the arms as the joint is expanded.

toggle switch *n.* A switch that uses a toggle joint with a spring to open or close an electric circuit as an attached lever is pushed through a small arc.

To·gliat·ti also **Tol·yat·ti** (tōl-yä′tē, tô-lyät′tē). A city of western Russia on the Volga River northwest of Kuibyshev. It is a manufacturing center. Population, 594,000.

To·go (tō′gō′). A country of western Africa on the Gulf of Guinea. It became a French colony in 1922 and gained independence in 1960. Lomé is the capital and the largest city. Population, 2,742,945.

togue (tōg) *n.* See **lake trout.** [Canadian French, from Micmac *atoghwaasu.*]

to·he·ro·a (tō′ə-rō′ə) *n., pl.* **toheroa** or **-ro·as.** A large edible marine clam *(Amphidesma ventricosum)* native to New Zealand. [Maori.]

To·ho·no O′o·dham (tō-hō′nō ō′ə-däm) *n., pl.* **Tohono O′odham** or **Tohono O′o·dhams.** See **Papago.**

toil¹ (toil) *intr.v.* **toiled, toil·ing, toils. 1.** To labor continuously; work strenuously. **2.** To proceed with difficulty: *toiling over the mountains.* **—toil** *n.* **1.** Exhausting labor or effort: *"A bit of the blackest and coarsest bread is . . . the sole recompense and the sole profit attaching to so arduous a toil"* (George Sand). See Synonyms at **work. 2.** *Archaic.* Strife; contention. [Middle English *toilen,* from Anglo-Norman *toiler,* to stir about, from Latin *tudiculāre,* from *tudicula,* a machine for bruising olives, diminutive of *tudēs,* hammer.] **—toil′er** *n.*

toil² (toil) *n.* **1.** Something that binds, snares, or entangles one; an entrapment. Often used in the plural: *caught in the toils of despair.* **2.** *Archaic.* A net for trapping game. [French *toile,* cloth, from Old French *teile,* from Latin *tēla,* web. See **teks-** in Appendix.]

toile (twäl) *n.* A sheer fabric, such as linen or cotton. [French. See TOIL².]

toile de Jouy (də zhwē′) *n., pl.* **toiles de Jouy** (twäl). A usually light-colored fabric printed with a scenic pattern or design often used in upholstery or for curtains. [French, after *Jouy-en-Josas,* a town of north-central France.]

toi·let (toi′lĭt) *n.* **1.a.** A fixture for defecation and urination, consisting of a bowl fitted with a hinged seat and connected to a waste pipe and a flushing apparatus; a privy. **b.** A room or booth containing such a fixture. **2.** The act or process of dressing or grooming oneself. **3.** Dress; attire; costume. **4.** The cleansing of a body area as part of a surgical or medical procedure. **5.** *Archaic.* A dressing table. [French *toilette,* clothes bag, from Old French *tellette,* diminutive of *teile,* cloth. See TOIL².]

toilet paper *n.* Thin, absorbent paper, usually in rolls, used to clean oneself after defecation or urination. Also called *toilet tissue.*

toi·let·ry (toi′lĭ-trē) *n., pl.* **-ries.** An article, such as toothpaste or a hairbrush, used in personal grooming or dressing.

toi·lette (twä-lĕt′) *n.* **1.** The act or process of dressing or grooming oneself; toilet. **2.** A person's dress or style of dress. **3.** A gown or costume. [French. See TOILET.]

toilet tissue *n.* See **toilet paper.**

toilet training *n.* The process of training a child to use a toilet for defecation and urination.

toilet water *n.* A scented liquid with a high alcohol content used in bathing or applied as a skin freshener.

toil·some (toil′səm) *adj.* Characterized by or requiring toil. **—toil′some·ly** *adv.* **—toil′some·ness** *n.*

To·jo Hi·de·ki (tō′jō′ hē′dĕ-kē). Originally Tojo Eiki. 1884–1948. Japanese army officer and politician who ruled as dictator (1941–1944) during World War II and was executed as a war criminal.

to·ka·mak (tô′kə-măk′, tŏk′ə-) *n.* A doughnut-shaped chamber used in fusion research in which a plasma is heated and confined by magnetic fields. [Russian, from *to(roidal′naya) kam(era s) ak(sial′nym magnitnym polem),* toroidal chamber with axial magnetic field.]

To·ka·ra Islands (tō-kär′ə, -kä′rä). A group of islands of Japan in the northern Ryukyu group south of Kyushu.

To·kay (tō-kā′) *n.* **1.** A variety of grape originally grown near Tokaj (formerly Tokay), a town of eastern Hungary. **2.** A wine made from these grapes.

toke (tōk) *Slang. n.* A puff on a cigarette, a marijuana cigarette, or a pipe containing hashish or another mind-altering substance. **—toke** *tr. & intr.v.* **toked, tok·ing, tokes.** To puff or smoke (a marijuana cigarette, for example) or to engage in such activity. [Perhaps from Spanish *toque,* a hit, a turn, from *tocar,* to touch, from Vulgar Latin **toccāre.*]

To·ke·lau Islands (tō′kə-lou′). An island group of the central Pacific Ocean in the northern Ryukyu Islands north of Samoa. They became part of New Zealand in 1948.

to·ken (tō′kən) *n.* **1.** Something serving as an indication, a proof, or an expression of something else; a sign: *"Tears are queer tokens of happiness"* (Eugene O'Neill). See Synonyms at **sign. 2.** Something that signifies or evidences authority, validity, or identity: *The scepter is a token of regal status.* **3.** A distinguishing feature or characteristic. **4.** One that represents a group, as an employee whose presence is used to deflect from the employer criticism or accusations of discrimination. **5.** A keepsake or souvenir. **6.** A piece of stamped metal used as a substitute for currency: *subway tokens.* **—token** *tr.v.* **-kened, -ken·ing, -kens.** To betoken or symbolize; portend. **—token** *adj.* **1.** Done as an indication or a pledge: *a token payment.* **2.a.** Perfunctory; minimal: *a token gesture of reconciliation; token resistance.* **b.** Merely symbolic: *a token woman on the board of directors.* ***—idioms.*** **by the same token.** In like manner; similarly. **in token of.** As an indication of: *a ring given in token of love.* [Middle English, from Old English *tācen.* See **deik-** in Appendix.]

to·ken·ism (tō′kə-nĭz′əm) *n.* **1.** The policy of making only a perfunctory effort or symbolic gesture toward the accomplishment of a goal, such as racial integration. **2.** The practice of hiring or appointing a token number of people from underrepresented groups in order to deflect criticism or comply with affirmative action rules: *"Tokenism does not change stereotypes of social systems but works to preserve them, since it dulls the revolutionary impulse"* (Mary Daly).

To·khar·i·an (tō-kâr′ē-ən, -kär′-, -kăr′-) *n.* Variant of **Tocharian.**

To·klas (tō′kləs), **Alice B.** 1877–1967. American writer remembered as the secretary and longtime companion of Gertrude Stein. Her works include cookbooks and a volume of memoirs.

to·kol·o·gy (tō-kŏl′ə-jē) *n.* Variant of **tocology.**

to·ko·no·ma (tō′kə-nō′mə) *n.* A niche or an alcove in a Japanese home for displaying a flower arrangement, kakemono, or other piece of art. [Japanese : *toko,* alcove + *no,* of + *ma,* room.]

Tok Pis·in (tŏk′ pĭs′ĭn) *n.* A pidgin based on English and spoken in Papua New Guinea. [Pidgin English : TALK + PIDGIN.]

To·ku·shi·ma (tō′kə-shē′mä). A city of eastern Shikoku, Japan, on the Inland Sea. It is a major port and manufacturing center. Population, 257,886.

To·ky·o (tō′kē-ō′, -kyō). Formerly **E·do** (ĕd′ō). The capital and largest city of Japan, in east-central Honshu on **Tokyo Bay,** an inlet of the Pacific Ocean. Founded in the 12th century as Edo, Tokyo became the imperial capital in 1868. Much of the city was destroyed by an earthquake in 1923 and by bombing raids during World War II. Population, 8,353,674.

to·la (tō′lə, tō-lä′) *n.* A unit of weight used in India, equal to the weight of one silver rupee (11.7 grams or 180 troy grains). [Hindi *tolā,* from Sanskrit *tulā,* weight. See **tele-** in Appendix.]

tol·booth also **toll·booth** (tōl′bo͞oth′) *n. Scots.* A prison; a jail. [Middle English *tolbothe,* town hall containing customs offices and prison cells : *tol,* toll; see TOLL¹ + *bothe,* booth; see BOOTH.]

Tol·bu·khin (tôl-bo͞o′kĭn, -KHĭn). A city of northeast Bulgaria north of Varna. It is a commercial center. Population, 105,000.

tol·bu·ta·mide (tŏl-byo͞o′tə-mīd′) *n.* A white powder, $C_{12}H_{18}N_2O_3S$, that lowers the level of sugar in the blood and is used in the treatment of diabetes. [TOL(U) + BUT– + AMIDE.]

told (tōld) *v.* Past tense and past participle of **tell.**

tole also **tôle** (tōl) *n.* A lacquered or enameled metalware, usually gilded and elaborately painted. [French *tôle,* sheet metal, variant of *table,* table, slab, from Old French, from Latin *tabula,* board.]

To·le·do¹ (tə-lē′dō). **1.** *(also* tô-lĕ′thō). A city of central Spain near the Tagus River south-southwest of Madrid. It fell to the Romans in 193 B.C. and was later the capital of the Visigoth kingdom (534–712). As a Moorish capital (712–1031) it was a center of Arab and Hebrew learning. Population, 57,778. **2.** A city of northwest Ohio on Lake Erie. Incorporated in 1837, it is one of the major shipping centers of the Great Lakes. Population, 354,635.

To·le·do² also **to·le·do** (tə-lē′dō) *n., pl.* **-dos.** A fine-tempered sword or steel sword blade made in Toledo, Spain.

tol·er·a·ble (tŏl′ər-ə-bəl) *adj.* **1.** Capable of being tolerated; endurable. **2.** Fairly good; passable. See Synonyms at **average.** **—tol′er·a·bil′i·ty, tol′er·a·ble·ness** *n.* **—tol′er·a·bly** *adv.*

tol·er·ance (tŏl′ər-əns) *n.* **1.** The capacity for or the practice of recognizing and respecting the beliefs or practices of others.

2.a. Leeway for variation from a standard. **b.** The permissible deviation from a specified value of a structural dimension, often expressed as a percent. **3.** The capacity to endure hardship or pain. **4.** *Medicine.* **a.** Physiological resistance to a poison. **b.** The capacity to absorb a drug continuously or in large doses without adverse effect; diminution in the response to a drug after prolonged use. **5.a.** Acceptance of a tissue graft or transplant without immunological rejection. **b.** Unresponsiveness to an antigen that normally produces an immunological reaction. **6.** The ability of an organism to resist or survive infection by a parasitic or pathogenic organism.

tol·er·ant (tŏl′ər-ənt) *adj.* **1.** Inclined to tolerate the beliefs, practices, or traits of others; forbearing. See Synonyms at **broad-minded. 2.** Able to withstand or endure an adverse environmental condition: *plants tolerant of extreme heat.* [French *tolérant,* from Latin *tolerāns,* present participle of *tolerāre,* to bear. See TOLERATE.] **—tol′er·ant·ly** *adv.*

tol·er·ate (tŏl′ə-rāt′) *tr.v.* **-at·ed, -at·ing, -ates. 1.** To allow without prohibiting or opposing; permit. **2.** To recognize and respect (the rights, beliefs, or practices of others). **3.** To put up with; endure. See Synonyms at **bear**[1]. **4.** *Medicine.* To have tolerance for (a substance or pathogen). [Latin *tolerāre, tolerāt-,* to bear. See **tele-** in Appendix.] **—tol′er·a′tive** *adj.* **—tol′er·a′tor** *n.*

tol·er·a·tion (tŏl′ə-rā′shən) *n.* **1.** Tolerance with respect to the actions and beliefs of others: *"Toleration . . . is the greatest gift of the mind"* (Helen Keller). **2.** Official recognition of the rights of individuals and groups to hold dissenting opinions, especially on religion.

tol·i·dine (tŏl′ĭ-dēn′) *n.* Any of several isomeric bases, $C_{14}H_{16}N_2$, derived from toluene, one of which is used as a reagent to test for gold and for chlorine in water. [TOL(UENE) + -ID(E) + -INE[2].]

Tol·kien (tōl′kēn′, tŏl′-), **J(ohn) R(onald) R(euel).** 1892–1973. British philologist and writer of the fantasies *The Hobbit* (1937) and *The Lord of the Rings* (1954–1955).

toll[1] (tōl) *n.* **1.** A fixed charge or tax for a privilege, especially for passage across a bridge or along a road. **2.** A charge for a service, such as a long-distance telephone call. **3.** The amount or extent of loss or destruction, as of life, health, or property, caused by a disaster. **—toll** *tr.v.* **tolled, toll·ing, tolls. 1.** To exact as a toll. **2.** To charge a fee for using (a structure, such as a bridge). [Middle English, from Old English, variant of *toln,* from Medieval Latin *tolōnīum,* from Latin *telōnēum,* tollbooth, from Greek *telōneion,* from *telōnēs,* tax collector, from *telos,* tax. See **tele-** in Appendix.]

toll[2] (tōl) *v.* **tolled, toll·ing, tolls.** *—tr.* **1.** To sound (a large bell) slowly at regular intervals. **2.** To announce or summon by tolling. *—intr.* To sound in slowly repeated single tones. **—toll** *n.* **1.** The act of tolling. **2.** The sound of a bell being struck. [Middle English *tollen,* to ring an alarm, perhaps from *tollen,* to entice, pull, variant of *tillen,* from Old English *-tyllan.*]

toll·booth[1] (tōl′bo͞oth′) *n.* A booth where a toll is collected. Also called *tollhouse.*

toll·booth[2] (tōl′bo͞oth′) *n.* Variant of **tolbooth.**

toll bridge *n.* A bridge at which a toll is charged for crossing.

toll call *n.* A telephone call for which a higher rate is charged than that standard for a local call.

toll·gate (tōl′gāt′) *n.* **1.** A gate barring passage to a road, tunnel, or bridge until a toll is collected. **2.** A tollbooth equipped with a gate.

toll·house (tōl′hous′) *n.* **1.** A house adjoining a tollgate and occupied by a toll collector. **2.** See **tollbooth**[1].

tollhouse cookie *n.* A cookie made with flour, brown sugar, semisweet chocolate chips, and often chopped nuts.

Tol·stoy or **Tol·stoi** (tōl′stoi, tŏl′-, təl-stoi′), Count **Leo** or **Lev Nikolayevich.** 1828–1910. Russian writer and philosopher whose great novels *War and Peace* (1864–1869) and *Anna Karenina* (1873–1876) offer extraordinary detail and profound psychological insights. His later theories of ethics and morality recommended nonparticipation in and passive resistance to evil. **—Tol·stoy′an, Tol·stoi′an** *adj.*

Tol·tec (tōl′tĕk′, tŏl′-) *n., pl.* **Toltec** or **-tecs.** A member of a Nahuatl-speaking people of central and southern Mexico whose empire flourished from the 10th century until it collapsed under invasion by the Aztecs in the 12th century. **—Toltec** also **Tol·tec·an** (-tĕk′ən, tŏl-) *adj.* Of or relating to the Toltec or their culture. [Spanish *tolteca,* from Nahuatl *toltecatl,* artisan, mechanic.]

to·lu (tə-lo͞o′) *n.* Balsam of Peru. [Spanish *tolú,* after *Tolú,* a seaport of northwest Colombia.]

tol·u·ate (tŏl′yo͞o-āt′) *n.* A salt or an ester of toluic acid. [TOLU(IC ACID) + -ATE[2].]

To·lu·ca (tə-lo͞o′kə, tō-lo͞o′kä). A city of south-central Mexico west of Mexico City. Established as a settlement by Hernando Cortés in 1530, it is a commercial center. Population, 199,778.

tol·u·ene (tŏl′yo͞o-ēn′) also **tol·u·ol** (-ôl′, -ōl′, -ŏl′) *n.* A colorless flammable liquid, $CH_3C_6H_5$, obtained from coal tar or petroleum and used in aviation fuel and other high-octane fuels, in dyestuffs, explosives, and as a solvent for gums and lacquers. Also called *methylbenzene.* [TOLU (from which it was originally obtained) + -ENE.]

to·lu·ic acid (tə-lo͞o′ĭk) *n.* Any of three isomeric acids, $C_8H_8O_2$, derived from toluene. [TOLU(ENE) + -IC.]

to·lu·i·dine (tə-lo͞o′ĭ-dēn′) *n.* Any of three isomeric compounds, C_7H_9N, used to make dyes. [TOLU(ENE) + -ID(E) + -INE[2].]

tol·u·ol (tŏl′yo͞o-ôl′, -ōl′, -ŏl′) *n.* Variant of **toluene.**

Tol·yat·ti (tōl-yä′tē, tô-lyät′tē). See **Togliatti.**

tol·yl (tŏl′əl) *n.* The group C_7H_7, derived from toluene. Also called *cresyl.* [TOL(U) + -YL.]

tom (tŏm) *n.* The male of various animals, especially a male cat or turkey. [*Tom,* nickname for *Thomas.*]

Tom (tŏm) *n. Slang.* An Uncle Tom.

♦**tom·a·hawk** (tŏm′ə-hôk′) *n.* **1.** A light ax formerly used as a tool or weapon by certain Native American peoples. See Regional Note at **pone. 2.** A similar implement or weapon. **—tomahawk** *tr.v.* **-hawked, -hawk·ing, -hawks.** To strike with or as if with a tomahawk. [Virginia Algonquian *tamahaac.*]

to·mal·ley (tə-măl′ē, tŏm′ăl′ē) *n., pl.* **-leys.** The soft, green liver of cooked lobster, considered a delicacy. [Galibi *tamali.*]

Tom and Jer·ry (jĕr′ē) *n., pl.* **Tom and Jer·ries.** A hot drink consisting of rum or another liquor, a beaten egg, milk or water, sugar, and spices. [After Corinthian *Tom* and *Jerry* Hawthorn, characters in *Life in London,* a novel by Pierce Egan (1772–1849).]

to·ma·til·lo (tō′mə-tē′yō, -tēl′yō) *n., pl.* **-los.** A species of ground cherry *(Physalis ixocarpa)* native to Mexico, widely naturalized in eastern North America, and having an edible, yellow to purple viscid fruit. [American Spanish, diminutive of *tomate,* tomato. See TOMATO.]

to·ma·to (tə-mā′tō, -mä′-) *n., pl.* **-toes. 1.a.** A widely cultivated South American plant *(Lycopersicon esculentum)* having edible, fleshy, usually red fruit. **b.** The fruit of this plant. **2.** *Slang.* A woman regarded as attractive. [Alteration of Spanish *tomate,* from Nahuatl *tomatl.*]

WORD HISTORY: It has been said that the real contributions to world civilization were made by the unknown inhabitants of the Americas who domesticated plants such as the potato and squash and not by the great pre-Columbian civilizations, including that of the Aztecs. The tomato was another contribution, its name coming ultimately from the Nahuatl language spoken by the Aztecs as well as by other groups in Mexico and Central America. The Spanish, who conquered the area, brought back the tomato to Spain and, borrowing the Nahuatl word *tomatl* for it, named it *tomate,* a form shared in French, Portuguese, and early Modern English. *Tomate,* first recorded in 1604, gave way to *tomato,* a form created in English either because it was assumed to be Spanish or under the influence of the word *potato.* In any case, as is well known, people resisted eating this New World food at first because its membership in the Nightshade family made it suspect, but it is now eaten throughout the world while Aztec civilization is memorialized by ruins.

tomato fruit·worm (fro͞ot′wûrm′) *n.* The destructive larva of a noctuid moth *(Heliothis zea)* of the United States that burrows into the fruit of tomato plants.

tomato hornworm *n.* The destructive larva of a North American hawk moth *(Manduca quinquemaculata)* that feeds on the leaves of tomato plants.

tomb (to͞om) *n.* **1.** A grave or other place of burial. **2.** A vault or chamber for burial of the dead. **3.** A monument commemorating the dead. [Middle English, from Old French *tombe,* from Late Latin *tumba,* from Greek *tumbos.* See **teuə-** in Appendix.]

tom·bac also **tam·bac** or **tam·bak** (tŏm′băk) *n.* An alloy of copper with zinc and sometimes other metals, used in making inexpensive jewelry. [French, from Dutch *tombak,* from Malay *tĕmbaga.*]

Tom·baugh (tŏm′bô′), **Clyde William.** Born 1906. American astronomer who discovered the planet Pluto (1930).

Tom·big·bee (tŏm-bĭg′bē). A river, about 644 km (400 mi) long, rising in northeast Mississippi and flowing generally southward through western Alabama to join the Alabama River and form the Mobile River.

tom·bo·lo (tŏm′bə-lō′) *n., pl.* **-los.** A sandbar that connects an island to the mainland or to another island. [Italian, from Latin *tumulus,* mound. See TUMULUS.]

tom·boy (tŏm′boi′) *n.* A girl considered boyish or masculine in behavior or manner.

tomb·stone (to͞om′stōn′) *n.* A gravestone.

Tomb·stone (to͞om′stōn′). A city of southeast Arizona north-northwest of Bisbee. After silver was discovered here in 1877, Tombstone became one of the richest and most lawless frontier mining towns. Population, 1,632.

tom·cat (tŏm′kăt′) *n.* A male cat. **—tomcat** *intr.v.* **-cat·ted, -cat·ting, -cats.** *Slang.* To be sexually active with more than one partner. Used of men.

tom·cod (tŏm′kŏd′) *n., pl.* **tomcod** or **-cods.** Either of two edible marine fishes, *Microgadus tomcod* of North American Atlantic waters or *M. proximus* of northern Pacific waters, related to and resembling the cod.

Tom Col·lins (kŏl′ĭnz) *n.* A drink consisting of gin, lemon or lime juice, carbonated water, and sugar. [From the name *Tom Collins.*]

Tom, Dick, and Har·ry (tŏm′ dĭk′ ən hăr′ē) *n. Informal.*

tollbooth[1]

Leo Tolstoy

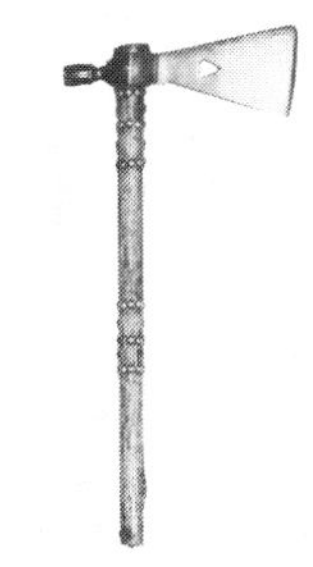
tomahawk
Oglala Sioux tomahawk

ă pat	oi boy
ā pay	ou out
âr care	o͝o took
ä father	o͞o boot
ĕ pet	ŭ cut
ē be	ûr urge
ĭ pit	th thin
ī pie	*th* this
îr pier	hw which
ŏ pot	zh vision
ō toe	ə about, item
ô paw	♦ regionalism

Stress marks: ′ (primary); ′ (secondary), as in **dictionary** (dĭk′shə-nĕr′ē)

Anybody at all; a member of the public at large: *It's not a smart idea to admit every Tom, Dick, and Harry to the party.*

tome (tōm) *n.* **1.** One of the books in a work of several volumes. **2.** A book, especially a large or scholarly one. [French, from Latin *tomus,* from Greek *tomos,* a cutting, section, from *temnein,* to cut. See **tem-** in Appendix.]

–tome *suff.* **1.** Part; area; segment: *dermatome.* **2.** Cutting instrument: *microtome.* [New Latin *-tomus,* from Greek *-tomos,* a cutting, from *tomos.* See TOME.]

to·men·ta (tō-mĕn′tə) *n. Anatomy & Biology.* Plural of **tomentum.**

to·men·tose (tō-mĕn′tōs′, tō′mən-) *adj. Biology.* Covered with short, dense, matted hairs. [New Latin *tōmentōsus,* from Latin *tōmentum,* cushion stuffing.]

to·men·tum (tō-mĕn′təm) *n., pl.* **-ta** (-tə). **1.** *Anatomy.* A network of extremely small blood vessels passing between the pia mater and the cerebral cortex. **2.** *Biology.* A covering of closely matted woolly hairs. [Latin *tōmentum,* cushion stuffing.]

tom-tom

tom·fool (tŏm′fo͞ol′) *n.* A person considered stupid or foolish. **—tomfool** *adj.* Extremely foolish or stupid.

tom·fool·er·y (tŏm-fo͞o′lə-rē) *n., pl.* **-ies. 1.** Foolish behavior. **2.** Something trivial or foolish; nonsense.

tom·my also **Tom·my** (tŏm′ē) *n., pl.* **-mies.** *Chiefly British.* A British Soldier. [Short for *Tommy Atkins,* from *Thomas Atkins,* a name often used on sample forms.]

Tommy gun *n. Informal.* A Thompson submachine gun.

tom·my·rot (tŏm′ē-rŏt′) *n. Informal.* Utter foolishness; nonsense. [Dialectal *tommy,* fool (from *Tom,* nickname for *Thomas*) + ROT.]

to·mog·ra·phy (tō-mŏg′rə-fē) *n.* A technique for making detailed x-rays of a predetermined plane section of a solid object while blurring out the images of other planes. [Greek *tomos,* section; see TOME + –GRAPHY.] **—to′mo·gram′** (tō′mə-grăm′) *n.* **—to′mo·graph′** (-grăf′) *n.* **—to′mo·graph′ic** *adj.*

to·mor·row (tə-môr′ō, -mŏr′ō) *n.* **1.** The day following today. **2.** The near future. **—tomorrow** *adv.* On or for the day following today: *"I won't think of it now. . . . I'll think of it tomorrow"* (Margaret Mitchell). [Middle English *to morow,* from Old English *tō morgenne,* in the morning : *tō,* at, on; see TO + *morgenne,* dative of *morgen,* morning.]

Tonegawa Susumu
Photographed in 1987

tom·pi·on (tŏm′pē-ən) *n.* Variant of **tampion.**

Tomp·kins (tŏmp′kĭnz, tŏm′-), **Daniel D.** 1774–1825. Vice President of the United States (1817–1825) under James Monroe.

Tomsk (tŏmsk, tômsk). A city of central Russia northeast of Novosibirsk. It is a major river port and an industrial center. Population, 475,000.

Tom Thumb *n.* **1.** A hero of English folklore, who was no bigger than his father's thumb. **2.** A person of very small physical stature.

♦**tom·tit** (tŏm′tĭt′) *n.* A small bird, such as a titmouse. See Regional Note at **tit¹.**

tom-tom (tŏm′tŏm′) also **tam-tam** (tŭm′tŭm′, tăm′tăm′) *n.* **1.** Any of various small-headed drums, usually long and narrow, that are beaten with the hands. **2.** A monotonous rhythmical drumbeat or similar sound. [Hindi *ṭamṭam,* probably of imitative origin.]

–tomy *suff.* Act of cutting; incision: *gastrotomy.* [New Latin *-tomia,* from Greek, from *tomos,* a cutting, from *temnein,* to cut. See **tem-** in Appendix.]

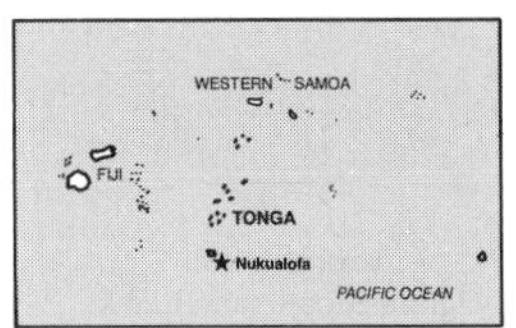

Tonga

ton (tŭn) *n. Abbr.* **t., tn. 1.** A unit of weight equal to 2,000 pounds (0.907 metric ton or 907.18 kilograms). Also called *net ton, short ton.* **2.** A unit of weight equal to 2,240 pounds (1.016 metric tons or 1,016.05 kilograms). Also called *long ton.* **3.** A metric ton. See table at **measurement. 4.** A unit of capacity for cargo in maritime shipping, normally estimated at 40 cubic feet. **5.** A unit of internal capacity of a ship equal to 100 cubic feet. **6.** A unit for measuring the displacement of ships, equal to 35 cubic feet, and supposed to equal the volume taken by a long ton of seawater. **7.** *Informal.* A very large quantity: *tons of fan mail.* [Middle English *tonne,* a measure of weight. See TUN.]

to·nal (tō′nəl) *adj.* Of or relating to tones, a tone, or tonality. **—to′nal·ly** *adv.*

to·nal·i·ty (tō-năl′ĭ-tē) *n., pl.* **-ties. 1.** *Music.* **a.** A system or an arrangement of seven tones built on a tonic key. **b.** The arrangement of all the tones and chords of a composition in relation to a tonic. **2.** The scheme or interrelation of the tones in a painting.

Ton·a·wan·da (tŏn′ə-wŏn′də). A city of western New York, an industrial suburb of Buffalo. Population, 18,693.

ton·do (tŏn′dō, tôn′-) *n., pl.* **-dos** also **-di** (-dē). A round painting, relief, or similar work of art. [Italian, short for *rotondo,* round, from Latin *rotundus.* See ROTUND.]

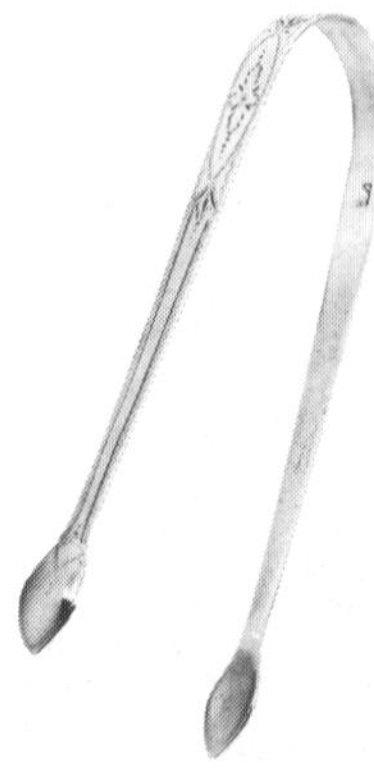

tongs

tone (tōn) *n.* **1.** *Music.* **a.** A sound of distinct pitch, quality, and duration; a note. **b.** The interval of a major second in the diatonic scale; a whole step. **c.** A recitational melody in a Gregorian chant. **2. a.** The quality or character of sound. **b.** The characteristic quality or timbre of a particular instrument or voice. **3. a.** The pitch of a word used to determine its meaning or to distinguish differences in meaning. **b.** The particular or relative pitch of a word, phrase, or sentence. **4.** Manner of expression in speech or writing: *took an angry tone with the reporters.* **5.** A general quality, effect, or atmosphere: *a room with an elegant tone.* **6.** *Color.* **a.** A color or shade of color: *light tones of blue.* **b.** Quality of color: *The green wallpaper had a particularly somber tone.* **7.** The general effect in painting of light, color, and shade. **8.** *Physiology.* **a.** The normal state of elastic tension or partial contraction in resting muscles. **b.** Normal firmness of a tissue or an organ. **—tone** *v.* **toned, ton·ing, tones.** —*tr.* **1.** To give a particular tone or inflection to. **2.** To soften or change the color of (a painting or photographic negative, for example). **3.** To sound monotonously; intone. —*intr.* **1.** To assume a particular color quality. **2.** To harmonize in color. **—*phrasal verbs.* tone down.** To make less vivid, harsh, or violent; moderate. **tone up.** To make or become brighter or more vigorous. [Middle English *ton,* from Old French, from Latin *tonus,* from Greek *tonos,* a stretching. See **ten-** in Appendix.]

tone arm *n.* The arm of a phonograph turntable that holds the cartridge.

tone cluster *n. Music.* A dissonant group of close notes played at the same time.

tone color *n. Music.* The timbre of a singing voice or an instrument.

tone control *n.* A circuit or device in an amplifier designed to increase or decrease the amplification in a specific frequency range without affecting other frequencies.

tone-deaf (tōn′dĕf′) *adj.* Unable to distinguish differences in musical pitch.

To·ne·ga·wa Su·su·mu (tô-nĕ′gä-wä so͞o-so͞o′mo͞o). Born 1939. Japanese molecular biologist. He won a 1987 Nobel Prize for discovering how certain cells of the immune system can genetically rearrange themselves to produce diverse antibodies.

tone language *n.* A language that distinguishes meanings among words of similar form by variations in pitch and tone.

tone·less (tōn′lĭs) *adj.* **1.** Lacking tone. **2.** Lacking vitality; listless. **—tone′less·ly** *adv.* **—tone′less·ness** *n.*

ton·eme (tō′nēm) *n.* A type of phoneme that occurs in languages that use tone to convey differences in lexical meaning.

tone poem *n. Music.* See **symphonic poem.**

ton·er (tō′nər) *n.* One that tones, as: **a.** A chemical bath used to change the color of a photographic print or to preserve black-and-white prints or movie film. **b.** A powdery ink used dry or suspended in a liquid to produce a photocopy. **c.** A mildly astringent cream or lotion used to refresh the skin.

tone row (rō) *n. Music.* A unique, arbitrary series of notes used in the 12-tone system of composition.

ton·ey (tō′nē) *adj.* Variant of **tony.**

tong¹ (tông, tŏng) *tr.v.* **tonged, tong·ing, tongs.** To seize, hold, or manipulate with tongs. [Back-formation from TONGS.]

tong² (tông, tŏng) *n.* **1.** A Chinese association or political party. **2.** An association or a secret society of Chinese in the United States, believed to be involved in organized crime. [Chinese (Cantonese), assembly hall, familial relationship between cousins, equivalent to Mandarin *táng.*]

Ton·ga (tŏng′gə) also **Friend·ly Islands** (frĕnd′lē). A country in the southwest Pacific Ocean east of Fiji comprising about 150 islands, some 36 of which are inhabited. It became a British protectorate in 1900 and gained independence in 1970. Nukualofa is the capital and the largest city. Population, 96,592.

Ton·gan (tŏng′gən, tŏng′ən) *adj.* Of or relating to Tonga or its people, language, or culture. **—Tongan** *n.* **1.** A native or inhabitant of Tonga. **2.** The Polynesian language of Tonga.

tongs (tôngz, tŏngz) *pl.n. (used with a sing. or pl. verb).* A grasping device consisting of two arms joined at one end by a pivot or hingelike scissors. [Middle English *tonges,* pl. of *tonge,* from Old English *tang, tong.*]

tongue (tŭng) *n.* **1. a.** The fleshy, movable, muscular organ, attached in most vertebrates to the floor of the mouth, that is the principal organ of taste, an aid in chewing and swallowing, and, in human beings, an important organ of speech. **b.** An analogous organ or part in invertebrate animals, as in certain insects or mollusks. **2.** The tongue of an animal, such as a cow, used as food. **3.** A spoken language or dialect. **4. a.** Speech; talk: *If there is goodness in your heart, it will come to your tongue.* **b.** The act or power of speaking: *She had no tongue to answer.* **c. tongues.** Speech or vocal sounds produced in a state of religious ecstasy. **d.** Style or quality of utterance: *her sharp tongue.* **5.** The bark or baying of a hunting dog that sees game: *The dog gave tongue when the fox came through the hedge.* **6.** Something resembling a tongue in shape or function, as: **a.** The vibrating end of a reed in a wind instrument. **b.** A flame. **c.** The flap of material under the laces or buckles of a shoe. **d.** A spit of land; a promontory. **e.** A bell clapper. **f.** The harnessing pole attached to the front axle of a horse-drawn vehicle. **7.** A protruding strip along the edge of a board that fits into a matching groove on the edge of another board. **—tongue** *v.* **tongued, tongu·ing, tongues.** —*tr.* **1.** *Music.* To separate or articulate (notes played on a brass or wind instrument) by shutting off the stream of air with the tongue. **2.** To touch or lick with the tongue. **3. a.** To provide (a board) with a tongue. **b.** To join by means of a tongue and groove. **4.** *Archaic.* To scold. —*intr.* **1.** *Music.* To articulate notes on a brass or wind instrument. **2.** To project: *a spit of land tonguing into the bay.* **—*idioms.* hold (one's) tongue.** To be or keep silent. **lose (one's) tongue.** To lose the capacity to speak, as from shock. **on the tip of (one's) tongue.** On the verge of being recalled or expressed. [Middle English, from Old English *tunge.* See **dṇghū** in Appendix.]

tongue and groove *n.* A joint made by fitting a tongue on the edge of a board into a matching groove on another board.

tongue depressor *n.* A thin blade for pressing down the tongue during a medical examination of the mouth and throat; a spatula.

tongue·fish (tŭng′fĭsh′) *n., pl.* **tonguefish** or **-fish·es.** Any of various marine flatfishes of the family Cynoglossidae, having the posterior part of the body tapering to a point. [From its tongue-shaped body.]

tongue-in-cheek (tŭng′ĭn-chēk′) *adj.* Meant or expressed ironically or facetiously.

tongue-lash·ing (tŭng′lăsh′ĭng) *n. Informal.* A scolding.

tongue·less (tŭng′lĭs) *adj.* **1.** Having no tongue. **2.** Lacking the faculty of speech; mute. **3.** Speechless; silent.

tongue-tie (tŭng′tī′) *n.* Restricted mobility of the tongue resulting from abnormal shortness of the frenum. **—tongue-tie** *tr.v.* **-tied, -ty·ing, -ties.** To make tongue-tied.

tongue-tied (tŭng′tīd′) *adj.* **1.** Speechless or confused in expression, as from shyness, embarrassment, or astonishment. **2.** Affected with tongue-tie.

tongue twister *n.* **1.** A word or group of words difficult to articulate rapidly, usually because of a succession of similar consonantal sounds, as in *Shall she sell seashells?* **2.** Something difficult to pronounce.

tongue worm *n.* Any of numerous tongue-shaped, soft-bodied, colorless invertebrates of the phylum Pentastoma that live embedded in the lungs, nostrils, or nasal sinuses of various mammals, reptiles, and birds, especially in tropical and subtropical regions. Also called *pentastome.*

tongu·ing (tŭng′ĭng) *n. Music.* Interruption of the wind stream through an instrument by movement of the tongue in order to articulate notes.

–tonia *suff.* Degree or state of tonicity: *myotonia.* [New Latin, from Latin *tonus.* See TONE.]

♦**ton·ic** (tŏn′ĭk) *n.* **1.** An agent, such as a medication, that restores or increases body tone. **2.** An invigorating, refreshing, or restorative agent or influence. **3.a.** Quinine water. **b.** *Boston.* See **soft drink. 4.** *Music.* The first note of a diatonic scale; the keynote. **5.** A tonic accent. **—tonic** *adj.* **1.** Producing or stimulating physical, mental, or emotional vigor. **2.a.** *Physiology.* Of, relating to, or producing tone or tonicity in muscles or tissue: *a tonic reflex.* **b.** *Medicine.* Characterized by continuous tension or contraction of muscles: *a tonic convulsion or spasm.* **3.** *Music.* Of or based on the keynote. **4.** Stressed, as a syllable; accented. [New Latin *tonicus,* of tension or tone, from Greek *tonikos,* capable of extension, from *tonos,* a stretching, tone. See TONE.] **—ton′i·cal·ly** *adv.*

♦***REGIONAL NOTE:*** Generic terms for carbonated soft drinks vary widely in the United States. Probably the two most common words competing for precedence are *soda,* used in the northeast United States, and *pop,* used from the Midwest westward. In the South all soft drinks, regardless of the flavor or brand name, are referred to as *cold drinks.* Speakers in Boston and its environs have a term of their own: *tonic.* Such a variety of regional equivalents is unusual for a product for which advertising is so aggressive and universal; usually advertising has the effect of squeezing out regional variants. On the other hand, because there are so many types and flavors of soft drinks, perhaps no single generic word has ever emerged to challenge the regionalisms.

tonic accent *n. Linguistics.* A stress produced by a change, especially a rise, in pitch as distinguished from increased volume. Also called *pitch accent.*

to·nic·i·ty (tō-nĭs′ĭ-tē) *n., pl.* **-ties. 1.** Normal firmness or functional readiness in body tissues or organs. **2.** The sustained partial contraction of resting or relaxed muscles.

tonic sol-fa *n. Music.* A system of notation that is based on relationships between tones in a key and that replaces the usual staff notation with solmization syllables, such as *do, re,* and *mi,* or their abbreviations.

to·night (tə-nīt′) *adv.* On or during the present or coming night. **—tonight** *n.* This night or the night of this day. [Middle English *to night,* from Old English *tō niht,* at night : *tō,* at, on; see TO + *niht,* night; see NIGHT.]

ton·ka bean (tŏng′kə) *n.* **1.** A tropical South American tree *(Dipteryx odorata)* having pulpy, egg-shaped, one-seeded pods and fragrant seeds used as a substitute for vanilla and for flavoring tobacco and candies. **2.** The seed of this tree. [Perhaps from Galibi *tonka.*]

Ton·kin (tŏn′kĭn′, tŏng′-). A historical region of southeast Asia on the **Gulf of Tonkin,** an arm of the South China Sea, now forming most of northern Vietnam. It was part of French Indochina from 1887 to 1946. **—Ton′kin·ese′** (-ēz′, -ēs′) *adj. & n.*

Ton·le Sap (tŏn′lā săp′, săp′). A lake of central Cambodia. It is the largest lake in southeast Asia.

ton-mile (tŭn′mīl′) *n.* A unit of freight transportation equivalent to a ton of freight moved one mile.

ton·nage (tŭn′ĭj) *n.* **1.** The number of tons of water that a ship displaces when afloat. **2.** The capacity of a merchant ship in units of 100 cubic feet. **3.** A duty or charge per ton on cargo, as at a port or canal. **4.** The total shipping of a country or port, figured in tons, with reference to carrying capacity. **5.** Weight measured in tons. [TON + –AGE. Sense 3, Middle English, from Old French, from *tonne,* tun. See TONNE.]

tonne (tŭn) *n.* A metric ton. [French, from Old French, tun, from Late Latin *tunna,* probably of Celtic origin.]

ton·neau (tə-nō′, tŏn′ō′) *n., pl.* **-neaus.** The rear seating compartment of an early type of automobile. [French, from Old French *tonnel,* cask. See TUNNEL.]

to·nom·e·ter (tō-nŏm′ĭ-tər) *n.* **1.** Any of various instruments for measuring pressure or tension. **2.** An instrument for measuring hydrostatic pressure within the eyeball, used in the detection of glaucoma. **3.** *Music.* An instrument, such as a graduated set of tuning forks, used to determine the pitch or vibration rate of tones. [Greek *tonos,* tension; see TONE + –METER.] **—to′no·met′ric** (tō′nə-mĕt′rĭk) *adj.* **—to·nom′e·try** *n.*

to·no·plast (tō′nə-plăst′) *n.* The cytoplasmic membrane that surrounds a vacuole of a plant cell. Also called *vacuolar membrane.* [Greek *tonos,* tension; see **ten-** in Appendix + –PLAST.]

ton·sil (tŏn′səl) *n.* A small oral mass of lymphoid tissue, especially either of two such masses embedded in the lateral walls of the opening between the mouth and the pharynx, of uncertain function, but believed to help protect the body from respiratory infections. [From Latin *tōnsillae,* tonsils.] **—ton′sil·lar** *adj.*

tonsill– *pref.* Variant of **tonsillo–.**

ton·sil·lec·to·my (tŏn′sə-lĕk′tə-mē) *n., pl.* **-mies.** Surgical removal of tonsils or a tonsil.

ton·sil·li·tis (tŏn′sə-lī′tĭs) *n.* Inflammation of the tonsils. **—ton′sil·lit′ic** (-lĭt′ĭk) *adj.*

tonsillo– or **tonsill–** *pref.* Tonsil: *tonsillectomy.* [From Latin *tōnsillae,* tonsils.]

ton·sil·lot·o·my (tŏn′sə-lŏt′ə-mē) *n., pl.* **-mies.** Surgical incision of a tonsil.

ton·so·ri·al (tŏn-sôr′ē-əl, -sōr-) *adj.* Of or relating to barbering or a barber. [From Latin *tōnsōrius,* from *tōnsor,* barber, from *tōnsus,* past participle of *tondēre,* to shear. See **tem-** in Appendix.]

ton·sure (tŏn′shər) *n.* **1.** The act of shaving the head or part of the head, especially as a preliminary to becoming a priest or a member of a monastic order. **2.** The part of a monk's or priest's head that has been shaved. **—tonsure** *tr.v.* **-sured, -sur·ing, -sures.** To shave the head of. [Middle English, from Old French, from Medieval Latin *tōnsūra,* from Latin, a shearing, from *tōnsus,* past participle of *tondēre,* to shear. See **tem-** in Appendix.]

ton·tine (tŏn′tēn′, tŏn-tēn′) *n.* **1.** An investment plan in which participants buy shares in a common fund and receive an annuity that increases every time a participant dies, with the entire fund going to the final survivor or to those who survive after a specified time. **2.** Each member's share of a tontine. **3.** The subscribers to a tontine. [French, after Lorenzo *Tonti* (1635–1690?), Italian-born French banker.]

to·nus (tō′nəs) *n., pl.* **-nus·es.** Body or muscular tone; tonicity. [Latin, tone. See TONE.]

ton·y also **ton·ey** (tō′nē) *adj.* **-i·er, -i·est.** *Informal.* Marked by an expensive, luxurious, or exclusive manner or quality. [From TONE.]

To·ny (tō′nē) *n., pl.* **-nys.** An annual award for outstanding achievement in the theater. [After *Tony,* nickname of Antoinette PERRY.]

too (to͞o) *adv.* **1.** In addition; also: *He's coming along too.* See Synonyms at **also. 2.** More than enough; excessively: *She worries too much.* **3.** To a regrettable degree: *My error was all too apparent.* **4.** Very; extremely; immensely: *He's only too willing to be of service.* **5.** *Informal.* Indeed; so: *You will too do it!* [Middle English *to,* from Old English *tō,* to, furthermore. See **de-** in Appendix.]

USAGE NOTE: A number of commentators have objected to the use of *not too* as an equivalent of "not very," as in *She was not too pleased with the results.* In many contexts this construction is entirely idiomatic and should pass without notice: *It wasn't too long ago that deregulation was being hailed as the savior of the savings and loan industry. It was not too bright of them to build in an area where rock slides occur.* In these cases *not too* adds a note of ironic understatement. • Negation of *too* by *can't* may sometimes lead to ambiguities, as in *You can't check your child's temperature too often,* which may mean either that the temperature should be checked only occasionally or that it should be checked as frequently as possible. • *Too* meaning "in addition" or "also" is sometimes used to introduce a sentence: *There has been a cutback in federal subsidies. Too, rates have been increasing.* This usage cannot be called incorrect, but some critics consider it awkward.

took (to͝ok) *v.* Past tense of **take.**

tool (to͞ol) *n.* **1.** A device, such as a saw, used to perform or facilitate manual or mechanical work. **2.a.** A machine, such as a lathe, used to cut and shape machine parts or other objects. **b.** The cutting part of such a machine. **3.** Something regarded as necessary to the carrying out of one's occupation or profession: *Words are the tools of our trade.* **4.** Something used in the performance of an operation; an instrument: *"Modern democracies have the fiscal and monetary tools . . . to end chronic slumps and galloping inflations"* (Paul A. Samuelson). **5.** *Vulgar Slang.* A penis. **6.** A person used to carry out the designs of another; a dupe. **7.a.** A bookbinder's hand stamp. **b.** A design impressed

ă pat	oi boy
ā pay	ou out
âr care	o͝o took
ä father	o͞o boot
ĕ pet	ŭ cut
ē be	ûr urge
ĭ pit	th thin
ī pie	*th* this
îr pier	hw which
ŏ pot	zh vision
ō toe	ə about, item
ô paw	♦ regionalism

Stress marks: ′ (primary); ′ (secondary), as in **dictionary** (dĭk′shə-nĕr′ē)

on a book cover by such a stamp. **8.** *Computer Science.* An application program in some computer systems. **—tool** *v.* **tooled, tool·ing, tools.** *—tr.* **1.** To form, work, or decorate with a tool. **2.** To ornament (a book cover) with a bookbinder's tool. **3.** *Slang.* To drive (a vehicle): *tooled the car at 80 miles an hour.* *—intr.* **1.** To work with a tool. **2.** *Slang.* To drive or ride in a vehicle: *tooled up and down the roads.* ***—phrasal verb.*** **tool up.** To provide an industry or a factory with machinery and tools suitable for a particular job. [Middle English, from Old English *tōl,* possibly from Old Norse.]

SYNONYMS: *tool, instrument, implement, utensil, appliance.* These nouns refer to devices used in the performance of work. *Tool* applies broadly to a device that facilitates work; specifically it denotes a small manually operated device, such as a file, of the kind employed by carpenters and plumbers: *a box full of tools for repair jobs. Instrument* refers especially to one of the relatively small precision tools, such as a stethoscope or supersonic drill, used by trained professionals such as doctors and dentists: *had to sterilize all the instruments. Implement* is the preferred term for tools used in agriculture and certain building trades: *rakes, hoes, and other implements. Utensil* often refers to an implement, such as a pot or spoon, used in doing household work: *cooking utensils laid out on the table. Appliance* most frequently denotes a power-driven device, such as a toaster or refrigerator, that performs a specific function: *a store selling modern appliances.*

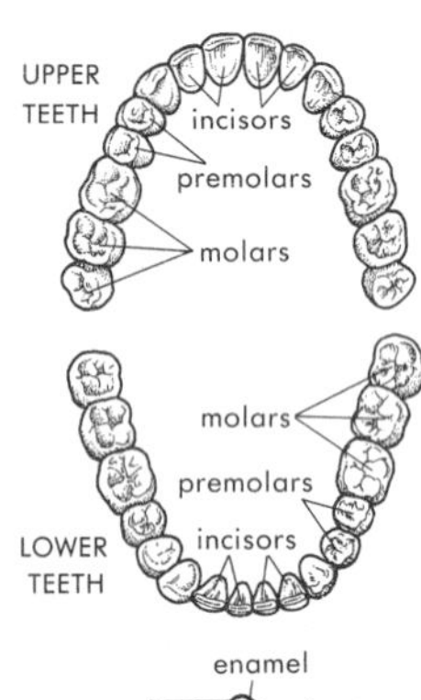

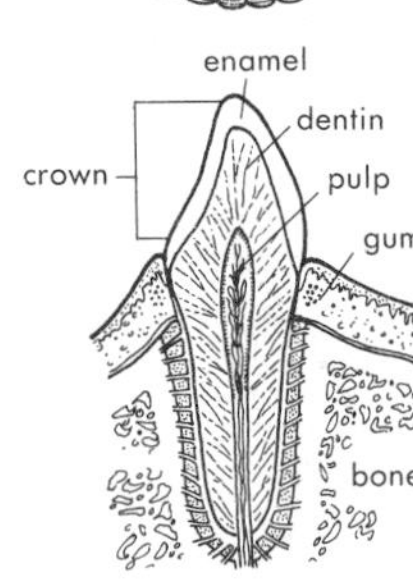

tooth
Top: Permanent teeth of an adult human
Bottom: Cross section of an incisor

tool·box (to͞ol′bŏks′) *n.* A case for carrying or storing tools.

tool·ing (to͞o′lĭng) *n.* **1.** Work or ornamentation done with tools, especially stamped or gilded designs on leather. **2.** The process of providing a factory with machinery in preparation for production.

tool·mak·er (to͞ol′mā′kər) *n.* A skilled machinist trained in making and repairing tools and parts.

Toombs (to͞omz), **Robert Augustus.** 1810–1885. American politician. A U.S. representative (1845–1853) and senator (1853–1861) from Georgia, he was an outspoken supporter of the states' right to permit slavery.

toon (to͞on) *n.* **1.** A tall tree *(Cedrela toona)* of tropical Asia and Australia, having dark red, aromatic wood. **2.** The wood of this tree. [Hindi *tūn,* from Sanskrit *tunnaḥ.*]

toot (to͞ot) *v.* **toot·ed, toot·ing, toots.** *—intr.* **1.** To sound a horn or whistle in short blasts. **2.** To make the sound of a horn or whistle blown in short blasts or a sound resembling it. **3.** *Slang.* To snort cocaine. *—tr.* **1.** To blow or sound (a horn or whistle). **2.** To sound (a blast, for example) on a horn or whistle. **3.** *Slang.* To snort (cocaine). **—toot** *n.* **1.** A blast, as of a horn. **2.** *Slang.* A drinking binge. **3.** *Slang.* Cocaine, especially a small amount snorted at one time. [Ultimately of imitative origin.] **—toot′er** *n.*

tooth (to͞oth) *n., pl.* **teeth** (tēth). **1.a.** One of a set of hard, bonelike structures rooted in sockets in the jaws of vertebrates, typically composed of a core of soft pulp surrounded by a layer of hard dentin that is coated with cement or enamel at the crown and used for biting or chewing food or as a means of attack or defense. **b.** A similar structure in invertebrates, such as one of the pointed denticles or ridges on the exoskeleton of an arthropod or the shell of a mollusk. **2.** A projecting part resembling a tooth in shape or function, as on a comb, gear, or saw. **3.** A small, notched projection along a margin, especially of a leaf. Also called *dent.* **4.** A rough surface, as of paper or metal. **5.a.** Something that injures or destroys with force. Often used in the plural: *the teeth of the blizzard.* **b. teeth.** Effective means of enforcement; muscle: *"This . . . puts real teeth into something where there has been only lip service"* (Ellen Convisser). **6.** Taste or appetite: *She always had a sweet tooth.* **—tooth** (to͞oth, to͞oth) *v.* **toothed, tooth·ing, tooths.** *—tr.* **1.** To furnish (a tool, for example) with teeth. **2.** To make a jagged edge on. *—intr.* To become interlocked; mesh. ***—idioms.*** **get** (or **sink) (one's) teeth into.** *Slang.* To be actively involved in; get a firm grasp of. **show** (or **bare) (one's) teeth.** To express a readiness to fight; threaten defiantly. **to the teeth.** Lacking nothing; completely: *armed to the teeth; dressed to the teeth.* [Middle English, from Old English *tōth.* See **dent-** in Appendix.]

WORD HISTORY: Eating, biting, teeth, and dentists are all related, as is well known, but the relationship goes further than one might think, that is, into the roots of the words *eat, tooth,* and *dentist.* The Proto-Indo-European root **ed–,* meaning "to eat" and the source of our word *eat,* originally meant "to bite." A participial form of **ed–* in this sense was **dent–,* "biting," which came to mean "tooth." Our word *tooth* comes from **dont–,* a form of **dent–,* with sound changes that resulted in the Germanic word **tanthuz.* This word became Old English *tōth* and Modern English *tooth.* Meanwhile the Proto-Indo-European form **dent–* itself became in Latin *dēns* (stem *dent–*), "tooth," from which is derived our word *dentist.* We find a descendant of another Proto-Indo-European form **(o)dont–* in the word *orthodontist.*

tooth·ache (to͞oth′āk′) *n.* An aching pain in or near a tooth.

toothache tree *n.* An aromatic North American shrub or tree *(Zanthoxylum americanum)* whose dried bark has medicinal uses. Also called *Northern prickly ash.*

tooth and nail *adv.* With every available resource; with unrelenting effort: *"Bureaucrats would correctly see this as a curb on their power and would fight tooth and nail against it"* (George R. Packard).

tooth·brush (to͞oth′brŭsh′) *n.* A brush used for cleaning teeth.

toothed (to͞otht, to͞othd) *adj.* Having teeth, especially of a certain number or type. Often used in combination: *saw-toothed.*

toothed whale *n.* Any of various whales of the suborder Odontoceti, having numerous conical teeth.

tooth fairy *n.* A fairy supposed to leave money under a child's pillow in place of a baby tooth that has just fallen out.

tooth·less (to͞oth′lĭs) *adj.* **1.** Lacking teeth. **2.** Lacking force; ineffectual. **—tooth′less·ly** *adv.* **—tooth′less·ness** *n.*

tooth·paste (to͞oth′pāst′) *n.* A paste for cleaning teeth.

tooth·pick (to͞oth′pĭk′) *n.* A small piece of wood or other material for removing food particles from between the teeth.

tooth·pow·der (to͞oth′pou′dər) *n.* Powder for cleaning teeth.

tooth shell *n.* Any of various burrowing marine mollusks of the class Scaphopoda, having a long, tapering, slightly curved tubular shell. Also called *scaphopod, tusk shell.*

tooth·some (to͞oth′səm) *adj.* **1.** Delicious; luscious: *a toothsome pie.* See Synonyms at **delicious. 2.** Pleasant; attractive: *a toothsome offer.* **3.** Sexually attractive or exciting. **—tooth′some·ly** *adv.* **—tooth′some·ness** *n.*

tooth·wort (to͞oth′wûrt′, -wôrt′) *n.* **1.** Any of several eastern North American plants of the genus *Cardamine,* such as the crinkleroot, having fleshy rhizomes and palmately divided leaves. **2.** A parasitic European plant *(Lathraea squamaria)* having scaly cream-colored or pink stems and pinkish flowers. [From its tooth-shaped scales.]

tooth·y (to͞o′thē) *adj.* **-i·er, -i·est.** Having or showing prominent teeth. **—tooth′i·ly** *adv.*

too·tle (to͞ot′l) *intr.v.* **-tled, -tling, -tles. 1.** To toot softly and repeatedly, as on a flute. **2.** *Informal.* To walk or drive in a leisurely manner; amble: *spent the morning tootling around town.* **—tootle** *n.* The act or sound of tooting softly and repeatedly, as on a flute. ***—phrasal verb.*** **tootle off.** *Informal.* To depart; go. [Frequentative of TOOT.]

toots (to͞ots) *n.* *Slang.* Babe; sweetie. [Perhaps short for TOOTSIE.]

toot·sie (to͞ot′sē) *n.* *Slang.* **1.** Toots. **2.** A girl or young woman. [Origin unknown.]

toot·sy (to͞ot′sē) *n., pl.* **-sies.** *Slang.* A person's foot. [Alteration of *footsy,* from FOOT.]

top¹ (tŏp) *n.* **1.** The uppermost part, point, surface, or end. **2.** The crown of the head: *from top to toe.* **3.** The part of a plant, such as a rutabaga, that is above the ground. **4.** Something, such as a lid or cap, that covers or forms an uppermost part. **5.** The upper half of a two-piece garment, especially a sweater or knit shirt. **6.** *Nautical.* A platform enclosing the head of each mast of a sailing ship, to which the topmast rigging is attached. **7.** The highest degree, pitch, or point; the peak, acme, or zenith: *"It had come at a time when he was not feeling at the top of his form"* (Anthony Powell). **8.a.** The highest position or rank: *at the top of her profession.* **b.** A person in this position. **9.** *Games.* The highest card or cards in a suit or hand. **10.** The best part. **11.** The earliest part or beginning: *She played the piece again, from the top.* **12.** *Baseball.* The first half of an inning. **13.** *Sports.* **a.** A stroke that lands above the center of a ball, as in golf or tennis, giving it a forward spin. **b.** A forward spin on a ball resulting from such a stroke. **—top** *adj.* **1.** Situated at the top: *the top shelf.* **2.** Of the highest degree, quality, or amount: *in top form.* **3.** In a position of preeminence: *the top historian in her department.* **—top** *v.* **topped, top·ping, tops.** *—tr.* **1.** To form, furnish with, or serve as a top. **2.** To reach the top of. **3.** To go over the top of. **4.** To exceed or surpass. **5.** To be at the head of: *She topped her class.* **6.** To remove the top or uppermost part from; crop: *topped the fruit trees.* **7.** *Sports.* **a.** To strike the upper part of (a ball), giving it forward spin. **b.** To make (a stroke) in this way. *—intr.* To make a finish, an end, or a conclusion. ***—phrasal verbs.*** **top off. 1.** To fill up (a container), especially when it is almost full to begin with. **2.** To finish up. **top out. 1.** To put the framework for the top story on (a building). **2.** To fill up (a ship, for example). **3.** To cease rising: *Interest rates topped out at 16 percent.* **4.** *Informal.* To give up one's career just as one becomes highly successful. ***—idioms.*** **off the top of (one's) head.** *Informal.* In an impromptu way: *She recited the poem off the top of her head.* **on top. 1.** At the highest point or peak. **2.** In a dominant, controlling, or successful position. **on top of.** *Informal.* **1.** In control of. **2.** Fully informed about: *a senator who is always on top of the issues.* **3.** In addition to; besides: *On top of this, several other benefits are being offered.* **4.** Following closely on; coming immediately after: *Hail came on top of a violent thunderstorm.* **on top of the world.** *Informal.* In a position of great happiness or success. **over the top. 1.** Surpassing a goal or quota. **2.** Over the breastwork, as an attack in trench warfare: *"a whole battalion, onto the beachhead, over the top"* (Margaret Atwood). [Middle English, from Old English.]

top² (tŏp) *n.* A toy having one end tapered to a point, allowing it to be spun, as by suddenly pulling a string wound around it. [Middle English, from Old English.]

top– *pref.* Variant of **topo–.**

to·paz (tō′păz′) *n.* **1.a.** A colorless, blue, yellow, brown, or pink aluminum silicate mineral, often found in association with granitic rocks and valued as a gemstone, especially in the brown and pink varieties. **b.** Any of various yellow gemstones, especially a yellow variety of sapphire or corundum. **2.** A light yellow variety of quartz. **3.** Either of two South American hummingbirds *(Topaza pyra* or *T. pella)* having colorful plumage. [Middle English *topace,* from Old French, from Latin *topazus,* from Greek *topazos.*]

top banana *n. Slang.* **1.** The main comic in a burlesque show. **2.** The head person, as of a group or project. [So called from the presentation of a banana to the comedian who has the punch line in a three-man burlesque routine.]

top boot *n.* A high boot usually having its upper part made of a different material or with leather of a contrasting color or texture.

top•coat (tŏp′kōt′) *n.* A lightweight overcoat.

top dog *n. Slang.* One considered to have the dominant position or highest authority, especially as a result of a competitive victory. **—top′-dog′** (tŏp′dôg′, -dŏg′) *adj.*

top-drawer (tŏp′drôr′) *adj.* Of the highest importance, rank, privilege, or merit.

top-dress (tŏp′drĕs′) *tr.v.* **-dressed, -dress•ing, -dress•es. 1.** To cover (a road surface) with loose material that is not worked in. **2.** To cover (farmland) with fertilizer.

top dressing *n.* **1.** A covering of loose gravel on a road. **2.** A covering of manure or other fertilizer spread on soil without being plowed under.

tope[1] (tōp) *tr. & intr.v.* **toped, top•ing, topes.** To drink (liquor) habitually and excessively or engage in such drinking. [Possibly from obsolete *tope,* interjection used in proposing a toast.]

tope[2] (tōp) *n.* A small, rough-skinned, widely distributed shark *(Galeorhinus galeus)* having an elongated conical snout. [Origin unknown.]

tope[3] (tōp) *n.* A dome-shaped monument, used to house Buddhist relics or to commemorate significant facts of Buddhism or Jainism. Also called *stupa.* [Hindi *top,* probably from Prakrit *thūpo,* from Sanskrit *stūpaḥ,* tuft of hair, crown of the head, stupa.]

to•pec•to•my (tə-pĕk′tə-mē) *n., pl.* **-mies.** Surgical removal of specific areas of the frontal lobe of the cerebral cortex as a treatment of certain mental disorders. [TOP(O)– + –ECTOMY.]

to•pee (tō-pē′, tō′pē) *n.* Variant of **topi**[1].

To•pe•ka (tə-pē′kə). The capital of Kansas, in the northeast part of the state west of Kansas City. Founded in 1854, it became capital when Kansas was admitted to the Union in 1861. Population, 115,266.

top•er (tō′pər) *n.* A chronic drinker.

top•flight (tŏp′flīt′) *adj. Informal.* First-rate; excellent.

top•gal•lant (tə-găl′ənt, tŏp-) *adj.* **1.** *Nautical.* Of, relating to, or being the mast above the topmast, its sails, or its rigging. **2.** Raised above adjacent parts or structures.

top gun *n. Slang.* One who performs at the pinnacle of professional ability; one who is the best at what one does.

top-ham•per also **top ham•per** (tŏp′hăm′pər) *n.* **1.** *Nautical.* Weight or materials, such as rigging, cables, and spars stored either aloft or on the upper decks. **2.** Cumbersome, unnecessary matter.

top hat *n.* A man's hat having a narrow brim and a tall cylindrical crown, usually made of silk. Also called *high hat.*

top-heav•y (tŏp′hĕv′ē) *adj.* **-i•er, -i•est. 1.** Likely to topple because of an uneven distribution of weight, with the majority being at the top. **2.** *Accounting.* Overcapitalized. **3.** Having a disproportionately large number of administrators. **—top′-heav′i•ness** *n.*

To•phet (tō′fĕt′, -fĭt) *n.* **1.** *Judaism.* The underworld where wicked souls suffer torment after death. **2.** An extremely unpleasant or painful condition or place. [Middle English, from Hebrew *tōpet,* a place where children were burned.]

top-hole (tŏp′hōl′) *adj. Chiefly British.* First-rate; excellent.

to•phus (tō′fəs) *n., pl.* **-phi** (-fī). **1.** *Pathology.* A deposit of urates in the skin and tissue around a joint or in the external ear, occurring in gout. Also called *chalkstone.* **2.** A concretion of mineral salts and organic matter deposited on the surface of the teeth. [Latin *tōphus,* tufa.]

to•pi[1] also **to•pee** (tō-pē′, tō′pē) *n., pl.* **-pis** also **-pees.** A pith helmet worn for protection against sun and heat. [Hindi *ṭopī,* hat.]

to•pi[2] (tō′pē) *n., pl.* **topi** or **-pis.** A sassaby *(Damaliscus lunatus* subsp. *topi)* of eastern Africa having a glossy dark brown coat. [Probably of Swahili origin.]

to•pi•ar•y (tō′pē-ĕr′ē) *adj.* Of or characterized by the clipping or trimming of live shrubs or trees into decorative shapes, as of animals. **—topiary** *n., pl.* **-ies. 1.** Topiary work or art. **2.** A topiary garden. [Latin *topiārius,* from *topia,* ornamental gardening, from Greek *topia,* pl. of *topion,* field, diminutive of *topos,* place.]

top•ic (tŏp′ĭk) *n.* **1.** The subject of a speech, an essay, a thesis, or a discourse. **2.** A subject of discussion or conversation. **3.** A subdivision of a theme, a thesis, or an outline. See Synonyms at **subject.** [Obsolete *topic,* rhetorical argument, sing. of *Topics,* title of a work by Aristotle, from Latin *Topica,* from Greek *Topika,* commonplaces, from neuter pl. of *topikos,* of a place, from *topos,* place.]

top•i•cal (tŏp′ĭ-kəl) *adj.* **1.** Of or belonging to a particular location or place; local. **2.** Currently of interest; contemporary. **3.** *Medicine.* Of or applied to an isolated or localized area of the body. **4.** Of, arranged by, or relating to a particular topic or topics. [From Greek *topikos,* from *topos,* place.] **—top′i•cal′i•ty** (-kăl′ĭ-tē) *n.* **—top′i•cal•ly** *adv.*

topic sentence *n.* The sentence within a paragraph or discourse that states the main thought, often placed at the beginning.

top•knot (tŏp′nŏt′) *n.* **1.** A crest or knot of hair or feathers on the crown of the head. **2.** A decorative ribbon or bow worn as a headdress.

top•less (tŏp′lĭs) *adj.* **1.** Having no top: *a collection of topless jars.* **2.** So high as to appear to extend out of sight: *the topless Alps.* **3.** Of, relating to, or wearing a garment that does not cover the breasts.

top-lev•el (tŏp′lĕv′əl) *adj.* **1.** Of or relating to people of the highest office or rank. **2.** Of or relating to the highest office or rank: *a top-level job.*

top•loft•y (tŏp′lôf′tē, -lŏf′-) *adj.* **-i•er, -i•est.** Haughty; pretentious. **—top′loft′i•ness** *n.*

top•mast (tŏp′məst, -măst′) *n. Nautical.* The mast below the topgallant mast in a square-rigged ship and highest in a fore-and-aft-rigged ship.

top•min•now (tŏp′mĭn′ō) *n.* **1.** Any of several small New World freshwater fishes of the genus *Fundulus,* related to the killifishes. **2.** Any of various small viviparous New World fishes of the family Poeciliidae, of fresh or brackish waters. [So called because it swims near the surface of the water.]

top•most (tŏp′mōst′) *adj.* Highest; uppermost.

top•notch (tŏp′nŏch′) *adj. Informal.* First-rate; excellent.

topo– or **top–** *pref.* Place; region: *toponymy.* [Greek, from *topos,* place.]

topog. *abbr.* topography.

to•pog•ra•pher (tə-pŏg′rə-fər) *n.* **1.** One who is skilled in topography. **2.** One who describes and maps the surface features of geographic regions.

to•pog•ra•phy (tə-pŏg′rə-fē) *n., pl.* **-phies.** *Abbr.* **topog. 1.** Detailed, precise description of a place or region. **2.** Graphic representation of the surface features of a place or region on a map, indicating their relative positions and elevations. **3.** A description or an analysis of a structured entity, showing the relations among its components: *In the topography of the economy, several depressed areas are revealed.* **4. a.** The surface features of a place or region. **b.** The surface features of an object: *The topography of a crystal.* **5.** The surveying of the features of a place or region. **6.** The study or description of an anatomical region or part. **—top′o•graph′** (tŏp′ə-grăf′) *n.* **—top′o•graph′ic** (-grăf′ĭk), **top′o•graph′i•cal** (-ĭ-kəl) *adj.* **—top′o•graph′i•cal•ly** *adv.*

to•poi (tō′poi) *n.* Plural of **topos.**

to•pol•o•gy (tə-pŏl′ə-jē) *n., pl.* **-gies. 1.** Topographic study of a given place, especially the history of a region as indicated by its topography. **2.** *Medicine.* The anatomical structure of a specific area or part of the body. **3.** *Mathematics.* The study of the properties of geometric figures or solids that are not normally affected by changes in size or shape. **—top′o•log′ic** (tŏp′ə-lŏj′ĭk), **top′o•log′i•cal** (-ĭ-kəl) *adj.* **—top′o•log′i•cal•ly** *adv.* **—to•pol′o•gist** *n.*

top•o•nym (tŏp′ə-nĭm′) *n.* **1.** A place name. **2.** A name derived from a place or region. [Back-formation from TOPONYMY.] **—top′o•nym′ic, top′o•nym′i•cal** *adj.*

to•pon•y•my (tə-pŏn′ə-mē) *n., pl.* **-mies. 1. a.** The place names of a region or language. **b.** The study of such place names. **2.** *Anatomy.* Nomenclature with respect to a region of the body rather than to organs or structures.

to•pos (tō′pōs, -pŏs) *n., pl.* **-poi** (-poi). A traditional theme or motif; a literary convention. [Greek, short for *(koinos) topos,* (common)place.]

top•o•type (tŏp′ə-tīp′) *n. Biology.* A specimen of an organism taken from the type locality of that species.

top•per (tŏp′ər) *n.* **1.** One that removes tops or puts tops on. **2. a.** One that is exceedingly or surpassingly good of its kind. **b.** *Slang.* Something, such as a witticism, that surpasses all that has gone before. **3.** A woman's short, lightweight coat. **4.** *Slang.* A top hat.

top•ping (tŏp′ĭng) *n.* **1.** A sauce, frosting, or garnish for food. **2.** A part or layer that forms the top. **3. toppings.** The cropped parts of plants or trees after pruning. **—topping** *adj.* **1.** Highest in rank or eminence. **2.** *Chiefly British.* First-rate; excellent.

top•ple (tŏp′əl) *v.* **-pled, -pling, -ples.** —*tr.* To push or throw over; overturn or overthrow. See Synonyms at **overthrow.** —*intr.* **1.** To totter and fall. **2.** To lean over as if about to fall. [Frequentative of TOP[1].]

top quark *n. Abbr.* **t** A hypothetical quark with a charge of +⅔ and a mass more than 100,000 times that of the electron. Also called *truth quark.* See table at **subatomic particle.**

top round *n.* A cut of meat, such as a steak or roast, taken from the inner section of a round of beef.

tops (tŏps) *adj. Slang.* First-rate; excellent: *Her new novel is tops.*

top hat

topiary

ă pat	oi boy
ā pay	ou out
âr care	ŏŏ took
ä father	ōō boot
ĕ pet	ŭ cut
ē be	ûr urge
ĭ pit	th thin
ī pie	*th* this
îr pier	hw which
ŏ pot	zh vision
ō toe	ə about, item
ô paw	♦ regionalism

Stress marks: ′ (primary); ′ (secondary), as in **dictionary** (dĭk′shə-nĕr′ē)

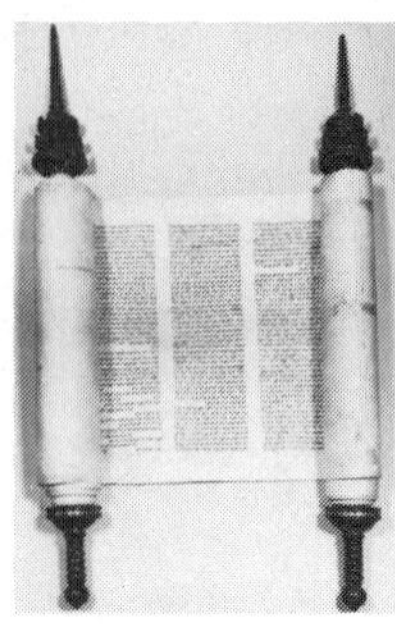

Torah
18th-century Torah scroll

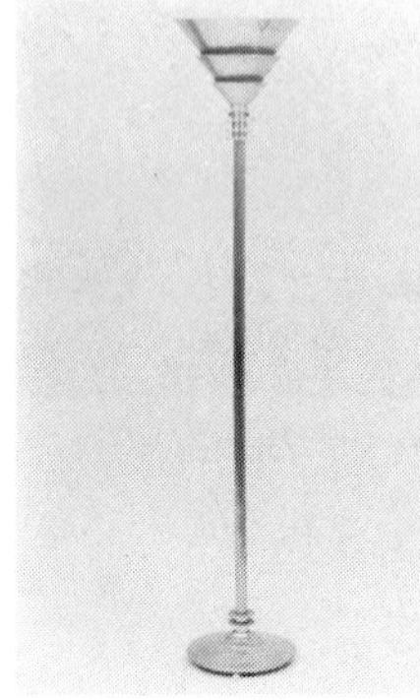

torchère
c. 1932 aluminum torchère, designed by Walter von Nessen (1889–1943) with modifications by Eliel Saarinen (1873–1950)

torii
The Grand Torii of Itsukushima, Japan

tornado

top·sail (tŏp′səl, -sāl′) *n. Nautical.* **1.** A square sail set above the lowest sail on the mast of a square-rigged ship. **2.** A triangular or square sail set above the gaff of a lower sail on a fore-and-aft-rigged ship.

topsail schooner *n. Nautical.* A schooner carrying two or more square topsails on its foremast.

top-se·cret (tŏp′sē′krĭt) *adj.* Containing information, the unauthorized disclosure of which poses the gravest threat to national security.

top·side (tŏp′sīd′) *n.* **1.** Often **topsides.** *Nautical.* The surface of a ship's hull above the water line. **2.** The highest position of authority. **—topside** *adv. & adj.* **1.** *Nautical.* On or to the upper parts of a ship; on deck. **2.** In a position of authority.

top·sid·er (tŏp′sī′dər) *n.* One who is at the highest level of authority.

Top-Sid·er (tŏp′sī′dər). A trademark used for a soft leather or canvas shoe with a rubber sole. This trademark often occurs in print in the plural: *"Slightly beat-up Top-Siders complete the look"* (New York Times). "[He] *strides through his domain in designer jeans and Top-Siders"* (Fortune).

top·soil (tŏp′soil′) *n.* The upper part of the soil. **—topsoil** *tr.v.* **-soiled, -soil·ing, -soils.** To remove the surface layer of soil from (land).

top·spin (tŏp′spĭn′) *n. Sports.* Forward rotation imparted to a ball by a stroke, as in tennis.

top·stitch (tŏp′stĭch′) *tr.v.* **-stitched, -stitch·ing, -stitch·es.** To sew a row of stitching close to the seam or edge of (a garment) on the outer side of the fabric.

top·sy-tur·vy (tŏp′sē-tûr′vē) *adv.* **1.** With the top downward and the bottom up; upside-down. **2.** In a state of utter disorder or confusion: *"turning our ordered life topsy-turvy"* (Anne Tyler). **—topsy-turvy** *adj.* **-vi·er, -vi·est.** Being in a confused or disordered condition. **—topsy-turvy** *n., pl.* **-vies.** The quality, the condition, or an instance of confusion or chaos. [Probably from TOP[1] + obsolete *terve,* to overturn (from Middle English *terven*).] **—top′sy-tur′vi·ly** *adv.* **—top′sy-tur′vi·ness** *n.*

toque (tōk) *n.* **1.** A woman's small, brimless, close-fitting hat. **2.** A plumed velvet cap with a full crown and small rolled brim, worn in 16th-century France. [French, from Spanish *toca,* perhaps from Arabic **ṭâqa,* from Old Persian *tāq,* veil, shawl.]

tor (tôr) *n.* **1.** A high rock or pile of rocks on the top of a hill. **2.** A rocky peak or hill. [Middle English, from Old English *torr,* probably of Celtic origin.]

To·rah also **to·rah** (tôr′ə, tōr′ə, toir′ə, tô-rä′) *n. Judaism.* **1.** The entire body of religious law and learning including both sacred literature and oral tradition. **2.** A scroll of parchment containing the first five books of the Hebrew Scriptures, used in a synagogue during services. **3.** The first five books of the Hebrew Scriptures. See table at **Bible.** [Hebrew *tôrâ,* law, instruction.]

Tor·bay (tôr-bā′, tôr′bā′). A borough of southwest England east-northeast of Plymouth. It is in a popular seaside resort area. Population, 112,400.

tor·bern·ite (tôr′bər-nīt′) *n.* A green radioactive mineral that is a hydrous crystalline phosphate of uranium and copper. [After *Torbern* Olof Bergman (1735–1784), Swedish chemist.]

torch (tôrch) *n.* **1.a.** A portable light produced by the flame of a stick of resinous wood or of a flammable material wound about the end of a stick of wood; a flambeau. **b.** *Chiefly British.* A flashlight. **2.** Something that serves to illuminate, enlighten, or guide. **3.** *Slang.* An arsonist. **4.** A portable apparatus that produces a very hot flame by the combustion of gases, used in welding and construction. **—torch** *tr.v.* **torched, torch·ing, torch·es.** *Slang.* To cause to burn or undergo combustion, especially with extraordinary rapidity, force, or thoroughness. [Middle English *torche,* from Old French, from Vulgar Latin **torca,* alteration of Latin *torqua,* variant of *torquēs,* torque, from Latin *torquēre,* to twist. See **terkʷ-** in Appendix.]

torch·bear·er (tôrch′bâr′ər) *n.* **1.** One that carries a torch. **2.** One, such as the leader of a government, who imparts knowledge, truth, or inspiration to others.

tor·chère (tôr-shâr′) also **tor·chier** or **tor·chiere** (-chîr′) *n.* A usually tall floor lamp with a bowl-shaped part that diffuses the light or directs it upward. [French, from *torche,* torch. See TORCH.]

tor·chon lace (tôr′shŏn′) *n.* Lace made of coarse linen or cotton thread twisted in simple geometric patterns. [French *torchon,* duster, from Old French, from *torche,* twisted straw, torch. See TORCH.]

torch song *n. Music.* A sentimental love song, typically one in which the singer laments a lost love. **—torch singer** *n.*

torch·wood (tôrch′wo͝od′) *n.* **1.** Any of several tropical American trees of the genus *Amyris,* especially *A. balsamifera,* having resinous wood that burns with a torchlike flame. **2.** The wood of any of these trees.

tore[1] (tôr, tōr) *v.* Past tense of **tear[1].**

tore[2] (tôr, tōr) *n. Mathematics.* See **torus** (sense 4). [French, from Latin *torus.*]

tor·e·a·dor (tôr′ē-ə-dôr′) *n.* A matador; a bullfighter. [Spanish, from *torear,* to fight bulls, from *toro,* bull, from Latin *taurus.* See **tauro-** in Appendix.]

to·re·ro (tə-râr′ō, tô-rĕ′rō) *n., pl.* **-ros.** A matador or one of the supporting team. [Spanish, from Late Latin *taurārius,* from Latin *taurus,* bull. See **tauro-** in Appendix.]

to·reu·tics (tə-ro͞o′tĭks) *n. (used with a sing. verb).* The art of working metal or other materials by the use of embossing and chasing to form minute detailed reliefs. [From Greek *toreutikos,* of metal work, from *toreutos,* worked in relief, from *toreuein,* to work in relief, from *toreus,* a boring tool. See **terə-[1]** in Appendix.] **—to·reu′tic** *adj.*

to·ri (tôr′ī, tōr′ī) *n.* Plural of **torus.**

tor·ic (tôr′ĭk, tōr′-) *adj.* Of, relating to, or shaped like a torus or part of a torus.

to·ri·i (tôr′ē-ē′, tōr′-) *n., pl.* **torii.** The gateway of a Shinto temple, consisting of two uprights supporting a concave crosspiece with projecting ends and a straight crosspiece beneath it. [Japanese : *tori,* bird + *i-* (from *iru,* to dwell).]

To·ri·no (tô-rē′nô). See **Turin.**

tor·ment (tôr′mĕnt′) *n.* **1.** Great physical pain or mental anguish. **2.** A source of harassment, annoyance, or pain. **3.** The torture inflicted on prisoners under interrogation. **—torment** (tôr-mĕnt′, tôr′mĕnt′) *tr.v.* **-ment·ed, -ment·ing, -ments.** **1.** To cause to undergo great physical pain or mental anguish. See Synonyms at **afflict. 2.** To agitate or upset greatly. **3.** To annoy, pester, or harass. [Middle English, from Old French, from Latin *tormentum* (from *torquēre,* to twist. See **terkʷ-** in Appendix).] **—tor·ment′ing·ly** *adv.*

tor·men·til (tôr′mən-tĭl′) *n.* A perennial Eurasian plant *(Potentilla erecta)* having yellow flowers and astringent roots. [Middle English *tormentille,* from Medieval Latin *tormentilla,* feminine diminutive of Latin *tormentum,* torment (from its use as an analgesic). See TORMENT.]

tor·men·tor also **tor·ment·er** (tôr-mĕn′tər, tôr′mĕn′-) *n.* **1.** One that torments. **2.** A hanging at each side of a stage directly behind the proscenium that serves to block the wing area and sidelights from the audience. **3.** A sound-absorbent screen used on a movie set, used to prevent echo.

torn (tôrn, tōrn) *v.* Past participle of **tear[1].**

tor·na·do (tôr-nā′dō) *n., pl.* **-does** or **-dos.** **1.** A rotating column of air usually accompanied by a funnel-shaped downward extension of a cumulonimbus cloud and having a vortex several hundred yards in diameter whirling destructively at speeds of up to 500 miles (800 kilometers) per hour. **2.** A violent thunderstorm in western Africa or nearby Atlantic waters. **3.** A whirlwind or hurricane. [Alteration (perhaps influenced by Spanish *tornar,* to turn) of Spanish *tronada,* thunderstorm, from *tronar,* to thunder, from Latin *tonāre.* See **(s)tenə-** in Appendix.] **—tor·na′dic** (-nā′dĭk, -năd′ĭk) *adj.*

Tor·ne (tôr′nə) also **Tor·ni·o** (tôr′nē-ō′). A river of northern Sweden rising near the Norwegian border in **Lake Torne** and flowing about 402 km (250 mi) generally southeast to the Gulf of Bothnia. It forms the Swedish-Finnish border in its lower course.

tor·nil·lo (tôr-nĭl′ō, -nē′ō) *n., pl.* **-los.** See **screw bean.** [American Spanish, from Spanish, small lathe, screw, diminutive of *torno,* lathe, from Latin *tornus.* See TURN.]

Tor·ni·o (tôr′nē-ō′). See **Torne.**

to·roid (tôr′oid′, tōr′-) *n.* **1.** *Mathematics.* **a.** A surface generated by a closed curve rotating about, but not intersecting or containing, an axis in its own plane. **b.** A solid having such a surface. **2.** A body having the shape of a toroid. [TOR(US) + -OID.] **—to·roi′dal** (tô-roid′l) *adj.*

To·ron·to (tə-rŏn′tō). The capital and largest city of Ontario, Canada, in the southern part of the province on Lake Ontario. Originally a French trading post, it was founded as York by the British in 1793 and renamed as Toronto in 1834. Toronto is an important Great Lakes port and an industrial center. Population, 599,217.

to·rose (tôr′ōs′, tōr′-) *adj.* Cylindrical and having ridges or swellings. [Latin *torōsus,* from *torus,* knot, bulge.]

♦**tor·pe·do** (tôr-pē′dō) *n., pl.* **-does.** **1.** A cigar-shaped, self-propelled underwater projectile launched from a submarine, an aircraft, or a ship and designed to detonate on contact with or in the vicinity of a target. **2.** Any of various submarine explosive devices, especially a submarine mine. **3.** A small explosive placed on a railroad track that is fired by the weight of the train to sound a warning of an approaching hazard. **4.** An explosive fired in an oil or gas well to begin or increase the flow. **5.** A small firework consisting of some gravel wrapped in tissue paper with a percussion cap that explodes when thrown against a hard surface. **6.** See **electric ray. 7.** *Slang.* A professional assassin or thug. **8.** *Chiefly New Jersey.* See **submarine** (sense 2). See Regional Note at **submarine. —torpedo** *tr.v.* **-doed, -do·ing, -does.** **1.** To attack, strike, or sink with a torpedo. **2.** To destroy decisively; wreck: *torpedo efforts at reform.* [Latin *torpēdō,* numbness; electric ray, crampfish, from *torpēre,* to be stiff. See **ster-[1]** in Appendix.]

torpedo boat *n.* A small, fast, thinly plated warship equipped for firing torpedoes.

tor·pe·do-boat destroyer (tôr-pē′dō-bōt′) *n.* A large, heavily armed torpedo boat used in combat especially against other torpedo boats.

torpedo tube *n.* A tube in the hull of a submarine or another naval vessel through which torpedoes are launched.

tor·pid (tôr′pĭd) *adj.* **1.** Deprived of the power of motion or feeling; benumbed. **2.** Dormant; hibernating. **3.** Lethargic; apathetic. See Synonyms at **inactive.** [Latin *torpidus,* from *torpēre,* to be stiff. See **ster-[1]** in Appendix.] **—tor′pid·ly** *adv.*

tor·pid·i·ty (tôr-pĭd′ĭ-tē) *n.* The quality or state of being torpid. See Synonyms at **lethargy.**

tor·por (tôr′pər) *n.* **1.** A state of mental or physical inactivity or insensibility. **2.** Lethargy; apathy. See Synonyms at **lethargy. 3.** The dormant, inactive state of a hibernating or estivating animal. [Latin, from *torpēre,* to be stiff. See **ster-[1]** in Appendix.] **—tor′po·rif′ic** (-pə-rĭf′ĭk) *adj.*

tor·quate (tôr′kwāt′) *adj. Zoology.* Having a ringlike or collarlike band or marking about the neck. [Latin *torquātus,* from *torquēs,* collar. See TORQUE[2].]

torque[1] (tôrk) *n.* **1.** The moment of a force; the measure of a force's tendency to produce torsion and rotation about an axis, equal to the vector product of the radius vector from the axis of rotation to the point of application of the force. **2.** A turning or twisting force. **—torque** *tr.v.* **torqued, torqu·ing, torques.** To impart torque to. [From Latin *torquēre,* to twist. See **terkʷ-** in Appendix.] **—torqu′er** *n.* **—torque′y** *adj.*

torque[2] (tôrk) *n.* A collar, a necklace, or an armband made of a strip of twisted metal, worn by the ancient Gauls, Germans, and Britons. [French, from Old French, from Latin *torquēs,* from *torquēre,* to twist. See **terkʷ-** in Appendix.]

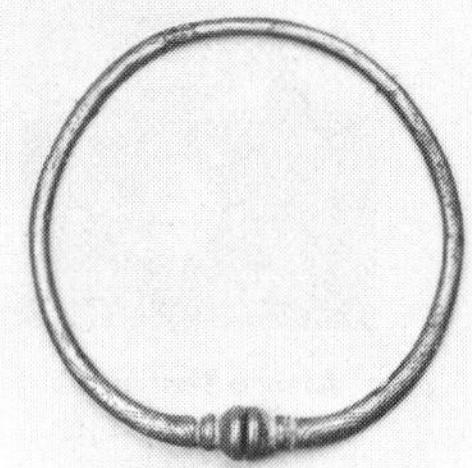

torque[2]
Fourth- to second-century B.C. Celtic bronze torque

torque converter *n.* A mechanical or hydraulic device for changing the ratio of torque to speed between the input and output shafts of a mechanism.

Tor·que·ma·da (tôr′kə-mä′də, tôr′kĕ-mä′*thä*), **Tomás de.** 1420–1498. Spanish Dominican monk who was appointed grand inquisitor by Pope Innocent VIII (1487). Under his authority, thousands of Jews, suspected witches, and others were killed or tortured during the Spanish Inquisition.

tor·ques (tôr′kwēz′) *n. Zoology.* A band of feathers, hair, or coloration around the neck. [Latin *torquēs,* collar. See TORQUE[2].]

torr (tôr) *n., pl.* **torr.** A unit of pressure that is equal to approximately 1.316×10^{-3} atmosphere or 1,333 pascals. [After Evangelista TORRICELLI.]

Tor·rance (tôr′əns, tŏr′-). A city of southern California south of Los Angeles. Founded c. 1912, it is a manufacturing center. Population, 131,497.

Tor·re An·nun·zi·a·ta (tôr′ā ə-no͞on′sē-ä′tə, tôr′rĕ ä-no͞on′tsē-ä′tä). A city of southern Italy on the Bay of Naples. Founded in the 14th century, the city was destroyed by an eruption of Vesuvius in 1631. Population, 57,097.

Torre de Cer·re·do (də sə-rā′dō, *thĕ* sĕ-rĕ′*thô*). A mountain, 2,649.8 m (8,688 ft) high, of the Cantabrian Mountains in northwest Spain. It is the highest elevation in the range.

Torre del Gre·co (dĕl grĕk′ō). A city of southern Italy on the Bay of Naples near Mount Vesuvius. It is a fishing port and tourist resort. Population, 102,890.

Tor·rens (tôr′ənz, tŏr′-). A salt lake of south-central Australia north-northwest of Adelaide.

tor·rent (tôr′ənt, tŏr′-) *n.* **1.** A turbulent, swift-flowing stream. **2.** A heavy downpour; a deluge. **3.** A heavy, uncontrolled outpouring: *a torrent of insults; torrents of mail.* [Latin *torrēns, torrent-,* from present participle of *torrēre,* to burn. See **ters-** in Appendix.]

tor·ren·tial (tô-rĕn′shəl, tə-) *adj.* **1.** Resembling, flowing in, or forming torrents: *torrential mountain streams; a torrential downpour.* **2.** Resulting from the action of fast-flowing streams: *torrential erosion.* **3.** Flowing or surging abundantly; wild: *torrential applause.* **—tor·ren′tial·ly** *adv.*

Tor·re·ón (tôr′ē-ōn′, -rĕ-ôn′). A city of northern Mexico west of Monterrey. Founded in 1893, it is an agricultural center. Population, 328,086.

Tor·res Strait (tôr′ĭs). A strait between New Guinea and Cape York Peninsula of northeast Australia. It connects the Arafura Sea with the Coral Sea.

Tor·reys Peak (tôr′ēz, tŏr′-). A mountain, 4,351.4 m (14,267 ft) high, in the Front Range of the Rocky Mountains in central Colorado.

Tor·ri·cel·li (tôr′ə-chĕl′ē, tôr′ē-), **Evangelista.** 1608–1647. Italian mathematician and physicist who invented the mercury barometer.

tor·rid (tôr′ĭd, tŏr′-) *adj.* **-er, -est. 1.** Parched with the heat of the sun; intensely hot. **2.** Scorching; burning: *the torrid noonday sun.* **3.** Passionate; ardent: *a torrid love scene.* **4.** Hurried; rapid: *set a torrid pace; torrid economic growth.* [Latin *torridus,* from *torrēre,* to parch. See **ters-** in Appendix.] **—tor·rid′i·ty, tor′rid·ness** *n.* **—tor′rid·ly** *adv.*

Tor·rid Zone (tôr′ĭd, tŏr′-). The central latitude zone of the earth, between the Tropic of Cancer and the Tropic of Capricorn.

Tor·ri·jos Her·re·ra (tôr-rē′hôs ĕr-rĕ′rä), **Omar.** 1929–1981. Panamanian military and political leader who seized power in a coup d'état and ruled as a virtual dictator (1968–1981).

Tor·ring·ton (tôr′ĭng-tən, tŏr′-). A city of northwest Connecticut west of Hartford. The process of milk homogenization was invented here. Population, 30,987.

tor·sade (tôr-säd′, -săd′) *n.* A decorative trimming of twisted ribbon or cord, used especially on hats. [French, from *tors,* from Vulgar Latin *-*torsus,* alteration of Latin *tortus,* past participle of *torquēre,* to twist. See **terkʷ-** in Appendix.]

Tór·shavn (tôr′shouN′). The capital of the Faeroe Islands, on southeast Straymoy Island. It is a major port and shipping center. Population, 14,443.

tor·si (tôr′sē) *n.* A plural of **torso.**

tor·sion (tôr′shən) *n.* **1.a.** The act of twisting or turning. **b.** The condition of being twisted or turned. **2.** The stress or deformation caused when one end of an object is twisted in one direction and the other end is held motionless or twisted in the opposite direction. [Middle English *torcion,* wringing pain in the bowels, from Old French *torsion,* from Late Latin *torsiō, torsiōn-,* a wringing pain, variant of Latin *tortiō,* from *tortus,* past participle of *torquēre,* to twist. See TORSADE.] **—tor′sion·al** *adj.* **—tor′sion·al·ly** *adv.*

torsion balance *n.* An instrument with which small forces, as of electricity or magnetism, are measured by means of the torsion they produce in a wire or slender rod.

torsion bar *n.* A part of an automotive suspension consisting of a bar that twists to maintain stability.

tor·so (tôr′sō) *n., pl.* **-sos** or **-si** (-sē). **1.** The human body excluding the head and limbs; trunk. **2.** A statue of the human body with the head and limbs omitted or removed. **3.** A truncated or unfinished thing. [Italian, trunk of a statue, from Old Italian, stalk, stem, from Vulgar Latin **tursus,* from Latin *thyrsus,* stem. See THYRSUS.]

tort (tôrt) *n. Law.* Damage, injury, or a wrongful act done willfully, negligently, or in circumstances involving strict liability, but not involving breach of contract, for which a civil suit can be brought. [Middle English, injury, from Old French, from Medieval Latin *tortum,* from Latin, neuter past participle of *torquēre,* to twist. See **terkʷ-** in Appendix.]

torte (tôrt, tôr′tə) *n.* A rich cake made with many eggs and little flour and usually containing chopped nuts. [Probably German, perhaps from Italian *torta,* cake, tart, from Late Latin *tōrta,* a kind of bread.]

tor·tel·li·ni (tôr′tl-ē′nē) *n.* Small ring-shaped pasta stuffed usually with meat or cheese and served in soup or with a sauce. [Italian, diminutive of *tortelli,* a kind of pasta, pl. diminutive of *torta,* cake, from Late Latin *torta,* a kind of bread.]

tor·ti·col·lis (tôr′tĭ-kŏl′ĭs) *n.* A contracted state of the neck muscles producing an unnatural position of the head. Also called *wryneck.* [New Latin : Latin *tortus,* twisted, past participle of *torquēre,* to twist; see **terkʷ-** in Appendix + *collum,* neck; see **kʷel-[1]** in Appendix.] **—tor′ti·col′lar** (-kŏl′ər) *adj.*

tor·til·la (tôr-tē′yə) *n.* A thin disk of unleavened bread made from cornmeal or wheat flour, baked on a hot surface, and usually served topped with or rolled around beans, ground meat, or cheese. [American Spanish, diminutive of Spanish *torta,* cake, from Late Latin *torta,* a kind of bread.]

tortoise
Galápagos giant tortoise
Geochelone elephantopus

tor·toise (tôr′tĭs) *n.* **1.a.** Any of various terrestrial turtles, especially one of the family Testudinidae, characteristically having thick clublike hind limbs and a high, rounded carapace. **b.** *Chiefly British.* A terrestrial or freshwater chelonian. **2.** One that moves slowly; a laggard. [Alteration (influenced by PORPOISE) of Middle English *tortuce,* from Medieval Latin *tortūca,* alteration of Late Latin *tartarūcha,* feminine of *tartarūchus,* of the underworld. See TURTLE[1].]

tortoise beetle *n.* Any of several small beetles of the subfamily Cassidinae, shaped somewhat like a tortoise and having soft, fleshy larvae that eat the leaves of trees.

tor·toise·shell also **tor·toise-shell** or **tor·toise shell** (tôr′tĭs-shĕl′) *n.* **1.a.** The mottled, horny, translucent, brownish covering of the carapace of certain tortoises or turtles, especially the hawksbill, used to make combs, jewelry, and other articles. **b.** A synthetic imitation of natural tortoiseshell. **2.** See **hawksbill. 3.** A domestic cat having fur with brown, black, and yellowish markings. **4.** Any of several butterflies, chiefly of the genus *Nymphalis,* having wings with orange, black, and brown markings. **—tor′toise·shell′** *adj.*

Tor·to·la (tôr-tō′lə). An island of the West Indies east of Puerto Rico. It is the largest of the British Virgin Islands.

tor·tri·cid (tôr′trĭ-sĭd) *n.* Any of various small, thick-bodied moths of the family Tortricidae, including the leaf rollers, having larvae that feed on the leaves of trees such as oak, pine, and larch. **—tortricid** *adj.* Of or belonging to the family Tortricidae. [From New Latin *Tortricidae,* family name, from *Tortrix, Tortric-,* type genus. See TORTRIX.]

tor·trix (tôr′trĭks) *n.* A moth of the family Tortricidae; a tortricid. [New Latin *Tortrix,* genus name, from Latin *tortus,* past participle of *torquēre,* to twist. See TORTUOUS.]

Tor·tu·ga (tôr-to͞o′gə). An island in the West Indies off northern Haiti. It was a pirate refuge in the 17th century.

tor·tu·os·i·ty (tôr′cho͞o-ŏs′ĭ-tē) *n., pl.* **-ties. 1.** The quality or condition of being tortuous; twistedness or crookedness. **2.** A bent or twisted part, passage, or thing.

tor·tu·ous (tôr′cho͞o-əs) *adj.* **1.** Having or marked by repeated turns or bends; winding or twisting: *a tortuous road through the mountains.* **2.** Not straightforward; circuitous; devious: *a tortuous plot; tortuous reasoning.* **3.** Highly involved; complex: *tortuous legal procedures.* [Middle English, from Anglo-Norman, from Latin *tortuōsus,* from *tortus,* a twisting, from past participle of *torquēre,* to twist. See **terkʷ-** in Appendix.] **—tor′tu·ous·ly** *adv.* **—tor′tu·ous·ness** *n.*

USAGE NOTE: Although *tortuous* and *torturous* both come from the Latin word *torquēre,* "to twist," their primary meanings are

ă pat	oi boy
ā pay	ou out
âr care	o͝o took
ä father	o͞o boot
ĕ pet	ŭ cut
ē be	ûr urge
ĭ pit	th thin
ī pie	*th* this
îr pier	hw which
ŏ pot	zh vision
ō toe	ə about, item
ô paw	♦ regionalism

Stress marks: **′** (primary); ′ (secondary), as in **dictionary** (dĭk′shə-nĕr′ē)

Arturo Toscanini
Photographed in the 1930's

totem pole
Tlingit totem pole

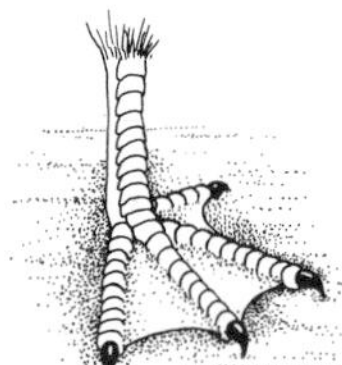
totipalmate
Totipalmate foot

toucan

distinct. *Tortuous* means "twisting" (*a tortuous road*) or by extension "complex" or "devious." *Torturous* refers primarily to torture and the pain associated with it. However, *torturous* also can be used in the sense of "twisted" or "strained," and *tortured* is an even stronger synonym: *tortured reasoning*.

tor·ture (tôr′chər) *n.* **1.a.** Infliction of severe physical pain as a means of punishment or coercion. **b.** An instrument or a method for inflicting such pain. **2.** Excruciating physical or mental pain; agony: *the torture of waiting in suspense.* **3.** Something causing severe pain or anguish. **—torture** *tr.v.* **-tured, -tur·ing, -tures. 1.** To subject (a person or an animal) to torture. **2.** To bring great physical or mental pain upon (another). See Synonyms at **afflict. 3.** To twist or turn abnormally; distort: *torture a rule to make it fit a case.* [Middle English, from Old French, from Late Latin *tortūra,* from Latin *tortus,* past participle of *torquēre,* to twist. See TORTUOUS.] **—tor′tur·er** *n.*

tor·tur·ous (tôr′chər-əs) *adj.* **1.** Of, relating to, or causing torture. **2.** Twisted; strained. See Usage Note at **tortuous. —tor′tur·ous·ly** *adv.*

tor·u·la (tôr′yə-lə, -ə-lə, tŏr′-) *n., pl.* **-lae** (-lē′, -lī′) or **-las.** Any of a group of fungi similar to the yeasts but lacking asci, many of which ferment sugars and are commonly found in dairy products. Also called *torula yeast.* [New Latin *Torula,* fungus genus, feminine diminutive of *torus,* bulge.]

To·ruń (tôr′o͞on′, -o͞on′yə). A city of north-central Poland on the Vistula River northwest of Warsaw. Founded by the Teutonic Knights in 1231, it became part of the kingdom of Poland in 1454. Toruń was taken by Sweden (1703) and Prussia (1793 and 1815) before being returned to Poland in 1919. Population, 186,200.

to·rus (tôr′əs, tōr′-) *n., pl.* **to·ri** (tôr′ī, tōr′ī). **1.** *Architecture.* A large convex molding, semicircular in cross section, located at the base of a classical column. **2.** *Anatomy.* A bulging or rounded projection or swelling. **3.** *Botany.* The receptacle of a flower. **4.** *Mathematics.* A toroid generated by a circle; a surface having the shape of a doughnut. In this sense, also called *tore.* [Latin, bulge, knot, torus.]

To·ry (tôr′ē, tōr′ē) *n., pl.* **-ries. 1.a.** A member of a British political party, founded in 1689, that was the opposition party to the Whigs and has been known as the Conservative Party since about 1832. **b.** A member of a Conservative Party, as in Canada. **2.** An American who, during the period of the American Revolution, favored the British side. Also called *Loyalist.* **3.** Often **tory.** A supporter of traditional political and social institutions against the forces of democratization or reform; a political conservative. [Irish Gaelic *tóraidhe,* robber, from Old Irish *tóir,* pursuit. See **ret-** in Appendix.] **—To′ry** *adj.* **—To′ry·ism** *n.*

Tos·ca·ni·ni (tŏs′kə-nē′nē, tôs′kä-), **Arturo.** 1867–1957. Italian conductor of the Metropolitan Opera (1908–1921), the New York Philharmonic (1928–1936), and many other orchestras worldwide.

toss (tôs, tŏs) *v.* **tossed, toss·ing, toss·es.** *—tr.* **1.** To throw lightly or casually or with a sudden slight jerk: *tossed the letter in the wastebasket.* See Synonyms at **throw. 2.** To throw, fling, or heave continuously about; pitch to and fro: *boats that were tossed by the storm.* **3.** To mix (a salad) lightly so as to cover with dressing. **4.** To discuss informally; bandy: *tossed the idea around.* **5.** To move or lift (the head) with a sudden motion: *"tossing their heads in sprightly dance"* (William Wordsworth). **6.** To disturb or agitate; upset. **7.** To throw to the ground: *ducked the blow and tossed his opponent.* **8.a.** To flip (coins) in order to decide an issue. **b.** To flip coins with: *I'll toss you to see who goes first.* *—intr.* **1.** To be thrown here and there; be flung to and fro. **2.** To move about restlessly; twist and turn: *toss in one's sleep.* **3.** To flip a coin to decide an issue. **—toss** *n.* **1.** The act of tossing or the condition of being tossed. **2.** The distance that something is or can be tossed. **3.** An abrupt upward movement, as of the head. **4.** A flipping of a coin to decide an issue: *The home team won the toss and elected to kick off.* ***—phrasal verbs.*** **toss down.** *Informal.* To drink in one draft by suddenly tilting. **toss off.** *Informal.* **1.** To drink up in one draft. **2.** To do or finish effortlessly or casually: *"technicians who can toss off the Romantic blockbusters with stupendous speed and ease"* (Annalyn Swan). [Middle English *tossen,* possibly of Scandinavian origin.] **—toss′er** *n.*

toss·pot (tôs′pŏt′, tŏs′-) *n.* A drunkard.

toss·up (tôs′ŭp′, tŏs′-) *n. Informal.* **1.** An even chance or choice: *It is a tossup whether we will win or lose.* **2.** The flipping of a coin to decide an issue.

tos·ta·da (tō-stä′də) or **tos·ta·do** (-dō) *n., pl.* **-das** or **-dos.** A tortilla or tortilla chip deep-fried until crisp. [American Spanish, from Spanish, feminine past participle of *tostar,* to toast, from Vulgar Latin **tostāre.* See TOAST[1].]

tot[1] (tŏt) *n.* **1.** A small child. **2.** A small amount, as of liquor. [Origin unknown.]

tot[2] (tŏt) *tr.v.* **tot·ted, tot·ting, tots.** To total: *totted up the bill.*

to·tal (tōt′l) *n.* **1.** *Abbr.* **tot.** An amount obtained by addition; a sum. **2.** A whole quantity; an entirety. **—total** *adj.* **1.** Of, relating to, or constituting the whole; entire. See Synonyms at **whole. 2.** Complete; utter; absolute: *total concentration; a total effort; a total fool.* **—total** *v.* **-taled, -tal·ing, -tals** or **-talled, -tal·ling, -tals.** *—tr.* **1.** To determine the total of; add up. **2.** To equal a total of; amount to. **3.** *Slang.* To wreck completely; demolish: *survived the crash but totaled the car.* *—intr.* To add up; amount: *It totals to three dollars.* [Middle English, whole, from Old French, from Medieval Latin *tōtālis,* from Latin *tōtus.* See **teutā-** in Appendix.]

total eclipse *n.* An eclipse in which the entire surface of a celestial body is obscured.

to·tal·i·tar·i·an (tō-tăl′ĭ-târ′ē-ən) *adj.* Of, relating to, being, or imposing a form of government in which the political authority exercises absolute and centralized control over all aspects of life, the individual is subordinated to the state, and opposing political and cultural expression is suppressed: *"A totalitarian regime crushes all autonomous institutions in its drive to seize the human soul"* (Arthur M. Schlesinger, Jr.). **—totalitarian** *n.* A practitioner or supporter of such a government. [TOTAL + (AUTHOR)ITARIAN.] **—to·tal′i·tar′i·an·ism** *n.*

to·tal·i·ty (tō-tăl′ĭ-tē) *n., pl.* **-ties. 1.** The quality or state of being total: *appalled by the totality of the destruction.* **2.** An aggregate amount; a sum. **3.** The phase of an eclipse when it is total.

to·tal·i·za·tor (tōt′l-ĭ-zā′tər) *n.* A machine for computing and showing totals, especially a pari-mutuel machine showing the total number and amounts of bets at a racetrack.

to·tal·ize (tōt′l-īz′) *tr.v.* **-ized, -iz·ing, -iz·es.** To make or combine into a total. **—to′tal·i·za′tion** (-ĭ-zā′shən) *n.*

to·tal·iz·er (tōt′l-ī′zər) *n.* A pari-mutuel machine.

to·tal·ly (tōt′l-ē) *adv.* Entirely; wholly; completely.

tote[1] (tōt) *tr.v.* **tot·ed, tot·ing, totes.** *Informal.* **1.** To haul; lug. **2.** To have on one's person; pack: *toting guns.* **—tote** *n.* **1.** *Informal.* A load; a burden. **2.** A tote bag. [Perhaps (via Black West African English) of Bantu origin; akin to Kongo *-tota,* to pick up, Swahili *-tuta,* to pile up, carry.] **—tot′a·ble** *adj.* **—tot′er** *n.*

tote[2] (tōt) *tr.v.* **tot·ed, tot·ing, totes.** *Informal.* **1.** To determine the total of; add up. **2.** To sum up; summarize.

tote[3] (tōt) *n. Informal.* A pari-mutuel machine. [Short for TOTALIZATOR.]

tote bag *n.* A large handbag or shopping bag.

tote board *n.* A large, usually electrically operated board that displays changing numerical information, such as betting payoffs or voting results.

to·tem (tō′təm) *n.* **1.a.** An animal, a plant, or a natural object serving among certain tribal or traditional peoples as the emblem of a clan or family and sometimes revered as its founder, ancestor, or guardian. **b.** A representation of such an object. **c.** A social group having a common affiliation to such an object. **2.** A venerated emblem or symbol: *"grew up with the totems and taboos typical of an Irish Catholic kid in Boston"* (Connie Paige). [Ojibwa *nindoodem,* my totem.] **—to·tem′ic** (-tĕm′ĭk) *adj.*

to·tem·ism (tō′tə-mĭz′əm) *n.* **1.** A belief in totems or in kinship through common affiliation to a totem. **2.** A social system based on affiliations to totems. **—to′tem·ist** *n.* **—to′tem·is′tic** *adj.*

totem pole *n.* **1.** A post carved and painted with a series of totemic symbols and erected before a dwelling, as among certain Native American peoples of the northwest coast of North America. **2.** *Slang.* A hierarchy: *low on the totem pole.*

toth·er or **t'oth·er** (tŭth′ər) *pron. & adj. Informal.* The other. [From Middle English *the tother,* alteration of *thet other,* that other : *thet,* the (from Old English *thæt;* see THAT) + *other,* other; see OTHER.]

to·ti·pal·mate (tō′tĭ-păl′māt′) *adj.* Having webbing that connects each of the four anterior toes, as in water birds such as pelicans and gannets. [Latin *tōtus,* whole; see TOTAL + PALMATE.] **—to′ti·pal·ma′tion** *n.*

to·tip·o·ten·cy (tō-tĭp′ə-tən-sē, tō′tĭ-pōt′n-sē) also **to·tip·o·tence** (tō-tĭp′ə-təns, tō′tĭ-pōt′ns) *n., pl.* **-cies** also **-ten·ces.** The ability of a cell, such as an egg, to give rise to unlike cells and thus to develop into or generate a new organism or part. [Latin *tōtus,* whole; see TOTAL + POTENCY.] **—to·tip′o·tent** *adj.*

tot·ter (tŏt′ər) *intr.v.* **-tered, -ter·ing, -ters. 1.a.** To sway as if about to fall. **b.** To appear about to collapse: *an empire that had begun to totter.* **2.** To walk unsteadily or feebly; stagger. [Middle English *toteren,* perhaps of Scandinavian origin.] **—tot′ter** *n.* **—tot′ter·er** *n.* **—tot′ter·y** *adj.*

tou·can (to͞o′kăn′, -kän′, to͞o-kăn′, -kän′) *n.* Any of various tropical American birds of the family Ramphastidae, having brightly colored plumage and a very large bill and feeding mainly on small fruits. [French, from Portuguese *tucano* or Spanish *tucán,* both from Tupi *tucano,* bird.]

tou·ca·net (to͞o′kə-nĕt′, to͞o′kə-nĕt′) *n.* Any of several small toucans of the genus *Aulacorhynchus,* that range from Mexico to Peru, especially at high altitudes along the Andes.

touch (tŭch) *v.* **touched, touch·ing, touch·es.** *—tr.* **1.** To cause or permit a part of the body, especially the hand or fingers, to come in contact with so as to feel: *reached out and touched the smooth stone.* **2.a.** To bring something into light contact with: *touched the sore spot with a probe.* **b.** To bring (one thing) into light contact with something else: *grounded the radio by touching a wire to it; touching fire to a fuse.* **3.** To press or push lightly; tap: *touched a control to improve the TV picture; touched 19 on the phone to get room service.* **4.** To lay hands on in violence: *I never touched him!* **5.** To eat or drink; taste: *She didn't touch her food.* **6.** To disturb or move by handling: *Just don't touch anything in my room!* **7.a.** To meet without going beyond; adjoin:

the ridge where his property touches mine. **b.** *Mathematics.* To be tangent to. **c.** To come up to; reach: *when the thermometer touches 90°.* **d.** To match in quality; equal: *Rival artists can't touch her work at its best.* **8.** To deal with, especially in passing; treat briefly or allusively: *some remarks touching recent events.* **9.** To be pertinent to; concern: *environmental problems that touch us all.* **10.** To affect the emotions of; move to tender response: *an appeal that touched us deeply.* **11.** To injure slightly: *plants touched by frost.* **12.** To color slightly; tinge: *a white petal touched with pink.* **13.a.** To draw with light strokes. **b.** To change or improve by adding fine lines or strokes. **14.** To stamp (tested metal). **15.** *Slang.* To wheedle a loan or handout from: *touched a friend for five dollars.* **16.a.** *Archaic.* To strike or pluck the keys or strings of (a musical instrument). **b.** To play (a musical piece). —*intr.* **1.** To touch someone or something. **2.** To be or come into contact: *Don't let the live wires touch.* **—touch** *n.* **1.** The act or an instance of touching. **2.** The physiological sense by which external objects or forces are perceived through contact with the body. **3.** A sensation experienced in touching something with a characteristic texture: *felt the touch of snowflakes on her face.* **4.** A light push; a tap: *an electric switch that requires just a touch.* **5.** A discernible mark or effect left by contact with something. **6.** A small change or addition, or the effect achieved by it: *Candlelight provided just the right touch.* **7.** A suggestion, hint, or tinge: *a touch of jealousy.* **8.** A mild attack: *a touch of the flu.* **9.** A small amount; a dash: *a touch of paprika.* **10.a.** A manner or technique of striking the keys of a keyboard instrument: *He types quickly, using a light touch.* **b.** The resistance to pressure characteristic of the keys of a keyboard: *an old piano with uneven touch.* **11.** A characteristic way of doing things: *recognized my friend's touch in the choice of the card.* **12.** A facility; a knack: *lose one's touch.* **13.** The state of being in contact or communication: *kept in touch with several classmates; out of touch with current trends.* **14.** An official stamp indicating the quality of a metal product. **15.** *Slang.* **a.** The act of approaching someone for a loan or handout. **b.** A prospect for a loan or handout: *a generous person, a soft touch for beggars.* **16.** *Sports.* The area just outside the sidelines in Rugby and soccer. ***—phrasal verbs.* touch down.** To make contact with the ground; land: *The spacecraft touched down on schedule.* **touch off. 1.** To cause to explode; fire. **2.** To initiate; trigger: *disclosures that touched off a public uproar.* **3.** To describe or portray with deft precision. **touch on** (or **upon). 1.** To deal with (a topic) in passing. **2.** To pertain to; concern. **3.** To approach being; verge on: *frenzy that touched on clinical insanity.* **touch up.** To improve by making minor corrections, changes, or additions. ***—idiom.* touch base** (or **bases).** *Informal.* To renew a line of communication: *"He went out of his way to touch base with a broad cross section of . . . residents"* (George B. Merry). [Middle English *touchen,* from Old French *touchier,* perhaps of imitative origin.] **—touch′a·ble** *adj.* **—touch′a·ble·ness** *n.* **—touch′er** *n.*

SYNONYMS: *touch, feel, finger, handle, palpate, paw.* The central meaning shared by these verbs is "to bring the hands or fingers into contact with so as to give or receive a physical sensation": *gently touched my hand; felt the runner's pulse; fingering his worry beads; handle a bolt of fabric; palpating the patient's abdomen; fans pawing a celebrity's arm.* See also Synonyms at **affect**[1].

touch-and-go (tŭch′ən-gō′) *adj.* Dangerous and uncertain in nature or outcome; precarious; delicate: *major surgery followed by a touch-and-go recovery.*

touch·back (tŭch′băk′) *n. Football.* A play in which the defensive team recovers and downs the ball behind its own goal line after the ball has been kicked or passed there by the team on offense. No points are scored, and the ball is put back in play by the recovering team on its own 20-yard line.

touch·down (tŭch′doun′) *n.* **1.** *Abbr.* **TD, td** *Football.* An act of carrying, receiving, or gaining possession of the ball across the opponent's goal line for a score of six points. **2.** The contact, or moment of contact, of a landing aircraft or spacecraft with the landing surface. [From the earlier practice of touching the ball to the ground behind the goal line.]

tou·ché (to͞o-shā′) *interj.* Used to acknowledge a hit in fencing or a successful criticism or an effective point in argument. [French, from past participle of *toucher,* to hit or wound in fencing, from Old French *touchier,* to touch. See TOUCH.]

touched (tŭcht) *adj.* **1.** Emotionally affected; moved: *very touched by the stranger's kindness.* **2.** Somewhat demented or mentally unbalanced.

touch football *n. Sports.* A variety of football played without protective clothing usually on an improvised field, in which ball carriers are downed by touching instead of tackling.

touch·hole (tŭch′hōl′) *n.* The opening in early firearms and cannons through which the powder was ignited.

touch·ing (tŭch′ĭng) *adj.* Eliciting or capable of eliciting sympathy or tenderness. See Synonyms at **moving. —touching** *prep.* Concerning; about. **—touch′ing·ly** *adv.* **—touch′ing·ness** *n.*

touch·line (tŭch′līn′) *n. Sports.* Either of the sidelines bordering the playing field in soccer and Rugby.

touch-me-not (tŭch′mē-nŏt′) *n.* **1.** See **jewelweed. 2.** See **sensitive plant** (sense 1). [From the bursting of ripe seedpods when touched.]

touch·stone (tŭch′stōn′) *n.* **1.** A hard black stone, such as jasper or basalt, formerly used to test the quality of gold or silver by comparing the streak left on the stone by one of these metals with that of a standard alloy. **2.** An excellent quality or example that is used to test the excellence or genuineness of others: *"the qualities of courage and vision that are the touchstones of leadership"* (Henry A. Kissinger). See Synonyms at **standard.**

touch-tone also **touch·tone** (tŭch′tōn′) —*adj.* Of, relating to, or being a telephone with which the user places calls by pressing push buttons that generate and transmit tones of differing pitch, these tones corresponding to the digits of the number being called. —*n.* A touch-tone telephone.

touch-type (tŭch′tīp′) *intr. & tr.v.* **-typed, -typ·ing, -types.** To engage in typing or type (a document, for example) without having to look at the keyboard, the fingers having been trained to locate the keys by position. **—touch′-typ′ist** *n.*

touch·up (tŭch′ŭp′) *n.* The act or an instance of finishing or improving by small changes, corrections, or additions.

touch·wood (tŭch′wo͝od′) *n.* Material, such as decayed wood, that is used as tinder; punk. [From its being easy to ignite.]

touch·y (tŭch′ē) *adj.* **-i·er, -i·est. 1.** Tending to take offense with slight cause; oversensitive. **2.** Requiring special tact or skill in handling; delicate: *a touchy situation.* **3.** Highly sensitive to touch. Used of a body part. **4.** Easily ignited; flammable. **—touch′i·ly** *adv.* **—touch′i·ness** *n.*

tough (tŭf) *adj.* **tough·er, tough·est. 1.** Able to withstand great strain without tearing or breaking; strong and resilient: *a tough all-weather fabric.* **2.** Hard to cut or chew: *tough meat.* **3.** Physically hardy; rugged: *tough mountaineers; a tough cop.* See Synonyms at **strong. 4.** Severe; harsh: *a tough winter.* **5.a.** Aggressive; pugnacious. **b.** Inclined to violent or disruptive behavior; rowdy or rough: *a tough street group.* **6.** Demanding or troubling; difficult: *skipping the toughest questions.* **7.** Strong-minded; resolute: *a tough negotiator.* **8.** *Slang.* Unfortunate; too bad: *a tough break.* **9.** *Slang.* Fine; great. **—tough** *n.* A violent or rowdy person; a hoodlum or thug. ***—idiom.* tough it out.** *Slang.* To get through despite hardship; endure: *"It helps if one was raised to tough it out"* (Gail Sheehy). [Middle English, from Old English *tōh.*] **—tough′ly** *adv.* **—tough′ness** *n.*

tough·en (tŭf′ən) *tr. & intr.v.* **-ened, -en·ing, -ens.** To make or become tough. See Synonyms at **harden. —tough′en·er** *n.*

tough·ie (tŭf′ē) *n. Informal.* **1.** A thug; a tough. **2.** A difficult problem.

tough-mind·ed (tŭf′mīn′dĭd) *adj.* Facing facts and difficulties with strength and determination; realistic and resolute. **—tough′-mind′ed·ly** *adv.* **—tough′-mind′ed·ness** *n.*

Tou·lon (to͞o-lôɴ′). A city of southeast France on the Mediterranean Sea east-southeast of Marseille. First mentioned in the third century A.D. as a Roman naval station, it became part of France in 1481. Population, 179,423.

Tou·louse (to͞o-lo͞oz′). A city of southern France on the Garonne River southeast of Bordeaux. Originally part of Roman Gaul, it was the capital of the Visigoths (419–507) and the Carolingian kingdom of Aquitaine (781–843). Toulouse was a cultural center of medieval Europe. Population, 347,995.

Tou·louse-Lau·trec (to͞o-lo͞os′lō-trĕk′, to͞o-lo͞oz′-), **Henri de.** 1864–1901. French artist who portrayed the music halls and cafés of Montmartre in his paintings, lithographs, and posters, including *La Goulue at the Moulin Rouge* (1892).

tou·pee (to͞o-pā′) *n.* **1.** A partial wig or hairpiece worn to cover a bald spot. **2.** A curl or lock of hair worn during the 18th century as a topknot on a periwig. [French *toupet,* diminutive of Old French *toupe,* tuft of hair, from Frankish **top.*]

tour (to͝or) *n.* **1.** A trip with visits to various places of interest for business, pleasure, or instruction. **2.** A group organized for such a trip or for a shorter sightseeing excursion. **3.** A brief trip to or through a place for the purpose of seeing it: *a tour of the house.* **4.** A journey to fulfill a round of engagements in several places: *a pianist on a concert tour.* **5.** A shift, as in a factory. **6.** A period of duty at a single place or job. **—tour** *v.* **toured, tour·ing, tours.** —*intr.* **1.** To travel from place to place, especially for pleasure. **2.** To travel among various places while fulfilling engagements. —*tr.* **1.** To make a tour of: *toured Europe last summer; officials touring the scene of the disaster.* **2.** To present (a play, for example) on a tour. [Middle English, a turn, from Old French (influenced by *tourner,* to turn about), from Latin *tornus,* lathe. See TURN.] **—tour′er** *n.*

tou·ra·co also **tu·ra·co** (to͝or′ə-kō′) *n., pl.* **-cos.** Any of various weak-flying, cuckoolike African birds of the family Musophagidae, many of which have brightly colored plumage and long tails. [French, perhaps of West African origin.]

Tou·raine (to͞o-rān′, -rĕn′). A historical region and former province of west-central France. Taken by the English in 1152, it was recaptured by Philip II of France in 1204 and incorporated into the royal domain by Henry III.

Tou·rane (to͞o-rän′). See **Da Nang.**

tour·bil·lion (to͝or-bĭl′yən) *n.* **1.a.** A whirlwind. **b.** A vortex, as of a whirlwind or whirlpool. **2.** A skyrocket that has a spiral flight. [Middle English *turbilloun,* from Old French *torbeillon,* ultimately from Latin *turbō,* from Greek *turbē,* noise, confusion. See TURBID.]

Tour·coing (to͞or-kwăɴ′). A city of northern France northeast of Lille near the Belgian border. It is an important textile center. Population, 96,908.

ă pat	oi boy
ā pay	ou out
âr care	o͝o took
ä father	o͞o boot
ĕ pet	ŭ cut
ē be	ûr urge
ĭ pit	th thin
ī pie	*th* this
îr pier	hw which
ŏ pot	zh vision
ō toe	ə about, item
ô paw	♦ regionalism

Stress marks: ′ (primary); ′ (secondary), as in **dictionary** (dĭk′shə-nĕr′ē)

tour de force (to͝or′ də fôrs′, fōrs′) *n., pl.* **tours de force** (to͝or′). A feat requiring great virtuosity or strength, often deliberately undertaken for its difficulty: *"In an extraordinary structural tour de force the novel maintains a dual focus"* (Julian Moynahan). [French : *tour,* turn, feat + *de,* of + *force,* strength.]

Tou·rette's syndrome (to͞o-rĕts′) or **Tou·rette syndrome** (-rĕt′) *n.* A severe neurological disorder characterized by multiple facial and other body tics, usually beginning in childhood or adolescence and often accompanied by grunts and compulsive utterances, as of interjections and obscenities. Also called *Gilles de la Tourette syndrome.* [After Georges Gilles de la *Tourette* (1857–1904), French physician.]

François Dominique Toussaint L'Ouverture

tour·ing (to͝or′ĭng) *n.* Travel, as on a bicycle or on skis, for pleasure rather than competition.

touring car *n.* A large open automobile for five or more people, popular in the 1920's.

tour·ism (to͝or′ĭz′əm) *n.* **1.** The practice of traveling for pleasure. **2.** The business of providing tours and services for tourists.

tour·ist (to͝or′ĭst) *n.* One who travels for pleasure. **—tour·is′tic** *adj.* **—tour′ist·y** *adj.*

tourist class *n.* The lowest class of accommodations on some passenger ships and airplanes.

tourist trap *n.* A place, such as a shop or resort area, that offers overpriced goods and services to tourists.

tour·ma·line also **tur·ma·line** (to͝or′mə-lĭn, -lēn′) *n.* A complex crystalline silicate containing aluminum, boron, and other elements, used in electronic instrumentation and, especially in its green, clear, and blue varieties, as a gemstone. [French, from Singhalese *toramalli,* carnelian.]

tower
Eiffel Tower,
Paris, France

tour·na·ment (to͝or′nə-mənt, tûr′-) *n.* **1.** A series of contests in which a number of contestants compete and the one that prevails through the final round or that finishes with the best record is declared the winner. **2.** A medieval martial sport in which two groups of mounted and armored combatants fought against each other with blunted lances or swords. [Middle English *tournement,* a medieval sport, from Old French *torneiement,* from *torneier,* to tourney. See TOURNEY.]

tour·ne·dos (to͝or′nə-dō′) *n., pl.* **tour·ne·dos** (-dō′, -dōz′). A fillet of beef cut from the tenderloin, often bound in bacon or suet for cooking. [French : *tourner,* to turn (from Old French; see TURN) + *dos,* the back (from Latin *dorsum*).]

tour·ney (to͝or′nē, tûr′-) *intr.v.* **-neyed, -ney·ing, -neys.** To compete in a tournament. **—tourney** *n., pl.* **-neys.** A tournament. [Middle English *torneien,* from Old French *torneier,* from Vulgar Latin **tornizāre,* to turn around, from Latin *tornāre,* to turn in a lathe. See TURN.]

tour·ni·quet (to͝or′nĭ-kĭt, tûr′-) *n.* A device, typically a tightly encircling bandage, used to check bleeding by temporarily stopping the flow of blood through a large artery in a limb. [French : *tourner,* to turn (from Old French; see TURN) + *-iquet,* diminutive suff. (from Old French).]

Tours (to͝or). A city of west-central France on the Loire River. Dating to pre-Roman times, it was a prosperous silk-manufacturing town from the 15th century to the 17th century and a Huguenot stronghold until the revocation of the Edict of Nantes in 1685. Population, 132,209.

tou·sle (tou′zəl) *tr.v.* **-sled, -sling, -sles.** To disarrange or rumple; dishevel. **—tousle** *n.* A disheveled mass, as of hair. [Middle English *touselen,* frequentative of *tousen,* to pull roughly.]

Tous·saint L'Ou·ver·ture (to͞o-săN′ lo͞o-vĕr-tür′), **François Dominique.** 1743?–1803. Haitian revolutionary who with the help of the French led a force that expelled the British and Spanish from Haiti (1798).

tout (tout) *v.* **tout·ed, tout·ing, touts.** *—intr.* **1.** To solicit customers, votes, or patronage, especially in a brazen way. **2.** To obtain and deal in information on racehorses. *—tr.* **1.** To solicit or importune: *street vendors who were touting pedestrians.* **2.** To obtain or sell information on (a racehorse or stable) for the guidance of bettors. **3.** To promote or praise energetically; publicize: *"Projects for . . . construction of a deep-water route . . . to reach ports in the continent's industrial heartland had been widely touted"* (Kenneth McNaught). **—tout** *n.* **1.** One who obtains information on racehorses and their prospects and sells it to bettors. **2.** One who solicits customers brazenly or persistently: *"The administration of the nation's literary affairs falls naturally into the hands of touts and thieves"* (Lewis H. Lapham). [Middle English *tuten,* to peer.] **—tout′er** *n.*

to·va·rich or **to·va·rish** (tə-vär′ĭch, -ĭsh, -ĭshch) *n.* A comrade. [Russian *tovarishch,* from Old Russian *tovarishchĭ,* sing. of *tovarishchi,* business associates, from Old Turkic *tavar ishchi,* businessman, merchant : *tavar,* wealth, trade + *ishchi,* one who works (from *ish,* work, business).]

towhee
Pipilo erythrophthalmus

tow¹ (tō) *tr.v.* **towed, tow·ing, tows.** To draw or pull behind by a chain or line: *a tugboat towing a barge.* See Synonyms at **pull.** **—tow** *n.* **1.a.** The act or an instance of towing. **b.** The condition of being towed: *a car with a trailer in tow.* **2.** Something, such as a tugboat, that tows. **3.** Something, such as a barge or car, that is towed. **4.** A rope or cable used in towing. ***—idiom.*** **in tow.** **1.** Under close guidance; in one's charge: *The new girl was taken in tow by an older student.* **2.** As a companion or follower: *came to dinner with a friend in tow.* [Middle English *towen,* from Old English *togian.* See **deuk-** in Appendix.] **—tow′a·ble** *adj.* **—tow′er** *n.*

♦**tow²** (tō) *n.* Coarse broken flax or hemp fiber prepared for spinning. See Regional Note at **gunnysack.** [Middle English, possibly from Old English *tōw-,* spinning.]

tow·age (tō′ĭj) *n.* **1.** The act or service of towing. **2.** A charge for towing.

to·ward (tôrd, tōrd, tə-wôrd′) also **to·wards** (tôrdz, tōrdz, tə-wôrdz′) *prep.* **1.** In the direction of: *driving toward home.* **2.** In a position facing: *had his back toward me.* **3.** Somewhat before in time: *It began to rain toward morning.* **4.** With regard to; in relation to: *an optimistic attitude toward the future.* **5.** In furtherance or partial fulfillment of: *contributed five dollars toward the bill.* **6.** By way of achieving; with a view to: *efforts toward peace.* **—toward** (tôrd, tōrd) *adj.* **1.** Favoring success or a good outcome; propitious. **2.** Often **towards.** Happening soon; imminent. **3.** *Obsolete.* Being quick to understand or learn. [Middle English, from Old English *tōweard* : *tō,* to; see TO + *-weard,* -ward.]

USAGE NOTE: Some critics have tried to discern a semantic distinction between *toward* and *towards,* but the difference is entirely dialectal. *Toward* is more common in American English; *towards* is the predominant form in British English.

to·ward·ly (tôrd′lē, tōrd′-) *adj. Archaic.* **1.** Appearing likely to succeed; promising. **2.** Advantageous; favorable. **—to·ward′li·ness** *n.*

to·wards (tôrdz, tōrdz, tə-wôrdz′) *prep.* Variant of **toward.** **—towards** *adj.* Variant of **toward** (sense 2).

tow-a·way zone (tō′ə-wā′) *n.* A no-parking zone from which motor vehicles may be towed away.

♦**tow bag** *n. Eastern North Carolina.* See **gunnysack.** See Regional Note at **gunnysack.**

tow·boat (tō′bōt′) *n. Nautical.* **1.** See **tugboat.** **2.** A powerful, shallow-draft boat with a broad bow, intended to push barges on rivers and canals.

tow·el (tou′əl) *n.* A piece of absorbent cloth or paper used for wiping or drying. **—towel** *v.* **-eled, -el·ing, -els** or **-elled, -el·ling, -els.** *—tr.* To wipe or rub dry with a towel. *—intr.* To dry oneself with a towel. [Middle English *towaille,* from Old French *toaille,* of Germanic origin.]

tow·el·ette (tou′ə-lĕt′) *n.* A small, usually moistened piece of paper or cloth used for cleansing.

tow·el·ing also **tow·el·ling** (tou′ə-lĭng) *n.* Any of various fabrics of cotton or linen used for making towels.

tow·er (tou′ər) *n.* **1.** A building or part of a building that is exceptionally high in proportion to its width and length. **2.** A tall, slender structure used for observation, signaling, or pumping. **3.** One that conspicuously embodies strength, firmness, or another virtue. **—tower** *intr.v.* **-ered, -er·ing, -ers.** **1.** To appear at or rise to a conspicuous height; loom: *"There he stood, grown suddenly tall, towering above them"* (J.R.R. Tolkien). See Synonyms at **rise.** **2.** To fly directly upward before swooping or falling. Used of certain birds. **3.** To demonstrate great superiority; be preeminent: *towers over other poets of the day.* [Middle English *tur, tour, towr,* from Old English *torr* and from Old French *tur,* both from Latin *turris,* probably from Greek *tursis, turris.*]

tow·er·ing (tou′ər-ĭng) *adj.* **1.** Of imposing height. See Synonyms at **high.** **2.** Outstanding; preeminent: *a towering intellect.* **3.** Very great or intense: *a towering rage.* **—tow′er·ing·ly** *adv.*

tow·head (tō′hĕd′) *n.* **1.a.** A head of white-blond hair resembling tow. **b.** A person having such hair. **2.** A sandbar or a low-lying alluvial island in a river, especially one with a stand of trees. **—tow′head′ed** *adj.*

tow·hee (tō′hē, tō-hē′) *n.* **1.** A North American bird *(Pipilo erythrophthalmus)* that ranges from southern Canada to Mexico and has black, white, and rust-colored plumage in the male. Also called *chewink, ground robin.* **2.** Any of several finches of the genera *Pipilo* or *Chlorura,* found in the western United States. [Imitative of the song of some of these birds.]

tow·line (tō′līn′) *n.* A line used in towing a vessel or vehicle.

town (toun) *n.* **1.a.** *Abbr.* **t., T., tn.** A population center, often incorporated, larger than a village and usually smaller than a city. **b.** The residents of such a population center: *The whole town disagreed with the mayor.* **2.** A township. **3.** *Informal.* A city: *New York is a big town.* **4.** *Chiefly British.* A rural village that has a market or fair periodically. **5.** The commercial district or center of an area: *going into town for shopping. —attributive.* Often used to modify another noun: *town streets; town populations.* ***—idiom.*** **on the town.** *Informal.* In spirited pursuit of the entertainment offered by a town or city. [Middle English, from Old English *tūn,* enclosed place, village. See **dhū-no-** in Appendix.]

town clerk *n.* A public official in charge of keeping the records of a town.

town crier *n.* **1.** A person formerly employed by a town to proclaim announcements in the streets. **2.** *Informal.* A gossip.

town hall *n.* A building that contains the offices of the public officials of a town and that houses the town council and courts.

town·house or **town house** (toun′hous′) *n.* **1.** A residence in a city. **2.** One of a row of houses connected by common side walls.

town·ie also **town·y** (tou′nē) *n., pl.* **-ies.** *Informal.* A permanent resident of a town, especially a resident of a college town who is academically unaffiliated with the local college or university.

town manager *n.* An administrator appointed to manage the government of a town.

town meeting *n.* A legislative assembly of townspeople.

town·scape (toun′skāp′) *n.* **1.** The appearance of a town or city; an urban scene: *"The high school . . . once dominated American townscapes the way the cathedral dominated medieval European cities"* (Dennis A. Williams). **2.** A depiction of an urban scene.

Town·send (toun′zənd), **Francis Everett.** 1867–1960. American physician and social reformer whose plan for a government-sponsored old-age pension was a precursor of the Social Security Act of 1935.

Town·send's solitaire (toun′zəndz) *n.* A long-tailed, short-billed thrush *(Myadestes townsendi)* of western North America, living mostly in woody mountainous areas and noted for its clear, ringing song. [After John Kirk *Townsend* (1809–1851), American ornithologist.]

towns·folk (tounz′fōk′) *pl.n.* The people of a town.

Town·shend (toun′zənd), **Charles.** 1725–1767. British politician who as Chancellor of the Exchequer (1766) and acting prime minister sponsored the Townshend Acts (1767), which levied duties on many items imported to the American colonies. Strong resistance to the acts led to the repeal of all the duties, except for the tax on tea.

town·ship (toun′shĭp′) *n. Abbr.* **t., T., twp., tp. 1.** A subdivision of a county in most northeast and Midwest U.S. states, having the status of a unit of local government with varying governmental powers; a town. **2.** A public land surveying unit of 36 sections or 36 square miles. **3.** An ancient administrative division of a large parish in England. **4.** A racially segregated area in South Africa established by the government as a residence for people of color.

towns·man (tounz′mən) *n.* **1.** A man who is a resident of a town. **2.** A man who is a fellow resident of one's town.

towns·peo·ple (tounz′pē′pəl) *pl.n.* The inhabitants or citizens of a town or city.

towns·wom·an (tounz′wo͝om′ən) *n.* **1.** A woman who is a resident of a town. **2.** A woman who is a fellow resident of one's town.

town·y (tou′nē) *n. Informal.* Variant of **townie.**

tow·path (tō′păth′, -päth′) *n.* A path along a canal or river used by animals towing boats.

♦ **tow sack** *n. Upper Southern U.S.* See **gunnysack.** See Regional Note at **gunnysack.**

Tow·son (tou′sən). A city of northern Maryland, a residential and industrial suburb of Baltimore. Population, 51,083.

tox– *pref.* Variant of **toxi–.**

tox·al·bu·min (tŏk′săl-byo͞o′mĭn) *n.* Any of various toxic proteins obtained from certain plants and bacterial cultures.

tox·a·phene (tŏk′sə-fēn′) *n.* A toxic solid compound, $C_{10}H_{10}Cl_8$, used as an insecticide. [TOX(I)– + (C)A(M)PHENE.]

tox·e·mi·a (tŏk-sē′mē-ə) *n.* A condition in which the blood contains toxins produced by body cells at a local source of infection or derived from the growth of microorganisms. Also called *blood poisoning.* **—tox·e′mic** *adj.*

toxi– or **toxo–** or **tox–** *pref.* Poison; poisonous: *toxalbumin.* [From Latin *toxicum.* See TOXIC.]

tox·ic (tŏk′sĭk) *adj.* **1.** Of, relating to, or caused by a toxin or other poison: *a toxic condition; toxic hepatitis.* **2.** Capable of causing injury or death, especially by chemical means; poisonous: *food preservatives that are toxic in concentrated amounts; a dump for toxic industrial wastes.* See Synonyms at **poisonous. —toxic** *n.* A toxic chemical or other substance. [Late Latin *toxicus,* from Latin *toxicum,* poison, from Greek *toxikon,* poison for arrows, poison, from neuter of *toxikos,* of a bow, from *toxon,* bow, from Old Persian **taxša-,* an arrow.] **—tox′i·cal·ly** *adv.*

toxic– *pref.* Variant of **toxico–.**

tox·i·cant (tŏk′sĭ-kənt) *n.* A poison or poisonous agent. **—toxicant** *adj.* Poisonous; toxic.

tox·ic·i·ty (tŏk-sĭs′ĭ-tē) *n., pl.* **-ties. 1.** The quality or condition of being toxic. **2.** The degree to which a substance is toxic.

toxico– or **toxic–** *pref.* Poison: *toxicosis.* [From Latin *toxicum.* See TOXIC.]

tox·i·co·gen·ic (tŏk′sĭ-kō-jĕn′ĭk) *adj.* **1.** Producing poison or toxic substances. **2.** Derived from or containing toxic matter.

tox·i·col·o·gy (tŏk′sĭ-kŏl′ə-jē) *n.* The study of the nature, effects, and detection of poisons and the treatment of poisoning. **—tox′i·co·log′i·cal** (-kə-lŏj′ĭ-kəl), **tox′i·co·log′ic** (-ĭk) *adj.* **—tox′i·co·log′i·cal·ly** *adv.* **—tox′i·col′o·gist** *n.*

tox·i·co·sis (tŏk′sĭ-kō′sĭs) *n., pl.* **-ses** (-sēz). A diseased condition resulting from poisoning.

toxic shock syndrome *n. Abbr.* **TSS** An acute infection characterized by high fever, a sunburnlike rash, vomiting, and diarrhea, followed in severe cases by shock, that is caused by a toxin-producing strain of the common bacterium *Staphylococcus aureus,* occurring chiefly among young menstruating women who use vaginal tampons.

tox·i·gen·ic (tŏk′sə-jĕn′ĭk) *adj.* Producing poison; toxicogenic. **—tox′i·ge·nic′i·ty** (-jə-nĭs′ĭ-tē) *n.*

tox·in (tŏk′sĭn) *n.* A poisonous substance, especially a protein, that is produced by living cells or organisms and is capable of causing disease when introduced into the body tissues but is often also capable of inducing neutralizing antibodies or antitoxins.

tox·in-an·ti·tox·in (tŏk′sĭn-ăn′tĭ-tŏk′sĭn) *n.* A mixture of a toxin and its antitoxin with a slight excess of toxin, formerly used as a vaccine.

toxo– *pref.* Variant of **toxi–.**

tox·oid (tŏk′soid′) *n.* A substance that has been treated to destroy its toxic properties but retains the capacity to stimulate production of antitoxins, used in immunization.

tox·o·plas·ma (tŏk′sə-plăz′mə) *n.* Any of various parasitic sporozoans of the genus *Toxoplasma,* including some that cause disease in birds and mammals.

tox·o·plas·mo·sis (tŏk′sō-plăz-mō′sĭs) *n., pl.* **-mo·ses** (-mō′sēz). A disease caused by the sporozoan *Toxoplasma gondii,* especially: **a.** A congenital disease characterized by lesions of the central nervous system that can cause blindness and brain damage. **b.** An acquired disease characterized by fever, swollen lymph nodes, and lesions in the liver, heart, lungs, and brain.

♦ **toy** (toi) *n.* **1.** An object for children to play with. **2.** Something of little importance; a trifle. **3.** An amusement; a pastime: *thought of the business as a toy.* **4.** A small ornament; a bauble. **5.** A diminutive thing or person. **6.** A dog of a very small breed or of a variety smaller than the standard variety of its breed. **7.** *Scots.* A loose covering for the head, formerly worn by women. **8.** *Chiefly Southern U.S.* A shooter marble. *—attributive.* Often used to modify another noun: *a toy truck; a toy stove; a toy chest.* **—toy** *intr.v.* **toyed, toy·ing, toys. 1.** To amuse oneself idly; trifle: *a cat toying with a mouse.* **2.** To treat something casually or without seriousness: *toyed with the idea of writing a play.* See Synonyms at **flirt.** [Middle English *toye,* amorous play, a piece of fun.]

To·ya·ma (tō-yä′mä). A city of west-central Honshu, Japan, on **Toyama Bay,** an inlet of the Sea of Japan. Toyama is noted for its patent medicine industry. Population, 314,111.

♦ **toy line** *n. Chiefly Southern U.S.* The line used in a game of marbles.

Toyn·bee (toin′bē), **Arnold Joseph.** 1889–1975. British historian and educator who studied cyclical patterns in the growth and decline of civilizations. His most famous work is the 12-volume *Study of History* (1934–1961).

To·yo·ha·shi (tô′yō-hä′shē). A city of south-central Honshu, Japan, on the Pacific Ocean southeast of Nagoya. It is a textile-manufacturing center. Population, 287,700.

toy·on (toi′ŏn′) *n.* An evergreen Californian shrub *(Heteromeles arbutifolia),* having leathery leaves, small white flowers in large panicles, and red, fleshy, berrylike fruit. Also called *Christmas berry.* [Spanish *tollon,* from Greek *tolon.*]

To·yo·na·ka (tô′yō-nä′kä). A city of southern Honshu, Japan, a mainly residential suburb of Osaka. Population, 413,219.

To·yo·ta (toi-ō′tə, tô-yô′tä). A city of south-central Honshu, Japan, east-southeast of Nagoya. It is an industrial center. Population, 308,106.

tp. *abbr.* Township.

t.p. *abbr. Printing.* Title page.

TPA or **tPA** *abbr.* Tissue plasminogen activator.

tpk. *abbr.* Turnpike.

TR or **T-R** *abbr.* Transmit-receive.

tr. *abbr.* **1.** *Grammar.* Transitive. **2. a.** Translated. **b.** Translation; translator. **3.** Transpose; transposition. **4.** Treasurer. **5.** Troop. **6.** *Law.* Trust; trustee.

tra·be·at·ed (trā′bē-ā′tĭd) also **tra·be·ate** (-bē-ĭt, -āt′) *adj. Architecture.* Having horizontal beams or lintels rather than arches. [From Latin *trabs,* beam. See **treb-** in Appendix.] **—tra′be·a′tion** *n.*

tra·bec·u·la (trə-bĕk′yə-lə) *n., pl.* **-lae** (-lē′). **1.** A small supporting beam or bar. **2. a.** *Anatomy.* Any of the supporting strands of connective tissue projecting into an organ and constituting part of the framework of that organ. **b.** Any of the fine spicules forming a network in cancellous bone. [Latin, diminutive of *trabs,* beam. See **treb-** in Appendix.] **—tra·bec′u·lar** *adj.*

Trab·zon (trăb-zŏn′, träb-zôn′) or **Treb·i·zond** (trĕb′ĭ-zŏnd′). A city of northeast Turkey on the Black Sea. Founded in the eighth century B.C., the city was part of the Roman, Byzantine, Trebizond, and Ottoman empires. Population, 108,403.

trace¹ (trās) *n.* **1. a.** A visible mark, such as a footprint, made or left by the passage of a person, an animal, or a thing. **b.** Evidence or an indication of the former presence or existence of something; a vestige. **2.** A barely perceivable indication; a touch: *spoke with a trace of sarcasm.* **3. a.** An extremely small amount. **b.** A constituent, such as a chemical compound or element, present in quantities less than a standard limit. **4.** A path or trail that has been beaten out by the passage of animals or people. **5.** A way or route followed. **6.** A line drawn by a recording instrument, such as a cardiograph. **7.** *Mathematics.* **a.** The point at which a line, or the curve in which a surface, intersects a coordinate plane. **b.** The sum of the elements of the principal diagonal of a matrix. **8.** An engram. **—trace** *v.* **traced, trac·ing, trac·es.** *—tr.* **1.** To follow the course or trail of: *trace a wounded*

ă pat	oi boy
ā pay	ou out
âr care	o͝o took
ä father	o͞o boot
ĕ pet	ŭ cut
ē be	ûr urge
ĭ pit	th thin
ī pie	*th* this
îr pier	hw which
ŏ pot	zh vision
ō toe	ə about, item
ô paw	♦ regionalism

Stress marks: **′** (primary); ′ (secondary), as in **dictionary** (dĭk′shə-nĕr′ē)

tracery
South transept of the Cathedral of Notre Dame, Paris

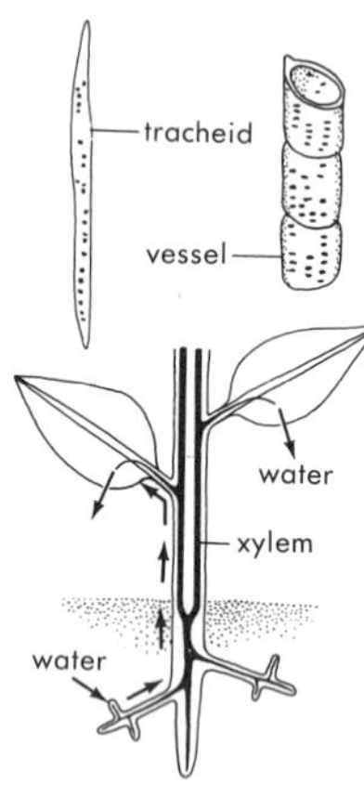

tracheid

track and field
Top: Foot race
Bottom: Long jump by Carl Lewis in 1987

deer; tracing missing persons. **2.** To ascertain the successive stages in the development or progress of: *tracing the life cycle of an insect; trace the history of a family.* **3.** To locate or discover by searching or researching evidence: *trace the cause of a disease.* **4.** To draw (a line or figure); sketch; delineate. **5.** To form (letters) with special concentration or care. **6.** To copy by following lines seen through a sheet of transparent paper. **7.a.** To imprint (a design) by pressure with an instrument on a superimposed pattern. **b.** To make a design or series of markings on (a surface) by such pressure on a pattern. **8.** To record (a variable), as on a graph. —*intr.* **1.** To make one's way along a trail or course: *traced through the files.* **2.** To have origins; be traceable: *linguistic features that trace to West Africa.* [Middle English, track, from Old French, from *tracier,* to make one's way, from Vulgar Latin **trāctiāre,* from Latin *trāctus,* a dragging, course, from past participle of *trahere,* to draw.] **—trace′a·bil′i·ty, trace′a·ble·ness** *n.* **—trace′a·ble** *adj.* **—trace′a·bly** *adv.*

SYNONYMS: *trace, vestige, track, trail.* These nouns denote a visible sign or perceptible indication of the passage or former presence of something. *Trace* applies to both physical and immaterial evidence: *I immediately recognized the charred traces of a fire. Despite his excellent English, he still retains the faint trace of a French accent. Vestige* refers to a surviving remnant of what once existed or is past: *"long lines of edifices, vestiges of whose ruins may still be found"* (William Hickling Prescott); *"vestiges of a very universal custom"* (Henry Hallam). *Track* usually denotes a mark or succession of marks, as footprints, left by something that has passed: *Archaeologists excavated fossilized dinosaur tracks from the riverbed. Trail* can refer to the tracks of a person or an animal, especially one being hunted: *"We came across the recent trails of but two of the animals we were after"* (Theodore Roosevelt).

trace[2] (trās) *n.* **1.** One of two side straps or chains connecting a harnessed draft animal to a vehicle or whiffletree. **2.** A bar or rod, hinged at either end to another part, that transfers movement from one part of a machine to another. [Middle English *trais,* from Old French, pl. of *trait,* a hauling, harness strap, from Latin *trāctus,* a hauling, from past participle of *trahere,* to haul.]

trace element *n.* **1.** A chemical element required in minute quantities by an organism to maintain proper physical functioning. **2.** A minute quantity or amount: *"The trace elements of belief vanish when it becomes apparent that the . . . officer . . . never has suffered the indignity of combat"* (Lewis H. Lapham).

trac·er (trā′sər) *n.* **1.a.** One who is employed to locate missing goods or persons. **b.** An investigation or inquiry organized to trace missing goods or persons. **2.** Any of several instruments used in making tracings or in imprinting designs by tracing. **3.** A tracer bullet. **4.** *Chemistry.* An identifiable substance, such as a dye or a radioactive isotope, that is introduced into a biological or mechanical system and can be followed through the course of a process, providing information on the pattern of events in the process or on the redistribution of the parts or elements involved. In this sense, also called *label.*

tracer bullet *n.* A bullet that leaves a luminous or smoky trail.

trac·er·y (trā′sə-rē) *n., pl.* **-ies.** Ornamental work of interlaced and branching lines, especially the lacy openwork in a Gothic window. [From TRACE[1].] **—trac′er·ied** *adj.*

trache– *pref.* Variant of **tracheo–.**

tra·che·a (trā′kē-ə) *n., pl.* **-che·ae** (-kē-ē′) or **-che·as. 1.** *Anatomy.* A thin-walled tube of cartilaginous and membranous tissue descending from the larynx to the bronchi and carrying air to the lungs. Also called *windpipe.* **2.** *Zoology.* One of the internal respiratory tubes of insects and some other terrestrial arthropods. **3.** *Botany.* One of the tubular conductive vessels in the xylem of vascular plants. [Middle English *trache,* from Medieval Latin *trāchēa,* from Late Latin *trāchīa,* from Greek *(artēria) trakheia,* rough (artery), trachea, from feminine of *trakhus,* rough.] **—tra′che·al** *adj.*

tra·che·ate (trā′kē-āt′, -ĭt) *adj.* Having tracheae. Used of arthropods. **—tracheate** *n.* A tracheate arthropod.

tra·che·id (trā′kē-ĭd, -kēd′) *n. Botany.* A cell in the xylem of vascular plants. **—tra·che′i·dal** (trā-kē′ĭ-dl, -kēd′l) *adj.*

tra·che·i·tis (trā′kē-ī′tĭs) *n.* Inflammation of the trachea.

tracheo– or **trache–** *pref.* Trachea: *tracheid.* [New Latin *trāchēo-,* from Medieval Latin *trāchēa.* See TRACHEA.]

tra·che·o·bron·chi·al (trā′kē-ō-brŏng′kē-əl) *adj.* Of or relating to the trachea and the bronchi.

tra·che·o·e·soph·a·ge·al (trā′kē-ō′ĭ-sŏf′ə-jē′əl) *adj.* Of or relating to the trachea and the esophagus.

tra·che·ole (trā′kē-ōl′) *n.* One of the fine branching tubes of the trachea of an insect, which penetrates the tissues to provide oxygen. [TRACHE(A) + *-ole,* diminutive suff. (from French, from Latin *-olus*).] **—tra·che′o·lar** (-ə-lər) *adj.*

tra·che·o·phyte (trā′kē-ə-fīt′) *n.* Any of various vascular plants, including seed plants and ferns, having a conducting system of xylem and phloem. [From New Latin *Tracheophyta,* division name : TRACHEO– + Greek *phuta,* pl. of *phuton,* plant; see **bheuə-** in Appendix.]

tra·che·os·co·py (trā′kē-ŏs′kə-pē) *n., pl.* **-pies.** Examination of the interior of the trachea, as with a laryngoscope. **—tra′che·o·scop′ic** (-ə-skŏp′ĭk) *adj.*

tra·che·os·to·my (trā′kē-ŏs′tə-mē) *n., pl.* **-mies. 1.a.** Surgical construction of a respiratory opening in the trachea. **b.** The opening so made. **2.** A tracheotomy performed in order to insert a catheter or tube into the trachea, especially to facilitate breathing.

tra·che·ot·o·my (trā′kē-ŏt′ə-mē) *n., pl.* **-mies.** The act or procedure of cutting into the trachea through the neck, as to make an artificial opening for breathing.

tra·cho·ma (trə-kō′mə) *n.* A contagious disease of the conjunctiva and cornea, caused by the gram-negative bacterium *Chlamydia trachomatis* and characterized by inflammation, hypertrophy, and formation of granules of adenoid tissue. It is a major cause of blindness in Asia and Africa. [New Latin *trachōma,* from Greek *trakhōma,* from *trakhus,* rough.] **—tra·cho′ma·tous** (-kō′mə-təs) *adj.*

tra·chyte (trā′kīt′, trăk′īt′) *n.* A light-colored igneous rock consisting essentially of alkali feldspar. [French, from Greek *trakhus,* rough.] **—tra·chyt′ic** (trə-kĭt′ĭk) *adj.*

trac·ing (trā′sĭng) *n.* **1.** A reproduction made by superimposing a transparent sheet and copying the lines of the original on it. **2.** A graphic record made by a recording instrument, such as a cardiograph or seismograph.

track (trăk) *n.* **1.a.** A mark or succession of marks left by something that has passed. See Synonyms at **trace[1]. b.** A path, route, or course indicated by such marks: *an old wagon track through the mountains.* **2.** A path along which something moves; a course: *following the track of an airplane on radar.* **3.a.** A course of action; a method of proceeding: *on the right track for solving the puzzle.* **b.** An intended or proper course: *putting a stalled project back on track.* **4.** A succession of ideas; a train of thought. **5.** Awareness of something occurring or passing: *keeping track of the score; lost all track of time.* **6.** *Sports.* **a.** A course laid out for running or racing. **b.** Athletic competition on such a course; track events. **c.** Track and field. **7.** A rail or set of parallel rails upon which railroad cars or other vehicles run. **8.** A metal groove or ridge that holds, guides, and reduces friction for a moving device or apparatus. **9.** Any of several courses of study to which students are assigned according to ability, achievement, or needs: *academic, vocational, and general tracks.* **10.a.** A distinct path, as along a length of film or magnetic tape, on which sound or other information is recorded. **b.** A distinct selection from a sound recording, such as a phonograph record or compact disk, usually containing an individual work or part of a larger work: *the title track of an album.* **c.** One of the separate sound recordings that are combined so as to be heard simultaneously, as in stereophonic sound reproduction: *mixed the vocal track and instrumental track.* **—track** *v.* **tracked, track·ing, tracks.** —*tr.* **1.** To follow the tracks of; trail: *tracking game through the forest.* **2.** To pursue successfully: *"When, like a running grave, time tracks you down"* (Dylan Thomas). **3.** To move over or along; traverse. **4.** To carry on the shoes and deposit: *tracked mud on the rug.* **5.** To observe or monitor the course of (aircraft, for example), as by radar. **6.** To observe the progress of; follow: *tracking the company's performance daily.* **7.** To equip with a track. **8.** To assign (a student) to a curricular track. —*intr.* **1.** To move along a track. **2.** To follow a course; travel. **3.** To keep a constant distance apart. Used of a pair of wheels. **4.** To be in alignment. **—*idiom.* in (one's) tracks.** Exactly where one is standing: *stopped him right in his tracks.* [Middle English *trak,* from Old French *trac,* perhaps of Germanic origin.] **—track′a·ble** *adj.* **—track′er** *n.*

track·age (trăk′ĭj) *n.* **1.** Railway tracks. **2.a.** The right of one railroad company to use the track system of another. **b.** The charge for this right.

track and field *n. Sports.* Athletic events performed on a running track and the field associated with it. **—track′-and-field′** (trăk′ən-fēld′) *adj.*

track event *n. Sports.* A running event at a track meet as distinguished from a field event.

track·ing (trăk′ĭng) *n.* The placing of students in any of several courses of study according to ability, achievement, or needs.

tracking poll *n.* An opinion poll in which the same sample, such as a small number of voters, is questioned periodically to measure shifts in opinion.

tracking shot *n.* A movie sequence made by a camera moving steadily on a track or dolly.

tracking station *n.* A station for observing the path of and maintaining contact with an object in the atmosphere or in space especially by means of radar or radio.

track·less (trăk′lĭs) *adj.* **1.** Not running on tracks or rails. **2.** Unmarked by trails or paths.

trackless trolley *n.* A trolley bus.

track light *n.* A light mounted on and movable along an electrified metal track. **—track lighting** *n.*

track·man (trăk′mən) *n.* A worker employed to maintain or inspect railroad tracks.

track meet *n. Sports.* A track-and-field competition between two or more teams.

track record *n. Informal.* A record of actual performance or accomplishment: *a job applicant with an excellent track record.*

track·side (trăk′sīd′) *n.* The area near a track, especially a racetrack. —*attributive.* Often used to modify another noun: *trackside betting; trackside seats.*

track·suit (trăk′so͞ot′) *n.* A loose-fitting jacket and pants worn by athletes and exercisers usually before and after workouts.

track·walk·er (trăk′wô′kər) *n.* A worker employed to inspect a section of railroad track.

tract[1] (trăkt) *n.* **1.a.** An expanse of land or water. **b.** A specified or limited area of land: *developing a 30-acre tract.* **2.** *Anatomy.* **a.** A system of organs and tissues that together perform a specialized function: *the alimentary tract.* **b.** A bundle of nerve fibers having a common origin, termination, and function. **3.** *Archaic.* A stretch or lapse of time. [Middle English, period of time, from Latin *tractus,* course, space, period of time, from past participle of *trahere,* to draw.]

tract[2] (trăkt) *n.* A leaflet or pamphlet containing a declaration or an appeal, especially one put out by a religious or political group. [Middle English *tracte,* treatise, probably short for Latin *tractātus,* from past participle of *tractāre,* to discuss, frequentative of *trahere,* to draw.]

tract[3] (trăkt) *n.* The verses from Scripture sung during Lent or on Ember days after the gradual in the Roman Catholic Mass. [Middle English *tracte,* from Medieval Latin *tractus,* from Latin, a drawing out (from its being an uninterrupted solo). See TRACT[1].]

trac·ta·ble (trăk′tə-bəl) *adj.* **1.** Easily managed or controlled; governable. See Synonyms at **obedient. 2.** Easily handled or worked; malleable. [Latin *tractābilis,* from *tractāre,* to manage, frequentative of *trahere,* to draw.] **—trac′ta·bil′i·ty, trac′ta·ble·ness** *n.* **—trac′ta·bly** *adv.*

Trac·tar·i·an·ism (trăk-târ′ē-ə-nĭz′əm) *n.* The religious opinions and principles of the founders of the Oxford movement, put forth in a series of 90 pamphlets entitled *Tracts for the Times,* published at Oxford, England (1833–1841). **—Trac·tar′i·an** *adj. & n.*

trac·tate (trăk′tāt′) *n.* A treatise; an essay. [Latin *tractātus.* See TRACT[2].]

tract house *n.* One of numerous houses of similar or complementary design built on a tract of land. **—tract housing** *n.*

trac·tile (trăk′təl, -tīl′) *adj.* Capable of being drawn out in length; ductile: *a tractile metal.* [From Latin *tractus,* past participle of *trahere,* to draw.] **—trac·til′i·ty** (-tĭl′ĭ-tē) *n.*

trac·tion (trăk′shən) *n.* **1.a.** The act of drawing or pulling, especially the drawing of a vehicle or load over a surface by motor power. **b.** The condition of being drawn or pulled. **2.** Pulling power, as of a draft animal or an engine. **3.** Adhesive friction, as of a wheel on a track or a tire on a road. **4.** *Medicine.* A sustained pull applied mechanically especially to the arm, leg, or neck so as to correct fractured or dislocated bones, overcome muscle spasms, or relieve pressure. [Medieval Latin *tractiō, tractiōn-,* from Latin *tractus,* past participle of *trahere,* to pull, draw.] **—trac′tion·al** *adj.*

trac·tive (trăk′tĭv) *adj.* Serving to pull or draw; exerting traction. [From Latin *tractus,* past participle of *trahere,* to draw.]

trac·tor (trăk′tər) *n.* **1.** A vehicle, powered by a gasoline or diesel motor, having large heavily treaded tires, and used in mowing, farming, or other applications. **2.** A truck having a cab and no body, used for pulling large vehicles such as vans or trailers. **3.** Something that pulls or draws. **4.a.** An airplane propeller mounted in front of the supporting surfaces. **b.** An airplane having such a propeller. **5.** A toothed mechanism that automatically advances perforated continuous-form paper through a computer printer. [From Latin *tractus,* past participle of *trahere,* to draw.]

tractor feed *n.* *Computer Science.* A mechanism for automatically advancing continuous-form paper through a printer by means of two or more toothed tractors that catch the perforations along the edges of the paper.

trac·tor-trail·er (trăk′tər-trā′lər) *n.* A truck consisting of a tractor attached to a semitrailer or trailer, used for transporting loads.

Tra·cy (trā′sē). A city of west-central California south-southwest of Stockton. Population, 18,428.

Tracy, Spencer. 1900–1967. American actor known for his film partnership with Katharine Hepburn and his performances in *Captains Courageous* (1937) and *Boys' Town* (1938), for which he won Academy Awards.

trade (trād) *n.* **1.** The business of buying and selling commodities; commerce. See Synonyms at **business. 2.** The people working in or associated with a business or an industry: *a textile-exporting publication for the trade.* **3.** The customers of a specified business or industry; clientele. **4.** The act or an instance of buying or selling; transaction. **5.** An exchange of one thing for another. **6.** An occupation, especially one requiring skilled labor; craft: *the building trades, including carpentry, masonry, plumbing, and electrical installation.* **7.** Often **trades.** The trade winds. Used with *the.* **—trade** *v.* **trad·ed, trad·ing, trades.** —*intr.* **1.** To engage in buying and selling for profit. **2.** To make an exchange of one thing for another. **3.** To shop or buy regularly: *trades at the local supermarket.* —*tr.* **1.** To give in exchange for something else: *trade farm products for manufactured goods; will trade my ticket for yours.* **2.** To buy and sell (stock, for example). **3.** To pass back and forth: *We traded jokes.* **—*phrasal verbs.* trade down.** To trade something in for something else of lower value or price: *bought a new, smaller car, trading the old one down for economy.* **trade in.** To surrender or sell (an old or used item), using the proceeds as partial payment on a new purchase. **trade on.** To put to calculated and often unscrupulous advantage; exploit: *children of celebrities who trade on their family names.* **trade up.** To trade something in for something else of greater value or price: *The value of our house soared, enabling us to trade up to a larger place.* [Middle English, course, from Middle Low German.] **—trad′a·ble** *adj.*

trade acceptance *n.* A bill of exchange for the amount of a purchase drawn by the seller on the purchaser, bearing the purchaser's signature and specifying time and place of payment.

trade book *n.* A book published for distribution to the general public through booksellers.

trade·craft (trād′krăft′) *n.* The methods used in clandestine operations such as espionage.

trade discount *n.* A discount on the list price granted by a manufacturer or wholesaler to buyers in the same trade.

trade edition *n.* An edition of a book published for distribution to the general public through booksellers.

trade-in (trād′ĭn′) *n.* **1.** Merchandise accepted as partial payment for a new purchase. **2.** A transaction involving such merchandise.

trade language *n.* A language, especially a pidgin, used by speakers of different native languages for communication in commercial trade.

trade-last (trād′lăst′) *n.* *Informal.* A favorable remark that one has overheard about another person and offers to repeat to that person in exchange for a compliment overheard about oneself.

trade·mark (trād′märk′) *n.* **1.** *Abbr.* **TM** A name, symbol, or other device identifying a product, officially registered and legally restricted to the use of the owner or manufacturer. **2.** A distinctive characteristic by which a person or thing comes to be known: *the shuffle and snicker that became the comedian's trademark.* **—trademark** *tr.v.* **-marked, -mark·ing, -marks. 1.** To label (a product) with proprietary identification. **2.** To register (something) as a trademark.

trade name *n.* **1.** A name used to identify a commercial product or service, which may or may not be registered as a trademark. Also called *brand name.* **2.** The name by which a commodity, service, or process is known to the trade. **3.** The name under which a business firm operates.

trade·off or **trade-off** (trād′ôf′, -ŏf′) *n.* An exchange of one thing in return for another, especially relinquishment of one benefit or advantage for another regarded as more desirable: *"a fundamental trade-off between capitalist prosperity and economic security"* (David A. Stockman).

trade paperback *n.* A paperback book that is typically of better production quality, larger size, and higher price than a mass-market edition, intended for sale in bookstores.

trad·er (trā′dər) *n.* **1.** One that trades; a dealer: *a gold trader; a trader in bonds.* **2.** *Nautical.* A ship employed in foreign trade.

trade rat *n.* See **pack rat** (sense 1).

trade route *n.* A route used by traveling traders or merchant ships.

trade school *n.* A secondary school that offers instruction in skilled trades; a vocational school.

trade secret *n.* A secret formula, method, or device that gives one an advantage over competitors.

trades·man (trādz′mən) *n.* **1.** A man engaged in retail trade. **2.** A craftsman.

trades·peo·ple (trādz′pē′pəl) *pl.n.* **1.** People engaged in retail trade. **2.** Skilled workers.

trade union *n.* *Abbr.* **T.U.** A labor union, especially one limited in membership to people in the same trade. **—trade unionism** *n.* **—trade unionist** *n.*

trade wind (wĭnd) *n.* Any of a consistent system of prevailing winds occupying most of the tropics, constituting the major component of the general circulation of the atmosphere, and blowing northeasterly in the Northern Hemisphere and southeasterly in the Southern Hemisphere. Often used in the plural. [From obsolete *to blow trade,* to blow in a regular course, from TRADE, regular course (obsolete).]

trad·ing card (trā′dĭng) *n.* A card with a picture or design printed on it, often one of a set collected and traded by children.

trading post *n.* A station or store in a sparsely settled area established by traders to barter supplies for local products.

trading stamp *n.* A stamp given by a retailer to a buyer for a purchase of a specified amount and intended to be redeemed in quantity for merchandise.

tra·di·tion (trə-dĭsh′ən) *n.* **1.** The passing down of elements of a culture from generation to generation, especially by oral communication. **2.a.** A mode of thought or behavior followed by a people continuously from generation to generation; a custom or usage. **b.** A set of such customs and usages viewed as a coherent body of precedents influencing the present: *followed family tradition in dress and manners.* See Synonyms at **heritage. 3.** A body of unwritten religious precepts. **4.** A time-honored practice or set of such practices. **5.** *Law.* Transfer of property to another. [Middle English *tradicion,* from Old French, from Latin *trāditiō, trāditiōn-,* from *trāditus,* past participle of *trādere,* to hand over, deliver, entrust : *trā-, trāns-,* trans- + *dare,* to give; see **dō-** in Appendix.]

tra·di·tion·al (trə-dĭsh′ə-nəl) *adj.* Of, relating to, or in accord with tradition: *the traditional handshake; a traditional wedding ceremony.* **—tra·di′tion·al·ly** *adv.*

tra·di·tion·al·ism (trə-dĭsh′ə-nə-lĭz′əm) *n.* **1.** Adherence to tradition, especially in cultural or religious practice. **2.** *Phi-*

tractor

tractor-trailer

Spencer Tracy

ă pat	oi boy
ā pay	ou out
âr care	ŏŏ took
ä father	ōō boot
ĕ pet	ŭ cut
ē be	ûr urge
ĭ pit	th thin
ī pie	*th* this
îr pier	hw which
ŏ pot	zh vision
ō toe	ə about, item
ô paw	♦ regionalism

Stress marks: **′** (primary); ′ (secondary), as in **dictionary** (dĭk′shə-nĕr′ē)

losophy. A system holding that all knowledge is derived from original divine revelation and is transmitted by tradition. **—tra·di′tion·al·ist** *adj. & n.* **—tra·di′tion·al·is′tic** *adj.*

tra·di·tion·al·ize (trə-dĭsh′ə-nə-līz′) *tr.v.* **-ized, -iz·ing, -iz·es.** To make traditional.

trad·i·tor (trăd′ĭ-tər) *n., pl.* **-to·res** (-tôr′ēz, -tōr′-). One of the early Christians who betrayed fellow Christians during the Roman persecutions. [Middle English *traditour,* betrayer, from Latin *trāditor,* from *trāditus,* past participle of *trādere,* to betray, hand over. See TRADITION.]

tra·duce (trə-do͞os′, -dyo͞os′) *tr.v.* **-duced, -duc·ing, -duc·es.** To cause humiliation or disgrace to by making malicious and false statements. See Synonyms at **malign.** [Latin *trādūcere,* to lead as a spectacle, dishonor : *trā-, trāns-,* trans- + *dūcere,* to lead; see **deuk-** in Appendix.] **—tra·duce′ment** *n.* **—tra·duc′er** *n.* **—tra·duc′ing·ly** *adv.*

tra·du·cian·ism (trə-do͞o′shə-nĭz′əm, -dyo͞o′-) *n. Theology.* The belief that the soul is inherited from the parents along with the body. [From Late Latin *trādūciānus,* believer in traducianism, from *trādux, trāduc-,* inheritance, from Latin, vine-branch trained for propagation, from *trādūcere,* to lead across. See TRADUCE.] **—tra·du′cian·ist** *adj. & n.* **—tra·du′cian·is′tic** *adj.*

Tra·fal·gar (trə-făl′gər), **Cape.** A cape on the southwest coast of Spain northwest of the Strait of Gibraltar. The British navy under Adm. Horatio Nelson defeated the French and Spanish fleets off Cape Trafalgar in 1805.

tragopan
Satyr tragopan
Tragopan satyra

traf·fic (trăf′ĭk) *n.* **1.a.** The commercial exchange of goods; trade. **b.** Illegal or improper commercial activity: *drug traffic on city streets.* **2.a.** The business of moving passengers and cargo through a transportation system. See Synonyms at **business. b.** The amount of cargo or number of passengers conveyed. **3.a.** The passage of people, vehicles, or messages along routes of transportation or communication. **b.** Vehicles or pedestrians in transit: *heavy traffic on the turnpike; stopped oncoming traffic to let the children cross.* **4.** Social or verbal exchange; communication: *Refused further traffic with the estranged friend.* **—traffic** *intr.v.* **-ficked, -fick·ing, -fics.** To carry on trade or other dealings: *trafficked in liquidation merchandise; traffic with gangsters.* [French *trafic,* from Old French *trafique,* from Old Italian *traffico,* from *trafficare,* to trade, perhaps from Catalan *trafegar,* to decant, from Vulgar Latin **trānsfaecāre* : *trāns-,* trans- + *faex, faec-,* dregs; see FECES.] **—traf′fick·er** *n.*

traffic circle *n.* A circular one-way road at a junction of thoroughfares, facilitating an uninterrupted flow of traffic.

traffic island *n.* A raised area over which cars may not pass, placed at a junction of thoroughfares or between opposing traffic lanes.

traffic light *n.* A road signal for directing vehicular traffic by means of colored lights, typically red for stop, green for go, and yellow for proceed with caution. Also called *stoplight, traffic signal.*

trag·a·canth (trăg′ə-kănth′, trăj′-) *n.* **1.** Any of various thorny shrubs of the genus *Astragalus,* especially *A. gummifer,* of the Middle East, yielding a gum used in pharmacy, adhesives, and textile printing. **2.** The gum of this plant. [Latin *tragacantha,* from Greek *tragakantha* : *tragos,* goat + *akantha,* thorn.]

tra·ge·di·an (trə-jē′dē-ən) *n.* **1.** A writer of tragedies. **2.** One who performs tragic roles in the theater.

tra·ge·di·enne (trə-jē′dē-ĕn′) *n.* A woman who performs tragic roles in the theater. [French, feminine of *tragédien,* tragedian, from Old French *tragedian,* from *tragedie,* tragedy. See TRAGEDY.]

trag·e·dy (trăj′ĭ-dē) *n., pl.* **-dies. 1.a.** A drama or literary work in which the main character is brought to ruin or suffers extreme sorrow, especially as a consequence of a tragic flaw, a moral weakness, or an inability to cope with unfavorable circumstances. **b.** The genre made up of such works. **c.** The art or theory of writing or producing these works. **2.** A play, film, television program, or other narrative work that portrays or depicts calamitous events and has an unhappy but meaningful ending. **3.** A disastrous event, especially one involving distressing loss or injury to life: *an expedition that ended in tragedy, with all hands lost at sea.* **4.** A tragic aspect or element. [Middle English *tragedie,* from Old French, from Latin *tragoedia,* from Greek *tragōidia* : *tragos,* goat + *ōidē,* song; see **wed-**[2] in Appendix.]

tra·gi (trā′gī, -jī) *n.* Plural of **tragus.**

trag·ic (trăj′ĭk) *adj.* **1.** Relating to or characteristic of dramatic tragedy or tragedies: *tragic plays; the tragic hero.* **2.** Writing or performing in tragedy: *a tragic poet.* **3.** Having the elements of tragedy; involving death, grief, or destruction: *a tragic accident.* [Latin *tragicus,* from Greek *tragikos,* from *tragos,* goat.]

trag·i·cal (trăj′ĭ-kəl) *adj.* Tragic: *"You take too tragical a view of matters"* (John Fowles). *"He assumes a sudden look of tragical sobriety"* (Scott Turow). **—trag′i·cal·ly** *adv.* **—trag′i·cal·ness** *n.*

tragic flaw *n.* A flaw in the character of the protagonist of a tragedy that brings the protagonist to ruin or sorrow.

tragic irony *n.* Dramatic irony in a tragedy.

trag·i·com·e·dy (trăj′ĭ-kŏm′ĭ-dē) *n., pl.* **-dies. 1.** A drama combining elements of tragedy and comedy. **2.** The genre made up of such works. **3.** An incident or a situation having both comic and tragic elements. [French *tragicomédie,* from Italian *tragicommedia,* from Late Latin *tragicōmoedia,* short for Latin *tragicocōmoedia* : *tragicus,* tragic; see TRAGIC + *cōmoedia,* comedy; see COMEDY.] **—trag′i·com′ic** (-kŏm′ĭk), **trag′i·com′i·cal** (-ĭ-kəl) *adj.* **—trag′i·com′i·cal·ly** *adv.*

trag·o·pan (trăg′ə-păn′) *n.* Any of several Asian pheasants of the genus *Tragopan,* the male of which has a brightly colored wattle and two blue hornlike appendages on the head. [Latin *tragopān,* fabulous bird, from Greek : *tragos,* goat + *Pan,* Pan; see PAN.]

tra·gus (trā′gəs) *n., pl.* **-gi** (-gī, -jī). **1.** The projection of skin-covered cartilage in front of the meatus of the external ear. **2.** Any of the hairs growing at the entrance to the meatus of the external ear. [New Latin, from Greek *tragos,* goat, hairy part of the ear.]

trail (trāl) *v.* **trailed, trail·ing, trails.** *—tr.* **1.** To allow to drag or stream behind, as along the ground: *The dog ran off, trailing its leash.* **2.** To drag (the body, for example) wearily or heavily. **3.a.** To follow the traces or scent of, as in hunting; track. **b.** To follow the course taken by; pursue: *trail a fugitive.* **4.** To follow behind: *several cruisers trailed by an escorting destroyer.* **5.** To lag behind (an opponent): *trailed the league leader by four games.* *—intr.* **1.** To drag or be dragged along, brushing the ground: *The queen's long robe trailed behind.* **2.** To extend, grow, or droop loosely over a surface: *vines trailing through the garden.* **3.** To drift in a thin stream: *smoke trailing from a dying fire.* **4.** To become gradually fainter; dwindle: *His voice trailed off in confusion.* **5.** To walk or proceed with dragging steps; trudge. **6.** To be behind in competition; lag: *trailing by two goals in the second period.* **—trail** *n.* **1.** Something that hangs loose and long: *Trails of ticker tape floated down from office windows.* **2.** Something that is drawn along or follows behind; a train: *the senator, followed by a trail of reporters.* **3.** A succession of things that come afterward or are left behind: *left a trail of broken promises.* **4.a.** A mark or trace left by something that has moved or been dragged by. See Synonyms at **trace**[1]. **b.** A succession of such marks indicating a course taken; a track: *the trail of a hunted animal.* **5.a.** A marked or beaten path, as through woods or wilderness. **b.** An overland route: *the pioneers' trail across the prairies.* **6.** The part of a gun carriage that rests or slides on the ground. **7.** The act of trailing. [Middle English *trailen,* probably from Old French *trailler,* to hunt without a foreknown course, from Vulgar Latin **trāgulāre,* to make a deer double back and forth, perhaps alteration (influenced by Latin *trāgula,* dragnet) of Latin *trahere,* to pull, draw.]

trail bike *n.* A small motorcycle with rugged tires and suspension, designed for cross-country, off-road riding.

trail·blaz·er (trāl′blā′zər) *n.* **1.** One that blazes a trail. **2.** An innovative leader in a field; a pioneer.

trail·blaz·ing (trāl′blā′zĭng) *adj.* Suggestive of one that blazes a trail; setting out in a promising new direction; pioneering or innovative: *trailblazing research; a trailblazing new technique.*

trail·break·er (trāl′brā′kər) *n.* A trailblazer.

trail·er (trā′lər) *n.* **1.** A large transport vehicle designed to be hauled by a truck or tractor. **2.** A furnished van drawn by a truck or an automobile and used when parked as a dwelling or an office. **3.a.** A short filmed advertisement for a movie. **b.** A short, blank strip of film at the end of a reel. **—trailer** *v.* **-ered, -er·ing, -ers.** *—tr.* To transport by a trailer: *trailered the boat to the beach.* *—intr.* To travel or live in a trailer. **—trail′er·a·ble** *adj.*

trailer park *n.* An area in which parking space for house trailers is rented, usually providing utilities and services. Also called *trailer camp.*

trail·head (trāl′hĕd′) *n.* The place where a trail begins.

trail·ing arbutus (trā′lĭng) *n.* A low-growing evergreen shrub *(Epigaea repens)* of eastern North America, having leathery leaves and clusters of fragrant pink or white flowers. Also called *mayflower.*

trailing edge *n.* The rearmost edge of a structure that moves, as an airfoil.

trail·side (trāl′sīd′) *n.* The area beside a trail. *—attributive.* Often used to modify another noun: *a trailside picnic; a trailside condominium.*

train (trān) *n.* **1.** *Abbr.* **tn.** A series of connected railroad cars pulled or pushed by one or more locomotives. **2.** A long line of moving people, animals, or vehicles. **3.** The personnel, vehicles, and equipment following and providing supplies and services to a combat unit. **4.** A part of a gown that trails behind the wearer. **5.** A staff of people following in attendance; a retinue. **6.a.** An orderly succession of related events or thoughts; a sequence. See Synonyms at **series. b.** A series of consequences wrought by an event; aftermath. **7.** A set of linked mechanical parts: *a train of gears.* **8.** A string of gunpowder that acts as a fuse for exploding a charge. **—train** *v.* **trained, train·ing, trains.** *—tr.* **1.** To coach in or accustom to a mode of behavior or performance. **2.** To make proficient with specialized instruction and practice. See Synonyms at **teach. 3.** To prepare physically, as with a regimen: *train athletes for track-and-field competition.* **4.** To cause (a plant or one's hair) to take a desired course or shape, as by manipulating. **5.** To focus on or aim at (a goal, mark, or target); direct. See Synonyms at **aim. 6.** To let drag behind; trail. *—intr.* **1.** To give or undergo a course of training: *trained daily for the marathon.* **2.** To travel by railroad train. [Middle English, trailing part of a gown, from Old French, from *trainer,* to drag, from Vulgar Latin **tragīnāre,* from **tragere,* to pull, back-formation from *trāctus,* past participle of Latin *trahere.*] **—train′a·bil′i·ty** *n.* **—train′a·ble** *adj.*

train·band (trān′bănd′) *n.* A company of trained militia in England or America from the 16th to the 18th century. [Contraction of *trained band.*]

train·bear·er (trān′bâr′ər) *n.* An attendant who holds up the train of a robe or gown, as in a procession.

train·ee (trā-nē′) *n.* One who is being trained. **—train·ee′ship′** *n.*

train·er (trā′nər) *n.* **1.** One who trains, especially one who coaches athletes, racehorses, or show animals. **2.** A contrivance or an apparatus used in training. **3.** A member of a naval gun crew who trains cannons horizontally.

train·ing (trā′nĭng) *n. Abbr.* **tng. 1.** The process or routine of one who trains. **2.** The state of being trained.

training school *n.* **1.** A school that gives practical vocational and technical instruction. **2.** A detention home that offers vocational training to juvenile offenders.

training table *n. Sports.* A table, as in a mess hall, providing planned meals for athletes in training.

train·load (trān′lōd′) *n.* The number of occupants or the amount of material that a passenger or freight train can hold.

train·man (trān′mən) *n.* A member of the operating crew on a railroad train, especially the brakeman.

train oil *n.* Oil obtained from the blubber of a whale or other marine animal. [Middle English *trane,* from Middle Dutch, tear, drop, train oil. See **dakru-** in Appendix.]

traipse (trāps) *intr.v.* **traipsed, traips·ing, traips·es.** To walk or tramp about; gad. [Origin unknown.]

trait (trāt) *n.* **1.** A distinguishing feature, as of a person's character. See Synonyms at **quality. 2.** A genetically determined characteristic or condition: *a recessive trait.* **3.a.** A stroke with or as if with a pencil. **b.** A slight degree or amount, as of a quality; a touch or trace: *a sermon with a trait of humor.* [Middle English, shot, from Old French, something drawn, shot, from Latin *trāctus,* a drawing out, line. See TRACT[1].]

trai·tor (trā′tər) *n.* One who betrays one's country, a cause, or a trust, especially one who commits treason. [Middle English, from Old French, from Latin *trāditor, trāditōr-,* from *trāditus,* past participle of *trādere,* to betray. See TRADITION.]

trai·tor·ous (trā′tər-əs) *adj.* **1.** Having the character of a traitor; disloyal. **2.** Constituting treason: *a traitorous act.* See Synonyms at **faithless. —trai′tor·ous·ly** *adv.* **—trai′tor·ous·ness** *n.*

Tra·jan (trā′jən). A.D. 53–117. Roman emperor (98–117) whose reign was marked by an extensive building program and compassionate treatment of the poor.

tra·ject (trə-jĕkt′) *tr.v.* **-ject·ed, -ject·ing, -jects.** To transmit. [Latin *trāiicere, trāiect-,* to throw across : *trā-, trāns-,* trans- + *iacere,* to throw; see **yē-** in Appendix.] **—tra·jec′tion** *n.*

tra·jec·to·ry (trə-jĕk′tə-rē) *n., pl.* **-ries. 1.a.** The path of a projectile or other moving body through space. **b.** A chosen course or a course taken: *"a moral trajectory, a style of aspiration"* (Lance Morrow). **2.** *Mathematics.* A curve that cuts all of a given family of curves or surfaces at the same angle. [New Latin *trāiectōria,* feminine of *trāiectōrius,* from Latin *trāiectus,* past participle of *trāiicere,* to throw across. See TRAJECT.]

Tra·lee (trə-lē′). An urban district of southwest Ireland at the head of **Tralee Bay,** an inlet of the Atlantic Ocean. Tralee is a seaport and manufacturing center. Population, 16,495.

tram[1] (trăm) *n.* **1.** *Chiefly British.* **a.** A streetcar. **b.** A streetcar line. **2.** A cable car, especially one suspended from an overhead cable. **3.** A four-wheeled, open, box-shaped wagon or iron car run on tracks in a coal mine. **—tram** *tr.v.* **trammed, tram·ming, trams.** To move or convey in a tram. [Scots, shaft of a barrow, probably from Middle Flemish.]

tram[2] (trăm) *n.* **1.** An instrument for gauging and adjusting machine parts; a trammel. **2.** Accurate mechanical adjustment: *The device is in tram.* **—tram** *tr.v.* **trammed, tram·ming, trams.** To adjust or align (mechanical parts) with a trammel. [Short for TRAMMEL.]

tram[3] (trăm) *n.* A heavy silk thread used for the weft, or cross threads, in fine velvet or silk. [Middle English, contrivance, from Old French *traime,* contrivance, weft, from Latin *trāma,* weft, woof.]

tram·car (trăm′kär′) *n.* **1.** *Chiefly British.* A streetcar. **2.** A coal car in a mine.

tram·line (trăm′līn′) *n. Chiefly British.* A streetcar line.

tram·mel (trăm′əl) *n.* **1.** A shackle used to teach a horse to amble. **2.** Something that restricts activity, expression, or progress; a restraint. **3.** A vertically set fishing net of three layers, consisting of a finely meshed net between two nets of coarse mesh. **4.** An instrument for describing ellipses. **5.** An instrument for gauging and adjusting parts of a machine; a tram. **6.** An arrangement of links and a hook in a fireplace for raising and lowering a kettle. **—trammel** *tr.v.* **-meled, -mel·ing, -mels** or **-melled, -mel·ling, -mels. 1.** To enmesh in or as if in a fishing net. See Synonyms at **hamper**[1]. **2.** To hinder the activity or free movement of. [Middle English *tramale,* a kind of net, from Old French *tramail,* from Late Latin *trēmaculum* : Latin *trēs,* three; see **trei-** in Appendix + Latin *macula,* mesh.] **—tram′mel·er** *n.*

tra·mon·tane (trə-mŏn′tān′, trăm′ən-tān′) *adj.* **1.** Dwelling beyond or coming from the far side of the mountains, especially the Alps as viewed from Italy. **2.** From another country; foreign. **—tramontane** *n.* **1.** A person who lives beyond the mountains. **2.** A foreigner; a stranger. **3.** A cold north wind in Italy. [Italian *tramontano,* from Latin *trānsmontānus* : *trāns-,* trans- + *montā-nus,* of a mountain; see MOUNTAIN.]

tramp (trămp) *v.* **tramped, tramp·ing, tramps.** —*intr.* **1.** To walk with a firm, heavy step; trudge. **2.a.** To travel on foot; hike. **b.** To wander about aimlessly. —*tr.* **1.** To traverse on foot: *tramp the fields.* **2.** To tread down; trample: *tramp down snow.* **—tramp** *n.* **1.a.** A heavy footfall. **b.** The sound produced by heavy walking or marching. **2.** A walking trip; a hike. **3.** One who travels aimlessly about on foot, doing odd jobs or begging for a living; a vagrant. **4.a.** A prostitute. **b.** A person regarded as promiscuous. **5.** *Nautical.* A tramp steamer. **6.** A metal plate attached to the sole of a shoe for protection, as when spading ground. [Middle English *trampen,* to walk heavily, from Middle Low German.] **—tramp′er** *n.* **—tramp′ish** *adj.* **—tramp′y** *adj.*

tram·ple (trăm′pəl) *v.* **-pled, -pling, -ples.** —*tr.* **1.** To beat down with the feet so as to crush, bruise, or destroy; tramp on. **2.** To treat harshly or ruthlessly: *would trample anyone who got in their way.* —*intr.* **1.** To tread heavily or destructively: *trampling on the flowers.* **2.** To inflict injury as if by treading heavily: *"trampling on the feelings of those about you"* (Thornton Wilder). **—trample** *n.* The action or sound of trampling. [Middle English *tramplen,* frequentative of *trampen,* to tramp. See TRAMP.] **—tram′pler** *n.*

tram·po·line (trăm′pə-lēn′, -lĭn) *n. Sports.* A strong, taut sheet, usually of canvas, attached with springs to a metal frame and used for gymnastic springing and tumbling. [Spanish *trampolín* and Italian *trampolino* (Italian, from Spanish), from *tràmpoli,* stilts, of Germanic origin.] **—tram′po·lin′er, tram′po·lin′ist** *n.*

tramp steamer *n. Nautical.* A commercial vessel that has no regular schedule but takes on and discharges cargo whenever hired to do so.

tram·way (trăm′wā′) *n.* **1.** A track or way for trams, as in a mine. **2.** *Chiefly British.* A streetcar line. **3.** A cable or system of cables for a cable car.

trance (trăns) *n.* **1.** A hypnotic, cataleptic, or ecstatic state. **2.** Detachment from one's physical surroundings, as in contemplation or daydreaming. **3.** A semiconscious state, as between sleeping and waking; a daze. **—trance** *tr.v.* **tranced, tranc·ing, tranc·es.** To put into a trance; entrance. [Middle English *traunce,* from Old French *transe,* passage, fear, vision, from *transir,* to die, be numb with fear, from Latin *trānsīre,* to go over or across. See TRANSIENT.] **—trance′like′** *adj.*

trance channeling *n.* Channeling. **—trance channeler** *n.*

tran·quil (trăng′kwəl, trăn′-) *adj.* **1.** Free from commotion or disturbance. See Synonyms at **calm. 2.** Free from anxiety, tension, or restlessness; composed. **3.** Steady; even: *a tranquil flame.* [Middle English *tranquill,* from Latin *tranquillus.* See **k^w^eiə-** in Appendix.] **—tran′quil·ly** *adv.* **—tran′quil·ness** *n.*

tran·quil·i·ty (trăng-kwĭl′ĭ-tē, trăn-) *n.* Variant of **tranquillity.**

tran·quil·ize also **tran·quil·lize** (trăng′kwə-līz′, trăn′-) *v.* **-ized, -iz·ing, -iz·es** also **-lized, -liz·ing, -liz·es.** —*tr.* **1.** To make tranquil; pacify: *"Nothing contributes so much to tranquilize the mind as a steady purpose"* (Mary Wollstonecraft Shelley). **2.** To sedate or relieve of anxiety or tension by the administration of a drug. —*intr.* **1.** To become tranquil; relax. **2.** To have a calming or soothing effect. **—tran′quil·i·za′tion** (-kwə-lĭ-zā′shən) *n.*

tran·quil·iz·er (trăng′kwə-lī′zər, trăn′-) *n.* **1.** One that serves to tranquilize, as soothing music. **2.** Any of various depressant drugs used to reduce tension or anxiety and to treat psychotic states.

tran·quil·li·ty or **tran·quil·i·ty** (trăng-kwĭl′ĭ-tē, trăn-) *n.* The quality or state of being tranquil; serenity.

tran·quil·lize (trăng′kwə-līz′, trăn′-) *v.* Variant of **tranquilize.**

trans. *abbr.* **1.** Transaction. **2.** Transfer. **3.** *Grammar.* Transitive. **4.a.** Translated. **b.** Translation; translator. **5.** Transportation. **6.** Transpose; transposition. **7.** Transverse.

trans– *pref.* **1.** Across; on the other side; beyond: *transpolar.* **2.** Through: *transcontinental.* **3.** Change; transfer: *transliterate.* **4.** Having a pair of identical atoms on opposite sides of two atoms linked by a double bond. Used of a geometric isomer: *trans-butene.* [From Latin *trāns-,* from *trāns,* across, beyond, through. See **terə-**[2] in Appendix.]

trans·act (trăn-săkt′, -zăkt′) *v.* **-act·ed, -act·ing, -acts.** —*tr.* To do, carry on, or conduct: *transact business over the phone; transacting trade agreements.* —*intr.* To conduct business: *transacting with foreign leaders.* [Latin *trānsigere, trānsāct-* : *trāns-,* trans- + *agere,* to drive, do; see **ag-** in Appendix.] **—trans·ac′tor** *n.*

transactinide *adj.* Of or belonging to the series of elements whose atomic numbers are greater than 103.

trans·ac·tion (trăn-săk′shən, -zăk′-) *n. Abbr.* **trans. 1.** The act of transacting or the fact of being transacted. **2.** Something transacted, especially a business agreement or exchange. **3.** Communication involving two or more people that affects all those involved; personal interaction: *"a rich sense of the transaction between writer and reader"* (William Zinsser). **4. transactions.** A

ă pat	oi boy
ā pay	ou out
âr care	o͝o took
ä father	o͞o boot
ĕ pet	ŭ cut
ē be	ûr urge
ĭ pit	th thin
ī pie	*th* this
îr pier	hw which
ŏ pot	zh vision
ō toe	ə about, item
ô paw	♦ regionalism

Stress marks: **′** (primary); ′ (secondary), as in **dictionary** (dĭk′shə-nĕr′ē)

record of business conducted at a meeting; proceedings. **—trans·ac′tion·al** *adj.*

transactional analysis *n. Abbr.* **TA** A system of psychotherapy that analyzes personal relationships and interactions in terms of conflicting or complementary ego states that correspond to the roles of parent, child, and adult.

trans·ac·ti·vate (trăns-ăk′tə-vāt′, tranz-) *tr.v.* **-vat·ed, -vat·ing, -vates.** To stimulate (a host cell) to replicate the genetic components of a virus. Used of a viral protein. **—trans′-ac·ti·va′tion** *n.* **—trans·ac′ti·va′tor** *n.*

Trans A·lai (trăns′ ə-lī′, trănz′). A range of the Pamir Mountains in eastern Tadzhikistan and southern Kirghiz rising to 7,138.5 m (23,405 ft).

trans·al·pine (trăns-ăl′pīn′, trănz-) *adj.* Relating to, living on, or coming from the other side of the Alps, especially as viewed from Italy.

Trans·al·pine Gaul (trăns-ăl′pīn′ gôl′, trănz-). The part of ancient Gaul northwest of the Alps, including modern France and Belgium.

trans·am·i·nase (trăns-ăm′ə-nās′, -nāz′, trănz-) *n.* Any of a group of enzymes that catalyze transamination.

trans·am·i·na·tion (trăns-ăm′ə-nā′shən, trănz-) *n.* **1.** Transfer of an amino group from one chemical compound to another. **2.** Transposition of an amino group within a chemical compound.

trans·at·lan·tic (trăns′ət-lăn′tĭk, trănz′-) *adj.* **1.** Situated on or coming from the other side of the Atlantic Ocean. **2.** Spanning or crossing the Atlantic Ocean.

trans·ax·le (trăns-ăk′səl, trănz-) *n.* An automotive part that combines the transmission and the differential and is used on vehicles with front-wheel drive. [TRANS(MISSION) + AXLE.]

Trans·cau·ca·sia (trăns′kô-kā′zhə, -zhē-ə, trănz′-). A region of Georgia, Armenia, and Azerbaijan between the Caucasus Mountains and the borders of Turkey and Iran. **—Trans′cau·ca′sian** *adj.* & *n.*

trans·ceiv·er (trăn-sē′vər) *n.* A transmitter and receiver housed together in a single unit and having some circuits in common, often for portable or mobile use. [TRANS(MITTER) + (RE)CEIVER.]

tran·scend (trăn-sĕnd′) *v.* **-scend·ed, -scend·ing, -scends.** *—tr.* **1.** To pass beyond the limits of: *emotions that transcend understanding.* **2.** To be greater than, as in intensity or power; surpass: *love that transcends infatuation.* See Synonyms at **excel. 3.** To exist above and independent of (material experience or the universe): *"One never can see the thing in itself, because the mind does not transcend phenomena"* (Hilaire Belloc). *—intr.* To be transcendent; excel. [Middle English *transcenden,* from Old French *transcendre,* from Latin *trānscendere* : *trāns-,* trans- + *scandere,* to climb; see **skand-** in Appendix.]

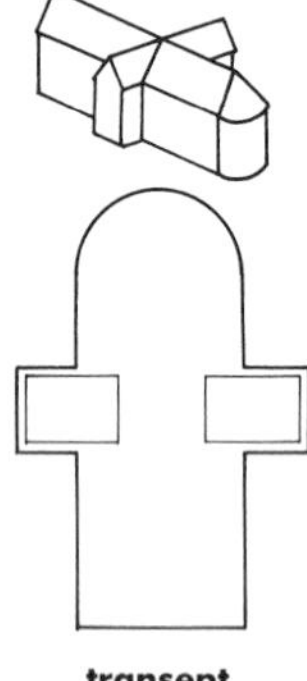

transept

tran·scen·dent (trăn-sĕn′dənt) *adj.* **1.** Surpassing others; preeminent or supreme. **2.** Lying beyond the ordinary range of perception: *"fails to achieve a transcendent significance in suffering and squalor"* (National Review). **3.** *Philosophy.* **a.** Transcending the Aristotelian categories. **b.** In Kant's theory of knowledge, being beyond the limits of experience and hence unknowable. **4.** Being above and independent of the material universe. Used of the Deity. **—tran·scen′dence, tran·scen′den·cy** *n.* **—tran·scen′dent·ly** *adv.*

tran·scen·den·tal (trăn′sĕn-dĕn′tl) *adj.* **1.** *Philosophy.* **a.** Concerned with the a priori or intuitive basis of knowledge as independent of experience. **b.** Asserting a fundamental irrationality or supernatural element in experience. **2.** Surpassing all others; superior. **3.** Beyond common thought or experience; mystical or supernatural. **4.** *Mathematics.* **a.** Not capable of being determined by any combination of a finite number of equations with rational integral coefficients. **b.** Not expressible as an integer or as the root or quotient of integers. Used of numbers, especially nonrepeating infinite decimals. **—tran′scen·den′tal·ly** *adv.*

tran·scen·den·tal·ism (trăn′sĕn-dĕn′tl-ĭz′əm) *n.* **1.** A philosophy associated with Kant, holding that one must transcend empiricism or what is experienced in order to ascertain the a priori principles of all knowledge. **2.** A literary and philosophical movement, associated with Ralph Waldo Emerson and Margaret Fuller, asserting the existence of an ideal spiritual reality that transcends the empirical and scientific and is knowable through intuition. **3.** The quality or state of being transcendental. **—tran′scen·den′tal·ist** *n.*

transcendental meditation *n. Abbr.* **T.M.** A technique of meditation derived from Hindu traditions that promotes deep relaxation through the use of a mantra.

trans·con·ti·nen·tal (trăns′kŏn-tə-nĕn′tl) *adj.* Spanning or crossing a continent.

tran·scribe (trăn-skrīb′) *tr.v.* **-scribed, -scrib·ing, -scribes. 1.** To make a full written or typewritten copy of (dictated material, for example). **2.** *Computer Science.* To transfer (information) from one recording and storing system to another. **3.** *Music.* To adapt or arrange (a composition) for a voice or an instrument other than the original. **4.** To record, usually on tape, for broadcast at a later date. **5.** *Linguistics.* To represent (speech sounds) by phonetic symbols. **6.** To translate or transliterate. **7.** *Biology.* To cause (DNA or RNA) to undergo transcription. [Latin *trānscrībere* : *trāns-,* trans- + *scrībere,* to write; see **skribh-** in Appendix.] **—tran·scrib′a·ble** *adj.* **—tran·scrib′er** *n.*

tran·script (trăn′skrĭpt′) *n.* **1.** Something transcribed, especially a written, typewritten, or printed copy: *the transcript of court testimony; an academic transcript.* **2.** *Biology.* A sequence of RNA produced by transcription. [Middle English, from Medieval Latin *trānscrīptum,* from Latin, neuter past participle of *trānscrībere,* to transcribe. See TRANSCRIBE.]

tran·scrip·tase (trăn-skrĭp′tās, -tāz) *n.* **1.** A polymerase that catalyzes the formation of RNA from a DNA template in the process of transcription. **2.** Reverse transcriptase.

tran·scrip·tion (trăn-skrĭp′shən) *n.* **1.** The act or process of transcribing. **2.** Something that has been transcribed, especially: **a.** *Music.* An adaptation of a composition. **b.** A recorded radio or television program. **c.** *Linguistics.* A representation of speech sounds in phonetic symbols. **3.** *Biology.* The process by which messenger RNA is synthesized from a DNA template resulting in the transfer of genetic information from the DNA molecule to the messenger RNA. **—tran·scrip′tion·al** *adj.* **—tran·scrip′tion·al·ly** *adv.* **—tran·scrip′tion·ist** *n.*

trans·cul·tu·ra·tion (trăns′kŭl-chə-rā′shən) *n.* Cultural change induced by introduction of elements of a foreign culture.

trans·cur·rent (trăns-kûr′ənt, -kŭr′-) *adj.* Extending or running transversely.

trans·cu·ta·ne·ous (trăns′kyo͞o-tā′nē-əs) *adj.* Transdermal.

trans·der·mal (trăns-dûr′məl, trănz-) *n.* Through or by way of the skin: *transdermal inoculation; transdermal medication.*

transdermal patch *n.* A medicated adhesive pad that is placed on the skin to deliver a time-release dose of medication through the skin into the bloodstream. Also called *skin patch.*

trans·duce (trăns-do͞os′, -dyo͞os′, trănz-) *tr.v.* **-duced, -duc·ing, -duc·es. 1.** To convert (energy) from one form to another. **2.** To transfer (genetic material or characteristics) from one bacterial cell to another. Used of a bacteriophage or plasmid. [Back-formation from TRANSDUCER.]

trans·duc·er (trăns-do͞o′sər, -dyo͞o′-, trănz-) *n.* A substance or device, such as a piezoelectric crystal, microphone, or photoelectric cell, that converts input energy of one form into output energy of another. [From Latin *trānsdūcere,* to transfer : *trāns-,* trans- + *dūcere,* to lead; see **deuk-** in Appendix.]

trans·duc·tant (trăns-dŭk′tənt, trănz-) *n.* A bacterial cell into which genetic material has been transduced.

trans·duc·tion (trăns-dŭk′shən, trănz-) *n. Genetics.* Transfer of genetic material or characteristics from one bacterial cell to another by a bacteriophage or plasmid. [From Latin *transductus,* past participle of *trānsdūcere,* to transfer. See TRANSDUCER.] **—trans·duc′tion·al** *adj.*

tran·sect (trăn-sĕkt′) *tr.v.* **-sect·ed, -sect·ing, -sects.** To divide by cutting transversely. [TRANS– + –SECT.] **—tran·sec′-tion** *n.*

tran·sept (trăn′sĕpt′) *n. Architecture.* **1.** The transverse part of a cruciform church, crossing the nave at right angles. **2.** Either of the two lateral arms of such a part. [New Latin *trānseptum* : Latin *trāns-,* trans- + Latin *saeptum,* partition; see SEPTUM.]

tran·se·unt (trăn′sē-ənt) *adj. Philosophy.* Productive of effects outside the mind. [Latin *trānsiēns, trānseunt-,* present participle of *trānsīre,* to go over. See TRANSIENT.]

transf. *abbr.* **1.** Transfer. **2.** Transferred.

trans·fec·tion (trăns-fĕk′shən) *n.* Infection of a cell with purified viral nucleic acid, resulting in subsequent replication of the virus in the cell. [TRANS– + (IN)FECTION.] **—trans·fect′** *v.*

trans·fer (trăns-fûr′, trăns′fər) *v.* **-ferred, -fer·ring, -fers.** *—tr.* **1.** To convey or cause to pass from one place, person, or thing to another. **2.** *Law.* To make over the possession or legal title of; convey. **3.** To convey (a design, for example) from one surface to another, as by impression. *—intr.* **1.** To move oneself from one location or job to another. **2.** To withdraw from one educational institution or course of study and enroll in another. **3.** To change from one public conveyance to another: *transferred to another bus.* **—transfer** (trăns′fər) *n. Abbr.* **trans., transf., tfr. 1.** Also **trans·fer·al** (trăns-fûr′əl). The conveyance or removal of something from one place, person, or thing to another. **2.** One who transfers or is transferred, as to a new school. **3.** A design conveyed by contact from one surface to another. **4. a.** A ticket entitling a passenger to change from one public conveyance to another as part of one trip. **b.** A place where such a change is made. **5.** Also **transferal.** *Law.* A conveyance of title or property from one person to another. [Middle English *transferren,* from Old French *transferer,* from Latin *trānsferre* : *trāns-,* trans- + *ferre,* to carry; see **bher-**[1] in Appendix.] **—trans·fer′a·bil′i·ty** *n.* **—trans·fer′a·ble, trans·fer′ra·ble** *adj.* **—trans·fer′rer** *n.*

trans·fer·al (trăns-fûr′əl) *n.* **1.** Variant of **transfer** (sense 1). **2.** *Law.* Variant of **transfer** (sense 5).

trans·fer·ase (trăns′fə-rās′, -rāz′) *n.* Any of various enzymes that catalyze the transfer of a chemical group, such as a phosphate or an amine, from one molecule to another.

trans·fer·ee (trăns′fə-rē′) *n.* **1.** *Law.* One to whom a conveyance of title or property is made. **2.** One who is transferred.

trans·fer·ence (trăns-fûr′əns, trăns′fər-əns) *n.* **1. a.** The act or process of transferring. **b.** The fact of being transferred. **2.** In psychoanalysis, the process by which emotions and desires originally associated with one person, such as a parent or sibling, are unconsciously shifted to another person, especially to the analyst. **—trans′fer·en′tial** (trăns′fə-rĕn′shəl) *adj.*

transfer factor *n.* A polypeptide secreted by lymphocytes that is capable of transferring immunity from one cell or individual to another.

trans·fer·or (trăns′fə-rôr′) *n. Law.* One who conveys a title or property.

trans·fer·rin (trăns-fĕr′ĭn) *n.* A beta globulin in blood serum that combines with and transports iron. [TRANS– + FERR(O)– + –IN.]

transfer RNA *n.* One of a class of RNA molecules that transport amino acids to ribosomes for incorporation into a polypeptide undergoing synthesis. Also called *tRNA.*

trans·fig·u·ra·tion (trăns-fĭg′yə-rā′shən) *n.* **1.a.** A marked change in form or appearance; a metamorphosis. **b.** A change that glorifies or exalts. **2. Transfiguration. a.** The sudden emanation of radiance from the person of Jesus that occurred on the mountain. **b.** The Christian feast commemorating this event, observed on August 6 and, in the Eastern Orthodox Church, on August 19.

trans·fig·ure (trăns-fĭg′yər) *tr.v.* **-ured, -ur·ing, -ures. 1.** To alter the outward appearance of; transform. See Synonyms at **convert. 2.** To exalt or glorify. [Middle English *transfiguren,* from Old French *transfigurer,* from Latin *trānsfigūrāre* : *trāns-,* trans- + *figūra,* form; see **dheigh-** in Appendix.] **—trans·fig′ure·ment** *n.*

trans·fi·nite (trăns-fī′nīt′) *adj.* Going beyond the finite.

transfinite number *n. Mathematics.* A number that is greater than any finite number.

trans·fix (trăns-fĭks′) *tr.v.* **-fixed, -fix·ing, -fix·es. 1.** To pierce with or as if with a pointed weapon. **2.** To fix fast; impale **3.** To render motionless, as with terror, amazement, or awe. [Latin *trānsfīgere, trānsfīx-* : *trāns-,* trans- + *fīgere,* to pierce, fasten; see **dhīgʷ-** in Appendix.] **—trans·fix′ion** (-fĭk′shən) *n.*

trans·form (trăns-fôrm′) *v.* **-formed, -form·ing, -forms.** *—tr.* **1.** To change markedly the appearance or form of: *"A thick, fibrous fog had transformed the trees into ghosts and the streetlights into soft, haloed moons"* (David Michael Kaplan). **2.** To change the nature, function, or condition of; convert. See Synonyms at **convert. 3.** *Mathematics.* To subject to a transformation. **4.** *Linguistics.* To subject (a construction) to a transformation. **5.** *Electricity.* To subject to the action of a transformer. **6.** *Genetics.* To subject (a bacterial cell) to transformation. *—intr.* To undergo a transformation. **—transform** (trăns′fôrm′) *n.* The result, especially a mathematical quantity or linguistic construction, of a transformation. [Middle English *transformen,* from Old French *transformer,* from Latin *trānsfōrmāre* : *trāns-,* trans- + *fōrma,* form.] **—trans·form′a·ble** *adj.*

trans·for·ma·tion (trăns′fər-mā′shən, -fôr-) *n.* **1.a.** The act or an instance of transforming. **b.** The state of being transformed. **2.** A marked change, as in appearance or character, usually for the better. **3.** *Mathematics.* **a.** Replacement of the variables in an algebraic expression by their values in terms of another set of variables. **b.** A mapping of one space onto another or onto itself. **4.** *Linguistics.* **a.** The process of converting a syntactic construction into a semantically equivalent construction according to the rules shown to generate the syntax of the language. **b.** A construction derived by such transformation; a transform. **5.** *Genetics.* Alteration of a bacterial cell by introduction of DNA from another cell or from a virus. **—trans·form′a·tive** (-fôr′mə-tĭv) *adj.*

trans·for·ma·tion·al grammar (trăns′fər-mā′shə-nəl, -fôr-) *n. Abbr.* **TG** *Linguistics.* A grammar that accounts for the constructions of a language by linguistic transformations and phrase structures, especially generative transformational grammar.

trans·form·er (trăns-fôr′mər) *n.* A device used to transfer electric energy from one circuit to another, especially a pair of multiply wound, inductively coupled wire coils that effect such a transfer with a change in voltage, current, phase, or other electric characteristic.

trans·fuse (trăns-fyo͞oz′) *tr.v.* **-fused, -fus·ing, -fus·es. 1.** To pour (something) out of one vessel into another. **2.** To cause to be instilled or imparted: *transfused a love of learning to her children.* **3.** To diffuse through; permeate: *a glade that was transfused with sunlight.* **4.** *Medicine.* To administer a transfusion of or to. [Middle English *transfusen,* to transmit, from Latin *trānsfundere, trānsfūs-,* to transfuse : *trāns-,* trans- + *fundere,* to pour; see **gheu-** in Appendix.] **—trans·fus′er** *n.* **—trans·fus′i·ble, trans·fus′a·ble** *adj.* **—trans·fu′sive** (-fyo͞o′sĭv, -zĭv) *adj.*

trans·fu·sion (trăns-fyo͞o′zhən) *n.* **1.** The act or process of transfusing. **2.** *Medicine.* The transfer of whole blood or blood products from one individual to another. **—trans·fu′sion·al** *adj.*

trans·gen·ic (trăns-jĕn′ĭk, trănz-) *adj.* Carrying genes transferred from another species or breed: *a transgenic animal; transgenic chickens.*

trans·gress (trăns-grĕs′, trănz-) *v.* **-gressed, -gress·ing, -gress·es.** *—tr.* **1.** To go beyond or over (a limit or boundary); exceed or overstep: *"to make sure that her characters didn't transgress the parameters of ordinariness"* (Ron Rosenbaum). **2.** To act in violation of (the law, for example). *—intr.* **1.** To commit an offense by violating a law or command; sin. **2.** To spread over land, especially over the land along a subsiding shoreline. Used of the sea. [Middle English *transgressen,* from Old French *transgresser,* from Latin *trānsgredī, trānsgress-,* to step across : *trāns-,* trans- + *gradī,* to go; see **ghredh-** in Appendix.] **—trans·gress′i·ble** *adj.* **—trans·gres′sive** *adj.* **—trans·gres′sive·ly** *adv.* **—trans·gres′sor** *n.*

trans·gres·sion (trăns-grĕsh′ən, trănz-) *n.* **1.** A violation of a law, command, or duty: *"The same transgressions should be visited with equal severity on both man and woman"* (Elizabeth Cady Stanton). See Synonyms at **breach. 2.** The exceeding of due bounds or limits. **3.** The spread of the sea over land along a subsiding shoreline.

tran·ship (trăn-shĭp′) *v.* Variant of **transship.**

trans·hu·mance (trăns-hyo͞o′məns, trănz-) *n.* Transfer of livestock from one grazing ground to another, as from lowlands to highlands, with the changing of seasons. [French, from *transhumer,* to move livestock seasonally, from Spanish *trashumar* : Latin *trāns-,* trans- + Latin *humus,* ground; see **dhghem-** in Appendix.] **—trans·hu′mant** *adj. & n.*

tran·sience (trăn′shəns, -zhəns, -zē-əns) also **tran·sien·cy** (-shən-sē, -zhən-, -zē-ən-) *n.* The state or quality of being transient.

tran·sient (trăn′shənt, -zhənt, -zē-ənt) *adj.* **1.** Passing with time; transitory: *"the transient beauty of youth"* (Lydia M. Child). **2.** Remaining in a place only a brief time: *transient laborers.* **3.** *Physics.* Decaying with time, especially as a simple exponential function of time. **—transient** *n.* **1.** One that is transient, especially a hotel guest or boarder who stays for only a brief time. **2.** *Physics.* A transient phenomenon or property, especially a transient electric current. [Alteration of Latin *trānsiēns, trānseunt-,* present participle of *trānsīre,* to go over : *trāns,* over; see **tere-**[2] in Appendix + *īre,* to go; see **ei-** in Appendix.] **—tran′sient·ly** *adv.*

SYNONYMS: *transient, transitory, ephemeral, fleeting, fugitive, momentary, evanescent.* These adjectives mean lasting, existing, or staying for a short time. *Transient* usually refers to what remains only briefly: *We stayed at the inn as transient guests. "The moods were many and transient"* (W.H. Hudson). *Transitory* more often means inherently short-lived or impermanent: *"This false world is but transitory"* (William Dunbar). *"Action is transitory—a step, a blow,/The motion of a muscle, this way or that—/'Tis done"* (William Wordsworth). *Ephemeral,* which in its original sense means living or lasting only for a day, implies conspicuously brief existence or duration: *"the old universal truths lacking which any story is ephemeral and doomed"* (William Faulkner). *Fleeting* is applied to what slips away swiftly, often more swiftly than one would wish: *"Art is long, and Time is fleeting"* (Henry Wadsworth Longfellow). *Fugitive* especially describes what is elusive or quickly fades: *"I cannot praise a fugitive . . . virtue, unexercised and unbreathed, that never sallies out and sees her adversary"* (John Milton). *Momentary* implies the brevity of or as if of a single moment: *I had some momentary misgivings that were quickly resolved. Evanescent* suggests that something disappears like vapor: *"The incidents which give excellence to biography are of a volatile and evanescent kind"* (Samuel Johnson).

transient ischemic attack *n.* A temporary blockage of the blood supply to the brain caused by a blood clot and usually lasting ten minutes or less, during which dizziness, blurring of vision, numbness on one side of the body, and other symptoms of a stroke may occur. Also called *ministroke.*

trans·il·lu·mi·na·tion (trăns′ĭ-lo͞o′mə-nā′shən, trănz′-) *n. Medicine.* The passing of a light through the walls of a body part or organ to facilitate medical inspection. **—trans′il·lu′mi·nate′** (-lo͞o′mə-nāt′) *v.* **—trans′il·lu′mi·na′tor** *n.*

tran·sis·tor (trăn-zĭs′tər, -sĭs′-) *n.* **1.** A small electronic device containing a semiconductor and having at least three electrical contacts, used in a circuit as an amplifier, a detector, or a switch. **2.** A transistor radio. [TRANS(FER) + (RES)ISTOR.]

tran·sis·tor·ize (trăn-zĭs′tə-rīz′, -sĭs′-) *tr.v.* **-ized, -iz·ing, -iz·es.** To equip (an electronic circuit or device) with transistors.

transistor radio *n.* A small portable radio using transistorized circuitry.

tran·sit (trăn′sĭt, -zĭt) *n. Abbr.* **t. 1.** The act of passing over, across, or through; passage. **2.** Conveyance of people or goods from one place to another, especially on a local public transportation system. **3.** A transition or change, as to a spiritual existence at death. **4.** *Astronomy.* **a.** The passage of a celestial body across the observer's meridian. **b.** The passage of a smaller celestial body or its shadow across the disk of a larger celestial body. **5.** A surveying instrument similar to a theodolite that measures horizontal and vertical angles. **—transit** *v.* **-sit·ed, -sit·ing, -sits.** *—tr.* **1.** To pass over, across, or through: *aircraft transiting the United States and Canada.* **2.** To revolve (the telescope of a surveying transit) about its horizontal transverse axis in order to reverse its direction. *—intr. Astronomy.* To make a transit. [Middle English *transite,* from Latin *trānsitus,* from past participle of *trānsīre,* to go across. See TRANSIENT.]

tran·si·tion (trăn-zĭsh′ən, -sĭsh′-) *n.* **1.** Passage from one form, state, style, or place to another. **2.a.** Passage from one subject to another in discourse. **b.** A word, phrase, sentence, or series of sentences connecting one part of a discourse to another. **3.** *Music.* **a.** A modulation, especially a brief one. **b.** A passage connecting two themes. **—tran·si′tion·al, tran·si′tion·ar′y** (-zĭsh′-ə-nĕr′ē) *adj.* **—tran·si′tion·al·ly** *adv.*

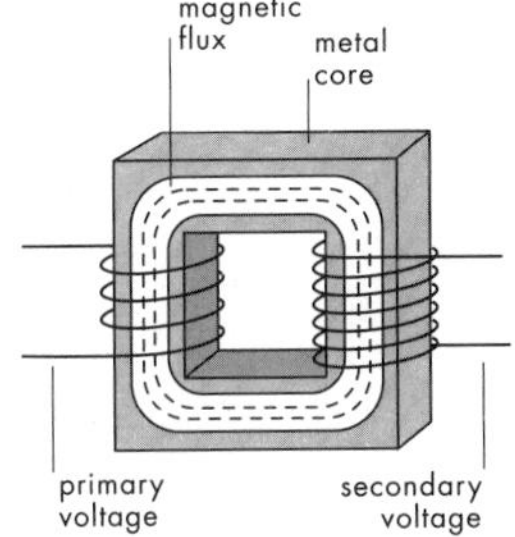

transformer
Iron core transformer

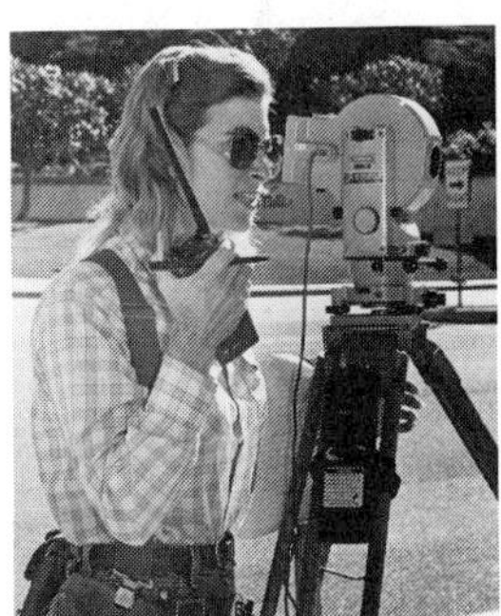

transit

ă pat	oi boy
ā pay	ou out
âr care	o͝o took
ä father	o͞o boot
ĕ pet	ŭ cut
ē be	ûr urge
ĭ pit	th thin
ī pie	*th* this
îr pier	hw which
ŏ pot	zh vision
ō toe	ə about, item
ô paw	♦ regionalism

Stress marks: ′ (primary); ′ (secondary), as in **dictionary** (dĭk′shə-nĕr′ē)

transition element *n.* Any of the metallic elements that have an incomplete inner electron shell and that serve as transitional links between the most and the least electropositive in a series of elements. They are characterized by multiple valences, colored compounds, and the ability to form stable complex ions.

transition metal *n.* A transition element.

transition region *n.* A zone in a seed plant where the vascular tissue of the root changes into the vascular tissue of the stem.

tran·si·tive (trăn′sĭ-tĭv, -zĭ-) *adj.* **1.** *Abbr.* **t., tr., trans.** *Grammar.* Expressing an action that is carried from the subject to the object; requiring a direct object to complete meaning. Used of a verb or verb construction. **2.** Characterized by or involving transition. **—transitive** *n. Abbr.* **t., tr., trans.** *Grammar.* A transitive verb. [Late Latin *trānsitīvus,* passing over, from *trānsitus,* past participle of *trānsīre,* to go over. See TRANSIENT.] **—tran′si·tive·ly** *adv.* **—tran′si·tive·ness, tran′si·tiv′i·ty** *n.*

transit lounge *n.* A waiting room in an airport used typically by international travelers on layovers.

tran·si·to·ry (trăn′sĭ-tôr′ē, -tōr′ē, trăn′zĭ-) *adj.* Existing or lasting only a short time; short-lived or temporary: *"the disorder of his life: the succession of cities, of transitory loves"* (Carson McCullers). See Synonyms at **transient.** [Middle English *transitorie,* from Old French *transitoire,* from Late Latin *trānsitōrius,* from Latin, having a passageway, from *trānsitus,* passage. See TRANSIT.] **—tran′si·to′ri·ly** *adv.* **—tran′si·to′ri·ness** *n.*

Trans·jor·dan (trăns′jôr′dn, trănz′-). See **Jordan. —Trans′jor·da′ni·an** (-jôr-dā′nē-ən) *adj. & n.*

Trans·kei (trăns-kā′, -kī′). An internally self-governing Black African homeland in southeast South Africa on the Indian Ocean coast. It was designated a semiautonomous territory in 1963 and granted nominal independence in 1976. Umtata is the capital. Population, 2,400,000. **—Trans·kei′an** *adj. & n.*

transl. *abbr.* **1.** Translated. **2.** Translation.

trans·late (trăns-lāt′, trănz-, trăns′lāt′, trănz′-) *v.* **-lat·ed, -lat·ing, -lates.** *—tr.* **1.** To render in another language. **2.a.** To put into simpler terms; explain or interpret. **b.** To express in different words; paraphrase. **3.a.** To change from one form, function, or state to another; convert or transform: *translate ideas into reality.* **b.** To express in another medium. **4.** To transfer from one place or condition to another. **5.** To forward or retransmit (a telegraphic message). **6.a.** *Ecclesiastical.* To transfer (a bishop) to another see. **b.** *Theology.* To convey to heaven without death. **7.** *Physics.* To subject (a body) to translation. **8.** *Biology.* To subject (messenger RNA) to translation. **9.** *Archaic.* To enrapture. *—intr.* **1.a.** To make a translation. **b.** To work as a translator. **2.** To admit of translation. **3.** To be changed or transformed in effect. Often used with *into* or *to: "Today's low inflation and steady growth in household income translate into more purchasing power"* (Thomas G. Exter). [Middle English *translaten,* from Old French *translater,* from Latin *trānslātus,* past participle of *trānsferre,* to transfer : *trāns-,* trans- + *lātus,* brought; see **telə-** in Appendix.] **—trans·lat′a·bil′i·ty, trans·lat′a·ble·ness** *n.* **—trans·lat′a·ble** *adj.*

transom

trans·la·tion (trăns-lā′shən, trănz-) *n. Abbr.* **tr., trans., transl. 1.a.** The act or process of translating, especially from one language into another. **b.** The state of being translated. **2.** A translated version of a text. **3.** *Physics.* Motion of a body in which every point of the body moves parallel to and the same distance as every other point of the body; nonrotational displacement. **4.** *Biology.* The process by which messenger RNA directs the amino acid sequence of a growing polypeptide during protein synthesis. **—trans·la′tion·al** *adj.*

trans·la·tor (trăns-lā′tər, trănz-, trăns′lā′tər, trănz′-) *n. Abbr.* **tr., trans. 1.** One that translates, especially one employed to render written works into another language. **2.** An interpreter. **—trans′la·to′ri·al** (-lə-tôr′ē-əl, -tōr′-) *adj.*

trans·lit·er·ate (trăns-lĭt′ə-rāt′, trănz-) *tr.v.* **-at·ed, -at·ing, -ates.** To represent (letters or words) in the corresponding characters of another alphabet. [TRANS– + Latin *littera, lītera,* letter + –ATE[1].] **—trans·lit′er·a′tion** *n.*

trans·lo·cate (trăns-lō′kāt′, trănz-) *tr.v.* **-cat·ed, -cat·ing, -cates. 1.** To cause to change from one place or position to another; displace. **2.** To transfer (a chromosomal segment) to a new position; cause to undergo translocation.

trans·lo·ca·tion (trăns′lō-kā′shən, trănz′-) *n.* **1.** A change of location. **2.** *Genetics.* **a.** A transfer of a chromosomal segment to a new position, especially on a nonhomologous chromosome. **b.** A chromosomal segment that is translocated.

trans·lu·cent (trăns-lo͞o′sənt, trănz-) *adj.* **1.** Transmitting light but causing sufficient diffusion to prevent perception of distinct images. **2.** Clear; lucid. [Latin *trānslūcēns, trānslūcent-,* present participle of *trānslūcēre,* to shine through : *trāns-,* trans- + *lūcēre,* to shine; see **leuk-** in Appendix.] **—trans·lu′cence, trans·lu′cen·cy** *n.* **—trans·lu′cent·ly** *adv.*

trans·lu·nar (trăns′lo͞o′nər, trănz′-, trăns-lo͞o′-, trănz-) *adj.* Extending beyond the moon or the moon's orbit around Earth.

trans·ma·rine (trăns′mə-rēn′, trănz′-) *adj.* **1.** Crossing the sea. **2.** Beyond or coming from across the sea. [Latin *trānsmarīnus* : *trāns-,* trans- + *marīnus,* of the sea; see MARINE.]

trans·mem·brane (trăns-mĕm′brān, trănz-) *adj.* Passing or occurring across a membrane.

trans·mi·grant (trăns-mī′grənt, trănz-) *n.* **1.** One that transmigrates. **2.** One in transit through a country on the way to the country in which one intends to settle.

trans·mi·grate (trăns-mī′grāt′, trănz-) *intr.v.* **-grat·ed, -grat·ing, -grates. 1.** To migrate. **2.** To pass into another body after death. Used of the soul. [Latin *trānsmigrāre, trānsmigrāt-* : *trāns-,* trans- + *migrāre,* to migrate; see MIGRATE.] **—trans·mi′gra′tor** *n.* **—trans·mi′gra·to′ry** (-mī′grə-tôr′ē, -tōr′ē) *adj.*

trans·mi·gra·tion (trăns′mī-grā′shən, trănz′-) *n.* **1.** The act or process of transmigrating. **2.** The passing of a soul into another body after death; reincarnation. **—trans′mi·gra′tion·ism** *n.*

trans·mis·si·ble (trăns-mĭs′ə-bəl, trănz-) *adj.* That can be transmitted: *transmissible messages; transmissible signals.* **—trans·mis′si·bil′i·ty** *n.*

trans·mis·sion (trăns-mĭsh′ən, trănz-) *n.* **1.a.** The act or process of transmitting. **b.** The fact of being transmitted. **2.** Something, such as a message, that is transmitted. **3.** An automotive assembly of gears and associated parts by which power is transmitted from the engine to a driving axle. Also called *gearbox.* **4.** The sending of a signal, picture, or other information from a transmitter. [Latin *trānsmissiō, trānsmissiōn-,* a sending across, from *trānsmissus,* past participle of *trānsmittere,* to transmit. See TRANSMIT.] **—trans·mis′sive** (-mĭs′ĭv) *adj.*

trans·mis·som·e·ter (trăns′mĭ-sŏm′ĭ-tər, trănz′-) *n.* A device used to measure transmission of light through a medium. [TRANSMISS(ION) + –METER.] **—trans′mis·som′e·try** *n.*

trans·mit (trăns-mĭt′, trănz-) *v.* **-mit·ted, -mit·ting, -mits.** *—tr.* **1.** To send from one person, thing, or place to another; convey. See Synonyms at **send[1]. 2.** To cause to spread; pass on: *transmit an infection.* **3.** To impart or convey to others by heredity or inheritance; hand down. **4.** To pass along (news or information); communicate. **5.a.** *Electronics.* To send (a signal), as by wire or radio. **b.** *Physics.* To cause (a disturbance) to propagate through a medium. **6.** To convey (force or energy) from one part of a mechanism to another. *—intr.* To send out a signal. [Middle English *transmitten,* from Latin *trānsmittere* : *trāns-,* trans- + *mittere,* to send.] **—trans·mit′ta·ble** *adj.*

trans·mit·tal (trăns-mĭt′l, trănz-) *n.* The act or process of transmitting; a transmission.

trans·mit·tance (trăns-mĭt′ns, trănz-) *n.* **1.** A transmission. **2.** *Physics.* The ratio of the radiant energy transmitted to the total radiant energy incident on a given body.

trans·mit·ter (trăns-mĭt′ər, trănz-) *n.* **1.** One that transmits: *a transmitter of disease; a transmitter of tall tales.* **2.a.** An electronic device that generates and amplifies a carrier wave, modulates it with a meaningful signal derived from speech or other sources, and radiates the resulting signal from an antenna. **b.** The portion of a telephone that converts the incident sounds into electrical impulses that are conveyed to a remote receiver. **c.** A telegraphic sending instrument.

trans·mit·ter-re·ceiv·er (trăns-mĭt′ər-rĭ-sē′vər, trănz-) *n.* An electronic device that both transmits and receives communications signals.

trans·mog·ri·fy (trăns-mŏg′rə-fī′, trănz-) *tr.v.* **-fied** (-fīd′), **-fy·ing, -fies** (-fīz′). To change into a different shape or form, especially one that is fantastic or bizarre. See Synonyms at **convert.** [Origin unknown.] **—trans·mog′ri·fi·ca′tion** (-fĭ-kā′shən) *n.*

trans·mon·tane (trăns-mŏn′tān′, trănz-, trăns′mŏn-tān′, trănz′-) *adj.* Tramontane. [Latin *trānsmontānus.* See TRAMONTANE.]

trans·mun·dane (trăns′mŭn-dān′, trănz′-, trăns-mŭn′dā′, trănz-) *adj.* Existing or extending beyond the physical world.

trans·mu·ta·tion (trăns′myo͞o-tā′shən, trănz′-) *n.* **1.a.** The act or an instance of transmuting; transformation. **b.** The state of being transmuted. **2.** *Physics.* Transformation of one element into another by one or a series of nuclear reactions. **3.** The supposed conversion of base metals into gold or silver in alchemy. **—trans′mu·ta′tion·al, trans·mut′a·tive** (-myo͞o′tə-tĭv) *adj.*

trans·mute (trăns-myo͞ot′, trănz-) *v.* **-mut·ed, -mut·ing, -mutes.** *—tr.* To change from one form, nature, substance, or state into another; transform: *"the tendency to transmute what has become customary into what has been divinely ordained"* (Suzanne LaFollette). See Synonyms at **convert.** *—intr.* To undergo transmutation. [Middle English *transmuten,* from Latin *trānsmūtāre* : *trāns-,* trans- + *mūtāre,* to change; see **mei-[1]** in Appendix.] **—trans·mut′a·bil′i·ty, trans·mut′a·ble·ness** *n.* **—trans·mut′a·ble** *adj.* **—trans·mut′a·bly** *adv.* **—trans·mut′er** *n.*

trans·na·tion·al (trăns-năsh′ə-nəl, trănz-) *adj.* **1.** Reaching beyond or transcending national boundaries: *"the transnational ramifications of terror networks"* (Emanuel Litvinoff). **2.** Relating to or involving several nations or nationalities: *transnational organizations.*

trans·o·ce·an·ic (trăns′ō-shē-ăn′ĭk, trănz′-) *adj.* **1.** Situated beyond or on the other side of the ocean. **2.** Spanning or crossing the ocean.

tran·som (trăn′səm) *n.* **1.a.** A horizontal crosspiece over a door or between a door and a window above it. **b.** A small hinged window above a door or another window. **2.** A horizontal dividing bar of wood or stone in a window. **3.** A lintel. **4.** *Nautical.* **a.** Any of several transverse beams affixed to the sternpost of a wooden ship and forming part of the stern. **b.** The aftermost transverse structural member in a steel ship, including the floor, frame, and beam assembly at the sternpost. **c.** The stern of a square-sterned boat when it is a structural member. **5.** The horizontal beam on a cross or gallows. [Middle English *traunsom,* probably alteration of Latin *trānstrum,* cross-beam, from *trāns,* across. See TRANS–.]

tran·son·ic (trăn-sŏn′ĭk) *adj.* Of or relating to aerodynamic flow or flight conditions at speeds close to the speed of sound. [TRAN(S)– + SONIC.]

transp. *abbr.* Transportation.

trans·pa·cif·ic (trăns′pə-sĭf′ĭk, trănz′-) *adj.* **1.** Situated on or coming from the other side of the Pacific Ocean. **2.** Spanning or crossing the Pacific Ocean.

trans·par·en·cy (trăns-pâr′ən-sē, -păr′-) *n., pl.* **-cies. 1.** A transparent object, especially a photographic slide that is viewed by light shining through it from behind or by projection. **2.** Also **trans·par·ence** (-pâr′əns, -păr′-). The quality or state of being transparent.

trans·par·ent (trăns-pâr′ənt, -păr′-) *adj.* **1.** Capable of transmitting light so that objects or images can be seen as if there were no intervening material. See Synonyms at **clear. 2.** Permeable to electromagnetic radiation of specified frequencies, as to visible light or radio waves. **3.** So fine in texture that it can be seen through; sheer. See Synonyms at **airy. 4.a.** Easily seen through or detected; obvious: *transparent lies.* **b.** Free from guile; candid or open: *transparent sincerity.* **5.** *Obsolete.* Shining through; luminous. [Middle English, from Old French, from Medieval Latin *trānspārēns, trānspārent-,* present participle of *trānspārēre,* to show through : Latin *trāns-,* trans- + Latin *pārēre,* to show.] **—trans·par′ent·ly** *adv.* **—trans·par′ent·ness** *n.*

trans·per·son·al (trăns-pûr′sə-nəl, trănz-) *adj.* Transcending or reaching beyond the personal or individual.

tran·spic·u·ous (trăn-spĭk′yo͞o-əs) *adj.* Easily understood or seen through: *transpicuous motives.* [From New Latin *trānspicuus,* from Latin *trānspicere,* to see through : *trāns-,* trans- + *specere,* to look at; see **spek-** in Appendix.]

tran·spi·ra·tion (trăn′spə-rā′shən) *n.* The act or process of transpiring, especially through the stomata of plant tissue or the pores of the skin. **—tran′spi·ra′tion·al** *adj.*

tran·spire (trăn-spīr′) *v.* **-spired, -spir·ing, -spires.** *—tr.* To give off (vapor containing waste products) through the pores of the skin or the stomata of plant tissue. *—intr.* **1.** To become known; come to light. **2.** *Usage Problem.* To come about; happen or occur. **3.** To give off vapor containing waste products, as through animal or plant pores. [French *transpirer,* from Medieval Latin *trānspīrāre* : Latin *trāns-,* trans- + Latin *spīrāre,* to breathe.]

USAGE NOTE: *Transpire* has been used since the mid-18th century in the sense "leak out, become publicly known," as in *Despite efforts to hush the matter up, it soon transpired that the colonels had met with the rebel leaders.* This usage was objected to as a Gallicism when it was first introduced but has long been standard. The more common use of *transpire* to mean "occur" or "happen" has had a more troubled history. Though it dates at least to the beginning of the 19th century, it has been the object of critical opprobrium for more than a hundred years, charged with being both pretentious and unetymological. There is some sign that resistance to this sense of *transpire* is abating, however. In a 1969 survey the usage was acceptable only to 38 percent of the Usage Panel; in the most recent survey it was acceptable to 58 percent in the sentence *All of these events transpired after last week's announcement* (though many of the Panelists who accepted the usage also remarked that it was pretentious or pompous).

trans·pla·cen·tal (trăns′plə-sĕn′tl) *adj.* Passing through or occurring across the placenta: *a transplacental infection.* **—trans′pla·cen′tal·ly** *adv.*

trans·plant (trăns-plănt′) *v.* **-plant·ed, -plant·ing, -plants.** *—tr.* **1.** To uproot and replant (a growing plant). **2.** To transfer from one place or residence to another; resettle or relocate. **3.** *Medicine.* To transfer (tissue or an organ) from one body or body part to another. *—intr.* To be capable of undergoing transplantation. **—transplant** (trăns′plănt′) *n.* **1.** The act or process of transplanting. **2.** Something transplanted. **3.** *Medicine.* An operation in which tissue or an organ is transplanted: *undergo a heart transplant; surgical transplant of a cornea.* [Middle English *transplaunten,* from Old French *transplanter,* from Late Latin *trānsplantāre* : Latin *trāns,* trans- + Latin *plantāre,* to plant; see **plat-** in Appendix.] **—trans·plant′a·ble** *adj.* **—trans′plan·ta′tion** *n.* **—trans·plant′er** *n.*

trans·po·lar (trăns-pō′lər) *adj.* Extending across or crossing either of the Polar Regions.

tran·spond·er (trăn-spŏn′dər) *n.* A radio or radar transmitter-receiver activated for transmission by reception of a predetermined signal. [TRAN(SMITTER) + (RE)SPONDER.]

trans·pon·tine (trăns-pŏn′tīn′) *adj.* **1.** Situated on the other side of a bridge. **2.** Similar to or characteristic of melodramas once performed in London theaters located south of the Thames River.

trans·port (trăns-pôrt′, -pōrt′) *tr.v.* **-port·ed, -port·ing, -ports. 1.** To carry from one place to another; convey. **2.** To move to strong emotion; carry away; enrapture. See Synonyms at **enrapture. 3.** To send abroad to a penal colony; deport. See Synonyms at **banish. —transport** (trăns′pôrt′, -pōrt′) *n.* **1.** The act of transporting; conveyance. **2.** The condition of being transported by emotion; rapture. See Synonyms at **ecstasy. 3.** A ship or an aircraft used to transport troops or military equipment. **4.** A vehicle, such as an aircraft, used to transport passengers, mail, or freight. **5.** A system for transporting passengers: *public transport.* **6.** A deported convict. [Middle English *transporten,* from Old French *transporter,* from Latin *trānsportāre* : *trāns-,* trans- + *portāre,* to carry; see **per-**[2] in Appendix.] **—trans·port′a·bil′i·ty** *n.* **—trans·port′a·ble** *adj.* **—trans·port′er** *n.* **—trans·por′tive** *adj.*

trans·por·ta·tion (trăns′pər-tā′shən) *n. Abbr.* **trans., transp. 1.a.** The act or an instance of transporting. **b.** The state of being transported. **2.** A means of conveyance. **3.** The business of conveying passengers or goods. **4.** A charge for public conveyance; fare. **5.** Deportation to a penal colony.

trans·pose (trăns-pōz′) *v.* **-posed, -pos·ing, -pos·es.** *Abbr.* **tr., trans.** *—tr.* **1.** To reverse or transfer the order or place of; interchange. **2.** To put into a different place or order: *transpose the words of a sentence.* See Synonyms at **reverse. 3.** *Mathematics.* To move (a term) from one side of an algebraic equation to the other side, reversing its sign to maintain equality. **4.** *Music.* To write or perform (a composition) in a key other than the original or given key. **5.** To render into another language. **6.** To alter in form or nature; transform. *—intr.* **1.** *Music.* To write or perform music in a different key. **2.** To admit of being transposed. **—transpose** *n. Mathematics.* A matrix formed by interchanging the rows and columns of a given matrix. [Middle English *transposen,* to transform, from Old French *transposer,* alteration (influenced by *poser,* to put, place; see POSE[1]) of Latin *trānspōnere,* to transfer : *trāns-,* trans- + *pōnere,* to place; see **apo-** in Appendix.] **—trans·pos′a·ble** *adj.*

trans·po·si·tion (trăns′pə-zĭsh′ən) *n. Abbr.* **tr., trans. 1.a.** The act or an instance of transposing. **b.** The state of being transposed. **2.** Something transposed. **3.** *Genetics.* Transfer of a segment of DNA to a new position on the same or another chromosome, plasmid, or cell. **—trans′po·si′tion·al** *adj.*

trans·po·son (trăns-pō′zŏn) *n.* A segment of DNA that is capable of moving to a new position within the same or another chromosome, plasmid, or cell and thereby transferring genetic properties such as resistance to antibiotics. [TRANSPOS(ITION) + –ON[1].]

trans·sex·u·al (trăns-sĕk′sho͞o-əl) *n.* **1.** One whose primary sexual identification is with the opposite sex. **2.** One who has undergone a sex change. **—trans·sex′u·al** *adj.* **—trans·sex′u·al·ism, trans·sex′u·al′i·ty** (-ăl′ĭ-tē) *n.*

trans·ship (trăns-shĭp′) also **tran·ship** (trăn-shĭp′) *tr. & intr.v.* **-shipped, -ship·ping, -ships.** To transfer or be transferred from one conveyance to another for reshipment. **—trans·ship′ment** *n.*

trans·tho·rac·ic (trăns′thə-răs′ĭk) *adj.* Across or through the thoracic cavity or chest wall. **—trans′tho·rac′i·cal·ly** *adv.*

tran·sub·stan·ti·ate (trăn′səb-stăn′shē-āt′) *tr.v.* **-at·ed, -at·ing, -ates. 1.** To change (one substance) into another; transmute. **2.** *Theology.* To change the substance of (the Eucharistic bread and wine) into the body and blood of Jesus. [Medieval Latin *trānsubstantiāre, trānsubstantiāt-* : Latin *trāns-,* trans- + Latin *substantia,* substance; see SUBSTANCE.]

tran·sub·stan·ti·a·tion (trăn′səb-stăn′shē-ā′shən) *n.* **1.** Conversion of one substance into another. **2.** *Theology.* The doctrine holding that the bread and wine of the Eucharist are transformed into the body and blood of Jesus, although their appearances remain the same. **—tran′sub·stan′ti·a′tion·al·ist** *n.*

tran·su·date (trăn-so͞o′dāt′, -syo͞o′-, trăn′so͞o-dāt′, -syo͞o-) also **tran·su·da·tion** (trăn′so͞o-dā′shən, -syo͞o-) *n.* **1.** A product of the process of transudation. **2.** A substance that transudes.

tran·sude (trăn-so͞od′, -syo͞od′, -zo͞od′, -zyo͞od′) *intr.v.* **-sud·ed, -sud·ing, -sudes.** To pass through pores or interstices in the manner of perspiration. [New Latin *trānsūdāre* : Latin *trāns-,* trans- + Latin *sūdāre,* to sweat; see **sweid-** in Appendix.] **—tran·su′da·to′ry** (trăn-so͞o′də-tôr′ē, -tōr′ē, -syo͞o′-) *adj.*

trans·u·ran·ic (trăns′yo͞o-răn′ĭk, -rā′nĭk, trănz′-) also **trans·u·ra·ni·um** (-rā′nē-əm) *adj.* Having an atomic number greater than 92. [TRANS– + URAN(IUM) + –IC.]

trans·u·re·thral (trăns′yo͞o-rē′thrəl, trănz′-) *adj. Medicine.* Performed through or by way of the urethra: *a transurethral resection.*

Trans·vaal (trăns-väl′, trănz-). A region of northeast South Africa. Inhabited by Bantu-speaking Black Africans, the area was settled by Boer farmers who formed an independent state, called the South African Republic, in the 1850's. Great Britain annexed the territory in 1877, but the discovery of gold in 1886 led to an influx of settlers, further tensions between the British and the Boers, and the eventual formation of the Transvaal as a crown colony (1900) after the Boer War. Transvaal became a part of South Africa in 1910.

trans·val·ue (trăns-văl′yo͞o, trănz-) *tr.v.* **-ued, -u·ing, -ues.** To evaluate by a new standard or principle, especially by one that varies from conventional standards. **—trans·val′u·a′tion** *n.*

trans·ver·sal (trăns-vûr′səl, trănz-) *adj.* Transverse. **—transversal** *n. Mathematics.* A line that intersects a system of other lines.

trans·verse (trăns-vûrs′, trănz-, trăns′vûrs′, trănz′-) *adj. Abbr.* **trans.** Situated or lying across; crosswise. **—transverse** *n.*

ă pat	oi boy
ā pay	ou **out**
âr care	o͝o took
ä father	o͞o boot
ĕ pet	ŭ cut
ē be	ûr urge
ĭ pit	th thin
ī pie	*th* this
îr pier	hw which
ŏ pot	zh vision
ō toe	ə about, item
ô paw	♦ regionalism

Stress marks: ′ (primary); ′ (secondary), as in **dictionary** (dĭk′shə-nĕr′ē)

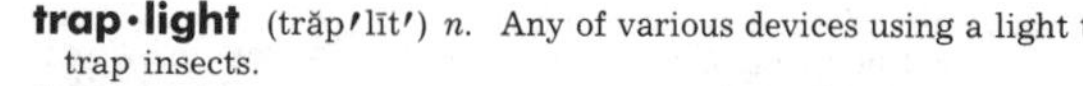

Abbr. **trans.** Something, such as a part or beam, that is transverse. [Latin *trānsversus,* from past participle of *trānsvertere,* to turn across : *trāns-,* trans- + *vertere,* to turn; see **wer-**[2] in Appendix.] —**trans·verse′ly** *adv.* —**trans·verse′ness** *n.*

transverse colon *n.* The part of the colon that lies across the upper part of the abdominal cavity.

transverse flute *n. Music.* See **flute** (sense 1a).

transverse process *n.* A process projecting outward from the side of a vertebra.

trans·ves·tite (trăns-vĕs′tīt′, trănz-) *n.* A person who dresses and acts in a style or manner traditionally associated with the opposite sex. [German *Transvestit* : Latin *trāns-,* trans- + Latin *vestīre,* to dress; see TRAVESTY.] —**trans·ves′tism** (-tĭz′əm), **trans·ves′ti·tism** (-tĭ-tĭz′əm) *n.*

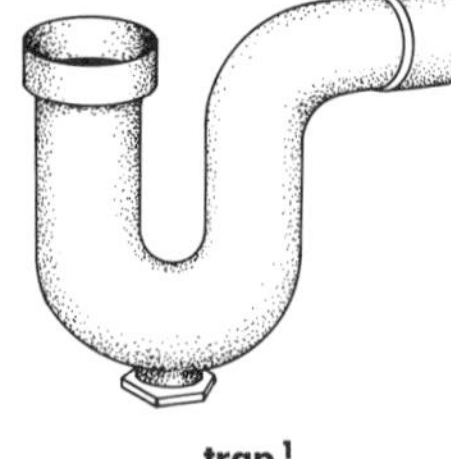

trap[1]
Drainpipe trap

Tran·syl·va·nia (trăn′sĭl-vān′yə, -vā′nē-ə). A historical region of western Romania bounded by the Transylvanian Alps and the Carpathian Mountains. Part of the Roman province of Dacia after A.D. 107, it was later overrun by Germanic peoples and came under Hungarian rule in 1003. Transylvania passed to various powers over the following centuries and finally became part of modern-day Romania after World War II. —**Tran′syl·va′ni·an** *adj. & n.*

Transylvanian Alps. A range of the southern Carpathian Mountains in central Romania rising to 2,544.6 m (8,343 ft).

trap[1] (trăp) *n.* **1.** A contrivance for catching and holding animals, as a concealed pit or a clamplike device that springs shut suddenly. **2.** A stratagem for catching or tricking an unwary person. **3.** A device for sealing a passage against the escape of gases, especially a U-shaped or S-shaped bend in a drainpipe that prevents the return flow of sewer gas by means of a water barrier. **4.** *Sports.* **a.** A device that hurls clay pigeons into the air in trapshooting. **b.** A land hazard or bunker on a golf course; a sand trap. **c. traps.** A measured length of roadway over which electronic timers register the speed of a racing vehicle, such as a dragster. **5.** A light two-wheeled carriage with springs. **6.** A trap door. **7. traps.** *Music.* Percussion instruments, such as snare drums and cymbals, especially in a jazz band. **8.** *Slang.* The human mouth. —**trap** *v.* **trapped, trap·ping, traps.** —*tr.* **1.** To catch in or as if in a trap; ensnare. See Synonyms at **catch. 2.** To place in a confining or embarrassing position. **3.** To seal off (gases) by a trap. **4.** To furnish with traps or a trap. —*intr.* **1.** To set traps for game. **2.** To engage in trapping furbearing animals. [Middle English, from Old English *træppe.*]

trapeze artist

trap[2] (trăp) *Informal. n.* Personal belongings or household goods. Often used in the plural. —**trap** *tr.v.* **trapped, trap·ping, traps.** To furnish with trappings. [Middle English *trap,* trapping, perhaps alteration of Old French *drap,* cloth, from Late Latin *drappus.*]

trap[3] (trăp) *n.* Any of several dark, fine-grained igneous rocks often used in making roads. [Swedish *trapp,* from *trappa,* step, from Middle Low German *trappe.*]

tra·pan (trə-păn′) *v.* Variant of **trepan**[2].

Tra·pa·ni (trä′pə-nē, -pä-). A city of northwest Sicily, Italy, on the Mediterranean Sea west-southwest of Palermo. An important Carthaginian naval base, it fell to Rome in 241 B.C. Population, 61,900.

trap door *n.* A hinged or sliding door in a floor, roof, or ceiling.

trap-door spider (trăp′dôr′, -dōr′) *n.* Any of various insect-eating spiders of the family Ctenizidae, found in warm climates, that construct a silk-lined burrow concealed by a hinged lid.

tra·peze (tră-pēz′, trə-) *n. Sports.* **1.** A short horizontal bar suspended from two parallel ropes, used for exercises or for acrobatic stunts. **2.** An article of women's clothing, such as a jacket, dress, or coat, that is cut so as to hang down from the shoulders and swing out and away around the hips and legs. [French *trapèze,* from Late Latin *trapezium,* trapezoid. See TRAPEZIUM.]

trapeze artist *n. Sports.* One that performs on a trapeze.

tra·pe·zi·a (trə-pē′zē-ə) *n.* A plural of **trapezium.**

tra·pe·zi·form (trə-pē′zə-fôrm′) *adj.* Shaped like a trapezium: *a trapeziform thorax.*

tra·pe·zi·um (trə-pē′zē-əm) *n., pl.* **-zi·ums** or **-zi·a** (-zē-ə). **1.** A quadrilateral having no parallel sides. **2.** *Chiefly British.* A trapezoid. **3.** A bone in the wrist at the base of the thumb. [Late Latin *trapezium,* trapezoid, from Greek *trapezion,* diminutive of *trapeza,* table : *tra-,* four; see **kʷetwer-** in Appendix + *peza,* foot; see **ped-** in Appendix.]

tra·pe·zi·us (trə-pē′zē-əs) *n., pl.* **-us·es.** Either of two large, flat, triangular muscles running from the base of the occiput to the middle of the back that support and make it possible to raise the head and shoulders. [New Latin, from Late Latin *trapēzium,* trapezium (from the shape of the muscles paired). See TRAPEZIUM.]

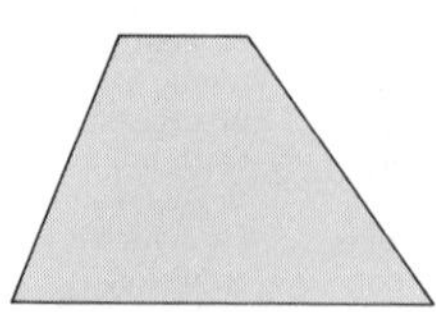

trapezoid

tra·pe·zo·he·dron (trə-pē′zō-hē′drən, trăp′ĭ-zō-) *n., pl.* **-drons** or **-dra** (-drə). Any of several forms of crystal with trapeziums as faces. [TRAPEZ(IUM) + -HEDRON.]

trap·e·zoid (trăp′ĭ-zoid′) *n.* **1.** A quadrilateral having two parallel sides. **2.** A small bone in the wrist, situated near the base of the index finger. [New Latin *trapezoidēs,* from Greek *trapezoeidēs,* trapezium-shaped : *trapeza,* table; see TRAPEZIUM + *-oeidēs,* -oid.] —**trap′e·zoid′, trap′e·zoi′dal** (-zoid′l) *adj.*

trap gun *n. Sports.* A shotgun designed for trapshooting.

trap house *n. Sports.* The enclosure housing the spring traps used in trapshooting and skeet.

trap·light (trăp′līt′) *n.* Any of various devices using a light to trap insects.

trap·per (trăp′ər) *n.* One who traps animals for their fur.

trap·ping (trăp′ĭng) *n.* **1.** Often **trappings.** An ornamental covering or harness for a horse; a caparison. **2. trappings. a.** Articles of dress or adornment, especially accessories. **b.** Characteristic or symbolic signs: *all the trappings of power.*

Trap·pist (trăp′ĭst) *n.* A member of the main, reformed branch of Cistercian monks, characterized by austerity and a vow of silence, established in 1664 at La Trappe Monastery in northwest France. —**Trap′pist** *adj.*

trap·shoot·ing (trăp′sho͞o′tĭng) *n.* Shooting at clay pigeons hurled into the air from spring traps. —**trap′shoot′er** *n.*

tra·pun·to (trə-po͝on′tō) *n., pl.* **-tos.** Quilting in which the design is outlined with two or more rows of running stitches and then padded from the underside to achieve a raised effect. [Italian, from past participle of *trapungere,* to embroider : Latin *trāns-,* trans- + Latin *pungere,* to prick; see **peuk-** in Appendix.]

trash (trăsh) *n.* **1.a.** Worthless or discarded material or objects; refuse or rubbish. **b.** Something broken off or removed to be discarded, especially plant trimmings. **c.** The refuse of sugar cane after extraction of the juice. **2.a.** Empty words or ideas. **b.** Worthless or offensive literary or artistic material. **3.** A person or group of people regarded as worthless or contemptible. —**trash** *tr.v.* **trashed, trash·ing, trash·es. 1.** *Slang.* **a.** To throw away; discard: *"Ideas and works of art . . . get bought and trashed as quickly as razor blades"* (New York). **b.** To wreck or destroy by or as if by vandalism; reduce to trash or ruins. **c.** To beat up; assault. **d.** To subject to scathing criticism or abuse; attack verbally: *"The . . . professor trashes conservative . . . proposals as well as liberal nostrums"* (Michael Marien). **2.a.** To remove twigs or branches from. **b.** To cut off the outer leaves of (growing sugar cane). [Probably of Scandinavian origin; akin to Norwegian dialectal *trask.*]

trash fish *n.* A fish considered to have little value as a food fish and therefore typically discarded whenever caught.

trash·y (trăsh′ē) *adj.* **-i·er, -i·est. 1.** Resembling or containing trash; cheap or worthless: *trashy merchandise.* **2.** In very poor taste or of very poor quality: *"There was a special pathos . . . within . . . her trashy tales"* (James Wolcott). —**trash′i·ly** *adv.* —**trash′i·ness** *n.*

Tra·si·me·no (trä′zə-mā′nō, -zē-mĕ′-), **Lake.** A lake in central Italy west of Perugia. Hannibal defeated a Roman force here in 217 B.C.

trass (trăs) *n.* A light-colored tuff used in hydraulic cement. [Dutch *tras,* short for obsolete *terras, tiras,* possibly from Italian *terrazzo,* stone chips. See TERRAZZO.]

trat·to·ri·a (trä′tə-rē′ə, trät′tô-rē′ä) *n., pl.* **-ri·as** or **-ri·e** (-rē′ĕ). An informal restaurant or tavern serving simple Italian dishes. [Italian, from *trattore,* host, from *trattare,* to treat, from Latin *tractāre.* See TREAT.]

Trau·bel (trou′bəl), **Helen.** 1903–1972. American operatic soprano who performed with the New York Metropolitan Opera from 1939 to 1953.

trau·ma (trou′mə, trô′-) *n., pl.* **-mas** or **-ma·ta** (-mə-tə). **1.** *Medicine.* A serious injury or shock to the body, as from violence or an accident. **2.** *Psychiatry.* An emotional wound or shock that creates substantial, lasting damage to the psychological development of a person, often leading to neurosis. —*attributive.* Often used to modify another noun: *a trauma center; a trauma team.* [Greek. See **terə-**[1] in Appendix.] —**trau·mat′ic** (-măt′ĭk) *adj.* —**trau·mat′i·cal·ly** *adv.*

trau·ma·tism (trou′mə-tĭz′əm, trô′-) *n.* **1.** The physical or psychological condition produced by a trauma. **2.** A wound or an injury.

trau·ma·tize (trou′mə-tīz′, trô′-) *tr.v.* **-tized, -tiz·ing, -tiz·es. 1.** To wound or injure (a tissue), as in a surgical operation. **2.** To subject to psychological trauma.

trau·ma·tol·o·gy (trou′mə-tŏl′ə-jē, trô′-) *n.* The branch of medicine that deals with the treatment of serious wounds, injuries, and disabilities. —**trau′ma·to·log′i·cal** *adj.* —**trau′ma·tol′o·gist** *n.*

trav. *abbr.* **1.** Traveler. **2.** Travels.

tra·vail (trə-vāl′, trăv′āl′) *n.* **1.** Work, especially when arduous or involving painful effort; toil. See Synonyms at **work. 2.** Tribulation or agony; anguish. **3.** The labor of childbirth. —**travail** *intr.v.* **-vailed, -vail·ing, -vails. 1.** To work strenuously; toil. **2.** To be in the labor of childbirth. [Middle English, from Old French, from *travailler,* to work hard, from Vulgar Latin **tripāliāre,* to torture with a tripalium, from Late Latin *tripālium,* instrument of torture, probably from Latin *tripālis,* having three stakes : *tri-,* tri- + *pālus,* stake; see **pag-** in Appendix.]

trave (trāv) *n.* **1.** *Architecture.* **a.** A crossbeam. **b.** A section, as of a ceiling, formed by crossbeams. **2.** A wooden frame used to confine a horse being shod. [Middle English, from Old French, from Latin *trabs, trab-.* See **treb-** in Appendix.]

trav·el (trăv′əl) *v.* **-eled, -el·ing, -els** or **-elled, -el·ling, -els.** —*intr.* **1.** To go from one place to another, as on a trip; journey. **2.** To go from place to place as a salesperson or an agent. **3.** To be transmitted, as light or sound; move or pass. **4.** To advance or proceed. **5.** To go about in the company of a particular group; associate: *travels in wealthy circles.* **6.** To move along a course, as in a groove. **7.** To admit of being transported without loss of quality: *Some wines travel poorly.* **8.** *Informal.* To move swiftly. **9.** *Basketball.* To walk or run illegally while holding the ball. —*tr.* To pass or journey over or through; traverse: *travel the roads of Europe.* **—travel** *n.* **1.** The act or process of traveling; movement or passage from one place to another. **2. travels. a.** A series of journeys. **b.** An account of one's journeys. **3.** Activity or traffic along a route or through a given point. [Middle English *travelen,* alteration of *travailen,* to toil, from Old French *travailler.* See TRAVAIL.]

travel agency *n.* A business that attends to the details of transportation, itinerary, and accommodations for travelers. Also called *travel bureau.* **—travel agent** *n.*

trav•eled or **trav•elled** (trăv′əld) *adj.* **1.** Having made journeys; experienced in travel. **2.** Frequented by travelers: *a heavily traveled road.*

trav•el•er or **trav•el•ler** (trăv′əl-ər, trăv′lər) *n. Abbr.* **trav. 1.** One who travels or has traveled, as to distant places. **2.** *Chiefly British.* A traveling salesperson. **3.** *Nautical.* **a.** A metal ring that moves freely back and forth on a rope, rod, or spar. **b.** The rope, rod, or spar on which such a ring moves.

trav•el•er's check (trăv′əl-ərz, trăv′lərz) *n., pl.* **traveler's checks** or **travelers' checks.** An internationally redeemable draft purchased in various denominations from a bank or traveler's aid company and valid only with the purchaser's endorsement against his or her original signature on the draft.

trav•el•ers' diarrhea also **trav•el•er's diarrhea** (trăv′-əl-ərz, trăv′lərz) *n.* Diarrhea and abdominal cramps occurring among travelers to foreign countries where sanitation is poor, commonly caused by a toxin-producing strain of the bacterium *Escherichia coli.*

trav•el•ing salesman (trăv′ə-lĭng, trăv′lĭng) *n.* A man who travels throughout a given territory to solicit business orders or sell merchandise.

trav•el•ler (trăv′əl-ər, trăv′lər) *n.* Variant of **traveler.**

trav•e•logue also **trav•e•log** (trăv′ə-lôg′, -lŏg′) *n.* **1.** A lecture illustrated by travel slides or films. **2.** A narrated film about travels.

Tra•ven (trä′vən), **B.** Probable original name Berick Traven Torsvan. 1890–1969. American-born writer who is best known for his novel *The Treasure of the Sierra Madre* (1935).

Trav•ers (trăv′ərz), **P(amela) L.** Born 1906. Australian-born British writer of children's stories, including *Mary Poppins* (1934).

tra•verse (trə-vûrs′, trăv′ərs) *v.* **-versed, -vers•ing, -vers•es.** —*tr.* **1.** To travel or pass across, over, or through. **2.** To move to and fro over; cross and recross. **3.** *Sports.* To go up, down, or across (a slope) diagonally, as in skiing. **4.** To cause to move laterally on a pivot; swivel: *traverse an artillery piece.* **5.** To extend across; cross: *a bridge that traverses a river.* **6.** To look over carefully; examine. **7.** To go counter to; thwart. **8.** *Law.* **a.** To deny formally (an allegation of fact by the opposing party) in a suit. See Synonyms at **deny. b.** To join issue upon (an indictment). **9.** To survey by traverse. **10.** *Nautical.* To brace (a yard) fore and aft. —*intr.* **1.** To move to the side or back and forth. **2.** To turn laterally; swivel. **3.** *Sports.* **a.** To go up, down, or across a slope diagonally or in a zigzag manner, as in skiing. **b.** To slide one's blade with pressure toward the hilt of the opponent's foil in fencing. **—trav•erse** (trăv′ərs, trə-vûrs′) *n.* **1.** A passing across, over, or through. **2.** A route or path across or over. **3.** Something that lies across, especially: **a.** An intersecting line; a transversal. **b.** *Architecture.* A structural crosspiece; a transom. **c.** A gallery, deck, or loft crossing from one side of a building to the other. **d.** A railing, curtain, screen, or similar barrier. **e.** A defensive barrier across a rampart or trench, as a bank of earth thrown up to protect against enfilade fire. **4.** Something that obstructs and thwarts; an obstacle. **5.** *Nautical.* The zigzag route of a vessel forced by contrary winds to sail on different courses. **6.** *Sports.* A zigzag or diagonal course on a steep slope, as in skiing. **7. a.** A lateral movement, as of a lathe tool across a piece of wood. **b.** A part of a mechanism that moves in this manner. **c.** The lateral swivel of a mounted gun. **8.** A line established by sighting in surveying a tract of land. **9.** *Law.* A formal denial of the opposing party's allegation of fact in a suit. **—trav•erse** (trăv′ərs, trə-vûrs′) *adj.* Lying or extending across; transverse. [Middle English *traversen,* from Old French *traverser,* from Vulgar Latin **trāversāre,* from Late Latin *trānsversāre,* from Latin *trānsversus,* transverse. See TRANSVERSE.] **—tra•vers′a•ble** *adj.* **—tra•vers′al** *n.* **—tra•vers′er** *n.*

trav•erse rod (trăv′ərs) *n.* A horizontal rod having a mechanism by which attached draperies can be drawn with a pull cord.

trav•er•tine (trăv′ər-tēn′, -tĭn) *n.* **1.** A light-colored porous calcite, $CaCO_3$, deposited from solution in ground or surface waters and forming, among other deposits, stalactites and stalagmites. **2.** A compact calcium carbonate used as a facing material in construction. [French, from Italian *travertino,* alteration of *tivertino,* from Latin *(lapis) tīburtīnus,* (stone) of Tibur (Tivoli), an ancient city of central Italy.]

trav•es•ty (trăv′ĭ-stē) *n., pl.* **-ties. 1.** An exaggerated or grotesque imitation, such as a parody of a literary work. **2.** A debased or grotesque likeness: *a travesty of justice.* See Synonyms at **caricature. —travesty** *tr.v.* **-es•tied** (-ĭ-tēd), **-es•ty•ing, -es•ties** (-ĭ-stēz). To make a travesty of; parody or ridicule. [From obsolete, disguised, burlesqued, from French *travesti,* past participle of *travestir,* to disguise, parody, from Italian *travestire* : Latin *trāns-,* trans- + Latin *vestīre,* to dress (from *vestis,* garment; see **wes-**[2] in Appendix).]

Trav•is (trăv′ĭs), **William Barret.** 1809–1836. American military leader who commanded the Texans who died in the defense of the Alamo (1836).

tra•vois (trə-voi′, trăv′oi′) also **tra•voise** (trə-voiz′, trăv′-oiz′) *n., pl.* **tra•vois** (trə-voiz′, trăv′oiz′) also **tra•vois•es** (trə-voi′zĭz, trăv′oi′zĭz). A frame slung between trailing poles and pulled by a dog or horse, formerly used by Plains Indians as a conveyance for goods and belongings. [Canadian French, alteration of obsolete *travoy,* from *travail,* cart-shaft, from French, frame for restraining horses, alteration of Late Latin *tripālium,* device with three stakes, probably from Latin *tripālis,* having three stakes. See TRAVAIL.]

trawl (trôl) *n.* **1.** A trawl net. **2.** See **setline. —trawl** *v.* **trawled, trawl•ing, trawls.** —*tr.* To catch (fish) with a trawl. —*intr.* **1.** To fish with a trawl. **2.** To troll. [Possibly Middle English *trawelle,* perhaps from Middle Dutch *tragel,* dragnet, possibly from Latin *trāgula,* from *trahere,* to drag.]

trawl•er (trô′lər) *n.* **1.** *Nautical.* A vessel used for trawling. **2.** One who trawls.

trawl line *n.* See **setline.**

trawl net *n.* A large tapered fishing net that is towed along the sea bottom.

tray (trā) *n.* **1.** A shallow, flat receptacle with a raised edge or rim, used for carrying, holding, or displaying articles. **2.** A shallow, flat receptacle with its contents: *took the patient a dinner tray.* [Middle English, from Old English *trēg.* See **deru-** in Appendix.]

tra•zo•done (trā′zə-dōn′) *n.* A white, odorless, crystalline compound, $C_{19}H_{23}Cl_2N_5O$, used as an antidepressant. [TR(I)– + AZO– + (PYRI)D(INE) + –ONE.]

treach•er•ous (trĕch′ər-əs) *adj.* **1.** Marked by betrayal of fidelity, confidence, or trust; perfidious. See Synonyms at **faithless. 2.** Not to be relied on; not dependable or trustworthy. **3.** Marked by unforeseen hazards; dangerous or deceptive: *treacherous waters.* **—treach′er•ous•ly** *adv.* **—treach′er•ous•ness** *n.*

treach•er•y (trĕch′ə-rē) *n., pl.* **-ies. 1.** Willful betrayal of fidelity, confidence, or trust; perfidy. **2.** The act or an instance of such betrayal. [Middle English *trecherie,* from Old French, from *trichier,* to trick, probably from Vulgar Latin **triccāre.* See TRICK.]

trea•cle (trē′kəl) *n.* **1.** Cloying speech or sentiment. **2.** *Chiefly British.* Molasses. **3.** A medicinal compound formerly used as an antidote for poison. [Middle English *triacle,* antidote for poison, from Old French, from Latin *thēriaca,* from Greek *thēriakē (antidotos),* (antidote against) wild animals, feminine of *thēriakos,* of wild animals, from *thērion,* diminutive of *thēr,* beast. See **ghwer-** in Appendix.]

trea•cly (trē′klē) *adj.* Cloyingly sweet or sentimental.

tread (trĕd) *v.* **trod** (trŏd), **trod•den** (trŏd′n) or **trod, tread•ing, treads.** —*tr.* **1.** To walk on, over, or along. **2.** To press beneath the feet; trample. **3.** To subdue harshly or cruelly; crush. **4.** To form by walking or trampling: *tread a path.* **5.** To execute by walking or dancing: *tread a measure.* **6.** To copulate with. Used of a male bird. —*intr.* **1. a.** To go on foot; walk. **b.** To set down the foot; step. **2.** To press, crush, or injure something by or as if by trampling. Often used with *on* or *upon: trod on her feelings.* **3.** To copulate. Used of birds. **—tread** *n.* **1. a.** The act, manner, or sound of treading. **b.** An instance of treading; a step. **2.** The upper horizontal part of a step in a staircase. **3. a.** The part of a wheel or tire that makes contact with the road or rails. **b.** The grooved face of a tire. **4.** The part of a shoe sole that touches the ground. **—*idioms.* tread the boards.** To act on the stage: *"We who tread the boards are not the only players of parts in this world"* (John Fowles). **tread water. 1.** To keep the head above water while in an upright position by pumping the legs. **2.** To expend effort but make little or no progress to achievement of a goal or an end. [Middle English *treden,* from Old English *tredan.*] **—tread′less** *adj.*

tread•le (trĕd′l) *n.* A pedal or lever operated by the foot for circular drive, as in a potter's wheel or sewing machine. **—treadle** *intr.v.* **-led, -ling, -les.** To work a treadle. [Middle English *tredel,* from Old English, step of a stair, from *tredan,* to tread.] **—tread′ler** *n.*

tread•mill (trĕd′mĭl′) *n.* **1. a.** A mechanism rotated by people treading on the moving steps of a wheel. **b.** A similar device operated by an animal treading an endless sloping belt. **2.** An exercise device consisting of an endless moving belt on which a person can walk or jog while remaining in one place. **3.** A monotonous task or set of tasks seeming to have no end.

treas. *abbr.* Treasurer; treasury.

trea•son (trē′zən) *n.* **1.** Violation of allegiance toward one's country or sovereign, especially the betrayal of one's country by waging war against it or by consciously and purposely acting to aid its enemies. **2.** A betrayal of trust or confidence. [Middle English, from Anglo-Norman *treson,* from Latin *trāditiō, trāditiōn-,* a handing over. See TRADITION.]

trea•son•a•ble (trē′zə-nə-bəl) *adj.* Relating to, constituting, or involving treason: *a treasonable act such as espionage.* **—trea′son•a•ble•ness** *n.* **—trea′son•a•bly** *adv.*

trea•son•ous (trē′zə-nəs) *adj.* Treasonable. **—trea′son•ous•ly** *adv.*

travois
Photograph by
Edward Sheriff Curtis
(1868–1952)

trawler
Oil painting
by Ellery F. Thompson
(1899–1986)

treadmill
Exercise treadmill

ă pat	oi boy
ā pay	ou out
âr care	o͝o took
ä father	o͞o boot
ĕ pet	ŭ cut
ē be	ûr urge
ĭ pit	th thin
ī pie	*th* this
îr pier	hw which
ŏ pot	zh vision
ō toe	ə about, item
ô paw	♦ regionalism

Stress marks: ′ (primary); ′ (secondary), as in **dictionary** (dĭk′shə-nĕr′ē)

treas•ure (trĕzh′ər) *n.* **1.** Accumulated or stored wealth in the form of money, jewels, or other valuables. **2.** Valuable or precious possessions of any kind. **3.** One considered especially precious or valuable. **—treasure** *tr.v.* **-ured, -ur•ing, -ures. 1.** To keep or regard as precious; value highly. See Synonyms at **appreciate. 2.** To accumulate and store away, as for future use. [Middle English *tresure,* from Old French *tresor,* from Latin *thēsaurus,* from Greek *thēsauros.*] **—treas′ur•a•ble** *adj.*

treasure house *n.* A place where items of great value are stored or can be found.

treasure hunt *n. Games.* A game in which the players attempt to find hidden articles by means of a series of clues.

Treas•ure Island (trĕzh′ər). An artificial island of San Francisco Bay in western California. Built for the Golden Gate International Exposition in 1939, it became a U.S. Navy base in 1941.

treas•ur•er (trĕzh′ər-ər) *n. Abbr.* **tr., treas.** One who has charge of funds or revenues, especially the chief financial officer of a government, a corporation, or an association. [Middle English *tresurer,* from Anglo-Norman *tresorer,* from Late Latin *thēsaurārius,* from Latin, of treasure, from *thēsaurus,* treasure. See TREASURE.]

treble clef

treas•ure-trove (trĕzh′ər-trōv′) *n.* **1.** Treasure found hidden. **2.** *Law.* Silver or gold in the form of bullion, plate, or money that is found hidden and has no known owner. **3.** A discovery of great value. [Anglo-Norman *tresor trove* : Old French *tresor,* treasure; see TREASURE + Old French *trove,* past participle of *trover,* to find; see TROVER.]

treas•ur•y (trĕzh′ə-rē) *n., pl.* **-ies.** *Abbr.* **treas. 1.** A place in which treasure is kept. **2.** A place in which private or public funds are received, kept, managed, and disbursed. **3.** Public funds or revenues. **4.** A collection of literary or artistic treasures: *a treasury of English verse.* **5. Treasury. a.** The department of a government in charge of the collection, management, and expenditure of the public revenue. **b.** A security, such as a note, issued by the U.S. Treasury. [Middle English *tresorie,* from Old French, from *tresor,* treasure. See TREASURE.]

Treasury bill *n.* A short-term obligation of the U.S. Treasury having a maturity period of one year or less and sold at a discount from face value.

Treasury bond *n.* A long-term obligation of the U.S. Treasury having a maturity period of more than ten years and paying interest semiannually.

Treasury note *n.* An intermediate-term obligation of the U.S. Treasury having a maturity period of one to ten years and paying interest semiannually.

tree frog
Anderson tree frog
Hyla andersonii

treat (trēt) *v.* **treat•ed, treat•ing, treats.** —*tr.* **1.** To act or behave in a specified manner toward. **2.** To regard and handle in a certain way. Often used with *as*: *treated the matter as a joke.* **3.** To deal with in writing or speech; discuss: *a book that treats all aspects of health care.* **4.** To deal with or represent artistically in a specified manner or style: *treats the subject poetically.* **5. a.** To provide with food, entertainment, or gifts at one's own expense: *treated her sister to the theater.* **b.** To give (someone or oneself) something pleasurable: *treated herself to a day in the country.* **6.** To subject to a process, an action, or a change, especially to a chemical or physical process or application. **7. a.** To give medical aid to (someone): *treated many patients in the emergency room.* **b.** To give medical aid to counteract (a disease or condition): *treated malaria with quinine.* —*intr.* **1.** To deal with a subject or topic in writing or speech. Often used with *of*: *The essay treats of courtly love.* **2.** To pay for another's entertainment, food, or drink. **3.** To engage in negotiations, as to reach a settlement or agree on terms: *"Both sides nonetheless are quite willing to treat with* [the king]*"* (Gregory J. Wallance). **—treat** *n.* **1.** Something, such as one's food or entertainment, that is paid for by someone else. **2.** A source of a special delight or pleasure: *A day in the country is a real treat for a city person.* [Middle English *tretien,* from Old French *traitier,* from Latin *tractāre,* frequentative of *trahere,* to draw.] **—treat′er** *n.*

SYNONYMS: *treat, deal, handle.* The central meaning shared by these verbs is "to act in a specified way with regard to someone or something": *treats his guests with courtesy; dealt rationally with the problem; handling a case with discretion.* See also Synonyms at **confer.**

treat•a•ble (trē′tə-bəl) *adj.* Possible to treat; responsive to treatment: *a treatable disorder.*

trea•tise (trē′tĭs) *n.* **1.** A systematic, usually extensive written discourse on a subject. **2.** *Obsolete.* A tale or narrative. [Middle English *treatis,* from Anglo-Norman *tretiz,* alteration of *treteiz,* from Vulgar Latin **tractāticius,* from Latin *tractātus,* past participle of *tractāre,* to drag about, deal with. See TREAT.]

treat•ment (trēt′mənt) *n.* **1. a.** The act, manner, or method of handling or dealing with someone or something: *"the right to equal treatment in the criminal and juvenile justice system"* (Susan C. Ross). **b.** *Informal.* The usual methods of dealing with a given situation: *gave the opposing team the treatment.* **2. a.** Administration or application of remedies to a patient or for a disease or an injury; medicinal or surgical management; therapy. **b.** The substance or remedy so applied.

trea•ty (trē′tē) *n., pl.* **-ties. 1. a.** A formal agreement between two or more states, as in reference to terms of peace or trade. **b.** The document in which such an agreement is set down. **2.** A contract or an agreement. **3.** *Obsolete.* **a.** Negotiation for the purpose of reaching an agreement. **b.** An entreaty. [Middle English *tretee,* from Old French *traite,* from Latin *tractātus,* discussion, from past participle of *tractāre,* to drag about, deal with. See TREAT.]

treaty port *n.* A port kept open for foreign trade according to the terms of a treaty, especially formerly in China, Korea, and Japan.

Treb•bia (trĕb′yä). A river, about 113 km (70 mi) long, of northwest Italy flowing northward to the Po River. Hannibal defeated the Romans on the banks of the river in 218 B.C.

Treb•i•zond (trĕb′ĭ-zŏnd′). **1.** A former Greek empire occupying much of the land bordering the Black Sea. It was founded as an offshoot of the Byzantine Empire by Alexius I Comnenus in 1204 and retained its autonomy until it was conquered by Ottoman Turks in 1461. **2.** See **Trabzon.**

treb•le (trĕb′əl) *adj.* **1.** Triple: *"treble reason for loving as well as working while it is day"* (George Eliot). **2.** *Music.* Relating to or having the highest part, voice, or range. **3.** High-pitched; shrill. **—treble** *n.* **1.** *Music.* **a.** The highest part, voice, instrument, or range. **b.** A singer or player that performs this part. **2.** A high, shrill sound or voice. **—treble** *tr. & intr.v.* **-led, -ling, -les.** To make or become triple. [Middle English, from Old French, from Medieval Latin *triplum,* from Latin, neuter of *triplus,* triple. See TRIPLE.] **—treb′le•ness** *n.* **—treb′ly** (trĕb′lē) *adv.*

treble clef *n. Music.* A symbol indicating that the second line from the bottom of a staff represents the pitch of G above middle C. Also called *G clef.*

treb•u•chet (trĕb′yə-shĕt′) also **treb•uc•ket** (-ə-kĕt′) *n.* A medieval catapult for hurling heavy stones. [Middle English, from Old French, from *trebucher,* to overthrow : *tre-,* over (from Latin *trāns-;* see TRANS–) + *but,* trunk of the body (of Germanic origin).]

tre•cen•to (trā-chĕn′tō) *n.* The 14th century, especially with reference to Italian art and literature. [Italian, from *(mil) trecento,* (one thousand) three hundred : *tre,* three (from Latin *trēs;* see **trei-** in Appendix) + *cento,* hundred (from Latin *centum;* see **dekm̥** in Appendix).]

tree (trē) *n.* **1. a.** A perennial woody plant having a main trunk and usually a distinct crown. **b.** A plant or shrub resembling a tree in form or size. **2.** Something, such as a clothes tree, that resembles a tree in form. **3.** A wooden beam, post, stake, or bar used as part of a framework or structure. **4.** A saddletree. **5.** A diagram showing a family lineage; a family tree. **6.** *Archaic.* **a.** A gallows. **b.** The cross on which Jesus was crucified. **—tree** *tr.v.* **treed, tree•ing, trees. 1.** To force up a tree: *Dogs treed the raccoon.* **2.** *Informal.* To force into a difficult position; corner. **3.** To supply with trees: *a field that had been treed with oak saplings.* **4.** To stretch (a shoe or boot) onto a shoetree. **—*idiom.* up a tree.** *Informal.* In a situation of great difficulty or perplexity; helpless. [Middle English, from Old English *trēow.* See **deru-** in Appendix.] **—tree′less** *adj.*

Tree (trē), Sir **Herbert Beerbohm.** 1853–1917. British actor and theatrical producer who founded the Royal Academy of Dramatic Art (1904).

tree farm *n.* An area of forest land on which trees are grown for commercial use.

tree fern *n.* Any of various tropical treelike ferns having a woody, trunklike stem and a terminal crown of large, pinnately divided fronds.

tree frog *n.* Any of various small arboreal frogs of the family Hylidae having long toes terminating in adhesive disks. Also called *tree toad.*

tree heath *n.* A Mediterranean evergreen shrub or small tree *(Erica arborea)* having fragrant, white flowers grouped in large terminal panicles. It is the source of briarroot.

tree•hop•per (trē′hŏp′ər) *n.* Any of numerous, generally small, often oddly shaped homopterous insects of the family Membracidae, found mostly in the tropics and having mouthparts adapted to sucking the sap from trees.

tree house *n.* A structure built among the limbs of a tree, usually for recreation.

tree line *n.* **1.** The limit of northern or southern latitude beyond which trees will not grow except as stunted forms. **2.** See **timberline.**

tre•en (trē′ən) *n.* Cookware, tableware, or eating utensils made of wood. [From Middle English, made of wood, from Old English *trēowen,* from *trēow,* tree. See TREE.]

tree•nail or **tre•nail** (trē′nāl′, trĕn′əl, trŭn′əl) also **trun•nel** (trŭn′əl) *n.* A wooden peg that swells when wet and is used to fasten timbers, especially in shipbuilding.

tree-of-heav•en (trē′əv-hĕv′ən) *n.* A deciduous, rapidly growing tree *(Ailanthus altissima)* native to China, having sweetish, fetid male flowers and widely planted in the United States as a street tree because of its resistance to pollution, disease, and insects.

tree of knowledge *n.* The tree in the Garden of Eden whose forbidden fruit Adam and Eve tasted.

tree of life *n., pl.* **trees of life. 1.** A tall palm *(Mauritia flexuosa)* of northern South America having large fan-shaped leaves and used for food, fiber, and building. **2.** A tree in the Garden of Eden whose fruit, if eaten, gave everlasting life.

tree poppy *n.* An evergreen shrub *(Dendromecon rigidum)* of southern California and northern Baja California, having minutely toothed, lance-shaped leaves and showy yellow flowers.

tree shrew *n.* Any of various small squirrellike arboreal mammals of the family Tupaiidae found in southeast Asia, India, and southern China. Though sometimes placed in a separate taxonomic order, tree shrews are thought to be related to both insectivores and primates.

tree snail *n.* Any of various tropical snails of the genus *Liguus,* having a colorful shell in the shape of a teardrop.

tree sparrow *n.* **1.** A sparrow *(Spizella arborea)* of northern North America having a reddish-brown crown and a dark spot on the breast. **2.** A European sparrow *(Passer montanus)* related to the house sparrow.

tree squirrel *n.* See **squirrel** (sense 1).

tree surgery *n.* Treatment of diseased or damaged trees by filling cavities and pruning and bracing branches. **—tree surgeon** *n.*

tree toad *n.* See **tree frog.**

tree tobacco *n.* A South American shrub or small tree *(Nicotiana glauca)* naturalized in the United States and having yellow flowers and thick, rubbery, oval or lance-shaped leaves.

tree·top (trē′tŏp′) *n.* The uppermost part of a tree.

tref (trāf) *adj.* *Judaism.* Unclean and unfit for consumption according to dietary law; not kosher. [Yiddish *treyf,* from Hebrew *ṭĕrēpâ,* carrion, from *ṭārap,* to tear.]

tre·foil (trē′foil′, trĕf′oil′) *n.* **1.** Any of various plants of the genera *Trifolium, Lotus,* and related genera of the pea family, having compound trifoliate leaves. **2.** An ornament, a symbol, or an architectural form having the appearance of a trifoliate leaf. [Middle English, from Anglo-Norman *trifoil,* from Latin *trifolium* : *tri-,* tri- + *folium,* leaf; see **bhel-**[3] in Appendix.]

tre·ha·la (trĭ-hä′lə) *n.* A sugarlike, edible substance obtained from the pupal case of an Old World beetle of the genus *Larinus.* [New Latin *trehāla,* from Turkish *tīqāla,* from Persian *tīghāl.*]

tre·ha·lase (trĭ-hä′lās′, -lāz′) *n.* An enzyme that catalyzes the hydrolysis of trehalose.

tre·ha·lose (trĭ-hä′lōs′, -lōz′) *n.* A sweet-tasting, crystalline disaccharide, $C_{12}H_{22}O_{11}$, found in trehala and in many fungi.

treil·lage (trĕ-yäzh′, trā′lĭj) *n.* Latticework, especially a trellis for a vine. [French, from Old French *treille,* bower supported by trelliswork, from Latin *trichila,* bower, arbor.]

trek (trĕk) *intr.v.* **trekked, trek·king, treks. 1.** To make a slow or arduous journey. **2.** To journey on foot, especially to hike through mountainous areas. **3.** *South African.* To travel by ox wagon. **—trek** *n.* **1.** A journey or leg of a journey, especially when slow or difficult. **2.** *South African.* A journey by ox wagon, especially a migration such as that of the Boers from 1835 to 1837. [Afrikaans, to travel by ox wagon, from Dutch *trekken,* to travel, from Middle Dutch *trecken,* to pull.] **—trek′ker** *n.*

WORD HISTORY: Fans of *Star Trek* and others may be interested to know that the word *trek* originally had to do with a slow journey by a very different mode of transportation, a wagon drawn by oxen. *Trek* was borrowed into English in South Africa, where the word was used by speakers of Afrikaans for a journey by ox wagon. The British, who at the turn of the century were to seize control of South Africa from the descendants of the original Dutch settlers, borrowed the word *trek* during the 19th century. *Trek* is recorded earliest in 1822 in the compound *trektow,* "a rope joining the wagon pole and the yoke to which oxen were fastened." *Trek* in this compound is either the noun or the stem of the corresponding verb in Afrikaans, *trekken.* The earliest recorded use of the noun by itself is found in 1849, where it means "a stage in a journey by ox wagon." The word has long since migrated from South African into general English—and into space travel.

trel·lis (trĕl′ĭs) *n.* **1.** A structure of open latticework, especially one used as a support for vines and other creeping plants. **2.** An arbor or arch made of latticework. **—trellis** *tr.v.* **-lised, -lis·ing, -lis·es. 1.** To provide with a trellis, especially to train (a vine) on a trellis. **2.** To make (something) in the form of a trellis. [Middle English *trelis,* from Old French, from Vulgar Latin **trilīcius,* from Latin *trilīx, trilīc-,* woven with three threads : *tri-,* tri- + *līcium,* thread.]

trel·lis·work (trĕl′ĭs-wûrk′) *n.* Latticework.

trem·a·tode (trĕm′ə-tōd′) *n.* Any of numerous flatworms of the class Trematoda, including both external and internal parasites of animal hosts, that have a thick outer cuticle and one or more suckers or hooks for attaching to host tissue. Also called *fluke.* **—trematode** *adj.* Of or belonging to the Trematoda. [From New Latin *Trematoda,* class name, from Greek *trēmatōdēs,* having holes, from *trēma, trēmat-,* perforation. See **terə-**[1] in Appendix.]

trem·a·to·di·a·sis (trĕm′ə-tō-dī′ə-sĭs) *n.* Infestation or infection with trematodes, often caused by ingestion of inadequately cooked food.

trem·ble (trĕm′bəl) *intr.v.* **-bled, -bling, -bles. 1.** To shake involuntarily, as from excitement, weakness, or anger; quake. See Synonyms at **shake. 2.** To feel fear or anxiety: *I tremble at the very thought of it.* **3.** To vibrate or quiver: *leaves trembling in the breeze.* **—tremble** *n.* **1.** The act or state of trembling. **2.** Often **trembles.** A convulsive fit of shaking. Often used with *the.* **3. trembles** *(used with a sing. verb).* **a.** An infectious viral disease of sheep that is transmitted by the tick *Ixodes ricinus* and affects the nervous system, causing galloping and trotting by little leaps and often prolonged trembling. Also called *louping ill.* **b.** Poisoning of domestic animals, especially cattle and sheep, caused by eating white snakeroot or rayless goldenrod and characterized by muscular tremors and weakening. Also called *milk sickness.* [Middle English *tremblen,* from Old French *trembler,* from Vulgar Latin **tremulāre,* from Latin *tremulus,* trembling. See TREMULOUS.] **—trem′bler** *n.* **—trem′bling·ly** *adv.* **—trem′bly** *adj.*

tre·men·dous (trĭ-mĕn′dəs) *adj.* **1.a.** Extremely large in amount, extent, or degree; enormous: *a tremendous task.* See Synonyms at **enormous. b.** *Informal.* Marvelous; wonderful: *had a tremendous night at the theater last night.* **2.** Capable of making one tremble; terrible. [From Latin *tremendus,* gerundive of *tremere,* to tremble.] **—tre·men′dous·ly** *adv.* **—tre·men′dous·ness** *n.*

trem·o·lite (trĕm′ə-līt′) *n.* A white to dark gray amphibole mineral, $Ca_2Mg_5Si_8O_{22}(OH)_2$, typically occurring in aggregates and used as a substitute for asbestos and in paints and ceramics. [French *trémolite,* after *Tremola,* a valley in the Swiss Alps.]

trem·o·lo (trĕm′ə-lō′) *n., pl.* **-los.** *Music.* **1.a.** A tremulous effect produced by rapid repetition of a single tone. **b.** A similar effect produced by rapid alternation of two tones. **2.** A device on an organ for producing a tremulous effect. **3.** A vibrato in singing, often excessive or poorly controlled. [Italian, from Latin *tremulus,* tremulous. See TREMULOUS.]

trem·or (trĕm′ər) *n.* **1.** A shaking or vibrating movement, as of the earth. **2.** A trembling or quivering effect: *a tremor of aspen leaves.* **3.** An involuntary trembling or quivering, as from nervous agitation or weakness. **4.** A nervous quiver or thrill: *felt a tremor of joy.* **5.** A state or feeling of nervous agitation or tension. **6.** A tremulous sound; a quaver. [Middle English, terror, from Old French, from Latin, a trembling, from *tremere,* to tremble.]

trem·u·lant (trĕm′yə-lənt) *adj.* Tremulous; trembling.

trem·u·lous (trĕm′yə-ləs) *adj.* **1.** Marked by trembling, quivering, or shaking. **2.** Timid or fearful; timorous. [From Latin *tremulus,* from *tremere,* to tremble.] **—trem′u·lous·ly** *adv.* **—trem′u·lous·ness** *n.*

tre·nail (trē′nāl′, trĕn′əl, trŭn′əl) *n.* Variant of **treenail.**

trench (trĕnch) *n.* **1.** A deep furrow or ditch. **2.** A long, narrow ditch embanked with its own soil and used for concealment and protection in warfare. **3.** A long, steep-sided valley on the ocean floor. **—trench** *v.* **trenched, trench·ing, trench·es.** —*tr.* **1.** To cut a trench in. **2.** To fortify with trenches. **3.** To place in a trench. **4.** To make a cut in; carve. —*intr.* **1.** To dig trenches or a trench. **2.** To verge or encroach. Often used with *on* or *upon.* [Middle English *trenche,* from Old French, from *trenchier,* to cut, perhaps from Vulgar Latin **trincāre,* variant of Latin *truncāre,* from *truncus,* trunk. See **terə-**[2] in Appendix.]

Trench (trĕnch), **Richard Chenevix.** 1807–1886. British poet and philologist whose works include *On the Study of Words* (1851) and *English Past and Present* (1855).

trench·ant (trĕn′chənt) *adj.* **1.** Keen; incisive: *a trenchant comment.* **2.** Forceful, effective, and vigorous: *a trenchant argument.* See Synonyms at **incisive. 3.** Caustic; cutting: *trenchant criticism.* **4.** Distinct; clear-cut. [Middle English, from Old French, cutting, from present participle of *trenchier,* to cut. See TRENCH.] **—trench′an·cy** *n.* **—trench′ant·ly** *adv.*

trench coat *n.* A belted raincoat in a military style, having straps on the shoulders and deep pockets.

trench·er[1] (trĕn′chər) *n.* **1.** A wooden board or platter on which food is carved or served. **2.** *Archaic.* The pleasure of the table; food. [Middle English *trenchur,* from Anglo-Norman *trenchour,* from *trencher,* to cut, perhaps from Vulgar Latin **trincāre.* See TRENCH.]

trench·er[2] (trĕn′chər) *n.* One that digs trenches.

trench·er·man (trĕn′chər-mən) *n.* **1.** A hearty eater. **2.** *Archaic.* One who frequents another's table; a hanger-on or parasite.

trench fever *n.* An acute infectious disease characterized by chills and fever, caused by the microorganism *Rickettsia quintana* and transmitted by the louse *Pediculus humanus.* [From its occurrence among soldiers in trenches.]

trench foot *n.* A condition of the foot resembling frostbite, caused by prolonged exposure to cold and dampness and often affecting soldiers in trenches. [From its occurrence among soldiers in trenches.]

trench mortar *n.* See **mortar** (sense 3a).

trench mouth *n.* A painful infection of the mouth and throat characterized by ulcerations of the mucous membranes, bleeding, and foul breath. It is caused by the bacterium *Fusobacterium fusiforme* in combination with the spirochete *Treponema vincentii.* Also called *Vincent's angina, Vincent's infection.* [From its occurrence among soldiers in trenches.]

trend (trĕnd) *n.* **1.** The general direction in which something tends to move. **2.** A general tendency or inclination. See Synonyms at **tendency. 3.** Current style; vogue: *the latest trend in fashion.* **—trend** *intr.v.* **trend·ed, trend·ing, trends. 1.** To extend, incline, or veer in a specified direction: *The prevailing wind trends east-northeast.* **2.** To show a general tendency; tend: *"The gender gap was trending down"* (James J. Kilpatrick). [From Middle English *trenden,* to revolve, from Old English *trendan.*]

trefoil
Early 18th-century American silver salver by Edward Winslow (1669–1753) of Boston, Massachusetts

trellis

ă pat	oi boy
ā pay	ou out
âr care	o͝o took
ä father	o͞o boot
ĕ pet	ŭ cut
ē be	ûr urge
ĭ pit	th thin
ī pie	*th* this
îr pier	hw which
ŏ pot	zh vision
ō toe	ə about, item
ô paw	♦ regionalism

Stress marks: **′** (primary); ′ (secondary), as in **dictionary** (dĭk′shə-nĕr′ē)

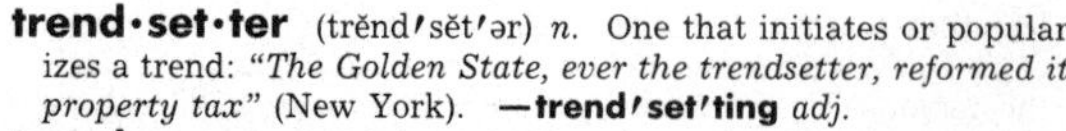

trend·set·ter (trĕnd′sĕt′ər) *n.* One that initiates or popularizes a trend: *"The Golden State, ever the trendsetter, reformed its property tax"* (New York). **—trend′set′ting** *adj.*

trend·y (trĕn′dē) *Informal. adj.* **-i·er, -i·est.** Of or in accord with the latest fad or fashion: *trendy clothes.* See Synonyms at **fashionable. —trendy** *n., pl.* **-ies.** One who is drawn to and represents the latest trends: *"International trendies have spread the word about the area's new nightclubs"* (Lynn Langway). **—trend′i·ly** *adv.* **—trend′i·ness** *n.*

Trent (trĕnt) also **Tren·to** (trĕn′tō). A city of northern Italy northwest of Venice. Probably founded in the fourth century B.C., it was the site of the Council of Trent (1545–1563), which established the foundations of the Counter Reformation. Population, 98,833.

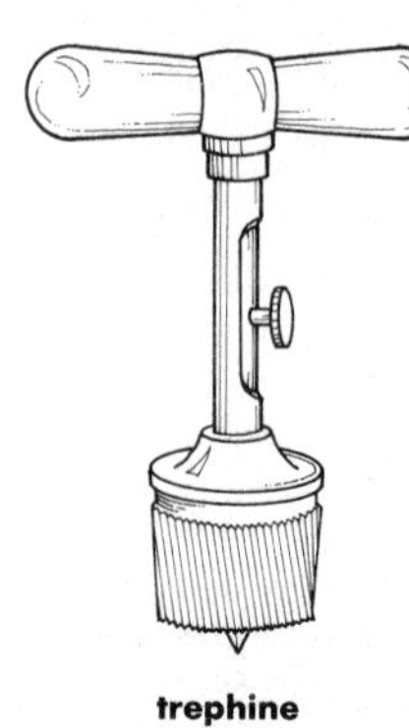

trephine

Tren·ti·no-Al·to-A·di·ge (trĕn-tē′nō-äl′tō-ä′dē-jĕ′). A region of northeast Italy bordering on Switzerland and Austria. Annexed by Austria in 1814, it was ceded to Italy in sections between 1866 and 1919.

Tren·to (trĕn′tō). See **Trent.**

Tren·ton (trĕn′tən). **1.** A city of southeast Michigan, a suburb of Detroit. Population, 22,762. **2.** The capital of New Jersey, in the west-central part of the state on the Delaware River northeast of Philadelphia. Settled c. 1679 by Quakers, it was the site of a pivotal battle in the American Revolution in which George Washington's troops captured a Hessian encampment in a surprise attack (December 26, 1776). Population, 92,124.

Trent River. **1.** A river, about 241 km (150 mi) long, of southeast Ontario, Canada. It is part of the **Trent Canal** system, about 386 km (240 mi) long, that connects Lake Ontario with Georgian Bay. **2.** A river, about 274 km (170 mi) long, of central England flowing generally northeast to join the Ouse River and form the Humber estuary.

tre·pan[1] (trĭ-păn′) *n.* **1.** A rock-boring tool used in mining for sinking shafts. **2.** *Medicine.* A trephine. **—trepan** *tr.v.* **-panned, -pan·ning, -pans.** **1.** To bore (a shaft) with a trepan. **2.** *Medicine.* To trephine. [Middle English *trepane,* surgical crown saw, from Medieval Latin *trepanum,* from Greek *trupanon,* borer, from *trupan,* to pierce, from *trupē,* hole. See **tere-**[1] in Appendix.] **—trep′a·na′tion** (trĕp′ə-nā′shən) *n.*

tre·pan[2] (trĭ-păn′) also **tra·pan** (trə-) *Archaic.*—*tr.v.* **-panned, -pan·ning, -pans.** To trap; ensnare. —*n.* **1.** A trickster. **2.** A trick or snare. [Origin unknown.]

tre·pang (trĭ-păng′) *n.* A sea cucumber of the genus *Holothuria* of the southern Pacific and Indian oceans, dried or smoked for use as an ingredient in soup, especially in China and Indonesia. Also called *bêche-de-mer.* [Malay *tĕripang.*]

tre·phine (trĭ-fīn′) *Medicine. n.* A surgical instrument having circular, sawlike edges, used to cut out disks of bone, usually from the skull. **—trephine** *tr.v.* **-phined, -phin·ing, -phines.** To operate on with a trephine. [French *tréphine,* from obsolete English *trefine,* from Latin *trēs fīnēs,* three ends : *trēs,* three; see **trei-** in Appendix + *fīnēs,* pl. of *fīnis,* end.] **—treph′i·na′tion** (trĕf′ə-nā′shən) *n.*

trep·id (trĕp′ĭd) *adj.* Timid; timorous. [Latin *trepidus,* anxious.]

trep·i·da·tion (trĕp′ĭ-dā′shən) *n.* **1.** A state of alarm or dread; apprehension. See Synonyms at **fear. 2.** An involuntary trembling or quivering. [Latin *trepidātiō, trepidātiōn-,* from *trepidātus,* past participle of *trepidāre,* to be in a state of confusion, from *trepidus,* anxious.]

trep·o·ne·ma (trĕp′ə-nē′mə) *n., pl.* **-ma·ta** (-mə-tə) or **-mas.** Any of a group of spirochetes of the genus *Treponema,* including those that cause syphilis, pinta, and yaws. [New Latin *Treponema,* genus name : Greek *trepein,* to turn; see **trep-** in Appendix + Greek *nēma,* thread; see **(s)nē-** in Appendix.] **—trep′o·ne′mal, trep′o·nem′a·tous** (-nĕm′ə-təs) *adj.*

trep·o·ne·ma·to·sis (trĕp′ə-nē′mə-tō′sĭs) *n., pl.* **-ses** (-sēz). An infection or a disease caused by a treponema.

trep·o·neme (trĕp′ə-nēm′) *n.* A treponema.

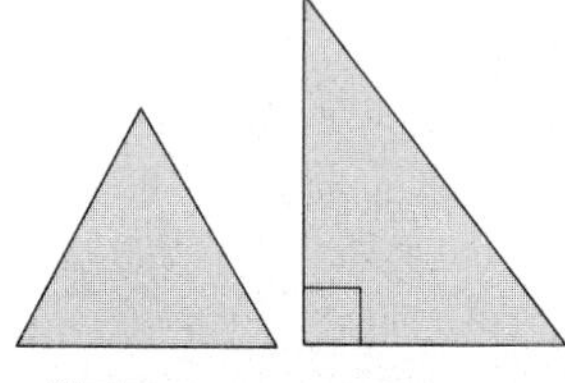

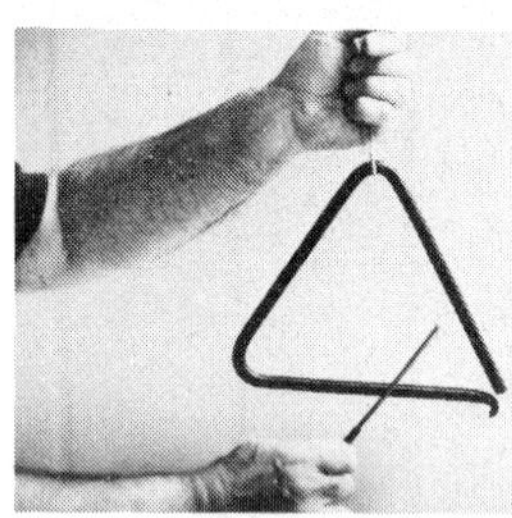

triangle
Top: Equilateral triangle (*left*) and right triangle (*right*)
Bottom: Musical instrument

tres·pass (trĕs′pəs, -păs′) *intr.v.* **-passed, -pass·ing, -pass·es.** **1.** To commit an offense or a sin; transgress or err. **2.** *Law.* To commit an unlawful injury to the person, property, or rights of another, with actual or implied force or violence, especially to enter onto another's land wrongfully. **3.** To infringe on the privacy, time, or attention of another: *"I must . . . not trespass too far on the patience of a good-natured critic"* (Henry Fielding). **—trespass** (trĕs′păs′, -pəs) *n.* **1.** Transgression of a moral or social law, code, or duty. **2.** *Law.* **a.** The act of trespassing. **b.** A suit brought for trespassing. **3.** An intrusion or infringement on another. See Synonyms at **breach.** [Middle English *trespassen,* from Old French *trespasser* : *tres-,* over (from Latin *trāns-;* see TRANS–) + *passer,* to pass; see PASS.] **—tres′pass·er** *n.*

tress (trĕs) *n.* **1.** A long lock or ringlet of hair. **2.** *Archaic.* A plait or braid of hair. [Middle English *tresse,* from Old French, perhaps from Vulgar Latin **trichia, tricia,* rope, braid, from Greek *trikhia,* rope, from *thrix, trikh-,* hair.]

tres·tle (trĕs′əl) *n.* **1.** A horizontal beam or bar held up by two pairs of divergent legs and used as a support. **2.** A framework consisting of vertical, slanted supports and horizontal crosspieces supporting a bridge. [Middle English *trestel,* from Old French, alteration of Vulgar Latin **trāstellum, trānstellum,* diminutive of Latin *trānstrum,* beam. See TRANSOM.]

tres·tle·tree (trĕs′əl-trē′) *n. Nautical.* One of a pair of horizontal beams set into a masthead to support the crosstrees.

tres·tle·work (trĕs′əl-wûrk′) *n.* A trestle or system of trestles, as that supporting a bridge.

tret·i·noin (trĕt′ĭ-noin′) *n.* An isomer of retinoic acid, used in the treatment of acne. [T(RANS–), type of chemical bond + *retinoic acid* (RETINO– + –IC) + –IN.]

tre·val·ly (trə-văl′ē) *n., pl.* **-lies.** An Australian food fish of the genus *Caranx.* [Perhaps alteration of CAVALLA.]

Tre·vel·yan (trə-vĕl′yən, -vĭl′-), Sir **George Otto.** 1838–1928. British historian and politician who was secretary for Ireland (1882–1884) and Scotland (1886 and 1892–1895) and wrote the four-volume *American Revolution* (1899–1907). His son **George Macaulay Trevelyan** (1876–1962) was a historian and biographer whose works include three books on Garibaldi (1907–1911).

Trèves (trĕv). See **Trier.**

Tre·vi·no (trə-vē′no), **Lee.** Born 1939. American golfer who won the U.S. Open (1968 and 1971), the British Open (1971 and 1972), and the Professional Golfers' Association title (1974 and 1984).

Tre·vi·so (trə-vē′zō, trĕ-). A city of northeast Italy north-northwest of Venice. An ancient Roman town, it was later the seat of a Lombard duchy and passed to Venice in the 14th century. Population, 87,089.

trews (tro͞oz) *pl.n.* Close-fitting trousers, usually of tartan. [Variant of obsolete *trouse.* See TROUSER.]

trey (trā) *n., pl.* **treys.** *Games.* A card, die, or domino with three pips. [Middle English *treye,* from Old French *treie,* from Latin *tria,* neuter of *trēs,* three. See **trei-** in Appendix.]

tri– *pref.* **1.** Three: *trilobate.* **2.a.** Occurring at intervals of three: *trimonthly.* **b.** Occurring three times during: *triweekly.* [Middle English, from Latin and Greek; see **trei-** in Appendix.]

tri·a·ble (trī′ə-bəl) *adj.* **1.** That can be tried or tested: *a triable plan.* **2.** *Law.* Subject to judicial examination: *a triable case.* **—tri′a·ble·ness** *n.*

tri·ac·id (trī-ăs′ĭd) *adj.* **1.** Capable of reacting with three molecules of a monobasic acid. Used of a base. **2.** Containing three replaceable hydrogen atoms. Used of an acid or acid salt. **—triacid** *n.* An acid containing three replaceable hydrogen atoms.

tri·ad (trī′ăd′, -əd) *n.* **1.** A group of three. **2.** *Music.* A chord of three tones, especially one built on a given root tone plus a major or minor third and a perfect fifth. **3.** A section of a Pindaric ode consisting of the strophe, antistrophe, and epode. [Late Latin *trias, triad-,* from Greek, the number three. See **trei-** in Appendix.] **—tri·ad′ic** (trī-ăd′ĭk) *adj.*

tri·age (trē-äzh′, trē′äzh′) *n.* **1.** A process for sorting injured people into groups based on their need for or likely benefit from immediate medical treatment. Triage is used on the battlefield, at disaster sites, and in hospital emergency rooms when limited medical resources must be allocated. **2.** A system used to allocate a scarce commodity, such as food, only to those capable of deriving the greatest benefit from it. [French, from *trier,* to sort, from Old French.]

tri·al (trī′əl, trīl) *n.* **1.** *Law.* Examination of evidence and applicable law by a competent tribunal to determine the issue of specified charges or claims. **2.a.** The act or process of testing, trying, or putting to the proof: *a trial of one's faith.* **b.** An instance of such testing, especially as part of a series of tests or experiments. **3.** An effort or attempt: *succeeded on the third trial.* **4.** A state of pain or anguish that tests patience, endurance, or belief: *"the fiery trial through which we pass"* (Abraham Lincoln). **5.** A trying, troublesome, or annoying person or thing: *The child was a trial to his parents.* **6.** A preliminary competition or test to determine qualifications, as in a sport. **—trial** *adj.* **1.** Of, relating to, or used in a trial. **2.** Attempted or advanced on a provisional or experimental basis: *a trial separation.* **3.** Made or done in the course of a trial or test. ***—idioms.* on trial.** In the process of being tried, as in a court of law. **trial by fire.** A test of one's abilities, especially the ability to perform well under pressure. [Middle English *triall,* a testing, from Anglo-Norman *trial,* from *trier,* to sort, try.]

SYNONYMS: *trial, affliction, crucible, ordeal, tribulation, visitation.* The central meaning shared by these nouns is "distress or suffering that severely tests resiliency and character": *no consolation in their hour of trial; the affliction of a bereaved family; the crucible of revolution; the ordeal of being an innocent murder suspect; domestic tribulations; an epidemic considered to be a visitation.* See also Synonyms at **burden**[1]**.**

trial and error *n.* A method of reaching a correct solution or satisfactory result by trying out various means or theories until error is sufficiently reduced or eliminated. **—tri′al-and-er′ror** (trī′əl-ən-ĕr′ər, trīl′-) *adj.*

trial balance *n. Abbr.* **t.b.** A statement of all the open debit and credit items in a double-entry ledger, made to test their equality.

trial balloon *n.* An idea or a plan advanced tentatively to test public reaction. [From the use of balloons to test weather conditions.]

trial jury *n. Law.* See **petit jury.**

tri·a·logue (trī′ə-lôg′, -lŏg′) *n.* A conversation or discussion in which three people or groups participate. [TRI– + (DI)ALOGUE.]

trial run *n.* A test, as of performance or acceptance.

tri·am·cin·o·lone (trī′ăm-sĭn′ə-lōn′) *n.* A synthetic glucocorticoid, $C_{21}H_{27}FO_6$, used as an anti-inflammatory drug in the treatment of allergic and respiratory disorders. [Perhaps from TRI– + AM(YL) + *cin(ene),* a turpene + *(prednis)olone,* a corticoid.]

tri·an·gle (trī′ăng′gəl) *n.* **1.a.** The plane figure formed by connecting three points not in a straight line by straight line segments; a three-sided polygon. **b.** Something shaped like such a figure: *a triangle of land.* **2.** Any of various flat, three-sided drawing and drafting guides, used especially to draw straight lines at specific angles. **3.** *Music.* A percussion instrument consisting of a piece of metal in the shape of a triangle open at one angle. **4.** A relationship involving three people, especially a ménage à trois. [Middle English, from Old French, from Latin *triangulum,* from neuter of *triangulus,* three-angled : *tri-,* tri- + *angulus,* angle.]

tri·an·gu·lar (trī-ăng′gyə-lər) *adj.* **1.** Of, relating to, or shaped like a triangle. **2.** Having a triangle for a base: *a triangular pyramid.* **3.** Relating to or involving three entities, such as three people, objects, or ideas. **—tri·an′gu·lar′i·ty** (-lăr′ĭ-tē) *n.* **—tri·an′gu·lar·ly** *adv.*

tri·an·gu·late (trī-ăng′gyə-lāt′) *tr.v.* **-lat·ed, -lat·ing, -lates. 1.** To divide into triangles. **2.** To survey by triangulation. **3.** To make triangular. **4.** To measure by using trigonometry. **—triangulate** (trī-ăng′gyə-lĭt) *adj.* **1.** Of or relating to triangles; triangular. **2.** Made up of or marked with triangles.

tri·an·gu·la·tion (trī-ăng′gyə-lā′shən) *n.* **1.a.** A surveying technique in which a region is divided into a series of triangular elements based on a line of known length so that accurate measurements of distances and directions may be made by the application of trigonometry. **b.** The network of triangles so laid out. **2.** The location of an unknown point, as in navigation, by the formation of a triangle having the unknown point and two known points as the vertices.

Tri·an·gu·lum (trī-ăng′gyə-ləm) *n.* A constellation in the northern sky near Aries and Andromeda. [Latin *triangulum,* triangle. See TRIANGLE.]

Triangulum Aus·tra·le (ô-strā′lē) *n.* A constellation in the polar region of the southern sky near Apus and Norma. [New Latin : Latin *triangulum,* triangle + Latin *austrālis,* southern.]

tri·ar·chy (trī′är′kē) *n., pl.* **-chies. 1.** Government by three people; a triumvirate. **2.** A country governed by three rulers.

Tri·as·sic (trī-ăs′ĭk) *adj.* Of, belonging to, or being the geologic time, system of rocks, and sedimentary deposits of the first period of the Mesozoic Era, after the Permian Period of the Paleozoic Era and before the Jurassic Period of the Mesozoic Era. See table at **geologic time. —Triassic** *n.* The Triassic Period or its system of deposits. [Late Latin *trias,* triad (from the subdivision of this period into three parts); see TRIAD + –IC.]

tri·ath·lete (trī-ăth′lēt) *n. Sports.* One who competes in a triathlon.

tri·ath·lon (trī-ăth′lən, -lŏn′) *n. Sports.* An athletic contest in which participants compete without stopping in three successive events, usually long-distance swimming, bicycling, and running. [TRI– + (DEC)ATHLON.]

tri·a·tom·ic (trī′ə-tŏm′ĭk) *adj.* **1.** Containing three atoms per molecule. **2.** Containing three replaceable atoms or radicals.

tri·ax·i·al (trī-ăk′sē-əl) *adj.* Having three axes. **—tri·ax′i·al′i·ty** (-ăl′ĭ-tē) *n.*

tri·a·zine (trī′ə-zēn′, trī-ăz′ēn′) *n.* **1.** Any of three isomeric compounds, $C_3H_3N_3$, each having three carbon and three nitrogen atoms in a six-membered ring. **2.** A compound derived from one of these isomers.

tri·a·zole (trī′ə-zōl′, trī-ăz′ōl′) *n.* Any of several compounds with composition $C_2H_3N_3$, having a five-membered ring of two carbon atoms and three nitrogen atoms.

trib. *abbr.* Tributary.

trib·ade (trĭb′əd) *n.* A lesbian. [French, from Latin *tribas, tribad-,* from Greek, from *tribein,* to rub. See TRIBOLOGY.] **—trib′a·dism** *n.*

trib·al (trī′bəl) *adj.* Of, relating to, or characteristic of a tribe. **—trib′al·ly** *adv.*

trib·al·ism (trī′bə-lĭz′əm) *n.* **1.** The organization, culture, or beliefs of a tribe. **2.** A strong feeling of identity with and loyalty to one's tribe or group. **—trib′al·ist** *n.* **—trib′al·is′tic** *adj.*

tri·ba·sic (trī-bā′sĭk) *adj.* **1.** Containing three replaceable hydrogen atoms per molecule. Used of an acid. **2.** Containing three univalent basic atoms or radicals per molecule. Used of a base or salt.

tribe (trīb) *n.* **1.** A unit of social organization consisting of a number of families, clans, or other groups who share a common ancestry, culture, and leadership. **2.** A political, ethnic, or ancestral division of ancient states and cultures, especially: **a.** Any of the three divisions of the ancient Romans, namely, the Latin, Sabine, and Etruscan. **b.** Any of the 12 divisions of ancient Israel. **c.** A phyle of ancient Greece. **3.** A group of people sharing an occupation, an interest, or a habit: *a tribe of graduate students.* **4.** *Informal.* A large family. **5.** *Biology.* A taxonomic category placed between a subfamily and a genus or between a suborder and a family and usually containing several genera. [Middle English, from Old French *tribu,* from Latin *tribus,* division of the Roman people, perhaps of Etruscan origin, or possibly from *tri-,* three; see **trei-** in Appendix.]

tribes·man (trībz′mən) *n.* **1.** A man who is a member of one's own tribe. **2.** A member of an aboriginal people living in tribes.

tribes·peo·ple (trībz′pē′pəl) *pl.n.* **1.** The people of one's own tribe. **2.** An aboriginal people living in tribes: *the tribespeople of the Kalahari Desert.*

tribes·wom·an (trībz′wo͝om′ən) *n.* **1.** A woman who is a member of one's own tribe. **2.** A woman who is a member of an aboriginal people living in tribes.

tri·bo·e·lec·tric·i·ty (trī′bō-ĭ-lĕk-trĭs′ĭ-tē, -ē′lĕk-, trĭb′ō-) *n., pl.* **-ties.** An electrical charge produced by friction between two objects. [Greek *tribos,* a rubbing, from *tribein,* to rub; see **terə-**[1] in Appendix + ELECTRICITY.] **—tri′bo·e·lec′tric** *adj.*

tri·bol·o·gy (trī-bŏl′ə-jē, trĭb-) *n.* The science of the mechanisms of friction, lubrication, and wear of interacting surfaces that are in relative motion. [Greek *tribos,* a rubbing (from Greek *tribein,* to rub; see **terə-**[1] in Appendix) + –LOGY.] **—tri′bo·log′i·cal** (trī′bə-lŏj′ĭ-kəl, trĭb′ə-) *adj.* **—tri·bol′o·gist** *n.*

tri·brach (trī′brăk′) *n.* A metrical foot having three short or unstressed syllables. [Latin *tribrachys,* from Greek *tribrakhus* : *tri-,* tri- + *brakhus,* short; see **mregh-u-** in Appendix.]

tri·bro·mo·eth·a·nol (trī-brō′mō-ĕth′ə-nôl′, -nōl′, -nŏl′) *n.* A white crystalline compound, CBr_3CH_2OH, that has a slight aromatic odor and taste and is used as a basal anesthetic.

trib·u·la·tion (trĭb′yə-lā′shən) *n.* **1.** Great affliction, trial, or distress; suffering: *the tribulations of the persecuted.* See Synonyms at **trial. 2.** An experience that tests one's endurance, patience, or faith. See Synonyms at **burden**[1]. [Middle English *tribulacioun,* from Old French *tribulacion,* from Latin *trībulātiō, trībulātiōn-,* from *trībulātus,* past participle of *trībulāre,* to oppress, from Latin *trībulum,* threshing-sledge. See **terə-**[1] in Appendix.]

tri·bu·nal (trī-byo͞o′nəl, trĭ-) *n.* **1.** *Law.* **a.** A seat or court of justice. **b.** The bench on which a judge or other presiding officer sits in court. **2.** A committee or board appointed to adjudicate in a particular matter. **3.** Something that has the power to determine or judge: *the tribunal of public opinion.* [Middle English, from Old French, from Latin *tribūnal,* judge's platform, from *tribūnus,* tribune. See TRIBUNE[1].]

trib·u·nate (trĭb′yə-nāt′, trĭ-byo͞o′nĭt) *n.* The rank, office, dignity, or authority of a tribune.

trib·une[1] (trĭb′yo͞on′, trĭ-byo͞on′) *n.* **1.** An officer of ancient Rome elected by the plebeians to protect their rights from arbitrary acts of the patrician magistrates. **2.** A protector or champion of the people. [Middle English, from Old French *tribun,* from Latin *tribūnus,* from *tribus,* tribe. See TRIBE.] **—trib′u·nar′y** (trĭb′yə-nĕr′ē) *adj.*

trib·une[2] (trĭb′yo͞on′, trĭ-byo͞on′) *n.* A raised platform or dais from which a speaker addresses an assembly. [French, from Old French, part of a church, speaking platform, from Old Italian *tribuna,* from Medieval Latin *tribūna,* alteration of Latin *tribūnal.* See TRIBUNAL.]

trib·u·tar·y (trĭb′yə-tĕr′ē) *adj.* **1.** Making additions or yielding supplies; contributory. **2.** Paid in tribute. **3.** Paying tribute: *a tributary colony.* **—tributary** *n., pl.* **-ies.** *Abbr.* **trib. 1.** A stream that flows into a larger stream or other body of water. **2.** A ruler or nation that pays tribute. [Middle English *tributarie,* paying tribute, from Latin *tribūtārius,* from *tribūtum,* tribute. See TRIBUTE.]

trib·ute (trĭb′yo͞ot) *n.* **1.** A gift, payment, declaration, or other acknowledgment of gratitude, respect, or admiration: *put up a plaque as a tribute to his generosity.* **2.** Evidence attesting to some praiseworthy quality or characteristic: *Her home is a tribute to her good taste.* **3.a.** A payment in money or other valuables made by one ruler or nation to another in acknowledgment of submission or as the price of protection or security. **b.** A tax imposed for such payment. **4.** Any payment exacted for protection. **5.a.** A payment or tax given by a feudal vassal to an overlord. **b.** The obligation to make such a payment. [Middle English *tribut,* from Old French, from Latin *tribūtum,* from neuter past participle of *tribuere,* to pay, distribute, from *tribus,* tribe. See TRIBE.]

tri·cam·er·al (trī-kăm′ər-əl) *adj.* Of or being a legislature composed of three chambers. [TRI– + Latin *camera,* chamber; see CAMERA + –AL[1].]

tri·car·box·yl·ic (trī′kär-bŏk-sĭl′ĭk) *adj.* Having three carboxyl groups.

tricarboxylic acid cycle *n.* See **Krebs cycle.**

trice (trīs) *n.* A very short period of time; an instant: *came back in a trice.* **—trice** *tr.v.* **triced, tric·ing, tric·es.** *Nautical.* To hoist and secure with a rope: *trice a sail.* [From Middle English *(at a) trise,* at one pull, from *trisen,* to hoist, from Middle Dutch *trīsen,* from *trīse,* pulley. V., from Middle English *trisen.*]

tri·cen·ten·ni·al (trī′sĕn-tĕn′ē-əl) *adj.* Tercentenary. **—tricentennial** *n.* A tercentenary event or celebration.

tri·ceps (trī′sĕps′) *n., pl.* **-ceps·es** (-sĕp′sĭz) also **triceps.** A large three-headed muscle running along the back of the upper arm and serving to extend the forearm. [From Latin, three-headed : *tri-,* tri- + *caput,* head; see **kaput-** in Appendix.]

tri·cer·a·tops (trī-sĕr′ə-tŏps′) *n.* A herbivorous dinosaur of the genus *Triceratops,* of the Cretaceous Period, having a bony plate covering the neck, a large horn above either eye, and a

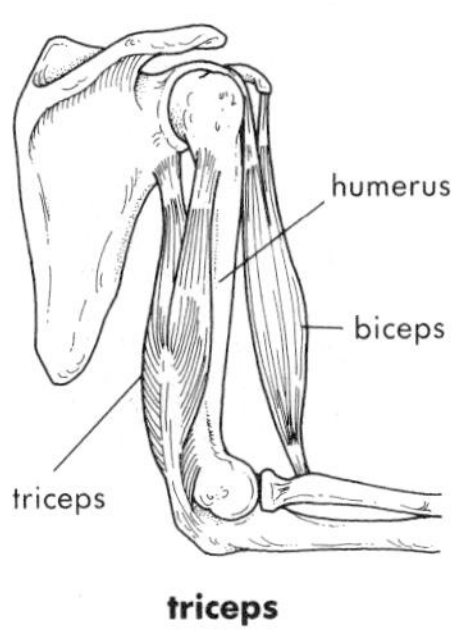

triceps

triceratops

ă pat	oi boy
ā pay	ou out
âr care	o͝o took
ä father	o͞o boot
ĕ pet	ŭ cut
ē be	ûr urge
ĭ pit	th thin
ī pie	*th* this
îr pier	hw which
ŏ pot	zh vision
ō toe	ə about, item
ô paw	♦ regionalism

Stress marks: ′ (primary); ′ (secondary), as in **dictionary** (dĭk′shə-nĕr′ē)

tricorn

smaller horn on the nose. [New Latin *Triceratops,* genus name : Greek *tri-,* tri- + Greek *keras, kerat-,* horn; see **ker-**[1] in Appendix + Greek *ōps,* eye, face; see **okʷ-** in Appendix.]

trich– *pref.* Variant of **tricho–.**

tri·chi·a·sis (trĭ-kī′ə-sĭs) *n.* A condition of ingrowing hairs about an orifice, especially ingrowing eyelashes.

tri·chi·na (trĭ-kī′nə) *n., pl.* **-nae** (-nē) or **-nas.** A small, slender parasitic nematode worm *(Trichinella spiralis)* that infests the intestines of various mammals and whose larvae move through the bloodstream, becoming encysted in muscles. [New Latin, from Greek *trikhinē,* feminine of *trikhinos,* hairy, from *thrix, trikh-,* hair.]

trich·i·nize (trĭk′ə-nīz′) *tr.v.* **-nized, -niz·ing, -niz·es.** To infect with trichinae. **—trich′i·ni·za′tion** (-nĭ-zā′shən) *n.*

trich·i·no·sis (trĭk′ə-nō′sĭs) *n.* A disease caused by eating undercooked meat, usually pork, that contains trichinae, which develop as adults in the intestines and as larvae in the muscles, causing intestinal disorders, fever, nausea, muscular pain, and edema of the face.

tri·chi·nous (trĭ-kī′nəs, trĭk′ə-nəs) *adj.* **1.** Containing trichinae: *trichinous pork.* **2.** Of or relating to trichinae or trichinosis: *a trichinous infection.*

trich·ite (trĭk′īt′) *n.* A small, dark, needle-shaped crystal. **—tri·chit′ic** (trĭ-kĭt′ĭk) *adj.*

tri·chlor·eth·yl·ene (trī′klôr-ĕth′ə-lēn′, -klōr-) *n.* Variant of **trichloroethylene.**

tri·chlor·fon (trī-klôr′fŏn′, -klōr′-) *n.* A colorless crystalline compound, $C_4H_8Cl_3O_4P$, used as an agricultural insecticide. [TRI– + CHLOR(O)– + *-fon* (from *phosphonate,* a chemical compound).]

tri·chlo·ride (trī-klôr′īd′, -klōr′-) also **tri·chlo·rid** (-klôr′ĭd, -klōr′-) *n.* A compound containing three chlorine atoms per molecule.

tri·chlo·ro·a·ce·tic acid (trī-klôr′ō-ə-sē′tĭk, -klōr′-) *n.* A colorless, deliquescent, corrosive, crystalline compound, CCl_3COOH, used as a herbicide and topically as an astringent and antiseptic.

tri·chlo·ro·eth·yl·ene (trī-klôr′ō-ĕth′ə-lēn′, -klōr′-) also **tri·chlor·eth·yl·ene** (trī′klôr-, -klōr-) *n.* A heavy, colorless, toxic liquid, $CHCl{:}CCl_2$, used to degrease metals, as an extraction solvent for oils and waxes, as a refrigerant, in dry cleaning, and as a fumigant.

tricho– or **trich–** *pref.* Hair; thread; filament: *trichocyst.* [Greek *trikho-,* from *thrix, trikh-,* hair.]

trich·o·cyst (trĭk′ə-sĭst′) *n.* A stinging or grasping organ in the outer cytoplasm of certain protozoans, especially ciliates, consisting of a threadlike or bristlelike filament that can be discharged suddenly from a minute capsule. **—trich′o·cys′tic** *adj.*

trich·o·gyne (trĭk′ə-jīn′, -gīn′) *n.* A hairlike terminal process forming the receptive part of the female reproductive structure in certain fungi or algae.

trich·oid (trĭk′oid′, trī′koid′) *adj.* Resembling hair.

trich·ome (trĭk′ōm′, trī′kōm′) *n.* A hairlike or bristlelike outgrowth, as from the epidermis of a plant. [Greek *trikhōma,* growth of hair, from *trikhoun,* to cover with hair, from *thrix, trikh-,* hair.] **—tri·chom′ic** (trĭ-kŏm′ĭk, -kō′mĭk, trī-) *adj.*

trident
Detail of a bell krater showing Poseidon holding a trident

trich·o·mo·nad (trĭk′ə-mō′năd′) *n.* Any of various flagellate protozoans of the genus *Trichomonas,* occurring as parasites in the digestive and urogenital tracts of vertebrates. [New Latin *Trichomonas, Trichomonad-,* genus name : TRICHO– + Late Latin *monas, monad-,* unit; see MONAD.] **—trich′o·mo·nad′al** (-năd′l), **trich′o·mon′al** (-mō′nəl) *adj.*

trich·o·mo·ni·a·sis (trĭk′ə-mə-nī′ə-sĭs) *n., pl.* **-ses** (-sēz′). **1.** A vaginal inflammation caused by a trichomonad *(Trichomonas vaginalis)* and resulting in a refractory discharge and itching. **2.** An infection caused by trichomonads, as a disease of cattle that commonly results in infertility or abortion in infected cows.

tri·chop·ter·an (trī-kŏp′tər-ən) *n.* An insect of the order Trichoptera, constituting the caddis flies. [From New Latin *Trichoptera,* order name : Greek *trikho-,* tricho- + Greek *-ptera,* pl. of *-pteros,* winged (from *pteron,* wing; see –PTER).]

tri·cho·sis (trĭ-kō′sĭs) *n., pl.* **-ses** (-sēz). Any disease of or affecting the hair.

tri·chot·o·my (trī-kŏt′ə-mē) *n., pl.* **-mies. 1.** Division into three parts or elements. **2.** A system based on three parts or elements. [New Latin *trichotomia* : Greek *trikha,* in three parts; see **trei-** in Appendix + New Latin *-tomia,* -tomy.] **—tri·chot′o·mous** *adj.* **—tri·chot′o·mous·ly** *adv.*

–trichous *suff.* Having a specified kind of hair or hairlike part: *peritrichous.* [From Greek *-trikhos,* from *thrix, trikh-,* hair.]

tri·chro·ism (trī′krō-ĭz′əm) *n.* The property possessed by certain minerals of exhibiting three different colors when viewed from three different directions under white lights. [From Greek *trikhroos,* three-colored : *tri-,* tri- + *khrōs,* color.] **—tri·chro′ic** *adj.*

tri·chro·mat (trī′krō-măt′) *n.* A person who has trichromatic vision.

tri·chro·mat·ic (trī′krō-măt′ĭk) also **tri·chrome** (trī′krōm′) or **tri·chro·mic** (trī-krō′mĭk) *adj.* **1.** Of, relating to, or having three colors, as in photography or printing. **2.** Having perception of the three primary colors, as in normal vision: *trichromatic vision; a trichromatic individual.* **—tri·chro′ma·tism** (trī-krō′mə-tĭz′əm) *n.*

trich·u·ri·a·sis (trĭk′yə-rī′ə-sĭs) *n., pl.* **-ses** (-sēz). Infestation of the large intestine with whipworms of the genus *Trichuris.* [New Latin *Trichuris,* genus name (TRICH(O)– + Greek *oura,* tail; see **ors-** in Appendix) + –IASIS.]

trick (trĭk) *n.* **1.** An act or a procedure intended to achieve an end by deceptive or fraudulent means. See Synonyms at **artifice. 2.** A mischievous action; a prank. **3.** A stupid, disgraceful, or childish act or performance. **4. a.** A peculiar trait or characteristic; a mannerism: *"Mimicry is the trick by which a moth or other defenseless insect comes to look like a wasp"* (Marston Bates). **b.** A peculiar event with unexpected, often deceptive results: *"One of history's cruelest tricks is to take words that sounded good at the time and make them sound pretty stupid"* (David Owen). **c.** A deceptive or illusive appearance; an illusion: *a trick of sunlight.* **5. a.** A special skill; a knack: *Is there a trick to getting this window to stay up?* **b.** A convention or specialized skill peculiar to a particular field of activity: *learned the tricks of the winemaking trade.* **6.** A feat of magic or legerdemain. **7.** A difficult, dexterous, or clever act designed to amuse. **8.** *Games.* **a.** All the cards played in a single round, one from each player. **b.** One such round. **9. a.** A period or turn of duty, as at the helm of a ship. **b.** *Slang.* A prison term. **10.** *Slang.* **a.** An act of prostitution. **b.** A prostitute's customer. **c.** A session carried out by a prostitute with a client. **11.** *Slang.* A robbery or theft. **—trick** *tr. & intr.v.* **tricked, trick·ing, tricks.** To cheat or deceive or to practice trickery or deception. **—trick** *adj.* **1.** Of, relating to, or involving tricks. **2.** Capable of performing tricks: *a trick dog.* **3.** Designed or made for doing a trick or tricks: *trick cards; trick dice.* **4.** Weak, defective, or liable to fail: *a trick knee.* ***—phrasal verb.*** **trick out** (or **up**). *Informal.* To ornament or adorn, often garishly: *was all tricked out in beads and fringe.* ***—idioms.*** **do** (or **turn**) **the trick.** To bring about the desired result. **how's tricks.** *Informal.* Used to make a friendly inquiry about a person or that person's affairs. **not miss a trick.** To be extremely alert: *The teacher was known for not missing a trick.* [Middle English *trik,* from Old North French *trique,* from *trikier,* to deceive, probably from Vulgar Latin **triccāre,* from Latin *trīcārī,* to play tricks, from *trīcae,* tricks.] **—trick′er** *n.*

trick·er·y (trĭk′ə-rē) *n., pl.* **-ies.** The practice or use of tricks; deception by stratagem.

trick·ish (trĭk′ĭsh) *adj.* Characterized by or tending to use tricks or trickery. **—trick′ish·ly** *adv.* **—trick′ish·ness** *n.*

trick·le (trĭk′əl) *v.* **-led, -ling, -les.** *—intr.* **1.** To flow or fall in drops or in a thin stream. **2.** To move or proceed slowly or bit by bit: *The audience trickled in.* *—tr.* To cause to trickle. **—trickle** *n.* **1.** The act or condition of trickling. **2.** A slow, small, or irregular quantity that moves, proceeds, or occurs intermittently. [Middle English *triklen,* perhaps variant of *striklen,* frequentative of *striken,* to flow. See STRIKE.]

trickle charge *n.* An electric charge supplied to a storage battery at a continuous low rate to keep it fully charged.

trick·le-down also **trick·le·down** (trĭk′əl-doun′) *adj.* Of or relating to the trickle-down theory: *the trickle-down effect.*

trickle-down theory *n.* A theory in economics that financial benefits accorded to big business enterprises will in turn pass down to smaller businesses and consumers.

trick or treat *interj.* Used as a greeting by children when trick-or-treating.

trick-or-treat (trĭk′ər-trēt′) *intr.v.* **-treat·ed, -treat·ing, -treats.** To engage in the practice of asking for treats on Halloween and threatening to play tricks on those who refuse.

trick·ster (trĭk′stər) *n.* One that swindles or plays tricks.

trick·sy (trĭk′sē) *adj.* **-si·er, -si·est. 1.** Smartly attired; dapper. **2.** Sportive; mischievous. **3.** Crafty; cunning; devious. **4.** Likely to cause trouble and therefore requiring special care or skilled, delicate treatment.

trick·y (trĭk′ē) *adj.* **-i·er, -i·est. 1.** Given to or characterized by trickery. See Synonyms at **sly. 2.** Requiring caution or skill: *a tricky recipe.* **—trick′i·ly** *adv.* **—trick′i·ness** *n.*

tri·clin·ic (trī-klĭn′ĭk) *adj.* Having three unequal axes intersecting at oblique angles. Used of certain crystals.

tri·clin·i·um (trī-klĭn′ē-əm) *n., pl.* **-i·a** (-ē-ə). **1.** A couch facing three sides of a rectangular table, used by the ancient Greeks, Etruscans, and Romans for reclining at meals. **2.** A room containing such a couch or couches; a dining room. [Latin *trīclīnium,* from Greek *triklinion,* diminutive of *triklinos,* room with three couches : *tri-,* three; see **trei-** in Appendix + *klinē,* couch; see **klei-** in Appendix.]

tri·col·or (trī′kŭl′ər) *n.* **1.** A flag having three colors. **2.** Also **Tricolor.** The French flag. **—tricolor** also **tri·col·ored** (-ərd) *adj.* Having three colors.

tri·corn also **tri·corne** (trī′kôrn′) *—n.* A hat having the brim turned up on three sides. *—adj.* Having three corners, horns, or projections. [French *tricorne,* from Latin *tricornis,* three-horned : *tri-,* tri- + *cornū,* horn; see **ker-**[1] in Appendix.]

tri·cor·nered (trī′kôr′nərd) *adj.* Having three corners.

tri·cos·tate (trī-kŏs′tāt′) *adj.* Having three costae.

tri·cot (trē′kō) *n.* **1.** A plain, warp-knitted cloth of any of various yarns. **2.** A soft, ribbed cloth of wool or a wool blend, usually used for dresses. [French, from *tricoter,* to knit, from Old French, to beat, run, from *tricote,* short thick stick, diminutive of *estrique, trique,* stick for leveling measures of grain, from *es-*

triquier, to strike off, of Germanic origin. See **streig-** in Appendix.]

tric·o·tine (trĭk′ə-tēn′, trē′kə-) *n.* A sturdy, worsted fabric with a double twill, used for dresses and suits. [French, from *tricot,* tricot. See TRICOT.]

tri·crot·ic (trī-krŏt′ĭk) *adj. Medicine.* Having three waves or elevations to one beat of the pulse. [From Greek *trikrotos,* having a triple beat : *tri-,* three; see **trei-** in Appendix + *krotein,* to beat.] **—tri′cro·tism** (trī′krə-tĭz′əm) *n.*

tri·cus·pid (trī-kŭs′pĭd) *n.* An organ or a part, especially a tooth, having three cusps. **—tricuspid** also **tri·cus·pi·dal** (-pĭ-dəl) or **tri·cus·pi·date** (-pĭ-dāt′) *adj.* **1.** Having three cusps, especially a molar tooth. **2.** Of or relating to the tricuspid valve. [From Latin *tricuspis, tricuspid-,* having three points : *tri-,* tri- + *cuspis,* point.]

tricuspid valve *n.* The three-segmented valve of the heart that keeps blood in the right ventricle from flowing back into the right atrium.

tri·cy·cle (trī′sĭk′əl, -sĭ-kəl) *n.* A vehicle, used especially by small children, that has three wheels, one at the front and two at the back, and is usually propelled by pedals. [French : *tri-,* three (from Greek *tri-;* see TRI–) + Greek *kuklos,* wheel; see CYCLE.]

tri·cy·clic (trī-sī′klĭk, -sĭk′lĭk) *adj. Chemistry.* Having or being a molecular structure that contains three closed rings: *a tricyclic molecule.* **—tricyclic** *n.* A tricyclic antidepressant drug.

tri·dac·tyl (trī-dăk′təl) also **tri·dac·ty·lous** (-tə-ləs) *adj.* Having three toes, claws, or similar parts on each limb. [Greek *tridaktulos,* three-fingered : *tri-,* tri-; see **trei-** in Appendix + *daktulos,* finger.]

tri·dent (trīd′nt) *n.* **1.** A long, three-pronged fork or weapon, especially a three-pronged spear used for fishing. **2.** *Greek & Roman Mythology.* The three-pronged spear carried by Neptune or Poseidon. **—trident** also **tri·den·tate** (trī-dĕn′tāt) *adj.* Having three teeth, prongs, or similar protrusions. [Middle English, from Old French, from Latin *tridēns, trident-* : *tri-,* tri- + *dēns,* tooth; see **dent-** in Appendix.]

Tri·den·tine (trī-dĕn′tīn′, -tēn′) *adj.* **1.** Of or relating to an ecumenical council held by the Roman Catholic Church in Trent, Italy, from 1545 to 1563. **2.** Of or relating to the decrees, reforms, or results of that council: *the Tridentine Catechism.* **—Tridentine** *n.* A Roman Catholic who rigorously conforms to the Tridentine Creed formulated at that council. [Medieval Latin *Tridentīnus,* from Latin, area around Tridentum, from *Tridentum* (Trent).]

tri·di·men·sion·al (trī′dĭ-mĕn′shə-nəl, -dī-) *adj.* Of, relating to, or having three dimensions.

tried (trīd) *v.* Past tense and past participle of **try.** **—tried** *adj.* **1.** Thoroughly tested and proved to be good or trustworthy. **2.** Made to undergo trials or distress. Often used in combination: *a much-tried teacher.*

tried and true *adj.* Tested and proved to be worthy or good.

tri·en·ni·al (trī-ĕn′ē-əl) *adj.* **1.** Occurring every third year. **2.** Lasting three years. **—triennial** *n.* **1.** A third anniversary. **2.** A ceremony or celebration occurring every three years. [From Latin *triennis,* from *triennium,* triennium. See TRIENNIUM.] **—tri·en′ni·al·ly** *adv.*

tri·en·ni·um (trī-ĕn′ē-əm) *n., pl.* **-en·ni·ums** or **-en·ni·a** (-ĕn′ē-ə). A period of three years. [Latin : *tri-,* tri- + *annus,* year; see **at-** in Appendix.]

tri·er (trī′ər) *n.* **1.a.** One that tries; a test or tester. **b.** One who keeps attempting something despite failure. **2.** *Law.* One who examines and settles a case; a judge or juror. **3.a.** An instrument or a device that sifts, filters, or separates ore or grain, for example, from impurities. **b.** An instrument or a device, such as a tube or siphon, for taking samples of wine, for example.

Trier (trîr) also **Trèves** (trĕv). A city of southwest Germany on the Moselle River near the Luxembourg border. Settled by the Treveri, an eastern Gaulish people, it was an important commercial center under the Romans and later as part of the Holy Roman Empire. The city was under French control from 1797 until 1815. Population, 94,190.

tri·er·arch (trī′ə-rärk′) *n.* **1.** The captain of a Greek trireme. **2.** An Athenian who outfitted and maintained a trireme as a part of his civic duties. [Latin *triērarchus,* from Greek *triērarkhos* : *triērēs,* trireme; see **trei-** in Appendix + *arkhos,* ruler; see –ARCH.]

tri·er·ar·chy (trī′ə-rär′kē) *n., pl.* **-chies.** **1.** The authority or office of the commander of a trierarch. **2.** The ancient Athenian system whereby individual citizens furnished and maintained triremes as a part of their public duty.

tries (trīz) *v.* Third person singular present tense of **try.** **—tries** *n.* Plural of **try.**

Tri·este (trē-ĕst′, -ĕs′tē). A city of extreme northeast Italy on the **Gulf of Trieste,** an inlet of the Gulf of Venice at the head of the Adriatic Sea. Held by Austria from 1382 until 1919, Trieste became in 1947 the center of the **Free Territory of Trieste** administered by the United Nations. In 1954 the city and the northern zone of the territory were returned to Italy; the remainder of the area became part of Yugoslavia. Population, 251,380.

tri·fa·cial (trī-fā′shəl) *adj.* Trigeminal.

tri·fec·ta (trī-fĕk′tə) *n. Sports & Games.* A system of betting in which the bettor must pick the first three winners in the correct sequence. Also called *triple.* [TRI– + (PER)FECTA.]

tri·fid (trī′fĭd′) *adj.* Divided or cleft into three narrow parts or lobes: *a trifid tail; a trifid organ.* [Latin *trifidus* : *tri-,* tri- + *findere, fid-,* to split.]

tri·fle (trī′fəl) *n.* **1.** Something of little importance or value. **2.** A small amount; a jot. **3.** A dessert typically consisting of plain or sponge cake soaked in sherry, rum, or brandy and topped with layers of jam or jelly, custard, and whipped cream. **4.a.** A moderately hard variety of pewter. **b. trifles.** Utensils made from this variety of pewter. **—trifle** *v.* **-fled, -fling, -fles.** *—intr.* **1.** To deal with something as if it were of little significance or value. **2.** To act, perform, or speak with little seriousness or purpose; jest. **3.** To play or toy with something: *She trifled with my affections.* See Synonyms at **flirt.** *—tr.* To waste (time or money, for example). **—*idiom.* a trifle.** Very little; somewhat: *a trifle stingy.* [Middle English *trufle, trifle,* from Old French *trufle,* mockery, diminutive of *truffe,* deception.] **—tri′fler** (trī′flər) *n.*

trifoliate

tri·fling (trī′flĭng) *adj.* **1.** Of slight worth or importance. See Synonyms at **trivial.** **2.** Frivolous or idle. **—tri′fling·ly** *adv.*

tri·flu·ra·lin (trī-flo͝or′ə-lĭn) *n.* A crystalline compound, $C_{13}H_{16}F_3N_3O_4$, used as a herbicide. [TRI– + FLU(O)R(O)– + A(N-I)LIN(E).]

tri·fo·cal (trī-fō′kəl, trī′fō′-) *adj.* **1.** Having three focal lengths. **2.** Having one section that corrects for distant vision, a second section that corrects for medium vision, and a third that corrects for near vision, as an eyeglass lens. **—trifocal** *n.* **1.** A lens having three focal lengths. **2. trifocals.** Eyeglasses having trifocal lenses.

tri·fo·li·ate (trī-fō′lē-ĭt) also **tri·fo·li·at·ed** (-ā′tĭd) *adj.* Having three leaves or leaflike parts, as in the trillium.

tri·fo·li·o·late (trī-fō′lē-ə-lāt′) *adj.* Having three leaflets, as a leaf of clover or string bean.

tri·fo·ri·um (trī-fôr′ē-əm, -fōr′-) *n., pl.* **-fo·ri·a** (-fôr′ē-ə, -fōr′-). *Architecture.* A gallery of arches above the side-aisle vaulting in the nave of a church. [Medieval Latin, a gallery in Canterbury Cathedral (later taken to mean "with three openings").]

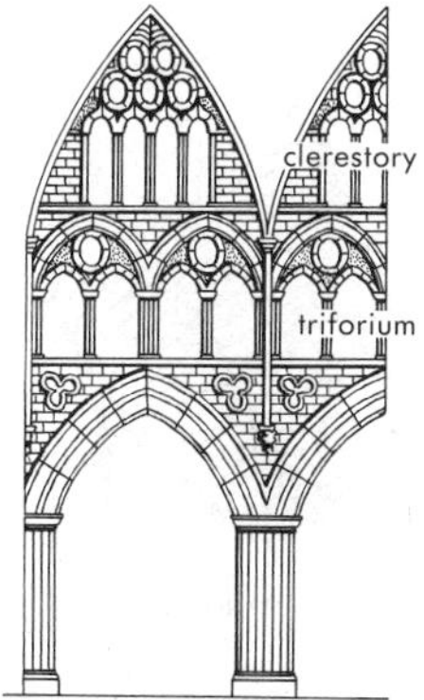

triforium

tri·formed (trī′fôrmd′) also **tri·form** (-fôrm′) *adj.* Having three different forms or parts.

tri·fur·cate (trī-fûr′kĭt, -kāt′, trī′fər-kāt′) also **tri·fur·cat·ed** (trī′fər-kā′tĭd) *adj.* Having three forks or branches: *trifurcate antennae; trifurcate ribs.* **—tri′fur·ca′tion** *n.*

trig¹ (trĭg) *adj.* **1.** Smart and trim, as in appearance. See Synonyms at **neat¹.** **2.** Being in good condition. **—trig** *tr.v.* **trigged, trig·ging, trigs.** To make trim or neat, especially in dress. [Middle English, true, from Old Norse *tryggr,* loyal, true. See **deru-** in Appendix.] **—trig′ly** *adv.* **—trig′ness** *n.*

trig² (trĭg) *tr.v.* **trigged, trig·ging, trigs.** **1.** To stop (a wheel) from rolling, as with a wedge. **2.** To prop up; support. **—trig** *n.* A wedge or other braking device. [Perhaps of Scandinavian origin; akin to Old Norse *tryggr,* firm. See TRIG¹.]

trig. *abbr. Mathematics.* **1.** Trigonometric. **2.** Trigonometry.

tri·gem·i·nal (trī-jĕm′ə-nəl) *adj.* Of or relating to the trigeminal nerves; trifacial.

trigeminal nerve *n.* Either of the fifth pair of cranial nerves, having sensory and motor functions in the face, teeth, mouth, and nasal cavity. Also called *trigeminus.*

trigeminal neuralgia *n.* Paroxysmal shooting pains of the facial area around one or more branches of the trigeminal nerve, of unknown cause, but often precipitated by irritation of the affected area. Also called *tic douloureux.*

tri·gem·i·nus (trī-jĕm′ə-nəs) *n., pl.* **-ni** (-nī′). See **trigeminal nerve.** [New Latin, from Latin, born as three twins, triple : *tri-,* tri- + *geminus,* twin.]

trig·ger (trĭg′ər) *n.* **1.a.** The lever pressed by the finger to discharge a firearm. **b.** A similar device used to release or activate a mechanism. **2.** An event that precipitates other events. **3.** *Electronics.* A pulse or circuit that initiates the action of another component. **—trigger** *tr.v.* **-gered, -ger·ing, -gers.** **1.** To set off; initiate: *a high-level meeting that triggered bitter bureaucratic debates.* **2.** To fire or explode (a weapon or an explosive charge). [Dutch *trekker,* from Middle Dutch *trecker,* from *trecken,* to pull.]

trig·ger·fish (trĭg′ər-fĭsh′) *n., pl.* **triggerfish** or **-fish·es.** Any of various brightly colored fishes of the family Balistidae of warm coastal waters, having a roundish body and an erectile spine on the anterior dorsal fin that locks upright when the fish is threatened.

trig·ger-hap·py (trĭg′ər-hăp′ē) *adj. Slang.* **1.** Having a tendency or desire to shoot a firearm before adequately identifying the target. **2.** Inclined to react violently at the slightest provocation.

trig·ger·man (trĭg′ər-mən) *n.* **1.** An underworld gunman who in premeditation shoots a victim. **2.** A gunman; a shooter: *"Where is the moral justification . . . in offering the platoon survivors—the actual triggermen—immunity?"* (Nelson DeMille).

tri·glyc·er·ide (trī-glĭs′ə-rīd′) *n.* A naturally occurring ester of three fatty acids and glycerol that is the chief constituent of fats and oils.

tri·glyph (trī′glĭf′) *adj. Architecture.* An ornament in a Doric frieze, consisting of a projecting block having on its face two parallel vertical glyphs or grooves and two half grooves or chamfers on either vertical end, that separates the metopes. [Latin *trīglyphus,* from Greek *trigluphos* : *tri-,* three; see **trei-** in Appendix + *gluphē,* carving; see GLYPH.] **—tri·glyph′ic** *adj.*

ă pat	oi boy
ā pay	ou out
âr care	o͝o took
ä father	o͞o boot
ĕ pet	ŭ cut
ē be	ûr urge
ĭ pit	th thin
ī pie	*th* this
îr pier	hw which
ŏ pot	zh vision
ō toe	ə about, item
ô paw	♦ regionalism

Stress marks: ′ (primary); ′ (secondary), as in **dictionary** (dĭk′shə-nĕr′ē)

trilithon
Stonehenge, Salisbury Plain, England

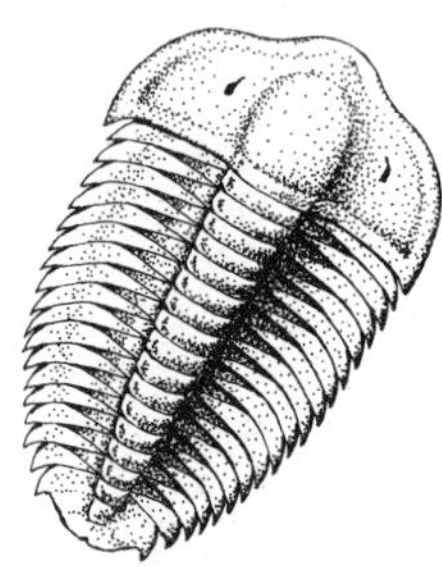
trilobite

Trimurti

tri·gon (trī′gŏn′) *n.* **1.** *Music.* A triangular lyre or harp of Roman and Greek antiquity. **2.** See **triplicity** (sense 3). **3.** *Archaic.* A triangle. [Latin *trigōnum,* from Greek *trigōnon,* from neuter of *trigōnos,* triangular : *tri-,* tri- + *gōnia,* angle; see -GON.]

trigon. *abbr.* **1.** Trigonometric. **2.** Trigonometry.

trigonometric function *n. Mathematics.* A function of an angle expressed as the ratio of two of the sides of a right triangle that contains that angle; the sine, cosine, tangent, cotangent, secant, and cosecant. Also called *circular function.*

trig·o·nom·e·try (trĭg′ə-nŏm′ĭ-trē) *n. Abbr.* **trig., trigon.** *Mathematics.* The branch of mathematics that deals with the relationships between the sides and the angles of triangles and the calculations based on them, particularly the trigonometric functions. [New Latin *trigōnometria* : Greek *trigōnon,* triangle; see TRIGON + Greek *-metria,* -metry.] **—trig′o·no·met′ric** (-nə-mĕt′rĭk), **trig′o·no·met′ri·cal** (-rĭ-kəl) *adj.* **—trig′o·no·met′ri·cal·ly** *adv.*

tri·gram (trī′grăm′) *n.* **1.** A figure composed of three solid or interrupted parallel lines, especially as used in Chinese philosophy or divination according to the I Ching. **2.** See **trigraph** (sense 3). **—tri′gram·mat′ic** (-grə-măt′ĭk) *adj.* **—tri′gram·mat′i·cal·ly** *adv.*

tri·graph (trī′grăf′) *n.* **1.** Three letters spelling one consonant, vowel, or diphthong, such as *Sch* in *Schiller* or *igh* in *high* or *thigh.* **2.** A group of three letters, especially of frequent occurrence in a given language, as *the* or *ing* in English or *gli* in Italian. **3.** Any combination of three letters of an alphabet. In this sense, also called *trigram.*

tri·graph·ic (trī-grăf′ĭk) *adj.* **1.** Of, relating to, or being a trigraph. **2.** Of, relating to, or being a substitution or procedure by groups of three characters or elements at a time in encoding, decoding, or cryptanalysis. **—tri·graph′i·cal·ly** *adv.*

tri·he·dra (trī-hē′drə) *n.* A plural of **trihedron.**

tri·he·dral (trī-hē′drəl) *adj.* Having or formed by three planes meeting at a point. **—trihedral** *n.* See **trihedron.**

tri·he·dron (trī-hē′drən) *n., pl.* **-drons** or **-dra** (-drə). A figure formed by three planes meeting at a point. Also called *trihedral.*

tri·hy·brid (trī-hī′brĭd) *n. Genetics.* The hybrid of parents that differ at only three gene loci, for which each parent is homozygous.

tri·i·o·do·thy·ro·nine (trī′ī-ō′dō-thī′rə-nēn′, -ī-ŏd′ō-) *n.* A thyroid hormone, $C_{15}H_{12}I_3NO_4$, similar to thyroxine but more potent, used in the treatment of hypothyroidism. [TRI– + IODO– + *thyronine* (THYR(O)– + –ON(E) + –INE[2]).]

trike (trīk) *n. Informal.* A tricycle.

tri·lat·er·al (trī-lăt′ər-əl) *adj.* Having or involving three sides, countries, or parties. [From Latin *trilaterus* : *tri-,* tri- + *latus, later-,* side.] **—tri·lat′er·al·ly** *adv.*

tri·lat·er·al·ism (trī-lăt′ər-ə-lĭz′əm) *n.* **1.** The practice of engaging in three-party relations, agreements, or negotiations. **2.** The political and economic policy of encouraging friendly relations among three nations or regions, especially the United States, Western Europe, and Japan, or North America, Europe, and the Pacific Rim. **—tri·lat′er·al·ist** *n.*

tril·by (trĭl′bē) *n., pl.* **tril·bies.** A soft felt hat with a deeply creased crown. [After the novel *Trilby* by George du Maurier, because such a hat was worn in the original London stage production.]

tri·lin·e·ar (trī-lĭn′ē-ər) *adj.* Relating to, having, or bounded by three lines.

tri·lin·gual (trī-lĭng′gwəl) *adj.* **1.** Using or able to use three languages, especially with equal or nearly equal fluency. **2.** Of, relating to, or expressed in three languages. **—trilingual** *n.* A person who is able to use three languages, especially with equal fluency. **—tri·lin′gual·ism** *n.*

tri·lit·er·al (trī-lĭt′ər-əl) *adj.* Consisting of three letters, especially of three consonants. Used chiefly of roots in Semitic languages. **—triliteral** *n.* **1.** A three-letter word or word element. **2.** A triliteral root or word.

tri·lith·on (trī-lĭth′ŏn, trī′lĭ-thŏn′) also **tri·lith** (trī′lĭth) *n.* A prehistoric structure consisting of two large stones set upright to support a third on their tops. [Greek, neuter of *trilithos,* having three stones : *tri-,* tri- + *lithos,* stone.]

trill (trĭl) *n.* **1.** A fluttering or tremulous sound, as that made by certain birds; a warble. **2.** *Music.* **a.** The rapid alternation of two tones either a whole or a half tone apart. **b.** A vibrato. **3.** *Linguistics.* **a.** A rapid vibration of one speech organ against another, as of the tongue against the alveolar ridge in Spanish *rr.* **b.** A speech sound pronounced with such a vibration. **—trill** *v.* **trilled, trill·ing, trills.** *—tr.* **1.** To sound, sing, or play with a trill. **2.** To articulate (a sound) with a trill. *—intr.* To produce or give forth a trill. [Italian *trillo,* from *trillare,* to trill, ultimately probably of imitative origin.]

Tril·ling (trĭl′ĭng), **Lionel.** 1905–1975. American literary critic whose works include *Beyond Culture* (1965) and *Sincerity and Authenticity* (1972).

tril·lion (trĭl′yən) *n.* **1.** The cardinal number equal to 10^{12}. **2.** *Chiefly British.* The cardinal number equal to 10^{18}. [French : *tri-,* third power (from Latin *tri-,* tri-) + *(m)illion,* million (from Old French *milion;* see MILLION).] **—tril′lion** *adj.*

tril·lionth (trĭl′yənth) *n.* **1.** The ordinal number matching the number one trillion in a series. **2.** One of a trillion equal parts. **—tril′lionth** *adv. & adj.*

tril·li·um (trĭl′ē-əm) *n.* Any of various plants of the genus *Trillium,* of North America, the Himalaya Mountains, and eastern Asia, usually having a single cluster of three leaves and a variously colored, three-petaled flower. Also called *birthroot, wakerobin.* [New Latin *Trillium,* genus name, probably from Swedish *trilling,* triplet (from its three leaves), from obsolete Swedish *tri,* three, from Old Swedish *thrīr.* See **trei-** in Appendix.]

tri·lo·bate (trī-lō′bāt′) or **tri·lo·bat·ed** (-bā′tĭd) also **tri·lobed** (trī′lōbd′) *adj.* Having three lobes, as certain leaves.

tri·lo·bite (trī′lə-bīt′) *n.* Any of numerous extinct marine arthropods of the class Trilobita, of the Paleozoic Era, having a segmented body divided by grooves into three vertical lobes and found as fossils throughout the world. [New Latin *Trilobītēs,* former class name, from Greek *trilobos,* three-lobed : *tri-,* tri- + *lobos,* lobe.] **—tri′lo·bit′ic** (-bĭt′ĭk) *adj.*

tri·loc·u·lar (trī-lŏk′yə-lər) *adj.* Having three chamberlike divisions or cavities, as the capsule of a plant or the heart of a reptile.

tril·o·gy (trĭl′ə-jē) *n., pl.* **-gies.** A group of three dramatic or literary works related in subject or theme. [Greek *trilogia,* series of three related tragedies : *tri-,* tri- + *-logia,* -logy.]

trim (trĭm) *v.* **trimmed, trim·ming, trims.** *—tr.* **1.** To make neat or tidy by clipping, smoothing, or pruning: *trimmed his moustache.* **2. a.** To remove (excess) by cutting: *trim a budget.* **b.** To remove the excess from by or as if by cutting: *trimmed off the rotten wood.* **3.** To ornament; decorate. **4.** *Informal.* **a.** To thrash; beat. **b.** To defeat soundly. **c.** To cheat. **d.** To rebuke; scold. **5.** *Nautical.* **a.** To adjust (the sails and yards) so that they receive the wind properly. **b.** To balance (a ship) by shifting its cargo or contents. **6.** To balance (an aircraft) in flight by regulating the control surfaces and tabs. **7.** To furnish or equip. *—intr.* **1.** *Nautical.* **a.** To be in or retain equilibrium. **b.** To make sails and yards ready for sailing. **2. a.** To affect or maintain cautious neutrality. **b.** To fashion one's views for momentary popularity or advantage. **—trim** *n.* **1. a.** State of order, arrangement, or appearance; condition: *in good trim.* **b.** A condition of good health or fitness. **2. a.** Exterior ornamentation, such as moldings or framework, on a building or vehicle. **b.** Decoration or ornament, as for clothing. **3.** Material used in commercial window displays. **4.** Dress or equipment. **5.** Excised or rejected material, such as film that has been cut in editing. **6.** Personal quality; character. **7.** A cutting or clipping to make neat: *My hair needs a trim.* **8.** *Nautical.* **a.** The readiness of a vessel for sailing with regard to ballast, sails, and yards. **b.** The balance of a ship. **c.** The difference between the draft at the bow and at the stern. **9.** The position of an aircraft relative to its horizontal axis. **—trim** *adj.* **trim·mer, trim·mest. 1. a.** In good or neat order. **b.** In good physical condition; fit; slim. **2.** Having lines, edges, or forms of neat and pleasing simplicity. See Synonyms at **neat**[1]. **—trim** *adv.* In a trim manner. [Middle English *trimmen,* to make firm, from Old English *trymman,* from *trum,* strong. See **deru-** in Appendix.] **—trim′ly** *adv.* **—trim′ness** *n.*

tri·ma·ran (trī′mə-răn′) *n. Nautical.* A fast sailboat with three parallel hulls. [TRI– + (CATA)MARAN.]

Trim·ble (trĭm′bəl), **Robert.** 1777–1828. American jurist who served as an associate justice of the U.S. Supreme Court (1826–1828).

tri·mer (trī′mər) *n.* A molecule formed by combining three identical smaller molecules. [TRI– + (POLY)MER.] **—tri·mer′ic** (-mĕr′ĭk) *adj.*

trim·er·ous (trĭm′ər-əs) *adj.* **1.** Having three similar segments or parts. **2.** *Botany.* Having flower parts, such as petals, sepals, and stamens, in sets of three. **—trim′er·ism** *n.*

tri·mes·ter (trī-mĕs′tər, trī′mĕs′-) *n.* **1.** A period or term of three months. **2.** One of three terms into which an academic year is divided in some universities and colleges. [French *trimestre,* from Latin *trimēstris,* of three months : *tri-,* tri- + *mēnsis,* month; see **mē-**[2] in Appendix.] **—tri·mes′tral** (-trəl), **tri·mes′tri·al** (-trē-əl) *adj.*

trim·e·ter (trĭm′ĭ-tər) *n.* A line of verse consisting of three metrical feet. [Late Latin, from Latin *trimetrus,* from Greek *trimetros* : *tri-,* tri- + *metron,* measure; see METER[1].] **—tri·met′ric** (trī-mĕt′rĭk), **tri·met′ri·cal** (-rĭ-kəl) *adj.*

tri·meth·a·di·one (trī-mĕth′ə-dī′ōn′) *n.* A white crystalline substance, $C_6H_9NO_3$, used as an anticonvulsant in the treatment of epilepsy. [TRI– + METH(YL) + DI–[1] + –ONE.]

tri·met·ro·gon (trī-mĕt′rə-gŏn′) *n.* A system of aerial photography in which one vertical and two oblique photographs are simultaneously taken for use in topographic mapping. [TRI– + *Metrogon,* a kind of camera lens.]

trim·mer (trĭm′ər) *n.* **1. a.** One that trims: *a hedge trimmer.* **b.** A device or machine, such as a lumber trimmer, that is used for trimming. **2.** One who changes one's opinions, especially political opinions, to suit the needs of the moment. **3.** *Electronics.* A variable component used to make fine adjustments to capacity or resistance. **4.** *Architecture.* A beam across an opening, such as a hearth, into which the ends of joists can be fitted.

trim·ming (trĭm′ĭng) *n.* **1.** The act of one that trims. **2.** Something added as decoration or ornament, especially a band of lace or embroidery on clothing. **3. trimmings.** Accessories; extras: *roast turkey with all the trimmings.* **4. trimmings.** Scraps or material removed when something is trimmed. **5.** *Informal.* A sound defeat, beating, or punishment.

tri·mo·lec·u·lar (trī′mə-lĕk′yə-lər) *adj.* Relating to or formed from three molecules.

tri·month·ly (trī-mŭnth′lē) *adj.* Done, occurring, or appearing every three months. **—tri·month′ly** *adv.*

tri·morph (trī′môrf′) *n.* **1.** A substance that occurs in three distinct crystalline forms. **2.** One of the crystalline forms in which a trimorphic substance occurs.

tri·mor·phic (trī-môr′fĭk) also **tri·mor·phous** (-fəs) *adj.* **1.** *Biology.* Having or occurring in three differing forms. **2.** *Chemistry.* Crystallizing in three distinct forms. **—tri·mor′phi·cal·ly** *adv.* **—tri·mor′phism** *n.*

Tri·mur·ti (trĭ-mo͝or′tē) *n.* *Hinduism.* The triad of gods consisting of Brahma the creator, Vishnu the preserver, and Shiva the destroyer as the three highest manifestations of the one ultimate reality. [Sanskrit *trimūrtiḥ* : *tri-*, three; see **trei-** in Appendix + *mūrtiḥ*, form.]

tri·nal (trī′nəl) *adj.* Having three parts; threefold. [Late Latin *trīnālis*, from Latin *trīnus*, trine. See TRINE.]

tri·na·ry (trī′nə-rē) *adj.* Consisting of three parts or proceeding by threes; ternary. [Late Latin *trīnārius*, from Latin *trīnus*, trine. See TRINE.]

trine (trīn) *adj.* **1.** Threefold; triple. **2. a.** Of or relating to an astrologically favorable positioning of two celestial bodies 120° apart. **b.** In astrology, situated 120° apart. **—trine** *n.* **1.** A group of three. **2.** In astrology, the aspect of two planets when 120° apart. **3. Trine.** *Theology.* See **Trinity** (sense 2). [Middle English, from Old French, from Latin *trīnus*, sing. of *trīnī*, three each. See **trei-** in Appendix.]

Trin·i·dad (trĭn′ĭ-dăd′). An island of Trinidad and Tobago in the Atlantic Ocean off northeast Venezuela. First sighted by Columbus in 1498, it was not settled until the 1570's and was a frequent target for Dutch, French, and British buccaneers. Ceded to Great Britain in 1802, Trinidad was joined with Tobago in 1888 to form the colony of Trinidad and Tobago (1898). **—Trin′i·dad′i·an** *adj. & n.*

Trinidad and To·ba·go (tə-bā′gō). A country of the southeast West Indies in the Atlantic Ocean off northeast Venezuela. It comprises the islands of Trinidad and Tobago, which became independent in 1962. Port of Spain, on Trinidad, is the capital. Population, 1,059,825.

Trin·i·tar·i·an (trĭn′ĭ-târ′ē-ən) *adj.* **1. a.** Of or relating to the Christian Trinity. **b.** Believing or professing belief in the Christian Trinity or the doctrine of the Trinity. **2. trinitarian.** Having three members, parts, or facets. **—Trinitarian** *n.* **1.** One who believes in the Christian doctrine of the Trinity. **2.** A member of a Roman Catholic religious congregation founded in 1198 and now devoted to teaching, nursing, and pastoral work. **—Trin′i·tar′i·an·ism** *n.*

tri·ni·tro·ben·zene (trī-nī′trō-bĕn′zēn′, -bĕn-zēn′) *n.* A yellow crystalline compound, $C_6H_3(N_3O_2)_3$, derived from trinitrotoluene and used as an explosive.

tri·ni·tro·cre·sol (trī-nī′trō-krē′sôl′, -sōl′, -sŏl′) *n.* A yellow crystalline compound, $(NO_2)_3C_6H(CH_3)OH$, used in high explosives.

tri·ni·tro·phe·nol (trī-nī′trō-fē′nôl′, -nôl′, -nŏl′) *n.* Picric acid.

tri·ni·tro·tol·u·ene (trī-nī′trō-tŏl′yo͞o-ēn′) also **tri·ni·tro·tol·u·ol** (-ôl′, -ōl′, -ŏl′) *n.* TNT.

trin·i·ty (trĭn′ĭ-tē) *n., pl.* **-ties. 1.** A group consisting of three closely related members. Also called *triunity.* **2. Trinity.** *Theology.* The union of three divine persons, the Father, Son, and Holy Spirit, in one God. Also called *Trine.* **3. Trinity.** Trinity Sunday. [Middle English *trinite*, from Old French, from Latin *trīnitās*, from *trīnus*, trine. See TRINE.]

Trinity River. A river, about 821 km (510 mi) long, of eastern Texas formed near Dallas by the juncture of three forks and flowing generally southeast to **Trinity Bay,** an arm of Galveston Bay.

Trinity Sunday *n.* The first Sunday after Pentecost, celebrated by a feast in honor of the Trinity.

trin·ket (trĭng′kĭt) *n.* **1.** A small ornament, such as a piece of jewelry. **2.** A trivial thing; a trifle. [Origin unknown.]

tri·no·mi·al (trī-nō′mē-əl) *adj.* **1.** Consisting of three names or terms, as a taxonomic designation. **2.** *Mathematics.* Consisting of three terms. **—trinomial** *n.* **1.** A three-part taxonomic designation indicating genus, species, and subspecies or variety, such as *Brassica oleracea botrytis*, the cauliflower. **2.** *Mathematics.* An algebraic expression consisting of three terms connected by plus or minus signs. [TRI– + (BI)NOMIAL.] **—tri·no′mi·al·ism** *n.*

tri·nu·cle·o·tide (trī-no͞o′klē-ə-tīd′, -nyo͞o′-) *n.* A triplet of nucleotides; a codon.

tri·o (trē′ō) *n., pl.* **-os. 1.** A group of three people or things joined or associated. **2.** *Music.* **a.** A composition for three performers. **b.** The group performing such a composition. **c.** The middle section of a minuet or scherzo, a march, or of various dance forms. [French, composition for three voices, from Italian : *tri-*, three (from Latin; see **trei-** in Appendix) + *(du)o*, duet; see DUO.]

tri·ode (trī′ōd′) *n.* A highly evacuated electron tube containing an anode, a cathode, and a control grid.

tri·ol (trī′ôl′, -ōl′, -ŏl′) *n.* A chemical compound containing three hydroxyl groups.

tri·o·let (trē′ə-lĭt, trī′-, trē′ə-lā′) *n.* A poem or stanza of eight lines with a rhyme scheme *abaaabab*, in which the fourth and seventh lines are the same as the first, and the eighth line is the same as the second. [French, diminutive of *trio*, trio. See TRIO.]

tri·ose (trī′ōs′) *n.* One of a group of monosaccharides that contain three carbon atoms.

tri·ox·ide (trī-ŏk′sīd′) also **tri·ox·id** (-ŏk′sĭd) *n.* An oxide containing three oxygen atoms per molecule.

trip (trĭp) *n.* **1.** A going from one place to another; a journey. **2.** A stumble or fall. **3.** A maneuver causing someone to stumble or fall. **4.** A mistake. **5.** *Slang.* **a.** A hallucinatory experience induced by a psychedelic drug: *an acid trip.* **b.** An intense, stimulating, or exciting experience: *a power trip.* **6.** *Slang.* **a.** A usually temporary but absorbing interest: *a health food trip.* **b.** A certain way of life or situation: *"deny that his reclusiveness is some sort of deliberate star trip"* (Patricia Bosworth). **7.** A light or nimble tread. **8. a.** A device, such as a pawl, for triggering a mechanism. **b.** The action of such a device. **—trip** *v.* **tripped, trip·ping, trips.** *—intr.* **1.** To stumble. **2.** To move nimbly with light, rapid steps; skip. **3.** To be released, as a tooth on an escapement wheel in a watch. **4.** To make a trip. **5.** *Slang.* To have a drug-induced hallucination. *—tr.* **1.** To cause to stumble or fall. **2.** To trap or catch in an error or inconsistency. **3.** To release a catch, trigger, or switch, thereby setting something in operation. **4.** *Nautical.* **a.** To raise (an anchor) from the bottom. **b.** To tip or turn (a yardarm) into a position for lowering. **c.** To lift (an upper mast) in order to remove the fid before lowering. ***—idioms.*** **trip the light fantastic.** To dance. **trip up on.** To make a mistake: *tripped up on the last question.* [Middle English, act of tripping, from *trippen*, to trip, from Old French *tripper*, to stamp the foot, of Germanic origin.]

tri·pal·mi·tin (trī-păl′mĭ-tĭn) *n.* See **palmitin.**

tri·par·tite (trī-pär′tīt) *adj.* **1.** Composed of or divided into three parts. **2.** Relating to or executed by three parties: *a tripartite agreement.*

tri·par·ti·tion (trī′pär-tĭsh′ən) *n.* Division into three parts or among three parties: *the tripartition of Poland among Austria, Prussia, and Russia in the 18th century.*

tripe (trīp) *n.* **1.** The light-colored, rubbery lining of the stomach of cattle or other ruminants, used as food. **2.** *Informal.* Something of no value; rubbish. [Middle English, from Old French *tripes*, intestines, tripe.]

tri·ped·al (trī-pĕd′l) *adj.* Having three feet or legs; tripodal.

tri·pep·tide (trī-pĕp′tīd) *n.* A peptide containing three amino acids.

tri·pet·al·ous (trī-pĕt′l-əs) *adj.* *Botany.* Having three petals.

trip ham·mer also **trip·ham·mer** or **trip-ham·mer** (trĭp′hăm′ər) *n.* A heavy, power-operated hammer that is lifted by a cam or lever and then dropped.

tri·phen·yl·meth·ane (trī-fĕn′əl-mĕth′ān′, -fē′nəl-) *n.* A colorless crystalline hydrocarbon, $(C_6H_5)_3CH$, from which a large number of synthetic dyes are derived by substitution.

tri·phib·i·an (trī-fĭb′ē-ən) *adj.* Designed to operate on land, water, or in air. **—triphibian** *n.* A triphibian aircraft. [TRI– + (AM)PHIBIAN.]

tri·phos·phate (trī-fŏs′fāt′) *n.* A salt or an ester containing three phosphate groups.

tri·phos·pho·py·ri·dine nucleotide (trī-fŏs′fō-pîr′ĭ-dēn′) *n.* NADP.

triph·thong (trĭf′thông′, -thŏng′, trĭp′-) *n.* *Linguistics.* A compound vowel sound resulting from the succession of three simple ones and functioning as a unit, as (wou) in *wow.* [TRI– + (DI)PHTHONG.] **—triph·thon′gal** (-thông′əl, -thŏng′əl) *adj.*

tri·pin·nate (trī-pĭn′āt′) *adj.* *Botany.* Divided into pinnae that are subdivided into smaller, further subdivided leaflets or lobes, as in many ferns. **—tri·pin′nate′ly** *adv.*

tripl. *abbr.* Triplicate.

tri·plane (trī′plān′) *n.* An airplane with wings placed above each other in three levels.

tri·ple (trĭp′əl) *adj.* **1.** Consisting of three parts. **2.** Three times as many or as much. **3.** Repeated three times. **4.** *Music.* Characterized by three beats in a measure. **—triple** *n.* **1.** A number or quantity three times as great as another. **2.** A group or set of three; a triad. **3.** *Baseball.* See **three-base hit. 4.** *Sports & Games.* See **trifecta. —triple** *v.* **-pled, -pling, -ples.** *—tr.* To make three times as great in number or amount. *—intr.* **1.** To be or become three times as great in number or amount. **2.** *Baseball.* To make a three-base hit. [Middle English, from Old French, from Latin *triplus* (on the model of Greek *triploos*) : Latin *tri-*, three; see **trei-** in Appendix + *-plus*, -fold; see **pel-**[2] in Appendix.]

triple bond *n.* A covalent bond in which three electron pairs are shared between two atoms.

Tri·ple Crown (trĭp′əl) *n.* **1.** *Sports & Games.* An unofficial championship title attained by a horse that wins the three traditional races for a specified category. **2.** *Baseball.* An unofficial championship title achieved by a player who is at the head of the league in batting average, home runs, and runs batted in.

tri·ple-deck·er (trĭp′əl-dĕk′ər) *n.* *Informal.* Something, such as a structure or sandwich, that has three decks, floors, or layers.

tri·ple-head·er also **tri·ple·head·er** (trĭp′əl-hĕd′ər) *n.* *Sports.* A contest consisting of three games or events in a row.

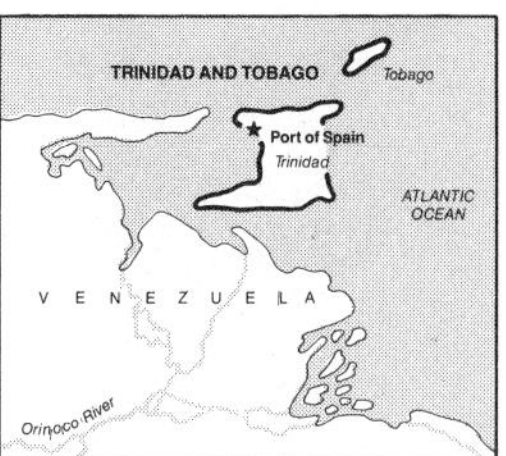

Trinidad and Tobago

Trinity
Detail from *The Book of Hours of Catherine of Cleves*

triplane
Fokker Dr-I
World War I fighter

ă pat	oi boy
ā pay	ou out
âr care	o͝o took
ä father	o͞o boot
ĕ pet	ŭ cut
ē be	ûr urge
ĭ pit	th thin
ī pie	*th* this
îr pier	hw which
ŏ pot	zh vision
ō toe	ə about, item
ô paw	♦ regionalism

Stress marks: **′** (primary); ′ (secondary), as in **dictionary** (dĭk′shə-nĕr′ē)

tripod
12th- to 11th-century B.C. Chinese bronze wine vessel

triple measure *n. Music.* See **triple time.**

triple play *n. Baseball.* A defensive play in which three putouts are executed during one turn at bat on two base runners and the batter, thereby ending suddenly the offensive threat and the inning.

triple rhyme *n.* A rhyme involving three syllables, as in *vanity/humanity.*

trip•let (trĭp′lĭt) *n.* **1.** A group or set of three of one kind. **2.** One of three children born at one birth. **3.** A group of three lines of verse. **4.** *Music.* A group of three notes having the time value of two notes of the same kind. Also called *tercet.* **5.** *Physics.* A multiplet with three components. **6.** *Genetics.* A unit of three successive nucleotides in a molecule of DNA or RNA that codes for a specific amino acid; a codon or anticodon. [TRIPL(E) + (DOUBL)ET.]

tri•ple•tail (trĭp′əl-tāl′) *n.* Any of several chiefly marine percoid fishes of the family Lobotidae, especially *Lobotes surinamensis,* of warm waters of the western Atlantic, having prominent dorsal and anal fins that resemble extra tails.

triple time *n. Music.* A time or rhythm having three beats to the measure, with the accent on the first beat. Also called *triple measure.* **—tri′ple-time′** (trĭp′əl-tīm′) *adj.*

tri•plex (trĭp′lĕks′, trī′plĕks′) *adj.* **1.** Composed of three parts; threefold; triple. **2.** Having three apartments, divisions, or floors: *a triplex apartment building; a triplex cinema.* **—triplex** *n.* Something, such as an apartment, that is triplex: *We live in a triplex.* [Latin. See **trei-** in Appendix.]

trip•li•cate (trĭp′lĭ-kĭt) *n. Abbr.* **tripl.** One of a set of three identical objects or copies. **—triplicate** (-kāt′) *tr.v.* **-cat•ed, -cat•ing, -cates.** *Abbr.* **tripl. 1.** To make threefold; triple. **2.** To make three identical copies of. [From Middle English, triple, from Latin *triplicātus,* past participle of *triplicāre,* to triple, from *triplex, triplic-,* threefold. See TRIPLEX.] **—trip′li•cate•ly** *adv.* **—trip′li•ca′tion** *n.*

tri•plic•i•ty (trĭ-plĭs′ĭ-tē, trī-) *n., pl.* **-ties. 1.** The quality or condition of being triple. **2.** A group or set of three. **3.** In astrology, one of four groups of the zodiac, each consisting of three signs separated from each other by 12°. In this sense, also called *trigon.* [Middle English, three signs of zodiac, from Late Latin *triplicitās,* triplicity, from Latin *triplex, triplic-,* triplex. See TRIPLEX.]

trip•lo•blas•tic (trĭp′lō-blăs′tĭk) *adj.* Having three germ layers. Used of the vertebrate embryo. [Greek *triploos,* triple; see **pel-**[2] in Appendix + -BLASTIC.]

trip•loid (trĭp′loid′) *Genetics. adj.* Having three times the haploid number of chromosomes in the cell nucleus: *triploid somatic cells.* **—triploid** *n.* A triploid organism or cell. **—trip′loi•dy** *n.*

trip•ly (trĭp′lē) *adv.* **1.** In three ways: *As an actor, a singer, and a juggler, she was triply qualified for the role.* **2.** To a triple degree: *a triply redundant navigational system.* **3.** Three times: *Prices were triply inflated.*

tri•pod (trī′pŏd′) *n.* **1.** A three-legged object, such as a caldron, stool, or table. **2.** An adjustable three-legged stand, as for supporting a transit or camera. [Latin *tripūs, tripod-,* from Greek *tripous,* three-footed : *tri-,* tri- + *pous,* foot; see -POD.] **—trip′o•dal** (trĭp′ə-dl, trī′pŏd′l) *adj.*

trip•o•li (trĭp′ə-lē) *n., pl.* **-lis.** A porous, lightweight, siliceous sedimentary rock composed of the shells of diatoms or radiolarians or of finely weathered chert, used as an abrasive and a polish. [French, probably after TRIPOLI, Lebanon.]

Trip•o•li (trĭp′ə-lē). **1.** A historical region of northern Africa roughly coextensive with the ancient region of Tripolitania. It became part of the Barbary States in the 16th century and later passed to Turkey and Italy. **2.** A city of northwest Lebanon on the Mediterranean Sea north-northeast of Beirut. Probably founded after the seventh century B.C., it was capital of a Phoenician federation and later flourished under the Seleucid and Roman empires. Tripoli was captured by the Arabs in A.D. 638 and taken by the Crusaders in 1109 after a long siege. Population, 198,000. **3.** The capital and largest city of Libya, in the northwest part of the country on the Mediterranean Sea. Settled by Phoenicians from Tyre, it has Roman and Byzantine remains. Population, 858,500. **—Tri•pol′i•tan** (trĭ-pŏl′ĭ-tn) *adj. & n.*

Tri•pol•i•ta•ni•a (trĭ-pŏl′ĭ-tā′nē-ə, -tān′yə, trĭp′ə-lĭ-). A historical region of northern Africa bordering on the Mediterranean Sea. Originally a Phoenician colony, it was later held by Carthage, Numidia, and Rome (after 46 B.C.). Tripolitania fell to the Vandals in A.D. 435, to the Arabs in the seventh century, and to the Ottoman Turks in 1553. **—Tri•pol′i•ta′ni•an** *adj. & n.*

tri•pos (trī′pŏs′) *n., pl.* **-pos•es.** Any of the examinations for the B.A. degree with honors at Cambridge University in England. [Alteration of Latin *tripūs, tripod-,* tripod (from the stool upon which a degree holder was appointed to sit and dispute humorously with candidates for that degree). See TRIPOD.]

trip•per (trĭp′ər) *n.* **1.** *Slang.* One who is undergoing a hallucinatory experience induced by a psychedelic drug. **2.** A tripping or triggering device on a mechanism. **3.** *Chiefly British.* One who is taking a short pleasure trip.

trip•pet (trĭp′ĭt) *n.* A cam or projection in a mechanism designed to strike another part at regular intervals. [Middle English *tripet,* piece of wood used in a game, from *trippen,* to trip. See TRIP.]

trip•ping•ly (trĭp′ĭng-lē) *adv.* Lightly and easily; fluently.

triptych
14th-century French ivory

trip•tane (trĭp′tān′) *n.* A colorless liquid antiknock additive, C_7H_{16}, used in aviation fuels. [Shortening and alteration of *trimethylbutane* : TRI- + METHYL + BUTANE.]

trip•tych (trĭp′tĭk) *n.* **1.** A hinged writing tablet consisting of three leaves, used in ancient Rome. **2.** A work consisting of three painted or carved panels that are hinged together. [From Greek *triptukhos,* threefold : *tri-,* tri- + *ptux, ptukh-,* fold.]

trip•wire (trĭp′wīr′) *n.* **1.** A wire stretched near ground level to trip or ensnare an enemy. **2.** A wire or line that activates a weapon, trap, or camera, for example, when pulled. **3.** A relatively small frontline military force whose involvement in hostilities will trigger the use of a larger force: *"a demilitarized West Bank, with an Israeli military tripwire on the Jordan"* (New Statesman).

tri•que•trous (trī-kwē′trəs, -kwĕt′rəs) *adj.* Three-edged; having three salient angles: *triquetrous mandibles.* [From Latin *triquetrus,* three-cornered : *tri-,* tri- + *-quetrus,* -cornered.]

tri•que•trum (trī-kwē′trəm, -kwĕt′rəm) *n., pl.* **-que•tra** (-kwē′trə, -kwĕt′rə). A bone of the wrist in the proximal row of carpal bones. [Latin, neuter of *triquetrus,* three-cornered. See TRIQUETROUS.] **—tri•que′tral** (-trəl) *adj.*

tri•reme (trī′rēm′) *n. Nautical.* An ancient Greek or Roman galley or warship, having three tiers of oars on each side. [Latin *trirēmis* : *tri-,* tri- + *rēmus,* oar; see **erə-** in Appendix.]

tri•sac•cha•ride (trī-săk′ə-rīd′, -rĭd) *n.* A carbohydrate that yields three monosaccharides upon hydrolysis.

tri•sect (trī′sĕkt′, trī-sĕkt′) *tr.v.* **-sect•ed, -sect•ing, -sects.** To divide into three equal parts. **—tri′sec′tion** (trī′sĕk′shən, trī-sĕk′-) *n.* **—tri′sec′tor** (trī′sĕk′tər, trī-sĕk′-) *n.*

tri•sep•al•ous (trī-sĕp′ə-ləs) *adj. Botany.* Having three sepals. Used of the calyx of a flower.

tris•kai•dek•a•pho•bi•a (trĭs′kī-dĕk′ə-fō′bē-ə, trĭs′kĭ-) *n.* An abnormal fear of the number 13. [Greek *triskaideka,* thirteen (*treis, tris,* three; see **trei-** in Appendix + *kai,* and + *deka,* ten; see DECA-) + PHOBIA.]

tri•skel•i•on (trī-skĕl′ē-ən, trĭ-) also **tri•skele** (trī′skēl′, trĭs′kēl′) *n., pl.* **-skel•i•a** (-skĕl′ē-ə) also **-skeles.** A figure consisting of three curved lines or branches, or three stylized human arms or legs, radiating from a common center. [New Latin, from Greek *triskelēs,* three-legged : *tri-,* tri- + *skelos,* leg.]

tris•mus (trĭz′məs) *n.* See **lockjaw** (sense 2). [New Latin, from Greek *trismos,* a grinding.] **—tris′mic** (-mĭk) *adj.*

tris•oc•ta•he•dron (trĭs-ŏk′tə-hē′drən) *n., pl.* **-drons** or **-dra** (-drə). *Mathematics.* A solid figure having 24 equal faces, every three of which correspond to one face of an octahedron. [Greek *tris,* thrice; see **trei-** in Appendix + OCTAHEDRON.] **—tris•oc′ta•he′dral** (-drəl) *adj.*

tri•so•di•um (trī-sō′dē-əm) *adj.* Containing three sodium atoms.

tri•so•my (trī-sō′mē, trī′sō′-) *n., pl.* **-mies.** The condition of having three copies of a given chromosome in each somatic cell rather than the normal number of two. [TRI- + -SOM(E)[3] + -Y[2].] **—tri′some′** *n.* **—tri•so′mic** *adj.*

trisomy 21 *n.* See **Down syndrome.**

Tris•tan (trĭs′tən, -tän′, -tăn′) or **Tris•tram** (-trəm) *n.* In Arthurian legend, a knight who fell in love with the Irish princess Iseult, who was betrothed to his uncle King Mark of Cornwall.

Tris•tan da Cun•ha (trĭs′tən də ko͞o′nə). An island and volcanic island group of the southern Atlantic Ocean between southern Africa and southern South America. Discovered by the Portuguese in 1506, the islands were annexed by Great Britain in 1816 and are now administered as a dependency of St. Helena.

triste (trēst) *adj.* Sad; wistful. [Middle English, from Old French, from Latin *tristis.*]

tri•ste•a•rin (trī-stē′ə-rĭn, -stîr′ĭn) *n.* See **stearin** (sense 1).

trist•ful (trĭst′fəl) *adj.* Sorrowful; gloomy. [Middle English : *triste,* sad; see TRISTE + *-ful,* -ful.] **—trist′ful•ly** *adv.* **—trist′ful•ness** *n.*

tris•tich (trĭs′tĭk) *n.* A strophe, stanza, or poem consisting of three lines. [TRI- + (DI)STICH.]

Tris•tram (trĭs′trəm) *n.* Variant of **Tristan.**

tri•sul•fide (trī-sŭl′fīd′) *n.* A sulfide containing three sulfur atoms per molecule.

tri•syl•la•ble (trī′sĭl′ə-bəl) *n. Linguistics.* A three-syllable word. **—tri′syl•lab′ic** (-sĭ-lăb′ĭk), **tri′syl•lab′i•cal** (-ĭ-kəl) *adj.* **—tri′syl•lab′i•cal•ly** *adv.*

tri•tan•o•pi•a (trī′tə-nō′pē-ə) *n.* A visual defect characterized by the inability to discern blue and yellow. [Greek *tritos,* third; see **trei-** in Appendix + Greek *anōpia,* blindness (*an-,* not; see A-[1] + *-ōpia,* -opia).]

trite (trīt) *adj.* **trit•er, trit•est. 1.** Lacking power to evoke interest through overuse or repetition; hackneyed. **2.** *Archaic.* Frayed or worn out by use. [Latin *trītus,* from past participle of *terere,* to wear out. See **terə-**[1] in Appendix.] **—trite′ly** *adv.* **—trite′ness** *n.*

SYNONYMS: *trite, hackneyed, shopworn, stereotyped, threadbare, stale, banal.* These adjectives describe something, such as writing or speech, that lacks appeal or power because it lacks freshness. *Trite, hackneyed,* and *shopworn* imply overfamiliarity resulting from overuse or repetition; the terms often suggest reduction of something once forceful to an empty formula or cliché:

a trite saying; a soap opera with a hackneyed plot; shopworn slogans. Stereotyped refers to what is so lacking in originality or creative force that it seems a mechanical reproduction: *stereotyped phrases of condolence. Threadbare* suggests that something has been overworked until it is worn out: *a threadbare argument. Stale* implies that something has lost novelty or interest because it has been overused or because it is dated or passé: *stale jokes. Banal* applies to what is commonplace or inane: *banal lyrics.*

tri·the·ism (trīʹthē-ĭzʹəm) *n. Theology.* The belief that the Father, Son, and Holy Spirit are three separate and distinct gods, heretical in orthodox Christianity. **—triʹthe·ist** *n.* **—triʹthe·isʹtic, triʹthe·isʹti·cal** *adj.*

trit·i·ca·le (trĭtʹĭ-kāʹlē) *n.* **1.** A hardy hybrid of wheat and rye having a high yield. **2.** The grains of this hybrid. [Latin *trīticum,* wheat (from *trītus,* past participle of *terere,* to rub, thresh; see TRITE) + *sēcale,* rye.]

trit·i·um (trĭtʹē-əm, trĭshʹē-) *n.* A rare radioactive hydrogen isotope with atomic mass 3 and half-life 12.5 years, prepared artificially for use as a tracer and as a constituent of hydrogen bombs. [From Greek *tritos,* third. See **trei-** in Appendix.]

tri·ton¹ (trītʹn) *n.* Any of various chiefly tropical marine gastropod mollusks of the family Cymatiidae, having a pointed, spirally twisted, often colorfully marked shell. [Latin *Trītōn,* Triton (from representations of the sea god holding a conch shell). See TRITON.]

tri·ton² (trīʹtŏnʹ) *n.* The nucleus of tritium, consisting of two neutrons and one proton. [TRIT(IUM) + –ON¹.]

Tri·ton (trītʹn) *n.* **1.** *Greek Mythology.* A god of the sea, son of Poseidon and Amphitrite, portrayed as having the head and trunk of a man and the tail of a fish. **2.** *Astronomy.* The satellite of Neptune that is second in distance from the planet. [Latin *Trītōn,* from Greek.]

tri·tone (trīʹtōnʹ) *n. Music.* An interval composed of three whole tones. [Medieval Latin *tritonus,* from Greek *tritonos,* having three tones : *tri-,* three; see **trei-** in Appendix + *tonos,* tone; see TONE.]

trit·u·rate (trĭchʹə-rātʹ) *tr.v.* **-rat·ed, -rat·ing, -rates.** To rub, crush, grind, or pound into fine particles or a powder; pulverize. **—triturate** (-ər-ĭt) *n.* A triturated substance, especially a powdered drug. [Late Latin *trītūrāre, trītūrāt-,* to thresh, from Latin *trītūra,* a threshing, from *trītus,* past participle of *terere,* to thresh. See **terə-¹** in Appendix.] **—tritʹu·ra·ble** *adj.* **—tritʹu·raʹtor** *n.*

trit·u·ra·tion (trĭchʹə-rāʹshən) *n.* **1.** The act or process of triturating. **2.** The composing of a dental amalgam by mortar and pestle.

tri·umph (trīʹəmf) *intr.v.* **-umphed, -umph·ing, -umphs. 1.** To be victorious or successful; win. **2.** To rejoice over a success or victory; exult. **3.** To receive honors upon return from a victory in ancient Rome. Used of a general. **—triumph** *n.* **1.** The fact of being victorious; victory or conquest. See Synonyms at **victory. 2.** A noteworthy or spectacular success. **3.** Exultation or rejoicing over victory or success. **4.** A public celebration in ancient Rome to welcome a returning victorious commander and his army. **5.** *Obsolete.* A public celebration or spectacular pageant. [Middle English *triomfen,* from Old French *triumpher,* from Latin *triumphāre,* from *triumphus,* triumph, (probably via Etruscan) from Greek *thriambos,* hymn to Dionysus.]

tri·um·phal (trī-ŭmʹfəl) *adj.* **1.** Relating to or having the nature of a triumph. **2.** Celebrating or commemorating a victory or triumph: *a triumphal arch; a triumphal ode.*

tri·umph·al·ism (trī-ŭmʹfə-lĭzʹəm) *n.* The attitude or belief that a particular doctrine, especially a religion or political theory, is superior to all others. **—tri·umphʹal·ist** *n.*

tri·um·phant (trī-ŭmʹfənt) *adj.* **1.** Exulting in success or victory. **2.** Victorious; conquering. **3.** *Archaic.* Triumphal. **4.** *Obsolete.* Magnificent; splendid. **—tri·umʹphant·ly** *adv.*

tri·um·vir (trī-ŭmʹvər) *n., pl.* **-virs** or **-vi·ri** (-və-rīʹ). **1.** One of three men sharing public administration or civil authority in ancient Rome. **2.** One of three people sharing public administration or civil authority. [Middle English, from Latin, back-formation from *triumvirī,* board of three, from *trium virum,* of three men : *trium,* genitive pl. of *trēs,* three; see **trei-** in Appendix + *virum,* variant of *virōrum,* genitive pl. of *vir,* man. See **wī-ro-** in Appendix.] **—tri·umʹvi·ral** *adj.*

tri·um·vi·rate (trī-ŭmʹvər-ĭt) *n.* **1.** Government by triumvirs. **2.** The office or term of a triumvir. **3.** A body or group of triumvirs. **4.** An association or a group of three. In this sense, also called *troika.* [Latin *triumvirātus,* from *triumvirī,* board of three. See TRIUMVIR.]

tri·um·vi·ri (trī-ŭmʹvə-rīʹ) *n.* A plural of **triumvir.**

tri·une (trīʹyo͞onʹ) *adj.* Being three in one. Used especially of the Christian Trinity. **—triune** *n.* A trinity. [TRI– + Latin *ūnus,* one; see **oi-no-** in Appendix.]

tri·u·ni·ty (trī-yo͞oʹnĭ-tē) *n., pl.* **-ties.** See **trinity** (sense 1).

tri·va·lent (trī-vāʹlənt) *adj.* Having valence 3. **—tri·vaʹlence, tri·vaʹlen·cy** *n.*

tri·valve (trīʹvălvʹ) *adj.* Having three valves.

Tri·van·drum (trə-vănʹdrəm). A city of southwest India on the Arabian Sea south-southwest of Bangalore. It is a port and manufacturing center. Population, 483,086.

triv·et (trĭvʹĭt) *n.* **1.** A metal stand with short feet, used under a hot dish on a table. **2.** A three-legged stand made of metal, used for supporting cooking vessels in a hearth. [Middle English *trevet,* stand for cooking vessels, from Old English *trefet,* probably alteration (influenced by Old English *thrifēte,* three-footed) of Latin *tripēs, triped-* : *tri-,* tri- + *pēs,* foot; see **ped-** in Appendix.]

triv·i·a¹ (trĭvʹē-ə) *pl.n. (used with a sing. or pl. verb).* Insignificant or inessential matters; trifles. [Latin *trivia,* neuter pl. of *trivium,* crossroads, gutter (influenced by TRIVIAL). See TRIVIUM.]

triv·i·a² (trĭvʹē-ə) *n.* Plural of **trivium.**

triv·i·al (trĭvʹē-əl) *adj.* **1.** Of little significance or value. **2.** Ordinary; commonplace. **3.** Concerned with or involving trivia. **4.** *Biology.* Relating to or designating a species; specific. **5.** *Mathematics.* **a.** Of, relating to, or being the solution of an equation in which every variable is equal to zero. **b.** Of, relating to, or being the simplest possible case; self-evident. [Middle English *trivialle,* of the trivium (from Medieval Latin *triviālis,* from *trivium,* trivium; see TRIVIUM) and Latin *triviālis,* ordinary (from *trivium,* crossroads).] **—trivʹi·al·ly** *adv.*

SYNONYMS: *trivial, trifling, paltry, petty, picayune.* These adjectives all apply to what is small and unimportant. *Trivial* refers principally to what is so insignificant as to be utterly commonplace or unremarkable: *"I think all Christians . . . agree in the essential articles, and that their differences are trivial, and rather political than religious"* (Samuel Johnson). Something *trifling* is so unimportant or so small as to be scarcely worth notice: *"I regret the trifling narrow contracted education of the females of my own country"* (Abigail Adams). *Paltry* especially describes what falls so far short of what is required or desired that it arouses contempt: *"He . . . considered the prize too paltry for the lives it must cost"* (John Lothrop Motley). *Petty* can refer to what is of minor or secondary significance or size; the term can suggest meanness of spirit: *"Our knights are limited to petty enterprises"* (Sir Walter Scott). *"Always give your best, never get discouraged, never be petty"* (Richard M. Nixon). What is *picayune* is of negligible value or importance: *Giving a police officer a free meal may be against the law, but it seems to be a picayune infraction.*

WORD HISTORY: *Trivial Pursuit* is an etymologically sound name, because roads and traveling, which might involve pursuit, are involved in the origin of the word *trivial.* The history of *trivial* begins with the Latin word *trivium,* formed from the prefix *tri–,* "consisting of three of the things named," and *via,* "road." *Trivium* meant "the meeting place of three roads, especially as a place of public resort." Hence it also had a pejorative sense, which we express by the phrase *the gutter,* as in "His manners were formed in the gutter." The adjective *triviālis,* derived from *trivium,* meant "appropriate to the street corner, commonplace, vulgar." *Trivial* entered Middle English in senses that need not detain us here, first being recorded in a sense identical to that of *triviālis* in 1589. Shortly after that *trivial* is recorded in the sense most familiar to us, "of little importance or significance."

triv·i·al·i·ty (trĭvʹē-ălʹĭ-tē) *n., pl.* **-ties. 1.** The quality or condition of being trivial. **2.** Something trivial.

triv·i·al·ize (trĭvʹē-ə-līzʹ) *tr.v.* **-ized, -iz·ing, -iz·es.** To reduce to triviality: *"one of the deep perceptions of a feminism which looks with fresh eyes on all that has been trivialized, devalued, forbidden, or silenced"* (Adrienne Rich). **—trivʹi·al·i·za·ʹtion** (-ə-lĭ-zāʹshən) *n.*

trivial name *n.* **1.** A common or vernacular name as distinguished from a specific name, as *chimpanzee* for *Pan troglodytes.* **2.** See **specific epithet. 3.** *Chemistry.* A common, historic, or convenient name for a substance, derived often from the source in which the substance was discovered, but unsystematic and not used in modern official nomenclature, as *sucrose* for *α-D-Glucopyranosyl β-D-fructo-furanoside.*

triv·i·um (trĭvʹē-əm) *n., pl.* **-i·a** (-ē-ə). The lower division of the seven liberal arts in medieval schools, consisting of grammar, logic, and rhetoric. [Medieval Latin, from Latin, crossroads : *tri-,* tri- + *via,* road; see **wegh-** in Appendix.]

tri·week·ly (trī-wēkʹlē) *adj.* **1.** Happening, done, or appearing three times a week. **2.** Happening, done, or appearing every three weeks. **—triweekly** *adv.* **1.** Three times a week. **2.** Every three weeks. **—triweekly** *n., pl.* **-lies.** A periodical published triweekly.

-trix *suff.* **1.** A female that is connected with a specified thing: *testatrix.* **2.** A geometric point, line, or surface: *directrix.* [Middle English, from Latin *-trīx,* feminine of *-tor,* noun suff.]

tRNA (tēʹär-ĕn-āʹ) *n.* See **transfer RNA.**

Tro·as (trōʹăsʹ) also **Tro·ad** (-ădʹ). An ancient region of northwest Asia Minor surrounding the city of Troy. It formed the setting for the events recounted in the *Iliad.*

Tro·bri·and Islands (trōʹbrē-ăndʹ, -ändʹ). An island group of Papua New Guinea in the Solomon Sea off eastern New Guinea. The islands were occupied by Allied forces in June 1943.

tro·car (trōʹkärʹ) *n.* A sharp-pointed surgical instrument, used with a cannula to puncture a body cavity for fluid aspiration. [French *trocart* : *trois,* three (from Old French, from Latin *trēs;* see **trei-** in Appendix) + *carre,* side of an instrument (from Old French, from *carrer,* to square, from Latin *quadrāre,* from *quadrum,* square; see **kʷetwer-** in Appendix).]

tro·cha·ic (trō-kāʹĭk) *adj.* Of, relating to, or consisting of trochees. [Latin *trochāicus,* from Greek *trokhaikos,* from *trokhaios,* trochee. See TROCHEE.] **—tro·chaʹic** *n.*

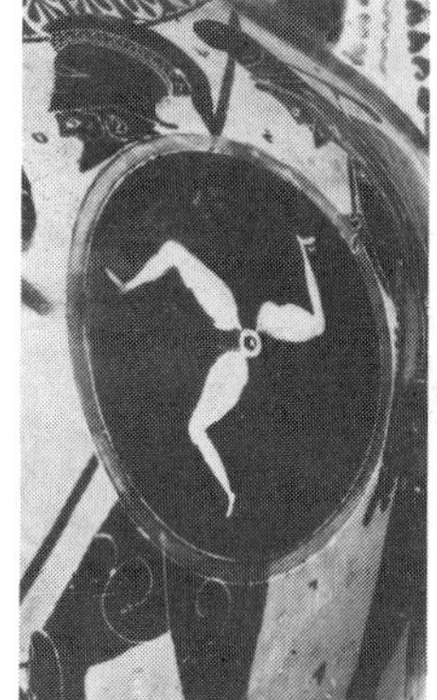

triskelion
Detail of an amphora showing triskelion pattern on a warrior's shield

Triton

ă pat	oi boy
ā pay	ou out
âr care	o͝o took
ä father	o͞o boot
ĕ pet	ŭ cut
ē be	ûr urge
ĭ pit	th thin
ī pie	*th* this
îr pier	hw which
ŏ pot	zh vision
ō toe	ə about, item
ô paw	♦ regionalism

Stress marks: ʹ (primary); ʹ (secondary), as in **dictionary** (dĭkʹshə-nĕrʹē)

Trojan horse
Engraving after a painting by Henri Paul Motte (1846–1922)

trombone

trophy

tro·chal (trō′kəl) *adj.* Shaped like or resembling a wheel, as the ciliated ring of a rotifer. [From Greek *trokhos,* wheel. See TROCHE.]

tro·chan·ter (trō-kăn′tər) *n.* **1.** Any of several bony processes on the upper part of the femur of many vertebrates. **2.** The second proximal segment of the leg of an insect. [New Latin, from Greek *trokhantēr,* ball of the hip joint, from *trekhein,* to run.] **—tro·chan′ter·al, tro′chan·ter′ic** (trō′kən-tĕr′ĭk, -kăn-) *adj.*

tro·che (trō′kē) *n.* A small, circular medicinal lozenge; a pastille. [Back-formation from Middle English *trocis, troches* (taken as pl.), from Old French *trocisse,* from Late Latin *trochiscus,* from Greek *trokhiskos,* diminutive of *trokhos,* wheel, from *trekhein,* to run.]

tro·chee (trō′kē) *n.* A metrical foot consisting of a stressed syllable followed by an unstressed syllable, as in *season,* or of a long syllable followed by a short syllable. [French *trochée,* from Latin *trochaeus,* from Greek *trokhaios,* from *trokhos,* a running, from *trekhein,* to run.]

troch·le·a (trŏk′lē-ə) *n., pl.* **-le·ae** (-lē-ē′). An anatomical structure that resembles a pulley, especially the part of the distal end of the humerus that articulates with the ulna. [Latin, system of pulleys, from Greek *trokhileia;* akin to *trekhein,* to run.]

troch·le·ar (trŏk′lē-ər) *adj.* **1.** Of, resembling, or situated near a trochlea. **2.** Of or relating to the trochlear nerve. **3.** *Botany.* Shaped like a pulley.

trochlear nerve *n.* Either of the fourth pair of cranial nerves that innervate the superior oblique muscles of the eyeballs.

tro·choid (trō′koid′, trŏk′oid′) *n.* A curve traced by a point on or connected with a circle as the circle rolls along a fixed straight line. **—trochoid** also **tro·choi·dal** (trō-koid′l, trŏk-oid′l) *adj.* **1.** Capable of or exhibiting rotation about a central axis. **2.** Permitting rotation, as a pulley or pivot. [Greek *trokhoeidēs,* wheellike : *trokhos,* wheel; see TROCHEE + *-oeidēs,* -oid.] **—tro·choi′dal·ly** *adv.*

troch·o·phore (trŏk′ə-fôr′, -fōr′) *n.* The small, free-swimming, ciliated aquatic larva of various invertebrates, including certain mollusks and annelids. [Greek *trokhos,* wheel (from *trekhein,* to run) + –PHORE.]

trod (trŏd) *v.* Past tense and a past participle of **tread.**

trod·den (trŏd′n) *v.* A past participle of **tread.**

trof·fer (trŏf′ər, trô′fər) *n.* An inverted, usually metal trough suspended from a ceiling as a fixture for fluorescent lighting tubes. [Alteration of TROUGH.]

trog·lo·dyte (trŏg′lə-dīt′) *n.* **1. a.** A member of a fabulous or prehistoric race of people that lived in caves, dens, or holes. **b.** A person considered to be reclusive, reactionary, out of date, or brutish. **2. a.** An anthropoid ape, such as a gorilla or chimpanzee. **b.** An animal that lives underground, as an ant or a worm. [From Latin *Trōglodytae,* a people said to be cave dwellers, from Greek *Trōglodutai,* alteration (influenced by *trōglē,* hole, and *-dutai,* those who enter) of *Trōgodutai.*] **—trog′lo·dyt′ic** (-dĭt′ĭk), **trog′lo·dyt′i·cal** (-ĭ-kəl) *adj.*

tro·gon (trō′gŏn′) *n.* Any of various colorful tropical or subtropical birds of the family Trogonidae, which includes the quetzal. [Greek *trōgōn,* present participle of *trōgein,* to gnaw. See **terə-¹** in Appendix.]

troi·ka (troi′kə) *n.* **1.** A Russian carriage drawn by a team of three horses abreast. **2.** See **triumvirate** (sense 4). [Russian *troĭka,* from *troe,* group of three. See **trei-** in Appendix.]

Troi·lus (troi′ləs, trō′ə-ləs) *n.* A son of King Priam of Troy, depicted as Cressida's lover in medieval romance.

Trois Ri·vières or **Trois-Rivières** (trwä rē-vyĕr′). A city of southern Quebec, Canada, at the confluence of the St. Lawrence and St. Maurice rivers. Founded in 1634, it is a manufacturing center with a pulp and paper industry. Population, 50,466.

Tro·jan (trō′jən) *n.* **1.** A native or inhabitant of ancient Troy. **2.** A person of courageous determination or energy. [Middle English, from Latin *Trōiānus,* from *Trōia,* Troy, from Greek *Trōia,* from *Trōs,* the mythical founder of Troy.] **—Tro′jan** *adj.*

Trojan horse *n.* **1.** A subversive group or device placed within enemy ranks. **2.** The hollow wooden horse in which, according to legend, Greeks hid and gained entrance to Troy, later opening the gates to their army. **3.** *Computer Science.* A set of instructions hidden inside a legitimate program, causing a computer to perform illegitimate functions.

Trojan War *n. Greek Mythology.* The ten-year war waged against Troy by the Greeks, caused by the abduction of Helen by Paris and resulting in the burning and destruction of Troy.

troll¹ (trōl) *v.* **trolled, troll·ing, trolls.** *—tr.* **1. a.** To fish for by trailing a baited line from behind a slowly moving boat. **b.** To fish in by trailing a baited line: *troll the lake for bass.* **c.** To trail (a baited line) in fishing. **2.** *Slang.* To patrol (an area) in search for someone or something: "[Criminals] *troll bus stations for young runaways*" (Pete Axthelm). **3.** *Music.* **a.** To sing in succession the parts of (a round, for example). **b.** To sing heartily: *troll a carol.* **4.** To roll or revolve. *—intr.* **1.** To fish by trailing a line, as from a moving boat. **2. a.** To wander about; ramble. **b.** *Slang.* To patrol an area in search for someone or something. **3.** *Music.* To sing heartily or gaily. **4.** To roll or spin around. **—troll** *n.* **1. a.** The act of trolling for fish. **b.** A lure, such as a spoon or spinner, that is used for trolling. **2.** *Music.* A vocal composition in successive parts; a round. [Middle English *trollen,* to wander about, from Old French *troller,* of Germanic origin.] **—troll′er** *n.*

troll² (trōl) *n.* A supernatural creature of Scandinavian folklore, variously portrayed as a friendly or mischievous dwarf or as a giant, that lives in caves, in the hills, or under bridges. [Ultimately from Old Norse.]

trol·ley also **trol·ly** (trŏl′ē) *—n., pl.* **-leys** also **-lies. 1.** A streetcar. **2.** A device that collects electric current from an underground conductor, an overhead wire, or a third rail and transmits it to the motor of an electric vehicle. **3.** A small truck or car operating on a track and used in a mine, quarry, or factory for conveying materials. **4.** A wheeled carriage, cage, or basket that is suspended from and travels on an overhead track. **5.** *Chiefly British.* A cart. *—tr. & intr.v.* **-leyed, -ley·ing, -leys** also **-lied,** (-lēd), **-ly·ing, -lies** (-lēz). To convey (passengers) or travel by trolley. [Probably from TROLL¹.]

trolley bus *n.* An electric bus that does not run on tracks and is powered by electricity from an overhead wire.

trolley car *n.* A streetcar.

trol·lop (trŏl′əp) *n.* **1.** A woman regarded as slovenly or untidy; a slattern. **2.** A strumpet. [Perhaps from TROLL¹, to roll about, wallow.]

Trol·lope (trŏl′əp), **Anthony.** 1815–1882. British writer best known for a series of novels set in the imaginary county of Barsetshire, including *Barchester Towers* (1857) and *The Last Chronicle of Barset* (1867). **—Trol·lo·pi·an** (trə-lŏp′ē-ən, -lō′pē-, trŏl′ə-pē′-) *adj.*

trol·ly (trŏl′ē) *n. & v.* Variant of **trolley.**

trom·bic·u·li·a·sis (trŏm-bĭk′yə-lī′ə-sĭs) also **trom·bic·u·lo·sis** (-lō′sĭs) *n.* Infestation with chiggers. [New Latin *Trombicula,* genus of mites, diminutive of *Trombidium* + –IASIS.]

trom·bone (trŏm-bōn′, trəm-, trŏm′bōn′) *n. Music.* **1.** A brass instrument consisting of a long cylindrical tube bent upon itself twice, ending in a bell-shaped mouth, and having a movable U-shaped slide for producing different pitches. **2.** A member of an orchestra who plays the trombone. [French, from Italian, augmentative of *tromba,* trumpet, of Germanic origin.] **—trom·bon′ist** *n.*

trom·mel (trŏm′əl) *n.* A revolving cylindrical sieve used for screening or sizing rock and ore. [German, from Middle High German *trummel,* diminutive of *trumme,* drum, probably of imitative origin.]

tromp (trŏmp) *v.* **tromped, tromp·ing, tromps.** *Informal.* *—intr.* **1.** To walk heavily and noisily; tramp. **2.** To apply heavy foot pressure on something: *tromped on the accelerator and sped off.* *—tr.* **1.** To trample underfoot. **2.** To defeat soundly; trounce. [Alteration of TRAMP.]

trompe (trŏmp) *n.* An apparatus in which water falling through a perforated pipe entrains air into and down the pipe to produce an air blast for a furnace or forge. [French, from Old French, trumpet. See TRUMP².]

trompe l'oeil (trômp′ loi′) *n., pl.* **trompe l'oeils** (loi′). **1.** A style of painting that gives an illusion of photographic reality. **2.** A painting or effect created in this style. [French : *trompe,* third person sing. present tense of *tromper,* to deceive + *le,* the + *oeil,* eye.]

–tron *suff.* **1.** Vacuum tube: *dynatron.* **2.** Device for manipulating subatomic particles: *betatron.* [Greek, instrumental noun suff.]

tro·na (trō′nə) *n.* A natural vitreous gray or white mineral, $Na_2CO_3 \cdot NaHCO_3 \cdot 2H_2O$, used as a source of sodium compounds. [Swedish, probably from Arabic dialectal *ṭrōn,* variant of Arabic *naṭrūn,* natron. See NATRON.]

Trond·heim (trŏn′hām′, trôn′-). A city of central Norway on **Trondheim Fjord,** an inlet of the Norwegian Sea. Founded in 997, it was the capital of Norway until 1380. Population, 134,652.

troop (tro͞op) *n. Abbr.* **tr., trp. 1.** A group or company of people, animals, or things. See Synonyms at **band², flock¹. 2. a.** A group of soldiers. **b. troops.** Military units; soldiers. **3.** A unit of at least five Boy Scouts or Girl Scouts under the guidance of an adult leader. **4.** A great many; a lot. **—troop** *intr.v.* **trooped, troop·ing, troops. 1.** To move or go as a throng. **2.** To assemble or move in crowds. **3.** To consort; associate. [French *troupe,* from Old French *trope,* probably from Vulgar Latin **troppu-.*]

troop·er (tro͞o′pər) *n.* **1. a.** A member of a unit of cavalry. **b.** A cavalry horse. **2. a.** A mounted police officer. **b.** A state police officer.

troop·ship (tro͞op′shĭp′) *n.* A ship for transporting troops.

troost·ite (tro͞o′stīt′) *n.* A white or colored crystalline mineral, a variety of willemite, in which the zinc is partly replaced by manganese. [After Gerard *Troost* (1776–1850), Dutch-born American geologist.]

trop. *abbr.* Tropic; tropical.

trop– *pref.* Variant of **tropo–.**

trope (trōp) *n.* **1. a.** The figurative use of a word or an expression, as metaphor or hyperbole. **b.** An instance of this use; a figure of speech. **2.** *Music.* A word or phrase interpolated as an embellishment in the sung parts of certain medieval liturgies. [Latin *tropus,* from Greek *tropos,* turn, figure of speech. See **trep-** in Appendix.] **—trop′i·cal** (trō′pĭ-kəl) *adj.*

troph– *pref.* Variant of **tropho–.**

troph·al·lax·is (trŏf′ə-lăk′sĭs, trō′fə-) *n., pl.* **-lax·es** (-lăk′sēz). Mutual exchange of food between adults and larvae of certain social insects such as bees or wasps. [TROPH(O)– + Greek

ă pat	oi boy
ā pay	ou out
âr care	o͝o took
ä father	o͞o boot
ĕ pet	ŭ cut
ē be	ûr urge
ĭ pit	th thin
ī pie	*th* this
îr pier	hw which
ŏ pot	zh vision
ō toe	ə about, item
ô paw	♦ regionalism

Stress marks: **′** (primary); ′ (secondary), as in **dictionary** (dĭk′shə-nĕr′ē)

allaxis, exchange (from *allassein,* to exchange, from *allos,* other; see **al-[1]** in Appendix).]

troph·ic (trŏf′ĭk, trō′fĭk) *adj.* **1.** Of or relating to nutrition. **2.** *Ecology.* Of or involving the feeding habits or food relationship of different organisms in a food chain.

–trophic *suff.* **1.** Of, relating to, or characterized by a specified kind of nutrition: *polytrophic.* **2.** Acting on something specified: *gonadotrophic.* [From TROPHIC.]

trophic level *n. Ecology.* A group of organisms that occupy the same position in a food chain.

tropho– or **troph–** *pref.* Nutrition; nutritive: *trophoblast.* [Greek, from *trophē,* from *trephein,* to nourish.]

tro·pho·blast (trō′fə-blăst′) *n.* The outermost layer of cells of the blastocyst that attaches the fertilized ovum to the uterine wall and serves as a nutritive pathway for the embryo. Also called *trophoderm.* **—tro′pho·blas′tic** *adj.*

tro·pho·derm (trō′fə-dûrm′) *n.* See **trophoblast.**

tro·pho·zo·ite (trō′fə-zō′īt′) *n.* A protozoan, especially of the class Sporozoa, in the active stage of its life cycle.

tro·phy (trō′fē) *n., pl.* **-phies. 1.a.** A prize or memento, such as a cup or plaque, received as a symbol of victory, especially in sports. **b.** A specimen or part, such as a lion's head, preserved as a token of a successful hunt. **c.** A memento, as of one's personal achievements. **d.** The spoils of war, dedicated in classical antiquity with an inscription to a deity and set up as a temporary monument on or near a battlefield, hung or placed in an existing temple, or housed in a permanent, new structure. **2.** *Architecture.* An ornamental marble carving or bronze casting depicting a group of weapons or armor placed upon a square or circular base. [French *trophée,* from Old French *trophee,* from Latin *trophaeum,* monument to victory, variant of *tropaeum,* from Greek *tropaion,* from neuter of *tropaios,* of defeat, from *tropē,* a turning, rout. See **trep-** in Appendix.]

–trophy *suff.* Nutrition; growth: *hypertrophy.* [Greek *-trophia,* from *trophē,* from *trephein,* to nourish.]

trop·ic (trŏp′ĭk) *n. Abbr.* **trop. 1.a.** Either of two parallels of latitude on the earth, one 23°27′ north of the equator and the other 23°27′ south of the equator, representing the points farthest north and south at which the sun can shine directly overhead and constituting the boundaries of the Torrid Zone. **b. Tropics** or **tropics.** The region of the earth's surface lying between these latitudes. **2.** *Astronomy.* Either of two corresponding parallels of celestial latitude that are the limits of the apparent northern and southern passages of the sun. **—tropic** *adj. Abbr.* **trop.** Of or relating to the Tropics; tropical. [Middle English *tropik,* from Old French *tropique,* from Late Latin *tropicus,* from Latin, of a turn, from Greek *tropikos,* from *tropē,* a turning. See **trep-** in Appendix.]

–tropic *suff.* **1.** Turning or changing in a specified way or in response to a specified stimulus: *heliotropic.* **2.** Affecting or attracted to something specified: *gonadotropic.* [From Greek *tropē,* a turning. See TROPIC.]

trop·i·cal (trŏp′ĭ-kəl) *adj. Abbr.* **trop. 1.** Of, occurring in, or characteristic of the Tropics. **2.** Hot and humid; torrid. **—tropical** *n.* A tropical plant. **—trop′i·cal·ly** *adv.*

tropical almond *n.* See **Indian almond.**

tropical cyclone *n.* A cyclone originating over tropical oceans, characterized by violent rainstorms and winds with velocities of up to 320 kilometers (200 miles) per hour.

tropical fish *n.* Any of various small, brightly colored fishes native to tropical waters and often kept in home aquariums.

tropical storm *n.* A cyclonic storm having winds ranging from approximately 48 to 121 kilometers (30 to 75 miles) per hour.

tropical year *n.* See **solar year.**

trop·ic·bird (trŏp′ĭk-bûrd′) *n.* Any of several predominantly white, swift-flying sea birds of the genus *Phaethon,* of warm regions, having small weak legs and a pair of long, slender, central tail feathers.

tropic of Cancer *n.* The parallel of latitude 23°27′ north of the equator, the northern boundary of the Torrid Zone, and the most northerly latitude at which the sun can shine directly overhead.

tropic of Capricorn *n.* The parallel of latitude 23°27′ south of the equator, the southern boundary of the Torrid Zone, and the most southerly latitude at which the sun can shine directly overhead.

tro·pine (trō′pēn′, -pĭn) also **tro·pin** (-pĭn) *n.* A white, crystalline, poisonous alkaloid, $C_8H_{15}NO$, obtained chiefly by hydrolysis of atropine. [From ATROPINE.]

tro·pism (trō′pĭz′əm) *n.* The turning or bending movement of an organism or a part toward or away from an external stimulus, such as light, heat, or gravity. [From –TROPISM.] **—tro′pic, tro·pis′tic** *adj.* **—tro·pis′ti·cal·ly** *adv.*

–tropism *suff.* Tropism: *phototropism.* [From Greek *tropē,* a turning. See –TROPIC.]

tropo– or **trop–** *pref.* **1.** Turning; change: *troposphere.* **2.** Tropism: *tropotaxis.* [Greek, from *tropē,* turn. See **trep-** in Appendix.]

tro·po·col·la·gen (trō′pə-kŏl′ə-jən, trŏp′ə-) *n.* The molecular component of a collagen fiber, consisting of three polypeptide chains coiled around each other.

tro·pol·o·gy (trō-pŏl′ə-jē) *n., pl.* **-gies. 1.** The use of tropes in speech or writing. **2.** A mode of biblical interpretation insisting on the morally edifying sense of tropes in the Scriptures. [Late Latin *tropologia,* from Late Greek : Greek *tropos,* trope; see TROPE + Greek *-logia,* -logy.] **—tro′po·log′ic** (trō′pə-lŏj′ĭk, trŏp′ə-), **tro′po·log′i·cal** (-ĭ-kəl) *adj.* **—tro′po·log′i·cal·ly** *adv.*

tro·po·my·o·sin (trō′pə-mī′ə-sĭn, trŏp′ə-) *n.* Any of a group of muscle proteins that bind to molecules of actin and troponin to regulate the interaction of actin and myosin.

tro·po·nin (trō′pə-nĭn, trŏp′ə-) *n.* A calcium-regulated protein in muscle tissue occurring in three subunits with tropomyosin. [TROPO(MYOSI)N + –IN.]

tro·po·pause (trō′pə-pôz′, trŏp′ə-) *n.* The boundary between the troposphere and the stratosphere varying in altitude from approximately 8 kilometers (5 miles) at the poles to approximately 18 kilometers (11 miles) at the equator.

tro·po·phyte (trō′pə-fīt′, trŏp′ə-) *n.* A plant adapted to climatic conditions in which periods of heavy rainfall alternate with periods of drought. **—tro′po·phyt′ic** (-fĭt′ĭk) *adj.*

tro·po·sphere (trō′pə-sfîr′, trŏp′ə-) *n.* The lowest region of the atmosphere between the earth's surface and the tropopause, characterized by decreasing temperature with increasing altitude. **—tro′po·spher′ic** (-sfîr′ĭk, -sfĕr′-) *adj.*

tro·po·tax·is (trō′pə-tăk′sĭs, trŏp′ə-) *n.* The movement or orientation of an organism in response to two stimuli, especially lights, by means of different sense organs. **—tro′po·tac′tic** (-tăk′tĭk) *adj.* **—tro′po·tac′ti·cal·ly** *adv.*

–tropous *suff.* Turning in a specified way or from a specified stimulus: *amphitropous.* [From Greek *-tropos,* of turning, from *tropos,* changeable, from *trepein,* to turn. See **trep-** in Appendix.]

–tropy *suff.* The state of turning in a specified way or from a specified stimulus: *thixotropy.* [Greek *-tropia,* from *-tropos,* -tropous.]

trot (trŏt) *n.* **1.a.** The gait of a horse or other four-footed animal, between a walk and a canter in speed, in which diagonal pairs of legs move forward together. **b.** A ride on a horse at this pace. **2.** A gait of a person, faster than a walk; a jog. **3.** *Sports.* A race for trotters. **4.** See **pony** (sense 4). **5. trots.** *Informal.* Diarrhea. Used with *the.* **6.** A toddler. **7.** *Archaic.* An old woman; a crone. **—trot** *v.* **trot·ted, trot·ting, trots.** *—intr.* **1.** To go or move at a trot. **2.** To proceed rapidly; hurry. *—tr.* To cause to move at a trot. ***—phrasal verb.*** **trot out.** *Informal.* To bring out and show for inspection or admiration: *"His novel trots out an Irish president named Finn"* (Charles E. Claffey). [Middle English, from Old French, from *troter,* to trot, of Germanic origin.]

troth (trôth, trŏth, trōth) *n.* **1.a.** Betrothal. **b.** One's pledged fidelity. **2.** Good faith; fidelity. **—troth** *tr.v.* **trothed, troth·ing, troths.** To pledge or betroth. [Middle English *trouthe, trothe,* variant of *treuthe,* from Old English *trēowth,* truth. See **deru-** in Appendix.]

troth·plight (trôth′plīt′, trŏth′-, trōth′-) *Archaic. n.* A betrothal. **—trothplight** *tr.v.* **-plight·ed, -plight·ing, -plights.** To betroth.

trot·line (trŏt′līn′) *n.* See **setline.** [Perhaps from TROT.]

Trot·sky or **Trot·ski** (trŏt′skē, trôt′-), **Leon.** 1879–1940. Russian revolutionary theoretician. A leader of the Bolshevik Revolution (1917), he was later expelled from the Communist Party (1927) and banished (1929) for his opposition to the authoritarianism of Stalin and his emphasis on world revolution. His writings include *Literature and Revolution* (1925) and *My Life* (1930). Trotsky was murdered while in exile in Mexico.

Trots·ky·ism (trŏt′skē-ĭz′əm) *n.* The political and economic theories of Communism advocated by Leon Trotsky and his followers, usually including the principle of worldwide revolution. **—Trots′ky·ist, Trots′ky·ite′** (-īt′) *n.*

trot·ter (trŏt′ər) *n.* **1.** A horse that trots, especially one trained for harness racing. **2.** *Informal.* A foot, especially the foot of a pig or sheep prepared as food.

trou·ba·dour (tro͞o′bə-dôr′, -dōr′, -do͝or′) *n.* **1.** One of a class of 12th-century and 13th-century lyric poets in Provence, northern Italy, and northern Spain, who composed songs in langue d'oc often about courtly love. **2.** A strolling minstrel. [French, from Provençal *trobador,* from Old Provençal, from *trobar,* to compose, perhaps from Vulgar Latin **tropāre,* from Late Latin *tropus,* trope, song, from Latin, trope. See TROPE.]

trou·ble (trŭb′əl) *n.* **1.** A state of distress, affliction, danger, or need: *in trouble with the police.* **2.** A cause or source of distress, disturbance, or difficulty: *One trouble after another delayed the job.* **3.** An effort, especially one that causes inconvenience or bother: *went to a lot of trouble to find this book.* **4.** A condition of pain, disease, or malfunction: *heart trouble.* **—trouble** *v.* **-led, -ling, -les.** *—tr.* **1.** To agitate; stir up. **2.** To afflict with pain or discomfort. **3.** To cause mental agitation or distress to; worry. **4.** To inconvenience; bother: *May I trouble you to close the window?* *—intr.* To take pains: *They trouble over every detail.* [Middle English, from Old French, from *troubler,* to trouble, from Vulgar Latin **turbulāre,* alteration (influenced by Latin *turbula,* small group, diminutive of *turba,* crowd) of Late Latin *turbidāre,* from Latin *turbidus,* confused. See TURBID.] **—trou′bler** *n.* **—trou′bling·ly** *adv.*

SYNONYMS: *trouble, ail, distress, worry.* The central meaning shared by these verbs is "to cause anxious uneasiness in": *suffers memory lapses that trouble her children; asked him what's ailing*

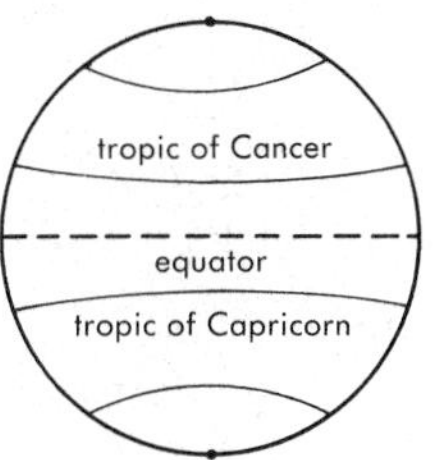

tropic

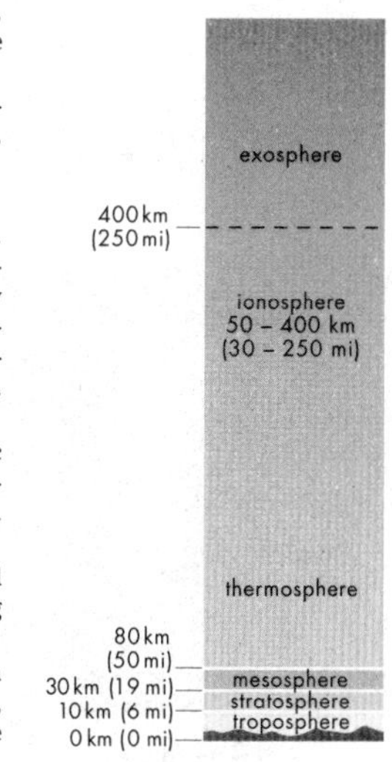

troposphere

Leon Trotsky
Photographed c. 1917

trough
Feeding trough

trowel
Top: Corner trowel
Center: Pointing trowel
Bottom: Finishing trowel

Pierre Trudeau

him; a turn of events that has distressed us; has a high fever that worries the doctor. See also Synonyms at **effort.**

---

trou·ble·mak·er (trŭb′əl-mā′kər) *n.* One that stirs up trouble or strife.

trou·ble·shoot also **trou·ble-shoot** (trŭb′əl-sho͞ot′) —*v.* **-shot** (-shŏt′), **-shoot·ing, -shoots.** —*intr.* To work or serve as a troubleshooter. —*tr.* To investigate as a troubleshooter and eliminate or settle problems with: *"cited the service it performed in trouble-shooting an employee problem"* (Vance Packard).

trou·ble·shoot·er also **trou·ble-shoot·er** (trŭb′əl-sho͞o′tər) *n.* **1.** A worker whose job is to locate and eliminate sources of trouble, as in mechanical operations. **2.** A mediator skilled in settling disputes especially of a diplomatic, political, or industrial nature.

trou·ble·some (trŭb′əl-səm) *adj.* **1.** Causing trouble or anxiety; worrisome. **2.** Difficult; trying. **—trou′ble·some·ly** *adv.* **—trou′ble·some·ness** *n.*

trouble spot *n.* A location or site of possible difficulty: *"They suggested that arms control negotiations should not be convened until Soviet behavior in the world's trouble spots improved"* (Charles William Maynes).

trou·blous (trŭb′ləs) *adj.* **1.a.** Full of trouble. **b.** Uneasy; troubled. **2.** Causing trouble; troublesome.

trough (trôf, trŏf) *n.* **1.a.** A long, narrow, generally shallow receptacle for holding water or feed for animals. **b.** Any of various similar containers for domestic or industrial use, such as kneading or washing. **2.** A gutter under the eaves of a roof. **3.** A long, narrow depression, as between waves or ridges. **4.** A low point in a business cycle or on a statistical graph. **5.** *Meteorology.* An elongated region of relatively low atmospheric pressure, often associated with a front. **6.** *Physics.* A minimum point in a wave or an alternating signal. [Middle English, from Old English *trog.* See **deru-** in Appendix.]

trounce (trouns) *v.* **trounced, trounc·ing, trounc·es.** —*tr.* **1.** To thrash; beat. **2.** To defeat decisively. —*intr.* To censure something or someone forcefully: *"I was out to trounce on every digression and indiscretion conducted (or should I say semiconducted) in this performance"* (Robert Maxwell Stern). [Origin unknown.]

troupe (tro͞op) *n.* A company or group, especially of touring actors, singers, or dancers. See Synonyms at **band**[2]. **—troupe** *intr.v.* **trouped, troup·ing, troupes.** To tour with a theatrical company. [French, troop. See TROOP.]

troup·er (tro͞o′pər) *n.* **1.** A member of a theatrical company. **2.** A veteran actor or performer. **3.** A reliable, uncomplaining, often hard-working person.

trou·pi·al (tro͞o′pē-əl) *n.* Any of several tropical American birds of the genus *Icterus,* related to the orioles and New World blackbirds, especially *I. icterus,* having orange and black plumage. [French *troupiale,* from *troupe,* flock. See TROOP.]

trou·ser also **trow·ser** (trou′zər) —*n.* An outer garment for covering the body from the waist to the ankles, divided into sections to fit each leg separately, worn especially by men and boys. Often used in the plural. —*adj.* Of, designed for, or to be found on trousers: *trouser legs; trouser cuffs.* [Back-formation from *trousers,* alteration of obsolete *trouse,* from Scottish Gaelic *triubhas.*]

trous·seau (tro͞o′sō, tro͞o-sō′) *n., pl.* **-seaux** (-sōz, -sōz′) or **-seaus.** The possessions, such as clothing and linens, that a bride assembles for her marriage. [French, from Old French, diminutive of *trousse,* bundle. See TRUSS.]

trout (trout) *n., pl.* **trout** or **trouts. 1.a.** Any of various freshwater or anadromous food and game fishes of the family Salmonidae, especially of the genera *Salmo* and *Salvelinus,* usually having a streamlined, speckled-body with small scales. **b.** Any of various similar but unrelated fishes, such as the troutperch. **2.** *Chiefly British.* An elderly woman regarded as being silly. [Middle English *troute,* from Old English *trūht,* from Late Latin *tructa,* perhaps from Greek *trōktēs,* a kind of sea fish with sharp teeth, from *trōgein,* to gnaw. See **tere-**[1] in Appendix.]

trout lily *n.* See **dogtooth violet.** [Probably from its speckled leaves.]

troutperch (trout′pûrch′) *n., pl.* **troutperch** or **-perch·es.** A small North American freshwater fish *(Percopsis omiscomaycus)* having a translucent body, an adipose fin, and fine saw-toothed edges on its scales.

trou·vère (tro͞o-vâr′) also **trou·veur** (-vûr′, -vœr′) *n.* One of a class of poet-musicians flourishing in northern France in the 12th and 13th centuries, who composed chiefly narrative works, such as the chansons de geste, in langue d'oïl. [French, from Old French *trovere,* from *trover,* to compose, from Vulgar Latin **tropāre.* See TROUBADOUR.]

Trou·ville (tro͞o-vēl′) or **Trou·ville-sur-Mer** (-so͞or-mĕr′, -sür-). A town of northwest France on the English Channel south of Le Havre. It is a popular resort. Population, 6,008.

trove (trōv) *n.* A collection of valuable items discovered or found; a treasure-trove. [Short for (TREASURE-)TROVE.]

tro·ver (trō′vər) *n. Law.* A common-law action to recover damages for property illegally withheld or wrongfully converted to use by another. [From Anglo-Norman, to compose, invent, find, probably from Vulgar Latin **tropāre.* See TROUBADOUR.]

trow (trō) *intr.v.* **trowed, trow·ing, trows. 1.** *Archaic.* To think. **2.** *Obsolete.* To suppose. [Middle English *trowen,* from Old English *trēowian,* to trust. See **deru-** in Appendix.]

trow·el (trou′əl) *n.* **1.** A flat-bladed hand tool for leveling, spreading, or shaping substances such as cement or mortar. **2.** A small implement with a pointed, scoop-shaped blade used for digging, as in setting plants. **—trowel** *tr.v.* **-eled, -el·ing, -els** or **-elled, -el·ling, -els.** To spread, smooth, form, or scoop with a trowel. [Middle English *trowell,* from Old French *truele,* from Late Latin *truella,* diminutive of Latin *trua,* ladle.] **—trow′el·er, trow′el·ler** *n.*

trow·ser (trou′zər) *n.* Variant of **trouser.**

troy (troi) *adj. Abbr.* **t** Of or expressed in troy weight. [Middle English *troye,* after TROYES.]

Troy (troi). **1.** Also **Il·i·on** (ĭl′ē-ən, -ŏn′) or **Il·i·um** (-ē-əm). An ancient city of northwest Asia Minor near the Dardanelles River. Originally a Phrygian city dating from the Bronze Age, it is the legendary site of the Trojan War and was captured and destroyed by Greek forces c. 1200 B.C. The ruins of Troy were discovered by Heinrich Schliemann in 1871. **2.** A city of southeast Michigan, a residential and industrial suburb of Detroit. Population, 67,102. **3.** A city of eastern New York on the Hudson River northeast of Albany. Settled in the 1780's, it is a manufacturing center with a clothing industry. Population, 56,638. **4.** A city of west-central Ohio north of Dayton. It is a processing center. Population, 19,086.

Troyes (trwä). A city of northeast France on the Seine River east-southeast of Paris. A pre-Roman town, it was a prosperous commercial center in the Middle Ages and was noted for its annual fairs, which set standards of weights and measures for all of Europe. Population, 63,581.

troy weight *n.* A system of units of weight in which the grain is the same as in the avoirdupois system and the pound contains 12 ounces, 240 pennyweights, or 5,760 grains.

trp. *abbr.* Troop.

tru·an·cy (tro͞o′ən-sē) also **tru·ant·ry** (-ən-trē) *n., pl.* **-cies** also **-ries.** The act or condition of being absent without permission.

tru·ant (tro͞o′ənt) *n.* **1.** One who is absent without permission, especially from school. **2.** One who shirks work or duty. **—truant** *adj.* **1.** Absent without permission, especially from school. **2.** Idle, lazy, or neglectful. **—truant** *intr.v.* **-ant·ed, -ant·ing, -ants.** To be truant. [Middle English, beggar, from Old French. See **tere-**[1] in Appendix.]

truant officer *n.* An official who investigates unauthorized absences from school.

tru·ant·ry (tro͞o′ən-trē) *n.* Variant of **truancy.**

truce (tro͞os) *n.* **1.** A temporary cessation or suspension of hostilities by agreement of the opposing sides; an armistice. **2.** A respite from a disagreeable state of affairs. **—truce** *tr. & intr.v.* **truced, truc·ing, truc·es.** To end or be ended with a truce. [Middle English *trewes,* pl. of *trewe,* treaty, pledge, from Old English *trēow.* See **deru-** in Appendix.]

Tru·chas Peaks (tro͞o′chəs). Three mountains in northern New Mexico northeast of Santa Fe, rising to 3,998.6 m (13,110 ft) at **North Truchas Peak.**

Tru·cial O·man (tro͞o′shəl ō-män′). See **United Arab Emirates.**

truck[1] (trŭk) *n. Abbr.* **tk. 1.** Any of various heavy motor vehicles designed for carrying or pulling loads. **2.** A two-wheeled barrow for moving heavy objects by hand. **3.** A wheeled platform, sometimes equipped with a motor, for conveying loads in a warehouse or freight yard. **4.** One of the swiveling frames of wheels under each end of a railroad car or trolley car. **5.** A set of bookshelves mounted on four wheels or casters, used in libraries. **6.** *Nautical.* A small piece of wood placed at the top of a mast or flagpole, usually having holes through which halyards can be passed. **7.** *Chiefly British.* A railroad freight car without a top. —*attributive.* Often used to modify another noun: *truck drivers; truck transport.* **—truck** *v.* **trucked, truck·ing, trucks.** —*tr.* To transport by truck. —*intr.* **1.** To carry goods by truck. **2.** To drive a truck. **3.** *Slang.* To move or travel in a steady but easy manner. [Short for TRUCKLE, or from Latin *trochus,* iron hoop (from Greek *trokhos,* wheel).]

truck[2] (trŭk) *v.* **trucked, truck·ing, trucks.** —*tr.* **1.** To exchange; barter. **2.** To peddle. —*intr.* To have dealings or commerce; traffic. **—truck** *n.* **1.** Articles of commerce; trade goods. **2.** Garden produce raised for the market. **3.** *Informal.* Worthless goods; stuff or rubbish. *"Look at your hands. And look at your mouth. What is that truck?"* (Mark Twain). **4.** Barter; exchange. **5.** *Informal.* Dealings; business: *We'll have no further truck with them.* [Middle English *trukien,* from Old North French *troquer.*]

truck·age (trŭk′ĭj) *n.* **1.** Transportation of goods by truck. **2.** A charge for transportation by truck.

Truck·ee (trŭk′ē). A river, about 193 km (120 mi) long, rising in eastern California and flowing east and northeast into northwest Nevada.

truck·er (trŭk′ər) *n.* **1.** One who drives a truck. **2.** One that is engaged in trucking goods.

truck farm *n.* A farm producing vegetables for the market. [From TRUCK[2].] **—truck farmer** *n.* **—truck farm′ing** *n.*

truck·le (trŭk′əl) *n.* A small wheel or roller; a caster. **—truckle** *intr.v.* **-led, -ling, -les.** To be servile or submissive. See Synonyms at **fawn**[1]. [Middle English *trocle,* pulley, from Anglo-

Norman, from Latin *trochlea,* system of pulleys. See TROCHLEA.] **—truck′ler** *n.*

truckle bed *n.* A trundle bed.

truck·load (trŭk′lōd′) *n.* The quantity that a truck can hold.

truck stop *n.* An establishment that sells fuel for trucks and usually maintains a restaurant for truck drivers.

truc·u·lence (trŭk′yə-ləns) also **truc·u·len·cy** (-lən-sē) *n.* **1.** A disposition or apparent disposition to fight, especially fiercely. **2.** Ferociously cruel actions or behavior.

truc·u·lent (trŭk′yə-lənt) *adj.* **1.** Disposed to fight; pugnacious. **2.** Expressing bitter opposition; scathing: *a truculent speech against the new government.* **3.** Disposed to or exhibiting violence or destructiveness; fierce. [Latin *truculentus,* from *trux, truc-,* fierce. See **terə-**[2] in Appendix.] **—truc′u·lent·ly** *adv.*

Tru·deau (tro͞o-dō′, tro͞o′dō′), **Pierre Elliott.** Born 1919. Canadian prime minister (1968–1979 and 1980–1984) whose administration was marked by efforts to contain the French separatist movement in Quebec and by the Constitution Act of 1982, which granted Canada full independence.

trudge (trŭj) *intr.v.* **trudged, trudg·ing, trudg·es.** To walk in a laborious, heavy-footed way; plod. **—trudge** *n.* A long, tedious walk. [Origin unknown.] **—trudg′er** *n.*

trudg·en also **trudg·eon** (trŭj′ən) *n. Sports.* A swimming stroke in which an alternating overarm movement is combined with a scissors kick. [After John *Trudgen* (1852–1902), British swimmer.]

true (tro͞o) *adj.* **tru·er, tru·est. 1.a.** Consistent with fact or reality; not false or erroneous. See Synonyms at **real**[1]. See Usage Note at **fact. b.** Truthful. **2.** Real; genuine. See Synonyms at **authentic. 3.** Reliable; accurate: *a true prophecy.* **4.** Faithful, as to a friend, vow, or cause; loyal. See Synonyms at **faithful. 5.** Sincerely felt or expressed; unfeigned: *true grief.* **6.** Fundamental; essential: *his true motive.* **7.** Rightful; legitimate: *the true heir.* **8.** Exactly conforming to a rule, standard, or pattern: *trying to sing true B.* **9.** Accurately shaped or fitted: *a true wheel.* **10.** Accurately placed, delivered, or thrown. **11.** Quick and exact in sensing and responding. **12.** Determined with reference to the earth's axis, not the magnetic poles: *true north.* **13.** Conforming to the definitive criteria of a natural group; typical: *The horseshoe crab is not a true crab.* **14.** Narrowly particularized; highly specific: *spoke of probity in the truest sense of the word.* **—true** *adv.* **1.** In accord with reality, fact, or truthfulness. **2.** Unswervingly; exactly: *The archer aimed true.* **3.** So as to conform to a type, standard, or pattern. **—true** *tr.v.* **trued, tru·ing** or **true·ing, trues.** To position (something) so as to make it balanced, level, or square: *trued up the long planks.* **—true** *n.* **1.** Truth or reality. Used with *the.* **2.** Proper alignment or adjustment: *out of true.* [Middle English *trewe,* from Old English *trēowe,* firm, trustworthy. See **deru-** in Appendix.] **—true′ness** *n.*

true believer *n.* One who is deeply, sometimes fanatically devoted to a cause, an organization, or a person: *"a band of true believers bonded together against all those who did not agree with them"* (Theodore Draper).

true bill *n. Law.* A bill of indictment endorsed by a grand jury.

true-blue (tro͞o′blo͞o′) *adj.* Loyal or faithful; staunch. [From the adoption of the color blue by 17th-century Scottish Presbyterians in opposition to the Royalists' red.]

true·born (tro͞o′bôrn′) *adj.* Being authentically or genuinely such by birth.

true bug *n.* A wingless or four-winged insect of the order Hemiptera, especially of the suborder Heteroptera, including the bedbug, louse, and chinch bug, having mouthparts adapted for piercing and sucking.

true-false test (tro͞o′fôls′) *n.* A test in which statements are to be marked either true or false.

true-life (tro͞o′līf′) *adj.* Presenting conditions and especially human relationships accurately; true to life: *a true-life romance.*

true·love (tro͞o′lŭv′) *n.* One's beloved; a sweetheart.

true lovers' knot *n.* See **love knot.**

true·pen·ny (tro͞o′pĕn′ē) *n., pl.* **-nies.** An honest, trustworthy person.

true rhyme *n.* See **perfect rhyme** (sense 1).

true rib *n.* Any of the ribs that are attached to the sternum by a costal cartilage, especially any of the seven upper ribs on either side of the thorax in human beings.

true seal *n.* See **earless seal.**

Truf·faut (tro͞o-fō′), **François.** 1932–1984. French New Wave filmmaker whose works include *The 400 Blows* (1959) and *Jules and Jim* (1961).

truf·fle (trŭf′əl) *n.* **1.** Any of various fleshy, ascomycetous, edible fungi, chiefly of the genus *Tuber,* that grow underground on or near the roots of trees and are valued as a delicacy. **2.** Any of various chocolate confections, especially one made of a mixture including chopped nuts, rolled into balls and covered with cocoa powder. [Alteration of French *trufe,* from Old French, from Old Provençal *trufa,* from Vulgar Latin **tūfera,* truffles, from dialectal variant of Latin *tūber,* lump. See **teuə-** in Appendix.]

tru·ism (tro͞o′ĭz′əm) *n.* A self-evident truth. See Synonyms at **cliché. —tru·is′tic** (tro͞o-ĭs′tĭk) *adj.*

Tru·ji·llo (tro͞o-hē′ō, -yō). A city of northwest Peru northwest of Lima. Founded in 1534, it was provisional capital of Peru in 1825 and is now a processing center. Population, 202,469.

Trujillo Mo·li·na (mō-lē′nə, -nä), **Rafael Leónidas.** 1891–1961. Dominican soldier and dictator who ran unopposed for president in 1930 and controlled the country until his assassination in 1961.

Truk Islands (trŭk, tro͝ok). An island group of the western Pacific Ocean in the central Caroline Islands. Site of a major Japanese naval base in World War II, the islands are part of the U.S. Trust Territory of the Pacific Islands.

trull (trŭl) *n.* A prostitute; a harlot. [Perhaps from German *Trulle,* from Middle High German *trulle;* akin to Old Norse, creature, troll.]

tru·ly (tro͞o′lē) *adv.* **1.** Sincerely; genuinely: *We are truly sorry for the inconvenience.* **2.** Truthfully; accurately: *reported the matter truly.* **3.** Indeed: *truly ugly.* **4.** Properly: *not truly civilized.*

Tru·man (tro͞o′mən), **Elizabeth.** Known as "Bess." 1885–1982. First Lady of the United States (1945–1953) as the wife of President Harry S. Truman. She was a valued adviser to her husband.

Bess Truman
Photographed in 1948

Truman, Harry S. 1884–1972. The 33rd President of the United States (1945–1953). He authorized the use of the atomic bomb against Japan (1945), implemented the Marshall Plan (1948), initiated the establishment of NATO (1949), and ordered U.S. involvement in the Korean War (1950–1953).

Harry S. Truman
Photographed c. 1945

Trum·bo (trŭm′bō), **Dalton.** 1905–1976. American screenwriter who was blacklisted and imprisoned for his refusal to participate in the anti-Communist investigations of the House Un-American Activities Committee. His screenplays include *Spartacus* (1960) and *The Fixer* (1968).

Trum·bull (trŭm′bəl). A town of southwest Connecticut north of Bridgeport. It is a residential community with varied industries. Population, 32,989.

Trumbull[1], **John.** 1750–1831. American poet noted for his satirical works, including *The Progress of Dulness* (1772–1773).

Trumbull[2], **John.** 1756–1843. American painter of historical scenes, such as *The Battle of Bunker's Hill* (1786) and *The Declaration of Independence* (1786–1797).

Trumbull, Jonathan. 1710–1785. American politician. As governor of Connecticut (1769–1784) he provided supplies and support for the Continental Army during the American Revolution.

trump[1] (trŭmp) *n.* **1.** *Games.* **a.** *Often* **trumps.** A suit in card games that outranks all other suits for the duration of a hand. **b.** A card of such a suit. **c.** A trump card. **2.** A key resource to be used at an opportune moment. **3.** *Informal.* A reliable or admirable person. **—trump** *v.* **trumped, trump·ing, trumps.** *—tr.* **1.** *Games.* To take (a card or trick) with a trump. **2.** To get the better of (an adversary or a competitor, for example) by using a key, often hidden resource. *—intr. Games.* To play a trump. ***—phrasal verb.* trump up.** To devise fraudulently: *trumped up a charge of conspiracy.* [Alteration of TRIUMPH.]

WORD HISTORY: The history of the word *trump* gives meaning to this seemingly nonsensical word and also relates to the history of the game of bridge. *Trump* is an alteration of the word *triumph* used in special senses that are now obsolete. These senses, first recorded in a sermon of 1529 by the English prelate Hugh Latimer, are "a card game" and "trump" as it is used in card games. In the same 1529 text one may find the first instances of *trump,* used in the same two senses as *triumph.* From *trump* and other games came the card game whist, which in turn developed into bridge. The term *trump* survived even though the game of trump did not.

trump[2] (trŭmp) *n. Music.* A trumpet. [Middle English *trompe,* from Old French. See TRUMPET.]

trumpet

trump card *n.* **1.** *Games.* A card in the trump suit, held in reserve for winning a trick. **2.** A key resource to be used at the opportune moment; a trump: "[They] *seem determined to use the agreement as a trump card to obtain . . . all the advantages they feel they deserve"* (Christian Science Monitor).

trump·er·y (trŭm′pə-rē) *n., pl.* **-ies. 1.** Showy but worthless finery; bric-a-brac. **2.** Nonsense; rubbish. **3.** Deception; trickery; fraud. [Middle English *trompery,* deceit, from Old French *tromperie,* from *tromper,* to deceive.]

trum·pet (trŭm′pĭt) *n.* **1.a.** *Music.* A soprano brass wind instrument consisting of a long metal tube looped once and ending in a flared bell, the modern type being equipped with three valves for producing variations in pitch. **b.** Something shaped or sounding like this instrument. **2.** *Music.* An organ stop that produces a tone like that of the brass wind instrument. **3.** A resounding call, as that of the elephant. **—trumpet** *v.* **-pet·ed, -pet·ing, -pets.** *—intr.* **1.** *Music.* To play a trumpet. **2.** To give forth a resounding call. *—tr.* To sound or proclaim loudly. [Middle English *trumpette,* from Old French *trompette,* diminutive of *trompe,* horn, from Old High German *trumpa.*]

trumpet creeper *n.* A deciduous woody vine *(Campsis radicans)* of the eastern United States, having opposite compound leaves and trumpet-shaped reddish-orange flowers. Also called *trumpet vine.*

trum·pet·er (trŭm′pĭ-tər) *n.* **1.** *Music.* One who plays the trumpet. **2.** One who announces something, as a herald. **3.** Any of several large cranelike birds of the genus *Psophia* of tropical South America, having a loud resonant call. **4.a.** The trumpeter swan. **b.** A variety of domestic pigeon having a shell-shaped crest and heavily feathered feet.

ă pat	oi boy
ā pay	ou out
âr care	o͝o took
ä father	o͞o boot
ĕ pet	ŭ cut
ē be	ûr urge
ĭ pit	th thin
ī pie	*th* this
îr pier	hw which
ŏ pot	zh vision
ō toe	ə about, item
ô paw	♦ regionalism

Stress marks: ′ (primary); ′ (secondary), as in **dictionary** (dĭk′shə-nĕr′ē)

trundle bed
Pulled out from underneath a canopied bed

truss bridge

Sojourner Truth
Photographed c. 1870

trumpeter swan *n.* A large white swan *(Olor buccinator)* of western North America, having a loud buglelike call.

trumpet honeysuckle *n.* A vine *(Lonicera sempervirens)* of the eastern United States, having tubular reddish flowers.

trumpet vine *n.* See **trumpet creeper.**

trun·cate (trŭng′kāt′) *tr.v.* **-cat·ed, -cat·ing, -cates. 1.** To shorten by or as if by cutting off. See Synonyms at **shorten. 2.** To shorten (a number) by dropping one or more digits after the decimal point. **3.** To replace (the edge of a crystal) with a plane face. **—truncate** *adj.* **1.** Appearing to terminate abruptly, as a leaf of a tulip tree or a coiled gastropod shell that lacks a spire. **2.** Truncated. [Latin *truncāre, truncāt-,* from *truncus,* trunk. See **tere-**[2] in Appendix.] **—trun′cate′ly** *adv.* **—trun·ca′tion** *n.*

trun·ca·ted (trŭng′kā′tĭd) *adj.* **1.** Having the apex cut off and replaced by a plane, especially one parallel to the base. Used of a cone or pyramid. **2.a.** Lacking one or more syllables, especially in the final foot; catalectic. **b.** Lacking an initial or final syllable. Used of a line of verse. **3.** Truncate.

trun·cheon (trŭn′chən) *n.* **1.** A short stick carried by police; a billy club. **2.** A staff carried as a symbol of office or authority; a baton. **3.** *Obsolete.* **a.** A heavy club; a cudgel. **b.** A thick cutting from a plant, as for grafting. [Middle English *tronchon,* piece broken off, club, from Old North French, from Vulgar Latin **trunciō, trunciōn-,* from Latin *truncus,* trunk. See TRUNK.] **—trun′cheon** *v.*

trun·dle (trŭn′dl) *n.* **1.** A small wheel or roller. **2.** The motion or noise of rolling. **3.** A trundle bed. **4.** A low-wheeled cart; a dolly. **—trundle** *v.* **-dled, -dling, -dles.** *—tr.* **1.** To push or propel on wheels or rollers: *"I doubt if Emerson could trundle a wheelbarrow through the streets"* (Henry David Thoreau). **2.** To spin; twirl. *—intr.* To move along by or as if by rolling or spinning. [Variant of dialectal *trendle,* wheel, from Middle English, from Old English *trendel,* circle.] **—trun′dler** *n.*

trundle bed *n.* A low bed on casters that can be rolled under another bed for storage.

trunk (trŭngk) *n.* **1.a.** The main woody axis of a tree. **b.** *Architecture.* The shaft of a column. **2.a.** The body of a human being or an animal excluding the head and limbs. **b.** The thorax of an insect. **3.** A proboscis, especially the long prehensile proboscis of an elephant. **4.a.** A main body, apart from tributaries or appendages. **b.** The main stem of a blood vessel or nerve apart from the branches. **5.** A trunk line. **6.** A chute or conduit. **7.** *Nautical.* **a.** A shaft connecting two or more decks. **b.** The housing for the centerboard of a vessel. **8.** *Nautical.* **a.** Any of certain structures projecting above part of a main deck, as: **b.** A covering over the hatches of a ship. **c.** An expansion chamber on a tanker. **d.** A cabin on a small boat. **9.a.** A covered compartment for luggage and storage, generally at the rear of an automobile. **b.** A large packing case or box that clasps shut, used as luggage or for storage. **10. trunks.** Shorts worn for swimming or other athletics. [Middle English *trunke,* from Old French *tronc,* from Latin *truncus.* See **tere-**[2] in Appendix.]

trunk·fish (trŭngk′fĭsh′) *n., pl.* **trunkfish** or **-fish·es.** Any of various colorful tropical marine fishes of the family Ostraciidae, having a body enclosed in bony armorlike plates with only the mouth, eyes, fins, and vent exposed. Also called *boxfish.*

trunk hose *pl.n.* Short, ballooning breeches, extending from the waist to midthigh, worn by men in Europe in the 16th and 17th centuries. [Perhaps from obsolete *trunk,* to cut off, from Latin *truncāre.* See TRUNCATE.]

trunk line *n.* **1.** A direct line between two telephone switchboards. **2.** The main line of a communications or transportation system.

trunk show *n.* A traveling collection of designer clothing or jewelry, displayed in various stores.

trun·nel (trŭn′əl) *n.* Variant of **treenail.**

trun·nion (trŭn′yən) *n.* A pin or gudgeon, especially either of two small cylindrical projections on a cannon forming an axis on which it pivots. [French *trognon,* stump.]

truss (trŭs) *n.* **1.** *Medicine.* A supportive device, usually consisting of a pad with a belt, worn to prevent enlargement of a hernia or the return of a reduced hernia. **2.a.** A rigid framework, as of wooden beams or metal bars, designed to support a structure, such as a roof. **b.** *Architecture.* A bracket. **3.** Something gathered into a bundle; a pack. **4.** *Nautical.* An iron fitting by which a lower yard is secured to a mast. **5.** *Botany.* A compact cluster of flowers at the end of a stalk. **—truss** *tr.v.* **trussed, truss·ing, truss·es. 1.** To tie up or bind tightly. **2.** To bind or skewer the wings or legs of (a fowl) before cooking. **3.** To support or brace with a truss. [Middle English *trusse,* bundle, from Old French *trousse,* from *torser, trousser,* to truss, possibly from Vulgar Latin **torsāre,* from **torsus,* variant of Latin *tortus,* past participle of *torquēre,* to twist. See **terkʷ-** in Appendix.]

truss bridge *n.* A bridge supported by trusses.

trust (trŭst) *n.* **1.** Firm reliance on the integrity, ability, or character of a person or thing. **2.** Custody; care. **3.** Something committed into the care of another; charge. **4.a.** The condition and resulting obligation of having confidence placed in one: *violated a public trust.* **b.** One in which confidence is placed. **5.** Reliance on something in the future; hope. **6.** Reliance on the intention and ability of a purchaser to pay in the future; credit. **7.** *Abbr.* **tr.** *Law.* **a.** A legal title to property held by one party for the benefit of another. **b.** The confidence reposed in a trustee when giving the trustee legal title to property to administer for another, together with the trustee's obligation regarding that property and the beneficiary. **c.** The property so held. **8.** A combination of firms or corporations for the purpose of reducing competition and controlling prices throughout a business or an industry. **—trust** *v.* **trust·ed, trust·ing, trusts.** *—intr.* **1.** To have or place reliance; depend: *Trust in the Lord. Trust to destiny.* **2.** To be confident; hope. **3.** To sell on credit. *—tr.* **1.** To have or place confidence in; depend on. **2.** To expect with assurance; assume: *I trust that you will be on time.* **3.** To believe: *I trust what you say.* **4.** To place in the care of another; entrust. **5.** To grant discretion to confidently: *Can I trust them with the boat?* **6.** To extend credit to. ***—idiom.* in trust.** In the possession or care of a trustee. [Middle English *truste,* perhaps from Old Norse *traust,* confidence. See **deru-** in Appendix.] **—trust′er** *n.*

SYNONYMS: *trust, faith, confidence, reliance, dependence.* These nouns denote a feeling of certainty that a person or thing will not fail. *Trust* implies depth and assurance of feeling that is often based on inconclusive evidence: *The new President said he would try to justify the trust the electorate had placed in him. Faith* connotes unquestioning, often emotionally charged belief: *"Faith and knowledge lean largely upon each other in the practice of medicine"* (Peter M. Latham). *"Often enough our faith beforehand in an uncertified result is the only thing that makes the result come true"* (William James). *Confidence,* which suggests less emotional intensity, frequently implies stronger grounds for assurance: *"Confidence is a plant of slow growth in an aged bosom: youth is the season of credulity"* (William Pitt). *Reliance* connotes a confident and trustful commitment to another: *"What reliance could they place on the protection of a prince so recently their enemy?"* (William Hickling Prescott). *Dependence* suggests reliance on the help or support of another to whom one is often subordinate: *"I fared like a distressed Prince who calls in a powerful Neighbor to his Aid . . . when I had once called him in, I could not subsist without Dependence on him"* (Richard Steele). See also Synonyms at **care, rely.**

trust·bust·er (trŭst′bŭs′tər) *n. Informal.* One that seeks to prosecute or dissolve business trusts. **—trust′bust′ing** *adj. & n.*

trust company *n.* A commercial bank or other corporation that manages trusts.

trus·tee (trŭ-stē′) *n.* **1.** *Abbr.* **tr.** *Law.* One, such as a bank, that holds legal title to property in order to administer it for a beneficiary. **2.** A member of a board elected or appointed to direct the funds and policy of an institution. **3.** A country responsible for supervising a trust territory. See Usage Note at **-ee**[1]. **—trustee** *tr. & intr.v.* **-teed, -tee·ing, -tees.** To place (property) in the care of a trustee or to function or serve as a trustee.

trus·tee·ship (trŭ-stē′shĭp′) *n.* **1.** The position or function of a trustee. **2.a.** Administration of a territory by a country or countries so commissioned by the United Nations. **b.** See **trust territory.**

trust·ful (trŭst′fəl) *adj.* Inclined to believe or confide readily; full of trust. **—trust′ful·ly** *adv.* **—trust′ful·ness** *n.*

trust fund *n.* Property, especially money and securities, held or settled in trust.

trust territory *n. Abbr.* **TT** A colony or territory placed under the administration of a country or countries by commission of the United Nations. Also called *trusteeship.*

trust·wor·thy (trŭst′wûr′thē) *adj.* **-thi·er, -thi·est.** Warranting trust; reliable. See Synonyms at **reliable. —trust′wor′thi·ly** *adv.* **—trust′wor′thi·ness** *n.*

trust·y (trŭs′tē) *adj.* **-i·er, -i·est.** Meriting trust; trustworthy. See Synonyms at **reliable. —trusty** *n., pl.* **-ies. 1.** A convict regarded as worthy of trust and therefore granted special privileges. **2.** A trusted person. **—trust′i·ly** *adv.* **—trust′i·ness** *n.*

truth (tro͞oth) *n., pl.* **truths** (tro͞o*th*z, tro͞oths). **1.** Conformity to fact or actuality. **2.** A statement proven to be or accepted as true. **3.** Sincerity; integrity. **4.** Fidelity to an original or a standard. **5.** Reality; actuality. **6. Truth.** *Christian Science.* God. [Middle English *trewthe,* loyalty, from Old English *trēowth.* See **deru-** in Appendix.]

SYNONYMS: *truth, veracity, verity, verisimilitude.* These nouns refer to the quality of being in accord with fact or reality. *Truth* is a comprehensive term that in all of its nuances implies accuracy and honesty: *"Every man is fully satisfied that there is such a thing as truth, or he would not ask any questions"* (Charles S. Peirce). *"We seek the truth, and will endure the consequences"* (Charles Seymour). *Veracity* is adherence to the truth: *"Veracity is the heart of morality"* (Thomas H. Huxley). *Verity* often applies to an enduring or repeatedly demonstrated truth: *"beliefs that were accepted as eternal verities"* (James Harvey Robinson). *Verisimilitude* is the quality of having the appearance of truth or reality: *"merely corroborative detail, intended to give artistic verisimilitude to an otherwise bald and unconvincing narrative"* (W.S. Gilbert).

Truth, Sojourner. 1797?–1883. American abolitionist and feminist. Born into slavery, she was freed in 1827 and became a leading preacher against slavery and for the rights of women.

truth·ful (tro͞oth′fəl) *adj.* **1.** Consistently telling the truth; honest. **2.** Corresponding to reality; true. **—truth′ful·ly** *adv.* **—truth′ful·ness** *n.*

truth quark *n.* See **top quark.**

truth serum *n.* Any of various hypnotic or anesthetic drugs, such as scopolamine or thiopental sodium, used to induce a subject under questioning to talk without inhibition.

truth table *n. Logic.* A table that displays the truth-value of a compound sentence as a function of the varying truth-values of its components.

truth-val·ue (tro͞oth′văl′yo͞o) *n. Logic.* The truth or falsity of a statement or sentence.

try (trī) *v.* **tried** (trīd), **try·ing, tries** (trīz). —*tr.* **1.** To make an effort to do or accomplish (something); attempt: *tried to ski.* **2.** To taste, sample, or otherwise test in order to determine strength, effect, worth, or desirability: *Try this casserole. Try the door.* **3.** *Law.* **a.** To examine or hear (evidence or a case) by judicial process. **b.** To put (an accused person) on trial. **4.** To subject to great strain or hardship; tax: *The last steep ascent tried my every muscle.* **5.** To melt (lard, for example) to separate out impurities; render. **6.** To smooth, fit, or align accurately. —*intr.* To make an effort; strive. —**try** *n., pl.* **tries** (trīz). An attempt; an effort. —***phrasal verbs.* try on. 1.** To don (a garment) to test its fit. **2.** To test or use experimentally. **try out. 1.** To undergo a competitive qualifying test, as for a job or athletic team. **2.** To test or use experimentally. —***idiom.* try (one's) hand.** To attempt to do something for the first time: *I tried my hand at skiing.* [Middle English *trien,* from Old French *trier,* to pick out, from Vulgar Latin **triāre.*]

USAGE NOTE: The phrase *try and* is commonly used as a substitute for *try to,* as in *Could you try and make less noise?* A number of grammarians have labeled the construction incorrect. To be sure, associated with informal style, the usage strikes an inappropriately conversational note in formal writing. In the most recent survey 65 percent of the Usage Panel rejected the use in writing of the sentence *Why don't you try and see if you can work the problem out between yourselves?* See Usage Note at **and.**

try·ing (trī′ĭng) *adj.* Causing strain, hardship, or distress. —**try′ing·ly** *adv.*

try·out (trī′out′) *n.* **1.** A test to ascertain the qualifications of applicants, as for an athletic team or for a theatrical role. **2.** An experimental performance of a play before its official opening.

try·pan·o·some (trĭ-păn′ə-sōm′) *n.* Any of various parasitic flagellate protozoans of the genus *Trypanosoma,* transmitted to the vertebrate bloodstream, lymph, and spinal fluid by certain insects and often causing diseases such as sleeping sickness and nagana. [From New Latin *Trypanosoma,* genus name : Greek *trupanon,* auger (from *trupan,* to bore, from *trupē,* hole; see **terə-**[1] in Appendix) + Greek *sōma,* body; see –SOME[3].] —**try·pan′o·so′mal, try·pan′o·som′ic** (-sŏm′ĭk).

try·pan·o·so·mi·a·sis (trĭ-păn′ə-sō-mī′ə-sĭs) *n., pl.* **-ses** (-sēz′). A disease or an infection caused by a trypanosome.

try·pars·a·mide (trĭ-pär′sə-mīd′) *n.* A white crystalline powder, $C_8H_{10}AsN_2NaO_4$, used in the treatment of trypanosomiasis. [TRYP(ANOSOME) + ARS(ENIC) + AMIDE.]

tryp·sin (trĭp′sĭn) *n.* An enzyme of pancreatic juice that hydrolyzes proteins to form smaller polypeptide units. [Perhaps Greek *tripsis,* a rubbing (from its having been first obtained by rubbing a pancreas with glycerin), from *tribein,* to rub see **terə-**[1] in Appendix + –IN.] —**tryp′tic** (-tĭk) *adj.*

tryp·sin·o·gen (trĭp-sĭn′ə-jən) *n.* The inactive precursor of trypsin, produced by the pancreas and converted to trypsin in the small intestine by enterokinase.

tryp·ta·mine (trĭp′tə-mēn′) *n.* A crystalline substance, $C_{10}H_{12}N_2$, that is formed in plant and animal tissues from tryptophan and is an intermediate in various metabolic processes. [TRYPT(OPHAN) + AMINE.]

tryp·to·phan (trĭp′tə-făn′) also **tryp·to·phane** (-fān′) *n.* An essential amino acid, $C_{11}H_{12}N_2O_2$, formed from proteins during the digestive process by the action of proteolytic enzymes. [*tryptic,* of trypsin; see TRYPSIN + –PHAN(E).]

try·sail (trī′səl, -sāl′) *n. Nautical.* A small fore-and-aft sail hoisted abaft the foremast and mainmast in a storm to keep a ship's bow to the wind. [From obsolete *try,* a lying to, heaving to.]

try square *n.* A carpenter's tool consisting of a ruled metal straightedge set at right angles to a straight piece, used for measuring and marking square work.

tryst (trĭst) *n.* **1.** An agreement, as between lovers, to meet at a certain time and place. **2.** A meeting or meeting place that has been agreed on. See Synonyms at **engagement.** —**tryst** *intr.v.* **tryst·ed, tryst·ing, trysts.** To keep a tryst. [Middle English *trist,* from Old French *triste,* a waiting place (in hunting). See **deru-** in Appendix.] —**tryst′er** *n.*

T.S. or **t.s.** *abbr.* Tensile strength.

tsa·de (tsä′də, -dē) *n.* Variant of **sadhe.**

Tsa·na (tsä′nə, -nä), **Lake.** See Lake **Tana.**

tsar (zär, tsär) *n.* Variant of **czar** (sense 1). See Usage Note at **czar.**

tsats·ke (tsäts′kə) *n.* Variant of **chachka.**

Tse·lin·o·grad (tsə-lĭn′ə-grăd′, tsĭ-lyĭ-nə-grät′). A city of north-central Kazakhstan north-northwest of Karaganda. It is a railroad junction in a mining region. Population, 262,000.

tset·se disease (tsĕt′sē, tsē′tsē) *n.* See **nagana.**

tsetse fly also **tzet·ze fly** (tsĕt′sē, tsē′tsē) *n.* Any of several two-winged bloodsucking African flies of the genus *Glossina,* often carrying and transmitting pathogenic trypanosomes to human beings and livestock. [Afrikaans, from Sotho (Setswana) *tsêtsê.*]

WORD HISTORY: By its spelling a word such as *tsetse* proclaims that it has not passed into English by the usual channels. We must look to Africa, the home of the more than 20 species of fly known by the term *tsetse,* for its source. The word comes into English from Setswana, a language spoken by the Tswana people, who live in Botswana and western South Africa. The term passed from Setswana into Afrikaans and from there into English, being first recorded in 1849. The first instance of the word in English refers to the death of horses and oxen caused by this insect, which transmits diseases to human beings and animals. The first instance of the compound *tsetse fly* is found in 1865.

T.Sgt. *abbr.* Technical sergeant.

TSH *abbr.* Thyroid-stimulating hormone.

Tshi·lu·ba (chĭ-lo͞o′bə) *n.* See **Luba** (sense 2).

T-shirt also **tee shirt** (tē′shûrt′) *n.* **1.** A short-sleeved, collarless undershirt. **2.** An outer shirt of a design similar to the T-shirt. [From its being shaped like the letter *T* when spread out.]

tsim·mes or **tzim·mes** (tsĭm′ĭs) *n.* **1.** A stew of vegetables or fruits cooked slowly over very low heat. **2.** *Informal.* A state of confusion. [Yiddish *tsimes* : Middle High German *ze, zuo,* to, for (from Old High German; see **de-** in Appendix) + Middle High German *imbiz,* light meal (from Old High German, from *enbizzan,* to eat : *in,* in; see **en** in Appendix + *bīzan, bizzan,* to bite; see **bheid-** in Appendix).]

Tsi·mshi·an (chĭm′shē-ən, tsĭm′-) *n., pl.* **Tsimshian** or **-ans. 1. a.** A Native American people inhabiting a coastal area of western British Columbia and extreme southeast Alaska. **b.** A member of this people. **2.** The family of languages spoken by the Tsimshian and related peoples.

Tsi·nan (jē′nän′). See **Jinan.**

Tsing·hai (tsĭng′hī′). See **Qinghai.**

Tsing·tao (tsĭng′dou′). See **Qingdao.**

Tsi·tsi·har (tsē′tsē′här′). See **Qiqihar.**

tsk (*a t-like sound produced by suction rather than plosion; conventional spelling pronunciation,* tĭsk) *interj.* Used to express disappointment or sympathy. —**tsk** *n.* A sucking noise made by suddenly releasing the tongue from the hard palate, used to express disappointment or sympathy. —**tsk** *v.*

tsp. or **tsp** *abbr.* Teaspoon; teaspoonful.

T-square (tē′skwâr′) *n.* A rule having a short, sometimes sliding, perpendicular crosspiece at one end, used by drafters for establishing and drawing parallel lines.

TSS *abbr.* Toxic shock syndrome.

Tsu·ga·ru Strait (tso͞o-gä′ro͞o). A channel between Honshu and Hokkaido in northern Japan.

tsu·na·mi (tso͞o-nä′mē) *n., pl.* **-mis.** A very large ocean wave caused by an underwater earthquake or volcanic eruption. [Japanese : *tsu,* port + *nami,* wave.] —**tsu·na′mic** *adj.*

tsu·ris also **tzu·ris** (tso͝or′ĭs, tsûr′-) *n. Informal.* Trouble; aggravation. [Yiddish *tsores,* pl. of *tsure,* from Hebrew *ṣarā.*]

Tsu·shi·ma (tso͞o-shē′mə, tso͞o′shē-mä′). Two islands of southwest Japan in Korea Strait between Kyushu and southeast South Korea. They are separated from Kyushu by **Tsushima Strait,** the site of a major naval battle (May 1905) in the Russo-Japanese War in which the Russian fleet was largely destroyed.

tsu·tsu·ga·mu·shi disease (tso͞o′tso͞o-gə-mo͞o′shē) *n.* See **scrub typhus.** [Japanese *tsutsugamushi,* typhus mite : *tsutsuga,* illness + *mushi,* tick.]

Tswa·na (tswä′nə, swä′-) *n., pl.* **Tswana** or **-nas. 1.** A member of a Bantu people inhabiting Botswana and western South Africa. Also called *Batswana, Bechuana.* **2.** The Sotho language of the Tswana. Also called *Setswana.*

Tt *abbr. Bible.* Titus.

TT *abbr.* **1.** Telegraphic transfer. **2.** Teletypewriter. **3.** Transit time. **4.** Trust territory.

T-top (tē′tŏp′) *n.* An automobile roof with removable panels.

TTY *abbr.* Teletypewriter.

Tu. *abbr.* Tuesday.

T.U. *abbr.* **1.** Trade union. **2.** Transmission unit.

Tu·a·mo·tu Archipelago (to͞o′ə-mō′to͞o). An island group of French Polynesia in the southern Pacific Ocean east of Tahiti. The islands were annexed by France in 1881.

Tuan (twän) *n.* Used in Malay as a form of respectful address for a man, equivalent to sir or mister. [Malay.]

Tua·reg (twä′rĕg′) *n., pl.* **Tuareg** or **-regs.** A member of a Moslem, Berber-speaking people inhabiting the western and central Sahara and western Sahel of northwest Africa. [Arabic *Tawāriq.*]

tu·a·ta·ra (to͞o′ə-tär′ə) *n.* A lizardlike reptile *(Sphenodon punctatus)* that is found only on certain islands off New Zealand and is the sole extant member of the Rhynchocephalia, an order that flourished during the Mesozoic Era. Also called *sphenodon.* [Maori *tuatàra* : *tua,* back + *tàra,* spine.]

tub (tŭb) *n.* **1. a.** An open, flat-bottomed vessel, usually round and typically wider than it is deep, used for washing, packing, or storing. **b.** The amount that such a vessel can hold. **c.** The contents of such a vessel. **2. a.** A bathtub. **b.** *Informal.* A bath taken in a bathtub. **3.** *Informal.* A wide, clumsy, slow-moving boat.

try square

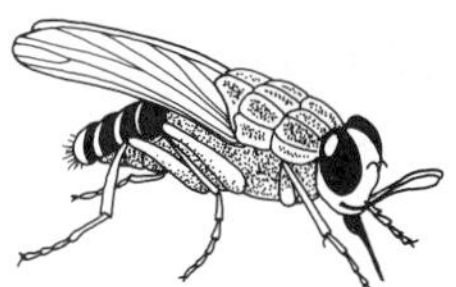

tsetse fly

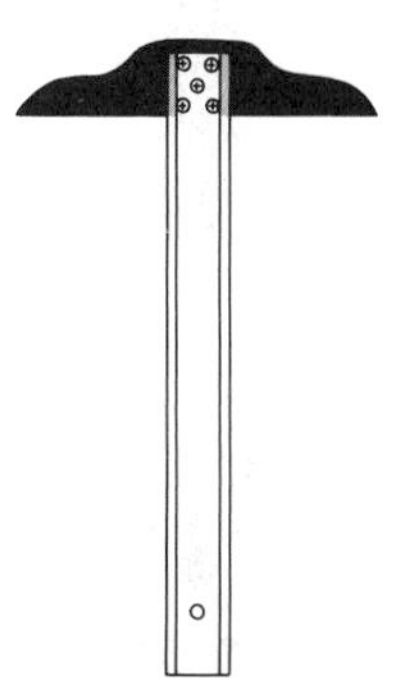

T-square

ă pat	oi boy
ā pay	ou out
âr care	o͝o took
ä father	o͞o boot
ĕ pet	ŭ cut
ē be	ûr urge
ĭ pit	th thin
ī pie	*th* this
îr pier	hw which
ŏ pot	zh vision
ō toe	ə about, item
ô paw	♦ regionalism

Stress marks: **′** (primary); ′ (secondary), as in **dictionary** (dĭk′shə-nĕr′ē)

tuba

tube pan

tuberose¹
Polianthes tuberosa

ă pat oi boy
ā pay ou out
âr care ŏŏ took
ä father ōō boot
ĕ pet ŭ cut
ē be ûr urge
ĭ pit th thin
ī pie *th* this
îr pier hw which
ŏ pot zh vision
ō toe ə about, item
ô paw ♦ regionalism

Stress marks: ′ (primary); ′ (secondary), as in **dictionary** (dĭk′shə-nĕr′ē)

4.a. A bucket used for conveying ore or coal up a mine shaft. **b.** A coal car used in a mine. **—tub** *v.* **tubbed, tub·bing, tubs.** —*tr.* **1.** To pack or store in a tub. **2.** To wash or bathe in a tub. —*intr.* To take a bath. [Middle English, from Middle Dutch or Middle Low German.] **—tub′ba·ble** *adj.* **—tub′ber** *n.*

tu·ba (to͞o′bə, tyo͞o′-) *n. Music.* **1.** A large, valved, brass wind instrument with a bass pitch. **2.** A reed stop in an organ, having eight-foot pitch. [Italian, from Latin, trumpet; akin to *tubus,* tube.] **—tu′ba·ist, tu′bist** *n.*

tu·bal (to͞o′bəl, tyo͞o′-) *adj.* Of, relating to, or occurring in a tube, such as the fallopian tube or the eustachian tube.

tubal ligation *n.* A method of female sterilization in which the fallopian tubes are surgically tied.

tu·bate (to͞o′bāt′, tyo͞o′-) *adj.* Forming or having a tube.

tub·by (tŭb′ē) *adj.* **-bi·er, -bi·est. 1.** Short and fat. **2.** Having a dull sound; lacking resonance. **—tub′bi·ness** *n.*

tube (to͞ob, tyo͞ob) *n.* **1.a.** A hollow cylinder, especially one that conveys a fluid or functions as a passage. **b.** An organic structure having the shape or function of a tube; a duct: *a bronchial tube.* **2.** A small, flexible cylindrical container sealed at one end and having a screw cap at the other, for pigments, toothpaste, or other pastelike substances. **3.** *Music.* The cylindrical part of a wind instrument. **4.** *Electronics.* **a.** An electron tube. **b.** A vacuum tube. **5.** *Botany.* The lower, cylindrical part of a gamopetalous corolla or a gamosepalous calyx. **6.** *Chiefly British.* A subway; an underground. **7.** A tunnel. **8.** An inner tube. **9.** *Slang.* **a.** Television: *What's on the tube?* **b.** A television set. **—tube** *v.* **tubed, tub·ing, tubes.** —*tr.* **1.** To provide with a tube; insert a tube in. **2.** To place in or enclose in a tube. —*intr. Informal.* To float down a stream or river for recreation in an inner tube: *went tubing on Sunday afternoon.* **—*idiom.* down the tubes** (or **tube).** *Slang.* Into a state of failure or ruin: *saw all her plans go down the tubes.* [French, from Old French, from Latin *tubus.*]

tu·bec·to·my (to͞o-bĕk′tə-mē, tyo͞o-) *n., pl.* **-mies.** See **salpingectomy.**

tube foot *n.* One of the numerous external, fluid-filled muscular tubes of echinoderms, such as the starfish or sea urchin, serving as organs of locomotion, food handling, and respiration.

tube·less tire (to͞ob′lĭs, tyo͞ob′-) *n.* A pneumatic vehicular tire in which the air is held in the assembly of casing and rim without an inner tube.

tube·nose (to͞ob′nōz′, tyo͞ob′-) *n.* A small marine fish *(Aulorhynchus flavidum)* similar to the stickleback, ranging from southern California to Alaska.

tube pan *n.* A round pan with a hollow cylindrical or conical projection in the middle, used for baking or molding foods in the shape of a ring.

tu·ber (to͞o′bər, tyo͞o′-) *n.* **1.** *Botany.* A swollen, fleshy, usually underground stem, such as the potato, bearing buds from which new plant shoots arise. **2.** *Biology.* A rounded projection or swelling; a tubercle. [Latin *tūber,* lump. See **teuə-** in Appendix.]

tu·ber·cle (to͞o′bər-kəl, tyo͞o′-) *n.* **1.** *Pathology.* A nodule or swelling, especially a mass of lymphocytes and epithelioid cells forming the characteristic lesion of tuberculosis. **2.** A small, rounded prominence or process, such as a wartlike excrescence on the roots of some leguminous plants or a knoblike process in the skin or on a bone. [Latin *tūberculum,* diminutive of *tūber,* lump. See TUBER.]

tubercle bacillus *n. Abbr.* **t.b., T.B.** A rod-shaped aerobic bacterium *(Mycobacterium tuberculosis)* that causes tuberculosis.

tu·ber·cu·lar (to͞o-bûr′kyə-lər, tyo͞o-) *adj.* **1.** Of, relating to, or covered with tubercles; tuberculate. **2.** Of, relating to, or affected with tuberculosis. **—tubercular** *n.* A person having tuberculosis.

tu·ber·cu·late (to͞o-bûr′kyə-lĭt, tyo͞o-) also **tu·ber·cu·la·ted** (-lā′tĭd) *adj.* **1.** Having or affected with tubercles. **2.** Tubercular. **—tu·ber′cu·late·ly** *adv.* **—tu·ber′cu·la′tion** *n.*

tu·ber·cu·lin (to͞o-bûr′kyə-lĭn, tyo͞o-) *n.* A sterile liquid containing proteins extracted from cultures of tubercle bacilli and used in tests for tuberculosis. [Latin *tūberculum,* tubercle; see TUBERCLE + -IN.]

tuberculin test *n.* Any of various tests used to determine past or present infection with the tubercle bacillus and based on hypersensitivity to tuberculin.

tu·ber·cu·loid (to͞o-bûr′kyə-loid′, tyo͞o-) *adj.* **1.** Resembling tuberculosis. **2.** Resembling a tubercle.

tu·ber·cu·lo·sis (to͞o-bûr′kyə-lō′sĭs, tyo͞o-) *n. Abbr.* **TB, T.B. 1.** An infectious disease of human beings and animals caused by the tubercle bacillus and characterized by the formation of tubercles on the lungs and other tissues of the body, often developing long after the initial infection. **2.** Tuberculosis of the lungs, characterized by the coughing up of mucus and sputum, fever, weight loss, and chest pain. [Latin *tūberculum,* tubercle; see TUBERCLE + -OSIS.]

tu·ber·cu·lous (to͞o-bûr′kyə-ləs, tyo͞o-) *adj.* **1.** Of, relating to, or having tuberculosis. **2.** Of, affected with, or caused by tubercles. **—tu·ber′cu·lous·ly** *adv.*

tube·rose¹ (to͞ob′rōz′, tyo͞ob′-, to͞o′bə-) *n.* A tuberous perennial Mexican herb *(Polianthes tuberosa)* having grasslike leaves and cultivated for its highly fragrant white flowers. [From New Latin *tūberōsa,* species name, from feminine of Latin *tūberōsus,* full of lumps, from *tūber,* lump. See TUBER.]

tu·ber·ose² (to͞o′bə-rōs′, tyo͞o′-) *adj.* Variant of **tuberous.**

tu·ber·os·i·ty (to͞o′bə-rŏs′ĭ-tē, tyo͞o′-) *n., pl.* **-ties. 1.** The quality or condition of being tuberous. **2.** A projection or protuberance, especially one at the end of a bone for the attachment of a muscle or tendon.

tu·ber·ous (to͞o′bər-əs, tyo͞o′-) also **tu·ber·ose** (-bə-rōs′) *adj.* **1.** Producing or bearing tubers. **2.** Being or resembling a tuber: *a tuberous root.*

tube·worm (to͞ob′ wûrm′, tyo͞ob′-) *n.* Any of various annelids living within tubular cases that they secrete or glue together from grit.

tu·bic·o·lous (to͞o-bĭk′yə-ləs, tyo͞o-) *adj.* Inhabiting a tube or tubular structure: *a tubicolous marine worm.*

tu·bi·fex (to͞o′bə-fĕks′, tyo͞o′-) *n., pl.* **tubifex** or **-fex·es.** Any of various small, slender, reddish freshwater worms of the genus *Tubifex,* often used as food for tropical aquarium fish. [New Latin *Tubifex,* genus name : Latin *tubus,* tube + Latin *-fex,* maker; see **dhē-** in Appendix.]

tub·ing (to͞o′bĭng, tyo͞o′-) *n.* **1.a.** Tubes considered as a group. **b.** A system of tubes. **c.** A piece or length of tube. **2.** Tubular fabric, such as that used for making pillowcases. **3.** *Informal.* The sport or recreation of floating down a stream or river in an inner tube.

Tü·bing·en (to͞o′bĭng-ən, tü′-). A city of southwest Germany on the Neckar River south of Stuttgart. Its university was founded in 1477. Population. 75,333.

Tub·man (tŭb′mən), **Harriet.** 1820?–1913. American abolitionist. Born a slave on a Maryland plantation, she escaped to the North in 1849 and became the most renowned conductor on the Underground Railroad, leading more than 300 slaves to freedom.

Tubman, William Vacanarat Shadrach. 1895–1971. Liberian politician. As president of Liberia (1944–1971) he modernized the country and maintained a close relationship with the United States.

tu·bo·cu·ra·rine (to͞o′bō-ko͞o-rä′rĭn, -rēn′, -kyo͞o, tyo͞o′-) *n.* **1.** An alkaloid that is the active component of curare. **2.** The chloride of this alkaloid, $C_{38}H_{44}Cl_2N_2O_6$, used as a muscle relaxant. [Latin *tubus,* tube (from the practice of shipping it in bamboo tubes) + *curarine* (CURARE + -INE²).]

tu·bo·plas·ty (to͞o′bō-plăs′tē, tyo͞o′-) *n., pl.* **-ties.** Surgical repair of one or both fallopian tubes.

tub-thump (tŭb′thŭmp′) *intr.v.* **-thumped, -thump·ing, -thumps.** *Slang.* To argue for or promote something vigorously: *"is tub-thumping for a six-month limit on the legislative session"* (David Nyhan). **—tub′-thump′er** *n.*

Tu·bu·a·i Islands (to͞ob-wä′ē, to͞o′bo͞o-ī′). An island group of southern French Polynesia in the southern Pacific Ocean south of Tahiti. Visited by Capt. James Cook in 1769 and 1777, the islands were annexed by France between 1850 and 1889.

tu·bu·lar (to͞o′byə-lər, tyo͞o′-) *adj.* **1.** Of or relating to a tube. **2.** Constituting or consisting of tubes or a tube. **3.** Shaped like a tube. **—tu′bu·lar′i·ty** (-lăr′ĭ-tē) *n.* **—tu′bu·lar·ly** *adv.*

tu·bu·late (to͞o′byə-lĭt, -lāt′, tyo͞o′-) also **tu·bu·lat·ed** (-lā′tĭd) *adj.* **1.** Formed into or resembling a tube; tubular. **2.** Having a tube. [Latin *tubulātus,* from *tubulus,* diminutive of *tubus,* tube.] **—tu′bu·la′tion** *n.* **—tu′bu·la′tor** *n.*

tu·bule (to͞o′byo͞ol, tyo͞o′-) *n.* A very small tube or tubular structure. [Latin *tubulus,* diminutive of *tubus,* tube.]

tu·bu·lif·er·ous (to͞o′byə-lĭf′ər-əs, tyo͞o′-) *adj.* Having or consisting of tubules.

tu·bu·li·flo·rous (to͞o′byə-lə-flôr′əs, -flōr′-, tyo͞o′-) *adj.* Having flowers or florets with tubular corollas.

tu·bu·lin (to͞o′byə-lĭn, tyo͞o′-) *n.* A globular protein that is the basic structural constituent of microtubules.

tu·bu·lous (to͞o′byə-ləs, tyo͞o′-) *adj.* **1.** Shaped like a tube; tubular. **2.a.** Composed of tubes. **b.** Having tubular parts. **—tu′bu·lous·ly** *adv.*

Tu·ca·na (to͞o-kā′nə, -kä′-, tyo͞o-) *n.* A constellation in the polar region of the Southern Hemisphere near Indus and Hydrus, containing the smaller Magellanic Clouds. [Tupi *tucana,* toucan.]

Tuch·man (tŭck′mən), **Barbara Wertheim.** 1912–1989. American historian who won a Pulitzer Prize for *The Guns of August* (1962) and for *Stilwell and the American Experience in China* (1971).

tu·chun (to͞o′cho͞on′, do͞o′jün′) *n., pl.* **-chuns** or **tuchun.** A Chinese provincial military governor. [Chinese (Mandarin) *dū jūn* : *dū,* to supervise + *jūn,* army.]

tuck¹ (tŭk) *v.* **tucked, tuck·ing, tucks.** —*tr.* **1.** To make one fold or several folds in. **2.** To gather up and fold, thrust, or turn in so as to secure or confine: *She tucked her scarf into her blouse.* **3.a.** To put in a snug spot. **b.** To put in an out-of-the-way, snug place: *a cabin that was tucked among the pines.* **c.** To store in a safe spot; save: *tuck away a bit of lace; tuck away millions.* **4.a.** To draw in; contract: *He tucked his chin into his chest.* **b.** *Sports.* To bring (a body part) into a tuck position. —*intr.* To make tucks. **—tuck** *n.* **1.** The act of tucking. **2.** A flattened pleat or fold, especially a very narrow one stitched in place. **3.** *Nautical.* The part of a ship's hull under the stern where the ends of the bottom planks come together. **4.** *Sports.* **a.** A bodily position used in some sports, such as diving, in which the knees are bent, the thighs are drawn close to the chest, and the hands are clasped around the shins. **b.** A position in skiing in which the skier squats while holding the poles parallel to the ground and under the arms. **5.** *Chiefly British.* Food, especially sweets and pastry.

—phrasal verbs. tuck away. *Informal.* To consume (food) heartily. **tuck in.** To make (a child, for example) secure in bed for sleep, especially by tucking bedclothes into the bed. [Middle English *tukken,* possibly from Middle Low German or Middle Dutch *tocken, tucken.*]

tuck² (tŭk) *n.* A beat or tap, especially on a drum. [From Middle English *tukken,* to beat a drum, from Old North French *toquer,* to strike, from Vulgar Latin **toccāre.*]

tuck³ (tŭk) *n. Archaic.* A slender sword; a rapier. [Perhaps from French dialectal *étoc,* from Old French *estoc,* of Germanic origin.]

tuck⁴ (tŭk) *n.* Energy; vigor. [Origin unknown.]

tuck·a·hoe (tŭkʹə-hōʹ) *n.* **1.** Any of various plants or plant parts used by certain Native American peoples as food, especially the edible root of certain arums or the sclerotium of certain fungi. **2.** See **arrow arum.** [Of Virginia Algonquian origin.]

tuck·er¹ (tŭkʹər) *n.* **1.** One that tucks, especially an attachment on a sewing machine for making tucks. **2.** A piece of linen or frill of lace formerly worn by women around the neck and shoulders.

tuck·er² (tŭkʹər) *tr.v.* **-ered, -er·ing, -ers.** *Informal.* To make weary; exhaust. [Perhaps from TUCK¹.]

Tuck·er (tŭkʹər), **Benjamin Ricketson.** 1854–1939. American anarchist whose own writings and translations of Proudhon and Bakunin influenced radical thought before World War I.

Tucker, Sophie. 1884–1966. Russian-born American entertainer known for her flamboyant vaudeville performances and her signature tune, "Some of These Days."

tuck·er-bag (tŭkʹər-băgʹ) *n. Australian.* A bag for carrying food, used by a traveler in the bush or by a swagman. [From Australian English *tucker,* food, provisions, from TUCK¹.]

tuck·et (tŭkʹĭt) *n. Music.* A trumpet fanfare. [Probably from obsolete *tuk,* from Middle English, from *tukken,* to beat a drum. See TUCK².]

tuck-point (tŭkʹpointʹ) *tr.v.* **-point·ed, -point·ing, -points.** To point (grooved mortar joints) with a thin ridge of fine lime mortar or putty.

tuck-shop (tŭkʹshŏpʹ) *n. Chiefly British.* A shop where candy and other sweets are sold; a confectionery. [From British slang *tuck,* food, sweets, from TUCK¹.]

Tuc·son (to͞oʹsŏnʹ). A city of southeast Arizona south-southeast of Phoenix. A Spanish mission was founded nearby in 1700, and the present city was first settled in 1775 as a walled presidio. It became part of the United States after the Gadsen Purchase (1853) and served as territorial capital from 1867 until 1877. Population, 330,537.

Tu·cu·mán (to͞oʹkə-mänʹ, -ko͞o-). See **San Miguel de Tucumán.**

-tude *suff.* Condition, state, or quality: *exactitude.* [French, from Old French, from Latin *-tūdō, -tūdin-.*]

Tu·dor¹ (to͞oʹdər, tyo͞oʹ-). English ruling dynasty (1485–1603), including Henry VII and his descendants Henry VIII, Edward VI, Mary I, and Elizabeth I.

Tu·dor² (to͞oʹdər, tyo͞oʹ-) *adj.* **1.** Of or relating to the royal house of Tudor. **2.a.** Of, relating to, or characteristic of the period of the Tudors. **b.** Of, relating to, or characteristic of an architectural style derived from this period, having exposed beams as a typical feature.

Tudor, Antony. 1909–1987. British-born American dancer and choreographer known for his psychological ballets, such as *Undertow* (1945) and *The Leaves Are Fading* (1975).

Tues·day (to͞ozʹdē, -dāʹ, tyo͞ozʹ-) *n. Abbr.* **T., Tu., Tue., Tues.** The third day of the week. [Middle English *Tuesdai,* from Old English *Tīwesdæg,* Tiu's day : *Tīwes,* genitive of *Tīw,* Tiu; see TIU + *dæg,* day (translation of Latin *diēs Mārtis,* Mars' day); see DAY.]

tu·fa (to͞oʹfə, tyo͞oʹ-) *n.* **1.** The calcareous and siliceous rock deposits of springs, lakes, or ground water. **2.** See **tuff.** [Obsolete Italian, from Latin *tōfus.*] **—tu·faʹceous** (-fāʹshəs) *adj.*

tuff (tŭf) *n.* A rock composed of compacted volcanic ash varying in size from fine sand to coarse gravel. Also called *tufa.* [French *tuf,* from Old French, from Old Italian *tufo,* tufa. See TUFA.] **—tuff·aʹceous** (tŭ-fāʹshəs) *adj.*

tuf·fet (tŭfʹĭt) *n.* **1.** A clump or tuft of grass. **2.** A low seat, such as a stool. [Alteration of TUFT.]

tuft (tŭft) *n.* **1.** A short cluster of elongated strands, as of yarn, hair, or grass, attached at the base or growing close together. **2.** A dense clump, especially of trees or bushes. **3.** A goatee. **—tuft** *v.* **tuft·ed, tuft·ing, tufts.** *—tr.* **1.** To furnish or ornament with tufts or a tuft. **2.** To pass threads through the layers of (a quilt, mattress, or upholstery), securing the thread ends with a knot or button. *—intr.* **1.** To separate or form into tufts. **2.** To grow in a tuft. [Middle English, probably alteration of Old French *tofe,* from Late Latin *tufa,* helmet crest, or of Germanic origin.] **—tuftʹer** *n.* **—tuftʹy** *adj.*

tuft·ed duck (tŭfʹtĭd) *n.* An Old World duck *(Aythya fuligula)* having a short, plump body and a crest on its head, the male of which has mostly black plumage.

tufted titmouse *n.* A bluish-gray titmouse *(Parus bicolor)* of the eastern and southern United States, having a crest on its head and brown flanks.

tug (tŭg) *v.* **tugged, tug·ging, tugs.** *—tr.* **1.** To pull at vigorously; strain at. **2.** To move by pulling with great effort or exertion; drag. **3.** *Nautical.* To tow by tugboat. *—intr.* **1.** To pull hard: *tugged at her boots.* See Synonyms at **pull. 2.** To toil or struggle; strain. **3.** To vie; contend. **—tug** *n.* **1.** A strong pull or pulling force: *the tug of the sea.* **2.** A contest; a struggle: *a tug between loyalty and desire.* **3.a.** *Nautical.* A tugboat. **b.** A land, air, or space vehicle that moves or tows other vehicles: *an airplane tug.* **4.** A rope, chain, or strap used in hauling, especially a harness trace. [Middle English *tuggen,* from Old English *tēon.* See **deuk-** in Appendix.] **—tugʹger** *n.*

tug·boat (tŭgʹbōtʹ) *n. Nautical.* A small powerful boat designed for towing or pushing larger vessels. Also called *towboat.*

Tu·ge·la Falls (to͞o-gāʹlə). A series of five waterfalls in the **Tugela River,** about 483 km (300 mi) long, of eastern South Africa. The falls have a total drop of 915 m (3,000 ft).

tug of war *n., pl.* **tugs of war. 1.** *Games.* A contest of strength in which two teams tug on opposite ends of a rope, each trying to pull the other across a dividing line. **2.** A struggle for supremacy: *a political tug of war between those in favor of the new legislation and those against it.*

tu·grik (to͞oʹgrĭk) *n.* See table at **currency.** [Mongolian *dughurik,* wheel, tugrik.]

tu·i (to͞oʹē) *n., pl.* **-is.** A honeyeater *(Prosthemadera novaeseelandiae)* of New Zealand, having dark plumage with white feathers on the throat. Also called *parson bird.* [Maori *tūī.*]

tuille (twēl) *n.* A steel plate used in medieval armor for protecting the thigh. [Middle English *toile,* from Old French *teuille, tuille,* from Latin *tēgula,* tile. See **(s)teg-** in Appendix.]

tu·i·tion (to͞o-ĭshʹən, tyo͞o-) *n.* **1.** A fee for instruction, especially at a formal institution of learning. **2.** Instruction; teaching. **3.** *Archaic.* Guardianship. *—attributive.* Often used to modify another noun: *tuition payments; tuition assistance.* [Middle English *tuicion,* protection, from Old French, from Latin *tuitiō, tuitiōn-,* from *tuitus,* past participle of *tuērī,* to protect.] **—tu·iʹtion·al, tu·iʹtion·arʹy** (-ĭshʹə-nĕrʹē) *adj.*

Tu·la (to͞oʹlə). **1.** A town of central Mexico north of Mexico City. Impressive Toltec ruins have been discovered on the site. Population, 10,720. **2.** A city of western Russia south of Moscow. First mentioned in 1146, it was an important fortress in the 16th century and became an armament-manufacturing center in 1712. Population, 532,000.

Tu·lare (to͞o-lârʹē, -lârʹ). A city of south-central California southeast of Fresno in the San Joaquin Valley. It is a processing center. Population, 22,475.

tu·la·re·mi·a (to͞oʹlə-rēʹmē-ə, tyo͞oʹ-) *n.* An infectious disease caused by the bacterium *Francisella tularensis* that chiefly affects rodents but can also be transmitted to human beings through the bite of various insects or contact with infected animals. In human beings, the disease is characterized by intermittent fever and swelling of the lymph nodes. Also called *rabbit fever.* [New Latin, after *Tulare,* a county of south-central California.] **—tuʹla·reʹmic** *adj.*

♦**tu·le** (to͞oʹlē) *n.* **1.** Any of several bulrushes of the genus *Scirpus,* growing in marshy lowlands of the southwest United States. **2. tu·les** (to͞oʹlēz). *Northern California.* Marshy or swampy land. Also called ♦*tule land.* [American Spanish, from Nahuatl *tollin,* reed.]

♦ ***REGIONAL NOTE:*** Low, swampy land is *tules* or *tule land* in the parlance of northern California. When the Spanish colonized Mexico and Central America, they borrowed from the native inhabitants the Nahuatl word *tollin,* "bulrush." The English-speaking settlers of the West in turn borrowed the Spanish word *tule* to refer to certain varieties of bulrushes native to California. Eventually the meaning of the word was extended to the marshy land where the bulrushes grew.

tu·lip (to͞oʹlĭp, tyo͞oʹ-) *n.* **1.** Any of several bulbous plants of the genus *Tulipa,* native chiefly to Asia and widely cultivated for their showy, variously colored flowers. **2.** The flower of any of these plants. [French *tulipe,* alteration of *tulipan,* from Ottoman Turkish *tülbend,* muslin, gauze.]

WORD HISTORY: Although we associate tulips with Holland and windmills, the history of the word takes us on an odyssey to the Middle East, where the tulip is associated with turbans and whence the flower was brought to Europe in the 16th century. The word *tulip,* which earlier in English appeared in such forms as *tulipa* or *tulipant,* comes to us by way of French *tulipe* and its obsolete form *tulipan* or by way of Modern Latin *tulīpa,* from Ottoman Turkish *tülbend,* "muslin, gauze." (Our word *turban,* first recorded in English in the 16th century, can also be traced to Ottoman Turkish *tülbend.*) The Turkish word for gauze, with which turbans can be wrapped, seems to have been used for the flower because a fully opened tulip was thought to resemble a turban.

tulip tree *n.* **1.** A tall, deciduous, eastern North American tree *(Liriodendron tulipifera)* having large, tuliplike green and orange flowers, aromatic twigs, and yellowish, easily worked wood. Also called *poplar.* **2.** See **African tulip tree.**

tu·lip·wood (to͞oʹlĭp-wo͝odʹ, tyo͞oʹ-) *n.* **1.** The wood of the tulip tree. **2.** The irregularly striped, ornamental wood of any of several related or similar trees.

tulle (to͞ol) *n.* A fine, often starched net of silk, rayon, or nylon,

Harriet Tubman

tugboat
Towing the *Queen Elizabeth II* into Victoria harbor, Hong Kong

tulip

tulip tree
Liriodendron tulipifera

used especially for veils, tutus, or gowns. [French, after *Tulle*, a city of south-central France.]

tul·li·bee (tŭl′ə-bē′) *n.* A large, thick-backed cisco *(Coregonus artedi* or *Leucichthys artedi)* of the Great Lakes. [Canadian French *toulibi*, from Ojibwa dialectal **oto·lipi·*.]

Tul·sa (tŭl′sə). A city of northeast Oklahoma on the Arkansas River northeast of Oklahoma City. A port and manufacturing center, it grew rapidly after the discovery of oil nearby in the early 20th century. Population, 360,919.

Tul·si Das (tōōl′sē däs′). 1543?–1623. Hindu poet whose *Ramcaritmanas* is considered one of the greatest works of Hindi literature.

tum·ble (tŭm′bəl) *v.* **-bled, -bling, -bles.** —*intr.* **1.** To perform acrobatic feats such as somersaults, rolls, or twists. **2.a.** To fall or roll end over end: *The kittens tumbled over each other.* **b.** To spill or roll out in confusion or disorder: *Schoolchildren tumbled out of the bus.* **c.** To pitch headlong; fall: *tumbled on the ice.* **d.** To proceed haphazardly. **3.a.** To topple, as from power or a high position; fall. **b.** To collapse: *The walls came tumbling down.* **c.** To drop: *Prices tumbled.* **4.** To come upon accidentally; happen on: *We tumbled on a first-rate restaurant.* **5.** *Slang.* To come to a sudden understanding; catch on: *I finally tumbled to the reality that I was being cheated.* —*tr.* **1.** To cause to fall; bring down: *a scandal that tumbled the government.* **2.** To put, spill, or toss haphazardly: *tumbled the extra parts into a box.* **3.** To toss or whirl in a drum, tumbler, or tumbling box. —**tumble** *n.* **1.** An act of tumbling; a fall. **2.** Confusion; disorder. [Middle English *tumblen*, frequentative of *tumben*, to dance about, from Old English *tumbian*.]

tum·ble·bug (tŭm′bəl-bŭg′) *n.* Any of various dung beetles, especially of the genera *Canthon* and *Phanaeus*, that roll up balls of fresh dung, inside which the female deposits her eggs and on which the larvae feed.

tum·ble·down (tŭm′bəl-doun′) *adj.* Being in such bad repair as to seem in danger of collapsing; very dilapidated or rickety: *a tumbledown shack.*

tum·ble-dry (tŭm′bəl-drī′) *tr. & intr.v.* **-dried** (-drīd′), **-dry·ing, -dries** (-drīz′). To make or become dry by rolling about in the heated rotating drum of a clothes dryer.

tum·ble·home (tŭm′bəl-hōm′) *n. Nautical.* The inward curve of a ship's topsides. [From TUMBLE, to slope inward (obsolete).]

tumbler
c. 1695 American engraved silver tumbler

tum·bler (tŭm′blər) *n.* **1.** One that tumbles, especially an acrobat or a gymnast. **2.a.** A drinking glass, originally with a rounded bottom. **b.** A flat-bottomed glass having no handle, foot, or stem. **c.** The contents of such a drinking glass. **3.** A toy made with a weighted, rounded base so that it can rock over and then right itself. **4.** One of a breed of domestic pigeons characteristically tumbling or somersaulting in flight. **5.** A piece in a gunlock that forces the hammer forward by action of the mainspring. **6.** The part in a lock that releases the bolt when moved by a key. **7.a.** The drum of a clothes dryer. **b.** A tumbling box. **8.a.** A projecting piece on a revolving or rocking part in a mechanism that transmits motion to the part it engages. **b.** The rocking frame that moves a gear into place in a selective transmission, as in an automobile.

♦**tumbleset** (tŭm′bəl-sĕt′) *n. Lower Southern U.S.* See **somersault** (sense 1). [Blend of TUMBLE and *somerset* (alteration of *somersaut*, variant of SOMERSAULT).]

♦ ***REGIONAL NOTE:*** The Lower Southern word *tumbleset* for *somersault* combines *tumble* with *–set*, which at first glance seems not to have any relationship to *–sault* in *somersault*. However, *–set* is an old *l*-less variant of *–sault* (from Latin *saltus*, "a leap") that has been an alternative pronunciation throughout the word's history; hence, the variant *somerset*. *Somer–* is an alteration of Old French *sobre–*, from Latin *supra*, "over." In the word *tumbleset*, as in a folk etymology, *somer–*, part of a compound word that no longer bears any meaning for the speakers, has been replaced by *tumble*, a word that makes more sense in the context.

tum·ble·weed (tŭm′bəl-wēd′) *n.* Any of various densely branched annual plants, such as amaranth and Russian thistle, that break off from the roots at the end of the growing season and are rolled about by the wind.

tum·bling (tŭm′blĭng) *n. Sports.* Gymnastics, such as somersaults, rolls, and handsprings, performed without the use of specialized apparatus.

tumbling box *n.* A revolving drum in which objects are dried, reduced in size, polished, or cleaned. Also called *tumbling barrel.*

tum·brel or **tum·bril** (tŭm′brəl) *n.* **1.** A two-wheeled cart, especially a farmer's cart that can be tilted to dump a load. **2.** A crude cart used to carry condemned prisoners to their place of execution, as during the French Revolution. [Middle English *tumberell*, from Old French *tomberel*, from *tomber*, to let fall, perhaps of Germanic origin.]

tu·me·fa·cient (tōō′mə-fā′shənt, tyōō′-) *adj.* Producing or tending to produce swelling or tumefaction. [Latin *tumefaciēns*, *tumefacient-*, present participle of *tumefacere*, to tumefy : *tumēre*, to swell; see **teuə-** in Appendix + *facere*, to make; see **dhē-** in Appendix.]

tu·me·fac·tion (tōō′mə-făk′shən, tyōō′-) *n.* **1.a.** The act or process of puffing or swelling. **b.** A swollen condition. **2.** A puffy or swollen part. [French *tuméfaction*, from Latin *tumefacere*, to tumefy. See TUMEFACIENT.] —**tu′me·fac′tive** (-tĭv) *adj.*

tu·me·fy (tōō′mə-fī′, tyōō′-) *intr & tr.v.* **-fied** (-fīd′), **-fy·ing, -fies** (-fīz′). To swell or cause to swell. [French *tuméfier*, Latin *tumefacere*. See TUMEFACTION.]

tu·mes·cence (tōō-mĕs′əns, tyōō-) *n.* **1.a.** A swelling or an enlarging. **b.** A swollen condition. **2.** A swollen part or organ.

tu·mes·cent (tōō-mĕs′ənt, tyōō-) *adj.* **1.** Somewhat tumid. **2.** Becoming swollen; swelling. [Latin *tumēscēns*, *tumēscent-*, present participle of *tumēscere*, to begin to swell, inchoative of *tumēre*, to swell. See **teuə-** in Appendix.]

tu·mid (tōō′mĭd, tyōō′-) *adj.* **1.** Swollen; distended. Used of a body part or organ. **2.** Of a bulging shape; protuberant. **3.** Overblown; bombastic: *tumid political prose.* [Latin *tumidus*, from *tumēre*, to swell. See **teuə-** in Appendix.] —**tu·mid′i·ty, tu′mid·ness** *n.* —**tu′mid·ly** *adv.*

tumm·ler (tōōm′lər) *n.* **1.** One, such as a social director or an entertainer, who encourages guest or audience participation. **2.** One who incites others to action. [Yiddish *tumler*, from *tumlen*, to make a racket.]

tum·my (tŭm′ē) *n., pl.* **-mies.** *Informal.* The human stomach or belly. [Baby-talk alteration of STOMACH.]

tu·mor (tōō′mər, tyōō′-) *n.* **1.** An abnormal growth of tissue resulting from uncontrolled, progressive multiplication of cells and serving no physiological function; a neoplasm. **2.** A swollen part; a swelling. [Middle English *tumour*, from Latin *tumor*, from *tumēre*, to swell. See **teuə-** in Appendix.] —**tu′mor·al, tu′mor·ous** *adj.*

tu·mor·i·gen·e·sis (tōō′mər-ə-jĕn′ĭ-sĭs, tyōō′-) *n., pl.* **-ses** (-sēz′). Formation or production of tumors.

tu·mor·i·gen·ic (tōō′mər-ə-jĕn′ĭk, tyōō′-) *adj.* Capable of causing tumors. —**tu′mor·i·ge·nic′i·ty** (-jə-nĭs′ĭ-tē) *n.*

tumor necrosis factor *n.* A protein produced by macrophages in the presence of an endotoxin and shown experimentally to be capable of attacking and destroying cancerous tumors.

♦**tump¹** (tŭmp) *v.* **tumped, tump·ing, tumps.** *Chiefly Southern U.S.* —*tr.* To overturn. Often used with *over*: *You're about to tump that thing over.* —*intr.* To fall over. Often used with *over*: *Is that wheelbarrow going to tump over?* [Probably akin to TUMBLE.]

♦ ***REGIONAL NOTE:*** The verb *tump*, used almost invariably with *over* in the intransitive sense "to fall over" and the transitive sense "to overturn," is in common use in the South. The editors of the *Dictionary of American Regional English* have collected evidence of its use in Arkansas, Texas, and Kentucky; it is also common in Alabama, Tennessee, and Georgia. This example supplied by *DARE* is typical: *"When he brushed against the coffee table his Coke tumped over"* (Little Rock, Arkansas, informant). But another citation, taken from Gregory Jaynes's parody of detective fiction, "In New York State: Who Poisoned the Pudding?" in the June 17, 1985, issue of *Time*, indicates that *tump* may not be exclusively Southern: *"At the end he tumps over into his rice pudding, poisoned. Whodunit?"* As for its ultimate origin, *tump* is probably related to *tumble* as a separate development from the same Old English verb *tumbian*.

tump² (tŭmp) *n.* **1.** A mound. **2.** A clump of trees, shrubs, or grass. [Origin unknown.]

tump·line (tŭmp′līn′) *n.* A strap slung across the forehead or the chest to support a load carried on the back. [*tump* (alteration of *mattump*, of Southern New England Algonquian origin) + LINE¹.]

tu·mu·lar (tōō′myə-lər, tyōō′-) *adj.* Relating to or having the shape of a tumulus.

tu·mu·li (tōō′myə-lī′, tyōō′-) *n.* Plural of **tumulus.**

tu·mu·lose (tōō′myə-lōs′, tyōō′-) also **tu·mu·lous** (-ləs) *adj.* Having many mounds or small hills. [Latin *tumulōsus*, from *tumulus*, mound. See TUMULUS.] —**tu′mu·los′i·ty** (-lŏs′ĭ-tē) *n.*

tu·mult (tōō′mŭlt′, tyōō′-) *n.* **1.** The din and commotion of a great crowd. **2.a.** A disorderly commotion or disturbance. **b.** A tempestuous uprising; a riot. **3.** Agitation of the mind or emotions: *"I spend much time in a tumult of anger and disbelief"* (Scott Turow). [Middle English *tumulte*, from Latin *tumultus*.]

tu·mul·tu·ar·y (tōō-mŭl′chōō-ĕr′ē, tyōō-) *adj.* Marked by haste, confusion, disorder, and irregularity. [Latin *tumultuārius*, from *tumultus*, commotion. See TUMULT.]

tu·mul·tu·ous (tōō-mŭl′chōō-əs, tyōō-) *adj.* **1.** Characterized by tumult; noisy and disorderly: *tumultuous applause.* **2.** Tending to cause tumult. **3.** Confusedly or violently agitated. —**tu·mul′tu·ous·ly** *adv.* —**tu·mul′tu·ous·ness** *n.*

tu·mu·lus (tōō′myə-ləs, tyōō′-) *n., pl.* **-li** (-lī′). An ancient grave mound; a barrow. [Latin. See **teuə-** in Appendix.]

tun (tŭn) *n.* **1.** A large cask for liquids, especially wine. **2.** A measure of liquid capacity, especially one equivalent to approximately 252 gallons (954 liters). [Middle English, from Old English *tunne*, possibly of Celtic origin.]

Tun. *abbr.* Tunisia; Tunisian.

tu·na¹ (tōō′nə, tyōō′-) *n., pl.* **tuna** or **-nas.** **1.a.** Any of various often large scombroid marine food and game fishes of the genus *Thunnus* and related genera, many of which, including *T. thynnus* and the albacore, are commercially important sources of canned fish. Also called *tunny.* **b.** Any of several related fishes, such as the bonito. **2.** The edible flesh of tuna, often canned or processed. In this sense, also called *tuna fish.* [American Spanish, from Spanish *atún,* from Arabic *at-tūn,* the tuna, from Latin *thunnus.* See TUNNY.]

tu•na² (to͞o′nə, tyo͞o′-) *n.* **1.** Any of several flat-jointed tropical American cacti of the genus *Opuntia,* which includes the prickly pears, especially *O. tuna* of Jamaica, having yellow flowers and edible red fruit. **2.** The edible fruit of any of these cacti. Also called *cactus pear.* [American Spanish, from Taino.]

tun•a•ble also **tune•a•ble** (to͞o′nə-bəl, tyo͞o′-) *adj.* **1.** That can be tuned: *a tunable wind instrument; a tunable radio.* **2.** *Archaic.* Tuneful. **—tun′a•ble•ness** *n.* **—tun′a•bly** *adv.*

tuna fish *n.* See **tuna¹** (sense 2).

tun•dra (tŭn′drə) *n.* A treeless area between the icecap and the tree line of Arctic regions, having a permanently frozen subsoil and supporting low-growing vegetation such as lichens, mosses, and stunted shrubs. [Russian, from Sami *tūndar,* flat-topped hill.]

tune (to͞on, tyo͞on) *n.* **1.** *Music.* **a.** A melody, especially a simple and easily remembered one. **b.** A song. **c.** Correct pitch. **d.** The state of being properly adjusted for pitch: *a piano out of tune.* **e.** Agreement in pitch: *play in tune with the piano.* **f.** *Obsolete.* A musical tone. **2.a.** Concord or agreement; harmony: *in tune with the times.* **b.** *Archaic.* Frame of mind; disposition. **3.** *Electronics.* Adjustment of a receiver or circuit for maximum response to a given signal or frequency. **—tune** *v.* **tuned, tun•ing, tunes.** *—tr.* **1.a.** *Music.* To put into proper pitch: *tuned the violin.* **b.** *Archaic.* To utter musically; sing. **2.** To adopt or adjust, especially in order to bring into harmony. **3.** *Electronics.* **a.** To adjust (a receiver) to a desired frequency. **b.** To adjust (a circuit) so as to make it resonant with a given input signal. **4.** To adjust (an engine, for example) for maximum usability or performance. *—intr.* To become attuned. ***—phrasal verbs.*** **tune in. 1.** *Electronics.* To adjust a receiver to receive signals at a particular frequency or a particular program. **2.** *Slang.* To make or become aware or responsive: *"Nobody tunes in to what anybody else is saying"* (Bruce Allen). **tune out. 1.** *Electronics.* To adjust a receiver so as not to receive a particular signal. **2.** *Slang.* **a.** To disassociate oneself from one's environment: *"The average reader, used to seeing the world in three-dimensional color, tunes out"* (Carlin Romano). **b.** To become unresponsive to; ignore: *tuned out the children's screaming.* **tune up. 1.** *Music.* To adjust an instrument to a desired pitch or key. **2.** To adjust a machine so as to put it into proper condition. **3.** To prepare (oneself) for a specified activity. ***—idiom.*** **to the tune of.** To the sum or extent of: *produced profits to the tune of about $20 million.* [Middle English, variant of *tone,* tone. See TONE.]

tune•a•ble (to͞o′nə-bəl, tyo͞o′-) *adj.* Variant of **tunable.**

tune•ful (to͞on′fəl, tyo͞on′-) *adj.* **1.** Full of tune; melodious. **2.** Producing musical sounds. **—tune′ful•ly** *adv.* **—tune′ful•ness** *n.*

tune•less (to͞on′lĭs, tyo͞on′-) *adj.* **1.** Deficient in melody; not tuneful. **2.** Producing no music; silent. **—tune′less•ly** *adv.* **—tune′less•ness** *n.*

tun•er (to͞o′nər, tyo͞o′-) *n.* **1.** One that tunes: *a piano tuner.* **2.** A device for tuning, especially an electronic circuit or device used to select signals at a specific radio frequency for amplification and conversion to sound.

tune•smith (to͞on′smĭth′, tyo͞on′-) *n.* *Music.* One who composes melodies, especially for popular songs.

tune-up (to͞on′ŭp′, tyo͞on′-) *n.* **1.** An adjustment, as of a motor or an engine, made to improve working order or efficiency. **2.** An engine warm-up.

tung oil (tŭng) *n.* A yellow or brownish oil extracted from the seeds of the tung tree and used as a drying agent in varnishes and paints and for waterproofing. Also called *Chinawood oil.*

tung-oil tree (tŭng′oil′) *n.* The tung tree.

tung•state (tŭng′stāt′) *n.* A salt of tungstic acid.

tung•sten (tŭng′stən) *n.* *Symbol* **W** A hard, brittle, corrosion-resistant, gray to white metallic element extracted from wolframite, scheelite, and other minerals, having the highest melting point and lowest vapor pressure of any metal. Tungsten and its alloys are used in high-temperature structural materials; in electrical elements, notably lamp filaments; and in instruments requiring thermally compatible glass-to-metal seals. Atomic number 74; atomic weight 183.85; melting point 3,410°C; boiling point 5,900°C; specific gravity 19.3 (20°C); valence 2, 3, 4, 5, 6. Also called *wolfram.* See table at **element.** [Swedish : *tung,* heavy (from Old Norse *thungr*) + *sten,* stone (from Old Norse *steinn;* see **stei-** in Appendix).] **—tung•sten′ic** (-stĕn′ĭk) *adj.*

tungsten carbide *n.* An extremely hard, fine gray powder whose composition is WC, used in tools, dies, wear-resistant machine parts, and abrasives.

tungsten lamp *n.* An incandescent electric lamp with a tungsten filament.

tungsten steel *n.* A very hard, heat-resistant steel containing tungsten.

tung•stic (tŭng′stĭk) *adj.* Of, relating to, or containing tungsten, especially with valence 6.

tungstic acid *n.* A yellow powder, H_2WO_4, used in textiles and plastics.

tung•stite (tŭng′stīt′) *n.* A yellow or yellowish-green mineral, essentially WO_3, often occurring with tungsten ores.

tung tree *n.* Any of several eastern Asian trees of the genus *Aleurites,* especially *A. montana* and *A. fordii,* cultivated for their seeds that yield a commercially valuable drying oil. [Chinese (Mandarin) *tóng.*]

Tun•gus (to͝ong-go͞oz′, tŭn-) *n., pl.* **Tungus** or **-gus•es.** See **Evenki.** [Russian, from East Turkic *tunguz,* wild pig, boar, from Old Turkic *tonguz.*]

Tun•gus•ic (to͝ong-go͞o′zĭk, tŭn-) *n.* A subfamily of the Altaic languages in eastern Siberia and northern Manchuria that includes Tungus and Manchu. Also called *Manchu-Tungus.* **—Tungusic** *adj.* Of or relating to Tungusic or its speakers.

Tun•gus•ka (to͝ong-go͞o′skə, to͞on-). The name of three rivers of central Russia. The **Upper Tunguska** is the lower course of the Angara River. The **Lower Tunguska** flows about 3,218 km (2,000 mi) north and west to the Yenisei River. The **Stony Tunguska,** about 1,609 km (1,000 mi) long, flows generally west-northwest to the Yenisei.

tu•nic (to͞o′nĭk, tyo͞o′-) *n.* **1.a.** A loose-fitting garment, sleeved or sleeveless, extending to the knees and worn by men and women especially in ancient Greece and Rome. **b.** A medieval surcoat. **2.a.** A long, plain, close-fitting military jacket, usually with a stiff high collar. **b.** A long, plain, sleeved or sleeveless blouse. **c.** A short pleated and belted dress worn by women for some sports. **3.** *Anatomy.* A coat or layer enveloping an organ or a part. **4.** *Botany.* A loose, membranous outer covering of a bulb or corm, as of the onion, tulip, or crocus. **5.** See **tunicle.** [Middle English *tunik,* from Old French *tunique,* from Latin *tunica,* probably of Semitic origin.]

tu•ni•ca (to͞o′nĭ-kə, tyo͞o′-) *n., pl.* **-cae** (-kē′, -sē′). An enclosing membrane or layer of tissue. [Latin, tunic. See TUNIC.]

tu•ni•cate (to͞o′nĭ-kĭt, -kāt′, tyo͞o′-) *n.* Any of various chordate marine animals of the subphylum Tunicata or Urochordata having a cylindrical or globular body enclosed in a tough outer covering and including the sea squirts and salps. **—tunicate** *adj.* **1.** Of or relating to the tunicates. **2.** *Anatomy.* Having a tunic. **3.** *Botany.* Having a tunic, as the bulb of an onion. [Latin *tunicātus,* past participle of *tunicāre,* to clothe with a tunic, from *tunica,* tunic. See TUNIC.]

tu•ni•cle (to͞o′nĭ-kəl, tyo͞o′-) *n.* A sleeved outer vestment reaching to the knees, worn over the alb by a subdeacon or sometimes under the dalmatic by a bishop or cardinal. Also called *tunic.* [Middle English, from Latin *tunicula,* diminutive of *tunica,* tunic. See TUNIC.]

tun•ing fork (to͞o′nĭng, tyo͞o′-) *n.* A small two-pronged metal device that when struck produces a sound of fixed pitch that is used as a reference, as in tuning musical instruments.

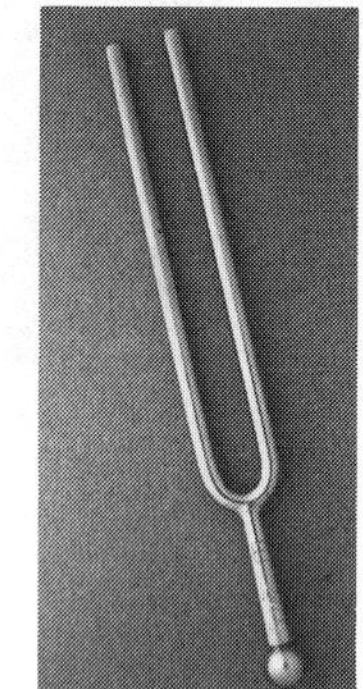

tuning fork

Tu•nis (to͞o′nĭs, tyo͞o′-). **1.** A former Barbary state on the northern coast of Africa south and west of the ancient city of Carthage. It was conquered by the Turks in 1575 and later became a French protectorate (1881). **2.** The capital and largest city of Tunisia, in the northern part of the country on the **Gulf of Tunis,** an inlet of the Mediterranean Sea. It occupies a site near the ruins of ancient Carthage. Population, 550,404.

Tu•ni•sia (to͞o-nē′zhə, -shə, -nĭzh′ə, -nĭsh′ə, tyo͞o-). *Abbr.* **Tun.** A country of northern Africa bordering on the Mediterranean Sea. The region was settled in the 12th century B.C. by Phoenicians, was later controlled by Romans, Carthaginians, and Turks, among others, and became a French protectorate in 1881. Full independence was achieved in 1956. Tunis is the capital and the largest city. Population, 5,588,209.

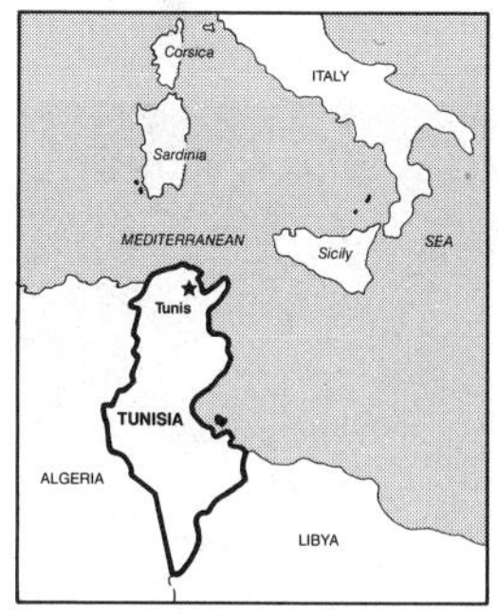

Tunisia

Tu•ni•sian (to͞o-nē′zhən, -shən, -nĭzh′ən, -nĭsh′-, tyo͞o-) *adj.* *Abbr.* **Tun.** Of or relating to Tunisia or Tunis or their inhabitants. **—Tunisian** *n.* A native or inhabitant of Tunisia or Tunis.

tun•nel (tŭn′əl) *n.* **1.** An underground or underwater passage. **2.** A passage through or under a barrier. **3.** *Obsolete.* The main flue on a chimney. **—tunnel** *v.* **-neled, -nel•ing, -nels** or **-nelled, -nel•ling, -nels.** *—tr.* **1.** To make a tunnel through or under. **2.** To produce, shape, or dig in the form of a tunnel. *—intr.* To make a tunnel. [Middle English *tonel,* tubular net, from Old French *tonnelle,* diminutive of *tonne,* tun, possibly of Celtic origin.] **—tun′nel•er, tun′nel•ler** *n.*

tunnel disease *n.* See **ancylostomiasis.**

tunnel vision *n.* **1.** Vision in which the visual field is severely constricted, as from within a tunnel looking out. **2.** An extremely narrow point of view; narrow-mindedness.

Tun•ney (tŭn′ē), **James Joseph.** Known as "Gene." 1898–1978. American prizefighter who won the world heavyweight championship in 1926 by defeating Jack Dempsey, defeated him again in 1927, and retired as champion in 1928.

tun•ny (tŭn′ē) *n., pl.* **tunny** or **-nies.** See **tuna¹** (sense 1a). [Italian *tonno* or French *thon,* both from Old Provençal *ton,* from Latin *thynnus,* from Greek *thunnos.*]

tup (tŭp) *n.* **1.** *Chiefly British.* A male sheep; a ram. **2.** A heavy metal body, especially the head of a power hammer. **—tup** *v.* **tupped, tup•ping, tups.** *—tr.* To copulate with (a ewe). Used of a ram. *—intr.* To copulate with a ewe. [Middle English *tupe.*]

tu•pe•lo (to͞o′pə-lō′, tyo͞o′-) *n., pl.* **-los.** **1.** Any of several trees of the genus *Nyssa,* especially *N. aquatica,* of the southeast United States, having soft, light wood. **2.** The wood of this tree. [Probably Creek *'topilwa : íto,* tree + *opílwa,* swamp.]

Tu•pe•lo (to͞o′pə-lō′, tyo͞o′-). A city of northeast Mississippi north-northwest of Columbus. It was the site of a Civil War battle (July 14, 1864) in which Union forces defeated the Confederate troops led by Gen. Nathan B. Forrest. Population, 23,905.

ă pat	oi boy
ā pay	ou out
âr care	o͝o took
ä father	o͞o boot
ĕ pet	ŭ cut
ē be	ûr urge
ĭ pit	th thin
ī pie	*th* this
îr pier	hw which
ŏ pot	zh vision
ō toe	ə about, item
ô paw	♦ regionalism

Stress marks: **′** (primary); ′ (secondary), as in **dictionary** (dĭk′shə-nĕr′ē)

Tu·pi (to͞o′pē, to͞o-pē′) *n., pl.* **Tupi** or **-pis. 1.** A member of any of a group of South American Indian peoples living along the coast of Brazil, in the Amazon River valley, and in Paraguay. **2.** The Tupian language of the Tupi.

Tu·pi·an (to͞o′pē-ən, to͞o-pē′-) *n.* **1.** A subdivision of Tupi-Guarani that includes Tupi. **2.** A member of a Tupian-speaking people. **—Tupian** *adj.* Of or relating to Tupian or to a Tupian-speaking people.

Tu·pi-Gua·ra·ni (to͞o-pē′gwär-ə-nē′, to͞o′pē-) *n.* A language family widely spread throughout the Amazon River valley, coastal Brazil, and northeast South America. **—Tu·pi′-Gua·ra·ni′, Tu·pi′-Gua·ra·ni′an** *adj.*

tup·pence (tŭp′əns) *n.* Variant of **twopence.**

tup·pen·ny (tŭp′nē) *n. Chiefly British.* **—tuppenny** *adj.* Variant of **twopenny.**

Tup·per (tŭp′ər), Sir **Charles.** 1821–1915. Canadian politician who helped establish Nova Scotia as a province of Canada (1867) and served as prime minister (1896).

Tu·pun·ga·to (to͞o′po͝ong-gä′tō). A mountain, 6,804.6 m (22,310 ft) high, in the Andes on the Chile-Argentina border east of Santiago, Chile.

tuque (to͞ok, tyo͞ok) *n.* A knitted woolen cap in the form of a cylindrical bag often with tapered ends that is worn with one end tucked into the other. [Canadian French, from French *toque,* toque. See TOQUE.]

turban

tu quo·que (to͞o kwō′kwē, -kwā, tyo͞o) *n.* A retort accusing an accuser of a similar offense or similar behavior. [Latin *tū quoque,* you also : *tū,* you + *quoque,* also.]

Tur. *abbr.* Turkey; Turkish.

tu·ra·co (to͝or′ə-kō′) *n.* Variant of **touraco.**

Tu·ra·ni·an (to͞o-rā′nē-ən, -rä′-, tyo͞o-) *adj.* Of or relating to the Ural-Altaic languages or to the peoples who speak them. **—Turanian** *n.* **1.** See **Ural-Altaic. 2.** A member of any of the peoples who speak languages of the Ural-Altaic group. [From Persian *Tūrān,* Turkistan.]

tur·ban (tûr′bən) *n.* **1.** A traditionally Moslem headdress consisting of a long scarf of linen, cotton, or silk that is wound around a small cap or directly around the head. **2.** A woman's close-fitting hat that consists of material wound around a small inner cap. [French *turbant,* from Italian *turbante,* from Ottoman Turkish *tülbend,* muslin, gauze.]

tur·ba·ry (tûr′bə-rē) *n., pl.* **-ries.** A place where peat can be dug; a peat bog. [Middle English *turbarie,* from Anglo-Norman *turberie,* from Medieval Latin *turbāria,* from *turba,* turf, of Germanic origin.]

tur·bel·lar·i·an (tûr′bə-lâr′ē-ən) *n.* Any of various free-living chiefly aquatic ciliate flatworms of the class Turbellaria, which includes the common planarians of the genus *Dugesia.* **—turbellarian** *adj.* Of or belonging to the Turbellaria. [From New Latin *Turbellāria,* class name, from Latin *turbella,* bustle, diminutive of *turba,* turmoil (from the motion of their cilia in the water). See TURBID.]

tur·bid (tûr′bĭd) *adj.* **1.** Having sediment or foreign particles stirred up or suspended; muddy: *turbid water.* **2.** Heavy, dark, or dense, as smoke or fog. **3.** In a state of turmoil; muddled: *turbid feelings.* [Latin *turbidus,* disordered, from *turba,* turmoil, probably from Greek *turbē.*] **—tur′bid·ly** *adv.* **—tur′bid·ness, tur·bid′i·ty** *n.*

tureen
Mid 18th-century porcelain tureen with cover

tur·bi·dim·e·ter (tûr′bĭ-dĭm′ĭ-tər) *n.* An instrument for measuring the loss in intensity of a light beam through a solution that contains suspended particulate matter. **—tur′bi·di·met′ric** (-də-mĕt′rĭk) *adj.* **—tur′bi·di·met′ri·cal·ly** *adv.* **—tur′bi·dim′e·try** *n.*

tur·bi·nal (tûr′bə-nəl) *adj.* Having the shape of a cone resting on its apex. **—turbinal** *n. Anatomy.* A turbinate bone. [From Latin *turbō, turbin-,* spinning top. See TURBINE.]

tur·bi·nate (tûr′bə-nĭt, -nāt′) also **tur·bi·nat·ed** (-nā′tĭd) *adj.* **1.** Shaped like a top. **2.** Spinning like a top. **3.** *Zoology.* Spiral and decreasing sharply in diameter from base to apex. Used especially of shells. **4.** *Anatomy.* Of, relating to, or designating a small curved bone that extends horizontally along the lateral wall of the nasal passage in higher vertebrates. [Latin *turbinātus,* from *turbō, turbin-,* spinning top. See TURBINE.]

tur·bi·na·tion (tûr′bə-nā′shən) *n.* A turbinate formation.

tur·bine (tûr′bĭn, -bīn′) *n.* Any of various machines in which the kinetic energy of a moving fluid is converted to mechanical power by the impulse or reaction of the fluid with a series of buckets, paddles, or blades arrayed about the circumference of a wheel or cylinder. [French, from Latin *turbō, turbin-,* spinning top, perhaps from Greek *turbē,* turmoil.]

tur·bit (tûr′bĭt) *n.* Any of a breed of domestic pigeons having a small crested head and a ruffled breast. [Origin unknown.]

turbo– *pref.* **1.** Turbine: *turbocharger.* **2.** Driven by a turbine: *turbojet.* [From TURBINE.]

tur·bo·charg·er (tûr′bō-chär′jər) *n.* See **turbosupercharger. —tur′bo·charged′** *adj.*

tur·bo·fan (tûr′bō-făn′) *n.* **1.** A turbojet engine in which a fan supplements the total thrust by forcing air directly into the hot turbine exhaust. **2.** An aircraft in which a turbofan is used.

tur·bo·jet (tûr′bō-jĕt′) *n.* **1.** A jet engine having a turbine-driven compressor and developing thrust from the exhaust of hot gases. **2.** An aircraft in which a turbojet is used.

tur·bo·prop (tûr′bō-prŏp′) *n.* **1.** A turbojet engine used to drive an external propeller. **2.** An aircraft in which a turboprop is used. Also called *propjet.*

tur·bo·ram·jet (tûr′bō-răm′jĕt′) *n.* **1.** A turbojet engine that can be operated as a ramjet. **2.** An aircraft in which a turboramjet is used.

tur·bo·su·per·charg·er (tûr′bō-so͞o′pər-chär′jər) *n.* A supercharger that uses an exhaust-driven turbine to maintain air-intake pressure especially in high-altitude aircraft. Also called *turbocharger.* **—tur′bo·su′per-charged′** *adj.*

tur·bot (tûr′bət) *n., pl.* **turbot** or **-bots. 1.** A European flatfish, *Scophthalmus maximus,* that has a brown, knobby upper side and is prized as food. **2.** Any of various flatfishes similar or related to this fish. [Middle English *turbut,* from Old French *tourbout,* probably of Scandinavian origin; akin to Old Swedish *törnbut* : *törn,* thorn + *but,* flatfish; see **bhau-** in Appendix.]

tur·bu·lence (tûr′byə-ləns) *n.* **1.** The state or quality of being turbulent: *times of turbulence and confusion.* **2.** *Physics.* Turbulent flow. **3.** An eddying motion of the atmosphere that interrupts the flow of wind.

tur·bu·lent (tûr′byə-lənt) *adj.* **1.** Violently agitated or disturbed; tumultuous: *turbulent rapids.* **2.** Having a chaotic or restless character or tendency: *a turbulent period in history.* **3.** Causing unrest or disturbance; unruly: *turbulent, revolutionary undercurrents.* [Middle English, from Old French, from Latin *turbulentus,* from *turba,* turmoil. See TURBID.] **—tur′bu·lent·ly** *adv.*

turbulent flow *n. Physics.* The motion of a fluid having local velocities and pressures that fluctuate randomly.

Tur·co·man (tûr′kə-mən) *n. & adj.* Variant of **Turkmen.**

turd (tûrd) *n. Vulgar Slang.* **1.** A piece of excrement. **2.** A person regarded as contemptible. [Middle English, from Old English *tord.* See **der-** in Appendix.]

tu·reen (to͞o-rēn′, tyo͞o-) *n.* A broad, deep, usually covered dish used for serving foods such as soups or stews. [French *terrine,* from Old French, from feminine of *terrin,* earthen, from Vulgar Latin **terrīnus,* from Latin *terra,* earth. See **ters-** in Appendix.]

Tu·renne (to͞o-rĕn′, tü-), Vicomte de. Title of Henri de La Tour d'Auvergne. 1611–1675. French military leader noted for his campaigns in France and Italy (1635–1642) during the Thirty Years' War and for his victory in the Battle of the Dunes (1658).

turf (tûrf) *n., pl.* **turfs** also **turves** (tûrvz). **1.a.** A surface layer of earth containing a dense growth of grass and its matted roots; sod. **b.** An artificial substitute for such a grassy layer, as on a playing field. **2.** A piece cut from a layer of earth or sod. **3.** A piece of peat that is burned for use as fuel. **4.** *Slang.* **a.** The range of the authority or influence of a person, group, or thing; a bailiwick: *"a bureaucracy like any other, chiefly concerned with turf, promotions, the budget, and protecting the retirement system"* (Harper's). **b.** A geographical area; a territory. **c.** The area claimed by a gang, as of youths, as its personal territory. **5.** *Sports.* **a.** A racetrack. **b.** The sport or business of racing horses. **—turf** *tr.v.* **turfed, turf·ing, turfs. 1.** To spread with turf: *turfed the front yard.* **2.** *Chiefly British.* To discard or eject. **3.** *Slang.* To kill: *"These guys can't . . . make sure nobody gets turfed"* (Scott Turow). [Middle English, from Old English.] **—turf′y** *adj.*

Tur·ge·nev (to͝or-găn′yəf, -gĕn′-, to͝or-gyĕ′nyĭf), **Ivan Sergeevich.** 1818–1883. Russian writer whose works include the collection of stories *A Sportsman's Sketches* (1852), plays, such as *A Month in the Country* (1850), and novels, most notably *Fathers and Sons* (1862).

tur·ges·cence (tûr-jĕs′əns) *n.* **1.a.** The condition of being swollen. **b.** The process of swelling. **2.** Pomposity; self-importance. [From Latin *turgēscere,* to begin to swell, inchoative of *turgēre,* to be swollen.] **—tur·ges′cent** *adj.*

tur·gid (tûr′jĭd) *adj.* **1.** Excessively ornate or complex in style or language; grandiloquent: *turgid prose.* **2.** Swollen or distended, as from a fluid; bloated: *a turgid bladder; turgid veins.* [Latin *turgidus,* from *turgēre,* to be swollen.] **—tur·gid′i·ty, tur′gid·ness** *n.* **—tur′gid·ly** *adv.*

tur·gor (tûr′gər, -gôr′) *n.* **1.** The state of being turgid. **2.** *Biology.* The normal fullness or tension produced by the fluid content of blood vessels, capillaries, and plant or animal cells. [Late Latin, from Latin *turgēre,* to be swollen.]

Tur·got (to͝or-gō′, tür-), **Anne Robert Jacques.** 1727–1781. French economist. Appointed controller general under Louis XVI (1774), he was dismissed (1776) after proposing reforms that were unpopular with the aristocracy.

Tu·rin (to͝or′ĭn, tyo͝or′-) also **To·ri·no** (tô-rē′nô). A city of northwest Italy on the Po River west-southwest of Milan. An important Roman town, it was later a Lombard duchy and the capital of the kingdom of Sardinia (1720–1861). It was also the first capital of the new kingdom of Italy. Population, 1,103,520.

tu·ri·on (to͝or′ē-ŏn′, tyo͝or′-) *n.* A thick, fleshy, young shoot or sucker, such as an emerging stem of asparagus. [Latin *turiō, turiōn-.*]

Turk (tûrk) *n.* **1.** A native or inhabitant of Turkey. **2.** A member of the principal ethnic group of modern-day Turkey or, formerly, of the Ottoman Empire. **3.** A member of any of the Turkic-speaking peoples. **4.** A Moslem. [Middle English, from Old French *Turc,* from Turkish *Türk,* from Old Turkic *türk,* strong.]

Turk. *abbr.* Turkey; Turkish.

Tur•ka•na (tər-kăn′ə, to͝or-kä′nə), **Lake.** Also **Lake Ru•dolf** (ro͞o′dŏlf′). A lake of northwest Kenya in the Great Rift Valley bordering on Ethiopia.

Tur•ke•stan (tûr′kĭ-stăn′, -stän′). See **Turkistan.**

tur•key (tûr′kē) *n., pl.* **-keys. 1.a.** A large North American bird *(Meleagris gallopavo)* that has brownish plumage and a bare, wattled head and neck and is widely domesticated for food. **b.** A related bird *(Agriocharis ocellata)* of Mexico and Central America, brilliantly colored and having eyelike spots on its tail. **2.** *Slang.* **a.** A person considered inept or undesirable. **b.** A failure, especially a failed theatrical production or movie. **3.** *Sports.* Three consecutive strikes in bowling. ***—idiom.*** **talk turkey.** *Informal.* To speak frankly and get down to the basic facts of a matter. [After TURKEY, from a confusion with the guinea fowl, once believed to have originated in Turkish territory.]

Tur•key (tûr′kē). *Abbr.* **Tur., Turk.** A country of southwest Asia and southeast Europe between the Mediterranean and the Black seas. One of the oldest inhabited regions in the world, Turkey was the center of the Ottoman Empire for more than 600 years. Its modern history dates to the rise of the Young Turks (after 1908) and the collapse of the empire in 1918. Under the leadership of Kemal Atatürk, a republic was proclaimed in 1923. Ankara is the capital and Istanbul the largest city. Population, 44,736,957.

turkey buzzard *n.* See **turkey vulture.**

turkey cock *n.* **1.** A male turkey. **2.** A strutting, conceited person.

Turkey red *n.* *Color.* A moderate red.

turkey trot *n.* A ragtime dance characterized by a springy walk with the feet well apart and a swinging up-and-down movement of the shoulders.

turkey vulture *n.* A New World vulture *(Cathartes aura)* having dark plumage and a bare red head and neck similar to that of the turkey. Also called *turkey buzzard.*

Tur•ki (tûr′kē) *adj.* Of or relating to the Turkic language subfamily, especially the eastern Turkic languages, or their speakers. **—Turki** *n., pl.* **Turki** or **-kis. 1.** The Turkic language subfamily, especially the eastern Turkic languages. **2.** A member of a Turki-speaking people. [Persian *turkī,* from *Turk,* Turk, from Turkish *Türk.* See TURK.]

Turk•ic (tûr′kĭk) *n.* A subfamily of the Altaic language family that includes Turkish. **—Turkic** *adj.* **1.** Of or relating to Turkic or the peoples who speak Turkic. **2.** Turkish.

Turk•ish (tûr′kĭsh) *adj. Abbr.* **Tur., Turk.** Of or relating to Turkey or its peoples, languages, or cultures. **—Turkish** *n. Abbr.* **Tur., Turk.** Ottoman Turkish.

Turkish bath *n.* **1.a.** A steam bath that induces heavy perspiration in the bather and is followed by a shower and massage. **b.** An establishment where facilities are available for Turkish baths. **2.** An extremely hot place.

Turkish coffee *n.* A strong, usually sweetened brew of pulverized coffee.

Turkish delight *n.* A candy usually consisting of jellylike cubes covered with powdered sugar.

Turkish Empire. See **Ottoman Empire.**

Turkish towel *n.* A thick towel with a nap of uncut pile.

Turk•ism (tûr′kĭz′əm) *n.* The culture, religion, or social system of the Turks.

Tur•ki•stan also **Tur•ke•stan** (tûr′kĭ-stăn′, -stän′). A historical region of west-central Asia extending east from the Caspian Sea to the border of China and south from the Aral Sea into Afghanistan. It has long been a crossroads for trade and conquest between East and West.

Turk•men (tûrk′mĕn, -mən) also **Tur•ko•man** or **Tur•co•man** (tûr′kə-mən) *—n., pl.* **Turkmen** or **-mens** also **-ko•mans** or **-co•mans. 1.** A member of a traditionally nomadic Turkic people inhabiting Turkmenistan and neighboring areas in Iran and Afghanistan. **2.** The Turkic language of the Turkmen. *—adj.* Of or relating to the Turkmen or their language or culture. [Medieval Latin *Turcomannus,* from Persian *Turkmān,* from *turkmān,* like a Turk, from *Turk,* Turk. See TURKI.]

Turk•men•i•stan (tûrk′mĕn-ĭ-stăn′, -stän′). A region of west-central Asia east of the Caspian Sea. Inhabited by Turkic-speaking peoples since the tenth century, it was annexed by Russia in 1881 and became a constituent republic in 1925. Ashkhabad is the capital. Population, 3,189,000.

Turks and Cai•cos Islands (tûrks; kā′kəs, kī′kōs). Two island groups of the British West Indies in the Atlantic Ocean in the southeast part of the Bahama Islands. The islands were a dependency of Jamaica after 1848 and became a crown colony in 1962.

Turk's-cap lily (tûrks′kăp′) *n.* **1.** Either of two North American lilies, *Lilium michauxii* or *L. superbum,* having nodding, orange-red, spotted flowers with a reflexed perianth. **2.** See **martagon.**

Turk's-head (tûrks′hĕd′) *n.* A turban-shaped knot made by winding a smaller rope around a larger one.

Tur•ku (to͝or′ko͞o′). A city of southwest Finland on the Baltic Sea west of Helsinki. Settled in the early 13th century, it was the capital of Finland until 1812. Turku is now a major seaport and manufacturing center. Population, 162,282.

Tur•lock (tûr′lŏk′). A city of central California southeast of Modesto. It is the center of an irrigated farming region. Population, 26,291.

tur•ma•line (to͝or′mə-lĭn, -lēn′) *n.* Variant of **tourmaline.**

tur•mer•ic (tûr′mər-ĭk) *n.* **1.** A widely cultivated tropical plant *(Curcuma domestica)* of India, having yellow flowers and an aromatic, somewhat fleshy rhizome. **2.** The powdered rhizome of this plant, used as a condiment and a yellow dye. **3.** Any of several other plants having similar rhizomes. [Alteration of Middle English *termeryte,* from Old French *terre-merite,* saffron, from Medieval Latin *terra merita* : Latin *terra,* earth; see **ters-** in Appendix + Latin *merita,* feminine past participle of *merēre,* to deserve; see **(s)mer-**[2] in Appendix.]

turmeric paper *n.* Paper saturated with turmeric and used to detect the presence of alkalis, which turn the paper brown, or boric acid, which turns it red-brown.

tur•moil (tûr′moil′) *n.* A state of extreme confusion or agitation; commotion or tumult: *a country in turmoil over labor strikes.* [Origin unknown.]

◆**turn** (tûrn) *v.* **turned, turn•ing, turns.** *—tr.* **1.** To cause to move around an axis or a center; cause to rotate or revolve. **2.** To cause to move around in order to achieve a result, such as opening, closing, tightening, or loosening: *turn the key; turn a screw.* **3.** To alter or control the functioning of (a mechanical device, for example) by the use of a rotating or similar movement: *Please turn the iron to a hotter setting.* **4.** To perform or accomplish by rotating or revolving: *turn a somersault.* **5.a.** To change the position of so that the underside becomes the upper side: *turn the steak; turn a page.* **b.** To spade or plow (soil) to bring the undersoil to the surface. **c.** To reverse and resew the material of (a collar, for example). **6.** To revolve in the mind; meditate on; ponder. **7.a.** To give a rounded form to (wood, for example) by rotating against a cutting tool. **b.** To give a rounded shape to (clay, for example) by rotating and shaping with the hands or tools. **c.** To give a rounded form to: *turn a heel in knitting a sock.* **d.** To give distinctive, artistic, or graceful form to: *"They know precisely how to turn a dramatic line or phrase that is guaranteed to make the evening news"* (William Safire). **8.a.** To change the position of by traversing an arc of a circle; pivot: *turned his chair toward the speaker.* **b.** To cause (a scale) to move up or down so as to register weight: *Even a feather will turn a delicate scale.* **9.a.** To fold, bend, or twist (something). **b.** To change the position or disposition of by folding, bending, or twisting: *Turn the design right side up on all your jacket buttons. Turn the hat inside out.* **c.** To make a bend or curve in: *He could turn a bar of steel.* **d.** To blunt or dull (the edge of a cutting instrument). **e.** To injure by twisting: *turn an ankle.* **f.** To upset or make nauseated: *That story turns my stomach.* **10.** To change the direction or course of: *turn the car to the left.* **11.a.** To divert or deflect: *turn a stampede.* **b.** To reverse the course of; cause to retreat: *"Then turn your forces from this paltry siege/And stir them up against a mightier task"* (Shakespeare). **12.** To make a course around or about: *turn a corner.* **13.** To change the purpose, intention, or content of by persuasion or influence: *His speech turned my thinking.* **14.** To change the order or disposition of; unsettle: *"Sudden prosperity had turned* [his] *head"* (Macaulay). **15.a.** To set in a specified way or direction by or as if by rotating or pivoting; point: *turn the antenna east.* **b.** To present in a specified direction by or as if by rotating or pivoting: *turn one's face to the wall.* **16.a.** To aim or focus; train: *turn one's gaze to the sky.* **b.** To devote or apply (oneself, for example) to something: *She turned herself to music.* **17.** To cause to act or go against; make antagonistic: *News of the scandal turned public opinion against the candidate.* **18.** To cause to go in a specific direction; direct: *They turned their way back.* **19.** To send, drive, or let go: *turn the bully out of the bar; turned the dog loose.* **20.** To pour, let fall, or otherwise release (contents) from or into a receptacle: *Turn the dough onto a floured board.* **21.** To cause to take on a specified character, nature, identity, or appearance; change or transform. Used with *to* or *into: water that had been turned to ice; turn a rundown house into a show place.* **22.** To make sour; ferment: *Lack of refrigeration turned the milk.* **23.** To affect or change the color of: *Autumn turns the green leaves golden.* **24.** To exchange; convert. Used with *to* or *into: turns her singing talent into extra money.* **25.** To keep in circulation; sell and restock: *We turned a great deal of merchandise during the holidays.* **26.** To get by buying and selling: *turn a fair profit.* **27.** *Slang.* To perform (an act of prostitution): *turning tricks.* *—intr.* **1.** To move around an axis or a center; rotate or revolve. **2.** To have a sensation of revolving or whirling, especially as a result of dizziness or giddiness. **3.** To change position from side to side or back and forth: *I tossed and turned all night.* **4.** To progress through pages so as to arrive at a given place: *Please turn to page 361.* **5.a.** To operate a lathe. **b.** To be formed on a lathe: *a softwood that turns easily.* **6.** To direct one's way or course: *The truck turned into the service station. We turned off the highway at the first exit.* **7.** To change or reverse one's way, course, or direction: *Too tired to go farther, we turned toward home.* **8.** To have a specific reaction or effect, especially when adverse. **9.** To change one's actions or attitudes adversely; become hostile or antagonistic: *The once servile peasants turned against the cruel king.* **10.** To attack suddenly and violently with no apparent motive: *The tiger turned on the animal trainer.* **11.** To channel one's attention, interest, or thought toward or away from something: *"In the spring a young man's fancy lightly turns to thoughts of love"* (Tennyson). **12.** To devote or apply oneself to something, as to a field of study: *Un-*

Turkey

ă pat — oi boy
ā pay — ou out
âr care — o͝o took
ä father — o͞o boot
ĕ pet — ŭ cut
ē be — ûr urge
ĭ pit — th thin
ī pie — *th* this
îr pier — hw which
ŏ pot — zh vision
ō toe — ə about, item
ô paw — ◆ regionalism

Stress marks: ′ (primary); ′ (secondary), as in **dictionary** (dĭk′shə-nĕr′ē)

successful in mathematics, the student turned to biology. **13.** To convert to a religion. **14.** To switch one's loyalty from one side or party to another. **15.** To have recourse to a person or thing for help, support, or information. **16.** To depend on something for success or failure; hinge: *"The election would turn not on ideology but on competence"* (George F. Will). **17.a.** To change so as to be; become: *His hair turned gray. I am a lawyer turned novelist.* **b.** To change; become transformed. Used with *to* or *into*: *The sky turned to pink at dawn. The night turned into day.* **c.** To reach and pass (a certain age, for example): *My niece has turned three.* **18.** To become sour: *The milk turned because we did not refrigerate it.* **19.** To change color: *The leaves have turned.* **20.** To be stocked and sold: *This merchandise will turn easily.* **21.** To become dull or blunt by bending back. Used of the edge of a cutting instrument. **—turn** *n.* **1.** The act of turning or the condition of being turned; rotation or revolution. **2.** A change of direction, motion, or position: *Make a left turn at the corner.* **3.** A place, as in a road or path, where a change in direction occurs; a curve: *a sharp turn in the road.* **4.** A departure or deviation, as in a trend: *a strange turn of events.* **5.** A point marking the end of one period of time and the beginning of the next: *the turn of the century.* **6.a.** A chance or an opportunity. **b.** One of a series of such opportunities accorded people in succession or in scheduled order: *waiting for her next turn at bat.* **7.** A period of participation: *a turn at wrestling.* **8.a.** An attack of illness or severe nervousness. **b.** *Informal.* A momentary shock or scare: *I had quite a turn when I first heard the crash.* **9.** A characteristic mood, style, or habit; a natural inclination: *a curious and speculative turn of mind.* **10.** A propensity or an adeptness: *a turn for carpentry.* **11.** A distinctive, graceful, or artistic expression or arrangement of words: *the poetic turn of a phrase.* **12.a.** A movement or development in a particular direction: *a turn for the worse.* **b.** A variation of a given kind or type: *"His muse occasionally takes a humorous and satirical turn"* (Albert C. Baugh). **13.** A deed or an action having a good or bad effect on another: *"He thought some friend had done him an ill turn"* (Stephen Crane). **14.** Advantage or purpose: *It served his turn.* **15.** A short walk or excursion out and back: *took a turn in the park.* **16.** A distortion in shape. **17.** The condition of being twisted or wound. **18.a.** A winding of one thing about another. **b.** A single wind or convolution, as of wire on a spool. **19.** Something that winds or turns around a center axis. **20.** *Music.* A figure or an ornament consisting of four or more notes in rapid succession and including in addition to the principal note the one that is a degree above and the one that is a degree below it. **21.** A brief theatrical act or stage appearance. **22.** A transaction on the stock market involving both a sale and a purchase. **23.** *South Atlantic U.S.* The amount that can be carried in the arms in one load: *a turn of firewood.* **—*phrasal verbs.*** **turn away. 1.** To send away; dismiss: *turned away the salesperson.* **2.** To repel: *The poor location of the condominium turned away many prospective buyers.* **3.** To avert; deflect: *turned away all criticism.* **turn back. 1.** To reverse one's direction of motion: *stopped on the road and had to turn back.* **2.** To drive back and away: *turned back the uninvited comers.* **3.** To halt the advance of: *managed to turn back the advancing army.* **4.** To fold down: *Turn back the corner of the page to save your place in the book.* **turn down. 1.** To diminish the speed, volume, intensity, or flow of: *Turn down the radio, please.* **2.** To reject or refuse, as a person, advice, or a suggestion: *We politely turned down the invitation.* **3.** To fold or be capable of folding down: *turn a collar down; a collar that turns down.* **turn in. 1.** To hand in; give over: *turned in the final exam.* **2.** To inform on or deliver: *The criminal turned herself in.* **3.** To produce: *turns in a consistent performance every day.* **4.** *Informal.* To go to bed: *I turned in early last night.* **turn off. 1.** To stop the operation, activity, or flow of; shut off: *turned off the television.* **2.** *Slang.* **a.** To affect with dislike, displeasure, or revulsion: *That song really turns me off.* **b.** To affect with boredom: *The play turned the audience off.* **c.** To lose or cause to lose interest; withdraw: *turning off to materialism.* **d.** To cease paying attention to: *Unable to leave my seat, I turned off the boring speaker and thought about vacation.* **3.** To divert; deflect. **4.** *Chiefly British.* To dismiss (an employee). **turn on. 1.** To cause to begin the operation, activity, or flow of: *Turn on the light bulb.* **2.** To begin to display, employ, or exude: *turn on the charm.* **3.** *Slang.* **a.** To take or cause to take a mind-altering drug, especially for the first time. **b.** To be or cause to become interested, pleasurably excited, or stimulated. Often used with *to*: *My uncle turned me on to jazz. She turned on to surfing this summer.* **c.** To excite or become excited sexually. **turn out. 1.** To shut off: *turned out the lights.* **2.** To arrive or assemble, as for a public event or entertainment: *A large group of protesters have turned out.* **3.** To produce, as by a manufacturing process; make: *an assembly line turning out cars.* **4.** To be found to be, as after experience or trial: *The rookie turned out to be the best hitter on the team.* **5.** To end up; result: *The cake turned out beautifully.* **6.** To equip; outfit: *troops that were turned out beautifully.* **7.** *Informal.* To get out of bed. **8.** To evict; expel: *The tenants were turned out.* **turn over. 1.** To bring the bottom to the top or vice versa; invert. **2.a.** To shift the position of, as by rolling from one side to the other. **b.** To shift one's position by rolling from one side to the other. **3.** To rotate; cycle: *The engine turned over but wouldn't start.* **4.** To think about; consider: *She turned over the problem in her mind.* **5.** To transfer to another; surrender: *turned over the illegal funds.* **6.** To do business to the extent or amount of: *turn over a million dollars a year.* **7.** To seem to lurch or heave convulsively: *My stomach turned over.* **turn to.** To begin work: *If you quit dawdling and just turn to, the cleaning will be done in a day.* **turn up. 1.** To increase the speed, volume, intensity, or flow of: *turn up the public-address system.* **2.a.** To find: *She turned up the missing papers under her blotter.* **b.** To be found: *The papers will turn up sooner or later.* **3.** To make an appearance; arrive: *Several old friends turned up at the reunion.* **4.** To fold or be capable of folding up: *turning up his cuffs; cuffs that will turn up.* **5.** To happen unexpectedly: *Something turned up and I was unable to go.* **6.** To be evident: *Her name constantly turns up in art circles.* **—*idioms.*** **at every turn.** In every place; at every moment. **by turns.** One after another; alternately: *"From the . . . testimony emerges a man by turns devious and honest, vulgar and gallant, scatterbrained and shrewd"* (Life). **in turn.** In the proper order or sequence. **out of turn. 1.** Not in the proper order or sequence. **2.** At an inappropriate time or in an inappropriate manner: *I may be speaking out of turn, but you might like to know that your attire does not conform to the dress code here.* **to a turn.** To a precise degree; perfectly: *The roast was done to a turn.* **turn a blind eye.** To refuse to see or recognize something: *turned a blind eye to government corruption.* **turn a deaf ear.** To refuse to listen to or hear something: *turned a deaf ear to the protests.* **turn a hair.** To become afraid or upset: *didn't turn a hair during the bank robbery.* **turn (one's) back on. 1.** To deny; reject. **2.** To abandon; forsake. **turn (one's) hand.** To apply oneself, as to a task: *turned her hand to writing the dissertation; was lazy and wouldn't turn his hand.* **turn (one's) head. 1.** To cause to become infatuated. **2.** To cause to become egotistical and conceited: *Success has turned his head.* **turn over a new leaf.** To change, as one's attitude or conduct, for the better. **turn tail.** To run away. **turn the** (or **a**) **corner.** To reach and surpass a midpoint or milestone. **turn the other cheek.** To respond to insult or injury by patiently eschewing retaliation. **turn the scales.** To offset the balance of a situation. **turn the tables.** To reverse a situation and gain the upper hand. **turn turtle.** To capsize or turn upside-down: *Our sailboat turned turtle during the squall.* **turn up (one's) nose.** To regard (something) with disdain or scorn: *turned up her nose at the food.* [Middle English *turnen,* from Old English *turnian, tyrnan* and Old French *torner,* both from Latin *tornāre,* to turn in a lathe, from *tornus,* lathe, from Greek *tornos.* See **terə-¹** in Appendix.]

SYNONYMS: *turn, rotate, revolve, gyrate, spin, whirl, circle, eddy, swirl.* These verbs all mean to move or cause to move in a circle. *Turn,* the most general, means to move in a circular course: *a planet turning on its axis; turned and stared at me. Rotate* usually involves movement around an object's own axis or center: *The top rotated with decreasing speed as the spring wound down. Revolve* can have the same meaning as *rotate,* while in certain contexts it is distinguished from *rotate* as involving orbital movement: *The earth revolves around the sun. Gyrate* usually refers to revolving in or as if in a spiral course: *waltzers gyrating giddily.* To *spin* is to rotate rapidly, often within a narrow compass: *"He . . . spun round, flung up his arms, and fell on his back, shot through"* (John Galsworthy). *Whirl* applies to rapid or forceful revolution or rotation: *whirling snowflakes. Circle* refers to circular or approximately circular motion: *sea gulls circling above the ocean. Eddy* usually denotes rapid circular movement like that of a whirlpool: *Storm clouds eddied overhead. Swirl,* often interchangeable with *eddy,* sometimes connotes a graceful undulation, spiral, or whorl: *The flood waters swirled wildly under the bridge. The milliner swirled tulle lavishly above the brim of the hat.* See also Synonyms at **resort.**

turn·a·bout (tûrnʹə-boutʹ) *n.* **1.** The act of turning about and facing or moving in the opposite direction. **2.** A shift or change in opinion, loyalty, or allegiance. **3.** A dance or party to which girls invite boys.

turn·a·round (tûrnʹə-roundʹ) *n.* **1.** A space, as in a driveway, permitting the turning around of a vehicle. **2.** The act or an instance of turning about and facing or moving in the opposite direction; a reversal: *Stock prices fell in the morning but rallied in a dramatic afternoon turnaround.* **3.** A shift or change in opinion, loyalty, or allegiance. **4.a.** The process of or time needed for loading, unloading, and servicing a ship, an airplane, or other vehicle. **b.** The process of or time needed for performing a task, especially receiving, completing, and returning an assignment.

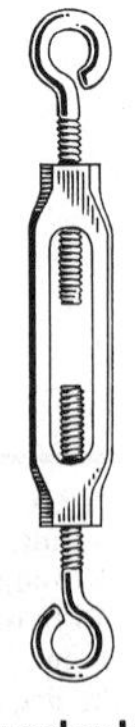

turnbuckle

turn·buck·le (tûrnʹbŭkʹəl) *n.* A metal coupling device consisting of an oblong piece internally threaded at both ends into which the two sections of a threaded rod are screwed in order to adjust the tension of the rod.

turn·coat (tûrnʹkōtʹ) *n.* One who traitorously switches allegiance.

turn·down (tûrnʹdounʹ) *n.* **1.** A rejection. **2.** One who has been turned down or rejected. **3.** Something that is folded down, as on a garment. **4.** A downturn. **—turndown** *adj.* Being or capable of being turned or folded down: *a turndown collar.*

turned-on (tûrndʹŏnʹ, -ônʹ) *adj. Slang.* **1.** Highly aware of and responsive to what is fashionable and up-to-date. **2.a.** Pleasantly excited or stimulated. **b.** Sexually aroused. **c.** Under the influence of a mind-altering drug.

turn·er¹ (tûrʹnər) *n.* One that turns, especially a person who operates a lathe or similar device.

turn·er² (tûrʹnər) *n. Sports.* A tumbler or gymnast, especially a member of a turnverein. [German, from *turnen,* to do gymnastics, from Old High German *turnēn,* to turn, from Latin *tornāre,* to turn in a lathe. See TURN.]

Tur·ner (tûr′nər), **Frederick Jackson.** 1861–1932. American historian who emphasized the importance of the frontier in American history.

Turner, Joseph Mallord William. 1775–1851. British painter whose abstract treatment of light, color, and space influenced the French impressionists. Among his works are *Sun Rising Through Vapour* (1807) and *Rain, Steam, and Speed* (1844).

Turner, Nat. 1800–1831. American slave leader who organized about 70 followers and led a rebellion in Virginia, during which approximately 50 whites were killed (1831). He was subsequently captured and executed.

Tur·ner's syndrome (tûr′nərz) *n.* A congenital condition of females associated with a defect or an absence of an X chromosome, characterized by short stature, sexual underdevelopment, and other physical abnormalities. [After Henry Hubert *Turner* (1892–1970), American endocrinologist.]

turn·er·y (tûr′nə-rē) *n., pl.* **-ies.** The work or workshop of a lathe operator.

turn·ing (tûr′nĭng) *n.* **1.** A deviation from a straight course; a turn. **2. a.** The shaping of metal or wood on a lathe. **b. turnings.** Shavings produced in shaping metal on a lathe.

turning point *n.* **1.** The point at which a very significant change occurs; a decisive moment. **2.** *Mathematics.* A maximum or minimum point on a curve.

tur·nip (tûr′nĭp) *n.* **1.** A widely cultivated Eurasian plant *(Brassica rapa)* of the mustard family, having a large, fleshy, edible yellow or white root. **2.** The root of this plant, eaten as a vegetable. [*tur-,* of unknown origin + dialectal *nepe,* turnip (from Middle English, from Old English *nǣp,* from Latin *nāpus*).]

turnip cabbage *n.* See **kohlrabi.**

tur·nip-root·ed celery (tûr′nĭp-ro͞otĭd, -ro͞ot′ĭd) *n.* See **celeriac.**

turn·key (tûrn′kē′) *n., pl.* **-keys.** The keeper of the keys in a prison; a jailer. **—turnkey** *adj.* **1.** Supplied, installed, or purchased in a condition ready for immediate use, occupation, or operation: *a turnkey computer system; a turnkey housing project; a turnkey factory.* **2.** Of or relating to something supplied, installed, or purchased in this manner: *a turnkey agreement.*

turn·off (tûrn′ôf′, -ŏf′) *n.* **1.** A branch of a road or path leading away from a main thoroughfare, especially an exit on a highway. **2.** The act or an instance of turning off. **3.** *Slang.* **a.** One that is distasteful: *The evening was a real turnoff.* **b.** Something that causes loss of interest.

turn-on (tûrn′ŏn′, -ôn′) *n.* *Slang.* Something that causes pleasure or excitement: *"The real turn-on . . . is that he is a visionary as well as a scientist"* (Village Voice).

turn·out (tûrn′out′) *n.* **1.** The number of people gathered for a particular event or purpose; attendance: *The peace march attracted a large turnout.* **2.** A number of things produced; output. **3.** The act or an instance of turning out. **4.** *Chiefly British.* **a.** A labor strike. **b.** A laborer on strike. **5.** An array of equipment; an outfit. **6.** An outfit of a carriage with its horse or horses; equipage. **7.** A railroad siding. **8.** A widening in a highway to allow vehicles to pass or park. **9.** The rotation of a dancer's legs from the hip sockets in classical ballet.

turn·o·ver (tûrn′ō′vər) *n.* *Abbr.* **t.o.** **1.** The act of turning over; an upset or overthrow. **2.** An abrupt change; a reversal. **3.** A small pastry made by covering one half of a piece of dough with fruit, preserves, or other filling and folding the other half over on top. **4. a.** The number of times a particular stock of goods is sold and restocked during a given period of time. **b.** The amount of business transacted during a given period of time. **c.** The number of shares of stock sold on the market during a given period of time. **5. a.** The number of workers hired by an establishment to replace those who have left in a given period of time. **b.** The ratio of this number to the number of employed workers. **6.** *Sports.* A loss of possession of the ball to the opposing team, as by a misplay or an infraction of the rules. **—turnover** *adj.* Capable of being turned or folded down or over: *a turnover collar.*

turn·pike (tûrn′pīk′) *n.* *Abbr.* **tnpk., tpk.** **1.** A toll road, especially an expressway with tollgates. **2.** A tollgate. [Middle English *turnepike,* spiked barrier : *turnen,* to turn; see TURN + *pike,* sharp point; see PIKE[5].]

turn signal *n.* See **directional signal.**

turn·sole (tûrn′sōl′) *n.* **1.** Any of various plants that move or are believed to move in response to the sun. **2.** See **heliotrope** (sense 1a). [Middle English *turnesole,* purple dye obtained from the plant, from Old French *tournesol,* from Old Italian *tornasole,* heliotrope : *tornare,* to turn (from Latin *tornāre;* see TURN) + *sole,* sun (from Latin *sōl;* see **sāwel-** in Appendix).]

turn·spit (tûrn′spĭt′) *n.* **1. a.** One that turns a roasting spit. **b.** A roasting spit that can be turned. **2.** A dog formerly used in a treadmill to turn a roasting spit.

turn·stile (tûrn′stīl′) *n.* **1.** A mechanical device used to control passage from one public area to another, typically consisting of several horizontal arms supported by and radially projecting from a central vertical post and allowing only the passage of individuals on foot. **2.** A similar structure that permits the passage of an individual once a charge has been paid or that counts the number of individuals passing through.

turn·stone (tûrn′stōn′) *n.* Either of two wading birds, *Arenaria interpres,* a widely distributed species that is dark brown above with large areas of chestnut and black, or *A. melanocephala,* having black and white plumage, that breeds along the coast of Alaska and winters from there to Baja California. [From its method of finding food.]

turn·ta·ble (tûrn′tā′bəl) *n.* **1. a.** The circular horizontal rotating platform of a phonograph on which the record is placed. **b.** A phonograph exclusive of amplifying circuitry and speakers. **2.** A circular horizontal rotating platform equipped with a railway track, used for turning locomotives, as in a roundhouse. **3.** A rotating platform or disk, such as a lazy Susan.

turn·up (tûrn′ŭp′) *n.* Something, such as the cuff on a trouser leg, that is turned up or can be turned up. **—turnup** *adj.* Turned up or capable of being turned up.

turn·ver·ein (tûrn′və-rīn′, to͝orn′-) *n.* *Sports.* A club of tumblers or gymnasts. [German : *turnen,* to do gymnastics; see TURNER[2] + *Verein,* club (from obsolete *vereine,* back-formation from Middle High German *vereinen,* to unite : *ver-,* intensive pref., from Old High German *far-;* see **per**[1] in Appendix + *einen,* to make one, from *ein,* one, from Old High German; see **oi-no-** in Appendix).]

tur·pen·tine (tûr′pən-tīn′) *n.* **1.** A thin volatile essential oil, $C_{10}H_{16}$, obtained by steam distillation or other means from the wood or exudate of certain pine trees and used as a paint thinner, solvent, and medicinally as a liniment. Also called *oil of turpentine, spirit of turpentine.* **2.** The sticky mixture of resin and volatile oil from which turpentine is distilled. **3.** A brownish-yellow resinous liquid obtained from the terebinth. **—turpentine** *tr.v.* **-tined, -tin·ing, -tines.** **1.** To apply turpentine to or mix turpentine with. **2.** To extract turpentine from (a tree). [Middle English, resin of the terebinth, from Old French *terebentine,* from Latin *terebinthina (rēsīna),* terebinth (resin), from Greek *terebinthinē,* feminine of *terebenthinos,* from *terebinthos,* terebinth tree.] **—tur′pen·tin′ic** (-tĭn′ĭk), **tur′pen·tin′ous** (-tĭn′əs) *adj.*

turnip
Brassica rapa

tur·pi·tude (tûr′pĭ-to͞od′, -tyo͞od′) *n.* **1.** Depravity; baseness. **2.** A base act. [Middle English, from Old French, from Latin *turpitūdō,* from *turpis,* shameful.]

turps (tûrps) *pl.n.* *(used with a sing. verb).* *Informal.* Turpentine. [Shortening and alteration of TURPENTINE.]

tur·quoise (tûr′kwoiz′, -koiz′) *n.* **1.** A blue to blue-green mineral of aluminum and copper, mainly $CuAl_6(PO_4)_4(OH)_8 \cdot 4H_2O$, prized as a gemstone in its polished blue form. **2.** *Color.* A light to brilliant bluish green. [Middle English *turkeis* and French *turquoise,* both from Old French *(pierre) turqueise,* Turkish (stone), turquoise, feminine of *turqueis,* Turkish, from *Turc,* Turk. See TURK.] **—tur′quoise′** *adj.*

tur·ret (tûr′ĭt, tŭr′-) *n.* **1.** A small tower or tower-shaped projection on a building. **2. a.** A low, heavily armored structure, usually rotating horizontally, containing mounted guns and their gunners or crew, as on a warship or tank. **b.** A domelike gunner's enclosure projecting from the fuselage of a combat aircraft. **3.** A tall wooden structure mounted on wheels and used in ancient warfare by besiegers to scale the walls of an enemy fortress. **4.** An attachment for a lathe consisting of a rotating cylindrical block holding various cutting tools. **5.** A rotating device holding various lenses, as for a microscope, allowing easy switching from one lens to another. [Middle English *turet,* from Old French *torete,* diminutive of *tor,* tower. See TOWER.]

tur·ret·ed (tûr′ĭ-tĭd, tŭr′-) *adj.* **1.** Furnished with turrets or a turret. **2.** Having the shape or form of a turret, as certain long-spired gastropod shells.

tur·tle[1] (tûr′tl) *n.* **1.** Any of various aquatic or terrestrial reptiles of the order Testudines (or Chelonia), having horny toothless jaws and a bony or leathery shell into which the head, limbs, and tail can be withdrawn in most species. **2.** *Chiefly British.* A sea turtle. **—turtle** *intr.v.* **-tled, -tling, -tles.** **1.** To hunt for turtles, especially as an occupation. **2.** *Nautical.* To capsize. [Perhaps from French *tortue,* from Old French, from Medieval Latin **tortūca,* perhaps alteration of Vulgar Latin **tartarūca,* feminine of **tartarūcus,* of Tartarus, from Late Latin *tartarūchus,* from Late Greek *tartaroukhos,* occupying Tartarus : *Tartaros,* Tartarus + *ekhein,* to hold; see EUNUCH.] **—tur′tler** *n.*

turtle[1]
Florida box turtle
Terrapene carolina bauri

tur·tle[2] (tûr′tl) *n.* *Archaic.* A turtledove. [Middle English, from Old English, from Latin *turtur,* probably of imitative origin.]

tur·tle[3] (tûr′tl) *n.* A turtleneck.

tur·tle·back (tûr′tl-băk′) *n.* Something shaped like the back of a turtle, especially: **a.** *Nautical.* An arched structure erected over the deck of a ship as protection from heavy seas. **b.** *Archaeology.* A stone tool with a convex side. **—tur′tle·back′, tur′tle·backed′** *adj.*

tur·tle·dove (tûr′tl-dŭv′) *n.* **1.** A small, slender European dove *(Streptopelia turtur)* having a white-edged tail and a soft, purring voice. **2.** See **mourning dove.**

tur·tle·head (tûr′tl-hĕd′) *n.* Any of several perennial North American herbs of the genus *Chelone,* especially *C. glabra,* having a white or pink bilabiate corolla with a bearded lower lip. Also called *snakehead.* [From the shape of its flowers.]

tur·tle·neck (tûr′tl-nĕk′) *n.* **1.** A high, tubular, turned-down collar that fits closely about the neck. **2.** A garment, such as a sweater, that has this type of collar.

turves (tûrvz) *n.* A plural of **turf.**

Tus·ca·loo·sa (tŭs′kə-lo͞o′sə). A city of west-central Alabama southwest of Birmingham. Established in 1819 on the site of

ă pat	oi boy
ā pay	ou out
âr care	o͝o took
ä father	o͞o boot
ĕ pet	ŭ cut
ē be	ûr urge
ĭ pit	th thin
ī pie	*th* this
îr pier	hw which
ŏ pot	zh vision
ō toe	ə about, item
ô paw	♦ regionalism

Stress marks: ′ (primary); ′ (secondary), as in **dictionary** (dĭk′shə-nĕr′ē)

tusk
Bull walrus

Tutankhamen

tutu

a Creek village, it was the state capital from 1826 to 1846. Population, 75,143.

Tus·can (tŭs′kən) *adj.* **1.** Of or relating to Tuscany, its people, or their language. **2.** *Architecture.* Of or relating to the Tuscan order. **—Tuscan** *n.* **1.** A native or inhabitant of Tuscany. **2.a.** Any of the dialects of Italian spoken in Tuscany. **b.** The standard literary form of Italian. [Middle English, from Latin *Tuscānus,* Etruscan, from *Tuscus,* an Etruscan.]

Tuscan order *n. Architecture.* A classical order similar to Roman Doric but having columns with an unfluted shaft and a simplified base, capital, and entablature.

Tus·ca·ny (tŭs′kə-nē′). A region of northwest Italy between the northern Apennines and the Ligurian and Tyrrhenian seas. Inhabited in ancient times by the Etruscans, it fell to Rome in the mid-fourth century B.C. Tuscany was a grand duchy under the Medicis (1569–1860) and subsequently became united with the kingdom of Sardinia.

Tus·ca·ro·ra (tŭs′kə-rôr′ə, -rōr′ə) *n., pl.* **Tuscarora** or **-ras. 1.a.** A Native American people formerly inhabiting parts of North Carolina, with present-day populations in western New York and southeast Ontario, Canada. The Tuscarora migrated northward in the 18th century, joining the Iroquois confederacy in 1722 and adopting aspects of the Iroquois culture. **b.** A member of this people. **2.** The Iroquoian language of the Tuscarora.

tu·sche (to͝osh′ə) *n.* A black liquid used for drawing in lithography and as a resist in etching and silk-screen work. [German, back-formation from *tuschen,* to lay on colors, from French *toucher,* from Old French *tochier, touchier,* to touch. See TOUCH.]

Tus·cu·lum (tŭs′kə-ləm, -kyə-). A city of ancient Latium southeast of modern-day Rome, Italy. Pliny the Younger, Cicero, and the emperors Nero and Titus were among the prominent Romans who built villas here.

tush¹ (tŭsh) *interj.* Used to express mild reproof, disapproval, or admonition.

♦**tush²** (tŭsh) *n.* **1.** A canine tooth, especially of a horse. **2.** *Chiefly Southern U.S.* See **tusk** (sense 1). [Middle English *tusche,* from Old English *tūsc.* See TUSK.]

tush³ (to͝osh) *n. Slang.* The buttocks. [Alteration of Yiddish *tokhes,* from Hebrew *taḥat,* under, buttocks.]

tush·y also **tush·ie** (to͝osh′ē) *n., pl.* **-ies.** *Slang.* The buttocks. [From TUSH³.]

♦**tusk** (tŭsk) *n.* **1.** An elongated, pointed tooth, usually one of a pair, extending outside of the mouth in certain animals such as the walrus, elephant, or wild boar. Also called ♦*tush.* **2.** A long, projecting tooth or toothlike part. **—tusk** *tr. & intr.v.* **tusked, tusk·ing, tusks.** To gore or dig with the tusks or a tusk. [Middle English *tux, tusce,* from Old English *tūx, tūsc,* canine tooth. See **dent-** in Appendix.] **—tusked** *adj.*

Tus·ke·gee (tŭs-kē′gē). A city of eastern Alabama east of Montgomery. It is the seat of the Tuskegee Institute, founded by Booker T. Washington in 1881. Population, 12,716.

tusk·er (tŭs′kər) *n.* An animal, such as a wild boar, that has tusks.

tusk shell *n.* See **tooth shell.**

tus·sah (tŭs′ə, tŭs′ô′) also **tus·sore** (tŭs′ôr′, -ōr′) *n.* **1.** An Asian silkworm, the larva of a large saturniid moth *(Antheraea paphia),* that produces a coarse brownish or yellowish silk. **2.** The silk produced by this worm or a fabric woven from it. [Hindi *tasar,* from Sanskrit *tasaram,* shuttle (probably from the shape of its cocoon).]

tus·sie-mus·sie (tŭs′ē-mŭs′ē) or **tuz·zy-muz·zy** (tŭz′ē-mŭz′ē) *n., pl.* **-sies** or **-zies. 1.** A small bouquet of flowers; a nosegay. **2.** A cone-shaped holder for such a bouquet. [Middle English *tussemose,* perhaps reduplication of **tusse.*]

tus·sis (tŭs′ĭs) *n., pl.* **-ses** (-sēz). A cough. [Latin.] **—tus′sal** (tŭs′əl) *adj.*

tus·sle (tŭs′əl) *intr.v.* **-sled, -sling, -sles.** To struggle roughly; scuffle. **—tussle** *n.* A rough or vigorous struggle; a scuffle. [Middle English *tussillen,* frequentative of *-tousen,* to pull roughly.]

tus·sock (tŭs′ək) *n.* **1.** A clump or tuft, as of growing grass. **2.** A tuft of hair or feathers. [Origin unknown.] **—tus′sock·y** *adj.*

tussock moth *n.* Any of various dull-colored moths of the family Lymantriidae, the caterpillars of which have tufts of hair along the back and are often destructive to deciduous trees.

tus·sore (tŭs′ôr′, -ōr′) *n.* Variant of **tussah.**

Tus·tin (tŭs′tĭn). A city of southern California, a residential and manufacturing suburb in the Greater Los Angeles area. Population, 32,073.

tut (*a* t-*like sound produced by suction rather than plosion; conventional spelling pronunciation,* tŭt) *interj.* Used to express annoyance, impatience, or mild reproof: *"Tut, tut, child! . . . Everything's got a moral, if only you can find it"* (Lewis Carroll). **—tut** *n. & v.*

Tut·ankh·a·men (to͞ot′äng-kä′mən). fl. c. 1358 B.C. King of Egypt during the XVIII Dynasty. His tomb was found almost intact by Howard Carter in 1922.

tu·tee (to͞o-tē′, tyo͞o-) *n.* One that is being tutored. [*tut(or)* + -EE¹.]

tu·te·lage (to͞ot′l-ĭj, tyo͞ot′-) *n.* **1.** The capacity or activity of a guardian; guardianship. **2.** The capacity or activity of a tutor; instruction or teaching. **3.** The state of being under the direction of a guardian or tutor. [Latin *tūtēla* (from *tūtus,* variant past participle of *tuērī,* to guard) + -AGE.]

tu·te·lar·y (to͞ot′l-ĕr′ē, tyo͞ot′-) also **tu·te·lar** (to͞ot′l-ər, -är′, tyo͞ot′-) *—adj.* **1.** Being or serving as a guardian or protector: *tutelary gods.* **2.** Of or relating to a guardian or guardianship. *—n., pl.* **-lar·ies** also **-lars.** One that serves as a guardian or protector. [From Latin *tūtēlārius,* guardian, from *tūtēla,* tutelage. See TUTELAGE.]

tu·tor (to͞o′tər, tyo͞o′-) *n.* **1.a.** A private instructor. **b.** One that gives additional, special, or remedial instruction. **2.** A teacher or teaching assistant in some universities and colleges having a rank lower than that of an instructor. **3.** A graduate, usually a fellow, responsible for the supervision of an undergraduate at some British universities. **4.** *Law.* The legal guardian of a minor and of the minor's property. **—tutor** *v.* **-tored, -tor·ing, -tors.** *—tr.* **1.** To act as a tutor to; instruct or teach privately. **2.** To have the guardianship, tutelage, or care of. *—intr.* **1.** To function as a tutor. **2.** To be instructed by a tutor; study under a tutor. [Middle English *tutour,* from Old French, from Latin *tūtor,* from *tūtus,* variant past participle of *tuērī,* to guard.]

tu·to·ri·al (to͞o-tôr′ē-əl, -tōr′-, tyo͞o-) *adj.* Of or relating to tutors or a tutor. **—tutorial** *n.* Something that provides special, often individual instruction, especially: **a.** A book or class that provides instruction in a particular area. **b.** *Computer Science.* A program that instructs the user of a system or software package by simulating the capabilities of the system or software.

tut·ti (to͞o′tē) *Music. adv. & adj.* All. Used chiefly as a direction to indicate that all performers are to take part. **—tutti** *n., pl.* **-tis.** A passage of ensemble music intended to be executed by all the performers simultaneously. [Italian, pl. of *tutto,* all, from Vulgar Latin **tōttus,* variant of Latin *tōtus.* See **teutā-** in Appendix.]

tut·ti-frut·ti (to͞o′tē-fro͞o′tē) *n., pl.* **-tis. 1.** A confection, especially ice cream, containing a variety of chopped and usually candied fruits. **2.** A flavoring simulating the flavor of many fruits. **—tutti-frutti** *adj.* Having a combination of fruit flavors. [Italian : *tutti,* pl. of *tutto,* all + *frutti,* pl. of *frutto,* fruit.]

tut-tut (*two* t-*like sounds produced by suction rather than plosion; conventional spelling pronunciation,* tŭt′tŭt′) *intr.v.* **-tut·ted, -tut·ting, -tuts.** To express annoyance, impatience, or mild reproof: *"those fussy fellows at the State Department tut-tutting about lack of reform in the political system"* (John Hughes). [Imitative.]

tut·ty (tŭt′ē) *n., pl.* **-ties.** An impure zinc oxide obtained as a sublimate from the flues of zinc-smelting furnaces and used as a polishing powder. [Middle English *tutie,* from Old French, from Arabic *tūtiyā,* from Persian, from Sanskrit *tuttham,* blue vitriol.]

tu·tu (to͞o′to͞o) *n.* A short skirt, often consisting of many layers of gathered sheer fabric, worn by ballerinas. [French, perhaps alteration of *cucu,* baby-talk reduplication of *cul,* buttocks. See CULOTTE.]

Tu·tu (to͞o′to͞o), **Desmond.** Born 1931. South African prelate. A leader in the antiapartheid struggle, he has been a prominent advocate of international economic sanctions against South Africa. He won the 1984 Nobel Peace Prize.

Tu·tu·i·la (to͞o′to͞o-ē′lə). An island of American Samoa in the southwest-central Pacific Ocean. It is the largest island in the group.

Tu·va·lu (to͞o-vä′lo͞o, to͞o′və-lo͞o′). Formerly **El·lice Islands** (ĕl′ĭs). An island country of the western Pacific Ocean north of Fiji. Organized as a British protectorate in 1892, the islands became part of the Gilbert and Ellice Islands colony in 1915 and achieved independence in 1978. Fongafale, on Funafuti Island, is the capital. Population, 7,349.

tux (tŭks) *n. Informal.* A tuxedo.

tux·e·do (tŭk-sē′dō) *n., pl.* **-dos** or **-does. 1.** A man's dress jacket, usually black with satin or grosgrain lapels, worn for formal or semiformal occasions. Also called *dinner jacket.* **2.** A complete outfit including this jacket, trousers usually with a silken stripe down the side, a bow tie, and often a cummerbund. [Short for *Tuxedo coat,* after a country club at *Tuxedo* Park, a village of southeast New York.] **—tux·e′doed** *adj.*

Tux·tla Gu·tiér·rez (to͞os′tlə go͞o-tyĕr′ĕs). A city of southeast Mexico near the Isthmus of Tehuantepec. It is an agricultural trade center. Population, 131,096.

tu·yère (twē-yâr′) *n.* The pipe, nozzle, or other opening through which air is forced into a blast furnace or forge to facilitate combustion. [French, from Old French, from *tuyau,* pipe, probably of Germanic origin.]

tuz·zy-muz·zy (tŭz′ē-mŭz′ē) *n.* Variant of **tussie-mussie.**

TV (tē′vē′) *n., pl.* **TVs** or **TV's.** Television.

TVA *abbr.* Tennessee Valley Authority.

TV dinner *n.* A frozen prepared meal that needs only to be heated before serving.

twa (twä, twô) *n., adj. & pron. Scots.* Two. [Middle English, variant of *two.* See TWO.]

twad·dle (twŏd′l) *intr.v.* **-dled, -dling, -dles.** To talk foolishly; prate. **—twaddle** *n.* Foolish, trivial, or idle talk or chatter. [Probably variant of dialectal *twattle,* perhaps alteration of TATTLE.] **—twad′dler** *n.*

twain (twān) *n., adj. & pron.* Two. [Middle English *tweien, twaine,* from Old English *twēgen.* See **dwo-** in Appendix.]

Twain (twān), **Mark.** See Samuel Langhorne **Clemens.**

twang (twăng) *v.* **twanged, twang·ing, twangs.** *—intr.* **1.** To emit a sharp, vibrating sound, as the string of a musical instrument does when it is plucked. **2.** To resound with a sharp, vibrating sound. **3.** To speak in a strongly nasal tone of voice. —*tr.* **1.** To cause to make a sharp, vibrating sound: *twanged the car antenna.* **2.** To utter with a strongly nasal tone of voice. —**twang** *n.* **1.** A sharp, vibrating sound, as that of a plucked string. **2.** A strongly nasal tone of voice, especially as a peculiarity of certain regional dialects. [Imitative.] —**twang′y** *adj.*

'twas (twŭz, twŏz, twəz *when unstressed*). It was.

twat (twŏt) *n. Obscene.* **1.** The vulva. **2.** Used as a disparaging term for a woman. [Origin unknown.]

tway·blade (twā′blād′) *n.* Any of numerous small terrestrial orchids of the genera *Liparis* and *Listera,* having usually two basal leaves and a terminal cluster of greenish or purplish flowers. [Obsolete *tway,* two (short for Middle English *twaine;* see TWAIN) + BLADE (translation of Medieval Latin *bifolium,* two-leaf).]

tweak (twēk) *tr.v.* **tweaked, tweak·ing, tweaks. 1.** To pinch, pluck, or twist sharply. **2.** To adjust; fine-tune. —**tweak** *n.* A sharp, twisting pinch. [Probably variant of dialectal *twick,* from Middle English *twikken,* from Old English *twiccian.*] —**tweak′y** *adj.*

twee (twē) *adj. Chiefly British.* Overly precious or nice. [Alteration of *tweet,* baby-talk alteration of SWEET.]

tweed (twēd) *n.* **1.** A coarse, rugged, often nubby woolen fabric made in any of various twill weaves and used chiefly for casual suits and coats. **2. tweeds.** Clothing made of this fabric. [Alteration (possibly influenced by the river TWEED) of Scots *tweel,* twill, from Middle English *twile.* See TWILL.]

WORD HISTORY: Calling the word *tweed* an alteration of the form *tweel* obscures the fact that in this case, as in many others, human error has helped create a word. *Tweed* is indeed possibly the result of a misreading of *tweel,* an originally Scots form of *twill. Tweed* also could be a misreading of an abbreviated form of *tweeled,* a form of *twilled.* Association with *Tweed,* the name of the river that is part of the border between England and Scotland, helped support the misreading, which was originally a trade name. The word is said to have first been used around 1831, but it is not recorded until 1847. Thus had it not been for the misreading, the tweedy look might have been the tweely look or the tweeledy look.

Tweed (twēd). A river, 156 km (97 mi) long, of southeast Scotland forming part of the Scottish-English border. It flows eastward to the North Sea and has rich salmon fisheries.

Tweed, William Marcy. Known as "Boss Tweed." 1823–1878. American politician. The Democratic boss of New York City in the 1860's, he defrauded the city of millions of dollars before being exposed and convicted (1873).

twee·dle·dum and twee·dle·dee (twēd′l-dŭm′ ən twēd′l-dē′) *n.* Two people or two groups resembling each other so closely that they are practically indistinguishable. [After *Tweedledum* and *Tweedledee,* names of two proverbial rival fiddlers, of imitative origin.]

tweed·y (twē′dē) *adj.* **-i·er, -i·est. 1.** Made of tweed. **2.** Wearing tweeds. **3.** *Informal.* Suggestive of casual, informal taste, habits, and lifestyle: *"He's rumpled and tweedy . . . and you get the feeling that if he were preparing to drink a martini, he might casually stir it with his finger"* (Phil McCombs).

'tween (twēn) *prep.* Between.

tweet (twēt) *n.* A weak chirping sound, as of a young or small bird. —**tweet** *intr.v.* **tweet·ed, tweet·ing, tweets.** To utter a weak chirping sound. [Imitative.]

tweet·er (twē′tər) *n.* A small loudspeaker designed to reproduce high-pitched sounds in a high-fidelity audio system.

tweeze (twēz) *tr.v.* **tweezed, tweez·ing, tweez·es.** To handle or extract with tweezers. [Back-formation from TWEEZERS.]

tweez·er (twē′zər) *n.* Tweezers.

tweez·ers (twē′zərz) *pl.n.* (*used with a sing. or pl. verb*). Small pincers, usually of metal, used for plucking or handling small objects. [From obsolete *tweezes,* pl. of *tweeze,* a case for tweezers or other small instruments, alteration of *etweese,* from French *étuis,* pl. of *étui.* See ÉTUI.]

twelfth (twĕlfth) *n.* **1.** The ordinal number matching the number 12 in a series. **2.** One of 12 equal parts. **3.** *Music.* **a.** A 12-degree interval in a diatonic scale. **b.** A tone 12 degrees below or above a given tone. [Middle English *twelfthe,* alteration of Old English *twelfta.* See **dwo-** in Appendix.] —**twelfth** *adv. & adj.*

Twelfth Day (twĕlfth) *n. Ecclesiastical.* Epiphany.

Twelfth Night *n.* January 5, the eve of Epiphany and the beginning of Carnival, celebrated as a holiday in parts of Europe and the United States and marked by feasting, merrymaking, and the lighting of bonfires.

twelve (twĕlv) *n.* **1.** The cardinal number equal to the sum of 11 + 1. **2.** The twelfth in a set or sequence. **3. Twelve.** *Bible.* See table at **Bible.** [Middle English, from Old English *twelf.* See **dwo-** in Appendix.] —**twelve** *adj. & pron.*

twelve·mo (twĕlv′mō′) *n., pl.* **-mos.** *Printing.* See **duodecimo** (sense 1).

twelve·month (twĕlv′mŭnth′) *n.* A year.

twelve·pen·ny nail (twĕlv′pĕn′ē) *n.* A nail 3¼ inches (8.25 centimeters) long. [From the original price per hundred.]

twelve-tone (twĕlv′tōn′) *adj. Music.* Relating to, consisting of, or based on an atonal arrangement of the traditional 12 chromatic tones.

twen·ti·eth (twĕn′tē-ĭth, twŭn′-) *n.* **1.** The ordinal number matching the number 20 in a series. **2.** One of 20 equal parts. —**twen′ti·eth** *adv. & adj.*

twen·ty (twĕn′tē, twŭn′-) *n.* **1.** The cardinal number equal to 2 × 10. **2. twenties. a.** *Often* **Twenties.** The decade from 20 to 29 in a century. **b.** A decade or the numbers from 20 to 29: *The children are now in their twenties. The temperature dipped into the twenties.* [Middle English, from Old English *twēntig.* See **dwo-** in Appendix.] —**twen′ty** *adj. & pron.*

twen·ty-one (twĕn′tē-wŭn′, twŭn′-) *n. Games.* See **blackjack** (sense 3).

twen·ty-twen·ty or **20/20** (twĕn′tē-twĕn′tē, twŭn′tē-twŭn′tē) *adj.* Having normal visual acuity. [From a method of testing vision by reading charts at a distance of 20 feet.]

'twere (twûr). It were: *"to hold as 'twere the mirror up to nature"* (Shakespeare).

twerp also **twirp** (twûrp) *n. Slang.* A person regarded as insignificant and contemptible. [Origin unknown.]

Twi (chwē, chē) *n.* A variety of the Akan language spoken in Ghana.

twi·bill (twī′bĭl′) *n. Archaic.* **1.** A battle-ax with two cutting edges. **2.** A mattock with one blade like an ax and the other like an adz. [Middle English, from Old English : *twi-,* two; see **dwo-** in Appendix + *bil,* billhook.]

twice (twīs) *adv.* **1.** In two cases or on two occasions; two times: *I rewrote the essay twice.* **2.** In doubled degree or amount: *twice as many.* [Middle English, from Old English *twiga.* See **dwo-** in Appendix.]

twice-laid (twīs′lād′) *adj.* Made from strands of old or used rope. Used of rope.

twice-told (twīs′tōld′) *adj.* Very familiar because of repeated telling: *"'Tis hard to . . . lend fresh interest to a twice-told tale"* (Byron).

twid·dle (twĭd′l) *v.* **-dled, -dling, -dles.** —*tr.* To turn over or around idly or lightly; fiddle with: *"Couples are twiddling swizzle sticks while waiting for their tables"* (Bryan Miller). —*intr.* **1.** To trifle with something. **2.** To be busy about trifles. **3.** To twirl or rotate without purpose. —**twiddle** *n.* The act or an instance of twiddling. —***idiom.*** **twiddle (one's) thumbs.** To do little or nothing; be idle. [Possibly blend of TWIST and FIDDLE.] —**twid′dler** *n.*

twig¹ (twĭg) *n.* **1.** A young shoot representing the current season's growth of a woody plant. **2.** Any small, leafless branch of a woody plant. [Middle English, from Old English *twigge.* See **dwo-** in Appendix.]

twig² (twĭg) *v.* **twigged, twig·ging, twigs.** *Chiefly British.* —*tr.* **1.** To observe or notice. **2.** To understand or figure out: *"The layman has twigged what the strategist twigged almost two decades ago"* (Manchester Guardian Weekly). —*intr.* To be or become aware of the situation; understand: *"As Europe is now twigging, the best breeding ground for innovators who know how to do business is often big, competitive companies"* (Economist). [Irish Gaelic *tuigim,* I understand, from Old Irish *tuicse,* variant of *to-ucc-,* to understand.]

twig³ (twĭg) *n. Chiefly British.* The current style; the fashion. [Origin unknown.]

twig borer *n.* Any of various small beetles or moths whose larvae bore into the twigs of certain trees, especially fruit trees.

twig·gy (twĭg′ē) *adj.* **-gi·er, -gi·est. 1.** Resembling a twig or twigs, as in slenderness or fragility. **2.** Abounding in twigs: *a twiggy branch.*

twi·light (twī′līt′) *n.* **1. a.** The diffused light from the sky during the early evening or early morning when the sun is below the horizon and its light is refracted by the earth's atmosphere. **b.** The time of the day when the sun is just below the horizon, especially the period between sunset and dark. **2.** Dim or diffused illumination. **3.** A period or condition of decline following growth, glory, or success: *in the twilight of his life.* **4.** A state of ambiguity or obscurity. —*attributive.* Often used to modify another noun: *the twilight glow of the sky; a twilight area in the interpretation of the Constitution.* [Middle English *twilighte* : Old English *twi-,* two, half; see **dwo-** in Appendix + Old English *līht,* light; see LIGHT¹.]

twilight sleep *n.* An amnesic condition characterized by insensibility to pain without loss of consciousness, induced by an injection of morphine and scopolamine, especially to relieve the pain of childbirth.

twilight zone *n.* An area of ambiguity between two distinct states or conditions: *a twilight zone between good and evil.*

twill (twĭl) *n.* **1.** A fabric with diagonal parallel ribs. **2.** The weave used to produce such a fabric. —**twill** *tr.v.* **twilled, twill·ing, twills.** To weave (cloth) so as to produce a pattern of diagonal parallel ribs. [Middle English *twile,* from Old English *twilīc,* woven of double thread. See **dwo-** in Appendix.]

twin (twĭn) *n.* **1.** One of two offspring born at the same birth. **2.** One of two identical or similar people, animals, or things; a counterpart. **3. twins.** *Mineralogy.* Two interwoven crystals that are mirror images of each other. **4.** A twin-size bed. —**twin** *adj.* **1.** Being two or one of two offspring born at the same birth: *twin sisters.* **2.** Being two or one of two identical or similar people, animals, or things: *twin executives; twin cities; a twin bed.* **3.**

Desmond Tutu

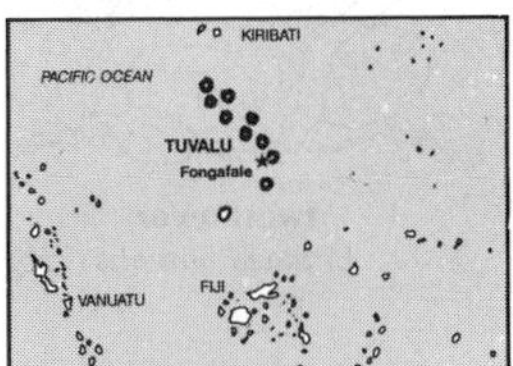

Tuvalu

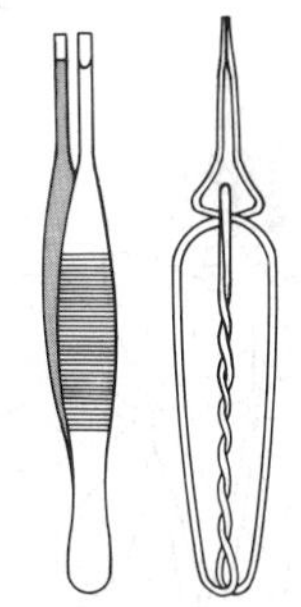

tweezers
Left: Thumb tweezers
Right: Soldering tweezers

ă pat | oi boy
ā pay | ou out
âr care | ŏŏ took
ä father | ōō boot
ĕ pet | ŭ cut
ē be | ûr urge
ĭ pit | th thin
ī pie | *th* this
îr pier | hw which
ŏ pot | zh vision
ō toe | ə about, item
ô paw | ♦ regionalism

Stress marks: ′ (primary); ′ (secondary), as in **dictionary** (dĭk′shə-nĕr′ē)

Consisting of two identical or similar parts: *a twin lamp fixture.* **—twin** *v.* **twinned, twin·ning, twins.** *—intr.* **1.a.** To give birth to twins. **b.** *Archaic.* To be one of twin offspring. **2.** To be paired or coupled. *—tr.* **1.** To pair or couple. **2.** To provide a match or counterpart to. [Middle English, from Old English *twinn,* twofold. See **dwo-** in Appendix.]

twin·ber·ry (twĭn′bĕr′ē) *n.* **1.** See **partridgeberry. 2.** A deciduous North American shrub *(Lonicera involucrata)* having shiny purple-black berries and paired flowers with a yellow tubular corolla.

twin bill *n.* **1.** A double feature. **2.** *Sports.* A double-header, especially in baseball.

twin·born (twĭn′bôrn′) *adj.* Born a twin or twins: *twinborn sisters.*

twine (twīn) *v.* **twined, twin·ing, twines.** *—tr.* **1.** To twist together (threads, for example); intertwine. **2.** To form by twisting, intertwining, or interlacing. **3.** To encircle or coil about: *The fence post was twined by vines.* **4.** To wind, coil, or wrap around something: *"She was twining a wisp of hair very slowly around her fingers"* (Anne Tyler). *—intr.* **1.** To become twisted, interlaced, or interwoven. **2.** To go in a winding course; twist about: *a stream twining through the forest.* **—twine** *n.* **1.** A strong string or cord made of two or more threads twisted together. **2.** Something formed by twining: *a twine of dough.* **3.** A tangle; a knot. [Middle English *twinen,* from *twin,* twine, from Old English *twīn,* double thread. See **dwo-** in Appendix.] **—twin′er** *n.*

twinflower
Linnaea borealis

twin-en·gine (twĭn′ĕn′jĭn) *adj.* Powered by two engines: *a twin-engine aircraft.*

Twin Falls (twĭn). A city of south-central Idaho west of Pocatello near the **Twin Falls** of the Snake River. The southern falls are a source of hydroelectric power. The city is a processing and trade center. Population, 26,209.

twin·flow·er (twĭn′flou′ər) *n.* A shrubby, creeping evergreen plant *(Linnaea borealis)* of northern regions, having roundish, opposite leaves and paired, bell-shaped, pinkish flowers.

twinge (twĭnj) *n.* **1.** A sharp, sudden physical pain. See Synonyms at **pain. 2.** A mental or emotional pain: *a twinge of guilt.* **—twinge** *v.* **twinged, twing·ing, twing·es.** *—tr.* **1.** To cause to feel a sharp pain. **2.** *Obsolete.* To tweak; pinch. *—intr.* To feel a twinge or twinges. [From Middle English *twengen,* to pinch, from Old English *twengan.*]

twi·night (twī′nīt′) *adj.* *Baseball.* Relating to or being a double-header in which the first game begins in late afternoon. [TWI(LIGHT) + NIGHT.]

twin·jet (twĭn′jĕt′) *n.* An aircraft powered by two jet engines.

twin·kle (twĭng′kəl) *v.* **-kled, -kling, -kles.** *—intr.* **1.** To shine with slight, intermittent gleams, as distant lights or stars; flicker; glimmer. See Synonyms at **flash. 2.** To be bright or sparkling, as with merriment or delight: *eyes that twinkled with joy.* **3.** To blink or wink the eyes. See Synonyms at **blink. 4.** To move about or to and fro rapidly and gracefully; flit. *—tr.* To emit (light) in slight, intermittent gleams. **—twinkle** *n.* **1.** A slight, intermittent gleam of light; a sparkling flash; a glimmer. **2.** A sparkle of merriment or delight in the eye. **3.** A brief interval; a twinkling. **4.** A rapid to-and-fro movement. [Middle English *twinklen,* from Old English *twinclian,* frequentative of *twincan,* to blink.] **—twin′kler** *n.* **—twink′ly** *adj.*

twinleaf
Jeffersonia diphylla

twin·kling (twĭng′klĭng) *n.* **1.** The act of blinking. **2.** A blink or twinkle: *the twinkling of a starry sky.* **3.** The time it takes to blink once; an instant: *disappeared in the twinkling of an eye.*

twin·leaf (twĭn′lēf′) *n., pl.* **-leaves** (-lēvz′). An eastern North American woodland plant *(Jeffersonia diphylla)* having basal leaves deeply cleft into two kidney-shaped lobes and a solitary white flower borne on a long scape.

twinned (twĭnd) *adj.* **1.** Born two in a single birth. **2.** Paired or coupled with something identical or similar. **3.** *Mineralogy.* Formed by the process of twinning. Used of crystals.

twin·ning (twĭn′ĭng) *n.* **1.** The bearing of twins. **2.** A pairing or union of two similar or identical objects. **3.** *Mineralogy.* The formation of twin crystals.

Twin Peaks. A mountain, 3,153.7 m (10,340 ft) high, in the Salmon River Mountains of central Idaho.

Twins (twĭnz) *pl.n. (used with a sing. verb).* See **Gemini** (senses 1, 2a).

twin-screw (twĭn′skro͞o′) *adj.* *Nautical.* Having two propellers, one on either side of the keel, that usually revolve in opposite directions.

twin-size (twĭn′sīz′) *adj.* **1.** Measuring about 39 by 75 inches (99 by 190 centimeters). Used of a bed: *a twin-size bed.* **2.** Being of a size that will fit such a bed: *twin-size sheets.* [From *twin bed,* one of a matching pair of single beds.]

twirl (twûrl) *v.* **twirled, twirl·ing, twirls.** *—tr.* **1.** To rotate or revolve briskly; swing in a circle; spin: *twirled a baton to lead the band.* **2.** To twist or wind around: *twirl thread on a spindle.* *—intr.* **1.** To move or spin around rapidly, suddenly, or repeatedly: *The pinwheel twirled in the breeze.* **2.** To whirl or turn suddenly; make an about-face: *twirled in the direction of the noise.* **3.** *Baseball.* To pitch. **—twirl** *n.* **1.** The act of twirling or the condition of being twirled; a quick spinning or twisting. **2.** Something twirled; a twist: *a twirl of cotton candy.* [Origin unknown.] **—twirl′er** *n.*

twirp (twûrp) *n.* *Slang.* Variant of **twerp.**

twist (twĭst) *v.* **twist·ed, twist·ing, twists.** *—tr.* **1.a.** To wind together (two or more threads, for example) so as to produce a single strand. **b.** To form in this manner: *twist a length of rope from strands of hemp.* **2.** To wind or coil (vines or rope, for example) about something. **3.** To interlock or interlace: *twist flowers in one's hair.* **4.** To make (one's way) in a tortuous manner: *twisted my way through the briar patch.* **5.** To turn so as to face another direction: *twisted their heads around at the sound of the doorbell.* **6.** To impart a spiral or coiling shape to, as by turning the ends in opposite directions: *twisting wire into a loop.* **7.a.** To turn or open by turning: *twisted off the bottle cap.* **b.** To pull, break, or snap by turning: *twist off a dead branch.* **8.** To wrench or sprain: *twist one's wrist.* **9.** To alter the normal aspect of; contort: *twist one's mouth into a wry smile.* **10.** To alter or distort the intended meaning of: *The cross-examiner twisted the words of the witness.* See Synonyms at **distort. 11.** To alter or distort the mental, moral, or emotional character of: *The trauma twisted the child's outlook.* *—intr.* **1.** To be or become twisted. **2.** To move or progress in a winding course; meander: *The river twisted toward the sea.* **3.** To squirm; writhe: *twist with pain.* **4.** To rotate or revolve. **5.** To dance the twist. **6.** To move so as to face in another direction. **—twist** *n.* **1.** Something twisted or formed by twisting, especially: **a.** A length of yarn, cord, or thread, especially a strong silk thread used mainly to bind the edges of buttonholes. **b.** Tobacco leaves processed into the form of a rope or roll. **c.** A loaf of bread or other bakery product made from pieces of dough twisted together. **d.** A sliver of citrus peel twisted over or dropped into a beverage for flavoring. **2.** The act of twisting or the condition of being twisted; a spin, twirl, or rotation. **3.** *Sports.* **a.** A complete rotation of the body around its vertical axis, as in diving and gymnastics. **b.** A spinning motion given to a ball when thrown or struck in a specific way. **4.a.** The state of being twisted into a spiral; torsional stress or strain. **b.** The degree or angle of torsional stress. **5.a.** A contortion or distortion of the body, especially the face. **b.** A distortion of meaning: *gave my words a misleading twist.* **6.** A sprain or wrench, as of an ankle. **7.** A change in direction; a turn: *a sharp twist in the path.* **8.** An unexpected change in a process or a departure from a pattern, often producing a distortion or perversion: *a twist of fate; a story with a quirky twist.* **9.** A personal inclination or eccentricity; a penchant or flaw: *an odd twist to his character.* **10.** A dance characterized by vigorous gyrations of the hips and arms. ***—idiom.* twist (someone's) arm.** *Slang.* To coerce by or as if by physical force: *If you twist my arm, I'll stay for a second beer.* [Middle English *twisten,* from *twist,* a divided object, fork, rope, from Old English *-twist.* See **dwo-** in Appendix.] **—twist′a·bil′i·ty** *n.* **—twist′a·ble** *adj.* **—twist′ing·ly** *adv.* **—twist′y** *adj.*

twist drill *n.* A drill having deep helical grooves along the shank from the point.

twist·er (twĭs′tər) *n.* **1.** One that twists, as in the manufacture of rope or yarn. **2.** *Sports.* A ball thrown or batted with a twist. **3.** *Informal.* **a.** A cyclone. **b.** A tornado.

twit (twĭt) *tr.v.* **twit·ted, twit·ting, twits.** To taunt, ridicule, or tease, especially for embarrassing mistakes or faults. See Synonyms at **ridicule. —twit** *n.* **1.** The act or an instance of twitting. **2.** A reproach, gibe, or taunt. **3.** *Slang.* A person regarded as foolishly annoying. [Short for obsolete *atwite,* from Middle English *atwiten,* from Old English *ætwītan* : *æt,* at; see AT[1] + *wītan,* to reproach; see **weid-** in Appendix.] **—twit′ter** *n.*

twitch (twĭch) *v.* **twitched, twitch·ing, twitch·es.** *—tr.* To draw, pull, or move suddenly and sharply; jerk: *I twitched my fishing line.* *—intr.* **1.** To move jerkily or spasmodically. See Synonyms at **jerk[1]. 2.** To ache sharply from time to time; twinge. **—twitch** *n.* **1.** A sudden involuntary or spasmodic muscular movement: *a twitch of the eye.* **2.** A sudden pulling; a tug: *The fish gave my line a twitch.* **3.** A looped cord used to restrain a horse by tightening it around the animal's upper lip. [Middle English *twicchen;* possibly akin to Low German *twikken.*] **—twitch′ing·ly** *adv.* **—twitch′y** *adj.*

twitch·y (twĭch′ē) *adj.* **-i·er, -i·est. 1.** Characterized by jerky or spasmodic motion: *the twitchy whiskers of a cat.* **2.** Nervous; jittery. **—twitch′i·ly** *adv.* **—twitch′i·ness** *n.*

twite (twīt) *n.* A small songbird *(Carduelis flavirostris)* of northern Great Britain and Scandinavia that resembles the linnet. [Imitative of its call.]

twit·ter (twĭt′ər) *v.* **-tered, -ter·ing, -ters.** *—intr.* **1.** To utter a succession of light chirping or tremulous sounds; chirrup. **2.a.** To speak rapidly and in a tremulous manner: *twittering over office gossip.* **b.** To giggle nervously; titter. **3.** To tremble with nervous agitation or excitement. *—tr.* To utter or say with a twitter: *twittered a greeting.* **—twitter** *n.* **1.a.** The light chirping sound made by certain birds. **b.** A similar sound, especially light, tremulous speech or laughter. **2.** Agitation or excitement; flutter. [Middle English *twiteren,* ultimately of imitative origin.] **—twit′ter·er** *n.* **—twit′ter·y** *adj.*

twixt also **'twixt** (twĭkst) *prep.* Betwixt.

two (to͞o) *n.* **1.** The cardinal number equal to the sum of 1 + 1. **2.** The second in a set or sequence. **3.** Something having two parts, units, or members, especially a playing card, the face of a die, or a domino with two pips. ***—idiom.* in two.** Into two separate parts; in half: *cut the sandwich in two.* [Middle English, from Old English *twā.* See **dwo-** in Appendix.] **—two** *adj. & pron.*

two-bag·ger (to͞o′băg′ər) *n.* *Baseball.* See **two-base hit.**

two-base hit (to͞o′bās′) *n.* *Baseball.* A hit enabling the batter to reach second base. Also called *double, two-bagger.*

two-bit (to͞o′bĭt′) *adj.* **1.** *Informal.* Costing or worth 25 cents: *a two-bit cigar.* **2.** *Slang.* Worth very little; petty or insignificant: *a two-bit thief.*

two bits *pl.n.* **1.** *Informal.* Twenty-five cents. **2.** *Slang.* A petty sum.

two-by-four (to͞o′bī-fôr′, -fōr′, to͞o′bə-) *adj.* **1.** Measuring two units by four units, especially inches. **2.** *Slang.* Small in size; boxed in or cramped: *a two-by-four apartment.* **—two-by-four** *n.* A length of lumber that is 2 inches thick and 4 inches wide, or that is trimmed to slightly smaller dimensions.

two cents worth *n. Informal.* A usually unsolicited opinion on a subject: *offered my two cents worth on the new policy.*

two-di·men·sion·al (to͞o′dĭ-mĕn′shə-nəl, -dī-) *adj.* **1.** Having only two dimensions, especially length and width. **2.** Lacking the requisite or expected range or depth: *a movie with two-dimensional characters.*

two-edged (to͞o′ĕjd′) *adj.* **1.** Having two keen edges. **2.** Being such that two contrasting meanings, effects, or interpretations are possible: *a two-edged compliment.*

two-faced (to͞o′fāst′) *adj.* **1.** Having two faces or surfaces. **2.** Hypocritical or double-dealing; deceitful. **—two′-fac′ed·ly** (-fā′sĭd-lē, -fāst′lē) *adv.* **—two′-fac′ed·ness** *n.*

two·fer (to͞o′fər) *n. Informal.* **1.** A coupon offering two items, especially tickets for a play, for the price of one. **2.** An offer, a deal, or an arrangement in which a single expense yields a dual return: *Going to a wedding in New Orleans during Mardi Gras was a twofer.* **3.** One who belongs to two minority groups and can be counted, as by an employer, as part of two quotas. [Shortening and alteration of *two for (the price of one).*]

two-fist·ed (to͞o′fĭs′tĭd) *adj.* **1.** Using or able to use two fists: *a two-fisted backhand stroke in tennis.* **2.** *Informal.* Characterized by great vigor, energy, or enthusiasm: *a two-fisted drinker; a two-fisted card player.*

two-grained spelt (to͞o′grānd′) *n.* See **emmer.**

two-hand·ed (to͞o′hăn′dĭd) *adj.* **1.** Requiring the use of two hands at once: *a two-handed sledgehammer.* **2.** Made to be operated by two people: *a two-handed crosscut saw.* **3.** Able to use both hands with equal facility; ambidextrous. **4.** Having two hands.

two-mast·er (to͞o′măs′tər) *n. Nautical.* A sailing vessel having two masts.

two-name (to͞o′nām′) *adj.* Relating to or being a commercial paper bearing the signatures of two persons liable for the obligation.

two·pence or **tup·pence** (tŭp′əns) *n.* **1.a.** *Chiefly British.* Two pennies regarded as a monetary unit. **b.** A very small amount; a whit: *didn't care twopence about politics.* **2.** *pl.* **two·pence** or **-penc·es** A British coin worth two pennies.

two·pen·ny (tŭp′ə-nē, to͞o′pĕn′ē) *adj.* **1.** Worth or costing two pennies: *twopenny candy.* **2.** Cheap; worthless.

two-phase (to͞o′fāz′) *adj. Electricity.* Relating to two alternating currents with phases at 90°.

two-piece (to͞o′pēs′) *adj.* Made in or consisting of two parts or pieces. **—two-piece** *n.* A garment, such as a swimsuit, consisting of two parts.

two-ply (to͞o′plī′) *adj.* **1.** Made of two interwoven layers. **2.** Consisting of two thicknesses or strands: *two-ply yarn.*

two-seat·er (to͞o′sē′tər) *n.* A vehicle seating two people.

Two Sic·i·lies (to͞o sĭs′ə-lēz). A former kingdom comprising Sicily and Naples. The two territories were ruled jointly at various times and were united in 1816. Garibaldi conquered the kingdom in 1860 and annexed it to Italy.

two·some (to͞o′səm) *n.* **1.** Two people or things together; a pair or couple. **2.** *Sports.* A round of golf played by two people.

two-spot (to͞o′spŏt′) *n.* **1.** *Games.* A playing card bearing two spots or pips; a deuce. **2.** *Slang.* **a.** A two-dollar bill. **b.** Two dollars.

two-step (to͞o′stĕp′) *n.* **1.** A ballroom dance in 2/4 time, characterized by long, sliding steps. **2.** The music for this dance.

two-time (to͞o′tīm′) *tr.v.* **-timed, -tim·ing, -times.** *Slang.* **1.** To be unfaithful to (a spouse or lover). **2.** To deceive; double-cross. **—two′-tim′er** *n.*

two-toed sloth (to͞o′tōd′) *n.* See **sloth** (sense 2b).

two-tone (to͞o′tōn′) or **two-toned** (-tōnd′) *adj.* Having two colors or two shades of a single color.

two-way (to͞o′wā′) *adj.* **1.a.** Affording passage in two directions: *a two-way street.* **b.** Moving in two directions: *two-way traffic.* **2.a.** Permitting communication in two directions: *a two-way radio.* **b.** Permitting flow in two directions: *a two-way valve.* **3.a.** Expressive of or involving mutual action, relationship, or responsibility. **b.** Involving two participants: *a two-way treaty.*

two-wheel·er (to͞o′hwē′lər, -wē′-) *n.* A vehicle with two wheels, especially a bicycle.

twp. *abbr.* Township.

TWX *abbr.* Teletypewriter exchange.

TX *abbr.* Texas.

-ty *suff.* Condition; quality: *realty.* [Middle English *-te,* from Old French, from Latin *-tās.*]

Ty·chy (tĭk′ē). A town of south-central Poland south of Katowice. It was largely developed as a resettlement community after World War II. Population, 181,800.

ty·coon (tī-ko͞on′) *n.* **1.** A wealthy and powerful businessperson or industrialist; a magnate. **2.** Used formerly as a title for a Japanese shogun. [Japanese *taikun,* title of a shogun, of Chinese origin.]

WORD HISTORY: Business tycoons may consider themselves captains or even princes of industry, but by virtue of being called *tycoons,* they have already achieved princely status, at least from an etymological point of view. *Tycoon* came into English from Japanese, which had borrowed the title, meaning "great prince," from Chinese. Use of the word was intended to make the shogun, the commander in chief of the Japanese army, more impressive to foreigners (his official title *shōgun* merely meant "general"). In fact, the shogun actually ruled Japan, although he was supposedly acting for the emperor. When Matthew C. Perry opened Japan to the West in 1854, he negotiated with the shogun, thinking him to be the emperor. The shogun's title, *taikun,* was brought back to the United States after Perry's visit. Abraham Lincoln's cabinet members used *tycoon* as an affectionate nickname for the President. The word soon came to be used for business and industry leaders—perhaps at times for those who had as much right to such an impressive title as did the shogun. The word itself now has an old-fashioned sound, but when we encounter it, we should think back to the days of Commodore Perry and President Lincoln, both of whom were real tycoons in their own ways.

ty·ing (tī′ĭng) *v.* Present participle of **tie.**

tyke also **tike** (tīk) *n.* **1.** A small child, especially a boy. **2.** A mongrel or cur. **3.** *Chiefly British.* A man considered uncouth or mean; a boor. [Middle English, mongrel, from Old Norse *tīk,* bitch.]

ty·lec·to·my (tī-lĕk′tə-mē) *n., pl.* **-mies.** Surgical removal of a lump, especially a cancerous one. [Greek *tulos,* lump; see **teuə-** in Appendix + -ECTOMY.]

Ty·le·nol (tī′lə-nôl′, -nŏl′). A trademark used for a brand of acetaminophen.

Ty·ler (tī′lər). A city of northeast Texas east-southeast of Dallas. It is a refining and manufacturing center noted for its rose-growing industry. Population, 70,508.

Tyler, John. 1790–1862. The 10th President of the United States (1841–1845), who succeeded to office after the death of President William Henry Harrison. His administration was marked by the annexation of Texas (1845).

John Tyler
Detail of an 1842 portrait by George Peter Alexander Healy (1813?–1894)

Tyler, Royall. 1757–1826. American jurist and writer considered the founder of American drama. His plays include *The Contrast* (first produced 1787).

Tyler, Wat. Died 1381. English revolutionary who led the Peasants' Revolt against Richard II's poll tax in June 1381. The uprising ended when he was killed.

ty·lose (tī′lōs) *n. Botany.* A balloonlike outgrowth of a parenchyma cell through a pit into the cavity of a plant vessel. Also called *tylosis.* [French.]

ty·lo·sin (tī′lə-sĭn′) *n.* An antibiotic, $C_{46}H_{77}NO_{17}$, obtained from the actinomycete *Streptomyces fradiae* and used to treat respiratory infections in animals. [Origin unknown.]

ty·lo·sis[1] (tī-lō′-sĭs) *n., pl.* **-ses** (-sēz). **1.** Inflammation of the eyelids, characterized by thickening and hardening of the edges. **2.** A thickening of the horny layer of the skin as a result of chronic pressure or friction. [New Latin *tylōsis,* from Greek *tulōsis,* a making callous : *tulos,* callus; see **teuə-** in Appendix + *-ōsis,* -osis.]

ty·lo·sis[2] (tī-lō′sĭs) *n., pl.* **-ses** (-sēz). *Botany.* See **tylose.**

tym·bal (tĭm′bəl) *n.* Variant of **timbal.**

tym·pan (tĭm′pən) *n.* **1.** *Printing.* A padding, as of paper or cloth, placed over the platen of a press to regulate the pressure on the sheet being printed. **2.** *Architecture.* A tympanum. **3.** A tightly stretched sheet or membrane, as on the head of a drum. [Middle English *timpan,* drum, from Old English *timpana,* from Latin *tympanum,* from Greek *tumpanon.*]

tym·pa·na (tĭm′pə-nə) *n.* A plural of **tympanum.**

tym·pa·nal (tĭm′pə-nəl) *adj. Anatomy.* Variant of **tympanic** (sense 2).

tym·pa·ni (tĭm′pə-nē) *pl.n. Music.* Variant of **timpani.**

tym·pan·ic (tĭm-păn′ĭk) *adj.* **1.** Relating to or resembling a drum. **2.** Also **tym·pa·nal** (tĭm′pə-nəl). *Anatomy.* Of or relating to the middle ear or eardrum. [From Latin *tympanum,* drum. See TYMPANUM.]

tympanic bone *n.* The part of the temporal bone of the skull that partially encloses the middle ear and supports the eardrum.

tympanic cavity *n.* A large, irregularly shaped cavity of the middle ear.

tympanic membrane *n. Anatomy.* See **eardrum.**

tym·pa·nist (tĭm′pə-nĭst) *n. Music.* Variant of **timpanist.**

tym·pa·ni·tes (tĭm′pə-nī′tēz) *n.* A distention of the abdomen resulting from the accumulation of gas or air in the intestine or peritoneal cavity. Also called *tympany.* [Middle English, from Late Latin *tympanītēs,* from Greek *tumpanitēs,* from *tumpanon,* drum.] **—tym′pa·nit′ic** (-nĭt′ĭk) *adj.*

tym·pa·ni·tis (tĭm′pə-nī′tĭs) *n.* Inflammation of the inner ear. [TYMPAN(UM) + -ITIS.]

tym·pa·no·plas·ty (tĭm′pə-nə-plăs′tē, -nō-) *n., pl.* **-ties.** Surgical repair or reconstruction of the middle ear. [TYMPAN(UM) + -PLASTY.]

ă pat	oi boy
ā pay	ou out
âr care	o͝o took
ä father	o͞o boot
ĕ pet	ŭ cut
ē be	ûr urge
ĭ pit	th thin
ī pie	*th* this
îr pier	hw which
ŏ pot	zh vision
ō toe	ə about, item
ô paw	♦ regionalism

Stress marks: ′ (primary); ′ (secondary), as in **dictionary** (dĭk′shə-nĕr′ē)

tympanum

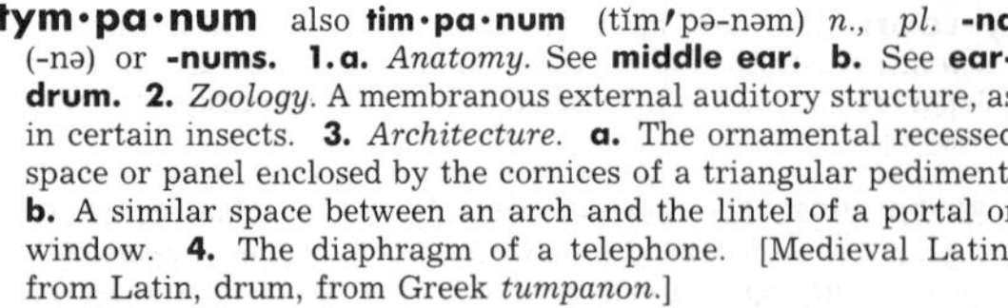

tym·pa·num also **tim·pa·num** (tĭm′pə-nəm) *n., pl.* **-na** (-nə) or **-nums. 1.a.** *Anatomy.* See **middle ear. b.** See **eardrum. 2.** *Zoology.* A membranous external auditory structure, as in certain insects. **3.** *Architecture.* **a.** The ornamental recessed space or panel enclosed by the cornices of a triangular pediment. **b.** A similar space between an arch and the lintel of a portal or window. **4.** The diaphragm of a telephone. [Medieval Latin, from Latin, drum, from Greek *tumpanon.*]

tym·pa·ny (tĭm′pə-nē) *n., pl.* **-nies. 1.** *Archaic.* Inflated manner or style; bombast. **2.** See **tympanites.** [Medieval Latin *tympanias,* tympanites, from Greek *tumpanias,* from *tumpanon,* drum.]

Tyn·dale also **Tin·dal** or **Tin·dale** (tĭn′dl), **William.** 1494?–1536. English religious reformer and martyr whose translation of the New Testament was the basis of the King James Bible.

Tyn·dall (tĭn′dl), **John.** 1820–1893. Irish-born British physicist known for his work on the transparency of gases and the absorption by gases of radiant heat.

Tyndall, Mount. A mountain, 4,275.8 m (14,019 ft) high, in the Sierra Nevada of south-central California.

Tyn·dar·e·us (tĭn-dâr′ē-əs) *n. Greek Mythology.* A king of Sparta and the husband of Leda.

Tyne (tīn). A river, about 129 km (80 mi) long, of northern England flowing eastward to the North Sea.

Tyne·mouth (tīn′mouth′, -məth). A borough of northeast England on the North Sea at the mouth of the Tyne River. It is a port, shipbuilding center, and seaside resort. Population, 200,100.

typ. *abbr.* Typographer; typography.

typ·al (tī′pəl) *adj.* Of, relating to, or serving as a type; typical.

type (tīp) *n.* **1.** A number of people or things having in common traits or characteristics that distinguish them as a group or class. **2.** The general character or structure held in common by a number of people or things considered as a group or class. **3.** A person or thing having the features of a group or class. **4.** An example or a model having the ideal features of a group or class; an embodiment: *"He was the perfect type of a military dandy"* (Joyce Cary). **5.** A person regarded as exemplifying a particular profession, rank, or social group: *a group of executive types; a restaurant frequented by tourist types.* **6.** A figure, representation, or symbol of something to come, such as an event in the Old Testament that foreshadows another in the New Testament. **7.a.** A taxonomic group, especially a genus or species, chosen as the representative example in characterizing the larger taxonomic group to which it belongs. **b.** The specimen on which the original description and naming of a taxon is based. **8.** *Printing.* **a.** A small block of metal or wood bearing a raised letter or character on the upper end that leaves a printed impression when inked and pressed on paper. **b.** Such pieces considered as a group. **c.** Printed or typewritten characters; print. **d.** A size or style of printed or typewritten characters; a typeface: *a sans-serif type.* **9.** A pattern, a design, or an image impressed or stamped onto the face of a coin. **—type** *v.* **typed, typ·ing, types.** *—tr.* **1.** To write (something) with a typewriter; typewrite. **2.** To determine the antigenic characteristics of (a blood or tissue sample). **3.** To typecast. **4.** To represent or typify. **5.** To prefigure. *—intr.* To write with a typewriter; typewrite. [Middle English, symbol, from Late Latin *typus,* type, from Latin, image, from Greek *tupos,* impression.]

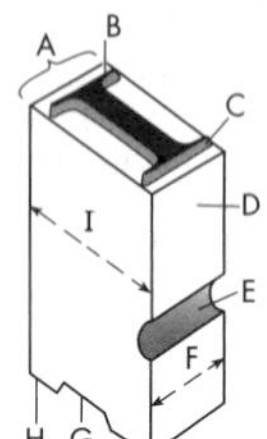

type
A. Face
B. Serif
C. Beard
D. Body
E. Nick
F. Set width
G. Groove
H. Foot
I. Point size

SYNONYMS: *type, kind, sort, nature, character, ilk.* These nouns refer to groups of people or things regarded as constituting a class because of their shared attributes or characteristics. *Type* in strict usage implies such similarity in traits among members of the group that the group is clearly and unmistakably distinguished from all others: *"I seem to discern six types* [of judicial writing] *which divide themselves from one another with measurable distinctness"* (Benjamin N. Cardozo). *Kind* can refer to a class whose members are linked by innate characteristics: *"Material objects are of two kinds, atoms and compounds of atoms"* (Lucretius). Often, however, *type* and *kind,* like *sort,* are applied when the resemblance or relationship is not precisely defined: *I don't enjoy that type of show. "What kind of people do they think we are?"* (Winston S. Churchill). *"Here dies the dusky torch of Mortimer,/ Chok'd with ambition of the meaner sort"* (Shakespeare). *Nature* in this comparison refers to native or inherent traits: *Most of the articles in the magazine are of a didactic nature. Character* emphasizes qualities peculiar to individual members of a group: *Her criticism had the character of a bit of kindly advice. Ilk* refers, often disparagingly, to classification by character, disposition, point of view, or standing: *a larcenous tendency restricted to shady operators and others of that ilk.*

type A or **Type A** *—adj.* Of or relating to a behavior pattern characterized by tenseness, impatience, and aggressiveness, often resulting in stress-related symptoms such as insomnia and indigestion and possibly increasing the risk of heart disease. *—n., pl.* **type A's** or **Type A's.** One who exhibits this behavior pattern.

type B or **Type B** *—adj.* Of or relating to a behavior pattern characterized by a relaxed manner, patience, and friendliness that possibly decreases one's risk of heart disease. *—n., pl.* **type B's** or **Type B's.** One who exhibits this behavior pattern.

type bar *n.* One of the thin movable bars on many typewriters and some computer printers that carry the letters or characters.

type·cast (tīp′kăst′) *tr.v.* **-cast, -cast·ing, -casts. 1.** To cast in an acting role akin or natural to one's own personality or fitted to one's physical appearance. **2.** To assign (a performer) repeatedly to the same kind of part.

Tyr

type·face (tīp′fās′) *n. Printing.* **1.a.** The surface of a block of type that makes the impression. **b.** The impression made by this surface. **2.** The size or style of the letter or character on a block of type. **3.** The full range of type of the same design.

type genus *n. Abbr.* **t.g.** The taxonomic genus that is designated as representative of the family to which it belongs.

type-high (tīp′hī′) *adj. Printing.* As high as the standard height of type, measured from the face to the foot, 23.3 millimeters (0.9186 inch).

type locality *n.* **1.** *Biology & Paleontology.* The place or source where a holotype or type specimen was found. **2.** *Geology.* The place or region in which a rock, series of rock, or formation is typically exposed.

type metal *n. Printing.* An alloy used for making metal type, consisting mainly of lead, antimony, and tin.

type·script (tīp′skrĭpt′) *n.* **1.** A typewritten copy, as of a manuscript. **2.** Typewritten matter. [TYPE + (MANU)SCRIPT.]

type·set (tīp′sĕt′) *tr.v.* **-set, -set·ting, -sets.** *Printing.* To set (written material) into type; compose. **—type′set′ter** *n.*

type-site (tīp′sīt′) *n.* An archaeological site regarded as definitively characteristic of a particular culture and whose name is often applied to the culture.

type species *n.* The taxonomic species that is designated as representative of the genus to which it belongs.

type specimen *n.* The individual specimen used as a basis for determining the characteristics of a species.

type·style or **type style** (tīp′stīl′) *n. Printing.* A specific style of type, as Roman.

type·write (tīp′rīt′) *v.* **-wrote** (-rōt′), **-writ·ten** (-rĭt′n), **-writ·ing, -writes. —typewrite** *intr. & tr.v.* To engage in writing or to write (matter) with a typewriter. [Back-formation from TYPEWRITER.]

type·writ·er (tīp′rī′tər) *n.* **1.** A writing machine that produces characters similar to typeset print by means of a manually operated keyboard that actuates a set of raised types, which strike the paper through an inked ribbon. **2.** *Printing.* A typestyle like that of typewritten copy.

type·writ·ing (tīp′rī′tĭng) *n.* **1.** The act, process, or skill of using a typewriter. **2.** Copy produced on a typewriter; typescript.

type·writ·ten (tīp′rĭt′n) *v.* Past participle of **typewrite.**

type·wrote (tīp′rōt′) *v.* Past tense of **typewrite.**

typh·li·tis (tĭf-lī′tĭs). Inflammation of the cecum of the large intestine. [Greek *tuphlon,* cecum, from neuter of *tuphlos,* blind + -ITIS.] **—typh·lyt′ic** (-lĭt′ĭk) *adj.*

typh·lol·o·gy (tĭf-lŏl′ə-jē) *n.* The medical study of blindness. [Greek *tuphlos,* blind + -LOGY.]

typh·lo·sole (tĭf′lə-sōl′) *n. Zoology.* A longitudinal fold of the intestinal wall in certain invertebrates and lower vertebrates that increases the absorptive and digestive surface area of the intestine. [Greek *tuphlos,* blind + Greek *sōlēn,* pipe.]

ty·pho·gen·ic (tī′fə-jĕn′ĭk) *adj.* Causing typhus.

ty·phoid (tī′foid′) *n.* Typhoid fever. **—typhoid** also **ty·phoi·dal** (tī-foid′l) *adj.* Of, relating to, or resembling typhoid fever. [TYPH(US) + -OID.]

typhoid fever *n.* An acute, highly infectious disease caused by a bacillus *(Salmonella typhi)* transmitted chiefly by contaminated food or water and characterized by high fever, headache, coughing, intestinal hemorrhaging, and rose-colored spots on the skin. Also called *enteric fever.*

ty·phoi·din (tī-foi′dĭn) *n.* A culture of typhoid bacilli, used to test for the presence of typhoid fever.

Ty·phoid Mar·y (tī′foid′ mâr′ē) *n.* A person from whom something undesirable or deadly spreads to those nearby. [After *Mary* Mallon, a carrier of typhoid.]

Ty·phon (tī′fŏn′) *n. Greek Mythology.* A monster with one hundred heads, thrown by Zeus into Tartarus.

ty·phoon (tī-fo͞on′) *n.* A tropical cyclone occurring in the western Pacific or Indian oceans. [Probably alteration of Chinese (Cantonese) *toi fung* : Mandarin *tái,* great + Mandarin *fēng,* wind.]

WORD HISTORY: Perhaps few words better illustrate the polyglot background of English than *typhoon,* with its Chinese, Arabic, East Indian, and Greek background. The Greek word *typhon,* both the name of the father of the winds and a common noun meaning "whirlwind, typhoon," was borrowed into Arabic (as was many a Greek word during the Middle Ages, when Arabic learning both preserved the classical heritage and expanded upon it, passing it on to Europe). *Ṭūfān,* the Arabic version of the Greek word, passed into languages spoken in India, where Arabic-speaking Moslem invaders had settled in the 11th century. Thus the descendant of the Arabic word, passing into English (first recorded in 1588) through an Indian language and appearing in English in forms such as *touffon* and *tufan,* originally referred specifically to a severe storm in India. China, another great empire, gave us yet another word for a storm, in this case the hurricane that occurred in the waters around China. This Chinese word in its Cantonese form, *toi fung,* was similar to our Arabic borrowing and is first recorded in English guise as *tuffoon* in 1699. The various forms coalesced and finally became *typhoon.*

ty·phus (tīʹfəs) *n.* Any of several forms of infectious disease caused by rickettsia, especially those transmitted by fleas, lice, or mites, and characterized generally by severe headache, sustained high fever, depression, delirium, and the eruption of red rashes on the skin. Also called *prison fever, ship fever, typhus fever.* [New Latin, from Greek *tuphos,* stupor arising from a fever, vapor, from *tuphein,* to smoke.] **—tyʹphous** (-fəs) *adj.*

typ·i·cal (tĭpʹĭ-kəl) *adj.* **1.** Exhibiting the qualities, traits, or characteristics that identify a kind, class, group, or category: *a typical suburban community.* See Synonyms at **normal. 2.** Of or relating to a representative specimen; characteristic or distinctive. **3.** Conforming to a type: *a composition typical of the baroque period.* **4.** Also **typ·ic** (-ĭk). Of the nature of, constituting, or serving as a type; emblematic. [Late Latin *typicālis,* from *typicus,* from Greek *tupikos,* from *tupos,* impression.] **—typʹi·cal·ly** *adv.* **—typʹi·cal·ness, typʹi·calʹi·ty** (-kălʹĭ-tē) *n.*

typ·i·fy (tĭpʹə-fīʹ) *tr.v.* **-fied** (-fīdʹ), **-fy·ing, -fies** (-fīzʹ). **1.** To serve as a typical example of; embody the essential characteristics of: *a painting that typifies the artist's work.* **2.** To represent by an image, a form, or a model; symbolize or prefigure. **—typʹi·fi·caʹtion** (-fĭ-kāʹshən) *n.* **—typʹi·fiʹer** *n.*

typ·ist (tīʹpĭst) *n.* One who operates a typewriter.

ty·po (tīʹpō) *n., pl.* **-pos.** *Informal.* A typographical error.

typo. *abbr. Printing.* Typographer; typography.

ty·pog·ra·pher (tī-pŏgʹrə-fər) *n. Abbr.* **typ., typo.** *Printing.* One that sets written material into type; a compositor or printer.

typographical error *n. Printing.* A mistake in printing, typesetting, or typing, especially one caused by striking an incorrect key on a keyboard.

ty·pog·ra·phy (tī-pŏgʹrə-fē) *n., pl.* **-phies.** *Abbr.* **typ., typo.** *Printing.* **1.a.** The art and technique of printing with movable type. **b.** The composition of printed material from movable type. **2.** The arrangement and appearance of printed matter. [French *typographie,* from Medieval Latin *typographia* : Greek *tupos,* impression + Latin *-graphia,* -graphy.] **—tyʹpo·graphʹi·cal** (tīʹpə-grăfʹĭ-kəl), **tyʹpo·graphʹic** (-grăfʹĭk) *adj.* **—tyʹpo·graphʹi·cal·ly** *adv.*

ty·pol·o·gy (tī-pŏlʹə-jē) *n., pl.* **-gies. 1.** The study or systematic classification of types that have characteristics or traits in common. **2.** A theory or doctrine of types, as in scriptural studies. **—tyʹpo·logʹi·cal** (tīʹpə-lŏjʹĭ-kəl), **tyʹpo·logʹic** (-lŏjʹĭk) *adj.* **—tyʹpo·logʹi·cal·ly** *adv.* **—ty·polʹo·gist** *n.*

Tyr (tîr) *n. Mythology.* A Norse god of war, son of Odin. [Old Norse *Tȳr.* See **deiw-** in Appendix.]

ty·ra·mine (tīʹrə-mēnʹ) *n.* A colorless crystalline amine, $C_8H_{11}NO$, found in mistletoe, putrefied animal tissue, certain cheeses, and ergot and also produced synthetically, used in medicine as a sympathomimetic agent. [TYR(OSINE) + AMINE.]

ty·ran·ni·cal (tĭ-rănʹĭ-kəl, tī-) also **ty·ran·nic** (-rănʹĭk) *adj.* **1.** Of or relating to a tyrant or tyranny: *a tyrannical government.* **2.** Characteristic of a tyrant or tyranny; despotic and oppressive: *a tyrannical supervisor.* **—ty·ranʹni·cal·ly** *adv.* **—ty·ranʹni·cal·ness** *n.*

tyr·an·nize (tĭrʹə-nīzʹ) *v.* **-nized, -niz·ing, -niz·es.** —*tr.* To treat tyrannically; oppress. —*intr.* **1.** To exercise absolute power: *"So it is the nature of such persons to insult and tyrannize over little people"* (Henry Fielding). **2.** To rule as a tyrant. [Middle English, from Old French *tyranniser,* from tyran, *tyrant.* See TYRANT.] **—tyrʹan·nizʹer** *n.* **—tyrʹan·nizʹing·ly** *adv.*

ty·ran·no·saur (tĭ-rănʹə-sôrʹ, tī-) also **ty·ran·no·saur·us** (tĭ-rănʹə-sôrʹəs, tī-) *n.* A large carnivorous dinosaur of the Upper Cretaceous Period of North America, characterized by small forelimbs and a large head. [New Latin *Tyrannosaurus,* genus name : Greek *turannos,* tyrant + Greek *sauros,* lizard.]

tyr·an·nous (tĭrʹə-nəs) *adj.* Characterized by tyranny; despotic. **—tyrʹan·nous·ly** *adv.*

tyr·an·ny (tĭrʹə-nē) *n., pl.* **-nies. 1.** A government in which a single ruler is vested with absolute power. **2.** The office, authority, or jurisdiction of an absolute ruler. **3.** Absolute power, especially when exercised unjustly or cruelly: *"I have sworn . . . eternal hostility against every form of tyranny over the mind of man"* (Thomas Jefferson). **4.a.** Use of absolute power. **b.** A tyrannical act. **5.** Extreme harshness or severity; rigor. [Middle English *tyrannie,* from Old French, from Late Latin *tyrannia,* from Greek *turannia,* from *turannos,* tyrant.]

ty·rant (tīʹrənt) *n.* **1.** An absolute ruler who governs without restrictions. **2.** A ruler who exercises power in a harsh, cruel manner. **3.** An oppressive, harsh, arbitrary person. [Middle English, from Old French, alteration of *tyran,* from Latin *tyrannus,* from Greek *turannos.*]

tyrannosaur
Tyrannosaurus rex

tyrant flycatcher *n.* See **flycatcher** (sense 2).

tyre (tīr) *n. Chiefly British.* Variant of **tire**[2].

Tyre (tīr). An ancient Phoenician city on the eastern Mediterranean Sea in present-day southern Lebanon. The capital of Phoenicia after the 11th century B.C., it was a flourishing commercial center noted for its purple dyestuffs and rich, silken clothing. Tyre was besieged and captured by Alexander the Great in 332 B.C. and was finally destroyed by Moslems in A.D. 1291.

Tyr·i·an purple (tĭrʹē-ən) *n.* A reddish dyestuff obtained from the bodies of certain mollusks of the genus *Murex* and highly prized in ancient times. [After TYRE.]

ty·ro also **ti·ro** (tīʹrō) *n., pl.* **-ros.** A beginner in learning something. See Synonyms at **amateur.** [Medieval Latin *tȳrō,* squire, variant of Latin *tīrō,* recruit.]

ty·ro·ci·dine also **ty·ro·ci·din** (tīʹrə-sīdʹn) *n.* A polypeptide antibiotic, produced by the soil microorganism *Bacillus brevis,* that is a major constituent of tyrothricin. [TYRO(THRICIN) + (GRAMI)CID(IN) + -INE[2].]

Ty·rol or **Ti·rol** (tə-rōlʹ, tī-, tīʹrōlʹ). A region of the eastern Alps in western Austria and northern Italy. Inhabited in ancient times by Celtic peoples, the Tyrol constantly passed back and forth, in whole or in part, between Austria and Italy in the 1800's. Its present division dates from the Treaty of St. Germain in 1919. The Tyrolean Alps are a popular tourist area. **—Ty·rolʹle·an, Tyrʹo·leseʹ** (tĭrʹə-lēzʹ, -lēsʹ, tīʹrə-) *adj. & n.*

Tzu Hsi

ty·ros·i·nase (tī-rŏsʹə-nāsʹ, -nāzʹ) *n.* A copper-containing enzyme of plant and animal tissues that catalyzes the production of melanin and other pigments from tyrosine by oxidation, as in the blackening of a peeled or sliced potato exposed to air.

ty·ro·sine (tīʹrə-sēnʹ) *n.* A white crystalline amino acid, $C_9H_{11}NO_3$, that is derived from the hydrolysis of proteins such as casein and is a precursor of epinephrine, thyroxine, and melanin. [Greek *turos,* cheese; see **teuə-** in Appendix + -INE[2].]

ty·ro·thri·cin (tīʹrō-thrīʹsĭn) *n.* A gray-brown mixture consisting mainly of tryocidine and gramicidin, used as a topical antibiotic in treating infections caused by gram-positive bacteria. [New Latin *Tyrothrix,* former bacteria genus name (Greek *turos,* cheese; see **teuə-** in Appendix + Greek *thrix,* hair) + -IN.]

Tyr·rhe·ni·an Sea (tə-rēʹnē-ən). An arm of the Mediterranean Sea between the Italian peninsula and the islands of Corsica, Sardinia, and Sicily. The Strait of Messina connects it with the Ionian Sea.

Tyu·men (tyo͞o-mĕnʹ). A city of west-central Russia east of Sverdlovsk. Founded in 1585, it is the oldest Russian settlement east of the Ural Mountains. Population, 425,000.

tzar (zär, tsär) *n.* Variant of **czar** (sense 1). See Usage Note at **czar.**

Tze·kung (tsŭʹko͝ongʹ, dzŭʹgo͝ongʹ). See **Zigong.**

Tze·po (tsŭʹpōʹ, dzŭʹbōʹ). See **Zibo.**

tzet·ze fly (tsĕtʹsē, tsēʹtsē) *n.* Variant of **tsetse fly.**

tzim·mes (tsĭmʹĭs) *n.* Variant of **tsimmes.**

Tzu Hsi (tso͞oʹ shēʹ). 1835–1908. The dowager empress of China (1861–1908) who was hostile to foreign influences in China and supported the Boxer Rebellion (1898–1900).

tzu·ris (tso͝orʹĭs, tsûrʹ-) *n.* Variant of **tsuris.**

ă pat	oi boy
ā pay	ou out
âr care	o͝o took
ä father	o͞o boot
ĕ pet	ŭ cut
ē be	ûr urge
ĭ pit	th thin
ī pie	*th* this
îr pier	hw which
ŏ pot	zh vision
ō toe	ə about, item
ô paw	♦ regionalism

Stress marks: ʹ (primary); ʹ (secondary), as in **dictionary** (dĭkʹshə-nĕrʹē)

Uu

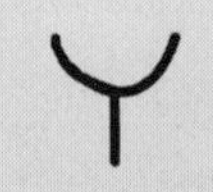

Phoenician
The Phoenicians used a single sign for the initial sound in *wāw,* "hook" or "peg," and the related vowel *u.*

Early Greek
This sign was altered into two different shapes by the Greeks. One form became *digamma,* the ancestor of Roman F (see F); the other was used for the vowel sound *u.*

Roman
The Romans adopted the second form for both *u* and *w* sounds, simplifying its shape to V. The letter U originated in the early Middle Ages as a cursive version of V. It was not until the 16th century that the two forms were used systematically to distinguish between the vowel *u* and the consonant *v* (see V).

u¹ or **U** (yo͞o) *n., pl.* **u's** or **U's. 1.** The 21st letter of the modern English alphabet. **2.** Any of the speech sounds represented by the letter *u.* **3.** The 21st in a series. **4.** Something shaped like the letter U.

u² *abbr. Physics.* Up quark.

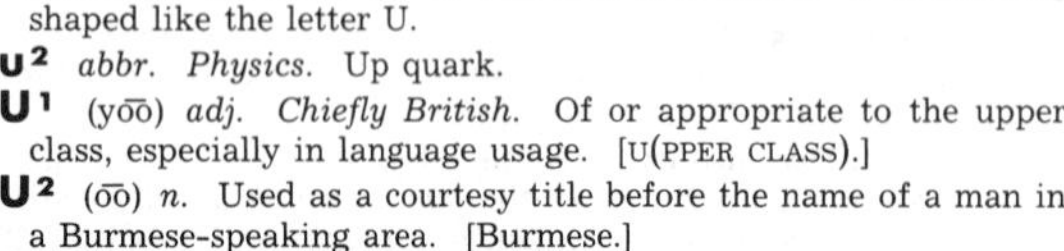

U¹ (yo͞o) *adj. Chiefly British.* Of or appropriate to the upper class, especially in language usage. [U(PPER CLASS).]

U² (o͞o) *n.* Used as a courtesy title before the name of a man in a Burmese-speaking area. [Burmese.]

U³ 1. The symbol for the element **uranium. 2.** The symbol for **internal energy.**

u. *abbr.* **1.** Or **U.** Uncle. **2.** Unit. **3.** Or **U.** Upper.

U. or **U** *abbr.* University.

U.A.E. *abbr.* United Arab Emirates.

U.A.R. *abbr.* United Arab Republic.

Uau·pés (wou-pĕs′). In its upper course called **Vau·pés** (vou-păs′, -pĕs′). A river of northwest South America rising in south-central Colombia and flowing about 805 km (500 mi) east-southeast through northwest Brazil to the Río Negro.

UAW or **U.A.W.** *abbr.* **1.** United Automobile, Aerospace, and Agricultural Implement Workers. **2.** United Automobile Workers.

U·ban·gi (yo͞o-băng′gē, o͞o-bäng′-). A river of central Africa flowing about 1,126 km (700 mi) along the northwest border of Zaire to the Congo River.

U·be·ra·ba (o͞o′bĭ-rä′bə, -bä). A city of eastern Brazil west of Belo Horizonte. Population, 180,228.

U·ber·lân·di·a (o͞o′bĭr-län′dē-ə, -dyä). A city of eastern Brazil west-northwest of Belo Horizonte. Population, 230,185.

u·bi·e·ty (yo͞o-bī′ĭ-tē) *n.* The condition of being located in a particular place. [Latin *ubī,* where; see UBIQUITY + –TY.]

u·bi·qui·none (yo͞o′bĭ-kwĭ-nōn′, -kĭn′ōn) *n.* A quinone compound that serves as an electron carrier between flavoproteins and in cellular respiration. [Latin *ubī(que),* everywhere; see UBIQUITY + QUINONE.]

u·biq·ui·tous (yo͞o-bĭk′wĭ-təs) *adj.* Being or seeming to be everywhere at the same time; omnipresent: *"plodded through the shadows fruitlessly like an ubiquitous spook"* (Joseph Heller). **—u·biq′ui·tous·ly** *adv.* **—u·biq′ui·tous·ness** *n.*

u·biq·ui·ty (yo͞o-bĭk′wĭ-tē) *n.* Existence or apparent existence everywhere at the same time; omnipresence: *"the repetitiveness, the selfsameness, and the ubiquity of modern mass culture"* (Theodor Adorno). [New Latin *ubīquitās,* from Latin *ubīque,* everywhere : *ubī,* where; see **kʷo-** in Appendix + *-que,* and, generalizing particle; see **kʷe** in Appendix.]

U-boat (yo͞o′bōt′) *n.* A submarine of the German navy. [Translation of German *U-Boot,* short for *Unterseeboot* : *unter,* under (from Middle High German *under,* from Old High German *untar;* see **ṇdher-** in Appendix) + *See,* sea (from Middle High German *sē,* from Old High German) + *Boot,* boat.]

U-bolt (yo͞o′bōlt′) *n.* A bolt shaped like the letter U, fitted with threads and a nut at each end.

UBV photometry (yo͞o′bē-vē′) *n.* Photometry used to obtain stellar magnitudes by comparing observed magnitudes to a standard sequence of stars. [U(LTRAVIOLET) + B(LUE) + V(ISUAL).]

u.c. also **UC** *abbr. Printing.* Uppercase.

U·ca·ya·li (o͞o′kä-yä′lē). A river of eastern Peru flowing about 1,609 km (1,000 mi) northward to join the Marañón River and form the Amazon River.

Uc·cel·lo (o͞o-chĕl′ō), **Paolo.** Originally Paolo di Dono. 1397–1475. Italian painter of the Florentine school known for his experimentation with perspective.

Uc·cle (o͞ok′lə, ü′klə). A city of central Belgium, a manufacturing suburb of Brussels. Population, 75,675.

UCMJ *abbr.* Uniform Code of Military Justice.

UCS *abbr.* Universal character set.

UDC *abbr.* Universal decimal system.

ud·der (ŭd′ər) *n.* A baglike organ containing the mammary glands, characteristic of certain female mammals, such as cows, sheep, and goats. [Middle English, from Old English *ūder.* See **eue-dh-r** in Appendix.]

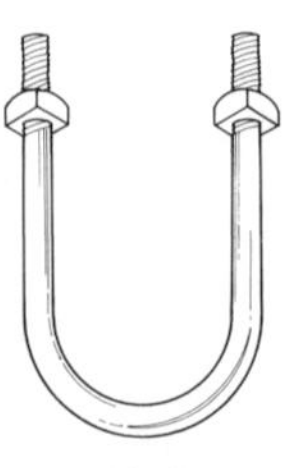

U-bolt

U·di·ne (o͞o′dē-nā′). A city of northeast Italy northeast of Venice. It was the headquarters (1915–1917) of the Italian army in World War I. Population, 101,264.

u·do (o͞o′dō) *n., pl.* **u·dos.** A perennial Japanese plant *(Aralia cordata)* having bipinnately compound leaves and young shoots that are cooked and eaten as a vegetable. [Japanese.]

u·dom·e·ter (yo͞o-dŏm′ĭ-tər) *n.* See **rain gauge.** [Latin *ūdus,* wet (contraction of *ūvidus*) + –METER.]

Ue·le (wĕl′ē, wĕl′ā). A river, about 1,126 km (700 mi) long, of northern Zaire flowing westward as a tributary of the Ubangi River.

U·fa (o͞o-fä′). A city of western Russia in the southern Ural Mountains at the confluence of the Belaya and **Ufa** rivers. The Ufa flows about 965 km (600 mi) northwest and southwest. The city was founded as a fortress (1586) and is now a major industrial center. Population, 1,064,000.

UFO (yo͞o′ĕf-ō′) *n., pl.* **UFOs** or **UFO's.** An unidentified flying object.

u·fol·o·gy (yo͞o-fŏl′ə-jē) *n.* The study of unidentified flying objects. [UFO + –LOGY.] **—u′fo·log′i·cal** (yo͞o′fə-lŏj′ĭ-kəl) *adj.* **—u·fol′o·gist** *n.*

U·gan·da (yo͞o-găn′də, o͞o-gän′-dä). A country of east-central Africa. Inhabited in Paleolithic and Neolithic times, the region was an important conglomeration of native states by the 14th century but became a British protectorate in 1894. Uganda achieved its independence in 1962. Kampala is the capital and the largest city. Population, 12,636,179. **—U·gan′dan** *adj. & n.*

U·ga·rit (o͞o′gə-rēt′). An ancient city of western Syria on the Mediterranean Sea. It flourished as a trade center from c. 1450 to 1195 B.C. but was destroyed soon after by an earthquake.

U·ga·rit·ic (o͞o′gə-rĭt′ĭk, yo͞o′-) *n.* The Semitic language of Ugarit. **—U′ga·rit′ic** *adj.*

ugh (ŭg, ŭk) *interj.* Used to express horror, disgust, or repugnance.

Ug·li (ŭg′lē). A trademark used for a citrus fruit produced by a cross of a grapefruit, an orange, and a tangerine and having a loose, wrinkled yellowish rind.

ug·li·fy (ŭg′lə-fī′) *tr.v.* **-fied** (-fīd′), **-fy·ing, -fies** (-fīz′). To make ugly; disfigure. **—ug′li·fi·ca′tion** (-fĭ-kā′shən) *n.* **—ug′li·fi′er** *n.*

♦ **ug·ly** (ŭg′lē) *adj.* **-li·er, -li·est. 1.** Displeasing to the eye; unsightly. **2.a.** Repulsive or offensive; objectionable: *an ugly remark.* **b.** *Chiefly Southern U.S.* Rude: *Don't be ugly to your grandparents.* **c.** *New England.* Unmanageable. Used of animals, especially cows or horses. **3.** Morally reprehensible; bad. **4.** Threatening or ominous: *ugly black clouds in the sky.* **5.a.** Likely to cause embarrassment or trouble: *"Public opinion in both nations could take an ugly turn"* (George R. Packard). **b.** Marked by or inclined to anger or bad feelings; cross or disagreeable: *an ugly temper; an ugly scene.* **—ugly** *n., pl.* **-lies.** *Informal.* One that is ugly. [Middle English, frightful, repulsive, from Old Norse *uggligr,* from *uggr,* fear.] **—ug′li·ly** *adv.* **—ug′li·ness** *n.*

SYNONYMS: *ugly, hideous, ill-favored, unsightly.* The central meaning shared by these adjectives is "offensive to the sense of sight": *ugly furniture; a hideous scar; an ill-favored countenance; an unsightly billboard.*
ANTONYM: *beautiful.*

♦ ***REGIONAL NOTE:*** The standard sense of the adjective *ugly* becomes figurative in the common expression *an ugly temper.* Regional American speech shares this figurative sense and makes it even more specific. In New England *ugly* as applied to animals, especially large farm animals such as cows and horses, means "balky, hard to manage." In the South, on the other hand, *ugly* with the specific sense of "rude" is used of persons: *Don't be ugly, son.* Interestingly, the word *clever* (senses 4 through 6) follows the same regional pattern as *ugly:* in New England the specialized senses refer to animals; in the South, to persons.

ugly duckling *n.* One that is considered ugly or unpromising at first but has the potential of becoming beautiful or admirable in maturity. [After *The Ugly Duckling,* a story by Hans Christian Andersen.]

U·gri·an (o͞o′grē-ən, yo͞o′-) *n.* **1.** A member of a group of Finno-Ugric peoples of western Siberia and Hungary, including the Magyars. **2.** Ugric. [From Old Russian *Ugre,* Hungarians, of Turkic origin.] **—U′gri·an** *adj.*

U·gric (o͞o′grĭk, yo͞o′-) *n.* The branch of the Finno-Ugric subfamily of languages that includes Hungarian. **—U′gric** *adj.*

ug·some (ŭg′səm) *adj.* Disgusting; loathsome. [Middle English : *uggen,* to fear (from Old Norse *ugga,* from *uggr,* fear) + *-some,* characterized by; see –SOME[1].] **—ug′some·ness** *n.*

UGT *abbr.* Urgent (telegram).

uh (ŭ) *interj.* Used to express hesitation or uncertainty.

uhf or **UHF** *abbr.* Ultrahigh frequency.

uh-huh (ə-hŭ′) *interj. Informal.* Used to express agreement or an answer in the affirmative.

uh·lan also **u·lan** (o͞o′län′, yo͞o′lən) *n.* One of a body of horse cavalry that formed part of the former Polish army, and later, the former German army. [German, from Polish *ulan,* from Turkish *oğlan,* youth, from *oğul,* son.]

Uh·land (o͞o′länt′), **Johann Ludwig.** 1787–1862. German romantic poet known for his lyrical ballads and plays, including *Ludwig the Bavarian* (1819).

uh-uh (ŭN′ŭN′) *interj. Informal.* Used to express disagreement or an answer in the negative.

Ui·gur also **Ui·ghur** (wē′go͝or) *n., pl.* **Uigur** or **-gurs** also **Uighur** or **-ghurs. 1.** A member of a mainly agricultural Turkic people inhabiting the Xinjiang region in China. **2.** The Turkic language of the Uigurs. [Uigur.] **—Ui·gu′ri·an** (-go͝or′ē-ən), **Ui·gu′ric** (-go͝or′ĭk) *adj.*

u·in·ta·ite (yo͞o-ĭn′tə-īt′) *n.* A natural black bitumen used in the manufacture of acid, alkali, and waterproof coatings. [After the UINTA (MOUNTAINS).]

U·in·ta Mountains (yo͞o-ĭn′tə). A range of the Rocky Mountains extending about 193 km (120 mi) eastward from northeast Utah to southwest Wyoming.

uit·land·er (oit′län′dər, īt′-) *n. South African.* **1.** An outlander; a foreigner. **2. Uitlander.** A native of Great Britain who resided in either of the former republics of the Orange Free State and Transvaal. [Afrikaans, from Middle Dutch *utelander,* from *utelant,* foreign land : *ute,* out; see **ud-** in Appendix + *land,* land; see **lendh-** in Appendix.]

Uj·jain (o͞o′jīn′). A city of west-central India east of Ahmadabad. A Hindu pilgrimage site, it is one of the oldest cities in India and was a noted center of Sanskrit learning from c. A.D. 120 to c. 395. Population, 278,454.

U·jung Pan·dang (o͞o-jo͝ong′ pän-däng′). Formerly **Ma·kas·sar** or **Ma·ka·sar** (mə-kăs′ər). A city of central Indonesia on southwest Celebes Island. First visited by the Portuguese in 1512, it was settled by the Dutch in 1607. Population, 709,038.

U.K. or **UK** *abbr.* United Kingdom.

u·kase (yo͞o-kās′, -kāz′, yo͞o′kās′, -kāz′) *n.* **1.** An authoritative order or decree; an edict. **2.** A proclamation of a czar having the force of law in imperial Russia. [French, from Russian *ukaz,* decree, from Old Church Slavonic *ukazŭ,* a showing, proof : *u-,* at, to + *kazati,* to point out, show.]

uke (yo͞ok) *n. Music.* A ukulele.

U·kraine (yo͞o-krān′). A region of eastern Europe. Inhabited in early times by Scythians and Sarmatians, the area was ruled by a number of conquerors until it came under the control of Lithuania in the mid-14th century. The Ukraine later passed to Poland and then to Russia (between 1680 and 1793). A short-lived independent republic was proclaimed in 1918. It was designated a constituent republic in 1922. Kiev is the capital. Population, 50,840,000.

U·krain·i·an (yo͞o-krā′nē-ən) *n.* **1.** A native or inhabitant of the Ukraine. **2.** The Slavic language of the Ukrainians, which is closely related to Russian. **—U·krain′i·an** *adj.*

♦**u·ku·le·le** (yo͞o′kə-lā′lē, o͞o′kə-) *n. Music.* A small four-stringed guitar popularized in Hawaii. [Hawaiian *'ukulele* : *'uku,* flea + *lele,* jumping.]

♦***REGIONAL NOTE:*** The word *ukulele* is one of a small stock of Polynesian borrowings into American English. Other Hawaiian words now common in American English are *aloha* (a greeting or farewell) and *luau* (an outdoor picnic usually featuring a whole barbecued pig). *Haole,* a word common in Hawaii itself but not well known on the American mainland, is the Hawaiian word for a white resident of Hawaii.

u·la·ma (o͞o′lə-mä′) *n.* Variant of **ulema.**

u·lan (o͞o′län′, yo͞o′lən) *n.* Variant of **uhlan.**

U·lan Ba·tor (o͞o′län bä′tôr′). The capital and largest city of Mongolia, in the north-central part of the country. It was founded as a monastery town in 1649. Population, 488,200.

U·la·no·va (o͞o-lä′nə-və), **Galina.** Born 1910. Russian-born dancer who was a prima ballerina with the Bolshoi Ballet from 1944 to 1962.

U·lan-U·de (o͞o′län-o͞o-dā′, o͞o-län′o͞o-dĕ′). A city of south-central Russia near Lake Baikal and the Mongolian border. Founded as a Cossack fortress in 1649, it is a transportation hub and a processing and manufacturing center. Population, 335,000.

-ular *suff.* Of, relating to, or resembling: *tubular.* [Latin *-ulāris,* from *-ulus,* diminutive suff.]

Ul·bricht (o͞ol′brĭkt, -brĭKHt), **Walter.** 1893–1973. German politician who was general secretary of East Germany's Socialist Unity Party (1953–1971) and chairman of the council of state (1960–1973). He ordered the building of the Berlin Wall (1961).

ul·cer (ŭl′sər) *n.* **1.** A lesion of the skin or a mucous membrane such as the one lining the stomach or duodenum that is accompanied by formation of pus and necrosis of surrounding tissue, usually resulting from inflammation or ischemia. **2.** A corrupting condition or influence. [Middle English, from Old French *ulcere,* from Latin *ulcus, ulcer-.*]

ul·cer·ate (ŭl′sə-rāt′) *v.* **-at·ed, -at·ing, -ates.** *—intr.* To develop an ulcer; become ulcerous. *—tr.* To cause ulceration of. **—ul′cer·a′tive** (-sə-rā′tĭv, -sər-ə-tĭv) *adj.*

ul·cer·a·tion (ŭl′sə-rā′shən) *n.* **1.** Development of an ulcer. **2.** An ulcer or an ulcerous condition.

ul·cer·o·gen·ic (ŭl′sə-rō-jĕn′ĭk) *adj.* Tending to cause an ulcer.

ul·cer·ous (ŭl′sər-əs) *adj.* **1.** Of the nature of ulcers or an ulcer. **2.** Having ulcers or an ulcer. **—ul′cer·ous·ly** *adv.* **—ul′cer·ous·ness** *n.*

-ule *suff.* Small one: *valvule.* [French, from Latin *-ulus, -ula, -ulum,* diminutive suff.]

u·le·ma or **u·la·ma** (o͞o′lə-mä′) *pl.n.* Moslem scholars trained in Islam and Islamic law. [Turkish *'ulemā,* from Arabic *'ulamā',* wise men, from pl. of *'alim,* wise, learned, from *'alimā,* to know.]

u·lex·ite (yo͞o′lĭk-sīt′, yo͞o-lĕk′-) *n.* A white mineral, $NaCaB_5O_9·8H_2O$, that forms rounded masses of very fine needle-shaped crystals. [After G.L. *Ulex,* 19th-century German chemist.]

ul·lage (ŭl′ĭj) *n.* **1.** The amount of liquid within a container that is lost, as by leakage, during shipment or storage. **2.** The amount by which a container, such as a bottle, cask, or tank, falls short of being full. [Middle English *ulage,* from Old French *ouillage,* from *ouiller,* to fill up a cask, from *ouil,* eye, bunghole, from Latin *oculus,* eye. See **okʷ-** in Appendix.] **—ul′laged** *adj.*

Ulm (o͝olm). A city of southern Germany on the Danube River southeast of Stuttgart. First mentioned in 854, it was later a free imperial city and reached the height of its influence in the 15th century. Population, 98,604.

ul·na (ŭl′nə) *n., pl.* **-nas** or **-nae** (-nē). *Anatomy.* **1.** The bone extending from the elbow to the wrist on the side opposite to the thumb in human beings. **2.** A corresponding bone in the forelimb of other vertebrates. [Latin, elbow, forearm. See **el-** in Appendix.] **—ul′nar** *adj.*

Ul·pi·an (ŭl′pe-ən) Died A.D. 228. Roman jurist who wrote prolifically on many aspects of law.

Ul·san (o͞ol′sän′). A city of southwest South Korea on Korea Strait north-northeast of Pusan. Population, 345,700.

ul·ster (ŭl′stər) *n.* A loose, long overcoat made of heavy, rugged fabric and often belted. [After ULSTER.]

Ul·ster (ŭl′stər). A historical region and ancient kingdom of northern Ireland. Largely annexed by the English Crown during the reign of James I, it is now divided between Ireland and Northern Ireland, which is often called Ulster.

ult. *abbr.* **1.** Ultimate. **2.** Ultimately. **3.** Ultimo.

ul·te·ri·or (ŭl-tîr′ē-ər) *adj.* **1.** Lying beyond what is evident, revealed, or avowed, especially being concealed intentionally so as to deceive: *an ulterior motive.* **2.** Lying beyond or outside the area of immediate interest. **3.** Occurring later; subsequent. [Latin, farther, comparative of **ulter,* on the other side. See **al-**[1] in Appendix.] **—ul·te′ri·or·ly** *adv.*

ul·ti·ma (ŭl′tə-mə) *n. Linguistics.* The last syllable of a word. [Latin, feminine of *ultimus,* last. See ULTIMATE.]

ul·ti·ma·ta (ŭl′tə-mā′tə, -mä′tə) *n.* A plural of **ultimatum.**

ul·ti·mate (ŭl′tə-mĭt) *adj. Abbr.* **ult. 1.** Being last in a series, process, or progression: *"As the ultimate arbiter of the Constitution, the Supreme Court occupies a central place in our scheme of government"* (Richard A. Epstein). **2.** Fundamental; elemental: *an ultimate truth.* **3. a.** Of the greatest possible size or significance; maximum: *Has the ultimate diamond been found?* **b.** Representing or exhibiting the greatest possible development or sophistication: *the ultimate bicycle.* **c.** Utmost; extreme: *the ultimate insult.* **4.** Being most distant or remote; farthest. See Synonyms at **last**[1]. **5.** Eventual: *hoped for ultimate victory.* **—ultimate** *n.* **1.** The basic or fundamental fact, element, or principle. **2.** The final point; the conclusion. **3.** The greatest extreme; the maximum: *actions that represented the ultimate in political expediency.* [Latin *ultimātus,* past participle of *ultimāre,* to come to an end, from *ultimus,* last, superlative of **ulter,* on the other side. See **al-**[1] in Appendix.]

ul·ti·mate·ly (ŭl′tə-mĭt-lē) *adv. Abbr.* **ult.** At last; in the end; eventually.

ultima Thu·le (tho͞o′lē) *n.* **1.** The northernmost region of the habitable world as thought of by ancient geographers. **2.** A distant territory or destination. **3.** A remote goal or ideal: *"the ultima Thule of technology, the ne plus ultra . . . the answer to every earthly problem"* (John Gould). [Latin *ultima Thūlē* : *ultima,* feminine of *ultimus,* farthest + *Thūlē,* Thule.]

ul·ti·ma·tum (ŭl′tə-mā′təm, -mä′-) *n., pl.* **-tums** or **-ta**

Uganda

Galina Ulanova

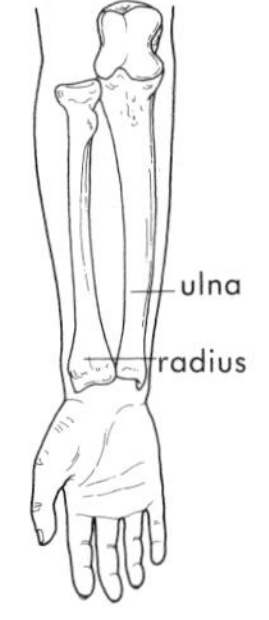

ulna

ă pat | oi boy
ā pay | ou out
âr care | o͝o took
ä father | o͞o boot
ĕ pet | ŭ cut
ē be | ûr urge
ĭ pit | th thin
ī pie | *th* this
îr pier | hw which
ŏ pot | zh vision
ō toe | ə about, item
ô paw | ♦ regionalism

Stress marks: **′** (primary); ′ (secondary), as in **dictionary** (dĭk′shə-nĕr′ē)

(-tə). **1.** A final statement of terms made by one party to another. **2.** A statement, especially in diplomatic negotiations, that expresses or implies the threat of serious penalties if the terms are not accepted. [New Latin, from neuter of Latin *ultimātus,* last. See ULTIMATE.]

ul·ti·mo (ŭl′tə-mō′) *adv. Abbr.* **ult.** In or of the month before the present one. [Latin *ultimō (mēnse),* in the last (month), ablative of *ultimus,* last. See ULTIMATE.]

ul·tra (ŭl′trə) *adj.* Immoderately adhering to a belief, fashion, or course of action; extreme. **—ultra** *n.* An extremist. [French, from Latin *ultrā-,* ultra-.]

ultra– *pref.* **1.** Beyond; on the other side of: *ultraviolet.* **2.** Beyond the range, scope, or limit of: *ultrasonic.* **3.** Beyond the normal or proper degree; excessively: *ultraconservative.* [Latin *ultrā-,* from *ultrā,* beyond. See **al-**[1] in Appendix.]

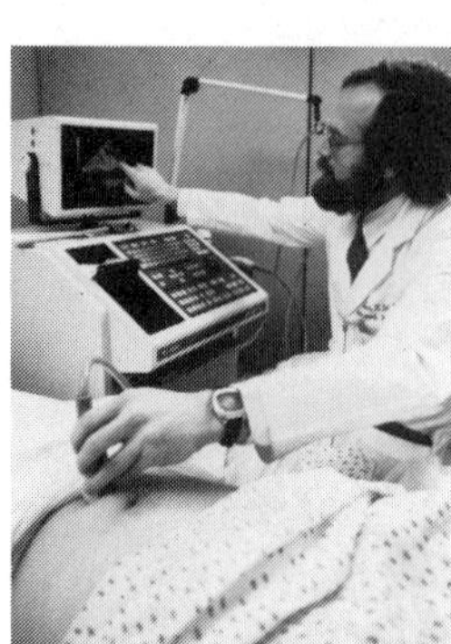
ultrasonograph

ul·tra·ba·sic (ŭl′trə-bā′sĭk) *adj. Geology.* Containing magnesium and iron and only a very small amount of silica. Used of igneous rock.

ul·tra·cen·tri·fuge (ŭl′trə-sĕn′trə-fyo͞oj′) *n.* A high-velocity centrifuge used in the separation of colloidal or submicroscopic particles. **—ul′tra·cen·trif′u·gal** (-trĭf′yə-gəl, -trĭf′ə-gəl) *adj.* **—ul′tra·cen·trif′u·gal·ly** *adv.* **—ul′tra·cen′tri·fu·ga′tion** (-fyo͞o-gā′shən) *n.*

ul·tra·con·ser·va·tive (ŭl′trə-kən-sûr′və-tĭv) *adj.* Conservative to an extreme, especially in political beliefs; reactionary. **—ultraconservative** *n.* One who is extremely conservative. **—ul′tra·con·ser′va·tism** *n.*

ul·tra·di·an (ŭl-trā′dē-ən) *adj.* Relating to or exhibiting periodic physiological activity that occurs more than once every 24 hours. [ULTRA– + (CIRCA)DIAN.]

ul·tra·fiche (ŭl′trə-fēsh′) *n.* A microfiche on which material is reduced by a factor of 100 or more. Also called *ultramicrofiche.*

ul·tra·fil·tra·tion (ŭl′trə-fĭl-trā′shən) *n.* The filtration of a colloidal substance through a semipermeable medium that allows only the passage of small molecules.

ul·tra·high (ŭl′trə-hī′) *adj.* Exceedingly high.

ultrahigh frequency *n. Abbr.* **uhf, UHF** A band of radio frequencies from 300 to 3,000 megahertz.

ul·tra·ism (ŭl′trə-ĭz′əm) *n.* Extremism, especially in politics or government; radicalism. **—ul′tra·ist** *n.*

ul·tra·lib·er·al (ŭl′trə-lĭb′ər-əl, -lĭb′rəl) *adj.* Liberal to an extreme, especially in political beliefs; radical. **—ultraliberal** *n.* One who is extremely liberal.

ul·tra·light (ŭl′trə-līt′, ŭl′trə-līt′) *n.* A recreational aircraft that is constructed of lightweight materials such as aluminum, graphite compositions, or high-strength plastics, having an engine of 15 to 40 horsepower and resembling a motorized hang glider with wings. **—ul′tra·light′** *adj.*

ul·tra·maf·ic (ŭl′trə-măf′ĭk) *adj. Geology.* Ultrabasic.

ul·tra·mar·a·thon (ŭl′trə-măr′ə-thŏn′) *n. Sports.* A cross-country footrace with distances of 30 miles (48 kilometers) or more. **—ul′tra·mar′a·thon′er** *n.*

ul·tra·ma·rine (ŭl′trə-mə-rēn′) *n.* **1.a.** A blue pigment made from powdered lapis lazuli. **b.** A similar pigment made synthetically by heating clay, sodium carbonate, and sulfur together. **2.** *Color.* A vivid or strong blue to purplish blue. **—ultramarine** *adj.* **1.** *Color.* Of the color ultramarine. **2.** Of or from a place beyond the sea. [From Medieval Latin *ultrāmarīnus,* from beyond the sea : Latin *ultrā,* ultra- + Latin *marīnus,* of the sea (from *mare,* sea; see **mori-** in Appendix).]

ul·tra·mi·cro·fiche (ŭl′trə-mī′krō-fēsh′, -krə-) *n.* See **ultrafiche.**

ul·tra·mi·crom·e·ter (ŭl′trə-mī-krŏm′ĭ-tər) *n.* An extremely accurate micrometer.

ul·tra·mi·cro·scope (ŭl′trə-mī′krə-skōp′) *n.* A microscope with high-intensity illumination used to study very minute objects, such as colloidal particles that scatter the light and appear as bright spots against a dark background. **—ul′tra·mi·cros′co·py** (-krŏs′kə-pē) *n.*

ul·tra·mi·cro·scop·ic (ŭl′trə-mī′krə-skŏp′ĭk) *adj.* **1.** Too minute to be seen with an ordinary microscope. **2.** Of or relating to an ultramicroscope.

ul·tra·mi·cro·tome (ŭl′trə-mī′krə-tōm′) *n.* A microtome for cutting very thin sections of material for use in electron microscopy. **—ul′tra·mi·crot′o·my** (-mī-krŏt′ə-mē) *n.*

ul·tra·mil·i·tant (ŭl′trə-mĭl′ĭ-tənt) *adj.* Militant to an extreme. **—ultramilitant** *n.* One who is extremely militant.

ul·tra·min·i·a·ture (ŭl′trə-mĭn′ē-ə-cho͝or′, -chər, -mĭn′ə-) *adj.* Subminiature. **—ul′tra·min′i·a·tur·ize′** (-īz′) *v.* **—ul′tra·min′i·a·tur·i·za′tion** (-chə-rĭ-zā′shən) *n.*

ul·tra·mod·ern (ŭl′trə-mŏd′ərn) *adj.* Extremely modern in ideas or style; completely up-to-date. **—ul′tra·mod′ern·ism** *n.* **—ul′tra·mod′ern·ist** *n.* **—ul′tra·mod′ern·is′tic** *adj.*

ul·tra·mon·tane (ŭl′trə-mŏn′tān′, -mŏn-tān′) *adj.* **1.** Of or relating to peoples or regions lying beyond the mountains, especially the Alps. **2.** *Roman Catholic Church.* **a.** Supporting the authority of the papal court over national or diocesan authority. **b.** Relating to or supporting the doctrine of papal supremacy. **—ultramontane** *n.* **1.** One who lives beyond the mountains, especially south of the Alps. **2.** Often **Ultramontane.** *Roman Catholic Church.* One who advocates support of papal policy in ecclesiastical and political matters. [Medieval Latin *ultrāmontānus* : Latin *ultrā-,* ultra- + Latin *montānus,* of mountains (from *mōns, mont-,* mountain; see **men-**[2] in Appendix).]

ul·tra·mon·ta·nism or **Ul·tra·mon·ta·nism** (ŭl′trə-mŏn′tə-nĭz′əm) *n. Roman Catholic Church.* The policy that absolute authority in the Church should be vested in the pope. **—ul′tra·mon′ta·nist** *n.*

ul·tra·mun·dane (ŭl′trə-mŭn′dān′, -mŭn-dān′) *adj.* Extending or being beyond the world or the limits of the universe. [Latin *ultrāmundānus* : *ultrā-,* ultra- + *mundānus,* of the world; see MUNDANE.]

ul·tra·na·tion·al·ism (ŭl′trə-năsh′ə-nə-lĭz′əm) *n.* Extreme nationalism, especially when opposed to international cooperation. **—ul′tra·na′tion·al** *adj.* **—ul′tra·na′tion·al·ist** *n.* **—ul′tra·na′tion·al·is′tic** *adj.*

ul·tra·pure (ŭl′trə-pyo͝or′) *adj.* Exceedingly pure.

ul·tra·short (ŭl′trə-shôrt′) *adj.* **1.** Of or relating to radio waves with a wavelength less than 10 meters (33 feet). **2.** Of extremely short duration: *an ultrashort flash.* **3.** Extremely short: *an ultrashort skirt.*

ul·tra·son·ic (ŭl′trə-sŏn′ĭk) *adj.* **1.** Of or relating to acoustic frequencies above the range audible to the human ear, or above approximately 20,000 hertz. **2.** Of, relating to, or involving ultrasound. **—ul′tra·son′i·cal·ly** *adv.*

ul·tra·son·ics (ŭl′trə-sŏn′ĭks) *n.* *(used with a sing. verb).* **1.** The acoustics of ultrasonic sound. **2.** The science and technology that deals with the study and application of ultrasound.

ul·tra·son·o·gram (ŭl′trə-sŏn′ə-grăm′, -sō′nə-) *n.* See **sonogram.**

ul·tra·son·o·graph (ŭl′trə-sŏn′ə-grăf′, -sō′nə-) *n.* An apparatus for producing images obtained by ultrasonography.

ul·tra·so·nog·ra·phy (ŭl′trə-sə-nŏg′rə-fē) *n.* Diagnostic imaging in which ultrasound is used to visualize an internal body structure or a developing fetus. Also called *echography.* [ULTRASON(IC) + –GRAPHY.] **—ul′tra·so·nog′ra·pher** *n.* **—ul′tra·son′o·graph′ic** (-sŏn′ə-grăf′ĭk, -sō′nə-) *adj.*

ul·tra·so·phis·ti·cat·ed (ŭl′trə-sə-fĭs′tĭ-kā′tĭd) *adj.* Very sophisticated.

ul·tra·sound (ŭl′trə-sound′) *n.* **1.** Ultrasonic sound. **2.** *Medicine.* The use of ultrasonic waves for diagnostic or therapeutic purposes, specifically to visualize an internal body structure, monitor a developing fetus, or generate localized deep heat to the tissues. *—attributive.* Often used to modify another noun: *ultrasound pictures; ultrasound waves; an ultrasound test.*

ul·tra·struc·ture (ŭl′trə-strŭk′chər) *n. Biology.* The detailed structure of a biological specimen, such as a cell, a tissue, or an organ, that can be observed only by electron microscopy. Also called *fine structure.*

ul·tra·thin (ŭl′trə-thĭn′) *adj.* Very thin.

ul·tra·vi·o·let (ŭl′trə-vī′ə-lĭt) *adj. Abbr.* **UV, U.V.** Of or relating to the range of invisible radiation wavelengths from about 4 nanometers, on the border of the x-ray region, to about 380 nanometers, just beyond the violet in the visible spectrum. **—ultraviolet** *n.* Ultraviolet light or the ultraviolet part of the spectrum.

ultraviolet lamp *n.* A lamp, especially a mercury-vapor lamp, that produces ultraviolet light.

ul·tra·vi·rus (ŭl′trə-vī′rəs) *n., pl.* **-rus·es.** See **filterable virus.**

U·lugh Muz·tagh (o͞o′lə məz-tä′, -täg′). A mountain, 7,729 m (25,341 ft) high, of the Kunlun Mountains in western China.

ul·u·late (ŭl′yə-lāt′, yo͞ol′-) *intr.v.* **-lat·ed, -lat·ing, -lates.** To wail or lament loudly. [Latin *ululāre, ululāt-,* ultimately of imitative origin.] **—ul′u·lant** (-lənt) *adj.* **—ul′u·la′tion** *n.*

Ul·ya·novsk (o͞ol-yä′nəfsk). A city of western Russia on the Volga River east-southeast of Moscow. Founded in 1648 on the site of an earlier fort, it was the birthplace of V.I. Lenin. Population, 544,000.

U·lys·ses (yo͞o-lĭs′ēz′) *n. Mythology.* Odysseus.

um also **umm** (ŭm, əm) *interj.* Used to express doubt or uncertainty or to fill a pause when hesitating in speaking.

U·ma·til·la (yo͞o′mə-tĭl′ə) *n., pl.* **Umatilla** or **-las. 1.a.** A Native American people of northeast Oregon. **b.** A member of this people. **2.** The dialect of Sahaptin spoken by the Umatilla.

U·may·yad (o͞o-mī′ăd) or **Om·mi·ad** also **O·may·yad** (ō-mī′ăd). The first dynasty of Arab caliphs (661–750).

um·bel (ŭm′bəl) *n.* A flat-topped or rounded flower cluster in which the individual flower stalks arise from about the same point, as in the geranium, milkweed, onion, and chive. [New Latin *umbella,* from Latin, parasol, diminutive of *umbra,* shadow.]

um·bel·late (ŭm′bə-lāt′, ŭm-bĕl′ĭt) also **um·bel·lat·ed** (-bə-lā′tĭd) *adj.* Having, forming, or of the nature of an umbel. **—um′bel·late′ly** *adv.*

um·bel·let (ŭm′bə-lĭt) *n. Botany.* A secondary umbel in a compound umbel, as in the carrot. Also called *umbellule.*

um·bel·lif·er (ŭm-bĕl′ə-fər) *n.* An umbelliferous plant.

um·bel·lif·er·ous (ŭm′bə-lĭf′ər-əs) *adj. Botany.* Bearing umbels.

um·bel·lule (ŭm′bəl-yo͞ol′, ŭm-bĕl′-) *n. Botany.* See **umbellet.** [New Latin *umbellula,* diminutive of *umbella,* umbel. See UMBEL.]

um·ber (ŭm′bər) *n.* **1.** A natural brown earth containing ferric oxide and manganese oxides, used as pigment. **2.** *Color.* Any of the shades of brown produced by umber in its various states. **—umber** *adj.* **1.** Of or related to umber. **2.** *Color.* Having a brownish color. **—umber** *tr.v.* **-bered, -ber·ing, -bers.** To darken with or as if with umber. [French *(terre d')ombre* or Italian *(terra di) ombra,* shadow (earth), both possibly from alteration (influenced by *ombre* and *ombra,* shadow, from Latin *umbra*) of Latin *Umbria,* a region of ancient Italy.]

um·bil·i·cal (ŭm-bĭl′ĭ-kəl) *adj.* **1.** Of, relating to, or resembling a navel or an umbilical cord. **2.** Located near the central area of the abdomen. **—umbilical** *n. Aerospace.* An umbilical cord. **—um·bil′i·cal·ly** *adv.*

umbilical cord *n.* **1.a.** *Anatomy.* The flexible cordlike structure connecting a fetus at the navel with the placenta and containing two umbilical arteries and one vein that transport nourishment to the fetus and remove its wastes. **b.** A source or means of support or sustenance: *"All the umbilical cords of dependency still exist because the public wants them"* (David A. Stockman). **2.** *Aerospace.* **a.** Any of various external electrical lines or fluid tubes that supply a rocket before launch. **b.** The line that supplies an astronaut with oxygen and in some cases with communications while outside the spacecraft.

umbilical hernia *n.* A usually self-correcting hernia of the intestines in which protrusion occurs through the abdominal wall in the region of the navel.

um·bil·i·cate (ŭm-bĭl′ĭ-kĭt) also **um·bil·i·cat·ed** (-kā′tĭd) *adj.* **1.** Having a central mark or depression resembling a navel. **2.** Having a navel. **—um·bil′i·ca′tion** *n.*

um·bil·i·cus (ŭm-bĭl′ĭ-kəs, ŭm′bə-lī′kəs) *n., pl.* **-ci** (-sī′). **1.** See **navel** (sense 1). **2.** *Biology.* A small opening or depression similar to a navel, as the hollow at the base of the shell of some gastropod mollusks, one of the openings in the shaft of a feather, or the hilum of a seed. [Latin *umbilīcus.* See **nobh-** in Appendix.]

um·bo (ŭm′bō) *n., pl.* **um·bo·nes** (ŭm-bō′nēz) or **um·bos. 1.** The boss or knob at the center of a shield. **2.a.** *Biology.* A knoblike protuberance arising from a surface, as the prominence near the hinge of a bivalve shell or the projection at the scale tip of a seed-bearing cone. **b.** *Anatomy.* A small projection at the center of the outer surface of the eardrum. [Latin *umbō, umbōn-.* See **nobh-** in Appendix.] **—um′bo·nal** (ŭm′bə-nəl, ŭm-bō′-nəl), **um·bon′ic** (ŭm-bŏn′ĭk) *adj.*

um·bo·nate (ŭm′bə-nāt′, ŭm-bō′nĭt) *adj.* Having or resembling a knob or knoblike protuberance.

um·bo·nes (ŭm-bō′nēz) *n.* A plural of **umbo.**

um·bra (ŭm′brə) *n., pl.* **-bras** or **-brae** (-brē). **1.** A dark area, especially the blackest part of a shadow from which all light is cut off. See Synonyms at **shade. 2.** *Astronomy.* **a.** The completely dark portion of the shadow cast by the earth, moon, or other body during an eclipse. **b.** The darkest region of a sunspot. [Latin, shadow.] **—um′bral** *adj.*

um·brage (ŭm′brĭj) *n.* **1.** Offense; resentment: *took umbrage at their rudeness.* **2.a.** Something that affords shade. **b.** Shadow or shade. See Synonyms at **shade. 3.** A vague or indistinct indication; a hint. [Middle English, shade, from Old French, from Latin *umbrāticum,* neuter of *umbrāticus,* of shade, from Latin *umbra,* shadow.]

um·bra·geous (ŭm-brā′jəs) *adj.* **1.** Affording or forming shade; shady. **2.** Easily offended; irritable. **—um·bra′geous·ly** *adv.* **—um·bra′geous·ness** *n.*

um·brel·la (ŭm-brĕl′ə) *n.* **1.** A device for protection from the weather consisting of a collapsible, usually circular canopy mounted on a central rod. **2.a.** Something that covers or protects. **b.** Air cover, especially during a military operation. **3.** Something that encompasses or covers many different elements or groups. **4.** *Zoology.* The gelatinous, rounded mass that is the major part of the body of most jellyfish. [Italian *ombrella,* from Late Latin *umbrella,* alteration (influenced by *umbra,* shade) of Latin *umbella,* parasol. See UMBEL.] **—um·brel′la·less** *adj.*

umbrella bird *n.* Any of several tropical American birds of the genus *Cephalopterus,* especially *C. ornatus,* having a retractile, umbrellalike black crest and a long, feathered wattle.

umbrella leaf *n.* A perennial herb *(Diphylleia cymosa)* of the southeast United States, having a broad, peltate basal leaf, a terminal cluster of white flowers, and small blue berries.

umbrella palm *n.* An Australian palm tree *(Hedyscepe canterburyana)* cultivated as an ornamental for its feathery, drooping leaves with silvery-blue sheaths.

♦ **umbrella plant** *n.* **1.** A widely cultivated, ornamental, robust sedge *(Cyperus alternifolius)* native to Madagascar and Mauritius, having long triangular leafless stems, a terminal umbrellalike cluster of grasslike leaves, and a compound umbel of spikelets with drooping rays. **2.** *Midland U.S.* The May apple.

umbrella tree *n.* **1.** Either of two trees, *Magnolia fraseri* or *M. tripetala,* of the southeast United States, having large leaves clustered in an umbrellalike form at the ends of the branches. **2.** An Australian evergreen tree *(Brassaia actinophylla),* having palmately compound leaves and widely cultivated in its smaller forms as a houseplant. **3.** See **schefflera.**

um·brette (ŭm-brĕt′) *n.* See **hammerhead** (sense 3). [New Latin *umbretta,* species name, from French *ombrette,* shadow, diminutive of *ombre,* shade, from Old French, from Latin *umbra.*]

Um·bri·a (ŭm′brē-ə, o͞om′brē-ä). A region of central Italy in the Apennines. Occupied by the Umbrians in ancient times, it later fell to the Etruscans and then the Romans (c. 300 B.C.). After passing to various powers, Umbria came under the control of the papacy in the 16th century and joined Sardinia in 1860.

Um·bri·an (ŭm′brē-ən) *adj.* Of or relating to Umbria. **—Umbrian** *n.* **1.** The Italic language of ancient Umbria. **2.** A native or inhabitant of Umbria.

Um·bri·el (ŭm′brē-əl′) *n.* The satellite of Uranus that is third in distance from the planet. [After *Umbriel,* a character in *The Rape of the Lock* by Alexander Pope.]

Um·bun·du (o͝om-bo͞on′do͞o, əm-) *n.* See **Mbundu** (sense 2).

U·me (o͞o′mə, ü′mə). A river, about 459 km (285 mi) long, of northern Sweden flowing southeast into the Gulf of Bothnia.

u·mi·ak also **oo·mi·ak** (o͞o′mē-ăk′) *n. Nautical.* A large open Eskimo boat made of skins stretched on a wooden frame, usually propelled by paddles. [Canadian and Greenlandic Eskimo *umiaq.*]

um·laut (o͝om′lout′) *Linguistics. n.* **1.a.** A change in a vowel sound caused by partial assimilation especially to a vowel or semivowel occurring in the following syllable. **b.** A vowel sound changed in this manner. Also called *vowel mutation.* **2.** The diacritic mark (¨) placed over a vowel to indicate an umlaut, especially in German. **—umlaut** *tr.v.* **-laut·ed, -laut·ing, -lauts. 1.** To modify by umlaut. **2.** To write or print (a vowel) with an umlaut. [German : *um-,* around, alteration (from Middle High German *umb-,* from *umbe,* from Old High German *umbi;* see **ambhi** in Appendix) + *Laut,* sound (from Middle High German *lūt,* from Old High German *hlūt;* see **kleu-** in Appendix).]

Um·nak Island (o͞om′năk′). An island of southwest Alaska in the east-central Aleutian Islands. It is separated from Unalaska Island by **Umnak Pass.**

ump (ŭmp) *Sports. n.* An umpire. **—ump** *intr.v.* **umped, ump·ing, umps.** To serve as an umpire.

um·pir·age (ŭm′pīr′ĭj, -pər-ĭj) *n.* **1.** The position, function, or authority of an umpire. **2.** A ruling or decision of an umpire.

um·pire (ŭm′pīr′) *n.* **1.** *Sports.* A person appointed to rule on plays, especially in baseball. **2.** A person appointed to settle a dispute that arbitrators have been unable to resolve. See Synonyms at **judge. —umpire** *v.* **-pired, -pir·ing, -pires.** —*tr.* To act as referee for; rule or judge. —*intr.* To be or act as a referee or an arbitrator. [Middle English *(an) oumpere,* (an) umpire, alteration of *(a) noumpere,* a mediator, from Old French *nonper* : *non-,* non- + *per,* equal, even, paired (from Latin *pār;* see PAIR).]

WORD HISTORY: The anguished, hostile cry "Kill the ump" could have been "kill the nump" had it not been for the linguistic process known as false splitting or juncture loss. In the case of *umpire* we can almost see the process in action if we study the *Middle English Dictionary* entry for *noumpere,* the Middle English ancestor of our word. Noumpere comes from the Old French *nonper,* made up of *non,* "not," and *per,* "equal," as is someone who is requested to act as arbiter of a dispute between two people; that is, the arbiter is not paired with one of them. In Middle English the earliest recorded form is *noumper* (about 1350). The earliest dated form without an *n* in the entry is *owmpere* (a Middle English variant spelling), in a text composed in 1440. How the *n* was lost can be seen if we compare the sequence *a noounpier* in a text written in 1426–1427 with the sequence *an Oumper* from a text written probably around 1475. The *n* of *noumpere* became attached to the indefinite article, giving us *an* instead of *a* and, eventually, *umpire* instead of **numpire.*

ump·teen (ŭmp′tēn′, ŭm′-) *adj. Informal.* Relatively large but unspecified in number: *umpteen reasons; umpteen guests.* [Slang *ump(ty),* dash in Morse code (of imitative origin) + *-teen* (as in THIRTEEN).] **—ump′teenth′** *adj.*

Um·ta·ta (o͞om-tä′tə). The capital of Transkei, in the west-central part of the homeland. It was founded in 1860 as a military post. Population, 30,000.

UMW *abbr.* United Mine Workers.

UN or **U.N.** *abbr.* United Nations.

un–¹ *pref.* **1.** Not: *unhappy.* **2.** Opposite of; contrary to: *unrest.* [Middle English, from Old English. See **ne** in Appendix.]

USAGE NOTE: There is occasional uncertainty as to the choice between the prefixes *un–* and *in–*. In general, the native English form *un–* is the more widely applicable. It is the usual choice with simple stems, as in *unfair, unclean, uneven,* or *unripe,* and with words bearing native English endings: *unceasing, unmindful, unwealthy, unselfish,* or *unwholesome. In–* is used primarily with established words originally having Latin endings: *inaccurate, incapacity, indivisible, insignificant, illegal, impossible,* or *irregular.* Sometimes the addition of a Latinate suffix to a word changes it from the *un–* category to the *in–* category: thus, we have *unable, unequal, unjust, undivided,* and *unstable* but *inability, inequality, injustice, indivisible,* and *instability.* A few words with Latinate suffixes do take *un–*: *unadventurous, unceremonious, unconditional,* and *unconventional.* A few stems appear with both prefixes with distinctions of meaning. *Inhuman* means "brutal, monstrous," while *unhuman* means "not of human form, superhuman." • When used with adjectives, *un–* often has a sense distinct from that of *non–*. *Non–* picks out the set of things that are not in the category denoted by the stem to which it is attached, whereas *un–* picks out properties unlike those of the prototypical exemplars of the category. Thus *nonmilitary personnel* are those

umbrella

umbrella bird

ă pat	oi boy
ā pay	ou out
âr care	o͝o took
ä father	o͞o boot
ĕ pet	ŭ cut
ē be	ûr urge
ĭ pit	th thin
ī pie	*th* this
îr pier	hw which
ŏ pot	zh vision
ō toe	ə about, item
ô paw	♦ regionalism

Stress marks: ′ (primary); ′ (secondary), as in **dictionary** (dĭk′shə-nĕr′ē)

who are not members of the military, but one who is *unmilitary* is unlike a typical soldier in dress, habits, or attitudes.

---

un–[2] *pref.* **1.** To reverse or undo the result of a specified action: *unbind.* **2. a.** To deprive of or remove a specified thing: *unfrock.* **b.** To release, free, or remove from: *unyoke.* **3.** Used as an intensive: *unloose.* [Middle English, from Old English *on-*, alteration (influenced by *un-*, not; see UN–[1]) of *ond-, and-, an-*, against, opposing. See **ant-** in Appendix.]

USAGE NOTE: Strictly speaking, the intensive use of *un–* in words such as *unloose, unravel, unthaw, unstrip,* or *unrid* is redundant: *unloose* has exactly the same sense as *loose; unravel,* as *ravel;* and so on. For this reason, many grammarians have suggested that the prefix be avoided, although they allow that it is well established in certain cases, such as *unloose* and *unravel,* and has been used by reputable writers: *"Pretended patriotism unstripped of its mask"* (Oliver Goldsmith). *"The weak wanton Cupid/Shall from your neck unloose his amorous fold"* (Shakespeare). Some constructions require the prefixed form: *During the storm all the insulation came unstripped* (not *stripped*).

---

un·a·bashed (ŭn′ə-băsht′) *adj.* **1.** Not disconcerted or embarrassed; poised. **2.** Not concealed or disguised; obvious: *unabashed disgust.* **—un′a·bash′ed·ly** (-băsh′ĭd-lē) *adv.*

un·a·bat·ed (ŭn′ə-bā′tĭd) *adj.* Sustaining an original intensity or maintaining full force with no decrease: *an unabated wind storm; a battle fought with unabated violence.* **—un′a·bat′ed·ly** *adv.*

un·a·ble (ŭn-ā′bəl) *adj.* **1.** Lacking the necessary power, authority, or means; not able; incapable: *unable to get to town without a car.* **2.** Lacking mental or physical capability or efficiency; incompetent: *unable to walk.*

un·a·bridged (ŭn′ə-brĭjd′) *adj.* Containing the original content; not condensed. Used of books, articles, and documents.

un·ac·cent·ed (ŭn-ăk′sĕn-tĭd) *adj. Linguistics.* **1.** Having no diacritical mark. Used of a word, syllable, or letter. **2.** Having weak stress or no stress.

un·ac·cept·a·ble (ŭn′ĭk-sĕp′tə-bəl, -ăk-) *adj.* Not acceptable; unsatisfactory. **—un′ac·cept′a·bil′i·ty** *n.* **—un′ac·cept′a·bly** *adv.*

un·ac·com·mo·dat·ed (ŭn′ə-kŏm′ə-dā′tĭd) *adj.* **1.** Not adapted or accommodated: *new arrivals who were unaccommodated to the heat of the tropics.* **2.** Lacking accommodations: *an unaccommodated guest.*

un·ac·com·pa·nied (ŭn′ə-kŭm′pə-nēd) *adj.* **1.** Going or acting without companions or a companion: *unaccompanied children on a flight.* **2.** *Music.* Performed or scored without accompaniment.

un·ac·com·plished (ŭn′ə-kŏm′plĭsht) *adj.* **1.** Not completed or done; unfinished. **2.** Lacking special skills or abilities; unpolished, as in the social graces.

un·ac·count·a·ble (ŭn′ə-koun′tə-bəl) *adj.* **1.** Impossible to account for; inexplicable: *unaccountable absences; unaccountable errors.* **2.** Free from accountability; not responsible: *an executive unaccountable to anyone but the president.* **—un′ac·count′a·bil′i·ty, un′ac·count′a·ble·ness** *n.* **—un′ac·count′a·bly** *adv.*

un·ac·count·ed-for (ŭn′ə-koun′tĭd-fôr′) *adj.* **1.** Not explained, understood, or taken into account. **2.** Missing or absent without explanation, as from a roll call or after a military operation.

un·ac·cred·it·ed (ŭn′ə-krĕd′ĭ-tĭd) *adj.* **1.** Not having the proper credentials; unauthorized: *an unaccredited school.* **2.** Not being ascribed to a source: *an unaccredited quotation.*

un·ac·cus·tomed (ŭn′ə-kŭs′təmd) *adj.* **1.** Not common or usual: *"The legislature has produced a new budget of unaccustomed austerity"* (People). **2.** Not being habituated. Used with *to*: *is still unaccustomed to a life of stress.* **—un′ac·cus′tomed·ly** *adv.* **—un′ac·cus′tomed·ness** *n.*

un·a·chiev·a·ble (ŭn′ə-chē′və-bəl) *adj.* Impossible to achieve or attain: *an unachievable goal.*

un·ac·knowl·edged (ŭn′ăk-nŏl′ĭjd) *adj.* Not accepted or recognized: *an unacknowledged inventor; an unacknowledged greeting.*

u·na cor·da (o͞o′nə kôr′də) *adv. & adj. Music.* With the soft pedal of the piano depressed. Used chiefly as a direction. [Italian : *una,* one + *corda,* string (so called because depressing the soft pedal causes only one string to be struck of the two or three provided for each note).]

un·ac·quaint·ed (ŭn′ə-kwān′tĭd) *adj.* **1.** Not familiar or acquainted with another. **2.** Not informed or knowledgeable: *unacquainted with the legal issues at hand.*

un·ad·dressed (ŭn-ə-drĕst′) *adj.* **1.** Not brought up for discussion or solution: *questions that remain unaddressed.* **2.** Not containing the required address: *unaddressed letters.*

un·ad·just·ed (ŭn′ə-jŭs′tĭd) *adj.* **1.** Not having been adjusted to conform to new data or information: *an unadjusted figure of 8.5 percent.* **2.** Not having adapted to new conditions: *several unadjusted refugees.* **3.** Needing to be made operable or accurate by adjusting or regulating: *an unadjusted clock that is running fast.*

un·a·dopt·a·ble (ŭn′ə-dŏp′tə-bəl) *adj.* Difficult to place in an adoptive home.

un·a·dorned (ŭn′ə-dôrnd′) *adj.* Without adornment or embellishment; simple or plain.

un·a·dul·ter·at·ed (ŭn′ə-dŭl′tə-rā′tĭd) *adj.* **1.** Not mingled or diluted with extraneous matter; pure. See Synonyms at **pure. 2.** Out-and-out; utter: *the unadulterated truth.*

un·ad·ven·tur·ous (ŭn′ăd-vĕn′chər-əs) *adj.* Not inclined to undertake new, risky enterprises.

un·ad·ver·tised (ŭn-ăd′vûr-tīzd′) *adj.* Not having been advertised to the public: *unadvertised sale merchandise.*

un·ad·vised (ŭn′əd-vīzd′) *adj.* **1.** Having received no advice; not informed. **2.** Carried out without careful deliberation; imprudent: *took the unadvised measure of going public with the accusations.* **—un′ad·vis′ed·ly** (-vī′zĭd-lē) *adv.* **—un′ad·vis′ed·ness** *n.*

un·af·fect·ed (ŭn′ə-fĕk′tĭd) *adj.* **1.** Not changed, modified, or affected. **2.** Marked by lack of affectation; genuine. See Synonyms at **naive, sincere. —un′af·fect′ed·ly** *adv.* **—un′af·fect′ed·ness** *n.*

un·af·fil·i·at·ed (ŭn′ə-fĭl′ē-ā′tĭd) *adj.* Not associated with another or others as a subordinate, subsidiary, or member; independent.

un·af·ford·a·ble (ŭn′ə-fôr′də-bəl) *adj.* Too expensive: *medical care that has become unaffordable for many.* **—un′af·ford′a·bil′i·ty** *n.* **—un′af·ford′a·bly** *adv.*

un·a·fraid (ŭn′ə-frād′) *adj.* Feeling, exhibiting, or expressing no fear.

u·nai (yo͞o′nô, o͞o′nou) *n.* Variant of **unau.**

un·aid·ed (ŭn-ā′dĭd) *adj.* Carried out or functioning without aid or assistance: *made an unaided attempt to climb the sheer cliff.*

Un·a·las·ka Island (ŭn′ə-lăs′kə). An island of southwest Alaska in the eastern Aleutian Islands southwest of Unimak Island. It was discovered c. 1759 by Russian explorers and used as a fur-trading center.

un·al·ien·a·ble (ŭn-āl′yə-nə-bəl, -ā′lē-ə-) *adj.* Not to be separated, given away, or taken away; inalienable: *"All of them . . . claim unalienable dignity as individuals"* (Garrison Keillor).

un·a·ligned (ŭn′ə-līnd′) *adj.* Nonaligned: *unaligned nations.*

un·al·loyed (ŭn′ə-loid′) *adj.* **1.** Not in mixture with other metals; pure. **2.** Complete; unqualified: *unalloyed blessings; unalloyed relief.* **—un′al·loy′ed·ly** (-loi′ĭd-lē) *adv.*

un·al·ter·a·ble (ŭn-ôl′tər-ə-bəl) *adj.* Impossible to alter: *the unalterable season of bitter cold in Siberia.* **—un·al′ter·a·bil′i·ty, un·al′ter·a·ble·ness** *n.* **—un·al′ter·a·bly** *adv.*

un·am·big·u·ous (ŭn′ăm-bĭg′yo͞o-əs) *adj.* Having or exhibiting no ambiguity or uncertainty; clear: *"As a horror, apartheid . . . is absolutely unambiguous. There are . . . no shades of interpretation or circumstances to weigh that might make coming to a moral judgment more difficult"* (Mario Vargas Llosa). **—un′am·big′u·ous·ly** *adv.*

un-A·mer·i·can (ŭn′ə-mĕr′ĭ-kən) *adj.* Considered contrary to the institutions or principles of the United States.

U·na·mi (o͞o-nä′mē, yo͞o-năm′ē) *n., pl.* **Unami** or **-mis. 1.** One of the two Algonquian languages of the Delaware peoples, originally spoken in central and southern New Jersey, eastern Pennsylvania, and northern Delaware. **2.** A speaker of this language.

U·na·mu·no (o͞o′nə-mo͞o′nō, -nä-), **Miguel de.** 1864–1936. Spanish philosopher and writer primarily concerned with the conflict between reason and faith and the solitary nature of human existence.

unan. *abbr.* Unanimous.

un·an·a·lyz·a·ble (ŭn-ăn′ə-lī′zə-bəl) *adj.* Difficult or impossible to analyze: *unanalyzable data.*

un·a·neled (ŭn′ə-nēld′) *adj. Archaic.* Not having received extreme unction.

u·na·nim·i·ty (yo͞o′nə-nĭm′ĭ-tē) *n.* The condition of being unanimous.

u·nan·i·mous (yo͞o-năn′ə-məs) *adj. Abbr.* **unan. 1.** Sharing the same opinions or views; being in complete harmony or accord. **2.** Based on or characterized by complete assent or agreement. [From Latin *ūnanimus* : *ūnus,* one; see **oi-no-** in Appendix + *animus,* mind; see **ane-** in Appendix.] **—u·nan′i·mous·ly** *adv.* **—u·nan′i·mous·ness** *n.*

un·an·swer·a·ble (ŭn-ăn′sər-ə-bəl) *adj.* Impossible to answer or refute; incontrovertible: *unanswerable accusations.* **—un·an′swer·a·bil′i·ty, un·an′swer·a·ble·ness** *n.* **—un·an′swer·a·bly** *adv.*

un·an·tic·i·pat·ed (ŭn′ăn-tĭs′ə-pā′tĭd) *adj.* **1.** Not anticipated: *unanticipated problems.* **2.** *Usage Problem.* Not having been expected; unexpected: *unanticipated guests.* See Usage Note at **anticipate. —un′an·tic′i·pat′ed·ly** *adv.*

un·a·pol·o·get·ic (ŭn′ə-pŏl′ə-jĕt′ĭk) *adj.* Unwilling to make or express an apology; not feeling apologetic. **—un′a·pol′o·get′i·cal·ly** *adv.*

un·ap·peal·a·ble (ŭn′ə-pē′lə-bəl) *adj.* Not subject to appeal: *an unappealable grievance; an unappealable sentence of life imprisonment.* **—un′ap·peal′a·bly** *adv.*

un·ap·peal·ing (un′ə-pē′lĭng) *adj.* Not appealing to the senses, as in appearance, taste, or aroma. **—un′ap·peal′ing·ly** *adv.*

un·ap·peas·a·ble (ŭn′ə-pē′zə-bəl) *adj.* Impossible to appease or satisfy: *unappeasable thirst and hunger.* **—un′ap·peas′a·bly** *adv.*

un·ap·pe·tiz·ing (ŭn-ăp′ĭ-tī′zĭng) *adj.* Not appetizing in appearance, aroma, or taste. **—un·ap′pe·tiz′ing·ly** *adv.*

un·ap·pre·ci·at·ed (un′ə-prē′shē-ā′tĭd) *adj.* **1.** Not recognized, as to quality or worth: *an unappreciated gesture of good will.* **2.** Not having risen in price or value: *an unappreciated investment.*

un·ap·pre·cia·tive (ŭn′ə-prē′shə-tĭv, -shē-ā′tĭv) *adj.* Not feeling or exhibiting appreciation. **—un′ap·pre′cia·tive·ly** *adv.*

un·ap·proach·a·ble (ŭn′ə-prō′chə-bəl) *adj.* **1.** Not friendly; aloof: *an unapproachable executive.* **2.** Not accessible; inapproachable: *an unapproachable chalet high in the Alps.* **—un′ap·proach′a·bil′i·ty, un′ap·proach′a·ble·ness** *n.* **—un′ap·proach′a·bly** *adv.*

un·ap·pro·pri·at·ed (ŭn′ə-prō′prē-ā′tĭd) *adj.* **1.** Not designated for a specific use. **2.** Not possessed by, spoken for, or formally assigned to a particular person or organization.

un·ap·proved (ŭn′ə-pro͞ovd′) *adj.* Not approved or sanctioned: *an unapproved vaccine; an unapproved protest march.*

un·apt (ŭn-ăpt′) *adj.* **1.** Not suitable or appropriate. **2.** Not likely or liable. **—un·apt′ly** *adv.* **—un·apt′ness** *n.*

un·ar·gu·a·ble (ŭn-är′gyo͞o-ə-bəl) *adj.* Not open to argument or further discussion: *the plain, unarguable facts.* **—un·ar′gu·a·bly** *adv.*

un·arm (ŭn-ärm′) *tr.v.* **-armed, -arm·ing, -arms.** To divest of armor or arms; disarm.

un·armed (ŭn-ärmd′) *adj.* **1.a.** Lacking weapons or armor; defenseless. **b.** Not carrying, using, or displaying arms: *an unarmed spotter plane; unarmed robbery.* **2.** *Biology.* Having no thorns, spines, teeth, claws, or other protective parts.

un·ar·tic·u·lat·ed (ŭn′är-tĭk′yə-lā′tĭd) *adj.* **1.a.** Not articulated: *our unarticulated fears.* **b.** Not carefully or thoroughly thought out. **2.** *Biology.* Not having joints or segments.

un·a·shamed (ŭn′ə-shāmd′) *adj.* **1.** Feeling or showing no remorse, shame, or need for apology. **2.** Exhibiting no embarrassment; unabashed: *lived in unashamed luxury.* **—un′a·sham′ed·ly** (-shā′mĭd-lē) *adv.* **—un′a·sham′ed·ness** *n.*

un·asked (ŭn-ăskt′) *adj.* **1.** Not asked: *Several unasked questions remain.* **2.** Not invited: *Unasked guests arrived at the party.* **3.** Not requested: *Such unasked suggestions are less than welcome.*

un·as·sail·a·ble (ŭn′ə-sā′lə-bəl) *adj.* **1.** Impossible to dispute or disprove; undeniable: *unassailable truths.* **2.** Not subject to attack or seizure; impregnable: *an unassailable fortress.* **—un′as·sail′a·bil′i·ty, un′as·sail′a·ble·ness** *n.* **—un′as·sail′a·bly** *adv.*

un·as·sem·bled (ŭn′ə-sĕm′bəld) *adj.* Made or manufactured with parts or sections ready to be joined or fitted together before use: *working with unassembled metal shelving.*

un·as·ser·tive (ŭn′ə-sûr′tĭv) *adj.* Not assertive; reserved. **—un′as·ser′tive·ly** *adv.* **—un′as·ser′tive·ness** *n.*

un·as·sist·ed (ŭn′ə-sĭs′tĭd) *adj.* **1.** Not having assistance; unaided. **2.** *Baseball.* Of, relating to, or being a play handled by only one fielder.

un·as·sum·ing (ŭn′ə-so͞o′mĭng) *adj.* Exhibiting no pretensions, boastfulness, or ostentation; modest. **—un′as·sum′ing·ly** *adv.* **—un′as·sum′ing·ness** *n.*

un·at·tached (ŭn′ə-tăcht′) *adj.* **1.** Not joined, especially to surrounding tissue. **2.a.** Not committed to or dependent on another person, group, or organization. **b.** Not engaged, married, or involved in a serious sexual or romantic relationship. **3.** *Law.* Not possessed or seized as security.

un·at·tain·a·ble (ŭn′ə-tā′nə-bəl) *adj.* Impossible to attain: *unattainable goals.* **—un′at·tain′a·bil′i·ty, un′at·tain′a·ble·ness** *n.* **—un′at·tain′a·bly** *adv.*

un·at·tend·ed (ŭn′ə-tĕn′dĭd) *adj.* **1.** Not being attended to, looked after, or watched: *an unattended fire.* **2.** Having no attendants: *unattended gasoline pumps.* **3.** Not being paid attention to or listened to: *an unattended question.*

un·at·test·ed (ŭn′ə-tĕs′tĭd) *adj.* Not attested: *a series of unattested quotations.*

un·at·trib·ut·ed (ŭn′ə-trĭb′yo͞o-tĭd) *adj.* Not attributed to a source, creator, or possessor: *an unattributed opinion.*

u·nau also **u·nai** (yo͞o′nô, o͞o′nou) *n., pl.* **u·naus** also **u·nais.** See **sloth** (sense 2b). [Portuguese, from Tupi *unáu*, lazy.]

un·au·dit·ed (ŭn-ô′dĭ-tĭd) *adj.* Not having been audited: *an unaudited financial statement.*

un·a·vail·a·ble (ŭn′ə-vā′lə-bəl) *adj.* Not available, accessible, or at hand. **—un′a·vail′a·bil′i·ty** *n.*

un·a·vail·ing (ŭn′ə-vā′lĭng) *adj.* Not availing; ineffectual or useless. See Synonyms at **futile. —un′a·vail′ing·ly** *adv.* **—un′a·vail′ing·ness** *n.*

u·na vo·ce (yo͞o′nə vō′sē, o͞o′nə vō′kā) *adv.* With one voice; unanimously. [Latin *ūnā vōce* : *ūnā*, feminine ablative of *ūnus*, one + *vōce*, ablative of *vōx*, voice.]

un·a·void·a·ble (ŭn′ə-voi′də-bəl) *adj.* Impossible to avoid; inevitable. See Synonyms at **certain. —un′a·void′a·bil′i·ty, un′a·void′a·ble·ness** *n.* **—un′a·void′a·bly** *adv.*

un·a·ware (ŭn′ə-wâr′) *adj.* Not aware or cognizant. **—unaware** *adv.* Unawares. **—un′a·ware′ly** *adv.* **—un′a·ware′ness** *n.*

USAGE NOTE: *Unaware*, followed by *of* (expressed or implied), is the usual adjectival form modifying a noun or pronoun or following a linking verb: *Unaware of the difficulty, I went ahead. He was unaware of my presence. Unawares* is the usual adverbial form: *The rain caught them unawares* (without warning). *They came upon it unawares* (without design or plan).

un·a·wares (ŭn′ə-wârz′) *adv.* **1.** By surprise; unexpectedly: *"Sorrow comes to all, and to the young it comes with bittered agony because it takes them unawares"* (Abraham Lincoln). **2.** Without forethought or plan. See Usage Note at **unaware.**

unb. *abbr.* Unbound.

un·backed (ŭn-băkt′) *adj.* **1.** Lacking backing or support. **2.** Not having a back. **3.** Never having been ridden, as a horse.

un·baked (ŭn-bākt′) *adj.* Not having been baked or cooked, especially in an oven: *unbaked bricks; an unbaked pie crust.*

un·bal·ance (ŭn-băl′əns) *tr.v.* **-anced, -anc·ing, -anc·es. 1.** To upset the balance, stability, or equilibrium of: *"By being too good a singer, too hell-bent an actress, and too strong a presence, the star unbalances the proceedings"* (John Simon). **2.** To derange (the mind). **—unbalance** *n.* The condition of being unbalanced. **—un·bal′ance·a·ble** *adj.*

un·bal·anced (ŭn-băl′ənst) *adj.* **1.** Not in balance or in proper balance. **2.a.** Mentally deranged. **b.** Not exhibiting sound judgment; irrational. **3.** *Accounting.* Not satisfactorily adjusted so that debit and credit correspond.

un·bal·last·ed (ŭn-băl′ə-stĭd) *adj.* **1.** Not stabilized or properly stabilized by ballast. **2.** Unsteady; wavering.

un·bar (ŭn-bär′) *tr. & intr.v.* **-barred, -bar·ring, -bars.** To remove the bars from or become unbarred.

un·bat·ed (ŭn-bā′tĭd) *adj.* **1.** Unabated. **2.** *Archaic.* Not blunted by a guard on the tip, as a sword or fencing foil.

unbd. *abbr.* Unbound.

un·bear·a·ble (ŭn-bâr′ə-bəl) *adj.* So unpleasant, distasteful, or painful as to be intolerable: *unbearable heat.* **—un·bear′a·ble·ness** *n.* **—un·bear′a·bly** *adv.*

un·beat·a·ble (ŭn-bē′tə-bəl) *adj.* Impossible to defeat or surpass: *an unbeatable team; an unbeatable sales record.* **—un·beat′a·bly** *adv.*

un·beat·en (ŭn-bēt′n) *adj.* **1.** Not defeated: *an unbeaten football team.* **2.** Not traversed before; untrodden: *an unbeaten path through jungle growth.* **3.** Not beaten or pounded, as in cooking: *unbeaten eggs.*

un·be·com·ing (ŭn′bĭ-kŭm′ĭng) *adj.* **1.** Not appropriate, attractive, or flattering: *an unbecoming dress.* **2.** Not in accord with the standards implied by one's character or position: *conduct unbecoming an officer.* See Synonyms at **improper. —un′be·com′ing·ly** *adv.* **—un′be·com′ing·ness** *n.*

un·be·got·ten (ŭn′bĭ-gŏt′n) *adj.* **1.** Not yet begotten; as yet unborn. **2.** Self-existent; eternal.

un·be·known (ŭn′bĭ-nōn′) *adj.* Occurring or existing without the knowledge of; unknown: *a crisis unbeknown to us.* [UN–[1] + obsolete *beknown*, known (from Middle English *beknowen*, past participle of *beknowen*, to get to know, from Old English *becnāwan* : *be-*, be- + *cnāwan*, to know; see KNOW).]

un·be·knownst (ŭn′bĭ-nōnst′) *adj.* Unbeknown. **—unbeknownst** *adv.* Without the knowledge of a specified party. Used with *to*: *Our cousin had been ill for years, unbeknownst to the family.* [UNBEKNOWN + *-st* (as in *amongst*).]

un·be·lief (ŭn′bĭ-lēf′) *n.* Lack of belief or faith, especially in religious matters.

un·be·liev·a·ble (ŭn′bĭ-lē′və-bəl) *adj.* Not to be believed; incredible: *unbelievable luck.* **—un′be·liev′a·bly** *adv.*

un·be·liev·er (ŭn′bĭ-lē′vər) *n.* One who lacks belief or faith, especially in a particular religion; a nonbeliever.

un·be·liev·ing (ŭn′bĭ-lē′vĭng) *adj.* Not believing; doubting: *The incident occurred right before our unbelieving eyes.* **—un′be·liev′ing·ly** *adv.* **—un′be·liev′ing·ness** *n.*

un·belt·ed (ŭn-bĕl′tĭd) *adj.* **1.** Made or designed to be worn without a belt: *an unbelted jacket.* **2.** Not having or using a seat belt: *tests of unbelted dummies at various impact speeds.*

un·bend (ŭn-bĕnd′) *v.* **-bent** (-bĕnt′), **-bend·ing, -bends.** —*tr.* **1.** To release from mental tension, strain, or formality; relax. **2.** To release (a bow, for example) from flexure or tension. **3.** *Nautical.* To untie or loosen (a rope or sail). **4.** To straighten (something crooked or bent): *unbend a paper clip.* —*intr.* **1.** To become less tense; relax. **2.** To become less strict. **3.** To become straight. **—un·bend′a·ble** *adj.*

un·bend·ing (ŭn-bĕn′dĭng) *adj.* **1.** Not yielding; inflexible: *an unbending will to dominate.* **2.** Aloof and often antisocial; extremely reserved: *an unbending manner.* **—un·bend′ing·ly** *adv.*

un·bent (ŭn-bĕnt′) *v.* Past tense and past participle of **unbend.**

un·bi·ased also **un·bi·assed** (ŭn-bī′əst) *adj.* Without bias or prejudice; impartial. See Synonyms at **fair[1]. —un·bi′ased·ly** *adv.* **—un·bi′ased·ness** *n.*

un·bid·den (ŭn-bĭd′n) also **un·bid** (-bĭd′) *adj.* Not invited, asked, or requested; unasked: *unbidden guests; comments unbid and unwelcome.*

un·billed (ŭn-bĭld′) *adj.* **1.** Not having been billed or charged for: *unbilled medical charges.* **2.** Appearing, as in a movie, without being credited: *an unbilled walk-on.*

un·bind (ŭn-bīnd′) *tr.v.* **-bound** (-bound′), **-bind·ing, -binds. 1.** To untie or unfasten, as wrappings or bindings. **2.** To release from restraints or bonds; free.

un·bleached (ŭn-blēcht′) *adj.* Not bleached or whitened: *unbleached flour; unbleached linen.*

un·blem·ished (ŭn-blĕm′ĭsht) *adj.* Lacking blemishes or faults: *an unblemished peach; an unblemished political record.*

un·blenched (ŭn-blĕncht′) *adj.* Undaunted; unflinching.

un·blessed also **un·blest** (ŭn-blĕst′) *adj.* **1.** Deprived of a blessing. **2.** Unholy. **—un·bless′ed·ness** (-blĕs′ĭd-nĭs) *n.*

un·blink·ing (ŭn-blĭng′kĭng) *adj.* **1.** Without blinking: *an unblinking stare.* **2.** Without visible emotion: *an unblinking answer to a very personal question.* **3.** Fearless in facing reality: *engaged in unblinking self-analysis.* **—un·blink′ing·ly** *adv.*

un·block (ŭn-blŏk′) *tr.v.* **-blocked, -block·ing, -blocks.** To remove or clear an obstruction from: *unblock a road; unblock a coronary artery.*

un·blush·ing (ŭn-blŭsh′ĭng) *adj.* **1.** Lacking shame or embarrassment. See Synonyms at **shameless. 2.** Not blushing. **—un·blush′ing·ly** *adv.* **—un·blush′ing·ness** *n.*

un·bod·ied (ŭn-bŏd′ēd) *adj.* **1.** Having no body or form; incorporeal. **2.** Being disembodied.

un·bolt (ŭn-bōlt′) *tr.v.* **-bolt·ed, -bolt·ing, -bolts.** To release the bolts of (a door, for example); unlock.

un·bolt·ed[1] (ŭn-bōl′tĭd) *adj.* Not bolted or fastened.

un·bolt·ed[2] (ŭn-bōl′tĭd) *adj.* Not sifted: *unbolted flour.*

un·born (ŭn-bôrn′) *adj.* **1.** Not yet born: *an unborn child.* **2.** Not yet appeared; future: *unborn inventions.*

un·bos·om (ŭn-bo͝oz′əm, -bo͞o′zəm) *v.* **-omed, -om·ing, -oms.** —*tr.* **1.** To confide (one's thoughts or feelings). **2.** To relieve (oneself) of troublesome thoughts or feelings. —*intr.* To reveal one's thoughts or feelings. **—un·bos′om·er** *n.*

un·bound (ŭn-bound′) *v.* Past tense and past participle of **unbind. —unbound** *adj.* **1.** *Abbr.* **unb., unbd.** Not bound: *unbound manuscripts; an unbound book.* **2.** Freed from bonds or restraints; released: *an unbound captive.*

un·bound·ed (ŭn-boun′dĭd) *adj.* **1.** Having no boundaries or limits: *unbounded space.* **2.** Not kept within bounds; unrestrained: *unbounded enthusiasm.* **—un·bound′ed·ly** *adv.* **—un·bound′ed·ness** *n.*

un·bowed (ŭn-boud′) *adj.* **1.** Not bowed; unbent. **2.** Not subdued; unyielding: *"My head is bloody but unbowed"* (W.E. Henley).

un·brace (ŭn-brās′) *tr.v.* **-braced, -brac·ing, -brac·es. 1.** To set free by removing bands or braces. **2.** To release from tension; relax. **3.** To make slack; weaken.

un·brand·ed (ŭn-brăn′dĭd) *adj.* Not branded or carrying a brand name: *unbranded cattle; unbranded merchandise.*

un·break·a·ble (un-brā′kə-bəl) *adj.* **1.** Impossible to break; able to withstand rough usage: *unbreakable dinnerware.* **2.** Able to withstand an attempt to break. Used of a horse. **—unbreakable** *n.* An article or object that is not easily broken. **—un·break′a·ble·ness** *n.* **—un·break′a·bly** *adv.*

un·breath·a·ble (ŭn-brē′*th*ə-bəl) *adj.* Not fit or suitable to be breathed: *unbreathable exhaust fumes.*

un·bred (ŭn-brĕd′) *adj.* **1.** Not instructed; untaught. **2.** Not yet bred: *an unbred mare.* **3.** *Obsolete.* Ill-bred; impolite.

un·bridge·a·ble (ŭn-brĭj′ə-bəl) *adj.* Impossible to span: *an unbridgeable chasm; unbridgeable differences.* **—un·bridge′a·bly** *adv.*

un·bri·dle (ŭn-brīd′l) *tr.v.* **-dled, -dling, -dles. 1.** To free from restriction or restraint. **2.** To free from a bridle.

un·bri·dled (ŭn-brīd′ld) *adj.* **1.** Unrestrained; uncontrolled: *unbridled anger.* **2.** Not wearing or being fitted with a bridle: *an unbridled pony.* **—un·bri′dled·ly** *adv.*

un·bro·ken (ŭn-brō′kən) *adj.* **1.** Not tampered with; intact: *an unbroken dozen.* **2.** Not violated or breached: *unbroken promises.* **3.** Uninterrupted; continuous: *unbroken silence.* **4.** Not tamed or broken to harness: *unbroken horses.* **5.** Not disordered or disturbed: *unbroken family ties.* **—un·bro′ken·ly** *adv.* **—un·bro′ken·ness** *n.*

un·buck·le (ŭn-bŭk′əl) *v.* **-led, -ling, -les.** —*tr.* To loosen or undo the buckle or buckles of. —*intr.* **1.** To undo buckles. **2.** *Informal.* To relax.

un·budg·ing (ŭn-bŭj′ĭng) *adj.* Not moving or willing to move from a position or place: *unbudging honesty; an unbudging foe.* **—un·budg′ing·ly** *adv.*

un·build (un-bĭld′) *v.* **-built** (-bĭlt′), **-build·ing, -builds.** —*tr.* To dismantle, take apart, or demolish; raze. —*intr.* To dismantle something built.

un·build·a·ble (ŭn-bĭl′də-bəl) *adj.* **1.** That cannot be built: *an unbuildable house, given the eccentric design.* **2.** Unsuitable to be built upon: *unbuildable wetlands.*

un·built (ŭn-bĭlt′) *v.* Past tense and past participle of **unbuild.**

un·bun·dling (ŭn-bŭn′dlĭng) *n.* The separate pricing of goods and services.

un·bur·den (ŭn-bûr′dn) *tr.v.* **-dened, -den·ing, -dens.** To free from or relieve of a burden or trouble: *unburden one's mind.*

un·but·ton (ŭn-bŭt′n) *v.* **-toned, -ton·ing, -tons.** —*tr.* **1.** To unfasten the buttons of. **2.** To free or remove (a button) from a buttonhole. **3.** To open as if by unbuttoning: *unbutton the hatches.* —*intr.* To undo buttons.

un·caged (ŭn-kājd′) *adj.* **1.** Not being confined in or as if in a cage: *uncaged birds.* **2.** Having been released from a cage: *an uncaged lion in the arena.*

un·cal·cu·lat·ed (ŭn-kăl′kyə-lā′tĭd) *adj.* Not thought out in advance; spontaneous.

un·cal·cu·lat·ing (ŭn-kăl′kyə-lā′tĭng) *adj.* Not using or involving calculation.

un·called-for (ŭn-kôld′fôr′) *adj.* **1.** Not required or requested; unwanted: *uncalled-for suggestions.* **2.** Not justified or deserved; unwarranted: *uncalled-for rudeness.*

un·can·ny (ŭn-kăn′ē) *adj.* **-ni·er, -ni·est. 1.** Peculiarly unsettling, as if of supernatural origin or nature; eerie. See Synonyms at **weird. 2.** So keen and perceptive as to seem preternatural. **—un·can′ni·ly** *adv.* **—un·can′ni·ness** *n.*

un·cap (ŭn-kăp′) *v.* **-capped, -cap·ping, -caps.** —*tr.* To remove the cap or covering of. —*intr.* To remove one's head covering as a sign of deference.

un·cared-for (ŭn-kârd′fôr′) *adj.* Not looked after; neglected.

un·car·ing (ŭn-kâr′ĭng) *adj.* Devoid of concern or sympathy.

Un·cas (ŭng′kəs). 1588?–1683? Native American leader who rebelled against his father's leadership of the Pequot and with his followers formed the Mohegan tribe.

un·caused (ŭn-kôzd′) *adj.* Existing without a perceptible cause; spontaneous.

un·ceas·ing (ŭn-sē′sĭng) *adj.* Not stopping; continuous. **—un·ceas′ing·ly** *adv.* **—un·ceas′ing·ness** *n.*

un·cel·e·brat·ed (ŭn-sĕl′ə-brā′tĭd) *adj.* **1.** Not famous or well known; obscure. **2.** Not formally or officially honored.

un·cen·sored (ŭn-sĕn′sərd) *adj.* Not examined, expurgated, or given a rating for inclusion of improper or inappropriate material: *received uncensored correspondence from a theater of military operations; sells uncensored movies and novels.*

un·cer·e·mo·ni·ous (ŭn-sĕr′ə-mō′nē-əs) *adj.* **1.** Without the due formalities; abrupt: *an unceremonious departure.* **2.** Not ceremonious; informal: *an unceremonious speech.* **—un·cer′e·mo′ni·ous·ly** *adv.* **—un·cer′e·mo′ni·ous·ness** *n.*

un·cer·tain (ŭn-sûr′tn) *adj.* **1.** Not known or established; questionable: *domestic changes of great if uncertain consequences.* **2.** Not determined; undecided: *uncertain plans.* **3.** Not having sure knowledge: *an uncertain recollection of the sequence of events.* **4.a.** Subject to change; variable: *uncertain weather.* **b.** Unsteady; fitful: *uncertain light.* **—un·cer′tain·ly** *adv.* **—un·cer′tain·ness** *n.*

un·cer·tain·ty (ŭn-sûr′tn-tē) *n., pl.* **-ties. 1.** The condition of being uncertain; doubt. **2.** Something uncertain: *the uncertainties of modern life.* **3.** *Statistics.* The estimated amount or percentage by which an observed or calculated value may differ from the true value.

SYNONYMS: *uncertainty, doubt, dubiety, skepticism, suspicion, mistrust.* These nouns all refer to the condition of being unsure about someone or something. *Uncertainty,* the least forceful, merely denotes a lack of assurance or conviction: *I regarded my decision with growing uncertainty. Doubt* and *dubiety* imply a questioning state of mind that leads to hesitation in accepting a premise or in making a decision: *"Doubt is part of all religion"* (Isaac Bashevis Singer). *On this point there can be no dubiety. Skepticism* generally suggests an instinctive or habitual tendency to question and demand proof, as of truth or merit: *"A wise skepticism is the first attribute of a good critic"* (James Russell Lowell). *Suspicion* is doubt as to the innocence, truth, integrity, honesty, or soundness of someone or something; the word often suggests an uneasy feeling that the person or thing is evil: *"I had rather take my chance that some traitors will escape detection than spread abroad a spirit of general suspicion and distrust"* (Learned Hand). *Mistrust* denotes lack of trust or confidence, as in a person's motives, arising from suspicion: *Corporate leaders viewed the economist's recommendations with mistrust.*

uncertainty principle *n.* A principle in quantum mechanics holding that increasing the accuracy of measurement of one observable quantity increases the uncertainty with which other quantities may be known.

un·cer·ti·fied (ŭn-sûr′tə-fīd′) *adj.* Not officially verified, guaranteed, or registered; not certified: *an uncertified check; an uncertified teacher.*

un·chain (ŭn-chān′) *tr.v.* **-chained, -chain·ing, -chains.** To release from or as if from chains or bonds; set free. **—un·chain′a·ble** *adj.*

un·chal·lenge·a·ble (ŭn-chăl′ən-jə-bəl) *adj.* Not open to challenge: *unchallengeable facts; an unchallengeable legal position.* **—un·chal′lenge·a·bly** *adv.*

un·change·a·ble (ŭn-chān′jə-bəl) *adj.* Not to be altered; immutable: *the unchangeable seasons.* **—un·change′a·bil′i·ty, un·change′a·ble·ness** *n.* **—un·change′a·bly** *adv.*

un·chang·ing (ŭn-chān′jĭng) *adj.* Remaining the same; showing or undergoing no change: *unchanging weather patterns; unchanging friendliness.* —**un·chang′ing·ly** *adv.* —**un·chang′ing·ness** *n.*

un·char·ac·ter·is·tic (ŭn′kăr-ək-tə-rĭs′tĭk) *adj.* Unusual or atypical: *an uncharacteristic display of anger.* —**un′char·ac·ter·is′ti·cal·ly** *adv.*

un·charged (ŭn-chärjd′) *adj.* **1.** Not loaded. Used of a weapon. **2.** *Law.* **a.** Not being formally accused. **b.** Not subject to a charge. Used of land. **3.** Lacking electric charge.

un·char·i·ta·ble (ŭn-chăr′ĭ-tə-bəl) *adj.* **1.** Exhibiting no charity or generosity. **2.** Unfair or unkind: *uncharitable remarks.* —**un·char′i·ta·ble·ness** *n.* —**un′char′i·ta·bly** *adv.*

un·chart·ed (ŭn-chär′tĭd) *adj.* **1.** Not charted or recorded on a map or plan: *uncharted waterways; the uncharted desert.* **2.** Unknown: *The nation's geopolitical strategy is yet uncharted.*

un·chaste (ŭn-chāst′) *adj.* **-chast·er, -chast·est.** Not chaste or modest. —**un·chaste′ly** *adv.* —**un·chaste′ness, un·chas′ti·ty** (-chăs′tĭ-tē) *n.*

un·checked (ŭn-chĕkt′) *adj.* **1.** Not held in check; unrestrained: *an unchecked flow of water; an unchecked temper.* **2.** Not checked for accuracy, efficiency, flaws: *an unchecked list.*

un·chris·tian (ŭn-krĭs′chən) *adj.* **1.** Not in accord with the spirit or principles of Christianity. **2.** Not Christian. **3.** Uncivilized; barbaric.

un·church (ŭn-chûrch′) *tr.v.* **-churched, -church·ing, -church·es. 1.** To expel from a church or from church membership; excommunicate. **2.** To deprive (a congregation, sect, or building) of the status of a church.

un·ci (ŭn′sī) *n.* Plural of **uncus.**

un·cial also **Un·cial** (ŭn′shəl, -sē-əl) —*adj.* Of or relating to a style of writing characterized by somewhat rounded capital letters and found especially in Greek and Latin manuscripts of the fourth to the eighth century A.D. —*n.* **1.** A style of writing characterized by somewhat rounded capital letters. It provided the model from which most of the capital letters in the modern Latin alphabet are derived. **2.** A capital letter written in this style. [From Late Latin *unciālēs (litterae),* inch-high (letters), uncials, pl. of Latin *unciālis,* inch-high, from *uncia,* a twelfth part, ounce, inch. See **oi-no-** in Appendix.]

un·ci·form (ŭn′sə-fôrm′) *adj.* Shaped like a hook. —**unciform** *n.* See **hamate.** [Latin *uncus,* hook + —FORM.]

un·ci·nar·i·a (ŭn′sə-nâr′ē-ə) *n.* See **hookworm.** [New Latin *Uncīnāria,* hookworm genus, from Latin *uncīnus,* barb. See UNCINATE.]

un·ci·nate (ŭn′sə-nāt′, -nĭt) *adj.* Bent at the end like a hook. [Latin *uncīnātus,* from *uncīnus,* barb, from *uncus,* hook.]

un·cir·cu·lat·ed (ŭn-sûr′kyə-lā′tĭd) *adj.* Not circulated or in circulation: *uncirculated coins; uncirculated air.*

un·cir·cum·cised (ŭn-sûr′kəm-sīzd′) *adj.* **1.** Not circumcised. **2. a.** Not Jewish; Gentile. **b.** Not Christian. —**un·cir′cum·ci′sion** (-sĭzh′ən) *n.*

un·civ·il (ŭn-sĭv′əl) *adj.* **1.** Discourteous; rude: *"The street was quiet; slamming the car door seemed an uncivil disturbance"* (Anthony Hyde). **2.** *Archaic.* Uncivilized; barbarous. —**un·civ′il·ly** *adv.* —**un·civ′il·ness** *n.*

un·civ·i·lized (ŭn-sĭv′ə-līzd′) *adj.* Not civilized; barbarous. —**un·civ′i·liz′ed·ly** (-lī′zĭd-lē, -līzd′lē) *adv.* —**un·civ′i·liz′ed·ness** *n.*

un·clad (ŭn-klăd′) *adj.* Not wearing clothes; naked.

un·claimed (ŭn-klāmd′) *adj.* Not claimed: *unclaimed luggage at the airport terminal.*

un·clasp (ŭn-klăsp′) *v.* **-clasped, -clasp·ing, -clasps.** —*tr.* **1.** To release or loosen the clasp of. **2.** To release or loosen from a clasp or an embrace. —*intr.* **1.** To become unfastened. **2.** To release or relax a clasp or grasp; let go.

un·clas·si·fied (ŭn-klăs′ə-fīd′) *adj.* **1.** Not placed or included in a class or category: *unclassified mail.* **2.** Of, relating to, or being official matter not requiring the application of security safeguards: *unclassified defense documentation.*

un·cle (ŭng′kəl) *n.* **1.** *Abbr.* **u., U. a.** The brother of one's mother or father. **b.** The husband of one's aunt. **2.** Used as a form of address for an older man, especially by children. **3.** A kindly counselor. **4.** *Slang.* A pawnbroker. **5. Uncle.** Uncle Sam. —***idiom.* cry** (or **say**) **uncle.** *Informal.* To indicate a willingness to give up a fight or surrender: *Members of the gang held him down until at last he cried uncle.* [Middle English, from Anglo-Norman, from Latin *avunculus,* maternal uncle. See **awo-** in Appendix.] —**un′cle·less** *adj.*

un·clean (ŭn-klēn′) *adj.* **-clean·er, -clean·est. 1.** Foul or dirty. **2.** Morally defiled; unchaste. **3.** Ceremonially impure. —**un·clean′ness** *n.*

un·clean·ly (ŭn-klĕn′lē) *adj.* **-li·er, -li·est.** Unclean. —**uncleanly** (-klēn′-) *adv.* In an unclean manner. —**un·clean′li·ness** *n.*

un·clear (ŭn-klîr′) *adj.* **-clear·er, -clear·est.** Not clearly defined; not explicit.

un·clench (ŭn-klĕnch′) *v.* **-clenched, -clench·ing, -clench·es.** —*tr.* To loosen from a clenched position; relax: *unclench one's fists.* —*intr.* To become unclenched.

Uncle Sam (săm) *n.* *Abbr.* **U.S., US 1.** The government of the United States, often personified by a representation of a tall, thin man having a white beard and wearing a blue swallow-tailed coat, red-and-white-striped trousers, and a tall hat with a band of stars: *"intent on giving states greater incentive to save both their dollars and Uncle Sam's"* (New York Times). **2.** The American nation or its people. [From *U.S.,* abbr. of UNITED STATES.]

WORD HISTORY: Obvious explanations of word origins often meet resistance simply because they are dull compared with less reliable ones. Such a conclusion seems justified on the basis of the disagreement about the origin of the name *Uncle Sam.* The term is first recorded in the Troy, New York, *Post* of September 7, 1813, and right along with it is found the explanation that "The letters U.S. on the government waggons, &c are supposed to have given rise to it." Nonetheless, attempts have since been made to connect the name to such people as Samuel Wilson, an army yard inspector of Troy, New York. None of these attempts, including the one involving Samuel Wilson, has been successful. This expansion of initials was carried yet further with those in the name U.S. Grant, which were variously explained as "Unconditional Surrender," "United We Stand," "United States," and "Uncle Sam."

Uncle Tom (tŏm) *n.* *Offensive.* A Black person who is regarded as being humiliatingly subservient or deferential to white people. [After *Uncle Tom,* a character in *Uncle Tom's Cabin,* a novel by Harriet Beecher Stowe.]

Uncle Tom·ism (tŏm′ĭz′əm) *n.* *Offensive.* Deferential, subservient behavior and attitudes believed characteristic of an Uncle Tom: *"Some will seek 'status' through renewed acquiescence and Uncle Tomism"* (Alvin F. Poussaint).

un·cloak (ŭn-klōk′) *tr.v.* **-cloaked, -cloak·ing, -cloaks. 1.** To remove a cloak or cover from. **2.** To expose; reveal.

un·clog (ŭn-klŏg′) *tr.v.* **-clogged, -clog·ging, -clogs.** To clear a blockage from (a drain, for example).

un·close (ŭn-klōz′) *v.* **-closed, -clos·ing, -clos·es.** —*tr.* **1.** To open. **2.** To disclose. —*intr.* **1.** To be opened. **2.** To undergo disclosure.

un·clothe (ŭn-klōth′) *tr.v.* **-clothed, -cloth·ing, -clothes.** To remove the clothing or cover from; strip.

un·clut·tered (ŭn-klŭt′ərd) *adj.* Not being cluttered; orderly: *a neat, uncluttered room; an uncluttered mind.*

un·co (ŭng′kō) *Scots. adj.* So unusual as to be surprising; uncanny. —**unco** *n., pl.* **-cos. 1.** An unusual or amazing person. **2.** A stranger. **3. uncos.** News. —**unco** *adv.* To an excessive degree; remarkably. [Middle English *unkow,* variant of *uncouth,* strange. See UNCOUTH.]

un·coat·ed (ŭn-kō′tĭd) *adj.* **1.** Not furnished with or wearing a coat. **2.** Not being covered with a layer: *an uncoated pill; uncoated paper.*

un·coil (ŭn-koil′) *tr. & intr.v.* **-coiled, -coil·ing, -coils.** To unwind or untwist or to become unwound or untwisted.

un·col·lect·ed (ŭn′kə-lĕk′tĭd) *adj.* Not having been collected; ungathered: *uncollected garbage; uncollected thoughts.*

un·com·fort·a·ble (ŭn-kŭm′fər-tə-bəl, -kŭmf′tə-) *adj.* **1.** Experiencing physical discomfort. **2.** Ill at ease; uneasy. **3.** Causing anxiety; disquieting. —**un·com′fort·a·ble·ness** *n.* —**un·com′fort·a·bly** *adv.*

un·com·mer·cial (ŭn′kə-mûr′shəl) *adj.* **1.** Not engaged in or involving trade or commerce. **2.** Not in accord with the spirit or methods of commerce. **3.** Uneconomical.

un·com·mit·ted (ŭn′kə-mĭt′ĭd) *adj.* Not pledged to a specific cause or course of action: *an uncommitted delegate.*

un·com·mon (ŭn-kŏm′ən) *adj.* **-er, -est. 1.** Not common; rare. **2.** Wonderful; remarkable. —**un·com′mon·ly** *adv.* —**un·com′mon·ness** *n.*

un·com·mu·ni·ca·tive (ŭn′kə-myo͞o′nĭ-kā′tĭv, -kə-tĭv) *adj.* Not communicative. See Synonyms at **silent.** —**un′com·mu′ni·ca′tive·ly** *adv.* —**un′com·mu′ni·ca′tive·ness** *n.*

Un·com·pah·gre Peak (ŭn′kəm-pä′grē). A mountain, 4,364.2 m (14,309 ft) high, in the San Juan Mountains of southwest Colorado. It is the highest elevation in the range.

un·com·pen·sat·ed (ŭn-kŏm′pən-sā′tĭd) *adj.* Not having been compensated; serving without compensation; unpaid.

un·com·pet·i·tive (ŭn′kəm-pĕt′ĭ-tĭv) *adj.* Not competitive; not liking or inclined to compete. —**un′com·pet′i·tive·ly** *adv.* —**un′com·pet′i·tive·ness** *n.*

un·com·plain·ing (ŭn′kəm-plā′nĭng) *adj.* Showing patience and tolerance. —**un′com·plain′ing·ly** *adv.*

un·com·plet·ed (ŭn′kəm-plē′tĭd) *adj.* As yet unfinished.

un·com·pli·cat·ed (ŭn-kŏm′plĭ-kā′tĭd) *adj.* **1.** Not complex or involved; simple: *found an uncomplicated solution to the problem.* **2.** Not involving medical complications.

un·com·pli·men·ta·ry (ŭn′kŏm-plə-mĕn′tə-rē, -mĕn′trē) *adj.* Not complimentary; derogatory.

un·com·pre·hend·ing (ŭn′kŏm-prĭ-hĕn′dĭng) *adj.* Not understanding; having little or no comprehension. —**un′com·pre·hend′ing·ly** *adv.*

un·com·pro·mis·a·ble (ŭn-kŏm′prə-mī′zə-bəl) *adj.* That cannot be compromised: *uncompromisable honesty.*

un·com·pro·mis·ing (ŭn-kŏm′prə-mī′zĭng) *adj.* Unwilling to grant concessions or negotiate; inflexible: *took an uncompromising stance during the peace talks; displayed uncompromising honesty.* —**un·com′pro·mis′ing·ly** *adv.*

Uncle Sam
World War I poster painted by James Montgomery Flagg

ă pat	oi boy
ā pay	ou out
âr care	o͝o took
ä father	o͞o boot
ĕ pet	ŭ cut
ē be	ûr urge
ĭ pit	th thin
ī pie	*th* this
îr pier	hw which
ŏ pot	zh vision
ō toe	ə about, item
ô paw	♦ regionalism

Stress marks: ′ (primary); ′ (secondary), as in **dictionary** (dĭk′shə-nĕr′ē)

un·com·put·er·ized (ŭn′kəm-pyo͞o′tə-rīzd′) *adj. Computer Science.* Not equipped with or using computers.

un·con·ceiv·a·ble (ŭn′kən-sē′və-bəl) *adj.* Inconceivable: *unconceivable beauty.* —**un′con·ceiv′a·ble·ness** *n.* —**un′con·ceiv′a·bly** *adv.*

un·con·cern (ŭn′kən-sûrn′) *n.* **1.** Lack of interest; indifference. **2.** Lack of worry or apprehensiveness.

un·con·cerned (ŭn′kən-sûrnd′) *adj.* **1.** Not interested; indifferent. See Synonyms at **indifferent. 2.** Not anxious or apprehensive; unworried. —**un′con·cern′ed·ly** (-sûr′nĭd-lē) *adv.* —**un′con·cern′ed·ness** *n.*

un·con·di·tion·al (ŭn′kən-dĭsh′ə-nəl) *adj.* Without conditions or limitations; absolute: *demanded unconditional surrender.* —**un′con·di′tion·al·ly** *adv.* —**un′con·di′tion·al·ness, un′con·di′tion·al′i·ty** (-dĭsh′ə-năl′ĭ-tē) *n.*

un·con·di·tioned (ŭn′kən-dĭsh′ənd) *adj.* **1.** Unconditional. **2.** *Psychology.* Not dependent on or resulting from conditioning; unlearned or natural. —**un′con·di′tioned·ness** *n.*

unconditioned response *n. Psychology.* A natural, usually unvarying response evoked by a stimulus in the absence of learning or conditioning.

unconditioned stimulus *n. Psychology.* A stimulus that evokes an unconditioned response.

un·con·form·a·ble (ŭn′kən-fôr′mə-bəl) *adj.* **1.** Incapable of conformity; not conforming. **2.** *Geology.* Showing unconformity. —**un′con·form′a·bil′i·ty, un′con·form′a·ble·ness** *n.* —**un′con·form′a·bly** *adv.*

un·con·for·mi·ty (ŭn′kən-fôr′mĭ-tē) *n., pl.* **-ties. 1.** Lack of conformity; nonconformity. **2.** *Geology.* A surface of erosion between rock layers of different ages indicating that deposition was not continuous.

un·con·gen·ial (ŭn′kən-jēn′yəl) *adj.* **1.** Not compatible or sympathetic, as in character. See Synonyms at **inconsistent. 2.** Not appropriate; unsuitable. **3.** Not pleasing; disagreeable. —**un′con·ge′ni·al′ity** (-jē′nē-ăl′ĭ-tē) *n.*

un·con·nect·ed (ŭn′kə-nĕk′tĭd) *adj.* **1.** Not joined or connected. **2.** Not coherent; disconnected: *unconnected sentences.* —**un′con·nect′ed·ly** *adv.* —**un′con·nect′ed·ness** *n.*

un·con·quer·a·ble (ŭn-kŏng′kər-ə-bəl) *adj.* Impossible to overcome or defeat: *unconquerable obstacles to success; an unconquerable faith.* —**un·con′quer·a·bly** *adv.*

un·con·scion·a·ble (ŭn-kŏn′shə-nə-bəl) *adj.* **1.** Not restrained by conscience; unscrupulous: *unconscionable behavior.* **2.** Beyond prudence or reason: *unconscionable spending.* —**un·con′scion·a·ble·ness** *n.* —**un·con′scion·a·bly** *adv.*

un·con·scious (ŭn-kŏn′shəs) *adj.* **1.** Lacking awareness and the capacity for sensory perception; not conscious. **2.** Temporarily lacking consciousness. **3.** Occurring in the absence of conscious awareness or thought: *unconscious resentment; unconscious fears.* **4.** Without conscious control; involuntary or unintended: *an unconscious mannerism.* —**unconscious** *n.* The division of the mind in psychoanalytic theory containing elements of psychic makeup, such as memories or repressed desires, that are not subject to conscious perception or control but that often affect conscious thoughts and behavior. —**un·con′scious·ly** *adv.* —**un·con′scious·ness** *n.*

un·con·sid·ered (ŭn′kən-sĭd′ərd) *adj.* Not reasoned or considered; rash: *an unconsidered remark.*

un·con·sol·i·dat·ed (ŭn′kən-sŏl′ĭ-dā′tĭd) *adj.* Not yet consolidated: *unconsolidated subsidiaries.*

un·con·sti·tu·tion·al (ŭn′kŏn-stĭ-to͞o′shə-nəl, -tyo͞o′-) *adj.* Not in accord with the principles set forth in the constitution of a nation or state. —**un′con·sti·tu′tion·al′i·ty** (-shə-năl′ĭ-tē) *n.* —**un′con·sti·tu′tion·al·ly** *adv.*

un·con·struct·ed (ŭn′kən-strŭk′tĭd) *adj.* Designed or made with little or no interfacing, padding, or lining to produce a loose, soft shape. Used of apparel: *an unconstructed jacket.*

un·con·tam·i·nat·ed (ŭn′kən-tăm′ə-nā′tĭd) *adj.* Not contaminated: *uncontaminated blood.*

un·con·test·ed (ŭn′kən-tĕs′tĭd) *adj.* Not contested: *an uncontested divorce; the uncontested leader.*

un·con·trol·la·ble (ŭn′kən-trō′lə-bəl) *adj.* Impossible to control or govern: *an uncontrollable urge for a chocolate bar; uncontrollable rebels.* —**un′con·trol′la·bil′i·ty, un′con·trol′la·ble·ness** *n.* —**un′con·trol′la·bly** *adv.*

un·con·trolled (ŭn′kən-trōld′) *adj.* Not under control, discipline, or governance. —**un′con·trolled′ness** *n.*

un·con·tro·ver·sial (ŭn′kŏn-trə-vûr′shəl, -sē-əl) *adj.* Engendering no controversy. —**un′con·tro·ver′sial·ly** *adv.*

un·con·ven·tion·al (ŭn′kən-vĕn′shə-nəl) *adj.* Not adhering to convention; out of the ordinary. —**un′con·ven′tion·al′i·ty** (-shə-năl′ĭ-tē) *n.* —**un′con·ven′tion·al·ly** *adv.*

un·con·vinc·ing (ŭn′kən-vĭn′sĭng) *adj.* Not convincing: *gave an unconvincing excuse.* —**un′con·vinc′ing·ly** *adv.* —**un′con·vinc′ing·ness** *n.*

un·cooked (ŭn-ko͝okt′) *adj.* Not cooked; raw.

un·cool (ŭn-ko͞ol′) *adj. Slang.* **1.** Lacking assurance, self-control, or sophistication. **2.** Not in accord with the standards or mores of a specified group: *"trying to teach children simply to reject drugs as uncool"* (Larry Martz).

un·co·op·er·a·tive (ŭn′kō-ŏp′ər-ə-tĭv, -ŏp′rə-tĭv, -ŏp-ə-rā′tĭv) *adj.* Not cooperative: *an uncooperative witness.* —**un′co·op′er·a·tive·ly** *adv.* —**un′co·op′er·a·tive·ness** *n.*

un·co·or·di·nat·ed (ŭn′kō-ôr′dn-ā′tĭd) *adj.* **1.** Lacking physical or mental coordination. **2.** Lacking planning, method, or organization. —**un′co·or′di·nat′ed·ly** *adv.*

un·cork (ŭn-kôrk′) *tr.v.* **-corked, -cork·ing, -corks. 1.** To draw the cork from. **2.** To free from a sealed or constrained state.

un·cor·rect·ed (ŭn′kə-rĕk′tĭd) *adj.* Not corrected: *an uncorrected manuscript; a host of uncorrected abuses.*

un·cor·rob·o·rat·ed (ŭn′kə-rŏb′ə-rā′tĭd) *adj.* Not corroborated: *uncorroborated testimony.*

un·count·a·ble (ŭn-koun′tə-bəl) *adj.* Too many to be counted; innumerable: *an uncountable number of tourists.*

un·count·ed (ŭn-koun′tĭd) *adj.* **1.** Not counted: *The uncounted money is in the safe.* **2.** Uncountable; innumerable: *There are uncounted reasons for my declining the invitation.*

un·cou·ple (ŭn-kŭp′əl) *v.* **-pled, -pling, -ples.** —*tr.* **1.** To disconnect. **2.** To set loose or release from a couple. —*intr.* To come or break loose. —**un·cou′pler** *n.*

un·couth (ŭn-ko͞oth′) *adj.* **1.** Crude; unrefined. **2.** Awkward or clumsy; ungraceful. **3.** *Archaic.* Foreign; unfamiliar. [Middle English, unknown, strange, from Old English *uncūth* : *un-*, not; see UN–[1] + *cūth*, known; see **gnō-** in Appendix.] —**un·couth′ly** *adv.* —**un·couth′ness** *n.*

un·cov·e·nant·ed (ŭn-kŭv′ə-nən-tĭd) *adj.* **1.** Not bound by a covenant. **2.** Not promised or guaranteed by a covenant.

un·cov·er (ŭn-kŭv′ər) *v.* **-ered, -er·ing, -ers.** —*tr.* **1.** To remove the cover from: *uncovered the saucepan.* **2.** To manifest or disclose; reveal: *uncovered new evidence.* **3.** To remove the hat from, as in respect or reverence. —*intr.* **1.** To remove a cover. **2.** To bare the head in respect or reverence.

un·cov·ered (ŭn-kŭv′ərd) *adj.* **1.** Having no cover or protection. **2.** Lacking the protection of insurance or collateral security. **3.** Bareheaded.

uncovered option *n.* See **naked option.**

un·cre·at·ed (ŭn′krē-ā′tĭd) *adj.* **1.** Not having been created; not yet in existence. **2.** Existing of itself; uncaused.

un·cred·it·ed (ŭn-krĕd′ĭ-tĭd) *adj.* **1.** Not having been credited, as on a ledger: *an uncredited deposit.* **2.** Not having been accorded due recognition: *an uncredited discovery.*

un·crewed (ŭn-kro͞od′) *adj.* Not having a crew; crewless: *uncrewed missile launch.*

un·crit·i·cal (ŭn-krĭt′ĭ-kəl) *adj.* **1.** Not critical; undiscriminating or indulgent. **2.** Not using critical standards or methods, as in evaluation. —**un·crit′i·cal·ly** *adv.*

un·cross (ŭn-krôs′, -krŏs′) *tr.v.* **-crossed, -cross·ing, -cross·es.** To move (one's legs, for example) from a crossed position.

un·crowd·ed (ŭn-krou′dĭd) *adj.* Not crowded: *an uncrowded museum; an uncrowded bus.*

un·crowned (ŭn-kround′) *adj.* **1.** Yet to be crowned: *an uncrowned queen.* **2.** Having the power or influence of a monarch or other prominent figure but not the title: *the uncrowned king of the espionage world.*

unc·tion (ŭngk′shən) *n.* **1.** The act of anointing as part of a religious, ceremonial, or healing ritual. **2.** An ointment or oil; a salve. **3.** Something that serves to soothe; a balm. **4.** Affected or exaggerated earnestness, especially in choice and use of language. [Middle English, from Latin *ūnctiō, ūnctiōn-*, from *ūnctus*, past participle of *unguere*, to anoint.]

unc·tu·ous (ŭngk′cho͞o-əs) *adj.* **1.** Characterized by affected, exaggerated, or insincere earnestness: *"the unctuous, complacent court composer who is consumed with envy and self-loathing"* (Rhoda Koenig). **2.** Having the quality or characteristics of oil or ointment; slippery. **3.** Containing or composed of oil or fat. **4.** Abundant in organic materials; soft and rich: *unctuous soil.* [Middle English, from Old French *unctueus*, from Medieval Latin *ūnctuōsus*, from Latin *ūnctum*, ointment, from neuter past participle of *unguere*, to anoint.] —**unc′tu·ous·ly** *adv.* —**unc′tu·ous·ness, unc′tu·os′i·ty** (-ŏs′ĭ-tē) *n.*

SYNONYMS: *unctuous, fulsome, oily, oleaginous, smarmy.* The central meaning shared by these adjectives is "insincerely, self-servingly, or smugly agreeable or earnest": *an ambitious and unctuous assistant; gave the dictator a fulsome introduction; oily praise; oleaginous hypocrisy; smarmy self-importance.*

un·cul·ti·vat·ed (ŭn-kŭl′tə-vā′tĭd) *adj.* **1.** Not cultivated by standard agricultural methods: *uncultivated vegetables; uncultivated ground.* **2.** Socially unpolished, uncultured, or unrefined.

un·cul·tured (ŭn-kul′chərd) *adj.* Not cultured or cultivated: *an uncultured coal-mining town; an uncultured brute.*

un·curl (ŭn-kûrl′) *v.* **-curled, -curl·ing, -curls.** —*tr.* To unwind from or as if from a curl, a coil, a spiral, or a curled position: *uncurled my fists.* —*intr.* To become unwound from a curl: *fern fronds uncurling in the spring air.*

un·cus (ŭng′kəs) *n., pl.* **un·ci** (ŭn′sī). *Biology.* A hook-shaped part or process. [Latin, hook.]

un·cut (ŭn-kŭt′) *adj.* **1.** Not cut: *uncut hair.* **2.** *Printing.* Having the page edge not slit or trimmed. Used of a book. **3.** Not cut or ground to a specific shape. Used of a gemstone. **4.** Not condensed, abridged, or shortened, as by an editor or a censor: *the uncut version of the scandalous story.* —**un·cut′ta·ble** *adj.*

un·dam·aged (ŭn-dăm′ĭjd) *adj.* Not damaged, injured, or harmed: *an undamaged nuclear reactor; undamaged feelings.*

un·damped (ŭn'dămpt') *adj.* **1.** *Physics.* Not tending toward a state of rest; not damped. Used of oscillations. **2.** Not stifled or discouraged; unchecked: *undamped ardor.*

un·dat·ed (ŭn-dā'tĭd) *adj.* **1.** Not marked with or showing a date: *an undated letter; an undated portrait.* **2.** Being such as to have long-lasting appeal without ever going out of style: *a classic, undated dress.*

un·daunt·a·ble (ŭn-dôn'tə-bəl, -dän'-) *adj.* Not admitting of discouragement: *undauntable heroism; undauntable optimism.*

un·daunt·ed (ŭn-dôn'tĭd, -dän'-) *adj.* Not discouraged or disheartened; resolutely courageous. See Synonyms at **brave.** —**un·daunt'ed·ly** *adv.* —**un·daunt'ed·ness** *n.*

un·de·bat·a·ble (ŭn'dĭ-bā'tə-bəl) *adj.* Closed to debate or further discussion: *undebatable facts.* —**un'de·bat'a·bly** *adv.*

un·de·ceive (ŭn'dĭ-sēv') *tr.v.* **-ceived, -ceiv·ing, -ceives.** To free from illusion or deception. —**un'de·ceiv'a·ble** *adj.* —**un'de·ceiv'a·bly** *adv.*

un·de·cid·ed (ŭn'dĭ-sī'dĭd) *adj.* **1.** Not yet determined or settled; open: *Our position on this bill is still undecided.* **2.** Not having reached a decision; uncommitted: *undecided voters.* —**undecided** *n., pl.* **-eds.** One, such as a voter, that has not yet reached a decision: *"Will this joint interview make up minds among the vast throng of undecideds?"* (William Safire). —**un'de·cid'ed·ly** *adv.* —**un'de·cid'ed·ness** *n.*

un·decked[1] (ŭn-dĕkt') *adj.* Not decorated; unornamented.

un·decked[2] (ŭn-dĕkt') *adj.* *Nautical.* Having no deck. Used of a ship.

un·de·clared (ŭn'dĭ-klârd') *adj.* **1.** Not having been formally declared: *an undeclared war.* **2.** Not having formally declared oneself: *an undeclared candidate.*

un·de·liv·er·a·ble (ŭn'dĭ-lĭv'ər-ə-bəl) *adj.* Difficult or impossible to deliver: *undeliverable mail.*

un·de·mon·stra·tive (ŭn'dĭ-mŏn'strə-tĭv) *adj.* Not disposed to expressions of feeling; reserved. —**un'de·mon'stra·tive·ly** *adv.* —**un'de·mon'stra·tive·ness** *n.*

un·de·ni·a·ble (ŭn'dĭ-nī'ə-bəl) *adj.* Difficult or impossible to deny; irrefutable: *undeniable facts.* —**un'de·ni'a·bly** *adv.* —**un'de·ni'a·ble·ness** *n.*

un·de·pend·a·ble (ŭn'dĭ-pĕn'də-bəl) *adj.* Not easily relied or depended on: *an undependable worker; an undependable lamp socket.* —**un'de·pend'a·bil'i·ty** *n.*

un·der (ŭn'dər) *prep.* **1.a.** In a lower position or place than: *a rug under a chair.* **b.** To or into a lower position or place than: *rolled the ball under the couch.* **2.** Beneath the surface of: *under the ground; swam under water.* **3.** Beneath the assumed surface or guise of: *traveled under a false name.* **4.** Less than; smaller than: *The jar's capacity is under three quarts.* **5.** Less than the required amount or degree of: *under voting age.* **6.** Inferior to in status or rank: *nine officers under me at headquarters.* **7.** Subject to the authority, rule, or control of: *under a dictatorship.* **8.** Subject to the supervision, instruction, or influence of: *under parental guidance.* **9.** Undergoing or receiving the effects of: *under constant care.* **10.** Subject to the restraint or obligation of: *under contract.* **11.** Within the group or classification of: *listed under biology.* **12.** In the process of: *under discussion.* **13.** In view of; because of: *under these conditions.* **14.** With the authorization of: *under the monarch's seal.* **15.** Sowed or planted with: *an acre under oats.* **16.** *Nautical.* Powered or propelled by: *under sail; under steam.* **17.** During the time conventionally assigned to (a sign of the zodiac): *born under Aries.* —**under** *adv.* **1.** In or into a place below or beneath: *struggled in the water but then slipped under.* **2.** In or into a subordinate or inferior condition or position. **3.** So as to be covered or enveloped. **4.** So as to be less than the required amount or degree. —**under** *adj.* **1.** Located or situated on a lower level or beneath something else: *the under parts of a machine.* **2.** Lower in rank, power, or authority; subordinate. **3.** Less than is required or customary: *an under dose of medication.* —***idiom.*** **out from under.** *Informal.* Free of worries or difficulties: *Credit counseling helped us get out from under.* [Middle English, from Old English. See **n̥dher-** in Appendix.]

under– *pref.* **1.** Beneath or below in position: *underground.* **2.** Inferior or subordinate in rank or importance: *undersecretary.* **3.** Less in degree, rate, or quantity than normal or proper: *undersized.* [Middle English, from Old English. See **n̥dher-** in Appendix.]

USAGE NOTE: Many compounds other than those entered here may be formed with *under–*. In forming compounds, *under–* is joined with the following element without a space or a hyphen: *underrate; undergrow.* Note, however, that the adjective *under* may combine with other words as a unit modifier. In such cases the words are joined by hyphens: *an under-the-table deal.*

un·der·a·chieve (ŭn'dər-ə-chēv') *intr.v.* **-chieved, -chiev·ing, -chieves.** To perform worse or achieve less success than expected. —**un'der·a·chieve'ment** *n.* —**un'der·a·chiev'er** *n.*

un·der·act (ŭn'dər-ăkt') *v.* **-act·ed, -act·ing, -acts.** —*tr.* **1.** To perform (a role) weakly or with insufficient expressiveness. **2.** To understate (a role) intentionally; underplay. —*intr.* To perform in an understated way.

un·der·age[1] (ŭn'dər-ĭj) *n.* **1.** An amount, as of money or goods actually on hand, that falls short of the listed amount in records or books of account. **2.** A deficient amount; a shortfall.

un·der·age[2] (ŭn'dər-āj') also **un·der·aged** (-ājd') *adj.* Below the customary or legal age, as for drinking or voting.

un·der·arm (ŭn'dər-ärm') *adj.* **1.** Located, placed, or used under the arm. **2.** *Sports.* Executed with the hand brought forward and up from below the level of the shoulder; underhand. —**underarm** *adv.* With an underarm motion or delivery. —**underarm** *n.* The armpit. —*attributive.* Often used to modify another noun: *underarm perspiration; underarm deodorant.*

un·der·bel·ly (ŭn'dər-bĕl'ē) *n., pl.* **-lies.** **1.** The soft belly or underside of an animal's body. Also called *underbody.* **2.** The vulnerable or weak part: *"the soft underbelly of the Axis"* (Winston S. Churchill). *"So much . . . can be learned from these and other neglected sources from the underbelly of traditional scholarship"* (Stephen Jay Gould).

un·der·bid (ŭn'dər-bĭd') *v.* **-bid, -bid·ding, -bids.** —*tr.* **1.** To bid lower than (a competitor). **2.** *Games.* To bid less than the full value of (one's hand) in bridge. —*intr.* To make an unnecessarily low bid. —**un'der-bid', un'der·bid'der** *n.*

un·der·bod·y (ŭn'dər-bŏd'ē) *n., pl.* **-ies.** **1.** See **underbelly** (sense 1). **2.** The under parts of the body of a motor vehicle.

un·der·boss (ŭn'dər-bôs', -bŏs') *n.* An assistant to a chief, especially in a crime syndicate.

un·der·bought (ŭn'dər-bôt') *v.* Past tense and past participle of **underbuy.**

un·der·bred (ŭn'dər-brĕd') *adj.* **1.** Poorly brought up; ill-bred. **2.** Of mixed breed; not thoroughbred.

un·der·brush (ŭn'dər-brŭsh') *n.* Small trees, shrubs, or similar plants growing beneath the taller trees in a forest.

un·der·buy (ŭn'dər-bī') *v.* **-bought** (-bôt'), **-buy·ing, -buys.** —*tr.* **1.** To buy less (of something) than one wants or needs. **2.** To buy at a lower price than a competitor. **3.** To buy (something) at less than a proper or expected price. —*intr.* **1.** To buy less of something than what is wanted or needed. **2.** To buy something at a price lower than proper or expected.

un·der·cap·i·tal·ize (ŭn'dər-kăp'ĭ-tl-īz') *tr.v.* **-ized, -iz·ing, -iz·es.** To supply (a business or government, for example) with so little capital that operations are hindered. —**un'der·cap'i·tal·i·za'tion** (-ĭ-zā'shən) *n.*

un·der·car·riage (ŭn'dər-kăr'ĭj) *n.* **1.** A supporting framework or structure, as for the body of a motor vehicle. **2.** The landing gear of an aircraft.

un·der·charge (ŭn'dər-chärj') *tr.v.* **-charged, -charg·ing, -charg·es.** **1.** To charge (a customer, for example) less than is customary or required. **2.** To load (a firearm) with an insufficient charge. —**undercharge** (ŭn'dər-chärj') *n.* An insufficient or improper charge.

un·der·class (ŭn'dər-klăs') *n.* The lowest societal stratum, usually composed of the disadvantaged: *"America can no longer afford racism and a neglect of the underclass"* (Lance Morrow). *"Divorced women and their children are becoming a new underclass"* (Barbara Fisher Williamson).

un·der·class·man (ŭn'dər-klăs'mən) *n.* A student in the freshman or sophomore class at a secondary school or college. Also called *lowerclassman.*

un·der·clothes (ŭn'dər-klōz', -klōthz') *pl.n.* Clothes worn next to the skin, beneath one's outer clothing. Also called *underclothing, underwear.*

un·der·cloth·ing (ŭn'der-klō'thĭng) *n.* See **underclothes.**

un·der·coat (ŭn'dər-kōt') *n.* **1.** A coat worn beneath another coat. **2.** A covering of short hairs lying underneath the longer outer hairs of an animal's coat. **3.** Also **un·der·coat·ing** (-kō'tĭng). **a.** A coat of sealing material applied to a surface before the outer coats, as of paint, are applied. **b.** The sealing material used for this purpose. **c.** A tarlike substance sprayed on the underside of a vehicle to prevent rusting. —**undercoat** *tr.v.* **-coat·ed, -coat·ing, -coats.** To apply an undercoat to.

un·der·cool (ŭn'dər-ko͞ol') *tr.v.* **-cooled, -cool·ing, -cools.** To supercool.

un·der·count (ŭn'dər-kount') *tr.v.* **-count·ed, -count·ing, -counts.** To record fewer than the actual number of (persons in a census, for example). —**un'der·count'** *n.*

un·der·cov·er (ŭn'dər-kŭv'ər) *adj.* **1.** Performed or occurring in secret: *an undercover investigation.* **2.** Engaged or employed in spying or secret investigation: *undercover FBI agents.*

un·der·croft (ŭn'dər-krôft', -krŏft') *n.* A crypt, especially one used for burial under a church. [Middle English : *under-,* under- + *croft,* crypt (from Middle Dutch *crofte,* from Medieval Latin *crupta,* from Latin *crypta,* crypt; see CRYPT).]

un·der·cur·rent (ŭn'dər-kûr'ənt, -kŭr'-) *n.* **1.** A current, as of air or water, below another current or beneath a surface. **2.** An underlying tendency, force, or influence often contrary to what is superficially evident; an intimation: *"The Gaucho began to talk, calmly but with an undercurrent of passion"* (Thomas Pynchon).

un·der·cut (ŭn'dər-kŭt') *v.* **-cut, -cut·ting, -cuts.** —*tr.* **1.** To diminish or destroy the province or effectiveness of; undermine: *"This celebration of opulence and wealth and power undercuts the character of the Statue of Liberty"* (Jesse Jackson). *"The partnership between the United States and Western Europe is undercut by diverging economic interests"* (Scott Sullivan). **2.** To sell at a lower price than or to work for lower wages or fees than (a competitor). **3.** To make a cut under or below. **4.** To create an overhang by cutting material away from, as in carving. **5.** *Sports.* **a.** To impart backspin to (a ball) by striking downward as well as

ă pat	oi boy
ā pay	ou out
âr care	o͝o took
ä father	o͞o boot
ĕ pet	ŭ cut
ē be	ûr urge
ĭ pit	th thin
ī pie	*th* this
îr pier	hw which
ŏ pot	zh vision
ō toe	ə about, item
ô paw	♦ regionalism

Stress marks: **'** (primary); ' (secondary), as in **dictionary** (dĭk'shə-nĕr'ē)

forward, as in golf and baseball. **b.** To cut or slice (a ball) with an underarm stroke, as in tennis. *—intr.* To engage in undercutting. **—undercut** (ŭn′dər-kŭt′) *n.* **1.a.** A cut made in the under part to remove material. **b.** The material so removed. **2.** A notch cut in a tree to direct its fall and insure a clean break. **3.** *Chiefly British.* The tenderloin of beef; the fillet. **4.** *Sports.* **a.** A spin given to a ball opposite to its direction of flight; a backspin. **b.** A cut or slice imparting such a spin. **c.** A cut or slice made with an underarm motion.

un·der·de·vel·oped (ŭn′dər-dĭ-vĕl′əpt) *adj.* **1.** Not adequately or normally developed; immature: *underdeveloped leaves and flowers.* **2.** Processed in too weak a developing solution, or for too short a time, or at too low a temperature to produce a normal degree of contrast. Used of film. **3.** Having a low level of economic productivity and technological sophistication within the contemporary range of possibility; developing: *underdeveloped countries.* **—un′der·de·vel′op·ment** *n.*

un·der·do (ŭn′dər-do͞o′) *tr.v.* **-did** (-dĭd′), **-done** (-dŭn′), **-do·ing, -does** (-dŭz′). To do to an insufficient degree, especially to cook for too short a time.

un·der·dog (ŭn′dər-dôg′, -dŏg′) *n.* **1.** One that is expected to lose a contest or struggle, as in sports or politics. **2.** One that is at a disadvantage.

un·der·done (ŭn′dər-dŭn′) *v.* Past participle of **underdo.** **—underdone** *adj.* Not sufficiently cooked.

un·der·draw·ers (ŭn′dər-drôrz′) *pl.n.* Undershorts.

un·der·dress (ŭn′dər-drĕs′) *n.* **1.** Apparel worn beneath outer garments; underclothing. **2.** An outer garment, such as a dress beneath a tunic or coat, that is worn as part of a costume or suit. **—underdress** (ŭn′dər-drĕs′) *intr.v.* **-dressed, -dress·ing, -dress·es. 1.** To dress too informally for the occasion. **2.** To dress without sufficient warmth.

un·der·drive (ŭn′dər-drīv′) *n.* A gearing device that causes the output drive shaft to rotate at a slower rate than the engine input shaft.

un·der·ed·u·cat·ed (ŭn′dər-ĕj′ə-kā′tĭd) *adj.* Poorly or insufficiently educated.

un·der·em·pha·size (ŭn′dər-ĕm′fə-sīz′) *tr.v.* **-sized, -siz·ing, -siz·es.** To fail to give enough emphasis to. **—un′der·em′pha·sis** (-sĭs) *n.*

un·der·em·ployed (ŭn′dər-ĕm-ploid′) *adj.* **1.** Employed only part-time when one needs and desires full-time employment. **2.** Inadequately employed, especially employed at a low-paying job that requires less skill or training than one possesses. **3.** Not fully or adequately used or employed. **—underemployed** *n.* *(used with a pl. verb).* Underemployed persons considered as a group. Used with *the.* **—un′der·em·ploy′ment** *n.*

un·der·en·dow (ŭn′dər-ĕn-dou′) *tr.v.* **-dowed, -dow·ing, -dows.** To supply with insufficient gifts or attributes, especially of money or features deemed attractive. **—un′der·en·dow′ment** *n.*

un·der·es·ti·mate (ŭn′dər-ĕs′tə-māt′) *tr.v.* **-mat·ed, -mat·ing, -mates.** To make too low an estimate of the quantity, degree, or worth of. **—underestimate** (-ĕs′tə-mĭt) *n.* An estimate that is or proves to be too low. **—un′der·es′ti·ma′tion** *n.*

un·der·ex·pose (ŭn′dər-ĭk-spōz′) *tr.v.* **-posed, -pos·ing, -pos·es. 1.** To expose (film) to light for too short a time or to light or radiation insufficient to produce normal image contrast. **2.** To provide with too little publicity. **—un′der·ex·po′sure** (-ĭk-spō′zhər) *n.*

un·der·feed (ŭn′dər-fēd′) *tr.v.* **-fed** (-fĕd′), **-feed·ing, -feeds. 1.** To feed insufficiently. **2.** To supply (an engine) with fuel from the underside.

un·der·flow (ŭn′dər-flō′) *n.* *Computer Science.* A data-processing error arising when a computed quantity is a smaller number than the device is capable of displaying.

un·der·foot (ŭn′dər-fo͝ot′) *adv.* **1.** Below or under the foot or feet; against the ground: *trampled the beans underfoot.* **2.** At or under the foot or feet; on the ground: *moist, cool, soft grass growing underfoot.* **3.** Hindering progress; in the way: *pets, toys, and children underfoot.*

un·der·fund (ŭn′dər-fŭnd′) *tr.v.* **-fund·ed, -fund·ing, -funds.** To provide insufficient funding for.

un·der·fur (ŭn′dər-fûr′) *n.* The soft, fine undercoat of certain mammals, such as otters, beavers, and seals.

un·der·gar·ment (ŭn′dər-gär′mənt) *n.* A garment worn under outer garments, especially one worn next to the skin.

un·der·gird (ŭn′dər-gûrd′) *tr.v.* **-gird·ed** or **-girt** (-gûrt′), **-gird·ing, -girds.** To support or strengthen from beneath.

un·der·glaze (ŭn′dər-glāz′) *n.* Coloring or decoration applied to pottery before glazing.

un·der·go (ŭn′dər-gō′) *tr.v.* **-went** (-wĕnt′), **-gone** (-gôn′, -gŏn′), **-go·ing, -goes** (-gōz′). **1.** To pass through; experience: *a house that is undergoing renovations.* See Synonyms at **experience. 2.** To endure; suffer: *undergo great hardship.*

un·der·grad (ŭn′dər-grăd′) *n. & adj.* *Informal.* Undergraduate.

un·der·grad·u·ate (ŭn′dər-grăj′o͞o-ĭt) *n.* **1.** A college or university student who has not yet received a bachelor's or similar degree. **2.** A high-school student who has not yet received a diploma. **—undergraduate** *adj.* **1.** Of, relating to, or characteristic of undergraduates: *undergraduate courses; undergraduate humor.* **2.** Having the standing of an undergraduate: *an undergraduate transfer student.*

underhand
Underhand softball pitch

un·der·ground (ŭn′dər-ground′) *adj.* **1.** Situated, occurring, or operating below the surface of the earth: *underground caverns; underground missile sites.* **2.a.** Hidden or concealed; clandestine: *underground resistance to the tyrant.* **b.** Of or relating to an organization involved in secret or illegal activity: *underground trade in weapons.* **3.** Of or relating to an avant-garde movement or its films, publications, and art, usually privately produced and of special appeal and often concerned with social or artistic experiment. **—underground** *n.* **1.** A clandestine, often nationalist, organization fostering or planning hostile activities against, or the overthrow of, a government in power, such as an occupying military government: *"an underground of dissident intellectuals"* (Kenneth L. Woodward). **2.** *Chiefly British.* A subway system. **3.** An avant-garde movement or publication. **—underground** (ŭn′dər-ground′) *adv.* **1.** Below the surface of the earth. **2.** In secret; stealthily. **—underground** *tr.v.* **-ground·ed, -ground·ing, -grounds.** To situate under the ground: *workers undergrounding telephone lines.*

Un·der·ground Railroad (ŭn′dər-ground′) *n.* **1.** A secret cooperative network that aided fugitive slaves in reaching sanctuary in the free states or in Canada in the years before the abolition of slavery in the United States. **2. underground railroad.** A secret cooperative network engaged in the clandestine movement and housing of fugitives, such as children removed illegally from the custody of a parent charged with child abuse.

un·der·grown (ŭn′dər-grōn′) *adj.* **1.** Not fully grown; puny. **2.** Covered with undergrowth.

un·der·growth (ŭn′dər-grōth′) *n.* **1.** Low-growing plants, saplings, and shrubs beneath trees in a forest. **2.** A growth of short, fine hairs underlying the longer and thicker outer hairs of an animal's coat; underfur or underwool. **3.** The condition of being less than fully grown.

un·der·hair (ŭn′dər-hâr′) *n.* A covering of soft downy hairs lying under the outer hairs of an animal's coat; an undercoat.

un·der·hand (ŭn′dər-hănd′) also **un·der·hand·ed** (ŭn′dər-hăn′dĭd) *—adj.* **1.** Marked by or done in a deceptive, secret, or sly manner; dishonest and sneaky. See Synonyms at **secret. 2.** *Sports.* Executed with the hand brought forward and up from below the level of the shoulder; underarm: *an underhand pitch; an underhand stroke.* *—adv.* **1.** With an underhand movement. **2.** In a sly and secret way. **—un′der·hand′** *n.* **—un′der·hand′ed·ly** *adv.* **—un′der·hand′ed·ness** *n.*

un·der·hung (ŭn′dər-hŭng′) *adj.* **1.a.** Protruding from beneath. **b.** Supported by or lying over something that projects. **2.** Resting on or mounted along a supporting track, as a sliding door on rollers. **3.** Underslung, as a machine. **4.** Having the lower jaw projecting beyond the upper jaw.

un·der·in·sure (ŭn′dər-ĭn-sho͝or′) *tr.v.* **-sured, -sur·ing, -sures.** To insure under a policy that provides inadequate benefits: *Be certain that you are not underinsured against catastrophic illness.* **—un′der·in·sur′ance** *n.*

un·der·kill (ŭn′dər-kĭl′) *n.* Insufficient force to defeat an enemy.

un·der·laid (ŭn′dər-lād′) *v.* Past tense and past participle of **underlay**[1]. **—underlaid** *adj.* **1.** Placed or laid underneath. **2.** Supported or raised by something from beneath; having an underlay.

un·der·lain (ŭn′dər-lān′) *v.* Past participle of **underlie.**

un·der·lay[1] (ŭn′dər-lā′) *tr.v.* **-laid** (-lād′), **-lay·ing, -lays. 1.** To put (one thing) under another. **2.** To provide with a base or support. **3.** *Printing.* To raise or support (the level of a bed) by inserting a piece of paper or other material under the type. **—underlay** (ŭn′dər-lā′) *n.* **1.** Something, such as felt under a carpet, that is underlaid. Also called *underlayment.* **2.** *Printing.* Paper or other material used to underlay.

un·der·lay[2] (ŭn′dər-lā′) *v.* Past tense of **underlie.**

un·der·lay·ment (ŭn′dər-lā′mənt) *n.* See **underlay**[1] (sense 1).

un·der·let (ŭn′dər-lĕt′) *tr.v.* **-let, -let·ting, -lets. 1.** To lease for less than the proper value. **2.** To sublet.

un·der·lie (ŭn′dər-lī′) *tr.v.* **-lay** (-lā′), **-lain** (-lān′), **-ly·ing, -lies. 1.** To be located under or below. **2.** To be the support or basis of; account for: *Many factors underlie my decision.* **3.** To constitute a prior financial claim over: *Dividends for preferred stock underlie those of common stock.*

un·der·line (ŭn′dər-līn′, ŭn′dər-līn′) *tr.v.* **-lined, -lin·ing, -lines. 1.** To draw a line under; emphasize or cause to stand out; underscore. **2.** To emphasize; stress. **—underline** (ŭn′dər-līn′) *n.* A line under something, such as a symbol, word, or phrase, used to indicate emphasis or italic type.

un·der·ling (ŭn′dər-lĭng) *n.* One of lesser rank or authority than another; a subordinate.

WORD HISTORY: People trying to build their vocabulary often study affixes, a not unreasonable way to proceed. But studying a group of words that share an affix can be fascinating in its own right in the way that studying common features in a photograph of an extended family can be fascinating. The suffix *–ling* is Germanic in origin and had several uses already in Old English. For example, it could be added to a noun to make a second noun that referred to something connected with or similar to the first noun; thus, adding the suffix to the Old English word *yrth,* "plough-land," produced the Old English word *yrthling,* "plowman." The suffix could also be added to an adjective to make a noun that referred to something having the quality denoted by the adjective: from Old English *dēore,* "dear, beloved," was derived *dēorling* (Modern English *darling*). Adding *–ling* to an adverb produced a noun referring to something having the position or condition denoted by the adverb: from Old English *under* came *underling.* The last use of the *–ling* family to be described here was actually borrowed from another Germanic source, Old Norse. The Old Norse version of the *–ling* suffix was used to form diminutives; thus, our word *gosling* was a borrowing in Middle English of an Old Norse word, *gæslingr,* "gosling."

---

un·der·lin·ing (ŭn′dər-lī′nĭng) *n.* **1.** The act of drawing a line under; underscoring. **2.** Emphasis or stress, as in instruction or argument.

un·der·lip (ŭn′dər-lĭp′) *n.* The lower lip.

un·der·ly·ing (ŭn′dər-lī′ĭng) *adj.* **1.** Lying under or beneath something: *underlying strata.* **2.** Basic; fundamental. **3.** Present but not obvious; implicit: *an underlying meaning.* **4.** Taking precedence; prior: *an underlying financial claim.*

un·der·mine (ŭn′dər-mīn′) *tr.v.* **-mined, -min·ing, -mines. 1.** To weaken by wearing away a base or foundation: *Water has undermined the stone foundations.* **2.** To weaken, injure, or impair, often by degrees or imperceptibly; sap: *Late hours can undermine one's health.* **3.** To dig a mine or tunnel beneath.

un·der·mod·u·late (ŭn′dər-mŏj′ə-lāt′) *tr.v.* **-lat·ed, -lat·ing, -lates.** To use a sound reproduction or transmission device less than optimally possible. **—un′der·mod′u·la′tion** *n.*

un·der·most (ŭn′dər-mōst′) *adj.* Lowest in position, rank, or place; bottom. **—undermost** *adv.* In or to the lowest place.

un·der·neath (ŭn′dər-nēth′) *adv.* **1.** In or to a place beneath; below. **2.** On the lower face or underside. **—underneath** *prep.* **1.** Under; below; beneath. **2.** Under the power or control of. **—underneath** *adj.* Lower; under. **—underneath** *n.* The part or side below or under. [Middle English *undernethe,* from Old English *underneothan* : *under,* under; see UNDER + *neothan,* below; see BENEATH.]

un·der·nour·ish (ŭn′dər-nûr′ĭsh, -nŭr′-) *tr.v.* **-ished, -ish·ing, -ish·es.** To provide with insufficient quantity or quality of nourishment to sustain proper health and growth. **—un′der·nour′ish·ment** *n.*

un·der·nu·tri·tion (ŭn′dər-no͞o-trĭsh′ən, -nyo͞o-) *n.* Inadequate nutrition resulting from lack of food or failure of the body to absorb or assimilate nutrients properly.

un·der·paid (ŭn′dər-pād′) *v.* Past tense and past participle of **underpay.**

un·der·pants (ŭn′dər-pănts′) *pl.n.* Briefs or shorts worn as underwear.

un·der·part (ŭn′dər-pärt′) *n.* **1.** A lower part or a portion of a lower part or underside, especially of an animal's body: *We recognized the robin by its reddish underparts.* **2.** A subordinate role, as in a play.

un·der·pass (ŭn′dər-păs′) *n.* **1.** A passage underneath something, especially a section of road that passes under another road or a railroad. **2.** An intersection formed in this way.

un·der·pay (ŭn′dər-pā′) *tr.v.* **-paid** (-pād′), **-pay·ing, -pays.** To pay insufficiently or less than is deserved. **—un′der·pay′ment** *n.*

un·der·per·form (ŭn′dər-pər-fôrm′) *v.* **-formed, -form·ing, -forms.** *—tr.* **1.** To perform not as well as (something else): *three stocks that underperformed the market as a whole.* **2.** To perform (a musical or theatrical work, for example) too seldom: *In recent years, her plays have been underperformed.* *—intr.* To exhibit a level of performance below the standard: *Mutual funds have underperformed during the last two quarters.* **—un′der·per·form′ance** *n.* **—un′der·per·form′er** *n.*

un·der·pin (ŭn′dər-pĭn′) *tr.v.* **-pinned, -pin·ning, -pins. 1.** To support from below, as with props, girders, or masonry. **2.** To give support or substance to: *"the public awareness that must underpin a sustained and concerted development effort for Africa and its youth"* (Barber B. Conable).

un·der·pin·ning (ŭn′dər-pĭn′ĭng) *n.* **1.** Material or masonry used to support a structure, such as a wall. **2.** Often **underpinnings.** A support or foundation. **3.** Often **underpinnings.** *Informal.* The human legs.

un·der·play (ŭn′dər-plā′, ŭn′dər-plā′) *v.* **-played, -play·ing, -plays.** *—tr.* **1.** To act (a role) subtly or with restraint. **2.** To present or deal with subtly or with restraint; play down. *—intr.* **1.** To act a role subtly or with restraint. **2.** *Games.* To play a low card while holding a higher card in the same suit.

un·der·plot (ŭn′dər-plŏt′) *n.* See **subplot** (sense 1).

un·der·pop·u·lat·ed (ŭn′dər-pŏp′yə-lā′tĭd) *adj.* Lacking the normal or required population density. **—un′der·pop·u·la′tion** *n.*

un·der·price (ŭn′dər-prīs′) *tr.v.* **-priced, -pric·ing, -pric·es. 1.** To price lower than the real, normal, or appropriate value. **2.** To sell at a lower price than (a competitor): *one store that underpriced others of its kind.*

un·der·priv·i·leged (ŭn′dər-prĭv′ə-lĭjd) *adj.* Lacking opportunities or advantages enjoyed by other members of one's community; deprived. **—un′der·priv′i·leged** *n.*

un·der·pro·duce (ŭn′dər-prə-do͞os′, -dyo͞os′) *v.* **-duced, -duc·ing, -duces.** *—tr.* To produce (goods, for example) at a level below full capacity or beneath the degree of demand. *—intr.* To produce goods, for example, in a quantity insufficient to meet demand. **—un′der·pro·duc′tion** (-dŭk′shən) *n.* **—un′der·pro·duc′tive** (-dŭk′tĭv) *adj.*

un·der·proof (ŭn′dər-pro͞of′) *adj. Abbr.* **UP** Having a smaller proportion of alcohol than proof spirit.

un·der·prop (ŭn′dər-prŏp′) *tr.v.* **-propped, -prop·ping, -props.** To prop (something) from below.

un·der·quote (ŭn′dər-kwōt′) *tr.v.* **-quot·ed, -quot·ing, -quotes. 1.** To offer (goods or services) for sale at a price lower than the official list or market price. **2.** To quote a lower price than that quoted by (another); undersell.

un·der·ran (ŭn′dər-răn′) *v.* Past tense of **underrun.**

un·der·rate (ŭn′dər-rāt′) *tr.v.* **-rat·ed, -rat·ing, -rates.** To rate too low; underestimate.

un·der·re·act (ŭn′dər-rē-ăkt′) *intr.v.* **-act·ed, -act·ing, -acts.** To react with insufficient enthusiasm, force, or emphasis. **—un′der·re·ac′tion** *n.*

un·der·re·port (ŭn′dər-rĭ-pôrt′, -pōrt′) *tr.v.* **-port·ed, -port·ing, -ports.** To report (income, for example) as being less than actually is the case.

un·der·rep·re·sent (ŭn′dər-rĕp′rĭ-zĕnt′) *tr.v.* **-sent·ed, -sent·ing, -sents.** To imply or suggest a lower amount, quantity, quality, or degree of than is actually present: *Management has seriously underrepresented the firm's financial problems.* **—un′der·rep′re·sen·ta′tion** *n.*

un·der·rep·re·sent·ed (ŭn′dər-rĕp′rĭ-zĕn′tĭd) *adj.* Insufficiently or inadequately represented: *the underrepresented minority groups, ignored by the government.*

un·der·run (ŭn′dər-rŭn′) *tr.v.* **-ran** (-răn′), **-run, -run·ning, -runs. 1.** To run, pass, or go beneath. **2.** *Nautical.* To haul (a line or cable) onto a boat for inspection or repair. **—underrun** *n.* **1.** Something that runs under, as: **a.** An amount or a quantity produced that is less than what has been estimated. **b.** The difference between this amount or quantity and what has been estimated. **2.** An undercurrent.

un·der·score (ŭn′dər-skôr′, -skōr′) *tr.v.* **-scored, -scor·ing, -scores. 1.** To underline. **2.** To emphasize; stress. **—underscore** *n.* A line drawn under writing to indicate emphasis or italic type.

un·der·sea (ŭn′dər-sē′) *adj.* Existing, relating to, or created for use beneath the surface of the sea: *undersea life; undersea cameras.* **—undersea** (ŭn′dər-sē′) also **un·der·seas** (-sēz′) *adv.* Beneath the surface of the sea.

un·der·sec·re·tar·y (ŭn′dər-sĕk′rə-tĕr′ē) *n., pl.* **-ies.** An official directly subordinate to a member of a cabinet. **—un′der·sec′re·tar′i·at** (-târ′ē-ĭt) *n.*

un·der·sell (ŭn′dər-sĕl′) *tr.v.* **-sold** (-sōld′), **-sell·ing, -sells. 1.** To sell goods for a lower price than (another seller): *undersell the competition.* **2.** To sell (something) at a price less than the actual value. **3.** To present (an idea, for example) with such mild or insufficient enthusiasm as to engender a lack of interest: *Now that our proposal has failed, it's obvious that we undersold it.* **—un′der·sell′er** *n.*

un·der·serve (ŭn′dər-sûrv′) *tr.v.* **-served, -serv·ing, -serves.** To supply with insufficient services, especially social and health services.

un·der·set (ŭn′dər-sĕt′) *n.* An ocean undercurrent.

un·der·sexed (ŭn′dər-sĕkst′) *adj.* Having less sexual desire or potency than what is regarded as normal.

un·der·shirt (ŭn′dər-shûrt′) *n.* An upper undergarment, typically having short or no sleeves, worn next to the skin under a shirt.

un·der·shoot (ŭn′dər-sho͞ot′) *v.* **-shot** (-shŏt′), **-shoot·ing, -shoots.** *—tr.* **1.** To shoot a projectile short of (a target). **2. a.** To start the approach of one's aircraft to (a landing area) too low or too soon. **b.** To land an aircraft short of (a landing area). *—intr.* **1.** To shoot short of a target. **2.** To land short of a landing area.

un·der·shorts (ŭn′dər-shôrts′) *pl.n.* Shorts or briefs worn as undergarments, especially those for a man; underpants.

un·der·shot (ŭn′dər-shŏt′) *v.* Past tense and past participle of **undershoot.** **—undershot** (ŭn′dər-shŏt′) *adj.* **1.** Driven by water passing from below, as a water wheel. **2.** Having the lower jaw or teeth projecting beyond the upper; underhung.

un·der·shrub (ŭn′dər-shrŭb′) *n.* A very low-growing shrub.

un·der·side (ŭn′dər-sīd′) *n.* **1.** The side or surface that is underneath; the bottom side. Also called *undersurface.* **2.** The side that is less desirable, reputable, or noble than the obverse: *"hunger, isolation, filth, the underside of* [a] *hellish regime"* (National Review).

un·der·sign (ŭn′dər-sīn′) *tr.v.* **-signed, -sign·ing, -signs.** To sign one's name at the bottom of (a letter or document).

un·der·signed (ŭn′dər-sīnd′) *adj.* **1.** Having signatures or a signature at the bottom or end. Used of documents. **2.** Signed at the bottom or end of a document: *the undersigned names.* **3.** Having placed one's signature at the bottom or end of a document: *You are undersigned on page 6.* **—undersigned** *n., pl.* **undersigned.** A signer whose name appears at the bottom or end of a document. Often used with *the.*

un·der·sized (ŭn′dər-sīzd′) also **un·der·size** (-sīz′) *adj.* Of less than normal or sufficient size.

ă pat	oi boy
ā pay	ou out
âr care	o͝o took
ä father	o͞o boot
ĕ pet	ŭ cut
ē be	ûr urge
ĭ pit	th thin
ī pie	*th* this
îr pier	hw which
ŏ pot	zh vision
ō toe	ə about, item
ô paw	♦ regionalism

Stress marks: **′** (primary); ′ (secondary), as in **dictionary** (dĭk′shə-nĕr′ē)

un·der·skirt (ŭn′dər-skûrt′) *n.* **1.** A skirt worn under another skirt; a petticoat. **2.** One skirt of a layered gown over which outer skirts are formed and draped.

un·der·sleeve (ŭn′dər-slēv′) *n.* **1.** A sleeve worn under another. **2.** An ornamental sleeve worn under another sleeve, designed to extend below or show through slashes in the outer sleeve.

un·der·slung (ŭn′dər-slŭng′) *adj.* **1.** Having springs attached to the axles from below. Used of a vehicle or of its frame. **2.** Supported from above. **3.** Having a low center of gravity.

un·der·soil (ŭn′dər-soil′) *n.* Soil below the ground surface.

un·der·sold (ŭn′dər-sōld′) *v.* Past tense and past participle of **undersell.**

un·der·spin (ŭn′dər-spĭn′) *n.* A backspin.

un·der·staff (ŭn′dər-stăf′) *tr.v.* **-staffed, -staff·ing, -staffs.** To supply with fewer employees than required: *Management was careful not to understaff the agency.*

un·der·stand (ŭn′dər-stănd′) *v.* **-stood** (-stŏŏd′), **-stand·ing, -stands.** —*tr.* **1.** To perceive and comprehend the nature and significance of; grasp. See Synonyms at **apprehend. 2.** To know thoroughly by close contact or long experience with: *That teacher understands children.* **3.a.** To grasp or comprehend the meaning intended or expressed by (another): *They have trouble with English, but I can understand them.* **b.** To comprehend the language, sounds, form, or symbols of. **4.** To know and be tolerant or sympathetic toward: *I can understand your point of view even though I disagree with it.* **5.** To learn indirectly, as by hearsay: *I understand his departure was unexpected.* **6.** To infer: *Am I to understand you are staying the night?* **7.** To accept (something) as an agreed fact: *It is understood that the fee will be 50 dollars.* **8.** To supply or add (words or a meaning, for example) mentally. —*intr.* **1.a.** To have understanding, knowledge, or comprehension. **b.** To have sympathy or tolerance. **2.** To learn something indirectly; gather. [Middle English *understanden,* from Old English *understandan* : *under-,* under- + *standan,* to stand; see **stā-** in Appendix.] **—un′der·stand′a·bil′i·ty** *n.* **—un′der·stand′a·ble** *adj.* **—un′der·stand′a·bly** *adv.*

un·der·stand·ing (ŭn′dər-stăn′dĭng) *n.* **1.** The quality or condition of one who understands; comprehension. **2.** The faculty by which one understands; intelligence. See Synonyms at **reason. 3.** Individual or specified judgment or outlook; opinion. **4.a.** A compact implicit between two or more people or groups. **b.** The matter implicit in such a compact. **5.** A reconciliation of differences; a state of agreement: *They finally reached an understanding.* **6.** A disposition to appreciate or share the feelings and thoughts of others; sympathy. **—understanding** *adj.* **1.** Characterized by or having comprehension, good sense, or discernment. **2.** Compassionate; sympathetic. **—un′der·stand′ing·ly** *adv.*

un·der·state (ŭn′dər-stāt′) *v.* **-stat·ed, -stat·ing, -states.** —*tr.* **1.** To state with less completeness or truth than seems warranted by the facts. **2.** To express with restraint or lack of emphasis, especially ironically or for rhetorical effect. **3.** To state (a quantity, for example) that is too low: *understate corporate financial worth.* —*intr.* To give an understatement.

un·der·stat·ed (ŭn′dər-stā′tĭd) *adj.* Exhibiting restrained good taste: *"The waiting room is comfortable and understated"* (Tony Schwartz). **—un′der·stat′ed·ly** *adv.*

un·der·state·ment (ŭn′dər-stāt′mənt, ŭn′dər-stāt′-) *n.* **1.** A disclosure or statement that is less than complete. **2.** Restraint or lack of emphasis in expression, as for rhetorical effect. **3.** Restraint in artistic expression.

un·der·steer (ŭn′dər-stîr′) *intr.v.* **-steered, -steer·ing, -steers.** To turn less sharply than the operator would expect. Used of vehicles, especially automobiles. **—understeer** *n.* **1.** An instance of understeering. **2.** A tendency to understeer.

un·der·stood (ŭn′dər-stŏŏd′) *v.* Past tense and past participle of **understand. —understood** *adj.* **1.** Agreed on; assumed: *the understood conditions of troop withdrawal.* **2.** Not expressed in writing; implied: *the understood provisos of a custody agreement.*

un·der·stra·tum (ŭn′dər-strā′təm, -străt′əm) *n., pl.* **-stra·ta** (-strā′tə, -străt′ə) or **-stra·tums.** A substratum.

un·der·stud·y (ŭn′dər-stŭd′ē) *v.* **-ied** (-ēd), **-y·ing, -ies** (-ēz). —*tr.* **1.** To study or know (a role) so as to be able to replace the regular performer when required. **2.** To act as an understudy to. —*intr.* To be engaged in studying a role so as to be able to replace the regular performer when required. **—understudy** *n., pl.* **-ies. 1.** A performer who understudies. **2.** A person trained to do the work of another.

un·der·sub·scribe (ŭn′dər-səb-skrīb′) *tr.v.* **-scribed, -scrib·ing, -scribes.** To subscribe for (something), leaving supply or accommodation still available: *This course is usually undersubscribed.* **—un′der·sub·scrip′tion** (-skrĭp′shən) *n.*

un·der·sup·ply (ŭn′dər-sə-plī′) *n., pl.* **-plies.** A supply smaller than what is appropriate or required. **—undersupply** (ŭn′dər-sə-plī′) *tr.v.* **-plied** (-plīd′), **-ply·ing, -plies** (-plīz′). To supply in an amount insufficient to what is appropriate or required: *undersupplied the troops with blankets; undersupplied blankets to the troops.*

un·der·sur·face (ŭn′dər-sûr′fəs) *n.* See **underside** (sense 1).

un·der·take (ŭn′dər-tāk′) *v.* **-took** (-tŏŏk′), **-tak·en, -tak·ing, -takes.** —*tr.* **1.** To take upon oneself; decide or agree to do: *undertake a task.* **2.** To pledge or commit (oneself) to: *undertake oneself to care for an elderly relative.* **3.** To set about; begin. **4.** *Obsolete.* To accept combat with. —*intr. Archaic.* To make oneself responsible. Used with *for.*

un·der·tak·er (ŭn′dər-tā′kər) *n.* **1.** (ŭn′dər-tā′kər). See **funeral director. 2.** One, especially an entrepreneur, that undertakes a task or job.

un·der·tak·ing (ŭn′dər-tā′kĭng) *n.* **1.** A task or an assignment undertaken; a venture. **2.** A guaranty, an engagement, or a promise. **3.** The profession or duties of a funeral director.

un·der-the-count·er (ŭn′dər-*thə*-koun′tər) *adv. & adj.* Transacted, given, or sold illicitly.

un·der-the-ta·ble (ŭn′dər-*thə*-tā′bəl) *adv. & adj.* Not straightforward; secret or underhand.

un·der·things (ŭn′dər-thĭngz′) *pl.n.* Underwear, especially of women or girls.

un·der·tint (ŭn′dər-tĭnt′) *n.* A slight or subtle tint.

un·der·tone (ŭn′dər-tōn′) *n.* **1.** An underlying or implied tendency or meaning; an undercurrent. **2.** A tone of low pitch or volume, especially of spoken sound. **3.** *Color.* **a.** A pale or subdued color. **b.** A color applied under or seen through another color.

un·der·took (ŭn′dər-tŏŏk′) *v.* Past tense of **undertake.**

un·der·tow (ŭn′dər-tō′) *n.* **1.** The seaward pull of receding waves after they break on a shore. **2.** A tendency, especially in thought or feeling, contrary to what seems the strongest: *"As she talks nostalgically of her days of glory . . . a poignant undertow emerges"* (Tina Brown).

un·der·trick (ŭn′dər-trĭk′) *n. Games.* A trick in card games, especially bridge, the loss of which prevents a declarer from making a contract.

un·der·trump (ŭn′dər-trŭmp′) *intr.v.* **-trumped, -trump·ing, -trumps.** *Games.* To play a trump lower than another card player's trump when trump has not been led.

un·der·val·ue (ŭn′dər-văl′yo͞o) *tr.v.* **-ued, -u·ing, -ues. 1.** To assign too low a value to; underestimate. **2.** To have too little regard or esteem for. **—un′der·val′u·a′tion** *n.*

un·der·vest (ŭn′dər-vĕst′) *n. Chiefly British.* An undershirt.

un·der·wa·ter (ŭn′dər-wô′tər, -wŏt′ər) *adj.* **1.** Relating to, occurring, used, or performed beneath the surface of water. **2.** Below the water line of a vessel. **—un′der·wa′ter** *adv.*

un·der way or **un·der·way** (ŭn′dər-wā′) *adv. & adj.* **1.** In motion or operation. **2.** Already commenced or initiated; in progress. **3.** *Nautical.* Neither anchored nor moored to a fixed object.

un·der·wear (ŭn′dər-wâr′) *n.* See **underclothes.**

un·der·weight (ŭn′dər-wāt′) *adj.* Weighing less than is normal, healthy, or required. **—underweight** *n.* Insufficiency of weight.

un·der·went (ŭn′dər-wĕnt′) *v.* Past tense of **undergo.**

un·der·whelm (ŭn′dər-hwĕlm′, -wĕlm′) *tr.v.* **-whelmed, -whelm·ing, -whelms.** To fail to excite, stimulate, or impress: *"He is just as entitled to be underwhelmed by the prospect of reigning over a fourth-class nation as the rest of us are by the prospect of living in it"* (Peter Jay). [UNDER– + (OVER)WHELM.]

un·der·wing (ŭn′dər-wĭng′) *n.* **1.** One of a pair of hind wings of an insect, such as a moth. **2.** Any of various noctuid moths of the genus *Calocala,* having brightly colored hind wings visible only during flight.

un·der·wood (ŭn′dər-wŏŏd′) *n.* Shrubs and small trees growing beneath taller trees; underbrush.

un·der·wool (ŭn′dər-wŏŏl′) *n.* The soft woolly undercoat of certain animals, especially sheep.

un·der·world (ŭn′dər-wûrld′) *n.* **1.** The part of society that is engaged in and organized for the purpose of crime and vice. **2.** A region, realm, or dwelling place conceived to be below the surface of the earth. **3.** The opposite side of the earth; the antipodes. **4.** *Greek & Roman Mythology.* The world of the dead, located below the world of the living; Hades. **5.** *Archaic.* The world beneath the heavens; the earth.

un·der·write (ŭn′dər-rīt′) *v.* **-wrote** (-rōt′), **-writ·ten** (-rĭt′n), **-writ·ing, -writes.** —*tr.* **1.** To assume financial responsibility for; guarantee against failure: *underwrite a theatrical production.* **2.a.** To sign (an insurance policy) so as to assume liability in case of specified losses. **b.** To insure. **c.** To insure against losses totaling (a given amount). **3.a.** To guarantee the purchase of (a full issue of stocks or bonds). **b.** To agree to buy the unsold part of (stock not yet sold publicly) at a fixed time and price. **4.a.** To write under or at the end of something. **b.** To subscribe to, especially to sign or endorse (a document). **5.** To support or agree to (a decision, for example). —*intr.* To act as an underwriter, especially to issue an insurance policy.

un·der·writ·er (ŭn′dər-rī′tər) *n. Abbr.* **UW** One that underwrites, especially: **a.** A person or firm engaged in the insurance business. **b.** An insurance agent who assesses the risk of enrolling an applicant for coverage or a policy. **c.** One that guarantees the purchase of a full issue of stocks or bonds.

un·der·writ·ten (ŭn′dər-rĭt′n) *v. Abbr.* **UW** Past participle of **underwrite.**

un·der·wrote (ŭn′dər-rōt′) *v.* Past tense of **underwrite.**

un·de·scend·ed testicle (ŭn′dĭ-sĕn′dĭd) *n.* A testicle that has remained within the inguinal canal and has not descended to the scrotum.

un·de·served (ŭn′dĭ-zûrvd′) *adj.* Not merited; unjustifiable or unfair. **—un′de·serv′ed·ly** (-zûr′vĭd-lē) *adv.*

un·de·sign·ing (ŭn′dĭ-zī′nĭng) *adj.* Having no ulterior motives; straightforward.

un·de·sir·a·ble (ŭn′dĭ-zīr′ə-bəl) *adj.* **1.** Not likely to please; objectionable: *undesirable intrusions.* **2.** Not wanted: *undesirable aliens.* **—undesirable** *n.* A person regarded as undesirable: *"men tentatively regarded as scoundrels—or at least as undesirables"* (New York). **—un′de·sir′a·bil′i·ty** *n.* **—un′de·sir′a·bly** *adv.*

un·de·ter·mined (ŭn′dĭ-tûr′mĭnd) *adj.* **1.** Not yet determined; undecided: *Our lawsuit is still undetermined.* **2.** Not specifically known or ascertained: *a fire of undetermined origin.*

un·did (ŭn-dĭd′) *v.* Past tense of **undo.**

un·dies (ŭn′dēz) *pl.n. Informal.* Underwear, especially for women or girls.

un·dig·ni·fied (ŭn-dĭg′nə-fīd′) *adj.* Lacking in or damaging to dignity.

un·dine (ŭn-dēn′, ŭn′dēn′) *n.* According to Paracelsus, a female water spirit who could earn a soul by marrying a mortal and bearing his child. [New Latin *undīna,* from Latin *unda,* wave. See **wed-**[1] in Appendix.]

un·dip·lo·mat·ic (ŭn-dĭp′lə-măt′ĭk) *adj.* Not tactful or diplomatic. **—un·dip′lo·mat′i·cal·ly** *adv.*

un·di·rect·ed (ŭn′dĭ-rĕk′tĭd, -dī-) *adj.* **1.** Having no object or purpose; not guided. **2.** Having no prescribed destination. Used of mail.

un·dis·charged (ŭn′dĭs-chärjd′) *adj.* **1.** Not fulfilled: *an undischarged obligation.* **2.** Not paid: *an undischarged debt.* **3.** Not unloaded. Used of a ship's cargo.

un·dis·crim·i·nat·ing (ŭn′dĭ-skrĭm′ə-nā′tĭng) *adj.* **1.** Lacking sensitivity, taste, or judgment. **2.** Indiscriminate.

un·dis·posed (ŭn′dĭ-spōzd′) *adj.* **1.** Not settled, removed, or resolved: *undisposed assets.* **2.** Disinclined; unwilling: *undisposed to help us.*

un·dis·tin·guished (ŭn′dĭ-stĭng′gwĭsht) *adj.* **1.a.** Marked by no peculiar quality; not distinguished; ordinary: *an undistinguished appearance.* **b.** Lacking particularly good qualities; mediocre: *an undistinguished performance.* **2.** Not separated from others into categories. **3.a.** Incapable of being noticed or perceived individually from others; indistinguishable: *an undistinguished cry amid all the uproar.* **b.** Unnoticed; unperceived: *an undistinguished face in the crowd.*

un·dis·turbed (ŭn′dĭ-stûrbd′) *adj.* Not disturbed; calm.

un·do (ŭn-do͞o′) *v.* **-did** (-dĭd′), **-done** (-dŭn′), **-do·ing** (-do͞o′ĭng), **-does** (-dŭz′). *—tr.* **1.** To reverse or erase; annul: *impossible to undo the suffering caused by the war.* **2.** To untie, disassemble, or loosen: *undo a shoelace.* **3.** To open (a parcel, for example); unwrap. **4.a.** To cause the ruin or downfall of; destroy. **b.** To throw into confusion; unsettle. **5.** *Obsolete.* To solve or interpret; unravel. *—intr.* To come open or unfastened. **—un·do′er** *n.*

un·dock (ŭn-dŏk′) *tr.v.* **-docked, -dock·ing, -docks. 1.** *Nautical.* To move (a ship) away from a dock. **2.** To uncouple (spacecraft).

un·doc·u·ment·ed (ŭn-dŏk′yə-mĕn′tĭd) *adj.* **1.** Not supported by written evidence: *undocumented income tax deductions; undocumented accusations.* **2.** Not having the needed documents, as for permission to live or work in a foreign country. **—undocumented** *n.* A person not having proper documentation, especially for immigration.

un·do·ing (ŭn-do͞o′ĭng) *v.* Present participle of **undo. —undoing** *n.* **1.** The act of unfastening or loosening. **2.a.** Ruin; destruction. **b.** The act of bringing to ruin. **c.** A cause or source of ruin; downfall: *Greed was his undoing.* **3.** The act of reversing or annulling something accomplished; a cancellation.

un·done (ŭn-dŭn′) *v.* Past participle of **undo.**

un·dou·ble (ŭn-dŭb′əl) *tr.v.* **-bled, -bling, -bles.** To unfold, as a piece of paper money.

un·doubt·ed (ŭn-dou′tĭd) *adj.* Accepted as beyond question. See Synonyms at **authentic. —un·doubt′ed·ly** *adv.*

un·draw (ŭn-drô′) *tr.v.* **-drew** (-dro͞o′), **-drawn** (-drôn′), **-draw·ing, -draws.** To draw to one side, as a curtain.

un·dreamed (ŭn-drēmd′) also **un·dreamt** (-drĕmt′) *adj.* Beyond what could be imagined; unimaginable. Often used with *of: undreamed luxuries; a peace undreamed of a generation ago.*

un·dress (ŭn-drĕs′) *v.* **-dressed, -dress·ing, -dress·es.** *—tr.* **1.** To remove the clothing of; disrobe. **2.** To remove the bandages from (a wound, for example). *—intr.* To take off one's clothing. **—undress** *n.* **1.** Informal attire or uniform. **2.a.** Nakedness or partial nakedness. **b.** Partial but incomplete dress.

un·dressed (ŭn-drĕst′) *adj.* **1.a.** Naked. **b.** Partially but not fully dressed. **2.** Not specially treated or processed: *undressed leather.* **3.a.** Not prepared for cooking or eating. Used of certain meats. **b.** Lacking sauce or dressing. Used of a salad. **4.** Not treated or bandaged: *an undressed wound.*

un·drew (ŭn-dro͞o′) *v.* Past tense of **undraw.**

Und·set (o͝on′sĕt′), **Sigrid.** 1882–1949. Danish-born Norwegian writer whose novels, including the trilogy *Kristin Lavransdatter* (1920–1922), concern Catholicism and the struggles of women. She won the 1928 Nobel Prize for literature.

un·due (ŭn-do͞o′, -dyo͞o′) *adj.* **1.** Exceeding what is appropriate or normal; excessive: *"I was grateful, without showing undue excitement"* (Katherine Mansfield). **2.** Not just, proper, or legal: *undue use of force.* **3.** Not yet payable or due: *an undue loan.*

un·du·lant (ŭn′jə-lənt, ŭn′dyə-, -də-) *adj.* Resembling waves in occurrence, appearance, or motion.

undulant fever *n.* See **brucellosis** (sense 1).

un·du·late (ŭn′jə-lāt′, ŭn′dyə-, -də-) *v.* **-lat·ed, -lat·ing, -lates.** *—tr.* **1.** To cause to move in a smooth wavelike motion. **2.** To give a wavelike appearance or form to. *—intr.* **1.** To move in waves or with a smooth, wavelike motion. See Synonyms at **swing. 2.** To have a wavelike appearance or form. **3.** To increase and decrease in volume or pitch as if in waves. **—undulate** (-lĭt, -lāt′) *adj.* Having a wavy outline or appearance: *leaves with undulate margins.* [From Late Latin *undula,* small wave, diminutive of Latin *unda,* wave. See **wed-**[1] in Appendix.] **—un′du·la·to′ry** (-lə-tôr′ē, -tōr′ē) *adj.*

un·du·la·tion (ŭn′jə-lā′shən, ŭn′dyə-, -də-) *n.* **1.** A regular rising and falling or movement to alternating sides; movement in waves. **2.** A wavelike form, outline, or appearance. **3.** One of a series of waves or wavelike segments.

un·du·ly (ŭn-do͞o′lē, -dyo͞o′-) *adv.* Excessively; immoderately: *unduly familiar with strangers.*

un·du·ti·ful (ŭn-do͞o′tĭ-fəl, -dyo͞o′-) *adj.* **1.** Lacking a sense of duty. **2.** Unreliable or disobedient. **—un·du′ti·ful·ly** *adv.* **—un·du′ti·ful·ness** *n.*

un·dy·ing (ŭn-dī′ĭng) *adj.* Endless; everlasting; immortal: *my undying gratitude.*

un·earned (ŭn-ûrnd′) *adj.* **1.** Not gained by work or service: *unearned income.* **2.** Not deserved: *unearned luck.* **3.** Not yet earned: *unearned interest.*

unearned increment *n.* The increase in property value resulting from factors independent of the owner, such as a general rise in demand for land, as opposed to increase of value earned directly by the efforts of the owner.

un·earth (ŭn-ûrth′) *tr.v.* **-earthed, -earth·ing, -earths. 1.** To bring up out of the earth; dig up. **2.** To bring to public notice; uncover.

un·earth·ly (ŭn-ûrth′lē) *adj.* **-li·er, -li·est. 1.** Not of this earth; preternatural; supernatural. **2.** Unnaturally strange and frightening; eerie. See Synonyms at **weird. 3.** Ridiculously unreasonable or uncustomary; absurd: *telephoned me at an unearthly hour.* **—un·earth′li·ness** *n.*

un·eas·y (ŭn-ē′zē) *adj.* **-i·er, -i·est. 1.** Lacking a sense of security; anxious or apprehensive: *The farmers were uneasy until it finally rained.* **2.** Affording no ease or reassurance: *an uneasy calm.* **3.a.** Awkward or unsure in manner; constrained: *uneasy with strangers.* **b.** Causing constraint or awkwardness: *an uneasy silence.* **4.** Not conducive to rest: *fell into a fitful, uneasy sleep.* **—un·ease′, un·eas′i·ness** *n.* **—un·eas′i·ly** *adv.*

un·ed·it·ed (ŭn-ĕd′ĭ-tĭd) *adj.* **1.** Not edited or revised. **2.** Not adapted for a special audience or purpose.

un·ed·u·cat·ed (ŭn-ĕj′ə-kā′tĭd) *adj.* Not educated. See Synonyms at **ignorant.**

un·e·lect·a·ble (ŭn′ĭ-lĕk′tə-bəl) *adj.* Being such that election, as to high office, is difficult or impossible: *The candidate's private life rendered him unelectable.*

un·e·mo·tion·al (ŭn′ĭ-mō′shə-nəl) *adj.* **1.** Not easily stirred or moved in feeling. **2.** Involving little or no emotion; rational. **—un′e·mo′tion·al·ly** *adv.*

un·em·ploy·a·ble (ŭn′ĕm-ploi′ə-bəl, -ĭm-) *adj.* Not able to find or hold a job. **—un′em·ploy′a·ble** *n.*

un·em·ployed (ŭn′ĕm-ploid′, -ĭm-) *adj.* **1.** Not having work; jobless. **2.** Not being used; idle. **—unemployed** *n.* One not having a job. Often used with *the.* **—un′em·ploy′ment** *n.*

unemployment compensation *n.* Financial compensation for unemployed workers, provided in the United States chiefly by state governments.

un-Eng·lish (ŭn-ĭng′glĭsh) *adj.* **1.** Not having the characteristics of British people or practices: *The purple shutters on her house had a decidedly un-English look.* **2.** Not in agreement with standard English usage.

un·e·qual (ŭn-ē′kwəl) *adj.* **1.** Not the same in any measurable aspect, such as extent or quantity. **2.** Not the same as another in rank or social position. **3.** Consisting of ill-matched opponents: *an unequal race.* **4.** Having unbalanced sides or parts; asymmetrical. **5.** Not even or consistent; variable. **6.** Not having the required abilities; inadequate: *"It was maddening to be unequal to many enterprises"* (D.H. Lawrence). **7.** Not fair. See Usage Note at **equal. —unequal** *n.* One that is not the equal of another. **—un·e′qual·ly** *adv.*

un·e·qualed also **un·e·qualled** (ŭn-ē′kwəld) *adj.* Not matched or paralleled by others of its kind; unrivaled.

un·e·quiv·o·cal (ŭn′ĭ-kwĭv′ə-kəl) *adj.* Admitting of no doubt or misunderstanding; clear and unambiguous: *an unequivocal success.* **—un′e·quiv′o·cal·ly** *adv.*

un·err·ing (ŭn-ûr′ĭng, -ĕr′ĭng) *adj.* Committing no mistakes; consistently accurate. **—un·err′ing·ly** *adv.*

UNESCO *abbr.* United Nations Educational, Scientific, and Cultural Organization.

un·es·sen·tial (ŭn′ĭ-sĕn′shəl) *adj.* Not necessary or important; dispensable. **—unessential** *n.* One that is unnecessary.

un·e·ven (ŭn-ē′vən) *adj.* **-er, -est. 1.a.** Not equal, as in size,

ă pat	oi boy
ā pay	ou out
âr care	o͝o took
ä father	o͞o boot
ĕ pet	ŭ cut
ē be	ûr urge
ĭ pit	th thin
ī pie	*th* this
îr pier	hw which
ŏ pot	zh vision
ō toe	ə about, item
ô paw	♦ regionalism

Stress marks: ′ (primary); ′ (secondary), as in **dictionary** (dĭk′shə-nĕr′ē)

length, or quality. **b.** Having ill-matched opponents: *an uneven contest.* **2.** Not consistent or uniform: *an uneven color.* **3.** Not smooth or level: *the uneven surface of a cobblestone road.* See Synonyms at **rough. 4.** Not straight or parallel: *uneven margins.* **5.** Of, relating to, or being an odd number. **6.** *Obsolete.* Not fair or equitable. **—un·e′ven·ly** *adv.* **—un·e′ven·ness** *n.*

un·e·vent·ful (ŭn′ĭ-vĕnt′fəl) *adj.* **1.** Lacking in significant events. **2.** Occurring without disruption. **—un′e·vent′ful·ly** *adv.* **—un′e·vent′ful·ness** *n.*

un·ex·am·pled (ŭn′ĭg-zăm′pəld) *adj.* Without precedent; unparalleled: *"Witchcraft blazed forth with unexampled virulence"* (Montague Summers).

un·ex·cep·tion·a·ble (ŭn′ĭk-sĕp′shə-nə-bəl) *adj.* Beyond any reasonable objection; irreproachable. **—un′ex·cep′tion·a·ble·ness** *n.* **—un′ex·cep′tion·a·bly** *adv.*

USAGE NOTE: *Unexceptional* and *unexceptionable* are sometimes confused. *Unexceptionable* is derived from the word *exception* in the sense "objection," as in the idiom *take exception.* Thus *unexceptionable* means "not open to any objection," as in *A judge's ethical standards should be unexceptionable. Unexceptional,* in contrast, is related to the common sense of *exception* and generally means "not exceptional, not varying from the usual," as in *Some judges' ethical standards have unfortunately been unexceptional.*

un·ex·cep·tion·al (ŭn′ĭk-sĕp′shə-nəl) *adj.* **1.** Not varying from a norm; usual. **2.** Not subject to exceptions; absolute. See Usage Note at **unexceptionable. —un′ex·cep′tion·al·ly** *adv.*

un·ex·pect·ed (ŭn′ĭk-spĕk′tĭd) *adj.* Coming without warning; unforeseen. **—un′ex·pect′ed·ly** *adv.* **—un′ex·pect′ed·ness** *n.*

un·ex·ploit·ed (ŭn′ĭk-sploi′tĭd) *adj.* Not exploited or developed.

un·ex·pres·sive (ŭn′ĭk-sprĕs′ĭv) *adj.* **1.** Not conveying the meaning intended or the emotion felt. **2.** *Obsolete.* Inexpressible. **—un′ex·pres′sive·ly** *adv.* **—un′ex·pres′sive·ness** *n.*

un·fad·ing (ŭn-fā′dĭng) *adj.* Retaining color, freshness, value, or usefulness. **—un·fad′ing·ly** *adv.*

un·fail·ing (ŭn-fā′lĭng) *adj.* **1.** Always able to supply more; inexhaustible: *an unfailing source of good stories.* **2.** Constant; unflagging: *unfailing loyalty.* **3.** Incapable of error; infallible. **—un·fail′ing·ly** *adv.* **—un·fail′ing·ness** *n.*

un·fair (ŭn-fâr′) *adj.* **-er, -est. 1.** Not just or evenhanded; biased: *an unfair call by an umpire.* **2.** Contrary to laws or conventions, especially in commerce; unethical: *unfair trading.* **—un·fair′ly** *adv.* **—un·fair′ness** *n.*

un·faith (ŭn-fāth′) *n.* Absence of faith, especially in religion.

un·faith·ful (ŭn-fāth′fəl) *adj.* **1.** Not adhering to promises, obligations, or allegiances; disloyal. See Synonyms at **faithless. 2.a.** Not true or constant to one's sexual partner. **b.** Not true to one's spouse; guilty of adultery. **3.** Not justly representing or reflecting the original; inaccurate. **4.** *Obsolete.* Deficient in or lacking religious faith; unbelieving. **—un·faith′ful·ly** *adv.* **—un·faith′ful·ness** *n.*

un·fa·mil·iar (ŭn′fə-mĭl′yər) *adj.* **1.** Not being acquainted with; not conversant: *unfamiliar with the roads here.* **2.** Not within one's knowledge; strange: *unfamiliar faces.* **—un′fa·mil·iar′i·ty** (-mĭl-yăr′ĭ-tē, -mĭl′ē-ăr′ĭ-tē) *n.* **—un′fa·mil′iar·ly** *adv.*

un·fash·ion·a·ble (ŭn-făsh′ə-nə-bəl) *adj.* **1.** Not in current fashion: *unfashionable attire.* **2.** Not socially approved: *an unfashionable part of town.* **—un·fash′ion·a·bly** *adv.*

un·fas·ten (ŭn-făs′ən) *v.* **-tened, -ten·ing, -tens.** —*tr.* To separate the connected parts of. —*intr.* To become loosened or separated.

un·fa·thered (ŭn-fä′*th*ərd) *adj.* **1.a.** Having no father; fatherless. **b.** Having no known father; illegitimate. **2.** Of uncertain origin or authenticity: *unfathered rumors.*

un·fath·om·a·ble (ŭn-făth′ə-mə-bəl) *adj.* **1.** Difficult or impossible to understand; incomprehensible: *unfathomable theories.* **2.** Difficult or impossible to measure: *the unfathomable depths.*

un·fa·vor·a·ble (ŭn-fā′vər-ə-bəl, -fāv′rə-bəl) *adj.* **1.** Likely to be a hindrance; disadvantageous: *unfavorable winds.* **2.** Having or showing opposition; adverse: *an unfavorable reaction.* **—un′fa′vor·a·ble·ness** *n.* **—un·fa′vor·a·bly** *adv.*

un·feel·ing (ŭn-fē′lĭng) *adj.* **1.** Having no physical feeling or sensation; insentient. **2.** Not sharing in the pleasures or pains of others; callous. **—un·feel′ing·ly** *adv.* **—un·feel′ing·ness** *n.*

un·feigned (ŭn′fānd′) *adj.* Not feigned; genuine. See Synonyms at **sincere. —un·feign′ed·ly** (ŭn-fā′nĭd-lē) *adv.*

un·fet·ter (ŭn-fĕt′ər) *tr.v.* **-tered, -ter·ing, -ters.** To set free or keep free from restrictions or bonds.

un·fin·ished (ŭn-fĭn′ĭsht) *adj.* **1.** Not brought to an end; incomplete: *unfinished business.* **2.** Not having received special processing, such as dyeing or varnishing: *unfinished furniture.*

un·fit (ŭn-fĭt′) *adj.* **1.** Not meant or adapted for a given purpose; inappropriate: *a solvent that is unfit for use on wood surfaces.* **2.** Below the required standard; unqualified: *an unfit parent.* **3.** Not in good physical or mental health. **—unfit** *tr.v.* **-fit·ted, -fit·ting, -fits.** To cause to be unsuited or unqualified: *"Having run for president . . . often unfits a man for lesser or more useful subsequent work"* (Garry Wills). **—un·fit′ly** *adv.* **—un·fit′ness** *n.*

un·fix (ŭn-fĭks′) *tr.v.* **-fixed, -fix·ing, -fix·es. 1.** To detach from what secures; unfasten. **2.** To cause to leave a tranquil condition; disturb.

un·flag·ging (ŭn-flăg′ĭng) *adj.* Not flagging; untiring. See Synonyms at **tireless. —un·flag′ging·ly** *adv.*

un·flap·pa·ble (ŭn-flăp′ə-bəl) *adj.* Persistently calm, whether when facing difficulties or experiencing success; not easily upset or excited: *"cherubic, unflappable, not quite successful in obscuring his penetrating intelligence behind the bland exterior of the perfect civil servant"* (Henry A. Kissinger). **—un·flap′pa·bil′i·ty** *n.* **—un·flap′pa·bly** *adv.*

un·flapped (ŭn-flăpt′) *adj.* Not upset or excited; calm: *"went about her business outwardly unflapped"* (Laurie Colwin).

un·flat·ter·ing (ŭn-flăt′ər-ĭng) *adj.* Acknowledging few or no good aspects; unfavorable: *gave the film an unflattering review.* **—un·flat′ter·ing·ly** *adv.*

un·fledged (ŭn-flĕjd′) *adj.* **1.** Not having the feathers necessary to fly. Used of a young bird. **2.** Inexperienced, immature, or untried.

un·flinch·ing (ŭn-flĭn′chĭng) *adj.* Showing neither fear nor indecision; resolute. **—un·flinch′ing·ly** *adv.* **—un·flinch′ing·ness** *n.*

un·fo·cused also **un·fo·cussed** (ŭn-fō′kəst) *adj.* **1.** Not brought into focus: *an unfocused lens.* **2.** Not centered on anything specific: *"my unfocused broodings about love and loyalty"* (John le Carré).

un·fold (ŭn-fōld′) *v.* **-fold·ed, -fold·ing, -folds.** —*tr.* **1.** To open and spread out (something folded); extend. **2.** To remove the coverings from; disclose to view. **3.** To reveal gradually by written or spoken explanation; make known. —*intr.* **1.a.** To become spread out; open out: *Spring flowers unfolded everywhere.* **b.** To develop, as if by spreading out: *A brilliant career unfolded.* **2.** To be revealed gradually to the understanding: *The solution to the problem unfolded as they spoke.* **—un·fold′ment** *n.*

un·fore·seen (ŭn′fər-sēn′, -fôr-) *adj.* Not felt or realized beforehand; unexpected: *unforeseen difficulties.*

un·for·get·ta·ble (ŭn′fər-gĕt′ə-bəl) *adj.* Earning a permanent place in the memory; memorable: *an unforgettable experience.* **—un′for·get′ta·bil′i·ty, un′for·get′ta·ble·ness** *n.* **—un′for·get′ta·bly** *adv.*

un·for·giv·ing (ŭn′fər-gĭv′ĭng) *adj.* **1.** Reluctant or refusing to forgive: *an unforgiving creditor.* **2.** Providing little or no opportunity to forestall undesired results of mistakes: *an unforgiving computer program.*

un·for·mat·ted (ŭn-fôr′măt′ĭd) *adj. Computer Science.* Of or relating to a disk that has not been prepared for writing or reading.

un·formed (ŭn-fôrmd′) *adj.* **1.** Having no definite shape or structure; unorganized. See Synonyms at **shapeless. 2.** Not yet developed to maturity: *"a headstrong, unformed young man"* (Rod Nordland). **3.** Not yet given a physical existence; uncreated.

un·for·tu·nate (ŭn-fôr′chə-nĭt) *adj.* **1.** Characterized by undeserved bad luck; unlucky. **2.** Causing misfortune; disastrous. **3.** Regrettable; deplorable: *an unfortunate lack of good manners.* **—unfortunate** *n.* A victim of bad luck. **—un·for′tu·nate·ly** *adv.* **—un·for′tu·nate·ness** *n.*

SYNONYMS: *unfortunate, hapless, ill-fated, ill-starred, luckless, unlucky.* The central meaning shared by these adjectives is "marked by, affected by, or promising bad fortune": *an unfortunate turn of events; a hapless victim; an ill-fated business venture; an ill-starred romance; a luckless prisoner; an unlucky accident.* ***ANTONYM:*** *fortunate.*

un·found·ed (ŭn-foun′dĭd) *adj.* **1.** Not based on fact or sound evidence. See Synonyms at **baseless. 2.** Not yet established. **—un·found′ed·ly** *adv.* **—un·found′ed·ness** *n.*

un·fre·quent·ed (ŭn-frē′kwən-tĭd, ŭn′frē-kwĕn′tĭd) *adj.* Receiving few or no travelers or visitors: *unfrequented inns.*

un·friend·ed (ŭn-frĕn′dĭd) *adj.* Having no friends.

un·friend·ly (ŭn-frĕnd′lē) *adj.* **-li·er, -li·est. 1.** Not disposed to friendship. **2.** Indicating a bad prospect; unfavorable: *unfriendly clouds.* **—un·friend′li·ness** *n.*

un·frock (ŭn-frŏk′) *tr.v.* **-frocked, -frock·ing, -frocks. 1.** To strip of priestly privileges and functions. **2.** To deprive of the right to practice a profession. **3.** To deprive of an honorary position.

un·fruit·ful (ŭn-fro͞ot′fəl) *adj.* **1.** Not bearing fruit or offspring; barren. **2.** Not productive of a good or useful result. See Synonyms at **sterile. —un·fruit′ful·ly** *adv.* **—un′fruit′ful·ness** *n.*

un·fund·ed (ŭn-fŭn′dĭd) *adj.* **1.** Not funded, as a floating debt. **2.** Not furnished with funds: *an unfunded project.*

un·furl (ŭn-fûrl′) *tr. & intr.v.* **-furled, -furl·ing, -furls.** To spread or open (something) out or become spread or opened out.

un·fuss·y (ŭn-fŭs′ē) *adj.* **1.** Not particular about or concerned with details. **2.** Not cluttered or complicated, as with extraneous matters or details.

un·gain·ly (ŭn-gān′lē) *adj.* **-li·er, -li·est. 1.** Lacking grace or ease of movement or form; clumsy. See Synonyms at **awkward. 2.** Difficult to move or use; unwieldy. [UN–[1] + *gainli,* proper (from Middle English, from *gain,* from Old Norse *gegn,* direct).] **—un·gain′li·ness** *n.*

Un·ga·va Bay (ŭn-gā′və, -gä′-). An inlet of Hudson Strait in northeast Quebec, Canada, between northern Labrador and **Ungava Peninsula,** which is bordered on the west by Hudson Bay.

un·gen·er·ous (ŭn-jĕn′ər-əs) *adj.* **1.** Slow or reluctant in giving, forgiving, or sharing; stingy. **2.** Harsh in judgment; unkind. **3.** Mean-spirited; ignoble. **—un·gen′er·ous·ly** *adv.*

un·girt (ŭn-gûrt′) *adj.* **1.** Having the belt or girdle removed or loosened. **2.** Loose or free; slack.

un·glue (ŭn-glo͞o′) *tr.v.* **-glued, -glu·ing, -glues.** To separate by or as if by dissolving a glue or other adhesive.

un·glued (ŭn-glo͞od′) *adj.* **1.** Loosened or separated; unfastened. **2.** *Slang.* In confused distress; upset. ***—idiom.* come unglued.** *Slang.* To lose one's composure.

un·god·ly (ŭn-gŏd′lē) *adj.* **-li·er, -li·est. 1.** Not revering God; impious. **2.** Sinful; wicked. **3.** Outrageous: *had to leave for work at an ungodly hour.* **—un·god′li·ness** *n.*

un·gov·ern·a·ble (ŭn-gŭv′ər-nə-bəl) *adj.* Incapable of being governed, restrained, or controlled. See Synonyms at **unruly. —un·gov′ern·a·ble·ness** *n.* **—un·gov′ern·a·bly** *adv.*

un·gra·cious (ŭn-grā′shəs) *adj.* **1.** Lacking social grace or graciousness; rude. **2.** Not welcome or acceptable; unattractive. **3.** *Archaic.* Evil; wicked. **—un·gra′cious·ly** *adv.* **—un·gra′cious·ness** *n.*

un·gram·mat·i·cal (ŭn′grə-măt′ĭ-kəl) *adj.* **1.** Not in accord with the rules of a prescriptive grammar. **2.** Not in accord with a language as used by a native speaker. **—un′gram·mat′i·cal′i·ty** (-kăl′ĭ-tē) *n.* **—un′gram·mat′i·cal·ly** *adv.*

un·grate·ful (ŭn-grāt′fəl) *adj.* **1.** Not feeling or exhibiting gratitude, thanks, or appreciation. **2.** Not agreeable or pleasant; repellent: *"I will not perform the ungrateful task of comparing cases of failure"* (Abraham Lincoln). **—un·grate′ful·ly** *adv.* **—un·grate′ful·ness** *n.*

un·gual (ŭng′gwəl) *adj.* **1.** Of, resembling, or bearing a hoof, nail, or claw. **2.** Of or relating to fingernails or toenails. [From Latin *unguis,* nail. See UNGUIS.]

un·guard·ed (ŭn-gär′dĭd) *adj.* **1.** Lacking protection or a guard; vulnerable: *an unguarded gate.* **2.** Displaying, having, or feeling no wariness: *an unguarded remark; an unguarded glance.* **—un·guard′ed·ly** *adv.* **—un·guard′ed·ness** *n.*

un·guent (ŭng′gwənt) *n.* A salve for soothing or healing; an ointment. [Middle English, from Latin *unguentum,* from *unguere,* to anoint.] **—un′guen·tar′y** (-tĕr′ē) *adj.*

un·gues (ŭng′gwēz) *n.* *Zoology & Botany.* Plural of **unguis.**

un·guic·u·late (ŭng-gwĭk′yə-lĭt, -lāt′) also **un·guic·u·lat·ed** (-lā′tĭd) *—adj.* **1.** Having or resembling nails or claws. **2.** *Zoology.* Having nails or claws, as opposed to hooves. Used of mammals. **3.** *Botany.* Having a claw-shaped base: *an unguiculate petal.* *—n.* *Zoology.* A mammal having nails or claws. [New Latin *unguiculātus,* from Latin *unguiculus,* fingernail, diminutive of *unguis.* See UNGUIS.]

un·guid·ed missile (ŭn′gī′dĭd) *n.* **1.** A missile lacking a guidance system. **2.** *Slang.* One that is insufficiently controlled in movements, words, or actions and that is potentially harmful: *Their sales manager is an unguided missile at meetings.*

un·guis (ŭng′gwĭs) *n., pl.* **-gues** (-gwēz). **1.** *Zoology.* A nail, claw, or hoof. **2.** *Botany.* The clawlike base of some petals. [Latin. See **nogh-** in Appendix.]

un·gu·late (ŭng′gyə-lĭt, -lāt′) *adj.* **1.a.** Having hoofs. **b.** Resembling hoofs; hooflike. **2.** Of or belonging to the former order Ungulata, now divided into the orders Perissodactyla and Artiodactyla and composed of the hoofed mammals such as horses, cattle, deer, swine, and elephants. **—ungulate** *n.* An ungulate mammal. [Latin *ungulātus,* from *ungula,* hoof, diminutive of *unguis,* nail. See UNGUIS.]

un·gu·li·grade (ŭng′gyə-lĭ-grād′) *adj.* Walking on hoofs. **—unguligrade** *n.* An unguligrade mammal. [Latin *ungula,* hoof; see UNGULATE + *-gradus,* walking; see PLANTIGRADE.]

un·hal·low (ŭn-hăl′ō) *tr.v.* **-lowed, -low·ing, -lows.** *Archaic.* To violate the holiness of; profane or desecrate.

un·hal·lowed (ŭn-hăl′ōd) *adj.* **1.** Not hallowed or consecrated. **2.a.** Lacking reverence; impious or irreligious. **b.** Not conforming to accepted ethical standards; immoral.

un·hand (ŭn-hănd′) *tr.v.* **-hand·ed, -hand·ing, -hands.** To remove one's hand from; let go.

un·hand·some (ŭn-hăn′səm) *adj.* **1.** Not attractive or beautiful; homely. **2.** Not courteous or in good taste; ungracious. **—un·hand′some·ly** *adv.* **—un·hand′some·ness** *n.*

un·hand·y (ŭn-hăn′dē) *adj.* **-i·er, -i·est. 1.** Difficult to handle or manage; unwieldy. **2.** Lacking manual skill or dexterity. **—un·hand′i·ly** *adv.* **—un·hand′i·ness** *n.*

un·hap·py (ŭn-hăp′ē) *adj.* **-pi·er, -pi·est. 1.** Not happy or joyful; sad or sorrowful: *unhappy over his friend's departure.* **2.** Not satisfied; displeased or discontented: *unhappy with her raise.* **3.** Not attended by or bringing good fortune; unlucky. **4.** Not suitable; inappropriate: *an unhappy choice of words.* **—un·hap′pi·ly** *adv.* **—un·hap′pi·ness** *n.*

un·har·ness (ŭn-här′nĭs) *tr.v.* **-nessed, -ness·ing, -ness·es. 1.** To remove the harness or similar equipment from. **2.** To release or liberate (energy or passions, for example). **3.** To remove the armor from (a wearer).

un·health·y (ŭn-hĕl′thē) *adj.* **-i·er, -i·est. 1.a.** Being in a state of ill health; sick. **b.** Characterized by or symptomatic of ill health: *an unhealthy pallor.* **c.** Causing or conducive to poor health; unwholesome: *an unhealthy diet.* **2.** Harmful to character or moral health; corruptive: *unhealthy reading material.* **3.** Characterized by or symptomatic of disturbed mental health: *took an unhealthy interest in violence and fires.* **4.** Of a risky nature; dangerous: *an unhealthy predicament.* **—un′health′i·ly** *adv.* **—un·health′i·ness** *n.*

un·heard (ŭn-hûrd′) *adj.* **1.** Not heard: *unheard pleas for help.* **2.** Not given a hearing; not listened to: *unheard objections.* **3.** *Archaic.* Not heard of; obscure.

un·heard-of (ŭn-hûrd′ŭv′, -ŏv′) *adj.* **1.** Not previously known; unknown. **2.** Without precedent; unparalleled. **3.** Highly offensive; outrageous or brazen.

un·hes·i·tat·ing (ŭn-hĕz′ĭ-tā′tĭng) *adj.* **1.** Prompt to act, move, or express oneself; ready: *I gave my unhesitating approval.* **2.** Unfaltering; steadfast. **—un·hes′i·tat′ing·ly** *adv.*

un·hinge (ŭn-hĭnj′) *tr.v.* **-hinged, -hing·ing, -hing·es. 1.** To remove from hinges. **2.** To remove the hinges from. **3.** To confuse; disrupt. **4.** To derange; unbalance: *He was unhinged by his wife's death.*

un·hip (ŭn-hĭp′) *adj.* *Slang.* Not aware of or following the latest fashions or developments.

un·his·tor·i·cal (ŭn′hĭ-stôr′ĭ-kəl, -stŏr′-) *adj.* Taking little or no account of history: *"It is simply unhistorical and self-indulgent to prosecute, convict, and condemn him by our own standards of civil rights, animal welfare, or women's rights"* (David Cannadine).

un·hitch (ŭn-hĭch′) *tr.v.* **-hitched, -hitch·ing, -hitch·es.** To release from or as if from a hitch; unfasten.

un·ho·ly (ŭn-hō′lē) *adj.* **-li·er, -li·est. 1.** Wicked; immoral. **2.** Not hallowed or consecrated. **3.** *Informal.* Outrageous: *took unholy risks to win the downhill race.* **—un·ho′li·ly** *adv.* **—un·ho′li·ness** *n.*

un·hook (ŭn-ho͝ok′) *tr.v.* **-hooked, -hook·ing, -hooks. 1.** To release or remove from or as if from a hook. **2.** To unfasten the hooks of.

un·hoped (ŭn-hōpt′) *adj.* *Archaic.* Not hoped or looked for.

un·hoped-for (ŭn-hōpt′fôr′) *adj.* Not expected or hoped for.

un·horse (ŭn-hôrs′) *tr.v.* **-horsed, -hors·ing, -hors·es. 1.** To cause to fall from a horse. **2.** To overthrow or dislodge; upset.

un·hou·seled (ŭn-hou′zəld) *adj.* *Archaic.* Not having received the Eucharist. Used of a dead or dying person.

uni– *pref.* Single; one: *unicycle.* [Latin *ūni-,* from *ūnus,* one. See **oi-no-** in Appendix.]

U·ni·at (yo͞o′nē-ăt′, -ĭt) also **U·ni·ate** (-ĭt, -āt′) *—adj.* Of or relating to any of several Eastern Christian churches that are in communion with the Roman Catholic Church but retain their own languages, rites, and codes of canon law. *—n.* A member of any of these churches. [Russian *uniyat,* from Polish *uniat,* the Union of Brest-Litovsk (1596), from *unija,* union, from Latin *ūniō, ūniōn-.* See UNION.]

u·ni·ax·i·al (yo͞o′nē-ăk′sē-əl) *adj.* **1.** Of, relating to, or affecting one axis. **2.** *Botany.* Of, relating to, or being a plant with one primary stem that has no branches and terminates in a flower. **3.** Having one direction along which double refraction of light does not take place. Used of a crystal.

u·ni·cam·er·al (yo͞o′nĭ-kăm′ər-əl) *adj.* Having or consisting of a single legislative chamber. [UNI– + Latin *camera,* chamber; see CAMERA + –AL[1].] **—u′ni·cam′er·al·ly** *adv.*

UNICEF *abbr.* United Nations Children's Fund (formerly United Nations International Children's Emergency Fund).

u·ni·cel·lu·lar (yo͞o′nĭ-sĕl′yə-lər) *adj.* Having or consisting of one cell; one-celled: *unicellular organisms.* **—u′ni·cel′lu·lar′i·ty** (-lăr′ĭ-tē, -lâr′-) *n.*

u·ni·col·or (yo͞o′nĭ-kŭl′ər) *adj.* Monochromatic.

u·ni·corn (yo͞o′nĭ-kôrn′) *n.* **1.a.** A fabled creature symbolic of virginity and usually represented as a horse with a single straight spiraled horn projecting from its forehead. **b.** *Heraldry.* A representation of this beast, having a horse's body, a stag's legs, a lion's tail, and a straight spiraled horn growing from its forehead, especially employed as a supporter for the Royal Arms of Great Britain or of Scotland. **2. Unicorn.** *Astronomy.* The constellation Monoceros. [Middle English *unicorne,* from Old French, from Late Latin *ūnicornis,* from Latin, having one horn : *ūnus,* one; see **oi-no-** in Appendix + *cornū,* horn; see **ker-**[1] in Appendix.]

unicorn plant *n.* Any of several annual North American herbs of the genus *Proboscidea,* having large leaves with long petioles and axillary racemes of large purple flowers and grown as an ornamental or for the young edible fruit that may be pickled like cucumbers.

u·ni·cos·tate (yo͞o′nĭ-kŏs′tāt′) *adj.* Having a single main costa, rib, or riblike part: *a unicostate leaf.*

u·ni·cus·pid (yo͞o′nĭ-kŭs′pĭd) *adj.* Having only one cusp. Used of a tooth. **—unicuspid** *n.* A unicuspid tooth.

u·ni·cy·cle (yo͞o′nĭ-sī′kəl) *n.* A vehicle consisting of a frame mounted over a single wheel and usually propelled by pedals. [UNI– + *-cycle,* perhaps on the model of BICYCLE.] **—u′ni·cy′clist** *n.*

un·i·den·ti·fied flying object (ŭn′ī-dĕn′tə-fīd′) *n.* **1.** A

unicorn
Detail of late 18th- to early 19th-century American watercolor and ink drawing of rampant unicorn

unicorn plant

unicycle

ă pat	oi boy
ā pay	ou out
âr care	o͝o took
ä father	o͞o boot
ĕ pet	ŭ cut
ē be	ûr urge
ĭ pit	th thin
ī pie	*th* this
îr pier	hw which
ŏ pot	zh vision
ō toe	ə about, item
ô paw	♦ regionalism

Stress marks: ′ (primary); ′ (secondary), as in **dictionary** (dĭk′shə-nĕr′ē)

flying or apparently flying object of an unknown nature, especially one suspected to have been sent by extraterrestrial beings. **2.** A flying saucer.

u·ni·di·rec·tion·al (yo͞o′nĭ-dĭ-rĕk′shə-nəl, -dī-) *adj.* Having, operating, or moving in one direction only: *a unidirectional microphone.*

u·ni·fac·to·ri·al (yo͞o′nə-făk-tôr′ē-əl, -tōr′-) *adj.* Involving, dependent on, or controlled by a single gene.

u·ni·fied field theory (yo͞o′nə-fīd′) *n.* A physical theory that combines the treatment of two or more types of fields in order to deduce previously unrecognized interrelationships, especially such a theory unifying the theories of nuclear, electromagnetic, and gravitational forces.

u·ni·fi·lar (yo͞o′nə-fī′lər) *adj.* Having or using only one filament, such as a thread or wire.

u·ni·fo·li·ate (yo͞o′nə-fō′lē-ĭt, -āt′) *adj. Botany.* Having a single leaf.

u·ni·fo·li·o·late (yo͞o′nĭ-fō′lē-ə-lāt′) *adj. Botany.* Compound in structure but having a single leaflet, as the leaf of a citrus plant.

u·ni·form (yo͞o′nə-fôrm′) *adj.* **1.** Always the same, as in character or degree; unvarying. **2.** Conforming to one principle, standard, or rule; consistent. **3.** Being the same as or consonant with another or others. **4.** Unvaried in texture, color, or design. See Synonyms at **steady.** —**uniform** *n.* **1.** A distinctive outfit intended to identify those who wear it as members of a specific group. **2.** One set of such an outfit. —**uniform** *tr.v.* **-formed, -form·ing, -forms. 1.** To make (something) uniform. **2.** To provide or dress with a uniform. [Latin *ūniformis* : *ūni-*, uni- + *forma,* shape.] —**u′ni·for′mi·ty, u′ni·form′ness** *n.* —**u′ni·form′ly** *adv.*

u·ni·for·mi·tar·i·an·ism (yo͞o′nə-fôr′mĭ-târ′ē-ə-nĭz′əm) *n.* The theory that all geologic phenomena may be explained as the result of existing forces having operated uniformly from the origin of the earth to the present time. —**u′ni·for′mi·tar′i·an** *adj. & n.*

u·ni·fy (yo͞o′nə-fī′) *tr. & intr.v.* **-fied** (-fīd), **-fy·ing, -fies** (-fīz). To make into or become a unit; consolidate. [French *unifier,* from Old French, from Late Latin *ūnificāre* : Latin *ūni-*, uni- + Latin *-ficāre,* -fy.] —**u′ni·fi′a·ble** *adj.* —**u′ni·fi·ca′tion** (-fĭ-kā′shən) *n.* —**u′ni·fi′er** *n.*

u·ni·lat·er·al (yo͞o′nə-lăt′ər-əl) *adj.* **1.** Of, on, relating to, involving, or affecting only one side: *"a unilateral advantage in defense"* (New Republic). **2.** Performed or undertaken by only one side: *unilateral disarmament.* **3.** Obligating only one of two or more parties, nations, or persons, as a contract or an agreement. **4.** Emphasizing or recognizing only one side of a subject. **5.** Having only one side. **6.** Tracing the lineage of one parent only: *a unilateral genealogy.* **7.** *Botany.* Having leaves, flowers, or other parts on one side only. —**u′ni·lat′er·al·ly** *adv.*

u·ni·lat·er·al·ism (yo͞o′nə-lăt′ər-ə-lĭz′əm) *n.* A tendency of nations to conduct their foreign affairs individualistically, characterized by minimal consultation and involvement with other nations, even their allies. —**u′ni·lat′er·a·list** *adj. & n.*

u·ni·lin·e·ar (yo͞o′nĭ-lĭn′ē-ər) *adj.* Of or developing in a progressive sequence usually from the primitive to the advanced.

u·ni·lin·gual (yo͞o′nĭ-lĭng′gwəl) *adj.* Making use of or written in one language only.

u·ni·lo·bar (yo͞o′nə-lō′bər, -bär′) *adj.* Having only one lobe.

u·ni·loc·u·lar (yo͞o′nə-lŏk′yə-lər) *adj. Botany.* Having a single compartment in the ovary or fruit, as in a melon.

U·ni·mak Island (yo͞o′nə-măk′). An island of southwest Alaska in the eastern Aleutian Islands separated from the Alaska Peninsula by a narrow strait.

un·im·pas·sioned (ŭn′ĭm-păsh′ənd) *adj.* Not impassioned; marked by a reasonable approach totally devoid of emotional influence or appeal: *answered the charges with an unimpassioned defense.*

un·im·peach·a·ble (ŭn′ĭm-pē′chə-bəl) *adj.* **1.** Difficult or impossible to impeach: *an unimpeachable witness.* **2.** Beyond reproach; blameless: *unimpeachable behavior.* **3.** Beyond doubt; unquestionable: *"works of such unimpeachable greatness"* (Musical Heritage Review). —**un′im·peach′a·bly** *adv.*

un·im·por·tant (ŭn′ĭm-pôr′tnt) *adj.* Not important; petty. —**un′im·por′tance** *n.*

un·im·proved (ŭn′ĭm-pro͞ovd′) *adj.* **1.** Not improved; not made better. **2.** Not made use of or put to advantage. **3.** Not built on or cultivated so as to increase in value. Used of land.

un·in·form·a·tive (ŭn′ĭn-fôr′mə-tĭv) *adj.* Providing little or no information. —**un′in·form′a·tive·ly** *adv.*

un·in·formed (ŭn′ĭn-fôrmd′) *adj.* Not having, showing, or making use of information; not informed: *uninformed voters; an uninformed decision.*

un·in·hab·it·a·ble (ŭn′ĭn-hăb′ĭ-tə-bəl) *adj.* Unfit for habitation: *an uninhabitable island.* —**un·in·hab′it·a·bil′i·ty** *n.*

un·in·hab·it·ed (ŭn′ĭn-hăb′ĭ-tĭd) *adj.* Having no residents; not inhabited.

un·in·hib·it·ed (ŭn′ĭn-hĭb′ĭ-tĭd) *adj.* **1.** Open and unrestrained: *uninhibited laughter.* **2.** Free from traditional social or moral constraints. —**un′in·hib′it·ed·ly** *adv.* —**un′in·hib′it·ed·ness** *n.*

un·in·i·ti·ate (ŭn′ĭ-nĭsh′ē-ĭt) *adj.* Not experienced. —**un′-in·i′ti·ate** *n.*

un·in·i·ti·at·ed (ŭn′ĭ-nĭsh′ē-ā′tĭd) *adj.* Not knowledgeable or skilled; inexperienced. —**uninitiated** *n.* An uninformed, unskilled, or inexperienced person or group of people. Often used with *the*: *"What's the difference, the uninitiated may ask, between eggshell white and wedding gown white?"* (Wall Street Journal).

un·in·spired (ŭn′ĭn-spīrd′) *adj.* Having no intellectual, emotional, or spiritual excitement; dull. See Synonyms at **dull.**

un·in·struct·ed (ŭn′ĭn-strŭk′tĭd) *adj.* **1.** Not educated or informed: *an uninstructed young mind.* **2.** Not provided with directives on how to vote or proceed: *an uninstructed representative at a political convention.*

un·in·sur·a·ble (ŭn′ĭn-sho͝or′ə-bəl) *adj.* That cannot be covered by insurance: *uninsurable risks; an uninsurable client.* —**un·in·sur′a·bil′i·ty** *n.*

un·in·sured (ŭn′ĭn-sho͝ord′) *adj.* Not covered by insurance: *an uninsured motorist.* —**uninsured** *n., pl.* **-sureds.** A party that is not insured.

un·in·tel·li·gent (ŭn′ĭn-tĕl′ə-jənt) *adj.* **1.** Having or displaying a lack of intelligence. **2.** Not invested with intelligence. —**un′in·tel′li·gence** *n.* —**un′in·tel′li·gent·ly** *adv.*

un·in·tel·li·gi·ble (ŭn′ĭn-tĕl′ĭ-jə-bəl) *adj.* Being such that understanding or comprehension is difficult or impossible; incomprehensible: *unintelligible remarks; an unintelligible prose passage.* —**un′in·tel′li·gi·bil′i·ty, un′in·tel′li·gi·ble·ness** *n.* —**un′in·tel′li·gi·bly** *adv.*

un·in·tend·ed (ŭn′ĭn-tĕn′dĭd) *adj.* Not deliberate or intentional; unplanned: *an unintended slight.*

un·in·ten·tion·al (ŭn′ĭn-tĕn′shə-nəl) *adj.* Not deliberate or intentional; inadvertent: *an unintentional pun.* —**un′in·ten′tion·al·ly** *adv.*

un·in·ter·est (ŭn-ĭn′trĭst, -tər-ĭst, -trĕst′) *n.* Lack of interest or concern; indifference.

un·in·ter·est·ed (ŭn-ĭn′trĭ-stĭd, -tər-ĭ-stĭd, -tə-rĕs′tĭd) *adj.* **1.a.** Without an interest: *uninterested parties.* **b.** Not having a financial interest. **2.** Marked by or exhibiting a lack of interest. See Synonyms at **indifferent.** See Usage Note at **disinterested.** —**un·in′ter·est·ed·ly** *adv.* —**un·in′ter·est·ed·ness** *n.*

un·in·ter·est·ing (ŭn-ĭn′trĭ-stĭng, -tər-ĭ-stĭng, -tə-rĕs′tĭng) *adj.* Arousing little or no interest or curiosity; boring. —**un·in′ter·est·ing·ly** *adv.*

u·ni·nu·cle·ate (yo͞o′nĭ-no͞o′klē-ĭt, -nyo͞o′-) *adj.* Having one nucleus.

un·in·vit·ed (ŭn′ĭn-vī′tĭd) *adj.* Not welcome or wanted.

un·in·vit·ing (ŭn′ĭn-vī′tĭng) *adj.* Not pleasant or attractive; disagreeable: *an uninviting prospect.* —**un′in·vit′ing·ly** *adv.*

un·in·volved (ŭn′ĭn-vŏlvd′) *adj.* Feeling or showing no interest or involvement; unconcerned: *an uninvolved bystander.*

un·ion (yo͞on′yən) *n.* **1.a.** The act of uniting or the state of being united. **b.** A combination so formed, especially an alliance or confederation of people, parties, or political entities for mutual interest or benefit. **2.** *Mathematics.* A set, every member of which is an element of one or another of two or more given sets. **3.** Agreement or harmony resulting from the uniting of individuals; concord. See Synonyms at **unity. 4.a.** The state of matrimony; marriage: *"The element that was to make possible such a union was trust in each other's love"* (Kate Chopin). **b.** Sexual intercourse. **5.a.** A combination of parishes for joint administration of relief for the poor in Great Britain. **b.** A workhouse maintained by such a union. **6.** A labor union. **7.** A coupling device for connecting parts, such as pipes or rods. **8.** A device on a flag or an ensign, occupying the upper inner corner or the entire field, that signifies the union of two or more sovereignties. **9.** Often **Union. a.** An organization at a college or university that provides facilities for recreation; a student union. **b.** A building housing such facilities. **10. Union.** The United States of America regarded as a national unit, especially during the Civil War. —**union** *adj.* **1. Union.** Of, relating to, or loyal to the United States of America during the Civil War: *a Union cause; a Union soldier.* **2.** Of or relating to a labor union or labor union organizing: *the union movement; union negotiations.* [Middle English, from Old French, from Late Latin *ūniō, ūniōn-*, from Latin *ūnus,* one. See **oi-no-** in Appendix.]

Union. A community of northeast New Jersey west-northwest of Elizabeth. Settled c. 1749 by colonists from Connecticut, it is a manufacturing center. Population, 50,184.

union catalog *n.* A library catalog combining in alphabetical sequence the contents of a number of catalogs or the contents of more than one library.

union church *n.* A local interdenominational church bringing together worshipers of different denominational backgrounds.

Union City. 1. A city of western California southeast of Oakland. It is a residential community with some manufacturing. Population, 39,406. **2.** A city of northeast New Jersey on the Hudson River adjoining Jersey City. Its varied manufactures include embroidery and perfumes. Population, 55,593.

un·ion·ism (yo͞on′yə-nĭz′əm) *n.* **1.** The principle or theory of forming a union. **2.** The principles, theory, or system of a union, especially a trade union. **3. Unionism.** Loyalty to the federal government during the Civil War.

un·ion·ist (yo͞on′yə-nĭst) *n.* **1.** One who believes in or supports a union or unionism. **2.** A member of a labor or trade union. **3. Unionist.** One loyal to the federal government during the Civil War. —**un′ion·is′tic** *adj.*

un·ion·ize (yo͞on′yə-nīz′) *v.* **-ized, -iz·ing, -iz·es.** —*tr.* **1.** To organize into a labor union. **2.** To cause to join a labor union. —*intr.* To organize or join a labor union. **—un′ion·i·za′tion** (-yə-nĭ-zā′shən) *n.* **—un′ion·iz′er** *n.*

union jack *n.* **1.** A flag consisting entirely of a union. **2. Union Jack.** The flag of the United Kingdom.

union label *n.* An identifying mark attached to a product indicating it has been produced by members of a trade union.

Union of So·vi·et Socialist Republics (sō′vē-ĕt′, -ĭt, sŏv′ē-, sō′vē-ĕt′). Commonly called **Soviet Union** or **Rus·sia** (rŭsh′ə). *Abbr.* **U.S.S.R., USSR** A former country of eastern Europe and northern Asia with coastlines on the Baltic and Black seas and the Arctic and Pacific oceans. It was established in December 1922 with the union of the Russian S.F.S.R (proclaimed after the Russian Revolution of 1917) and various other soviet republics, including Belorussia and the Ukraine. In 1991 a number of constituent republics, including Estonia and Latvia, gained their independence, and the U.S.S.R. was officially dissolved on December 31, 1991.

union shop *n.* A business or industrial establishment whose employees are required to be union members or to agree to join the union within a specified time. Also called *closed shop.*

union suit *n.* A one-piece undergarment combining shirt and long pants.

u·nip·a·rous (yo͞o-nĭp′ər-əs) *adj.* **1.** Producing only one egg or offspring at a time. **2.** Having produced only one offspring; primiparous. **3.** *Botany.* Forming a single axis at each branching, as certain flower clusters.

u·ni·per·son·al (yo͞o′nĭ-pûr′sə-nəl) *adj.* Manifested as or existent in the form of only one person: *a unipersonal spirit.*

u·ni·pla·nar (yo͞o′nĭ-plā′nər, -när′) *adj.* Situated or occurring in one plane.

u·ni·po·lar (yo͞o′nĭ-pō′lər) *adj.* **1.** Having, acting by means of, or produced by a single magnetic or electric pole. **2.** *Biology.* A single fibrous process. Used of a neuron. **—u′ni·po·lar′i·ty** (-pō-lăr′ĭ-tē, -pə-) *n.*

u·ni·po·tent (yo͞o-nĭp′ə-tənt) *adj.* Capable of developing into only one type of cell or tissue.

u·nique (yo͞o-nēk′) *adj.* **1.** Being the only one of its kind: *the unique existing example of Donne's handwriting.* See Synonyms at **single. 2.** Without an equal or equivalent; unparalleled. **3. a.** Characteristic of a particular category, condition, or locality: *a problem unique to coastal areas.* **b.** *Informal.* Unusual; extraordinary: *spoke with a unique accent.* [French, from Old French, from Latin *ūnicus.* See **oi-no-** in Appendix.] **—u·nique′ly** *adv.*

USAGE NOTE: Over the course of the century *unique* has become the paradigmatic example of the class of terms that do not allow comparison or modification by an adverb of degree such as *very, somewhat,* or *quite.* Thus, most grammarians believe that it is incorrect to say that something is *very unique* or *more unique than* something else, though phrases such as *nearly unique* and *almost unique* are acceptable. In the most recent survey the sentence *Her designs are quite unique in today's fashion scene* was unacceptable to 80 percent of the Usage Panel. • Critical objections to the comparison and degree modification of absolute terms date to the 18th century and have been applied to a wide group of adjectives including *equal, fatal, omnipotent, parallel, perfect,* and *unanimous.* According to the standard argument, such words denote properties that a thing either does or does not have but cannot have to a qualifiable degree. Thus if *unique* is properly used to mean "without equal or equivalent," something either is unique or it isn't, and phrases such as *very unique* and *more unique* can only betray a weakening of the sense to mean something like "unusual" or "distinctive." It is true that comparison and modification of *unique* are often associated with the style favored by copywriters, as in the advertisement announcing that *Omaha's most unique restaurant is now even more unique* or in the claim that a new automobile is *So unique, it's patented.* But modification of *unique* is also found in the work of reputable writers, where it may lack any connotations of hyperbole. A painting is described as *the most unique of Beckman's self-portraits,* and a travel writer states that *Chicago is no less unique an American city than New York or San Francisco.* The relative acceptability of these usages reflects the semantic subtlety of *unique* itself. If we were to use *unique* only according to the strictest criteria of logic, after all, we might freely apply the term to anything in the world since nothing is wholly equivalent to anything else. Clearly, then, when we say that a restaurant or painting is unique, we mean that it is worthy of inclusion in a class by itself according to certain implicit but generally accepted criteria. Thus a legitimately unique painting might be one that realizes an unparalleled aesthetic vision, but not one that is rendered only in pigments whose names begin with the letter *o;* and a legitimately unique restaurant might be one that serves 18th-century French cuisine according to the original recipes, not one that has been installed in a converted sardine cannery. Given this understanding, it is not inherently impossible to think of uniqueness as a matter of degree, in the sense that one painting or restaurant may be more or less worthy of inclusion in a class by itself than some other. • What is troubling about the copywriters' use of *unique* is not that the word has become a synonym for *unusual.* Rather, it is the copywriters who are using the word in conformity with strict logic. Uniqueness is claimed for a restaurant in virtue of some trivial properties of its decor or menu, or for a resort hotel that simply happens to have a singularly picturesque view of the bay. Though it may be true that such properties render these things *logically* unique, they do not constitute legitimate grounds for putting the things into a class by themselves according to the criteria ordinarily invoked when things are sorted into classes. In fact, the abuse of *unique* can be cloying even when no modification or comparison is involved; when we read an advertisement for a line of sportswear that features *a unique selection of colors,* we may suspect that the distinctive properties of the color selection are not so remarkable as the advertiser would have us believe. But it is not surprising that these uses of *unique* should lend themselves to promiscuous modification and comparison; for once it is granted that uniqueness can be claimed for any product or service that is somehow distinctive from all its competitors, it is inevitable that an increase in uniqueness will be seen in every minor innovation. See Usage Notes at **equal, infinite, parallel, perfect.**

u·ni·se·ri·ate (yo͞o′nĭ-sîr′ē-āt′, -ĭt) *adj.* Arranged in one row, as the seeds of a pea or string bean.

u·ni·sex (yo͞o′nĭ-sĕks′) *adj.* **1.** Designed for or suitable to both sexes: *unisex clothing; unisex hairstyles.* **2.** Not distinguished or distinguishable on the basis of sex; androgynous in appearance: *cultivated a unisex look.* **—unisex** *n.* Elimination or absence of sexual distinctions, especially in dress.

u·ni·sex·u·al (yo͞o′nĭ-sĕk′sho͞o-əl) *adj.* **1.** Of or relating to only one sex. **2.** Having only one type of sexual organ; not a hermaphrodite. **3.** *Botany.* Having either stamens or pistils but not both. **4.** Unisex. **—u′ni·sex′u·al′i·ty** (-ăl′ĭ-tē) *n.* **—u′ni·sex′u·al·ly** *adv.*

u·ni·son (yo͞o′nĭ-sən, -zən) *n.* **1.** *Music.* **a.** Identity of pitch; the interval of a perfect prime. **b.** The combination of parts at the same pitch or in octaves. **2.** The act or an instance of speaking the same words simultaneously by two or more speakers. **3.** An instance of agreement; concord. ***—idiom.* in unison. 1.** In complete agreement; harmonizing exactly. **2.** At the same time; at once. [Middle English, from Old French, from Medieval Latin *ūnisonus,* in unison, from Late Latin, monotonous : Latin *ūni-,* uni- + Latin *sonus,* sound; see **swen-** in Appendix.]

u·nit (yo͞o′nĭt) *n. Abbr.* **u. 1.** An individual, a group, a structure, or other entity regarded as an elementary structural or functional constituent of a whole. **2.** A group regarded as a distinct entity within a larger group. **3. a.** A mechanical part or module. **b.** An entire apparatus or the equipment that performs a specific function. **4.** A precisely specified quantity in terms of which the magnitudes of other quantities of the same kind can be stated. **5.** *Medicine.* The quantity of a vaccine, serum, drug, or other agent necessary to produce a specific effect. **6. a.** A fixed amount of scholastic study used as a basis for calculating academic credits, usually measured in hours of classroom instruction or laboratory work. **b.** A section of an academic course focusing on a selected theme: *a unit on Native Americans.* **7.** The number immediately to the left of the decimal point in the Arabic numeral system. **8.** *Mathematics.* The lowest positive whole number. [Back-formation from UNITY.]

Unit. *abbr.* **1.** Unitarian. **2.** Unitarianism.

u·ni·tard (yo͞o′nĭ-tärd′) *n.* A one-piece tight-fitting leotard and tights combination, sometimes with foot straps. [UNI– + (LEO)TARD.]

U·ni·tar·i·an (yo͞o′nĭ-târ′ē-ən) *n. Abbr.* **Unit. 1.** An adherent of Unitarian Universalism. **2.** A monotheist who is not a Christian. **3.** A Christian who is not a Trinitarian. [From New Latin *ūnitārius,* monotheist, from Latin *ūnitās,* unity. See UNITY.] **—U′ni·tar′i·an** *adj.* **—U′ni·tar′i·an·ism** *n.*

Unitarian Universalism *n.* A religious association derived from Christianity that considers God to be unipersonal, salvation to be granted to the entire human race, and reason and conscience to be the criteria for belief and practice. **—Unitarian Universalist** *adj. & n.*

u·ni·tar·y (yo͞o′nĭ-tĕr′ē) *adj.* **1.** Of or relating to a unit. **2.** Having the nature of a unit; whole. **3.** Based on or characterized by one or more units. **—u′ni·tar′i·ly** *adv.*

unit character *n. Genetics.* A character inherited in accordance with Mendel's law of segregation.

unit cost *n.* The cost of a given unit of a product.

u·nite (yo͞o-nīt′) *v.* **u·nit·ed, u·nit·ing, u·nites.** —*tr.* **1.** To bring together so as to form a whole. **2.** To combine (people) in interest, attitude, or action: *"the love that unites humanity"* (Germaine Greer). **3.** To join (a couple) in marriage. **4.** To cause to adhere. **5.** To have or demonstrate in combination: *She unites common sense with vision.* —*intr.* **1.** To become or seem to become joined, formed, or combined into a unit. **2.** To join and act together in a common purpose or endeavor. See Synonyms at **join. 3.** To be or become bound together by adhesion. [Middle English *uniten,* from Latin *ūnīre, ūnīt-,* from *ūnus,* one. See **oi-no-** in Appendix.]

u·nit·ed (yo͞o-nī′tĭd) *adj.* **1.** Combined into a single entity. **2.** Concerned with, produced by, or resulting from mutual action. **3.** Being in harmony; agreed. **—u·nit′ed·ness** *n.*

U·nit·ed Ar·ab E·mir·ates (yo͞o-nī′tĭd ăr′əb ĭ-mîr′ĭts, ĕm′ər-). Formerly **Tru·cial O·man** (tro͞o′shəl ō-män′). *Abbr.* **U.A.E.** A country of eastern Arabia, a federation of seven sheikdoms on the Persian Gulf and the Gulf of Oman. It was formed in 1971. Abu Dhabi is the capital. Population, 980,000.

Union Jack

unitard

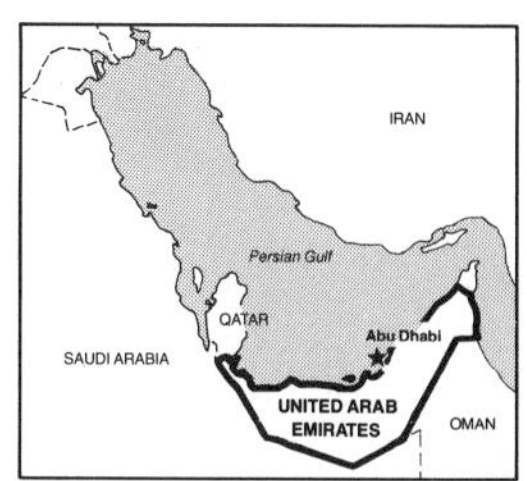

United Arab Emirates

ă pat	oi boy
ā pay	ou out
âr care	o͝o took
ä father	o͞o boot
ĕ pet	ŭ cut
ē be	ûr urge
ĭ pit	th thin
ī pie	*th* this
îr pier	hw which
ŏ pot	zh vision
ō toe	ə about, item
ô paw	♦ regionalism

Stress marks: ′ (primary); ′ (secondary), as in **dictionary** (dĭk′shə-nĕr′ē)

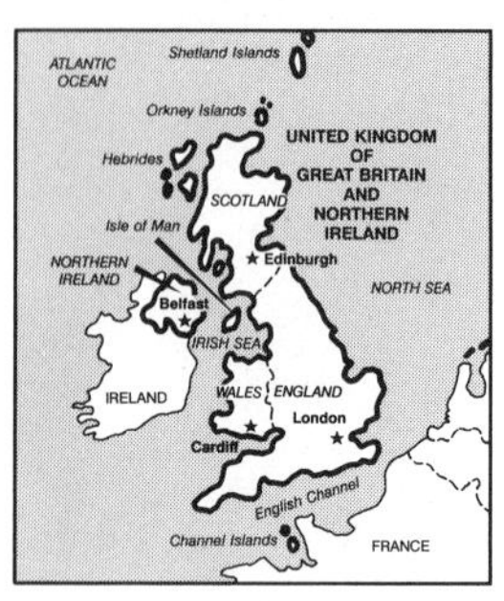

United Kingdom

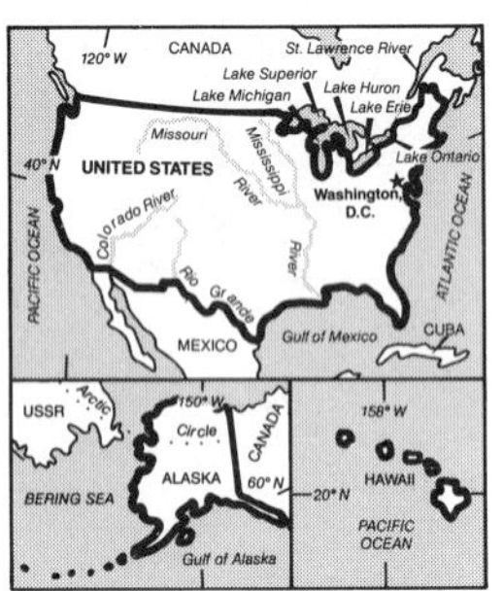

United States

United Arab Republic. *Abbr.* **U.A.R. 1.** A former union of Egypt and Syria that lasted from 1958 until 1961. Yemen also joined the union in 1958, thus creating the **United Arab States. 2.** See **Egypt.**

United Kingdom or **United Kingdom of Great Brit·ain and Northern Ire·land** (brĭt′n; īr′lənd). Commonly called **Great Britain** or **Britain.** *Abbr.* **U.K., UK.** A country of western Europe comprising England, Scotland, Wales, and Northern Ireland. Beginning with the kingdom of England, it was created by three acts of union: with Wales (1536), Scotland (1707), and Northern Ireland (1800). London is the capital and the largest city. Population, 55,648,994.

United Nations. *Abbr.* **UN, U.N.** An international organization composed of most of the countries of the world. It was founded in 1945 to promote peace, security, and economic development.

United States or **United States of A·mer·i·ca** (ə-mĕr′ĭ-kə). *Abbr.* **U.S., US, U.S.A., USA.** A country of central and northwest North America with coastlines on the Atlantic and Pacific oceans. It includes the noncontiguous states of Alaska and Hawaii and various island territories in the Caribbean Sea and Pacific Ocean. The original Thirteen Colonies declared their independence from Great Britain in 1776 and formed a government under the Articles of Confederation in 1781. A new constitution, adopted in 1787 and in effect after 1789, provided for a strong central government, and the nation soon began to expand westward. The Civil War (1861–1865) was a brief but tragic disruption in the unity of the nation. Since that time the United States has evolved into a vast, diversified economic power. Washington, D.C., is the capital and New York the largest city. Population, 226,549,010.

u·ni·tive (yo͞o′nĭ-tĭv, yo͞o-nī′-) *adj.* Serving to unite; tending to promote unity.

u·nit·ize (yo͞o′nĭ-tīz′) *tr.v.* **-ized, -iz·ing, -iz·es. 1.** To separate, classify, or package in units. **2.** To make or transform into a single unit. **—u′nit·i·za′tion** (yo͞o′nĭ-tĭ-zā′shən) *n.*

unit pric·ing (prī′sĭng) *n.* The pricing of goods on the basis of cost per unit of measure.

unit rule *n.* A rule holding that a state's entire vote must go to the candidate preferred by the majority of that state's delegates in a Democratic Party national convention.

u·ni·ty (yo͞o′nĭ-tē) *n., pl.* **-ties. 1.** The state or quality of being one; singleness. **2.** The state or quality of being in accord; harmony. **3. a.** The combination or arrangement of parts into a whole; unification. **b.** A combination or union thus formed. **4.** Singleness or constancy of purpose or action; continuity: *"In an army you need unity of purpose"* (Emmeline Pankhurst). **5. a.** An ordering of all elements in a work of art or literature so that each contributes to a unified aesthetic effect. **b.** The effect thus produced. **6.** One of the three principles of dramatic structure derived by French neoclassicists from Aristotle's *Poetics,* stating that a drama should have but one plot, which should take place in a single day and be confined to a single locale. **7.** *Mathematics.* **a.** The number 1. **b.** See **identity element.** [Middle English *unite,* from Old French, from Latin *ūnitās,* from *ūnus,* one. See **oi-no-** in Appendix.]

SYNONYMS: *unity, union, solidarity.* These nouns denote the condition of accord resulting from an identity or coincidence of interests, purposes, or sympathies among the members of a group. *Unity* implies agreement and collaboration among interdependent, usually varied components: *"Religion . . . calls for the integration of lands and peoples in harmonious unity"* (Vine Deloria, Jr.). *Union* connotes harmony, cohesiveness, and often unanimity among individuals united in a whole: *"All your strength is in your union./All your danger is in discord"* (Henry Wadsworth Longfellow). *Solidarity* refers to the community of objectives and responsibilities that enables a group of people to think and act as one: *"A downtrodden class . . . will never be able to make an effective protest until it achieves solidarity"* (H.G. Wells).

univ. *abbr.* **1.** Universal. **2.** Or **Univ.** University.

Univ. *abbr.* Universalist.

u·ni·va·lent (yo͞o′nĭ-vā′lənt) *adj.* **1.** *Chemistry.* **a.** Having valence 1. **b.** Having only one valence. **2.** *Genetics.* Of or relating to a chromosome that is not paired or united with its homologous chromosome during synapsis. **—univalent** *n. Genetics.* A univalent chromosome.

u·ni·valve (yo͞o′nĭ-vălv′) *adj.* **1.** Having a shell consisting of a single valve or piece. Used of a mollusk. **2.** Composed of a single valve or piece. Used of a shell. **—univalve** *n.* A univalve mollusk or shell.

universal joint

u·ni·ver·sal (yo͞o′nə-vûr′səl) *adj. Abbr.* **univ. 1.** Of, relating to, extending to, or affecting the entire world or all within the world; worldwide: *"This discovery of literature has as yet only partially penetrated the universal consciousness"* (Ellen Key). **2.** Including, relating to, or affecting all members of the class or group under consideration: *the universal skepticism of philosophers.* See Synonyms at **general. 3.** Applicable or common to all purposes, conditions, or situations: *a universal remedy.* **4.** Of or relating to the universe or cosmos; cosmic. **5.** Knowledgeable about or constituting all or many subjects; comprehensively broad. **6.** Adapted or adjustable to many sizes or mechanical uses. **7.** *Logic.* Encompassing all of the members of a class or group. Used of a proposition. **—universal** *n.* **1.** *Logic.* **a.** A universal proposition. **b.** A general or abstract concept or term considered absolute or axiomatic. **2.** A general or widely held principle, concept, or notion. **3.** A trait or pattern of behavior characteristic of all the members of a particular culture or of all human beings. **—u′ni·ver′sal·ly** *adv.* **—u′ni·ver′sal·ness** *n.*

universal coupling *n.* See **universal joint.**

universal donor *n.* A person who has group O blood and is therefore able to serve as a donor to a person of any other blood group in the ABO system.

u·ni·ver·sal·ism (yo͞o′nə-vûr′sə-lĭz′əm) *n.* **1. Universalism. a.** *Theology.* The doctrine of universal salvation. **b.** Unitarian Universalism. **2.** The condition of being universal; universality. **3.** A universal scope or range, as of knowledge.

U·ni·ver·sal·ist (yo͞o′nə-vûr′sə-lĭst) *n. Abbr.* **Univ.** An adherent of Unitarian Universalism. **—U′ni·ver′sal·ist** *adj.*

u·ni·ver·sal·is·tic (yo͞o′nə-vûr′sə-lĭs′tĭk) *adj.* Universal in character or scope: *universalistic values.*

u·ni·ver·sal·i·ty (yo͞o′nə-vər-săl′ĭ-tē) *n., pl.* **-ties. 1.** The quality, fact, or condition of being universal. **2.** Universal inclusiveness in scope or range, especially great or unbounded versatility of the mind.

u·ni·ver·sal·ize (yo͞o′nə-vûr′sə-līz′) *tr.v.* **-ized, -iz·ing, -iz·es.** To make universal; generalize. **—u′ni·ver′sal·i·za′tion** (-sə-lĭ-zā′shən) *n.*

universal joint *n.* A joint or coupling that allows parts of a machine not in line with each other limited freedom of movement in any direction while transmitting rotary motion. Also called *universal coupling.*

U·ni·ver·sal Product Code (yo͞o′nə-vûr′səl) *n. Abbr.* **UPC** A series of vertical bars of varying widths printed on consumer product packages and used especially for computerized inventory control. Also called *bar code.*

universal recipient *n.* A person who has group AB blood and is therefore able to receive blood from any other group in the ABO system.

universal set *n. Mathematics.* A set containing all elements of a problem under consideration.

universal time *n. Abbr.* **UT** The mean solar time for the meridian at Greenwich, England, used as a basis for calculating time throughout most of the world. Also called *Greenwich time.*

u·ni·verse (yo͞o′nə-vûrs′) *n.* **1.** All matter and energy, including Earth, the galaxies and all therein, and the contents of intergalactic space, regarded as a whole. **2. a.** The earth together with all its inhabitants and created things. **b.** The human race. **3.** The sphere or realm in which something exists or takes place. **4.** *Logic.* See **universe of discourse. 5.** *Statistics.* See **population** (sense 5). [Middle English, from Old French *univers,* from Latin *ūniversum,* from neuter of *ūniversus,* whole : *ūnus,* one; see **oi-no-** in Appendix + *versus,* past participle of *vertere,* to turn; see **wer-**[2] in Appendix.]

universe of discourse *n. Logic.* A class containing all the entities referred to in a discourse or an argument. Also called *universe.*

u·ni·ver·si·ty (yo͞o′nə-vûr′sĭ-tē) *n., pl.* **-ties.** *Abbr.* **univ., Univ., U., U 1.** An institution for higher learning with teaching and research facilities constituting a graduate school and professional schools that award master's degrees and doctorates and an undergraduate division that awards bachelor's degrees. **2.** The buildings and grounds of such an institution. **3.** The body of students and faculty of such an institution. [Middle English *universite,* from Old French, from Medieval Latin *ūniversitās,* from Latin, the whole, a corporate body, from *ūniversus,* whole. See UNIVERSE.]

WORD HISTORY: The universe in the word *university* is not the universe as we know it, though *university* is derived from the ancestor of our word *universe.* This ancestor, Latin *ūniversus,* was made up of *ūnus,* "one," and *versus,* "in a specified direction." *Ūniversus* thus literally meant "in one specified direction" but actually meant "the whole of, entire," and "regarded as a whole, regarded as a group." *Ūniversum,* the neuter singular of *ūniversus,* used as a noun, meant "the universe," as did the derivative *ūniversitās,* which also meant "a corporate body of persons, community." During the Middle Ages, when Latin continued to be used in areas such as government, religion, and education, the word *ūniversitās* was applied to the new corporate bodies of teachers and students, as at Salerno, Paris, and Oxford, that were the ancestors of our universities of today. Our word *university,* going back to the Latin word, is first recorded around 1300, with reference to this corporate body.

U·ni·ver·si·ty City (yo͞o′nə-vûr′sĭ-tē). A city of eastern Missouri, a suburb of St. Louis. Population, 42,738.

University Park. A city of northeast Texas, a residential suburb entirely surrounded by Dallas. Population, 22,254.

u·niv·o·cal (yo͞o-nĭv′ə-kəl) *adj.* Having only one meaning; unambiguous. **—univocal** *n.* A word or term having only one meaning. [From Late Latin *ūnivōcus* : Latin *ūni-,* uni- + Latin *vōx, vōc-,* voice; see **wekʷ-** in Appendix.] **—u·niv′o·cal·ly** *adv.*

UNIX (yo͞o′nĭks). A trademark used for a computer disk operating system.

un·joint (ŭn-joint′) *tr.v.* **-joint·ed, -joint·ing, -joints.** To dislocate a joint of; disjoint.

un·just (ŭn-jŭst′) *adj.* **1.** Violating principles of justice or fairness; unfair: *"monstrously unjust and socially harmful"* (Anna Garlin Spencer). **2.** *Archaic.* Faithless; dishonest. **—un·just′ly** *adv.* **—un·just′ness** *n.*

un·jus·ti·fi·a·ble (ŭn-jŭs′tə-fī′ə-bəl, ŭn′jŭs-tə-fī′-) *adj.* Impossible to excuse, pardon, or justify: *took an unjustifiable risk.* **—un·jus′ti·fi′a·bly** *adv.*

un·kempt (ŭn-kĕmpt′) *adj.* **1.a.** Not combed: *unkempt hair.* **b.** Not properly maintained; disorderly or untidy: *an unkempt garden.* See Synonyms at **sloppy. 2.** Unpolished; rude. [Middle English *unkemd* : *un-*, not; see UN–[1] + *kembed,* past participle of *kemben,* to comb (from Old English *cemban;* see **gembh-** in Appendix).]

un·ken·nel (ŭn-kĕn′əl) *tr.v.* **-neled, -nel·ing, -nels** or **-nelled, -nel·ling, -nels. 1.a.** To drive from a lair or den. **b.** To loose from a kennel. **2.** To bring to light; uncover or disclose.

un·kept (ŭn-kĕpt′) *adj.* **1.** Unkempt: *an unkept cemetery plot.* **2.** Not kept or fulfilled: *an unkept promise.*

un·kind (ŭn-kīnd′) *adj.* **-er, -est. 1.** Lacking kindness; inconsiderate or unsympathetic. **2.** Harsh; severe: *unkind winters.* **—un·kind′ness** *n.*

un·kind·ly (ŭn-kīnd′lē) *adj.* **-li·er, -li·est.** Not kindly; unkind. **—unkindly** *adv.* In an unkind manner. **—un·kind′li·ness** *n.*

un·kink (ŭn-kĭngk′) *v.* **-kinked, -kink·ing, -kinks.** *—tr.* To remove kinks from; make straight. *—intr.* To become relaxed.

un·knit (ŭn-nĭt′) *tr. & intr.v.* **-knit** or **-knit·ted, -knit·ting, -knits.** To unravel or undo (something knit or tied) or become unraveled or undone.

un·know·a·ble (ŭn-nō′ə-bəl) *adj.* Impossible to know, especially being beyond the range of human experience or understanding: *the unknowable mysteries of life.* **—un·know′a·bil′i·ty, un·know′a·ble·ness** *n.* **—un·know′a·ble** *n.* **—un·know′a·bly** *adv.*

un·know·ing (ŭn-nō′ĭng) *adj.* Not knowing; unaware. **—un·know′ing·ly** *adv.*

un·known (ŭn-nōn′) *adj.* **1.** Not known; unfamiliar: *a modern-day problem unknown in earlier times.* **2.a.** Not identified or ascertained: *received flowers from an unknown admirer.* **b.** Not established or verified. **3.** Not well known or widely known: *an unknown artist.* **—unknown** *n.* **1.a.** A person or thing that is unknown: *"the abyss of the unknown"* (Helena Petrovna Blavatsky). **b.** A person who is not well known, as to the general public: *cast an unknown in the starring role.* **2.** *Mathematics.* A quantity of unknown numerical value.

Un·known Soldier (ŭn′nōn′) *n.* An unidentified soldier killed in war and chosen to be interred with national honors as a representative of all those who died in a war.

un·la·bored (ŭn-lā′bərd) *adj.* **1.** Done with or requiring little effort; effortless. **2.** Not tilled or cultivated.

un·lace (ŭn-lās′) *tr.v.* **-laced, -lac·ing, -lac·es. 1.a.** To loosen or undo the lacing or laces of. **b.** To loosen or remove the clothing of. **2.** *Obsolete.* To disgrace.

un·lade (ŭn-lād′) *v.* **-lad·ed, -lad·ing, -lades.** *Nautical.* *—tr.* **1.** To unload (cargo) from a ship. **2.** To unload (a ship). *—intr.* To discharge a cargo.

un·laid (ŭn-lād′) *v.* *Nautical.* Past tense and past participle of **unlay.**

un·lash (ŭn-lăsh′) *tr.v.* **-lashed, -lash·ing, -lash·es.** To untie the lashing of; loose.

un·latch (ŭn-lăch′) *v.* **-latched, -latch·ing, -latch·es.** *—tr.* To unfasten or open by releasing the latch. *—intr.* To become unfastened or opened.

un·law·ful (ŭn-lô′fəl) *adj.* **1.** Not lawful; illegal. **2.** Contrary to accepted morality or convention; illicit. **3.** Of, relating to, or being a child or children born to unmarried parents. **—un·law′ful·ly** *adv.* **—un·law′ful·ness** *n.*

un·lay (ŭn-lā′) *v.* **-laid** (-lād′), **-lay·ing, -lays.** *Nautical.* *—tr.* To untwist the strands of (a rope). *—intr.* To untwist.

un·lead (ŭn-lĕd′) *tr.v.* **-lead·ed, -lead·ing, -leads. 1.** To remove the lead from. **2.** *Printing.* To extricate the leads from between (lines of type).

un·lead·ed (ŭn-lĕd′ĭd) *adj.* **1.** Not containing tetraethyl lead: *unleaded gasoline.* **2.** *Printing.* Not spaced or separated with lead, as lines of type.

un·learn (ŭn-lûrn′) *tr.v.* **-learned** also **-learnt** (-lûrnt′), **-learn·ing, -learns. 1.** To put (something learned) out of the mind; forget. **2.** To undo the effect of; put aside the practice of: *tried to unlearn smoking.*

un·learn·ed (ŭn-lûr′nĭd) *adj.* **1.** Not educated; ignorant or illiterate. See Synonyms at **ignorant. 2.** Not skilled or versed in a specified discipline. **3.** (-lûrnd′). Not acquired by training or studying: *an unlearned response.* **—un·learn′ed·ly** *adv.*

un·leash (ŭn-lēsh′) *tr.v.* **-leashed, -leash·ing, -leash·es.** To release or loose from or as if from a leash: *unleashed the guard dogs; unleashed his pent-up rage.*

un·leav·ened (ŭn-lĕv′ənd) *adj.* Made without yeast or any other leavening agent: *unleavened bread.*

un·less (ŭn-lĕs′) *conj.* Except on the condition that; except under the circumstances that: *"Exceptional talent does not always win its reward unless favored by exceptional circumstances"* (Mary Elizabeth Braddon). **—unless** *prep.* Except for; except. [Middle English *unlesse,* alteration (influenced by *un-*, not) of *on-lesse* : *on,* on; see ON + *lesse,* less; see LESS.]

un·let·tered (ŭn-lĕt′ərd) *adj.* **1.a.** Not adept at reading and writing; deficient in the knowledge that can be acquired from books. See Synonyms at **ignorant. b.** Illiterate. **2.** Having no lettering: *unlettered poster board.*

un·li·censed (ŭn-lī′sənst) *adj.* **1.** Having no official license. **2.** Done without permission; not authorized. **3.** Lacking moral restraint; unrestrained.

un·licked (ŭn-lĭkt′) *adj.* *Archaic.* **1.** Not licked clean. **2.** Not having proper shape or form.

un·like (ŭn-līk′) *adj.* **1.** Not alike; different: *For twins, they are very unlike.* **2.** Not equal, as in amount. **—unlike** *prep.* **1.** Different from; not like: *She's unlike the rest of her family.* **2.** Not typical of: *It's unlike him not to call.*

un·like·li·hood (ŭn-līk′lē-ho͝od′) *n.* **1.** The state of being unlikely or improbable; improbability. **2.** Something unlikely.

un·like·ly (ŭn-līk′lē) *adj.* **-li·er, -li·est. 1.** Not likely; improbable. **2.** Not promising; likely to fail. **—un·like′li·ness** *n.*

un·like·ness (ŭn-līk′nĭs) *n.* The quality or condition of being unlike. See Synonyms at **difference.**

un·lim·ber (ŭn-lĭm′bər) *v.* **-bered, -ber·ing, -bers.** *—tr.* **1.** To make ready for action. **2.** To detach (a gun or caisson) from its limber. *—intr.* To prepare something for action.

un·lim·it·ed (ŭn-lĭm′ĭ-tĭd) *adj.* **1.** Having no restrictions or controls: *an unlimited travel ticket.* **2.** Having or seeming to have no boundaries; infinite: *an unlimited horizon.* **3.** Without qualification or exception; absolute: *unlimited self-confidence.* **—un·lim′it·ed·ly** *adv.* **—un·lim′it·ed·ness** *n.*

un·link (ŭn-lĭngk′) *v.* **-linked, -link·ing, -links.** *—tr.* **1.** To disconnect the links of; unfasten. **2.** To separate as if by undoing links: *unlink arms.* *—intr.* To become unfastened.

un·list·ed (ŭn-lĭs′tĭd) *adj.* **1.** Not appearing on a list, especially not listed in a telephone directory. **2.** Relating to or being stock or securities not listed on a stock exchange.

un·lis·ten·a·ble (ŭn-lĭs′ə-nə-bəl) *adj.* Being such that listening with comfort or pleasure is impossible: *an unlistenable operatic solo; an unlistenable diatribe.*

un·liv·a·ble (ŭn-lĭv′ə-bəl) *adj.* Unfit for habitation; uninhabitable: *an unlivable apartment.*

un·live (ŭn-lĭv′) *tr.v.* **-lived, -liv·ing, -lives.** To undo the effects of; annul.

un·load (ŭn-lōd′) *v.* **-load·ed, -load·ing, -loads.** *—tr.* **1.a.** To remove the load or cargo from. **b.** To discharge (cargo or a load). **2.a.** To relieve of something burdensome or oppressive; unburden. **b.** To give expression to (one's troubles or feelings); pour forth. **3.** To remove the charge from (a firearm). **4.** To dispose of, especially by selling in great quantity; dump. *—intr.* To discharge a cargo or some other burden.

un·lock (ŭn-lŏk′) *v.* **-locked, -lock·ing, -locks.** *—tr.* **1.a.** To undo (a lock) by turning a key or corresponding part. **b.** To undo the lock of. **2.** To give access to; open. **3.** To set free; release: *The news unlocked a torrent of emotion.* **4.** To provide a key to; disclose or reveal: *unlock a mystery.* *—intr.* To become unfastened, loosened, or freed from something that restrains.

un·looked-for (ŭn-lo͝okt′fôr′) *adj.* Not expected; unforeseen: *unlooked-for riches.*

un·loose (ŭn-lo͞os′) *tr.v.* **-loosed, -loos·ing, -loos·es. 1.** To unfasten; untie. **2.** To set free from or as if from restraints. **3.** To relax: *unloosed my grip on the handlebars.*

un·loos·en (ŭn-lo͞o′sən) *tr.v.* **-ened, -en·ing, -ens.** To unloose.

un·love·ly (ŭn-lŭv′lē) *adj.* **-li·er, -li·est. 1.** Not deemed visually attractive. **2.** Not pleasant; disagreeable: *an unlovely ride to work on a crowded train.*

un·luck·y (ŭn-lŭk′ē) *adj.* **-i·er, -i·est. 1.** Subjected to or marked by misfortune. **2.** Resulting or likely to result in misfortune; inauspicious. See Synonyms at **unfortunate. 3.** Not producing the desired outcome; disappointing. **—un·luck′i·ly** *adv.* **—un·luck′i·ness** *n.*

un·made (ŭn-mād′) *adj.* Not made: *an unmade bed; plans still unmade.*

un·make (ŭn-māk′) *tr.v.* **-made** (-mād′), **-mak·ing, -makes. 1.** To deprive of position, rank, or authority; depose. **2.** To cause the ruin of; destroy. **3.** To alter the nature or characteristics of.

un·man (ŭn-măn′) *tr.v.* **-manned, -man·ning, -mans. 1.** To cause to give up manly courage or spirit. **2.** To take away virility from; emasculate.

un·man·age·a·ble (ŭn-măn′ĭ-jə-bəl) *adj.* Difficult or impossible to manage, as: **a.** Not submitting to discipline; unruly: *an unmanageable child.* **b.** Difficult to keep under control or within limits: *unmanageable traffic congestion; an unmanageable federal deficit.* **c.** Awkward; unwieldy: *unmanageable bundles.* **—un·man′age·a·bil′i·ty** *n.* **—un·man′age·a·bly** *adv.*

un·man·ly (ŭn-măn′lē) *adj.* **-li·er, -li·est. 1.a.** Dishonorable; degrading. **b.** Lacking courage; cowardly. **2.** Regarded as unbecoming to a man. **—un·man′li·ness** *n.*

un·manned (ŭn-mănd′) *adj.* **1.** Not crewed: *an unmanned spacecraft.* **2.** *Obsolete.* Not trained. Used of a hawk.

un·man·nered (ŭn-măn′ərd) *adj.* **1.** Lacking good manners; rude. **2.** Natural and unaffected. **—un·man′nered·ly** *adv.*

ă pat	oi boy
ā pay	ou out
âr care	o͝o took
ä father	o͞o boot
ĕ pet	ŭ cut
ē be	ûr urge
ĭ pit	th thin
ī pie	*th* this
îr pier	hw which
ŏ pot	zh vision
ō toe	ə about, item
ô paw	♦ regionalism

Stress marks: ′ (primary); **′** (secondary), as in **dictionary** (dĭk′shə-nĕr′ē)

un·man·ner·ly (ŭn-măn′ər-lē) *adj.* Ill-mannered; rude. **—un·man′ner·li·ness** *n.* **—un·man′ner·ly** *adv.*

un·marked (ŭn-märkt′) *adj.* **1.** Not bearing an identifying mark: *an unmarked police car; unmarked merchandise.* **2.** Not observed or noticed.

un·mar·ried (ŭn-măr′ēd) *adj.* Not married; having no spouse. **—unmarried** *n.* One who is not married.

un·mask (ŭn-măsk′) *v.* **-masked, -mask·ing, -masks.** *—tr.* **1.** To remove a mask from. **2.** To disclose the true character of; expose. *—intr.* To remove one's mask.

un·matched (ŭn-măcht′) *adj.* **1.** Not matched: *unmatched socks.* **2.** Without equal or rival; peerless: *unmatched skill.*

un·mean·ing (ŭn-mē′nĭng) *adj.* **1.** Devoid of meaning or sense; meaningless: *gave a vapid and unmeaning response to a difficult query.* **2.** Lacking intelligence or liveliness of expression; vacant: *an unmeaning face.* **—un·mean′ing·ly** *adv.*

un·meant (ŭn-mĕnt′) *adj.* Not intentional.

un·me·chan·i·cal (ŭn′mĭ-kăn′ĭ-kəl) *adj.* Lacking skill in the use of machinery and tools. **—un′me·chan′i·cal·ly** *adv.*

un·meet (ŭn-mēt′) *adj.* Not fitting or proper; unseemly.

un·men·tion·a·ble (ŭn-mĕn′shə-nə-bəl) *adj.* Not fit to be mentioned or discussed; unspeakable: *unmentionable words.* **—unmentionable** *n.* **1.** One that is not to be mentioned. **2. unmentionables.** Underwear. **—un·men′tion·a·ble·ness** *n.* **—un·men′tion·a·bly** *adv.*

un·mer·ci·ful (ŭn-mûr′sĭ-fəl) *adj.* **1.** Having or exhibiting no mercy; merciless. **2.** Exceeding a normal or reasonable limit; excessive: *unmerciful heat.* **—un·mer′ci·ful·ly** *adv.* **—un·mer′ci·ful·ness** *n.*

un·met (ŭn-mĕt′) *adj.* Not satisfied or fulfilled: *unmet demands.*

un·mind·ful (ŭn-mīnd′fəl) *adj.* Failing to give due heed, care, or attention; inattentive. See Synonyms at **forgetful.** **—un·mind′ful·ly** *adv.* **—un·mind′ful·ness** *n.*

un·mis·tak·a·ble (ŭn′mĭ-stā′kə-bəl) *adj.* Impossible to mistake or misinterpret; obvious: *unmistakable signs of illness.* **—un′mis·tak′a·bly** *adv.*

un·mit·i·gat·ed (ŭn-mĭt′ĭ-gā′tĭd) *adj.* **1.** Not diminished or moderated in intensity or severity; unrelieved: *unmitigated suffering.* **2.** Without qualification or exception: *an unmitigated lie.* **—un·mit′i·gat′ed·ly** *adv.* **—un·mit′i·gat′ed·ness** *n.*

un·mixed (ŭn-mĭkst′) *adj.* Free from other elements; pure: *unmixed pleasure; was not an unmixed blessing.* **—un·mix′ed·ly** (-mĭk′sĭd-lē) *adv.*

un·mold (ŭn-mōld′) *tr.v.* **-mold·ed, -mold·ing, -molds.** To remove from a mold: *unmold a lemon mousse.*

un·mo·lest·ed (ŭn′mə-lĕs′tĭd) *adj.* Not interfered with, disturbed, or harmed.

un·moor (ŭn-mo͝or′) *v.* **-moored, -moor·ing, -moors.** *—tr.* **1.** To release from or as if from moorings. **2.** *Nautical.* To release (a ship) from all but one anchor. *—intr.* To cast off moorings.

un·mor·al (ŭn-môr′əl, -mŏr′-) *adj.* **1.** Having no moral quality; amoral. **2.** Unrelated to moral or ethical considerations; nonmoral. **—un′mo·ral′i·ty** (-mə-răl′ĭ-tē, -mô-) *n.* **—un·mor′al·ly** *adv.*

un·mor·tise (ŭn-môr′tĭs) *tr.v.* **-tised, -tis·ing, -tis·es.** **1.** To loosen a mortised joint of. **2.** To separate.

un·mo·ti·vat·ed (ŭn-mō′tə-vā′tĭd) *adj.* Having no motive or incentive: *unmotivated students; an unmotivated episode in a movie.*

un·moved (ŭn-mo͞ovd′) *adj.* Emotionally unaffected.

un·mov·ing (ŭn-mo͞o′vĭng) *adj.* **1.** Not moving; motionless. **2.** Not affecting the emotions: *a curiously unmoving dramatic work.*

un·muf·fle (ŭn-mŭf′əl) *v.* **-fled, -fling, -fles.** *—tr.* To free from a garment or device that muffles. *—intr.* To remove or cast off something that muffles.

un·mu·si·cal (ŭn-myo͞o′zĭ-kəl) *adj.* **1.** Lacking in musical qualities, such as melody or harmony. **2.** Sounding harsh to the ear; dissonant. **3.** Not skilled or interested in music. **—un·mu′si·cal·ly** *adv.* **—un·mu′si·cal·ness** *n.*

un·muz·zle (ŭn-mŭz′əl) *tr.v.* **-zled, -zling, -zles.** **1.** To remove a muzzle from: *unmuzzle a dog.* **2.** *Informal.* To free from restraint or censorship: *unmuzzle the press.*

un·my·e·lin·at·ed (ŭn-mī′ə-lĭ-nā′tĭd) *adj.* Lacking a myelin sheath. Used of a nerve fiber.

un·name·a·ble or **un·nam·a·ble** (ŭn-nā′mə-bəl) *adj.* Not to be named or identified: *"We lived in dread of various unnameable calamities"* (Garrison Keillor).

un·nat·u·ral (ŭn-năch′ər-əl) *adj.* **1.** In violation of a natural law. **2.** Inconsistent with an individual pattern or custom. **3.** Deviating from a behavioral or social norm: *an unnatural attachment.* **4.** Contrived or constrained; artificial: *smiled in an unnatural manner.* **5.** In violation of natural feelings; inhuman. **—un·nat′u·ral·ly** *adv.* **—un·nat′u·ral·ness** *n.*

un·nec·es·sar·y (ŭn-nĕs′ĭ-sĕr′ē) *adj.* Not necessary; needless. **—un·nec′es·sar′i·ly** (-sâr′ə-lē) *adv.*

un·nerve (ŭn-nûrv′) *tr.v.* **-nerved, -nerv·ing, -nerves.** **1.** To deprive of fortitude, strength, or firmness of purpose. **2.** To make nervous or upset. **—un·nerv′ing·ly** *adv.*

un·nil·quad·i·um (yo͞o′nĭl-kwŏd′ē-əm) *n.* Element 104. [Latin *ūnus,* one; see UNION + *nīl,* nothing; see NIL + QUAD(RI)– + –IUM.]

un·nil·quin·ti·um (yo͞o′nĭl-kwĭn′tē-əm) *n.* Element 105. [Latin *ūnus,* one; see UNION + *nīl,* nothing; see NIL + *quīntus,* fifth; see QUINTET + –IUM.]

un·no·tice·a·ble (ŭn-nō′tĭ-sə-bəl) *adj.* Not readily noticeable. **—un·no′tice·a·bly** *adv.*

un·num·bered (ŭn-nŭm′bərd) *adj.* **1.** Innumerable; countless: *the unnumbered stars.* **2.** Not marked with an identifying number: *unnumbered pages.*

un·ob·jec·tion·a·ble (ŭn′əb-jĕk′shə-nə-bəl) *adj.* Raising no objections; acceptable: *unobjectionable goals.*

un·ob·struct·ed (ŭn′əb-strŭk′tĭd, -ŏb-) *adj.* Free from obstructions; clear: *an unobstructed view.*

un·ob·tru·sive (ŭn′əb-tro͞o′sĭv) *adj.* Not undesirably noticeable or blatant; inconspicuous. **—un′ob·tru′sive·ly** *adv.* **—un′ob·tru′sive·ness** *n.*

un·oc·cu·pied (ŭn-ŏk′yə-pīd′) *adj.* **1.a.** Not being used: *an unoccupied telephone booth.* **b.** Not inhabited: *an unoccupied house.* **2.** Not busy, employed, or engaged; idle.

un·of·fi·cial (ŭn′ə-fĭsh′əl) *adj.* **1.** Not official: *the unofficial election results.* **2.** Not acting officially: *an unofficial adviser.* **—un′of·fi′cial·ly** *adv.*

un·op·posed (ŭn′ə-pōzd′) *adj.* Not challenged by another: *The candidate was unopposed in the campaign.*

un·or·gan·ized (ŭn-ôr′gə-nīzd′) *adj.* **1.** Lacking order, system, or unity; disorganized. **2.** Having no organic qualities; inorganic. **3.** Not represented by a labor union.

un·o·rig·i·nal (ŭn′ə-rĭj′ə-nəl) *adj.* Lacking originality; trite.

un·or·na·ment (ŭn-ôr′nə-mĕnt′) *tr.v.* **-ment·ed, -ment·ing, -ments.** To divest of ornamentation; make unadorned.

un·or·tho·dox (ŭn-ôr′thə-dŏks′) *adj.* Breaking with convention or tradition; not orthodox. **—un·or′tho·dox′ly** *adv.* **—un·or′tho·dox′y** *n.*

un·os·ten·ta·tious (ŭn-ŏs′tĕn-tā′shəs, -tən-) *adj.* Not ostentatious; unpretentious. See Synonyms at **plain.** **—un·os′ten·ta′tious·ly** *adv.* **—un·os′ten·ta′tious·ness** *n.*

unp. *abbr.* **1.** Unpaged. **2.** Unpaginated.

un·pack (ŭn-păk′) *v.* **-packed, -pack·ing, -packs.** *—tr.* **1.** To remove the contents of (a suitcase, for example). **2.** To remove from a container, from packaging, or from packing. **3.** To remove a pack from (a pack animal). *—intr.* To unpack objects from a container.

un·paged (ŭn-pājd′) *adj.* *Abbr.* **unp.** Having no page numbers.

un·pag·i·nat·ed (ŭn-păj′ə-nā′tĭd) *adj.* Unpaged.

un·paid (ŭn-pād′) *adj.* **1.** Not yet paid: *unpaid bills.* **2.** Serving without pay; unsalaried: *unpaid research assistants.*

un·pal·at·a·ble (ŭn-păl′ə-tə-bəl) *adj.* **1.** Not pleasing to the taste: *an unpalatable meal.* **2.** Not pleasant or agreeable: *unpalatable truths.* **—un′pal·at·a·bil′i·ty** *n.* **—un·pal′at·a·bly** *adv.*

un·par·al·leled (ŭn-păr′ə-lĕld′) *adj.* Without parallel, equal, or match; unequaled.

un·par·lia·men·ta·ry (ŭn′pär-lə-mĕn′tə-rē, -mĕn′trē) *adj.* Not in accord with parliamentary procedure.

un·peo·ple (ŭn-pē′pəl) *tr.v.* **-pled, -pling, -ples.** To reduce sharply the population of (an area); depopulate.

un·peo·pled (ŭn-pē′pəld) *adj.* Uninhabited: *unpeopled Arctic wastelands.*

un·per·fo·rat·ed (ŭn-pûr′fə-rā′tĭd) *adj.* **1.** Lacking perforations. **2.** Imperforate. Used of a postage stamp.

un·per·son (ŭn′pûr′sən) *n.* A nonperson.

un·per·turbed (ŭn′pər-tûrbd′) *adj.* Calm and serene.

un·pick (ŭn-pĭk′) *tr.v.* **-picked, -pick·ing, -picks.** To undo (sewing) by removing stitches: *unpick a seam.*

un·pile (ŭn-pīl′) *tr.v.* **-piled, -pil·ing, -piles.** To remove from a pile.

un·pin (ŭn-pĭn′) *tr.v.* **-pinned, -pin·ning, -pins.** **1.** To remove pins or a pin from. **2.a.** To open or unfasten by or as if by removing pins. **b.** To free.

un·planned (ŭn-plănd′) *adj.* **1.** Not intended; unintentional. **2.a.** Having no particular purpose, organization, or structure; random. **b.** Not thought out or prepared in advance; spontaneous: *an unplanned adventure; an unplanned picnic.*

un·pleas·ant (ŭn-plĕz′ənt) *adj.* Not pleasing; disagreeable. **—un·pleas′ant·ly** *adv.*

un·pleas·ant·ness (ŭn-plĕz′ənt-nĭs) *n.* **1.** The quality or condition of being unpleasant. **2.** An unpleasant experience or situation.

un·pleas·ant·ry (ŭn-plĕz′ən-trē) *n., pl.* **-ries.** A disagreeable remark, situation, or act.

un·plug (ŭn-plŭg′) *tr.v.* **-plugged, -plug·ging, -plugs.** **1.a.** To remove a plug from. **b.** To free from an obstruction. **2.a.** To remove (an electric plug) from an outlet. **b.** To disconnect (an electric appliance) by removing a plug from an outlet.

un·plumbed (ŭn-plŭmd′) *adj.* **1.** Not measured or sounded with a plumb: *unplumbed ocean depths.* **2.** Not fully examined or explored: *unplumbed ideas.*

un·pol·ished (ŭn-pŏl′ĭsht) *adj.* **1.** Not polished, as: **a.** Not smooth and shiny: *unpolished shoes; unpolished gemstones.* **b.** Not elaborated, perfected, or completed: *an unpolished performance.* **c.** Not having attained a high degree of skill: *an unpolished tenor.* **2.a.** Lacking good manners or refinement. **b.** Natural and unsophisticated: *The service was friendly and unpolished.*

un·po·lit·i·cal (ŭn'pə-lĭt'ĭ-kəl) *adj.* Not politically structured, oriented, or focused; not interested in politics.

un·polled (ŭn-pōld') *adj.* **1.** Not interviewed in a poll. **2.** Not registered at the polls: *unpolled voters.*

un·pop·u·lar (ŭn-pŏp'yə-lər) *adj.* Lacking general approval or acceptance. **—un'pop·u·lar'i·ty** (-lăr'ĭ-tē) *n.*

un·prac·ticed (ŭn-prăk'tĭst) *adj.* **1.** Not yet tested or tried. **2.** Lacking the benefit of experience; unskilled.

un·prec·e·dent·ed (ŭn-prĕs'ĭ-dĕn'tĭd) *adj.* Having no previous example: *unprecedented economic growth.* **—un·prec'e·dent'ed·ly** *adv.*

un·pre·dict·a·ble (ŭn'prĭ-dĭk'tə-bəl) *adj.* Difficult to foretell or foresee: *unpredictable test results; unpredictable behavior.* **—unpredictable** *n.* Something difficult or impossible to foresee. **—un·pre·dict'a·bil'i·ty** *n.* **—un'pre·dict'a·bly** *adv.*

un·prej·u·diced (ŭn-prĕj'ə-dĭst) *adj.* Free from prejudice; impartial. See Synonyms at **fair**[1].

un·pre·med·i·tat·ed (ŭn'prĭ-mĕd'ĭ-tā'tĭd) *adj.* Not planned or thought out in advance. See Synonyms at **extemporaneous.** **—un'pre·med'i·tat'ed·ly** *adv.*

un·pre·pared (ŭn'prĭ-pârd') *adj.* **1.** Having made no preparations. **2.** Not equipped to meet a contingency. **3.** Impromptu: *unprepared remarks.* **—un'pre·par'ed·ly** (-pâr'ĭd-lē) *adv.* **—un'pre·par'ed·ness** (-pâr'ĭd-nĭs, -pârd'nĭs) *n.*

un·pre·pos·sess·ing (ŭn'prē-pə-zĕs'ĭng) *adj.* Failing to impress favorably; nondescript: *an unprepossessing little hotel.* **—un'pre·pos·sess'ing·ly** *adv.*

un·pre·tend·ing (ŭn'prĭ-tĕn'dĭng) *adj.* Unpretentious.

un·pre·ten·tious (ŭn'prĭ-tĕn'shəs) *adj.* Lacking pretention or affectation; modest. See Synonyms at **plain.** **—un'pre·ten'tious·ly** *adv.* **—un'pre·ten'tious·ness** *n.*

un·priced (ŭn-prīst') *adj.* Having no assigned price: *unpriced merchandise.*

un·prin·ci·pled (ŭn-prĭn'sə-pəld) *adj.* Lacking principles or moral scruples; unscrupulous: *unprincipled behavior.* **—un·prin'ci·pled·ness** *n.*

un·print·a·ble (ŭn-prĭn'tə-bəl) *adj.* Not proper for publication for legal or social reasons: *unprintable remarks.*

un·pro·duc·tive (ŭn'prə-dŭk'tĭv) *adj.* **1.** Not productive; idle. **2.** *Economics.* Adding nothing to exchangeable value. **—un'pro·duc'tive·ly** *adv.* **—un'pro·duc'tive·ness** *n.*

un·pro·fes·sion·al (ŭn'prə-fĕsh'ə-nəl) *adj.* **1.a.** Not in a profession. **b.** Not a qualified member of a professional group. **2.** Not conforming to the standards of a profession: *unprofessional behavior.* **3.** Characteristic of an amateur; inexpert. **—un'pro·fes'sion·al·ism** *n.* **—un'pro·fes'sion·al·ly** *adv.*

un·prof·it·a·ble (ŭn-prŏf'ĭ-tə-bəl) *adj.* **1.** Bringing in no profit or profits: *an unprofitable business venture.* **2.** Serving no useful purpose: *an unprofitable argument.* **—un·prof'it·a·bil'i·ty, un·prof'it·a·ble·ness** *n.* **—un·prof'it·a·bly** *adv.*

un·prom·is·ing (ŭn-prŏm'ĭ-sĭng) *adj.* Not likely to develop in a desirable manner: *an unpromising beginning to the relationship.* **—un·prom'is·ing·ly** *adv.*

un·pro·nounce·a·ble (ŭn'prə-noun'sə-bəl) *adj.* **1.** Difficult or impossible to pronounce correctly: *an unpronounceable last name.* **2.** Not fit to be mentioned.

un·pro·pi·tious (ŭn'prə-pĭsh'əs) *adj.* Unfavorable; inauspicious: *an unpropitious moment.* **—un'pro·pi'tious·ly** *adv.*

un·pro·vid·ed (ŭn'prə-vī'dĭd) *adj.* Not supplied, furnished, or equipped. **—un'pro·vid'ed·ly** *adv.*

un·pro·voked (ŭn'prə-vōkt') *adj.* Not provoked or prompted: *an unprovoked attack.*

un·pub·lish·a·ble (ŭn-pŭb'lĭ-shə-bəl) *adj.* Unfit for publication: *an unpublishable manuscript.*

un·put·down·a·ble (ŭn'po͝ot-dou'nə-bəl) *adj.* *Informal.* So well written and entertaining as to be difficult to put down: *"Unless the story is at once as unputdownable to a taxi driver as to a university professor, it is not good enough"* (Brian Burland).

un·qual·i·fied (ŭn-kwŏl'ə-fīd') *adj.* **1.** Lacking the proper or required qualifications: *unqualified for the job.* **2.** Not modified by conditions or reservations; absolute: *an unqualified refusal.* **—un·qual'i·fied'ly** *adv.*

un·quench·a·ble (ŭn-kwĕn'chə-bəl) *adj.* **1.** Impossible to slake or satisfy: *unquenchable thirst.* **2.** Impossible to suppress or destroy: *unquenchable enthusiasm.* **—un·quench'a·bly** *adv.*

un·ques·tion·a·ble (ŭn-kwĕs'chə-nə-bəl) *adj.* Beyond question or doubt; indisputable. See Synonyms at **authentic.** **—un·ques'tion·a·bil'i·ty, un'ques'tion·a·ble·ness** *n.* **—un·ques'tion·a·bly** *adv.*

un·ques·tioned (ŭn-kwĕs'chənd) *adj.* **1.** Not subjected to questioning; not interrogated. **2.** Being such as to debar questioning or doubts; indisputable. **3.** Not called into question or examination; not doubted.

un·ques·tion·ing (ŭn-kwĕs'chə-nĭng) *adj.* Not marked by or exhibiting uncertainty or indecision: *unquestioning faith.* **—un·ques'tion·ing·ly** *adv.*

un·qui·et (ŭn-kwī'ĭt) *adj.* **-er, -est.** **1.** Emotionally or mentally restless or uneasy. **2.** Characterized by unrest or disorder; turbulent. **—un·qui'et·ly** *adv.* **—un·qui'et·ness** *n.*

un·quote (ŭn-kwōt') *n.* Used by a speaker to indicate the end of a quotation.

un·raised (ŭn-rāzd') *adj.* Containing no yeast; not leavened: *an unraised doughnut.*

un·rav·el (ŭn-răv'əl) *v.* **-eled, -el·ing, -els** or **-elled, -el·ling, -els.** —*tr.* **1.a.** To undo or ravel the knitted fabric of. **b.** To separate (entangled threads). **2.** To separate and clarify the elements of (something mysterious or baffling); solve. See Synonyms at **solve.** —*intr.* To become unraveled.

un·reach·a·ble (ŭn-rē'chə-bəl) *adj.* Inaccessibly located or situated: *an unreachable canyon; an executive unreachable by telephone.* **—un·reach'a·bil'i·ty** *n.* **—un·reach'a·bly** *adv.*

un·read (ŭn-rĕd') *adj.* **1.** Not read, studied, or perused: *a book that is yet unread.* **2.a.** Having read little; lacking in knowledge acquired by reading. **b.** Not versed in a specified subject: *unread in anthropology.*

un·read·a·ble (ŭn-rē'də-bəl) *adj.* **1.** Not legible or decipherable; illegible: *unreadable handwriting.* **2.** Unsuitable for or not worth reading: *unreadable prose.* **3.** Not interesting; dull: *wholly unreadable statistics.* **4.** Incomprehensible; opaque: *an unreadable look in his eyes.* **—un·read'a·bil'i·ty** *n.*

un·read·y (ŭn-rĕd'ē) *adj.* **-i·er, -i·est.** **1.** Not ready or prepared. **2.** Slow to see or respond; not prompt. **—un·read'i·ly** *adv.* **—un·read'i·ness** *n.*

un·re·al (ŭn-rē'əl, -rēl') *adj.* **1.** Not real or substantial; illusory. **2.** *Slang.* So remarkable as to elicit disbelief; fantastic. **3.** Surreal.

un·re·al·is·tic (ŭn'rē-ə-lĭs'tĭk) *adj.* Not compatible with reality or fact; unreasonably idealistic: *unrealistic expectations.* **—un're·al·is'ti·cal·ly** *adv.*

un·re·al·i·ty (ŭn'rē-ăl'ĭ-tē) *n., pl.* **-ties.** **1.** The quality or state of being unreal. **2.** Something unreal, insubstantial, or imaginary. **3.** A lack of ability to deal with reality.

un·re·al·ized (ŭn-rē'ə-līzd') *adj.* Not brought to realization; not made actual or real: *unrealized aspirations.*

un·rea·son (ŭn-rē'zən) *n.* **1.** Absence or lack of reason; irrationality. **2.** Nonsense; absurdity.

un·rea·son·a·ble (ŭn-rē'zə-nə-bəl) *adj.* **1.** Not governed by reason: *an unreasonable attitude.* **2.** Exceeding reasonable limits; immoderate: *unreasonable demands.* **—un·rea'son·a·ble·ness** *n.* **—un·rea'son·a·bly** *adv.*

SYNONYMS: *unreasonable, irrational.* The central meaning shared by these adjectives is "not guided by or predicated on reason": *an unreasonable expectation; irrational fears.* See also Synonyms at **excessive.**
ANTONYM: *reasonable.*

un·rea·soned (ŭn-rē'zənd) *adj.* Not based on or guided by reason; unreasonable: *unreasoned prejudices.*

un·rea·son·ing (ŭn-rē'zə-nĭng) *adj.* Not governed or moderated by reason. **—un·rea'son·ing·ly** *adv.*

un·reck·on·a·ble (ŭn-rĕk'ə-nə-bəl) *adj.* Difficult or impossible to calculate; incalculable: *unreckonable distances.*

un·re·con·struct·ed (ŭn'rē-kən-strŭk'tĭd) *adj.* Not reconciled to social, political, or economic change; maintaining outdated attitudes, beliefs, and practices.

un·reel (ŭn-rēl') *tr. & intr.v.* **-reeled, -reel·ing, -reels.** To unwind (something) from or as if from a reel or become unwound.

un·reeve (ŭn-rēv') *v.* **-reeved** or **-rove** (-rōv'), **-reeved** or **-ro·ven** (-rō'vən), **-reev·ing, -reeves.** *Nautical.* —*tr.* To withdraw (a rope, for example) from an opening, such as a block or thimble. —*intr.* **1.** To become unreeved. **2.** To unreeve a rope.

un·re·flect·ing (ŭn'rĭ-flĕk'tĭng) *adj.* Marked by or exhibiting a lack of serious thought or consideration: *unreflecting impulses.* **—un're·flect'ing·ly** *adv.*

un·re·flec·tive (ŭn'rĭ-flĕk'tĭv) *adj.* Not reflective; unthinking. **—un're·flec'tive·ly** *adv.*

un·re·gen·er·ate (ŭn'rĭ-jĕn'ər-ĭt) *adj.* **1.a.** Not spiritually renewed or reformed; not repentant. **b.** Sinful; dissolute. **2.a.** Not reconciled to change; unreconstructed. **b.** Stubborn; obstinate. **—un're·gen'er·a·ble** *adj.* **—un're·gen'er·a·cy** (-ə-sē) *n.* **—un're·gen'er·ate·ly** *adv.*

un·re·hearsed (ŭn'rĭ-hûrst') *adj.* Not rehearsed. See Synonyms at **extemporaneous.**

un·re·lent·ing (ŭn'rĭ-lĕn'tĭng) *adj.* **1.** Having or exhibiting uncompromising determination; unyielding: *an unrelenting human rights worker.* **2.** Not diminishing in intensity, pace, or effort: *an unrelenting ice storm.* **—un're·lent'ing·ly** *adv.*

un·re·li·a·ble (ŭn'rĭ-lī'ə-bəl) *adj.* Marked by or exhibiting a lack of reliability. **—un're·li'a·bil'i·ty, un're·li'a·ble·ness** *n.* **—un're·li'a·bly** *adv.*

un·re·lieved (ŭn'rĭ-lēvd') *adj.* Utter; complete: *unrelieved boredom.* **—un're·liev'ed·ly** (-lē'vĭd-lē) *adv.*

un·re·lig·ious (ŭn'rĭ-lĭj'əs) *adj.* **1.** Indifferent to religion; irreligious. **2.** Not related to religion.

un·re·mark·a·ble (ŭn'rĭ-mär'kə-bəl) *adj.* Lacking distinction; ordinary. **—un're·mark'a·bly** *adv.*

un·re·marked (ŭn'rĭ-märkt') *adj.* Not noticed.

ă pat	oi boy
ā pay	ou out
âr care	o͝o took
ä father	o͞o boot
ĕ pet	ŭ cut
ē be	ûr urge
ĭ pit	th thin
ī pie	*th* this
îr pier	hw which
ŏ pot	zh vision
ō toe	ə about, item
ô paw	♦ regionalism

Stress marks: **'** (primary); ' (secondary), as in **dictionary** (dĭk'shə-nĕr'ē)

un·re·mit·ting (ŭn′rĭ-mĭt′ĭng) *adj.* Never slackening; persistent. **—un′re·mit′ting·ly** *adv.* **—un′re·mit′ting·ness** *n.*

un·re·pent·ant (ŭn′rĭ-pĕn′tənt) *adj.* Having or exhibiting no remorse. **—un′re·pent′ant·ly** *adv.*

un·re·proved (ŭn′rĭ-pro͞ovd′) *adj.* Not rebuked for a fault or misdeed.

un·re·quit·ed (ŭn′rĭ-kwī′tĭd) *adj.* Not reciprocated or returned in kind: *unrequited love; an unrequited injury.* **—un′re·quit′ed·ly** *adv.*

un·re·serve (ŭn′rĭ-zûrv′) *n.* Frankness of manner; candor.

un·re·served (ŭn′rĭ-zûrvd′) *adj.* **1.** Not held back for a particular person: *an unreserved seat.* **2.** Given without reservation; unqualified: *unreserved praise.* **3.** Exhibiting no reserve: *an unreserved grin of approval.* **—un′re·serv′ed·ly** (-zûr′vĭd-lē) *adv.* **—un′re·serv′ed·ness** *n.*

un·re·spon·sive (ŭn′rĭ-spŏn′sĭv) *adj.* Exhibiting a lack of responsiveness. **—un′re·spon′sive·ly** *adv.* **—un′re·spon′sive·ness** *n.*

un·rest (ŭn-rĕst′, ŭn′rĕst′) *n.* An uneasy or troubled condition: *social unrest.*

un·re·strained (ŭn′rĭ-strānd′) *adj.* **1.** Not controlled or held in check; immoderate: *unrestrained exploitation of natural resources.* **2.** Free of constraint; spontaneous and natural: *an unrestrained laugh.* **—un′re·strain′ed·ly** (-strā′nĭd-lē) *adv.* **—un′re·strain′ed·ness** *n.*

un·re·straint (ŭn′rĭ-strānt′) *n.* Want of or freedom from restraint.

un·rid·dle (ŭn-rĭd′l) *tr.v.* **-dled, -dling, -dles.** To solve or explain (a riddle or mystery). **—un·rid′dler** *n.*

un·ri·fled (ŭn-rī′fəld) *adj.* Having a smooth bore. Use of a gun barrel.

un·rig (ŭn-rĭg′) *tr.v.* **-rigged, -rig·ging, -rigs.** *Nautical.* To strip (a vessel) of rigging.

un·right·eous (ŭn-rī′chəs) *adj.* **1.** Not righteous; wicked. **2.** Not right or fair; unjust. **—un·right′eous·ly** *adv.* **—un·right′eous·ness** *n.*

un·rip (ŭn-rĭp′) *tr.v.* **-ripped, -rip·ping, -rips.** To separate or detach by ripping; rip open.

un·ripe (ŭn-rīp′) *adj.* **-rip·er, -rip·est. 1.** Not ripe or matured; immature. **2.** Not fully ready or prepared. **—un·ripe′ness** *n.*

un·ri·valed or **un·ri·valled** (ŭn-rī′vəld) *adj.* Having no rival or equal; incomparable.

un·roll (ŭn-rōl′) *v.* **-rolled, -roll·ing, -rolls.** *—tr.* **1.** To unwind and open (something rolled up). **2.** To unfold and present to view; reveal. *—intr.* To become unrolled.

un·roof (ŭn-ro͞of′, -ro͝of′) *tr.v.* **-roofed, -roof·ing, -roofs.** To remove the roof or covering of.

un·root (ŭn-ro͞ot′, -ro͝ot′) *tr.v.* **-root·ed, -root·ing, -roots.** To uproot.

un·round (ŭn-round′) *tr.v.* **-round·ed, -round·ing, -rounds.** *Linguistics.* To pronounce (a sound) with the lips in a flattened or neutral position.

un·rove (ŭn-rōv′) *v.* *Nautical.* A past tense of **unreeve.**

un·ro·ven (ŭn-rō′vən) *v.* *Nautical.* A past participle of **unreeve.**

UNRRA *abbr.* United Nations Relief and Rehabilitation Administration.

un·ruf·fled (ŭn-rŭf′əld) *adj.* **1.** Not agitated; calm. See Synonyms at **cool. 2.** Regular and smooth, as the surface of water.

un·ru·ly (ŭn-ro͞o′lē) *adj.* **-li·er, -li·est.** Difficult or impossible to discipline, control, or rule. [Middle English *unreuli* : *un-*, not; see UN–[1] + *reuli,* easy to govern (from *reule,* rule; see RULE).] **—un·ru′li·ness** *n.*

SYNONYMS: *unruly, ungovernable, intractable, refractory, recalcitrant, willful, headstrong, wayward.* These adjectives all mean resistant or marked by resistance to control. *Unruly* implies failure to submit to rule or discipline: *The little boy's parents think he is spirited, but his teacher finds him unruly.* One that is *ungovernable* is not capable of or amenable to being governed or restrained: *an ungovernable temper. Intractable* refers to what is obstinate and difficult to manage or control: *"Fox, as the less proud and intractable of the refractory pair, was preferred"* (Macaulay). *Refractory* implies stubborn resistance to control or authority: *as refractory as a mule.* One that is *recalcitrant* not only resists authority but rebels against it: *The university suspended the most recalcitrant demonstrators. Willful* and *headstrong* describe one obstinately bent on having his or her own way: *Willful people cannot tolerate the slightest frustration of their wishes. His headstrong daughter is destined to learn from her own mistakes.* One who is *wayward* willfully and often perversely departs from what is desired, advised, expected, or required in order to gratify his or her own impulses or inclinations: *"a lively child, who had been spoilt and indulged, and therefore was sometimes wayward"* (Charlotte Brontë).

UNRWA *abbr.* United Nations Relief and Works Agency.

uns. *abbr.* Unsymmetrical.

un·sad·dle (ŭn-săd′l) *v.* **-dled, -dling, -dles.** *—tr.* **1.** To remove a saddle from. **2.** To throw (a rider) from the saddle. Used of a horse. *—intr.* To remove a saddle from a horse.

un·safe (ŭn-sāf′) *adj.* **-saf·er, -saf·est.** Not safe; dangerous.

un·said (ŭn-sĕd′) *v.* Past tense and past participle of **unsay.** **—unsaid** *adj.* Not said, especially not uttered out loud: *Their unsaid objections were almost palpable to the rest of the group.*

un·san·i·tar·y (ŭn-săn′ĭ-tĕr′ē) *adj.* Not sanitary.

un·sat·is·fac·to·ry (ŭn-săt′ĭs-făk′tə-rē) *adj.* Not satisfactory; inadequate. **—un·sat′is·fac·to′ri·ly** *adv.* **—un·sat′is·fac·to′ri·ness** *n.*

un·sat·u·rate (ŭn-săch′ə-rĭt) *n.* An unsaturated compound.

un·sat·u·rat·ed (ŭn-săch′ə-rā′tĭd) *adj.* **1.** Of or relating to a compound, especially of carbon, containing atoms that share more than one valence bond: *unsaturated fats.* **2.** Capable of dissolving more of a solute at a given temperature.

un·sa·vor·y (ŭn-sā′və-rē) *adj.* **1.** Distasteful or disagreeable: *an unsavory task.* **2.** Not savory: *an unsavory meal.* **3.** Morally offensive: *an unsavory scandal.* **—un·sa′vor·i·ly** *adv.* **—un·sa′vor·i·ness** *n.*

un·say (ŭn-sā′) *tr.v.* **-said** (-sĕd′), **-say·ing, -says.** To retract (something said).

un·say·a·ble (ŭn-sā′ə-bəl) *adj.* Not readily spoken or expressed: *unsayable fears.* **—unsayable** *n.* **1.** Something not readily said. **2.** Something unfit to be said.

un·scathed (ŭn-skāthd′) *adj.* Not injured or harmed: *escaped the hurricane unscathed.*

un·schooled (ŭn-sko͞old′) *adj.* **1.** Not educated or instructed; having little or no formal schooling. **2.** Not the result of training; natural: *an artist of unschooled talents.*

un·sci·en·tif·ic (ŭn′sī-ən-tĭf′ĭk) *adj.* **1.** Not adhering to the principles of science. **2.** Not knowledgeable about science or the scientific method. **—un′sci·en·tif′i·cal·ly** *adv.*

un·scram·ble (ŭn-skrăm′bəl) *tr.v.* **-bled, -bling, -bles. 1.** To straighten out or disentangle (a jumble or tangle); resolve. **2.** To restore (a scrambled message) to intelligible form. **—un·scram′bler** *n.*

un·screw (ŭn-skro͞o′) *v.* **-screwed, -screw·ing, -screws.** *—tr.* **1.** To take out the screw or screws from. **2.** To loosen, adjust, or remove by rotating. *—intr.* To become or allow to become unscrewed.

un·script·ed (ŭn-skrĭp′tĭd) *adj.* Not adhering to or in accordance with a script written beforehand: *"his unscripted encounters with the press"* (Eleanor Clift).

un·scru·pu·lous (ŭn-skro͞o′pyə-ləs) *adj.* Devoid of scruples; oblivious to or contemptuous of what is right or honorable. **—un·scru′pu·lous·ly** *adv.* **—un·scru′pu·lous·ness** *n.*

un·seal (ŭn-sēl′) *tr.v.* **-sealed, -seal·ing, -seals.** To break or remove the seal of; open.

un·seam (ŭn-sēm′) *tr.v.* **-seamed, -seam·ing, -seams.** To undo the seams of.

un·search·a·ble (ŭn-sûr′chə-bəl) *adj.* Beyond search or investigation; inscrutable: *the unsearchable ways of the gods.* **—un·search′a·bly** *adv.*

un·sea·son·a·ble (ŭn-sē′zə-nə-bəl) *adj.* **1.** Not suitable to or appropriate for the season. **2.** Not characteristic of the time of year: *unseasonable weather.* **3.** Poorly timed; inopportune. **—un·sea′son·a·ble·ness** *n.* **—un·sea′son·a·bly** *adv.*

un·sea·soned (ŭn-sē′zənd) *adj.* **1.** Lacking experience and the knowledge gained from it; inexperienced. **2. a.** Inadequately aged or seasoned; not ripe or mature: *unseasoned wood.* **b.** Having no added seasoning: *unseasoned meat and carrots.*

un·seat (ŭn-sēt′) *tr.v.* **-seat·ed, -seat·ing, -seats. 1.** To remove from a seat, especially from a saddle. **2.** To dislodge from a location or position, especially to remove from office.

un·seem·ly (ŭn-sēm′lē) *adj.* **-li·er, -li·est. 1.** Not in accord with accepted standards of good taste; grossly improper. See Synonyms at **improper. 2.** Not suited to the circumstances; inappropriate. **—unseemly** *adv.* In an improper or inappropriate manner. **—un·seem′li·ness** *n.*

un·seen (ŭn-sēn′) *adj.* **1.** Not directly evident; invisible. **2.** Recognized or grasped without previous study; understood or done as soon as seen.

un·seg·re·gat·ed (ŭn-sĕg′rĭ-gā′tĭd) *adj.* Not segregated, especially not racially segregated.

un·se·lec·tive (ŭn′sĭ-lĕk′tĭv) *adj.* **1.** Not selective; indiscriminate. **2.** Marked by random selection.

un·self·cons·cious or **un·self-cons·cious** (ŭn′sĕlf-kŏn′shəs) *adj.* Not self-conscious; natural and genuine. **—un′self·cons′cious·ly** *adv.* **—un′self·cons′cious·ness** *n.*

un·sel·fish (ŭn-sĕl′fĭsh) *adj.* Generous or altruistic. **—un·sel′fish·ly** *adv.* **—un·sel′fish·ness** *n.*

un·sell (ŭn-sĕl′) *tr.v.* **-sold** (-sōld′), **-sell·ing, -sells.** To persuade not to believe in the advisability, worth, or truth of something.

un·set (ŭn-sĕt′) *adj.* **1.** Not yet firm or solidified: *unset gelatin; unset cement.* **2.** Not mounted in a setting: *an unset gem.*

un·set·tle (ŭn-sĕt′l) *v.* **-tled, -tling, -tles.** *—tr.* **1.** To displace from a settled condition; disrupt. **2.** To make uneasy; disturb. *—intr.* To become unsettled. **—un·set′tle·ment** *n.* **—un·set′tling·ly** *adv.*

un·set·tled (ŭn-sĕt′ld) *adj.* **1.** Not in a state of order or calmness; disturbed: *these unsettled times.* **2.** Likely to change or vary; variable: *unsettled weather.* **3. a.** Not determined or resolved: *an unsettled issue.* **b.** Uncertain or doubtful: *were still* *unsettled with respect to their future plans.* **4.** Not paid or adjusted; outstanding: *an unsettled bill.* **5.** Not populated; uninhabited: *unsettled territory.* **6.** Not fixed or established: *an unsettled lifestyle.*

un·sex (ŭn-sĕks′) *tr.v.* **-sexed, -sex·ing, -sex·es. 1.** To deprive of sexual capacity or sexual attributes. **2.** To castrate.

un·shack·le (ŭn-shăk′əl) *tr.v.* **-led, -ling, -les.** To free from or as if from shackles.

un·shak·a·ble (ŭn-shā′kə-bəl) *adj.* Incapable of being shaken: *unshakable faith.* **—un·shak′a·bly** *adv.*

un·shaped (ŭn-shāpt′) *adj.* **1.** Not shaped or formed. See Synonyms at **shapeless. 2.** Imperfectly shaped or formed.

un·shap·en (ŭn-shā′pən) *adj.* Unshaped.

un·sheathe (ŭn-shēth′) *tr.v.* **-sheathed, -sheath·ing, -sheathes.** To draw from or as if from a sheath or scabbard.

un·shell (ŭn-shĕl′) *tr.v.* **-shelled, -shell·ing, -shells.** To remove from a shell.

un·shift (ŭn-shĭft′) *intr.v.* **-shift·ed, -shift·ing, -shifts.** To release the shift key on a typewriter or computer keyboard.

un·ship (ŭn-shĭp′) *v.* **-shipped, -ship·ping, -ships.** —*tr. Nautical.* **1.** To unload from a ship; discharge. **2.** To remove (a piece of gear) from its proper place; detach: *unship an oar.* —*intr.* To become or be capable of becoming removed or detached.

un·shod (ŭn-shŏd′) *adj.* Not having or wearing shoes or a shoe: *unshod horses.*

un·sight·ed (ŭn-sī′tĭd) *adj.* Having no sight for aiming. Used of a firearm.

un·sight·ly (ŭn-sīt′lē) *adj.* **-li·er, -li·est.** Unpleasant or offensive to look at; unattractive. See Synonyms at **ugly. —un′sight′li·ness** *n.*

un·skilled (ŭn-skĭld′) *adj.* **1.** Lacking skill or technical training: *unskilled laborers.* **2.** Requiring no training or skill: *unskilled jobs; unskilled labor.* **3.** Exhibiting a lack of skill; inexpert: *an unskilled painting.*

un·skill·ful (ŭn-skĭl′fəl) *adj.* **1.** Unskilled; inexpert. **2.** *Obsolete.* Ignorant. **—un·skill′ful·ly** *adv.* **—un′skill′ful·ness** *n.*

un·sling (ŭn-slĭng′) *tr.v.* **-slung** (-slŭng′), **-sling·ing, -slings. 1.** To remove from a sling or a slung position: *unsling a backpack.* **2.** *Nautical.* To remove the slings of (a yard, for example).

un·snag (ŭn-snăg′) *tr.v.* **-snagged, -snag·ging, -snags.** To free of snags: *"unsnags fine legal problems for the lawyers presenting their cases"* (Savvy).

un·snap (ŭn-snăp′) *tr.v.* **-snapped, -snap·ping, -snaps.** To loosen, unfasten, or free by or as if by undoing snaps.

un·snarl (ŭn-snärl′) *tr.v.* **-snarled, -snarl·ing, -snarls.** To free of snarls; disentangle.

un·so·cia·ble (ŭn-sō′shə-bəl) *adj.* **1.** Not disposed to seek the company of others; reserved. **2.** Not congenial; incompatible. **3.** Not conducive to social exchange: *an unsociable atmosphere.* **—un·so′cia·bil′i·ty, un·so′cia·ble·ness** *n.* **—un-so′cia·bly** *adv.*

un·so·cial (ŭn-sō′shəl) *adj.* Having or showing a lack of desire for the company of others. **—un·so′cial·ly** *adv.*

un·sold (ŭn-sōld′) *v.* Past tense of **unsell.**

un·so·lic·it·ed (ŭn′sə-lĭs′ĭ-tĭd) *adj.* Not looked for or requested: *an unsolicited manuscript; unsolicited opinions.*

un·so·phis·ti·cat·ed (ŭn′sə-fĭs′tĭ-kā′tĭd) *adj.* Not sophisticated. See Synonyms at **naive. —un′so·phis′ti·cat′ed·ly** *adv.* **—un′so·phis′ti·ca′tion** *n.*

un·sought (ŭn-sôt′, ŭn′sôt′) *adj.* Not looked for or requested: *received some unsought advice.*

un·sound (ŭn-sound′) *adj.* **-er, -est. 1.** Not dependably strong or solid. **2.** Not physically or mentally healthy. **3.** Not true or logically valid; fallacious: *an unsound conclusion.* **—un·sound′ly** *adv.* **—un·sound′ness** *n.*

un·spar·ing (ŭn-spâr′ĭng) *adj.* **1.** Unmerciful; severe: *an unsparing superior officer; unsparing criticism.* **2.** Not frugal; generous. **—un·spar′ing·ly** *adv.* **—un·spar′ing·ness** *n.*

un·speak (ŭn-spēk′) *tr.v.* **-spoke** (-spōk′), **-spo·ken** (-spō′kən), **-speak·ing, -speaks.** *Obsolete.* To retract (something spoken); unsay.

un·speak·a·ble (ŭn-spē′kə-bəl) *adj.* **1.** Beyond description; inexpressible: *unspeakable happiness.* **2.** Inexpressibly bad or objectionable: *unspeakable poverty.* **3.** Not to be spoken: *unspeakable thoughts; an unspeakable word.* **—un·speak′a·ble·ness** *n.* **—un·speak′a·bly** *adv.*

SYNONYMS: *unspeakable, indefinable, indescribable, ineffable, inexpressible, unutterable.* The central meaning shared by these adjectives is "defying expression or description": *unspeakable misery; indefinable yearnings; indescribable beauty; ineffable ecstasy; inexpressible anguish; unutterable contempt.*

un·spe·cial·ized (ŭn-spĕsh′ə-līzd′) *adj.* Having no special function; without specialty or specialization.

un·sphere (ŭn-sfîr′) *tr.v.* **-sphered, -spher·ing, -spheres.** To remove from a sphere or position in the heavens.

un·spoke (ŭn-spōk′) *v.* Past tense of **unspeak.**

un·spo·ken (ŭn-spō′kən) *v.* Past participle of **unspeak. —unspoken** *adj.* Not orally articulated: *unspoken fears.*

un·sports·man·like (ŭn-spôrts′mən-līk′, -spōrts′-) *adj.* Not displaying the qualities or behavior befitting a good sport.

un·spot·ted (ŭn-spŏt′ĭd) *adj.* **1.** Having no spots. **2.** Morally upright. **—un·spot′ted·ness** *n.*

un·sta·ble (ŭn-stā′bəl) *adj.* **-bler, -blest. 1.a.** Tending strongly to change: *unstable weather.* **b.** Not constant; fluctuating: *unstable vital signs.* **2.a.** Fickle. **b.** Lacking control of one's emotions; characterized by unpredictable behavior. **3.** Not firmly placed; unsteady: *an unstable ladder.* **4.** *Chemistry.* **a.** Decomposing readily. **b.** Highly or violently reactive. **5.** *Physics.* **a.** Decaying with relatively short lifetime. Used of subatomic particles. **b.** Radioactive. **—un·sta′ble·ness** *n.* **—un·sta′bly** *adv.*

un·stead·y (ŭn-stĕd′ē) *adj.* **-i·er, -i·est. 1.** Not firm, solid, or securely in place; unstable. **2.** Marked by fluctuation or changeableness; inconstant: *an unsteady market.* **3.** Not even or regular; wavering: *an unsteady voice.* **—unsteady** *tr.v.* **-ied** (-ēd), **-y·ing, -ies** (-ēz). To cause to become unsteady. **—un·stead′i·ly** *adv.* **—un·stead′i·ness** *n.*

un·steel (ŭn-stēl′) *tr.v.* **-steeled, -steel·ing, -steels.** To make less obdurate or hardhearted; disarm.

un·step (ŭn-stĕp′) *tr.v.* **-stepped, -step·ping, -steps.** *Nautical.* To remove (a mast) from a step.

un·stick (ŭn-stĭk′) *tr.v.* **-stuck** (-stŭk′), **-stick·ing, -sticks.** To free from a condition of adhesion: *unstick the window.*

un·stint·ing (ŭn-stĭn′tĭng) *adj.* Bestowed liberally: *unstinting approval.* **—un·stint′ing·ly** *adv.*

un·stop (ŭn-stŏp′) *tr.v.* **-stopped, -stop·ping, -stops. 1.** To remove a stopper from. **2.** To remove an obstruction from; open. **3.** *Music.* To pull out the stops of (a pipe organ).

un·stop·pa·ble (ŭn-stŏp′ə-bəl) *adj.* Difficult or impossible to stop: *"This movement toward freedom is natural and unstoppable and good"* (Pauline Kael). **—un·stop′pa·bly** *adv.*

un·stopped (ŭn-stŏpt′) *adj.* **1.** Not stopped: *an era of unstopped progress in medicine.* **2.** *Linguistics.* Capable of being prolonged, as the consonants *z* and *l.*

un·strap (ŭn-străp′) *tr.v.* **-strapped, -strap·ping, -straps.** To loosen or remove a strap on or from.

un·strat·i·fied (ŭn-străt′ə-fīd′) *adj.* Lacking definite layers: *unstratified rock.*

un·stressed (ŭn-strĕst′) *adj.* **1.** *Linguistics.* Not stressed or accented: *an unstressed syllable in a word.* **2.** Not exposed or subjected to stress.

un·stri·at·ed (ŭn-strī′ā′tĭd) *adj.* Lacking striations.

un·string (ŭn-strĭng′) *tr.v.* **-strung** (-strŭng′), **-string·ing, -strings. 1.** To remove from a string. **2.** To unfasten or loosen the strings of. **3.** To deprive of composure or emotional stability; unnerve.

un·struc·tured (ŭn-strŭk′chərd) *adj.* **1.** Lacking a definite structure or organization; not formally organized or systematized. **2.** Not regulated or regimented: *an unstructured environment.* **3.** *Psychology.* Having no intrinsic or objective meaning; meaningful by subjective interpretation only: *unstructured inkblot tests.*

un·strung (ŭn-strŭng′) *v.* Past tense and past participle of **unstring. —unstrung** *adj.* **1.** Having a string or strings loosened or removed. **2.** Emotionally upset.

un·stuck (ŭn-stŭk′) *v.* Past tense and past participle of **unstick. —unstuck** *adj.* **1.** Freed from a condition of adhesion. **2.a.** Thrown into a state of disorder or confusion; undone. **b.** *Slang.* Emotionally upset or unbalanced.

un·stud·ied (ŭn-stŭd′ēd) *adj.* **1.** Not contrived for effect; natural: *unstudied grace.* **2.** Not gained by study or instruction: *unstudied talent.*

un·sub·stan·tial (ŭn′səb-stăn′shəl) *adj.* **1.** Lacking material substance; insubstantial. **2.** Lacking firmness or strength; flimsy. **3.** Lacking basis in fact. **—un′sub·stan′ti·al′i·ty** (-shē-ăl′ĭ-tē) *n.* **—un′sub·stan′tial·ly** *adv.*

un·suc·cess (ŭn′sək-sĕs′) *n.* Failure to achieve a desired end.

un·suc·cess·ful (ŭn′sək-sĕs′fəl) *adj.* **1.** Having an unfavorable outcome: *an unsuccessful business venture.* **2.** Failing to attain something desired or intended: *an unsuccessful entrepreneur.* **—un′suc·cess′ful·ly** *adv.* **—un′suc·cess′ful·ness** *n.*

un·suit·a·ble (ŭn-so͞o′tə-bəl) *adj.* Not appropriate: *unsuitable attire.* **—un·suit′a·bil′i·ty, un·suit′a·ble·ness** *n.* **—un·suit′a·bly** *adv.*

un·sung (ŭn-sŭng′) *adj.* **1.** Not honored or praised; uncelebrated: *a war won by unsung heroes.* **2.** *Music.* Not sung.

un·sus·cep·ti·ble (ŭn′sə-sĕp′tə-bəl) *adj.* Not susceptible to or admitting of: *unsusceptible to illegal entry.*

un·sus·pect·ed (ŭn′sə-spĕk′tĭd) *adj.* **1.** Not under suspicion. **2.** Not known to exist: *an unsuspected disease.* **—un′sus·pect′ed·ly** *adv.*

un·sus·pect·ing (ŭn′sə-spĕk′tĭng) *adj.* Not suspicious; trusting. **—un′sus·pect′ing·ly** *adv.*

un·swathe (ŭn-swŏth′, -swôth′, -swāth′) *tr.v.* **-swathed, -swath·ing, -swathes.** To remove the swathes or bindings from.

un·swear (ŭn-swâr′) *v.* **-swore** (-swôr′, -swōr′), **-sworn** (-swôrn′, -swōrn′), **-swear·ing, -swears.** *Archaic.* —*tr.* To retract (an oath), often by swearing another oath. —*intr.* To recant or retract something sworn.

un·swerv·ing (ŭn-swûr′vĭng) *adj.* **1.** Not veering or turning aside: *"a path . . . so straight and unswerving"* (Mary Wilkins Freeman). **2.** Constant, steady: *unswerving allegiance; unswerving devotion.* **—un·swerv′ing·ly** *adv.*

ă pat	oi boy
ā pay	ou out
âr care	o͝o took
ä father	o͞o boot
ĕ pet	ŭ cut
ē be	ûr urge
ĭ pit	th thin
ī pie	*th* this
îr pier	hw which
ŏ pot	zh vision
ō toe	ə about, item
ô paw	♦ regionalism

Stress marks: **′** (primary); ′ (secondary), as in **dictionary** (dĭk′shə-nĕr′ē)

un·swore (ŭn-swôr′, -swōr′) *v.* Past tense of **unswear.**

un·sworn (ŭn-swôrn′, -swōrn′) *v.* Past participle of **unswear.** —**unsworn** *adj.* Not having been asserted as true under oath: *unsworn statements by witnesses.*

un·sym·met·ri·cal (ŭn′sĭ-mĕt′rĭ-kəl) *adj. Abbr.* **uns.** Asymmetrical. —**un′sym·met′ri·cal·ly** *adv.*

un·tan·gle (ŭn-tăng′gəl) *tr.v.* **-gled, -gling, -gles. 1.** To free from a tangle; disentangle. See Synonyms at **extricate. 2.** To straighten out (something puzzling or complicated); resolve.

un·tapped (ŭn-tăpt′) *adj.* **1.** Not having been tapped: *an untapped cask of wine.* **2.** Not utilized: *untapped resources.*

un·taught (ŭn-tôt′) *adj.* **1.** Not instructed; ignorant. See Synonyms at **ignorant. 2.** Not acquired by instruction; natural.

un·teach (ŭn-tēch′) *tr.v.* **-taught** (-tôt′), **-teach·ing, -teach·es. 1.** To cause to forget or unlearn something. **2.** To teach the opposite or contrary of (something previously taught).

un·ten·a·ble (ŭn-tĕn′ə-bəl) *adj.* **1.** Being such that defense or maintenance is impossible: *an untenable position.* **2.** Being such that occupation or habitation is impossible: *untenable quarters.* —**un·ten′a·bil′i·ty, un·ten′a·ble·ness** *n.* —**un·ten′a·bly** *adv.*

Un·ter·mey·er (ŭn′tər-mī′ər), **Louis.** 1885–1977. American writer and editor of poetry anthologies, including *Modern American Poetry* (first published 1919).

un·thank·ful (ŭn-thăngk′fəl) *adj.* **1.** Not thankful; ungrateful. **2.** Not drawing thanks; unwelcome. —**un·thank′ful·ly** *adv.* —**un·thank′ful·ness** *n.*

un·think (ŭn-thĭngk′) *tr.v.* **-thought** (-thôt′), **-think·ing, -thinks.** To dismiss from the mind; disregard.

un·think·a·ble (ŭn-thĭng′kə-bəl) *adj.* **1.** Impossible to imagine; inconceivable: *an unthinkable amount of money.* **2.** Contrary to what is plausible or probable: *That this project would achieve ultimate success was unthinkable at the time.* **3.** Not to be thought of or considered; out of the question: *Raising taxes was politically unthinkable.* —**un·think′a·bil′i·ty, un·think′a·ble·ness** *n.* —**un·think′a·bly** *adv.*

un·think·ing (ŭn′thĭng′kĭng) *adj.* **1.** Not taking due thought; thoughtless or heedless: *proceeded, unthinking, into the trap.* **2.** Exhibiting a lack of thought: *unthinking bravado.* **3.** Incapable of the power of thought. —**un·think′ing·ly** *adv.* —**un·think′ing·ness** *n.*

un·thought (ŭn-thôt′) *v.* Past tense and past participle of **unthink.**

un·thread (ŭn-thrĕd′) *tr.v.* **-thread·ed, -thread·ing, -threads. 1.** To draw out the thread from. **2.** To find one's way out of (a labyrinth, for example).

un·throne (ŭn-thrōn′) *tr.v.* **-throned, -thron·ing, -thrones.** To depose from or as if from a throne.

un·ti·dy (ŭn-tī′dē) *adj.* **-di·er, -di·est. 1.** Not neat and tidy; sloppy. **2.** Disorderly and unorganized: *untidy financial affairs.* —**un·ti′di·ly** *adv.* —**un·ti′di·ness** *n.*

un·tie (ŭn-tī′) *v.* **-tied, -ty·ing** (-tī′ĭng), **-ties.** —*tr.* **1.** To undo or loosen (a knot or something knotted). **2.** To free from something that binds or restrains: *untie a horse from a tree.* **3.** To straighten out (difficulties, for example); resolve. —*intr.* To become untied.

un·til (ŭn-tĭl′) *prep.* **1.** Up to the time of: *We danced until dawn.* **2.** Before (a specified time): *She can't leave until Friday.* **3.** *Scots.* Unto; to. —**until** *conj.* **1.** Up to the time that: *We walked until it got dark.* **2.** Before: *You cannot leave until your work is finished.* **3.** To the point or extent that: *I talked until I was hoarse.* See Usage Note at **till**[2]. [Middle English : *un-*, up to (from Old Norse *und;* see **ant-** in Appendix) + *til,* till; see TILL[2].]

un·time·ly (ŭn-tīm′lē) *adj.* **-li·er, -li·est. 1.** Occurring or done at an inappropriate time; inopportune. **2.** Occurring too soon; premature: *an untimely death.* —**untimely** *adv.* **1.** Inopportunely. **2.** Prematurely. —**un·time′li·ness** *n.*

un·tir·ing (ŭn-tīr′ĭng) *adj.* **1.** Not tiring; tireless. **2.** Not ceasing despite fatigue or frustration; indefatigable: *untiring efforts.* See Synonyms at **tireless.** —**un·tir′ing·ly** *adv.*

un·ti·tled (ŭn-tīt′ld) *adj.* **1.** Not named: *an untitled story.* **2.** Not holding a title, as of nobility. **3.** Having no right or claim.

un·to (ŭn′to͞o) *prep.* **1.** To. **2.** Until: *a fast unto death.* **3.** By: *a place unto itself, quite unlike its surroundings.* [Middle English : *un-*, up to; see UNTIL + *to,* to; see TO.]

un·told (ŭn-tōld′) *adj.* **1.** Not told or revealed: *untold secrets.* **2.** Beyond description or enumeration: *untold suffering.*

un·touch·a·ble (ŭn-tŭch′ə-bəl) *adj.* **1.** Not to be touched. **2.** Out of reach; unobtainable. **3.** Being beyond the reach of criticism, impeachment, or attack. **4.** Loathsome or unpleasant to the touch. —**untouchable** also **Untouchable** *n. Hinduism.* **1.** The class, comprising numerous subclasses, that is excluded from and considered ritually unclean and defiling by the four Hindu classes. **2.** A member of this class. —**un·touch′a·bil′i·ty** *n.* —**un·touch′a·bly** *adv.*

un·to·ward (ŭn-tôrd′, -tōrd′) *adj.* **1.** Not favorable; unpropitious. **2.** Troublesome; adverse: *an untoward incident.* **3.** Hard to control; unruly. **4.** Improper; unseemly. **5.** *Archaic.* Awkward. —**un·to·ward′ly** *adv.* —**un·to·ward′ness** *n.*

un·tram·meled (ŭn-trăm′əld) *adj.* Not limited or restricted; unrestrained.

un·trav·eled (ŭn-trăv′əld) *adj.* **1.** Not traveled on: *untraveled back roads.* **2.a.** Not having traveled. **b.** Provincial; narrow-minded.

un·tread (ŭn-trĕd′) *tr.v.* **-trod** (-trŏd′), **-trod·den** (-trŏd′n) or **-trod, -tread·ing, -treads.** *Archaic.* To go back over (one's course); retrace.

un·tried (ŭn-trīd′) *adj.* **1.** Not attempted, tested, or proved. **2.** *Law.* Not tried in court.

un·trod (ŭn-trŏd′) *v.* Past tense and a past participle of **untread.**

un·trod·den (ŭn-trŏd′n) *v.* A past participle of **untread.**

un·trou·bled (ŭn-trŭb′əld) *adj.* **1.** Not disturbed or distracted. **2.** Without trouble or disturbance; calm: *untroubled sleep.* —**un·trou′bled·ness** *n.*

un·true (ŭn-tro͞o′) *adj.* **-tru·er, -tru·est. 1.** Contrary to fact; false. **2.** Deviating from a standard; not straight, even, level, or exact. **3.** Disloyal; unfaithful. —**un·tru′ly** *adv.*

un·truss (ŭn-trŭs′) *v.* **-trussed, -truss·ing, -truss·es.** *Archaic.* —*tr.* **1.** To unfasten; undo. **2.** To undress. —*intr.* To remove one's clothes, especially one's breeches.

un·truth (ŭn-tro͞oth′) *n.* **1.** Something untrue; a lie. **2.** The condition of being false. **3.** *Archaic.* Unfaithfulness.

un·truth·ful (ŭn-tro͞oth′fəl) *adj.* **1.** Contrary to truth. **2.** Given to falsehood; mendacious. See Synonyms at **dishonest.** —**un·truth′ful·ly** *adv.* —**un·truth′ful·ness** *n.*

un·tu·tored (ŭn-to͞o′tərd, -tyo͞o′-) *adj.* **1.** Having had no formal education or instruction. See Synonyms at **ignorant. 2.** Unsophisticated; unrefined.

un·twine (ŭn-twīn′) *v.* **-twined, -twin·ing, -twines.** —*tr.* **1.** To separate the twisted strands of: *untwine a rope.* **2.** To disentangle. —*intr.* To become untwined.

un·twist (ŭn-twĭst′) *v.* **-twist·ed, -twist·ing, -twists.** —*tr.* To loosen or separate (something twisted) by turning in the opposite direction; unwind. —*intr.* To become untwisted.

un·ty·ing (ŭn-tī′ĭng) *v.* Present participle of **untie.**

un·used (ŭn-yo͞ozd′, ŭn-yo͞ost′) *adj.* **1.** Not in use or put to use. **2.** Never having been used. **3.** Not accustomed: *unused to city traffic.*

un·u·su·al (ŭn-yo͞o′zho͞o-əl) *adj.* Not usual, common, or ordinary. —**un·u′su·al·ly** *adv.* —**un·u′su·al·ness** *n.*

un·ut·ter·a·ble (ŭn-ŭt′ər-ə-bəl) *adj.* **1.** That cannot or must not be uttered or expressed: *"I burned in the unutterable beauty of being alive"* (John Peale Bishop). See Synonyms at **unspeakable. 2.** Being such that pronunciation is impossible: *unutterable consonant clusters.* —**un·ut′ter·a·ble·ness** *n.* —**un·ut′ter·a·bly** *adv.*

un·val·ued (ŭn-văl′yo͞od) *adj.* **1.** Not prized or valued; unappreciated. **2.** Not appraised or assayed: *an unvalued gemstone.* **3.** *Obsolete.* Inestimable; invaluable.

un·var·nished (ŭn′vär′nĭsht) *adj.* **1.** Not coated with varnish: *unvarnished floors.* **2.** Stated or otherwise presented without any effort to soften or disguise; plain: *the unvarnished truth.*

un·veil (ŭn-vāl′) *v.* **-veiled, -veil·ing, -veils.** —*tr.* **1.** To remove a veil or covering from. **2.** To disclose; reveal. —*intr.* **1.** To take off one's veil. **2.** To reveal oneself.

un·voice (ŭn-vois′) *tr.v.* **-voiced, -voic·ing, -voic·es.** *Linguistics.* To devoice.

un·voiced (ŭn-voist′) *adj.* **1.** Not expressed or uttered: *unvoiced fears.* **2.** *Linguistics.* Voiceless: *unvoiced consonants.*

un·war·rant·a·ble (ŭn-wôr′ən-tə-bəl, -wŏr′-) *adj.* Not justifiable; inexcusable: *unwarrantable criticism.* —**un′war′rant·a·bly** *adv.*

un·war·rant·ed (ŭn-wôr′ən-tĭd, -wŏr′-) *adj.* Having no justification; groundless: *unwarranted interference.* See Synonyms at **baseless.**

un·war·y (ŭn-wâr′ē) *adj.* **-i·er, -i·est.** Not alert to danger or deception. —**un·war′i·ly** *adv.* —**un·war′i·ness** *n.*

un·washed (ŭn-wŏsht′, -wôsht′) *adj.* **1.** Not washed; unclean. **2.** Plebeian: *the unwashed masses.*

un·wea·ried (ŭn-wîr′ēd) *adj.* **1.** Not tired. **2.** Never wearying. See Synonyms at **tireless.** —**un·wea′ried·ly** *adv.*

un·wed (ŭn-wĕd′) *adj.* Not married.

un·well (ŭn-wĕl′) *adj.* **1.** Being in poor health; sick. **2.** Undergoing a menstrual cycle.

un·wept (ŭn-wĕpt′) *adj.* **1.** Not mourned or wept for: *the unwept dead.* **2.** Not yet shed: *unwept tears.*

un·whole·some (ŭn-hōl′səm) *adj.* **1.** Injurious to physical, mental, or moral health; unhealthy. **2.** Suggestive of disease or degeneracy: *an unwholesome pallor.* **3.** Offensive or loathsome. —**un·whole′some·ly** *adv.* —**un·whole′some·ness** *n.*

un·wield·y (ŭn-wēl′dē) *adj.* **-i·er, -i·est. 1.** Difficult to carry or manage because of bulk or shape: *an unwieldy parcel.* **2.** Clumsy; ungainly. —**un·wield′i·ly** *adv.* —**un·wield′i·ness** *n.*

un·willed (ŭn-wĭld′) *adj.* Involuntary; spontaneous.

un·will·ing (ŭn-wĭl′ĭng) *adj.* **1.** Not willing; hesitant or loath: *unwilling to face facts.* **2.** Done, given, or said reluctantly: *unwilling consent.* —**un·will′ing·ly** *adv.* —**un·will′ing·ness** *n.*

un·wind (ŭn-wīnd′) *v.* **-wound** (-wound′), **-wind·ing, -winds.** —*tr.* **1.** To reverse the winding or twisting of: *unwind a ball of yarn.* **2.** To separate the tangled parts of; disentangle. **3.** To free (someone) of nervous tension or pent-up energy. —*intr.* **1.**

To become unwound. **2.** To become free of nervous tension; relax: *liked to unwind with a cocktail before dinner.*

un·wis·dom (ŭn-wĭz′dəm) *n.* Lack of wisdom; imprudence or recklessness.

un·wise (ŭn-wīz′) *adj.* **-wis·er, -wis·est.** Lacking or exhibiting a lack of wisdom; foolish or imprudent: *an unwise decision.* **—un·wise′ly** *adv.*

un·wish (ŭn-wĭsh′) *tr.v.* **-wished, -wish·ing, -wish·es. 1.** To retract a wish for. **2.** *Obsolete.* To wish out of existence.

un·wit·ting (ŭn-wĭt′ĭng) *adj.* **1.** Not knowing; unaware: *an unwitting subject in an experiment.* **2.** Not intended; unintentional: *an unwitting admission of guilt.* [Middle English : *un-*, not; see UN–[1] + *witting,* present participle of *witten,* to know (from Old English *witan;* see **weid-** in Appendix).] **—un·wit′ting·ly** *adv.*

un·wont·ed (ŭn-wôn′tĭd, -wōn′-, -wŭn′-) *adj.* **1.** Not habitual or ordinary; unusual: *"Her unwonted breach of delicacy . . . perplexed him"* (George Meredith). **2.** Not accustomed; unused. **—un·wont′ed·ly** *adv.* **—un·wont′ed·ness** *n.*

un·work·a·ble (ŭn-wûr′kə-bəl) *adj.* Not workable, especially not capable of being put into practice successfully; not practicable: *an unworkable scheme.* **—un·work′a·bil′i·ty, un·work′a·ble·ness** *n.* **—un·work′a·bly** *adv.*

un·world·ly (ŭn-wûrld′lē) *adj.* **-li·er, -li·est. 1.** Not of this world; spiritual. **2.** Concerned with matters of the spirit or soul. **3.** Not wise to the ways of the world; naive: *"This now is the story of an unworldly young scientist"* (John Simon). **—un·world′li·ness** *n.*

un·worn (ŭn-wôrn′, -wōrn′) *adj.* **1.** Not worn out or worn away. **2.** Not worn before; new. **3.** Not stale or overused; fresh.

un·wor·thy (ŭn-wûr′thē) *adj.* **-thi·er, -thi·est. 1.a.** Insufficient in worth; undeserving: *a bad plan unworthy of our consideration.* **b.** Lacking value or merit; worthless. **2.** Not suiting or befitting: *"The acquaintances she had already formed were unworthy of her"* (Jane Austen). **3.** Vile; despicable. **—un·wor′thi·ly** *adv.* **—un·wor′thi·ness** *n.*

un·wound (ŭn-wound′) *v.* Past tense and past participle of **unwind.**

un·wrap (ŭn-răp′) *tr. & intr.v.* **-wrapped, -wrap·ping, -wraps.** To remove the wrapping or wrappings from or become unwrapped.

un·writ·ten (ŭn-rĭt′n) *adj.* **1.** Not written or recorded: *an unwritten agreement between friends.* **2.** Having authority based on custom, tradition, or usage rather than documentation: *an unwritten law.* **3.** Not written on; blank.

un·yield·ing (ŭn-yēl′dĭng) *adj.* **1.** Not bending; inflexible. **2.** Not giving way to pressure or persuasion; obdurate. **—un·yield′ing·ly** *adv.* **—un·yield′ing·ness** *n.*

un·yoke (ŭn-yōk′) *v.* **-yoked, -yok·ing, -yokes.** *—tr.* **1.** To release from or as if from a yoke. **2.** To separate; disjoin. *—intr.* **1.** To remove a yoke. **2.** *Archaic.* To stop working.

un·zip (ŭn-zĭp′) *tr. & intr.v.* **-zipped, -zip·ping, -zips.** To open or unfasten by means of a zipper or become unzipped.

up (ŭp) *adv.* **1.a.** In or to a higher position: *looking up.* **b.** In a direction opposite to the center of the earth or a comparable gravitational center: *up from the lunar surface.* **2.** In or to an upright position: *sat up in bed.* **3.a.** Above a surface: *coming up for air.* **b.** So as to detach or unearth: *pulling up weeds.* **c.** Above the horizon: *as the sun came up.* **4.** Into view or existence: *draw up a will.* **5.** Into consideration: *take up a new topic.* **6.** In or toward a position conventionally regarded as higher, as on a scale, chart, or map: *temperatures heading up; up in Canada.* **7.** To or at a higher price: *stocks that are going up.* **8.** So as to advance, increase, or improve: *Our spirits went up.* **9.** With or to a greater intensity, pitch, or volume: *turn the sound up.* **10.** Into a state of excitement or turbulence: *stir up; rouse up.* **11.** Completely; entirely: *drank it up in a gulp; fastened up the coat.* **12.** Used as an intensifier of the action of a verb: *typed up a list.* **13.** So as to approach; near: *came up and kissed me.* **14.** To a stop: *pulled up in front of the station.* **15.** Each; apiece: *The score was tied at 11 up.* **16.** Apart; into pieces: *tore it up.* **17.** *Nautical.* To windward. **—up** *adj.* **1.** Being above a former position or level; higher: *My grades are up. The pressure is up.* **2.a.** Out of bed: *was up by seven.* **b.** Standing; erect. **c.** Facing upward: *two cards up, one down; the up side of a tossed coin.* **3.** Raised; lifted: *a switch in the up position.* **4.** Moving or directed upward: *an up elevator.* **5.a.** Marked by increased excitement or agitation; aroused: *Our fighting spirit was up.* **b.** *Informal.* Cheerful; optimistic; upbeat. **c.** *Slang.* Happily excited; euphoric: *After receiving the award, the performer was really up.* **6.** *Informal.* Taking place; going on: *wondered what was up back home.* **7.** Being considered; under study: *a contract that is up for renewal.* **8.** Running as a candidate. **9.** On trial; charged: *The defendant is up for manslaughter.* **10.** Having been finished; over: *Your time is up.* **11.** *Informal.* **a.** Prepared; ready: *had to be up for the game.* **b.** Well informed; abreast: *not up on sports.* **12.** Functioning or capable of functioning normally; operational: *Their computers are now up.* **13.** *Sports.* Being ahead of one's opponent: *up two strokes in golf.* **14.** *Baseball.* At bat. **15.** As a bet; at stake. **16.** *Nautical.* Bound; headed: *a freighter up for Panama.* **—up** *prep.* **1.** From a lower to or toward a higher point on: *up the hill.* **2.** Toward or at a point farther along: *two miles up the road.* **3.** In a direction toward the source of: *up the Mississippi.* **4.** *Nautical.* Against: *up the wind.* **—up** *n.* **1.** An upward slope; a rise. **2.** An upward movement or trend. **3.** *Slang.* A feeling of excitement or euphoria. **—up** *v.* **upped, up·ping, ups.** *—tr.* **1.** To increase: *upped their fees; upping our output.* **2.** To raise to a higher level, especially to promote to a higher position. *—intr.* **1.** To get up; rise. **2.** *Informal.* To act suddenly or unexpectedly: *"She upped and perjured her immortal soul"* (Margery Allingham). **—*idioms.* on the up-and-up** (or **up and up**). *Informal.* Open and honest. **up against.** Confronted with; facing: *up against a strong opponent.* **up to. 1.** Occupied with, especially devising or scheming: *a prowler up to no good.* **2.** Able to do or deal with: *didn't feel up to a long drive.* **3.** Dependent on: *The success of this project is up to us.* **4.a.** As long as: *allowed up to two hours to finish the test.* **b.** As many as: *seed that yields up to 300 bushels per acre.* [Middle English *up,* upward, and *uppe,* on high, both from Old English. See **upo** in Appendix.]

UP *abbr.* Underproof.

up. *abbr.* Upper.

up– *pref.* **1.** Up; upward: *upheave.* **2.** Upper: *upland.* [Middle English, from Old English *ūp-, upp-.* See **upo** in Appendix.]

up-and-com·ing (ŭp′ən-kŭm′ĭng) *adj.* Showing signs of advancement and ambitious development: *an up-and-coming executive; an up-and-coming neighborhood.* **—up′-and-com′er** *n.*

up-and-down (ŭp′ən-doun′) *adj.* **1.** Characterized by or exhibiting an alternating upward and downward movement. **2.** Variable; changeable. **3.** Vertical.

U·pan·i·shad (o͞o-păn′ə-shăd′, o͞o-pä′nĭ-shäd′) *n.* Any of a group of philosophical treatises contributing to the theology of ancient Hinduism, elaborating on the earlier Vedas. [Sanskrit *upaniṣad* : *upa,* under, near; see **upo** in Appendix + *ni-,* down + *sīdati, sad-,* he sits; see **sed-** in Appendix.] **—U·pan′i·shad′ic** *adj.*

u·pas (yo͞o′pəs) *n.* **1.** A deciduous tree *(Antiaris toxicaria)* of tropical Africa and Asia that yields a latex used as an arrow poison. **2.** The poison obtained from this tree or from similar trees. [Malay *(pōhun) upas,* poison (tree), of Javanese origin.]

up·beat (ŭp′bēt′) *n. Music.* An unaccented beat, especially the last beat of a measure. **—upbeat** *adj. Informal.* **1.** Optimistic: *an upbeat business forecast.* **2.** Happy; cheerful.

up-bow (ŭp′bō′) *n. Music.* A stroke performed on a stringed instrument in which the bow is moved across the strings from its tip to its heel.

up·braid (ŭp-brād′) *tr.v.* **-braid·ed, -braid·ing, -braids.** To reprove sharply; reproach. See Synonyms at **scold.** [Middle English *upbreiden,* from Old English *ūpbrēdan,* to bring forward as a ground for censure : *ūp-,* up- + *bregdan,* to turn, lay hold of.] **—up·braid′er** *n.* **—up·braid′ing·ly** *adv.*

up·bring·ing (ŭp′brĭng′ĭng) *n.* The rearing and training received during childhood.

up·build (ŭp-bĭld′) *tr.v.* **-built** (-bĭlt′), **-build·ing, -builds.** To build up; increase or enlarge: *sand dunes that were upbuilt by the wind.* **—up·build′er** *n.*

UPC *abbr.* Universal Product Code.

up·cast (ŭp′kăst′) *adj.* Directed or thrown upward: *upcast volcanic ash.* **—upcast** *n.* **1.** Something cast upward. **2.** A ventilating shaft, as in a mine.

up·chuck (ŭp′chŭk′) *tr. & intr.v.* **-chucked, -chuck·ing, -chucks.** *Slang.* To vomit or experience vomiting.

up-close (ŭp′klōs′) *adj. Slang.* **1.** Being at very close range: *"his up-close coverage of the . . . hostage drama"* (Time). **2.** Exhibiting or providing great detail and depth of coverage because of close scrutiny: *"up-close glimpses of the big money, big deals, and big decisions of America's entrepreneurial giants"* (Harvard Business Review).

up·com·ing (ŭp′kŭm′ĭng) *adj.* Occurring soon; forthcoming.

up·coun·try (ŭp′kŭn′trē) *n.* An inland or upland region of a country. **—upcountry** *adj.* Of, located in, or coming from the upcountry. **—upcountry** *(also* ŭp-kŭn′trē) *adv.* In, to, or toward the upcountry.

up·date (ŭp-dāt′) *tr.v.* **-dat·ed, -dat·ing, -dates.** To bring up to date: *update a textbook; update the files.* **—update** (ŭp′dāt′) *n.* **1.** Information that updates. **2.** The act or an instance of bringing up to date.

Up·dike (ŭp′dīk′), **John Hoyer.** Born 1932. American writer particularly known for his tragicomic novels, such as *Rabbit, Run* (1960) and *Rabbit at Rest* (1990).

John Updike
Photographed in 1988

up·draft (ŭp′drăft′, -dräft′) *n.* An upward current of air.

up·end (ŭp-ĕnd′) *v.* **-end·ed, -end·ing, -ends.** *—tr.* **1.** To stand, set, or turn on one end: *upend an oblong box.* **2.** To overturn or overthrow. *—intr.* To be upended.

up-front or **up·front** (ŭp′frŭnt′) *adj. Informal.* **1.** Straightforward; frank: *"She is very up-front"* (Ronald Ferguson). **2.** Paid or due in advance: *up-front cash.* **—up′front′** *adv.* **—up′-front′ness** *n.*

up·grade (ŭp′grād′) *v.* **-grad·ed, -grad·ing, -grades.** *—tr.* **1.** To raise to a higher grade or standard: *upgrading their military defenses.* **2.** To improve the quality of (livestock) by selective breeding for desired characteristics. *—intr.* To exchange a possession for one of greater value or quality; trade up. **—upgrade** *n.* **1.** The act or instance of upgrading. **2.** Something that upgrades. **3.** An upward incline. **—upgrade** *adv. & adj.* Uphill. **—*idiom.* on the upgrade.** Improving or progressing.

up·growth (ŭp′grōth′) *n.* **1.** The process of growing upward. **2.** Upward development.

ă pat	oi boy
ā pay	ou out
âr care	o͝o took
ä father	o͞o boot
ĕ pet	ŭ cut
ē be	ûr urge
ĭ pit	th thin
ī pie	*th* this
îr pier	hw which
ŏ pot	zh vision
ō toe	ə about, item
ô paw	♦ regionalism

Stress marks: ′ (primary); ′ (secondary), as in **dictionary** (dĭk′shə-nĕr′ē)

up·heav·al (ŭp-hē′vəl) *n.* **1.a.** The process of being heaved upward. **b.** An instance of being so heaved. **2.** A sudden, violent disruption or upset: *"the psychic upheaval caused by war"* (Wallace Fowlie). **3.** *Geology.* A raising of a part of the earth's crust.

up·heave (ŭp-hēv′) *v.* **-heaved, -heav·ing, -heaves.** —*tr.* To lift forcefully from beneath; heave upward. —*intr.* To be lifted or thrust upward.

up·held (ŭp-hĕld′) *v.* Past tense and past participle of **uphold.**

up·hill (ŭp′hĭl′) *adj.* **1.** Located on high or higher ground: *an uphill mine entrance.* **2.** Going up a hill or slope: *an uphill climb.* **3.** Marked by difficulty or strong resistance; laborious: *an uphill election campaign against a popular incumbent.* —**uphill** (ŭp′hĭl′) *adv.* **1.** To or toward higher ground; up a slope. **2.** Against adversity; with difficulty: *struggling uphill to make ends meet.* —**uphill** *n.* An upward slope or incline.

up·hold (ŭp-hōld′) *tr.v.* **-held** (-hĕld′), **-hold·ing, -holds. 1.** To hold aloft; raise: *upheld the banner proudly.* **2.** To prevent from falling or sinking; support. **3.** To maintain or affirm against opposition. See Synonyms at **support.** —**up·hold′er** *n.*

up·hol·ster (ŭp-hōl′stər, ə-pōl′-) *tr.v.* **-stered, -ster·ing, -sters.** To supply (furniture) with stuffing, springs, cushions, and covering fabric. [Back-formation from UPHOLSTERER.]

up·hol·ster·er (ŭp-hōl′stər-ər, ə-pōl′-) *n.* One that upholsters furniture. [From obsolete *upholster,* from Middle English *upholdester* : *upholden,* to repair (*up,* up; see UP + *holden,* to hold; see HOLD[1]) + *-ster,* -ster.]

up·hol·ster·y (ŭp-hōl′stə-rē, -strē, ə-pōl′-) *n., pl.* **-ies. 1.** Fabric, stuffing, and other materials used in upholstering. **2.** The craft, trade, or business of upholstering.

UPI or **U.P.I.** *abbr.* United Press International.

Up·john (ŭp′jŏn′), **Richard.** 1802–1878. British-born American architect who was a leader of the Gothic revival.

up·keep (ŭp′kēp′) *n.* **1.** Maintenance in proper operation, condition, and repair. **2.** The cost of such maintenance.

up·land (ŭp′lənd, -lănd′) *n.* **1.** Land or an area of land of high elevation, especially when level. **2.** Land in the interior of a country. —**upland** *adj.* Of, relating to, or located in an upland.

Up·land (ŭp′lənd). A city of southern California east of Los Angeles. It is a processing center. Population, 47,647.

upland cotton *n.* A tropical American plant *(Gossypium hirsutum)* cultivated for the woolly lint that surrounds its seeds.

upland sandpiper
Bartramia longicauda

upland sandpiper *n.* A large brownish sandpiper *(Bartramia longicauda)* inhabiting the fields and uplands of eastern North America. Also called *upland plover.*

up·lift (ŭp-lĭft′) *tr.v.* **-lift·ed, -lift·ing, -lifts. 1.** To raise; elevate. **2.** To raise to a higher social, intellectual, or moral level or condition. **3.** To raise to spiritual or emotional heights; exalt: *music that uplifts the spirit.* —**uplift** (ŭp′lĭft′) *adj.* Uplifted. —**uplift** (ŭp′lĭft′) *n.* **1.** The act, process, or result of raising or lifting up. **2.** An effort or a movement to improve social, moral, or intellectual standards. **3.** *Geology.* An upheaval.

up·link (ŭp′lĭngk′) *n.* A transmission path by which radio or other signals are sent to an aircraft or a communications satellite.

up·load (ŭp′lōd′) *v.* **-load·ed, -load·ing, -loads.** *Computer Science.* —*tr.* To transfer (data or programs), usually from a peripheral computer or device to a central, often remote computer. —*intr.* To transfer data or programs to a central computer.

up·man·ship (ŭp′mən-shĭp′) *n.* One-upmanship.

up·mar·ket (ŭp′mär′kĭt) *adj.* Appealing to or designed for high-income consumers; upscale: *"He turned up in well-cut clothes . . . and upmarket felt hats"* (New Yorker).

up·most (ŭp′mōst′) *adj.* Uppermost.

U·po·lu (o͞o-pō′lo͞o). A volcanic island of Western Samoa in the southern Pacific Ocean. It is the site of Apia, the country's capital.

up·on (ə-pŏn′, ə-pôn′) *prep.* On. See Usage Note at **on.**

upright piano

up·per (ŭp′ər) *adj. Abbr.* **up., u., U. 1.** Higher in place, position, or rank: *the upper bunk; the upper half of the class.* **2.a.** Situated on higher ground: *upper regions.* **b.** Lying farther inland: *the upper Nile.* **c.** Northern: *the upper Midwest.* **3. Upper.** *Geology & Archaeology.* Of, relating to, or being a later division of the period named. —**upper** *n.* **1.** The part of a shoe or boot above the sole. **2.** *Informal.* An upper berth. **3. uppers.** *Informal.* The upper teeth or a set of upper dentures. **4.** *Slang.* **a.** A drug, especially an amphetamine, used as a stimulant. **b.** An exhilarating or euphoric experience. —***idiom.* on (one's) uppers.** *Informal.* Impoverished; destitute.

Upper Ar·ling·ton (är′lĭng-tən). A city of central Ohio, a residential suburb of Columbus. Population, 35,648.

upper atmosphere *n.* The part of the atmosphere above the troposphere.

Upper A·von (ā′vŏn, ā′vən, ăv′ən). See **Avon.**

upper bound *n. Mathematics.* A number that is greater than or equal to every number in a given set of real numbers.

Upper Cal·i·for·ni·a (kăl′ĭ-fôr′nyə, -fôr′nē-ə). See **Alta California.**

Upper Can·a·da (kăn′ə-də). A historical region and province of British North America. Roughly coextensive with southern Ontario, Canada, it was formed in 1791 and joined Lower Canada in 1841.

Upper Carboniferous *adj. & n. Geology.* Pennsylvanian.

up·per·case (ŭp′ər-kās′) *Printing. adj. Abbr.* **u.c., UC** Belonging to, set, or printed in capital letters; capital: *an uppercase A; uppercase titles.* —**uppercase** *tr.v.* **-cased, -cas·ing, -cas·es.** To print or set in uppercase letters.

upper class *n.* The highest socioeconomic class in a society. —**up′per-class′** (ŭp′ər-klăs′) *adj.*

up·per·class·man (ŭp′ər-klăs′mən) *n.* A student in the junior or senior class of a secondary school or college.

upper crust *n. Informal.* The highest social class or group. —**up′per-crust′** (ŭp′ər-krŭst′) *adj.*

up·per·cut (ŭp′ər-kŭt′) *n. Sports.* A swinging blow directed upward, as to a boxing opponent's chin.

Upper East Side. See **East Side.**

Upper E·gypt (ē′jĭpt). A region of ancient Egypt in the valley of the Nile River south of the delta area, which was known as Lower Egypt. The two regions were united c. 3100 B.C..

Upper En·ga·dine (ĕng′gə-dēn′). See **Engadine.**

upper hand *n.* A position of control or advantage.

upper house *n.* The branch of a bicameral legislature, such as the U.S. Senate, that is smaller and less broadly representative of the population.

Upper Klam·ath Lake (klăm′əth). A lake of south-central Oregon east of Medford. It is in a popular resort area.

up·per·most (ŭp′ər-mōst′) *adv. & adj.* In the highest position, place, or rank: *finished uppermost in the standings; the uppermost balcony.*

Upper New York Bay (no͞o yôrk′, nyo͞o). See **New York Bay.**

Upper Pa·lat·i·nate (pə-lăt′n-ĭt). See **Palatinate.**

Upper Peninsula. The northern part of Michigan between Lakes Superior and Michigan. It is separated from the Lower Peninsula by the Straits of Mackinac.

Upper Saint Clair (sānt clâr′). A community of southwest Pennsylvania, a suburb of Pittsburgh. Population, 19,023.

Upper Si·le·sia (sī-lē′zhə, -shə, sĭ-). See **Silesia.**

Upper Tun·gus·ka (to͝ong-go͞o′skə, to͞on-). See **Tunguska.**

Upper Vol·ta (vōl′tə, vŏl′-). See **Burkina Faso.** —**Upper Vol′tan** *adj. & n.*

up·pish (ŭp′ĭsh) *adj. Informal.* Uppity. —**up′pish·ly** *adv.* —**up′pish·ness** *n.*

up·pi·ty (ŭp′ĭ-tē) *adj. Informal.* Taking liberties or assuming airs beyond one's station; presumptuous: *"was getting a little uppity and needed to be slapped down"* (New York Times). [From UP.] —**up′i·ty·ness** *n.*

Upp·sa·la (ŭp′sə-lə, -sä′-, o͝op′sä′lä). A city of eastern Sweden north-northwest of Stockholm. Capital of a pre-Christian kingdom in the early Middle Ages, it became an episcopal see in 1164. Population, 152,579.

up quark *n. Abbr.* **u** A quark with a charge of +⅔ and a mass about 607 times that of the electron. It is a component of protons and neutrons. See table at **subatomic particle.**

up·raise (ŭp-rāz′) *tr.v.* **-raised, -rais·ing, -rais·es.** To raise or lift up; elevate.

up·rear (ŭp-rîr′) *v.* **-reared, -rear·ing, -rears.** —*tr.* To raise or lift up. —*intr.* To rise up.

up·right (ŭp′rīt′) *adj.* **1.a.** Being in a vertical position or direction: *an upright post.* See Synonyms at **vertical. b.** Erect in posture or carriage: *"She sat with grim determination, upright as a darning needle stuck in a board"* (Harriet Beecher Stowe). **2.** Adhering strictly to moral principles; righteous. —**upright** *adv.* Vertically: *walk upright.* —**upright** *n.* **1.** A perpendicular position; verticality. **2.** Something, such as a goal post, that stands upright. **3.** *Music.* An upright piano. —**up′right′ly** *adv.* —**up′right′ness** *n.*

upright piano *n. Music.* A piano having the strings mounted vertically in a rectangular case with the keyboard at a right angle to the case.

up·rise (ŭp-rīz′) *intr.v.* **-rose** (-rōz′), **-ris·en** (-rĭz′ən), **-ris·ing, -ris·es. 1.** To get up or stand up; rise. **2.** To go, move, or incline upward; ascend. **3.** To rise into view, especially from below the horizon. **4.** To increase in pitch or volume; swell. —**uprise** (ŭp′rīz′) *n.* **1.** The act or process of rising. **2.** An upward slope; an ascent.

up·ris·ing (ŭp′rī′zĭng) *n.* **1.** A sometimes limited popular revolt against a government or its policies. See Synonyms at **rebellion. 2.** The act or an instance of rising or rising up.

up·riv·er (ŭp′rĭv′ər) *adv. & adj.* Toward or near the source of a river; in the direction opposite to that of the current: *rowing upriver; upriver rapids.*

up·roar (ŭp′rôr′, -rōr′) *n.* **1.** A condition of noisy excitement and confusion; tumult. See Synonyms at **noise. 2.** A heated controversy. [Probably by folk etymology from Middle Low German *uprōr* : *up-,* up (from *up;* see **upo** in Appendix) + *rōr,* motion; see **kerə-** in Appendix.]

up·roar·i·ous (ŭp-rôr′ē-əs, -rōr′-) *adj.* **1.** Causing or accompanied by an uproar: *an uproarious New Year's celebration.* **2.** Loud and full; boisterous: *uproarious laughter.* **3.** Causing hearty laughter; hilarious: *uproarious stories.* —**up·roar′i·ous·ly** *adv.* —**up·roar′i·ous·ness** *n.*

up·root (ŭp-ro͞ot′, -ro͝ot′) *tr.v.* **-root·ed, -root·ing, -roots. 1.** To pull up (a plant and its roots) from the ground. **2.** To destroy or remove completely; eradicate. **3.** To force to leave an accustomed or native location. —**up·root′ed·ness** *n.* —**up·root′er** *n.*

up·rose (ŭp-rōz′) *v.* Past tense of **uprise.**

ups and downs (ŭps′ ən dounz′) *pl.n.* Alternating periods of good and bad fortune or spirits.

up·scale (ŭp′skāl′) *adj.* Of, intended for, or relating to high-income consumers: *an upscale neighborhood; upscale fashions.* **—upscale** (*also* ŭp-skāl′) *tr.v.* **-scaled, -scal·ing, -scales. 1.** To raise to a higher level; upgrade. **2.** To redesign or market for higher-income consumers: *"the upscaling of TV dinners* [to] *savory, low-calorie entrées"* (Bernice Kanner).

up·set (ŭp-sĕt′) *v.* **-set, -set·ting, -sets.** *—tr.* **1.** To cause to turn or tip over; capsize. **2.** To disturb the functioning, order, or course of: *Protesters upset the meeting by chanting and shouting.* **3.** To distress or perturb mentally or emotionally: *The bad news upset me.* **4.** To overthrow; overturn: *upset a will.* See Synonyms at **overthrow. 5.** (ŭp′sĕt′). To defeat unexpectedly (an opponent favored to win). **6.** To make (a heated metal bolt, for example) shorter and thicker by hammering on the end. *—intr.* **1.** To become overturned; capsize. **2.** To become disturbed. **—upset** (ŭp′sĕt′) *n.* **1.** The act of upsetting or the condition of being upset. **2.** A disturbance, disorder, or state of agitation. **3.** *Sports & Games.* A game or contest in which the favorite is defeated. **4.a.** A tool used for upsetting; a swage. **b.** An upset part or piece. **—upset** *adj.* **1.** Having been overturned; capsized. **2.** Exhibiting signs and symptoms of indigestion: *an upset stomach.* **3.** In a state of emotional or mental distress; distraught: *upset parents.* [Middle English *upsetten,* to set up : *up-,* up- + *setten,* to set; see SET[1].] **—up·set′ter** *n.* **—up·set′ting·ly** *adv.*

upset price *n.* The lowest price at which an item of property may be auctioned or sold at public sale. [Past participle of UPSET, to establish (obsolete).]

up·shift (ŭp′shĭft′) *intr.v.* **-shift·ed, -shift·ing, -shifts.** To shift a motor vehicle into a higher gear. **—up′shift′** *n.*

up·shot (ŭp′shŏt′) *n.* The final result. See Synonyms at **effect.** [Earlier *upshot,* the last shot in an archery contest.]

up·side (ŭp′sīd′) *n.* **1.** The upper side or portion. **2.** An advantageous aspect: *the upsides and downsides of home ownership.* **3.** An upward tendency, as in business profitability or in the prices of a stock. **—upside** *prep. Slang.* On: *"If you still didn't get it, well, sometimes you have to hit people upside the head . . . to get their attention"* (Howie Carr).

upside down *adv.* **1.** So that the upper or right side is down. **2.** In great disorder. [Alteration of Middle English *up so doun,* up as if down : *up,* up; see UP + *so,* as if; see SO[1] + *doun,* down; see DOWN[1].] **—up′side-down′** (ŭp′sīd-doun′) *adj.*

upside-down cake *n.* A single-layer cake baked with sliced fruit at the bottom, then served with the fruit side up.

up·si·lon (ŭp′sə-lŏn′, yo͞op′-) *n.* The 20th letter of the Greek alphabet. See table at **alphabet.** [Late Greek *u psilon,* simple u (from the fact that *oi* was given the same pronunciation in Late Greek as *u*), from *psilon,* neuter of *psilos,* simple (written with one letter as opposed to two).]

up·spring (ŭp-sprĭng′) *intr. v.* **-sprang** (-sprăng′) or **-sprung** (-sprŭng′), **-sprung, -spring·ing, -springs. 1.** To spring up, as from the soil. **2.** To come into being; arise.

up·stage (ŭp′stāj′) *adv.* Toward, at, or on the rear part of a stage. **—upstage** *adj.* **1.** Of or relating to the rear part of a stage. **2.** *Informal.* Haughty; aloof. **—upstage** (ŭp′stāj′) *n.* The rear part of a stage, away from the audience. **—upstage** (ŭp-stāj′) *tr.v.* **-staged, -stag·ing, -stag·es. 1.** To distract attention from (another performer) by moving upstage, thus forcing the other performer to face away from the audience. **2.** To divert attention or praise from; force out of the spotlight: *a vice president who repeatedly tried to upstage the president.* **3.** To treat haughtily. **—up·stag′er** *n.*

up·stairs (ŭp′stârz′) *adv.* **1.** Up the stairs: *raced upstairs.* **2.** To or on a higher floor: *went upstairs to go to bed.* **3.** To or at a higher level: *promoted upstairs to management.* **—upstairs** (ŭp′stârz′) *adj.* Of or located on an upper floor: *an upstairs bedroom.* **—upstairs** (ŭp′stârz′) *n.* (*used with a sing. verb*). The part of a building above the ground floor.

up·stand·ing (ŭp-stăn′dĭng, ŭp′stan′-) *adj.* **1.** Standing erect. **2.** Morally upright; honest. **—up·stand′ing·ness** *n.*

up·start (ŭp′stärt′) *n.* A person of humble origin who attains sudden wealth, power, or importance, especially one made immodest or presumptuous by the change; a parvenu. **—upstart** *adj.* **1.** Suddenly raised to a position of consequence. **2.** Self-important; presumptuous. **—upstart** (ŭp-stärt′) *tr.v.* **-start·ed, -start·ing, -starts.** To spring or start up suddenly.

up·state (ŭp′stāt′) *n.* The northerly section of a state in the United States. **—upstate** *adv. & adj.* To, from, or in the northerly section of a state. **—up′stat′er** *n.*

up·stream (ŭp′strēm′) *adv. & adj.* In the direction opposite to the current of a stream: *paddling upstream; upstream traffic.*

up·stroke (ŭp′strōk′) *n.* An upward stroke, as of a brush.

up·surge (ŭp-sûrj′) *intr.v.* **-surged, -surg·ing, -surg·es.** To surge up. **—upsurge** (ŭp′sûrj′) *n.* A rapid or abrupt rise: *an upsurge in violent crime.*

up·sweep (ŭp′swēp′) *n.* **1.** An upward curve or sweep. **2.** A hairdo that is smoothed upward in the back and piled on top of the head. **—upsweep** *tr.v.* **-swept** (-swĕpt′), **-sweep·ing, -sweeps.** To brush, curve, or sweep upward.

up·swing (ŭp′swĭng′) *n.* **1.** An upward swing or trend. **2.** An increase, as in movement or business activity.

up·take (ŭp′tāk′) *n.* **1.** A passage for drawing up smoke or air. **2.** Understanding; comprehension: *very quick on the uptake.*

up-tem·po also **up·tem·po** (ŭp′tĕm′pō) *Music.* *—n., pl.* **-pos.** A fast or lively tempo, as in jazz. *—adj.* Having a fast or lively tempo: *an up-tempo arrangement.*

up·throw (ŭp′thrō′) *n.* **1.** A throwing upward. **2.** *Geology.* An upward displacement of rock on one side of a fault.

up·tick (ŭp′tĭk′) *n.* **1.** An increase, especially a small or incremental one: *last week's uptick in interest rates.* **2.** A transaction in a stock market security above the price of the previous transaction. [From the indication of a rise in price of a stock by a plus sign on boards above stock market stations.]

up·tight (ŭp′tīt′) *adj. Slang.* **1.** Tense; nervous: *"She is both poised and uptight, both intellectually curious and submissively ladylike"* (Edward Klein). **2.** Financially pressed; destitute. **3.** Outraged; angry. **4.** Rigidly conventional, as in manners, opinions, and tastes. **—up′tight′ness** *n.*

up·time (ŭp′tīm′) *n.* The time during which a device, such as a computer, is functioning or available for use.

up-to-date (ŭp′tə-dāt′) *adj.* **1.** Informed of or reflecting the latest information or changes: *an up-to-date timetable.* **2.** Being in accord with the latest ideas, improvements, or styles: *up-to-date technology; up-to-date fashions.* **—up′-to-date′ness** *n.*

up-to-the-min·ute (ŭp′tə-*th*ə-mĭn′ĭt) *adj.* Constituting or including the very latest information: *up-to-the-minute news.*

up·town (ŭp′toun′) *n.* The upper part of a town or city. **—uptown** (ŭp′toun′) *adv.* To, toward, or in the upper part of a town or city. **—uptown** *adj.* Of, relating to, or located uptown. **—up′town′er** *n.*

up·trend (ŭp′trĕnd′) *n.* An upward trend; an upturn. **—up′trend′** *v.*

up·turn (ŭp′tûrn′, ŭp-tûrn′) *v.* **-turned, -turn·ing, -turns.** *—tr.* **1.** To turn up or over: *upturn the soil.* **2.** To upset; overturn. **3.** To direct upward: *upturned their gaze.* *—intr.* To turn over or up. **—upturn** (ŭp′tûrn′) *n.* An upward movement, curve, or trend, as in business activity.

up·ward (ŭp′wərd) *adv.* **1.** In, to, or toward a higher place, level, or position: *flying upward.* **2.** Toward a higher position in a hierarchy or on a socioeconomic scale: *a young executive moving upward fast.* **3.** To or toward the source, origin, or interior. **4.** Toward the head or upper parts: *bare from the waist upward.* **5.** Toward a higher amount, degree, or rank: *Prices soared upward.* **6.** Toward a later time or age: *from adolescence upward.* **—upward** *adj.* Directed toward a higher place or position: *upward movement.* **—*idiom.* upward** (or **upwards**) **of.** More than; in excess of: *"the onslaught of upwards of seventy divisions"* (Winston S. Churchill). **—up′ward·ly** *adv.* **—up′wards** *adv.*

upwardly mobile *adj.* Advancing or likely to advance in economic and social standing: *"They had considered her suitor unambitious, not sufficiently upwardly mobile"* (Maggie Scarf). **—upwardly mobile** *n.* (*used with a pl. verb*). Those regarded as advancing rapidly in economic and social standing. Used with *the.*

up·well (ŭp-wĕl′) *intr.v.* **-welled, -well·ing, -wells.** To rise from a lower or inner source; well up: *tears upwelling in my eyes.*

up·well·ing (ŭp-wĕl′ĭng, ŭp′wĕl′-) *n.* **1.** The act or an instance of rising up from or as if from a lower source: *an upwelling of emotion.* **2.** A process in which cold, often nutrient-rich waters from the ocean depths rise to the surface.

up·wind (ŭp′wĭnd′) *adv.* In or toward the direction from which the wind blows. **—up′wind′** *adj.*

Ur (ûr, o͝or). Known in biblical times as **Ur of the Chal·dees** (kăl′dēz′, kăl-dēz′). A city of ancient Sumer in southern Mesopotamia on a site in present-day southeast Iraq. One of the oldest cities in Mesopotamia, it was an important center of Sumerian culture after c. 3000 B.C. and the birthplace of Abraham. The city declined after the sixth century B.C.

ur–[1] *pref.* Variant of **uro–**[1]**.**

ur–[2] *pref.* Variant of **uro–**[2]**.**

URA *abbr.* Urban Renewal Administration.

u·ra·cil (yo͝or′ə-sĭl) *n.* A pyrimidine base, $C_4H_4N_2O_2$, that is an essential constituent of RNA. [UR(EA) + AC(ETIC) + *-il,* substance relating to.]

u·rae·mi·a (yo͞o-rē′mē-ə) *n.* Variant of **uremia.**

u·rae·us (yo͞o-rē′əs) *n.* The figure of the sacred serpent, an emblem of sovereignty depicted on the headdress of ancient Egyptian rulers and deities. [New Latin, from Late Greek *ouraios,* cobra, perhaps alteration (influenced by Greek *ouraios,* of the tail, from *oura,* tail; see URO–[2]) of Egyptian *y′rt.*]

uraeus

U·ral-Al·ta·ic (yo͝or′əl-ăl-tā′ĭk) *n.* A hypothetical language group that comprises the Uralic and Altaic language families. Also called *Turanian.* **—U′ral-Al·ta′ic** *adj.*

U·ral·ic (yo͞o-răl′ĭk) also **U·ra·li·an** (yo͞o-rā′lē-ən) *n.* A language family that comprises the Finno-Ugric and Samoyedic subfamilies. [After the URAL (MOUNTAINS).] **—U·ral′ic** *adj.*

U·ral Mountains (yo͝or′əl). A range of western Russia forming the traditional boundary between Europe and Asia and extending about 2,414 km (1,500 mi) from the Arctic Ocean southward to Kazakhstan.

Ural River. A river of western Russia and western Kazakhstan rising in the southern Ural Mountains and flowing about 2,533 km (1,574 mi) to the Caspian Sea.

ă pat	oi boy
ā pay	ou out
âr care	o͝o took
ä father	o͞o boot
ĕ pet	ŭ cut
ē be	ûr urge
ĭ pit	th thin
ī pie	*th* this
îr pier	hw which
ŏ pot	zh vision
ō toe	ə about, item
ô paw	♦ regionalism

Stress marks: ′ (primary); ′ (secondary), as in **dictionary** (dĭk′shə-nĕr′ē)

U·ralsk (yŏŏ-rălsk′, ōō-rälsk′). A city of northwest Kazakhstan on the Ural River west-northwest of Aktyubinsk. Founded by Cossacks c. 1622, it is a processing and manufacturing center. Population, 192,000.

uran– *pref.* Variant of **urano–.**

u·ra·ni·a (yŏŏ-rā′nē-ə, -rān′yə) *n.* Uranium dioxide. [New Latin *ūrania,* from URANIUM.]

U·ra·ni·a (yŏŏ-rā′nē-ə, -rān′yə) *n. Greek Mythology.* The muse of astronomy. [Latin *Ūrania,* from Greek *Ourania,* from *ouranos,* heaven.]

Urania
Holding her attributes, a compass and globe

u·ran·ic¹ (yŏŏ-răn′ĭk, -rā′nĭk) *adj.* Of or relating to the heavens; celestial. [From Greek *ouranos,* heaven.]

u·ran·ic² (yŏŏ-răn′ĭk, -rā′nĭk) *adj.* Of, relating to, or derived from uranium, especially with valence higher than in comparable uranous compounds.

u·ra·ni·nite (yŏŏ-rā′nə-nīt′) *n.* A complex brownish-black mineral, UO_2, forming the chief ore of uranium and containing variable amounts of radium, lead, thorium, and other elements. [German *Uranin* (from New Latin *ūranium,* uranium; see URANIUM) + –ITE¹.]

u·ra·ni·um (yŏŏ-rā′nē-əm) *n. Symbol* **U** A heavy silvery-white metallic element, radioactive and toxic, easily oxidized, and having 14 known isotopes of which U 238 is the most abundant in nature. The element occurs in several minerals, including uraninite and carnotite, from which it is extracted and processed for use in research, nuclear fuels, and nuclear weapons. Atomic number 92; atomic weight 238.03; melting point 1,132°C; boiling point 3,818°C; specific gravity 18.95; valence 2, 3, 4, 5, 6. See table at **element.** [New Latin *ūranium,* after URANUS.]

WORD HISTORY: The element uranium, whose discovery has been so vital to our nuclear age, owes its name to a preceding scientific discovery, that of the planet Uranus. Sir William Herschel, who discovered Uranus in 1781, named the planet *Georgium sīdus,* "the Georgian planet," in honor of George III. Some also called it *Herschel,* but convention prevailed and the planet came to be called *Uranus,* the name of a heavenly deity like the rest of the planets. Called Uranus in Latin mythology and Ouranos in Greek, this god of the heavens was chosen because he was the father of Saturn (Greek Kronos), the deity of the planet next in line, who was the father of Jupiter (Greek Zeus), the deity of the next planet. The name of this new planet was then used in the name of a new chemical element, *uranium,* discovered eight years later by M.H. Klaproth. Klaproth, a German scientist, gave it the Latin name *ūranium* in honor of the discovery of *Uranus. Uranium* passed into English shortly thereafter, being first recorded in the third edition of the *Encyclopedia Britannica,* published in 1797.

uranium 235 *n.* The uranium isotope with mass number 235 and half-life 7.13×10^8 years, fissionable with slow neutrons and capable in a critical mass of sustaining a chain reaction that can proceed explosively with appropriate mechanical arrangements.

uranium 238 *n.* The most common isotope of uranium, having mass number 238 and half-life 4.51×10^9 years, nonfissionable but irradiated with neutrons to produce fissionable plutonium 239.

uranium dioxide *n.* A black, highly toxic crystalline powder, UO_2, once used in ceramic glazes and gas mantles, now used primarily to pack nuclear fuel rods.

uranium trioxide *n.* A poisonous, radioactive orange powder, UO_3, used for uranium refining and as a coloring agent in ceramics.

urano– or **uran–** *pref.* Uranium: *uranyl.* [From URANIUM.]

u·ra·nous (yŏŏ-rā′nəs, yŏŏr′ə-nəs) *adj.* Of or relating to uranium, especially with valence lower than in comparable uranic compounds.

U·ra·nus (yŏŏr′ə-nəs, yŏŏ-rā′nəs) *n.* **1.** *Greek Mythology.* The earliest supreme god, a personification of the sky, who was the son and consort of Gaea and the father of the Cyclopes and Titans. **2.** The seventh planet from the sun, revolving about it every 84.07 years at a distance of approximately 2,869 million kilometers (1,790 million miles), having a mean equatorial diameter of 52,290 kilometers (32,480 miles) and a mass 14.6 times that of Earth. [Late Latin *Ūranus,* from Greek *ouranos,* heaven, Uranus.]

u·ra·nyl (yŏŏr′ə-nĭl, yŏŏ-rā′nəl) *n.* The divalent radical UO_2^{2+}.

u·rase (yŏŏr′ās′, -āz′) *n.* Variant of **urease.**

u·rate (yŏŏr′āt′) *n.* A salt of uric acid. [UR(IC ACID) + –ATE².]

U·ra·wa (ōō-rä′wə, -wä). A city of east-central Honshu, Japan, a commercial suburb of Tokyo. Population, 377,233.

ur·ban (ûr′bən) *adj.* **1.** Of, relating to, or located in a city. **2.** Characteristic of the city or city life. [Latin *urbānus,* from *urbs, urb-,* city.]

Urban II
1592 Italian woodcut

Ur·ban II (ûr′bən). Originally Odo of Lagery. 1042?–1099. Pope (1088–1099) who promoted the First Crusade.

Urban VI. Originally Bartolomeo Prignano. 1318?–1389. Pope (1378–1389) who precipitated the Great Schism by alienating the French cardinals, who in turn elected an antipope (1378).

Ur·ban·a (ûr-băn′ə). A city of east-central Illinois adjoining Champaign. Population, 35,978.

Ur·ban·dale (ûr′bən-dāl′). A city of south-central Iowa, a suburb of Des Moines. Population, 17,869.

urban district *n.* An administrative district of England, Wales, and Northern Ireland, usually composed of several densely populated communities, resembling a borough but lacking a borough charter.

ur·bane (ûr-bān′) *adj.* **-ban·er, -ban·est.** Polite, refined, and often elegant in manner. See Synonyms at **suave.** [Latin *urbānus,* of a city. See URBAN.] **—ur·bane′ly** *adv.*

urban forest *n.* A dense, widespread growth of trees and other plants covering an area of a city.

ur·ban·ism (ûr′bə-nĭz′əm) *n.* **1.** The culture or way of life of city dwellers. **2.** Urbanization.

ur·ban·ist (ûr′bə-nĭst) *n.* A specialist in the study and planning of cities. **—ur′ban·is′tic** *adj.* **—ur′ban·is′ti·cal·ly** *adv.*

ur·ban·ite (ûr′bə-nīt′) *n.* A city dweller.

ur·ban·i·ty (ûr-băn′ĭ-tē) *n., pl.* **-ties. 1.** Refinement and elegance of manner; polished courtesy. See Synonyms at **elegance. 2. urbanities.** Courtesies; civilities.

ur·ban·ize (ûr′bə-nīz′) *tr.v.* **-ized, -iz·ing, -iz·es.** To make urban in nature. **—ur′ban·i·za′tion** (-bə-nĭ-zā′shən) *n.*

ur·ban·ol·o·gist (ûr′bə-nŏl′ə-jĭst) *n.* A sociologist who specializes in the problems of cities and urban life. **—ur′ban·ol′o·gy** *n.*

urban renewal *n.* Rehabilitation of impoverished urban neighborhoods by large-scale renovation or reconstruction of housing and public works.

urban sprawl *n.* The unplanned, uncontrolled spreading of urban development into areas adjoining the edge of a city.

urban wind (wĭnd) *n.* A strong wind generated near or around a group of high-rise buildings, creating areas of intense air turbulence especially at street level.

ur·ce·o·late (ûr-sē′ə-lĭt, ûr′sē-ə-lāt′) *adj.* Shaped like an urn: *an urceolate corolla.* [New Latin *urceolātus,* from Latin *urceolus,* diminutive of *urceus,* jug.]

ur·chin (ûr′chĭn) *n.* **1.** A playful or mischievous youngster; a scamp. **2.** A sea urchin. **3.** A hedgehog. [Middle English *urchone,* hedgehog, from Old French *erichon,* from Vulgar Latin **ēriciō, ēriciōn-,* from Latin *ērīcius,* from *ēr.*]

Ur·du (ŏŏr′dōō, ûr′-) *n.* An Indic language that is the official literary language of Pakistan. It is written in an Arabic alphabet and is also widely used in India, chiefly by Moslems. [Urdu *urdū,* short for *zabān-i urdū* : Persian *zabān,* language, tongue + Persian *urdū,* camp, court (from Old Turkic *ordu,* residence, court).] **—Ur′du** *adj.*

–ure *suff.* **1.** Act; process; condition: *erasure.* **2.a.** Function; office: *judicature.* **b.** Body performing a function: *legislature.* [Middle English, from Old French, from Latin *-ūra.*]

u·re·a (yŏŏ-rē′ə) *n.* A water-soluble compound, $CO(NH_2)_2$, that is the major nitrogenous end product of protein metabolism and is the chief nitrogenous component of the urine in mammals and other organisms. Also called *carbamide.* [New Latin, from French *urée,* from *urine,* urine, from Old French, from Latin *ūrīna.* See URINE.]

u·re·a-for·mal·de·hyde resin (yŏŏ-rē′ə-fôr-măl′də-hīd′) *n.* Any of various thermosetting resins made by combining urea and formaldehyde and widely used to make molded household and industrial objects.

u·re·ase (yŏŏr′ē-ās′, -āz′) also **u·rase** (yŏŏr′ās′, -āz′) *n.* An enzyme that promotes the hydrolysis of urea to form ammonium carbonate. [URE(A) + –ASE.]

u·re·din·i·a (yŏŏr′ĭ-dĭn′ē-ə) *n.* Plural of **uredinium.**

u·re·din·i·o·spore (yŏŏr′ĭ-dĭn′ē-ə-spôr′, -spōr′) *n.* Variant of **uredospore.** [UREDINI(UM) + SPORE.]

u·re·din·i·um (yŏŏr′ĭ-dĭn′ē-əm) also **u·re·di·um** (yŏŏ-rē′dē-əm) *n., pl.* **-din·i·a** (-dĭn′ē-ə) also **-di·a** (-dē-ə). A reddish, pustulelike structure that is formed on the tissue of a plant infected by a rust fungus and produces uredospores. [New Latin *ūrēdinium,* from Latin *ūrēdō, ūrēdin-,* blight, from *ūrere,* to burn.]

u·re·do·spore (yŏŏ-rē′də-spôr′, -spōr′) also **u·re·din·i·o·spore** (yŏŏr′ĭ-dĭn′ē-ə-) *n.* A reddish spore that is produced in the uredinium of a rust fungus and that spreads to and infects other host plants. [URED(INIUM) + SPORE.]

u·re·do·stage (yŏŏ-rē′də-stāj′) *n.* The stage of a rust fungus in which uredinia are produced. [*uredinia,* pl. of UREDINIUM + STAGE.]

u·re·ide (yŏŏr′ē-īd′) *n.* Any of various derivatives of urea. [URE(A) + –IDE.]

u·re·mi·a also **u·rae·mi·a** (yŏŏ-rē′mē-ə) *n.* A toxic condition resulting from kidney disease in which there is retention in the bloodstream of waste products normally excreted in the urine. Also called *azotemia.* **—u·re′mic** *adj.*

u·re·o·tel·ic (yŏŏ-rē′ə-tĕl′ĭk, yŏŏr′ē-ō-) *adj.* Excreting urea as the chief component of nitrogenous waste. [URE(A) + TELIC.] **—u·re′o·tel′ism** (yŏŏ-rē′ə-tĕl′ĭz′əm, yŏŏr′ē-ŏt′l-ĭz′əm) *n.*

u·re·ter (yŏŏ-rē′tər, yŏŏr′ĭ-tər) *n.* The long, narrow duct that conveys urine from the kidney to the urinary bladder or cloaca. [New Latin *ūrētēr,* from Greek *ourētēr,* from *ourein,* to urinate.] **—u·re′ter·al, u′re·ter′ic** (yŏŏr′ĭ-tĕr′ĭk) *adj.*

u·re·thane (yŏŏr′ĭ-thān′) also **u·re·than** (-thăn′) *n.* **1.** A colorless or white crystalline compound, $CO(NH_2)OC_2H_5$, used in organic synthesis and formerly as a palliative treatment for leukemia. **2.** Any of several esters, other than the ethyl ester, of carbamic acid. [UR(O)–¹ + ETH(YL) + –ANE.]

u·re·thra (yŏŏ-rē′thrə) *n., pl.* **-thras** or **-thrae** (-thrē). The canal through which urine is discharged from the bladder in most mammals and through which semen is discharged in the male. [Late Latin *ūrēthra,* from Greek *ourēthra,* from *ourein,* to urinate.] **—u·re′thral** *adj.*

u·re·threc·to·my (yo͝or′ĭ-thrĕk′tə-mē) *n., pl.* **-mies.** Surgical removal of all or part of the urethra.

u·re·thri·tis (yo͝or′ĭ-thrī′tĭs) *n.* Inflammation of the urethra.

u·re·thro·scope (yo͝o-rē′thrə-skōp′) *n.* An instrument for examining the interior of the urethra. **—u′re·thros′co·py** (yo͝or′ə-thrŏs′kə-pē) *n.*

u·ret·ic (yo͝o-rĕt′ĭk) *adj.* Of or relating to urine; urinary. [Late Latin *ūrēticus,* from Greek *ourētikos,* from *ourein,* to urinate.]

U·rey (yo͝or′ē), **Harold Clayton.** 1893–1981. American chemist. He won a 1934 Nobel for his discovery of heavy hydrogen.

Ur·fa (o͝or-fä′). A city of southeast Turkey near the Syrian border. Founded as Edessa in ancient times, it was incorporated into the Ottoman Empire in 1637 and renamed Urfa. Population, 147,488.

urge (ûrj) *v.* **urged, urg·ing, urg·es.** *—tr.* **1.** To force or drive forward or onward; impel. **2.** To entreat earnestly and often repeatedly; exhort. **3.** To advocate earnestly the doing, consideration, or approval of; press for: *urge passage of the bill; a speech urging moderation.* **4.** To stimulate; excite: *"It urged him to an intensity like madness"* (D.H. Lawrence). **5.** To move or impel to action, effort, or speed; spur. *—intr.* **1.** To exert an impelling force; push vigorously. **2.** To present a forceful argument, claim, or case. **—urge** *n.* **1.** The act of urging. **2.a.** An impulse that prompts action or effort: *suppressed an urge to laugh.* **b.** An involuntary tendency to perform a given activity; an instinct: *"There is a human urge to clarify, rationalize, justify"* (Leonard Bernstein). [Latin *urgēre.*]

SYNONYMS: *urge, press, exhort, prod, prick.* These verbs mean to constrain or impel to action. *Urge* implies strong pressure or persuasion: *"Urged by an extreme necessity, he had come there to steal food"* (Joseph Conrad). *We urged her to reconsider the offer, but she refused. Press* suggests greater insistence, urgency, or importunity: *"Isaacs hesitated long, but as everyone pressed him in turn, he yielded at last"* (Francis Marion Crawford). *Exhort* stresses the use of earnest, urgent, often stirring admonition, advice, or appeal: *"He exhorted his crews to take a good night's rest, wind up their family affairs, and make their wills"* (Washington Irving). To *prod* is to goad to action as if by poking with a pointed instrument: *"She reverted to her resolution to change the town—awaken it, prod it, 'reform' it"* (Sinclair Lewis). *Prick* suggests driving as if with a spur: *"Honor pricks me on"* (Shakespeare).

ur·gen·cy (ûr′jən-sē) *n., pl.* **-cies. 1.** The quality or condition of being urgent; pressing importance: *the urgency of the call for help; pleading with urgency.* **2.** A pressing necessity.

ur·gent (ûr′jənt) *adj.* **1.** Compelling immediate action or attention; pressing. **2.** Insistent or importunate: *the urgent words "Hurry! Hurry!"* **3.** Conveying a sense of pressing importance: *an urgent message.* [Middle English, from Old French, from Latin *urgēns, urgent-,* present participle of *urgēre,* to urge.] **—ur′gent·ly** *adv.*

SYNONYMS: *urgent, pressing, imperative, exigent.* These adjectives are compared as they mean compelling immediate attention. *Urgent* often implies that a matter takes precedence over others: *"My business is too urgent to waste time on apologies"* (John Buchan). *Pressing* suggests an urgency that demands that prompt measures be taken: *"The danger now became too pressing to admit of longer delay"* (James Fenimore Cooper). *Imperative* implies a need or demand whose fulfillment cannot be evaded or deferred: *As more nations acquire nuclear weapons the necessity for preventing war becomes imperative.* Something *exigent* requires swift action or remedy: *Her family's needs make exigent demands on her time and energy.*

-urgy *suff.* Technique or process for working with: *zymurgy.* [New Latin *-ūrgia,* from Greek *-ourgia,* from *-ourgos,* working, from *ergon,* work. See **werg-** in Appendix.]

-uria *suff.* **1.** The condition of having a specified substance in the urine: *aciduria.* **2.** The condition of having a specified kind of urine: *polyuria.* [New Latin *-ūria,* from Greek *-ouria,* from *ouron,* urine.]

U·ri·ah (yo͝o-rī′ə). In the Old Testament, an officer in the Israelite army and the husband of Bathsheba. He was sent to die in battle so that David could marry his wife.

u·ric (yo͝or′ĭk) *adj.* Relating to, contained in, or obtained from urine.

uric acid *n.* A semisolid compound, $C_5H_4N_4O_3$, that is a nitrogenous end product of protein and purine metabolism and is the chief nitrogenous component of the urine in birds, terrestrial reptiles, and insects.

u·ri·co·sur·ic (yo͝or′ĭ-kə-so͝or′ĭk) *adj.* Promoting the excretion of uric acid in the urine. [From URIC + URIC.]

u·ri·co·tel·ic (yo͝or′ĭ-kō-tĕl′ĭk) *adj.* Excreting uric acid as the chief component of nitrogenous waste. **—u′ri·co·tel′ism** (-kō-tĕl′ĭz′əm, -kŏt′l-) *n.*

u·ri·dine (yo͝or′ĭ-dēn′) *n.* A white, odorless powder, $C_9H_{12}N_2O_6$, that is the nucleoside of uracil, important in carbohydrate metabolism, and used in biochemical experiments.

U·ri·el (yo͝or′ē-əl) *n.* One of the archangels named in the Apocrypha and in Hebrew tradition.

U·rim and Thum·mim (yo͝or′ĭm ən thŭm′ĭm, o͝or′ĭm; to͝om′ĭm) *pl.n.* Sacred objects carried inside the breastplate of the high priest of ancient Israel and used as oracular media to divine the will of God. [Partial translation of Hebrew *'ûrîm wĕtummîm.*]

urin- *pref.* Variant of **urino-.**

u·ri·nal (yo͝or′ə-nəl) *n.* **1.a.** A fixture, typically one attached upright to a wall, used by men for urinating. **b.** A room or other place containing facilities for urinating. **2.** A portable receptacle for urine. [Middle English, chamber pot, from Old French, from Late Latin *ūrīnāle,* neuter of *ūrīnālis,* pertaining to urine, from Latin *ūrīna,* urine. See URINE.]

u·ri·nal·y·sis (yo͝or′ə-năl′ĭ-sĭs) *n., pl.* **-ses** (-sēz′). *Medicine.* Laboratory analysis of urine, used to aid in the diagnosis of disease or to detect the presence of a specific substance, such as an illegal drug. [URIN(O)- + (AN)ALYSIS.]

u·ri·nar·y (yo͝or′ə-nĕr′ē) *adj.* **1.** Of or relating to urine, its production, function, or excretion. **2.** Of or relating to the organs involved in the formation and excretion of urine.

urinary bladder *n.* An elastic, muscular sac situated in the anterior part of the pelvic cavity in which urine collects before excretion.

urinary calculus *n.* A hard mass of mineral salts in the urinary tract. Also called *cystolith, urolith.*

urinary tract *n.* A continuous anatomical tract, including the kidneys, ureters, and urethra, involved in the formation and excretion of urine.

u·ri·nate (yo͝or′ə-nāt′) *intr.v.* **-nat·ed, -nat·ing, -nates.** To excrete urine. [Medieval Latin *ūrīnāre, ūrīnāt-,* from Latin *ūrīna,* urine. See URINE.] **—u′ri·na′tion** *n.* **—u′ri·na′tive** *adj.* **—u′ri·na′tor** *n.*

u·rine (yo͝or′ĭn) *n.* The waste product secreted by the kidneys that in mammals is a yellow to amber-colored, slightly acid fluid discharged from the body through the urethra. [Middle English, from Old French, from Latin *ūrīna.* See **wē-r-** in Appendix.]

u·ri·nif·er·ous (yo͝or′ə-nĭf′ər-əs) *adj.* Conveying urine.

urino- or **urin-** *pref.* Urine: *urinalysis.* [From Latin *ūrīna,* urine. See URINE.]

u·ri·no·gen·i·tal (yo͝or′ə-nō-jĕn′ĭ-tl) *adj.* Variant of **urogenital.**

u·ri·nom·e·ter (yo͝or′ə-nŏm′ĭ-tər) *n.* A hydrometer for measuring the specific gravity of urine.

u·ri·nous (yo͝or′ə-nəs) also **u·ri·nose** (-nōs) *adj.* Of, resembling, or containing urine.

Ur·mi·a (o͝or′mē-ə), **Lake.** A shallow saline lake of northwest Iran between Tabriz and the Turkish border. The city of **Urmia,** on the western side of the lake, is the reputed birthplace of Zoroaster. Population, 263,000.

urn
c. 1450 Flemish

urn (ûrn) *n.* **1.** A vase of varying size and shape, usually having a footed base or pedestal. **2.** A closed metal vessel having a spigot and used for warming or serving tea or coffee. **3.** *Botany.* The spore-bearing part of a moss capsule. [Middle English *urne,* from Latin *urna.*]

uro-¹ or **ur-** *pref.* **1.** Urine: *uric.* **2.** Urinary tract: *urology.* **3.** Urea: *urethane.* [New Latin, from Greek *ouro-,* from *ouron,* urine.]

uro-² or **ur-** *pref.* Tail: *urochord.* [New Latin, from Greek *ouro-,* from *oura.* See **ors-** in Appendix.]

u·ro·chord (yo͝or′ə-kôrd′) *n. Zoology.* A notochord limited to the caudal region, characteristic of the urochordates. [URO-² + CHORD².]

u·ro·chor·date (yo͝or′ə-kôr′dāt) *n.* A chordate marine animal of the subphylum Urochordata; a tunicate. **—urochordate** *adj.* Having a urochord.

u·ro·chrome (yo͝or′ə-krōm′) *n.* The yellow pigment responsible for the color of urine.

u·ro·dele (yo͝or′ə-dēl′) *n.* Any of various amphibians of the order Caudata, including the salamanders and newts, in which the larval tail persists in adult life. [From New Latin *Ūrodēla,* former order name : URO-² + Greek *dēlos,* visible; see PSYCHEDELIC.]

u·ro·gen·i·tal (yo͝or′ō-jĕn′ĭ-tl) also **u·ri·no·gen·i·tal** (yo͝or′ə-nō-) *adj.* Of, relating to, or involving both the urinary and genital structures or functions.

u·rog·e·nous (yo͝o-rŏj′ə-nəs) *adj.* **1.** Producing urine. **2.** Produced or derived from urine.

u·ro·gram (yo͝or′ə-grăm′) *n.* A radiograph of the urinary tract.

u·rog·ra·phy (yo͝o-rŏg′rə-fē) *n., pl.* **-phies.** Radiography of the urinary tract. **—u′ro·graph′ic** (yo͝or′ə-grăf′ĭk) *adj.*

u·ro·ki·nase (yo͝or′ō-kī′nās, -nāz) *n.* An enzyme in human urine that catalyzes the conversion of plasminogen to plasmin and is used in medicine to dissolve blood clots.

urol. *abbr.* **1.** Urological. **2.** Urology.

u·ro·lith (yo͝or′ə-lĭth′) *n.* See **urinary calculus. —u′ro·lith′ic** *adj.*

u·ro·lith·i·a·sis (yo͝or′ə-lĭ-thī′ə-sĭs) *n.* A diseased condition resulting from the formation of calculi in the urinary tract.

u·rol·o·gy (yo͝o-rŏl′ə-jē) *n. Abbr.* **urol.** The branch of medicine that deals with the diagnosis and treatment of diseases of the

ă pat	oi boy
ā pay	ou out
âr care	o͝o took
ä father	o͞o boot
ĕ pet	ŭ cut
ē be	ûr urge
ĭ pit	th thin
ī pie	*th* this
îr pier	hw which
ŏ pot	zh vision
ō toe	ə about, item
ô paw	♦ regionalism

Stress marks: ′ (primary); ′ (secondary), as in **dictionary** (dĭk′shə-nĕr′ē)

urinary tract and urogenital system. —**ur′o·log′ic** (yo͝or′ə-lŏj′ĭk), **ur′o·log′i·cal** (-ĭ-kəl) *adj.* —**u·rol′o·gist** *n.*

–uronic *suff.* Connected with urine: *hyaluronic acid.* [From Greek *ouron,* urine.]

u·ro·pod (yo͝or′ə-pŏd′) *n.* One of the last pair of posterior abdominal appendages of certain crustaceans, such as the lobster or shrimp. [URO–[2] + –POD.]

u·ro·py·gi·al gland (yo͝or′ə-pī′jē-əl, -pĭj′ē-) *n.* A large gland at the base of a bird's tail that secretes an oil used in preening. Also called *oil gland.*

u·ro·py·gi·um (yo͝or′ə-pī′jē-əm, -pĭj′ē-) *n.* The posterior part of a bird's body, from which the tail feathers grow. [New Latin, from Greek *ouropugion* : *ouro-,* tail; see URO–[2] + *pugē,* rump.] —**u′ro·py′gi·al** (-əl) *adj.*

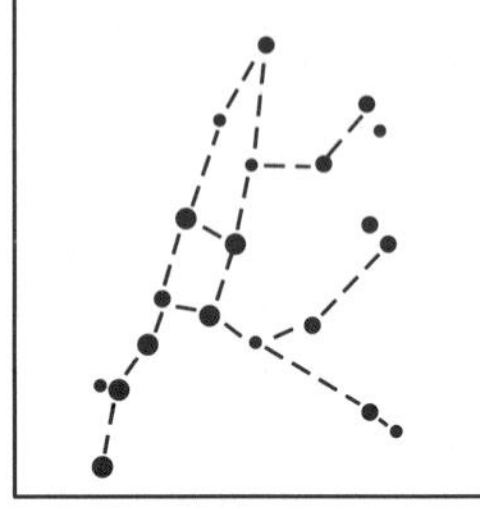

Ursa Major

u·ros·co·py (yo͞o-rŏs′kə-pē) *n., pl.* **-pies.** Examination of urine for diagnostic purposes.

u·ros·to·my (yo͞o-rŏs′tə-mē) *n., pl.* **-mies.** Surgical construction of an artificial excretory opening from the urinary tract.

–urous *suff.* Having a specified kind of tail: *anurous.* [From New Latin *-ūrus,* from Greek *-ouros,* from *oura,* tail. See **ors-** in Appendix.]

♦ **urp** (ûrp) *intr.v.* **urped, urp·ing, urps.** *Mississippi River Delta.* To vomit. [Imitative.]

Ur·quhart (ûr′kərt, -kärt′), Sir **Thomas.** 1611–1660. Scottish Royalist, writer, and translator of the works of Rabelais.

Ur·sa Major (ûr′sə) *n.* A constellation in the region of the north celestial pole near Draco and Leo, containing the seven stars that form the Big Dipper. Also called *Great Bear.* [Middle English, from Latin *Ursa Māior* : *ursa,* bear + *māior,* comparative of *magnus,* great.]

Ursa Minor *n.* A constellation having the shape of a ladle with Polaris at the tip of its handle. Also called *Little Bear.* [From Late Latin *minor Ursa* : *minor,* lesser + *ursa,* bear.]

ur·sine (ûr′sīn′) *adj.* Of or characteristic of bears or a bear. [Latin *ursīnus,* from *ursus,* bear. See **r̥tko-** in Appendix.]

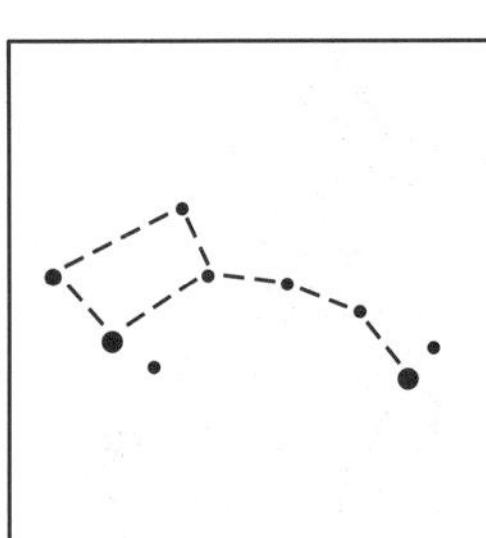

Ursa Minor

Ur·spra·che (o͞or′shprä′KHə) *n.* See **protolanguage.** [German : *ur-,* original (from Middle High German, out of, from Old High German; see **ud-** in Appendix) + *Sprache,* language, speech (from Middle High German *sprāche,* from Old High German *sprāhha*).]

Ur·su·line (ûr′sə-lĭn, -līn′, -lēn′, ûr′syə-) *n.* A member of an order of nuns of the Roman Catholic Church, founded in the early 16th century and devoted to the education of girls. —**Ursuline** *adj.* Of or belonging to the Ursulines. [After Saint *Ursula,* legendary British princess and martyr.]

ur·ti·cant (ûr′tĭ-kənt) *adj.* Causing itching or stinging. —**urticant** *n.* A substance that causes itching or stinging.

ur·ti·car·i·a (ûr′tĭ-kâr′ē-ə) *n.* See **hives.** [New Latin *urticāria,* from Latin *urtica,* nettle.] —**ur′ti·car′i·al** *adj.*

ur·ti·cate (ûr′tĭ-kāt′) *v.* **-cat·ed, -cat·ing, -cates.** —*tr.* To sting or whip with or as if with nettles. —*intr.* To produce a stinging or itching sensation. —**urticate** (-kĭt, -kāt′) *adj.* Characterized by the presence of hives. [Medieval Latin *urticāre, urticāt-,* from Latin *urtica,* nettle.]

ur·ti·ca·tion (ûr′tĭ-kā′shən) *n.* **1.** The formation or development of hives. **2.** The sensation of having been stung by nettles. **3.** A lashing with nettles formerly used to treat a paralyzed part of the body.

U·rua·pan (o͞or-wä′pən, -pän). A city of southwest-central Mexico west of Mexico City. Population, 122,828.

U·ru·bam·ba (o͞o′ro͞o-bäm′bə). A river of Peru rising in the Andes and flowing about 724 km (450 miles) north-northwest to join the Apurímac River and form the Ucayali River.

Uruguay

U·ru·guay (yo͝or′ə-gwī′, -gwā′, o͞o′ro͞o-gwī′). *Abbr.* **Urug.** A country of southeast South America on the Atlantic Ocean and the Río de la Plata. First settled in the 1600's, the region achieved its independence from Spain in 1814 and severed its union with Brazil in 1828. Montevideo is the capital and the largest city. Population, 2,788,429. —**U′ru·guay′an** *adj. & n.*

Uruguay River. A river of southeast South America rising in southern Brazil and flowing about 1,609 km (1,000 mi) west and south along the Brazil-Argentina border and the Argentina-Uruguay border to the Río de la Plata.

Ü·rüm·qi also **U·rum·chi** (o͞o-ro͞om′chē, ü′rüm′chē′). A city of northwest China in the Tien Shan. Population, 947,000.

u·rus (yo͝or′əs) *n., pl.* **u·rus·es.** An extinct wild ox *(Bos primigenius)* of Europe, northern Africa, and western Asia, believed to be the ancestor of domestic cattle. Also called *aurochs.* [Latin *ūrus,* of Germanic origin.]

u·ru·shi·ol (o͞o-ro͞o′shē-ôl′, -ōl′, -ŏl′) *n.* A toxic substance present in the resin or on the surface of plants of the genus *Rhus,* including poison ivy and the lacquer tree, from which a black Japanese lacquer is obtained. [Japanese *urushi,* lacquer + –OL[1].]

us (ŭs) *pron.* The objective case of **we. 1.** Used as the direct object of a verb: *She saw us on the subway.* **2.** Used as the indirect object of a verb: *They gave us free tickets.* **3.** Used as the object of a preposition: *This letter is addressed to us.* **4.** *Informal.* Used as a predicate nominative: *It's us.* See Usage Note at **we.** [Middle English, from Old English *ūs.* See **nes-**[2] in Appendix.]

u.s. *abbr. Latin.* **1.** Ubi supra (where mentioned above). **2.** Ut supra (as above).

U.S. or **US** *abbr.* **1.** Uncle Sam. **2.** Uniform System (of lens aperture). **3.** United States. **4.** United States highway.

USA *abbr.* **1.** Also **U.S.A.** United States Army. **2.** Or **U.S.A.** United States of America.

us·a·ble also **use·a·ble** (yo͞o′zə-bəl) *adj.* **1.** That can be used: *usable byproducts.* **2.** Fit for use; convenient to use: *usable spare parts; a usable reference book.* —**us′a·bil′i·ty, us′a·ble·ness** *n.* —**us′a·bly** *adv.*

USAF also **U.S.A.F.** *abbr.* United States Air Force.

us·age (yo͞o′sĭj, -zĭj) *n.* **1.a.** The act, manner, or amount of using; use: *the usage of a technical term; an instrument that measures water usage.* **b.** The act or manner of treating; treatment: *subjected the car to rough usage.* **2.** A usual, habitual, or accepted practice. See Synonyms at **habit. 3.** The way in which words or phrases are actually used, spoken, or written in a speech community. **4.** A particular expression in speech or writing: *a nonce usage.* [Middle English, from Old French, from *us,* from Latin *ūsus,* from past participle of *ūtī,* to use.]

us·ance (yo͞o′zəns) *n.* **1.** The length of time, established by custom and varying between countries, that is allowed for payment of a foreign bill of exchange. **2.** Use. **3.** Usage; custom. **4.** Interest paid on borrowed money. [Middle English, usage, from Old French, probably from Vulgar Latin **ūsantia,* from **ūsāns, *ūsant-,* present participle of **ūsāre,* frequentative of Latin *ūtī.*]

USAR *abbr.* United States Army Reserve.

USAREUR *abbr.* United States Army, Europe.

U.S.C. *abbr. Law.* United States Code.

U.S.C.A. *abbr. Law.* United States Code Annotated.

USCG also **U.S.C.G.** *abbr.* United States Coast Guard.

USDA *abbr.* United States Department of Agriculture.

use (yo͞oz) *v.* **used, us·ing, us·es.** —*tr.* **1.** To put into service or apply for a purpose; employ. **2.** To avail oneself of; practice: *use caution.* **3.** To conduct oneself toward; treat or handle: *"the peace offering of a man who once used you unkindly"* (Laurence Sterne). **4.** To seek or achieve an end by means of; exploit: *used their highly placed friends to gain access to the president; felt he was being used by seekers of favor.* **5.** To take or consume; partake of: *She rarely used alcohol.* —intr. (yo͞os, yo͞ost). Used in the past tense followed by *to* in order to indicate a former state, habitual practice, or custom: *Mail service used to be faster.* —**use** (yo͞os) *n.* **1.a.** The act of using; the application or employment of something for a purpose: *with the use of a calculator; skilled in the use of the bow and arrow.* **b.** The condition or fact of being used: *a chair in regular use.* **2.** The manner of using; usage: *learned the proper use of power tools.* **3.a.** The permission, privilege, or benefit of using something: *gave us the use of their summerhouse.* **b.** The power or ability to use something: *lost the use of one arm.* **4.** The need or occasion to use or employ: *have no use for these old clothes.* **5.** The quality of being suitable or adaptable to an end; usefulness: *tried to be of use in the kitchen.* **6.** A purpose for which something is used: *a tool with several uses; a pretty bowl, but of what use is it?* **7.** Gain or advantage; good: *There's no use in discussing it. What's the use?* **8.** Accustomed or usual procedure or practice. **9.** *Law.* **a.** Enjoyment of property, as by occupying or exercising it. **b.** The benefit or profit of lands and tenements of which the legal title and possession are vested in another. **c.** The arrangement establishing the equitable right to such benefits and profits. **10.** A liturgical form practiced in a particular church, ecclesiastical district, or community. **11.** *Obsolete.* Usual occurrence or experience. —***phrasal verb.* use up.** To consume completely: *used up all our money.* [Middle English *usen,* from Old French *user,* from Vulgar Latin **ūsāre,* frequentative of Latin *ūtī.*]

SYNONYMS: *use, employ, utilize.* These verbs mean to avail oneself of someone or something in order to make him, her, or it useful, functional, or beneficial. To *use* is to put into service or apply for a purpose: *uses a hearing aid; used the press secretary as spokesperson for the administration; using a stick to stir the paint. Employ* is often interchangeable with *use*: *She employed her education to maximum advantage.* Unlike *use,* however, the term can denote engaging or maintaining the services of another or putting another to work: *"When men are employed, they are best contented"* (Benjamin Franklin). *Utilize* is especially appropriate in the narrower sense of making something profitable or of finding new and practical uses for it: *In the 19th century waterpower was widely utilized to generate electricity.* See also Synonyms at **habit.**

use·a·ble (yo͞o′zə-bəl) *adj.* Variant of **usable.**

used (yo͞ozd) *adj.* **1.** Not new; secondhand: *a used car.* **2.** (*also* yo͞ost). Accustomed; habituated: *getting used to the cold weather; was used to driving a small car.*

use·ful (yo͞os′fəl) *adj.* **1.** Having a beneficial use; serviceable: *a useful kitchen gadget.* **2.** Having practical utility: *a useful job; useful members of society.* —**use′ful·ly** *adv.* —**use′ful·ness** *n.*

use·less (yo͞os′lĭs) *adj.* **1.** Being or having no beneficial use; futile or ineffective. **2.** Incapable of functioning or assisting; ineffectual: *He panics easily and is useless in an emergency.* See Synonyms at **futile.** —**use′less·ly** *adv.* —**use′less·ness** *n.*

us·er (yo͞o′zər) *n.* **1.** One that uses: *a user of public transportation.* **2.** *Law.* The exercise or enjoyment of a right or property. **3.** One who uses addictive drugs.

us·er-friend·ly (yo͞o′zər-frĕnd′lē) *adj.* **-li·er, -li·est.** Easy to use or learn to use: *"a user-friendly system designed for small* *businesses with no prior computer experience"* (Byte). *"The public ought to be aware of the complexity of making new tax forms user-friendly"* (New York Times). **—us′er-friend′li·ness** *n.*

us·er-un·friend·ly (yo͞o′zər-ŭn-frĕnd′lē) *adj.* **-li·er, -li·est.** Not easy to use or learn to use: *"renovating user-unfriendly JFK airport and rebuilding Brooklyn shipping"* (Stanley Brezenoff).

Ush·ant (ŭsh′ənt). An island of northwest France in the Atlantic Ocean off western Brittany. Naval battles between the French and the British occurred off the island in 1778 and 1794.

ush·er (ŭsh′ər) *n.* **1.** One who is employed to escort people to their seats, as in a theater, church, or stadium. **2.** A man who attends a bridal party at a wedding. **3.** One who serves as official doorkeeper, as in a courtroom or legislative chamber. **4.** An official whose duty is to make introductions between unacquainted persons or to precede persons of rank in a procession. **5.** *Archaic.* An assistant teacher in a school. **—usher** *v.* **-ered, -er·ing, -ers.** —*tr.* **1.** To serve as an usher to; escort. **2.** To lead or conduct. See Synonyms at **guide. 3.** To precede and introduce; inaugurate: *a celebration to usher in the new century.* —*intr.* To serve as an usher: *ushered at church.* [Middle English, doorkeeper, from Anglo-Norman *usser,* from Vulgar Latin **ūstiārius,* from Latin *ōstiārius,* from *ōstium,* door. See **ōs-** in Appendix.]

ush·er·ette (ŭsh′ə-rĕt′) *n.* A girl or woman employed to escort people to their seats, as in a theater or stadium. See Usage Note at **-ette.**

USIA *abbr.* United States Information Agency.

U.S.M. *abbr.* United States Mail.

USMC also **U.S.M.C.** *abbr.* United States Marine Corps.

USN also **U.S.N.** *abbr.* United States Navy.

USNA also **U.S.N.A.** *abbr.* United States Naval Academy.

us·ne·a (ŭs′nē-ə, ŭz′-) *n.* Any of various widely distributed lichens of the genus *Usnea,* characterized by a gray pendulous thallus. [From Arabic *'ušnah,* moss.]

us·nic acid (ŭs′nĭk) *n.* An antibacterial substance, $C_{18}H_{16}O_7$, obtained from lichens of the genus *Usnea,* especially *U. barbata.*

USNR *abbr.* United States Naval Reserve.

USO or **U.S.O.** *abbr.* United Service Organizations.

U.S.P. *abbr.* United States Pharmacopoeia.

Us·pal·la·ta Pass (o͞o′spä-yä′tə, -tä). A pass, about 3,813 m (12,500 ft) high, through the Andes between Mendoza, Argentina, and Santiago, Chile.

USPO also **U.S.P.O.** *abbr.* United States Post Office.

USPS also **U.S.P.S.** *abbr.* United States Postal Service.

us·que·baugh (ŭs′kwĭ-bô′, -bä′) *n.* *Irish & Scots.* Whiskey. [Scottish Gaelic *uisge beatha* and Irish Gaelic *uisce beatha,* water of life, whiskey (translation of Medieval Latin *aqua vītae*) : Old Irish *uisce,* water; see **wed-**[1] in Appendix + Old Irish *bethad,* genitive of *bethu,* life; see **gʷei-** in Appendix.]

U.S.S. *abbr.* **1.** United States Senate. **2.** *Nautical.* United States ship.

Ussh·er (ŭsh′ər), **James.** 1581–1656. Irish prelate and scholar who devised a scheme of biblical chronology that placed the Creation in the year 4004 B.C.

U.S.S.R. or **USSR** *abbr.* Union of Soviet Socialist Republics.

U·sti·nov (o͞o-stĭn′ôf). See **Izhevsk.**

Ust-Ka·me·no·gorsk (o͞ost′kə-mĕn′ə-gôrsk′, -myĭ-nə-). A city of northeast Kazakhstan on the Irtysh River southeast of Semipalatinsk. Population, 307,000.

usu. *abbr.* Usually.

u·su·al (yo͞o′zho͞o-əl) *adj.* **1.** Commonly encountered, experienced, or observed: *the usual summer heat.* **2.** Regularly or customarily used: *ended the speech with the usual expressions of thanks.* **3.** In conformity with regular practice or procedure: *Come at the usual time.* **—*idiom.* as usual.** As commonly or habitually happens: *As usual, I slept late that Saturday morning.* [Middle English, from Old French *usuel,* from Late Latin *ūsuālis,* from Latin *ūsus,* use, from past participle of *ūtī,* to use.] **—u′su·al·ly** *adv.* **—u′su·al·ness** *n.*

SYNONYMS: *usual, habitual, customary, accustomed.* These adjectives apply to what is expected or familiar because it occurs frequently or recurs regularly. *Usual* describes what accords with normal, common, or ordinary practice or procedure: *"The parson said the usual things about the sea—its blueness . . . its beauty"* (George du Maurier). *Habitual* implies repetition and force of habit: *"He who permits himself to tell a lie once, finds it much easier to do it a second and third time, till at length it becomes habitual"* (Thomas Jefferson). *Customary* and *accustomed* refer to conformity with the prevailing customs or conventions of a group or with an individual's own established practice: *"It is the customary fate of new truths to begin as heresies and to end as superstitions"* (Thomas H. Huxley). *She resolved the difficulty with her accustomed resourcefulness and tact.*

u·su·fruct (yo͞o′zə-frŭkt′, -sə-) *n.* *Law.* The right to use and enjoy the profits and advantages of something belonging to another as long as the property is not damaged or altered in any way. [Late Latin *ūsūfrūctus,* variant of Latin *ūsusfrūctus* : *ūsus,* use; see USUAL + *frūctus,* enjoyment; see FRUIT.]

u·su·fruc·tu·ar·y (yo͞o′zə-frŭk′cho͞o-ĕr′ē, -sə-) *Law. n., pl.* **-ies.** One that holds property by usufruct. **—usufructuary** *adj.* Of or relating to the nature of a usufruct.

U·su·ma·cin·ta (o͞o′sə-mə-sĭn′tə, -so͞o-mä-sēn′tä). A river, about 965 km (600 mi) long, of southeast Mexico.

u·su·rer (yo͞o′zhər-ər) *n.* One who lends money at interest, especially at an exorbitant or unlawfully high rate. [Middle English, from Anglo-Norman, from Late Latin *ūsūrārius,* moneylender, from Latin, interest-bearing, from *ūsūra,* usury. See USURY.]

u·su·ri·ous (yo͞o-zho͝or′ē-əs) *adj.* **1.** Practicing usury. **2.** Of or constituting usury: *usurious interest rates.* **—u·su′ri·ous·ly** *adv.* **—u·su′ri·ous·ness** *n.*

u·surp (yo͞o-sûrp′, -zûrp′) *v.* **-surped, -surp·ing, -surps.** —*tr.* **1.** To seize and hold (the power or rights of another, for example) by force and without legal authority. See Synonyms at **appropriate. 2.** To take over or occupy without right: *usurp a neighbor's land.* —*intr.* To seize another's place, authority, or possession wrongfully. [Middle English *usurpen,* from Old French *usurper,* from Latin *ūsūrpāre,* to take into use, usurp. See **reup-** in Appendix.] **—u·surp′er** *n.* **—u·surp′ing·ly** *adv.*

u·sur·pa·tion (yo͞o′sər-pā′shən, -zər-) *n.* **1.** The act of usurping, especially the wrongful seizure of royal sovereignty. **2.** A wrongful seizure or exercise of authority or privilege belonging to another; an encroachment: *"in our own day, gross usurpations upon the liberty of private life"* (John Stuart Mill).

u·su·ry (yo͞o′zhə-rē) *n., pl.* **-ries. 1.** The practice of lending money and charging the borrower interest, especially at an exorbitant or illegally high rate. **2.** An excessive or illegally high rate of interest charged on borrowed money. **3.** *Archaic.* Interest charged or paid on a loan. [Middle English, from Medieval Latin *ūsūria,* alteration of Latin *ūsūra,* from *ūsus,* use. See USUAL.]

ut (ŭt, o͞ot) *n.* *Music.* A syllable representing the tone C, otherwise represented by *do,* in the French system of solmization. [Middle English, from Medieval Latin. See GAMUT.]

UT *abbr.* **1.** Universal time. **2.** Or **Ut.** Utah.

U·tah (yo͞o′tô′, -tä′). *Abbr.* **UT, Ut.** A state of the western United States. It was admitted as the 45th state in 1896. First explored by the Spanish in 1540, the region was settled in 1847 by Mormons led by Brigham Young. Salt Lake City is the capital and the largest city. Population, 1,461,037. **—U′tah·an** *adj. & n.*

UTC *abbr.* Universal time coordinated.

ut dict. *abbr.* *Latin.* Ut dictum (as directed).

Ute (yo͞ot) *n., pl.* **Ute** or **Utes. 1.a.** A Native American people formerly inhabiting a large area of Colorado, Utah, and northern New Mexico, with present-day populations in northeast Utah and along the Colorado–New Mexico border. **b.** A member of this people. **2.** The Uto-Aztecan language of the Ute. [From *Utah,* Ute Indian, from American Spanish *Yuta;* akin to Southern Paiute *yuuttaci.*]

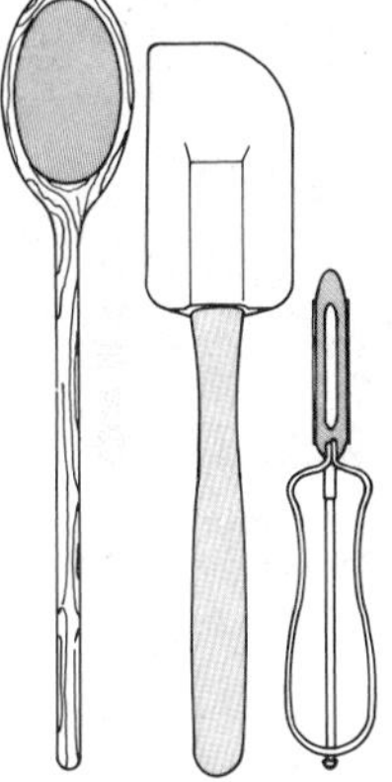

utensil
Left to right: Wooden spoon, spatula, and vegetable peeler

u·ten·sil (yo͞o-tĕn′səl) *n.* An instrument, an implement, or a container used domestically, especially in a kitchen. See Synonyms at **tool.** [Middle English, from Old French *utensile,* from Latin *ūtēnsilia,* utensils, from neuter pl. of *ūtēnsilis,* fit for use, from *ūtī,* to use.]

u·ter·i (yo͞o′tə-rī′) *n.* A plural of **uterus.**

u·ter·ine (yo͞o′tər-ĭn, -tə-rīn′) *adj.* **1.** Of, relating to, or in the region of the uterus: *the uterine canal; uterine contractions.* **2.** Having the same mother but different fathers. [Middle English, from Late Latin *uterīnus,* from Latin *uterus,* uterus.]

u·ter·us (yo͞o′tər-əs) *n., pl.* **u·ter·i** (yo͞o′tə-rī′) or **u·ter·us·es. 1.** A hollow muscular organ located in the pelvic cavity of female mammals in which the fertilized egg implants and develops. Also called *womb.* **2.** A corresponding part in other animals. [Middle English, from Latin.]

U Thant (o͞o thänt′, thănt′). See U **Thant.**

U·ther Pen·dra·gon (yo͞o′thər pĕn-drăg′ən, o͞o′-) *n.* In Arthurian legend, a king of Britain and the father of Arthur.

U·ti·ca (yo͞o′tĭ-kə). **1.** An ancient city of northern Africa on the Mediterranean Sea northwest of Carthage. According to tradition, it was founded c. 1100 B.C. by Phoenicians from Tyre. The city declined in the first century B.C. and was finally destroyed by the Arabs c. A.D. 700. **2.** A city of central New York east-northeast of Syracuse. Settled in 1773 on the site of Fort Schuyler (established in 1758), it developed as an industrial center after the opening of the Erie Canal in 1825. Population, 75,632.

util. *abbr.* Utility.

u·tile (yo͞ot′l, yo͞o′tīl′) *adj.* Useful. [Middle English, from Old French, from Latin *ūtilis.* See UTILITY.]

u·til·i·tar·i·an (yo͞o-tĭl′ĭ-târ′ē-ən) *adj.* **1.** Of, relating to, or in the interests of utility: *utilitarian considerations in industrial design.* **2.** Exhibiting or stressing utility over other values; practical: *plain, utilitarian kitchenware.* **3.** Of, characterized by, or advocating utilitarianism. **—utilitarian** *n.* One who advocates or practices utilitarianism. [UTILIT(Y) + -ARIAN.]

u·til·i·tar·i·an·ism (yo͞o-tĭl′ĭ-târ′ē-ə-nĭz′əm) *n.* **1.** The belief that the value of a thing or an action is determined by its utility. **2.** The ethical theory proposed by Jeremy Bentham and James Mill that all action should be directed toward achieving the greatest happiness for the greatest number of people. **3.** The quality of being utilitarian: *housing of bleak utilitarianism.*

u·til·i·ty (yo͞o-tĭl′ĭ-tē) *n., pl.* **-ties. 1.** The quality or condition of being useful; usefulness: *"I have always doubted the utility of these conferences on disarmament"* (Winston S. Churchill). **2.** A useful article or device. **3.** *Abbr.* **util. a.** A public utility. **b.** A commodity or service, such as electricity, water, or public transportation, that is provided by a public utility. **—utility** *adj.* **1.**

ă pat	oi boy
ā pay	ou out
âr care	o͝o took
ä father	o͞o boot
ĕ pet	ŭ cut
ē be	ûr urge
ĭ pit	th thin
ī pie	*th* this
îr pier	hw which
ŏ pot	zh vision
ō toe	ə about, item
ô paw	♦ regionalism

Stress marks: ′ (primary); ′ (secondary), as in **dictionary** (dĭk′shə-nĕr′ē)

Used, serving, or working in several capacities as needed, especially: **a.** Prepared to play any of the smaller theatrical roles on short notice: *a utility cast member.* **b.** Capable of playing as a substitute in any of several positions: *a utility infielder.* **2.** Designed for various often heavy-duty practical uses: *a utility knife; a utility vehicle.* **3.** Raised or kept for the production of a farm product rather than for show or as pets: *utility livestock.* **4.** Of the lowest U.S. Government grade: *utility beef.* [Middle English *utilite,* from Old French, from Latin *ūtilitās,* from *ūtilis,* useful, from *ūtī,* to use.]

u·til·ize (yo͞ot′l-īz′) *tr.v.* **-ized, -iz·ing, -iz·es.** To put to use, especially to find a profitable or practical use for. See Synonyms at **use.** [French *utiliser,* from Italian *utilizzare,* from *utile,* useful, from Latin *ūtilis,* from *ūtī,* to use.] **—u′til·iz′a·ble** *adj.* **—u′til·i·za′tion** (-ĭ-zā′shən) *n.* **—u′til·iz′er** *n.*

USAGE NOTE: A number of critics have remarked that *utilize* is an unnecessary substitute for *use.* It is true that many occurrences of *utilize* could be replaced by *use* with no loss to anything but pretentiousness, for example, in sentences such as *Barbara utilized* (prefer *used*) *questionable methods in her analysis* or *We hope that many commuters will continue to utilize* (prefer *use*) *mass transit after the bridge has reopened.* But *utilize* can mean "to find a profitable or practical use for." Thus the sentence *The teachers were unable to use the new computers* might mean only that the teachers were unable to turn the computers on, whereas the *The teachers were unable to utilize the new computers* suggests that the teachers could not find ways to employ the computers in instruction.

ut·most (ŭt′mōst′) *adj.* **1.** Being or situated at the most distant limit or point; farthest: *the utmost tip of the peninsula.* **2.** Of the highest or greatest degree, amount, or intensity; most extreme: *a matter of the utmost importance.* **—utmost** *n.* The greatest possible amount, degree, or extent; the maximum: *worked every day to the utmost of her abilities.* [Middle English, from Old English *ūtmest* : *ūt,* out; see **ud-** in Appendix + *-mest,* -most.]

U·to-Az·tec·an (yo͞o′tō-ăz′tĕk′ən) *n.* **1.** A language phylum of North and Central America that includes Ute, Hopi, Nahuatl, and Shoshone. **2.a.** A tribe speaking a Uto-Aztecan language. **b.** A member of such a tribe. **—Uto-Aztecan** *adj.* Of or relating to the Uto-Aztecans or to the languages spoken by them. [From UTE + AZTEC.]

u·to·pi·a (yo͞o-tō′pē-ə) *n.* **1.a.** Often **Utopia.** An ideally perfect place, especially in its social, political, and moral aspects. **b.** A work of fiction describing a utopia. **2.** An impractical, idealistic scheme for social and political reform. [New Latin *Ūtopia,* imaginary island in *Utopia* by Sir Thomas More : Greek *ou,* not, no + Greek *topos,* place.]

u·to·pi·an (yo͞o-tō′pē-ən) *adj.* **1.** Often **Utopian.** Of, relating to, describing or having the characteristics of a Utopia: *a Utopian island; Utopian novels.* **2.a.** Excellent or ideal but impracticable; visionary: *a utopian scheme for equalizing wealth.* **b.** Proposing impracticably ideal schemes. **—utopian** *n.* A zealous but impractical reformer of human society.

u·to·pi·an·ism also **U·to·pi·an·ism** (yo͞o-tō′pē-ə-nĭz′əm) *n.* The ideals or principles of a utopian; idealistic and impractical social theory.

U·trecht (yo͞o′trĕkt′, ü′trĕKHt). A city of central Netherlands south-southeast of Amsterdam. Dating to pre-Roman times, it was an important textile and commercial center during the Middle Ages. Population, 230,414.

u·tri·cle[1] (yo͞o′trĭ-kəl) *n.* **1.** A membranous sac contained within the labyrinth of the inner ear and connected with the semicircular canals. **2.** *Botany.* A small bladderlike one-seeded indehiscent fruit, as in the amaranth. [Latin *utriculus,* diminutive of *uter, utr-,* leather bottle, possibly from Greek *hudria,* water vessel, from *hudōr, hudr-,* water. See **wed-[1]** in Appendix.]

u·tri·cle[2] (yo͞o′trĭ-kəl) *n.* A small vestigial blind pouch of the prostate gland. [Latin *utriculus,* sac, diminutive of *uterus,* uterus.]

u·tric·u·lar[1] (yo͞o-trĭk′yə-lər) *adj.* **1.** Of, relating to, or resembling a utricle. **2.** Having one or more utricles.

u·tric·u·lar[2] (yo͞o-trĭk′yə-lər) *adj.* Relating to the uterus.

u·tric·u·lus (yo͞o-trĭk′yə-ləs) *n., pl.* **-li** (-lī′). A sac or pouch.

U·tril·lo (yo͞o-trĭl′ō, ü-trē-ō′), **Maurice.** 1883–1955. French painter known especially for his street scenes of Paris.

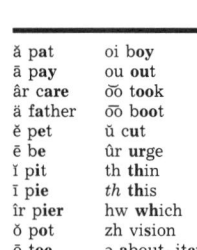

Maurice Utrillo
Photographed c. 1924

U·tsu·no·mi·ya (o͞ot′sə-nō′mē-ə, o͞o-tso͞o′nô-mē′yä). A city of central Honshu, Japan, north of Tokyo. It is a resort and tobacco-processing center. Population, 405,384.

ut·ter[1] (ŭt′ər) *tr.v.* **-tered, -ter·ing, -ters. 1.** To send forth with the voice: *uttered a cry.* **2.** To articulate (words); pronounce or speak. See Synonyms at **vent[1]. 3.** *Law.* To put (counterfeit money, for example) into circulation. **4.** To publish (a book, for example). **5.** *Obsolete.* To sell or deliver (merchandise) in trading. [Middle English *utteren,* partly from Middle Low German *uteren* (from *uter,* outer, comparative of *ūt,* out; see **ud-** in Appendix) and partly alteration (influenced by *utter,* outer; see UTTER[2]) of Middle English *outen,* to disclose (from *out,* out; see OUT).] **—ut′ter·a·ble** *adj.* **—ut′ter·er** *n.*

ut·ter[2] (ŭt′ər) *adj.* Complete; absolute; entire: *utter nonsense; utter darkness.* [Middle English, from Old English *ūtera,* outer. See **ud-** in Appendix.]

ut·ter·ance[1] (ŭt′ər-əns) *n.* **1.a.** The act of uttering; vocal expression. **b.** The power of speaking; speech: *as long as I have utterance.* **c.** A manner of speaking: *argued with forceful utterance.* **2.** Something uttered or expressed; a statement.

ut·ter·ance[2] (ŭt′ər-əns) *n.* The uttermost end or extremity; the bitter end. [Middle English, from Old French *outrance,* from *outrer,* to go beyond limits, from Vulgar Latin **ultrāre,* from Latin *ultrā,* beyond. See **al-[1]** in Appendix.]

ut·ter·ly (ŭt′ər-lē) *adv.* Completely; absolutely; entirely.

ut·ter·most (ŭt′ər-mōst′) *adj.* **1.** Utmost. **2.** Outermost. **—uttermost** *n.* The greatest amount or degree possible; the utmost. [Middle English : *utter,* outer; see UTTER[2] + *-most,* -most.]

U-turn (yo͞o′tûrn′) *n.* A turn, as by a vehicle, completely reversing the direction of travel.

UV also **U.V.** *abbr.* Ultraviolet.

u·va·rov·ite (yo͞o-vär′ə-vīt′, o͞o-) *n.* An emerald-green variety of garnet, $Ca_3Cr_2(SiO_4)_3$, found in chromium deposits. [After Count Sergei Semenovitch *Uvarov* (1785–1855), president of the St. Petersburg Academy.]

u·ve·a (yo͞o′vē-ə) *n.* The vascular middle layer of the eye constituting the iris, ciliary body, and choroid. [Medieval Latin *ūvea,* from Latin *ūva,* grape.] **—u′ve·al** *adj.*

u·ve·i·tis (yo͞o′vē-ī′tĭs) *n.* Inflammation of the uvea. [UVE(A) + -ITIS.]

u·vu·la (yo͞o′vyə-lə) *n.* A small, conical, fleshy mass of tissue suspended from the center of the soft palate. [Middle English, from Late Latin *ūvula,* diminutive of Latin *ūva,* grape (from the organ's shape).]

u·vu·lar (yo͞o′vyə-lər) *adj.* **1.** Of, relating to, or associated with the uvula. **2.** *Linguistics.* Articulated by vibration of the uvula or with the back of the tongue near or touching the uvula.

u·vu·li·tis (yo͞o′vyə-lī′tĭs) *n.* Inflammation of the uvula. [UVUL(A) + -ITIS.]

UW *abbr.* **1.** Underwriter. **2.** Underwritten.

ux. *abbr. Latin.* Uxor (wife).

UXB *abbr.* Unexploded bomb.

Ux·mal (o͞os-mäl′). An ancient ruined Mayan city of Yucatán in southeast Mexico. It flourished from 600 to 900. The ruins include many impressive structures, such as the Pyramid of the Magician.

ux·o·ri·al (ŭk-sôr′ē-əl, -sōr′-, ŭg-zôr′-, -zōr′-) *adj.* Of a wife; regarded as befitting a wife. [From Latin *uxōrius,* from *uxor, uxōr-,* wife.] **—ux·o′ri·al·ly** *adv.*

ux·o·ri·cide (ŭk-sôr′ĭ-sīd′, -sōr′-, ŭg-zôr′-, -zōr′-) *n.* **1.** The killing of a wife by her husband. **2.** A man who kills his wife. [Medieval Latin *uxōricīdium* : Latin *uxor, uxōr-,* wife + Latin *-cīdium,* -cide.]

ux·o·ri·ous (ŭk-sôr′ē-əs, -sōr′-, ŭg-zôr′-, -zōr′-) *adj.* Excessively submissive or devoted to one's wife. [From Latin *uxōrius,* from *uxor, uxōr-,* wife.] **—ux·o′ri·ous·ly** *adv.* **—ux·o′ri·ous·ness** *n.*

Uz·bek (o͞oz′bĕk′, ŭz′-) *n., pl.* **Uzbek** or **-beks. 1.** A member of a Turkic people inhabiting Uzbekistan and neighboring areas. **2.** The Turkic language of the Uzbeks. [Russian, from Uzbek *ŭzbek.*]

Uz·bek·i·stan (o͞oz-bĕk′ĭ-stăn′, -stän′, ŭz-). A region of west-central Asia. Settled in ancient times, it was conquered by Alexander the Great, Genghis Khan, and Tamerlane and finally overrun by Uzbek peoples in the early 16th century. Russia conquered the area in the 19th century. Split into various administrative territories after 1917, it was consolidated as a constituent republic in 1924. Tashkent is the capital. Population, 17,974,000.

ă pat	oi **boy**
ā pay	ou **out**
âr **care**	o͝o **took**
ä father	o͞o **boot**
ĕ pet	ŭ **cut**
ē be	ûr **urge**
ĭ pit	th **thin**
ī pie	*th* **this**
îr **pier**	hw **which**
ŏ pot	zh vision
ō **toe**	ə about, item
ô **paw**	♦ regionalism

Stress marks: ′ (primary); ′ (secondary), as in **dictionary** (dĭk′shə-nĕr′ē)

v or **V** (vē) *n., pl.* **v's** or **V's. 1.** The 22nd letter of the modern English alphabet. **2.** Any of the speech sounds represented by the letter *v.* **3.** The 22nd in a series. **4.** Something shaped like the letter V.

V[1] **1.** The symbol for the element **vanadium. 2.** *Electricity.* The symbol for **potential** (sense 5). **3.** Also **v** The symbol for the Roman numeral 5.

V[2] *abbr.* **1.** *Physics.* Velocity. **2.** Victory. **3.** *Electricity.* Volt. **4.** Volume (size or capacity).

V-1 (vē′wŭn′) *n.* A robot bomb deployed by the Germans in World War II. [German *Vergeltungswaffe eins,* retaliation weapon (number) one.]

V-2 (vē′to͞o′) *n.* A long-range liquid-fuel rocket used by the Germans as a ballistic missile in World War II. [German *Vergeltungswaffe zwei,* retaliation weapon (number) two.]

v. *abbr.* **1.** Verb. **2.** Verse. **3.** Version. **4.** *Printing.* Verso. **5.** Versus. **6.** Or **V.** Very (in titles). **7.** Vide. **8.** Or **V.** Village. **9.** Violin. **10.** Vocative. **11.** Voice. **12.** Volume (book). **13.** Vowel.

V. *abbr.* **1.** Venerable (in titles). **2.** Viscount; viscountess.

VA or **Va.** *abbr.* Virginia.

V.A. *abbr.* **1.** Also **VA** Veterans' Administration. **2.** Vicar apostolic.

Vaal (väl). A river rising in eastern South Africa and flowing about 1,207 km (750 mi) southwest to the Orange River.

VAB *abbr.* Voice answer back.

vac[1] (văk) *n. Informal.* A vacuum cleaner.

vac[2] (văk) *n. Informal.* A vacation.

vac. *abbr.* Vacuum.

va·can·cy (vā′kən-sē) *n., pl.* **-cies. 1.** The condition of being vacant or unoccupied. **2.** An empty or unoccupied space. **3.** A position, an office, or a place of accommodation that is unfilled or unoccupied. **4.** Emptiness of mind; inanity. **5.** A crystal defect caused by the absence of an atom, an ion, or a molecule in a crystal lattice. **6.** *Archaic.* A period of leisure; idleness.

va·cant (vā′kənt) *adj.* **1.** Containing nothing; empty. **2.** Without an incumbent or occupant; unfilled: *a vacant position.* **3.** Not occupied or put to use: *a vacant lot.* **4.** *Law.* Not claimed by an heir: *a vacant estate.* **5.a.** Lacking intelligence or knowledge: *a vacant mind.* **b.** Lacking expression; blank: *a vacant stare.* **6.** Not filled with any activity: *vacant hours.* See Synonyms at **empty.** [Middle English, from Old French, from Latin *vacāns, vacant-,* present participle of *vacāre,* to be empty. See **eu-[2]** in Appendix.] **—va′cant·ly** *adv.* **—va′cant·ness** *n.*

va·cate (vā′kāt′, vā-kāt′) *v.* **-cat·ed, -cat·ing, -cates.** —*tr.* **1.a.** To cease to occupy or hold; give up. **b.** To empty of occupants or incumbents. **2.** *Law.* To make void or annul; countermand: *vacate a death sentence.* —*intr.* To leave a job, an office, or a lodging. [Latin *vacāre, vacāt-,* to be empty. See **eu-[2]** in Appendix.]

va·ca·tion (vā-kā′shən, və-) *n.* **1.** A period of time devoted to pleasure, rest, or relaxation, especially one with pay granted to an employee. **2.a.** A holiday. **b.** A fixed period of holidays, especially one during which a school, court, or business suspends activities. **3.** *Archaic.* The act or an instance of vacating. **—vacation** *intr.v.* **-tioned, -tion·ing, -tions.** To take or spend a vacation. [Middle English *vacacioun,* from Old French *vacation,* from Latin *vacātiō, vacātiōn-,* freedom from occupation, from *vacātus,* past participle of *vacāre,* to be empty, at leisure. See **eu-[2]** in Appendix.] **—va·ca′tion·er, va·ca′tion·eer′** (-shə-nîr′) *n.* **—va·ca′tion·less** *adj.*

va·ca·tion·ist (vā-kā′shə-nĭst, və-) *n.* One who is on vacation.

va·ca·tion·land (vā-kā′shən-lănd′) *n.* A place with special attractions for those on vacation.

Vac·a·ville (văk′ə-vĭl′). A city of central California west-southwest of Sacramento. Population, 43,367.

vac·ci·nal (văk′sə-nəl, văk-sē′-) *adj.* **1.** Of or relating to vaccination or a vaccine. **2.** Induced by vaccination.

vac·ci·nate (văk′sə-nāt′) *v.* **-nat·ed, -nat·ing, -nates.** —*tr.* To inoculate with a vaccine in order to produce immunity to an infectious disease such as diphtheria or typhus. —*intr.* To perform vaccinations or a vaccination. **—vac′ci·na′tor** *n.*

vac·ci·na·tion (văk′sə-nā′shən) *n.* **1.** Inoculation with a vaccine in order to protect against a particular disease. **2.** A scar left on the skin by vaccinating.

vac·cine (văk-sēn′ văk′sēn′) *n.* **1.a.** A preparation of a weakened or killed pathogen, such as a bacterium or virus, or of a portion of the pathogen's structure that upon administration stimulates antibody production against the pathogen but is incapable of causing severe infection. **b.** A vaccine prepared from the cowpox virus and inoculated against smallpox. **2.** *Computer Science.* Software designed to detect and stop the progress of a computer virus. [From Latin *vaccīnus,* of cows, from *vacca,* cow.]

vac·ci·nee (văk′sə-nē′) *n.* One that has been vaccinated.

vac·cin·i·a (văk-sĭn′ē-ə) *n.* See **cowpox.** [New Latin *vaccīnia,* from Latin *vaccīnus,* of cows. See VACCINE.] **—vac·cin′i·al** *adj.*

vac·il·lant (văs′ə-lənt) *adj.* Undergoing vacillation; wavering.

vac·il·late (văs′ə-lāt′) *intr.v.* **-lat·ed, -lat·ing, -lates. 1.** To sway from one side to the other; oscillate. **2.** To swing indecisively from one course of action or opinion to another. See Synonyms at **hesitate.** [Latin *vacillāre, vacillāt-,* to waver.] **—vac′il·lat′ing·ly** *adv.* **—vac′il·la′tion** *n.* **—vac′il·la′tor** *n.*

vac·il·la·to·ry (văs′ə-lə-tôr′ē, -tōr′ē) *adj.* Inclined to waver; irresolute.

vac·u·a (văk′yo͞o-ə) *n.* A plural of **vacuum.**

va·cu·i·ty (vă-kyo͞o′ĭ-tē, və-) *n., pl.* **-ties. 1.** Total absence of matter; emptiness. **2.** An empty space; a vacuum. **3.** Total lack of ideas; emptiness of mind. **4.** Absence of meaningful occupation; idleness: *"the crew, being patient people, much given to slumber and vacuity"* (Washington Irving). **5.** The quality or fact of being devoid of something specified: *a vacuity of taste; a vacuity of emotions.* **6.** Something, especially a remark, that is pointless or inane: *a conversation full of vacuities.* [Middle English *vacuite,* from Old French, from Latin *vacuitās,* from *vacuus,* empty. See VACUUM.]

vacuolar membrane *n.* See **tonoplast.**

vac·u·o·lat·ed (văk′yo͞o-ō-lā′tĭd) also **vac·u·o·late** (-lāt′, -lĭt) *adj.* Containing vacuoles or a vacuole.

vac·u·ole (văk′yo͞o-ōl′) *n.* A small cavity in the cytoplasm of a cell, bound by a single member and containing water, food, or metabolic waste. [French, from Latin *vacuus,* empty. See VACUUM.] **—vac′u·o′lar** (-ō′lər, -lär′) *adj.* **—vac′u·o·la′tion** *n.*

vac·u·ous (văk′yo͞o-əs) *adj.* **1.** Devoid of matter; empty. **2.a.** Lacking intelligence; stupid. **b.** Devoid of substance or meaning; inane: *a vacuous comment.* **c.** Devoid of expression; vacant: *"The narrow, swinelike eyes were open, no more vacuous in death than they had been in life"* (Nicholas Proffitt). **3.** Lacking serious purpose or occupation; idle. See Synonyms at **empty.** [From Latin *vacuus,* empty. See VACUUM.] **—vac′u·ous·ly** *adv.* **—vac′u·ous·ness** *n.*

vac·u·um (văk′yo͞o-əm, -yo͞om, -yəm) *n., pl.* **-u·ums** or **-u·a** (-yo͞o-ə). *Abbr.* **vac. 1.a.** Absence of matter. **b.** A space empty of matter. **c.** A space relatively empty of matter. **d.** A space in which the pressure is significantly lower than atmospheric pressure. **2.** A state of emptiness; a void. **3.** A state of being sealed off from external or environmental influences; isolation. **4.** *pl.* **-uums.** A vacuum cleaner. **—vacuum** *adj.* **1.** Of, relating to, or used to create a vacuum. **2.** Containing air or other gas at a reduced pressure. **3.** Operating by means of suction or by maintaining a partial vacuum. **—vacuum** *tr. & intr.v.* **-umed, -um·ing, -umes.** To clean with or use a vacuum cleaner. [Latin, empty space, from neuter of *vacuus,* empty, from *vacāre,* to be empty. See **eu-[2]** in Appendix.]

vacuum bottle *n.* A bottle or flask having a vacuum between its inner and outer walls, designed to maintain the desired temperature of the contents.

vacuum casting *n.* The casting of metals under a vacuum.

vacuum cleaner *n.* An electrical appliance that cleans surfaces by suction.

Phoenician
The Phoenicians used a single sign for the initial sound in *wāw,* "hook" or "peg," and the related vowel *u.*

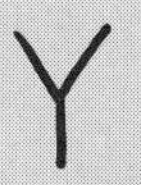

Early Greek
This sign was altered into two different shapes by the Greeks. One form became *digamma,* the ancestor of Roman F (see F); the other was used for the vowel sound *u.*

Roman
The Romans adopted the second form for both *u* and *w* sounds, simplifying its shape to V. In later Latin the *w* came to be pronounced as *v.* Not until the 16th century were the vowel and consonant consistently distinguished in writing by making separate letters of V and its cursive variant U.

vacuum drying *n.* Removal of liquid material from a solution or mixture under reduced air pressure, which results in drying at a lower temperature than is required at full pressure.

vacuum gauge *n.* A device for measuring pressures below atmospheric pressure.

vac·u·um-packed (văk′yo͞o-əm-păkt′, -yo͞om-, văk′yəm-) *adj.* **1.** Packed in an airtight container. **2.** Sealed under low pressure or a partial vacuum.

vacuum pump *n.* **1.** A pump used to evacuate an enclosure. **2.** See **pulsometer.**

vacuum tube *n. Abbr.* **VT** An electron tube from which all or most of the gas has been removed, permitting electrons to move with low interaction with any remaining gas molecules.

va·de me·cum (vä′dē mē′kəm, vä′dē mā′-) *n., pl.* **va·de me·cums. 1.** A useful thing that one constantly carries about. **2.** A book, such as a guidebook, for ready reference. [Latin *vāde mēcum,* go with me : *vāde,* sing. imperative of *vādere,* to go + *mē,* ablative sing. of *egō,* I + *cum,* with.]

V.Adm. or **VADM** *abbr.* Vice admiral.

va·dose (vā′dōs′) *adj.* Of, relating to, or being water that is located in the zone of aeration in the earth's crust above the ground water level. [Latin *vadōsus,* shallow, from *vadum,* a shallow, ford.]

Va·duz (vä-do͞ots′, fä-). The capital of Liechtenstein, in the western part of the country on the Rhine River. Destroyed during a conflict between Switzerland and the Holy Roman Empire (1499), it was rebuilt in the 1520's. Population, 4,927.

vag·a·bond (văg′ə-bŏnd′) *n.* **1.** A person without a permanent home who moves from place to place. **2.** A vagrant; a tramp. **3.** A wanderer; a rover. **—vagabond** *adj.* **1.** Of, relating to, or characteristic of a wanderer; nomadic. **2.** Aimless; drifting. **3.** Irregular in course or behavior; unpredictable. **—vagabond** *intr.v.* **-bond·ed, -bond·ing, -bonds.** To lead the life of a vagabond; roam about. [Middle English *vagabonde,* from Old French *vagabond,* from Late Latin *vagābundus,* wandering, from Latin *vagārī,* to wander, from *vagus,* wandering.] **—vag′a·bond′age** *n.* **—vag′a·bond′ism** *n.*

va·gal (vā′gəl) *adj.* Of or relating to the vagus nerve. **—va′gal·ly** *adv.*

va·ga·ry (vā′gə-rē, və-gâr′ē) *n., pl.* **-ries.** An extravagant or erratic notion or action. See Synonyms at **caprice.** [From Latin *vagārī,* to wander, from *vagus,* wandering.]

va·gi (vā′gī, -jī) *n.* Plural of **vagus.**

vag·ile (văj′əl, -īl) *adj.* Characterized by vagility; able to move about or disperse in a given environment: *a vagile animal species.* [Latin *vagus,* wandering + –ILE[1].]

va·gil·i·ty (və-jĭl′ĭ-tē, vă-) *n.* The capacity or tendency of an organism or a species to move about or disperse in a given environment.

va·gi·na (və-jī′nə) *n., pl.* **-nas** or **-nae** (-nē). **1.** *Anatomy.* **a.** The passage leading from the opening of the vulva to the cervix of the uterus in female mammals. **b.** A similar part in some invertebrates. **2.** *Botany.* A sheathlike structure, such as the leaf of a grass that surrounds a stem. [Latin *vāgīna,* sheath.]

vag·i·nal (văj′ə-nəl) *adj.* **1.** Of or relating to the vagina. **2.** Relating to or resembling a sheath. **—vag′i·nal·ly** *adv.*

vag·i·nate (văj′ə-nĭt, -nāt′) also **vag·i·nat·ed** (-nā′tĭd) *adj.* **1.** Forming or enclosed in a sheath. **2.** Resembling a sheath.

vag·i·nec·to·my (văj′ə-nĕk′tə-mē) *n., pl.* **-mies. 1.** Surgical removal of all or part of the vagina. **2.** Surgical removal of the serous membrane covering the testis and epididymus.

vag·i·nis·mus (văj′ə-nĭz′məs) *n.* A usually prolonged and painful contraction or spasm of the vagina. [New Latin : VAGIN(A) + Latin *-ismus,* -ism.]

vag·i·ni·tis (văj′ə-nī′tĭs) *n.* Inflammation of the vagina. Also called *colpitis.*

va·got·o·my (vā-gŏt′ə-mē) *n., pl.* **-mies.** Surgical division of fibers of the vagus nerve, used to diminish acid secretion of the stomach and control a duodenal ulcer. [VAG(US) + –TOMY.]

va·go·to·ni·a (vā′gə-tō′nē-ə) *n.* Overactivity or irritability of the vagus nerve, adversely affecting function of the blood vessels, stomach, and muscles. [VAG(US) + –TONIA.] **—va′go·ton′ic** (-tŏn′ĭk) *adj.*

valance

va·go·tro·pic (vā′gə-trō′pĭk, -trŏp′ĭk) *adj.* Affecting or acting on the vagus nerve. Used chiefly of a drug. [VAG(US) + –TROPIC.]

va·gran·cy (vā′grən-sē) *n., pl.* **-cies. 1.a.** The state of being a vagrant. **b.** The conduct or mode of existence of a vagrant. **c.** The offense of being a vagrant. **2.** A wandering in mind or thought.

va·grant (vā′grənt) *n.* **1.** One who wanders from place to place without a permanent home or a means of livelihood. **2.** A wanderer; a rover. **3.** One who lives on the streets and constitutes a public nuisance. **—vagrant** *adj.* **1.** Wandering from place to place and lacking any means of support. **2.** Wayward; unrestrained: *a vagrant impulse.* **3.** Moving in a random fashion; not fixed in place: *"Thanks to a vagrant current of the Gulf Stream, a stretch of the Kola coast is free of ice year round"* (Jack Beatty). [Middle English *vagraunt,* probably alteration of Old French *wacrant,* present participle of *wacrer,* to wander, of Germanic origin.] **—va′grant·ly** *adv.*

vague (vāg) *adj.* **vagu·er, vagu·est. 1.** Not clearly expressed; inexplicit. **2.** Not thinking or expressing oneself clearly. **3.** Lacking definite shape, form, or character; indistinct: *saw a vague outline of a building through the fog.* **4.** Not clear in meaning or application. See Synonyms at **ambiguous. 5.** Indistinctly felt, perceived, understood, or recalled; hazy: *a vague uneasiness.* [French, from Old French, wandering, from Latin *vagus.*] **—vague′ly** *adv.* **—vague′ness** *n.*

va·gus (vā′gəs) *n., pl.* **-gi** (-gī, -jī). The vagus nerve.

vagus nerve *n.* Either of the tenth and longest of the cranial nerves, passing through the neck and thorax into the abdomen and supplying sensation to part of the ear, the tongue, the larynx, and the pharynx, motor impulses to the vocal cords, and motor and secretory impulses to the abdominal and thoracic viscera. Also called *pneumogastric nerve.* [New Latin *(nervus) vagus,* wandering (nerve), from Latin.]

Váh (vä, väKH). A river, about 394 km (245 mi) long, of eastern and central Czechoslovakia flowing west and south to the Danube River.

va·hi·ne (vä-hē′nē, -nā) *n.* Variant of **wahine.**

vail[1] (vāl) *v.* **vailed, vail·ing, vails.** *Archaic.* —*tr.* **1.** To lower (a banner, for example). **2.** To doff (one's hat) as a token of respect or submission. —*intr.* **1.** To descend; lower. **2.** To doff one's hat. [Middle English *valen,* short for *avalen,* from Old French *avaler,* from *aval,* downward, from Latin *ad vallem,* to the valley : *ad,* ad- + *vallem,* accusative of *vallēs,* valley; see **wel-**[2] in Appendix.]

vail[2] (vāl) *n. Obsolete.* Variant of **veil.**

vain (vān) *adj.* **vain·er, vain·est. 1.** Not yielding the desired outcome; fruitless: *a vain attempt.* **2.** Lacking substance or worth: *vain talk.* **3.** Excessively proud of one's appearance or accomplishments; conceited. **4.** *Archaic.* Foolish. ***—idiom.* in vain. 1.** To no avail: *Our labor was in vain.* **2.** In an irreverent or disrespectful manner: *took the name of the Lord in vain.* [Middle English, from Old French, from Latin *vānus,* empty. See **eu-**[2] in Appendix.] **—vain′ly** *adv.* **—vain′ness** *n.*

SYNONYMS: *vain, empty, hollow, idle, nugatory, otiose.* The central meaning shared by these adjectives is "lacking value or substance": *vain regrets; empty pleasures; hollow threats; idle dreams; nugatory commentaries; an otiose belief in alchemy.* See also Synonyms at **futile.**

vain·glo·ri·ous (vān-glôr′ē-əs, -glōr′-) *adj.* **1.** Characterized by or exhibiting excessive vanity; boastful. **2.** Proceeding from vainglory. **—vain·glo′ri·ous·ly** *adv.* **—vain·glo′ri·ous·ness** *n.*

vain·glo·ry (vān′glôr′ē, -glōr′ē, vān-glôr′ē, -glōr′ē) *n., pl.* **-ries. 1.** Boastful, unwarranted pride in one's accomplishments or qualities. **2.** Vain, ostentatious display. [Middle English *vein glory,* from Old French *vaine gloire,* from Latin *vāna glōria,* empty pride : *vānus,* empty; see VAIN + *glōria,* glory, pride.]

vair (vâr) *n.* **1.** A fur, probably squirrel, much used in medieval times to line and trim robes. **2.** *Heraldry.* A representation of fur. [Middle English *vair,* from Old French *vair,* variegated, vair, from Latin *varius,* variegated.]

Vaish·na·va (vīsh′nə-və) *n. Hinduism.* One who worships Vishnu. [From Sanskrit *vaiṣṇava-,* relating to Vishnu, from *Viṣṇuḥ,* Vishnu.] **—Vaish′na·vism** (-vĭz′əm) *n.*

Vais·ya (vī′shə, vīsh′yə) *n.* **1.** The third of the four Hindu classes, comprising farmers, herders, artisans, merchants, and businessmen. **2.** A member of this class. [Sanskrit *vaiśyaḥ,* settler, homesteader, from *viśaḥ,* house. See **weik-**[1] in Appendix.]

val. *abbr.* **1.** Valley. **2.** Valuation; value.

Va·la·don (vä-lä-dôN′), **Suzanne.** 1865?–1938. French painter known for her characteristically strong depictions of the female nude and her many self-portraits, which reflect trends of postimpressionism and fauvism.

val·ance (văl′əns, vā′ləns) *n.* **1.** An ornamental drapery hung across a top edge, as of a bed, table, or canopy. **2.** A short drapery, decorative board, or metal strip mounted especially across the top of a window to conceal structural fixtures. **—valance** *tr.v.* **-anced, -anc·ing, -anc·es.** To supply with valances or a valance. [Middle English.]

Val·dai Hills also **Val·day Hills** (väl-dī′). An upland region of western Russia between St. Petersburg and Moscow. It forms the watershed for numerous rivers, including the Volga, the Western Dvina, and the Dnieper.

Val·de·mar I (väl′də-mär′). See **Waldemar I.**

Val·dez (văl-dēz′). A city of southern Alaska on an inlet of Prince William Sound. A military base during World War II, it is the southern terminus of the oil pipeline from Prudhoe Bay. An oil spill in the waters of the sound caused extensive environmental damage in 1989. Population, 3,079.

Val·di·via (väl-dē′vē-ə, bäl-dē′vyä). A city of south-central Chile near the Pacific Ocean south of Concepción. Founded in 1552, it grew rapidly after the arrival of German immigrants in the mid-19th century. Population, 100,046.

Val·do (văl′dō, väl′-), **Peter.** See Peter **Waldo.**

Val d'Or (văl′ dôr′, väl dôr′). A town of southwest Quebec, Canada, near the Ontario border. It is a mining and lumbering center. Population, 21,321.

Val·dos·ta (văl-dŏs′tə). A city of southern Georgia near the

Florida border east-northeast of Tallahassee. Settled in 1859, it is a processing and trade center. Population, 37,596.

vale¹ (vāl) *n.* A valley, often coursed by a stream; a dale. [Middle English, from Old French *val,* from Latin *vallēs.* See **wel-²** in Appendix.]

va·le² (vä′lē, wä′lā) *interj.* Used to express leave-taking or farewell. —**vale** *n.* A farewell. [Latin *valē,* sing. imperative of *valēre,* to be strong or well. See **wal-** in Appendix.]

val·e·dic·tion (văl′ĭ-dĭk′shən) *n.* **1.** An act of bidding farewell; a leave-taking. **2.** A speech or statement made as a farewell. [From Latin *valedictus,* past participle of *valedīcere,* to say farewell : *valē,* farewell; see VALE² + *dīcere,* to say; see **deik-** in Appendix.]

val·e·dic·to·ri·an (văl′ĭ-dĭk-tôr′ē-ən, -tōr′-) *n.* The student with the highest academic rank in a class who delivers the valedictory at graduation.

val·e·dic·to·ry (văl′ĭ-dĭk′tə-rē) *n., pl.* **-ries.** A closing or farewell statement or address, especially one delivered at graduation exercises. —**valedictory** *adj.* Of, relating to, or expressing a valedictory.

va·lence (vā′ləns) also **va·len·cy** (-lən-sē) *n., pl.* **-lenc·es** also **-len·cies. 1.** *Chemistry.* **a.** The combining capacity of an atom or a radical determined by the number of electrons that it will lose, add, or share when it reacts with other atoms. **b.** A positive or negative integer used to represent this capacity: *The valences of copper are 1 and 2.* **2.** *Immunology.* The number of components of an antigen molecule to which an antibody molecule can bind. **3.** *Psychology* The attraction or aversion that an individual feels toward a specific object or event. **4.** The capacity of something to unite, react, or interact with something else: *"I do not claim to know much more about novels than the writing of them, but I cannot imagine one set in the breathing world which lacks any moral valence"* (Robert Stone). [Latin *valentia,* capacity, from Latin *valēns, valent-,* present participle of *valēre,* to be strong. See **wal-** in Appendix.]

Va·lence (və-läɴs′, vă-). A city of southeast France on the Rhone River south of Lyons. Settled in Roman times, it was captured by the Visigoths in A.D. 413 and the Arabs c. 730. Population, 66,356.

valence electron *n.* An electron in an outer shell of an atom that can participate in forming chemical bonds with other atoms.

valence shell *n.* The outermost shell of an atom consisting of the valence electrons.

Va·len·ci·a (və-lĕn′shē-ə, -chə, -sē-ə). **1.** (*also* bä-lĕn′thyä). A region and former kingdom of eastern Spain on the Mediterranean coast south of Catalonia. Inhabited by Iberian peoples in early times, it was colonized by Greek and Carthaginian traders and fell to the Moors in the eighth century. The Cid ruled the region and the city of Valencia from 1094 until his death in 1099. **2.** (*also* bä-lĕn′thyä). A city of eastern Spain on the **Gulf of Valencia,** a wide inlet of the Mediterranean Sea. First mentioned as a Roman colony in 138 B.C., Valencia was taken by the Visigoths in A.D. 413 and the Moors in 714. Population, 785,273. **3.** (*also* bä-lĕn′syä). A city of northern Venezuela west-southwest of Caracas on the western shore of **Lake Valencia.** Founded in 1555, it is a major industrial center. Population, 523,000.

Va·len·ci·ennes¹ (və-lĕn′sē-ĕnz′, vä-läɴ-syĕn′). A city of northern France near the Belgian border southeast of Lille. An important medieval town, it became noted for its lace industry in the 15th century. Population, 40,275.

Va·len·ci·ennes² (və-lĕn′sē-ĕn′, -ĕnz′, văl′ən-sē-) *n.* A fine lace with a floral pattern.

va·len·cy (vā′lən-sē) *n.* Variant of **valence.**

Va·lens (vā′lənz, -lĕnz′). A.D. 328?–378. Emperor of Rome in the East (364–378) who ruled in conjunction with his brother Valentinian I in the West.

-valent *suff.* Having a specified valence or valences: *polyvalent.* [From VALENCE.]

val·en·tine (văl′ən-tīn′) *n.* **1.a.** A sentimental or humorous greeting card sent to a sweetheart, friend, or family member, for example, on Saint Valentine's Day. **b.** A gift sent as a token of love to one's sweetheart on Saint Valentine's Day. **2.** A person singled out especially as one's sweetheart on Saint Valentine's Day.

WORD HISTORY: Geoffrey Chaucer should perhaps receive honor as the real Saint Valentine. Although reference books abound with mention of Roman festivals from which Valentine's Day—the day for lovers—may be derived, Jack B. Oruch has shown that no evidence exists to support these connections and that Chaucer is most likely the first to link the saint's day with the custom of choosing sweethearts. No link between the day and lovers exists before the time of Chaucer and several literary contemporaries who also mention it, but after them the link becomes widespread, a circumstance that makes it seem likely that Chaucer, the most imaginative of the group, invented the tradition. The fullest and perhaps earliest description of the tradition occurs in Chaucer's *Parlement of Foules,* composed around 1380, which takes place "on Seynt Valentynes day,/Whan every foul cometh there to chese [choose] his make [mate]."

Val·en·tine (văl′ən-tīn′), Saint. fl. third century A.D. Roman Christian who according to tradition was martyred during the persecution of Christians by Emperor Claudius II. Another martyr named Valentine, who was bishop of Terni, a region in present-day central Italy, has also been suggested as the inspiration for our modern feast of Saint Valentine's Day.

Val·en·tine's Day or **Val·en·tines Day** (văl′ən-tīnz′) *n.* See **Saint Valentine's Day.**

Val·en·tin·ian I (văl′ən-tĭn′ē-ən, -tĭn′yən). A.D. 321–375. Emperor of Rome in the West (364–375) who ruled jointly with his brother Valens in the East.

Valentinian II. A.D. 371?–392. Emperor of Rome (375–392) who ruled jointly with Gratian in the East (375–383). He was driven from Italy (387) and assassinated in Vienna.

Valentinian III. A.D. 419–455. Emperor of Rome in the West (425–455) whose reign was marked by numerous raids by Germanic tribes.

Val·en·ti·no (văl′ĭn-tē′nō), **Rudolf.** 1895–1926. Italian-born American actor known for his romantic leading roles in silent films such as *The Sheik* (1921) and *Blood and Sand* (1922).

Rudolf Valentino

va·le·ri·an (və-lîr′ē-ən) *n.* **1.** A plant of the genus *Valeriana,* especially *V. officinalis,* native to Eurasia and widely cultivated for its small, fragrant, white to pink or lavender flowers and for use in medicine. **2.** The dried rhizomes of this plant, used medicinally as a sedative. [Middle English, from Old French *valeriane,* from Medieval Latin *valeriāna,* probably from feminine of Latin *Valeriānus,* of Valeria, Roman province where the plant originated.]

Va·le·ri·an (və-lîr′ē-ən). Died c. A.D. 260. Emperor of Rome (253–260) whose reign was marked by military and financial troubles. He was defeated by Persian forces (260) and died in captivity.

va·le·ric acid (və-lîr′ĭk, -lĕr′-) *n.* A colorless liquid, $C_5H_{10}O_2$, used in flavorings, perfumes, plasticizers, and pharmaceuticals. [From VALERIAN, from its occurrence in the plant's root.]

Va·lé·ry (văl′ə-rē′, vä-lā-rē′), **Paul Ambroise.** 1871–1945. French poet known for his dramatic dialogues, such as *La Jeune Parque* (1917), and symbolic works, including *Le Cimitière Marin* (1932).

val·et (văl′ĭt, văl′ā, vă-lā′) *n.* **1.** A man's male servant, who takes care of his clothes and performs other personal services. **2.** An employee, as in a hotel or on a ship, who performs personal services for guests or passengers. —**valet** *v.* **-et·ed, -et·ing, -ets.** —*tr.* To act as a personal servant to; attend. —*intr.* To work as a valet. [Middle English *valette,* from Old French *vaslet, valet,* servant, squire, from Vulgar Latin **vassellitus,* diminutive of **vassus,* vassal. See VASSAL.]

valet parking *n.* Parking arrangements provided by a commercial establishment, such as a restaurant, whereby patrons leave their cars at the entrance and attendants park and retrieve them.

val·e·tu·di·nar·i·an (văl′ĭ-to͞od′n-âr′ē-ən, -tyo͞od′-) *n.* A sickly or weak person, especially one who is constantly and morbidly concerned with his or her health: *"She affected to be spunky about her ailments and afflictions, but she was in fact an utterly self-centered valetudinarian"* (Louis Auchincloss). —**valetudinarian** *adj.* **1.** Chronically ailing; sickly. **2.** Constantly and morbidly concerned with one's health. [From Latin *valētūdinārius,* from *valētūdō, valētūdin-,* state of health, from *valēre,* to be strong or well. See **wal-** in Appendix.] —**val′e·tu′di·nar′i·an·ism** *n.*

val·e·tu·di·nar·y (văl′ĭ-to͞od′n-ĕr′ē, -tyo͞od′-) *adj.* Of, relating to, or typical of a valetudinarian. —**valetudinary** *n., pl.* **-ies.** A valetudinarian.

val·gus (văl′gəs) *adj.* **1.** Characterized by an abnormal outward turning of a bone, especially of the hip, knee, or foot. **2.** Knock-kneed. —**valgus** *n.* A valgus bone. [From Latin, bowlegged.] —**val′goid′** (-goid′) *adj.*

Val·hal·la (văl-hăl′ə, väl-hä′lə) also **Wal·hal·la** (wäl-hăl′ə, văl-, wäl-hä′lə, väl-) *n. Mythology.* The hall in which Odin received the souls of slain heroes. [Old Norse *Valhöll* : *valr,* the slain in battle; see **welə-** in Appendix + *höll, hall,* hall; see **kel-¹** in Appendix.]

Valhalla

val·iant (văl′yənt) *adj.* **1.** Possessing valor; brave. **2.** Marked by or done with valor. See Synonyms at **brave.** —**valiant** *n.* A brave person. [Middle English, from Old French *vaillant,* from Latin *valēns, valent-,* present participle of *valēre,* to be strong. See **wal-** in Appendix.] —**val′ian·cy, val′iance, val′iant·ness** *n.* —**val′iant·ly** *adv.*

val·id (văl′ĭd) *adj.* **1.** Well grounded; just: *a valid objection.* **2.** Producing the desired results; efficacious: *valid methods.* **3.** Having legal force; effective or binding: *a valid title.* **4.** *Logic.* **a.** Containing premises from which the conclusion may logically be derived: *a valid argument.* **b.** Correctly inferred or deduced from a premise: *a valid conclusion.* **5.** *Archaic.* Of sound health; robust. [French *valide,* from Old French, from Latin *validus,* strong, from *valēre,* to be strong. See **wal-** in Appendix.] —**va·lid′i·ty, val′id·ness** *n.* —**val′id·ly** *adv.*

SYNONYMS: *valid, sound, cogent, convincing, telling.* These adjectives describe assertions, arguments, conclusions, reasons, or intellectual processes that are persuasive because they are well founded, as in fact, logic. or rationality. What is *valid* is based on or borne out by truth or fact or has legal force: *a valid excuse; a valid claim.* What is *sound* is free from logical flaws or is based on valid reasoning: *a sound theory; sound principles.* Something co-

ă pat	oi boy
ā pay	ou out
âr care	o͝o took
ä father	o͞o boot
ĕ pet	ŭ cut
ē be	ûr urge
ĭ pit	th thin
ī pie	*th* this
îr pier	hw which
ŏ pot	zh vision
ō toe	ə about, item
ô paw	♦ regionalism

Stress marks: **′** (primary); ′ (secondary), as in **dictionary** (dĭk′shə-nĕr′ē)

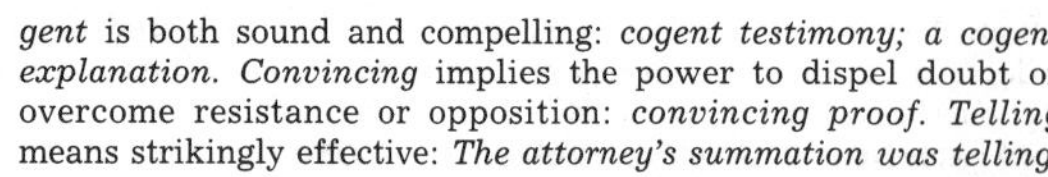
gent is both sound and compelling: *cogent testimony; a cogent explanation. Convincing* implies the power to dispel doubt or overcome resistance or opposition: *convincing proof. Telling* means strikingly effective: *The attorney's summation was telling.*

val·i·date (văl′ĭ-dāt′) *tr.v.* **-dat·ed, -dat·ing, -dates. 1.** To declare or make legally valid. **2.** To mark with an indication of official sanction. **3.** To establish the soundness of; corroborate. See Synonyms at **confirm.** **—val′i·da′tion** *n.*

val·ine (văl′ēn′, vā′lēn′) *n.* An essential amino acid, $C_5H_{11}NO_2$. [VAL(ERIC ACID) + –INE[2].]

val·in·o·my·cin (văl′ə-nō-mī′sĭn) *n.* An antibiotic, $C_{54}H_{90}N_6O_{18}$, produced by the actinomycete B *Streptomyces fulvissimus,* that increases the transport of potassium across cell membranes. [VALIN(E) + –MYCIN.]

va·lise (və-lēs′) *n.* A small piece of hand luggage. [French, from Italian *valigia.*]

Val·i·um (văl′ē-əm). A trademark used for diazepam.

Valkyrie

Val·kyr·ie (văl-kîr′ē, -kī′rē, văl′kə-rē) also **Wal·kyr·ie** (wäl-kîr′ē, -kī′rē, văl-, wäl′kə-rē, văl′-) *n. Mythology.* Any of Odin's handmaidens who conducted the souls of the slain to Valhalla. [Old Norse *Valkyrja.* See **wela-** in Appendix.]

Val·la·do·lid (văl′ə-də-lĭd′, bä′lyä-*thô*-lē*th*′). A city of northwest-central Spain north-northwest of Madrid. It became the chief residence of the Castilian court in the mid-15th century and was the site of the marriage of Ferdinand and Isabella in 1469. Population, 331,404.

val·la·tion (vă-lā′shən) *n.* **1.** An earthwork wall used for military defense; a rampart. **2.** The process of planning or erecting earth fortifications. [Late Latin *vallātiō, vallātiōn-,* from Latin *vallātus,* past participle of *vallāre,* to surround with a rampart, from *vallum,* rampart, from *vallus,* stake.] **—val′la·to′ry** (văl′ə-tôr′ē, -tōr′ē) *adj.*

val·lec·u·la (vă-lĕk′yə-lə, və-) *n., pl.* **-lae** (-lē′). A shallow groove, depression, or furrow, as between the hemispheres of the brain. [Late Latin, diminutive of Latin *vallēs,* valley.] **—val·lec′u·lar, val·lec′u·late** (-lĭt, -lāt′) *adj.*

Val·le d'A·os·ta (vä′lā dä-ō′stə, -ô′stä). A region of northwest Italy bordering on France and Switzerland. Separated from Piedmont in the 1940's, it has a predominantly French linguistic and cultural heritage.

Val·le·jo (və-lā′ō, -hō). A city of western California on San Pablo Bay north of Oakland. It is a trade and processing center and has a large naval shipyard, founded by Adm. David Farragut in 1854. Population, 80,188.

Val·let·ta (və-lĕt′ə). The capital of Malta, on the northeast coast of the main island. Dating to the 16th century, it contains many relics of the Knights of Malta. Population, 14,013.

val·ley (văl′ē) *n., pl.* **-leys.** *Abbr.* **val. 1.** An elongated lowland between ranges of mountains, hills, or other uplands, often having a river or stream running along the bottom. **2.** An extensive area of land drained or irrigated by a river system. **3.** A depression or hollow resembling or suggesting a valley, as the point at which the two slopes of a roof meet. [Middle English *valey,* from Old French *valee,* from Vulgar Latin **vallāta,* from Latin *vallēs.* See **wel-**[2] in Appendix.] **—val′leyed** *adj.*

vambrace
c. 1550 Spanish

Val·ley East (văl′ē). A town of central Ontario, Canada, a suburb of Sudbury. Population, 20,433.

valley fever *n.* See **coccidioidomycosis.**

Val·ley·field (văl′ē-fēld′). A city of southern Quebec, Canada, on the St. Lawrence River southwest of Montreal. It is a port of entry and an industrial center. Population, 29,574.

Valley Forge. A village of southeast Pennsylvania on the Schuylkill River northwest of Philadelphia. It was the site of the Continental Army headquarters from December 1777 to June 1778. The encampment was subjected to severe winter weather that caused extensive illness and suffering.

Valley of Ten Thou·sand Smokes (tĕn′ thou′zənd smōks′). A volcanic region of southwest Alaska at the upper end of the Alaska Peninsula. It was formed by the eruption of Mount Katmai in 1912 and continues to emit hot gases through countless cracks in the surface.

Valley of the Kings (kĭngz). A narrow valley of east-central Egypt surrounding the site of ancient Thebes between Karnak and Luxor. The valley contains the tombs of numerous pharaohs of the XVIII, XIX, and XX Dynasties, including that of Tutankhamen.

Valley Stream. A village of southeast New York on southwest Long Island. It is mainly residential. Population, 35,769.

Va·lois[1] (văl′wä, väl-wä′). A French ruling dynasty (1328–1589) that succeeded the Capetian line when Philip VI ascended to the throne.

Va·lois[2] (văl′wä′, väl-wä′). A historical region and former duchy of northern France. A county from the 10th to the 12th century, it was an appanage of the royal house of Valois after 1285.

va·lo·ni·a (və-lō′nē-ə, -lōn′yə) *n.* The dried acorn cups of an oak tree *(Quercus aegilops)* of the eastern Mediterranean, used chiefly in tanning and dyeing. [Italian *vallonia,* from Modern Greek *balania,* pl. of *balani,* acorn, from Greek *balanos.*]

val·or (văl′ər) *n.* Courage and boldness, as in battle; bravery. [Middle English *valour,* from Old French, from Late Latin *valor,* from Latin *valēre,* to be strong. See **wal-** in Appendix.]

val·or·ize (văl′ə-rīz′) *tr.v.* **-ized, -iz·ing, -iz·es. 1.** To establish and maintain the price of (a commodity) by governmental action. **2.** To give or assign a value to: *"The prophets valorized history"* (Mircea Eliade). [Portuguese *valorizar,* from *valor,* value, from Late Latin. See VALOR.] **—val′or·i·za′tion** (-ər-ĭ-zā′shən) *n.*

val·or·ous (văl′ər-əs) *adj.* Marked by or possessing great personal bravery; valiant. See Synonyms at **brave.** **—val′or·ous·ly** *adv.* **—val′or·ous·ness** *n.*

val·our (văl′ər) *n. Chiefly British.* Variant of **valor.**

Val·pa·rai·so (văl′pə-rī′zō). **1.** Also **Val·pa·ra·í·so** (bäl′-pä-rä-ē′sô). A city of central Chile on the Pacific Ocean west-northwest of Santiago. Founded in 1536, it has frequently been subject to severe earthquakes. The modern city developed as an industrial center and the chief port of Chile in the early 20th century. Population, 265,355. **2.** A city of northwest Indiana southeast of Gary. It is a manufacturing and educational center. Population, 22,247.

val·pro·ate (văl-prō′āt) *n.* An anticonvulsive drug, $C_8H_{15}NaO_2$, given orally in the treatment of epilepsy. [*valpro(ic acid)* (VAL(ERIC ACID) + PRO(PYL) + –IC) + –ATE[2].]

Val·sal·va maneuver (văl-săl′və) *n.* **1.** Expiratory effort when the mouth is closed and the nostrils are pinched shut, which forces air into the eustachian tubes and increases pressure on the inside of the eardrum. **2.** Expiratory effort against a closed glottis, which increases pressure within the thoracic cavity and thereby impedes venous return of blood to the heart. [After Antonio Maria *Valsalva* (1666–1723), Italian anatomist.]

val·u·a·ble (văl′yo͞o-ə-bəl, văl′yə-) *adj.* **1.** Having considerable monetary or material value for use or exchange: *a valuable diamond.* **2.** Of great importance, use, or service: *valuable information; valuable advice.* **3.** Having admirable or esteemed qualities or characteristics: *a valuable friend.* **—valuable** *n.* A personal possession, such as a piece of jewelry, having a relatively high monetary value. Often used in the plural. **—val′u·a·ble·ness** *n.* **—val′u·a·bly** *adv.*

val·u·ate (văl′yo͞o-āt′) *tr.v.* **-at·ed, -at·ing, -ates.** To set a value for; appraise. [Back-formation from VALUATION.]

val·u·a·tion (văl′yo͞o-ā′shən) *n. Abbr.* **val. 1.** The act or process of assessing value or price; an appraisal. **2.** Assessed value or price. **3.** An estimation of worth, merit, or character: *set a high valuation on friendship.* **—val′u·a′tion·al** *adj.*

val·u·a·tor (văl′yo͞o-ā′tər) *n.* One that estimates values; an appraiser.

val·ue (văl′yo͞o) *n. Abbr.* **val. 1.** An amount, as of goods, services, or money, considered to be a fair and suitable equivalent for something else; a fair price or return. **2.** Monetary or material worth: *the fluctuating value of gold and silver.* **3.** Worth in usefulness or importance to the possessor; utility or merit: *the value of an education.* **4.** A principle, standard, or quality considered worthwhile or desirable: *"The speech was a summons back to the patrician values of restraint and responsibility"* (Jonathan Alter). **5.** Precise meaning or import, as of a word. **6.** *Mathematics.* An assigned or calculated numerical quantity. **7.** *Music.* The relative duration of a tone or rest. **8.** *Color.* The relative darkness or lightness of a color: *"I establish the colors and principal values by organizing the painting into three values—dark, medium . . . and light"* (Joe Hing Lowe). **9.** *Linguistics.* The sound quality of a letter or diphthong. **10.** One of a series of specified values: *issued a stamp of new value.* **—value** *tr.v.* **-ued, -u·ing, -ues. 1.** To determine or estimate the worth or value of; appraise. **2.** To regard highly; esteem. See Synonyms at **appreciate. 3.** To rate according to relative estimate of worth or desirability; evaluate: *valued health above money.* **4.** To assign a value to (a unit of currency, for example). [Middle English, from Old French, from feminine past participle of *valoir,* to be strong, be worth, from Latin *valēre.* See **wal-** in Appendix.] **—val′u·er** *n.*

val·ue-add·ed (văl′yo͞o-ăd′ĭd) *adj.* Of or relating to the estimated value that is added to a product or material at each stage of its manufacture or distribution: *"Unlike the steel or aluminum industries, where heavier profits come from value-added fabrication, mining is the most lucrative stage of copper production"* (Forbes).

value-added tax *n. Abbr.* **VAT, V.A.T.** A tax on the estimated market value added to a product or material at each stage of its manufacture or distribution, ultimately passed on to the consumer.

val·ued policy (văl′yo͞od) *n.* An insurance policy requiring the insurer to pay the insured the full face value of the policy in the event of total loss, regardless of the actual value of the lost property.

value judgment *n.* A judgment that assigns a value, as to an object or action; a subjective evaluation.

val·ue·less (văl′yo͞o-lĭs) *adj.* Having no value; worthless. **—val′ue·less·ness** *n.*

val·var (văl′vər) *adj.* Valvular.

val·vate (văl′vāt′) *adj.* **1.** Having valvelike parts. **2.** *Botany.* **a.** Meeting at the edges without overlapping, as some petals do. **b.** Opening by valves, as the capsule of a lily or iris.

valve (vălv) *n.* **1.** *Anatomy.* A membranous structure in a hollow organ or passage, as in an artery or a vein, that folds or closes to prevent the return flow of the body fluid passing through it. **2. a.** Any of various devices that regulate the flow of gases, liquids, or loose materials through piping or through apertures by opening, closing, or obstructing ports or passageways. **b.** The movable control element of such a device. **c.** *Music.* A device in a brass wind instrument that permits change in pitch by a rapid varying of the air column in a tube. **3.** *Biology.* **a.** One of the paired, hinged shells of certain mollusks and of brachiopods. **b.** One of the two silicified halves of the cell wall of a diatom. **c.** The entire, one-piece shell of a snail and certain other mollusks. **4.** *Botany.* **a.** One of the sections into which the wall of a seedpod or other dehiscent fruit splits. **b.** A lidlike covering of an anther. **5.** *Chiefly British.* An electron tube or a vacuum tube. **6.** *Archaic.* Either half of a double or folding door. **—valve** *tr.v.* **valved, valv•ing, valves. 1.** To provide with a valve. **2.** To control by means of a valve. [Middle English, leaf of a door, from Latin *valva.* See **wel-**[2] in Appendix.] **—valve′less** *adj.*

valve-in-head engine (vălv′ĭn-hĕd′) *n.* An internal-combustion engine, as in some automobiles, that has the inlet and exhaust valves in the cylinder head instead of in the engine block.

val•vu•la (văl′vyə-lə) *n.* Variant of **valvule.**

val•vu•lar (văl′vyə-lər) *adj.* Relating to, having, or operating by means of valves or valvelike parts.

val•vule (văl′vyo͞ol′) also **val•vu•la** (-vyə-lə) *n., pl.* **-vules** also **-vu•lae** (-vyə-lē′). A small valve or valvelike structure.

val•vu•li•tis (văl′vyə-lī′tĭs) *n.* Inflammation of a valve, especially a cardiac valve.

val•vu•lo•plas•ty (văl′vyə-lə-plăs′tē) *n., pl.* **-ties.** Plastic surgery to repair a valve, especially a heart valve.

vam•brace (văm′brās′) *n.* Armor used to protect the forearm. [Middle English *vambras,* from Anglo-Norman *vauntbras* : *vaunt* (variant of Old French *avaunt,* before; see VANGUARD) + *bras,* arm; see BRACER[2].]

va•moose (vă-mo͞os′, və-) *intr.v.* **-moosed, -moos•ing, -moos•es.** *Slang.* To leave hurriedly. [From Spanish *vamos,* let's go, from Latin *vādāmus,* first person pl. subjunctive of *vādere,* to go.]

vamp[1] (vămp) *n.* **1.** The upper part of a boot or shoe covering the instep and sometimes extending over the toe. **2. a.** Something patched up or refurbished. **b.** Something rehashed, as a book based on old material. **3.** *Music.* An improvised accompaniment. **—vamp** *v.* **vamped, vamp•ing, vamps.** *—tr.* **1.** To provide (a shoe) with a new vamp. **2.** To patch up (something old); refurbish. **3.** To put together; fabricate or improvise: *With no hard news available about the summit meeting, the reporters vamped up questions based only on rumor.* **4.** *Music.* To improvise (an accompaniment, for example) for a solo. *—intr. Music.* To improvise simple accompaniment or variation of a tune. [Middle English *vampe,* sock, from Old French *avanpie* : *avaunt,* before; see VANGUARD + *pie,* foot (from Latin *pēs;* see **ped-** in Appendix).] **—vamp′er** *n.*

vamp[2] (vămp) *Informal. n.* An unscrupulous, seductive woman who uses her sex appeal to entrap and exploit men. **—vamp** *v.* **vamped, vamp•ing, vamps.** *—tr.* To seduce or exploit (someone) in the manner of a vamp. *—intr.* To play the part of a vamp. [Short for VAMPIRE.] **—vamp′ish** *adj.* **—vamp′ish•ly** *adv.* **—vamp′y** *adj.*

vam•pire (văm′pīr′) *n.* **1.** A reanimated corpse that is believed to rise from the grave at night to suck the blood of sleeping people. **2.** A person, such as an extortionist, who preys upon others. **3.** A vampire bat. [French, from German *Vampir,* of Slavic origin.] **—vam•pir′ic** (văm-pîr′ĭk), **vam•pir′i•cal** (-ĭ-kəl), **vam′pir′ish** (-ĭsh) *adj.*

WORD HISTORY: Dracula might terrify some younger members in the audience of a horror film, but we know he is an imaginary creature. The word *vampire,* however, comes to us from other words and other times, when these bloodsucking reanimated corpses were considered real. The word entered English by way of French (*vampire*) and German (*Vampir*), but it came into German from an Old West Slavic source of the form **vŭmpir.* The word *vampire* is first recorded in English in a work written before 1734.

vampire bat *n.* **1.** Any of various tropical American bats of the family Desmodontidae that bite mammals and birds to feed on their blood and that often carry diseases such as rabies. **2.** Any of various other bats, as those of the family Megadermatidae, erroneously believed to feed on blood.

vampire bat

vam•pir•ism (văm′pīr-ĭz′əm) *n.* **1.** Belief in vampires. **2.** The behavior of a vampire.

van[1] (văn) *n.* **1. a.** An enclosed boxlike motor vehicle having rear or side doors and side panels especially for transporting people. **b.** A covered or enclosed truck or wagon often used for transporting goods or livestock. **2.** *Chiefly British.* A closed railroad car used for carrying baggage or freight. **—van** *v.* **vanned, van•ning, vans.** *—tr.* To transport by van: *vanned the horses to the racetrack.* *—intr.* To drive or travel in a van: *vanned around the country.* [Short for CARAVAN.]

van[2] (văn) *n.* The vanguard; the forefront. [Short for VANGUARD.]

van[3] (văn) *n.* **1.** A wing. **2.** *Archaic.* A winnowing device, such as a fan. [Middle English, from Old English *fann* and Old French *van,* both from Latin *vannus.* See **wet-**[1] in Appendix.]

Van (văn, vän), **Lake.** A salt lake of eastern Turkey. The largest lake in the country, it has no known outlet.

van•a•date (văn′ə-dāt′) *n.* Any of three anions, VO_3, VO_4, or V_2O_7, containing pentavalent vanadium. [VANAD(IUM) + -ATE[2].]

va•na•dic acid (və-nā′dĭk, -năd′ĭk) *n.* **1.** An acid containing a vanadate group, especially HVO_3, H_3VO_4, or $H_4V_2O_7$, not existing in a pure state. **2.** See **vanadium pentoxide.**

va•na•di•nite (və-năd′n-īt′, -năd′-, văn′ə-dē′nīt′) *n.* A red, yellow, or brown mineral, essentially an ore of vanadium and lead. [VANAD(IUM) + -IN + -ITE[1].]

va•na•di•um (və-nā′dē-əm) *n. Symbol* **V** A bright white, soft, ductile metallic element found in several minerals, notably vanadinite and carnotite, having good structural strength and used in rust-resistant high-speed tools, as a carbon stabilizer in some steels, as a titanium-steel bonding agent, and as a catalyst. Atomic number 23; atomic weight 50.942; melting point 1,890°C; boiling point 3,000°C; specific gravity 6.11; valence 2, 3, 4, 5. See table at **element.** [From Old Norse *Vanadīs,* the goddess Freya. See **wen-**[1] in Appendix.]

vanadium pentoxide *n.* A yellow to red crystalline powder, V_2O_5, used as a catalyst in various organic reactions and as a starting material for other vanadium salts. Also called *vanadic acid.*

vanadium steel *n.* Steel alloyed with vanadium for added strength, hardness, and high-temperature stability.

Van Al•len belt (văn ăl′ən) *n.* Either of two zones of high-intensity particulate radiation trapped in Earth's magnetic field and surrounding the planet, beginning at an altitude of about 800 kilometers (500 miles) and extending tens of thousands of kilometers into space. [After James Alfred *Van Allen* (born 1914), American physicist.]

Van•brugh (văn′brə, văn-bro͞o′), Sir **John.** 1664–1726. English playwright and architect who wrote *The Provok'd Wife* (produced 1697) and designed Blenheim Palace.

Van Bu•ren (văn byo͞or′ən), **Martin.** 1782–1862. The eighth President of the United States (1837–1841). A powerful Democrat from New York, he served in the U.S. Senate (1821–1828), as secretary of state (1829–1831), and as Vice President (1833–1837) under Andrew Jackson before being elected President in 1836. He unsuccessfully sought reelection in 1840 and 1848.

Martin Van Buren

van•co•my•cin (văng′kə-mī′sĭn, văn′kə-) *n.* An antibiotic, $C_{66}H_{75}Cl_2N_9O_{24}$, produced by the actinomycete *Streptomyces orientalis,* found in Indonesian and Indian soil, and effective against staphylococci and spirochetes. [*vanco-* (of unknown origin) + -MYCIN.]

Van•cou•ver (văn-ko͞o′vər). **1.** A city of southwest British Columbia, Canada, on the Strait of Georgia opposite Vancouver Island. The largest city in the province, it is a major port, commercial and industrial center, and railroad hub. Population, 414,281. **2.** A city of southwest Washington on the Columbia River opposite Portland, Oregon. Founded as Fort Vancouver by the Hudson's Bay Company in the 1820's, it is a deep-water port with shipyards, lumber mills, and other processing facilities. Population, 42,834.

Vancouver, George. 1757–1798. British navigator who led an expedition to the coasts of Australia, New Zealand, and the Hawaiian Islands (1791–1792) and to the Pacific coast of North America (1792–1794).

Vancouver, Mount. A peak, 4,873.6 m (15,979 ft) high, in the St. Elias Mountains of southwest Yukon Territory, Canada, near the border of Alaska.

Vancouver Island. An island of southwest British Columbia, Canada, in the Pacific Ocean separated from the mainland by the Strait of Georgia and Queen Charlotte Strait. The Strait of Juan de Fuca flows between the southern end of the island and the coastline of northwest Washington. First sighted by Spanish explorers in 1774 and visited by Capt. James Cook in 1778, it was named in honor of Capt. George Vancouver, who circumnavigated the island in 1792.

Van•dal (văn′dl) *n.* **1. vandal.** One who willfully or maliciously defaces or destroys public or private property. **2.** A member of a Germanic people that overran Gaul, Spain, and northern Africa in the fourth and fifth centuries A.D. and sacked Rome in 455. [Latin *Vandalus,* probably of Germanic origin.] **—Van•dal′ic** (văn-dăl′ĭk) *adj.*

van•dal•ism (văn′dl-ĭz′əm) *n.* Willful or malicious destruction of public or private property. **—van′dal•is′tic** *adj.*

van•dal•ize (văn′dl-īz′) *tr.v.* **-ized, -iz•ing, -iz•es.** To destroy or deface (public or private property) willfully or maliciously. **—van′dal•i•za′tion** (-ĭ-zā′shən) *n.*

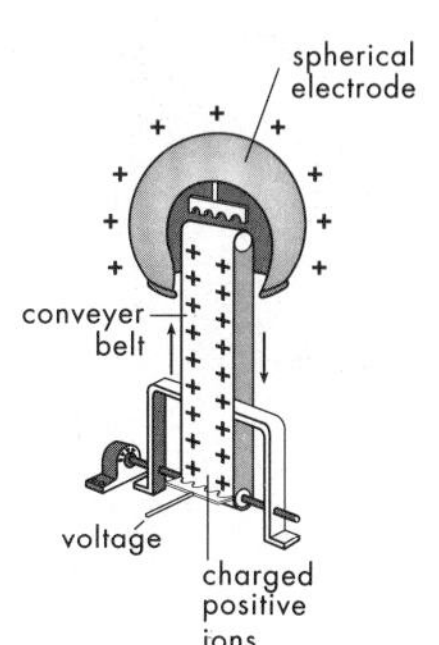

Van de Graaff generator

Van de Graaff generator (văn′ də grăf′) *n.* An electrostatic generator in which an electric charge is either removed from or transferred to a large hollow spherical electrode by a rapidly moving belt, accelerating particles to energies of about ten million electron volts. [After Robert Jemison *Van de Graaff* (1901–1967), American physicist.]

Van•der•bilt (văn′dər-bĭlt′), **Cornelius.** Known as "Commodore Vanderbilt." 1794–1877. American transportation promoter and financier who amassed a great fortune through railroad and shipping interests. His heirs included his son **William Henry** (1821–1885), a financier and philanthropist, and William Henry's sons **Cornelius** (1843–1899), a railroad director; **William Kissam** (1849–1920), a railroad executive and philanthropist; **Frederick William** (1856–1938), a railroad manager; and **George Washington** (1862–1914), who commissioned Biltmore, located in Asheville, North Carolina, the largest private home in America.

Van Der Ro•he (văn dər rō′ə, fān). See Ludwig **Mies Van Der Rohe.**

ă pat	oi boy
ā pay	ou out
âr care	o͝o took
ä father	o͞o boot
ĕ pet	ŭ cut
ē be	ûr urge
ĭ pit	th thin
ī pie	*th* this
îr pier	hw which
ŏ pot	zh vision
ō toe	ə about, item
ô paw	♦ regionalism

Stress marks: ′ (primary); ′ (secondary), as in **dictionary** (dĭk′shə-nĕr′ē)

Sir Anthony Vandyke
Self-portrait

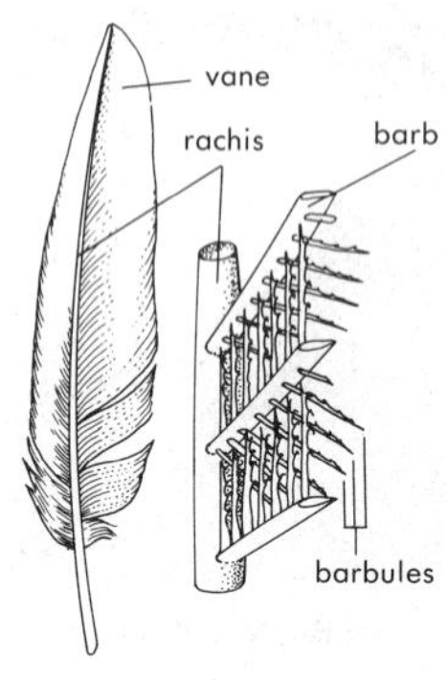

vane

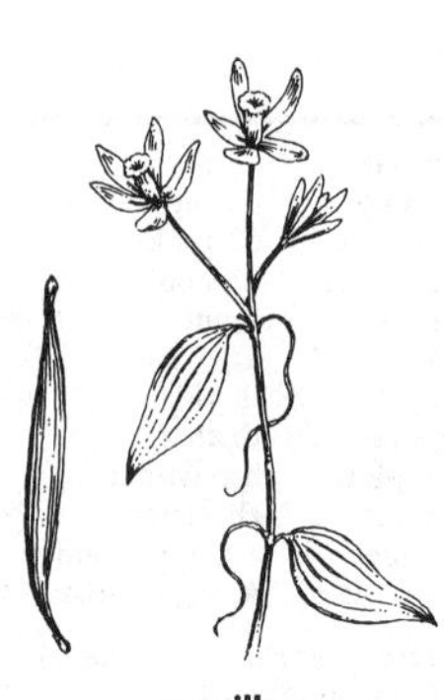
vanilla

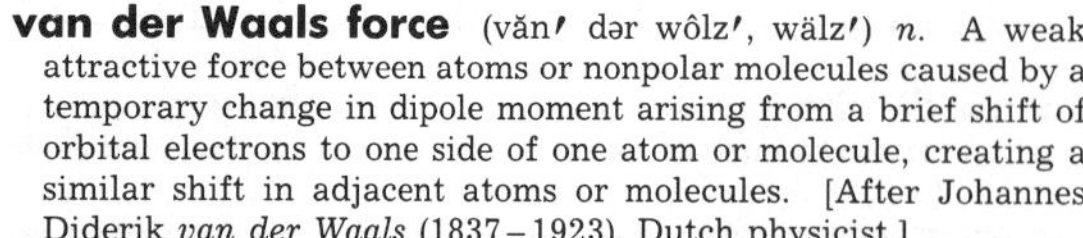
van der Waals force (văn′ dər wôlz′, wälz′) *n.* A weak attractive force between atoms or nonpolar molecules caused by a temporary change in dipole moment arising from a brief shift of orbital electrons to one side of one atom or molecule, creating a similar shift in adjacent atoms or molecules. [After Johannes Diderik *van der Waals* (1837–1923), Dutch physicist.]

Van De·van·ter (văn′ də-văn′tər), **Willis.** 1859–1941. American jurist who served as an associate justice of the U.S. Supreme Court (1910–1937).

Van Die·men's Land (văn dē′mənz, vän). See **Tasmania.**

van Dong·en (văn dŏng′ən, vän dông′ən), **Kees.** 1877–1968. Dutch artist known for his fauvist paintings of elegant Parisian women.

Van Dor·en (văn dôr′ən, dōr′-), **Carl Clinton.** 1885–1950. American literary critic, editor, and writer whose biography of Benjamin Franklin (1938) won a Pulitzer Prize. His brother **Mark** (1894–1972), a prolific writer and critic, is best known for his poetry, including *That Shining Place* (1969).

Van Dyck (văn dīk′), Sir **Anthony.** See Sir Anthony **Vandyke.**

Van·dyke (văn-dīk′) *n.* **1.** A Vandyke beard. **2.** A Vandyke collar. **3.a.** A V-shaped point that is part of a decorative border or edging. **b.** A border made up of such points.

Vandyke or **Van Dyck** (văn dīk′), Sir **Anthony.** 1599–1641. Flemish painter whose numerous portraits, including many of the English court, are remarkable for their dignity and gentle emotion.

Vandyke beard *n.* A short, pointed beard. [After Sir Anthony VANDYKE.]

Vandyke brown *n. Color.* A moderate to grayish brown. [After Sir Anthony VANDYKE.] **—Van·dyke′-brown′** (văn-dīk′broun′) *adj.*

Vandyke collar *n.* A large collar of linen or lace having a deeply indented or scalloped edge. [After Sir Anthony VANDYKE.]

vane (vān) *n.* **1.** A weathervane. **2.** Any of several usually relatively thin, rigid, flat, or sometimes curved surfaces radially mounted along an axis, as a blade in a turbine or a sail on a windmill, that is turned by or used to turn a fluid. **3.** The flattened, weblike part of a feather, consisting of a series of barbs on either side of the shaft. **4.a.** The movable target on a leveling rod. **b.** A sight on a quadrant or compass. **5.** One of the metal guidance or stabilizing fins attached to the tail of a bomb or other missile. [Middle English, variant of obsolete *fane,* from Old English *fana,* flag. See **pan-** in Appendix.]

Vane (vān), Sir **Henry** or **Harry.** 1613–1662. English politician and colonial administrator who was governor of Massachusetts (1636–1637) and a leading Parliamentarian during the English Civil War. He was tried and executed for high treason after the restoration of the monarchy.

Vä·nern (vā′nərn, vĕ′-). A lake of southwest Sweden. It is the largest lake in the country and navigable for small oceangoing ships via the Göta Canal.

van Eyck (văn īk′), **Jan.** 1390?–1441. Flemish painter who is considered the founder of the Flemish school and the pioneer of modern oil painting techniques. His minutely detailed and brilliantly colored works include *Giovanni Arnolfini and His Wife* (1434) and the altarpiece *Mystic Lamb* (1432), begun by his brother **Hubert** (1366?–1426).

vang (văng) *n. Nautical.* A guy running from the peak of a gaff or derrick to the deck. [Dutch, a catch, from *vangen,* to catch. See **pag-** in Appendix.]

van Gogh (văn gō′, gôKH′, vän KHôKH′), **Vincent.** 1853–1890. Dutch postimpressionist painter whose early works, such as *The Potato Eaters* (1885), portray peasant life in somber, dark colors. His later works, including numerous self-portraits, a series of sunflower paintings (1888), and *Starry Night* (1889), are characterized by bold, rhythmic brush strokes and vivid colors. His long struggle with depression ended in suicide.

van·guard (văn′gärd) *n.* **1.** The foremost position in an army or a fleet advancing into battle. **2.a.** The foremost or leading position in a trend or movement. **b.** Those occupying a foremost position. [Middle English *vandgard,* from *avant garde,* from Old French : *avaunt,* before (from Latin *abante;* see ADVANCE) + *garde,* guard (from *garder,* to guard; see GUARD).] **—van′guard·ism** *n.* **—van′guard·ist** *n.*

Va·nier (văn-yā′). A city of southeast Ontario, Canada, a suburb of Ottawa on the Ottawa River. Population, 18,792.

va·nil·la (və-nĭl′ə) *n.* **1.** Any of various tropical American vines of the genus *Vanilla* in the orchid family, especially *V. planifolia,* cultivated for its long narrow seedpods from which a flavoring agent is obtained. **2.** The seedpod of this plant. Also called *vanilla bean.* **3.** A flavoring extract prepared from the cured seedpods of this plant or produced synthetically. **—vanilla** *adj.* **1.** Flavored with vanilla: *vanilla pudding.* **2.** Relatively unoriginal, unexciting, or uninspiring; ordinary: *"We went through a period of vanilla cars"* (Charles Jordan). [Spanish *vainilla,* diminutive of *vaina,* sheath (from the shape of its seedpods), from Latin *vāgīna.*]

vanilla bean *n.* See **vanilla** (sense 2).

vanilla plant *n.* A fragrant perennial herb *(Carphephorus odoratissimus)* of the southeast United States, having numerous lavender to purple flower heads.

va·nil·lic (və-nĭl′ĭk) *adj.* Of, relating to, or derived from vanilla or vanillin.

va·nil·lin (və-nĭl′ĭn, văn′ə-lĭn) *n.* A white or yellowish crystalline compound, $C_8H_8O_3$, found in vanilla beans and certain balsams and resins and used in perfumes, flavorings, and pharmaceuticals.

Va·nir (vä′nîr′) *pl.n. Mythology.* An early race of Norse gods who dwelt with the Aesir in Asgard. [Old Norse. See **wen-**[1] in Appendix.]

van·ish (văn′ĭsh) *intr.v.* **-ished, -ish·ing, -ish·es. 1.a.** To pass out of sight, especially quickly; disappear. See Synonyms at **disappear. b.** To pass out of existence. **2.** *Mathematics.* To become zero. Used of a function or variable. [Middle English *vanisshen,* alteration of Old French *esvanir, esvaniss-,* from Vulgar Latin **exvanīre,* alteration of Latin *ēvānēscere* : *ē-, ex-,* ex- + *vānēscere,* to vanish (from *vānus,* empty; see **eu-**[2] in Appendix).] **—van′ish·er** *n.* **—van′ish·ing·ly** *adv.* **—van′ish·ment** *n.*

van·ish·ing point (văn′ĭ-shĭng) *n.* **1.** A point in a drawing at which parallel lines drawn in perspective converge or seem to converge. **2.** A point at which a thing disappears or ceases to exist.

van·i·ty (văn′ĭ-tē) *n., pl.* **-ties. 1.** The quality or condition of being vain. **2.** Excessive pride in one's appearance or accomplishments; conceit. See Synonyms at **conceit. 3.** Lack of usefulness, worth, or effect; worthlessness. **4.a.** Something that is vain, futile, or worthless. **b.** Something about which one is vain or conceited. **5.** A vanity case. **6.** See **dressing table. 7.** A bathroom cabinet that encloses a basin and its water lines and drain, usually furnished with shelves and drawers underneath for storage of toiletries. [Middle English *vanite,* from Old French, from Latin *vānitās,* from *vānus,* empty. See **eu-**[2] in Appendix.]

vanity case *n.* **1.** A small handbag or case used by women for carrying cosmetics or toiletries. **2.** A woman's compact.

Van·i·ty Fair also **van·i·ty fair** (văn′ĭ-tē) *n.* A place or scene of ostentation or empty, idle amusement and frivolity. [From *Vanity Fair,* the fair in *Pilgrim's Progress* by John Bunyan.]

vanity plate *n.* A license plate for a motor vehicle bearing a combination of letters or numbers selected by the purchaser.

vanity press *n.* A publisher that publishes a book at the expense of the author.

vanity telephone number *n.* A telephone number with a combination of letters selected by the purchaser.

van·load (văn′lōd′) *n.* The quantity, as of passengers or goods, that a van can carry.

van·pool (văn′po͞ol′) *n.* An arrangement by which commuters travel together in a van. **—vanpool** *tr. & intr.v.* **-pooled, -pool·ing, -pools.** To transport or be transported in a vanpool. **—van′pool′er** *n.*

van·quish (văng′kwĭsh, văn′-) *tr.v.* **-quished, -quish·ing, -quish·es. 1.a.** To defeat or conquer in battle; subjugate. **b.** To defeat in a contest, conflict, or competition. **2.** To overcome or subdue (an emotion, for example); suppress: *Success vanquished their fears.* See Synonyms at **defeat.** [Middle English *vaynquisshen,* from Old French *vainquir, vainquiss-,* from Latin *vincere.* See **weik-**[3] in Appendix.] **—van′quish·a·ble** *adj.* **—van′quish·er** *n.* **—van′quish·ment** *n.*

Van Rens·se·laer (văn rĕn′sə-lîr′, rĕn′sə-lər, văn rĕn′sə-lär′), **Killian** or **Kiliaen.** 1595–1644. Dutch merchant who was a founder of the Dutch West India Company (1621) and established Rensselaerswyck (1635), the only successful privately held colony in America, on his estate in present-day upstate New York.

Van Rensselaer, Stephen. 1764–1839. American army officer and politician. A descendant of Killian Van Rensselaer, he inherited the family estate in New York, saw military action in the War of 1812, and was an early advocate of the Erie Canal project.

Van·taa (vän′tä). A city of southern Finland, a suburb of Helsinki. Population, 141,991.

van·tage (văn′tĭj) *n.* **1.a.** An advantage in a competition or conflict; superiority. **b.** A position, condition, or opportunity that is likely to provide superiority or an advantage. **2.** A position that affords a broad overall view or perspective, as of a place or situation. **3.** *Sports.* An advantage. [Middle English, from Anglo-Norman, short for Old French *avantage,* advantage. See ADVANTAGE.]

van't Hoff (vänt hôf′, hŏf′), **Jacobus Hendricus.** 1852–1911. Dutch chemist. He won a 1901 Nobel Prize for his pioneering work in stereochemistry and thermodynamics.

Va·nu·a Le·vu (və-no͞o′ə lĕv′o͞o). A volcanic island of Fiji in the southern Pacific Ocean northeast of Viti Levu. Sugar cane is important to the island's economy.

Va·nu·a·tu (vä′no͞o-ä′to͞o). Formerly **New Heb·ri·des** (no͞o hĕb′rĭ-dēz′, nyo͞o). An island country of the southern Pacific Ocean east of northern Australia. The islands were first sighted by the Portuguese in 1606 and charted by Capt. James Cook in 1774. Under joint French and British control after 1906, New Hebrides achieved independence as Vanuatu in 1980. Vila is the capital. Population, 138,000. **—Va′nu·a′tu·an** *adj. & n.*

Van Vleck (văn vlĕk′), **John Hasbrouck.** 1899–1980. American physicist. He shared a 1977 Nobel Prize for developments in computer memory.

Van·zet·ti (văn-zĕt′ē, vän-dzĕt′tē), **Bartolomeo.** 1888–1927. Italian-born American anarchist who with Nicola Sacco was convicted of a double murder and sentenced to death (1921). Despite the circumstantial nature of the evidence against them and worldwide protest at the political overtones of the proceedings, the two were executed in 1927.

vap·id (văp′ĭd, vā′pĭd) *adj.* **1.** Lacking liveliness, animation, or interest; dull: *vapid conversation.* **2.** Lacking taste, zest, or flavor; flat: *vapid beer.* [Latin *vapidus.*] **—va·pid′i·ty, vap′id·ness** *n.* **—vap′id·ly** *adv.*

va·por (vā′pər) *n.* **1.** Barely visible or cloudy diffused matter, such as mist, fumes, or smoke, suspended in the air. **2.a.** The state of a substance that exists below its critical temperature and that may be liquefied by application of sufficient pressure. **b.** The gaseous state of a substance that is liquid or solid under ordinary conditions. **3.a.** The vaporized form of a substance for use in industrial, military, or medical processes. **b.** A mixture of a vapor and air, as the explosive gasoline-air mixture burned in an internal-combustion engine. **4.** *Archaic.* **a.** Something insubstantial, worthless, or fleeting. **b.** A fantastic or foolish idea. **5. vapors.** *Archaic.* **a.** Exhalations within a bodily organ, especially the stomach, supposed to affect the mental or physical condition. Used with *the.* **b.** A nervous disorder such as depression or hysteria. Used with *the.* **—vapor** *v.* **-pored, -por·ing, -pors.** —*tr.* To vaporize. —*intr.* **1.** To give off vapor. **2.** To evaporate. **3.** To engage in idle, boastful talk. [Middle English *vapour,* from Anglo-Norman, from Latin *vapor, vapōr-.*] **—va′por·er** *n.*

va·por·es·cence (vā′pə-rĕs′əns) *n.* Formation of vapor.

va·por·if·ic (vā′pə-rĭf′ĭk) *adj.* **1.** Producing or turning to vapor. **2.** Having the nature of vapor; vaporous.

va·por·ing (vā′pər-ĭng) *adj.* Foolishly bombastic; boastful. **—vaporing** *n.* Boastful or bombastic talk or behavior: *"All his . . . dreams of fame were the vaporings of a shoddy aesthete without talent"* (Thomas Wolfe). **—va′por·ing·ly** *adv.*

va·por·ish (vā′pər-ĭsh) *adj.* **1.** Suggestive of or resembling vapor. **2.** *Archaic.* Affected by the vapors; given to spells of hysteria or low spirits. **—va′por·ish·ness** *n.*

va·por·ize (vā′pə-rīz′) *tr. & intr.v.* **-ized, -iz·ing, -iz·es.** To convert or be converted into vapor. **—va′por·iz′a·ble** *adj.* **—va·por·i·za′tion** (-ĭ-zā′shən) *n.*

va·por·iz·er (vā′pə-rī′zər) *n.* One that vaporizes, especially a device used to vaporize medicine for inhalation.

vapor lock *n.* A pocket of vaporized gasoline in the fuel line of an internal-combustion engine that obstructs the normal flow of fuel. **—va′por-lock′** (vā′pər-lŏk′) *v.*

va·por·ous (vā′pər-əs) *adj.* **1.** Relating to or resembling vapor. **2.a.** Producing vapors; volatile. **b.** Giving off or full of vapors. **3.** Insubstantial, vague, or ethereal: *"the imponderable mysterious and vaporous illusions of twilight"* (John C. Powys). See Synonyms at **airy. 4.** Extravagantly fanciful; high-flown: *vaporous conjecture.* **—va′por·os′i·ty** (vā′pə-rŏs′ĭ-tē), **va′por·ous·ness** (-pər-əs-nĭs) *n.* **—va′por·ous·ly** *adj.*

vapor pressure *n.* The pressure exerted by a vapor in equilibrium with its solid or liquid phase.

vapor trail *n.* See **contrail.**

va·por·ware (vā′pər-wâr′) *n.* *Computer Science.* New software that has been announced or marketed but has not been produced.

va·por·y (vā′pə-rē) *adj.* Vaporous.

va·pour (vā′pər) *n. & v.* *Chiefly British.* Vapor.

♦ **va·que·ro** (vä-kâr′ō) *n., pl.* **-ros.** *Chiefly Texas.* See **cowboy** (sense 1). [Spanish, from *vaca,* cow, from Latin *vacca.*]

♦ ***REGIONAL NOTE:*** Used chiefly in southwest and central Texas to mean a ranch hand or cowboy, the word *vaquero* is a direct loan from Spanish; that is, it is spelled and pronounced, even by English speakers, much as it would be in Spanish. In California, however, the same word was Anglicized to *buckaroo.* Craig M. Carver, author of *American Regional Dialects,* points out that the two words also reflect cultural differences between cattlemen in Texas and California. The Texas vaquero was typically a bachelor who hired on with different outfits, while the California buckaroo usually stayed on the same ranch where he was born or had grown up and raised his own family there.

var. *abbr.* **1.** Variable. **2.** Variant. **3.** Variation. **4.** Variety. **5.** Various.

va·ra (vär′ə) *n.* **1.** A Spanish, Portuguese, and Latin-American unit of linear measure varying from about 81 to 109 centimeters (32 to 43 inches). **2.** A square vara. [Spanish and Portuguese, rod, both from Latin *vāra,* forked pole, from *vārus,* bent.]

va·rac·tor (və-răk′tər, vă-) *n.* A semiconductor device in which the capacitance is sensitive to the applied voltage at the boundary of the semiconductor material and an insulator. [VAR(YING) + (RE)ACT(ANCE) + –OR[1].]

Va·ra·na·si (və-rä′nə-sē) also **Be·na·res** (bə-när′əs, -ēz) or **Ba·na·ras** (bə-när′əs). A city of northeast-central India on the Ganges River southeast of Lucknow. One of India's oldest cities, it is a sacred Hindu pilgrimage site with some 1,500 temples, palaces, and shrines. Population, 708,647.

Var·dar (vär′där′). A river, about 386 km (240 mi) long, rising in southeast Yugoslavia and flowing southward to an arm of the Aegean Sea in northeast Greece.

Va·re·se (və-rā′sē, vä-rĕ′zĕ). A city of northern Italy northwest of Milan. It is the center of a resort area. Population, 90,285.

Va·rèse (və-rāz′, vä-rĕz′), **Edgard.** 1883–1965. French-born American composer of arrhythmic and atonal works, including early examples of electronic music.

Var·gas (vär′gəs), **Getulio Dornelles.** 1883–1954. Brazilian politician who led a successful revolution (1930) and was president (1930–1945 and 1951–1954) until resigning from office under pressure from the military.

Var·gas Llo·sa (vär′gəs yō′sə, bär′gäs yô′sä), **Mario.** Born 1936. Peruvian writer known for his stylistically innovative and complex novels, such as *The Green House* (1966) and *The War of the End of the World* (1984), which often concern the political and social climate of his homeland.

vari– *pref.* Variant of **vario–.**

var·i·a (vâr′ē-ə, văr′-) *n.* A miscellany, especially of literary works. [Latin, from neuter pl. of *varius,* various.]

var·i·a·bil·i·ty (vâr′ē-ə-bĭl′ĭ-tē, văr′-) *n., pl.* **-ties.** The quality, state, or degree of being variable or changeable.

var·i·a·ble (vâr′ē-ə-bəl, văr′-) *adj.* *Abbr.* **var. 1.a.** Likely to change or vary; subject to variation; changeable. **b.** Inconstant; fickle. **2.** *Biology.* Tending to deviate, as from a normal or recognized type; aberrant. **3.** *Mathematics.* Having no fixed quantitative value. **—variable** *n.* *Abbr.* **var. 1.** Something that varies or is prone to variation. **2.** *Astronomy.* A variable star. **3.** *Mathematics.* **a.** A quantity capable of assuming any of a set of values. **b.** A symbol that represents such a quantity. For example, in the expression $a^2 + b^2 = c^2$, *a, b,* and *c* are variables. **—var′i·a·ble·ness** *n.* **—var′i·a·bly** *adv.*

variable cost *n.* A cost that fluctuates directly with output changes.

variable field *n.* *Computer Science.* A field of data that may be varied in length according to need.

variable logic *n.* *Computer Science.* A form of internal machine logic that may be changed to match programming formats.

var·i·a·ble-rate mortgage (vâr′ē-ə-bəl-rāt′, văr′-) *n.* *Abbr.* **VRM** A mortgage that is renegotiable at periodic intervals. The interest rate may be raised or lowered and is indexed to the prevailing market rates.

variable star *n.* A star whose brightness varies because of internal changes or periodic eclipsing of mutually revolving stars.

var·i·ance (vâr′ē-əns, văr′-) *n.* **1.a.** The act of varying. **b.** The state or quality of being variant or variable; a variation. **c.** A difference between what is expected and what actually occurs. **2.** The state or fact of differing or of being in conflict. See Synonyms at **discord. 3.** *Law.* **a.** A discrepancy between two statements or documents in a proceeding. **b.** License to engage in an act contrary to a usual rule: *a zoning variance.* **4.** *Statistics.* The square of the standard deviation. **5.** *Chemistry.* The number of thermodynamic variables, such as temperature and pressure, required to specify a state of equilibrium of a system, given by the phase rule. **—*idiom.* at variance.** In a state of discrepancy; differing: *The facts are at variance with your story.*

var·i·ant (vâr′ē-ənt, văr′-) *adj.* **1.** Having or exhibiting variation; differing. **2.** Tending or liable to vary; variable. **3.** Deviating from a standard, usually by only a slight difference. **—variant** *n.* *Abbr.* **var.** Something that differs in form only slightly from something else, as a different spelling or pronunciation of the same word. [Middle English, from Old French, from Latin *variāns, variant-,* present participle of *variāre,* to vary. See VARY.]

var·i·ate (vâr′ē-ĭt, -āt′, văr′-) *n.* *Statistics.* A random variable with a numerical value that is defined on a given sample space. [From Latin *variātus,* past participle of *variāre,* to vary. See VARY.]

var·i·a·tion (vâr′ē-ā′shən, văr′-) *n.* *Abbr.* **var. 1.a.** The act, process, or result of varying. **b.** The state or fact of being varied. See Synonyms at **difference. 2.** The extent or degree to which something varies: *a variation of ten pounds in weight.* **3.** Magnetic declination. **4.** Something slightly different from another of the same type. **5.** *Biology.* **a.** Marked difference or deviation from the normal or recognized form, function, or structure. **b.** An organism or a plant exhibiting such difference or deviation. **6.** *Mathematics.* A function that relates the values of one variable to those of other variables. **7.** *Music.* **a.** A form that is an altered version of a given theme, diverging from it by melodic ornamentation and by changes in harmony, rhythm, or key. **b.** One of a series of forms based on a single theme. **8.** A solo dance, especially one forming part of a larger work. **—var′i·a′tion·al** *adj.*

varic– *pref.* Variant of **varico–.**

var·i·ce·al (văr′ĭ-sē′əl) *adj.* Of, relating to, or caused by a varix or varices: *variceal hemorrhage.*

var·i·cel·la (văr′ĭ-sĕl′ə) *n.* See **chickenpox.** [New Latin, diminutive of *variola,* variola. See VARIOLA.] **—var′i·cel′loid′** (-sĕl′oid′) *adj.*

var·i·cel·late (văr′ĭ-sĕl′ĭt, -āt) *adj.* Having small varices, as certain gastropod shells.

var·i·cel·la-zos·ter virus (văr′ĭ-sĕl′ə-zŏs′tər) *n.* A herpesvirus that causes chickenpox and shingles.

var·i·ces (văr′ĭ-sēz′) *n.* Plural of **varix.**

varico– or **varic–** *pref.* Varix; varicose vein: *varicosis.* [From Latin *varix, varic-,* varix.]

var·i·co·cele (văr′ĭ-kō-sēl′) *n.* A varicose condition of veins of the spermatic cord or the ovaries, forming a soft tumor. [VARICO– + –CELE[1].]

vanishing point

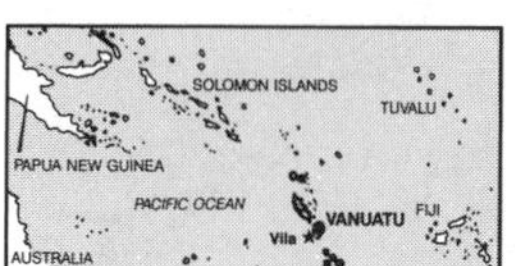

Vanuatu

ă pat	oi boy
ā pay	ou out
âr care	ŏŏ took
ä father	ōō boot
ĕ pet	ŭ cut
ē be	ûr urge
ĭ pit	th thin
ī pie	*th* this
îr pier	hw which
ŏ pot	zh vision
ō toe	ə about, item
ô paw	♦ regionalism

Stress marks: **′** (primary); ′ (secondary), as in **dictionary** (dĭk′shə-nĕr′ē)

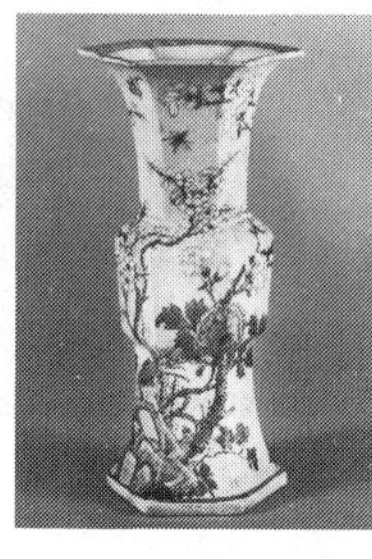

vase
Enamel on porcelain biscuit, dating from the reign (1662–1722) of the emperor Kangxi (1654–1722)

vat

var·i·col·ored (vâr′ĭ-kŭl′ərd, văr′-) *adj.* Having a variety of colors; variegated.

var·i·cose (văr′ĭ-kōs′) *adj.* **1.** Abnormally swollen or knotted: *varicose veins.* **2.** Relating to or causing unusual swelling. **3.** Resembling a varix on the surface of a shell. [Latin *varicōsus,* from *varix, varic-,* swollen vein.]

var·i·co·sis (văr′ĭ-kō′sĭs) *n., pl.* **-ses** (-sēz). **1.** The condition of being varicose. **2.** Formation of varices.

var·i·cos·i·ty (văr′ĭ-kŏs′ĭ-tē) *n., pl.* **-ties. 1.** Varicosis. **2.** A varicose enlargement or swelling. **3.** The condition of having varicose veins.

var·i·cot·o·my (văr′ĭ-kŏt′ə-mē) *n., pl.* **-mies.** Surgical removal of varicose veins.

var·ied (vâr′ēd, văr′-) *adj.* **1.** Having or consisting of various kinds or forms; diverse. See Synonyms at **miscellaneous. 2.** Having been modified or altered. **3.** Of several colors; varicolored or variegated. **—var′ied·ly** *adv.*

varied thrush *n.* A bird *(Ixoreus naevius)* of western North America that resembles the robin but has a black stripe across the breast.

var·i·e·gate (vâr′ē-ĭ-gāt′, vâr′ĭ-gāt′, văr′-) *tr.v.* **-gat·ed, -gat·ing, -gates. 1.** To change the appearance of, especially by marking with different colors; streak. **2.** To give variety to; make varied. [From Late Latin *variegātus,* past participle of *variegāre* : Latin *varius,* various + *agere,* to do, drive; see **ag-** in Appendix.] **—var′i·e·ga′tor** *n.*

var·i·e·gat·ed (vâr′ē-ĭ-gā′tĭd, vâr′ĭ-gā′-, văr′-) *adj.* **1.** Having streaks, marks, or patches of a different color or colors; varicolored: *"If they recall the Colosseum . . . it is only as a showcase for cats more variegated than any fevered artist's mind could imagine"* (Michael Mewshaw). **2.** Distinguished or characterized by variety; diversified.

var·i·e·ga·tion (vâr′ē-ĭ-gā′shən, vâr′ĭ-gā′-, văr′-) *n.* The state of being variegated; diversified coloration.

va·ri·e·tal (və-rī′ĭ-tl) *adj.* Of, indicating, or characterizing a variety, especially a biological variety. **—varietal** *n.* A wine made principally from one variety of grapes and carrying the name of that grape. [From VARIETY.] **—va·ri′e·tal·ly** *adv.*

va·ri·e·ty (və-rī′ĭ-tē) *n., pl.* **-ties.** *Abbr.* **var. 1.** The quality or condition of being various or varied; diversity. **2.** A number or collection of varied things, especially of a particular group; an assortment: *brought home a variety of snacks.* **3.** A group that is distinguished from other groups by a specific characteristic or set of characteristics. **4.** *Biology.* **a.** A taxonomic subdivision of a species consisting of naturally occurring or selectively bred populations or individuals that differ from the remainder of the species in certain minor characters. **b.** An organism, especially a plant, belonging to such a subdivision. **5.** A variety show. [French *variété,* from Old French, from Latin *varietās, varietāt-,* from *varius,* various.]

variety meat *n.* **1.** Meat, such as liver or sweetbreads, that has been taken from a part other than skeletal muscles. **2.** Meat, such as sausage, that has been processed.

variety show *n.* A theatrical entertainment consisting of successive unrelated acts, such as songs, dances, and comedy skits.

variety store *n.* A retail store that carries a large variety of usually inexpensive merchandise.

var·i·form (vâr′ə-fôrm′, văr′-) *adj.* Having a variety of forms; diversiform.

vario– or **vari–** *pref.* Variety; difference; variation: *variometer.* [From Latin *varius,* speckled.]

va·ri·o·la (və-rī′ə-lə, vâr′ē-ō′lə, văr′-) *n.* See **smallpox.** [New Latin, from Medieval Latin, pustule, from Latin *varius,* speckled.]

var·i·o·late (vâr′ē-ə-lāt′, văr′-) *adj.* Having pustules or marks like those of smallpox. **—variolate** *tr.v.* **-lat·ed, -lat·ing, -lates.** To inoculate with the smallpox virus.

var·i·ole (vâr′ē-ōl′) *n.* A small pocklike mark, as on an insect.

var·i·o·lite (vâr′ē-ə-līt′, văr′-) *n.* A basic rock whose pockmarked appearance is caused by the presence of numerous white, rounded, embedded spherules.

var·i·o·loid (vâr′ē-ə-loid′, văr′-, və-rī′ə-loid′) *n.* A mild form of smallpox occurring in people who have been previously vaccinated or who have had the disease.

va·ri·o·lous (və-rī′ə-ləs, vâr′ē-ō′-, văr′-) *adj.* Of, relating to, or affected with smallpox.

var·i·om·e·ter (vâr′ē-ŏm′ĭ-tər, văr′-) *n.* A variable inductor used to measure variations in terrestrial magnetism.

var·i·o·rum (vâr′ē-ôr′əm, -ōr′-, văr′-) *n.* **1.** An edition of the works of an author with notes by various scholars or editors. **2.** An edition containing various versions of a text. **—variorum** *adj.* Of or relating to a variorum edition or text. [From Latin *(ēditiō cum notīs) variōrum,* (edition with the notes) of various persons, genitive pl. of *varius,* various.]

var·i·ous (vâr′ē-əs, văr′-) *adj. Abbr.* **var. 1.a.** Of diverse kinds: *for various reasons.* **b.** Unlike; different. **2.** Being more than one; several. **3.** Many-sided; versatile: *a person of various skills.* **4.** Having a variegated nature or appearance. **5.** Being an individual or separate member of a class or group: *The various reports all agreed.* **6.** *Archaic.* Changeable; variable. **—various** *pron. (used with a pl. verb). Usage Problem.* Several different individuals. [From Latin *varius.*] **—var′i·ous·ly** *adv.* **—var′i·ous·ness** *n.*

USAGE NOTE: *Various* is sometimes used as a pronoun, as in *He spoke to various of the members.* It is not clear why this usage should be regarded as an error, since it is supported by analogy to the uses of quantifiers such as *few, many,* and *several.* But it has occasioned widespread critical objections; in an earlier survey the usage was found unacceptable by 91 percent of the Usage Panel.

var·i·sized (vâr′ĭ-sīzd′, văr′-) *adj.* Of different sizes.

var·ix (văr′ĭks) *n., pl.* **-i·ces** (-ĭ-sēz′). **1.** An abnormally dilated or swollen vein, artery, or lymph vessel. **2.** One of the longitudinal ridges on the surface of a gastropod shell. [Latin, swollen vein.]

var·let (vär′lĭt) *n.* **1.** An attendant or a servant. **2.** A knight's page. **3.** A rascal; a knave. [Middle English, from Old French, variant of *vaslet.* See VALET.]

var·let·ry (vär′lĭ-trē) *n., pl.* **-tries.** *Archaic.* **1.** A crowd of attendants or menials. **2.** A disorderly crowd; a rabble.

var·mint (vär′mĭnt) *n. Informal.* One that is considered undesirable, obnoxious, or troublesome. [Variant of VERMIN.]

Var·na (vär′nə). A city of eastern Bulgaria on the Black Sea north-northeast of Burgas. Founded in the sixth century B.C. as a Greek colony, it came under Turkish control in 1391 and was ceded to newly independent Bulgaria in 1878. Population, 297,000.

var·nish (vär′nĭsh) *n.* **1.a.** A paint containing a solvent and an oxidizing or evaporating binder, used to coat a surface with a hard, glossy, transparent film. **b.** The smooth coating or gloss resulting from the application of this paint. **2.a.** Something suggestive of or resembling varnish. **b.** A deceptively attractive external appearance; an outward show. **—varnish** *tr.v.* **-nished, -nish·ing, -nish·es. 1.** To cover with varnish. **2.** To give a smooth and glossy finish to. **3.** To give a deceptively attractive appearance to; gloss over. [Middle English *vernisshe,* from Old French *vernis,* from Medieval Latin *veronix, vernix,* sandarac resin, from Late Greek *verenikē,* from Greek *Berenikē,* Berenice (Benghazi), an ancient city of Cyrenaica.] **—var′nish·er** *n.*

varnish tree *n.* Any of several trees having milky juice used to make varnish.

va·room (və-ro͞om′, -ro͝om′) *n. & v.* Variant of **vroom.**

Var·ro (văr′ō), **Marcus Terentius.** 116–27 B.C. Roman scholar and encyclopedist who reputedly produced more than 600 volumes, covering nearly every field of knowledge.

var·si·ty (vär′sĭ-tē) *n., pl.* **-ties. 1.** The principal team representing a university, college, or school in sports, games, or other competitions. **2.** *Chiefly British.* A university. *—attributive.* Often used to modify another noun: *varsity football; a varsity letter.* [Alteration of UNIVERSITY.]

var·us (vâr′əs, văr′-) *n.* An abnormal position of a bone of the leg or foot. [From Latin *vārus,* crooked.]

varve (värv) *n. Geology.* A layer or series of layers of sediment deposited in a body of still water in one year. [Swedish *varv,* layer, from *varva,* to bend, from Old Norse *hverfa.*]

var·y (vâr′ē, văr′ē) *v.* **-ied** (-ēd), **-y·ing, -ies** (-ēz). *—tr.* **1.** To make or cause changes in the characteristics or attributes of; modify or alter. **2.** To give variety to; make diverse: *vary one's diet.* **3.** To introduce under new aspects; express in a different manner: *vary a musical tempo.* *—intr.* **1.** To undergo or show change: *The temperature varied throughout the day.* **2.** To be different; deviate: *vary from established patterns of behavior.* See Synonyms at **differ. 3.** To undergo successive or alternate changes in attributes or qualities: *Foliage varies with the seasons.* [Middle English *varien,* to undergo change, from Old French *varier,* from Latin *variāre,* from *varius,* various.] **—var′y·ing·ly** *adv.*

var·y·ing hare (vâr′ē-ĭng, văr′-) *n.* See **snowshoe rabbit.**

vas (văs) *n., pl.* **va·sa** (vā′zə). *Anatomy.* A vessel or duct. [Latin *vās,* vessel.]

vas– *pref.* Variant of **vaso–.**

va·sa (vā′zə) *n.* Plural of **vas.**

vasa def·er·en·ti·a (dĕf′ə-rĕn′shē-ə) *n.* Plural of **vas deferens.**

vasa ef·fer·en·ti·a (ĕf′ə-rĕn′shē-ə) *n.* Plural of **vas efferens.**

va·sal (vā′səl, -zəl) *adj.* Of, relating to, or connected with a vessel or duct of the body.

Va·sa·ri (və-zär′ē, -sär′ē, vä-zä′rē), **Giorgio.** 1511–1574. Italian painter, architect, and art historian who wrote *Lives of the Most Imminent Italian Architects, Painters, and Sculptors* (1550), a history of Renaissance art.

vas·cu·la (văs′kyə-lə) *n.* Plural of **vasculum.**

vas·cu·lar (văs′kyə-lər) *adj. Biology.* Of, characterized by, or containing vessels that carry or circulate fluids, such as blood, lymph, or sap through the body of an animal or a plant. [From Latin *vāsculum,* diminutive of *vās,* vessel.] **—vas′cu·lar′i·ty** (-lăr′ĭ-tē) *n.*

vascular bundle *n. Botany.* A strand of primary conductive plant tissue consisting essentially of xylem and phloem. Also called *fibrovascular bundle.*

vascular cambium *n. Botany.* A lateral meristem that produces secondary xylem to the inside and secondary phloem to the outside.

vas·cu·lar·i·za·tion (văs′kyə-lər-ĭ-zā′shən) *n.* **1.** The process of vascularizing; the formation of vessels, especially blood

ă pat	oi boy
ā pay	ou out
âr care	o͝o took
ä father	o͞o boot
ĕ pet	ŭ cut
ē be	ûr urge
ĭ pit	th thin
ī pie	*th* this
îr pier	hw which
ŏ pot	zh vision
ō toe	ə about, item
ô paw	♦ regionalism

Stress marks: **′** (primary); ′ (secondary), as in **dictionary** (dĭk′shə-nĕr′ē)

vessels. **2.** *Medicine.* An abnormal or pathological formation of blood vessels.

vas·cu·lar·ize (văs′kyə-lə-rīz′) *tr. & intr.v.* **-ized, -iz·ing, -iz·es.** To make or become vascular.

vascular plant *n.* Any of various plants, such as the ferns and seed-bearing plants, in which the phloem transports sugar and the xylem transports water and salts.

vascular tissue *n.* The supportive and conductive tissue in plants, consisting of xylem and phloem.

vas·cu·la·ture (văs′kyə-lə-cho͝or′, -chər) *n.* Arrangement of blood vessels in the body or in an organ or a body part.

vas·cu·li·tis (văs′kyə-lī′tĭs) *n.* Inflammation of a vessel of the body.

vas·cu·lum (văs′kyə-ləm) *n., pl.* **-la** (-lə). A small box or case used for carrying collected plant specimens. [Latin *vāsculum,* small vessel. See VASCULAR.]

vas def·er·ens (văs′ dĕf′ər-ənz, -ə-rĕnz′) *n., pl.* **va·sa def·er·en·ti·a** (vā′zə dĕf′ə-rĕn′shē-ə). The main duct through which semen is carried from the epididymis to the ejaculatory duct. [New Latin *vās dēferēns* : *vās,* duct + Latin *dēferēns,* carrying away.]

vase (vās, vāz, väz) *n.* An open container, as of glass or porcelain, used for holding flowers or for ornamentation. [French, from Latin *vās,* vessel.]

va·sec·to·mize (və-sĕk′tə-mīz′, vā-zĕk′-) *tr.v.* **-mized, -miz·ing, -miz·es.** To perform a vasectomy on.

va·sec·to·my (və-sĕk′tə-mē, vă-zĕk′-) *n., pl.* **-mies.** Surgical removal of all or part of the vas deferens, usually as a means of sterilization.

vas ef·fer·ens (văs′ ĕf′ər-ənz, -ə-rĕnz′) *n., pl.* **va·sa ef·fer·en·ti·a** (vā′zə ĕf′ə-rĕn′shē-ə). Any of a number of small ducts that carry semen from the testis to the epididymis. [New Latin *vās efferēns* : *vās,* duct + Latin *efferēns,* carrying out.]

Vas·e·line (văs′ə-lēn′, văs′ə-lēn′). A trademark used for a brand of petroleum jelly.

Vash·on Island (văsh′ŏn). An island of west-central Washington in Puget Sound between Seattle and Tacoma.

vaso– or **vas–** *pref.* **1.** Blood vessel: *vasoconstriction.* **2.** Vas deferens: *vasectomy.* [From Latin *vās,* vessel.]

va·so·ac·tive (vā′zō-ăk′tĭv) *adj.* Causing constriction or dilation of blood vessels. **—va′so·ac·tiv′i·ty** *n.*

va·so·con·stric·tion (vā′zō-kən-strĭk′shən) *n.* Constriction of a blood vessel, as by a nerve or drug. **—vas′o·con·stric′tive** *adj.*

va·so·con·stric·tor (vā′zō-kən-strĭk′tər) *n.* Something, such as a nerve or drug, that causes vasoconstriction.

va·so·dil·a·tion (vā′zō-dī-lā′shən, -dĭ-) also **va·so·dil·a·ta·tion** (-dĭl′ə-tā′shən, -dī′lə-) *n.* Dilation of a blood vessel, as by the action of a nerve or drug.

va·so·di·la·tor (vā′zō-dī-lā′tər, -dĭ-, -dī′lā-) *n.* Something, such as a nerve or drug, that causes vasodilation.

va·so·li·ga·tion (vā′zō-lī-gā′shən) *n.* Surgical ligation of the vas deferens as a means of sterilization. **—va′so·li′gate** (-lī′găt) *v.*

va·so·mo·tor (vā′zō-mō′tər) *adj.* Relating to, causing, or regulating constriction or dilation of blood vessels.

va·so·pres·sin (vā′zō-prĕs′ĭn) *n.* A hormone secreted by the posterior lobe of the pituitary gland that constricts blood vessels, raises blood pressure, and reduces excretion of urine. Also called *antidiuretic hormone.*

va·so·pres·sor (vā′zō-prĕs′ər) *adj.* Of, relating to, or causing constriction of blood vessels. **—vasopressor** *n.* An agent that causes a rise in blood pressure.

va·so·spasm (vā′zō-spăz′əm) *n.* A sudden constriction of a blood vessel, causing a reduction in blood flow. **—va′so·spas′tic** (-spăs′tĭk) *adj.*

va·so·va·gal (vā′zō-vā′gəl) *adj.* Relating to or involving blood vessels and the vagus nerve.

vas·sal (văs′əl) *n.* **1.** A person who held land from a feudal lord and received protection in return for homage and allegiance. **2.** A bondman; a slave. **3.** A subordinate or dependent. [Middle English, from Old French, from Vulgar Latin *vassallus, from *vassus, of Celtic origin. See **upo** in Appendix.]

vas·sal·age (văs′ə-lĭj) *n.* **1.** The condition of being a vassal. **2.** The service, homage, and fealty required of a vassal. **3.** A position of subordination or subjection; servitude.

Vas·sar (văs′ər), **Matthew.** 1792–1868. American merchant and philanthropist who was an advocate of higher education for women and endowed Vassar College (1861).

vast (văst) *adj.* **vast·er, vast·est.** **1.** Very great in size, number, amount, or quantity. **2.** Very great in area or extent; immense. **3.** Very great in degree or intensity. See Synonyms at **enormous.** **—vast** *n. Archaic.* An immense space. [Latin *vastus.*] **—vast′ly** *adv.* **—vast′ness** *n.*

Väs·ter·ås (vĕs′tə-rōs′). A city of eastern Sweden west-northwest of Stockholm. Founded before 1000, it was an important medieval city and a center of the Swedish Reformation. Population, 117,658.

vas·ti·tude (văs′tĭ-to͞od′, -tyo͞od′) also **vas·ti·ty** (-tē) *n.* Immensity. [Latin *vastitūdō,* from *vastus,* vast.]

vast·y (văs′tē) *adj.* **-i·er, -i·est.** *Archaic.* Vast.

vat (văt) *n.* A large vessel, such as a tub, cistern, or barrel, used to hold or store liquids. **—vat** *tr.v.* **vat·ted, vat·ting, vats.** To put into or treat in a vat. [Middle English, variant of *fat,* from Old English *fæt.*]

VAT or **V.A.T.** *abbr.* Value-added tax.

Vat. *abbr.* Vatican.

vat dye *n.* A dye, such as indigo, that produces a fast color by impregnating fiber with a reduced soluble form that is then oxidized to an insoluble form. **—vat′-dyed′** (văt′dīd′) *adj.*

vat·ic (văt′ĭk) also **vat·i·cal** (-ĭ-kəl) *adj.* Of or characteristic of a prophet; oracular. [From Latin *vātēs,* seer. See **wet-**[1] in Appendix.]

Vat·i·can (văt′ĭ-kən) *n. Abbr.* **Vat.** **1.** The official residence of the pope in Vatican City. **2.** The papal government; the papacy. [Latin *Vaticānus (mōns),* the Vatican (Hill).]

Vatican City. An independent papal state on the Tiber River within Rome, Italy. Created by the Lateran Treaty signed by Pope Pius XI and Victor Emmanuel III of Italy in 1929, it issues its own currency and postage stamps and has its own newspaper and broadcasting facilities. Population, 736.

Vatican City

Vat·i·can·ism (văt′ĭ-kə-nĭz′əm) *n.* The policies and authority of the papacy.

va·tic·i·nal (vă-tĭs′ə-nəl, və-) *adj.* Prophetic.

va·tic·i·nate (vă-tĭs′ə-nāt′, və-) *v.* **-nat·ed, -nat·ing, -nates.** —*tr.* To prophesy; foretell. See Synonyms at **foretell.** —*intr.* To be a prophet. [Latin *vāticinārī, vāticināt-,* from *vātēs,* seer. See VATIC.] **—va·tic′i·na′tor** *n.*

va·tic·i·na·tion (vă-tĭs′ə-nā′shən, və-) *n.* **1.** The act of prophesying. **2.** A prediction; a prophecy.

Vät·tern (vĕt′ərn). A lake of south-central Sweden southeast of Lake Vänern. It is connected with the Baltic by the Göta Canal.

va·tu (vä′to͞o) *n.* See table at **currency.** [Native word in Vanuatu.]

vau (väv, vôv) *n.* Variant of **vav.**

Vau·ban (vō-bäN′), Marquis **Sébastien Le Prestre de.** 1633–1707. French military engineer who revolutionized fortification and siege strategies during the reign of Louis XIV.

Sarah Vaughan
Photographed in 1960

vaude·ville (vôd′vĭl′, vōd′-, vô′də-) *n.* **1. a.** Stage entertainment offering a variety of short acts such as slapstick turns, song-and-dance routines, and juggling performances. **b.** A theatrical performance of this kind; a variety show. **2.** A light comic play that often includes songs, pantomime, and dances. **3.** *Music.* A popular, often satirical song. [French, alteration of Old French *vaudevire,* occasional or topical light popular song, possibly short for *chanson du Vau de Vire,* song of Vau de Vire, a valley of northwest France, or perhaps : dialectal *vauder,* to go + *virer,* to turn; see VEER[1].]

vaude·vil·lian (vôd-vĭl′yən, vōd-, vô′də-) *n.* One, especially a performer, who works in vaudeville. **—vaude·vil′lian** *adj.*

Vau·dois (vō-dwä′) *pl.n.* See **Waldenses.** [French, from Old French *vaudeis,* from Medieval Latin *Waldēnsēs.* See WALDENSES.]

Vaughan (vôn, vän). A town of southeast Ontario, Canada, a suburb of Toronto. Population, 29,674.

Vaughan (vôn), **Henry.** Known as "the Silurist." 1622–1695. Welsh metaphysical poet whose works include *Silex Scintillans* (1650–1655).

Vaughan, Sarah. 1924–1990. American jazz singer known for her complex bebop phrasing and her scat-singing virtuosity.

Vaughan Wil·liams (wĭl′yəmz), **Ralph.** 1872–1958. British composer who was influenced by folk tunes and Tudor music. His works include nine symphonies, the ballet *Job* (1930), and the opera *The Pilgrim's Progress* (1951).

vault[1] (vôlt) *n.* **1. a.** An arched structure, usually of stone, brick, or concrete, forming the supporting structure of a ceiling or roof. **b.** An arched overhead covering, such as the sky, that resembles the architectural structure in form. **2.** A room or space, such as a cellar or storeroom, with arched walls and ceiling, especially when underground. **3.** A room or compartment, often built of steel, for the safekeeping of valuables: *a bank vault.* **4.** A burial chamber, especially when underground. **5.** *Anatomy.* An arched part of the body, especially the top part of the skull. **—vault** *tr.v.* **vault·ed, vault·ing, vaults.** **1.** To construct or supply with an arched ceiling; cover with a vault. **2.** To build or make in the shape of a vault; arch. [Middle English *vaute,* from Old French, from Vulgar Latin *volvita, *volta, from feminine of *volvitus, arched, alteration of Latin *volūtus,* past participle of *volvere,* to roll. See **wel-**[2] in Appendix.]

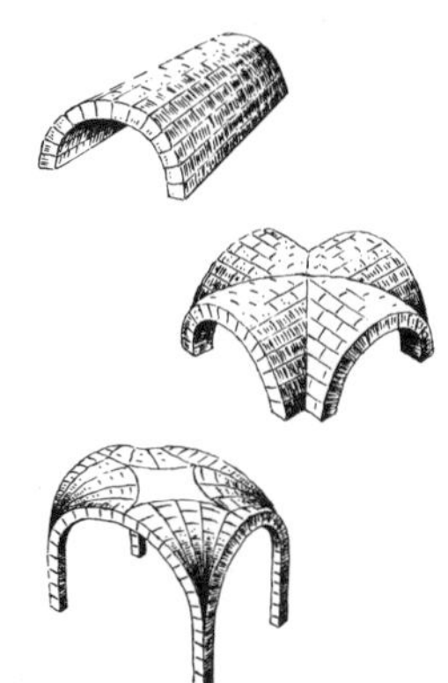
vault[1]
Top: Barrel vault
Center: Groin vault
Bottom: Fan vault

vault[2] (vôlt) *v.* **vault·ed, vault·ing, vaults.** —*tr.* To jump or leap over, especially with the aid of a support such as the hands or a pole. —*intr.* **1.** To jump or leap, especially with the use of the hands or a pole. **2.** To accomplish something as if by leaping suddenly or vigorously: *vaulted into a position of wealth.* **—vault** *n.* The act of vaulting; a jump. [Obsolete French *volter,* from Old French, from Old Italian *voltare,* from Vulgar Latin *volvitāre, frequentative of Latin *volvere,* to turn, roll. See **wel-**[2] in Appendix.] **—vault′er** *n.*

vault·ing[1] (vôl′tĭng) *n.* Something vaulted or arched.

vault·ing[2] (vôl′tĭng) *adj.* **1.** Leaping upward or over. **2.** Reaching too far; exaggerated: *his vaulting ambition.* **3.** Employed in leaping over: *a vaulting pole.*

vaunt (vônt, vŏnt) *v.* **vaunt·ed, vaunt·ing, vaunts.** —*tr.* To speak boastfully of; brag about. —*intr.* To speak boastfully; brag. See Synonyms at **boast**[1]. **—vaunt** *n.* **1.** A boastful remark.

2. Speech of extravagant self-praise. [Middle English *vaunten,* from Old French *vanter,* from Late Latin *vānitāre,* to talk frivolously, frequentative of Latin *vānāre,* from *vānus,* empty. See **eu-**[2] in Appendix.] **—vaunt′er** *n.* **—vaunt′ing·ly** *adv.*

vaunt-cour·i·er (vônt′ko͝or′ē-ər, -kûr′-, kŭr′-, vŏnt′-) *n. Archaic.* A person, such as a herald, sent in advance. [Short for obsolete French *avaunt-courier* : Old French *avaunt,* in front; see VANGUARD + Old French *courrier,* messenger; see COURIER.]

Vau·pés (vou-pās′, -pĕs′). See **Uaupés.**

Vaux (vôks), **Calvert.** 1824–1895. British-born American landscape architect who was a designer of Central Park in New York City.

vav also **vau** or **waw** (väv, vôv) *n.* The sixth letter of the Hebrew alphabet. See table at **alphabet.** [Hebrew *wāw,* hook.]

vav·a·sor also **vav·a·sour** (văv′ə-sôr′, -sōr′, -so͝or′) *n.* A feudal tenant who ranked directly below a baron or peer. [Middle English *vavasour,* from Old French, from Medieval Latin *vavassor,* possibly contraction of *vassus vassōrum,* vassal of vassals : *vassus,* vassal (from Vulgar Latin **vassus;* see VASSAL) + *vassōrum,* genitive pl. of *vassus,* vassal.]

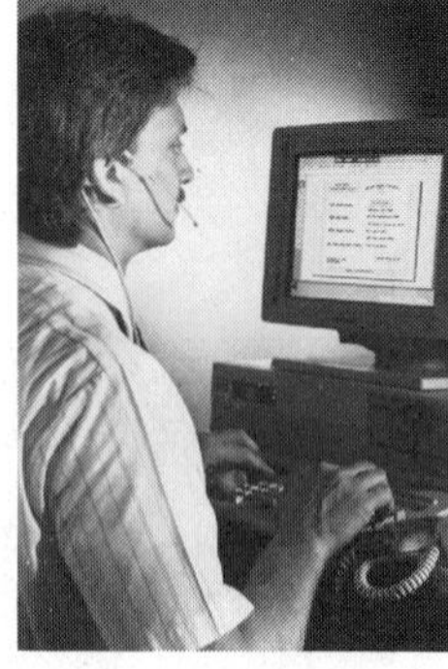

VDT

vb. *abbr.* Verb; verbal.

VC also **V.C.** *abbr.* Vietcong.

V.C. *abbr.* **1.** Vice-chairman; vice-chairperson. **2.** Vice chancellor. **3.** Vice consul. **4.** Victoria Cross.

VCR (vē′sē-är′) *n., pl.* **VCR's.** An electronic device for recording and playing back video images and sound on a videocassette. [*V(ideo)c(assette) r(ecorder).*]

VD also **V.D.** *abbr.* Venereal disease.

v.d. *abbr.* **1.** Vapor density. **2.** Various dates.

V-day (vē′dā′) *n.* A day of victory, as at the conclusion of a war. [V(ICTORY) + DAY.]

VDT (vē′dē-tē′) *n., pl.* **VDT's.** *Computer Science.* An output device using the screen of a cathode-ray tube to display data and graphic images. [*V(ideo) d(isplay) t(erminal).*]

've. Have: *I've been invited.*

veal (vēl) *n.* **1.** The meat of a calf. **2.** Also **veal·er** (vē′lər). A calf raised to be slaughtered for food. [Middle English *veel,* from Old French, from Latin *vitellus,* diminutive of *vitulus,* calf. See **wet-**[2] in Appendix.]

Veb·len (vĕb′lən), **Oswald.** 1880–1960. American mathematician noted for his work on projective geometry and topology.

Veblen, Thorstein Bunde. 1857–1929. American economist who described a fundamental conflict between the provision of goods and the making of money. In his popular study *The Theory of the Leisure Class* (1899) he coined the phrase *conspicuous consumption.*

vec·tor (vĕk′tər) *n.* **1.** *Mathematics.* **a.** A quantity, such as velocity, completely specified by a magnitude and a direction. **b.** A one-dimensional array. **c.** An element of a vector space. **2.** *Pathology.* An organism, such as a mosquito or tick, that carries disease-causing microorganisms from one host to another. **3.** *Genetics.* A bacteriophage, a plasmid, or another agent that transfers genetic material from one location to another. **4.** A force or an influence. **—vector** *tr.v.* **-tored, -tor·ing, -tors.** To guide (a pilot or an aircraft, for example) by means of radio communication according to vectors. [Latin, carrier, from *vehere, vect-,* to carry. See **wegh-** in Appendix.] **—vec·to′ri·al** (vĕk-tôr′ē-əl, -tōr′-) *adj.*

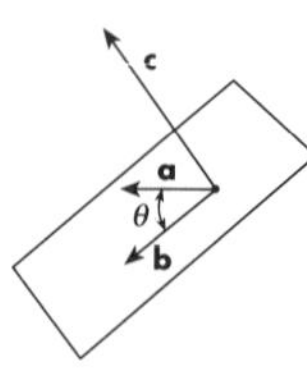

vector product
$c = a \times b$

vector product *n. Mathematics.* A vector, C, that has magnitude equal to the product of the magnitudes of two vectors, A and B, and the sine of the angle between A and B. It is perpendicular to the plane of A and B and in a right-handed coordinate system directed so that a right-handed rotation about C carries A into B through an angle not greater than 180°. Also called *cross product.*

vector space *n. Mathematics.* A system consisting of a set of generalized vectors and a field of scalars, having the same rules for vector addition and scalar multiplication as physical vectors and scalars.

Ve·da (vā′də, vē′-) *n. Hinduism.* Any of the oldest Hindu sacred texts, composed in Sanskrit and gathered into four collections. [Sanskrit *vedaḥ,* sacred lore, knowledge, Veda. See **weid-** in Appendix.]

Ve·dan·ta (vĭ-dän′tə, -dăn′-) *n. Hinduism.* The system of philosophy that further develops the implications in the Upanishads that all reality is a single principle, Brahman, and teaches that the believer's goal is to transcend the limitations of self-identity and realize one's unity with Brahman. [Sanskrit *vedāntaḥ,* complete knowledge of the Veda : *vedaḥ,* Veda; see VEDA + *antaḥ,* end; see **ant-** in Appendix.] **—Ve·dan′tic** *adj.* **—Ve·dan′tism** *n.* **—Ve·dan′tist** *n.*

V-E Day (vē′ē′) *n.* May 8, 1945, the day on which the Allies announced the surrender of German forces in Europe. [*V(ictory) in) E(urope) Day.*]

Ved·da also **Ved·dah** (vĕd′ə) *n., pl.* **Vedda** or **-das** also **Veddah** or **-dahs.** A member of the earliest people of Sri Lanka, originally forest-dwelling hunters but now almost completely assimilated into the modern Singhalese population. [Singhalese, hunter.]

ve·dette also **vi·dette** (vĭ-dĕt′) *n.* **1.** A mounted sentinel stationed in advance of an outpost. **2.** A small scouting boat used to observe and report on an opposing naval force. [French, from Italian *vedetta,* alteration (influenced by *vedere,* to see) of *veletta,* probably from Spanish *vela,* watch, from *velar,* to watch, from Latin *vigilāre,* to watch through the night, from *vigil,* awake. See **weg-** in Appendix.]

Ve·dic (vā′dĭk, vē′-) *adj.* Of or relating to the Veda or Vedas, the variety of Sanskrit in which they are written, or the Hindu culture that produced them. **—Vedic** *n.* The early Sanskrit in which the Vedas are written.

vee (vē) *n.* The letter *v.*

vee-jay (vē′jā′) *n.* A video jockey. [V(IDEO) + (D)EEJAY.]

vee·na (vē′nə) *n. Music.* Variant of **vina.**

veep (vēp) *n. Slang.* A vice president. [Pronunciation of *V.P.,* abbr. of VICE PRESIDENT.]

veer[1] (vîr) *v.* **veered, veer·ing, veers.** *—intr.* **1.** To turn aside from a course, direction, or purpose; swerve: *"a sequence of adventures that veered between tragedy and bleak farce"* (Anthony Haden-Guest). See Synonyms at **swerve. 2.** To shift clockwise in direction, as from north to northeast. Used of the wind. **3.** *Nautical.* To change the course of a ship by turning the stern to the wind while advancing to windward; wear ship. *—tr.* **1.** To alter the direction of; turn: *veered the car sharply to the left.* **2.** *Nautical.* To change the course of (a ship) by turning the stern windward. **—veer** *n.* A change in direction; a swerve. [French *virer,* from Old French.]

veer[2] (vîr) *tr.v.* **veered, veer·ing, veers.** *Nautical.* To let out or release (a line or an anchor train). [Middle English *veren,* from Middle Dutch *vieren.* See **per**[1] in Appendix.]

vee·ry (vîr′ē) *n., pl.* **-ries.** A New World thrush *(Hylocichla fuscescens)* having a reddish-brown head, back, and tail and an indistinctly spotted breast. Also called *Wilson's thrush.* [Possibly imitative of its song.]

veg. *abbr.* Vegetable.

Ve·ga (vē′gə, vā′-) *n.* The brightest star in the constellation Lyra. [Medieval Latin, from Arabic *(al nasr) al wāqi',* the falling (vulture), Vega.]

Vega (vā′gə, bĕ′gä), **Lope de.** 1562–1635. Spanish playwright whose enormous body of works, including *Fuenteovejuna* (c. 1619), established the national drama of Spain. Nearly 500 of his more than 2,000 plays are extant.

veg·an (vē′gən, vĕj′ən) *n.* A vegetarian whose diet consists of plant products only. [Short for VEGETARIAN.] **—veg′an·ism** *n.*

veg·e·ta·ble (vĕj′tə-bəl, vĕj′ĭ-tə-) *n. Abbr.* **veg. 1.a.** A plant cultivated for an edible part, such as the root of the beet, the leaf of spinach, or the flower buds of broccoli or cauliflower. **b.** The edible part of such a plant. **c.** A member of the vegetable kingdom; a plant. **2.** A person who is regarded as dull, passive, or unresponsive. **—vegetable** *adj.* **1.** Of, relating to, or derived from plants or a plant. **2.** Suggestive of or resembling a plant. **3.** Growing or multiplying like plants. [From Middle English, living and growing as plants do, from Old French, from Medieval Latin *vegetābilis,* from Late Latin, enlivening, from Latin *vegetāre,* to enliven, from *vegetus,* lively, from *vegēre,* to enliven. See **weg-** in Appendix.]

WORD HISTORY: When the speaker in Andrew Marvell's "To his Coy Mistress" tells his mistress that "Had we but world enough, and time . . . /My vegetable love should grow/Vaster than empires and more slow," he "makes one think of pumpkins and eternity in one breath," as one critic has playfully suggested. However, *vegetable* in this case is used figuratively in the sense, "having the property of life and growth, as does a plant." This use is based on the ancient religious and philosophical notion of the tripartite soul as interpreted by the Scholastics: the *vegetative* soul common to plants, animals, and humans; the *sensitive* soul common to animals and humans; and the *rational* soul, found only in humans. "Vegetable love" in Marvell's poem is thus a love that grows, takes nourishment, and reproduces, although it grows slowly. Marvell's use illustrates the original sense of *vegetable,* first recorded in the 15th century. In a work published in 1582 we find recorded for the first time the adjective use of *vegetable* familiar to us, "having to do with plants." In a work of the same date appears the first instance of *vegetable* as a noun, meaning "a plant." It is not until the 18th century that we find the noun and adjective used in the more restricted way associated with the injunction "Eat your vegetables."

vegetable ivory *n.* A hard, ivorylike material obtained from the ivory nut and used in making small objects such as buttons.

vegetable marrow *n. Chiefly British.* Marrow squash.

vegetable oil *n.* Any of various oils obtained from plants and used in food products and industrially.

vegetable oyster *n.* See **salsify.**

vegetable silk *n.* Any of several silky fibers from the seed pods of certain plants, such as the kapok.

vegetable sponge *n.* See **loofa** (sense 2).

vegetable tallow *n.* **1.** Any of various waxy fats obtained from certain plants, such as the bayberry, and used in making soap and candles. **2.** See **Chinese tallow tree.**

vegetable wax *n.* A waxy substance of plant origin, as that obtained from certain palm trees.

veg·e·tal (vĕj′ĭ-tl) *adj.* **1.** Of, relating to, or characteristic of plants. **2.** Relating to growth rather than to sexual reproduction; vegetative. [Middle English, from Medieval Latin *vegetālis,* from Latin *vegetāre,* to enliven. See VEGETABLE.]

vegetal pole *n. Embryology.* The portion of an egg opposite the animal pole that contains most of the yolk.

veg·e·tar·i·an (vĕj′ĭ-târ′ē-ən) *n.* **1.** One who practices vegetarianism. **2.** A herbivore. **—vegetarian** *adj.* **1.** Of or relating to vegetarianism or vegetarians. **2.** Consisting primarily or wholly of vegetables and vegetable products: *a vegetarian diet.* [VEGET(ABLE) + –ARIAN.]

veg·e·tar·i·an·ism (vĕj′ĭ-târ′ē-ə-nĭz′əm) *n.* The practice of subsisting on a diet composed primarily or wholly of vegetables, grains, fruits, nuts, and seeds, with or without eggs and dairy products.

veg·e·tate (vĕj′ĭ-tāt′) *intr.v.* **-tat·ed, -tat·ing, -tates. 1.** To grow or sprout as a plant does. **2.** *Pathology.* To grow in size or spread abnormally. **3.** To exist in a state of physical or mental inactivity or insensibility. [Latin *vegetāre, vegetāt-,* to enliven. See VEGETABLE.]

veg·e·ta·tion (vĕj′ĭ-tā′shən) *n.* **1.** The act or process of vegetating. **2.** The plants of an area or a region; plant life: *The vegetation is lush on the Hawaiian Islands.* **3.** *Pathology.* An abnormal growth on the body. **—veg′e·ta′tion·al** *adj.*

veg·e·ta·tive (vĕj′ĭ-tā′tĭv) also **veg·e·tive** (-ĭ-tĭv) *adj.* **1.** Of, relating to, or characteristic of plants or their growth. **2.** *Biology.* **a.** Of, relating to, or capable of growth. **b.** Of, relating to, or functioning in processes such as growth or nutrition rather than sexual reproduction. **c.** Of or relating to asexual reproduction, such as fission or budding.

veg·gie also **veg·ie** (vĕj′ē) *n. Informal.* A vegetable.

ve·he·ment (vē′ə-mənt) *adj.* **1.** Characterized by forcefulness of expression or intensity of emotion or conviction; fervid: *a vehement denial.* See Synonyms at **intense. 2.** Marked by or full of vigor or energy; strong: *a vehement storm.* [Middle English, from Old French, from Latin *vehemēns, vehement-,* perhaps from *vehere,* to carry. See **wegh-** in Appendix.] **—ve′he·mence, ve′he·men·cy** *n.* **—ve′he·ment·ly** *adv.*

ve·hi·cle (vē′ĭ-kəl) *n.* **1.a.** A device or structure for transporting persons or things; a conveyance: *a space vehicle.* **b.** A self-propelled conveyance that runs on tires; a motor vehicle. **2.** A medium through which something is transmitted, expressed, or accomplished: *His novels are a vehicle for his political views.* **3.** The concrete or specific word or phrase that is applied to the tenor of a metaphor and gives the metaphor its figurative power, as *walking shadow* in *"Life's but a walking shadow"* (Shakespeare). **4.** A play, role, or piece of music used to display the special talents of one performer or company. **5.** A substance of no therapeutic value used to convey an active medicine for administration. **6.** A substance, such as oil, in which paint pigments are mixed for application. [Latin *vehiculum,* from *vehere,* to carry. See **wegh-** in Appendix.]

ve·hic·u·lar (vē-hĭk′yə-lər) *adj.* **1.** Of, relating to, or intended for vehicles, especially motor vehicles. **2.** Serving as a vehicle: *a vehicular contrivance.*

Ve·ii (vē′ī). An ancient city of Etruria north of modern-day Rome, Italy. A powerful member of the Etruscan League, it was almost constantly at war with Rome and finally succumbed in 396 B.C. after a ten-year siege.

veil (vāl) *n.* **1.** A length of cloth worn by women over the head, shoulders, and often the face. **2.** A length of netting attached to a woman's hat or headdress, worn for decoration or to protect the head and face. **3.a.** The part of a nun's headdress that frames the face and falls over the shoulders. **b.** The life or vows of a nun. **4.a.** A piece of light fabric hung to separate or conceal what is behind it; a curtain. **b.** Something that conceals, separates, or screens like a curtain: *a veil of secrecy.* **5.** *Biology.* A membranous covering or part, as that on the developing fruiting body of certain mushrooms; a velum. **—veil** *tr.v.* **veiled, veil·ing, veils. 1.** To cover with or as if with a veil: *Dense fog veiled the bridge.* **2.** To conceal or disguise. [Middle English, from Old North French, from Latin *vēla,* pl. of *vēlum,* a covering.]

veiled (vāld) *adj.* **1.** Covered with a veil: *the veiled head of a bride.* **2.** Concealed or disguised as if with a veil: *"slur-footed ironies, veiled jokes, tiptoe malices"* (Edith Wharton).

veil·ing (vā′lĭng) *n.* **1.** A veil. **2.** Sheer material, such as gauze or fine lace, used for veils.

vein (vān) *n.* **1.a.** *Anatomy.* Any of a branching system of membranous tubes that carry blood to the heart. **b.** A blood vessel. **2.** *Botany.* One of the vascular bundles or ribs that form the branching framework of conducting and supporting tissues in a leaf or other expanded plant organ. Also called *nervure.* **3.** *Zoology.* One of the horny ribs that stiffen and support the wing of an insect. Also called *nervure.* **4.** *Geology.* A regularly shaped and lengthy occurrence of an ore; a lode. **5.** A long, wavy strip of a different shade or color, as in wood or marble, or as mold in cheese. **6.** A fissure, crack, or cleft. **7.** A pervading character or quality; a streak: *"All through the interminable narrative there ran a vein of impressive earnestness"* (Mark Twain). See Synonyms at **streak. 8.a.** A transient attitude or mood. **b.** A particular turn of mind: *spoke later in a more serious vein.* **—vein** *tr.v.* **veined, vein·ing, veins. 1.** To supply or fill with veins. **2.** To mark or decorate with veins. [Middle English *veine,* from Old French, from Latin *vēna.*] **—vein′al** *adj.*

veined (vānd) *adj.* Having veins or showing veinlike markings.

vein·ing (vā′nĭng) *n.* Distribution or arrangement of veins or veinlike markings.

vein·let (vān′lĭt) *n.* A small or secondary vein, as on the wing of an insect.

vein·stone (vān′stōn′) *n.* Mineral matter in a vein exclusive of the ore; gangue.

vein·ule (vān′yo͞ol) *n.* A small vein.

vein·y (vā′nē) *adj.* **-i·er, -i·est.** Full of or exhibiting veins; veined.

vel. *abbr.* **1.** Vellum. **2.** Velocity.

ve·la (vē′lə) *n. Biology, Anatomy, & Zoology.* Plural of **velum.**

Ve·la (vē′lə, vā′-) *n.* A constellation in the Southern Hemisphere near Pyxis and Carina. [Latin *vēla,* pl. of *vēlum,* a covering.]

ve·la·men (və-lā′mən) *n., pl.* **-lam·i·na** (-lăm′ə-nə). **1.** *Anatomy.* A membranous covering or partition; velum. **2.** *Botany.* The spongy, multiple epidermis that covers the aerial roots of epiphytic orchids and certain other plants and is capable of absorbing atmospheric moisture. [Latin, covering, from *vēlāre,* to cover, from *vēlum,* a covering.] **—vel′a·men′tous** (vĕl′ə-mĕn′təs) *adj.*

ve·lar (vē′lər) *adj.* **1.a.** Of or relating to a velum. **b.** Concerning or using the soft palate. **2.** *Linguistics.* Articulated with the back of the tongue touching or near the soft palate, as (g) in *good* and (k) in *cup.* **—velar** *n. Linguistics.* A velar sound.

ve·lar·ize (vē′lə-rīz′) *tr.v.* **-ized, -iz·ing, -iz·es.** *Linguistics.* To articulate (a sound) by retracting the back of the tongue toward the soft palate. **—ve′lar·i·za′tion** (-lər-ĭ-zā′shən) *n.*

ve·late (vē′lāt′, -lĭt) *adj. Biology.* Having or covered by a velum or veil.

Ve·láz·quez (və-läs′kĕs, bĕ-läth′kĕth), **Diego Rodríguez de Silva y.** 1599–1660. Spanish painter whose works, including portraits, notably of Pope Innocent X (1650), historical scenes, such as *The Surrender of Breda* (1635), still lifes, and genre scenes, display his extraordinary technique and mastery of light.

Vel·bert (fĕl′bərt). A city of west-central Germany in the Ruhr Valley northeast of Düsseldorf. It is a manufacturing center specializing in iron goods. Population, 89,261.

Vel·cro (vĕl′krō). A trademark used for a fastening tape consisting of a strip of nylon with a surface of minute hooks that fasten to a corresponding strip with a surface of uncut pile, used especially on cloth products, such as outerwear, luggage, and athletic shoes. This trademark sometimes occurs in print in lowercase: *"dart boards with velcro balls for darts"* (American Banker). It also occurs as a verb: *"We might Velcro the camera to the window, to steady it"* (Washington Post). The trademark occurs in figurative contexts as well: *"Many colleges and universities have adopted a Velcro approach to curriculum design: sticking additional requirements on a base of distribution requirements"* (New York Times). *"In the early stages of a romance—the Velcro period—intimacy is rarely an issue"* (Chicago Tribune).

veldt also **veld** (vĕlt, fĕlt) *n.* Any of the open grazing areas of southern Africa. [Afrikaans *veld,* from Middle Dutch, field. See **pela-²** in Appendix.]

Ve·li·a (vē′lē-ə). See **Elea.**

ve·li·ger (vē′lə-jər, vĕl′ə-) *n.* A larval stage of a mollusk characterized by the presence of a velum. [New Latin *vēliger* : *vēlum,* velum; see VELUM + Latin *gerere,* to bear.]

vel·le·i·ty (vĕ-lē′ĭ-tē, və-) *n., pl.* **-ties. 1.** Volition at its lowest level. **2.** A mere wish or inclination. [New Latin *velleitās,* from Latin *velle,* to wish. See **wel-¹** in Appendix.]

Vel·lore (və-lôr′, -lōr′). A town of southeast India west-southwest of Madras. The Sepoy Mutiny began here in 1806. Population, 174,247.

vel·lum (vĕl′əm) *n. Abbr.* **vel. 1.a.** A fine parchment made from calfskin, lambskin, or kidskin and used for the pages and binding of books. **b.** A work written or printed on this parchment. **2.** A heavy off-white fine-quality paper resembling this parchment. [Middle English *velim,* from Old French *velin,* from *veel,* calf. See VEAL.]

ve·lo·ce (vā-lō′chā) *adv. Music.* Rapidly. Used chiefly as a direction. [Italian, from Latin *vēlōx, vēlōc-,* rapid. See VELOCITY.]

ve·lo·cim·e·ter (vē′lō-sĭm′ĭ-tər, vĕl′ō-) *n.* A device for measuring the speed of sound in water. [VELOCI(TY) + –METER.]

ve·loc·i·pede (və-lŏs′ə-pēd′) *n.* **1.** A tricycle. **2.a.** Any of several early bicycles having pedals attached to the front wheel. **b.** An early bicycle propelled by pushing the feet along the ground while straddling the vehicle. [French *vélocipède* : Latin *vēlōx, vēlōc-,* fast; see VELOCITY + Latin *pēs, ped-,* foot; see –PED.]

ve·loc·i·ty (və-lŏs′ĭ-tē) *n., pl.* **-ties. 1.** *Abbr.* **vel.** Rapidity or speed of motion; swiftness. **2.** *Abbr.* **V** *Physics.* A vector quantity whose magnitude is a body's speed and whose direction is the body's direction of motion. **3.a.** The rate of speed of action or occurrence. **b.** The rate at which money changes hands in an economy. [Middle English *velocite,* from Old French, from Latin *vēlōcitās,* from *vēlōx, vēlōc-,* fast. See **weg-** in Appendix.]

ve·lour or **ve·lours** (və-lo͝or′) *n., pl.* **-lours** (-lo͝orz′). **1.** A closely napped fabric resembling velvet, used chiefly for clothing and upholstery. **2.** A felt resembling velvet, used in making hats. [Alteration of French *velours,* velvet, from Old French *velour,* alteration of *velous,* from Old Provençal *velos,* from Latin *villōsus,* hairy, from *villus,* shaggy hair. See VELVET.]

ve·lou·té (və-lo͞o-tā′) *n.* A white sauce made of chicken, veal, or fish stock thickened with a roux of flour and butter. [French, from Old French *vellute,* velvety, from *velous,* velvet. See VELOUR.]

veil

velocipede

ă pat	oi boy
ā pay	ou out
âr care	o͝o took
ä father	o͞o boot
ĕ pet	ŭ cut
ē be	ûr urge
ĭ pit	th thin
ī pie	*th* this
îr pier	hw which
ŏ pot	zh vision
ō toe	ə about, item
ô paw	♦ regionalism

Stress marks: ′ (primary); ′ (secondary), as in **dictionary** (dĭk′shə-nĕr′ē)

ve·lum (vē′ləm) *n., pl.* **-la** (-lə). **1.** *Biology.* A covering or partition of thin membranous tissue, such as the veil of a mushroom or a membrane of the brain. **2.** *Anatomy.* The soft palate. **3.** *Zoology.* A ciliated swimming organ that develops in certain larval stages of most marine gastropod mollusks. [Latin, veil.]

ve·lure (vĕ-lo͝or′, vĕl′yər) *n. Obsolete.* Velvet or a velvetlike fabric. [Alteration of French *velours.* See VELOUR.]

ve·lu·ti·nous (və-lo͞ot′n-əs) *adj.* Covered with dense, soft, silky hairs. [From New Latin *velūtīnus,* from Medieval Latin *velūtum,* velvet, from Vulgar Latin **villūtus.* See VELVET.]

♦ **vel·vet** (vĕl′vĭt) *n.* **1.** A soft fabric, such as silk, rayon, or nylon, having a smooth, dense pile and a plain underside. **2.a.** Something suggesting the smooth surface of velvet. **b.** Smoothness; softness. **3.** The soft, furry covering on the developing antlers of deer. **4.** *Informal.* **a.** The winnings of a gambler. **b.** A profit or gain beyond what is expected or due. **5.** *New England.* See **milk shake** (sense 1). See Regional Note at **milk shake.** [Middle English *veluet,* probably from Old Provençal, from Vulgar Latin **villūtittus,* diminutive of **villūtus,* from Latin *villus,* shaggy hair, nap.]

vender

velvet ant *n.* Any of various brightly colored wasps of the family Mutillidae, the females of which are wingless and have a coat of velvety hair.

vel·vet·een (vĕl′vĭ-tēn′) *n.* A cotton pile fabric resembling velvet. [From VELVET.]

vel·vet·leaf (vĕl′vĭt-lēf′) *n.* A tropical Asian annual herb *(Abutilon theophrasti)* naturalized in the United States, having large, velvety, heart-shaped leaves and yellow flowers. It is an important fiber plant in northern China. Also called *China jute.*

velvet plant *n.* See **mullein.** [From its dense, velvety hairs.]

velvet worm *n.* See **onychophoran.**

vel·vet·y (vĕl′vĭ-tē) *adj.* **-i·er, -i·est. 1.** Suggestive of the texture of velvet; soft and smooth: *velvety skin.* **2.** Smooth-tasting; mellow: *a velvety sherry.*

Ven. *abbr.* **1.** Venerable. **2.** Venezuela.

ven– *pref.* Variant of **veno–.**

ve·na (vē′nə) *n., pl.* **-nae** (-nē). *Anatomy.* A vein. [Middle English, from Latin *vēna.*]

vena ca·va (kā′və) *n., pl.* **venae ca·vae** (kā′vē). Either of two large veins that drain blood from the upper body and from the lower body and empty into the right atrium of the heart. [New Latin *vēna cava* : Latin *vēna,* vein + Latin *cava,* hollow.]

ve·nae (vē′nē) *n. Anatomy.* Plural of **vena.**

ve·nal (vē′nəl) *adj.* **1.a.** Open to bribery; mercenary: *a venal police officer.* **b.** Capable of betraying honor, duty, or scruples for a price; corruptible. **2.** Marked by corrupt dealings, especially bribery: *a venal administration.* **3.** Obtainable for a price. [Latin *vēnālis,* from *vēnum,* sale. See **wes-**[3] in Appendix.] **—ve′nal·ly** *adv.*

ve·nal·i·ty (vē-năl′ĭ-tē) *n., pl.* **-ties.** Susceptibility to bribery or corruption, as in the use of a position of trust for dishonest gain.

ve·nat·ic (vē-năt′ĭk) also **ve·nat·i·cal** (-ĭ-kəl) *adj.* **1.** Of or relating to hunting. **2.** Engaging in hunting for sport or livelihood. [Latin *vēnāticus,* from *vēnātus,* past participle of *vēnārī,* to hunt. See **wen-**[1] in Appendix.]

ve·na·tion (vē-nā′shən, vĕ-) *n.* **1.** Distribution or arrangement of a system of veins, as in a leaf blade or the wing of an insect. **2.** The veins of such a system considered as a group. **—ve·na′tion·al** *adj.*

vend (vĕnd) *v.* **vend·ed, vend·ing, vends.** —*tr.* **1.a.** To sell by means of a vending machine. **b.** To sell, especially by peddling. **2.** To offer (an idea, for example) for public consideration. —*intr.* To engage in selling. [Latin *vēndere,* alteration of *vēnumdare* : *vēnum,* sale; see **wes-**[3] in Appendix + *dare,* to give; see **dō-** in Appendix.]

Ven·da (vĕn′də). An internally self-governing Black African homeland in northeast South Africa near the Zimbabwe border. It was granted limited self-government in 1962 and nominal independence in 1979. Thohoyandou is the capital. Population, 374,000.

Venezuela

vend·a·ble (vĕn′də-bəl) *adj.* Variant of **vendible.**

ven·dace (vĕn′dĭs, -dās) *n., pl.* **vendace** or **-dac·es. 1.** A small whitefish *(Coregonus vandesius)* of Scotland. **2.** A closely related whitefish *(C. gracilior)* of the Lake District of England. [Probably French *vandoise,* a kind of fish, from Old French *vendoise,* probably of Celtic origin.]

vend·ee (vĕn-dē′) *n.* One to whom something is sold; a buyer.

vend·er or **ven·dor** (vĕn′dər) *n.* **1.** One that sells or vends: *a street vender; vendors of cheap merchandise.* **2.** A vending machine.

ven·det·ta (vĕn-dĕt′ə) *n.* **1.** A feud between two families or clans that arises out of a slaying and is perpetuated by retaliatory acts of revenge; a blood feud. **2.** A bitter, destructive feud. [Italian, from Latin *vindicta,* revenge. See VINDICTIVE.]

vend·i·ble also **vend·a·ble** (vĕn′də-bəl) —*adj.* **1.** Suitable or fit for sale; salable: *vendible items of food.* **2.** *Obsolete.* Venal. —*n.* Something that can be sold.

vend·ing machine (vĕn′dĭng) *n.* A coin-operated machine that dispenses merchandise.

Ven·dôme (väɴ-dōm′), Duc de. Title of Louis Joseph de Bourbon. 1654–1712. French general who commanded Spanish troops in northern Italy (1710) during the War of the Spanish Succession.

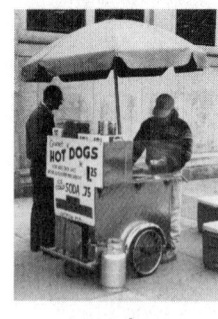

ven·dor (vĕn′dər) *n.* Variant of **vender.**

ven·due (vĕn′do͞o, -dyo͞o, vĕn-do͞o′, -dyo͞o′) *n.* A public sale; an auction. [Dutch *vendu,* from obsolete French *vendue,* sale, from Old French, feminine past participle of *vendre,* to sell. See VEND.]

ve·neer (və-nîr′) *n.* **1.** A thin surface layer, as of finely grained wood, glued to a base of inferior material. **2.** Any of the thin layers glued together to make plywood. **3.** A decorative facing, as of brick. **4.** A deceptive, superficial show; a façade: *a veneer of friendliness.* **—veneer** *tr.v.* **-neered, -neer·ing, -neers. 1.** To overlay (a surface) with a thin layer of a fine or decorative material. **2.** To glue together (layers of wood) to make plywood. **3.** To conceal, as something common or crude, with a deceptively attractive outward show. [Alteration of obsolete *faneering,* from German *Furnierung,* from *furnieren,* to furnish, veneer, from French *fournir,* to furnish, from Old French *furnir,* of Germanic origin. See **per**[1] in Appendix.] **—ve·neer′er** *n.*

ven·e·na·tion (vĕn′ə-nā′shən) *n.* **1.** Introduction of a venom into animal tissue. **2.** The poisoned condition produced by a venom. [From Latin *venēnātus,* past participle of *venēnāre,* to poison, from Latin *venēnum,* venom. See VENOM.]

ve·nene (və-nēn′, vĕn′ēn) *n.* **1.** A preparation of snake venoms used in medicine, especially in the treatment of epilepsy. **2.** Variant of **venin.** [From Latin *venēnum,* venom. See VENOM.]

ve·ne·punc·ture (vē′nĭ-pŭngk′chər, vĕn′ĭ-) *n.* Variant of **venipuncture.**

ven·er·a·ble (vĕn′ər-ə-bəl) *adj.* **1.** Commanding respect by virtue of age, dignity, character, or position. See Synonyms at **elderly. 2.** Worthy of reverence, especially by religious or historical association: *venerable relics.* **3. Venerable.** *Abbr.* **Ven., V. a.** *Roman Catholic Church.* Used as a form of address for a dead person who has reached the first stage of canonization. **b.** Used as a form of address for an archdeacon in the Anglican Church or the Episcopal Church. **—ven′er·a·ble·ness, ven′er·a·bil′i·ty** *n.* **—ven′er·a·bly** *adv.*

ven·er·ate (vĕn′ə-rāt′) *tr.v.* **-at·ed, -at·ing, -ates.** To regard with respect, reverence, or heartfelt deference. See Synonyms at **revere**[1]. [Latin *venerārī, venerāt-,* to venerate, from *venus, vener-,* love, desire. See **wen-**[1] in Appendix.] **—ven′er·a′tor** *n.*

ven·er·a·tion (vĕn′ə-rā′shən) *n.* **1.** The act of venerating. **2.** Profound respect or reverence: *"The veneration of man has been misdirected"* (Lucretia Mott). See Synonyms at **honor. 3.** The condition or status of one who is venerated. **—ven′er·a′tion·al** *adj.*

ve·ne·re·al (və-nîr′ē-əl) *adj.* **1.a.** Transmitted by sexual intercourse. **b.** Of or relating to a sexually transmitted disease. **2.** Of or relating to sexual intercourse. **3.** Of or relating to the genitals. [Middle English *venereall e,* from Latin *venereus,* from *venus, vener-,* desire, love. See **wen-**[1] in Appendix.]

venereal disease *n. Abbr.* **VD, V.D.** Any of several contagious diseases, such as syphilis and gonorrhea, contracted through sexual intercourse; a sexually transmitted disease.

venereal wart *n.* See **genital wart.**

ve·ne·re·ol·o·gy (və-nîr′ē-ŏl′ə-jē) *n.* The study of sexually transmitted diseases. [VENERE(AL) + –LOGY.] **—ve·ne′re·o·log′i·cal** (-ə-lŏj′ĭ-kəl) *adj.* **—ve·ne′re·ol′o·gist** *n.*

ven·er·y[1] (vĕn′ə-rē) *n., pl.* **-ies.** *Archaic.* **1.** Indulgence in or pursuit of sexual activity. **2.** The act of sexual intercourse. [Middle English *venerie,* from Old French, from Medieval Latin *veneria,* from Latin *venus, vener-,* desire, love. See **wen-**[1] in Appendix.]

ven·er·y[2] (vĕn′ə-rē) *n., pl.* **-ies.** *Archaic.* The act or sport of hunting; the chase. [Middle English *venerie,* from Old French, from *vener,* to hunt, from Latin *vēnārī.* See **wen-**[1] in Appendix.]

ven·e·sec·tion (vĕn′ĭ-sĕk′shən, vē′nĭ-) *n.* See **phlebotomy.** [New Latin *venae sectiō, venae sectiōn-* : Latin *vēnae,* genitive sing. of *vēna,* vein + Latin *sectiō,* cutting; see SECTION.]

Ve·ne·ti·a (və-nē′shē-ə, -shə). A historical region of northern Italy and northwest Yugoslavia. An ancient Roman territory including Istria and the lands between the Po River and the Alps, it was named after the Veneti, a people who settled the area in c. 1000 B.C. Part of the region was ceded to Yugoslavia in 1947.

Ve·ne·tian (və-nē′shən) *adj.* Of or relating to Venice, Italy, or its people, language, or culture. **—Venetian** *n.* **1.** A native or inhabitant of Venice, Italy. **2.** The variety of Italian spoken in Venice. [Medieval Latin *Venetiānus,* from *Venetia,* Venice.]

ve·ne·tian blind or **Ve·ne·tian blind** (və-nē′shən) *n.* A window blind consisting of a number of thin horizontal adjustable slats that overlap when closed.

venetian blue *n. Color.* A strong blue to greenish blue.

Venetian glass *n.* A fine, often colored and ornamented glassware made in or near Venice, Italy.

venetian red *n. Color.* A deep to strong reddish brown.

Ve·ne·to (vĕn′ĕ-tō′). A region of northeast Italy bordering on the Adriatic Sea. Dominated by Venice since the early 15th century, it passed to Austria in 1797 and was awarded to Italy in 1866.

Ven·e·zue·la (vĕn′ə-zwā′lə, -zwē′-). *Abbr.* **Ven., Venez.** A country of northern South America on the Caribbean Sea. In 1499 a Spanish explorer first applied the name, meaning "little Venice," to an offshore island where the inhabitants raised their huts above the water on stilts, and the name was then used for the mainland area. Dominated by Spain after the 16th century, Venezuela was liberated by Simón Bolívar in 1821, although it was not formally separated from Colombia until 1830. Caracas is the capital and the largest city. Population, 14,515,885. **—Ven′e·zue′lan** *adj. & n.*

Venezuela, Gulf of. An inlet of the Caribbean Sea between northwest Venezuela and northern Colombia. It extends southward as Lake Maracaibo.

venge (vĕnj) *tr.v.* **venged, veng·ing, veng·es.** *Archaic.* To avenge. [Middle English *vengen,* from Old French *vengier.* See VENGEANCE.]

ven·geance (vĕn′jəns) *n.* Infliction of punishment in return for a wrong committed; retribution: *"Something of vengeance I had tasted for the first time. An aromatic wine it seemed"* (Charlotte Brontë). **—*idiom.* with a vengeance. 1.** With great violence or force. **2.** To an extreme degree: *December has turned cold with a vengeance.* [Middle English, from Old French, from *vengier,* to avenge, from Latin *vindicāre.* See VINDICATE.]

venge·ful (vĕnj′fəl) *adj.* **1.** Desiring vengeance; vindictive. See Synonyms at **vindictive. 2.** Indicating or proceeding from a desire for revenge. **3.** Serving to exact vengeance. **—venge′ful·ly** *adv.* **—venge′ful·ness** *n.*

V-en·gine (vē′ĕn′jən) *n.* An internal-combustion engine having cylinders arranged so that pairs form V shapes.

veni– *pref.* Variant of **veno–.**

ve·ni·al (vē′nē-əl, vēn′yəl) *adj.* **1.** Easily excused or forgiven; pardonable: *a venial offense.* **2.** *Roman Catholic Church.* Minor, therefore warranting only temporal punishment. [Middle English, from Old French, from Late Latin *veniālis,* from Latin *venia,* forgiveness. See **wen-**[1] in Appendix.] **—ve′ni·al′i·ty** (vē′nē-ăl′ĭ-tē, vēn-yăl′-), **ve′ni·al·ness** (vē′nē-əl-nĭs, vēn′yəl-) *n.* **—ve′ni·al·ly** *adv.*

venial sin *n. Roman Catholic Church.* An offense that is judged to be minor or committed without deliberate intent and thus does not estrange the soul from the grace of God.

Ven·ice (vĕn′ĭs). A city of northeast Italy on islets within a lagoon in the **Gulf of Venice,** a wide inlet of the northern Adriatic Sea. Founded in the 5th century A.D. by refugees fleeing the Lombard invaders who had gained control of the mainland, it became a major maritime power by the 13th century and spread its influence over northern Italy by the 15th century. Its territories were gradually lost to the Turks, and in 1797 it passed to Austria. Venice was ceded to Italy in 1866. Population, 332,775.

ven·in (vĕn′ĭn, vē′nĭn) also **ve·nene** (və-nēn′, vĕn′ēn) *n.* Any of various toxic substances found in the venom of snakes. [VEN(OM) + –IN.]

ve·ni·punc·ture also **ve·ne·punc·ture** (vē′nĭ-pŭngk′chər, vĕn′ĭ-) *n.* Puncture of a vein, as for drawing blood, intravenous feeding, or administration of medicine.

ve·ni·re (və-nī′rē, -nîr′ē) *n. Law.* **1.** A writ issued by a judge to a sheriff directing the summons of prospective jurors. Also called *venire facias.* **2.** The panel of prospective jurors from which a jury is selected. [Short for Middle English *venire facias,* from Medieval Latin *venīre (faciās),* (you should cause) to come, a phrase used in the writ, from Latin. See **gʷā-** in Appendix.]

venire fa·ci·as (fā′shē-əs, -ăs′) *n. Law.* See **venire** (sense 1). [Middle English. See VENIRE.]

ve·ni·re·man (və-nī′rē-mən, -nîr′ē-) *n. Law.* A person summoned to jury duty under a venire.

ven·i·son (vĕn′ĭ-sən, -zən) *n.* **1.** The flesh of a deer used as food. **2.** *Archaic.* The flesh of a game animal used as food. [Middle English *veneson,* from Old French, from Latin *vēnātiō, vēnātiōn-,* hunting, from *vēnātus,* past participle of *vēnārī,* to hunt. See **wen-**[1] in Appendix.]

Venn diagram (vĕn) *n.* A diagram using circles to represent an operation in set theory, with the position and overlap of the circles indicating the relationships between the sets. [After John *Venn* (1834–1923), British logician.]

veno– or **veni–** or **ven–** *pref.* Vein: *venipuncture.* [From Latin *vēna.*]

ve·no·gram (vē′nə-grăm′) *n.* A radiograph of a vein after injection of a radiopaque substance.

ve·nog·ra·phy (vĭ-nŏg′rə-fē) *n.* Radiography of veins or a vein after injection of a radiopaque substance. Also called *phlebography.*

ven·om (vĕn′əm) *n.* **1.** A poisonous secretion of an animal, such as a snake, spider, or scorpion, usually transmitted by a bite or sting. **2.** A poison. **3.** Malice; spite. [Middle English *venim,* from Old French, from Vulgar Latin **venīmen,* from Latin *venēnum,* poison. See **wen-**[1] in Appendix.]

ven·om·ous (vĕn′ə-məs) *adj.* **1.a.** Secreting and transmitting venom: *a venomous snake.* **b.** Full of or containing venom. **2.** Malicious; spiteful: *a venomous remark.* See Synonyms at **poisonous. —ven′om·ous·ly** *adv.* **—ven′om·ous·ness** *n.*

ve·nose (vē′nōs′) *adj.* **1.** Having noticeable veins or veinlike markings. **2.** Venous. [Latin *vēnōsus,* from *vēna,* vein.]

ve·nos·i·ty (vē-nŏs′ĭ-tē) *n.* The quality or condition of being venous or venose.

ve·nous (vē′nəs) *adj.* **1.** *Physiology.* Of or contained in the veins: *venous blood; venous circulation.* **2.** Having numerous veins, as a leaf or the wings of an insect. [From Latin *vēnōsus,* from *vēna,* vein.] **—ve′nous·ly** *adv.* **—ve′nous·ness** *n.*

vent[1] (vĕnt) *n.* **1.** A means of escape or release from confinement; an outlet: *give vent to one's anger.* **2.** An opening permitting the escape of fumes, a liquid, a gas, or steam. **3.** The small hole at the breech of a gun through which the charge is ignited. **4.** *Zoology.* The excretory opening of the digestive tract in animals such as birds, reptiles, amphibians, and fish. **5.** *Geology.* **a.** The opening of a volcano in the earth's crust. **b.** An opening on the ocean floor that emits hot water and dissolved minerals. **—vent** *tr.v.* **vent·ed, vent·ing, vents. 1.** To give often forceful expression or utterance to. **2.** To release or discharge (steam, for example) through an opening. **3.** To provide with a vent. [Partly from French *vent* (from Old French) and partly alteration of French *évent* (from Old French *esvent,* from *esventer,* to let out air, from Vulgar Latin **exventāre* : Latin *ex-;* see EX– + Latin *ventus,* wind; see **wē-** in Appendix).] **—vent′er** *n.*

SYNONYMS: *vent, express, utter, voice, air.* These verbs mean to give outlet to thoughts or emotions. To *vent* is to unburden oneself of a strong pent-up emotion: *"She was jealous . . . and glad of any excuse to vent her pique"* (Edward G.E.L. Bulwer-Lytton). *Express,* a more comprehensive term, refers to communication both by verbal and by nonverbal means: *can't express the idea adequately in words; expressed her affection with a hug; "expressing emotion in the form of art"* (T.S. Eliot). *Utter* involves vocal expression; it may imply speech but can also refer to inarticulate sounds: *"The words were uttered in the hearing of Montezuma"* (William Hickling Prescott). *"The Canon uttered a resounding sigh"* (John Galsworthy). *Voice* denotes the expression in speech or writing of the outlook or viewpoint of a person or, often, of a group: *The judge voiced her satisfaction that the jury had reached a verdict. The majority leader rose to voice the party's opposition to the bill.* To *air* is to give vent to and often to show off one's feelings, beliefs, or ideas: *He wants a forum where he can air his favorite theory.*

vent[2] (vĕnt) *n.* A slit in a garment, as in the back seam of a pocket. [Middle English *vente,* alteration (probably influenced by Old French *vent,* wind) of *fente,* from Old French, slit, from *fendre,* to split open, from Latin *findere.* See FISSION.]

vent·age (vĕn′tĭj) *n.* A small opening; a vent.

ven·tail (vĕn′tāl′) *n.* The lower movable part of the front of a medieval helmet, fitting over the mouth or neck. [Middle English, from Old French *vantail,* from *vent,* wind, from Latin *ventus.* See **wē-** in Appendix.]

ven·ter (vĕn′tər) *n.* **1.** *Anatomy.* **a.** The abdomen. **b.** The prominent fleshy portion of a muscle. **c.** A cavity or hollowed surface, especially of a bone. **2.** *Zoology.* A part in lower forms of animal life corresponding to the abdomen of mammals. **3.** *Botany.* The swollen lower portion of an archegonium containing the egg. **4.** *Law.* The uterus of a woman as the source of offspring. [Anglo-Norman, from Latin.]

ven·ti·fact (vĕn′tə-făkt′) *n.* A stone that has been shaped, polished, or faceted by wind-driven sand. [Latin *ventus,* wind; see VENT[1] + (ARTI)FACT.]

ven·ti·late (vĕn′tl-āt′) *tr.v.* **-lat·ed, -lat·ing, -lates. 1.** To admit fresh air into (a mine, for example) to replace stale or noxious air. **2.** To circulate through and freshen: *A sea breeze ventilated the rooms.* **3.** To provide with a vent, as for airing. **4.** To expose (a substance) to the circulation of fresh air, as to retard spoilage. **5.** To expose to public discussion or examination: *The students ventilated their grievances.* **6.** To aerate or oxygenate (blood). [Middle English *ventilaten,* to blow away, from Latin *ventilāre, ventilāt-,* to fan, from *ventulus,* diminutive of *ventus,* wind. See **wē-** in Appendix.] **—ven′ti·la′tion** *n.*

ven·ti·la·tor (vĕn′tl-ā′tər) *n.* **1.** A device that circulates fresh air and expels stale or foul air. **2.** *Medicine.* A respirator. **—ven′ti·la·to′ry** (vĕn′tl-ə-tôr′ē, -tōr′ē) *adj.*

ventr– *pref.* Variant of **ventro–.**

ven·trad (vĕn′trăd) *adv.* Toward the ventral side or surface.

ven·tral (vĕn′trəl) *adj.* **1.** *Anatomy.* **a.** Relating to or situated on or close to the abdomen; abdominal. **b.** Relating to or situated on or close to the anterior aspect of the human body or the lower surface of the body of an animal. **2.** *Botany.* Of or on the lower or inner surface of an organ that faces the axis; adaxial. **—ventral** *n.* **1.** A ventral fin. **2.** The abdominal segment of an insect. [Late Latin *ventrālis,* from Latin *venter, ventr-,* belly.] **—ven′tral·ly** *adv.*

ventral fin *n. Zoology.* A fin, such as a pelvic fin or an anal fin, that is found on the ventral side of a fish.

ventral root *n.* The part of a spinal nerve, consisting of motor fibers, that arises from the anterior section of the spinal cord.

ven·tri·cle (vĕn′trĭ-kəl) *n.* A small cavity or chamber within a body or an organ, especially: **a.** The chamber on the left side of the heart that receives arterial blood from the left atrium and contracts to force it into the aorta. **b.** The chamber on the right side of the heart that receives venous blood from the right atrium and forces it into the pulmonary artery. **c.** Any of the interconnecting cavities of the brain. [Middle English, from Old French *ventricule,* from Latin *ventriculus,* diminutive of *venter,* belly.]

ven·tri·cose (vĕn′trĭ-kōs′) also **ven·tri·cous** (-kəs) *adj.* Inflated, swollen, or distended, especially on one side: *the ventricose gullet of an insect.* [New Latin *ventricōsus,* from Latin *venter, ventr-,* belly.] **—ven′tri·cos′i·ty** (-kŏs′ĭ-tē) *n.*

ă pat	oi boy
ā pay	ou out
âr care	ŏŏ took
ä father	ōō boot
ĕ pet	ŭ cut
ē be	ûr urge
ĭ pit	th thin
ī pie	*th* this
îr pier	hw which
ŏ pot	zh vision
ō toe	ə about, item
ô paw	♦ regionalism

Stress marks: ′ (primary); ′ (secondary), as in **dictionary** (dĭk′shə-nĕr′ē)

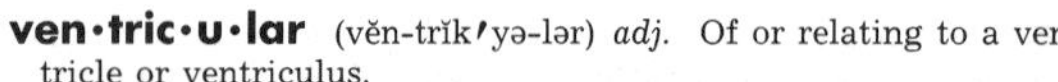

Venus
Fourth-century B.C. Roman, after a sculpture by Praxiteles

ven·tric·u·lar (vĕn-trĭk′yə-lər) *adj.* Of or relating to a ventricle or ventriculus.

ventricular fibrillation *n.* An often fatal form of arrhythmia characterized by rapid, irregular fibrillar twitching of the ventricles of the heart in place of normal contractions, resulting in a loss of pulse.

ven·tric·u·lus (vĕn-trĭk′yə-ləs) *n., pl.* **-li** (-lī′). **1.** A hollow digestive organ, especially the stomach of certain insects or the gizzard of a bird. **2.** The digestive cavity in the body of a sponge. [Latin, diminutive of *venter,* belly.]

ven·tri·lo·qui·al (vĕn′trə-lō′kwē-əl) *adj.* Of, relating to, or practicing ventriloquism. **—ven′tri·lo′qui·al·ly** *adv.*

ven·tril·o·quism (vĕn-trĭl′ə-kwĭz′əm) also **ven·tril·o·quy** (-kwē) *n.* The art of projecting one's voice so that it seems to come from another source, as from a wooden figure. [From Latin *ventriloquus,* speaking from the belly : Latin *venter, ventr-,* belly + *loquī,* to speak; see **tolk**ʷ**-** in Appendix.] **—ven·tril′o·quist** (-kwĭst) *n.* **—ven·tril′o·quis′tic** *adj.*

ven·tril·o·quize (vĕn-trĭl′ə-kwīz′) *intr.v.* **-quized, -quiz·ing, -quiz·es.** To practice ventriloquism.

ven·tril·o·quy (vĕn-trĭl′ə-kwē) *n.* Variant of **ventriloquism.**

ventro– or **ventr–** *pref.* Ventral: *ventrolateral.* [From Latin *venter, ventr-,* belly.]

ven·tro·dor·sal (vĕn′trō-dôr′səl) *adj.* Both ventral and dorsal; extending from a ventral to a dorsal surface. **—ven′tro·dor′sal·ly** *adv.*

ven·tro·lat·er·al (vĕn′trō-lăt′ər-əl) *adj.* Both ventral and lateral; extending from a ventral to a lateral surface. **—ven′tro·lat′er·al·ly** *adv.*

ven·tro·me·di·al (vĕn′trō-mē′dē-əl) *adj.* Both ventral and medial; extending toward the ventral surface and the median line. **—ven′tro·me′di·al·ly** *adv.*

Ven·tu·ra (vĕn-cho͝or′ə, -to͝or′ə). A city of southern California on the Pacific Ocean west of Los Angeles. It was founded as the mission of San Buenaventura (still the official name of the city) in 1782. Population, 74,393.

ven·ture (vĕn′chər) *n.* **1.** An undertaking that is dangerous, daring, or of uncertain outcome. **2.** A business enterprise involving some risk in expectation of gain. **3.** Something, such as money or cargo, at hazard in a risky enterprise. **—venture** *v.* **-tured, -tur·ing, -tures.** *—tr.* **1.** To expose to danger or risk: *ventured her entire fortune.* **2.** To brave the dangers of: *ventured the high seas in a small boat.* **3.** To express at the risk of denial, criticism, or censure: *"I would venture to guess that Anon., who wrote so many poems without signing them, was often a woman"* (Virginia Woolf). *—intr.* **1.** To take a risk; dare. **2.** To proceed despite possible danger or risk: *ventured into the wilderness.* ***—idiom.*** **at a venture.** By mere chance or fortune; at random. [Middle English, chance, short for *aventure,* adventure. See ADVENTURE.] **—ven′tur·er** *n.*

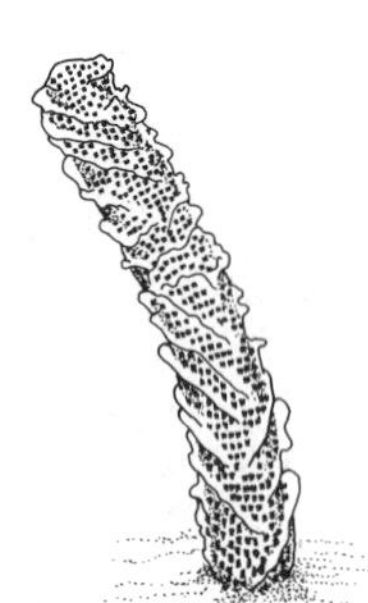

Venus's flower basket

venture capital *n.* Money made available for investment in innovative enterprises or research, especially in high technology, in which both the risk of loss and the potential for profit may be considerable. Also called *risk capital.* **—venture capitalist** *n.*

ven·ture·some (vĕn′chər-səm) *adj.* **1.** Disposed to venture or to take risks; daring. See Synonyms at **adventurous. 2.** Involving risk or danger; hazardous. **—ven′ture·some·ly** *adv.* **—ven′ture·some·ness** *n.*

ven·tu·ri (vĕn-to͝or′ē) *n., pl.* **-ris. 1.** A short tube with a constricted throat used to determine fluid pressures and velocities by measurement of differential pressures generated at the throat as a fluid traverses the tube. **2.** A constricted throat in the air passage of a carburetor, causing a reduction in pressure that results in fuel vapor being drawn out of the carburetor bowl. [After Giovanni Battista *Venturi* (1746–1822), Italian physicist.]

Ven·tur·i (vĕn-to͝or′ē), **Robert Charles.** Born 1925. American architect who led the postmodern reaction to functionalism. His eclectic, sometimes humorous designs often incorporate historical references.

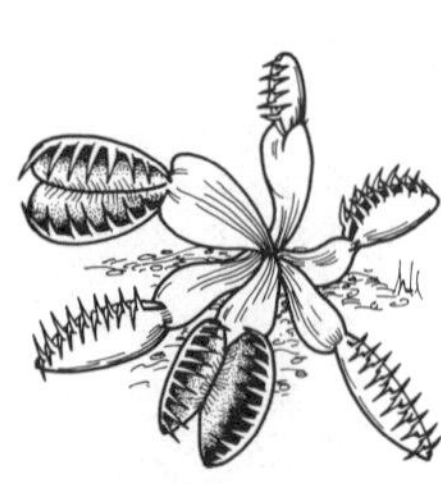

Venus's-flytrap
Dionaea muscipula

ven·tur·ous (vĕn′chər-əs) *adj.* Venturesome. **—ven′tur·ous·ly** *adv.* **—ven′tur·ous·ness** *n.*

ven·ue (vĕn′yo͞o) *n.* **1.** *Law.* **a.** The locality where a crime is committed or a cause of action occurs. **b.** The locality or political division from which a jury is called and in which a trial is held. **c.** The clause within a declaration naming the locality in which a trial will be held. **d.** The clause in an affidavit naming the place where it was sworn to. **2. a.** The scene or setting in which something takes place; a locale: *"that non-cinematic venue of popular nightmares, the discotheque"* (P.J. O'Rourke). **b.** A place for large gatherings, as a sports stadium. [Middle English, attack, from Old French, a coming, attack, from feminine past participle of *venir,* to come, from Latin *venīre.* See **g**ʷ**ā-** in Appendix.]

ven·ule (vĕn′yo͞ol, vēn′-) *n.* A small vein, especially one joining capillaries to larger veins. [Latin *vēnula,* diminutive of *vēna,* vein.] **—ven′u·lar** (-yə-lər) *adj.*

Ve·nus (vē′nəs) *n.* **1.** *Roman Mythology.* The goddess of sexual love and physical beauty. **2.** The second planet from the sun, having an average radius of 6,052 kilometers (3,760 miles), a mass 0.815 times that of Earth, and a sidereal period of revolution about the sun of 224.7 days at a mean distance of approximately 108.1 million kilometers (67.2 million miles). [Middle English, from Old English, from Latin, love, Venus. See **wen-**[1] in Appendix.]

Venus flytrap *n.* Variant of **Venus's-flytrap.**

Ve·nu·sian (vĭ-no͞o′zhən, -shē-ən, -nyo͞o′-) *adj.* Of, relating to, or characteristic of the planet Venus. **—Venusian** *n.* A hypothetical inhabitant of the planet Venus.

Ve·nus's flower basket (vē′nə-sĭz) *n.* A sponge of the genus *Euplectella,* living in deep marine waters of the East Indies and the eastern Asian coast and having a cylindrical skeleton of glassy, intricate latticework.

Ve·nus's-fly·trap (vē′nəs-flī′trăp′, vē′nə-sĭz-) or **Venus flytrap** *n.* An insectivorous plant *(Dionaea muscipula)* of the coastal plain of the Carolinas, having sensitive, hinged, marginally bristled, two-lobed leaf blades that close and entrap insects.

Venus's girdle *n.* A large ribbon-shaped ctenophore *(Cestum veneris)* having a jellylike bluish-green iridescent body.

Ve·nus's-hair (vē′nə-sĭz-hâr′) *n.* A maidenhair fern *(Adiantum capillus-veneris)* of warm moist regions, having slender blackish stalks, bipinnately compound fronds, and marginal sori.

Ve·nus's-look·ing-glass (vē′nə-sĭz-lo͝ok′ĭng-glăs′) *n.* A European annual plant *(Legousia speculum-veneris)* having small, blue or white star-shaped flowers.

ver. *abbr.* **1.** Verse. **2.** Version.

ve·ra·cious (və-rā′shəs) *adj.* **1.** Honest; truthful. **2.** Accurate; precise. [From Latin *vērāx, vērāc-,* from *vērus.* See **wēro-** in Appendix.] **—ve·ra′cious·ly** *adv.* **—ve·ra′cious·ness** *n.*

ve·rac·i·ty (və-răs′ĭ-tē) *n., pl.* **-ties. 1.** Adherence to the truth; truthfulness. See Synonyms at **truth. 2.** Conformity to fact or truth; accuracy or precision: *a report of doubtful veracity.* **3.** Something that is true. [Medieval Latin *vērācitās,* from Latin *vērāx, vērāc-,* true. See VERACIOUS.]

Ve·ra·cruz (vĕr′ə-kro͞oz′, bä′rä-kro͞os′). A city of east-central Mexico on the Gulf of Mexico east of Puebla. Founded in 1599 on a site visited earlier (1519) by Hernando Cortés, it was frequently sacked by buccaneers in the 17th and 18th centuries. U.S. troops led by Gen. Winfield Scott captured the city in 1847 during the Spanish-American War. Population, 284,822.

♦**ve·ran·da** or **ve·ran·dah** (və-răn′də) *n.* A porch or balcony, usually roofed and often partly enclosed, extending along the outside of a building. Also called ♦*gallery.* [Hindi *varaṇḍā,* from Persian *bar āmadaḥ,* coming out, or from Portuguese *varanda* (perhaps ultimately from Vulgar Latin *barra, barrier, bar).]

ve·rat·ri·dine (və-răt′rĭ-dēn′) *n.* A yellowish-white, amorphous powdered alkaloid, $C_{36}H_{51}NO_{11}$, obtained from sabadilla seeds and from the rhizome of hellebore. [VERATR(INE) + –ID(E) + –INE[2].]

ver·a·trine (vĕr′ə-trēn′, -trĭn) *n.* A poisonous mixture of colorless crystalline alkaloids extracted from sabadilla seeds and formerly used medicinally as a counterirritant. [New Latin *vērātrīna,* from *Vērātrum,* genus name of a hellebore, from Latin *vērātrum,* hellebore.]

verb (vûrb) *n. Abbr.* **v., vb. 1. a.** The part of speech that expresses existence, action, or occurrence in most languages. **b.** Any of the words within this part of speech, as *be, run,* or *conceive.* **2.** A phrase or other construction used as a verb. [Middle English *verbe,* from Old French, from Latin *verbum,* word, verb. See **wer-**[5] in Appendix.]

ver·bal (vûr′bəl) *adj. Abbr.* **vb. 1.** Of, relating to, or associated with words: *a verbal picture.* **2. a.** Concerned with words only rather than with content or ideas: *a merely verbal distinction.* **b.** Consisting of words alone without action: *a verbal confrontation.* **3.** Expressed in spoken rather than written words; oral: *a verbal contract.* **4.** Corresponding word for word; literal: *a verbal translation.* **5.** *Grammar.* **a.** Relating to, having the nature or function of, or derived from a verb. **b.** Used to form verbs: *a verbal suffix.* **6.** Of or relating to proficiency in the use and understanding of words: *a verbal aptitude test.* **—verbal** *n. Grammar.* A verbal noun or adjective. [Middle English, from Old French, from Late Latin *verbālis,* from Latin *verbum,* word. See VERB.] **—ver′bal·ly** *adv.*

USAGE NOTE: *Verbal* has been used to refer to spoken, as opposed to written, communication by reputable writers since the 16th century, and the usage cannot be considered incorrect. But critics are right to observe that this use of *verbal* may sometimes invite confusion with the use meaning "by linguistic means." Thus the phrase *modern technologies for verbal communication* may refer only to devices such as radio, the telephone, and the loudspeaker, or also may refer to devices such as the telegraph, the teletype, and the fax machine. In such contexts the word *oral* is always available to convey the narrower sense of communication by spoken means.

verbal adjective *n.* An adjective that is derived from a verb and that in some constructions, participial phrases for example, preserves the verb's syntactic features, such as transitivity and the capability of taking nominal or verbal complements.

ver·bal·ism (vûr′bə-lĭz′əm) *n.* **1. a.** An expression in words; a word or phrase. **b.** The manner in which something is phrased; wording. **2.** A wordy phrase or sentence that has little meaning. **3.** Abundant use of words without conveying much meaning.

ver·bal·ist (vûr′bə-lĭst) *n.* **1.** One skilled in the use of words.

2. One who favors words over ideas or substance. **—ver′bal·is′tic** *adj.*

ver·bal·ize (vûr′bə-līz′) *v.* **-ized, -iz·ing, -iz·es.** *—tr.* **1.** To express in words. **2.** *Grammar.* To convert to use as a verb: *verbalized the noun* contact. *—intr.* **1.** To express oneself in words. **2.** To be verbose. **—ver′bal·i·za′tion** (-bə-lĭ-zā′shən) *n.* **—ver′bal·iz′er** *n.*

verbal noun *n.* A noun that is derived from a verb and usually preserves the verb's syntactic features, such as transitivity or the capability of taking nominal or verbal complements.

ver·ba·tim (vər-bā′tĭm) *adj.* Using exactly the same words; corresponding word for word: *a verbatim report of the conversation.* **—verbatim** *adv.* In exactly the same words; word for word: *repeated their dialogue verbatim.* [Middle English, from Medieval Latin *verbātim,* from Latin *verbum,* word. See VERB.]

ver·be·na (vər-bē′nə) *n.* **1.** Any of various New World plants of the genus *Verbena,* especially one of several species cultivated for their showy spikes of variously colored flowers. Also called *vervain.* **2.** Any of several similar plants, such as the lemon verbena. [Latin *verbēna,* sacred foliage. See **wer-**[2] in Appendix.]

ver·bi·age (vûr′bē-ĭj, -bĭj) *n.* **1.** An excess of words for the purpose; wordiness. **2.** The manner in which something is expressed in words: *software verbiage.* [French, from Old French *verbier,* to chatter, from *verbe,* word, from Latin *verbum.* See VERB.]

verb·i·fy (vûr′bə-fī′) *tr.v.* **-fied** (-fīd′), **-fy·ing, -fies** (-fīz′). To use (a noun, for example) as a verb.

ver·big·er·a·tion (vər-bĭj′ə-rā′shən) *n.* Obsessive repetition of meaningless words and phrases, especially as a symptom of mental illness. [From Latin *verbigerātus,* past participle of *verbigerāre,* to chat, dispute : *verbum,* word; see VERB + *-gerāre,* frequentative of *gerere,* to carry.]

ver·bose (vər-bōs′) *adj.* Using or containing a great and usually an excessive number of words; wordy. See Synonyms at **talkative, wordy.** [Middle English *verbous, from Latin *verbōsus,* from *verbum,* word. See VERB.] **—ver·bose′ly** *adv.* **—ver·bose′ness, ver·bos′i·ty** (-bŏs′ĭ-tē) *n.*

ver·bo·ten (vər-bōt′n, fĕr-) *adj.* Forbidden; prohibited. [German, past participle of *verbieten,* to forbid, from Middle High German, from Old High German *farbiotan.* See **bheudh-** in Appendix.]

ver·dant (vûr′dnt) *adj.* **1.** Green with vegetation; covered with green growth. **2.** *Color.* Green in hue. **3.** Lacking experience or sophistication; naive. [French *verdoyant,* from Old French, present participle of *verdoyer,* to become green, from Vulgar Latin **viridiāre,* from Latin *viridis,* green.] **—ver′dan·cy** *n.* **—ver′dant·ly** *adv.*

verd antique also **verde antique** (vûrd) *n.* A dull green, mottled or veined serpentine used in interior decoration. [Obsolete French, from Italian *verde antico* : *verde,* green + *antico,* antique.]

Verde (vûrd), **Cape.** A peninsula of western Senegal projecting into the Atlantic Ocean. First sighted by the Portuguese in 1445, it is the westernmost point of Africa.

ver·der·er also **ver·der·or** (vûr′dər-ər) *n.* A man serving as an official in charge of the royal forests of medieval England. [Anglo-Norman, from *verd,* green, from Latin *viridis.*]

Ver·de River (vûr′dē, vĕr′-). A river, about 306 km (190 mi) long, of central Arizona flowing southeast to the Salt River.

Ver·di (vâr′dē), **Giuseppe.** 1813–1901. Italian composer of operas, including *La Traviata* (1853), *Aïda* (1871), and *Otello* (1887). He is credited with raising Italian opera to its fullest artistic form.

ver·dict (vûr′dĭkt) *n.* **1.** *Law.* The finding of a jury in a trial. **2.** An expressed conclusion; a judgment or an opinion: *the verdict of history.* [Middle English *verdit,* from Anglo-Norman : *ver,* true (from Latin *vērus;* see **wēro-** in Appendix) + *dit,* speech (from Latin *dictum,* from neuter past participle of *dīcere,* to say; see **deik-** in Appendix).]

ver·di·gris (vûr′dĭ-grēs′, -grĭs′, -grē′) *n.* **1.** A blue or green powder consisting of basic cupric acetate used as a paint pigment and fungicide. **2.** A green patina or crust of copper sulfate or copper chloride formed on copper, brass, and bronze exposed to air or seawater for long periods of time. [Middle English *vertegrez,* from Old French *verte grez,* alteration of *vert-de-Grice* : *verd,* green; see VERDURE + *de,* of (from Latin *dē;* see DE–) + *Grice,* Greece.]

Ver·di·gris (vûr′dĭ-grĭs). A river, about 451 km (280 mi) long, of southeast Kansas and northeast Oklahoma flowing generally southward to the Arkansas River.

ver·din (vûr′dn) *n.* A small grayish bird *(Auriparus flaviceps)* of Mexico and the southwest United States, having a yellowish head and throat. [French, bunting, from *vert,* green, from Old French *verd.* See VERDURE.]

ver·di·ter (vûr′dĭ-tər) *n.* Either of two basic carbonates of copper, used as a blue or green pigment. [Middle English, alteration of Old French *verd de terre,* green of earth : *verd,* green; see VERDURE + *de,* of; see VERDIGRIS + *terre,* earth (from Latin *terra;* see **ters-** in Appendix).]

Ver·dun (vər-dŭn′, vĕr-dœn′). **1.** A city of southern Quebec, Canada, a residential suburb of Montreal on Montreal Island. Population, 61,287. **2.** A city of northeast France on the Meuse River west of Metz. Dating to Roman times and an important Carolingian commercial center, it was the site of a prolonged World War I battle (February–December 1916) in which French forces repelled a massive German offensive. The total casualties have been estimated at more than 700,000. Population, 21,516.

ver·dure (vûr′jər) *n.* **1.a.** The lush greenness of flourishing vegetation. **b.** Vigorous greenery. **2.** A fresh or flourishing condition: *the verdure of childhood.* [Middle English, from Old French, from *verd,* green, from Latin *viridis.*] **—ver′dur·ous** *adj.* **—ver′dur·ous·ness** *n.*

Ve·re·shcha·gin (vĕr′əsh-shä′gĭn, vyĭ-rĭsh-chä′gyĭn), **Vasili Vasilievich.** 1842–1904. Russian painter many of whose works, most notably *Apotheosis of War* (1871), are realistic and symbolic denunciations of warfare.

verge[1] (vûrj) *n.* **1.** The extreme edge or margin; a border. See Synonyms at **border. 2.a.** An enclosing boundary. **b.** The space enclosed by such a boundary. **3.** The point beyond which an action, a state, or a condition is likely to begin or occur; the brink: *on the verge of tears; a nation on the verge of economic prosperity.* **4.** *Architecture.* The edge of the tiling that projects over a roof gable. **5.** *Chiefly British.* The shoulder of a road. **6.** A rod, wand, or staff carried as an emblem of authority or office. **7.** *Obsolete.* The rod held by a feudal tenant while swearing fealty to a lord. **8.** The spindle of a balance wheel in a clock or watch, especially such a spindle in a clock with vertical escapement. **9.** The male organ of copulation in certain invertebrates. **—verge** *intr.v.* **verged, verg·ing, verg·es. 1.** To approach the nature or condition of something specified; come close. Used with *on: a brilliance verging on genius.* **2.** To be on the edge or border: *Her land verges on the neighboring township.* [Middle English, from Old French, rod, ring, from Latin *virga,* rod, strip.]

verge[2] (vûrj) *intr.v.* **verged, verg·ing, verg·es. 1.** To slope or incline. **2.** To tend to move in a particular direction: *"the Neoclassicism . . . away from which they subsequently verged"* (Hugh Honour). **3.** To pass or merge gradually: *dusk verging into night.* [Latin *vergere.* See **wer-**[2] in Appendix.]

verg·er (vûr′jər) *n. Chiefly British.* **1.** One who carries the verge or other emblem of authority before a scholastic, legal, or religious dignitary in a procession. **2.** One who takes care of the interior of a church and acts as an attendant during ceremonies.

Ver·gil (vûr′jəl). See **Virgil.**

ver·glas (vĕr-glä′) *n.* A thin coating of ice, as on rock. [French, from Old French *verre-glaz* : *verre,* glass (from Latin *vitrum*) + *glas, glace,* ice (from Vulgar Latin **glacia,* from Latin *glaciēs;* see GLACÉ).]

ve·rid·i·cal (və-rĭd′ĭ-kəl) also **ve·rid·ic** (-rĭd′ĭk) *adj.* **1.** Truthful; veracious. **2.** Coinciding with fact or reality; genuine or real. [From Latin *vēridicus* : *vērus,* true; see **wēro-** in Appendix + *dīcere,* to say; see **deik-** in Appendix.] **—ve·rid′i·cal′i·ty** (-kăl′ĭ-tē) *n.* **—ve·rid′i·cal·ly** *adv.*

ver·i·fi·a·ble (vĕr′ə-fī′ə-bəl) *adj.* Possible to verify: *a verifiable account of the incident; verifiable sales data.* **—ver′i·fi′a·bil′i·ty, ver′i·fi′a·ble·ness** *n.* **—ver′i·fi′a·bly** *adv.*

ver·i·fi·ca·tion (vĕr′ə-fĭ-kā′shən) *n.* **1.** The act of verifying or the state of being verified. **2.a.** A confirmation of truth or authority. **b.** The evidence for such a confirmation. **c.** A formal assertion of validity. **3.** *Law.* An affidavit that attests to the truth of a pleading. **—ver′i·fi·ca′tive** *adj.*

ver·i·fy (vĕr′ə-fī′) *tr.v.* **-fied** (-fīd′), **-fy·ing, -fies** (-fīz′). **1.** To prove the truth of by presentation of evidence or testimony; substantiate. **2.** To determine or test the truth or accuracy of, as by comparison, investigation, or reference: *conducted experiments to verify the hypothesis.* See Synonyms at **confirm. 3.** *Law.* **a.** To affirm formally or under oath. **b.** To append a verification to (a pleading); conclude with a verification. [Middle English *verifien,* from Old French *verifier,* from Medieval Latin *vērificāre* : Latin *vērus,* true; see **wēro-** in Appendix + Latin *-ficāre,* -fy.] **—ver′i·fi′er** *n.*

ver·i·ly (vĕr′ə-lē) *adv.* **1.** In truth; in fact. **2.** With confidence; assuredly. [Middle English *verraily,* from *verrai,* true. See VERY.]

ver·i·sim·i·lar (vĕr′ə-sĭm′ə-lər) *adj.* Appearing to be true or real; probable. [From Latin *vērīsimilis* : *vērī,* genitive of *vērum,* truth, from neuter sing. of *vērus,* true; see **wēro-** in Appendix + *similis,* similar; see SIMILAR.] **—ver′i·sim′i·lar·ly** *adv.*

ver·i·si·mil·i·tude (vĕr′ə-sĭ-mĭl′ĭ-to͞od′, -tyo͞od′) *n.* **1.** The quality of appearing to be true or real. See Synonyms at **truth. 2.** Something that has the appearance of being true or real. [Latin *vērīsimilitūdō,* from *vērīsimilis,* verisimilar. See VERISIMILAR.] **—ver′i·si·mil′i·tu′di·nous** (-to͞od′n-əs, -tyo͞od′-) *adj.*

ver·ism (vĕr′ĭz′əm) *n.* Realism in art and literature. [Italian *verismo* : *vero,* true (from Latin *vērus;* see **wēro-** in Appendix) + *-ismo,* system of principles (from Latin *-ismus,* -ism).] **—ver′ist** *n.* **—ve·ris′tic** (və-rĭs′tĭk) *adj.*

ve·ris·mo (və-rĭz′mō) *n.* **1.** Verism. **2.** An artistic movement of the late 19th century, originating in Italy and influential especially in grand opera, marked by the use of common, everyday themes often treated in a melodramatic manner. [Italian. See VERISM.]

ver·i·ta·ble (vĕr′ĭ-tə-bəl) *adj.* Being truly so called; real or genuine: *"Her tea . . . was set forth with as much grace as if she had been a veritable guest to her own self"* (Mary Wilkins Freeman). [Middle English, from Old French, from *verite,* truth. See VERITY.] **—ver′i·ta·ble·ness** *n.* **—ver′i·ta·bly** *adv.*

vé·ri·té (vā-rē-tā′) *n.* Cinéma vérité.

Giuseppe Verdi
1886 pastel portrait by
Giovanni Boldini
(1845–1931)

verdin
Auriparus flaviceps

ă pat	oi boy
ā pay	ou out
âr care	o͝o took
ä father	o͞o boot
ĕ pet	ŭ cut
ē be	ûr urge
ĭ pit	th thin
ī pie	*th* this
îr pier	hw which
ŏ pot	zh vision
ō toe	ə about, item
ô paw	♦ regionalism

Stress marks: **′** (primary); ′ (secondary), as in **dictionary** (dĭk′shə-nĕr′ē)

ver·i·ty (vĕr′ĭ-tē) *n., pl.* **-ties. 1.** The quality or condition of being true, factual, or real. **2.** Something, such as a statement, principle, or belief, that is true, especially an enduring truth: *"The mind once suddenly aware of a verity for the first time immediately invents it again"* (Agnes Sligh Turnbull). See Synonyms at **truth.** [Middle English *verite,* truth, from Old French, from Latin *vēritās,* from *vērus,* true. See **wēro-** in Appendix.]

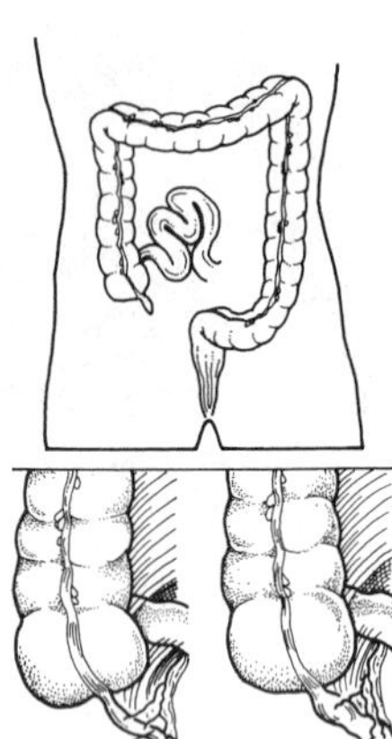

vermiform appendix

ver·juice (vûr′jo͞os′) *n.* **1.** The acidic juice of crab apples or other sour fruit, such as unripe grapes. **2.** Sourness, as of disposition. [Middle English *verjus,* from Old French *vertjus* : *verd,* unripe; see VERDURE + *jus,* juice; see JUICE.]

Ver·kho·yansk Range (vĕr′kə-yänsk′, vĭr-KHô-). A mountain chain of northeast Russia parallel to and east of the lower Lena River. The lowest temperature for an inhabited area, −68°C (−90°F), was recorded here on February 6, 1933.

Ver·laine (vĕr-lān′, -lĕn′), **Paul.** 1844–1896. French symbolist poet whose works, noted for their fine lyricism, include *Romances sans Paroles* (1874) and *Sagesse* (1881).

Ver·meer (vər-mîr′, -mâr′), **Jan.** Also known as Jan van der Meer. 1632–1675. Dutch painter noted for his interior genre scenes, in which he used to great effect his mastery of lighting and color. His works include *The Lacemaker* (c. 1664).

ver·meil (vûr′məl, -māl′) *n.* **1.** *Color.* Vermilion or a similar bright red color. **2.** (vĕr-mā′). Gilded silver, bronze, or copper. **—vermeil** *adj. Color.* Bright red in color. [Middle English *vermail,* from Old French *vermeil,* from Late Latin *vermiculus,* a kind of red worm, from Latin, grub, diminutive of *vermis,* worm. See **wer-²** in Appendix.]

vermi– *pref.* Worm: *vermicide.* [From Latin *vermis,* worm. See **wer-²** in Appendix.]

ver·mi·cel·li (vûr′mĭ-chĕl′ē, -sĕl′ē) *n.* Pasta made in long strands thinner than spaghetti. [Italian, pl. of *vermicello,* diminutive of *verme,* worm, from Latin *vermis.* See **wer-²** in Appendix.]

WORD HISTORY: We are now going to open an etymological can of worms by discussing the origin of the word *vermicelli.* This word, like the food itself, is Italian in origin. Italian *vermicelli* is the plural of *vermicello,* a diminutive of *verme,* "worm," from the Latin word *vermis,* having the same sense. Perhaps you might prefer spaghetti instead; the word *spaghetti* is derived from the Italian plural of the diminutive of *spago,* "string."

ver·mi·cide (vûr′mĭ-sīd′) *n.* An agent used to kill worms. **—ver′mi·cid′al** (-sīd′l) *adj.*

ver·mic·u·lar (vər-mĭk′yə-lər) *adj.* **1.** Having the shape or motion of a worm. **2.** Having wormlike markings; vermiculate. **3.** Caused by or relating to worms. [Medieval Latin *vermiculāris,* from Latin *vermiculus,* diminutive of *vermis,* worm. See **wer-²** in Appendix.] **—ver·mic′u·lar·ly** *adv.*

ver·mic·u·late (vər-mĭk′yə-lāt′) *tr.v.* **-lat·ed, -lat·ing, -lates.** To adorn or decorate with wavy or winding lines. **—vermiculate** (-lĭt, -lāt′) *adj.* **1.** Bearing wavy, wormlike lines. **2.** Having a wormlike motion; twisting or wriggling. **3.** Sinuous; tortuous. **4.** Infested with worms; worm-eaten. [Latin *vermiculārī, vermiculāt-,* from *vermiculus,* diminutive of *vermis,* worm. See VERMICULAR.]

ver·mic·u·la·tion (vər-mĭk′yə-lā′shən) *n.* **1.** Motion resembling that of a worm, especially the wavelike contractions of the intestine; peristalsis. **2.** Wormlike marks or carvings, as in a mosaic or masonry. **3.** The condition of being worm-eaten.

vernier caliper

ver·mic·u·lite (vər-mĭk′yə-līt′) *n.* Any of a group of micaceous hydrated silicate minerals related to the chlorites and used in heat-expanded form as insulation and as a planting medium. [Latin *vermiculus,* diminutive of *vermis,* worm; see VERMICULAR + –ITE[1].]

ver·mi·form (vûr′mə-fôrm′) *adj.* Resembling or having the long, thin, cylindrical shape of a worm.

vermiform appendix *n.* A narrow vestigial process projecting from the cecum in the lower right-hand part of the abdomen of some mammals, including human beings. Also called *vermiform process.*

ver·mi·fuge (vûr′mə-fyo͞oj′) *n.* A medicine that expels intestinal worms. **—vermifuge** *adj.* Causing expulsion of intestinal worms; anthelmintic.

ver·mil·ion also **ver·mil·lion** (vər-mĭl′yən) *—n.* **1.** A bright red mercuric sulfide used as a pigment. **2.** *Color.* A vivid red to reddish orange. In this sense, also called *Chinese red, cinnabar.* *—adj. Color.* Of a vivid red to reddish orange. *—tr.v.* **-ioned, -ion·ing, -ions** also **-lioned, -lion·ing, -lions.** To color or dye (something) in the hue vermilion. [Middle English *vermelion,* from Old French *vermeillon,* from *vermeil.* See VERMEIL.]

ver·min (vûr′mĭn) *n., pl.* **vermin. 1.** Various small animals or insects, such as rats or cockroaches, that are destructive, annoying, or injurious to health. **2.** Animals that prey on game, such as foxes or weasels. **3.a.** A person considered loathsome or highly offensive. **b.** Such people considered as a group. [Middle English, from Old French, from Vulgar Latin **vermīnum,* from Latin *vermis,* worm. See **wer-²** in Appendix.]

ver·mi·na·tion (vûr′mə-nā′shən) *n.* Infestation by vermin, especially parasitic vermin.

ver·min·ous (vûr′mə-nəs) *adj.* **1.** Of, relating to, or caused by vermin: *verminous diseases.* **2.** Infested with vermin. **3.** Of the nature of vermin; repulsive. **—ver′min·ous·ly** *adv.*

ver·miv·o·rous (vər-mĭv′ər-əs) *adj.* Feeding on worms or insect vermin. Used of a bird.

Ver·mont (vər-mŏnt′). *Abbr.* **VT, Vt.** A state of the northeast United States bordering on Canada. It was admitted as the 14th state in 1791. Explored by Samuel de Champlain in 1609, the region was first permanently settled by the British in 1724. Claims to the area were relinquished by Massachusetts in 1781, New Hampshire in 1782, and New York in 1790. Montpelier is the capital and Burlington the largest city. Population, 511,456. **—Ver·mont′er** *n.*

ver·mouth (vər-mo͞oth′) *n.* A sweet or dry wine flavored with aromatic herbs and used chiefly in mixed drinks. [French *vermout,* from German *Wermut,* from Middle High German *wermuot,* wormwood, from Old High German *wermuota.*]

ver·nac·u·lar (vər-năk′yə-lər) *n.* **1.** The standard native language of a country or locality. **2.** The everyday language spoken by a people as distinguished from the literary language. See Synonyms at **dialect. 3.** The idiom of a particular trade or profession: *in the legal vernacular.* **4.** An idiomatic word, phrase, or expression. **5.** The common, nonscientific name of a plant or an animal. **—vernacular** *adj.* **1.** Native to or commonly spoken by the members of a particular country or region. **2.** Using the native language of a region, especially as distinct from the literary language: *a vernacular poet.* **3.** Relating to or expressed in the native language or dialect. **4.** Of, relating to, or characteristic of the style of architecture and decoration common in a particular region, culture, or period. **5.** Occurring or existing in a particular locality; endemic: *a vernacular disease.* **6.** Relating to or designating the common, nonscientific name of a plant or an animal. [From Latin *vernāculus,* native, from *verna,* native slave, perhaps of Etruscan origin.] **—ver·nac′u·lar·ly** *adv.*

ver·nac·u·lar·ism (vər-năk′yə-lə-rĭz′əm) *n.* A vernacular word or expression.

ver·nac·u·lar·ize (vər-năk′yə-lə-rīz′) *tr.v.* **-ized, -iz·ing, -iz·es.** To translate into the everyday language spoken by a people: *vernacularized the liturgy.*

ver·nal (vûr′nəl) *adj.* **1.** Of, relating to, or occurring in the spring. **2.** Characteristic of or resembling spring. **3.** Fresh and young; youthful. [Latin *vērnālis,* from *vērnus,* from *vēr,* spring. See **wesr̥** in Appendix.] **—ver′nal·ly** *adv.*

vernal equinox *n.* **1.** The point at which the ecliptic intersects the celestial equator, the sun having a northerly motion. **2.** The moment at which the sun passes through the vernal equinox, occurring on about March 21 in the Northern Hemisphere and marking the beginning of spring.

ver·nal·i·za·tion (vûr′nə-lĭ-zā′shən) *n.* Subjection of seeds or seedlings to low temperature in order to hasten plant development and flowering.

ver·na·tion (vər-nā′shən) *n.* The arrangement of the young leaves within a bud. [New Latin *vērnātiō, vērnātiōn-,* from Latin *vērnātus,* past participle of *vērnāre,* to flourish, from *vērnus,* vernal. See VERNAL.]

Verne (vûrn, vĕrn), **Jules.** 1828–1905. French writer who is considered the founder of modern science fiction. His novels include *Journey to the Center of the Earth* (1864) and *Around the World in Eighty Days* (1873).

Ver·ner's Law (vûr′nərz, vĕr′-) *n. Linguistics.* A law stating essentially that Proto-Germanic noninitial voiceless fricatives in voiced environments became voiced when the previous syllable was unstressed in Proto-Indo-European. [After Karl Adolph *Verner* (1846–1896), Danish philologist.]

ver·ni·er (vûr′nē-ər) *n.* **1.** A small, movable auxiliary graduated scale attached parallel to a main graduated scale, calibrated to indicate fractional parts of the subdivisions of the larger scale, and used on certain precision instruments to increase accuracy in measurement. **2.** An auxiliary device designed to facilitate fine adjustments or measurements on precision instruments. Also called *vernier scale.* **—vernier** *adj.* Of or relating to a vernier. [After Pierre *Vernier* (1580?–1637), French mathematician.]

vernier caliper *n.* A measuring instrument consisting of an L-shaped frame with a linear scale along its longer arm and an L-shaped sliding attachment with a vernier, used to read directly the dimension of an object represented by the separation between the inner or outer edges of the two shorter arms.

vernier rocket *n.* A small rocket engine used primarily to make fine adjustments in velocity and trajectory.

vernier scale *n.* See **vernier.**

ver·nis·sage (vĕr′nĭ-säzh′) *n.* A private showing held before the opening of an art exhibition. [French, from *vernis,* varnish, from Old French. See VARNISH.]

ver·nix (vûr′nĭks) *n.* A waxy white protective substance covering the skin of a fetus. [Short for VERNIX CASEOSA.]

vernix ca·se·o·sa (kā′sē-ō′sə) *n.* Vernix. [New Latin *vernix cāseōsa* : *vernix,* varnish + *cāseōsa,* cheeselike.]

Ver·non (vûr′nən). **1.** A city of southern British Columbia, Canada, near the northern end of Okanagan Lake. It is a processing center in a lumbering region. Population, 19,987. **2.** A town of northern Connecticut northeast of Hartford. Settled c. 1726, it is a manufacturing center. Population, 27,974.

Ve·ro Beach (vîr′ō). A city of eastern Florida on the Indian River lagoon north-northwest of West Palm Beach. It is a fishing resort in a citrus-growing area. Population, 16,176.

Ve·ro·na (və-rō′nə). A city of northern Italy on the Adige River west of Venice. The original settlement on the site was conquered by Rome in 89 B.C. Verona became an independent republic in A.D. 1107 and formed the powerful Veronese League in 1164. It became part of Italy in 1866. Population, 261,208. **—Ve′ro·nese′** (vĕr′ə-nēz′, -nēs′) *adj. & n.*

Ve·ro·ne·se (vĕr′ə-nā′sē, -zē, vĕ′rô-nĕ′zĕ), **Paolo.** Originally Paola Caliari. 1528–1588. Italian painter of the Venetian school. His large, richly colored, harmonious works include *Rape of Europa* (1576).

ve·ron·i·ca¹ (və-rŏn′ĭ-kə) *n.* Any of various plants of the genus *Veronica,* which includes the speedwells. [New Latin *Veronica,* genus name.]

ve·ron·i·ca² (və-rŏn′ĭ-kə) *n.* **1.a.** According to popular legend, an image of the face of Jesus as impressed on the handkerchief offered to him by Saint Veronica on the road to Calvary. **b.** The handkerchief itself. **2.** A cloth bearing a representation of Jesus's face. [Medieval Latin, perhaps alteration of *vēra īconica,* true image : Latin *vēra,* feminine of *vērus,* true; see VERY + Latin *īconica,* feminine of *īconicus,* of an image (from Greek *eikonikos,* from *eikōn,* image; see ICON).]

ve·ron·i·ca³ (və-rŏn′ĭ-kə) *n.* A maneuver in bullfighting in which the matador stands with both feet fixed in position and swings the cape slowly away from the charging bull. [Spanish, from *veronica,* the veronica (from the gesture Saint Veronica made), from Medieval Latin. See VERONICA².]

Vé·ro·nique (vâr′ə-nēk′, vā-rô-) *adj.* Served with a sauce containing white seedless grapes: *sole Véronique.* [French, probably after *Véronique,* an opera by André Messager (1853–1929).]

Ver·ra·za·no or **Ver·raz·za·no** (vĕr′ə-zä′nō, -rä-tsä′nô), **Giovanni da.** 1485?–1528? Italian explorer of the Atlantic coast of North America.

Ver·roc·chio (və-rō′kē-ō, vĕr-rôk′kyô), **Andrea del.** Originally Andrea di Michele di Francesco Cione. 1435–1488. Florentine sculptor and painter who was a tutor of Leonardo da Vinci and is best known for a magnificent equestrian statue in Verona.

ver·ru·ca (və-ro͞o′kə) *n., pl.* **-cae** (-kē). **1.** *Medicine.* A wart. **2.** *Biology.* A wartlike projection, as on the back of a toad or on some leaves. [Latin *verrūca.*]

ver·ru·cose (və-ro͞o′kōs′) also **ver·ru·cous** (-kəs) *adj.* Covered with warts or wartlike projections. [Latin *verrūcōsus,* from *verrūca,* wart.]

vers *abbr. Mathematics.* Versed sine.

Ver·sailles (vər-sī′, vĕr-). A city of north-central France west-southwest of Paris. It is best known for its magnificent palace, built by Louis XIV in the mid-17th century, where the treaty ending World War I was signed in 1919. Population, 91,494.

ver·sant (vûr′sənt) *n.* **1.** The slope of a side of a mountain or mountain range. **2.** The general slope of a region. [French, present participle of *verser,* to turn, from Old French, from Latin *versāre,* to turn frequently. See VERSATILE.]

ver·sa·tile (vûr′sə-təl, -tīl′) *adj.* **1.** Capable of doing many things competently. **2.** Having varied uses or serving many functions: *"The most versatile of vegetables is the tomato"* (Craig Claiborne). **3.** Variable or inconstant; changeable: *a versatile temperament.* **4.** *Biology.* Capable of moving freely in all directions, as the antenna of an insect, the toe of an owl, or the loosely attached anther of a flower. [Latin *versātilis,* from *versātus,* past participle of *versāre,* to turn. See **wer-²** in Appendix.] **—ver′sa·tile·ly** *adv.* **—ver′sa·til′i·ty** (-tĭl′ĭ-tē), **ver′sa·tile·ness** (-təl-nĭs, -tīl′-) *n.*

SYNONYMS: *versatile, all-around, many-sided, multifaceted, multifarious.* The central meaning shared by these adjectives is "having many aspects, uses, or abilities": *a versatile writer; an all-around athlete; a many-sided subject; a multifaceted undertaking; multifarious interests.*

verse¹ (vûrs) *n.* **1.** *Abbr.* **ver., v. a.** A single metrical line in a poetic composition; one line of poetry. **b.** A division of a metrical composition, such as a stanza of a poem or hymn. **c.** A poem. **2.** Metrical or rhymed composition as distinct from prose; poetry. **3.a.** The art or work of a poet. **b.** A group of poems: *read a book of satirical verse.* **4.** Metrical writing that lacks depth or artistic merit. **5.** A particular type of metrical composition, such as blank verse or free verse. **6.** One of the numbered subdivisions of a chapter in the Bible. **—verse** *tr. & intr.v.* **versed, vers·ing, vers·es.** To versify or engage in versifying. [Middle English *vers,* from Old English *fers* and from Old French *vers,* both from Latin *versus,* from past participle of *vertere,* to turn. See **wer-²** in Appendix.]

verse² (vûrs) *tr.v.* **versed, vers·ing, vers·es.** To familiarize by study or experience: *He versed himself in philosophy.* [Latin *versāre.* See VERSATILE.]

versed (vûrst) *adj.* Acquainted through study or experience; knowledgeable or skilled: *She is well versed in classical languages.*

versed cosine *n. Abbr.* **covers.** *Mathematics.* A trigonometric function of an angle equal to one minus the sine of that angle. Also called *coversine.* [VERSED (SINE) + COSINE.]

versed sine *n. Abbr.* **vers.** *Mathematics.* A trigonometric function of an angle equal to one minus the cosine of that angle. Also called *versine.* [Translation of New Latin *sinus versus* : *sinus,* sine + Latin *versus,* past participle of *vertere,* to turn.]

ver·si·cle (vûr′sĭ-kəl) *n.* **1.** A short verse. **2.** A short sentence spoken or chanted by a priest and followed by a response from the congregation. [Middle English, from Latin *versiculus,* diminutive of *versus,* verse. See VERSE¹.]

ver·si·col·or (vûr′sĭ-kŭl′ər) also **ver·si·col·ored** (-kŭl′ərd) *adj.* **1.** Having a variety of colors; variegated. **2.** Changing in color; iridescent. [Latin : *versus,* past participle of *vertere,* to turn; see VERSE¹ + *color,* color; see COLOR.]

ver·si·fi·er (vûr′sə-fī′ər) *n.* One who versifies. See Synonyms at **poet.**

ver·si·fy (vûr′sə-fī′) *v.* **-fied** (-fīd′), **-fy·ing, -fies** (-fīz′). *—tr.* **1.** To change from prose into metrical form. **2.** To treat or tell in verse: *versify stories from the Bible.* *—intr.* To write verses. [Middle English *versifien,* from Old French *versifier,* from Latin *versificāre* : *versus,* verse; see VERSE¹ + *-ficāre,* -fy.] **—ver′si·fi·ca′tion** (-fĭ-kā′shən) *n.*

ver·sine (vûr′sīn′) *n. Mathematics.* See **versed sine.** [Contraction of VERSED SINE.]

ver·sion (vûr′zhən, -shən) *n. Abbr.* **ver., v. 1.** A description or an account from one point of view, especially as opposed to another: *Your version of the accident differs from mine.* **2.a.** A translation from another language. **b.** Often **Version.** A translation of the entire Bible or a part of it. **3.** A particular form or variation of an earlier or original type: *a modern version of the one-room schoolhouse.* **4.** An adaptation of a work of art or literature into another medium or style: *the film version of a famous novel.* **5.** *Medicine.* **a.** Manipulation of a fetus in the uterus to bring it into a desirable position for delivery. **b.** Deflection of an organ, such as the uterus, from its normal position. [French, from Old French, act of turning, from Medieval Latin *versiō, versiōn-,* from Latin *versus,* past participle of *vertere,* to turn. See **wer-²** in Appendix.] **—ver′sion·al** *adj.*

vers li·bre (vĕr lē′brə) *n.* Free verse. [French : *vers,* verse + *libre,* free.]

ver·so (vûr′sō) *n., pl.* **-sos. 1.** *Abbr.* **v., vo.** *Printing.* A left-hand page of a book or the reverse side of a leaf, as opposed to the recto. **2.** The back of a coin or medal. [New Latin *versō (foliō),* (with the page) turned, verso, from Latin *versō,* ablative of *versus,* past participle of *vertere,* to turn. See VERSION.]

verst (vûrst) *n.* A Russian measure of linear distance equivalent to about two thirds of a mile. [French *verste* or German *Werst,* both from Russian *versta.* See **wer-²** in Appendix.]

ver·sus (vûr′səs, -səz) *prep. Abbr.* **v., vs. 1.** Against: *the plaintiff versus the defendant; Army versus Navy.* **2.** As the alternative to or in contrast with: *"freedom of information versus invasion of privacy"* (Ian Hamilton). [Middle English, from Medieval Latin, from Latin, turned, toward, from past participle of *vertere,* to turn. See **wer-²** in Appendix.]

vert (vûrt) *n.* **1.** *Heraldry.* The color green. **2.a.** Green vegetation that can serve as cover for deer. Used in English forest law. **b.** The right to cut such vegetation. [Middle English *verte,* from Anglo-Norman, feminine of *verd.* See VERDERER.]

vert. *abbr.* **1.** Vertebrate. **2.** Vertical.

ver·te·bra (vûr′tə-brə) *n., pl.* **-brae** (-brā′, -brē′) or **-bras.** Any of the bones or cartilaginous segments forming the spinal column. [Middle English, from Latin, from *vertere,* to turn. See **wer-²** in Appendix.]

ver·te·bral (vûr′tə-brəl, vər-tē′brəl) *adj.* **1.** Of, relating to, or of the nature of a vertebra. **2.** Having or consisting of vertebrae. **3.** Having a spinal column. **—ver′te·bral·ly** *adv.*

vertebral canal *n.* See **spinal canal.**

vertebral column *n.* See **spinal column.**

ver·te·brate (vûr′tə-brĭt, -brāt′) *adj.* **1.** Having a backbone or spinal column. **2.** Of or characteristic of vertebrates or a vertebrate. **—vertebrate** *n. Abbr.* **vert.** A member of the subphylum Vertebrata, a primary division of the phylum Chordata that includes the fishes, amphibians, reptiles, birds, and mammals, all of which are characterized by a segmented spinal column and a distinct, well-differentiated head. [Latin *vertebrātus,* having joints, from *vertebra,* vertebra. See VERTEBRA.]

ver·te·bra·tion (vûr′tə-brā′shən) *n.* Division into segments like those of the spinal column; vertebral formation.

ver·tex (vûr′tĕks′) *n., pl.* **-tex·es** or **-ti·ces** (-tĭ-sēz′). **1.** The highest point; the apex or summit: *the vertex of a mountain.* **2.** *Anatomy.* **a.** The highest point of the skull. **b.** The top of the head. **3.** *Astronomy.* The highest point reached in the apparent motion of a celestial body. **4.** *Mathematics.* **a.** The point at which the sides of an angle intersect. **b.** The point on a triangle or pyramid opposite to and farthest away from its base. **c.** A point on a polyhedron common to three or more sides. [Latin, whirling column, vertex, from *vertere,* to turn. See **wer-²** in Appendix.]

ver·ti·cal (vûr′tĭ-kəl) *adj. Abbr.* **vert. 1.** Being or situated at right angles to the horizon; upright. **2.** Situated at the vertex or highest point; directly overhead. **3.** *Anatomy.* Of or relating to the vertex of the head. **4.** *Economics.* Relating to or involving all stages from production to sale: *vertical integration.* **5.** Relating to or composed of elements at different levels, as of society. **—vertical** *n.* **1.** Something vertical, as a line, plane, or circle. **2.** A vertical position. [Late Latin *verticālis,* overhead, from Latin *vertex, vertic-,* highest point. See VERTEX.] **—ver′ti·cal′i·ty** (-kăl′ĭ-tē), **ver′ti·cal·ness** (-kəl-nĭs) *n.* **—ver′ti·cal·ly** *adv.*

SYNONYMS: *vertical, upright, perpendicular, plumb.* These adjectives are compared as they mean being at or approximately at

veronica²
c. 1480 painting
by Hans Memling

Giovanni da Verrazano

ă pat	oi boy
ā pay	ou out
âr care	o͝o took
ä father	o͞o boot
ĕ pet	ŭ cut
ē be	ûr urge
ĭ pit	th thin
ī pie	*th* this
îr pier	hw which
ŏ pot	zh vision
ō toe	ə about, item
ô paw	♦ regionalism

Stress marks: ′ (primary); ′ (secondary), as in **dictionary** (dĭk′shə-nĕr′ē)

right angles to the horizon or to level ground. *Vertical* and especially *upright* are often used to signify contrast with what is horizontal; the terms do not always imply an exact right angle: *wallpaper with vertical stripes; an upright column. Perpendicular* and *plumb* are generally used to specify an angle of precisely 90 degrees: *a perpendicular escarpment; careful to make the doorjambs plumb.*

---

vertical angle *n. Mathematics.* Either of two angles formed by two intersecting lines and lying on opposite sides of the point of intersection.

vertical circle *n.* A great circle on the celestial sphere that passes through the zenith and the nadir and thus is perpendicular to the horizon.

vertical file *n.* A collection of resource materials, such as pamphlets, clippings from periodicals, and mounted photographs, arranged for ready reference, as in a library or an archive.

vertical union *n.* An industrial union.

ver·ti·ces (vûr′tĭ-sēz′) *n.* A plural of **vertex.**

ver·ti·cil (vûr′tĭ-sĭl′) *n.* A circular arrangement, as of flowers, leaves, or hairs, growing about a central point; a whorl. [Latin *verticillus,* the whorl of a spindle, diminutive of *vertex, vertic-,* highest point. See VERTEX.]

ver·ti·cil·las·ter (vûr′tĭ-sə-lăs′tər) *n.* A cymose inflorescence resembling a whorl but actually arising in the axils of opposite bracts, as in most mints. [New Latin *verticillastēr* : Latin *verticillus,* whorl; see VERTICIL + Latin *astēr,* star; see ASTER.] **—ver′ti·cil·las′trate′** (-trāt′) *adj.*

ver·ti·cil·late (vûr′tĭ-sĭl′ĭt, -āt′) also **ver·ti·cil·lat·ed** (-sĭl′ā′tĭd) *adj.* Arranged in or forming whorls or a whorl. **—ver′ti·cil′late·ly** *adv.* **—ver′ti·cil·la′tion** *n.*

ver·tig·i·nous (vər-tĭj′ə-nəs) *adj.* **1.** Turning about an axis; revolving or whirling. **2.** Affected by vertigo; dizzy. See Synonyms at **giddy. 3.** Tending to produce vertigo: *"my small mind contained in earthly human limits, not lost in vertiginous space and elements unknown"* (Diana Cooper). **4.** Inclined to change quickly; unstable. [From Latin *vertīgō, vertīgin-,* a whirling, from *vertere,* to turn. See VERSION.] **—ver·tig′i·nous·ly** *adv.* **—ver·tig′i·nous·ness** *n.*

ver·ti·go (vûr′tĭ-gō′) *n., pl.* **-goes** or **-gos. 1.a.** The sensation of dizziness. **b.** An instance of such a sensation. **2.** A confused, disoriented state of mind. [Middle English, from Latin *vertīgō,* from *vertere,* to turn. See **wer-**[2] in Appendix.]

ver·tu (vər-to͞o′) *n.* Variant of **virtu.**

ver·vain (vûr′vān′) *n.* See **verbena** (sense 1). [Middle English *verveine,* from Old French, from Latin *verbēna,* leafage. See VERBENA.]

verve (vûrv) *n.* **1.** Energy and enthusiasm in the expression of ideas, especially in artistic performance or composition: *The play lacks verve.* **2.** Vitality; liveliness. See Synonyms at **vigor. 3.** *Archaic.* Aptitude; talent. [French, from Old French, fanciful expression, probably from Vulgar Latin **verva,* from Latin *verba,* pl. of *verbum,* word. See **wer-**[5] in Appendix.]

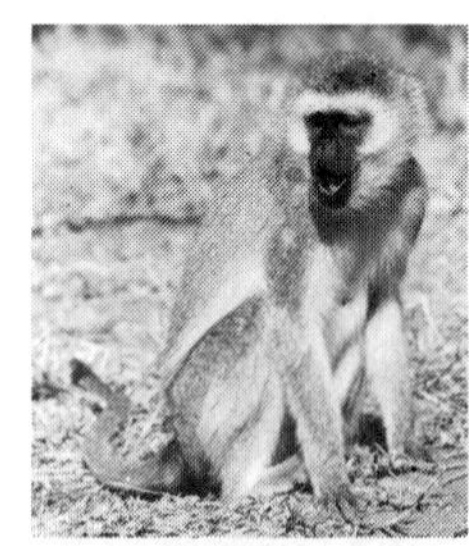

vervet
Cercopithecus aethiops

ver·vet (vûr′vĭt) *n.* A small, long-tailed African monkey *(Cercopithecus aethiops)* having a yellowish-brown or greenish coat. [French : *vert,* green (from Old French *verd;* see VERDURE) + *grivet,* grivet.]

Ver·woerd (fər-vo͞ort′), **Hendrik Frensch.** 1901–1966. South African politician who as prime minister (1958–1966) pursued a policy of apartheid and removed South Africa from the British Commonwealth (1961). He was assassinated in Cape Town.

ver·y (vĕr′ē) *adv.* **1.** In a high degree; extremely: *very happy; very much admired.* **2.** Truly; absolutely: *the very best advice; attended the very same schools.* **3. Very.** *Abbr.* **v., V.** Used in titles: *the Very Reverend Jane Smith.* **—very** *adj.* **-i·er, -i·est. 1.** Complete; absolute: *at the very end of his career; the very opposite.* **2.** Being the identical one; selfsame: *the very question she asked yesterday.* See Synonyms at **same. 3.** Used to emphasize the importance of the thing named: *"The very essence of artistic expression is invention"* (Irving R. Kaufman). **4.** Being particularly suitable or appropriate: *the very item needed to increase sales.* **5.** Being precisely as stated: *the very center of town.* **6.** Mere: *The very thought is frightening.* **7.** Actual: *caught in the very act of stealing.* **8.** Genuine; true: *"Like very sanctity, she did approach"* (Shakespeare). [Middle English *verrai,* from Old French *verai,* true, from Vulgar Latin **vērācus,* from Latin *vērāx, vērāc-,* from Latin *vērus.* See **wēro-** in Appendix.]

USAGE NOTE: In general usage *very* is not used alone to modify a past participle. Thus we may say of a book, for example, that it has been *very much praised, very much criticized, very much applauded,* or whatever, but not that it has been *very praised, very criticized,* or *very applauded.* However, many past participle forms do double duty as adjectives, in which case modification by a bare *very,* or by analogous adverbs such as *quite,* is acceptable: there can be no objection to phrases such as *a very creased handkerchief, a very celebrated singer,* or *a very polished performance.* In some cases there is disagreement as to whether a particular participle can be used properly as an adjective: over the years objections have been raised as to the use of *very* by itself with *delighted, interested, annoyed, pleased, disappointed,* and *irritated.* All these words are now well established as adjectives, as indicated by the fact that they can be used attributively (*a delighted audience, a pleased look, a disappointed young man*) as well as by other syntactic criteria. But the status of other participles is still in flux. Some speakers accept phrases such as *very appreciated, very astonished,* or *very heartened,* while others prefer alternatives using *very much.* What is more, some participles allow treatment as adjectives in one sense but not another: one may speak of *a very inflated reputation,* for example, but not, ordinarily, of *a very inflated balloon.* As a result, there is no sure way to tell which participles may be modified by a bare *very*—syntactic tests such as the use of the participle as an attributive adjective will themselves yield different judgments for different speakers—and writers must trust their ears. When in doubt, the use of *very much* is generally the safer alternative.

♦ **very close veins** *pl.n. Chiefly Southern U.S.* Varicose veins. [By folk etymology from *varicose veins.*]

♦ ***REGIONAL NOTE:*** A linguistic process called folk etymology is observed frequently in regional U.S. dialects. Folk etymology causes an unfamiliar and difficult word to be replaced with a similar-sounding word or phrase whose meaning happens to coincide in a way that makes sense. In this manner, *varicose veins* becomes *very close veins* in the speech of many elderly and rural Southerners. The Latinate *varicose,* not a part of their ordinary vocabulary, sounds like *very close,* which certainly describes the location of these blood vessels just under the skin. Nurses at the East Alabama Medical Center in Lee County, Alabama, report that folk etymologies for medical terms are extremely common among their patients.

---

very high frequency *n. Abbr.* **vhf, VHF.** A band of radio frequencies falling between 30 and 300 megahertz.

Ver·y Large Array (vĕr′ē) *n. Abbr.* **VLA.** A Y-shaped pattern of radio telescopes in New Mexico with a radius of 21 kilometers (13 miles).

very large scale integration *n. Abbr.* **VLSI.** *Electronics.* Technology that enables the placement of more than 100,000 integrated circuits on a single semiconductor chip.

very low frequency *n. Abbr.* **vlf, VLF.** A band of radio frequencies falling between 3 and 30 kilohertz.

Ver·y pistol (vĕr′ē, vîr′ē) *n.* A pistol used for firing colored signal flares. [After Edward Wilson *Very* (1847–1910), American naval officer.]

Ve·sa·li·us (vĭ-sā′lē-əs, -zā′-), **Andreas.** 1514–1564. Flemish anatomist and surgeon who is considered the founder of modern anatomy. His major work, *On the Structure of the Human Body* (1543), was based on meticulous dissection of cadavers.

Ve·sey (vē′zē), **Denmark.** 1767?–1822. American insurrectionist. A freed slave in South Carolina, he was implicated in the planning of a large uprising of slaves and was hanged. The event led to more stringent slave codes in many Southern states.

ve·si·ca (və-sī′kə, -sē′-) *n., pl.* **-cae** (-kē, -sē). A bladder, especially the urinary bladder or the gallbladder. [Latin *vēsīca.*] **—ves′i·cal** (vĕs′ĭ-kəl) *adj.*

ves·i·cant (vĕs′ĭ-kənt) *n.* A blistering agent, especially mustard gas, used in chemical warfare. **—vesicant** *adj.* Causing blisters.

vesica pis·cis (pī′sĭs, pĭs′ĭs) *n.* A pointed oval shape used in medieval Christian art as an aureole to surround a sacred figure. [New Latin *vēsīca piscis* : Latin *vēsīca,* bladder + Latin *piscis,* genitive of *piscis,* fish (from the resemblance in shape).]

ves·i·cate (vĕs′ĭ-kāt′) *tr. & intr.v.* **-cat·ed, -cat·ing, -cates.** To blister or become blistered. [New Latin *vēsīcāre, vēsīcāt-,* from Latin *vēsīca,* bladder, blister.] **—ves′i·ca′tion** *n.*

ves·i·ca·to·ry (vĕs′ĭ-kə-tôr′ē, -tōr′ē) *adj.* Vesicant. **—vesicatory** *n., pl.* **-ries.** A vesicant.

ves·i·cle (vĕs′ĭ-kəl) *n.* **1.** A small bladderlike cell or cavity. **2.** *Anatomy.* A small sac or cyst, especially one containing fluid. **3.** *Pathology.* A serum-filled blister formed in or beneath the skin. **4.** *Geology.* A small cavity formed in volcanic rock by entrapment of a gas bubble during solidification. [Middle English, from Old French *vesicule,* from Latin *vēsīcula,* diminutive of *vēsīca,* bladder, blister.]

ve·sic·u·lar (vĕ-sĭk′yə-lər, və-) *adj.* **1.** Of or relating to vesicles. **2.** Composed of or containing vesicles. **3.** Having the form of a vesicle. **—ve·sic′u·lar·ly** *adv.*

vesicular exanthema *n.* An acute, highly infectious viral disease of swine characterized by formation of vesicles on the snout, the mucous membranes of the mouth, and the feet.

vesicular stomatitis *n.* An acute viral disease of cattle, swine, and horses, transmitted by mosquitoes and other insects and having symptoms resembling those of foot-and-mouth disease and vesicular exanthema.

ve·sic·u·late (vĕ-sĭk′yə-lāt′, və-) *tr. & intr.v.* **-lat·ed, -lat·ing, -lates.** To make or become vesicular. **—vesiculate** (-lĭt, -lāt′) *adj.* Full of or bearing vesicles; vesicular. **—ve·sic′u·la′tion** *n.*

Ves·pa·sian (vĕs-pā′zhən, -zhē-ən). A.D. 9–79. Emperor of Rome (69–79) who brought prosperity to the empire, reformed the army, was a patron of the arts, and began the building of the Colosseum.

ves·per (vĕs′pər) *n.* **1.** A bell that summons worshipers to ves-

ă pat	oi boy
ā pay	ou out
âr care	o͝o took
ä father	o͞o boot
ĕ pet	ŭ cut
ē be	ûr urge
ĭ pit	th thin
ī pie	*th* this
îr pier	hw which
ŏ pot	zh vision
ō toe	ə about, item
ô paw	♦ regionalism

Stress marks: **′** (primary); ′ (secondary), as in **dictionary** (dĭk′shə-nĕr′ē)

pers. **2. Vesper.** The evening star, especially Venus. **3.** *Archaic.* Evening. [Middle English, evening star, from Latin, evening. See **wes-pero-** in Appendix.]

ves·per·al (vĕs′pər-əl) *Ecclesiastical. n.* **1.** A book containing the words and hymns to be used at vespers. **2.** A covering used to protect an altar cloth between services. **—vesperal** *adj.* Of or relating to vesper or vespers.

ves·pers also **Ves·pers** (vĕs′pərz) *pl.n.* *(used with a sing. or pl. verb).* **1.a.** The sixth of the seven canonical hours. **b.** A worship service held in the late afternoon or evening in many Western Christian churches. **c.** The time of day appointed for this service. **2.** Evensong. **3.** *Roman Catholic Church.* A service held on Sundays or holy days that includes the office of vespers. [Obsolete French *vespres,* from Old French, from Medieval Latin *vesperās,* evening service, from Latin, accusative pl. of *vespera,* evening, variant of *vesper.* See VESPER.]

vesper sparrow *n.* A North American sparrow *(Pooecetes gramineus)* having white markings on its outer tail feathers. [From its singing in the evening.]

ves·per·til·i·o·nid (vĕs′pər-tĭl′ē-ə-nĭd) *n.* Any of various widely distributed insect-eating bats of the family Vespertilionidae, characterized by a long tail. **—vespertilionid** *adj.* Of or belonging to the family Vespertilionidae. [From New Latin *Vespertiliōnidae,* family name, from *Vespertiliō, Vespertiliōn-,* type genus, from Latin *vespertiliō,* bat, from *vesper,* evening. See **wes-pero-** in Appendix.]

ves·per·tine (vĕs′pər-tīn′) also **ves·per·ti·nal** (vĕs′pər-tī′nəl) *adj.* **1.** Of, relating to, or occurring in the evening. **2.** *Botany.* Opening or blooming in the evening. **3.** *Zoology.* Becoming active in the evening, as bats and owls; crepuscular. [Latin *vespertīnus,* from *vesper,* evening. See VESPER.]

ves·pi·ar·y (vĕs′pē-ĕr′ē) *n., pl.* **-ies.** A nest or colony of wasps or hornets. [Latin *vespa,* wasp + (AP)IARY.]

ves·pid (vĕs′pĭd) *n.* Any of various widely distributed social insects of the family Vespidae, which includes certain wasps, hornets, and yellow jackets. **—vespid** *adj.* Of or belonging to the family Vespidae. [From New Latin *Vespidae,* family name, from *Vespa,* type genus, from Latin *vespa,* wasp.]

ves·pine (vĕs′pīn′) *adj.* Of, relating to, or resembling a wasp. [From Latin *vespa,* wasp.]

Ves·puc·ci (vĕs-po͞o′chē, -pyo͞o′-), **Amerigo.** Latin name Americus Vespucius. 1454–1512. Italian navigator and explorer of the South American coast. America was named in his honor.

ves·sel (vĕs′əl) *n.* **1.** A hollow utensil, such as a cup, vase, or pitcher, used as a container, especially for liquids. **2.a.** *Nautical.* A craft, especially one larger than a rowboat, designed to navigate on water. **b.** An airship. **3.** *Anatomy.* A duct, canal, or other tube that contains or conveys a body fluid: *a blood vessel.* **4.** *Botany.* One of the tubular conductive structures of xylem, consisting of dead cylindrical cells that are attached end to end and connected by perforations. They are found in nearly all flowering plants. **5.** A person seen as the agent or embodiment, as of a quality: *a vessel of mercy.* [Middle English, from Old French, from Late Latin *vāscellum,* diminutive of Latin *vāsculum,* diminutive of *vās,* vessel.]

vest (vĕst) *n.* **1.** A sleeveless garment, often having buttons down the front, worn usually over a shirt or blouse and sometimes as part of a three-piece suit. **2.** A waist-length, sleeveless garment worn for protection: *a thick, down vest; a bulletproof vest.* **3.** A fabric trim worn to fill in the neckline of a woman's garment; a vestee. **4.** *Chiefly British.* An undershirt. **5.a.** *Archaic.* Clothing; raiment. **b.** *Obsolete.* An ecclesiastical vestment. **—vest** *v.* **vest·ed, vest·ing, vests.** *—tr.* **1.** To place (authority, property, or rights, for example) in the control of a person or group, especially to give someone an immediate right to present or future possession or enjoyment of (an estate, for example). Used with *in*: *vested his estate in his daughter.* **2.** To invest or endow (a person or group) with something, such as power or rights. Used with *with*: *vested the council with broad powers; vests its employees with full pension rights after five years of service.* **3.** To clothe or robe, as in ecclesiastical vestments. *—intr.* **1.** To become legally vested. **2.** To dress oneself, especially in ecclesiastical vestments. [French *veste,* robe, from Italian *vesta,* from Latin *vestis,* garment. See **wes-**[2] in Appendix.]

Ves·ta (vĕs′tə) *n.* **1.** *Roman Mythology.* The goddess of the hearth, worshiped in a temple containing the sacred fire tended by the vestal virgins. **2.** The brightest of all the asteroids and the fourth to be discovered. [Latin. See **wes-**[1] in Appendix.]

ves·tal (vĕs′təl) *adj.* **1.** *Roman Mythology.* **a.** Of or relating to Vesta. **b.** Relating to or characteristic of the vestal virgins. **2.** Chaste; pure. **—vestal** *n.* **1.** *Roman Mythology.* A priest who tended the sacred fire of Vesta in ancient Rome. **2.** A woman who is a virgin. **3.** A nun.

vestal virgin *n.* *Roman Mythology.* One of the women who tended the sacred fire in the temple of Vesta in ancient Rome. They acted as priests to Vesta and remained celibate during their servitude.

vest·ed (vĕs′tĭd) *adj.* **1.** *Law.* Settled, fixed, or absolute; being without contingency: *a vested right.* **2.** Dressed or clothed, especially in ecclesiastical vestments.

vested interest *n.* **1.** *Law.* A right or title, as to present or future possession of an estate, that can be conveyed to another. **2.** A fixed right granted to an employee under a pension plan. **3.** A special interest in protecting or promoting that which is to one's own personal advantage. **4. vested interests.** Those groups that seek to maintain or control an existing system or activity from which they derive private benefit.

vest·ee (vĕ-stē′) *n.* A garment worn by women as a blouse front under a sweater or jacket. [From VEST.]

ves·ti·ar·y (vĕs′tē-ĕr′ē, -chē-) *adj.* Of or relating to clothes. **—vestiary** *n., pl.* **-ies.** A dressing room, cloakroom, or vestry. [Latin *vestiārius,* from *vestis,* garment. See VEST. N., from Middle English *vestiarie,* from Old French, from Medieval Latin *vestiārium,* from Latin, wardrobe, from neuter of *vestiārius,* of clothes.]

vesper sparrow
Pooecetes gramineus

ves·tib·u·lar (vĕ-stĭb′yə-lər) *adj.* Of, relating to, or serving as a vestibule.

vestibular nerve *n.* A division of the acoustic nerve that conducts impulses related to maintaining balance to the brain.

ves·ti·bule (vĕs′tə-byo͞ol′) *n.* **1.** A small entrance hall or passage between the outer door and the interior of a house or building. **2.** An enclosed area at the end of a passenger car on a railroad train. **3.** *Anatomy.* A cavity, chamber, or channel that leads to or is an entrance to another cavity: *the vestibule to the ear.* [Latin *vestibulum.*]

ves·tige (vĕs′tĭj) *n.* **1.** A visible trace, evidence, or sign of something that once existed but exists or appears no more. See Synonyms at **trace**[1]. **2.** *Biology.* A rudimentary or degenerate, usually nonfunctioning, structure that is the remnant of an organ or a part that was fully developed or functioning in a preceding generation or an earlier stage of development. [French, from Old French, from Latin *vestīgium.*]

ves·tig·i·a (vĕ-stĭj′ē-ə) *n.* *Biology.* Plural of **vestigium.**

ves·tig·i·al (vĕ-stĭj′ē-əl, -stĭj′əl) *adj.* **1.** Of, relating to, or constituting a vestige. **2.** *Biology.* Occurring or persisting as a rudimentary or degenerate structure. **—ves·tig′i·al·ly** *adv.*

ves·tig·i·um (vĕ-stĭj′ē-əm) *n., pl.* **-i·a** (-ē-ə). *Biology.* A vestige. [Latin *vestīgium,* footprint.]

Amerigo Vespucci
Portrait by
an unknown artist

vest·ing (vĕs′tĭng) *n.* The granting to an employee of credits toward a pension even if separated from the job before retirement.

vest·ment (vĕst′mənt) *n.* **1.** A garment, especially a robe or gown worn as an indication of office or state. **2.** *Ecclesiastical.* Any of the ritual robes worn by members of the clergy, acolytes, or other assistants at services or rites, especially a garment worn at the celebration of the Eucharist. [Middle English *vestement,* from Old French *vestment,* from Latin *vestīmentum,* from *vestīre,* to clothe, from *vestis,* garment. See VEST.] **—vest·ment′al** (-mĕn′tl) *adj.*

vest-pock·et (vĕst′pŏk′ĭt) *adj.* **1.** Small enough to fit into a vest pocket: *a vest-pocket book.* **2.** Very small; diminutive.

vest-pocket park *n.* A very small park set in a heavily populated urban area.

ves·try (vĕs′trē) *n., pl.* **-tries.** **1.** A room in or attached to a church where the clergy put on their vestments and where these robes and other sacred objects are stored; a sacristy. **2.** A room in a church used for meetings and classes. **3.** A committee of members elected to administer the temporal affairs of a parish. **4.** A business meeting of parishioners in a parish. [Middle English *vestrie,* probably from Anglo-Norman **vesterie,* alteration of Old French *vestiarie.* See VESTIARY.]

ves·try·man (vĕs′trē-mən) *n.* A man who is a member of a vestry.

ves·try·wo·man (vĕs′trē-wo͝om′ən) *n.* A woman who is a member of a vestry.

vest

ves·ture (vĕs′chər) *n.* **1.** Clothing; apparel. **2.** Something that covers or cloaks: *hills in a vesture of mist.* **—vesture** *tr.v.* **-tured, -tur·ing, -tures.** To cover with vesture; clothe. [Middle English, from Old French, from Vulgar Latin **vestītūra,* from Latin *vestītus,* past participle of *vestīre,* to clothe, from *vestis,* garment. See VEST.]

ve·su·vi·an (vĭ-so͞o′vē-ən) *n.* A slow-burning match formerly used for lighting cigars; a fusee. **—vesuvian** *adj.* Marked by sudden or violent outbursts: *a vesuvian temper.* [After Mount VESUVIUS.]

ve·su·vi·an·ite (vĭ-so͞o′vē-ə-nīt′) *n.* A green, brown, yellow, or blue metamorphic silicate mineral, $Ca_{10}Mg_2Al_4(SiO_4)_5(Si_2O_7)_2(OH)_4$. Also called *idocrase.*

Ve·su·vi·us (vĭ-so͞o′vē-əs), **Mount.** An active volcano, 1,281 m (4,200 ft) high, of southern Italy on the eastern shore of the Bay of Naples. A violent eruption in A.D. 79 destroyed the nearby city of Pompeii. **—Ve·su′vi·an** *adj.*

vet[1] (vĕt) *Informal. n.* A veterinarian. **—vet** *v.* **vet·ted, vet·ting, vets.** *—tr.* **1.** To subject to veterinary evaluation, examination, medication, or surgery. **2.** To subject to thorough examination or evaluation: *vet a manuscript.* *—intr.* To engage in the practice of veterinary medicine.

vet[2] (vĕt) *n.* *Informal.* A veteran.

vet. *abbr.* Veteran.

vetch (vĕch) *n.* Any of various herbs of the genus *Vicia,* having pinnately compound leaves that terminate in tendrils and small, variously colored flowers. [Middle English *vetche,* from Old North French *veche,* from Latin *vicia.* See **weik-**[2] in Appendix.]

vetch·ling (vĕch′lĭng) *n.* Any of several plants of the genus *Lathyrus,* having pinnately compound leaves, slender tendrils, and variously colored flowers.

veter. *abbr.* Veterinary.

vet·er·an (vĕt′ər-ən, vĕt′rən) *n.* *Abbr.* **vet.** **1.** A person who

vetch
Cow vetch
Vicia cracca

viaduct

is long experienced or practiced in an activity or a capacity: *a veteran of political campaigns.* **2.** A person who has served in the armed forces: *"Privilege, a token income . . . were allowed for veterans of both world wars"* (Mavis Gallant). **3.** An old soldier who has seen long service. **—veteran** *adj.* **1.** Having had long experience or practice: *a veteran actor.* **2.** Of or relating to former members of the armed forces: *veteran benefits.* [Latin *veterānus,* from *vetus, veter-,* old. See **wet-**[2] in Appendix.]

Vet·er·ans Day (vĕt′ər-ənz, vĕt′rənz) *n.* November 11, observed in the United States in honor of veterans of the armed services and in commemoration of the armistice that ended World War I in 1918. In 1954 it was renamed from Armistice Day and given the added significance of honoring veterans.

vet·er·i·nar·i·an (vĕt′ər-ə-nâr′ē-ən, vĕt′rə-) *n.* A person who practices veterinary medicine.

vet·er·i·nar·y (vĕt′ər-ə-nĕr′ē, vĕt′rə-) *adj. Abbr.* **veter.** Of or relating to veterinary medicine; concerned or connected with the medical or surgical treatment of animals, especially domestic animals. **—veterinary** *n., pl.* **-ies.** A veterinarian. [Latin *veterīnārius,* from *veterīnae,* beasts of burden, from feminine pl. of *veterīnus,* of beasts of burden. See **wet-**[2] in Appendix.]

veterinary medicine *n.* The branch of medicine that deals with the causes, diagnosis, and treatment of diseases and injuries of animals, especially domestic animals.

veterinary surgeon *n.* A veterinarian.

vet·i·ver (vĕt′ə-vər) *n.* **1.** A grass *(Vetiveria zizanioides)* of tropical India, cultivated for its aromatic roots that yield an oil used in perfumery. **2.** The roots of this plant. [French *vétiver,* from Tamil *veṭṭivēr* : *veṭṭi,* worthless + *vēru,* useless.]

vet·i·vert (vĕt′ə-vûrt′) *n.* The essential oil of the vetiver. [Alteration of VETIVER.]

Vet·lu·ga (vĕt-lo͞o′gə). A river, about 850 km (528 mi) long, of western Russia flowing generally southward to the Volga River.

ve·to (vē′tō) *n., pl.* **-toes. 1.a.** The vested power or constitutional right of one branch or department of government to refuse approval of measures proposed by another department, especially the power of a chief executive to reject a bill passed by the legislature and thus prevent or delay its enactment into law. **b.** Exercise of this right. **c.** An official document or message from a chief executive stating the reasons for rejection of a bill. **2.** An authoritative prohibition or rejection of a proposed or intended act. **—veto** *tr.v.* **-toed, -to·ing, -toes. 1.** To prevent (a legislative bill) from becoming law by exercising the power of veto. **2.** To forbid or prohibit authoritatively. [From Latin *vetō,* first person sing. present tense of *vetāre,* to forbid.] **—ve′to·er** *n.*

vex (vĕks) *tr.v.* **vexed, vex·ing, vex·es. 1.** To annoy, as with petty importunities; bother. See Synonyms at **annoy. 2.** To cause perplexity in; puzzle. **3.** To bring distress or suffering to; plague or afflict. **4.** To debate or discuss (a question, for example) at length. **5.** To toss about or shake up. [Middle English *vexen,* from Old French *vexer,* from Latin *vexāre.* See **wegh-** in Appendix.] **—vex′ed·ly** (vĕk′sĭd-lē) *adv.* **—vex′er** *n.* **—vex′ing·ly** *adv.*

vex·a·tion (vĕk-sā′shən) *n.* **1.** The act of annoying, irritating, or vexing. **2.** The quality or condition of being vexed; annoyance. **3.** A source of irritation or annoyance.

vex·a·tious (vĕk-sā′shəs) *adj.* **1.** Causing or creating vexation; annoying. **2.** Full of annoyance or distress; harassed. **3.** Intended to vex or annoy. **—vex·a′tious·ly** *adv.* **—vex·a′tious·ness** *n.*

vexed (vĕkst) *adj.* **1.** Irritated, distressed, or annoyed: *greatly vexed by their behavior; the vexed parents of an unruly teenager.* **2.** Much discussed or debated: *a vexed question.*

vex·il·la (vĕk-sĭl′ə) *n. Botany & Zoology.* Plural of **vexillum.**

vex·il·lar·y (vĕk′sə-lĕr′ē) *n., pl.* **-ies. 1.** A member of the oldest class of army veterans who served under a special standard in ancient Rome. **2.** A standard-bearer. **—vexillary** *adj.* Of or relating to a vexillum. [Latin *vexillārius,* from *vexillum,* flag. See VEXILLUM.]

vex·il·late (vĕk′sə-lĭt, -lāt′) *adj.* Having a vexillum.

vex·il·lol·o·gy (vĕk′sə-lŏl′ə-jē) *n.* The study of flags. **—vex·il′lo·log′ic** (vĕk-sĭl′ə-lŏj′ĭk), **vex·il′lo·log′i·cal** (-ĭ-kəl) *adj.* **—vex′il·lol′o·gist** *n.*

vex·il·lum (vĕk-sĭl′əm) *n., pl.* **vex·il·la** (vĕk-sĭl′ə). **1.** *Botany.* See **standard** (sense 8). **2.** *Zoology.* The weblike part of a feather; the vane. [Latin, flag, diminutive of *vēlum,* a covering.]

V.F. *abbr.* **1.** *Roman Catholic Church.* Vicar forane. **2.** Also **VF** Video frequency. **3.** Also **VF** Visual field.

VFD *abbr.* Volunteer fire department.

V format *n. Computer Science.* A method of presenting data processor output so that each record begins with an indication of its length. [V(ARIABLE).]

VFR *abbr.* Visual flight rules.

VFW also **V.F.W.** *abbr.* Veterans of Foreign Wars.

V.G. *abbr. Roman Catholic Church.* Vicar general.

vhf or **VHF** *abbr.* Very high frequency.

VI or **V.I.** *abbr.* Virgin Islands.

v.i. *abbr. Latin.* Vide infra (see below).

V.I. *abbr.* Volume indicator.

vi·a (vī′ə, vē′ə) *prep.* **1.** By way of: *went to Pittsburgh via Philadelphia.* **2.** By means of: *sent the letter via airmail.* [Latin *viā,* ablative of *via,* road. See **wegh-** in Appendix.]

vi·a·ble (vī′ə-bəl) *adj.* **1.** Capable of living, developing, or germinating under favorable conditions. **2.** Capable of living outside the uterus. Used of a fetus or newborn. **3.** Capable of success or continuing effectiveness; practicable: *a viable plan; a viable national economy.* See Synonyms at **possible.** [French, from *vie,* life, from Old French, from Latin *vīta.* See **g**[w]**ei-** in Appendix.] **—vi′a·bil′i·ty** *n.* **—vi′a·bly** *adv.*

Vi·a Do·lo·ro·sa (vī′ə dō′lə-rō′sə, vē′ə) *n.* **1.** A difficult course or experience. **2.** Jesus's route from Pilate's judgment hall to Calvary. [New Latin *via dolōrōsa* : Latin *via,* road + Late Latin *dolōrōsa,* sorrowful.]

vi·a·duct (vī′ə-dŭkt′) *n.* A series of spans or arches used to carry a road or railroad over a wide valley or over other roads or railroads. [Latin *via,* road; see VIA + (AQUE)DUCT.]

vi·al (vī′əl) *n.* A small container, usually with a closure, used especially for liquids. **—vial** *tr.v.* **-aled, -al·ing, -als** or **-alled, -al·ling, -als.** To put or keep in or as if in a vial. [Middle English *viole,* variant of *fiol.* See PHIAL.]

via me·di·a (mē′dē-ə, mĕd′ē-ə, mā′dē-ə) *n.* The middle course or way. [Latin : *via,* way + *media,* middle.]

vi·and (vī′ənd) *n.* **1.a.** An item of food. **b.** A very choice or delicious dish. **2. viands.** Provisions; victuals. [Middle English *viaunde,* from Old French *viande,* from Vulgar Latin **vīvanda,* alteration of Latin *vīvenda,* neuter pl. gerundive of Latin *vīvere,* to live. See **g**[w]**ei-** in Appendix.]

vi·at·ic (vī-ăt′ĭk) also **vi·at·i·cal** (-ĭ-kəl) *adj.* Of or relating to traveling, a road, or a way. [Latin *viāticus,* from *via,* road. See VIA.]

vi·at·i·cum (vī-ăt′ĭ-kəm, vē-) *n., pl.* **-ca** (-kə) or **-cums. 1.** *Ecclesiastical.* The Eucharist given to a dying person or one in danger of death. **2.** Supplies for a journey. [Late Latin *viāticum,* from Latin, traveling provisions, from neuter of *viāticus,* viatic. See VIATIC.]

vibe (vīb) *n. Slang.* A vibration. Often used in the plural: *good vibes; bad vibes.* [Short for VIBRATION.]

vibes (vībz) *pl.n. Music.* A vibraphone. [Shortening and alteration of VIBRAPHONE.]

vib·ist (vī′bĭst) *n. Music.* A person who plays the vibraphone.

vi·brac·u·lum (vī-brăk′yə-ləm) *n., pl.* **-la** (-lə). One of the long, whiplike, modified zooids on the surface of certain bryozoan colonies. [New Latin *vibrāculum,* from Latin *vibrāre,* to shake. See VIBRATE.] **—vi·brac′u·lar** (-lər) *adj.* **—vi·brac′u·loid′** (-loid′) *adj.*

vi·bra·harp (vī′brə-härp′) *n. Music.* See **vibraphone. —vi′bra·harp′ist** *n.*

vi·brant (vī′brənt) *adj.* **1.a.** Pulsing or throbbing with energy or activity: *the vibrant streets of a big city.* **b.** Vigorous, lively, and vital: *"a vibrant group that challenged the . . . system"* (Philip Taubman). **2.** Exhibiting or characterized by rapid, rhythmic movement back and forth or to and fro; vibrating. **3.** Produced as a result of vibration; resonant or resounding: *vibrant voices.* **4.** *Color.* Relatively high on the scale of brightness: *a vibrant hue.* **—vi′bran·cy, vi′brance** *n.* **—vi′brant·ly** *adv.*

vi·bra·phone (vī′brə-fōn′) *n. Music.* An instrument similar to a marimba but having metal bars and rotating disks in the resonators to produce a vibrato. Also called *vibraharp.* [Latin *vibrāre,* to shake; see VIBRATE + -PHONE.] **—vi′bra·phon′ist** *n.*

vi·brate (vī′brāt′) *v.* **-brat·ed, -brat·ing, -brates.** —*intr.* **1.** To move back and forth or to and fro, especially rhythmically and rapidly. See Synonyms at **swing. 2.** To feel a quiver of emotion. **3.** To shake or move with or as if with a slight quivering or trembling motion: *"Even as the film moved . . . to the more deadly fields of Vietnam, old hatreds vibrated in me"* (Loudon Wainwright). **4.** To produce a sound; resonate. **5.** To fluctuate or waver in making choices; vacillate. —*tr.* **1.** To cause to tremble or quiver. **2.** To cause to move back and forth rapidly. **3.** To produce (sound) by vibration. [Latin *vibrāre, vibrāt-.* See **weip-** in Appendix.]

vi·bra·tile (vī′brə-tl, -tīl′) *adj.* **1.** Characterized by vibration. **2.** Capable of or adapted to vibratory motion. [French, from Latin *vibrātus,* past participle of *vibrāre,* to vibrate. See VIBRATE.] **—vi′bra·til′i·ty** (-tĭl′ĭ-tē) *n.*

vi·bra·tion (vī-brā′shən) *n.* **1.a.** The act of vibrating. **b.** The condition of being vibrated. **2.** *Physics.* **a.** A rapid linear motion of a particle or of an elastic solid about an equilibrium position. **b.** A periodic process. **3.** A single complete vibrating motion; a quiver. **4.** *Slang.* A distinctive emotional aura or atmosphere regarded as being instinctively sensed or experienced. Often used in the plural: *"Miami gives off the same vibrations, the same portent of disaster, but with a difference"* (James Atlas). **—vi·bra′tion·al** *adj.*

vi·bra·tive (vī′brə-tĭv) *adj.* Variant of **vibratory.**

vi·bra·to (və-brä′tō, vī-) *n., pl.* **-tos.** *Music.* A tremulous or pulsating effect produced in an instrumental or vocal tone by barely perceptible minute and rapid variations in pitch. [Italian, from Late Latin *vibrātus,* a quivering, from Latin, past participle of *vibrāre,* to vibrate. See VIBRATE.]

vi·bra·tor (vī′brā′tər) *n.* **1.** Something that vibrates. **2.** An electrically operated device used for massage. **3.** An electrical device consisting basically of a vibrating conductor interrupting a current.

vi·bra·to·ry (vī′brə-tôr′ē, -tōr′ē) also **vi·bra·tive** (-tĭv) *adj.* **1.** Of, characterized by, or consisting of vibration. **2.** Causing vibration. **3.** Vibrating or capable of vibration.

vib·ri·o (vĭb′rē-ō′) *n., pl.* **-os.** Any of various short, motile, S-shaped or comma-shaped bacteria of the genus *Vibrio,* especially *V. cholerae,* which causes cholera. [New Latin *Vibriō,* genus name, from Latin *vibrāre,* to vibrate (from their vibratory motion). See VIBRATE.] **—vib′ri·oid′** (-oid′) *adj.*

vib·ri·o·sis (vĭb′rē-ō′sĭs) *n., pl.* **-ses** (-sēz). **1.** Infection with the bacterium *Vibrio parahaemolyticus,* often the result of eating undercooked seafood from contaminated waters. **2.** A venereal infection in cattle and sheep caused by the bacterium *Vibrio fetus,* often producing infertility or spontaneous abortion.

vi·bris·sa (vī-brĭs′ə, və-) *n., pl.* **-bris·sae** (-brĭs′ē). **1.** Any of the long, stiff hairs that project from the snout or brow of most mammals, as the whiskers of a cat. **2.** One of several long modified feathers that grow along the gape of the mouth of insect-eating birds. [From Late Latin *vibrissae,* nostril hairs, from *vibrāre,* to vibrate. See VIBRATE.]

vi·bron·ic (vī-brŏn′ĭk) *adj.* Of or relating to changes in molecular energy states associated with the vibrational energy of atoms. [VIBR(ATION) + (ELECTR)ONIC.]

vi·bur·num (vī-bûr′nəm) *n.* Any of various shrubs or trees of the genus *Viburnum,* having opposite leaves, showy terminal clusters of small white or pink flowers, and red or black drupes. [Latin *vīburnum,* a kind of shrub.]

vic. *abbr.* **1.** Vicar. **2.** Vicinity.

vic·ar (vĭk′ər) *n. Abbr.* **vic. 1.a.** The priest of a parish in the Church of England who receives a stipend or salary but does not receive the tithes of a parish. **b.** A cleric in charge of a chapel in the Episcopal Church of the United States. **c.** A cleric acting in the place of a rector or bishop in the Anglican Communion generally. **2.** *Roman Catholic Church.* A priest who acts for or represents another, often higher-ranking member of the clergy. [Middle English, from Old French *vicaire,* from Latin *vicārius,* vicarious, a substitute, from *vicis,* genitive of **vix,* change. See **weik-**[2] in Appendix.] **—vic′ar·ship′** *n.*

vic·ar·age (vĭk′ər-ĭj) *n.* **1.** The residence of a vicar. **2.** The benefice of a vicar. **3.** The duties or office of a vicar; a vicariate.

vicar apostolic *n., pl.* **vicars apostolic.** *Abbr.* **V.A.** *Roman Catholic Church.* **1.** A titular bishop who administers a region that is not yet a diocese as a representative of the Holy See. **2.** A titular bishop appointed to administer to a vacant see in which the succession of bishops has been interrupted. **3.** A bishop or an archbishop formerly delegated by the pope to act in his stead in a particular region.

vic·ar·ate (vĭk′ər-ĭt, -ə-rāt′) *n.* A vicariate.

vicar fo·rane (fô-rān′, fō-) *n., pl.* **vicars forane.** *Abbr.* **V.F.** *Roman Catholic Church.* A priest who by a bishop's appointment exercises limited jurisdiction over the clergy in a district of a diocese. [VICAR + Late Latin *forāneus,* living away, foreign; see FOREIGN.]

vicar general *n., pl.* **vicars general.** *Abbr.* **V.G. 1.** *Roman Catholic Church.* **a.** A priest acting as deputy to a bishop to assist him in the administration of his diocese. **b.** The head of a religious order. **2.** An ecclesiastical official in the Church of England, usually a layperson, who assists an archbishop or a bishop in administrative and judicial duties.

vi·car·i·al (vī-kâr′ē-əl, -kăr′-, vĭ-) *adj.* **1.** Of or relating to a vicar. **2.** Acting as or having the position of a vicar. **3.** Serving in the place of someone or something else.

vi·car·i·ance (vī-kâr′ē-əns, -kăr′-, vĭ-) *n. Biology.* The separation or division of a group of organisms by a geographic barrier, such as a mountain or a body of water, resulting in differentiation of the original group into new varieties or species. [From VICARIANT, from Latin *vicārius,* vicarious. See VICARIOUS.] **—vi·car′i·ant** *adj. & n.*

vi·car·i·ate (vī-kâr′ē-ĭt, -āt′, -kăr′-, vĭ-) *n.* **1.** The office or authority of a vicar. **2.** The district under a vicar's jurisdiction. [Medieval Latin *vicāriātus,* from Latin *vicārius,* a substitute. See VICAR.]

vi·car·i·ous (vī-kâr′ē-əs, -kăr′-, vĭ-) *adj.* **1.** Felt or undergone as if one were taking part in the experience or feelings of another: *read about mountain climbing and experienced vicarious thrills.* **2.** Endured or done by one person substituting for another: *vicarious punishment.* **3.a.** Acting or serving in place of someone or something else; substituted. **b.** Committed or entrusted to another, as powers or authority; delegated. **4.** *Physiology.* Occurring in or performed by a part of the body not normally associated with a certain function. [From Latin *vicārius.* See VICAR.] **—vi·car′i·ous·ly** *adv.* **—vi·car′i·ous·ness** *n.*

Vic·ar of Christ (vĭk′ər) *n. Roman Catholic Church.* The pope.

vice[1] (vīs) *n.* **1.a.** An evil, degrading, or immoral practice or habit. **b.** A serious moral failing. **c.** Wicked or evil conduct or habits; corruption. **2.** Sexual immorality, especially prostitution. **3.a.** A slight personal failing; a foible: *the vice of untidiness.* See Synonyms at **fault. b.** A flaw or an imperfection; a defect. **4.** A physical defect or weakness. **5.** An undesirable habit, such as crib-biting, in a domestic animal. **6. Vice. a.** A character representing generalized or particular vice in English morality plays. **b.** A jester or buffoon. [Middle English, from Old French, from Latin *vitium.*]

vice[2] (vīs) *n. & v.* Variant of **vise.**

vi·ce[3] (vī′sē, -sə) *prep.* In place of; replacing. [Latin, ablative of **vix,* change. See VICE–.]

vice– *pref.* One who acts in the place of another; deputy: *vice-chairman.* [Middle English *vice-,* from Old French, from Late Latin, from Latin *vice,* ablative of **vix,* change. See **weik-**[2] in Appendix.]

vice admiral (vīs) *n. Abbr.* **V. Adm., VADM. 1.** A commissioned rank in the U.S. Navy or Coast Guard that is above rear admiral and below admiral. **2.** One who holds this rank.

vice-ad·mir·al·ty (vīs-ăd′mər-əl-tē) *n., pl.* **-ties.** The office, rank, or command of a vice admiral.

vice chancellor (vīs) *n. Abbr.* **V.C. 1.** A deputy or an assistant chancellor in a university. **2.** A deputy to or a substitute for a head of state or an official bearing the title chancellor. **3.** *Law.* A judge in equity courts ranking below a chancellor. **—vice-chan′cel·lor·ship′** (vīs-chăn′sə-lər-shĭp′, -chăns′lər-) *n.*

vice consul (vīs) *n. Abbr.* **V.C.** A consular officer who is subordinate to and a deputy of a consul or consul general. **—vice-con′su·lar** (vīs-kŏn′sə-lər) *adj.* **—vice-con′su·late** (-sə-lĭt) *n.* **—vice-con′sul·ship′** (-səl-shĭp′) *n.*

vice·ge·ren·cy (vīs-jîr′ən-sē) *n., pl.* **-cies. 1.** The position, function, or authority of a vicegerent. **2.** A district under a vicegerent's jurisdiction.

vice·ge·rent (vīs-jîr′ənt) *n.* A person appointed by a ruler or head of state to act as an administrative deputy. [Medieval Latin *vicegerēns, vicegerent-* : Latin *vice,* ablative of **vix,* change; see VICE[3] + Latin *gerēns,* governing; see GERENT.] **—vice·ge′ral** (-jîr′əl) *adj.*

vic·e·nar·y (vĭs′ə-nĕr′ē) *adj.* **1.** Consisting of or relating to 20. **2.** Of, relating to, or being a notation system based on 20. [Latin *vīcēnārius,* from *vīcēnī,* twenty each, from *vīgintī,* twenty. See **wīkm̥tī** in Appendix.]

vi·cen·ni·al (vī-sĕn′ē-əl) *adj.* **1.** Happening once every 20 years. **2.** Existing or lasting for 20 years. [From Late Latin *vīcennium,* period of twenty years : Latin *vīciēns,* twenty times (from *vīgintī,* twenty; see VICENARY) + Latin *annus,* year; see **at-** in Appendix.]

Vi·cen·te Ló·pez (və-sĕn′tē lō′pĕz′, vē-sĕn′tĕ lô′pĕs). A city of east-central Argentina, an industrial suburb of Buenos Aires. Population, 289,815.

Vi·cen·za (vĭ-chĕn′sə, vē-chĕn′dzä). A city of northeast Italy west of Venice. Founded by Ligurians c. first century B.C., it became a free city in A.D. 1164 and passed to Austria in 1797. Vicenza joined the kingdom of Italy in 1866. Population, 113,931.

vice pres·i·dent or **vice-pres·i·dent** (vīs′prĕz′ĭ-dənt, -dĕnt′) *n. Abbr.* **VP, V.P. 1.** An officer ranking next below a president, usually empowered to assume the president's duties under conditions such as absence, illness, or death. **2.** A deputy to a president, especially in a corporation, in charge of a specific department or location: *vice president of sales.* **—vice-pres′i·den·cy** (vīs-prĕz′ĭ-dən-sē, -dĕn′-) *n.* **—vice-pres′i·den′tial** (-dĕn′shəl) *adj.*

vice·re·gal (vīs-rē′gəl) *adj.* Of or relating to a viceroy. **—vice·re′gal·ly** *adv.*

vice regent (vīs) *n.* One who acts as a regent's deputy. **—vice-re′gen·cy** (vīs-rē′jən-sē) *n.*

vice·reine (vīs′rān′) *n.* **1.** The wife of a viceroy. **2.** A woman who is the governor of a country, province, or colony, ruling as the representative of a sovereign. [French : *vice-,* vice (from Old French; see VICE[3]) + *reine,* queen (from Latin *rēgīna,* feminine of *rēx, rēg-,* king; see **reg-** in Appendix).]

vice·roy (vīs′roi′) *n.* **1.** A man who is the governor of a country, province, or colony, ruling as the representative of a sovereign. **2.** An orange and black North American butterfly *(Limenitis archippus),* resembling but somewhat smaller than the monarch. [French : *vice-,* vice; see VICEREINE + *roi,* king (from Latin *rēx, rēg-;* see **reg-** in Appendix).]

vice·roy·al·ty (vīs′roi′əl-tē, vīs-roi′-) *n., pl.* **-ties. 1.** The office, authority, or term of service of a viceroy. **2.** A district or province governed by a viceroy.

vice·roy·ship (vīs′roi-shĭp′) *n.* Viceroyalty.

vice squad (vīs) *n.* A police division charged with enforcement of laws dealing with various forms of vice, such as gambling and prostitution.

vi·ce ver·sa (vī′sə vûr′sə, vīs′) *adv. Abbr.* **v.v.** With the order or meaning reversed; conversely. [Latin *vice versā* : *vice,* ablative of **vix,* position + *versā,* feminine ablative of *versus,* past participle of *vertere,* to turn.]

WORD HISTORY: *Vice versa* is perhaps one of a handful of borrowings of foreign phrases that have worked their way so tightly into normal speech that one never thinks about their foreign origins or earlier meanings. *Versa* might be thought to be related to *reverse,* and so it is, both *versa* and *–verse* in *reverse* going back to the Latin verb *vertere,* "to turn." *Versa* actually goes back formally to *versus,* the past participle of *vertere,* while going back semanticallly to the sense "to reverse, change to the contrary." *Vice* is the ablative form of the noun **vix,* used in the sense "a reciprocal relation." The whole phrase then literally means "with the reciprocal relation having been reversed," or "with reversal of

ă pat	oi boy
ā pay	ou out
âr care	ŏŏ took
ä father	ōō boot
ĕ pet	ŭ cut
ē be	ûr urge
ĭ pit	th thin
ī pie	*th* this
îr pier	hw which
ŏ pot	zh vision
ō toe	ə about, item
ô paw	♦ regionalism

Stress marks: **′** (primary); ′ (secondary), as in **dictionary** (dĭk′shə-nĕr′ē)

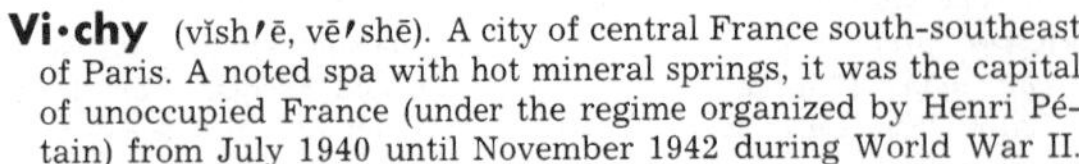
the regular order, conversely." The phrase is first recorded as an English usage in 1601.

victoria

Vi·chy (vĭsh′ē, vē′shē). A city of central France south-southeast of Paris. A noted spa with hot mineral springs, it was the capital of unoccupied France (under the regime organized by Henri Pétain) from July 1940 until November 1942 during World War II. Population, 30,527.

vi·chys·soise (vĭsh′ē-swäz′, vē′shē-) *n.* A thick, creamy potato soup flavored with leeks and onions, usually served cold. [French, from feminine of *vichyssois,* of Vichy.]

Vichy water *n.* **1.** A naturally effervescent mineral water from the springs at Vichy. **2.** A sparkling mineral water resembling this effervescent beverage.

vic·i·nage (vĭs′ə-nĭj) *n.* **1.a.** A limited region around a particular area; a vicinity. **b.** A number of places situated near each other and considered as a group. **2.** The residents of a particular neighborhood. **3.** The state of living in a neighborhood; proximity. [Middle English *vesinage,* from Old French, from *vesin,* neighboring, from Latin *vīcīnus.* See VICINITY.]

vic·i·nal (vĭs′ə-nəl) *adj.* **1.** Of, belonging to, or restricted to a limited area or neighborhood; local. **2.** Relating to or being a local road. **3.** *Mineralogy.* Approximating, resembling, or taking the place of a fundamental crystalline form or face. **4.** *Chemistry.* Of or relating to the consecutive positions of substituted elements or radicals on a benzene ring. [Latin *vīcīnālis,* from *vīcīnus,* neighboring. See VICINITY.]

vi·cin·i·ty (vĭ-sĭn′ĭ-tē) *n., pl.* **-ties.** *Abbr.* **vic. 1.** The state of being near in space or relationship; proximity: *two restaurants in close vicinity.* **2.** A nearby, surrounding, or adjoining region; a neighborhood. **3.** An approximate degree or amount: *houses priced in the vicinity of $200,000.* [Latin *vīcīnitās,* from *vīcīnus,* neighboring, from *vīcus,* neighborhood. See **weik-**[1] in Appendix.]

vi·cious (vĭsh′əs) *adj.* **1.** Having the nature of vice; evil, immoral, or depraved. **2.** Given to vice, immorality, or depravity. **3.** Spiteful; malicious: *vicious gossip.* **4.** Disposed to or characterized by violent or destructive behavior. See Synonyms at **cruel. 5.** Marked by an aggressive disposition; savage. Used chiefly of animals. **6.** Faulty, imperfect, or otherwise impaired by defects: *a forced, vicious style of prose.* **7.** Impure; foul. [Middle English, from Old French *vicieus,* from Latin *vitiōsus,* from *vitium,* vice.] **—vi′cious·ly** *adv.* **—vi′cious·ness** *n.*

Victoria[1]

vicious circle *n.* **1.** A situation in which the apparent solution of one problem in a chain of circumstances creates a new problem and increases the difficulty of solving the original problem. **2.** A condition in which a disorder or disease gives rise to another that subsequently affects the first. **3.** *Logic.* A fallacy in reasoning in which the premise is used to prove the conclusion, and the conclusion used to prove the premise. [Translation of New Latin *circulus vitiōsus,* circular argument : Medieval Latin *circulus,* circular argument + Latin *vitiōsus,* flawed, faulty.]

vi·cis·si·tude (vĭ-sĭs′ĭ-to͞od′, -tyo͞od′) *n.* **1.a.** A change or variation. **b.** The quality of being changeable; mutability. **2.** Often **vicissitudes.** One of the sudden or unexpected changes or shifts often encountered in one's life, activities, or surroundings. See Synonyms at **difficulty.** [Latin *vicissitūdō,* from *vicissim,* in turn, probably from *vicēs,* pl. of **vix,* change. See **weik-**[2] in Appendix.]

vi·cis·si·tu·di·nar·y (vĭ-sĭs′ĭ-to͞od′n-ĕr′ē, -tyo͞od′-) also **vi·cis·si·tu·di·nous** (-to͞od′n-əs, -tyo͞od′-) *adj.* Characterized by, full of, or subject to vicissitudes.

Vicks·burg (vĭks′bûrg′). A city of western Mississippi on bluffs above the Mississippi River west of Jackson. During the Civil War it was besieged from 1862 to 1863 and finally captured by troops led by Ulysses S. Grant on July 4, 1863. Population, 25,434.

Victoria Falls

vic·tim (vĭk′tĭm) *n.* **1.** One who is harmed or killed by another: *a victim of a mugging.* **2.** A living creature slain and offered as a sacrifice during a religious rite. **3.** One who is harmed by or made to suffer from an act, circumstance, agency, or condition: *victims of war.* **4.** A person who suffers injury, loss, or death as a result of a voluntary undertaking: *You are a victim of your own scheming.* **5.** A person who is tricked, swindled, or taken advantage of: *the victim of a cruel hoax.* [Latin *victima.*] **—vic′tim·hood′** (-ho͝od′) *n.*

vic·tim·ize (vĭk′tə-mīz′) *tr.v.* **-ized, -iz·ing, -iz·es. 1.** To subject to swindle or fraud. **2.** To make a victim of. **—vic′tim·i·za′tion** (-tə-mĭ-zā′shən) *n.* **—vic′tim·iz′er** *n.*

vic·tim·less crime (vĭk′tĭm-lĭs) *n.* An illegal act that is felt to have no direct or identifiable victim.

vic·tim·ol·o·gy (vĭk′tə-mŏl′ə-jē) *n.* The study of crime victims. **—vic′tim·ol′o·gist** *n.*

vic·tor (vĭk′tər) *n.* One who defeats an adversary; the winner in a fight, battle, contest, or struggle. [Middle English, from Old French *victeur,* from Latin *victor, victōr-,* from *victus,* past participle of *vincere,* to conquer. See **weik-**[3] in Appendix.]

Vic·tor Em·man·u·el I (vĭk′tər ĭ-măn′yo͞o-əl). 1759–1824. Sardinian king (1802–1821) whose kingdom was restored after the fall of Napoleon (1815). An uprising forced his abdication in 1821.

Victor Emmanuel II. 1820–1878. Italian king (1861–1878). He completed the unification of Italy by acquiring Venice (1866) and Rome (1870).

Victor Emmanuel III. 1869–1947. Italian king (1900–1946). He appointed Benito Mussolini prime minister in 1922 and did little to stop Italy's decline into a fascist state. He abdicated in 1946, and the monarchy was formally abolished in 1947.

vic·to·ri·a (vĭk-tôr′ē-ə, -tōr′-) *n.* **1.** A low, light four-wheeled carriage for two with a folding top and an elevated driver's seat in front. **2.** A touring car with a folding top usually covering only the rear seat. [After VICTORIA[1].]

Vic·to·ri·a[1] (vĭk-tôr′ē-ə, -tōr′-). 1819–1901. Queen of Great Britain and Ireland (1837–1901) and empress of India (1876–1901). Her sense of duty and strict moral code had great influence on 19th-century British society.

Vic·to·ri·a[2] (vĭk-tôr′ē-ə, -tōr′-). **1.** The capital of British Columbia, Canada, on southeast Vancouver Island at the eastern end of the Strait of Juan de Fuca. Founded in 1843 as a Hudson's Bay Company outpost, it became provincial capital in the late 1860's. Population, 64,379. **2.** The capital of Hong Kong, on the northwest coast of Hong Kong Island. It has extensive shipping facilities and is the seat of the University of Hong Kong (established 1911). Population, 1,183,621. **3.** The capital of Seychelles, on the northeast coast of Mahé Island on the Indian Ocean. Population, 23,000. **4.** A city of southeast Texas southeast of San Antonio. It is connected with the Intracoastal Waterway by a barge canal. Population, 50,695.

Victoria, Lake. Also **Victoria Ny·an·za** (nī-ăn′zə, nyän′-). A lake of east-central Africa bordered by Uganda, Kenya, and Tanzania. It was first sighted in 1858 by the British explorer John Speke, who was searching for the source of the Nile River.

Victoria Cross *n. Abbr.* **V.C.** A bronze Maltese cross, Britain's highest military award for conspicuous valor. [After VICTORIA[1].]

Victoria Day *n.* The last Monday before May 25, observed in Canada in commemoration of the birthday of Queen Victoria.

Victoria Falls. A waterfall, 108.3 m (355 ft) high, of south-central Africa in the Zambezi River between southwest Zambia and northwest Zimbabwe. The falls were discovered by David Livingstone in November 1855.

Victoria Island. An island of north-central Northwest Territories, Canada, in the Arctic Archipelago east of Banks Island. It was discovered in the late 1830's and explored by John Rae in 1851.

Victoria Land. A region of Antarctica bounded by Ross Sea and Wilkes Land. The mountainous area was discovered by Sir James Clark Ross during his 1839–1843 expedition.

Vic·to·ri·an (vĭk-tôr′ē-ən, -tōr′-) *adj.* **1.** Of, relating to, or belonging to the period of the reign of Queen Victoria: *a Victorian novel.* **2.** Relating to or displaying the standards or ideals of morality regarded as characteristic of the time of Queen Victoria: *Victorian manners.* **3.** Being in the highly ornamented, massive style of architecture, decor, and furnishings popular in 19th-century England. **—Victorian** *n.* A person belonging to or exhibiting characteristics typical of the Victorian period.

Vic·to·ri·an·a (vĭk-tôr′ē-ăn′ə, -ä′nə, -tōr′-) *n.* Material or a collection of materials of, relating to, or characteristic of the Victorian era.

Victoria Nile (nīl). A section of the Nile River, about 418 km (260 mi) long, between Lake Victoria and Lake Albert in central Uganda.

Vic·to·ri·an·ism (vĭk-tôr′ē-ə-nĭz′əm, -tōr′-) *n.* **1.** The state or quality of being Victorian, as in attitude, style, or taste. **2.** Something exhibiting Victorian characteristics.

Vic·to·ri·an·ize (vĭk-tôr′ē-ə-nīz′, -tōr′-) *tr.v.* **-ized, -iz·ing, -iz·es.** To make Victorian, as in character or style. **—Vic·to′ri·an·i·za′tion** (-ə-nĭ-zā′shən) *n.*

Victoria Ny·an·za (nī-ăn′zə, nyän′-). See Lake **Victoria.**

Vic·to·ri·a·ville (vĭk-tôr′ē-ə-vĭl′, -tōr′-). A town of southern Quebec, Canada, southeast of Trois Rivières. It is a manufacturing and processing center. Population, 21,838.

vic·to·ri·ous (vĭk-tôr′ē-əs, -tōr′-) *adj.* **1.** Being the winner in a contest or struggle: *the victorious army.* **2.** Characteristic of or expressing a sense of victory or fulfillment: *a victorious cheer.* **—vic·to′ri·ous·ly** *adv.* **—vic·to′ri·ous·ness** *n.*

vic·to·ry (vĭk′tə-rē) *n., pl.* **-ries.** *Abbr.* **V 1.** Defeat of an enemy or opponent. **2.** Success in a struggle against difficulties or an obstacle. **3.** The state of having triumphed. [Middle English, from Old French *victorie,* from Latin *victōria,* from *victor, victōr-,* victor. See VICTOR.]

SYNONYMS: *victory, conquest, triumph.* These nouns denote the fact of winning or the state of having won in a war, struggle, or competition. *Victory,* the most general term, refers especially to the final defeat of an enemy or opponent: *"Victory at all costs, victory in spite of all terror, victory however long and hard the road may be; for without victory there is no survival"* (Winston S. Churchill). *Conquest* connotes subduing, subjugating, or achieving mastery or control over someone or something: *"Conquest of illiteracy comes first"* (John Kenneth Galbraith). *Triumph* denotes a victory or success that is especially noteworthy because it is decisive, significant, or spectacular: *"If* [a man] *has a talent and learns somehow to use the whole of it, he has gloriously succeeded, and won a satisfaction and a triumph few men ever know"* (Thomas Wolfe).

vict·ual (vĭt′l) *n.* **1.** Food fit for human consumption. **2. victuals.** Food supplies; provisions. **—victual** *v.* **-ualed, -ual·ing,**

-uals or **-ualled, -ual·ling, -uals.** —*tr.* To provide with food. —*intr.* **1.** To lay in food supplies. **2.** To eat. [Alteration (influenced by Late Latin *vīctuālia,* provisions) of Middle English *vitaille,* from Old French, from Late Latin *vīctuālia,* provisions, from Latin, neuter pl. of *vīctuālis,* of nourishment, from Latin *vīctus,* nourishment, from past participle of *vīvere,* to live. See **gʷei-** in Appendix.]

vict·ual·er also **vict·ual·ler** (vĭt′l-ər) *n.* **1.** A supplier of victuals; a sutler. **2.** *Chiefly British.* An innkeeper. **3.** *Nautical.* A supply ship.

vi·cu·ña also **vi·cu·na** (vī-ko͞on′yə, -ko͞o′nə, -kyo͞o′nə, vĭ-) *n.* **1.** A llamalike ruminant mammal *(Vicugna vicugna)* of the central Andes, having fine, silky fleece. **2. a.** The fleece of this mammal. **b.** Fabric made from the fleece of this mammal. [Spanish, from Quechua *wikuña.*]

Vi·dal (vĭ-däl′), **Gore.** Born 1925. American writer noted for his cynical humor and his numerous accounts of society in decline. His works include the novel *Myra Breckinridge* (1968) and the play *The Best Man* (1960).

Vi·dal·ia onion (vĭ-dāl′yə) *n.* A large, white, sweet, delicately flavored onion, having a thin yellowish outer skin and poor storage qualities. [After *Vidalia,* a city of east-central Georgia.]

vi·de (vī′dē, vē′dā′, wē′-) *v. Abbr.* **v.** See. Used to direct a reader's attention. [Latin, sing. imperative of *vidēre,* to see. See **weid-** in Appendix.]

vi·del·i·cet (vĭ-dĕl′ĭ-sĕt′, vī-, wĭ-dā′lĭ-kĕt′) *adv. Abbr.* **viz.** That is; namely. Used to introduce examples, lists, or items. [Latin *vidēlicet,* contraction of *vidēre licet,* it is permitted to see : *vidēre,* to see; see VIDE + *licet,* it is permitted, third person sing. present tense of *licēre,* to be permitted.]

vid·e·o (vĭd′ē-ō′) *adj.* **1.** Of or relating to television, especially televised images. **2.** Of or relating to videotaped productions or videotape equipment and technology. —**video** *n., pl.* **-os. 1.** The visual portion of a televised broadcast. **2.** Television: *a star of stage, screen, and video.* **3.** A videocassette or videotape, especially one containing a recording of a movie, music performance, or television program, for playback on a television set. [From Latin *videō,* first person sing. present tense of *vidēre,* to see. See VIDE.]

video art *n.* See **artist's video.**

video camera *n.* A portable, hand-held camera resembling a movie camera but recording on videocassettes for playback on a television set.

vid·e·o·cas·sette (vĭd′ē-ō-kə-sĕt′, -kă-) *n.* A cassette containing blank or prerecorded videotape.

videocassette recorder *n.* A VCR.

vid·e·o·con·fer·ence (vĭd′ē-ō-kŏn′fər-əns, -frəns) *n.* A teleconference conducted via closed-circuit television. —**vid′e·o·con′fer·enc·ing** *n.*

vid·e·o·disk also **vid·e·o·disc** (vĭd′ē-ō-dĭsk′) *n.* A recording on disk of sounds and images, as of a movie, that can be played back on a television receiver. [Originally a German trademark.]

video display terminal *n.* A VDT.

video game *n.* An electronic or computerized game played by manipulating images on a display screen.

vid·e·o·gen·ic (vĭd′ē-ō-jĕn′ĭk) *adj.* Appearing to advantage on television; telegenic. [VIDEO + (PHOTO)GENIC.]

vid·e·og·ra·phy (vĭd′ē-ŏg′rə-fē) *n.* The art or practice of making one's own video shows or movies using a video camera. —**vid′e·og′ra·pher** *n.*

video jockey *n. Abbr.* **VJ.** One who announces, plays, and provides commentary on videotaped programs, especially music videos, as on television or at a discotheque.

vid·e·o·phile (vĭd′ē-ə-fīl′) *n.* One with an avid interest in watching television or videos or in making video recordings.

vid·e·o·phone (vĭd′ē-ō-fōn′) *n.* A telephone equipped for both audio and video transmission.

vid·e·o·tape (vĭd′ē-ō-tāp′) *n.* **1.** A relatively wide magnetic tape used to record visual images and associated sound for subsequent playback or broadcasting. **2.** A recording made on such a tape. —**videotape** *tr.v.* **-taped, -tap·ing, -tapes.** To make a videotape recording of.

videotape recorder *n. Abbr.* **VTR.** A device for making a videotape recording.

video terminal *n.* A VDT.

vid·e·o·tex (vĭd′ē-ō-tĕks′) also **vid·e·o·text** (-tĕkst′) *n.* A system in which computer-stored information is transmitted over television cables or telephone lines and displayed on home television screens or computer terminals, used for various services such as electronic banking, electronic mail, and home shopping. [VIDEO + TEX(T).]

video vérité *n.* A television filming or videotaping technique in which the subjects are portrayed with frank, unbiased realism, as for a documentary program. [VIDEO + (CINÉMA) VÉRITÉ.]

vi·dette (vĭ-dĕt′) *n.* Variant of **vedette.**

vid·i·con (vĭd′ĭ-kŏn′) *n.* A small television camera tube that forms a charge-density image on a photoconductive surface for subsequent electron-beam scanning. [VID(EO) + ICON(OSCOPE).]

vie (vī) *v.* **vied, vy·ing** (vī′ĭng), **vies.** —*intr.* To strive for victory or superiority; contend. See Synonyms at **rival.** —*tr.* **1.** *Archaic.* To offer in competition; match. **2.** *Obsolete.* To wager or bet. [Short for Middle English *envien,* from Old French *envier,* from Latin *invītāre,* to invite, give occasion for. See INVITE.]

Vi·en·na (vē-ĕn′ə). The capital and largest city of Austria, in the northeast part of the country on the Danube River. Originally a Celtic settlement, it became the official residence of the house of Hapsburg in 1278 and a leading cultural center in the 18th century, particularly under the reign (1740–1780) of Maria Theresa. Vienna was designated the capital of Austria in 1918. Population, 1,524,510.

Vienna sausage *n.* A small sausage resembling a frankfurter, often served as an hors d'oeuvre. [After VIENNA, Austria.]

Vienne (vyĕn). A river, about 349 km (217 mi) long, of southwest-central France flowing generally northwest to the Loire River.

Vi·en·nese (vē′ə-nēz′, -nēs′) *adj.* Relating to or characteristic of Vienna, Austria. —**Viennese** *n., pl.* **Viennese. 1.** A native or inhabitant of Vienna. **2.** The variety of German spoken in Vienna.

Vien·tiane (vyĕn-tyän′). The capital and largest city of Laos, in the north-central part of the country on the Mekong River and the Thailand border. It became the capital of the French protectorate of Laos in 1899 and later the capital of independent Laos. Population, 210,000.

Vier·sen (fîr′zən). A city of west-central Germany west of Düsseldorf. It is a processing and manufacturing center with a textile industry. Population, 78,784.

Viet. *abbr.* **1.** Vietnam. **2.** Vietnamese.

Viet·cong also **Viet Cong** (vē-ĕt′kŏng′, -kông′, vē′ĭt-, vyĕt′-) —*n., pl.* **Vietcong** also **Viet Cong.** *Abbr.* **VC, V.C.** A Vietnamese belonging to or supporting the National Liberation Front of the former country South Vietnam. —*adj.* Of or relating to the Vietcong. [Vietnamese, short for *Viet Nam Cong San,* Vietnamese Communist.]

Viet·minh also **Viet Minh** (vē-ĕt′mĭn′, vyĕt′-, vē′ĭt-) —*n., pl.* **Vietminh** also **Viet Minh.** A member of the Vietnamese army that defeated the Japanese and the French between 1941 and 1954. —*adj.* Of or relating to the Vietminh. [Vietnamese, short for *Viet Nam Doc Lap Dong Minh Hoi,* Vietnam Federation of Independence.]

Viet·nam (vē-ĕt′näm′, -năm′, vē′ĭt-, vyĕt′-). *Abbr.* **Viet.** A country of southeast Asia in eastern Indochina on the South China Sea. Ruled by China from 221 B.C. to A.D. 939 and from 1407 to 1428, it was occupied by the French in the 19th century. After the fall of the French garrison at Dien Bien Phu in 1954, it was partitioned into **North Vietnam** and **South Vietnam.** The country was reunited in July 1976 after the end of the Vietnam War. Hanoi is the capital and Ho Chi Minh City the largest city. Population, 52,741,766.

Viet·nam·ese (vē-ĕt′nə-mēz′, -mēs′, vē′ĭt-, vyĕt′-) *adj.* Of or relating to Vietnam or its people, language, or culture. —**Vietnamese** *n., pl.* **Vietnamese.** *Abbr.* **Viet. 1.** A native or inhabitant of Vietnam. **2.** The language of the largest ethnic group in Vietnam and the official language of the nation.

Viet·nam·i·za·tion (vē-ĕt′nə-mĭ-zā′shən, vyĕt′-, vē′ĭt-) *n.* During the Vietnam War, the U.S. program of turning over to the South Vietnamese government responsibility for waging the conflict, in order to implement withdrawal of U.S. military personnel.

Viet·nam·ize (vē-ĕt′nə-mīz′, vyĕt′-, vē′ĭt-) *tr.v.* **-ized, -iz·ing, -iz·es.** To turn over responsibility for (military operations, for example) to the South Vietnamese: *"a policy of Vietnamizing the actual fighting"* (C.L. Sulzberger).

Vietnam War *n.* A protracted military conflict (1954–1975) between the Communist forces of North Vietnam supported by China and the Soviet Union and the non-Communist forces of South Vietnam supported by the United States.

view (vyo͞o) *n.* **1.** An examination or inspection: *used binoculars to get a better view.* **2.** A systematic survey; coverage: *a view of Romantic poetry.* **3.** An individual and personal perception, judgment, or interpretation; an opinion: *In his view, aid to the rebels should be suspended.* See Synonyms at **opinion. 4.** Field of vision: *The aircraft has disappeared from view.* **5.** A scene or vista: *the view from the tower.* **6.** A picture of a landscape: *a view of Paris, done in oils.* **7.** A way of showing or seeing something, as from a particular position or angle: *a side view of the house.* **8.** Something kept in sight as an aim or intention: *"The pitch of the roof had been calculated with a view to the heavy seasonal rains"* (Caroline Alexander). **9.** Expectation; chance: *The measure has no view of success.* —**view** *tr.v.* **viewed, view·ing, views. 1.** To look at; watch: *view an exhibit of etchings.* **2. a.** To examine or inspect: *viewed the house they were thinking of buying.* **b.** To survey or study mentally; consider. **3.** To think of in a particular way; regard: *doesn't view herself as a success; viewed their efforts unfavorably.* See Synonyms at **see**[1]. —***idioms.* in view of.** Taking into account; in consideration of. **on view.** Placed so as to be seen; exhibited. [Middle English *vewe,* from Anglo-Norman, from feminine past participle of *veoir,* to see, from Latin *vidēre.* See **weid-** in Appendix.] —**view′a·ble** *adj.*

view·da·ta (vyo͞o′dā′tə, -dăt′ə, dä′tə) *n.* An interactive videotex system in which information can be retrieved or transmitted over television cables or telephone lines.

view·er (vyo͞o′ər) *n.* **1.** One that views, especially an onlooker or spectator. **2.** Any of various optical devices used to facilitate the viewing of photographic transparencies by illuminating or

vicuña
Vicugna vicugna

video game

Vietnam

ă pat	oi boy
ā pay	ou out
âr care	o͝o took
ä father	o͞o boot
ĕ pet	ŭ cut
ē be	ûr urge
ĭ pit	th thin
ī pie	*th* this
îr pier	hw which
ŏ pot	zh vision
ō toe	ə about, item
ô paw	♦ regionalism

Stress marks: ′ (primary); ′ (secondary), as in **dictionary** (dĭk′shə-nĕr′ē)

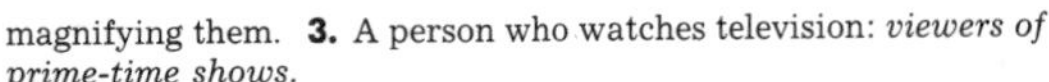

magnifying them. **3.** A person who watches television: *viewers of prime-time shows.*

view·er·ship (vyo͞oʹər-shĭpʹ) *n.* A television audience, especially of a particular kind or extent: *a largely male viewership.*

view·find·er (vyo͞oʹfīnʹdər) *n.* A device on a camera that indicates, either optically or electronically, what will appear in the field of view of the lens.

view hal·loo (vyo͞oʹ hə-lo͞oʹ) *n.* A strident call given during a fox hunt to indicate that the fox has been seen breaking cover.

♦**view·ing** (vyo͞oʹĭng) *n.* **1.** The act of seeing, watching, or examining carefully. **2.** The act or an instance of watching a movie or television. **3.** *Pennsylvania.* See **wake**[1] (sense 2). —**viewing** *adj.* Engaged in watching a movie or television: *a poll of the viewing audience.*

view·less (vyo͞oʹlĭs) *adj.* **1.** Providing no view. **2.** Not having or expressing opinions or views. —**viewʹless·ly** *adv.*

view·point (vyo͞oʹpointʹ) *n.* A position from which something is observed or considered; a point of view.

view·y (vyo͞oʹē) *adj.* **-i·er, -i·est. 1.** Exhibiting extravagant or visionary opinions. **2.** Conspicuous or striking; showy.

Élisabeth Vigée-Lebrun
Detail of a c. 1781 oil on canvas self-portrait (25½″ × 21¼″)

Vi·gée-Le·brun (vē-zhāʹlə-brœɴʹ), **(Marie Louise) Élisabeth.** 1755–1842. French painter noted for her portraits, especially those of Marie Antoinette and the royal family.

vi·ges·i·mal (vī-jĕsʹə-məl) *adj.* **1.** Twentieth. **2.** Proceeding or occurring in intervals of 20. **3.** Based on or relating to 20. [From Latin *vīgēsimus,* variant of *vīcēsimus,* twentieth, from *vīgintī,* twenty. See **wīkm̥tī** in Appendix.]

vig·il (vĭjʹəl) *n.* **1.a.** A watch kept during normal sleeping hours. **b.** The act or a period of observing; surveillance. **2.** The eve of a religious festival as observed by devotional watching. **3.** Often **vigils.** Ritual devotions observed on the eve of a holy day. [Middle English *vigile,* a devotional watching, from Old French, from Latin *vigilia,* wakefulness, watch, from *vigil,* awake. See **weg-** in Appendix.]

vig·i·lance (vĭjʹə-ləns) *n.* Alert watchfulness.

vigilance committee *n.* A volunteer group of citizens that without authority assumes powers such as pursuing and punishing those suspected of being criminals or offenders.

vig·i·lant (vĭjʹə-lənt) *adj.* On the alert; watchful. See Synonyms at **aware.** [Middle English, from Old French, from Latin *vigilāns, vigilant-,* present participle of *vigilāre,* to be watchful. See VIGILANTE.] —**vigʹi·lant·ly** *adv.*

vig·i·lan·te (vĭjʹə-lănʹtē) *n.* **1.** One who takes or advocates the taking of law enforcement into one's own hands. **2.** A member of a vigilance committee. [Spanish, watchman, vigilante, from Latin *vigilāns, vigilant-,* present participle of *vigilāre,* to be watchful, from *vigil,* watchful. See **weg-** in Appendix.] —**vigʹi·lanʹtism** (-lănʹtĭz-əm), **vigʹi·lanʹte·ism** (-tē-ĭzʹəm) *n.*

vigil light *n.* **1.** A small candle kept burning in the chancel of Christian churches to symbolize the presence of the Holy Sacrament; an altar light. **2.** A candle lighted by a worshiper for a special devotional purpose. **3.** A light or candle kept burning at a shrine or before an icon.

Pancho Villa

vi·gnette (vĭn-yĕtʹ) *n.* **1.** A decorative design placed at the beginning or end of a book or chapter of a book or along the border of a page. **2.** An unbordered picture, often a portrait, that shades off into the surrounding color at the edges. **3.a.** A short, usually descriptive literary sketch. **b.** A short scene or incident, as from a movie. —**vignette** *tr.v.* **-gnet·ted, -gnet·ting, -gnettes. 1.** To soften the edges of (a picture) in vignette style. **2.** To describe in a brief way. [French, from Old French, diminutive of *vigne,* vine (from the use of vine tendrils in decorative borders). See VINE.]

vi·gnet·ter (vĭn-yĕtʹər) *n.* **1.** A device used to print photographs and illustrations with borders that fade gradually into the background. **2.** Also **vi·gnet·tist** (-ĭst). One who makes or specializes in the making of vignettes.

Vi·gno·la (vēn-yōʹlə, vē-nyôʹlä), **Giacomo da.** Originally Giacomo da Barozzi or **Barozio.** 1507–1573. Italian architect best known for his influential treatise *Rule of the Five Orders of Architecture* (1562).

Vi·gny (vēn-yēʹ), Comte **Alfred Victor de.** 1797–1863. French writer. A leader of the romantic school, he wrote several volumes of poetry, including *Les Destinées* (1864).

Vi·go (vēʹgō, bēʹgô). A city of northwest Spain on the **Bay of Vigo,** an inlet of the Atlantic Ocean. Vigo is a naval base and major shipping and fishing center. Population, 277,460.

vig·or (vĭgʹər) *n.* **1.** Physical or mental strength, energy, or force. **2.** The capacity for natural growth and survival, as of plants or animals. **3.** Strong feeling; enthusiasm or intensity. **4.** Legal effectiveness or validity. [Middle English, from Old French, from Latin *vigor, vigōr-,* from *vigēre,* to be lively. See **weg-** in Appendix.]

SYNONYMS: *vigor, dash, punch, verve, vim, vitality.* The central meaning shared by these nouns is "a quality of spirited force or energy": *intellectual vigor; played the piano with dash; an editorial with real punch; painted with verve; arguing with his usual vim; a decreased mental vitality.*

vig·o·rish (vĭgʹər-ĭsh) *n. Slang.* **1.a.** A charge taken on bets, as by a bookie or gambling establishment. **b.** The rate or amount of such a charge. **2.** Interest, especially excessive interest, paid to a moneylender. [Yiddish slang, from Russian *vyigrysh,* winnings : *vy-,* out; see **ud-** in Appendix + *-igrysh,* as in *proigrysh,* a loss (from *igrat',* to play).]

vig·o·ro·so (vĭgʹə-rōʹsō, -zō, vēʹgə-) *adv. & adj. Music.* With emphasis and spirit. Used chiefly as a direction. [Italian, from Medieval Latin *vigōrōsus,* from Latin *vigor, vigōr-,* vigor. See VIGOR.]

vig·or·ous (vĭgʹər-əs) *adj.* **1.** Strong, energetic, and active in mind or body; robust. See Synonyms at **healthy. 2.** Marked by or done with force and energy. See Synonyms at **active.** —**vigʹor·ous·ly** *adv.* —**vigʹor·ous·ness** *n.*

vig·our (vĭgʹər) *n. Chiefly British.* Variant of **vigor.**

Vi·ja·ya·wa·da (vĭjʹə-yə-wäʹdə, vēʹjə-). Formerly **Bez·wa·da** (bĕz-wäʹdə). A city of southeast India east-southeast of Hyderabad. It is a trade center and transportation hub. Population, 454,577.

Vi·king (vīʹkĭng) *n.* **1.** One of a seafaring Scandinavian people who plundered the coasts of northern and western Europe from the eighth through the tenth century. **2.** A Scandinavian. [Old Norse *vīkingr,* perhaps from *vīk,* creek, inlet.]

vil. *abbr.* Village.

Vi·la (vēʹlə). The capital of Vanuatu, in the southwest Pacific Ocean. It was a Japanese base during World War II. Population, 13,067.

vi·la·yet (vēʹlä-yĕtʹ) *n.* An administrative division of Turkey. [Turkish *vilāyet,* from Arabic *wilāyah,* province, from *waliya,* to administer.]

vile (vīl) *adj.* **vil·er, vil·est. 1.** Loathsome; disgusting: *vile language.* **2.** Unpleasant or objectionable: *vile weather.* See Synonyms at **offensive. 3.a.** Contemptibly low in worth or account; second-rate. **b.** Of mean or low condition. **4.** Miserably poor and degrading; wretched: *a vile existence.* **5.** Morally depraved; ignoble or wicked: *a vile conspiracy.* [Middle English, from Old French, from Latin *vīlis.*] —**vileʹly** *adv.* —**vileʹness** *n.*

vil·i·fy (vĭlʹə-fīʹ) *tr.v.* **-fied** (-fīdʹ), **-fy·ing, -fies** (-fīzʹ). To make vicious and defamatory statements about. See Synonyms at **malign.** [Middle English *vilifien,* from Late Latin *vīlificāre,* to hold cheap : Latin *vīlis,* worthless + Latin *-ficāre,* -fy.] —**vilʹi·fi·caʹtion** (-fĭ-kāʹshən) *n.* —**vilʹi·fiʹer** *n.*

vil·i·pend (vĭlʹə-pĕndʹ) *tr.v.* **-pend·ed, -pend·ing, -pends. 1.** To view or treat with contempt; despise. **2.** To speak ill of; disparage. [Middle English *vilipenden,* from Old French *vilipender,* from Latin *vīlipendere* : *vīlis,* worthless + *pendere,* to consider, weigh; see **(s)pen-** in Appendix.]

vil·la (vĭlʹə) *n.* **1.** The often large, luxurious country house of a well-to-do person. **2.** A country estate with a substantial house. **3.** *Chiefly British.* A house in a middle-class suburb. [Italian, from Latin *villa.* See **weik-**[1] in Appendix.]

Vil·la (vēʹə, bēʹyä), **Francisco.** Known as "Pancho." 1877?–1923. Mexican revolutionary leader who ran unsuccessfully for the presidency after the Mexican Revolution (1910) and later attempted to oust (1914–1915) President Venustiano Carranza.

vil·lage (vĭlʹĭj) *n. Abbr.* **v., V., vil. 1.** A small group of dwellings in a rural area, usually ranking in size between a hamlet and a town. **2.** In some U.S. states, an incorporated community smaller in population than a town. **3.** The inhabitants of a village; villagers. **4.** A group of bird or animal habitations suggesting a village. —*attributive.* Often used to modify another noun: *a village square; the village green.* [Middle English, from Old French, from Latin *villāticum,* farmstead, from neuter of *villāticus,* of a villa or farmstead, from Latin *villa,* country house, farm. See **weik-**[1] in Appendix.]

vil·lag·er (vĭlʹə-jər) *n.* An inhabitant of a village.

Vil·la·her·mo·sa (vēʹə-ĕr-mōʹsə, bēʹyä-). A city of southeast Mexico east of the Isthmus of Tehuantepec. It was founded in the 16th century near the site of an Olmec settlement. Population, 158,216.

vil·lain (vĭlʹən) *n.* **1.** A wicked or evil person; a scoundrel. **2.** A dramatic or fictional character who is typically at odds with the hero. **3.** (*also* vĭlʹānʹ, vĭ-lānʹ). Variant of **villein. 4.** Something said to be the cause of particular trouble or an evil: *poverty, the villain in the increase of crime.* **5.** *Obsolete.* A peasant regarded as vile and brutish. [Middle English *vilein,* feudal serf, person of coarse feelings, from Old French, from Vulgar Latin **villānus,* feudal serf, from Latin *villa,* country house. See **weik-**[1] in Appendix.]

vil·lain·age (vĭlʹə-nĭj) *n.* Variant of **villeinage.**

vil·lain·ess (vĭlʹə-nĭs) *n.* A woman who is a villain.

vil·lain·ous (vĭlʹə-nəs) *adj.* **1.a.** Appropriate to a villain, as in wickedness or depravity: *a villainous plot.* **b.** Being or manifesting the nature of a villain: *a villainous band of thieves.* **2.** Highly undesirable or offensive; obnoxious. —**vilʹlain·ous·ly** *adv.* —**vilʹlain·ous·ness** *n.*

vil·lain·y (vĭlʹə-nē) *n., pl.* **-ies. 1.** Baseness of mind or character. **2.** Viciousness of conduct or action. **3.** A treacherous or vicious act.

Vil·la-Lo·bos (vēʹlə-lōʹbōs, vēʹlä-lôʹbo͝os), **Heitor.** 1887–1959. Brazilian composer whose works, including symphonies, operas, and songs, were influenced by Brazilian folk traditions.

vil·la·nelle (vĭlʹə-nĕlʹ) *n.* A 19-line poem of fixed form consisting of five tercets and a final quatrain on two rhymes, with the first and third lines of the first tercet repeated alternately as a refrain closing the succeeding stanzas and joined as the final couplet of the quatrain. [French, from Italian *villanella,* from feminine of *villanello,* rustic, from *villano,* peasant, from Vulgar Latin **vīllānus,* from Latin *vīlla,* country house. See **weik-**[1] in Appendix.]

Vil·la Park (vĭl′ə). A village of northeast Illinois, a residential suburb of Chicago. Population, 23,185.

Vil·lard (vĭ-lär′, -lärd′), **Henry.** 1835–1900. German-born American journalist and railroad magnate. He was president of the Northern Pacific Railroad (1881–1884) and formed (1890) the company that later became General Electric. His son **Oswald Garrison Villard** (1872–1949), a journalist and editor, was president of the *New York Evening Post* (1900–1918) and owner of *The Nation* (1918–1935).

vil·lat·ic (vĭ-lăt′ĭk) *adj.* Rustic; rural. [Latin *vīllāticus,* of a farmstead. See VILLAGE.]

Vil·la·vi·cen·ci·o (vē′ə-vĭ-sĕn′sē-ō′, bē′yä-vē-sĕn′syô). A city of central Colombia southeast of Bogotá. It is a trade and processing center in an agricultural region. Population, 159,808.

vil·lein also **vil·lain** (vĭl′ən, -ān′, vĭ-lān′) *n.* One of a class of feudal serfs who held the legal status of freemen in their dealings with all people except their lord. [Middle English *vilein.* See VILLAIN.]

vil·lein·age also **vil·lain·age** (vĭl′ə-nĭj) *n.* **1.** The legal status or condition of a villein. **2.** The legal tenure by which a villein held land.

Vil·lel·la (və-lĕl′ə), **Edward.** Born 1936. American ballet dancer. He joined the New York City Ballet in 1957 and won acclaim for his roles in *Prodigal Son* (1965) and *Rubies* (1967).

Ville·ur·banne (vē′lər-băn′, vēl-ür-bän′). A city of southeast France, an industrial suburb of Lyons. Population, 115,960.

vil·li (vĭl′ī) *n. Biology & Botany.* Plural of **villus.**

Vil·liers (vĭl′ərz, -yərz), **George.** See **Buckingham.**

vil·li·form (vĭl′ə-fôrm′) *adj.* Having the form of villi.

Vil·ling·en-Schwen·ning·en (fĭl′ĭng-ən-shvĕn′ĭng-ən). A city of southwest Germany south-southwest of Stuttgart. Founded in 999, it is a manufacturing center. Population, 76,600.

Vil·lon (vē-yôɴ′), **François.** 1431–1463? French poet. His satirical lyrics are contained in *Le Petit Testament* (c. 1456) and *Le Testament* (c. 1461).

vil·lose (vĭl′ōs′) *adj. Biology & Botany.* Variant of **villous.**

vil·los·i·ty (vĭ-lŏs′ĭ-tē) *n., pl.* **-ties. 1.** The condition of being villous. **2.** A villous formation, surface, or coating. **3.** A villus.

vil·lous (vĭl′əs) also **vil·lose** (-ōs′) *adj.* **1.** *Biology.* Of, relating to, resembling, or covered with villi. **2.** *Botany.* Covered with soft, shaggy unmatted hairs. [From Latin *villōsus,* hairy, from *villus,* shaggy hair.] **—vil′lous·ly** *adv.*

vil·lus (vĭl′əs) *n., pl.* **vil·li** (vĭl′ī). **1.** *Biology.* A minute projection arising from a mucous membrane, especially: **a.** One of the numerous vascular projections of the small intestine. **b.** One of the fingerlike projections of the chorion that contribute to the formation of the placenta in mammals. **2.** *Botany.* A fine, hairlike epidermal outgrowth. [Latin, shaggy hair.]

Vil·ni·us (vĭl′nē-əs) or **Vil·na** (-nə). The capital of Lithuania, in the southeast part of the country east-southeast of Kaunas. Founded in the 10th century, it was frequently devastated by plagues, fires, and invasions from the 15th to the 18th century. Vilnius passed to Russia in 1795. Population, 544,000.

Vil·yu·i (vĭl-yo͞o′ē). A river of eastern Russia flowing about 2,446 km (1,520 mi) eastward to the Lena River.

vim (vĭm) *n.* Ebullient vitality and energy. See Synonyms at **vigor.** [Latin, accusative of *vīs.* See **weiə-** in Appendix.]

Vim·i·nal (vĭm′ə-nəl). One of the seven hills of ancient Rome. The baths of Diocletian were built at the foot of the hill. **—Vim′i·nal** *adj.*

VIN *abbr.* Vehicle identification number.

vin– *pref.* Variant of **vini–.**

vi·na also **vee·na** (vē′nə) *n. Music.* A stringed instrument of India that has a long, fretted fingerboard with resonating gourds at each end. [Hindi *vīṇā,* from Sanskrit.]

vi·na·ceous (vī-nā′shəs, vĭ-) *adj.* Having the color of red wine. [From Latin *vīnāceus,* refuse from wine pressing, from *vīnum,* wine.]

Vi·ña del Mar (vēn′yə dĕl mär′, bē′nyä *th*ĕl). A city of central Chile, a resort and residential suburb of Valparaiso on the Pacific Ocean. Population, 244,899.

vin·ai·grette (vĭn′ĭ-grĕt′) *n.* **1.** A small decorative bottle or container with a perforated top, used for holding an aromatic preparation such as smelling salts. **2.** A cold sauce or dressing made of vinegar or lemon juice and oil flavored with finely chopped onions, herbs, and other seasonings. [French, from Old French, diminutive of *vinaigre,* vinegar. See VINEGAR.]

vi·nasse (vĭ-năs′, vĭ-) *n.* The residue left in a still after the process of distillation. [French, from Provençal *vinassa,* from Latin *vīnācea,* from feminine of *vīnāceus.* See VINACEOUS.]

vin·blas·tine (vĭn-blăs′tēn′) *n.* An alkaloid, $C_{46}H_{58}N_4O_9$, obtained from the Madagascar periwinkle and used as an antineoplastic drug. [New Latin *Vinca,* periwinkle genus (short for Latin *pervinca,* periwinkle; see PERIWINKLE[2]) + English *leukoblast,* a developing leukocyte (LEUKO– + –BLAST) + –INE[2].]

Vin·cennes. 1. (văɴ-sĕn′). A city of north-central France east of Paris. Its 14th-century castle was once a royal residence and later a state prison. Population, 42,870. **2.** (vĭn-sĕnz′). A city of southwest Indiana on the Wabash River south of Terre Haute. The oldest city in the state, it was founded as a mission and fur-trading post by the French in the early 18th century. Population, 20,857.

Vin·cent de Paul (vĭn′sənt də pôl), Saint. 1581–1660. French ecclesiastic who founded the Congregation of the Mission (1625) and the Daughters of Charity (1633).

Vin·cent's angina (vĭn′sənts) *n.* See **trench mouth.** [After Jean Hyacinthe *Vincent* (1862–1950), French physician.]

Vincent's infection *n.* See **trench mouth.** [After Jean Hyacinthe *Vincent* (1862–1950), French physician.]

vin·ci·ble (vĭn′sə-bəl) *adj.* Capable of being overcome or defeated: *a vincible army.* [Latin *vincibilis,* from *vincere,* to conquer. See **weik-**[3] in Appendix.] **—vin′ci·bil′i·ty** *n.* **—vin′ci·bly** *adv.*

vin·cris·tine (vĭn-krĭs′tēn′) *n.* An alkaloid, $C_{46}H_{56}N_4O_{10}$, obtained from the Madagascar periwinkle, used as an antineoplastic drug especially in the treatment of acute leukemia. [New Latin *Vinca,* periwinkle genus; see VINBLASTINE + Latin *crista,* crest; see CREST + –INE[2].]

vin·cu·lum (vĭng′kyə-ləm) *n., pl.* **-lums** or **-la** (-lə). **1.** *Mathematics.* A bar drawn over two or more algebraic terms to indicate that they are to be treated as a single term. **2.** *Anatomy.* A ligament that limits the movement of an organ or a part. **3.** A bond or tie. [Latin, bond, tie, from *vincīre,* to tie.]

Vin·dhya Range (vĭn′dyə). A chain of hills in central India extending east-northeast for about 965 km (600 mi) and rising to approximately 915 m (3,000 ft).

vin·di·ca·ble (vĭn′dĭ-kə-bəl) *adj.* Possible to vindicate: *a vindicable claim; vindicable objections.*

vin·di·cate (vĭn′dĭ-kāt′) *tr.v.* **-cat·ed, -cat·ing, -cates. 1.** To clear of accusation, blame, suspicion, or doubt with supporting arguments or proof: *"Our society permits people to sue for libel so that they may vindicate their reputations"* (Irving R. Kaufman). **2.** To provide justification or support for: *vindicate one's claim.* **3.** To justify or prove the worth of, especially in light of later developments. **4.** To defend, maintain, or insist on the recognition of (one's rights, for example). **5.** To exact revenge for; avenge. [Latin *vindicāre, vindicāt-,* from *vindex, vindic-,* surety, avenger. See **deik-** in Appendix.] **—vin′di·ca′tor** *n.*

vin·di·ca·tion (vĭn′dĭ-kā′shən) *n.* **1.** The act of vindicating or condition of being vindicated. **2.** The defense, such as evidence or argument, that serves to justify a claim or deed.

vin·di·ca·to·ry (vĭn′dĭ-kə-tôr′ē, -tōr′ē) *adj.* **1.** Affording vindication; justifying. **2.** Exacting retribution; punitive.

vin·dic·tive (vĭn-dĭk′tĭv) *adj.* **1.** Disposed to seek revenge; revengeful. **2.** Marked by or resulting from a desire to hurt; spiteful. [From Latin *vindicta,* vengeance, from *vindex, vindic-,* surety, avenger. See VINDICATE.] **—vin·dic′tive·ly** *adv.* **—vin·dic′tive·ness** *n.*

SYNONYMS: *vindictive, vengeful, revengeful.* These adjectives mean desiring or proceeding from a desire for revenge. *Vindictive* suggests gratuitous or unmotivated rancor and a disposition to retaliate for wrongs, real or imagined: *"He seemed to take a vindictive pleasure in punishing the least shortcomings"* (Mark Twain). *"Like many men whose self-love is wounded . . . he felt vindictive"* (George Meredith). *Vengeful* and *revengeful* imply the impulse to inflict or the infliction of suffering or punishment as retribution for evil or an injury: *"the vengeful massacre of Toulon"* (Joseph Conrad). *"I had a keen, revengeful sense of the insult"* (Nathaniel Hawthorne).

vine (vīn) *n.* **1.a.** A weak-stemmed plant that derives its support from climbing, twining, or creeping along a surface. **b.** The stem of such a plant. **2.a.** A grapevine. **b.** Grapevines considered as a group: *products of the vine.* **—vine** *intr.v.* **vined, vin·ing, vines.** To form or develop like a vine. [Middle English, from Old French *vigne,* from Latin *vīnea,* from feminine of *vīneus,* of wine, from *vīnum,* wine.]

vine·dress·er (vīn′drĕs′ər) *n.* One that cultivates and prunes grapevines.

vin·e·gar (vĭn′ĭ-gər) *n.* **1.** An impure dilute solution of acetic acid obtained by fermentation beyond the alcohol stage and used as a condiment and preservative. **2.** Sourness of speech or mood; ill temper. **3.** Liveliness and enthusiasm; vim. [Middle English *vinegre,* from Old French *vinaigre* : *vin,* wine (from Latin *vīnum*) + *aigre,* sour (from Vulgar Latin **acrus,* from Latin *ācer;* see **ak-** in Appendix).]

vinegar eel *n.* A minute nematode worm *(Anguillula aceti)* that feeds on the organisms causing fermentation in vinegar. Also called *vinegar worm.*

vinegar fly *n.* See **fruit fly** (sense 1).

vin·e·gar·ish (vĭn′ĭ-gər-ĭsh, -grĭsh) *adj.* Variant of **vinegary.**

vin·e·gar·roon (vĭn′ĭ-gə-ro͞on′) also **vin·e·ga·rone** (-rōn′) *n.* A large whip scorpion *(Mastigoproctus giganteus)* of the southern United States and Mexico that emits a strong odor of vinegar when disturbed. [American Spanish *vinagrón,* from Spanish *vinagre,* vinegar, from Old Spanish, from Old French *vinaigre.* See VINEGAR.]

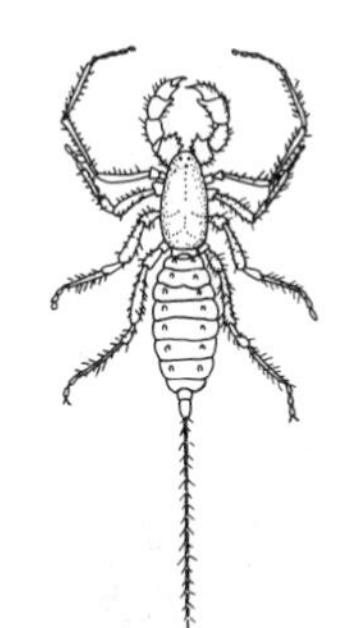

vinegarroon
Mastigoproctus giganteus

ă pat	oi boy
ā pay	ou out
âr care	o͝o took
ä father	o͞o boot
ĕ pet	ŭ cut
ē be	ûr urge
ĭ pit	th thin
ī pie	*th* this
îr pier	hw which
ŏ pot	zh vision
ō toe	ə about, item
ô paw	♦ regionalism

Stress marks: ′ (primary); ′ (secondary), as in **dictionary** (dĭk′shə-nĕr′ē)

viola da gamba
18th-century Swedish

vinegar worm *n.* See **vinegar eel.**

vin·e·gar·y (vĭn′ĭ-gə-rē, -grē) also **vin·e·gar·ish** (-gər-ĭsh, -grĭsh) *adj.* **1.** Having the taste, smell, or nature of vinegar. **2.** Unpleasant and irascible.

Vine·land (vīn′lənd). A city of southern New Jersey south-southwest of Camden. It is a trade, manufacturing, and processing center. Population, 53,753.

vin·er·y (vī′nə-rē) *n., pl.* **-ies.** An area or a greenhouse for growing vines.

vine·yard (vĭn′yərd) *n.* **1.** Ground planted with cultivated grapevines. **2.** A sphere of spiritual, mental, or physical endeavor.

vine·yard·ist (vĭn′yər-dĭst) *n.* One who owns or manages a vineyard.

vingt-et-un (văN′tā-oeN′) *n. Games.* See **blackjack** (sense 3). [French, twenty-one : *vingt,* twenty + *et,* and + *un,* one.]

vini– or **vino–** or **vin–** *pref.* Wine: *vinic.* [From Latin *vīni-,* from *vīnum.*]

vi·nic (vī′nĭk) *adj.* Of, contained in, or derived from wine.

vin·i·cul·ture (vĭn′ĭ-kŭl′chər, vī′nĭ-) *n.* Viticulture. **—vin′i·cul′tur·al** *adj.* **—vin′i·cul′tur·ist** *n.*

vin·i·fy (vĭn′ə-fī′) *tr.v.* **-fied** (-fīd′), **-fy·ing, -fies** (-fīz′). To convert (the juice of grapes, for example) into wine by the process of fermentation. **—vin′i·fi·ca′tion** (-fĭ-kā′shən) *n.*

Vin·land (vĭn′lənd). An unidentified coastal region of northeast North America visited by Norse voyagers as early as c. 1000. The region, variously located from Labrador to New Jersey, was named for the grapes growing plentifully in the area.

violet
Marsh blue violet
Viola cucullata

Vin·ni·tsa (vĭn′ĭ-tsə, vyē′nĭ-). A city of western Ukraine southwest of Kiev. Founded in the 14th century, it passed to Russia in 1793 and is now a processing center and railroad junction. Population, 367,000.

vi·no (vē′nō) *n., pl.* **-nos.** Wine. [Italian and Spanish, both from Latin *vīnum.*]

vino– *pref.* Variant of **vini–.**

Vi·no·gra·doff (vĭn′ə-grăd′ôf′, vē′nə-grä′dəf), Sir **Paul Gavrilovich.** 1854–1925. Russian-born British jurist and historian. His works include *Growth of the Manor* (1905) and *Historical Jurisprudence* (1920–1922).

vi·nom·e·ter (vĭ-nŏm′ĭ-tər, vī-) *n.* A hydrometer used to determine the percentage of alcohol in a wine.

vin or·di·naire (văN ôr-dē-nâr′) *n., pl.* **vins or·di·naires** (văNz′ ôr-dē-nâr′). An inexpensive red table wine. [French : *vin,* wine + *ordinaire,* ordinary.]

vi·nos·i·ty (vī-nŏs′ĭ-tē) *n., pl.* **-ties.** The distinctive body, color, and taste of wine. [Late Latin *vīnōsitās,* from Latin *vīnōsus,* vinous. See VINOUS.]

vi·nous (vī′nəs) *adj.* **1.** Of, relating to, or made with wine. **2.** Affected or caused by the consumption of wine. **3.** Having the color of wine. [Latin *vīnōsus,* from *vīnum,* wine.] **—vi′nous·ly** *adv.*

violin

Vin·son (vĭn′sən), **Carl.** 1883–1981. American legislator. He was elected as a U.S. representative from Georgia in 1914, a post he held for a record 60 years.

Vinson, Frederick Moore. 1890–1953. American jurist who served as the chief justice of the U.S. Supreme Court (1946–1953).

Vinson Mas·sif (mă-sēf′). A peak, 5,142.3 m (16,860 ft) high, in the Ellsworth Mountains of western Antarctica. It is the highest elevation in the range.

vin·tage (vĭn′tĭj) *n.* **1.** The yield of wine or grapes from a vineyard or district during one season. **2.** Wine, usually of high quality, identified as to year and vineyard or district of origin. **3.** The year or place in which a wine is bottled. **4. a.** The harvesting of a grape crop. **b.** The initial stages of winemaking. **5.** *Informal.* **a.** A group or collection of people or things sharing certain characteristics. **b.** A year or period of origin: *a car of 1942 vintage.* **c.** Length of existence; age. **—vintage** *adj.* **1.** Of or relating to a vintage. **2.** Characterized by excellence, maturity, and enduring appeal; classic. **3.** Old or outmoded. **4. a.** Of the best: *played songs that were vintage Cole Porter.* **b.** Of the most distinctive: *"It was vintage Nixon: the fear of confrontation; the indirect approach; the acute insight"* (Henry A. Kissinger). [Middle English, from Anglo-Norman, alteration (influenced by *viniter,* vintner) of Old French *vendange,* from Latin *vīndēmia* : *vīnum,* grapes + *dēmere,* to take off (*dē,* de- + *emere,* to obtain; see **em-** in Appendix).]

viper

vin·tag·er (vĭn′tə-jər) *n.* A producer or harvester of wine grapes.

vintage year *n.* **1.** The year in which a vintage wine is produced. **2.** A year of outstanding achievement or success.

vint·ner (vĭnt′nər) *n.* **1.** A wine merchant. **2.** One who makes wine. [Middle English *vineter,* from Old French *vinetier,* from Medieval Latin *vīnētārius,* from Latin *vīnētum,* vineyard, from *vīnum,* wine.]

vin·y (vī′nē) *adj.* **-i·er, -i·est. 1.** Of, relating to, or having the nature of vines. **2.** Overgrown with or abounding in vines.

vi·nyl (vī′nəl) *n.* **1.** The univalent chemical radical CH_2CH, derived from ethylene. **2.** Any of various compounds containing the vinyl radical, typically highly reactive, easily polymerized, and used as basic materials for plastics. **3.** Any of various typically tough, flexible, shiny plastics, often used for coverings and clothing. [VIN(I)– + –YL.] **—vi·nyl′ic** (-nĭl′ĭk) *adj.*

vinyl chloride *n.* A flammable gas, CH_2:CHCl, used as a monomer for polyvinyl chloride.

vi·ol (vī′əl) *n. Music.* **1.** Any of a family of stringed instruments, chiefly of the 16th and 17th centuries, having a fretted fingerboard, usually six strings, and a flat back and played with a curved bow. **2.** See **viola da gamba** (sense 1). [Alteration of Middle English *viel,* from Old French *viole, vielle,* from Old Provençal *viola.* See VIOLA[1].]

vi·o·la[1] (vē-ō′lə) *n. Music.* **1.** A stringed instrument of the violin family, slightly larger than a violin, tuned a fifth lower, and having a deeper tone. **2.** An organ stop usually of eight-foot or four-foot pitch yielding stringlike tones. [Italian, from Old Provençal, probably of imitative origin.] **—vi·o′list** *n.*

vi·o·la[2] (vī-ō′lə, vē-, vī′ə-lə) *n.* A plant of the genus *Viola,* which includes the violets and pansies, especially a variety having flowers resembling violets in size and shape and pansies in coloration. [Middle English, from Latin.]

vi·o·la·ble (vī′ə-lə-bəl) *adj.* That can be violated: *a violable rule; a violable contract.* **—vi′o·la·bil′i·ty, vi′o·la·ble·ness** *n.* **—vi′o·la·bly** *adv.*

vi·o·la da brac·cio (vē-ō′lə də brä′chō) *n., pl.* **viola da braccios.** *Music.* A stringed instrument of the viol family with approximately the range of the viola. [Italian : *viola,* viol + *da,* of, for + *braccio,* arm.]

viola da gam·ba (gäm′bə, găm′-) *n. Music.* **1.** A stringed instrument, the bass of the viol family, with approximately the range of the cello. Also called *bass viol, gamba, viol.* **2.** An organ stop of eight-foot pitch yielding tones similar to those of the viola da gamba. [Italian : *viola,* viol + *da,* of, for + *gamba,* leg.]

viola d'a·mo·re (dä-môr′ā, -mōr′ā, -môr′ē, -mōr′ē) *n. Music.* A stringed instrument, the tenor of the viol family, having six or seven stopped strings and an equal number of sympathetic strings that produce a characteristic silvery tone. [Italian : *viola,* viol + *da,* of + *amore,* love.]

vi·o·late (vī′ə-lāt′) *tr.v.* **-lat·ed, -lat·ing, -lates. 1.** To break or disregard (a law or promise, for example). **2.** To assault (a person) sexually. **3.** To do harm to (property or qualities considered sacred); desecrate or defile. **4.** To disturb rudely or improperly; interrupt: *violated our privacy.* [Middle English *violaten,* from Latin *violāre, violāt-,* from *vīs, vi-,* force. See **weiə-** in Appendix.] **—vi′o·la′tive** *adj.* **—vi′o·la′tor** *n.*

vi·o·la·tion (vī′ə-lā′shən) *n.* The act or an instance of violating or the condition of being violated. See Synonyms at **breach.**

vi·o·lence (vī′ə-ləns) *n.* **1.** Physical force exerted for the purpose of violating, damaging, or abusing: *crimes of violence.* **2.** The act or an instance of violent action or behavior. **3.** Intensity or severity, as in natural phenomena; untamed force: *the violence of a hurricane.* **4.** Abusive or unjust exercise of power. **5.** Abuse or injury to meaning, content, or intent: *do violence to a text.* **6.** Vehemence of feeling or expression; fervor.

vi·o·lent (vī′ə-lənt) *adj.* **1.** Marked by, acting with, or resulting from great force: *a violent attack.* **2.** Having or showing great emotional force: *violent dislike.* **3.** Marked by intensity; extreme: *violent pain; a violent squall.* See Synonyms at **intense. 4.** Caused by unexpected force or injury rather than by natural causes: *a violent death.* **5.** Tending to distort or injure meaning, phrasing, or intent. [Middle English, from Old French, from Latin *violentus,* from *vīs, vi-,* force. See **weiə-** in Appendix.] **—vi′o·lent·ly** *adv.*

violent storm *n. Meteorology.* See **storm** (sense 2).

vi·o·let (vī′ə-lĭt) *n.* **1. a.** Any of various low-growing herbs of the genus *Viola,* having short-spurred, irregular flowers that are characteristically purplish-blue but sometimes yellow or white. **b.** Any of several similar plants, such as the African violet. **2.** *Color.* The hue of the short-wave end of the visible spectrum, evoked in the human observer by radiant energy with wavelengths of approximately 380 to 420 nanometers; any of a group of colors, reddish-blue in hue, that may vary in lightness and saturation. [Middle English, from Old French *violete,* diminutive of *viole,* from Latin *viola.*]

vi·o·lin (vī′ə-lĭn′) *n. Abbr.* **v.** *Music.* A stringed instrument played with a bow, having four strings tuned at intervals of a fifth, an unfretted fingerboard, and a shallower body than the viol and capable of great flexibility in range, tone, and dynamics. [Italian *violino,* diminutive of *viola,* viola. See VIOLA[1].] **—vi′o·lin′ist** *n.* **—vi′o·lin·is′tic** *adj.*

vi·o·lin·mak·er (vī′ə-lĭn′mā′kər) *n.* One who designs and crafts violins, especially as a profession. **—vi′o·lin′mak′ing** *n.*

Viol·let-le-Duc (vē′ə-lā′lə-do͞ok′, -dyo͞ok′, vyô-lĕ′lə-dük′), **Eugène Emmanuel.** 1814–1879. French architect. A leader of the Gothic revival in France, he designed the restoration of the city of Carcassonne and supervised the refurbishment of many medieval buildings, including Notre Dame in Paris.

vi·o·lon·cel·lo (vē′ə-lən-chĕl′ō, vī′ə-) *n., pl.* **-los.** *Music.* A cello. [Italian, diminutive of *violone,* violone. See VIOLONE.] **—vi′o·lon·cel′list** *n.*

vi·o·lo·ne (vē′ə-lō′nā) *n. Music.* A 16-foot organ stop yielding stringlike tones similar to those of a cello. [Italian, augmentative of *viola,* viola. See VIOLA[1].]

vi·o·my·cin (vī′ə-mī′sĭn) *n.* An antibiotic, $C_{23}H_{36}N_{12}O_8$, produced by the actinomycete *Streptomyces puniceus,* used in the treatment of tuberculosis. [VIO(LET) + –MYCIN (from the color of the soil mold).]

vi·os·ter·ol (vī-ŏs′tə-rôl′, -rōl′, -rŏl′) *n.* Ergosterol activated by ultraviolet irradiation; vitamin D_2. [(ULTRA)VIO(LET) + (ERGO)STEROL.]

VIP (vē′ī-pē′) *n., pl.* **VIPs.** *Informal.* A person of great importance or influence, especially a dignitary who commands special treatment. [*v(ery) i(mportant) p(erson).*]

vi·per (vī′pər) *n.* **1.** Any of several venomous Old World snakes of the family Viperidae, having a single pair of long, hollow fangs and a thick, heavy body. Also called *adder.* **2.** A pit viper. **3.** A venomous or supposedly venomous snake. **4.** A person regarded as malicious or treacherous. [Middle English *vipere,* from Old French, from Latin *vīpera,* snake, contraction of **vīvipera* : *vīvus,* alive; see **gʷei-** in Appendix + *parere,* to give birth; see **perə-**[1] in Appendix.]

vi·per·fish (vī′pər-fĭsh′) *n.* **viperfish** or **-fish·es.** Any of various small deep-sea fish of the family Chauliodontidae, having fanglike teeth, a long first ray of the dorsal fin, and photophores along the sides.

vi·per·ine (vī′pə-rīn′) *adj.* Of, resembling, or characteristic of a viper.

vi·per·ish (vī′pər-ĭsh) *adj.* Spiteful or malicious; venomous: *a viperish retort.*

vi·per·ous (vī′pər-əs) *adj.* **1.** Suggestive of or related to a viper. **2.** Venomous; malicious. **—vi′per·ous·ly** *adv.*

vi·per's bugloss (vī′pərz) *n.* Any of various Eurasian plants of the genus *Echium,* including the blueweed, having bright blue to white flowers, bristly foliage, and a dense scorpioid inflorescence.

vir– *pref.* Variant of **viro–.**

vi·ra·go (və-rä′gō, -rā′-, vîr′ə-gō′) *n., pl.* **-goes** or **-gos. 1.** A woman regarded as noisy, scolding, or domineering. **2.** A large, strong, courageous woman. [Latin *virāgō,* from *vir,* man. See **wī-ro-** in Appendix.] **—vi·rag′i·nous** (və-răj′ə-nəs) *adj.*

vi·ral (vī′rəl) *adj.* Of, relating to, or caused by a virus. **—vi′ral·ly** *adv.*

vir·e·lay (vîr′ə-lā′) *n.* Any of several medieval French verse and song forms, especially one in which each stanza has two rhymes, the end rhyme recurring as the first rhyme of the following stanza. [Middle English *virelai,* from Old French, alteration (influenced by *lai,* lay) of *vireli,* song refrain.]

vi·re·mi·a (vī-rē′mē-ə) *n.* The presence of viruses in the bloodstream. **—vi·re′mic** (-mĭk) *adj.*

vir·e·o (vîr′ē-ō′) *n., pl.* **-os.** Any of various small insect-eating New World songbirds of the genus *Vireo,* having grayish or greenish plumage. [Latin *vireō,* a kind of bird, from *virēre,* to be green.]

vi·res·cence (və-rĕs′əns, vī-) *n.* The state or process of becoming green, especially the abnormal development of green coloration in plant parts normally not green.

vi·res·cent (və-rĕs′ənt, vī-) *adj.* **1.** Becoming green. **2.** Somewhat green; greenish. [Latin *virēscēns, virēscent-,* present participle of *virēscere,* to become green, inchoative of *virēre,* to be green.]

vi·res ma·jo·res (vī′rēz mə-jôr′ēz, -jŏr′-) *n. Law.* Plural of **vis major.**

vir·ga (vûr′gə) *n.* Wisps of precipitation streaming from a cloud but evaporating before reaching the ground. [Latin, twig, virga.]

vir·gate[1] (vûr′gāt′) *adj.* Shaped like a wand or rod; straight, long, and slender. [Latin *virgātus,* made of twigs, from *virga,* twig.]

vir·gate[2] (vûr′gĭt) *n.* An early English measure of land area of varying value, often equal to about 30 acres (12 hectares). [Medieval Latin *virgāta,* from feminine of Latin *virgātus,* relating to a rod. See VIRGATE[1].]

Vir·gil also **Ver·gil** (vûr′jəl). 70–19 B.C. Roman poet. His greatest work is the epic poem *Aeneid,* which tells of the wanderings of Aeneas after the sack of Troy. **—Vir·gil′i·an** (vûr-jĭl′ē-ən, -jĭl′yən) *adj.*

vir·gin (vûr′jĭn) *n.* **1.** A person who has not experienced sexual intercourse. **2.** A chaste or unmarried woman; a maiden. **3.** An unmarried woman who has taken religious vows of chastity. **4. Virgin.** The Virgin Mary. **5.** *Zoology.* **a.** A female animal that has not copulated. **b.** A female bee, wasp, or other insect that produces fertile eggs without copulating. **—virgin** *adj.* **1.** Of, relating to, or being a virgin; chaste. **2.** Being in a pure or natural state; unsullied: *virgin snow.* **3.** Unused, uncultivated, or unexplored: *virgin territory.* **4.** Existing in native or raw form; not processed or refined. **5.** Happening for the first time; initial. **6.** Obtained directly from the first pressing: *virgin olive oil.* [Middle English, from Old French *virgine,* from Latin *virgō, virgin-.*]

Virgin *n.* See **Virgo** (senses 1, 2a).

vir·gin·al[1] (vûr′jə-nəl) *adj.* **1.** Relating to, characteristic of, or befitting a virgin; chaste. **2.** Remaining in a state of virginity. **3.** Untouched or unsullied; fresh. **4.** *Zoology.* Virgin. **—vir′gin·al·ly** *adv.*

vir·gin·al[2] (vûr′jə-nəl) *n. Music.* A small, legless rectangular harpsichord popular in the 16th and 17th centuries. Often used in the plural. Also called *pair of virginals.* [From VIRGIN (perhaps from its being associated with female performers).]

virgin birth *n. Theology.* The doctrine that Jesus was miraculously begotten by God and born of the Virgin Mary without the agency of a human father.

Vir·gin·ia (vər-jĭn′yə). *Abbr.* **VA, Va.** A state of the eastern United States on Chesapeake Bay and the Atlantic Ocean. It was admitted as one of the original Thirteen Colonies in 1788. Early colonizing attempts (1584–1587) by Sir Walter Raleigh failed, but in 1607 colonists dispatched by the London Company established the first permanent settlement at Jamestown (May 13). Virginia was a prime force in the move for independence and was the site of Lord Cornwallis's surrender in 1781. Virginia seceded in April 1861 and was the scene of many major battles during the Civil War, including the final campaigns that led to the surrender of Gen. Robert E. Lee. Richmond is the capital and Norfolk the largest city. Population, 5,346,797. **—Vir·gin′ian** *adj. & n.*

Virginia Algonquian *n.* The extinct Eastern Algonquian language of eastern Virginia.

Virginia Beach. An independent city of southeast Virginia on the Atlantic Ocean east of Norfolk. Mainly residential, it is a popular resort. Population, 262,199.

Virginia bluebell *n.* See **Virginia cowslip.**

Virginia City. A town of southwest Montana south of Helena. It was founded in 1863 after the discovery of gold and soon became notorious as a rowdy mining town. Virginia City is now a tourist center, with many restored structures.

Virginia cowslip *n.* An eastern North American plant *(Mertensia virginica)* having clusters of showy, nodding blue flowers. Also called *Virginia bluebell.*

Virginia creeper *n.* A North American climbing vine *(Parthenocissus quinquefolia)* having palmately compound leaves with five leaflets and bluish-black berries. Also called *woodbine.*

Virginia deer *n.* See **white-tailed deer.**

Virginia fence *n.* See **worm fence.**

Virginia ham *n.* A lean hickory-smoked ham with dark red meat.

vir·gin·ia·my·cin (vər-jĭn′yə-mī′sĭn) *n.* Any of several antibacterial substances derived from an actinomycete related to *Streptomyces virginiae,* used chiefly as an additive in animal feed. [New Latin *virginiae,* specific epithet + –MYCIN.]

Virginia rail *n.* A small reddish-brown American rail *(Rallus limicola)* having a long, slender bill.

Virginia reel *n.* An American country-dance in which couples perform various steps together to the instructions of a caller.

Virgin Islands. 1. *Abbr.* **V.I.** A group of islands of the northeast West Indies east of Puerto Rico. They are divided politically into the **British Virgin Islands** to the northeast and the Virgin Islands of the United States to the southwest. The islands were first sighted and named by Christopher Columbus in 1493. **2.** *Abbr.* **VI, V.I.** Officially **Virgin Islands of the United States.** A United States territory constituting the southwest group of the Virgin Islands. The islands were purchased from the Dutch in 1917 because of their strategic location at the approach to the Panama Canal. Charlotte Amalie, on St. Thomas Island, is the capital. Population, 96,569.

vir·gin·i·ty (vər-jĭn′ĭ-tē) *n., pl.* **-ties. 1.** The quality or condition of being a virgin. **2.** The state of being pure, unsullied, or untouched.

Virgin Mary *n.* The mother of Jesus.

Virgin River. A river, about 322 km (200 mi) long, of southwest Utah and southeast Nevada flowing generally southwest and south to Lake Mead.

vir·gin's bower (vûr′jĭnz) *n.* Any of several climbing plants of the genus *Clematis,* especially *C. virginiana,* of eastern North America, having clusters of white flowers and a cluster of seedlike fruits each with a feathery, persistent style. Also called *old-man's-beard.*

virgin wool *n.* Wool that has not previously been used in manufacture.

Vir·go (vûr′gō) *n.* **1.** A constellation in the region of the celestial equator between Leo and Libra. Also called *Virgin.* **2. a.** The sixth sign of the zodiac in astrology. Also called *Virgin.* **b.** *pl.* **-gos.** One who is born under this sign. [Middle English, from Latin, virgin, the constellation Virgo.] **—Vir′go·an** *adj. & n.*

vir·gu·late (vûr′gyə-lĭt, -lāt′) *adj.* Shaped like a small rod. [From Latin *virgula,* small rod, from *virga,* rod.]

vir·gule (vûr′gyo͞ol) *n. Printing.* A diagonal mark (/) used especially to separate alternatives, as in *and/or,* to represent the word *per,* as in *miles/hour,* and to indicate the ends of verse lines printed continuously, as in *Old King Cole/Was a merry old soul.* [French, comma, obelus, from Late Latin *virgula,* accentual mark, from Latin, obelus, diminutive of *virga,* rod.]

vi·ri·cide (vī′rĭ-sīd′) also **vi·ru·cide** (vī′rə-) *n.* An agent that inhibits or destroys viruses. [VIR(US) + –CIDE.] **—vi′ri·cid′al** (-sīd′l) *adj.*

vir·id (vîr′ĭd) *adj.* Bright green with or as if with vegetation; verdant. [Latin *viridis,* from *virēre,* to be green.]

vir·i·des·cent (vîr′ĭ-dĕs′ənt) *adj.* Green or slightly green. [Late Latin *viridēscēns, viridēscent-,* present participle of *viridēscere,* to become green, from *viridis,* green. See VIRID.] **—vir′i·des′cence** *n.*

vi·rid·i·an (və-rĭd′ē-ən) *n.* A durable bluish-green pigment. [From Latin *viridis,* green. See VIRID.]

vi·rid·i·ty (və-rĭd′ĭ-tē) *n.* **1. a.** The quality or condition of being green; greenness. **b.** The green color of vegetation or leaves. **2.** Innocence or inexperience.

vireo
Philadelphia vireo
Vireo philadelphicus

virginal[2]
Early 17th-century Flemish by Andries Ruckers (1579–1640?)

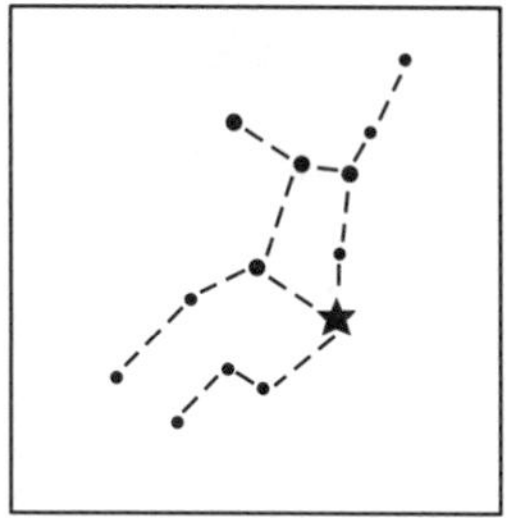

Virgo

ă pat	oi boy
ā pay	ou out
âr care	o͝o took
ä father	o͞o boot
ĕ pet	ŭ cut
ē be	ûr urge
ĭ pit	th thin
ī pie	*th* this
îr pier	hw which
ŏ pot	zh vision
ō toe	ə about, item
ô paw	♦ regionalism

Stress marks: ′ (primary); ′ (secondary), as in **dictionary** (dĭk′shə-nĕr′ē)

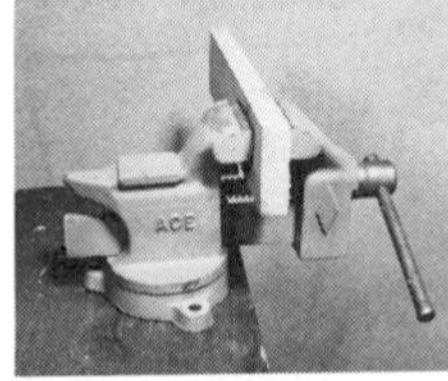

vise

Vishnu
Tenth-century bronze

vir·ile (vîr′əl, -īl′) *adj.* **1.** Of, relating to, or having the characteristics of an adult male. **2.** Having or showing masculine spirit, strength, vigor, or power. See Synonyms at **male.** **3.** Capable of performing sexually as a male; potent. [Middle English, from Old French *viril,* from Latin *virīlis,* from *vir,* man. See **wī-ro-** in Appendix.]

vir·il·ism (vîr′ə-lĭz′əm) *n.* The presence of male secondary sexual characteristics in a female.

vi·ril·i·ty (və-rĭl′ĭ-tē) *n.* **1.** The quality or state of being virile; manly character. **2.** Masculine vigor; potency.

vir·i·li·za·tion (vîr′ə-lĭ-zā′shən) *n.* Development of male secondary sexual characteristics. —**vir′il·ize′** (-ə-līz′) *v.*

vi·ri·on (vī′rē-ŏn′, vîr′ē-) *n.* A complete viral particle, consisting of RNA or DNA surrounded by a protein shell and constituting the infective form of a virus. [VIR(US) + -ON[1].]

viro– or **vir–** *pref.* Virus; virogenesis. [From VIRUS.]

vi·ro·gene (vī′rə-jēn′) *n.* A gene capable of specifying the synthesis of a virus in a cell.

vi·ro·gen·e·sis (vī′rō-jĕn′ĭ-sĭs, -rə-) *n., pl.* **-ses** (-sēz′). Production or formation of a virus. —**vi′ro·ge·net′ic** (-jə-nĕt′ĭk), —**vi′ro·gen′ic** (-jĕn′ĭk) *adj.*

vi·roid (vī′roid′) *n.* An infectious particle, similar to but smaller than a virus, that consists solely of a strand of RNA and is capable of causing disease in plants.

vi·rol·o·gy (vī-rŏl′ə-jē) *n.* The study of viruses and viral diseases. —**vi′ro·log′i·cal** (vī′rə-lŏj′ĭ-kəl), **vi′ro·log′ic** (-ĭk) *adj.* —**vi·rol′o·gist** *n.*

vi·ro·sis (vī-rō′sĭs) *n., pl.* **-ses** (-sēz). A disease caused by a virus.

vir·tu (vər-to͞o′, vîr-) also **ver·tu** (vər-) *n.* **1.** A knowledge or love of or taste for fine objects of art. **2.** Production of objects of art, especially fine antique objets d'art. [Italian *virtù,* virtue, virtu, from Latin *virtūs,* excellence, virtue. See VIRTUE.]

vir·tu·al (vûr′cho͞o-əl) *adj.* **1.** Existing or resulting in essence or effect though not in actual fact, form, or name: *the virtual extinction of the buffalo.* **2.** Existing in the mind, especially as a product of the imagination. Used in literary criticism of text. [Middle English *virtuall,* effective, from Medieval Latin *virtuālis,* from Latin *virtūs,* excellence. See VIRTUE.] —**vir′tu·al′i·ty** (-ăl′ĭ-tē) *n.*

virtual focus *n.* The point from which divergent rays of reflected or refracted light seem to have emanated, as from the image of a point in a plane mirror.

virtual image *n.* An image from which rays of reflected or refracted light appear to diverge, as from an image seen in a plane mirror.

vir·tu·al·ly (vûr′cho͞o-ə-lē) *adv.* **1.** In fact or to all purposes; practically: *The city was virtually paralyzed by the transit strike.* **2.** Almost but not quite; nearly: *"Virtually everyone gets a headache now and then"* (People).

virtual machine *n. Computer Science.* A computer designed to replicate copies of its entire hardware-software interface so that two operating systems can be run on a single computer.

virtual memory *n. Computer Science.* Computer memory, separate from the main memory of a specific machine, that can be used as an extension of the machine's main memory.

vir·tue (vûr′cho͞o) *n.* **1.a.** Moral excellence and righteousness; goodness. **b.** An example or kind of moral excellence: *the virtue of patience.* **2.** Chastity, especially in a girl or woman. **3.** A particularly efficacious, good, or beneficial quality; advantage: *a plan with the virtue of being practical.* **4.** Effective force or power: *believed in the virtue of prayer.* **5. virtues.** *Theology.* The fifth of the nine orders of angels. **6.** *Obsolete.* Manly courage; valor. —***idiom.* by** (or **in**) **virtue of.** On the grounds or basis of; by reason of: *well off by virtue of a large inheritance.* [Middle English *vertu,* from Old French, from Latin *virtūs,* manliness, excellence, goodness, from *vir,* man. See **wī-ro-** in Appendix.]

vir·tu·o·sa (vûr′cho͞o-ō′sə, -zə) *n.* A woman who is a virtuoso. [Italian, feminine of *virtuoso,* virtuoso. See VIRTUOSO.]

vir·tu·o·si (vûr′cho͞o-ō′sē) *n.* A plural of **virtuoso.**

vir·tu·os·i·ty (vûr′cho͞o-ŏs′ĭ-tē) *n., pl.* **-ties. 1.** The technical skill, fluency, or style exhibited by a virtuoso. **2.** An appreciation for or interest in fine objects of art.

vir·tu·o·so (vûr′cho͞o-ō′sō, -zō) *n., pl.* **-sos** or **-si** (-sē). **1.** A musician with masterly ability, technique, or personal style. **2.** A person with masterly skill or technique in the arts. **3.** A person who experiments or investigates in the arts and sciences; a savant. —**virtuoso** *adj.* Exhibiting the ability, technique, or personal style of a virtuoso: *a virtuoso performance.* [Italian, skilled, of great worth, virtuoso, from Late Latin *virtuōsus,* virtuous, from Latin *virtūs,* excellence. See VIRTUE.] —**vir′tu·o′sic** (-ō′sĭk, -zĭk) *adj.* —**vir′tu·o′si·cal·ly** *adv.*

vir·tu·ous (vûr′cho͞o-əs) *adj.* **1.** Having or showing virtue, especially moral excellence: *led a virtuous life.* **2.** Possessing or characterized by chastity; pure: *a virtuous woman.* See Synonyms at **moral.** —**vir′tu·ous·ly** *adv.* —**vir′tu·ous·ness** *n.*

vi·ru·cide (vī′rə-sīd′) *n.* Variant of **viricide.**

vir·u·lent (vîr′yə-lənt, vîr′ə-) *adj.* **1.a.** Extremely infectious, malignant, or poisonous. Used of a disease or toxin. **b.** Capable of causing disease by breaking down protective mechanisms of the host. Used of a pathogen. **2.** Bitterly hostile or antagonistic; hateful: *virulent criticism.* See Synonyms at **poisonous.** **3.** Intensely irritating, obnoxious, or harsh. [Middle English, from Latin *vīrulentus,* from *vīrus,* poison.] —**vir′u·lence, vir′u·len·cy** *n.* —**vir′u·lent·ly** *adv.*

vir·u·lif·er·ous (vîr′yə-lĭf′ər-əs, vîr′ə-) *adj.* Carrying or containing a virus: *viruliferous aphids.* [VIRUL(ENCE) + -FEROUS.]

vi·rus (vī′rəs) *n., pl.* **-rus·es. 1.a.** Any of various simple submicroscopic parasites of plants, animals, and bacteria that often cause disease and that consist essentially of a core of RNA or DNA surrounded by a protein coat. Unable to replicate without a host cell, viruses are typically not considered living organisms. **b.** A disease caused by a virus. **2.** Something that poisons one's soul or mind: *the pernicious virus of racism.* **3.** *Computer Science.* A computer virus. [Latin *vīrus,* poison.]

Vis (vēs). An island of western Yugoslavia off the Dalmatian coast south-southwest of Split. Major naval battles occurred off the island in 1811 and 1866. In the first, the British defeated the French; in the second, the Austrians defeated the Italians.

vis. *abbr.* **1.** Visibility. **2.** Visual.

Vis. *abbr.* **1.** Viscount. **2.** Viscountess.

vi·sa (vē′zə) *n.* An official authorization appended to a passport, permitting entry into and travel within a particular country or region. —**visa** *tr.v.* **-saed, -sa·ing, -sas. 1.** To endorse or ratify (a passport). **2.** To give a visa to. [French, short for Latin *(carta) vīsa,* (the document has been) seen, from feminine past participle of *vidēre,* to see. See **weid-** in Appendix.]

vis·age (vĭz′ĭj) *n.* **1.** The face or facial expression of a person; countenance. See Synonyms at **face.** **2.** Appearance; aspect: *the bleak visage of winter.* [Middle English, from Old French, from *vis,* from Latin *vīsus,* appearance, from past participle of *vidēre,* to see. See **weid-** in Appendix.]

Vi·sa·kha·pat·nam (vĭ-sä′kə-pŭt′nəm) or **Vi·sha·kha·pat·nam** (-shä′-) also **Vi·za·ga·pa·tam** (vĭ-zä′gə-pŭt′əm). A city of eastern India on the Bay of Bengal northeast of Madras. Established by the English as a trading post in 1683, it is a health resort and processing center with a protected harbor and shipping facilities. Population, 565,321.

Vi·sa·lia (vī-săl′yə). A city of south-central California southeast of Fresno. Agricultural products of the San Joaquin Valley are important to its economy. Population, 49,729.

vis·ard (vĭz′ərd, -ärd′) *n.* Variant of **vizard.**

vis-à-vis (vē′zə-vē′) *prep.* **1.** Face to face with; opposite to. **2.** Compared with. **3.** In relation to. —**vis-à-vis** *adv.* Face to face. —**vis-à-vis** *n., pl.* **vis-à-vis** (-vēz′, -vē′). **1.** One that is face to face with or opposite to another. **2.** A date or an escort, as at a party. **3.** One that has the same functions and characteristics as another; a counterpart. [French : *vis,* face + *à,* to.] —**vis′-à-vis′** *adj.*

Vi·sa·yan (vĭ-sī′ən) *n.* **1.** A member of the largest ethnic group indigenous to the Philippines, found in the Visayan Islands. **2.** The Austronesian language of the Visayans. —**Vi·say′an** *adj.*

Visayan Islands. An island group of the central Philippines in and around the **Visayan Sea** between Luzon and Mindanao.

Vis·by (vĭz′bē, vēs′bü). A city of southeast Sweden on western Gotland Island on the Baltic Sea. It was a member of the Hanseatic League and a commercial center from the 10th to the 14th century but declined after its capture by the Danes in 1362. Visby was a pirate stronghold for the next two centuries and passed to Sweden in 1645. Population, 20,100.

vis·ca·cha (vĭ-skä′chə) *n.* Any of several gregarious, burrowing South American rodents of the genera *Lagostomus* and *Lagidium,* related to and resembling the chinchilla. [Spanish *vizcacha,* from Quechua *wiskácha.*]

vis·cer·a (vĭs′ər-ə) *pl.n.* **1.** The soft internal organs of the body, especially those contained within the abdominal and thoracic cavities. **2.** The intestines. [Latin *vīscera,* pl. of *vīscus.*]

vis·cer·al (vĭs′ər-əl) *adj.* **1.** Relating to, situated in, or affecting the viscera. **2.** Perceived in or as if in the viscera; profound: *"The scientific approach to life is not really appropriate to states of visceral anguish"* (Anthony Burgess). **3.** Instinctive: *visceral needs.* See Synonyms at **instinctive.** —**vis′cer·al·ly** *adv.*

vis·cer·o·mo·tor (vĭs′ər-ə-mō′tər) *adj.* Producing or related to movements of the viscera.

vis·cid (vĭs′ĭd) *adj.* **1.** Thick and adhesive. Used of a fluid. **2.** Covered with a sticky or clammy coating. [Late Latin *viscidus,* from Latin *viscum,* mistletoe, birdlime made from mistletoe berries.] —**vis·cid′i·ty, vis′cid·ness** *n.* —**vis′cid·ly** *adv.*

vis·com·e·ter (vĭ-skŏm′ĭ-tər) *n.* An instrument used to measure viscosity. Also called *viscosimeter.* [Short for VISCOSIMETER.] —**vis′co·met′ric** (vĭs′kə-mĕt′rĭk) *adj.* —**vis·com′e·try** *n.*

Vis·con·ti (vĭs-kŏn′tē, vēs-kôn′-), **Gian Galeazzo.** 1351?–1402. Milanese leader who conquered Siena (1399), Perugia (1400), and Bologna (1402) and was a noted patron of the arts.

vis·cose (vĭs′kōs′) *n.* **1.** A thick, golden-brown viscous solution of cellulose xanthate, used in the manufacture of rayon and cellophane. **2.** Viscose rayon. —**viscose** *adj.* **1.** Viscous. **2.** Of, relating to, or made from viscose. [VISC(OUS) + -OSE[2]. Adj., sense 1, Middle English, viscous, from Late Latin *viscōsus,* from *viscum,* mistletoe, birdlime made from mistletoe berries.]

viscose rayon *n.* A rayon made by reconverting cellulose from a soluble xanthate form to tough fibers by washing in acid.

vis·co·sim·e·ter (vĭs′kə-sĭm′ĭ-tər) *n.* See **viscometer.** —**vis·cos′i·met′ric** (vĭ-skŏs′ə-mĕt′rĭk) *adj.*

vis·cos·i·ty (vĭ-skŏs′ĭ-tē) *n., pl.* **-ties. 1.** The condition or property of being viscous. **2.** *Physics.* Coefficient of viscosity.

vis·count (vī′kount′) *n. Abbr.* **V., Vis., Visct. 1.** A nobleman ranking below an earl or a count and above a baron. **2.** Used as a title for such a nobleman. [Middle English, from Old French *visconte,* from Medieval Latin *vicecomes, vicecomit-* : Late Latin *vice-,* vice; see VICE– + Late Latin *comes,* occupant of any state office; see COUNT[2].]

vis·count·cy (vī′kount′sē) *n., pl.* **-cies.** The rank, title, or dignity of a viscount. Also called *viscounty.*

vis·count·ess (vī′koun′tĭs) *n. Abbr.* **V., Vis., Visct. 1.** The wife or widow of a viscount. **2.** A noblewoman holding the rank of viscount in her own right.

Vis·count Mel·ville Sound (vī′kount mĕl′vĭl′, -vəl). An arm of the Arctic Ocean between Victoria and Melville islands in northern Northwest Territories, Canada.

vis·count·y (vī′koun′tē) *n., pl.* **-ies.** See **viscountcy.**

vis·cous (vĭs′kəs) *adj.* **1.** Having relatively high resistance to flow. **2.** Viscid. [Middle English, from Old French, from Late Latin *viscōsus.* See VISCOSE.] **—vis′cous·ly** *adv.* **—vis′cous·ness** *n.*

Visct. *abbr.* **1.** Viscount. **2.** Viscountess.

vis·cus (vĭs′kəs) *n.* Singular of **viscera.**

vise also **vice** (vīs) *—n.* A clamping device of metal or wood, usually consisting of two jaws closed or opened by a screw or lever, used in carpentry or metalworking to hold a piece in position. *—tr.v.* **vised, vis·ing, vis·es** also **viced, vic·ing, vic·es.** To hold or compress in or as if in a vise. [Middle English *vis,* screwlike device, from Old French, screw, from Latin *vītis,* vine (from its spiral wrappings). See **wei-** in Appendix.]

Vi·sha·kha·pat·nam (vĭ-shä′kə-pŭt′nəm). See **Visakhapatnam.**

Vi·shin·ski (vĭ-shĭn′skē), **Andrei Yanuarievich.** 1883–1954. Soviet jurist and diplomat. As chief Soviet prosecutor (1935–1939) he conducted the infamous Great Purge trials. He later served as a Soviet delegate to the United Nations (1946–1954) and as foreign minister (1949–1953).

Vish·nu (vĭsh′no͞o) *n. Hinduism.* One of the principal Hindu deities, worshiped as the protector and preserver of worlds. Vishnu is often conceived as a member of the triad including also Brahma and Shiva.

vis·i·bil·i·ty (vĭz′ə-bĭl′ĭ-tē) *n., pl.* **-ties. 1.** The fact, state, or degree of being visible. **2.** *Abbr.* **vis.** The greatest distance under given weather conditions to which it is possible to see without instrumental assistance. **3.a.** The capability of being easily observed: *an executive with high visibility.* **b.** The capability of providing a clear, unobstructed view: *a windshield with good visibility.*

vis·i·ble (vĭz′ə-bəl) *adj.* **1.** Possible to see; perceptible to the eye: *a visible object.* **2.a.** Obvious to the eye: *a visible change of expression.* **b.** Being often in the public view; conspicuous. **3.** Manifest; apparent: *no visible solution to the problem.* **4.** On hand; available: *a visible supply.* **5.** Constructed or designed to keep important parts in easily accessible view: *a visible file.* **6.** Represented visually, as by symbols. [Middle English, from Old French, from Latin *vīsibilis,* from *vīsus,* past participle of *vidēre,* to see. See VISION.] **—vis′i·ble·ness** *n.* **—vis′i·bly** *adv.*

visible speech *n.* A system of phonetic notation used as an aid for teaching speech to hearing-impaired people and consisting of diagrams of the organs of speech in the various positions required to articulate sounds.

Vis·i·goth (vĭz′ĭ-gŏth′) *n.* A member of the western Goths that invaded the Roman Empire in the fourth century A.D. and settled in France and Spain, establishing a monarchy that lasted until the early eighth century. [Late Latin *Visigothī,* the Visigoths. See **wes-pero-** in Appendix.] **—Vis′i·goth′ic** *adj.*

vi·sion (vĭzh′ən) *n.* **1.a.** The faculty of sight; eyesight: *poor vision.* **b.** Something that is or has been seen. **2.** Unusual competence in discernment or perception; intelligent foresight: *a leader of vision.* **3.** The manner in which one sees or conceives of something. **4.** A mental image produced by the imagination. **5.** The mystical experience of seeing as if with the eyes the supernatural or a supernatural being. **6.** A person or thing of extraordinary beauty. **—vision** *tr.v.* **-sioned, -sion·ing, -sions.** To see in or as if in a vision; envision. [Middle English, from Old French, from Latin *vīsiō, vīsiōn-,* from *vīsus,* past participle of *vidēre,* to see. See **weid-** in Appendix.] **—vi′sion·al** *adj.* **—vi′sion·al·ly** *adv.*

vi·sion·ar·y (vĭzh′ə-nĕr′ē) *adj.* **1.** Characterized by vision or foresight. **2.a.** Having the nature of fantasies or dreams; illusory. **b.** Existing in imagination only; imaginary. **3.a.** Characterized by or given to apparitions, prophecies, or revelations. **b.** Given to daydreams or reverie; dreamy. **4.a.** Not practicable or realizable; utopian: *visionary schemes for getting rich.* **b.** Tending to envision things in perfect but unrealistic form; idealistic. **—visionary** *n., pl.* **-ies. 1.** One who is given to impractical or speculative ideas; a dreamer. **2.** One who has visions; a seer. **—vi′sion·ar′i·ness** *n.*

vi·sion·less (vĭzh′ən-lĭs) *adj.* **1.** Lacking the faculty of sight; blind. **2.** Lacking intelligent foresight or imagination; uninspired: *visionless bureaucrats.*

vision quest *n.* A period of spiritual seeking among certain Native American peoples, often undertaken as a puberty rite, that typically involves isolation, fasting, and the inducement of a trance state for the purpose of attaining guidance or knowledge from supernatural forces.

vis·it (vĭz′ĭt) *v.* **-it·ed, -it·ing, -its.** *—tr.* **1.a.** To call on socially: *visit friends.* **b.** To go to see or spend time at (a place) with a certain intent: *visit a museum; visited London.* **c.** To stay with as a guest. **d.** To go to see in an official or professional capacity: *visited the dentist; a priest visiting his parishioners.* **2.** To go or come to: *visits the bank on Fridays.* **3.** To go to see in order to aid or console: *visit the sick and dying.* **4.** To make itself known to or seize fleetingly: *was visited by a bizarre thought.* **5.a.** To afflict or assail: *A plague visited the village.* **b.** To inflict punishment on or for; avenge: *The sins of the ancestors were visited on their descendants.* *—intr.* **1.** To make a visit. **2.** *Informal.* To converse or chat: *Stay and visit with me for a while.* **—visit** *n.* **1.** The act or an instance of visiting a person, place, or thing. **2.** A stay or sojourn as a guest. **3.** The act of visiting in a professional capacity. **4.** The act of visiting in an official capacity, such as an inspection or examination. [Middle English *visiten,* from Old French *visiter,* from Latin *vīsitāre,* frequentative of *vīsere,* frequentative of *vidēre,* to see. See VISION.]

vis·it·a·ble (vĭz′ĭ-tə-bəl) *adj.* **1.** Subject to inspection or visitation: *a hospital that was visitable by state officials.* **2.** Accessible or open: *a wildlife preserve visitable only during the summer months.*

vis·i·tant (vĭz′ĭ-tənt) *n.* **1.** A visitor; a guest. **2.** A supernatural being; a ghost or specter. **3.** A migratory bird that stops in a particular place for a limited period of time. **—visitant** *adj.* Visiting. [Latin *vīsitāns, vīsitant-,* present participle of *vīsitāre,* to go to see. See VISIT.]

vis·i·ta·tion (vĭz′ĭ-tā′shən) *n.* **1.** The act or an instance of visiting or an instance of being visited: *rules governing visitation at a prison.* **2.** An official visit for the purpose of inspection or examination, as of a bishop to a diocese. **3.** The right of a parent to visit a child as specified in a divorce or separation order. **4.a.** A visit of punishment or affliction or of comfort and blessing regarded as being ordained by God. **b.** A calamitous event or experience; a grave misfortune. See Synonyms at **trial. 5.** The appearance or arrival of a supernatural being. **6. Visitation.** *Roman Catholic Church.* **a.** The visit of the Virgin Mary to her cousin Elizabeth. **b.** July 2, observed in commemoration of this event. **—vis′i·ta′tion·al** *adj.*

vis·i·ta·to·ri·al (vĭz′ĭ-tə-tôr′ē-əl, -tōr′-) *adj.* **1.** Of or relating to an official visitor or visit. **2.** Having the right or power of visitation.

vis·it·ing card (vĭz′ĭ-tĭng) *n.* See **calling card.**

visiting fireman *n. Informal.* **1.** An important visitor who is entertained impressively. **2.** A visitor, especially a tourist or conventioneer, thought to be a free spender.

visiting nurse *n.* A registered nurse employed by a public health agency or hospital to promote community health and especially to visit and administer treatment to sick people in their homes.

visiting professor *n.* A professor on leave who is invited to serve as a member of the faculty of another college or university for a limited period of time, often an academic year.

visiting teacher *n.* A teacher affiliated with a public school system who visits and instructs sick or handicapped children in the area.

vis·i·tor (vĭz′ĭ-tər) *n.* One that visits: *Sunday afternoon visitors; lost the game to the visitors.*

vis ma·jor (vĭs mā′jər) *n., pl.* **vi·res ma·jo·res** (vī′rēz mə-jôr′ēz, -jōr′-). *Law.* An overwhelming force of nature having unavoidable consequences that under certain circumstances can exempt one from the obligations of a contract. [Latin *vīs māior* : *vīs,* force + *māior,* greater.]

Vi·so (vē′zō), **Mount.** A peak, 3,843.6 m (12,602 ft) high, of northwest Italy in the Cottian Alps near the French border. It is the highest elevation in the range.

vi·sor also **vi·zor** (vī′zər) *—n.* **1.** A piece projecting from the front of a cap to shade or protect the eyes. **2.** A fixed or movable shield against glare attached above the windshield of an automotive vehicle. **3.** The front piece of the helmet of a suit of armor, capable of being raised and lowered and designed to protect the eyes, nose, and forehead. **4.** A means of concealment or disguise; a mask. *—tr.v.* **-sored, -sor·ing, -sors** also **-zored, -zor·ing, -zors.** To provide or protect with a visor. [Alteration of Middle English *viser,* from Anglo-Norman, from *vis,* face, from Latin *vīsus,* appearance. See VISAGE.]

vis·ta (vĭs′tə) *n.* **1.a.** A distant view or prospect, especially one seen through an opening, as between rows of buildings or trees. **b.** An avenue or other passage affording such a view. **2.** An awareness of a range of time, events, or subjects; a broad mental view: *"the deep and sweeping vistas these pioneering critics opened up"* (Arthur C. Danto). [Italian, from feminine past participle of *vedere,* to see, from Latin *vidēre.* See **weid-** in Appendix.]

VISTA *abbr.* Volunteers In Service To America.

Vis·tu·la (vĭs′chə-lə, -cho͞o-). A river of Poland, about 1,091 km (678 mi) long, rising near the Czechoslovakian border and flowing in an arc northeast, northwest, and north to the Gulf of Gdańsk.

vi·su·al (vĭzh′o͞o-əl) *adj. Abbr.* **vis. 1.** Of or relating to the sense of sight: *a visual organ; visual receptors on the retina.* **2.**

Visitation

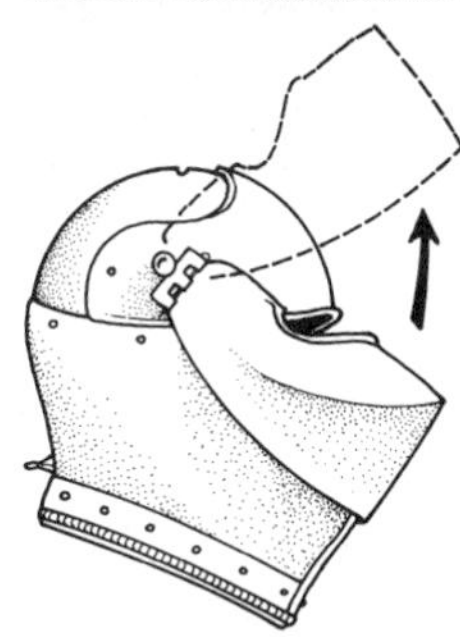

visor
Top: Of a cap
Bottom: Of a helmet

ă pat	oi boy
ā pay	ou out
âr care	o͝o took
ä father	o͞o boot
ĕ pet	ŭ cut
ē be	ûr urge
ĭ pit	th thin
ī pie	*th* this
îr pier	hw which
ŏ pot	zh vision
ō toe	ə about, item
ô paw	♦ regionalism

Stress marks: ′ (primary); ′ (secondary), as in **dictionary** (dĭk′shə-nĕr′ē)

Seen or able to be seen by the eye; visible: *a visual presentation.* **3.** Optical. **4.** Done, maintained, or executed by sight only: *visual navigation.* **5.** Having the nature of or producing an image in the mind: *a visual memory of the scene.* **6.** Of or relating to a method of instruction involving sight. **—visual** *n.* A picture, chart, or other presentation that appeals to the sense of sight, used in promotion or for illustration or narration. Often used in the plural: *an ad campaign with striking visuals; trying to capture a poem in a cinematic visual.* [Middle English, from Late Latin *vīsuālis,* from Latin *vīsus,* sight. See VISION.] **—vi′su·al·ly** *adv.* **—vi′su·al·ness, vi′su·al′i·ty** (-ăl′ĭ-tē) *n.*

visual acuity *n.* Sharpness of vision, especially as tested with a Snellen chart. Normal visual acuity based on the Snellen chart is 20/20.

visual aid *n.* An instructional aid, such as a scale model, filmstrip, or videotape, that presents information visually.

visual binary *n.* A binary star that can be seen as two stars with a telescope and sometimes with the unaided eye.

visual field *n. Abbr.* **V.F., VF** The space or range within which objects are visible to the immobile eyes at a given time. Also called *field of vision.*

vi·su·al·ize (vĭzh′o͞o-ə-līz′) *v.* **-ized, -iz·ing, -iz·es.** *—tr.* **1.** To form a mental image of; envisage: *tried to visualize the scene as it was described.* **2.** To make visible. *—intr.* To form a mental image. **—vi′su·al·i·za′tion** (-ə-lĭ-zā′shən) *n.*

vi·su·al·iz·er (vĭzh′o͞o-ə-lī′zər) *n.* One who visualizes, especially a person whose mental images are predominantly visual.

visual purple *n.* See **rhodopsin.**

vi·su·o·mo·tor (vĭzh′o͞o-ō-mō′tər) *adj.* Of or relating to motor activity dependent on or involving sight: *the visuomotor coordination required to write.* [VISU(AL) + MOTOR.]

vi·su·o·spa·tial (vĭsh′o͞o-ō-spā′shəl) *adj.* Of or relating to visual perception of spatial relationships among objects: *the visuospatial skills needed to complete a jigsaw puzzle.* [VISU(AL) + SPATIAL.]

vi·ta (vī′tə, vē′-) *n., pl.* **vi·tae** (vī′tē, vē′tī). **1.** A short biographical or autobiographical account. **2.** A curriculum vitae. [Latin *vīta,* life. See VITAL.]

vi·tal (vīt′l) *adj.* **1.** Of, relating to, or characteristic of life. See Synonyms at **living. 2.** Necessary to the continuation of life; life-sustaining: *a vital organ; vital nutrients.* **3.** Full of life; animated: *"The population of the teeming, vital slum . . . declined"* (Rick Hampson). **4.** Imparting life or animation; invigorating: *the sun's vital rays.* **5.** Necessary to continued existence or effectiveness; essential: *"Irrigation was vital to early civilization"* (William H. McNeill). *"A vital component of any democracy is a free labor movement"* (Bayard Rustin). **6.** Concerned with or recording data pertinent to lives: *vital records.* **7.** *Biology.* Used or done on a living cell or tissue: *vital dyes; vital staining.* **8.** Destructive to life; fatal: *a vital injury.* [Middle English, from Old French, from Latin *vītālis,* from *vīta,* life. See **gʷei-** in Appendix.] **—vi′tal·ly** *adv.* **—vi′tal·ness** *n.*

vital capacity *n.* The amount of air that can be forcibly expelled from the lungs after breathing in as deeply as possible.

vi·tal·ism (vīt′l-ĭz′əm) *n.* The theory or doctrine that life processes arise from or contain a nonmaterial vital principle and cannot be explained entirely as physical and chemical phenomena. **—vi′tal·ist** *adj. & n.* **—vi′tal·is′tic** *adj.*

vi·tal·i·ty (vī-tăl′ĭ-tē) *n., pl.* **-ties. 1.** The capacity to live, grow, or develop: *plants that lost their vitality when badly pruned.* **2.** Physical or intellectual vigor; energy. See Synonyms at **vigor. 3.** The characteristic, principle, or force that distinguishes living things from nonliving things. **4.** Power to survive: *the vitality of an old tradition.*

vi·tal·ize (vīt′l-īz′) *tr.v.* **-ized, -iz·ing, -iz·es. 1.** To endow with life; animate. **2.** To make more lively or vigorous; invigorate. **—vi′tal·i·za′tion** (-ĭ-zā′shən) *n.* **—vi′tal·iz′er** *n.*

vi·tals (vīt′lz) *pl.n.* **1.** The vital body organs. **2.** The parts essential to continued functioning, as of a system.

vital signs *pl.n.* The pulse rate, temperature, and respiratory rate of an individual.

vital statistics *pl.n.* Statistics concerning the important events in human life, such as births, deaths, marriages, and migrations.

vi·ta·mer (vī′tə-mər) *n.* One of two or more related chemical substances that fulfill the same specific vitamin function. [VITA(MIN) + (ISO)MER.] **—vi′ta·mer′ic** (-mĕr′ĭk) *adj.*

vi·ta·min (vī′tə-mĭn) *n.* Any of various fat-soluble or water-soluble organic substances essential in minute amounts for normal growth and activity of the body and obtained naturally from plant and animal foods. [Alteration of *vitamine* : Latin *vīta,* life; see **gʷei-** in Appendix + AMINE (so called because they were originally thought to be amines).] **—vi′ta·min′ic** *adj.*

vitamin A *n.* A fat-soluble vitamin or a mixture of vitamins, especially vitamin A_1 or a mixture of vitamins A_1 and A_2, occurring principally in fish-liver oils, milk, and some yellow and dark green vegetables, and functioning in normal cell growth and development. Its deficiency causes hardening and roughening of the skin, night blindness, and degeneration of mucous membranes. Also called *retinol.*

vitamin A_1 *n.* A yellow crystalline compound, $C_{20}H_{30}O$, extracted from egg yolks, milk, and cod-liver oil.

vitamin A_2 *n.* A golden yellow oil, $C_{20}H_{28}O$, occurring chiefly in the livers of freshwater fish and having about 40 percent of the biological activity of vitamin A_1.

vitamin B *n.* **1.** Vitamin B complex. **2.** A member of the vitamin B complex, especially thiamine.

vitamin B_1 *n.* See **thiamine.**

vitamin B_2 *n.* See **riboflavin.**

vitamin B_6 *n.* See **pyridoxine.**

vitamin B_{12} *n.* A complex compound containing cobalt, found especially in liver and widely used to treat pernicious anemia. Also called *cobalamin, cyanocobalamin, extrinsic factor.*

vitamin B_c *n.* See **folic acid.**

vitamin B complex *n.* A group of water-soluble vitamins including thiamine, riboflavin, niacin, pantothenic acid, biotin, pyridoxine, folic acid, inositol, and vitamin B_{12} and occurring chiefly in yeast, liver, eggs, and some vegetables. Also called *B complex.*

vitamin C *n.* See **ascorbic acid.**

vitamin D *n.* A fat-soluble vitamin occurring in several forms, especially vitamin D_2 or vitamin D_3, required for normal growth of teeth and bones, and produced in general by ultraviolet irradiation of sterols found in milk, fish, and eggs.

vitamin D_2 *n.* A white crystalline compound, $C_{28}H_{44}O$, produced by ultraviolet irradiation of ergosterol. Also called *calciferol, ergocalciferol.*

vitamin D_3 *n.* A colorless crystalline compound, $C_{27}H_{44}O$, found in fish-liver oils, irradiated milk, and all irradiated animal foodstuffs. It has essentially the same biological activity as vitamin D_2. Also called *cholecalciferol.*

vitamin E *n.* A fat-soluble vitamin, $C_{29}H_{50}O_2$, found chiefly in plant leaves, wheat germ oil, and milk and used to treat sterility and various abnormalities of the muscles, red blood cells, liver, and brain.

vitamin G *n.* Riboflavin.

vitamin H *n.* Biotin.

vitamin K *n.* A fat-soluble vitamin, occurring in leafy green vegetables, tomatoes, and egg yolks, that promotes blood clotting and prevents hemorrhaging. It exists in several related forms, such as K_1 and K_2.

vitamin K_1 *n.* A yellow viscous oil, $C_{31}H_{46}O_2$, found in leafy green vegetables or made synthetically, used by the body to form prothrombin and in veterinary medicine as an antidote to certain poisons.

vitamin K_2 *n.* A crystalline compound, $C_{41}H_{56}O_2$, isolated from putrefied fish meal or from various intestinal bacteria, used to stop hemorrhaging and in veterinary medicine as an antidote to certain poisons.

vitamin P *n.* A water-soluble vitamin, found as a crystalline substance especially in citrus juices, that functions as a bioflavonoid in promoting capillary resistance to hemorrhaging.

Vi·tebsk (vē′tĕpsk′, vyĕ′tyĭpsk). A city of northeast Belorussia on the Western Dvina River northeast of Minsk. First mentioned in 1021, it passed to Russia in 1772 and is now a port, railroad junction, and processing center. Population, 335,000.

vi·tel·lar·i·um (vĭt′l-âr′ē-əm, vīt′-) *n., pl.* **-i·ums** or **-i·a** (-ē-ə). A group of glands that secrete yolk around the egg in those invertebrates, such as worms, whose eggs do not contain yolk. [New Latin, from Latin *vitellus,* egg yolk. See VITELLUS.]

vi·tel·lin (vĭ-tĕl′ĭn, vī-) *n.* A protein found in egg yolk. [VITELL(US) + -IN.]

vi·tel·line (vĭ-tĕl′ĭn, -ēn′, vī-) *adj.* **1.** Of, relating to, or associated with the yolk of an egg: *the vitelline membrane.* **2.** *Color.* Having the yellow hue of an egg yolk; dull yellow. **—vitelline** *n.* The yolk of an egg. [VITELL(US) + -INE[1].]

vi·tel·lo·gen·e·sis (vĭt′l-ō-jĕn′ĭ-sĭs, vīt′-) *n.* Formation of the yolk of an egg. [VITELL(US) + -GENESIS.] **—vi′tel·lo·ge·net′ic** (-jə-nĕt′ĭk), **vi′tel·lo·gen′ic** (-jĕn′ĭk) *adj.*

vi·tel·lus (vĭ-tĕl′əs, vī-) *n., pl.* **-lus·es.** The yolk of an egg. [Latin, probably diminutive of *vitulus,* calf. See **wet-[2]** in Appendix.]

vi·ti·ate (vĭsh′ē-āt′) *tr.v.* **-at·ed, -at·ing, -ates. 1.** To reduce the value or impair the quality of. **2.** To corrupt morally; debase. **3.** To make ineffective; invalidate. See Synonyms at **corrupt.** [Latin *vitiāre, vitiāt-,* from *vitium,* fault.] **—vi′ti·a·ble** (vĭsh′ē-ə-bəl) *adj.* **—vi′ti·a′tion** *n.* **—vi′ti·a′tor** *n.*

vit·i·cul·ture (vĭt′ĭ-kŭl′chər, vī′tĭ-) *n.* The cultivation of grapes. [Latin *vītis,* vine; see **wei-** in Appendix + CULTURE.] **—vit′i·cul′tur·al** *adj.* **—vit′i·cul′tur·ist** *n.*

Vi·ti Le·vu (vē′tē lĕv′o͞o). The largest of the Fiji Islands, in the southwest Pacific Ocean. Suva, the capital of Fiji, is on the southeast coast of the island.

vit·i·li·go (vĭt′l-ī′gō, -ē′gō) *n., pl.* **-gos.** See **leukoderma.** [Latin *vitilīgō,* tetter.]

Vi·tim (vĭ-tēm′). A river of southeast Russia flowing about 1,834 km (1,140 mi) generally northeast and north to the Lena River.

Vi·to·ri·a (vĭ-tôr′ē-ə, -tōr′-, bē-tô′ryä). A city of north-central Spain south-southeast of Bilbao. Probably founded by the Visigoths in the sixth century A.D., it is a manufacturing and processing center. Population, 199,239.

Vi·tó·ri·a (vĭ-tôr′ē-ə, -tōr′-, vē-tô′ryä). A city of eastern Brazil on the Atlantic Ocean northeast of Rio de Janeiro. It was founded in 1535 and is now a major shipping and processing center. Population, 165,090.

vit·rec·to·my (vĭ-trĕk′tə-mē) *n.*, *pl.* **-mies.** Surgical removal of the vitreous humor from the eyeball. [VITR(EOUS) + -ECTOMY.]

vit·re·ous (vĭt′rē-əs) *adj.* **1.** Of, relating to, resembling, or having the nature of glass; glassy. **2.** Obtained or made from glass. **3.** Of or relating to the vitreous humor. **—vitreous** *n.* The vitreous humor. [From Latin *vitreus,* from *vitrum,* glass.] **—vit′re·os′i·ty** (-ŏs′ĭ-tē), **vit′re·ous·ness** (-əs-nĭs) *n.*

vitreous enamel *n.* See **porcelain enamel.**

vitreous humor *n.* The clear gelatinous substance that fills the eyeball between the retina and the lens.

vi·tres·cent (vĭ-trĕs′ənt) *adj.* **1.a.** Tending to turn into glass. **b.** Capable of being turned into glass. **2.** Resembling glass; vitreous. [Latin *vitrum,* glass + -ESCENT.] **—vi·tres′cence** *n.*

vit·ri·fy (vĭt′rə-fī′) *v.* **-fied** (-fīd′), **-fy·ing, -fies** (-fīz′). *—tr.* To change or make into glass or a glassy substance, especially through heat fusion. *—intr.* To become vitreous. [French *vitrifier,* from Medieval Latin *vitrificāre* : Latin *vitrum,* glass + Latin *-ficāre,* -fy.] **—vit′ri·fi′a·bil′i·ty** *n.* **—vit′ri·fi′a·ble** *adj.* **—vit′ri·fi·ca′tion** (-fĭ-kā′shən) *n.*

vi·trine (vē-trēn′) *n.* A glass-paneled cabinet or case for displaying articles such as china, objects d'art, or fine merchandise. [French, from *vitre,* pane of glass, from Old French, glass, window with multiple lights, from Latin *vitrum.*]

vitrine

vit·ri·ol (vĭt′rē-ōl′, -əl) *n.* **1.a.** See **sulfuric acid. b.** Any of various sulfates of metals, such as ferrous sulfate, zinc sulfate, or copper sulfate. **2.** Bitterly abusive feeling or expression. **—vitriol** *tr.v.* **-oled, -ol·ing, -ols** or **-olled, -ol·ling, -ols.** To expose or subject to vitriol. [Middle English, from Old French, from Medieval Latin *vitriolum,* from Late Latin *vitreolum,* neuter of *vitreolus,* of glass, from Latin *vitreus.* See VITREOUS.]

vit·ri·ol·ic (vĭt′rē-ŏl′ĭk) *adj.* **1.** Of, similar to, or derived from a vitriol. **2.** Bitterly scathing; caustic: *vitriolic criticism.*

Vi·tru·vi·us (vĭ-tro͞o′vē-əs). Originally Marcus Vitruvius Pollio. fl. first century B.C. Roman architect and writer. His *De Architectura* is the only surviving text on ancient architectural theory.

Vi·try-sur-Seine (vē-trē′so͝or-sĕn′, -sür-). A city of north-central France, an industrial suburb of Paris. Population, 85,263.

vit·ta (vĭt′ə) *n.*, *pl.* **vit·tae** (vĭt′ē). **1.** *Zoology.* A streak or band of color, as on the bill of a bird. **2.** *Botany.* An oil tube in the fruit of certain plants, such as the carrot or parsley. [Latin, headband, ribbon. See **wei-** in Appendix.] **—vit′tate′** (vĭt′āt′) *adj.*

vit·tle (vĭt′l) *n. & v.* *Non-Standard.* Variant of **victual** (sense 2).

vit·u·line (vĭch′ə-līn′) *adj.* Of, relating to, or resembling veal or a calf. [Latin *vitulīnus,* from *vitulus,* calf. See VITELLUS.]

vi·tu·per·ate (vī-to͞o′pə-rāt′, -tyo͞o′-, vĭ-) *v.* **-at·ed, -at·ing, -ates.** *—tr.* To rebuke or criticize harshly or abusively; berate. See Synonyms at **scold.** *—intr.* To use harshly abusive language; rail. [Latin *vituperāre, vituperāt-.*] **—vi·tu′per·a′tor** *n.*

vi·tu·per·a·tion (vī-to͞o′pə-rā′shən, -tyo͞o′-, vĭ-) *n.* **1.** The act or an instance of vituperating; abusive censure. **2.** Sustained, harshly abusive language; invective.

vi·tu·per·a·tive (vī-to͞o′pər-ə-tĭv, -tyo͞o′-, -pə-rā′-, vĭ-) *adj.* Using, containing, or marked by harshly abusive censure. **—vi·tu′per·a·tive·ly** *adv.* **—vi·tu′per·a·tive·ness** *n.*

vi·va (vē′və, -vä′) *interj.* Used to express acclamation, salute, or applause. [Italian and Spanish, (long) live, both from Latin *vīva,* third person sing. present subjunctive of *vīvere,* to live. See **gʷei-** in Appendix.]

vi·va·ce (vē-vä′chā) *adv. & adj. Music.* In a lively or vivacious manner. Used chiefly as a direction. [Italian, from Latin *vīvāx, vīvāc-,* vivacious. See VIVACIOUS.]

vi·va·cious (vĭ-vā′shəs, vī-) *adj.* Full of animation and spirit; lively: *a charming and vivacious host.* [From Latin *vīvāx, vīvāc-,* from *vīvere,* to live. See **gʷei-** in Appendix.] **—vi·va′cious·ly** *adv.* **—vi·va′cious·ness** *n.*

vi·vac·i·ty (vĭ-văs′ĭ-tē, vī-) *n.* The quality or condition of being vivacious; liveliness: *"the light and vivacity that laugh in the eyes of a child"* (Charles Dickens).

Vi·val·di (vĭ-väl′dē, -vôl′-), **Antonio Lucio.** 1675?–1741. Italian composer and violinist. He is best known for his lively concertos, particularly *The Four Seasons* (1725), a set of four violin concertos.

vi·van·dière (vē′väɴ-dyâr′) *n.* A woman who accompanies troops to sell them food, supplies, and liquor. [French, feminine of *vivandier,* from Old French, alteration (influenced by Medieval Latin *vīvenda,* provisions) of *viandier,* from *viande,* food. See VIAND.]

vi·var·i·um (vī-vâr′ē-əm) *n.*, *pl.* **-i·ums** or **-i·a** (-ē-ə). A place, especially an indoor enclosure, for keeping and raising living animals and plants under natural conditions for observation or research. [Latin *vīvārium,* from neuter of *vīvārius,* of living creatures, from *vīvus,* alive. See VIVIFY.]

vi·va vo·ce (vī′və vō′sē, vē′və) *adv. & adj.* By word of mouth: *a report submitted viva voce; a viva voce examination.* [Medieval Latin *vīvā vōce,* with the living voice : Latin *vīvā,* feminine ablative sing. of *vīvus,* living + Latin *vōce,* ablative of *vōx,* voice.]

vi·vax (vī′văks) *n.* **1.** The protozoan *(Plasmodium vivax)* that causes the most common form of malaria. **2.** Malaria caused by this protozoan, characterized by the occurrence of febrile paroxysms about every 48 hours. [From New Latin *vīvāx,* species name, from Latin, lively. See VIVACIOUS.]

vi·ver·rid (vī-vĕr′ĭd) *adj. & n.* Viverrine. [From New Latin *Vīverridae,* family name, from *Vīverra,* type genus. See VIVERRINE.]

vi·ver·rine (vī-vĕr′ĭn, -īn′) *adj.* Of or belonging to the family Viverridae, which includes small carnivorous mammals such as the civets and mongooses. **—viverrine** *n.* A member of the Viverridae. [New Latin *vīverrīnus,* from *Vīverra,* type genus, from Latin *vīverra,* ferret.]

viv·id (vĭv′ĭd) *adj.* **-er, -est. 1.** Perceived as bright and distinct; brilliant: *a vivid star.* **2.a.** Having intensely bright colors: *a vivid tapestry.* **b.** Having a very high degree of saturation: *a vivid purple.* **3.** Full of the vigor and freshness of immediate experience. **4.a.** Evoking lifelike images within the mind; heard, seen, or felt as if real: *a vivid description.* See Synonyms at **graphic. b.** Active in forming lifelike images: *a vivid imagination.* [Latin *vīvidus,* from *vīvere,* to live. See **gʷei-** in Appendix.] **—viv′id·ly** *adv.* **—viv′id·ness** *n.*

viv·i·fy (vĭv′ə-fī′) *tr.v.* **-fied, -fy·ing, -fies. 1.** To give or bring life to; animate: *vivify a puppet; vivifying the brown grasslands.* **2.** To make more lively, intense, or striking; enliven: *A smile may vivify a face.* [Middle English *vivifien,* from Old French *vivifier,* from Late Latin *vīvificāre* : Latin *vīvus,* alive; see **gʷei-** in Appendix + Latin *-ficāre,* -fy.] **—viv′i·fi·ca′tion** (-fĭ-kā′shən) *n.* **—viv′i·fi′er** *n.*

vi·vip·a·rous (vī-vĭp′ər-əs, vĭ-) *adj.* **1.** *Zoology.* Giving birth to living offspring that develop within the mother's body. Most mammals and some other animals are viviparous. **2.** *Botany.* **a.** Germinating or producing seeds that germinate before becoming detached from the parent plant, as in the mangrove. **b.** Producing bulbils or new plants rather than seed, as in the tiger lily. [From Latin *vīviparus* : *vīvus,* alive; see **gʷei-** in Appendix + *-parus,* -parous.] **—vi′vi·par′i·ty** (vī′və-păr′ĭ-tē, vĭv′ə-) *n.* **—vi·vip′a·rous·ly** *adv.*

viv·i·sect (vĭv′ĭ-sĕkt′) *v.* **-sect·ed, -sect·ing, -sects.** *—tr.* To perform vivisection on (an animal). *—intr.* To practice vivisection. [Back-formation from VIVISECTION.] **—viv′i·sec′tor** *n.*

viv·i·sec·tion (vĭv′ĭ-sĕk′shən, vĭv′ĭ-sĕk′-) *n.* The act or practice of cutting into or otherwise injuring living animals, especially for the purpose of scientific research. [Latin *vīvus,* alive; see VIVIFY + (DIS)SECTION.] **—viv′i·sec′tion·al** *adj.* **—viv′i·sec′tion·al·ly** *adv.* **—viv′i·sec′tion·ist** *n.*

vix·en (vĭk′sən) *n.* **1.** A female fox. **2.** A woman regarded as quarrelsome, shrewish, or malicious. [Middle English *fixen,* from Old English *fyxe.*] **—vix′en·ish** *adj.* **—vix′en·ish·ly** *adv.* **—vix′en·ish·ness** *n.*

viz. *abbr.* Videlicet.

Vi·za·ga·pa·tam (vĭ-zä′gə-pŭt′əm). See **Visakhapatnam.**

viz·ard also **vis·ard** (vĭz′ərd, -ärd′) *n.* **1.** A visor or mask. **2.** A disguise. [Alteration of obsolete *vizar,* from Middle English *viser.* See VISOR.]

Viz·ca·í·no (vĭz-kä-ē′nō, bēth-kä-), **Sebastián.** 1550?–1615? Spanish explorer who was the first European to make a systematic exploration of the California coast (1602–1603).

vi·zier (vĭ-zîr′, vĭz′yər) *n.* A high officer in a Moslem government, especially in the Ottoman Empire. [Turkish *vezīr,* from Arabic *wazīr,* minister, from *wazara,* to bear, carry.] **—vi·zier′ate** (vĭ-zîr′ĭt, -āt′, vĭz′yər-ĭt, -yə-rāt′) *n.* **—vi·zier′i·al** *adj.*

vi·zor (vī′zər) *n. & v.* Variant of **visor.**

vizs·la (vĭzh′lä) *n.* Any of a Hungarian breed of short-haired, medium-sized hunting dogs having a deep rust-gold coat and a docked tail. [Probably from Czech *vyžle,* a hunting dog.]

VJ *abbr.* Video jockey.

V-J Day (vē′jā′) *n.* August 15, 1945, the day on which the Allies announced the surrender of Japanese forces during World War II. [*V(ictory in) J(apan) Day.*]

VL *abbr.* Vulgar Latin.

VLA *abbr. Astronomy.* Very Large Array.

Vlaar·ding·en (vlär′dĭng-ən). A city of southwest Netherlands, a port and industrial suburb of Rotterdam. Population, 76,466.

Vla·di·mir (vlăd′ə-mîr′, vlə-dyē′mĭr). A city of west-central Russia east of Moscow. Probably founded in the 10th century, it came under the control of Moscow during the 15th century. Population, 331,000.

Vlad·i·vos·tok (vlăd′ə-və-stŏk′, -vŏs′tŏk′, vlə-dyə-və-stôk′). A city of extreme southeast Russia on an arm of the Sea of Japan. It has been a naval base since 1872 and grew rapidly after the completion of the Trans-Siberian Railroad in the early 1900's. Population, 600,000.

Vla·minck (vlä-măɴk′), **Maurice de.** 1876–1958. French artist. A leading exponent of fauvism, he is noted for his stormy, aggressive landscapes.

VLBI *abbr. Astronomy.* Very long baseline interferometry.

VLCC *abbr.* Very large crude (oil) carrier.

VLDL (vē′ĕl-dē′ĕl) *n.* A lipoprotein containing a very large proportion of lipids to protein and carrying most cholesterol from the liver to the tissues. [*v(ery) l(ow) d(ensity) l(ipoprotein).*]

ă pat	oi boy
ā pay	ou out
âr care	o͝o took
ä father	o͞o boot
ĕ pet	ŭ cut
ē be	ûr urge
ĭ pit	th thin
ī pie	*th* this
îr pier	hw which
ŏ pot	zh vision
ō toe	ə about, item
ô paw	♦ regionalism

Stress marks: ′ (primary); ′ (secondary), as in **dictionary** (dĭk′shə-nĕr′ē)

vlf or **VLF** *abbr.* Very low frequency.

Vlis·sing·en (vlĭs′ĭng-ən) also **Flush·ing** (flŭsh′ĭng). A city of southwest Netherlands on an island in the Schelde estuary and the North Sea. Chartered in 1247, it was one of the first Dutch towns to rebel against Spain (1572). Population, 26,500.

Vlo·rë (vlôr′ə, vlōr′ə) **Vlo·ne** (vlō′nə). A city of southwest Albania on **Vlorë Bay,** an inlet of the Adriatic Sea. The independence of Albania was proclaimed in Vlorë on November 28, 1912. Population, 61,100.

VLSI *abbr. Electronics.* Very large scale integration.

Vl·ta·va (vŭl′tə-və, vəl′tä-vä). A river, about 434 km (270 mi) long, of western Czechoslovakia flowing southeast then north to the Elbe River.

V.M.D. *abbr. Latin.* Veterinariae Medicinae Doctor (Doctor of Veterinary Medicine).

V-neck (vē′nĕk′) *n.* A V-shaped neckline, as of a sweater.

VO *abbr.* Verbal order.

vo. *abbr. Printing.* Verso.

VOA *abbr.* Voice of America.

voc. *abbr.* **1.** Vocational. **2.** Vocative.

vocab. *abbr.* Vocabulary.

vo·ca·ble (vō′kə-bəl) *Linguistics. n.* A word considered only as a sequence of sounds or letters rather than as a unit of meaning. **—vocable** *adj.* Capable of being voiced or spoken. [French, from Old French, from Latin *vocābulum,* name, from *vocāre,* to call. See **wekʷ-** in Appendix.]

vo·cab·u·lar·y (vō-kăb′yə-lĕr′ē) *n., pl.* **-ies.** *Abbr.* **vocab. 1.** All the words of a language. **2.** The sum of words used by, understood by, or at the command of a particular person or group. See Synonyms at **diction. 3.** A list of words and often phrases, usually arranged alphabetically and defined or translated; a lexicon or glossary. **4.** A supply of expressive means; a repertoire of communication: *a dancer's vocabulary of movement.* [French *vocabulaire,* from Old French, from Medieval Latin *vocābulārium,* from neuter of *vocābulārius,* of words, from Latin *vocābulum,* name. See VOCABLE.]

vo·cal (vō′kəl) *adj.* **1.** Of or relating to the voice: *the vertebrate vocal organs; a vocal defect.* **2.** Uttered or produced by the voice. **3.** Having a voice; capable of emitting sound or speech. **4.** Full of voices; resounding: *a playground vocal with the shouts and laughter of children.* **5.** Tending to express oneself often or freely; outspoken: *a vocal critic of city politics.* **6.** *Linguistics.* **a.** Of or resembling vowels; vocalic. **b.** Voiced. **7.** *Music.* Of, relating to, or performed by singing: *vocal training; vocal music.* **—vocal** *n.* **1.** A vocal sound. **2.** *Music.* A popular composition for a singer, often with instrumental accompaniment. [Middle English, from Old French, from Latin *vōcālis, from vōx, vōc-,* voice. See **wekʷ-** in Appendix.] **—vo′cal·ly** *adv.* **—vo′cal·ness** *n.*

vocal cords *pl.n.* Either of two pairs of bands or folds of mucous membrane in the throat that project into the larynx. The lower pair vibrate when pulled together and when air is passed up from the lungs, thereby producing vocal sounds. The upper, thicker pair are not involved in voice production.

vocal folds *pl.n.* Vocal cords.

vo·cal·ic (vō-kăl′ĭk) *adj. Linguistics.* **1.** Containing, marked by, or consisting of vowels. **2.** Of, relating to, or having the nature of a vowel. **—vo·cal′i·cal·ly** *adv.*

vo·cal·ise¹ (vō′kə-lēz′) *n. Music.* An exercise, a composition, or an arrangement in which a performer sings sol-fa syllables or other meaningless vocal sounds rather than a text. [French, from *vocaliser,* to vocalize, from *vocal,* vocal, from Old French. See VOCAL.]

vo·cal·ise² (vō′kə-līz′) *v. Chiefly British.* Variant of **vocalize.**

vo·cal·ism (vō′kə-lĭz′əm) *n.* **1.** Use of the voice in speaking or singing. **2.** *Music.* The act, technique, or art of singing. **3.** *Linguistics.* **a.** A vowel sound. **b.** A system of vowels used in a language or dialect. **—vo′cal·is′tic** *adj.*

vo·cal·ist (vō′kə-lĭst) *n. Music.* A singer. **—vo′ca·lis′tic** *adj.*

vo·cal·ize (vō′kə-līz′) *v.* **-ized, -iz·ing, -iz·es.** *—tr.* **1.** To produce with the voice. **2.** To give voice to; articulate: *vocalize popular sentiment.* **3.** To mark (a vowelless Hebrew text, for example) with vowel points. **4.** *Linguistics.* **a.** To change (a consonant) into a vowel during articulation. **b.** To voice. *—intr.* **1.a.** To use the voice. **b.** *Music.* To sing. **2.** *Linguistics.* To be changed into a vowel. **—vo′cal·i·za′tion** (-kə-lĭ-zā′shən) *n.* **—vo′cal·iz′er** *n.*

vocal tic *n.* An involuntary, abrupt, and inappropriate grunt, bark, or other exclamation or utterance, occurring especially in Tourette's syndrome.

vo·ca·tion (vō-kā′shən) *n.* **1.** A regular occupation, especially one for which a person is particularly suited or qualified. **2.** An inclination, as if in response to a summons, to undertake a certain kind of work, especially a religious career; a calling. [Middle English *vocacioun,* divine call to a religious life, from Old French *vocation,* from Latin *vocātiō, vocātiōn-,* a calling, from *vocātus,* past participle of *vocāre,* to call. See **wekʷ-** in Appendix.]

vo·ca·tion·al (vō-kā′shə-nəl) *adj. Abbr.* **voc. 1.** Of or relating to a vocation or vocations: *vocational counseling.* **2.** Relating to, providing, or undergoing training in a special skill to be pursued in a trade: *vocational students learning to operate a lathe.* **—vo·ca′tion·al·ly** *adv.*

vo·ca·tion·al·ism (vō-kā′shə-nə-lĭz′əm) *n.* The stressing of vocational training in education. **—vo·ca′tion·al·ist** *n.*

vocational school *n.* A school, especially one on a secondary level, that offers instruction and practical introductory experience in skilled trades such as mechanics, carpentry, plumbing, and construction.

voc·a·tive (vŏk′ə-tĭv) *adj.* **1.** Relating to, characteristic of, or used in calling. **2.** *Abbr.* **voc., v.** Relating to or being a grammatical case used in Latin and certain other languages to indicate the person or thing being addressed. **—vocative** *n. Abbr.* **voc., v. 1.** The vocative case. **2.** A word in the vocative case. [Middle English *vocatif,* from Old French, from Latin *vocātīvus (cāsus),* vocative (case), from *vocātus,* past participle of *vocāre,* to call. See VOCATION.] **—voc′a·tive·ly** *adv.*

vo·cif·er·ant (vō-sĭf′ər-ənt) *adj.* Noisy and insistent; vociferous.

vo·cif·er·ate (vō-sĭf′ə-rāt′) *tr. & intr.v.* **-at·ed, -at·ing, -ates.** To utter (something) or cry out loudly and vehemently, especially in protest. [Latin *vōciferārī, vōciferāt-* : *vōx, vōc-,* voice; see VOICE + *ferre,* to carry; see **bher-¹** in Appendix.] **—vo·cif′er·a′tion** *n.* **—vo·cif′er·a′tor** *n.*

vo·cif·er·ous (vō-sĭf′ər-əs) *adj.* Making, given to, or marked by noisy and vehement outcry. **—vo·cif′er·ous·ly** *adv.* **—vo·cif′er·ous·ness** *n.*

SYNONYMS: *vociferous, blatant, boisterous, strident, clamorous.* These adjectives all mean conspicuously and usually offensively loud. *Vociferous* suggests a noisy outcry, as of vehement protest: *vociferous complaints. Blatant* connotes coarse or vulgar noisiness: *"Up rose a blatant Radical"* (Walter Bagehot). *Boisterous* implies unrestrained noise, tumult, and often rowdiness, as that arising from high spirits: *boisterous mirth. Strident* stresses offensive harshness, shrillness, or discordance: *a strident voice.* Something *clamorous* is both vociferous and sustained: *a clamorous uproar.*

vo·cod·er (vō′kō′dər) *n.* An electronic device or system for synthesizing speech. [VO(ICE) + COD(E) + –ER¹.]

vod·ka (vŏd′kə) *n.* An alcoholic liquor originally distilled from fermented wheat mash but now also made from a mash of rye, corn, or potatoes. [Russian, diminutive of *voda,* water. See **wed-¹** in Appendix.]

vo·doun or **vo·dun** (vō-do͞on′) *n.* See **voodoo** (sense 1). [Haitian Creole, from Ewe *vodu* or Fon *vodun.*]

vogue (vōg) *n.* **1.** The prevailing fashion, practice, or style: *Hoop skirts were once the vogue.* **2.** Popular acceptance or favor; popularity: *a party game no longer in vogue.* See Synonyms at **fashion.** [French, from Old French, probably from *voguer,* to sail, row. See **wegh-** in Appendix.]

WORD HISTORY: The history of the word *vogue* takes us back from the abstract world of fashion to the concrete actions of moving in a vehicle and rowing a boat, demonstrating how sense can change dramatically over time even though it flows, as it were, in the same channel. The history of *vogue* begins with the Indo-European root **wegh–,* meaning "to go, transport in a vehicle." Among many other forms derived from this root was the Germanic stem **wēga–,* "water in motion." From this stem came the Old Low German verb *wogōn,* meaning "to sway, rock." This verb passed into Old French as *voguer,* which meant "to sail, row." The Old French word yielded the noun *vogue,* which probably literally meant "a rowing," and so "a course," and figuratively "reputation" and then "reputation of fashionable things" or "prevailing fashion," which involve courses, so to speak. The French passed the noun on to us, it being first recorded in English in 1571.

vogu·ish (vō′gĭsh) *adj.* **1.** Fashionable; chic: *a suit of voguish cut.* **2.** Temporarily in frequent use; faddish: *voguish terminology.* **—vogu′ish·ly** *adv.* **—vogu′ish·ness** *n.*

Vo·gul (vō′go͝ol) *n., pl.* **Vogul** or **-guls. 1.** A member of a people inhabiting the region of the Ob River in western Siberia, closely related to the Ostyak. **2.** The Ugric language of this people.

voice (vois) *n. Abbr.* **v. 1.a.** The sound produced by the vocal organs of a vertebrate, especially a human being. **b.** The ability to produce such sounds. **2.** A specified quality, condition, or pitch of vocal sound: *a hoarse voice; the child's piping voice.* **3.** *Linguistics.* Expiration of air through vibrating vocal cords, used in the production of vowels and voiced consonants. **4.** A sound resembling or reminiscent of vocal utterance: *the murmuring voice of the forest.* **5.** *Music.* **a.** Musical sound produced by vibration of the human vocal cords and resonated within the throat and head cavities. **b.** The quality or condition of a person's singing: *a baritone in excellent voice.* **c.** A singer: *a choir of excellent voices.* **d.** One of the individual parts or strands in a composition: *a fugue for four voices; string voices carrying the melody.* Also called *voice part.* **6.a.** Expression; utterance: *gave voice to their feelings at the meeting.* **b.** A medium or an agency of expression: *a newsletter that serves as a neighborhood voice.* **c.** The right or opportunity to express a choice or an opinion: *a territory that has a voice, but not a vote, in Congress.* **7.** *Grammar.* A property of verbs or a set of verb inflections indicating the relation between the subject and the action expressed by the verb: *"Birds build nests" uses the active voice; "nests built by birds" uses the passive voice.* **8.** The distinctive style or manner of expression of an author or a character in a book. **—voice** *tr.v.* **voiced, voic·ing, voic·es. 1.** To give voice to; utter: *voice a grievance.* See Synonyms at **vent**[1]. **2.** *Linguistics.* To pronounce with vibration of the vocal cords. **3.** *Music.* **a.** To provide (a composition) with voice parts. **b.** To regulate the tone of (the pipes of an organ, for example). **—*idiom.* with one voice.** In complete agreement; unanimously: *Our group rejected the proposal with one voice.* [Middle English, from Old French *vois,* from Latin *vōx, vōc-.* See **wekʷ-** in Appendix.]

voice box *n.* The larynx.

voiced (voist) *adj.* **1.** Having a voice or a specified kind of voice. Often used in combination: *harsh-voiced.* **2.** *Linguistics.* Uttered with vibration of the vocal cords, as the consonants *b* and *d.* **—voiced′ness** (voist′nĭs, voi′sĭd-) *n.*

voice·ful (vois′fəl) *adj.* Having a voice, especially a loud voice; resounding. **—voice′ful·ness** *n.*

voice·less (vois′lĭs) *adj.* **1.** Having no voice; mute. **2.** *Linguistics.* Uttered without vibration of the vocal cords, as the consonants *t* and *p.* **—voice′less·ly** *adv.* **—voice′less·ness** *n.*

voice-o·ver or **voice·o·ver** (vois′ō′vər) *n.* The voice of an unseen narrator, or of an on-screen character not seen speaking, in a movie or a television broadcast.

voice part *n.* *Music.* **1.** A part or strand of a composition written for the human voice. **2.** See **voice** (sense 5d).

voice·print (vois′prĭnt′) *n.* An electronically recorded graphic representation of a person's voice, in which the configuration for any given utterance is uniquely characteristic of the individual speaker.

voic·er (voi′sər) *n.* **1.** One that voices: *a voicer of criticism.* **2.** *Music.* A specialist in regulating the tone of organ pipes.

voic·ing (voi′sĭng) *n.* **1.** The act, practice, or production of one that voices. **2.** *Music.* Tonal quality of an instrument in an ensemble, especially a jazz ensemble, or of the ensemble as a whole.

void (void) *adj.* **1.** Containing no matter; empty. **2.** Not occupied; unfilled. **3.** Completely lacking; devoid: *void of understanding.* See Synonyms at **empty. 4.** Ineffective; useless. **5.** Having no legal force or validity; null: *a contract rendered void.* **6.** *Games.* Lacking cards of a particular suit in a dealt hand. **—void** *n.* **1.a.** An empty space. **b.** A vacuum. **2.** An open space or a break in continuity; a gap. **3.** A feeling or state of emptiness, loneliness, or loss. **4.** *Games.* Absence of cards of a particular suit in a dealt hand: *a void in hearts.* **—void** *v.* **void·ed, void·ing, voids.** *—tr.* **1.** To take out (the contents of something); empty. **2.** To excrete (body wastes). **3.** To leave; vacate. **4.** To make void or of no validity; invalidate: *issued a new passport and voided the old one.* *—intr.* To excrete body wastes. [Middle English, from Old French *voide,* feminine of *voit,* from Vulgar Latin **vocitus,* alteration of Latin *vacīvus, vocīvus,* variant of *vacuus,* from *vacāre,* to be empty. See **eu-**[2] in Appendix.] **—void′er** *n.*

void·a·ble (voi′də-bəl) *adj.* That can be voided and especially annulled: *voidable contracts.* **—void′a·ble·ness** *n.*

void·ance (void′ns) *n.* **1.** The act of voiding. **2.** The condition of being vacant; emptiness.

void·ed (voi′dĭd) *adj.* *Heraldry.* Having the central area cut out or left vacant, leaving a narrow border or an outline: *a voided lozenge.*

voi·là (vwä-lä′) *interj.* Used to call attention to or express satisfaction with a thing shown or accomplished: *Mix the ingredients, chill, and—voilà!—a light, tasty dessert.* [French : *voi,* second person sing. imperative of *voir,* to see (from Old French; see VOYEUR) + *là,* there (from Old French *la, lai,* probably from Latin *illāc,* by that way : *illa,* that, feminine of *ille;* see **al-**[1] in Appendix + *-ce,* deictic particle).]

voile (voil) *n.* A light, plain-weave, sheer fabric of cotton, rayon, silk, or wool used especially for making dresses and curtains. [French, from Old French *veile,* veil, from Latin *vēla,* neuter pl. of *vēlum,* covering.]

voir dire (vwär dîr′) *n.* *Law.* A preliminary examination of prospective jurors or witnesses under oath to determine their competence or suitability. [Anglo-Norman, to speak the truth : Latin *vērus,* true; see **wēro-** in Appendix + Latin *dīcere,* to say; see **deik-** in Appendix.]

voix cé·leste (vwä′ sā-lĕst′) *n., pl.* **voix cé·lestes** (sā-lĕst′). *Music.* An organ stop that produces a gentle tremolo effect. Also called *vox angelica.* [French : *voix,* voice + *céleste,* celestial.]

vol. *abbr.* **1.** Volcano. **2.** Volume. **3.** Volunteer.

Vo·lans (vō′lănz′) *n.* A constellation in the polar region of the celestial Southern Hemisphere near Carina and Dorado. [Latin *volāns,* present participle of *volāre,* to fly.]

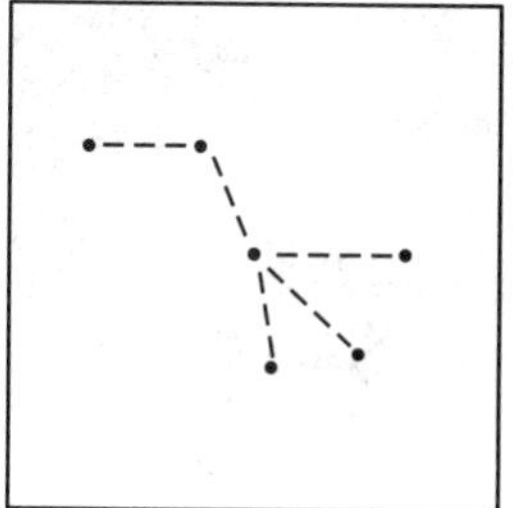

Volans

vo·lant (vō′lənt) *adj.* **1.** Flying or capable of flying. **2.** Moving quickly or nimbly; agile. **3.** *Heraldry.* Depicted with the wings extended as in flying. [Latin *volāns, volant-,* present participle of *volāre,* to fly. Sense 3, from French, from Old French, present participle of *voler,* to fly, from Latin *volāre.*]

Vo·la·pük (vō′lə-po͝ok′, -pük′, vŏl′ə-) *n.* An artificial international language based on English. [Volapük : *vol,* world (alteration of English WORLD) + *pük,* speech (alteration of English SPEECH).]

vo·lar (vō′lər) *adj.* Of or relating to the sole of the foot or the palm of the hand. [From Latin *vola,* sole, palm.]

vol·a·tile (vŏl′ə-tl, -tīl′) *adj.* **1.** *Chemistry.* **a.** Evaporating readily at normal temperatures and pressures. **b.** That can be readily vaporized. **2.a.** Tending to vary often or widely, as in price: *the ups and downs of volatile stocks.* **b.** Inconstant; fickle: *a flirt's volatile affections.* **c.** Lighthearted; flighty: *in a volatile mood.* **d.** Ephemeral; fleeting. **3.** Tending to violence; explosive: *a volatile situation with troops and rioters eager for a confrontation.* **4.** Flying or capable of flying; volant. [French, from Old French, from Latin *volātilis,* flying, from *volātus,* past participle of *volāre,* to fly.] **—vol′a·tile** *n.* **—vol′a·til′i·ty** (-tĭl′ĭ-tē), **vol′a·tile·ness** (-tl-nĭs, -tīl′-) *n.*

volatile oil *n.* A rapidly evaporating oil, especially an essential oil, that does not leave a stain.

vol·a·til·ize (vŏl′ə-tl-īz′) *intr. & tr.v.* **-ized, -iz·ing, -iz·es. 1.** To become or make volatile. **2.** To evaporate or cause to evaporate. **—vol′a·til·iz′a·ble** *adj.* **—vol′a·til·i·za′tion** (-ĭ-zā′shən) *n.* **—vol′a·til·iz′er** *n.*

vol-au-vent (vô′lō-väɴ′) *n.* A light pastry shell filled with a ragout of meat or fish. [French : *vol,* flight + *à,* with + *le,* the + *vent,* wind.]

vol·can·ic (vŏl-kăn′ĭk, vôl-) *adj.* **1.** Of, resembling, or caused by a volcano or volcanoes: *a volcanic peak; volcanic islands.* **2.** Produced by or discharged from a volcano: *volcanic ash.* **3.** Characterized by the presence of volcanoes. **4.** Powerfully explosive: *a volcanic temper.* **—vol·can′i·cal·ly** *adv.*

volcanic glass *n.* Natural glass produced by the cooling of molten lava too quickly to permit crystallization.

vol·ca·nism (vŏl′kə-nĭz′əm) also **vul·ca·nism** (vŭl′-) *n.* **1.** Volcanic force or activity. **2.** The phenomena associated with volcanic activity.

vol·ca·nize (vŏl′kə-nīz′) *tr.v.* **-nized, -niz·ing, -niz·es.** To subject to or change by the effects of volcanic heat. **—vol′ca·ni·za′tion** (-nĭ-zā′shən) *n.*

vol·ca·no (vŏl-kā′nō) *n., pl.* **-noes** or **-nos.** *Abbr.* **vol. 1.a.** An opening in the earth's crust through which molten lava, ash, and gases are ejected. **b.** A similar opening on the surface of another planet. **2.** A mountain formed by the materials ejected from a volcano. [Italian, from Spanish *volcán* or Portuguese *volcão,* probably from Latin *vulcānus,* from *Volcānus,* Vulcan.]

vol·ca·no·gen·ic (vŏl′kə-nə-jĕn′ĭk, vôl′-) *adj.* Of volcanic origin.

Vol·ca·no Islands (vŏl-kā′nō). A group of Japanese islands in the northwest Pacific Ocean north of the Mariana Islands. Annexed by Japan in the late 19th century, the islands were administered by the United States from 1945 until 1968.

vol·ca·nol·o·gy (vŏl′kə-nŏl′ə-jē, vôl′-) also **vul·ca·nol·o·gy** (vŭl′-) *n.* The scientific study of volcanoes and volcanic phenomena. **—vol′ca·no·log′i·cal** (-nə-lŏj′ĭ-kəl) *adj.* **—vol′ca·nol′o·gist** *n.*

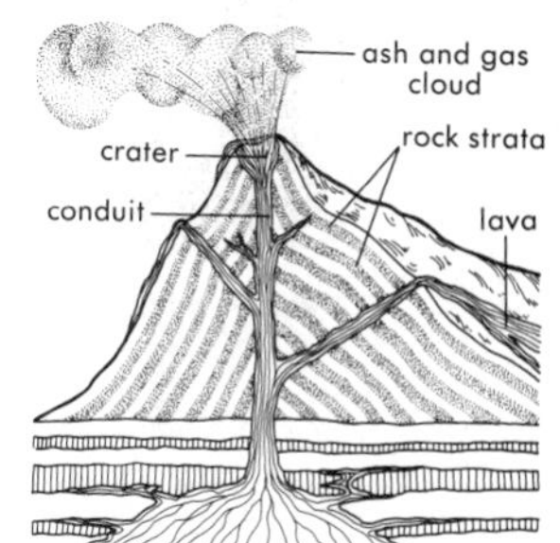

volcano
Cutaway view of an erupting volcano

vole[1] (vōl) *n.* Any of various rodents of the genus *Microtus* and related genera, resembling rats or mice but having a shorter tail and limbs and a heavier body. [Short for obsolete *volemouse,* perhaps from Norwegian **vollmus* : Old Norse *völlr,* field + Old Norse *mūs,* mouse.]

vole[2] (vōl) *n.* *Games.* The winning of all the tricks during the play of one hand, as of bridge; a grand slam. [French, probably from *voler,* to fly, from Old French, from Latin *volāre,* to fly.]

Vol·ga (vŏl′gə, vôl′-, vōl′-). A river of western Russia rising in the Valdai Hills northwest of Moscow and flowing about 3,701 km (2,300 mi) generally east and south to the Caspian Sea. It is the longest river of Europe and the main commercial waterway of Russia. The Volga is linked by canals and other rivers to the Baltic Sea.

Vol·go·grad (vŏl′gə-grăd′, vôl′-, vŭl-gə-grät′). Formerly **Sta·lin·grad** (stä′lĭn-grăd′, stə-lyĭn-grät′). A city of southwest Russia on the Volga River east of Voroshilovgrad. Founded in 1589 as a defensive stronghold named Tsaritsyn, it was renamed Stalingrad in 1925 and Volgograd in 1961. The city was besieged and severely damaged during a prolonged battle in World War II, with extensive casualties of both German and Soviet troops. Population, 974,000.

vol·i·tant (vŏl′ĭ-tnt) *adj.* **1.** Flying or capable of flying. **2.** Moving about rapidly. [Latin *volitāns, volitant-,* present participle of *volitāre,* to fly to and fro, frequentative of *volāre,* to fly.]

vol·i·ta·tion (vŏl′ĭ-tā′shən) *n.* **1.** The act of flying; flight. **2.** The ability to fly. **—vol′i·ta′tion·al** *adj.*

vo·li·tion (və-lĭsh′ən) *n.* **1.** The act or an instance of making a conscious choice or decision. **2.** A conscious choice or decision. **3.** The power or faculty of choosing; the will. [French, from Medieval Latin *volitiō, volitiōn-,* from Latin *velle, vol-,* to wish. See **wel-**[1] in Appendix.] **—vo·li′tion·al** *adj.* **—vo·li′tion·al·ly** *adv.*

vol·i·tive (vŏl′ĭ-tĭv) *adj.* **1.** Of, relating to, or originating in the will. **2.** Expressing a wish or permission.

volks·lied (fōks′lēt′, fôlk′s-) *n., pl.* **-lie·der** (-lē′dər). *Music.* A folk song. [German : *Volks,* genitive of *Volk,* people (from Middle High German *volc,* from Old High German *folc;* see **pele-**[1] in Appendix) + *Lied,* song; see LIED.]

vol·ley (vŏl′ē) *n., pl.* **-leys. 1.a.** A simultaneous discharge of a number of missiles. **b.** The missiles thus discharged. **2.** A bursting forth of many things together: *a volley of oaths.* **3.** *Sports.* **a.** The flight of a ball before it touches the ground: *kicked the soccer ball on the volley.* **b.** A shot, especially in tennis, made by striking the ball before it touches the ground. **—volley** *v.* **-leyed, -ley·ing, -leys.** *—tr.* **1.** To discharge in or

ă pat	oi boy
ā pay	ou out
âr care	o͝o took
ä father	o͞o boot
ĕ pet	ŭ cut
ē be	ûr urge
ĭ pit	th thin
ī pie	*th* this
îr pier	hw which
ŏ pot	zh vision
ō toe	ə about, item
ô paw	♦ regionalism

Stress marks: ′ (primary); ′ (secondary), as in **dictionary** (dĭk′shə-nĕr′ē)

as if in a volley: *volley musket shots at the attackers.* **2.** *Sports.* To strike (a tennis ball, for example) before it touches the ground. —*intr.* **1.** To be discharged in or as if in a volley. **2.** *Sports.* To make a volley, especially in tennis. **3.** To move rapidly, forcefully, or loudly like missiles: *The hailstones volleyed down. Charges and countercharges volleyed through the courtroom.* [French *volée,* from Old French, from Vulgar Latin **volāta,* from Latin *volāre,* to fly.] **—vol′ley·er** *n.*

volleyball

vol·ley·ball (vŏl′ē-bôl′) *n. Sports.* **1.** A game played by two teams on a rectangular court divided by a high net, in which both teams use up to three hits to ground the ball on the opposing team's side of the net. **2.** The large inflated ball used in this game. **—vol′ley·ball′er** *n.*

Vo·log·da (vô′ləg-də). A city of western Russia north-northeast of Moscow. It was founded in the mid-12th century by merchants from Novgorod and passed to Moscow in 1478. Population, 269,000.

Vó·los (vō′lŏs′, vô′lôs). A city of eastern Greece in Thessaly on the **Gulf of Vólos,** an inlet of the Aegean Sea. Vólos is a major port and an industrial, commercial, and transportation center. Population, 171,378.

vol·plane (vŏl′plān′, vôl′-) *intr.v.* **-planed, -plan·ing, -planes. 1.a.** To glide toward the earth in an airplane with the engine cut off. **b.** To glide toward the earth with the engine cut off. Used of an airplane. **2.** To make one's way or go by gliding. **—volplane** *n.* The act or an instance of volplaning. [From French *vol plané,* gliding flight : *vol,* flight (from Old French, from *voler,* to fly; see VOLLEY) + *plané,* gliding, past participle of *planer,* to glide; see PLANE³.]

Vol·sci (vŏl′skē, vŏl′sī, -sē, -shē) *pl.n.* A people of ancient Italy whose territory was conquered by the Romans in the fourth century B.C.

Vol·scian (vŏl′shən, vôl′skē-ən) *adj.* Of or relating to the Volsci or their language. **—Volscian** *n.* **1.** The Italic language of the Volsci. **2.** A member of the Volsci.

Vol·stead (vŏl′stĕd′, vôl′-, vōl′-), **Andrew John.** 1860–1947. American legislator. As a U.S. representative from Minnesota (1903–1923) he sponsored the Volsted Act (1919), prohibiting the sale, manufacture, and transportation of alcoholic beverages.

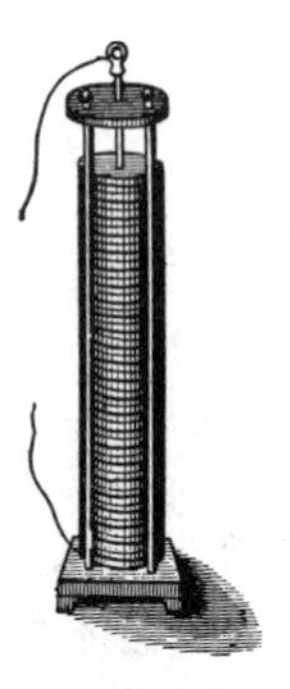

voltaic pile

volt¹ (vōlt) *n. Abbr.* **V** The International System unit of electric potential and electromotive force, equal to the difference of electric potential between two points on a conducting wire carrying a constant current of one ampere when the power dissipated between the points is one watt. See table at **measurement.** [After Count Alessandro VOLTA.]

volt² also **volte** (vōlt, vôlt) *n. Sports.* **1.** A circular movement executed by a horse in manège. **2.** A sudden movement made in avoiding a thrust in fencing. [French *volte,* from Italian *volta,* turn, from *voltare,* to turn, leap. See VAULT².]

Vol·ta (vŏl′tə, vōl′-, vôl′-). A river formed in central Ghana by the confluence of the White Volta and the Black Volta and flowing about 467 km (290 mi) southward through artificial **Lake Volta** to the Bight of Benin in the Gulf of Guinea.

Vol·ta (vōl′tə, vôl′tä), Count **Alessandro.** 1745–1827. Italian physicist who invented the first electric battery (1800). The volt is named in his honor.

volt·age (vōl′tĭj) *n.* Electromotive force or potential difference, usually expressed in volts.

voltage divider *n.* A number of resistors in series provided with taps at certain points to make available a fixed or variable fraction of the applied voltage.

vol·ta·ic (vŏl-tā′ĭk, vōl-, vôl-) *adj.* **1.** Of, relating to, or being electricity or electric current produced by chemical action; galvanic. **2.** Producing electricity by chemical action. [After Count Alessandro VOLTA.]

voltaic battery *n.* An electric battery composed of a primary cell or cells.

voltaic cell *n.* See **primary cell.**

voltaic couple *n.* Two dissimilar conductors in contact or in the same electrolytic solution, resulting in a difference of potential between them. Also called *galvanic couple.*

voltaic pile *n.* A source of electricity consisting of a number of alternating disks of two different metals separated by acid-moistened pads, forming primary cells connected in series.

Voltaire
1778 bust by
Jean Antoine Houdon

Vol·taire (vōl-târ′, vŏl-, vôl-tĕr′). Pen name of François Marie Arouet. 1694–1778. French philosopher and writer whose works epitomize the Age of Enlightenment, often attacking injustice and intolerance. He wrote *Candide* (1759) and the *Philosophical Dictionary* (1764).

vol·ta·ism (vŏl′tə-ĭz′əm, vōl′-, vôl′-) *n.* See **galvanism** (sense 1). [VOLTA(IC) + -ISM.]

volt·am·me·ter (vōl-tăm′mē′tər, vōlt′ăm′-) *n.* An instrument for measuring electrical current or potential.

volt-am·pere (vōlt′ăm′pîr′) *n.* A unit of electric power equal to the product of one volt and one ampere, equivalent to one watt.

Vol·ta Re·don·da (vôl′tä rĭ-dōn′də, -dôN′dä). A city of eastern Brazil on the Paraíba River west-northwest of Rio de Janeiro. Founded in 1941, it is the center of a major steel industry. Population, 180,126.

volte (vōlt, vôlt) *n. Sports.* Variant of **volt².**

volte-face (vôlt-fäs′, vôl′tə-) *n.* A reversal, as in policy; an about-face. [French, from Italian *voltafaccia* : *volta* (from *voltare,* to turn; see VAULT²) + *faccia,* face (from Vulgar Latin **facia;* see FACE).]

volt·me·ter (vōlt′mē′tər) *n.* An instrument, such as a galvanometer, for measuring potential differences in volts.

vol·u·ble (vŏl′yə-bəl) *adj.* **1.** Marked by a ready flow of speech; fluent. See Synonyms at **talkative. 2.a.** Turning easily on an axis; rotating. **b.** *Botany.* Twining or twisting. [Middle English, moving easily, from Old French, from Latin *volūbilis,* revolving, fluent, from *volvere,* to roll. See **wel-²** in Appendix.] **—vol′u·bil′i·ty, vol′u·ble·ness** *n.* **—vol′u·bly** *adv.*

vol·ume (vŏl′yo͞om, -yəm) *n.* **1.** *Abbr.* **vol., v. a.** A collection of written or printed sheets bound together; a book. **b.** One of the books of a work printed and bound in more than one book. **c.** A series of issues of a periodical, usually covering one calendar year. **d.** A unit of written material assembled together and cataloged in a library. **2.** *Abbr.* **vol., v.** A roll of parchment; a scroll. **3.** *Abbr.* **V a.** The amount of space occupied by a three-dimensional object or region of space, expressed in cubic units. **b.** The capacity of such a region or of a specified container, expressed in cubic units. **4.a.** Amount; quantity: *a low volume of business; a considerable volume of lumber.* **b.** A large amount. Often used in the plural: *volumes of praise.* **5.a.** The amplitude or loudness of a sound. **b.** A control, as on a radio, for adjusting amplitude or loudness. [Middle English, from Old French, from Latin *volūmen,* roll of writing, from *volvere,* to roll. See **wel-²** in Appendix.]

vol·umed (vŏl′yo͞omd, -yəmd) *adj.* **1.** Consisting of a volume or volumes. Often used in combination: *a large-volumed edition; a many-volumed novel.* **2.** Formed or moving in rolling or rounded masses: *volumed smoke.*

vol·u·me·ter (vŏl′yo͞o-mē′tər) *n.* Any of several instruments for measuring the volume of liquids, solids, or gases. [VOLU(ME) + -METER.]

vol·u·met·ric (vŏl′yo͞o-mĕt′rĭk) *adj.* Of or relating to measurement by volume. [VOLU(ME) + -METRIC.] **—vol′u·met′ri·cal·ly** *adv.*

volumetric analysis *n.* **1.** Quantitative analysis using accurately measured titrated volumes of standard chemical solutions. **2.** Analysis of a gas by volume.

vo·lu·mi·nous (və-lo͞o′mə-nəs) *adj.* **1.** Having great volume, fullness, size, or number: *a voluminous trunk; a voluminous cloud.* **2.** Filling or capable of filling a large volume or many volumes: *the voluminous court record of the long trial.* **3.** Ample or lengthy in speech or writing. **4.** Having many coils; winding. [Late Latin *volūminōsus,* having many folds, from Latin *volūmen, volūmin-,* roll of writing. See VOLUME.] **—vo·lu′mi·nos′i·ty** (-nŏs′ĭ-tē), **vo·lu′mi·nous·ness** (-nəs-nĭs) *n.* **—vo·lu′mi·nous·ly** *adv.*

vol·un·ta·rism (vŏl′ən-tə-rĭz′əm) *n.* **1.** The use of or reliance on voluntary action to maintain an institution, carry out a policy, or achieve an end. **2.** A theory or doctrine that regards the will as the fundamental principle of the individual or of the universe. **—vol′un·ta·rist** *n.* **—vol′un·ta·ris′tic** *adj.*

vol·un·tar·y (vŏl′ən-tĕr′ē) *adj.* **1.** Arising from or acting on one's own free will. **2.** Acting, serving, or done willingly and without constraint or expectation of reward: *a voluntary hostage; voluntary community work.* **3.** Normally controlled by or subject to individual volition: *Respiration is voluntary.* **4.** Capable of making choices; having the faculty of will. **5.** Supported by contributions or charitable donations rather than by government appropriations: *voluntary hospitals.* **6.** *Law.* **a.** Without legal obligation or consideration: *a voluntary conveyance of property.* **b.** Done deliberately; intentional: *voluntary manslaughter.* **—voluntary** *n., pl.* **-ies. 1.** *Music.* **a.** A short piece of music, often improvised on a solo instrument, played as an introduction to a larger work. **b.** A piece for solo organ, often improvised, played before, during, or after a religious service. **2.** A volunteer. [Middle English, from Latin *voluntārius,* from *voluntās,* choice, from *velle, vol-,* to wish. See **wel-¹** in Appendix.] **—vol′un·tar′i·ly** (-târ′ə-lē) *adv.* **—vol′un·tar′i·ness** *n.*

SYNONYMS: *voluntary, intentional, deliberate, willful, willing.* These adjectives mean being or resulting from one's own free will. *Voluntary* implies the operation of unforced choice: *"Ignorance, when it is voluntary, is criminal"* (Samuel Johnson). *Intentional* applies to something undertaken to further a plan or realize an aim: *"In whatsoever houses I enter, I will enter to help the sick, and I will abstain from all intentional wrongdoing and harm"* (Hippocratic Oath). *Deliberate* stresses premeditation and full awareness of the character and consequences of one's acts: *"In life courtesy and self-possession, and in the arts style, are the sensible impressions of the free mind, for both arise out of a deliberate shaping of all things"* (William Butler Yeats). *Willful* implies deliberate, headstrong persistence in a self-determined course of action: *a willful waste of time. Willing* suggests ready or cheerful acquiescence in the proposals or requirements of another: *"The first requisite of a good citizen . . . is that he shall be able and willing to pull his weight"* (Theodore Roosevelt).

vol·un·tar·y·ism (vŏl′ən-tĕr′ē-ĭz′əm) *n.* Reliance on voluntary contributions rather than government funds, as for churches or schools; voluntarism. **—vol′un·tar′y·ist** *n.*

voluntary muscle *n.* Muscle, such as striated muscle, normally controlled by individual volition.

vol·un·teer (vŏl′ən-tîr′) *n. Abbr.* **vol. 1.** A person who performs or offers to perform a service of his or her own free will: *an* *information booth stuffed by volunteers; hospital volunteers.* **2.** *Law.* **a.** A person who renders aid, performs a service, or assumes an obligation voluntarily. **b.** A person who holds property under a deed made without consideration. **3.** *Botany.* A cultivated plant growing from self-sown or accidentally dropped seed. **—volunteer** *adj.* **1.** Being, consisting of, or done by volunteers: *volunteer firefighters; volunteer tutoring.* **2.** *Botany.* Growing from self-sown or accidentally dropped seed. Used of a cultivated plant or crop. **—volunteer** *v.* **-teered, -teer•ing, -teers.** *—tr.* To give or offer to give voluntarily: *volunteered their services; volunteer to give blood.* *—intr.* **1.** To perform or offer to perform a service of one's own free will. **2.** To do charitable or helpful work without pay: *Many retirees volunteer in community service and day care centers.* [Obsolete French *voluntaire,* from Old French, voluntary, from Latin *voluntārius.* See VOLUNTARY.]

vol•un•teer•ism (vŏl′ən-tîr′ĭz′əm) *n.* Use of or reliance on volunteers, especially to perform social or educational work in communities.

vo•lup•tu•ar•y (və-lŭp′cho͞o-ĕr′ē) *n., pl.* **-ies.** A person whose life is given over to luxury and sensual pleasures; a sensualist: *"an adventurous voluptuary, angling in all streams for variety of pleasures"* (Thomas De Quincey). [French *voluptuaire,* from Old French, from Late Latin *voluptuārius,* variant of Latin *voluptārius,* devoted to pleasure, from *voluptās,* pleasure. See **wel-**[1] in Appendix.] **—vo•lup′tu•ar′y** *adj.*

vo•lup•tu•ous (və-lŭp′cho͞o-əs) *adj.* **1.** Giving, characterized by, or suggesting ample, unrestrained pleasure to the senses: *voluptuous sculptural forms; a voluptuous ripe fruit; a full, voluptuous figure.* **2.a.** Devoted to or indulging in sensual pleasures. **b.** Directed toward or anticipating sensual pleasure: *voluptuous thoughts.* **c.** Arising from or contributing to the satisfaction of sensuous or sensual desires. See Synonyms at **sensuous.** [Middle English, from Old French *voluptueux,* from Latin *voluptuōsus,* full of pleasure, from *voluptās,* pleasure. See **wel-**[1] in Appendix.] **—vo•lup′tu•ous•ly** *adv.* **—vo•lup′tu•ous•ness** *n.*

vo•lute (və-lo͞ot′) *n.* **1.** A spiral, scroll-like ornament such as that used on an Ionic capital. **2.a.** A spiral formation, such as one of the whorls of a gastropod shell. **b.** Any of various marine gastropod mollusks of the family Volutidae, having a spiral, often colorfully marked shell. [French, from Italian *voluta,* from Latin *volūta,* from feminine past participle of *volvere,* to turn, roll. See **wel-**[2] in Appendix.] **—vo•lut′ed** (-lo͞o′tĭd) *adj.*

vol•u•tin (vŏl′yə-tĭn, və-lo͞ot′n) *n.* A granular substance that stains easily with a basic dye and is often rich in phosphorus, found in the cytoplasm of various bacterial and fungal cells. [German, from New Latin *(Spirillum) volūtāns,* species of bacterium in which it was first found, from Latin *volūtāns,* present participle of *volūtāre,* to roll around, frequentative of *volvere,* to roll. See **wel-**[2] in Appendix.]

vo•lu•tion (və-lo͞o′shən) *n.* **1.** A turn or twist about a center; a spiral. **2.** *Zoology.* One of the whorls of a spiral gastropod shell. [From Latin *volūtus,* past participle of *volvere,* to turn. See VOLUTE.]

vol•va (vŏl′və, vôl′-) *n.* A cuplike structure around the base of the stalk of certain fungi. [Latin, a covering. See **wel-**[2] in Appendix.] **—vol′vate′** (-vāt′) *adj.*

vol•vent (vŏl′vənt) *n.* A pear-shaped nematocyst that ejects a thick thread which coils around and immobilizes prey. [From Latin *volvēns, volvent-,* present participle of *volvere,* to turn. See VOLVOX.]

vol•vox (vŏl′vŏks′, vôl′-) *n.* Any of various freshwater green algae of the genus *Volvox* that form hollow, spherical multicellular colonies. [New Latin *Volvox,* genus name, from Latin *volvere,* to roll. See **wel-**[2] in Appendix.]

vol•vu•lus (vŏl′vyə-ləs, vôl′-) *n.* Abnormal twisting of the intestine causing obstruction. [New Latin, from Latin *volvere,* to turn. See VOLVOX.]

Volzh•skiy (vôlzh′skē, vôlsh′-). A city of southwest Russia on the Volga River, a manufacturing suburb of Volgograd. Population, 245,000.

vo•mer (vō′mər) *n.* A thin flat bone forming the inferior and posterior part of the nasal septum and dividing the nostrils in most vertebrates. [Latin *vōmer,* plowshare.] **—vo′mer•ine′** (-mə-rīn′) *adj.*

vom•i•ca (vŏm′ĭ-kə) *n., pl.* **-cae** (-sē′). **1.** Profuse expectoration of putrid matter. **2.a.** An abnormal pus-containing cavity, usually in a lung, caused by deterioration of tissue. **b.** The pus contained in such a cavity. [Latin, ulcer, from *vomere,* to vomit. See VOMIT.]

vom•it (vŏm′ĭt) *v.* **-it•ed, -it•ing, -its.** *—intr.* **1.** To eject part or all of the contents of the stomach through the mouth, usually in a series of involuntary spasmic movements. **2.** To be discharged forcefully and abundantly; spew or gush: *The dike burst, and the flood waters vomited forth.* *—tr.* **1.** To eject (contents of the stomach) through the mouth. **2.** To eject or discharge in a gush; spew out: *a volcano that vomited lava and ash.* **—vomit** *n.* **1.** The act or an instance of ejecting matter from the stomach through the mouth. **2.** Matter ejected from the stomach through the mouth. **3.** An emetic. [Middle English *vomiten,* from Latin *vomitāre,* frequentative of *vomere.* See **weme-** in Appendix.] **—vom′it•er** *n.*

vom•i•tive (vŏm′ĭ-tĭv) *adj.* Relating to or causing vomiting. **—vomitive** *n.* An emetic.

vom•i•to•ry (vŏm′ĭ-tôr′ē, -tōr′ē) *adj.* Inducing vomiting; vomitive. **—vomitory** *n., pl.* **-ries. 1.** Something that induces vomiting. **2.** An aperture through which matter is discharged. **3.** One of the passageways of an amphitheater or a stadium leading from the outside wall or passageway to the seats.

vom•i•tu•ri•tion (vŏm′ĭ-chə-rĭsh′ən, -ĭ-to͞o-) *n.* Forceful attempts at vomiting without bringing up the contents of the stomach; retching. [VOMIT + (MICT)URITION.]

vom•i•tus (vŏm′ĭ-təs) *n.* Vomited matter. [Latin, from past participle of *vomere,* to vomit. See VOMIT.]

Von•ne•gut (vŏn′ĭ-gət), **Kurt, Jr.** Born 1922. American writer whose works show compassion and humor in the midst of the violence and alienation of modern life. His novels include *Cat's Cradle* (1963) and *Slaughterhouse Five* (1969).

Von Neu•mann (vŏn noi′män′), **John.** 1903–1957. Hungarian-born American mathematician noted for his contributions to game theory and quantum theory.

von Wil•le•brand's disease (vŏn wĭl′ə-brăndz′, fôn vĭl′ə-bränts′) *n.* A hereditary disease characterized by prolonged bleeding from the skin and mucous surfaces caused by abnormalities of the capillaries. [After Erik Adolf *von Willebrand* (1870–1949), Finnish physician.]

voo•doo (vo͞o′do͞o) *n., pl.* **-doos. 1.** A religion practiced chiefly in Caribbean countries, especially Haiti, syncretized from Roman Catholic ritual elements and the animism and magic of Dahomean slaves, in which a supreme God rules a large pantheon of local and tutelary deities, deified ancestors, and saints, who communicate with believers in dreams, trances, and ritual possessions. Also called *vodoun.* **2.** A charm, fetish, spell, or curse holding magic power for adherents of voodoo. **3.** A practitioner, priest, or priestess of voodoo. Also called *hoodoo.* **—voodoo** *tr.v.* **-dooed, -doo•ing, -doos.** To place under the influence of a spell or curse; bewitch. [Louisiana French *voudou,* from Ewe *vodu* and Fon *vodun.*] **—voo′doo** *adj.*

voo•doo•ism (vo͞o′do͞o-ĭz′əm) *n.* **1.** The practice and doctrines of voodoo. **2.** The practice of sorcery or witchcraft. **—voo′doo•ist** *n.* **—voo′doo•is′tic** *adj.*

vo•ra•cious (vô-rā′shəs, və-) *adj.* **1.** Consuming or eager to consume great amounts of food; ravenous. **2.** Having or marked by an insatiable appetite for an activity or a pursuit; greedy: *a voracious reader.* [From Latin *vorāx, vorāc-,* from *vorāre,* to swallow, devour.] **—vo•ra′cious•ly** *adv.* **—vo•rac′i•ty** (-răs′ĭ-tē), **vo•ra′cious•ness** (-rā′shəs-nĭs) *n.*

SYNONYMS: *voracious, gluttonous, rapacious, ravenous.* The central meaning shared by these adjectives is "having or marked by boundless greed": *a voracious observer of the political scene; a gluttonous appetite; rapacious demands; ravenous for power.*

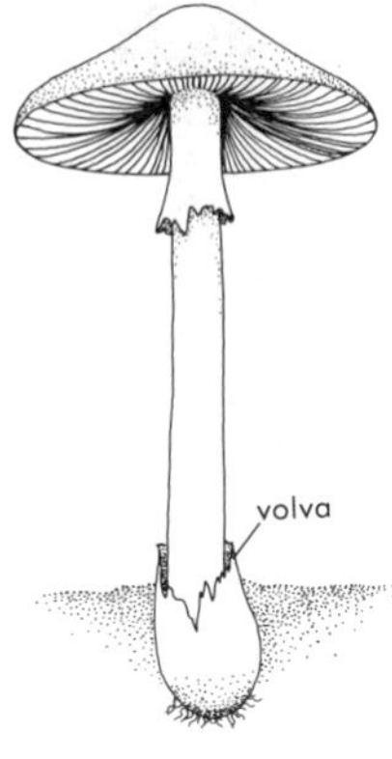

volva

Vor•ku•ta (vôr-ko͞o′tə, vôr′ko͞o-tä). A city of northwest Russia above the Arctic Circle. It was founded in 1932 to accommodate extensive penal-labor camps. The camps were reportedly closed after the death of Stalin in 1953. Population, 108,000.

vor•la•ge (fôr′lä′gə, fōr′-) *n.* *Sports.* A posture assumed in skiing in which the skier leans forward from the ankles, usually without lifting the heels. [German : *vor,* forward, before (from Middle High German, from Old High German *fora;* see **per**[1] in Appendix) + *Lage,* stance (from Middle High German *lāge,* from Old High German *lāga,* act of laying; see **legh-** in Appendix).]

Vo•ro•nezh (və-rô′nĭsh). A city of western Russia on the Don River southwest of Lipetsk. Founded as a frontier fortress in 1586, it was a shipbuilding center during the reign of Peter the Great. Population, 850,000.

Vo•ro•shi•lov (vôr′ə-shē′lôf′, -ləf), **Kliment Efremovich.** 1881–1969. Soviet military and political leader. He fought in the civil war (1918–1920) following the Russian Revolution of 1917 and later served as a member of the politburo (1926–1960) and as commissar for defense (1925–1940).

Vo•ro•shi•lov•grad (vôr′ə-shē′ləf-grăd′, və-rə-shē-ləf-grät′). A city of western Ukraine in the Donets Basin southeast of Kharkov. A coal-mining center, it was founded c. 1795. Population, 497,000.

-vorous *suff.* Eating; feeding on: *vermivorous.* [From Latin *-vorus,* from *vorāre,* to swallow, devour.]

Vor•ster (fôr′stər), **Balthazar Johannes.** 1915–1983. South African political leader who served as prime minister from 1966 to 1978.

vor•tex (vôr′tĕks′) *n., pl.* **-tex•es** or **-ti•ces** (-tĭ-sēz′). **1.** A spiral motion of fluid within a limited area, especially a whirling mass of water or air that sucks everything near it toward its center. **2.** A place or situation regarded as drawing into its center all that surrounds it: *"As happened with so many theater actors, he was swept up in the vortex of Hollywood"* (New York Times). [Latin *vortex, vortic-,* variant of *vertex,* from *vertere,* to turn. See **wer-**[2] in Appendix.]

vor•ti•cal (vôr′tĭ-kəl) *adj.* Of, relating to, or moving in a vortex; whirling. **—vor′ti•cal•ly** *adv.*

vor•ti•cel•la (vôr′tĭ-sĕl′ə) *n., pl.* **-cel•lae** (-sĕl′ē) or **-cel•las.** Any of various ciliate protozoans of the genus *Vorticella,* having a bell-shaped body and living underwater on a slender stalk often attached to a plant or other object. [New Latin *Vorticella,* genus name, from Latin *vortex, vortic-,* vortex. See VORTEX.]

vor•ti•ces (vôr′tĭ-sēz′) *n.* A plural of **vortex.**

ă pat	oi boy
ā pay	ou out
âr care	o͝o took
ä father	o͞o boot
ĕ pet	ŭ cut
ē be	ûr urge
ĭ pit	th thin
ī pie	*th* this
îr pier	hw which
ŏ pot	zh vision
ō toe	ə about, item
ô paw	♦ regionalism

Stress marks: ′ (primary); ′ (secondary), as in **dictionary** (dĭk′shə-nĕr′ē)

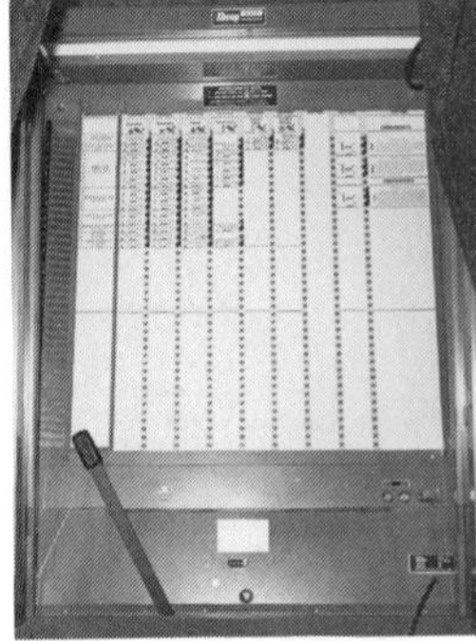
voting machine

vor·ti·cism (vôr′tĭ-sĭz′əm) *n.* A short-lived English movement in art and literature that arose in 1914 and was heavily influenced by cubism and futurism.

vor·ti·cose (vôr′tĭ-kōs′) *adj.* Vortical.

vor·tig·i·nous (vôr-tĭj′ə-nəs) *adj.* Vortical. [Blend of VORTEX and VERTIGINOUS.]

Vosges (vōzh). A mountain range of northeast France extending about 193 km (120 mi) parallel to the Rhine River. The mountains have rounded or nearly flat summits.

vo·ta·ry (vō′tə-rē) *n., pl.* **-ries. 1.a.** A person bound by vows to live a life of religious worship or service. **b.** A devout adherent of a cult or religion; a committed worshiper: *the votaries of Aphrodite.* **2.** A person who is fervently devoted, as to a leader or an ideal; a faithful follower. **3.** A person who is filled with enthusiasm, as for a pursuit or hobby; an enthusiast. [From Latin *vōtum,* vow. See VOTE.]

SYNONYMS: *votary, devotee, habitué.* These nouns refer to one who is devoted to a person, a cause, or an activity. Both *votary* and *devotee* originally referred to religious dedication but can also denote attachment to a pursuit such as a branch of learning or enthusiasm for something such as a hobby: *"the cultured votary of science"* (Francis Marion Crawford). *"The almighty dollar, that great object of universal devotion throughout our land, seems to have no genuine devotees in these peculiar villages"* (Washington Irving). A *habitué* regularly frequents a place, especially one offering a particular pleasurable activity: *a habitué of the racetrack.*

votive
c. 520–510 B.C. votive statuette of Hermes carrying a ram

vote (vōt) *n.* **1.a.** A formal expression of preference for a candidate for office or for a proposed resolution of an issue. **b.** A means by which such a preference is made known, such as a raised hand or a marked ballot. **2.** The number of votes cast in an election or to resolve an issue: *a heavy vote in favor of the bill.* **3.** A group of voters alike in some way: *the Black vote; the rural vote.* **4.** The act or process of voting: *took a vote on the issue.* **5.** The result of an election or a referendum. **6.** The right to participate as a voter; suffrage. **—vote** *v.* **vot·ed, vot·ing, votes.** *—intr.* **1.** To express one's preference for a candidate or for a proposed resolution of an issue; cast a vote: *voted yes on the motion; voting against the measure.* **2.** To express a choice or an opinion. *—tr.* **1.** To express one's preference for by vote: *voted the straight Republican ticket.* **2.** To decide the disposition of by vote, as by electing or defeating: *vote in a new mayor; voted out their representative; vote down the amendment.* **3.** To bring into existence or make available by vote: *vote new funds for a program.* **4.** To be guided by in voting: *vote one's conscience.* **5.** To declare or pronounce by general consent: *voted the play a success.* **6.** *Informal.* To state as a preference or an opinion: *I vote we eat out tonight.* ***—idiom.* vote with (one's) feet.** *Slang.* To indicate a preference or an opinion by leaving or entering a particular locale: *"If older cities are allowed to decay and contract, can citizens who vote with their feet . . . hope to find better conditions anywhere else?"* (Melinda Beck). [Middle English, vow, from Latin *vōtum,* from neuter past participle of *vovēre,* to vow.] **—vot′a·ble, vote′a·ble** *adj.* **—vot′er** *n.*

vote getter *n. Informal.* A candidate successful in attracting votes: *a runoff between the two top vote getters.*

vote·less (vōt′lĭs) *adj.* Having no vote; denied a vote or the right to vote.

vot·ing machine (vō′tĭng) *n.* An apparatus for use in polling places that mechanically records and counts votes.

vo·tive (vō′tĭv) *adj.* **1.** Given or dedicated in fulfillment of a vow or pledge: *a votive offering.* **2.** Expressing or symbolizing a wish, desire, or vow: *a votive prayer; votive candles.* [Latin *vōtīvus,* from *vōtum,* vow. See VOTE.] **—vo′tive·ly** *adv.*

votive Mass *n. Roman Catholic Church.* A Mass differing from the one prescribed for the day, said for a specific purpose or at the discretion of the priest.

vou. *abbr.* Voucher.

V sign
Sir Winston Churchill in 1953

vouch (vouch) *v.* **vouched, vouch·ing, vouch·es.** *—intr.* **1.** To give personal assurances; give a guarantee: *vouch for an old friend's trustworthiness.* **2.** To constitute supporting evidence; give substantiation: *a candidate whose strong record vouches for her ability.* *—tr.* **1.** To substantiate by supplying evidence; prove: *charges that he could not vouch.* **2.** *Law.* To summon as a witness to give warranty of title. **3.** To refer to (an authority, for example) in support or corroboration; cite. **4.** To assert; declare. **—vouch** *n. Obsolete.* A declaration of opinion; an assertion. [Middle English *vouchen,* to summon to court, warrant, from Anglo-Norman *voucher,* probably from Vulgar Latin **vocitāre,* alteration of Latin *vocitāre,* frequentative of *vocāre,* to call. See **wekʷ-** in Appendix.]

vouch·er (vou′chər) *n. Abbr.* **vou. 1.** A piece of substantiating evidence; a proof. **2.** A written record of an expenditure, a disbursement, or a completed transaction. **3.** A written authorization or certificate, especially one exchangeable for cash or representing a credit against future expenditures. **—voucher** *tr.v.* **-ered, -er·ing, -ers. 1.** To substantiate or authenticate with evidence. **2.** To prepare a voucher for: *properly vouchering each transaction.* **3.** To issue a voucher to: *a company that vouchers employees when the payroll cannot be met.*

vouch·safe (vouch-sāf′, vouch′sāf′) *tr.v.* **-safed, -saf·ing, -safes.** To condescend to grant or bestow (a privilege, for example); deign. See Synonyms at **grant.** [Middle English *vouchen sauf,* to warrant as safe : *vouchen,* to warrant; see VOUCH + *sauf,* safe; see SAFE.] **—vouch·safe′ment** *n.*

vous·soir (vo͞o-swär′) *n.* One of the wedge-shaped stones forming the curved parts of an arch or a vaulted ceiling. [French, from Old French *vossoir,* from Vulgar Latin **volsōrium,* from **volsus,* past participle of Latin *volvere,* to turn, roll. See **wel-²** in Appendix.]

Vou·vray (vo͞o-vrā′) *n.* A dry white table wine from central France. [After *Vouvray,* a village of west-central France.]

vow¹ (vou) *n.* **1.** An earnest promise to perform a specified act or behave in a certain manner, especially a solemn promise to live and act in accordance with the rules of a religious order: *take the vows of a nun.* **2.** A declaration or an assertion. **—vow** *v.* **vowed, vow·ing, vows.** *—tr.* **1.** To promise solemnly; pledge. See Synonyms at **promise. 2.** To make a pledge or threat to undertake: *vowing revenge on their persecutors.* *—intr.* To make a vow; promise. [Middle English *vou,* from Old French, from Latin *vōtum.* See VOTE.] **—vow′er** *n.*

vow² (vou) *tr.v.* To declare or assert: *"Well, I vow it is as fine a boy as ever was seen!"* (Henry Fielding). [Short for AVOW.]

vow·el (vou′əl) *n. Abbr.* **v. 1.** A speech sound created by the relatively free passage of breath through the larynx and oral cavity, usually forming the most prominent and central sound of a syllable. **2.** A letter, such as *a, e, i, o, u,* and sometimes *y* in the English alphabet, that represents a vowel. [Middle English *vowelle,* from Old French *vouel,* from Latin *(littera) vōcālis,* sounding (letter), from *vōx, vōc-,* voice. See **wekʷ-** in Appendix.]

vowel fracture *n. Linguistics.* Breaking.

vow·el·ize (vou′ə-līz′) *tr.v.* **-ized, -iz·ing, -iz·es.** To provide with vowel points. **—vow′el·i·za′tion** (-ə-lĭ-zā′shən) *n.*

vowel mutation *n. Linguistics.* See **umlaut** (sense 1).

vowel point *n.* Any of a number of diacritical marks written above or below consonants to indicate a preceding or following vowel in languages that are usually written without vowel letters, as Hebrew and Arabic.

vox an·gel·i·ca (vŏks′ ăn-jĕl′ĭ-kə) *n., pl.* **vox an·gel·i·cas.** *Music.* See **voix céleste.** [New Latin *vōx angelica* : Latin *vōx,* voice + Late Latin *angelicus,* angelic.]

vox hu·ma·na (hyo͞o-mā′nə, -mä′-, -măn′ə) *n., pl.* **vox hu·ma·nas.** *Music.* An organ reed stop that produces tones imitative of the human voice. [New Latin *vōx hūmāna* : Latin *vōx,* voice + Latin *hūmānus,* human.]

vox pop·u·li (pŏp′yə-lī′, -lē) *n.* Popular opinion or sentiment. [Latin *vōx populī* : *vōx,* voice + *populī,* genitive of *populus,* people.]

voy·age (voi′ĭj) *n.* **1.** A long journey, as: **a.** A journey by sea to a foreign or distant land. **b.** A journey by land to distant parts. **c.** A journey through outer space. **2.** Often **voyages. a.** The events of a journey of exploration or discovery considered as material for a narrative. **b.** Such a narrative. **—voyage** *v.* **-aged, -ag·ing, -ag·es.** *—intr.* To make a voyage. *—tr.* To sail across; traverse: *voyaged the western ocean.* [Middle English, from Old French *veyage,* from Late Latin *viāticum,* a journey, from Latin, provisions for a journey, from neuter of *viāticus,* of a journey, from *via,* road. See **wegh-** in Appendix.] **—voy′ag·er** *n.*

voy·a·geur (voi′ə-zhûr′, vwä′yä-zhœr′) *n., pl.* **-geurs** (-zhûr′, -zhœr′). A woodsman, boatman, or guide employed by a fur company to transport goods and supplies between remote stations in Canada or the U.S. Northwest. [French, traveler, from *voyager,* to travel, from *voyage,* journey, from Old French *veyage.* See VOYAGE.]

voy·eur (voi-yûr′) *n.* **1.** A person who derives sexual gratification from observing the naked bodies or sexual acts of others, especially from a secret vantage point. **2.** An obsessive observer of sordid or sensational subjects. [French, from Old French, one who lies in wait, from *voir,* to see, from Latin *vidēre,* to see. See **weid-** in Appendix.] **—voy·eur′ism** *n.* **—voy′eur·is′tic** *adj.* **—voy′eur·is′ti·cal·ly** *adv.*

Voz·ne·sen·ski (vŏz′nə-sĕn′skē), **Andrei.** Born 1933. Soviet poet whose collections of verse include *Parabola* (1960) and *The Triangular Pear* (1962).

VP *abbr.* **1.** Variable pitch. **2.** Verb phrase. **3.** Or **V.P.** Vice president.

Vra·tsa (vrät′sə, vrä′tsä). A city of northwest Bulgaria north-northeast of Sofia. It is a commercial center and railroad junction. Population, 77,000.

Vree·land (vrē′lənd), **Diana Dalziel.** 1903–1989. French-born American editor and fashion expert. She was editor in chief of *Vogue* (1963–1971) and a special consultant to the Costume Institute of the Metropolitan Museum of Art (1972–1989).

VRM *abbr.* Variable-rate mortgage.

vroom (vro͞om, vro͝om) also **va·room** (və-ro͞om′, -ro͝om′) *—n.* The loud, roaring noise of an engine operating at high speed. *—intr.v.* **vroomed, vroom·ing, vrooms** also **va·roomed, va·room·ing, va·rooms.** To move noisily at high speed in or as if in a motor vehicle. [Imitative.]

vs. *abbr.* Versus.

v.s. *abbr. Latin.* Vide supra (see above).

V.S. *abbr.* Veterinary surgeon.

V sign *n.* A hand sign indicating victory, solidarity, or approval, formed by holding the raised index and middle fingers in the shape of a V.

vss. *abbr.* **1.** Verses. **2.** Versions.

V/STOL *abbr.* Vertical short takeoff and landing.

VT *abbr.* **1.** Vacuum tube. **2.** Variable time. **3.** Also **Vt.** Vermont.

VT fuze (vē′tē′) *n.* See **proximity fuze.** [*v(ariable) t(ime) fuze.*]

VTOL *abbr.* Vertical takeoff and landing.

VTR *abbr.* Videotape recorder.

vug (vŭg, vo͝og) *n.* A small cavity in a rock or vein, often with a mineral lining of different composition from that of the surrounding rock. [Cornish *vooga.*]

Vuil·lard (vwē-yär′), **(Jean) Édouard.** 1868–1940. French postimpressionist painter whose works include *Public Gardens* (1894) and *Characters in Interiors* (1896).

Vul. *abbr.* Vulgate.

Vul·can (vŭl′kən) *n. Roman Mythology.* The god of fire and metalworking. [Latin *Volcānus, Vulcānus.*]

vul·ca·ni·an (vŭl-kā′nē-ən) *adj.* **1.** *Geology.* Of, relating to, or originating from an explosive volcanic eruption. **2. Vulcanian.** *Roman Mythology.* Of or relating to Vulcan. **3.** Of or relating to metalworking or craft.

vul·ca·nism (vŭl′kə-nĭz′əm) *n.* Variant of **volcanism.**

vul·ca·nite (vŭl′kə-nīt′) *n.* A hard rubber produced by vulcanization.

vul·ca·nize (vŭl′kə-nīz′) *tr.v.* **-nized, -niz·ing, -niz·es.** To improve the strength, resiliency, and freedom from stickiness and odor of (rubber, for example) by combining with sulfur or other additives in the presence of heat and pressure. **—vul′ca·niz′a·ble** *adj.* **—vul′ca·ni·za′tion** (-nĭ-zā′shən) *n.* **—vul′ca·niz′er** *n.*

vul·ca·nol·o·gy (vŭl′kə-nŏl′ə-jē) *n.* Variant of **volcanology. —vul′ca·nol′o·gist** *n.*

vulg. *abbr.* Vulgar.

Vulg. *abbr.* Vulgate.

vul·gar (vŭl′gər) *adj.* **1.** Of or associated with the great masses of people; common. **2.** *Abbr.* **vulg.** Spoken by or expressed in language spoken by the common people; vernacular: *the technical and vulgar names for an animal species.* **3.a.** Deficient in taste, delicacy, or refinement. **b.** Marked by a lack of good breeding; boorish. **c.** Offensively excessive in self-display or expenditure; ostentatious: *the huge vulgar houses and cars of the newly rich.* **4.** *Abbr.* **vulg.** Crudely indecent. See Synonyms at **coarse.** [Middle English, from Latin *vulgāris,* from *vulgus,* the common people.] **—vul′gar·ly** *adv.* **—vul′gar·ness** *n.*

WORD HISTORY: The word *vulgar* brings to mind off-color jokes, but this was not always so. Ironically the word *vulgar* is itself an example of pejoration, the process by which the semantic status of a word changes for the worse over a period of time. The ancestor of *vulgar,* the Latin word *vulgāris* (from *vulgus,* "the common people"), meant "of or belonging to the common people, everyday," as well as "belonging to or associated with the lower orders." *Vulgāris* also meant "ordinary," "common (of vocabulary, for example)," and "shared by all." Its only sense of the sort we might expect was related to the notion of general sharing, that is, "sexually promiscuous." Our word, first recorded in a work composed in 1391, entered English during the Middle English period, and in Middle English and later English we find not only the senses mentioned above but also related senses. What is common can be seen as debased, and in the 17th century we begin to find instances of *vulgar* that made very explicit what was already implicit. *Vulgar* now meant "deficient in taste, delicacy, or refinement." From such use *vulgar* has gone downhill, and at present "crudely indecent" is probably one of the first senses of *vulgar* that occurs to many when the word is used.

vul·gar·i·an (vŭl-gâr′ē-ən) *n.* A vulgar person, especially one who makes a conspicuous display of wealth. See Synonyms at **boor.**

vul·gar·ism (vŭl′gə-rĭz′əm) *n.* **1.** Vulgarity. **2.a.** A crudely indecent word or phrase; an obscenity. **b.** A word, phrase, or manner of expression used chiefly by uneducated people.

vul·gar·i·ty (vŭl-găr′ĭ-tē) *n., pl.* **-ties. 1.** The quality or condition of being vulgar. **2.** Something, such as an act or expression, that offends good taste or propriety.

vul·gar·ize (vŭl′gə-rīz′) *tr.v.* **-ized, -iz·ing, -iz·es. 1.** To make vulgar; debase: *"What appalls him is the sheer cheesiness of TV iniquity. Television has even vulgarized hell"* (Jack Kroll). **2.** To disseminate widely; popularize. **—vul′gar·i·za′tion** (-gər-ĭ-zā′shən) *n.* **—vul′gar·iz′er** *n.*

Vul·gar Latin (vŭl′gər) *n. Abbr.* **VL** The common speech of the ancient Romans, which is distinguished from standard literary Latin and is the ancestor of the Romance languages.

vul·gate (vŭl′gāt′, -gĭt) *n.* **1.** The common speech of a people; the vernacular. **2.** A widely accepted text or version of a work. **3. Vulgate.** *Abbr.* **Vulg., Vul.** The Latin edition or translation of the Bible made by Saint Jerome at the end of the fourth century A.D., now used in a revised form as the Roman Catholic authorized version. [Medieval Latin *Vulgāta,* from Late Latin *vulgāta (ēditiō),* popular (edition), from Latin, feminine past participle of *vulgāre,* to make known to all, from *vulgus,* the common people.]

vul·ner·a·ble (vŭl′nər-ə-bəl) *adj.* **1.a.** Susceptible to physical injury. **b.** Susceptible to attack: *"We are vulnerable both by water and land, without either fleet or army"* (Alexander Hamilton). **c.** Open to censure or criticism; assailable. **2.a.** Liable to succumb, as to persuasion or temptation. **b.** *Games.* In a position to receive greater penalties or bonuses as a result of having won one game of a rubber. Used of bridge partners. [Late Latin *vulnerābilis,* wounding, from Latin *vulnerāre,* to wound, from *vulnus, vulner-,* wound. See **wele-** in Appendix.] **—vul′ner·a·bil′i·ty, vul′ner·a·ble·ness** *n.* **—vul′ner·a·bly** *adv.*

vul·ner·ar·y (vŭl′nə-rĕr′ē) *adj.* Used in the healing or treating of wounds. **—vulnerary** *n., pl.* **-ies.** A remedy used in healing or treating wounds. [Latin *vulnerārius,* from *vulnus, vulner-,* wound. See VULNERABLE.]

Vul·pec·u·la (vŭl-pĕk′yə-lə) *n.* A constellation in the celestial Northern Hemisphere near Cygnus and Sagitta. [New Latin, from Latin *vulpēcula,* diminutive of *vulpēs,* fox. See VULPINE.]

vul·pec·u·lar (vŭl-pĕk′yə-lər) *adj.* Vulpine.

vul·pine (vŭl′pīn′) *adj.* **1.** Of, resembling, or characteristic of a fox. **2.** Cunning. [Latin *vulpīnus,* from *vulpēs,* fox. See **wl̥p-ē-** in Appendix.]

vul·ture (vŭl′chər) *n.* **1.** Any of various large birds of prey of the New World family Cathartidae or of the Old World family Accipitridae, characteristically having dark plumage and a featherless head and neck and generally feeding on carrion. **2.** A person of a rapacious, predatory, or profiteering nature. [Middle English, from Old French *voltour,* from Latin *vultur.*]

vul·tur·ine (vŭl′chə-rīn′) also **vul·tur·ous** (-chər-əs) *adj.* **1.** Of, relating to, or characteristic of a vulture. **2.** Rapacious; predatory.

vul·va (vŭl′və) *n., pl.* **-vae** (-vē). The external genital organs of the female, including the labia majora, labia minora, clitoris, and vestibule of the vagina. [Latin, womb, covering. See **wel-²** in Appendix.] **—vul′val, vul′var** (-vər, -vär′) *adj.* **—vul′vate′** (-vāt′, -vĭt) *adj.* **—vul′vi·form′** (-və-fôrm′) *adj.*

vul·vec·to·my (vŭl-vĕk′tə-mē) *n., pl.* **-mies.** Surgical removal of the vulva.

vul·vi·tis (vŭl-vī′tĭs) *n.* Inflammation of the vulva.

vul·vo·vag·i·ni·tis (vŭl′vō-văj′ə-nī′tĭs) *n.* Inflammation of the vulva and vagina.

♦ **vum** (vŭm) *interj. New England.* Used to express surprise. [Alteration of VOW².]

♦ ***REGIONAL NOTE:*** A New Englander expressing surprise is liable to say, *"Well, I vum!"* This odd-sounding word is in fact an alteration of the verb *vow* that goes back to the days of the American Revolution. It is also heard simply as *"Vum!"* or as a sort of past participle: *"I'll be vummed!"* A southern equivalent is *swanny,* also meaning "swear": *Now, I swanny!* According to the *Oxford English Dictionary,* the word *swanny* derives from the dialect of the North of England: *Is' wan ye,* "I shall warrant ye."

vv. *abbr.* Verses.

v.v. *abbr.* Vice versa.

Vyat·ka (vyät′kə). A river, about 1,368 km (850 mi) long, of western Russia rising in the foothills of the Ural Mountains and flowing west, south, and southeast to the Kama River.

Vy·borg (vē′bôrg′, -bərk). A city of northwest Russia northwest of St. Petersburg on the Gulf of Finland near the Finnish border. A Swedish castle was built here in 1293 and captured by Russian forces in 1710. Population, 80,000.

Vy·cheg·da (vĭch′ĭg-də). A river, about 1,126 km (700 mi) long, of northwest Russia flowing generally westward to the Northern Dvina River.

vy·ing (vī′ĭng) *v.* Present participle of **vie.**

Vulcan

vulture
Rüppell's griffon vulture
Gyps rueppellii

ă pat	oi boy
ā pay	ou out
âr care	o͝o took
ä father	o͞o boot
ĕ pet	ŭ cut
ē be	ûr urge
ĭ pit	th thin
ī pie	*th* this
îr pier	hw which
ŏ pot	zh vision
ō toe	ə about, item
ô paw	♦ regionalism

Stress marks: ′ (primary); ′ (secondary), as in **dictionary** (dĭk′shə-nĕr′ē)

Phoenician

The Phoenicians used a single sign for the initial sound in *wāw,* "hook" or "peg," and the related vowel *u.*

Early Greek

This sign was altered into two different shapes by the Greeks. One form became *digamma,* the ancestor of Roman F (see F); the other was used for the vowel sound *u.*

Roman

The Romans adopted the second form for both *u* and *w* sounds, simplifying its shape to V. As its name indicates, the letter W is in origin a "double u" (VV), often used in inscriptions from around the first century A.D. to represent the *w* sound in Germanic or Celtic names.

w[1] or **W** (dŭb′əl-yo͞o, -yo͞o) *n., pl.* **w's** or **W's. 1.** The 23rd letter of the modern English alphabet. **2.** Any of the speech sounds represented by the letter *w.* **3.** The 23rd in a series. **4.** Something shaped like the letter W.

w[2] *abbr. Physics.* Work.

W[1] The symbol for the element **tungsten.** [German *Wolfram.* See WOLFRAM.]

W[2] *abbr.* **1.** *Electricity.* Watt. **2.** Also **W.** or **w** or **w.** West; western.

w. *abbr.* **1.** Week. **2.** Weight. **3.** Wide. **4.** Width. **5.** Wife. **6.** With.

W. *abbr.* **1.** Wednesday. **2.** Welsh.

WA *abbr.* **1.** Washington. **2.** With average.

WAAC *abbr.* Women's Army Auxiliary Corps.

WAAF *abbr.* Women's Auxiliary Air Force.

Waal (väl). The southern branch of the Lower Rhine River in southern Netherlands, rising near the German border and flowing about 84 km (52 mi) generally westward to join the Maas River.

Wa·ba·na·ki (wä′bə-nä′kē) *n., pl.* **Wabanaki** or **-kis.** See **Abenaki.**

Wa·bash (wô′băsh′). A river of the east-central United States rising in western Ohio and flowing about 764 km (475 mi) generally southwest across Indiana and southward on the Indiana-Illinois border to the Ohio River.

wab·ble (wŏb′əl) *v. & n.* Variant of **wobble.**

WAC[1] or **Wac** (wăk) *n.* A member of the Women's Army Corps, organized during World War II, but now no longer a separate branch.

WAC[2] *abbr.* Women's Army Corps.

Wace (wās, wäs). fl. 12th century. Anglo-Norman poet whose adaptation of Arthurian legend, *Roman de Brut* (1155), was the first to mention the Round Table.

wack (wăk) *n. Slang.* A person regarded as eccentric. [Back-formation from WACKY.]

wack·o (wăk′ō) also **whack·o** (hwăk′ō, wăk′ō) *n., pl.* **-os.** *Slang.* A person regarded as eccentric: *"a catchy pop portrait of a wacko who talks to himself in French"* (Phoebe Hoban). [Alteration of WACKY.] **—wack′o** *adj.*

wack·y (wăk′ē) also **whack·y** (hwăk′ē, wăk′ē) *adj.* **-i·er, -i·est.** *Slang.* **1.** Eccentric: *a wacky person.* **2.** Crazy; silly: *a wacky outfit.* [Variant of *whacky,* probably from the phrase *out of whack.* See WHACK.] **—wack′i·ly** *adv.* **—wack′i·ness** *n.*

Wa·co (wā′kō). A city of east-central Texas south of Dallas–Fort Worth. A shipping and industrial center, it is also the seat of Baylor University (established 1845). Population, 101,261.

wad (wŏd) *n.* **1.** A small mass of soft material, often folded or rolled, used for padding, stuffing, or packing. **2.** A compressed ball, roll, or lump, as of tobacco. **3.a.** A plug, as of cloth or paper, used to retain a powder charge in a muzzleloading gun or cannon. **b.** A disk, as of felt or paper, used to keep the powder and shot in place in a shotgun cartridge. **4.** *Informal.* A large amount: *a wad of troubles.* **5.** *Informal.* **a.** A sizable roll of paper money. **b.** A considerable amount of money. **—wad** *v.* **wad·ded, wad·ding, wads.** *—tr.* **1.** To compress into a wad. **2.** To pad, pack, line, or plug with wadding. **3.a.** To hold (shot or powder) in place with a wad. **b.** To insert a wad into (a firearm). *—intr.* To form into a wad. [Origin unknown.]

Wad·den·zee (väd′n-zā′). An inlet of the North Sea off northern Netherlands between the Ijsselmeer and the West Frisian Islands.

♦**wad·die** (wŏd′ē) *n. Western U.S.* Variant of **waddy**[2]**.**

wad·ding (wŏd′ĭng) *n.* **1.a.** A wad. **b.** Wads considered as a group. **2.** A soft layer of fibrous cotton or wool used for padding or stuffing. **3.** Material for gun wads.

wad·dle (wŏd′l) *intr.v.* **-dled, -dling, -dles. 1.** To walk with short steps that tilt the body from side to side. **2.** To walk heavily and clumsily with a pronounced sway. **—waddle** *n.* A swaying gait. [Frequentative of WADE.] **—wad′dler** *n.*

wad·dy[1] (wŏd′ē) *Australian. n., pl.* **-dies.** A heavy straight stick or club thrown as a weapon by aborigines. **—waddy** *tr.v.* **-died** (wŏd′ēd), **-dy·ing, -dies** (wŏd′ēz). To strike with a waddy. [Dharuk (Aboriginal language of southeast Australia) *wadi.*]

wad·dy[2] also **wad·die** (wŏd′ē) *n., pl.* **-dies.** *Western U.S.* **1.** See **cowboy** (sense 1). **2.** A cattle rustler. [Origin unknown.]

wade (wād) *v.* **wad·ed, wad·ing, wades.** *—intr.* **1.** To walk in or through water or something else that similarly impedes normal movement. **2.** To make one's way arduously: *waded through a boring report.* *—tr.* To cross or pass through (water, for example) with difficulty: *wade a swift creek.* **—wade** *n.* The act or an instance of wading. ***—phrasal verb.*** **wade in** (or **into**)**.** To plunge into, begin, or attack resolutely and energetically: *waded into the task.* [Middle English *waden,* from Old English *wadan.*]

Wade (wād), **Benjamin Franklin.** 1800–1878. American politician who served as a U.S. senator from Ohio (1851–1869) and jointly authored the Wade-Davis Manifesto (1864), which declared the primacy of Congress in matters of the Reconstruction.

wad·er (wā′dər) *n.* **1.** See **wading bird. 2. waders.** Waterproof hip boots or trousers worn especially while fishing.

wa·di also **wa·dy** (wä′dē) *n., pl.* **-dis** also **-dies. 1.a.** A valley, gully, or streambed in northern Africa and southwest Asia that remains dry except during the rainy season. **b.** A stream that flows through such a channel. **2.** An oasis. [Arabic *wādī.*]

wad·ing bird (wā′dĭng) *n.* A long-legged bird, such as a crane, heron, or stork, that frequents shallow water, especially in search of food. Also called *wader.*

wa·dy (wä′dē) *n.* Variant of **wadi.**

WAF[1] or **Waf** (wăf) *n.* A member of the Women in the Air Force, organized after World War II, but now no longer a separate branch. [Abbreviation of *Women in the Air Force.*]

WAF[2] *abbr.* Women in the Air Force.

wa·fer (wā′fər) *n.* **1.** A small, thin, crisp cake, biscuit, or candy. **2.** *Ecclesiastical.* A small, thin disk of unleavened bread used in the Eucharist. **3.** *Pharmacology.* A flat tablet of rice paper or dried flour paste encasing a powdered drug. **4.** A small disk of adhesive material used as a seal for papers. **5.** *Electronics.* A small, thin, circular slice of a semiconducting material, such as pure silicon, on which an integrated circuit can be formed. **—wafer** *tr.v.* **-fered, -fer·ing, -fers. 1.** To seal or fasten together with a disk of adhesive material. **2.** *Pharmacology.* To prepare in the form of wafers. **3.** *Electronics.* To divide into wafers. [Middle English *wafre,* from Anglo-Norman, variant of Old North French *waufre,* of Germanic origin. See **webh-** in Appendix.]

waff (wăf, wäf) *Scots. v.* **waffed, waff·ing, waffs. —waff** *intr. & tr.v.* To wave or flutter or to cause to do so. **—waff** *n.* **1.** A waving or fluttering motion. **2.** A gust of air; a waft. [Middle English *waffen,* to wave, alteration of *waven.* See WAVE.]

waf·fle[1] (wŏf′əl) *n.* A light, crisp battercake baked in a waffle iron. [Dutch *wafel,* from Middle Dutch *wāfel.* See **webh-** in Appendix.]

waf·fle[2] (wŏf′əl) *Informal. v.* **-fled, -fling, -fles.** *—intr.* To speak or write evasively. *—tr.* To speak, write, or act evasively about. **—waffle** *n.* Evasive or vague speech or writing. [Probably frequentative of obsolete *waff,* to yelp, probably of imitative origin.] **—waf′fler** *n.* **—waf′fling·ly** *adv.* **—waf′fly** *adj.*

waffle iron *n.* An appliance having hinged, indented plates that impress a grid pattern into waffle batter as it bakes.

waft (wäft, wăft) *v.* **waft·ed, waft·ing, wafts.** *—tr.* **1.** To cause to go gently and smoothly through the air or over water. **2.** To convey or send floating through the air or over water. *—intr.* To float easily and gently, as on the air; drift: *"It was a heat that wafted from streets, rolled between buildings and settled over sidewalks"* (Sarah Lyall). **—waft** *n.* **1.** Something, such as an odor, that is carried through the air. **2.** A light breeze; a rush of air. **3.** The act of fluttering or waving. **4.** *Nautical.* **a.** A flag used for signaling or indicating wind direction. **b.** A signal with a flag. In this sense, also called *waif.* [Back-formation from *wafter,* convoy ship, alteration of Middle English *waughter,* from Middle Dutch or Middle Low German *wachter,* a guard, from *wachten,* to guard. See **weg-** in Appendix.] **—waft′er** *n.*

wag¹ (wăg) *v.* **wagged, wag·ging, wags.** —*intr.* **1.** To move briskly and repeatedly from side to side, to and fro, or up and down. **2.** To move rapidly in talking. Used of the tongue. **3.** To walk with a clumsy sway; waddle. **4.** *Archaic.* To be on one's way; depart. —*tr.* To move (a body part) rapidly from side to side or up and down, as in playfulness, agreement, admonition, or chatter. —**wag** *n.* The act or motion of wagging: *a farewell wag of the hand.* [Middle English *waggen.* See **wegh-** in Appendix.] —**wag′ger** *n.*

wag² (wăg) *n.* A humorous or droll person; a wit. [Perhaps from WAG¹.]

wage (wāj) *n.* **1.** Payment for labor or services to a worker, especially remuneration on an hourly, daily, or weekly basis or by the piece. **2. wages.** The portion of the national product that represents the aggregate paid for all contributing labor and services as distinguished from the portion retained by management or reinvested in capital goods. **3.** Often **wages.** *(used with a sing. or pl. verb).* A fitting return; a recompense: *the wages of sin.* —**wage** *tr.v.* **waged, wag·ing, wag·es.** To engage in (a war or campaign, for example). [Middle English, from Old North French, of Germanic origin.]

wage earner *n.* **1.** One who works for wages. **2.** One whose earnings support or help support a household.

wa·ger (wā′jər) *n.* **1.** *Games.* **a.** An agreement under which each bettor pledges a certain amount to the other depending on the outcome of an unsettled matter. **b.** A matter bet on; a gamble. **2.** Something staked on an uncertain outcome; a bet. See Synonyms at **bet. 3.** *Archaic.* A pledge of personal combat to resolve an issue or a case. —**wager** *v.* **-gered, -ger·ing, -gers.** —*tr.* To risk or stake (an amount or a possession) on an uncertain outcome; bet. —*intr.* To make a bet. [Middle English, from Anglo-Norman *wageure,* from Old North French *wagier,* to pledge, from *wage,* pledge. See WAGE.] —**wa′ger·er** *n.*

wage scale *n.* The scale of wages paid to employees for the various jobs within an industry, a factory, or a company.

wage·work·er (wāj′wûr′kər) *n.* A wage earner.

wag·ger·y (wăg′ə-rē) *n., pl.* **-ies. 1.** Waggish behavior or spirit; drollery. **2.** A droll remark or act.

wag·gish (wăg′ĭsh) *adj.* Characteristic of or resembling a wag; jocular or witty. See Synonyms at **playful.** —**wag′gish·ly** *adv.* —**wag′gish·ness** *n.*

wag·gle (wăg′əl) *v.* **-gled, -gling, -gles.** —*tr.* To move (an attached part, for example) with short, quick motions: *waggled her foot impatiently.* —*intr.* To move shakily; wobble: *waggled down the steps.* [Middle English *wagelen,* frequentative of *waggen.* See WAG¹.] —**wag′gly** *adj.*

Wag·ner (väg′nər), **Richard.** 1813–1883. German composer known especially for his romantic operas, often based on Germanic legends. Among his works are *Tannhäuser* (1845) and the tetralogy *Der Ring des Nibelungen* (1853–1874).

Wag·ner (wăg′nər), **Robert Ferdinand.** 1877–1953. German-born American politician. A U.S. senator from New York (1927–1949), he sponsored important social legislation, most notably the National Labor Relations Act (1935).

Wag·ner·i·an (väg-nîr′ē-ən) *adj.* Of, relating to, or characteristic of Richard Wagner, his music dramas, or his theories. —**Wagnerian** *n.* **1.** An admirer or a disciple of Wagner. **2.** A performer of Wagner's music, especially a vocalist or conductor.

wag·on (wăg′ən) *n.* **1.** A four-wheeled, usually horse-drawn vehicle with a large rectangular body, used for transporting loads. **2. a.** A light automotive transport or delivery vehicle. **b.** A station wagon. **c.** A police patrol wagon. **3.** A child's low, four-wheeled cart hauled by a long handle that governs the direction of the front wheels. **4.** A small table or tray on wheels used for serving drinks or food: *a dessert wagon.* **5.** *Chiefly British.* An open railway freight car. —*attributive.* Often used to modify another noun: *a wagon wheel; a wagon driver.* —**wagon** *v.* **-oned, -on·ing, -ons.** —**wagon** *tr. & intr.v.* To transport or undergo transportation by wagon. —***idioms.*** **off the wagon.** *Slang.* No longer abstaining from alcoholic beverages. **on the wagon.** *Slang.* Abstaining from alcoholic beverages. [Middle English *waggin,* from Middle Dutch *wagen.* See **wegh-** in Appendix.]

Wag·on (wăg′ən) *n.* The Big Dipper.

wag·on·er (wăg′ə-nər) *n.* One who drives a wagon.

Wag·on·er (wăg′ə-nər) *n.* Auriga.

wa·gon-lit (vä′gôN-lē′) *n., pl.* **wa·gons-lits** or **wa·gon-lits** (vä′gôN-lē′). A sleeping car on a European railroad train. [French : *wagon,* railroad car (from English WAGON) + *lit,* bed (from Old French, from Latin *lectus;* see **legh-** in Appendix).]

wag·on·load (wăg′ən-lōd′) *n.* The amount that a wagon can hold.

wa·gons-lits (vä′gôN-lē′) *n.* A plural of **wagon-lit.**

wagon train *n.* A line or train of wagons traveling cross-country.

Wa·gram (vä′gräm′). A town of northeast Austria northeast of Vienna. Napoleon defeated the Austrians here in July 1809.

wag·tail (wăg′tāl′) *n.* Any of various chiefly Old World birds of the family Motacillidae, having a slender body with a long tail that constantly wags.

Wah·ha·bi or **Wa·ha·bi** (wä-hä′bē) *n., pl.* **-bis.** A member of a Moslem sect founded by Abdul Wahhab (1703–1792), known for its strict observance of the Koran and flourishing mainly in Arabia. —**Wah·ha′bism** (-bĭz′əm) *n.*

Wa·hi·a·wa (wä′hē-ə-wä′). A city of central Oahu, Hawaii, northwest of Honolulu. Population, 17,598.

wa·hi·ne (wä-hē′nē, -nā′) also **va·hi·ne** (vä-) *n.* **1.** A Polynesian woman or wife. **2.** *Sports.* A woman surfer. [Hawaiian.]

wa·hoo¹ (wä-ho͞o′, wä′ho͞o) *n., pl.* **-hoos.** A deciduous shrub or small tree *(Euonymus atropurpurea)* of eastern North America, having small purplish flowers, pink fruit, and scarlet arillate seeds. [Dakota *wāhu.*]

wa·hoo² (wä-ho͞o′, wä′ho͞o) *n., pl.* **-hoos. 1.** An elm tree *(Ulmus alata)* of the southeast United States, having twigs with winged, corky edges. **2.** Any of several similar trees. [Origin unknown.]

wa·hoo³ (wä-ho͞o′, wä′ho͞o) *n., pl.* **wahoo** or **-hoos.** A tropical marine food and game fish *(Acanthocybium solanderi)* of the mackerel family, having a pointed snout, narrow body, and long dorsal fin. [Origin unknown.]

♦**wa·hoo⁴** (wä′ho͞o′) *Chiefly Western U.S. interj.* Used to express exuberance. —**wahoo** *n., pl.* **-hoos.** An exuberant cry: *He let out a wahoo.* Also called ♦*rebel yell.*

Wah·pe·ku·te (wä′pə-ko͞o′tē) *n., pl.* **Wahpekute** or **-tes. 1.** A Native American people of the Santee branch of the Sioux. **2.** A member of this people.

Wah·pe·ton (wô′pĭ-tn) *n., pl.* **Wahpeton** or **-tons. 1.** A Native American people of the Santee branch of the Sioux. **2.** A member of this people.

wah-wah also **wa-wa** (wä′wä′) *n. Music.* **1.** A wavering sound produced by alternately covering and uncovering the bell of a trumpet or trombone with a mute. **2.** A similar sound produced by means of an electronic attachment, as on an electric guitar, operated by a foot pedal. [Imitative.] —**wah′-wah′** *adj.*

waif¹ (wāf) *n.* **1. a.** A homeless person, especially a forsaken or orphaned child. **b.** An abandoned young animal. **2.** Something found and unclaimed, as an object cast up by the sea. [Middle English, ownerless property, stray animal, from Anglo-Norman, probably of Scandinavian origin. See **weip-** in Appendix.]

waif² (wāf) *n. Nautical.* See **waft** (sense 4). [Probably of Scandinavian origin. See **weip-** in Appendix.]

Wai·ki·ki (wī′kĭ-kē′). A famous beach and resort district of Oahu Island, Hawaii, southeast of Honolulu.

wail (wāl) *v.* **wailed, wail·ing, wails.** —*intr.* **1.** To grieve or protest loudly and bitterly; lament. See Synonyms at **cry. 2.** To make a prolonged, high-pitched sound suggestive of a cry: *The wind wailed through the trees.* —*tr. Archaic.* To lament over; bewail. —**wail** *n.* **1.** A long, loud, high-pitched cry, as of grief or pain. **2.** A long, loud, high-pitched sound: *the wail of a siren.* **3.** A loud, bitter protest: *A wail of misery went up when new parking restrictions were announced.* [Middle English *wailen,* probably of Scandinavian origin; akin to Old Norse *vāla, vǣla.*] —**wail′er** *n.* —**wail′ing·ly** *adv.*

wail·ful (wāl′fəl) *adj.* **1.** Resembling a wail; mournful. **2.** Issuing a sound resembling a wail. —**wail′ful·ly** *adv.*

Wail·ing Wall (wā′lĭng) *n. Judaism.* See **Western Wall.**

wain (wān) *n.* A large open farm wagon. [Middle English, from Old English *wǣn, wægn.* See **wegh-** in Appendix.]

Wain (wān) *n.* The Big Dipper.

wain·scot (wān′skət, -skŏt′, -skōt′) *n.* **1.** A facing or paneling, usually of wood, applied to the walls of a room. **2.** The lower part of an interior wall when finished in a material different from that of the upper part. —**wainscot** *tr.v.* **-scot·ed, -scot·ing, -scots** or **-scot·ted, -scot·ting, -scots.** To line or panel (a room or wall) with wainscoting. [Middle English, from Middle Dutch *waghenscot* : perhaps *waghen, wagen,* wagon (from the quality of wood used for carriagework); see WAGON + *scot,* partition; see **skeud-** in Appendix.]

wain·scot·ing or **wain·scot·ting** (wān′skə-tĭng, -skŏt′ĭng, -skō′tĭng) *n.* **1.** A wainscoted wall or walls; paneling. **2.** Material, such as wood, used for wainscoting.

wain·wright (wān′rīt′) *n.* One that builds and repairs wagons.

Wai·pa·hu (wī-pä′ho͞o). A city of southern Oahu, Hawaii, on the northwest shore of Pearl Harbor. Population, 29,200.

waist (wāst) *n.* **1. a.** The part of the human trunk between the bottom of the rib cage and the pelvis. **b.** The narrow part of the abdomen of an insect. **2. a.** The part of a garment that encircles the waist of the body. **b.** The upper part of a garment, extending from the shoulders to the waistline, especially the bodice of a woman's dress. **c.** A blouse. **d.** A child's undershirt. **3.** The middle section or part of an object, especially when narrower than the rest. **4.** *Nautical.* The middle part of the deck of a ship between the forecastle and the quarterdeck. [Middle English *wast,* perhaps from Old English **wæst,* growth, size. See **aug-** in Appendix.] —**waist′less** *adj.*

waist·band (wāst′bănd′) *n.* A band of material encircling and fitting the waist of a garment, such as trousers or a skirt.

waist·cloth (wāst′klôth′, -klŏth′) *n.* A loincloth.

waist·coat (wĕs′kĭt, wāst′kōt′) *n.* **1.** A garment formerly worn by men under a doublet. **2.** *Chiefly British.* A short, sleeveless, collarless garment worn especially over a shirt and often under a suit jacket; a vest. —**waist′coat′ed** *adj.*

waist·line (wāst′līn′) *n.* **1. a.** A line thought of as encircling the body at the waist. **b.** The measurement of this line. **2. a.** The point or line at which the skirt and bodice of a dress join. **b.** The part of a garment that covers the narrowest part of the waist or

waders

Richard Wagner
Photographed in 1865

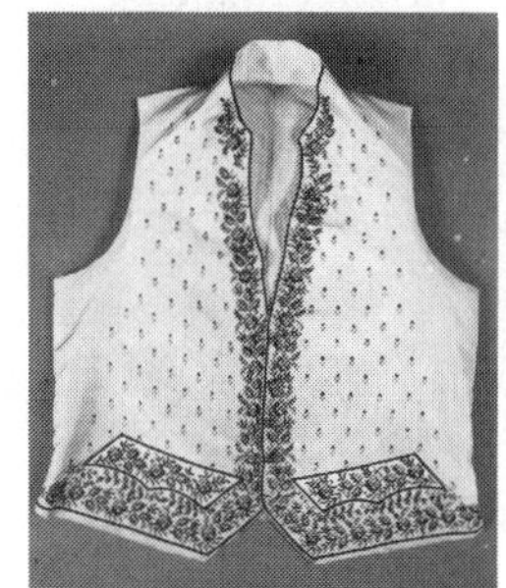

waistcoat

ă pat	oi boy
ā pay	ou out
âr care	o͝o took
ä father	o͞o boot
ĕ pet	ŭ cut
ē be	ûr urge
ĭ pit	th thin
ī pie	*th* this
îr pier	hw which
ŏ pot	zh vision
ō toe	ə about, item
ô paw	♦ regionalism

Stress marks: ′ (primary); ′ (secondary), as in **dictionary** (dĭk′shə-nĕr′ē)

the part above or below it as the current fashion demands.

♦ **wait** (wāt) *v.* **wait·ed, wait·ing, waits.** —*intr.* **1.a.** To remain or rest in expectation: *waiting for the guests to arrive.* See Synonyms at **stay**[1]. **b.** To tarry until another catches up. **2.** To remain or be in readiness: *lunch waiting on the table.* **3.** To remain temporarily neglected, unattended to, or postponed: *The trip will have to wait.* **4.** To work as a waiter or waitress. —*tr.* **1.** To remain or stay in expectation of; await: *wait one's turn.* **2.** *Informal.* To delay (a meal or an event); postpone: *They waited lunch for us.* **3.** To be a waiter or waitress at: *wait tables.* —**wait** *n.* **1.** The act of waiting or the time spent waiting. **2.** *Chiefly British.* **a.** One of a group of musicians employed, usually by a city, to play in parades or public ceremonies. **b.** One of a group of musicians or carolers who perform in the streets at Christmastime. —***phrasal verbs.*** **wait on** (or **upon**). **1.** To serve the needs of; be in attendance on. **2.** To make a formal call on; visit. **3.** To follow as a result; depend on. **4.** To await: *They're waiting on my decision.* **wait out.** To delay until the termination of: *wait out a war; waited out the miniskirt craze.* **wait up. 1.** To postpone going to bed in anticipation of something or someone. **2.** *Informal.* To stop or pause so that another can catch up: *Let's wait up for the stragglers.* [Middle English *waiten,* from Old North French *waitier,* to watch, of Germanic origin. See **weg-** in Appendix.]

USAGE NOTE: For more than a hundred years critics have stigmatized the use of *wait on* (and somewhat less frequently *wait upon*) to mean roughly "await" or "wait for," as in *We are still waiting on the committee vote.* This use is so widespread in both educated speech and reputable writing that the traditional objections have come to seem unnecessary.

wake[2]

wait-a-bit (wāt′ə-bĭt′) *n.* Any of several plants having sharp, often hooked thorns. Also called *wait-a-minute.* [Translation of Afrikaans *wag-'n-bietjie.*]

wait-a-minute (wāt′ə-mĭn′ĭt) *n.* See **wait-a-bit.**

Waite (wāt), **Morrison Remick.** 1816–1888. American jurist who served as the chief justice of the U.S. Supreme Court (1874–1888).

wait·er (wā′tər) *n.* **1.** One who serves at a table, as in a restaurant. **2.** A tray or salver.

wait·ing (wā′tĭng) *n.* **1.** The act of remaining inactive or stationary. **2.** A period of time spent waiting. —***idiom.*** **in waiting.** In attendance, especially at a royal court.

waiting game *n.* The stratagem of deferring action and allowing the passage of time to work in one's favor.

waiting list *n.* A list of persons waiting, as for an appointment or filling a vacancy.

waiting room *n.* A room, as in a railroad station or physician's office, for the use of people waiting.

wait·per·son (wāt′pûr′sən) *n., pl.* **-per·sons** or **-peo·ple** (-pē′pəl). A waiter or waitress.

wait·ress (wā′trĭs) *n.* A woman who serves at a table, as in a restaurant. See Usage Note at **-ess.**

wait·ron (wā′trən) *n.* A waiter or waitress: *"The dining room staff is as comfortable with making you comfortable as the typical modern waitron is uncomfortable"* (Washington Post). [Alteration of WAITER.]

Alice Walker

waive (wāv) *tr.v.* **waived, waiv·ing, waives. 1.** To give up (a claim or right) voluntarily; relinquish. See Synonyms at **relinquish. 2.** To refrain from insisting on or enforcing (a rule or penalty, for example); dispense with: *"The original ban on private trading had long since been waived"* (William L. Schurz). **3.** To put aside or off temporarily; defer. [Middle English *weiven,* to abandon, from Anglo-Norman *weyver,* from *waif,* ownerless property. See WAIF[1].]

waiv·er (wā′vər) *n.* **1.a.** Intentional relinquishment of a right, claim, or privilege. **b.** The document that evidences such relinquishment. **2.** A dispensation, as from a rule or penalty. **3.** A deferment. [Anglo-Norman *weyver,* from *weyver,* to abandon. See WAIVE.]

wa·ka·me (wä-kä′mĕ) *n.* A brown seaweed *(Undaria pinnatifida)* native to the coasts of China, Japan, and Korea, having a short stipe and pinnately divided blades, extensively used in oriental cooking. [Japanese.]

Wa·kash·an (wä-kăsh′ən, wô′kə-shăn′) *n.* A family of North American Indian languages spoken by the Nootka and other peoples of Washington and British Columbia. [Ultimately from Nootka *waakaash,* bravo!] —**Wa′kash·an** *adj.*

Wa·ka·ya·ma (wä′kə-yä′mə). A city of southern Honshu, Japan, south-southwest of Osaka on the Inland Sea. It is a railroad hub and a manufacturing center. Population, 401,357.

♦ **wake**[1] (wāk) *v.* **woke** (wōk) or **waked** (wākt), **waked** or **wok·en** (wō′kən), **wak·ing, wakes.** —*intr.* **1.a.** To cease to sleep; become awake: *overslept and woke late.* **b.** To stay awake: *Bears wake for spring, summer, and fall and hibernate for the winter.* **c.** To be brought into a state of awareness or alertness: *suddenly woke to the danger we were in.* **2.** To keep watch or guard, especially over a corpse. —*tr.* **1.** To rouse from sleep; awaken. **2.** To stir, as from a dormant or inactive condition; rouse: *wake old animosities.* **3.** To make aware of; alert: *The shocking revelations finally woke me to the facts of the matter.* **4.a.** To keep a vigil over. **b.** To hold a wake over. —**wake** *n.* **1.** A watch; a vigil. **2.** A watch over the body of a deceased person before burial, sometimes accompanied by festivity. Also called ♦*viewing.* **3. wakes** *(used with a sing. or pl. verb). Chiefly British.* **a.** A parish festival held annually, often in honor of a patron saint. **b.** An annual vacation. [Middle English *wakien, waken,* from Old English *wacan,* to wake up, and *wacian,* to be awake, keep watch; see **weg-** in Appendix.] —**wak′er** *n.*

USAGE NOTE: The pairs *wake, waken* and *awake, awaken* have formed a bewildering array since the Middle English period. All four words have similar meanings, though there are some differences in use. Only *wake* is used in the sense "to be awake," as in expressions like *waking* (not *wakening*) *and sleeping, every waking hour. Wake* is also more common than *waken* when used together with *up;* and *awake* and *awaken* never occur in this context: *She woke up* (rarely *wakened up;* never *awakened up* or *awoke up*). Some writers have suggested that *waken* should be used only transitively and *awaken* only intransitively, but there is ample literary precedent for usages such as *He wakened early* and *They did not awaken her.* In figurative senses *awake* and *awaken* are more prevalent: *With the governor's defeat the party awoke to the strength of the opposition to its position on abortion. The scent of the azaleas awakened my memory of his unexpected appearance that afternoon years ago.*

♦ ***REGIONAL NOTE:*** Regional American dialects vary in the way that certain verbs form their principal parts. Northern dialects seem to favor forms that change the internal vowel in the verb—hence *dove* for the past tense of *dive,* and *woke* for *wake: They woke up with a start.* Southern dialects, on the other hand, tend to prefer forms that add an *-ed* to form the past tense and the past participle of these same verbs: *The children dived into the swimming hole. The baby waked up early.*

wake[2] (wāk) *n.* **1.** The visible track of turbulence left by something moving through water: *the wake of a ship.* **2.** A track, course, or condition left behind something that has passed: *The war left destruction and famine in its wake.* —***idiom.*** **in the wake of. 1.** Following directly on. **2.** In the aftermath of; as a consequence of. [Possibly from Middle Low German, hole in the ice, of Scandinavian origin; akin to Old Norse *vök.*]

Wake·field (wāk′fēld′). **1.** A borough of north-central England east-northeast of Manchester. In the Battle of Wakefield (1460) Richard Plantagenet, the third duke of York (1411–1460), was slain by Lancastrian forces in the Wars of the Roses. **2.** A town of eastern Massachusetts, a residential and industrial suburb of Boston. Population, 24,895.

wake·ful (wāk′fəl) *adj.* **1.a.** Not sleeping or not able to sleep. **b.** Without sleep; sleepless. **2.** Watchful; alert. —**wake′ful·ly** *adv.* —**wake′ful·ness** *n.*

Wake Island (wāk). An island of the western Pacific Ocean between Hawaii and Guam. Annexed by the United States in 1898, it was a commercial air base and later a military base. Wake Island was held by the Japanese from 1941 to 1945.

wake·less (wāk′lĭs) *adj.* Unbroken. Used of sleep.

wak·en (wā′kən) *v.* **-ened, -en·ing, -ens.** —*tr.* **1.** To rouse from sleep; awake: *The noise wakened me.* **2.** To rouse from a quiescent or inactive state; stir. —*intr.* To become awake; wake up: *I plan to waken at six o'clock tomorrow.* See Usage Note at **wake**[1]. [Middle English *wakenen,* from Old English *wæcnan.* See **weg-** in Appendix.] —**wak′en·er** *n.*

wake-rob·in (wāk′rŏb′ĭn) *n.* **1.** See **trillium. 2.** Any of various North American aroid plants that bloom early in the spring.

wak·ing (wā′kĭng) *adj.* Marked by full consciousness, awareness, and alertness: *worked every moment of my waking hours.*

Waks·man (wăks′mən), **Selman Abraham.** 1888–1973. Russian-born American microbiologist. He won a 1952 Nobel Prize for discovering the antibiotic streptomycin.

Wa·la·chi·a (wə-lā′kē-ə, wŏ-). See **Wallachia.**

Wa·la·pai (wä′lə-pī′) *n.* Variant of **Hualapai.**

Wał·brzych (välb′zhĭk′, -zhĭkн′). A city of southwest Poland southwest of Wroclaw. A coal-mining center, it passed from Germany to Poland after 1945. Population, 138,000.

Wald (wôld), **Lillian D.** 1867–1940. American nurse and social reformer who founded a public-health service, the Henry Street Settlement, in New York City (1893).

Wal·de·mar I (wôl′də-mär′, väl′-) or **Val·de·mar I** (väl′-). Known as "Waldemar the Great." 1131–1182. Danish king (1157–1182) who extended his realm and gained recognition for the hereditary rule of his family.

Wal·den Pond (wôl′dən). A pond of northeast Massachusetts near Concord. Henry David Thoreau lived in a cabin near the pond from 1845 to 1847.

Wal·den·ses (wŏl-dĕn′sēz, wôl-) *pl.n.* A Christian sect of dissenters that originated in southern France in the late 12th century and adopted Calvinist doctrines in the 16th century. Also called *Vaudois.* [Medieval Latin *Waldēnsēs,* after Peter WALDO.] —**Wal·den′sian** (-shən) *adj. & n.*

Wald·heim (wôld′hīm′, vält′-), **Kurt.** Born 1918. Austrian diplomat and politician. After serving as secretary-general of the United Nations (1972–1981), he was elected president of Austria in 1986 despite worldwide controversy over his alleged Nazi affiliations during World War II.

Wal·do (wôl′dō, wäl′-) or **Val·do** (văl′-, väl′-), **Peter.** Also known as Peter or Pierre Valdès. fl. 12th century. French religious leader who founded the Waldenses and was excommunicated in 1184.

Wal·dorf salad (wôl′dôrf′) *n.* A salad of diced raw apples, celery, and walnuts mixed with mayonnaise. [After the *Waldorf-*Astoria Hotel in New York City.]

wale (wāl) *n.* **1.** A mark raised on the skin, as by a whip; a weal or welt. **2. a.** One of the parallel ribs or ridges in the surface of a fabric such as corduroy. **b.** The texture or weave of such a fabric: *a wide wale.* **3.** *Nautical.* **a.** A gunwale. **b.** One of the heavy planks or strakes extending along the sides of a wooden ship. **—wale** *tr.v.* **waled, wal·ing, wales.** To raise marks on (the skin), as by whipping. [Middle English, from Old English, variant of *walu.* See **wel-²** in Appendix.]

Wal·er also **wal·er** (wā′lər) *n.* A light saddle horse of mixed breed developed in Australia and exported to the British military forces in India during the 19th century. [After New South *Wales*, a state of southeast Australia.]

Wales (wālz). A principality of the United Kingdom on the western peninsula of the island of Great Britain. Incorporated with England since the Act of Union (1536), Wales has maintained its own distinct culture and a strong nationalist sentiment. Cardiff is the capital and the largest city. Population, 2,790,462.

Wa·le·sa (wä-lĕn′sə, vä-wĕn′sä), **Lech.** Born 1943. Polish labor leader. He won the 1983 Nobel Peace Prize for his leadership of the independent trade union Solidarity. In 1990 he was elected president of Poland.

Wal·hal·la (wăl-hăl′ə, văl-, wäl-hä′lə, väl-) *n. Mythology.* Variant of **Valhalla.**

walk (wôk) *v.* **walked, walk·ing, walks.** *—intr.* **1.** To move over a surface by taking steps with the feet at a pace slower than a run: *a baby learning to walk; a horse walking around a riding ring.* **2. a.** To go or travel on foot: *walked to the store.* **b.** To go on foot for pleasure or exercise; stroll: *walked along the beach looking for shells.* **c.** To move in a manner suggestive of walking: *saw a woodpecker walking up the tree trunk.* **3.** To conduct oneself or behave in a particular manner; live: *walks in majesty and pride.* **4.** To appear as a supernatural being: *The specter of famine walks through the land.* **5.** *Slang.* **a.** To go out on strike. **b.** To resign from one's job abruptly; quit. **6. a.** *Baseball.* To go to first base after the pitcher has thrown four balls. **b.** *Basketball.* To move illegally while holding the ball; travel. **7.** *Obsolete.* To be in constant motion. *—tr.* **1.** To go on or pass over, on, or through by walking: *walk the financial district of a city.* **2.** To bring to a specified condition by walking: *They walked me to exhaustion.* **3.** To cause to walk or proceed at a walk: *walk a horse uphill.* **4.** To accompany in walking; escort on foot: *walk the children home; walked me down the hall.* **5.** To traverse on foot in order to survey or measure; pace off: *walked the bounds of the property.* **6.** To move (a heavy or cumbersome object) in a manner suggestive of walking: *walked the bureau into the hall.* **7.** *Baseball.* To allow (a batter) to go to first base by pitching four balls. **—walk** *n.* **1. a.** The gait of a human being or other biped in which the feet are lifted alternately with one part of a foot always on the ground. **b.** The gait of a quadruped in which at least two feet are always touching the ground, especially the gait of a horse in which the feet touch the ground in the four-beat sequence of near hind foot, near forefoot, off hind foot, off forefoot. **c.** The self-controlled extravehicular movement in space of an astronaut. **2.** The act or an instance of walking, especially a stroll for pleasure or exercise. **3. a.** The rate at which one walks; a walking pace. **b.** The characteristic way in which one walks. **4.** The distance covered or to be covered in walking. **5.** A place, such as a sidewalk or promenade, on which one may walk. **6.** A route or circuit particularly suitable for walking: *one of the prettiest walks in the area.* **7. a.** *Baseball.* Base on balls. **b.** *Basketball.* The act or an instance of moving illegally with the ball; traveling. **8.** *Sports.* **a.** A track event in which contestants compete in walking a specified distance. **b.** Race walking. **9.** An enclosed area designated for the exercise or pasture of livestock. **10. a.** An arrangement of trees or shrubs planted in widely spaced rows. **b.** The space between such rows. ***—phrasal verbs.*** **walk out.** **1.** To go on strike. **2.** To leave suddenly, often as a signal of disapproval. **walk over.** *Informal.* **1.** To treat badly or contemptuously. **2.** To gain an easy or uncontested victory. **walk through.** To perform (a play, for example) in a perfunctory fashion, as at a first rehearsal. ***—idioms.*** **walk away from.** **1.** To outdo, outrun, or defeat with little difficulty. **2.** To survive (an accident) with very little injury. **walk off with.** **1.** To win easily or unexpectedly. **2.** To steal. **walk on air.** To feel elated. **walk out on.** To desert or abandon. **walk the plank.** To be forced, as by pirates, to walk off a plank extended over the side of a ship so as to drown. [Middle English *walken,* from Old English *wealcan,* to roll. See **wel-²** in Appendix.] **—walk′a·bil′i·ty** *n.* **—walk′a·ble** *adj.*

walk·a·bout (wôk′ə-bout′) *n.* **1.** *Australian.* A temporary return to traditional aboriginal life, taken especially between periods of work or residence in white society and usually involving a period of travel through the bush. **2.** A walking trip. **3.** *Chiefly British.* A public stroll taken by an important person, such as a monarch, among a group of people for greeting and conversation.

walk·a·way (wôk′ə-wā′) *n.* **1.** An easily won contest or victory. **2.** Something that is easy and presents no difficulties. See Synonyms at **breeze¹.**

walk·er (wô′kər) *n.* **1.** One that walks, especially a contestant in a footrace. **2.** A frame device used to support someone, such as an infant learning to walk or a convalescent learning to walk again. **3.** A shoe specially designed for walking comfortably. Often used in the plural.

Wal·ker (wô′kər), **Alice.** Born 1944. American writer whose works include the novels *Meridian* (1976) and *The Color Purple* (1982).

Walker, James John. Known as "Jimmy." 1881–1946. American politician who was the mayor of New York City from 1926 to 1932, when charges of corruption forced his resignation.

Walker, Sarah Breedlove. 1867–1919. American businesswoman who developed a straightening agent for hair (1905) and built the most successful Black-owned company of her day.

walk·ie-talk·ie also **walk·y-talk·y** (wô′kē-tô′kē) *n., pl.* **-ies.** A battery-powered portable sending and receiving radio set.

walkie-talkie

walk-in (wôk′ĭn′) *adj.* **1.** Large enough to admit entrance: *a walk-in closet.* **2.** Located so as to be entered directly from the street: *a walk-in apartment.* **—walk-in** *n.* **1.** A room large enough to admit entrance. **2.** An easily won victory, especially in an election. **3.** *Slang.* **a.** One who walks in without having an appointment. **b.** One, such as a spy, who initiates defection from one's own country to another, usually hostile country, without having been encouraged to do so.

walk·ing (wô′kĭng) *adj.* Regarded as having the capabilities or qualities of a specified object: *a teacher who is a walking dictionary.*

walking bass (bās) *n. Music.* A repetitive bass figure composed of nonsyncopated eighth notes, used in jazz.

walking catfish *n.* A freshwater catfish *(Clarius batrachus),* native to southeast Asia, that is able to breathe out of water and travel short distances on land.

walking delegate *n.* A trade union official appointed to inspect and confer with local unions or to serve as a representative of a union in dealings with an employer.

walking fern *n.* An eastern North American fern *(Camptosorus rhizophyllus)* having undivided fronds that often take root at the tip.

walking horse *n.* A Tennessee walking horse.

walking leaf *n.* **1.** A walking fern. **2.** See **leaf insect.**

walking papers *pl.n. Slang.* A notice of discharge or dismissal.

walking stick *n.* **1.** A cane or staff used as an aid in walking. **2.** A stick insect, especially a widely distributed North American species *(Diapheromera femorata)* that is brown to greenish and usually inhabits deciduous trees.

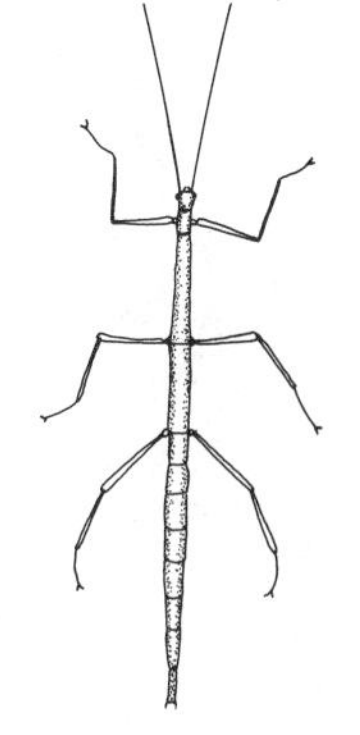

walking stick
Top: Wooden staff
Bottom: Diapheromera femorata

Walk·man (wôk′măn′, -mən). A trademark used for a pocket-sized audiocassette player, radio, or combined unit with lightweight earphones.

walk of life *n., pl.* **walks of life.** An occupation, a profession, or a social class: *People from all walks of life supported the cause.*

walk-on (wôk′ŏn′, -ôn′) *n.* **1.** A minor role in a theatrical production, usually without speaking lines. **2.** A performer playing such a role.

walk·out (wôk′out′) *n.* **1.** A labor strike. **2.** The act of leaving or quitting a meeting, a company, or an organization, especially as a sign of protest.

walk·o·ver (wôk′ō′vər) *n.* **1.** *Sports.* **a.** An easy or uncontested win in a competition. **b.** A horserace with only one horse entered, won by the mere formality of walking the length of the track. **2.** A walkaway. See Synonyms at **breeze¹.**

walk-through (wôk′thro͞o′) *n.* **1.** A brief rehearsal, as of a play or role, performed usually in an early stage of production. **2.** A television rehearsal during which no cameras are used.

walk·up also **walk-up** (wôk′ŭp′) *n.* **1.** An apartment house or office building with no elevator. **2.** An apartment or office in a building with no elevator.

walk·way (wôk′wā′) *n.* A passage or path for walking.

Wal·kyr·ie (wäl-kîr′ē, -kī′rē, väl-, wäl′kə-rē, väl′-) *n.* Variant of **Valkyrie.**

walk·y-talk·y (wô′kē-tô′kē) *n.* Variant of **walkie-talkie.**

wall (wôl) *n.* **1.** An upright structure of masonry, wood, plaster, or other building material serving to enclose, divide, or protect an area, especially a vertical construction forming an inner partition or exterior siding of a building. **2.** Often **walls.** A continuous structure of masonry or other material forming a rampart and built for defensive purposes. **3.** A structure of stonework, cement, or other material built to retain a flow of water. **4. a.** Something resembling a wall in appearance, function, or construction, as the exterior surface of a body organ or part: *the abdominal wall.* **b.** Something resembling a wall in impenetrability or strength: *a wall of silence; a wall of fog.* **c.** An extreme or desperate condition or position, such as defeat or ruin: *driven to the wall by poverty.* **5.** *Sports.* The vertical surface of an ocean wave in surfing. **—wall** *tr.v.* **walled, wall·ing, walls.** **1.** To enclose, surround, or fortify with or as if with a wall: *wall up an old window.* See Synonyms at **enclose.** **2.** To divide or separate with or as if with a wall: *wall off half a room.* **3.** To enclose within a wall; immure. **4.** To block or close (an opening or a passage, for example) with or as if with a wall. ***—idioms.*** **off the wall.** *Slang.* **1.** Extremely unconventional. **2.** Without foundation; ridiculous: *an accusation that is really off the wall.* **up the wall.** *Slang.* Into a state of extreme frustration, anger, or distress: *tensions that are driving me up the wall.* **writing** (or **handwriting**) **on the wall.** An ominous indication of the course of future

ă pat	oi boy
ā pay	ou out
âr care	o͝o took
ä father	o͞o boot
ĕ pet	ŭ cut
ē be	ûr urge
ĭ pit	th thin
ī pie	*th* this
îr pier	hw which
ŏ pot	zh vision
ō toe	ə about, item
ô paw	♦ regionalism

Stress marks: **′** (primary); ′ (secondary), as in **dictionary** (dĭk′shə-nĕr′ē)

wallaby

events: *saw the writing on the wall and fled the country.* [Middle English, from Old English *weall,* from Latin *vallum,* palisade, from *vallus,* stake.] **—wall′less** *adj.*

wal·la (wä′lä, wŏl′ə) *n.* Variant of **wallah.**

wal·la·by (wŏl′ə-bē) *n., pl.* **-bies** or **wallaby.** Any of various marsupials of the genus *Wallabia* and related genera, of Australia and adjacent islands, related to the kangaroos but generally smaller and often having a colorful coat. [Dharuk (Aboriginal language of southeast Australia) *walaba.*]

Wal·lace (wŏl′ĭs), **Alfred Russel.** 1823–1913. British naturalist who developed a concept of evolution that paralleled the work of Charles Darwin.

Wallace, De Witt. 1889–1981. American publisher who with his wife **Lila Bell Acheson Wallace** (1889–1984) founded *Reader's Digest* in 1922.

Wallace, George Corley. Born 1919. American politician. A three-time governor of Alabama (1963–1967, 1971–1979, and 1983–1987), he ran unsuccessfully for the presidency in 1968 and 1972.

Wallace, Henry Agard. 1888–1965. Vice President of the United States (1941–1945) under Franklin D. Roosevelt. He ran for President in 1948 on the Progressive Party ticket.

Wallace, Lewis. Known as "Lew." 1827–1905. American general and writer known especially for his novel *Ben Hur* (1880).

Wallace, Sir **William.** 1272?–1305. Scottish patriot who led resistance against the English and briefly gained control of Scotland in 1298.

Wal·la·chi·a also **Wa·la·chi·a** (wə-lā′kē-ə, wŏ-). A historical region of southeast Romania between the Transylvanian Alps and the Danube River. Founded as a principality c. 1290, it was ruled by Turkey from 1387 until it was united with Moldavia to form Romania (1861). **—Wal·la′chi·an** *adj. & n.*

wal·lah also **wal·la** (wä′lä, wŏl′ə) *n.* **1.** One employed in a particular occupation or activity: *a kitchen wallah; rickshaw wallahs.* **2.** An important person in a particular field or organization: *"the Ritz, a favorite haunt of Republican wallahs"* (John Robinson). **3.** *Chiefly British.* A man; a chap. [From Hindi *-wālā,* pertaining to, connected with.]

wal·la·roo (wŏl′ə-ro͞o′) *n., pl.* **-roos** or **wallaroo.** A large kangaroo *(Macropus robustus)* having reddish or gray fur and living in the hilly regions of Australia. [Dharuk (Aboriginal language of southeast Australia) *walaru.*]

Wal·la Wal·la (wŏl′ə wŏl′ə). A city of southeast Washington near the Oregon border south-southwest of Spokane. Founded in 1856 near the site of an army fort, it is a manufacturing center in an agricultural region. Population, 25,618.

wall·board (wôl′bôrd′, -bōrd′) *n.* See **plasterboard.**

wall creeper *n.* A long-billed crimson and gray Old World bird *(Tichodroma muraria),* of alpine regions, that feeds on insects on rocky cliffs.

Wal·len·stein (wŏl′ən-stīn′, väl′ən-shtīn′), **Albrecht Eusebius Wenzel von.** Duke of Friedland and Mecklenburg. 1583–1634. Austrian military leader who fought for the Hapsburgs during the Thirty Years' War (1618–1648).

Wal·ler (wŏl′ər), **Edmund.** 1606–1687. English poet known for his harmonious love lyrics, including "Go, Lovely Rose" (1645).

Waller, Thomas Wright. Known as "Fats." 1904–1943. American jazz musician and composer whose many songs include "Honeysuckle Rose" and "Ain't Misbehavin' " (both 1929).

wal·let (wŏl′ĭt) *n.* A flat pocket-sized folding case, usually made of leather, for holding paper money, cards, or photographs; a billfold. [Middle English *walet,* knapsack, possibly from Old North French **walet,* roll, knapsack. See **wel-**[2] in Appendix.]

wall·eye (wôl′ī′) *n.* **1.** An eye with a light-colored iris or a white or opaque cornea. **2.** *Pathology.* **a.** The condition of having a dense white opacity of the cornea. **b.** A form of strabismus in which the visual axis of one eye deviates from that of the other. **3.** *pl.* **walleye** or **-eyes** A freshwater food and game fish *(Stizostedium vitreum)* of North America, having large staring eyes. Also called *dory, walleyed pike.* [Back-formation from WALLEYED.]

walnut

wall·eyed (wôl′īd′) *adj.* **1.** Having a walleye. **2.** *Pathology.* Affected with walleye. **3.a.** Having large bulging or staring eyes. **b.** *Slang.* Having eyes with greatly distended pupils. **4.** *Slang.* Intoxicated; drunk. [Middle English *wawileyed,* from Old Norse *vagl-eygr* : *vagl,* film over the eye; see **wegh-** in Appendix + *auga,* eye; see **ok**ʷ**-** in Appendix.]

walleyed pike *n.* See **walleye** (sense 3).

walleyed pollack *n.* A food fish *(Theragra chalcogramma)* of the northern Pacific related to the pollack.

wall fern *n.* A low-growing Eurasian fern *(Polypodium vulgare)* characterized by creeping stems that form dense mats.

wall·flow·er (wôl′flou′ər) *n.* **1.a.** Any of numerous herbs of the genus *Erysimum* of the mustard family, having fragrant yellow, orange, or brownish flowers. **b.** Any of several perennial herbs of the genus *Cheiranthus,* especially *C. cheiri.* **2.** One who does not participate in the activity at a social event because of shyness or unpopularity. **3.** A security, a company, or an industry that is out of favor with investors.

WORD HISTORY: The *Cheiranthus cheiri,* with its sweet-smelling yellow, red, or brown flowers, came to be called the *wallflower* because it was noted for growing on surfaces such as old walls, rocks, and quarries. This plant name is first recorded in 1578. It is not known who first observed a likeness between this delicate, fragrant flower and the unpartnered women sitting along the wall at a dance, but the figurative sense is first found in an 1820 work by Mrs. Campbell Praed entitled *County Ball.* The word, although originally used only to describe women, has become unisex, and of course one can be a wallflower without having a wall in the vicinity.

wall hanging *n.* A flat decorative object, such as a tapestry, a rug, or an antique map, hung against a wall.

Wal·ling·ford (wŏl′ĭng-fərd). A town of southern Connecticut north-northeast of New Haven. Population, 37,274.

Wal·lis and Fu·tu·na Islands (wŏl′ĭs; fo͞o-to͞o′nə). A French overseas territory consisting of two groups of islands in the southwest Pacific northeast of Fiji. Controlled by the French from 1842, the islands became an overseas territory in 1961.

Wal·lo·ni·a (wä-lō′nē-ə). A French-speaking region of southern Belgium. It was granted limited autonomy in 1980.

Wal·loon (wŏ-lo͞on′) *n.* **1.** One of a French-speaking people of Celtic descent inhabiting southern and southeast Belgium and adjacent regions of France. **2.** The dialect of French spoken by these people. [French *Wallon,* from Old French, of Germanic origin.]

wal·lop (wŏl′əp) *Informal. v.* **-loped, -lop·ing, -lops.** *—tr.* **1.** To beat soundly; thrash. **2.** To strike with a hard blow. **3.** To defeat thoroughly. *—intr.* **1.** To move in a rolling, clumsy manner; waddle. **2.** To boil noisily. Used of a liquid. **—wallop** *n.* **1.** A hard or severe blow. **2.a.** The ability to strike a powerful blow: *has a punch that delivers a wallop.* **b.** The capacity to create a forceful effect: *"Tarragon's narrow, tender green leaves pack a strong wallop of anise"* (Marc Wortman). *"Therein lies the novel's emotional wallop and moral message"* (George F. Will). [Middle English *walopen,* to gallop, from Old North French **waloper.* See **wel-**[1] in Appendix.] **—wal′lop·er** *n.*

wal·lop·ing (wŏl′ə-pĭng) *Informal. adj.* **1.** Very large; huge: *a walloping fish.* **2.** Very fine; impressive: *a walloping success.* **—walloping** *adv.* Used as an intensive: *a walloping huge lie.* **—walloping** *n.* A sound thrashing or defeat.

wal·low (wŏl′ō) *intr.v.* **-lowed, -low·ing, -lows.** **1.** To roll the body about indolently or clumsily in or as if in water, snow, or mud. **2.** To luxuriate; revel: *wallow in self-righteousness.* **3.** To be plentifully supplied: *wallowing in money.* **4.** To move with difficulty in a clumsy or rolling manner; flounder: *"The car wallowed back through the slush, with ribbons of bright water trickling down the windshield from the roof"* (Anne Tyler). **5.** To swell or surge forth; billow. **—wallow** *n.* **1.** The act or an instance of wallowing. **2.a.** A pool of water or mud where animals go to wallow. **b.** The depression, pool, or pit produced by wallowing animals. **3.** A condition of degradation or baseness. [Middle English *walowen,* from Old English *wealwian.* See **wel-**[2] in Appendix.] **—wal′low·er** *n.*

wall·pa·per (wôl′pā′pər) *n.* Paper often colored and printed with designs and pasted to a wall as a decorative covering. **—wallpaper** *v.* **-pered, -per·ing, -pers.** *—tr.* To cover with or as if with wallpaper. *—intr.* To decorate a wall or room with wallpaper.

wall plate *n.* **1.** A horizontal timber situated along the top of a wall at the level of the eaves for bearing the ends of joists or rafters. **2.** A plate used to attach a bracket or similar device to a wall.

wall plug *n.* An electric socket, usually located in a wall, that is connected to and used as a source of electric power.

wall rock *n.* The rock that forms the walls of a vein or lode.

wall rue *n.* A small, delicate fern *(Asplenium ruta-muraria)* that grows on rocks or in rocky crevices.

Wall Street (wôl) *n.* The controlling financial interests of the United States. [After *Wall Street* in New York City.] **—Wall′-Street′er** (wôl′strē′tər) *n.*

wall-to-wall (wôl′tə-wôl′) *adj.* **1.** Completely covering a floor: *wall-to-wall carpeting.* **2.** *Informal.* **a.** Present or spreading throughout an entire area: *wall-to-wall people at the reception.* **b.** Found everywhere or including everything; pervasive: *wall-to-wall luxury.* **—wall-to-wall** *n.* A carpet that completely covers a floor.

wal·nut (wôl′nŭt′, -nət) *n.* **1.a.** Any of several deciduous trees of the genus *Juglans,* having pinnately compound leaves and a round, sticky outer fruit wall that encloses a nutlike stone with an edible seed. **b.** The stone or the ridged or corrugated seed of such a tree. **2.** The hard, dark brown wood of any of these trees, used for gunstocks and in cabinetwork. [Middle English *walnot,* from Old English *wealhhnutu* : *wealh,* Celt, foreigner + *hnutu,* nut.] **—wal′nut** *adj.*

Wal·nut Creek (wôl′nŭt′, -nət). A city of western California northeast of Oakland. Population, 53,643.

Wal·pole (wôl′pōl′, wŏl′-). A town of eastern Massachusetts southwest of Boston. Settled in 1659, it is a manufacturing center and the site of a large state prison. Population, 18,859.

Walpole, Horace or **Horatio.** Fourth Earl of Orford. 1717–1797. British writer and historian whose correspondence and memoirs provide valuable information about his era. He wrote *The Castle of Otranto* (1764), the first Gothic novel in English.

Walpole, Sir **Hugh Seymour.** 1884–1941. New Zealand-born

British writer known for his novels, including *The Herries Chronicle* (1930–1933).

Walpole, Sir **Robert.** First Earl of Orford. 1676–1745. English politician who as first lord of the treasury and Chancellor of the Exchequer (1715–1717 and 1721–1742) led the Whig administration and was regarded as Britain's first prime minister, although the office was not officially recognized until 1905.

Wal·pur·gis Night (väl-pŏŏr′gĭs) *n.* **1.a.** The eve of May Day, observed in some European countries and in some Scandinavian communities in the United States in celebration of spring and marked by music, singing, and bonfires. **b.** The eve of Beltane, believed by medieval Christians to be the occasion of a witches' Sabbath. **2.** An episode or a situation having the quality of nightmarish wildness. [Partial translation of German *Walpurgisnacht* : *Walpurgis,* Saint Walpurga (died 779) + *Nacht,* night.]

wal·rus (wôl′rəs, wŏl′-) *n., pl.* **walrus** or **-rus·es.** A large marine mammal *(Odobenus rosmarus)* of Arctic regions, related to the seals and having two long tusks, tough wrinkled skin, and four flippers. Also called *sea horse.* [Dutch, of Scandinavian origin.]

walrus mustache *n.* A bushy, drooping mustache.

Wal·sall (wôl′sôl′, -səl). A borough of west-central England northwest of Birmingham. It is a mining and manufacturing center. Population, 267,500.

Wal·ter (väl′tər), **Bruno.** 1876–1962. German conductor noted for his interpretations of Mozart and Mahler.

Wal·ter Mit·ty (wôl′tər mĭt′ē) *n.* An ordinary, often ineffectual person who indulges in fantastic daydreams of personal triumphs. [After the main character in "The Secret Life of *Walter Mitty*" by James Thurber.]

Wal·tham (wôl′thăm′, -thəm). A city of eastern Massachusetts west of Boston. It is a manufacturing center and the seat of Brandeis University (established 1947). Population, 58,200.

Wal·ther von der Vo·gel·wei·de (väl′tər fôn der fō′gəl-vī′də). 1170?–1230? German minnesinger whose lyrics reflected his religious and political views.

Wal·ton (wôl′tən), **Ernest Thomas Sinton.** Born 1903. Irish physicist who with Sir John Cockcroft succeeded in splitting the atom (1931). They shared a 1951 Nobel Prize for their contributions to nuclear physics.

Walton, Izaak. 1593–1683. English writer primarily known for *The Compleat Angler* (1653), a literary treatise on fishing.

Walton, Sir **William Turner.** 1902–1983. British composer of orchestral works and chamber music, including *Façade* (1923), an extravaganza accompanying poems by Edith Sitwell.

Walton and Wey·bridge (wā′brĭj). A district of southeast England, a residential suburb of London. Population, 113,000.

waltz (wôlts, wôls) *n.* **1.a.** A ballroom dance in triple time with a strong accent on the first beat. **b.** A piece of music for this dance. **c.** An instrumental or vocal composition in triple time. **2.** *Informal.* Something that presents no difficulties and can be accomplished with little effort. **—waltz** *v.* **waltzed, waltz·ing, waltz·es.** —*intr.* **1.** To dance the waltz. **2.** *Slang.* To move unhesitantly, briskly, and with aplomb: *always waltzes into the office 30 minutes late.* **3.** *Informal.* To accomplish a task, a chore, or an assignment with little effort: *waltzed through the exams.* —*tr.* **1.** To dance the waltz with. **2.** *Slang.* To lead or force to move briskly and purposefully; march: *waltzed them into the principal's office.* [German *Walzer,* from *walzen,* to turn about, from Middle High German *walzen,* to roll, from Old High German *walzan.* See **wel-**[2] in Appendix.] **—waltz′er** *n.*

Wal·vis Bay (wôl′vĭs). An inlet of the Atlantic Ocean on the western coast of Namibia. The town of **Walvis Bay** (population 11,600) and the surrounding area constitute an exclave of South Africa.

wam·ble (wŏm′bəl, wăm′-) *intr.v.* **-bled, -bling, -bles. 1.** To move in a weaving, wobbling, or rolling manner. **2.** To turn or roll. Used of the stomach. **—wamble** *n.* **1.** A wobble or roll. **2.** An upset stomach. [Middle English *wamelen,* to feel nausea. See **weme-** in Appendix.] **—wam′bli·ness** *n.* **—wam′bling·ly** *adv.* **—wam′bly** *adj.*

Wam·pa·no·ag (wäm′pə-nō′ăg) *n., pl.* **Wampanoag** or **-ags. 1.a.** A Native American people formerly inhabiting eastern Rhode Island and southeast Massachusetts, including Martha's Vineyard and Nantucket, with present-day descendants in this same area. **b.** A member of this people. **2.** The Algonquian language of the Wampanoag, a variety of Massachusett. [Narragansett, those of the east.] **—Wam′pa·no′ag′** *adj.*

wam·pum (wŏm′pəm, wôm′-) *n.* **1.** Small cylindrical beads made from polished shells and fashioned into strings or belts, formerly used by certain Native American peoples as currency and jewelry or for ceremonial exchanges between groups. Also called *peag.* **2.** *Informal.* Money. [Short for WAMPUMPEAG.]

wam·pum·peag (wŏm′pəm-pēg′, wôm′-) *n.* White shell beads used as wampum. [Massachusett.]

wan (wŏn) *adj.* **wan·ner, wan·nest. 1.** Unnaturally pale, as from physical or emotional distress. **2.** Suggestive or indicative of weariness, illness, or unhappiness; melancholy: *a wan expression.* **—wan** *intr.v.* **wanned, wan·ning, wans.** To become pale. [Middle English, pale, gloomy, from Old English *wann,* gloomy, dark.] **—wan′ly** *adv.* **—wan′ness** *n.*

Wan·a·ma·ker (wŏn′ə-mā′kər), **John.** 1838–1922. American merchant whose men's clothing business grew into one of the first department stores.

wand (wŏnd) *n.* **1.** A thin supple rod, twig, or stick. **2.** A slender rod carried as a symbol of office in a procession; a scepter. **3.** *Music.* A conductor's baton. **4.** A stick or baton used by a magician, conjurer, or diviner. **5.** A pipelike attachment that lengthens the handle of a device or tool: *a vacuum cleaner that has two extension wands.* **6.** *Sports.* A six-foot by two-foot slat used as an archery target. [Middle English, from Old Norse *vöndr.*]

wan·der (wŏn′dər) *v.* **-dered, -der·ing, -ders.** —*intr.* **1.** To move about without a definite destination or purpose. **2.** To go by an indirect route or at no set pace; amble: *wander toward town.* **3.** To proceed in an irregular course; meander. **4.** To go astray: *wander from the path of righteousness.* **5.** To lose clarity or coherence of thought or expression. —*tr.* To wander across or through: *wander the forests and fields.* **—wander** *n.* The act or an instance of wandering; a stroll. [Middle English *wanderen,* from Old English *wandrian.*] **—wan′der·er** *n.* **—wan′der·ing·ly** *adv.*

SYNONYMS: *wander, ramble, roam, rove, range, meander, stray, gallivant, gad.* These verbs mean to move about at random or without destination or purpose. *Wander* and *ramble* stress the absence of a fixed course or goal: *She wandered into the room. "An old man's wit may wander"* (Tennyson). *"They would go off together, rambling along the river"* (John Galsworthy). *"Be not . . . rambling in thought"* (Marcus Aurelius). *Roam* and *rove* emphasize freedom of movement, often over a wide area: *"Herds of horses and cattle roamed at will over the plain"* (George W. Cable). *"For ten long years I roved about, living first in one capital, then another"* (Charlotte Brontë). *Range* suggests wandering in all directions: *"a large hunting party known to be ranging the prairie"* (Francis Parkman). *"The talk ranged over literary and publishing matters of mutual interest"* (Edward Bok). *Meander* suggests leisurely, sometimes aimless wandering over an irregular or winding course: *"He meandered to and fro . . . observing the manners and customs of Hillport society"* (Arnold Bennett). *Stray* refers to deviation from a proper course: *"He gave . . . strict directions . . . not to allow any of the men to stray"* (J.A. Froude). *"I ask pardon, I am straying from the question"* (Oliver Goldsmith). *Gallivant* refers to wandering about in search of pleasure: *The students gallivanted all over New York City during the class trip. Gad* suggests restless, pointless wandering: *My parents wanted me to stop gadding about unaccompanied in foreign cities.*

wan·der·ing albatross (wŏn′dər-ĭng) *n.* A large, mostly white albatross *(Diomedea exulans)* of southern seas, having long narrow wings whose spread is regarded as the largest of any living bird.

wandering Jew *n.* Any of three trailing plants, *Tradescantia albiflora, T. fluminensis,* or *Zebrina pendula,* native to tropical America, having usually variegated foliage and widely grown as houseplants.

Wan·der·ing Jew (wŏn′dər-ĭng) *n.* A Jew of medieval legend condemned to wander until the Day of Judgment for having mocked Jesus on the day of the Crucifixion.

wan·der·lust (wŏn′dər-lŭst′) *n.* A very strong or irresistible impulse to travel. [German : *wandern,* to wander (from Middle High German) + *Lust,* desire (from Middle High German, from Old High German; see **las-** in Appendix.)]

wan·der·oo (wŏn′də-rōō′) *n., pl.* **wanderoo** or **-oos.** A monkey *(Macaca silenus)* of south-central Asia, having a glossy black coat and a ruff of gray hair about the face. [From Singhalese *vandaru,* pl. of *vandurā,* monkey, from Sanskrit *vānaraḥ,* forest dweller, from *vanam,* forest. See **wen-**[1] in Appendix.]

wand·flow·er (wŏnd′flou′ər) *n.* See **galax.**

wane (wān) *intr.v.* **waned, wan·ing, wanes. 1.** To decrease gradually in size, amount, intensity, or degree; decline. **2.** To exhibit a decreasing illuminated area from full moon to new moon. **3.** To approach an end. **—wane** *n.* **1.** The act or process of gradually declining or diminishing. **2.a.** A time or phase of gradual decrease. **b.** The period of the decrease of the moon's illuminated visible surface. **3.** A defective edge of a board caused by remaining bark or a beveled end. ***—idiom.* on the wane.** In a period of decline or decrease: *"The tide was near the turn and already the day was on the wane"* (James Joyce). [Middle English *wanen,* from Old English *wanian.* See **eu-**[2] in Appendix.]

Wang Jing·wei (wäng′ jĕng′wā′) also **Wang Ching-wei** (chĕng′-). 1883–1944. Chinese politician. An assistant to Sun Yat-sen, he abandoned the Nationalists (1938) and was premier of the Japanese puppet government in occupied China (1940–1944).

wan·gle (wăng′gəl) *v.* **-gled, -gling, -gles.** *Informal.* —*tr.* **1.** To make, achieve, or get by contrivance: *wangled a job for which she had no training.* **2.** To manipulate or juggle, especially fraudulently. **3.** To extricate (oneself) from difficulty. —*intr.* **1.** To use indirect, tricky, or fraudulent methods. **2.** To extricate oneself by subtle or indirect means, as from difficulty; wriggle. [Origin unknown.] **—wang′le** *n.* **—wang′ler** *n.*

♦**wan·i·gan** or **wan·ni·gan** (wŏn′ĭ-gən) also **wan·gun** (wŏn′gən, wăng′-) *n.* **1.** *New England & Upper Northern U.S.* **a.** A boat or small chest equipped with supplies for a lumber camp. **b.** Provisions for a camp or cabin. **2.** *Alaska.* **a.** A small house, bunkhouse, or shed mounted on skids and towed behind a tractor train as eating and sleeping quarters for a work crew. **b.** An addition built onto a trailer house for extra living or storage space. [Ojibwa *waanikaan,* storage pit.]

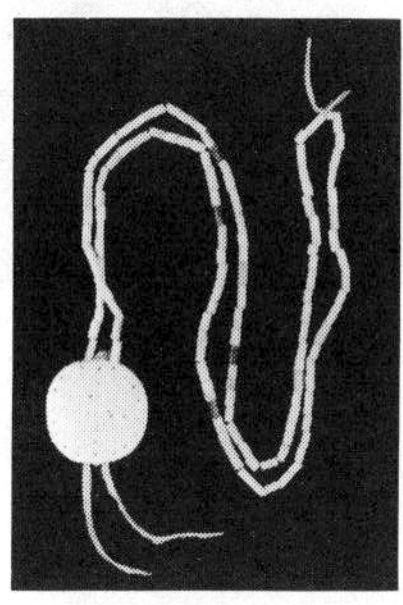

wampum
Huron wampum necklace

ă pat	oi boy
ā pay	ou out
âr care	ŏŏ took
ä father	ōō boot
ĕ pet	ŭ cut
ē be	ûr urge
ĭ pit	th thin
ī pie	*th* this
îr pier	hw which
ŏ pot	zh vision
ō toe	ə about, item
ô paw	♦ regionalism

Stress marks: ′ (primary); ′ (secondary), as in **dictionary** (dĭk′shə-nĕr′ē)

wapiti
Cervus canadensis

warbler

war bonnet

♦ ***REGIONAL NOTE:*** *Wanigan* is apparently borrowed from Ojibwa *waanikaan,* "storage pit," from the verb *waanikkee–,* "to dig a hole in the ground." Nineteenth-century citations in the *Oxford English Dictionary* indicate that the word was then associated chiefly with the speech of Maine. It denoted a storage chest containing small supplies for a lumber camp, a boat outfitted to carry such supplies, or, as in Algonquian, the camp equipment and provisions. In Alaska, on the western edge of the vast territory inhabited by Algonquian-speaking tribes, the same word was borrowed into English to indicate a little temporary hut, usually built on a log raft to be towed to wherever men were working. According to Russell Tabbert of the University of Alaska, *wanigan* is still used in the northernmost regions of Alaska to mean "a small house, bunkhouse, or shed mounted on skids" to be dragged along behind a tractor train as a place for a work crew to eat and sleep. However, Tabbert notes that in southeast Alaska, where mobile homes are a common option for housing, *wanigan* now means an addition built onto a trailer house for extra living or storage space. Classified advertisements for trailer homes frequently mention *wanigans.*

Wan•kel engine (väng′kəl, wäng′-, wăng′-) *n.* A rotary internal-combustion engine in which a triangular rotor turning in a specially shaped housing performs the functions allotted to the pistons of a conventional engine, thereby allowing great savings in weight and moving parts. [After Felix *Wankel* (1902–1988), German engineer.]

want (wŏnt, wônt) *v.* **want•ed, want•ing, wants.** —*tr.* **1.** To desire greatly; wish for: *They want to leave.* **2.** To be without; lack. See Synonyms at **lack. 3.** To be in need of; require: *"'Your hair wants cutting,' said the Hatter"* (Lewis Carroll). **4.a.** To request the presence or assistance of: *You are wanted by your office.* **b.** To seek with intent to capture: *The fugitive is wanted by the police.* **5.a.** To have a desire for. See Synonyms at **desire. b.** To have an inclination toward; like: *Say what you want, but be tactful.* —*intr.* **1.** To have need: *wants for nothing.* **2.** To be destitute or needy. **3.** To be disposed; wish: *Call me daily if you want.* —**want** *n.* **1.** The condition or quality of lacking something usual or necessary: *stayed home for want of anything better to do.* **2.** Pressing need; destitution: *lives in want.* **3.** Something desired: *a person of few wants and needs.* **4.** A defect of character; a fault. —***phrasal verbs.* want in.** *Slang.* **1.** To desire greatly to enter: *The dog wants in.* **2.** To wish to join a project, business, or other undertaking. **want out.** *Slang.* **1.** To desire greatly to leave: *The cat wants out.* **2.** To wish to leave a project, a business, or other undertaking. [Middle English *wanten,* to be lacking, from Old Norse *vanta.* See **eu-**[2] in Appendix.] —**want′er** *n.* —**want′less** *adj.* —**want′less•ness** *n.*

USAGE NOTE: When *want* is followed immediately by an infinitive construction, it does not take *for: I want you to go* (not *want for you*). When *want* and the infinitive are separated in the sentence, however, *for* is used: *What I want is for you to go. I want very much for you to go.* See Usage Note at **wish.**

want ad *n. Informal.* A classified advertisement.

Wan•tagh (wŏn′tô′). A town of southeast New York on the southern shore of Long Island. Population, 22,300.

want•ing (wŏn′tĭng, wôn′-) *adj.* **1.** Absent; lacking. **2.** Not measuring up to standards or expectations. —**wanting** *prep.* **1.** Without. **2.** Minus; less: *an hour wanting 15 minutes.*

wan•ton (wŏn′tən) *adj.* **1.** Immoral or unchaste; lewd. **2.a.** Gratuitously cruel; merciless. **b.** Marked by unprovoked, gratuitous maliciousness; capricious and unjust: *wanton destruction.* **3.** Unrestrainedly excessive: *wanton extravagance; wanton depletion of oil reserves.* **4.** Luxuriant; overabundant: *wanton tresses.* **5.** Frolicsome; playful. **6.** Undisciplined; spoiled. **7.** *Obsolete.* Rebellious; refractory. —**wanton** *v.* **-toned, -ton•ing, -tons.** —*intr.* To act, grow, or move in a wanton manner; be wanton. —*tr.* To waste or squander extravagantly. —**wanton** *n.* **1.** One who is immoral, lewd, or licentious. **2.** One that is playful or frolicsome. **3.** One that is undisciplined or spoiled. [Middle English *wantowen* : *wan-,* not, lacking (from Old English; akin to *wana,* lack; see WANE) + *towen,* past participle of *teen,* to bring up (from Old English *tēon,* to lead, draw; see **deuk-** in Appendix).] —**wan′ton•ly** *adv.* —**wan′ton•ness** *n.*

wap•en•take (wŏp′ən-tāk′, wăp′-) *n.* A historical subdivision of some northern counties in England, corresponding roughly to the hundred in other shires. [Middle English, from Old English *wæpengetæc,* from Old Norse *vāpnatak,* act of taking weapons : *vāpna,* genitive pl. of *vāpn,* weapon + *tak,* act of taking (from *taka,* to take).]

wap•i•ti (wŏp′ĭ-tē) *n., pl.* **wapiti** or **-tis.** A large light brown or grayish-brown North American deer *(Cervus canadensis)* having long, branching antlers. Also called *American elk, elk.* [Shawnee *waapiti.*]

Wap•pin•ger (wä′pĭn-jər). *n., pl.* **Wappinger** or **-gers. 1.** A Native American people formerly inhabiting the east bank of the Hudson River from Poughkeepsie to Manhattan and closely related to the Munsee-speaking peoples. The Wappinger dispersed to other Native American groups after warfare with the Dutch in the mid-17th century. **2.** A member of this people. [Of Algonquian origin.]

Wap•si•pin•i•con (wŏp′sə-pĭn′ĭ-kən). A river rising in southern Minnesota and flowing about 410 km (255 mi) generally southeast through eastern Iowa to the Mississippi River.

war (wôr) *n.* **1.a.** A state of open, armed, often prolonged conflict carried on between nations, states, or parties. **b.** The period of such conflict. **c.** The techniques and procedures of war; military science. **2.a.** A condition of active antagonism or contention: *a war of words; a price war.* **b.** A concerted effort or campaign to combat or put an end to something considered injurious: *the war against acid rain.* —**war** *intr.v.* **warred, war•ring, wars. 1.** To wage or carry on warfare. **2.** To be in a state of hostility or rivalry; contend. —***idiom.* at war.** In an active state of conflict or contention. [Middle English *warre,* from Old North French *werre,* of Germanic origin. See **wers-** in Appendix.]

WORD HISTORY: A piece of liverwurst may perhaps help us gain some insight into the nature of war, at least into the semantic history of the word *war. War* and the *–wurst* part of *liverwurst* can be traced back to the same Indo-European root, *wers–,* "to confuse, mix up." In the Germanic family of the Indo-European languages, this root gave rise to several words having to do with confusion or mixture of various kinds. In the case of the ancestry of *war,* the hypothetical Germanic stem **werza–,* "confusion," became **werra–,* which passed into Old French, a language descended from spoken Latin but supplemented by more than 200 words borrowed from the Frankish invaders of the 5th century. From the Germanic stem came both the form *werre* in Old North French, the form borrowed into English in the 12th century, and *guerre* (the source of *guerilla*) in the rest of the Old French-speaking area. Both forms meant "war," a very confused condition indeed. Meanwhile another Indo-European form derived from the same Indo-European root had developed into Old High German *wurst,* meaning "sausage," from an underlying sense of "mixture," which is, of course, related to the sense of the root "to confuse, mix up." Modern German *wurst* was borrowed into English in the 19th century, first by itself (recorded in 1855) and then as part of the word *liverwurst* (1869), the liver being a translation of German *leber* in *leberwurst.*

war. *abbr.* Warrant.

Wa•ran•gal (wə-rŭng′gəl, wôr′əng-). A city of southeast India northeast of Hyderabad. It was the capital of the Telugu Kingdom in the 12th century. Population, 335,150.

war baby *n.* A child born during wartime, especially during World War I or World War II.

War•beck (wôr′bĕk′), **Perkin.** 1474?–1499. Flemish pretender to the English throne. Posing as Richard, Duke of York, the murdered son of Edward IV, he landed in Cornwall (1497), proclaimed himself king, and proceeded to London, where he was captured and hanged by supporters of Henry VII.

War Between the States (wôr) *n.* See **civil war** (sense 3).

war•ble[1] (wôr′bəl) *v.* **-bled, -bling, -bles.** —*tr. Music.* To sing (a note or song, for example) with trills, runs, or other melodic embellishments. —*intr.* **1.** *Music.* To sing with trills, runs, or quavers. **2.** To be sounded in a trilling or quavering manner. —**warble** *n. Music.* The act or an instance of singing with trills, runs, or quavers. [Middle English *werbelen,* from Old North French *werbler,* of Germanic origin.]

war•ble[2] (wôr′bəl) *n.* **1.a.** An abscessed boillike swelling on the back of cattle, deer, and certain other animals, caused by the larva of a warble fly. **b.** The warble fly, especially in its larval stage. **2.** A hard lump of tissue on a riding horse's back caused by rubbing of the saddle. [Probably of Scandinavian origin; akin to obsolete Swedish *varbulde.*]

warble fly *n.* Any of several large hairy flies of the family Oestridae having larvae that form warbles under the skin of cattle and certain other animals.

war•bler (wôr′blər) *n.* **1.** Any of various small New World songbirds of the family Parulidae, many of which have brightly colored plumage or markings, as the redstart and the chat. Also called *wood warbler.* **2.** Any of various small, often brownish or grayish Old World songbirds of the family Silviidae, as the blackcap and the whitethroat. **3.** *Music.* One that warbles; a singer.

war•bling vireo (wôr′blĭng) *n.* A small vireo *(Vireo gilvus)* with a whitish breast, noted for its pleasant warble.

war bonnet *n.* A ceremonial headdress used by some Plains Indians consisting of a cap or band and a trailing extension decorated with erect feathers.

war bride *n.* A woman who marries a serviceman during wartime.

War•burg (wôr′bərg′, vär′bo͝ork′), **Otto Heinrich.** 1883–1970. German biochemist. He won a 1931 Nobel Prize for research on the respiration of cells.

war chest *n.* **1.** An accumulation of funds to finance a war effort. **2.** A fund reserved for a particular purpose such as a political campaign.

war correspondent *n.* A journalist, reporter, or commentator assigned to report directly from a war or combat zone.

war crime *n.* Any of various crimes, such as genocide or the mistreatment of prisoners of war, committed during a war and considered in violation of the conventions of warfare. —**war criminal** *n.*

war cry *n.* **1.** A cry uttered by combatants as they attack; a battle cry. **2.** A phrase or slogan used to rally people to a cause.

ward (wôrd) *n.* **1.** A division of a city or town, especially an electoral district, for administrative and representative purposes. **2.** A district of some English and Scottish counties corresponding roughly to the hundred or the wapentake. **3. a.** A room in a hospital usually holding six or more patients. **b.** A division in a hospital for the care of a particular group of patients: *a maternity ward.* **4.** One of the divisions of a penal institution, such as a prison. **5.** An open court or area of a castle or fortification enclosed by walls. **6. a.** *Law.* A minor or incompetent person placed under the care or protection of a guardian or court. **b.** A person under the protection or care of another. **7.** The state of being under guard; custody. **8.** The act of guarding or protecting; guardianship. **9.** A means of protection; a defense. **10.** A defensive movement or attitude, especially in fencing; a guard. **11. a.** The projecting ridge of a lock or keyhole that prevents the turning of a key other than the proper one. **b.** The notch cut into a key that corresponds to such a ridge. **—ward** *tr.v.* **ward•ed, ward•ing, wards.** To guard; protect. ***—phrasal verb.* ward off. 1.** To turn aside; parry: *ward off an opponent's blows.* **2.** To try to prevent; avert: *took vitamins to ward off head colds.* [Middle English, action of guarding, from Old English *weard,* a watching, keeper. See **wer-**[3] in Appendix.]

Ward (wôrd), **(Aaron) Montgomery.** 1843–1913. American merchant who established (1872) the mail-order business that bears his name.

Ward, Artemus[1]**.** 1727–1800. American Revolutionary general who directed Massachusetts troops in the siege of Boston, until George Washington relieved him of the command and drove the British from the city (1776).

Ward, Artemus[2]**.** See Charles Farrar **Browne.**

Ward, Barbara. Baroness Jackson of Lodsworth. 1914–1981. British economist, conservationist, and writer whose works on ecology and political economy include *Spaceship Earth* (1966).

Ward, Mary Augusta Arnold. Known as Mrs. Humphry Ward. 1851–1920. British writer whose novels include *Robert Elsmere* (1888).

Ward, Nathaniel. Pen name Theodore de la Guard. 1578?–1652. English clergyman and writer in America. He is primarily known for *The Simple Cobler of Aggawam in America* (1645).

-ward or **-wards** *suff.* **1. a.** In a specified direction in time or space: *downward.* **b.** Toward a specified place or position: *skyward.* **2. a.** Occurring or situated in a specified direction: *leftward.* **b.** Having a direction toward a specified place or position: *landward.* [Middle English, from Old English *-weard.* See **wer-**[2] in Appendix.]

war dance *n.* A tribal dance performed before a battle or as a celebration after a victory.

ward•ed (wôr′dĭd) *adj.* Having notches or ridges. Used of a key or lock.

war•den (wôrd′n) *n.* **1.** The chief administrative official of a prison. **2.** An official charged with the enforcement of certain laws and regulations: *an air raid warden.* **3.** *Chiefly British.* **a.** The chief executive official in charge of a port or market. **b.** Any of various crown officers having administrative duties. **c.** One of the governing officials of certain colleges, schools, guilds, or hospitals; a trustee. **4.** The chief executive of a borough in certain states. **5.** A churchwarden. [Middle English *wardein,* from Old North French, from *warder,* to guard, of Germanic origin. See **wer-**[3] in Appendix.] **—war′den•ship′** *n.*

war•den•ry (wôrd′n-rē) *n., pl.* **-ries.** The office, duties, or jurisdiction of a warden.

ward•er[1] (wôr′dər) *n.* **1.** A guard, porter, or watcher of a gate or tower. **2.** *Chiefly British.* A prison guard. [Middle English, from Anglo-Norman *wardere,* from Old North French *warder,* to guard. See WARDEN.] **—war′der•ship′** *n.*

ward•er[2] (wôr′dər) *n.* A baton formerly used by a ruler or commander as a symbol of authority and to signal orders. [Middle English, possibly from *warden,* to ward, from Old English *weardian.* See **wer-**[3] in Appendix.]

ward heeler *n. Informal.* A worker for the ward organization of a political machine.

ward•robe (wôr′drōb′) *n.* **1.** A tall cabinet, closet, or small room built to hold clothes. **2.** Garments considered as a group, especially all the articles of clothing that belong to one person. **3. a.** The costumes belonging to a theater or theatrical troupe. **b.** The place in which theatrical costumes are kept. **4.** The department in charge of wearing apparel, jewelry, and accessories in a royal or noble household. [Middle English *warderobe,* from Old North French : *warder,* to guard; see **wer-**[3] in Appendix + *robe,* garment; see ROBE.]

ward•room (wôrd′ro͞om′, -ro͝om′) *n.* **1.** The common recreation area and dining room for the commissioned officers on a warship. **2.** The commissioned officers on a warship.

-wards *suff.* Variant of **-ward.**

ward•ship (wôrd′shĭp′) *n.* **1.** The state of being in the charge of a guardian. **2.** Custody; guardianship.

ware[1] (wâr) *n.* **1.** Articles of the same general kind, made of a specified material or used in a specific application. Often used in combination: *earthenware, silverware; hardware, software.* **2. a.** An article of commerce. **b.** An immaterial asset or benefit, such as a service or personal accomplishment, regarded as an article of commerce. [Middle English, from Old English *waru,* goods. See **wer-**[3] in Appendix.]

ware[2] (wâr) *tr.v.* **wared, war•ing, wares.** *Archaic.* To beware of. **—ware** *adj. Obsolete.* **1.** Watchful; wary. **2.** Aware. [Middle English *waren,* from Old English *warian;* see **wer-**[3] in Appendix. Adj., Middle English. See WARY.]

Ware•ham (wâr′əm, -hăm′). A town of southeast Massachusetts on Buzzards Bay northeast of New Bedford. It is a resort town in a cranberry-growing region. Population, 18,457.

ware•house (wâr′hous′) *n. Abbr.* **whs. 1.** A place in which goods or merchandise are stored; a storehouse. **2.** *Chiefly British.* A large, usually wholesale shop. **—warehouse** (*also* -houz′) *tr.v.* **-housed, -hous•ing, -hous•es. 1.** To place or store in a warehouse, especially in a bonded or government warehouse. **2.** To institutionalize (people) in usually deficient housing and in conditions in which medical, educational, psychiatric, and social services are below par or absent: *"has felt forced to warehouse hundreds of children in temporary shelters"* (Justine Wise Polier). **—ware′hous′er** (-hou′zər) *n.*

ware•room (wâr′ro͞om′, -ro͝om′) *n.* A room used for the storage or display of goods or wares.

war•fare (wôr′fâr′) *n.* **1. a.** The waging of war against an enemy; armed conflict. **b.** Military operations marked by a specific characteristic: *guerrilla warfare; chemical warfare.* **2.** A state of disharmony or conflict; strife: *constant spousal warfare in the household.* **3.** Acts undertaken to destroy or undermine the strength of another: *political warfare.* [Middle English : *warre,* war; see WAR + *fare,* journey (from Old English *faru,* from *faran,* to journey; see FARE).]

war•fa•rin (wôr′fər-ĭn) *n.* A white crystalline compound, $C_{19}H_{16}O_4$, used to kill rodents and medicinally as a blood anticoagulant. [*W(isconsin) A(lumni) R(esearch) F(oundation)* + (COUM)ARIN.]

war game *n.* **1.** An often physical or electronic simulation of a military operation involving two or more forces and using rules, data, and procedures designed to depict an actual or assumed situation. **2.** A simulation of a proposed plan of action or a strategy, intended to test its validity when challenged.

war-game (wôr′gām′) *v.* **-gamed, -gam•ing, -games.** *—intr.* To engage in a war game. *—tr.* To simulate (a military operation or a proposed plan of action) in order to test effectiveness under actual or assumed conditions. **—war gamer** *n.*

war hawk *n.* **1.** A member of the 12th U.S. Congress (1811–1813) who advocated war with Great Britain. **2.** One who advocates war; a hawk.

war•head (wôr′hĕd′) *n.* A part of the armament system in the forward part of a projectile, such as a guided missile, rocket, torpedo, bomb, or other munition, that contains either a nuclear or thermonuclear system, a high explosive system, chemical or biological agents, or inert materials intended to inflict damage on a target.

War•hol (wôr′hôl′, -hōl′), **Andy.** 1930?–1987. American artist. A leader of the pop art movement, he produced paintings and silk-screen prints of commonplace images, such as soup cans and photographs of celebrities.

Andy Warhol

war•horse also **war-horse** (wôr′hôrs′) *n.* **1.** A horse used in combat; a charger. **2.** *Informal.* One who has been through many battles, struggles, or fights. **3.** *Informal.* A musical or dramatic work that has been performed so often that it has become hackneyed.

war•like (wôr′līk′) *adj.* **1.** Belligerent; hostile. **2. a.** Of or relating to war; martial. **b.** Indicative of or threatening war.

war•lock (wôr′lŏk′) *n.* A male witch, sorcerer, wizard, or demon. [Middle English *warloghe,* from Old English *wǣrloga,* oath-breaker : *wǣr,* pledge; see **wēro-** in Appendix + *-loga,* liar (from *lēogan,* to lie; see **leugh-** in Appendix).]

war•lord (wôr′lôrd′) *n.* A military commander exercising civil power in a region, whether in nominal allegiance to the national government or in defiance of it. **—war′lord′ism** *n.*

warm (wôrm) *adj.* **warm•er, warm•est. 1.** Somewhat hotter than temperate; having or producing a comfortable and agreeable degree of heat; moderately hot: *a warm climate.* **2.** Having the natural heat of living beings: *a warm body.* **3.** Preserving or imparting heat: *a warm overcoat.* **4.** Having or causing a sensation of unusually high body heat, as from exercise or hard work; overheated. **5.** Marked by enthusiasm; ardent: *warm support.* **6.** Characterized by liveliness, excitement, or disagreement; heated: *a warm debate.* **7.** Marked by or revealing friendliness or sincerity; cordial: *warm greetings.* **8.** Loving; passionate: *a warm embrace.* **9.** Excitable, impetuous, or quick to be aroused: *a warm temper.* **10.** *Color.* Predominantly red or yellow in tone: *a warm sunset.* **11.** Recently made; fresh: *a warm trail.* **12.** Close to discovering, guessing, or finding something, as in certain games. **13.** *Informal.* Uncomfortable because of danger or annoyance: *Things are warm for the bookies.* **—warm** *v.* **warmed, warm•ing, warms.** *—tr.* **1.** To raise slightly in temperature; make warm: *warmed the rolls a bit more; warm up the house.* **2.** To make zealous or ardent; enliven. **3.** To fill with pleasant emotions: *We were warmed by the sight of home.* *—intr.* **1.** To become warm: *The rolls are warming in the oven.* **2.** To become ardent, enthusiastic, or animated: *began to warm to the subject.* **3.** To become kindly disposed or friendly: *She felt the audience warming to her.* **—warm** *n. Informal.* A warming or heating. ***—phrasal verb.* warm up. 1.** *Sports.* To prepare for an athletic event by exercising, stretching, or practicing for a short time beforehand. **2.** To make or become ready for an event or operation. **3.** To make more enthusiastic, excited, or animated. **4.** To ap-

ă pat	oi boy
ā pay	ou out
âr care	o͝o took
ä father	o͞o boot
ĕ pet	ŭ cut
ē be	ûr urge
ĭ pit	th thin
ī pie	*th* this
îr pier	hw which
ŏ pot	zh vision
ō toe	ə about, item
ô paw	♦ regionalism

Stress marks: **′** (primary); ′ (secondary), as in **dictionary** (dĭk′shə-nĕr′ē)

warming pan
c. 1700–1750
Scandinavian

proach a state of confrontation or violence. [Middle English, from Old English *wearm.*] —**warm′er** *n.* —**warm′ish** *adj.* —**warm′ly** *adv.* —**warm′ness** *n.*

warm-blood·ed (wôrm′blŭd′ĭd) *adj.* **1.** *Zoology.* Maintaining a relatively constant and warm body temperature independent of environmental temperature; homeothermic. **2.** Ardent; passionate. —**warm′-blood′ed·ness** *n.*

warmed-o·ver (wôrmd′ō′vər) *adj.* **1.** Warmed up; reheated: *warmed-over tidbits.* **2.** Not new, fresh, or spontaneous; stale.

warm front *n.* A front along which an advancing mass of warm air rises over a mass of cold air.

warm-heart·ed (wôrm′här′tĭd) *adj.* Marked by kindness, sympathy, and generosity. —**warm′heart′ed·ly** *adv.* —**warm′heart′ed·ness** *n.*

warm·ing pan (wôr′mĭng) *n.* A metal pan with a cover and a long handle, designed to hold hot liquids or coals and used to warm a bed.

war·mon·ger (wôr′mŭng′gər, -mŏng′-) *n.* One who advocates or attempts to stir up war. —**war′mon′ger·ing** *adj.* & *n.*

war·mouth (wôr′mouth′) *n., pl.* **-mouths** (-mouthz′, -mouths′) or **warmouth.** A freshwater sunfish *(Lepomis gulosus)* of the eastern and midwestern United States, having an olive color, a large mouth, and minute teeth on its tongue. [Origin unknown.]

warmth (wôrmth) *n.* **1.** The state, sensation, or quality of producing or having a moderate degree of heat: *an agreeable warmth in the house.* **2.a.** Friendliness, kindness, or affection: *human warmth.* **b.** Excitement or intensity, as of love or passion; ardor. **3.** *Color.* The glowing effect produced by using predominantly red or yellow hues. [Middle English, from Old English **wiermthu,* from *wearm,* warm.]

warm-up or **warm·up** (wôrm′ŭp′) —*n.* **1.a.** The act or procedure of warming up. **b.** A period spent in warming up. **2.** Often **warm-ups** or **warm·ups.** Clothing, such as a sweat suit, made or designed to be worn before or after participation in an athletic event. —*attributive.* Often used to modify another noun: *a warm-up session; a warmup jacket.*

warn (wôrn) *v.* **warned, warn·ing, warns.** —*tr.* **1.** To make aware in advance of actual or potential harm, danger, or evil. **2.** To admonish as to action or manners. **3.** To notify (a person) to go or stay away: *warned them off the posted property.* **4.** To notify or apprise in advance: *They called and warned me that they might be delayed.* —*intr.* To give a warning. [Middle English *warnen,* from Old English *warnian.* See **wer-**[4] in Appendix.]

SYNONYMS: *warn, caution, forewarn.* These verbs mean to give someone notice of and put the person on guard against actual or possible danger or risk. *Warn,* the most inclusive, implies well-timed notice that causes a person to be alert, vigilant, or wary: *"My father was warned by the neighbors that we were in great danger"* (W.H. Hudson). *Caution* often suggests a warning that calls for the use of circumspection or prudence, as in avoiding unpleasant consequences: *The Secretary of State cautioned that terrorism would be countered by retaliatory action. Forewarn* intensifies the sense of advance notice: *Forewarned is forearmed.*

War·ner (wôr′nər), **Charles Dudley.** 1829–1900. American writer and editor best known for his collaboration on *The Gilded Age* (1873) with Mark Twain.

Warner, Harry Morris. 1881–1958. American filmmaker who with his brothers **Albert** (1884–1967), **Samuel Louis** (1887–1927), and **Jack** (1892–1978) founded Warner Brothers Pictures, which produced the first talkie, *The Jazz Singer* (1927).

Warner Rob·ins (rŏb′ĭnz). A city of central Georgia south of Macon. It was incorporated in 1943. Population, 39,839.

warn·ing (wôr′nĭng) *n.* **1.** An intimation, a threat, or a sign of impending danger or evil. **2.a.** Advice to beware. **b.** Counsel to desist from a specified undesirable course of action. **3.** A cautionary or deterrent example. **4.** Something, such as a signal, that warns. See Synonyms at **alarm.** —**warning** *adj.* Acting or serving to warn: *a warning light; warning words.* —**warn′ing·ly** *adv.*

warning coloration *n.* The conspicuously recognizable markings of an animal, such as a skunk, that serve to warn off potential predators. Also called *aposematic coloration.*

war of nerves *n., pl.* **wars of nerves.** A conflict marked by psychological tactics, such as intimidation and threats, that is intended primarily to confuse one's enemy and erode that enemy's morale.

warp (wôrp) *v.* **warped, warp·ing, warps.** —*tr.* **1.** To turn or twist (wood, for example) out of shape. **2.** To turn from a correct or proper course; deflect. **3.** To affect unfavorably, unfairly, or wrongly; bias. See Synonyms at **bias. 4.** To arrange (strands of yarn or thread) so that they run lengthwise in weaving. **5.** *Nautical.* To move (a vessel) by hauling on a line that is fastened to or around a piling, an anchor, or a pier. —*intr.* **1.** To become bent or twisted out of shape: *The wooden frame warped in the humidity.* **2.** To turn aside from a true, correct, or natural course; go astray. See Synonyms at **distort. 3.** *Nautical.* To move a vessel by hauling on a line that is fastened to or around a piling, an anchor, or a pier. —**warp** *n.* **1.** The state of being twisted or bent out of shape. **2.** A distortion or twist, especially in a piece of wood. **3.** A mental or moral twist, aberration, or deviation. **4.** The threads that run lengthwise in a woven fabric, crossed at right angles to the woof. **5.** Warp and woof. **6.** *Nautical.* A towline used in warping a vessel. [Middle English *werpen,* from Old English *weorpan,* to throw away. See **wer-**[2] in Appendix.] —**warp′er** *n.*

war paint *n.* **1.** Pigments applied to the face or body in preparation for battle, as in certain tribal societies. **2.** *Informal.* Cosmetics such as lipstick, rouge, or mascara.

warp and woof *n.* The underlying structure on which something is built; a base or foundation: *"profound dislocations throughout the entire warp and woof of the American economy"* (David A. Stockman).

war party *n.* **1.** A band of warriors engaged in fighting or raiding an enemy. Used especially of Native Americans. **2.** A usually blatantly patriotic political party supporting a war.

war·path (wôr′păth′, -päth′) *n.* **1.** A course that leads to warfare or battle. **2.** A hostile course or mood: *The chef is on the warpath today.*

war·plane (wôr′plān′) *n.* A combat aircraft.

war·rant (wôr′ənt, wŏr′-) *n. Abbr.* **war., wrnt. 1.** Authorization or certification; sanction, as given by a superior. **2.** Justification for an action or a belief; grounds: *"He almost gives his failings as a warrant for his greatness"* (Garry Wills). **3.** Something that provides assurance or confirmation; a guarantee or proof: *a warrant of authenticity; a warrant for success.* **4.** An order that serves as authorization, especially: **a.** A voucher authorizing payment or receipt of money. **b.** *Law.* A judicial writ authorizing an officer to make a search, a seizure, or an arrest or to execute a judgment. **5.a.** A warrant officer. **b.** A certificate of appointment given to a warrant officer. —**warrant** *tr.v.* **-rant·ed, -rant·ing, -rants. 1.** To guarantee or attest to the quality, accuracy, or condition of. **2.** To guarantee or attest to the character or reliability of; vouch for. **3.a.** To guarantee (a product). **b.** To guarantee (a purchaser) indemnification against damage or loss. **4.** To guarantee the immunity or security of. **5.** To provide adequate grounds for; justify. See Synonyms at **justify. 6.** To grant authorization or sanction to (someone); authorize or empower. **7.** *Law.* To guarantee clear title to (real property). [Middle English *warant,* from Old North French, of Germanic origin. See **wer-**[4] in Appendix.] —**war′rant·a·bil′i·ty, war′rant·a·ble·ness** *n.* —**war′rant·a·ble** *adj.* —**war′rant·a·bly** *adv.* —**war′rant·less** *adj.*

war·ran·tee (wôr′ən-tē′, wŏr′-) *n.* One to whom a warranty is made or a warrant is given.

war·rant·er (wôr′ən-tər, -tôr′, wŏr′-) *n.* Variant of **warrantor.**

warrant officer *n. Abbr.* **WO, W.O.** A military officer, usually a skilled technician or a helicopter pilot, intermediate in rank between a noncommissioned officer and a commissioned officer, having authority by virtue of a warrant.

war·ran·tor (wôr′ən-tər, -tôr′, wŏr′-) also **war·rant·er** (-tər) *n.* One that makes a warrant or gives a warranty to another.

war·ran·ty (wôr′ən-tē, wŏr′-) *n., pl.* **-ties. 1.** Official authorization, sanction, or warrant. **2.** Justification or valid grounds for an act or a course of action. **3.** *Law.* **a.** An assurance by the seller of property that the goods or property are as represented or will be as promised. **b.** The insured's guarantee that the facts are as stated in reference to an insurance risk or that specified conditions will be fulfilled to keep the contract effective. **c.** A covenant by which the seller of land binds himself or herself and his or her heirs to defend the security of the estate conveyed. **d.** A judicial writ; a warrant. **4.** A guarantee given to the purchaser by a company stating that a product is reliable and free from known defects and that the seller will, without charge, repair or replace defective parts within a given time limit and under certain conditions. [Middle English *warantie,* from Old North French, from feminine past participle of *warantir,* to guarantee, from *warant,* warrant. See **wer-**[4] in Appendix.]

war·ren (wôr′ən, wŏr′-) *n.* **1.a.** An area where rabbits live in burrows. **b.** A colony of rabbits. See Synonyms at **flock**[1]. **2.** An enclosure for small game animals. **3.a.** An overcrowded living area. **b.** A mazelike place where one may easily become lost: *a warren of narrow, dark alleys and side streets.* [Middle English *warenne,* from Old North French, enclosure. See **wer-**[4] in Appendix.]

War·ren (wôr′ən, wŏr′-). **1.** A city of southeast Michigan, an industrial suburb of Detroit. Population, 161,134. **2.** A city of northeast Ohio northwest of Youngstown. It is a manufacturing center. Population, 56,629.

Warren, Earl. 1891–1974. American jurist who served as the chief justice of the U.S. Supreme Court (1953–1969).

Warren, Joseph. 1741–1775. American physician and patriot who instructed Paul Revere and William Dawes to make their ride to Lexington (April 18, 1775) and was killed in the Battle of Bunker Hill (June 17, 1775).

Warren, Robert Penn. 1905–1989. American writer and critic primarily known for his poetry. His works include the novel *All the King's Men* (1946) and many poetry collections, such as *Promises* (1957). In 1985 he was appointed the first U.S. poet laureate.

war·ren·er (wôr′ə-nər, wŏr′-) *n.* **1.** One who owns or keeps a rabbit warren. **2.** A gamekeeper.

War·rens·ville Heights (wôr′ĭnz-vĭl′, wŏr′-). A city of northeast Ohio, a suburb of Cleveland. Population, 16,565.

War·ring·ton (wôr′ĭng-tən, wŏr′-). A borough of west-central

ă **pat**	oi **boy**
ā **pay**	ou **out**
âr **care**	ŏŏ **took**
ä **father**	ōō **boot**
ĕ **pet**	ŭ **cut**
ē **be**	ûr **urge**
ĭ **pit**	th **thin**
ī **pie**	*th* **this**
îr **pier**	hw **which**
ŏ **pot**	zh **vision**
ō **toe**	ə **about, item**
ô **paw**	♦ **regionalism**

Stress marks: **′** (primary); ′ (secondary), as in **dictionary** (dĭk′shə-nĕr′ē)

England east of Liverpool on the Mersey River. It is a manufacturing center. Population, 168,600.

war·ri·or (wôr′ē-ər, wŏr′-) *n.* One who is engaged in or experienced in battle. [Middle English *werreour,* from Old North French *werreieur,* from *werreier,* to make war, from *werre,* war. See WAR.]

war·saw (wôr′sô) *n.* A large grouper *(Epinephelus nigritus)* of warm Atlantic waters off the southeast coast of the United States. [Perhaps alteration of American Spanish *guasa,* a kind of sea bass.]

War·saw (wôr′sô′). The capital of Poland, in the east-central part of the country on the Vistula River. Founded in the 13th century, it replaced Cracow as Poland's capital in 1596. Warsaw was ruled by Russia as an independent kingdom (1815–1917) and became capital of Poland again in 1918. Population, 1,649,000.

war·ship (wôr′shĭp′) *n.* A combat ship. Also called *man-of-war.*

wart (wôrt) *n.* **1.a.** A hard, rough lump growing on the skin, caused by infection with certain viruses and occurring typically on the hands or feet. **b.** A similar growth or protuberance, as on a plant. **2.** A genital wart. **3.a.** One that resembles or is likened to a wart, especially in unattractiveness or smallness. **b.** An imperfection; a flaw. **—*idiom.* warts and all.** *Slang.* All defects and imperfections notwithstanding: *We love and respect you for what you are, warts and all.* [Middle English, from Old English *wearte.*] **—wart′ed, wart′y** *adj.*

War·ta (vär′tə, -tä). A river, about 764 km (475 mi) long, rising in south-central Poland northwest of Cracow and flowing generally north and west to the Oder River.

wart hog also **wart·hog** (wôrt′hôg′, -hŏg′) *n.* A wild African hog *(Phacochoerus aethiopicus)* that has two tusks and wartlike growths on the face.

war·time (wôr′tīm′) *n.* A period during which a war is in progress. *—attributive.* Often used to modify another noun: *wartime rationing; wartime marriages.*

wart plant *n.* See **haworthia.** [From the tubercles on the leaves of many species.]

War·wick (wôr′wĭk). A city of east-central Rhode Island on Narragansett Bay south of Providence. Settled in 1643, it is a manufacturing center and a summer resort. Population, 87,123.

War·wick (wŏr′ĭk), Earl of. Title of Richard Neville. Known as "the Kingmaker." 1428–1471. English military and political leader who fought for the Yorkists during the Wars of the Roses and secured the throne for Edward IV (1461). He then changed allegiance and restored the Lancastrian Henry VI to the throne (1470). Warwick was killed in the Battle of Barnet.

war·y (wâr′ē) *adj.* **-i·er, -i·est. 1.** On guard; watchful: *taught to be wary of strangers.* **2.** Characterized by caution: *a wary glance at the black clouds.* [Middle English *ware,* from Old English *wær.* See **wer-**[3] in Appendix.] **—war′i·ly** *adv.* **—war′i·ness** *n.*

was (wŭz, wŏz; wəz *when unstressed*) *v.* First and third person singular past indicative of **be.** [Middle English, from Old English *wæs.* See **wes-**[1] in Appendix.]

♦**wash** (wŏsh, wôsh) *v.* **washed, wash·ing, wash·es.** *—tr.* **1.a.** To cleanse, using water or other liquid, usually with soap, detergent, or bleach, by immersing, dipping, rubbing, or scrubbing: *wash one's hands; wash windows.* **b.** To soak, rinse out, and remove (dirt or stain) with or as if with water: *wash grease out of overalls.* **2.** To make moist or wet; drench: *Tears washed the child's cheeks.* **3.** To flow over, against, or past: *waves that washed the sandy shores.* **4.** To carry, erode, remove, or destroy by the action of moving water: *Heavy rains washed the topsoil away.* **5.** To rid of corruption or guilt; cleanse or purify: *wash sins away.* **6.** To cover or coat with a watery layer of paint or other coloring substance. **7.** *Chemistry.* **a.** To purify (a gas) by passing through or over a liquid, as to remove soluble matter. **b.** To pass a solvent, such as distilled water, through (a precipitate). **8.** To separate constituents of (an ore) by immersion in or agitation with water. **9.** To cause to undergo a swirling action: *washed the tea around in the cup.* *—intr.* **1.** To cleanse something in or by means of water or other liquid. **2.a.** To undergo washing without fading or other damage: *This fabric will wash.* **b.** *Informal.* To hold up under examination; be convincing: *"That [proclamation], of course, will not wash"* (John Hughes). **3.** To flow, sweep, or beat with a characteristic lapping sound: *Waves washed over the pilings.* **4.** To be carried away, removed, or drawn by the action of water. **—wash** *n.* **1.** The act or process of washing or cleansing. **2.** A quantity of articles washed or intended for washing: *The wash is on the back porch.* **3.** Waste liquid; swill. **4.** Fermented liquid from which liquor is distilled. **5.** A preparation or product used in washing or coating. **6.** A cosmetic or medicinal liquid, such as a mouthwash. **7.a.** A thin layer of water color or India ink spread on a drawing. **b.** A light tint or hue: *"a wash of red sunset"* (Thomas Pynchon). **8.a.** A rush or surge of water or waves. **b.** The sound of this rush or surge. **9.a.** Removal or erosion of soil by the action of moving water. **b.** A deposit of recently eroded debris. **10.a.** Low or marshy ground washed by tidal waters. **b.** A stretch of shallow water. **11.** *Western U.S.* The dry bed of a stream. **12.** Turbulence in air or water caused by the motion or action of an oar, propeller, jet, or airfoil. **13.** *Informal.* An activity, action, or enterprise that yields neither marked gain nor marked loss: "[The company] *doesn't do badly. That is, it's a wash"* (Harper's). **—wash** *adj.* **1.** Used for washing. **2.** Being such that washing is possible; washable. **—*phrasal verbs.* wash down. 1.** To clean by washing with water from top to bottom: *wash down the walls.* **2.** To follow the ingestion of (food, for example) with the ingestion of a liquid: *washed the cake down with coffee.* **wash out. 1.a.** To remove or be removed by washing. **b.** To cause to fade by laundering: *color that had been washed out by bleach.* **2.** To carry or wear away or be carried or worn away by the action of moving water: *The river rose and washed out the dam. The road has washed out five miles down the mountain.* **3.** To deplete or become depleted of vitality: *By evening, I was washed out from overwork.* **4.** To eliminate or be eliminated as unsatisfactory: *a football player who was washed out; an officer candidate who washed out after one month.* **5.** To cause (an event) to be rained out. **wash up. 1.** To wash one's hands and face. **2.** *Chiefly British.* To wash dishes after a meal. **3.** To burn out; exhaust: *She's all washed up as an editor.* **—*idioms.* come out in the wash.** *Slang.* **1.** To be revealed eventually: *The real reasons for her resignation will come out in the wash.* **2.** To turn out well in the end: *Don't worry: this project will come out in the wash.* **wash (one's) hands of. 1.** To refuse to accept responsibility for. **2.** To abandon; renounce. [Middle English *washen,* from Old English *wacsan, wæscan.* See **wed-**[1] in Appendix.]

wart hog
Phacochoerus aethiopicus

Wash (wŏsh, wôsh). An inlet of the North Sea off east-central England. The Wash has a dredged ship channel.

Wash. *abbr.* Washington.

wash·a·ble (wŏsh′ə-bəl, wôsh′-) *adj.* Capable of being washed without fading or other injury: *washable wool.* **—wash′a·bil′i·ty** *n.*

wash-and-wear (wŏsh′ən-wâr′, wôsh′-) *adj.* Treated so as to be easily or quickly washed or rinsed clean and to require little or no ironing. Used of clothes and linens: *a wash-and-wear shirt.*

wash·ba·sin (wŏsh′bā′sən, wôsh′-) *n.* See **washbowl.**

wash·board (wŏsh′bôrd′, -bōrd′, wôsh′-) *n.* **1.a.** A board having a corrugated surface on which clothes can be rubbed in the process of laundering. **b.** *Music.* A similar board used as a percussion instrument. **2.** A board fastened to a wall at the floor; a baseboard. **3.** *Nautical.* A thin plank fastened to the side of a boat or to the sill of a port to keep out the sea and the spray.

washboard

wash·bowl (wŏsh′bōl′, wôsh′-) *n.* A basin that can be filled with water for use in washing oneself. Also called *washbasin.*

wash·cloth (wŏsh′klôth′, -klŏth′, wôsh′-) *n.* A small, usually square cloth of absorbent material used for washing the face or body. Also called *facecloth, washrag.*

wash·day (wŏsh′dā′, wôsh′-) *n.* A day set aside for doing household washing.

wash drawing *n.* A drawing or painting in which washes of color are used.

washed-out (wŏsht′out′, wôsht′-) *adj.* **1.** Lacking color or intensity; faded. **2.** Exhausted or tired-looking. **3.** Having dropped a project or an enterprise or having been dropped from one: *a washed-out officer candidate.*

washed-up (wŏsht′ŭp′, wôsht′-) *adj.* **1.** No longer successful or needed; finished. **2.** Ready to give up in disgust.

wash·er (wŏsh′ər, wô′shər) *n.* **1.** One who washes: *a washer of clothes; a washer of windows.* **2.** An appliance used for washing, especially: **a.** A washing machine. **b.** An automatic dishwasher. **3.** A flat disk, as of metal, plastic, rubber, or leather, placed beneath a nut or at an axle bearing or a joint to relieve friction, prevent leakage, or distribute pressure.

wash·er·wom·an (wŏsh′ər-wo͝om′ən, wô′shər-) also **wash·wom·an** (wŏsh′wo͝om′ən, wôsh′-) *n.* A woman who washes clothes and linens for a living.

wash·ing (wŏsh′ĭng, wô′shĭng) *n.* **1.** The act or process of one that washes. **2.** Articles washed or intended to be washed at one time: *the week's washing.* **3.** The residue after an ore or other material has been washed. **4.** Often **washings.** The liquid used to wash something.

washing machine *n.* A usually automatic machine for washing clothes and linens.

washing soda *n.* A hydrated sodium carbonate used as a general cleanser.

Wash·ing·ton (wŏsh′ĭng-tən, wô′shĭng-). **1.** *Abbr.* **WA, Wash.** A state of the northwest United States on the Pacific Ocean. It was admitted as the 42nd state in 1889. Originally explored by Capt. James Cook (1778), Washington was the object of a dispute between England and the United States until 1846, when its northern border was set at the 49th parallel. Olympia is the capital and Seattle the largest city. Population, 4,132,204. **2.** The capital of the United States, on the Potomac River between Virginia and Maryland and coextensive with the District of Columbia. It was designed by Pierre L'Enfant and became the capital in 1800. Population, 638,432. **3.** A city of southwest Pennsylvania southwest of Pittsburgh. Settled in 1769, it is the seat of Washington and Jefferson College (first chartered 1787). Population, 18,363. **—Wash′ing·to′ni·an** (wŏsh′ĭng-tō′nē-ən, wô′shĭng-) *adj. & n.*

Booker T. Washington
c. 1895 photograph by
Elmer Chickering
(died 1915)

Washington, Booker T(aliaferro). 1856–1915. American educator. Born into slavery, he acquired an education after emancipation and became the principal of Tuskegee Institute, which flourished under his tutelage (1881–1915).

Washington, Bushrod. 1762–1829. American jurist who

George Washington
1795 portrait by Rembrandt Peale

Martha Washington
Early 19th-century portrait by an unknown artist

washstand
c. 1820–1830 American

wasp

served as an associate justice of the U.S. Supreme Court (1798–1829).

Washington, George. 1732–1799. American military leader and the first President of the United States (1789–1797). Commander of the American forces in the Revolutionary War (1775–1783), he presided over the Second Constitutional Convention (1787) and was elected President of the fledgling country (1789).

Washington, Lake. A lake in west-central Washington on the eastern boundary of Seattle.

Washington, Martha Dandridge Custis. 1731–1802. First Lady of the United States (1789–1797) as the wife of President George Washington.

Washington, Mount. A mountain, 1,917.8 m (6,288 ft) high, of eastern New Hampshire in the White Mountains.

Wash·ing·ton's Birthday (wŏsh′ĭng-tənz, wô′shĭng-) *n.* February 22, formerly observed to commemorate the birth of George Washington in 1732. This holiday is now included in the observances of Presidents' Day.

Wash·i·ta (wŏsh′ĭ-tô′, wô′shĭ-). A river rising in northwest Texas and flowing about 724 km (450 mi) generally east-southeast across Oklahoma to the Red River.

wash·out (wŏsh′out′, wôsh′-) *n.* **1.a.** Erosion of a relatively soft surface, such as a roadbed, by a sudden gush of water, as from a downpour or floods. **b.** A channel produced by such erosion. **2.a.** A total failure or disappointment. **b.** One who fails to measure up to a standard, especially one who fails a course of training or study.

wash·rag (wŏsh′răg′, wôsh′-) *n.* See **washcloth.**

wash·room (wŏsh′ro͞om′, -ro͝om′, wôsh′-) *n.* A bathroom, especially one in a public place.

wash sale *n.* The illegal buying of stock by a seller's agents to give the impression of an active market.

wash·stand (wŏsh′stănd′, wôsh′-) *n.* **1.** A stand designed to hold a basin and pitcher of water for washing. **2.** A stationary bathroom sink.

wash·tub (wŏsh′tŭb′, wôsh′-) *n.* A tub used for washing clothes.

wash·wom·an (wŏsh′wo͝om′ən, wôsh′-) *n.* Variant of **washerwoman.**

wash·y (wŏsh′ē, wô′shē) *adj.* **-i·er, -i·est.** **1.** Watery; diluted: *washy tea.* **2.** Lacking strength or intensity: *a washy handshake; washy prose.* **—wash′i·ness** *n.*

was·n't (wŭz′ənt, wŏz′-). Was not.

wasp (wŏsp, wôsp) *n.* Any of numerous social or solitary insects, chiefly of the superfamilies Vespoidea and Sphecoidea, having a slender body with a constricted abdomen, two pairs of membranous wings, mouths adapted for biting or sucking, and in the females an ovipositor often modified as a sting. [Middle English *waspe,* from Old English *wæps, wæsp.*]

Wasp or **WASP** (wŏsp, wôsp) *n.* A white Protestant of Anglo-Saxon ancestry. [W(HITE) + A(NGLO-)S(AXON) + P(ROTESTANT).]

wasp·ish (wŏs′pĭsh) *adj.* **1.** Of, relating to, or suggestive of a wasp. **2.** Easily irritated or annoyed; irascible. **3.** Indicative of irritation, annoyance, or spite: *a waspish remark.* **—wasp′ish·ly** *adv.* **—wasp′ish·ness** *n.*

wasp waist *n.* A very slender waist or one that is tightly corseted. **—wasp′-waist′ed** (wŏsp′wās′tĭd, wôsp′-) *adj.*

wasp·y (wŏs′pē) *adj.* **-i·er, -i·est.** Characteristic of a wasp.

was·sail (wŏs′əl, wŏ-sāl′) *n.* **1.a.** A salutation or toast given in drinking someone's health or as an expression of good will at a festivity. **b.** The drink used in such toasting, commonly ale or wine spiced with roasted apples and sugar. **2.** A festivity characterized by much drinking. **—wassail** *v.* **-sailed, -sail·ing, -sails.** —*tr.* To drink to the health of; toast. —*intr.* To engage in or drink a wassail. [Middle English, contraction of *wæshæil,* be healthy, from Old Norse *ves heill* : *ves,* imperative sing. of *vera,* to be; see **wes-**[1] in Appendix + *heill,* healthy; see **kailo-** in Appendix.] **—was′sail·er** *n.*

Was·ser·mann reaction (wä′sər-mən) *n.* A complement-fixing reaction to the Wassermann test.

Wassermann test *n.* A diagnostic test for syphilis involving the fixation or inactivation of a complement by an antibody in a blood serum sample. [After August von *Wassermann* (1866–1925), German bacteriologist.]

wast (wŏst; wəst *when unstressed*) *v.* *Archaic.* A second person singular past tense of **be.**

wast·age (wā′stĭj) *n.* **1.** Loss by deterioration, wear, or destruction: *"Disease and desertion still caused much greater wastage than battle"* (Theodore Ropp). **2.** The gradual process of wasting. **3.** An amount that is wasted or lost by wear.

waste (wāst) *v.* **wast·ed, wast·ing, wastes.** —*tr.* **1.** To use, consume, spend, or expend thoughtlessly or carelessly. **2.** To cause to lose energy, strength, or vigor; exhaust, tire, or enfeeble: *Disease wasted his body.* **3.** To fail to take advantage of or use for profit; lose: *waste an opportunity.* **4.a.** To destroy completely. **b.** *Slang.* To kill; murder. —*intr.* **1.** To lose energy, strength, weight, or vigor; become weak or enfeebled: *wasting away from an illness.* **2.** To pass without being put to use: *Time is wasting.* **—waste** *n.* **1.** The act or an instance of wasting or the condition of being wasted: *a waste of talent; gone to waste.* **2.** A place, region, or land that is uninhabited or uncultivated; a desert or wilderness. **3.** A devastated or destroyed region, town, or building; a ruin. **4.a.** A useless or worthless byproduct, as from a manufacturing process. **b.** Something, such as steam, that escapes without being used. **5.** Garbage; trash. **6.** The undigested residue of food eliminated from the body; excrement. **—waste** *adj.* **1.** Regarded or discarded as worthless or useless: *waste trimmings.* **2.** Used as a conveyance or container for refuse: *a waste bin.* **3.** Excreted from the body: *waste matter.* **—*idiom.* waste (one's) breath.** To gain or accomplish nothing by speaking. [Middle English *wasten,* from Old North French *waster,* from Latin *vāstāre,* to make empty, from *vāstus,* empty. See **eu-**[2] in Appendix.]

SYNONYMS: *waste, blow, consume, dissipate, fritter, squander.* The central meaning shared by these verbs is "to spend or expend without restraint and often to no avail": *wasted her inheritance; blew a fortune on a shopping spree; time and money consumed in litigation; dissipating their energies in pointless argument; frittering away her entire allowance; squandered his literary talent on writing commercials.*
ANTONYM: *save.*

waste·bas·ket (wāst′băs′kĭt) *n.* An open-topped container for rubbish.

wast·ed (wā′stĭd) *adj.* **1.** Not profitably used or maintained: *a wasted inheritance.* **2.** Needless or superfluous: *These are wasted words.* **3.** Deteriorated; ravaged: *a wasted landscape.* **4.** Frail and enfeebled, as from prolonged illness; emaciated. See Synonyms at **haggard.** **5.** *Slang.* Under the influence of a mind-altering drug. **6.** *Archaic.* Having elapsed.

waste·ful (wāst′fəl) *adj.* Marked by or inclined to waste; extravagant. **—waste′ful·ly** *adv.* **—waste′ful·ness** *n.*

waste·land (wāst′lănd′) *n.* **1.** Land that is desolate, barren, or ravaged. **2.** A place, an era, or an aspect of life considered as lacking in spiritual, aesthetic, or other humanizing qualities; a vacuum: *a cultural wasteland.*

waste·pa·per (wāst′pā′pər) *n.* Discarded paper.

waste pipe *n.* A pipe that carries off liquid waste.

waste product *n.* **1.** Useless or worthless debris produced during or as a result of a manufacturing or other process. **2.** Organic waste matter such as urine, feces, or dead cells.

wast·er (wā′stər) *n.* **1.** One that wastes: *a waster of time; a waster of money.* **2.** One that lays waste; a destroyer: *a waster of enemy cities.*

waste·wa·ter (wāst′wô′tər, -wŏt′ər) *n.* Water that has been used, as for washing, flushing, or in a manufacturing process, and so contains waste products; sewage.

wast·ing (wā′stĭng) *adj.* **1.** Gradually deteriorating; declining: *the wasting process of erosion.* **2.** Sapping the strength, energy, or substance of the body; emaciating: *a wasting disease.* **—wast′ing·ly** *adv.*

wasting asset *n.* A fixed asset, such as a mine or an oil well, that diminishes in value over time.

wast·rel (wā′strəl) *n.* **1.** One who wastes, especially one who wastes money; a profligate. **2.** An idler or a loafer. [WAST(E) + *-rel* (as in SCOUNDREL).]

wa·tap (wă-tăp′, wä-) also **wa·ta·pe** (-tä′pē) *n.* A stringy thread made from the roots of various conifers and used by certain Native American peoples in sewing and weaving. [Ojibwa *wadab.*]

watch (wŏch) *v.* **watched, watch·ing, watch·es.** —*intr.* **1.** To look or observe attentively or carefully; be closely observant: *watching for trail markers.* **2.** To look and wait expectantly or in anticipation: *watch for an opportunity.* **3.** To act as a spectator; look on: *stood by the road and watched.* **4.** To stay awake at night while serving as a guard, sentinel, or watcher. **5.** To stay alert as a devotional or religious exercise; keep vigil. —*tr.* **1.** To look at steadily; observe carefully or continuously: *watch a parade.* **2.** To keep a watchful eye on; guard: *watched the prisoner all day.* **3.** To observe the course of mentally; keep up on or informed about: *watch the price of gold.* **4.** To tend (a flock, for example). See Synonyms at **tend**[2]. **—watch** *n.* **1.** The act or process of keeping awake or mentally alert, especially for the purpose of guarding. **2.a.** The act of observing closely or the condition of being closely observed; surveillance. **b.** A period of close observation, often in order to discover something: *a watch during the child's illness.* **3.** A person or group of people serving, especially at night, to guard or protect. **4.** The post or period of duty of a guard, sentinel, or watcher. **5.** Any of the periods into which the night is divided; a part of the night. **6.** *Nautical.* **a.** Any of the periods of time into which the day aboard ship is divided and during which a part of the crew is assigned to duty. **b.** The members of a ship's crew on duty during a specific watch. **c.** A chronometer on a ship. **7.a.** A period of wakefulness, especially one observed as a religious vigil. **b.** A funeral wake. **8.** A small portable timepiece, especially one worn on the wrist or carried in the pocket. **9.** A flock of nightingales. See Synonyms at **flock**[1]. **—*phrasal verbs.* watch out.** To be careful or on the alert; take care. **watch over.** To be in charge of; superintend. **—*idioms.* watch it.** To be careful: *had to watch it when I stepped onto the ice.* **watch (one's) step.** **1.** To act or proceed with care and caution. **2.** To behave as is demanded, required, or appropriate. [Middle English *wacchen,* from Old English *wæccan,* to watch, be awake. See **weg-** in Appendix.]

watch·band (wŏch′bănd′) *n.* A band of leather, cloth, metal, or plastic with an adjustable clasp that holds a wristwatch in place.

watch cap *n.* A dark blue knitted cap worn in cold weather, especially by enlisted naval personnel.

watch·case (wŏch′kās′) *n.* The casing for the mechanism of a watch.

watch·dog (wŏch′dôg′, -dŏg′) *n.* **1.** A dog trained to guard people or property. **2.** One who serves as a guardian or protector against waste, loss, or illegal practices. **—watch′dog′** *v.*

watch·er (wŏch′ər) *n.* **1.** One that watches or observes: *a fire watcher; a China watcher.* **2.** One who keeps vigil, as at a sick person's bedside.

watch·eye (wŏch′ī′) *n.* Walleye, especially in dogs.

watch fire *n.* A fire kept burning at night, as for a signal or by a guard.

watch·ful (wŏch′fəl) *adj.* **1.** Closely observant or alert; vigilant: *kept a watchful eye on the clock.* See Synonyms at **aware, careful. 2.** *Archaic.* Not sleeping; awake. **—watch′ful·ly** *adv.* **—watch′ful·ness** *n.*

watch glass *n.* **1.** A shallow glass dish used as a beaker cover or an evaporating surface. **2.** A concavo-convex glass or plastic disk used to cover the face of a watch.

watch·mak·er (wŏch′mā′kər) *n.* One that makes or repairs watches.

watch·man (wŏch′mən) *n.* A man who is employed to stand guard or keep watch.

watch night *n.* **1.** New Year's Eve. **2.** A religious service held on New Year's Eve.

watch·tow·er (wŏch′tou′ər) *n.* An observation tower on which a guard or lookout is stationed to keep watch, as for enemies, for forest fires, or over prisoners.

watch·word (wŏch′wûrd′) *n.* **1.** A prearranged reply to a challenge, as from a guard or sentry; a password. **2.** A rallying cry: *Let our watchword be freedom.*

wa·ter (wô′tər, wŏt′ər) *n.* **1.** A clear, colorless, odorless, and tasteless liquid, H_2O, essential for most plant and animal life and the most widely used of all solvents. Freezing point 0°C (32°F); boiling point 100°C (212°F); specific gravity (4°C) 1.0000; weight per gallon (15°C) 8.337 pounds (3.772 kilograms). **2.a.** Any of various forms of water: *waste water.* **b.** *Often* **waters.** Naturally occurring mineral water, as at a spa. **3.a.** A body of water such as a sea, lake, river, or stream. **b. waters.** A particular stretch of sea or ocean, especially that of a state or country: *escorted out of British waters.* **4.a.** A supply of water: *had to turn off the water while repairing the broken drain.* **b.** A water supply system. **5.a.** Any of the liquids present in or passed out of the body, such as urine, perspiration, tears, or saliva. **b.** The fluid surrounding a fetus in the uterus; amniotic fluid. **6.** An aqueous solution of a substance, especially a gas: *ammonia water.* **7.** A wavy finish or sheen, as of a fabric or metal. **8.a.** The valuation of the assets of a business firm beyond their real value. **b.** Stock issued in excess of paid-in capital. **9.a.** The transparency and luster of a gem. **b.** A level of excellence. **—water** *v.* **-tered, -ter·ing, -ters.** *—tr.* **1.** To pour or sprinkle water on; make wet: *watered the garden.* **2.a.** To give drinking water to. **b.** To lead (an animal) to drinking water. **3.** To dilute or weaken by adding water: *a bar serving whiskey that had been watered.* **4.** To give a sheen to the surface of (silk, linen, or metal). **5.** To increase (the number of shares of stock) without increasing the value of the assets represented. **6.** To irrigate (land). *—intr.* **1.** To produce or discharge fluid, as from the eyes. **2.** To salivate in anticipation of food: *The wonderful aroma from the kitchen makes my mouth water.* **3.** To take on a supply of water, as a ship. **4.** To drink water, as an animal. ***—phrasal verb.* water down.** To reduce the strength or effectiveness of: *"It seemed clear by late autumn that the ban would be significantly watered down or removed altogether before the trade bill became law"* (George R. Packard). ***—idioms.* above water.** Out of difficulty or trouble. **water under the bridge.** A past occurrence, especially something unfortunate, that cannot be undone or rectified: *All that is now just water under the bridge.* [Middle English, from Old English *wæter.* See **wed-**[1] in Appendix.] **—wa′ter·er** *n.*

water arum *n.* See **calla** (sense 2).

water ash *n.* See **stinking ash.**

water bag *n.* The membranous sac filled with amniotic fluid that protects a fetus during pregnancy. Also called *bag of waters.*

water ballet *n.* **1.** The art of dancelike movement in water; synchronized swimming. **2.** A performance or competition of this swimming.

water bear *n.* See **tardigrade.**

Wa·ter Bearer (wô′tər, wŏt′ər) *n.* See **Aquarius** (senses 1, 2a).

wa·ter·bed (wô′tər-bĕd′, wŏt′ər-) *n.* A bed with a mattress made of a tough plastic that is filled with water.

water beetle *n.* Any of various aquatic beetles, especially of the family Dytiscidae, having a smooth oval body and flattened and fringed hind legs adapted for swimming.

water bird *n.* A swimming or wading bird.

water biscuit *n.* A biscuit made of flour and water.

water blister *n.* A blister having watery contents without blood or pus.

water bloom *n.* A growth of algae at or near the surface of a body of water, such as a pond.

water boatman *n.* Any of various aquatic insects of the families Corixidae and Notonectidae, having long oarlike hind legs adapted for swimming.

wa·ter·borne (wô′tər-bôrn′, -bōrn′, wŏt′ər-) *adj.* **1.** Floating on or supported by water; afloat. **2.** Transported by water: *waterborne freight.* **3.** Transmitted in water: *waterborne disease-causing microorganisms.*

water brash *n.* Regurgitation of watery acid.

wa·ter·buck (wô′tər-bŭk′, wŏt′ər-) *n., pl.* **waterbuck** or **-bucks.** Any of several African antelopes of the genus *Kobus,* having curved, ridged horns and frequenting swamps, rivers, and other bodies of water. [Translation of Afrikaans *waterbok.*]

water buffalo *n.* A large buffalo *(Bubalus bubalis)* of Asia, often domesticated especially as a draft animal and having large, spreading horns. Also called *carabao, water ox.*

water bug *n.* **1.** Any of various aquatic insects, especially the water boatman and certain backswimmers. **2.** A large cockroach.

Wat·er·bury (wô′tər-bĕr′ē, wŏt′ər-). A city of west-central Connecticut north-northwest of New Haven. Incorporated as a town in 1686 and as a city in 1853, it is today a manufacturing center. Population, 103,266.

wa·ter·bus (wô′tər-bŭs′, wŏt′ər-) *n., pl.* **-bus·es** or **-bus·ses.** *Nautical.* A large motorboat used for carrying passengers on rivers or canals.

water cal·trop (kăl′trəp) *n.* See **water chestnut** (sense 1).

water cannon *n.* A truck-mounted apparatus that fires water at high pressure, used especially to disperse crowds or control rioters.

water chestnut *n.* **1.** A floating aquatic plant *(Trapa natans)* native to Eurasia and Africa, bearing four-pronged, nutlike fruit and grown as a pond or aquarium ornamental. Also called *caltrop, water caltrop.* **2.a.** A tropical Asian aquatic sedge *(Eleocharis dulcis)* having an edible corm and cylindrical leaves. **b.** The succulent corm of this plant, used in Asian cooking. **c.** Also called *Chinese water chestnut.*

water chinquapin *n.* A North American aquatic plant *(Nelumbo lutea)* related to the lotus and the water lilies and having large shield-shaped aerial leaves, large pale-yellow flowers, and edible nutlike seeds.

water clock *n.* A clepsydra.

water closet *n.* *Abbr.* **W.C.** A room or booth containing a toilet and often a washbowl.

water clover *n.* See **pepperwort** (sense 1).

wa·ter·col·or (wô′tər-kŭl′ər, wŏt′ər-) *n.* **1.a.** A paint composed of a water-soluble pigment. **b.** A work that is executed through the use of this paint. **2.** The art of using watercolors. **—wa′ter·col′or** *adj.* **—wa′ter·col′or·ist** *n.*

wa·ter-cool (wô′tər-ko͞ol′, wŏt′ər-) *tr.v.* **-cooled, -cool·ing, -cools.** To cool (an engine) with water.

water cooler *n.* A device for cooling and dispensing drinking water.

wa·ter·course (wô′tər-kôrs′, -kōrs′, wŏt′ər-) *n.* **1.** A natural or artificial channel through which water flows. **2.** A stream or river.

wa·ter·craft (wô′tər-krăft′, wŏt′ər-) *n.* **1.** *Sports.* Skill in boating, swimming, or other water-related sports. **2.** *Nautical.* **a.** A boat or ship. **b.** Water vehicles considered as a group.

wa·ter·cress (wô′tər-krĕs′, wŏt′ər-) *n.* **1.** A pungent perennial Eurasian herb *(Rorippa nasturtium-aquaticum)* of the mustard family, growing in freshwater ponds and streams and used in salads and as a garnish. **2.** Any of several related aquatic plants.

water cure *n.* Hydropathy or hydrotherapy.

water cycle *n.* The cycle of evaporation and condensation that controls the distribution of Earth's water as it evaporates from bodies of water, condenses, precipitates, and returns to those bodies of water. Also called *hydrologic cycle.*

♦ **water dog** *n.* **1.** A dog that takes easily to the water, especially one trained for hunting waterfowl. **2.** *Informal.* A person who feels at home in or on the water. **3.** Often **wa·ter·dog** (wô′tər-dôg′, -dŏg′, wŏt′ər-). See **mud puppy** (sense 1). **4.** *Western U.S.* Any of several large salamanders.

♦ **wa·ter·dog·ging** (wô′tər-dô′gĭng, -dŏg′ĭng, wŏt′ər-) *n.* *Western U.S.* The collecting of salamanders out of drinking troughs to use for fishing bait.

wa·tered-down (wô′tərd-doun′, wŏt′ərd-) *adj.* Diminished in force or effect: *"at concert strength and tempo, rather than at a watered-down dance pace"* (Women's Wear Daily).

Wa·ter·ee (wô′tə-rē, wŏt′ə-). A river, about 233 km (145 mi) long, of central South Carolina flowing southward to form the Santee River. Its upper course, in North Carolina, is called the Catawba River.

water elm *n.* See **planer tree.**

wa·ter·fall (wô′tər-fôl′, wŏt′ər-) *n.* A steep descent of water from a height; a cascade.

wa·ter·find·er (wô′tər-fīn′dər, wŏt′ər-) *n.* A dowser.

water flea *n.* Any of various small aquatic crustaceans of the order Cladocera, especially the daphnid, that typically swim with jerking, flealike motions.

Wa·ter·ford (wô′tər-fərd, wŏt′ər-). **1.** A borough of southeast Ireland south-southwest of Dublin. A major port, Waterford was famous in the 18th and 19th centuries for its glass-manufacturing industry. Population, 38,473. **2.** A town of southeast Connecticut

wasp waist
c. 1900 photograph of Anna Held

watchtower

waterbuck

ă pat	oi boy
ā pay	ou out
âr care	o͝o took
ä father	o͞o boot
ĕ pet	ŭ cut
ē be	ûr urge
ĭ pit	th thin
ī pie	*th* this
îr pier	hw which
ŏ pot	zh vision
ō toe	ə about, item
ô paw	♦ regionalism

Stress marks: **′** (primary); ′ (secondary), as in **dictionary** (dĭk′shə-nĕr′ē)

on Long Island Sound. Settled c. 1653, it is a residential community. Population, 17,843.

wa·ter·fowl (wô′tər-foul′, wŏt′ər-) *n., pl.* **waterfowl** or **-fowls. 1.** A water bird, especially a swimming bird. **2.** Swimming game birds, such as ducks and geese, considered as a group.

wa·ter·front (wô′tər-frŭnt′, wŏt′ər-) *n.* **1.** Land abutting a body of water. **2.** The part of a town or city that abuts water, especially a district of wharves where ships dock. —*attributive.* Often used to modify another noun: *waterfront docks.*

water gap *n.* A transverse cleft in a mountain ridge through which a stream flows.

water gas *n.* A fuel gas containing about 50 percent carbon monoxide, 40 percent hydrogen, and small amounts of methane, carbon dioxide, and nitrogen, made by passing steam and air over heated coke or coal.

water gate *n.* **1.** See **floodgate** (sense 1). **2.** A gate that provides access to a body of water.

Wa·ter·gate (wô′tĕr-gāt′, wŏt′ər-) *n.* A scandal involving abuse of power by public officials, violation of the public trust, bribery, contempt of Congress, and attempted obstruction of justice. [After *Watergate,* a building complex in Washington, D.C., the site of illegal activities (1972) that gave rise to such a scandal.]

water gauge *n.* An instrument indicating the level of water, as in a boiler, tank, reservoir, or stream.

water glass *n.* **1.** A drinking glass or goblet. **2.** An open tube or box having a glass bottom for making observations below the surface of the water. **3.** See **sodium silicate. 4.** A water gauge made of glass. **5.** See **clepsydra.**

water gun *n.* See **squirt gun.**

water hammer *n.* **1.** A banging noise heard in a water pipe following an abrupt alteration of the flow with resultant pressure surges. **2.** A banging noise in steam pipes, caused by steam bubbles entering a cold pipe partially filled with water.

water hemlock *n.* Any of several poisonous, heavy-scented, perennial herbs of the genus *Cicuta,* especially *C. maculata,* of marshy areas in eastern and central North America, having compound umbels of small white flowers and bipinnately compound leaves.

water hen *n.* Any of various water birds of the family Rallidae, as the gallinule, rail, or coot, that inhabit marshland.

water hole *n.* **1.** A small natural depression in which water collects, especially a pool where animals come to drink. **2.** *Informal.* A watering hole.

water horehound *n.* Any of various perennial herbs of the genus *Lycopus* in the mint family, native to the North Temperate Zone and Australia.

water hyacinth *n.* A tropical American herb *(Eichhornia crassipes)* forming dense floating masses in ponds and streams and having large bluish-purple flowers and leafstalks with greatly inflated bases.

water ice *n.* A dessert made of finely crushed ice that has been sweetened and flavored.

wa·ter·ing can (wô′tər-ĭng, wŏt′ər-) *n.* See **watering pot.**

watering hole *n. Informal.* A social gathering place, such as a bar or saloon, where drinks are served: *"a Warsaw restaurant that was once a cosmopolitan watering hole for actors and writers"* (Newsweek).

watering place *n.* **1.** A place where animals find water to drink. **2.** A health resort with mineral springs; a spa. **3.** *Informal.* A watering hole.

watering pot *n.* A vessel, usually having a long spout with a perforated nozzle, used to water plants. Also called *watering can.*

wa·ter·ish (wô′tər-ĭsh, wŏt′ər-) *adj.* Resembling water; watery.

water jacket *n.* A casing containing water circulated by a pump, used around a part to be cooled, especially in water-cooled internal-combustion engines.

wa·ter-jack·et (wô′tər-jăk′ĭt, wŏt′ər-) *tr.v.* **-et·ed, -et·ing, -ets.** To encase in or provide with a water jacket.

wa·ter·leaf (wô′tər-lēf′, wŏt′ər-) *n., pl.* **-leafs.** Any of various North American herbs of the genus *Hydrophyllum,* having pinnately lobed leaves and terminal, cymose clusters of white or purplish flowers.

wa·ter·less (wô′tər-lĭs, wŏt′ər-) *adj.* **1.** Lacking water; dry. **2.** Not requiring water, as a cooling system.

water level *n.* **1.** The level of the surface of a body of water. **2.** *Geology.* See **water table** (sense 2). **3.** The water line of a ship.

water lily *n.* Any of various cosmopolitan aquatic herbs of the genus *Nymphaea,* having floating leaves and showy, variously colored flowers, especially *N. odorata,* with fragrant, many-petaled white or pinkish flowers. Also called *pond lily.*

water line *n. Abbr.* **w.l., WL 1.** *Nautical.* **a.** The line on the hull of a ship to which the surface of the water rises. **b.** Any of several lines parallel to this line, marked on the hull of a ship, and indicating the depth to which the ship sinks under various loads. **2.** A line or stain, as one left on a sea wall, indicating the height to which water has risen or may rise; a watermark.

wa·ter·log (wô′tər-lôg′, -lŏg′, wŏt′ər-) *tr.v.* **-logged, -log·ging, -logs. 1.** To make (a boat, for example) heavy and unwieldy by flooding with water. **2.** To saturate with water and make soggy or unusable. [Back-formation from WATERLOGGED.]

wa·ter·logged (wô′tər-lôgd′, -lŏgd′, wŏt′ər-) *adj.* **1.** *Nautical.* Heavy and sluggish in the water because of flooding, as in the hold: *a waterlogged ship.* **2.** Soaked or saturated with water: *waterlogged fields; waterlogged docking.* [WATER + LOGGED, past participle of LOG[1], to accumulate in a ship: used of water.]

wa·ter·loo (wô′tər-lo͞o′, wŏt′ər-, wô′tər-lo͞o′, wŏt′ər-) *n., pl.* **-loos.** A final, crushing defeat. [After WATERLOO, Belgium.]

Wa·ter·loo (wô′tər-lo͞o′, wŏt′ər-, wô′tər-lo͞o′, wŏt′ər-). **1.** A town of central Belgium near Brussels. Napoleon met his final defeat in the Battle of Waterloo (June 18, 1815). **2.** A city of southeast Ontario, Canada, a manufacturing suburb of Kitchener. Population, 24,933. **3.** A city of northeast Iowa northwest of Cedar Rapids. First settled in 1845, it is a trade center in an agricultural region. Population, 75,985.

water main *n.* A principal pipe in a system of pipes for conveying water, especially one installed underground.

wa·ter·man (wô′tər-mən, wŏt′ər-) *n.* A boatman.

wa·ter·mark (wô′tər-märk′, wŏt′ər-) *n. Abbr.* **wmk. 1.a.** A mark showing the greatest height to which water has risen. **b.** A line indicating the heights of high and low tide. **2.a.** A translucent design impressed on paper during manufacture and visible when the paper is held to the light. **b.** The metal pattern that produces this design. —*tr.* **-marked, -mark·ing, -marks. 1.** To mark (paper) with a watermark. **2.** To impress (a pattern or design) as a watermark.

wa·ter·mel·on (wô′tər-mĕl′ən, wŏt′ər-) *n.* **1.** An African vine *(Citrullus lanatus)* cultivated for its large, edible fruit. **2.** The fruit of this plant, having a hard green rind and sweet, watery pink or reddish flesh.

water milfoil *n.* Any of various cosmopolitan aquatic herbs of the genus *Myriophyllum,* having feathery, finely dissected submersed leaves and entire or toothed emersed leaves.

water mill *n.* A mill with machinery that is driven by water.

water moccasin *n.* **1.** A semiaquatic pit viper *(Agkistrodon piscivorus)* of lowlands and swampy regions of the southern United States. Also called *cottonmouth.* **2.** Any of various similar but harmless water snakes.

water mold *n.* Any of various parasitic or saprobic fungi of the phylum Oomycota, living chiefly in fresh water or moist soil.

water nymph *n. Mythology.* A nymph, such as a naiad or Nereid, living in or near water.

water oak *n.* Any of various oak trees that grow in wetlands, especially *Quercus nigra,* of eastern North America.

water of crystallization *n.* Water in chemical combination with a crystal, necessary for the maintenance of crystalline properties but capable of being removed by sufficient heat.

water of hydration *n.* Water chemically combined with a substance in such a way that it can be removed, as by heating, without substantially changing the chemical composition of the substance.

water on the brain *n.* Hydrocephalus.

water ouzel *n.* See **dipper** (sense 2).

water ox *n.* See **water buffalo.**

water parting *n.* See **watershed** (sense 1).

water pennywort *n.* Any of various creeping perennial herbs of the genus *Hydrocotyle* in the parsley family, having orbicular leaves and small, white or greenish flowers grouped in umbels. Also called *navelwort.*

water pepper *n.* A perennial herb *(Polygonum hydropiperoides)* growing in marshes and bogs of the United States, having reddish stems, clusters of small greenish flowers, and acrid-tasting leaves.

water pipe *n.* **1.** A pipe that is a conduit for water. **2.** An apparatus for smoking, such as a hookah, in which the smoke is drawn through a container of water or ice and cooled before inhaling.

water pipit *n.* A North American pipit *(Anthus spinoletta)* with a dark unstreaked back and an elaborate musical song.

water pistol *n.* See **squirt gun.**

water plantain *n.* Any of various aquatic herbs of the genus *Alisma,* having panicles with whorled branches and small, three-petaled, white or pinkish flowers.

water polo *n. Sports.* A water sport with two teams of swimmers each of which tries to pass a ball into the other's goal.

wa·ter·pow·er (wô′tər-pou′ər, wŏt′ər-) *n.* **1.a.** The energy produced by running or falling water that is used for driving machinery, especially for generating electricity. **b.** A source of such energy, as a waterfall. **2.** A water right owned by a mill.

wa·ter·proof (wô′tər-pro͞of′, wŏt′ər-) *adj.* **1.** Impervious to or unaffected by water. **2.** Made of or coated or treated with rubber, plastic, or a sealing agent to prevent penetration by water. —**waterproof** *n.* **1.** A material or fabric that is impervious to water. **2.** *Chiefly British.* A raincoat or other such outer garment. —**waterproof** *tr.v.* **-proofed, -proof·ing, -proofs.** To make impervious to water.

water purslane *n.* **1.** Any of various aquatic annual herbs of the genus *Peplis,* especially *P. diandra,* of the eastern and central United States, having small greenish flowers. **2.** A marsh or wetland herb *(Ludwigia palustris)* having reddish stems and small reddish flowers.

water rail *n.* A brownish Old World rail *(Rallus aquaticus)* with a long, red bill, living in marshy, warm coastal areas of the Pacific.

water lily

water line

water polo

ă pat	oi boy
ā pay	ou out
âr care	o͝o took
ä father	o͞o boot
ĕ pet	ŭ cut
ē be	ûr urge
ĭ pit	th thin
ī pie	*th* this
îr pier	hw which
ŏ pot	zh vision
ō toe	ə about, item
ô paw	♦ regionalism

Stress marks: ′ (primary); ′ (secondary), as in **dictionary** (dĭk′shə-nĕr′ē)

water rat *n.* **1.a.** Any of various semiaquatic rodents, especially *Neofiber alleni,* of Florida and southern Georgia, closely related to and resembling the muskrat. **b.** See **muskrat** (sense 1). **2.** *Slang.* A petty thief or ruffian who frequents waterfronts.

wa·ter-re·pel·lent (wô′tər-rĭ-pĕl′ənt, wŏt′ər-) *adj.* Resistant to penetration by water but not entirely waterproof.

wa·ter-re·sis·tant (wô′tər-rĭ-zĭs′tənt, wŏt′ər-) *adj.* Water-repellent.

water right *n.* **1.** The right to draw water from a particular source, such as a lake, an irrigation canal, or a stream. Often used in the plural. **2.** *Nautical.* The right to navigate on particular waters.

Wa·ters (wô′tərz, wŏt′ərz), **Ethel.** 1896–1977. American actress and singer who began in vaudeville and became popular on Broadway and in films, such as *The Sound and the Fury* (1959).

water sapphire *n.* A clear blue cordierite often used as a gemstone.

wa·ter·scape (wô′tər-skāp′, wŏt′ər-) *n.* A seascape.

water scorpion *n.* Any of various aquatic insects of the family Nepidae, having a large breathing tube projecting from the posterior part of the abdomen and inflicting a painful sting.

wa·ter·shed (wô′tər-shĕd′, wŏt′ər-) *n.* **1.** A ridge of high land dividing two areas that are drained by different river systems. Also called *water parting.* **2.** The region draining into a river, river system, or other body of water. **3.** A critical point that marks a division or a change of course; a turning point: *"a watershed in modern American history, a time that . . . forever changed American social attitudes"* (Robert Reinhold). [Probably translation of German *Wasserscheide* : *Wasser,* water + *Scheide,* divide, parting.]

water shield *n.* **1.** A cosmopolitan aquatic herb *(Brasenia schreberi)* having floating elliptic or ovate leaves and purplish flowers. **2.** Any of several New World aquatic herbs of the genus *Cabomba,* having entire, alternate floating leaves and finely divided, opposite or whorled submersed leaves.

wa·ter-sick (wô′tər-sĭk′, wŏt′ər-) *adj.* Unproductive because of excessive irrigation: *water-sick soil.*

wa·ter·side (wô′tər-sīd′, wŏt′ər-) *n.* Land bordering a body of water; a bank or shore. **—waterside** *adj.* **1.** Of, relating to, or situated at the waterside. **2.** Living or working along the waterside.

water ski *n. Sports.* A broad ski used for skiing on water.

wa·ter-ski (wô′tər-skē′, wŏt′ər-) *intr.v.* **-skied, -ski·ing, -skis.** *Sports.* To ski on water while being towed by a motorboat. **—wa′ter-ski′er** *n.* **—wa′ter-ski′ing** *n.*

water snake *n.* **1.** Any of various nonvenomous snakes of the genus *Natrix,* living in or frequenting freshwater streams and ponds. **2.** Any of various aquatic or semiaquatic snakes.

wa·ter-sol·u·ble (wô′tər-sŏl′yə-bəl, wŏt′ər-) *adj. Chemistry.* Soluble in water.

water spaniel *n.* A large spaniel of a breed characterized by a curly, water-resistant coat, often used in hunting to retrieve waterfowl.

wa·ter·spout (wô′tər-spout′, wŏt′ər-) *n.* **1.** A tornado or lesser whirlwind occurring over water and resulting in a funnel-shaped whirling column of air and spray. **2.** A hole or pipe from which water is discharged.

water sprite *n.* A sprite or nymph that inhabits or haunts a body of water.

water strider *n.* Any of various insects of the family Gerridae, having long, slender legs with which they support themselves on the surface of water. Also called *skater.*

water supply *n.* **1.** The water available for a community or region. **2.** The source and delivery system of such water.

water system *n.* **1.** A river and all its tributaries. **2.** A water supply.

water table *n.* **1.** A projecting ledge, molding, or stringcourse along the side of a building, designed to throw off rainwater. **2.** The level below which the ground is completely saturated with water. In this sense, also called *water level.*

water thrush *n.* Either of two brownish New World warblers *(Seiurus noveboracensis* or *S. motacilla)* living near streams and ponds.

wa·ter·tight (wô′tər-tīt′, wŏt′ər-) *adj.* **1.** So tightly made that water cannot enter or escape. **2.** Having no flaws or loopholes; impossible to fault, refute, or evade: *a watertight alibi; a watertight contract.*

water tower *n.* **1.** A standpipe or elevated tank used as a reservoir or for maintaining equal pressure in a water system. **2.** A firefighting apparatus for lifting hoses to the upper levels of a tall structure.

Wa·ter·town (wô′tər-toun′, wŏt′ər-). **1.** A town of western Connecticut near Waterbury. Set off from Waterbury in 1780, it is a manufacturing center. Population, 19,489. **2.** A town of eastern Massachusetts, a residential suburb of Boston. Population, 34,384. **3.** A city of northern New York north of Syracuse. Settled c. 1800, it is a manufacturing center. Population, 27,861. **4.** A city of southeast Wisconsin east-northeast of Madison. Population, 18,113.

water turkey *n.* See **anhinga.**

water vapor *n.* Water in a gaseous state, especially when diffused as a vapor in the atmosphere and at a temperature below boiling point.

wa·ter-vas·cu·lar system (wô′tər-văs′kyə-lər, wŏt′ər-) *n.* A system of water-filled canals derived from the coelom that connects the tube feet of echinoderms.

Wa·ter·ville (wô′tər-vĭl′, wŏt′ər-). A city of southern Maine north of Augusta. Settled in 1754, it is the seat of Colby College (founded 1813). Population, 17,779.

wa·ter·way (wô′tər-wā′, wŏt′ər-) *n. Nautical.* **1.** A navigable body of water, such as a river, channel, or canal. **2.** A channel at the edge of a ship's deck to drain away water.

wa·ter·weed (wô′tər-wēd′, wŏt′ər-) *n.* Any of various submersed aquatic herbs of the genus *Elodea,* native to the New World, having opposite or whorled one-nerved narrow leaves and small axillary flowers.

water wheel *n.* **1.** A wheel propelled by falling or running water and used to power machinery. **2.** A wheel with buckets attached to its rim for raising water.

water wings *pl.n.* A device consisting of a pair of joined inflatable waterproof bags that fits under the arms of a person, especially a child learning to swim, and provides buoyancy.

water witch *n.* One who claims to be able to find underground water by means of a divining rod; a dowser.

wa·ter·works (wô′tər-wûrks′, wŏt′ər-) *pl.n.* **1.a.** *(used with a sing. or pl. verb).* The water system, including reservoirs, tanks, buildings, pumps, and pipes, that supplies water to a city, town, or other municipality. **b.** *(used with a sing. verb).* A single unit, such as a pumping station, within such a system. **2.** *(used with a sing. verb).* An exhibition of moving water, such as a fountain or cascade. **3.** *(used with a pl. verb). Informal.* Tears: *turned on the waterworks.*

wa·ter·y (wô′tə-rē, wŏt′ə-) *adj.* **-i·er, -i·est.** **1.** Filled with, consisting of, or soaked with water; wet or soggy: *watery soil.* **2.** Containing too much water; diluted: *watery soup.* **3.** Suggestive of water, as in being thin, pale, or liquid: *watery sunshine.* **4.** Lacking force or substance; weak or insipid: *watery prose.* **5.** Secreting or discharging water or watery fluid, especially as a symptom of disease. **—wa′ter·i·ness** *n.*

Wat·lings Island (wät′lĭngz). See **San Salvador**[1].

WATS *abbr.* Wide-Area Telecommunications Service.

Wat·son (wŏt′sən), **James Dewey.** Born 1928. American biologist who with Francis Crick proposed a spiral model, the double helix, for the molecular structure of DNA. He shared a 1962 Nobel Prize for advances in the study of genetics.

Watson, Thomas Augustus. 1854–1934. American telephone pioneer who assisted Alexander Graham Bell in his experiments and was the leader of research and engineering for Bell Telephone Company (1877–1881).

Wat·son-Crick model (wät′sən-krĭk′) *n.* A three-dimensional model of the DNA molecule, consisting of two polynucleotide strands wound in the form of a double helix and joined in a ladderlike fashion by hydrogen bonds between the purine and pyrimidine bases. [After James Dewey WATSON and Francis Henry Compton CRICK.]

Wat·son·ville (wŏt′sən-vĭl′). A city of western California east-southeast of Santa Cruz. Founded in 1852, it is an agricultural processing center. Population, 23,543.

watt (wŏt) *n. Abbr.* **W.** *Electricity.* An International System unit of power equal to one joule per second. See table at **measurement.** [After James WATT.]

WORD HISTORY: One might well ask how many European scientists it takes to turn on a light bulb. If we think in terms of the names used for various units in the International, or meter-kilogram-second, System, a fair number are involved. Alphabetically arranged, these units are the *ampere,* named for the French scientist André Marie Ampère (1775–1836); the *coulomb,* after the French scientist Charles A. de Coulomb (1736–1806); the *farad* and the *faraday,* after the British scientist Michael Faraday (1791–1867); the *joule,* after the British scientist James P. Joule (1818–1889); the *newton,* after the British scientist Sir Isaac Newton (1642–1727); the *ohm,* after the German scientist Georg S. Ohm (1789–1854); the *volt,* after the Italian scientist Count Alessandro Volta (1745–1827); and the *watt,* after the British scientist James Watt (1736–1819). Definitions such as that of *ohm,* "a unit of electrical resistance equal to that of a conductor in which a current of one ampere is produced by a potential of one volt across its terminals," take on more human connotations when we think of how human contributions to the study of electricity are memorialized in them. The dates of first recorded use of the terms in English are as follows: *ampere,* 1881; *coulomb,* 1881; *farad,* 1861; *faraday,* 1904; *joule,* 1882; *newton,* 1904; *ohm,* 1870 (suggested in 1861); *volt,* 1873; and *watt,* 1882.

Watt (wŏt), **James.** 1736–1819. British engineer and inventor who made fundamental improvements in the steam engine, resulting in the modern, high-pressure steam engine (patented 1769).

watt·age (wŏt′ĭj) *n.* **1.** An amount of power, especially electric power, expressed in watts or kilowatts. **2.** The electric power required by an appliance or a device.

Wat·teau (wŏ-tō′, vä-), **Jean Antoine.** 1684–1721. French painter noted for his exuberant scenes of gallantry, such as *The Embarkation for Cythera* (1717).

water spaniel
Irish water spaniel

water tower

water wheel
Overshot water wheel

Watson-Crick model

wattle

Evelyn Waugh
Photographed in the 1950's

Wat·ter·son (wô′tər-sən, wŏt′ər-), **Henry.** Known as "Marse Henry." 1840–1921. American editor of the *Louisville Courier-Journal* (1868–1918). He exerted great political influence and served as a U.S. representative from Kentucky (1876–1877).

watt-hour (wŏt′our′) *n. Abbr.* **WH, W-hr.** A unit of energy, especially electrical energy, equal to the work done by one watt acting for one hour and equivalent to 3,600 joules.

wat·tle (wŏt′l) *n.* **1.a.** A construction of poles intertwined with twigs, reeds, or branches, used for walls, fences, and roofs. **b.** Material used for such construction. **2.** A fleshy, wrinkled, often brightly colored fold of skin hanging from the neck or throat, characteristic of certain birds, such as chickens or turkeys, and some lizards. **3.** *Botany.* Any of various Australian trees or shrubs of the genus *Acacia.* **—wattle** *tr.v.* **-tled, -tling, -tles. 1.** To construct from wattle. **2.** To weave into wattle. [Middle English *wattel,* from Old English *watel,* hurdle.] **—wat′tled** *adj.*

wattle and daub *n.* An interweaving of rods and twigs overlaid with clay and used as a building material.

wat·tle·bird (wŏt′l-bûrd′) *n.* Any of several honeyeaters of the genus *Anthochaera,* having wattles on either side of the head.

watt·me·ter (wŏt′mē′tər) *n. Abbr.* **wm.** An instrument for measuring in watts the power flowing in a circuit.

Watts (wŏts). A district of Los Angeles, California. It was the scene of severe racial tensions and violence in 1965.

Watts, Isaac. 1674–1748. English poet, theologian, and hymn writer whose poems include *The Psalms of David Imitated* (1719).

Waugh (wô), **Evelyn (Arthur Saint John).** 1903–1966. British writer whose satirical novels, such as *Vile Bodies* (1930), lampoon high society. His later works, notably *Brideshead Revisited* (1945), reflect his interest in Roman Catholicism.

Wau·ke·gan (wô-kē′gən). A city of northeast Illinois on Lake Michigan north of Chicago. A major lake port, Waukegan is also an industrial center. Population, 67,653.

Wau·ke·sha (wô′kə-shô′). A city of southeast Wisconsin west of Milwaukee. It was a health resort after the Civil War and is now a manufacturing center. Population, 50,319.

Wau·sau (wô′sô′). A city of north-central Wisconsin west-northwest of Green Bay. Settled in 1839, it grew as a lumber town and now has diversified industries. Population, 32,426.

Wau·wa·to·sa (wô′wə-tō′sə). A city of southeast Wisconsin, an industrial suburb of Milwaukee. Population, 51,308.

wave (wāv) *v.* **waved, wav·ing, waves.** *—intr.* **1.** To move freely back and forth or up and down in the air, as branches in the wind. **2.** To make a signal with an up-and-down or back-and-forth movement of the hand or an object held in the hand: *waved as she drove by.* **3.** To have an undulating or wavy form; curve or curl: *Her hair waves naturally.* *—tr.* **1.** To cause to move back and forth or up and down, either once or repeatedly: *She waved a fan before her face.* **2.a.** To move or swing as in giving a signal: *He waved his hand.* See Synonyms at **flourish. b.** To signal or express by waving the hand or an object held in the hand: *We waved good-bye.* **c.** To signal (a person) to move in a specified direction: *The police officer waved the motorist into the right lane.* **3.** To arrange into curves, curls, or undulations: *wave one's hair.* **—wave** *n.* **1.a.** A ridge or swell moving through or along the surface of a large body of water. **b.** A small ridge or swell moving across the interface of two fluids and dependent on surface tension. **2.** Often **waves.** The sea: *vanished beneath the waves.* **3.** Something that suggests the form and motion of a wave in the sea, especially: **a.** A moving curve or succession of curves in or on a surface; an undulation: *waves of wheat in the wind.* **b.** A curve or succession of curves, as in the hair. **c.** A curved shape, outline, or pattern. **4.** A movement up and down or back and forth: *a wave of the hand.* **5.a.** A surge or rush, as of sensation: *a wave of nausea; a wave of indignation.* **b.** A sudden great rise, as in activity or intensity: *a wave of panic selling on the stock market.* **c.** A rising trend that involves large numbers of individuals: *a wave of conservatism.* **d.** One of a succession of mass movements: *the first wave of settlers.* **e.** A maneuver in which fans at a sports event simulate an ocean wave by rising quickly in sequence with arms upraised and then quickly sitting down again in a continuous rolling motion. **6.** A widespread, persistent meteorological condition, especially of temperature: *a heat wave.* **7.** *Physics.* **a.** A disturbance traveling through a medium by which energy is transferred from one particle of the medium to another without causing any permanent displacement of the medium itself. **b.** A graphic representation of the variation of such a disturbance with time. **c.** A single cycle of such a disturbance. [Middle English *waven,* from Old English *wafian.* See **webh-** in Appendix.] **—wav′er** *n.*

Wave (wāv) *n.* A member of the women's reserve of the U.S. Navy, organized during World War II, but now no longer a separate branch. [*W(omen) A(ccepted for) V(olunteer) E(mergency Service).*]

wave·band (wāv′bănd′) *n.* A range of frequencies, especially radio frequencies, such as those assigned to communication transmissions.

wave equation *n.* **1.** A partial differential equation used to represent wave motion. **2.** The fundamental equation of wave mechanics.

wave·form (wāv′fôrm′) *n.* The mathematical representation of a wave, especially a graph obtained by plotting a characteristic of the wave against time.

wave front *n.* The continuous line or surface including all the points in space reached by a wave or vibration at the same instant as it travels through a medium.

wave function *n.* A mathematical function used in quantum mechanics to describe the propagation of the wave associated with any particle or group of particles.

wave·guide (wāv′gīd′) *n.* A system of material boundaries in the form of a solid dielectric rod or dielectric-filled tubular conductor capable of guiding high-frequency electromagnetic waves.

wave·length (wāv′lĕngkth′, -lĕngth′) *n. Abbr.* **WL.** The distance between one peak or crest of a wave of light, heat, or other energy and the next corresponding peak or crest. **—*idiom.* on the same wavelength.** *Informal.* In complete accord; in harmony: *"a fluid . . . production in which author, director, designer and cast seem to be working on the same wavelength"* (James Lardner).

wave·let (wāv′lĭt) *n.* A small wave; a ripple.

Wa·vell (wā′vəl), **Archibald Percival.** First Earl Wavell. 1883–1950. British field marshal who routed Italian forces in North Africa (1940–1941) before being defeated by the Germans.

wave mechanics *n. (used with a sing. or pl. verb).* A theory that ascribes characteristics of waves to subatomic particles and attempts to interpret physical phenomena on this basis.

wave number *n.* The number of waves per unit distance in a series of waves of a given wavelength; the reciprocal of the wavelength.

wave-par·ti·cle duality (wāv′pär′tĭ-kəl) *n.* The exhibition of both wavelike and particlelike properties by a single entity, as of both diffraction and linear propagation by light.

wa·ver (wā′vər) *intr.v.* **-vered, -ver·ing, -vers. 1.** To move unsteadily back and forth. See Synonyms at **swing. 2.a.** To exhibit irresolution or indecision; vacillate: *wavered over buying a house.* See Synonyms at **hesitate. b.** To become unsteady or unsure; falter: *His resolve began to waver.* **3.** To tremble or quaver in sound, as of the voice or a musical note. **4.** To flicker or glimmer, as light. **—waver** *n.* The act of wavering. [Middle English *waveren.* See **webh-** in Appendix.] **—wa′ver·er** *n.* **—wa′ver·ing·ly** *adv.*

WAVES *abbr.* Women Accepted for Volunteer Emergency Service.

wave train *n. Physics.* A succession of similar wave pulses.

wave trap *n.* An electronic filtering device designed to exclude unwanted signals or interference from a receiver.

wav·y (wā′vē) *adj.* **-i·er, -i·est. 1.** Abounding or rising in waves: *a wavy sea.* **2.** Marked by or moving in a wavelike form or motion; sinuous. **3.** Having curls, curves, or undulations: *wavy hair.* **4.** Characteristic or suggestive of waves. **5.** Wavering; unstable. **—wav′i·ly** *adv.* **—wav′i·ness** *n.*

waw (väv, vôv) *n.* Variant of **vav.**

wa-wa (wä′wä′) *n. Music.* Variant of **wah-wah.**

wax¹ (wăks) *n.* **1.a.** Any of various natural, oily or greasy heat-sensitive substances, consisting of hydrocarbons or esters of fatty acids that are insoluble in water but soluble in most organic solvents. **b.** Beeswax. **c.** Cerumen. **2.a.** A solid plastic or pliable liquid substance, such as ozocerite or paraffin, originating from petroleum and found in rock layers and used in paper coating, as insulation, in crayons, and often in medicinal preparations. **b.** A preparation containing wax used for polishing floors and other surfaces. **3.** A resinous mixture used by shoemakers to rub on thread. **4.** A phonograph record. **5.** Something suggestive of wax in being impressionable or readily molded. **—wax** *adj.* Made of wax: *a wax candle.* **—wax** *tr.v.* **waxed, wax·ing, wax·es. 1.** To coat, treat, or polish with wax. **2.** *Informal.* To make a phonograph record of. [Middle English, from Old English *weax.*]

wax² (wăks) *intr.v.* **waxed, wax·ing, wax·es. 1.** To increase gradually in size, number, strength, or intensity. **2.** To show a progressively larger illuminated area, as the moon does in passing from new to full. **3.** To grow or become as specified: *"could afford . . . to wax sentimental over their heritage"* (John Simon). [Middle English *waxen,* from Old English *weaxan.* See **aug-** in Appendix.]

♦ **wax bean** *n.* A variety of string bean having yellow pods. Also called ♦ *butter bean.*

wax·ber·ry (wăks′bĕr′ē) *n.* The waxy fruit of the wax myrtle or the snowberry.

wax·bill (wăks′bĭl′) *n.* Any of various tropical Old World birds of the genus *Estrilda* and related genera, having a short, often brightly colored waxy beak.

waxed paper (wăkst) *n.* Wax paper.

wax·en (wăk′sən) *adj.* **1.** Made of or covered with wax. **2.** Pale or smooth as wax: *waxen skin.* **3.** Weak, pliable, or impressionable: *waxen minds.*

wax·er (wăk′sər) *n.* One that polishes with or applies wax.

wax insect *n.* Any of various scale insects that secrete a waxy substance, especially a Chinese species *(Ericerus pe-la)* bred commercially for the production of candles.

wax moth *n.* See **bee moth.**

wax museum *n.* A place where life-size wax figures, usually of famous people, are exhibited.

wax myrtle *n.* An evergreen shrub *(Myrica cerifera)* of the southeast United States, having usually serrate leaves and small, berrylike fruit with a waxy coating.

wax palm *n.* Any of several palm trees that yield wax, as *Copernica prunifera,* the source of carnauba wax, or *Ceroxylon alpinum* of South America.

wax paper *n.* Paper that has been made moistureproof by treatment with wax, used especially in cooking and for wrapping food for storage.

wax plant *n.* A southeast Asian tropical vine *(Hoya carnosa)* having waxy white or pinkish flowers.

wax vine *n.* See **hoya.**

wax·wing (wăks′wĭng′) *n.* Any of several birds of the genus *Bombycilla,* having crested heads, grayish-brown plumage, and waxy red tips on the wing feathers.

wax·work (wăks′wûrk′) *n.* **1.** The art of modeling in wax. **2.** A figure made of wax, especially a life-size wax effigy of a famous person. **3. waxworks.** *(used with a sing. or pl. verb).* An exhibition of wax figures in a museum.

wax·y (wăk′sē) *adj.* **-i·er, -i·est. 1.** Resembling wax, especially: **a.** Pale. **b.** Smooth and lustrous. **c.** Pliable or impressionable. **2.** Consisting of, abounding in, or covered with wax. **3.** *Pathology.* Containing amyloid deposits, as an organ.

way (wā) *n.* **1.a.** A road, path, or highway affording passage from one place to another. **b.** An opening affording passage: *This door is the only way into the attic.* **2.a.** Space to proceed: *cleared the way for the parade.* **b.** Opportunity to advance: *opened the way to peace.* **3.** A course that is or may be used in going from one place to another: *tried to find the shortest way home.* **4.** Progress or travel along a certain route or in a specific direction: *on his way north.* **5.** A course of conduct or action: *tried to take the easy way out.* **6.** A manner or method of doing: *several ways of solving this problem; had no way to reach her.* **7.** A usual or habitual manner or mode of being, living, or acting: *the American way of life.* **8.** An individual or personal manner of behaving, acting, or doing: *Have it your own way.* **9.** Also **ways** (wāz) *(used with a sing. verb). Informal.* Distance: *The travelers have come a long way. That village is a good ways off.* **10.a.** A specific direction: *He glanced my way.* **b.** A participant. Often used in combination: *a three-way conversation.* **11.a.** An aspect, a particular, or a feature: *resembles his father in many ways; in no way comparable.* **b.** Nature or category: *not much in the way of a plot.* **12.** Freedom to do as one wishes: *if I had my way.* **13.** An aptitude or a facility: *She certainly does have a way with words.* **14.** A state or condition: *He is in a bad way financially.* **15.** Vicinity: *Drop in when you're out our way.* **16.** Often **ways.** A longitudinal strip on a surface that serves to guide a moving machine part. **17. ways** *(used with a sing. or pl. verb). Nautical.* The timbered structure on which a ship is built and from which it slides when launched. **—way** *adv. Informal.* **1.** By a great distance or to a great degree; far: *way off base; way over budget.* **2.** From this place; away: *Go way.* ***—idioms.*** **by way of. 1.** Through; via: *flew to the Far East by way of the polar route.* **2.** As a means of: *made no comment by way of apology.* **go out of one's** (or **the) way.** To inconvenience oneself in doing something beyond what is required. **in a way. 1.** To a certain extent; with reservations: *I like the new styles, in a way.* **2.** From one point of view: *In a way, you're right.* **in the way.** In a position to obstruct, hinder, or interfere. **on one's** (or **the) way.** In the process of coming, going, or traveling: *She is on her way out the door. Winter is on the way.* **on the way.** On the route of a journey: *met him on the way to town; ran into them on the way.* **out of the way. 1.** In such a position as not to obstruct, hinder, or interfere. **2.** Taken care of; disposed of: *some details to get out of the way first.* **3.** In a remote location. **4.** Of an unusual character; remarkable. **5.** Improper; amiss: *said nothing out of the way.* [Middle English, from Old English *weg.* See **wegh-** in Appendix.]

SYNONYMS: *way, route, course, passage, pass, artery.* These nouns refer to paths leading from one place or point to another. *Way* is the least specific: *"Many ways meet in one town"* (Shakespeare). *We made our way on foot. Show me the way home. Route* refers to a planned, well-established, or regularly traveled way: *"They know the routes . . . of the trappers; where to waylay them"* (Washington Irving). *"Their one purpose of speed over the great ocean routes was achieved by perfect balance of spars and sails to the curving lines of the smooth black hull"* (Samuel Eliot Morison). *Course* suggests the path or channel taken by something, such as a river or a satellite, that moves: *"the stars in their courses"* (Judges 5:20); *"earth's diurnal course"* (William Wordsworth). *Passage* denotes a traversal over, across, or through something: *The yacht continued its passage with favorable winds. The passage between the buildings is dark and cramped. Pass* usually refers to a way affording passage around, over, or through a barrier: *"They had reached one of those very narrow passes between two tall stones"* (George Eliot). An *artery* is a main route for the circulation of traffic into which local routes flow: *The city council voted to close the central artery for extensive repairs.* See also Synonyms at **method.**

USAGE NOTE: In American English *ways* is often used as an equivalent of *way* in phrases such as *a long ways to go.* The usage is not incorrect but is widely regarded as informal.

way·bill (wā′bĭl′) *n. Abbr.* **w.b., W.B.** A document giving details and instructions relating to a shipment of goods.

Way·cross (wā′krôs′, -krŏs′). A city of southeast Georgia southwest of Savannah. Population, 19,371.

way·far·er (wā′fâr′ər) *n.* One who travels, especially on foot. [Middle English *weifarere* : *wei,* way; see WAY + *faren,* to go on a journey (from Old English *faran;* see **per-**[2] in Appendix).]

way·far·ing (wā′fâr′ĭng) *n.* Traveling, especially on foot. [From Middle English *waifaringe,* journeying, from Old English *wegfarende* : *weg,* way; see WAY + *farende,* present participle of *faran,* to go on a journey; see **per-**[2] in Appendix.] **—way′far′ing** *adj.*

wayfaring tree *n.* A deciduous Eurasian shrub *(Viburnum lantana)* having cymes of white flowers and berries that turn from red to black. [Short for *wayfaring man's tree.*]

way·lay (wā′lā′) *tr.v.* **-laid** (-lād′), **-lay·ing, -lays. 1.** To lie in wait for and attack from ambush. See Synonyms at **ambush. 2.** To accost or intercept unexpectedly. **—way′lay′er** *n.*

Wayne (wān). **1.** A city of southeast Michigan, a manufacturing suburb of Detroit. Population, 21,159. **2.** A town of northern New Jersey west of Paterson. Population, 46,474.

Wayne, Anthony. Called "Mad Anthony." 1745–1796. American Revolutionary general who was involved in numerous campaigns, including the Battles of Brandywine (1777) and Monmouth (1778). His seizure of Stony Point, a British defense post (1779), displayed the tactical audacity that gave rise to his nickname.

Wayne, James Moore. 1790–1867. American jurist who served as an associate justice of the U.S. Supreme Court (1835–1867).

Wayne, John. Known as "Duke." 1907–1979. American film actor who played tough heroes in Westerns such as *Stagecoach* (1939), *Red River* (1948), and *True Grit* (1969), for which he won an Academy Award.

John Wayne

way-out (wā′out′) *adj. Slang.* Very unconventional, unusual, or strange.

way·point (wā′point′) *n.* A point between major points on a route, as along a track.

ways (wāz) *n. (used with a sing. verb). Informal.* Variant of **way** (sense 9). See Usage Note at **way.**

–ways *suff.* In a specified way, manner, direction, or position: *sideways.* [Middle English, from *weies, wais,* in such a way, from Old English *weges* : *weg,* way; see WAY + *-es,* gen. sing. suff.; see –s[3].]

ways and means *pl.n.* **1.** Methods and resources available to accomplish an end, especially to meet expenses. **2.** Methods and means, especially legislation, for raising revenue needed by a government.

way·side (wā′sīd′) *n.* The side or edge of a road, way, path, or highway. **—wayside** *adj.* Situated at or near the side of a road, way, path, or highway: *a wayside inn.* ***—idioms.*** **fall by the wayside.** To fail to continue; give up. **go by the wayside.** To be set aside or discarded because of other considerations.

way station *n.* A station between principal stations on a route, as of a railroad.

way·ward (wā′wərd) *adj.* **1.** Given to or marked by willful, often perverse deviation from what is desired, expected, or required in order to gratify one's own impulses or inclinations. See Synonyms at **contrary, unruly. 2.** Swayed or prompted by caprice; unpredictable. [Middle English, short for *awaiward,* turned away, perverse : *awai,* away; see AWAY + *-ward,* -ward.] **—way′ward·ly** *adv.* **—way′ward·ness** *n.*

way·worn (wā′wôrn′, -wōrn′) *adj.* Wearied by traveling.

Wa·zir·i·stan (wə-zîr′ĭ-stăn′, -stän′). A mountainous region of northwest Pakistan on the Afghanistan border, divided into **North Waziristan** and **South Waziristan.**

wa·zoo (wä-zo͞o′) *n. Vulgar Slang.* The anus. [Perhaps alteration of KAZOO.]

Wb *abbr. Physics.* Weber.

w.b. *abbr.* **1.** Water ballast. **2.** Also **W.B.** Waybill. **3.** Westbound.

W.B. *abbr.* Weather bureau.

WBC *abbr.* White blood cell.

WbN *abbr.* West by north.

WbS *abbr.* West by south.

W.C. *abbr.* **1.** Water closet. **2.** Without charge.

WCTU also **W.C.T.U.** *abbr.* Woman's Christian Temperance Union.

WD also **W.D.** *abbr.* War Department.

wd. *abbr.* **1.** Wood. **2.** Word.

we (wē) *pron.* **1.** Used by the speaker or writer to indicate the speaker or writer along with another or others as the subject: *We made it to the lecture hall on time. We are planning a trip to Arizona this winter.* **2.** Used instead of *I,* especially by a sovereign or by a writer wishing to maintain an impersonal tone. **3.** Used to refer to people in general, including the speaker or writer: *"How can we enter the professions and yet remain civilized human beings?"* (Virginia Woolf). **4.** Used instead of *you* in direct address, especially to imply a patronizing camaraderie with the addressee: *How are we feeling today?* [Middle English, from Old English *wē.* See **we-** in Appendix.]

USAGE NOTE: When the pronoun is followed by an appositive noun phrase, the form *us* is frequently encountered where grammatical correctness would require *we,* as in *Us owners* (properly *We owners) will have something to say about the contract.* Less

ă pat	oi boy
ā pay	ou out
âr care	o͝o took
ä father	o͞o boot
ĕ pet	ŭ cut
ē be	ûr urge
ĭ pit	th thin
ī pie	*th* this
îr pier	hw which
ŏ pot	zh vision
ō toe	ə about, item
ô paw	♦ regionalism

Stress marks: ′ (primary); ′ (secondary), as in **dictionary** (dĭk′shə-nĕr′ē)

frequently, *we* is substituted for *us,* as in *For we students, it's a no-win situation.* Both usages should be avoided. See Usage Notes at **be, I**[1].

weak (wēk) *adj.* **weak·er, weak·est.** **1.** Lacking physical strength, energy, or vigor; feeble. **2.** Likely to fail under pressure, stress, or strain; lacking resistance: *a weak link in a chain.* **3.** Lacking firmness of character or strength of will. **4.** Lacking the proper strength or amount of ingredients: *weak coffee.* **5.** Lacking the ability to function normally or fully: *a weak heart.* **6.** Lacking aptitude or skill: *a weak student; weak in math.* **7.** Lacking or resulting from a lack of intelligence. **8.** Lacking persuasiveness; unconvincing: *a weak argument.* **9.** Lacking authority or the power to govern. **10.** Lacking potency or intensity: *weak sunlight.* **11.** *Linguistics.* **a.** Of, relating to, or being those verbs in Germanic languages that form a past tense and past participle by means of a dental suffix, as *start, started; have, had; bring, brought.* **b.** Of, relating to, or being the inflection of nouns or adjectives in Germanic languages with a declensional suffix that historically contained an *n.* **12.** Unstressed or unaccented in pronunciation or poetic meter. Used of a word or syllable. **13.** Designating a verse ending in which the metrical stress falls on a word or syllable that is unstressed in normal speech, such as a preposition. **14.** Tending downward in price: *a weak market for oil stocks.* [Middle English *weike,* from Old Norse *veikr,* pliant. See **weik-**[2] in Appendix.]

weasel

SYNONYMS: *weak, feeble, frail, fragile, infirm, decrepit, debilitated.* These adjectives mean lacking or showing a lack of strength. *Weak,* the most widely applicable, implies lack of physical, mental, or spiritual strength or deficiency of will or purpose: *"These poor wretches . . . were so weak they could hardly sit to their oars"* (Daniel Defoe). *"Like all weak men he laid an exaggerated stress on not changing one's mind"* (W. Somerset Maugham). *Feeble* suggests pathetic or grievous physical or mental weakness or hopeless inadequacy: *a feeble patient; a feeble intellect; a feeble effort. "We, who were the tall pine of the forest, have become a feeble plant and need your protection"* (Red Jacket). *Frail* implies delicacy, as of constitution, or lack of ability to endure or withstand: *"an aged thrush, frail, gaunt, and small,/In blast-beruffled plume"* (Thomas Hardy). *"Frail is our happiness, if this be so"* (John Milton). What is *fragile* is easily broken, damaged, or destroyed: *"a fragile dewdrop"* (John Keats). *"This city is for the King, whose body is fragile, a very unhealthy city"* (Lord Dunsany). *Infirm* implies enfeeblement: *"a poor, infirm, weak, and despis'd old man"* (Shakespeare). *Decrepit* describes what is worn out or broken down by hard use or the passage of time: *"childhood, manhood, and decrepit age"* (Francis Quarles). *Debilitated* suggests a gradual impairment of energy or strength: *Her already debilitated constitution is being further weakened by overwork and smoking.*

weathercock
c. 1770 American copper weathercock by Thomas Drowne (1715–1796) from the spire of Dr. Bentley's East Church in Salem, Massachusetts

weak·en (wē′kən) *tr. & intr.v.* **-ened, -en·ing, -ens.** To make or become weak or weaker. **—weak′en·er** *n.*

weak·fish (wēk′fĭsh′) *n., pl.* **weakfish** or **-fish·es.** A marine food and game fish *(Cynoscion regalis)* of North American Atlantic waters. Also called *squeteague.* [Obsolete Dutch *weekvis* : *week,* soft (from Middle Dutch *weec;* see **weik-**[2] in Appendix) + Dutch *vis,* fish (from Middle Dutch).]

weak interaction *n.* A fundamental interaction between elementary particles that is several orders of magnitude weaker than the electromagnetic interaction and is responsible for some particle decay, nuclear beta decay, and neutrino absorption and emission. Also called *weak force.*

weak-kneed (wēk′nēd′) *adj.* Lacking strength of character or purpose.

weak·ling (wēk′lĭng) *n.* One of weak constitution or character.

weak·ly (wēk′lē) *adj.* **-li·er, -li·est.** Delicate in constitution; frail or sickly. **—weakly** *adv.* **1.** With little physical strength or force. **2.** With little strength of character. **—weak′li·ness** *n.*

weak-mind·ed (wēk′mīn′dĭd) *adj.* **1.** Having or exhibiting a lack of judgment or conviction. **2.** Foolish; silly. **3.** *Offensive.* Of less than normal intellect. **—weak′-mind′ed·ness** *n.*

weak·ness (wēk′nĭs) *n.* **1.** The condition or quality of being weak. **2.** A personal defect or failing. See Synonyms at **fault. 3.a.** A special fondness or inclination: *has a weakness for fast cars.* **b.** Something of which one is excessively fond or desirous: *Ice cream is his weakness.*

weak·on (wē′kŏn′) *n.* Either of two bosons, the W particle or the Z particle, that are quanta of the weak interaction. See table at **subatomic particle.**

weak sister *n. Slang.* **1.** A weak or undependable member of a group. **2.** A person regarded as timid or indecisive.

weal[1] (wēl) *n.* **1.** Prosperity; happiness: *in weal and woe.* **2.** The welfare of the community; the general good: *the public weal.* [Middle English *wele,* from Old English *wela.* See **wel-**[1] in Appendix.]

weal[2] (wēl) *n.* A ridge on the flesh raised by a blow; a welt. [Alteration (influenced by WHEAL) of WALE.]

weald (wēld) *n. Chiefly British.* **1.** A woodland. **2.** An area of open rolling upland. [From *Weald,* a once-forested area in southeast England, from Old English *wald, weald,* forest.]

wealth (wĕlth) *n.* **1.a.** An abundance of valuable material possessions or resources; riches. **b.** The state of being rich; affluence. **2.** All goods and resources having value in terms of exchange or use. **3.** A great amount; a profusion: *a wealth of advice.* [Middle English *welthe,* from *wele,* from Old English *wela.* See **wel-**[1] in Appendix.]

wealth·y (wĕl′thē) *adj.* **-i·er, -i·est.** **1.** Having wealth; rich. See Synonyms at **rich. 2.** Marked by abundance: *a wealthy land.* **3.** Well supplied: *wealthy in compassion.* **—wealth′i·ly** *adv.* **—wealth′i·ness** *n.*

wean (wēn) *tr.v.* **weaned, wean·ing, weans.** **1.** To accustom (the young of a mammal) to take nourishment other than by suckling. **2.** To detach from that to which one is strongly habituated or devoted: *She weaned herself from cigarettes.* **3.** *Usage Problem.* To be raised on. [Middle English *wenen,* from Old English *wenian.* See **wen-**[1] in Appendix.]

USAGE NOTE: In recent years *weaned on* has come to be widely used in the sense "raised on," as in *Moviegoers weaned on the* Star Trek *TV series will doubtless find the film to their liking.* A few critics have objected to this usage on the grounds that *wean* refers literally to a detachment from a source of nourishment. But the process of weaning involves a substitution of some other form of nourishment for mother's milk; thus it is sometimes said that a child is *weaned onto* or *on sugar water.* Hence a sentence like *Paul was weaned on Dixieland* may suggest metaphorically that Paul's exposure to Dixieland began from the time he stopped nursing, that is, from a very early age.

wean·ling (wēn′lĭng) *n.* A newly weaned child or young animal. **—weanling** *adj.* Newly weaned.

weap·on (wĕp′ən) *n. Abbr.* **wpn.** **1.** An instrument of attack or defense in combat, as a gun, missile, or sword. **2.** *Zoology.* A part or an organ, such as a claw or stinger, used by an animal in attack or defense. **3.** A means used to defend against or defeat another: *Logic was her weapon.* **—weapon** *tr.v.* **-oned, -on·ing, -ons.** To supply with weapons or a weapon; arm. [Middle English *wepen,* from Old English *wǣpen.*]

weap·on·eer (wĕp′ə-nîr′) *n.* **1.** One who prepares a nuclear weapon for release. **2.** One who designs weapons, especially nuclear weapons. **—weap′on·eer′ing** *n.*

weap·on·ry (wĕp′ən-rē) *n.* **1.** Weapons considered as a group. **2.** The design and production of weapons.

weap·ons system (wĕp′ənz) *n.* Weapons together with the materiel necessary for their use against an enemy.

♦**wear** (wâr) *v.* **wore** (wôr, wōr), **worn** (wôrn, wōrn), **wear·ing, wears.** —*tr.* **1.** To carry or have on the person as covering, adornment, or protection: *wearing a jacket; must wear a seat belt.* **2.** To carry or have habitually on the person, especially as an aid: *wears glasses.* **3.** To display in one's appearance: *always wears a smile.* **4.** To bear, carry, or maintain in a particular manner: *wears her hair long.* **5.** To fly or display (colors). Used of a ship, jockey, or knight. **6.** To damage, diminish, erode, or consume by long or hard use, attrition, or exposure. Often used with *away, down,* or *off: rocks worn away by the sea; shoes worn down at the heels.* **7.** To produce by constant use, attrition, or exposure: *eventually wore hollows in the stone steps.* **8.** To bring to a specified condition by long use or attrition: *wore the clothes to rags; pebbles worn smooth.* **9.** To fatigue, weary, or exhaust: *Your incessant criticism has worn my patience.* **10.** *Nautical.* To make (a sailing ship) come about with the wind aft. —*intr.* **1.a.** To last under continual or hard use: *a fabric that will wear.* **b.** To last through the passage of time: *a friendship that wears well.* **2.** To break down or diminish through use or attrition: *The rear tires began to wear.* **3.** To pass gradually or tediously: *The hours wore on.* **4.** *Nautical.* To come about with stern to windward. **—wear** *n.* **1.** The act of wearing or the state of being worn; use: *The coat has had heavy wear.* **2.** Clothing, especially of a particular kind or for a particular use. Often used in combination: *rainwear; footwear.* **3.** Gradual impairment or diminution resulting from use or attrition. **4.** The ability to withstand impairment from use or attrition: *The engine has plenty of wear left.* **—*phrasal verbs.*** **wear down.** To break down or exhaust by relentless pressure or resistance. **wear off.** To diminish gradually in effect: *The drug wore off.* **wear out.** **1.** To make or become unusable through long or heavy use. **2.** To use up or consume gradually. **3.** To exhaust; tire. **4.** *Chiefly Southern U.S.* To punish by spanking: *I'm going to wear you out!* **—*idioms.*** **wear the pants** (or **trousers**). *Informal.* To exercise controlling authority in a household. **wear thin.** **1.** To be weakened or eroded gradually: *Her patience is wearing thin.* **2.** To become less convincing, acceptable, or popular, as through repeated use: *excuses that are wearing thin.* [Middle English *weren,* from Old English *werian.* See **wes-**[2] in Appendix.] **—wear′er** *n.*

wear·a·bil·i·ty (wâr′ə-bĭl′ĭ-tē) *n.* The ability of a garment to withstand prolonged wear.

wear·a·ble (wâr′ə-bəl) *adj.* **1.** Suitable for wear: *wearable shoes for the summer.* **2.** Suitable for easy wear: *wearable evening clothes.* **—wearable** *n.* Something that can be worn, especially a garment. Often used in the plural.

wear and tear (târ) *n.* Loss, damage, or depreciation resulting from ordinary use and exposure.

wea·ri·ful (wîr′ē-fəl) *adj.* **1.** Causing weariness; tedious. **2.** Fatigued; exhausted. **—wea′ri·ful·ly** *adv.*

wea·ri·less (wîr′ē-lĭs) *adj.* Displaying or feeling no fatigue;

ă pat	oi boy
ā pay	ou out
âr care	ŏŏ took
ä father	ōō boot
ĕ pet	ŭ cut
ē be	ûr urge
ĭ pit	th thin
ī pie	*th* this
îr pier	hw which
ŏ pot	zh vision
ō toe	ə about, item
ô paw	♦ regionalism

Stress marks: ′ (primary); ′ (secondary), as in **dictionary** (dĭk′shə-nĕr′ē)

tireless. See Synonyms at **tireless.** **—wea′ri·less·ly** *adv.* **—wea′ri·less·ness** *n.*

wear·ing¹ (wâr′ĭng) *adj.* Intended to be worn: *wearing apparel.*

wear·ing² (wâr′ĭng) *adj.* Causing fatigue; tiring: *a wearing visit.*

wea·ri·some (wîr′ē-səm) *adj.* Causing physical or mental fatigue; tedious or tiresome. **—wea′ri·some·ly** *adv.* **—wea′ri·some·ness** *n.*

wea·ry (wîr′ē) *adj.* **-ri·er, -ri·est. 1.** Physically or mentally fatigued. **2.** Expressive of or prompted by fatigue: *a weary smile.* **3.** Having one's interest, forbearance, or indulgence worn out: *weary of delays.* **4.** Causing fatigue; tiresome: *a weary wait.* **—weary** *tr. & intr.v.* **wea·ried** (wîr′ēd), **wea·ry·ing, wea·ries** (wîr′ēz). To make or become weary. See Synonyms at **tire¹.** [Middle English *weri,* from Old English *wērig.*] **—wea′ri·ly** *adv.* **—wea′ri·ness** *n.*

wea·sand (wē′zənd) *n.* The gullet or throat. [Middle English *wesand,* perhaps from Old English **wǣsend,* variant of *wāsand.*]

wea·sel (wē′zəl) *n.* **1.** Any of various carnivorous mammals of the genus *Mustela,* having a long slender body, a long tail, short legs, and brownish fur that in many species turns white in winter. **2.** A person regarded as sneaky or treacherous. **—weasel** *intr.v.* **-seled, -sel·ing, -sels** also **-selled, -sel·ling, -sels.** To be evasive; equivocate. ***—phrasal verb.*** **weasel out.** *Informal.* To back out of a situation or commitment in a sneaky or cowardly manner. [Middle English *wesele,* from Old English *wesle.*]

weasel word *n.* A word of an equivocal nature used to deprive a statement of its force or to evade a direct commitment. [From the weasel's habit of sucking the contents out of an egg without breaking the shell.]

weath·er (wĕth′ər) *n.* **1.** The state of the atmosphere at a given time and place, with respect to variables such as temperature, moisture, wind velocity, and barometric pressure. **2.a.** Adverse or destructive atmospheric conditions, such as high winds or heavy rain: *encountered weather five miles out to sea.* **b.** The unpleasant or destructive effects of such atmospheric conditions: *protected the house from the weather.* **3. weathers.** Changes of fortune: *had known him in many weathers.* **—weather** *v.* **-ered, -er·ing, -ers.** *—tr.* **1.** To expose to the action of the elements, as for drying, seasoning, or coloring. **2.** To discolor, disintegrate, wear, or otherwise affect adversely by exposure. **3.** To come through (something) safely; survive: *weather a crisis.* **4.** To slope (a roof, for example) so as to shed water. **5.** *Nautical.* To pass to the windward of despite bad weather. *—intr.* **1.** To show the effects, such as discoloration, of exposure to the elements: *The walls of the barn had weathered.* **2.** To withstand the effects of weather: *a house paint that weathers well.* **—weather** *adj.* **1.** *Nautical.* Of or relating to the windward side of a ship; windward. **2.** Relating to or used in weather forecasting: *a weather plane.* ***—idioms.*** **make heavy weather of.** To exaggerate the difficulty of something to be done. **under the weather. 1.** Somewhat indisposed; slightly ill. **2.** *Informal.* **a.** Intoxicated; drunk. **b.** Suffering from a hangover; crapulous. [Middle English *weder, wether,* from Old English *weder.* See **wē-** in Appendix.]

weather balloon *n.* A balloon used to carry instruments aloft to gather meteorological data in the atmosphere.

weath·er-beat·en (wĕth′ər-bēt′n) *adj.* **1.** Worn by exposure to the weather. **2.** Tanned and coarsened from being outdoors: *a weather-beaten face.*

weath·er·board (wĕth′ər-bôrd′, -bōrd′) *n.* See **clapboard.**

weath·er·board·ing (wĕth′ər-bôr′dĭng, -bōr′-) *n.* Clapboards considered as a group; siding.

weath·er-bound (wĕth′ər-bound′) *adj.* Delayed, halted, or kept indoors by bad weather.

weather bureau *n. Abbr.* **W.B.** An agency responsible for the gathering and interpreting of meteorological data for weather study and forecasts.

weath·er·cast (wĕth′ər-kăst′) *n.* A broadcast of weather conditions. [WEATHER + (FORE)CAST.] **—weath′er·cast′er** *n.*

weath·er·cock (wĕth′ər-kŏk′) *n.* **1.** A weathervane, especially one in the form of a rooster. **2.** One that is very changeable or fickle. **—weathercock** *intr.v.* **-cocked, -cock·ing, -cocks.** To have a tendency to veer in the direction of the wind. Used of an aircraft or a missile.

weather deck *n. Nautical.* A ship's deck that is open to the sky.

weath·ered (wĕth′ərd) *adj.* **1.** Worn, stained, or warped by or as if by exposure to weather; seasoned: *a house of weathered shingles.* **2.** *Architecture.* Sloped to shed water: *a weathered masonry joint.* ***—phrasal verb.*** **weather in.** To experience or cause to experience weather conditions that prevent movement: *The squadron is weathered in because of dense fog. Such a storm will weather the fleet in.*

weather eye *n.* An eye quick to recognize signs of changes in the weather. ***—idiom.*** **keep a** (or **one's**) **weather eye open.** To keep watch; stay alert.

weath·er·glass (wĕth′ər-glăs′) *n.* An instrument, such as a barometer, that indicates changes in atmospheric conditions.

weath·er·ing (wĕth′ər-ĭng) *n.* Any of the chemical or mechanical processes by which rocks exposed to the weather undergo changes in character and break down.

weath·er·ize (wĕth′ə-rīz′) *tr.v.* **-ized, -iz·ing, -iz·es.** To protect (a structure) against cold weather, as with insulation.

weath·er·ly (wĕth′ər-lē) *adj. Nautical.* Able to sail close to the wind with little drift to leeward. **—weath′er·li·ness** *n.*

weather map *n.* A map or chart depicting the meteorological conditions over a specific geographic area at a specific time.

weath·er·proof (wĕth′ər-pro͞of′) *adj.* Capable of withstanding exposure to weather without damage. **—weatherproof** *tr.v.* **-proofed, -proof·ing, -proofs.** To make weatherproof. **—weath′er·proof′ness** *n.*

weather ship *n. Nautical.* An oceangoing vessel equipped to make meteorological observations.

weather station *n.* A facility or location where meteorological data are gathered, recorded, and released.

weath·er-strip (wĕth′ər-strĭp′) *tr.v.* **-stripped, -strip·ping, -strips.** To fit or equip with weather stripping.

weather strip·ping (strĭp′ĭng) *n.* **1.** A narrow piece of material, such as plastic, rubber, felt, or metal, installed around doors and windows to protect an interior from external extremes in temperature. **2.** This material considered as a unit.

weath·er·vane (wĕth′ər-vān′) *n.* A device for indicating wind direction.

weath·er-wise (wĕth′ər-wīz′) *adj.* Skilled in predicting shifts, as in the weather or public opinion.

weath·er·worn (wĕth′ər-wôrn′, -wōrn′) *adj.* Weatherbeaten.

weave (wēv) *v.* **wove** (wōv), **wo·ven** (wō′vən), **weav·ing, weaves.** *—tr.* **1.a.** To make (cloth) by interlacing the threads of the weft and the warp on a loom. **b.** To interlace (threads, for example) into cloth. **2.** To construct by interlacing or interweaving strips or strands of material: *weave a basket.* **3.a.** To interweave or combine (elements) into a complex whole: *wove the incidents into a story.* **b.** To contrive (something complex or elaborate) in this way: *weave a tale.* **4.** To introduce (another element) into a complex whole; work in: *wove folk tunes into the symphony.* **5.** To spin (a web, for example). **6.** *past tense* **weaved.** To make (a path or way) by winding in and out or from side to side: *weaved our way through the heavy traffic.* *—intr.* **1.a.** To engage in weaving; make cloth. **b.** To work at a loom. **2.** *past tense* **weaved.** To move in and out or sway from side to side. **—weave** *n.* The pattern, method of weaving, or construction of a fabric: *a twill weave; a loose weave.* [Middle English *weven,* from Old English *wefan.* See **webh-** in Appendix.]

weav·er (wē′vər) *n.* **1.** One that weaves: *a weaver of fine rugs.* **2.** A weaverbird.

weav·er·bird (wē′vər-bûrd′) *n.* Any of various chiefly tropical Old World birds of the family Ploceidae, similar to the finches and characterized by the ability to build complex communal nests of intricately woven vegetation. Also called *weaver finch.*

weav·er's hitch (wē′vərz) *n. Nautical.* A sheet bend. Also called *weaver's knot.*

web (wĕb) *n.* **1.a.** A woven fabric, especially one on a loom or just removed from it. **b.** The structural part of cloth. **2.** A latticed or woven structure: *A web of palm branches formed the roof of the hut.* **3.** A structure of delicate, threadlike filaments characteristically spun by spiders or certain insect larvae. **4.** Something intricately contrived, especially something that ensnares or entangles: *caught in a web of lies.* **5.** A complex, interconnected structure or arrangement: *a web of telephone wires.* **6.** A radio or television network. **7.** A membrane or fold of skin connecting the toes, as of certain amphibians, birds, and mammals. **8.** The barbs on each side of the shaft of a bird's feather; a vane. **9.** *Architecture.* The surface between the ribs of a ribbed vault. **10.** A metal sheet or plate connecting the heavier sections, ribs, or flanges of a structural element. **11.** A thin metal plate or strip, as the bit of a key or the blade of a saw. **12.** A large continuous roll of paper, such as newsprint, either in the process of manufacture or as it is fed into a web press. **—web** *tr.v.* **webbed, web·bing, webs. 1.** To provide with a web. **2.** To cover or envelop with a web. **3.** To ensnare in a web. [Middle English, from Old English. See **webh-** in Appendix.]

Webb, Sidney James. First Baron Passfield. 1859–1947. British sociologist and economist who was a founder of the London School of Economics (1895). He and his wife, **Beatrice Potter Webb** (1858–1943), were central members of the Fabian Society and together wrote *The History of Trade Unionism* (1894).

webbed (wĕbd) *adj.* Having or connected by a web.

web·bing (wĕb′ĭng) *n.* **1.** A strong, narrow, closely woven fabric used especially for seat belts and harnesses or in upholstery. **2.** Something forming a web.

web·by (wĕb′ē) *adj.* **-bi·er, -bi·est.** Consisting of, resembling, or having webs or a web.

web·er (wĕb′ər, vā′bər) *n. Abbr.* **Wb.** *Physics.* The SI unit of magnetic flux equal to the magnetic flux that in linking a circuit of one turn produces in it an electromotive force of one volt as it is uniformly reduced to zero within one second. See table at **measurement.** [After Wilhelm Eduard WEBER.]

We·ber (vā′bər), **Ernst Heinrich.** 1795–1878. German physiologist and psychologist who studied sensory response and is considered a founder of experimental psychology.

Weber, Baron **Karl Maria Friedrich Ernst von.** 1786–1826. German composer who is considered the founder of German romantic opera. His works include *Der Freischütz* (1821).

We·ber (vā′bər), **Max¹.** 1864–1920. German sociologist and a

weathering

weathervane

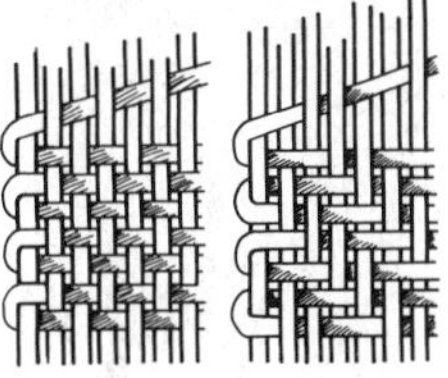

weave
Top: Weaving a tapestry
Bottom: Plain weave design (*left*) and twilled weave design (*right*)

Daniel Webster
20th-century portrait by Adrian Lamb

pioneer of the analytical method of sociology. His works include *The Protestant Ethic and the Spirit of Capitalism* (1904–1905).

We·ber (wĕb′ər), **Max[2].** 1881–1961. Russian-born American painter whose abstract works helped introduce the European avant-garde movements of the early 20th century to American art.

We·ber (vā′bər), **Wilhelm Eduard.** 1804–1891. German physicist noted for his study of terrestrial magnetism.

We·bern (vā′bərn), **Anton Friedrich Wilheim von.** 1883–1945. Austrian composer whose works, characterized by brevity and tonal dissonance, include a concerto for nine instruments (1934).

web·foot (wĕb′fo͝ot′) *n., pl.* **-feet** (-fēt′). **1.** A foot with webbed toes. **2.** An animal with webbed feet.

web-foot·ed (wĕb′fo͝ot′ĭd) *adj.* Having feet with webbed toes.

web member *n.* One of the structural elements connecting the top and bottom flanges of a lattice girder or the outside members of a truss.

web press *n. Printing.* A rotary press that prints on a continuous roll of paper.

web spinner *n.* Any of various social insects of the order Embioptera, having two-winged males and wingless females, both of which produce silk from glands in the front legs.

web·ster (wĕb′stər) *n. Obsolete.* A weaver of cloth. [Middle English, from Old English *webbestre,* feminine of *webba,* weaver, from *webb,* web. See **webh-** in Appendix.]

Web·ster (wĕb′stər), **Daniel.** 1782–1852. American politician. A U.S. representative from New Hampshire (1813–1817) and later a representative (1823–1827) and senator (1827–1841 and 1845–1850) from Massachusetts, he was a noted orator who espoused preservation of the Union.

Webster, John. 1580?–1625? English playwright whose works include *The Duchess of Malfi* (c. 1613).

Webster, Noah. 1758–1843. American lexicographer whose *Spelling Book* (1783) helped standardize American spelling. His major work, *An American Dictionary of the English Language,* was originally published in 1828.

Webster Groves. A city of eastern Missouri, a mainly residential suburb of St. Louis. Population, 23,097.

web-toed (wĕb′tōd′) *adj.* Web-footed.

web·worm (wĕb′wûrm′) *n.* Any of various usually destructive caterpillars that construct webs.

♦ **weck** (wĕk) *n. Buffalo.* See **kümmelweck.** [German dialectal, wedge-shaped roll, from Middle High German *wecke,* from Old High German, wedge.]

wed (wĕd) *v.* **wed·ded, wed** or **wed·ded, wed·ding, weds.** —*tr.* **1.** To take as a spouse; marry. **2.** To perform the marriage ceremony for; join in matrimony. **3.** To unite closely: *a style that weds form and function.* —*intr.* To take a spouse; marry. [Middle English *wedden,* from Old English *weddian.*]

Wed. *abbr.* Wednesday.

we'd (wēd). **1.** We had. **2.** We should. **3.** We would.

wed·ded (wĕd′ĭd) *adj.* **1.** Joined in marriage. **2.** Of or relating to marriage: *wedded bliss.* **3.** Closely attached or devoted: *a person completely wedded to a profession.*

Wed·dell Sea (wĭ-dĕl′, wĕd′l). A sea of the southern Atlantic Ocean off western Antarctica east of the Antarctic Peninsula.

wed·ding (wĕd′ĭng) *n.* **1.a.** The act of marrying. **b.** The ceremony or celebration of a marriage. **2.** The anniversary of a marriage: *a silver wedding.* **3.** The act or an instance of joining closely: *a wedding of ideas.* —*attributive.* Often used to modify another noun: *a wedding gown; wedding guests.*

wedding band *n.* See **wedding ring.**

wedding cake *n.* An elaborately decorated cake usually arranged in tiers and having white icing.

wed·ding-cake (wĕd′ĭng-kāk′) *adj.* Of, relating to, or having a highly ornate architectural style.

wedding ring *n.* **1.** A ring, often a plain gold or platinum band, given by the groom to the bride during the wedding ceremony. **2.** A similar ring often given by the bride to the groom. Also called *wedding band.*

we·del (vād′l) *intr.v.* **-deled, -del·ling, -dels.** *Sports.* To ski on snow by means of wedeln. [Back-formation from WEDELN.]

we·deln (vād′ln) *n. Sports.* A snow skiing style in which the skier executes a series of short, quick, parallel turns by moving the backs of the skis from side to side at a constant speed. [German, from *wedeln,* to wag the tail, fan, from Middle High German *wadelen, wedelen,* from *wadel, wedel,* fan, tuft of hair, from Old High German *wadal, wedil.* See **wet-[1]** in Appendix.]

wedge

♦ **wedge** (wĕj) *n.* **1.** A piece of material, such as metal or wood, thick at one edge and tapered to a thin edge at the other for insertion in a narrow crevice, used for splitting, tightening, securing, or levering. **2.a.** Something shaped like a wedge: *a wedge of pie.* **b.** *Downstate New York.* See **submarine** (sense 2). See Regional Note at **submarine. c.** A wedge-shaped formation, as in football or ground warfare. **3.a.** Something that intrudes and causes division or disruption: *His nomination drove a wedge into party unity.* **b.** Something that forces an opening or a beginning: *a wedge in the war on poverty.* **4.** *Meteorology.* See **ridge** (sense 4). **5.** *Sports.* An iron golf club with a very slanted face, used to lift the ball, as from sand. **6.** One of the triangular characters of cuneiform writing. —**wedge** *v.* **wedged, wedg·ing, wedg·es.** —*tr.* **1.** To split or force apart with or as if with a wedge. **2.** To

weeping willow
Salix babylonica

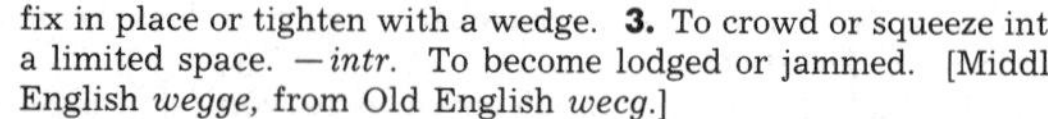

fix in place or tighten with a wedge. **3.** To crowd or squeeze into a limited space. —*intr.* To become lodged or jammed. [Middle English *wegge,* from Old English *wecg.*]

wedg·ie (wĕj′ē) *n.* A shoe having a wedge-shaped heel joined to a half sole so as to form a continuous undersurface. Often used in the plural. [Originally a trademark.]

Wedg·wood (wĕj′wo͝od′). A trademark used for a type of pottery made by Josiah Wedgwood and his successors.

Wedgwood, Josiah. 1730–1795. British potter who improved the materials and processes of pottery. The wares from his factory (founded 1759) are among the finest examples of British earthenware and neoclassical vases.

wed·lock (wĕd′lŏk′) *n.* The state of being married; matrimony. —***idiom.* out of wedlock.** Of parents not legally married to each other: *born out of wedlock.* [Middle English *wedlocke,* from Old English *wedlāc* : *wedd,* pledge + *-lāc,* n. suff. expressing activity.]

Wednes·day (wĕnz′dē, -dā′) *n. Abbr.* **W., Wed.** The fourth day of the week. [Middle English, from Old English *Wōdnesdæg,* Woden's day. See **wet-[1]** in Appendix.]

WORD HISTORY: We say the names of the days of the week constantly, but for most of us they are nonsense syllables. The seven-day system we use is based on the ancient astrological notion that the seven celestial bodies (the sun, the moon, Mars, Mercury, Jupiter, Venus, and Saturn) revolving around stationary Earth influence what happens on it and that each of these celestial bodies controls the first hour of the day named after it. This system was brought into Hellenistic Egypt from Mesopotamia, where astrology had been practiced for millenniums and where seven had always been a propitious number. In A.D. 321 the Emperor Constantine the Great grafted this astrological system onto the Roman calendar, made the first day of this new week a day of rest and worship for all, and imposed the following sequence and names to the days of the week: *Diēs Sōlis,* "Sun's Day"; *Diēs Lūnae,* "Moon's Day"; *Diēs Martis,* "Mars's Day"; *Diēs Mercuriī,* "Mercury's Day"; *Diēs Jovis,* "Jove's Day" or "Jupiter's Day"; *Diēs Veneris,* "Venus's Day"; and *Diēs Saturnī,* "Saturn's Day." This new Roman system was adopted with modifications throughout most of western Europe: in the Germanic languages, such as Old English, the names of four of the Roman gods were converted into those of the corresponding Germanic gods. Therefore in Old English we have the following names (with their Modern English developments): *Sunnandæg,* Sunday; *Mōnandæg,* Monday; *Tīwesdæg,* Tuesday (the god Tiu, like Mars, was a god of war); *Wōdnesdæg,* Wednesday (the god Woden, like Mercury, was quick and eloquent); *Thunresdæg,* Thursday (the god Thunor in Old English or Thor in Old Norse, like Jupiter, was lord of the sky; Old Norse *Thōrsdagr* influenced the English form); *Frīgedæg,* Friday (the goddess Frigg, like Venus, was the goddess of love); and *Sæternesdæg,* Saturday.

wee (wē) *adj.* **we·er, we·est. 1.** Very small; tiny. See Synonyms at **small. 2.** Very early: *the wee hours of the morning.* —**wee** *n. Scots.* A short time; a little bit. [Middle English *wei, we,* a small amount, small, from Old English *wǣge, wēg,* weight. See **wegh-** in Appendix.]

weed[1] (wēd) *n.* **1.a.** A plant considered undesirable, unattractive, or troublesome, especially one growing where it is not wanted, as in a garden. **b.** Rank growth of such plants. **2.** A water plant, especially seaweed. **3.** The leaves or stems of a plant as distinguished from the seeds: *dill weed.* **4.** Something useless, detrimental, or worthless, especially an animal unfit for breeding. **5.** *Slang.* **a.** Tobacco. **b.** A cigarette. **c.** Marijuana. —**weed** *v.* **weed·ed, weed·ing, weeds.** —*tr.* **1.** To clear of weeds. **2.** To remove (weeds). Often used with *out*: *weed out dandelions.* **3.** To eliminate as unsuitable or unwanted. Often used with *out*: *weed out unqualified applicants.* —*intr.* To remove weeds. [Middle English, from Old English *wēod,* herb, grass, weed.]

weed[2] (wēd) *n.* **1.** A token of mourning, as a black band worn on a man's hat or sleeve. **2. weeds.** The black mourning clothes of a widow. **3.** Often **weeds.** An article of clothing; a garment. [Middle English *wede,* garment, from Old English *wǣd.*]

Weed (wēd), **Thurlow.** 1797–1882. American journalist and politician. Editor of the *Albany Evening Journal* (1830–1862), he exerted great political influence as a leader of the Whig Party and later of the Republican Party.

weed·er (wē′dər) *n.* One that removes weeds.

weed·y (wē′dē) *adj.* **-i·er, -i·est. 1.** Full of or consisting of weeds: *a weedy lawn.* **2.** Resembling or characteristic of a weed: *a weedy plant.* **3.** Of a scrawny build; spindly or gawky. —**weed′i·ly** *adv.* —**weed′i·ness** *n.*

Wee·haw·ken (wē-hô′kən). A township of northeast New Jersey on the Hudson River opposite New York City. The duel in which Aaron Burr mortally wounded Alexander Hamilton took place here on July 11, 1804. Population, 13,383.

week (wēk) *n. Abbr.* **w., wk. 1.a.** A period of seven days: *a week of rain.* **b.** A seven-day calendar period, especially one starting with Sunday and continuing through Saturday: *this week.* **2.a.** A week designated by an event or a holiday occurring within it: *commencement week.* **b.** A week dedicated to a particular cause or institution: *Home Safety Week.* **3.** The part of a calendar week devoted to work, school, or business: *working a three-day week.* **4.a.** One week from a specified day: *I'll see you*

Friday week. **b.** One week ago from a specified day: *It was Friday week that we last met.* [Middle English *weke,* from Old English *wicu.* See **weik-**[2] in Appendix.]

week·day (wēk′dā′) *n.* Any day of the week except Sunday, or often except Saturday and Sunday. —*attributive.* Often used to modify another noun: *weekday meetings; a weekday commute.*

week·end (wēk′ĕnd′) *n.* The end of the week, especially the period from Friday evening through Sunday evening. —*attributive.* Often used to modify another noun: *a weekend job; a weekend cottage.* **—weekend** *intr.v.* **-end·ed, -end·ing, -ends.** To spend weekends or a weekend.

week·end·er (wēk′ĕn′dər) *n.* **1.** One who vacations or visits on a weekend. **2.** A small suitcase or bag for carrying clothing and toiletries for a weekend.

week·long (wēk′lông′, -lŏng′) *adj.* Continuing through the week: *a weeklong conference.*

week·ly (wēk′lē) *adv. Abbr.* **wkly. 1.** Once a week. **2.** Every week. **3.** By the week. **—weekly** *adj. Abbr.* **wkly. 1.** Of or relating to a week. **2.** Occurring, appearing, or done once a week or every week. **3.** Computed by the week: *a weekly rate.* **—weekly** *n., pl.* **-lies.** *Abbr.* **wkly.** A publication issued once a week.

week·night (wēk′nīt′) *n.* A night of the week exclusive of Saturday and Sunday.

Weems (wēmz), **Mason Locke.** Known as "Parson Weems." 1759–1825. American cleric known for his fictionalized biography of George Washington (1800), a later edition of which contains the story of Washington chopping down a cherry tree.

ween (wēn) *tr.v.* **weened, ween·ing, weens.** *Archaic.* To think; suppose. [Middle English *wenen,* from Old English *wēnan.* See **wen-**[1] in Appendix.]

ween·ie (wē′nē) *n.* **1.** *Informal.* A wiener. **2.** *Slang.* A person, especially a man, who is regarded as being weak and ineffectual.

wee·ny (wē′nē) *adj.* **-ni·er, -ni·est.** *Informal.* Very small; tiny. [Perhaps blend of WEE and TINY.]

weep (wēp) *v.* **wept** (wĕpt), **weep·ing, weeps.** —*tr.* **1.** To shed (tears) as an expression of emotion: *weep bitter tears of remorse.* **2.** To express grief or anguish for; lament: *wept the death of the child.* **3.** To bring to a specified condition by weeping: *She wept herself into a state of exhaustion.* **4.** To exude or let fall (drops of liquid): *"cuts the jellied milk into tiny, soft curds that weep whey"* (Kit Snedaker). —*intr.* **1.** To express emotion, such as grief or sadness, by shedding tears. See Synonyms at **cry. 2.** To mourn or grieve: *wept for the dead.* **3.** To emit or run with drops of liquid: *a sore that weeps.* **—weep** *n.* A period or fit of weeping. Often used in the plural. [Middle English *wepen,* from Old English *wēpan.*]

weep·er (wē′pər) *n.* **1.** One that weeps. **2.** A hired mourner. **3.** A badge of mourning, such as a black hatband or veil. **4.** A hole or pipe in a wall to allow water to run off. **5.** *Informal.* A highly sentimental artistic, cinematic, or dramatic work.

weep·ie (wē′pē) *n. Informal.* A work, especially a film or play, that is excessively sentimental.

weep·ing (wē′pĭng) *adj.* **1.** Shedding tears; tearful. **2.** Dropping rain: *weeping clouds.* **3.** Having slender, drooping branches.

weeping willow *n.* A widely cultivated deciduous tree *(Salix babylonica)* native to China, having long, slender, drooping branches and narrow leaves.

weep·y (wē′pē) *adj.* **-i·er, -i·est.** Weeping or inclined to weep; tearful.

wee·ver (wē′vər) *n.* Any of several marine fishes of the family Trachinidae, having venomous spines on the gill cover and first dorsal fin. [Old North French *wivre,* serpent, weever. See WYVERN.]

wee·vil (wē′vəl) *n.* Any of numerous beetles, of the superfamily Curculionoidea, especially the snout beetle, that characteristically have a downward-curving snout and are destructive to nuts, fruits, stems, and roots. [Middle English *wevel,* from Old English *wifel.* See **webh-** in Appendix.]

weft (wĕft) *n.* **1. a.** The horizontal threads interlaced through the warp in a woven fabric; woof. **b.** Yarn used for the weft. **2.** Woven fabric. [Middle English, from Old English *wefta.* See **webh-** in Appendix.]

We·ge·ner (vā′gə-nər), **Alfred Lothar.** 1880–1930. German geophysicist, meteorologist, and explorer who proposed the theory of continental drift.

Wei (wā). Name of several Chinese dynasties ruling from A.D. 220 to 265 and from 386 to 556.

wei·ge·la (wī-gē′lə, -jē′-, wī′jə-) *n.* Any of various deciduous shrubs of the genus *Weigela* of Asia, especially *W. florida,* widely cultivated for its pink, white, or red flowers. [New Latin, genus name, after Christian E. *Weigel* (1748–1831), German physician.]

weigh[1] (wā) *v.* **weighed, weigh·ing, weighs.** —*tr.* **1.** To determine the weight of by or as if by using a scale or balance. **2.** To measure or apportion (a certain quantity) by or as if by weight. Often used with *out: weighed out a pound of cheese.* **3. a.** To balance in the mind in order to make a choice; ponder or evaluate: *weighed the alternatives and decided to stay.* **b.** To choose carefully or deliberately: *weigh one's words.* **4.** *Nautical.* To raise (anchor). —*intr.* **1.** To be of a specific weight. **2.** To have consequence or importance: *The decision weighed heavily against us.* See Synonyms at **count**[1]. **3.** To press heavily. Used with *on* or *upon: Guilt weighed on him.* **4.** *Nautical.* To raise anchor. **—*phrasal verbs.* weigh down. 1.** To cause to bend down with added weight: *vines that were weighed down with grapes.* **2.** To burden or oppress: *were weighed down with cares; responsibilities that wore me down.* **weigh in. 1.** *Sports.* To be weighed before or after an athletic contest. **2.** To have one's baggage weighed, as at an airport. **3.** *Slang.* To enter as a participant: *She weighed in with some pertinent facts.* [Middle English *weien,* from Old English *wegan.* See **wegh-** in Appendix.] **—weigh′er** *n.*

weigh[2] (wā) *n. Nautical.* Way. Used in the phrase *under weigh.* [Variant of WAY.]

weight (wāt) *n. Abbr.* **w., wt. 1.** A measure of the heaviness of an object. **2.** The force with which a body is attracted to Earth or another celestial body, equal to the product of the object's mass and the acceleration of gravity. **3. a.** A unit measure of gravitational force: *a table of weights and measures.* **b.** A system of such measures: *avoirdupois weight; troy weight.* **4.** The measured heaviness of a specific object: *a two-pound weight.* **5.** An object used principally to exert a force by virtue of its gravitational attraction to Earth, especially: **a.** A metallic solid used as a standard of comparison in weighing. **b.** An object used to hold something else down. **c.** A counterbalance in a machine. **d.** *Sports.* A heavy object, such as a dumbbell, lifted for exercise or in athletic competition. **6.** *Statistics.* A factor assigned to a number in a computation, as in determining an average, to make the number's effect on the computation reflect its importance. **7.** Burden; oppressiveness. **8.** The greater part; preponderance: *The weight of the evidence is against the defendant.* **9. a.** Influence, importance, or authority: *Her approval carried great weight.* See Synonyms at **importance. b.** Ponderous quality: *the weight of the speaker's words.* **10.** *Sports.* A classification according to comparative lightness or heaviness. Often used in combination: *a heavyweight boxer.* **11.** The heaviness or thickness of a fabric in relation to a particular season or use. Often used in combination: *a summerweight jacket.* **—weight** *tr.v.* **weight·ed, weight·ing, weights. 1.** To add to, by or as if by attaching a weight; make heavy or heavier. **2.** To load down, burden, or oppress. **3.** To increase the weight or body of (fabrics) by treating with chemicals. **4.** *Mathematics & Statistics.* To assign weights or a weight to. **5.** To cause to have a slant or bias: *weighted the rules in favor of homeowners.* **6.** *Sports.* To assign to (a horse) the weight it must carry as a handicap in a race. **—*idiom.* by weight.** According to weight rather than volume or other measure. [Middle English *wight,* from Old English *wiht.* See **wegh-** in Appendix.]

weight·ed (wā′tĭd) *adj. Statistics.* Adjusted to reflect value or proportion: *a weighted average.*

weight·less (wāt′lĭs) *adj.* **1.** Having little or no weight. **2.** Not experiencing the effects of gravity; being in a state of free fall. **—weight′less·ly** *adv.* **—weight′less·ness** *n.*

weight lift·er or **weight·lift·er** (wāt′lĭf′tər) *n. Sports.* One who lifts heavy weights for exercise or in an athletic competition.

weight·lift·ing (wāt′lĭf′tĭng) *n. Sports.* The lifting of heavy weights in a prescribed manner as an exercise or in athletic competition.

weight·y (wā′tē) *adj.* **-i·er, -i·est. 1.** Having considerable weight; heavy. See Synonyms at **heavy. 2.** Burdensome; oppressive: *weighty problems.* **3.** Of great consequence; momentous: *the weighty matters before the delegates at the peace talks.* **4.** Having great power or influence: *a weighty argument.* **5.** Solemn; serious: *weighty music.* **—weight′i·ly** *adv.* **—weight′i·ness** *n.*

Wei He (wā′ hə′). A river of central China flowing about 724 km (450 mi) generally eastward to the Huang He (Yellow River).

Weil (vāl), **Simone.** 1909–1943. French philosopher and mystic who viewed suffering as a means of unity with God. Her works include *Waiting for God,* published posthumously.

Weill (wīl, vīl), **Kurt.** 1900–1950. German-born composer who collaborated with Bertolt Brecht on *The Rise and Fall of the City of Mahagonny* (1927) and *The Threepenny Opera* (1928).

Weil's disease (vīlz, wīlz) *n.* A severe form of leptospirosis in human beings that is characterized by jaundice, fever, muscle pain, and a tendency to hemorrhage. [After Adolf *Weil* (1848–1916), German physician.]

Wei·mar (wī′mär′, vī′-). A city of central Germany southwest of Leipzig. First mentioned in 975, it became the capital of the duchy of Saxe-Weimar in 1547 and developed as the most important cultural center in Germany after 1775. In 1919 the German National Assembly met here and established the **Weimar Republic,** which lasted until 1933. Population, 64,007.

Wei·mar·an·er (vī′mə-rä′nər, wī′-) *n.* Any of a large breed of hunting dog having a smooth grayish coat that originated in Germany. [German, after WEIMAR.]

weir (wîr) *n.* **1.** A fence or wattle placed in a stream to catch or retain fish. **2.** A dam placed across a river or canal to raise or divert the water, as for a millrace, or to regulate or measure the flow. [Middle English *were,* from Old English *wer.* See **wer-**[4] in Appendix.]

weird (wîrd) *adj.* **weird·er, weird·est. 1.** Of, relating to, or suggestive of the preternatural or supernatural. **2.** Of a strikingly odd or unusual character; strange. **3.** *Archaic.* Of or relating to fate or the Fates. **—weird** *n.* **1. a.** Fate; destiny. **b.** One's assigned lot or fortune, especially when evil. **2.** Often **Weird.** *Greek & Roman Mythology.* One of the Fates. [Middle English *werde,* fate, having power to control fate, from Old English *wyrd,* fate. See **wer-**[2] in Appendix.] **—weird′ly** *adv.* **—weird′ness** *n.*

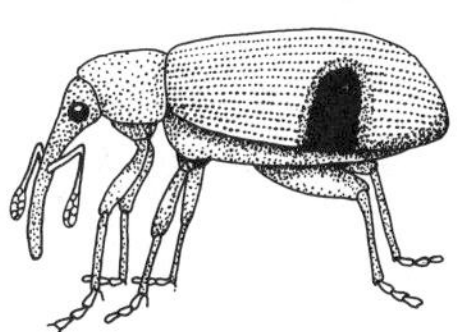

weevil
Strawberry weevil
Anthonomus signatus

Weimaraner

ă pat	oi boy
ā pay	ou out
âr care	ŏŏ took
ä father	ōō boot
ĕ pet	ŭ cut
ē be	ûr urge
ĭ pit	th thin
ī pie	*th* this
îr pier	hw which
ŏ pot	zh vision
ō toe	ə about, item
ô paw	♦ regionalism

Stress marks: ′ (primary); ′ (secondary), as in **dictionary** (dĭk′shə-nĕr′ē)

SYNONYMS: *weird, eerie, uncanny, unearthly.* These adjectives refer to what is of a mysteriously strange, usually frightening nature. *Weird* may suggest the operation of supernatural influences, but it may also be applied to what is merely odd or unusual: *"The person of the house gave a weird little laugh"* (Charles Dickens). *"There is a weird power in a spoken word"* (Joseph Conrad). Something *eerie* inspires inexplicable fear or uneasiness that seems to result from a sinister influence: *"At nightfall on the marshes, the thing was eerie and fantastic to behold"* (Robert Louis Stevenson). *Uncanny* refers to what is unnatural and peculiarly unsettling: *"The queer stumps . . . had uncanny shapes, as of monstrous creatures, whose eyes seemed to peer out at you"* (John Galsworthy). Something *unearthly* seems so strange as to come from or belong to another world: *"He could hear the unearthly scream of some curlew piercing the din"* (Henry Kingsley).

weird·ie also **weird·y** (wîr′dē) *n., pl.* **-ies.** *Slang.* A strange person, event, or thing.

weird·o (wîr′dō) *n., pl.* **-oes.** *Slang.* **1.** A person regarded as being very strange or eccentric. **2.** A deranged, potentially dangerous person.

Weir·ton (wîr′tn). A city of northern West Virginia in the Panhandle on the Ohio River north-northeast of Wheeling. Its first steel mills were built in 1909. Population, 24,736.

weis·en·hei·mer (wīz′ən-hī′mər) *n. Informal.* Variant of **wisenheimer.**

Weis·mann (vīs′män′), **August Friedrich Leopold.** 1834–1914. German biologist who asserted that hereditary characteristics are transmitted by a germinal plasm.

Weis·mann·ism (wīs′mə-nĭz′əm, vīs′män-ĭz′əm) *n. Genetics.* The theory that all heritable characteristics arise in the germ plasm and that acquired characteristics cannot be inherited. [After August Friedrich Leopold WEISMANN.]

Weiz·mann (wīts′mən, vīts′män), **Chaim Azriel.** 1874–1952. Polish-born Israeli chemist and politician who was the first president of Israel (1948–1952).

we·jack (wē′jăk) *n.* See **fisher** (sense 2a). [Cree *oček.*]

we·ka (wē′kə, wā′-) *n.* A flightless bird *(Gallirallus australis)* of New Zealand, having mottled brown plumage and short legs. [Maori.]

welch (wĕlch) *v.* Variant of **welsh.**

Welch (wĕlch, wĕlsh), **Joseph Nye.** 1890–1960. American lawyer who represented the U.S. Army during the 1954 Senate subcommittee hearings concerning charges of subversion brought by Senator Joseph McCarthy.

Orson Welles

wel·come (wĕl′kəm) *adj.* **1.** Received with pleasure and hospitality into one's company or home: *a welcome guest.* **2.** Giving pleasure or satisfaction; agreeable or gratifying: *a welcome respite from hard work.* **3.** Cordially or willingly permitted or invited: *You are welcome to join us.* **4.** Freely granted one's courtesy. Used to acknowledge an expression of gratitude. **—welcome** *n.* **1.** A cordial greeting or hospitable reception given to an arriving person. **2.** A reception upon arrival: *gave the stranger an unfriendly welcome.* **3.** The state of being welcome: *Don't overstay your welcome.* **—welcome** *tr.v.* **-comed, -com·ing, -comes. 1.** To greet, receive, or entertain (another or others) cordially or hospitably. **2.** To receive or accept gladly: *would welcome a little privacy.* **—welcome** *interj.* Used to greet cordially a visitor or recent arrival. ***—idiom.*** **wear out (one's) welcome.** To visit so often or stay so long as to become a nuisance. [Middle English, alteration (influenced by *wel,* well) of Old English *wilcuma,* welcome guest, welcome. See **gʷā-** in Appendix.] **—wel′come·ly** *adv.* **—wel′come·ness** *n.* **—wel′com·er** *n.*

weld¹ (wĕld) *v.* **weld·ed, weld·ing, welds.** *—tr.* **1.** To join (metals) by applying heat, sometimes with pressure and sometimes with an intermediate or filler metal having a high melting point. **2.** To bring into close association or union. *—intr.* To be capable of being welded. **—weld** *n.* **1.** The union of two metal parts by welding. **2.** The joint formed by welding. [Alteration (probably influenced by WELLED, past participle of WELL¹) of WELL¹, to weld (obsolete and dialectal).] **—weld′er, wel′dor** *n.*

weld² (wĕld) also **wold** (wōld) *n.* **1.** See **dyer's rocket. 2.** The yellow dye obtained from dyer's rocket. [Middle English *welde.*]

Weld (wĕld), **Theodore Dwight.** 1803–1895. American abolitionist whose pamphlet *Slavery As It Is* (1839) inspired Harriet Beecher Stowe's novel *Uncle Tom's Cabin.*

weld·ment (wĕld′mənt) *n.* A unit composed of an assemblage of pieces welded together.

wel·fare (wĕl′fâr′) *n.* **1.a.** Health, happiness, and good fortune; well-being. **b.** Prosperity. **2.** Welfare work. **3.** Financial or other aid provided, especially by the government, to people in need. *—attributive.* Often used to modify another noun: *a welfare hotel; welfare families.* ***—idiom.*** **on welfare.** Receiving regular assistance from the government or private agencies because of need. [Middle English, from *wel faren,* to fare well, from Old English *wel faran* : *wel,* well; see WELL² + *faran,* to get along; see FARE.]

Wel·fare Island (wĕl′fâr′). See **Roosevelt Island** (sense 1).

welfare state *n.* **1.** A social system whereby the state assumes primary responsibility for the welfare of its citizens, as in matters of health care, education, employment, and social security. **2.** A nation in which such a system operates.

welfare work *n.* Organized efforts by a community, an organization, or an agency to improve the socioeconomic conditions of disadvantaged groups in society. **—welfare worker** *n.*

wel·far·ism (wĕl′fâr-ĭz′əm) *n.* The policies, practices, and attitudes associated with a welfare state. **—wel′far·ist** *n.*

wel·kin (wĕl′kĭn) *n.* **1.** The vault of heaven; the sky. **2.** The upper air. [Middle English *welken,* from Old English *wolcen, weolcen,* cloud.]

well¹ (wĕl) *n.* **1.** A deep hole or shaft sunk into the earth to obtain water, oil, gas, or brine. **2.** A container or reservoir for a liquid, such as ink. **3.a.** A place where water issues from the earth; a spring or fountain. **b.** A mineral spring. **c. wells.** A watering place; a spa. **4.** An abundant source: *a well of information.* **5.** An open space extending vertically through the floors of a building, as for stairs or ventilation. **6.** *Nautical.* An enclosure in a ship's hold for the pumps. **7.** A cistern with a perforated bottom in the hold of a fishing vessel for keeping fish alive. **8.** An enclosed space for receiving and holding something, such as the wheels of an airplane when retracted. **9.** *Chiefly British.* The central space in a law court, directly in front of the judge's bench, where the counsel or solicitor sits. **—well** *v.* **welled, well·ing, wells.** *—intr.* **1.** To rise to the surface, ready to flow: *Tears welled in my eyes.* **2.** To rise or surge from an inner source: *Anger welled up in me.* *—tr.* To pour forth. [Middle English *welle,* from Old English *welle.* See **wel-²** in Appendix.]

well² (wĕl) *adv.* **bet·ter** (bĕt′ər), **best** (bĕst). **1.** In a good or proper manner: *behaved well.* **2.** Skillfully or proficiently: *dances well.* **3.** Satisfactorily or sufficiently: *slept well.* **4.** Successfully or effectively: *gets along well with people.* **5.** In a comfortable or affluent manner: *lived well.* **6.** In a manner affording benefit or gain; advantageously: *married well.* **7.** With reason or propriety; reasonably: *can't very well say no.* **8.** In all likelihood; indeed: *You may well need your umbrella.* **9.** In a prudent or sensible manner: *You would do well to say nothing more.* **10.** In a close or familiar manner: *knew them well.* **11.** In a favorable or approving manner: *spoke well of them.* **12.** Thoroughly; completely: *well cooked; cooked well.* **13.** Perfectly; clearly: *I well understand your intentions.* **14.** To a suitable or appropriate degree: *well pleased.* **15.** To a considerable extent or degree: *well over the estimate.* **16.** With care or attention: *listened well.* **17.** Entirely; fully: *well worth seeing.* **—well** *adj.* **better, best. 1.** In a satisfactory condition; right or proper: *All is well.* **2.a.** Not ailing, infirm, or diseased; healthy. See Synonyms at **healthy. b.** Cured or healed, as a wound. **3.a.** Advisable; prudent: *It would be well not to ask.* **b.** Fortunate; good: *It is well that you stayed.* **—well** *interj.* **1.** Used to introduce a remark, resume a narrative, or fill a pause during conversation. **2.** Used to express surprise. ***—idioms.*** **as well. 1.** In addition; also: *mentioned other matters as well.* **2.** With equal effect: *I might as well go.* **in well with.** *Informal.* In a position to influence or be favored by: *He's in well with management.* [Middle English *wel,* from Old English. See **wel-¹** in Appendix.]

USAGE NOTE: Used as an adjective applied to people, *well* usually refers to a state of health, whereas *good* has a much wider range of senses. It has always been a first principle of grammatical criticism that there should be no difference without a distinction, and perhaps for this reason, some critics have insisted that the expression *feel good* cannot be used in reference to health. It is true that there is a distinction between *feel well* and *feel good,* but both can be applied to a state of health. Thus a patient suffering from a chronic disease might appropriately say to a doctor *I feel good today,* which implies a relative lack of physical discomfort. By contrast, *I feel well today* would be appropriate if the patient believes that the ailment has disappeared. See Usage Note at **good.**

we'll (wēl). **1.** We will. **2.** We shall.

well·a·day (wĕl′ə-dā′) *interj. & n. Archaic.* Variant of **wellaway.**

well-ad·just·ed (wĕl′ə-jŭs′tĭd) *adj.* Having adapted or conformed suitably to new conditions: *a well-adjusted new student.*

Wel·land (wĕl′ənd). A city of southeast Ontario, Canada, on the **Welland Ship Canal,** 44.4 km (27.6 mi) long, which connects Lake Erie with Lake Ontario and bypasses Niagara Falls. The current canal, completed in 1932, replaced a canal originally built between 1824 and 1833. Population, 45,448.

well-ap·point·ed (wĕl′ə-poin′tĭd) *adj.* Having a full array of suitable equipment or furnishings: *a well-appointed kitchen; a well-appointed suite.*

well·a·way (wĕl′ə-wā′) *Archaic. interj.* Used to express woe or distress. **—wellaway** *n., pl.* **-ways.** A lamentation. [Middle English, alteration (influenced by *well,* well, and *awai,* away) of Old English *weilāwei,* alteration (influenced by Old Scandinavian **wei,* woe) of *wā lā wā* : *wā,* woe; see WOE + *lā,* lo; see LO.]

well-bal·anced (wĕl′băl′ənst) *adj.* **1.** Evenly proportioned, balanced, or regulated. **2.** Mentally stable; sensible or sound.

well-be·ing (wĕl′bē′ĭng) *n.* The state of being healthy, happy, or prosperous; welfare.

well-born (wĕl′bôrn′) *adj.* Of good lineage or stock.

well-bred (wĕl′brĕd′) *adj.* **1.** Of good upbringing; well-mannered and refined. **2.** Of good breed. Used of animals.

well-de·fined (wĕl′dĭ-fīnd′) *adj.* **1.** Having definite and distinct lines or features: *a well-defined silhouette.* **2.** Accurately and unambiguously stated or described: *a well-defined argument.*

well-dis·posed (wĕl′dĭ-spōzd′) *adj.* Disposed to be kindly, friendly, or sympathetic.

well-done (wĕl′dŭn′) *adj.* Cooked all the way through: *a well-done steak.*

Welles (wĕlz), **(George) Orson.** 1915–1985. American filmmaker and actor who directed and starred in *Citizen Kane* (1941). His other films include *Touch of Evil* (1958) and *The Trial* (1962).

Welles, Gideon. 1802–1878. American editor and politician. A founder of the Republican Party (1854), he established a partisan newspaper, the *Hartford Evening Press* (1856), and was U.S. secretary of the navy (1861–1869) during the Civil War.

Welles·ley (wĕlz′lē). A town of eastern Massachusetts west-southwest of Boston. It is a residential community and the seat of Wellesley College (established 1870). Population, 27,209.

Wellesley, First Marquis. Title of Richard Colley Wellesley. 1760–1842. British politician and colonial administrator who expanded the British Empire in India and sought reconciliation between Protestants and Catholics in Ireland.

well-fa·vored (wĕl′fā′vərd) *adj.* Handsome; attractive.

well-fed (wĕl′fĕd′) *adj.* **1.** Adequately or properly nourished. **2.** Overfed; fat.

well-fixed (wĕl′fĭkst′) *adj. Informal.* Financially secure; well-to-do.

well-found (wĕl′found′) *adj.* Properly furnished or equipped.

well-found·ed (wĕl′foun′dĭd) *adj.* Based on sound judgment, reasoning, or evidence; adequately substantiated: *well-founded suspicions.*

well-groomed (wĕl′gro͞omd′) *adj.* **1.** Attentive to details of dress; meticulously neat. **2.** Carefully tended or curried: *a well-groomed horse.* **3.** Trim and tidy: *a well-groomed lawn.*

well-ground·ed (wĕl′groun′dĭd) *adj.* **1.** Adequately versed in a subject. **2.** Having a sound basis; well-founded.

well-han·dled (wĕl′hăn′dəld) *adj.* **1.** Managed well. **2.** Showing signs of much handling.

well·head (wĕl′hĕd′) *n.* **1.** The source of a well or stream. **2.** A principal source; a fountainhead. **3.** The structure built over a well.

well-heeled (wĕl′hēld′) *adj.* Having plenty of money; prosperous.

Wel·ling·ton (wĕl′ĭng-tən). The capital of New Zealand, on an inlet of Cook Strait in southern North Island. It supplanted Auckland as capital in 1865. Population, 133,200.

Wellington, First Duke of. Title of Arthur Wellesley. Known as "the Iron Duke." 1769–1852. British general and politician. Commander of British troops during the Peninsular War (1808–1814), he defeated Napoleon at Waterloo (1815), thus ending the Napoleonic Wars. As prime minister (1828–1830) he passed the Catholic Emancipation Act (1829).

Wellington boot *n.* **1.** A boot extending to the top of the knee in front but cut low in back. **2.** *Chiefly British.* A waterproof boot of rubber or sometimes leather reaching to below the knee and worn in wet or muddy conditions. [After First Duke of WELLINGTON.]

well-in·ten·tioned (wĕl′ĭn-tĕn′shənd) *adj.* Marked by or having good intentions: *a well-intentioned but clumsy waiter; well-intentioned criticism.*

well-knit (wĕl′nĭt′) *adj.* Strongly knit, especially strongly and firmly constructed: *a well-knit theatrical production.*

well-known (wĕl′nōn′) *adj.* **1.** Widely known; famous: *a well-known performer.* **2.** Fully known: *well-known facts.*

well-man·nered (wĕl′măn′ərd) *adj.* Polite; courteous.

well-mean·ing (wĕl′mē′nĭng) *adj.* Well-intentioned.

well-meant (wĕl′mĕnt′) *adj.* Kindly or honestly intended: *well-meant admonitions.*

well·ness (wĕl′nĭs) *n. Usage Problem.* Good physical and mental health, especially when maintained by proper diet, exercise, and habits. —*attributive. Usage Problem.* Often used to modify another noun: *wellness programs; a wellness clinic.*

USAGE NOTE: It can be argued that *wellness* serves a useful function as a means of describing a state that includes not just physical health but fitness and emotional well-being. The word is first recorded in 1654 but has never been given the acceptance of its antonym *illness.* In the most recent survey 68 percent of the Usage Panel found the word unacceptable in the sentence *A number of corporations have implemented employee wellness programs, aimed at enhancing spiritual values, emotional stability, fitness, and nutrition.*

well-nigh (wĕl′nī′) *adv.* Nearly; almost.

well-off (wĕl′ôf′, -ŏf′) *adj.* **1.** Well-to-do. **2.** In fortunate circumstances. [OFF, circumstanced, probably from the phrase *to come well off,* to emerge from in good circumstances.]

well-read (wĕl′rĕd′) *adj.* Knowledgeable through having read extensively.

well-round·ed (wĕl′roun′dĭd) *adj.* **1.** Comprehensively developed and well-balanced in a range or variety of aspects: *a well-rounded scholar; a well-rounded curriculum.* **2.** Having a fully developed or shapely figure.

Wells (wĕlz), **H(erbert) G(eorge).** 1866–1946. British writer. Particularly known for his science-fiction novels, such as *The Time Machine* (1895) and *The War of the Worlds* (1898), he also wrote popular accounts of history and science.

Wells, Ida Bell. 1862–1931. American journalist and reformer who campaigned nationwide against lynching and founded the Negro Fellowship League in 1910.

well-spo·ken (wĕl′spō′kən) *adj.* **1.** Chosen or expressed with aptness or propriety. **2.** Courteous in speech.

well·spring (wĕl′sprĭng′) *n.* **1.** The source of a stream or spring. **2.** A source: *a wellspring of ideas.*

well-thought-of (wĕl-thôt′ŭv′, -ŏv′) *adj.* Regarded with respect; esteemed.

well-tim·bered (wĕl′tĭm′bərd) *adj.* **1.** Having a good framework or structure. **2.** Covered with a good growth of timber.

well-timed (wĕl′tīmd′) *adj.* Occurring or done at an opportune time: *a well-timed remark.* See Synonyms at **opportune.**

well-to-do (wĕl′tə-do͞o′) *adj.* Prosperous; affluent; well-off. **—well-to-do** *n. (used with a pl. verb).* Affluent or wealthy people: *Demonstrators protested that the tax bill favored the well-to-do.* [From the phrase *well to do in the world* : WELL[2], prosperous, affluent + TO, for + DO[1], doing.]

Duke of Wellington

well-turned (wĕl′tûrnd′) *adj.* **1.** Shapely: *a well-turned ankle.* **2.** Concisely or aptly expressed: *a well-turned phrase.* **3.** Expertly rounded or turned: *a well-turned bedpost.*

well-wish·er (wĕl′wĭsh′ər) *n.* One who extends good wishes to another. **—well′-wish′ing** *adj. & n.*

well-worn (wĕl′wôrn′, -wōrn′) *adj.* **1.** Showing signs of much wear or use. **2.** Repeated too often; trite or hackneyed. **3.** Carried or worn in a becoming manner: *well-worn fame.*

welsh (wĕlsh, wĕlch) also **welch** (wĕlch) *intr.v.* **welshed, welsh·ing, welsh·es** also **welched, welch·ing, welch·es.** *Informal.* **1.** To swindle a person by not paying a debt or wager. **2.** To fail to fulfill an obligation. [Origin unknown.] **—welsh′er** *n.*

Welsh (wĕlsh, wĕlch) *adj. Abbr.* **W.** Of or relating to Wales or its people, language, or culture. **—Welsh** *n.* **1.** The people of Wales. **2.** The Celtic language of Wales. In this sense, also called *Cymric.* [Middle English *Walische,* from Old English *Wælisc,* from *Wealh,* Welshman, Celt, perhaps of Celtic origin.]

Welsh corgi *n.* Either of two breeds of dog that originated in Wales, having a long body, short legs, and a foxlike head.

Welsh corgi

Welsh·man (wĕlsh′mən, wĕlch′-) *n.* A man who is a native or inhabitant of Wales.

Welsh rabbit *n.* A dish made of melted cheese, milk or cream, seasonings, and sometimes ale, served hot over toast or crackers.

Welsh rare·bit (râr′bĭt) *n.* Welsh rabbit.

Welsh springer spaniel *n.* Any of a breed of medium-sized dog that originated in Wales and has a silky red and white coat.

Welsh terrier *n.* Any of a breed of terrier originating in Wales and having a wiry black and tan coat.

Welsh·wom·an (wĕlsh′wo͝om′ən, wĕlch′-) *n.* A woman who is a native or inhabitant of Wales.

welt (wĕlt) *n.* **1.** A strip, as of leather or other material, stitched into a shoe between the sole and the upper. **2.** A tape or covered cord sewn into a seam as reinforcement or trimming; welting. **3.a.** A ridge or bump on the skin caused by a lash or blow or sometimes by an allergic reaction. **b.** A lash or blow producing such a mark. **—welt** *tr.v.* **welt·ed, welt·ing, welts. 1.** To reinforce or trim with a welt or welting. **2.** To beat severely; flog. **3.** To raise welts or a welt on. [Middle English *welte.*]

Welt·an·schau·ung (vĕlt′än′shou′o͝ong) *n., pl.* **-ungs** or **-ung·en** (-o͝ong-ən). A comprehensive philosophy of the world or of human life. [German : *Welt,* world (from Middle High German *wërlt,* from Old High German *weralt;* see **wi-ro-** in Appendix) + *Anschauung,* view (from Middle High German *anschouwunge,* observation, mystical contemplation : *an-,* on, at, from Old High German *ana-;* see ANLAGE + *schouwunge,* look, from *schouwen,* to look at, from Old High German *scouwōn;* see **keu-** in Appendix).]

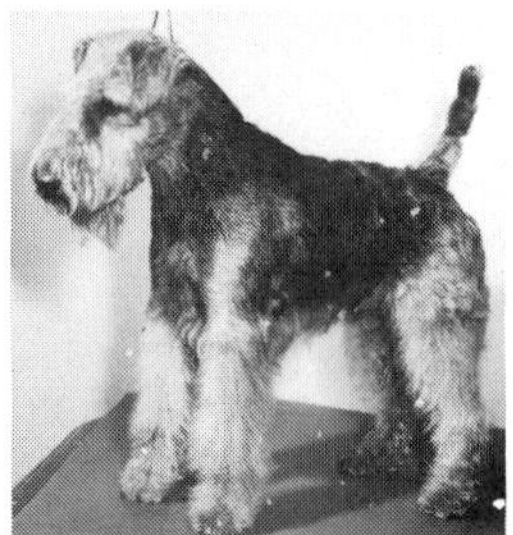
Welsh terrier

wel·ter (wĕl′tər) *n.* **1.** A confused mass; a jumble: *a welter of papers and magazines.* **2.** Confusion; turmoil. **—welter** *intr.v.* **-tered, -ter·ing, -ters. 1.** To wallow, roll, or toss about, as in mud or high seas. **2.** To lie soaked in a liquid. **3.** To roll and surge, as the sea. [From Middle English *welteren,* to toss about, as in high seas, from Middle Low German or Middle Dutch; see **wel-**[2] in Appendix.]

wel·ter·weight (wĕl′tər-wāt′) *n. Sports.* **1.** A professional boxer weighing between 135 and 147 pounds (approximately 61–66.5 kilograms), heavier than a lightweight and lighter than a middleweight. **2.** A contestant in various other sports in a similar weight class. [From *welter,* heavyweight boxer, perhaps from WELT.]

Welt·schmerz (vĕlt′shmĕrts′) *n.* Sadness over the evils of the world, especially as an expression of romantic pessimism. [German : *Welt,* world; see WELTANSCHAUUNG + *Schmerz,* pain (from Middle High German *smërze,* from Old High German *smerzo*).]

Wel·ty (wĕl′tē), **Eudora.** Born 1909. American writer known for her tales of rural Southern life.

wen[1] (wĕn) *n.* A harmless cyst, especially on the scalp or face, containing the fatty secretion of a sebaceous gland. [Middle English, from Old English. See **wen-**[2] in Appendix.]

wen[2] (wĕn) *n.* Variant of **wynn.**

We·natch·ee (wə-năch′ē). A city of central Washington on the Columbia River north-northeast of Yakima. It is a processing cen-

ă pat	oi boy
ā pay	ou out
âr care	o͝o took
ä father	o͞o boot
ĕ pet	ŭ cut
ē be	ûr urge
ĭ pit	th thin
ī pie	*th* this
îr pier	hw which
ŏ pot	zh vision
ō toe	ə about, item
ô paw	♦ regionalism

Stress marks: ′ (primary); ′ (secondary), as in **dictionary** (dĭk′shə-nĕr′ē)

ter in a fertile valley noted for apples. Population, 17,257.

Wen·ces·laus (wĕn′sĭ-slôs′) or **Wen·zel** (vĕn′tsəl). 1361–1419. Holy Roman emperor and king of Germany (1378–1400) and Bohemia (1378–1419). He was deposed as emperor and king by the German electors.

wench (wĕnch) *n.* **1.** A young woman or girl, especially a peasant girl. **2.** A woman servant. **3.** A sexually promiscuous woman; a prostitute. **—wench** *intr.v.* **wenched, wench·ing, wench·es. 1.** To engage in promiscuous sex with women. Used of a man. **2.** To consort with women prostitutes. Used of a man. [Middle English, short for *wenchel,* child, from Old English *wencel.*] **—wench′er** *n.*

Mae West
Photographed in the 1930's

Wen·chow (wĕn′chou′, wŭn′jō′). See **Wenzhou.**

wend (wĕnd) *v.* **wend·ed, wend·ing, wends.** *—tr.* To proceed on or along; go: *wend one's way home.* *—intr.* To go one's way. [Middle English *wenden,* from Old English *wendan.*]

Wend (wĕnd) *n.* One of a Slavic people inhabiting Saxony and Brandenburg. Also called *Sorb, Sorbian.* [German *Wende,* from Middle High German *Winde, Wende,* from Old High German *Winid.* See **wen-**[1] in Appendix.] **—Wend** *adj.*

Wend·ish (wĕn′dĭsh) *adj.* Of or relating to the Wends or their language. **—Wendish** *n.* The Slavic language of the Wends. Also called *Sorbian.*

went (wĕnt) *v.* **1.** Past tense of **go**[1]. **2.** *Archaic.* A past tense and a past participle of **wend.** [Middle English, from Old English *wende,* past tense and past participle of *wendan,* to go.]

wen·tle·trap (wĕnt′l-trăp′) *n.* Any of various marine snails of the family Epitoniidae, having a tapering, usually white spiral shell. [Dutch *wenteltrap,* from Middle Dutch *wendeltrappe* : *wendel,* winding (from *wenden,* to wind) + *trappe,* stairs.]

Wen·zel (vĕn′tsəl). See **Wenceslaus.**

Wen·zhou (wŭn′jō′) also **Wen·chow** (wĕn′chou′, wŭn′jō′). A city of eastern China near the East China Sea south of Shanghai. Founded in the fourth century A.D., it was opened to foreign trade in 1876. Population, 325,000.

wept (wĕpt) *v.* Past tense and past participle of **weep.**

were (wûr) *v.* **1.** Second person singular and plural and first and third person plural past indicative of **be. 2.** Past subjunctive of **be.** See Usage Notes at **if, wish.** [Middle English *were, weren,* from Old English *wǣre, wǣren, wǣron.* See **wes-**[1] in Appendix.]

we're (wîr). We are.

were·gild (wûr′gĭld′) *n.* Variant of **wergeld.**

were·n't (wûrnt, wûr′ənt). Were not.

were·wolf also **wer·wolf** (wâr′wo͝olf′, wîr′-, wûr′-) *n.* A person transformed into a wolf or capable of assuming the form of a wolf. [Middle English, from Old English *werewulf* : *wer,* man; see **wī-ro-** in Appendix + *wulf,* wolf; see WOLF.]

Wer·fel (vĕr′fəl), **Franz.** 1890–1945. Austrian writer whose works include the novel *Song of Bernadette* (1941).

wer·geld (wûr′gĕld′) also **wer·gild** or **were·gild** (-gĭld′) *n.* In Anglo-Saxon and Germanic law, a price set upon a person's life on the basis of rank and paid as compensation by the family of a slayer to the kindred or lord of a slain person to free the culprit of further punishment or obligation and to prevent a blood feud. [Middle English *wargeld,* from Old English *wergeld* : *wer,* man; see **wī-ro-** in Appendix + *geld,* payment.]

wer·ner·ite (wûr′nə-rīt′) *n.* See **scapolite.** [After Abraham Gottlob *Werner* (1750–1817), German mineralogist.]

Wer·ner's syndrome (vĕr′nərz) *n.* A hereditary disease of young adults that is characterized by short stature, early graying, cataracts, vascular disorders, and generally premature aging and death. [After Carl W.O. *Werner,* 20th-century German physician.]

Wer·nick·e's area (vĕr′nĭ-kēz, -kəz) *n.* An area in the posterior temporal lobe of the left hemisphere of the brain involved in the recognition of spoken words. [After Karl *Wernicke* (1848–1905), German neurologist.]

Wernicke's encephalopathy *n.* A disease of the brain caused by a deficiency of thiamine, usually associated with chronic alcoholism and characterized by loss of muscular coordination, abnormal eye movements, confusion, and forgetfulness. [After Karl *Wernicke* (1848–1905), German neurologist.]

Wer·ra (vĕr′ə). A river rising in central Germany and flowing about 291 km (181 mi) generally northward to join the Fulda River and form the Weser.

wert (wûrt) *v. Archaic.* A second person singular past indicative and past subjunctive of **be.** [Blend of WAST and WERE.]

Wert·mül·ler (vĕrt′myo͞o′lər), **Lina.** Born c. 1926. Italian filmmaker whose works include *The Seduction of Mimi* (1972) and *Swept Away* (1974).

wer·wolf (wâr′wo͝olf′, wîr′-, wûr′-) *n.* Variant of **werewolf.**

We·ser (vā′zər). A river, about 483 km (300 mi) long, of central and northwest Germany, flowing generally northward to the North Sea through a long estuary.

wes·kit (wĕs′kĭt) *n.* A waistcoat. [Variant of WAISTCOAT.]

Wes·la·co (wĕs′lə-kō′). A city of extreme southern Texas northwest of Brownsville. Population, 19,331.

Wes·ley (wĕs′lē, wĕz′-), **John.** 1703–1791. British religious leader who founded Methodism (1738). His brother **Charles** (1707–1788) wrote thousands of hymns, including "Hark, the Herald Angels Sing."

Wes·ley·an (wĕs′lē-ən, wĕz′-) *adj.* Of or relating to John or Charles Wesley or to Methodism. **—Wesleyan** *n.* A Methodist. **—Wes′ley·an·ism** *n.*

Wes·sex (wĕs′ĭks). A region and ancient Anglo-Saxon kingdom of southern England. According to tradition, the kingdom was founded by the Saxon conquerors of Britain and at its greatest extent occupied the territory between the English Channel and the Thames River.

west (wĕst) *n. Abbr.* **W, W., w, w. 1.a.** The cardinal point on the mariner's compass 270° clockwise from due north and directly opposite east. **b.** The direction opposite to the direction of the earth's axial rotation. **2.** An area or a region lying in the west. **3.** Often **West. a.** The western part of the earth, especially Europe and the Western Hemisphere. **b.** The western part of a region or country. **4.** Often **West. a.** A former region of the United States west of the Allegheny Mountains. **b.** The region of the United States west of the Mississippi River. **c.** The noncommunist countries of Europe and the Americas. **—west** *adj. Abbr.* **W, W., w, w. 1.** To, toward, of, facing, or in the west. **2.** Originating in or coming from the west: *a gentle west wind.* **—west** *adv. Abbr.* **W, W., w, w.** In, from, or toward the west. [Middle English, from Old English. See **wes-pero-** in Appendix.]

West, Benjamin. 1738–1820. American painter. The first American to study art in Italy (1760–1763), he settled in England and quickly became a prominent artist. *The Death of General Wolfe* (1770) is among his most important works.

West, Mae. 1892?–1980. American actress known for her sultry stage persona. Her films include *I'm No Angel* (1933) and *My Little Chickadee* (1940).

West, Nathanael. Pen name of Nathan Weinstein 1903–1940. American writer known for his novels of dark comedy, such as *Miss Lonelyhearts* (1933) and *The Day of the Locust* (1939).

West, Dame **Rebecca.** Pen name of Cicily Isabel Fairfield Andrews. 1892–1983. British writer and critic whose works include psychological novels, such as *The Judge* (1922).

West Af·ri·ca (ăf′rĭ-kə). A region of western Africa between the Sahara Desert and the Gulf of Guinea. It was largely controlled by colonial powers until the 20th century. **—West Af′ri·can** *adj. & n.*

West Al·lis (ăl′ĭs). A city of southeast Wisconsin, a residential and industrial suburb of Milwaukee. Population, 63,982.

West Atlantic *n.* The westernmost branch of the Niger-Congo language family.

West Bab·y·lon (băb′ə-lən, -lŏn′). A community of southeast New York on southern Long Island west of Bay Shore. It is mainly residential. Population, 32,500.

West Bank (băngk). A disputed territory of southwest Asia between Israel and Jordan west of the Jordan River. Part of Jordan after 1949, it has been occupied by Israel since 1967.

West Bend (bĕnd). A city of southeast Wisconsin north-northwest of Milwaukee. Population, 21,484.

West Ber·lin (bər-lĭn′). See **Berlin. —West Ber·lin′er** *n.*

West Bes·kids (bĕs′kĭdz, bĕs-kēdz′). See **Beskids.**

west·bound (wĕst′bound′) *adj. Abbr.* **w.b.** Going toward the west.

West Briton *n. Offensive.* A native Irishman or Irishwoman whose sympathies lie toward England: *"To say you'd write for a rag like that. I didn't think you were a West Briton"* (James Joyce). **—West British** *adj.*

west by north *n. Abbr.* **WbN.** The direction or point on the mariner's compass halfway between due west and west-northwest, or 78°45′ west of due north. **—west by north** *adv. & adj. Abbr.* **WbN.** Toward or from west by north.

west by south *n. Abbr.* **WbS.** The direction or point on the mariner's compass halfway between due west and west-southwest, or 101°15′ west of due north. **—west by south** *adv. & adj. Abbr.* **WbS.** Toward or from west by south.

West·ches·ter (wĕst′chĕs′tər). A village of northeast Illinois, a suburb of Chicago. Population, 17,730.

West Ches·ter (chĕs′tər). A borough of southeast Pennsylvania west of Philadelphia. It is primarily residential with some light industry. Population, 17,435.

West Coast. A region of the western United States bordering on the Pacific Ocean and including Washington, Oregon, and California.

West Co·vi·na (kō-vē′nə). A city of southern California east of Los Angeles. It is mainly residential. Population, 80,094.

West Des Moines (dĭ moin′). A city of south-central Iowa, a manufacturing suburb of Des Moines. Population, 21,894.

West End. The western section of central London, England, noted for its fashionable districts and its shops and theaters.

west·er (wĕs′tər) *n.* A strong wind coming from the west. **—wester** *intr.v.* **-ered, -er·ing, -ers.** To move westward. Used of the sun, the moon, or a star. [Middle English *westren,* from *west,* west. See WEST.]

west·er·ly (wĕs′tər-lē) *adj.* **1.** Situated toward the west. **2.** Coming or being from the west: *westerly winds.* **—westerly** *n., pl.* **-lies.** A storm or wind coming from the west. [Middle English, from *wester,* western, from Old English *westra.* See **wes-pero-** in Appendix.] **—west′er·ly** *adv.*

Wes·ter·ly (wĕs′tər-lē). A town of extreme southwest Rhode Island on the border of Connecticut east of New London. It was first settled in 1648. Population, 18,580.

west•ern (wĕs′tərn) *adj.* *Abbr.* **W, W., w, w.** **1.** Situated in, toward, or facing the west. **2.** Coming from the west: *western breezes.* **3.** Native to or growing in the west. **4.** Often **Western.** Of, relating to, or characteristic of western regions or the West. **5. Western.** Of, relating to, or descended from those Christian churches that use or formerly used Latin as their liturgical language. **—western** *n.* Often **Western.** A novel, film, or television or radio program about frontier life in the American West. [Middle English, from Old English *westerne.* See **wes-pero-** in Appendix.] **—west′ern•ness** *n.*

Western Bug (bo͞og, bo͝ok). See **Bug** (sense 1).

Western Dvi•na (dvē-nä′). See **Dvina** (sense 2).

Western Empire or **Western Ro•man Empire** (rō′mən). The western section of the Roman Empire, first set apart in A.D. 286 by Emperor Diocletian and later (395) formalized after the death of Theodosius I. It comprised Italy, Spain, Gaul, Britain, Illyricum, and northern Africa and lasted until 476.

west•ern•er also **West•ern•er** (wĕs′tər-nər) *n.* A native or inhabitant of the west, especially the western United States.

Western Eu•rope (yo͝or′əp). The countries of western Europe, especially those that are allied with the United States and Canada in the North Atlantic Treaty Organization (established 1949).

Western Ghats (gôts). See **Ghats.**

Western Hemisphere. The half of the earth comprising North America, Mexico, Central America, and South America.

western honey mesquite *n.* See **mesquite** (sense a). [From the high sugar content of its pods.]

Western Islands. See **Hebrides.**

west•ern•ize (wĕs′tər-nīz′) *tr.v.* **-ized, -iz•ing, -iz•es.** To convert to the customs of Western civilization. **—west′ern•i•za′tion** (wĕs′tər-nĭ-zā′shən) *n.*

west•ern•most (wĕs′tərn-mōst′) *adj.* Farthest west.

western omelet *n.* An omelet cooked with diced ham, chopped green pepper, and onion.

Western Reserve. A region of northeast Ohio bordering on Lake Erie. It was retained by Connecticut after other western claims were ceded to the U.S. Congress in 1786. Much of the area was given or sold to immigrants from Connecticut (1786–1800), and the remainder of the territory was ceded to Ohio in 1800 and became part of the Northwest Territory.

Western Ro•man Empire (rō′mən). See **Western Empire.**

western saddle *n.* See **stock saddle.**

Western Sa•ha•ra (sə-hâr′ə, -hăr′ə, -hä′rə) also **Span•ish Sahara** (spăn′ĭsh). A region of northwest Africa on the Atlantic coast. First visited by Portuguese navigators in 1434, it was claimed as a protectorate by Spain in 1884. The territory was partly annexed in 1976 and partly occupied in 1979 by Morocco.

Western Sa•mo•a (sə-mō′ə). An island country of the southern Pacific Ocean comprising the western Samoa Islands. The islands were awarded to Germany in 1899 but came under the control of New Zealand in 1914. They achieved independence in 1962. Apia is the capital. Population, 156,349.

western sandwich *n.* A sandwich having a western omelet as a filling.

Western Shoshone *n.* See **Shoshone** (sense 1b).

western tanager *n.* A tanager *(Piranga ludoviciana)* of western North America, the male of which is yellow with a red head and a black back.

Western Wall *n.* *Judaism.* A remnant of the western wall of the second Temple in Jerusalem, traditionally a site of pilgrimage, lamentation, and prayer. Also called *Wailing Wall.*

Wes•ter•ville (wĕs′tər-vĭl′). A city of central Ohio, an industrial suburb of Columbus. Population, 23,414.

West•field (wĕst′fēld′). **1.** A city of southwest Massachusetts, a residential and industrial suburb of Springfield. Population, 36,465. **2.** A town of northeast-central New Jersey southwest of Newark. It is a residential community. Population, 30,447.

West Fri•sian Islands (frĭzh′ən, frē′zhən). See **Frisian Islands.**

West Germanic *n.* A subdivision of the Germanic languages that includes High German, Low German, Yiddish, Dutch, Afrikaans, Flemish, Frisian, and English.

West Ger•ma•ny (jûr′mə-nē). A former country of central Europe bordering on the North Sea. It was part of Germany until 1945, when the country was divided into U.S., French, British, and Soviet zones of occupation. In 1949 the three western zones were reconstituted as West Germany; the Soviet zone became East Germany. West Germany was reunified with East Germany in October 1990. **—West Ger′man** *adj. & n.*

West Hart•ford (härt′fərd). A town of central Connecticut, a residential suburb of Hartford. Population, 61,301.

West Ha•ven (hā′vən). A city of southern Connecticut, a residential suburb of New Haven. Population, 53,184.

West Highland white terrier *n.* A small white terrier with upright ears and tail, developed in Scotland from Cairn, Scottish, and Skye terriers.

West Hol•ly•wood (hŏl′ē-wo͝od′). A community of southern California northeast of Beverly Hills. Population, 35,703.

West In•dies (ĭn′dēz). *Abbr.* **W.I.** An archipelago between southeast North America and northern South America, separating the Caribbean Sea from the Atlantic Ocean and including the Greater Antilles, the Lesser Antilles, and the Bahama Islands. Several of the islands were originally sighted and explored by Columbus during his voyages of 1492–1504. The first permanent European settlement was made by the Spanish on Hispaniola in 1496. During the colonial period the English, French, and Dutch also laid claim to various islands, and the United States acquired Puerto Rico and part of the Virgin Islands in the late 19th and early 20th centuries. **—West In′di•an** *adj. & n.*

West Indies Federation. A group of ten former British colonies in the West Indies, including Jamaica, Trinidad and Tobago, and Barbados. It was established in 1958 and slated for independence in 1962 but broke up in May 1962 because of economic disagreements among the members. Some of the islands later formed the British-sponsored **West Indies Associated States,** which was gradually disbanded as the islands achieved independence in the 1970's and early 1980's.

west•ing (wĕs′tĭng) *n.* **1.** The difference in longitude between two positions as a result of a movement to the west. **2.** Progress toward the west. [From WEST.]

West•ing•house (wĕs′tĭng-hous′), **George.** 1846–1914. American engineer and manufacturer who received more than 400 patents for his many inventions, including the air brake (1869).

West Jor•dan (jôr′dn). A city of northern Utah, a suburb of Salt Lake City. Population, 26,794.

West La•fay•ette (lä′fē-ĕt′, lăf′ē-). A city of western Indiana on the Wabash River opposite Lafayette. It is the seat of Purdue University (established 1869). Population, 21,247.

West•lake (wĕst′lāk′). A city of northeast Ohio, a manufacturing suburb of Cleveland. Population, 19,483.

West•land (wĕst′lənd). A city of southeast Michigan, a suburb of Detroit. Population, 84,603.

West Mem•phis (mĕm′fĭs). A city of eastern Arkansas near the Mississippi River west of Memphis, Tennessee. It is a shipping and processing center. Population, 28,198.

West Mif•flin (mĭf′lĭn). A borough of southwest Pennsylvania, an industrial suburb of Pittsburgh on the Monongahela River. Population, 26,279.

West•min•ster (wĕst′mĭn′stər). **1.** Officially **City of Westminster.** A borough of Greater London in southeast England on the Thames River. It includes the principal offices of the British government, especially along Whitehall and Downing streets. **2.** A city of southern California, a residential suburb of Long Beach. Population, 71,133. **3.** A city of north-central Colorado, a suburb of Denver. Population, 50,211.

West•mont (wĕst′mŏnt′). **1.** A community of southern California, a residential suburb between Los Angeles and Long Beach. Population, 27,916. **2.** A village of northeast Illinois, a residential suburb of Chicago. Population, 16,718.

West•more•land (wĕst-môr′lənd, -mōr′-), **William Childs.** Born 1914. American general who was the senior commander of American troops in Vietnam (1964–1968).

West•mount (wĕst′mount′). A city of southern Quebec, Canada, a suburb of Montreal. Population, 20,480.

West New York (no͞o yôrk′, nyo͞o). A town of northeast New Jersey on the Hudson River opposite Manhattan. It is a residential community with varied light industries. Population, 39,194.

west-north•west (wĕst′nôrth′wĕst′, -nôr-wĕst′) *n.* *Abbr.* **WNW** The direction or point on the mariner's compass halfway between due west and northwest, or 67°30′ west of due north. **—west-northwest** *adj.* *Abbr.* **WNW** To, toward, of, facing, or in the west-northwest. **—west-northwest** *adv.* *Abbr.* **WNW** In, from, or toward the west-northwest.

Wes•ton (wĕs′tən), **Edward.** 1886–1958. American photographer whose stark, realistic images of landscapes and nudes influenced photographic art.

West Or•ange (ôr′ĭnj, ŏr′-). A town of northeast New Jersey, a residential suburb of Newark. Population, 39,510.

West Pak•i•stan (păk′ĭ-stăn′, pä′kĭ-stän′). A former region of Pakistan (after 1947) separated by about 1,609 km (1,000 mi) from East Pakistan, formerly East Bengal. In 1971 East Pakistan declared its independence as Bangladesh, and West Pakistan became the sole territory governed by Pakistan.

West Palm Beach (päm). A city of southeast Florida opposite Palm Beach. Henry M. Flagler developed the city as a commercial center for Palm Beach in 1893. Population, 62,530.

West Pen•sa•co•la (pĕn′sə-kō′lə). A community of northwest Florida, a suburb of Pensacola in the Florida Panhandle. Population, 24,571.

West•pha•lia (wĕst-fāl′yə, -fā′lē-ə). A historical region and former duchy of west-central Germany east of the Rhine River. The duchy was created in the 12th century and was administered for many centuries by ecclesiastical princes, especially the archbishop of Cologne. The Peace of Westphalia (1648) marked the end of the Thirty Years' War. Napoleon seized the area in 1807 and designated a portion of it as the kingdom of Westphalia, to be ruled by his brother Jérôme. The region became part of Prussia after 1815. **—West•pha′lian** *adj. & n.*

West Point. A U.S. military installation in southeast New York on the western bank of the Hudson River north of New York City. It has been a military post since 1778 and the seat of the U.S. Military Academy since 1802.

West•port (wĕst′pôrt′, -pōrt′). A town of southwest Connecticut on Long Island Sound. First settled in 1645, it is a residential community and summer resort. Population, 25,290.

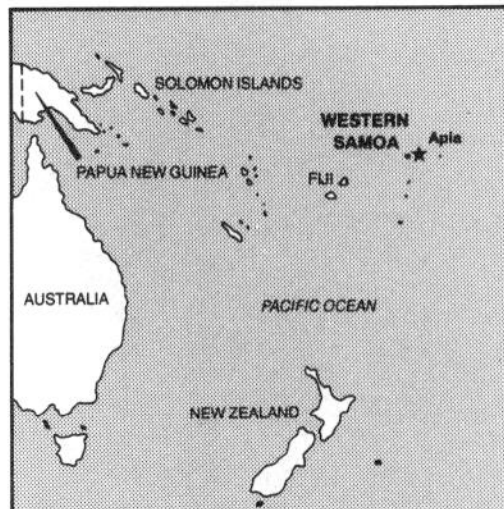

Western Samoa

Western Wall
With the Dome of the Rock in the background

West Highland white terrier

ă pat	oi boy
ā pay	ou out
âr care	o͝o took
ä father	o͞o boot
ĕ pet	ŭ cut
ē be	ûr urge
ĭ pit	th thin
ī pie	*th* this
îr pier	hw which
ŏ pot	zh vision
ō toe	ə about, item
ô paw	♦ regionalism

Stress marks: **′** (primary); ′ (secondary), as in **dictionary** (dĭk′shə-nĕr′ē)

wet suit

West Prus·sia (prŭsh′ə). A historical region of northeast Germany between Pomerania and East Prussia south of the Baltic Sea. Most of the territory was awarded to Poland in 1919 but reannexed by Germany in 1939. In 1945 West Prussia again became part of Poland.

West Saint Paul (sānt pôl′). A city of southeast Minnesota, an industrial suburb of St. Paul. Population, 18,527.

West Saxon *n.* **1.** The dialect of Old English used in southern England that was the chief literary dialect of England before the Norman Conquest. **2.** One of the Saxons inhabiting Wessex during the centuries before the Norman Conquest.

West Side. The western part of Manhattan Island in New York City bordering on the Hudson River. It includes a theater and entertainment district and many residential areas.

west-south·west (wĕst′south′wĕst′, -sou-wĕst′) *n. Abbr.* **WSW** The direction or point on the mariner's compass halfway between due west and southwest, or 112°30′ west of due north. **—west-southwest** *adj. Abbr.* **WSW** To, toward, of, facing, or in the west-southwest. **—west-southwest** *adv. Abbr.* **WSW** In, from, or toward the west-southwest.

West Spring·field (sprĭng′fēld′). **1.** A town of southwest Massachusetts, a manufacturing suburb of Springfield. Population, 27,042. **2.** A community of northeast Virginia, a residential suburb of Alexandria. Population, 16,000.

West Van·cou·ver (văn-ko͞o′vər). A city of southwest British Columbia, Canada, a suburb of Vancouver. Population, 35,728.

West Vir·gin·ia (vər-jĭn′yə). *Abbr.* **WV, W.Va.** A state of the east-central United States. It was admitted as the 35th state in 1863. West Virginia was part of Virginia until the area refused to endorse the ordinance of secession in 1861. Charleston is the capital and the largest city. Population, 1,950,258. **—West Vir·gin′ian** *adj. & n.*

west·ward (wĕst′wərd) *adv. & adj.* Toward, to, or in the west. **—westward** *n.* A westward direction, point, or region. **—west′ward·ly** *adv. & adj.* **—west′wards** *adv.*

West War·wick (wŏr′ĭk, wôr′wĭk). A town of east-central Rhode Island south-southwest of Providence. Textile manufacturing is important to its economy. Population, 27,026.

♦**wet** (wĕt) *adj.* **wet·ter, wet·test. 1.** Covered or soaked with a liquid, such as water. **2.** Not yet dry or firm: *wet paint.* **3.** Stored or preserved in liquid. **4.** Used or prepared with water or other liquids. **5.a.** Rainy, humid, or foggy: *wet weather.* **b.** Characterized by frequent or heavy precipitation: *a wet climate.* **6.** *Informal.* Allowing the sale of alcoholic beverages: *a wet county.* **—wet** *n.* **1.** Something that wets; moisture. **2.** Rainy or snowy weather: *go out into the wet.* **3.** *Informal.* One who supports the legality of the production and sale of alcoholic beverages. **4. wets.** *Chicago.* French fries served with gravy. **—wet** *v.* **wet** or **wet·ted, wet·ting, wets.** *—tr.* **1.** To make wet; dampen: *wet a sponge.* **2.** To make (a bed or one's clothes) wet by urinating. *—intr.* To become wet. ***—idioms.*** **all wet.** *Slang.* Entirely mistaken. **wet behind the ears.** Inexperienced; green. **wet (one's) whistle.** *Informal.* To take a drink. [Middle English, from Old English *wǣt.* See **wed-**[1] in Appendix.]

SYNONYMS: *wet, damp, moist, dank, humid.* These adjectives mean covered with or saturated with liquid. *Wet* describes not only what is covered or soaked (*a wet sidewalk; a wet sponge*) but also what is not yet dry (*wet paint*). *Damp* and *moist* both mean slightly wet, but *damp* often implies an unpleasant clamminess: *a cold, damp cellar; a moist breeze. Dank* emphasizes disagreeable, often unhealthful wetness: *a dank cave; dank tropical forests. Humid* refers to an unpleasantly high degree of moisture in the atmosphere: *hot, humid weather.*

wet·back (wĕt′băk′) *n. Offensive Slang.* Used as a disparaging term for a Mexican, especially a laborer who crosses the U.S. border illegally. [From the fact that the Rio Grande is a common entry point.]

wet blanket *n. Informal.* One that discourages enjoyment or enthusiasm.

wet cell *n.* A primary cell having a liquid electrolyte.

wet dream *n.* An erotic dream accompanied by ejaculation of semen.

wet fly *n.* An artificial fly used in fishing that floats beneath the water's surface when cast.

weth·er (wĕth′ər) *n.* A castrated ram. [Middle English, from Old English. See **wet-**[2] in Appendix.]

Weth·ers·field (wĕth′ərz-fēld′). A town of central Connecticut, a suburb of Hartford on the Connecticut River. It was first settled by English colonists in 1634. Population, 26,013.

wet·land (wĕt′lănd′) *n.* A lowland area, such as a marsh or swamp, that is saturated with moisture, especially when regarded as the natural habitat of wildlife: *a program to preserve our state's wetlands.*

wet monsoon *n. Meteorology.* A monsoon.

wet·ness (wĕt′nĭs) *n.* **1.** The condition of being wet. **2.** Moisture. **3.** Rainy or persistently damp weather.

wet nurse *n.* **1.** A woman who suckles another woman's child. **2.** One who treats another with excessive care or solicitude.

wet-nurse (wĕt′nûrs′) *tr.v.* **-nursed, -nurs·ing, -nurs·es. 1.** To serve as wet nurse for. **2.** To treat with excessive care.

wet pack *n.* A therapeutic pack moistened in hot or cold water.

wet suit *n.* A tight-fitting permeable suit worn in cold water, as by skin divers, to retain body heat.

wet·ter (wĕt′ər) *n.* One that wets.

Wet·ter·horn Peak (vĕt′ər-hôrn′). A mountain, 4,274.6 m (14,015 ft), in the San Juan Mountains of southwest Colorado.

wet·ting agent (wĕt′ĭng) *n.* A substance that reduces the surface tension of a liquid, causing the liquid to spread across or penetrate more easily the surface of a solid.

we've (wēv). We have.

Wey·den (wīd′n, vīd′n), **Rogier van der.** Also known as Roger de la Pasture. 1400?–1464. Flemish painter noted for his religious works, including *The Deposition* (c. 1435).

Wey·mouth (wā′məth). A town of eastern Massachusetts, a manufacturing suburb of Boston. Population, 55,601.

wf or **w.f.** *abbr. Printing.* Wrong font.

WFTU *abbr.* World Federation of Trade Unions.

w.g. *abbr.* Wire gauge.

WH *abbr.* Watt-hour.

wh. *abbr.* White.

whack (hwăk, wăk) *v.* **whacked, whack·ing, whacks.** *—tr.* To strike (someone or something) with a sharp blow; slap. *—intr.* To deal a sharp, resounding blow. **—whack** *n.* **1.** A sharp, swift blow. **2.** The sound made by a sharp, swift blow. ***—phrasal verb.*** **whack off.** *Vulgar Slang.* To masturbate. ***—idioms.*** **have (or take) a whack at.** *Informal.* To attempt. **out of whack.** *Informal.* Out of order; not functioning correctly. **whacked out.** *Slang.* **1.** Exhausted. **2.** Crazy. **3.** Under the influence of a mind-altering drug. [Probably imitative.]

whack·ing (hwăk′ĭng, wăk′-) *Chiefly British. adj.* Superlative; excellent. **—whacking** *adv.* Used as an intensive.

whack·o (hwăk′ō, wăk′ō) *n. Slang.* Variant of **wacko.**

whack·y (hwăk′ē, wăk′ē) *adj. Slang.* Variant of **wacky.**

whale[1] (hwāl, wāl) *n.* **1.** Any of various marine mammals of the order Cetacea, having the general shape of a fish with forelimbs modified to form flippers, a tail with horizontal flukes, and one or two blowholes for breathing, especially one of the very large species as distinguished from the smaller dolphins and porpoises. **2.** *Informal.* An impressive example: *a whale of a story.* **—whale** *intr.v.* **whaled, whal·ing, whales.** To engage in the hunting of whales. [Middle English, from Old English *hwæl.*]

whale[2] (hwāl, wāl) *v.* **whaled, whal·ing, whales.** *—tr.* To strike or hit repeatedly and forcefully; thrash. *—intr.* To attack vehemently: *The poet whaled away at the critics.* [Origin unknown.]

whale·back (hwāl′băk′, wāl′-) *n. Nautical.* A steamship with the bow and upper deck rounded so as to shed water.

whale·boat (hwāl′bōt′, wāl′-) *n. Nautical.* **1.** A long rowboat, pointed at both ends and designed to move and turn swiftly, formerly used in the pursuit and harpooning of whales. **2.** A boat similar to such a rowboat in size and shape; a whaler.

whale·bone (hwāl′bōn′, wāl′-) *n.* **1.** The elastic, horny material forming the fringed plates that hang from the upper jaw of baleen whales and strain plankton from the water. Also called *baleen.* **2.** An object made of this material.

whalebone whale *n.* See **baleen whale.**

whale oil *n.* A yellowish oil obtained from whale blubber, formerly used in making soap and candles and as a lubricating oil.

whal·er (hwā′lər, wā′-) *n.* **1.** One that hunts or processes whales. **2.** *Nautical.* A whaling ship. **3.** *Nautical.* A whaleboat.

Whales (hwālz, wālz), **Bay of.** An inlet of the Ross Sea in the Ross Ice Shelf of Antarctica.

whale shark *n.* A very large shark *(Rhincodon typus)* of warm marine waters, having a spotted body, small teeth, and a network of rakelike sieves extending from its gills for straining plankton from the water.

whal·ing (hwā′lĭng, wāl′-) *n.* The business or practice of hunting, killing, and processing whales.

wham (hwăm, wăm) *n.* **1.** A forceful, resounding blow. **2.** The sound of such a blow; a thud. **—wham** *v.* **whammed, wham·ming, whams.** *—tr.* To strike or smash into with resounding impact. *—intr.* To smash with great force. [Imitative.]

wham·mo (hwăm′ō, wăm′ō) *interj. Slang.* Used to indicate the startling abruptness of a sound, an action, or an event: *"The alarm goes off and—whammo!—we're all at our assigned stations"* (Meg Greenfield). [Alteration of WHAM.]

wham·my (hwăm′ē, wăm′ē) *n., pl.* **-mies.** *Slang.* A supernatural spell for subduing an adversary; a hex: *put the whammy on someone.* [Perhaps from WHAM.]

whang[1] (hwăng, wăng) *n.* **1.** A thong or whip of hide or leather. **2.a.** A lashing blow, as of a whip. **b.** The sound of such a blow. **—whang** *tr.v.* **whanged, whang·ing, whangs. 1.** To beat or whip with a thong. **2.** To beat with a sharp blow or blows. [Dialectal variant of Middle English *thong, thwang,* thong. See THONG.]

whang[2] (hwăng, wăng) *Informal. v.* **whanged, whang·ing, whangs.** *—tr.* To strike so as to produce a loud, reverberant noise. *—intr.* To produce a loud, reverberant noise. **—whang** *n.* A loud, reverberant noise. [Imitative.]

whang·ee (hwăng-gē′, wăng′-) *n.* **1.** Any of several Asian bamboos of the genus *Phyllostachys.* **2.** A walking stick made from the woody stem of any of these bamboos. [Chinese (Mandarin) *huáng lí* : *huáng* (short for *huáng zhú* : *huáng,* yellow + *zhú,* bamboo) + *lí,* a kind of bramble.]

wharf (hwôrf, wôrf) *n., pl.* **wharves** (hwôrvz, wôrvz) or **wharfs.** *Abbr.* **whf. 1.** A landing place or pier where ships may tie up and load or unload. **2.** *Obsolete.* A shore or riverbank. **—wharf** *v.* **wharfed, wharf·ing, wharfs.** *—tr.* **1.** To moor (a vessel) at a wharf. **2.** To take to or store (cargo) on a wharf. **3.** To furnish, equip, or protect with wharves or a wharf. *—intr.* To berth at a wharf. [Middle English, from Old English *hwearf.*]

wharf·age (hwôr′fĭj, wôr′fĭj) *n.* **1.a.** The use of wharves or a wharf. **b.** The charges for this usage. **2.** A group of wharves.

wharf·in·ger (hwôr′fĭn-jər, wôr′-) *n.* One who owns or manages a wharf. [Alteration of WHARFAGE + -ER[1].]

wharf rat *n.* **1.** A rat that infests wharves and ships. **2.** *Slang.* A person who frequents wharves.

Whar·ton (hwôr′tn, wôr′-), **Edith Newbold Jones.** 1862–1937. American writer whose works include subtle satires on New York society, such as *The House of Mirth* (1905), and the short, tragic novel *Ethan Frome* (1911).

wharves (hwôrvz, wôrvz) *n.* A plural of **wharf.**

what (hwŏt, hwŭt, wŏt, wŭt; hwət, wət *when unstressed*) *pron.* **1.a.** Which thing or which particular one of many: *What are you having for dinner? What did she say?* **b.** Which kind, character, or designation: *What are these objects?* **c.** One of how much value or significance: *What are possessions to a dying man?* **2.a.** That which; the thing that: *Listen to what I tell you.* **b.** Whatever thing that: *come what may.* **3.** *Informal.* Something: *I'll tell you what.* **4.** *Non-Standard.* Which, who, or that: *It's the poor what gets the blame.* **—what** *adj.* **1.** Which one or ones of several or many: *What college are you attending? You should know what musical that song is from.* **2.** Whatever: *They soon repaired what damage had been done.* **3.** How great; how astonishing: *What a fool!* **—what** *adv.* How much; in what respect; how: *What does it matter?* **—what** *conj.* That: *I don't know but what I'll go.* **—what** *interj.* **1.** Used to express surprise, incredulity, or other strong and sudden excitement. **2.** *Chiefly British.* Used as a tag question, often to solicit agreement. ***—idioms.*** **what for.** *Informal.* A scolding or strong reprimand: *The teacher gave the tardy student what for.* **what have you.** What remains and need not be mentioned: *a room full of chairs, lamps, radios, and what have you.* **what if. 1.** What would occur if; suppose that. **2.** What does it matter if. **what it takes.** The necessary expertise or qualities needed for success: *She has what it takes to be a doctor.* **what's what.** *Informal.* The fundamentals and details of a situation or process; the true state or condition. **what with.** Taking into consideration; because of: *"I've often wondered why some good crime writer . . . hasn't taken up with New Orleans, what with its special raffishness, its peculiar flavor of bonhomie and a slightly suspect charm"* (Walker Percy). [Middle English, from Old English *hwæt.* See **k^wo-** in Appendix.]

USAGE NOTE: When *what* is the subject of a clause, it may be construed as singular or plural, depending on the sense. It is singular when taken as the equivalent of *that which* or *the thing which,* as in *I see what* seems *to be a dead tree;* and it is plural when it is taken as the equivalent of *those which* or *the things which,* as in *He sometimes makes what* seem *to be gestures of aloofness.* • When a *what* clause is itself the subject of a sentence, it may be construed as singular or plural, but the conditions governing this choice are somewhat more complicated. In general, a *what* clause will be taken as a plural when the clause contains an explicit indication of its own plurality. There are two principal cases. First, the clause is plural if *what* is the subject of the clause and the verb of the clause is itself plural: *What* seem *to be two dead trees* are *blocking the road. What most* surprise *me* are *the inflammatory remarks at the end of his article.* If the verb in the *what* clause does not anticipate the plural sense of the predicate in this way, a singular verb is generally used in the main clause as well, though the plural is sometimes found: *What truly* commands *respect* is (sometimes *are*) *a large navy and a resolute foreign policy.* Second, the *what* clause is treated as plural when its predicate contains a plural noun phrase that unambiguously establishes the plurality of the clause as a whole, as in *What traditional grammarians called "predicates"* are *called "verb phrases" by modern linguists. What the Romans established as military outposts* were *later to become important trading centers.* In the absence of explicit plural marking of either of these types in a subject *what* clause, the clause is usually treated as singular for the purposes of agreement, regardless of the sense: *What she held in her lap* was *four kittens. What the apparent diamonds turned out to be* was *paste.* In some cases, however, a clause with *what* as the subject may be treated as singular or plural, depending on a subtle distinction of sense. In *What* excite *him most* are *money and power,* the implication is that money and power are distinct elements; in *What* excites *him most* is *money and power,* the implication is that money and power are taken as constituting a single entity. See Usage Note at **which.**

what·cha·ma·call·it (hwŏch′ə-mə-kôl′ĭt, hwŭch′-, wŏch′-, wŭch′-) also **what·cha·ma·call·um** (-əm) *n.* An item or a thing that is unnamed or unnamable. [Alteration of *what you may call it.*]

what·ev·er (hwŏt-ĕv′ər, hwŭt-, wŏt-, wŭt-) *pron.* **1.** Everything or anything that: *Do whatever you please.* **2.** What amount that; the whole of what: *Whatever is left over is yours.* **3.** No matter what: *Whatever happens, we'll meet here tonight.* **4.** Also what ever. *Informal.* Which thing or things; what: *Whatever does he mean?* **—whatever** *adj.* **1.** Of any number or kind; any: *Whatever requests you make will be granted.* **2.** All of; the whole of: *She applied whatever strength she had left to the task.* **3.** Of any kind at all: *No campers whatever may use the lake before noon.*

USAGE NOTE: Both *whatever* and *what ever* can be used in sentences such as *Whatever* (or *What ever*) *made her say that?* Critics have occasionally objected to the one-word form, but it is supported by extensive precedent in reputable writing. The same is true of the forms *whoever, whenever, wherever,* and *however* when these expressions are used similarly. In adjectival uses only the one-word form is used: *Take whatever* (not *what ever*) *books you need.* • When a clause beginning with *whatever* is the subject of a sentence, no comma should be used: *Whatever you do is right.* Otherwise, a comma may be used: *Whatever you do, don't burn the toast.* • When the phrase preceding a restrictive clause is introduced by *whichever* or *whatever, that* should not be used in formal writing. It is regarded as incorrect to write *whatever book that you want to look at;* one should write instead *Whatever book you want to look at will be sent to your office* or *Whichever book costs less* (not *that costs less*) *is fine with us.* See Usage Notes at **however, that.**

Phillis Wheatley
1773 engraving by an unknown artist

what·not (hwŏt′nŏt′, hwŭt′-, wŏt′-, wŭt′-) *n.* **1.** A minor or unspecified object or article. **2.** A set of light, open shelves for ornaments. **—whatnot** *pron.* Any of various additional or unspecified things or items: *"family differences, differing social origins, and whatnot"* (George F. Kennan).

what·so·ev·er (hwŏt′sō-ĕv′ər, hwŭt′-, wŏt′-, wŭt′-) *pron.* Whatever. **—whatsoever** *adj.* Whatever: *no power whatsoever.*

wheal (hwēl, wēl) *n.* A small swelling on the skin, as from an insect bite, that usually itches or burns. [Probably alteration of WALE.]

wheat (hwēt, wēt) *n.* **1.** Any of various annual cereal grasses of the genus *Triticum* of the Mediterranean region and southwest Asia, especially *T. aestivum,* widely cultivated in temperate regions in many varieties for its commercially important edible grain. **2.** The grain of any of these grasses, ground to produce flour used in breadstuffs and pasta. [Middle English *whete,* from Old English *hwǣte.* See **kweit-** in Appendix.]

wheat bread *n.* A bread made from a mixture of white and whole-wheat flours.

wheat·ear (hwēt′îr′, wēt′-) *n.* A small thrush *(Oenanthe oenanthe)* having a gray back, buff breast, and white rump, found in open areas of most northern regions. [Back-formation from earlier *wheatears* (taken as pl.) : probably by folk etymology from WHITE + ARSE.]

wheat·en (hwēt′n, wēt′n) *adj.* Of, relating to, or derived from wheat.

wheat germ *n.* The vitamin-rich embryo of the wheat kernel that is separated before milling for use as a cereal or food supplement.

Wheat·ley (hwēt′lē, wēt′-), **Phillis.** 1753?–1784. African-born American poet considered the first widely recognized Black writer in America.

Whea·ton (hwēt′n, wēt′n). A city of northeast Illinois west of Chicago. Settled in the 1830's, it is mainly residential. Population, 43,043.

Wheat Ridge (hwēt′, wēt′). A city of north-central Colorado, a residential suburb of Denver. Population, 30,293.

wheat rust *n.* **1.** A destructive disease of wheat caused by a rust fungus. **2.** Any of several rust fungi of the genus *Puccinia* that cause this disease.

Wheat·stone bridge (hwēt′stōn′, wēt′-) also **Wheat·stone's bridge** (-stōnz′) *n.* An instrument or a circuit consisting of four resistors or their equivalent in series, used to determine the value of an unknown resistance when the other three resistances are known. [After Sir Charles *Wheatstone* (1802–1875), British physicist and inventor.]

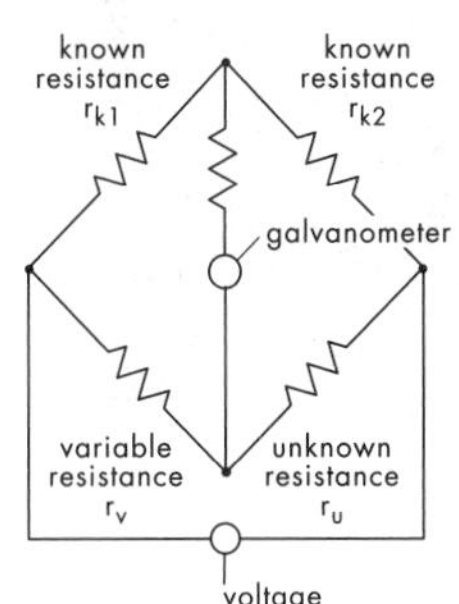

Wheatstone bridge

wheat·worm (hwēt′wûrm′, wēt′-) *n.* A small nematode worm *(Anguina tritici)* that is parasitic on and destructive to wheat.

whee (hwē, wē) *interj.* Used to express extreme pleasure.

whee·dle (hwēd′l, wēd′l) *v.* **-dled, -dling, -dles.** *—tr.* **1.** To persuade or attempt to persuade by flattery or guile; cajole. **2.** To obtain through the use of flattery or guile: *a swindler who wheedled my life savings out of me.* *—intr.* To use flattery or cajolery to achieve one's ends. [Origin unknown.] **—whee′dler** *n.* **—whee′dling·ly** *adv.*

wheel (hwēl, wēl) *n.* **1.** A solid disk or a rigid circular ring connected by spokes to a hub, designed to turn around an axle passed through the center. **2.** Something resembling such a disk or ring in appearance or movement or having a wheel as its principal part or characteristic, as: **a.** The steering device on a vehicle. **b.** A potter's wheel. **c.** A water wheel. **d.** A spinning wheel. **e.** *Games.* A device used in roulette and other games of chance. **f.** A firework that rotates while burning. **g.** *Informal.* A bicycle. **h.** An instrument to which a victim was bound for torture during the Middle Ages. **3. wheels.** Forces that provide energy, movement, or direction: *the wheels of commerce.* **4.** The act or process of turning; revolution or rotation. **5.** A military maneuver executed in order to change the direction of movement of

ă pat	oi boy
ā pay	ou out
âr care	ŏŏ took
ä father	ōō boot
ĕ pet	ŭ cut
ē be	ûr urge
ĭ pit	th thin
ī pie	*th* this
îr pier	hw which
ŏ pot	zh vision
ō toe	ə about, item
ô paw	♦ regionalism

Stress marks: ′ (primary); ′ (secondary), as in **dictionary** (dĭk′shə-nĕr′ē)

wheelbarrow

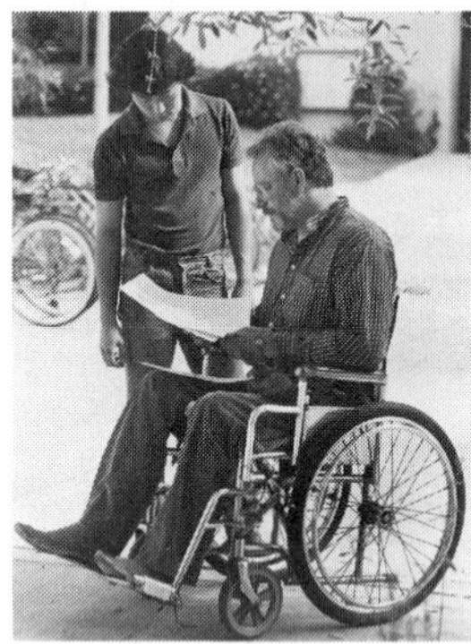

wheelchair

wheelie

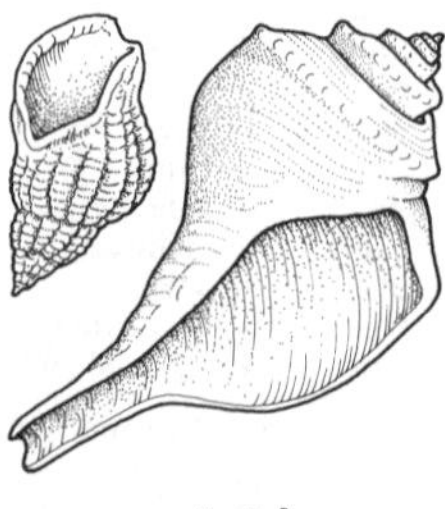

whelk[1]

a formation, as of troops or ships, in which the formation is maintained while the outer unit describes an arc and the inner or center unit remains stationary as a pivot. **6. wheels.** *Slang.* A motor vehicle or access thereto: *Do you have wheels tonight?* **7.** *Slang.* A person with a great deal of power or influence: *thinks he's a wheel because he works in the state government.* **—wheel** *v.* **wheeled, wheel·ing, wheels.** *—tr.* **1.** To roll, move, or transport on wheels or a wheel. **2.** To cause to turn around or as if around a central axis; revolve or rotate. **3.** To provide with wheels or a wheel. *—intr.* **1.** To turn around or as if around a central axis; revolve or rotate. **2.** To roll or move on or as if on wheels or a wheel. **3.** To fly in a curving or circular course: *A flock of gulls wheeled just above the dock.* **4.** To turn or whirl around in place; pivot: *"The boy wheeled and the fried eggs leaped from his tray"* (Ivan Gold). **5.** To reverse one's opinion or practice: *One can never tell when she'll wheel about on that subject.* ***—idioms.*** **at** (or **behind**) **the wheel. 1.** Operating the steering mechanism of a vehicle; driving. **2.** Directing or controlling; in charge. **wheel and deal.** *Informal.* To engage in the advancement of one's own interests, especially in a canny, aggressive, or unscrupulous way. [Middle English, from Old English *hwēol.* See **k^wel-[1]** in Appendix.]

wheel and axle *n.* A simple machine consisting of an axle to which a wheel is fastened so that torque applied to the wheel winds a rope or chain onto the axle, yielding a mechanical advantage equal to the ratio of the diameter of the wheel to that of the axle.

wheel·bar·row (hwēl′băr′ō, wēl′-) *n.* A one- or two-wheeled vehicle with handles at the rear, used to convey small loads.

wheel·base (hwēl′bās′, wēl′-) *n.* The distance from the center of the front wheel to that of the rear wheel in a motor vehicle, usually expressed in inches.

wheel bug *n.* A large assassin bug *(Arilus cristatus)* of North America that has a notched, wheellike projection on the back of the thorax and preys on other insects.

wheel·chair also **wheel chair** (hwēl′châr′, wēl′-) *n.* A chair mounted on large wheels for the use of a sick or disabled person.

wheeled (hwēld, wēld) *adj.* Having wheels or a wheel. Often used in combination: *a three-wheeled bike.*

wheel·er (hwē′lər, wē′-) *n.* **1.** One that wheels. **2.** A thing that moves on or is equipped with wheels or a wheel. Often used in combination: *a three-wheeler; a paddle-wheeler.* **3.** A wheel horse.

Whee·ler (hwē′lər, wē′-), **Joseph.** 1836–1906. American Confederate general and politician. One of the South's most popular and aggressive commanders, he later served as U.S. representative from Georgia (1881–1883 and 1885–1900) and sought reconciliation between the North and South.

Wheeler, William Almon. 1819–1887. Vice President of the United States (1877–1881) under Rutherford B. Hayes.

wheel·er-deal·er (hwē′lər-dē′lər, wē′-) *n. Informal.* One who advances one's own interests by canny, aggressive, or unscrupulous behavior.

wheel horse *n.* **1.** The horse in a team that follows the leader and is harnessed nearest the front wheels. **2.** A diligent, dependable worker, especially in a political organization.

wheel·house (hwēl′hous′, wēl′-) *n. Nautical.* See **pilothouse.**

wheel·ie (hwē′lē, wē-) *n.* A stunt in which the front wheel or wheels of a vehicle, such as a bicycle or motorcycle, are raised so that the vehicle is balanced momentarily on its rear wheel or wheels. [Diminutive of WHEEL.]

Wheel·ing (hwē′lĭng, wē′-). **1.** A village of northeast Illinois, a suburb of Chicago. Population, 23,266. **2.** A city of northwest West Virginia in the Panhandle on the Ohio River southwest of Pittsburgh, Pennsylvania. Settled in 1769, it was the state capital from 1863 to 1870 and from 1875 to 1885. Population, 43,070.

wheel lock *n.* **1.** A firing mechanism in certain obsolete small arms, in which a small wheel produces sparks by revolving against a flint. **2.** A firearm using such a mechanism.

wheel·man (hwēl′mən, wēl′-) *n.* **1.** *Nautical.* One who steers a ship; a helmsman. **2.** The driver of an automobile, especially of a getaway car. **3.** A bicyclist.

wheels·man (hwēlz′mən, wēlz′-) *n.* A wheelman.

wheel·work (hwēl′wûrk′, wēl′-) *n.* An arrangement of gears or wheels in a mechanical device.

wheel·wright (hwēl′rīt′, wēl′-) *n.* One that builds and repairs wheels.

wheeze (hwēz, wēz) *v.* **wheezed, wheez·ing, wheez·es.** *—intr.* **1.** To breathe with difficulty, producing a hoarse whistling sound. **2.** To make a sound resembling laborious breathing. *—tr.* To produce or utter with a hoarse whistling sound: *The old locomotive wheezed steam.* **—wheeze** *n.* **1.** A wheezing sound. **2.** *Informal.* An old joke. [Middle English *whesen,* probably from Old Norse *hvæsa,* to hiss. See **kwes-** in Appendix.] **—wheez′er** *n.* **—wheez′ing·ly** *adv.*

wheez·y (hwē′zē, wē′-) *adj.* **-i·er, -i·est. 1.** Given to wheezing. **2.** Producing a wheezing sound. **—wheez′i·ly** *adv.* **—wheez′i·ness** *n.*

whelk[1] (hwĕlk, wĕlk) *n.* Any of various large, mostly edible marine snails of the family Buccinidae, having a pointed, spiral shell, especially *Buccinum undatum,* which is commonly eaten in Europe. [Middle English *welke, whelke,* from Old English *weoloc.* See **wel-[2]** in Appendix.]

whelk[2] (hwĕlk, wĕlk) *n.* An inflamed swelling, such as a pimple or pustule. [Middle English *whelke,* from Old English *hwylca;* akin to *hwelian,* to suppurate.] **—whelk′y** *adj.*

whelm (hwĕlm, wĕlm) *tr.v.* **whelmed, whelm·ing, whelms. 1.** To cover with water; submerge. **2.** To overwhelm. [Middle English *whelmen,* to overturn, probably alteration (influenced by *helmen,* to cover, from Old English *helmian*) of *whelven,* from Old English *-hwelfan,* as in *āhwelfan,* to cover over.]

whelp (hwĕlp, wĕlp) *n.* **1.** A young offspring of a mammal, such as a dog or wolf. **2.a.** A child; a youth. **b.** An impudent young fellow. See Usage Note at **adage. 3.a.** A tooth of a sprocket wheel. **b.** *Nautical.* Any of the ridges on the barrel of a windlass or capstan. **—whelp** *v.* **whelped, whelp·ing, whelps.** *—intr.* To give birth to whelps or a whelp. *—tr.* To give birth to (whelps or a whelp). [Middle English, from Old English *hwelp.*]

when (hwĕn, wĕn) *adv.* At what time: *When will we leave?* **—when** *conj.* **1.** At the time that: *in the spring, when the snow melts.* **2.** As soon as: *I'll call you when I get there.* **3.** Whenever: *When the wind blows, all the doors rattle.* **4.** During the time at which; while: *When I was young, I was sick all the time.* **5.** Whereas; although: *She stopped short when she ought to have continued.* **6.** Considering that; if: *How can he get good grades when he won't study?* **—when** *pron.* What or which time: *Since when has this been going on?* **—when** *n.* The time or date: *Have they decided the where and when?* [Middle English, from Old English *hwenne.* See **k^wo-** in Appendix.]

USAGE NOTE: In informal style *when* is often used after *be* in definitions: *A dilemma is when you don't know which way to turn.* The construction is useful, but it is widely regarded as incorrect or as unsuitable for formal discourse. In formal style there is no alternative but to rephrase such definitions: *A dilemma is a situation in which you don't know which way to turn. You are in a dilemma when you don't know which way to turn.*

when·as (hwĕn-ăz′, wĕn-) *conj. Archaic.* **1.** When. **2.** Whereas.

whence (hwĕns, wĕns) *adv.* **1.** From where; from what place: *Whence came this traveler?* **2.** From what origin or source: *Whence comes this splendid feast?* **—whence** *conj.* **1.** Out of which place; from or out of which. **2.** By reason of which; from which: *The dog was coal black, whence the name Shadow.* [Middle English *whennes* : *whenne,* whence (from Old English *hwanon;* see **k^wo-** in Appendix) + *-es,* genitive sing. suff.; see –S[3].]

USAGE NOTE: The construction *from whence* has been criticized as redundant since the 18th century. It is true that *whence* incorporates the sense of *from: a remote village, whence little news reached the wider world.* But *from whence* has been used steadily by reputable writers since the 14th century, most notably in the King James Bible: *"I will lift up mine eyes unto the hills, from whence cometh my help"* (Psalms). It is difficult to label as incorrect a construction with such respectable antecedents. Still, it may be observed that *whence* (like *thence*) is most often used nowadays to impart an archaic or highly formal tone to a passage, and that this effect is probably better realized if the archaic syntax of the word—without *from*—is preserved as well.

whence·so·ev·er (hwĕns′sō-ĕv′ər, wĕns′-) *adv.* From whatever place or source. **—whencesoever** *conj.* From any place or source that.

when·ev·er (hwĕn-ĕv′ər, wĕn-) *adv.* **1.** At whatever time. **2.** Also **when ever.** When. See Usage Note at **whatever. —whenever** *conj.* **1.** At whatever time that: *We can leave whenever you're ready.* **2.** Every time that: *The child smiles whenever the puppy appears.*

when·so·ev·er (hwĕn′sō-ĕv′ər, wĕn′-) *adv.* At whatever time at all; whenever. **—whensoever** *conj.* Whenever.

where (hwâr, wâr) *adv.* **1.** At or in what place: *Where is the telephone?* **2.** In what situation or position: *Where would we be without your help?* **3.** From what place or source: *Where did you get this idea?* **4.** To what place; toward what end: *Where is this argument leading?* **—where** *conj.* **1.** At what or which place: *She moved to the city, where jobs are available.* **2.a.** In a place in which: *He lives where the climate is mild.* **b.** In any place or situation in which; wherever: *Where there's smoke, there's fire.* **3.a.** To a place in which: *We should go where it is quieter.* **b.** To a place or situation in which: *They will go where they are happy.* **—where** *n.* **1.** The place or occasion: *We know the when but not the where of it.* **2.** What place, source, or cause: *Where are you from?* [Middle English, from Old English *hwǣr.* See **k^wo-** in Appendix.]

USAGE NOTE: When *where* is used to refer to a point of origin, the preposition *from* is required: *Where did she come from?* When it is used to refer to a point of destination, the preposition *to* is generally superfluous: *Where is she going?* (preferable to *Where is she going to?*). When it is used to refer to the place at which an event or a situation is located, the use of *at* is widely regarded as regional or colloquial: *Where is the station?* (not *Where is the station at?*). The idiomatic phrase *where it's at,* widely used in the 1960's to refer to "the current state of things," is now largely passé, except when used for stylistic effect: *"Generally, I knew* *where he was at, but couldn't always tell where he was coming from"* (Robert M. Adams). See Usage Note at **why.**

---

where·a·bouts (hwâr′ə-bouts′, wâr′-) *adv.* About where; in, at, or near what location: *Whereabouts do you live?* **—whereabouts** *n.* *(used with a sing. or pl. verb).* Approximate location: *His whereabouts is a matter of conjecture. Her whereabouts are still unknown.*

where·as (hwâr-ăz′, wâr-) *conj.* **1.** It being the fact that; inasmuch as. **2.** While at the same time. **3.** While on the contrary. **—whereas** *n.* **1.** An introductory statement to a formal document; a preamble. **2.** A conditional statement.

where·at (hwâr-ăt′, wâr-) *conj.* **1.** Toward or at which. **2.** As a result or consequence of; whereupon.

where·by (hwâr-bī′, wâr-) *conj.* In accordance with which; by or through which.

where ever *adv.* Variant of **wherever** (sense 2).

where·fore (hwâr′fôr′, -fōr′, wâr′-) *adv.* **1.** For what purpose or reason; why. **2.** Therefore. **—wherefore** *n.* A purpose or cause: *wanted to know all the whys and wherefores.*

where·from (hwâr′frŭm′, -frŏm′, wâr′-) *conj.* From which.

where·in (hwâr-ĭn′, wâr-) *adv.* In what way; how: *Wherein have we sinned?* **—wherein** *conj.* **1.** In which location; where: *the country wherein those people live.* **2.** During which. **3.** In what way; how: *showed them wherein they were wrong.*

where·in·to (hwâr-ĭn′to͞o, wâr-) *conj.* Into which.

where·of (hwâr-ŏv′, -ŭv′, wâr-) *conj.* **1.** Of what: *I know whereof I speak.* **2.a.** Of which: *ancient pottery whereof many examples are lost.* **b.** Of whom. **—whereof** *adv. Archaic.* Of what.

where·on (hwâr-ŏn′, -ôn′, wâr-) *adv. Archaic.* On which or what: *"the ground whereon she trod"* (John Milton).

where·so·ev·er (hwâr′sō-ĕv′ər, wâr′-) *conj.* In, to, or from whatever place at all; wherever.

where·through (hwâr′thro͞o′, wâr′-) *conj.* Through, because of, or during which.

where·to (hwâr′to͞o′, wâr′-) *adv.* To what place; toward what end. **—whereto** *conj.* To which.

where·un·to (hwâr-ŭn′to͞o, wâr-) *adv. & conj.* Whereto.

where·up·on (hwâr′ə-pŏn′, -pôn′, wâr′-) *conj.* **1.** On which. **2.** In close consequence of which: *The instructor entered the room, whereupon we got to our feet.*

wher·ev·er (hwâr-ĕv′ər, wâr-) *adv.* **1.** In or to whatever place: *used red pencil wherever needed.* **2.** Also **where ever.** Where: *Where ever have you been so long?* See Usage Note at **whatever.** **—wherever** *conj.* In or to whichever place or situation: *He seems to make enemies wherever he goes.*

where·with (hwâr′wĭth′, -wĭth′, wâr′-) *pron.* The thing or things with which. **—wherewith** *conj.* By means of which. **—wherewith** *adv. Obsolete.* With what or which.

where·with·al (hwâr′wĭth-ôl′, -wĭth-, wâr′-) *n.* The necessary means, especially financial means: *didn't have the wherewithal to survive an economic downturn.* **—wherewithal** *conj.* Wherewith. **—wherewithal** *pron.* Wherewith.

wher·ry (hwĕr′ē, wĕr′ē) *n., pl.* **-ries.** *Nautical.* **1.** A light, swift rowboat built for one person and often used in racing. **2.** A sailing barge used in East Anglia. [Middle English *whery.*]

whet (hwĕt, wĕt) *tr.v.* **whet·ted, whet·ting, whets. 1.** To sharpen (a knife, for example); hone. **2.** To make more keen; stimulate: *The frying bacon whetted my appetite.* **—whet** *n.* **1.** The act of whetting. **2.** Something that whets. **3.** *Informal.* An appetizer. [Middle English *whetten,* from Old English *hwettan.*]

wheth·er (hwĕth′ər, wĕth′-) *conj.* **1.** Used in indirect questions to introduce one alternative: *We should find out whether the museum is open.* See Usage Notes at **doubt, if. 2.** Used to introduce alternative possibilities: *Whether she wins or whether she loses, this is her last tournament.* **3.** Either: *He passed the test, whether by skill or luck.* **—whether** *pron. Archaic.* Which: *"We came in full View of a great Island or Continent, (for we knew not whether)"* (Jonathan Swift). ***—idiom.* whether or no.** Regardless of circumstances. [Middle English, from Old English *hwether.* See **k^wo-** in Appendix.]

whet·stone (hwĕt′stōn′, wĕt′-) *n.* A hard, fine-grained stone for honing tools. Also called *snakestone.*

whew (hwyo͞o, hwo͞o, hwyo͞o *unvoiced*) *interj.* Used to express strong emotion, such as relief or amazement.

whey (hwā, wā) *n.* The watery part of milk that separates from the curds, as in the process of making cheese. [Middle English, from Old English *hwæg.*] **—whey′ey** *adj.*

whey-face (hwā′fās′, wā′-) *n.* A person with a pallid face.

whf. *abbr.* Wharf.

which (hwĭch, wĭch) *pron.* **1.** What particular one or ones: *Which of these is yours?* **2.** The one or ones previously mentioned or implied, specifically: **a.** Used as a relative pronoun in a clause that provides additional information about the antecedent: *my house, which is small and old.* **b.** Used as a relative pronoun preceded by *that* or a preposition in a clause that defines or restricts the antecedent: *that which he needed; the subject on which she spoke.* **c.** Used instead of *that* as a relative pronoun in a clause that defines or restricts the antecedent: *The movie which was shown later was better.* **3.** Any of the things, events, or people designated or implied; whichever: *Choose which you like best.* **4.** A thing or circumstance that: *He left early, which was wise.* **—which** *adj.* **1.** What particular one or ones of a number of things or people: *Which part of town do you mean?* **2.** Any one or any number of; whichever: *Use which door you please.* **3.** Being the one or ones previously mentioned or implied: *It started to rain, at which point we ran.* [Middle English, from Old English *hwilc.* See **k^wo-** in Appendix.]

USAGE NOTE: The antecedent of *which* can sometimes be a sentence or clause, as opposed to a noun phrase, as in *She ignored him, which proved to be unwise. They swept the council elections, which could never have happened under the old rules.* Such examples are unexceptionable, but care should be taken that this usage does not cause ambiguities. The sentence *It emerged that Edna made the complaint, which surprised everybody* may mean either that the complaint was surprising or that it was surprising that Edna made it. The ambiguity can be avoided with paraphrases such as *It emerged that Edna made the complaint, a revelation that surprised everybody.* • In its use to refer to the contents of sentences and clauses, *which* should be used only when it is preceded by its antecedent. When the antecedent follows, *what* should be used, particularly in formal style: *Still, he has not said he will withdraw, which is more surprising* but *Still, what* (not *which*) *is more surprising, he has not said he will withdraw.* See Usage Notes at **that, what, whose.**

---

which·ev·er (hwĭch-ĕv′ər, wĭch-) *pron.* Whatever one or ones. **—whichever** *adj.* Being any one or any number of a group: *Read whichever books you please. It's a long trip whichever road you take.* See Usage Note at **whatever.**

which·so·ev·er (hwĭch′sō-ĕv′ər, wĭch′-) *pron. & adj.* Whichever.

whick·er (hwĭk′ər, wĭk′-) *intr.v.* **-ered, -er·ing, -ers.** To whinny. **—whicker** *n.* A whinny. [Imitative.]

whid·ah (hwĭd′ə, wĭd′ə) *n.* Variant of **whydah.**

Whid·bey Island (hwĭd′bē, wĭd′-). An island of northwest Washington in Puget Sound northwest of Everett.

whiff (hwĭf, wĭf) *n.* **1.** A slight, gentle gust of air; a waft: *a whiff of cool air.* **2.a.** A brief, passing odor carried in the air: *a whiff of perfume.* **b.** A minute trace: *"Humanity is unregenerable and hates the language of conformity, since conformity has a whiff of the inhuman about it"* (Anthony Burgess). **3.** An inhalation, as of air or smoke: *Take a whiff of this pipe.* **4.** *Baseball.* A strikeout. **—whiff** *v.* **whiffed, whiff·ing, whiffs.** *—intr.* **1.** To be carried in brief gusts; waft: *puffs of smoke whiffing from the chimney.* **2.** *Sports.* To swing at and miss a ball or puck. **3.** *Baseball.* To strike out. Used of a batter. *—tr.* **1.** To blow or convey in whiffs. **2.** To inhale through the nose; sniff: *a dog whiffing the air.* **3.** *Baseball.* To strike out (a batter). [Perhaps alteration of Middle English *weffe,* offensive smell.] **—whiff′er** *n.*

whif·fle (hwĭf′əl, wĭf′-) *v.* **-fled, -fling, -fles.** *—intr.* **1.** To move or think erratically; vacillate. **2.** To blow in fitful gusts; puff: *The wind whiffled through the trees.* **3.** To whistle lightly. *—tr.* To blow, displace, or scatter with gusts of air. [Perhaps frequentative of WHIFF.]

♦ **whif·fle·tree** (hwĭf′əl-trē, wĭf′-) *n.* *Northeastern U.S.* The pivoted horizontal crossbar to which the harness traces of a draft animal are attached and which is in turn attached to a vehicle or an implement. Also called *singletree, swingletree,* ♦*whippletree.* [Variant of WHIPPLETREE.]

♦ ***REGIONAL NOTE:*** *Whiffletree,* a term primarily used in the northeast United States, is derived from an older term *whippletree,* which is used in the Upper Northern states farther to the west. The fact that *whiffletree,* the newer term, is used in the Northeast, the older dialect area, illustrates the process of linguistic change. Even as the older word *whippletree* was spreading westward into a new dialect area, it was evolving into something different—*whiffletree*—in the area where it originated, as if the older dialect area were somehow trying to keep a step ahead.

Whig (hwĭg, wĭg) *n.* **1.** A member of an 18th- and 19th-century British political party that was opposed to the Tories. **2.** A supporter of the war against England during the American Revolution. **3.** A 19th-century American political party formed to oppose the Democratic Party and favoring high tariffs and a loose interpretation of the Constitution. [Probably short for *Whiggamore,* a member of a body of 17th-century Scottish Presbyterian rebels.] **—Whig′ger·y** *n.* **—Whig′gish** *adj.* **—Whig′gism** *n.*

while (hwīl, wīl) *n.* **1.** A period of time: *stay for a while; sang all the while.* See Usage Note at **awhile. 2.** The time, effort, or trouble taken in doing something: *The project wasn't worth my while.* **—while** *conj.* **1.** As long as; during the time that: *It was lovely while it lasted.* **2.** At the same time that; although: *While the grandparents love the children, they are strict with them.* **3.** Whereas; and: *The soles are leather, while the uppers are canvas.* **—while** *tr.v.* **whiled, whil·ing, whiles.** To spend (time) idly or pleasantly: *while the hours away.* [Middle English, from Old English *hwīl.* See **k^weiə-** in Appendix.]

whiles (hwīlz, wīlz) *conj. Archaic.* While. [Middle English : *while,* while; see WHILE + *-es,* genitive sing. suff.; see –s^3.]

whi·lom (hwī′ləm, wī′-) *adj.* Having once been; former: *the whilom editor in chief.* **—whilom** *adv. Archaic.* At a past time; formerly. [Middle English, at times, from Old English *hwīlum,* dative pl. of *hwīl,* time, while. See **k^weiə-** in Appendix.]

ă pat	oi boy
ā pay	ou out
âr care	o͝o took
ä father	o͞o boot
ĕ pet	ŭ cut
ē be	ûr urge
ĭ pit	th thin
ī pie	*th* this
îr pier	hw which
ŏ pot	zh vision
ō toe	ə about, item
ô paw	♦ regionalism

Stress marks: ′ (primary); ′ (secondary), as in **dictionary** (dĭk′shə-nĕr′ē)

whippet

whilst (hwĭlst, wĭlst) *conj. Chiefly British.* While. [Middle English *whilest,* alteration of *whiles,* whiles. See WHILES.]

whim (hwĭm, wĭm) *n.* **1.** A sudden or capricious idea; a fancy. **2.** Arbitrary thought or impulse: *governed by whim.* See Synonyms at **caprice. 3.** A vertical horse-powered drum used as a hoist in a mine. [Short for *whim-wham,* fanciful object.]

whim·brel (hwĭm′brəl, wĭm′-) *n.* A grayish-brown wading bird *(Numenius phaeopus)* having a white, heavily streaked breast. [Perhaps alteration of WHIMPER (from its cry).]

whim·per (hwĭm′pər, wĭm′-) *v.* **-pered, -per·ing, -pers.** —*intr.* **1.** To cry or sob with soft intermittent sounds; whine. See Synonyms at **cry. 2.** To complain. —*tr.* To utter in a whimper. **—whimper** *n.* A low, broken, sobbing sound; a whine. [Probably imitative.] **—whim′per·er** *n.* **—whim′per·ing·ly** *adv.*

whim·sey (hwĭm′zē, wĭm′-) *n.* Variant of **whimsy.**

whim·si·cal (hwĭm′zĭ-kəl, wĭm′-) *adj.* **1.** Determined by, arising from, or marked by whim or caprice. See Synonyms at **arbitrary. 2.** Erratic in behavior or degree of unpredictability: *a whimsical personality.* [From WHIMSY.] **—whim′si·cal·ly** *adv.*

whim·si·cal·i·ty (hwĭm′zĭ-kăl′ĭ-tē, wĭm′-) *n., pl.* **-ties. 1.** The quality or state of being whimsical. **2.** A whimsical idea or its expression; a caprice.

whim·sy also **whim·sey** (hwĭm′zē, wĭm′-) *n., pl.* **-sies** also **-seys. 1.** An odd or fanciful idea; a whim. See Synonyms at **caprice. 2.** A quaint or fanciful quality: *stories full of whimsy.* [Probably from *whim-wham,* fanciful object.]

whin[1] (hwĭn, wĭn) *n. Botany.* See **gorse.** [Middle English *whinne,* probably of Scandinavian origin.]

whin[2] (hwĭn, wĭn) *n.* A whinstone. [Middle English *quin.*]

whin·chat (hwĭn′chăt′, wĭn′-) *n.* A small brownish Old World songbird *(Saxicola rubetra)* often found in open country.

whine (hwīn, wīn) *v.* **whined, whin·ing, whines.** —*intr.* **1.** To utter a plaintive, high-pitched, protracted sound, as in pain, fear, supplication, or complaint. **2.** To complain or protest in a childish fashion. **3.** To produce a sustained noise of relatively high pitch: *jet engines whining.* —*tr.* To utter with a whine. **—whine** *n.* **1.** The act of whining. **2.** A whining sound. **3.** A complaint uttered in a plaintive tone. [Middle English *whinen,* from Old English *hwīnan,* to make a whizzing sound.] **—whin′er** *n.* **—whin′ing·ly** *adv.* **—whin′y, whin′ey** *adj.*

whin·ny (hwĭn′ē, wĭn′ē) *v.* **whin·nied** (hwĭn′ēd, wĭn′-), **whin·ny·ing, whin·nies** (hwĭn′ēz, wĭn′-). —*intr.* To neigh, as a horse, especially in a gentle tone. —*tr.* To express in a whinny. **—whinny** *n., pl.* **-nies.** The sound made in whinnying; a neigh. [Probably akin to WHINE, to whinny.]

whin·stone (hwĭn′stōn′, wĭn′-) *n.* Any of various hard, dark-colored rocks, especially basalt and chert.

whip (hwĭp, wĭp) *v.* **whipped** or **whipt** (hwĭpt, wĭpt), **whip·ping, whips.** —*tr.* **1.** To strike with repeated strokes, as with a strap or rod; lash. **2.a.** To punish or chastise by repeated striking with a strap or rod; flog. **b.** To afflict, castigate, or reprove severely: *"For nonconformity the world whips you with its displeasure"* (Ralph Waldo Emerson). **3.** To drive, force, or compel by flogging, lashing, or other means. **4.** To strike or affect in a manner similar to whipping or lashing: *Icy winds whipped my face.* **5.** To beat (cream or eggs, for example) into a froth or foam. **6.** *Informal.* To snatch, pull, or remove in a sudden manner: *He whipped off his cap.* **7.** To sew with a loose overcast or overhand stitch. **8.** To wrap or bind (a rope, for example) with twine to prevent unraveling or fraying. **9.** *Nautical.* To hoist by means of a rope passing through an overhead pulley. **10.** *Informal.* To defeat; outdo: *Our team can whip your team.* —*intr.* **1.** To move in a sudden, quick manner; dart. **2.** To move in a manner similar to a whip; thrash or snap about: *Branches whipped against the windows.* **—whip** *n.* **1.** An instrument, either a flexible rod or a flexible thong or lash attached to a handle, used for driving animals or administering corporal punishment. **2.** A whipping or lashing motion or stroke; a whiplash. **3.** A blow, wound, or cut made by or as if by whipping. **4.** Something, such as a long radio antenna on a motor vehicle, that is similar to a whip in form or flexibility. **5.** *Sports.* Flexibility, as in the shaft of a golf club. **6.** *Sports.* A whipper-in. **7.a.** A member of a legislative body, such as the U.S. Congress or the British Parliament, charged by his or her party with enforcing party discipline and ensuring attendance. **b.** A call issued to party members in a lawmaking body to ensure attendance at a particular time. **8.** A dessert made of sugar and stiffly beaten egg whites or cream, often with fruit or fruit flavoring: *prune whip.* **9.** An arm on a windmill. **10.** *Nautical.* A hoist consisting of a single rope passing through an overhead pulley. **11.** A ride in an amusement park, consisting of small cars that move in a rapid, whipping motion along an oval track. **—*phrasal verbs.* whip in.** To keep together, as members of a political party or hounds in a pack. **whip up. 1.** To arouse; excite: *whipped up the mob; whip up enthusiasm.* **2.** *Informal.* To prepare quickly: *whip up a light lunch.* **—*idiom.* whip into shape.** *Informal.* To bring to a specified state or condition, vigorously and often forcefully. [Middle English *wippen, whippen.* See **weip-** in Appendix.] **—whip′per** *n.*

whip·cord (hwĭp′kôrd′, wĭp′-) *n.* **1.** A worsted fabric with a distinct diagonal rib. **2.** A strong twisted or braided cord sometimes used in making whiplashes. **3.** Catgut.

whip hand *n.* **1.** A dominating position; advantage. **2.** The hand in which a whip is held.

whip·lash (hwĭp′lăsh′, wĭp′-) *n.* **1.** The lash of a whip. **2.** An injury to the cervical spine caused by an abrupt jerking motion of the head, either backward or forward. In this sense, also called *whiplash injury.*

whip·per-in (hwĭp′ər-ĭn′, wĭp′-) *n., pl.* **whip·pers-in** (hwĭp′ərz-, wĭp′-). **1.** *Sports.* A person who assists the huntsman in handling a pack of hounds in foxhunting. **2.** The whip in a legislative body.

whip·per·snap·per (hwĭp′ər-snăp′ər, wĭp′-) *n.* A person regarded as insignificant and pretentious. [Alteration (influenced by WHIP) of dialectal *snippersnapper.*]

whip·pet (hwĭp′ĭt, wĭp′-) *n.* Any of a breed of swift, short-haired dog developed in England for racing, resembling the greyhound but smaller. [Probably from WHIP.]

whip·ping (hwĭp′ĭng, wĭp′-) *n.* **1.** The act of one that whips. **2.** A thrashing administered especially as punishment. **3.** Material, such as cord or thread, used to lash or bind parts.

whipping boy *n.* **1.** A scapegoat. **2.** A boy formerly raised with a prince or other young nobleman and whipped for the latter's misdeeds.

Whip·ple (hwĭp′əl, wĭp′-), **George Hoyt.** 1878–1976. American pathologist. He shared a 1934 Nobel Prize for discovering that a diet of liver relieves anemia.

♦ **whip·ple·tree** (hwĭp′əl-trē′, wĭp′-) *n. Upper Northern U.S.* See **whiffletree.** See Regional Note at **whiffletree.** [Perhaps blend of dialectal *whippin,* whippletree, and SWINGLETREE.]

whip·poor·will (hwĭp′ər-wĭl′, wĭp′-, hwĭp′ər-wĭl′, wĭp′-) *n.* An insect-eating nocturnal North American bird *(Caprimulgus vociferus)* of the goatsucker family, having spotted brown feathers that blend with its woodland habitat. [Imitative of its call.]

whip·saw (hwĭp′sô′, wĭp′-) *n.* A narrow two-person crosscut saw. **—whipsaw** *tr.v.* **-sawed, -sawed** or **-sawn** (-sôn′), **-saw·ing, -saws. 1.** To cut with a whipsaw. **2.** *Games.* To win two bets from (a person) at one time, as in faro. **3.** To defeat or best in two ways at once: *"Our internal divisions handed the Soviet leadership an irresistible opportunity to whipsaw us"* (Henry A. Kissinger).

whip scorpion *n.* Any of various arachnids of the order Pedipalpi, such as the vinegarroon, that resemble scorpions but have a slender whiplike process on the abdomen and no poisonous sting.

whip snake *n.* **1.** Any of several slender nonvenomous New World snakes of the genus *Masticophis,* having a long tail that resembles a whip. **2.** Any of several similar or related snakes.

whip·stall (hwĭp′stôl′, wĭp′-) *n.* A usually intentional stall in which a small aircraft enters a vertical climb, pauses, slips backward momentarily, then drops nose downward.

whip·stitch (hwĭp′stĭch′, wĭp′-) *tr.v.* **-stitched, -stitch·ing, -stitch·es.** To sew with overcast stitches, as in finishing a fabric edge or binding two pieces of fabric together. **—whipstitch** *n.* A stitch made in this manner.

whipt (hwĭpt, wĭpt) *v.* A past tense and a past participle of **whip.**

whip·tail (hwĭp′tāl′) *n.* Any of various New World lizards of the genus *Cnemidophorus,* having a long, slender tail.

whip·worm (hwĭp′wûrm′, wĭp′-) *n.* A slender, whip-shaped, parasitic nematode worm *(Trichuris trichiura)* that often infests the intestine of human beings.

whir (hwûr, wûr) *v.* **whirred, whir·ring, whirs.** —*intr.* To move so as to produce a vibrating or buzzing sound. —*tr.* To cause to make a vibratory sound. **—whir** *n.* **1.** A sound of buzzing or vibration: *the whir of turning wheels.* **2.** Excited, noisy activity; bustle: *the whir of busy shoppers.* [Middle English *whirren,* probably of Scandinavian origin.]

whirl (hwûrl, wûrl) *v.* **whirled, whirl·ing, whirls.** —*intr.* **1.** To revolve rapidly about a center or an axis. See Synonyms at **turn. 2.** To rotate or spin rapidly: *The dancer whirled across the stage.* **3.** To turn rapidly, changing direction; wheel: *She whirled around to face him.* **4.** To have the sensation of spinning; reel: *My head is whirling with data.* **5.** To move circularly and rapidly in varied, random directions: *The wind whirled across the steppes.* —*tr.* **1.** To cause to rotate or turn rapidly: *whirl a baton.* **2.** To move or drive in a circular or curving course. **3.** To drive at high speed: *whirled the motorcycle around the corner.* **4.** *Obsolete.* To hurl. **—whirl** *n.* **1.** The act of rotating or revolving rapidly. **2.** Something, such as a cloud of dust, that whirls or is whirled. **3.** A state of confusion; tumult. **4.** A swift succession or round of events: *the social whirl.* **5.** A state of mental confusion or giddiness; dizziness: *My head is in a whirl.* **6.** *Informal.* A short trip or ride. **7.** *Informal.* A brief or experimental try: *Let's give the plan a whirl.* [Middle English *whirlen,* probably from Old Norse *hvirfla.*] **—whirl′er** *n.*

whirl·i·gig (hwûr′lĭ-gĭg′, wûr′-) *n.* **1.** Any of various spinning toys. **2.** A carousel; a merry-go-round. **3.** Something that continuously whirls. **4.** The whirligig beetle. [Middle English *whirlegigge* : *whirlen,* whirl; see WHIRL + *-gigge,* something that rotates, possibly of Scandinavian origin; akin to GIG [1].]

whirligig beetle *n.* Any of various gregarious beetles of the family Gyrinidae that circle about rapidly on the surface of water.

whirl·pool (hwûrl′po͞ol′, wûrl′-) *n.* **1.** A rapidly rotating current of water; a vortex. **2.a.** Turmoil; whirl. **b.** A magnetic, impelling force into which one may be pulled. **3.** A bathtub or pool having jets of warm water that can be directed toward a body part as for therapeutic purposes.

whirl•wind (hwûrl′wĭnd′, wûrl′-) *n.* **1.** A rapidly rotating, generally vertical column of air, such as a tornado, dust devil, or waterspout. **2.a.** A tumultuous, confused rush. **b.** A destructive force or thing. **—whirlwind** *adj.* Tumultuous or rapid: *a whirlwind political campaign.*

whirl•y•bird (hwûr′lē-bûrd′, wûr′-) *n. Informal.* A helicopter.

whirr (hwûr, wûr) *v. & n. Chiefly British.* Variant of **whir.**

whisk (hwĭsk, wĭsk) *v.* **whisked, whisk•ing, whisks.** *—tr.* **1.** To move or cause to move with quick light sweeping motions: *whisked crumbs off the table; whisked the children away.* **2.** To whip (eggs or cream). *—intr.* To move lightly, nimbly, and rapidly. **—whisk** *n.* **1.** A quick light sweeping motion. **2.** A whiskbroom. **3.** A small bunch, as of twigs or hair, attached to a handle and used in brushing. **4.** A kitchen utensil for whipping foodstuffs. [Middle English *wisken,* of Scandinavian origin.]

whisk•broom (hwĭsk′bro͞om′, -bro͝om′, wĭsk′-) *n.* A small short-handled broom used especially to brush clothes.

whisk•er (hwĭs′kər, wĭs′-) *n.* **1.a. whiskers.** The hair on a man's cheeks and chin. **b.** A single hair of a beard or mustache. **2.** One of the long stiff tactile bristles or hairs that grow near the mouth and elsewhere on the head of most mammals; a vibrissa. **3.** *Informal.* A narrow margin; a hairsbreadth: *The candidate lost the election by a whisker.* **4.** *Nautical.* One of two spars or booms projecting from the side of a bowsprit for spreading the jib or flying-jib guys. **5.** *Chemistry.* An extremely fine filamentary crystal with extraordinary shear strength and unusual electrical or surface properties. [Middle English *wisker,* anything that wisks, from *wisken,* to whisk. See WHISK.] **—whisk′ered, whisk′er•y** *adj.*

whis•key also **whis•ky** (hwĭs′kē, wĭs′-) *n., pl.* **-keys** also **whis•kies. 1.** An alcoholic liquor distilled from grain, such as corn, rye, or barley, and containing approximately 40 to 50 percent ethyl alcohol by volume. **2.** A drink of such liquor. [From USQUEBAUGH.]

USAGE NOTE: Either *whiskey* or, less frequently, *whisky* can be used to refer to spirits distilled in the United States. Some writers prefer to reserve *whisky* for spirits distilled in Great Britain, but there is no widespread agreement on this point.

WORD HISTORY: Whiskey, vodka, and water seem a potent, incompatible combination. However, all three words share a common Indo-European root, **wed–,* "water, wet." The differences between their present forms are partially explained by the fact that under certain conditions the Indo-European *e* could appear as *o,* or both *e* and *o* could disappear. *Water* is a native English word, which goes back by way of prehistoric Common Germanic **watar* to the Indo-European suffixed form **wodō(r),* with an *o. Vodka* is borrowed from Russian, in which *vodka* is a diminutive of *voda,* "water." *Voda* goes back to the Indo-European suffixed form **woda–. Whiskey* is a shortened form of *usquebaugh,* meaning "whiskey." English borrowed *usquebaugh* from Irish Gaelic *uisce beatha* and Scottish Gaelic *uisge beatha,* a compound whose members descend from Old Irish *uisce,* "water," and *bethad,* "of life," and mean literally "water of life." *Uisce* comes from the Indo-European form **udskio–* (without *e* or *o*).

whiskey jack *n.* See **gray jay.** [Alteration of *whiskey-john,* by folk etymology from Cree dialectal *wiiskachaan.*]

whiskey sour *n.* A cocktail made with whiskey, lemon juice, and sugar.

whis•ky (hwĭs′kē, wĭs′-) *n.* Variant of **whiskey.**

whis•per (hwĭs′pər, wĭs′-) *n.* **1.** Soft speech produced without full voice. **2.** Something uttered very softly. **3.** A secretly or surreptitiously expressed belief, rumor, or hint: *whispers of scandal.* **4.** A low rustling sound: *the whisper of wind in the pines.* **—whisper** *v.* **-pered, -per•ing, -pers.** *—intr.* **1.** To speak softly. **2.** To speak quietly and privately, as by way of gossip, slander, or intrigue. **3.** To make a soft rustling sound. *—tr.* **1.** To utter very softly. **2.** To say or tell privately or secretly. [From Middle English *whisperen,* to whisper, from Old English *hwisprian.*] **—whis′per•er** *n.* **—whis′per•y** *adj.*

whist (hwĭst, wĭst) *n. Games.* A card game ancestral to bridge, played with a full deck by two teams of two players, in which the last card dealt indicates trump, tricks of four cards are played, and a point is scored for each trick over six won by each team. [Alteration (perhaps influenced by the exclamation *whist,* silence!) of obsolete and dialectal *whisk,* perhaps from WHISK.]

whis•tle (hwĭs′əl, wĭs′-) *v.* **-tled, -tling, -tles.** *—intr.* **1.** To produce a clear musical sound by forcing air through the teeth or through an aperture formed by pursing the lips. **2.** To produce a clear, shrill, sharp musical sound by blowing on or through a device. **3.a.** To produce a high-pitched sound when moving swiftly through the air: *The stone whistled past my head.* **b.** To produce a high-pitched sound by the rapid movement of air through an opening or past an obstruction: *Wind whistled through the cracks in the windows.* **4.** To emit a shrill, sharp, high-pitched cry, as some birds and other animals. **5.** To summon by whistling. *—tr.* **1.** To produce by whistling: *whistle a tune.* **2.** To summon, signal, or direct by whistling. **3.** To cause to move with a whistling noise. **—whistle** *n.* **1.a.** A small wind instrument for making whistling sounds by means of the breath. **b.** A device for making whistling sounds by means of forced air or steam: *a factory whistle.* **2.** A sound produced by a whistling device or by whistling through the lips. **1.** A whistling sound, as of an animal or a projectile. **2.** The act of whistling. **3.** A whistling sound used to summon or command. ***—idioms.* blow the whistle.** *Slang.* To expose a wrongdoing in the hope of bringing it to a halt: *an attorney who blew the whistle on governmental corruption.* **whistle in the dark.** To attempt to keep one's courage up. [Middle English *whistlen,* from Old English *hwistlian.*]

whistle blower or **whis•tle-blow•er** or **whis•tle•blow•er** (hwĭs′əl-blō′ər, wĭs′-) *n. Slang.* One who reveals wrongdoing within an organization to the public or to those in positions of authority: *"The Pentagon's most famous whistleblower is . . . hoping to get another chance to search for government waste"* (Washington Post). **—whis′tle-blow′ing** *n.*

♦ **whistle pig** *n. Appalachian Mountains.* See **woodchuck.** See Regional Note at **woodchuck.**

whis•tler (hwĭs′lər, wĭs′-) *n.* **1.** One that whistles: *a whistler of popular tunes.* **2.a.** A marmot *(Marmota caligata)* of the mountains of northwest North America, having a grayish coat and a shrill, whistling cry. **b.** Any of various birds that produce a whistling sound. **c.** A horse having a respiratory disease characterized by wheezing. **3.** *Physics.* An electromagnetic wave of audio frequency produced by atmospheric disturbances such as lightning, having a characteristically decreasing frequency responsible for a whistling sound of descending pitch in detection equipment.

Whis•tler (hwĭs′lər, wĭs′-), **James Abbott McNeill.** 1834–1903. American painter whose subtle coloring and tonal harmony were influenced by musical aesthetics and Japanese art. His works include a portrait of his mother, entitled *Arrangement in Grey and Black* (1872).

whistle stop *n.* **1.** A town or station at which a train stops only if signaled. **2.** A brief appearance of a political candidate in a small town, traditionally on the observation platform of a train.

whis•tle-stop (hwĭs′əl-stŏp′, wĭs′-) *intr.v.* **-stopped, -stop•ping, -stops.** To conduct a political campaign by making brief appearances or speeches in a series of small towns.

whis•tling swan (hwĭs′lĭng, wĭs′-) *n.* A white North American swan *(Olor columbianus)* having a soft, musical trumpeting voice and a black beak with a yellow spot at the base.

whit (hwĭt, wĭt) *n.* The least bit; an iota: *doesn't give a whit what was said; not a whit afraid.* [Middle English, amount, from Old English *wiht.* See WIGHT[1].]

Whit•by (hwĭt′bē, wĭt′-). A town of southeast Ontario, Canada, on Lake Ontario northeast of Toronto. Population, 36,698.

white (hwīt, wīt) *n. Abbr.* **wh. 1.** *Color.* The achromatic color of maximum lightness; the color of objects that reflect nearly all light of all visible wavelengths; the complement or antagonist of black, the other extreme of the neutral gray series. Although typically a response to maximum stimulation of the retina, the perception of white appears always to depend on contrast. **2.** The white or nearly white part, as: **a.** The albumen of an egg. **b.** The white part of an eyeball. **c.** A blank unprinted area, as of an advertisement. **3.** One that is white or nearly white, as: **a. whites.** White trousers or a white outfit of a special nature: *tennis whites.* **b. whites.** The white dress uniform of the U.S. Navy or Coast Guard. **c.** A white wine. **d.** A white pigment. **e.** A white breed, species, or variety of animal. **f.** Also **White.** A member of a racial group of people having light skin coloration, especially one of European origin. See Usage Note at **black. g.** Often **whites.** Products of a white color, such as flour, salt, and sugar. **4.** *Games.* **a.** The white or light-colored pieces, as in chess. **b.** The player using these pieces. **5.a.** The outermost ring of an archery target. **b.** A hit in this ring. **6. whites.** *Pathology.* Leukorrhea. **7.** A politically ultraconservative or reactionary person. **—white** *adj.* **whit•er, whit•est.** *Abbr.* **wh. 1.** Being of the color white; devoid of hue, as new snow. **2.** Approaching the color white, as: **a.** Weakly colored; almost colorless; pale: *white wine.* **b.** Pale gray; silvery and lustrous: *white hair.* **c.** Bloodless; blanched. **3.** Light or whitish in color or having light or whitish parts. Used with animal and plant names. **4.** Also **White.** Of, relating to, or belonging to a racial group having light skin coloration, especially one of European origin: *voting patterns within the white population.* **5.** Not written or printed on; blank. **6.** Unsullied; pure. **7.** Habited in white: *white nuns.* **8.** Accompanied by or mantled with snow: *a white Christmas.* **9.a.** Incandescent: *white flames.* **b.** Intensely heated; impassioned: *white with fury.* **10.** Ultraconservative or reactionary. **11.** With milk added. Used of tea or coffee. **—white** *tr.v.* **whit•ed, whit•ing, whites. 1.** *Printing.* To create or leave blank spaces in (printed or illustrated matter). Often used with *out.* **2.** *Archaic.* **a.** To whiten; whitewash. **b.** To blanch. [Middle English, from Old English *hwīt.* See **kweit-** in Appendix.] **—white′ness** *n.*

White, Andrew Dickson. 1832–1918. American educator and diplomat who founded Cornell University with Ezra Cornell and was its first president (1868–1885).

White, Byron Raymond. Born 1917. American jurist who was appointed an associate justice of the U.S. Supreme Court in 1962.

White, Edward Douglass. 1845–1921. American jurist who served as an associate justice (1894–1910) and the chief justice (1910–1921) of the U.S. Supreme Court.

White, E(lwyn) B(rooks). 1899–1985. American writer and humorist who contributed essays, editorials, and parodies to the *New Yorker.* He also wrote *Charlotte's Web* (1952) and revised a 1918 writing manual, *The Elements of Style* (1959).

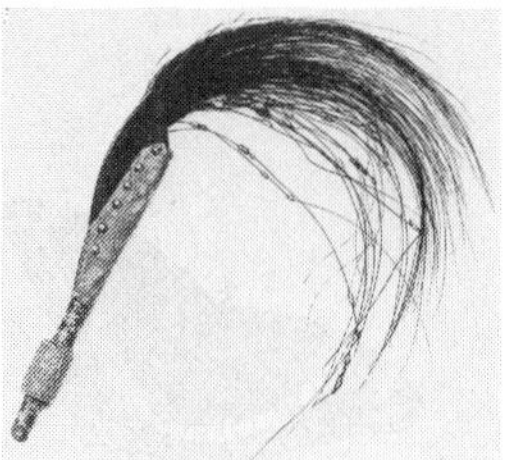

whisk

whisker
On a sea lion

ă pat	oi boy
ā pay	ou out
âr care	o͝o took
ä father	o͞o boot
ĕ pet	ŭ cut
ē be	ûr urge
ĭ pit	th thin
ī pie	*th* this
îr pier	hw which
ŏ pot	zh vision
ō toe	ə about, item
ô paw	♦ regionalism

Stress marks: ′ (primary); ′ (secondary), as in **dictionary** (dĭk′shə-nĕr′ē)

white admiral
Limenitis arthemis

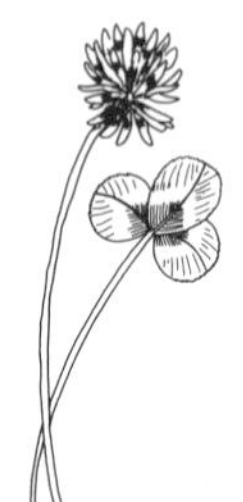

white clover
Trifolium repens

White House
Top: North Portico, facing Pennsylvania Avenue
Bottom: South Portico

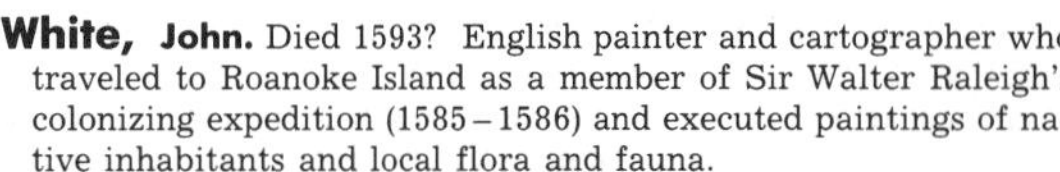

White, John. Died 1593? English painter and cartographer who traveled to Roanoke Island as a member of Sir Walter Raleigh's colonizing expedition (1585–1586) and executed paintings of native inhabitants and local flora and fauna.

White, Patrick. 1912–1990. Australian writer whose powerfully descriptive and original novels include *The Tree of Man* (1955) and *Voss* (1957). He won the 1973 Nobel Prize for literature.

White, Stanford. 1853–1906. American architect. A member of the prominent architectural firm McKim, Mead & White, he was particularly known for his ornate, eclectic designs.

White, T(erence) H(anbury). 1906–1964. British writer best known for the novel *The Once and Future King* (1958), a retelling of the Arthurian legend.

White, T(heodore) H(arold). 1915–1986. American political journalist noted for his commentaries on presidential elections, including *The Making of the President 1960* (1961).

White, Walter Francis. 1893–1955. American writer. The secretary of the NAACP (1931–1955), he wrote novels with racial themes, such as *Rising Wind* (1945).

White, William Allen. 1868–1944. American newspaper editor and writer noted for his politically influential editorials and for his autobiography (1946).

white admiral *n.* A nymphalid butterfly *(Limenitis arthemis)* of eastern North America, having a broad white band on blue-black wings.

white ant *n.* See **termite.**

white•bait (hwīt′bāt′, wīt′-) *n.* **1.** The young of various fishes, especially the herring, considered a delicacy when fried. **2.** Any of various similar or related small edible fishes.

white•bark pine (hwīt′bärk′, wīt′-) *n.* A prostrate shrub or tree *(Pinus albicaulis)* native to the mountains of Pacific North America and having small, purplish-brown, ovoid seed-bearing cones.

white bass (băs) *n.* A North American freshwater food fish *(Morone chrysops)* having a silvery color and blackish stripes on each side.

white bear *n.* See **polar bear.**

White Bear Lake (bâr′). A city of eastern Minnesota, a residential suburb of St. Paul. Population, 22,538.

white birch *n.* Any of several birch trees having white bark, as *Betula pendula* of Europe or the paper birch *B. papyrifera* of North America.

white blood cell *n. Abbr.* **WBC** Any of the colorless or white cells in the blood that have a nucleus and cytoplasm and help protect the body from infection and disease through specialized neutrophils, lymphocytes, and monocytes. Also called *leukocyte, white cell, white corpuscle.*

white book *n.* An official publication of a national government. [From its formerly being bound in white.]

♦**white bread** *n.* Bread made from finely ground, usually bleached wheat flour. Also called ♦*light bread.*

white bryony *n.* A climbing Eurasian vine *(Bryonia alba)* having lobed leaves, greenish-white flowers, and blackish berries.

white•cap (hwīt′kăp′, wīt′-) *n.* A wave with a crest of foam.

white cedar *n.* Either of two North American evergreen trees *(Thuja occidentalis* or *Chamaecyparis thyoides)* having light-colored wood.

white cell *n.* See **white blood cell.**

White Center. A community of west-central Washington, a suburb of Seattle. Population, 19,700.

white chip *n.* **1.** *Games.* A white disk used in poker as a betting token of minimal value. **2.** Something of minimal value or worth.

white cloud *n.* A small, brightly colored freshwater fish *(Tanichthys albonubes)* native to China and popular in home aquariums.

white clover *n.* A common European clover *(Trifolium repens)* widely naturalized in North America, having rounded white flower heads. Also called *Dutch clover.*

white-col•lar (hwīt′kŏl′ər, wīt′-) *adj.* Of or relating to workers whose work usually does not involve manual labor and who are often expected to dress with a degree of formality.

white corpuscle *n.* See **white blood cell.**

white crab *n.* See **ghost crab.**

white crappie *n.* A silvery, edible North American freshwater fish *(Pomoxis annularis)* related to the sunfish.

white-crowned sparrow (hwīt′kround′, wīt′-) *n.* A North American sparrow *(Zonotrichia leucophrys)* having a pearly gray breast and a black-and-white striped crown.

white daisy *n.* See **daisy** (sense 1).

whit•ed sepulcher (hwī′tĭd, wī′-) *n.* An evil person who pretends to be holy or good; a hypocrite. [From the simile applied by Jesus to hypocrites as exemplified by some scribes and Pharisees (Matthew 23:27).]

white dwarf *n.* A whitish star in a latter stage of development, having low luminosity, small size, and very great density.

white elephant *n.* **1.a.** A rare, expensive possession that is a financial burden to maintain. **b.** Something of dubious or limited value. **2.** An article, an ornament, or a household utensil no longer wanted by its owner. **3.** An endeavor or a venture that proves to be a conspicuous failure. **4.** A rare whitish or light-gray form of the Asian elephant, often regarded with special veneration in regions of southeast Asia and India.

white-eye (hwīt′ī′, wīt′ī′) *n.* Any of various small greenish birds of the genus *Zosterops* of Africa, southern Asia, and the Pacific islands, having a narrow ring of white feathers around each eye. Also called *silvereye.*

white•face (hwīt′fās′, wīt′-) *n.* **1.** White facial makeup: *a mime performing in whiteface.* **2.** A white-faced animal, especially a Hereford.

white-faced (hwīt′fāst′, wīt′-) *adj.* **1.** Having a pale face; pallid. **2.** Having a white face or a white patch extending from the muzzle to the forehead: *a white-faced antelope; white-faced cattle.*

white feather *n.* A sign of cowardice. ***—idiom.* show the white feather.** To act like a coward. [From the belief that a gamecock with a white feather in its tail was a poor fighter.]

White•field (hwĭt′fēld′, wĭt′-, hwīt′-, wīt′-), **George.** 1714–1770. British religious leader. A follower of John Wesley, he preached widely in the American colonies and was a central figure in the establishment of Methodism in America.

white•fish (hwīt′fĭsh′, wīt′-) *n., pl.* **whitefish** or **-fish•es. 1.a.** Any of various chiefly North American freshwater food fishes of the genus *Coregonus,* having a generally white or silvery color. **b.** Any of various similar or related fishes, such as the lake herring, whiting, or menhaden. **2.** See **beluga** (sense 2).

white flag *n.* A white cloth or flag signaling truce or surrender.

white-flow•ered gourd (hwīt′flou′ərd, wīt′-) *n.* See **calabash** (sense 1).

white•fly (hwīt′flī′, wīt′-) *n.* Any of various small whitish homopterous insects of the family Aleyrodidae, having long wings and a white waxy body, often injurious to plants.

white-foot•ed mouse (hwīt′fo͝ot′ĭd, wīt′-) *n.* A semidesert mouse *(Peromyscus leucopus)* of New Mexico that feeds on crop-damaging insects.

white fox *n.* The arctic fox in its winter color phase.

White Friar *n.* See **Carmelite** (sense 1). [From the color of the habit.]

white-fronted goose (hwīt′frŭn′tĭd, wīt′-) *n.* A gray-brown wild goose *(Anser albifrons)* of northern regions of Eurasia and North America, having yellow legs and a white area around the bill.

white frost *n.* See **hoarfrost.**

white gasoline *n.* Gasoline containing no tetraethyl lead.

white gold *n.* An alloy of gold and nickel, sometimes also containing palladium or zinc, having a pale platinumlike color.

White•hall¹ (hwīt′hôl′, wīt′-). A wide thoroughfare in London, England, running north and south between Trafalgar Square and the Houses of Parliament. Named after Whitehall Palace (1529–1698), the chief residence of the Court of London, it is noted for its government offices.

White•hall² (hwīt′hôl′, wīt′-). A city of central Ohio, an industrial suburb of Columbus. Population, 21,299.

White•hall³ (hwīt′hôl′, wīt′-) *n.* The British civil service. [After WHITEHALL¹.]

white•head (hwīt′hĕd′, wīt′-) *n.* See **milium.**

White•head (hwīt′hĕd′, wīt′-), **Alfred North.** 1861–1947. British mathematician and philosopher. A founder of mathematical logic, he wrote *Principia Mathematica* (1910–1913) with Bertrand Russell.

white-head•ed (hwīt′hĕd′ĭd, wīt′-) *adj.* **1.** Having white hair, fur, or plumage on the head: *white-headed elders; a white-headed bald eagle.* **2.** *Irish.* Favorite: *our white-headed child.*

white heat *n.* **1.** The temperature or physical condition of a white-hot substance. **2.** Intense emotion or excitement: *working at white heat to make the deadline.*

white hole *n.* A hypothetical hole in outer space from which energy, stars, and other celestial matter emerge or explode. [WHITE + (BLACK) HOLE.]

white hope *n.* **1.** Someone, especially a beginning competitor, whom supporters hope will achieve great success. **2.** A white prizefighter believed by fans to have a chance of defeating a Black champion.

White•horse (hwīt′hôrs′, wīt′-). The capital and largest city of Yukon Territory, Canada, in the southern part of the territory on the Yukon River. It was an important trading center during the Klondike gold rush (1897–1898) and has been the territorial capital since 1952. Population, 14,814.

white-hot (hwīt′hŏt′, wīt′-) *adj.* **1.** So hot as to glow with a bright white light. **2.** Zealous; fervid.

White House *n.* **1.** The executive branch of the U.S. government. **2.** The executive mansion of the President of the United States.

white iron pyrites *n.* See **marcasite** (sense 1).

white knight *n.* **1.** One that comes to the rescue; a savior. **2.** A person or company that rescues a targeted firm from a takeover attempt by buying the firm.

white-knuck•le (hwīt′nŭk′əl, wīt′-) *adj. Slang.* Characterized by tense nervousness or apprehension: *a white-knuckle emergency landing; white-knuckle time in the hospital waiting room.*

white lead (lĕd) *n.* A heavy white poisonous powder, essentially basic lead carbonate, used in paint pigments.

white leather also **whit·leath·er** (hwīt′lĕth′ər, wīt′-) *n.* A soft leather specially treated with salt and alum.

white lie *n.* A trivial, harmless, or well-intentioned untruth.

♦**white lightning** *n. Chiefly Southern U.S.* See **moonshine** (sense 3).

white list *n.* A list of people or organizations considered worthy of approval or acceptance. [WHITE + (BLACK)LIST.] —**white′-list′ed** (hwīt′lĭs′tĭd, wīt′-) *adj.*

white-liv·ered (hwīt′lĭv′ərd, wīt′-) *adj.* Cowardly.

white magic *n.* Magic or incantation practiced for good purposes or as a counter to evil.

white mahogany *n.* See **primavera¹** (sense 2).

White·man (hwīt′mən, wīt′-), **Paul.** 1890–1967. American conductor who introduced symphonic jazz to a general audience. He commissioned George Gershwin's *Rhapsody in Blue.*

white man's burden (mănz) *n.* The supposed responsibility of white people to govern and impart their culture to nonwhite people. [From *"The White Man's Burden,"* a poem by Rudyard Kipling.]

white marlin *n.* A small marlin *(Tetrapturus albidus)* of the western Atlantic, having silvery underparts.

white marriage *n.* A marriage without sexual relations.

white matter *n.* Whitish nerve tissue, especially of the brain and spinal cord, consisting chiefly of myelinated nerve fibers.

white meat *n.* Light-colored meat, especially of poultry.

white metal *n.* Any of various whitish alloys, such as pewter, that contain high percentages of tin or lead.

white mica *n.* See **muscovite.**

White Mountain. A peak, 4,345 m (14,246 ft) high, in the Sierra Nevada of east-central California.

White Mountains. A section of the Appalachian Mountains in northern New Hampshire rising to 1,917.8 m (6,288 ft).

white mulberry *n.* A deciduous Chinese tree *(Morus alba)* having edible whitish or purplish multiple fruit.

whit·en (hwīt′n, wīt′n) *tr. & intr.v.* **-ened, -en·ing, -ens.** To make or become white, especially by bleaching. —**whit′en·er** *n.*

white night *n.* **1.** A night without sleep. **2.** A night without full darkness, as during the summer in high latitudes.

White Nile (nīl). A section of the Nile River in eastern Africa flowing generally northward to Khartoum, where it joins the Blue Nile to form the Nile river proper.

white noise *n.* Acoustical or electrical noise of which the intensity is the same at all frequencies within a given band. [From the analogy with white light.]

white oak *n.* **1.** A large oak *(Quercus alba)* of eastern North America, having heavy, hard, light-colored wood. **2.** See **roble** (sense 1).

white·out (hwīt′out′, wīt′-) *n.* A polar weather condition caused by a heavy cloud cover over the snow, in which the light coming from above is approximately equal to the light reflected from below, characterized by absence of shadow, invisibility of the horizon, and discernibility of only very dark objects.

white paper *n.* **1.** A government report. **2.** An authoritative report on a major issue, as by a team of journalists.

White Pass. A pass, 880.8 m (2,888 ft) high, in the Coast Mountains between southeast Alaska and northwest British Columbia, Canada, north of Skagway.

white pepper *n.* Pepper ground from peppercorns from which the outer black layer has been removed.

white perch *n.* A small silver-colored food fish *(Roccus americanus)* of the Atlantic coast and freshwater streams of eastern North America.

white pine *n.* **1.** A timber tree *(Pinus strobus)* of eastern North America, having needles in clusters of five and durable, easily worked wood. **2.** The wood of this tree. **3.** Any of several other pines having needles in clusters of five.

white plague *n.* Tuberculosis, especially of the lungs.

White Plains. A city of southeast New York, a residential suburb of New York City. Population, 46,999.

white poplar *n.* A deciduous Eurasian tree *(Populus alba)* having palmately lobed leaves with whitish undersides. Also called *abele.*

white potato *n.* The edible tuber of the common potato.

white·print (hwīt′prĭnt′, wīt′-) *n.* A photomechanical copy, usually of a line drawing, in which black or colored lines appear on a white background.

white rat *n.* A domesticated albino variety of the Norway rat.

White River. **1.** A river of northern Arkansas and southern Missouri flowing about 1,110 km (690 mi) generally southeast to the Mississippi River. **2.** A river of northwest Nebraska and southern South Dakota flowing about 523 km (325 mi) northeast and east to the Missouri River.

white room *n.* See **clean room.**

White Rus·sia (rŭsh′ə). See **Belorussia.**

white sauce *n.* A sauce made with butter, flour, and milk, cream, or stock, used as a base for other sauces.

White Sea. A sea of northwest Russia, an inlet of the Barents Sea.

white shark *n.* The great white shark.

white slave *n.* A woman held unwillingly for purposes of prostitution.

white slaver *n.* A procurer of or trafficker in white slaves.

white slavery *n.* Forced prostitution.

white·smith (hwīt′smĭth′, wīt′-) *n.* **1.** One who works white metal. **2.** One who does finish work, such as polishing, on iron. [WHITE + (BLACK)SMITH.]

white snakeroot *n.* A poisonous eastern North American plant *(Eupatorium rugosum)* having opposite, heart-shaped leaves and flat-topped clusters of small white flower heads.

white space *n.* Space on a page or poster not covered by print or graphic matter.

white squall *n.* A sudden squall occurring in tropical or subtropical waters, characterized by the absence of a dark cloud and the presence of white-capped waves or broken water.

white squire *n.* An investor sympathetic to management who holds a large block of stock in a company that is or could be subject to a takeover unwanted by the management.

white stork *n.* The common stork *(Ciconia ciconia)* of Europe and Asia, having black and white plumage, a dark red bill, and pinkish-red legs.

white sturgeon *n.* A large freshwater food and sport fish *(Acipenser transmontanus)* of the American Pacific coast.

white supremacy *n.* The belief or theory that the white race is inherently superior to and therefore entitled to rule over all other races. —**white supremacist** *n.*

white·tail (hwīt′tāl′, wīt′-) *n.* See **white-tailed deer.**

white-tailed deer (hwīt′tāld′, wīt′-) *n.* A common North American deer *(Odocoileus virginianus)* having a grayish coat that turns reddish-brown in summer and a tail that is white on the underside. Also called *Virginia deer, whitetail.*

white·throat (hwīt′thrōt′, wīt′-) *n.* **1.** Either of two Old World songbirds *(Sylvia communis* or *S. curruca)* having brownish plumage and a white throat and belly. **2.** See **white-throated sparrow.**

white-throat·ed sparrow (hwīt′thrō′tĭd, wīt′-) *n.* A large North American sparrow *(Zonotrichia albicollis)* having a white patch on the throat, black and white stripes on the crown, and a distinctive song. Also called *whitethroat.*

white tie *n.* **1.** A white bow tie worn as a part of men's formal evening dress. **2.** Men's formal evening dress. —**white′-tie′** (hwīt′tī′, wīt′-) *adj.*

white trash *n. Offensive Slang.* Used as a disparaging term for a poor white person or poor white people.

white vitriol *n.* See **zinc sulfate.**

White Vol·ta (vŏl′tə, vōl′-, vôl′-). A river of Burkina Faso and northern Ghana flowing about 885 km (550 mi) southward to join the Black Volta and form the Volta River.

white·wall tire (hwīt′wôl′, wīt′-) *n.* A vehicular tire having a white sidewall.

white walnut *n.* See **butternut** (sense 1a).

white·wash (hwīt′wŏsh′, -wôsh′, wīt′-) *n.* **1.** A mixture of lime and water, often with whiting, size, or glue added, that is used to whiten walls, fences, or other structures. **2.** Concealment or palliation of flaws or failures. **3.** *Sports & Games.* A defeat in a game in which the loser scores no points. —**whitewash** *tr.v.* **-washed, -wash·ing, -wash·es.** **1.** To paint or coat with or as if with whitewash. **2.** To conceal or gloss over (wrongdoing, for example). See Synonyms at **palliate.** —**white′wash′er** *n.*

white water *n.* Turbulent or frothy water, as in rapids or surf.

white-wa·ter (hwīt′wô′tər, -wŏt′ər, wīt′-) *adj.* Of, relating to, intended for, or taking place on white water, especially in river rapids: *white-water rafting.*

white whale *n.* A small toothed whale *(Delphinapterus leucas),* chiefly of northern waters, that is white when full-grown. Also called *beluga, sea canary.*

white-winged dove (hwīt′wĭngd′, wīt′-) *n.* A large gray American dove *(Zenaida asiatica)* having a patch of white on each wing.

white-winged scoter *n.* A large, black North American diving duck *(Melanitta deglandi)* having a patch of white on each wing.

white·wood (hwīt′wo͝od′, wīt′-) *n.* **1.** Any of various deciduous trees such as the tulip tree, basswood, or cottonwood. **2.** The soft, light-colored wood of any of these trees.

whit·ey also **Whit·ey** (hwī′tē, wī′-) *n., pl.* **-eys.** *Offensive Slang.* Used as a disparaging term for a white person or white people.

whith·er (hwĭth′ər, wĭth′-) *adv.* To what place, result, or condition: *Whither are we wandering?* —**whither** *conj.* **1.** To which specified place or position: *landed on the shores whither the storm had tossed them.* **2.** To whatever place, result, or condition: *"Whither thou goest, I will go"* (Ruth 1:16). [Middle English, from Old English *hwider.* See **kʷo-** in Appendix.]

whith·er·so·ev·er (hwĭth′ər-sō-ĕv′ər, wĭth′-) *adv.* To whatever place; to any place whatsoever.

whit·ing¹ (hwī′tĭng, wī′-) *n.* A pure white grade of chalk that has been ground and washed for use in paints, ink, and putty. [Middle English *whityng,* from *whiten,* to whiten, from *white,* white. See WHITE.]

whit·ing² (hwī′tĭng, wī′-) *n., pl.* **whiting** or **-ings.** **1.** A food fish *(Merlangus merlangus)* of European Atlantic waters, related

white pine
Pinus strobus

white snakeroot
Eupatorium rugosum

whitewall tire

ă pat	oi boy
ā pay	ou out
âr care	o͝o took
ä father	o͞o boot
ĕ pet	ŭ cut
ē be	ûr urge
ĭ pit	th thin
ī pie	*th* this
îr pier	hw which
ŏ pot	zh vision
ō toe	ə about, item
ô paw	♦ regionalism

Stress marks: ′ (primary); ′ (secondary), as in **dictionary** (dĭk′shə-nĕr′ē)

Eli Whitney

to the cod. **2.** Any of several marine food fishes of the genera *Menticirrhus* and *Merluccius,* including the corbina and the silver hake, of North American coastal waters. [Middle English *whitynge,* from Middle Dutch *wijting.* See **kweit-** in Appendix.]

whit·ish (hwī′tĭsh, wī′-) *adj.* Somewhat white.

whit·leath·er (hwĭt′lĕth′ər, wĭt′-) *n.* Variant of **white leather.**

whit·low (hwĭt′lō, wĭt′-) *n.* See **felon**[2]. [Alteration of Middle English *whitflawe* : *white,* white (perhaps alteration of Middle Dutch *vijt,* abscess) + *flaue,* splinter, flaw; see FLAW[1].]

Whit·man (hwĭt′mən, wĭt′-), **Marcus.** 1802–1847. American frontier missionary who with his wife **Narcissa Prentiss** (1808–1847) established a missionary post in the Oregon region (1836), where they introduced Christianity, schooling, and medical advances to the Native Americans.

Whitman, Walt. 1819–1892. American poet whose great work *Leaves of Grass* (first published 1855), written in unconventional meter and rhyme, celebrates the self, universal brotherhood, and the greatness of democracy and the United States.

Whit·mon·day also **Whit-Mon·day** (hwĭt′mŭn′dē, -dā′, wĭt′-) *n.* The day after Whitsunday.

Whit·ney (hwĭt′nē, wĭt′-), **Eli.** 1765–1825. American inventor and manufacturer whose invention of the cotton gin (1793) revolutionized the cotton industry. He also established the first factory to assemble muskets with interchangeable parts, marking the advent of modern mass production.

Whitney, Mount. A peak, 4,420.7 m (14,494 ft) high, in the Sierra Nevada of east-central California. It is the highest elevation in the continental United States.

Whit·sun (hwĭt′sən, wĭt′-) *adj.* Of, relating to, or observed on Whitsunday or at Whitsuntide. [Middle English *whitsone,* back-formation from *whitsonday,* Whitsunday. See WHITSUNDAY.]

Whit·sun·day (hwĭt′sən-dē, -dā′, wĭt′-) *n.* See **Pentecost** (sense 1). [Middle English *whitsonday,* from Old English *hwīta sunnandæg,* White Sunday (from the white ceremonial robes worn on this day) : *hwīt,* white; see WHITE + *sunnandæg,* Sunday; see SUNDAY.]

Whit·sun·tide also **Whit·sun Tide** (hwĭt′sən-tīd′, wĭt′-) *n.* The week beginning on Whitsunday, especially the first three days of this week.

Whit·ta·ker (hwĭt′ə-kər, wĭt′-), **Charles Evans.** 1901–1973. American jurist who served as an associate justice of the U.S. Supreme Court (1957–1962).

Whit·ti·er (hwĭt′ē-ər, wĭt′-). A city of southern California east-southeast of Los Angeles. Founded by Quakers in 1887, it is a residential community with varied industries. Population, 69,717.

Whittier, John Greenleaf. 1807–1892. American poet. His early works, such as *Voices of Freedom* (1846), reflect his opposition to slavery, but he is best known for his nostalgic poems about New England, including *Snow-Bound* (1866).

Whit·ting·ton (hwĭt′ĭng-tən, wĭt′-), **Richard.** 1358?–1423. English merchant and mayor of London (1397–1399, 1406–1407, and 1419–1420).

whit·tle (hwĭt′l, wĭt′l) *v.* **-tled, -tling, -tles.** —*tr.* **1.a.** To cut small bits or pare shavings from (a piece of wood). **b.** To fashion or shape in this way: *whittle a toy boat.* **2.** To reduce or eliminate gradually, as if by whittling with a knife: *whittled down the debt by making small payments.* —*intr.* To cut or shape wood with a knife. [From Middle English *whyttel,* knife, variant of *thwitel,* from *thwiten,* to whittle, from Old English *thwītan,* to strike, whittle down.] —**whit′tler** *n.*

whiz also **whizz** (hwĭz, wĭz) —*v.* **whizzed, whiz·zing, whiz·zes.** —*intr.* **1.** To make a whirring or hissing sound, as of an object speeding through air. **2.** To move swiftly with or as if with such a sound; rush: *whizzed past on a ten-speed bike; as the days whizzed by.* —*tr.* To throw or spin rapidly: *The pitcher whizzed the ball to first.* —*n.* **1.** A whirring or hissing sound, as of an object speeding through air. **2.** A rapid passage or journey. **3.** *Informal.* One who has remarkable skill: *a whiz at all sorts of games.* [Imitative.]

whiz-bang also **whizz-bang** (hwĭz′băng′, wĭz′-) *Informal.*—*n.* One that is conspicuously effective, successful, or skillful: *a whiz-bang of a speech.* —*adj.* **1.** Conspicuously effective, successful, or skillful: *a whiz-bang ad campaign.* **2.** Very rapid and eventful; rushed: *whiz-bang pacing; a whiz-bang schedule.* [From *whizzbang,* a shell used in World War I that was heard only an instant before landing and exploding : WHIZ + BANG[1].]

whiz kid *n. Informal.* A young person who is exceptionally intelligent, innovatively clever, or precociously successful. [Alteration of *Quiz Kid,* a panelist on an early game show.]

whizz-bang (hwĭz′băng′, wĭz′-) *n.* & *adj.* Variant of **whiz-bang.**

who (ho͞o) *pron.* **1.** What or which person or persons: *Who left?* **2.** Used as a relative pronoun to introduce a clause when the antecedent is a person or persons or one to whom personality is attributed: *the visitor who came yesterday; our child, who is gifted; informed sources who denied the story.* **3.** The person or persons that; whoever: *Who believes that will believe anything.* [Middle English, from Old English *hwā.* See **kʷo-** in Appendix.]

USAGE NOTE: The traditional rules that determine the use of *who* and *whom* are relatively simple: *who* is used for a grammatical subject, where a nominative pronoun such as *I* or *he* would be appropriate, and *whom* is used elsewhere. Thus, we write *The actor who played Hamlet was there,* since *who* stands for the subject of *played Hamlet;* and *Who do you think is the best candidate?* where *who* stands for the subject of *is the best candidate.* But we write *To whom did you give the letter?* since *whom* is the object of the preposition *to;* and *The man whom the papers criticized did not show up,* since *whom* is the object of the verb *criticized.* • Considerable effort and attention are required to apply the rules correctly in complicated sentences. To produce correctly a sentence such as *I met the man whom the government had tried to get France to extradite,* we must anticipate when we write *whom* that it will function as the object of the verb *extradite,* several clauses distant from it. It is thus not surprising that writers from Shakespeare onward should often have interchanged *who* and *whom.* And though the distinction shows no signs of disappearing in formal style, strict adherence to the rules in informal discourse might be taken as evidence that the speaker or writer is paying undue attention to the form of what is said, possibly at the expense of its substance. In speech and informal writing *who* tends to predominate over *whom;* a sentence such as *Who did John say he was going to support?* will be regarded as quite natural, if strictly incorrect. By contrast, the use of *whom* where *who* would be required, as in *Whom shall I say is calling?* may be thought to betray a certain linguistic insecurity. • When the relative pronoun stands for the object of a preposition that ends a sentence, *whom* is technically the correct form: the strict grammarian will insist on *Whom* (not *who*) *did you give it to?* But grammarians since Noah Webster have argued that the excessive formality of *whom* in these cases is at odds with the relative informality associated with the practice of placing the preposition in final position and that the use of *who* in these cases should be regarded as entirely acceptable. • The relative pronoun *who* may be used in restrictive relative clauses, in which case it is not preceded by a comma, or in nonrestrictive clauses, in which case a comma is required. Thus, we may say either *The scientist who discovers a cure for cancer will be immortalized,* where the clause *who discovers a cure for cancer* indicates which scientist will be immortalized, or *The mathematician over there, who solved the four-color theorem, is widely known,* where the clause *who solved the four-color theorem* adds information about a person already identified by the phrase *the mathematician over there.* • Some grammarians have argued that only *who* and not *that* should be used to introduce a restrictive relative clause that identifies a person. This restriction has no basis either in logic or in the usage of the best writers; it is entirely acceptable to write either *the man that wanted to talk to you* or *the man who wanted to talk to you.* • The grammatical rules governing the use of *who* and *whom* apply equally to *whoever* and *whomever.* See Usage Notes at **else, that, whose.**

WHO *abbr.* World Health Organization.

whoa (hwō, wō) *interj.* Used as a command to stop, as to a horse.

who'd (ho͞od). **1.** Who would. **2.** Who had.

who·dun·it (ho͞o-dŭn′ĭt) *n. Informal.* A story dealing with a crime and its solution. [Alteration of *who done it?*]

who·ev·er (ho͞o-ĕv′ər) *pron.* **1.** Whatever person or persons: *Whoever comes will be welcomed.* **2.** Who: *Whoever could have dreamed of such a thing?* See Usage Notes at **whatever, who.**

whole (hōl) *adj.* **1.** Containing all components; complete: *a whole wardrobe for the tropics.* **2.** Not divided or disjoined; in one unit: *a whole loaf.* **3.** Constituting the full amount, extent, or duration: *The baby cried the whole trip home.* **4.a.** Not wounded, injured, or impaired; sound or unhurt: *escaped the fire with a whole skin.* **b.** Having been restored; healed: *a whole person again.* **5.** Having the same parents: *a whole sister.* **6.** *Mathematics.* Not fractional; integral. —**whole** *n.* **1.** A number, group, set, or thing lacking no part or element; a complete thing. **2.** An entity or a system made up of interrelated parts: *treating the human body as a whole.* —**whole** *adv. Informal.* Entirely; wholly: *a whole new idea.* —***idioms.*** **as a whole.** All parts or aspects considered; altogether: *disliked the acting but enjoyed the play as a whole.* **on the whole.** **1.** Considering everything: *on the whole, a happy marriage.* **2.** In most instances or cases; as a rule: *can expect sunny weather, on the whole.* [Middle English *hole,* unharmed, from Old English *hāl.* See **kailo-** in Appendix.] —**whole′ness** *n.*

SYNONYMS: *whole, all, entire, gross, total.* The central meaning shared by these adjectives is "including every constituent or individual": *a whole town devastated by an earthquake; all the class going on a field trip; entire freedom of choice; gross income; the total cost.*
ANTONYM: *partial.*

whole blood *n.* Blood drawn from the body from which no constituent, such as plasma or platelets, has been removed.

whole cloth *n.* Pure fabrication or fiction: *"He invented, almost out of whole cloth, what it means to be American"* (Ned Rorem). *"His account of being drugged, kidnapped and tortured was made up of whole cloth"* (George Carver). [From the fabrication of garments out of newly manufactured, full-sized pieces of cloth.]

whole gale *n. Meteorology.* A wind with a speed ranging from 55 to 63 miles (87 to 102 kilometers) per hour, according to the Beaufort scale.

whole·heart·ed (hōl′här′tĭd) *adj.* Marked by unconditional commitment, unstinting devotion, or unreserved enthusiasm: *wholehearted approval.* See Synonyms at **sincere.** —**whole′heart′ed·ly** *adv.* —**whole′heart′ed·ness** *n.*

whole hog *Slang. n.* The whole way; the fullest extent: *went the whole hog and ordered dessert.* —**whole hog** *adv.* Completely; unreservedly: *swallowed the official version whole hog.*

whole life insurance *n.* Insurance that provides death protection for the insured's entire lifetime.

whole milk *n.* Milk from which no constituent, such as fat, has been removed.

whole note *n. Music.* A note having, in common time, the value of four beats.

whole number *n. Mathematics.* Any of the set of numbers including zero and all negative and positive multiples of 1.

whole·sale (hōl′sāl′) *n. Abbr.* **whsle.** The sale of goods in large quantities, as for resale by a retailer. —**wholesale** *adj.* **1.** Of, relating to, or engaged in the sale of goods in large quantities for resale: *a wholesale produce market; wholesale goods; wholesale prices.* **2.** Made or accomplished extensively and indiscriminately; blanket: *wholesale destruction.* —**wholesale** *adv.* **1.** In large bulk or quantity. **2.** Extensively; indiscriminately. —**wholesale** *v.* **-saled, -sal·ing, -sales.** —*tr.* To sell in large quantities for resale. —*intr.* **1.** To engage in wholesale selling. **2.** To be sold wholesale. —**whole′sal′er** *n.*

whole·some (hōl′səm) *adj.* **-som·er, -som·est. 1.** Conducive to sound health or well-being; salutary: *simple, wholesome food.* **2.** Promoting mental, moral, or social health: *wholesome entertainment.* **3.** Enjoying or marked by physical, mental, or moral soundness; healthy. See Synonyms at **healthy.** [Middle English *holsom,* from Old English **hālsum.* See **kailo-** in Appendix.] —**whole′some·ly** *adv.* —**whole′some·ness** *n.*

whole-wheat (hōl′hwēt′, -wēt′) *adj.* **1.** Made from the entire grain of wheat, including the bran: *whole-wheat flour.* **2.** Made with whole-wheat flour: *whole-wheat bread.*

who'll (ho͞ol). **1.** Who will. **2.** Who shall.

whol·ly (hō′lē, hōl′lē) *adv.* **1.** Completely; entirely: *"The old American purposes are still wholly relevant"* (John F. Kennedy). **2.** Exclusively; solely.

whom (ho͞om) *pron.* The objective case of **who.** See Usage Note at **who.** [Middle English, from Old English *hwǣm, hwām.* See **kʷo-** in Appendix.]

whom·ev·er (ho͞om-ĕv′ər) *pron.* The objective case of **whoever.** See Usage Note at **who.**

whom·so·ev·er (ho͞om′sō-ĕv′ər) *pron.* The objective case of **whosoever.**

whoop (ho͞op, hwo͞op, wo͞op) *n.* **1.a.** A loud cry of exultation or excitement. **b.** A shout uttered by a hunter or warrior. **2.** A hooting cry, as of a bird. **3.** The paroxysmal gasp characteristic of whooping cough. —**whoop** *v.* **whooped, whoop·ing, whoops.** —*intr.* **1.** To utter a loud shout or cry. See Synonyms at **shout. 2.** To utter a hooting cry. **3.** To make the paroxysmal gasp characteristic of whooping cough. —*tr.* **1.** To utter with a whoop. **2.** To chase, call, urge on, or drive with a whoop: *whooping the cattle down the road.* —***idiom.* whoop it up.** *Slang.* **1.** To have a jolly, noisy celebration. **2.** To express or arouse enthusiasm; cheer: *conventioneers whooping it up for their candidate.* [From Middle English *whopen,* to whoop, variant of *hopen,* from Old French *hopper,* of imitative origin.]

whoop·ee (hwo͝op′ē, wo͝op′ē, hwo͞o′pē, wo͞o′-) *Slang. interj.* Used to express jubilance. —***idiom.* make whoopee.** *Slang.* **1.** To engage in a noisy, boisterous celebration. **2.** To make love. [Alteration of WHOOP.]

whoop·er (ho͞o′pər, hwo͞o′-, wo͞o′-) *n.* **1.** A whooping crane. **2.** An Old World swan *(Cygnus cygnus)* having a loud cry.

whoop·ing cough (ho͞o′pĭng, hwo͞o′-, wo͞o′-, ho͝op′ĭng) *n.* A highly contagious disease of the respiratory system, usually affecting children, that is caused by the bacterium *Bordetella pertussis* and is characterized in its advanced stage by spasms of coughing interspersed with deep, noisy inspirations. Also called *pertussis.*

whooping crane *n.* A large, long-legged North American bird *(Grus americana),* now very rare, having predominantly white plumage and a loud trumpeting cry.

whoops (hwo͝ops, wo͝ops, hwo͞ops, wo͞ops) also **woops** (wo͝ops, wo͞ops) *interj.* Used to express apology or mild surprise.

whoosh (hwo͞osh, wo͞osh, hwo͝osh, wo͝osh) *n.* **1.** A sibilant sound. **2.** A swift movement or flow; a rush or spurt. —**whoosh** *intr.v.* **whooshed, whoosh·ing, whoosh·es. 1.** To make a soft sibilant sound. **2.** To move or flow swiftly with or as if with such a sound. [Imitative.]

whop (hwŏp, wŏp) *tr.v.* **whopped, whop·ping, whops. 1.** To strike with a heavy blow. **2.** To defeat soundly; thrash. —**whop** *n.* A heavy blow; a sharp thud. [Middle English *whappen,* variant of *wappen,* to throw violently.]

whop·per (hwŏp′ər, wŏp′-) *n. Slang.* **1.** Something exceptionally big or remarkable. **2.** A gross untruth. [From WHOPPING.]

whop·ping (hwŏp′ĭng, wŏp′-) *Slang. adj.* Exceptionally large: *"yet another whopping pay raise"* (Lee Atwater). —**whopping** *adv.* Used as an intensive: *a whopping good joke.* [Present participle of WHOP.]

whore (hôr, hōr) *n.* **1.** A prostitute. **2.** A person considered sexually promiscuous. **3.** A person considered as having compromised principles for personal gain. —**whore** *intr.v.* **whored, whor·ing, whores. 1.** To associate or have sexual relations with prostitutes or a prostitute. **2.** To accept payment in exchange for sexual relations. **3.** To compromise one's principles for personal gain. [Middle English *hore,* from Old English *hōre.* See **kā-** in Appendix.]

WORD HISTORY: Derivatives of Indo-European roots often make strange bedfellows. A prime example is the case of **kā-,* "to like, desire." From the stem **kāro-* derived from this root came the prehistoric Common Germanic word **hōraz* with the underlying meaning "one who desires" and the effective meaning "adulterer." From this word came the Old English word *hōre,* the ancestor of Modern English *whore.* The same stem produced the Latin word *cārus,* "dear," from which came Modern English *caress, cherish,* and *charity,* the highest form of love. Contact with East Indian culture has added yet another pair of derivatives from this Indo-European root to the English language. From the stem **kāmo-* came the Sanskrit word *kāmaḥ,* "love, desire," from which are derived the English borrowings *Kama,* "the Hindu god of love," and *Kamasutra,* "a Sanskrit treatise on the rules of love and marriage according to Hindu law."

whooping crane
Grus americana

whore·dom (hôr′dəm, hōr′-) *n.* **1.** The practice of accepting payment in exchange for sexual relations; prostitution. **2.a.** Unlawful sexual relations. **b.** Promiscuous sex. **3.** *Bible.* Unfaithfulness to God; idolatry. [Middle English *hordom,* from Old Norse *hōrdōmr.* See **kā-** in Appendix.]

whore·house (hôr′hous′, hōr′-) *n.* A house of prostitution.

whore·mas·ter (hôr′măs′tər, hōr′-) *n.* **1.** A man who associates with or pays for sexual relations with prostitutes or a prostitute. **2.** A pimp.

whore·mong·er (hôr′mŭng′gər, -mŏng′-, hōr′-) *n.* A whoremaster.

whore·son (hôr′sən, hōr′-) *n.* An illegitimate child. —**whoreson** *adj.* Abominable.

whor·ish (hôr′ĭsh, hōr′-) *adj.* Of or characteristic of whores or a whore; lewd. —**whor′ish·ly** *adv.* —**whor′ish·ness** *n.*

whorl (hwôrl, wôrl, hwûrl, wûrl) *n.* **1.** A form that coils or spirals; a curl or swirl: *spread the icing in peaks and whorls.* **2.** *Botany.* An arrangement of three or more leaves, petals, or other organs radiating from a single node. **3.** *Zoology.* A single turn or volution of a spiral shell. **4.** One of the circular ridges or convolutions of a fingerprint. **5.** *Architecture.* An ornamental device, as in stonework or weaving, consisting of stylized vine leaves and tendrils. **6.** A small flywheel that regulates the speed of a spinning wheel. [Middle English *whorle,* alteration (influenced by *wharle,* variant of *whorlwyl,* from Middle Dutch *worvel*) of *whirle,* whirl, from *whirlen,* to whirl. See WHIRL.]

whorled (hwôrld, wôrld, hwûrld, wûrld) *adj.* Having or forming whorls or a whorl: *whorled flower parts.*

whort (hwûrt, wûrt) also **whor·tle** (hwûrt′l, wûrt′l) *n.* The whortleberry or its fruit. [Variant of dialectal *hurt.*]

whor·tle·ber·ry (hwûrt′l-bĕr′ē, wûrt′-) *n.* **1.** Either of two deciduous shrubs, *Vaccinium myrtillus,* of Eurasia, or *V. corymbosum,* of eastern North America, having edible blackish berries. **2.** The fruit of these plants. [Dialectal, variant of *hurtleberry.*]

whorl
Whorled leaves of northern bedstraw
Galium boreale

who's (ho͞oz). **1.** Who is. **2.** Who has.

whose (ho͞oz) *adj.* **1.** The possessive form of **who. 2.** The possessive form of **which.** [Middle English *whos,* from Old English *hwæs.* See **kʷo-** in Appendix.]

USAGE NOTE: It has sometimes been claimed that *whose* should be used only as the possessive form of *who* and should thus be restricted to animate antecedents, as in *a man whose power has greatly eroded.* But there is extensive literary precedent for the use of *whose* as the possessive of *which,* as in *The play, whose style is rigidly formal, is typical of the period.* In an earlier survey this example was acceptable to a large majority of the Usage Panel. The alternate form *of which* also can be used to this purpose, as in *The play, the style of which is rigidly formal, is typical of the period.* But as this example demonstrates, substituting *of which* for *whose* may result in stiltedness. See Usage Notes at **else, which, who.**

who·so·ev·er (ho͞o′sō-ĕv′ər) *pron.* Whoever.

who's who or **Who's Who** *n.* **1.** A reference work containing short biographical sketches of outstanding persons in a field: *a who's who of musicians.* **2.** The outstanding or best-known persons of a group.

W-hr *abbr.* Watt-hour.

whs. *abbr.* Warehouse.

whsle. *abbr.* Wholesale.

♦ **whup** (hwŭp, wŭp, hwo͝op, wo͝op) *v. Chiefly Southern U.S.* Variant of **whip.** [Scots, variant of WHIP.]

why (hwī, wī) *adv.* For what purpose, reason, or cause; with what intention, justification, or motive: *Why is the door shut? Why do birds sing?* —**why** *conj.* **1.** The reason, cause, or purpose for which: *I know why you left.* **2.** *Usage Problem.* On account of which; for which: *"The reason why* [regular verbs] *are called regular is that we can predict what all the other three forms are"* (Randolph Quirk). —**why** *n., pl.* **whys. 1.** The cause or intention underlying a given action or situation: *studying the whys of*

ă pat	oi boy
ā pay	ou out
âr care	o͝o took
ä father	o͞o boot
ĕ pet	ŭ cut
ē be	ûr urge
ĭ pit	th thin
ī pie	*th* this
îr pier	hw which
ŏ pot	zh vision
ō toe	ə about, item
ô paw	♦ regionalism

Stress marks: **′** (primary); ′ (secondary), as in **dictionary** (dĭk′shə-nĕr′ē)

wicker
Wicker carriage

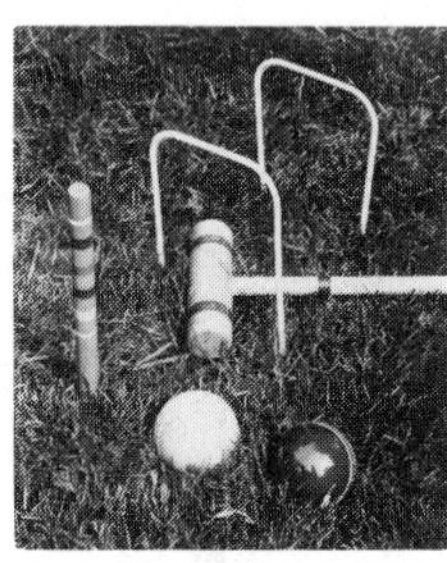
wicket

wickiup
1905 Apache

widow's walk

antisocial behavior. **2.** A difficult problem or question. **—why** *interj.* Used to express mild surprise, indignation, or impatience. [Middle English, from Old English *hwȳ.* See **kʷo-** in Appendix.]

USAGE NOTE: Many critics have held that *why* is redundant in the expression *the reason why,* as in *The reason why he accepted the nomination is not clear.* It is true that *why* could be eliminated from such examples with no loss to the sense, but the construction has been used by reputable English writers since the Renaissance. See Usage Note at **where.**

whyd·ah also **whid·ah** (hwĭd′ə, wĭd′ə) *n.* Any of several African weaverbirds of the genus *Vidua,* the male of which grows long, drooping, predominantly black tail feathers during the breeding season. Also called *widow bird.* [Probably alteration of WIDOW (BIRD).]

WI *abbr.* Wisconsin.

w.i. *abbr. Business.* When issued (financial stock).

W.I. *abbr.* **1.** West Indian. **2.** West Indies.

WIA *abbr.* Wounded in action.

Wic·ca (wĭk′ə) *n.* **1.** A pagan nature religion having its roots in pre-Christian western Europe and undergoing a 20th-century revival, especially in the United States and Great Britain. **2.** A group or community of believers or followers of this religion. [Old English *wicca,* necromancer. See WITCH.]

Wic·can (wĭk′ən) *adj.* Of or relating to Wicca: *the Wiccan religion; a Wiccan ritual.* **—Wiccan** *n.* A believer or follower of Wicca; a witch.

Wich·i·ta[1] (wĭch′ĭ-tô′) *n., pl.* **Wichita** or **-tas. 1.a.** A Native American confederacy formerly inhabiting south-central Kansas and later moving southward into Oklahoma and Texas, with a present-day population in southwest Oklahoma. **b.** A member of this confederacy. **2.** The Caddoan language of the Wichita. [Caddo *wiíc'ita.*]

Wich·i·ta[2] (wĭch′ĭ-tô′). A city of south-central Kansas on the Arkansas River southwest of Kansas City. It was founded in the 1860's and boomed as a cow town after the coming of the railroad in 1872. Population, 279,272.

Wichita Falls. A city of north-central Texas near the Oklahoma border northwest of Fort Worth. It prospered after the discovery of oil in the area in the early 20th century. Population, 94,201.

wick (wĭk) *n.* **1.** A cord or strand of loosely woven, twisted, or braided fibers, as on a candle or an oil lamp, that draws up fuel to the flame by capillary action. **2.** A piece of material that conveys liquid by capillary action. **—wick** *tr. & intr.v.* **wicked** (wĭkt), **wick·ing, wicks.** To convey or be conveyed by capillary action: *absorbent cloth that wicks moisture away from the skin; water gradually wicking up through the bricks.* [Middle English *wike,* from Old English *wēoce.*]

wick·ed (wĭk′ĭd) *adj.* **-er, -est. 1.** Evil by nature and in practice. See Synonyms at **bad**[1]. **2.** Playfully malicious or mischievous: *a wicked prank; a critic's wicked wit.* **3.** Severe and distressing: *a wicked cough; a wicked gash; wicked driving conditions.* **4.** Highly offensive; obnoxious: *a wicked stench.* **5.** *Slang.* Strikingly good, effective, or skillful: *a wicked curve ball; a wicked imitation.* **—wicked** *adv. Slang.* Used as an intensive: *"a . . . body suit, which she describes as wicked comfortable"* (Nathan Cobb). [Middle English, alteration of *wicke,* ultimately from Old English *wicca,* sorcerer. See WITCH.] **—wick′ed·ly** *adv.* **—wick′ed·ness** *n.*

wick·er (wĭk′ər) *n.* **1.** A flexible plant branch or twig, as of a willow, used in weaving baskets or furniture. **2.** Wickerwork. *—attributive.* Often used to modify another noun: *a wicker chair; a wicker birdcage.* [Middle English *wiker,* of Scandinavian origin. See **weik-**[2] in Appendix.]

wick·er·work (wĭk′ər-wûrk′) *n.* Work made of interlaced plant branches or twigs.

wick·et (wĭk′ĭt) *n.* **1.** A small door or gate, especially one built into or near a larger one. **2.** A small window or opening, often fitted with glass or a grating. **3.** A sluice gate for regulating the amount of water in a millrace or a canal or for emptying a lock. **4.** *Sports.* In cricket: **a.** Either of the two sets of three stumps, topped by bails, that forms the target of the bowler and is defended by the batsman. **b.** A batsman's innings, which may be terminated by the ball knocking the bails off the stumps. **c.** The termination of a batsman's innings. **d.** The period during which two batsmen are in together. **e.** See **pitch**[2] (sense 3). **5.** *Games.* Any of the small arches, usually made of wire, through which players try to drive their ball in croquet. [Middle English, from Old North French *wiket,* nook, wicket. See **weik-**[2] in Appendix.]

wick·et·keep·er (wĭk′ĭt-kē′pər) *n. Sports.* The cricket player positioned immediately behind the wicket in play.

wick·i·up also **wik·i·up** (wĭk′ē-ŭp′) *n.* A frame hut covered with matting, as of bark or brush, used by nomadic Native Americans of North America. [Fox *wiikiyaapi,* wigwam.]

Wick·liffe (wĭk′lĭf). A city of northeast Ohio, an industrial suburb of Cleveland on Lake Erie. Population, 16,790.

Wick·liffe or **Wic·lif** (wĭk′lĭf), **John.** See John **Wycliffe.**

wic·o·py (wĭk′ə-pē) *n., pl.* **-pies.** See **leatherwood** (sense 1). [Eastern Abenaki *wikəpi,* inner bark used for cordage.]

wid. *abbr.* **1.** Widow. **2.** Widower.

Wi·dal test (vē-däl′) *n.* A test of blood serum that uses an agglutination reaction to diagnose typhoid fever. [After Fernand *Widal* (1862–1929), French physician.]

wid·der·shins (wĭd′ər-shĭnz′) or **with·er·shins** (wĭth′-) *adv.* In a contrary or counterclockwise direction: *"The coracle whirled round, clockwise, then widdershins"* (Anthony Bailey). [Middle Low German *weddersinnes,* from Middle High German *widersinnes* : *wider,* back (from Old High German *widar;* see **wi-** in Appendix) + *sinnes,* in the direction of (from *sin,* direction, from Old High German; see **sent-** in Appendix).]

wide (wīd) *adj.* **wid·er, wid·est. 1.a.** *Abbr.* **w.** Having a specified extent from side to side: *a ribbon two inches wide.* **b.** Extending over a great distance from side to side; broad: *a wide road; a wide necktie.* **2.** Having great extent or range; including much or many: *a wide selection; granting wide powers; wide variations.* **3.** Fully open or extended: *look with wide eyes.* **4.a.** Being at a distance from a desired goal or point: *a shot that was wide of the mark; a claim that was wide of the truth.* **b.** *Baseball.* Outside. **5.** *Linguistics.* Lax. **—wide** *adv.* **wider, widest. 1.** Over a great distance; extensively: *traveled far and wide.* **2.** To the full extent; completely. **3.** So as to miss a target; astray. **—wide** *n. Sports.* A ball bowled outside of the batsman's reach, counting as a run for the batting team in cricket. [Middle English, from Old English *wīd.* See **wi-** in Appendix.] **—wide′ly** *adv.* **—wide′ness** *n.*

-wide *suff.* Extending or effective throughout a specified area or region: *statewide.* [From WIDE.]

wide-an·gle (wīd′ăng′gəl) *adj.* Of, having, or being a camera lens with a relatively short focal length that permits an angle of view wider than approximately 70°.

wide-a·wake (wīd′ə-wāk′) *adj.* **1.** Completely awake. **2.** Alert; watchful. **—wide-awake** *n.* See **sooty tern. —wide′-a·wake′ness** *n.*

wide-bod·ied (wīd′bŏd′ēd) *adj.* Being or relating to a jet aircraft having a wide fuselage with passenger seats divided by two lengthwise aisles.

wide-eyed (wīd′īd′) *adj.* **1.** Having the eyes completely opened, as in wonder. **2.** Innocent; credulous.

wid·en (wīd′n) *tr. & intr.v.* **wid·ened, wid·en·ing, wid·ens.** To make or become wide or wider. **—wid′en·er** *n.*

wide-o·pen (wīd′ō′pən) *adj.* **1.** Completely open: *a wide-open door.* **2.** Being without laws or law enforcement: *a wide-open frontier town.*

wide-rang·ing (wīd′rān′jĭng) *adj.* Covering a wide area; including much: *a pianist's wide-ranging repertoire.*

wide receiver *n. Football.* A receiver who usually lines up several yards to the side of the offensive formation.

wide·spread (wīd′sprĕd′) *adj.* **1.** Spread or scattered over a considerable extent: *widespread fallout from a nuclear explosion.* **2.** Occurring or accepted widely: *a widespread misunderstanding.*

wid·geon also **wi·geon** (wĭj′ən) *n., pl.* **widgeon** also **wigeon** or **-geons.** Either of two wild, freshwater ducks (*Anas americana* of North America or *A. penelope* of Europe) having a grayish or brownish back and a white belly and wing coverts. The European widgeon has a reddish-brown head and creamy crown, and the American widgeon has a shiny white crown. [Origin unknown.]

widg·et (wĭj′ĭt) *n.* **1.** A small mechanical device or control; a gadget. **2.** An unnamed or hypothetical manufactured article. [Perhaps alteration of GADGET.]

Wid·nes (wĭd′nĭs). A municipal borough of northwest England on the Mersey River east-southeast of Liverpool. It is a processing and manufacturing center. Population, 122,500.

wid·ow (wĭd′ō) *n.* **1.** *Abbr.* **wid.** A woman whose husband has died and who has not remarried. **2.** *Informal.* A woman whose husband is often away pursuing a sport or hobby. **3.** *Games.* An additional hand of cards dealt face down in some card games, to be used by the highest bidder. Also called *kitty.* **4.** *Printing.* **a.** A single, usually short line of type, as one ending a paragraph, carried over to the top of the next page or column. **b.** A short line at the bottom of a page, column, or paragraph. **—widow** *tr.v.* **-owed, -ow·ing, -ows.** To make a widow or widower of. [Middle English *widewe,* from Old English *widuwe.*]

widow bird *n.* See **whydah.** [From its black plumage.]

wid·ow·er (wĭd′ō-ər) *n. Abbr.* **wid.** A man whose wife has died and who has not remarried. [Middle English *widewer,* from *widewe,* widow. See WIDOW.]

wid·ow·er·hood (wĭd′ō-ər-ho͝od′) *n.* The condition or period of being a widower.

wid·ow·hood (wĭd′ō-ho͝od′) *n.* The condition or period of being a widow.

wid·ow's mite (wĭd′ōz) *n.* A small contribution made by one who has little. [From the widow who gave two small coins to the Temple treasury in the Gospel according to Saint Mark.]

widow's peak *n.* A V-shaped point formed by the hair at the middle of the human forehead. [From the superstition that it is a sign of early widowhood.]

widow's walk *n.* A railed, rooftop platform typically on a coastal house, originally designed to observe vessels at sea.

width (wĭdth, wĭth, wĭtth) *n.* **1.** The state, quality, or fact of being wide. **2.** *Abbr.* **w.** The measurement of the extent of something from side to side. **3.** A piece of material measured along its smaller dimension, especially a piece of fabric measured from selvage to selvage in sewing. [WIDE + –TH[2].]

width•wise (wĭdthʹwīzʹ, wĭthʹ-, wĭtthʹ-) *adv.* From side to side; in terms of width.

wield (wēld) *tr.v.* **wield•ed, wield•ing, wields. 1.** To handle (a weapon or tool, for example) with skill and ease. **2.** To exercise (authority or influence, for example) effectively. See Synonyms at **handle.** [Middle English *welden,* from Old English *wealdan,* to rule, and *wieldan,* to govern; see **wal-** in Appendix.] **—wieldʹa•ble** *adj.* **—wieldʹer** *n.*

wield•y (wēlʹdē) *adj.* **-i•er, -i•est.** Easily wielded or managed.

wie•ner (wēʹnər) *n.* **1.** Wienerwurst. **2.** A frankfurter. [German, short for *Wienerwurst.* See WIENERWURST.]

Wie•ner (wēʹnər), **Norbert.** 1894–1964. American mathematician who founded the field of cybernetics.

Wie•ner schnit•zel (vēʹnər shnĭtʹsəl) *n.* A breaded veal cutlet. [German : *Wiener,* of Vienna, Austria + *schnitzel,* cutlet.]

wie•ner•wurst (wēʹnər-wûrstʹ, -wo͝orstʹ) *n.* A smoked pork or beef sausage similar to a frankfurter. [German : *Wiener,* of Vienna, Austria + *Wurst,* sausage; see WURST.]

Wies•ba•den (vēsʹbädʹn). A city of west-central Germany on the Rhine River west of Frankfurt. Founded as a Celtic settlement in the third century B.C., it has been a noted spa since Roman times. Wiesbaden became a free imperial city c. A.D. 1242 and passed to Prussia in 1866. Population, 267,467.

Wie•sel (vēʹsəl), **Elie(zer).** Born 1928. Romanian-born writer and lecturer. A survivor of Nazi concentration camps, he is dedicated to preserving the memory of the Holocaust. He won the 1986 Nobel Peace Prize.

wife (wīf) *n., pl.* **wives** (wīvz). *Abbr.* **w.** A woman joined to a man in marriage; a female spouse. [Middle English, from Old English *wīf.*] **—wifeʹhoodʹ** *n.*

wife•ly (wīfʹlē) *adj.* Of or befitting a wife. **—wifeʹli•ness** *n.*

wig (wĭg) *n.* An artificial covering of human or synthetic hair worn on the head for personal adornment, as part of a costume, or to conceal baldness. **—wig** *tr.v.* **wigged, wig•ging, wigs.** To scold or censure. ***—phrasal verb.* wig out.** *Slang.* To make or become wildly excited or enthusiastic. [Short for PERIWIG.]

wig•an (wĭgʹən) *n.* A stiff fabric used for stiffening. [After WIGAN.]

Wig•an (wĭgʹən). A borough of northwest England northeast of Liverpool. An important market town in the Middle Ages, it is an industrial city in a coal-mining region. Population, 310,000.

wi•geon (wĭjʹən) *n.* Variant of **widgeon.**

Wig•gin (wĭgʹĭn), **Kate Douglas Smith.** 1856–1923. American writer of children's books, including *Rebecca of Sunnybrook Farm* (1903).

wig•gle (wĭgʹəl) *intr. & tr.v.* **-gled, -gling, -gles.** To move or cause to move from side to side with short irregular twisting motions: *wiggled restlessly in her chair; wiggle a finger at a waitron.* **—wiggle** *n.* A wiggling movement or course. ***—idiom.* get a wiggle on.** *Slang.* To hurry or hurry up. [Middle English *wiglen,* probably from Middle Low German *wiggelen,* to totter. See **wegh-** in Appendix.] **—wigʹgly** *adj.*

wig•gler (wĭgʹlər) *n.* **1.** One that wiggles: *a toddler who was a real wiggler on plane trips.* **2.** The larva or pupa of a mosquito.

Wig•gles•worth (wĭgʹəlz-wûrthʹ), **Michael.** 1631–1705. English-born American cleric and poet whose works include the popular poem *The Day of Doom* (1662).

wight[1] (wīt) *n. Obsolete.* A living being; a creature. [Middle English, from Old English *wiht.* See **wekti-** in Appendix.]

wight[2] (wīt) *adj. Archaic.* Valorous; brave. [Middle English, from Old Norse *vīgt,* neuter of *vīgr,* able to fight. See **weik-**[3] in Appendix.]

Wight (wīt), **Isle of.** An island in the English Channel off south-central England. It is a popular resort area and yachting center. Queen Victoria often stayed at the Osborne House near Cowes.

Wig•ner (wĭgʹnər), **Eugene Paul.** Born 1902. Hungarian-born American physicist. He shared a 1963 Nobel Prize for research on the structure of the atom and its nucleus.

wig•wag (wĭgʹwăgʹ) *v.* **-wagged, -wag•ging, -wags.** *—intr.* **1.** To move back and forth; wag steadily or rhythmically: *watched the pendulum wigwag.* **2.** To signal by waving an upraised arm, a flag, or a light, especially in accordance with a code. *—tr.* **1.** To move (something) back and forth steadily or rhythmically. **2.** To convey (a message or signal) by waving an upraised arm, a flag, or a light. **—wigwag** *n.* **1.** The act or practice of wigwagging. **2.** A message sent by this method. [Dialectal *wig,* to move + WAG[1].] **—wigʹwagʹger** *n.*

wig•wam (wĭgʹwŏmʹ) *n.* A Native American dwelling commonly having an arched or conical framework overlaid with bark, hides, or mats. [Eastern Abenaki *wikəwam.*]

wik•i•up (wĭkʹē-ŭpʹ) *n.* Variant of **wickiup.**

Wil•ber•force (wĭlʹbər-fôrsʹ, -fōrsʹ), **William.** 1759–1833. British politician. As a member of Parliament (1780–1825) he campaigned for the British abolition of slavery.

Wil•bur (wĭlʹbər), **Richard Purdy.** Born 1921. American poet whose works, including *Things of This World* (1956), adhere to formal conventions of rhyme and meter.

wild (wīld) *adj.* **wild•er, wild•est. 1.** Occurring, growing, or living in a natural state; not domesticated, cultivated, or tamed: *wild geese; edible wild plants.* **2.** Not inhabited or farmed: *remote, wild country.* **3.** Uncivilized or barbarous; savage. **4.a.** Lacking restraint; unruly: *wild children living in the streets.* **b.** Characterized by a lack of moral restraint; dissolute or licentious: *recalled his wild youth with remorse.* **5.** Disorderly; disarranged: *wild locks of long hair.* **6.** Full of, marked by, or suggestive of strong, uncontrolled emotion: *wild with jealousy; a wild look in his eye; a wild rage.* **7.** Extravagant; fantastic: *a wild idea.* **8.** Furiously disturbed or turbulent; stormy: *wild weather.* **9.** Risky; imprudent: *wild financial schemes.* **10.a.** Impatiently eager: *wild to get away for the weekend.* **b.** *Informal.* Highly enthusiastic: *just wild about the new music.* **11.** Based on little or no evidence or probability; unfounded: *wild accusations; a wild guess.* **12.** Deviating greatly from an intended course; erratic: *a wild bullet.* **13.** *Games.* Having an equivalence or value determined by the cardholder's choice: *playing poker with deuces wild.* **—wild** *adv.* In a wild manner: *growing wild; roaming wild.* **—wild** *n.* **1.** A natural or undomesticated state: *returned the zoo animals to the wild; plants that grow abundantly in the wild.* **2.** An uninhabited or uncultivated region: *the wilds of the northern steppes.* [Middle English *wilde,* from Old English.] **—wildʹly** *adv.* **—wildʹness** *n.*

Elie Wiesel

wild bergamot *n.* See **horsemint** (sense 1).

wild boar *n.* A wild pig *(Sus scrofa)* of Eurasia and northern Africa, having dark dense bristles. It is the ancestor of the domestic hog.

wild card *n.* **1.** *Games.* A card assigned specific values that could vary during a game and acquire any value assigned by its holder. **2.** *Slang.* An unpredictable or unforeseeable factor: *A surprise witness proved to be the wild card at the trial.*

wild carrot *n.* See **Queen Anne's lace.**

wild•cat (wīldʹkătʹ) *n.* **1.** Any of various wild felines of small to medium size, especially of the genus *Lynx,* including the bobcat and the caracal. **2.** Either of two small felines *(Felis silvestris* subsp. *silvestris* or subsp. *lybica)* of Europe, Asia, and Africa, often regarded as being the ancestor of the domestic cat. **3.a.** A quick-tempered person. **b.** A person regarded as fierce. **4.** An oil or natural-gas well drilled in an area not known to be productive. **5.** A workers' strike unauthorized by their union. **—wildcat** *adj.* **1.a.** Risky or unsound, especially financially. **b.** Issued by a financially irresponsible bank: *wildcat currency.* **c.** Operating or accomplished outside the norms of standard, ethical business procedures: *wildcat life insurance schemes.* **2.** Of, relating to, or being an oil or natural-gas well drilled speculatively in an area not known to be productive. **3.** Undertaken by workers without approval of the officials of their union: *a wildcat strike.* **—wildcat** *v.* **-cat•ted, -cat•ting, -cats.** *—tr.* To prospect for (oil, for example) in an area supposed to be unproductive. *—intr.* **1.** To prospect for oil or other minerals in an area not known to be productive. **2.** To go out on an unauthorized labor strike.

wigwam
Birch bark wigwam

wild•cat•ter (wīldʹkătʹər) *n.* **1.** One who is engaged in speculative mining or well drilling in areas not known to be productive. **2.** A promoter of speculative or fraudulent enterprises. **3.** A worker who participates in a wildcat strike.

wild celery *n.* See **eelgrass.**

Wilde (wīld), **Oscar (Fingal O'Flahertie Wills).** 1854–1900. Irish-born writer. Renowned as a wit, he achieved recognition with *The Picture of Dorian Gray* (1891), a novel. He also wrote plays, such as *The Importance of Being Earnest* (1895), and poetry, including *The Ballad of Reading Gaol* (1898).

wil•de•beest (wĭlʹdə-bēstʹ, vĭlʹ-) *n., pl.* **-beests** or **wildebeest.** See **gnu.** [Obsolete Afrikaans : Dutch *wild,* wild (from Middle Dutch *wilt*) + Dutch *beest,* beast (from Middle Dutch *beeste,* from Old French *beste;* see BEAST).]

wil•der (wĭlʹdər) *v.* **-dered, -der•ing, -ders.** *Archaic. —tr.* **1.** To lead astray; mislead. **2.** To bewilder; perplex. *—intr.* **1.** To lose one's way. **2.** To become bewildered. [Perhaps Middle English **wildren,* blend of *wilden,* to be wild (from *wilde,* wild; see WILD) and *wanderen,* to wander; see WANDER.] **—wilʹder•ment** *n.*

Wil•der (wĭlʹdər), **Billy.** Born 1906. Austrian-born American filmmaker whose works include *Double Indemnity* (1944), *Some Like It Hot* (1959), and *Fedora* (1978).

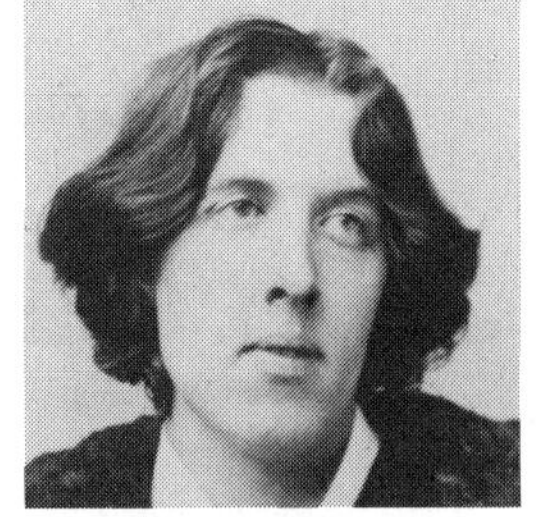

Oscar Wilde
Photographed in 1882

Wilder, Laura Ingalls. 1867–1957. American writer of novels, such as *Little House on the Prairie* (1935), based on her childhood on the American frontier.

Wilder, Thornton (Niven). 1897–1975. American writer whose works include novels, such as *The Bridge of San Luis Rey* (1927), and the theatrically innovative drama *Our Town* (1938).

wil•der•ness (wĭlʹdər-nĭs) *n.* **1.** An unsettled, uncultivated region left in its natural condition, especially: **a.** A large wild tract of land covered with dense vegetation or forests. **b.** An extensive area, such as a desert or an ocean, that is barren or empty; a waste. **c.** A piece of land set aside to grow wild. **2.** Something characterized by bewildering vastness, perilousness, or unchecked profusion: *the wilderness of the city; the wilderness of counterespionage; a wilderness of voices.* [Middle English, from Old English **willdēornes,* probably from *willdēor,* wild beast : *wilde,* wild + *dēor,* wild animal.]

WORD HISTORY: *Deer* comes from the Old English word *dēor,* meaning "beast." Clearly the word has narrowed in meaning and lost its general sense. But another word in English, *wilderness,* may point to this general sense of Old English *dēor.* The etymology of *wilderness* is variously given, but one etymology traces the

ă pat	oi boy
ā pay	ou out
âr care	o͝o took
ä father	o͞o boot
ĕ pet	ŭ cut
ē be	ûr urge
ĭ pit	th thin
ī pie	*th* this
îr pier	hw which
ŏ pot	zh vision
ō toe	ə about, item
ô paw	♦ regionalism

Stress marks: **ʹ** (primary); **ʹ** (secondary), as in **dictionary** (dĭkʹshə-nĕrʹē)

–*der–* of *wilderness* back to *dēor* and *wild–* back to Old English *wilde,* "wild." *Der–* may thus carry on *dēor* in its general sense, reminding us that wild beasts might be the only inhabitants of a wilderness. *Wilderness,* though it may have existed in Old English, is first found in 13th-century Middle English.

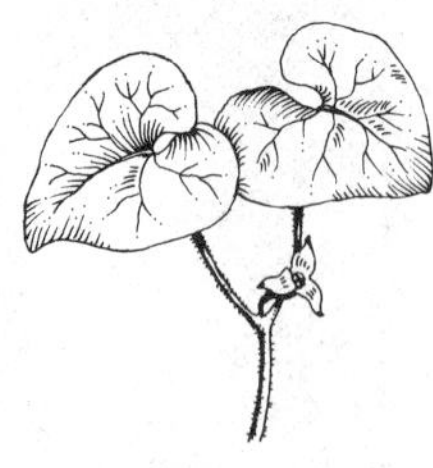

wild ginger

Wil•der•ness Road (wĭl′dər-nĭs). The principal route for westward migration in the United States from c. 1790 to 1840. Blazed largely by Daniel Boone in 1775, it stretched from Virginia to the Cumberland Gap and the Ohio River.

wild-eyed (wīld′īd′) *adj.* **1.** Glaring in or as if in anger, terror, or madness. **2.** Extreme and passionate in belief or advocacy.

wild fennel *n.* Any of various Mediterranean and western Asian annual herbs of the genus *Nigella,* having finely dissected leaves, showy white, blue, or yellow solitary flowers, and an aggregate fruit composed of several follicles. Also called *nigella.*

wild•fire (wīld′fīr′) *n.* **1.** A raging, rapidly spreading fire. **2.** Something that acts very quickly and intensely: *a land swept by the wildfire of revolution.* **3.** Lightning occurring without audible thunder. **4.** A luminosity that appears over swamps or marshes at night; ignis fatuus. **5.** A highly flammable material, such as Greek fire, once used in warfare.

wild•flow•er also **wild flow•er** (wīld′flou′ər) *n.* **1.** A flowering plant that grows in a natural, uncultivated state. **2.** The flower of such a plant.

wild•fowl (wīld′foul′) *n., pl.* **wildfowl** or **-fowls.** A wild game bird, such as a duck, goose, or quail.

wild turkey

wild geranium *n.* A North American woodland plant *(Geranium maculatum)* having rose-purple flowers. Also called *spotted cranesbill.*

wild ginger *n.* Any of various plants of the genus *Asarum,* especially *A. canadense* of North America, having broad leaves, a solitary brownish flower, and an aromatic root. Also called *heartleaf.*

wild goose *n.* Any of numerous species of undomesticated geese, as the Canada goose and the graylag.

wild-goose chase (wīld′go͞os′) *n.* A futile pursuit or search.

wild hyacinth *n.* See **eastern camass.**

wild indigo *n.* Any of several North American plants of the genus *Baptisia,* especially *B. tinctoria,* having trifoliate leaves and bright yellow flowers.

wild•ing (wīl′dĭng) *n.* **1.** A plant that grows wild or has escaped from cultivation, especially a wild apple tree or its fruit. **2.** A wild animal. **—wilding** *adj.* **1.** Growing wild; not cultivated. **2.** Undomesticated. [From WILD.]

wild•life (wīld′līf′) *n.* Wild animals and vegetation, especially animals living in a natural, undomesticated state.

wild lily of the valley *n.* A perennial woodland herb *(Maianthemum canadense)* of North America, having a terminal cluster of small fragrant white flowers.

wild•ling (wīld′lĭng) *n.* A wild plant or animal, especially a wild plant transplanted to a cultivated spot.

Tennessee Williams

wild marjoram *n.* See **marjoram.**

wild oat *n.* **1.** Often **wild oats.** An annual Eurasian grass *(Avena fatua)* related to the cultivated oat. **2. wild oats.** Misdeeds and indiscretions committed when young.

wild olive *n.* See **devilwood.**

wild pansy *n.* The heartsease.

wild pink *n.* A perennial herb *(Silene caroliniana)* native to the eastern United States, having pink or white flowers, opposite leaves, and glandular, hairy flower clusters.

wild pitch *n. Baseball.* An erratic pitch that the catcher cannot be expected to catch and that enables a base runner to advance.

wild rice *n.* **1.** A tall aquatic annual grass *(Zizania aquatica)* of North America, bearing edible grain. **2.** The grain of this plant.

wild rye *n.* Any of various grasses of the genus *Elymus* of the Northern Hemisphere.

wild turkey *n.* A wild variety of turkey, especially one from which the domesticated North American turkey is developed.

wild type *n.* The typical form of an organism, strain, gene, or characteristic as it occurs in nature, as distinguished from mutant forms that may result from selective breeding.

Wild West (wīld) *n.* The western United States during the period of its settlement, especially with reference to its lawlessness.

wild•wood (wīld′wo͝od′) *n.* A forest or wooded area in its natural state.

wile (wīl) *n.* **1.** A stratagem or trick intended to deceive or ensnare. See Synonyms at **artifice. 2.** A disarming or seductive manner, device, or procedure: *the wiles of a skilled negotiator.* **3.** Trickery; cunning. **—wile** *tr.v.* **wiled, wil•ing, wiles. 1.** To influence or lead by means of wiles; entice. **2.** To pass (time) agreeably: *wile away a Sunday afternoon.* [Middle English *wil,* from Old North French, from Old Norse *vēl,* trick, or of Low German origin.]

wil•ful (wĭl′fəl) *adj.* Variant of **willful.**

Wil•helm (vĭl′hĕlm). See William.

Wil•hel•mi•na (wĭl′ə-mē′nə, vĭl′hĕl-). 1880–1962. Queen of the Netherlands (1890–1948) who sought refuge in England during World War II but continued to encourage the Dutch resistance. In 1948 she abdicated in favor of her daughter Juliana.

Wil•helms•ha•ven (vĭl′hĕlmz-hä′fən). A city of northwest Germany on an inlet of the North Sea. It was a major naval base during World Wars I and II. Population, 97,495.

Wilkes (wĭlks), **Charles.** 1798–1877. American naval officer and explorer of Antarctica and the Pacific coast of North America. Wilkes Land was named after him.

Wilkes, John. 1727–1797. British political reformer noted for his published attacks on George III and for his support of the rights of American colonists.

Wilkes-Bar•re (wĭlks′băr′ē, -băr′ə). A city of northeast Pennsylvania on the Susquehanna River southwest of Scranton. It was settled in 1769. Population, 51,551.

Wilkes Land. A coastal region of Antarctica south of Australia. Most of the area has been included in Australia's Antarctic claims since 1936.

Wil•kins (wĭl′kĭnz), Sir **George Hubert.** 1888–1958. Australian aviator who was the first to explore the Arctic by air (1928).

Wilkins, Maurice Hugh Frederick. Born 1916. British biophysicist. He shared the 1962 Nobel Prize in physiology or medicine for advances in the study of DNA.

Wilkins, Roy. 1901–1981. American civil rights leader. Long associated with the NAACP, he asserted that racial equality should be achieved through the democratic process.

Wil•kins•burg (wĭl′kĭnz-bûrg′). A borough of southwest Pennsylvania, a suburb of Pittsburgh. Population, 23,669.

Wil•kin•son (wĭl′kĭn-sən), Sir **Geoffrey.** Born 1921. British chemist. He shared a 1973 Nobel Prize for research on pollutants in automobile exhaust.

will[1] (wĭl) *n.* **1. a.** The mental faculty by which one deliberately chooses or decides upon a course of action; volition. **b.** The act of exercising the will. **2. a.** Diligent purposefulness; determination: *a candidate with the will to win.* **b.** Self-control; self-discipline: *lacked the will to overcome the addiction.* **3.** A desire, purpose, or determination, especially of one in authority: *It is the sovereign's will that the prisoner be spared.* **4.** Deliberate intention or wish: *Let it be known that I took this course of action against my will.* **5.** Free discretion; inclination or pleasure: *wandered about, guided only by will.* **6.** Bearing or attitude toward others; disposition: *full of good will.* **7. a.** A legal declaration of how a person wishes his or her possessions to be disposed of after death. **b.** A legally executed document containing this declaration. **—will** *v.* **willed, will•ing, wills.** *—tr.* **1.** To decide on; choose. **2.** To yearn for; desire: *"She makes you will your own destruction"* (George Bernard Shaw). **3.** To decree, dictate, or order. **4.** To resolve with a forceful will; determine. **5.** To induce or try to induce by sheer force of will: *We willed the sun to come out.* **6.** To grant in a legal will; bequeath. *—intr.* **1.** To exercise the will. **2.** To make a choice; choose. ***—idiom.* at will.** Just as or when one wishes. [Middle English, from Old English *willa.* See **wel-**[1] in Appendix.]

will[2] (wĭl) *aux.v.* Past tense **would** (wo͝od). **1.** Used to indicate simple futurity: *They will appear later.* **2.** Used to indicate likelihood or certainty: *You will regret this.* **3.** Used to indicate willingness: *Will you help me with this package?* **4.** Used to indicate requirement or command: *You will report to me afterward.* **5.** Used to indicate intention: *I will too if I feel like it.* **6.** Used to indicate customary or habitual action: *People will talk.* **7.** Used to indicate capacity or ability: *This metal will not crack under heavy pressure.* **8.** Used to indicate probability or expectation: *That will be the messenger ringing.* **—will** *tr. & intr.v.* To wish; desire: *Do what you will. Sit here if you will.* See Usage Note at **shall.** [Middle English *willen,* to intend to, from Old English *willan.* See **wel-**[1] in Appendix.]

Wil•lam•ette (wə-lăm′ĭt). A river, about 473 km (294 mi) long, of northwest Oregon flowing generally northward to the Columbia River near Portland. The **Willamette Valley,** a fertile agricultural region, was first settled in the 1830's by pioneers traveling west along the Oregon Trail.

Wil•lard (wĭl′ərd), **Emma Hart.** 1787–1870. American educator who was an early proponent of higher education for women.

Willard, Frances Elizabeth Caroline. 1839–1898. American reformer. An ardent advocate of temperance and women's suffrage, she was the national president of the Woman's Christian Temperance Union (1879–1898).

willed (wĭld) *adj.* **1.** Having a will of a specified kind. Often used in combination: *weak-willed; iron-willed.* **2.** Determined by or proceeding from the will; deliberate: *"that most strained, willed, wooden, lifeless of novels"* (Joyce Carol Oates).

wil•lem•ite (wĭl′ə-mīt′) *n.* A colorless, vitreous to resinous, often fluorescent mineral, Zn_2SiO_4, a minor ore of zinc. [Dutch *willemit,* after *Willem* I (1772–1843), king of the Netherlands.]

Wil•lem•stad (vĭl′əm-stät′). The capital of the Netherlands Antilles, on the southern coast of Curaçao. Founded in 1634, it is a free port and an industrial center. Population, 43,547.

wil•let (wĭl′ĭt) *n.* A large grayish shore bird *(Catoptrophorus semipalmatus)* of North America, having black wings with a broad white stripe. [Imitative of its call.]

will•ful also **wil•ful** (wĭl′fəl) *adj.* **1.** Said or done on purpose; deliberate. See Synonyms at **voluntary. 2.** Obstinately bent on having one's own way. See Synonyms at **unruly. —will′ful•ly** *adv.* **—will′ful•ness** *n.*

Wil•liam (wĭl′yəm) also **Wil•helm** (vĭl′hĕlm). 1882–1951. German crown prince. The son of Emperor William II, he com-

ă pat	oi boy
ā pay	ou out
âr care	o͝o took
ä father	o͞o boot
ĕ pet	ŭ cut
ē be	ûr urge
ĭ pit	th thin
ī pie	*th* this
îr pier	hw which
ŏ pot	zh vision
ō toe	ə about, item
ô paw	♦ regionalism

Stress marks: ′ (primary); ′ (secondary), as in **dictionary** (dĭk′shə-nĕr′ē)

manded troops in the Battle of Verdun (1916) and renounced the crown at the close of World War I.

William I¹. Known as "William the Conqueror." 1027?–1087. King of England (1066–1087) and duke of Normandy (1035–1087). He led the Norman invasion of England (1066) after being promised the English throne by his cousin Edward the Confessor. He defeated Harold at the Battle of Hastings and as king adopted a feudal constitution.

William I² Prince of Orange. Known as "William the Silent." 1533–1584. Dutch stadholder (1579–1584) who was made governor of Holland, Zeeland, and Utrecht (1559) by Phillip II of Spain. Spurred by the Spanish persecution of Protestants, he led a revolt against Spanish rule (1568–1576).

William I³ also **Wilhelm I.** 1797–1888. King of Prussia (1861–1888) and emperor of Germany (1871–1888) whose reign was marked by war with Austria (1866), the Franco-Prussian War (1870–1871), and the wide reforms introduced by Bismarck.

William II¹. Known as "William Rufus." 1056?–1100. King of England (1087–1100). He was the second son of William the Conqueror, on whose death he succeeded to the throne.

William II² also **Wilhelm II.** 1859–1941. Emperor of Germany and king of Prussia (1888–1918). Grandson of Queen Victoria, he supported the Afrikaners in South Africa and Austria's demands on Serbia (1914). He was forced to abdicate at the end of World War I.

William III. Known as "William of Orange." 1650–1702. King of England, Scotland, and Ireland (1689–1702), Dutch stadholder (1672–1702), and prince of Orange. Married to Mary, daughter of James II, he was asked by the opponents of James to invade England (1688) and was proclaimed joint monarch with Mary (1689) after James fled.

William IV. Known as "the Sailor King." 1765–1837. King of Great Britain and Ireland (1830–1837). Son of George III and brother of George IV, he ascended to the throne after a long naval career.

William of Malmes·bur·y (mämz′bĕr′ē, -bə-rē, -brē). 1090?–1143? English monk and historian whose works include *Chronicle of the Kings of England,* written in Latin.

William of Orange. See **William III.**

Wil·liams (wĭl′yəmz), **Elizabeth.** Known as "Betty." Born 1943. Irish peace activist. She shared the 1976 Nobel Peace Prize for work in Northern Ireland's peace movement.

Williams, Roger. 1603?–1683. English cleric in America. After being expelled from Massachusetts for his criticism of Puritanism, he founded Providence (1636), a community based on religious freedom and democratic ideals, and obtained a royal charter for Rhode Island in 1663.

Williams, Tennessee. Originally Thomas Lanier Williams. 1911–1983. American playwright whose works include *The Glass Menagerie* (1944), *A Streetcar Named Desire* (1947), and *Cat on a Hot Tin Roof* (1955).

Williams, Theodore Samuel. Known as "Ted." Born 1918. American baseball player. Among the best hitters in the history of the game, he accrued 521 home runs and a .344 batting average as left fielder for the Boston Red Sox (1939–1960).

Williams, William Carlos. 1883–1963. American poet whose works include *Collected Poems* (1934).

Wil·liams·burg (wĭl′yəmz-bûrg′). A city of southeast Virginia northwest of Newport News. Settled c. 1632, it was the capital of Virginia from 1699 to 1779 but declined after the capital was moved to Richmond. In 1926 a large-scale restoration project, financed mainly by John D. Rockefeller, Jr., was begun, in which some 700 modern buildings were removed, 83 colonial buildings were renovated, and more than 400 buildings were reconstructed on their original sites. The city is the seat of William and Mary College (established 1693). Population, 9,870.

Wil·liam·son (wĭl′yəm-sən), **Mount.** A peak, 4,382.9 m (14,370 ft) high, in the Sierra Nevada of east-central California.

Wil·liams·port (wĭl′yəmz-pôrt′, -pōrt′). A city of central Pennsylvania north of Harrisburg. It developed as a lumbering center in the 19th century. Population, 33,401.

William the Conqueror. See **William I¹.**

wil·lies (wĭl′ēz) *pl.n. Slang.* Feelings of uneasiness. Often used with *the*: *The cave gave me the willies.* [Origin unknown.]

will·ing (wĭl′ĭng) *adj.* **1.** Disposed or inclined; prepared: *I am willing to overlook your mistakes.* **2.** Acting or ready to act gladly; eagerly compliant: *"The spirit indeed is willing, but the flesh is weak"* (Matthew 26:41). **3.** Done, given, accepted, or borne voluntarily or ungrudgingly. See Synonyms at **voluntary. 4.** Of or relating to exercise of the will; volitional. **—will′ing·ly** *adv.* **—will′ing·ness** *n.*

Wil·ling·bo·ro (wĭl′ĭng-bûr′ō, -bŭr′ō). A community of south-central New Jersey northeast of Camden. It is mainly residential. Population, 39,912.

wil·li·waw (wĭl′ē-wô′) *n.* **1.** A violent gust of cold wind blowing seaward from a mountainous coast, especially in the Straits of Magellan. **2.** A sudden gust of wind; a squall. [Origin unknown.]

Will·kie (wĭl′kē), **Wendell Lewis.** 1892–1944. American politician who was the Republican nominee for President in 1940.

will-o'-the-wisp (wĭl′ə-*thə*-wĭsp′) *n.* **1.** See **ignis fatuus** (sense 1). **2.** A delusive or misleading hope. [From the name *Will* (nickname for *William*).]

Wil·lough·by (wĭl′ə-bē). A city of northeast Ohio on Lake Erie northeast of Cleveland. Population, 19,329.

wil·low (wĭl′ō) *n.* **1.a.** Any of various deciduous trees or shrubs of the genus *Salix,* having usually narrow leaves, unisexual flowers borne in catkins, and strong lightweight wood. **b.** The wood of any of these trees. **2.** Something, such as a cricket bat, that is made from willow. **3.** A textile machine consisting of a spiked drum revolving inside a chamber fitted internally with spikes, used to open and clean unprocessed cotton or wool. **—willow** *tr.v.* **-lowed, -low·ing, -lows.** To open and clean (textile fibers) with a willow. [Middle English *wilowe,* from Old English *welig.* See **wel-²** in Appendix.]

willowware
c. 1820 English ceramic plate

Wil·low (wĭl′ō). A town of southern Alaska north of Anchorage. It has been proposed as a new state capital because of its central location.

Willow Grove. A community of southeast Pennsylvania, an industrial suburb of Philadelphia. Population, 21,300.

willow herb *n.* See **fireweed** (sense 1).

Wil·lo·wick (wĭl′ə-wĭk′). A city of northeast Ohio, a residential suburb of Cleveland on Lake Erie. Population, 17,834.

willow oak *n.* A deciduous timber tree *(Quercus phellos)* of the southern and central United States, having narrow, linear to oblong willowlike leaves.

willow ptarmigan *n.* The common ptarmigan *(Lagopus lagopus)* of Arctic regions, having brownish plumage that turns white in winter.

wil·low·ware (wĭl′ō-wâr′) *n.* Household china decorated with a blue-on-white design depicting a willow tree and often a river.

wil·low·y (wĭl′ō-ē) *adj.* **-i·er, -i·est. 1.** Planted with or abounding in willows. **2.** Resembling a willow tree, especially: **a.** Flexible; pliant. **b.** Tall, slender, and graceful.

will·pow·er or **will pow·er** (wĭl′pou′ər) *n.* The strength of will to carry out one's decisions, wishes, or plans.

Wills (wĭlz), **Helen Newington.** Also Helen Wills Moody. Born 1906. American tennis player who was the dominant woman player in the 1920's and 1930's.

Edith Wilson

wil·ly-nil·ly (wĭl′ē-nĭl′ē) *adv.* **1.** Whether desired or not: *After her boss fell sick, she willy-nilly found herself directing the project.* **2.** Without order or plan; haphazardly. **—willy-nilly** *adj.* **1.** Being or occurring whether desired or not: *willy-nilly cooperation.* **2.** Disordered; haphazard: *willy-nilly zoning laws.* [Alteration of *will ye* (or *he*), *nill ye* (or *he*), be you (*or* he) willing, be you (*or* he) unwilling.]

Wil·mette (wĭl-mĕt′). A village of northeast Illinois, a residential suburb of Chicago on Lake Michigan. Population, 28,229.

Wil·ming·ton (wĭl′mĭng-tən). **1.** A city of northeast Delaware on the Delaware River southwest of Philadelphia, Pennsylvania. It was founded as Fort Christina by Swedish settlers in 1638 and held by the Dutch from 1655 until 1664, when it was taken by the English. The name Wilmington dates from 1739. The city is now a manufacturing center with an extensive chemical industry. It is also the largest city in the state. Population, 70,195. **2.** A town of northeast Massachusetts, an industrial suburb of Boston. Population, 17,471. **3.** A city of southeast North Carolina on the Cape Fear River south-southeast of Raleigh. Settled c. 1730, it was used as a port by blockade runners during the Civil War. Population, 44,000.

Wil·son (wĭl′sən). A city of east-central North Carolina east of Raleigh. It is a trade and processing center. Population, 34,424.

Wilson, Charles Thomson Rees. 1869–1959. British physicist. He shared a 1927 Nobel Prize for devising the cloud chamber.

Wilson, Edith Bolling. 1872–1961. First Lady of the United States (1915–1921) as the second wife of President Woodrow Wilson. She was actively involved in government during the serious illness of her husband (1919–1920).

Ellen Wilson

Wilson, Edmund. 1895–1972. American literary critic whose influential works include *Axel's Castle* (1931), a study of the symbolist movement, and *Patriotic Gore* (1962), a critique of literature from the Civil War era.

Wilson, Ellen Louise Axson. 1860–1914. First Lady of the United States (1913–1914) as the first wife of President Woodrow Wilson. She died during Wilson's first term.

Wilson, Henry. 1812–1875. Vice President of the United States (1873–1875) under Ulysses S. Grant.

Wilson, James. 1742–1798. American Revolutionary patriot and jurist. A signer of the Declaration of Independence, he later served as an associate justice of the U.S. Supreme Court (1789–1798).

Wilson, (James) Harold. Baron Wilson of Rievaulx. Born 1916. British politician who served as prime minister (1964–1970 and 1974–1976). His administration was marked by turmoil in Rhodesia and Northern Ireland and resistance to a price and income policy. He resigned in 1976.

Wilson, Mount. 1. A mountain, 1,741.6 m (5,710 ft) high, in the San Gabriel Mountains of southwest California northeast of Pasadena. Its observatory was established in 1904. **2.** A peak, 4,345 m (14,246 ft) high, in the San Juan Mountains of southwest Colorado.

Wilson, Robert Woodrow. Born 1936. American physicist and radio astronomer. He shared a 1978 Nobel Prize for research on cosmic microwave radiation.

Wilson, (Thomas) Woodrow. 1856–1924. The 28th President of

Woodrow Wilson

wimple
Portrait of an Old Woman, c. 1468, by Hans Memling

winch

windbreak

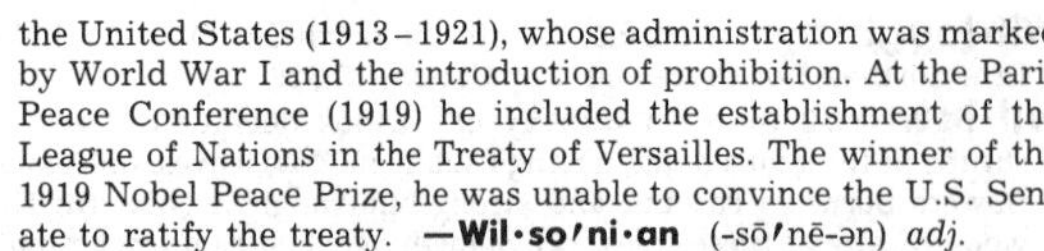

the United States (1913–1921), whose administration was marked by World War I and the introduction of prohibition. At the Paris Peace Conference (1919) he included the establishment of the League of Nations in the Treaty of Versailles. The winner of the 1919 Nobel Peace Prize, he was unable to convince the U.S. Senate to ratify the treaty. **—Wil·so′ni·an** (-sō′nē-ən) *adj.*

Wil·son's disease (wĭl′sənz) *n.* A rare hereditary disease caused by a defect in the body's ability to metabolize copper that results in an accumulation of copper deposits in organs such as the brain, liver, and kidneys. [After Samuel A.K. *Wilson* (1878–1937), British neurologist.]

Wilson's phalarope *n.* A grayish American wading bird *(Phalaropus tricolor)* with white underparts and a needlelike bill. [After Alexander *Wilson* (1766–1813), Scottish-born American ornithologist.]

Wilson's snipe *n.* A common North American snipe *(Capella gallinago* subsp. *delicata.)* [After Alexander *Wilson* (1766–1813), Scottish-born American ornithologist.]

Wilson's thrush *n.* See **veery.** [After Alexander *Wilson* (1766–1813), Scottish-born American ornithologist.]

Wilson's warbler *n.* A North American warbler *(Wilsonia pusilla)* with olive-green plumage, yellow underparts, and a black patch on top of the head. [After Alexander *Wilson* (1766–1813), Scottish-born American ornithologist.]

wilt[1] (wĭlt) *v.* **wilt·ed, wilt·ing, wilts.** *—intr.* **1.** To become limp or flaccid; droop: *plants wilting in the heat.* **2.** To feel or exhibit the effects of fatigue or exhaustion; weaken markedly: *"His brain wilted from hitherto unprecedented weariness"* (Vladimir Nabokov). *—tr.* **1.** To cause to droop or lose freshness. **2.** To deprive of energy or vigor; fatigue or exhaust. **—wilt** *n.* **1.** The act of wilting or the state of being wilted. **2.** Any of various plant diseases characterized by slow or rapid collapse of terminal shoots, branches, or entire plants. [Possibly alteration of dialectal *welk,* from Middle English *welken.*]

wilt[2] (wĭlt) *aux.v. Archaic.* A second person singular present tense of **will[2].**

Wil·ton (wĭl′tən) *n.* A carpet woven on a jacquard loom and having a velvety surface formed by the cut loops of a pile. [After *Wilton,* a municipal borough of south-central England.]

Wilt·shire (wĭlt′shîr, -shər) *n.* A white sheep of a breed originating in England, characterized by a long head with spiraling horns. [After *Wiltshire,* a county of south-central England.]

wi·ly (wī′lē) *adj.* **-li·er, -li·est.** Full of wiles; cunning. See Synonyms at **sly.** **—wil′i·ly** *adv.* **—wil′i·ness** *n.*

wim·ble (wĭm′bəl) *n.* Any of numerous hand tools for boring holes. [Middle English, from Anglo-Norman, probably from Middle Dutch *wimmel.* See **weip-** in Appendix.] **—wim′ble** *v.*

Wim·ble·don (wĭm′bəl-dən). A district of southern Greater London, England. It is the site of an annual tennis tournament.

wimp (wĭmp) *n. Slang.* A person who is regarded as weak or ineffectual: *"the impression that he is a colorless, indecisive wimp, and not a leader among men"* (James J. Kilpatrick). [Perhaps from WHIMPER.] **—wimp′ish** *adj.* **—wimp′y** *adj.*

wim·ple (wĭm′pəl) *n.* **1.** A cloth wound around the head, framing the face, and drawn into folds beneath the chin, worn by women in medieval times and as part of the habit of certain orders of nuns. **2.a.** A fold or pleat in cloth. **b.** A ripple, as on the surface of water. **c.** A curve or bend. **—wimple** *v.* **-pled, -pling, -ples.** *—tr.* **1.** To cover with or dress in a wimple. **2.** To cause to form folds, pleats, or ripples. *—intr.* **1.** *Archaic.* To form or lie in folds. **2.** To ripple. [Middle English *wimpel,* from Old English. See **weip-** in Appendix.]

Wims·hurst machine (wĭmz′hûrst′) *n.* An electrostatic generator having oppositely rotating mica or glass disks with metal carriers on which charges are produced by induction, used chiefly as a demonstration apparatus. [After James *Wimshurst* (1832–1903), British engineer.]

win (wĭn) *v.* **won** (wŭn), **win·ning, wins.** *—intr.* **1.** To achieve victory or finish first in a competition. **2.** To achieve success in an effort or a venture: *struggled to overcome the handicap and finally won.* *—tr.* **1.** To achieve victory or finish first in. **2.** To receive as a prize or reward for performance. **3.a.** To achieve or attain by effort: *win concessions in negotiations.* **b.** To obtain or earn (a livelihood, for example). See Synonyms at **earn[1].** **4.** To make (one's way) with effort. **5.** To reach with difficulty: *The ship won a safe port.* **6.** To take in battle; capture: *won the heights after a fierce attack.* **7.** To succeed in gaining the favor or support of; prevail on: *Her eloquence won over the audience.* **8.a.** To gain the affection or loyalty of. **b.** To appeal successfully to (someone's sympathy, for example). **c.** To persuade (another) to marry one: *He wooed and won her.* **9.a.** To discover and open (a vein or deposit) in mining. **b.** To extract from a mine or from mined ore. **—win** *n.* **1.a.** A victory, especially in a competition. **b.** First place in a competition. **2.** An amount won or earned. ***—phrasal verbs.*** **win out.** To succeed or prevail. **win through.** To overcome difficulties and attain a desired goal or end. ***—idiom.*** **win the day.** To be successful. [Middle English *winnen,* from Old English *winnan,* to fight, strive. See **wen-[1]** in Appendix.]

wince (wĭns) *intr.v.* **winced, winc·ing, winc·es.** To shrink or start involuntarily, as in pain or distress; flinch. **—wince** *n.* A shrinking or startled movement or gesture. [Middle English *wincen,* to kick, from Old North French **wencier,* variant of Old French *guencir,* of Germanic origin.] **—winc′er** *n.*

winch (wĭnch) *n.* **1.** A stationary motor-driven or hand-powered hoisting machine having a drum around which is wound a rope or chain attached to the load being lifted. **2.** The crank used to give motion to a grindstone or similar device. **—winch** *tr.v.* **winched, winch·ing, winch·es.** To move with or as if with a winch. [Middle English *winche,* pulley, from Old English *wince,* reel, roller.] **—winch′er** *n.*

Win·chell (wĭn′chəl), **Walter.** 1897–1972. American journalist whose newspaper column "On Broadway" (1924–1963) and radio newscasts (1932–1953) reported on entertainment and politics.

Win·ches·ter[1] (wĭn′chĕs′tər, -chĭ-stər). **1.** A municipal borough of south-central England southwest of London. The capital of the Anglo-Saxon kingdom of Wessex, it was an important center of learning that attracted many religious scholars after the Norman Conquest (1066). Population, 32,100. **2.** A town of northeast Massachusetts, a residential suburb of Boston. Population, 20,701. **3.** A community of southeast Nevada, a suburb of Las Vegas. Population, 19,728. **4.** An independent city of northern Virginia west-northwest of Washington, D.C. Settled c. 1744, it was an important military base during the French and Indian War and the Civil War, in which it changed hands a number of times. Population, 20,217.

Win·ches·ter[2] (wĭn′chĕs′tər, -chə-stər). A trademark used for a shoulder firearm.

Winck·el·mann (vĭng′kəl-män′), **Johann Joachim.** 1717–1768. German archaeologist and antiquary. Considered the father of archaeology, he was the first to study ancient art as history.

wind[1] (wĭnd) *n.* **1.a.** Moving air, especially a natural and perceptible movement of air parallel to or along the ground. **b.** A movement of air generated artificially, as by bellows or a fan. **2.a.** The direction from which a movement of air comes: *The wind is north-northwest.* **b.** A movement of air coming from one of the four cardinal points of the compass: *the four winds.* **3.** Moving air carrying sound, an odor, or a scent. **4.a.** Breath, especially normal or adequate breathing; respiration: *had the wind knocked out of them.* **b.** Gas produced in the stomach or intestines during digestion; flatulence. **5.** Often **winds.** *Music.* **a.** The brass and woodwinds sections of a band or an orchestra. **b.** Wind instruments or their players considered as a group. **6.a.** Something that disrupts or destroys: *the winds of war.* **b.** A tendency; a trend: *the winds of change.* **7.** Information, especially of something concealed; intimation: *Trouble will ensue if wind of this scandal gets out.* **8.a.** Speech or writing empty of meaning; verbiage. **b.** Futile or idle labor or thought. **—wind** *tr.v.* **wind·ed, wind·ing, winds.** **1.** To expose to free movement of air; ventilate or dry. **2.a.** To detect the smell of; catch a scent of. **b.** To pursue by following a scent. **3.** To cause to be out of or short of breath. **4.** To afford a recovery of breath: *stopped to wind and water the horses.* ***—idioms.*** **before the wind.** *Nautical.* In the same direction as the wind. **close to the wind.** *Nautical.* As close as possible to the direction from which the wind is blowing. **in the wind.** Likely to occur; in the offing: *Big changes are in the wind.* **near the wind.** **1.** *Nautical.* Close to the wind. **2.** Close to danger **off the wind.** *Nautical.* In a direction away from the wind. **on** (or **into** or **down) the wind.** *Nautical.* In the same or nearly the same direction as the wind. **under the wind.** **1.** *Nautical.* To the leeward. **2.** In a location protected from the wind. **up the wind.** *Nautical.* In a direction opposite or nearly opposite the wind. [Middle English, from Old English *wind.* See **wē-** in Appendix.]

wind[2] (wīnd) *v.* **wound** (wound), **wind·ing, winds.** *—tr.* **1.** To wrap (something) around a center or another object once or repeatedly: *wind string around a spool.* **2.** To wrap or encircle (an object) in a series of coils; entwine: *wound her injured leg with a bandage; wound the waist of the gown with lace and ribbons.* **3.a.** To go along (a curving or twisting course): *wind a path through the mountains.* **b.** To proceed on (one's way) with a curving or twisting course. **4.** To introduce in a disguised or devious manner; insinuate: *He wound a plea for money into his letter.* **5.** To turn (a crank, for example) in a series of circular motions. **6.a.** To coil the spring of (a mechanism) by turning a stem or cord, for example: *wind a watch.* **b.** To coil (thread, for example), as onto a spool or into a ball. **c.** To remove or unwind (thread, for example), as from a spool: *wound the line off the reel.* **7.** To lift or haul by means of a windlass or winch: *Wind the pail to the top of the well.* *—intr.* **1.** To move in or have a curving or twisting course: *a river winding through a valley.* **2.a.** To move in or have a spiral or circular course: *a column of smoke winding into the sky.* **b.** To be coiled or spiraled: *The vine wound about the trellis.* **3.** To be twisted or whorled into curved forms. **4.** To proceed misleadingly or insidiously in discourse or conduct. **5.** To become wound: *a clock that winds with difficulty.* **—wind** *n.* **1.** The act of winding. **2.** A single turn, twist, or curve. ***—phrasal verbs.*** **wind down.** *Informal.* **1.** To diminish gradually in energy, intensity, or scope: *The party wound down as guests began to leave.* **2.** To relax; unwind. **wind up.** **1.** To come or bring to a finish; end: *when the meeting wound up; wind up a project.* **2.** To put in order; settle: *wound up her affairs before leaving the country.* **3.** *Informal.* To arrive in a place or situation after or because of a course of action: *took a long walk and wound up at the edge of town; overspent and wound up in debt.* **4.** *Baseball.* To swing back the arm and raise the foot in preparation for pitching the ball. [Middle English *winden,* from Old English *windan.*]

wind[3] (wīnd, wĭnd) *tr.v.* **wind·ed** (wīn′dĭd, wĭn′-) or **wound** (wound), **wind·ing, winds.** *Music.* **1.** To blow (a wind instrument). **2.** To sound by blowing. [From WIND[1].] **—wind′er** *n.*

wind·age (wĭn′dĭj) *n.* **1.a.** The effect of wind on the course of a projectile. **b.** The point or degree at which the wind gauge or sight of a rifle or gun must be set to compensate for the effect of the wind. **c.** The difference in a given firearm between the diameter of the projectile fired and the diameter of the bore of the firearm. **2.** The disturbance of air caused by the passage of a fast-moving object, such as a railway train. **3.** *Nautical.* The part of the surface of a ship left exposed to the wind.

Win·daus (vĭn′dous′), **Adolf.** 1876–1959. German chemist. He won a 1928 Nobel Prize for conducting research on sterols and their connection with vitamins.

wind·bag (wĭnd′băg′) *n.* **1.** *Music.* The flexible air-filled chamber of a bagpipe, an accordion, or a similar wind instrument. **2.** *Slang.* A talkative person who communicates nothing of substance or interest.

wind·bell (wĭnd′bĕl′) *n.* **1.** A light bell that can be sounded by the wind. **2. wind-bells.** See **wind chimes.**

wind·blast (wĭnd′blăst′) *n.* **1.** An exceedingly strong gust of wind. **2.** The damaging effect of air friction on a pilot ejected from a high-speed aircraft.

wind·blown (wĭnd′blōn′) *adj.* **1.** Blown or dispersed by the wind: *windblown pollen.* **2.** Growing or shaped in a manner governed by the prevailing winds: *windblown scrub pines.* **3.** Cut short and curled or combed toward the front of the head: *a windblown hair style.*

wind-borne (wĭnd′bôrn′, -bōrn′) *adj.* Carried by the wind: *wind-borne ashes.*

wind·break (wĭnd′brāk′) *n.* A hedge, fence, or row of trees serving to lessen or break the force of the wind.

Wind·break·er (wĭnd′brā′kər). A trademark used for a warm outer jacket having close-fitting, often elastic, cuffs and waistband. This trademark often occurs in print in lowercase and in the plural: *"Whether a trenchcoat, balmacaan or windbreaker, it is a coverup that makes sense"* (New York Times). *"Politicians love photo opportunities featuring helicopters, devastation and nifty windbreakers"* (San Francisco Chronicle).

wind-bro·ken (wĭnd′brō′kən) *adj.* Suffering from the heaves or other impairment of breathing. Used of a horse.

wind·burn (wĭnd′bûrn′) *n.* A reddened irritation of the skin caused by long exposure to the wind. **—wind′burned′** *adj.*

wind-chill factor (wĭnd′chĭl′) *n.* The temperature of windless air that would have the same effect on exposed human skin as a given combination of wind speed and air temperature.

wind chimes (wĭnd) *pl.n.* An arrangement of small suspended pieces, as of glass, metal, or ceramic, hung loosely together so that they tinkle pleasingly when blown by the wind. Also called *windbells.*

wind cone (wĭnd) *n.* See **windsock.**

wind·ed (wĭn′dĭd) *adj.* **1.** Having breath or respiratory power of a specified kind. Often used in combination: *short-winded; broken-winded.* **2.** Out of breath: *a winded runner.*

wind·er[1] (wīn′dər) *n.* **1.** One that winds, especially a textile worker or machine that winds cloth or materials. **2.** An object, such as a spool or barrel, around which material is wound. **3.** A device, such as a key, for winding up a spring-driven mechanism. **4.** One of the steps of a winding staircase.

♦ **win·der**[2] (wĭn′dər) *n.* *Upper Southern U.S.* Variant of **window.** See Regional Note at **holler**[2].

Win·der·mere (wĭn′dər-mîr′), **Lake.** A lake of northwest England. It is a popular tourist area in the Lake District.

wind·fall (wĭnd′fôl′) *n.* **1.** A sudden, unexpected piece of good fortune or personal gain. **2.** Something, such as a ripened fruit, that has been blown down by the wind.

wind·flaw (wĭnd′flô′) *n.* A sudden gust or blast of wind.

wind·flow·er (wĭnd′flou′ər) *n.* See **anemone** (sense 1).

wind gap (wĭnd) *n.* A notch in the crest of a mountain ridge.

Wind·ham (wĭn′dəm). A town of east-central Connecticut north-northwest of Norwich. Population, 21,062.

wind harp (wĭnd) *n.* See **Aeolian harp.**

Wind·hoek (vĭnt′ho͝ok′). The capital of Namibia, in the central part of the country. Originally the headquarters of a Nama leader, it was occupied by German forces in 1885. Population, 88,700.

wind·ing (wīn′dĭng) *n.* **1.a.** Something wound about a center or an object: *an armature with its wire winding.* **b.** The way in which something is wound. **c.** One complete turn of something wound: *two windings of electrical tape.* **2.** A curve or bend, as of a road. **—winding** *adj.* **1.** Twisting or turning; sinuous. **2.** Spiral. **—wind′ing·ly** *adv.*

wind·ing-sheet (wīn′dĭng-shēt′) *n.* A sheet for wrapping a corpse; a shroud.

wind instrument (wĭnd) *n.* *Music.* An instrument, such as a clarinet, trumpet, or harmonica, in which sound is produced by the movement of an enclosed column of air, especially the breath.

wind·jam·mer (wĭnd′jăm′ər) *n.* *Nautical.* A large sailing ship.

wind·lass (wĭnd′ləs) *n.* Any of numerous hauling or lifting machines consisting of a horizontal cylinder turned by a crank or a motor so that a line attached to the load is wound around the cylinder. **—windlass** *tr.v.* **-lassed, -lass·ing, -lass·es.** To raise with a windlass. [Middle English *wyndlas,* alteration of *windas,* from Old Norse *vindāss* : *vinda,* to wind + *āss,* pole.]

win·dle·straw (wĭn′dl-strô′) *n.* *Chiefly British.* A thin, dried stalk of grass. [Old English *windelstrēaw* : *windel,* basket (from *windan,* to wind) + *strēaw,* straw; see STRAW.]

wind·mill (wĭnd′mĭl′) *n.* **1.** A machine that runs on the energy generated by a wheel of adjustable blades or slats rotated by the wind. **2.** Something, such as a toy pinwheel, similar to a windmill. **—windmill** *intr. & tr.v.* **-milled, -mill·ing, -mills.** To move or cause to move like the wheel of a windmill; rotate sweepingly. ***—idiom.*** **tilt at windmills.** To confront and engage in conflict with an imagined opponent or threat.

Win·dom Peak (wĭn′dəm). A mountain, 4,295 m (14,082 ft) high, in the San Juan Mountains of southwest Colorado.

win·dow (wĭn′dō) *n.* **1.a.** An opening constructed in a wall or roof that functions to admit light or air to an enclosure and is often framed and spanned with glass mounted to permit opening and closing. **b.** A framework enclosing a pane of glass for such an opening; a sash. **c.** A pane of glass or similar material enclosed in such a framework. **2.a.** An opening that resembles a window in function or appearance. **b.** The transparent panel on a window envelope. **3.** The area or space immediately behind a window, especially at the front of a shop. **4.** A means of access or observation: *St. Petersburg was Peter the Great's window onto the Baltic.* **5.** An interval of time during which an activity can or must take place: *a brief window of opportunity for a space mission; a window of vulnerability during which the air force was subject to attack.* **6.** Strips of foil dropped from an aircraft to confuse enemy radar; chaff. **7.** A range of electromagnetic frequencies that pass unobstructed through a planetary atmosphere. **8.** *Computer Science.* A small area on a screen in which a file or a part of a file can be displayed. **9.** *Aerospace.* **a.** A launch window. **b.** An area at the outer limits of the earth's atmosphere through which a spacecraft must pass in order to return safely. [Middle English, from Old Norse *vindauga* : *vindr,* air, wind; see **wē-** in Appendix + *auga,* eye; see **ok^{w}-** in Appendix.]

WORD HISTORY: The word *window* conceals a poetic image that is not at all transparent. Our word comes to us from the Scandinavian invaders and settlers of England in the early Middle Ages. Although we have no record of the exact word they gave us, it was related to Old Norse *vindauga,* "window," a compound made up of *vindr,* "wind," and *auga,* "eye," reflecting the fact that at one time windows contained no glass. In our time we have taken *window,* which has been recorded in the language for almost 800 years, in a figurative direction with phrases such as *launch window, weather window,* and *window of opportunity* or *vulnerability.* Rockets and missiles now travel through the "wind's eye."

window box *n.* **1.** A usually long, narrow box for growing plants, placed on a windowsill or ledge. **2.** One of the vertical grooves on the inner sides of a window frame for the weights that counterbalance the sash.

win·dow-dress·ing also **win·dow dress·ing** (wĭn′dō-drĕs′ĭng) *n.* **1.a.** Decorative exhibition of retail merchandise in store windows. **b.** Goods and trimmings used in such displays. **2.** A means of improving appearances or creating a falsely favorable impression: *Critics called the new users' fees a window-dressing for a tax increase.* **—win′dow-dress′er** *n.*

window envelope *n.* An envelope with a transparent panel that reveals the address on the enclosure.

win·dow·pane (wĭn′dō-pān′) *n.* A piece of glass in a window.

window shade *n.* An opaque fabric mounted to cover or expose a window.

win·dow-shop (wĭn′dō-shŏp′) *intr.v.* **-shopped, -shop·ping, -shops.** To look at merchandise in store windows or showcases without making purchases. **—win′dow-shop′per** *n.*

win·dow·sill (wĭn′dō-sĭl′) *n.* The horizontal member at the base of a window opening.

wind·pipe (wĭnd′pīp′) *n.* *Anatomy.* See **trachea** (sense 1).

Wind River Range (wĭnd). A section of the Rocky Mountains in west-central Wyoming rising to 4,210.2 m (13,804 ft).

Wind River Shoshone *n.* See **Shoshone** (sense 1c).

wind rose (wĭnd) *n.* A meteorological diagram depicting the distribution of wind direction and speed at a location over a period of time. [Translation of German *Windrose,* compass card : *Wind,* wind, air + *Rose,* rose.]

wind·row (wĭnd′rō′) *n.* **1.** A row, as of leaves or snow, heaped up by the wind. **2.** A long row of cut hay or grain left to dry in a field before being bundled. **—windrow** *tr.v.* **-rowed, -row·ing, -rows.** To arrange into a windrow. **—wind′row′er** *n.*

wind·sail·ing (wĭnd′sā′lĭng) *n.* *Sports.* See **windsurfing.** [WIND(SURFING) + (BOARD)SAILING.]

wind·screen (wĭnd′skrēn′) *n.* **1.** A screen for protection against the wind. **2.** *Chiefly British.* The windshield of a motor vehicle.

wind·shake (wĭnd′shāk′) *n.* A crack or separation between growth rings in timber, attributed to the straining of tree trunks in high winds.

wind shear (wĭnd) *n.* A change in wind direction and speed between slightly different altitudes, especially a sudden downdraft.

wind·shield (wĭnd′shēld′) *n.* **1.** A framed pane of usually curved glass or other transparent shielding located in front of the

windmill
Top: Water-pumping windmill in Colorado
Bottom: Grain-grinding windmill in La Mancha, Spain

ă pat	oi boy
ā pay	ou out
âr care	o͝o took
ä father	o͞o boot
ĕ pet	ŭ cut
ē be	ûr urge
ĭ pit	th thin
ī pie	*th* this
îr pier	hw which
ŏ pot	zh vision
ō toe	ə about, item
ô paw	♦ regionalism

Stress marks: ′ (primary); ′ (secondary), as in **dictionary** (dĭk′shə-nĕr′ē)

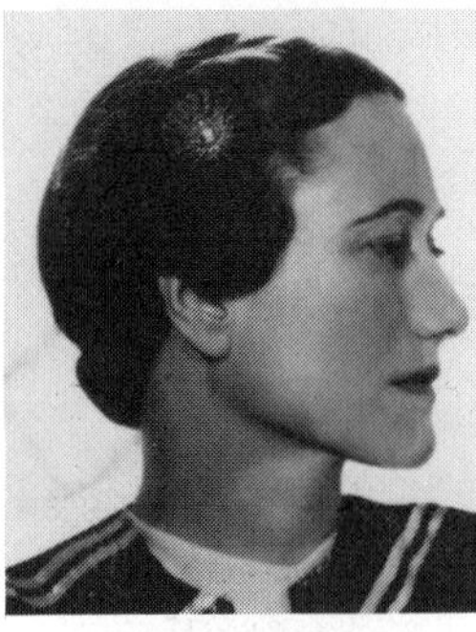
Duchess of Windsor
Photographed by
Cecil Beaton

occupants of a vehicle to protect them from the wind. **2.** A shield placed to protect an object from the wind.

wind·sock (wĭnd′sŏk′) *n.* A tapered, open-ended sleeve pivotally attached to a standard, that indicates the direction of the wind blowing through it. Also called *air sock, wind cone, wind sleeve.*

Wind·sor[1] (wĭn′zər). Ruling house of Great Britain (since 1917), including George V and his descendants Edward VIII, George VI, and Elizabeth II.

Wind·sor[2] (wĭn′zər). **1.** A city of southeast Ontario, Canada, on the Detroit River opposite Detroit, Michigan. Settled by the French after 1701, it is a port of entry and an industrial center. Population, 192,083. **2.** A municipal borough of south-central England on the Thames River southwest of London. Windsor Castle has been a royal residence since the time of William the Conqueror. Population, 28,700. **3.** A town of northern Connecticut north of Hartford. Settled c. 1635, it is the oldest town in the state. Population, 25,204.

Windsor, Duke of. See **Edward VIII.**

Windsor, Wallis Warfield. Duchess of Windsor. 1896–1986. American divorcée who married the Duke of Windsor, formerly Edward VIII of England, in 1937.

Windsor chair *n.* A wooden chair having a high spoked back, outward-slanting legs connected by a crossbar, and a saddle seat. [After WINDSOR[2], England.]

Windsor chair
c. 1795 American

Windsor knot *n.* A wide, triangular slipknot used to tie a four-in-hand necktie. [Perhaps after the Duke of WINDSOR.]

Windsor tie *n.* A wide silk necktie tied in a loose bow.

wind sprint (wĭnd) *n. Sports.* A sprint run repeatedly to develop breath and endurance.

wind·storm (wĭnd′stôrm′) *n.* A storm with high winds or violent gusts but little or no rain.

wind·suck·ing (wĭnd′sŭk′ĭng) *n.* The injurious habit of swallowing air. Used of horses. **—wind′suck·er** *n.*

wind·surf (wĭnd′sûrf′) *intr.v.* **-surfed, -surf·ing, -surfs.** *Sports.* To engage in windsurfing.

Wind·surf·er (wĭnd′sûr′fər). A trademark used for a brand of sailboard.

wind·surf·ing (wĭnd′sûr′fĭng) *n. Sports.* The sport of sailing while standing on a sailboard. Also called *boardsailing, windsailing.*

wind·swept (wĭnd′swĕpt′) *adj.* Exposed to or swept by winds: *windswept moors.*

wind tee (wĭnd) *n.* A large weathervane with a horizontal T-shaped wind indicator, commonly found at airfields.

wind tunnel (wĭnd) *n.* A chamber through which air is forced at controlled velocities in order to study the effects of aerodynamic flow around airfoils, scale models, or other objects.

wind-up or **wind·up** (wīnd′ŭp′) *—n.* **1.a.** The act of bringing something to an end. **b.** A concluding part; a conclusion. **2.** *Baseball.* The movements of a pitcher, including the swinging back of the arm and the raising of the forward foot, preparatory to pitching the ball. *—adj.* Operated by a spring that is wound up by hand.

windsurfing

wind·ward (wĭnd′wərd) *adj.* **1.** Of or moving toward the quarter from which the wind blows. **2.** Of or on the side exposed to the wind or to prevailing winds. **—windward** *adv.* In a direction from which the wind blows; against the wind. **—windward** *n.* The direction from which the wind blows. **—*idiom.* to windward.** Into or to an advantageous position.

Wind·ward Islands (wĭnd′wərd). An island group of the southeast West Indies, including the southern group of the Lesser Antilles from Martinique south to Grenada.

Windward Passage. A channel between eastern Cuba and northwest Haiti connecting the Atlantic Ocean with the Caribbean Sea.

wind·y (wĭn′dē) *adj.* **-i·er, -i·est. 1.** Characterized by or abounding in wind: *a windy night.* **2.** Open to the wind; unsheltered: *a windy terrace.* **3.** Swift, forceful, or variable: *windy haste.* **4.a.** Lacking substance; empty: *windy promises.* **b.** Given to or characterized by prolonged talk; verbose: *a windy speaker.* **5.** Flatulent. **—wind′i·ly** *adv.* **—wind′i·ness** *n.*

wine (wīn) *n.* **1.a.** A beverage made of the fermented juice of any of various kinds of grapes, usually containing from 10 to 15 percent alcohol by volume. **b.** A beverage made of the fermented juice of any of various other fruits or plants. **2.** Something that intoxicates or exhilarates. **3.** *Color.* The color of red wine. **—wine** *v.* **wined, win·ing, wines.** *—tr.* To provide or entertain with wine. *—intr.* To drink wine. [Middle English, from Old English *wīn,* from Latin *vīnum.*]

wine cooler

wine·bib·bing (wīn′bĭb′ĭng) *adj.* Given to much drinking of wine. **—winebibbing** *n.* Habitual drinking of wine. **—wine′bib′ber** *n.*

wine cellar *n.* **1.** A place for storing wine. **2.** A stock of wines.

wine cooler *n.* **1.** A container, such as an ice-filled bucket or chest, for cooling wine. **2.** A bottled mixture of wine, fruit juice, and sometimes soda water.

wine·glass (wīn′glăs′) *n.* A glass, usually with a stem, from which wine is drunk.

wine·grow·er (wīn′grō′ər) *n.* One that owns a vineyard and produces wine.

wine·mak·ing (wīn′mā′kĭng) *n.* The art and science of making wine. **—wine′mak′er** *n.* **—wine′mak′ing** *adj.*

wine palm *n.* Any of various palm trees having sap or juice from which wine is made.

wine·press (wīn′prĕs′) *n.* **1.** A vat in which the juice is pressed from grapes. **2.** A machine or device that presses the juice from grapes.

win·er·y (wī′nə-rē) *n., pl.* **-ies.** An establishment at which wine is made.

Wine·sap (wīn′săp′) *n.* A variety of apple having fruit with dark red skin.

wine·skin (wīn′skĭn′) *n.* A bag made from the skin of a goat for example, and used for holding and dispensing wine.

wine taster *n.* **1.** One who evaluates the quality of wine by tasting it, especially on a professional basis. **2.** A small bowl used to hold wine for tasting.

wine·tast·ing (wīn′tā′stĭng) *n.* A gathering of people to taste and compare a number of wines.

wine·y (wī′nē) *adj.* Variant of **winy.**

wing (wĭng) *n.* **1.** One of a pair of movable organs for flying, as the feather-covered modified forelimb of a bird or the skin-covered modified digits of the forelimb of a bat. **2.** Any of usually four membranous organs for flying that extend from the thorax of an insect. **3.** A winglike organ or structure used for flying, as the folds of skin of a flying squirrel or the enlarged pectoral fin of a flying fish. **4.** *Botany.* **a.** A thin or membranous extension, such as of the fruit of the elm, maple, or ash or of the seed of the pine. **b.** One of the lateral petals of the flower of a pea or of most plants in the pea family. **5.** *Informal.* An arm of a human being. **6.** An airfoil whose principal function is providing lift, especially either of two such airfoils symmetrically positioned on each side of the fuselage of an aircraft. **7.** Something that resembles a wing in appearance, function, or position relative to a main body. **8.a.** The act or manner of flying. **b.** A means of flight or of rapid ascent. **9.a.** Something, such as a weathervane, that is moved by or moves against the air. **b.** The sail of a ship. **10.** *Chiefly British.* The fender of a motor vehicle. **11.** A folding section, as of a double door or of a movable partition. **12.** Either of the two side projections on the back of a wing chair. **13.a.** A flat of theatrical scenery projecting onto the stage from the side. **b. wings.** The unseen backstage area on either side of the stage of a proscenium theater. **14.** A structure attached to and connected internally with the side of a main building. **15.** A section of a large building devoted to a specific purpose: *the children's wing of the hospital.* **16.** A group affiliated with or subordinate to an older or larger organization. **17.a.** Either of two groups with opposing views within a larger group; a faction. **b.** A section of a party, legislature, or community holding distinct, especially dissenting, political views: *the conservative wing.* **18.a.** Either the left or right flank of an army or a naval fleet. **b.** An air force unit larger than a group but smaller than a division. **19.** *Sports.* Either of the forward positions played near the sideline, especially in hockey. **20. wings.** An outspread pair of stylized bird's wings worn as insignia by qualified pilots or air crew members. **—wing** *v.* **winged, wing·ing, wings.** *—intr.* To move on or as if on wings; fly. *—tr.* **1.a.** To furnish with wings. **b.** To cause or enable to fly or speed swiftly along. **2.** To feather (an arrow). **3.a.** To pass over or through with or as if with wings. **b.** To carry or transport by or as if by flying. **c.** To effect or accomplish by flying. **4.** To throw or dispatch (a ball, for example). **5.a.** To wound the wing of (a game bird, for example). **b.** To wound superficially, as in an appendage. **6.** To furnish with side or subordinate extensions, as a building or an altarpiece. **—*idioms.* in the wings. 1.** In the stage wings, unseen by the audience. **2.** Close by in the background; available at short notice: *a presidential candidate waiting in the wings.* **on the wing.** In flight; flying. **take wing.** To fly off; soar away. **under (one's) wing.** Under one's protection; in one's care. **wing it.** *Informal.* To improvise: *She hadn't studied for the exam, so she decided to wing it.* [Middle English *wenge, winge,* of Scandinavian origin. See **wē-** in Appendix.]

wing and wing *adv. Nautical.* With sails extended on both sides.

wing·back (wĭng′băk′) *n. Football.* **1.** A back positioned on offense behind or outside of an end. **2.** The position played by such a back.

wing·bow (wĭng′bō′) *n.* A distinctive mark of color on the bend of a bird's wing, especially in domestic fowl.

wing case *n.* See **elytron.**

wing chair also **wing·chair** (wĭng′châr′) *n.* An armchair with a high back from which project large, enclosing side pieces.

wing·ding (wĭng′dĭng′) *n. Informal.* A lavish or lively party or celebration. [Origin unknown.]

winged (wĭngd, wĭng′ĭd) *adj.* **1.a.** Having wings or winglike appendages. **b.** Having wings of a specified kind. Often used in combination: *broken-winged; big-winged.* **2.** Moving on or as if on wings; flying. **3.** Soaring as if with wings; elevated or sublime. **4.** Swift; fleet.

winged bean *n.* See **asparagus pea.**

wing-foot·ed (wĭng′fo͝ot′ĭd) *adj.* **1.** Having winged feet. **2.** Swift; fleet.

wing·less (wĭng′lĭs) *adj.* Having no wings or only rudimentary wings. **—wing′less·ness** *n.*

wing·let (wĭng′lĭt) *n.* **1.** A small or rudimentary wing. **2.** A short, almost vertical stabilizing fin projecting from the tip of an aircraft wing.

wing loading *n.* The gross weight of an airplane divided by the wing area. Used in stress analysis.

wing·man (wĭng′mən) *n.* A pilot whose plane is positioned behind and outside the leader in a formation of flying aircraft.

wing nut *n.* A nut with winglike projections for thumb and forefinger leverage in turning. Also called *thumbnut.*

wing·o·ver (wĭng′ō′vər) *n.* A flight maneuver or stunt in which an airplane enters a climbing turn until almost stalled and is allowed to fall while the turn is continued until normal flight is attained in a direction opposite the original heading.

wing·span (wĭng′spăn′) *n.* **1.** The linear distance between the extremities of an airfoil. **2.** Wingspread.

wing·spread (wĭng′sprĕd′) *n.* The distance between the tips of the wings, as of a bird or an insect, when fully extended.

wing·tip also **wing tip** (wĭng′tĭp′) *n.* **1.a.** An often perforated shoe part that covers the toe and extends backward along the sides of the shoe from a point at the center. **b.** A style of shoe having such a tip. **2.** The tip of the wing of a bird, a bat, an insect, or another animal. **3.** The extreme edge of a wing, as of an aircraft.

wink (wĭngk) *v.* **winked, wink·ing, winks.** —*intr.* **1.** To close and open the eyelid of one eye deliberately, as to convey a message, signal, or suggestion. **2.** To close and open the eyelids of both eyes; blink. See Synonyms at **blink. 3.** To shine fitfully; twinkle: *Harbor lights were winking in the distance.* —*tr.* **1.** To close and open (an eye or the eyes) rapidly. **2.** To signal or express by winking. —**wink** *n.* **1.a.** The act of winking. **b.** A signal or hint conveyed by winking. **2.** The very brief time required for a wink; an instant. **3.** A quick closing and opening of the eyelids; a blink. **4.** A gleam or twinkle. **5.** *Informal.* A brief period of sleep. —***phrasal verbs.*** **wink at.** To pretend not to see: *winked at corruption in the ministry.* **wink out.** To come to a close; end. [Middle English *winken,* to close one's eyes, from Old English *wincian.*]

wink·er (wĭng′kər) *n.* One that winks, as: **a.** A blinder for a horse. **b.** *Informal.* An eye. **c.** *Informal.* An eyelash.

win·kle¹ (wĭng′kəl) *n. Zoology.* A periwinkle.

win·kle² (wĭng′kəl) *tr.v.* **-kled, -kling, -kles.** *Chiefly British.* To pry, extract, or force from a place or position. Often used with *out.* [From WINKLE¹ (from the process of extracting periwinkles from their shells).]

win·na·ble (wĭn′ə-bəl) *adj.* Possible to win or achieve: *a winnable election campaign; winnable games.* —**win′na·bil′i·ty** *n.*

Win·ne·ba·go (wĭn′ə-bā′gō) *n., pl.* **Winnebago** or **-gos** or **-goes. 1.a.** A Native American people formerly inhabiting the Green Bay area of Wisconsin, with present-day populations in Wisconsin and Nebraska. **b.** A member of this people. **2.** The Siouan language of the Winnebago. [Fox *wiinepyeekooha,* those of the dirty water.]

Winnebago, Lake. A lake of eastern Wisconsin traversed by the Fox River. It is a popular recreation area.

win·ner (wĭn′ər) *n.* One that wins, especially a victor in sports or a notably successful person.

win·ner's circle (wĭn′ərz) *n., pl.* **winners' circles.** *Sports.* An enclosed area at a racetrack where the winning horse and jockey are brought for awards and publicity.

win·ning (wĭn′ĭng) *adj.* **1.a.** Of or relating to the act of winning: *drew the winning number in the lottery.* **b.** Successful; victorious: *the winning entry; the winning team.* **2.** Attractive; charming: *a winning personality; a winning smile.* —**winning** *n.* **1.** The act of one that wins; victory. **2.** Often **winnings.** Something won, especially money. **3.** A section of a mine that has been recently prepared or opened for working. —**win′ning·ly** *adv.* —**win′ning·ness** *n.*

win·ning·est (wĭn′ĭng-ĭst) *adj. Slang.* More successful or winning more often than any others: *"It was one of America's winningest days for women"* (Christian Science Monitor).

winning gallery *n. Sports.* A winning opening in court tennis below the side penthouse and on the hazard side of the net.

winning opening *n. Sports.* Any of three openings in court tennis into which a played ball may be hit, thus affording the player a point.

winning post *n. Sports.* The post at the end of a racecourse.

Win·ni·peg (wĭn′ə-pĕg′). The capital and largest city of Manitoba, Canada, in the southeast part of the province at the confluence of the Red and Assiniboine rivers. Founded as a fur-trading post, it developed rapidly after the coming of the railroad in 1881. Population, 564,473.

Winnipeg, Lake. A lake of south-central Manitoba, Canada. A remnant of the glacial Lake Agassiz, it is now a popular resort area surrounded by valuable timberlands.

Win·ni·pe·go·sis (wĭn′ə-pĭ-gō′sĭs), **Lake.** A lake of southwest Manitoba, Canada, west of Lake Winnipeg. It drains southward into Lake Manitoba and has important fisheries.

Winnipeg River. A river, about 322 km (200 mi) long, of southwest Ontario and southeast Manitoba, Canada, flowing northwest to Lake Winnipeg.

Win·ni·pe·sau·kee (wĭn′ə-pĭ-sô′kē), **Lake.** A lake of east-central New Hampshire. It is in a popular resort area.

win·now (wĭn′ō) *v.* **-nowed, -now·ing, -nows.** —*tr.* **1.a.** To separate the chaff from (grain) by means of a current of air. **b.** To rid of undesirable parts. **2.** To blow (chaff) off or away. **3.** To blow away; scatter. **4.** To blow on; fan: *a breeze winnowing the tall grass.* **5.** To examine closely in order to separate the good from the bad; sift. **6.a.** To separate or get rid of (an undesirable part); eliminate: *winnowing out the errors in logic.* **b.** To sort or select (a desirable part); extract. —*intr.* **1.** To separate grain from chaff. **2.** To separate the good from the bad. —**winnow** *n.* **1.** A device for winnowing grain. **2.** An act of winnowing. [Middle English *winnewen,* alteration of *windwen,* from Old English *windwian,* from *wind,* wind. See WIND¹.] —**win′now·er** *n.*

win·o (wī′nō) *n., pl.* **-os.** *Slang.* An indigent wine-drinking alcoholic.

Wi·no·na (wĭ-nō′nə). A city of southeast Minnesota on the Mississippi River southeast of St. Paul. Population, 25,075.

Win·slow (wĭnz′lō), **Edward.** 1595–1655. English colonial administrator who traveled to America on the *Mayflower* and served as governor of Plymouth Colony (1633, 1636, and 1644).

win·some (wĭn′səm) *adj.* Charming, often in a childlike or naive way. [Middle English *winsum,* from Old English *wynsum* : from *wynn,* joy; see **wen-¹** in Appendix + *-sum,* characterized by; see -SOME¹.] —**win′some·ly** *adv.* —**win′some·ness** *n.*

Win·ston-Sa·lem (wĭn′stən-sā′ləm). A city of north-central North Carolina north-northeast of Charlotte. Salem was founded by Moravians in 1766, and Winston was established in 1849; the cities were consolidated in 1913. Population, 131,885.

win·ter (wĭn′tər) *n.* **1.** The usually coldest season of the year, occurring between autumn and spring, extending in the Northern Hemisphere from the winter solstice to the vernal equinox, and popularly considered to be constituted by December, January, and February. **2.** A year as expressed through the recurrence of the winter season. **3.** A period of time characterized by coldness, misery, barrenness, or death. —**winter** *adj.* **1.** Of, relating to, occurring in, or appropriate to the season of winter: *winter blizzards; winter attire.* **2.** Grown during the season of winter: *winter herbs.* —**winter** *v.* **-tered, -ter·ing, -ters.** —*intr.* **1.** To spend the winter: *wintered in Arizona.* **2.** To feed in winter. Used with *on: deer wintering on cedar bark.* —*tr.* To lodge, keep, or care for during the winter: *wintering the sheep in the stable.* [Middle English, from Old English. See **wed-¹** in Appendix.] —**win′ter·ish** *adj.*

WORD HISTORY: Winter, spring, summer, fall. It is not too difficult to see how the season names *spring* and *fall* came into being, but without some background information it is impossible to tell what the origins of the words *winter* and *summer* are. *Summer* goes back to the Indo-European root **sem-*, meaning "summer." From a suffixed form of this root came the prehistoric Common Germanic word **sumaraz*, the ancestor of Old English *sumor* and its descendant, Modern English *summer.* This is the only Indo-European root referring to a season that has survived in an English name for a season. Of the other three, **wesr-*, "spring," has produced words such as *vernal; ghyem-*, "winter," has given us words such as *hibernate;* and *esen-*, "harvest, fall," has yielded *earn* (from the prehistoric Common Germanic word **aznōn*, "to do harvest work, serve"). *Winter* does, however, go back to the Indo-European root *wed-*, "water, wet." From the form *we-n-d-* of this root with the nasal infix *-n-* was derived the Germanic word **wintruz*, with the underlying meaning "wet season" and the literal meaning "winter." The Germanic word is the source of Old English *winter,* the ancestor of Modern English *winter.*

winter aconite *n.* Any of various Eurasian herbs of the genus *Eranthis,* especially *E. hyemalis,* having palmately dissected leaves and a solitary yellow flower that blooms in winter or early spring.

win·ter·ber·ry (wĭn′tər-bĕr′ē) *n.* **1.** Any of several North American shrubs of the genus *Ilex,* having showy red berries. **2.** See **black alder** (sense 1).

winter break *n.* A period of recess, usually lasting one week, during the winter term at school.

winter cherry *n.* A frequently cultivated Eurasian plant *(Physalis alkekengi)* having small red berries enclosed in inflated papery, orange-red seed cases. Also called *Chinese lantern plant.*

winter cress *n.* Any of various herbs of the genus *Barbarea* of the mustard family, having pinnately divided basal leaves and yellow flowers.

win·ter-feed (wĭn′tər-fēd′) *tr.v.* **-fed** (-fĕd′), **-feed·ing, -feeds.** To feed (livestock) when grazing is not possible.

winter flounder *n.* A dark, rusty brown flounder *(Pseudopleuronectes americanus)* of the North American Atlantic coast, prized especially in winter as a food fish.

win·ter·green (wĭn′tər-grēn′) *n.* **1.a.** A low-growing, creeping evergreen plant *(Gaultheria procumbens)* of North America, having solitary, nodding white flowers, aromatic leaves, and spicy, edible scarlet berries. Also called *checkerberry, teaberry.* **b.** An oil or a flavoring obtained from this plant. **2.** Any of several similar or related plants, such as the pipsissewa. [Translation of Dutch *wintergroen.*]

Win·ter Ha·ven (wĭn′tər hā′vən). A city of central Florida east of Lakeland. Population, 21,119.

win·ter·ize (wĭn′tə-rīz′) *tr.v.* **-ized, -iz·ing, -iz·es.** To prepare or equip (an automobile or a house, for example) for winter weather. —**win′ter·i·za′tion** (-tĕr-ĭ-zā′shən) *n.*

winepress

wing chair
c. 1750–1770 American

ă **pat**	oi **boy**
ā **pay**	ou **out**
âr **care**	o͝o **took**
ä **father**	o͞o **boot**
ĕ **pet**	ŭ **cut**
ē **be**	ûr **urge**
ĭ **pit**	th **thin**
ī **pie**	*th* **this**
îr **pier**	hw **which**
ŏ **pot**	zh **vision**
ō **toe**	ə **about, item**
ô **paw**	♦ **regionalism**

Stress marks: **′** (primary); ′ (secondary), as in **dictionary** (dĭk′shə-nĕr′ē)

wire fox terrier

win·ter·kill (wĭn′tər-kĭl′) *v.* **-killed, -kill·ing, -kills.** —*tr.* To kill (plants, for example) by exposing to extremely cold winter weather. —*intr.* To die from exposure to cold winter weather. Used especially of plants. —**winterkill** *n.* Death, as of plants, resulting from exposure to winter weather.

winter melon *n.* See **honeydew melon.** [Translation of Chinese *dōng guā* : *dōng,* winter + *guā,* melon.]

Winter Park. A city of central Florida north of Orlando. It is a tourist center in a citrus-growing area. Population, 22,314.

winter purslane *n.* An annual plant *(Montia perfoliata)* of western North America, having small white flowers and fleshy leaves sometimes eaten in salads. Also called *miner's lettuce.*

winter savory *n.* See **savory²** (sense 2).

winter solstice *n.* In the Northern Hemisphere, the solstice that occurs on or about December 22.

♦**winter squash** *n.* Any of several thick-rinded varieties of squash, such as the acorn squash, that can be stored for long periods. Also called ♦*hubbard squash.*

Win·ter·thur (vĭn′tər-to͝or′). A city of northern Switzerland northeast of Zurich. It passed to the Hapsburgs in 1264 and became a free imperial city in 1415. Population, 84,600.

win·ter·time (wĭn′tər-tīm′) *n.* The season of winter.

winter wheat *n.* Wheat planted in the autumn and harvested the following spring or early summer.

winter wren *n.* A small wren *(Troglodytes troglodytes)* having a short tail and black bars on the belly.

Win·throp (wĭn′thrəp). A town of eastern Massachusetts, a resort and residential suburb of Boston. Population, 19,294.

Winthrop, John. 1588–1649. English colonial administrator who was the first governor of Massachusetts Bay Colony, serving seven terms between 1629 and 1649. His son **John** (1606–1676) was three times governor of Connecticut (1636, 1657, and 1659–1676), and his grandson **John** (1638–1707), born in America, was also governor of Connecticut (1698–1707).

win·try (wĭn′trē) also **win·ter·y** (wĭn′tə-rē) *adj.* **-tri·er, -tri·est** also **-ter·i·er, -ter·i·est. 1.** Belonging to or characteristic of winter; cold. **2.** Suggestive of winter, as in coldness: *a wintry welcome.* —**win′tri·ly** *adv.* —**win′tri·ness** *n.*

win·y or **wine·y** (wī′nē) *adj.* **-i·er, -i·est.** Having the qualities or taste of wine; heady or intoxicating.

winze (wĭnz) *n.* An inclined or vertical shaft or passage between levels in a mine. [Alteration of obsolete *winds,* probably from WIND², apparatus for winding.]

wipe (wīp) *tr.v.* **wiped, wip·ing, wipes. 1.a.** To subject to light rubbing or friction, as with a cloth or paper, in order to clean or dry. **b.** To clean or dry by rubbing: *wiped my feet before I went inside.* **c.** To rub, move, or pass (a cloth, for example) over a surface. **2.a.** To remove by or as if by rubbing: *wipe off dirt; wipe away grease.* **b.** To blot out completely, as from the memory. **3.a.** To spread or apply by or as if by wiping: *wiped furniture polish over the table.* **b.** To form (a joint) in plumbing by spreading solder with a piece of cloth or leather. —**wipe** *n.* **1.** The act or an instance of wiping. **2.** Something, such as a towel or tissue, used for wiping. **3.** A cam that activates another part; a wiper. **4.a.** A blow or swipe. **b.** *Informal.* A jeer; a gibe. **5.** A shift from one scene in a film or movie to another, effected by means of a line passing across the screen. —***phrasal verb.* wipe out. 1.** To destroy or be destroyed completely. **2.** *Slang.* To murder. **3.** *Sports.* To lose one's balance and fall or jump off a surfboard. [Middle English *wipen,* from Old English *wīpian.* See **weip-** in Appendix.]

wiped-out (wīpt′out′) *adj. Slang.* Totally exhausted.

wipe·out (wīp′out′) *n.* **1.a.** The act or an instance of wiping out. **b.** Complete destruction. **2.** *Sports.* A fall from a surfboard.

wip·er (wī′pər) *n.* **1.** One that wipes. **2.** Something, such as a towel, used for wiping. **3.** A device designed for wiping, as on an automobile windshield. **4.** A projecting cam, as on a rotating shaft, that activates another machine part. **5.** *Electricity.* A movable electrical contact, as in a rheostat.

wire (wīr) *n.* **1.** A usually pliable metallic strand or rod made in many lengths and diameters, sometimes clad and often electrically insulated, used chiefly for structural support or to conduct electricity. **2.** A group of wire strands bundled or twisted together as a functional unit; cable. **3.** Something resembling a wire, as in slenderness or stiffness. **4.** An open telephone connection. **5.** *Slang.* A hidden microphone, as on a person's body or in a building. **6.a.** A telegraph service. **b.** A telegram or cablegram. **7.** *Computer Science.* A pin in the print head of a computer printer. **8.** The screen on which sheets of paper are formed in a papermaking machine. **9.** *Sports.* The finish line of a racetrack. **10. wires. a.** The system of strings employed in manipulating puppets in a show. **b.** Hidden controlling influences. **11.** *Slang.* A pickpocket. **12.** Fencing made of usually barbed wire. —**wire** *v.* **wired, wir·ing, wires.** —*tr.* **1.** To bind, connect, or attach with wires or a wire. **2.** To string (beads, for example) on wire. **3.** To equip with a system of electrical wires. **4.** *Slang.* To install electronic eavesdropping equipment in (a room, for example). **5.** To send by telegraph: *wired her congratulations.* **6.** To send a telegram to. —*intr.* To send a telegram. —***idioms.* down to the wire.** *Informal.* To the very end, as in a race or contest. **under the wire. 1.** *Sports.* At the finish line. **2.** *Informal.* Just in the nick of time; at the last moment. [Middle English, slender metal rod, from Old English *wīr.* See **wei-** in Appendix.] —**wir′a·ble** *adj.*

wired (wīrd) *adj.* **1.** Equipped with a system of wires, as for electric or telephone connections. **2.** *Slang.* Equipped with hidden electronic eavesdropping devices: *a wired hotel room.* **3.a.** Reinforced or supported by wires. **b.** Tied or bound up with wire: *wired bundles of newspaper.* **4.** *Slang.* Well connected, as with high-ranking members of an organization. **5.** *Slang.* Very stimulated or excited, as from a stimulant or a rush of adrenaline.

wire·draw (wīr′drô′) *tr.v.* **-drew** (-dro͞o′), **-drawn** (-drôn′), **-draw·ing, -draws. 1.** To draw (metal) into wire. **2.** To treat (a subject, for example) with great length, excessive detail, or overrefinement; spin out. —**wire′draw′er** *n.*

wire·drawn (wīr′drôn′) *adj.* Overly subtle and particularized, such as comparisons or points in an argument.

wire·drew (wīr′dro͞o′) *v.* Past tense of **wiredraw.**

wire fox terrier *n.* Any of a breed of small fox terrier developed in northern England, having a rough, wiry, white coat with patches of black or tan. Also called *wirehair, wirehaired terrier.*

wire gauge *n.* **1.** A gauge for measuring the diameter of wire, usually consisting of a disk having variously sized slots in its periphery or a long graduated plate with similar slots along its edge. **2.** A standardized system of wire sizes.

wire glass *n.* Sheet glass reinforced with wire netting. Also called *safety glass.*

wire·grass (wīr′grăs′) *n.* Any of various grasses, such as Bermuda grass, having tough wiry roots or rootstocks.

wire·hair (wīr′hâr′) *n.* See **wire fox terrier.**

wire·haired (wīr′hârd′) *adj.* Having a coat of stiff, wiry hair. Used especially of breeds of dogs.

wirehaired point·ing griffon (poin′tĭng) *n.* Any of a breed of medium-sized hunting dog originating in the Netherlands, having a rough steel-gray coat with patches of chestnut.

wirehaired terrier *n.* See **wire fox terrier.**

wire·less (wīr′lĭs) *adj.* **1.** Having no wires: *a wireless security system.* **2.** *Chiefly British.* Of or relating to radio or communication by radiotelegraphy or radiotelephony. —**wireless** *n.* **1.** A radio telegraph or radiotelephone system. **2.** A message transmitted by wireless telegraph or telephone. **3.** *Chiefly British.* Radio. —**wireless** *tr. & intr.v.* **-lessed, -less·ing, -less·es.** To communicate with or send communications by wireless.

wireless telegraphy *n.* Telegraphy by radio rather than by long-distance transmission lines. Also called *wireless telegraph.*

wireless telephone *n.* See **radiotelephone.**

wire·man (wīr′mən) *n.* **1.** One who works with electric wiring. **2.** *Slang.* One who taps telephone lines; a wiretapper.

Wire·pho·to (wīr′fō′tō). A trademark used for a photograph electrically transmitted over telephone wires.

wire·pull·er (wīr′po͝ol′ər) *n.* **1.** *Slang.* One who uses subterfuge, private influence, or underhand means to reach a goal. **2.** One who pulls wires, as of puppets. —**wire′pull′ing** *n.*

wir·er (wīr′ər) *n.* **1.** One that wires: *a wirer of fences.* **2.** A trapper who uses wire traps to snare game.

wire rope *n.* Rope made of twisted strands of wire.

wire service *n.* A news-gathering organization that distributes syndicated copy electronically to subscribers.

wire·tap (wīr′tăp′) *n.* **1.** A concealed listening or recording device connected to a communications circuit. **2.** The act of installing such a device. —**wiretap** *v.* **-tapped, -tap·ping, -taps.** —*tr.* **1.** To connect a concealed listening or recording device to. **2.** To monitor (a telephone line) by means of such a device. —*intr.* To install a concealed listening or recording device or use it to monitor communications. —**wire′tap′per** *n.*

wire·walk·er (wīr′wô′kər) *n.* An acrobat who walks on a wire tightrope.

wire·work (wīr′wûrk′) *n.* **1.** Something made of wire or wires. **2.** The skill of walking on a wire tightrope.

wire·worm (wīr′wûrm′) *n.* **1.** The yellowish, hard-bodied larva of various click beetles that feeds on the roots and seedlings of many crop plants. **2.** Any of various millipedes.

wir·ing (wīr′ĭng) *n.* **1.** The act of attaching, connecting, or installing electric wires. **2.** A system of electric wires.

wir·ra (wĭr′ə) *interj. Irish.* Used to express sorrow or concern. [From Irish Gaelic *a Muire,* Virgin Mary : *a,* O + *Muire,* Mary.]

wir·y (wīr′ē) *adj.* **-i·er, -i·est. 1.** Of or relating to wire. **2.** Resembling wire in form or quality, especially in stiffness: *wiry red hair.* **3.** Sinewy and lean: *He had a wiry build.* **4.** Produced by or as if by wire being vibrated. Used of sounds: *a wiry tone.* —**wir′i·ly** *adv.* —**wir′i·ness** *n.*

Wis·con·sin¹ (wĭs-kŏn′sĭn). *Abbr.* **WI, Wis.** A state of the north-central United States. It was admitted as the 30th state in 1848. First settled by the French, the region was ceded to Great Britain in 1763 and became part of the Northwest Territory in 1787. Madison is the capital and Milwaukee the largest city. Population, 4,705,642. —**Wis·con′sin·ite′** *n.*

Wis·con·sin² (wĭs-kŏn′sĭn) *adj. Geology.* Of or relating to the fourth glacial stage of the Pleistocene Epoch in North America. [After WISCONSIN¹.]

Wisconsin Rapids. A city of central Wisconsin south of Wausau on the Wisconsin River. Population, 17,995.

Wisconsin River. A river of central and southwest Wisconsin flowing about 692 km (430 mi) to the Mississippi River.

wis·dom (wĭz′dəm) *n.* **1.** Understanding of what is true, right, or lasting; insight: *"One cannot have wisdom without living life"*

(Dorothy McCall). **2.** Common sense; good judgment: *"It is a characteristic of wisdom not to do desperate things"* (Henry David Thoreau). **3.a.** The sum of scholarly learning through the ages; knowledge: *"In those homely sayings was couched the collective wisdom of generations"* (Maya Angelou). **b.** Wise teachings of the ancient sages. **4.** A wise outlook, plan, or course of action. **5. Wisdom.** *Bible.* Wisdom of Solomon. [Middle English, from Old English *wīsdōm.* See **weid-** in Appendix.]

Wisdom of Jesus, the Son of Si·rach (sī′răk′) *n. Bible.* Ecclesiasticus.

Wisdom of Solomon *n. Bible.* See table at **Bible.**

wisdom tooth *n.* One of four rearmost molars on each side of the upper and lower jaw in human beings. Wisdom teeth are the last teeth to erupt, typically in early adulthood. [Translation of New Latin *dēns sapientiae* : *dēns,* tooth + *sapientiae,* genitive of *sapientia,* wisdom.]

wise¹ (wīz) *adj.* **wis·er, wis·est. 1.** Having wisdom or discernment for what is true, right, or lasting; sagacious: *a wise leader.* **2.a.** Exhibiting common sense; prudent: *a wise decision.* **b.** Shrewd; crafty. **3.** Having great learning; erudite. **4.** Provided with information; informed. Used with *to: was wise to the politics of the department.* **5.** *Slang.* Rude and disrespectful; impudent. —***phrasal verb.* wise up.** *Slang.* To make or become aware, informed, or sophisticated. [Middle English, from Old English *wīs.* See **weid-** in Appendix.] **—wise′ly** *adv.* **—wise′ness** *n.*

wise² (wīz) *n.* Method or manner of doing; way: *in no wise; in any wise.* [Middle English, from Old English *wīse.* See **weid-** in Appendix.]

Wise (wīz), **Isaac Mayer.** 1819–1900. Bohemian-born American religious leader who united Reform Jewish organizations in the United States.

Wise, Stephen Samuel. 1874–1949. Hungarian-born American religious leader who founded the World Jewish Congress (1936).

–wise *suff.* **1.** In a specified manner, direction, or position: *clockwise.* **2.** *Usage Problem.* With reference to; in regard to: *profitwise.* [Middle English, from Old English *-wīsan,* from *-wīse,* manner. See WISE².]

USAGE NOTE: The suffix *–wise* has a long history of use to mean "in the manner or direction of," as in *clockwise, otherwise,* and *slantwise.* Since the 1930's, however, the suffix has been widely used in the vaguer sense of "with reference to," as in *This has not been a good year saleswise. Taxwise, it is an unattractive arrangement.* From their introduction, these usages were associated with the more informal prose of the newsmagazines, and 50 years later the usages still show no sign of achieving critical respectability. In an earlier survey the examples cited were unacceptable to the large majority of the Usage Panel. The suffix may save a few syllables, but in most writing there is no alternative to paraphrases such as *This has not been a good year with respect to sales. As far as taxes are concerned, it is an unattractive arrangement.*

wise·a·cre (wīz′ā′kər) *n. Slang.* A person regarded as being disagreeably egotistical and self-assured. [Alteration of Middle Dutch *wijsseggher,* soothsayer, translation of Middle High German *wīssage,* from Old High German *wīssago, wīzzago,* seer. See **weid-** in Appendix.]

wise·ass also **wise-ass** (wīz′ăs′) *n. Vulgar Slang.* A smart aleck.

wise·crack (wīz′krăk′) *Slang. n.* A flippant, typically sardonic remark or retort. See Synonyms at **joke. —wisecrack** *intr.v.* **-cracked, -crack·ing, -cracks.** To make or utter a wisecrack. **—wise′crack′er** *n.*

wise guy *n. Slang.* A smart aleck.

wise man *n.* **1.** One of the magi who paid homage to the baby Jesus; a magus. **2.** A sage.

wis·en·heim·er also **weis·en·heim·er** (wī′zən-hī′mər) *n. Informal.* A smart aleck. [WISE¹ + German *-enheimer* (as in surnames such as *Oppenheimer*).]

wi·sent (vē′zənt) *n.* The European bison *(Bison bonasus)* having a smaller and higher head than the North American bison. Also called *aurochs.* [German, from Middle High German, from Old High German *wisunt.*]

wish (wĭsh) *n.* **1.** A desire, longing, or strong inclination for a specific thing. **2.** An expression of a desire, longing, or strong inclination; a petition. **3.** Something desired or longed for. **—wish** *v.* **wished, wish·ing, wish·es.** *—tr.* **1.** To long for; want. See Synonyms at **desire. 2.** To entertain or express wishes for; bid: *He wished her good night.* **3.** To call or invoke upon: *I wish them luck.* **4.** To order or entreat: *I wish you to go.* **5.** To impose or force; foist: *They wished a hard job on her.* *—intr.* **1.** To have or feel a desire: *wish for the moon.* **2.** To express a wish. [Middle English *wissh,* from *wisshen,* to wish, from Old English *wȳscan.* See **wen-¹** in Appendix.] **—wish′er** *n.*

USAGE NOTE: *Wish* is widely used as a polite substitute for *want* with infinitives: *Do you wish to sit at a table on the terrace? Anyone who wishes to may leave now.* This usage is consonant with formal style, where it is natural to treat the desires of others with exaggerated deference. The corresponding use of *wish* with a noun-phrase object is less frequent, though it cannot be regarded as incorrect: *Anyone who wishes an aisle seat should see an attendant.* Both usages are likely to sound stilted in informal style, however. • When *wish* precedes a subordinate clause containing a contrary-to-fact statement, strict grammatical correctness requires that one use *were* rather than *was: I wish I were* (not *was*) *lighter on my feet.* Many writers continue to insist on this rule, but precedent for using the indicative *was* in such clauses can be found in the works of many writers, including King Alfred and Jonathan Swift. See Usage Notes at **if, want.**

wish·bone (wĭsh′bōn′) *n.* **1.** The forked bone anterior to the breastbone of most birds, formed by the fusion of the clavicles. **2.** *Football.* An offensive formation in which the halfbacks are positioned behind and to the left and right of the fullback. [From the superstition that when two people pull the bone apart a wish will be fulfilled for the person who retains the longer piece.]

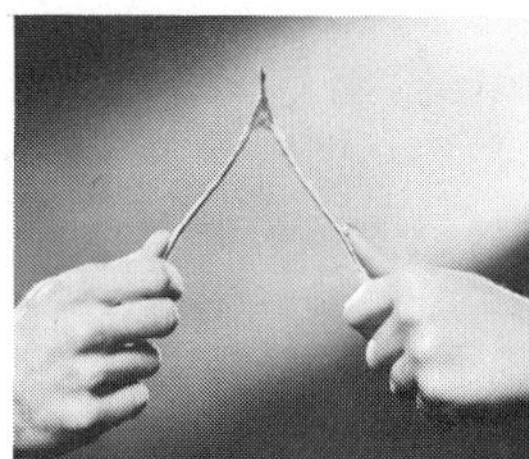

wishbone

wish·ful (wĭsh′fəl) *adj.* Having or expressing a wish or longing. **—wish′ful·ly** *adv.* **—wish′ful·ness** *n.*

wish fulfillment *n.* **1.** Gratification of a desire. **2.** In psychoanalytic theory, the satisfaction of a desire or an impulse through a dream, a fantasy, or other exercise of the imagination.

wishful thinking *n.* Identification of one's wishes or desires with reality.

wish list *n. Informal.* An often mental list of things wanted.

wish-wash (wĭsh′wŏsh′, -wôsh′) *n. Informal.* **1.** Speech or writing deemed banal or foolish. **2.** A thin, watery drink. [Reduplication of WASH.]

wish·y-wash·y (wĭsh′ē-wŏsh′ē, -wô′shē) *adj.* **-i·er, -i·est.** *Informal.* **1.** Thin and watery, as tea or soup; insipid. **2.** Lacking in strength of character or purpose; ineffective. [Reduplication of *washy,* thin, watery, from WASH.] **—wish′y-wash′i·ness** *n.*

Wis·kott-Al·drich syndrome (wĭs′kŏt-ôl′drĭch, -ŏl′-, vĭs′-) *n.* A hereditary, sex-linked, recessive disorder characterized by chronic eczema, recurring infections, and a decrease in the number of white blood cells and platelets. [After Alfred *Wiskott* (1898–1978), German pediatrician, and Robert Anderson *Aldrich* (born 1917), American physician.]

wisp (wĭsp) *n.* **1.** A small bunch or bundle, as of straw, hair, or grass. **2.a.** One that is thin, frail, or slight. **b.** A thin or faint streak or fragment, as of smoke or clouds. **3.** A fleeting trace or indication; a hint: *a wisp of a smile.* **4.** A flock of birds, especially snipe. See Synonyms at **flock¹. 5.** See **ignis fatuus** (sense 1). **—wisp** *v.* **wisped, wisp·ing, wisps.** *—tr.* To twist into wisps or a wisp. *—intr.* To drift in wisps: *smoke wisping from chimneys.* [Middle English.] **—wisp′i·ly** *adv.* **—wisp′i·ness** (wĭs′pē-nĭs) *n.* **—wisp′y** *adj.*

wist (wĭst) *v.* Past tense and past participle of **wit².**

Wis·ter (wĭs′tər), **Owen.** 1860–1938. American writer known for his novel *The Virginian* (1902).

wis·ter·i·a (wĭ-stîr′ē-ə) also **wis·tar·i·a** (wĭ-stâr′-) *n.* Any of several climbing woody vines of the genus *Wisteria* in the pea family, having pinnately compound leaves and drooping racemes of showy purplish or white flowers. [New Latin *Wisteria,* genus name, after Caspar *Wistar* (1761–1818), American physician.]

wisteria

wist·ful (wĭst′fəl) *adj.* **1.** Full of wishful yearning. **2.** Pensively sad; melancholy. [From obsolete *wistly,* intently.] **—wist′ful·ly** *adv.* **—wist′ful·ness** *n.*

wit¹ (wĭt) *n.* **1.** The natural ability to perceive and understand; intelligence. **2.a.** Often **wits.** Keenness and quickness of perception or discernment; ingenuity: *living by one's wits.* **b. wits.** Sound mental faculties; sanity: *scared out of my wits.* **3.a.** The ability to perceive and express in an ingeniously humorous manner the relationship between seemingly incongruous or disparate things: *"Wit has truth in it; wisecracking is simply calisthenics with words"* (Dorothy Parker). **b.** One noted for this ability, especially one skilled in repartee. **c.** A person of exceptional intelligence. —***idioms.* at (one's) wits' end.** At the limit of one's mental resources; utterly at a loss. **have** (or **keep**) **(one's) wits about (one).** To remain alert or calm, especially in a crisis. [Middle English, from Old English. See **weid-** in Appendix.]

SYNONYMS: *wit, humor, repartee, sarcasm, irony.* These nouns are compared as they denote forms of expression that elicit amusement or laughter. *Wit* implies intellectual keenness and the ability to perceive and express in a diverting, often pointed way analogies between essentially dissimilar things; *humor,* on the other hand, suggests the faculty of recognizing what is amusing, comical, incongruous, or absurd and using it as the basis for expression: *"Humor is, as it were, the growth of nature and accident; wit is the product of art and fancy"* (William Hazlitt). *Repartee* implies a facility for answering swiftly and cleverly: *"framing comments . . . that would be sure to sting and yet leave no opening for repartee"* (H.G. Wells). *Sarcasm* is a form of caustic wit intended to wound or ridicule another: *"Sarcasm I now see to be, in general, the language of the Devil; for which reason I have, long since, as good as renounced it"* (Thomas Carlyle). *Irony* is a form of expression in which an intended meaning is the opposite of the literal meaning of the words used: *"A drayman in a passion* [a rage] *calls out, 'You are a pretty fellow,' without suspecting that he is uttering irony"* (Macaulay). See also Synonyms at **mind.**

wit² (wĭt) *v.* **wist** (wĭst), **wit·ting** (wĭt′ĭng), first and third person singular present tense **wot** (wŏt). *Archaic.* *—tr.* To be or become aware of; learn. *—intr.* To know. —***idiom.* to wit.** That is to say; namely. [Middle English, from Old English *witan.* See **weid-** in Appendix.]

ă pat	oi boy
ā pay	ou out
âr care	o͝o took
ä father	o͞o boot
ĕ pet	ŭ cut
ē be	ûr urge
ĭ pit	th thin
ī pie	*th* this
îr pier	hw which
ŏ pot	zh vision
ō toe	ə about, item
ô paw	♦ regionalism

Stress marks: ′ (primary); ′ (secondary), as in **dictionary** (dĭk′shə-nĕr′ē)

wit·an (wĭt′än) *pl.n.* **1.** The members of the witenagemot in Anglo-Saxon England. **2.** The witenagemot. [Old English, pl. of *wita,* councilor. See WITENAGEMOT.]

witch (wĭch) *n.* **1.** A woman popularly believed to have supernatural powers and practice sorcery, and often believed to be aided by spirits or a familiar. **2.** A believer or follower of Wicca; a Wiccan. **3.** A hag. **4.** *Informal.* A woman or girl considered bewitching. **5.** One particularly skilled or competent at one's craft: *"A witch of a writer,* [she] *is capable of developing an intensity that verges on ferocity"* (Peter S. Prescott). **—witch** *v.* **witched, witch·ing, witch·es.** *—tr.* **1.** To work or cast a spell on; bewitch. **2.** To cause, bring, or effect by witchcraft. *—intr.* To use a divining rod to find underground water or minerals; dowse. [Middle English *wicche,* from Old English *wicce,* witch, and *wicca,* wizard, sorcerer; see **weg-** in Appendix.] **—witch′er·y** (-ə-rē) *n.* **—witch′y** *adj.*

witch·craft (wĭch′krăft′) *n.* **1.** Magic; sorcery. **2.** Wicca. **3.** A magical or irresistible influence, attraction, or charm.

witch doctor *n. Anthropology.* A shamanistic healer, a sorcerer, or a prophet, especially among African peoples. Not in scientific use.

witch elm *n.* Variant of **wych elm.** [Alteration of WYCH ELM.]

witch·es′ brew (wĭch′ĭz) *n.* A powerful or terrifying concoction.

witch·es′ broom (wĭch′ĭz) *n.* An abnormal brushlike growth of weak, closely clustered shoots or branches on a tree, such as the hackberry, caused by fungi or viruses.

witches′ Sabbath *n.* A meeting of witches, supposed by medieval Christians to be a demonic orgy.

witch grass *n.* **1.** An annual North American grass *(Panicum capillare)* having branching, purplish panicles. **2.** See **couch grass.** [Probably alteration of QUITCH GRASS.]

witch hazel *n.* **1.** Any of several deciduous shrubs or small trees of the genus *Hamamelis,* especially *H. virginiana,* of eastern North America, having yellow flowers that bloom in late autumn or winter. **2.** An alcoholic solution containing an extract of the bark and leaves of this plant, applied externally as a mild astringent. [Alteration of obsolete *wych,* wych elm; see WYCH ELM + HAZEL.]

witch-hunt (wĭch′hunt′) *n.* An investigation carried out ostensibly to uncover subversive activities but actually used to harass and undermine those with differing views. **—witch′-hunt′er** *n.* **—witch′-hunt′ing** *adj. & n.*

witch·ing (wĭch′ĭng) *adj.* **1.** Relating to or characteristic of witchcraft. **2.** Having the power to charm or enchant; bewitching. **—witching** *n.* Witchcraft; sorcery. **—witch′ing·ly** *adv.*

witch moth *n.* Any of several large noctuid moths of the genus *Erebus* of the southern United States and tropical America. [From its nocturnal habits.]

witch of Ag·ne·si (än-yā′zē) *n. Mathematics.* A planar cubic curve that is symmetric about the y-axis and that approaches the x-axis as an asymptote. Its equation is $x^2y = 4a^2(2a - y)$, where a is a constant. [WITCH (translation of Italian *avversiera, versiera,* confused with *versiera,* curve, turning, from New Latin *versōria,* from Latin *versus,* turned, reversed, past participle of *vertere,* to turn; see VERSE[1]) + Maria Gaetana *Agnesi* (1718–1799), Italian mathematician.]

wite (wīt) *n. Scots.* Blame; fault. [Middle English, from Old English *wīte,* penalty. See **weid-** in Appendix.]

wit·e·na·ge·mot (wĭt′n-ə-gə-mōt′) *n.* An Anglo-Saxon advisory council to the king, composed of about 100 nobles, prelates, and other officials, convened at intervals to discuss administrative and judicial affairs. [Old English *witena gemōt,* meeting of councilors : *witena,* genitive pl. of *wita,* councilor; see **weid-** in Appendix + *gemōt,* meeting (*ge-,* collective pref.; see **kom** in Appendix + *mōt,* meeting).]

with (wĭth, wĭth) *prep. Abbr.* **w. 1.** In the company of; accompanying: *Did you go with her?* **2.** Next to; alongside of: *stood with the rabbi; sat with the family.* **3.a.** Having as a possession, an attribute, or a characteristic: *arrived with bad news; a man with a moustache.* **b.** Used as a function word to indicate accompanying detail or condition: *just sat there with his mouth open.* **4.a.** In a manner characterized by: *performed with skill; spoke with enthusiasm.* **b.** In the performance, use, or operation of: *had trouble with the car.* **5.** In the charge or keeping of: *left the cat with the neighbors.* **6.** In the opinion or estimation of: *if it's all right with you.* **7.a.** In support of; on the side of: *I'm with anyone who wants to help the homeless.* **b.** Of the same opinion or belief as: *He is with us on that issue.* **8.** In the same group or mixture as; among: *planted onions with the carrots.* **9.** In the membership or employment of: *plays with a symphony orchestra; is with a publishing company.* **10.a.** By the means or agency of: *eat with a fork; made us laugh with his jokes.* **b.** By the presence or use of: *a pillow stuffed with feathers; balloons filled with helium.* **11.** In spite of: *With all her experience, she could not get a job.* **12.** In the same direction as: *sail with the wind; flow with the river.* **13.** At the same time as: *gets up with the birds.* **14.a.** In regard to: *We are pleased with her decision. They are disgusted with the status quo.* **b.** Used as a function word to indicate a party to an action, a communicative activity, or an informal agreement or settlement: *played with the dog; had a talk with the class; lives with an aunt.* **15.** In comparison or contrast to: *a dress identical with the one her sister just bought.* **16.** Having received: *With her permission, he left. I escaped with just a few bruises.* **17.a.** And; plus: *My books, with my brother's, make a sizable library. We had turkey with all the trimmings.* **b.** Inclusive of; including: *comes to $29.95 with postage and handling.* **18.** In opposition to; against: *wrestling with an opponent.* **19.** As a result or consequence of: *trembling with fear; sick with the flu.* **20.** So as to be touching or joined to: *coupled the first car with the second; linked arms with their partners.* **21.** So as to be free of or separated from: *parted with her husband.* **22.** In the course of: *We grow older with the hours.* **23.** In proportion to: *wines that improve with age.* **24.** In relationship to: *at ease with my peers.* **25.** As well as; in favorable comparison to: *She could sing with the best of them.* **26.** According to the experience or practice of: *With me, it is a question of priorities.* **27.** Used as a function word to indicate close association: *With the advent of the rockets, the Space Age began.* **—*idiom.* in with.** *Informal.* In league or association with: *He is in with the wrong crowd.* [Middle English, with, against, from, from Old English. See **wi-** in Appendix.]

USAGE NOTE: *With* does not have the conjunctive force of *and.* Consequently, in the following example the verb is governed by the singular subject and remains singular: *The governor, with his aides, is expected at the fair on Monday.* See Usage Note at **and.**

with·al (wĭth-ôl′, wĭth-) *adv.* **1.** In addition; besides: *"And, withal, a wider publicity was given to thought-provoking ideas"* (Holbrook Jackson). **2.** Despite that; nevertheless. **3.** *Archaic.* Therewith. **—withal** *prep. Archaic.* With. Used after its object at the end of a sentence or clause. [Middle English : *with,* with; see WITH + *al,* all; see ALL.]

with·draw (wĭth-drô′, wĭth-) *v.* **-drew** (-dro͞o′), **-drawn** (-drôn′), **-draw·ing, -draws.** *—tr.* **1.a.** To take back or away; remove. **b.** To remove (money) from an account. **c.** To turn away (one's gaze, for example). **d.** To draw aside: *withdrew the curtain.* **2.a.** To remove from consideration or participation: *withdrew her application; withdrew his son from the race.* **b.** To recall or retract: *withdrew the accusation.* *—intr.* **1.a.** To move or draw back; retire. **b.** To retreat from a battlefield. **2.a.** To remove oneself from active participation: *withdrew from the competition.* **b.** To become detached from social or emotional involvement. **3.** To recall or remove a motion from consideration in parliamentary procedure. **4.a.** To discontinue the use of an addictive substance. **b.** To adjust physiologically and mentally to this discontinuation. [Middle English *withdrawen* : *with,* away from; see WITH + *drawen,* to pull; see DRAW.] **—with·draw′a·ble** *adj.* **—with·draw′er** *n.*

with·draw·al (wĭth-drô′əl, wĭth-) *n.* **1.** The act or process of withdrawing, as: **a.** A retreat or retirement. **b.** Retreat of a military force in the face of enemy attack or after a defeat. **c.** Detachment, as from social or emotional involvement. **d.** A removal from a place or position of something that has been deposited. **2.a.** Discontinuation of the use of an addictive substance. **b.** The physiological and mental readjustment that accompanies such discontinuation. **3.** The act or an instance of retracting or revoking: *feared the withdrawal of his parents' permission.*

with·drawn (wĭth-drôn′, wĭth-) *v.* Past participle of **withdraw. —withdrawn** *adj.* **1.** Not readily approached; remote. **2.a.** Not friendly or sociable; aloof. **b.** Emotionally unresponsive and detached; introverted. **—with·drawn′ness** *n.*

with·drew (wĭth-dro͞o′, wĭth-) *v.* Past tense of **withdraw.**

withe (wĭth, wĭth, wīth) *n.* A tough, supple twig, especially of willow, used for binding things together; a withy. [Middle English, from Old English *withthe.* See **wei-** in Appendix.]

with·er (wĭth′ər) *v.* **-ered, -er·ing, -ers.** *—intr.* **1.** To dry up or shrivel from or as if from loss of moisture. **2.** To lose freshness; droop. *—tr.* **1.** To cause to shrivel or fade. **2.** To render speechless or incapable of action; stun: *withered the noisy student with a glance.* [Alteration of Middle English *widderen,* perhaps variant of *wederen,* to weather, from *weder,* weather. See WEATHER.]

with·ered (wĭth′ərd) *adj.* Shriveled, shrunken, or faded from or as if from loss of moisture or sustenance: *"the battle to keep his withered dreams intact"* (Time).

with·er·ing (wĭth′ər-ĭng) *adj.* Tending to overwhelm or destroy; devastating: *withering sarcasm.* **—with′er·ing·ly** *adv.*

with·er·ite (wĭth′ə-rīt′) *n.* A white, yellow, or gray mineral, chiefly $BaCO_3$. [German *Witherit,* after William *Withering* (1741–1799), British physician.]

withe rod *n.* An eastern North American deciduous shrub *(Viburnum cassinoides)* having clusters of small white flowers and bluish-black edible fruit. Also called *Appalachian tea, teaberry.*

with·ers (wĭth′ərz) *pl.n.* The high part of the back of a horse or similar animal, located between the shoulder blades. [Possibly from obsolete *wither-,* against (from the strain exerted on them when a horse draws a load), from Middle English, from Old English *wither-.* See **wi-** in Appendix.]

with·er·shins (wĭth′ər-shĭnz′) *adv.* Variant of **widdershins.**

With·er·spoon (wĭth′ər-spo͞on′), **John.** 1723–1794. Scottish-born American cleric, educator, and Revolutionary leader. A signer of the Declaration of Independence, he was president (1768–1794) of the college that became Princeton University.

with·hold (wĭth-hōld′, wĭth-) *v.* **-held** (-hĕld′), **-hold·ing, -holds.** *—tr.* **1.** To keep in check; restrain. **2.** To refrain from giving, granting, or permitting. See Synonyms at **keep. 3.** To deduct (withholding tax) from an employee's salary. *—intr.* To refrain or forbear. [Middle English *witholden* : *with,* away from;

see WITH + *holden,* to hold; see HOLD[1].] **—with·hold′er** *n.*

with·hold·ing tax (wĭth-hōl′dĭng, wĭth-) *n.* A portion of an employee's wages or salary withheld by the employer as partial payment of the employee's income tax.

with·in (wĭth-ĭn′, wĭth-) *adv.* **1.** In or into the inner part; inside. **2.** Inside the mind, heart, or soul; inwardly. **—within** *prep.* **1.** In the inner part or parts of; inside: *resentment seething within him.* **2.a.** Inside the limits or extent of in time or distance: *arrived within two days; stayed within earshot; within ten miles of home.* **b.** Inside the fixed limits of; not beyond: *lived within her income.* **c.** In the scope or sphere of: *acted within the law; within the medical profession.* **d.** Inside a specified amount or degree: *The team had pulled to within five points of winning.* **—within** *n.* An inner position, place, or area: *treachery from within.* [Middle English *withinne,* from Old English *withinnan* : *with,* with; see WITH + *innan,* from within (from *in,* in; see IN[1]).]

with·in·doors (wĭth-ĭn′dôrz′, -dōrz′, wĭth-) *adv.* Into or inside a house or other building; indoors.

with-it (wĭth′ĭt′, wĭth-) *adj. Slang.* **1.** Interested in and sensitive to the latest styles and trends; up-to-date. **2.** Streetwise and knowing; savvy.

♦ **with·out** (wĭth-out′, wĭth-) *adv.* **1.** On the outside: *a sturdy structure within and without.* **2.** With something absent or lacking: *had to do without.* **—without** *prep. Abbr.* **w/o 1.a.** Not having; lacking: *a family without a car.* **b.** Not accompanied by; in the absence of: *volunteered without hesitation; spoke without thinking.* **2.** At, on, to, or toward the outside or exterior of: *standing without the door.* **—without** *conj. Regional.* Unless: *"You don't know about me without you have read a book by the name of* The Adventures of Tom Sawyer*"* (Mark Twain). [Middle English *withoute,* from Old English *withūtan* : *with,* with; see WITH + *ūtan,* from without (from *ūt,* out; see OUT).]

with·out·doors (wĭth-out′dôrz′, -dōrz′, wĭth-) *adv.* Outside a house or other building; outdoors.

with·stand (wĭth-stănd′, wĭth-) *v.* **-stood** (-sto͝od′), **-stand·ing, -stands.** *—tr.* **1.** To oppose with force or resolution. **2.** To be successful in resisting. See Synonyms at **oppose.** *—intr.* To resist or endure successfully. [Middle English *withstanden,* from Old English *withstandan* : *with,* against; see WITH + *standan,* to stand; see STAND.] **—with·stand′er** *n.*

with·y (wĭth′ē, wĭth′ē) *adj.* **1.** Made of or as flexible as withes; tough. **2.** Wiry and agile. **—withy** *n., pl.* **-ies. 1.** A rope or band made of withes. **2.a.** A long flexible twig, as that of an osier. **b.** A tree or shrub having such twigs. [WITHE + –Y[1]. N., from Middle English *withye,* willow branch, from Old English *wīthig,* willow. See **wei-** in Appendix.]

wit·less (wĭt′lĭs) *adj.* Lacking intelligence or wit; foolish. **—wit′less·ly** *adv.* **—wit′less·ness** *n.*

wit·ling (wĭt′lĭng) *n.* **1.** One who aspires to wittiness. **2.** One who has little wit.

wit·loof (wĭt′lōf′) *n.* See **endive** (sense 2). [Dutch dialectal : *wit,* white (from Middle Dutch; see **kweit-** in Appendix) + *loof,* leaf (from Middle Dutch).]

wit·ness (wĭt′nĭs) *n.* **1.a.** One who can give a firsthand account of something seen, heard, or experienced: *a witness to the accident.* **b.** One who furnishes evidence. **2.** Something that serves as evidence; a sign. **3.** *Law.* **a.** One who is called on to testify before a court. **b.** One who is called on to be present at a transaction in order to attest to what takes place. **c.** One who signs one's name to a document for the purpose of attesting to its authenticity. **4.** An attestation to a fact, a statement, or an event; testimony. **5. Witness.** A member of the Jehovah's Witnesses. **—witness** *v.* **-nessed, -ness·ing, -ness·es.** *—tr.* **1.a.** To be present at or have personal knowledge of. **b.** To take note of; observe. **2.** To provide or serve as evidence of. See Synonyms at **indicate. 3.** To testify to; bear witness. **4.** To be the setting or site of: *This old auditorium has witnessed many ceremonies.* **5.** To attest to the legality or authenticity of by signing one's name to. *—intr.* **1.** To furnish or serve as evidence; testify. **2.** To testify to one's religious beliefs. [Middle English, from Old English, from *wit,* knowledge. See WIT[1].] **—wit′ness·er** *n.*

witness box *n. Chiefly British.* A witness stand.

witness stand *n. Law.* A stand or an enclosed area in a courtroom from which a witness presents testimony.

wit·ted (wĭt′ĭd) *adj.* Having wit or comprehension. Often used in combination: *keen-witted; dull-witted.* **—wit′ted·ness** *n.*

Wit·ten (vĭt′n). A city of west-central Germany on the Ruhr River east-southeast of Essen. Chartered in 1825, it is an industrial center. Population, 102,195.

Wit·ten·berg (wĭt′n-bûrg′, vĭt′n-bĕrk′). A city of east-central Germany on the Elbe River east of Dessau. Martin Luther made the city the center of the Protestant Reformation when he nailed his 95 theses to the door of the Schlosskirche in 1517. Population, 54,306.

Witt·gen·stein (vĭt′gən-shtīn′, -stīn), **Ludwig.** 1889–1951. Austrian-born British philosopher noted for his analyses of language and meaning. Among his writings are *Tractatus Logico-Philosophicus* (1921) and *Philosophical Investigations* (1953).

wit·ti·cism (wĭt′ĭ-sĭz′əm) *n.* A witty remark. See Synonyms at **joke.** [WITT(Y) + (CRIT)ICISM.]

wit·ting (wĭt′ĭng) *adj.* **1.** Aware or conscious of something. **2.** Done intentionally or with premeditation; deliberate. **—witting** *v.* Present participle of **wit[2]. —witting** *n. Chiefly British.* **1.** Knowledge or awareness; cognizance. **2.** Information obtained and passed on; news. **—wit′ting·ly** *adv.*

wit·tol (wĭt′l) *n. Archaic.* A man who tolerates his wife's infidelity. [Middle English *wetewold* : *weten,* to know (from Old English *witan;* see WIT[2]) + *(coke)wold,* cuckold; see CUCKOLD.]

wit·ty (wĭt′ē) *adj.* **-ti·er, -ti·est. 1.** Possessing or demonstrating wit in speech or writing; very clever and humorous. **2.** Characterized by or having the nature of wit; funny or jocular: *a witty saying.* **3.** Quick to discern and express amusing insights or relationships. **4.** Entertainingly and strikingly clever or original in concept, design, or performance: *a witty sculpture; witty choreography.* **—wit′ti·ly** *adv.* **—wit′ti·ness** *n.*

Wit·wa·ters·rand (wĭt-wô′tərz-rănd′, -ränd′, -wŏt′ərz-). Often called **Rand** (rănd). A region of northeast South Africa between the Vaal River and Johannesburg. It has been a rich gold-mining area since the discovery of gold in 1886.

wive (wīv) *v.* **wived, wiv·ing, wives.** *—tr.* **1.** To marry as a wife. **2.** To provide a wife for. *—intr.* To marry a woman. [Middle English *wiven,* from Old English *wīfian,* from *wīf,* woman.]

wi·vern (wī′vərn) *n. Heraldry.* Variant of **wyvern.**

wives (wīvz) *n.* Plural of **wife.**

wiz (wĭz) *n. Informal.* A person considered exceptionally gifted or skilled. [Short for WIZARD.]

wiz·ard (wĭz′ərd) *n.* **1.** One who practices magic; a sorcerer or magician. **2.** A skilled or clever person: *a wizard at math.* **3.** *Archaic.* A sage. **—wizard** *adj.* **1.** *Chiefly British.* Excellent. **2.** *Archaic.* Of or relating to wizards or wizardry. [Middle English *wisard* : *wise,* wise; see WISE[1] + *-ard,* pejorative suff.; see –ARD.]

wiz·ard·ly (wĭz′ərd-lē) *adj.* **1.** Having the qualities or attributes of a wizard. **2.** Astonishingly remarkable in design, performance, or execution; fabulous: *wizardly lighting and special effects.*

wiz·ard·ry (wĭz′ər-drē) *n., pl.* **-ries. 1.** The art, skill, or practice of a wizard; sorcery. **2.a.** A power or an effect that appears magical by its capacity to transform: *computer wizardry.* **b.** Great ability or adroitness in a pursuit.

wiz·en (wĭz′ən) *v.* **-ened, -en·ing, -ens.** *—intr.* To dry up; wither or shrivel. *—tr.* To cause to wither, shrivel, or dry up. **—wizen** *adj.* Shriveled or dried up; withered: *"There would be a day when his face would be wrinkled and wizen"* (Oscar Wilde). [Middle English *wisenen,* from Old English *wisnian.*]

wiz·ened (wĭz′ənd) *adj.* Withered; wizen.

wk. *abbr.* **1.** Week. **2.** Work.

wkly. *abbr.* Weekly.

WL *abbr.* **1.** Or **w.l.** Water line. **2.** Wavelength.

Wlo·cla·wek (vlôt-slä′vĕk). A city of central Poland on the Vistula River west-northwest of Warsaw. It was founded in the 12th century, passed to Russia in 1815, and reverted to Poland after World War I. Population, 115,300.

wm. *abbr.* Wattmeter.

wmk. *abbr.* Watermark.

WNW *abbr.* West-northwest.

wo (wō) *n. Archaic.* Variant of **woe.**

WO or **W.O.** *abbr.* Warrant officer.

w/o *abbr.* Without.

woad (wōd) *n.* **1.** An annual Old World plant *(Isatis tinctoria)* in the mustard family, formerly cultivated for its leaves that yield a blue dye. **2.** The dye obtained from this plant. [Middle English *wode,* from Old English *wād.*]

woad·wax·en (wōd′wăk′sən) *n.* See **dyer's greenweed.** [Alteration of WOODWAXEN.]

wob·ble also **wab·ble** (wŏb′əl) *—v.* **-bled, -bling, -bles.** *—intr.* **1.** To move or rotate with an uneven or rocking motion or unsteadily from side to side. **2.** To tremble or quaver: *The child's voice wobbled with emotion.* **3.** To waver or vacillate in one's opinions or feelings. *—tr.* To cause to wobble. *—n.* **1.** The act or an instance of wobbling; unsteady motion. **2.** A tremulous, uncertain tone or sound: *a vocal wobble.* [Probably from Low German *wabbeln.* See **webh-** in Appendix.] **—wob′bler** *n.*

wob·bly (wŏb′lē) *adj.* **-bli·er, -bli·est.** Tending to wobble; unsteady. **—wob′bli·ness** *n.*

Wo·burn (wō′bərn, wo͞o′-). A city of northeast Massachusetts, an industrial suburb of Boston. Population, 36,626.

w.o.c. *abbr.* Without compensation.

Wode·house (wo͝od′hous′), **P(elham) G(renville).** 1881–1975. British writer known for his humorous novels and stories that feature the aristocrat Bertie Wooster and his butler Jeeves.

Wo·den also **Wo·dan** (wōd′n) *n. Mythology.* An Anglo-Saxon god identified with Odin. [Middle English, from Old English *Wōden.* See **wet-**[1] in Appendix.]

Wod·zi·slaw Sla·ski (vô-jē′swäf shlôN′skē). A city of southern Poland southwest of Katowice. It is a rail junction and manufacturing center. Population, 107,700.

woe (wō) *n.* **1.** Deep distress or misery, as from grief; wretchedness. See Synonyms at **regret. 2.** Misfortune; calamity: *economic and political woes.* **—woe** *interj.* Used to express sorrow or dismay. [Middle English *wa, wo,* from Old English *wā,* woe!]

woe·be·gone (wō′bĭ-gôn′, -gŏn′) *adj.* **1.** Affected with or marked by deep sorrow, grief, or wretchedness. See Synonyms at **sad. 2.** Of an inferior or deplorable condition: *a rundown, woebegone old shack.* [Middle English *wo begon,* beset with woe : *wo,* woe; see WOE + *begon,* past participle of *begon,* to beset (from Old

ă pat	oi boy
ā pay	ou out
âr care	o͝o took
ä father	o͞o boot
ĕ pet	ŭ cut
ē be	ûr urge
ĭ pit	th thin
ī pie	*th* this
îr pier	hw which
ŏ pot	zh vision
ō toe	ə about, item
ô paw	♦ regionalism

Stress marks: **′** (primary); ′ (secondary), as in **dictionary** (dĭk′shə-nĕr′ē)

English *begān* : *bī, be-,* be- + *gān,* to go; see GO[1].] **—woe′be·gone′ness** *n.*

woe·ful also **wo·ful** (wō′fəl) *adj.* **1.** Affected by or full of woe; mournful. **2.** Causing or involving woe. **3.** Deplorably bad or wretched: *woeful treatment of the accused; woeful errors in judgment.* **—woe′ful·ly** *adv.* **—woe′ful·ness** *n.*

wog (wŏg) *n. Chiefly British & Offensive Slang.* Used as a disparaging term for a person of color, especially a foreigner from the Middle East or Asia. [Probably short for GOLLIWOG.]

wok (wŏk) *n.* A metal pan having a rounded bottom, used for frying and steaming in Asian cooking. [Chinese (Cantonese).]

♦ **woke** (wōk) *v.* A past tense of **wake[1].** See Regional Note at **wake[1].**

wok·en (wō′kən) *v.* A past participle of **wake[1].**

Wo·king (wō′kĭng). An urban district of southeast England, a mainly residential suburb of London. Population, 81,800.

wold[1] (wōld) *n.* An unforested rolling plain; a moor. [Middle English, from Old English *weald,* forest.]

wold[2] (wōld) *n.* Variant of **weld[2].**

Wolds (wōldz). A range of chalk hills in northeast England along both banks of the Humber River.

wolf
Tundra wolf
Canis lupus tundarum

wolf (wo͝olf) *n., pl.* **wolves** (wo͝olvz). **1.a.** Either of two carnivorous mammals of the family Canidae, especially the gray wolf of northern regions, that typically live and hunt in hierarchical packs and prey on livestock and game animals. **b.** The fur of such an animal. **c.** Any of various similar or related mammals, such as the hyena. **2.** The destructive larva of any of various moths, beetles, or flies. **3.** One that is regarded as predatory, rapacious, and fierce. **4.** *Slang.* A man given to paying unwanted sexual attention to women. **5.** *Music.* **a.** A harshness in some tones of a bowed stringed instrument produced by defective vibration. **b.** Dissonance in some intervals of a keyboard instrument tuned to a system of unequal temperament. **—wolf** *tr.v.* **wolfed, wolf·ing, wolfs.** To eat greedily or voraciously: *"The town's big shots were . . . wolfing down the buffet"* (Ralph Ellison). **—*idioms.* keep the wolf from the door.** *Slang.* To avoid the privation and suffering resulting from a lack of money: *Both spouses had to take jobs in order to keep the wolf from the door.* **wolf at the door.** Creditors or a creditor. **wolf in sheep's clothing.** One who feigns congeniality while actually holding malevolent intentions. [Middle English, from Old English *wulf.* See **wl̥kʷo-** in Appendix.]

Wolf, Friedrich August. 1759–1824. German classical scholar who proposed that the *Iliad* and the *Odyssey* are the work of several authors.

Wolf, Hugo. 1860–1903. Austrian composer known for his musical settings of the poetry of Goethe and Italian and Spanish writers and for the opera *Der Corregidor* (1895).

wolf·ber·ry (wo͝olf′bĕr′ē) *n.* A deciduous shrub *(Symphoricarpos occidentalis)* of western North America, having white berries and pinkish, bell-shaped flowers.

Wolf Cub (wo͝olf) *n. Chiefly British.* A Cub Scout.

wolf dog *n.* **1.** A dog trained to hunt wolves. **2.** The hybrid offspring of a dog and a wolf.

Wolfe (wo͝olf), **James.** 1727–1759. British general in Canada. He defeated the French at Quebec (1759) but was mortally wounded in the battle.

Wolfe, Thomas (Clayton). 1900–1938. American writer who is best known for his two autobiographical novels, *Look Homeward, Angel* (1929) and *You Can't Go Home Again* (1940).

Wolfe, Thomas (Kennerly). Known as "Tom." Born 1931. American writer. A leading exponent of New Journalism, he has written extensively on popular culture.

wolverine
Gulo gulo

wolf eel *n.* A Pacific wolf fish *(Anarrhichthys ocellatus)* having a long body and a pointed tail.

Wolff (vôlf), **Kaspar Friedrich.** 1733–1794. German anatomist noted for his pioneering work in embryology.

Wolff·i·an body (wo͝ol′fē-ən) *n. Biology.* See **mesonephros.** [After Kaspar Friedrich WOLFF.]

Wolffian duct *n. Biology.* The embryonic duct of the mesonephros, which in the male becomes the vas deferens and in both sexes gives rise to the ureter. [After Kaspar Friedrich WOLFF.]

wolf fish *n.* Any of several northern marine fishes of the family *Anarhichadidae,* having sharp teeth and powerful jaws.

wolf·hound (wo͝olf′hound′) *n.* Any of various large dogs, such as the Irish wolfhound or the borzoi, trained to hunt wolves or other large game.

wolf·ish (wo͝ol′fĭsh) *adj.* **1.** Of or relating to wolves. **2.a.** Suggestive of or resembling a wolf. **b.** Fierce or rapacious. **—wolf′ish·ly** *adv.* **—wolf′ish·ness** *n.*

wolf pack *n.* A group of submarines that attack a single vessel or a convoy.

wolf·ram (wo͝ol′frəm) *n.* See **tungsten.** [German, wolframite, tungsten : probably *Wolf,* wolf (from Middle High German, from Old High German; see **wl̥kʷo-** in Appendix) + *-ram* (from Middle High German *rām,* dirt).]

wolf·ram·ite (wo͝ol′frə-mīt′) *n.* Any of several red-brown to black minerals with the general formula $(Fe,Mn)WO_4$, which constitute a major source of tungsten.

wolfs·bane (wo͝olfs′bān′) *n.* **1.** See **monkshood** (sense 2). **2.** Any of several poisonous perennial herbs of the genus *Aconitum,* especially *A. lycoctonum,* having broad, rounded leaves, elongate racemes, and purple-lilac flowers.

Wolfs·burg (wo͝olfs′bûrg′, vôlfs′bo͝ork′). A city of north-central Germany northeast of Brunswick. It grew after the establishment of a Volkswagen automobile factory in the late 1930's. Population, 122,099.

wolf spider *n.* Any of various spiders of the family Lycosidae that stalk prey on the ground and do not spin webs, especially a common small species *(Lycosa tarentula)* of southern Europe found on beaches and in woods.

wolf whistle *n.* A typically two-note whistle made by a boy or man as an expression of sexual attention, often unsolicited, to a girl or woman. **—wolf whistle** *v.*

Wol·las·ton (wo͝ol′ə-stən), **William Hyde.** 1766–1828. British chemist and physicist who discovered palladium (1803) and rhodium (1804).

wol·las·ton·ite (wo͝ol′ə-stə-nīt′) *n.* A white to gray mineral, essentially $CaSiO_3$, found in metamorphic rocks and used in ceramics, paints, plastics, and cements. [After William Hyde WOLLASTON.]

Wol·las·ton Lake (wo͝ol′ə-stən, wŏl′-). A lake of northeast Saskatchewan, Canada, draining into the Churchill and Mackenzie river systems.

Wol·lon·gong (wo͝ol′ən-gŏng′, -gông′). A city of southeast Australia on the Tasman Sea south-southwest of Sydney. It is an iron and steel center. Population, 176,500.

Woll·stone·craft (wo͝ol′stən-krăft′, -kräft′), **Mary.** In full Mary Wollstonecraft Godwin. 1759–1797. British writer and reformer noted for *Vindication of the Rights of Women* (1792), considered the first important feminist essay.

Wo·lof (wō′lŏf′) *n.* **1.** A member of a West African people primarily inhabiting coastal Senegal. **2.** The West Atlantic language of this people, widely used as a lingua franca in Senegal.

Wol·sey (wo͝ol′zē), **Thomas.** 1475?–1530. English prelate and politician. The influential chief adviser to Henry VIII, he fell from favor after failing to secure papal approval of Henry's divorce from Catherine of Aragon (1529).

Wol·ver·hamp·ton (wo͝ol′vər-hămp′tən, -hăm′-). A borough of west-central England northwest of Birmingham. It is a highly industrialized city. Population, 256,500.

wol·ver·ine (wo͝ol′və-rēn′, wo͝ol′və-rēn′) *n.* **1.** A solitary, burrowing carnivorous mammal *(Gulo gulo)* of northern forest regions, related to the weasel and having a heavyset body, short legs, and dark fur with a bushy tail. Also called *carcajou, glutton, skunk bear.* **2. Wolverine.** A native or inhabitant of Michigan. [Probably from WOLF.]

wolves (wo͝olvz) *n.* Plural of **wolf.**

wom·an (wo͝om′ən) *n., pl.* **wom·en** (wĭm′ĭn). **1.** An adult female human being. **2.** Women considered as a group; womankind: *"Woman feels the invidious distinctions of sex exactly as the black man does those of color"* (Elizabeth Cady Stanton). **3.** An adult female human being belonging to a specified occupation, group, nationality, or other category. Often used in combination: *Englishwoman; congresswoman; saleswoman.* **4.** Feminine quality or aspect; womanliness. **5.** A female servant or subordinate. **6.** *Informal.* **a.** A wife. **b.** A lover or sweetheart. **7.** A representative, as of a company. —*attributive.* Often used to modify another noun: *a woman athlete; a woman electrician.* **—*idioms.* (one's) own woman.** Independent in judgment or action: *She has always been her own woman.* **to a woman.** Without exception. [Middle English, from Old English *wimman,* variant of *wīfman* : *wīf,* woman + *man,* person; see MAN.]

woman about town *n., pl.* **women about town.** A sophisticated and socially active woman who frequents fashionable places.

wom·an·ful·ly (wo͝om′ən-fŭl′ē) *adv.* With the characteristic grace, strength, or purposefulness of a woman: *"I will trample . . . upon all the prickles of the impossibilities and flatten them womanfully"* (Maria Edgeworth).

wom·an·hood (wo͝om′ən-ho͝od′) *n.* **1.** The state or time of being a woman. **2.** The composite of qualities thought to be appropriate to or representative of women. **3.** Women considered as a group: *"The true worth of a race must be measured by the character of its womanhood"* (Mary McLeod Bethune).

wom·an·ish (wo͝om′ə-nĭsh) *adj.* **1.** Of, characteristic of, or natural to a woman. See Synonyms at **feminine. 2.** Resembling, imitative of, or suggestive of a woman. **—wom′an·ish·ly** *adv.* **—wom′an·ish·ness** *n.*

wom·an·ist (wo͝om′ən-ĭst) *adj.* Having or expressing a belief in or respect for women and their talents and abilities beyond the boundaries of race and class: *"Womanist . . . tradition assumes, because of our experiences during slavery, that black women already are capable"* (Alice Walker). **—womanist** *n.* One whose beliefs or actions are informed by womanist ideals. **—wom′an′ism** *n.*

wom·an·ize (wo͝om′ə-nīz′) *v.* **-ized, -iz·ing, -iz·es.** —*intr.* To pursue women lecherously. —*tr.* To give female characteristics to; feminize. **—wom′an·iz′er** *n.*

wom·an·kind (wo͝om′ən-kīnd′) *n.* Women considered as a group.

wom·an·like (wo͝om′ən-līk′) *adj.* **1.** Resembling a woman: *a womanlike stone image.* **2.** Belonging to or befitting a woman.

wom·an·ly (wo͝om′ən-lē) *adj.* **-li·er, -li·est. 1.** Having qualities generally attributed to a woman. **2.** Belonging to or representative of a woman; feminine: *womanly attire.* See Synonyms at **feminine.** —**wom′an·li·ness** *n.*

woman of the house *n., pl.* **women of the house.** The primary woman of a household.

woman of the world *n., pl.* **women of the world.** A sophisticated, worldly woman.

wom·an·pow·er (wo͝om′ən-pou′ər) *n.* Power in terms of the women available to a particular group or required for a particular task.

woman suffrage *n.* **1.** The right of women to vote; exercise of the franchise by women. **2.** A movement to promote and secure such rights.

wom·an-to-wom·an (wo͝om′ən-tə-wo͝om′ən) *adj.* Characterized by direct interaction between or among women: *woman-to-woman talks; a woman-to-woman conference.*

womb (wo͞om) *n.* **1.** See **uterus** (sense 1). **2.a.** A place where something is generated. **b.** An encompassing, protective hollow or space. **3.** *Obsolete.* The belly. [Middle English, from Old English *wamb.*] —**wombed** *adj.*

wom·bat (wŏm′băt′) *n.* Any of several stocky, burrowing, Australian marsupials of the family Vombatidae, resembling a small bear and feeding mainly on grass, leaves, and roots. [Dharuk (Aboriginal language of southeast Australia) *wambat*[y].]

wom·en (wĭm′ĭn) *n.* Plural of **woman.**

wom·en·folk (wĭm′ĭn-fōk′) also **wom·en·folks** (-fōks′) *pl.n.* **1.** Women considered as a group. **2.** The women of a community or family.

wom·en·kind (wĭm′ən-kīnd′) *n.* Womankind.

wom·en's movement (wĭm′ĭnz) *n.* A loosely organized movement in the United States beginning in the late 1960's and focusing chiefly on women's roles as wage earners, women's control of their own sexuality, an end to violence against women, and ratification of the Equal Rights Amendment: *"The women's movement brought new possibilities for social change, particularly for women"* (Art in America).

women's rights *pl.n.* **1.** Socioeconomic, political, and legal rights for all women equal to those of men. **2.** A movement in support of these rights.

women's room *n.* A restroom for women.

wom·en's studies also **Wom·en's Studies** (wĭm′ĭnz) *n.* *(used with a sing. or pl. verb).* An academic curriculum focusing on the roles and contributions of women in fields such as literature, history, and the social sciences.

women's wear *n.* Clothing for women.

wom·er·a (wŏm′ər-ə) *n.* Variant of **woomera.**

won¹ (wŭn, wŏn) *intr.v.* **wonned, won·ning, wons.** *Archaic.* To dwell or abide. [Middle English *wonen,* from Old English *wunian.* See **wen-¹** in Appendix.]

won² (wôn) *n., pl.* **won.** See table at **currency.** [Korean.]

won³ (wŭn) *v.* Past tense and past participle of **win.**

won·der (wŭn′dər) *n.* **1.a.** One that arouses awe, astonishment, surprise, or admiration; a marvel: *"The decision of one age or country is a wonder to another"* (John Stuart Mill). **b.** The emotion aroused by something awe-inspiring, astounding, or marvelous: *gazed with wonder at the northern lights.* **2.** An event inexplicable by the laws of nature; a miracle. **3.** A feeling of puzzlement or doubt. **4.** Often **Wonder.** A monumental human creation regarded with awe, especially one of seven monuments of the ancient world that appeared on various lists of late antiquity. —**wonder** *v.* **-dered, -der·ing, -ders.** —*intr.* **1.a.** To have a feeling of awe or admiration; marvel: *"She wondered at all the things civilization can teach a woman to endure"* (Frances Newman). **b.** To have a feeling of surprise. **2.** To be filled with curiosity or doubt. —*tr.* To feel curiosity or be in doubt about: *wondered what was going on.* —**wonder** *adj.* **1.a.** Arousing awe or admiration. **b.** Wonderful. **2.** Far superior to anything formerly recognized or foreseen. —***idiom.*** **for a wonder.** As a cause for surprise; surprisingly. [Middle English, from Old English *wundor.*] —**won′der·er** *n.*

SYNONYMS: *wonder, marvel, miracle, phenomenon, prodigy, sensation.* The central meaning shared by these nouns is "one that evokes amazement or admiration": *saw the wonders of Paris; a marvel of modern technology; a miracle of culinary art; organ transplantation, a phenomenon of medical science; a musical prodigy; a performance that was the sensation of the season.*

wonder drug *n.* See **miracle drug.**

won·der·ful (wŭn′dər-fəl) *adj.* **1.** Capable of eliciting wonder; astonishing: *"The . . . whale is one of the most wonderful animals in the world"* (Charles Darwin). **2.** Admirable; excellent: *"The spirit of the movement was wonderful. It was joyous and grave at the same time"* (Christabel Pankhurst). —**won′der·ful·ly** *adv.* —**won′der·ful·ness** *n.*

won·der·ing (wŭn′dər-ĭng) *adj.* Feeling or expressing awe, admiration, amazement, or surprise. —**won′der·ing·ly** *adv.*

won·der·land (wŭn′dər-lănd′) *n.* **1.** A marvelous imaginary realm. **2.** A marvelous real place or scene.

won·der·ment (wŭn′dər-mənt) *n.* **1.** Astonishment, awe, or surprise. **2.** Something that produces wonder; a marvel. **3.** Puzzlement or curiosity.

won·der·work (wŭn′dər-wûrk′) *n.* A marvelous or miraculous act, work, or achievement; a marvel. —**won′der·work′er** *n.* —**won′der·work′ing** *adj.*

won·drous (wŭn′drəs) *adj.* Remarkable or extraordinary; wonderful. —**wondrous** *adv. Archaic.* To a wonderful or remarkable extent. —**won′drous·ly** *adv.* —**won′drous·ness** *n.*

wonk (wŏngk) *n. Slang.* A student who studies excessively; a grind. [Origin unknown.]

won·ky (wŏng′kē) *adj.* **-ki·er, -ki·est.** *Chiefly British.* **1.** Shaky; feeble. **2.** Wrong; awry. [Probably alteration of dialectal *wanky,* alteration of *wankle,* from Middle English *wankel,* from Old English *wancol,* unsteady.]

Won·san (wŭn′sän′). A city of southeast North Korea on the Sea of Japan east of Pyongyang. Opened to foreign trade in 1883, it is a major port and naval base. Population, 350,000.

wont (wônt, wōnt, wŭnt) *adj.* **1.** Accustomed or used: *"The poor man is wont to complain that this is a cold world"* (Henry David Thoreau). **2.** Likely: *chaotic as holidays are wont to be.* —**wont** *n.* Customary practice; usage. See Synonyms at **habit.** —**wont** *v.* **wont** or **wont·ed, wont·ing, wonts.** —*tr.* To make accustomed to. —*intr.* To be in the habit of doing something. [Middle English, past participle of *wonen,* to be used to, dwell. See WON¹.]

won't (wōnt). Will not.

wont·ed (wôn′tĭd, wōn′-, wŭn′-) *adj.* Accustomed; usual: *striding along with her wonted purposefulness.* —**wont′ed·ly** *adv.* —**wont′ed·ness** *n.*

won ton or **won·ton** (wŏn′tŏn′) *n.* **1.** A noodle-dough dumpling filled typically with spiced minced pork or other ground meat, usually boiled in soup or fried and eaten as a side dish. **2.** Soup containing such dumplings. [Chinese (Cantonese) *wan tan.*]

woo (wo͞o) *v.* **wooed, woo·ing, woos.** —*tr.* **1.** To seek the affection of with intent to romance. **2.a.** To seek to achieve; try to gain. **b.** To tempt or invite. **3.** To entreat, solicit, or importune. —*intr.* To court a woman. Used of a man. [Middle English *wowen,* from Old English *wōgian.*] —**woo′er** *n.*

wood¹ (wo͝od) *n. Abbr.* **wd. 1.a.** The secondary xylem of trees and shrubs, lying beneath the bark and consisting largely of cellulose and lignin. **b.** This tissue, often cut and dried especially for use as building material and fuel. **2.** Often **woods.** A dense growth of trees; a forest. **3.** An object made of wood, especially: **a.** *Music.* A woodwind. **b.** *Sports.* A golf club used to hit long shots, having a wooden head numbered one to five in order of increasing loft. —**wood** *v.* **wood·ed, wood·ing, woods.** —*tr.* **1.** To fuel with wood. **2.** To cover with trees; forest. —*intr.* To gather or be supplied with wood. —**wood** *adj.* **1.** Made or consisting of wood; wooden. **2.** Used or suitable for cutting, storing, or working with wood. **3. woods.** Living, growing, or present in forests: *woods animals; a woods path.* —***idiom.*** **out of the woods.** *Informal.* Free of a difficult or hazardous situation. [Middle English *wode,* from Old English *wudu.*]

wood² (wo͝od) *adj. Archaic.* Mentally unbalanced; insane. [Middle English, from Old English *wōd.* See **wet-¹** in Appendix.]

Wood (wo͝od), **Grant.** 1892–1942. American artist noted for his paintings based on life in the Midwest, especially *American Gothic* (1930).

Wood, Leonard. 1860–1927. American military leader who was chief of staff of the U.S. Army (1910–1914) and governor-general of the Philippines (1921–1927).

wood alcohol *n.* See **methanol.**

wood anemone *n.* Either of two plants, *Anemone quinquefolia* of eastern North America or *A. nemorosa* of Eurasia, having deeply divided leaves and a solitary, showy, white to crimson flower.

wood betony *n.* See **lousewort.**

wood·bin (wo͝od′bĭn′) *n.* A box for holding firewood.

wood·bine (wo͝od′bīn′) *n.* **1.** Any of various climbing vines, especially a Mediterranean honeysuckle *(Lonicera periclymenum)* having yellowish flowers. **2.** See **Virginia creeper.** [Middle English *wodebinde,* from Old English *wudubinde* : *wudu,* wood + *binde,* wreath (from *bindan,* to bind; see **bhendh-** in Appendix).]

wood·block (wo͝od′blŏk′) *n.* **1.** See **woodcut. 2.** Also **wood block.** *Music.* A hollow block of wood struck with a drumstick to produce percussive effects in an orchestra.

wood·bor·er (wo͝od′bôr′ər, -bōr′ər) *n.* Any of various insects, insect larvae, or mollusks that bore into wood. —**wood′bor′ing** *adj.*

Wood·bridge (wo͝od′brĭj′). **1.** A city of northeast New Jersey south-southwest of Elizabeth. Settled in 1665, it is an industrial center. Population, 16,400. **2.** A community of northwest Virginia, a suburb of Washington, D.C. Population, 35,000.

Wood·bur·y (wo͝od′bĕr′ē, -bə-rē), **Helen Laura Sumner.** 1876–1933. American social economist noted for her studies of labor and woman suffrage.

Woodbury, Levi. 1789–1851. American jurist who served as an associate justice of the U.S. Supreme Court (1845–1851).

wood·carv·ing (wo͝od′kär′vĭng) *n.* **1.** The art of creating or decorating objects of wood by carving with a sharp, hand-held tool. **2.** A carved wood object. —**wood′carv′er** *n.*

wood·chat (wo͝od′chăt′) *n.* An Old World shrike *(Lanius senator)* having black and white plumage with a reddish crown.

wood·chop·per (wo͝od′chŏp′ər) *n.* One who chops wood, especially one who chops down trees. —**wood′chop′ping** *n.*

♦**wood·chuck** (wo͝od′chŭk′) *n.* A common burrowing rodent

wombat
Common wombat
Vombatus ursinus

woodchuck
Marmota monax

ă pat	oi boy
ā pay	ou out
âr care	o͝o took
ä father	o͞o boot
ĕ pet	ŭ cut
ē be	ûr urge
ĭ pit	th thin
ī pie	*th* this
îr pier	hw which
ŏ pot	zh vision
ō toe	ə about, item
ô paw	♦ regionalism

Stress marks: **′** (primary); ′ (secondary), as in **dictionary** (dĭk′shə-nĕr′ē)

(Marmota monax) of northern and eastern North America, having a short-legged, heavy-set body and grizzled brownish fur. Also called *groundhog,* ♦*whistle pig.* [By folk etymology, probably of New England Algonquian origin.]

♦ ***REGIONAL NOTE:*** The woodchuck goes by several names in the United States. The most famous of these is *groundhog,* under which name all the legends about the animal's hibernation have accrued. In the Appalachian Mountains the woodchuck is known as a *whistle pig.* The word *woodchuck* is probably a folk etymology of a New England Algonquian word—that is, English-speaking settlers "translated" the Indian word into a compound of two words that made sense to them in light of the animal's habitat.

Victoria Woodhull

wood coal *n.* **1.** Charcoal. **2.** Lignite.

wood·cock (wo͝od′kŏk′) *n., pl.* **woodcock** or **-cocks.** Either of two related game birds, *Scolopax rusticola* of the Old World or *Philohela minor* of North America, having brownish plumage, short legs, and a long bill.

wood·craft (wo͝od′krăft′) *n.* **1.** Skill and experience in matters relating to the woods, as hunting, fishing, or camping. **2.** The act, process, or art of carving or fashioning objects from wood.

wood·craft·er (wo͝od′krăf′tər) *n.* One who carves or fashions objects from wood. —**wood′craft′ing** *n.*

wood·cut (wo͝od′kŭt′) *n.* **1.** A block of wood on whose surface a design for printing is engraved along the grain. **2.** A print made from a woodcut. Also called *woodblock, woodprint.*

wood·cut·ter (wo͝od′kŭt′ər) *n.* One that cuts wood.

wood·cut·ting (wo͝od′kŭt′ĭng) *n.* **1.** The act, activity, or job of cutting wood. **2.** The art or process of making woodcuts.

wood duck *n.* A brightly colored American duck *(Aix sponsa)* that nests in hollow trees and the male of which is noted for its large crest.

wood·ed (wo͝od′ĭd) *adj.* Covered with trees or woods: *a wooded area near the highway; a heavily wooded tract.*

wood·en (wo͝od′n) *adj.* **1.** Made or consisting of wood. **2.** Stiff and unnatural; without spirit: *a wooden performance; a wooden smile.* **3.** Clumsy and awkward; ungainly. —**wood′en·ly** *adv.* —**wood′en·ness** *n.*

woodpecker
Common flicker
Colaptes auratus

wood engraving *n.* **1.a.** A block of wood on whose surface a design for printing is engraved across the end grain. **b.** A print made from a wood engraving. **2.** The art or process of making wood engravings.

wood·en·head (wo͝od′n-hĕd′) *n.* A person regarded as stupid. —**wood′en-head′ed** *adj.*

wooden Indian *n.* A cigar-store Indian.

wood·en·ware (wo͝od′n-wâr′) *n.* Articles, such as kitchenware, furniture, or ornaments, made of wood.

wood frog *n.* A North American frog *(Rana sylvatica)* that inhabits damp woodlands and has a brown masklike patch running from snout to ears.

wood grouse *n.* See **capercaillie.**

wood hoopoe *n.* Any of several tropical and southern African birds of the family Phoeniculidae, similar to the hoopoe but having metallic plumage, long graduated tails, and no crest.

Wood·hull (wo͝od′hŭl′), **Victoria Clafin.** 1838–1927. American reformer. An outspoken advocate of woman suffrage and free love, she was the first woman to run for the U.S. presidency (1872).

wood hyacinth *n.* See **bluebell** (sense 1).

wood ibis *n.* Any of several large, mainly white wading birds of the subfamily Mycteriinae, related to and resembling the storks, especially the New World species *Mycteria americana,* which inhabits wooded areas of tropical and subtropical America. Also called *flinthead, wood stork.*

wood·ie (wo͝od′ē) *n.* Variant of **woody²**.

wood·land (wo͝od′lənd, -lănd′) *n.* Land having a cover of trees and shrubs. —**woodland** *adj.* **1.** Of, relating to, or constituting woodland. **2.** Living, growing, or present in woodland: *woodland flowers.* —**wood′land·er** (-lən-dər) *n.*

Wood·land (wo͝od′lənd). A city of north-central California west-northwest of Sacramento. It is a manufacturing center in an agricultural area. Population, 30,235.

woodland caribou *n.* A large dark brown caribou with a light muzzle and heavily palmate antlers, inhabiting forested areas of Canada and the northwest United States.

wood·lark (wo͝od′lärk′) *n.* An Old World songbird *(Lullula arborea)* resembling the skylark.

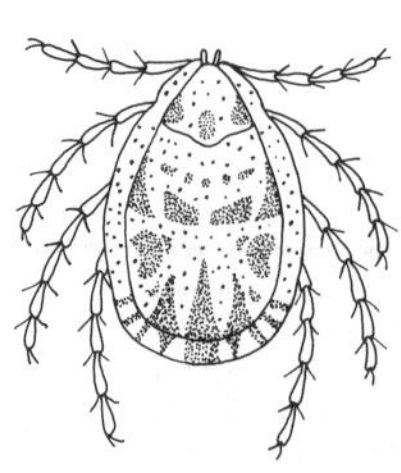

wood tick
Rocky Mountain wood tick
Dermacentor andersoni

wood lot or **wood·lot** (wo͝od′lŏt′) *n.* A usually private area restricted to the growing of forest trees, especially for building material or fuel.

wood louse *n.* See **sow bug.**

wood·man (wo͝od′mən) *n.* A woodsman.

Wood·mere (wo͝od′mîr). A town of southeast New York on western Long Island. It is mainly residential. Population, 19,700.

wood mouse *n.* A mouse, such as a deer mouse, that commonly lives in woodlands.

wood·note (wo͝od′nōt′) *n.* **1.** A song or call characteristic of a woodland bird. **2.** Natural, spontaneous verbal utterance.

wood nymph *n.* **1.** A nymph of the forest; a dryad. **2.** Any of several tropical hummingbirds of the genera *Thalurania* and *Cyanophaia.* **3.** Any of various butterflies of the family Satyridae, especially *Cercyonis pegala,* having brownish wings with dark eyespots.

♦**wood·peck·er** (wo͝od′pĕk′ər) *n.* Any of various usually brightly colored birds of the family Picidae, having strong claws and a stiff tail adapted for clinging to and climbing trees and a chisellike bill for drilling through bark and wood. Also called ♦*peckerwood.*

wood pewee *n.* Either of two small pewees, *Contopus virens* of the eastern United States or *C. sordidulus* of western North America, living in wooded areas.

wood pigeon *n.* A large pigeon *(Columba palumbus)* of Europe and Asia, having a white band on each wing. Also called *ringdove.*

wood·pile (wo͝od′pīl′) *n.* A pile of wood, especially when used for fuel.

wood·print (wo͝od′prĭnt′) *n.* See **woodcut.**

wood pulp *n.* Pulp made from wood, used especially to make paper.

wood pussy *n. Slang.* A skunk.

wood rabbit *n.* See **cottontail.**

wood rat *n.* See **pack rat** (sense 1).

Wood·ridge (wo͝od′rĭj′). A village of northeast Illinois west of Chicago. Population, 22,322.

wood·ruff (wo͝od′rəf, -rŭf′) *n.* **1.** A fragrant perennial herb *(Galium odoratum)* native to Eurasia and North Africa and widely cultivated as a shade ground cover, having small white flowers and narrow leaves used for flavoring wine and in sachets. Also called *sweet woodruff.* **2.** Any of various plants of the genus *Asperula,* having whorled leaves and small funnel-shaped flowers. [Middle English *woderofe,* from Old English *wudurofe* : *wudu,* wood + *-rofe,* of unknown meaning.]

Woods (wo͝odz), **Lake of the.** A lake of southwest Ontario and southwest Manitoba, Canada, and northern Minnesota.

Woods, William Burnham. 1824–1887. American jurist who served as an associate justice of the U.S. Supreme Court (1880–1887).

♦**woods colt** (wo͝odz) *n. Chiefly Southern U.S.* See **old-field colt.** See Regional Note at **old-field colt.**

wood·shed (wo͝od′shĕd′) *n.* A shed in which firewood is stored. —**woodshed** *intr.v.* **-shed·ded, -shed·ding, -sheds.** *Slang.* To practice on a musical instrument.

wood shot *n. Sports.* **1.** A golf shot made with a wood. **2.** A stroke in racket games made with the frame of the racket instead of the strings.

wood·si·a (wo͝od′zē-ə) *n.* Any of several small tufted ferns of the genus *Woodsia,* having pinnately divided fronds and growing in cool, rocky areas. [After Joseph *Woods* (1776–1864), British botanist.]

woods·man (wo͝odz′mən) *n.* A man who works or lives in the woods or is versed in woodcraft; a forester.

wood sorrel *n.* See **oxalis.**

wood spirits *pl.n. (used with a sing. or pl. verb).* See **methanol.**

Wood·stock (wo͝od′stŏk′). **1.** A city of southern Ontario, Canada, on the Thames River west-southwest of Toronto. It is a manufacturing center. Population, 26,603. **2.** A village of southeast New York south-southwest of Albany. In 1969 a large rock music festival named after the village was held at another small town in the Catskill Mountains. Population, 1,073.

wood stork *n.* See **wood ibis.**

wood sugar *n.* See **xylose.**

woods·y (wo͝od′zē) *adj.* **-i·er, -i·st.** Of, relating to, characteristic of, or suggestive of the woods.

wood tar *n.* A viscous black fluid that is a byproduct of the destructive distillation of wood and is used in pitch, preservatives, and medicines.

wood thrush *n.* A large, plump thrush *(Hylocichla mustelina)* of wooded areas of eastern North America, having a reddish-brown head and a spotted, cream-colored breast.

wood tick *n.* Any of various ticks of the genus *Dermacentor,* which transmit the microorganism that causes Rocky Mountain spotted fever and tularemia in human beings.

wood·turn·ing (wo͝od′tûr′nĭng) *n.* The art or process of shaping wood into forms on a lathe. —**wood′turn′er** *n.*

wood vinegar *n.* See **pyroligneous acid.**

wood warbler *n.* See **warbler** (sense 1).

Wood·ward (wo͝od′wərd), **C(omer) Vann.** Born 1908. American historian whose works include *Origins of the New South* (1951) and *The Strange Career of Jim Crow* (1955).

Woodward, Robert Burns. 1917–1979. American chemist. He won a 1965 Nobel Prize for work in synthesizing complicated organic compounds.

wood·wax·en (wo͝od′wăk′sən) *n.* See **dyer's greenweed.** [Middle English *wodewaxen,* from Old English *wuduweaxe* : *wudu,* wood + *weaxan,* to grow; see WAX².]

wood·wind (wo͝od′wĭnd′) *n. Music.* **1.** A wind instrument, such as a bassoon, clarinet, flute, oboe, or saxophone, in which sound is produced by the vibration of reeds in or by the passing of air across the mouthpiece. **2. woodwinds. a.** The section of a band or an orchestra composed of woodwind instruments. **b.**

Woodwind instruments or their players considered as a group.

wood·work (wo͝od′wûrk′) *n.* Objects made of or work done in wood, especially wooden interior fittings in a house, as moldings, doors, staircases, or windowsills. —***idiom.* out of the woodwork.** Out of obscurity or a place of seclusion: *People were coming out of the woodwork to apply for the plummy job.*

wood·work·ing (wo͝od′wûr′kĭng) *n.* The act, art, or trade of working with wood. —*attributive.* Often used to modify another noun: *a woodworking shop; woodworking tools.* —**wood′work′er** *n.*

wood·worm (wo͝od′wûrm′) *n.* A worm or an insect larva that bores into wood.

wood·y¹ (wo͝od′ē) *adj.* **-i·er, -i·est. 1.** Forming or consisting of wood; ligneous: *woody tissue.* **2.** Marked by the presence of wood or xylem: *woody plants.* **3.** Characteristic or suggestive of wood: *a woody smell.* **4.** Abounding in trees; wooded.

wood·y² Also **wood·ie** (wo͝od′ē) *n., pl.* **-ies.** A station wagon with exterior wood paneling. —**wood′i·ness** *n.*

woof¹ (wo͝of, wo͞of) *n.* **1.** The threads that run crosswise in a woven fabric, at right angles to the warp threads. **2.** The texture of a fabric. [Alteration (influenced by WARP) of Middle English *oof,* from Old English *ōwef* : *ō-, on,* on; see ON + *wefan,* to weave; see **webh-** in Appendix.]

woof² (wo͝of) *n.* **1.** The characteristically deep, gruff bark of a dog. **2.** A sound similar to a woof. —**woof** *intr.v.* **woofed, woof·ing, woofs.** To make this sound. [Imitative.]

woof·er (wo͝of′ər) *n.* A loudspeaker designed to reproduce bass frequencies. [From WOOF².]

wool (wo͝ol) *n.* **1.a.** The dense, soft, often curly hair forming the coat of sheep and certain other mammals, such as the goat and alpaca, consisting of cylindrical fibers of keratin covered by minute overlapping scales and much valued as a textile fabric. **b.** A material or garment made of this hair. **2.** The furry hair of some insect larvae, such as the caterpillar. **3.** A filamentous or fibrous covering or substance suggestive of the texture of true wool. [Middle English *wolle,* from Old English *wull.*] —**wool** *adj.*

wool·en also **wool·len** (wo͝ol′ən) —*adj.* **1.** Made or consisting of wool. **2.** Of or relating to the production or marketing of woolen goods. —*n.* Fabric or clothing made from wool. Often used in the plural.

Woolf (wo͝olf), **(Adeline) Virginia (Stephen).** 1882–1941. British writer whose works include fiction written in an experimental stream-of-consciousness style, such as *Mrs. Dalloway* (1925) and *To the Lighthouse* (1927), and collections of essays, such as *A Room of One's Own* (1929).

wool fat *n.* **1.** See **wool grease. 2.** See **lanolin.**

wool·gath·er (wo͝ol′găth′ər) *intr.v.* **-ered, -er·ing, -ers.** To engage in fanciful daydreaming. —**wool′gath′er·er** *n.*

wool·gath·er·ing (wo͝ol′găth′ər-ĭng) *n.* Indulgence in fanciful daydreams. —**woolgathering** *adj.* Indulging in fanciful daydreams.

wool grease *n.* A fatty, pale yellow wax that coats the fibers of sheep's wool and yields lanolin. Also called *wool fat.*

wool·grow·er (wo͝ol′grō′ər) *n.* One that raises sheep or other animals for the production of wool. —**wool′grow′ing** *n.*

Wooll·cott (wo͝ol′kət, -kŏt′), **Alexander.** 1887–1943. American drama critic and journalist whose collections of essays include *While Rome Burns* (1934) and *Long, Long Ago* (1943).

wool·len (wo͝ol′ən) *adj. & n.* Variant of **woolen.**

Wool·ley (wo͝ol′ē), Sir **Charles Leonard.** 1880–1960. British archaeologist who led excavations at Carchemish (1912–1914 and 1919) and Ur (1922–1934).

wool·ly also **wool·y** (wo͝ol′ē) —*adj.* **-li·er, -li·est** also **-i·er, -i·est. 1.a.** Relating to, consisting of, or covered with wool. **b.** Resembling wool. **2.a.** Lacking sharp detail or clarity: *woolly television reception.* **b.** Mentally or intellectually disorganized or unclear: *woolly thinking.* **3.** Having the characteristics of the rough, generally lawless atmosphere of the American frontier: *wild and woolly.* —*n., pl.* **-lies** also **-ies. 1.** A garment made of wool, especially an undergarment of knitted wool. **2.** *Australia.* A sheep. —**wool′li·ness** *n.*

woolly bear *n.* The hairy caterpillar of any of various moths, especially that of the North American tiger moth *Isia isabella,* having a reddish-brown middle stripe and black at either end.

wool·ly-head·ed (wo͝ol′ē-hĕd′ĭd) *adj.* **1.** Having hair that looks or feels like wool. **2.** Vague or muddled: *wooly-headed ideas.*

wool·sack (wo͝ol′săk′) *n.* **1.** A sack for wool. **2.** The official seat of the Lord Chancellor in the House of Lords.

wool shed *n.* A building or complex of buildings in which sheep are sheared and wool is prepared for shipment to market.

wool·skin (wo͝ol′skĭn′) *n.* A sheepskin with the wool still on it.

wool-sort·er's disease (wo͝ol′sôr′tərz) *n.* A pulmonary form of anthrax that results from the inhalation of spores of the bacterium *Bacillus anthracis* in the wool of contaminated sheep.

wool-sta·pler (wo͝ol′stā′plər) *n.* **1.** A dealer in wool. **2.** One who sorts wool by the quality of the staple or fiber. —**wool′-sta′pling** *adj. & n.*

Wool·worth (wo͝ol′wûrth′), **Frank Winfield.** 1852–1919. American merchant. Starting in 1879, he built a successful national chain of five-and-tens.

wool·y (wo͝ol′ē) *adj. & n.* Variant of **woolly.**

woom·er·a (wo͞om′ər-ə) also **wom·er·a** (wŏm′-) *n.* A hooked wooden stick used by aboriginal peoples of Australia for hurling a spear or dart. [Dharuk (Aboriginal language of southeast Australia) *wumara.*]

Woon·sock·et (wo͞on-sŏk′ĭt, wo͞on′sŏk′-). A city of northern Rhode Island north-northwest of Providence near the Massachusetts border. It was settled c. 1666. Population, 45,914.

woops (wo͝ops, wo͞ops) *interj.* Variant of **whoops.**

Woo·ster (wo͝os′tər). A city of north-central Ohio southwest of Akron. It is a manufacturing center. Population, 19,289.

wooz·y (wo͞o′zē, wo͝oz′ē) *adj.* **-i·er, -i·est. 1.** Dazed or confused. **2.** Dizzy or queasy. [Possibly from alteration of *boozy,* drunken, from BOOZE.] —**wooz′i·ly** *adv.* —**wooz′i·ness** *n.*

wop (wŏp) *n. Offensive Slang.* Used as a disparaging term for an Italian. [Italian dialectal *guappo,* thug, from Spanish *guapo,* handsome, dashing, braggart, bully, from French dialectal *wape,* rogue, from Latin *vappa,* flat wine, scoundrel.]

Worces·ter¹ (wo͝os′tər). **1.** A borough of west-central England on the Severn River south-southwest of Birmingham. Oliver Cromwell and the Parliamentarian army gained their final victory over Charles II and the Scottish army here on September 3, 1651. Population, 73,900. **2.** A city of central Massachusetts west of Boston. Population, 161,799.

Worces·ter² (wo͝os′tər). A trademark used for a fine porcelain made in Worcester, England.

Worcester, Joseph Emerson. 1784–1865. American lexicographer. The publication of his *Comprehensive Pronouncing and Explanatory Dictionary of the English Language* (1830) brought charges of plagiarism from Noah Webster and started the battle known as the "Dictionary War."

Worces·ter·shire (wo͝os′tər-shîr, -shər) *n.* A piquant sauce of soy, vinegar, and spices.

word (wûrd) *n. Abbr.* **wd. 1.** A sound or a combination of sounds, or its representation in writing or printing, that symbolizes and communicates a meaning and may consist of a single morpheme or of a combination of morphemes. **2.** Something said; an utterance, a remark, or a comment: *May I say a word about that?* **3.** *Computer Science.* A set of bits constituting the smallest unit of addressable memory. **4. words.** Discourse or talk; speech: *Actions speak louder than words.* **5. words.** *Music.* The text of a vocal composition; lyrics. **6.** An assurance or a promise; sworn intention: *She has kept her word.* **7.a.** A command or direction; an order: *gave the word to retreat.* **b.** A verbal signal; a password or watchword. **8.a.** News: *Any word on your promotion?* See Synonyms at **news. b.** Rumor: *Word has it they're divorcing.* **9. words.** Hostile or angry remarks made back and forth. **10. Word. a.** See **Logos** (sense 3). **b.** The Scriptures; the Bible. —**word** *tr.v.* **word·ed, word·ing, words.** To express in words: *worded the petition carefully.* —***idioms.* at a word.** In immediate response. **good word. 1.** A favorable comment: *She put in a good word for me.* **2.** Favorable news. **have no words for.** To be unable to describe or talk about. **in a word.** In short; in summary: *In a word, the situation is serious.* **in so many words. 1.** In precisely those words; exactly: *hinted at impending indictments but did not say it in so many words.* **2.** Speaking candidly and straightforwardly: *In so many words, the weather has been beastly.* **of few words.** Not conversational or loquacious; laconic: *a person of few words.* **of (one's) word.** Displaying personal dependability: *a woman of her word.* **take at (one's) word.** To be convinced of another's sincerity and act in accord with his or her statement: *We had to take them at their word that the job would be done on time.* **upon my word.** Indeed; really. [Middle English, from Old English. See **wer-⁵** in Appendix.]

word·age (wûr′dĭj) *n.* **1.** Words considered as a group. **2.** The use of an excessive number of words; verbiage. **3.** The number of words used, as in a novel. **4.** Wording.

word association test *n. Psychology.* A test in which the subject is asked to respond to a given word with the first word that comes to mind or with a predetermined type of word, such as an antonym.

word blindness *n.* See **alexia.** —**word′-blind′** (wûrd′blīnd′) *adj.*

word·book (wûrd′bo͝ok′) *n.* A lexicon, vocabulary, or dictionary.

word deafness *n.* A form of aphasia in which the meaning of ordinary spoken words becomes incomprehensible.

word for word *adv.* In exactly the same words; verbatim. —**word′-for-word′** (wûrd′fər-wûrd′) *adj.*

word-hoard (wûrd′hôrd′, -hōrd′) *n.* The sum of words one uses or understands; a vocabulary.

word·ing (wûr′dĭng) *n.* The act or style of expressing in words. See Synonyms at **diction.**

word·less (wûrd′lĭs) *adj.* **1.** Not expressed in words; unspoken. *wordless animosity; wordless joy.* **2.** Inarticulate; silent: *wordless spectators.* —**word′less·ly** *adv.* —**word′less·ness** *n.*

word·mon·ger (wûrd′mŭng′gər, -mŏng′-) *n.* A writer or speaker who uses language pretentiously or carelessly. —**word′mon′ger·ing** *n.*

word of mouth *n.* Spoken communication: *News of their success spread by word of mouth.* —**word′-of-mouth′** (wûrd′-əv-mouth′) *adj.*

woofer

Virginia Woolf
Photographed in 1902 by George Charles Beresford (1864–1938)

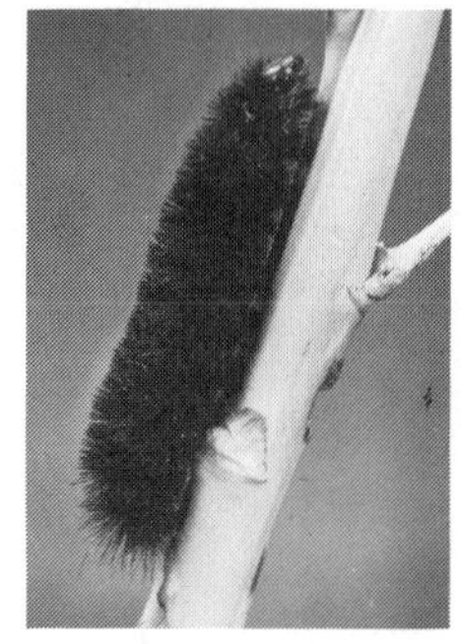

woolly bear
Isabella tiger moth caterpillar
Pyrrharctia isabella

ă pat	oi boy
ā pay	ou out
âr care	o͝o took
ä father	o͞o boot
ĕ pet	ŭ cut
ē be	ûr urge
ĭ pit	th thin
ī pie	*th* this
îr pier	hw which
ŏ pot	zh vision
ō toe	ə about, item
ô paw	♦ regionalism

Stress marks: **′** (primary); ′ (secondary), as in **dictionary** (dĭk′shə-nĕr′ē)

word order *n.* The syntactic arrangement of words in a sentence, clause, or phrase.

word•play or **word play** (wûrd′plā′) *n.* **1.** Witty or clever verbal exchange; repartee. **2.** The act or an instance of playing on words.

word proc•ess•ing (prŏs′ĕs′ĭng, prō′sĕs′-) *n. Abbr.* **WP** *Computer Science.* The creation, input, editing, and production of documents and texts by means of computer systems. **—word′-proc′ess** (wûrd′prŏs′ĕs, -prō′sĕs) *v.* **—word′-proc′ess•ing** *adj.*

word processor *n. Abbr.* **WP** *Computer Science.* A computer system either specially designed for or capable of word processing.

word•smith (wûrd′smĭth′) *n.* **1.** A fluent and prolific writer, especially one who writes professionally. **2.** An expert on words.

word square *n. Games.* A set of words arranged in a square such that they read the same horizontally and vertically. Also called *acrostic.*

Words•worth (wûrdz′wûrth′), **William.** 1770–1850. British poet whose most important collection, *Lyrical Ballads* (1798), published jointly with Samuel Taylor Coleridge, helped establish romanticism in England. **—Words•worth′i•an** *adj.*

word•y (wûr′dē) *adj.* **-i•er, -i•est. 1.** Relating to or consisting of words; verbal. **2.** Tending to use, using, or expressed in more words than are necessary to convey meaning. **—word′i•ly** *adv.* **—word′i•ness** *n.*

SYNONYMS: *wordy, diffuse, long-winded, prolix, verbose.* The central meaning shared by these adjectives is "given to using or marked by the use of an excessive number of words": *a wordy apology; a diffuse historical novel; a long-winded speaker; a prolix, tedious lecturer; verbose correspondence.*

wore (wôr, wōr) *v.* Past tense of **wear.**

work (wûrk) *n. Abbr.* **wk. 1.** Physical or mental effort or activity directed toward the production or accomplishment of something. **2.a.** A job; employment: *looking for work.* **b.** A trade, profession, or other means of livelihood. **3.a.** Something that one is doing, making, or performing, especially as an occupation or undertaking; a duty or task: *begin the day's work.* **b.** An amount of such activity either done or required: *a week's work.* **4.a.** The part of a day devoted to an occupation or undertaking: *met her after work.* **b.** One's place of employment: *Should I call you at home or at work?* **5.a.** Something that has been produced or accomplished through the effort, activity, or agency of a person or thing: *This story is the work of an active imagination. Erosion is the work of wind, water, and time.* **b.** Full action or effect of an agency: *The sleeping pills did their work.* **c.** An act; a deed: *"I have seen all the works that are done under the sun; and, behold, all is vanity"* (Ecclesiastes 1:14). **6.a.** An artistic creation, such as a painting, sculpture, or literary or musical composition; a work of art. **b. works.** The output of a writer, an artist, or a musician considered or collected as a whole: *the works of Shakespeare.* **7.a. works.** Engineering structures, such as bridges or dams. **b.** A fortified structure, such as a trench or fortress. **8.a.** Needlework, weaving, lacemaking, or a similar textile art. **b.** A piece of such textile art. **9.** A material or piece of material being processed in a machine during manufacture: *work to be turned in the lathe.* **10. works** *(used with a sing. or pl. verb).* A factory, plant, or similar building or complex of buildings where a specific type of business or industry is carried on. Often used in combination: *a steelworks.* **11. works.** Internal mechanism: *the works of a watch.* **12.** The manner, style, or quality of working or treatment; workmanship. **13.** *Abbr.* **w** *Physics.* The transfer of energy from one physical system to another, especially the transfer of energy to a body by the application of a force that moves the body in the direction of the force. It is calculated as the product of the force and the distance through which the body moves and is expressed in joules, ergs, and foot-pounds. **14. works.** *Theology.* Moral or righteous acts or deeds: *salvation by faith rather than works.* **15. works. a.** *Informal.* The full range of possibilities; everything. Used with *the*: *ordered a pizza with the works.* **b.** *Slang.* A thorough beating or other severe treatment. Used with *the*: *took him outside and gave him the works.* **—work** *adj.* Of, relating to, designed for, or engaged in work. **—work** *v.* **worked** also **wrought** (rôt), **work•ing, works.** *—intr.* **1.** To exert oneself physically or mentally in order to do, make, or accomplish something. **2.** To be employed; have a job. **3.a.** To function; operate: *How does this latch work?* **b.** To function or operate in the desired or required way: *The telephone hasn't worked since the thunderstorm.* **4.a.** To have a given effect or outcome: *Our friendship works best when we speak our minds.* **b.** To have the desired effect or outcome; prove successful: *This recipe seems to work.* **5.** To exert an influence. Used with *on* or *upon*: *worked on her to join the group.* **6.** To arrive at a specified condition through gradual or repeated movement: *The stitches worked loose.* **7.** To proceed or progress slowly and laboriously: *worked through the underbrush.* **8.** To move in an agitated manner, as with emotion: *Her mouth worked with fear.* **9.** To behave in a specified way when handled or processed: *Not all metals work easily.* **10.** To ferment. **11.** *Nautical.* **a.** To strain in heavy seas so that the joints give slightly and the fastenings become slack. Used of a boat or ship. **b.** To sail against the wind. **12.** To undergo small motions that result in friction and wear: *The gears work against each other.* *—tr.* **1.** To cause or effect; bring about: *working miracles.* **2.** To cause to operate or function; actuate, use, or manage: *worked the controls; can work a lathe.* **3.** To shape or forge: *worked the metal into a sculpture.* **4.** To make or decorate by needlework: *work a sampler.* **5.** To solve (a problem) by calculation and reasoning. **6.** To knead, stir, or otherwise manipulate in preparation: *Work the dough before shaping it.* **7.** To bring to a specified condition by gradual or repeated effort or work: *finally worked the window open; worked the slaves to death.* **8.** To make, achieve, or pay for by work or effort: *worked her way to the top; worked his passage on the ship.* **9.** *Informal.* To arrange or contrive. Often used with *it*: *worked it so that her weekends are free.* **10.** To make productive; cultivate: *work a farm.* **11.** To cause to work: *works his laborers hard.* **12.** To excite or provoke: *worked the mob into a frenzy.* **13.** *Informal.* **a.** To gratify, cajole, or enchant artfully, especially for the purpose of influencing: *The politician worked the crowd. The comedian worked the room with flawless rhythm.* **b.** To use or manipulate to one's own advantage; exploit: *learned how to work the system; worked his relatives for sympathy.* **14.** To carry on an operation or a function in or through: *the agent who works that area; working the phones for donations.* **15.** To ferment (liquor, for example). ***—phrasal verbs.*** **work in. 1.** To insert or introduce: *worked in a request for money.* **2.** To make an opening for, as in a schedule: *said the doctor would try to work her in.* **3.** To cause to be inserted by repeated or continuous effort. **work into. 1.** To insert or introduce into. **2.** To make an opening for (someone or something) in: *worked a few field trips into the semester's calendar.* **3.** To cause to be inserted in by repeated or continuous effort: *worked the pick into the lock.* **work off.** To get rid of by work or effort: *work off extra pounds; work off a debt.* **work out. 1.** To accomplish by work or effort. **2.** To find a solution for; solve: *worked out the equations; worked out their personal differences.* **3.** To formulate or develop: *work out a plan.* **4.** To discharge (an obligation or a debt) with labor in place of money. **5.** To prove successful, effective, or satisfactory: *The new strategy may not work out.* **6.** To have a specified result: *The ratio works out to an odd number. It worked out that everyone left on the same train.* **7.** To engage in strenuous exercise for physical conditioning. **8.** To exhaust (a mine, for example). **work over. 1.** To do for a second time; rework. **2.** *Slang.* To inflict severe physical damage on; beat up. **work up. 1.** To arouse the emotions of; excite. **2.a.** To increase one's skill, responsibility, efficiency, or status through work: *worked up to 30 sit-ups a day; worked up to store manager.* **b.** To intensify gradually: *The film works up to a thrilling climax.* **3.** To develop or produce by mental or physical effort: *worked up a patient profile; worked up an appetite.* ***—idioms.*** **at work. 1.** Engaged in labor; working: *I'm at work on a new project now.* **2.** In operation: *inflationary forces at work in the economy.* **in the works.** In preparation; under development: *has a novel in the works.* **out of work.** Without a job; unemployed. **put in work.** To perform labor or duties, as on a specified project: *put in work on the plastering.* **work both sides of the street.** To engage in double-dealing; be duplicitous. **work like a charm.** To function very well or have a very good effect or outcome. **work (one's) fingers to the bone.** To labor extremely hard; toil or travail. [Middle English, from Old English *weorc.* See **werg-** in Appendix.]

SYNONYMS: *work, labor, toil, drudgery, travail.* These nouns refer to physical or mental effort expended to produce or accomplish something. *Work* is the most widely applicable; it can refer both to the activity and the output of persons, machines, and the forces of nature: *"Which of us . . . is to do the hard and dirty work for the rest—and for what pay?"* (John Ruskin). *"A work that aspires . . . to the condition of art should carry its justification in every line"* (Joseph Conrad). *Labor* usually implies human work, especially of a hard physical or intellectual nature: *"a youth of labor with an age of ease"* (Oliver Goldsmith); *"where men must beg with bated breath for leave to . . . garner the fruits of their own labors"* (Roger Casement). *Toil* applies principally to strenuous, fatiguing labor: *"I have nothing to offer but blood, toil, tears and sweat"* (Winston S. Churchill). *Drudgery* suggests dull, wearisome, or monotonous work: *"the drudgery of penning definitions and marking quotations for transcription"* (Macaulay). *Travail* connotes arduous work involving pain or suffering: *"I have had my labor for my travail"* (Shakespeare).

Work (wûrk), **Henry Clay.** 1832–1884. American songwriter noted for his Union compositions during the Civil War, including "Babylon Is Fallen" (1863).

work•a•ble (wûr′kə-bəl) *adj.* **1.** Capable of being worked, dealt with, or handled. **2.** Capable of being put into effective operation; practicable or feasible. See Synonyms at **possible. —work′a•bil′i•ty, work′a•ble•ness** *n.* **—work′a•bly** *adv.*

work•a•day (wûr′kə-dā′) *adj.* **1.** Relating to or suited for working days; everyday. **2.** Mundane; commonplace: *"the practical, workaday world, of . . . ordinary undistinguished things"* (Lionel Trilling). [From Middle English *werkeday,* workday : *work,* work; see WORK + *day,* day; see DAY.]

work•a•hol•ic (wûr′kə-hô′lĭk, -hŏl′ĭk) *n.* One who has a compulsive and unrelenting need to work. **—work′a•hol′ism** *n.*

work•bench (wûrk′bĕnch′) *n.* A sturdy table or bench at which manual work is done, as by a machinist or jeweler.

work•boat (wûrk′bōt′) *n. Nautical.* A boat used for work rather than for recreation, transportation, or military purposes.

work•book (wûrk′bo͝ok′) *n.* **1.** A booklet containing problems and exercises that a student may work directly on the pages. **2.** A manual containing operating instructions, as for an appliance or a machine. **3.** A book in which a record is kept of work proposed or accomplished.

work camp *n.* **1.** See **prison camp** (sense 2). **2.** A camp where volunteers, often from religious organizations, work together on community service projects.

work•day (wûrk′dā′) *n.* **1.** A day on which work is usually done. **2.** The part of the day during which one works: *an eight-hour workday.* **—workday** *adj.* Workaday.

work•er (wûr′kər) *n.* **1.a.** One who works at a particular occupation or activity: *an office worker.* **b.** One who does manual or industrial labor. **2.** A member of the working class. **3.** A member of a colony of social insects such as ants, bees, wasps, or termites, usually a sterile female but often a sexually immature individual of either sex, that performs specialized work such as building the nest, collecting and storing food, and feeding other members of the colony.

work•er-priest (wûr′kər-prēst′) *n.* *Roman Catholic Church.* A priest, especially in France, who spends time in secular employment for missionary purposes.

work•ers' compensation (wûr′kərz) *n.* Payments required by law to be made to an employee who is injured or disabled in connection with work.

work ethic *n.* A set of values based on the moral virtues of hard work and diligence.

work•fare (wûrk′fâr′) *n.* A form of welfare in which able-bodied adults receiving aid are required to perform public-service work. [WORK + (WEL)FARE.]

work farm *n.* A correctional facility that operates as a farm worked by prisoners.

work•flow (wûrk′flō′) *n.* **1.** The flow or progress of work done by a company, an industry, a department, or a person. **2.** The rate at which such flow or progress takes place.

work•folk (wûrk′fōk′) also **work•folks** (-fōks′) *pl.n.* Laborers, especially farm workers.

work force or **work•force** (wûrk′fôrs′, -fōrs′) *n.* **1.** The workers employed in a specific project or activity. **2.** All the people working or available to work, as in a nation, a company, an industry, or on a project.

work function *n.* The minimum amount of energy required to remove an electron from the surface of a metal.

work hardening *n.* The increase in strength that accompanies plastic deformation of a metal.

work•horse (wûrk′hôrs′) *n.* **1.** Something, such as a machine, that performs dependably under heavy or prolonged use: *"the 50-year-old DC-3 . . . one of aviation's most effective workhorses"* (Christian Science Monitor). **2.** A horse that is used for labor rather than for racing or riding. **3.** *Informal.* A person who works tirelessly, especially at difficult or time-consuming tasks.

work•house (wûrk′hous′) *n.* **1.** A prison in which limited sentences are served at manual labor. **2.** *Chiefly British.* A poorhouse.

work•ing (wûr′kĭng) *adj.* **1.a.** Performing work: *a working committee.* **b.** Operating or functioning as required: *a working flashlight.* **2.** Having a paying job; employed: *working mothers.* **3.a.** Spent at work: *a working life of 40 years.* **b.** Taken while continuing to work: *a working vacation.* **4.a.** Sufficient to allow action: *a working majority.* **b.** Adequate for practical use: *a working knowledge of Spanish.* **5.** Serving as a basis or guide for further work: *a working hypothesis.* **—working** *n.* **1.** Often **workings.** The manner in which something operates or functions: *the workings of the mind.* **2.** Often **workings.** The parts of a mine or quarry that have been or are being excavated.

working capital *n.* **1.** The assets of a business that can be applied to its operation. **2.** The amount of current assets that exceeds current liabilities.

working class *n.* The part of society consisting of those who work for wages, especially manual or industrial laborers. **—work′ing-class′** (wûr′kĭng-klăs′) *adj.*

working day *n.* A workday.

working dog *n.* Any of various breeds of dogs developed or trained to do useful work, such as herding animals, pulling wagons or sleds, or guarding property.

working fluid *n.* A working substance that is a fluid.

working girl *n.* **1.** A young woman who works. **2.** *Slang.* A woman prostitute.

work•ing•man (wûr′kĭng-măn′) *n.* **1.** A man who works for wages. **2.** A man who performs heavy manual or industrial labor.

working papers *pl.n.* Legal documents certifying the right to employment of a minor or an alien.

working storage *n.* *Abbr.* **WS** *Computer Science.* The section of computer storage reserved for data to be temporarily stored during the running of a program.

working substance *n.* A substance, such as a fluid, used to effect a thermodynamic or other change in a system.

work•ing•wom•an (wûr′kĭng-wo͝om′ən) *n.* A woman who works for wages.

work in progress *n.*, *pl.* **works in progress.** A yet incomplete artistic, theatrical, or musical work, often made available for public viewing or listening.

work•load (wûrk′lōd′) *n.* **1.** The amount of work assigned to or expected from a worker in a specified time period. **2.** The amount of work that a machine produces or can produce in a specified time period.

work•man (wûrk′mən) *n.* **1.** A man who performs manual or industrial labor for wages. **2.** A craftsman or an artisan.

work•man•like (wûrk′mən-līk′) *adj.* Befitting a skilled artisan or craftsperson; skillfully done.

work•man•ship (wûrk′mən-shĭp′) *n.* **1.** The skill of a craftsperson or an artisan. **2.** The quality of something made, as by an artisan: *a silver tray of excellent workmanship.* **3.** Something made or produced by a workman. **4.** The product of effort or endeavor.

work•men's compensation (wûrk′mənz) *n.* Workers' compensation.

work of art *n.*, *pl.* **works of art.** **1.** A product of the fine arts, especially a painting or sculpture. **2.** Something likened to a fine artistic work, as by reason of beauty or craft.

work•out (wûrk′out′) *n.* **1.** A session of exercise or practice to improve fitness, as for athletic competition. **2.** A strenuous test of ability and endurance.

work•peo•ple (wûrk′pē′pəl) *pl.n.* *Chiefly British.* Those who work for wages; workers.

work•place also **work place** (wûrk′plās′) *n.* **1.** A place, such as an office or a factory, where people are employed. **2.** The work setting in general: *"one of the last male bastions of the American workplace"* (Wall Street Journal).

work release *n.* A correctional program under which prisoners are permitted employment outside a prison while serving their sentences. **—work′-re•lease′** (wûrk′rĭ-lēs′) *adj.*

work•room (wûrk′ro͞om′, -ro͝om′) *n.* A room where work is done.

work sheet or **work•sheet** (wûrk′shēt′) *n.* **1.** A sheet of paper on which work records are kept. **2.** A sheet of paper on which preliminary notes or computations are set down.

work•shop (wûrk′shŏp′) *n.* **1.** A room, an area, or a small establishment where manual or light industrial work is done. **2.** An educational seminar or series of meetings emphasizing interaction and exchange of information among a usually small number of participants: *a creative writing workshop.*

work song *n.* *Music.* A song sung to accompany work, typically having a steady rhythm.

work•space (wûrk′spās′) *n.* An area used or allocated for one's work, as in an office.

work•sta•tion (wûrk′stā′shən) *n.* An area, as in an office, outfitted with equipment and furnishings for one worker, often including a computer or computer terminal.

work stoppage *n.* A cessation of work by a group of employees as a means of protest.

work-stud•y (wûrk′stŭd′ē) *adj.* Of, relating to, or being an academic program that enables high-school or college students to gain work experience and make money while continuing their studies.

work•ta•ble (wûrk′tā′bəl) *n.* A table designed for a specific kind of task or activity, such as needlework or the graphic arts.

worktable
c. 1790–1810 sewing table

work•up (wûrk′ŭp′) *n.* A thorough medical examination for diagnostic purposes.

work•week (wûrk′wēk′) *n.* The hours or days worked in a week: *a four-day workweek.*

work•wom•an (wûrk′wo͝om′ən) *n.* A woman who performs manual or industrial labor for wages.

world (wûrld) *n.* **1.** The earth. **2.** The universe. **3.** The earth with its inhabitants. **4.** The inhabitants of the earth; the human race. **5.a.** Humankind considered as social beings; human society: *turned her back on the world.* **b.** People as a whole; the public: *The event amazed the world.* **6.** Often **World.** A specified part of the earth: *the Western World.* **7.** A part of the earth and its inhabitants as known at a given period in history: *the ancient world.* **8.** A realm or domain: *the animal world; the world of imagination.* **9.a.** A sphere of human activity or interest: *the world of sports.* **b.** A class or group of people with common characteristics or pursuits: *the scientific world.* **10.** A particular way of life: *the world of the homeless.* **11.** All that relates to or affects the life of a person: *He saw his world collapse about him.* **12.** Secular life and its concerns: *a man of the world.* **13.a.** Human existence; life: *brought a child into the world.* **b.** A state of existence: *the next world.* **14.** Often **worlds.** A large amount; much: *did her a world of good; candidates that are worlds apart on foreign policy.* **15.** A celestial body such as a planet: *the possibility of life on other worlds.* **—world** *adj.* **1.** Of or relating to the world: *a world champion.* **2.** Involving or extending throughout the entire world: *a world crisis.* **—*idioms.* for all the world.** In all respects; precisely: *She looked for all the world like a movie star.* **in the world.** Used as an intensive: *How in the world did they manage? I never in the world would have guessed.* **out of this world.** *Informal.* Extraordinary; superb: *The dinner was out of this world.* **the world over.** Throughout the world: *known the world over.* **world without end.** Forever. [Middle English, from Old English *weorold.* See **wī-ro-** in Appendix.]

world-beat•er (wûrld′bē′tər) *n.* One that is markedly superior to all others, as in the ability to succeed.

world-class (wûrld′klăs′) *adj.* **1.** Ranking among the foremost in the world; of an international standard of excellence; of

ă pat	oi boy
ā pay	ou out
âr care	o͝o took
ä father	o͞o boot
ĕ pet	ŭ cut
ē be	ûr urge
ĭ pit	th thin
ī pie	*th* this
îr pier	hw which
ŏ pot	zh vision
ō toe	ə about, item
ô paw	♦ regionalism

Stress marks: ′ (primary); ′ (secondary), as in **dictionary** (dĭk′shə-nĕr′ē)

worm fence

the highest order: *a world-class figure skater.* **2.** *Usage Problem.* Great, as in importance, concern, or notoriety.

USAGE NOTE: The adjective *world-class* became current as a result of its original use to describe athletes capable of performing at an international level of competition, as in *A ten-second time would put him in the first rank of world-class sprinters.* In recent years it has been extended to mean "of an international standard of excellence" and has been applied to a wide variety of categories. When used of things that naturally admit such comparison, the extended use of the word is generally acceptable to the Usage Panel. In the most recent survey 65 percent accepted the description *world-class restaurant,* and 53 percent accepted *world-class sports car.* But the expression is not generally accepted as a vague way of emphasizing magnitude or degree. The sentence *Johann Sebastian Bach's 300th birthday will rank as a world-class anniversary* was acceptable to only 7 percent, and only 4 percent accepted a description of AIDS as *a world-class tragedy.*

world line *n.* The path in space-time traveled by an elementary particle for the time and distance that it retains its identity.

world·ling (wûrld′lĭng) *n.* One who is absorbed by worldly pursuits and pleasures.

world·ly (wûrld′lē) *adj.* **-li·er, -li·est. 1.** Of, relating to, or devoted to the temporal world. **2.** Sophisticated; cosmopolitan: *"an experienced and worldly man who had been almost everywhere"* (Willa Cather). **—worldly** *adv.* In a worldly manner. **—world′li·ness** *n.*

world·ly-mind·ed (wûrld′lē-mīn′dĭd) *adj.* Absorbed in the affairs of this world. **—world′ly-mind′ed·ness** *n.*

world·ly-wise (wûrld′lē-wīz′) *adj.* Experienced in the ways of the world.

world power *n.* A nation or other political entity having the power to influence the course of world events.

world-re·nowned (wûrld′rĭ-nound′) *adj.* Widely known and acclaimed.

World Series *n. Baseball.* A series of baseball games played each fall between the winning teams of the American League and the National League to decide the championship of the major leagues.

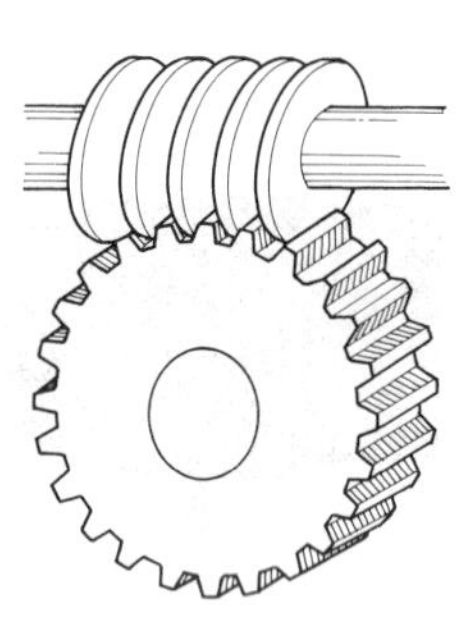
worm gear

world's fair (wûrldz) *n.* A large exposition featuring exhibits, as of arts and crafts and products of industry and agriculture, provided by countries from around the world.

world-shak·ing (wûrld′shā′kĭng) *adj.* Of great significance or consequence.

world soul *n.* A spiritual principle having the same relation to the physical world as the human soul does to the body; the animating force of the world.

world-view or **world·view** (wûrld′vyo͞o′) *n.* **1.** The overall perspective from which one sees and interprets the world. **2.** A collection of beliefs about life and the universe held by an individual or a group. [Translation of German *Weltanschauung.*]

World War I *n. Abbr.* **WWI** A war fought from 1914 to 1918, in which Great Britain, France, Russia, Belgium, Italy, Japan, the United States, and other allies defeated Germany, Austria-Hungary, Turkey, and Bulgaria.

World War II *n. Abbr.* **WWII** A war fought from 1939 to 1945, in which Great Britain, France, the Soviet Union, the United States, China, and other allies defeated Germany, Italy, and Japan.

world-wea·ry (wûrld′wîr′ē) *adj.* **-ri·er, -ri·est.** Tired of the world; bored with life. **—world′-wea′ri·ness** *n.*

world·wide (wûrld′wīd′) *adj.* Involving or extending throughout the entire world: *a worldwide epidemic.* **—worldwide** *adv.* Throughout the world: *distributed worldwide.*

worm (wûrm) *n.* **1.** Any of various invertebrates, as those of the phyla Annelida, Nematoda, Nemertea, or Platyhelminthes, having a long, flexible, rounded or flattened body, often without obvious appendages. **2.** Any of various crawling insect larvae, such as a grub or a caterpillar, having a soft, elongated body. **3.** Any of various unrelated animals, such as the shipworm or the slowworm, resembling a worm in habit or appearance. **4. a.** Something, such as the thread of a screw or the spiral condenser in a still, that resembles a worm in form or appearance. **b.** The spirally threaded shaft of a worm gear. **5.** An insidiously tormenting or devouring force: *"felt the black worm of treachery growing in his heart"* (Mario Puzo). **6.** A person regarded as pitiable or contemptible. **7. worms.** *Pathology.* Infestation of the intestines or other parts of the body with worms or wormlike parasites; helminthiasis. **8.** *Computer Science.* A program that replicates itself and interferes with software function or destroys stored information. **—worm** *v.* **wormed, worm·ing, worms.** *—tr.* **1.** To make (one's way) with or as if with the sinuous crawling motion of a worm. **2.** To work (one's way or oneself) subtly or gradually; insinuate: *She wormed her way into his confidence.* **3.** To elicit by artful or devious means. Usually used with *out of: wormed a confession out of the suspect.* **4.** To cure of intestinal worms. **5.** *Nautical.* To wrap yarn or twine spirally around (rope). *—intr.* **1.** To move in a manner suggestive of a worm. **2.** To make one's way by artful or devious means: *He can't worm out of this situation.* [Middle English, from Old English *wurm,* variant of *wyrm.* See **wer-^{2}** in Appendix.]

worm-eat·en (wûrm′ēt′n) *adj.* **1.** Bored through or gnawed by worms. **2.** Decayed; rotten. **3.** Antiquated; decrepit.

worm fence *n.* A fence of crossed rails supporting one another and forming a zigzag pattern. Also called *snake fence, Virginia fence.*

worm gear *n.* **1.** A gear consisting of a spirally threaded shaft and a wheel with marginal teeth that mesh into it. **2.** The toothed wheel of this gear; a worm wheel.

worm·grass (wûrm′grăs′) *n.* See **pinkroot.** [From its use as a vermifuge.]

worm·hole (wûrm′hōl′) *n.* A hole made by a burrowing worm.

worm lizard *n.* Any of various small, legless, burrowing lizards of the family Amphisbaenidae, resembling worms and found chiefly in tropical regions.

Worms (wûrmz, vôrms). A city of southwest Germany on the Rhine River north-northwest of Mannheim. Originally a Celtic settlement, it was the site of the Diet of Worms (1521) in which Martin Luther refused to recant his beliefs and was outlawed by the Roman Catholic Church. Population, 72,610.

worm screw *n.* The spirally threaded shaft of a worm gear.

worm·seed (wûrm′sēd′) *n.* **1.** A tropical American plant *(Chenopodium ambrosioides)* yielding an oil used as an anthelmintic. **2.** Any of several other plants used as an anthelmintic.

worm's-eye view (wûrmz′ī′) *n.* A view from below or from an inferior position.

worm snake *n.* A small, harmless burrowing snake *(Carphophis amoena)* of the central and eastern United States, usually living under stones or logs and feeding chiefly on earthworms.

worm wheel *n.* The toothed wheel of a worm gear.

worm·wood (wûrm′wo͝od′) *n.* **1.** Any of several aromatic plants of the genus *Artemisia,* especially *A. absinthium,* native to Europe, yielding a bitter extract used in making absinthe and in flavoring certain wines. **2.** Something embittering. [Middle English, alteration of *wermod,* from Old English *wermōd.*]

worm·y (wûr′mē) *adj.* **-i·er, -i·est. 1.** Infested with or damaged by worms. **2.** Suggestive of a worm. **—worm′i·ness** *n.*

worn (wôrn, wōrn) *v.* Past participle of **wear. —worn** *adj.* **1.** Affected by wear or use. **2.** Impaired or damaged by wear or use: *the worn pockets on a jacket.* **3.** Showing the wearing effects of overwork, care, worry, or suffering. See Synonyms at **haggard.** [Middle English, past participle of *weren,* to wear. See WEAR.]

worn-out (wôrn′out′, wōrn′-) *adj.* **1.** Worn or used until no longer usable or effective. **2.** Thoroughly exhausted; spent.

wor·ri·ment (wûr′ē-mənt, wŭr′-) *n.* **1.** The act or an instance of worrying. **2.** A source of anxiety; a worry.

wor·ri·some (wûr′ē-səm, wŭr′-) *adj.* **1.** Causing worry or anxiety. **2.** Tending to worry; anxious. **—wor′ri·some·ly** *adv.*

wor·ry (wûr′ē, wŭr′ē) *v.* **wor·ried** (wûr′ēd, wûr′-), **wor·ry·ing, wor·ries** (wûr′ēz, wŭr′-). *—intr.* **1.** To feel uneasy or concerned about something; be troubled. See Synonyms at **brood. 2.** To pull or tear at something with or as if with the teeth. **3.** To proceed doggedly in the face of difficulty or hardship; struggle: *worried along at the problem.* *—tr.* **1.** To cause to feel anxious, distressed, or troubled. See Synonyms at **trouble. 2.** To bother or annoy, as with petty complaints. **3. a.** To seize with the teeth and shake or tug at repeatedly: *a dog worrying a bone.* **b.** To attack roughly and repeatedly; harass. **c.** To touch, move, or handle idly; toy with: *worrying the loose tooth with his tongue.* **—worry** *n., pl.* **-ries. 1.** The act of worrying or the condition of being worried; persistent mental uneasiness. See Synonyms at **anxiety. 2.** A source of nagging concern or uneasiness. ***—idiom.* not to worry.** There is nothing to worry about; there is no need to be concerned: *"But not to worry: it all . . . falls into place in the book's second half, where the language is plainer"* (Hallowell Bowser). [Middle English *werien, worien,* to strangle, from Old English *wyrgan.* See **wer-^{2}** in Appendix.] **—wor′ri·er** *n.*

WORD HISTORY: "Don't worry" is a much milder injunction than it once would have been, for the word *worry* has softened its sense greatly over the course of its history. Its Old English ancestor, *wyrgan,* meant "to strangle." Its Middle English descendant, *worien,* kept this sense and developed the new sense "to grasp by the throat with the teeth and lacerate" or "to kill or injure by biting and shaking." This is the way wolves or dogs might attack sheep, for example. In the 16th century *worry* began to be used in the sense "to harass, as by rough treatment or attack," or "to assault verbally," and in the 17th century the word took on the sense "to bother, distress, or persecute." It was a small step from this sense to the main modern senses "to cause to feel anxious or distressed" and "to feel troubled or uneasy," first recorded in the 19th century.

worry beads *pl.n.* A string of beads for fingering in times of worry, boredom, or tension.

wor·ry·wart (wûr′ē-wôrt′, wŭr′-) *n.* One who worries excessively and needlessly.

worse (wûrs) *adj.* Comparative of **bad^{1}, ill. 1.** More inferior, as in quality, condition, or effect. **2.** More severe or unfavorable. **3.** Being further from a standard; less desirable or satisfactory. **4.** Being in poorer health; more ill. **—worse** *n.* Something that is worse: *Of the two routes, the eastern one is the worse. She was accused of cheating on exams, lying, and worse.* **—worse** *adv.* Comparative of **badly, ill.** In a worse manner; to a worse degree. ***—idiom.* for better or (for) worse.** Whether the situation or consequences be good or ill: *For better or worse, he trusts everyone.* [Middle English, from Old English *wyrsa.* See **wers-** in Appendix.]

wors·en (wûr′sən) *tr. & intr.v.* **-ened, -en·ing, -ens.** To make or become worse.

wors·er (wûr′sər) *adv. & adj. Non-Standard.* Worse.

wor·ship (wûr′shĭp) *n.* **1.a.** The reverent love and devotion accorded a deity, an idol, or a sacred object. **b.** The ceremonies, prayers, or other religious forms by which this love is expressed. **2.** Ardent devotion; adoration. **3.** Often **Worship.** *Chiefly British.* Used as a form of address for magistrates, mayors, and certain other dignitaries: *Your Worship.* **—worship** *v.* **-shiped, -ship·ing, -ships** or **-shipped, -ship·ping, -ships.** *—tr.* **1.** To honor and love as a deity. **2.** To regard with ardent or adoring esteem or devotion. See Synonyms at **revere**[1]. *—intr.* **1.** To participate in religious rites of worship. **2.** To perform an act of worship. [Middle English *worshipe,* worthiness, honor, from Old English *weorthscipe : weorth,* worth; see WORTH[1] + *-scipe,* -ship.] **—wor′ship·er, wor′ship·per** *n.*

wor·ship·ful (wûr′shĭp-fəl) *adj.* **1.** Given to or expressive of worship; reverent. **2.** *Chiefly British.* Used as a respectful form of address. **—wor′ship·ful·ly** *adv.* **—wor′ship·ful·ness** *n.*

wor·sle·ya (wûrz′lē-ə) *n.* A bulbous Brazilian plant *(Worsleya rayneri)* having lilac-colored, dark-spotted flowers and black seeds. [After Arthington *Worsley,* 19th–20th century British botanist and civil engineer.]

worst (wûrst) *adj.* Superlative of **bad**[1], **ill. 1.** Most inferior, as in quality, condition, or effect. **2.** Most severe or unfavorable. **3.** Being furthest from an ideal or a standard; least desirable or satisfactory. **—worst** *adv.* Superlative of **badly, ill.** In the worst manner or degree. **—worst** *tr.v.* **worst·ed, worst·ing, worsts.** To gain the advantage over; defeat. **—worst** *n.* Something that is worst. ***—idioms.* at (the) worst.** Under the most negative circumstances, estimation, or interpretation: *At worst, the storm will make us postpone the trip.* **get** (or **have**) **the worst of it.** To suffer a defeat or disadvantage. **if (the) worst comes to (the) worst.** If the very worst thing happens. **in the worst way.** *Informal.* Very much; a great deal: *wanted to be elected in the worst way.* [Middle English, from Old English *wyrsta.* See **wers-** in Appendix.]

worst-case (wûrst′kās′) *adj.* Most unfavorable; being or involving the worst possibility: *"has exceeded even the worst-case estimate of his harshest critics"* (Alan Cranston).

wor·sted (wo͝os′tĭd, wûr′stĭd) *n.* **1.** Firm-textured, compactly twisted woolen yarn made from long-staple fibers. **2.** Fabric made from such yarn. [Middle English, variant of *worthstede,* after *Worthstede* (Worstead), a village of eastern England.] **—wor′sted** *adj.*

wort[1] (wûrt, wôrt) *n.* A plant. Often used in combination: *liverwort; milkwort.* [Middle English, from Old English *wyrt.* See **wrād-** in Appendix.]

wort[2] (wûrt, wôrt) *n.* An infusion of malt that is fermented to make beer. [Middle English, from Old English *wyrt.* See **wrād-** in Appendix.]

worth[1] (wûrth) *n.* **1.** The quality that renders something desirable, useful, or valuable: *the worth of higher education.* **2.** Material or market value: *stocks having a worth of ten million dollars.* **3.** A quantity of something that may be purchased for a specified sum or by a specified means: *ten dollars' worth of natural gas; wanted their money's worth.* **4.** Wealth; riches: *her net worth.* **5.** Quality that commands esteem or respect; merit: *a person of great worth.* **—worth** *adj.* **1.** Equal in value to something specified: *worth its weight in gold.* **2.** Deserving of; meriting: *a proposal not worth consideration.* **3.** Having wealth or riches amounting to: *a person worth millions.* ***—idioms.* for all (one) is worth.** To the utmost of one's powers or ability. **for what it's worth.** Even though it may not be important or valuable: *Here's my advice, for what it's worth.* [Middle English, from Old English *weorth.* See **wer-**[2] in Appendix.]

worth[2] (wûrth) *intr.v.* **worthed, worth·ing, worths.** *Archaic.* To befall; betide: *"Howl ye, Woe worth the day!"* (Ezekiel 30:2). [Middle English *worthen,* from Old English *weorthan.* See **wer-**[2] in Appendix.]

Wor·thing (wûr′*th*ĭng). A borough of southeast England on the English Channel south-southwest of London. Population, 92,600.

worth·less (wûrth′lĭs) *adj.* **1.** Lacking worth; of no use or value. **2.** Low; despicable. **—worth′less·ly** *adv.* **—worth′less·ness** *n.*

worth·while (wûrth′hwīl′, -wīl′) *adj.* Sufficiently valuable or important to be worth one's time, effort, or interest. **—worth′while′ness** *n.*

wor·thy (wûr′*th*ē) *adj.* **-thi·er, -thi·est. 1.** Having worth, merit, or value; useful or valuable. **2.** Honorable; admirable: *a worthy fellow.* **3.** Having sufficient worth; deserving: *worthy to be revered; worthy of acclaim.* **—worthy** *n., pl.* **-thies.** An eminent person. **—wor′thi·ly** *adv.* **—wor′thi·ness** *n.*

-worthy *suff.* **1.** Of sufficient worth for: *creditworthy.* **2.** Suitable or safe for: *crashworthy.* [From WORTHY.]

wot (wŏt) *v.* First and third person singular present tense of **wit**[2].

Wo·tan (vō′tän′) *n. Mythology.* A German god identified with Odin. [German, from Middle High German, from Old High German *Wuotan.* See **wet-**[1] in Appendix.]

Wouk (wōk), **Herman.** Born 1915. American writer whose novels include *The Caine Mutiny* (1951), for which he won a Pulitzer Prize, and *The Winds of War* (1971).

would (wo͝od) *aux.v.* Past tense of **will**[2]. **1.** Used after a statement of desire, request, or advice: *I wish you would stay.* **2.** Used to make a polite request: *Would you go with me?* **3.** Used to indicate uncertainty: *It would seem to be getting warmer.* See Usage Note at **if.**

would-be (wo͝od′bē′) *adj.* Desiring, attempting, or professing to be: *"Would-be home buyers will have a somewhat easier time getting loans"* (Wall Street Journal).

would·n't (wo͝od′nt). Would not.

wouldst (wo͝odst) or **would·est** (wo͝od′ĭst) *v. Archaic.* Second person singular past tense of **will**[2].

wound[1] (wo͞ond) *n.* **1.** An injury, especially one in which the skin or other external surface is torn, pierced, cut, or otherwise broken. **2.** An injury to the feelings. **—wound** *v.* **wound·ed, wound·ing, wounds.** *—tr.* To inflict wounds or a wound on. *—intr.* To inflict wounds or a wound: *harsh criticism that wounds.* [Middle English, from Old English *wund.* See **wen-**[2] in Appendix.] **—wound′ed·ly** *adv.* **—wound′ing·ly** *adv.*

wound[2] (wound) *v.* Past tense and past participle of **wind**[2].

wound[3] (wound) *v. Music.* A past tense and a past participle of **wind**[3].

Wound·ed Knee (wo͞on′dĭd nē′). A creek of southwest South Dakota. Almost 200 Native Americans were massacred here by U.S. troops on December 29, 1890.

wound·wort (wo͞ond′wûrt′, -wôrt′) *n.* **1.** See **betony** (sense 1). **2.** Any of several plants formerly used to treat wounds.

wove (wōv) *v.* Past tense of **weave.**

wo·ven (wō′vən) *v.* Past participle of **weave. —woven** *adj.* Made by weaving: *a finely woven rug.* **—woven** *n.* Material or a fabric made by weaving.

wove paper *n.* Paper made on a closely woven wire roller or mold and having a faint mesh pattern. [Variant past participle of WEAVE.]

Wo·vo·ka (wō-vō′kə). Also called Jack Wilson. 1858?–1932. Paiute religious leader who founded the Ghost Dance movement. The movement faded when a number of its followers, thought to have supernatural protection, were massacred at Wounded Knee (1890).

wow[1] (wou) *Informal. interj.* Used to express wonder, amazement, or great pleasure. **—wow** *n.* An outstanding success. **—wow** *tr.v.* **wowed, wow·ing, wows.** To have a strong, usually pleasurable effect on: *a performance that wowed us.*

wow[2] (wou) *n.* Slow variation in the pitch of a sound reproduction resulting from variations in the speed of the recording or reproducing equipment. [Imitative.]

wow·ser (wou′zər) *n. Australian & New Zealand.* A person regarded as obnoxiously puritanical. [Possibly from dialectal *wow,* to howl, complain, of imitative origin.]

WP *abbr.* **1.** Weather permitting. **2.** Word processing; word processor. *Computer Science.*

WPA *abbr.* Work Projects Administration.

W particle *n.* A massive elementary particle, existing in positively and negatively charged forms, that is the quantum of weak interactions in which the charges of participating particles change. See table at **subatomic particle.**

wpm or **w.p.m.** *abbr.* Words per minute.

wpn. *abbr.* Weapon.

WRAC or **W.R.A.C.** *abbr.* Women's Royal Army Corps.

wrack[1] also **rack** (răk) *n.* **1.** Destruction or ruin. **2.** A remnant or vestige of something destroyed. [Middle English, from Old English *wræc,* punishment (influenced by Middle Dutch *wrak,* shipwreck).]

wrack[2] also **rack** (răk) *—n.* **1.a.** Wreckage, especially of a ship cast ashore. **b.** *Chiefly British.* Violent destruction of a building or vehicle. **2.a.** Dried seaweed. **b.** Marine vegetation, especially kelp. *—v.* **wracked, wrack·ing, wracks** also **racked, rack·ing, racks.** *—tr.* To cause the ruin of; wreck. *—intr.* To be wrecked. [Middle English *wrak,* from Middle Dutch.]

WRAF or **W.R.A.F.** *abbr.* Women's Royal Air Force.

wraith (rāth) *n.* **1.** An apparition of a living person that appears as a portent just before that person's death. **2.** The ghost of a dead person. **3.** Something shadowy and insubstantial. [Origin unknown.]

Wran·gel Island (răng′gəl, vrăn′gyĭl). An island of northeast Russia in the Arctic Ocean northwest of the Bering Strait.

Wran·gell (răng′gəl), **Mount.** A peak, 4,319.7 m (14,163 ft) high, of the central Wrangell Mountains in southern Alaska.

Wrangell Mountains. A mountain range of southern Alaska extending from the Copper River to the Canadian border. Mount Bona, at 5,032.5 m (16,500 ft), is the highest peak.

wran·gle (răng′gəl) *v.* **-gled, -gling, -gles.** *—intr.* To quarrel noisily or angrily; bicker. See Synonyms at **argue.** *—tr.* **1.** To win or obtain by argument. **2.** To herd (horses or other livestock). **—wrangle** *n.* **1.** The act of wrangling. **2.** An angry, noisy argument or dispute. [Middle English *wranglen,* of Middle Low German origin. See **wer-**[2] in Appendix.]

wran·gler (răng′glər) *n.* **1.** One who wrangles or quarrels. **2.** A cowboy or cowgirl, especially one who tends saddle horses.

ă pat	oi boy
ā pay	ou out
âr care	o͝o took
ä father	o͞o boot
ĕ pet	ŭ cut
ē be	ûr urge
ĭ pit	th thin
ī pie	*th* this
îr pier	hw which
ŏ pot	zh vision
ō toe	ə about, item
ô paw	♦ regionalism

Stress marks: ′ (primary); ′ (secondary), as in **dictionary** (dĭk′shə-nĕr′ē)

wren

Christopher Wren
Detail of a 1711 painting by Sir Godfrey Kneller

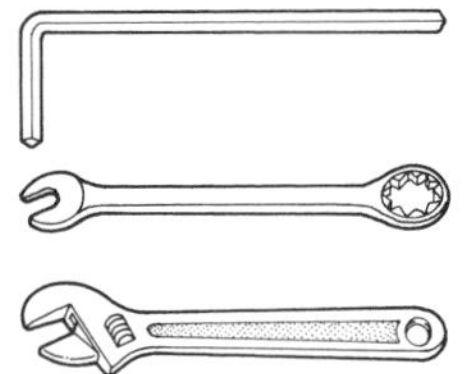

wrench
Top: Allen wrench
Center: Open-end box wrench
Bottom: Adjustable wrench

wrestling

wrap (răp) *v.* **wrapped** or **wrapt** (răpt), **wrap·ping, wraps.** —*tr.* **1.** To arrange or fold (something) about as cover or protection: *She wrapped her fur coat closely about herself.* **2.** To cover, envelop, or encase, as by folding or coiling something about: *wrapped my head in a scarf.* **3.** To enclose, especially in paper, and fasten: *wrap a package; wrapped up the peelings.* **4.** To clasp, fold, or coil about something: *She wrapped her arms about his neck.* **5.** To envelop and obscure: *Fog wrapped the city.* **6.** To surround or involve in a specified quality or atmosphere: *The plan was wrapped in secrecy.* **7.** To engross: *She was wrapped in thought.* —*intr.* **1.** To coil or twist about or around something: *The flag wrapped around the pole.* **2.** To put on warm clothing. Usually used with *up.* **3.** To conclude filming: *The movie is scheduled to wrap next week.* —**wrap** *n.* **1.** A garment to be wrapped or folded about a person, especially an outer garment such as a robe, cloak, shawl, or coat. **2.** A blanket. **3.** A wrapping or wrapper. **4.** The completion of filming on a movie. —***phrasal verb.* wrap up. 1.** To bring to a conclusion; settle finally or successfully: *wrap up a business deal.* **2.** To summarize; recapitulate. —***idioms.* under wraps.** *Informal.* Secret or concealed: *"The news was kept under wraps for the three-day weekend"* (Boston Globe). **wrapped up in. 1.** Completely immersed or absorbed in: *She is wrapped up in her studies.* **2.** Involved in: *They were wrapped up in criminal activities.* [Middle English *wrappen.* See **wer-**[2] in Appendix.]

wrap·a·round (răp′ə-round′) *adj.* **1.** Designed to be wrapped around the body and fastened: *a wraparound skirt.* **2.** Shaped to curve around the sides: *a wraparound windshield.* —**wraparound** *n.* **1.** A garment that is open to the side and is wrapped around the body. **2.** Something that encompasses or laps over something else.

wrap·per (răp′ər) *n.* **1.** That in which an object is wrapped or covered, as: **a.** The material, such as paper, in which something is wrapped: *a candy wrapper.* **b.** The material encircling a magazine or newspaper sent by mail. **c.** A book jacket. **d.** The tobacco leaf covering a cigar. **2.** A loose dressing gown or negligee. **3.** One that wraps, as a store employee who wraps parcels.

wrap·ping (răp′ĭng) also **wrap·pings** (-ĭngz) *n.* The material in which something is wrapped.

wrapt (răpt) *v.* A past tense and a past participle of **wrap.**

wrap-up (răp′ŭp′) *n.* **1.** A brief final summary, as of the news. **2.** A concluding or final action: *the wrap-up of a campaign.*

wrasse (răs) *n.* Any of numerous chiefly tropical, often brightly colored marine fishes of the family Labridae, having spiny fins, thick lips, and powerful jaws, and often valued for food. [Cornish *gwragh* and Welsh *gwrach,* old woman.]

wrath (răth, räth) *n.* **1.** Forceful, often vindictive anger. See Synonyms at **anger. 2.a.** Punishment or vengeance as a manifestation of anger. **b.** Divine retribution for sin. —**wrath** *adj. Archaic.* Wrathful. [Middle English, from Old English *wrǣththu,* from *wrāth,* angry. See **wer-**[2] in Appendix.]

wrath·ful (răth′fəl, räth′-) *adj.* **1.** Full of wrath; fiercely angry. **2.** Proceeding from or expressing wrath: *wrathful vengeance.* See Synonyms at **angry.** —**wrath′ful·ly** *adv.* —**wrath′ful·ness** *n.*

wreak (rēk) *tr.v.* **wreaked, wreak·ing, wreaks. 1.** To inflict (vengeance or punishment) upon a person. **2.** To express or gratify (anger, malevolence, or resentment); vent. **3.** To bring about; cause: *wreak havoc.* **4.** *Archaic.* To take vengeance for; avenge. [Middle English *wreken,* from Old English *wrecan.*]

USAGE NOTE: *Wreak* is sometimes confused with *wreck,* perhaps because the wreaking of damage may leave a wreck: *The storm wreaked* (not *wrecked*) *havoc along the coast.* The past tense and past participle of *wreak* is *wreaked,* not *wrought,* which is an alternative past tense and past participle of *work.*

wreath (rēth) *n., pl.* **wreaths** (rēthz, rēths). **1.a.** A ring or circlet of flowers, boughs, or leaves worn on the head, placed on a memorial, or hung as a decoration. **b.** A representation of this ring or circlet, as in woodwork. **2.** A curling or circular form: *a wreath of smoke.* [Middle English *wrethe,* from Old English *writha,* band. See **wer-**[2] in Appendix.]

wreathe (rēth) *v.* **wreathed, wreath·ing, wreathes.** —*tr.* **1.** To twist or entwine into a wreath. **2.** To twist or curl into a wreathlike shape or contour. **3.** To crown, decorate, or encircle with or as if with a wreath. **4.** To coil or curl. **5.** To form a wreath or wreathlike shape around. —*intr.* **1.** To assume the form of a wreath. **2.** To curl, writhe, or spiral: *The smoke wreathed upward.* [From WREATH.]

wreck (rĕk) *n.* **1.** The act of wrecking or the state of being wrecked; destruction. **2.** Accidental destruction of a ship; a shipwreck. **3.a.** The stranded hulk of a severely damaged ship. **b.** Fragments of a ship or its cargo cast ashore by the sea after a shipwreck; wreckage. **4.** The remains of something that has been wrecked or ruined. **5.** Something shattered or dilapidated. **6.** A person who is physically or mentally broken down or worn out. —**wreck** *v.* **wrecked, wreck·ing, wrecks.** —*tr.* **1.** To cause the destruction of in or as if in a collision. **2.** To dismantle or raze; tear down. **3.** To cause to undergo ruin or disaster. See Synonyms at **blast, ruin.** See Usage Note at **wreak.** —*intr.* **1.** To suffer destruction or ruin; become wrecked. **2.** To work as a wrecker. [Middle English *wrek,* from Anglo-Norman *wrec,* of Scandinavian origin; akin to Old Norse *rec,* wreckage.]

wreck·age (rĕk′ĭj) *n.* **1.** The act of wrecking or the state of being wrecked. **2.** Something wrecked. **3.** The debris of something wrecked.

wreck·er (rĕk′ər) *n.* **1.** One that wrecks or destroys: *a wrecker of dreams.* **2.a.** One who is in the business of demolishing old buildings. **b.** One who dismantles cars for salvage. **3.a.** A person, vehicle, or piece of equipment employed in recovering or removing wrecks, especially a truck with a hoist and towing apparatus used in towing disabled or wrecked vehicles. **b.** One that salvages wrecked cargo or parts. **4.a.** One who lures a vessel to destruction, as by a display of lights on a rocky coastline, in order to plunder it. **b.** A plunderer.

wreck·ing bar (rĕk′ĭng) *n.* A small crowbar with a claw at one end and a slight curve at the other end.

wren (rĕn) *n.* **1.** Any of various small brownish songbirds of the family Troglodytidae, having rounded wings, a slender bill, and a short, often erect tail. **2.** Any of various similar unrelated songbirds. [Middle English *wrenne,* from Old English *wrenna.*]

Wren (rĕn) *n.* A member of the Women's Royal Naval Service.

Wren, Sir **Christopher.** 1632–1723. English architect who designed more than 50 London churches, most notably Saint Paul's Cathedral (1675–1710).

wrench (rĕnch) *n.* **1.** A sudden sharp, forcible twist or turn. **2.** An injury produced by twisting or straining. **3.** A sudden tug at one's emotions; a surge of compassion, sorrow, or anguish. **4.a.** A break or parting that causes emotional distress. **b.** The pain so associated: *felt a wrench when he was parted from his children.* **5.** A distortion in the original form or meaning of something written or spoken; twisted interpretation. **6.** Any of various hand or power tools with fixed or adjustable jaws for gripping, turning, or twisting objects such as nuts, bolts, or pipes. —**wrench** *v.* **wrenched, wrench·ing, wrench·es.** —*tr.* **1.a.** To twist or turn suddenly and forcibly. **b.** To twist and sprain: *I wrenched my knee.* **2.a.** To force free by pulling at; yank. See Synonyms at **jerk**[1]. **b.** To pull with a wrench. **3.** To pull at the feelings or emotions of; distress: *It wrenched her to watch them go.* **4.** To distort or twist the original character or import of: *wrenched the text to prove her point.* —*intr.* To give a wrench, twist, or turn. [From Middle English *wrenchen,* to twist, from Old English *wrencan.* See **wer-**[2] in Appendix.] —**wrench′ing·ly** *adv.*

wren tit also **wren-tit** (rĕn′tĭt′) *n.* A small grayish-brown songbird *(Chamaea fasciata)* of the western United States, resembling both a wren and a titmouse and found usually in low scrub or chaparral.

wrest (rĕst) *tr.v.* **wrest·ed, wrest·ing, wrests. 1.** To obtain by or as if by pulling with violent twisting movements: *wrested the book out of his hands; wrested the islands from the settlers.* **2.** To usurp forcefully: *wrested power from the monarchy.* **3.** To extract by or as if by force, twisting, or persistent effort; wring: *wrest the meaning from an obscure poem.* **4.a.** To distort or twist the nature or meaning of: *wrested the words out of context.* **b.** To divert to an improper use; misapply. —**wrest** *n.* **1.** The act of wresting. **2.** *Music.* A small tuning key for the wrest pins of a stringed instrument. [Middle English *wresten,* from Old English *wrǣstan,* to twist. See **wer-**[2] in Appendix.] —**wrest′er** *n.*

wres·tle (rĕs′əl) *v.* **-tled, -tling, -tles.** —*intr.* **1.** To contend by grappling and attempting to throw or immobilize one's opponent, especially under contest rules. **2.** To contend or struggle: *wrestling with budget cuts.* **3.** To strive in an effort to master something: *wrestle with one's conscience.* —*tr.* **1.a.** To take part in (a wrestling match). **b.** To take part in a wrestling match with. **2.** To move or lift with great effort: *wrestled the piano up the stairs.* **3.** To throw (a calf) for branding. —**wrestle** *n.* **1.** The act or a bout of wrestling. **2.** A struggle. [Middle English *wrestlen,* from Old English **wrǣstlian,* frequentative of *wrǣstan,* to twist. See **wer-**[2] in Appendix.] —**wres′tler** *n.*

wres·tling (rĕs′lĭng) *n.* *Sports.* A sport in which two competitors attempt to throw or immobilize each other by grappling.

wrest pin *n.* *Music.* One of the pins to which the strings of a musical instrument, especially of a keyboard instrument, are attached and by turning which they are tuned.

wretch (rĕch) *n.* **1.** A miserable, unfortunate, or unhappy person. **2.** A person regarded as base, mean, or despicable: *"a stony adversary, an inhuman wretch"* (Shakespeare). [Middle English *wrecche,* from Old English *wrecca,* exile, wretch.]

wretch·ed (rĕch′ĭd) *adj.* **-er, -est. 1.** In a deplorable state of distress or misfortune; miserable: *"the wretched prisoners huddling in the stinking cages"* (George Orwell). **2.** Characterized by or attended with misery or woe: *a wretched life.* **3.** Of a poor or mean character; dismal: *a wretched building.* **4.** Contemptible; despicable: *wretched treatment of the patients.* **5.** Of very inferior quality: *wretched prose.* [Middle English *wrecched,* from *wrecche,* wretch. See WRETCH.] —**wretch′ed·ly** *adv.*

wri·er (rī′ər) *adj.* A comparative of **wry.**

wri·est (rī′ĭst) *adj.* A superlative of **wry.**

wrig·gle (rĭg′əl) *v.* **-gled, -gling, -gles.** —*intr.* **1.** To turn or twist the body with sinuous writhing motions; squirm. **2.** To proceed with writhing motions. **3.** To worm one's way into or out of a situation; insinuate or extricate oneself by sly or subtle means. —*tr.* **1.** To move with a wriggling motion: *wriggle a toe.* **2.** To make (one's way, for example) by or as if by wriggling: *He wriggled his way into favor.* —**wriggle** *n.* **1.** A wriggling movement. **2.** A sinuous path, line, or marking. [Middle English *wrigglen,* perhaps from Middle Low German *wriggeln.* See **wer-**[2] in Appendix.] **—wrig′gly** *adj.*

wrig·gler (rĭg′lər) *n.* **1.** The larva of a mosquito. **2.** One that wriggles or squirms.

wright (rīt) *n.* One that constructs or repairs something. Often used in combination: *a playwright; a shipwright.* [Middle English, from Old English *wryhta.* See **werg-** in Appendix.]

Wright (rīt), **Frances.** Known as "Fanny." 1795–1852. Scottish-born American reformer who lectured nationwide on women's rights, birth control, and public education and wrote *Views of Society and Manners in America* (1823).

Wright, Frank Lloyd. 1869–1959. American architect whose distinctive style, based on natural forms, had a great influence on the modern movement in architecture. His designs include private homes and the Guggenheim Museum in New York City (1943–1959).

Wright, Orville. 1871–1948. American aviation pioneer who with his brother **Wilbur** (1867–1912) invented the airplane. On December 17, 1903, near Kitty Hawk, North Carolina, they made the first sustained flights in a heavier-than-air vehicle.

Wright, Richard. 1908–1960. American writer whose powerful fiction explores the oppression suffered by Black Americans. His works include *Native Son* (1940) and *Black Boy* (1945).

Wright, Willard Huntington. Pen name S.S. Van Dine. 1888–1939. American writer of detective novels, including *The Canary Murder Case* (1927) and *The Casino Murder Case* (1934).

wring (rĭng) *v.* **wrung** (rŭng), **wring·ing, wrings.** *—tr.* **1.** To twist, squeeze, or compress, especially so as to extract liquid. Often used with *out.* **2.** To extract (liquid) by twisting or compressing. Often used with *out.* **3.** To wrench or twist forcibly or painfully: *wring the neck of a chicken.* **4.** To clasp and twist or squeeze (one's hands), as in distress. **5.** To clasp firmly and shake (another's hand), as in congratulation. **6.** To cause distress to; affect with painful emotion: *a tale that wrings the heart.* **7.** To obtain or extract by applying force or pressure: *wrung the truth out of the recalcitrant witness.* *—intr.* To writhe or squirm, as in pain. **—wring** *n.* The act or an instance of wringing; a squeeze or twist. [Middle English *wringen,* from Old English *wringan.* See **wer-**[2] in Appendix.]

wring·er (rĭng′ər) *n.* One that wrings, especially a device in which laundry is pressed between rollers to extract water. ***—idiom.* put (someone) through the wringer.** *Slang.* To subject to a severe trial or ordeal.

wrin·kle (rĭng′kəl) *n.* **1.** A small furrow, ridge, or crease on a normally smooth surface, caused by crumpling, folding, or shrinking. **2.** A line or crease in the skin, as from age. **3.** *Informal.* A clever trick, method, or device, especially one that is new and different; an innovation. **—wrinkle** *v.* **-kled, -kling, -kles.** *—tr.* **1.** To make wrinkles or a wrinkle in. **2.** To draw up into wrinkles; pucker: *wrinkled her nose in disdain.* *—intr.* To form wrinkles. [Middle English, back-formation from *wrinkled,* wrinkled, probably from Old English *gewrinclod,* past participle of *gewrinclian,* to wind, crease. See **wer-**[2] in Appendix.] **—wrin′kly** *adj.*

wrist (rĭst) *n.* **1.a.** The joint between the hand and the forearm. **b.** See **carpus** (sense 1). **2.** The part of a sleeve or glove that encircles the wrist. [Middle English, from Old English. See **wer-**[2] in Appendix.]

wrist·band (rĭst′bănd′) *n.* A band, as on a long sleeve or a wristwatch, that encircles the wrist.

wrist·let (rĭst′lĭt) *n.* **1.** A band of material worn round the wrist for warmth or support. **2.** A bracelet.

wrist·lock (rĭst′lŏk′) *n.* *Sports.* A wrestling hold in which an opponent's wrist is gripped and twisted to immobilize the opponent.

wrist pin *n.* A pin that attaches one end of a connecting rod to a wheel, crank, or piston. Also called *gudgeon pin.*

wrist·watch (rĭst′wŏch′) *n.* A watch worn on a band that fastens about the wrist.

writ[1] (rĭt) *n.* **1.** *Law.* A written order issued by a court, commanding the party to whom it is addressed to perform or cease performing a specified act. **2.** Writings: *holy writ.* [Middle English, from Old English.]

writ[2] (rĭt) *v.* A past tense and a past participle of **write.**

write (rīt) *v.* **wrote** (rōt), **writ·ten** (rĭt′n) also **writ** (rĭt), **writ·ing, writes.** *—tr.* **1.a.** To form (letters, words, or symbols) on a surface such as paper with an instrument such as a pen. **b.** To spell: *How do you write your name?* **2.** To form (letters or words) in cursive style. **3.** To compose and set down, especially in literary or musical form: *write a poem; write a prelude.* **4.** To draw up in legal form; draft: *write a will.* **5.** To fill in or cover with writing: *write a check; wrote five pages in an hour.* **6.** To express in writing; set down: *write one's thoughts.* **7.** To communicate by correspondence: *wrote that she was planning to visit.* **8.** To underwrite, as an insurance policy. **9.** To depict clearly; mark: *"Utter dejection was written on every face"* (Winston S. Churchill). **10.** To ordain or prophesy: *It was written that the empire would fall.* **11.** *Computer Science.* To record (data) on a storage device. *—intr.* **1.** To trace or form letters, words, or symbols on paper or another surface. **2.** To produce written material, such as articles or books. **3.** To compose a letter; communicate by mail. ***—phrasal verbs.* write down. 1.** To set down in writing. **2.** To reduce in rank, value, or price. **3.** To disparage in writing. **4.** To write in a conspicuously simple or condescending style: *felt he had to write down to his students.* **write in. 1.** To cast a vote by inserting (a name not listed on a ballot). **2.** To insert in a text or document: *wrote in an apology at the end of the note.* **3.** To communicate with an organization by mail: *write in with a completed entry form.* **write off. 1.** To reduce to zero the book value of (an asset that has become worthless). **2.** To cancel from accounts as a loss. **3.** To consider as a loss or failure: *wrote off the rainy first day of the vacation.* **write out. 1.** To express or compose in writing: *write out a request.* **2.** To write in full or expanded form: *All abbreviations are to be written out.* **write up. 1.** To write a report or description of, as for publication. **2.** To bring (a journal, for example) up to date. **3.** To overstate the value of (assets). **4.** To report (someone) in writing, as for breaking the law: *wrote him up for speeding.* ***—idioms.* write (one's) own ticket.** To set one's own terms or course of action entirely according to one's own needs or wishes: *a generous scholarship that lets recipients write their own ticket.* **writ large.** Signified, expressed, or embodied in a greater or more prominent magnitude or degree: *"The man was no more than the boy writ large"* (George Eliot). [Middle English *writen,* from Old English *wrītan.*]

write-down (rīt′doun′) *n.* *Accounting.* A reduction of the entered value of an asset.

write-in (rīt′ĭn′) *n.* **1.** A vote cast by writing in the name of a candidate not on the ballot. **2.** A candidate voted for in this way.

write-off (rīt′ôf′, -ŏf′) *n.* *Accounting.* **1.a.** A cancellation of an item in account books. **b.** The amount canceled or lost. **2.** A reduction or depreciation of the entered value of an item.

writ·er (rī′tər) *n.* One who writes, especially as an occupation.

writ·er·ly (rī′tər-lē) *adj.* Of, relating to, characteristic of, or befitting a writer: *"set a standard of writerly craft for that . . . well-wrought magazine"* (Newsweek).

writ·er's block (rītərz) *n.* A usually temporary psychological inability to begin or continue work on a piece of writing.

writer's cramp *n., pl.* **writers' cramps.** A cramp or spasm of the muscles of the fingers, hand, and forearm during writing.

write-up (rīt′ŭp′) *n.* **1.** A published account, review, or notice, especially a favorable one. **2.** *Accounting.* An intentional overevaluation of a corporation's assets.

writhe (rīth) *v.* **writhed, writh·ing, writhes.** *—intr.* **1.** To twist, as in pain, struggle, or embarrassment. **2.** To move with a twisting or contorted motion. **3.** To suffer acutely. *—tr.* To cause to twist or squirm; contort. **—writhe** *n.* The act or an instance of writhing; a contortion. [Middle English *writhen,* from Old English *wrīthan.* See **wer-**[2] in Appendix.] **—writh′er** *n.*

SYNONYMS: *writhe, agonize, squirm.* The central meaning shared by these verbs is "to twist and turn in discomfort or suffering": *writhing in pain; agonized over the impending examination; squirming in embarrassment.*

writ·ing (rī′tĭng) *n.* **1.** The act of one who writes. **2.** Written form: *Put it in writing.* **3.** Handwriting; penmanship. **4.** Something written, especially: **a.** Meaningful letters or characters that constitute readable matter. **b.** A written work, especially a literary composition. **5.** The occupation or style of a writer. **6. Writings** *(used with a sing. or pl. verb). Bible.* The third of the three divisions of the Hebrew Bible, usually composed of Psalms, Proverbs, Job, Song of Solomon, Ruth, Lamentations, Ecclesiastes, Esther, Daniel, Ezra, Nehemiah, and Chronicles. See table at **Bible.**

writing paper *n.* Paper on which to write, especially in ink.

writ of election *n., pl.* **writs of election.** A writ issued by a governor or other executive authority requiring that an election be held, especially a special election to fill a vacancy.

writ of error *n., pl.* **writs of error.** *Law.* A writ commissioning an appellate court to review the proceedings of another court and correct the judgment given if deemed necessary.

writ of prohibition *n., pl.* **writs of prohibition.** *Law.* An order issued by a higher court commanding a lower court to cease from proceeding in some matter not within its jurisdiction.

writ of summons *n., pl.* **writs of summons.** *Law.* A writ directing a person to appear in court to answer a complaint.

writ·ten (rĭt′n) *v.* Past participle of **write.**

wrnt. *abbr.* Warrant.

Wro·claw (vrôt′släf′) also **Bres·lau** (brĕs′lou). A city of southwest Poland on the Oder River. It was a member of the Hanseatic League (1368–1474) before passing to the Hapsburgs (1526) and Prussia (1742). Wroclaw was assigned to Poland by the Potsdam Conference (1945). Population, 636,000.

wrong (rông, rŏng) *adj.* **1.** Not in conformity with fact or truth; incorrect or erroneous. **2.a.** Contrary to conscience, morality, or law; immoral or wicked. **b.** Unfair; unjust. **3.** Not required, intended, or wanted: *took a wrong turn.* **4.** Not fitting or suitable; inappropriate or improper: *said the wrong thing.* **5.** Not in accord with established usage, method, or procedure: *the wrong way to shuck clams.* **6.** Not functioning properly; out of order. **7.** Unacceptable or undesirable according to social convention. **8.** Designating the side, as of a garment, that is less finished and not intended to show: *socks worn wrong side out.* **—wrong** *adv.* **1.** In a wrong manner; mistakenly or erroneously. **2.** In a wrong course or direction. **3.** Immorally or unjustly: *She acted wrong to lie.* **4.** In an unfavorable way. See Synonyms at **amiss.** **—wrong** *n.* **1.a.** An unjust or injurious act. **b.** Something contrary to

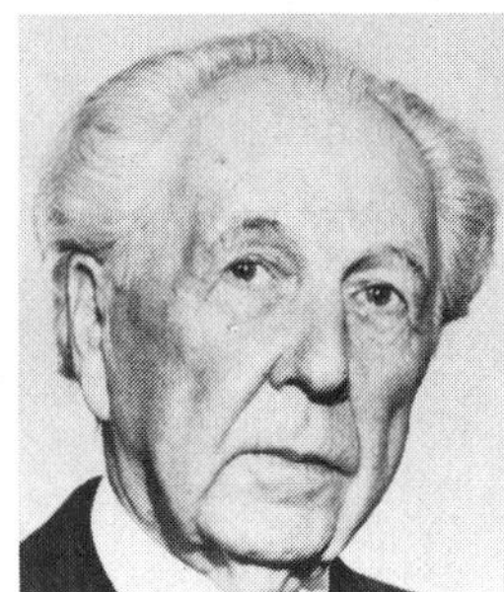

Frank Lloyd Wright

Wright Brothers
Top: Orville Wright
Bottom: Wilbur Wright

wristwatch

ă pat	oi boy
ā pay	ou out
âr care	ŏŏ took
ä father	ōō boot
ĕ pet	ŭ cut
ē be	ûr urge
ĭ pit	th thin
ī pie	*th* this
îr pier	hw which
ŏ pot	zh vision
ō toe	ə about, item
ô paw	♦ regionalism

Stress marks: **′** (primary); ′ (secondary), as in **dictionary** (dĭk′shə-nĕr′ē)

wrought iron

Wyandotte[2]
Columbian Wyandotte hen

Andrew Wyeth
Photographed in 1987

ă pat	oi boy
ā pay	ou out
âr care	o͝o took
ä father	o͞o boot
ĕ pet	ŭ cut
ē be	ûr urge
ĭ pit	th thin
ī pie	*th* this
îr pier	hw which
ŏ pot	zh vision
ō toe	ə about, item
ô paw	♦ regionalism

Stress marks: ′ (primary); ′ (secondary), as in **dictionary** (dĭk′shə-nĕr′ē)

ethics or morality. **2.a.** An invasion or a violation of another's legal rights. **b.** *Law.* A tort. See Synonyms at **injustice. 3.** The condition of being in error or at fault: *in the wrong.* **—wrong** *tr.v.* **wronged, wrong·ing, wrongs. 1.** To treat unjustly or injuriously. **2.** To discredit unjustly; malign. **3.** To treat dishonorably; violate. **—*idioms.* do (someone) wrong.** *Informal.* To be unfaithful or disloyal. **go wrong. 1.** To take a wrong turn or make a wrong move. **2.** To go astray morally. **3.** To go amiss; turn out badly. [Middle English, of Scandinavian origin. See **wer-[2]** in Appendix.] **—wrong′er** *n.* **—wrong′ly** *adv.*

wrong·do·er (rông′do͞o′ər, rŏng′-) *n.* One who does wrong, especially morally or ethically. **—wrong′do′ing** *n.*

wrong·ful (rông′fəl, rŏng′-) *adj.* **1.** Wrong; unjust: *wrongful criticism.* **2.** Unlawful: *wrongful death.* **—wrong′ful·ly** *adv.* **—wrong′ful·ness** *n.*

wrong-head·ed (rông′hĕd′ĭd, rŏng′-) *adj.* Stubbornly defiant of what is right or reasonable; obstinately perverse in judgment or opinion. **—wrong′-head′ed·ly** *adv.* **—wrong′-head′ed·ness** *n.*

wrote (rōt) *v.* Past tense of **write.**

wroth (rôth) *adj.* Wrathful; angry. [Middle English, from Old English *wrāth.* See **wer-[2]** in Appendix.]

wrought (rôt) *v.* A past tense and a past participle of **work.** **—wrought** *adj.* **1.** Put together; created: *a carefully wrought plan.* **2.** Shaped by hammering with tools. Used chiefly of metals or metalwork. **3.** Made delicately or elaborately. [Middle English *wroght,* from Old English *geworht,* past participle of *wyrcan,* to work. See **werg-** in Appendix.]

wrought iron *n.* An easily welded and forged iron that is a mechanical mixture of refined metallic iron with 1 to 3 percent siliceous slag.

wrought-up also **wrought up** (rôt′ŭp′) *adj.* Agitated; excited.

wrung (rŭng) *v.* Past tense and past participle of **wring.**

wry (rī) *adj.* **wri·er, wri·est** or **wry·er, wry·est. 1.** Dryly humorous, often with a touch of irony. **2.** Temporarily twisted in an expression of distaste or displeasure: *made a wry face.* **3.** Abnormally twisted or bent to one side; crooked: *a wry nose.* **4.** Being at variance with what is right, proper, or suitable; perverse. [From Middle English *wrien,* to turn, from Old English *wrīgian.* See **wer-[2]** in Appendix.] **—wry′ly** *adv.* **—wry′ness** *n.*

wry·neck (rī′nĕk′) *n.* **1.** Either of two small Old World woodpeckers *(Jynx torquilla* or *J. ruficollis),* having a sharply pointed bill and the habit of twisting the head and neck into contortions. **2.a.** See **torticollis. b.** A person with torticollis.

WS *abbr. Computer Science.* Working storage.

WSW *abbr.* West-southwest.

wt. *abbr.* Weight.

Wu·han (wo͞o′hän′). A city of east-central China on the Yangtze River (Chang Jiang). It is the industrial, commercial, and transportation center of central China and the capital of Hubei province. Population, 3,400,000.

Wu·hu (wo͞o′ho͞o′). A city of east-central China on the Yangtze River (Chang Jiang) south-southwest of Nanjing. It is a commercial center and a deep-water port. Population, 360,000.

Wu Jiang (wo͞o′ jyäng′). A river rising in south-central China and flowing about 805 km (500 mi) east and north to the Yangzte River (Chang Jiang).

wul·fen·ite (wo͝ol′fə-nīt′) *n.* A usually yellow to orange-brown mineral, $PbMoO_4$, used as a molybdenum ore. [German *Wulfenit,* after Franz X. von *Wulfen* (1728–1805), Austrian mineralogist.]

wun·der·kind (vo͝on′dər-kĭnd′, wŭn′-) *n., pl.* **-kin·der** (-kĭn′dər). **1.** A child prodigy. **2.** A person of remarkable talent or ability who achieves great success at an early age. [German : *Wunder,* wonder, prodigy (from Middle High German, from Old High German *wuntar*) + *Kind,* child; see KINDERGARTEN.]

Wup·per·tal (vo͝op′ər-täl′). A city of west-central Germany north-northeast of Düsseldorf. Population, 379,393.

wurst (wûrst, wo͝orst) *n.* Sausage. [German, from Middle High German, from Old High German. See **wers-** in Appendix.]

Würt·tem·berg (wûr′təm-bûrg′, vür′təm-bĕrk′). A historical region and former kingdom of southwest Germany. A duchy after 1495, it was a kingdom from 1806 to 1918 and came under German sovereignty in 1934.

Würz·burg (wûrts′bûrg′, vürts′bo͝ork′). A city of south-central Germany on the Main River. Originally a Celtic settlement, it is an industrial center. Population, 129,995.

wu·shu also **wu shu** (wo͞o′sho͞o′) *n.* The Chinese martial arts. [Chinese (Mandarin) *wǔ shù* : *wǔ,* martial + *shù,* skill, art.]

Wu·xi also **Wu·sih** (wo͞o′shē′). A city of eastern China between Shanghai and Nanjing. Population, 696,300.

WV *abbr.* West Virginia.

W.Va. *abbr.* West Virginia.

WVS *abbr.* Women's Voluntary Service.

WWI *abbr.* World War I.

WWII *abbr.* World War II.

WY *abbr.* Wyoming.

Wy·an·dot also **Wy·an·dotte** (wī′ən-dŏt′) *n., pl.* **Wyandot** or **-dots** also **Wyandotte** or **-dottes. 1.a.** A Native American people formed of groups displaced by the destruction of the Huron confederacy in the mid-17th century, formerly located in Ohio and the upper Midwest and now living in northeast Oklahoma. **b.** A member of this people. **2.** The Iroquoian language of the Wyandot. [Wyandot *wădát,* tribal name.]

Wy·an·dotte[1] (wī′ən-dŏt′). A city of southeast Michigan, an industrial suburb of Detroit. Population, 34,006.

Wy·an·dotte[2] (wī′ən-dŏt′) *n.* **1.** A medium-sized domestic chicken of a breed developed in North America for its eggs and meat. **2.** Variant of **Wyandot.**

Wy·att or **Wy·at** (wī′ət), Sir **Thomas.** 1503–1542. English diplomat and poet noted for introducing the sonnet form into English literature.

wych elm also **witch elm** (wĭch) *n.* A Eurasian elm *(Ulmus glabra)* often planted as a shade tree. [From Middle English *wiche,* from Old English *wice.* See **weik-[2]** in Appendix.]

Wych·er·ley (wĭch′ər-lē), **William.** 1640?–1716. English comic playwright and satirist whose plays include *The Country Wife* (1675) and *The Plain Dealer* (1676).

Wyc·liffe also **Wick·liffe** or **Wyc·lif** or **Wic·lif** (wĭk′lĭf), **John.** 1328?–1384. English theologian and religious reformer. His rejection of the biblical basis of papal power and dispute with the doctrine of the transubstantiation of the host anticipated the Protestant Reformation.

wye (wī) *n.* **1.** The letter *y.* **2.** An object shaped like a Y.

Wy·eth (wī′ĭth), **Andrew.** Born 1917. American painter whose realistic canvases depict stark rural scenes. His major works include *Christina's World* (1948) and *Tenant Farmer* (1961). His father, **Newell Convers Wyeth** (1882–1945), was also a painter and a book illustrator.

Wy·ler (wī′lər), **William.** 1902–1981. American filmmaker who directed such film classics as *Jezebel* (1938), *Wuthering Heights* (1939), and *Ben Hur* (1959).

Wy·lie (wī′lē), **Elinor Morton Hoyt.** 1885–1928. American writer best remembered for her poems, especially those collected in *Nets to Catch the Wind* (1921).

wynn or **wen** (wĕn) *n.* An Old English rune having the sound (w) and used in Old English and Middle English writing. [Old English. See **wen-[1]** in Appendix.]

Wy·o·ming (wī-ō′mĭng). **1.** *Abbr.* **WY, Wyo.** A state of the western United States. It was admitted as the 44th state in 1890. Acquired by the United States as part of the Louisiana Purchase (1803), Wyoming became a ranching center after the Union Pacific Railroad was established (1868). Cheyenne is the capital and the largest city. Population, 469,557. **2.** A city of west-central Michigan, a suburb of Grand Rapids. Population, 59,616.

WYSIWYG (wĭz′ē-wĭg′) *Computer Science. adj.* Relating to or being a word-processing or desktop publishing system in which the screen displays text exactly as it will be printed. **—WYSIWYG** *n.* A WYSIWYG system, effect, or screen display. [*w(hat) y(ou) s(ee) i(s) w(hat) y(ou) g(et).*]

Wy·szyń·ski (vĭ-shĭn′skē), **Stefan.** 1901–1981. Polish prelate whose agreements with Soviet authorities brought greater religious freedom to Poland.

wy·vern also **wi·vern** (wī′vərn) *n. Heraldry.* A two-legged dragon having wings and a barbed tail. [Alteration of Middle English *wyvere,* viper, from Old North French *wivre,* from Latin *vīpera.* See VIPER.]

x[1] or **X** (ĕks) —*n., pl.* **x's** or **X's. 1.** The 24th letter of the modern English alphabet. **2.** Any of the speech sounds represented by the letter *x*. **3.** The 24th in a series. **4.** Something shaped like the letter X. **5.** A mark inscribed to represent the signature of one who is unable to sign one's name. **6.** An unknown or unnamed factor, thing, or person. —*tr.v.* **x'd, x'ing, x's** or **X'd, X'ing, X's. 1.** To mark or sign with an X. **2.** To delete, cancel, or obliterate with a series of X's. Often used with *out.*

x[2] *Mathematics.* The symbol for **abscissa.**

X[1] (ĕks) *n.* A movie rating that allows admission to no one under the age of 17. —*attributive.* Often used to modify another noun: *an X movie.*

X[2] **1.** *Electricity.* The symbol for **reactance. 2.** Also **x.** The symbol for the Roman numeral 10.

X[3] *abbr.* **1.** Christ (Greek Χριστος, Christos). **2.** Christian. **3.** Or **x.** Experimental. **4.** Extra.

x. *abbr. Business.* Ex.

Xan·a·du (zăn′ə-do͞o′, -dyo͞o′) *n.* An idyllic, beautiful place. [After *Xanadu,* a place in "Kubla Khan," a poem by Samuel Taylor Coleridge.]

xanth– *pref.* Variant of **xantho–.**

xan·than gum (zăn′thən) *n.* A natural gum of high molecular weight produced by culture fermentation of glucose and used as a stabilizer in commercial food preparation. [From New Latin *Xanthomonas (campestris),* name of the bacterium used to produce it : Greek *xanthos,* yellow (from its color) + Greek *monas,* monad; see MONAD.]

xan·thate (zăn′thāt′) *n.* A salt of a xanthic acid, especially a simple xanthic acid salt, as of sodium or potassium, used as a flotation collector for copper, silver, and gold.

xan·thene (zăn′thēn′) *n.* A yellow crystalline organic compound, $CH_2(C_6H_4)_2O$, that is soluble in ether and is used as a fungicide and in organic synthesis.

xan·thic acid (zăn′thĭk) *n.* Any of various unstable acids of the form ROC(S)SH, in which R is usually an alkyl radical. [From the yellow color of its salts.]

xan·thine (zăn′thēn′, -thĭn) *n.* **1.** A yellowish-white, crystalline purine base, $C_5H_4N_4O_2$, that is a precursor of uric acid and is found in blood, urine, muscle tissue, and certain plants. **2.** Any of several derivatives of this compound.

Xan·thip·pe (zăn-thĭp′ē, -tĭp′ē) or **Xan·tip·pe** (-tĭp′ē). Fifth century B.C. Greek woman. The wife of Socrates, she is traditionally described as shrewish and scolding.

xantho– or **xanth–** *pref.* **1.** Yellow: *xanthine.* **2.** Xanthic acid: *xanthate.* [Greek, yellow, from *xanthos.*]

xan·tho·chroid (zăn′thə-kroid′) *adj.* Having a light complexion and light hair. **—xanthochroid** *n.* A person having a light complexion and light hair. [New Latin *xanthŏchroi,* yellow-haired, fair-skinned people (Greek *xantho-,* xantho- + Greek *ōkhroi,* pl. of *ōkhros,* pale) + –OID.] **—xan′tho·chro′ic** (-krō′ĭk) *adj.*

xan·tho·ma (zăn-thō′mə) *n., pl.* **-mas** or **-ma·ta** (-mə-tə). A yellowish-orange, lipid-filled nodule or papule in the skin, often on an eyelid or over a joint. **—xan·thom′a·tous** (-thŏm′ə-təs) *adj.*

xan·tho·ma·to·sis (zăn′thō-mə-tō′sĭs) *n.* A metabolic disorder characterized by excessive accumulation of lipids in the body and a resulting spread of xanthomas. [New Latin *xanthōma, xanthōmat-,* xanthoma (XANTHO– + –OMA) + –OSIS.]

xan·tho·phore (zăn′thə-fôr′, -fōr′) *n.* A chromatophore that contains a yellow pigment.

xan·tho·phyll (zăn′thə-fĭl′) *n.* **1.** A yellow carotenoid pigment, $C_{40}H_{56}O_2$, found with chlorophyll in green plants and identical with lutein. **2.** Any of various related yellow pigments. **—xan′tho·phyl′lic, xan′tho·phyl′lous** *adj.*

xan·thous (zăn′thəs) *adj.* **1.** *Color.* Yellow. **2.** Having light brown or yellowish skin.

xan·thop·ter·in (zăn-thŏp′tər-ĭn) *n.* A yellow pigment in the wings of certain butterflies and moths, found also in the urine of mammals.

Xan·thus (zăn′thəs). An ancient city of Lycia in present-day southwest Turkey. It was besieged and taken by the Persians (c. 546 B.C.) and the Romans (c. 42 B.C.). Both times the residents destroyed the city before surrendering.

Xan·tip·pe (zăn-tĭp′ē). See **Xanthippe.**

Xa·ve·ri·an Brother (zə-vĕr′ē-ən) *n. Roman Catholic Church.* A member of a congregation of lay brothers dedicated to education. [After Saint Francis XAVIER.]

Xa·vi·er (zā′vē-ər, zăv′ē-), Saint **Francis.** 1506–1552. Spanish Jesuit missionary. A cofounder of the Jesuit order (1534) with Ignatius of Loyola, he established missionaries in Japan, Ceylon, and the East Indies.

x-ax·is (ĕks′ăk′sĭs) *n., pl.* **x-ax·es** (-ăk′sēz). *Mathematics.* **1.** The horizontal axis of a two-dimensional Cartesian coordinate system. **2.** One of three axes in a three-dimensional Cartesian coordinate system.

XC or **X-C** *abbr. Sports.* Cross-country.

X-chro·mo·some (ĕks′krō′mə-sōm′) *n.* The sex chromosome associated with female characteristics, occurring paired in the female and single in the male sex-chromosome pair.

XD *abbr.* Ex dividend.

x-dis·ease (ĕks′dĭ-zēz′) *n.* Hyperkeratosis of cattle caused by ingestion of a toxic substance, especially one of uncertain origin or chemical composition.

x-div. *abbr.* Ex dividend.

Xe The symbol for the element **xenon.**

xe·bec also **ze·bec** or **ze·beck** (zē′bĕk′) *n. Nautical.* A small three-masted Mediterranean vessel with both square and triangular sails. [French *chebec,* probably from Catalan *xabec,* from Arabic dialectal *šabbāk.*]

xen– *pref.* Variant of **xeno–.**

xe·ni·a (zē′nē-ə, zēn′yə) *n. Botany.* The direct effect on a hybrid plant produced by the transfer of pollen from one strain to the endosperm of a different strain. [New Latin, from Greek, hospitality, from *xenos,* guest, stranger. See XENO–.]

Xen·ia (zēn′yə, zē′nē-ə). A city of southwest-central Ohio east-southeast of Dayton. It is a manufacturing center. Population, 24,653.

xeno– or **xen–** *pref.* **1.** Stranger; foreigner: *xenophobia.* **2.** Strange; foreign; different: *xenolith.* [New Latin, from Greek, from *xenos,* stranger. See **ghos-ti-** in Appendix.]

xen·o·bi·ot·ic (zĕn′ə-bī-ŏt′ĭk, zē′nə-) *adj.* Foreign to the body or to living organisms. Used of chemical compounds. **—xenobiotic** *n.* A xenobiotic chemical, such as a pesticide.

xen·o·blast (zĕn′ə-blăst′, zē′nə-) *n.* A mineral deposit that has developed during metamorphism without developing crystal-line faces.

xen·o·cryst (zĕn′ə-krĭst′, zē′nə-) *n.* A crystal foreign to the igneous rock in which it occurs. [XENO– + CRYST(AL).]

xen·o·di·ag·no·sis (zĕn′ə-dī′əg-nō′sĭs, zē′nə-) *n., pl.* **-ses** (-sēz). Diagnosis of an infectious disease at an early stage by exposing a presumably infected individual or tissue to a clean, laboratory-bred mosquito, tick, or other vector and then examining the vector for the presence of the infective microorganism. **—xen′o·di·ag·nos′tic** (-nŏs′tĭk) *adj.*

xe·nog·a·my (zĭ-nŏg′ə-mē) *n., pl.* **-mies.** *Botany.* Transfer of pollen from one plant to another; cross-pollination. **—xe·nog′a·mous** *adj.*

xen·o·ge·ne·ic (zĕn′ə-jə-nē′ĭk, -nā′-, zē′nə-) *adj.* Derived or obtained from an organism of a different species: *a xenogeneic tissue graft; xenogeneic antibodies.*

xen·o·gen·e·sis (zĕn′ə-jĕn′ĭ-sĭs, zē′nə-) *n.* **1.** The supposed production of offspring markedly different from either parent. **2.** See **alternation of generations. —xen′o·ge·net′ic** (-jə-nĕt′ĭk), **xen′o·gen′ic** (-jĕn′ĭk) *adj.*

xen·o·graft (zĕn′ə-grăft′, zē′nə-) *n.* See **heterograft.**

xen·o·lith (zĕn′ə-lĭth′, zē′nə-) *n.* A rock fragment foreign to the igneous mass in which it occurs.

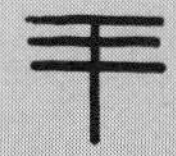

Phoenician
Although its earliest origins are disputed, the letter X appears to have affinities with the Semitic *samekh,* which stood for the sound *s.*

Early Greek
In West Greek it was used, at first together with the *sigma* (see S) and then on its own, to stand for the combination *ks.*

Roman
The Romans inherited it by way of the Etruscans with the same value.

Saint Francis Xavier
17th-century Hispano-Philippine carved ivory head

Xerxes I
Fifth-century B.C. low relief from Persepolis, widely recognized as Xerxes the Great

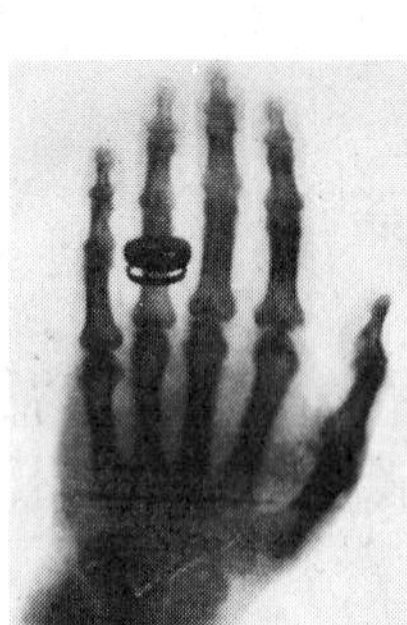

x-ray
One of the earliest x-rays taken, showing the left hand of Bertha Roentgen (died 1919)

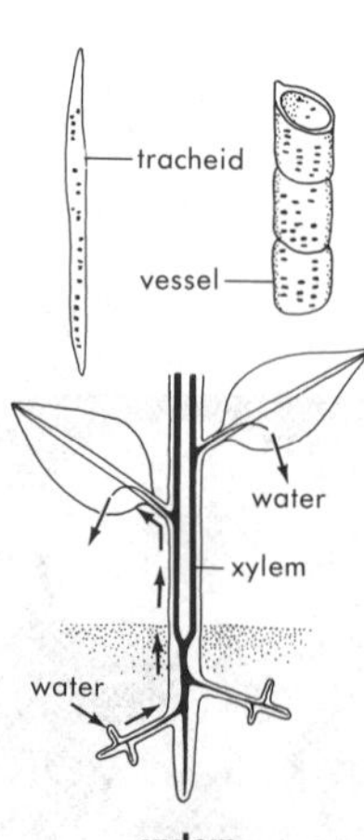

xylem

xe·non (zē′nŏn′) *n. Symbol* **Xe** A colorless, odorless, highly unreactive gaseous element found in minute quantities in the atmosphere, extracted commercially from liquefied air and used in stroboscopic, bactericidal, and laser-pumping lamps. Atomic number 54; atomic weight 131.30; melting point −111.9°C; boiling point −107.1°C; density (gas) 5.887 grams per liter; specific gravity (liquid) 3.52 (−109°C). See table at **element.** [From Greek, neuter of *xenos,* foreign, strange. See XENO–.]

Xe·noph·a·nes (zə-nŏf′ə-nēz′). 560?–478? B.C. Greek philosopher who was a founder of the Eleatic school.

xen·o·phile (zĕn′ə-fīl′, zē′nə-) *n.* A person attracted to that which is foreign, especially to foreign peoples, manners, or cultures. **—xen′o·phil′i·a** (-fĭl′ē-ə) *n.* **—xe·noph′i·lous** (zĕ-nŏf′ə-ləs, zē-) *adj.*

xen·o·phobe (zĕn′ə-fōb′, zē′nə-) *n.* A person unduly fearful or contemptuous of that which is foreign, especially of strangers or foreign peoples. **—xen′o·pho′bi·a** *n.* **—xen′o·pho′bic** *adj.*

Xen·o·phon (zĕn′ə-fən, -fŏn′). 430?–355? B.C. Greek soldier and writer. A disciple of Socrates, he joined Cyrus the Younger in an attack on Persia. After the death of Cyrus, Xenophon led the Greeks to the Black Sea, an ordeal he recounted in *Anabasis.*

xer– *pref.* Variant of **xero–.**

xer·arch (zîr′ärk′) *adj.* Originating in a dry habitat, such as a rocky shore, cliff, or desert. Used of a sere. [XER(O)– + Greek *arkhē,* beginning.]

xer·ic (zĕr′ĭk, zîr′-) *adj.* Of, characterized by, or adapted to an extremely dry habitat. **—xer′i·cal·ly** *adv.* **—xe·ric′i·ty** (zĕ-rĭs′ĭ-tē) *n.*

xero– or **xer–** *pref.* Dry; dryness: *xeroderma.* [Greek *xēro-,* from *xēros,* dry.]

xer·o·der·ma (zîr′ō-dûr′mə) also **xe·ro·der·mi·a** (-mē-ə) *n.* Excessive or abnormal dryness of the skin, as in ichthyosis.

xeroderma pig·men·to·sum (pĭg′mən-tō′səm) *n.* A rare hereditary skin disorder caused by a defect in the enzymes that repair DNA damaged by ultraviolet light. [New Latin *xēroderma pigmentōsum* : *xēroderma,* xeroderma + *pigmentōsus,* of pigment.]

xe·rog·ra·phy (zĭ-rŏg′rə-fē) *n.* A dry photographic or photocopying process in which a negative image formed by a resinous powder on an electrically charged plate is electrically transferred to and thermally fixed as positive on a paper or other copying surface. **—xe·rog′ra·pher** *n.* **—xer′o·graph′ic** (zîr′ə-grăf′ĭk) *adj.* **—xer′o·graph′i·cal·ly** *adv.*

xe·roph·i·lous (zĭ-rŏf′ə-ləs) *adj.* Flourishing in or adapted to a dry, hot environment. **—xe·roph′i·ly** *adv.*

xer·oph·thal·mi·a (zîr′əf-thăl′mē-ə) *n.* Extreme dryness and thickening of the conjunctiva, often resulting from a deficiency of vitamin A. **—xer′oph·thal′mic** *adj.*

xer·o·phyte (zîr′ə-fīt′) *n.* A plant adapted to living in a dry, arid habitat; a desert plant. **—xer′o·phyt′ic** (-fĭt′ĭk) *adj.* **—xer′o·phyt′i·cal·ly** *adv.* **—xer′o·phyt′ism** (-fī′tĭz-əm, -fī-tĭz′-) *n.*

xe·ro·sere (zîr′ə-sîr′) *n.* A succession of ecological communities originating in a dry habitat.

xe·ro·sis (zĭ-rō′sĭs) *n., pl.* **-ses** (-sēz). **1.** Abnormal dryness, especially of the skin, eyes, or mucous membranes. **2.** The normal hardening of aging tissue.

xer·o·ther·mic (zîr′ə-thûr′mĭk) *adj.* **1.** Both dry and hot: *a xerothermic climate.* **2.** Adapted to or flourishing in an environment that is both dry and hot: *xerothermic organisms.*

Xer·ox (zîr′ŏks). A trademark used for a photocopying process or machine employing xerography. This trademark often occurs in print in uppercase or lowercase as a verb, an adjective, and a noun: *"Juicy stories circulated . . . in a book proposal that was Xeroxed and read as an alternate beach book in the Hamptons"* (Washington Post). *"Letters you send should be xeroxed after you sign them"* (Progressive Architecture). *"To walk around the . . . campus during the strike was to be confronted with their fact sheets, their xeroxed research summaries and news clips"* (San Francisco Chronicle). *"The group's teacher . . . asked the children how they would feel if they received a Xeroxed thank-you card"* (New York Times). *"He reaches inside his windbreaker to his shirt pocket. He has four or five sheets of foolscap, xeroxes, I see, of court documents"* (Scott Turow). The trademark sometimes occurs in print in figurative contexts: *"Her performance was Xeroxed from her imagination"* (Chicago Tribune). *"And of course sequels are nothing new: Andy Hardy and Nick Charles, for instance, were Xeroxed shamelessly in earlier days"* (Boston Globe).

Xer·xes I (zûrk′sēz). Known as "Xerxes the Great." 519?–465 B.C. King of Persia (486–465) who organized a vast army that defeated the Greeks at Thermopylae and destroyed Athens (480). After the defeat of his navy at Salamis (480) and of his army at Plataea (479), he retreated to Persia, where he was assassinated.

x-height (ĕks′hīt′) *n. Printing.* The height of a lowercase x.

Xho·sa also **Xo·sa** (kō′sä, -zə) *n., pl.* **Xhosa** or **-sas** also **Xosa** or **-sas. 1.** A member of a Bantu people inhabiting the eastern part of Cape Province, South Africa. **2.** The Nguni language of this people, closely related to Zulu.

xi (zī, sī, ksē) *n.* **1.** The 14th letter of the Greek alphabet. See table at **alphabet. 2.** See **xi hyperon.** [Greek *xei.*]

XI *abbr. Business.* Ex interest.

Xia or **Hsia** (shyä). The first Chinese dynasty (traditionally dated c. 2205–1766 B.C.). No historical documents or archaeological evidence has been found to corroborate the legends about this dynasty.

Xia·men (shyä′mən) also **A·moy** (ä-moi′). A city of eastern China east-northeast of Guangzhou. One of the earliest seats of European commerce in China, it is a major harbor and a manufacturing center. Population, 350,000.

Xi'an (shē′än′, shyän) also **Si·an** (sē′än′, shē′-) or **Hsian** (shyän). A city of central China southwest of Beijing. The capital (221–206 B.C.) of the Qin dynasty, it is a major commercial center and the capital of Shaanxi province. Population, 1,730,000.

Xiang Jiang (shyäng′ jyäng′) also **Siang Kiang** (syäng′ kyäng′, shyäng′) or **Hsiang Kiang** (shyäng′). A river, about 1,150 km (715 mi) long, flowing generally northward from southeast China. Its valley has important mineral resources.

Xiang·tan (shyäng′tän′) also **Siang·tan** (syäng′-, shyäng′-). A city of south-central China on the Xiang Jiang south-southwest of Changsha. It is an industrial center. Population, 350,000.

xi hyperon *n.* Either of two subatomic particles in the baryon family, one neutral and one negatively charged, with masses of 2,573 and 2,585 times that of the electron and average lifetimes of 2.9×10^{-10} and 1.6×10^{-10} second. Also called *xi.* See table at **subatomic particle.**

Xi Jiang (shē′ jyäng′) also **Si Kiang** (sē′ kyäng′, shē′). A river, about 2,011 km (1,250 mi) long, rising in southeast China and flowing generally eastward to the South China Sea near Guangzhou.

Xin·gu (shēng-go͞o′). A river of central and northern Brazil rising in several streams and flowing about 1,979 km (1,230 mi) generally northward to the Amazon River at the head of the Amazon delta.

Xi·ning (shē′nĭng′). A city of central China north-northeast of Chengdu. The capital of Qinghai province, it has long been a commercial center on the caravan route to Xizang (Tibet). Population, 400,000.

Xin·jiang Uy·gur (shĭn′jyäng′ wē′gər) also **Sin·kiang Ui·ghur** or **Sin·kiang Ui·gur** (sĭn′kyäng′ wē′gər, shĭn′jyäng′). An autonomous region of extreme western China. It came under Chinese control in the 16th century and was the site of a conflict between China and the Soviet Union in 1969. Ürümqi is the capital. Population, 13,610,000.

Xin·xiang (shĭn′shyäng′). A city of eastern China south-southeast of Taiyuan. It is a rail center. Population, 325,000.

xiph·i·ster·num (zĭf′ĭ-stûr′nəm) *n., pl.* **-na** (-nə). The posterior and smallest of the three divisions of the sternum, below the gladiolus and the manubrium. Also called *xiphoid, xiphoid process.* [Greek *xiphos,* sword + STERNUM.]

xiph·oid (zĭf′oid′) *adj.* **1.** Shaped like a sword. **2.** Of or relating to the xiphisternum. **—xiphoid** *n.* See **xiphisternum.** [Greek *xiphoeidēs* : *xiphos,* sword + *-oeidēs,* -oid.]

xiphoid process *n.* See **xiphisternum.**

xiph·o·su·ran (zĭf′ə-so͝or′ən) *n.* An arthropod of the order Xiphosura, which includes the horseshoe crab and many extinct forms. **—xiphosuran** *adj.* Of or belonging to the order Xiphosura. [From New Latin *Xiphosūra,* order name : Greek *xiphos,* sword + Greek *-oura,* neuter pl. of *-ouros,* -urous.]

Xi·zang (shē′dzäng′) or **Ti·bet** (tə-bĕt′). An autonomous region of China in the southwest part of the country north and west of the Himalaya Mountains. Controlled by China since 1720, it became an autonomous province in 1951 and was formally proclaimed an autonomous region in 1965. Xizang is a center of Buddhism, but many Buddhists have fled since the 1950's to escape religious persecution. Lhasa is the capital. Population, 1,990,000.

x-ir·ra·di·ate (ĕks′ĭ-rā′dē-āt′) *tr.v.* **-at·ed, -at·ing, -ates.** To expose or subject to x-ray radiation. **—x′-ir·ra′di·a′tion** *n.*

XL *abbr.* **1.** Extra large. **2.** Extra long.

X·mas (krĭs′məs, ĕks′məs) *n. Usage Problem.* Christmas. [From *X,* the Greek letter chi, abbreviation of *Khristos,* Christ. See CHRIST.]

USAGE NOTE: *Xmas* has been used for hundreds of years in religious writing, where the *X* is understood to represent a Greek chi, the first letter of Χριστος, "Christ"; in this use it is parallel to other forms like *Xtian,* "Christian." But the letter *X,* or especially *x,* is nowadays more frequently interpreted as a mathematical variable than as a Greek letter, as indicated by the common pronunciation of the form *Xmas* as (ĕks′məs). Thus, while the word is etymologically innocent of the charge that it omits Christ from Christmas, it is now generally understood only as an informal shortening. In an earlier survey 88 percent of the Usage Panel rejected the use of *Xmas* in writing.

Xo·sa (kō′sä, -zə) *n.* Variant of **Xhosa.**

x-ra·di·a·tion (ĕks′rā′dē-ā′shən) *n.* **1.** Treatment with or exposure to x-rays. **2.** Radiation composed of x-rays.

X-rat·ed (ĕks′rā′tĭd) *adj.* **1.** Having the rating X: *an X-rated movie.* **2.** Vulgar, obscene, or explicit in the treatment of sex: *an X-rated novel; X-rated graffiti.*

X rating *n.* A classification assigned to movies that feature explicit sex or violence and that may not be viewed by persons under 17 years of age.

x-ray also **X-ray** or **x ray** or **X ray** (ĕks′rā′) *n.* **1.a.** A relatively high-energy photon with wavelength in the approximate range from 0.01 to 10 nanometers. **b.** A stream of such photons, used for their penetrating power in radiography, radiology, radiotherapy, and scientific research. Often used in the plural. Also called *roentgen ray.* **2.** A photograph taken with x-rays. —**x-ray** also **X-ray** *tr.v.* **x-rayed, x-ray·ing, x-rays** also **X-rayed, X-ray·ing, X-rays. 1.** To irradiate with x-rays. **2.** To photograph with x-rays.

x-ray astronomy *n.* The branch of astronomy that deals with the properties of celestial bodies as indicated by the x-rays they emit.

x-ray burster *n.* Any of several celestial phenomena characterized by the emission of very powerful bursts of x-radiation in cycles lasting from a few seconds to a few minutes.

x-ray crystallography *n.* The study of crystal structure by means of x-ray diffraction.

x-ray diffraction *n.* The scattering of x-rays by crystal atoms, producing a diffraction pattern that yields information about the structure of the crystal.

x-ray microscope *n.* An instrument using x-rays to render a highly magnified image.

x-ray star *n.* A celestial object, especially a star, that emits a major portion of its radiation in x-rays.

x-ray therapy *n.* Medical treatment using controlled doses of x-ray radiation.

x-ray tube *n.* A vacuum tube containing electrodes that accelerate electrons and direct them to a metal anode, where their impacts produce x-rays.

Xu·thus (zo͞o′thəs) *n. Greek Mythology.* The ancestor of the Ionian Greeks.

Xu·zhou (sho͞o′jō′) also **Sü·chow** (so͞o′chou′, sü′jō′). A city of eastern China north-northwest of Nanjing. It is a manufacturing center. Population, 806,400.

xyl– *pref.* Variant of **xylo–.**

xy·lan (zī′lən) *n.* A yellow, water-soluble, gummy polysaccharide found in plant cell walls and yielding xylose upon hydrolysis.

xy·lem (zī′ləm) *n.* The supporting and water-conducting tissue of vascular plants, consisting primarily of tracheids and vessels; woody tissue. [German, from Greek *xulon,* wood.]

xy·lene (zī-lēn′, zī′lēn′) also **xy·lol** (zī′lôl′, -lōl′) *n.* **1.** Any of three flammable isomeric hydrocarbons, $C_6H_4(CH_3)_2$, obtained from wood and coal tar. **2.** A mixture of xylene isomers used as a solvent in making lacquers and rubber cement and as an aviation fuel.

xy·li·dine (zī′lĭ-dēn′, -dĭn, zĭl′ĭ-) *n.* **1.** Any of six toxic isomers, $(CH_3)_2C_6H_3NH_2$, derived from xylene, used chiefly as dye intermediates. **2.** Any of various mixtures of xylidine isomers.

xylo– or **xyl–** *pref.* **1.** Wood: *xylograph.* **2.** Xylene: *xylidine.* [Greek *xulo-,* from *xulon,* wood.]

xy·lo·graph (zī′lə-grăf′) *n.* **1.** An engraving on wood. **2.** An impression from a woodblock. —**xylograph** *tr.v.* **-graphed, -graph·ing, -graphs.** To print from a wood engraving. —**xy·log′ra·pher** (-lŏg′rə-fər) *n.*

xy·log·ra·phy (zī-lŏg′rə-fē) *n.* **1.** Wood engraving, especially of an early period. **2.** The art of printing texts or illustrations, sometimes with color, from woodblocks, as distinct from typography. —**xy′lo·graph′ic** (-lə-grăf′ĭk), **xy′lo·graph′i·cal** (-ĭ-kəl) *adj.* —**xy′lo·graph′i·cal·ly** *adv.*

xy·loid (zī′loid′) *adj.* Of or similar to wood.

xy·lol (zī′lôl′, -lōl′) *n.* Variant of **xylene.**

xy·lo·phage (zī′lə-fāj′) *n.* A xylophagous organism.

xy·loph·a·gous (zī-lŏf′ə-gəs) *adj.* **1.** Feeding on wood, as certain insects or insect larvae. **2.** Destructive to wood, as certain crustaceans or fungi.

xy·lo·phone (zī′lə-fōn′) *n. Music.* A percussion instrument consisting of a mounted row of wooden bars graduated in length to sound a chromatic scale, played with two small mallets. —**xy′lo·phon′ist** *n.*

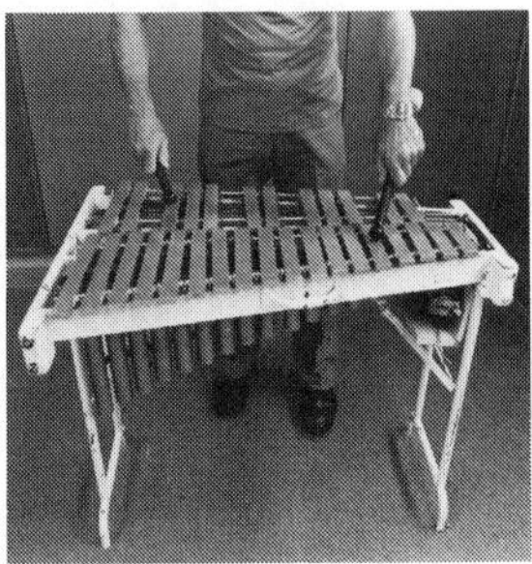

xylophone

WORD HISTORY: *Xylophone* is a word one expects to encounter in the X section of any children's alphabet book. It is there because it is one of the few words beginning with *x* that a child or most anyone else would know. Recognition of *xerophagy,* "the eating of dry food, especially as a form of fasting practiced in the early Christian Church and chiefly in the Eastern churches today," or *xylotomy,* "the preparation of sections of wood for microscopic study" is not to be expected. Most of the English words beginning with *x,* including these obscurities, are of Greek origin, the *x,* pronounced (z), representing the Greek letter xi. In the case of *xylophone, xylo–* is a form meaning "wood," derived from Greek *xulon,* "wood," and *–phone* represents Greek *phōnē,* "voice, sound," the same element found in words such as *telephone, microphone,* and *megaphone.* Our famous *x* word is first recorded in the April 7, 1866, edition of the *Athenaeum:* "A prodigy . . . who does wonderful things with little drumsticks on a machine of wooden keys, called the 'xylophone.' "

xy·lose (zī′lōs′) *n.* A white crystalline sugar, $C_5H_{10}O_5$, used in dyeing and tanning and in diabetic diets. Also called *wood sugar.*

xy·lot·o·my (zī-lŏt′ə-mē) *n., pl.* **-mies.** Preparation of sections of wood for microscopic study. —**xy·lot′o·mist** *n.*

XY recorder (eks′wī′) *n. Computer Science.* An output device that sketches the relationship between two variables onto a grid of plane rectangular coordinates.

xys·ter (zĭs′tər) *n.* A surgical instrument for scraping bones. [Greek *xustēr,* scraper, from *xuein,* to scrape.]

ă pat	oi boy
ā pay	ou out
âr care	o͝o took
ä father	o͞o boot
ĕ pet	ŭ cut
ē be	ûr urge
ĭ pit	th thin
ī pie	*th* this
îr pier	hw which
ŏ pot	zh vision
ō toe	ə about, item
ô paw	♦ regionalism

Stress marks: **′** (primary); ′ (secondary), as in **dictionary** (dĭk′shə-nĕr′ē)

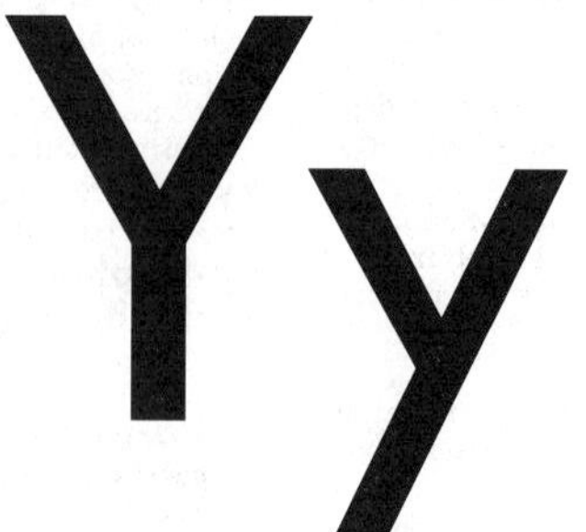

Phoenician
The Phoenicians used a single sign for the initial sound in *wāw*, "hook" or "peg," and the related vowel *u*.

Early Greek
This sign was altered into two different shapes by the Greeks. One form became *digamma*, the ancestor of Roman F (see F), while the other (*upsilon*) was used for the vowel sound *u*.

Roman
Early Latin applied the second form (see V) to both *u* and *w* sounds, but when scholars began importing words from classical Greek around the first century B.C., they borrowed the Greek letter *upsilon* again to represent the Attic pronunciation *ü*, sometimes calling it *y graeca*, "Greek y." Once this *ü* merged with *i* in Vulgar Latin, Y often became merely another way to spell *i* and its related semivowel *y*, much as it is in modern English. The English name is based on the letter's shape: it was earlier spelled *wī*, from Latin *uī*, that is, V + I.

y[1] or **Y** (wī) *n., pl.* **y's** or **Y's. 1.** The 25th letter of the modern English alphabet. **2.** Any of the speech sounds represented by the letter *y*. **3.** Something shaped like the letter Y. **4.** The 25th in a series.

y[2] *Mathematics.* The symbol for **ordinate.**

y[3] or **Y** *abbr.* Yen.

Y[1] **1.** The symbol for the element **yttrium. 2.** *Electricity.* The symbol for **admittance** (sense 3). **3.** *Physics.* The symbol for **hypercharge.**

Y[2] *abbr.* Yeoman.

y. *abbr.* Year.

–y[1] or **–ey** *suff.* **1.** Characterized by; consisting of: *clayey.* **2.a.** Like: *summery.* **b.** To some degree; somewhat; rather: *chilly.* **3.** Tending toward; inclined toward: *sleepy.* [Middle English, from Old English *-ig.*]

–y[2] *suff.* **1.** Condition; state; quality: *jealousy.* **2.a.** Activity: *cookery.* **b.** Instance of a specified action: *entreaty.* **3.a.** Place for an activity: *cannery.* **b.** Result or product of an activity: *laundry.* **4.** Collection; body; group: *soldiery.* [Middle English *-ie,* from Old French, from Latin *-ia.* Sense 2b, ultimately from Latin *-ium.*]

–y[3] or **–ie** *suff.* **1.** Small one: *doggy.* **2.** Dear one: *sweetie.* **3.** One having to do with or characterized by: *townie.* [Middle English *-ie, -y.*]

YA *abbr.* Young adult.

yab·ber (yăb′ər) *Australian. n.* Jabber. **—yabber** *tr. & intr.v.* **-bered, -ber·ing, -bers.** To jabber (something) or engage in jabbering. [From Australian pidgin, probably from Wuywurung, Aboriginal language of southeast Australia *yaba,* to talk.]

Ya·blo·no·vy Range (yä′blə-nə-vē′). A mountain chain of southeast Russia extending northeast from near the Mongolian border.

yacht (yät) *Nautical. n.* Any of various relatively small sailing or motor-driven vessels, generally with smart, graceful lines, used for pleasure cruises or racing. **—yacht** *intr.v.* **yacht·ed, yacht·ing, yachts.** To sail, cruise, or race in a yacht. [Probably obsolete Norwegian *jagt,* from Middle Low German *jacht,* short for *jachtschip* : *jagen,* to chase (from Old High German *jagōn*) + *schip,* ship.]

yacht club *n. Nautical.* A club that promotes and supports yachting and boating.

yacht·ing (yä′tĭng) *n. Nautical.* The activity of sailing in yachts.

yachts·man (yäts′mən) *n. Nautical.* A man who owns or sails a yacht.

yachts·wom·an (yäts′wo͝om′ən) *n.* A woman who owns or sails a yacht.

yack (yăk) *v. & n. Slang.* Variant of **yak**[2]**.**

yack·e·ty-yak (yăk′ĭ-tē-yăk′) *n. Slang.* Prolonged, sometimes senseless talk. [Imitative.]

YAG (yăg) *n.* A hard synthetic yttrium aluminum garnet used in laser technology and as a gemstone. [Y(TTRIUM) + A(LUMINUM) + G(ARNET)[1].]

ya·gi (yä′gē, yăg′ē) *n., pl.* **-gis.** A directional radio and television antenna consisting of a horizontal conductor with several insulated dipoles parallel to and in the plane of the conductor. [After Hidetsugu *Yagi* (1886–1976), Japanese electrical engineer.]

ya·hoo (yä′ho͞o, yā′-) *n., pl.* **-hoos.** A person regarded as crude or brutish. See Synonyms at **boor.** [From *Yahoo,* member of a race of brutes having human form in *Gulliver's Travels* by Jonathan Swift.] **—ya′hoo·ism** *n.*

Yah·weh (yä′wā, -wĕ) also **Yah·veh** (-vā, -vĕ) or **Jah·veh** (yä′vā, -vĕ) or **Jah·weh** (yä′wā, -wĕ) *n.* A name for God assumed by modern scholars to be a rendering of the pronunciation of the Tetragrammaton. [Hebrew.]

Yah·wist (yä′wĭst) also **Yah·vist** (-vĭst) *n.* The author of the earliest sources of the Hexateuch in which God is called Yahweh. **—Yah·wis′tic** *adj.*

yak[1] (yăk) *n.* **1.** A wild, shaggy-haired ox *(Bos grunniens)* of the mountains of central Asia. **2.** A domesticated yak, used as a work animal or raised for meat and milk. [Tibetan *gyag.*]

yak[2] also **yack** (yăk) *Slang.—intr.v.* **yakked, yak·king, yaks** also **yacked, yack·ing, yacks.** To talk persistently and meaninglessly; chatter. —*n.* Prolonged, sometimes senseless talk; chatter. [Imitative.]

Ya·ki·ma[1] (yăk′ə-mô, -mə) *n., pl.* **Yakima** or **-mas. 1.a.** A Native American people inhabiting south-central Washington. **b.** A member of this people. **2.** The dialect of Sahaptin spoken by the Yakima.

Ya·ki·ma[2] (yăk′ə-mô′, -mə). A city of south-central Washington southeast of Seattle. It is a trade, processing, and shipping center for an irrigated agricultural region. Population, 49,286.

Yakima River. A river, about 327 km (203 mi) long, of central and southeast Washington rising in the Cascade Range and flowing generally southeast to the Columbia River.

ya·ki·to·ri (yä′kĭ-tôr′ē, -tōr′ē) *n.* A dish consisting of bite-sized marinated chicken pieces that are grilled on small skewers. [Japanese : *yaki,* roasting + *tori,* bird.]

yak·ow (yăk′ou) *n.* The hybrid offspring of a yak and a cow. [YAK[1] + COW[1].]

Ya·kut (yä-ko͞ot′) *n., pl.* **Yakut** or **-kuts. 1.** A member of a people inhabiting the region of the Lena River in eastern Siberia. **2.** The Turkic language of the Yakut. **—Ya·kut′** *adj.*

Ya·kutsk (yə-ko͞otsk′). A city of east-central Russia on the Lena River. Founded as a fort in 1632, it is a port and processing center. Population, 180,000.

ya·ku·za (yä′ko͞o-zä′) *n., pl.* **yakuza. 1.** A loose alliance of Japanese criminal organizations and illegal enterprises. **2.** A Japanese gangster. [Japanese, good-for-nothing, gambler, racketeer.]

Yale (yāl), **Elihu.** 1649–1721. Colonial-born English merchant and philanthropist who made a series of contributions to the Collegiate School in Connecticut, which was renamed in Yale's honor (1718).

Yale, Mount. A peak, 4,329.8 m (14,196 ft) high, in the Sawatch Range of the Rocky Mountains in central Colorado.

♦ **y'all** (yôl) *pron. Chiefly Southern U.S.* Variant of **you-all.** See Regional Note at **you-all.**

Ya·long Jiang (yä′lo͝ong′ jyäng′). A river of south-central China flowing about 1,287 km (800 mi) generally southward to the Yangtze River (Chang Jiang).

Yal·ow (yăl′ō), **Rosalyn Sussman.** Born 1921. American medical physicist. She shared a 1977 Nobel Prize for research on hormones.

Yal·ta (yôl′tə). A city of southeast Ukraine in the southern Crimea on the Black Sea. A popular resort, it was the site of an Allied conference (attended by Franklin D. Roosevelt, Winston Churchill, and Joseph Stalin) in February 1945. Population, 86,000.

Ya·lu Jiang (yä′lo͞o′ jyäng′). A river, about 805 km (500 mi) long, forming part of the North Korea–China border.

♦ **yam** (yăm) *n.* **1.** Any of numerous chiefly tropical vines of the genus *Dioscorea,* many of which have edible tuberous roots. **2.** The starchy root of any of these plants, used in the tropics as food. **3.** *Chiefly Southern U.S.* See **sweet potato** (sense 1). See Regional Note at **goober.** [Portuguese *inhame* or obsolete Spanish *igname, ñame,* both from Portuguese and English Creole *nyam,* to eat, of West African origin; akin to Fulani *nyami,* to eat, Wolof *ñam,* food, to eat, or Mandingo (Bambara) *ñambu,* manioc.]

Ya·ma·mo·to (yä′mə-mō′tō, -mä-), **Isoroku.** 1884–1943. Japanese naval officer who planned Japan's naval strategies during World War II, including the attack on Pearl Harbor (1941).

Ya·ma·ni (yə-mä′nē, yä-), **Ahmed Zaki.** Born 1930. Saudi Arabian oil minister who was a central figure in the founding of OPEC (1960).

Ya·ma·see (yä′mə-sē′) *n., pl.* **Yamasee** or **-sees. 1.** A Native American people formerly inhabiting parts of coastal Georgia and South Carolina. The Yamasee dispersed to other Native American groups after conflict with English colonists in the early 18th century. **2.** A member of this people.

Yam·bol (yăm′bōl′). A city of southeast Bulgaria east of Stara Zagora. It was under Turkish rule from the 15th to the 19th century. Population, 91,000.

ya·men (yä′mən) *n.* The office or residence of an official in the Chinese Empire. [Chinese (Mandarin) *yámen* : *yá,* magistracy (from *yá,* tooth, flag with a serrated edge) + *mén,* gate.]

yam·mer (yăm′ər) *Informal. v.* **-mered, -mer·ing, -mers.** —*intr.* **1.** To complain peevishly or whimperingly; whine. **2.** To talk volubly and loudly. —*tr.* To utter or say in a complaining or clamorous tone. **—yammer** *n.* The act of yammering. [Middle English *yameren,* to lament, probably from Middle Flemish *jammeren,* to be sorrowful.] **—yam′mer·er** *n.*

Yam·pa (yăm′pə). A river, about 402 km (250 mi) long, of northwest Colorado flowing north then west to the Green River near the Utah border.

Ya·na (yä′nə). A river, about 1,207 km (750 mi) long, of northeast Russia flowing north to the Laptev Sea.

Yan·cey (yăn′sē), **William Lowndes.** 1814–1863. American politician who was an early and influential proponent of Southern secession from the Union.

yang (yăng) *n.* The active, masculine cosmic principle in Chinese dualistic philosophy. [Chinese (Mandarin) *yáng,* sun, light, masculine element.]

Yang Chen Ning (yäng′ chĕn′ nĭng′, jœn′). Born 1922. Chinese-born American physicist. He shared a 1957 Nobel Prize for disproving the principle of conservation of parity.

Yang·chow (yäng′jō′). See **Yangzhou.**

Yang·chü·an (yäng′chwän′, -chü′än′). See **Yangquan.**

Yan·gon (yäɴ′gôɴ′). See **Rangoon.**

Yang·quan (yäng′chwän′) also **Yang·chü·an** (-chwän′, -chü′än′). A city of eastern China southwest of Beijing. It is an industrial center in a coal and iron area. Population, 325,000.

Yang·tze River (yăng′sē′, -tsē′, yäng′dzə′) or **Chang Jiang** (chäng′ jyäng′). The longest river of China and of Asia, flowing about 5,551 km (3,450 mi) from Xizang (Tibet) to the East China Sea. The river has been an important trade and transportation route since ancient times.

Yang·zhou also **Yang·chow** (yäng′jō′). A city of east-central China on the Grand Canal. It was a capital of China in the sixth century A.D. and an important literary and cultural center. Marco Polo was governor of the city from 1282 to 1285. Population, 255,000.

yank (yăngk) *v.* **yanked, yank·ing, yanks.** —*tr.* **1.** To pull with a quick, strong movement; jerk: *yanked the emergency cord.* **2.** *Slang.* To extract or remove abruptly: *yanked the starting pitcher early in the game.* —*intr.* To pull on something suddenly. See Synonyms at **jerk**[1]. **—yank** *n.* A sudden vigorous pull; a jerk. [Origin unknown.]

Yank (yăngk) *n. Informal.* A Yankee.

Yan·kee (yăng′kē) *n.* **1.** A native or inhabitant of New England. **2.** A native or inhabitant of a northern U.S. state, especially a Union soldier during the Civil War. **3.** A native or inhabitant of the United States. [Origin unknown.] **—Yan′kee·dom** *n.*

WORD HISTORY: *Yankee* is an excellent example of a widely known word whose origins cannot be determined. The best hypothesis is that *Yankee* comes from Dutch *Janke,* a nickname for *Jan,* "John." Evidence can be found in the *Oxford English Dictionary* that the forms *Yankey, Yanky,* and *Yankee* were used as surnames or nicknames in the 17th century. The word *Yankee* is first found in one of our modern senses in 1758, the sense being "a New Englander." The 17th-century nickname for *Jan* was derisive, and the first instances of our word show the term being used derisively by the British for New Englanders. After the Battle of Lexington (1775) New Englanders dignified the name. The British were responsible for application of the term to all Americans (a use first recorded around 1784); and Southerners, for application of the term to Northerners (first recorded in 1817).

Yankee Doodle *n.* A Yankee. [From the title of a song popular during the Revolutionary War.]

Yan·kee·ism (yăng′kē-ĭz′əm) *n.* A Yankee custom, characteristic, usage, or pronunciation.

Yank·ton (yăngk′tən) *n., pl.* **Yankton** or **-tons. 1.** A division of the Sioux people formerly inhabiting northern Minnesota, now located mainly in the eastern Dakotas. The Yankton and Yanktonai occupy a middle position between the Santee and Teton divisions of the Sioux. **2.** A member of this division.

Yank·to·nai (yăngk′tə-nī′) *n., pl.* **Yanktonai** or **-nais.** A division of the Sioux people formerly inhabiting northern Minnesota, now located mainly in North and South Dakota and eastern Montana.

Yao (you) *n., pl.* **Yao** or **Yaos. 1.** A member of a people related to the Hmong and inhabiting southern China, northern Laos, Thailand, and Vietnam. **2.** The Miao-Yao language of the Yao.

Ya·oun·dé (yä-o͞on-dā′). The capital of Cameroon, in the south-central part of the country. It was founded in 1888 as an ivory-trading post. Population, 561,000.

yap (yăp) *v.* **yapped, yap·ping, yaps.** —*intr.* **1.** To bark sharply or shrilly; yelp. **2.** *Slang.* To talk noisily or stupidly; jabber. —*tr.* To utter by yapping. **—yap** *n.* **1.** A sharp, shrill bark; a yelp. **2.** *Slang.* Noisy, stupid talk; jabber. **3.** *Slang.* The mouth: *Shut your yap.* **4.** *Slang.* A person regarded as stupid, crude, or loud. [Probably imitative.] **—yap′per** *n.*

Yap (yăp, yäp). An island group in the western Caroline Islands of the western Pacific Ocean. Discovered by the Spanish in 1791, it became part of a Japanese mandate after 1920 and fell to U.S. forces in 1945.

ya·pok (yə-pŏk′) *n.* An aquatic opossum *(Chironectes minimus)* of tropical America, having dense fur, webbed hind feet, and a long tail. [After the *Oyapock,* a river of northern South America.]

Ya·qui (yä′kē) *n., pl.* **Yaqui** or **-quis. 1.a.** A Native American people of Sonora, a state of northwest Mexico, now also located in southern Arizona. Many Yaqui sought asylum in the United States in the early 19th century because of conflict with the Mexican government. **b.** A member of this people. **2.** The Uto-Aztecan language of the Yaqui. [Spanish, from Yaqui *hiaki.*]

yar·bor·ough (yär′bûr′ō, -bŭr′ō, -bər-ə) *n. Games.* A bridge or whist hand containing no honor cards. [After Charles Anderson Worsley, Second Earl of *Yarborough* (1809–1897), said to have bet 1,000 to 1 that such a hand would not occur.]

yard[1] (yärd) *n.* **1.** *Abbr.* **yd** A fundamental unit of length in both the U.S. Customary System and the British Imperial System, equal to 3 feet, or 36 inches (0.9144 meter). See table at **measurement. 2.** *Nautical.* A long tapering spar slung to a mast to support and spread the head of a square sail, lugsail, or lateen. [Middle English *yerde,* stick, unit of measure, from Old English *gerd.*]

yard[2] (yärd) *n.* **1.** A tract of ground adjacent to, surrounding, or surrounded by a building or group of buildings. **2.** A tract of ground, often enclosed, used for a specific work, business, or other activity. **3.** An area where railroad trains are made up and cars are switched, stored, and serviced on tracks and sidings. **4.a.** A winter pasture for deer or other grazing animals. **b.** An enclosed tract of ground in which animals, such as chickens or pigs, are kept. **—yard** *v.* **yarded, yard·ing, yards.** —*tr.* To enclose, collect, or put into or as if into a yard. —*intr.* To be gathered into or as if into a yard. [Middle English, from Old English *geard.* See **gher-**[1] in Appendix.]

yard·age[1] (yär′dĭj) *n.* **1.** An amount or length measured in yards. **2.** Cloth sold by the yard.

yard·age[2] (yär′dĭj) *n.* **1.** The use of a livestock yard at a station in the process of transporting cattle by railroad. **2.** A fee paid for such usage.

yard·arm (yärd′ärm′) *n. Nautical.* Either end of a yard of a square sail.

yard bird *n. Slang.* **1.a.** An untrained military recruit. **b.** A soldier confined to a restricted area or assigned menial tasks as a punishment. **2.** A convict; a prisoner.

yard goods *pl.n.* See **piece goods.**

yard grass *n.* Any of several weedy African grasses of the genus *Eleusine,* having usually digitately grouped spikes and flattened spikelets. Also called *goose grass.*

yard-long bean (yärd′lông′, -lŏng′) *n.* A type of cowpea *(Vigna unguiculata* subsp. *sesquipedalis)* in the pea family, native to southern Asia, having drooping fruits that reach up to a yard long. Also called *asparagus bean.*

yard·man (yärd′mən) *n.* A man employed in a yard, especially a railroad yard.

yard·mas·ter (yärd′măs′tər) *n.* A railroad employee in charge of a yard.

yard of ale *n., pl.* **yards of ale. 1.** A slender glass shaped like a horn that is about three feet tall and holds about three pints. **2.** The amount of liquid that a yard of ale can hold.

yard sale *n.* A sale of used household belongings on the front or back lawn of a house.

yard·stick (yärd′stĭk′) *n.* **1.** A graduated measuring stick one yard in length. **2.** A test or standard used in measurement, comparison, or judgment. See Synonyms at **standard.**

yare (yâr) *adj.* **1.** Agile; lively. **2.** *Nautical.* Responding easily; maneuverable. Used of a vessel. **3.** *Archaic.* Ready; prepared. **—yare** *adv. Archaic.* Soon; quickly. [Middle English, from Old English *gearo,* ready.] **—yare′ly** *adv.*

Yar·kant He (yär-känt′ hə′, -känt′) also **Yar·kand River** (-kănd′, -känd′). A river, about 805 km (500 mi) long, of northwest China rising in the Karakoram Range and flowing generally northeast to the Tarim He.

Yar·mouth (yär′məth). A town of southeast Massachusetts on south-central Cape Cod east of Barnstable. It is a resort and processing center. Population, 18,449.

yar·mul·ke also **yar·mel·ke** (yär′məl-kə, yä′məl-) *n.* A skullcap worn by Jewish men and boys, especially those adhering to Orthodox or Conservative Judaism. [Yiddish, from Polish and Ukranian *yarmulka,* possibly from Turkish *yağmurluk,* rain clothing, from *yağmur,* rain.]

yarn (yärn) *n.* **1.** A continuous strand of twisted threads of natural or synthetic material, such as wool or nylon, used in weaving or knitting. **2.** *Informal.* A long, often elaborate narrative of real or fictitious adventures; an entertaining tale. **—yarn** *intr.v.* **yarned, yarn·ing, yarns.** *Informal.* To tell an entertaining tale or series of tales. [Middle English, from Old English *gearn.* See **ghere-** in Appendix.]

Ya·ro·slavl (yär′ə-slä′vəl, yə-rə-). A city of west-central Russia on the Volga River northeast of Moscow. Traditionally

yam

yang
Yang (*left*) and yin (*right*)

ă pat	oi boy
ā pay	ou out
âr care	o͝o took
ä father	o͞o boot
ĕ pet	ŭ cut
ē be	ûr urge
ĭ pit	th thin
ī pie	*th* this
îr pier	hw which
ŏ pot	zh vision
ō toe	ə about, item
ô paw	♦ regionalism

Stress marks: ′ (primary); ′ (secondary), as in **dictionary** (dĭk′shə-nĕr′ē)

yashmak

founded in 1010, it was annexed by Moscow in 1463. Population, 626,000.

yar•row (yăr′ō) *n.* Any of several plants of the genus *Achillea* of the composite family, especially *A. millefolium,* native to Eurasia, having finely dissected foliage and flat corymbs of usually white flower heads. Also called *achillea, milfoil.* [Middle English *yarowe,* from Old English *gearwe.*]

yash•mak also **yash•mac** (yäsh-mäk′, yăsh′măk) *n.* A veil worn by Moslem women to cover the face in public. [Turkish.]

Ya•strzem•ski (yə-strĕm′skē), **Carl.** Born 1939. American baseball player. A left fielder for the Boston Red Sox (1961–1983), he won the American League Triple Crown and most valuable player award in 1967.

yat•a•ghan also **yat•a•gan** (yăt′ə-găn′, -gən) or **at•a•ghan** (ăt′-) *n.* A Turkish sword or scimitar having a double-curved blade and an eared pommel, but lacking a handle guard. [Turkish *yatağan.*]

yaup (yôp) *v. & n.* Variant of **yawp.**

yau•pon (yô′pən) *n.* An evergreen holly *(Ilex vomitoria)* of the southeast United States, having lustrous red or sometimes yellow fruit, whose dried leaves are used to make a bitter tea. Also called *cassina.* [Catawba *yă′pă.*]

Ya•va•pai (yăv′ə-pī′, yä′və-) *n., pl.* **Yavapai** or **-pais. 1.a.** A Native American people inhabiting western Arizona. **b.** A member of this people. **2.** The Yuman language of the Yavapai.

yaw (yô) *v.* **yawed, yaw•ing, yaws.** —*intr.* **1.** *Nautical.* To swerve off course momentarily or temporarily: *The ship yawed as the heavy wave struck abeam.* **2.** To turn about the vertical axis. Used of an aircraft, a spacecraft, or a projectile. **3.** To move unsteadily; weave. —*tr.* To cause to yaw. **—yaw** *n.* **1.** The act of yawing. **2.** Extent of yawing, measured in degrees. [Perhaps of Scandinavian origin.]

yawl (yôl) *n.* *Nautical.* **1.** A two-masted fore-and-aft-rigged sailing vessel similar to the ketch but having a smaller jigger mast stepped abaft the rudder. Also called *dandy.* **2.** A ship's small boat, crewed by rowers. [Dutch *jol,* possibly from Low German *jolle.*]

yawn (yôn) *v.* **yawned, yawn•ing, yawns.** —*intr.* **1.** To open the mouth wide with a deep inhalation, usually involuntarily from drowsiness, fatigue, or boredom. **2.** To open wide; gape: *The chasm yawned at our feet.* —*tr.* To utter wearily, while or as if while yawning: *yawned his disapproval of the silly venture.* **—yawn** *n.* **1.** The act of yawning. **2.** A fatigued or bored response. **3.** *Informal.* One that provokes yawns; a bore: *The movie was one big yawn.* [Middle English *yanen,* alteration of *yonen, yenen,* from Old English *geonian.*] **—yawn′er** *n.*

yawn•ing (yô′nĭng) *adj.* Gaping open; cavernous: *a yawning abyss.* **—yawn′ing•ly** *adv.*

yawp also **yaup** (yôp) —*intr.v.* **yawped, yawp•ing, yawps** also **yauped, yaup•ing, yaups. 1.** To utter a sharp cry; yelp. **2.** To talk loudly, raucously, or coarsely. —*n.* **1.** A bark; a yelp. **2.** Loud or coarse talk or utterance: *"I sound my barbaric yawp over the roofs of the world"* (Walt Whitman). [Middle English *yolpen,* possible variant of *yelpen.* See YELP.] **—yawp′er** *n.*

yaws (yôz) *pl.n. (used with a sing. or pl. verb).* A highly contagious tropical disease that chiefly affects children, caused by the spirochete *Treponema pertenue* and characterized by raspberry-like sores, especially on the hands, feet, and face. Also called *frambesia.* [From American Spanish *yaya,* sore, from Carib *yaya,* disease.]

y-ax•is (wī′ăk′sĭs) *n., pl.* **y-ax•es** (wī′ăk′sēz). *Mathematics.* **1.** The vertical axis of a two-dimensional Cartesian coordinate system. **2.** One of three axes in a three-dimensional Cartesian coordinate system.

Ya•zoo (yə-zo͞o′, yăz′o͞o). A river, 302.5 km (188 mi) long, of west-central Mississippi flowing generally southwest to the Mississippi River above Vicksburg.

Yb The symbol for the element **ytterbium.**

YB *abbr.* Yearbook.

Y-chro•mo•some (wī′krō′mə-sōm′) *n.* The sex chromosome associated with male characteristics, occurring with one X-chromosome in the male sex-chromosome pair.

y•clept or **y•cleped** (ĭ-klĕpt′, ī-klĕpt′) *v.* A past participle of **clepe.** [Middle English *icleped,* from Old English *geclepod,* past participle of *gecleopian,* to call : *ge-,* participial pref.; see **kom** in Appendix + *cleopian,* to call.]

yd *abbr.* Yard (measurement).

ye[1] (thē) *def.art. Archaic.* The. [Misreading of *ye,* from Middle English *þe,* spelling of *the,* the (using the letter thorn).]

ye[2] (yē) *pron.* **1.** *(used with a pl. verb). Archaic.* You. **2.** *(used with a sing. verb). Archaic.* You. [Middle English, from Old English *gē.* See **yu-** in Appendix.]

yea (yā) *adv.* **1.** Yes; aye. **2.** Indeed; truly: *They have spoken, yea, shouted their reply.* **—yea** *n.* **1.** An affirmative statement or vote. **2.** One who votes affirmatively. [Middle English, from Old English *gēa.* See **i-** in Appendix.]

yeah (yĕ′ə, yă′ə, yâ-) *adv. Informal.* Yes. [Variant of YEA.]

yean (yēn) *v.* **yeaned, yean•ing, yeans.** —*intr.* To bear young. Used of sheep and goats. —*tr.* To give birth to; bear. Used of sheep and goats. [Middle English *iyenen, yenen,* from Old English **geēanian* : *ge-,* verb pref.; see YCLEPT + *ēanian,* to bear young.]

William Butler Yeats
Photographed in 1932

yean•ling (yēn′lĭng) *n.* The young of a sheep or goat; a lamb or kid. **—yeanling** *adj.* Newly born; infant.

year (yîr) *n. Abbr.* **yr., y. 1.a.** The period of time during which the earth completes a single revolution around the sun, consisting of 365 days, 5 hours, 49 minutes, and 12 seconds of mean solar time. In the Gregorian calendar the year begins on January 1 and ends on December 31 and is divided into 12 months, 52 weeks, and 365 or 366 days. Also called *calendar year.* **b.** A period approximately equal to a year in other calendars. **c.** A period of approximately the duration of a calendar year: *We were married a year ago.* **2.** A sidereal year. **3.** A solar year. **4.** A period equal to the calendar year but beginning on a different date: *a tax-reckoning year; a farming year.* **5.** A specific period of time, usually shorter than 12 months, devoted to a special activity: *the academic year.* **6. years.** Age, especially old age: *I'm feeling my years.* **7. years.** An indefinitely long period of time: *it's been years since we saw her.* [Middle English *yere,* from Old English *gēar.* See **yēr-** in Appendix.]

year•book (yîr′bo͝ok′) *n. Abbr.* **YB 1.** A documentary, memorial, or historical book published every year, containing information about the previous year. **2.** A usually bound publication compiled by the graduating class of a school or college, recording the year's events and typically containing photographs of students and faculty.

Yeard•ley (yärd′lē), Sir **George.** 1587?–1627. English colonial administrator who as governor of Virginia (1619–1621 and 1626–1627) convoked the first representative assembly in the New World (1619).

year-end also **year•end** (yîr′ĕnd′) —*n.* The end of a year. —*adj.* Occurring or done at the end of the year: *a year-end audit.*

year•ling (yîr′lĭng) *n.* **1.** An animal that is one year old or has not completed its second year. **2.** A thoroughbred racehorse one year old dating from January 1 of the year in which it was foaled. **—yearling** *adj.* Being one year old.

year•long (yîr′lông′, -lŏng′) *adj.* Lasting one year.

year•ly (yîr′lē) *adj.* Occurring once a year or every year; annual. **—yearly** *adv.* Once a year; annually. **—yearly** *n., pl.* **-lies.** A publication issued once a year.

yearn (yûrn) *intr.v.* **yearned, yearn•ing, yearns. 1.** To have a strong, often melancholy desire. **2.** To feel deep pity, sympathy, or tenderness: *yearned over the poor child's fate.* [Middle English *yernen,* from Old English *geornan, giernan.* See **gher-**[2] in Appendix.] **—yearn′er** *n.* **—yearn′ing•ly** *adv.*

SYNONYMS: *yearn, long, pine, hanker, hunger, thirst.* These verbs mean to have a strong desire for something. *Yearn* and *long* both stress earnest, heartfelt, often melancholy desire, as for the return of something lost or the attainment of something unfulfilled or beyond reach: *"She yearned for reconciliation"* (W.H. Hudson). *"You don't really long for another country. You long for something in yourself that you don't have, or haven't been able to find"* (John Cheever). *Pine* implies a lingering, often nostalgic desire that saps strength or spirit: *"Like all sailors ashore, I at last pined for the billows"* (Herman Melville). *Hanker* refers to a persistent or restless desire: *"What business had he to be hankering after this girl at all!"* (John Galsworthy). *Hunger* and *thirst* are applied to compelling desire likened to the need for food or drink: *The child hungered for approval. Actors thirst for acclaim.*

yearn•ing (yûr′nĭng) *n.* A persistent, often wistful or melancholy desire; a longing: *yearnings for romance and adventure.*

year-round (yîr′round′) *adj.* Existing, active, or continuous throughout the year: *a year-round resort.*

yea-say•er (yā′sā′ər) *n.* **1.** One who is confidently affirmative in attitude. **2.** One who uncritically agrees.

yeast (yēst) *n.* **1.a.** Any of various unicellular fungi of the genus *Saccharomyces,* especially *S. cerevisiae,* reproducing by budding and from ascospores and capable of fermenting carbohydrates. **b.** Any of various similar fungi. **2.** Froth consisting of yeast cells together with the carbon dioxide they produce in the process of fermentation, present in or added to fruit juices and other substances in the production of alcoholic beverages. **3.** A commercial preparation in either powdered or compressed form, containing yeast cells and inert material such as meal and used especially as a leavening agent or as a dietary supplement. **4.** Foam; froth. **5.** An agent of ferment or activity: *political agitators who are the yeast of revolution.* See Synonyms at **catalyst. —yeast** *intr.v.* **yeast•ed, yeast•ing, yeasts. 1.** To ferment. **2.** To froth or foam. [Middle English *yeest,* from Old English *gist.* See **yes-** in Appendix.]

yeast•y (yē′stē) *adj.* **-i•er, -i•est. 1.** Of, similar to, or containing yeast: *a yeasty froth; yeasty bread dough; a yeasty home-brewed beer.* **2.** Causing or characterized by unrest or agitation; turbulent: *the yeasty days before the new government was established.* **3.** Frothy; frivolous: *a yeasty comedy.* **4.** Full of productivity or vitality; exuberantly creative. **—yeast′i•ly** *adv.* **—yeast′i•ness** *n.*

Yeats (yāts), **William Butler.** 1865–1939. Irish writer who is considered among the greatest poets of the 20th century. A founder of the Irish National Theatre Company at the Abbey Theatre, Dublin, he wrote many short plays, including *The Countess Cathleen* (1892). His poetry, published in collections such as *The Winding Stair* (1929), ranges from early love lyrics to the complex symbolist works of his later years. He won the 1923 Nobel Prize for literature. **—Yeats′i·an** *adj.*

yech or **yecch** (yĕκʜ, yŭκʜ, yĕk) *interj.* Used to express contempt or disgust. [Imitative.]

yegg (yĕg) *n. Slang.* A thief, especially a burglar or safecracker. [Origin unknown.]

yel. *abbr. Color.* Yellow.

yell (yĕl) *v.* **yelled, yell·ing, yells.** *—intr.* To cry out loudly, as in pain, fright, surprise, or enthusiasm. *—tr.* To utter or express with a loud cry; shout. See Synonyms at **shout.** **—yell** *n.* **1.** A loud cry; a shout. **2.** A rhythmic cheer chanted in unison by a group: *a college yell.* [Middle English *yellen,* from Old English *giellan, gellan.* See **ghel-**[1] in Appendix.] **—yell′er** *n.*

♦**yel·low** (yĕl′ō) *n.* **1.a.** *Abbr.* **yel.** *Color.* The hue of that portion of the visible spectrum lying between orange and green, evoked in the human observer by radiant energy with wavelengths of approximately 570 to 590 nanometers; any of a group of colors of a hue resembling that of ripe lemons and varying in lightness and saturation; one of the subtractive primaries; one of the psychological primary hues. **b.** A pigment or dye having this hue. **c.** Something that has this hue. **2.** *Chiefly Southern U.S.* The yolk of an egg. **3.** *Western U.S.* Gold. Used formerly by prospectors. **4. yellows.** Any of various plant diseases usually caused by fungi of the genus *Fusarium* or viruses of the genus *Chlorogenus* and characterized by yellow or yellowish discoloration. **—yellow** *adj.* **-er, -est. 1.** *Color.* Of the color yellow. **2.a.** Having a yellow-brown skin color. **b.** *Offensive.* Of or being a person of Asian origin. **3.** *Slang.* Cowardly. **—yellow** *tr. & intr.v.* **-lowed, -low·ing, -lows.** To make or become yellow: *documents that had been yellowed by age; clouds that yellow in the evening light.* [Middle English *yelow,* from Old English *geolu.* See **ghel-**[2] in Appendix.] **—yel′low·ness** *n.*

yel·low-bel·lied (yĕl′ō-bĕl′ēd) *adj.* **1.** Having a belly that is yellow or yellowish. Used of certain birds, for example. **2.** *Slang.* Cowardly. **—yel′low-bel′ly** *n.*

yellow-bellied sapsucker *n.* A showy sapsucker *(Sphyrapicus varius)* having a yellowish belly and in the male a bright scarlet crown and throat.

yellow bile *n. Archaic.* Choler.

yellow birch *n.* A North American deciduous tree *(Betula alleghaniensis)* having aromatic twigs, yellowish bark that peels off in thin flakes, and hard, light-colored wood used for furniture and flooring.

yel·low·bird (yĕl′ō-bûrd′) *n.* Any of various yellow or mostly yellow birds, such as the goldfinch or the yellow warbler.

yel·low-breast·ed chat (yĕl′ō-brĕs′tĭd) *n.* A large North American warbler *(Icteria virens)* having a bright yellow throat and breast, noted for its highly variable song.

yel·low·cake (yĕl′ō-kāk′) *n.* The concentrated oxide of uranium formed in the milling of uranium ore.

yel·low-dog contract (yĕl′ō-dôg′, -dŏg′) *n.* An employer-employee contract, no longer legal, by which the employee agrees not to join a union while employed.

yellow enzyme *n.* Any of various flavoproteins that take part in oxidation-reduction.

yellow fever *n.* An infectious tropical disease caused by an arbovirus transmitted by mosquitoes of the genera *Aedes,* especially *A. aegypti,* and *Haemagogus,* characterized by high fever, jaundice, and dark-colored vomit resulting from gastrointestinal hemorrhaging. Also called *yellow jack.*

yel·low-fe·ver mosquito (yĕl′ō-fē′vər) *n.* See **aedes.**

yel·low·fin tuna (yĕl′ō-fĭn′) *n.* A commercially important tuna *(Thunnus albacares)* with bright yellow fins and many scales, found in warm parts of the Atlantic and Pacific oceans.

yel·low-green alga (yĕl′ō-grēn′) *n.* An alga of the division Chrysophyta, plastids of which contain golden yellow pigments that mask the chlorophyll.

yel·low·ham·mer (yĕl′ō-hăm′ər) *n.* **1.** A small bunting *(Emberiza citrinella)* of Europe and western Asia having bright yellow plumage on the head, neck, and breast. **2.** See **yellow-shafted flicker.** [By folk etymology from earlier *yelambre,* perhaps from Middle English **yelwambre* : *yelow,* yellow; see YELLOW + Old English *amore,* a kind of bird.]

yel·low·ish (yĕl′ō-ĭsh) *adj. Color.* Somewhat yellow; tinged with yellow. **—yel′low·ish·ness** *n.*

yellow jack *n.* **1.** A yellowish-silver carangid food fish *(Caranx bartholomaei)* of western Atlantic and Caribbean waters. **2.** *Nautical.* A yellow flag hoisted on a ship to request pratique or warn of disease on board. **3.** See **yellow fever.**

yellow jacket *n.* Any of several small social wasps of the family *Vespidae,* having yellow and black markings and usually making nests in the ground or within the hollows of trees.

yellow jessamine *n.* See **Carolina jasmine.**

yellow journalism *n.* Journalism that exploits or exaggerates the news to create sensations and attract readers. [From the use of yellow ink in printing "Yellow Kid," a cartoon strip in the *New York World,* a newspaper noted for sensationalism.]

Yel·low·knife (yĕl′ō-nīf′). The capital of Northwest Territories, Canada, on the northern shore of Great Slave Lake. It was founded in 1935 after the discovery of gold and silver in the area and became the provincial capital in 1967. Population, 9,483.

yel·low·legs (yĕl′ō-lĕgz′) *n., pl.* **yellowlegs.** Either of two North American wading birds *(Tringa melanoleuca* or *T. flavipes)* having yellow legs and a long narrow bill.

yellow ocher *n.* **1.** A yellow pigment, usually containing limonite. **2.** *Color.* A moderate orange with yellow overtones.

yellow pages or **Yellow Pages** *pl.n.* A volume or section of a telephone directory that lists businesses, services, or products alphabetically according to field. [So called because they are usually printed on yellow paper.]

yellow perch *n.* A North American perch *(Perca flavescens)* having golden yellow sides marked by broad, dark vertical bars, much valued as a food and game fish.

yellow peril or **Yellow Peril** *n. Offensive.* Threatened expansion of Asian populations as magnified in the Western imagination.

yellow pine *n.* **1.** See **shortleaf pine. 2.** See **longleaf pine. 3.** The wood of either of these pines.

yellow poplar *n.* The tulip tree.

yellow rain *n.* A powdery, poisonous, yellow substance reported as dropping from the air in southeast Asia and found to be the excrement of wild honeybees contaminated by a fungal toxin.

Yellow River. See **Huang He.**

Yellow Sea. An arm of the Pacific Ocean between the Chinese mainland and the Korean Peninsula. It connects with the East China Sea to the south.

yel·low-shaft·ed flicker (yĕl′ō-shăf′tĭd) *n.* A large woodpecker *(Colaptes auratus)* of eastern North America, having a black crescent on the breast, a white rump, and yellow shafts in the wing and tail feathers. Also called *yellowhammer.*

yellow sheet *n. Slang.* A criminal record.

yellow spot *n.* See **macula lutea.**

Yel·low·stone (yĕl′ō-stōn′). A river, about 1,080 km (671 mi) long, of northwest Wyoming and southern and eastern Montana. It flows northward through **Yellowstone Lake** and **Yellowstone National Park** then east and northeast to the Missouri River. The park includes numerous geysers, including Old Faithful.

yel·low·tail (yĕl′ō-tāl′) *n.* **1.** Any of several large marine game fishes of the genus *Seriola,* having a yellow or yellowish tail, such as *S. dorsalis,* of coastal waters of southern California and Mexico. **2.** Any of several other fishes having a yellowish tail, as the silver perch.

yel·low·throat (yĕl′ō-thrōt′) *n.* Any of several small New World warblers of the genus *Geothlypis,* especially *G. trichas,* having a brownish back, yellow throat, and, in the male, a black facial mask.

yel·low-throat·ed vireo (yĕl′ō-thrō′tĭd) *n.* A vireo *(Vireo flavifrons)* of eastern North America, having a green back, bright yellow throat and breast, and a pair of white bars on each wing.

yellow-throated warbler *n.* A warbler *(Dendroica dominica)* of the southern United States, having a gray back, yellow throat and breast, and a white belly.

yellow warbler *n.* A small New World warbler *(Dendroica petechia)* having mostly yellow plumage with chestnut streaks along the sides.

yel·low·weed (yĕl′ō-wēd′) *n.* Any of various plants, such as the dyer's rocket, having yellow flowers.

yel·low·wood (yĕl′ō-wo͝od′) *n.* **1.a.** A deciduous tree *(Cladrastis lutea)* of the southeast United States, having pinnately compound leaves, drooping clusters of white flowers, and yellow wood yielding a yellow dye. **b.** The wood of this tree. **2.** Any of various trees having yellow wood.

yel·low·y (yĕl′ō-ē) *adj.* Somewhat yellow; yellowish.

yelp (yĕlp) *v.* **yelped, yelp·ing, yelps.** *—intr.* To utter a short, sharp bark or cry: *excited dogs yelping; yelped in pain when the bee stung.* *—tr.* To utter by yelping. **—yelp** *n.* A short, sharp cry or bark. [Middle English *yelpen,* to cry aloud, from Old English *gelpan, gielpan,* to boast. See **ghel-**[1] in Appendix.] **—yelp′er** *n.*

Yem·en (yĕm′ən, yā′mən). A country of southwest Asia at the southern tip of the Arabian peninsula. It was formed when Yemen (or North Yemen) merged with Southern Yemen in May 1990. Sana is the capital and Aden the largest city. Population, 8,959,000. **—Yem′en·ite′, Yem′e·ni** (ə-nē) *adj. & n.*

yen[1] (yĕn) *n.* A strong desire or inclination; a yearning or craving. **—yen** *intr.v.* **yenned, yen·ning, yens.** To have a strong desire or inclination; yearn. [Cantonese *yem.*]

yen[2] (yĕn) *n., pl.* **yen.** *Abbr.* **y, Y** See table at **currency.** [Japanese *en,* from Chinese (Mandarin) *yuán,* dollar.]

Ye·ni·sei (yĕn′ĭ-sā′, yĭ-nĭ-syā′). A river of central Russia flowing about 4,023 km (2,500 mi) westward and generally north to the Kara Sea through **Yenisei Bay,** a long estuary.

yen·ta (yĕn′tə) *n. Slang.* A person, especially a woman, who is regarded as meddlesome or gossipy. [Yiddish *yente,* back-formation from the woman's name *Yente,* alteration of *Yentl,* from Old Italian *Gentile,* from *gentile,* amiable, highborn, from Latin *gentilis,* of the same clan. See GENTLE.]

yeo. *abbr.* Yeoman; yeomanry.

yeo·man (yō′mən) *n. Abbr.* **yeo., Y 1.a.** An attendant, a servant, or a lesser official in a royal or noble household. **b.** A yeoman of the guard. **2.** A petty officer performing chiefly clerical duties in the U.S. Navy. **3.** An assistant or other subordinate, as of a sheriff. **4.** A diligent, dependable worker. **5.** A farmer who cultivates his own land, especially a member of a former class of small freeholding farmers in England. **—yeoman** *adj.* **1.** Of,

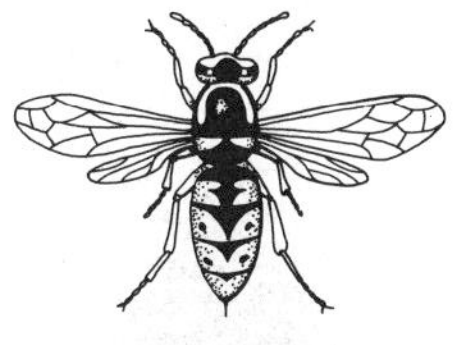

yellow jacket
Vespula maculifrons

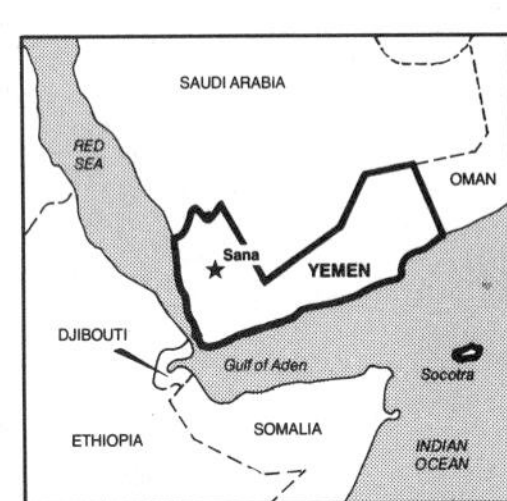

Yemen

ă pat — oi boy
ā pay — ou out
âr care — o͝o took
ä father — o͞o boot
ĕ pet — ŭ cut
ē be — ûr urge
ĭ pit — th thin
ī pie — *th* this
îr pier — hw which
ŏ pot — zh vision
ō toe — ə about, item
ô paw — ♦ regionalism

Stress marks: **′** (primary); ′ (secondary), as in **dictionary** (dĭk′shə-nĕr′ē)

relating to, or ranking as a yeoman. **2.** Sturdy, staunch, or workmanlike: *did yeoman service.* [Middle English *yoman*, perhaps from Old English **gēaman*, from Old Frisian *gāman*, villager.]

yeoman of the guard *n., pl.* **yeomen of the guard.** A member of a ceremonial guard attending the British sovereign and royal family and also guarding the Tower of London.

yeo·man·ry (yō′mən-rē) *n., pl.* **-ries. 1.** The class of yeomen; small freeholding farmers. **2.** *Abbr.* **yeo.** A British volunteer cavalry force organized in 1761 to serve as a home guard and later incorporated into the Territorial Army.

yep (yĕp) *adv. Informal.* Yes. [Alteration of YES.]

yer·ba bue·na (yâr′bə bwā′nə, yûr′bə) *n.* An aromatic perennial herb *(Satureja douglasii)* of the mint family, having crenate opposite leaves and white or purplish axillary flowers. [Spanish : *yerba*, herb + *buena*, good.]

yerba ma·té (mä′tā, mä-tā′) *n.* See **maté** (sense 2). [American Spanish : *yerba*, herb + *mate*, maté.]

yew

yerba san·ta (săn′tə) *n.* Any of various western North American evergreen shrubs of the genus *Eriodictyon*, having purple or white flowers borne in coiled cymes and a funnel-shaped corolla. [Spanish : *yerba*, herb + *santa*, holy.]

Ye·re·van also **E·re·van** or **E·ri·van** (yĕ′rĭ-vän′). The capital of Armenia, in the west-central part of the republic. An ancient city founded on the site of a fortress established in the eighth century B.C., it was strategically important as a trade center on caravan routes linking Transcaucasia and India after the seventh century A.D. Population, 1,133,000.

Yer·kes (yûr′kēz), **Charles Tyson.** 1837–1905. American financier who owned the syndicate of companies that developed the Chicago transit system.

Yerkes, Robert Mearns. 1876–1956. American psychobiologist who studied the intelligence of humans and primates.

Yerk·ish (yûr′kĭsh) *n.* An artificial language using geometric forms to represent words, created for experimental communication between chimpanzees and human beings. [After Robert Mearns YERKES.]

yer·sin·i·a (yər-sĭn′ē-ə) *n., pl.* **-i·ae** (-ē-ē′). A gram-negative bacillus of the genus *Yersinia* that causes various animal diseases. [From New Latin *Yersinia*, genus name, after Alexandre Émile Jean *Yersin* (1863–1943), Swiss-born French bacteriologist.]

yer·sin·i·o·sis (yər-sĭn′ē-ō′sĭs) *n.* An intestinal disease with symptoms resembling those of appendicitis, occurring chiefly in children and young adults and caused by a species of yersinia *(Yersinia enterocolitica)* that infects human beings and animals.

yes (yĕs) *adv.* It is so; as you say or ask. Used to express affirmation, agreement, positive confirmation, or consent. **—yes** *n., pl.* **yes·es. 1.** An affirmative or consenting reply. **2.** An affirmative vote or voter. **—yes** *tr.v.* **yessed, yes·sing, yes·es.** To give an affirmative reply to. [Middle English, from Old English *gēse*, so be it! : probably *gēa*, so; see **i-** in Appendix + *sīe*, may it be so; see **es-** in Appendix.]

WORD HISTORY: The word *yes* is a good example of how an ordinary and frequently used word can have a complex etymology. We can trace *yes* back to two Indo-European roots, **i–*, a pronominal stem, and **es–*, "to be." From two extended forms of **i–*, **yām* and **yāi*, came the prehistoric Common Germanic forms **jā* and *jai*, which gave us Old English *geā*, an affirmative particle, the source of Modern English *yea*. The Indo-European root **es–* is the source of our forms *am* and *is*. From the stem **sī–* used to make verb forms in the optative mood, a mood used to express a wish, came the Germanic form **sijai–*, which gave us Old English *sīe*, "may it be so." This form, unlike the sources of *am* and *is*, died out, but before disappearing it had combined with Old English *gēa* to form the compound *gēse*, the ancestor of our word *yes*. This *sīe* was destined to have even more of a triumph. Until around 1600 *yea* was used to respond to positive expressions, whereas *yes* was used to respond to negative expressions. After that time *yes* became a response to both positive and negative expressions, *yea* surviving primarily in voice votes.

Ye·se·nin or **E·se·nin** (yĭ-sā′nyĭn, -syĕ′-), **Sergei Aleksandrov.** 1895–1925. Russian poet whose works lament the passing of rural life in Russia.

ye·shi·va or **ye·shi·vah** (yə-shē′və) *n. Judaism.* **1.** An institute of learning where students study the Talmud. **2.** An elementary or secondary school with a curriculum that includes religion and culture as well as general education. [Hebrew *yĕšîbâ*, from *yāšab*, to sit down.]

yes man *n. Informal.* One who slavishly agrees with a superior; a sycophant.

yester– *pref.* Yesterday: *yestermorning.* [Middle English, from Old English *geostran*. See **dhgh(y)es-** in Appendix.]

yes·ter·day (yĕs′tər-dā′, -dē) *n.* **1.** The day before the present day. **2.** Also **yesterdays.** Time in the past, especially the recent past. **—yesterday** *adv.* **1.** On the day before the present day. **2.** A short while ago. [Middle English, from Old English *geostran dæg* : *geostran*, yesterday; see YESTER– + *dæg*, day; see DAY.]

yes·ter·eve·ning (yĕs′tər-ēv′nĭng) also **yes·ter·eve** (-ēv′) or **yes·ter·e·ven** (-ē′vən) *n.* The evening of yesterday. **—yes′ter·eve′ning** *adv.*

yes·ter·morn·ing (yĕs′tər-môr′nĭng) also **yes·ter·morn** (-môrn′) *n.* Yesterday morning. **—yes′ter·morn′ing** *adv.*

yes·ter·night (yĕs′tər-nīt′) *n.* Last night. **—yes′ter·night′** *adv.*

yes·ter·year (yĕs′tər-yîr′) *n.* **1.** The year before the present year. **2.** Time past; yore. **—yes′ter·year′** *adv.*

yes·treen (yĕs-trēn′) *n. Scots.* Yesterday evening.

yet (yĕt) *adv.* **1.** At this time; for the present: *isn't ready yet.* **2.** Up to a specified time; thus far: *The end had not yet come.* **3.** At a future time: *may yet change his mind.* **4.** Besides; in addition: *returned for yet another helping.* **5.** Still more; even *a yet sadder tale.* **6.** Nevertheless: *young yet wise.* **—yet** *conj.* And despite this; nevertheless: *She said she would be late, yet she arrived on time.* **—*idiom.* as yet.** Up to the present time; up to now. [Middle English, from Old English *gīet*. See **i-** in Appendix.]

USAGE NOTE: In formal style *yet* in the sense "up to now" requires that the accompanying verb be in the present perfect, rather than in the simple past: *He hasn't started yet,* not *He didn't start yet.*

ye·ti (yĕt′ē) *n., pl.* **-tis.** See **abominable snowman.** [Alteration of Tibetan *miti* : *mi*, person + *ti*, a kind of animal.]

Yev·tu·shen·ko (yĕv′tə-shĕng′kō, yĭf-to͞o-shĕn′kə), **Yevgeny Aleksandrovich.** Born 1933. Soviet antiestablishment poet. Much of his work, including "Babi Yar" (1961) and "The Heirs of Stalin" (1962), is critical of Soviet government and society.

yew (yo͞o) *n.* **1.** Any of several poisonous evergreen trees or shrubs of the genus *Taxus*, having scarlet cup-shaped seeds and flat needles that are dark green above and yellowish below. **2.** The wood of any of these trees, especially the durable, fine-grained wood of the Old World species *Taxus baccata*, used in cabinetmaking and for archery bows. [Middle English, from Old English *īw*.]

Ygg·dra·sil also **Yg·dra·sil** (ĭg′drə-sĭl, üg′-) *n. Mythology.* The great ash tree that holds together earth, heaven, and hell by its roots and branches in Norse mythology.

YHWH also **YHVH** or **JHVH** or **JHWH** (yo͞od′hā′väv′hā′, yä′wā, yä′wĕ) *n.* The Tetragrammaton representing the name of God.

yid (yĭd) *n. Offensive Slang.* Used as a disparaging term for a Jew. [Yiddish, from Middle High German *jüde*. See YIDDISH.]

Yid·dish (yĭd′ĭsh) *n.* The language historically of Ashkenazic Jews of Central and Eastern Europe, resulting from a fusion of elements derived principally from medieval German dialects and secondarily from Hebrew and Aramaic, various Slavic languages, and Old French and Old Italian. [Yiddish *yidish*, Jewish, Yiddish, from Middle High German *jüdisch*, Jewish, from *jude*, *jüde*, Jew, from Old High German *judo*, from Latin *Jūdaeus*. See JEW.] **—Yid′dish** *adj.* **—Yid′dish·ism** *n.*

yield (yēld) *v.* **yield·ed, yield·ing, yields.** *—tr.* **1.a.** To give forth by or as if by a natural process, especially by cultivation: *a field that yields many bushels of corn.* **b.** To furnish as return for effort or investment; be productive of: *an investment that yields high percentages.* **2.a.** To give over possession of, as in deference or defeat; surrender. **b.** To give up (an advantage, for example) to another; concede. *—intr.* **1.a.** To give forth a natural product; be productive. **b.** To produce a return for effort or investment: *bonds that yield well.* **2.a.** To give up, as in defeat; surrender or submit. **b.** To give way to pressure or force: *The door yielded to a gentle push.* **c.** To give way to argument, persuasion, influence, or entreaty: *The child pleaded, but the parents wouldn't yield.* **d.** To give place, as to one that is superior: *She yields to no one in her condemnation of violence.* **—yield** *n.* **1.a.** An amount yielded or produced; a product. **b.** A profit obtained from an investment; a return. **2.** The energy released by an explosion, especially by a nuclear explosion, expressed in units of weight of TNT required to produce an equivalent release: *The atomic bomb dropped on Hiroshima had a yield of 20 kilotons.* [Middle English *yielden*, from Old English *geldan*, to pay.] **—yield′er** *n.*

SYNONYMS: *yield, relent, bow, defer, submit, capitulate, succumb.* These verbs all mean to give in to what one can no longer oppose or resist. *Yield* has the widest application: *yield to an enemy; wouldn't yield to reason; yielded to desire. "The child . . . soon yielded to the drowsiness"* (Charles Dickens). To *relent* is to moderate the harshness or severity of an attitude or decision with respect to another over whom one has authority or influence: *"The captain at last relented, and told him that he might make himself at home"* (Herman Melville). *Bow* suggests giving way in defeat or through courtesy: *"Bow and accept the end/Of a love"* (Robert Frost). To *defer* is to yield out of respect or in recognition of another's authority, knowledge, or judgment: *"Philip . . . had the good sense to defer to the long experience and the wisdom of his father"* (William Hickling Prescott). *Submit* implies giving way out of necessity, as after futile or unsuccessful resistance: *"What must the King do now? Must he submit?"* (Shakespeare). *Capitulate* implies surrender to pressure, force, compulsion, or inevitability: *"I will be conquered; I will not capitulate* [to illness]*"* (Samuel Johnson). *Succumb* strongly suggests submission to something overpowering or overwhelming: *"I didn't succumb without a struggle to my uncle's allurements"* (H.G. Wells). See also Synonyms at **produce, relinquish.**

yield·ing (yēl′dĭng) *adj.* Inclined to give way to pressure, argument, or influence; docile. **—yield′ing·ly** *adv.* **—yield′ing·ness** *n.*

yin (yĭn) *n.* The passive, female cosmic principle in Chinese dualistic philosophy. [Chinese (Mandarin) *yīn,* moon, shade, femininity.]

Yin·chuan also **Yin·chwan** (yĭn′chwän′). A city of north-central China west-southwest of Beijing. In the 13th century Marco Polo visited the city, which is now the capital of Ningxia Hiuzu province. Population, 200,000.

yip (yĭp) *n.* A sharp, high-pitched bark; a yelp. **—yip** *intr.v.* **yipped, yip·ping, yips.** To emit a sharp, high-pitched bark; yelp. [Perhaps Middle English *yippe,* a cheeping sound, from *yippen,* to cheep, of imitative origin.]

yipe (yīp) also **yipes** (yīps) *interj. Informal.* Used to express surprise, fear, or dismay.

yip·pee (yĭp′ē) *interj. Informal.* Used to express elation.

-yl *suff.* An organic acid radical: *carbonyl.* [French *-yle,* from Greek *hulē,* wood, matter.]

y·lang-y·lang or **i·lang-i·lang** (ē′läng-ē′läng) *n.* **1.** A tropical Asian tree *(Cananga odorata)* having fragrant greenish-yellow flowers that yield an oil used in perfumery. **2.** An oil or a perfume obtained from this tree. [Tagalog *ilang-ilang.*]

y·lem (ī′ləm) *n.* A form of matter hypothesized by proponents of the big bang theory to have existed before the formation of the chemical elements. [Middle English, universal matter, from Old French *ilem,* from Medieval Latin *hȳlem,* accusative of *hȳlē,* matter, from Greek *hulē.*]

YMCA or **Y.M.C.A.** *abbr.* Young Men's Christian Association.

YMHA or **Y.M.H.A.** *abbr.* Young Men's Hebrew Association.

yo (yō) *interj. Slang.* Used as a greeting or to attract someone's attention.

yob (yŏb) *n. Chiefly British.* A rowdy, destructive youth; a hooligan or ruffian. [Alteration of BOY (spelled backward).]

YOB *abbr.* Year of birth.

yock (yŏk, yŭk) *Slang. intr.v.* **yocked, yock·ing, yocks.** To laugh or joke, especially boisterously. **—yock** *n.* A loud laugh or joke: *"It contains a few yocks, but the humor . . . never emerges"* (Variety). [Imitative.]

yo·del (yōd′l) *Music. v.* **-deled, -del·ing, -dels** or **-delled, -del·ling, -dels.** *—intr.* To sing so that the voice fluctuates rapidly between the normal chest voice and a falsetto. *—tr.* To sing (a song) by yodeling. **—yodel** *n.* A song or cry that is yodeled. [German *jodeln,* from German dialectal *jo,* exclamation of delight, of imitative origin.] **—yo′del·er** *n.*

yodh (yo͝od, yôd) *n.* The tenth letter of the Hebrew alphabet. See table at **alphabet.** [Hebrew *yôd,* from *yād,* hand.]

yo·ga (yō′gə) *n.* **1.** Also **Yoga.** A Hindu discipline aimed at training the consciousness for a state of perfect spiritual insight and tranquillity. **2.** A system of exercises practiced as part of this discipline to promote control of the body and mind. [Hindi, from Sanskrit *yogaḥ,* union, joining. See **yeug-** in Appendix.] **—yo′gic** (-gĭk) *adj.*

yogh (yōKH) *n.* The Middle English letter ȝ. [Middle English, possibly from Old English *īw, ēoh,* yew.]

yo·ghurt or **yo·ghourt** (yō′gərt) *n.* Variants of **yogurt.**

yo·gi (yō′gē) *n., pl.* **-gis.** One who practices yoga. [Hindi, from Sanskrit *yogī,* from *yogaḥ,* union. See YOGA.]

yo·gurt also **yo·ghurt** or **yo·ghourt** (yō′gərt) *n.* A custardlike food with a tart flavor, prepared from milk curdled by bacteria, especially *Lactobacillus bulgaricus* and *Streptococcus thermophilus,* and often sweetened or flavored with fruit. [Turkish *yoğurt.*]

Yog·ya·kar·ta (yŏg′yə-kär′tə, jôk′jä-, jŏk′yə-). See **Jogjakarta.**

yo·him·bine (yō-hĭm′bēn′) *n.* A poisonous alkaloid, $C_{21}H_{26}N_2O_3$, derived from the bark of a tree, *Corynanthe yohimbe,* and formerly used as an aphrodisiac, a local anesthetic, and a mydriatic. [New Latin *yohimbe,* specific epithet of *Corynanthe yohimbe,* species of tree from which it is derived (of Cameroonian Bantu origin; akin to Duala *djombe*) + -INE².]

yoicks (yoiks) also **hoicks** (hoiks) *interj.* Used as a hunting cry to urge hounds after a fox.

yoke (yōk) *n.* **1.a.** A crossbar with two U-shaped pieces that encircle the necks of a pair of oxen or other draft animals working together. **b.** *pl.* **yoke** or **yokes.** A pair of draft animals, such as oxen, joined by a yoke. See Synonyms at **couple. c.** A bar used with a double harness to connect the collar of each horse to the pole of a wagon or coach. **2.** A frame designed to be carried across a person's shoulders with equal loads suspended from each end. **3.** *Nautical.* A crossbar on a ship's rudder to which the steering cables are connected. **4.** A clamp or vise that holds a machine part in place or controls its movement or that holds two such parts together. **5.** A piece of a garment that is closely fitted, either around the neck and shoulders or at the hips, and from which an unfitted or gathered part of the garment is hung. **6.** Something that connects or joins together; a bond or tie. **7.** *Electronics.* A series of two or more magnetic recording heads fastened securely together for playing or recording on more than one track simultaneously. **8.a.** Any of various emblems of subjugation, such as a structure made of two upright spears with a third laid across them, under which conquered enemies of ancient Rome were forced to march in subjection. **b.** The condition of being subjugated by or as if by a conqueror; subjugation or bondage: *14th-century Russia under the Tartar yoke; the yoke of drug addiction.* **—yoke** *v.* **yoked, yok·ing, yokes.** *—tr.* **1.** To fit or join with a yoke. **2.a.** To harness a draft animal to. **b.** To harness (a draft animal) to a vehicle or an implement. **3.** To join securely as if with a yoke; bind: *partners who were yoked together for life.* **4.** To force into heavy labor, bondage, or subjugation. *—intr.* To become joined securely. [Middle English, from Old English *geoc.* See **yeug-** in Appendix.]

yo·kel (yō′kəl) *n.* A rustic; a bumpkin. [Origin unknown.]

Yo·ko·ha·ma (yō′kə-hä′mə, yô′kô-hä′mä). A city of southeast Honshu, Japan, on the western shore of Tokyo Bay. It was a small fishing village when Matthew Perry visited it in 1854 but was chosen as a site for foreign settlement in 1859 and grew rapidly thereafter. Almost entirely destroyed by an earthquake and fire in 1923, it was quickly rebuilt and modernized. The city is now a leading port and an industrial center. Population, 2,992,644.

Yo·ko·su·ka (yō′kə-so͞o′kə, yô′kô-so͞o′kä). A city of southeast Honshu, Japan, on Tokyo Bay. It is a naval base with shipyards and ironworks. Population, 427,087.

Yo·kuts (yō′kŭts) *n., pl.* **Yokuts. 1.a.** A group of Native American peoples formerly inhabiting the southern San Joaquin Valley and adjacent foothills of the Sierra Nevada, with present-day descendants in the same area. **b.** A member of this group. **2.** Any or all of the languages of the Yokuts peoples.

yolk (yōk) *n.* **1.a.** The yellow, usually spherical portion of an egg of a bird or reptile, surrounded by the albumen and serving as nutriment for the developing young. **b.** A corresponding portion of the egg of other animals, consisting of protein and fat which serve as the primary source of nourishment for the early embryo and protoplasmic substances from which the embryo develops. **2.** A greasy substance found in unprocessed sheep's wool. [Middle English *yolke,* from Old English *geolca,* from *geolu,* yellow. See YELLOW.] **—yolk′y** *adj.*

yolk sac *n.* A membranous sac attached to an embryo, providing early nourishment in the form of yolk in bony fishes, sharks, reptiles, birds, and primitive mammals and functioning as the circulatory system of the human embryo before internal circulation begins.

yolk stalk *n.* A narrow ductlike part that connects the yolk sac to the middle of the digestive tract of an embryo.

Yom Kip·pur (yôm′ kĭp′ər, yōm′, yŏm′, yôm′ kē-po͝or′) *n. Judaism.* A holy day observed on the tenth day of Tishri and marked by fasting and prayer for the atonement of sins. Also called *Day of Atonement.* [Hebrew *yôm kippûr* : *yôm,* day + *kippûr,* atonement (from *kipper,* to cover, atone).]

♦**yon** (yŏn) *adv. & adj.* Yonder. **—yon** *pron. Regional.* That one or those yonder. [Middle English, short for *yond,* yond; see YOND, and *yonder,* yonder; see YONDER. Pron., Middle English, from Old English *geon.* See **i-** in Appendix.]

yond (yŏnd) *adv. & adj. Archaic.* Yonder. [Middle English, from Old English *geond.* See **i-** in Appendix.]

♦**yon·der** (yŏn′dər) *adv.* In or at that indicated place: *the house over yonder.* **—yonder** *adj.* Being at an indicated distance, usually within sight: *"Yonder hills," he said, pointing.* **—yonder** *pron.* One that is at an indicated place, usually within sight. [Middle English, from *yond,* yond. See YOND.]

♦ ***REGIONAL NOTE:*** The adverb *yonder,* from Old English *geond,* is not exclusively Southern but is more frequently used there than in any other region of the United States, and not only by older or uneducated speakers. *Yonder* is not merely a Southern synonym for *there,* which in the South tends to mean "only a few feet from the speaker." *Yonder* carries with it an inherent sense of distance farther than "there" and is used if the person or thing indicated can be seen at all: *the shed over yonder.* Or it might be nearby but completely out of sight, as in the next room.

yo·ni (yō′nē) *n., pl.* **-nis.** *Hinduism.* A stylized vulva worshipped as a symbol of a goddess or Shakti. [Sanskrit *yoniḥ,* womb, abode, source.]

Yon·kers (yŏng′kərz). A city of southeast New York north of New York City. First inhabited by the Dutch in the mid-1600's, it is a residential and manufacturing center. Population, 195,351.

yoo-hoo (yo͞o′ho͞o′) *interj.* Used to call someone at a distance or to gain someone's attention.

Yor·ba Lin·da (yôr′bə lĭn′də). A city of southern California southeast of Los Angeles. It is the site of the presidential library of Richard M. Nixon (dedicated 1990). Population, 28,254.

yore (yôr, yōr) *n.* Time long past: *days of yore.* [Middle English, long ago, time long past, from Old English *gēara, geāra,* long ago, from genitive pl. of *gēar,* year. See YEAR.]

York¹ (yôrk). Ruling house of England (1461–1485), including Edward IV, Edward V, and Richard III. During the Wars of the Roses its symbol was a white rose. **—York′ist** *adj. & n.*

York². **1.** A borough of northern England on the Ouse River east-northeast of Leeds. Originally a Celtic settlement, it was later held by Romans, Angles, Danes, and Normans. During the Middle Ages the city was a prosperous wool market and an educational center. Its archbishopric is second only to Canterbury in importance. Population, 101,600. **2.** A city of southern Pennsylvania south-southeast of Harrisburg. Settled in 1735, it was the meeting place

yin
Yin (*right*) and yang (*left*)

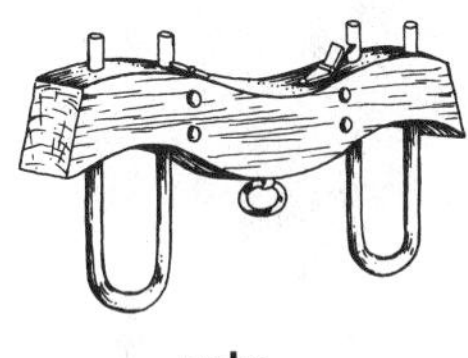

yoke

ă pat	oi boy
ā pay	ou out
âr care	o͝o took
ä father	o͞o boot
ĕ pet	ŭ cut
ē be	ûr urge
ĭ pit	th thin
ī pie	*th* this
îr pier	hw which
ŏ pot	zh vision
ō toe	ə about, item
ô paw	♦ regionalism

Stress marks: ′ (primary); ′ (secondary), as in **dictionary** (dĭk′shə-nĕr′ē)

of the Continental Congress in 1777–1778 during the British occupation of Philadelphia. Population, 44,619.

York, Alvin Cullum. Known as "Sergeant York." 1887–1964. American World War I hero famed for his single-handed attack on a German post, during which he captured 132 of the enemy.

York, Cape. 1. The northernmost point of Australia, on Torres Strait at the tip of Cape York Peninsula. **2.** A cape of northwest Greenland in northern Baffin Bay. It was used as an exploration base by Robert E. Peary, who discovered its iron meteorites.

Yorkshire terrier

Yorke Peninsula (yôrk). A narrow peninsula of southern Australia bounded by Spencer Gulf.

York River. An estuary, about 64 km (40 mi) long, of eastern Virginia flowing southeast into Chesapeake Bay.

York•shire (yôrk′shîr, -shər). A historical region and former county of northern England. It was an important area during Roman times and later became part of the kingdom of Northumbria.

Yorkshire pudding *n.* A popoverlike quick bread served with roast beef, made by baking a batter of eggs, flour, and milk in the drippings of the beef. [After YORKSHIRE.]

Yorkshire terrier *n.* Any of a breed of toy terrier developed in Yorkshire and having a long, silky bluish-gray coat.

York•town (yôrk′toun′). A village of southeast Virginia on the York River north of Newport News. It was the site of Cornwallis's surrender of the British forces (1781) in the American Revolution. During the Civil War Union troops occupied the town after a siege lasting from April to May 1862.

Yo•ru•ba (yôr′ə-bə, yō′rōō-bä) *n., pl.* **Yoruba** or **-bas. 1.** A member of a West African people living chiefly in southwest Nigeria. **2.** The South Central Niger-Congo language of this people. **—Yo′ru•ban** *adj.*

Yo•sem•i•te Valley (yō-sĕm′ĭ-tē). A valley of east-central California along the Merced River. It is surrounded by **Yosemite National Park** and includes many noted waterfalls, including **Yosemite Falls,** with a total drop of 739.6 m (2,425 ft).

Yo•shi•hi•to (yō′shĭ-hē′tō, yô′shē-hē′tô). 1879–1926. Emperor of Japan (1912–1926) whose reign was marked by World War I and Japan's increased international influence.

Andrew Young
Photographed in the late 1980's

♦you (yōō) *pron.* **1.** Used to refer to the one or ones being addressed: *I'll lend you the book. You shouldn't work so hard. Does she telephone you from San Francisco?* See Regional Note at **you-all. 2.** Used to refer to an indefinitely specified person; one: *You can't win them all.* [Middle English, from Old English *ēow,* dative and accusative of *gē,* ye, you. See **yu-** in Appendix.]

♦you-all (yōō′ôl′) also **y'all** (yôl) *pron. Chiefly Southern U.S.* You. Used in addressing two or more people or referring to two or more people, one of whom is addressed.

♦*REGIONAL NOTE:* The single most famous feature of southern United States dialects is the pronoun *you-all,* probably heard more often in its variant *y'all. You* and *you-all* preserve the singular/plural distinction that English used to have in *thou/you. You-all* functions with perfect grammatical regularity as a second person plural pronoun, taking its own possessive *you-all's* (or less frequently, *your-all's,* where both parts of the word are inflected for possession): *You-all's voices sound alike.* Southerners do not, as is sometimes believed, use *you-all* or *y'all* for both singular and plural *you.* A single person may only be addressed as *you-all* if the speaker implies in the reference other persons not present: *Did you-all* [you and others] *have dinner yet?*

you'd (yōōd). **1.** You had. **2.** You would.

you'll (yōōl, yōōl; yəl *when unstressed*). **1.** You will. **2.** You shall.

Brigham Young

young (yŭng) *adj.* **young•er, young•est. 1.** Being in an early period of life, development, or growth. **2.** Newly begun or formed; not advanced: *The evening is still young.* **3.** Of, belonging to, or suggestive of youth or early life: *He is young for his age.* **4.** Vigorous or fresh; youthful. **5.** Lacking experience; immature: *a young hand at plowing.* **6.** Being the junior of two people having the same name. **7.** *Geology.* Being of an early stage in a geologic cycle. Used of bodies of water and land formations. **—young** *n.* **1.** Young persons considered as a group; youth: *entertainment for the young.* **2.** Offspring: *a lioness with her young.* **—*idiom.* with young.** Pregnant. [Middle English *yong,* from Old English *geong.* See **yeu-** in Appendix.] **—young′ness** *n.*

SYNONYMS: *young, youthful, adolescent, immature, juvenile, puerile, green.* These adjectives are compared as they mean of, relating to, characteristic of, or being in an early period of growth or development. *Young* is the most general of the terms: *a young child. Youthful* suggests characteristics, such as enthusiasm, freshness, or energy, that are associated with youth: *youthful ardor. Adolescent* specifically implies the characteristics of those in the period between childhood and maturity: *adolescent insecurity. Immature* applies to what is not yet fully grown or developed; the term sometimes suggests that someone falls short of an expected level of maturity: *an emotionally immature adult. Juvenile* connotes immaturity, often childishness: *the juvenile pranks of the conventioneers. Puerile* is used derogatorily to suggest silliness, foolishness, or infantilism: *a puerile joke. Green* implies lack of training or experience and sometimes callowness: *The crew couldn't deal with the emergency. They were all green recruits.*

Young (yŭng), **Andrew Jackson Jr.** Born 1932. American diplomat and politician. Director of the Southern Christian Leadership Conference (1964–1970), he later served as U.S. ambassador to the United Nations (1977–1979) and as mayor of Atlanta (1981–1989).

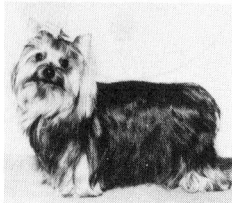

Young, Brigham. 1801–1877. American religious leader who directed the Mormon Church after the assassination (1884) of its founder, Joseph Smith. He led an exodus of the Mormons from their troubled settlement in Illinois to the site of present-day Salt Lake City, Utah, where they established a permanent home for the church (1847).

Young, Denton True. Known as "Cy." 1867–1955. American baseball player. A pitcher for 22 seasons, he won 515 games, including 76 shutouts, 3 no-hit games, and the first perfect game in modern baseball (1904).

Young, Edward. 1683–1765. English poet known for his dramatic monologue *Night Thoughts on Life, Death, and Immortality* (1742–1745).

Young, Lester Willis. Known as "Pres." 1909–1959. American jazz musician whose innovative tenor saxophone style greatly influenced jazz improvisation.

Young, Thomas. 1773–1829. British physician, physicist, and Egyptologist who revived the wave theory of light and postulated the three-color theory of color vision. He also helped decipher the hieroglyphics on the Rosetta Stone.

Young, Whitney Moore, Jr. 1921–1971. American civil rights leader who was executive director of the National Urban League (1961–1971).

young•ber•ry (yŭng′bĕr′ē) *n.* **1.** A trailing, prickly hybrid between a blackberry and a dewberry *(Rubus ursinus* cv. *Young)* of the rose family, cultivated in the western United States. **2.** The edible, dark red berry of this plant. [After B.M. *Young* (fl. 1905), American fruit grower.]

young•ish (yŭng′ĭsh) *adj.* Somewhat young.

young•ling (yŭng′lĭng) *n.* A young person, animal, or plant.

young•ster (yŭng′stər) *n.* **1.** A young person; a child or youth. **2.** A young animal. **3.** A member of the second-year class in the U.S. Naval Academy.

Youngs•town (yŭngz′toun′). A city of northeast Ohio east of Akron. It is a major center of iron and steel production with extensive manufacturing facilities. Population, 115,436.

Young Turk *n.* **1.** A young progressive or insurgent member of a collective enterprise, such as a political party. **2.** A member of a Turkish reformist and nationalist political party active in the early 20th century. [After the *Young Turks,* a late 19th- and early 20th-century revolutionary party in Turkey.]

young•'un (yŭng′ən) *n. Informal.* A young one; a child.

youn•ker (yŭng′kər) *n.* **1.** A young man. **2.** A child. [Obsolete Dutch *jonchere,* young nobleman, from Middle Dutch : *jonc,* young; see **yeu-** in Appendix + *here,* lord.]

your (yŏŏr, yôr, yōr; yər *when unstressed*) *adj.* The possessive form of **you.** *Abbr.* **yr. 1.** Used as a modifier before a noun: *your boots; your accomplishments.* **2.** A person's; one's: *The light switch is on your right.* **3.** *Informal.* Used with little or no sense of possession to indicate a type familiar to the listener: *not one of your two-bit philosophers.* [Middle English, from Old English *ēower,* genitive of *gē,* ye. See YOU.]

you're (yŏŏr; yər *when unstressed*). You are.

yours (yŏŏrz, yôrz, yōrz) *pron. (used with a sing. or pl. verb).* **1.** Used to indicate the one or ones belonging to you: *The larger boots are yours. If I can't find my book, I'll take yours.* **2.** Used often with an adverbial modifier in the complimentary close of a letter: *Sincerely yours.* **—*idiom.* yours truly.** I, myself, or me: *"Let me talk about a typical day in the life of yours truly"* (Robert A. Spivey). [Middle English, from *your,* your. See YOUR.]

your•self (yŏŏr-sĕlf′, yôr-, yōr-, yər-) *pron.* **1.** That one identical with you. **a.** Used reflexively as the direct or indirect object of a verb or as the object of a preposition: *Did you buy yourself a gift?* **b.** Used for emphasis: *You yourself were certain of the facts.* **c.** Used in an absolute construction: *In office yourself, you helped push the bill along.* **2.** Your normal or healthy condition: *Are you feeling yourself again?* See Usage Note at **myself.**

your•selves (yŏŏr-sĕlvz′, yôr-, yōr-, yər-) *pron.* **1.** Those ones identical with you. **a.** Used reflexively as the direct or indirect object of a verb or as the object of a preposition: *Help yourselves. Have yourselves a good time. You should all watch out for yourselves.* **b.** Used for emphasis: *You should take care of the matter yourselves.* **c.** Used in an absolute construction: *Yourselves having run the race, you four should receive the prize.* **2.** Your normal or healthy condition: *Just relax and be yourselves.* See Usage Note at **myself.**

youth (yōōth) *n., pl.* **youths** (yōōths, yōōthz). **1.a.** The condition or quality of being young. **b.** An early period of development or existence: *a nation in its youth.* **2.** The time of life between childhood and maturity. **3.a.** A young person, especially a young male in late adolescence. **b.** *(used with a sing. or pl. verb).* Young people considered as a group. **4.** *Geology.* The first stage in the erosion cycle. [Middle English *youthe,* from Old English *geoguth.* See **yeu-** in Appendix.]

youth•ful (yōōth′fəl) *adj.* **1.** Characterized by youth; young. **2.** Of, relating to, or characteristic of youth. **3.** Marked by or possessing characteristics, such as vigor, freshness, or enthusiasm, that are associated with youth. See Synonyms at **young. 4.** In an early stage of development; new. **5.** *Geology.* Young: *a youthful streambed.* **—youth′ful·ly** *adv.* **—youth′ful·ness** *n.*

youth hostel *n.* A supervised, inexpensive lodging place for young travelers.

♦**you-uns** (yo͞o′ənz) *pron. Upper Southern U.S.* You. Used in addressing two or more people. [YOU + dialectal *uns,* people, variant of *ones,* pl. of ONE.]

you've (yo͞ov). You have.

yow (you) *interj.* Used to express alarm, pain, or surprise.

yowl (youl) *v.* **yowled, yowl·ing, yowls.** *—intr.* To utter a long, loud, mournful cry; wail. *—tr.* To say or utter with a yowl. **—yowl** *n.* A long, loud, mournful cry; a wail. [Middle English *yowlen,* probably of imitative origin.]

yo-yo (yō′yō′) *n., pl.* **-yos. 1.** A toy consisting of a flattened spool wound with string that is spun down from and reeled up to the hand by motions of the wrist. **2.** *Informal.* One that undergoes frequent abrupt shifts or reversals, as of opinion or emotion; a vacillator. **3.** *Slang.* A person regarded as stupid or objectionable. **—yo-yo** *intr.v.* **-yoed, -yo·ing, -yos.** *Informal.* To undergo frequent abrupt shifts or reversals. [Originally a trademark.]

Y·pres (ē′prə). See **Ieper.**

Yp·si·lan·ti (ĭp′sə-lăn′tē). A city of southeast Michigan west-southwest of Detroit. Founded on the site of a Native American village and French trading post, it is a residential, commercial, and industrial center. Population, 24,031.

Y·quem (ē-kĕm′) *n.* A sweet white wine from the Sauternes region of southwest France. [After Château d'*Yquem,* an estate in southwest France.]

yr. *abbr.* **1.** Year. **2.** Younger. **3.** Your.

Y.T. *abbr.* Yukon Territory.

yt·ter·bi·a (ĭ-tûr′bē-ə) *n.* See **ytterbium oxide.** [New Latin, from YTTERBIUM.]

yt·ter·bi·um (ĭ-tûr′bē-əm) *n. Symbol* **Yb** A soft, bright, silvery rare-earth element occurring in two allotropic forms and used as an x-ray source for portable irradiation devices, in some laser materials, and in some special alloys. Atomic number 70; atomic weight 173.04; melting point 824°C; boiling point 1,196°C; specific gravity 6.972 or 6.54 (25°C) depending on allotropic form; valence 2, 3. See table at **element.** [After *Ytterby,* a town in Sweden.] **—yt·ter′bic** (-bĭk) *adj.*

ytterbium oxide *n.* A colorless hygroscopic compound, Yb_2O_3, used in certain alloys. Also called *ytterbia.*

yt·tri·a (ĭt′rē-ə) *n.* See **yttrium oxide.** [New Latin, after *Ytterby.* See YTTERBIUM.]

yt·tri·um (ĭt′rē-əm) *n. Symbol* **Y** A silvery metallic element, not a rare earth but occurring in nearly all rare-earth minerals, used in various metallurgical applications, notably to increase the strength of magnesium and aluminum alloys. Atomic number 39; atomic weight 88.905; melting point 1,522°C; boiling point 3,338°C; specific gravity 4.45 (25°C); valence 3. See table at **element.** [From YTTRIA.] **—yt′tric** (ĭt′rĭk) *adj.*

yttrium oxide *n.* A yellowish powder, Y_2O_3, used in optical glasses, ceramics, and color-television tubes. Also called *yttria.*

yu·an (yo͞o-än′, yüän) *n., pl.* **yuan** or **-ans.** See table at **currency.** [Chinese (Mandarin) *yuán,* dollar.]

Yu·an (yo͞o′än′, yüän). A Chinese dynasty (1271–1368) established by the Mongolian ruler Kublai Khan at Peking (Beijing). It was superseded by the Ming dynasty.

Yuan Jiang (jyäng′). See **Red River** (sense 1).

Yuan Shi·gai also **Yuan Shih-k'ai** (shē′kī′). 1859–1916. Chinese politician. Authorized by China's final imperial edict to create a republican government, he was named president but ruled as a dictator (1912–1916).

Yu·ba City (yo͞o′bə). A city of north-central California north of Sacramento. It is a processing center in an agricultural region. Population, 18,736.

Yu·cai·pa (yo͞o-kī′pə). A community of southern California in the foothills of the San Bernardino Mountains east of Los Angeles. It is a processing center. Population, 20,000.

Yu·ca·tán (yo͞o′kə-tăn′, -tän′). A peninsula mostly in southeast Mexico between the Caribbean Sea and the Gulf of Mexico. The region includes many Mayan and Toltec sites and is separated from western Cuba by the **Yucatán Channel.**

Yuc·a·tec (yo͞o′kə-tĕk′) *n., pl.* **Yucatec** or **-tecs. 1.** A member of a Mayan people inhabiting the Yucatán Peninsula. **2.** The Mayan language of the Yucatec.

yuc·ca (yŭk′ə) *n.* Any of various evergreen plants of the genus *Yucca,* native to the warmer regions of North America, having often tall stout stems and a terminal cluster of white flowers. [From New Latin *Iucca,* genus name, from Spanish *yuca,* cassava, from Taino.]

yucca moth *n.* A small white moth *(Tegeticula alba)* of North America that pollinates the yucca plant and at the same time lays its eggs in the ovaries of the flower.

Yu·chi (yo͞o′chē) *n., pl.* **Yuchi** or **-chis. 1.a.** A Native American people formerly inhabiting northern Georgia and eastern Tennessee, politically included in the Creek confederacy since the 19th century. **b.** A member of this people. **2.** The language of the Yuchi. [Probably Cherokee *yutsi.*]

yuck (yŭk) *interj. Slang.* Used to express rejection or strong disgust.

yuck·y (yŭk′ē) *adj.* **-i·er, -i·est.** *Slang.* Repugnant; disgusting. **—yuck′i·ness** *n.*

Yug. *abbr.* Yugoslavian.

Yu·ga (yo͝og′ə) *n. Hinduism.* One of the four ages constituting a cycle of history. [Sanskrit *yugam,* yoke, pair, era. See **yeug-** in Appendix.]

Yugo. *abbr.* Yugoslavian.

Yu·go·sla·vi·a (yo͞o′gō-slä′vē-ə). A country of southeast Europe bordering on the Adriatic Sea. It was formed in 1918 as the Kingdom of Serbs, Croats, and Slovenes after the collapse of the Austro-Hungarian Empire and was renamed Yugoslavia in 1929. Under the leadership of Marshal Tito the country became a Communist-led regime after World War II. Belgrade is the capital and the largest city. Population, 22,427,595. **—Yu′go·sla′vi·an** *adj. & n.*

Yu·ka·wa (yo͞o-kä′wä), **Hideki.** 1907–1981. Japanese physicist. He won a 1949 Nobel Prize for mathematically predicting the existence of the meson.

Yu·kon (yo͞o′kŏn′). A city of central Oklahoma west of Oklahoma City. It is a processing center. Population, 17,112.

Yukon River. A river flowing about 3,218 km (2,000 mi) from southern Yukon Territory, Canada, through Alaska to the Bering Sea. It was a major route to the Klondike during the gold rush of 1897–1898.

Yukon Territory. *Abbr.* **Y.T.** A territory of northwest Canada east of Alaska. It joined the Confederacy in 1898. The region was first explored by fur traders in the 1840's and was acquired by Canada from the Hudson's Bay Company in 1870. Whitehorse is the capital and the largest city. Population, 23,153.

Yukon Time *n.* Alaska Standard Time.

yu·lan (yo͞o′lăn, yü′län′) *n.* A deciduous Chinese tree *(Magnolia heptapeta)* often cultivated for its large, cup-shaped, fragrant white flowers. [Chinese (Mandarin) *yùlán* : *yù,* jade + *lán,* orchid.]

Yule (yo͞ol) *n.* Christmas, or the season or feast celebrating Christmas. [Middle English *yole,* from Old English *geōl.*]

yule log (yo͞ol) *n.* A large log traditionally burned in a fireplace at Christmas.

Yule·tide (yo͞ol′tīd′) *n.* The Christmas season.

Yu·ma[1] (yo͞o′mə) *n., pl.* **Yuma** or **-mas. 1.a.** A Native American people inhabiting an area along the lower Colorado River, formerly on both banks but now mainly on the California side. **b.** A member of this people. **2.** The Yuman language of the Yuma. Also called *Quechan.* [Spanish, from Papago *yuumi.*]

Yu·ma[2] (yo͞o′mə). A city of southwest Arizona on the Colorado River and the California border. It is a resort and processing center in a gold-mining region. Population, 42,433.

Yu·man (yo͞o′mən) *n.* A language family constituting the languages of the Yuma and Mohave peoples and other Native American languages of western Arizona and adjacent parts of California and Mexico. **—Yu′man** *adj.*

yum·my (yŭm′ē) *adj.* **-mi·er, -mi·est.** *Slang.* **1.** Very pleasing to the taste or smell; delicious. See Synonyms at **delicious. 2.** Delightful; delicious. [From *yum,* the sound of smacking the lips.] **—yum′mi·ness** *n.*

Yun·nan (yo͞o′nän′). A province of south-central China bordering on Vietnam, Laos, and Burma. The region was overrun by Mongols in 1253 and became part of China in the 17th century. Kunming is the capital. Population, 34,060,000.

Yu·pik (yo͞o′pĭk) *n., pl.* **Yupik** or **-piks. 1.** A member of a group of Eskimoan peoples inhabiting coastal areas of western Alaska and extreme northeast U.S.S.R. **2.** The group of Eskimoan languages spoken by the Yupik.

yup·pie also **Yup·pie** (yŭp′ē) *n. Informal.* A young city or suburban resident with a well-paid professional job and an affluent, materialistic lifestyle. [Y(OUNG) + U(RBAN) + P(ROFESSIONAL), influenced by *yippie,* politically active hippie.] **—yup′pie·dom** *n.*

Yu·rok (yo͝or′ŏk) *n., pl.* **Yurok** or **-roks. 1.a.** A Native American people inhabiting northwest California along the Pacific coast and lower Klamath River. **b.** A member of this people. **2.** The language of this people, distantly related to Algonquian.

yurt (yûrt) *n.* A circular, domed, portable tent used by the nomadic Mongols of central Asia. [Russian *yurta,* of Turkic origin.]

YWCA or **Y.W.C.A.** *abbr.* Young Women's Christian Association.

YWHA or **Y.W.H.A.** *abbr.* Young Women's Hebrew Association.

y·wis (ĭ-wĭs′) *adv.* Variant of **iwis.**

yucca
Yucca rigida

Yugoslavia

yurt
In the Gobi Desert

ă pat	oi boy
ā pay	ou out
âr care	o͝o took
ä father	o͞o boot
ĕ pet	ŭ cut
ē be	ûr urge
ĭ pit	th thin
ī pie	*th* this
îr pier	hw which
ŏ pot	zh vision
ō toe	ə about, item
ô paw	♦ regionalism

Stress marks: ′ (primary); ′ (secondary), as in **dictionary** (dĭk′shə-nĕr′ē)

Zz

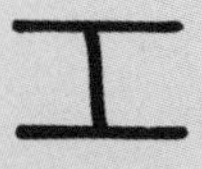

Phoenician
The Phoenician alphabet used a sign called *zayin* to stand for the sound *z*.

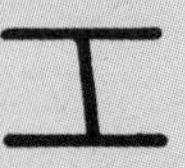

Early Greek
The Greeks adopted this symbol for their *z* and renamed it *zēta* to rhyme with *ēta* (see H).

Z

Roman
The letter was not needed in native Latin words, and its position in the alphabet was taken by G when the Romans adapted the west Greek-Etruscan script for their own use (see G). But when scholars began borrowing vocabulary from Greek around the first century B.C., they also imported the letters Y and Z to help in transcribing the Greek words.

z or **Z** (zē) *n., pl.* **z's** or **Z's. 1.** The 26th letter of the modern English alphabet. **2.** Any of the speech sounds represented by the letter *z*. **3.** The 26th in a series. **4.** Something shaped like the letter Z.

Z 1. The symbol for **atomic number. 2.** The symbol for **impedance.**

z. *abbr.* **1.** Zero. **2.** Zone.

Zaan·dam (zän-dăm′, -däm′). A city of western Netherlands west-northwest of Amsterdam. Peter the Great lived here in 1697 while he was studying shipbuilding. Population, 128,413.

za·ba·glio·ne (zä′bəl-yō′nē, -bäl-yô′nĕ) *n.* A dessert or sauce consisting of egg yolks, sugar, and wine or liqueur beaten until thick and served hot or cold. Also called *sabayon.* [Italian, variant of *zabaione,* ultimately from Illyrian *sabaium,* beer.]

Zab·rze (zäb′zhĕ). A city of south-central Poland west of Katowice. Founded in the 13th century, it passed to Prussia in 1742 and was ceded to Poland in 1945. Population, 198,000.

Zach·a·ri·as (zăk′ə-rī′əs) also **Zech·a·ri·ah** (zĕk′ə-rī′ə). In the New Testament, the husband of Elizabeth and the father of John the Baptist.

zaf·fer also **zaf·fre** (zăf′ər) *n.* An impure oxide of cobalt, used to produce a blue color in enamel and in the making of smalt. [Italian *zaffera,* from Old French *safre,* perhaps alteration of *safir,* sapphire; see SAPPHIRE, or from Arabic *ṣufr,* yellow copper, brass.]

zaf·tig or **zof·tig** (zäf′tĭk, -tĭg) *adj.* **1.** Full-bosomed. **2.** Having a full, shapely figure. [Yiddish *zaftik,* juicy, from Middle High German *saftec,* from *saft,* juice, from Old High German *saf.*]

zag (zăg) *n.* One of a series of sharp turns or reversals: *many zigs and zags in the mountain road; the zigs and zags of the stock market.* **—zag** *intr.v.* **zagged, zag·ging, zags. 1.** To turn or change direction suddenly. Usually used in contrast to *zig*: *The runner zigged when he should have zagged.* **2.** To behave erratically or indecisively. Usually used with *zig*: *zigging and zagging for years over the question of disarmament.* [From ZIGZAG.]

Za·gorsk (zə-gôrsk′). A city of west-central Russia northeast of Moscow. It developed around a monastery founded in 1340. Population, 112,000.

Za·greb (zä′grĕb). A city of northwest Yugoslavia on the Sava River north-northwest of Belgrade. Long the chief city of Croatia, it was a center of the Yugoslavian nationalist movement in the 19th century. Population, 768,700.

Za·greus (zā′grōōs, -grē-əs) *n. Greek Mythology.* The son of Zeus and Persephone who was slain by the Titans and reborn as Dionysus.

Zag·ros Mountains (zăg′rəs). A range of western Iran forming the western and southern border of the central Iranian plateau and rising to 4,550.6 m (14,920 ft).

Za·har·i·as (zə-hăr′ē-əs), **Mildred Ella Didrikson.** See Mildred Ella **Didrikson.**

zai·bat·su (zī′bät-sōō′) *n., pl.* **zaibatsu. 1.** A powerful family-controlled commercial combine of Japan. **2.** A Japanese conglomerate or cartel. [Japanese : *zai,* wealth (from Chinese *cái*) + *batsu,* powerful person or family (from Chinese *fá*).]

zai·kai (zī′kī′) *n.* The commercial and financial community of Japan. [Japanese : *zai,* wealth + *-kai,* community.]

zaire (zī′ĭr, zä-îr′) *n.* See table at **currency.** [Portuguese, the Congo River, from Kongo *n-zadi,* large river.]

Zaire (zī′ĭr, zä-îr′). Formerly (1885–1908) **Con·go Free State** (kŏng′gō) and (1908–1960) **Bel·gian Congo** (bĕl′jən), **Congo.** A country of central Africa astride the equator. Inhabited since ancient times, the region came under the control of Leopold II of Belgium in the late 1870's and was annexed outright in 1908. Full independence was achieved in 1960. Kinshasa is the capital and the largest city. Population, 29,671,407. **—Za·ir′e·an, Za·ir′i·an** *adj. & n.*

Zaire

Zaire River. See **Congo River.**

Za·ma (zā′mə, zä′mä). An ancient town of northern Africa southwest of Carthage in present-day northern Tunisia. The Romans decisively defeated Hannibal here in the final battle of the Second Punic War (202 B.C.).

Zam·be·zi (zăm-bē′zē). A river, about 2,735 km (1,700 mi) long, of central and southern Africa rising in northwest Zambia and flowing south and west to the Mozambique Channel.

Zam·bi·a (zăm′bē-ə). A country of south-central Africa. Under British jurisdiction after 1889, it became a protectorate in 1924 and achieved independence in 1964. Lusaka is the capital and the largest city. Population, 5,661,801. **—Zam′bi·an** *adj. & n.*

za·mi·a (zā′mē-ə) *n.* Any of various chiefly tropical American cycads of the genus *Zamia,* having a thick, usually underground trunk, palmlike terminal leaves, and seeds borne in woody cones. [New Latin *Zamia,* genus name, from misreading of *(nucēs) azāniae,* pine cone (nuts), probably from Greek *azainein,* to dry up, from *azein,* to dry. See **as-** in Appendix.]

zam·in·dar also **zem·in·dar** (zăm′ən-där′, zĕm′-, zə-mēn-där′) *n.* **1.** An official in precolonial India assigned to collect the land taxes of his district. **2.** A landholder in British colonial India responsible for collecting and paying to the government the taxes on the land under his jurisdiction. [Hindi *zamīndār,* from Persian : *zamīn,* earth; see **dhghem-** in Appendix + *-dār,* -holder; see **dher-** in Appendix.]

zam·in·dar·i also **zem·in·dar·y** (zăm′ən-där′ē, zĕm′-, zə-mēn-) *n., pl.* **-is** also **-ies. 1.** The system of tax collection by zamindars. **2.** The area administered by a zamindar. [Hindi *zamīndārī,* from Persian, from *zamīndār,* zamindar. See ZAMINDAR.]

za·na·na (zə-nä′nə) *n.* Variant of **zenana.**

zan·der (zăn′dər) *n., pl.* **zander** or **-ders.** A common European pikeperch *(Stizostedion lucioperca)* valued as a food fish. [German, from Low German *Sander.*]

Zanes·ville (zānz′vĭl′). A city of east-central Ohio east of Columbus. Incorporated in 1800, it was state capital from 1810 to 1812. Population, 28,655.

Zang·will (zăng′gwĭl′, -wĭl′), **Israel.** 1864–1926. British writer and Zionist whose works include the novel *Children of the Ghetto* (1892) and the play *Melting Pot* (1908).

Zan·uck (zăn′ək), **Darryl Francis.** 1902–1979. American motion-picture producer whose works include *The Jazz Singer* (1927), the first feature-length film with sound sequences.

za·ny (zā′nē) *n., pl.* **-nies. 1.** A ludicrous, buffoonish character in old comedies who attempts feebly to mimic the tricks of the clown. **2.** A comical person given to extravagant or outlandish behavior. **—zany** *adj.* **-ni·er, -ni·est. 1.** Ludicrously comical; clownish. **2.** Comical because of incongruity or strangeness; bizarre. [French *zani,* from Italian dialectal *zanni,* from *Zanni,* variant of Italian *Gianni,* nickname for *Giovanni,* John, the name of servants who act as clowns in commedia dell'arte.] **—za′ni·ly** *adv.* **—za′ni·ness** *n.*

Zan·zi·bar (zăn′zə-bär′). **1.** A region of eastern Africa, comprising **Zanzibar Island** and several adjacent islands off the northeast coast of Tanzania. Formerly a British protectorate, it became an independent sultanate in December 1963 and a republic after an uprising in January 1964. In April 1964 it joined Tanganyika to form a new republic that was renamed Tanzania in October 1964. **2.** A city of Tanzania on the western coast of Zanzibar Island. Founded in the 16th century as a Portuguese trading post, it was a major center of the East African ivory trade in the 19th century. Population, 110,699.

zap (zăp) *Slang. v.* **zapped, zap·ping, zaps.** *—tr.* **1.a.** To destroy or kill with a burst of gunfire, flame, or electric current. **b.** To kill or destroy as if by shooting. **c.** To strike suddenly and forcefully as if with a projectile or weapon: *"His . . . narrative runs marvelously on and on, zapping the reader with often surprising and . . . painful glimpses"* (Publishers Weekly). **d.** To expose to radiation; irradiate: *"perfect for those who can't bring themselves to zap food in a microwave"* (John F. Mariani). **2.** To attack (an enemy) with heavy firepower; strafe or bombard. **3.** To use a remote control device to switch (channels on a television) or to turn off (a television set). *—intr.* To move swiftly; zoom. **—zap** *n.* Something that imparts excitement or great interest. **—zap** *interj.* **1.** Used to imitate a sound made by a gun when fired. **2.** Used to indicate a sudden occurrence. [Imitative.]

Za·pa·ta (zə-pä′tə, sä-pä′tä), **Emiliano.** 1879?–1919. Mexican revolutionary who led a revolt (1910–1919) for agrarian reforms, during which he captured Mexico City three times.

Zapata mustache *n.* A mustache that curves downward on each side. [After Emiliano ZAPATA.]

za·pa·te·a·do (zä′pə-tä-ä′dō, thä′pä-tä-ä′thô, sä′-) *n., pl.* **-dos. 1.** The rhythmic stamping of the heels characteristic of Spanish flamenco dances. **2.** A Spanish flamenco dance in which the performer stamps rhythmically with the heels. [Spanish, from *zapatear,* to tap with the shoe, from *zapato,* shoe.]

Za·po·pan (zä′pō-pän′, sä′pô-). A city of southwest Mexico west of Guadalajara. It is the center of a cattle-raising region. Population, 345,390.

Za·po·ro·zhe (zä′pə-rô′zhə, zə-pə-rô′zhyĕ). Formerly **A·lek·san·drovsk** (ăl′ĭk-săn′drəfsk, ə-lĭk-sän′-). A city of southern Ukraine on the Dnieper River west of Donetsk. It was founded in 1770 on the site of a Cossack camp. Population, 852,000.

Za·po·tec (zä′pə-tĕk′, sä′pô-) *n., pl.* **Zapotec** or **-tecs. 1.a.** A member of a Mesoamerican Indian people centered at Monte Albán in southern Mexico, whose civilization reached its height around A.D. 300–900. **b.** A modern-day descendant of this people. **2.** Any of a group of related languages spoken in southern Mexico. [Spanish *Zapoteco,* from Nahuatl *tzapotēcah,* pl. of *tzapotēcatl,* person from Tzapotlan, from *Tzapotlān,* place name : *tzapotl,* sapodilla + *tlān,* place.] **—Za′po·tec′** *adj.*

zap·per (zăp′ər) *n. Slang.* **1.** A destructive device, especially one that destroys by means of electric current or radiation: *a bug zapper.* **2.** A remote-control device for switching a television set on and off and for changing channels.

zap·py (zăp′ē) *adj.* **-pi·er, -pi·est.** *Slang.* Lively: *a zappy advertisement.*

Za·ra·go·za (zăr′ə-gō′zə, thä′rä-gô′thä). See **Saragossa.**

Zar·a·thu·stra (zăr′ə-thōō′strə). See **Zoroaster.**

za·re·ba also **za·ree·ba** (zə-rē′bə) *n.* **1.** An enclosure of bushes or stakes protecting a campsite or village in northeast Africa. **2.** A campsite or village protected by such an enclosure. [Arabic *zarībah,* pen for cattle.]

zarf (zärf) *n.* A chalicelike holder for a hot coffee cup, typically made of ornamented metal, used in the Middle East. [Arabic *ẓarf,* container.]

Za·ri·a (zä′rē-ə). A city of north-central Nigeria south-southwest of Kano. It is a processing center in a cotton-growing region. Population, 267,300.

zas·tru·ga (ză-strōō′gə, zä-) *n.* Variant of **sastruga.**

zax (zăks) *n.* A tool similar to a hatchet, used for cutting and dressing roofing slates. [Variant of *sax,* from Middle English, knife, from Old English *seax.* See **sek-** in Appendix.]

z-ax·is (zē′ăk′sĭs) *n., pl.* **z-ax·es** (zē′ak′sēz). *Mathematics.* One of three axes in a three-dimensional Cartesian coordinate system.

za·yin (zä′yĭn) *n.* The seventh letter of the Hebrew alphabet. See table at **alphabet.** [Hebrew, from Aramaic.]

za·zen (zä′zĕn′) *n.* Meditation as practiced in Zen Buddhism. [Japanese : *za,* to sit down + *zen,* silent meditation; see ZEN BUDDHISM.]

Zc *abbr. Bible.* Zechariah.

zeal (zēl) *n.* Enthusiastic devotion to a cause, an ideal, or a goal and tireless diligence in its furtherance. See Synonyms at **passion.** [Middle English *zele,* from Old French *zel,* from Late Latin *zēlus,* from Greek *zēlos.*]

Zea·land (zē′lənd). See **Sjaelland.**

zeal·ot (zĕl′ət) *n.* **1.a.** One who is zealous, especially excessively so. **b.** A fanatically committed person. See Synonyms at **fanatic. 2. Zealot.** A member of a Jewish movement of the first century A.D. that fought against Roman rule in Palestine as incompatible with strict monotheism. [Middle English *zelote,* from Latin *zēlōtēs,* from Greek, from *zēlos,* zeal.]

zeal·ot·ry (zĕl′ə-trē) *n.* Excessive zeal; fanaticism.

zeal·ous (zĕl′əs) *adj.* Filled with or motivated by zeal; fervent. **—zeal′ous·ly** *adv.* **—zeal′ous·ness** *n.*

ze·a·tin (zē′ə-tĭn) *n.* A cytokinin originally isolated from young corn kernels and found later in various other plants. [New Latin *Zea,* corn genus; see ZEIN + –IN.]

ze·bec or **ze·beck** (zē′bĕk′) *n. Nautical.* Variant of **xebec.**

Zeb·e·dee (zĕb′ĭ-dē′). In the New Testament, a fisherman whose sons James and John became disciples of Jesus.

ze·bra (zē′brə) *n.* **1.** Any of several swift, wild, horselike African mammals of the genus *Equus,* having distinctive overall markings of alternating white and black or brown stripes. **2.** The zebra butterfly. [Italian, from Old Portuguese *zevro, zevra,* wild ass.]

zebra butterfly *n.* A butterfly *(Heliconius charitonius)* of the southern United States, having a black body marked with yellow stripes.

zebra crossing *n. Chiefly British.* A pedestrian crosswalk. [So called because it is marked with white stripes.]

zebra danio *n.* See **zebra fish.**

zebra finch *n.* A small Australian bird *(Poephila guttata)* having black and white striped markings and popular as a cage bird.

zebra fish *n.* A small freshwater tropical fish *(Brachydanio rerio)* of India, having horizontal dark blue and silvery stripes and popular in home aquariums. Also called *zebra danio.*

ze·bra·wood (zē′brə-wŏŏd′) *n.* **1.** Any of several African or tropical American trees having striped wood. **2.** The wood of any of these trees, used in cabinetmaking.

ze·brine (zē′brīne′) *adj.* Related to, resembling, or characteristic of a zebra.

ze·broid (zē′broid′) *adj.* Zebrine. **—zebroid** *n.* The hybrid offspring of a zebra and a horse.

ze·bu (zē′bōō, -byōō) *n.* A domesticated ox *(Bos indicus)* of Asia and eastern Africa, having a prominent hump on the back and a large dewlap. [French *zébu.*]

Zeb·u·lon also **Zeb·u·lun** (zĕb′yə-lən). In the Old Testament, a son of Jacob and Leah and the forebear of one of the tribes of Israel.

zec·chi·no (zĕ-kē′nō) also **zec·chin** or **zech·in** (zĕk′ĭn) *n., pl.* **-ni** (-nē) or **-nos** also **-chins** or **-ins.** See **sequin** (sense 2). [Italian. See SEQUIN.]

Zech·a·ri·ah¹ (zĕk′ə-rī′ə) *n. Abbr.* **Zc, Zech.** *Bible.* **1.** A Hebrew prophet of the sixth century B.C. **2.** See table at **Bible.** [Hebrew *Zĕkaryāh* : *zekar',* remembrance + *Yāh,* God.]

Zech·a·ri·ah² (zĕk′ə-rī′ə). See **Zacharias.**

zed (zĕd) *n. Chiefly British.* The letter *z.* [Middle English, from Old French *zede,* from Late Latin *zēta,* zeta, from Greek. See ZETA.]

Zed·e·ki·ah (zĕd′ĭ-kī′ə). Sixth century B.C. The last king of Judah (597–586 B.C.). He revolted unsuccessfully (588–586) against Nebuchadnezzar II and was sent to captivity in Babylon, where he died.

zed·o·ar·y (zĕd′ō-ĕr′ē) *n., pl.* **-ies. 1.** An Indian plant *(Curcuma zedoaria)* having yellow flowers, purple bracts, and starchy tuberous rhizomes. **2.** The dried rhizomes of this plant, used as a condiment and in perfumes, medicines, and cosmetics. [Middle English *zeduarie,* from Medieval Latin *zeduāria,* from Arabic *zadwār,* from Persian.]

ze·donk (zē′dŏngk′, -dŭngk′, -dôngk′) *n.* The hybrid offspring of a male zebra and a female donkey. [ZE(BRA) + DONK(EY).]

zee (zē) *n.* The letter *z.*

Zee·land (zē′lənd, zā′länt). A historical region of southwest Netherlands bordering on Belgium and the North Sea. Part of Holland after the tenth century, it later became a separate county but continued to be ruled by the counts of Holland.

Zee·man (zā′män′), **Pieter.** 1865–1943. Dutch physicist. He shared a 1902 Nobel Prize for researching the influence of magnetism on radiation.

Zeeman effect *n.* The splitting of single spectral lines of an emission spectrum into three or more polarized components when the radiation source is in a magnetic field. [After Pieter ZEEMAN.]

ze·in (zē′ĭn) *n.* A prolamine protein derived from corn, used in the manufacture of various plastics, coatings, and lacquers. [New Latin *Zea,* corn genus (from Latin *zēa,* emmer, from Greek *zeia,* one-seeded wheat, barley; see **yewo-** in Appendix) + –IN.]

Zeit·geist (tsīt′gīst′, zīt′-) *n.* The spirit of the time; the taste and outlook characteristic of a period or generation: *"It's easy to see how a student . . . in the 1940's could imbibe such notions. The Zeitgeist encouraged Philosopher-Kings"* (James Atlas). [German : *Zeit,* time (from Middle High German *zīt,* from Old High German; see **dā-** in Appendix) + *Geist,* spirit; see POLTERGEIST.]

zek (zĕk) *n.* An inmate of a Soviet labor camp. [Russian, from abbr. for *zaklyuchënnyĭ,* prisoner, from past passive participle of *zaklyuchat',* to imprison, from *klyuch,* key, from Old Church Slavonic *ključĭ.*]

zem·in·dar (zăm′ən-där′, zĕm′-, zə-mēn-där′) *n.* Variant of **zamindar.**

zem·in·dar·y (zăm′ən-där′ē, zĕm′-, zə-mēn-) *n.* Variant of **zamindari.**

zemst·vo (zĕmst′vō, zyĕm′stvə) *n., pl.* **-vos.** An elective council responsible for the local administration of a provincial district in czarist Russia. [Russian, from Old Russian *zemĭ,* land. See **dhghem-** in Appendix.]

Zen (zĕn) *n.* Zen Buddhism.

ze·na·na also **za·na·na** (zə-nä′nə) *n.* The part of a house in southwest Asia reserved for the women of the household. [Hindi *zenāna,* from Persian, from *zan,* woman. See **gʷen-** in Appendix.]

Zen Buddhism *n.* A Chinese and Japanese school of Mahayana Buddhism that asserts that enlightenment can be attained through meditation, self-contemplation, and intuition rather than through faith and devotion. [Japanese *zen,* from Chinese (Mandarin) *chán,* meditation, from Pali *jhānaṃ,* from Sanskrit *dhyānam,* from *dhyāti,* he meditates.] **—Zen Buddhist** *n.*

Zend (zĕnd) *n.* The Zend-Avesta.

Zend-A·ves·ta (zĕn′də-vĕs′tə) *n.* The entire body of sacred writings of the Zoroastrian religion. [French, from Persian *zandavastā,* from *Avesta-va-zend,* Avesta with an interpretation : Middle Persian *apastāk,* text + Middle Persian *va,* with + Middle Persian *zend,* interpretation.] **—Zend′-A·ves·ta′ic** (-vĕs-tā′ĭk) *adj.*

ze·ner diode or **Ze·ner diode** (zē′nər) *n.* A silicon semiconductor device used as a voltage regulator because of its ability to maintain an almost constant voltage with a wide range of currents. [After Clarence Melvin *Zener* (born 1905), American physicist.]

Zeng·er (zĕng′gər, -ər), **John Peter.** 1697–1746. German-

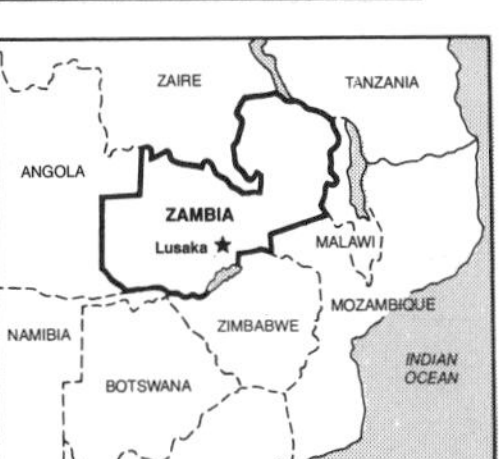

Zambia

Emiliano Zapata

zareba

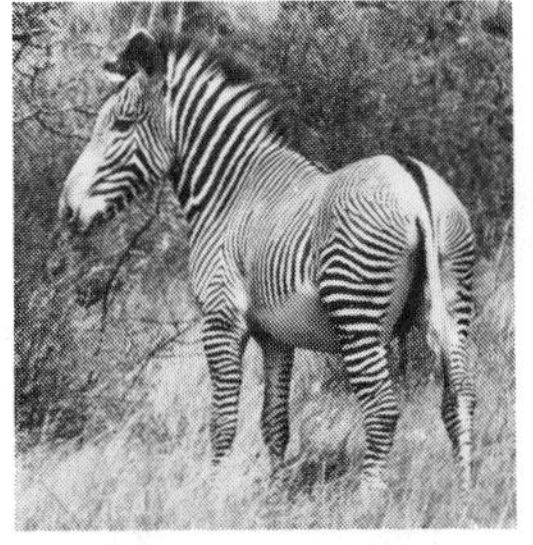

zebra
Grevy's zebra
Equus grevyi

ă pat	oi boy
ā pay	ou out
âr care	ŏŏ took
ä father	ōō boot
ĕ pet	ŭ cut
ē be	ûr urge
ĭ pit	th thin
ī pie	*th* this
îr pier	hw which
ŏ pot	zh vision
ō toe	ə about, item
ô paw	♦ regionalism

Stress marks: ′ (primary); ′ (secondary), as in **dictionary** (dĭk′shə-nĕr′ē)

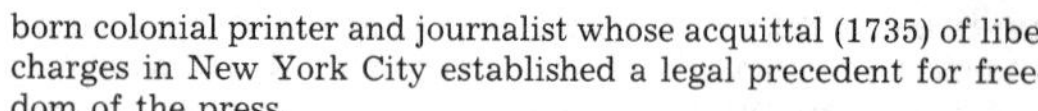

born colonial printer and journalist whose acquittal (1735) of libel charges in New York City established a legal precedent for freedom of the press.

ze•nith (zē′nĭth) *n.* **1.** The point on the celestial sphere that is directly above the observer. **2.** The upper region of the sky. **3.** The highest point above the observer's horizon attained by a celestial body. **4.** The point of culmination; the peak: *the zenith of her career.* See Synonyms at **summit.** [Middle English *senith,* from Old French *cenith,* from Medieval Latin, from Arabic *samt (ar-ra's),* path (over the head).]

zeppelin
The *Graf Zeppelin* at Lakehurst, New Jersey

Ze•no of Cit•i•um (zē′nō, sĭt′ē-əm). 335?–263? B.C. Greek philosopher who founded the Stoic school, teaching that virtue is necessarily good and that objects of desire are morally ambiguous.

Zeno of E•le•a (ē-lē′ə). 495?–430? B.C. Greek philosopher who formulated numerous paradoxes that challenged the ideas of pluralism and the existence of motion and change.

ze•o•lite (zē′ə-līt′) *n.* Any one of a family of hydrous aluminum silicate minerals, whose molecules enclose cations of sodium, potassium, calcium, strontium, or barium, or a corresponding synthetic compound, used chiefly as molecular filters and ion-exchange agents. [Swedish *zeolit,* from Greek *zein,* to boil (from its swelling and boiling under the blowpipe). See **yes-** in Appendix.]

♦**zep** (zĕp) *n. Chiefly New Jersey.* See **submarine** (sense 2). See Regional Note at **submarine.** [Possibly short for ZEPPELIN (from its shape).]

Zeph•a•ni•ah (zĕf′ə-nī′ə) *n. Abbr.* **Zeph., Zp** *Bible.* **1.** A Hebrew prophet of the seventh century B.C. **2.** See table at **Bible.**

zeph•yr (zĕf′ər) *n.* **1.** The west wind. **2.** A gentle breeze. **3.** Any of various soft, light fabrics, yarns, or garments. Something that is airy, insubstantial, or passing. [Middle English *Zephirus,* Zephyrus, from Latin *Zephyrus,* from Greek *Zephuros.*]

zephyr lily *n.* Any of several plants of the genus *Zephyranthes,* native to tropical America, having grasslike leaves and solitary, funnel-shaped, variously colored flowers. Also called *fairy lily, rain lily.*

Zeph•y•rus (zĕf′ər-əs) *n. Greek Mythology.* A god personifying the gentle west wind.

zep•pe•lin also **Zep•pe•lin** (zĕp′ə-lĭn) *n.* A rigid airship having a long cylindrical body supported by internal gas cells. [After Count Ferdinand von ZEPPELIN.]

Zeus

Zep•pe•lin (zĕp′ə-lĭn, zĕp′lĭn, tsĕp′ə-lēn′), Count **Ferdinand von.** 1838–1917. German inventor who designed and manufactured the first motorized, rigid-frame dirigible balloon (1900).

Zer•matt (tsĕr-măt′). A village of southern Switzerland in the Pennine Alps northwest of the Matterhorn. It is a noted tourist resort. Population, 3,548.

ze•ro (zîr′ō, zē′rō) *n., pl.* **-ros** or **-roes.** *Abbr.* **z. 1.** The numerical symbol 0; a cipher. **2.** *Mathematics.* **a.** An element of a set that when added to any other element in the set produces a sum identical with the element to which it is added. **b.** A cardinal number indicating the absence of any or all units under consideration. **c.** An ordinal number indicating an initial point or origin. **d.** An argument at which the value of a function vanishes. **3.** The temperature indicated by the numeral 0 on a thermometer. **4.** A sight setting that enables a firearm to shoot on target. **5.** *Informal.* One having no influence or importance; a nonentity: *a manager who was a total zero.* **6.** The lowest point: *His prospects were approaching zero.* **7.** A zero-coupon bond. **8.** *Informal.* Nothing; nil: *Today I accomplished zero.* **—zero** *adj.* **1.** Of, relating to, or being zero. **2.a.** Having no measurable or otherwise determinable value. **b.** *Informal.* Absent, inoperative, or irrelevant in specified circumstances: *"The town has . . . practically no opportunities for amusement, zero culture"* (Robert M. Adams). **3.** *Meteorology.* **a.** Designating a ceiling not more than 16 meters (52 feet) high. **b.** Limited in horizontal visibility to no more than 55 meters (180 feet). **—zero** *tr.v.* **-roed, -ro•ing, -roes.** To adjust (an instrument or a device) to zero value. ***—phrasal verb.*** **zero in. 1.a.** To aim or concentrate firepower on an exact target location. **b.** To adjust the aim or sight of by repeated firings. **2.** To converge intently; close in: *The children zeroed in on the display of toys in the store window.* [Italian, from alteration of Medieval Latin *zephirum,* from Arabic *ṣifr,* nothing, cipher.]

ze•ro-base (zîr′ō-bās′, zē′rō-) or **ze•ro-based** (-bāst′) *adj.* Having each expenditure or item justified as to need or cost: *"Zero-base budgeting requires its practitioners to justify every dollar they spend"* (Wall Street Journal).

Zhou Enlai

ze•ro-cou•pon (zîr′ō-ko͞o′pŏn, -kyo͞o′-, zē′rō-) *adj.* Paying no interest to the holder until maturity or sale: *a zero-coupon bond; a zero-coupon certificate of deposit.*

ze•ro-de•fect (zîr′ō-dē′fĕkt′, -dĭ-fĕkt′, zē′rō-) *adj.* Having no flaws or errors: *a zero-defect political campaign.*

zero gravity *n.* The condition of apparent weightlessness occurring when the centrifugal force on a body exactly counterbalances the gravitational attraction on it.

zero hour *n.* The scheduled time for the start of an operation or action, especially a combat operation of great size.

ze•ro-point energy (zîr′ō-point′, zē′rō-) *n.* The irreducible minimum energy possessed by a substance at absolute zero temperature.

zero population growth *n. Abbr.* **ZPG** The limiting of population increase to the number of live births needed to replace the existing population.

ze•ro-rate (zîr′ō-rāt′, zē′rō-) *tr.v.* **-rat•ed, -rat•ing, -rates.** *Chiefly British.* To exempt from paying a value-added tax.

ze•ro-sum game (zîr′ō-sŭm′, zē′rō-) *n.* A situation in which a gain by one person or side must be matched by a loss by another person or side: *"It's not a zero-sum game in which either youth or pensioners must lose"* (Earl W. Foell).

zest (zĕst) *n.* **1.a.** Flavor or interest; piquancy. **b.** The outermost part of the rind of an orange or a lemon, used as flavoring. **2.** Spirited enjoyment; gusto: *"At 53 he retains all the heady zest of adolescence"* (Kenneth Tynan). **—zest** *tr.v.* **zest•ed, zest•ing, zests.** To give zest, charm, or spirit to. [Obsolete French, orange or lemon peel.] **—zest′ful** *adj.* **—zest′ful•ly** *adv.* **—zest′ful•ness** *n.*

SYNONYMS: *zest, gusto, relish.* The central meaning shared by these nouns is "keen, hearty pleasure or appreciation": *ate with zest; telling a joke with gusto; has no relish for repetitive work.*

ze•ta (zā′tə, zē′-) *n.* The sixth letter of the Greek alphabet. See table at **alphabet.** [Greek *zēta,* of Phoenician origin; akin to Hebrew *zayin.*]

Ze•thus also **Ze•thos** (zē′thəs) *n. Greek Mythology.* The twin brother of Amphion.

zeug•ma (zo͞og′mə) *n.* **1.** A construction in which a single word, especially a verb or an adjective, is applied to two or more nouns when its sense is appropriate to only one of them or to both in different ways, as in *He took my advice and my wallet.* **2.** Syllepsis. [Latin, from Greek, a joining, bond. See **yeug-** in Appendix.]

Zeus (zo͞os) *n. Greek Mythology.* The principal god of the Greek pantheon, ruler of the heavens, and father of other gods and mortal heroes. [Greek. See **deiw-** in Appendix.]

Zeux•is (zo͞ok′sĭs). Fifth century B.C. Greek artist who was among the first Athenians to use shading, thereby achieving a degree of realism hitherto unknown in Greek painting.

Ze•ya (zā′yə, zyĕ′-). A river of southeast Russia flowing about 1,287 km (800 mi) south and southeast to the Amur River.

Zhang•jia•kou (jäng′jyä′kō′) also **Kal•gan** (käl′gän′). A city of northeast China near the Great Wall northwest of Beijing. It was a commercial and military center under the Ming and Manchu dynasties. Population, 350,000.

Zhan•jiang also **Chan•chiang** (jän′jyäng′) or **Chan•kiang** (chän′kyäng′). A city of southeast China southwest of Guangzhou on an inlet of the South China Sea. It is a seaport and trade center with varied industries. Population, 300,000.

Zhao Kuang•yin or **Chao K'uang-yin** (jou′ kwäng′yĭn′). 927–976. Emperor of China (960–976) who founded the Song dynasty and unified much of China.

Zhao Zi•yang (jou′ dzē-yäng′) or **Chao Tzu-yang** (jou′ dzo͞o-). Born 1919. Chinese politician. Purged from the Communist Party in the Cultural Revolution, he was reinstated (1971), served as premier (1980–1987), and was appointed general secretary of the Communist Party (1987). He was dismissed in 1989 for showing support for prodemocracy demonstrators.

Zhda•nov (zhdä′nəf). A city of southeast Ukraine on the Sea of Azov. Founded in 1779, it is a port with extensive iron and steel works. Population, 522,000.

Zhe•jiang (jœ′jyäng′) also **Che•kiang** (chŭ′kyäng′, jə′-gyäng′). A province of eastern China on the East China Sea. It was a cultural center of early China and now is one of the most densely populated regions in the country. Hangzhou is the capital. Population, 40,300,000.

Zheng•zhou also **Cheng•chow** (jŭng′jō′, jœng′-). A city of east-central China south-southwest of Beijing. An important railroad junction and industrial center, it is the capital of Henan province. Population, 1,000,000.

Zhen•jiang (jŭn′jyäng′, jœn′-) also **Chin•kiang** (chĭn′-kyäng′, jĭn′gyäng′). A city of eastern China on the Grand Canal east of Nanjing. It was an important trade center during the Ming and Manchu dynasties. Population, 250,000.

Zhi•to•mir (zhĭ-tô′mîr). A city of western Ukraine west of Kiev. First mentioned in 1240, it was a way station on the trade route between Scandinavia and Constantinople, passed to Lithuania (1320) and Poland (1569), and was incorporated into Russia in the late 1770's. Population, 275,000.

Zhou or **Chou** or **Chow** (jō). A Chinese dynasty (traditionally dated 1122–221 B.C.) characterized by great intellectual achievements, including the rise of Confucianism and Taoism and the writing of the oldest known Chinese literature.

Zhou En•lai or **Chou En-lai** (jō′ ĕn-lī′). 1898–1976. Chinese revolutionary and politician. A leader of the Chinese Communist Party, he was the first prime minister (1949–1976) and foreign minister (1949–1958) of China.

Zhu De or **Chu Teh** (jo͞o′ də′). 1886–1976. Chinese military leader who took part in a Communist rebellion that marked the birth of the Chinese Red Army (1927). He commanded the Communist forces until 1954.

Zhu Jiang (jo͞o′ jyäng′) also **Can•ton River** (kăn′tŏn′, kăn′-tŏn′) or **Chu Kiang** (cho͞o′ kyäng′, jo͞o′ gyäng′). A river, about 177 km (110 mi) long, of southeast China flowing into the South China Sea.

Zhu•kov (zho͞o′kəf), **Georgi Konstantinovich.** 1896–1974. Soviet army officer. As chief of staff during World War II, he directed the counteroffensive at Stalingrad, relieved Leningrad (1942–1943), and captured Berlin (April 1945).

Zi·a ul-Haq (zē′ə o͞ol-hăk′, -häk′), **Mohammad.** 1924–1988. Pakistani politician. An army general, he led the military coup d'état that overthrew President Ali Bhutto (1977). As president (1978–1988) he postponed general elections, had Bhutto executed, and introduced strict Islamic law.

zib·e·line or **zib·el·line** (zĭb′ə-lēn′, -līn′) *n.* **1.** A thick, lustrous, soft fabric of wool and other animal hair, such as mohair, having a silky nap. **2.** The sable or its fur. [French, sable, from Italian *zibellino,* of Slavic origin.]

zib·et also **zib·eth** (zĭb′ĭt) *n.* A civet cat *(Viverra zibetha)* of India and southeast Asia. [Medieval Latin *zibethum* or Italian *zibetto,* both from Arabic *zabād,* civet.]

Zi·bo (dzē′bō′) also **Tze·po** (tsŭ′pō′, dzŭ′bō′). A city of eastern China east of Jinan. Population, 762,500.

zi·do·vu·dine (zĭ-dō′vyo͞o-dēn′) *n.* See **azidothymidine.** [Alteration of (A)ZIDO(THYMI)DINE.]

Zieg·feld (zĭg′fĕld′, -fēld′, zēg′-), **Florenz.** 1869–1932. American theatrical producer famed for his extravagant revues known as the *Ziegfeld Follies,* which were produced annually from 1907 to 1931 (except 1926, 1928, and 1929).

Zie·gler (zē′glər, tsē′-), **Karl Waldemar.** 1898–1973. German chemist. He shared a 1963 Nobel Prize for research on polymers.

Zie·lo·no Gó·ra (zhĕ-lô′nə go͝or′ə). A city of western Poland west of Łódź. Founded in the 13th century, it was assigned to Poland by the Postdam Conference in 1945. Population, 109,400.

zig (zĭg) *n.* One of a series of sharp turns or reversals: *The zigs and zags of foreign policy.* **—zig** *intr.v.* **zigged, zig·ging, zigs. 1.** To turn or change direction suddenly. Usually used in contrast to *zag: When your opponent zigs, zag!* **2.** To behave erratically or indecisively. Usually used with *zag: The market has zigged and zagged for months.* [From ZIGZAG.]

zig·gu·rat (zĭg′ə-răt′) *n.* A temple tower of the ancient Assyrians and Babylonians, having the form of a terraced pyramid of successively receding stories. [Assyrian *zigguratu,* summit.]

Zi·gong (dzē′go͝ong′) also **Tze·kung** (tsŭ′ko͝ong′, dzŭ′-go͝ong′). A city of south-central China west of Chongqing. It is an oil and natural gas center. Population, 450,000.

zig·zag (zĭg′zăg′) *n.* **1.a.** A line or course that proceeds by sharp turns in alternating directions. **b.** One of a series of such sharp turns. **2.** Something, such as a road or design, that exhibits one or a series of sharp turns. **—zigzag** *adj.* Moving in or having a zigzag. **—zigzag** *adv.* In a zigzag manner or pattern. **—zigzag** *v.* **-zagged, -zag·ging, -zags.** *—intr.* To move in or form a zigzag: *a destroyer zigzagging to evade torpedos.* *—tr.* To cause to move in or form a zigzag. [French, alteration of *zic-zac,* from German *Zickzack,* perhaps reduplication of *Zacke,* tooth, cog, from Middle High German *zacke,* point, nail.]

zig·zag·ger (zĭg′zăg′ər) *n.* **1.** One that zigzags. **2.** A sewing-machine attachment for sewing zigzag stitches.

zilch (zĭlch) *Slang. n.* **1.** Zero; nothing. **2.** A person regarded as being insignificant; a nonentity. **—zilch** *adj.* Amounting to nothing; nil: *"Business was zilch"* (New York). [Origin unknown.]

zill (zĭl) *n. Music.* One of a pair of round metal cymbals attached to the fingers and struck together for rhythm and percussion in belly dancing. [Turkish *zil,* cymbals.]

zil·lion (zĭl′yən) *n. Informal.* An extremely large, indefinite number. [On the model of *million, billion,* etc.]

zil·lion·aire (zĭl′yə-nâr′) *n. Informal.* One having an immense, incalculable amount of wealth. [ZILLION + (MILLION)AIRE.]

Zim·bab·we¹ (zĭm-bäb′wē, -wā). A ruined city of southeast Zimbabwe south of Harare. First occupied by Iron Age peoples in the third century A.D., it was rediscovered c. 1870 and is believed by some to be the site of King Solomon's mines.

Zim·bab·we² (zĭm-bäb′wē, -wā). Formerly **Rho·de·sia** (rō-dē′zhə). A country of southern Africa. Administered by the British South Africa Company from 1889 to 1923, it became a British protectorate in 1923 and declared itself independent in 1965, although independence was not formally granted by Great Britain until 1980. Harare is the capital and the largest city. Population, 7,539,000. **—Zim·bab′we·an** *adj. & n.*

Zim·ba·list (zĭm′bə-lĭst′), **Efrem.** 1889–1985. Russian-born American violinist noted for his pure intonation.

Zim·mer·mann (zĭm′ər-mən, tsĭm′ər-män′), **Arthur.** 1864–1940. German diplomat whose intercepted telegram to Mexico (1917), offering alliance with Germany and aid in regaining lost territories in the United States, precipitated American involvement in World War I.

zinc (zĭngk) *n. Symbol* **Zn** A bluish-white, lustrous metallic element that is brittle at room temperature but malleable with heating. It is used to form a wide variety of alloys including brass, bronze, various solders, and nickel silver, in galvanizing iron and other metals, for electric fuses, anodes, and meter cases, and in roofing, gutters, and various household objects. Atomic number 30; atomic weight 65.37; melting point 419.4°C; boiling point 907°C; specific gravity 7.133 (25°C); valence 2. See table at **element.** **—zinc** *tr.v.* **zinced, zinc·ing, zincs** or **zincked, zinck·ing, zincks.** To coat or treat with zinc; galvanize. [German *Zink,* possibly from *Zinke,* spike (so called because it becomes jagged in the furnace), from Middle High German *zinke,* from Old High German *zinko.*]

zinc·ate (zĭng′kāt′) *n.* A salt of zinc hydroxide, such as $Zn(OH)_2$.

zinc blende *n.* See **sphalerite.**

zinc·ite (zĭng′kīt′) *n.* A red to yellow-orange zinc ore, ZnO.

zinck·en·ite (zĭng′kə-nīt′) *n.* Variant of **zinkenite.**

zinc·o·graph (zĭng′kə-grăf′) *n.* **1.** A prepared zinc plate used in zincography. **2.** A print or picture obtained from a zincograph.

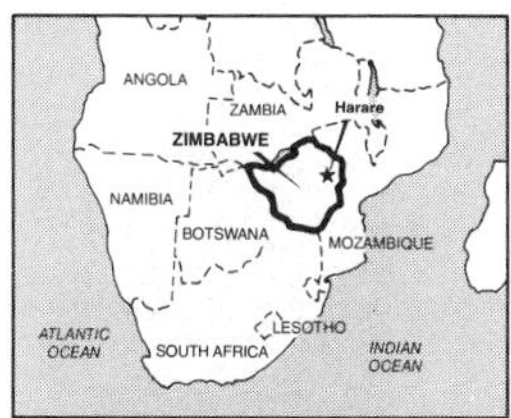

Zimbabwe²

zinc·og·ra·phy (zĭng-kŏg′rə-fē) *n.* The process of engraving zinc printing plates. **—zinc·og′ra·pher** *n.* **—zinc′o·graph′ic** (zĭng′kə-grăf′ĭk), **zinc′o·graph′i·cal** (-ĭ-kəl) *adj.*

zinc ointment *n.* A salve consisting of about 20 percent zinc oxide with beeswax or paraffin and petrolatum, used in the treatment of skin disorders.

zinc oxide *n.* An amorphous white or yellowish powder, ZnO, used as a pigment, in compounding rubber, in the manufacture of plastics, and in pharmaceuticals and cosmetics. Also called *Chinese white, zinc white.*

zinc oxide ointment *n.* Zinc ointment.

zinc spinel *n.* See **gahnite.**

zinc sulfate *n.* A colorless crystalline compound, $ZnSO_4 \cdot 7H_2O$, used medicinally as an emetic and astringent, as a fungicide, and in wood and skin preservatives. Also called *white vitriol.*

zinc white *n.* See **zinc oxide.**

zin·fan·del also **Zin·fan·del** (zĭn′fən-dĕl′) *n.* A dry red California table wine similar to claret. [Origin unknown.]

zing (zĭng) *n.* A brief high-pitched humming or buzzing sound, such as that made by a swiftly passing object or a taut vibrating string. **—zing** *v.* **zinged, zing·ing, zings.** *—intr.* **1.** To make a zing. **2.** To move swiftly with or as if with a zing: *an arrow zinging toward its target.* **3.** *Informal.* To be vivacious or lively: *a conversation zinging along.* *—tr. Informal.* **1.** To attack verbally; criticize sharply: *zing an opponent in a debate.* **2.** To strike suddenly. [Imitative.]

zing·er (zĭng′ər) *n. Informal.* **1.** A witty, often caustic remark. **2.** A sudden shock, revelation, or turn of events.

zing·y (zĭng′ē) *adj.* **-i·er, -i·est.** *Informal.* **1.** Pleasantly stimulating: *"The times are good. The living is easy. The vibes are zingy"* (Saturday Review). **2.** Exceptionally attractive or appealing: *a zingy gown.*

zink·en·ite also **zinck·en·ite** (zĭng′kə-nīt′) *n.* A dark gray mineral, $Pb_6Sb_{14}S_{27}$. [German *Zinkenit,* after J.K.L. *Zinken* (1790–1862), German mineralogist.]

zinnia

♦**zin·ni·a** (zĭn′ē-ə) *n.* Any of various plants of the genus *Zinnia,* native to tropical America, especially *Z. elegans,* widely cultivated for its showy, rayed, variously colored flower heads. Also called ♦*old maid,* ♦*old maid flower.* [New Latin *Zinnia,* genus name, after Johann Gottfried *Zinn* (1727–1759), German botanist.]

Zi·nov·iev (zĭ-nō′vē-ĕf′, zyĭ-nôf′yĭf), **Grigori Evseyevich.** 1883–1936. Soviet politician. A close colleague of Lenin, he shared power with Kamenev and Stalin after Lenin's death (1924). Joining Trotsky and Kamenev in opposition to Stalin, he was expelled from the party (1927) and was ultimately executed during a Stalinist purge.

Zins·ser (zĭn′sər), **Hans.** 1878–1940. American bacteriologist and pioneer immunologist who helped develop immunization against varieties of typhus fever (1930).

Zin·zen·dorf (zĭn′zən-dôrf′, tsĭn′tsən-), Count **Nikolaus Ludwig von.** 1700–1760. German theologian who founded the Moravian Church (1722).

Zi·on¹ (zī′ən). A city of northeast Illinois on Lake Michigan north of Waukegan. It was founded in 1901 as a communal settlement with a theocratic government. Population, 17,861.

Zi·on² (zī′ən) also **Si·on** (sī′ən) *n.* **1.a.** The historic land of Israel as a symbol of the Jewish people. **b.** The Jewish people; Israel. **2.** A place or religious community regarded as sacredly devoted to God. **3.** An idealized, harmonious community; utopia. [Middle English *Sion,* from Old English, from Late Latin *Siōn,* from Greek *Seiōn,* from Hebrew *ṣiyôn.*]

Zi·on·ism (zī′ə-nĭz′əm) *n.* An organized movement of world Jewry that arose in Europe in the late 19th century with the aim of reconstituting a Jewish state in Palestine. Modern Zionism is concerned with the development and support of the state of Israel. **—Zi′on·ist** *adj. & n.* **—Zi′on·is′tic** *adj.*

zip (zĭp) *n.* **1.** A brief, sharp, hissing sound. **2.** Energy; vim. **3.** A zipper. **4.** *Slang.* Nothing; nil; zero: *received zip for money after doing the job for them.* **—zip** *v.* **zipped, zip·ping, zips.** *—intr.* **1.a.** To move with a sharp, hissing sound. **b.** To move or act with a speed that suggests such a sound: *The cars zipped by endlessly.* **2.** To act or proceed swiftly and energetically: *zipped through her homework.* **3.** To become fastened or unfastened by a zipper. *—tr.* **1.** To give speed and force to. **2.** To impart life or zest to. **3.** To fasten or unfasten with a zipper. [Imitative.]

ZIP code (zĭp). A service mark used for a system designed to expedite the sorting and delivery of mail by assigning a series of numbers to each delivery area in the United States.

zip gun *n. Slang.* A crude homemade pistol.

zip·per (zĭp′ər) *n.* A fastening device consisting of parallel rows of metal, plastic, or nylon teeth on adjacent edges of an opening that are interlocked by a sliding tab. [From ZIP.]

ă pat	oi boy
ā pay	ou out
âr care	o͝o took
ä father	o͞o boot
ĕ pet	ŭ cut
ē be	ûr urge
ĭ pit	th thin
ī pie	*th* this
îr pier	hw which
ŏ pot	zh vision
ō toe	ə about, item
ô paw	♦ regionalism

Stress marks: ′ (primary); ′ (secondary), as in **dictionary** (dĭk′shə-nĕr′ē)

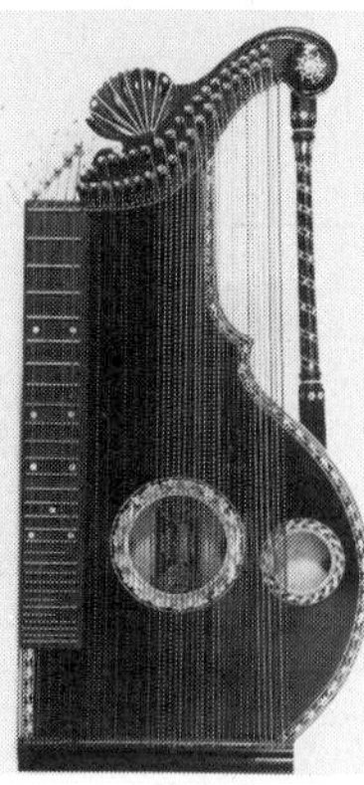
zither

WORD HISTORY: The word *zipper* is an example of what the owners of trademarks try to prevent. Registered in 1925, *zipper* was originally a B.F. Goodrich trademark for overshoes with fasteners. A Goodrich executive is said to have slid the fastener up and down on the boot and exclaimed, "Zip 'er up," from the zipping sound made by the device. The noun *zip* and the verb *zip,* referring to a light sharp sound or to motion accompanied by that kind of sound, were already in existence (*zip* as a noun was first recorded in 1875; as a verb, in 1852). The two words owed their origin to the imitation by speakers of the sound made by a rapidly moving object. As the fastener that "zipped" came to be used in other articles, its name became generalized. B.F. Goodrich sued to protect its trademark but was allowed to retain proprietary rights over it only for its *Zipper Boots.* The word *zipper* had moved out into the world of common nouns.

zip·pered (zĭp′ərd) *adj.* **1.** Having or equipped with zippers or a zipper: *a coat with zippered pockets.* **2.** Closed or fastened with or as if with a zipper.

zip·py (zĭp′ē) *adj.* **-pi·er, -pi·est.** Full of energy; lively.

zir·ca·loy (zûr′kə-loi′) *n.* A stable, corrosion-resistant zirconium alloy. [ZIRC(ONIUM) + AL(L)OY.]

zir·con (zûr′kŏn′) *n.* A brown to colorless mineral, $ZrSiO_4$, which is heated, cut, and polished to form a brilliant blue-white gem. [German *Zirkon,* from Arabic *zarqūn,* minium, from Aramaic *sīrīqūn,* from Greek *surikon,* from Persian *āzargūn,* fire color, from *zar,* gold.]

zir·co·ni·a (zûr-kō′nē-ə) *n.* Cubic zirconia. [New Latin, from ZIRCON.]

zir·co·ni·um (zûr-kō′nē-əm) *n. Symbol* **Zr** A lustrous, grayish-white, strong, ductile metallic element obtained primarily from zircon and used chiefly in ceramic and refractory compounds, as an alloying agent, and in nuclear reactors as a highly corrosion-resistant alloy. Atomic number 40; atomic weight 91.22; melting point 1,852°C; boiling point 3,578°C; specific gravity 6.56 (20°C); valence 2, 3, 4. See table at **element.**

zirconium oxide *n.* A hard white amorphous powder, ZrO_2, derived from zirconium and also found naturally, used chiefly in pigments, refractories, and ceramics and as an abrasive.

zit (zĭt) *n. Slang.* A pimple. [Origin unknown.]

zith·er (zĭth′ər, zĭth′-) also **zith·ern** (-ərn) *n. Music.* An instrument composed of a flat sound box with about 30 to 40 strings stretched over it and played horizontally with the fingertips or a plectrum. [German, from Middle High German *zitter, from Old High German *zitera,* from Latin *cithara,* cithara, from Greek *kithara.*] **—zith′er·ist** *n.*

zi·ti (zē′tē) *n.* Medium-sized tubular pasta. [Italian, from pl. of *zito,* boy.]

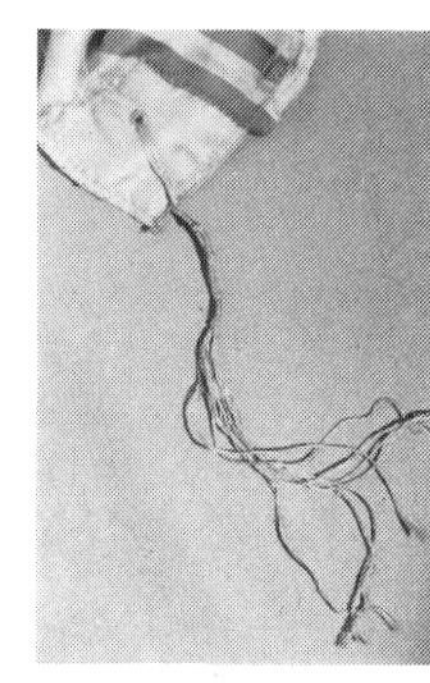
zizith

zi·zith (tsē-tsēt′, tsĭt′sĭs) *pl.n. Judaism.* The tassels or fringes of thread on the corners of a garment, especially a prayer shawl, worn by men as prescribed by ritual law. [Hebrew *ṣîṣit.*]

Žiž·ka (zhĭsh′kə, -kä), Count **Jan.** 1376?–1424. Bohemian military leader who commanded the Hussite forces (1420–1424) during the Hussite Wars against Catholic forces.

Zl *abbr.* Zloty.

Zla·to·ust (zlä′tə-o͞ost′, zlə-). A city of western Russia in the southern Ural Mountains west of Chelyabinsk. It is a rail junction and metallurgical center. Population, 204,000.

Z line *n.* Any of the dark, thin protein bands to which actin filaments are attached in a striated muscle fiber and that mark the boundaries of adjoining contractile units.

zlo·ty (zlô′tē) *n., pl.* **zloty** or **-tys.** *Abbr.* **Zl** See table at **currency.** [Polish *złoty,* golden, zloty, from *złoto,* gold. See **ghel-**[2] in Appendix.]

Zn The symbol for the element **zinc.**

zo– *pref.* Variant of **zoo–.**

zo·a (zō′ə) *n.* A plural of **zoon**[1].

zo·ar·i·um (zō-âr′ē-əm) *n., pl.* **-i·ums** also **-i·a** (-ē-ə). The aggregate of zooids that make up a colonial or compound organism. **—zo·ar′i·al** (-ē-əl) *adj.*

zo·ca·lo (sō′kə-lō′, sô′-) *n., pl.* **-los.** A town square or plaza, especially in Mexico. [American Spanish *zócalo,* from Spanish, socle, from Italian *zoccolo.* See SOCLE.]

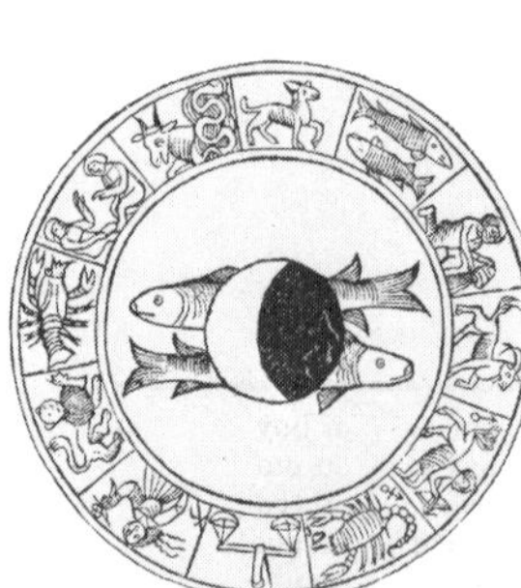
zodiac
16th-century German

zo·di·ac (zō′dē-ăk′) *n.* **1.a.** *Astronomy.* A band of the celestial sphere extending about 8° to either side of the ecliptic that represents the path of the principal planets, the moon, and the sun. **b.** In astrology, this band divided into 12 equal parts called signs, each 30° wide, bearing the name of a constellation for which it was originally named but with which it no longer coincides owing to the precession of the equinoxes. **c.** A diagram or figure representing the zodiac. **2.** A complete circuit; a circle. [Middle English, from Old French *zodiaque,* from Latin *zōdiacus,* from Greek *zōidiakos (kuklos),* (circle) of the zodiac, from *zōidion,* small represented figure, zodiacal sign, diminutive of *zōion,* living being. See ZOON[1].] **—zo·di′a·cal** (-dī′ə-kəl) *adj.*

zodiacal light *n.* A faint, hazy cone of light, often visible in the west just after sunset or in the east just before sunrise, apparently caused by the reflection of sunlight from meteoric particles in the plane of the ecliptic.

zo·e·a (zō-ē′ə) *n., pl.* **-e·ae** (-ē′ē) or **-e·as.** A larval form of crabs and other decapod crustaceans, characterized by one or more spines on the carapace and rudimentary limbs on the abdomen and thorax. [New Latin, from Greek *zōē,* life. See AZO–.]

zof·tig (zäf′tĭk, -tĭg) *adj.* Variant of **zaftig.**

Zog I (zōg). 1895–1961. King of Albania (1928–1946) who fled the country after Italy's invasion (1939) and later abdicated.

–zoic *suff.* **1.** Relating to a specified manner of animal existence: *holozoic.* **2.** Of or relating to a specified geologic era: *Archeozoic.* [From Greek *zōikos,* of animals, from *zōion,* living being. See **gʷei-** in Appendix.]

zoi·site (zoi′sīt′) *n.* A gray, brown, or pink mineral, $Ca_2Al_3(SiO_4)_3(OH)$, used in ornamental stonework. [German *Zoisit,* after Baron Sigismund *Zois* von Edelstein (1747–1819), Slovenian noble.]

Zo·la (zō′lə, zō-lä′), **Émile.** 1840–1902. French writer and critic who was a leading proponent of naturalism in fiction. His works include *Les Rougon-Macquart* (1871–1893), a series of 20 novels, and "J'Accuse" (1898), a defense of Alfred Dreyfus.

zom·bie also **zom·bi** (zŏm′bē) *n., pl.* **zom·bies** also **zom·bis.** **1.** A snake god of voodoo cults in West Africa, Haiti, and the southern United States. **2.a.** A supernatural power or spell that according to voodoo belief can enter into and reanimate a corpse. **b.** A corpse revived in this way. **3.** One who looks or behaves like an automaton. **4.** A tall mixed drink made of various rums, liqueur, and fruit juice. [Caribbean French and English Creole, from Kimbundu *n-zumbi,* ghost, departed spirit.]

zo·nal (zō′nəl) also **zo·na·ry** (-nə-rē) *adj.* **1.** Of or associated with a zone. **2.** Divided into zones. **—zo′nal·ly** *adv.*

zo·na pel·lu·ci·da (zō′nə pə-lo͞o′sĭ-də, pĕl-yo͞o′-) *n.* The thick, solid, transparent outer membrane of a developed mammalian ovum. Also called *oolemma.* [New Latin *zōna pellūcida* : Latin *zōna,* belt, girdle + Latin *pellūcidus,* transparent.]

zo·na·ry (zō′nə-rē) *adj.* Variant of **zonal.**

zo·nate (zō′nāt′) also **zo·nat·ed** (-nā′tĭd) *adj.* Having zones; belted, striped, or ringed.

zo·na·tion (zō-nā′shən) *n.* **1.** Arrangement or formation in zones; zonate structure. **2.** *Ecology.* The distribution of organisms in biogeographic zones.

zone (zōn) *n. Abbr.* **z.** **1.** An area or a region distinguished from adjacent parts by a distinctive feature or characteristic. **2.a.** Any of the five regions of the surface of the earth that are loosely divided according to prevailing climate and latitude, including the Torrid Zone, the North and South Temperate zones, and the North and South Frigid zones. **b.** A similar division on any other planet. **c.** *Mathematics.* A portion of a sphere bounded by the intersections of two parallel planes with the sphere. **3.** *Ecology.* An area characterized by distinct physical conditions and populated by communities of certain kinds of organisms. **4.** *Anatomy.* A ringlike or cylindrical growth or structure. **5.** *Geology.* A region or stratum distinguished by composition or content. **6.** A section of an area or a territory established for a specific purpose, as a section of a city restricted to a particular type of building, enterprise, or activity: *a residential zone.* See Synonyms at **area.** **7.** An area of a given radius within which a uniform rate is charged, as for transportation or shipping. **8.** *Computer Science.* **a.** A region on a punch card or on magnetic tape in which nondigital information is recorded. **b.** A section of storage to be used for a particular purpose. **9.** *Archaic.* A belt or girdle. **—zone** *tr.v.* **zoned, zon·ing, zones.** **1.** To divide into zones. **2.** To designate or mark off into zones. **3.** To surround or encircle with or as if with a belt or girdle. [Latin *zōna,* girdle, from Greek *zōnē.*]

zone melting *n.* A purification technique for crystalline substances in which a heating system passes slowly over a bar of the material to be refined, creating a molten region that carries impurities with it across the bar. Also called *zone refining.*

zone of accumulation *n. Geology.* See **B-horizon.**

zone of illuviation *n. Geology.* See **B-horizon.**

zone of leach·ing (lē′chĭng) *n. Geology.* See **A-horizon.**

zone re·fin·ing (rĭ-fī′nĭng) *n.* See **zone melting.**

zone·time (zōn′tīm′) *n. Nautical.* The standard time throughout a time zone that is the actual time at the meridian on which the time zone is based.

zonk (zôngk, zŏngk) *v.* **zonked, zonk·ing, zonks.** *Slang.* *—tr.* **1.** To stupefy; stun. **2.** To intoxicate with drugs or alcohol: *"zonk their patients with tranquilizers"* (Psychology Today). *—intr.* To become intoxicated with drugs or alcohol. [Origin unknown.]

zon·ule (zōn′yo͞ol) *n.* A small zone, as of a ligament.

zoo (zo͞o) *n., pl.* **zoos.** **1.** A park or an institution in which living animals are kept and usually exhibited to the public. Also called *zoological garden.* **2.** *Slang.* A place or situation marked by confusion or disorder: *The bus station is a zoo on Fridays.* [Short for ZOOLOGICAL GARDEN.]

zoo– or **zo–** *pref.* **1.** Animal; animal kingdom: *zoography.* **2.** Motile: *zoospore.* [Greek *zōo-, zōio-,* from *zōion,* living being. See **gʷei-** in Appendix.]

zo·o·chlor·el·la (zō′ə-klə-rĕl′ə) *n., pl.* **-chlor·el·las** also **-chlor·el·lae** (-klə-rĕl′ē). Any of numerous unicellular green algae that live symbiotically within the cells of other organisms, especially those of many freshwater invertebrates.

zo·o·chore (zō′ə-kôr′, -kōr′) *n.* A plant dispersed by animals.

zo·o·flag·el·late (zō′ə-flăj′ə-lĭt, -lāt′) *n.* A flagellated protist that ingests food and lacks chlorophyll.

zo·o·gen·ic (zō′ə-jĕn′ĭk) also **zo·og·e·nous** (zō-ŏj′ə-nəs) *adj.* Originating in or produced by animals.

zo·o·ge·og·ra·phy (zō′ə-jē-ŏg′rə-fē) *n.* The biological study of the geographic distribution of animals, especially the causes and effects of such distribution. **—zo′o·ge·og′ra·pher** *n.* **—zo′o·ge′o·graph′ic** (-ə-grăf′ĭk), **zo′o·ge′o·graph′i·cal** (-ĭ-kəl) *adj.* **—zo′o·ge′o·graph′i·cal·ly** *adv.*

zo·o·gle·a also **zo·o·gloe·a** (zō′ə-glē′ə) *n., pl.* **-gle·ae** (-glē′ē′) or **-gle·as** also **-gloe·ae** (-glē′ē′) or **-gloe·as.** An aggregate of bacteria forming a jellylike mass with cell walls swollen by the absorption of water or other fluid. [ZOO– + New Latin *gloea,* gum (from Medieval Greek *gloia, glia,* gum, glue, from Greek *gloios*).] **—zo′o·gle′al** *adj.*

zo·og·ra·phy (zō-ŏg′rə-fē) *n.* The biological description of animals and their habitats. **—zo′o·graph′ic** (-ə-grăf′ĭk), **zo′o·graph′i·cal** (-ĭ-kəl) *adj.*

zo·oid (zō′oid′) *n.* **1.** *Biology.* **a.** An organic cell or organized body that has independent movement within a living organism, especially a motile gamete such as a spermatozoon. **b.** An independent animallike organism produced asexually, as by budding or fission. **2.** *Zoology.* One of the distinct individuals forming a colonial animal such as a bryozoan or hydrozoan. **—zo·oid′al** (-oid′l) *adj.*

zoo·keep·er (zo͞o′kē′pər) *n.* One who takes care of animals in a zoo.

zool. *abbr.* Zoological; zoology.

zo·ol·a·try (zō-ŏl′ə-trē) *n.* Worship of animals. **—zo·ol′a·ter** *n.* **—zo·ol′a·trous** *adj.*

zo·o·log·i·cal (zō′ə-lŏj′ĭ-kəl) also **zo·o·log·ic** (-lŏj′ĭk) *adj. Abbr.* **zool. 1.** Of or relating to animals or animal life. **2.** Of or relating to zoology. **—zo′o·log′i·cal·ly** *adv.*

zoological garden *n.* See **zoo** (sense 1).

zo·ol·o·gy (zō-ŏl′ə-jē) *n., pl.* **-gies.** *Abbr.* **zool. 1.** The branch of biology that deals with animals and animal life, including the study of the structure, physiology, development, and classification of animals. **2.** The animal life of a particular area or period: *the zoology of Alaska; the zoology of the Pleistocene.* **3.** The characteristics of a particular animal group or category: *the zoology of mammals.* **4.** A book or scholarly work on zoology. **—zo·ol′o·gist** *n.*

zoom (zo͞om) *v.* **zoomed, zoom·ing, zooms.** *—intr.* **1. a.** To make a continuous low-pitched buzzing or humming sound. **b.** To move while making such a sound. **2.** To climb suddenly and sharply. Used of an airplane. **3.** To move about rapidly; swoop. **4. a.** To move a camera lens rapidly toward or away from a subject. **b.** To simulate such a movement, as by means of a zoom lens. *—tr.* To cause to zoom. **—zoom** *n.* The act or sound of zooming. [Imitative.]

zo·om·e·try (zō-ŏm′ĭ-trē) *n., pl.* **-tries.** Measurement and comparison of the sizes and proportions of animals or animal parts. **—zo′o·met′ric** (-ə-mĕt′rĭk), **zo′o·met′ri·cal** (-rĭ-kəl) *adj.* **—zo′o·met′ri·cal·ly** *adv.*

zoom lens *n.* A camera lens whose focal length can be rapidly changed, allowing rapid change in the size of an image.

zo·o·mor·phism (zō′ə-môr′fĭz′əm) *n.* **1.** Attribution of animal characteristics or qualities to a god. **2.** Use of animal forms in symbolism, literature, or graphic representation. **—zo′o·mor′phic** *adj.*

zo·on[1] (zō′ŏn′) *n., pl.* **zo·ons** or **zo·a** (zō′ə). **1.** An animal developed from a fertilized egg. **2.** One of the distinct individuals that join to form a compound or colonial animal; a zooid. [New Latin *zōon,* from Greek *zōion, zōon,* living being. See **gʷei-** in Appendix.]

♦ **zoon**[2] (zo͞on) *intr.v.* **zooned, zoon·ing, zoons.** *Chiefly Southern U.S.* To fly with a humming or buzzing sound. [Probably imitative.]

–zoon *suff.* Animal; independently moving organic unit: *spermatozoon.* [New Latin *-zōon,* from Greek *zōion, zōon,* living being. See **gʷei-** in Appendix.]

zo·on·o·sis (zō-ŏn′ə-sĭs) *n., pl.* **-ses** (-sēz′). A disease of animals, such as rabies or psittacosis, that can be transmitted to human beings. [New Latin : ZOO– + *-nosis,* alteration (influenced by –OSIS) of Greek *nosos,* disease.]

zo·o·par·a·site (zō′ə-păr′ə-sīt′) *n.* A parasitic animal. **—zo′o·par·a·sit′ic** (-sĭt′ĭk) *adj.*

zo·oph·a·gous (zō-ŏf′ə-gəs) *adj.* Feeding on animal matter.

zo·o·phile (zō′ə-fīl′) *n.* A lover of animals, especially one opposed to vivisection.

zo·oph·i·lism (zō-ŏf′ə-lĭz′əm) also **zo·oph·i·ly** (-ə-lē) or **zo·o·phil·i·a** (zō′ə-fĭl′ē-ə) *n.* Attraction to or affinity for animals. **—zo′o·phil′ic** (zō′ə-fĭl′ĭk) *adj.*

zo·oph·i·lous (zō-ŏf′ə-ləs) *adj.* Pollinated by animals.

zo·oph·i·ly (zō-ŏf′ə-lē) *n.* Variant of **zoophilism.**

zo·o·pho·bi·a (zō′ə-fō′bē-ə) *n.* An abnormal fear of animals. **—zo′o·phobe′** (-fōb′) *n.*

zo·o·phyte (zō′ə-fīt′) *n.* Any of various invertebrate animals, such as a sea anemone or sponge, that attach to surfaces and superficially resemble plants. **—zo′o·phyt′ic** (-fĭt′ĭk), **zo′o·phyt′i·cal** (-ĭ-kəl) *adj.*

zo·o·plank·ter (zō′ə-plăngk′tər) *n.* One of the animal organisms constituting zooplankton.

zo·o·plank·ton (zō′ə-plăngk′tən) *n.* Plankton that consists of animals, including the corals, rotifers, sea anemones, and jellyfish. **—zo′o·plank·ton′ic** (-tŏn′ĭk) *adj.*

zo·o·plas·ty (zō′ə-plăs′tē) *n., pl.* **-ties.** Surgical transfer of tissue from an animal to a human being. **—zo′o·plas′tic** *adj.*

zo·o·sperm (zō′ə-spûrm′) *n.* See **spermatozoon.**

zo·o·spo·ran·gi·um (zō′ə-spə-răn′jē-əm) *n., pl.* **-gi·a** (-jē-ə). A sporangium in which zoospores develop.

zo·o·spore (zō′ə-spôr′, -spōr′) *n.* A motile, flagellated asexual spore, as of certain algae and fungi. Also called *swarm spore.* **—zo′o·spor′ic** (-spôr′ĭk, -spŏr′-), **zo′o·spor′ous** (zō′ə-spôr′əs, -spōr′-, zō-ŏs′pər-əs) *adj.*

zo·os·ter·ol (zō-ŏs′tə-rôl′, -rōl′, -rŏl′) *n.* A sterol, such as cholesterol, that is produced by animals rather than plants.

zo·o·tech·nics (zō′ə-tĕk′nĭks) *n. (used with a sing. or pl. verb).* Zootechny.

zo·o·tech·ny (zō′ə-tĕk′nē) *n.* The domestication, breeding, and improvement of animals; the technology of animal husbandry. [ZOO– + Greek *tekhnē,* art; see TECHNICAL.] **—zo′o·tech′ni·cal** *adj.* **—zo′o·tech·ni′cian** (-nĭsh′ən) *n.*

zo·ot·o·my (zō-ŏt′ə-mē) *n., pl.* **-mies. 1.** The anatomy of animals. **2.** Dissection of animals. **—zo′o·tom′ic** (zō′ə-tŏm′ĭk), **zo′o·tom′i·cal** (-ĭ-kəl) *adj.* **—zo·ot′o·mist** *n.*

zo·o·tox·in (zō′ə-tŏk′sĭn) *n.* A toxin of animal origin.

zoot suit (zo͞ot) *n. Slang.* A man's suit popular during the early 1940's, characterized by full-legged, tight-cuffed trousers and a long coat with wide lapels and heavily padded, wide shoulders. [Probably from an alteration of SUIT.]

zo·o·xan·thel·la (zō′ə-zăn-thĕl′ə) *n., pl.* **-thel·lae** (-thĕl′ē). Any of various yellow-green algae that live symbiotically within the cells of other organisms, such as those of certain radiolarians and marine invertebrates. [New Latin : ZOO– + XANTH(O)– + *-ella,* diminutive suff.]

Zor·ach (zō′răk′, -räk′, -räkh′), **William.** 1887–1966. Lithuanian-born American sculptor whose simple, monumental works include *Builders of the Future* (1939).

zo·ri (zôr′ē, zōr′ē) *n., pl.* **zori** or **-ris.** A flat sandal with thongs, usually made of straw or leather. [Japanese *zōri* : *sō,* grass, straw + *ri,* sole.]

zor·ille also **zor·il** (zôr′ĭl, zŏr′-) or **zo·ril·la** (zə-rĭl′ə) *n.* A carnivorous African mammal *(Ictonyx striatus)* related to the weasel but resembling the skunk in appearance and in its method of defense. [French, from Spanish *zorrillo,* skunk, diminutive of *zorro,* fox, from Old Spanish, idler, vagabond, fox.]

Zorn (sôrn, zôrn), **Anders Leonhard.** 1860–1920. Swedish artist noted for his sculptures and his paintings and etchings of landscapes, nudes, and genre scenes.

Zo·ro·as·ter (zôr′ō-ăs′tər, zŏr′-) **Zar·a·thu·stra** (zăr′ə-tho͞o′strə). Sixth century B.C. Persian prophet who founded Zoroastrianism. Little is known about his life.

Zo·ro·as·tri·an·ism (zôr′ō-ăs′trē-ə-nĭz′əm) *n.* The religious system founded in Persia by Zoroaster and set forth in the Zend-Avesta, teaching the worship of Ormazd in the context of a universal struggle between the forces of light and of darkness. **—Zo′ro·as′tri·an** *adj. & n.*

Zor·ril·la y Mo·ral (zə-rē′ə ē mə-räl′, thô-rē′lyä ē mô-räl′), **José.** 1817–1893. Spanish writer whose romantic works include the play *Don Juan Tenorio* (1844) and the unfinished narrative poem *Granada* (1852).

zos·ter (zŏs′tər) *n.* **1.** A belt or girdle worn by men in ancient Greece. **2.** Herpes zoster. [Greek *zōstēr,* girdle.]

Zou·ave (zo͞o-äv′, zwäv) *n.* **1.** A member of a French infantry unit, formerly composed of Algerian recruits, characterized by colorful uniforms and precision drilling. **2.** A member of a group patterned after the French Zouaves, especially a member of such a unit of the Union Army in the U.S. Civil War. [French, from Berber *Zwāwa,* an Algerian tribe.]

zounds (zoundz) *interj.* Used to express anger, surprise, or indignation. [Shortening and alteration of *God's wounds!*]

zoy·sia (zoi′shə, -zhə, -sē-ə, -zē-ə) *n.* Any of several creeping grasses of the genus *Zoysia,* native to southeast Asia and New Zealand and widely cultivated for lawns. [New Latin *Zoysia,* genus name, after Karl von *Zois* zu Laubach (1756–1800?), Austrian botanist.]

Zp *abbr. Bible.* Zephaniah.

Z particle *n.* A massive elementary particle, electrically neutral, that is the quantum of weak interactions in which the charges of participating particles do not change. See table at **subatomic particle.**

ZPG *abbr.* Zero population growth.

Zr The symbol for the element **zirconium.**

Z score *n. Statistics.* A measure of the distance in standard deviations of a sample from the mean.

zuc·chet·to (zo͞o-kĕt′ō, tso͞ok-kĕt′tô) *n., pl.* **-tos.** *Roman Catholic Church.* A skullcap worn by clerics, varying in color with the rank of the wearer. [Italian, variant of *zucchetta,* diminutive of *zucca,* gourd, head. See ZUCCHINI.]

zuc·chi·ni (zo͞o-kē′nē) *n., pl.* **zucchini** or **-nis.** A variety of squash having an elongated shape and a smooth, thin, dark green rind. [Italian, pl. of *zucchino,* diminutive of *zucca,* gourd, from Late Latin *cucutia.*]

Zug·spit·ze (zo͞og′spĭt-sə, tso͞ok′shpĭt-). A mountain, 2,964.9 m (9,721 ft) high, in the Bavarian Alps of south-central Germany.

Zug·un·ru·he (tso͞ok′o͞on-ro͞o′hə) *n.* The migratory drive in

Émile Zola

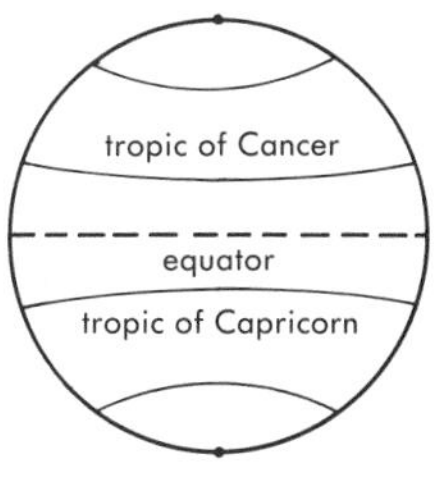

zone

zucchini

ă pat	oi boy
ā pay	ou out
âr care	o͝o took
ä father	o͞o boot
ĕ pet	ŭ cut
ē be	ûr urge
ĭ pit	th thin
ī pie	*th* this
îr pier	hw which
ŏ pot	zh vision
ō toe	ə about, item
ô paw	♦ regionalism

Stress marks: ′ (primary); ′ (secondary), as in **dictionary** (dĭk′shə-nĕr′ē)

Ulrich Zwingli

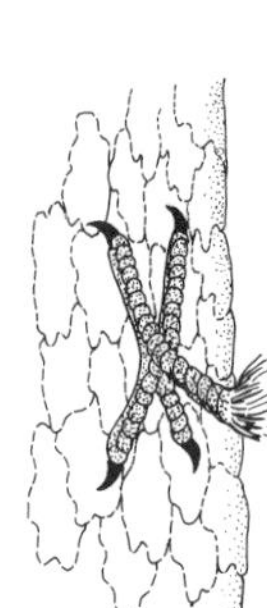

zygodactyl

ă pat	oi boy
ā pay	ou out
âr care	o͝o took
ä father	o͞o boot
ĕ pet	ŭ cut
ē be	ûr urge
ĭ pit	th thin
ī pie	*th* this
îr pier	hw which
ŏ pot	zh vision
ō toe	ə about, item
ô paw	♦ regionalism

Stress marks: **ʹ** (primary); ʹ (secondary), as in **dictionary** (dĭkʹshə-nĕrʹē)

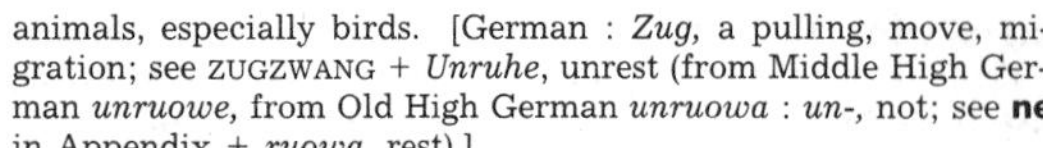

animals, especially birds. [German : *Zug,* a pulling, move, migration; see ZUGZWANG + *Unruhe,* unrest (from Middle High German *unruowe,* from Old High German *unruowa* : *un-,* not; see **ne** in Appendix + *ruowa,* rest).]

zug·zwang (tso͝okʹtsvängʹ) *n. Games.* A situation in a chess game in which a player is forced to make an undesirable or disadvantageous move. [German *Zugzwang* : *Zug,* pull, move (from Middle High German *zuc,* pull, from Old High German, from *ziohan,* to pull; see **deuk-** in Appendix) + *Zwang,* compulsion (from Middle High German *twanc,* from Old High German).]

Zui·der Zee (zīʹdər zēʹ, zāʹ, zoiʹdər zāʹ). A former shallow inlet of the North Sea in northeast Netherlands. Originally a lake, it was joined with the North Sea by heavy flooding. A dike, completed in 1932, turned the southern section into the Ijsselmeer, which has largely been reclaimed for agriculture.

Zuk·er·man (zo͞oʹkər-mən), **Pinchas.** Born 1948. Israeli violinist noted particularly for his performance of chamber music.

Zu·lu (zo͞oʹlo͞o) *n., pl.* **Zulu** or **-lus. 1.** A member of a Bantu people of southeast Africa, primarily inhabiting northeast Natal province in South Africa. **2.** The Nguni language of this people, closely related to Xhosa. **—Zuʹlu** *adj.*

Zu·lu·land (zo͞oʹlo͞o-lăndʹ). A historical region of northeast South Africa. Settled by members of a Bantu nation, it was annexed by the British in 1887.

Zu·ni (zo͞oʹnē) also **Zu·ñi** (-nyē, -nē) *n., pl.* **Zuni** or **-nis** also **Zuñi** or **-ñis. 1.a.** A Pueblo people located in western New Mexico. **b.** A member of this people. **2.** The language of the Zuni.

Zu·ni·an (zo͞oʹnē-ən) or **Zu·ñi·an** (zo͞onʹyē-) *n.* A language family consisting only of Zuni. **—Zuʹni·an, Zuʹñi·an** *adj.*

Zur·ba·rán (zo͞orʹbä-ränʹ, tho͞orʹ-), **Francisco de.** 1598–1664. Spanish painter noted for his simple naturalism. His works include still lifes and religious scenes.

Zu·rich (zo͝orʹĭk). A city of northeast Switzerland at the northern tip of the **Lake of Zurich.** Founded before Roman times, Zurich became a free imperial city after 1218 and joined the Swiss Confederation in 1351. In the 16th century it was a center of the Swiss Reformation under the leadership of Ulrich Zwingli. Today it is the largest city in the country. Population, 354,500.

Zweig (zwīg, swīg, tsvīk), **Arnold.** 1887–1968. German-born writer. A Zionist, he wrote about Judaism, the persecution of the Jews, and war. His works include the novel *The Case of Sergeant Grischa* (1927).

Zweig, Stefan. 1881–1942. Austrian writer of poetry, fiction, and sensitive psychoanalytic biographies, notably *Three Masters* (1920), a study of Balzac, Dickens, and Dostoyevsky.

Zwick·au (zwĭkʹou, tsvĭkʹ-). A city of east-central Germany south of Leipzig. Chartered in the early 13th century, it was a free imperial city from 1290 to 1323. Population, 120,486.

zwie·back (swēʹbăkʹ, -bäkʹ, swīʹ-, zwēʹ-, zwīʹ-) *n.* A usually sweetened bread baked first as a loaf and later cut into slices and toasted. [German : *zwie-,* twice (from Middle High German *zwi-,* from Old High German; see **dwo-** in Appendix) + *backen,* to bake (from Middle High German, from Old High German *bahhan, bakkan*).]

Zwing·li (zwĭngʹlē, swĭngʹ-, tsvĭngʹ-), **Ulrich** or **Huldreich.** 1484–1531. Swiss religious reformer whose sermons on the absolute authority of the Bible (1519) marked the beginning of the Reformation in Switzerland.

Zwing·li·an (zwĭngʹlē-ən, swĭngʹ-, tsvĭngʹ-) *adj.* Of or relating to Ulrich Zwingli or to his theological system, especially his doctrine that the physical body of Jesus is not present in the Eucharist and that the ceremony is merely a symbolic commemoration of Jesus's death. **—Zwinglian** *n.* A follower of Zwingli. **—Zwingʹli·an·ism** *n.*

zwit·ter·i·on (zwĭtʹər-īʹən, swĭtʹ-, tsvĭtʹ-) *n. Physics.* A molecule carrying both a positive and a negative charge. [German : *Zwitter,* hybrid (from Middle High German *zwitarn,* from Old High German, from *zwi-,* twice; see **dwo-** in Appendix) + *ion,* ion (from Greek; see ION).] **—zwitʹter·i·onʹic** (-ī-ŏnʹĭk) *adj.*

Zwol·le (zwôlʹə, zvôlʹə). A city of northern Netherlands on the Ijssel River. Thomas à Kempis lived at a monastery nearby for more than 60 years. Population, 87,340.

Zwor·y·kin (zwôrʹĭ-kĭn, zvôrʹyə-), **Vladimir Kosma.** 1889–1982. Russian-born American physicist and inventor of the iconoscope (1923), the first practical television camera.

zy·de·co (zīʹdĭ-kōʹ) *n. Music.* Popular music of southern Louisiana that combines French dance melodies, elements of Caribbean music, and the blues, played by small groups featuring the guitar, the accordion, and a washboard. [From Louisiana French, possibly alteration of *Les haricots (sont pas salé),* name of a song, pl. of French *haricot,* bean. See HARICOT[1].]

zyg– *pref.* Variant of **zygo–.**

zyg·a·poph·y·sis (zĭgʹə-pŏfʹĭ-sĭs, zīʹgə-) *n., pl.* **-ses** (-sēzʹ). One of two usually paired processes of the neural arch of a vertebra that articulates with corresponding parts of adjacent vertebrae. **—zygʹap·o·physʹe·al, zygʹap·o·physʹi·al** (zĭgʹăp-ə-fĭzʹē-əl, zīʹgăp-) *adj.*

zygo– or **zyg–** *pref.* **1.** Yoke; pair: *zygodactyl.* **2.** Union: *zygospore.* [New Latin, from Greek *zugo-,* from *zugon,* yoke. See **yeug-** in Appendix.]

zy·go·dac·tyl (zīʹgə-dăkʹtĭl, zĭgʹə-) *adj.* Having two toes projecting forward and two projecting backward, as certain climbing birds. **—zygodactyl** *n.* A zygodactyl bird, such as a parrot.

zy·go·dac·ty·lous (zīʹgə-dăkʹtə-ləs, zĭgʹə-) *adj.* Zygodactyl.

zy·go·gen·e·sis (zīʹgō-jĕnʹĭ-sĭs) *n., pl.* **-ses** (-sēzʹ). Reproduction involving the formation of a zygote. **—zyʹgo·ge·netʹic** (-jə-nĕtʹĭk) *adj.*

zy·go·ma (zī-gōʹmə, zĭ-) *n., pl.* **-ma·ta** (-mə-tə) or **-mas. 1.** The zygomatic bone. **2.** The zygomatic arch. **3.** The zygomatic process. [New Latin *zygōma, zygōmat-,* from Greek *zugōma,* bolt, from *zugoun,* to join. See **yeug-** in Appendix.]

zy·go·mat·ic (zīʹgə-mătʹĭk, zĭgʹə-) *adj.* Of, relating to, or located in the area of the zygoma: *a zygomatic muscle.*

zygomatic arch *n.* The bony arch in vertebrates that extends along the side or front of the skull beneath the eye socket and that is formed by the zygomatic bone and the zygomatic process of the temporal bone.

zygomatic bone *n.* A small bone in vertebrates on each side of the face socket, forming the prominence of the cheek. Also called *cheekbone.*

zygomatic process *n.* Any of three processes that articulate with the zygomatic bone, especially the process from the temporal bone that articulates to form the zygomatic arch.

zy·go·mor·phic (zīʹgə-môrʹfĭk, zĭgʹə-) also **zy·go·mor·phous** (-fəs) *adj.* Bilaterally symmetrical. Used of organisms or parts. **—zyʹgo·morʹphism** *n.*

zy·go·sis (zī-gōʹsĭs, zĭ-) *n., pl.* **-ses** (-sēz). The union of gametes to form a zygote; conjugation.

zy·gos·i·ty (zī-gŏsʹĭ-tē) *n.* The genetic condition of a zygote, especially with respect to its being a homozygote or a heterozygote.

zy·go·spore (zīʹgə-spôrʹ, -spōrʹ, zĭgʹə-) *n.* A large multinucleate spore formed by union of similar gametes, as in algae or fungi.

zy·gote (zīʹgōtʹ) *n.* **1.** The cell formed by the union of two gametes, especially a fertilized ovum before cleavage. **2.** The organism that develops from a zygote. [From Greek *zugōtos,* yoked, from *zugoun,* to yoke. See **yeug-** in Appendix.] **—zy·gotʹic** (-gŏtʹĭk) *adj.* **—zy·gotʹi·cal·ly** *adv.*

zy·go·tene (zīʹgə-tēnʹ) *n.* The stage in prophase of meiosis during which homologous chromosomes become paired. [French *zygotène* : *zygo-,* pair (from New Latin; see ZYGO–) + *-tène,* ribbon (from Latin *taenia;* see TAENIA).]

–zygous *suff.* Having a zygotic constitution of a specified kind: *heterozygous.* [From Greek *-zugos,* yoked, from *zugon,* yoke. See **yeug-** in Appendix.]

zym– *pref.* Variant of **zymo–.**

zy·mase (zīʹmāsʹ, -māzʹ) *n.* The enzyme complex in yeasts that catalyzes the breakdown of sugar into alcohol and carbon dioxide.

–zyme *suff.* Enzyme: *lysozyme.* [From Greek *zumē,* leaven.]

zymo– or **zym–** *pref.* **1.** Fermentation: *zymurgy.* **2.** Enzyme: *zymogram.* [New Latin, from Greek *zumē,* leaven.]

zy·mo·gen (zīʹmə-jən) *n.* See **proenzyme.**

zy·mo·gen·ic (zīʹmə-jĕnʹĭk) also **zy·mog·e·nous** (zī-mŏjʹə-nəs) *adj.* **1.** Of or relating to a zymogen. **2.** Capable of causing fermentation. **3.** Enzyme-producing.

zy·mo·gram (zīʹmə-grămʹ) *n.* A strip or band of electrophoretic medium showing the pattern of enzymes or isoenzymes after their separation by electrophoresis.

zy·mol·o·gy (zī-mŏlʹə-jē) *n.* The chemistry of fermentation. **—zyʹmo·logʹic** (-mə-lŏjʹĭk), **zyʹmo·logʹi·cal** (-ĭ-kəl) *adj.* **—zy·molʹo·gist** *n.*

zy·mol·y·sis (zī-mŏlʹĭ-sĭs) *n.* Fermentation. **—zyʹmo·lytʹic** (-mə-lĭtʹĭk) *adj.*

zy·mom·e·ter (zī-mŏmʹĭ-tər) *n.* See **zymoscope.**

zy·mo·san (zīʹmə-sănʹ) *n.* An insoluble carbohydrate from the cell wall of yeast, used especially in the immunoassay of properdin. [ZYMOS(IS) + –AN[2].]

zy·mo·scope (zīʹmə-skōpʹ) *n.* An instrument used to determine fermentation efficiency by measurement of carbon dioxide produced. Also called *zymometer.*

zy·mo·sis (zī-mōʹsĭs) *n., pl.* **-ses** (-sēz). **1.** Fermentation. **2.** *Medicine.* **a.** The process of infection. **b.** An infectious disease, especially one caused by a fungus. [Greek *zumōsis,* from *zumoun,* to leaven, from *zumē,* leaven.] **—zy·motʹic** (-mŏtʹĭk) *adj.* **—zy·motʹi·cal·ly** *adv.*

zy·mur·gy (zīʹmûrʹjē) *n.* The branch of chemistry that deals with fermentation processes, as in brewing.

zyz·zy·va (zĭzʹə-və) *n.* Any of various tropical American weevils of the genus *Zyzzyva,* often destructive to plants. [New Latin *Zyzzyva,* genus name, probably from *Zyzza,* former genus of leafhoppers.]

INDO-EUROPEAN AND THE INDO-EUROPEANS

CALVERT WATKINS

After the initial identification of a prehistoric language underlying the modern Indo-European family and the foundation of the science of comparative linguistics, the detailed reconstruction of Proto-Indo-European proceeded by stages still fascinating to observe. The main outlines of the reconstructed language were already seen by the end of the 1870's, but it was only during the course of the 20th century that certain of these features received general acceptance. The last decades of the 20th century have happily witnessed a resurgence of Indo-European studies, catalyzed by advances in linguistic theory and by an increase in the available data, which have resulted in a picture of the reconstructed protolanguage that is, in a word, "tighter." The grammar of Indo-European today is more tightly organized and more sharply focused, at all levels. There are fewer loose ends, fewer hazy areas, and those that do remain are more clearly identified as such. New etymologies continue to be made, and older etymologies undergo revision to incorporate new evidence or better analyses. The attention to detail in reconstruction in this revised Roots Appendix reflects these ongoing developments in the field: Indo-European studies are alive with excitement, growth, and change.

AN EXAMPLE OF RECONSTRUCTION

Before proceeding with a survey of the lexicon and culture of the Indo-Europeans (see page 2084), it may be helpful to give a concrete illustration of the method used to reconstruct the Proto-Indo-European vocabulary, followed by a brief description of some of the main features of the Proto-Indo-European language. This example will serve as an introduction to the comparative method and indicate as well the high degree of precision that the techniques of reconstruction permit.

A number of Indo-European languages show a similar word for the kinship term "daughter-in-law": Sanskrit *snuṣā́*, Old English *snoru*, Old Church Slavonic *snŭkha* (Russian *snokhá*), Latin *nurus*, Greek *nuós* and Armenian *nu*. All of these forms, called *cognates*, provide evidence for the phonetic shape of the prehistoric Indo-European word for "daughter-in-law" that is their common ancestor. Sanskrit, Germanic, and Slavic agree in showing an Indo-European word that began with *sn-*. We know that an Indo-European *s* was lost before *n* in other words in Latin, Greek, and Armenian, so we can confidently assume that Latin *nurus*, Greek *nuós* and Armenian *nu* also go back to an Indo-European **sn-*. (Compare Latin *nix* [stem *niv-*], "snow," with English SNOW, which preserves the *s*.) This principle is spoken of as the *regularity of sound correspondences*; it is basic to the sciences of etymology and comparative linguistics.

Sanskrit, Latin, Greek, and Armenian agree in showing the first vowel as *-u-*. We know from other examples that Slavic *ŭ* regularly corresponds to Sanskrit *u* and that in this position Germanic *o* (of Old English *snoru*) has been changed from an earlier *u*. It is thus justifiable to reconstruct an Indo-European word beginning **snu-*.

For the consonant originally following **snu-*, closer analysis is required. The key is furnished first by the Sanskrit form, for we know there is a rule in Sanskrit that *s* always changes to *ṣ* (a *sh*-like sound) after the vowel *u*. Therefore a Sanskrit *snuṣ-* must go back to an earlier **snus-*. In the same position, after *u*, an old *s* changes to *kh* (like the *ch* in Scottish *loch* or German *ach*) in Slavic; hence the Slavic word, too, reflects **snus-*. In Latin always, and in Germanic under certain conditions, an old *-s-* between vowels went to *-r-*. For this reason Latin *nurus* and Old English *snoru* may go back to older **snus-* (followed by a vowel) as well. In Greek and Armenian, on the other hand, an old *-s-* between vowels disappeared entirely, as we know from numerous instances. Greek *nuós* and Armenian *nu* (stem *nuo-*) thus regularly presuppose the same earlier form, **snus-* (followed by a vowel). All the comparative evidence agrees, then, on the Indo-European root form **snus-*.

For the ending, the final vowels of Sanskrit *snuṣā́*, Old English *snoru*, and Slavic *snŭkha* all presuppose earlier *-ā (*snus-ā)*, which is the ordinary feminine ending of these languages. On the other hand, Latin *nurus*, Greek *nuós* and Armenian *nu* (stem *nuo-*) all regularly presuppose the earlier ending **-os (*snus-os)*. We have an apparent impasse; but the way out is given by the gender of the forms in Greek and Latin. They are feminine, even though most nouns in Latin *-us* and Greek *-os* are masculine.

Feminine nouns in Latin *-us* and Greek *-os*, since they are an abnormal type, cannot have been created afresh; they must have been inherited. This suggests that the original Indo-European form was **snusos*, of feminine gender. On the other hand, the commonplace freely formed ending for feminine nouns was **-ā*. It is reasonable to suggest that the three languages Sanskrit, Germanic, and Slavic replaced the peculiar feminine ending **-os* (because that ending was normally masculine) with the normal ordinary feminine ending **-ā*, and thus that the oldest form of the word was **snusos* (feminine).

One point remains to be ascertained: the accent. Of those four language groups that reflect the Indo-European accent, Sanskrit, (Balto-)Slavic, Greek, and Germanic, the first three are agreed in showing a form accented on the last syllable: *snuṣā́, snokhá, nuós*. The Germanic form is equally precise, however, since the rule is that old *-s-* went to *-r-* (Old English *snoru*) only if the accented syllable came after the *-s-*.

On this basis we may add the finishing touch to our reconstruction: the full form of the word for "daughter-in-law" in Indo-European is **snusós*.

It is noteworthy that no single language in the family preserves this word intact. In every language, in every tradition in the Indo-European family, the word has been somehow altered from its original shape. It is the comparative method that permits us to explain the different forms in this variety of languages by the reconstruction of a unitary common prototype, a common ancestor.

PROTO-INDO-EUROPEAN GRAMMAR: SOUNDS AND FORMS

A large part of the success of the comparative method with the Indo-European family is due to the number and the precision of the agreements among the languages, not only in the regular sound correspondences of the roots but even more strikingly so in the particulars of morphology, the forms of language in their grammatical function. Consider the partial paradigms of the words for "dog" *(*kwon-)* and "to kill" *(*gʷhen-)*:

	Hittite	**Greek**	**Vedic**
nominative	*kuwas*	*kúōn*	*ś(u)vā́*
accusative	*kuwanan*	*kúna*	*śvā́nam*
genitive	*kūnas*	*kunós*	*śúnas*

	Lithuanian	**Old Irish**	**Proto-Indo-European**
nominative	*šuõ*	*cú*	**k(u)wō(n)*
accusative	*šùnį*	*coin*	**kwónm̥*
genitive	*šuñs*	*con*	**kunés*

	Hittite	**Vedic**	**PIE**
third singular present indicative	*kuenzi*	*hánti*	**gʷhén-ti*
third plural present indicative	*kunanzi*	*ghnánti*	**gʷhn-énti*

The agreement of detail in sound correspondences (see the chart on pages 2092–2093), in vowel alternations and their distribution, in the accent, in the grammatical forms (endings), and in the syntactic functions is little short of astounding.

SPEECH SOUNDS AND THEIR ALTERNATIONS. The system of *sounds* in Proto-Indo-European was rich in stop consonants. There was an unvoiced series, *p, t, k, kʷ* (like the *qu* of *quick*), a voiced series, *b, d, g, gʷ*, and a voiced aspirate or "murmured" series, *bh, dh, gh, gʷh,* pronounced like the voiced series but followed by a puff of breath. (Some scholars would reinterpret the traditional voiced series as an unvoiced ejective, or glottalized, one. While this new "glottalic theory" accounts for some typological difficulties, it introduces more problems than it solves. In this work, as in most current handbooks, Indo-European forms appear in their traditional shape.) If the language was rich in stop consonants, it was correspondingly poor in continuants, or fricatives, such as English *f, v, th, s,* and *z,* having only *s,* which was voiced to *z* before voiced stop consonants. It had as well three so-called *laryngeals* or *h*-like sounds, all of which are written here as schwa, or *ə* (equivalent notations are *H* or *h*). The sound is preserved as such (at least in part) only in Hittite and the other Anatolian languages in cuneiform documents from the second millennium B.C. Compare Hittite *pahs-*, "to protect," coming directly from Indo-European **paə-s-* (PASTOR). In all the other languages of the family, its former presence in a word can only be deduced from indirect evidence such as the contractions discussed immediately below. Elucidation of the details of these laryngeals remains one of the most interesting problems confronting Indo-Europeanists today.

Proto-Indo-European had two nasals, *m* and *n,* two liquids, *r* and *l,* and the glides *w* and *y.* A salient characteristic of Indo-European was that these sounds could function both as consonants and as vowels. Their consonantal value was as in English. As vowels, symbolized *m̥, n̥, l̥,* and *r̥,* the liquids and nasals sounded much like the final syllables of English *bottom, button, bottle,* and *butter.* The vocalic counterparts of *w* and *y* were the vowels *u* and *i.* The laryngeals too could function both as consonants and as vowels: their consonantal value was that of *h*-like sounds, while as vowels they were varieties of schwa, much like the final syllable of English *sofa*; hence the choice of schwa to represent laryngeals in this Appendix.

The other vowels of Indo-European were *e, o,* and *a.* These, as well as *i* and *u,* occurred both long and short, as did the diphthongs *ei, oi, ai, eu, ou, au.* (All vowels are pronounced as in Latin or Italian.) Since we can distinguish chronological layers in Proto-Indo-European, it can be said that a number of the long vowels of later Indo-European resulted from the contraction of early Indo-European short vowels with a following *ə.* Already in Proto-Indo-European itself, two of the three laryngeals had the property of "coloring" an adjacent fundamental vowel *e* to *a* and *o,* respectively, before the contractions took place. Thus the root **pa-,**"to protect," is contracted from older **paə-*, with "a-coloring"; the root **dō-,** "to give," is contracted from older **doə-*, with "o-coloring"; and the root **dhē-,** "to set, put," is contracted from older **dheə-*, without coloring. The fundamental vowel in each of these roots, as in most Indo-European roots, was originally *e.* In scholarly usage it is now customary to write the noncoloring laryngeal as $ə_1$ (or h_1), thus **dheə*$_1$*-*; the a-coloring laryngeal as $ə_2$ (or h_2), thus **paə*$_2$*-*; and the o-coloring laryngeal as $ə_3$ (or h_3), thus **doə*$_3$*-*. This typographically cumbersome notation has been simplified in the Appendix, since the vowel before the schwa is sufficient to distinguish the three in the cases of contraction to a long vowel, and in other positions in most languages other than Greek the three merge to one. No systematic notice has been taken in this Appendix of word-initial laryngeals before vowels (amply attested in Hittite), since the root forms with initial vowel are readily convertible by the student. Thus **ant-,** "front, forehead," from **ə$_2$ant-*, **əant-* (Hittite *hant-*, "front, forehead"); **op-,** "to work, produce in abundance," from **ə$_3$op-*, **əop-* (Hittite *happ-in-ant-*, "rich"); and **ed-,** "to eat," from **ə$_1$ed-*, **əed-* (Hittite *ed-*, "to eat").

A characteristic feature of Indo-European was the system of vocalic *alternations* termed *apophony* or *ablaut.* This was a set of internal vowel changes expressing different morphological functions. A clear reflex of this feature is preserved in the English strong verbs, where, for example, the vocalic alternations between *write* and *wrote, give* and *gave,* express the present and past tenses. Ablaut in Indo-European affected the vowels *e* and *o.* The fundamental form was *e;* this *e* could appear as *o* under certain conditions, and in other conditions both *e* and *o* could disappear entirely. On this basis we speak of given forms in Indo-European as exhibiting, respectively, the *e-grade* (or *full grade*), the *o-grade,* or the *zero grade.* The *e* and the *o* might furthermore occur as long *ē* or *ō,* termed the *lengthened grade.*

To illustrate: the Indo-European root **ped-,** "foot," appears in the e-grade in Latin *ped-* (PEDAL), but in the o-grade in Greek *pod-* (PODIATRIST). Germanic **fōtuz* (FOOT) reflects the lengthened o-grade **pōd-*. The zero grade of the same root shows no vowel at all: **pd-*, a form attested in Sanskrit.

When the zero grade involved a root with one of the sounds *m, n, r, l, w,* or *y* (collectively termed *resonants*), the resonant would regularly appear in its vocalic function, forming a syllable. We have the e-grade root **senk^w-** in English SINK, the o-grade form **sonk^w-* in SANK, and the zero-grade form **sn̥k^w-* in SUNK.

In the paradigms cited earlier, the word for "dog," **kwon-,** appears in the o-grade in the accusative case **kwón-(m̥),* in the zero grade in the genitive case **kun-(és),* and in the lengthened o-grade in the nominative case **kwō(n).* Note that the nonsyllabic resonant *w* appears as the vowel *u* when it becomes syllabic. The verb "to kill," **g^{w}hen-,** appears in the e-grade in the third singular **g^{w}hén-(ti),* and in the zero grade in the third plural **g^{w}hn-(énti).* It appears in the o-grade **g^{w}hon-* in Germanic **ban-ōn-* (BANE). The *n* of the zero grade **g^{w}hn-* becomes syllabic *(n̥)* before a consonant: **g^{w}hn̥(tyā́-)* becoming Germanic **gundjō* (GUN).

In the case of roots with long vowels arising from contraction with *ə*, the ablaut can be most clearly understood by referring to the older, uncontracted forms. Thus **pā-,** "to protect," contracted from **paə-*, has a zero grade **pə-*; **dō-,** "to give," contracted from **doə-*, has a zero grade **də-*; **dhē-,** "to place," contracted from **dheə-*, has a zero grade **dhə-*. The fundamental vowel of the full grade disappears in the zero grade, and only the *ə* remains. Long *ū* and long *ī* could also arise from contraction: full grade **peuə-,** "to purify," has a zero grade **puə-* contracted to **pū-* (PURE); full grade **peiə-,** "to be fat, swell," has a zero grade **piə-* contracted to **pī-* (IRISH).

GRAMMATICAL FORMS AND SYNTAX. Proto-Indo-European was a highly inflected language. Grammatical relationships and the syntactic function of words in the sentence were indicated primarily by variations in the endings of the words. Nouns had different endings for different cases, such as the subject and the direct object of the verb, the possessive, and many other functions, and for the different numbers, namely the singular, plural, and a special dual number for objects occurring in pairs. Verbs had different endings for the different persons (first, second, third) and numbers (singular, plural, dual), for the voices active and passive (or middle, a sort of reflexive), as well as special affixes for a rich variety of tenses, moods, and categories such as causative-transitive *(*-éyo-)* and stative-intransitive *(*-ē-)* verbs. Practically none of this rich inflection is preserved in Modern English, but it has left its trace in many formations in Germanic and in other languages such as Latin and Greek. These are noted in the Appendix where they are relevant.

With the exception of the numbers five to ten and a group of particles including certain conjunctions and quasi-adverbial forms, all Indo-European words underwent inflection. The structure of all inflected words, regardless of part of speech, was the same: *root* plus one or more *suffixes* plus *ending.* Thus the word **ker-wo-s,* "a stag," is composed of the root **ker-[1],** "horn," plus the noun suffix *-wo-*, plus the nominative singular ending *-s*. The root contained the basic semantic kernel, the underlying notion, which the suffix could modify in various ways. It was primarily the suffix that determined the part of speech of the word. Thus a single root like **prek-,** "to ask," could, depending on the suffix, form a verb **pr̥k-sko-*, "to ask" (Latin *poscere*), a noun **prek-*, "prayer" (Latin *precēs*), and an adjective **prok-o-*, "asking" (underlying Latin *procus,* "suitor"). Note that **prek-, *prok-,* and **pr̥k-* have, respectively, e-grade, o-grade, and zero grade.

The root could undergo certain modifications. *Extensions* or *enlargements* did not affect the basic meaning and simply reflect formal variations between languages. *Suffixes* had more specific values. There were verbal suffixes that made nouns into verbs and others that marked different types of action, like transitive and intransitive. There were nominal suffixes that made agent nouns, abstract nouns, verbal nouns and verbal adjectives, and nouns of instrument and other functions.

The root plus the suffix or suffixes constituted the *stem.* The stems represented the basic lexical stock of Indo-European, the separate words of its dictionary. Yet a single root would commonly furnish a large number of derivative stems with different suffixes, both nominal and verbal, much as English *love* is both noun and verb as well as the base of such derivatives as *lovely, lover,* and *beloved.* For this reason it is customary to group such collections of derivatives, in a variety of Indo-European languages, under the root on which they are built. The root entries of the Appendix are arranged in this way, with derivatives that exhibit similar suffixes forming subgroups consisting of Indo-European stems or words.

Indo-European made extensive use of suffixation in the formation of words but had very few prefixes. The use of such prefixes ("preverbs") as Latin *ad-, con-, de-, ex-* (ADVENT, CONVENE, DERIVE, EXPRESS) or Germanic *be-* (BECOME, BEGET) can be shown to be a development of the individual languages after the breakup of the common language. In Indo-European such "compounds" represented two independent words, a situation still reflected in Hittite and the older Sanskrit of the Vedas (the sacred books of the ancient Hindus) and surviving in isolated remnants in Greek and Latin.

An important technique of word formation in Indo-European was *composition,* the combining of two separate words or notions into a single word. Such forms were and continue to be built on underlying simple sentences; an example in English would be "he is someone who *cuts wood,*" whence "he is a *woodcutter.*" It is in the area of composition that English has most faithfully preserved the ancient Indo-European patterns of word formation, by continuously forming them anew, re-creating them. Thus *housewife* is immediately analyzable into *house* + *wife,* a so-called descriptive compound in which the first member modifies the second; the same elements compounded in Old English, *hūs* + *wīf,* have been preserved as an indivisible unit in *hussy.* Modern English has many different types of compound, such as *catfish, housewife, woodcutter, pickpocket,* or *blue-eyed*; exactly similar types may be found in the other Germanic languages and in Sanskrit, Greek, Latin, Celtic, and Slavic.

The comparative study of Indo-European poetics has shown that such compounds were considered particularly apt for elevated, formal styles of discourse; they are a salient characteristic especially of Indo-European poetic language. In addition, it is amply clear that in Indo-European society the names of individual persons – at least in the priestly and ruling (or warrior) classes – were formed by such two-member compounds. Greek names like *Sophocles,* "famed for wisdom," Celtic names like *Vercingetorix,* "warrior-king," Slavic names like *Mstislav,* "famed for vengeance," Old Persian names like *Xerxes,* "ruling men," and Germanic names like *Bertram,* "bright raven," are all compounds. The type goes as far back as Proto-Indo-European, even if the individual names do not. English family names continue the same tradition with such types as *Cartwright* and *Shakespeare,* as do those of other languages, like Irish *(O')Toole,* "having the people's valor."

SEMANTICS. A word of caution should be entered about the semantics of the roots. It is perhaps more hazardous to attempt to reconstruct meaning than to reconstruct linguistic form, and the meaning of a root can only be extrapolated from the meanings of its descendants. Often these diverge sharply from one another, and the scholar is reduced in practice to inferring only what seems a reasonable, or even merely possible, semantic common denominator. The result is that reconstructed words and particularly roots are often assigned hazy, vague, or unspecific meanings. This is doubtless quite illusory; a portmanteau meaning for a root should not be confused with the specific meaning of a derivative of that root at a particular time and place. The apparent haziness in meaning of a given Indo-European root often simply reflects the fact that with the passage of several thousand years the different words derived from this root in divergent languages have undergone semantic changes that are no longer recoverable in detail.

LEXICON AND CULTURE

The reconstruction of a *protolanguage* – the common ancestor of a family of spoken or attested languages – has a further implication. Language is a social fact; languages are not spoken in a vacuum but by human beings living in a society. When we have reconstructed a protolanguage, we have also necessarily established the existence of a prehistoric society, a speech community that used that protolanguage. The existence of Proto-Indo-European presupposes the existence, in some fashion, of a society of Indo-Europeans.

Language is intimately linked to culture in a complex fashion; it is at once the expression of culture and a part of it. Especially the lexicon of a language – its dictionary – is a face turned toward culture. Though by no means a perfect mirror, the lexicon of a language remains the single most effective way of approaching and understanding the culture of its speakers. As such, the contents of the Indo-European lexicon provide a remarkably clear view of the whole culture of an otherwise unknown prehistoric society.

The evidence that archaeology can provide is limited to material remains. But human culture is not confined to material artifacts alone. The reconstruction of vocabulary can offer a fuller, more interesting view of the culture of a prehistoric people than archaeology precisely because it includes nonmaterial culture.

Consider the case of religion. To form an idea of the religion of a people, archaeologists proceed by inference, examining temples, sanctuaries, idols, votive objects, funerary offerings, and other material remains. But these may not be forthcoming; archaeology is, for example, of little or no utility in understanding the religion of the ancient Hebrews. Yet, for the Indo-European-speaking society, we can reconstruct with certainty the word for "god," **deiw-os,* and the two-word name of the chief deity of the pantheon, **dyeu-pəter-* (Latin *Jūpiter,* Greek *Zeus patēr,* Sanskrit *Dyaus pitar,* and Luvian *Tatis Tiwaz*). The forms **dyeu-* and **deiw-os* are both derivatives of a root **deiw-,** meaning "to shine," which appears in the word for "day" in numerous languages (Latin *diēs*; but English DAY is not related). The notion of deity was therefore linked to the notion of the bright sky.

The second element of the name of the chief god, **dyeu-pəter-,* is the general Indo-European word for father, used not in the sense of father as parent but with the meaning of the adult male who is head of the household, the sense of Latin *pater familias.* For the Indo-Europeans the society of the gods was conceived in the image of their own society as patriarchal. The reconstructed words **deiw-os* and **dyeu-pəter-* alone tell us more about the conceptual world of the Indo-Europeans than a roomful of graven images.

The comparative method enables us to construct a basic vocabulary for the society of speakers of Proto-Indo-European that extends to virtually all aspects of their culture. This basic vocabulary is, to be sure, not uniform in its attestation. Most Indo-European words are found only in some of the attested languages, not in all, which suggests that they may well have been formed only at a period later than the oldest common Indo-European we can reconstruct. There are also dialectal words that are limited in the area of their extension, as in the case of an important sociological term such as the word for "people," **teutā-,** which is confined to the western branches: Italic, Celtic, and Germanic. (It is the base of German *Deutsch* and of DUTCH and TEUTONIC.) In cases such as these, where a word is attested in several traditions, it is still customary to call it Indo-European, even though it may not date from the remotest reconstructible time. It is in this sense, universally accepted by scholars, that the term *Indo-European* has been used in this Appendix.

We may examine the contents of this Indo-European lexicon, which aside from its inherent interest permits us to ascertain many characteristics of Indo-European society. It is remarkable that by far the greater part of this reconstructed vocabulary is preserved in native or borrowed derivatives in Modern English.

GENERAL TERMS. It is appropriate to begin with a sampling of basic terms in the lexicon, which have no special cultural value but attest to the richness of the tradition. All are widespread in the family. There are two verbs expressing existence, **es-** and **bheuə-**, found in English IS, Latin *esse*, and English BE, Latin *fu-tūrus* (FUTURE), respectively. There are verbs meaning "to sit" (**sed-**), "to lie" (**legh-, kei-¹**), and "to stand" (**stā-**). There are a number of verbs of motion, like **gʷā-**, "to come," **ei-**, "to go," **terə-²**, "to cross over," **sekʷ-¹**, "to follow," **kei-**, "to set in motion," and the variants of "rolling or turning motion" in **wel-**, **wer-**, and **kʷel-¹**.

Reconstructions are by no means confined to general, imprecise meanings such as these; we have also such specific semantic values as **nes-¹**, "to return safely home" (NOSTALGIA).

The notion of carrying is represented by the widespread root **bher-¹** (BEAR¹), found in every branch except Anatolian. This root is noteworthy in that it formed a phrase **nŏ-men- bher-**, "to bear a name," which is reconstructible from several traditions, including English. This phrase formed a counterpart to **nŏ-men- dhē-**, "to give a name," with the verb **dhē-**, "to set, put," in Sanskrit, Greek, and Slavic tradition. The persistence of these expressions attests the importance of the name-giving ritual in Indo-European society.

For the notions of eating and drinking, the roots **ed-** and **pō(i)-** are most widespread. The metaphor in "drunk, intoxicated," seems to have been created independently a number of times in the history of the Indo-European languages; Latin *ēbrius*, "drunk" (INEBRIATED), was without etymology until a cognate turned up in the Hittite verb meaning "to drink"; both are derived from the root **ēgʷh-**.

The verb "to live" was **gʷei-**; it formed an adjective **gʷī-wos*, "alive," which survives in English QUICK, whose original sense is seen in the biblical phrase *the quick and the dead*. For the notion of begetting or giving birth there are two roots, **tek-** and the extremely widely represented **genə-**, which appears not only as a verb but also in various nominal forms like **gen-os*, "race," and the prototypes of English KIN and KIND.

A number of qualitative adjectives are attested that go back to the protolanguage. Some come in semantic pairs: **sen-**, "old," and **newo-**, "new"; also **sen-**, "old," and **yeu-**, "youthful vigor"; **tenu-*, "thin" (under **ten-**), and **tegu-**, "thick"; **gʷerə-¹**, "heavy," and **legʷh-**, "light." There are also the two prefixes **su-**, "good, well-," and **dus-**, "bad, ill-," in the Greek forms borrowed as EU- and DYS-. But normally adjectives denoting value judgments like "good" and "bad" are not widespread in the family and are subject to replacement; English *good*, Latin *bonus*, and Greek *agathos* have nothing to do with each other, and each is confined to its own branch of the family.

The personal pronouns belong to the very earliest layer of Indo-European that can be reached by reconstruction. Their forms are unlike those of any other paradigms in the language; they have been called the "Devonian rocks" of Indo-European. The lack of any formal resemblance in English between the subject case (nominative) I and the object case (accusative) ME is a direct and faithful reflection of the same disparity in Proto-Indo-European, respectively **eg** *(*egō)* and **me-¹**. The other pronouns are **tu-** *(*te-)*, "thou," **nes-²** or **we-**, "we," and **yu-**, "you." No pronouns for the third person were in use.

The cognate languages give evidence for demonstrative and interrogative pronouns. Both have also developed into relative pronouns in different languages. The most persistent and widespread pronominal stems are **to-** and **kʷo-**, which are preserved in the English demonstrative and interrogative-relative pronouns and adverbs beginning with *th-* (THIS, THEN) and *wh-* (WHO, WHICH, WHEN).

All the languages of the family show some or all of the Indo-European numerals. The language had a decimal system. There is complete agreement on the numerals from two to ten: **dwo-** *(*duwō)*, **trei-** *(*treyes)*, **kʷetwer-** *(*kʷetwores)*, **penkʷe, s(w)eks, septm̥, oktō(u), newn̥, dekm̥.** For the numeral "one" the dialects vary. We have a root **sem-¹** in some derivatives, while the western Indo-European languages Germanic, Celtic, and Latin share the form **oi-no-.** The word for "hundred," formed from **dekm̥**, "ten," was **(d)km̥tom*. No common form for "thousand" or any other higher number can be reconstructed for the protolanguage.

NATURE AND THE PHYSICAL ENVIRONMENT. A large number of terms relating to time, weather, seasons, and natural surroundings can be reconstructed from the daughter languages, some of which permit certain inferences about the homeland of the Indo-European-speaking people before the period of migrations took them to the different localities where they historically appear.

There are several words for "year," words that relate to differing conceptions of the passage of time. Such are **yēr-** (YEAR), related to words denoting activity; **wet-²**, the year as a measure of the growth of a domestic animal (WETHER, basically "yearling"); and **at-** in Latin *annus* (ANNUAL), from a verb meaning "to go," referring to the year as passage or change. The seasons were distinguished in Indo-European: **ghei-**, "winter," **wes-r̥**, "spring," and **sem-²**, "summer."

The lunar month was a unit of time. The word for "month" *(*mēns-)* is in some languages identical with the word for "moon," in others a derivative of it, as in Germanic **mēnōth-* from **mēnōn-*. "Moon/month" in Indo-European is a derivative of the verb "to measure," **mē-².** The adjective **sen-** *(*seno-)*, "old," was also used for the waning of the moon, on the evidence of several languages.

The other celestial bodies recognized were the sun, **sāwel-**, and the stars, **ster-³.** There is evidence from several traditions for similar designations of the constellation Ursa Major, though these may not go back to the earliest Indo-European times. The movement of the sun dictated the names for the points of the compass. The word east is derived from the verbal root **aus-**, "to shine," as is the word for "dawn" (Latin *Aurora*), deified since Indo-European times on the evidence of Greek, Lithuanian, and Sanskrit. The setting sun furnished the word for "evening" and "west": **wes-pero-.** The most widespread of the words for "night" was **nekʷ-t-.** Words for "day" include **agh-** and such dialectal creations as Latin *diēs*.

The Indo-Europeans knew snow in their homeland; the word **sneigʷh-** is nearly ubiquitous. Curiously enough, however, the word for "rain" varies among the different branches; we have words of differing distribution such as **seuə-².**

Conceptions of the sky, or heaven, were varied in the different dialects. As we have seen, the root **deiw-** occurs widely as the divine bright sky. On the other hand, certain languages viewed the heavens as basically cloudy; **nebh-** is "sky" in Balto-Slavic and Iranian but "cloud" elsewhere. Another divine natural phenomenon is illustrated by the root **(s)tenə-,** "thunder," and the name of the Germanic god THOR.

A word for the earth can be reconstructed as **dhghem-** *(*dheghom).* Other terms of lesser distribution, like **kaito-,** designated forest or uncultivated land. Swampy or boggy terrain was apparently also familiar, judging from the evidence of the root **pelə-**[1]**.** But since none of these runs through the whole family, it would not be justifiable to infer anything from them regarding the terrain of a hypothetical original homeland of the Indo-Europeans.

On the other hand, from the absence of a general word for "sea" we may deduce that the Indo-Europeans were originally an inland people. The root **mori-** is attested dialectally (MERE), but it may well have referred to a lake or other smaller body of water. Transportation by or across water was, however, known to the Indo-Europeans, since most of the languages attest an old word for "boat" or "ship," **nāu-,** probably propelled by oars or a pole (**erə-,** "to row").

The names for a number of different trees are widely enough attested to be viewed as Proto-Indo-European in date. The general term for "tree" and "wood" was **deru-.** The original meaning of the root was doubtless "to be firm, solid," and from it is derived not only the family of English TREE but also that of English TRUE. Note that the semantic evolution has here been from the general to the particular, from "solid" to "tree" (and even "oak" in some dialects), and not the other way around.

There are very widely represented words for the beech tree, **bhāgo-,** and the birch, **bherəg-.** These formerly played a significant role in attempts to locate the original homeland of the Indo-Europeans, since their distribution is geographically distinct. But their ranges may have changed over several millenniums, and, more important, the same word may have been applied to entirely different species of tree. Thus the Greek and Latin cognates of BEECH designate a kind of oak found in the Mediterranean lands.

Indo-European had a generic term for "wild animal," **ghwer-** (FERAL). The wolf was known and evidently feared; its name is subject to taboo deformation (the conscious alteration of the form of a tabooed word, as in English *goldderned, dad-burned*). The variant forms **wl̥kʷo-,** **lupo-*, and **wl̥p-** (also "fox") are all found. The name of the bear was likewise subject to a hunter's taboo: the animal could not be mentioned by its real name on the hunt. The southern Indo-European languages have the original form, **r̥tko-** (Latin *ursus,* Greek *arktos*), but all the northern languages have a substitute term. In Slavic the bear is the "honey-eater," in Germanic the "brown one" (BEAR[2], and note also BRUIN).

The BEAVER was evidently known (**bhi-bhru-*, from **bher-**[2]), at least in Europe, and the MOUSE (**mūs-**) then as now was ubiquitous. The HARE, probably named from its color (**kas-,** "gray"), is also widespread. Domesticated animals are discussed below.

A generic term for "fish" existed, **dhghū-* (also **peisk-* in Europe). The salmon (**laks-**) and the eel *(*angʷi-)* were known, the latter also in the meaning "snake." Several birds were known, including the crane (**gerə-**[2]) and the eagle (**or-**). The generic term for "bird" was **awi-** (Latin *avis*), and from this was derived the well-represented word for "egg," **ōwyo-*.

The names for a number of insects can be reconstructed in the protolanguage, including the wasp *(*wopsā),* the hornet (**krəs-r̥o-*, a derivative of **ker-**[1]**,** "head," from the shape of the insect), and the fly *(*mū-).* The bee (**bhei-**) was particularly important as the producer of honey, for which we have the common Indo-European name **melit-** (MILDEW). Honey was the only source of sugar and sweetness (**swād-,** "sweet," is ancient), and notably was the base of the only certain Indo-European alcoholic beverage, **medhu-,** which in different dialects meant both MEAD ("wine" in Greece and Anatolia) and "honey."

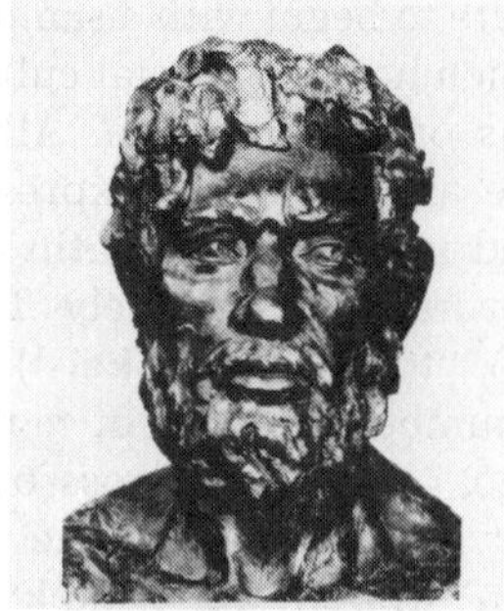

Reconstructed male and female heads (Dnieper-Donets culture, c. 4000 B.C.)

PEOPLE AND SOCIETY. For human beings themselves, a number of terms were employed, with different nuances of meaning. The usual terms for "man" and "woman" are **wiro-** (VIRILE) and **gʷenā-* from **gʷen-** (GYNECOLOGY). For "person" in general, the oldest word was apparently **manu-* (**man-**[1]), as preserved in English MAN and in Slavic and Sanskrit. In other dialects we find interesting metaphorical expressions, which attest a set of religious concepts opposing the gods as immortal and celestial to humankind as mortal and terrestrial. Humans are either **mortos,* "mortal" (**mer-,** "to die"), or **dhghomyo-,* "earthling" (**dhghem-,** "earth").

The parts of the body belong to the basic layer of vocabulary and are for the most part faithfully preserved in Indo-European languages. Such are **ker-**[1]**,** "head" (also **kaput-** in dialects, doubtless a more colloquial word), **genu-**[2]**,** "chin, jaw," **dent-,** "tooth," **okʷ-,** "to see," whence "eye," **ous-,** "ear," **nas-,** "nose," **leb-,** "lip," **bhrū-,** "brow," **ōs-,** "mouth," and **dn̥ghū-,** "tongue." The word for "foot" is attested everywhere (**ped-**), while that for "hand" differs according to dialect; the most widespread is **ghes-r̥-* (CHIRO-).

Internal organs were also named in Indo-European times, including the heart (**kerd-**), womb *(*gʷelbh-),* gall (**ghel-**[2]), and liver (**yekʷr̥**). The male sexual organs, **pes-** and **ergh-*, are common patrimony, as is **ors-,** "backside."

A large number of kinship terms have been reconstructed. They are agreed in pointing to a society that was patriarchal, patrilocal (the bride leaving her household to join that of her husband's family), and patrilineal (descent reckoned by the male line). "Father" and "head of the household" are one: **pəter-,** with his spouse, the **māter-.** These terms are ultimately derived from the baby-talk syllables *pa(pa)* and *ma(ma),* but the kinship-term suffix *-ter* shows that they had a sociological significance over and above this in the Indo-European family. Related terms are found for the grandfather (**awo-**) and the maternal uncle *(*awon-),* and correspondingly the term **nepōt-** (feminine **neptī-*) applied to both grandson (perhaps originally "daughter's son") and nephew ("sister's son"). English SON and DAUGHTER clearly reflect Indo-European **sūnu-* (from **seuə-**[1]) and **dhughəter-.**

Male blood relations were designated as **bhrāter-**

Reconstructed hillfort at Vučedol in eastern Croatia (c. 3000 B.C.)

(BROTHER), which doubtless extended beyond those with a common father or mother; the Greek cognate means "fellow member of a clanlike group." The female counterpart was **swesor-** (SISTER), probably literally "the female member of the kin group," with a feminine suffix **-sor-* and the root **s(w)e-**, designating the self, one's own group.

While there exist many special terms for relatives by marriage on the husband's side, like **daiwer-**, "husband's brother," fewer corresponding terms on the wife's side can be reconstructed for the protolanguage. The terms vary from dialect to dialect, providing good evidence for the patrilocal character of marriage.

The root **dem-** denoted both the house (Latin *domus*) and the household as a social unit. The father of the family (Latin *pater familias*) was the "master of the house" (Greek *despotēs*) or simply "he of the house" (Latin *dominus*). A larger unit was the village, designated by the word **weik-¹**. The community may have been grouped into divisions by location; this seems to be the basic meaning of the **dā-mo-* (from **dā-**) in Greek *dēmos,* people (DEMOCRACY).

Human settlements were frequently built on the top of high places fortified for defense, a practice taken by Indo-European migrants into central and western Europe and into Italy and Greece, as confirmed by archaeological finds. Words for such fortified high places vary; there are **pelə-³**, variant **poli-* (ACROPOLIS), the Celtic word for "ring fort," **dhūno-** (TOWN), and **bhergh-²** (*-burg* in place names).

ECONOMIC LIFE AND TECHNOLOGY. A characteristic of Indo-European and other archaic societies was the principle of exchange and reciprocal gift-giving. The presentation of a gift entailed the obligation of a countergift, and the acts of giving and receiving were equivalent. They were simply facets of a single process of generalized exchange, which assured the circulation of wealth throughout the society.

This principle has left clear traces in the Indo-European vocabulary. The root **dō-** of Latin *dōnāre* means "to give" in most dialects but in Hittite means "to take." The root **nem-** is "to distribute" in Greek (NEMESIS), but in German it means "to take," and the cognate of English GIVE (**ghabh-**) has the meaning "to take" in Irish. The notion of exchange predominates in the roots **mei-** and **gher-²**. The GUEST (**ghos-ti-**) in Indo-European times was the person with whom one had mutual obligations of hospitality. But he was also the stranger, and the stranger in an uncertain and warring tribal society may well be hostile: the Latin cognate *hostis* means "enemy."

The Indo-Europeans practiced agriculture and the cultivation of cereals. We have several terms of Indo-European antiquity for grain: **gr̥ə-no-** (CORN), **yewo-**, and **pūro-*, which may have designated wheat or spelt. Of more restricted distribution is **bhares-**, "barley." A root for grinding is attested, **melə-** (MEAL², MILL). Another Indo-European term is **sē-**, "to sow," not found in Greek, Armenian, or Indo-Iranian. The verb "to plow" is **arə-*, again a common European term, with the name of the plow, **arətrom.* Other related roots are **yeug-**, "to yoke," and **kerp-**, "to gather, pluck" (HARVEST). The root **gʷerə-¹**, "heavy," is the probable base of **gʷerə-nā-*, "hand mill" (QUERN). The term is found throughout the Indo-European-speaking world, including India.

Stockbreeding and animal husbandry were an important part of Indo-European economic life. The names for all the familiar domesticated animals are present throughout the family: **gʷou-**, "cow" and "bull," **owi-**, "sheep," **agʷh-no-*, "swine," and **porko-**, "farrow." The domestic dog was ancient (**kwon-**). The common Indo-European name of the horse, **ekwo-**, is probably derived from the adjective **ōku-**, "swift." The expansion and migration of the Indo-European-speaking peoples in the later third and early second millenniums B.C. is intimately bound up with the diffusion of the horse. The verbal root **demə-**, "to force," acquired the special sense of "to tame horses," whence English TAME. Stock was a source and measure of wealth; the original sense of **peku-** was probably "wealth, riches," as in Latin *pecunia,* which came to mean "wealth in cattle" and finally "cattle" proper.

The verbal roots **pā-**, "to protect," and **kʷel-¹**, "to revolve, move around," are widely used for the notion of herding or watching over stock, and it is interesting to note that the metaphor of the god or priest watching over humankind like a shepherd (Latin *pāstor*) over his flock occurs in many Indo-European dialects as well as outside Indo-European.

Roots indicating a number of technical operations are attested in most of the languages of the family. One such is **teks-**, which in some dialects means "to fabricate, especially by working with an ax," but in others means "to weave" (TEXTILE). The root **dheigh-**, meaning "to mold, shape," is applied both to bread (DOUGH) and to mud or clay, whence words for both pottery and mud walls (Iranian **pari-daiza,* "walled around," borrowed into Greek as the word that became English PARADISE.)

The house (**dem-**) included a **dhwer-** (DOOR), which probably referred originally to the gateway into the enclosure of the household. The house would have had a central hearth, denoted in some languages by **as-** (properly a verb, "to burn"). Fire itself was known by two words, one of animate gender (**egni-*, Latin *ignis*) and one neuter (**pūr-**, Greek *pur*).

Indo-European had a verb "to cook" (**pekʷ-**, also having the notion "to ripen"). Other household activities included spinning (**[s]nē-**), weaving (**webh-**), and sewing (**syū-**). The verb **wes-²** (WEAR) is ancient and everywhere attested.

The Indo-Europeans knew metal and metallurgy, to judge from the presence of the word **ayes-* in Sanskrit, Germanic, and Latin. The term designated copper and perhaps bronze. Iron is a latecomer, technologically, and the terms for it vary from dialect to dialect. Latin has *ferrum,*

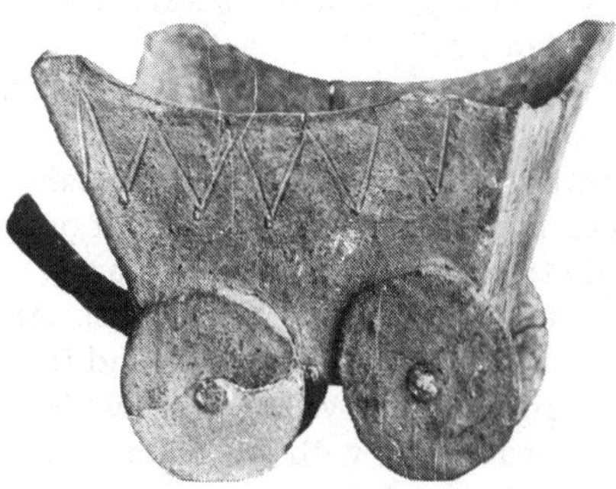

Clay model of wagon from Budakalász, Hungary (c. 2800 B.C.)

while the Germanic and Celtic term was **isarno-*, properly "holy (metal)," from **eis-,** doubtless so called because the first iron was derived from small meteorites. Gold, **ghel-²,** probably "yellow (metal)," was known from ancient times, though the names for it vary. Silver was **arg-,** with various suffixes, doubtless meaning "white (metal)."

It was probably not long before the dispersal of the Proto-Indo-European community that the use of the wheel and wheeled transport was adopted. Despite the existence of widespread word families, most terms relating to wheeled vehicles seem to be metaphors formed from already existing words, rather than original, unanalyzable ones. So NAVE, or hub of the wheel (**nobh-**), is the same word as NAVEL. This is clearly the case with WHEEL itself, where the widespread **kʷ(e)-kʷl-o-* is an expressive derivative of a verb (**kʷel-¹**) meaning "to revolve or go around." Other words for "wheel" are dialectal and again derivative, such as Latin *rota* from a verbal root **ret-,** "to run." The root **wegh-,** "to go, transport in a vehicle" (WAGON), is attested quite early, though not in Hittite. This evidence for the late appearance of the wheel agrees with archaeological findings that date the distribution of the wheel in Europe to the latter part of the fifth millennium B.C., the latest possible date for the community of Proto-Indo-European proper.

IDEOLOGY. We pointed out earlier that the great advantage of the lexicon as an approach to culture and history is that it is not confined to material remains. Words exist for natural phenomena, objects, and things that can be found in nature or identified from their material remains. But there are also words for ideas, abstractions, and relations. The Indo-European protolanguage is particularly rich in such vocabulary items.

A number of verbs denoting mental activity are found. The most widespread is **men-¹,** preserved in English MIND. Other derivatives refer to remembering, warning (putting in mind), and thinking in general. A root notable for the diversity of its derivatives is **med-,** which may be defined as "to take the appropriate measures." Reflexes of this verb range in meaning from "rule," through "measure" (MODICUM, from Latin), to "physician" (Latin *medicus*).

The notions of government and sovereignty were well represented. The presence of the old word for tribal king, **reg-* (**reg-**), only in the extreme east (RAJAH) and the extreme west (Latin *rēx*, Celtic *-rīx*) virtually guarantees its presence in the earliest Indo-European society. (Here is an example of the phenomenon of marginal or peripheral conservation of a form lost in the central innovating area.) Roman tradition well attests the sacral character of kingship among the Indo-Europeans. The functions of king and priest were different aspects of a single function of sovereignty. It is this that is symbolized by the divine name **dyeu-pəter-* (**deiw-**), the chief of the gods.

Another aspect of the function of sovereignty is the sphere of the law. There is an old word, **yewes-,** probably for "religious law," in Latin *iūs*. Latin *lēx* is also ancient (**leg-** or **legh-**), though the details of its etymology are uncertain. In a society that emphasized the principle of exchange and reciprocity, it is scarcely surprising that the notion of contractual obligation should be well represented. Several roots specify the notion of "bond": **bhendh-, ned-,** and **leig-,** all of which have derivatives with technical legal meanings in various languages. The verb **kʷei-¹** meant "to pay compensation for an injury." Its derivative noun **kʷoinā* was borrowed from Doric Greek into the most ancient Roman law as Latin *poena* and *pūnīre,* whence English PUNISH and a host of legal terms. The Greek word for "justice," *dikē,* is derived from the notion of "boundary marker" (**deik-**).

Indo-European is particularly rich in religious vocabulary. An important form, which is also found only in the peripheral languages Sanskrit, Latin, and Celtic, is the two-word metaphoric phrase **kred-dhē-*, literally "to put (**dhē-**) heart (**kerd-**)." The two words have been joined together in the western languages, as in Latin *crēdō,* "I believe." Here a term of the most ancient pagan religion has been taken over by Christianity. A common word for religious "formulation," **bhregh-men-*, is preserved in *Brahmin,* a member of the priestly class, from Sanskrit.

Oral prayers, requests of the deity, and other ritual utterances must have played a significant role in Indo-European religion. We have already seen **prek-** (PRAY), and note also the roots **wegʷh-* (in Latin *vovēre,* to vow), **sengʷh-** (SING), and **gwerə-²,** which in Latin *grātia* (GRACE) has had a new life in Christianity.

The root **spend-** has the basic meaning of "to make an offering or perform a rite," whence "to engage oneself by a ritual act." Its Latin derivative *spondēre* means "to promise" (SPOUSE).

A hint of Indo-European metaphysics appears in the word **aiw-,** "vital force," whence "long life, the eternal re-creation of life, eternity" (EON). It is noteworthy that the idea of "holy" is intimately bound up with that of "whole, healthy," in a number of forms: **kailo-** (WHOLE and HOLY) and **solə-,** whence Latin *salvus* (SALVATION). An ancient root relating solely to religion is **sak-** (SACRED).

In conclusion we may add that poetry and a tradition of poetics are also common patrimony in most of the Indo-European traditions. The hymns of the Rig-Veda are composed in meters related to those used by the Greek poets, and the earliest verse forms found among the Celts and the Slavs go back to the same Indo-European source. Many, perhaps most, of the stylistic figures and embellishments of poetic language that we associate with "classical" poetics and rhetoric can be shown, by the comparative method, to have their roots in Indo-European poetics itself.

A number of metaphorical expressions appear to be creations of ancient, even Indo-European date. Latin *terra,* "earth" (TERRAN), is historically a transferred epithet, "dry (land)," from **ters-,** "to dry," whose English descendant is THIRST. One securely reconstructible Indo-European place name rests squarely on a metaphor: **Pīwer-iā* in Greek *Pieria* (PIERIAN SPRING) and *Īwer-ion-*, the prehistoric Celtic name for Ireland (Gaelic *Éire, Érin*), both continue an Indo-European feminine adjective **pīwer-iə,* "fat," metaphori-

Stele from Kernosovka in the Crimea

cally "fertile," from **peiə-,** the same root that gives English FAT.

Most interesting are the cases where it is possible to reconstruct from two or more traditions (usually including Homer and the Rig-Veda) a poetic phrase or formula consisting of two members. Such are the expressions "imperishable fame," **klewos n̥dhg^{w}hitom* (**kleu-**); "holy (mental) force," **isərom menos* (**eis-, men-**[1]); and the "weaver (or crafter) of words," the Indo-European poet himself, **wek^{w}ōm teks-on* (**wek^w-, teks-**). The immortality of the gods (**n̥-mr̥to-*, from **mer-**) is emphasized anew by the vivid verb phrase **nek-**[1] **terə-**[2]**,** "to overcome death," appearing in the Greek word *nektar,* the drink of the gods. And at least one three-member formula (in the sense of the word in traditional oral poetry) can be reconstructed for the poetic language of prayer, on the combined evidence of four languages, Latin, Umbrian, Avestan, and Sanskrit: "Protect, keep safe, man and cattle!" (**pā- wī-ro- peku**).

CONCLUSION

This survey has touched on only a representative sample of the available reconstructed Indo-European lexicon and has made no attempt to cite the mass of evidence in all the languages of the family, ancient and modern, for these reconstructions.

For this essay, we have given only the information about Indo-European culture that could be derived from language and lexicon alone. Other disciplines serve to fill out and complete the picture to be gathered from the study of vocabulary: archaeology, prehistory, comparative religion, and the history of institutions.

Archaeologists have not in fact succeeded in locating the Indo-Europeans. An artifact other than a written record is silent on the language of its user, and prehistoric Eurasia offers an abundant choice of culture areas. Archaeologists are generally agreed that the so-called Kurgan peoples, named after the Russian word for their characteristic "barrow" or "tumulus" grave structure, spoke an Indo-European language. The correlation between the Kurgan cultural features described by archaeologists and the Indo-European lexicon are striking: for example, small tribal units (**teutā-**) ruled by powerful chieftains (**reg-**), a predominantly pastoral (**pā-**) economy including horse (**ekwo-**) breeding (**demə-**) and plant cultivation (**yewo-**), and architectural features such as a small subterranean or aboveground rectangular hut (**dom-*, **dem-**) of timber uprights (**kli-t-*, **klei-,** and **stu-t-*, **stā-,** still with us in English STUD).

Some time around the middle of the fifth millennium B.C., these people expanded from the steppe zone north of the Black Sea and beyond the Volga into the Balkans and adjacent areas. These Kurgan peoples bore a new mobile and aggressive culture into Neolithic Europe, and it is not unreasonable to associate them with the coming of the Indo-Europeans. But the Kurgan peoples' movement into Europe took place in distinct waves from the fifth to the third millennium B.C. The earliest so far discovered might be compatible with a reasonable date for Proto-Indo-European, that is, a date sufficiently long ago for a single language to develop into forms as divergent as Mycenaean Greek and Hittite as they are historically attested by the middle of the second millennium B.C. But the subsequent Kurgan immigrations, after 4000 B.C., are too late to be regarded as incursions of speakers of undifferentiated Proto-Indo-European. The archaeological evidence for the later waves of Kurgan migrations points to their having had an Indo-European culture, but the languages spoken by the later Kurgan peoples must have been already differentiated Indo-European dialects, some of which would doubtless evolve into some of the historical branches of the family tree. We must be content to recognize the Kurgan peoples as speakers of certain Indo-European languages and as sharing a common Indo-European cultural patrimony. The ultimate "cradle" of the Indo-Europeans may well never be known, and language remains the best and fullest evidence for prehistoric Indo-European society. It is the comparative method in historical linguistics that can illumine not only ancient ways of life but also ancient modes of thought.

GUIDE TO THE APPENDIX

This Dictionary carries the etymology of the English language to its logical and natural conclusion, for if the documentary history of words is of interest and value, so is their reconstructed prehistory. The historical component is given in the etymologies, after the definitions in the main body of the Dictionary. This Appendix supplies the prehistoric component, tracing the ultimate Indo-European derivations of those English words that are descended from a selected group of Indo-European roots.

The form given in **boldface** type at the head of each entry is, unless otherwise identified, an Indo-European root in its basic form; this is followed by a list of some of its more important Modern English descendants. The entry proper begins with a repetition of the basic root form, followed in some cases by one or more variants, also in boldface type. The basic meaning or meanings of the root are given immediately after the entry form and its variants (but see the cautionary note under "Semantics" in the preceding essay). Meanings that are different parts of speech are separated by a semicolon:

kei-[1]. To lie; bed, couch; beloved, dear.

pelə-[2]. Flat; to spread.

leg-. To collect; with derivatives meaning "to speak."

After the basic meaning there may appear further information about the phonological shape or nature of the root:

skei-. To cut, split. Extension of **sek-.**

k^{w}r̥mi-. Worm. Rhyme word to **wr̥mi-*, worm (see **wer-[2]**).

pā-. To protect, feed. Contracted from **paə-*.

līk-. Body, form; like, same. Germanic root.

Most, but not all, of the additional information is self-explanatory. In the first two examples, the boldface forms **sek-** and **wer-[2]** are cross-references to those roots, which are main entries in this Appendix. Every boldface form appearing in the text of an entry is such a cross-reference. In the example **pā-** the form **paə-* represents an older root form; the nature of these contractions is explained in the preceding essay under "Speech Sounds and their Alternations." The entries **līk-, nēhw-iz,** and **re-** are not, strictly speaking, Indo-European, since they are represented in only one branch of the family, but they are included within boldface brackets because of the number of English words among their descendants.

The text of each entry describes in detail the development of Modern English words from the root. Each section of an entry begins with a list, in SMALL CAPITALS, of the Modern English words derived from a particular form of the root. The simple (uncompounded) derivatives are given first; the compounds follow, separated from them by a semicolon. Parentheses indicate that the etymology of a word in the main body of the Dictionary contains a cross-reference to the etymology at another entry. In some cases no further semantic or morphological development needs to be explained, and the *lemma,* the historically attested representative of the root, is immediately given:

awi-. Bird. **I. 1.** AVIAN . . . from Latin *avis,* bird.

Much more commonly, however, intermediate developments require explanation. These intermediate stages are reconstructions representing a word stem in Indo-European that is necessary to explain the lemma following it (see the section "Grammatical Forms and Syntax" in the preceding essay). The reconstructed forms are not historically attested; they are preceded by an asterisk (*) to note this fact. Sometimes earlier or later developments of the intermediate forms are given in parentheses, as in the example of **stā-** below. In these cases the symbol < is used to mean "derived from" and the symbol > is used to mean "developed into." The following terms are used to describe typical morphological processes of Indo-European:

Full-grade form: A form with e-vocalism (the basic form); so identified for descriptive contrast.

O-grade form: A form with o-vocalism:

nek^{w}-t- . . . O-grade form **nok^{w}-t-*.

Zero-grade form: A form with zero-vocalism:

men-[1] . . . **I.** Zero-grade form **mn̥-*.

Lengthened-grade form: A form with lengthened vocalism:

ked- . . . **1.** Lengthened-grade form **kēd-*.

Secondary full-grade form: A new full-grade form created by inserting the fundamental vowel *e* in the zero-grade form of an extended root:

stā- . . . **V.** Zero-grade extended root **stū-* (< **stuə-*). . . . **VI.** Secondary full-grade form **steuə-*.

Basic form: The unchanged root; so identified for descriptive contrast.

Suffixed form: A form with one or more suffixes, written with an internal hyphen:

laks- . . . Suffixed form **laks-o-*.

maghu- . . . Suffixed form **magho-ti-*.

mel-[2] . . . **1.** Suffixed (comparative) form **mel-yos-*.

Prefixed form: A form with a prefix, written with an internal hyphen:

op- . . . **6.** . . . from prefixed form **co-op-*.

Extended form: A form with an extension or enlargement, written without internal hyphens:

pel-[5] . . . **II.** Extended form **pelə-*.

Nasalized form: A form with a nasal infix, written with internal hyphens:

tag- . . . **1.** Nasalized form **ta-n-g-*.

Reduplicated form: A form prefixed by its own initial consonant followed by a vowel:

segh- . . . **5.** Reduplicated form **si-sgh-*.

Expressive form: A form with "expressive gemination" (doubling of the final consonant), written without internal hyphens:

gal- . . . **3.** Expressive form **gall-*.

Compound Form: A form compounded with a form of another root, written with internal hyphens:

dem- . . . **3.** Compound **dems-pot-*.

Shortened form: A form with shortened vocalism:

syū- . . . **III.** Suffix shortened form **syu-men-*.

Reduced form: A form with loss of one or more sounds:

ghesor- . . . Reduced form **ghesr-*.

Oldest root form: A root form showing a laryngeal (ə) in a position, typically at the beginning or end of a root, where it is preserved in only a few Indo-European languages, such as Greek or Hittite:

ster-[3] . . . **3.** Oldest root form **əster-*.

Variant form: A form altered in any way other than those described in the above categories:

deru- . . . **2.** Variant form *dreu-*.

These terms can be combined freely to describe in as much detail as necessary the development from the root to the lemma.

dhē(i)- . . . **1.** Suffixed reduced form **dhē-mnā-*. FEMALE, FEMININE; EFFEMINATE, from Latin *fēmina*, woman (< "she who suckles").

gerə-[1] . . . **1.** Suffixed lengthened-grade form **gērə-s-*. AGERATUM, GERIATRICS, from Greek *gēras*, old age.

petə- . . . **2.** Suffixed (stative) variant zero-grade form **pat-ē-*. PATENT, PATULOUS, from Latin *patēre*, to be open.

In order to emphasize the fact that English belongs to the Germanic branch of Indo-European and give precedence to directly inherited words in contrast to words borrowed from other branches, the intermediate stages in Germanic etymologies are covered in fuller detail. The Common or Proto-Germanic (here called simply Germanic) forms underlying English words are always given. Where no other considerations intervene, Germanic is given first of the Indo-European groups, and Old English is given first within Germanic, although this order of precedence is not rigidly applied.

The final item in most entries is an abbreviated reference, in brackets, to Julius Pokorny's *Indogermanisches Etymologisches Wörterbuch* (Bern, 1959). This, the standard work of reference and synthesis in the Indo-European field, carries a full range of the actual comparative material on which the roots are reconstructed. Our Appendix presents only those aspects of the material that are directly relevant to English. For example, the English word MANY is found at the root **menegh-,** "copious." This entry describes the transition of the Indo-European form through Germanic **managa-* to Old English *manig, mænig,* "many." It does not cite the evidence on which this assertion is based, but it refers to "Pokorny *men(e)gh-* 730." The entry *men(e)gh-* on page 730 in Pokorny's dictionary cites, in addition to the Old English word, the forms attested in Sanskrit, Celtic, Gothic, Old High German, Old Norse, Slavic, and Lithuanian, from which the reconstruction of the root was made. These references should serve as a reminder that the information given in this Appendix is assertive rather than expository and that the evidence and evaluation upon which its assertions are based are not presented here.

Symbols: * unattested
< derived from
> developed into

INDO-EUROPEAN SOUND CORRESPONDENCES

Probably the most basic element of language change is a gradual shift in the way individual speech sounds are pronounced. As the Indo-European speech community expanded over the centuries into new territories, local dialectal variations gave rise to increasingly divergent language families. This table shows the historical development of sounds from Proto-Indo-European to the principal older Indo-European languages. For example, reading down the first column, it can be seen that Proto-Indo-European initial **p** remains **p** in Latin, but it is lost entirely in Old Irish and becomes **f** in Germanic and consequently in Old English: thus Indo-European ***pəter-**, meaning "father," becomes Latin *pater*, Old Irish *athir*, and Common Germanic ***fadar**, Old English *fæder*. A more precise way of describing this relationship is to say that initial **p** in Proto-Indo-European corresponds to **p** in Latin, to **f** in Germanic and Old English, and to

	CONSONANTS															
	STOPS												CONTINUANT	LARYNGEALS		
	UNVOICED				VOICED				VOICED ASPIRATE							
INDO-EUROPEAN	p	t	k	k^w	b	d	g	g^w	bh	dh	gh	g^wh	s	$ə_1$	$ə_2$	$ə_3$
HITTITE	p	t	k	ku	p	t	k	ku	p	t	k	ku	s	—*	h	h
TOCHARIAN	p	t/c/ts	k/ś	k/ś	p	t/c/ts	k/ś	k/ś	p	t/c/ts	k/ś	k/ś	s/ṣ	—	—	—
SANSKRIT	p	t	ś	k/c	b	d	j	g/j	bh	dh	h	gh/h	s/ṣ	—	—	—
AVESTAN	p	t	s	k/c	b	d	z	g/j	b	d	g/z	g/j	h	—	—	—
OLD PERSIAN	p	t	th	k	b	d	d/z	g/j	b	d	g/d	g/j	h	—	—	—
OLD CHURCH SLAVONIC	p	t	s	k/č/c	b	d	z	g/ž/z	b	d	z	g/ž/z	s	—	—	—
LITHUANIAN	p	t	s	k	b	d	z	g	b	d	z	g	s	—	—	—
ARMENIAN	h	th	s	kh	p	t	c	k	b	d	z(j)	g	h	—	—	—
GREEK	p	t	k	p/t/k	b	d	g	b/d/g	ph	th	kh	ph/th/kh	h	—	—	—
LATIN	p	t	c	qu	b	d	g	v	f(b)	f(d)	h	f	s	—	—	—
OLD IRISH	—*	t	c	c	b	d	g	b	b	d	g	g	s	—	—	—
COMMON GERMANIC	f	th	h	hw	p	t	k	kw/k	b	d	g	b/g	s	—	—	—
GOTHIC	f	th	h(j)	hw/w	p	t	k	q	b	d	g	b/g	s	—	—	—
OLD NORSE†	f	th	h	hv	p	t	k	kv	b	d	g	b/g	s	—	—	—
OLD HIGH GERMAN†	f	d	h	hw/w	p/pf	z	k	qu	b	t/d	g	b/g	s	—	—	—
MIDDLE DUTCH†	v	th/d	h	w	p	t	k	qu	b	d	g	b/g	s	—	—	—
OLD ENGLISH†	f	th	h	hw	p	t	c	cw/c	b	d	g	b/g	s	—	—	—

zero in Old Irish. The correspondences shown in the table are regular: they always occur as stated unless specific factors intervene. This table shows only the initial consonants and vowels in initial syllables, which are generally the simplest elements involved in sound change. All other phonetic elements including stress and environment also show regular correspondences, but often with considerable complexity.

NOTES:

*— equals zero: p was lost in Old Irish.
w was lost in Greek.
y was lost in Old Irish, Old Norse.
Initial laryngeals are preserved only in Hittite.

†The effects of umlaut are not considered.

SONORANTS						VOWELS													
NASALS		LIQUIDS		GLIDES		SHORT					LONG					SYLLABIC SONORANTS			
m	n	r	l	y/i	w/u	e	o	a	i	u	ē (eə)	ō (oə)	ā (aə)	ī (iə)	ū (uə)	m̥	n̥	r̥	l̥
m	n	r	l	y	w	ei	a/ha	a/ha	i	u	e/i	a	a/ah	i	u/uh	am	an	ar	al
m	n	r	l	y	w	ä	e	ā	ä/i	ä/u	e	o,ā	o,ā	i	u	äm	än	är	äl
m	n	r/l	l/r	y	v	a	a/ā	a	i	u	ā	ā	ā	ī	ū	a	a	ṛ	ṛ
m	n	r	l	y	v	a	a/ā	a	i	u	ā	ā	ā	ī	ū	a	a	ərə	ərə
m	n	r	l	y	v	a	a/ā	a	i	u	ā	ā	ā	ī	ū	a	a	(a)r	(a)r
m	n	r	l	j	v	e	o	o	ĭ	ŭ	e	a	a	i	u	ę	e	rŭ	lŭ
m	n	r	l	j	v	e	a	a	i	u	ė	uo	o	y	u	im	in	ir	il
m	n	r	l	y	g/v	e	o	a	i	u	i	u	a	i	u	am	an	ar	ał
m	n	r	l	h/z	–*	e	o	a	i	u	ē	ō	ā/ē	ī	ū	a	a	ar/ra	al/la
m	n	r	l	i/j	v	e	o	a	i	u	ē	ō	ā	ī	ū	em	en	or	ul
m	n	r	l	–*	f	e/i	o/u	a	i/e	u/o	ī	ā	ā	ī	ū	(*am)e	(*an)e	ri	li
m	n	r	l	j	w	e	a	a	i	u	ē	ō	ā	ī	ū	um	un	ur	ul
m	n	r	l	j	w	i/ai	a	a	i/e	u	ē	ō	ō	ī	ū	um	un	aur	ul
m	n	r	l	–*	v	e	a	a	i/e	u/o	ā	ō	ō	ī	ū	um	un	ur/or	ul/ol
m	n	r	l	j	w	e	a	a	i/e	u/o	ā	uo	uo	ī	ū	um	un	ur/or	ul/ol
m	n	r	l	g	w	e	a	a	i/e	u/o	ē	ō	ō	ī	ū	um	un	ur/or	ul/ol
m	n	r	l	g(y)	w	e	æ/a	æ/a	i/e	u/o	ǣ	ō	ō	ī	ū	um	un	ur/or	ul/ol

App.

INDO-EUROPEAN ROOTS

ad-. Important derivatives are *at*[1] and *aid.*

ad-. To, near, at. **1.** ADO, AT[1], from Old English *æt,* near, by, at, and from Middle English *at,* "to," from Old Norse *at,* both from Germanic **at.* **2.** AD-, -AD; (ADJUVANT), AID, AMOUNT, (PARAMOUNT), from Latin *ad, ad-,* to, toward. [Pokorny 1. *ad-* 3.]

ag-. Important derivatives are *act, agent, agile, ambiguous, essay, exact, navigate,* and *agony.*

ag-. To drive, draw, move. **1.** ACT, AGENDUM, AGENT, AGILE, AGITATE; (ALLEGE), AMBAGE, AMBIGUOUS, (ASSAY), (CACHE), COAGULUM, COGENT, ESSAY, EXACT, (EXAMINE), (EXIGENT), FUMIGATE, FUSTIGATE, INTRANSIGENT, LEVIGATE, LITIGATE, NAVIGATE, OBJURGATE, PRODIGALITY, RETROACTIVE, SQUAT, TRANSACT, VARIEGATE, from Latin *agere,* to do, act, drive, conduct, lead, weigh. **2.** -AGOGUE, AGONY; ANAGOGE, (ANTAGONIZE), CHORAGUS, DEMAGOGUE, EPACT, GLUCAGON, HYPNAGOGIC, MYSTAGOGUE, PEDAGOGUE, PROTAGONIST, STRATAGEM, SYNAGOGUE, from Greek *agein,* to drive, lead, weigh. **3.** Suffixed form **ag-to-.* AMBASSADOR, EMBASSAGE, (EMBASSY), from Latin *ambactus,* servant, from Celtic **amb(i)-ag-to-,* "one who goes around" (**ambi,* around; see **ambhi**). **4.** Suffixed form **ag-ti-,* whence adjective **ag-ty-o-,* "weighty." AXIOM; AXIOLOGY, CHRONAXIE, from Greek *axios,* worth, worthy, of like value, weighing as much. **5.** Possibly suffixed form **ag-ro-,* driving, pursuing, grabbing. PELLAGRA, PODAGRA, from Greek *agra,* a seizing. [Pokorny *aĝ-* 4.] Derivative **agro-.**

agh-. Important derivatives are *day, today,* and *dawn.*

agh-. A day (considered as a span of time). **a.** DAY; DAISY, TODAY, from Old English *dæg,* day; **b.** LANDTAG, from Old High German *tag,* day; **c.** DAWN, from Old English denominative *dagian,* to dawn. **a, b,** and **c** all from Germanic **dagaz* (with initial *d-* of obscure origin), day. [Pokorny *agher-* 7.]

agro-. Important derivatives are *acre, pilgrim,* and *agro-.*

agro-. Field. Probably a derivative of **ag-,** "to drive." **1.** ACRE, from Old English *æcer,* field, acre, from Germanic **akraz.* **2.** AGRARIAN; AGRICULTURE, PEREGRINE, (PILGRIM), from Latin *ager* (genitive *agrī*), earlier **agros,* district, property, field. **3.** AGRIA, AGRO-; (AGROSTOLOGY), ONAGER, STAVESACRE, from Greek *agros,* field, and *agrios,* wild. [In Pokorny *aĝ-* 4.]

ais-. An important derivative is *ask.*

ais-. To wish, desire. Suffixed form **ais-sk-.* ASK, from Old English *āscian, ācsian,* to ask, seek, from Germanic **aiskōn.* [Pokorny 1. *ais-* 16.]

aiw-. Important derivatives are *no*[1]*, ever, every, never, medieval, age, eternal,* and *eon.*

aiw-. Vital force, life, long life, eternity; also "endowed with the acme of vital force, young." **1.a.** NO[1], from Old English *ā,* ever; **b.** AUGHT[1], from Old English *āwiht, āuht,* anything, "ever a creature"; **c.** EVER; EVERY, NEVER, from Old English *ǣfre* (second element obscure), ever; **d.** AYE[2]; NAY, from Old Norse *ei,* ever. **a, c,** and **d** all from extended form in Germanic **aiwi;* **b** from Germanic **aiwi* + **wihti,* "ever a thing, anything" (**wihti-,* thing; see **wekti-**). **2.a.** Suffixed form **aiw-o-.* COEVAL, LONGEVITY, MEDIEVAL, PRIMEVAL, from Latin *aevum,* age, eternity; **b.** suffixed form **aiwo-tā(ti)-.* AGE; COETANEOUS, from Latin *aetās* (stem *aetāti-*), age; **c.** suffixed form **aiwo-t-erno-.* ETERNAL; SEMPITERNAL, from Latin *aeternus,* eternal. **3.** Suffixed form **aiw-en-.* EON, from Greek *aiōn,* age, vital force. [Pokorny *aiu̯-* 17.] See also **yuwen-* under **yeu-.**

ak-. Important derivatives are *edge, acute, hammer, heaven, acrid, eager*[1]*, vinegar, acid, acme, acne, acro-,* and *oxygen.*

ak-. Sharp. **1.** Suffixed form **ak-yā-.* **a.** EDGE, from Old English *ecg,* sharp side, from Germanic **agjō;* **b.** EGG[2], from Old Norse *eggja,* to incite, goad, from Germanic **agjan.* **2.** Suffixed form **ak-u-.* **a.** EAR[2], from Old English *æhher, ēar,* spike, ear of grain, from Germanic **ahuz-;* **b.** ACICULA, (ACUITY), ACUMEN, ACUTE, AGLET, EGLANTINE, from Latin *acus,* needle; **c.** ACEROSE, from Latin *acus,* chaff. **3.** Suffixed form **ak-i-.* ACIDANTHERA, from Greek *akis,* needle. **4.** Suffixed form **ak-men-,* stone, sharp stone used as a tool, with metathetic variant **ka-men-,* with variants: **a.** **ka-mer-.* HAMMER, from Old English *hamor,* hammer, from Germanic **hamaraz;* **b.** **ke-men-* (probable variant). HEAVEN, from Old English *heofon, hefn,* heaven, from Germanic **hibin-,* "the stony vault of heaven," dissimilated form of **himin-.* **5.** Suffixed form **ak-onā-,* independently created in: **a.** AWN, from Old Norse *ögn,* ear of grain, and Old English *agen,* ear of grain, from Germanic **aganō,* and **b.** PARAGON, from Greek *akonē,* whetstone. **6.** Suffixed lengthened form **āk-ri-.* ACERATE, ACRID, ACRIMONY, EAGER[1]; CARVACROL, VINEGAR, from Latin *ācer,* sharp, bitter. **7.** Suffixed form **ak-ri-bhwo-.* ACERBIC, EXACERBATE, from Latin *acerbus,* bitter, sharp, tart. **8.** Suffixed (stative) form **ak-ē-.* ACID, from Latin *acēre,* to be sharp. **9.** Suffixed form **ak-ēto-.* (ACETABULUM), (ACETIC), ACETUM; ESTER, from Latin *acētum,* vinegar. **10.** Suffixed form **ak-mā-.* ACME, (ACNE), from Greek *akmē,* point. **11.** Suffixed form **ak-ro-.* ACRO-; (ACROBAT), ACROMION, from Greek *akros,* topmost. **12.** Suffixed o-grade form **ok-ri-.* MEDIOCRE, from Latin *ocris,* rugged mountain. **13.** Suffixed o-grade form **ok-su-.* AMPHIOXUS, OXALIS, OXYGEN, OXYURIASIS, PAROXYSM, from Greek *oxus,* sharp, sour. [Pokorny 2. *ak̑-* 18, 3. *k̑em-* 556.]

akʷ-ā-. Important derivatives are *island, aquatic, ewer,* and *sewer*[1]*.*

akʷ-ā-. Water. **1.** ISLAND, from Old English *īg, īeg,* island, from Germanic **aujō,* "thing on the water," from **agwjō.* **2.** AQUA, AQUARELLE, AQUARIUM, AQUATIC, AQUI-, EWER, GOUACHE; SEWER[1], from Latin *aqua,* water. [Pokorny *akʷā-* 23.]

al-[1]**.** Important derivatives are *alarm, alert, ultimate, ultra-, alternate, adulterate, other, else, alien, alibi,* and *parallel.*

al-[1]**.** Beyond. **1.** Variant **ol-,* "beyond." **a.** Suffixed forms **ol-se-, *ol-so-.* ALARM, ALERT, ALLIGATOR, EL NIÑO, VOILÀ, from Latin *ille* (feminine *illa,* neuter *illud*), "yonder," that, from Old Latin *ollus;* **b.** suffixed forms **ol-s, *ol-tero-.* OUTRÉ, ULTERIOR, ULTIMATE, ULTRA-, UTTERANCE[2], from Latin *uls, *ulter, ultrā,* beyond. **2.** Suffixed form **al-tero-,* "other of two." **a.** ALTER, ALTERCATE, ALTERNATE, ALTRUISM; SUBALTERN, from Latin *alter,* other, other of two; **b.** ADULTERATE, (ADULTERINE), (ADULTERY), from Latin *adulterāre,* to commit adultery with, pollute, probably from the phrase *ad alterum,* "(approaching) another (unlawfully)" (*ad-,* to; see **ad-**); **c.** variant suffixed form **an-tero-,* "other (of two)." OTHER, from Old English *ōther,* other, from Germanic **antharaz.* **3.** Extended form **alyo-,* "other of more than two." **a.** ELSE; ELDRITCH, from Old English *el-, elles,* else, otherwise, from Germanic **aljaz* (with adverbial suffix); **b.** ALIAS, ALIEN; ALIBI, ALIQUOT, HIDALGO, from Latin *alius,* other of more than two; **c.** ALLO-; ALLEGORY, ALLELOMORPH, ALLELOPATHY, MORPHALLAXIS, PARALLAX, PARALLEL, TROPHALLAXIS, from Greek *allos,* other. [Pokorny 1. *al-* 24, 2. *an-* 37.]

al-[2]**.** Important derivatives are *old, elder*[1]*, haughty, altitude, enhance, exalt, adolescent, alumnus, coalesce,* and *prolific.*

al-[2]**.** To grow, nourish.
I. Suffixed (participial) form **al-to-,* "grown." **1.a.** ALDERMAN, OLD, from Old English *eald, ald,* old; **b.** ELDER[1], from Old English (comparative) *ieldra, eldra,* older, elder; **c.** ELDEST, from Old English (superlative) *ieldesta, eldesta,* eldest; **d.** (see **wī-ro-**) Germanic compound **wer-ald-,* "life or age of man." **a, b, c,** and **d** all from Germanic **alda-.* **2.** ALT, ALTO, HAUGHTY, HAWSER; ALTIMETER, ALTIPLANO, ALTITUDE, ALTOCUMULUS, ALTOSTRATUS, ENHANCE, EXALT, (HAUTBOY), from Latin *altus,* high, deep.
II. ADOLESCENT, (ADULT), ALIBLE, ALIMENT, ALIMONY, ALTRICIAL, ALUMNUS; COALESCE, from Latin *alere,* to nourish.
III. Suffixed (causative) form **ol-eye-.* ABOLISH, from Latin *abolēre,* to retard the growth of, abolish (*ab-,* from; see **apo-**).
IV. Compound form **pro-al-* (*pro-,* forth; see **per**[1]). PROLAN, PROLETARIAN, PROLIFEROUS, PROLIFIC, from Latin *prōlēs,* offspring.
V. Extended form **aldh-.* ALTHEA, from Greek *althein, althainein,* to get well. [Pokorny 2. *al-* 26.]

al-[3]**.** Important derivatives are *all* and *also.*

al-[3]**.** All. Germanic and Celtic root. **1.** Suffixed form **al-na-.* ALL; ALSO, from Old English *all, eall, eal-, al-,* all, from Germanic **allaz.* **2.** (see **man-**[1]) Germanic prefix **ala-,* all, in **Ala-manniz,* "all men."

albho-. Important derivatives are *elf, oaf, albino, album, auburn,* and *daub.*

albho-. White. **1.a.** ELF, from Old English *ælf,* elf; **b.** OAF, from Old Norse *alfr,* elf; **c.** OBERON, from Old French *Auberon,* from a source akin to Old High German *Alberich.* **a, b,** and **c** all possibly from Germanic **albiz, *albaz,* if meaning "white ghostly apparitions." **2.** ELFIN, from Old English *-elfen,* elf, possibly from Germanic **albinjō.* **3.** ABELE, ALB, ALBEDO, ALBESCENT, ALBINO, ALBITE, ALBUM, ALBUMEN, AUBADE, AUBURN; DAUB, from Latin *albus,* white. [Pokorny *albho-* 30.]

alu-. An important derivative is *ale.*

alu-. In words related to sorcery, magic, possession, and intoxication. Suffixed form **alu-t-.* ALE, from Old English *(e)alu,* ale, from Germanic **aluth-.* [Pokorny *alu-* 33.]

ambhi. Important derivatives are *by*[1], *be-*, *ambi-*, and *amphi-*.

---

ambhi. Also **m̥bhi.** Around. Probably derived from *ant-bhi.* See **ant-.** **1.** Reduced form **bhi.* **a.** BY[1]; ABAFT, BUT, from Old English *bi, bī, be,* by; **b.** BE-, from Old English *be-,* on all sides, be-, also intensive prefix; **c.** BELEAGUER, from Middle Dutch *bie,* by; **d.** BIVOUAC, from Old High German *bi,* by, at. **a, b, c,** and **d** all from Germanic **bi, *bi-* (intensive prefix). **2.a.** EMBER DAY, from Old English *ymbe,* around; **b.** OMBUDSMAN, from Old Norse *um(b),* about, around; **c.** UMLAUT, from Old High German *umbi,* around. **a, b,** and **c** all from Germanic **umbi.* **3.a.** AMBI-, from Latin *ambi-,* around, about; **b.** (ALLEY[1]); AMBULATE, FUNAMBULIST, (PREAMBLE), from Latin *amb-,* around, about, in *ambulāre,* to go about, walk (**alāre,* to go). **4.** AMPHI-, from Greek *amphi,* around, about. **5.** (see **ag-**) Celtic **ambi.* [Pokorny *ambhi* 34.]

---

an-. Important derivatives are *on, acknowledge, alike, aloft, onslaught,* and *ana-.*

---

an-. On. Extended form **ana.* **1.a.** ON; (ACKNOWLEDGE), ALIKE, from Old English *an, on, a,* on, and prefixed *on-;* **b.** ALOFT, AMISS, from Old Norse *ā,* in, on; **c.** ANLAGE, ANSCHLUSS, from Old High German *ana-,* on; **d.** ONSLAUGHT, from Middle Dutch *aen,* on. **a, b, c,** and **d** all from Germanic **ana, *anō.* **2.** ANA[2], ANA-, from Greek *ana,* on, up, at the rate of. [Pokorny 4. *an* 39.]

---

anə-. Important derivatives are *anima, animal, animus, equanimity,* and *unanimous.*

---

anə-. To breathe. Suffixed form **anə-mo-.* **a.** ANIMA, ANIMADVERT, ANIMAL, ANIMATE, (ANIMATO), ANIMISM, ANIMOSITY, ANIMUS; EQUANIMITY, LONGANIMITY, MAGNANIMOUS, PUSILLANIMOUS, UNANIMOUS, from Latin *animus,* reason, mind, spirit, and *anima,* soul, spirit, life, breath; **b.** ANEMO-, from Greek *anemos,* wind. [Pokorny 3. *an(ə)-* 38.]

---

angh-. Important derivatives are *anger, anxious, anguish,* and *angina.*

---

angh-. Tight, painfully constricted, painful. **1.** AGNAIL, (HANGNAIL), from Old English *ang-nægl,* "painful spike (in the flesh)," corn, excrescence (*nægl,* spike; see **nogh-**), from Germanic **ang-,* compressed, hard, painful. **2.** Suffixed form **anghos-.* ANGER, from Old Norse *angr,* sorrow, grief, from Germanic **angaz.* **3.** Suffixed form **angh-os-ti-.* ANGST[1], from Old High German *angust,* anxiety, from Germanic **angusti-.* **4.** ANXIOUS, from Latin *angere,* to strangle, torment. **5.** Suffixed form **angh-os-to-.* ANGUISH, from Latin *angustus,* narrow. **6.** QUINSY, from Greek *ankhein,* to squeeze, embrace. **7.** ANGINA, from Greek *ankhonē,* a strangling. [Pokorny *an̂gh-* 42.]

---

ansu-. Important derivatives are *Aesir* and *Ormazd.*

---

ansu-. Spirit, demon. **1.** AESIR, from Old Norse *āss,* god, from Germanic **ansu-.* **2.** Suffixed reduced form **n̥su-ro-.* AHURA MAZDA, (ORMAZD), from Avestan *ahura-,* spirit, lord. [Pokorny *ansu-* 48.]

---

ant-. Important derivatives are *along, end, ante-, advance, anti-, antic, antique,* and *until.*

---

ant-. Front, forehead.
I. Inflected form (locative singular) **anti,* "against," with derivatives meaning in front of, before; also end. **1.** UN-[2]; ALONG, from Old English *and-,* indicating opposition, from Germanic **andi-* and **anda-.* **2.** END, from Old English *ende,* end, from Germanic **andja-.* **3.** ANCIENT[1], ANTE, ANTE-, ANTERIOR; ADVANCE, from Latin *ante,* before, in front of, against. **4.** ANTI-; ENANTIOMER, ENANTIOMORPH, from Greek *anti,* against, and *enantios,* opposite. **5.** Compound form **anti-ək^{w}o-,* "appearing before, having prior aspect" (**ək^{w}-,* appearance; see **ok^{w}-**). ANTIC, ANTIQUE, from Latin *antīquus,* former, antique. **6.** Reduced form **n̥ti-.* **a.** UNTIL, from Old Norse *und,* until, unto; **b.** ELOPE, from Middle Dutch *ont-,* away from. Both **a** and **b** from Germanic **und-.* **7.** Variant form **anto-.* VEDANTA, from Sanskrit *antaḥ,* end.
II. Probable inflected form (ablative plural) **antbhi,* "from both sides," whence **ambhi.* See **ambhi-.** [Pokorny *ant-s* 48.]

---

apo-. Important derivatives are *of, off, ebb, apo-, after, post-, deposit, dispose, impose, oppose, position, positive, post*[2], *post*[3], and *suppose.*

---

apo-. Also **ap-.** Off, away. **1.a.** OF, OFF, OFFAL, from Old English *of, æf,* off; **b.** EBB, from Old English *ebba,* low tide; **c.** ABLAUT, from Old High German *aba,* off, away from; **d.** AFT; ABAFT, from Old English *æftan,* behind, from Germanic **aftan-.* **a, b, c,** and **d** all from Germanic **af.* **2.** AB-[1], from Latin *ab, ab-,* away from. **3.** APO-, from Greek *apo,* away from, from. **4.** Suffixed (comparative) form **ap(o)-tero-.* AFTER, from Old English *æfter,* after, behind, from Germanic **aftar-.* **5.** Suffixed form **ap-t-is-.* EFTSOONS, from Old English *eft,* again, from Germanic **aftiz.* **6.** Suffixed form **apu-ko-.* AWKWARD, from Old Norse *öfugr,* turned backward, from Germanic **afug-.* **7.** Possible variant root form **po(s),* on, in. **a.** POGROM, from Russian *po,* at, by, next to; **b.** POST-, POSTERIOR; (POSTMORTEM), PREPOSTEROUS, PUISNE, (PUNY), from Latin *post,* behind, back, afterward; **c.** APPOSITE, (APPOSITION), COMPONENT, (COMPOSE), (COMPOSITE), (COMPOSITION), (COMPOUND), CONTRAPPOSTO, DEPONE, DEPOSIT, DISPOSE, EXPOUND, IMPOSE, INTERPOSE, OPPOSE, POSITION, POSITIVE, POST[2], POST[3], POSTICHE, POSTURE, PREPOSITION, PROPOSE, PROVOST, REPOSIT, SUPPOSE, TRANSPOSE, from Latin *pōnere,* to put, place, from **po-sinere* (*sinere,* to leave, let; of obscure origin). [Pokorny *apo-* 53.]

---

ar-. Important derivatives are *arm*[1], *arm*[2], *army, alarm, disarm, harmony, art*[1], *artist, inert, article, aristocracy, order, ordinary, ornate, adorn, rate*[1], *ratio, reason, read, hatred, riddle*[2], *rite, arithmetic,* and *rhyme.*

---

ar-. Also **arə-.** To fit together.
I. Basic form **arə-.* **1.** Suffixed form **ar(ə)-mo-.* **a.** ARM[1], from Old English *earm,* arm, from Germanic **armaz;* **b.** ARM[2], (ARMADA), ARMADILLO, ARMATURE, ARMOIRE, ARMY; ALARM, DISARM, from Latin *arma,* tools, arms; **c.** ARMILLARY SPHERE, from Latin *armus,* upper arm. **2.** Suffixed form **ar(ə)-smo-.* HARMONY, from Greek *harmos,* joint, shoulder. **3.** Suffixed form **ar(ə)-ti-.* **a.** ART[1], ARTISAN, ARTIST; INERT, (INERTIA), from Latin *ars* (stem *art-*), art, skill, craft; **b.** further suffixed form **ar(ə)-ti-o-.* ARTIODACTYL, from Greek *artios,* fitting, even. **4.** Suffixed form **ar(ə)-tu-.* ARTICLE, from Latin *artus,* joint. **5.** Suffixed form **ar(ə)-to-.* COARCTATE, from Latin *artus,* tight. **6.** Suffixed form **ar(ə)-dhro-.* ARTHRO-; ANARTHROUS, DIARTHROSIS, ENARTHROSIS, SYNARTHROSIS, from Greek *arthron,* joint. **7.** Suffixed (superlative) form **ar(ə)-isto-.* ARISTOCRACY, from Greek *aristos,* best.
II. Possibly suffixed variant form (or separate root) **ōr-dh-.* **1.** ORDAIN, ORDER, ORDINAL, ORDINANCE, ORDINARY, ORDINATE, ORDO; COORDINATION, INORDINATE, SUBORDINATE, from Latin *ōrdō,* order (originally a row of threads in a loom). **2.** EXORDIUM, PRIMORDIAL, from Latin *ōrdīrī,* to begin to weave. **3.** ORNAMENT, ORNATE; ADORN, SUBORN, from Latin *ōrnāre,* to adorn.
III. Variant or separate root **rē-* (< **reə-*). **1.** RATE[1], RATIO, REASON; (ARRAIGN), from Latin *rērī,* to consider, confirm, ratify. **2.** Suffixed form **rē-dh-.* **a.** *(i)* READ, REDE, from Old English *rǣdan,* to advise; *(ii)* HATRED, KINDRED, from Old English *rǣden,* condition. Both *(i)* and *(ii)* from Germanic **rēdan;* **b.** *(i)* RATHSKELLER, from Old High German *rāt,* counsel; *(ii)* RIDDLE[2], from Old English *rǣdels(e),* opinion, riddle. Both *(i)* and *(ii)* from Germanic **rēdaz.* **3.** Zero-grade form **rə-.* (see **dekm̥**) Germanic **radam,* number.
IV. Variant (or separate root) **rī-.* **1.** Suffixed form **rī-tu-.* RITE, from Latin *rītus,* rite, custom, usage. **2.** Suffixed form **(a)rī-dhmo-.* ARITHMETIC, LOGARITHM, from Greek *arithmos,* number, amount. **3.** RHYME, from a Germanic source akin to Old High German *rīm,* number, series. [Pokorny 1. *ar-* 55.]

---

arg-. An important derivative is *argue.*

---

arg-. To shine; white; the shining or white metal, silver. **1.** Suffixed form **arg-ent-.* ARGENT, ARGENTINE, from Latin *argentum,* silver. **2.** Suffixed form **arg-i-l(l)-.* ARGIL, from Greek *argillos,* white clay. **3.** Suffixed form **arg-u-ro-.* LITHARGE, (PYRARGYRITE), from Greek *arguros,* silver. **4.** Suffixed form **arg-i-n-.* ARGININE, from Greek *arginoeis,* brilliant, bright-shining. **5.** Extended form **argu-,* brilliance, clarity, ARGUE, from Latin denominative *arguere,* to make clear, demonstrate. **6.** Suffixed form **arg-ro-.* **a.** (see **pel-**[1]). Greek *argos* (< **argros*), white; **b.** AGRIMONY, possibly from Greek *argos,* white. [Pokorny *ar(e)ĝ-* 64.]

---

as-. Important derivatives are *ash*[1], *arid, ardent, arson,* and *azalea.*

---

as-. To burn, glow. **1.** Extended form **asg-.* ASH[1], from Old English *æsce, asce,* ash, from Germanic **askōn-.* **2.** Suffixed form **ās-ā-.* ARA, from Latin *āra,* altar, hearth. **3.** Suffixed (stative) form **ās-ē-.* **a.** ARID, from Latin *āridus,* dry, parched, from *ārēre,* to be dry; **b.** ARDENT, ARDOR, ARSON, from Latin *ārdēre,* to burn, be on fire, from *āridus,* parched. **4.** Extended form **asd-.* **a.** ZAMIA, from Greek *azein,* to dry; **b.** AZALEA, from Greek *azaleos,* dry. [Pokorny *as-* 68.]

---

at-. Important derivatives are *annual, anniversary, millennium,* and *perennial.*

---

at-. To go; with Germanic and Latin derivatives meaning a year (conceived as "the period gone through, the revolving year"). Suffixed form **at-no-.* ANNALS, ANNUAL, ANNUITY; ANNIVERSARY, BIENNIUM, DECENNIUM, MILLENNIUM, PERENNIAL, QUADRENNIUM, QUINDECENNIAL, QUINQUENNIUM, SEPTENNIAL, SEXENNIAL, SUPERANNUATED, TRIENNIUM, VICENNIAL, from Latin *annus,* year. [Pokorny *at-* 69.]

āter-. Important derivatives are *atrium* and *atrocious.*

āter-. Fire. **1.** Suffixed zero-grade form **ātr-o-.* ATRABILIOUS, from Latin *āter* (feminine *ātra*), black (< "blackened by fire"). **2.** Suffixed zero-grade form **ātr-yo-.* ATRIUM, from Latin *ātrium,* forecourt, hall, atrium (perhaps originally the place where the smoke from the hearth escaped through a hole in the roof). **3.** Compound shortened zero-grade form **atro-ək^{w}-* (**ək^{w}-,* "looking"; see **ok^{w}-**). ATROCIOUS, from Latin *ătrōx,* "black-looking," frightful. [Pokorny *āt(e)r-* 69.]

---

au-. Important derivatives are *audible, audience, audio-, audit, auditorium, obey, aesthetic,* and *anesthesia.*

---

au-. To perceive. Compound forms **aw-dh-, *awis-dh-,* "to place perception" (see **dhē-**). **1.** Suffixed form **awisdh-yo-* or **awdh-yo-.* AUDIBLE, AUDIENCE, AUDILE, AUDIO-, AUDIT, AUDITION, AUDITOR, AUDITORIUM, AUDITORY, OYEZ; OBEY, SUBAUDITION, from Latin *audīre,* to hear. **2.** AESTHETIC; ANESTHESIA, from Greek *aisthanesthai,* to feel. [Pokorny 8. *au̯-* 78.]

---

aug-. Important derivatives are *nickname, wax*[2], *auction, augment, author, inaugurate,* and *auxiliary.*

---

aug-. To increase. Variant **(a)weg-* (< **əweg-*). **1.** EKE[1], from Old English *ēacan, ēcan,* to increase; **b.** NICKNAME, from Old English *ēaca,* an addition. Both **a** and **b** from Germanic **aukan.* **2.** Variant extended forms **wogs-, *wegs-.* **a.** WAX[2], from Old English *weaxan,* to grow, from Germanic **wahsan;* **b.** WAIST, from Old English **wæst,* growth, hence perhaps waist, size, from Germanic **wahs-tu-.* **3.** Form **aug-ē-.* AUCTION, AUGEND, AUGMENT, AUTHOR, (AUTHORIZE), (OCTROI), from Latin *augēre,* to increase. **4.** AUGUR; INAUGURATE, from Latin *augur,* diviner (< "he who obtains favorable presage" < "divine favor, increase"). **5.** AUGUST, from Latin *augustus,* majestic, august. **6.** Suffixed form **aug-s-.* **a.** AUXILIARY, from Latin *auxilium,* aid, support, assistance; **b.** AUXIN, AUXESIS from Greek *auxein, auxanein,* to increase. [Pokorny *au̯eg-* 84.]

---

aus-. Important derivatives are *east, Easter,* and *aurora.*

---

aus-. To shine. **1.a.** EAST, from Old English *ēast,* east (< "the direction of the sunrise"); **b.** OSTMARK, from Old High German *ōstan,* east. Both **a** and **b** from Germanic **aust-.* **2.a.** EASTERN, from Old English *ēasterne,* eastern; **b.** OSTROGOTH, from Late Latin *ostro-,* eastern. Both **a** and **b** from Germanic **austra-.* **3.** EASTER, from Old English *ēastre,* Easter, from Germanic **austrōn-,* a dawn-goddess whose holiday was celebrated at the vernal equinox. **4.** Possibly in AUSTRO-[1], from Latin *auster,* the south wind, formally identical to the Germanic forms in **2** and **3,** but the semantics are unclear. **5.** Probably suffixed form **ausōs-,* dawn, also Indo-European goddess of the dawn. **a.** AURORA, from Latin *aurōra,* dawn; **b.** EO-, EOS; EOSIN, from Greek *ēōs,* dawn. [Pokorny *au̯es-* 86.]

awi-. Important derivatives are *aviation, bustard, osprey, ostrich, auspice, cockney, oval, ovary, ovum,* and *caviar.*

awi-. Bird.
I. 1. AVIAN, AVIARY, AVIATION; AVICULTURE, AVIFAUNA, BUSTARD, OCARINA, OSPREY, OSTRICH, from Latin *avis,* bird. **2.** Compound **awi-spek-,* "observer of birds" (**spek-,* to see; see **spek-**). AUSPICE, from Latin *auspex,* augur.
II. Possible derivatives are the Indo-European words for egg, **ōwyo-, *əyo-.* **1.a.** COCKNEY, from Old English *ǣg,* egg; **b.** EGG^{1}, from Old Norse *egg,* egg. Both **a** and **b** from Germanic **ajja(m).* **2.** OVAL, OVARY, OVATE, OVI-, OVOLO, OVULE, OVUM, from Latin *ōvum,* egg. **3.** OO-, from Greek *ōion,* egg. **4.** CAVIAR, from a source akin to Middle Persian *khāyak,* egg, from Old Iranian **āvyaka-,* diminutive of **avya-.* [Pokorny *au̯ei-* 86.]

awo-. Important derivatives are *avuncular* and *uncle.*

awo-. An adult male relative other than one's father. **1.** ATAVISM, from Latin *avus,* grandfather. **2.** AVUNCULAR, UNCLE, from Latin *avunculus,* maternal uncle. **3.** AYAH, from Latin *avia,* grandmother. [Pokorny *au̯o-s* 89.]

ayer-. Important derivatives are *early* and *ere.*

ayer-. Day, morning. **1.a.** EARLY, ERE, OR^{2}, from Old English *ǣr,* before; **b.** OR^{2}, from Old Norse *ār,* before. Both **a** and **b** from Germanic **airiz.* **2.** ERST, from Old English *ǣrest,* earliest, from Germanic (superlative) **airistaz.* [Pokorny *ai̯er-* 12.]

ayes-. An important derivative is *era.*

ayes-. A metal, copper or bronze. AENEOUS, ERA, from Latin *aes,* bronze, money. [Pokorny *ai̯os-* 15.]

bak-. Important derivatives are *imbecile* and *bacterium.*

bak-. Staff used for support. **1.** BACILLUS, BAGUETTE, (BAIL^{4}), (BAILEY); BACULIFORM, DEBACLE, IMBECILE, possibly from Latin *baculum,* rod, walking stick. **2.** BACTERIUM; (CORYNEBACTERIUM), from Greek *baktron,* staff. [Pokorny *bak-* 93.]

bel-. Derivatives are *Bolshevik* and *debilitate.*

bel-. Strong. **1.** Suffixed o-grade form **bol-iyo-.* BOLSHEVIK, from Russian *bol'shoĭ,* large. **2.** Prefixed form **dē-bel-i-,* "without strength" (*dē-,* privative prefix; see **de-**). DEBILITATE, DEBILITY, from Latin *dēbilis,* weak. [Pokorny 2. *bel-* 96.]

bhā-^{1}. Important derivatives are *beacon, beckon, berry, banner, photo-, fantasy,* and *phase.*

bhā-^{1}. To shine. Contracted from **bhaə-.* **1.** Suffixed zero-grade form **bhə-w-.* **a.** BEACON, from Old English *bēac(e)n,* beacon; **b.** BECKON, from Old English denominative *bēcnan, bēcnian,* to make a sign, beckon; **c.** BUOY, from Old French *boue,* buoy. **a, b,** and **c** all from Germanic **baukna-,* beacon, signal. **2.a.** BERRY; MULBERRY, from Old English *berie, berige,* berry, and Old High German *beri,* berry; **b.** FRAMBESIA, from Old French *framboise,* raspberry, alteration of Frankish **brām-besi,* "bramble berry." Both **a** and **b** from Germanic **bazja-,* berry (< "bright-colored fruit"), perhaps from **bhā-^{1}. 3.a.** BANDOLEER, from Spanish *banda,* sash; **b.** BANNER, (BANNERET^{1}), (BANNERET^{2}), from Late Latin *bandum,* banner, standard. Both **a** and **b** from Germanic **bandwa-,* "identifying sign," banner, standard, sash, also "company united under a (particular) banner." **4.** Suffixed form **bhə-w-es-.* PHOS-, PHOT, PHOTO-; PHOSPHORUS, from Greek *phōs* (stem *phōt-*), light. **5.** Extended and suffixed form **bhə-n-yo-.* FANTASY, (PANT), -PHANE, PHANTASM, (PHANTOM), PHASE, PHENO-, PHENOMENON; DIAPHANOUS, EMPHASIS, EPIPHANY, HIEROPHANT, PHANEROGAM, (PHANTASMAGORIA), PHOSPHENE, SYCOPHANT, THEOPHANY, (TIFFANY), from Greek *phainein,* "to bring to light," cause to appear, show, and *phainesthai* (passive), "to be brought to light," appear, with zero-grade noun *phasis* (**bhə-ti-*), an appearance. [Pokorny 1. *bhā-* 104.]

bhā-^{2}. Important derivatives are *fable, fate, infant, preface, prophet, abandon, banish, bandit, fame, phono-, symphony, confess,* and *blame.*

bhā-^{2}. To speak. Contracted from **bhaə-.* **1.** FABLE, FATE; AFFABLE, (FANTOCCINI), INEFFABLE, INFANT, (INFANTRY), PREFACE, from Latin *fārī,* to speak. **2.** -PHASIA; APOPHASIS, PROPHET, from Greek *phanai,* to speak. **3.a.** BAN^{1}, from Old English *bannan,* to summon, proclaim, and Old Norse *banna,* to prohibit, curse; **b.** BANAL, BANNS; ABANDON, from Old French *ban,* feudal jurisdiction, summons to military service, proclamation, Old French *bandon,* power, and Old English *gebann,* proclamation; **c.** BANISH, from Old French *banir,* to banish; **d.** CONTRABAND, from Late Latin *bannus, bannum,* proclamation; **e.** BANDIT, from Italian *bandire,* to muster, band together (< "to have been summoned"). **a, b, c, d,** and **e** all from Germanic suffixed form **ban-wan, *bannan,* to speak publicly (used of particular kinds of proclamation in feudal or prefeudal custom; "to proclaim under penalty, summon to the levy, declare outlaw"). **4.** Suffixed form **bhā-ni-.* **a.** BOON^{1}, from Old Norse *bōn,* prayer, request; **b.** BEE^{1}, perhaps from Old English *bēn,* prayer, from a Scandinavian source akin to Old Norse *bōn,* prayer. Both **a** and **b** from Germanic **bōni-.* **5.** Suffixed form **bhā-ma.* **a.** FAME, FAMOUS; DEFAME, INFAMOUS, from Latin *fāma,* talk, reputation, fame; **b.** EUPHEMISM, from Greek *phēmē,* saying, speech. **6.** Suffixed o-grade form **bhō-nā.* PHONE^{2}, -PHONE, PHONEME, PHONETIC, PHONO-, -PHONY; ANTHEM, (ANTIPHON), APHONIA, CACOPHONOUS, EUPHONY, SYMPHONY, from Greek *phōnē,* voice, sound, and (denominative) *phōnein,* to speak. **7.** Suffixed zero-grade form **bhə-to-.* CONFESS, PROFESS, from Latin *fatērī,* to acknowledge, admit. **8.** (BLAME), BLASPHEME, from Greek *blasphēmos,* evil-speaking, blasphemous (first element obscure). [Pokorny 2. *bhā-* 105.]

bha-bhā-. An important derivative is *bean.*

bha-bhā-. Broad bean. **1.** FAVA BEAN, from Latin *faba,* broad bean. **2.** Variant form **bha-un-.* BEAN, from Old English *bēan,* broad bean, bean of any kind, from Germanic **baunō.* **3.** Possible suffixed form **bha-ko-.* PHACOEMULSIFICATION, from Greek *phakos,* lentil. [Pokorny *bhabhā* 106.]

bhad-. Important derivatives are *better* and *best.*

bhad-. Good. **1.** BETTER, from Old English *betera,* better, from Germanic (comparative) **batizō.* **2.** BEST, from Old English *bet(e)st,* best, from Germanic (superlative) **batistaz.* **3.** BOOT^{2}, from Old English *bōt,* remedy, aid, from Germanic noun **bōtō.* **4.** BATTEN^{1}, ultimately from Old Norse *batna,* to improve, from Germanic verb **batnan,* to become better. [Pokorny *bhād-* 106.]

bhag-. Derivatives are *phago-* and *-phagous.*

bhag-. To share out, apportion, also to get a share. **1.** -PHAGE, -PHAGIA, PHAGO-, -PHAGOUS, from Greek *phagein,* to eat (< "to have a share of food"). **2.** NEBBISH, from a Slavic source akin to Czech *neboh,* poor, unfortunate, from Common Slavic **ne-bogŭ,* poor ("un-endowed"). **3.** PAGODA; BHAGAVAD-GITA, from Sanskrit *bhagaḥ,* good fortune. **4.** Extended form **bhags-.* BAKSHEESH, (BUCKSHEE), from Persian *bakhshīdan,* to give, from Avestan *bakhsh-.* [Pokorny 1. *bhag-* 107.]

bhāghu-. An important derivative is *bough.*

bhāghu-. Arm. BOUGH, from Old English *bōg, bōh,* bough, from Germanic **bōguz.* [Pokorny *bhāghú-s* 108.]

bhāgo-. Important derivatives are *book, buckwheat,* and *beech.*

bhāgo-. Beech tree. **1.a.** BOOK, from Old English *bōc,* written document, composition; **b.** BUCKWHEAT, from Middle Dutch *boek,* beech; **c.** BOKMÅL, from Norwegian *bok,* book. **a, b,** and **c** all from Germanic **bōkō,* beech, also "beech staff for carving runes on" (an early Germanic writing device). **2.** BEECH, from Old English *bēce,* beech, from Germanic **bōkjōn-.* [Pokorny *bhāgo-s* 107.]

bhardh-ā-. Important derivatives are *beard, barb^{1},* and *barber.*

bhardh-ā-. Beard. **1.** BEARD, from Old English *beard,* beard, from Germanic **bardaz.* **2.** HALBERD, from Old High German *barta,* beard, ax, from Germanic **bardō,* beard, also hatchet, broadax. **3.** BARB^{1}, BARBEL^{1}, BARBELLATE, BARBER, (BARBETTE), BARBICEL, BARBULE; REBARBATIVE, from Latin *barba,* beard. [Pokorny *bhardhā* 110.]

bhares-. Important derivatives are *barley, barn,* and *farina.*

bhares-. Also **bhars-.** Barley. **1.a.** BARN, from Old English *bere,* barley, from Germanic **bariz-;* **b.** BARLEY, from Old English *bærlic,* barley-like, barley, from Germanic **barz-.* **2.** FARINA, (FARINACEOUS), (FARRAGINOUS), FARRAGO, from Latin *far* (stem *farr-*), spelt, grain. [Pokorny *bhares-* 111.]

bhau-. Important derivatives are *beat, buttock, halibut, butt^{1}, button,* and *refute.*

bhau-. To strike. Contracted from **bhaəu-.* **1.** BEAT, from Old English *bēatan,* to beat, from Germanic **bautan.* **2.** BEETLE^{3}, from Old English *bȳtl,* hammer, mallet, from Germanic **bautilaz,* hammer. **3.** BASTE^{3}, probably from a Scandinavian source akin to Old Norse *beysta,* to beat, denominative from Germanic **baut-sti-.* **4.** BUTTOCK, from Old English diminutive *buttuc,* end, strip of land, from Germanic **būtaz.* **5.a.** HALIBUT, from Middle Dutch *butte,* flatfish; **b.** TURBOT, from a Scandinavian source akin to Old Swedish *but,* flatfish. Both **a** and **b** from Germanic **butt-,* name for a flatfish. **6.** (BOUTON), BUTT^{1}, BUTTON, BUTTRESS; ABUT, REBUT, SACKBUT, from Old French *bo(u)ter,* to strike, push, from Germanic **buttan.* **7.** Zero-grade form **bhū-* (**bhuə-*) with verbal suffix *-tā-.* **a.** CONFUTE, from Latin *cōnfūtāre,* to check, suppress, restrain (*com-,* intensive prefix; see **kom**); **b.** REFUTE, from Latin *refūtāre,* to drive back, rebut (*re-,* back; see **re-**). **8.** Possibly reduced suffixed form **bhu-tu-* (**bhəu-*). FOOTLE, from Latin *futuere,* to have intercourse with (a woman). [Pokorny 1. *bhau-* 112.]

bheg^{w}-. Derivatives are *-phobe* and *-phobia.*

bheg^{w}-. To run. **1.** BECK^{2}, from Old Norse *bekkr,* a stream, from Germanic **bakjaz,* a stream. **2.** -PHOBE, -PHOBIA, from Greek *phobos,* panic, flight, fear, from *phebesthai,* to flee in terror. [Pokorny *bheg$^{u̯}$-* 116.]

bhei-. An important derivative is *bee^{1}.*

bhei-. A bee. BEE^{1}, from Old English *bēo,* a bee, from Germanic suffixed form **bīōn-.* [Pokorny *bhei-* 116.]

bheid-. Important derivatives are *beetle^{1}, bite, bit^{1}, bitter, bait^{1}, boat,* and *fission.*

bheid-. To split; with Germanic derivatives referring to biting (hence also to eating and to hunting) and woodworking. **1.a.** BEETLE^{1}, BITE, from Old English *bītan,* to bite; **b.** TSIMMES, from Old High German *bīzan, bizzan,* to bite. Both **a** and **b** from Germanic **bītan.* **2.** Zero-grade form **bhid-.* **a.** BIT^{2}, from Old English *bite,* a bite, sting, from Germanic **bitiz;* **b.** (*i*) BIT^{1}, from Old English *bita,* a piece bitten off, morsel; (*ii*) BITT, from a Germanic source akin to Old Norse *biti,* bit, crossbeam. Both (*i*) and (*ii*) from Germanic **bitōn-;* **c.** suffixed form **bhid-ro-.* BITTER, from Old English *bit(t)er,* "biting," sharp, bitter. **3.** O-grade form **bhoid-.* **a.** BAIT^{1}, from Old Norse *beita* (verb), to hunt with dogs, and *beita* (noun), pasture, food; **b.** ABET, from Old French *beter,* to harass with dogs. Both **a** and **b** from Germanic **baitjan.* **4.** BATEAU, BOAT; (BOATSWAIN), from Old English *bāt,* boat, from Germanic **bait-,* a boat (< "dugout canoe" or "split planking"). **5.** Nasalized zero-grade form **bhi-n-d-* -FID, FISSI-, (FISSILE), (FISSION), (FISSURE), from Latin *findere,* to split. [Pokorny *bheid-* 116.]

bheidh-. Important derivatives are *bide, abide, fiancé, affidavit, confide, confident, defy, federal, faith, fidelity,* and *infidel.*

bheidh-. To trust, confide, persuade. **1.** BIDE; ABIDE, (ABODE), from Old English *bīdan,* to wait, stay, from Germanic **bīdan,* to await (< "to await trustingly, expect, trust"), probably from **bheidh-. 2.** FIANCÉ, FIDUCIAL, (FIDUCIARY); AFFIANCE, (AFFIANT), (AFFIDAVIT), (CONFIDANT), CONFIDE, (CONFIDENT), (DEFIANCE), DEFY, DIFFIDENT, from Latin *fīdere,* to trust, confide, and *fīdus,* faithful. **3.** Suffixed o-grade form **bhoidh-es-.* FEDERAL, FEDERATE; CONFEDERATE, from Latin *foedus* (stem *foeder-*), treaty, league. **4.** Zero-grade form **bhidh-.* FAITH,

FEALTY, FIDELITY; INFIDEL, PERFIDY, from Latin *fidēs,* faith, trust. [Pokorny *bheidh-* 117.]

bhel-[1]. Important derivatives are *blue, bleach, bleak[1], blaze[1], blemish, blind, blend, blond, blank, blanket, blush, black, flagrant,* and *flame.*

bhel-[1]. To shine, flash, burn; shining white and various bright colors.
I. 1. BELUGA, from Russian *belyĭ,* white. **2.** PHALAROPE, from Greek *phalaros,* having a white spot.
II. 1. Suffixed variant form **bhlē-wo-.* BLUE, from Old French *bleu,* blue, from Germanic **blēwaz,* blue. **2.** Suffixed zero-grade form **bhlə-wo-.* FLAVESCENT, FLAVO-; (FLAVIN), (FLAVONE), (FLAVOPROTEIN), from Latin *flāvus,* golden or reddish yellow.
III. Various extended Germanic forms. **1.** BLEACH, from Old English *blǣcan,* to bleach, from Germanic **blaikjan,* to make white. **2.** BLEAK[1], from Old Norse *bleikr,* shining, white, from Germanic **blaikaz,* shining, white. **3.** BLITZKRIEG, from Old High German *blecchazzen,* to flash, lighten, from Germanic **blikkatjan.* **4.a.** BLAZE[1], from Old English *blæse,* torch, bright fire; **b.** BLESBOK, from Middle Dutch *bles,* white spot; **c.** BLEMISH, from Old French *ble(s)mir,* to make pale. **a, b,** and **c** all from Germanic **blas-,* shining, white. **5.a.** BLIND; (BLINDFOLD), (PURBLIND), from Old English *blind,* blind; **b.** BLENDE, from Old High German *blentan,* to blind, deceive; **c.** BLEND, from Old Norse *blanda,* to mix; **d.** BLOND, from Old French *blond,* blond. **a, b, c,** and **d** all from Germanic **blendaz,* clouded, and **bland-, *bland-ja-,* to mix, mingle (< "make cloudy"). **6.a.** BLENCH[1], from Old English *blencan,* to deceive; **b.** BLANCH, BLANK, BLANKET; BLANCMANGE, from Old French *blanc,* white. Both **a** and **b** from Germanic **blenk-, *blank-,* to shine, dazzle, blind. **7.** BLUSH, from Old English *blyscan,* to glow red, from Germanic **blisk-,* to shine, burn.
IV. Extended form **bhleg-,* to shine, flash, burn. **1.** O-grade form *bhlog-.* BLACK, from Old English *blæc,* black, from Germanic **blakaz,* burned. **2.** Zero-grade form **bhl̥g-.* **a.** FULGENT, FULGURATE; EFFULGENT, FOUDROYANT, REFULGENT, from Latin *fulgēre,* to flash, shine, and *fulgur,* lightning; **b.** FULMINATE, from Latin *fulmen* (< **fulg-men*), lightning, thunderbolt. **3.a.** FLAGRANT; CONFLAGRANT, (CONFLAGRATION), DEFLAGRATE, from Latin *flagrāre,* to blaze; **b.** (FLAMBÉ), (FLAMBEAU), (FLAMBOYANT), FLAME, FLAMINGO, FLAMMABLE; INFLAME, from Latin *flamma* (< **flag-ma*), a flame. **4.** PHLEGM, PHLEGMATIC, PHLEGETHON, from Greek *phlegein,* to burn. **5.** O-grade form **bhlog-.* PHLOGISTON, PHLOX; PHLOGOPITE, from Greek *phlox,* a flame, also a wallflower. [Pokorny 1. *bhel-* 118, *bheleg-* 124, *bhleu-(k)-* 159.]

bhel-[2]. Important derivatives are *bowl[1], bulk[1], boulevard, boulder, bull[1], phallus, ball[1], balloon, ballot, bold,* and *fool.*

bhel-[2]. To blow, swell; with derivatives referring to various round objects and to the notion of tumescent masculinity. **1.** Zero-grade form *bhl̥-.* **a.** BOWL[1], from Old English *bolla,* pot, bowl; **b.** BOLE, from Old Norse *bolr,* tree trunk; **c.** BULK, from Old Norse *bulki,* cargo (< "rolled-up load"); **d.** ROCAMBOLE, from Old High German *bolla,* ball; **e.** (BOULEVARD), BULWARK, from Middle High German *bole,* beam, plank; **f.** BOLL, from Middle Dutch *bolle,* round object; **g.** BILTONG, from Middle Dutch *bille,* buttock; **h.** BOULDER, from a Scandinavian source akin to Swedish *bullersten,* "rounded stone," boulder, from **buller-,* "round object." **a, b, c, d, e, f, g,** and **h** all from Germanic **bul-.* **2.** Suffixed zero-grade form **bhl̥-n-.* **a.** BULL[1], from Old Norse *boli,* bull, from Germanic **bullōn-,* bull; **b.** BULLOCK, from Old English *bulluc,* bull, from Germanic **bulluka-;* **c.** PHALLUS, ITHYPHALLIC, from Greek *phallos,* phallus; **d.** FULL[2], from Latin *fullō,* a fuller, possibly from **bhel-[2]**. **3.** O-grade form **bhol-.* **a.** BOLLIX, from Old English *beallucas,* testicles; **b.** BALL[1], from Old English **beall,* ball; **c.** BILBERRY, probably from a Scandinavian source akin to Danish *bolle,* round roll; **d.** BALLOON, BALLOT, (BALLOTTEMENT), from Italian dialectal *balla,* ball; **e.** PALL-MALL, from Italian *palla,* ball; **f.** BALE[1], from Old French *bale,* rolled-up bundle. **a, b, c, d, e,** and **f** all from Germanic **ball-.* **4.** Possibly suffixed o-grade form **bhol-to-.* **a.** BOLD, from Old English *bald, beald,* bold; **b.** BAWD, from Old Low German *bald,* bold. Both **a** and **b** from Germanic **balthaz,* bold. **5.** Suffixed o-grade form **bhol-n-.* FILS[2], FOLLICLE, FOOL; (FOLLICULITIS), from Latin *follis,* bellows, inflated ball. **6.** BALEEN, from Greek *phal(l)aina,* whale, possibly from **bhel-[2]**. **7.** PHELLEM; PHELLODERM, PHELLOGEN, from Greek *phellos,* cork, cork oak, conceivably from **bhel-[2]** (but more likely unrelated). [Pokorny 3. *bhel-* 120.] (The following derivatives of this root are entered separately: **bhel-[3], bhelgh-, bhleu-.**)

bhel-[3]. Important derivatives are *foliage, folio, bloom[1], blossom, flora, flour, flourish, flower, bleed, blood, bless,* and *blade.*

bhel-[3]. To thrive, bloom. Possibly from **bhel-[2]**.
I. Suffixed o-grade form **bhol-yo-,* leaf. **1.** FOIL[2], (FOLIAGE), FOLIO, FOLIUM; (CINQUEFOIL), DEFOLIATE, EXFOLIATE, FEUILLETON, FOLIICOLOUS, MILFOIL, PERFOLIATE, PORTFOLIO, TREFOIL, from Latin *folium,* leaf. **2.** (-PHYLL), PHYLLO-, -PHYLLOUS; CHERVIL, GILLYFLOWER, PODOPHYLLIN, from Greek *phullon,* leaf.
II. Extended form **bhlē-* (< **bhleə-*). **1.** O-grade form **bhlō-.* **a.** suffixed form **bhlō-w-.* BLOW[3], from Old English *blōwan,* to flower, from Germanic **blō-w-;* **b.** *(i)* BLOOM[1], from Old Norse *blōm, blōmi,* flower, blossom; *(ii)* BLOOM[2], from Old English *blōma,* a hammered ingot of iron (semantic development obscure). Both *(i)* and *(ii)* from Germanic suffixed form **blō-mōn-;* **c.** BLOSSOM, from Old English *blōstm, blōstma,* flower, blossom, from Germanic suffixed form **blō-s-;* **d.** FERRET[2], (FLORA), FLORA, (FLORAL), FLORIATED, FLORID, FLORIN, FLORIST, -FLOROUS, (FLOUR), FLOURISH, FLOWER; (CAULIFLOWER), DEFLOWER, EFFLORESCE, ENFLEURAGE, FLORIGEN, from Latin *flōs* (stem *flōr-*), flower, from Italic suffixed form **flō-s-;* **e.** suffixed form *bhlō-to-:* *(i)* BLEED, BLOOD, from Old English *blōd,* blood; *(ii)* BLESS, from Old English *bloedsian, blētsian,* to consecrate, from Germanic **blōdisōn,* to treat or hallow with blood. Both *(i)* and *(ii)* from Germanic **blō-dam,* possibly from **bhel-[3]** in the meaning "swell, gush, spurt." **2.** EMBLEMENTS, from Medieval Latin *blādum, bladium,* produce of the land, grain, from Germanic suffixed form **blē-da-.* **3.** Suffixed zero-grade form **bhlə-to-.* BLADE, from Old English *blæd,* leaf, blade, from Germanic **bladaz.* [Pokorny 4. *bhel-* 122.]

bhelgh-. Important derivatives are *bellows, belly, billow, budget,* and *bulge.*

bhelgh-. To swell. Extension of **bhel-[2]**. **1.** O-grade form **bholgh-.* BELLOWS, BELLY, from Old English *bel(i)g, bælig,* bag, bellows, from Germanic **balgiz.* **2.** Zero-grade form **bhl̥gh-.* BILLOW, from Old Norse *bylgja,* a wave, from Germanic **bulgjan.* **3.** Zero-grade form **bhl̥gh-.* BOLSTER, from Old English *bolster,* cushion, from Germanic **bulgstraz.* **4.** O-grade form **bholgh-.* BUDGET, BULGE, from Latin *bulga,* leather sack, from Celtic **bolg-.* [Pokorny *bhelgh-* 125.]

bhendh-. Important derivatives are *bind, bend[1], band[1], bond,* and *bundle.*

bhendh-. To bind. **1.a.** BIND; WOODBINE, from Old English *bindan,* to bind; **b.** BINDLESTIFF, from Old High German *binten,* to bind. Both **a** and **b** from Germanic **bindan.* **2.** BANDANNA, from Sanskrit *bandhati,* he ties. **3.** O-grade form **bhondh-.* **a.** BEND[2]; RIBBON, from Old English *bend,* band, and Old French *bende,* band; **b.** BEND[1], from Old English *bendan,* to bend; **c.** BAND[1], BOND, from Old Norse *band,* band, fetter; **d.** BAND[1], from Old French *bande,* bond, tie, link. **a, b, c,** and **d** all from Germanic **band-.* **4.** Suffixed form **bhond-o-.* BUND[1]; (CUMMERBUND), from Old Iranian *banda-,* bond, fetter. **5.** Zero-grade form **bhn̥dh-.* **a.** BUND[2], from Middle High German *bunt,* league; **b.** BUNDLE, from Middle Dutch *bondel,* sheaf of papers, bundle. Both **a** and **b** from Germanic **bund-.* [Pokorny *bhendh-* 127.]

bher-[1]. Important derivatives are *bear[1], burden[1], birth, bring, fertile, differ, offer, prefer, suffer, transfer, furtive,* and *metaphor.*

bher-[1]. To carry; also to bear children. **1.a.** *(i)* BEAR[1], from Old English *beran,* to carry; *(ii)* FORBEAR[1], from Old English *forberan,* to bear, endure (*for-,* for-; see **per[1]**). Both *(i)* and *(ii)* from Germanic **beran;* **b.** BIER, from Old English *bēr, bǣr,* bier, and Old French *biere* bier, both from Germanic **bērō;* **c.** BORE[3], from Old Norse *bāra,* wave, billow, from Germanic **bēr-.* **2.a.** BAIRN, from Old English *bearn,* child, from Germanic **barnam;* **b.** BARROW[1], from Old English *bearwe,* basket, wheelbarrow, from Germanic **barwōn-.* **3.a.** BURLY, from Old English **borlic,* excellent, exalted (< "borne up"), from Germanic **bur-;* **b.** BURDEN[1], from Old English *byrthen,* burden, from Germanic **burthinja;* **c.** BIRTH, from a source akin to Old Norse *burdhr,* birth, from Germanic **burthiz;* **d.** BIRR[1], from Old Norse *byrr,* favorable wind, perhaps from Germanic **burja-.* **4.** Compound root **bhrenk-,* to bring (< **bher-* + **enk-,* to reach; see **nek-[2]**). BRING, from Old English *bringan,* to bring, from Germanic **brengan.* **5.** -FER, FERTILE; AFFERENT, CIRCUMFERENCE, CONFER, (DEFER[1]), DEFER[2], DIFFER, EFFERENT, INFER, OFFER, PREFER, (PROFFER), REFER, SUFFER, TRANSFER, VOCIFERATE, from Latin *ferre,* to carry. **6.** OPPROBRIUM, from Latin *probrum,* a reproach (< **pro-bhr-o-,* "something brought before one"; *pro-,* before; see **per[1]**). **7.** Probably lengthened o-grade form **bhōr-.* FERRET[1], FURTIVE, FURUNCLE; (FURUNCULOSIS), from Latin *fūr,* thief. **8.** FERETORY, -PHORE, -PHORESIS, -PHOROUS; AMPHORA, ANAPHORA, DIAPHORESIS, EUPHORIA, METAPHOR, PERIPHERY, PHEROMONE, TELPHER, TOCOPHEROL, from Greek *pherein,* to carry, with o-grade noun *phoros,* a carrying. **9.** PARAPHERNALIA, from Greek *phernē,* dowry ("something brought by a bride"). **10.** SAMBAL, from Sanskrit *bharati,* he carries, brings. [Pokorny 1. *bher-* 128.]

bher-[2]. Important derivatives are *brown, burnish, beaver[1],* and *bear[2].*

bher-[2]. Bright, brown. **1.** Suffixed variant form **bhrū-no-.* **a.** BROWN, from Old English *brūn,* brown; **b.** BRUIN, from Middle Dutch *bruun;* **c.** BRUNET, BURNET, BURNISH, from Old French *brun,* shining, brown. **a, b,** and **c** all from Germanic **brūnaz.* **2.** Reduplicated form **bhibhru-, *bhebhru-,* "the brown animal," beaver. BEAVER[1], from Old English *be(o)for,* beaver, from Germanic **bebruz.* **3.** BEAR[2], from Old English *bera,* bear, from Germanic **berō,* "the brown animal," bear. **4.** BERSERKER, from Old Norse *björn,* bear, from Germanic **bernuz.* [Pokorny 5. *bher-* 136.]

bherəg-. Important derivatives are *bright* and *birch.*

bherəg-. To shine; bright, white. **1.** BRIGHT, from Old English *beorht,* bright, from Germanic **berhtaz,* bright. **2.** "The white tree," the birch (also the ash). **a.** BIRCH, (BIRK), from Old English *birc(e),* birch, from Germanic **birkjōn-;* **b.** probably suffixed zero-grade form **bhrag-s-.* FRAXINELLA, from Latin *fraxinus,* ash tree. [Pokorny *bherəg-* 139.]

bhergh-[1]. Important derivatives are *bury, burial, borrow,* and *bargain.*

bhergh-[1]. To hide, protect. **1.a.** (see **kʷel-[1]**) Germanic compound **h(w)als-berg-,* "neck-protector," gorget (**h(w)alsaz,* neck); **b.** (see **sker-[1]**) Germanic compound **skēr-berg-,* "sword-protector," scabbard (**skēr-,* sword). Both **a** and **b** from Germanic **bergan.* **2.** Zero-grade form **bhr̥gh-.* **a.** BURY, from Old English *byrgan,* to bury, from Germanic **burgjan;* **b.** BURIAL, from Old English *byrgels,* burial, from Germanic derivative **burgisli-.* **3.a.** BORROW, from Old English *borgian,* to borrow, from Germanic **borgēn,* to pledge, lend, borrow; **b.** BARGAIN, from Old French *bargaignier,* to haggle, from Germanic derivative **borganjan.* [Pokorny *bhergh-* 145.]

bhergh-[2]. Important derivatives are *iceberg, bourgeois, burglar, force, fort, comfort, effort, enforce,* and *fortify.*

bhergh-[2]. High; with derivatives referring to hills and hill-forts. **1.a.** BARROW[2], from Old English *beorg,* hill; **b.** ICEBERG, from Middle Dutch *bergh,* mountain. Both **a** and **b** from Germanic **bergaz,* hill, mountain. **2.** (see **koro-**) Germanic compound **harja-bergaz,* "army-hill," hill-fort (**harjaz,* army). **3.** BELFRY, from Old French *berfroi,* tower, from Germanic compound **berg-frij-,* "high place of safety," tower (**frij-,* peace, safety; see **prī-**). **4.** Zero-grade form **bhr̥gh-.* **a.** BOROUGH, BURG, from Old English *burg, burh, byrig,* (fortified) town; **b.** BURGHER, from Old High German *burg,* fortress; **c.** BURGOMASTER, from Middle Dutch *burch,* town; **d.** BOURG, (BOURGEOIS), BURGLAR; FAUBOURG, from Late Latin *burgus,* fortified place, and Old French *burg,* borough. **a, b, c,** and **d** all from Germanic **burgs,* hill-fort. **5.** Possibly suffixed zero-grade form **bhr̥gh-to-.* FORCE, FORT, (FORTALICE), FORTE[1], FORTE[2], FORTIS, (FORTISSIMO), FORTITUDE, FORTRESS; COMFORT, DEFORCE, EFFORT, (ENFORCE), FORTIFY, (PIANOFORTE), (REINFORCE), from Latin *fortis,* strong (but this is also possibly from **dher-**). [Pokorny *bheregh-* 140.]

bhes-. Important derivatives are *psyche, psychic,* and *psycho-.*

bhes-. To breathe. Probably imitative. Zero-grade form **bhs-.* PSYCHE, PSYCHIC, PSYCHO-; METEMPSYCHOSIS, from Greek *psukhē,* spirit, soul, from *psukhein* (< **bhs-ū-kh-*), to breathe. [Pokorny 2. *bhes-* 146.]

bheudh-. Important derivatives are *bid, forbid, bode*[1], and *Buddha*[2].

bheudh-. To be aware, to make aware. **1.a.** BID, from Old English *bēodan,* to proclaim; **b.** FORBID, from Old English *forbēodan,* to forbid; **c.** VERBOTEN, from Old High German *farbiotan,* to forbid. **a, b,** and **c** all from Germanic **(for)beudan* (**for,* before; see **per**[1]). **2.** BODE[1], from Old English *bodian,* to announce, from *boda,* messenger, from Germanic **budōn-:* **3.** BEADLE, from Old English *bydel,* herald, messenger, and Old High German *butil,* herald, both from Germanic **budilaz,* herald. **4.** OMBUDSMAN, from Old Norse *bodh,* command, from Germanic **budam.* **5.** BUDDHA[2]; BODHISATTVA, BO TREE, from Sanskrit *bodhati,* he awakes, is enlightened, becomes aware, and *bodhiḥ,* perfect knowledge. [Pokorny *bheudh-* 150.]

bheuə-. Important derivatives are *be, husband, booth, build, future, neighbor,* and *beam.*

bheuə-. Also **bheu-.** To be, exist, grow.
I. Extended forms **bhwiy(o)-, *bhwī-.* **1.** BE, from Old English *bēon,* to be, from Germanic **biju,* I am, will be. **2.** FIAT, from Latin *fierī,* to become. **3.** Possibly suffixed form **bhwī-lyo-.* (see **dhē(i)-**) Latin *fīlius,* son.
II. Lengthened o-grade form **bhōw-.* **a.** BONDAGE, BOUND[4]; BUSTLE[1], HUSBAND, from Old Norse *būa,* to live, prepare, and *būask,* to make oneself ready (*-sk,* reflexive suffix; **see s(w)e-**); **b.** BAUHAUS, from Old High German *būan,* to dwell; **c.** BOOTH, from Middle English *bothe,* market stall, from a Scandinavian source akin to Old Danish *bōth,* dwelling, stall. **a, b,** and **c** all from Germanic **bōwan.*
III. Zero-grade form **bhu-.* **1.a.** BUILD, from Old English *byldan,* to build, from *bold,* dwelling, house, from Germanic **buthla;* **b.** BOODLE, from Middle Dutch *bōdel,* riches, property, from alternate Germanic form **bōthla.* **2.** PHYSIC, PHYSICS, PHYSIO-, PHYSIQUE, -PHYTE, PHYTO-, (PHYTON); APOPHYSIS, DIAPHYSIS, DIPHYODONT, EPIPHYSIS, EUPHUISM, HYPOPHYSIS, IMP, MONOPHYSITE, NEOPHYTE, PERIPHYTON, SYMPHYSIS, TRACHEOPHYTE, from Greek *phuein,* to bring forth, make grow, *phutos, phuton,* a plant, and *phusis,* growth, nature. **3.** Suffixed form **bhu-tā-.* EISTEDDFOD, from Welsh *bod,* to be. **4.** Suffixed form **bhu-tu-.* FUTURE, from Latin *futūrus,* "that is to be," future.
IV. Zero-grade form **bhū-* (< **bhuə-*). **1.a.** BOWER[1], from Old English *būr,* "dwelling space," bower, room; **b.** NEIGHBOR, from Old English *gebūr,* dweller (*ge-,* collective prefix; see **kom**); **c.** BOER, BOOR, from Middle Dutch *gheboer, ghebuer,* peasant. **a, b,** and **c** all from Germanic **būram,* dweller, especially farmer. **2.** BYRE, from Old English *bȳre,* stall, hut, from Germanic **būrjam,* dwelling. **3.** BYLAW, from a Scandinavian source akin to Old Norse *bȳr,* settlement, from Germanic **būwi-.* **4.** Suffixed form **bhū-lo-.* PHYLE, PHYLETIC, PHYLUM; PHYLOGENY, from Greek *phulon,* tribe, class, race, and *phulē,* tribe, clan.
V. Suffixal forms in Latin. **1.** (see **dwo-**) Latin *dubius,* doubtful, and *dubitāre,* to doubt, from **du-bhw-io-.* **2.** (see **per**[1]) Latin *probus,* upright, from **pro-bhw-o-,* "growing well or straightforward." **3.** (see **uper**) Latin *superbus,* superior, proud, from **super-bhw-o-,* "being above."
VI. a. BEAM, from Old English *bēam,* tree, beam; **b.** BOOM[2], from Middle Dutch *boom,* tree; **c.** BUMPKIN[1], from Flemish *boom,* tree. **a, b** and **c** all from Germanic **baumaz* (and **bagmaz*), tree (? < "growing thing"), possibly from **bheuə-.** [Pokorny *bheu-* 146.]

bheug-. Important derivatives are *bow*[3], *bow*[2], and *bog.*

bheug-. To bend; with derivatives referring to bent, pliable, or curved objects.
I. Variant form **bheugh-* in Germanic **beug-.* **1.a.** BEE[2], from Old English *bēag,* a ring; **b.** BAGEL, from Old High German *boug,* a ring. Both **a** and **b** from Germanic **baugaz.* **2.a.** BOW[3], from Old English *boga,* a bow, arch; **b.** (see **el-**) Germanic compound **alino-bugōn-,* "bend of the forearm," elbow (**alino-,* forearm); **c.** BOW[1], from a source akin to Middle Low German *boog,* bow of a boat. **a, b,** and **c** all from Germanic **bugōn-.* **3.** BOW[2], BUXOM, from Old English *būgan,* to bend, from Germanic *būgan.* **4.** BAIL[3], from Middle English *beil,* a handle, perhaps from Old English **bēgel* or from a Scandinavian source akin to Old Swedish **bøghil,* both from Germanic **baugil-.* **5.** BIGHT, from Old English *byht,* a bend, angle, from Germanic **buhtiz.*
II. BOG, from Scottish and Irish Gaelic *bog,* soft, from Celtic **buggo-,* "flexible." [Pokorny 3. *bheug-* 152.]

bhlē-. Important derivatives are *blow*[1], *bladder, blast, flavor,* and *inflate.*

bhlē-. Also **bhlā-.** To blow. Possibly identical to **bhel-**[3] **II** **bhlē-* above. **1.** BLOW[1], from Old English *blāwan,* to blow, from Germanic suffixed form **blē-w-.* **2.a.** BLADDER, from Old English *blǣdre,* blister, bladder; **b.** BLATHER, from Old Norse *bladhra* (noun), bladder, and *bladhra* (verb), to prattle. Both **a** and **b** from Germanic suffixed form **blēdram,* "something blown up." **3.a.** BLAST, from Old English *blǣst,* a blowing, blast; **b.** ISINGLASS, from Middle Dutch *blas(e),* a bladder; **c.** BLASÉ, BLAZE[3], from Middle Dutch *blāsen,* to blow up, swell. **a, b** and **c** all from Germanic extended form **blēs-.* **4.** Variant form **bhlā-.* FLABELLUM, FLATUS, FLAVOR; AFFLATUS, CONFLATE, (DEFLATE), INFLATE, SOUFFLÉ, from Latin *flāre,* to blow. [In Pokorny 3. *bhel-* 120.]

bhleu-. Important derivatives are *bloat, fluctuate, fluent, fluid, affluent,* and *influence.*

bhleu-. To swell, well up, overflow. Extension of **bhel-**[2]. **1.** BLOAT, from Old Norse *blautr,* soft, wet, from Germanic **blaut-,* possibly from **bhleu-.** **2.** Extended form **bhleug*^{w}*-.* FLUCTUATE, FLUENT, FLUERIC, FLUID, FLUME, FLUOR, (FLUORO-), (FLUSH[2]), FLUVIAL, FLUX; AFFLUENT, CONFLUENT, EFFLUENT, (EFFLUVIUM), (EFFLUX), (FLUORIDE), FLUVIOMARINE, INFLUENCE, (INFLUENZA), MELLIFLUOUS, REFLUX, SUPERFLUOUS, from Latin *fluere,* to flow, and *-fluus,* flowing. **3.** Zero-grade form **bhlu-.* PHLYCTENA, from Greek *phluein, phluzein,* to boil over. **4.** PHLOEM, from Greek *phloos, phloios,* tree bark (< "swelling with growth"), possibly from **bhleu-.** [Pokorny *bhleu-* 158.]

bhoso-. An important derivative is *bare*[1].

bhoso-. Naked. **a.** BARE[1], from Old English *bær,* bare; **b.** BALLAST, from Old Swedish and Old Danish *bar,* bare. Both **a** and **b** from Germanic **bazaz.* [Pokorny *bhoso-s* 163.]

bhrāter-. Important derivatives are *brother, fraternal,* and *pal.*

bhrāter-. Brother, male agnate. **1.a.** BROTHER, from Old English *brōthor,* brother; **b.** BULLY[1], from Middle Dutch *broeder,* brother. Both **a** and **b** from Germanic **brōthar-.* **2.** FRA, FRATERNAL, FRIAR; CONFRERE, FRATRICIDE, from Latin *frāter,* brother. **3.** PHRATRY, from Greek *phratēr,* fellow member of a clan. **4.** PAL, from Sanskrit *bhrātā, bhrātar-,* brother. [Pokorny *bhrāter-* 163.]

bhreg-. Important derivatives are *break, breach, fraction, fracture, fragile, fragment, frail*[1], *infringe,* and *suffrage.*

bhreg-. To break. **1.a.** BREAK, from Old English *brecan,* to break; **b.** BREACH, from Old English *brēc,* a breaking; **c.** (BRASH[2]), BRECCIA, from Italian *breccia,* breccia, rubble, breach in a wall, from Old High German **brehha,* from *brehhan,* to break; **d.** BRAY[2], from Old French *breier,* to break; **e.** BRIOCHE, from Old French *brier,* dialectal variant of *broyer,* to knead. **a, b, c, d,** and **e** all from Germanic **brekan.* **2.** BRACKEN, (BRAKE[4]), from Middle English *brake(n),* bracken, probably from a Scandinavian source akin to Old Norse **brakni,* undergrowth; **b.** BRAKE[5], from Middle Low German *brake,* thicket. Both **a** and **b** from Germanic **brak-,* bushes (< "that which impedes motion"). **3.** BRAKE[2], from Middle Low German *brake,* flax brake, from Germanic **brāk-,* crushing instruments. **4.** Nasalized zero-grade form **bhr̥-n-g-.* (FRACTED), FRACTION, (FRACTIOUS), FRACTURE, FRAGILE, FRAGMENT, FRAIL[1], FRANGIBLE; ANFRACTUOUS, CHAMFER, DEFRAY, DIFFRACTION, (INFRACT), INFRANGIBLE, INFRINGE, OSSIFRAGE, REFRACT, (REFRAIN[2]), (REFRINGENT), SAXIFRAGE, SEPTIFRAGAL, from Latin *frangere,* to break. **5.a.** SUFFRAGAN, SUFFRAGE, from Latin *suffrāgium,* the right to vote, from *suffrāgārī,* to vote for (? < "to use a broken piece of tile as a ballot"); **b.** IRREFRAGABLE, from Latin *refrāgārī,* to vote against. [Pokorny 1. *bhreĝ-* 165.]

bhreu-. Important derivatives are *brew, bread, broth, brood, breed, ferment,* and *fervent.*

bhreu-. To boil, bubble, effervesce, burn; with derivatives referring to cooking and brewing.
I. 1. BREW, from Old English *brēowan,* to brew, from Germanic **breuwan,* to brew. **2.** BREAD, from Old English *brēad,* piece of food, bread, from Germanic **braudam,* (cooked) food, (leavened) bread. **3.a.** BROTH, from Old English *broth,* broth; **b.** BREWIS, BROIL[2], from Vulgar Latin **brodum,* broth. Both **a** and **b** from Germanic **brudam,* broth.
II. Variant form **bhrē-.* **1.a.** BROOD, from Old English *brōd,* offspring, brood; **b.** BREED, from Old English *brēdan,* to beget or cherish offspring, breed, from Germanic denominative **brōdjan,* to rear young. Both **a** and **b** from Germanic derivative **brōd-ō,* "a warming," hatching, rearing of young. **2.a.** BRATWURST, SAUERBRATEN, from Old High German *brāt, brāto,* roast meat; **b.** BRAWN, from Old French *braon,* meat. Both **a** and **b** from Germanic derivative **brēd-ōn-,* roast flesh. Both **1** and **2** from Germanic **brēdan,* to warm.
III. a. Variant form **bhres-.* BRAISE, BRAZE[2], (BRAZIER[2]), BREEZE[2], from Old French *brese,* burning coal, ember; **b.** BRACIOLA, from Italian dialectal *bras'a,* burning coal. Both **a** and **b** from Germanic **bres-.*
IV. Reduced form **bher-,* especially in derivatives referring to fermentation. **1.a.** Suffixed form **bhermen-,* yeast. BARM, (BARMY), from Old English *beorma,* yeast, from Germanic **bermōn-;* **b.** further suffixed form **bhermen-to-.* FERMENT, from Latin *fermentum,* yeast. **2.** Extended form **bherw-.* FERVENT, FERVID, (FERVOR); DEFERVESCENCE, EFFERVESCE, from Latin *fervēre,* to be boiling or fermenting.
V. As a very archaic word for a spring. **1.** Suffixed zero-grade form **bhru-n(e)n-.* BOURN[1], BURN[2], from Old English *burn, burna,* spring, stream, from Germanic **brunnōn-.* **2.** Suffixed form **bhrēw-r̥.* PHREATIC, from Greek *phrear,* spring. [Pokorny *bh(e)reu-* 143, 2. *bher-* 132.]

bhrū-. Important derivatives are *brow* and *bridge*[1].

bhrū-. Eyebrow. Contracted from **bhruə-.* **1.** BROW, from Old English *brū-,* eyebrow, eyelid, eyelash, from Germanic **brūs.* **2.** Possibly in the sense of a beam of wood, and perhaps a log bridge. BRIDGE[1], from Old English *brycg(e),* bridge, from Germanic **brugjō* (with cognates in Celtic and Slavic). [Pokorny 1. *bhrū-* 172, 2. *bhrū-* 173.]

dā-. Important derivatives are *democracy, epidemic, demon, tide*[1], and *time.*

dā-. To divide. Contracted from **daə-.*
I. Suffixed form **dā-mo-,* perhaps "division of society." DEME, DEMOS, DEMOTIC; DEMAGOGUE, DEMIURGE, DEMOCRACY, DEMOGRAPHY, ENDEMIC, EPIDEMIC, PANDEMIC, from Greek *dēmos,* people, land.
II. Variants **dai-, *dī-,* from extended root **daəi-.* **1.** Root form **dai-.* GEODESY, from Greek *daiesthai,* to divide. **2.** Suffixed form **dai-mon-,* divider, provider. DEMON, from Greek *daimōn,* divinity. **3.** Suffixed variant form **dī-ti-.* **a.** TIDE[1]; EVENTIDE, from Old English *tīd,* time, season; **b.** TIDE[2], from Old English denominative *tīdan,* to happen (< "to occur in time"); **c.** TIDING, from Old Norse *tīdhr,* occurring; **d.** ZEITGEIST, from Old High German *zīt,* time. **a, b, c,** and **d** all from Germanic **tīdiz,* division of time. **4.** Suffixed variant form **dī-mon-.* TIME, from Old English *tīma,* time, period, from Germanic **tīmōn-.* [Pokorny *dā-* 175.]

dail-. Important derivatives are *deal*[1] and *ordeal.*

dail-. To divide. Northern Indo-European root extended from **da(ə)i-* (see **dā-**). **1.** DEAL[1], from Old English *dǣlan,* to share, from Germanic **dailjan.* **2.** DOLE[1], from Old English *dāl,* portion, lot, from Germanic **dailaz.* **3.** ORDEAL, from Old English *ordāl,* trial by ordeal, from Germanic prefixed form **uz-dailjam,* "a portioning out," judgment (**uz-,* out; see **ud-**). **4.** FIRKIN, from Middle Dutch *deel,* part, from Germanic **dailiz.* [In Pokorny *dā-* 175.]

daiwer-. A derivative is *levirate.*

daiwer-. Husband's brother. LEVIRATE, from Latin *lēvir,* husband's brother. [Pokorny *dāi̯u̯ēr* 179.]

dakru-. An important derivative is *tear*[2].

dakru-. Tear. **1.a.** TEAR[2], from Old English *tēar, tehher,* tear; **b.** TRAIN OIL, from Middle Dutch *trane,* tear, drop. Both **a** and **b** from Germanic *tahr-, *tagr-. **2.** Suffixed form *dakru-mā. LACHRYMAL, from Latin *lacrima* (Old Latin *dacruma*), tear. [Pokorny *dakru-* 179.]

de-. Important derivatives are *to, too, de-,* and *deteriorate.*

de-. Demonstrative stem, base of prepositions and adverbs. **1.a.** TO, TOO, from Old English *tō,* to; **b.** TSIMMES, from Old High German *zuo, ze,* to; **c.** TATTOO[1], from Middle Dutch *toe,* to, shut. **a, b,** and **c** all from Germanic *tō. **2.** DE-, from Latin *dē, dē-,* from, perhaps from **de-.** **3.** (see **kʷo-**) Latin *quandō,* when. **4.** DETERIORATE, from Latin *dēterior,* worse. **5.** (see **bel-**) Latin *dēbilis,* weak. **6.** EISTEDDFOD, from Welsh *eistedd,* sitting, from Celtic *eks-dī-sedo- (*dī- from *dē-). [Pokorny *de-, do-* 181.]

deik-. Important derivatives are *teach, token, digit, toe, dictate, addict, condition, predict, preach, index, indicate, judge, prejudice, revenge,* and *disk.*

deik-. To show, pronounce solemnly; also in derivatives referring to the directing of words or objects. **I.** Variant *deig-. **1.** O-grade form *doig-. **a.** TEACH, from Old English *tǣcan,* to show, instruct, from Germanic *taikjan, to show; **b.** *(i)* TOKEN, from Old English *tācen, tācn,* sign, mark; *(ii)* BETOKEN, from Old English *tācnian,* to signify; *(iii)* TETCHY, from Gothic *taikns,* sign; *(iv)* TACHISME, from Old French *tache, teche,* mark, stain. *(i), (ii), (iii),* and *(iv)* all from Germanic *taiknam. **2.** DIGIT, from Latin *digitus,* finger (< "pointer," "indicator"). **II.** Basic form *deik-. **1.** Possibly o-grade form *doik-. TOE, from Old English *tā, tahe,* toe, from Germanic *taihwō. **2.** Basic form *deik-. DICTATE, DICTION, DICTUM, DITTO, DITTY; ADDICT, BENEDICTION, CONDITION, CONTRADICT, EDICT, FATIDIC, (INDICT), INDITE, INTERDICT, JURIDICAL, JURISDICTION, MALEDICT, PREDICT, VALEDICTION, VERDICT, VERIDICAL, VOIR DIRE, from Latin *dīcere,* to say, tell. **3.** Zero-grade form *dik-ā-. ABDICATE, DEDICATE, PREACH, PREDICATE, from Latin *dicāre,* to proclaim. **4.** Agential suffix *-dik-. **a.** INDEX, INDICATE, from Latin *index,* indicator, forefinger (*in-,* toward; see **en**); **b.** JUDGE, JUDICIAL; PREJUDICE, from Latin *iūdex* (< *yewes-dik-), judge, "one who shows or pronounces the law" (*iūs,* law; see **yewes-**); **c.** (VENDETTA), VINDICATE; (AVENGE), REVENGE, from Latin *vindex* (first element obscure), surety, claimant, avenger. **5.** DEICTIC; APODICTIC, PARADIGM, POLICY[2], from Greek *deiknunai,* to show, with *deigma* (*deik-mn̥), sample, pattern. **6.** Zero-grade form *dik-. DISK; DICTYOSOME, from suffixed form *dik-skos, from Greek *dikein,* to throw (< "to direct an object"). **7.** Form *dikā. DICAST; SYNDIC, THEODICY, from Greek *dikē,* justice, right, court case. [Pokorny *dei̯ḱ-* 188.]

deiw-. Important derivatives are *Tuesday, deity, divine, jovial, July, Jupiter, Zeus, dial, diary, dismal, journey,* and *psychedelic.*

deiw-. To shine (and in many derivatives, "sky, heaven, god"). **I.** Noun *deiwos, god. **1.a.** TIU, (TUESDAY), from Old English *Tīw* (genitive *Tīwes),* god of war and sky; **b.** TYR, from Old Norse *Tȳr,* sky god. Both **a** and **b** from Germanic *Tīwaz. **2.** DEISM, DEITY, DEUS, JOSS; ADIEU, DEIFIC, from Latin *deus,* god. **3.** DIVA, DIVINE, from Latin *dīvus,* divine, god. **4.** DIVES, from Latin *dīves,* rich (< "fortunate, blessed, divine"). **5.** Suffixed zero-grade form *diw-yo-, heavenly. DIANA, from Latin *Diāna,* moon goddess. **6.** DEVI; DEODAR, DEVANAGARI, from Sanskrit *devaḥ,* god, and *deva-,* divine. **II.** Variant *dyeu-, Jove, the name of the god of the bright sky, head of the Indo-European pantheon. **1.** JOVE, JOVIAL, from Latin *Iovis,* Jupiter, or *Iov-,* stem of *Iuppiter,* Jupiter. **2.** JULY, from Latin *Iūlius,* "descended from Jupiter" (name of a Roman gens), from derivative *iou-il-. **3.** Vocative compound *dyeu-pəter-, "O father Jove" (*pəter-, father; see **pəter-**). JUPITER, from Latin *Iuppiter, Iūpiter,* head of the Roman pantheon. **4.** DIONE, ZEUS; DIOSCURI, from Greek *Zeus* (genitive *Dios*), Zeus. **III.** Variant *dyē- (< *dyeə-). DIAL, DIARY, DIET[2], DISMAL, DIURNAL; ADJOURN, CIRCADIAN, (JOURNAL), (JOURNEY), MERIDIAN, (POSTMERIDIAN), QUOTIDIAN, SOJOURN, from Latin *diēs,* day. **IV.** Variant *deiə-. PSYCHEDELIC, from Greek *dēlos,* (< *deyalos), clear. [Pokorny 1. *dei-* 183.]

dek-. Important derivatives are *decent, doctor, doctrine, document, dogma, paradox, decorate, dainty, dignity, disdain, indignant, disciple,* and *discipline.*

dek-. To take, accept. **1.** Suffixed (stative) form *dek-ē-. DECENT, from Latin *decēre,* to be fitting (< "to be acceptable"). **2.** Suffixed (causative) o-grade form *dok-eye-. **a.** DOCENT, DOCILE, DOCTOR, DOCTRINE, DOCUMENT, from Latin *docēre,* to teach (< "to cause to accept"); **b.** DOGMA, (DOGMATIC); DOCETISM, DOXOLOGY, HETERODOX, ORTHODOX, PARADOX, from Greek *dokein,* to appear, seem, think (< "to cause to accept or be accepted"). **3.** Suffixed form *dek-es-. **a.** (DÉCOR), DECORATE, from Latin *decus,* grace, ornament; **b.** DECOROUS, from Latin *decor,* seemliness, elegance, beauty. **4.** Suffixed form *dek-no-. DAINTY, DEIGN, DIGNITY, CONDIGN, DIGNIFY, DISDAIN, INDIGN, (INDIGNANT), (INDIGNATION), from Latin *dignus,* worthy, deserving, fitting. **5.** Reduplicated form *di-dk-ske-. DISCIPLE, (DISCIPLINE), from Latin *discere,* to learn. **6.** (DOWEL), PANDECT, SYNECDOCHE, from Greek *dekhesthai,* to accept. **7.** DIPLODOCUS, from Greek *dokos,* beam, support. [Pokorny 1. *deḱ-* 189.]

dekm̥. Important derivatives are *ten, December, decimal, dime, dozen, dean, decade, tenth, hundred, cent, century,* and *percent.*

dekm̥. Ten. **I.** Basic form *dekm̥. **1.a.** TEN, from Old English *tīen,* ten; **b.** (see **oktō(u)**) Old Norse *tjan,* ten. Both **a** and **b** from Germanic *tehun. **2.** EIGHTEEN, FIFTEEN, FOURTEEN, NINETEEN, SEVENTEEN, SIXTEEN, THIRTEEN, from Old English suffix *-tēne, -tīne, -tȳne,* ten, -teen, from Germanic *tehan. **3.** DECEMBER, DECEMVIR, DECI-, DECIMAL, DECIMATE, DECUPLE, DICKER, DIME; (DECENNARY), DECENNIUM, DECUSSATE, DOZEN, DUODECIMAL, OCTODECIMO, SEXTODECIMO, from Latin *decem,* ten. **4.** (DENARIUS), DENARY, (DENIER[2]), from irregular Latin distributive *dēnī,* by tens, ten each (formed by analogy with *nōnī,* nine each). **5.** DEAN, DECA-, DECADE, (DOYEN); DECAGON, DECALOGUE, DODECAGON, from Greek *deka,* ten. **II.** Extended form *dekm̥t-. (see **dwo-**) Old English *-tig,* ten, from Germanic *-tig. **III.** Ordinal number *dekm̥to-. TENTH, (TITHE), from Old English *teogotha, tēotha,* tenth, from Germanic *teguntha-. **IV.** Suffixed zero-grade form *-dkm̥-tā̆, reduced to *-km̥tā̆, and lengthened o-grade form *-dkōm-tā̆, reduced to *-kontā̆. **1.** NONAGENARIAN, OCTOGENARIAN, SEPTUAGINT, SEXAGENARY, from Latin *-gintā,* ten times. **2.** PENTECOST, from Greek *-konta,* ten times. **V.** Suffixed zero-grade form *dkm̥-tom, hundred, reduced to *km̥tom. **1.** HUNDRED, from Old English *hundred,* hundred (*-red,* from Germanic *radam, number; see **ar-**), from Germanic *hundam, hundred. **2.** (see **teuə-**) Germanic *thūs-hundi, "swollen hundred," thousand. **3.** CENT, CENTAL, CENTAVO, (CENTENARIAN), CENTENARY, CENTESIMAL, CENTI-, CENTIME, (CENTNER), CENTUM, CENTURY; CENTENNIAL, CINQUECENTO, PERCENT, QUATTROCENTO, SEICENTO, (SEN[2]), (SENITI), SEXCENTENARY, TRECENTO, from Latin *centum,* hundred. **4.** HECATOMB, HECTO-, from Greek *hekaton,* a hundred (? dissimilated from *hem-katon, one hundred; see **sem-**[1]). **5.** STOTINKA, from Old Church Slavonic *sŭto,* hundred. **6.** SATEM, from Avestan *satəm,* hundred. [Pokorny *deḱm̥* 191.] See also compound root **wīkm̥tī.**

del-[1]**.** Important derivatives are *linger, long*[1], *long*[2], *length, Lent, longitude, lunge,* and *prolong.*

del-[1]**.** Long. Probably extended and suffixed zero-grade form *dlon-gho-. **1.a.** LONG[1], from Old English *lang, long,* long; **b.** LANGLAUF, from Old High German *lang,* long; **c.** BELONG, from Old English *gelang,* along; **d.** LONG[2], from Old English denominative *langian,* to grow longer, yearn for, from Germanic *langōn; **e.** LINGER, from Old English *lengan,* to prolong (possibly influenced by Old Norse *lengja,* to lengthen), from Germanic *langjan, to make long; **f.** LOMBARD, from Latin compound *Longobardus, Langobardus* (with Germanic ethnic name *Bardi). **a, b, c, d, e,** and **f** all from Germanic *langaz, long. **2.a.** LENGTH, from Old English *lengthu,* length; **b.** LENT, from Old English *lengten, lencten,* spring, Lent, from West Germanic *langitinaz, lengthening of day; **c.** LING[1], from Middle English *lenge, ling,* ling, from a Low German source akin to Dutch *lenghe, linghe,* "long one." **a, b,** and **c** all from Germanic abstract noun *langithō. **3.** LONGERON, LONGITUDE; ELOIGN, (ELONGATE), LONGEVITY, LUNGE, OBLONG, PROLONG, PURLOIN, from Latin *longus,* long. **4.** Possibly suffixed variant *dl̥ə-gho-. DOLICHOCEPHALIC, DOLICHOCRANIAL, from Greek *dolikhos,* long. [Pokorny 5. *del-* 196.]

del-[2]**.** Important derivatives are *tell, tale,* and *talk.*

del-[2]**.** To recount, count. **1.** TELL, from Old English *tellan,* to count, recount, from Germanic *taljan. **2.** TALL, from Old English *getæl,* quick, ready, from West Germanic *(ge-)tala-. **3.a.** TALE, from Old English *talu,* story; **b.** TAAL[2], from Middle Dutch *tāle,* speech, language. Both **a** and **b** from Germanic *talō. **4.** TALK, from Middle English *talken,* to talk, from a source probably akin to Old English denominative *talian,* to tell, relate. **5.** DOLERITE, SEDULOUS, from Greek *dolos,* ruse, snare, perhaps from **del-**[2]. [Pokorny 1. *del-* 193.]

dem-. Important derivatives are *dome, domestic, danger, domain, dominate,* and *timber.*

dem-. House, household. **1.** Suffixed o-grade form *dom-o-, dom-u-, house. **a.** DOME, DOMESTIC, DOMICILE; MAJOR-DOMO, from Latin *domus,* house; **b.** suffixed form *dom-o-no-. DAME, DAN[2], DANGER, DOM, DOMAIN, DOMINATE, DOMINICAL, DOMINIE, DOMINION, (DOMINO[1]), DOMINO[2], DON[1], DUNGEON; (MADAM), MADAME, MADEMOISELLE, MADONNA, PREDOMINATE, from Latin *dominus,* master of a household (feminine *domina).* **2.** Possibly lengthened-grade form *dōm-m̥. DOME, from Greek *dōma,* house. **3.** Compound *dems-pot-, "house-master" (*-pot-, powerful; see **poti-**). DESPOT, from Greek *despotēs,* master, lord. **4.** Root form *dem(ə)-, to build (possibly a separate root). **a.** TIMBER, from Old English *timber,* building material, lumber, from Germanic *timram; **b.** TOFT, from Old Norse *topt,* homestead, from Germanic *tumftō. [Pokorny *dem-* 198.]

demə-. Important derivatives are *tame, daunt, adamant,* and *diamond.*

demə-. To constrain, force, especially to break in (horses). **1.** Suffixed o-grade form *dom(ə)-o-. TAME, from Old English *tam,* domesticated, from Germanic *tamaz. **2.** O-grade form *domə-. DAUNT; INDOMITABLE, from Latin *domāre,* to tame, subdue. **3.** Zero-grade form *dm̥ə-. ADAMANT, (DIAMOND), from Greek *daman,* to tame (> *adamas,* unconquerable, from *n̥-dm̥ə-nt-). [Pokorny *(demə-), domə-* 199.]

dent-. Important derivatives are *tooth, tusk, dental, dandelion,* and *indent*[1].

dent-. Tooth. (Originally participle of **ed-** in the earlier meaning "to bite".) **1.** O-grade form *dont-. TOOTH, from Old English *tōth,* tooth, from Germanic *tanthuz. **2.** Zero-grade form *dn̥t-. TUSK, from Old English *tūsc, tūx,* canine tooth, from Germanic *tunth-sk-. **3.** Full-grade form *dent-. DENTAL, DENTATE, DENTI-, DENTICLE, DENTIST; DANDELION, EDENTATE, EDENTULOUS, INDENT[1], (INDENTURE), TRIDENT, from Latin *dēns* (stem *dent-*), tooth. **4.** O-grade variant form *(o)dont-. -ODON, -ODONT, ODONTO-; CERATODUS, MASTODON, from Greek *odōn, odous,* tooth. [In Pokorny *ed-* 287.]

der-. Important derivatives are *tear*[1], *tart*[2], *turd, epidermis, drab*[1], and *drape.*

der-. To split, peel, flay; with derivatives referring to skin and leather. **1.** TEAR[1], from Old English *teran,* to tear, from Germanic *teran. **2.** TART[1], from Old English *teart,* sharp, severe, from Germanic *ter-t. **3.** Suffixed zero-grade form *dr̥-tom, "something separated or discarded." TURD, from Old English *tord,* turd, from Germanic *turdam, turd. **4.** Reduplicated form *de-dr-u-. TETTER, from Old English *tet(e)r,* eruption, skin disease. **5.** DERRIS, from Greek *derris,* leather covering. **6.** Suffixed form *der-mn̥. -DERM, DERMA[1], -DERMA, DERMATO-; EPIDERMIS, from Greek *derma,* skin. [Pokorny 4. *der-* 206.]

deru-. Important derivatives are *tree, truce, true, truth, trust, tray, trough, trim, tar*[1], *endure,* and *druid.*

deru-. Also **dreu-.** To be firm, solid, steadfast;

hence specialized senses "wood," "tree," and derivatives referring to objects made of wood. **1.** Suffixed variant form *drew-o-. **a.** TREE, from Old English _trēow,_ tree, from Germanic _*trewam;_ **b.** TRUCE, from Old English _trēow,_ pledge, from Germanic _*treuwō._ **2.** Variant form _dreu-._ **a.** TRUE, from Old English _trēowe,_ firm, true; **b.** TROW, from Old English _trēowian, trūwian,_ to trust; **c.** TRIG[1], from Old Norse _tryggr,_ firm, true; **d.** TROTH, TRUTH; BETROTH, from Old English _trēowth_ faith, loyalty, truth, from Germanic abstract noun _*treuwithō;_ **e.** TRUST, from Old Norse _traust,_ confidence, firmness, from Germanic abstract noun _*traustam;_ **f.** TRYST, from Old French _triste,_ waiting place (< "place where one waits trustingly"), probably from a source akin to Old Norse denominative _treysta,_ to trust, make firm. **a, b, c, d, e,** and **f** all from Germanic _*treuwaz._ **3.** Variant form _*drou-._ TRAY, from Old English _trēg, trīg,_ wooden board, from Germanic _*traujam._ **4.** Suffixed zero-grade form _*dru-ko-._ TROUGH, from Old English _trog,_ wooden vessel, tray, from Germanic _*trugaz._ **5.** Suffixed zero-grade form _*dru-mo-._ **a.** TRIM, from Old English _trum,_ firm, strong; **b.** SHELTER, from Old English _truma,_ troop. Both **a** and **b** from Germanic _*trum-._ **6.** Variant form _*derw-._ TAR[1], from Old English _te(o)ru,_ resin, pitch (obtained from the pine tree), from Germanic _*terw-._ **7.** Suffixed variant form _*drū-ro-._ DOUR, DURAMEN, DURESS, DURUM; (DURA MATER), ENDURE, INDURATE, OBDURATE, from Latin _dūrus,_ hard (many of whose English derivatives represent a semantic cross with Latin _dūrāre,_ to last long; see **deuə-**). **8.** Lengthened zero-grade form _*drū-._ DRUPE, DRYAD; DRYOPITHECINE, GERMANDER, HAMADRYAD, from Greek _drus,_ oak. **9.** Reduplicated form _*der-drew-,_ dissimilated with suffix in _*der-drew-on._ DENDRO-, DENDRON; PHILODENDRON, RHODODENDRON, from Greek _dendron,_ tree. **10.** DRUID, from Latin _druides,_ druids, probably from Celtic compound _*dru-wid-,_ "strong seer" (_*wid-,_ seeing; see **weid-**), the Celtic priestly caste. **11.** O-grade form _*doru-._ DEODAR, from Sanskrit _dāru,_ wood, timber. [Pokorny _deru-_ 214.]

deu-[1]**.** An important derivative is _tire_[1].

deu-[1]**.** To lack, be wanting. **1.** Possibly suffixed form _*deu-s-._ **a.** TIRE[1], from Old English _tēorian, tyrian,_ to fail, tire (< "to fall behind"), from Germanic _*teuzōn;_ **b.** DEONTOLOGY, from Greek _dein,_ to lack, want. **2.** Suffixed form _*deu-tero-._ DEUTERO- ; DEUTERAGONIST, (DEUTERIUM), DEUTERONOMY, from Greek _deuteros,_ "missing," next, second. [Pokorny 3. _deu-_ 219.] (For suffixed zero-grade form _*du-s-,_ combining form of _*dew-es-,_ a lack, see **dus-**.)

deu-[2]**.** Important derivatives are _bonus, bounty, benefactor, benefit, benign, beauty, embellish, dynamic, dynamite,_ and _dynasty._

deu-[2]**.** To do, perform, show favor, revere. **1.** Suffixed form _*dw-enos._ BONBON, BONITO, BONUS, BOON[2], BOUNTY; BONANZA, BONHOMIE, DEBONAIR, from Latin _bonus,_ good (< "useful, efficient, working"). **2.** Adverbial form _*dw-enē._ BENEDICTION, BENEFACTION, (BENEFACTOR), (BENEFIC), (BENEFICENCE), (BENEFIT), BENEVOLENT, (BENIGN), (HERB BENNET), from Latin _bene,_ well. **3.** Diminutive _*dw-en-elo-._ BEAU, BEAUTY, BELLE; BELDAM, BELLADONNA, BELVEDERE, EMBELLISH, from Latin _bellus,_ handsome, pretty, fine. **4.** Possibly suffixed zero-grade form _*dw-eye-._ (BEATITUDE); BEATIFIC, (BEATIFY), from Latin _beāre,_ to make blessed. **5.** Possible (but unlikely for formal and semantic reasons) suffixed zero-grade form _*du-nə-._ DYNAMIC, (DYNAMITE), DYNAST, (DYNASTY); AERODYNE, from Greek _dunasthai,_ to be able. [Pokorny 2. _deu-_ 218.]

deuə-. Important derivatives are _durable, duration,_ and _during._

deuə-. Also **dwaə-.** Long (in duration). Suffixed zero-grade form _*dū-ro-_ (< _*duə-ro-_). DURABLE, DURANCE, DURATION, DURING; PERDURABLE, THERMODURIC, from Latin _dūrāre,_ to last. [In Pokorny 3. _deu-_ 219.]

deuk-. Important derivatives are _tug, wanton, tow_[1]_, tie, team, dock_[1]_, duct, duke, abduct, conduct, deduce, introduce, produce, reduce, subdue,_ and _educate._

deuk-. To lead. **1.a.** TUG; WANTON, from Old English _tēon,_ to pull, draw, lead; **b.** ZUGZWANG, from Old High German _ziohan,_ to pull. Both **a** and **b** from Germanic _*teuhan._ **2.** Suffixed zero-grade form _*duk-ā-._ TOW[1], from Old English _togian,_ to draw, drag, from Germanic _*tugōn._ **3.** Suffixed o-grade form _*douk-eyo-._ TIE, from Old English _*tīegan, tīgan,_ to bind. **4.** Suffixed o-grade form _*douk-mo-._ TEAM, from Old English _tēam,_ descendant, family, race, brood, team, from Germanic _*tau(h)maz._ **5.** TEEM[1], from Old English _tēman, tīeman,_ to beget, from Germanic denominative _*tau(h)mjan._ **6.** Basic form _*deuk-._ DOGE, DOUCHE, (DUCAL), (DUCAT), (DUCE), (DUCHESS), (DUCHY), DUCT, DUCTILE, DUKE; (ABDUCENS), ABDUCT, ADDUCE, CIRCUMDUCTION, (CON[3]), (CONDOTTIERE), CONDUCE, (CONDUCT), DEDUCE, (DEDUCT), EDUCE, (ENDUE), INDUCE, INTRODUCE, PRODUCE, (REDOUBT), REDUCE, SEDUCE, SUBDUCTION, SUBDUE, TRADUCE, TRANSDUCER, from Latin _dūcere,_ to lead. **7.** Suffixed zero-grade form _*duk-ā-._ EDUCATE, from Latin _ēducāre,_ to lead out, bring up (_ē-_ < _ex-,_ out; see **eghs**). [Pokorny _deuk-_ 220.]

dhē-. Important derivatives are _do_[1]_, deed, doom, -dom, deem, fact, factor, fashion, feat_[1]_, feature, affair, affect_[1]_, affection, amplify, benefit, defeat, defect, effect, efficient, infect, justify, modify, notify, perfect, profit, qualify, sacrifice, face, surface, difficulty, thesis,_ and _theme._

dhē-. To set, put. Contracted from _*dheə-._ **1.** O-grade form _*dhō-._ DO[1]; FORDO, from Old English _dōn,_ to do, from Germanic _*dōn._ **2.** Suffixed form _*dhē-ti-,_ "thing laid down or done, law, deed." DEED, from Old English _dǣd,_ doing, deed, from Germanic _*dēdiz._ **3.** Suffixed o-grade form _*dhō-mo-._ **a.** DOOM, from Old English _dōm,_ judgment (< "thing set or put down"); **b.** -DOM, from Old English _-dōm,_ abstract suffix indicating state, condition, or power; **c.** (see **kā-**) Old Norse _-dōmr,_ condition; **d.** DUMA, from Russian _Duma,_ Duma, from a Germanic source akin to Gothic _dōms,_ judgment; **e.** DEEM, from Old English _dēman,_ to judge, from Germanic denominative _dōmjan._ **a, b, c, d,** and **e** all from Germanic _dōmaz._ **4.** Suffixed o-grade form _*dhō-t-._ (see **sak-**) Latin _sacerdōs,_ priest, "performer of sacred rites." **5.** Zero-grade form _*dhə-._ **a.** prefixed form _*kom-dhə-._ ABSCOND, INCONDITE, RECONDITE, SCONCE[2], from Latin _condere,_ to put together, establish, preserve (_*kom,_ together; see **kom**); **b.** prefixed and suffixed form _*kom-dh(ə)-yo-._ CONDIMENT, from Latin _condīre,_ to season, flavor; **c.** compound _*kred-dhə-._ (see **kerd-**) **6.** Suffixed zero-grade form _dhə-k-._ **a.** -FACIENT, FACT, FACTION[1], -FACTION, FACTITIOUS, FACTITIVE, FACTOR, FASHION, FEASIBLE, FEAT[1], FEATURE, (FETISH), -FIC, (-FY), HACIENDA; AFFAIR, AFFECT[1], (AFFECT[2]), (AFFECTION), (AMPLIFY), ARTIFACT, ARTIFICE, (BEATIFIC), BENEFACTION, (BENEFIC), (BENEFICE), (BENEFICENCE), (BENEFIT), CHAFE, COMFIT, CONFECT, (CONFETTI), COUNTERFEIT, (DEFEASANCE), DEFEAT, DEFECT, (DEFICIENT), (DISCOMFIT), (EDIFICE), (EDIFY), EFFECT, (EFFICACIOUS), (EFFICIENT), FACSIMILE, FACTOTUM, FORFEIT, INFECT, (JUSTIFY), MALEFACTOR, (MALFEASANCE), MANUFACTURE, MISFEASANCE, (MODIFY), (MOLLIFY), (NIDIFY), (NOTIFY), (NULLIFY), OFFICINAL, ORIFICE, PERFECT, (PETRIFY), (PLUPERFECT), PONTIFEX, PREFECT, (PROFICIENT), PROFIT, PUTREFY, (QUALIFY), RAREFY, (RECTIFY), REFECT, (REFECTORY), RUBEFACIENT, SACRIFICE, SATISFY, SPINIFEX, SUFFICE, (SUFFICIENT), SURFEIT, TUBIFEX, TUMEFACIENT, (VIVIFY), from Latin _facere_ (< _*fak-yo-_), to do, make, and Latin combining form _-fex_ (< _*-fak-s_), "maker"; **b.** FAÇADE, FACE, (FACET), (FACIAL), FACIES; (DEFACE), EFFACE, (SURFACE), from Latin derivative _faciēs,_ shape, face (< "form imposed on something"); **c.** OFFICE, from Latin compound _officium_ (< _*opi-fici-om_), service, duty, business, performance of work (_*opi-,_ work; see **op-**); **d.** further suffixed form _*dhə-k-li-._ FACILE, (FACILITATE), FACULTY, DIFFICULTY, from Latin _facilis_ (< Old Latin _facul_), feasible, easy. **7.** Suffixed zero-grade form _*dhə-s-_ (probably identical with zero-grade of **dhēs-**). NEFARIOUS, from Latin _fās,_ divine law, right. **8.** MULTIFARIOUS, OMNIFARIOUS, from Latin _-fāriam,_ adverbial suffix, as in _bifāriam,_ in two places, parts, double, from _*dwi-dh(ə)-,_ "making two" (_*dwi-,_ two; see **dwo-**). **9.** Reduplicated form _*dhi-dhə-._ THESIS, THETIC; ANATHEMA, ANTITHESIS, DIATHESIS, EPENTHESIS, EPITHET, HYPOTHESIS, METATHESIS, PARENTHESIS, PROSTHESIS, PROTHESIS, SYNTHESIS, from Greek _tithenai,_ to put, with zero-grade noun _thesis_ (_*dhə-ti-_), a placing, and verbal adjective _thetos_ (_*dhə-to-_), placed. **10.** Suffixed form _*dhē-k-._ THECA, TICK[3]; AMPHITHECIUM, APOTHECARY, (APOTHECIUM), BIBLIOTHECA, (BODEGA), (BOUTIQUE), CLEISTOTHECIUM, ENDOTHECIUM, PERITHECIUM, from Greek _thēkē,_ receptacle. **11.** Suffixed zero-grade form _*dhə-mn̥._ (THEMATIC), THEME, from Greek _thema,_ "thing placed," proposition. **12.** Reduplicated form _*dhe-dhē-._ SANDHI, from Sanskrit _dadhāti,_ he places. **13.** Basic form _*dhē-._ PURDAH, from Old Persian _dā-,_ to place. **14.** Suffixed form _*dhē-to-,_ set down, created. (see **s(w)e-**) Old Iranian compound _*khvatō-dāta-,_ created from oneself. **15.** Reduced form _*dh-._ (see **au-**) [Pokorny 2. _dhē-_ 235.]

dhē(i)-. Important derivatives are _female, feminine, fawn_[2]_, fetus, fennel,_ and _affiliate._

dhē(i)-. To suck. Contracted from _*dheə(i)-._ **1.** Suffixed reduced form _*dhē-mnā-._ FEMALE, FEMININE; EFFEMINATE, from Latin _fēmina,_ woman (< "she who suckles"). **2.** Suffixed reduced form _*dhē-to-._ FAWN[2], (FETAL), FETUS; EFFETE, (FETICIDE), SUPERFETATE, from Latin _fētus,_ pregnancy, childbearing, offspring, with adjective _fētus, fēta,_ pregnant. **3.** Suffixed reduced form _*dhē-kwondo-._ FECUND, from Latin _fēcundus,_ fruitful. **4.** Suffixed reduced form _*dhē-no-._ FENNEL, FINOCHIO; (FENUGREEK), SAINFOIN, from Latin _fēnum, faenum,_ hay (< "produce"). **5.** Perhaps suffixed zero-grade form _*dhī-lyo-_ (< _*dhiə-lyo-_). FILIAL, FILIATE; FILS[1]; AFFILIATE, HIDALGO, from Latin _fīlius,_ son, and _fīlia,_ daughter (but these are equally possibly from the root **bheuə-**). **6.** Suffixed reduced form _*dhē-lo-._ FELLATIO, from Latin _fēlāre, fellāre,_ to suck. **7.** Suffixed reduced form _*dhē-l-īk-._ FELICITATE, FELICITY; FELICIFIC, INFELICITY, from Latin _fēlīx,_ fruitful, fertile, lucky, happy. **8.** Suffixed reduced form _*dhē-lā-._ ENDOTHELIUM, EPITHELIUM, (MESOTHELIUM), from Greek _thēlē,_ nipple. **9.** Suffixed reduced form _*dhē-l-u-._ THEELIN, from Greek _thēlus,_ female. [Pokorny _dhē(i)-_ 241.]

dheigh-. Important derivatives are _dairy, lady, dough, figure, faint, fiction, effigy,_ and _paradise._

dheigh-. To form, build. **1.** DAIRY, from Old English _dǣge,_ bread kneader, from Germanic _*daigjōn-._ **2.** LADY, from Old English compound _hlǣfdige,_ mistress of a household (< "bread kneader"; _hlāf,_ bread, loaf), from Germanic _*dīg-._ **3.** Suffixed o-grade form _*dhoigh-o-._ **a.** DOUGH, from Old English _dāg,_ dough; **b.** TEIGLACH, from Old High German _teic,_ dough. Both **a** and **b** from Germanic _*daigaz._ **4.** Suffixed zero-grade form _*dhigh-ūrā._ FIGURE; CONFIGURE, DISFIGURE, PREFIGURE, TRANSFIGURE, from Latin _figūra,_ form, shape (< "result of kneading"). **5.** Nasalized zero-grade form _*dhi-n-gh-._ (FAINT), FEIGN, (FEINT), FICTILE, FICTION, FIGMENT; EFFIGY, from Latin _fingere,_ to shape. **6.** Probable nasalized zero-grade form _*dhi-n-g(h)-._ THIGMOTAXIS, THIXOTROPY, from Greek _thinganein,_ to touch. **7.** Suffixed o-grade form _*dhoigh-o-._ PARADISE, from Avestan _daēza-,_ wall (originally made of clay or mud bricks). [Pokorny _dheigh-_ 244.]

dher-. Important derivatives are _farm, firm_[1]_, confirm,_ and _throne._

dher-. To hold firmly, support. **1.** Suffixed form _*dher-mo-._ FARM, FERMATA, FIRM[1], FIRM[2], (FIRMAMENT); AFFIRM, CONFIRM, INFIRM, (INFIRMARY), from Latin _firmus,_ firm, strong. **2.** Perhaps extended form _*dhergh-._ (see **bhergh-**[2]) Latin _fortis,_ strong (but this is also possibly from **bhergh-**[2]). **3.** Suffixed zero-grade form _*dhr-ono-._ THRONE, from Greek _thronos,_ seat, throne (< "support"). **4.** Suffixed form _*dher-mn̥._ DHARMA, from Sanskrit _dharma,_ statute, law (< "that which is established firmly"). **5.** Suffixed form _*dher-eno-._ DHARNA, from Prakrit _dharaṇa,_ a holding firm. **6.** Suffixed o-grade form _*dhor-o-._ SIRDAR, TAHSILDAR, ZAMINDAR, from Iranian _dāra-,_ holding, whence Persian _-dār._ [Pokorny 2. _dher-_ 252.]

dhers-. An important derivative is _dare._

dhers-. To venture, be bold. O-grade form _*dhors-_ and zero-grade form _*dhr̥s-._ DARE, (DURST), from Old English _dearr_ and _durst,_ first and third person singular present and past indicative of _durran,_ to venture, respectively from Germanic _*dors-_ and _*durs-._ [Pokorny _dhers-_ 259.]

dhēs-. Important derivatives are _fair_[2]_, feast, festival, fanatic, profane, atheism,_ and _enthusiasm._

dhēs-. Root of words in religious concepts. Contracted from _dheəs-._ Possibly an extension of **dhē-.** **1.** Suffixed form _*dhēs-yā._ FAIR[2], FERIA, from Latin _fēriae_ (< Old Latin _fēsiae_), holidays. **2.** Suffixed form _*dhēs-to-._ FEAST, (-FEST), (FESTAL), FESTIVAL,

FESTIVE, (FESTOON), (FETE), (FIESTA); (GABFEST), OKTOBERFEST, from Latin *fēstus,* festive. **3.** Suffixed zero-grade form **dhəs-no-.* FANATIC; PROFANE, from Latin *fānum,* temple. **4.** Suffixed zero-grade form **dhəs-o-.* THEO-; APOTHEOSIS, ATHEISM, ENTHUSIASM, PANTHEON, POLYTHEISM, from Greek *theos* (< **thes-os*), god. [Pokorny *dhēs-* 259.]

dheu-[1]. An important derivative is *dew.*

dheu-[1]. To flow. **a.** DEW, from Old English *dēaw,* dew; **b.** SUNDEW, from Middle Dutch *dau,* dew; **c.** (see **melit-**) Germanic compound **melith-dauwaz,* "honeydew." **a, b,** and **c** all from Germanic **dauwaz,* dew. [Pokorny 1. *dheu-* 259.]

dheu-[2]. Important derivatives are *dead, death, die[1],* and *dwindle.*

dheu-[2]. To die. **1.** Suffixed o-grade form **dhou-to-.* DEAD, from Old English *dēad,* dead, from Germanic **daudaz.* **2.** Suffixed o-grade form **dhou-tu-.* DEATH, from Old English *dēath,* death, from Germanic **dauthuz.* **3.** Suffixed o-grade form **dhow-yo-.* DIE[1], from Old Norse *deyja,* to die. **4.** Suffixed extended zero-grade form **dhwī-no-.* DWINDLE, from Old English *dwīnan,* to diminish, languish, from Germanic **dwīnan.* [Pokorny 2. *dheu-* 260.] See **dhū-no-.**

dheub-. Important derivatives are *deep, depth, dip,* and *dive.*

dheub-. Deep, hollow. **1.** DEEP, (DEPTH), from Old English *dēop,* deep, from Germanic **deupaz.* **2.** DIP, from Old English *dyppan,* to immerse, dip, from Germanic expressive denominative **duppjan.* **3.** Parallel root form **dheubh-.* DIVE, from Old English *dȳfan,* to dip, and *dūfan,* to sink, dive, from Germanic verb **dūbjan,* from **deub-, *dub-.* [Pokorny *dheu-b-* 267.]

dheugh-. Derivatives are *doughty* and *Pentateuch.*

dheugh-. To produce something of utility. **1.** DOUGHTY, from Old English *dyhtig, dohtig,* strong (< "productive"), from Germanic extended form **duht-.* **2.** Suffixed form **dheugh-os-.* HEPTATEUCH, (HEXATEUCH), PENTATEUCH, from Greek *teukhos* (< **theukhos*), gear, anything produced, tool, container, scroll. [Pokorny *dheugh-* 271.]

dhghem-. Important derivatives are *bridegroom, chamomile, humble, homage, homicide,* and *human.*

dhghem-. Earth. **1.** Suffixed zero-grade form **(dh)ghm̥-on-,* "earthling." BRIDEGROOM, from Old English *guma,* man, from Germanic **gumōn-.* **2.** O-grade form **dh(e)ghom-.* CHTHONIC; AUTOCHTHON, from Greek *khthōn,* earth. **3.** Zero-grade form **dhghm̥-.* CHAMAEPHYTE, CHAMELEON, CHAMOMILE, GERMANDER, from Greek *khamai,* on the ground. **4.** Suffixed o-grade form **(dh)ghom-o-.* HUMBLE, (HUMILIATE), (HUMILITY), HUMUS[1]; EXHUME, INHUME, TRANSHUMANCE, from Latin *humus,* earth. **5.** Suffixed o-grade form **(dh)ghom-on-,* "earthling." **a.** HOMAGE, HOMBRE[1], HOMINID, HOMO[1], HOMUNCULUS, OMBRE; BONHOMIE, HOMICIDE, from Latin *homō,* human being, man; **b.** HUMAN, (HUMANE), from Latin *hūmānus,* human, kind, humane (in part from **dhghem-**). **6.** Suffixed form **(dh)ghem-yā.* CHERNOZEM, SIEROZEM, ZEMSTVO, from Old Russian *zemĭ,* land, earth. **7.** Full-grade form **(dh)ghem-.* ZAMINDAR, from Persian *zamīn,* earth, land. [Pokorny *ĝhđem-* 414.]

dhgh(y)es-. An important derivative is *yesterday.*

dhgh(y)es-. Yesterday. Suffixed (comparative) form **(dh)ghes-ter-.* YESTER-, (YESTERDAY), from Old English *geostran, giestran,* "yester-," from Germanic **ges-ter-.* [Pokorny *ĝhđi̯es* 416.]

dhīgʷ-. Important derivatives are *dike[1], ditch, dig, fix,* and *prefix.*

dhīgʷ-. To stick, fix. **1.a.** DIKE[1], DITCH, from Old English *dīc,* trench, moat; **b.** DIG, from Middle English *diggen,* to dig, from a source perhaps akin to Old French *digue,* trench. Both **a** and **b** from Germanic **dīk-.* **2.** FIBULA, FICHU, FINCA, FIX, (FIXATE), (FIXITY), (FIXTURE); AFFIX, ANTEFIX, CRUCIFY, INFIX, MICROFICHE, PREFIX, SUFFIX, TRANSFIX, from Latin *fīgere,* to fasten, fix. [Pokorny *dhēigᵘ-* 243.]

dhreg-. Important derivatives are *drink, drench,* and *drown.*

dhreg-. To draw, glide. **1.** DRINK, from Old English *drincan,* to drink, from nasalized Germanic form **drenkan,* to draw into the mouth, drink. **2.** DRENCH, from Old English *drencan,* to soak, from nasalized o-grade Germanic causative form **drankjan,* "to cause to drink." **3.** DROWN, from a Scandinavian or late Old English source similar to Old Norse *drukkna,* to drown, from Germanic zero-grade suffixed form **drunk-nōn.* [Pokorny *dhreĝ-* 273.]

dhreibh-. Important derivatives are *drive* and *drift.*

dhreibh-. To drive, push; snow. **1.** DRIVE, DROVE[2], from Old English *drīfan,* to drive, rush, from Germanic **drīban.* **2.** DRIFT, from Middle English *drift,* drove, herd, akin to Old Norse *drift,* snowdrift, and Middle Dutch *drift,* herd, from Germanic zero-grade suffixed form **driftiz.* [Pokorny *dhreibh-* 274.]

dhreu-. Important derivatives are *drizzle, dreary, drowse, drop, droop,* and *drip.*

dhreu-. To fall, flow, drip, droop. **1.** Extended form **dhreus-.* DRIZZLE, from Old English *-drysnian* (in *gedrysnian,* to pass away, vanish), from zero-grade Germanic derived verb **drus-inōn.* **2.** Extended o-grade form **dhrous-.* **a.** DREARY, from Old English *drēor,* flowing blood, from Germanic **drauzaz;* **b.** DROWSE, from Old English *drūsian,* to be sluggish, from Germanic **drūsjan.* **3.** Extended zero-grade form **dhrub-.* **a.** DROP, from Old English *dropa,* drop, from Germanic **drupan;* **b.** DROOP, from Old Norse *drūpa,* to hang down, from Germanic **drūpōn,* to let fall; **c.** DRIP, from Middle English *drippen,* to drip, drop, from an unattested Old English **dryppan* or another source akin to Old English *droppa,* drop, from Germanic geminated **drupp-.* **4.** Suffixed zero-grade form **dhrubh-yo-.* LITHOTRIPTER, (LITHOTRITY), from Greek *thruptein,* to crumble. [Pokorny *dhreu-* 274.]

dhughəter-. An important derivative is *daughter.*

dhughəter-. Daughter. DAUGHTER, from Old English *dohtor,* daughter, from Germanic **dohtēr.* [Pokorny *dhug(h)əter-* 277.]

dhū-no-. Important derivatives are *down[1], dune,* and *town.*

dhū-no-. Enclosed, fortified place. Derivative of a verb **dhuə-,* "to close, finish," probably related to **dheu-[2],** "to die." **1.a.** DOWN[1], DOWN[3], from Old English *dūn,* hill; **b.** DUNE, from Middle Dutch *dūne,* sandy hill. Both **a** and **b** from Germanic **dūnaz,* possibly from **dhū-no-.** **2.** TOWN, from Old English *tūn,* enclosed place, homestead, village, from Germanic **tūnaz,* fortified place, borrowed from Celtic **dūn-o-,* hill, stronghold. [In Pokorny 4. *dheu-* 261.]

dhwer-. Important derivatives are *door, foreign, forest, forfeit,* and *forum.*

dhwer-. Door, doorway (usually in plural). Originally an apophonic noun **dhwor, *dhur-,* in the plural, designating the entrance to the enclosure (**dhwor-o-*) surrounding the house proper. **1.** Zero-grade form **dhur-* in suffixed forms **dhur-n̥s* (accusative plural) and **dhur-o-* (neuter). DOOR, from Old English *duru,* door (feminine, originally plural), and *dor,* door (neuter), respectively from Germanic **durunz* and **duram.* **2.** Suffixed o-grade form **dhwor-āns* (accusative plural). FOREIGN, from Latin *forās,* (toward) out of doors, outside. **3.** Suffixed o-grade form **dhwor-ois* (locative plural). FOREST; (AFFOREST), FAUBOURG, FORECLOSE, FORFEIT, from Latin *forīs,* (being) out of doors. **4.** Suffixed o-grade form **dhwor-o-.* FORENSIC, FORUM, from Latin *forum,* marketplace (originally the enclosed space around a home). **5.** DURBAR, from Old Persian *duvara-,* door, gate. **6.** Zero-grade form **dhur-.* THYROID, from Greek *thura,* door. [Pokorny *dhu̯ĕr-* 278.]

dn̥ghū-. Important derivatives are *tongue, language,* and *linguist.*

dn̥ghū-. Tongue. **1.a.** TONGUE, from Old English *tunge,* tongue; **b.** BILTONG, from Middle Dutch *tonghe,* tongue. Both **a** and **b** from Germanic **tungōn-.* **2.** LANGUAGE, LANGUET, LIGULA, LIGULE, LINGO, LINGUA, LINGUIST; (BILINGUAL), from Latin *lingua* (< Old Latin *dingua*), tongue, language. [Pokorny *dn̥ghū* 223.]

dō-. Important derivatives are *date, add, betray, edition, rent[1], surrender, tradition, traitor, vend, donation, pardon, endow, dose,* and *antidote.*

dō-. To give. Contracted from **doə-.* **1.a.** Zero-grade form **də-.* DADO, DATE[1], DATIVE, DATUM, DIE[2]; ADD, (BETRAY), EDITION, PERDITION, RENDER, (RENT[1]), (SURRENDER), TRADITION, (TRAITOR), (TREASON), VEND, from Latin *dare,* to give; **b.** (see **4**) Greek *dosis,* something given. **2.** Suffixed form **dō-no-.* DONATION, (DONATIVE), (DONOR); CONDONE, PARDON, from Latin *dōnum,* gift. **3.** Suffixed form **dō-t(i)-.* **a.** DOT[2], DOWAGER, DOWER, (DOWRY); ENDOW, from Latin *dōs* (genitive *dōtis*), dowry; **b.** DACHA, from Russian *dacha,* gift, dacha, from Slavic **datja;* **c.** SAMIZDAT, from Russian *samizdat,* samizdat, from *dat',* to give. **4.** Suffixed form **dō-ro-.* LOBSTER THERMIDOR, from Greek *dōron,* gift. **5.** Reduplicated form **di-dō-.* DOSE; ANECDOTE, ANTIDOTE, APODOSIS, EPIDOTE, from Greek *didonai,* to give, with zero-grade noun *dosis* (< **də-ti-*), something given. [Pokorny *dō-* 223.]

dus-. A derivative is *dys-.*

dus-. Bad, evil; mis- (used as a prefix). Derivative of **deu-[1].** DYS-, from Greek *dus-,* bad. [Pokorny *dus-* 227.]

dwo-. Important derivatives are *two, twelve, twilight, biscuit, twist, twice, twenty, twine, between, twin, binary, combine, twig[1], diploma, deuce[1], dozen, dual, duet, double, duplicate, doubt,* and *dubious.*

dwo-. Two.
I. Variant form **duwo.* **1.a.** TWO, from Old English *twā,* two (nominative feminine and neuter); **b.** TWAIN, from Old English *twēgen,* two (nominative and accusative masculine). Both **a** and **b** from Germanic **twa,* two. **2.** TWELFTH, TWELVE, from Old English *twelf,* twelve, and *twelfta,* twelfth, from Germanic compound **twa-lif-,* "two left (over from ten)," twelve (**-lif-,* left; see **leikʷ-**).
II. Adverbial form **dwis* and combining form **dwi-.* **1.a.** TWIBILL, TWILIGHT, from Old English *twi-,* two; **b.** ZWIEBACK, ZWITTERION, from Old High German *zwi-,* twice. Both **a** and **b** from Germanic **twi-.* **2.** BI-[1], BIS; BALANCE, BAROUCHE, BEZEL, BISCUIT, from Latin *bis* (combining form *bi-*), twice. **3.** DI-[1], from Greek *dis* (combining form *di-*), twice. **4.** TWIST, from Old English *-twist,* divided object, fork, rope, from Germanic **twis.* **5.** TWICE, from Old English *twige, twiga,* twice, from Germanic **twiyes.* **6.** TWENTY, from Old English *twēntig,* twenty, from Germanic compound **twēgentig,* "twice ten" (**-tig,* ten; see **dekm̥**). **7.** TWINE, from Old English *twīn,* double thread, from Germanic **twīhna,* double thread, twisted thread. **8.** BETWEEN, BETWIXT, (TWIXT), from Old English *betwēonum* and *betweox, betwix,* between, from Germanic compounds **bi-twīhna* and **bi-twisk,* "at the middle point of two" (*bi,* at, by; see **ambhi**). **9.** TWILL, from Old English *twilic,* woven of double thread, from Germanic compound **twilic-,* "two-threaded fabric." **10.** Suffixed form **dwis-no-.* **a.** TWIN, from Old English *twinn, getwinn,* two by two, twin, from Germanic **twisnaz,* double; **b.** BI-, BINAL, BINARY; COMBINE, from Latin *bīnī,* two by two, two each. **11.** Suffixed form **dwi-ko-.* TWIG[1], from Old English *twigge,* a branch, from Germanic **twig(g)a,* a fork. **12.** Compound **dwi-plo-,* twofold (**-plo-,* -fold; see **pel-[2]**). DIPLO-, DIPLOE, DIPLOID, DIPLOMA; ANADIPLOSIS, from Greek *diploos, diplous,* twofold. **13.** Suffixed reduplicated form **dwi-du-mo-.* DIDYMIUM, DIDYMOUS; EPIDIDYMIS, TETRADYMITE, from Greek *didumos,* double, the testicles. **14.** Suffixed form **dwi-gha.* DICHASIUM, DICHO-, from Greek *dikha,* in two.
III. Inflected form **duwō.* **1.** DEUCE[1], DOZEN, DUAL, DUET, DUO, DUO-; DUODECIMAL, from Latin *duo,* two. **2.** DUAD, DYAD; DODECAGON, HENDIADYS, from Greek *duo, duō,* two.
IV. Variant form **du-.* **1.** Compound **du-plo-,* twofold (**-plo-,* -fold; see **pel-[2]**). DOUBLE, (DOUBLET), DOUBLOON, DUPLE, from Latin *duplus,* double. **2.** Compound **du-plek-,* twofold (**-plek-,* -fold; see **plek-**). DUPLEX, DUPLICATE, DUPLICITY; CONDUPLICATE, from Latin *duplex,* double. **3.** Suffixed form **du-bhw-io-.* DOUBT, DUBIOUS; (REDOUBTABLE), from Latin *dubius,* doubtful (< "hesitating between two alternatives"), and *dubitāre,* to be in doubt. [Pokorny *du̯ō(u)-* 228.]

ed-. Important derivatives are *eat, etch,* and *edible.*

ed-. To eat; original meaning "to bite." See **dent-. 1.a.** EAT, from Old English *etan,* to eat; **b.** ETCH, from Old High German *ezzen,* to feed on, eat; **c.** ORT, from Middle Dutch *eten,* to eat; **d.** FRET[1], from Old English *fretan,* to devour, from Germanic compound **fra-etan,* to eat up (**fra-,* completely; see **per[1]**). **a, b, c,** and **d** all from Germanic **etan.* **2.** EDACIOUS, EDIBLE, ESCAROLE, ESCULENT, ESURIENT; COMEDO, COMESTIBLE, OBESE, from Latin *edere,* to eat. **3.** PRANDIAL, from Latin compound *prandium* (syncopated from **pram-ed-ium*), "first meal," lunch (**pram-,* first; see **per[1]**). **4.** Suffixed form **ed-un-ā.* ANODYNE, PLEURODYNIA, from Greek *odunē,* pain (< "gnawing care"). **5.** SAMOYED, from Russian *-ed,* eater. [Pokorny *ed-* 287.]

eg. Important derivatives are *I* and *ego.*

eg. I. Nominative form of the personal pronoun of the first person singular. For oblique forms see **me-[1]. 1.** I, from Old English *ic,* I, from Germanic **ek.* **2.** Extended form **egō.* EGO, (EGOIST), (EGOTISM), from Latin *ego,* I. [Pokorny *eĝ-* 291.]

eghs. Important derivatives are *ex-, exotic, external, extra-, strange,* and *extreme.*

eghs. Out. **1.** Variant **eks.* **a.** EX[1], EX-, from Latin *ex, ex-,* out of, away from; **b.** ECTO-, EXO-, EXOTERIC, EXOTIC; ELECTUARY, SYNECDOCHE, from Greek *ex, ek,* out of, from. **2.** Suffixed (comparative) variant form **eks-tero-.* EXTERIOR, EXTERNAL, EXTRA-, STRANGE, from Latin *exter,* outward (feminine ablative *exterā, extrā,* on the outside). **3.** Suffixed (superlative) form. EXTREME, from Latin *extrēmus,* outermost (**-mo-,* superlative suffix). **4.** Suffixed form **eghs-ko-.* ESCHATOLOGY, from Greek *eskhatos,* outermost, last. **5.** EISTEDDFOD, from Welsh *eistedd,* sitting, from Celtic **eks-dī-sedo-.* **6.** SAMIZDAT, from Russian *iz,* from, out of, from Balto-Slavic **iz.* [Pokorny *eĝhs* 292.]

ēg^{w}h-. A derivative is *inebriate.*

ēg^{w}h-. To drink. Suffixed form **ēg^{w}h-r-yo-.* **a.** INEBRIATE, from Latin *ēbrius,* drunk; **b.** (see **s(w)e-**) Latin compound *sōbrius* (*sē,* without).

ei-. Important derivatives are *ambition, circuit, exit[2], issue, perish, sudden, transit, ion, commence, initial, janitor,* and *January.*

ei-. To go. **1.** Full-grade form **ei-.* **a.** ADIT, AMBIENT, (AMBITION), CIRCUIT, COITUS, COMITIA, EXIT, INTROIT, ISSUE, OBITUARY, PERISH, PRAETOR, PRETERIT, SEDITION, (SUBITO), SUDDEN, (TRANCE), TRANSIENT, (TRANSIT), (TRANSITIVE), from Latin *īre,* to go; **b.** ION; ANION, CATION, DYSPROSIUM, from Greek *ienai,* to go. **2.** Suffixed zero-grade form **i-t-.* **a.** further suffixed form **i-t-yo-.* COMMENCE, INITIAL, INITIATE, from Latin *initium,* entrance, beginning (*in-,* in; see **en**); **b.** COUNT[2], COUNTY; CONCOMITANT, CONSTABLE, (VISCOUNT), from Latin *comes* (stem *comit-*), companion (< "one who goes with another"; *com-,* with; see **kom**). **3.** Suffixed form **i-ter.* ERRANT, EYRE, ITINERANT, ITINERARY, from Latin *iter,* journey. **4.** Extended form **yā-* (< **yaə-*) in suffixed forms **yā-no-, *yā-nu-.* **a.** JANITOR, JANUARY, JANUS, from Latin *iānus,* archway, and *Iānus,* god of doors and of the beginning of a year; **b.** HINAYANA, MAHAYANA, from Sanskrit *yānam,* way (in Buddhism, "mode of knowledge," "vehicle"). [Pokorny 1. *ei-* 293.]

ēik-. Important derivatives are *ought[1], owe, own,* and *freight.*

ēik-. To be master of, possess. **1.** OUGHT[1], OWE, from Old English *āgan,* to possess, from Germanic **aigan,* to possess. **2.** OWN, from Old English *āgen,* one's own, from Germanic participial form **aiganaz,* possessed, owned. **3.** FRAUGHT, FREIGHT, from Middle Low German and Middle Dutch *vrecht, vracht,* "earnings," hire for a ship, freight, from Germanic prefixed form **fra-aihtiz,* absolute possession, property (**fra-,* intensive prefix; see **per[1]**). [Pokorny *ēik-* 298.]

eis-. Important derivatives are *irate, hierarchy,* and *iron.*

eis-. In words denoting passion. **1.** Suffixed form **eis-ā-.* IRASCIBLE, IRATE, IRE, from Latin *īra,* anger. **2.** Suffixed zero-grade form **is-(ə)ro-,* powerful, holy. HIERATIC, HIERO-; HIERARCH, (HIERARCHY), HIEROGLYPHIC, HIEROPHANT, from Greek *hieros,* "filled with the divine," holy. **3.a.** IRON, from Old English *īse(r)n, īren,* iron; **b.** GISARME, SPIEGELEISEN, from Old High German *īsarn, īsan,* iron. Both **a** and **b** from Germanic **īsarno-,* "holy metal" (possibly from Celtic). **4.** Suffixed o-grade form **ois-tro-,* madness. ESTRUS; (ESTRONE), from Greek *oistros,* gadfly, goad, anything causing madness. [Pokorny 1. *eis-* 299.]

ekwo-. Derivatives are *equestrian* and *hippopotamus.*

ekwo-. Horse. Probably originally derived from **ōku-. 1.** EQUESTRIAN, EQUINE, EQUITANT, (EQUITATION); EQUISETUM, from Latin *equus,* horse. **2.** EOHIPPUS, HIPPOCAMPUS, HIPPOCRENE, HIPPODROME, HIPPOGRIFF, HIPPOPOTAMUS, from Greek *hippos,* horse. [Pokorny *eḱu̯o-s* 301.]

el-. An important derivative is *elbow.*

el-. Elbow, forearm. Extended o-grade form **olinā,* elbow. **a.** ELL[2], from Old English *eln,* forearm, cubit, from Germanic **alinō;* **b.** ELBOW, from Old English *elnboga,* elbow, from Germanic compound **alino-bugōn-,* "bend of the forearm," elbow (**bugōn-,* bend, bow; see **bheug-**); **c.** ULNA, from Latin *ulna,* forearm; **d.** lengthened variant form **ōlenā-.* OLECRANON, from Greek *ōlenē,* elbow. [Pokorny 8. *el-* 307.]

em-. Important derivatives are *example, exempt, premium, prompt, ransom, redeem, sample, vintage, assume, consume,* and *resume.*

em-. To take, distribute. **1.** ADEMPTION, EXAMPLE, (EXEMPLARY), (EXEMPLIFY), (EXEMPLUM), (EXEMPT), (IMPROMPTU), PEREMPTORY, PREEMPTION, PREMIUM, PROMPT, (RANSOM), REDEEM, (REDEMPTION), (SAMPLE), VINTAGE, from Latin *emere,* to obtain, buy. **2.** SUMPTUARY, (SUMPTUOUS); ASSUME, CONSUME, PRESUME, RESUME, SUBSUME, from Latin *sūmere* (< **sus(e)m-*), to take, obtain, buy (*sus-,* variant of *sub-,* up from under; see **upo**). [Pokorny *em-* 310.]

en. Important derivatives are *in[1], inner, en-[1], intro-, enter, intimate[2], industry, episode,* and *and.*

en. In. **1.a.** IN[1] (preposition), from Old English *in,* in; **b.** IN[1] (adverb), from Old English *inn,* into, *inne,* inside; **c.** INN, from Old English *inn,* habitation, inn; **d.** TSIMMES, from Old High German *in,* in; **e.** INNER, from Old English *innera,* farther in, inner, from Germanic (comparative) **inn(e)ra;* **f.** *(i)* BEN, from Old English *binnan,* within; *(ii)* BILANDER, from Middle Dutch *binnen,* within (*be,* by; see **ambhi** + *innan,* in, within). Both *(i)* and *(ii)* from Germanic **innan.* **a, b, c, d, e,** and **f** all from Germanic **in.* **2.** EN-[1], IN-[2], from Latin *in, in-,* in, into. **3.** EN-[2]; ENKEPHALIN, PARENCHYMA, PARENTHESIS, from Greek *en, en-.* **4.** Suffixed form **en-t(e)ro-.* **a.** INTRO-; INTRODUCE, INTROIT, INTROMIT, INTRORSE, INTROSPECT, from Latin *intrō,* inward, within; **b.** ENTER, INTRA-; (INTRADOS), from Latin *intrā,* inside, within; **c.** INTERIM, INTRINSIC, from Latin *interim,* meanwhile, with ablative suffix *-im; intrīnsecus,* on the inside, from *int(e)rim* + *secus,* alongside (see **sek^{w}-[1]**). **5.** Suffixed form **en-ter.* ENTRAILS, INTER-, INTERIOR, INTERNAL, from Latin *inter, inter-,* between, among. **6.** INTIMA, INTIMATE[2], from Latin (superlative) *intimus,* innermost (**-mo-,* superlative suffix). **7.** Extended form **en-do.* **a.** INDUSTRY, from Latin *industrius,* diligent (**stru-,* to construct; see **ster-[2]**); **b.** INDIGENT, from Latin *indigēre,* to be in need (*egēre,* to be in need). Both **a** and **b** from *indu-,* within, from Old Latin *endo;* **c.** ENDO-, from Greek *endo, endo-,* within. **8.** Suffixed form **en-tos.* **a.** DEDANS, INTESTINE, INTINE, INTUSSUSCEPTION, from Latin *intus,* within, inside; **b.** ENTO-, from Greek *entos,* within. **9.** Suffixed form **en-tero-.* (ENTERIC), ENTERO-, ENTERON; DYSENTERY, EXENTERATE, MESENTERY, from Greek *enteron,* intestine. **10.** Extended form **ens.* **a.** EPISODE, from Greek *eis,* into; **b.** suffixed form **ens-ō.* ESOTERIC, from Greek *esō,* within. **11.** Possibly suffixed zero-grade form **n̥-dha.* AND, from Old English *and,* and, from Germanic **anda, *unda.* [Pokorny 1. *en* 311.]

epi. An important derivative is *epi-.*

epi. Also **opi.** Near, at, against. **1.** OB-, from Latin *ob, ob-,* before, to, against. **2.** EPI-, from Greek *epi,* on, over, at. **3.** OPISTHOBRANCH, OPISTHOGNATHOUS, from Greek *opisthen,* behind, at the back. **4.** Zero-grade **pi,* on. (see **sed-**) Greek *piezein,* to press tight. **5.** OBLAST, from Russian *oblast',* oblast, from Old Church Slavonic *ob,* on. **6.** Prefix **op-* in **op-wer-yo-,* to cover over (see **wer-[4]**). [Pokorny *epi* 323.]

er-[1]. Important derivatives are *are[1], earnest[1], orient, origin, original,* and *abort.*

er-[1]. To move, set in motion. **1.** ARE[1], ART[2], from Old English *eart* and *aron,* second person singular and plural present of *bēon,* to be, from Germanic **ar-, *or-, *art(a),* to be, exist, probably from **er-[1]. 2.** EARNEST[1], from Old English *eornoste,* zealous, serious, from Germanic suffixed form **er-n-os-ti-,* perhaps from **er-[1]. 3.** Suffixed form **or-yo-.* ORIENT, ORIGIN, (ORIGINAL); ABORT, from Latin *orīrī,* to arise, appear, be born. **4.** Suffixed form **or-smā-.* HORMONE, from Greek *hormē,* impulse, onrush. [Pokorny 3. *er-* 326; *ergh-* 339.]

er-[2]. An important derivative is *earth.*

er-[2]. Earth, ground. Extended form **ert-.* **a.** EARTH, from Old English *eorthe,* earth; **b.** AARDVARK, AARDWOLF, from Middle Dutch *aerde, eerde,* earth. Both **a** and **b** from Germanic **erthō.* [Pokorny 4. *er-* 332.]

erə-. Important derivatives are *row[2]* and *rudder.*

erə-. To row. **1.** Variant form **rē-* (< **reə-*). **a.** ROW[2], from Old English *rōwan,* to row, from Germanic **rō-;* **b.** suffixed form **rō-tro-.* RUDDER, RUSSIAN, from Old English *rōther* and Old Norse *rōdhr,* steering oar, both from Germanic **rōthra,* rudder; **c.** suffixed form **rē-smo-.* BIREME, REMEX, TRIREME, from Latin *rēmus,* oar. **2.** Oldest variant form **əreə-* becoming **erē-.* TRIERARCH, from Greek *triērēs,* trireme. [Pokorny 1. *erə-* 338.]

ers-. Important derivatives are *race[2], erratic,* and *error.*

ers-. To be in motion. **1.** Variant form **rēs-.* RACE[2], from Old Norse *rās,* rushing, from Germanic **rēs-.* **2.** Form **ers-ā-.* ERR, ERRATIC, ERRATUM, ERRONEOUS, ERROR; ABERRATION, from Latin *errāre,* to wander. [Pokorny 2. *ere-s-* 336.]

es-. Important derivatives are *am[1], is, yes, soothe, sin[1], essence, absent, interest, present[1],* and *proud.*

es-. To be. **1.** Athematic first person singular form **es-mi.* AM[1], from Old English *eam, eom,* am, from Germanic **izm(i).* **2.** Athematic third person singular form **es-ti.* IS, from Old English *is,* is, from Germanic **ist(i).* **3.** Optative stem **sī-.* YES, from Old English *gēse,* yes, (*gēa,* yea; see **i-** + *sīe*), from *sīe,* may it be (so), from Germanic **sijai-.* **4.** Participial form **sont-,* being, existing, hence real, true. **a.** SOOTH, SOOTHE, from Old English *sōth,* true, from Germanic **santhaz;* **b.** suffixed (collective) zero-grade form **sn̥t-yā,* "that which is." SIN[1], from Old English *synn,* sin, from Germanic **sun(d)jō,* sin (< "it is true," "the sin is real"); **c.** SUTTEE; BODHISATTVA, SATYAGRAHA, from Sanskrit *sat-, sant-,* existing, true, virtuous. **5.** Basic form **es-.* ENTITY, ESSENCE; ABSENT, (IMPROVE), INTEREST, OSSIA, PRESENT[1], (PRESENT[2]), PROUD, (QUINTESSENCE), (REPRESENT), from Latin *esse,* to be. **6.** Basic form **es-.* -ONT, ONTO-; (-BIONT), HOMOIOUSIAN, PAROUSIA, (SCHIZONT), from Greek *einai* (present participle *ont-,* being), to be (in *pareinai,* to be present). **7.** Suffixed form **es-ti-.* SWASTIKA, from Sanskrit *svas-ti-,* "well-being" (see **su-**). [Pokorny *es-* 340.] See extension **(e)su-.**

(e)su-. A derivative is *eu-.*

(e)su-. Good. Suffixed form of **es-.** EU-, from Greek *eu-,* well, combining form of *eus,* good. [Pokorny *esu-s* 342.] See **su-.**

eu-[1]. A derivative is *endue.*

eu-[1]. To dress. **1.** ENDUE, from Latin *induere,* to don (*ind-,* variant of *in-,* in, on; see **en**). **2.** EXUVIAE, from Latin *exuere,* to doff (*ex-,* off; see **eghs**). **3.** REDUVIID, from Latin *reduvia,* fragment (*red-,* back, in reverse; see **re-**). [Pokorny 2. *eu-* 346.] See extension **wes-[2].**

eu-[2]. Important derivatives are *wane, want, vanish,*

vacant, vacation, vacuum, void, avoid, evacuate, and _waste._

eu-[2]. Lacking, empty. Extended forms _*euə-, *wā-, *wə-._ **1.** Suffixed form _*wə-no-._ **a.** WANE, from Old English _wanian,_ to lessen, and _wana,_ lack, from Germanic _*wanēn;_ **b.** WANT, from Old Norse _vanta,_ to lack, from North Germanic _*wanatōn._ **2.** Suffixed form _*wā-no-._ VAIN, VANITY, VAUNT; EVANESCE, VANISH, from Latin _vānus,_ empty. **3.** Extended form _*wak-._ VACANT, VACATE, VACATION, (VACUITY), VACUUM, VOID; (AVOID), (DEVOID), EVACUATE, from Latin _vacāre_ (variant _vocāre_), to be empty. **4.** Extended and suffixed form _*wās-to-._ WASTE; DEVASTATE, from Latin _vāstus,_ empty, waste. [Pokorny 1. _eu-_ 345.]

euə-dh-r̥. Derivatives are _udder_ and _exuberant._

euə-dh-r̥. Udder. Related to **wē-r-**. **1.** Suffixed zero-grade form _*ūdh-r̥._ UDDER, from Old English _ūder,_ udder, from Germanic _*ūdr-._ **2.** Suffixed o-grade form _*oudh-r̥._ (EXUBERANT), EXUBERATE, from Latin adjective _ūber,_ fertile, derived from _ūber,_ "breast." [Pokorny _ēudh-_ 347.]

gal-. Important derivatives are _call_ and _clatter._

gal-. To call, shout. **1.** CALL, from Old Norse _kalla,_ to call, from Germanic expressive form _*kall-._ **2.** CLATTER, from Old English _*clatrian,_ to clatter, from Germanic _*klat-._ **3.** Expressive form _*gall-._ GALLINACEOUS, (GALLINULE), from Latin _gallus,_ cock (< "the calling bird"; but probably also associated with _Gallus,_ Gallic, as if to mean "the bird of Gaul," the cock being archaeologically attested as an important symbol in the iconography of Roman and pre-Roman Gaul). **4.** Suffixed form _*gal-so-._ GLASNOST, from a Slavic source akin to Old Church Slavonic _glasŭ,_ voice. **5.** Reduplicated form _gal-gal-._ GLAGOLITIC, from a Slavic source akin to Old Church Slavonic _glagolu,_ word. [Pokorny 2. _gal-_ 350.]

gāu-. Important derivatives are _gaudy[1], joy, enjoy,_ and _rejoice._

gāu-. To rejoice; also to have religious fear or awe. Contracted from _*gaəu-._ **1.** Suffixed form _*gau-d-ē-._ GAUD, (GAUDY[1]), GAUDY[2], JOY; ENJOY, REJOICE, from Latin _gaudēre,_ to rejoice. **2.** Form (with nasal infix) _*gə-n-u-._ GANOID, from Greek _ganusthai,_ to rejoice. [Pokorny _gāu-_ 353.]

gel-. Important derivatives are _chill, cold, cool, jelly,_ and _glacier._

gel-. Cold; to freeze. **1.** CHILL, from Old English _c(i)ele,_ chill, from Germanic _*kaliz,_ coldness. **2.** COLD, from Old English _ceald,_ cold, from Germanic _*kaldaz,_ cold. **3.a.** COOL, from Old English _cōl,_ cold, cool; **b.** KEEL[3], from Old English _cēlan,_ to cool, from Germanic _*kōljan,_ to cool. Both **a** and **b** from Germanic _*kōl-,_ cool. **4.** Suffixed form _*gel-ā-._ GELATIN, GELATION, JELLY; CONGEAL, from Latin _gelāre,_ to freeze. **5.** Suffixed form _*gel-u-._ GELID, from Latin _gelū,_ frost, cold. **6.** Probably suffixed zero-grade form _*gl̥-k-._ (GLACÉ), GLACIAL, GLACIATE, GLACIER, GLACIS, from Latin _glaciēs,_ ice. [Pokorny 3. _gel(ə)-_ 365.]

gembh-. Important derivatives are _comb, unkempt,_ and _gem._

gembh-. Tooth, nail.
I. Suffixed o-grade form _*gombh-o-._ **1.a.** COMB, KAME, from Old English _comb, camb,_ comb; **b.** CAM, from Dutch _kam,_ cog, comb; **c.** UNKEMPT, from Old English _cemban,_ to comb, from Germanic denominative _*kambjan,_ to comb. **a, b,** and **c** all from Germanic _*kambaz,_ comb. **2.** GOMPHOSIS, from Greek _gomphos,_ tooth, peg, bolt.
II. Suffixed zero-grade form _*gm̥bh-ō/n-._ OAKUM, from Old English _ā-cumba,_ oakum.
III. CHIME[2], from Old English _cim-, cimb-,_ rim (only in compounds), from Germanic _*kimb-,_ perhaps from **gembh-**.
IV. Possibly suffixed form _*gembh-mā._ GEM, GEMMA, GEMMATE, GEMMULE, from Latin _gemma,_ bud, hence gem. [Pokorny _ĝembh-_ 369.]

gemə-. Derivatives are _gamete, -gamous,_ and _-gamy._

gemə-. To marry. Suffixed zero-grade form _*gm̥ə-o-._ GAMETE, GAMO-, -GAMOUS, -GAMY, from Greek _gamos,_ marriage. [Pokorny _ĝem(e)-_ 369.]

genə-. Important derivatives are _kin, king, kind[1], kind[2], gentle, general, generate, genius, engine, genuine, germ, genital, pregnant, nation, native,_ and _nature._

genə-. Also **gen-**. To give birth, beget; with derivatives referring to aspects and results of procreation and to familial and tribal groups. **1.** Suffixed zero-grade form _*gn̥-yo-._ **a.** KIN; KINDRED, from Old English _cyn(n),_ race, family, kin; **b.** KING, from Old English _cyning,_ king, from Germanic _*kuningaz,_ king. Both **a** and **b** from Germanic _*kunjam,_ family. **2.** Suffixed zero-grade form _*gn̥-t-._ **a.** KIND[2], from Old English _cynd, gecynd(e),_ origin, birth, race, family, kind, from Germanic _*kundjaz,_ family, race; **b.** KIND[1], from Old English _gecynde,_ natural, native, fitting (_ge-,_ collective prefix; see **kom**), from Germanic _*kundiz,_ natural, native; **c.** Suffixed form _*gn̥-ti-._ GENS, (GENTEEL), (GENTILE), GENTLE; GENDARME, from Latin _gēns_ (stem _gent-_), race, clan; **d.** KINDERGARTEN, KRISS KRINGLE, from Old High German _kind,_ child, from Germanic secondary full-grade variant _*kentham._ **3.** Suffixed full-grade form _*gen-es-._ **a.** GENDER, GENERAL, GENERATE, (GENERATION), GENERIC, GENEROUS, GENRE, GENUS; CONGENER, DEGENERATE, (ENGENDER), MISCEGENATION, from Latin _genus_ (stem _gener-_), race, kind; **b.** GENE; ALLOGENEIC, GENEALOGY, GENOCIDE, GENOTYPE, HETEROGENEOUS, SYNGENEIC, from Greek _genos_ and _genea,_ race, family; **c.** -GEN, -GENY; EPIGENE, from Greek suffix _-genēs,_ "-born." **4.** Suffixed full-grade form _*gen-yo-._ **a.** GENIAL[1], GENIUS; (CONGENIAL), from Latin _genius,_ procreative divinity, inborn tutelary spirit, innate quality; **b.** ENGINE, INGENIOUS, from Latin _ingenium,_ inborn character (_in-,_ in; see **en**). **5.** Suffixed full-grade form _*gen-ā-._ INDIGEN, (INDIGENOUS), from Latin _indigena,_ born in (a place), indigenous (_indu-,_ within; see **en**). **6.** Suffixed full-grade form _*genə-wo-._ (GENUINE), INGENUOUS, from Latin _ingenuus,_ born in (a place), native, natural, freeborn (_in-,_ in; see **en**). **7.** Suffixed full-grade form _*gen-men-._ GERM, GERMAN[2], (GERMANE), GERMINAL, GERMINATE, from dissimilated Latin _germen,_ shoot, bud, embryo, germ. **8.** Suffixed secondary zero-grade form _*gnə-ti-._ GENESIS, -GENESIS, from Greek _genesis,_ birth, beginning. **9.** Reduplicated form _*gi-gn-._ GENITAL, GENITIVE, GENITOR, GENT[1], (GINGERLY); CONGENITAL, PRIMOGENITOR, PRIMOGENITURE, PROGENITOR, (PROGENY), from Latin _gignere_ (past participle _genitus_), to beget. **10.** Suffixed zero-grade form _*-gn-o-._ BENIGN, MALIGN, from Latin _benignus,_ good-natured, kindly (_bene,_ well; see **deu-[2]**), and _malignus,_ evil-natured, malevolent (_male,_ ill; see **mel-[3]**). **11.** Zero-grade form _*gn̥ə-_ becoming _*gnā-._ PREGNANT[1], from Latin _praegnās,_ pregnant (_prae-,_ before; see **per[1]**). **12.** Suffixed zero-grade form _*gn̥ə-sko-_ becoming _*gnā-sko-._ NAIVE, NASCENT, NATAL, NATION, NATIVE, NATURE, NÉE, NOËL; (ADNATE), AGNATE, COGNATE, CONNATE, ENATE, INNATE, NEONATE, PUISNE, (PUNY), RENAISSANCE, from Latin _gnāscī, nāscī_ (present participle _nāscēns,_ past participle _gnātus, nātus_), to be born. **13.** Suffixed o-grade form _*gon-o-._ GONAD, GONO-, -GONY; ARCHEGONIUM, EPIGONE, from Greek _gonos_ (combining form _-gonos_), child, procreation, seed. **14.** Zero-grade form _*gn̥-._ (see **kʷr̥mi-**) Sanskrit _kr̥mi-ja-,_ "produced by worms," from _ja-._ [Pokorny 1. _ĝen-_ 373.]

genu-[1]. Important derivatives are _knee, kneel,_ and _diagonal._

genu-[1]. Knee; also angle. **1.** Variant form _*gneu-._ **a.** KNEE, from Old English _cnēo,_ knee, from Germanic _*knewam;_ **b.** KNEEL, from Old English _cnēowlian,_ to kneel, from Germanic _*knewljan._ **2.** Basic form _*genu-._ GENICULATE, GENUFLECT, from Latin _genū,_ knee. **3.** O-grade form _*gonu._ POLYGONUM, PYCNOGONID, from Greek _gonu,_ knee. **4.** Suffixed variant form _*gōnw-yə-._ -GON, GONION; AMBLYGONITE, DIAGONAL, GONIOMETER, ORTHOGONAL, from Greek _gōnia,_ angle, corner. [Pokorny 1. _ĝenu-_ 380.]

genu-[2]. An important derivative is _chin._

genu-[2]. Jawbone, chin. **1.** Form _*genw-._ CHIN, from Old English _cin(n),_ chin, from Germanic _*kinnuz._ **2.** Basic form _*genu-._ GENIAL[2], from Greek _genus,_ jaw, chin. **3.** Suffixed variant form _*gnə-dho-._ GNATHAL, GNATHIC, -GNATHOUS; CHAETOGNATH, from Greek _gnathos,_ jaw. **4.** Variant form _*g(h)enu-._ HANUMAN, from Sanskrit _hanu,_ jaw. [Pokorny 2. _ĝenu-_ 381.]

ger-. Important derivatives are _cram, congregate, segregate,_ and _category._

ger-. To gather. **1.** Extended form _*grem-._ CRAM, from Old English _crammian,_ to stuff, cram, from Germanic _*kramm-._ **2.** Reduplicated form _*gre-g-._ GREGARIOUS; AGGREGATE, CONGREGATE, EGREGIOUS, SEGREGATE, from Latin _grex_ (stem _greg-_), herd, flock. **3.** Earliest forms _*əger-, *əgor-ā-._ AGORA[1], AGORAPHOBIA, ALLEGORY, CATEGORY, PANEGYRIC, from Greek _ageirein,_ to assemble, and _aguris, agora,_ marketplace. [Pokorny 1. _ger-_ 382.]

gerbh-. Important derivatives are _carve, crab[1], crawl[1], gram[1], grammar, diagram, paragraph,_ and _program._

gerbh-. To scratch. **1.** CARVE, from Old English _ceorfan,_ to cut, from Germanic _*kerban._ **2.** KERF, from Old English _cyrf,_ a cutting (off), from zero-grade Germanic form _*kurbiz._ **3.** Variant form _*grebh-._ **a.** CRAB[1], from Old English _crabba,_ a crab, from Germanic _*krab(b)-;_ **b.** CRAYFISH, from Old High German _kerbiz,_ edible crustacean, from Germanic _*krabiz-;_ **c.** CRAWL[1], from Old Norse _krafla,_ to crawl, from Germanic _*krab-,_ perhaps from **gerbh-**. **4.** Zero-grade form _*gr̥bh-._ GRAFFITO, GRAM[1], -GRAM, GRAMMAR, -GRAPH, -GRAPHER, GRAPHIC, -GRAPHY; AGRAPHA, AGRAPHIA, ANAGRAM, DIAGRAM, EPIGRAM, (EPIGRAPH), GRAPHITE, (ICONOGRAPHY), PARAGRAPH, PARALLELOGRAM, PROGRAM, PSEUDEPIGRAPHA, TETRAGRAMMATON, (TOPOGRAPHY), from Greek _graphein,_ to scratch, draw, write, _gramma_ (< _*gr̥bh-mn̥_), a picture, written letter, piece of writing, and _grammē,_ a line. [Pokorny _gerebh-_ 392.]

gerə-[1]. An important derivative is _geriatrics._

gerə-[1]. To grow old. **1.** Suffixed lengthened-grade form _*gērə-s-._ AGERATUM, GERIATRICS, from Greek _gēras,_ old age. **2.** Suffixed form _*gerə-ont-._ GERONTO-, from Greek _gerōn_ (stem _geront-_), old man. [Pokorny _ger-_ 390.]

gerə-[2]. Important derivatives are _crow[1], crack, crane, cranberry, pedigree,_ and _geranium._

gerə-[2]. To cry hoarsely; also the name of the crane.
I. Words meaning "to cry hoarsely"; also words denoting the crow. **1.a.** CROW[1], from Old English _crāwe,_ a crow; **b.** CROW[2], from Old English _crāwan,_ to crow; **c.** CRACK, from Old English _cracian,_ to resound; **d.** CRACKNEL, from Middle Dutch _krāken,_ to crack; **e.** CRAKE, from Old Norse _krāka,_ a crow; **f.** CROON, from Middle Dutch _krōnen,_ to groan, lament. **a, b, c, d, e,** and **f** all from Germanic _*krē-._ **2.** CUR, from Middle English _curre,_ cur. akin to Old Norse _kurra,_ to growl, from Germanic _*kur(r)-,_ possibly from **gere-[2]** (but more likely imitative).
II. Words denoting a crane. **1.a.** CRANE, from Old English _cran,_ crane; **b.** CRANBERRY, from Middle Low German _kran,_ crane. Both **a** and **b** from Germanic _*kran-,_ crane. **2.** Extended form _*grū-._ GRUS; PEDIGREE, from Latin _grūs,_ crane. **3.** Suffixed variant form _*grā-k-._ GRACKLE, from Latin _grāculus,_ jackdaw. **4.** Suffixed extended form _*gerə-no-._ GERANIUM, from Greek _geranos,_ crane. [Pokorny 2. _ger-_ 383.]

geus-. Important derivatives are _choose, choice,_ and _disgust._

geus-. To taste, choose. **1.a.** CHOOSE, from Old English _cēosan, ceōsan,_ to choose, from Germanic _*keusan;_ **b.** CHOICE, from a Germanic source akin to Gothic _kausjan,_ to test, taste, from Germanic causative _*kausjan._ **2.** Zero-grade _*gus-._ (see **welə-**) Old Norse _Valkyrja,_ "chooser of the slain," Valkyrie (_valr,_ the slain), from Germanic _*kur-_ from _*kuz-._ **3.** Suffixed zero-grade form _*gus-tu-._ **a.** (GUST[2]), GUSTO; RAGOUT, from Latin _gustus,_ taste; **b.** DEGUST, DISGUST, from Latin _gustāre,_ to taste. [Pokorny _ĝeus-_ 399.]

ghabh-. Important derivatives are _give, forgive, gift, able, habit, exhibit, inhabit, malady, prohibit, debt, due, duty,_ and _endeavor._

ghabh-. Also **ghebh-**. To give or receive. **1.** Form _*ghebh-._ **a.** GIVE, from Old English _giefan,_ to give, and Old Norse _gefa,_ to give; **b.** FORGIVE, from Old English _forgi(e)fan,_ to give, give up, leave off (anger), remit, forgive, from Germanic compound _*fargeban,_ to give away (_*far-,_ away; see **per[1]**). Both **a** and **b** from Germanic _*geban._ **2.** Suffixed form _*ghebh-ti-_, something given (or received). GIFT, from Old Norse _gipt, gift_, a gift, from Germanic _*giftiz_. **3.** O-grade form _*ghobh-_. GAVEL[2], from Old English _gafol_, tribute, tax, debt, from Germanic _*gab-ulam_, something paid (or received). **4.** Form _*ghabh-ē-_. **a.** ABLE, BINNACLE, HABILE, HABIT, HABITABLE, (HABITANT), (HABITAT); (COHABIT), EXHIBIT, INHABIT, INHIBIT, MALADY, PREBEND, PROHIBIT, (PROVENDER), from Latin _habēre_, to hold, possess, have, handle (> _habitāre_, to dwell); **b.** DEBENTURE, (DEBIT), DEBT, DEVOIR, DUE, (DUTY); (ENDEAVOR), from Latin _dēbēre_, to owe (_dē-_, away from; see **de-**). [Pokorny _ghabh-_ 407.] Compare **kap-**.

ghans-. Important derivatives are _goose[1], gosling_, and _gander_.

ghans-. Goose. **1.a.** GOOSE[1]; (GOSHAWK), from Old English _gōs_ (nominative plural _gēs_), goose; **b.** GOSLING, from Old Norse _gās_, goose; **c.** GUNSEL, from Old High German _gans_, goose; **d.** GONZO, from Spanish _ganso_, goose, from a Germanic source akin to Old High German _gans_, goose. **a, b, c,** and **d** all from Germanic _*gans-_ (nominative plural _*gansiz_). **2.** GANDER, from Old English _ganra, gandra_, gander, from Germanic _*gan(d)rōn-_. **3.** GANNET, from Old English _ganot_, gannet, from Germanic _*ganōtōn-_. **4.** Suffixed form _*ghans-er-_. ANSERINE; MERGANSER, from Latin _ānser_ (< _*hanser_), goose. **5.** Basic form _*ghans-_. CHENOPOD, from Greek _khēn_, goose. [Pokorny _ĝhans-_ 412.]

ghē-. Important derivatives are _go, ago, heir, heritage, inherit_, and _gait_.

ghē-. To release, let go; (in the middle voice) to be released, go. Contracted from _*gheə-_. **1.** GO; AGO, FOREGO[1], FORGO, from Old English _gān_, to go, from Germanic variant form _*gaian_. **2.** Suffixed form _*ghē-ro-_. HEIR, HEREDITAMENT, HEREDITY, (HERITAGE); INHERIT, from Latin _hērēs_, heir (? < "orphan" < "bereft"). **3.** Possibly suffixed o-grade form _*ghō-ro-_, "empty space." **a.** CHOROGRAPHY, from Greek _khōros_, place, country, particular spot; **b.** -CHORE; ANCHORITE, from Greek denominative _khōrein_, to move, go, spread about, make room for; **c.** CHORIPETALOUS, from Greek _khōris, khōri_, apart, separate. **4.** Possible suffixed zero-grade form _*ghə-t(w)ā-_. **a.** GAIT, GATE[2]; RUNAGATE, from Old Norse _gata_, path, street; **b.** (GANTLET[1]), GAUNTLET[2], from Old Swedish _gata_, lane. Both **a** and **b** from Germanic _*gatwōn-_, a going. **5.** Suffixed zero-grade form _*ghə-no-_. HINAYANA, from Sanskrit _hīna-_, inferior, verbal adjective of _jahāti_, he leaves, lets go (< reduplicated _*ghe-ghē-ti, *ghe-gheə-ti_). [Pokorny 1. _ĝhē-_ 418.]

ghebh-el-. Derivatives are _gable_ and _cephalic_.

ghebh-el-. Head. **1.** GABLE, from Old Norse _gafl_, gable, from Germanic _*gablaz_, top of a pitched roof. **2.** Form _*kephal-_, dissimilated from _*khephal-_. CEPHALIC, CEPHALO-, -CEPHALOUS; ENCEPHALO-, ENKEPHALIN, HYDROCEPHALUS, from Greek _kephalē_, head. [Pokorny _ghebh-el-_ 423.]

ghedh-. Important derivatives are _good, together_, and _gather_.

ghedh-. To unite, join, fit. **1.** Lengthened o-grade form _*ghōdh-_. GOOD, from Old English _gōd_, good, from Germanic _*gōdaz_, "fitting, suitable." **2.** TOGETHER, from Old English _tōgædere_, together (_tō_, to; see **de-**), from Germanic _*gadurī_, "in a body." **3.** GATHER, from Old English _gad(e)rian_, to gather, from Germanic _*gadurōn_, "to come or bring together." [Pokorny _ghedh-_ 423.]

ghei-. An important derivative is _hibernate_.

ghei-. Theoretical base of _*ghyem-, *ghiem-_, winter. **1.** Form _*ghiem-_. HIEMAL, from Latin _hiems_, winter. **2.** Suffixed variant form _*gheim-ri-no-_. HIBERNACULUM, HIBERNATE, from Latin _hībernus_, pertaining to winter. **3.** Suffixed zero-grade form _*ghim-r̥-yə_, "female animal one year (winter) old." CHIMERA, from Greek _khimaira_, she-goat. [Pokorny 2. _ĝhei-_ 425.]

ghel-[1]. Important derivatives are _yell, yelp_, and _nightingale_.

ghel-[1]. To call. **1.a.** YELL, from Old English _gellan, giellan_, to sound, shout; **b.** YELP, from Old English _gielpan_, to boast, exult; **c.** NIGHTINGALE, from Old English _galan_, to sing. **a, b,** and **c** all from Germanic _*gel-, *gal-_. **2.** Reduplicated form _*ghi-ghl-_. CICHLID, from Greek _kikhlē_, thrush, later also the name for a kind of wrasse (a sea fish that has bright colors and jagged waving fins, reminiscent of the plumage of a bird). **3.** CELANDINE, from Greek _khelidwōn, khelidōn_, the swallow. [Pokorny _ghel-_ 428.]

ghel-[2]. Important derivatives are _yellow, gold, arsenic, gall[1], melancholy, gleam, glimpse, glimmer, glitter, glass, glare[1], glad, glee, glow_, and _glide_.

ghel-[2]. To shine; with derivatives referring to colors, bright materials (probably "yellow metal"), and bile or gall.

I. Words denoting colors. **1.** Suffixed form _*ghel-wo-_. YELLOW, from Old English _geolu_, yellow, from Germanic _*gelwaz_. **2.** Suffixed variant form _*ghlō-ro-_. CHLORO-; CHLORITE[1], from Greek _khlōros_, green, greenish yellow. **3.** Suffixed variant form _*ghlo-wo-_. CHLOASMA, from Greek _khloos_ (< _*khlo-wo-s_), greenish color. **4.** O-grade form _*ghol-_. PODZOL, from Russian _zola_, ashes (from their color). **5.** Suffixed form _*ghel-i-_. HARE KRISHNA, from Sanskrit _hari-_, tawny yellow. **6.** Possibly suffixed zero-grade form _*ghl̥-wo-_. GRISEOFULVIN, from Latin _fulvus_, tawny, perhaps from **ghel-[2]** (with dialectal _f-_ as in _fel_, gall).

II. Words denoting gold. **1.** Suffixed zero-grade form _*ghl̥-to-_. **a.** GOLD, from Old English _gold_, gold; **b.** GILD[1], from Old English _gyldan_, to gild, from Germanic denominative verb _*gulthjan_; **c.** GUILDER, GULDEN, from Middle Dutch _gulden_, golden; **d.** GOWAN, from Middle English _gollan_, yellow flower, possibly from a source akin to Old Norse _gullinn_, golden. **a, b, c,** and **d** all from Germanic _*gultham_, gold. **2.** Suffixed o-grade form _*ghol-to-_. ZLOTY, from Polish _zioto_, gold. **3.** Suffixed full-grade form _*ghel-no-_. ARSENIC, from Syriac _zarnīkā_, orpiment, from Middle Iranian _*zarnik-_, from Old Iranian _*zarna-_, golden.

III. Words denoting bile. **1.** Suffixed o-grade form _*ghol-no-_. GALL[1], from Old English _gealla_, gall, from Germanic _*gallōn-_, bile. **2.** Suffixed o-grade form _*ghol-ā_. CHOLE-, CHOLER, (CHOLERA); ACHOLIA, MELANCHOLY, from Greek _kholē_, bile. **3.** Suffixed full-grade form _*ghel-n-_. FELON[2], from Latin _fel_, bile.

IV. A range of Germanic words (where no preforms are given, the words are late creations). **1.** GLEAM, from Old English _glǣm_, bright light, gleam, from Germanic _*glaimiz_. **2.** GLIMPSE, from Middle English _glimsen_, to glimpse, from a source akin to Middle High German _glimsen_, to gleam. **3.** GLANCE[1], GLINT, from Middle English _glent_, a glint, and _glenten_, to shine, from a source akin to Swedish dialectal _glinta_, to shine. **4.** GLIMMER, from Middle English _glimeren_, to glimmer, from a source akin to Swedish _glimra_, glimmer. **5.** GLITTER, from Old Norse _glitra_, to shine. **6.** GLITZ, from Old High German _glīzan_, to sparkle. **7.** GLISTEN, from Old English _glisnian_, to shine. **8.** GLISTER, from Middle Dutch _glinsteren_ or Middle Low German _glisteren_, to shine. **9.** GLASS, GLAZE, (GLAZIER), from Old English _glæs_, glass, from Germanic _*glasam_, glass. **10.** GLARE[1], from Middle English _glaren_, to glitter, stare, from a source akin to Middle Low German _glaren_, to glisten, from Germanic _*glaz-_. **11.** GLOSS[1], from a source perhaps akin to Icelandic _glossi_, a spark. **12.** GLANCE[2], from Old High German _glanz_, bright. **13.** GLEG, from Old Norse _glöggr_, clear-sighted. **14.** GLAD, from Old English _glæd_, shining, joyful, from Germanic _*gladaz_. **15.** GLEE, from Old English _glēo_, sport, merriment, from Germanic _*gleujam_. **16.a.** GLEED, from Old English _glēd_, ember; **b.** GLOGG, from Swedish _glöd_, ember. Both **a** and **b** from Germanic _*glō-di-_. **17.a.** GLOW, from Old English _glōwan_, to glow; **b.** GLOWER, from Middle English _gloren_, to gleam, stare, probably from a source akin to Norwegian dialectal _glora_, to gleam, stare; **c.** GLOAT, from a source perhaps akin to Old Norse _glotta_, to smile (scornfully). **a, b,** and **c** all from Germanic _*glō-_. **18.** GLOAMING, from Old English _glōm_, twilight, from Germanic _*glō-m-_. **19.a.** GLIDE, from Old English _glīdan_, to slip, glide; **b.** GLISSADE, from Old French _glier_, to glide; **c.** GLITCH, from Old High German _glītan_, to glide; **d.** GLEDE, from Old English _glida_, kite (< "gliding, hovering bird"), from derivative Germanic _*glidōn-_. **a, b, c,** and **d** all from Germanic _*glīdan_, to glide, possibly distantly related to **ghel-[2]**. **20.** GLIB, from a source possibly akin to Middle Low German _glibberich_, slippery. [Pokorny 1. _ĝhel-_ 429.]

ghend-. Important derivatives are _get, forget, guess, prison, apprehend, comprehend, surprise_, and _prey_.

ghend-. Also **ghed-.** To seize, take. **1.a.** GET, from Old Norse _geta_, to get; **b.** BEGET, from Old English _beg(i)etan_, to get, beget, from Germanic compound _*bigetan_, to acquire (_*bi-_, intensive prefix; see **ambhi**); **c.** FORGET, from Old English _forg(i)etan_, to forget, from Germanic compound _*fer-getan_, "to lose one's hold," forget (_*fer-_, prefix denoting rejection; see **per[1]**). **a, b,** and **c** all from Germanic _*getan_. **2.** GUESS, from Middle English _gessen_, to guess, from a Scandinavian source akin to Old Swedish _gissa_, to guess, from Germanic _*getisōn_, "to try to get," aim at. **3.** Basic form _*ghend-_. PREHENSILE, PREHENSION, PRISON, PRIZE[2], (PRIZE[3]), (PRY[2]); APPREHEND, (APPRENTICE), (APPRISE), COMPREHEND, (COMPRISE), EMPRISE, ENTERPRISE, (ENTREPRENEUR), MISPRISION[1], PREGNABLE, REPREHEND, (REPRISAL), (REPRISE), SURPRISE, from Latin _prendere, prehendere_, to get hold of, seize, grasp (_pre-, prae-_, before; see **per[1]**). **4.** Form _*ghed-_. PREDATORY, PREY, SPREE; DEPREDATE, OSPREY, from Latin _praeda_, booty (< _*prai-heda_, "something seized before"; _prai-, prae-_, before; see **per[1]**). [Pokorny _ghend-_ 437.]

gher-[1]. Important derivative are _girdle, yard[2], orchard, kindergarten, garden, court, courteous, choir_, and _choral_.

gher-[1]. To grasp, enclose; with derivatives meaning "enclosure." **1.** Suffixed zero-grade form _*ghr̥-dh-_. **a.** GIRD[1], from Old English _gyrdan_, to gird, from Germanic _*gurdjan_; **b.** GIRDLE, from Old English _gyrdel_, girdle; **c.** GIRTH, from Old Norse _gjördh_, girdle, girth. **2.** Suffixed o-grade form _*ghor-to-_ or (in Germanic) _*ghor-dho-_, an enclosure. **a.** _(i)_ YARD[2]; ORCHARD, from Old English _geard_, enclosure, garden, yard; _(ii)_ GARTH, from Old Norse _gardhr_, garden, yard; _(iii)_ KINDERGARTEN, from Old High German _garto_, garden; _(iv)_ GARDEN, from Old North French _gart_, garden; _(v)_ HANGAR, from Old French _hangard_, shelter, possibly from Germanic _*haimgardaz_ (_*haimaz_, home; see **tkei-**); _(vi)_ (see **medhyo-**) Germanic compound _*midja-gardaz_, "middle zone," earth. _(i), (ii), (iii), (iv), (v),_ and _(vi)_ all from Germanic _*gardaz_; **b.** HORTICULTURE, ORTOLAN, from Latin _hortus_, garden. **3.** Prefixed and suffixed zero-grade form _*ko(m)-ghr̥-ti-_ (_*ko(m)-_, collective prefix, "together"; see **kom**). COHORT, CORTEGE, COURT, (COURTEOUS), COURTESAN, (COURTESY), (COURTIER), (CURTILAGE), (CURTSY), from Latin _cohors_ (stem _cohort-_), enclosed yard, company of soldiers, multitude. **4.** Perhaps suffixed o-grade form _*ghor-o-_. (CHOIR), (CHORAL), (CHORALE), CHORIC, (CHORISTER), CHORUS, HORA; CHORAGUS, TERPSICHORE, from Greek _khoros_, dancing ground (? perhaps originally a special enclosure for dancing), dance, dramatic chorus. [Pokorny 4. _ĝher-_ 442, _ĝherdh-_ 444.]

gher-[2]. Important derivatives are _yearn, greedy, exhort_, and _charisma_.

gher-[2]. To like, want. **1.** Suffixed form _*gher-n-_. YEARN, from Old English _giernan, gyrnan_, to strive, desire, yearn, from Germanic _*gernjan_. **2.** Possibly extended form _*ghrē-_. **a.** GREEDY, from Old English _grǣdig_, hungry, covetous, greedy, from Germanic _*grēdigaz_, hungry, formed from _*grēduz_, hunger; **b.** CATACHRESIS, CHRESARD, CHRESTOMATHY, from Greek _khrēsthai_, to lack, want, use, from _khrē_, it is necessary. **3.** Suffixed zero-grade form _*ghr̥-to-_. HORTATIVE; EXHORT, from Latin _hortārī_, to urge on, encourage (< "to cause to strive or desire"). **4.** Suffixed zero-grade form _*ghr̥-i-_. CHARISMA; EUCHARIST, from Greek _kharis_, grace, favor. **5.** Suffixed zero-grade form _*ghr̥-yo-_. CHERVIL, from Greek _khairein_, to rejoice, delight in. [Pokorny 1. _ĝher-_ 440.]

gherə-. Important derivatives are _yarn, hernia_, and _cord_.

gherə-. Gut, entrail. **1.** Suffixed form _*gherə-no-_. YARN, from Old English _gearn_, yarn, from Germanic _*garnō_, string. **2.** Suffixed form _*gherə-n-_. HERNIA, from Latin _hernia_, "protruded viscus," rupture, hernia. **3.** Suffixed o-grade form _*ghorə-d-_. (CHORD[2]), CORD, (CORDON); HARPSICHORD, TETRACHORD, from Greek _khordē_, gut, string. **4.** O-grade form _*ghorə-_. CHORION, from Greek _khorion_, intestinal membrane, afterbirth. **5.** Possible suffixed zero-grade form _*ghr̥ə-u-_. HARUSPEX, from Latin _haruspex_, "he who inspects entrails," diviner (_-spex_, "he who sees" < _*spek-_, "to see"; see **spek-**), but perhaps borrowed from Etruscan. [Pokorny 5. _ĝher-_ 443.]

gheslo-. Important derivatives are *kilo-, mile,* and *million.*

gheslo-. Seen by some as a base for words meaning "thousand." **1.** Suffixed form **ghesl-yo-.* CHILIAD, KILO-, from Greek *khilioi,* thousand. **2.** MIL, MILE, MILLENARY, MILLESIMAL, MILLI-, MILLIARY, MILLIME, MILLION; MILFOIL, MILLENNIUM, MILLEPORE, MILLIPEDE, from Latin *mīlle,* thousand, which has been analyzed as **smī-,* "one" + a form **ghslī-,* but is of obscure origin. [Pokorny *ĝhéslo-* 446.]

ghesor-. Important derivatives are *surgeon* and *surgery.*

ghesor-. Hand. Reduced form **ghesr-.* CHIRO-; (CHIRURGEON), ENCHIRIDION, (SURGEON), SURGERY, from Greek *kheir,* hand. [Pokorny 1. *ĝhesor-* 447.]

gheu-. Important derivatives are *gut, funnel, fusion, confuse, refund*[1], and *refuse*[1].

gheu-. To pour, pour a libation.
I. Extended form **gheud-.* **1.** Zero-grade form **ghud-.* GUT, from Old English *guttas,* intestines, from Germanic **gut-.* **2.** Nasalized zero-grade form **ghu-n-d-.* FOISON, FONDANT, (FONDUE), (FONT[2]), FOUND[2], (FUNNEL), FUSE[2], FUSILE, FUSION; AFFUSION, CIRCUMFUSE, CONFOUND, (CONFUSE), DIFFUSE, EFFUSE, INFUSE, PERFUSE, PROFUSE, REFUND, (REFUSE[1]), (REFUSE[2]), SUFFUSE, TRANSFUSE, from Latin *fundere,* to melt, pour out.
II. Extended form **gheus-.* **1.a.** GUST[1], from Old Norse *gustr,* a cold blast of wind, from Germanic suffixed form **gustiz;* **b.** GUSH, from Middle English *gushen,* to gush, perhaps akin to Icelandic *gusa,* to gush. Both **a** and **b** from Germanic zero-grade form **gus-.* **2.** GEYSER, from Old Norse *geysa,* to gush, from Germanic suffixed o-grade form **gausjan.* **3.a.** Suffixed zero-grade form **ghus-mo-.* (CHYME); ECCHYMOSIS, from Greek *khumos,* juice; **b.** suffixed zero-grade form **ghus-lo-.* CHYLE, from Greek *khulos,* juice.
III. Suffixed form **gheu-ti-.* FUTILE, from Latin *fūtilis,* "(of a vessel) easily emptied, leaky," hence untrustworthy, useless.
IV. Basic form **gheu-.* CHOANOCYTE, PARENCHYMA, from Greek *khein,* to pour, with o-grade noun *khoanē,* funnel. [Pokorny *ĝheu-* 447.]

gheu(ə)-. Important derivatives are *god* and *giddy.*

gheu(ə)-. To call, invoke. Suffixed zero-grade form **ghu-to-,* "the invoked," god. **a.** GOD, from Old English *god,* god; **b.** GIDDY, from Old English *gydig, gidig,* possessed, insane, from Germanic **gud-igaz,* possessed by a god; **c.** GÖTTERDÄMMERUNG, from Old High German *got,* god. **a, b,** and **c** all from Germanic **gudam,* god. [Pokorny *ĝhau-* 413.]

ghos-ti-. Important derivatives are *guest, hostile, hospital, host*[1], and *hostage.*

ghos-ti-. Stranger, guest, host; properly "someone with whom one has reciprocal duties of hospitality." **1.** Basic form **ghos-ti-.* **a.** GUEST, from Old Norse *gestr,* guest, from Germanic **gastiz;* **b.** HOST[2], HOSTILE, from Latin *hostis,* enemy (< stranger). **2.** Compound **ghos-pot-, *ghos-po(d)-,* "guest-master," one who symbolizes the relationship of reciprocal obligation (**pot-,* master; see **poti-**). HOSPICE, HOSPITABLE, HOSPITAL, (HOSPITALITY), HOST[1], (HOSTAGE), (HOSTEL), (HOSTLER), from Latin *hospes* (stem *hospit-*), host, guest, stranger. **3.** Suffixed zero-grade form **ghs-en-wo-.* XENO-; EUXENITE, PYROXENE, from Greek *xenos,* guest, host, stranger. [Pokorny *ghosti-s* 453.]

ghrē-. Important derivatives are *grow, green,* and *grass.*

ghrē-. To grow, become green. Contracted from **ghreə-.* **1.** O-grade form **ghrō-.* GROW, from Old English *grōwan,* to grow, from Germanic **grō(w)an.* **2.** Suffixed o-grade form **ghrō-n-yo-.* GREEN, from Old English *grēne,* green, from Germanic **grōnjaz,* green. **3.** Suffixed zero-grade form **ghrə-so-.* GRASS, GRAZE[1], from Old English *græs,* grass, from Germanic **grasam,* grass. [Pokorny *ghrē-* 454.]

ghrebh-[1]. Important derivatives are *grasp* and *grab*[1].

ghrebh-[1]. To seize, reach. **1.** Zero-grade form **ghr̥bh-.* SATYAGRAHA, from Sanskrit *gr̥bhṇāti, gr̥hṇāti,* he seizes. **2.a.** GRASP, from Middle English *graspen,* to grasp; **b.** GRAB[1], from Middle Dutch or Middle Low German *grabben,* to seize. Both **a** and **b** from parallel (imitative) Germanic creations with base **grab-, *grap-.* [Pokorny 1 *ghrebh-* 455.]

ghrebh-[2]. Important derivatives are *engrave, grave*[1], *grub,* and *groove.*

ghrebh-[2]. To dig, bury, scratch. **1.** O-grade form **ghrobh-.* **a.** *(i)* GRAVE[3], (ENGRAVE), from Old English *grafan,* to dig, engrave, scratch, carve; *(ii)* GRABEN, from Old High German *graban,* to dig; *(iii)* GRAVLAX, from Swedish *grava,* to bury; *(iv)* GRAVURE, from Old French *graver,* to engrave. *(i), (ii), (iii),* and *(iv)* all from Germanic **graban;* **b.** GRAVE[1], from Old English *græf,* trench, grave, from Germanic **grabam.* **2.** GRUB, from Old English **grybban,* to dig, from Germanic **grub(b)jan* (with secondary ablaut). **3.** GROOVE, from Middle Dutch *groeve,* ditch, from Germanic **grōbō.* [Pokorny 2. *ghrebh-* 455.]

ghredh-. Important derivatives are *congress, progress, grade, degrade,* and *degree.*

ghredh-. To walk, go. Suffixed zero-grade form **ghr̥dh-yo-.* **a.** GRESSORIAL; AGGRESS, CONGRESS, DEGRESSION, DIGRESS, EGRESS, INGRESS, PINNIGRADE, PLANTIGRADE, PROGRESS, REGRESS, RETROGRADE, RETROGRESS, TRANSGRESS, from Latin *gradī* (past participle *gressus*), to walk, go; **b.** GRADE; CENTIGRADE, DEGRADE, DEGREE, from Latin *gradus* (< deverbative **grad-u-*), step, stage, degree, rank. [Pokorny *ghredh-* 456.]

ghrēi-. Important derivatives are *grisly, grime, Christ, christen, Christian,* and *Christmas.*

ghrēi-. To rub. **1.** GRISLY, from Old English *grislīc,* terrifying, from Germanic **gris-,* to frighten (< "to grate on the mind"). **2.** GRIME, from Middle English *grime,* grime, from a source akin to Middle Dutch *grīme,* grime, from Germanic **grīm-,* smear. **3.** Extended form **ghrīs-.* CHRISM, CHRIST, (CHRISTEN), (CHRISTIAN); (CHRISTMAS), CREAM, from Greek *khriein,* to anoint. [Pokorny *ghrēi-* 457.]

ghrendh-. Important derivatives are *grind, grist,* and *refrain*[1].

ghrendh-. To grind. **1.** GRIND, from Old English *grindan,* to grind, from Germanic **grindan.* **2.** GRIST, from Old English *grīst,* the action of grinding, from Germanic **grinst-,* a grinding. **3.** (FRAISE), FRENULUM, FRENUM; REFRAIN[1], from Latin *frendere,* to grind. **4.** Variant form **ghrend-.* CHONDRO-; HYPOCHONDRIA, MITOCHONDRION, from Greek *khondros,* granule, groats, hence cartilage, sometimes but improbably regarded as from **ghrendh-.** [Pokorny *ghren-* 459.]

ghwer-. Important derivatives are *feral, fierce, ferocious,* and *treacle.*

ghwer-. Wild beast. **1.** Suffixed form **ghwer-o-.* FERAL, FIERCE, from Latin *ferus,* wild. **2.** Compound **ghwero-ək^{w}-,* "of wild aspect" (**-ək^{w}-,* "-looking"; see **ok^{w}-**). FEROCIOUS, from Latin *ferōx* (stem *ferōc-*), fierce. **3.** Lengthened-grade form **ghwēr-.* TREACLE; CHALICOTHERE, DINOTHERE, THEROPOD, from Greek *thēr,* wild beast. [Pokorny *ĝhu̯er-* 493.]

gleubh-. Important derivatives are *cleave*[1], *clove*[2], *clever,* and *hieroglyphic.*

gleubh-. To tear apart, cleave.
I. Basic form **gleubh-.* **1.** CLEAVE[1], from Old English *clēofan,* to split, cleave, from Germanic **kleuban.* **2.** Probably o-grade **gloubh-.* CLEVER, from Middle English *cliver,* nimble, skillful, perhaps akin to East Frisian *klüfer, klifer,* skillful, and Old Norse *kleyfr,* easy to split, from Germanic **klaubri-.*
II. Zero-grade form **glubh-.* **1.a.** CLOVE[2], from Old English *clufu,* clove (of garlic); **b.** KLOOF, from Middle Dutch *clove,* a cleft; **c.** CLEVIS, from a Scandinavian source akin to Old Norse *klofi,* a cleft. **a, b,** and **c** all from Germanic **klub-,* a splitting. **2.** CLEFT, from Old English *geclyft,* fissure, from Germanic **klufti-* (**klub-ti-*). **3.** GLYPH, GLYPTIC; ANAGLYPH, HIEROGLYPHIC, from Greek *gluphein,* to carve. **4.** Suffixed zero-grade form **glubh-mā-.* GLUME, from Latin *glūma,* husk of grain. [Pokorny *gleubh-* 401.]

gnō-. Important derivatives are *know, can*[1], *cunning, uncouth, notice, recognize, ignore, noble, diagnosis,* and *narrate.*

gnō-. To know. Contracted from **gnoə-.* **1.** Variant form **gnē-,* contracted from **gnēə-.* KNOW, from Old English *cnāwan,* to know, from Germanic **knē(w)-.* **2.** Zero-grade form **gn̥ə-.* **a.** CAN[1], CON[2], CUNNING, from Old English *cunnan,* to know, know how to, be able to, from Germanic **kunnan* (Old English first and third singular *can* from Germanic **kann* from o-grade **gonə-*); **b.** KEN, KENNING, from Old English *cennan,* to declare, and Old Norse *kenna,* to know, name (in a formal poetic metaphor), from Germanic causative verb **kannjan,* to make known; **c.** (COUTH); UNCOUTH, from Old English *cūth,* known, well-known, usual, excellent, familiar, from Germanic **kunthaz;* **d.** KITH AND KIN, from Old English *cȳth(the), cȳththu,* knowledge, acquaintance, friendship, kinfolk, from Germanic **kunthithō.* **3.** Suffixed form **gnō-sko-.* NOTICE, NOTIFY, NOTION, NOTORIOUS; (ACQUAINT), COGNITION, (COGNIZANCE), (CONNOISSEUR), (QUAINT), RECOGNIZE, from Latin *(g)nōscere, cognōscere,* to get to know, get acquainted with. **4.** Suffixed form **gnō-ro-.* IGNORANT, IGNORE, from Latin *ignōrāre,* not to know, to disregard (*i-* for *in-,* not; see **ne**). **5.** Suffixed form **gnō-dhli-.* NOBLE, from Latin *nōbilis,* knowable, known, famous, noble. **6.** Reduplicated and suffixed form **gi-gnō-sko-.* GNOME[2], GNOMON, GNOSIS; AGNOSIA, DIAGNOSIS, PATHOGNOMONIC, PHYSIOGNOMY, PROGNOSIS, from Greek *gignōskein,* to know, think, judge, with *gnōsis* (< **gnō-ti-*), knowledge, inquiry, and *gnōmōn,* judge, interpreter. **7.** Suffixed zero-grade form **gn̥ə-ro-.* NARRATE, from Latin *narrāre* (< **gnarrāre*), to tell, relate, from *gnārus,* knowing, expert. **8.** Traditionally but improbably referred here are: **a.** NOTE; ANNOTATE, CONNOTE, PROTHONOTARY, from Latin *nota,* a mark, note, sign, cipher, shorthand character; **b.** NORM, NORMA, NORMAL; ABNORMAL, ENORMOUS, from Latin *norma,* carpenter's square, rule, pattern, precept, possibly from an Etruscan borrowing of Greek *gnōmōn,* carpenter's square, rule. [Pokorny 2. *ĝen-* 376.]

gr̥ə-no-. Important derivatives are *corn*[1], *kernel, grain, granite,* and *grenade.*

gr̥ə-no-. Grain. **1.a.** CORN[1], from Old English *corn,* grain; **b.** KERNEL, from Old English derivative noun *cyrnel,* seed, pip; **c.** EINKORN, from Old High German *korn,* grain. **a, b,** and **c** all from Germanic **kornam.* **2.** (GARNER), GRAIN, GRAM[2], GRANADILLA, GRANARY, GRANGE, GRANITE, GRANULE, (GRENADE); FILIGREE, POMEGRANATE, from Latin *grānum,* grain. [In Pokorny *ĝer-* 390.]

g^{w}ā-. Important derivatives are *come, welcome, become, adventure, convene, convenient, event, invent, prevent, revenue, souvenir, base*[1], *basis, acrobat,* and *diabetes.*

g^{w}ā-. Contracted from **g^{w}aə-.* Also **g^{w}em-.** To go, come. **1.a.** COME, from Old English *cuman,* to come; **b.** WELCOME, from Old English *wilcuma,* a welcome guest, and *wilcume,* the greeting of welcome, from Germanic compound **wil-kumōn-,* a desirable guest (**wil-,* desirable; see **wel-[1]**), from **kumōn-,* he who comes, a guest; **c.** BECOME, from Old English *becuman,* to become, from Germanic compound **bi-kuman,* to arrive, come to be (**bi-,* intensive prefix; see **ambhi**). **a, b,** and **c** all from Germanic **kuman.* **2.** Suffixed form **g^{w}(e)m-yo-.* VENIRE, VENUE; ADVENT, (ADVENTITIOUS), (ADVENTURE), (AVENUE), CIRCUMVENT, CONTRAVENE, CONVENE, (CONVENIENT), (CONVENT), (CONVENTICLE), (CONVENTION), (COVEN), (COVENANT), EVENT, INTERVENE, INVENT, (MISADVENTURE), PARVENU, PREVENIENT, PREVENT, PROVENANCE, (PROVENIENCE), REVENANT, REVENUE, SOUVENIR, SUBVENTION, SUPERVENE, from Latin *venīre,* to come. **3.** Suffixed zero-grade form **g^{w}m̥-yo-.* BASE[1], BASIS; ABASIA, ACROBAT, ADIABATIC, AMPHISBAENA, ANABAENA, BATOPHOBIA, (DIABASE), DIABETES, HYPERBATON, KATABATIC, STEREOBATE, STYLOBATE, from Greek *bainein,* to go, walk, step, with *basis* (< **g^{w}m̥-ti-*), a stepping, tread, base, *-batos* (< **g^{w}m̥-to-*), going, and *-batēs* (< **g^{w}ə-to-,* zero-grade of **g^{w}ā-*), agential suffix, "one that goes or treads, one that is based." **4.** Suffixed zero-grade form **g^{w}(ə)-u-* in compound form **pres-g^{w}u-,* "going before" (see **per[1]**). **5.** Basic form **g^{w}ā-.* BEMA, from Greek *bēma,* step, seat, raised platform. **6.** JUGGERNAUT, from Sanskrit *jigāti,* he goes. [Pokorny *g^{u}ā-* 463.]

gʷei-. Important derivatives are *quick, vivid, revive, survive, vital, vitamin, whiskey, bio-, amphibious, microbe,* and *hygiene.*

gʷei-. Also **gʷeiə-.** To live.
I. Suffixed zero-grade form **gʷi-wo-, *gʷī-wo-* (< **gʷiə-wo-*), living. **1.a.** QUICK, QUICKSILVER, from Old English *cwic, cwicu,* living, alive; **b.** (COUCH GRASS), QUITCH GRASS, from Old English *cwice,* couch grass (so named from its rapid growth). Both **a** and **b** from Germanic **kwi(k)waz.* **2.a.** VIVIFY, VIVIPAROUS, from Latin *vīvus,* living, alive; **b.** VIAND, VICTUAL, VIVA, VIVACIOUS, VIVID; CONVIVIAL, REVIVE, SURVIVE, from Latin denominative *vīvere,* to live. **3.** AZOTH, from Sanskrit *jīva-,* alive. **4.** Further suffixed form **gʷī-wo-tā.* VIABLE, VITAL; VITAMIN, from Latin *vīta,* life. **5.** Further suffixed form **gʷi-wo-tūt-.* USQUEBAUGH, (WHISKEY), from Old Irish *bethu,* life.
II. Suffixed zero-grade form **gʷiə-o-.* BIO-, BIOTA, BIOTIC; AEROBE, AMPHIBIAN, ANABIOSIS, CENOBITE, DENDROBIUM, MICROBE, RHIZOBIUM, SAPROBE, SYMBIOSIS, from Greek *bios,* life (> *biotē,* way of life).
III. Variant form **gʷyō-* (< **gʷyoə-*). **1.** AZO-, (DIAZO), from Greek *zoē,* life. **2.** Suffixed form **gʷyō-yo-.* -ZOIC, ZOO-, ZOON[1], -ZOON, from Greek *zōon, zōion,* living being, animal.
IV. Prefixed and suffixed form **su-gʷiə-es-,* "having good life" (**su-,* well; see **su-**). HYGIENE, from Greek *hugiēs,* healthy.
V. QUIVER[1], from Old English *cwifer-,* nimble, possibly from **gʷei-.** [Pokorny 3. *gᵘei̯-* 467.]

gʷelə-. Important derivatives are *devil, emblem, metabolism, parable, parliament, parlor, problem, symbol, ball*[2], *ballad, ballet,* and *kill*[1].

gʷelə-. Also **gʷel-.** To throw, reach, with further meaning to pierce.
I. Words denoting to throw, reach. Variant **gʷlē-,* contracted from **gʷleə-.* **1.** Suffixed zero-grade form **gʷl̥-n-ə-.* **a.** BALLISTA; AMPHIBOLE, ASTROBLEME, BOLIDE, DEVIL, (DIABOLIC), EMBLEM, EPIBOLY, (HYPERBOLA), HYPERBOLE, METABOLISM, (PALAVER), PARABLE, (PARABOLA), (PARLEY), (PARLIAMENT), (PARLOR), (PAROL), (PAROLE), PROBLEM, SYMBOL, from Greek *ballein,* to throw (with o-grade **bol-* and variant **blē-*); **b.** BALL[2], (BALLAD), (BALLET), BAYADERE, from Greek *ballizein,* to dance. **2.** Suffixed o-grade form **gʷolə-ā.* BOLOMETER, from Greek *bolē,* beam, ray. **3.** Possible suffixed o-grade form *gʷol(ə)-sā.* BOULE[1], ABULIA, from Greek *boulē,* determination, will (< "throwing forward of the mind"), council. **4.** Suffixed variant zero-grade form **gʷelə-mno-.* BELEMNITE, from Greek *belemnon,* dart, javelin.
II. Words denoting to pierce. **1.** Suffixed o-grade form **gʷol-eyo-.* **a.** QUELL, from Old English *cwellan,* to kill, destroy; **b.** QUAIL[2], from Middle Dutch *quelen,* to be ill, suffer. Both **a** and **b** from Germanic **kwaljan.* **2.** Suffixed zero-grade form **gʷl̥-yo-.* KILL[1], from Middle English *killen,* to kill, perhaps from Old English **cyllan,* to kill, from Germanic **kuljan.* **3.** Full-grade form **gʷel-.* BELONEPHOBIA, from Greek *belonē,* needle. [Pokorny 2. *gᵘel-* 471, 1. *gᵘel-* 470.]

gʷen-. An important derivative is *queen.*

gʷen-. Woman. **1.** Suffixed form **gʷen-ā-.* **a.** QUEAN, from Old English *cwene,* woman, prostitute, wife, from Germanic **kwenōn-;* **b.** BANSHEE, from Old Irish *ben,* woman; **c.** ZENANA, from Persian *zan,* woman. **2.** Suffixed lengthened-grade form **gʷēn-i-.* QUEEN, from Old English *cwēn,* woman, wife, queen, from Germanic **kwēniz,* woman, wife, queen. **3.** Suffixed zero-grade form **gʷn̥-ā-.* -GYNE, GYNO-, -GYNOUS, -GYNY; GYNECOCRACY, (GYNECOLOGY), GYNOECIUM, from Greek *gunē,* woman. [Pokorny *gᵘenā* 473.]

gʷerə-[1]**.** Important derivatives are *grave*[2], *grief, aggravate, baritone, guru, brute,* and *blitzkrieg.*

gʷerə-[1]**.** Heavy.
I. Zero-grade form **gʷr̥ə-.* **1.** Suffixed form **gʷr̥ə-u-i-.* GRAVE[2], GRAVID, GRAVITY, (GRIEF), GRIEVE; AGGRAVATE, (AGGRIEVE), from Latin *gravis,* heavy, weighty. **2.** Suffixed form **gʷr̥ə-u-.* **a.** BARITE, (BARIUM), BARYON, BARYTA; BARITONE, BARYCENTER, BARYSPHERE, CHARIVARI, from Greek *barus,* heavy; **b.** GURU, from Sanskrit *guru-,* heavy, venerable. **3.** Suffixed form **gʷr̥ə-es-.* BAR[2], BARO-; CENTROBARIC, ISALLOBAR, ISOBAR, from Greek *baros,* weight. **4.** Possibly **gʷrĭ-.* (see **ud-**) Greek compound **u(d)-bri-* from *bri-.*
II. Suffixed extended form **gʷrū-to-.* BRUT, BRUTE, from Latin *brūtus,* heavy, unwieldy, dull, stupid, brutish.
III. Suffixed extended form *gʷrī-g-.* **a.** BRIO, from Spanish *brio* and Provençal *briu,* vigor, from Celtic **brīg-o-,* strength; **b.** (BRIG), BRIGADE, (BRIGAND), (BRIGANTINE), from Old Italian *briga,* strife, from Celtic **brīg-ā-,* strife; **c.** BLITZKRIEG, SITZKRIEG, from Old High German *krēg, chrēg,* stubbornness, from Germanic **krīg-.*
IV. Suffixed full-grade form **gʷerə-nā-,* millstone. QUERN, from Old English *cweorn,* quern. [Pokorny 2. *gᵘer-* 476.]

gʷerə-[2]**.** Important derivatives are *grace, grateful, gratitude, agree, congratulate,* and *bard*[1].

gʷerə-[2]**.** To favor. **1.** Suffixed zero-grade form **gʷr̥ə-to-.* GRACE, GRATEFUL, GRATIFY, GRATIS, GRATITUDE, GRATUITOUS, (GRATUITY); AGREE, CONGRATULATE, DISGRACE, INGRATE, INGRATIATE, MAUGRE, from Latin *grātus,* pleasing, beloved, agreeable, favorable, thankful, with related suffixed forms **gʷr̥ə-ti-, *gʷr̥ə-t-ā-, *gʷr̥ə-t-olo-.* **2.** Possible suffixed zero-grade form **gʷr̥ə-d(h)o-,* "he who praises." BARD[1], from Welsh *bardd* and Scottish and Irish Gaelic *bard,* bard, from Celtic *bardo-,* bard (but this is possibly from **gʷerə-**[1]). [Pokorny 4. *gᵘer(ə)-* 478.]

gʷet-. Derivatives are *bequeath* and *quoth.*

gʷet-. To say, speak. **1.** Basic form **gʷet-.* BEQUEATH, QUOTH, from Old English *cwethan,* to say, speak, from Germanic **kwithan.* **2.** Suffixed form **gʷet-ti-.* BEQUEST, from Old English *-cwis,* will, from Germanic **kwessiz.* [Pokorny 2. *gᵘet-* 480.]

gʷhedh-. Important derivatives are *bid* and *bead.*

gʷhedh-. To ask, pray. **1.** Suffixed form **gʷhedh-yo-.* BID, from Old English *biddan,* to ask, pray, from Germanic **bidjan,* to pray, entreat. **2.** BEAD, from Old English *bed(u), gebed,* prayer (*ge-,* intensive and collective prefix; see **kom**), from Germanic **bidam,* entreaty. **3.** Suffixed form **gʷhedh-to-.* INFEST, MANIFEST, from Latin *-festus,* probably in *īnfestus,* hostile, (< **n̥-gʷhedh-to-,* "inexorable"; **n̥-,* not; see **ne**), and perhaps in *manifestus,* caught in the act, red-handed (*manus,* hand; see **man-**[2]). [Pokorny *gᵘhedh-* 488, 2. *bhedh-* 114.]

gʷhen-. Important derivatives are *bane, gun, defend, fence,* and *offend.*

gʷhen-. To strike, kill. **1.** O-grade **gʷhon-.* **a.** BANE, from Old English *bana,* slayer, cause of ruin or destruction; **b.** AUTOBAHN, from Middle High German *ban, bane,* way, road (? < "path hewn through woods"). Both **a** and **b** from Germanic suffixed form **ban-ōn-.* **2.** Suffixed zero-grade form **gʷhn̥-tyā-.* **a.** GUN, from Old Norse *gunnr,* war; **b.** GONFALON, from Italian *gonfalone,* standard, from Germanic compound **gund-fanōn-,* "battle flag" (**fanōn-,* flag; see **pan-**). Both **a** and **b** from Germanic **gund-jō,* war, battle. **3.** Suffixed form **gʷhen-do-.* **a.** DEFEND, (DEFENSE), (FENCE), from Latin *dēfendere,* to ward off (*dē-,* away; see **de-**); **b.** OFFEND, (OFFENSE), from Latin *offendere,* to strike against, be offensive, offend (*ob-,* against; see **epi**). **4.** Suffixed zero-grade form **gʷhn̥-tro-.* BEZOAR, from Persian *zahr,* poison, from Old Iranian **jathra-.* [Pokorny 2. *gᵘhen-(ə)-* 491, *bhen-* 126.]

gʷher-. Important derivatives are *burn*[1], *brand, brandy, brandish, forceps,* and *furnace.*

gʷher-. To heat, warm. **1.** Zero-grade **gʷhr-.* **a.** BURN[1], from Old English *beornan, byrnan* (intransitive) and *bærnan* (transitive), to burn; **b.** BRIMSTONE, from late Old English *brynstān,* "burning mineral," sulfur (*stān,* stone; see **stei-**); **c.** BRINDLED, from Old Norse *brenna,* to burn. **a, b,** and **c** all from Germanic **brennan* (intransitive) and *brannjan* (transitive), formed from **brenw-* with nasal suffix and analogical vocalism. **2.a.** BRAND, from Old English *brand,* piece of burning wood, sword; **b.** BRANDY, from Dutch *branden,* to burn, distill; **c.** BRANDISH, from Old French *brand,* sword; **d.** BRANDADE, from Old Provençal *brand,* sword. **a, b, c,** and **d** all from Germanic **brandaz,* a burning, a flaming torch, hence also a sword. **3.** Suffixed form **gʷher-mo-.* THERM, -THERM, THERMO-, -THERMY; HYPOTHERMIA, from Greek *thermos,* warm, hot, and *thermē,* heat. **4.** O-grade form **gʷhor-.* FORCEPS, FORCIPATE, from Latin *forceps,* pincers, fire tongs (< "that which holds hot things"; *-ceps,* agential suffix, "-taker"; see **kap-**). **5.** Suffixed o-grade form **gʷhor-no-.* **a.** FORNAX, FURNACE, HORNITO, from Latin *furnus, fornus, fornāx,* oven; **b.** FORNICATE, FORNIX, from Latin *fornix,* arch, vault (< "vaulted brick oven"), probably from **gʷher-.** [Pokorny *gᵘher-* 493, *bhereu-* 143.]

gʷhī-. Important derivatives are *filament, file*[1], and *profile.*

gʷhī-. Thread, tendon. Contracted from **gʷhiə-.* Suffixed form **gʷhī-slo-.* FILAMENT, FILAR, FILARIA, FILE[1], FILLET, FILOSE, FILUM; (DEFILE[2]), ENFILADE, FILIFORM, FILIGREE, FILOPLUME, PROFILE, PURFLE, from Latin *fīlum,* thread. [Pokorny *gᵘheia-* 489.]

gʷhrē-. Important derivatives are *breath* and *breathe.*

gʷhrē-. To smell, breathe. Contracted from **gʷhreə-.* BREATH, (BREATHE), from Old English *brǣth,* odor, exhalation, from Germanic suffixed form **brē-thaz.*

gʷhren-. Important derivatives are *frantic, frenetic, frenzy, phrase,* and *paraphrase.*

gʷhren-. To think. **1.** (FRANTIC), FRENETIC, (FRENZY), -PHRENIA, PHRENO-; (PHRENITIS), from Greek *phrēn,* the mind, also heart, midriff, diaphragm. **2.** Extended zero-grade root form **gʷhrn̥-d-.* PHRASE; HOLOPHRASTIC, METAPHRASE, PARAPHRASE, PERIPHRASIS, from Greek *phrazein,* to point out, show. [Pokorny *gᵘhren-* 496.]

gʷou-. Important derivatives are *cow*[1], *beef, bugle*[1], *bucolic,* and *butter.*

gʷou-. Ox, bull, cow. Nominative singular form **gʷōu-s.* **1.** COW[1], (KINE); COWSLIP, from Old English *cū, cȳ, cȳe,* cow, from Germanic **kōuz* (> **kūz*). **2.** BEEF, BOVINE, BUGLE[1], from Latin *bōs* (stem *bov-*), ox, bull, cow. **3.** BOÖTES, BOUSTROPHEDON, BUCOLIC, BUGLOSS, BULIMIA, BUPRESTID, BUTTER, (BUTYRIC), from Greek *bous,* ox, bull, cow. **4.** GAYAL, from Sanskrit *go-, gauḥ,* cow. **5.** Suffixed form **gʷōu-ro-.* GAUR, from Sanskrit *gauraḥ,* wild ox. **6.** Zero-grade suffixed form **gʷw-ā-.* HECATOMB, from Greek *hekatombē,* "sacrifice of a hundred oxen" (*hekaton,* hundred; see **dekm̥**). [Pokorny *gᵘōu-* 482.]

i-. Important derivatives are *yonder, yea, yes, yet, if, identity,* and *item.*

i-. Pronominal stem. **1.** ILK[1], from Old English *ilca,* same, from Germanic **is-līk-,* same (**līk-,* like; see **līk-**). **2.** YON, from Old English *geon,* that, from Germanic **jaino-, *jeno-.* **3.a.** YOND, (YONDER), from Old English *geond,* as far as, yonder, from Germanic **jend-;* **b.** BEYOND, from Old English *geondan,* beyond, from Germanic **jendana-.* **4.** Extended forms **yăm, *yăi.* YEA, YES, from Old English *gēa,* affirmative particle, and *gēse,* yes (see **es-**), from Germanic **jā, *jai.* **5.** YET, from Old English *gīet, gīeta* (preform uncertain), still. **6.** Relative stem **yo-* plus particle. IF, from Old English *gif,* if, from Germanic **ja-ba.* **7.** Basic form **i-,* with neuter **id-em.* ID, IDEM, (IDENTICAL), IDENTITY; (IDENTIFY), from Latin *is,* he (neuter *id,* it), and *īdem,* same. **8.** Suffixed form **i-tero-.* ITERATE; (REITERATE), from Latin *iterum,* again. **9.** Suffixed and extended form **it(ə)-em.* ITEM, from Latin *item,* thus, also. **10.** Stem **i-* plus locatival particle **-dha-i.* IBIDEM, from Latin *ibī-dem,* in the same place. **11.** Suffixed variant form **e-tero-.* (see **ko-**). [Pokorny 3. *e-* 281.]

kā-. Important derivatives are *whore, caress, charity,* and *cherish.*

kā-. To like, desire. Contracted from **kaə-.* **1.** Suffixed form **kā-ro-.* **a.** *(i)* WHORE, from Old English *hōre,* whore; *(ii)* WHOREDOM, from Old Norse compound *hōrdōmr,* whoredom (*-dōmr,* "condition"; see **dhē-**). Both *(i)* and *(ii)* from Germanic **hōraz* (feminine **hōrōn-*), "one who desires," adulterer; **b.** CARESS, CHARITY, CHERISH, from Latin *cārus,* dear. **2.** Suffixed form **kā-mo-.* KAMA; KAMASUTRA, from Sanskrit *kāmaḥ,* love, desire. [Pokorny *kā-* 515.]

kad-. Important derivatives are *cadaver, cadence, cascade, case*[1], *chance, chute, accident, decay, incident,* and *occasion.*

kad-. To fall. CADAVER, CADENCE, CADENT, CADUCOUS, CASCADE, CASE[1], CHANCE, CHUTE; ACCIDENT, DECAY, DECIDUOUS, ESCHEAT, INCIDENT, OCCASION, RECIDIVISM, from Latin *cadere,* to fall, die. [Pokorny 1. *kad-* 516.]

kaə-id-. Important derivatives are *cement, chisel, scissors, circumcise, concise, decide,* and *precise.*

kaə-id-. To strike. **1.** CAESURA, CEMENT, CESTUS[2], CHISEL, -CIDE, SCISSOR; ABSCISE, CIRCUMCISE, CONCISE, DECIDE, EXCISE[2], INCISE, PRECISE, RECISION, from Latin *caedere,* to cut, strike. **2.** CAELUM, from Latin *caelum* (? < **caedum*), sculptor's chisel. [Pokorny *(s)k(h)ai-* 917.]

kai-. Important derivatives are *hot* and *heat.*

kai-. Heat. Extended form **kaid-*. **a.** HOT, from Old English *hāt,* hot, from Germanic **haitaz;* **b.** HEAT, from Old English *hǣtu,* from Germanic **haitī-*. [Pokorny *kăi-* 519.]

kailo-. Important derivatives are *whole, wholesome, health, heal, holy,* and *hallow.*

kailo-. Whole, uninjured, of good omen. **1.a.** HALE[1], WHOLE, from Old English *hāl,* hale, whole; **b.** WHOLESOME, from Old English **hālsum* (> Middle English *holsom*), wholesome; **c.** (HAIL[2]); WASSAIL, from Old Norse *heill,* healthy. **a, b,** and **c** all from Germanic **hailaz.* **2.** HEALTH, from Old English *hǣlth,* health, from Germanic **hailithō.* **3.** HEAL, from Old English *hǣlan,* to heal, from Germanic **hailjan.* **4.a.** HOLY, from Old English *hālig,* holy, sacred; **b.** HALLOW, from Old English *hālgian,* to consecrate, bless, from Germanic derivative verb **hailagōn.* Both **a** and **b** from Germanic **hailagaz.* [Pokorny *kai-lo-* 520.]

kaito-. Important derivatives are *heath* and *heathen.*

kaito-. Forest, uncultivated land. **1.** HEATH, from Old English *hǣth,* heath, untilled land, from Germanic **haithiz.* **2.a.** HEATHEN, from Old English *hǣthen,* heathen, "savage" (< "one inhabiting uncultivated land"); **b.** HOYDEN, from Middle Dutch *heiden,* heathen. Both **a** and **b** from Germanic **haithinaz.* [Pokorny *kaito-* 521.]

kakka-. Derivatives are *poppycock* and *cacophony.*

kakka-. Also **kaka-.** To defecate. Root imitative of glottal closure. **1.** CUCKING STOOL, from Middle English *cukken,* to defecate, from a source akin to Old Norse **kūka,* to defecate. **2.** POPPYCOCK, from Latin *cacāre,* to defecate. **3.** CACO-; CACODYL, CACOËTHES, CACOPHONOUS, (CACOPHONY), from Greek *kakos,* bad. [Pokorny *kakka-* 521.]

kan-. Important derivatives are *hen, chant, accent, enchant, incentive,* and *charm.*

kan-. To sing. **1.** HEN, from Old English *hen(n),* hen, from Germanic **han(e)nī.* **2.** CANOROUS, CANT[2], CANTABILE, CANTATA, CANTICLE, CANTILLATE, (CANTO), CANTOR, CANZONE, CHANT; ACCENT, DESCANT, ENCHANT, (INCANTATION), INCENTIVE, PRECENTOR, RECANT, from Latin *canere,* to sing (> *cantāre,* to sing, frequentative of *canere*). **3.** OSCINE, from Latin *oscen,* a singing bird used in divination (< **obs-cen,* "one that sings before the augurs"; *ob-,* before; see **epi-**). **4.** Suffixed form **kan-men-*. CHARM, from Latin *carmen,* song, poem. [Pokorny *kan-* 525.]

kand-. Important derivatives are *candid, candidate, candle, candor, incandesce,* and *incense.*

kand-. To shine. **1.** Suffixed (stative) form **kand-ē-*. CANDENT, CANDID, (CANDIDA), (CANDIDATE), CANDLE, CANDOR; INCANDESCE, from Latin *candēre* to shine. **2.** (INCENDIARY), INCENSE[1], INCENSE[2] from Latin compound *incendere,* to set fire to, kindle (*in-,* in; see **en**), from transitive **candere,* to kindle. [Pokorny *kand-* 526.]

kap-. Important derivatives are *have, heavy, haven, hawk*[1]*, heave, cable, capable, caption, captive, catch, chase*[1]*, accept, conceive, deceive, except, intercept, municipal, occupy, participate, perceive, receive, recover, capsule,* and *chassis.*

kap-. To grasp.
I. Basic form **kap-*. **1.** HEDDLE, from Old English *hefeld,* thread used for weaving, heddle (a device which grasps the thread), from Germanic **haf-*. **2.** HAFT, from Old English *hæft,* handle, from Germanic **haftjam.* **3.** Form **kap-o-*. HAVE, from Old English *habban,* to have, hold, from Germanic **habai-,* **habēn.* **4.** HEAVY, from Old English *hefig,* heavy, from Germanic **hafigaz,* "containing something," having weight. **5.** HAVEN, from Old English *hæfen,* a haven, from Germanic **hafnō-,* perhaps "place that holds ships." **6.** HAWK[1], from Old English *h(e)afoc,* hawk, from Germanic **habukaz.* **7.** (see **per**[1]) Latin combining form *-ceps* (< **kap-s*), "taker." **8.** GAFF[1], from Provençal *gafar,* to seize, from Germanic **gaf-,* probably akin to **kap-.**
II. Suffixed form **kap-yo-*. **1.** HEAVE, from Old English *hebban,* to lift, from Germanic **hafjan.* **2.** CABLE, CAPABLE, CAPACIOUS, CAPIAS, CAPSTAN, CAPTION, CAPTIOUS, (CAPTIVATE), CAPTIVE, CAPTOR, CAPTURE, CATCH, (CHASE[1]), ACCEPT, ANTICIPATE, CONCEIVE, DECEIVE, EXCEPT, INCEPTION, (INCIPIENT), INTERCEPT, INTUSSUSCEPTION, MUNICIPAL, NUNCUPATIVE, OCCUPY, PARTICIPATE, PERCEIVE, PRECEPT, RECEIVE, (RECOVER), RECUPERATE, (RX), SUSCEPTIBLE, from Latin *capere,* to take, seize, catch.
III. Lengthened-grade variant form **kōp-*. **1.a.** BEHOOF, from Old English *behōf,* use, profit, need; **b.** BEHOOVE, from Old English *behōfian,* to have need of. Both **a** and **b** from Germanic compound **bi-hōf,* "that which binds," requirement, obligation (**bi-,* intensive prefix; see **ambhi**), from **hōf-*. **2.** COPEPOD, from Greek *kōpē,* oar, handle. [Pokorny *kap-* 527.] Compare **ghabh-.**

kaput-. Important derivatives are *head, cadet, capital*[1]*, caprice, captain, cattle, chapter, chief, biceps, decapitate, kerchief,* and *mischief.*

kaput-. Head. **1.a.** HEAD, from Old English *hēafod,* head; **b.** HETMAN, from Old High German *houbit,* head. Both **a** and **b** from Germanic **haubudam,* **haubidam.* **2.** CADET, CAPE[2], CAPITAL[1], CAPITAL[2], CAPITATE, CAPITATION, CAPITELLUM, (CAPITULATE), CAPITULUM, CAPO[1], (CAPO[2]), CAPRICE, CAPTAIN, CATTLE, CAUDILLO, (CHAPITER), CHAPTER, CHIEF, CHIEFTAIN, CORPORAL[2]; BICEPS, DECAPITATE, KERCHIEF, MISCHIEF, OCCIPUT, PRECIPITATE, RECAPITULATE, SINCIPUT, TRICEPS, from Latin *caput,* head [Pokorny *kap-ut-* 529.]

kar-. Important derivatives are *hard, standard, hardy*[1]*, cancer,* and *canker.*

kar-. Hard.
I. Variant form **ker-*. **1.** Suffixed o-grade form **kor-tu-*. **a.** HARD, from Old English *hard, heard,* hard; **b.** -ARD, from Germanic **-hart,* **-hard,* bold, hardy; **c.** STANDARD, from Old French *estandard,* rallying place, perhaps from Frankish **hard,* hard; **d.** HARDY[1], from Old French *hardir,* to make hard. **a, b, c,** and **d** all from Germanic **harduz.* **2.** Suffixed zero-grade form **kr̥t-es-,* from earlier full-grade form **kret-es-*. -CRACY, from Greek *kratos,* strength, might, power.
II. Possible basic form **kar-* in derivatives referring to things with hard shells. **1.** CAREEN, CARINA, from Latin *carīna,* keel of a ship, nutshell, possibly from **kar-.** **2.** KARYO-; EUCARYOTE, GILLYFLOWER, SYNKARYON, from Greek *karuon,* nut, possibly from **kar-.** **3.** Reduplicated form **kar-kr-o-*. (CANCER), CANKER, CHANCRE, from dissimilated Latin *cancer,* crab, cancer, constellation Cancer. **4.** Suffixed form **kar-k-ino-*. CARCINO-, CARCINOMA, from Greek *karkinos,* cancer, crab. [Pokorny 3. *kar-* 531.]

kas-. An important derivative is *hare.*

kas-. Gray. **1.a.** HARE, from Old English *hara,* hare; **b.** HASENPFEFFER, from Old High German *haso,* rabbit. Both **a** and **b** from Germanic **hazōn-,* **hasōn-*. **2.** Suffixed form **kas-no-*. CANESCENT, from Latin *cānus,* white, gray, grayed hair. [Pokorny *k̂as-* 533.]

kat-. A derivative is *cata-.*

kat-. Down. **1.** CATA-, from Greek *kata,* down, possibly from **kat-.** **2.** Suffixed form **kat-olo-*. CADELLE, from Latin *catulus,* young puppy, young of animals ("dropped"). [Pokorny 2. *kat-* 534.]

kau-. Important derivatives are *hew, haggle, hoe,* and *hay.*

kau-. To hew, strike. **1.a.** HEW, from Old English *hēawan,* to hew; **b.** HAGGLE, from Old Norse *högg-va,* to cut; **c.** HOE, from Old French *houe,* a hoe. **a, b,** and **c** all from Germanic **hawwan.* **2.** HAG[2], from a source akin to Old Norse *högg,* a gap, a cutting blow, from Germanic **hawwō.* **3.** HAY, from Old English *hīeg,* hay, cut grass, from Germanic **haujam.* **4.** Suffixed form **kau-do-*. INCUS, from Latin *cūdere* (< **caudere*), to strike, beat. [Pokorny *kāu-* 535.]

ked-. Important derivatives are *cease, cede, abscess, access, ancestor, concede, decease, exceed, precede, proceed, succeed,* and *necessary.*

ked-. To go, yield. **1.** Lengthened-grade form **kēd-*. CEASE, CEDE, CESSION; ABSCESS, ACCEDE, ACCESS, ANCESTOR, ANTECEDE, CONCEDE, (CONCESSION), DECEASE, EXCEED, INTERCEDE, PRECEDE, PREDECESSOR, PROCEED, RECEDE, RETROCEDE, SECEDE, SUCCEED, from Latin *cēdere,* to go, withdraw, yield. **2.** Prefixed and suffixed form **ne-ked-ti-,* "(there is) no drawing back" (**ne-,* not; see **ne**). NECESSARY, from Latin *necesse,* inevitable, unavoidable. [In Pokorny *sed-* 884.]

keg-. Important derivatives are *hook, heckle,* and *hack*[1].

keg-. Hook, tooth. **1.a.** HAKE, from Old English *haca,* hook, akin to Old Norse *haki,* hook; **b.** HARQUEBUS, from Middle Dutch *hake,* hook. Both **a** and **b** from Germanic **hakan-*. **2.a.** HOOK, from Old English *hōc,* hook; **b.** HOOKER[1], from Middle Dutch *hōk, hoec,* hook; **c.** HAČEK, from Old High German *hāko,* hook. **a, b,** and **c** all from Germanic lengthened form **hōka-*. **3.** HECKLE, from Middle Dutch *hekel,* hatchel, a flax comb with long metal hooklike teeth, from Germanic **hakila-*. **4.** HACK[1], from Old English *-haccian,* to hack to pieces as with a hooked instrument, from Germanic **hakkijan.* [Pokorny *keg-* 537.]

kei-¹. Important derivatives are *city, civic, civil,* and *cemetery.*

kei-¹. To lie; bed, couch; beloved, dear.
I. Basic form **kei-*. **1.** Suffixed form **kei-wo-*. **a.** HIND[3], from Old English *hīwan,* members of a household, from Germanic **hīwa-;* **b.** HIDE[3], from Old English *hīgid, hīd,* a measure of land (< "household"), from suffixed Germanic form **hīwidō.* **2.** Suffixed form **kei-wi-*. CITY, CIVIC, CIVIL, from Latin *cīvis,* citizen (< "member of a household"). **3.** Suffixed form **kei-liyo-*. CEILIDH, from Old Irish *céle,* companion.
II. O-grade form **koi-*. **1.** Suffixed form **koi-nā.* INCUNABULUM, from Latin *cūnae,* a cradle. **2.** Suffixed form **koi-m-ā.* CEMETERY, from Greek *koiman,* to put to sleep.
III. Suffixed zero-grade form **ki-wo-*. SHIVA, from Sanskrit *śiva-,* auspicious, dear. [Pokorny 1. *k̂ei-* 539.]

kei-². Important derivatives are *cite, excite, incite, resuscitate, solicitous,* and *kinetic.*

kei-². To set in motion.
I. Possibly extended o-grade from **koid-*. **1.** HIGHT, from Old English *hātan,* to call, summon, order, from Germanic **haitan.* **2.** Suffixed form **koid-ti-*. **a.** HEST, from Old English *hǣs,* a command, a bidding; **b.** BEHEST, from Old English compound *behǣs,* a vow, promise, command (*be-,* intensive prefix; see **ambhi**). Both **a** and **b** from Germanic **haissiz* from **hait-ti-* (but Germanic **hait-* of **1** and **2** is perhaps to be referred to a separate root **kaid-*).
II. Zero-grade form **ki-*. Suffixed iterative form **ki-eyo-*. CITE; EXCITE, INCITE, OSCITANCY, RESUSCITATE, SOLICITOUS, from Latin *ciēre* (past participle *citus*), with its frequentative *citāre,* to set in motion, summon.
III. Extended root **kyeu-*. Nasal infixed form **ki-n-eu-*. KINEMATICS, KINESICS, -KINESIS, KINETIC; CINEMATOGRAPH, HYPERKINESIA, KINESIOLOGY, KINESTHESIA, KININ, (TELEKINESIS), from Greek *kinein,* to move. [Pokorny *kēi-* 538.]

kekʷ-. A derivative is *copro-.*

kekʷ-. To excrete. Suffixed o-grade form **kokʷ-ro-*. COPRO-, from Greek *kopros,* dung. [Pokorny *k̂eku̯-* 544.]

kel-¹. Important derivatives are *hell, hall, hull, hole, hollow, holster, apocalypse, eucalyptus, helmet, occult, color, cell, cellar,* and *conceal.*

kel-[1]. To cover, conceal, save.
I. O-grade form *kol-. **1.a.** HELL, from Old English *hell*, hell; **b.** HEL, from Old Norse *Hel*, the underworld, goddess of death. Both **a** and **b** from Germanic *haljō, the underworld (< "concealed place"). **2.a.** HALL, from Old English *heall*, hall; **b.** VALHALLA, from Old Norse *höll*, hall. Both **a** and **b** from Germanic *hallō, covered place, hall. **3.** Suffixed form *kol-eyo-. COLEUS; COLEOPTERAN, COLEOPTILE, COLEORHIZA, from Greek *koleon, koleos*, sheath.
II. Zero-grade form *kl̥-. **1.a.** HOLD[2], HULL, from Old English *hulu*, husk, pod (< "that which covers"); **b.** HOLE, from Old English *hol*, a hollow; **c.** HOLLOW, from Old English *holh*, hole, hollow; **d.** HAUGH, from Old English *healh*, secret place, small hollow. **a, b, c,** and **d** all from Germanic *hul-. **2.a.** HOLSTER, from Old High German *hulft*, covering; **b.** HOUSING[2], from Medieval Latin *hultia*, protective covering. Both **a** and **b** from suffixed Germanic form *hulftī-. **3.** Suffixed form *kl̥-to-. (see **III. 2.** below) Latin *occultus*. **4.** Extended form *klā (< *kl̥ə-). CLANDESTINE, from Latin *clam*, in secret. **5.** Suffixed variant form *kal-up-yo-. CALYPSO[1], CALYPTRA; APOCALYPSE, EUCALYPTUS, from Greek *kaluptein*, to cover, conceal.
III. Full-grade form *kel-. **1.a.** HELM[2], from Old English *helm*, protection, covering; **b.** HELMET, from Middle English *helmet*, helmet, from a source akin to Frankish *helm, helmet. Both **a** and **b** from Germanic *helmaz, "protective covering." **2.** OCCULT, from Latin *occulere* < *ob-kel- (past participle *occultus* < *ob-kl̥-to-; see **II. 3.** above), to cover over (*ob-*, over; see **epi**). **3.** Suffixed form *kel-os-. COLOR, from Latin *color*, color, hue (< "that which covers"). **4.** Suffixed form *kel-nā-. CELL, CELLA, CELLAR, CELLARER; (RATHSKELLER), from Latin *cella*, storeroom, chamber. **5.** Suffixed form *kel-yo-. CILIUM, SEEL; SUPERCILIOUS, (SUPERCILIUM), from Latin *cilium*, lower eyelid.
IV. Lengthened-grade form *kēl-ā-. CONCEAL, from Latin *cēlāre*, to hide. [Pokorny 4. k̂el- 553.]

kel-[2]. Important derivatives are *hill, excel, culminate, colonel,* and *column*.

kel-[2]. To be prominent; hill. **1.** Zero-grade form *kl̥-. **a.** HILL, from Old English *hyll*, hill, from suffixed Germanic form *hul-ni-; **b.** HOLM, from Old Norse *hōlmr*, islet in a bay, meadow, from suffixed Germanic form *hul-ma-. **2.** Suffixed form *kel-d-. EXCEL, from Latin *excellere*, to raise up, elevate, also to be eminent (*ex-*, up out of; see **eghs**). **3.** O-grade form *kol-. **a.** COLOPHON, from Greek *kolophōn*, summit; **b.** suffixed form *kol(u)men-. CULMINATE, from Latin *culmen*, top, summit; **c.** extended and suffixed form *kolumnā. COLONEL, COLONNADE, COLUMN, from Latin *columna*, a projecting object, column. [Pokorny 1. kel- 544.]

kelə-[1]. Important derivatives are *lee, chafe, caldron, chowder, scald[1],* and *calorie*.

kelə-[1]. Warm. Variant *klē-, contracted from *kleə-. **1.** Suffixed variant form *klē-wo-. **a.** LEE, from Old English *hlēo, hlēow*, covering, protection (as from cold); **b.** LUKEWARM, from Old English *-hlēow*, warm. Both **a** and **b** from Germanic *hlēwaz. **2.** Suffixed zero-grade form *kl̥ə-ē-. **a.** CALENTURE, CHAFE; DECALESCENCE, INCALESCENT, NONCHALANT, RECALESCENCE, from Latin *calēre*, to be warm; **b.** CALDRON, CAUDLE, (CHOWDER); SCALD[1], from Latin derivative adjective *calidus*, warm. **3.** Suffixed zero-grade form *kl̥ə-os-. CALORIC, CALORIE; CALORECEPTOR, CALORIFIC, CALORIMETER, CALORIMETRY, from Latin *calor*, heat. [Pokorny 1. k̂el- 551.]

kelə-[2]. Important derivatives are *claim, clamor, acclaim, exclaim, reclaim, haul, council, calendar, clear, declare,* and *class*.

kelə-[2]. To shout.
I. Variant form *klā- (< *klaə-). **1.** LOW[2], from Old English *hlōwan*, to roar, low, from Germanic *hlō-. **2.** Suffixed form *klā-mā-. CLAIM, CLAMANT, CLAMOR; ACCLAIM, DECLAIM, EXCLAIM, PROCLAIM, RECLAIM, from Latin *clāmāre*, to call, cry out.
II. O-grade form *kolə-. **a.** KEELHAUL, from Middle Dutch *halen*, to haul, pull (? < "to call together, summon"); **b.** HALE[2], HAUL, from Old French *haler*, to haul. Both **a** and **b** from Germanic *halōn, to call.
III. Zero-grade form *kl̥ə- (> *kal-). **1.** Suffixed form *kal-yo-. CONCILIATE, COUNCIL, from Latin *concilium*, a meeting, gathering (< "a calling together"; *con-*, together; see **kom**). **2.** Suffixed form *kal-end-. CALENDAR, CALENDS, from Latin *kalendae*, the calends, the first day of the month, when it was publicly announced on which days the nones and ides of that month would fall. **3.** Suffixed form *kal-e-. ECCLESIA, PARACLETE, from Greek *kalein* (variant *klē-*), to call. **4.** Suffixed form *kal-ā-. INTERCALATE, NOMENCLATOR, from Latin *calāre*, to call, call out. **5.** Suffixed form *kl̥ə-ro- or suffixed variant form *klaə-ro- contracted to *klā-ro-. CLEAR, GLAIR; CHIAROSCURO, CLAIRVOYANT, DECLARE, ÉCLAIR, (ECLAIRCISSEMENT), from Latin *clārus*, bright, clear.
IV. Possibly extended zero-grade form *kl̥d-, becoming *klad- in suffixed form *klad-ti-. CLASS, from Latin *classis*, summons, division of citizens for military draft, hence army, fleet, also class in general. [Pokorny 6. kel- 548.]

ken-. An important derivative is *recent*.

ken-. Fresh, new, young. **1.** Suffixed form *ken-t-. RECENT, from Latin *recēns*, young, fresh, new (*re-*, again; see **re-**). **2.** Suffixed zero-grade form *kn̥-yo-. -CENE; CAINOTOPHOBIA, CENOZOIC, KAINITE, from Greek *kainos*, new, fresh. [Pokorny 3. ken- 563.]

kenk-. Important derivatives are *cinch, precinct,* and *succinct*.

kenk-. To gird, bind. Variant form *keng-. CINCH, CINCTURE, CINGULUM; ENCEINTE[1], ENCEINTE[2], PRECINCT, SHINGLES, SUCCINCT, from Latin *cingere*, to gird. [Pokorny 1. kenk- 565.]

kens-. Important derivatives are *censor* and *census*.

kens-. To proclaim, speak solemnly. Form *kensē-. CENSOR, CENSUS; RECENSION, from Latin *cēnsēre*, to judge, assess, estimate, tax. [Pokorny k̂ens- 566.]

kent-. Important derivatives are *center* and *eccentric*.

kent-. To prick, jab. **1.** CENTER; AMNIOCENTESIS, DICENTRA, ECCENTRIC, from Greek *kentein*, to prick. **2.** Suffixed form *kent-to-. CESTUS[1], from Greek *kestos*, belt, girdle. [Pokorny k̂ent- 567.]

ker-[1]. Important derivatives are *horn, cornea, corner, cornet, Capricorn, unicorn, hornet, reindeer, cranium, migraine, cheer, carrot, cervix, carat, rhinoceros,* and *cerebrum*.

ker-[1]. Horn, head; with derivatives referring to horned animals, horn-shaped objects, and projecting parts.
I. Zero-grade form *kr̥-. **1.** Suffixed form *kr̥-n-. **a.** *(i)* HORN, (HORNBEAM), from Old English *horn*, horn; *(ii)* ALPENHORN, ALTHORN, FLÜGELHORN, HORNBLENDE, from Old High German *horn*, horn. Both *(i)* and *(ii)* from Germanic *hurnaz; **b.** CORN[2], CORNEA, CORNEOUS, CORNER, CORNET, CORNICULATE, CORNU; BICORNUATE, CAPRICORN, CORNIFICATION, LAMELLICORN, LONGICORN, TRICORN, UNICORN, from Latin *cornū*, horn. **2.** Suffixed and extended form *kr̥s-n-. HORNET, from Old English *hyrnet*, hornet, from Germanic *hurznuta-. **3.** Suffixed form *kr-ei-. **a.** REINDEER, from Old Norse *hreinn*, reindeer, from Germanic *hraina-; **b.** RINDERPEST, from Old High German *hrind*, ox, from Germanic *hrinda-. **4.** Suffixed extended form *kr̥əs-no-. CRANIUM; MIGRAINE, OLECRANON, from Greek *kranion*, skull, upper part of the head. **5.** Suffixed form *kr̥-ə-. **a.** CHARIVARI; CHEER, from Greek *karē, kara*, head; **b.** CAROTID, from Greek *karoun*, to stupefy, be stupefied (< "to feel heavy-headed"); **c.** CARROT, from Greek *karōton*, carrot (from its hornlike shape). **6.** Possibly extended form *krī-. CRIOSPHINX, from Greek *krios*, ram.
II. Suffixed form *ker-wo-. **1.** CERVINE, SERVAL, from Latin *cervus*, deer. **2.** CERVIX, from Latin *cervīx*, neck.
III. Extended and suffixed form *keru-do-. **a.** HART, from Old English *heorot*, hart, stag; **b.** HARTEBEEST, from Middle Dutch *hert*, deer, hart. Both **a** and **b** from Germanic *herutaz.
IV. Extended form *kerəs-. **1.** CARAT, CERASTES, KERATO-; CERATODUS, CHELICERA, CLADOCERAN, KERATIN, MONOCEROS, RHINOCEROS, TRICERATOPS, from Greek *keras*, horn. **2.** SIRDAR, from Persian *sar*, head. **3.** Suffixed form *kerəs-ro. CEREBELLUM, CEREBRUM, SAVELOY, from Latin *cerebrum*, brain.
V. Extended o-grade form *koru-. **1.** CORYMB, from Greek *korumbos*, uppermost point (< "head"). **2.** CORYPHAEUS, from Greek *koruphē*, head. **3.** Suffixed form *koru-do-. CORYDALIS, from Greek *korudos*, crested lark. **4.** Suffixed form *koru-nā-. CORYNEBACTERIUM, from Greek *korunē*, club, mace. [Pokorny 1. k̂er- 574.]

ker-[2]. Important derivatives are *cereal, create, Creole, crescent, crew[1], concrete, decrease, increase, recruit,* and *sincere*.

ker-[2]. To grow. **1.** Suffixed form *ker-es-. CEREAL, CERES, from Latin *Cerēs*, goddess of agriculture, especially the growth of grain. **2.** Extended form *krē- (< *kreə-). **a.** suffixed form *krē-yā-. CREATE, CREOLE; PROCREATE, from Latin *creāre*, to bring forth, create, produce (< "to cause to grow"); **b.** suffixed form *krē-sko-. CRESCENDO, CRESCENT, CREW[1]; ACCRUE, (CONCRESCENCE), CONCRETE, DECREASE, EXCRESCENCE, INCREASE, RECRUIT, from Latin *crēscere*, to grow, increase. **3.** Suffixed o-grade form *kor-wo-, "growing," adolescent. DIOSCURI, HYPOCORISM, from Greek *kouros, koros*, boy, son, and *korē*, girl. **4.** Compound *sm̥-kēro-, "of one growth" (*sm̥-, same, one; see **sem-[1]**). SINCERE, from Latin *sincērus*, pure, clean. [Pokorny 2. k̂er- 577.]

ker-[3]. Important derivatives are *hearth, carbon, cremate,* and *ceramic*.

ker-[3]. Heat, fire. **1.** Suffixed form *ker-tā. HEARTH, from Old English *heorth*, hearth, from Germanic *herthō. **2.** Zero-grade form *kr̥-. **a.** CARBON, CARBUNCLE, from Latin *carbō*, charcoal, ember; **b.** extended form *krem-. CREMATE, from Latin *cremāre*, to burn. **3.** Possibly suffixed and extended form *kerə-mo-. CERAMIC, from Greek *keramos*, potter's clay, earthenware. **4.** Possibly variant extended form *krās-. CRASH[2], from Russian *krasit'*, to color. [Pokorny 3. ker(ə)- 571.]

kerd-. Important derivatives are *heart, cordial, courage, quarry[1], accord, discord, record, cardiac, credence, credible, credit,* and *grant*.

kerd-. Heart. **1.** Suffixed form *kerd-en-. HEART, from Old English *heorte*, heart, from Germanic *hertōn-. **2.** Zero-grade form *kr̥d-. **a.** CORDATE, CORDIAL, COURAGE, QUARRY[1]; ACCORD, CONCORD, CORDIFORM, DISCORD, MISERICORD, RECORD, from Latin *cor* (stem *cord-*), heart; **b.** suffixed form *kr̥d-yā-. CARDIA, CARDIAC, CARDIO-; ENDOCARDIUM, EPICARDIUM, MEGALOCARDIA, MYOCARDIUM, PERICARDIUM, from Greek *kardia*, heart, stomach, orifice. **3.** Possibly *kred-dhə-, "to place trust" (an old religious term; *dhə-, to do, place; see **dhē-**). CREDENCE, CREDIBLE, CREDIT, CREDO, CREDULOUS, GRANT; MISCREANT, RECREANT, from Latin *crēdere*, to believe. [Pokorny k̂ered- 579.]

kerə-. Important derivatives are *rare[2], uproar,* and *crater*.

kerə-. To mix, confuse, cook. **1.** Variant form *krā- (< *kraə-). **a.** RARE[2], from Old English *hrēr*, lightly boiled, half-cooked, possibly from **kerə-;** **b.** UPROAR, from Middle Low German *rōr*, motion. Both **a** and **b** from Germanic *hrōr-. **2.** Zero-grade form *kr̥ə-. **a.** suffixed form *kr̥ə-ti-. IDIOSYNCRACY; DYSCRASIA, from Greek *krasis*, a mixing; **b.** suffixed form *kr̥ə-ter-. CRATER, from Greek *kratēr*, mixing vessel. [Pokorny k̂erə- 582.]

kerp-. Important derivatives are *harvest, carpet, excerpt,* and *scarce*.

kerp-. To gather, pluck, harvest. Variant *karp-. **1.** HARVEST, from Old English *hærfest*, harvest, from Germanic *harbistaz. **2.** CARPET; EXCERPT, (SCARCE), from Latin *carpere*, to pluck. **3.** -CARP, CARPEL, CARPO-, -CARPOUS, from Greek *karpos*, fruit. [In Pokorny 4. sker- 938.]

kers-. Important derivatives are *corridor, courier, course, current, cursive, cursor, concur, discourse, excursion, incur, intercourse, occur, recur, car, career, cargo, carry, charge,* and *carpenter*.

kers-. To run. Zero-grade form *kr̥s-. **1.** CORRAL, CORRIDA, CORRIDOR, (CORSAIR), COURANTE, COURIER, COURSE, CURRENT, CURSIVE, CURSOR, CURULE; CONCOURSE, CONCUR, DECURRENT, DISCOURSE, EXCURSION, (HUSSAR), INCUR, INTERCOURSE, OCCUR, PERCURRENT, PRECURSOR, RECOURSE, RECUR, SUCCOR, from Latin *currere*, to run. **2.** Suffixed form *kr̥s-o-. **a.** CAR, CAREER, CARGO, CARICATURE, CARIOLE, (CARK), CAROCHE, (CARRY), CHARGE, CHARIOT; (DISCHARGE), from Latin *carrus*, a two-wheeled wagon; **b.** CARPENTER, from Latin *carpentum,* a two-wheeled carriage. Both **a** and **b** from Gaulish *carros,* a wagon, cart. [Pokorny 2. ḱers- 583.]

kes-. Important derivatives are *castrate, castle, caste, chaste, incest,* and *cashier.*

kes-. To cut. Variant *kas-. **1.** Suffixed form *kas-tro-. **a.** CASTRATE, from Latin *castrāre,* to castrate; **b.** ALCAZAR, CASTLE, from Latin *castrum,* fortified place, camp (perhaps "separated place"). **2.** Suffixed form *kas-to-. CASTE, CHASTE; CASTIGATE, INCEST, from Latin *castus,* chaste, pure (< "cut off from or free of faults"). **3.** Suffixed (stative) form *kas-ē-. CARET, from Latin *carēre,* "to be cut off from," lack. **4.** Extended geminated form *kasso-. (CASHIER), QUASH[1], from Latin *cassus,* empty, void. [Pokorny ḱes- 586.]

keu-. Important derivatives are *hear, acoustic, show, scavenger,* and *sheen.*

keu-. Also **əkeu-.** To perceive, see, hear. O-grade form *əkou-. **1.** Extended form *kous-. **a.** *(i)* HEAR, from Old English *hīeran,* to hear; *(ii)* HEARKEN, from Old English *he(o)rcnian,* to harken. Both *(i)* and *(ii)* from Germanic *hausjan; **b.** suffixed form *əkous-yo-. ACOUSTIC, from Greek *akouein,* to hear. **2.** Variant *skou-. **a.** *(i)* SHOW, from Old English *scēawian,* to look at; *(ii)* SCAVENGER, from Flemish *scauwen,* to look at; *(iii)* WELTANSCHAUUNG, from Old High German *scouwōn,* to look at. *(i), (ii),* and *(iii)* all from Germanic *skauwōn; **b.** SCONE, from Middle Dutch *schoon,* beautiful, bright (< "conspicuous, attractive"); **c.** SHEEN, from Old English *scīene,* bright, sheen, from Germanic *skauniz. [Pokorny 1. ḱeu- 587.]

keuə-. Important derivatives are *cave, cavern, concave, excavate, cumulus, accumulate,* and *church.*

keuə-. To swell; vault, hole.
I. O-grade form *kouə-. **1.** Basic form *kouə- becoming *kaw-. CAVE, CAVERN, CAVETTO, CAVITY; CONCAVE, EXCAVATE, from Latin *cavus,* hollow. **2.** Suffixed form *kow-ilo-.(-CELE[2]), CELIAC, -COEL, COELOM, from Greek *koilos,* hollow. **3.** Suffixed lengthened-grade form *kōw-o-. CODEINE, from Greek *kōos,* hollow place, cavity.
II. Zero-grade form *kū- (< *kuə-). **1.** Suffixed shortened form *ku-m-olo. CUMULATE, CUMULUS; ACCUMULATE, from Latin *cumulus,* heap, mass. **2.** Basic form *kū-. **a.** suffixed form *kū-ro-, "swollen," strong, powerful. CHURCH, (KIRK), KYRIE, from Greek *kurios* (vocative *kurie*), master, lord; **b.** suffixed form *kuw-eyo-. CYMA; PSEUDOCYESIS, from Greek *kuein,* to swell, and derivative *kuma* (< *kū-mn̥), " a swelling," wave; **c.** suffixed form *en-kū-yo- (*en, in; see **en-**). ENCEINTE[1]; from Latin *inciēns,* pregnant. [Pokorny 1. ḱeu- 592.]

klei-. Important derivatives are *decline, incline, recline, proclivity, lid, lean[1], client, clinic, climax, climate,* and *ladder.*

klei-. To lean.
I. Full-grade form *klei-. **1.** Suffixed form *klei-n-. DECLINE, INCLINE, RECLINE, from Latin *-clīnāre,* to lean, bend. **2.** Suffixed form *klei-tro-. CLITELLUM, from Latin *clītellae,* packsaddle, from diminutive of *clītra, litter. **3.** Suffixed form *klei-wo-. ACCLIVITY, DECLIVITY, PROCLIVITY, from Latin *clīvus,* a slope. **4.** Suffixed form *klei-tor-, "incline, hill." CLITORIS, from Greek feminine diminutive *kleitoris.*
II. Zero grade form *kli-. **1.** LID, from Old English *hlid,* cover, from Germanic *hlid-, "that which bends over," cover. **2.** Suffixed form *kli-n-. LEAN[1], from Old English *hlinian* and *hleonian,* to lean, from Germanic *hlinēn. **3.** Suffixed form *kli-ent-. CLIENT, from Latin *cliēns,* dependent, follower. **4.** Suffixed form *kli-to-. (see **ous-**) Latin *auscultāre,* "to hold one's ear inclined," to listen to, from *aus-klit-ā-. **5.** Suffixed form *kli-n-yo-. -CLINAL, CLINE, (-CLINE), (-CLINIC), CLINO-; ACLINIC LINE, ANACLISIS, CLINANDRIUM, ENCLITIC, MATRICLINOUS, PATROCLINOUS, PERICLINE, (PROCLITIC), from Greek *klinein,* to lean. **6.** Lengthened form *klī-. **a.** suffixed form *klī-n-ā. CLINIC; DICLINOUS, MONOCLINOUS, TRICLINIUM, from Greek *klinē,* bed; **b.** suffixed form *klī-m-. CLIMAX, from Greek *klimax,* ladder; **c.** suffixed form *klī-mn̥. CLIMATE, from Greek *klima,* sloping surface of the earth.
III. Suffixed o-grade form *kloi-tr-. LADDER, from Old English *hlǣd(d)er,* ladder, from Germanic *hlaidri-. [Pokorny ḱlei- 600.]

kleu-. Important derivatives are *leer, listen,* and *loud.*

kleu-. To hear.
I. Extended form *kleus-. LEER, from Old English *hlēor,* cheek (< "side of the face" < "ear"), from Germanic *hleuza-.
II. Zero-grade form *klu-. **1.** LIST[4], from Old English *hlystan,* to listen, from Germanic *hlustjan. **2.** LISTEN, from Old English *hlysnan,* to listen, from Germanic *hlusinōn. **3.** Suffixed lengthened form *klū-to-. **a.** LOUD, from Old English *hlūd,* loud; **b.** ABLAUT, UMLAUT, from Old High German *hlūt,* sound. Both **a** and **b** from Germanic *hlūdaz, "heard," loud.
III. Full-grade form *kleu-. **1.** Suffixed form *klew-yo-. CLIO, from Greek *kleiein,* to praise, tell. **2.** Suffixed form *klew-es-. HERCULES, from Latin *Herculēs,* from Greek *Hēraklēs, Hērakleēs.* **3.** Suffixed form *kleu-to-. SAROD, from Old Iranian *srauta-.* [Pokorny 1. ḱleu- 605.]

ko-. Important derivatives are *he[1], him, his, her, it, here, hence,* and *et cetera.*

ko-. Stem of demonstrative pronoun meaning "this."
I. Variant form *ki-. **1.a.** HE[1], from Old English *hē,* he; **b.** HIM, from Old English *him,* him (dative of *hē*); **c.** HIS, from Old English *his,* his (genitive of *hē*); **d.** HER, from Old English *hire,* her (dative and genitive of *heo,* she); **e.** IT, from Old English *hit,* it (neuter of *hē*); **f.** HERE, from Old English *hēr,* here; **g.** HENCE, from Old English *heonane, heonon,* from here. **a, b, c, d, e, f,** and **g** all from Germanic *hi-, **2.** Suffixed form *ki-tro-. HITHER, from Old English *hider,* hither, from Germanic *hi-thra-. **3.** Suffixed form *ki-s. CIS-, from Latin *cis,* on this side of.
II. Variant form *ke-. **1.** Preposed in *ke-etero- (*e-tero- , a second time, again; see **i-**). ET CETERA, from Latin *cēterus* (neuter plural *cētera*), the other part, that which remains. **2.** (see **nu-**) Postposed in Latin *-ce.*
III. **1.** BEHIND, HIND[1], from Old English *behindan,* in the rear, behind (*bi,* at; see **ambhi**). **2.** HINTERLAND, from Old High German *hintar,* behind. **3.** HINDER[1], from Old English *hindrian,* to check, hinder, from Germanic derivative verb *hindrōn, to keep back. **1, 2,** and **3** all from Germanic root *hind-, behind, attributed by some to this root (but more likely of obscure origin). [Pokorny 1. ko- 609.]

kō-. An important derivative is *cone.*

kō-. To sharpen, whet. Contracted from *koə-. **1.** Suffixed extended form *koəi-no-. HONE[1], from Old English *hān,* stone, from Germanic *hainō. **2.** CONE, CONIC; CONIFER, CONODONT, from Greek *kōnos,* cone, conical object (< "a sharp-pointed object"), perhaps from **kō-**. [Pokorny ḱēi- 541.]

kob-. Important derivatives are *happen, happy, hapless,* and *mishap.*

kob-. To suit, fit, succeed. HAP, (HAPPEN), (HAPPY); (HAPLESS), (MISHAP), from Old Norse *happ,* chance, good luck, from Germanic *hap-. [Pokorny kob- 610.]

kom. Important derivatives are *enough, co-, contra-, contrary, counter[1], country,* and *encouter.*

kom. Beside, near, by, with. **1.** ENOUGH, GEMOT, HANDIWORK, YCLEPT; WITENAGEMOT, from Old English *ge-,* with, also participial, collective, and intensive prefix, from Germanic *ga-, together, with (collective and intensive prefix and marker of the past participle). **2.** CUM; COONCAN, from Latin *cum, co-,* with. **3.** (CO-), COM-, from Old Latin *com,* with (collective and intensive prefix). **4.** (see **merg-**) British Celtic *kombrogos, fellow countryman, from Celtic *kom-, collective prefix. **5.** Suffixed form *kom-trā. (CON[1]), CONTRA-, CONTRARY, (COUNTER[1]), COUNTER-, COUNTRY; ENCOUNTER, from Latin *contrā,* against, opposite. **6.** Suffixed form *kom-yo-. COENO-; CENOBITE, EPICENE, KOINE, from Greek *koinos,* common, shared. **7.** Reduced form *ko- (see **gher-[1], mei-[1], smei-**). [Pokorny kom 612.]

konk-. Important derivatives are *hang* and *hinge.*

konk-. To hang. **1.a.** HANG, from Old English *hōn,* to hang; **b.** HANKER, from Dutch (dialectal) *hankeren,* to long for; **c.** HINGE, from Middle English *he(e)ng, hinge,* hinge, possibly related (ultimately from the base of Old English *hangian,* to hang). **a, b,** and **c** all from Germanic *hanhan (transitive), *hangēn* (intransitive), hang. **2.** Suffixed form *konk-t-ā-. CUNCTATION, from Latin *cūnctārī,* to delay. [Pokorny ḱenk- 566, ḱonk- 614.]

koro-. Important derivatives are *harbor, harbinger, herald, harry,* and *harangue.*

koro-. War; also war-band, host, army.
I. **1.** HERIOT, from Old English *here,* army. **2.** ARRIÈRE-BAN, from Old French *herban,* a summoning to military service (*ban,* proclamation, summons; see **bhā-[2]**). **3.a.** HARBOR, from Old English *herebeorg,* lodging; **b.** HARBINGER, from Old French *herberge,* lodging. Both **a** and **b** from Germanic compound *harja-bergaz, "army hill," hill-fort, later shelter, lodging, army quarters (*bergaz, hill; see **bhergh-[2]**). **4.** HERALD, from Anglo-Norman *herald,* from Germanic compound *harja-waldaz, "army commander" (*wald-, rule, power; see **wal-**). **5.** HARNESS, from Old French *harneis,* harness, from Germanic compound *harja-nestam, "army provisions" (*nestam, food for a journey; see **nes-[1]**). **1, 2, 3, 4,** and **5** all from Germanic *harjaz, army.
II. HARRY, from Old English *hergian,* to ravage, plunder, raid, from Germanic denominative *harjōn.
III. HARANGUE, from Old Italian *aringo, arringa,* public square, from Germanic compound *hari-hring, assembly, "host-ring" (*hringaz, ring; see **sker-[2]**). [Pokorny koro-s 615.]

kost-. Important derivatives are *coast, cutlet,* and *accost.*

kost-. Bone. Probably related to **ost-.** COAST, COSTA, COSTARD, COSTREL, CUESTA, CUTLET; ACCOST, INTERCOSTAL, STERNOCOSTAL, from Latin *costa,* rib, side. [Pokorny kost- 616.]

krei-. Important derivatives are *riddle[1], garble, crime, criminal, discriminate, certain, concern, decree, discern, excrement, secret, crisis, critic,* and *hypocrisy.*

krei-. To sieve, discriminate, distinguish. **1.** Basic form with variant instrumental suffixes. **a.** suffixed form *krei-tro-. RIDDLE[1], from Old English *hridder, hriddel,* sieve, from Germanic *hridra-, a sieve; **b.** suffixed form *krei-dhro-. CRIBRIFORM, GARBLE, from Latin *crībrum,* a sieve. **2.** Suffixed form *krei-men-. **a.** CRIME, (CRIMINAL); RECRIMINATE, from Latin *crīmen,* judgment, crime; **b.** DISCRIMINATE, from Latin *discrīmen,* distinction (*dis-,* apart). **3.** Suffixed zero-grade form *kri-no- (participial form *kri-to-). CERTAIN; CONCERN, DECREE, DISCERN, (EXCREMENT), EXCRETE, (INCERTITUDE), RECREMENT, SECERN, SECRET, from Latin *cernere* (perfect *crēvī;* past participle *crētus*), to sift, separate, decide. **4.** Suffixed zero-grade form *kri-n-yo-. CRISIS, CRITIC, CRITERION; APOCRINE, DIACRITIC, ECCRINE, ENDOCRINE, EPICRITIC, EXOCRINE, HEMATOCRIT, HYPOCRISY, from Greek *krinein,* to separate, decide, judge (> *krinesthai,* to explain). [Pokorny 4. sker-, Section II. 945.]

kreuə-. Important derivatives are *raw, pancreas, crude,* and *cruel.*

kreuə-. Raw flesh. **1.** Lengthened-grade form *krēw-. RAW, from Old English *hrēaw,* raw, from Germanic *hrēwaz. **2.** Suffixed form *krewə-s-. CREATINE, CREODONT, CREOSOTE, PANCREAS, from Greek *kreas,* flesh. **3.** Suffixed zero-grade form *krū-do- (< *kruə-do-). **a.** CRUDE; ECRU, RECRUDESCE, from Latin *crūdus,* bloody, raw; **b.** CRUEL, from Latin *crūdēlis,* cruel. [Pokorny 1. A. kreu- 621.]

kreus-. Important derivatives are *crust, crustacean,* and *crystal.*

kreus-. To begin to freeze, form a crust. **1.** Suffixed zero-grade form *krus-to-. **a.** CROUTON, CRUST, CRUSTACEAN, CRUSTACEOUS, CRUSTOSE; ENCRUST, from Latin *crusta,* crust; **b.** CRYSTAL, CRYSTALLINE, CRYSTALLO-, from Greek *krustallos,* ice, crystal. **2.** Suffixed zero-grade form *krus-es-. CRYO-, from Greek *kruos,* icy cold, frost. **3.** Suffixed zero-grade form *krus-mo-. CRYMOTHERAPY, from Greek *krumos,* icy cold, frost. [Pokorny 1. B. kreu- 621.]

ksun. Important derivatives are *syn-* and *sputnik.*

ksun. Preposition and preverb meaning "with." **1.**

SYN-, from Greek *sun, xun,* together, with. **2.** Basic form **su(n)-.* **a.** SOVIET, from Old Russian compound *sŭvětŭ,* assembly, from *sŭ(n)-,* with, together; **b.** SPUTNIK, from Russian *sputnik,* fellow traveler, sputnik (see **pent-**), from *so-, s-,* with, together, from *sŭ(n).* [In Pokorny 2. *sem-* 902.]

k^we. Derivatives are *sesqui-* and *ubiquity.*

k^we. And (enclitic). SESQUI-, UBIQUITY, from Latin *-que,* and. [Pokorny *k^ue* 635.]

k^wei-[1]. Important derivatives are *pain, penalty, punish, impunity,* and *subpoena.*

k^wei-[1]. To pay, atone, compensate. Suffixed o-grade form **k^woi-nā.* PAIN, PENAL, (PENALTY), PINE[2], PUNISH; IMPUNITY, PENOLOGY, (PUNITORY), (REPINE), SUBPOENA, from Greek *poinē,* fine, penalty. [Pokorny *k^uei-(t-)* 636.]

k^wei-[2]. Important derivatives are *cheetah, poem,* and *poet.*

k^wei-[2]. To pile up, build, make. O-grade form **k^woi-.* **a.** CHEETAH, from Sanskrit *kāyaḥ,* body; **b.** suffixed form **k^woi-wo-,* making, in denominative verb **k^woiw-eyo-.* POEM, POESY, POET, POETIC, -POIESIS, -POIETIC; EPOPEE, MYTHOPOEIC, ONOMATOPOEIA, PHARMACOPOEIA, PROSOPOPEIA, from Greek *poiein,* to make, create. [Pokorny 2. *k^uei-* 637.]

k^weiə-. Important derivatives are *while, tranquil, coy, quiet,* and *acquiesce.*

k^weiə-. To rest, be quiet.
I. Suffixed zero-grade variant form **k^wī-lo-* (< **k^wiə-lo-*). **1.a.** WHILE, from Old English *hwīl,* while; **b.** WHILOM, from Old English *hwīlum,* sometimes. Both **a** and **b** from Germanic **hwīlō.* **2.** TRANQUIL, from Latin *tranquillus,* tranquil (*trāns,* across, beyond; see **terə-[2]**), possibly from **k^weiə-.**
II. Variant form **k^wyē-* (< **k^wyeə-*). COY, QUIET; ACQUIESCE, REQUIEM, REQUIESCAT, from Latin *quiēs,* quiet, *requiēs,* rest, and *requiēscere,* to rest. [Pokorny *k^uei-* 638.]

kweit-. Important derivatives are *white* and *wheat.*

kweit-. White; to shine. **1.** Suffixed form **kweit-o-.* **a.** WHITE, from Old English *hwīt,* white; **b.** WITLOOF, from Middle Dutch *wit,* white; **c.** WHITING[2], from Middle Dutch *wijting,* whiting; **d.** EDELWEISS, from Old High German *hwīz, wīz,* white. **a, b, c,** and **d** all from Germanic **hwītaz.* **2.** Suffixed o-grade form **kwoit-yo-.* WHEAT, from Old English *hwǣte,* wheat (from the fine white flour it yields), from Germanic **hwaitjaz.* [Pokorny 3. *k̂u̯ei-* 628.]

k^wel-[1]. Important derivatives are *colony, cult, cultivate, culture, wheel, cycle, cyclone, bicycle, collar, pole[1], pulley,* and *bucolic.*

k^wel-[1]. To revolve, move around, sojourn, dwell.
I. Basic form **k^wel-.* COLONY, CULT, CULTIVATE, (CULTURE); INCULT, INQUILINE, SILVICOLOUS, from Latin *colere,* to till, cultivate, inhabit.
II. Suffixed form **k^wel-es-.* TELIC, (TELIUM), TELO-; ENTELECHY, TALISMAN, TELEOLOGY, (TELEOST), TELEUTOSPORE, from Greek *telos,* "completion of a cycle," consummation, perfection, end, result.
III. Suffixed reduplicated form **k^w(e)-k^wl-o-,* circle. **1.** WHEEL, from Old English *hwēol, hweogol,* wheel, from Germanic **hwewlaz.* **2.** CYCLE, CYCLO-, CYCLOID, CYCLONE, CYCLOSIS; (BICYCLE), ENCYCLICAL, EPICYCLE, from Greek *kuklos,* circle, wheel. **3.** CHAKRA, CHUKKER, from Sanskrit *cakram,* circle, wheel. **4.** Metathesized form **k^we-lk^w-o-.* CHARKHA, from Old Persian **carka-.*
IV. O-grade form **k^wol-.* **1.** Suffixed form **k^wol-so-,* "that on which the head turns," neck. **a.** *(i)* HAWSE, from Old Norse *hāls,* neck, ship's bow; *(ii)* RINGHALS, from Middle Dutch *hals,* neck; *(iii)* HAUBERK, from Old French *hauberc,* hauberk, from Germanic compound **h(w)als-berg-,* "neck-protector," gorget (**bergan,* to protect; see **bhergh-[1]**). *(i), (ii),* and *(iii)* all from Germanic **h(w)alsaz;* **b.** COL, COLLAR, COLLET, CULLET; ACCOLADE, DECOLLATE[1], DÉCOLLETÉ, MACHICOLATE, (MACHICOLATION), TORTICOLLIS, from Latin *collum,* neck. **2.** Suffixed form **k^wol-ā.* -COLOUS; PRATINCOLE, from Latin *-cola* and *incola,* inhabitant (*in-,* in; see **en**). **3.** Suffixed form **k^wol-o-.* **a.** ANCILLARY, from Latin *anculus,* "he who bustles about," servant (*an-,* short for *ambi-,* around, about; see **ambhi**); **b.** POLE[1], PULLEY, from Greek *polos,* axis of a sphere; **c.** BUCOLIC, from Greek *boukolos,* cowherd, from *-kolos,* herdsman. **4.** Suffixed form **kwol-es-* (probably a blend of o-grade **k^wol-o-* and expected e-grade **k^wel-es-*). CALASH, KOLACKY, from Slavic *kolo, koles-,* wheel. **5.** Suffixed o-grade form **k^wol-eno-.* (see **wes-[3]**) Old Iranian **vahā-carana-,* "sale-traffic," from **carana-,* trade, traffic. **6.** Suffixed zero-grade form **k^wl̥-i-.* PALIMPSEST, PALINDROME, PALINGENESIS, PALINODE, from Greek *palin,* again (< "revolving"). [Pokorny 1. *k^uel-* 639.]

k^wel-[2]. Derivatives are *tele-* and *paleo-.*

k^wel-[2]. Far (in space and time). **1.** Lengthened-grade form **k^wēl-.* TELE-, from Greek *tēle,* far off. **2.** Suffixed zero-grade form **k^wl̥-ai.* PALEO-, from Greek *palai,* long ago. [Pokorny 2. *k^uel-* 640.]

k^went(h)-. Important derivatives are *pathetic, pathos,* and *sympathy.*

k^went(h)-. To suffer. **1.** Suffixed form **k^wenth-es-.* NEPENTHE, from Greek *penthos,* grief. **2.** Zero-grade form **k^wn̥th-.* PATHETIC, PATHO-, PATHOS, -PATHY; APATHY, (PATHOGNOMONIC), SYMPATHY, from Greek *pathos,* suffering, passion, emotion, feelings. [Pokorny *k^uenth-* 641.]

k^wer-. An important derivative is *karma.*

k^wer-. To make. **1.** SANSKRIT, from Sanskrit *karoti,* he makes. **2.** Suffixed form **k^wer-ōr* with dissimilated form **k^wel-ōr.* PELORIA, from Greek *pelōr,* monster (perhaps "that which does harm"). **3.** Suffixed form **k^wer-əs-.* TERA-; (TERATOCARCINOMA), TERATOGEN, TERATOID, TERATOMA, from Greek *teras,* monster. **4.** Suffixed form **k^wer-mn̥.* KARMA, from Sanskrit *karma,* act, deed. [Pokorny *k^uer-* 641.]

kwes-. Important derivatives are *wheeze, quarrel[1], querulous,* and *cyst.*

kwes-. To pant, wheeze. **1.** WHEEZE, from Old Norse *hvæsa,* to hiss, from Germanic **hwēsjan.* **2.** QUARREL[1], QUERULOUS, from Latin *querī,* to complain. **3.** Suffixed zero-grade form **kus-ti-.* CYST, CYSTO-, from Greek *kustis,* bladder, bag (< "bellows"). [Pokorny *k̂u̯es-* 631.]

kwēt-. Important derivatives are *squash[2], discuss,* and *rescue.*

kwēt-. To shake. Zero-grade form **kwət-,* becoming **kwat-.* **a.** CASCARA, SCUTCH, SQUASH[2]; CONCUSS, DISCUSS, PERCUSS, RESCUE, SUCCUSSION, from Latin *quatere* (past participle *quassus,* in composition *-cussus*), to shake, strike; **b.** PASTE[1], from Greek *passein,* to sprinkle. [Pokorny *ku̯ēt-* 632.]

k^wetwer-. Important derivatives are *four, forty, fourteen, quatrain, squad, square, quadri-, quadrant, quarantine, tetra-, trapezium, fourth, farthing, quart,* and *quarter.*

k^wetwer-. Four.
I. O-grade form **k^wetwor-.* **1.a.** FOUR, from Old English *fēower,* four; **b.** FORTY, from Old English *fēowertig,* forty; **c.** FOURTEEN, from Old English *fēowertēne,* fourteen (*-tēne,* ten; see **dekm̥**). **a, b,** and **c** all from Germanic **fe(d)wor-,* probably from **k^wetwor-.* **2.** QUATRAIN; CATER-CORNERED, QUATTROCENTO, from Latin *quattuor,* four. **3.** CZARDAS, from Old Iranian *cathwārō,* four.
II. Multiplicatives **k^weturs, *k^wetrus,* and combining forms **k^wetur-, *k^wetru-.* **1.** CAHIER, (CARILLON), (CARNET), QUATERNARY, QUATERNION, QUIRE[1], from Latin *quater,* four times. **2.** CADRE, QUADRATE, QUADRILLE[1], QUARREL[2], QUARRY[2]; (SQUAD), SQUARE, TROCAR, from Latin *quadrum,* square. **3.** QUADRI-, from Latin *quadri-,* four. **4.** QUADRANT, from Latin *quadrāns,* a fourth part. **5.** QUARANTINE, from Latin *quadrāgintā,* forty (*-gintā,* ten times; see **dekm̥**). **6.** Variant form **k^wet(w)r̥-.* **a.** TETRA-, from Greek *tetra-,* four; **b.** TESSERA; DIATESSARON, from Greek *tessares, tettares* (genitive *tessarōn*), four; **c.** TETRAD, from Greek *tetras,* group of four; **d.** zero-grade form **k^wt(w)r̥-.* TRAPEZIUM, from Greek *tra-,* four.
III. Ordinal adjective **k^wetur-to-.* **1.a.** FOURTH, from Old English *fēortha, fēowertha,* fourth; **b.** FIRKIN, from Middle Dutch *veerde,* fourth; **c.** FARTHING, from Old English *fēorthing, fēorthung,* fourth part of a penny. **a, b,** and **c** all from Germanic **fe(d)worthōn-.* **2.** QUADRILLE[2], QUADROON, QUART, QUARTAN, QUARTER, QUARTO, from Latin *quārtus,* fourth, quarter. [Pokorny *k^uetu̯er-* 642.]

k^wo-. Important derivatives are *who, what, why, which, how, when, where, whether, neither, either, quorum, quip, quasi, quote, quotient, quantity, quality, neuter,* and *alibi.*

k^wo-. Also **k^wi-.** Stem of relative and interrogative pronouns. **1.a.** WHO, WHOSE, WHOM, from Old English *hwā, hwæs, hwǣm,* who, whose, whom, from Germanic personal pronouns **hwas, *hwasa, *hwam;* **b.** WHAT, from Old English *hwæt,* what, from Germanic pronoun **hwat;* **c.** WHY, from Old English *hwӯ,* why, from Germanic adverb **hwī;* **d.** WHICH, from Old English *hwilc, hwelc,* which, from Germanic relative pronoun **hwa-līk-* (**līk-,* body, form; see **līk-**); **e.** HOW, from Old English *hū,* how, from Germanic adverb **hwō;* **f.** *(i)* WHEN, from Old English *hwenne, hwanne,* when; *(ii)* WHENCE, from Old English *hwanon,* whence. Both *(i)* and *(ii)* from Germanic adverb **hwan-;* **g.** WHITHER, from Old English *hwider,* whither, from Germanic adverb **hwithrē;* **h.** WHERE, from Old English *hwǣr,* where, from Germanic adverb **hwar-.* **a, b, c, d, e, f, g,** and **h** all from Germanic **hwa-, *hwi-.* **2.a.** WHETHER; NEITHER, from Old English *hwæther, hwether,* which of two, whether; **b.** EITHER, from Old English *ǣghwæther, ǣther,* either, from Germanic phrase **aiwo gihwatharaz,* "ever each of two" (**aiwo, *aiwi,* ever; see **aiw-;** **gi-* from **ga-,* collective prefix; see **kom**). Both **a** and **b** from Germanic **hwatharaz.* **3.** QUA, QUIBBLE, QUORUM, from Latin *quī* (genitive plural *quōrum*), who. **4.** HIDALGO, QUIDDITY, QUIDNUNC, QUIP, from Latin *quid,* what, something. **5.** QUASI, from Latin *quasi,* as if (*quam* + *sī,* if; see **swo-**), from *quam,* as, than, how. **6.** QUODLIBET, from Latin *quod,* what. **7.** QUOTE, QUOTIDIAN, QUOTIENT; ALIQUOT, from Latin *quot,* how many. **8.** QUONDAM, from Latin *quom,* when. **9.** COONCAN, from Latin *quem,* whom. **10.** QUANTITY, from Latin *quantus,* how great. **11.** QUALITY, from Latin *quālis,* of what kind. **12.** CUE[2], from Latin *quandō,* when (from **k^wām* + *-dō,* to, til; see **de-**). **13.** NEUTER, from Latin *uter,* either of two. **14.** ALIBI, UBIQUITY, from Latin *ubi,* where, and *ibi,* there. **15.** CHEESE[3], from Old Persian **ciš-ciy,* something (< **k^wid-k^wid*). [Pokorny *k^uo-* 644.]

kwon-. Important derivatives are *cynic, hound, dachshund, canary, canine,* and *kennel[1].*

kwon-. Dog. **1.** CYNIC; CYNOSURE, PROCYON, QUINSY, from Greek *kuōn,* dog. **2.** Suffixed zero-grade form **kwn̥-to-.* **a.** HOUND, from Old English *hund,* dog; **b.** DACHSHUND, from Old High German *hunt,* dog; **c.** KEESHOND, from Middle Dutch *hond,* dog. **a, b,** and **c** all from Germanic **hundaz.* **3.** Nominative form **kwō.* CORGI, from Welsh *ci,* dog. **4.** Variant **kan-i-.* CANAILLE, CANARY, CANICULAR, CANINE, CHENILLE, KENNEL[1], from Latin *canis,* dog. [Pokorny *ku̯on-* 632.]

k^wrep-. Important derivatives are *midriff, corporal[1], corporate, corporeal, corps, corpse, corpuscle, corsage, corset,* and *leprechaun.*

k^wrep-. Body. **1.** Suffixed form **k^wrep-es-.* MIDRIFF, from Old English *hrif,* belly from Germanic **hrefiz-.* **2.** Suffixed zero-grade form **k^wr̥p-es-.* CORPORAL[1], CORPORAL[3], CORPORATE, CORPOREAL, CORPOSANT, CORPS, CORPSE, CORPULENCE, CORPUS, CORPUSCLE, CORSAGE, CORSE, CORSET; LEPRECHAUN, from Latin *corpus,* body, substance. [Pokorny 1. *krep-* 620.]

k^wr̥mi-. An important derivative is *crimson.*

k^wr̥mi-. Worm. Rhyme word to **wr̥mi-,* worm (see **wer-[2]**). (CRIMSON), KERMES, from Arabic *qirmiz,* kermes, borrowed from Sanskrit compound *kr̥mi-ja-,* "(red dye) produced by worms" (*ja-,* produced; see **genə-**), from *kr̥mi-,* worm. [Pokorny *k^ur̥mi-* 649.]

laks-. A derivative is *lox[1].*

laks-. Salmon. Suffixed form **laks-o-.* **a.** LOX[1], from Old High German *lahs,* salmon; **b.** GRAVLAX, from Swedish *lax,* salmon. Both **a** and **b** from Germanic **lahsaz.* [Pokorny *lak-* 653.]

las-. Important derivatives are *lust, wanderlust,* and *lascivious.*

las-. To be eager, wanton, or unruly. **1.a.** LUST, from Old English *lust,* lust; **b.** WANDERLUST, from Old High German *lust,* desire; **c.** LIST[5], from Old English *lystan,* to please, satisfy a desire, from Germanic denominative verb **lustjan.* **a, b,** and **c** all from suffixed Germanic zero-grade form **lustuz.* **2.** Suffixed form **las-ko-.* LASCIVIOUS, from Latin *lascīvus,* wanton, lustful. [Pokorny *las-* 654.]

lau-. An important derivative is *lucrative.*

lau-. Gain, profit. **1.** Suffixed form **lau-no-.* GUERDON, from Old High German *lōn,* reward from Germanic **launam.* **2.** Suffixed zero-grade form **lu-tlo-.* LUCRATIVE, LUCRE, from Latin *lucrum,* gain, profit. [Pokorny *lāu-* 655.]

lē-. Important derivatives are *let*[1], *liege, late, latter, last*[1], *alas,* and *lenient.*

lē-. To let go, slacken. Contracted from **leə-.*
I. Extended form **lēd-.* **1.a.** LET[1], from Old English *lǣtan,* to allow, leave undone, from Germanic **lētan;* **b.** LIEGE, from Late Latin *laetus,* semifree colonist, from Germanic derivative **lēthigaz,* freed. **2.** Zero-grade form **ləd-.* **a.** LATE, LATTER, LAST[1], from Old English *læt,* late, with its comparative *lætra,* latter, and its superlative *latost,* last, from Germanic **lataz;* **b.** LET[2], from Old English *lettan,* to hinder, impede (< "to make late"), from Germanic **latjan;* **c.** suffixed form **ləd-to-.* LASSITUDE; ALAS, from Latin *lassus,* tired, weary.
II. Suffixed basic form **lē-ni-.* LENIENT, LENIS, LENITIVE, LENITY, from Latin *lēnis,* soft, gentle. [Pokorny 3. *lē(i)-* 666.]

leb-. Important derivatives are *lip* and *labial.*

leb-. Lip. **1.** LIP, from Old English *lippa,* lip, from Germanic **lep-.* **2.** Variant form **lab-.* **a.** suffixed form **lab-yo-.* LABIAL, LABIUM, from Latin *labium,* lip; **b.** suffixed form **lab-ro-.* LABELLUM, LABRET, LABRUM, from Latin *labrum,* lip. [Pokorny *lĕb-* 655.]

leg-. Important derivatives are *leech*[1], *lectern, lecture, legend, legible, legion, lesson, coil*[1], *collect*[1], *diligent, elect, intelligent, neglect, sacrilege, select, lexicon, catalog, dialect, dialogue, eclectic, legal, legitimate, loyal, legislator, privilege, legacy, allege, colleague, delegate, relegate, logic, analogous, apology, epilogue, logarithm, prologue,* and *syllogism.*

leg-. To collect; with derivatives meaning "to speak." **1.** LEECH[1], from Old English *lǣce,* physician, from Germanic **lēkjaz,* enchanter, one who speaks magic words, perhaps from **leg-**. **2.** LECTERN, (LECTION), LECTURE, LEGEND, LEGIBLE, LEGION, LESSON; (COIL[1]), COLLECT[1], DILIGENT, ELECT, INTELLIGENT, NEGLECT, PRELECT, SACRILEGE, SELECT, SORTILEGE, from Latin *legere,* to gather, choose, pluck, read. **3.** LEXICON, LOGION, -LOGUE, -LOGY; ALEXIA, ANALECTS, ANTHOLOGY, CATALOG, DIALECT, (DIALOGUE), DYSLEXIA, ECLECTIC, HOROLOGE, PROLEGOMENON, from Greek *legein,* to gather, speak, with *logos,* speech (see **6**). **4.** Suffixed form **leg-no-.* LIGNEOUS, LIGNI-, from Latin *lignum,* wood, firewood (< "that which is gathered"). **5.** Possibly lengthened-grade form **lēg-.* **a.** LEGAL, LEGIST, LEGITIMATE, LEX, LOYAL; LEGISLATOR, PRIVILEGE, from Latin *lēx,* law (? < "collection of rules"); **b.** LEGACY, LEGATE; COLLEAGUE, (COLLEGIAL), DELEGATE, RELEGATE, from Latin denominative *lēgāre,* to depute, commission, charge (< "to engage by contract"; but possibly from **legh-**). **6.** Suffixed o-grade form **log-o-.* LOGIC, LOGISTIC, LOGO-, LOGOS, -LOGY; ANALOGOUS, APOLOGUE, APOLOGY, DECALOGUE, EPILOGUE, HOMOLOGOUS, LOGARITHM, PARALOGISM, PROLOGUE, SYLLOGISM, from Greek *logos,* speech, word, reason. [Pokorny *leĝ-* 658.]

legh-. Important derivatives are *lie*[1], *lay*[1], *ledge, ledger, lair, beleaguer, lees, low*[1], *litter, law, fellow,* and *outlaw.*

legh-. To lie, lay. **1.** Suffixed form **legh-yo-.* **a.** LIE[1], from Old English *licgan,* to lie, from Germanic **ligjan;* **b.** *(i)* LAY[1], LEDGE, (LEDGER), from Old English *lecgan,* to lay; *(ii)* BELAY, from Old English *belecgan,* to cover, surround (*be-,* over; see **ambhi**). Both *(i)* and *(ii)* from Germanic **lagjan.* **2.** Suffixed form **legh-ro-.* **a.** LAIR, from Old English *leger,* lair; **b.** LEAGUER[1]; BELEAGUER, from Middle Dutch *leger,* lair, camp; **c.** LAAGER, LAGER; (STALAG), from Old High German *legar,* bed, lair. **a, b,** and **c** all from Germanic **legraz.* **3.** LEES, from Medieval Latin *lia,* sediment, from Celtic **leg-yā-.* **4.** Lengthened-grade form **lēgh-.* LOW[1], from Old Norse *lāgr,* low, from Germanic **lēgaz,* "lying flat," low. **5.** Suffixed form **legh-to-.* COVERLET, LITTER; WAGON-LIT, from Latin *lectus,* bed. **6.** Suffixed o-grade form **logh-o-.* **a.** LAW; BYLAW, (DANELAW), from Old Norse **lagu, lag-,* law, "that which is set down"; **b.** FELLOW, from Old Norse *lag,* a laying down; **c.** OUTLAW, from Old Norse *lög,* law; **d.** ANLAGE, VORLAGE, from Old High German *lāga,* act of laying. **a, b, c,** and **d** all from Germanic **lagam.* **7.** LAGAN, from Old Norse *lögn,* dragnet (< "that which is laid down"), from Germanic **lag-īnō-.* **8.** Suffixed o-grade form **logh-o-.* LOCHIA, from Greek *lokhos,* childbirth, place for lying in wait. [Pokorny *legh-* 658, 2. *lēĝh-* 660.]

leg^{wh}-. Important derivatives are *light*[2], *leaven, lever, levity, alleviate, carnival, elevate, relieve, leprechaun,* and *lung.*

leg^{wh}-. Light, having little weight. **1.** Suffixed form **leg^{w}h-t-.* **a.** LIGHT[2], from Old English *līht, lēoht,* light; **b.** LIGHTER[2], from Old English *līhtan,* to lighten. Both **a** and **b** from Germanic **līht(j)az.* **2.** Suffixed form **leg^{w}h-u-i-.* LEAVEN, LEVER, LEVITY; ALLEVIATE, CARNIVAL, ELEVATE, LEGERDEMAIN, (MEZZO-RELIEVO), RELIEVE, from Latin *levis,* light, with its derivative *levāre,* to lighten, raise. **3.** Variant form **lag^{w}h-.* LEPRECHAUN, from Old Irish *lū-,* small. **4.** Nasalized form **l(e)ng^{w}h-.* LUNG, from Old English *lungen,* lungs (from their lightness), from Germanic **lung-.* **5.** (see **lei-**) Latin *oblīviscī,* to forget, attributed by some to this root, is more likely from **lei-**. [Pokorny *leg^{u}h-* 660.]

lei-. Important derivatives are *slime, slippery, slick, loam, slight, slip*[1], *oblivion,* and *liniment.*

lei-. Also **slei-.** Slimy. **1.a.** SLIME, from Old English *slīm,* slime; **b.** SLIPPERY, from Old English *slipor,* slippery; **c.** SLICK, from Old English **slice,* smooth; **d.** LIME[3], from Old English *līm,* cement, birdlime; **e.** LOAM, from Old English *lām,* loam; **f.** SLIGHT, from Middle English *slight,* slender, probably from a Scandinavian source akin to Old Norse *slēttr,* smooth, sleek; **g.** SLIP[1], from Middle English *slippen,* to slip, probably from a source akin to Middle Dutch and Middle Low German *slippen,* to slip, slip away; **h.** SCHLEP, from Middle Low German *slēpen,* to drag. **a, b, c, d, e, f, g,** and **h** all from Germanic **slī-* with various extensions. **2.** Suffixed form **lei-mo-.* LIMACINE, LIMICOLINE, from Latin *līmus,* slime. **3.** Suffixed form **lei-w-.* OBLIVION, OUBLIETTE, from Latin *oblīviscī,* to forget (< "to wipe, let slip from the mind"; *ob-,* away; see **epi**). **4.** Extended form **(s)leiə-,* with metathesis **(s)leə(i)-.* **a.** Zero-grade form with nasal infix **li-n-ə-.* LINIMENT, from Latin *linere* (perfect *lēvī*), to anoint; **b.** suffixed zero-grade form **lī-* (< **liə-*). LITOTES, from Greek *litos,* plain, simple; **c.** suffixed metathesized form **leə-wo-,* whence **lē-wo-.* LEVIGATE, from Latin *lēvis,* smooth. [Pokorny 3. *lei-* 662.]

leid-. Important derivatives are *ludicrous, allude, collude, delude, elude, illusion, interlude,* and *prelude.*

leid-. To play, jest. Suffixed o-grade form **loid-o-.* LUDIC, LUDICROUS; ALLUDE, COLLUDE, DELUDE, ELUDE, ILLUSION, INTERLUDE, PRELUDE, PROLUSION, from Latin *lūdus,* game, play, with its derivative *lūdere,* to play (but both words may possibly be from Etruscan). [Pokorny *leid-* 666.]

leig-. Important derivatives are *league*[1], *liable, lien, alloy, ally, furl, oblige, rally,* and *rely.*

leig-. To bind. **1.** LEECH[2], from Middle Low German *līk,* leech line, from Germanic **līk-.* **2.** Suffixed agent noun **l(e)ig-tor-.* LICTOR, from Latin *lictor,* lictor. **3.** Zero-grade form **lig-ā-.* LEAGUE[1], LEGATO, LIABLE, LIEN, LIGASE, LIGATE, LIGATURE; ALLOY, (ALLY), COLLIGATE, FURL, OBLIGE, (RALLY[1]), (RELIGION), RELY, from Latin *ligāre,* to bind. [Pokorny 4. *leig-* 668.]

leigh-. Important derivatives are *lick* and *lecher.*

leigh-. To lick. **1.** ELECTUARY, LICHEN, from Greek *leikhein,* to lick. **2.** Zero-grade form **ligh-.* **a.** LICK, from Old English *liccian,* to lick; **b.** LECHER, from Old French *lechier,* to live in debauchery. Both **a** and **b** from Germanic **likkōn.* **3.** Nasalized zero-grade form **li-n-gh-.* ANILINGUS, CUNNILINGUS, from Latin *lingere,* to lick. [Pokorny *leigh-* 668.]

leik^{w}-. Important derivatives are *eclipse, ellipsis, lend, loan, delinquent, derelict,* and *relinquish.*

leik^{w}-. To leave. **1.** Basic form **leik^{w}-.* ECLIPSE, ELLIPSIS, from Greek *leipein,* to leave. **2.** O-grade form **loik^{w}-.* **a.** suffixed form **loik^{w}-nes-.* LOAN, from Old Norse *lān,* loan, from Germanic **laihwniz;* **b.** LEND, from Old English *lǣnan,* to lend, loan from Germanic denominative **laihwnjan.* **3.** Zero-grade form **lik^{w}-.* **a.** (see **oi-no-**) Old English *endleofan,* eleven, from Germanic **ain-lif-,* "one left (beyond ten)"; **b.** (see **dwo-**) Old English *twelf,* twelve, from Germanic **twa-lif-,* "two left (beyond ten)." Both **a** and **b** from Germanic **-lif-,* left. **4.** Nasalized zero-grade form **li-n-k^{w}-.* DELINQUENT, (DERELICT), RELINQUISH, from Latin *linquere,* to leave. [Pokorny *leik^{u}-* 669.]

leip-. Important derivatives are *life, lively, live*[1], *leave*[1], and *liver*[1].

leip-. To stick, adhere; fat. **1.** LIFE, LIVELY, from Old English *līf,* life (< "continuance"), from Germanic **lībam.* **2.a.** LIVE[1], from Old English *lifian, libban,* to live; **b.** LEBENSRAUM, from Old High German *lebēn,* to live. Both **a** and **b** from Germanic **libēn.* **3.a.** LEAVE[1], from Old English *lǣfan,* to leave, have remaining; **b.** DELAY, RELAY, from Old French *laier,* to leave, from Frankish **laibjan.* Both **a** and **b** from o-grade Germanic causative **-laibjan.* **4.** LIVER[1], from Old English *lifer,* liver (formerly believed to be the blood-producing organ), from Germanic **librō.* **5.** Zero-grade form **lip-.* LIPO-, from Greek *lipos,* fat. **6.** Variant form **əleibh-.* ALIPHATIC; SYNALEPHA, from Greek *aleiphein,* to anoint with oil. [Pokorny *leip-* 670.]

leis-[1]. Important derivatives are *last*[2], *lore*[1], *learn,* and *delirium.*

leis-[1]. Track, furrow. **1.** O-grade form **lois-.* **a.** LAST[3], from Old English *lāst, lǣst,* sole, footprint, from Germanic **laist-;* **b.** LAST[2], from Old English *lǣstan,* to continue, from Germanic **laistjan,* "to follow a track"; **c.** suffixed form **lois-ā.* LORE,[1] from Old English *lār,* learning, from Germanic **laizō.* **2.** LEARN, from Old English *leornian,* to learn, from Germanic zero-grade form **liznōn,* "to follow a course (of study)." **3.** Suffixed full-grade form **leis-ā.* DELIRIUM, from Latin *līra,* a furrow. [Pokorny *leis-* 671.]

leis-[2]. Important derivatives are *least* and *less.*

leis-[2]. Small. LEAST, LESS, from Old English comparative *lǣs, lǣssa* and superlative *lǣst, lǣrest,* from Germanic comparative **lais-izō* and superlative **lais-ista-.*

leit-. Important derivatives are *lead*[1], *load, lode,* and *livelihood.*

leit-. To go forth, die. **1.** Suffixed o-grade form **loit-eyo-.* **a.** LEAD[1], from Old English *lǣdan,* to lead; **b.** LEITMOTIF, from Old High German *leitan,* to lead. Both **a** and **b** from Germanic **laidjan.* **2.** Suffixed variant o-grade form **loit-ā.* LOAD, LODE; LIVELIHOOD, from Old English *lād,* course, way, from Germanic **laidō.* [Pokorny *leit(h)-* 672.]

lendh-. Important derivatives are *land, landscape, hinterland,* and *lawn*[1].

lendh-. Open land. **a.** LAND; ISLAND, from Old English *land,* land; **b.** BILANDER, LANDSCAPE, UITLANDER, from Middle Dutch *land,* land; **c.** AUSLANDER, GELÄNDESPRUNG, HINTERLAND, LANDSMAN[2], from Old High German *lant,* land; **d.** LANDGRAVE, (LANDGRAVINE), from Middle Low German *lant,* country; **e.** LANDSMÅL, from Old Norse *land,* land; **f.** LAWN[1], from Old French *launde,* heath, pasture. **a, b, c, d,** and **e** all from Germanic **landam;* **f** from Germanic, or from Celtic **landā.* [Pokorny 3. *lendh-* 675.]

leu-. Important derivatives are *forlorn, -less, lose, loss, loose, analysis, paralysis, soluble, solve, absolute, absolve, dissolve,* and *resolve.*

leu-. To loosen, divide, cut apart.
I. Extended Germanic root **leus-.* **1.a.** LORN, (LOSEL), from Old English *-lēosan,* to lose; **b.** *(i)* FORLORN, from Old English *forlēosan,* to forfeit, lose; *(ii)* FORLORN HOPE, from Dutch *verliezen* (past participle *verloren*), to lose. Both *(i)* and *(ii)* from Ger-

manic **fer-leusan, *far-leusan (*fer-, *far-,* prefix denoting rejection or exclusion; see **per[1]**). Both **a** and **b** from Germanic **leusan.* **2.a.** LEASING, -LESS, from Old English *lēas,* "loose," free from, without, untrue, lacking; **b.** LOSE, (LOSS), from Old English *los,* loss; **c.** LOOSE, from Old Norse *lauss, louss,* loose; **d.** LOESS, from German dialectal *lösch,* loose. **a, b, c,** and **d** all from Germanic **lausaz.*
II. Basic form **leu-.* **1.** LAG[2], probably from a source akin to Swedish *lagg,* barrel stave (< "split piece of wood"), from Germanic **lawwō.* **2.** Zero-grade form **lu-.* **a.** LYO-, LYSIS, LYSO-, -LYTE, (LYTIC), -LYTIC; ANALYSIS, CATALYSIS, DIALYSIS, LYASE, PARALYSIS, TACHYLYTE, from Greek *luein,* to loosen, release, untie; **b.** LUES, from Latin *luēs,* plague, pestilence (< "dissolution, putrefaction"); **c.** prefixed form **se-lu- (se-,* apart; see **s(w)e-**). SOLUBLE, SOLUTE, SOLVE; ABSOLUTE, (ABSOLVE), ASSOIL, CONSOLUTE, DISSOLVE, RESOLVE, from Latin *solvere,* to loosen, untie. [Pokorny 2. *leu-* 681.]

leubh-. Important derivatives are *livelong, furlough, belief, believe, love,* and *libido.*

leubh-. To care, desire; love.
I. Suffixed form **leubh-o-.* LIEF; LEMAN, LIVELONG, from Old English *lēof,* dear, beloved, from Germanic **leubaz.*
II. O-grade form **loubh-.* **1.a.** LEAVE[2], from Old English *lēaf,* permission (< "pleasure, approval"); **b.** FURLOUGH, from Middle Dutch *verlof,* leave, permission *(ver-,* intensive prefix, from Germanic **fer-;* see **per[1]**); **c.** BELIEF, from Old English *geléafa,* belief, faith *(bi-,* about; see **ambhi**), from Germanic **galaubō (*ga-,* intensive prefix; see **kom**). **a, b,** and **c** all from Germanic **laubō.* **2.** BELIEVE, from Old English *gelēfan, belēfan,* to believe, trust *(be-,* about; see **ambhi**), from Germanic **galaubjan,* "to hold dear," esteem, trust *(*ga-,* intensive prefix; see **kom**).
III. Zero-grade form **lubh-.* **1.** Suffixed form **lubh-ā-.* LOVE, from Old English *lufu,* love, from Germanic **lubō.* **2.** Suffixed (stative) form **lubh-ē-.* QUODLIBET, from Latin *libēre,* to be dear, be pleasing. **3.** LIBIDO, from Latin *libīdō,* pleasure, desire. [Pokorny *leubh-* 683.]

leudh-. Important derivatives are *liberal, liberate, liberty, livery,* and *deliver.*

leudh-. To mount up, grow. **1.** Basic form **leudh-.* LANDSLEIT, from Old High German *liut,* person, people, from Germanic **liud-i-.* **2.** Suffixed form **leudh-ero-.* LIBERAL, LIBERATE, LIBERTINE, LIBERTY, LIVERY; DELIVER, from Latin *līber,* free (the precise semantic development is obscure). [Pokorny 1. *leudh-* 684.]

leu(ə)-. Important derivatives are *lye, lather, lotion, deluge, dilute,* and *latrine.*

leu(ə)-. To wash. **1.** Suffixed form **lou-kā.* LYE, from Old English *lēag,* lye, from Germanic **laugō.* **2.** Suffixed form **lou-tro-.* LATHER, from Old English *lēthran, līthran,* to lather. **3.** Variant form **law-.* **a.** LOMENT, LOTION; ABLUTION, ALLUVION, COLLUVIUM, DELUGE, DILUTE, (ELUANT), ELUTE, (ELUVIUM), from Latin *lavere,* to wash, with its derivative *-luere,* to wash; **b.** form **law-ā-.* LAVE, from Latin *lavāre,* to wash; **c.** LATRINE, from Latin *lavātrīna, lātrīna,* a bath, privy. **4.** O-grade form **lou-.* PYROLUSITE, from Greek *louein,* to wash. [Pokorny *lou-* 692.]

leugh-. Important derivatives are *warlock, belie,* and *lie[2].*

leugh-. To tell a lie. **1.a.** WARLOCK, from Old English *lēogan,* to lie; **b.** BELIE, from Old English *belēogan,* to deceive *(be-,* about; see **ambhi**). Both **a** and **b** from Germanic **leugan.* **2.** LIE[2], from Old English *lyge,* a lie, falsehood, from Germanic **lugiz.* [Pokorny *leugh-* 686.]

leuk-. Important derivatives are *light[1], luminary, luminous, illuminate, lunar, lunatic, luster, illustrate, lea, lucid, elucidate, translucent,* and *lynx.*

leuk-. Light, brightness.
I. Basic form **leuk-.* **1.** Suffixed form **leuk-to-.* **a.** LIGHT[1], from Old English *lēoht, līht,* light; **b.** LIGHTNING, from Old English *līhtan,* to shine, from Germanic **leuht-jan,* to make light. Both **a** and **b** from Germanic **leuhtam.* **2.** Unsuffixed form **leuk-.* LUCINA, LUCULENT, LUX; LUCIFER, (LUCIFERIN), from Latin *lūx,* light. **3.** Suffixed form **leuk-smen-.* LIMN, LUMEN, LUMINARY, LUMINOUS; ILLUMINATE, PHILLUMENIST, from Latin *lūmen,* light, opening. **4.** Suffixed form **leuk-snā-.* LUNA, LUNAR, LUNATE, LUNATIC, LUNE, LUNULA; SUBLUNARY, from Latin *lūna,* moon. **5.** Suffixed form **leuk-stro-.* **a.** LUSTER, (LUSTRUM), from Latin *lūstrum,* purification; **b.** ILLUSTRATE, from Latin *lūstrāre,* to purify, illuminate. **6.** Suffixed form **leuko-dhro-.* LUCUBRATE, from Latin *lūcubrāre,* to work by lamplight. **7.** Suffixed form **leuk-o-.* LEUKO-, from Greek *leukos,* clear, white.
II. O-grade form **louk-.* **1.** Suffixed form **louk-o-.* **a.** LEA, from Old English *lēah,* meadow (< "place where light shines"), from Germanic **lauhaz;* **b.** LEVIN, from Middle English *levin,* lightning, from Germanic **lauh-ubni-.* **2.** Suffixed (iterative) form **louk-eyo-.* LUCENT, LUCID; ELUCIDATE, NOCTILUCA, PELLUCID, RELUCENT, TRANSLUCENT, from Latin *lūcēre,* to shine.
III. Zero-grade form **luk-.* **1.** Suffixed form **luk-sno-.* LINK[2], LYCHNIS, from Greek *lukhnos,* lamp. **2.** LYNX, OUNCE[2], from Greek *lunx,* lynx (as if from its shining eyes), attributed by some to this root (but more likely of obscure origin). [Pokorny *leuk-* 687.]

[līk-. Important derivatives are *-ly[1], -ly[2], alike, like[2], each, likely, frolic,* and *like[1].*

līk-. Body, form; like, same. Germanic root. **1.** LYCH-GATE, from Old English *līc,* form, body. **2.** -LY[1], -LY[2], from Old English *-līc,* having the form of. **3.a.** ALIKE, LIKE[2], LIKELY, from Old English *gelīc,* similar, and Old Norse *(g)līkr,* like, both from Germanic **galīkaz;* **b.** EACH; EVERY, from Old English *ǣlc,* each, from Germanic phrase **aiwo galīkaz,* "ever alike" *(*aiwo, *aiwi,* ever; see **aiw-**). **4.** (see **i-**) Old English *ilca,* the same, from Germanic **islīk-.* **5.** ALIKE, from Old English *onlīc,* from Germanic **ana-līkaz.* **6.** FROLIC, from Middle Dutch *-lijc,* -like. **7.** LIKE[1], from Old English *līcian,* to please, from Germanic **līkjan.* **8.** (see **kʷo-**) Germanic **hwa-līk-,* which. [Pokorny 2. *lĕig-* 667.] **]**

līno-. Important derivatives are *line[1], linen, lingerie, lint,* and *linseed.*

līno-. Flax. **1.** Form **lino-.* LINOLEIC ACID, from Greek *linon,* flax. **2.** Form **līno-.* LINE[1], LINE[2], LINEN, LINGERIE, LININ, LINNET, LINT; CRINOLINE, LINSEED, from Latin *līnum,* flax, linen, thread. [Pokorny *lī-no-* 691.]

lūs-. An important derivative is *louse.*

lūs-. Louse. LOUSE, from Old English *lūs* louse, from Germanic **lūs-.* [Pokorny *lūs-* 692.]

mā-[1]. Important derivatives are *mature, premature,* and *matinee.*

mā-[1]. Good; with derivatives meaning "occurring at a good moment, timely, seasonable, early." **1.** Suffixed form **mā-tu-.* **a.** further suffixed form **mā-tu-ro-.* MATURE; IMMATURE, PREMATURE, from Latin *mātūrus,* seasonable, ripe, mature; **b.** further suffixed form **mā-tu-to-.* (MATINEE), MATINS, (MATUTINAL), from Latin *Mātūta,* name of the goddess of dawn. **2.** Suffixed form **mā-ni-.* **a.** MAÑANA, from Latin *māne,* (in) the morning; **b.** MANES, from Latin *mānis, mānus,* good. [Pokorny 2. *mā-* 693.]

mā-[2]. An important derivative is *mammal.*

mā-[2]. Mother. A linguistic near-universal found in many of the world's languages, often in reduplicated form. **1.** MAMMA[2], MAMMAL, MAMMILLA, from Latin *mamma,* breast. **2.** MAIA, MAIEUTIC, from Greek *Maia,* "good mother" (respectful form of address to old women), also nurse, probably from **mā-[2].** **3.** MAMA, more recently formed in the same way. [Pokorny 3. *mā-* 694.]

mag-. Important derivatives are *make, mason, match[1], mingle, among, mongrel, magma, mass,* and *amass.*

mag-. Also **mak-.** To knead, fashion, fit. **1.a.** *(i)* MAKE, from Old English *macian,* to make; *(ii)* MASON, from Old French *masson,* mason; *(iii)* MAQUILLAGE, from Middle Dutch *maken,* to make. *(i), (ii),* and *(iii)* all from Germanic verb **makōn,* to fashion, fit; **b.** MATCH[1], from Old English *gemæcca,* mate, spouse, from Germanic compound noun **ga-mak-(j)ōn-,* "one who is fitted with (another)" *(*ga-,* with, together; see **kom**). Both **a** and **b** from Germanic **mak-.* **2.a.** MINGLE, from Old English *mengan,* to mix; **b.** AMONG, MONGREL, from Old English *gemang,* mixture, crowd *(ge-,* together; see **kom**). Both **a** and **b** from Germanic nasalized form **mangjan,* to knead together. **3.** Suffixed form **mak-yo-.* MAGMA, from Greek *magma,* unguent, from *massein* (aorist stem *mag-*), to knead. **4.** Suffixed lengthened-grade form **māg-ya-.* MASS; (AMASS), MAZAEDIUM, from Greek *maza,* a (kneaded) lump, barley cake. **5.** Suffixed lengthened-grade form **māk-ero-.* MACERATE, from Latin *mācerāre,* to tenderize, to soften (food) by steeping. [Pokorny *maĝ-* 696, 2. *māk-* 698, *men(ə)k-* 730.]

magh-. Important derivatives are *may[1], dismay, might[1], main, machine, mechanic,* and *magic.*

magh-. To be able, have power. **1.a.** MAY[1], from Old English *magan,* to be able; **b.** DISMAY, from Old French *esmaier,* to frighten. Both **a** and **b** from Germanic **magan,* to be able. **2.** MIGHT[1], from Old English *miht,* power, from Germanic suffixed form **mah-ti-,* power. **3.** MAIN, from Old English *mægen,* power, from Germanic suffixed form **mag-inam,* power. **4.** Suffixed lengthened-grade form **māgh-anā-,* "that which enables." MACHINE, MECHANIC, (MECHANISM), (MECHANO-), from Greek (Attic) *mēkhanē,* (Doric) *mākhanā,* device. **5.** Possibly suffixed form **magh-u-.* (MAGIC), MAGUS, from Old Persian *maguš,* member of a priestly caste (< "mighty one"). [Pokorny *magh-* 695.]

maghu-. Important derivatives are *maid* and *maiden.*

maghu-. Young person of either sex. Suffixed form **magho-ti-.* **a.** MAID, MAIDEN, from Old English *mægden,* virgin; **b.** MATJES HERRING, from Dutch *maagd,* maid. Both **a** and **b** from Germanic **magadi-,* with diminutive **magadin-.* [Pokorny *maghos* 696.]

māk-. Important derivatives are *meager, emaciate,* and *macro-.*

māk-. Long, thin. Contracted from **maək-.* **1.** Zero-grade form **mək-* becoming **mak-* in suffixed form **mak-ro-.* **a.** MEAGER; EMACIATE, from Latin *macer,* thin; **b.** MACRO-, MACRON; AMPHIMACER, from Greek *makros,* long, large. **2.** Suffixed form **māk-es-.* MECOPTERAN, PARAMECIUM, from Greek *mēkos,* length. [Pokorny *māk-* 699.]

man-[1]. Important derivatives are *man, Norman[1], mannequin,* and *ombudsman.*

man-[1]. Also **mon-.** Man. **1.** Extended forms **manu-, *manw-.* **a.** MAN; NORMAN, from Old English *man(n)* (plural *menn*), man; **b.** FUGLEMAN, LANDSMAN[2], from Old High German *man,* man; **c.** MANIKIN, (MANNEQUIN), from Middle Dutch *man,* man; **d.** NORMAN[1], OMBUDSMAN, from Old Norse *madhr, mannr,* man; **e.** ALEMANNI, possibly from Germanic **Ala-manniz,* tribal name (< *"all men": **ala-,* all; see **al-[3]**). **a, b, c, d,** and **e** all from Germanic **manna-* (plural **manniz*). **2.** MENSCH, from Old High German *mennisco,* human, from Germanic adjective **manniska-,* human. **3.** MUZHIK, from Russian *muzh,* man, male, from Slavic suffixed form **mon-gyo-.* [Pokorny *manu-s* 700.]

man-[2]. Important derivatives are *manacle, manage, manner, manual, maintain, maneuver, manicure, manifest, manipulation, manufacture, manure, manuscript, mastiff, emancipate, mandate, command, commando, commend, countermand, demand,* and *recommend.*

man-[2]. Hand. **1.** MANACLE, MANAGE, (MANÈGE), MANNER, MANUAL, MANUBRIUM, MANUS; AMANUENSIS, MAINTAIN, MANEUVER, MANICOTTI, MANICURE, MANIFEST, MANIPLE, MANIPULATION, MANSUETUDE, MANUFACTURE, MANUMIT, MANURE, MANUSCRIPT, MASTIFF, MORTMAIN, QUADRUMANOUS, from Latin *manus,* hand. **2.** Suffixed form **man-ko-,* maimed in the hand. MANQUÉ, from Latin *mancus,* maimed, defective. **3.** EMANCIPATE, from Latin compound *manceps,* "he who takes by the hand," purchaser *(-ceps,* agential suffix, "taker"; see **kap-**). **4.** MANDAMUS, MANDATE; COMMAND, (COMMANDO), COMMEND, COUNTERMAND, DEMAND, (RECOMMEND), REMAND, from Latin compound *mandāre,* "to put into someone's hand," entrust, order *(-dere,* to put; see **dhē-**). [Pokorny *mə-r* 740.]

marko-. An important derivative is *mare[1].*

marko-. Horse. MARE[1], from Old English *mere, miere,* mare, from Germanic feminine **marhjōn-*. [Pokorny *marko-* 700.]

māter-. Important derivatives are *mother*[1], *maternal, maternity, matriculate, matrix, matron, matrimony, metropolis, material,* and *matter.*

māter-. Mother. Based ultimately on the baby-talk form **mā-**[2], with the kinship term suffix **-ter-*. **1.a.** MOTHER[1], from Old English *mōdor,* mother; **b.** MOTHER[2], from Middle Dutch *moeder,* mother. Both **a** and **b** from Germanic **mōdar-*. **2.** MATER, MATERNAL, MATERNITY, (MATRICULATE), MATRIX, MATRON; MADREPORE, MATRIMONY, from Latin *māter,* mother. **3.** METRO-; METROPOLIS, from Greek *mētēr,* mother. **4.** MATERIAL, MATTER, from Latin *māteriēs, māteria,* tree trunk (< "matrix," the tree's source of growth), hence hard timber used in carpentry, hence (by a calque on Greek *hulē,* wood, matter) substance, stuff, matter. **5.** DEMETER, from Greek compound *Dēmētēr,* name of the goddess of produce, especially cereal crops (*dē-*, possibly meaning "earth"). [Pokorny *māter-* 700.]

me-[1]. Important derivatives are *me, myself, mine*[2], and *my.*

me-[1]. Oblique form of the personal pronoun of the first person singular. For the nominative see **eg.** **1.** ME, MYSELF, from Old English *mē̆* (dative and accusative), from Germanic **mē̆-*. **2.** Possessive adjective **mei-no-*. **a.** MINE[2], MY, from Old English *mīn,* my; **b.** MYNHEER, from Middle Dutch *mijn,* my. Both **a** and **b** from Germanic **mīn-*. **3.** Possessive adjective **me-yo-*. MADAME, MONSIEUR, from Latin *meus,* mine. **4.** Genitive form **me-wo.* MAVOURNEEN, from Old Irish *mo,* my. [Pokorny 1. *me-* 702.]

me-[2]. Derivatives are *midwife* and *meta-*.

me-[2]. In the middle of. **1.** Suffixed form **me-dhi.* MIDWIFE, from Old English *mid,* among, with, from Germanic **mid-*. **2.** Suffixed form **me-ta.* META-, from Greek *meta,* between, with, beside, after. [Pokorny 2. *me-* 702.] See also **medhyo-.**

mē-[1]. Important derivatives are *mood*[1], *moral, morale,* and *morose.*

mē-[1]. Expressing certain qualities of mind. Contracted from **meə-*. **1.** Suffixed o-grade form **mō-to-*. *(i)* MOOD[1], from Old English *mōd,* mind, disposition; *(ii)* GEMÜTLICH, (GEMÜTLICHKEIT); BISMUTH, from Old High German *muot,* mind, spirit. Both *(i)* and *(ii)* from Germanic **mōthaz.* **2.** MORAL, (MORALE), MORES, MOROSE, from Latin *mōs* (< **mō-s-*), wont, humor, manner, custom, perhaps from **mē-**[1]. [Pokorny 5. *mē-* 704.]

mē-[2]. Important derivatives are *meal*[2], *piecemeal, measure, dimension, immense, meter*[1], *diameter, geometry, moon, Monday, month, menopause, menstruate,* and *semester.*

mē-[2]. To measure. Contracted from **meə-*.
I. Basic form *mē-*. **1.** Suffixed form **mē-lo-*. MEAL[2]; PIECEMEAL, from Old English *mǣl,* "measure, mark, appointed time, time for eating, meal," from Germanic **mēlaz.* **2.** Suffixed form **mē-ti-*. **a.** MEASURE, (MENSURAL); (COMMENSURATE), DIMENSION, IMMENSE, from Latin *mētīrī,* to measure; **b.** METIS, from Greek *mētis,* wisdom, skill. **3.** METER[1], METER[2], (METER[3]), -METER, METRICAL, -METRY; DIAMETER, GEOMETRY, ISOMETRIC, METROLOGY, METRONOME, SYMMETRY, from Greek *metron,* measure, rule, length, proportion, poetic meter, possibly from **mē-**[2] (but this is referred by some to **med-**).
II. Extended and suffixed forms **mēn-, *mēn-en-, *mēn-ōt-, *mēn-s-*, moon, month (an ancient and universal unit of time measured by the moon). **1.** MOON; (MONDAY), from Old English *mōna,* moon, from Germanic **mēnōn-*. **2.** MONTH, from Old English *mōnath,* month, from Germanic **mēnōth-*. **3.** AMENORRHEA, CATAMENIA, DYSMENORRHEA, EMMENAGOGUE, (MENARCHE), MENISCUS, (MENOPAUSE) from Greek *mēn, mēnē,* month. **4.** MENSES, MENSTRUAL, (MENSTRUATE); BIMESTRIAL, SEMESTER, TRIMESTER, from Latin *mēnsis,* month. [Pokorny 3. *mē-* 703, *mēnōt-* 731.]

mē-[3]. Important derivatives are *more* and *most.*

mē-[3]. Big. Contracted from **meə-*. **1.** Suffixed (comparative) form **mē-is-*. MORE, from Old English *māra,* greater, and *māre* (adverb), more, from Germanic **maizōn-*. **2.** Suffixed (superlative) form **mē-isto-*. MOST, from Old English *mǣst,* most, from Germanic **maista-*. **3.** Suffixed form **mē-ro-, *mē-ri-*. MÄRCHEN, from Old High German *māri,* news, narration. **4.** Suffixed o-grade form **mō-ro-*. CLAYMORE, from Gaelic *mōr,* big, great. [Pokorny 4. *mē-* 704.]

mē-[4]. Important derivatives are *mow*[2], *aftermath,* and *meadow.*

mē-[4]. To cut down grass or grain with a sickle or scythe. Contracted from **meə-*. **1.** MOW[2], from Old English *māwan,* to mow, from Germanic **mē-*. **2.** Suffixed form **mē-ti-*. AFTERMATH, from Old English *mǣth,* a mowing, a mown crop, from Germanic **mēdiz.* **3.** Suffixed form **mē-twā-*, a mown field. MEAD[2], MEADOW, from Old English *mǣd* (oblique case *mǣdwe*), meadow, from Germanic **mēdwō.* [Pokorny 2. *mē-* 703.]

med-. Important derivatives are *mete*[1], *medicine, remedy, meditate, modest, moderate, mode, model, modern, modify, module, mold*[1], *accomodate, commodity, must*[1], and *empty.*

med-. To take appropriate measures. **1.a.** METE[1], from Old English *metan,* to measure (out), from Germanic **metan;* **b.** MEET[2], from Old English *gemǣte,* "commensurate," fit (*ge-*, with; see **kom**), from Germanic derivative **mǣtō,* measure. **2.a.** MEDICAL, MEDICATE, (MEDICINE), (MEDICO); METHEGLIN, REMEDY, from Latin *medērī,* to look after, heal, cure; **b.** MEDITATE, from Latin *meditārī,* to think about, consider, reflect. **3.** Suffixed form **med-es-*. **a.** MODEST; IMMODEST, from Latin *modestus,* "keeping to the appropriate measure," moderate; **b.** MODERATE; IMMODERATE, from Latin *moderārī,* "to keep within measure," to moderate, control. Both **a** and **b** from Latin **modes-*, replacing **medes-* by influence of *modus* (see **5** below). **4.** MEDUSA, from Greek *medein,* to rule (feminine participle *medousa* < **medont-ia*). **5.** Suffixed o-grade form **mod-o-*. MODAL, MODE, MODEL, MODERN, MODICUM, MODIFY, MODULATE, MODULE, MODULUS, MOLD[1], (MOOD[2]), (MOULAGE); (ACCOMODATE), (COMMODE), COMMODIOUS, (COMMODITY), from Latin *modus,* measure, size, limit, manner, harmony, melody. **6.** Suffixed o-grade form **mod-yo-*. MODIOLUS, MUTCHKIN, from Latin *modius,* a measure of grain. **7.** Possibly lengthened o-grade form **mōd-*. **a.** MOTE[2], MUST[1], from Old English *mōtan,* to have occasion, to be permitted or obliged; **b.** EMPTY, from Old English *ǣmetta,* rest, leisure, from Germanic compound **ē-mōt-ja-* (prefix **ē-*, meaning uncertain, from Indo-European **ē, *ō,* to). Both **a** and **b** from Germanic **mōt-*, ability, leisure. [Pokorny 1. *med-* 705.]

medhu-. Important derivatives are *mead*[1] and *amethyst.*

medhu-. Honey; also mead. **1.** MEAD[1], from Old English *meodu,* mead, from Germanic **medu.* **2.** AMETHYST, METHYLENE, from Greek *methu,* wine. [Pokorny *médhu-* 707.]

medhyo-. Important derivatives are *mid*[1], *amid, middle, mean*[3], *medial, mediate, medium, intermediate, medieval, mediocre, mediterranean,* and *meridian.*

medhyo-. Middle. **1.a.** MID[1]; AMID, from Old English *midd(e),* middle; **b.** MIDDLE, from Old English *middel,* middle, from West Germanic diminutive form **middila-;* **c.** MIDGARD, from Old Norse *Midhgardhr,* Midgard, from Germanic compound **midja-gardaz,* "middle zone," name of the earth conceived as an intermediate zone lying between heaven and hell (**gardaz,* enclosure, yard; see **gher-**[1]). **a, b,** and **c** all from Germanic **midja-*. **2.** MEAN[3], MEDIAL, MEDIAN, MEDIASTINUM, MEDIATE, MEDIUM, MIZZEN, MOIETY, MULLION; INTERMEDIATE, MEDIEVAL, MEDIOCRE, MEDITERRANEAN, MERIDIAN, MILIEU, from Latin *medius,* middle, half. **3.** MESO-, from Greek *mesos,* middle. [Pokorny *medhi-* 706.] See also **me-**[2].

meg-. Important derivatives are *much, magnate, magnitude, magnum, magnanimous, magnificent, magnify, major, majority, mayor, majesty, maestro, magistrate, master, mister, mistress, maximum, May, mega-,* and *maharajah.*

meg-. Great. **1.a.** MICKLE, MUCH, from Old English *micel, mycel,* great; **b.** MICKLE, from Old Norse *mikill.* Both **a** and **b** from Germanic suffixed form **mik-ila-*. **2.** Suffixed form **mag-no-*. MAGNATE, MAGNITUDE, MAGNUM; MAGNANIMOUS, MAGNIFIC, (MAGNIFICENT), (MAGNIFICO), (MAGNIFY), MAGNILOQUENT, from Latin *magnus,* great. **3.** Suffixed (comparative) form **mag-yos-*. **a.** MAJOR, MAJORDOMO, MAJORITY, MAJUSCULE, MAYOR, from Latin *māior,* greater; **b.** MAESTOSO, MAJESTY, from Latin *māiestās,* greatness, authority; **c.** MAESTRO, MAGISTERIAL, MAGISTRAL, MAGISTRATE, MASTER, (MISTER), MISTRAL, (MISTRESS), from Latin *magister,* master, high official (< "he who is greater"). **4.** Suffixed (superlative) form **mag-samo-*. MAXIM, MAXIMUM, from Latin *maximus,* greatest. **5.** Suffixed (feminine) form **mag-ya-*, "she who is great." MAY, from Latin *Maia,* name of a goddess. **6.** Suffixed form **meg-ə-(l-)*. MEGA-, MEGALO-; ACROMEGALY, ALMAGEST, OMEGA, from Greek *megas* (stem *megal-*), great. **7.** Variant form **megh-* (< **meg-ə-*). MAHARAJAH, MAHARANI, MAHARISHI, MAHATMA, MAHAYANA, from Sanskrit *mahā-, mahat-*, great. [Pokorny *meĝ(h)-* 708.]

mei-[1]. Important derivatives are *permeate, mad, molt, mutate, commute, mutual, mis-*[1], *amiss, mistake, miss*[1], *common, communicate, communism, municipal, remunerate, immune, amoeba, migrate,* and *emigrate.*

mei-[1]. To change, go, move; with derivatives referring to the exchange of goods and services within a society as regulated by custom or law. **1.** MEATUS; CONGÉ, IRREMEABLE, PERMEATE, from Latin *meāre,* to go, pass. **2.** Suffixed o-grade form **moi-to-*. **a.** MAD, from Old English **gemǣdan,* to make insane or foolish, from Germanic **ga-maid-jan,* denominative from **ga-maid-az,* "changed (for the worse)," abnormal (**ga-*, intensive prefix; see **kom**); **b.** MEW[1], MOLT, MUTATE; COMMUTE, PERMUTE, REMUDA, TRANSMUTE, from Latin *mūtāre,* to change; **c.** MUTUAL, from Latin *mūtuus,* "done in exchange," borrowed, reciprocal, mutual. **3.** Suffixed extended zero-grade form **mit-to-*. **a.** MIS-[1], from Old English *mis-*, mis-, and Old French *mes-* (from Frankish **miss-*); **b.** AMISS, MISTAKE, from Old Norse *mis(s), mis(s)-*, miss, mis-; **c.** MISS[1], from Old English *missan,* to miss, from Germanic **missjan,* to go wrong. **a, b,** and **c** all from Germanic **missa-*, "in a changed manner," abnormally, wrongly. **4.** Suffixed o-grade form **moi-n-* in compound adjective **ko-moin-i-*, "held in common" (**ko-*, together; see **kom**). **a.** MEAN[2], (DEMEAN[2]), from Old English *gemǣne,* common, public, general, from Germanic **gamainiz;* **b.** COMMON, (COMMUNE[1]), COMMUNE[2], COMMUNICATE, (COMMUNISM), from Latin *commūnis,* common, public, general. **5.** Suffixed o-grade form **moi-n-es-*. **a.** MUNICIPAL, MUNIFICENT, REMUNERATE, from Latin *mūnus,* "service performed for the community," duty, work, "public spectacle paid for by a magistrate," gift; **b.** IMMUNE, from Latin *immūnis,* exempt from public service (*in-*, negative prefix; see **ne**). **6.** Extended form **(ə)meigʷ-*. **a.** AMOEBA, from Greek *ameibein,* to change; **b.** MIGRATE; EMIGRATE, from Latin *migrāre,* to change one's place of living. [Pokorny 2. *mei-*, 3. *mei-* 710, *meigᵘ-* 713, 2. *meit(h)-* 715.]

mei-[2]. Important derivatives are *menu, mince, minute*[2], *diminish, minor, minus, minimum, minestrone,* and *minister.*

mei-[2]. Small. **1.** MEIOSIS; MIOCENE, from Greek *meiōn,* less, lesser. **2.** (see **ne**) Latin *nimis,* too much, very (< **ne-mi-s,* "not little"; *ne-*, negative prefix). **3.** Suffixed zero-grade form **mi-nu-*. **a.** MENU, (MINCE), MINUEND, MINUTE[2]; COMMINUTE, DIMINISH, from Latin *minuere,* to reduce, diminish; **b.** MINOR, MINUS; MINUSCULE, from Latin *minor* (influenced by the comparative suffix *-or*), less, lesser, smaller; **c.** further suffixed (superlative) form **minu-mo-*. MINIMUM, from Latin *minimus,* least; **d.** MINESTRONE, MINISTER, MINISTRY, MYSTERY[2], from Latin *minister,* an inferior, servant (formed after *magister,* master; see **meg-**); **e.** MENSHEVIK, from Russian *men'she,* less. [Pokorny 5. *mei-* 711.]

meigh-. Important derivatives are *mist* and *mistletoe.*

meigh-. To urinate. **1.a.** MIST, from Old English *mist,* mist; **b.** MIZZLE[1], from Middle English *misellen,* to drizzle, from a source perhaps akin to Dutch dialectal *mieselen,* to drizzle; **c.** (MISSEL THRUSH), MISTLETOE, from Old English *mistel,* mistletoe, from Germanic diminutive form **mihst-ila-*, mistletoe (which is propagated through the droppings of the missel thrush). **a, b,** and **c** all from Germanic suffixed form **mih-stu-*, urine, hence mist, fine rain. **2.** Suffixed form **migh-tu-*. MICTURATE, from Latin *micturīre*, to want to urinate (desiderative of *meiere*, to urinate). [Pokorny *meik-* 713.]

meik-. Important derivatives are *meddle, medley, mestizo, miscellaneous, mix, mixture, pell-mell, promiscuous,* and *mash.*

meik-. To mix. **1.** Variant form **meig-*. AMPHIMIXIS, APOMIXIS, PANMICTIC, PANMIXIA, from Greek *mignunai*, to mix, with zero-grade noun *mixis* (< **mig-ti-*), a mingling. **2.** Suffixed zero-grade form **mik-sk-*. MEDDLE, (MEDLEY), (MELANGE), MESTIZO, MISCELLANEOUS, MISCIBLE, MIX, MIXTURE, MUSTANG; ADMIX, COMMIX, IMMIX, MISCEGENATION, (PELL-MELL), PROMISCUOUS, from Latin *miscēre* (past participle *mixtus*), to mix. **3.** MASH, from Old English **māsc, *māc, māx-*, mashed malt, from a possible Germanic form **maisk-*. [Pokorny *meiḱ-* 714.]

mei-no-. Important derivatives are *moan, bemoan,* and *mean*[1].

mei-no-. Opinion, intention. **1.** MOAN, from Old English **mān*, opinion, complaint, from Germanic **main-*. **2.** MEAN[1]; BEMOAN, from Old English *mǣnan*, to signify, tell, complain of, moan, from Germanic **mainjan*. [Pokorny *mei-no-* 714.]

mel-[1]. Important derivatives are *melt, malt, mollify, mollusk, bland, smelt*[1]*, enamel, mild,* and *mulch.*

mel-[1]. Soft; with derivatives referring to soft or softened materials of various kinds.
I. Extended form **meld-*. **1.** MELT, from Old English *meltan*, to melt, from Germanic **meltan*. **2.** MILT, from Old English *milte*, spleen, and Middle Dutch *milte*, milt, from Germanic **miltja-*, possibly from **mel-[1]**. **3.** MALT, from Old English *mealt*, malt, from Germanic **malta-*, possibly from **mel-[1]**. **4.** Suffixed variant form **mled-sno-*. BLENNY, from Greek *blennos*, slime, also a name for the blenny. **5.** Suffixed zero-grade form **mḷd-wi-*. MOIL, MOLLIFY, MOLLUSK, (MOUILLÉ); EMOLLIENT, from Latin *mollis*, soft. **6.** Possibly nasalized variant form **mlad-*. BLAND, BLANDISH, from Latin *blandus*, smooth, caressing, flattering, soft-spoken.
II. Variant form **smeld-*. **a.** SMELT[1], from Middle Dutch or Middle Low German *smelten*, to smelt; **b.** SCHMALTZ, from Old High German *smalz*, animal fat; **c.** SMALT, from Italian *smalto*, enamel, glaze; **d.** ENAMEL, from Old French *esmail*, enamel; **e.** SMELT[2], from Old English *smelt, smylt*, a marine fish, smelt, perhaps from **mel-[1]**. **a, b, c, d,** and **e** all from Germanic **smelt-*.
III. Extended form **meldh-*. **1.** MILD, from Old English *milde*, mild, from Germanic **mildja-*. **2.** MALTHA, from Greek *maltha*, a mixture of wax and pitch, possibly from **mel-[1]**.
IV. Suffixed form **mel-sko-*. MULCH, from Old English *mel(i)sc, mylsc*, mild, mellow, from Germanic **mil-sk-*.
V. Extended form **mḷək-*. BONANZA, CHONDROMALACIA, MALACOLOGY, OSTEOMALACIA, from Greek *malakos*, soft.
VI. MUTTON, from Old French *moton*, sheep, from Celtic **molto-*, sheep, possibly from **mel-[1]**.
VII. Suffixed zero-grade form **(ə)ml-u-*. AMBLYGONITE, AMBLYOPIA, from Greek *amblus*, blunt, dull, dim. [Pokorny 1. *mel-* 716.]

mel-[2]. Important derivatives are *ameliorate, multi-,* and *multitude.*

mel-[2]. Strong, great. **1.** Suffixed (comparative) form **mel-yos-*. (AMELIORATE), MELIORATE, MELIORISM, from Latin *melior*, better. **2.** Suffixed zero-grade form **mḷ-to-*. MOLTO, MULTI-, MULTITUDE, from Latin *multus*, much, many. [Pokorny 4. *mel-* 720.]

mel-[3]. Important derivatives are *mal-, malice, malign, dismal, malady, malefactor,* and *malevolent.*

mel-[3]. Bad. MAL-, MALICE, (MALIGN); DISMAL, MALADY, MALARIA, MALEDICT, MALEFACTOR, MALEFIC, MALENTENDU, MALEVOLENCE, MALVERSATION, from Latin *malus*, bad, and *male*, ill (> *malignus*, harmful). [Pokorny *mēlo-* 724.]

melə-. Important derivatives are *maelstrom, meal*[1]*, mill*[1]*, immolate, millet, malleable, mallet,* and *maul.*

melə-. Also **mel-.** To crush, grind; with derivatives referring to various ground or crumbling substances (such as flour) and to instruments for grinding or crushing (such as millstones). **1.** O-grade form **mol-*. MAELSTROM, from Middle Dutch *malen*, to whirl, from Germanic **mal-*. **2.** Full-grade form **mel-*. MEAL[1], from Old English *melu*, flour, meal, from Germanic suffixed form **mel-wa-*. **3.** Zero-grade form **mḷ-*. MOLD[3], (MOLDER), from Old English *molde*, soil, from Germanic suffixed form **mul-dō*. **4.** Full-grade form **mel-*. **a.** MILL[1], MOLA[2], MOLAR[2], MOLE[4], (MOULIN); EMOLUMENT, IMMOLATE, ORMOLU, from Latin *molere*, to grind (grain), and its derivative *mola*, a millstone, mill, coarse meal customarily sprinkled on sacrificial animals; **b.** possible suffixed form **mel-iyo-*. MEALIE, MILIUM, MILLET, from Latin *milium*, millet. **5.** Suffixed variant form **mal-ni-*. MALLEABLE, (MALLET), MALLEUS, MAUL; PALL-MALL, from Latin *malleus*, hammer, mallet. **6.** Zero-grade form **mḷ-*. AMYLUM, MYLONITE, from Greek *mulē, mulos*, millstone, mill. **7.** Possibly extended form **mlī-*. BLIN, BLINTZ, from Old Russian *blinŭ*, pancake. [Pokorny 1. *mel-* 716.]

melg-. Important derivatives are *emulsion, milk, galaxy, lacto-,* and *lettuce.*

melg-. To rub off; also to milk.
I. 1. Zero-grade form **mḷg-*. EMULSION, from Latin *mulgēre*, to milk. **2.** Full-grade form **melg-*. **a.** MILK, from Old English *meolc, milc*, milk; **b.** MILCH, from Old English *-milce*, milch, from Germanic suffixed form **meluk-ja-*, giving milk; **c.** MILCHIG, from Old High German *miluh*, milk. **a, b,** and **c** all from Germanic **melkan*, to milk, contaminated with an unrelated noun for milk, cognate with the Greek and Latin forms given in **II** below, to form the blend **meluk-*.
II. Included here to mark the unexplained fact that no common Indo-European noun for milk can be reconstructed is another root **g(a)lag-*, **g(a)lakt-*, milk, found only in: **a.** (GALACTIC), GALACTO-, GALAXY; AGALACTIA, POLYGALA, from Greek *gala* (stem *galakt-*), milk; **b.** (LACTATE), LACTEAL, LACTESCENT, LACTO-, LETTUCE, from Latin *lac* (stem *lact-*), milk; **c.** the blended Germanic form cited in **I. 2.** above. [Pokorny *mel̑ǵ-* 722, *glag-* 400.]

melit-. Important derivatives are *marmalade, mellifluous, molasses,* and *mildew.*

melit-. Honey. **1.** HYDROMEL, MARMALADE, MELILOT, OENOMEL, from Greek *meli*, honey. **2.a.** MELLIFEROUS, MELLIFLUOUS, MOLASSES, from Latin *mel* (stem *mell-*), honey, from **meld-*, syncopated from **melid-*; **b.** suffixed zero-grade form **mḷd-to-*, "honied." MOUSSE, from Latin *mulsus*, honey-sweet. **3.** MILDEW, from Old English *mildēaw*, honeydew, nectar, from Germanic compound **melith-dauwaz*, honeydew (a substance secreted by aphids on leaves; it was formerly imagined to be distilled from the air like dew; **dauwaz*, dew; see **dheu-[1]**), from **melith-*. [Pokorny *melit-* 723.]

men-[1]. Important derivatives are *mind, mental, mention, automatic, memento, comment, reminiscent, mania, mandarin, mint*[1]*, money, monitor, monster, monument, muster, admonish, demonstrate, premonition, summon, mosaic, Muse, museum, music, amnesia,* and *amnesty.*

men-[1]. To think; with derivatives referring to various qualities and states of mind and thought.
I. Zero-grade form **mṇ-*. **1.** Suffixed form **mṇ-ti-*. **a.** MIND, from Old English *gemynd*, memory, mind, from Germanic **ga-mundi-* (**ga-*, intensive prefix; see **kom**); **b.** MENTAL[1]; AMENT[2], DEMENT, from Latin *mēns* (stem *ment-*), mind; **c.** MENTION, from Latin *mentiō*, remembrance, mention. **2.** Suffixed form **mṇ-to-*. AUTOMATIC, from Greek *-matos*, "willing." **3.** Suffixed form **mṇ-yo-*. **a.** MAENAD, from Greek *mainesthai*, to be mad; **b.** AHRIMAN, from Avestan *mainiiuš*, spirit.
II. Full-grade form **men-*. **1.** Suffixed form **men-ti-*. **a.** MINNESINGER, from Old High German *minna*, love; **b.** MINIKIN, from Middle Dutch *minne*, love. Both **a** and **b** from Germanic **minthjō*. **2.a.** MEMENTO, from Latin reduplicated form *meminisse*, to remember; **b.** COMMENT, from Latin *comminīscī*, to contrive by thought (*com-*, intensive prefix; see **kom**); **c.** REMINISCENT, from Latin *reminīscī*, to recall, recollect (*re-*, again, back; see **re-**); **d.** MINERVA, from Latin *Minerva*, name of the goddess of wisdom, possibly from **men-[1]**. **3.a.** MENTOR, from Greek *Mentōr*, Mentor, man's name (probably meaning "adviser"); **b.** MANIA, MANIAC, MANIC, from Greek *mania*, madness; **c.** -MANCY, MANTIC, MANTIS, from Greek *mantis*, seer. **4.** MANDARIN, MANTRA, from Sanskrit *mantraḥ*, counsel, prayer, hymn.
III. O-grade form **mon-*. **1.** Suffixed (causative) form **mon-eyo-*. MONISH, MONITION, MONITOR, MONSTER, MONUMENT, MUSTER; ADMONISH, DEMONSTRATE, PREMONITION, SUMMON, from Latin *monēre*, to remind, warn, advise. **2.** Suffixed o-grade form **mon-twə*. MOSAIC, MUSE, MUSEUM, MUSIC, from Greek *Mousa*, a Muse.
IV. Extended form **mnā-*, contracted from **mnaə-*. **1.** AMNESIA, AMNESTY, ANAMNESIS, from Greek reduplicated form *mimnēskein*, to remember. **2.** MNEMONIC, from Greek *mnēmōn*, mindful.
V. Indo-European verb phrase **mens dhē-*, "to set mind" (see **dhē-**), underlying compound **mṇs-dhē-*. AHURA MAZDA, (ORMAZD), from Avestan *mazdā-*, wise. [Pokorny 3. *men-* 726, *mendh-* 730.]

men-[2]. Important derivatives are *mouth, menace, amenable, demean*[1]*, promenade, eminent, imminent, prominent, mount*[1]*, mountain,* and *amount.*

men-[2]. To project. **1.** Suffixed zero-grade form **mṇ-to-* in a western Indo-European word for a projecting body part, variously "chin, jaw, mouth." **a.** MOUTH, from Old English *mūth*, mouth, from Germanic **munthaz*; **b.** MENTAL[2], from Latin *mentum*, chin. **2.** MENACE, MINACIOUS; AMENABLE, DEMEAN[1], PROMENADE, from Latin *minae*, projecting points, threats. **3.** EMINENT, IMMINENT, PROMINENT, (PROMONTORY), from Latin *-minēre*, to project, jut, threaten. **4.** Suffixed o-grade form **mon-ti-*. MONS, (MONTAGNARD), MONTANE, MONTE, MONTICULE, MOUNT[1], MOUNT[2], MOUNTAIN; AMOUNT, ULTRAMONTANE, from Latin *mōns* (stem *mont-*), mountain. [Pokorny 1. *men-* 726, 2. *menth-* 732.]

men-[3]. Important derivatives are *manor, mansion, ménage, permanent,* and *remain.*

men-[3]. To remain. Variant suffixed (stative) form **man-ē-*. MANOR, MANSE, MANSION, (MÉNAGE); IMMANENT, PERMANENT, REMAIN, from Latin *manēre*, to remain. [Pokorny 5. *men-* 729.]

men-[4]. Important derivatives are *monastery, monk, mono-,* and *minnow.*

men-[4]. Small, isolated. **1.** MANOMETER, from Greek *manos*, rare, sparse. **2.** Suffixed o-grade form **mon-wo-*. MONAD, MONASTERY, MONK, MONO-; PSEUDOMONAD, from Greek *monos*, alone, single, sole. **3.** Possibly also suffixed form **men-i-*, a small fish. MINNOW, from Middle English *meneu*, a small fish, from a source akin to Old English *myne, mynwe*, minnow. [Pokorny 4. *men-* 728, *meni-* 731.]

mendh-. Important derivatives are *mathematical* and *mathematics.*

mendh-. To learn. Zero-grade form **mṇdh-*. MATHEMATICAL, (MATHEMATICS); CHRESTOMATHY, POLYMATH, from Greek *manthanein* (aorist stem *math-*), to learn. [Pokorny *mendh-* 730.]

menegh-. An important derivative is *many.*

menegh-. Copious. MANY, from Old English *manig, mænig*, many, from Germanic **managa-*. [Pokorny *men(e)gh-* 730.]

mer-. Important derivatives are *nightmare, mortar, mordant, morsel, remorse, morbid, murder, mortal, mortuary, mortgage, mortify, postmortem,* and *ambrosia.*

mer-. To rub away, harm.
I. 1. NIGHTMARE, from Old English *mare, mære*, goblin, incubus, from Germanic **marōn-*, goblin. **2.** MARASMUS; AMARANTH, from Greek *marainein*, to waste away, wither. **3.** Probably suffixed zero-grade form **mṛ- to-*, "ground down." MORTAR, from Latin *mortārium*, mortar. **4.** Possibly extended root **merd-*. MORDACIOUS, MORDANT, MORDENT, MORSEL; PREMORSE, REMORSE, from Latin *mordēre*, to bite. **5.** Possibly suffixed form **mor-bho-*. MORBID, from Latin *morbus*, disease (but this is more likely of unknown origin).
II. Possibly the same root, but more likely distinct, is **mer-*, "to die," with derivatives referring to death and to human beings as subject to death. **1.** Zero-grade form **mṛ-*. **a.** suffixed form **mṛ-tro-*. MURDER, from Old English *morthor*, murder, from Germanic suffixed form **mur-thra-*; **b.** suffixed form

*mr̥-ti-. MORT[1], MORTAL; AMORTIZE, MORTIFY, POST-MORTEM, from Latin *mors* (stem *mort-*), death; **c.** suffixed form *mr̥-yo-. MORIBUND, MORTUARY, MURRAIN, MORTGAGE, (MORTMAIN), from Latin *morī*, to die, with irregular past participle *mortuus* (< *mr̥-two-), replacing older *mr̥-to- (for which see **d**); **d.** prefixed and suffixed form *n̥-mr̥-to-, "undying, immortal." (*n̥-, negative prefix; see **ne**). *(i)* IMMORTAL, from Latin *immortālis; (ii)* AMBROSIA, from Greek *ambrotos*, immortal, divine (*a-* + *-mbrotos, brotos*, mortal); *(iii)* AMRITA, from Sanskrit *amr̥tam*, immortality (*a-* + *mr̥ta-*, dead). **2.** Suffixed o-grade form *mor-t-yo-. MANTICORE, from Greek *mantikhōras* (corrupted from *martiokhōras*), manticore, probably from Iranian compound *martiya-khvāra-, "man-eater" (*khvāra-, eating; see **swel-**), from Old Persian *martiya-* , a mortal man. [Pokorny 4. *mer-*, 5. *mer-* 735.]

merg-. Important derivatives are *mark[1], marquee, marquis, demarcation, mark[2], remark, march[1]*, and *margin*.

merg-. Boundary, border. **1.a.** MARK[1], from Old English *mearc*, boundary, landmark, sign, trace; **b.** MARGRAVE, from Middle Dutch *marc*, border; **c.** MARCH[2], (MARQUEE), MARQUIS, (MARQUISE), from Old French *marc, marche*, border country; **d.** MARCHESE, MARCHIONESS, from Medieval Latin *marca*, boundary, border; **e.** DEMARCATION, from Old Italian *marcare*, to mark out; **f.** MARK[2], from Old English *marc*, a mark of weight or money; **g.** MARKKA, from Swedish *mark*, a mark of money. **a, b, c, d, e, f,** and **g** all from Germanic *mark-, boundary, border territory; also to mark out a boundary by walking around it (ceremonially "beating the bounds"); also a landmark, boundary marker, and a mark in general (and in particular a mark on a metal currency bar, hence a unit of currency); these various meanings are widely represented in Germanic descendants and in Romance borrowings. **2.** MARQUETRY; REMARK, from Old Norse *merki*, a mark, from Germanic *markja-, mark, border. **3.** MARC, MARCH[1], from Frankish *markōn, to mark out, from Germanic denominative verb *markōn. **4.** MARGIN; EMARGINATE, from Latin *margō*, border, edge. **5.** Celtic variant form *mrog-, territory, land. CYMRY, from Welsh *Cymro*, Wales, from British Celtic *kombrogos, fellow countryman (*kom-, collective prefix; see **kom**), from *-brogos*, district. [Pokorny *mereĝ-* 738.]

meuə-. Important derivatives are *mob, mobile, moment, momentous, momentum, motif, motion, motive, motor, move, movement, commotion, emotion, promote, remote*, and *remove*.

meuə-. To push away. (MOB), MOBILE, MOMENT, (MOMENTOUS), MOMENTUM, MOSSO, (MOTIF), MOTION, MOTIVE, MOTOR, MOVE, (MOVEMENT); COMMOTION, EMOTION, PROMOTE, (REMOTE), (REMOVE), from Latin *movēre*, to move. [Pokorny 2. *meu-* 743.]

mori-. Important derivatives are *mere[2], mermaid, meerschaum, marsh, morass, marine, maritime*, and *ultramarine*.

mori-. Body of water; lake (?), sea (?). **1.a.** MERE[2]; (MERMAID), from Old English *mere*, sea, lake, pond; **b.** MARRAM, from a Scandinavian source akin to Old Norse *marr*, sea; **c.** MEERSCHAUM, from Old High German *mari*, sea. **a, b,** and **c** all from Germanic *mari-. **2.a.** MARSH, from Old English *mersc, merisc*, marsh; **b.** MORASS, from Old French *maresc, mareis*, marsh. Both **a** and **b** from Germanic *mariska-, water-logged land. **3.** MARE[2], (MARINARA), MARINE, MARITIME; BÊCHE-DE-MER, MARICULTURE, ORMER, ULTRAMARINE, from Latin *mare*, sea. [Pokorny *mori* 748.]

mregh-u-. Important derivatives are *brief, abbreviate, abridge, merry, mirth, brace, brassiere, pretzel*, and *embrace*.

mregh-u-. Short.
I. Suffixed form *mregh-w-i-. BRIEF, BRUMAL; ABBREVIATE, (ABRIDGE), from Latin *brevis*, short.
II. Zero-grade form *mr̥ghu-. **1.a.** MERRY, from Old English *myrge, mirige*, pleasant; **b.** MIRTH, from Old English *myrgth*, pleasure, joy, from Germanic *murgithō, pleasantness. Both **a** and **b** from Germanic *murgja-, short, also pleasant, joyful. **2.** BRACHY-; AMPHIBRACH, TRIBRACH, from Greek *brakhus*, short. **3.** BRACE, BRACERO, BRACHIUM, BRASSARD, BRASSIERE, PRETZEL; (EMBRACE), from Greek comparative *brakhiōn*, shorter, hence also "upper arm" (as opposed to the longer forearm). [Pokorny *mreghu-* 750.]

mūs-. Important derivatives are *mouse* and *muscle*.

mūs-. A mouse; also a muscle (from the resemblance of a flexing muscle to the movements of a mouse). **1.** MOUSE, from Old English *mūs* (plural *mȳs*), mouse, from Germanic *mūs- (plural *mūsiz). **2.** MURINE, MUSCLE, MUSTELINE, from Latin *mūs*, mouse. **3.** MYELO-, MYO-; EPIMYSIUM, MYOSOTIS, MYSTICETE, PERIMYSIUM, SYRINGOMYELIA, from Greek *mus*, mouse, muscle. [Pokorny *mūs* 752.]

nas-. Important derivatives are *nose, nuzzle, nostril, nasal, nasturtium*, and *pince-nez*.

nas-. Nose. **1.** NOSE, (NUZZLE); NOSTRIL, from Old English *nosu*, nose, from Germanic zero-grade form *nusō. **2.** NESS, from Old English *næss*, headland, from Germanic *nasja-. **3.** Lengthened-grade form *nās-. **a.** NARIS, from Latin *nāris*, nostril; **b.** expressive form *nāss-. NASAL, NASO-; NASTURTIUM, PINCE-NEZ, from Latin *nāsus*, nose. **4.** NARK[2], from Romany *nāk*, nose, from expressive Indo-Aryan form *nakka-. [Pokorny *nas-* 755, *neu-ks-* 768.]

nāu-. Important derivatives are *naval, navigate, navy, nausea, nautical, nautilus, noise*, and *astronaut*.

nāu-. Boat. Contracted from *naəu-. **1.** NACELLE, NAVAL, NAVE[1], NAVICULAR, NAVIGATE, (NAVY), from Latin *nāvis*, ship. **2.** NAUSEA, NAUTICAL, NAUTILUS, (NOISE); AERONAUT, AQUANAUT, ARGONAUT, ASTRONAUT, COSMONAUT, from Greek *naus*, ship, and *nautēs*, sailor. [Pokorny 1. *nāu-* 755.]

n̥dher-. Important derivatives are *under, inferior, infernal, inferno*, and *infra-*.

n̥dher-. Under. **1.a.** UNDER, UNDER-, from Old English *under*, under; **b.** U-BOAT, from Old High German *untar*, under. Both **a** and **b** from Germanic *under-. **2.** INFERIOR, from Latin *īnferus*, lower. **3.** INFERNAL, (INFERNO), from Latin *īnfernus*, lower. **4.** INFRA-, from Latin *īnfrā*, below. [Pokorny *n̥dhos* 771.]

ne. Important derivatives are *naught, naughty, neither, never, no[1], no[2], none, nor[1], not, nothing, nay, annul, nefarious, neuter, nice, null, nullify, annihilate, non-, neglect, negligee, negotiate, negate, deny*, and *renegade*.

ne. Not. **1.a.** NAUGHT, (NAUGHTY), NEITHER, NEVER, NILL, NO[1], NO[2], NONE, (NOR[1]), (NOT), (NOTHING), from Old English *ne*, not, and *nā*, no; **b.** NAY, from Old Norse *ne*, not; **c.** NIX[2], from Old High German *ne, ni*, not. **a, b,** and **c** all from Germanic *ne-, *na-. **2.** ANNUL, NEFARIOUS, NESCIENCE, NEUTER, (NICE), NULL, NULLIFY, NULLIPARA, from Latin *ne-*, not, and *nūllus*, none (*ne-* + *ūllus*, any; see **oi-no-**). **3.** NIMIETY, from Latin *nimis*, too much, excessively, very (< *ne-mi-s, "not little"; *mi-, little; see **mei-[2]**). **4.** NIHILISM, (NIHILITY), NIL; ANNIHILATE, from Latin *nihil, nīl*, nothing, contracted from *nihilum*, nothing (< *ne-hīlum, "not a whit, nothing at all"; *hīlum*, a thing, trifle; origin unknown). **5.** NON-, from Latin *nōn*, not (< *ne-oinom, not one thing"; *oino-, one; see **oi-no-**). **6.** NISI, from Latin *nisī*, unless (*nī*, not, from *nei + *sī*, if; see **swo-**). **7.a.** NEGLECT, (NEGLIGEE), NEGOTIATE, from Latin prefix *neg-*, not; **b.** NEGATE; ABNEGATE, DENY, RENEGADE, (RENEGE), from Latin *negāre*, to deny. Both **a** and **b** from Italic *nek, not. **8.** NEPENTHE, from Greek *nē-*, not. **9.** Zero-grade combining form *n̥-. **a.** *(i)* UN-[1], from Old English *un-*, not; *(ii)* ZUGUNRUHE, from Old High German *un-*, not. Both *(i)* and *(ii)* from Germanic *un-; **b.** IN-[1], from Latin *in-*, not; **c.** A-[1], (AN-), from Greek *a-, an-*, not; **d.** AHIMSA, AMRITA, from Sanskrit *a-, an-*, not. [Pokorny *ne* 756.]

nebh-. Important derivatives are *nebula, nebulous*, and *nimbus*.

nebh-. Cloud. **1.** Suffixed form *nebh-(e)lo-. **a.** NIFLHEIM, from Old Norse *nifl-*, "mist" or "dark," probably from Germanic *nibila-; **b.** NIBELUNG, from Old High German *Nibulunc, Nibilung*, from Germanic suffixed patronymic form *nibul-unga-, beside Old High German *nebul*, mist, fog, from Germanic *nebla-. **2.** Suffixed form *nebh-elā-. **a.** NEBULA, NEBULOUS, from Latin *nebula*, cloud; **b.** NEPHELINE; NEPHELOMETER, from Greek *nephelē*, cloud. **3.** Suffixed form *nebh-es-. NEPHOLOGY, from Greek *nephos*, cloud. **4.** Nasalized form *ne-m-bh-. NIMBUS, from Latin *nimbus*, rain, cloud, aura. [Pokorny *(enebh-)* 315.]

ned-. Important derivatives are *net[1], nettle, node, nodule, annex*, and *connect*.

ned-. To bind, tie. **1.** O-grade form *nod-. **a.** NET[1], from Old English *net(t)*, a net, from Germanic *nati-; **b.** NETTLE, from Old English *netel(e), netle*, nettle, from Germanic *nat-ilo, a nettle (nettles or plants of closely related genera such as hemp were used as a source of fiber); **c.** OUCH[2], from Anglo-Norman *nouch*, brooch, from Germanic *nat-sk-. **2.** Lengthened o-grade form *nōdo-. NODE, NODULE, NODUS; DÉNOUEMENT, from Latin *nōdus*, a knot. **3.** With re-formation of the root. NEXUS; (ADNEXA), ANNEX, CONNECT, from Latin *nectere* (past participle *nexus*), to tie, bind, connect. [Pokorny 1. *ned-* 758.]

[nēhw-iz. Important derivatives are *near, neighbor, next*, and *nigh*.

nēhw-iz. Near. Germanic root. NEAR, NEIGHBOR, NEXT, NIGH, from Old English *nēah*, near.**]**

nek-[1]. Important derivatives are *pernicious, nuisance, innocent, innocuous, noxious, obnoxious, necrosis, necromancy, nectar*, and *nectarine*.

nek-[1]. Death. **1.** INTERNECINE, PERNICIOUS, from Latin *nex* (stem *nec-*), death. **2.** Suffixed (causative) o-grade form *nok-eyo-. NOCENT, NOCUOUS, NUISANCE; INNOCENT, INNOCUOUS, from Latin *nocēre*, to injure, harm. **3.** Suffixed o-grade form *nok-s-. NOXIOUS; OBNOXIOUS, from Latin *noxa*, injury, hurt, damage entailing liability. **4.** Suffixed full-grade form *nek-ro-. NECRO-, NECROSIS; NECROMANCY, from Greek *nekros*, corpse. **5.** NECTAR, (NECTARINE), from Greek *nektar*, the drink of the gods, "overcoming death" (*tar-, overcoming; see **terə-[2]**). [Pokorny *neḱ-* 762.]

nek-[2]. Important derivatives are *enough* and *oncology*.

nek-[2]. To reach, attain.
I. O-grade form *nok-. ENOUGH, from Old English *genōg*, enough, from Germanic *ganōga-, sufficient, from *ga-nah, "suffices" (*ga-, intensive prefix; see **kom**).
II. Variant form *enk-. **1.** ONCOGENESIS, ONCOLOGY, from Greek *onkos*, a burden, mass, hence a tumor, from reduplicated *enenkein*, to carry. **2.** Compound root *bhrenk- (see **bher[1]**). [Pokorny *eneḱ-* 316.]

nek^w**-t-.** Important derivatives are *night, nocturnal*, and *equinox*.

nek^w**-t-.** Night. O-grade form *nok^w-t-. **1.** NIGHT, from Old English *niht, neaht*, night, from Germanic *naht-. **2.** NOCTI-, (NOCTURN), NOCTURNAL, EQUINOX, from Latin *nox* (stem *noct-*), night. **3.** NOCTUID, NOCTULE, from Latin *noctua*, night owl. **4.** NYCTALOPIA, NYCTITROPISM, from Greek *nux* (stem *nukt-*), night. [Pokorny *nek*^{u}*(t)-* 762.]

nem-. Important derivatives are *numb, nimble, nemesis, economy, astronomy, autonomous, metronome, nomad, number*, and *enumerate*.

nem-. To assign, allot; also to take. **1.a.** NIM, NUMB; (BENUMB), from Old English *niman*, to take, seize; **b.** NIMBLE, from Old English *næmel*, quick to seize, and *numol*, quick at learning, seizing; **c.** NIM[2], from Old High German *nëman*, to take. **a, b,** and **c** all from Germanic *nem-. **2.** NEMESIS; ECONOMY, from Greek *nemein*, to allot. **3.** O-grade form *nom-. **a.** NOME, -NOMY; ANOMIE, ANTINOMIAN, ANTINOMY, (ASTRONOMER), (ASTRONOMY), AUTONOMOUS, DEUTERONOMY, METRONOME, NOMOGRAPH, NOMOLOGY, NOMOTHETIC, NUMISMATIC, from Greek *nomos*, portion, usage, custom, law, division, district; **b.** NOMA, from Greek *nomē*, pasturage, grazing, hence a spreading, a spreading ulcer; **c.** NOMAD, from Greek *nomas*, wandering in search of pasture; **d.** NUMMULAR, NUMMULITE, from Greek *nomimos*, legal. **4.** Perhaps suffixed o-grade form *nom-eso-. NUMBER; ENUMERATE, SUPERNUMERARY, from Latin *numerus*, number, division. [Pokorny 1. *nem-* 763.]

nepōt-. Important derivatives are *nephew, nepotism*, and *niece*.

nepōt-. Grandson, nephew. Feminine *neptī-. NEPHEW, NEPOTISM, NIECE, from Latin *nepōs,* grandson, nephew, and *neptis,* granddaughter, niece. [Pokorny *nepōt-* 764.]

ner-[1]. Important derivatives are *Nordic, north, Norman[1], northern,* and *Norse.*

ner-[1]. Under, also on the left; hence, with an eastward orientation, north. Suffixed zero-grade form *nr̥-t(r)o-. **a.** NORDIC, NORTH, from Old English *north,* north; **b.** NORTHERN, from Old English *northerne,* northern; **c.** NORSE, from Middle Dutch *nort,* north; **d.** NORMAN[1], NORWEGIAN, from Old Norse *nordhr,* north. [Pokorny 2. *ner-* 765.]

ner-[2]. A derivative is *andro-.*

ner-[2]. Also **əner-.** Man; basic sense "vigorous, vital, strong." Oldest root form *əner-. ANDRO-, -ANDROUS, -ANDRY; PHILANDER, from Greek *anēr* (stem *andr-,* from zero-grade *ənr-), man. [Pokorny 1. *ner-(t)-* 765.]

nes-[1]. Important derivatives are *harness* and *nostalgia.*

nes-[1]. To return safely home. **1.** HARNESS, from Old French *harneis,* harness, possibly from a Germanic source akin to Old English, Old High German (in composition), and Old Norse *nest,* food for a journey, from Germanic *nes-tam. **2.** Suffixed o-grade form *nos-to-. NOSTALGIA, from Greek *nostos,* a return home. [Pokorny *nes-* 766.]

nes-[2]. Important derivatives are *us, our,* and *ours.*

nes-[2]. Oblique cases of the personal pronoun of the first person plural. For the nominative see **we-**. **1.** Zero-grade form *n̥s-. US, from Old English *ūs,* us (accusative), from Germanic *uns. **2.** Suffixed (possessive) zero-grade form *n̥s-ero-. OUR, OURS, from Old English *ūser, ūre,* our, from Germanic *unsara-. **3.** O-grade form *nos-, with suffixed (possessive) form *nos-t(e)ro-*. NOSTRUM; PATERNOSTER, from Latin *nōs,* we, and *noster,* our. [Pokorny 3. *ne-* 758.]

neu-. Important derivatives are *announce, denounce, enunciate, pronounce,* and *renounce.*

neu-. To shout. Suffixed (participial) o-grade form *now-ent-(yo-), "shouting." NUNCIO; ANNOUNCE, DENOUNCE, ENUNCIATE, PRONOUNCE, RENOUNCE, from Latin *nūntius,* "announcing," hence a messenger, also a message, and *nūntium,* message. [Pokorny 1. *neu-* 767.]

newn̥. Important derivatives are *nine, nineteen, ninety, ninth, November, novena,* and *noon.*

newn̥. Nine. **1.** NINE, NINETEEN, NINETY, NINTH, from Old English *nigon,* nine, with derivatives *nigontig,* ninety, and *nigontēne,* nineteen (*-tēne,* ten; see **dekm̥**), from Germanic *nigun, variant of *niwun. **2.** NOVEMBER, NOVENA; (NONAGENARIAN), from Latin *novem,* nine (< *noven, with *m* for *n* by analogy with the *m* of *septem,* seven, and *decem,* ten). **3.** Ordinal form *neweno-. NONA-, NONES, NOON; (NONAGON), (NONANOIC ACID), from Latin *nōnus,* ninth. **4.** Prothetic or prefixed forms *enewn̥, *enwn̥. ENNEAD, from Greek *ennea,* nine (< *ennewa, *enwa-). [Pokorny *e-neu̯en* 318.]

newo-. Important derivatives are *new, neo-, neon, nova, novel[1], novel[2], novelty, novice, innovate,* and *renovate.*

newo-. New. Related to **nu-**. **1.** Suffixed form *new-yo-. **a.** NEW, from Old English *nēowe, nīwe,* new; **b.** SPAN-NEW, from Old Norse *nȳr,* new. Both **a** and **b** from Germanic *neuja-. **2.** Basic form *newo-. NEO-, NEON, NEOTERIC; MISONEISM, from Greek *newos, neos,* new. **3.** Suffixed form *new-aro-. ANEROID, from Greek *nēron,* water, from *nēros,* fresh (used of fish and of water), contracted from *nearos,* young, fresh. **4.** Basic form *newo-. NOVA, NOVATION, NOVEL[1], NOVEL[2], (NOVELTY), NOVICE; INNOVATE, RENOVATE, from Latin *novus,* new. **5.** Suffixed form *new-er-ko-. NOVERCAL, from Latin *noverca,* stepmother (< "she who is new"). [Pokorny *neu̯os* 709.]

nobh-. Important derivatives are *nave[2], navel,* and *umbilicus.*

nobh-. Also **ombh-.** Navel; later also "central knob," boss of a shield, hub of a wheel. **1.a.** NAVE[2], from Old English *nafu, nafa,* hub of a wheel; **b.** AUGER, from Old English *nafogār,* auger, from Germanic compound *nabō-gaizaz, tool for piercing wheel hubs (*gaizaz, spear, piercing tool). Both **a** and **b** from Germanic *nabō. **2.** Variant form *ombh-. UMBO, from Latin *umbō,* boss of a shield. **3.** Suffixed form *nobh-alo-. NAVEL, from Old English *nafela,* navel, from Germanic *nabalō. **4.** Suffixed variant form *ombh-alo-. **a.** UMBILICUS; NOMBRIL, from Latin *umbilīcus,* navel; **b.** OMPHALOS, from Greek *omphalos,* navel. [Pokorny 1. *(enebh-)* 314.]

nogh-. An important derivative is *nail.*

nogh-. Also **ənogh-, ongh-.** Nail, claw. **1.** Suffixed (diminutive) form *nogh-ela-. NAIL, from Old English *nægl,* nail, from Germanic *nagla-. **2.** Form *ənogh-. ONYX; PARONYCHIA, PERIONYCHIUM, SARDONYX, from Greek *onux* (stem *onukh-*), nail. **3.** Variant form *ongh-. UNGUIS, from Latin *unguis,* nail, claw, hoof, with diminutive *ungula,* hoof, claw, talon (< *ongh-elā-). [Pokorny *onogh-* 780.]

nog^w-. Important derivatives are *naked, nude, denude, gymnasium,* and *gymnast.*

nog^w-. Naked. **1.** Suffixed forms *nog^w-eto-, *nog^w-oto-. NAKED, from Old English *nacod,* naked, from Germanic *nakweda-, *nakwada-. **2.** Suffixed form *nog^w-edo-. NUDE, NUDI-; DENUDE, from Latin *nūdus,* naked. **3.** Suffixed form *nog^w-mo-. GYMNASIUM, (GYMNAST); GYMNOSOPHIST, GYMNOSPERM, from Greek *gumnos,* naked. [Pokorny nog^u- 769.]

nō̆-men-. Important derivatives are *name, nominal, nominate, noun, ignominy, misnomer, pronoun, renown, anonymous, eponym, homonymous, metonymy, pseudonym,* and *synonymous.*

nō̆-men-. Name. Earlier form *(ə)noə-mn̥, zero-grade form *(ə)nə-men-. **1.** NAME, from Old English *nama,* name, from Germanic *namōn-. **2.** NOMINAL, NOMINATE, NOUN; AGNOMEN, (BINOMIAL), COGNOMEN, DENOMINATE, IGNOMINY, MISNOMER, NOMENCLATOR, NUNCUPATIVE, PRAENOMEN, (PRONOUN), RENOWN, from Latin *nōmen,* name, reputation. **3.** ONOMASTIC, -ONYM, -ONYMY; ANONYMOUS, ANTONOMASIA, EPONYM, (EPONYMOUS), EUONYMUS, HETERONYMOUS, HOMONYMOUS, METONYMY, METRONYMIC, ONOMATOPOEIA, (PARONOMASIA), PARONYMOUS, PATRONYMIC, PSEUDONYM, SYNONYMOUS, from Greek *onoma, onuma,* name. **4.** MONIKER, from Old Irish *ainm,* name. [Pokorny *en(o)mn̥-* 321.]

nu-. An important derivative is *now.*

nu-. Now. Related to **newo-**. **1.** NOW, from Old English *nū,* now. **2.** QUIDNUNC, from Latin *nunc,* now (< *nun-ce; *-ce,* a particle meaning "this," "here"; see **ko-**). [Pokorny *nu-* 770.]

od-. Important derivatives are *annoy, ennui, noisome,* and *odium.*

od-. To hate. ANNOY, ENNUI, (NOISOME), ODIUM, from Latin *ōdī,* I hate, and *odium,* hatred. [Pokorny 2. *od-* 773.]

oi-no-. Important derivatives are *a[1], an[1], once, one, alone, atone, lone, lonely, none, eleven, inch[1], ounce[1], union, unite, unity, unanimous, unicorn, universe, any,* and *unique.*

oi-no-. One, unique.
I. Basic form *oi-no-. **1.a.** (A[1]), AN[1], ONCE, ONE; (ALONE), ANON, (ATONE), (LONE), (LONELY), NONE, from Old English *ān,* one; **b.** ELEVEN, from Old English *endleofan,* eleven, from Germanic compound *ain-lif-, "one left (beyond ten)," eleven (*lif-, left over; see **leik^w-**); **c.** EINKORN, TURNVEREIN, from Old High German *ein,* one. **a, b,** and **c** all from Germanic *ainaz. **2.** UNI-, UNION, UNITE, UNITY; COADUNATE, TRIUNE, UNANIMOUS, UNICORN, UNIVERSE, from Latin *ūnus,* one. **3.** (see **ne**) Latin *nōn,* not (< *ne-oinom, "not one thing"; *ne,* not).
II. Suffixed form *oino-ko-. **a.** ANY, from Old English *ǣnig,* one, anyone, from Germanic *ainigaz; **b.** UNIQUE, from Latin *ūnicus,* sole, single. **c.** INCH[1], OUNCE[1], UNCIAL; (QUINCUNX), from Latin *uncia,* one twelfth of a unit (*unc-,* shortened form of *ūnc-).
III. Suffixed form *oino-lo-. (see **ne**) Latin *ūllus,* any. [In Pokorny *e-* 281.]

oktō(u). Important derivatives are *eight, octave, octet, October, octogenarian,* and *octopus.*

oktō(u). Eight. **1.a.** EIGHT, EIGHTEEN, EIGHTY, from Old English *eahta,* eight, with derivatives *eahtatig,* eighty, and *eahtatēne,* eighteen (*-tēne,* ten; see **dekm̥**); **b.** ATTO-, from Old Norse *āttjān,* eighteen (*tjān,* ten; see **dekm̥**). Both **a** and **b** from Germanic *ahtō. **2.** OCTANS, OCTANT, OCTAVE, OCTAVO, OCTET, OCTO-, OCTOBER, OCTONARY; OCTODECIMO, OCTOGENARIAN, from Latin *octō,* eight. **3.** OCTAD, OCTO-; OCTOPUS, from Greek *oktō,* eight. [Pokorny *ok̑tō* 775.]

ōku-. A derivative is *accipiter.*

ōku-. Swift. **1.** OXYTOCIC, from Greek *ōkus,* swift. **2.** Possibly altered zero-grade form *aku- in compound *aku-petro-, "swift-flying" (*pet-ro-, flying; see **pet-**). ACCIPITER, from Latin *accipiter,* hawk. [Pokorny *ōk̑u-s* 775.] See also **ekwo-.**

ok^w-. Important derivatives are *eye, daisy, window, eyelet, ocular, inoculate, monocle, myopia, autopsy, synopsis, optic,* and *optometry.*

ok^w-. To see. **1.a.** EYE; DAISY, from Old English *ēage,* eye; **b.** WALLEYED, WINDOW, from Old Norse *auga,* eye; **c.** OGLE, from Low German *oog, oge,* eye. **a, b,** and **c** all from Germanic *augōn- (with taboo deformation). **2.** Suffixed form *ok^w-olo-. **a.** EYELET, OCELLUS, OCULAR, OCULIST, ULLAGE; INOCULATE, MONOCLE, OCULOMOTOR, PINOCHLE, from Latin *oculus,* eye; **b.** INVEIGLE, from French *aveugle,* blind, from Gallo-Latin compound *ab-oculus, blind, modeled on Gaulish *ex-ops,* blind. **3.** Form *ok^w-s. METOPIC, MYOPIA, NYCTALOPIA, PELOPS, PHLOGOPITE, PYROPE, TRICERATOPS, from Greek *ōps,* eye (and stem *op-, to see). **4.** Suffixed form *ok^w-ti-. (OPSIN), -OPSIS, -OPSY; AUTOPSY, (IODOPSIN), (RHODOPSIN), SYNOPSIS, from Greek *opsis,* sight, appearance. **5.** Suffixed form *ok^w-to-. OPTIC; DIOPTER, OPTOMETRY, PANOPTIC, from Greek *optos,* seen, visible. **6.** Suffixed form *ok^w-ā. METOPE, from Greek *opē,* opening. **7.** Suffixed form *ok^w-mn̥. OMMATIDIUM, OMMATOPHORE, from Greek *omma* (< *opma), eye. **8.** Suffixed form *ok^w-tro-. CATOPTRIC, from Greek *katoptron,* "back-looker," mirror (*kata-,* down, back; see **kat-**). **9.** OPHTHALMO-; EXOPHTHALMOS, from Greek *ophthalmos,* eye (with taboo deformation). **10.** Zero-grade form *ək^w- (of oldest full-grade form *əok^w-). **a.** (see **ant-**) Latin *antīquus,* "appearing before, having prior aspect," former (*anti-, before); **b.** (see **āter-**) Latin *ātrōx,* "black-looking," frightful (*atro-, black); **c.** (see **ghwer-**) *ferōx,* "wild-looking," fierce (*ghwero-, wild). [Pokorny ok^u- 775.]

op-. Important derivatives are *opera[1], operate, opus, cooperate, inure, maneuver, manure, opulent, omni-, optimum, copious, copy,* and *cornucopia.*

op-. To work, produce in abundance. **1.** Suffixed form *op-es-. OPERA[1], OPERATE, OPEROSE, OPUS; COOPERATE, INURE, MANEUVER, MANURE, OFFICINAL, from Latin *opus* (stem *oper-*), work, with its denominative verb *operārī,* to work, and secondary noun *opera,* work. **2.** (see **dhē-**) Latin *officium,* service, duty, business (< *opi-fici-om, "performance of work"; *-fici-, doing). **3.** Suffixed form *op-en-ent-. OPULENT, from Latin dissimilated *opulentus,* rich, wealthy. **4.** Suffixed form *op-ni-. OMNI-, OMNIBUS; OMNIUM-GATHERUM, from Latin *omnis,* all (< "abundant"). **5.** Suffixed (superlative) form *op-tamo-. OPTIMUM, from Latin *optimus,* best (< "wealthiest"). **6.** COPIOUS, COPY; CORNUCOPIA, from Latin *cōpia,* profusion, plenty, from prefixed form *co-op- (*co-,* collective and intensive prefix; see **kom**). [Pokorny 1. *op-* 780.]

or-. Derivatives are *erne* and *ornitho-.*

or-. Large bird. **1.** Suffixed form *or-n-. ERNE, from Old English *earn,* eagle, from Germanic *arnuz, eagle. **2.** Suffixed form *or-n-īth-. ORNITHO-; AEPYORNIS, ICHTHYORNIS, NOTORNIS, from Greek *ornis* (stem *ornith-*), bird. [Pokorny 1. *er-* 325.]

orbh-. Important derivatives are *orphan* and *robot.*

orbh-. To put asunder, separate. Suffixed form *orbh-o-, "bereft of father," also "deprived of free status." **a.** ORPHAN, from Greek *orphanos,* orphaned; **b.** ROBOT, from Czech *robota,* compulsory labor, drudgery, from Old Church Slavonic *rabota,* servitude, from *rabŭ,* slave, from Old Slavic **orbŭ.* [Pokorny *orbho-* 781.]

ors-. Important derivatives are *ass*[2] and *squirrel.*

ors-. Buttocks, backside. **1.** Suffixed form **ors-o-.* **a.** ASS[2], from Old English *ærs, ears,* backside; **b.** DODO, from Middle Dutch *ærs,* backside, tail. Both **a** and **b** from Germanic **arsaz.* **2.** Suffixed form **ors-ā-.* **a.** URO-[2], -UROUS; ANTHURIUM, ANURAN, CYNOSURE, DASYURE, EREMURUS, OXYURIASIS, SQUIRREL, TRICHURIASIS, from Greek *oura,* tail; **b.** SILURID, from Greek *silouros,* sheatfish (< obscure first element + *oura*), probably from **ors-.** [Pokorny *ers-* 340.]

ōs-. Important derivatives are *oral* and *usher.*

ōs-. Mouth. **1.** ORAL, OS[1], OSCILLATE, OSCULATE, OSCULUM, OSTIARY, OSTIUM, USHER; INOSCULATE, ORIFICE, ORINASAL, OROTUND, OSCITANCY, (PERORAL), from Latin *ōs* (stem *ōr-*), mouth, face, orifice, and derivative *ōstium* (< suffixed form **ōs-to-*), door. **2.** AURIGA, from Latin *aurīga,* charioteer (< **ōr-ig-,* "he who manages the (horse's) bit"; *-īg-* , lengthened from *ig-,* driving, from **ag-;* see **ag-**), possibly from **ōs-.** [Pokorny 1. *ōus-* 784.]

ost-. Important derivatives are *ossify, osteo-, ostracize,* and *oyster.*

ost-. Bone. **1.** OS[2], OSSEOUS, OSSICLE, OSSUARY; OSSIFRAGE, OSSIFY, from Latin *os* (stem *oss-*), bone. **2.** OSTEO-; ENDOSTEUM, EXOSTOSIS, PERIOSTEUM, SYNOSTOSIS, TELEOST, from Greek *osteon,* bone. **3.** Suffixed form **ost-r-.* **a.** OSTRACIZE, OSTRACOD, from Greek *ostrakon,* shell, potsherd; **b.** OYSTER, from Greek *ostreon,* oyster; **c.** ASTRAGAL, ASTRAGALUS, from variant form in Greek *astragalos,* vertebra, ball of the ankle joint, knucklebone, Ionic molding. [Pokorny *ost(h)-* 783.]

ous-. Important derivatives are *ear*[1], *aural*[1], and *scout*[1].

ous-. Also **aus-.** Ear. **1.** Suffixed form **ous-en-.* EAR[1], from Old English *ēare,* ear, from Germanic **auzōn-.* **2.** Suffixed form **aus-i-.* AURAL[1], AURICLE; AURIFORM, ORMER, from Latin *auris,* ear. **3.** AUSCULTATION, SCOUT[1], from Latin *auscultāre,* to listen to (**aus-* + **kli-to-,* inclined; see **klei-**). **4.** Suffixed basic form **ous-os-.* **a.** OTIC, OTO-; MYOSOTIS, PAROTID GLAND, from Greek *ous* (stem *ōt-*), ear; **b.** (see **slēg-**) Greek *lagōs,* hare (< **lag-ous-,* "with drooping ears"; **lag-,* to droop). [Pokorny *ōus-* 785.]

owi-. Important derivatives are *ewe* and *ovine.*

owi-. Sheep. **1.** EWE, from Old English *ēwe, eōwu,* ewe, from Germanic **awi-.* **2.** OVINE, from Latin *ovis,* sheep. [Pokorny *ou̯i-s* 784.]

pā-. Important derivatives are *fodder, forage, fur, pabulum, food, feed, foster, pasture, antipasto, pester, repast, pastor, pantry, companion,* and *company.*

pā-. To protect, feed. Contracted from **paə-.* **1.** Suffixed form **pā-trom.* **a.** FODDER, from Old English *fōdor,* fodder; **b.** FORAGE, from Old French *feurre,* fodder; **c.** FUR, from Old French *forre, fuerre,* trimming made from animal skin, fur (< "sheath, case, lining"). **a, b,** and **c** all from Germanic **fōdram.* **2.** Suffixed form **pā-dhlom* (doublet of **pātrom*). PABULUM, from Latin *pābulum,* food, fodder. **3.** Extended form **pāt-.* **a.** FOOD, from Old English *fōda,* food, from Germanic **fōd-,* food; **b.** FEED, from Old English *fēdan,* to feed, from Germanic denominative **fōdjan,* to give food to; **c.** suffixed form **pāt-tro-.* FOSTER, from Old English *fōstor,* food, nourishment, from Germanic **fōstra-.* **4.** Extended form **pās-.* **a.** suffixed form **pās-sko-.* PASTURE; ANTIPASTO, REPAST, from Latin *pāscere,* to feed; **b.** suffixed form **pās-tor-.* PASTOR, PESTER, from Latin *pāstor,* shepherd; **c.** suffixed form **pās-t-ni-.* PANADA, PANATELA, PANNIER, (PANOCHA), PANTRY, PASTILLE, (PENUCHE); APPANAGE, COMPANION[1], (COMPANY), from Latin *pānis,* bread. **5.** Suffixed form **pā-tor-.* BEZOAR, from Persian *pād,* protecting against, from Iranian **pātar-* (Avestan *pātar-*). **6.** Suffixed form **pā-won-,* protector. SATRAP, from Old Persian *khshathra-pāvā,* protector of the province. [Pokorny *pā-* 787, 1. *pō(i)-* 839.]

pag-. Important derivatives are *fang, compact*[1], *impinge, pay*[1], *peace, appease, pacific, pacify, pact, pale*[1], *palisade, pole*[2], *impale, travail, travel, palette, pagan, peasant, page*[1], *pageant, propagate,* and *pectin.*

pag-. Also **pak-.** To fasten. **1.** Lengthened-grade form **pāk-.* FAY[1], from Old English *fēgan,* to fit closely, from Germanic **fōgjan,* to join, fit. **2.** Nasalized form **pa-n-g-,* also **pa-n-k-.* **a.** *(i)* FANG, from Old English *fang, feng,* plunder, booty, from Germanic **fangam, *fangiz; (ii)* VANG, from Dutch *vangen,* to catch, from remade Germanic verb **fangan; (iii)* NEWFANGLED, from Middle English **-fangel,* taken, akin to Old High German *-fangolon,* to close, from Germanic **fanglōn,* to grasp. *(i), (ii),* and *(iii)* all derivatives of Germanic **fanhan,* to seize; **b.** COMPACT[1], IMPINGE, from Latin *pangere,* to fasten. **3.** Root form **pă̄k-.* **a.** PACE[2], PAY[1], PEACE; APPEASE, PACIFIC, PACIFY, from Latin *pāx,* peace (< "a binding together by treaty or agreement"); **b.** PACT, from Latin *pacīscī,* to agree. **4.** Suffixed form **pak-slo-.* **a.** PALE[1], PALISADE, PAWL, PEEL[3], POLE[2]; IMPALE, TRAVAIL, (TRAVEL), from Latin *pālus,* stake (fixed in the ground); **b.** PALETTE, PEEL[2], from Latin *pāla,* spade, probably from **pag-.** **5.** Lengthened-grade form **pāg-.* **a.** PAGAN, PEASANT, from Latin *pāgus,* "boundary staked out on the ground," district, village, country; **b.** PAGE[1], PAGEANT, from Latin *pāgina,* "trellis to which a row of vines is fixed," hence (by metaphor) column of writing, page; **c.** PROPAGATE, from Latin *prōpāgāre,* to propagate (< "to fix before"; *prō-,* before, in front; see **per**[1]); **d.** PECTIN, PEGMATITE; AREOPAGUS, from Greek *pēgnunai,* to fasten, coagulate, with derivative *pagos* (< **pag-o-*), mass, hill. [Pokorny *pă̄k-* 787.]

pan-. Important derivatives are *vane, pane,* and *panel.*

pan-. Fabric. **1.a.** VANE, from Old English *fana,* flag, banner, weathercock; **b.** (see **gʷhen-**) Germanic compound **gund-fanōn-,* "battle-flag." Both **a** and **b** from Germanic **fanōn.* **2.** Extended form **panno-.* PANE, PANEL, from Latin *pannus,* piece of cloth, rag. [Pokorny *pan-* 788.]

pant-. Derivatives are *pan-* and *pancreas.*

pant-. All. Attested only in Tocharian and Greek. PAN-; DIAPASON, PANCRATIUM, PANCREAS, from Greek *pas* (neuter *pan,* stem *pant-*), all. [In Pokorny 1. *k̑eu-* 592.]

papa. Important derivatives are *papa* and *pope.*

papa. A child's word for "father," a linguistic near-universal found in many languages. **1.** PAPA, from French *papa,* father. **2.** PAPPUS, POPE, from Greek *pappas,* father, and *pappos,* grandfather. [Pokorny *pap(p)a* 789.]

past-. Important derivatives are *fast*[1], *steadfast, fasten, fast*[2], and *breakfast.*

past-. Solid, firm. **1.a.** FAST[1]; STEADFAST, from Old English *fæst,* fixed, firm; **b.** AVAST, from Middle Dutch *vast,* firm, fast. Both **a** and **b** from Germanic **fastuz,* firm, fast. **2.** FASTEN, from Old English *fæstnian,* to fasten, establish, from Germanic **fastinōn,* to make firm or fast. **3.** HANDFAST, from Old Norse *festa,* to fix, affirm, from Germanic causative **fastjan,* to make firm. **4.a.** FAST[2], from Old English *fæstan,* to abstain from food; **b.** BREAKFAST, from Old Norse *fasta,* to abstain from food. Both **a** and **b** from Germanic **fastēn,* to hold fast, observe abstinence. [Pokorny *pasto-* 789.]

pau-. Important derivatives are *few, paucity, paraffin, pauper, poor, poverty, foal, filly, pony, pullet, puerile, encyclopedia,* and *orthopedics.*

pau-. Few, little.
I. Adjectival form **pau-,* few, little. **1.** FEW, from Old English *fēawe,* few, from Germanic **fawaz.* **2.** Suffixed form **pau-ko-.* PAUCITY, POCO, from Latin *paucus,* little, few. **3.** Suffixed form **pau-ro-* in metathetical form **par-wo-.* PARAFFIN, PARVOVIRUS, from Latin *parvus,* little, small, neuter *parvum,* becoming *parum,* little, rarely. **4.** Compound **pau-paros,* producing little, poor (**par-os,* producing; see **pere-**[1]). PAUPER, POOR, POVERTY, from Latin *pauper,* poor.
II. Suffixed reduced variant form **pu-lo-,* young of an animal. **1.** FOAL, from Old English *fola,* young horse, colt, from Germanic **fulōn-.* **2.** FILLY, from Old Norse *fylja,* young female horse, from Germanic derivative **fuljō.*
III. Basic form **pau-* and variant form **pŭ̄-,* boy, child. **1.** Suffixed form **pu-ero-.* PUERILE, PUERPERAL, from Latin *puer,* child. **2.** Extended form **put-.* **a.** POLTROON, PONY, POOL[2], POULARD, PULLET; CATCHPOLE, from Latin *pullus* (< **putslo-*), young of an animal, chicken; **b.** PUSILLANIMOUS, from Latin *pusillus* (< **putslo-lo*), old diminutive of *pullus.* **3.** Suffixed form **paw-id-.* PEDO-[2]; ENCYCLOPEDIA, ORTHOPEDICS, from Greek *pais* (stem *paid-*), child (> *paideia,* education). [Pokorny *pōu-* 842.]

ped-. Important derivatives are *foot, fetter, fetlock, pawn*[2], *pedal, pedestrian, peon, pioneer, millipede, trivet, expedite, impede, impeach, pew, podium, octopus, platypus, podiatry, pajamas, fetch*[1], *impair, pessimism,* and *impeccable.*

ped-. Foot.
I. Nominal root. **1.** Lengthened o-grade form **pōd-.* FOOT, from Old English *fōt,* foot, from Germanic **fōt-.* **2.** Suffixed form **ped-ero-.* FETTER, from Old English *fetor, feter,* leg iron, fetter, from Germanic **feterō.* **3.** Suffixed form **ped-el-.* FETLOCK, from Middle English *fitlock, fetlock,* fetlock, from a Germanic source akin to Old High German *vizzelach,* fetlock, from Germanic **fetel-.* **4.** Basic form **ped-.* PAWN[2], -PED, PEDAL, PEDATE, PEDESTRIAN, PEDI-, PEDICEL, PEDUNCLE, (PEON), PES, PIONEER; MILLIPEDE, SESQUIPEDAL, (TRIPEDAL), TRIVET, VAMP[1], from Latin *pēs* (stem *ped-*), foot. **5.** Form **ped-yo-.* **a.** EXPEDITE, from Latin *expedīre,* to free from a snare (*ex-,* out of; see **eghs**); **b.** IMPEDE, from Latin *impedīre,* "to put in fetters, hobble, shackle," entangle, hinder (*in-,* in; see **en**). **6.** Suffixed form **ped-ikā.* IMPEACH, from Latin *pedica,* fetter, snare. **7.** O-grade form **pod-.* **a.** (PEW), -POD, PODITE, PODIUM; ANTIPODES, APODAL, APPOGGIATURA, APUS, LYCOPODIUM, MONOPODIUM, OCTOPUS, (PELECYPOD), PHALAROPE, PLATYPUS, PODAGRA, PODIATRY, PODOPHYLLIN, POLYP, (POLYPOD), SYMPODIUM, from Greek *pous* (stem *pod-*), foot; **b.** PODZOL, from Russian *pod,* under. **8.** Suffixed form **ped-ya.* TRAPEZIUM, from Greek *peza,* foot. **9.** Suffixed form **ped-o-.* **a.** PEDO-[1]; PARALLELEPIPED, from Greek *pedon,* ground, soil; **b.** (PAISA), (PICE), PIE[3], PUG[3], from Sanskrit *padam,* footstep, foot, and *pāt,* foot; **c.** PAJAMA, TEAPOY, from Middle Persian *pāī,* leg, foot; **d.** lengthened-grade form **pēd-o-.* *(i)* PILOT, from Greek *pēdon,* rudder, steering oar; *(ii)* DIAPEDESIS, from Greek *pēdan,* to leap. **10.** Suffixed form *ped-ī-.* CYPRIPEDIUM, from Greek *pedilon,* sandal.
II. Verbal root **ped-,* to walk, stumble, fall. **1.** FETCH[1], from Old English *fetian, feccean,* to bring back, from Germanic **fetēn.* **2.a.** Suffixed (comparative) form **ped-yos-.* PEJORATION; IMPAIR, from Latin *pēior,* worse (< "stumbling"); **b.** suffixed (superlative) form **ped-samo-.* PESSIMISM, from Latin *pessimus,* worst; **c.** suffixed form **ped-ko-.* PECCABLE, PECCADILLO, PECCANT; IMPECCABLE, from Latin *peccāre,* to stumble, sin. **a, b,** and **c** all from Latin **ped-.* [Pokorny 2. *pĕ̄d-* 790.]

pē(i)-. Important derivatives are *fiend, passion, passive, patient,* and *compassion.*

pē(i)-. Also **pē-, pī-.** To hurt. Contracted from **peə(i)-.* **1.** Suffixed (participial) form **pī-ont-* (< **piə-ont-*). FIEND, from Old English *fēond, fīond,* enemy, devil, from Germanic **fījand-,* hating, hostile. **2.** Possibly **pē-* in suffixed zero-grade **pə-to-.* PASSIBLE, PASSION, PASSIVE, PATIENT; COMPASSION, from Latin *patī,* to suffer. [Pokorny *pē(i)-* 792.]

peiə-. Important derivatives are *fat, pituitary, pine*[1], and *Irish.*

peiə-. To be fat, swell. **1.** Extended o-grade form **poid-.* FAT, from Old English *fǣt(t),* fat, from Germanic past participle **faitidaz,* fattened, from derivative verb **faitjan,* to fatten, from **faitaz,* plump, fat. **2.** Possibly suffixed zero-grade form **pī-tu-.* PIP[5], PITUITARY, from Latin *pītuīta,* moisture exuded from trees, gum, phlegm. **3.** Possibly suffixed zero-grade form **pī-nu-.* PINE[1], PINEAL, PINNACE, PIÑON, PINOT; PIÑA CLOTH, from Latin *pīnus,* pine tree (yielding a resin). **4.** Suffixed zero-grade form **pī-won-.* PROPIONIC ACID, from Greek *piōn,* fat. **5.** Suffixed zero-grade form **pī-wer-,* "fat, fertile." **a.** (ERSE), IRISH, from Old English *Īras,* the Irish, from **Īwer-iū,* the prehistoric Celtic name for Ireland; **b.**

PIERIAN SPRING, from Greek *Pieria,* a region of Macedonia, from **Pīwer-iā.* [Pokorny *pei(ə)-* 793.]

peig-. Important derivatives are *file*[2], *paint, picture, picturesque, pigment, pimento, pinto,* and *depict.*

peig-. Also **peik-.** To cut, mark (by incision). **1.** Alternate form **peik-.* FILE[2], from Old English *fīl,* file, from Germanic **fīhala,* cutting tool. **2.** Nasalized zero-grade form **pi-n-g-.* PAINT, PICTOR, PICTURE, PICTURESQUE, PIGMENT, PIMENTO, PINT, PINTO; DEPICT, PICTOGRAPH, from Latin *pingere,* to embroider, tattoo, paint, picture. **3.** Suffixed zero-grade form **pik-ro-.* PICRO-, from Greek *pikros,* sharp, bitter. **4.** O-grade form **poik-.* PLATY[2], POIKILOTHERM, from Greek *poikilos,* spotted, pied, various. [Pokorny 1. *peig-* 794.]

peku-. Important derivatives are *fellow, fee, pecuniary,* and *peculiar.*

peku-. Wealth, movable property. **1.a.** FELLOW, from Old Norse *fē,* property, cattle; **b.** FEE, from Old French *fie,* fief; **c.** FEUD[2], from Medieval Latin *feudum,* feudal estate. **a, b,** and **c** all from Germanic **fehu-.* **2.** PECORINO, from Latin *pecus,* cattle. **3.** Suffixed form **peku-n-.* PECUNIARY; IMPECUNIOUS, from Latin *pecūnia,* property, wealth. **4.** Suffixed form **peku-l-.* PECULATE, PECULIAR, from Latin *pecūlium,* riches in cattle, private property. [In Pokorny 2. *peḱ-* 797.]

pekʷ-. Important derivatives are *cook, cuisine, kitchen, apricot, biscuit, concoct, precocious, culinary, kiln, pumpkin, peptic,* and *dyspepsia.*

pekʷ-. To cook, ripen. **1.** Assimilated form (in Italic and Celtic) **kʷekʷ-.* **a.** COOK, CUISINE, KITCHEN, QUITTOR; APRICOT, BISCUIT, CONCOCT, DECOCT, PRECOCIOUS, RICOTTA, TERRA COTTA, from Latin *coquere,* to cook; **b.** CULINARY, KILN, from Latin *culīna,* kitchen, deformed from *coquīna.* **2.** PEPO; PUMPKIN, from Greek *pepōn,* ripe. **3.** PEPTIC, PEPTIZE; DRUPE, EUPEPTIC, PEPSIN, PEPTONE, from Greek *peptein,* to cook, ripen, digest (> *peptos,* cooked). **4.** DYSPEPSIA, from Greek *-pepsia,* digestion. **5.** PUKKA, from Sanskrit *pakva-,* ripe. [Pokorny *pekᵘ-* 798.]

pel-[1]**.** Important derivatives are *pale*[1], *pallid, pallor, appall, palomino, falcon,* and *poliomyelitis.*

pel-[1]**.** Pale. **1.** Suffixed variant form **pal-wo-.* **a.** *(i)* FALLOW DEER, from Old English *fealu, fealo,* reddish yellow; *(ii)* FAUVISM, from Frankish *falw-,* reddish-yellow. Both *(i)* and *(ii)* from Germanic **falwaz;* **b.** PALE[2], PALLID, PALLOR; APPALL, from Latin *pallēre,* to be pale; **c.** PALOMINO, from Latin *palumbēs* (influenced in form by Latin *columbus,* dove), ringdove, "gray-bird." **2.** Probably suffixed form **pel-ko-.* FALCON; (GYRFALCON), from Late Latin *falcō,* falcon, from Germanic **falkōn-,* falcon (< "gray bird"; but this is also possibly from the Late Latin). **3.** Suffixed extended form **peli-wo-.* **a.** PELOPS, from Greek *pelios,* dark; **b.** o-grade form **poli-wo-.* POLIOMYELITIS, from Greek *polios,* gray. **4.** PELARGONIUM, from Greek *pelargos* (< **pelawo-argos*), stork (< "black-white bird"; *argos,* white; see **arg-**), perhaps from **pel-**[1]. [Pokorny 6. *pel-* 804.]

pel-[2]**.** Important derivatives are *fold*[1], *-fold, multiple,* and *triple.*

pel-[2]**.** To fold. **1.** Extended o-grade form **polt-.* **a.** FOLD[1], from Old English *fealdan, faldan,* to fold; **b.** FALTBOAT, from Old High German *faldan,* to fold; **c.** FURBELOW, from Italian *falda,* fold, flap, pleat; **d.** *(i)* FALDSTOOL, from Medieval Latin compound *faldistolium,* folding chair; *(ii)* FAUTEUIL, from Old French *faldestoel,* faldstool. Both *(i)* and *(ii)* from Germanic compound **faldistōlaz,* "folding stool" (**stōlaz,* stool; see **stā-**); **e.** -FOLD, from Old English *-feald, -fald,* -fold, from Germanic combining form **-falthaz, *-faldaz.* **a, b, c, d,** and **e** all from Germanic **falthan, *faldan.* **2.** Combining form **-plo-.* **a.** DECUPLE, MULTIPLE, OCTUPLE, QUADRUPLE, QUINTUPLE, SEPTUPLE, (SEXTUPLE), TRIPLE, from Latin *-plus,* -fold (as in *triplus,* threefold); **b.** (-PLOID); TRIPLOBLASTIC, from Greek *-plos, -ploos,* -fold (as in *haploos,* single, and *triploos,* triple). [Pokorny 3. a. *pel-* 802.]

pel-[3]**.** Important derivatives are *film, pelt*[1], and *surplice.*

pel-[3]**.** Skin, hide. **1.** Suffixed form **pel-no-.* FELL[3], from Old English *fell,* skin, hide, from Germanic **felnam.* **2.** FILM, from Old English *filmen,* membrane, from Germanic suffixed form **fel-man-ja-.* **3.** Suffixed form **pel-ni-.* PELISSE, PELLICLE, (PELT[1]), PELTRY, PILLION; PELLAGRA, SURPLICE, from Latin *pellis,* skin. **4.** ERYSIPELAS, from Greek *-pelas,* skin. **5.** Suffixed form **pel-to-.* PELTATE, from Greek *peltē,* a shield (made of hide). [Pokorny 3. b. *pel-* 803.]

pel-[4]**.** An important derivative is *monopoly.*

pel-[4]**.** To sell. Lengthened o-grade form **pōl-.* BIBLIOPOLE, MONOPOLY, from Greek *pōlein,* to sell. [Pokorny 5. *pel-* 804.]

pel-[5]**.** Important derivatives are *anvil, felt*[1], *filter, pulsate, pulse*[1], *push, compel, expel, propel, repel, polish,* and *appeal.*

pel-[5]**.** To thrust, strike, drive.
I. Suffixed form **pel-de-.* **1.a.** ANVIL, from Old English *anfilt(e), anfealt,* anvil ("something beaten on"); **b.** *(i)* FELT[1], from Old English *felt,* felt; *(ii)* FILTER, from Medieval Latin *filtrum,* filter, piece of felt. Both *(i)* and *(ii)* from Germanic **feltaz, *filtiz,* compressed wool. Both **a** and **b** from Germanic **felt-, *falt-,* to beat. **2.** PELT[2], POUSSETTE, PULSATE, PULSE[1], PUSH; COMPEL, DISPEL, EXPEL, IMPEL, PROPEL, REPEL, from Latin *pellere* (past participle *pulsus*), to push, drive, strike. **3.a.** Suffixed o-grade form **pol-o-,* fuller of cloth. POLISH, from Latin *polīre,* to make smooth, polish (< "to full cloth"); **b.** suffixed o-grade form **pol-o-* (with different accentuation from the preceding), fulled (of cloth). INTERPOLATE, from Latin compound adjective *inter-polis* (also *interpolus*), refurbished (*inter-,* between; see **en**).
II. Extended form **pelə-.* **1.** Present stem **pelnā-.* **a.** APPEAL, from Latin *appellāre,* "to drive to," address, entreat, appeal, call (*ad-,* to; see **ad-**); **b.** COMPELLATION, from Latin *compellāre,* to accost, address (*com-,* intensive prefix; see **kom**). **2.** Possible suffixed zero-grade extended adverbial form **plə-ti-,* or locative plural **plə-si.* PLESIOSAUR, from Greek *plēsios,* near (< "pushed toward"), from pre-Greek **plāti* or **plāsi.* [Pokorny 2. a. *pel-* 801.]

pelə-[1]**.** Important derivatives are *full*[1], *fill, plenitude, plenty, replenish, folk, plural, plus, surplus, poly-, accomplish, complete, compliment, comply, deplete, expletive, implement, supply, plebeian,* and *plethora.*

pelə-[1]**.** To fill; with derivatives referring to abundance and multitude. Variant **plē-,* contracted from **pleə-.*
I. Zero-grade form **pḷə-.* **1.** Suffixed form **pḷə-no-* FULL[1], from Old English *full,* full, from Germanic **fulnaz, *fullaz,* full. **2.** FILL, from Old English *fyllan,* to fill (from Germanic derivative verb **fulljan,* to fill), and *fyllu,* full amount (from Germanic abstract noun **full-īnō-,* fullness). **3.** PLENARY, PLENITUDE, PLENTY, PLENUM; PLENIPOTENTIARY, REPLENISH, TERREPLEIN, from Latin *plēnus,* full, from Latin stem **plēno-,* replacing **plāno-* (influenced by Latin verb *plēre,* to fill; see **III. 1.** below). **4.** Suffixed form **pḷə-go-.* **a.** FOLK, from Old English *folc,* people; **b.** VOLKSLIED, from Old High German *folc,* people. Both **a** and **b** from Germanic **folkam.*
II. Suffixed form **p(e)lə-u-.* **1.** Obscure comparative form. PIÙ, PLURAL, PLUS; NONPLUS, PLUPERFECT, SURPLUS, from Latin *plūs,* more (Old Latin *plous*). See also **III. 4.** below. **2.** O-grade form **pol(ə)-u-.* POLY-; HOI POLLOI, from Greek *polus,* much, many. **3.** PALUDAL, PALUDISM, from Latin *palūs,* marsh, possibly from **pelə-**[1] (? < "inundated"; but probably rather from **pel-**[1]).
III. Variant form **plē-.* **1.** (ACCOMPLISH), COMPLETE, COMPLIMENT, (COMPLY), DEPLETE, EXPLETIVE, IMPLEMENT, REPLETE, SUPPLY, from Latin *plēre,* to fill. **2.** Possibly suffixed form **plē-dhw-.* (PLEBE), PLEBEIAN, PLEBS; PLEBISCITE, from Latin *plēbs, plēbēs,* the people, multitude. **3.** Suffixed form **plē-dhwo-.* PLETHORA; PLETHYSMOGRAPH, from Greek derivative verb *plēthein,* to be full. **4.** Suffixed adjective (positive) form **plē-ro-.* PLEROCERCOID, from Greek *plērēs,* full. **5.** Suffixed (comparative) form **plē-i(s)on-.* PLEO-, PLEONASM; PLEIOTAXY, PLEIOTROPISM, PLIOCENE, from Greek *pleōn, pleiōn,* more. **6.** Suffixed (superlative) form **plē-isto-.* PLEISTOCENE, from Greek *pleistos,* most.
IV. POORI, from Sanskrit *pūraḥ,* cake (< "that which fills or satisfies"), possibly from **pelə-**[1]. [Pokorny 1. *pel-* 798.]

pelə-[2]**.** Important derivatives are *field, floor, plain, plane*[1], *plane*[2], *explain, palm*[1], *palm*[2], *planet, plasma, plaster, plastic,* and *polka.*

pelə-[2]**.** Flat; to spread. Variant **plā-,* contracted from **plaə-.* **1.** Suffixed form **pel(ə)-tu-.* FIELD, from Old English *feld,* open field, from Germanic **felthuz,* flat land. **2.** Suffixed form **pel(ə)-t-es-* (by-form of **pel(ə)-tu-*). **a.** FELDSPAR, from Old High German *feld,* field; **b.** VELDT, from Middle Dutch *veld, velt,* field. Both **a** and **b** from Germanic **feltha-,* flat land. **3.** Variant form **plā-.* **a.** suffixed form **plā-ru-.* FLOOR, from Old English *flōr,* floor, from Germanic **flōruz,* floor; **b.** suffixed form **plā-no-.* LLANO, PIANO[2], PLAIN, PLANARIAN, PLANE[1], PLANE[2], PLANE[3], PLANISH, PLANO-, PLANULA; EXPLAIN, (PIANOFORTE), from Latin *plānus,* flat, level, even, plain, clear. **4.** Suffixed zero-grade form **pḷə-mā.* PALM[1], PALM[2], from Latin *palma* (< **palama*), palm of the hand. **5.** Possibly extended variant form **plan-.* **a.** PLANET; APLANATIC, from Greek *planasthai,* to wander (< "to spread out"); **b.** FLÂNEUR, from French *flâner,* to walk the streets idly, from a Germanic source akin to Old Norse *flana,* to wander aimlessly, from Germanic **flan-,* possibly from **pelə-**[2]. **6.** Suffixed zero-grade form **plə-dh-.* -PLASIA, PLASMA, -PLAST, PLASTER, PLASTIC, (PLASTID), -PLASTY; (DYSPLASIA), METAPLASM, (TOXOPLASMA), from Greek *plassein* (< **plath-yein*), to mold, "spread out." **7.** O-grade form **polə-.* **a.** POLYNYA, from Russian *polyĭ,* open; **b.** POLACK, POLKA, from Slavic *polje,* broad flat land, field. [Pokorny *pelə-* 805.] See also extensions **plāk-**[1] and **plat-.**

pelə-[3]**.** Important derivatives are *police, policy*[1], *politic,* and *metropolis.*

pelə-[3]**.** Citadel, fortified high place. POLICE, (POLICY[1]), POLIS, POLITIC, (POLITY); ACROPOLIS, COSMOPOLIS, COSMOPOLITE, MEGALOPOLIS, METROPOLIS, NECROPOLIS, POLICLINIC, PROPOLIS, from Greek *polis,* city. [In Pokorny 1. *pel-* 798.]

penkʷe. Important derivatives are *five, fifteen, penta-, pentad, pentagon, pentathlon, Pentecost, fifth, quintet, quintessence, finger, fist,* and *foist.*

penkʷe. Five.
I. Basic form **penkʷe.* **1.** Assimilated form **pempe.* **a.** FIVE; FIFTY, from Old English *fīf,* five, with derivative *fīftig,* fifty (*-tēne,* ten; see **dekṃ**); **b.** FIN[2], from Old High German *finf, funf,* five. Both **a** and **b** from Germanic **fimf.* **2.a.** FIFTEEN, from Old English *fīftēne,* fifteen; **b.** FEMTO-, from Old Norse *fimmtān,* fifteen. Both **a** and **b** from Germanic compound **fimftehun,* fifteen (**tehun,* ten; see **dekṃ**). **3.** Assimilated form **kʷenkʷe.* **a.** CINQUAIN, CINQUE, QUINQUE-; CINQUECENTO, (CINQUEFOIL), QUINCUNX, from Latin *quīnque,* five; **b.** KENO, QUINATE, from Latin distributive *quīnī,* five each; **c.** QUINDECENNIAL, from Latin compound *quīndecim,* fifteen (*decem,* ten; see **dekṃ**). **4.** PENTA-, PENTAD; PENSTEMON, (PENTAGON), (PENTAMETER), (PENTATHLON), from Greek *pente,* five. **5.** PUNCH[3]; PACHISI, from Sanskrit *pañca,* five.
II. Compound **penkʷe-(d)konta,* "five tens," fifty (**-(d)konta,* group of ten; see **dekṃ**). **1.** QUINQUAGENARIAN, QUINQUAGESIMA, from Latin *quīnquāginta,* fifty. **2.** PENTECOST, from Greek *pentēkonta,* fifty.
III. Ordinal adjective **penkʷ-to-.* **1.** FIFTH, from Old English *fīfta,* fifth, from Germanic **fimftōn-.* **2.** QUINT[1], QUINTAIN, QUINTET, QUINTILE; QUINTESSENCE, QUINTILLION, QUINTUPLE, from Latin *quīntus* (< **quinc-tos*), feminine *quīnta,* fifth.
IV. Suffixed form **penkʷ-ro-.* FINGER, from Old English *finger,* finger, from Germanic **fingwraz,* finger (< "one of five").
V. Suffixed reduced zero-grade form **pṇk-sti-.* **a.** FIST, from Old English *fȳst,* fist; **b.** FOIST, from Dutch *vuist,* fist. Both **a** and **b** from Germanic **funhstiz* [Pokorny *penkᵘe* 808, *pṇksti-* 839.]

pent-. Important derivatives are *find, pontiff, pontoon, punt*[1], *sputnik,* and *path.*

pent-. To tread, go. **1.** FIND, from Old English *findan,* to find, from Germanic **finthan,* to come upon, discover. **2.** Suffixed o-grade form **pont-i-.* **a.** PONS, PONTIFEX, PONTIFF, PONTINE, PONTOON, PUNT[1]; (TRANSPONTINE), from Latin *pōns* (stem *pont-*), bridge (earliest meaning, "way, passage," preserved in the priestly title *pontifex,* "he who prepares the way"; *-fex,* maker; see **dhē-**); **b.** SPUTNIK, from Russian *sputnik,* fellow traveler, sputnik, from *put',* path, way. **3.** Zero-grade form **pn̥t-*. PERIPATETIC, from Greek *patein,* to tread, walk. **4.** Suffixed zero-grade form **pn̥t-ə-*. **a.** PATH, from Old English *pæth,* path; **b.** FOOTPAD, from Middle Dutch *pad,* way, path. Both **a** and **b** from Germanic **patha-,* way, path, probably borrowed (? via Scythian) from Iranian **path-*. [Pokorny *pent-* 808.]

per[1]. Important derivatives are *far, paramount, paradise, for, forth, afford, further, foremost, former[2], first, prow, protein, proton, fore, forefather, before, from, furnish, veneer, purchase, prone, reciprocal, approach, reproach, approximate, probable, probe, proof, prove, approve, improve, pre-, private, privilege, privy, deprive, proper, property, appropriate, premier, primal, primary, primate, prime, primitive, prince, principal, principle, pristine,* and *priest.*

per[1]. Base of prepositions and preverbs with the basic meanings of "forward," "through," and a wide range of extended senses such as "in front of," "before," "early," "first," "chief," "toward," "against," "near," "at," "around."

I. Basic form **per* and extended form **peri*. **1.a.** TURNVEREIN, from Middle High German *vereinen,* to unite, from Old High German *far-;* **b.** VEER[2], from Middle Dutch *vieren,* to let out, slacken; **c.** (see **ghend-**) Germanic compound **fer-getan,* "to lose one's hold," forget. **d.** FRUMP, from Middle Dutch *verrompelen,* to wrinkle. **a, b, c,** and **d** all from Germanic **fer-, *far-,* used chiefly as an intensive prefix denoting destruction, reversal, or completion. **2.** Suffixed (comparative) form **per-ero-,* farther away. FAR, from Old English *feor(r),* far, from Germanic **fer(e)ra.* **3.** PER, PER-; PARAMOUNT, PARAMOUR, PARGET, PARVENU, from Latin *per,* through, for, by. **4.** PERI-; PERISSODACTYL, from Greek *peri,* around, near, beyond. **5.a.** PARADISE, from Avestan *pairi-,* around; **b.** PURDAH, from Old Persian *pari,* around, over; **c.** (see **wer-**) Old Iranian **pari-vāraka-,* protective. **a, b,** and **c** all from Old Iranian **pari-,* around. **6.** PERESTROIKA, from Old Russian *pere-,* around, again, from Slavic **per-*.

II. Zero-grade form **pr̥-*. **1.a.** FOR, from Old English *for,* before, instead of, on account of; **b.** FOR-, from Old English *for-,* prefix denoting destruction, pejoration, exclusion, or completion. Both **a** and **b** from Germanic **fur,* before, in. **2.** Extended form **pr̥t-*. FORTH; AFFORD, from Old English *forth,* from Germanic **furth-,* forward. **3.** Suffixed (comparative) form **pr̥-tero-*. FURTHER, from Old English *furthra, furthor,* farther away, from Germanic **furthera-*. **4.a.** Compound **pr̥-st-i-* (or **por-st-i-,* with o-grade form **por-*), "that which stands before," stake, post (see **stā-**); **b.** PORRECT, from Latin *por-,* forth, forward. Both **a** and **b** from Latin *por-* from **pr̥-*. **5.** Suffixed form **pr̥-sōd.* PARGET, from Latin *porrō,* forward.

III. Extended zero-grade form **prə-*. **1.** Suffixed (superlative) form **prə-mo-*. **a.** FOREMOST, FORMER[2], from Old English *forma,* first, foremost, from Germanic **fruma-, *furma-;* **b.** (see **ed-**) Latin compound *prandium,* "first meal," late breakfast, lunch (probably < **prām-d-ium* < **prəm-(e)d-yo-;* second element **-(e)d-,* to eat). **2.** Suffixed (superlative) form **prə-isto-*. FIRST, from Old English *fyrst, fyrest,* first, from Germanic **furista-,* foremost. **3.** Suffixed form **prə-wo-*. **a.** PROW, from Greek *prōira,* forward part of a ship, from analogically suffixed form **prōw-arya;* **b.** PROTEIN, PROTIST, PROTO-, PROTON, from Greek *prōtos,* first, foremost, from suffixed (superlative) form **prōw-ato-*. Both **a** and **b** from Greek **prōwo-,* first, foremost. **4.** Suffixed form **prə-i.* ARPENT, from Latin *arepennis,* half-acre (second element obscure), from Gaulish *ari* (combining form *are-*), before, from Celtic **(p)ari, *are.*

IV. Extended form **prə̆.* **1.a.** FORE, FORE-; (FOREFATHER), from Old English *fore, for,* before; **b.** VORLAGE, from Old High German *fora,* before; **c.** BEFORE, from Old English *beforan,* before, from Germanic prefixed and suffixed form **bi-fora-na,* in the front (**bi-,* at, by; see **ambhi**). **a, b,** and **c** all from Germanic **fura,* before. **2.** PARA-[1]; PALFREY, from Greek *para,* beside, alongside of, beyond.

V. Extended form **prŏ.* **1.a.** FRO; (FROWARD), from Old Norse *frā,* from, from Germanic **fra,* forward, away from; **b.** (see **ed-, ēik-**) Germanic **fra-,* completely. **2.** Suffixed form **prŏ-mo-*. **a.** FROM, from Old English *from,* from, from Germanic **fram,* from; **b.** FURNISH, VENEER, from Old French *f(o)urnir,* to supply, provide, from Germanic derivative verb **frumjan,* to further, from Germanic **frum,* forward; **c.** PRAM[2], from Czech *prám,* raft. **3.** Suffixed form **prō-wo-*. FRAU, (FRÄULEIN), from Old High German *frouwa,* lady, from Germanic **frōwō-,* lady, lengthened-grade feminine of **frawan-,* lord. **4.** Suffixed form **prō-wo-*. NAPRAPATHY, from Slavic *pravŭ,* right. **5.** PRO[1], PRO-[1], (PROUD); (IMPROVE), PURCHASE, from Latin *prō, prŏ-,* before, for, instead of. **6.** Suffixed form **prō-no-*. PRONE, from Latin *prōnus,* leaning forward. **7.** Possible suffixed form **pro-ko-*. RECIPROCAL, from Latin compound *reciprocus,* alternating, "backward and forward" (**re-ko-,* backward; see **re-**). **8.** Suffixed adverb **pro-kʷe.* **a.** APPROACH, (RAPPROCHEMENT), REPROACH, from Latin *prope,* near; **b.** suffixed form **prokʷ-inkʷo-*. PROPINQUITY, from Latin *propinquus,* near; **c.** suffixed (superlative) form **prokʷ-samo-*. PROXIMATE; APPROXIMATE, from Latin *proximus,* nearest. **9.** Compound **pro-bhw-o-,* growing well or straightforward (**bhw-o-,* to grow; see **bheuə-**). (PROBABLE), PROBE, PROBITY, (PROOF), PROVE; APPROVE, IMPROBITY, (REPROVE), from Latin *probus,* upright, good, virtuous. **10.** PRO-[2], from Greek *pro,* before, in front, forward. **11.** Suffixed (comparative) form **pro-tero-*. HYSTERON PROTERON, PROTEROZOIC, from Greek *proteros,* before, former. **12.** PRAKRIT, from Sanskrit *pra-* , before, forth. **13.** (see **wērə-**) Celtic **ro-,* intensive prefix, in **ro-wero-,* sufficiency.

VI. Extended forms **prai-, *prei-*. **1.** PRE-; PRETERIT, from Latin *prae,* before. **2.** Suffixed (comparative) form **prei-yos-*. PRIOR[2], from Latin *prior,* former, higher, superior. **3.** Suffixed form **prei-wo-*. **a.** PRIVATE, PRIVILEGE, PRIVITY, PRIVY; DEPRIVE, from Latin *prīvus,* single, alone (< "standing in front," "isolated from others"); **b.** PROPER, PROPERTY; APPROPRIATE, PROPRIOCEPTION, PROPRIOCEPTOR, from Latin *proprius,* one's own, particular (< *prō prīvō,* in particular, from the ablative of *prīvus,* single; *prō,* for; see **V. 5.**). **4.** Extended form **preis-*. **a.** Suffixed (superlative) form **preis-mo-*. *(i)* PREMIER, PRIMAL, PRIMARY, PRIMATE, PRIME, PRIMITIVE, PRIMO, PRIMUS; IMPRIMIS, PRIMAVERA[1], PRIMEVAL, PRIMIPARA, PRIMOGENITOR, PRIMOGENITURE, PRIMORDIAL, from Latin *prīmus* (< **prīsmus;* ablative plural *prīmīs*), first, foremost; *(ii)* PRINCE, PRINCIPAL, PRINCIPLE, from Latin compound *prīnceps,* "he who takes first place," leader, chief, emperor (*-ceps,* "-taker"; see **kap-**); **b.** suffixed form **preis-tano-*. PRISTINE, from Latin *prīstinus,* former, earlier, original.

VII. Extended form **pres-* in compound **pres-gʷu-,* "going before" (**gʷ-u-,* going; see **gʷā-**). PRESBYTER, (PRIEST); PRESBYOPIA, from Greek *presbus,* old, old man, elder.

VIII. Extended form **proti.* PROS-, from Greek *pros,* against, toward, near, at. [Pokorny 2. A. *per* 810.] Other possibly related forms are grouped under **per-[2], per-[3], per-[4], and per-[5].**

per-[2]. Important derivatives are *firth, fjord, fare, wayfarer, welfare, pore[2], emporium, ferry, fern, ford, port[1], opportune, porch, portal, portable, portage, porter[1], export, import, important, portfolio, rapport, report, sport, support,* and *transport.*

per-[2]. To lead, pass over. A verbal root belonging to the group of **per[1].**

I. Full-grade form **per-*. **1.** Suffixed form **per-tu-*. FIRTH, FJORD, from Old Norse *fjördhr,* an inlet, estuary, from Germanic **ferthuz,* place for crossing over, ford. **2.** Suffixed form **per-onā.* PERONEAL, from Greek *peronē,* pin of a brooch, buckle (< "that which pierces through"). **3.** Suffixed form **per-yo-*. DIAPIR, from Greek *peirein,* to pierce.

II. O-grade form **por-*. **1.a.** *(i)* FARE; WAYFARER, WAYFARING, (WELFARE), from Old English *faran,* to go on a journey, get along; *(ii)* FIELDFARE, from Old English *faran,* possibly altered by folk etymology in Old English, from an uncertain original; **b.** GABERDINE, from Old High German *faran,* to go, travel. Both **a** and **b** from Germanic **faran,* to go. **2.** Suffixed form **por-o-,* passage, journey. PORE[2]; EMPORIUM, POROMERIC, from Greek *poros,* journey, passage. **3.** Suffixed (causative) form **por-eyo-,* to cause to go, lead, conduct. FERRY, from Old English *ferian,* to transport, from Germanic **farjan,* to ferry. **4.** Lengthened-grade form **pōr-*. **a.** FERE, from Old English *(ge)fēra,* "fellow-traveler," companion (*ge-,* together, with; see **kom**), from Germanic suffixed form **fōr-ja-;* **b.** FÜHRER, from Old High German *fuoren,* to lead, from Germanic suffixed (causative) form **fōr-jan.* **5.** Possibly suffixed form **por-no-,* feather, wing (< "that which carries a bird in flight"). **a.** FERN, from Old English *fearn,* fern (having feathery fronds), from Germanic **farnō,* feather, leaf; **b.** PAN[2], from Sanskrit *parṇam,* leaf, feather.

III. Zero-grade form **pr̥-*. **1.** Suffixed form **pr̥-tu-,* passage. **a.** FORD, f[illegible] shallow place where one may [illegible] Germanic **furdu-;* **b.** PORT[1]; IM[illegible] TUNE, from Latin *portus,* harbor (<[illegible] Suffixed form **pr̥-tā.* PORCH, PORT[3], P[illegible] CULLIS, PORTER[2], PORTICO, PORTIÈRE, [illegible] from Latin *porta,* gate. **3.** Suffixed (deno[illegible] form **pr̥-to-*. PORT[5], PORTABLE, PORTAGE, [illegible] MENTO, PORTATIVE, PORTER[1]; COMPORT, DEPORT, [illegible] PORT, IMPORT, (IMPORTANT), PORTFOLIO, PURPOR[illegible] RAPPORT, REPORT, (SPORT), SUPPORT, TRANSPORT, from Latin *portāre,* to carry. [Pokorny 2. B. *per* 816.]

per-[3]. Important derivatives are *fear, peril, experience, experiment, expert, pirate,* and *empiric.*

per-[3]. To try, risk (< "to lead over," "press forward"). A verbal root belonging to the group of **per[1].** **1.** Lengthened grade **pēr-*. FEAR, from Old English *fǣr,* danger, sudden calamity, from Germanic **fēraz,* danger. **2.** Suffixed form **perī-tlo-*. (PARLOUS), PERIL, from Latin *perīclum, perīculum,* trial, danger. **3.** Suffixed form **per-yo-*. EXPERIENCE, EXPERIMENT, EXPERT, from Latin *experīrī,* to try, learn by trying (*ex-,* from; see **eghs**). **4.** Suffixed form **per-ya.* PIRATE; EMPIRIC, from Greek *peira,* trial, attempt. [Pokorny 2. E. *per* 818.]

per-[4]. Important derivatives are *press[1], pressure, print, compress, depress, express, imprint, oppress, repress, reprimand,* and *suppress.*

per-[4]. To strike. A verbal root possibly belonging to the group of **per[1].** Extended forms **prem-, *pres-*. PREGNANT[2], PRESS[1], PRESSURE, PRINT; APPRESSED, COMPRESS, DEPRESS, EXPRESS, IMPRESS[1], (IMPRINT), OPPRESS, REPRESS, (REPRIMAND), SUPPRESS, from Latin *premere* (past participle *pressus*), to press. [Pokorny 3. *per-* 818.]

per-[5]. Important derivatives are *interpret, praise, precious, price, appraise, appreciate, depreciate,* and *pornography.*

per-[5]. To traffic in, sell (< "to hand over," "distribute"). A verbal root belonging to the group of **per[1].** Base of two distinct extended roots.

I. Root form **pret-*. **1.** INTERPRET, from Latin compound *inter-pres* (stem *inter-pret-*), go-between, negotiator (*inter-,* between; see **en**). **2.** Suffixed form **pret-yo-*. PRAISE, PRECIOUS, PRICE; APPRAISE, (APPRECIATE), DEPRECIATE, from Latin *pretium,* price.

II. Root form **perə-*. Suffixed form **p(e)r-n-ə-,* with o-grade **por(ə)-nā.* PORNOGRAPHY, from Greek *pornē,* prostitute, from *pernanai,* to sell. [In Pokorny 2. C. *per* 817.]

perd-. Important derivatives are *fart* and *partridge.*

perd-. To fart. **1.** FART, from Old English **feortan,* to fart, from Germanic **fertan, *fartōn.* **2.** PARTRIDGE, from Greek *perdix,* partridge (which makes a sharp whirring sound when suddenly flushed). [Pokorny *perd-* 819.] See also **pezd-.**

perə-[1]. Important derivatives are *parade, pare, parry, apparatus, apparel, disparate, emperor, imperative, imperial, parachute, parasol, prepare, rampart, repair[1], separate, sever, several, parent,* and *repertory.*

perə-[1]. To produce, procure. Possibly the same root as **perə-[2].** See also **per-[5] II.** Zero-grade form **pr̥ə-* (becoming **par-* in Latin). **a.** root form **par-ā-*. PARADE, PARE, (PARLAY), PARRY, (PARURE); APPARATUS, (APPAREL), COMPRADOR, DISPARATE, EMPEROR, (IMPERATIVE), (IMPERIAL), (PARACHUTE), PARASOL, PREPARE, RAMPART, REPAIR[1], SEPARATE, (SEVER), (SEVERAL), from Latin *parāre,* to try to get, prepare, equip; **b.** suffixed form **par-yo-*. -PARA, PARENT, PARITY[2], -PAROUS, PARTURIENT, POSTPARTUM, REPERTORY, from Latin *parere, parīre,* to get, beget, give birth; **c.** suffixed form **par-o-,* producing, in compound **pau-paros,* producing little, poor (see **pau-**); **d.** suffixed form **par-ikā.* PARCAE, from Latin *Parcae,* the Fates (who assign one's destiny). [Pokorny 2. D. *per* 818.]

perə-[2]. Important derivatives are *parcel, parse, part, impart, repartee, portion, proportion, pair, par, parlay, peer[2], compare,* and *nonpareil.*

perə-[2]. To grant, allot (reciprocally, to get in return). Possibly the same root as **perə-[1].** See also **per-[5] II.** Zero-grade form **pr̥ə-* (becoming **par-* in

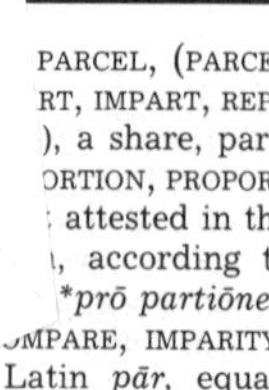

... PARCEL, (PARCE- ... RT, IMPART, REP- ...), a share, part; ... ORTION, PROPOR- ... attested in the ... , according to ... _*prō partiōne_); ... OMPARE, IMPARITY, ... om Latin _pār_, equal, ... [Pokorny 2. _per_, Section C.

...-. Important derivatives are _fir_ and _cork_.

perk^{w}u-. Oak. **1.** Zero-grade form _*pr̥k^{w}-_. FIR, probably from a Scandinavian source akin to Old Icelandic _fȳri_, fir, from Germanic _*furh-jōn-_. **2.** Assimilated form _*k^{w}erk^{w}u-_. CORK, QUERCETIN; QUERCITRON, from Latin _quercus_, oak. [Pokorny _perk^{u}u-s_ 822.]

pes-. Important derivatives are _pencil, penicillium,_ and _penis._

pes-. Penis. Suffixed form _*pes-ni-_. PENCIL, (PENICILLIUM), PENIS, from Latin _pēnis_ (< _*pesnis_), penis, tail. [Pokorny 3. _pes-_ 824.]

pet-. Important derivatives are _feather, petition, appetite, compete, perpetual, repeat, pen[1], propitious, ptomaine, symptom,_ and _hippopotamus._

pet-. Also **petə-**. To rush, fly. Variant _*ptē-_, contracted from _*pteə-_. **1.** Suffixed form _*pet-rā_. FEATHER, from Old English _fether_, feather, from Germanic _*fethrō_, feather. **2.** -PETAL, PETITION, PETULANT; APPETITE, COMPETE, IMPETUS, PERPETUAL, REPEAT, from Latin _petere_, to go toward, seek. **3.** Suffixed form _*pet-nā_. PANACHE, PEN[1], PENNA, PENNATE, PENNON, PIN, PINNA, PINNACLE, PINNATE, (PINNATI-), PINNULE; EMPENNAGE, from Latin _penna, pinna_, feather, wing. **4.** Suffixed form _*pet-ro-_ (see **ōku-**). **5.** Suffixed form _*pet-yo-_. PROPITIOUS, from Latin _propitius_, favorable, gracious, orginially a religious term meaning "falling or rushing forward," hence "eager," "well-disposed" (said of the gods; _prō-_, forward; see **per[1]**). **6.** Suffixed zero-grade form _*pt-ero-_. -PTER; ACANTHOPTERYGIAN, APTERYX, ARCHAEOPTERYX, COLEOPTERAN, MECOPTERAN, ORTHOPTERAN, PERIPTERAL, PLECOPTERAN, PTERIDOLOGY, PTERYGOID, from Greek _pteron_, feather, wing, and _pterux_, wing. **7.** Suffixed zero-grade form _*pt-ilo-_. COLEOPTILE, from Greek _ptilon_, soft feathers, down, plume. **8.** Suffixed variant form _*ptē-no-_. STEAROPTENE, from Greek _ptēnos_, winged, flying. **9.** Reduplicated form _*pi-pt-_. PTOMAINE, PTOSIS; ASYMPTOTE, PERIPETEIA, PROPTOSIS, SYMPTOM, from Greek _piptein_, to fall, with nominal derivatives _ptō-to-, ptō-ti-, ptō-ma_. **10.** O-grade form _*pot-_. HIPPOPOTAMUS, from Greek _potamos_ "rushing water," river (_-amo-_, Greek suffix). **11.** Suffixed form _*pet-tro-_. TALIPOT, from Sanskrit _pattram_, feather, leaf. [Pokorny 2. _pet-_ 826.]

petə-. Important derivatives are _fathom, patent, pace[1], pass, compass, expand, petal,_ and _pan[1]._

petə-. To spread. **1.** Suffixed o-grade form _*pot(ə)-mo-_. FATHOM, from Old English _fæthm_, fathom, from Germanic _*fathmaz_, "length of two arms stretched out." **2.** Suffixed (stative) variant zero-grade form _*pat-ē-_. PATENT, PATULOUS, from Latin _patēre_, to be open. **3.** Probably variant zero-grade form in remade nasalized form _*pat-no-_. PACE[1], (PAS), (PASS), PASSIM; (COMPASS), EXPAND, REPAND, from Latin _pandere_ (past participle _passus_ < _*pat-to-_), to spread out. **4.** Suffixed form _*pet-alo-_. PETAL, from Greek _petalon_, leaf. **5.** Suffixed form _*pet-ano-_. (PAELLA), PAN[1], PATEN, (PATINA[1]), (PATINA[2]), from Greek _patanē_ (? < _*petanā_), platter, "thing spread out." **6.** PETASOS, from Greek _petasos_, broad-brimmed hat, from Greek suffixed form _*peta-so-_. [Pokorny 1. _pet_ 824.]

peu-. Important derivatives are _putative, account, amputate, compute, count[1], dispute, impute, repute,_ and _pave._

peu-. To cut, strike, stamp. **1.** Suffixed (participial) zero-grade form _*pu-to_, cut, struck. **a.** PUTAMEN, PUTATIVE; (ACCOUNT), AMPUTATE, COMPUTE, COUNT[1], DEPUTE, DISPUTE, IMPUTE, REPUTE, from Latin _putāre_, to prune, clean, settle an account, think over, reflect; **b.** PIT[1], from Latin _puteus_, well, possibly from **peu-**. **2.** Variant form _*pau-_. **a.** suffixed form _*pau-yo_. PAVE, (PAVÉ), from Latin _pavīre_, to beat; **b.** suffixed (stative) form _*paw-ē-_. PAVID, from Latin _pavēre_, to fear (< "to be struck"); **c.** ANAPEST, from Greek _paiein_, to beat, perhaps from **peu-**. [Pokorny 3. _pēu-_ 827.]

peuə-. Important derivatives are _pure, purge, Puritan,_ and _expurgate._

peuə-. To purify, cleanse. Suffixed zero-grade form _*pū-ro-_ (< _*puə-ro_). POUR, PURE, PURGE, PURITAN; COMPURGATION, DEPURATE, EXPURGATE, (SPURGE), from Latin _pūrus_, pure, and _pūrgāre_, to purify (< _*pūr-igāre;_ second element _agere_, to drive; see **ag-**). [Pokorny 1. _peu-_ 827.]

peuk-. Important derivatives are _pugilism, pugnacious, impugn, poignant, point, pounce[1], punctuate, puncture, pungent, expunge,_ and _pygmy._

peuk-. Also **peug-**. To prick. Zero-grade form _*pug-_. **1.** Suffixed form _*pug-no-_. PONIARD, PUGILISM, PUGIL STICK, PUGNACIOUS; IMPUGN, OPPUGN, REPUGN, from Latin _pugil_, pugilist, and _pugnus_, fist, with denominative _pugnāre_, to fight with the fist. **2.** Nasalized zero-grade form _*pu-n-g-_. BUNG, POIGNANT, POINT, POINTILLISM, PONTIL, (POUNCE[1]), (POUNCE[3]), PUNCHEON[1], PUNCTUATE, PUNCTURE, PUNGENT; COMPUNCTION, EXPUNGE, SPONTOON, TRAPUNTO, from Latin _pungere_, to prick. **3.** (PYGMAEAN), PYGMY, from Greek _pugmē_, fist. [Pokorny _peuk̂-_ 828.]

pezd-. Derivatives are _fizzle_ and _petard._

pezd-. To fart. **1.** Suffixed form _*pezd-i-_. FEIST, FIZZLE, from Middle English _fisten_, to fart, from Germanic _*fistiz_, a fart. **2.** PETARD, from Latin _pēdere_, to fart. **3.** PEDICULAR, from Latin _pēdis_, louse (? < "foul-smelling insect"), possibly from **pezd-**. [Pokorny _pezd-_ 829, 2. _peis-_ 796.] See also **perd-**.

pəter-. Important derivatives are _father, forefather, padre, paternal, patrician, patrimony, patron, expatriate, perpetrate, patriot,_ and _patriarch._

pəter-. Father. **1.** FATHER; (FOREFATHER), from Old English _fæder_, father, from Germanic _*fadar_. **2.** PADRE, PATER, PATERNAL, PATRI-, PATRICIAN, PATRIMONY, PATRON, PÈRE; EXPATRIATE, PERPETRATE, from Latin _pater_, father. **3.** PATRI-, PATRIOT; ALLOPATRIC, EUPATRID, PATRIARCH, SYMPATRIC, from Greek _patēr_, father. [Pokorny _pətḗ(r)_ 829.]

plāk-[1]. Important derivatives are _fluke[1], flake[1], flaw[1], placebo, placid, plea, plead, pleasant, please, complacent, placate, plank, placenta,_ and _archipelago._

plāk-[1]. Also **plak-**. To be flat. Extension of **pelə-[2]**. **1.** FLOE, from Old Norse _flō_, layer, coating, from Germanic _*flōhō_. **2.** Variant form _*plāg-_. **a.** FLUKE[1], from Old English _flōc_, flatfish, from Germanic _*flōk-;_ **b.** FLAKE[1], from Middle English _flake_, flake, from a Scandinavian source probably akin to Norwegian _flak_, flat piece, flake, from Germanic _*flakaz;_ **c.** FLAKE[2], from Old Norse _flaki, fleki_, hurdle, from Germanic _*flak-_. **3.** Extended form _*plakā_. FLAG[4], FLAW[1], from Old Norse _flaga_, layer of stone, from Germanic _*flagō_. **4.** Possibly suffixed (stative) form _*plak-ē-_, to be calm (as of the flat sea). PLACEBO, PLACID, PLEA, (PLEAD), PLEASANT, PLEASE; COMPLACENT, from Latin _placēre_, to please, be agreeable. **5.** Root noun _*plak-_. (SUPPLICATE), SUPPLE, from Latin _supplex_, suppliant (whence denominative _supplicāre_, to beg humbly, first attested in Archaic Latin as _sub vos placō_, I entreat you; _sub_, under; see **upo.**) **6.** Lengthened suffixed form _*plāk-ā-_. PLACABLE, PLACATE, from Latin _plācāre_, to calm (causative of _placēre_). **7.** Nasalized form _*pla-n-k-_. PLANCHET, PLANK, from Latin _plancus_, flat, flat-footed. **8.** Variant form _*plag-_. **a.** PLAGIARY, from Latin _plaga_, net (? < "something extended"), perhaps from **plāk-[1]**; **b.** PLAGAL, PLAGIO-, PLAYA, from Greek _plagos_, side. **9.** Root form _*plak-_. PLACENTA, PLACOID; LEUKOPLAKIA, from Greek _plax_, flat, flat land, surface. **10.** Possible variant form _*pelag-_. PELAGIC; ARCHIPELAGO, from Greek _pelagos_, sea. [Pokorny 1. _plā-k-_ 831.]

plāk-[2]. Important derivatives are _fling, plaint, complain, plankton, plague, apoplexy,_ and _paraplegia._

plāk-[2]. To strike. **1.** Nasalized variant forms _*pla-n-k-, *pla-n-g-_. **a.** FLING, from Middle English _flingen_ to fling, from a Scandinavian source akin to Old Norse _flengja_, to flog, whip, from Germanic _*flang-;_ **b.** PLAINT, PLANGENT; COMPLAIN, from Latin _plangere_, to strike (one's own breast), lament; **c.** suffixed form _*plang-yo-_. PLANKTON, from Greek _plazein_, to drive away, turn aside. **2.** Variant form _*plāg-_. PLAGUE, from Latin _plāga_, a blow, stroke. **3.** Suffixed form _*plāk-yo-_. PLECTRUM, -PLEGIA, PLEXOR; APLOPLEXY, CATAPLEXY, PARAPLEGIA, from Greek _plēssein_, to beat, strike. [Pokorny 2. _plāk-_ 832.]

plat-. Important derivatives are _flat[1], flatter[1], flat[2], flounder[2], clan, plan, plant, supplant, place, plate, plateau, platitude,_ and _plaza._

plat-. To spread. Also _*plet-_. Extension of **pelə-[2]**. **1.** Variant form _*plad-_. **a.** FLAT[1], from Old Norse _flatr_, flat; **b.** FLATTER[1], from Old French _flater_, to flatter. Both **a** and **b** from Germanic _*flataz_, flat. **2.** Suffixed variant form _*plad-yo-_. FLAT[2], from Old English _flet(t)_, floor, dwelling, from Germanic _*flatjam_. **3.** Basic form _*plat-_. FLAN, from Late Latin _fladō_, flat cake, pancake, from Germanic _*flathō(n)_, flat cake. **4.** FLOUNDER[2], from Anglo-Norman _floundre_, flounder, from a Scandinavian source probably akin to Old Swedish _flundra_, flatfish, flounder, from Germanic nasalized suffixed form _*flu-n-th-r-jō-_. **5.** Nasalized form _*pla-n-t-_. CLAN, PLAN, PLANT, PLANTAIN[1], PLANTAR; PLANTIGRADE, SUPPLANT, TRANSPLANT, from Latin _planta_, sole of the foot, and denominative _plantāre_, to drive in with the sole of the foot, plant, whence _planta_, a plant. **6.** Suffixed zero-grade form _*pl̥t-u-_. PIAZZA, PLACE, PLAICE, PLANE[4], (PLANE TREE), PLATE, (PLATEAU), (PLATITUDE), (PLATY[2]), PLATY-, (PLAZA), from Greek _platus_, flat, broad. [Pokorny _plat-_ 833.]

plek-. Important derivatives are _flax, multiplex, plait, pliant, plight[1], ply[1], apply, complicate, deploy, display, employ, implicate, reply, complex,_ and _perplex._

plek-. To plait. Extension of **pel-[2]**. **1.** Suffixed o-grade form _*plok-so-_. FLAX, from Old English _fleax_, flax, from Germanic _*flahsam_, flax. **2.** Full-grade form _*plek-_. MULTIPLEX, from Latin _-plex_, -fold (in compounds such as _duplex_, twofold; see **dwo-**). **3.** PLAIT, PLIANT, PLICA, PLICATE, PLIGHT[1], PLISSÉ, PLY[1]; APPLY, COMPLICATE, COMPLICE, DEPLOY, DISPLAY, EMPLOY, EXPLICATE, IMPLICATE, REPLICATE, (REPLY), from Latin _plicāre_, to fold (also in compounds used as denominatives of words in _-plex_, genitive _-plicis_). **4.** Suffixed forms _*plek-to-_ and _*plek-t-to-_. PLEACH, PLEXUS; AMPLEXICAUL, COMPLECT, (COMPLEX), PERPLEXED, from Latin _plectere_ (past participle _plexus_), to weave, plait, entwine. **5.** PLECOPTERAN, PLECTOGNATH, from Greek _plekein_, to plait, twine, and _plektos_, twisted. [Pokorny _plek̂-_ 834.]

pleu-. Important derivatives are _plover, pulmonary, pneumonia, Pluto, flow, flood, fly[1], fly[2], flee, fledge, flight[1], fowl, fleet[1], fleet[2], float, flutter, flit,_ and _fluster._

pleu-. To flow.
I. Basic form _*pleu-_. **1.** (PLOVER), (PLUVIAL), PLUVIOUS, from Latin _pluere_, to rain. **2.** PLEUSTON, from Greek _pleusis_, sailing. **3.** Suffixed zero-grade form _*plu-elos_. PYELITIS, from Greek dissimilated _puelos_, trough, basin. **4.** Suffixed form _*pl(e)umon-_, "floater," lung(s). **a.** PULMONARY, from Latin _pulmō_ (< _*plumonēs_), lung(s); **b.** PNEUMO-, PNEUMONIA, PNEUMONIC, from Greek _pleumōn, pneumōn_ (influenced by _pneuma_, breath; see **pneu-**), lung. **5.** Suffixed o-grade form _*plou-to_. PLUTO; PLUTOCRACY, PLUTOGRAPHY, from Greek _ploutos_, wealth, riches (< "overflowing"). **6.** Lengthened o-grade form _*plō(u)-_. **a.** _(i)_ FLOW, from Old English _flōwan_, to flow; _(ii)_ FLUE[2], from Middle Dutch _vluwe_, fishnet, perhaps from **pleu-**. Both _(i)_ and _(ii)_ from Germanic _*flōwan_, to flow; **b.** suffixed form _*plō-tu-_. FLOOD, from Old English _flōd_, flood, from Germanic _*flōduz_, flowing water, deluge.
II. Extended form _*pleuk-_. **1.** FLY[1], from Old English _flēogan_, to fly, from Germanic _*fleugan_, to fly. **2.** FLY[2], from Old English _flēoge_, a fly, from Germanic _*fleugōn-_, flying insect, fly. **3.** FLEE, from Old English _flēon_, to flee, from Germanic _*fleuhan_, to run away, probably from **pleu-**. **4.** FLEY, from Old English _flȳgan, flēgan_, to put to flight, from Germanic causative _*flaugjan_. **5.** FLÈCHE, FLETCHER, from Old French _fleche_, arrow, from Germanic suffixed form _*fleug-ika_. **6.** Zero-grade form _*pluk-_. **a.** FLEDGE, from Old English _*flycge_, with feathers (only in _unfligge_, featherless), from Ger-

manic **flugja-,* feather; **b.** FLIGHT^1, FLIGHT^2, from Old English *flyht,* act of flying, and **flyht,* act of fleeing, escape, from Germanic suffixed form **flug-ti-;* **c.** FOWL, from Old English *fugol,* bird, from Germanic **fuglaz,* bird, dissimilated from possible (but unlikely) suffixed form **flug-laz;* **d.** FLÜGELHORN, FUGLEMAN, from Middle High German *vlügel,* wing, from Germanic suffixed form **flug-ila.* **III.** Extended form **pleud-.* **1.** FLEET^1, FLEET^2, from Old English *flēotan,* to float, swim (from Germanic **fleutan*), and Old Norse *fliōtr,* fleet, swift (from Germanic **fleutaz*). **2.** Zero-grade form **plud-.* **a.** *(i)* FLOAT, from Old English *flotian,* to float; *(ii)* FLOTSAM, from Old French *floter,* to float. Both *(i)* and *(ii)* from Germanic derivative **flotōn,* to float; **b.** FLOTILLA, from Old Norse *floti,* raft, fleet; **c.** FLUTTER, from Old English *floterian, flotorian,* to float back and forth (*-erian,* iterative and frequentative suffix); **d.** FLIT, from Old Norse *flytja,* to further, convey, from Germanic **flutjan,* to float. **a, b, c,** and **d** all from Germanic **flut-, *flot-.* **3.** FLUSTER, probably from a Scandinavian source akin to Icelandic *flaustr,* hurry, and *flaustra,* to bustle, from Germanic **flausta-,* contracted from suffixed form **flaut-stā-,* probably from **pleud-,* o-grade **ploud-.* [Pokorny *pleu-* 835, *pl(e)u-mon-* 837.]

pneu-. Important derivatives are *sneeze, snore, snort,* and *pneumatic.*

pneu-. To breathe. Imitative root. **1.** SNEEZE, from Old English *fnēosan,* to sneeze, from Germanic **fneu-s-.* **2.** SNORE, (SNORT), from Old English *fnora,* sneezing, from Germanic **fnu-s-.* **3.** APNEA, DIPNOAN, DYSPNEA, EUPNEA, HYPERPNEA, HYPOPNEA, POLYPNEA, TACHYPNEA, from Greek *pnein,* to breathe, with o-grade nouns *pnoia,* breathing, and *pnoē,* breath. **4.** Suffixed form **pneu-mn̥.* PNEUMA, PNEUMATIC, PNEUMATO-, PNEUMO-, from Greek *pneuma,* breath, wind, spirit. **5.** Germanic variant root **fnes-.* SNEER, from Old English *fnǣran,* to snort, gnash one's teeth. [Pokorny *pneu-* 838.]

pō(i)-. Important derivatives are *potable, poison, potion, beer, beverage, imbibe,* and *symposium.*

pō(i)-. To drink. Contracted from **poə(i)-.*
I. Basic form **pō(i)-.* **1.a.** Suffixed reduced form **pō-to-.* POTABLE, POTATION, POTATORY, from Latin *pōtus,* drunk; a drink (whence *pōtāre,* to drink); **b.** suffixed form **pō-ti-.* POISON, POTION, from Latin *pōtiō,* a drink. **2.** Reduplicated form **pi-pə-o-,* whence **pi-bo-,* assimilated to **bi-bo-.* BEER, BEVERAGE, BIB, BIBULOUS; IMBIBE, (IMBRUE), from Latin *bibere,* to drink. **3.** Suffixed zero-grade form **pə-ti-, *po-ti-.* SYMPOSIUM, from Greek *posis,* drink, drinking.
II. Zero-grade form **pī-* (< **piə-*). **1.** Suffixed form **pī-ro-.* PIROG, from Old Church Slavonic *pirŭ,* feast. **2.** Suffixed (nasal present) form **pī-no-.* PINOCYTOSIS, from Greek *pinein,* to drink. [Pokorny 2. *pō(i)-* 839.]

pōl-. Important derivatives are *feel, palpable, palpitate, catapult,* and *psalm.*

pōl-. To touch, feel, shake. **1.a.** FEEL, from Old English *fēlan,* to examine by touch, feel; **b.** SPRACHGEFÜHL, from Old High German *vuolen,* to feel. Both **a** and **b** from Germanic **fōljan,* to feel. **2.** Reduplicated zero-grade form **pal-p-.* **a.** PALP, from Latin *palpus,* a touching; **b.** PALPABLE, PALPATE^1, PALPITATE, from Latin *palpārī, palpāre,* to stroke gently, touch; **c.** PALPEBRA, from Latin *palpebra,* eyelid (< "that which shakes or moves quickly"). **3.** Perhaps suffixed zero-grade form **pal-yo-.* CATAPULT, from Greek *pallein,* to sway, brandish. **4.** Perhaps suffixed form **psal-yo-.* PSALM, PSALTERY, from Greek *psallein,* to pluck, play the harp (but more likely of imitative origin). [Pokorny 1. G. *pel-* 801.]

porko-. Important derivatives are *aardvark, porcelain, pork, porcupine,* and *porpoise.*

porko-. Young pig. **1.a.** FARROW^1, from Old English *fearh,* little pig; **b.** AARDVARK, from Middle Dutch diminutive form *varken,* small pig. Both **a** and **b** from Germanic **farhaz.* **2.** PORCELAIN, PORCINE, PORK; PORCUPINE, PORPOISE, from Latin *porcus,* pig. [Pokorny *porko-s* 841.]

poti-. Important derivatives are *possess, power, possible, potent,* and *impotent.*

poti-. Powerful; lord. **1.** PODESTA, POSSESS, POWER, from Latin *potis* (> **pots* > *pos-*), powerful, able. **2.** POSSIBLE, POTENT; (IMPOTENT), OMNIPOTENT, PREPOTENT, from Latin compound *posse,* to be able (contracted from *potis,* able + *esse,* to be; see **es-**). **3.** Form **pot-.* **a.** compound **ghos-pot-,* "guest-master," host (see **ghos-ti-**); **b.** compound **dems-pot-,* "house- master," ruler (see **dem-**). **4.** PADISHAH, from Old Persian *pati-,* master. [Pokorny *poti-s* 842.]

prek-. Important derivatives are *pray, prayer^1, precarious, deprecate,* and *postulate.*

prek-. To ask, entreat. **1.** Basic form **prek-.* PRAY, PRAYER^1, PRECARIOUS; DEPRECATE, IMPRECATE, from **prex,* prayer (attested only in the plural *precēs*), with Latin denominative *precārī,* to entreat, pray. **2.** Suffixed zero-grade form **pr̥k-sk-* becoming **pork-sk-,* contracted into **posk-* in suffixed form **posk-to,* contracted into **posto-.* POSTULATE; EXPOSTULATE, from Latin *postulāre,* to ask, request. [Pokorny 4. *perk̂-* 821.]

preus-. Important derivatives are *freeze, frost,* and *prurient.*

preus-. To freeze, burn. **1.** FREEZE, from Old English *frēosan,* to freeze, from Germanic **freusan,* to freeze. **2.** Suffixed zero-grade form **prus-to-.* FROST, from Old English *forst, frost,* frost, from Germanic **frustaz,* frost. **3.** Suffixed form **preus-i-.* PRURIENT, PRURIGO, PRURITUS, from Latin denominative *prūrīre,* to burn, itch, yearn for, from **preusis, *preuris,* act of burning. **4.** Suffixed zero-grade form **prus-wīnā.* PRUINOSE, from Latin *pruīna,* hoarfrost. [Pokorny *preus-* 846.]

prī-. Important derivatives are *free, filibuster, friend, afraid,* and *Friday.*

prī-. To love. Contracted from **priə-.* **1.** Suffixed form **priy-o-.* **a.** FREE, from Old English *frēo,* free, and *frēon, freogan,* to love, set free; **b.** (FILIBUSTER), FREEBOOTER, from Dutch *vrij,* free. Both **a** and **b** from Germanic **frijaz,* beloved, belonging to the loved ones, not in bondage, free, and **frijōn,* to love. **2.** Suffixed (participial) form **priy-ont-,* loving. FRIEND, from Old English *frīond, frēond,* friend, from Germanic **frijand-,* lover, friend. **3.** Suffixed shortened form **pri-tu-.* **a.** SIEGFRIED, from Old High German *fridu,* peace; **b.** AFFRAY, AFRAID, from Old French *esfreer,* to disturb, from Vulgar Latin **exfridāre,* to break the peace, from *ex-,* out, away (see **eghs**) + **fridāre,* to make peace, from Germanic **frithu-,* peace; **c.** (see **bhergh-^{2}**) Germanic compound **berg-frij-,* "high place of safety," from **frij-,* peace, safety. **a, b,** and **c** all from Germanic **frithuz,* peace. **4.** Suffixed feminine form **priy-ā,* beloved. **a.** FRIGG, from Old Norse *Frigg,* goddess of the heavens, wife of Odin; **b.** FRIDAY, from Old English *Frīgedæg,* Friday, from Germanic compound **frije-dagaz,* "day of Frigg" (translation of Latin *Veneris diēs,* "Venus's day"). Both **a** and **b** from Germanic **frijjō,* beloved, wife. [Pokorny *prāi-* 844.]

pŭ-. Important derivatives are *foul, filth, defile^1, fuzzy, putrid, potpourri, putrefy, purulent,* and *pus.*

pŭ-. To rot, decay. **1.** Suffixed form **pū-lo-.* **a.** FOUL, from Old English *fūl,* unclean, rotten; **b.** FULMAR, from Old Norse *fūll,* foul; **c.** FILTH, from Old English *fȳlth,* foulness, from Germanic abstract noun **fūlithō;* **d.** FILE^3; DEFILE^1, from Old English *fȳlan,* to sully, from Germanic denominative **fūljan,* to soil, dirty. **a, b, c,** and **d** all from Germanic **fūlaz,* rotten, filthy. **2.** Extended form **pug-.* FOG^2, from Middle English *fog, fogge,* aftermath grass, from a Scandinavian source probably akin to Icelandic *fūki,* rotten sea grass, and Norwegian *fogg,* rank grass, from Germanic **fuk-.* **3.** Extended variant form **pous-.* FUZZY, from Low German *fussig,* spongy, from Germanic **fausa-.* **4.** Suffixed form **pu-tri-.* PUTRESCENT, PUTRID; (OLLA PODRIDA), (POTPOURRI), PUTREFY, from Latin *puter* (stem *putri-*), rotten. **5.** Suffixed form **puw-os-.* **a.** PURULENT, PUS; SUPPURATE, from Latin *pūs,* pus; **b.** PYO-, from Greek *puon, puos,* pus. **6.** EMPYEMA, from Greek compound *empuein,* to suppurate (*en-,* in; see **en**). [Pokorny 2. *pŭ-* 848.]

pūr-. Important derivatives are *fire* and *pyre.*

pūr-. Fire. Contracted from **puər-,* zero-grade form of **pəwr̥.* **1.** FIRE, from Old English *fȳr,* fire, from Germanic suffixed form **fūr-i-.* **2.** PYRE, PYRETIC, PYRITES, PYRO-, PYRRHOTITE, PYROSIS; EMPYREAL, from Greek *pur,* fire. [Pokor

[re-. Important derivatives are *r*
rears.

re-. Also **red-.** Backward. Latin comb
conceivably from Indo-European **wret-,* m
cal variant of **wert-,* to turn (< "turned ba
extended form of **wer-^{2}.** **1.** RE-, from Lati
red-, backward, again. **2.** Suffixed form **re(d)-t*
RETRAL, RETRO-; ARREARS, REAR GUARD, REARWARD^2,
REREDOS, from Latin *retrō,* backward, back, behind. **3.** Suffixed form **re-ko-.* (see **per^1**) Latin *reciprocus,* "backward and forward."**]**

rē-. Important derivatives are *real^1* and *republic.*

rē-. To bestow, endow. Contracted from **reə-.* Suffixed form **reə-i-,* goods, wealth, property. RE^2, REAL^1, REBUS, REIFY, REPUBLIC, from Latin *rēs,* thing. [Pokorny 4. *rei-* 850.]

rēd-. Important derivatives are *rodent, corrode, erode, rostrum, rash^2, abrade,* and *erase.*

rēd-. To scrape, scratch, gnaw. **1.** O-grade form **rōd-.* **a.** RODENT; CORRODE, ERODE, from Latin *rōdere,* to gnaw; **b.** suffixed (instrumental) form **rōd-tro-.* ROSTRUM, from Latin *rōstrum,* beak, ship's bow. **2.** Possibly variant form **rād-.* **a.** RADULA, RASH^2, RASORIAL; ABRADE, CORRADE, ERASE, from Latin *rādere,* to scrape; **b.** suffixed (instrumental) form **rād-tro-.* RACLETTE, from Latin *rāstrum,* rake. [Pokorny 2. *rēd-* 854.]

reg-. Important derivatives are *right, realm, rector, rectum, regent, regime, regiment, region, correct, direct, erect, rectangle, rectify, surge, rich, regal, reign, royal, maharajah, rail^1, regular, regulate, rule, rake^1, rack^1, reckon, interrogate, prerogative,* and *reckless.*

reg-. To move in a straight line, with derivatives meaning "to direct in a straight line, lead, rule."
I. Basic form **reg-.* **1.** Suffixed form **reg-to-.* RIGHT, from Old English *riht,* right, just, correct, straight, from Germanic **rehtaz.* **2.** REALM, RECTITUDE, RECTO, RECTOR, RECTUM, REGENT, REGIME, REGIMENT, REGION; CORRECT, DIRECT, ERECT, (PORRECT), RECTANGLE, RECTIFY, RECTILINEAR, (RESURGE), (RISORGIMENTO), SURGE, from Latin *regere,* to lead straight, guide, rule (past participle *rēctus,* hence adjective *rēctus,* right, straight). **3.** ANORECTIC, ANOREXIA, from Greek *oregein,* to stretch out, reach out for (with prothetic vowel from oldest root form **əreg-*).
II. Lengthened-grade form **rēg-,* Indo-European word for a tribal king. **1.a.** BISHOPRIC, ELDRITCH, from Old English *rīce,* realm; **b.** RIKSMÅL, from Old Norse *rīki,* realm; **c.** REICHSMARK, from Old High German *rīchi,* realm; **d.** RICH, from Old English *rīce,* strong, powerful, and Old French *riche,* wealthy. **a, b, c,** and **d** all from Germanic **rīkja-,* from Celtic suffixed form **rīg-yo-.* **2.** REAL^2, REGAL, REGULUS, REIGN, ROYAL; REGICIDE, REGIUS PROFESSOR, VICEREINE, VICEROY, from Latin *rēx,* king (royal and priestly title). **3.** Suffixed form **rēg-en-.* RAJ, RAJAH, (RANI), (RYE^2); MAHARAJAH, MAHARANI, from Sanskrit *rājā, rājan-,* king, rajah (feminine *rājñī,* queen, rani), and *rājati,* he rules.
III. Suffixed lengthened-grade form **rēg-olā.* RAIL^1, REGLET, REGULAR, REGULATE, RULE, from Latin *rēgula,* straight piece of wood, rod.
IV. O-grade form **rog-.* **1.** RAKE^1, from Old English *raca, racu,* rake (implement with straight pieces of wood), from Germanic **rakō.* **2.** RACK^1, from Middle Dutch *rec,* framework, from Germanic **rak-.* **3.** RANK^2, from Old English *ranc,* straight, strong, hence haughty, overbearing, from Germanic **rankaz* (with nasal infix), possibly from **reg-.** **4.** RECKON, from Old English *gerecenian,* to arrange in order, recount (*ge-,* collective prefix; see **kom**), from Germanic **rakinaz,* ready, straightforward. **5.** Suffixed form **rog-ā-.* ROGATION, ROGATORY; ABROGATE, ARROGATE, CORVÉE, DEROGATE, INTERROGATE, PREROGATIVE, PROROGUE, SUBROGATE, SUPEREROGATE, from Latin *rogāre,* to ask (< "stretch out the hand"). **6.** Suffixed form **rog-o-.* ERGO, from Latin *ergō,* therefore, in consequence of, perhaps contracted from a Latin phrase **ē rogō,* "from the direction of" (*ē* < *ex,* out of; see **eghs**), from a possible Latin noun **rogus,* "extension, direction."
V. Lengthened o-grade form **rōg-.* **1.** RECK, Old English *rec(c)an,* to pay attention to, take care (formally influenced by Old English *reccan,* to extend, stretch out, from Germanic **rakjan*), from Germanic

…English *rēceléas*, … from Germanic …

…*ll, rival, rivulet,* …

…grade form *ri-… English *rinnan,* to …, to run (from Germanic … *ri-nw-an*), and from Old En… *ærnan, eornan,* to run (from second… Germanic causative *rannjan*); **b.** EMBER DAY, from Old English *ryne,* a running, from secondary Germanic derivative *runiz;* **c.** RENNET, from Old English *rynet, from secondary Germanic derivative *runita-*. **2.** Suffixed zero-grade form *ri-l-*. RILL, from Dutch *ril* or Low German *rille,* running stream, from Germanic *ril-*. **3.** Suffixed form *rei-wo-*. RIVAL, RIVULET; DERIVE, from Latin *rīvus,* stream. [Pokorny 3. *er-* 326.]

reidh-. Important derivatives are *ride, raid, road, ready,* and *array.*

reidh-. To ride.
I. Basic form *reidh-*. **1.a.** RIDE, from Old English *rīdan,* to ride; **b.** RITTER, from Middle Dutch *rīden,* to ride. Both **a** and **b** from Germanic *rīdan*. **2.** PALFREY, from Latin *verēdus,* post horse, from Celtic *wo-rēd-* (*wo-,* under; see **upo**).
II. O-grade form *roidh-*. **1.a.** RAID, ROAD, from Old English *rād,* a riding, road; **b.** RADDLE[1], from Middle High German *reidel,* rod between upright stakes (< "wooden horse"), possibly from **reidh-.** Both **a** and **b** from Germanic *raid-*. **2.** READY, from Old English *rǣde, gerǣde,* ready (< "prepared for a journey"), from Germanic *raid-ja-*, probably from **reidh-.** **3.** ARRAY, CURRY[1], from Vulgar Latin *-rēdāre,* to arrange, from Germanic *raidjan,* probably from **reidh-.** [Pokorny *reidh-* 861.]

reig-. Important derivatives are *reach, rigid,* and *rigor.*

reig-. To reach, stretch out. **1.** O-grade form *roig-*. REACH, from Old English *rǣcan,* to stretch out, reach, from Germanic *raikjan*. **2.** Possibly suffixed (stative) zero-grade form *rig-ē-*. RIGID, RIGOR, from Latin *rigēre,* to be stiff (? < "be stretched out"). [Pokorny *(reiĝ)* 862.]

rep-. Important derivatives are *rape[1], rapid, rapt, ravish,* and *surreptitious.*

rep-. To snatch. Suffixed zero-grade form *rap-yo-*. RAPACIOUS, RAPE[1], RAPID, RAPINE, RAPT, (RAVEN[2]), RAVIN, RAVISH; EREPSIN, (SUBREPTION), SURREPTITIOUS, from Latin *rapere,* to seize. [Pokorny *rep-* 865.]

ret-. Important derivatives are *Tory, rodeo, roll, rotary, rotate, rotund, roulette, round[1], control,* and *prune[2]*.

ret-. To run, roll. **1.** Prefixed form *to-wo-ret-*, "a running up to" (*to-,* to; *wo,* under, up, up from under; see **upo**). TORY, from Old Irish *tōir,* pursuit. **2.** Suffixed o-grade form *rot-ā-*. RODEO, ROLL, ROTA, ROTARY, ROTATE, ROTUND, (ROTUNDA), ROULETTE, ROUND[1], ROWEL; BAROUCHE, CONTROL, PRUNE[2], ROTIFORM, ROTOGRAVURE, from Latin *rota,* wheel. **3.** Suffixed (participial) form *ret-ondo-*. ROTUND, from Latin *rotundus,* round, probably from *retundus,* "rolling." [Pokorny *ret(h)-* 866.]

reudh-. Important derivatives are *red, rufous, robust, corroborate, rambunctious, ruddy, rust, rouge, rubeola, ruby, rubric,* and *russet.*

reudh-. Red, ruddy.
I. O-grade form *roudh-*. **1.a.** RED, from Old English *rēad,* red; **b.** RORQUAL, from Old Norse *raudhr,* red. Both **a** and **b** from Germanic *raudaz*. **2.** ROWAN, from a source akin to Old Norse *reynir,* mountain ash, rowan (from its red berries), from Germanic *raudnia-*. **3.** RUFESCENT, RUFOUS, from Latin *rūfus* (of dialectal Italic origin), reddish. **4.** RUBIGINOUS, from Latin *rōbus,* red. **5.** ROBLE, ROBORANT, ROBUST; CORROBORATE, (RAMBUNCTIOUS), from Latin *rōbur, rōbus,* red oak, hardness, and *rōbustus,* strong.
II. Zero-grade form *rudh-*. **1.** Form *rudh-ā-*. **a.** RUDDLE, from Old English *rudu,* red color; **b.** RUDDOCK, from Old English *rudduc,* robin; **c.** RUDDY, from Old English *rudig,* ruddy. **a, b,** and **c** all from Germanic *rudō*. **2.** Suffixed form *rudh-sto-*. RUST, from Old English *rūst* (also *rust?*), rust, from Germanic *rust-*. **3.** ROUGE, RUBEOLA, RUBY; RUBEFACIENT, from Latin *rubeus,* red. **4.** RUBICUND, from Latin *rubicundus,* red, ruddy. **5.** RUBIDIUM, from Latin *rubidus,* red. **6.** Suffixed (stative) form *rudh-ē-*. RUBESCENT, from Latin *rubēre,* to be red. **7.** Suffixed form *rudh-ro-*. **a.** RUBELLA, RUBRIC; BILIRUBIN, from Latin *ruber,* red; **b.** RUTILANT, from Latin *rutilus,* reddish; **c.** ERYTHEMA, ERYTHRO-, from Greek *eruthros,* red (with prothetic vowel, from oldest root form *əreudh-*); **d.** ERYSIPELAS, from possibly remade Greek *erusi-,* red, reddening. **8.** Suffixed form *rudh-to-*. RISSOLE, ROUX, RUSSET, from Latin *russus,* red. [Pokorny *reudh-* 872.]

reuə-. Important derivatives are *room, rummage, rural,* and *rustic.*

reuə-. To open; space. **1.** Suffixed variant form *rū-mo-* (< *ruə-mo-*). **a.** ROOM, from Old English *rūm,* space; **b.** LEBENSRAUM, from Old High German *rūm,* space; **c.** RUMMAGE, from Old Provençal *run,* ship's hold, space. **a, b,** and **c** all from Germanic *rūmaz;* **d.** REAM[2], from Old English *rȳman,* to widen, open up, from Germanic denominative *rūmjan*. **2.** Suffixed form *reu(ə)-es-*. RURAL, RUSTIC, from Latin *rūs,* "open land," the country. [Pokorny *reuə-, rū-* 874.]

reug-. An important derivative is *reek.*

reug-. To vomit, belch; smoke, cloud. **1.** REEK, from Old English *rēocan,* to smoke, reek, and *rēcan,* to fumigate, from Germanic *reukan*. **2.** Suffixed zero-grade form *rug-to-*. ERUCT, from Latin *ructāre,* to belch. [Pokorny 4. *reu-* 871.]

reup-. Important derivatives are *rip[1], bereave, rover, rob, robe, loot, usurp, rout[1], rupture, abrupt, bankrupt, corrupt, disrupt, erupt,* and *interrupt.*

reup-. Also **reub-.** To snatch.
I. Basic form *reub-*. RIP[1], from Flemish *rippen,* to rip, from Germanic *rupjan*.
II. O-grade form *roup-*. **1.a.** REAVE[1], from Old English *rēafian,* to plunder; **b.** BEREAVE, from Old English *berēafian,* to take away (*be-, bi-,* intensive prefix; see **ambhi**); **c.** ROVER[2], from Middle Dutch and Middle Low German *roven,* to rob. **a, b,** and **c** all from Germanic *(bi-)raubōn*. **2.a.** ROB, from Old French *rober,* to rob; **b.** RUBATO, from Italian *rubare,* to rob. Both **a** and **b** from a Romance borrowing from Germanic *raubōn,* to rob. **3.** ROBE, from Old French *robe,* robe (< "clothes taken as booty"), from Germanic *raubō,* booty. **4.** Suffixed form *roup-tro-*. LOOT, from Sanskrit *loptram,* booty. **5.** RUBLE, from Old Russian *rubiti,* to chop, hew, from Slavic *rubje/a-*.
III. Zero-grade form *rup-*. **1.** USURP, from Latin *ūsūrpāre* (< *ūsu-rup-; ūsus,* use, usage, from *ūtī,* to use), originally "to interrrupt the orderly acquisition of something by the act of using," whence to take into use, usurp. **2.** Nasalized form *ru-m-p-*. ROUT[1], RUPTURE; ABRUPT, BANKRUPT, CORRUPT, DISRUPT, ERUPT, INTERRUPT, IRRUPT, RUPICOLOUS, from Latin *rumpere,* to break. [Pokorny 2. *reu-* 868.]

r̥tko-. Important derivatives are *arctic* and *Arthur.*

r̥tko-. Bear. **1.** URSINE, from Latin *ursus,* bear (< *orcsos*). **2.** ARCTIC, ARCTURUS, from Greek *arktos,* bear. [Pokorny *r̥̂ko-s* 875.]

sā-. Important derivatives are *sad, sate[1], satiate, asset, satisfy, satire,* and *saturate.*

sā-. To satisfy. Contracted from *saə-*. **1.** Suffixed zero-grade form *sə-to-*. **a.** SAD, from Old English *sæd,* sated, weary, from Germanic *sadaz,* sated; **b.** SATE[1], from Old English *sadian,* to sate, from derivative Germanic verb *sadōn,* to satisfy, sate. **2.** Suffixed zero-grade form *sə-ti-*. SATIATE, SATIETY; (ASSAI[2]), ASSET, SATISFY, from Latin *satis,* enough, sufficient. **3.** Suffixed zero-grade form *sə-tu-ro-*. SATIRE, SATURATE, from Latin *satur,* full (of food), sated. **4.** Suffixed zero-grade form *sə-d-ro-*. HADRON, from Greek *hadros,* thick. [Pokorny *sā-* 876.]

sāg-. Important derivatives are *seek, sake[1], forsake, ransack, presage, sagacious,* and *hegemony.*

sāg-. To seek out. Contracted from *saəg-*. **1.** Suffixed form *sāg-yo-*. SEEK, from Old English *sēcan, sēcan,* to seek, from Germanic *sōkjan*. **2.** Suffixed form *sāg-ni-*. SOKE, from Old English *sōcn,* attack, inquiry, right of local jurisdiction, from Germanic *sōkniz*. **3.** Zero-grade form *səg-*. **a.** SAKE[1], from Old English *sacu,* lawsuit, case, from Germanic derivative noun *sakō,* "a seeking," accusation, strife; **b.** *(i)* FORSAKE, from Old English *forsacan,* to renounce, refuse (*for-,* prefix denoting exclusion or rejection; see **per[1]**); *(ii)* RANSACK, from Old Norse *saka,* to seek. Both *(i)* and *(ii)* from Germanic *sakan,* to seek, accuse, quarrel. Both **a** and **b** from Germanic *sak-*. **4.** Independent suffixed form *sāg-yo-*. PRESAGE, from Latin *sāgīre,* to perceive, "seek to know." **5.** Zero-grade form *səg-*. SAGACIOUS, from Latin *sagāx,* of keen perception. **6.** Suffixed form *sāg-eyo-*. EXEGESIS, HEGEMONY, from Greek *hēgeisthai,* to lead (< "to track down"). [Pokorny *sāg-* 876.]

sak-. Important derivatives are *sacred, consecrate, execrate, saint, sanctum,* and *sanctify.*

sak-. To sanctify. **1.** Suffixed form *sak-ro-*. **a.** SACRED; CONSECRATE, EXECRATE, from Latin *sacer,* holy, sacred, dedicated; **b.** compound *sakro-dhōt-*, "performer of sacred rites" (*-dhōt-,* doer; see **dhē-**). SACERDOTAL, from Latin *sacerdōs,* priest. **2.** Nasalized form *sa-n-k-*. SAINT, (SANCTUM); CORPOSANT, SACROSANCT, SANCTIFY, from Latin *sancīre* (past participle *sanctus*), to make sacred, consecrate. [Pokorny *sak-* 878.]

sal-. Important derivatives are *salt, silt, sauce, salad, salami, salary, saline, saltcellar,* and *saltpeter.*

sal-. Salt. **1.** Extended form *sald-*. **a.** suffixed form *sald-o-*. SALT, from Old English *sealt,* salt, from Germanic *saltam;* **b.** *(i)* SOUSE[1], from Old French *sous,* pickled meat; *(ii)* SILT, from Middle English *cylte,* fine sand, from a source probably akin to Danish and Norwegian *sylt,* salt marsh. Both *(i)* and *(ii)* from Germanic zero-grade suffixed extended form *sult-jō;* **c.** (SALSA), SAUCE, from Latin *sallere* (past participle *salsus* < *sald-to-*), to salt. **2.** SAL, SALAD, SALAMI, SALARY, SALI-, SALINE; SALTCELLAR, SALTPETER, from Latin *sāl* (genitive *salis*), salt. **3.** HALO-, from Greek *hals* (stem *hal-*), salt, sea. [Pokorny 1. *sal-* 878.]

sāwel-. Important derivatives are *sun, Sunday, south, southern, solar, parasol, solstice,* and *helium.*

sāwel-. Also **s(u)wel-, su(ə)el-, su(ə)en-, sun-.** The sun. Contracted from *saəwel-*. **1.** Variant forms *swen-, *sun-*. **a.** *(i)* SUN, from Old English *sunne,* sun; *(ii)* SUNDEW, from Middle Dutch *sonne,* sun. Both *(i)* and *(ii)* from Germanic *sunnōn-;* **b.** SUNDAY, from Old English *sunnandæg,* Sunday, from Germanic compound *sunnōn-dagaz,* "day of the sun" (translation of Latin *diēs sōlis*); **c.** SOUTH, SOUTHERN, from Old English *sūth,* south, and *sūtherne,* southern, from Germanic derivative *sunthaz,* "sun-side," south. **2.** Variant form *s(ə)wōl-*. SOL[3], SOL, SOLAR, SOLARIUM; GIRASOL, INSOLATE, PARASOL, SOLANINE, SOLSTICE, TURNSOLE, from Latin *sōl,* the sun. **3.** Suffixed form *sāwel-yo-*. HELIACAL, HELIO-, HELIUM; ANTHELION, APHELION, ISOHEL, PARHELION, PERIHELION, from Greek *hēlios,* sun. [Pokorny *sāwel-* 881.]

sē-. Important derivatives are *sow[1], seed, season, semen, seminary,* and *disseminate.*

sē-. To sow. Contracted from *seə-*. **1.** SOW[1], from Old English *sāwan,* to sow, from Germanic *sēan*. **2.** Suffixed form *sē-ti-*, sowing. **a.** SEED, from Old English *sǣd,* seed; **b.** COLZA, from Middle Dutch *saet* and Middle Low German *sāt,* seed. Both **a** and **b** from Germanic *sēdiz,* seed. **3.** Reduplicated zero-grade form *si-s(ə)-*. SEASON, from Latin *serere,* to sow, *satiō* (< *sə-tiō*), sowing. **4.** Suffixed form *sē-men-*, seed. SEMÉ, SEMEN, SEMINARY; DISSEMINATE, from Latin *sēmen,* seed. [In Pokorny 2. *sē(i)-* 889.]

sed-. Important derivatives are *sit, set[1], ersatz, settle, saddle, soot, seat, séance, sedentary, sediment, session, siege, assess, dissident, obsess, possess, preside, reside, subsidy, supersede, subside, sedate[1], soil[1],* and *chair.*

sed-. To sit. **1.** Suffixed form *sed-yo-*. **a.** SIT, from Old English *sittan,* to sit; **b.** SITZ BATH, SITZKRIEG, SITZMARK, from Old High German *sizzen,* to sit. Both **a** and **b** from Germanic *sitjan*. **2.** Suffixed (causative) o-grade form *sod-eyo-*. **a.** SET[1], from Old English *settan,* to place; **b.** BESET, from Old English *besettan,* to set near; **c.** ERSATZ, from Old High German *irsezzan,* to replace, from *sezzan,* to set. **a, b,** and **c** all from Germanic **(bi-)satjan,* to cause to sit, set. **3.** Suffixed form **sed-lo-,* seat. SETTLE, from Old English *setl,* seat, from Germanic **setlaz.* **4.** O-grade form **sod-.* SADDLE, from Old English *sadol,* saddle, from Germanic **sadulaz,* seat, saddle (perhaps from **sod-dhlo-*). **5.** Suffixed lengthened o-grade form **sōd-o-.* SOOT, from Old English *sōt,* soot (< "that which settles"), from Germanic **sōtam.* **6.** Suffixed lengthened-grade form *sēd-i-,* settler. COSSET, possibly from Old English *sǣta, -sǣte,* inhabitant(s), from Germanic **sāti-.* **7.** Suffixed lengthened-grade form **sēd-yo-.* SEAT, from Old Norse *sæti,* seat, from Germanic **(ge)sēt-jam,* seat (**ge-, *ga-,* collective prefix; see **kom**). **8.** Form **sed-ē-.* SÉANCE, SEDENTARY, SEDERUNT, SEDILE, SEDIMENT, SESSILE, SESSION, SEWER[2], SIEGE; ASSESS, ASSIDUOUS, DISSIDENT, (INSESSORIAL), INSIDIOUS, OBSESS, POSSESS, PRESIDE, RESIDE, SUBSIDY, SUPERSEDE, from Latin *sedēre,* to sit. **9.** Reduplicated form **si-zd-.* **a.** SUBSIDE, from Latin *sīdere,* to sit down, settle; **b.** SYNIZESIS, from Greek *hizein,* to sit down, settle down. **10.** Lengthened-grade form **sēd-.* SEE[2], from Latin *sēdēs,* seat, residence. **11.** Lengthened-grade form **sēd-ā-.* SEDATE[1], from Latin *sēdāre,* to settle, calm down. **12.** Suffixed o-grade form **sod-yo-.* SOIL[1], from Latin *solium,* throne, seat. **13.** Suffixed form **sed-rā-.* -HEDRON; CATHEDRA, (CHAIR), EPHEDRINE, EXEDRA, SANHEDRIN, TETRAHEDRON, from Greek *hedra,* seat, chair, face of a geometric solid. **14.** Prefixed and suffixed form **pi-sed-yo-,* to sit upon (**pi,* on; see **epi**). PIEZO-; ISOPIESTIC, from Greek *piezein,* to press tight. **15.** Basic form **sed-.* **a.** EDAPHIC, from Greek *edaphos,* ground, foundation (with Greek suffix *-aphos*); **b.** UPANISHAD, from Sanskrit *upaniṣad,* Upanishad, from *sad-;* **c.** TANIST, from Old Irish *tānaise,* designated successor, from Celtic **tānihessio-,* "one who is waited for," from **to-ad-ni-sed-tio,* from **to-ad-ni-sed-,* to wait for. **16.** Suffixed form **sed-o-,* sitting. EISTEDDFOD, from Welsh *eistedd,* sitting, from Celtic **eks-dī-sedo-* (see **eghs, de-**). [Pokorny *sed-* 884.]

segh-. Important derivatives are *hectic, eunuch, epoch, scheme, scholar, scholastic,* and *school*[1].

segh-. To hold. **1.** Suffixed form **segh-es-.* SIEGFRIED, from Old High German *sigu, sigo,* victory, from Germanic **sigiz-,* victory (< "a holding or conquest in battle"). **2.** HECTIC; CACHEXIA, CATHEXIS, ECHARD, ENTELECHY, EUNUCH, OPHIUCHUS, from Greek *ekhein,* to hold, possess, be in a certain condition, and *hexis,* habit, condition. **3.** O-grade form **sogh-.* EPOCH, from Greek *epokhē,* "a holding back," pause, cessation, position in time (*epi-,* on, at; see **epi**). **4.** Zero-grade form **sgh-.* **a.** SCHEME, from Greek *skhēma,* "a holding," form, figure; **b.** (SCHOLAR), SCHOLASTIC, SCHOLIUM, SCHOOL[1], from Greek *skholē,* "a holding back," stop, rest, leisure, employment of leisure in disputation, school. **5.** Reduplicated form **si-sgh-.* ISCHEMIA, from Greek *iskhein,* to keep back. [Pokorny *seĝh-* 888.]

sek-. Important derivatives are *scythe, saw*[1]*, sedge, Saxon, skin, secant, section, sector, segment, dissect, insect, intersect,* and *sickle.*

sek-. To cut. **1.** SCYTHE, from Old English *sīthe, sigthe,* sickle, from Germanic **segithō,* sickle. **2.** Suffixed o-grade form **sok-ā-.* SAW[1], from Old English *sagu, sage,* saw, from Germanic **sagō,* a cutting tool, saw. **3.** Suffixed o-grade form **sok-yo-.* SEDGE, from Old English *secg,* sedge, from Germanic **sagjaz,* "sword," plant with a cutting edge. **4.** Suffixed o-grade form **sok-so-.* SAXON, from Late Latin *Saxō,* (plural *Saxonēs*), a Saxon, from West Germanic tribal name **Saxon-,* Saxon, traditionally (but doubtfully) regarded as from Germanic **sahsam,* knife, sword (as if "warrior with knives"). **5.** Extended root **skend-,* to peel off, flay. SKIN, from Old Norse *skinn,* skin, from Germanic **skinth-.* **6.** Basic form **sek-.* SECANT, -SECT, SECTILE, SECTION, SECTOR, SEGMENT; DISSECT, INSECT, INTERSECT, RESECT, (TRANSECT), from Latin *secāre,* to cut. **7.** Lengthened-grade form **sēk-.* SICKLE, from Latin *sēcula,* sickle. **8.** Possible suffixed variant form **sak-so-.* **a.** ZAX, from Old English *seax,* knife; **b.** SAXATILE; SAXICOLOUS, SAXIFRAGE, from Latin *saxum,* stone (< "broken-off piece"?). [Pokorny 2. *sĕk-* 895, *sken-(d-)* 929.] See also extended roots **skei-, sker-**[1]**, sker-**[3]**.**

sekʷ-[1]**.** Important derivatives are *sect, sequel, sequence, sue, suitor, consequent, ensue, execute, persecute, prosecute, pursue, subsequent, sequester, second*[2]*, intrinsic, seal*[1]*, sign, assign, designate, insignia, resign, social, society, associate,* and *dissociate.*

sekʷ-[1]**.** To follow. **1.** SECT, SEGUE, SEGUIDILLA, SEQUACIOUS, SEQUEL, SEQUENCE, SUE, SUITOR; CONSEQUENT, ENSUE, EXECUTE, OBSEQUIOUS, PERSECUTE, PROSECUTE, (PURSUE), SUBSEQUENT, from Latin *sequī,* to follow. **2.** SEQUESTER, SEQUESTRUM, from Latin *sequester,* "follower," mediator, depositary. **3.** Suffixed (participial) form **sekʷ-ondo-.* SECOND[2], SECONDO, SECUND, SECUNDINES, from Latin *secundus,* following, coming next, second. **4.** Suffixed form **sekʷ-os,* following. EXTRINSIC, INTRINSIC, from Latin *secus,* along, alongside of. **5.** Suffixed form **sekʷ-no-.* SEAL[1], SEGNO, SIGN; ASSIGN, CONSIGN, DESIGNATE, INSIGNIA, RESIGN, from Latin *signum,* identifying mark, sign (< "standard that one follows"). **6.** Suffixed o-grade form **sokʷ-yo-.* SOCIABLE, SOCIAL, SOCIETY, SOCIO-; ASSOCIATE, CONSOCIATE, DISSOCIATE, from Latin *socius,* ally, companion (< "follower"). [Pokorny 1. *sekᵘ̯-* 896.]

sekʷ-[2]**.** Important derivatives are *see*[1] and *sight.*

sekʷ-[2]**.** To perceive, see. **1.** SEE[1], from Old English *sēon,* to see, from Germanic **sehwan,* to see. **2.** SIGHT, from Old English *sihth, gesiht,* vision, spectacle, from Germanic abstract noun **sih-tiz.* [Pokorny 2. *sekᵘ̯-* 897.]

sekʷ-[3]**.** Important derivatives are *say, saw*[2]*, saga,* and *scold.*

sekʷ-[3]**.** To say, utter. **1.** O-grade form **sokʷ-.* **a.** suffixed form **sokʷ-yo-.* SAY, from Old English *secgan,* to say, from Germanic **sagjan;* **b.** suffixed form **sokʷ-ā-.* *(i)* SAW[2], from Old English *sagu,* a saying, speech; *(ii)* SAGA, from Old Norse *saga,* a saying, narrative. Both *(i)* and *(ii)* from Germanic **sagō,* a saying. **2.** Perhaps suffixed zero-grade form **skʷ-e-tlo-,* narration. SCOLD, SKALD, from Middle English *scolde,* an abusive person, and Old Norse *skāld,* poet, "satirist" (to which the probable Scandinavian source of Middle English *scolde* is perhaps akin), from North Germanic **skathla.* [In Pokorny 2. *sekᵘ̯-* 897.]

sel-. Important derivatives are *salient, sally, sauté, assail, desultory, exult, insult, result, somersault,* and *salmon.*

sel-. To jump. **1.** Suffixed zero-grade form **sal-yo-.* **a.** SALACIOUS, SALIENT, SALLY, (SAUTÉ); ASSAIL, DESULTORY, DISSILIENT, EXULT, INSULT, RESILE, RESULT, SOMERSAULT, from Latin *salīre,* to leap; **b.** HALTER[2], from Greek *hallesthai,* to leap, jump. **2.** SALMON, from Latin *salmō* (borrowed from Gaulish), salmon (< "the leaping fish"), perhaps from **sel-.** [Pokorny 4. *sel-* 899.]

sem-[1]**.** Important derivatives are *simultaneous, assemble, ensemble, single, Sanskrit, same, anomalous, seem, seemly, some, similar, assimilate, resemble, simplicity,* and *simple.*

sem-[1]**.** One; also adverbially "as one," together with.
I. Full-grade form **sem-.* **1.a.** HENDECASYLLABIC, HENDIADYS, HENOTHEISM, HYPHEN, from Greek *heis* (< nominative singular masculine **hen-s* < **hem-s*), one; **b.** (see **dekm̥**) Greek *he-* in *hekaton,* one hundred (? dissimilated from **hem-katon*). Both **a** and **b** from Greek **hem-.* **2.** Suffixed form **sem-el-.* SIMULTANEOUS; ASSEMBLE, ENSEMBLE, from Latin *simul,* at the same time. **3.** Suffixed form **sem-golo-.* SINGLE, from Latin *singulus,* alone, single. **4.** Compound **sem-per-* (**per,* during, for; see **per**[1]). SEMPRE; SEMPITERNAL, from Latin *semper,* always, ever (< "once for all").
II. O-grade form **som-.* **1.** SAMSARA, SANDHI, SANSKRIT, from Sanskrit *sam,* together. **2.** Suffixed form **som-o-.* **a.** SAME, from Old Norse *samr,* same, from Germanic **samaz,* same; **b.** HOMEO-, HOMO-; ANOMALOUS, from Greek *homos,* same; **c.** HOMILY, from Greek *homilos,* crowd. **3.** Suffixed form **som-alo-.* HOMOLOGRAPHIC, from Greek *homalos,* like, even, level.
III. Lengthened o-grade form **sōm-.* **1.** Suffixed form **sōm-i-.* SEEM, SEEMLY, from Old Norse *sœmr,* fitting, agreeable (< "making one," "reconciling"), from Germanic **sōmiz.* **2.** Suffixed lengthened o-grade form **sōm-o-.* SAM[illegible] Russian *sam(o)-,* self.
IV. Zero-grade form **sm̥-.* **1.** [illegible] LUTHON, from Greek compound *a-ko*[illegible] panying (*a-* + *keleuthos,* way, path), [illegible] together. **2.** Compound form **sm̥-p*[illegible] -fold; see **pel-**[2]). HAPLOID, from Greek *hap*[illegible] *lous,* single, simple. **3.** Suffixed form **sm̥m*[illegible] SOME, from Old English *sum,* one, a certain one[illegible] -SOME[1], from Old English *-sum,* -like. Both **a** and [illegible] from Germanic **sumaz.* **4.** Suffixed form **sm̥m-alo-.* SIMILAR; ASSIMILATE, RESEMBLE, from Latin *similis,* of the same kind, like. **5.** Compound **sm̥-kēro-,* of one growing (see **ker-**[2]). **6.** Suffixed form **sm̥-tero-.* HETERO-, from Greek *heteros* (earlier *hateros*), one of two, other. **7.** Compound **sm̥-plek-,* "one-fold," simple (**plek-,* -fold; see **plek-**). SEMPLICE, SIMPLEX, SIMPLICITY, from Latin *simplex,* simple. **8.** Compound **sm̥-plo-,* "one-fold," simple (**-plo-,* -fold; see **pel-**[2]). SIMPLE, from Latin *simplus,* simple. **9.** Extended form **sm̥ma.* HAMADRYAD, from Greek *hama,* together with, at the same time. [Pokorny 2. *sem-* 902.]

sem-[2]**.** An important derivative is *summer*[1].

sem-[2]**.** Also **seme-.** Summer. Suffixed zero-grade form **sm̥ə-aro-.* SUMMER[1], from Old English *sumor,* summer, from Germanic **sumaraz.* [Pokorny 3. *sem-* 905.]

sēmi-. An important derivative is *semi-.*

sēmi-. Half. **1.** SAND-BLIND, from Old English *sām-,* half, from Germanic **sēmi-.* **2.** SEMI-, from Latin *sēmi-*, half. **3.** SESQUI-, SESTERCE, from Latin *sēmis,* half. **4.** HEMI-, from Greek *hēmi-* , half. [Pokorny *sēmi-* 905.]

sen-. Important derivatives are *senate, senescent, senile, senior, sir, sire,* and *surly.*

sen-. Old. SEIGNIOR, SENATE, SENECTITUDE, SENESCENT, SENILE, SENIOR, SENOPIA, (SIGNORY), (SIR), SIRE, (SURLY), from Latin *senex,* old, an elder. [Pokorny *sen(o)-* 907.]

sengʷh-. Important derivatives are *sing* and *song.*

sengʷh-. To sing, make an incantation. **1.a.** SING, from Old English *singan,* to sing; **b.** MEISTERSINGER, MINNESINGER, SINGSPIEL, from Old High German *singan,* to sing. Both **a** and **b** from Germanic **singan.* **2.** Suffixed o-grade form **songʷh-o-,* singing, song. SONG, from Old English *sang, song,* song, from Germanic **sangwaz.* [Pokorny *sengᵘ̯h-* 906.]

sent-. Important derivatives are *send*[1]*, godsend, scent, sense, sentence, sentinent, sentiment, sentinel, assent, consent, dissent,* and *resent.*

sent-. To head for, go. **1.** WIDDERSHINS, from Old High German *sin(d),* direction, from Germanic form **sinthaz.* **2.** Suffixed (causative) o-grade form **sont-eyo-.* SEND[1], from Old English *sendan,* to send, from Germanic **sandjan,* to cause to go. **3.** Suffixed o-grade form **sont-o-.* GODSEND, from Old English *sand,* message, messenger, from Germanic **sandaz,* that which is sent. **4.** Perhaps suffixed form **sent-yo-.* SCENT, SENSE, (SENSILLIUM), SENTENCE, SENTIENT, SENTIMENT, SENTINEL; ASSENT, CONSENT, DISSENT, PRESENTIMENT, RESENT, from Latin *sentīre,* to feel (< "to go mentally"). [Pokorny *sent-* 908.]

sep-. Important derivatives are *sage*[1]*, sapient, savant, savor, savvy,* and *insipid.*

sep-. To taste, perceive. Suffixed zero-grade form **sap-yo-.* SAGE[1], SAPID, SAPIENT, SAPOR, SAVANT, SAVOR, SAVVY; INSIPID, from Latin *sapere,* to taste, have taste, be wise. [Pokorny *sap-* 880.]

septm̥. Important derivatives are *seven, September,* and *septet.*

septm̥. Seven. **1.** SEVEN; SEVENTEEN, SEVENTY, from Old English *seofon,* seven, with derivatives *(hund)seofontig,* seventy, and *seofontīne,* seventeen (*-tīne,* ten; see **dekm̥**), from Germanic **sebum.* **2.** SEPTEMBER, SEPTENNIAL, SEPTET, SEPTUAGINT, SEPTUPLE; SEPTENTRION, from Latin *septem,* seven. **3.** HEBDOMAD, HEPTA-, HEPTAD, from Greek *hepta,* seven. [Pokorny *septm̥* 909.]

...nserve, observe, ...o.

...n *serw-. CON- ..., (RESERVOIR), ...e. **2.** Perhaps ...ōs-. HERO, from ...ny 2. *ser-* 910.]

...ves are *series, assert, exert, ...rcerer, sort, assort,* and *consort.*

...r-[2]**.** To line up. **1.** SERIES, SERTULARIAN; ASSERT, DESERT[3], DISSERTATE, EXERT, INSERT, from Latin *serere,* to arrange, attach, join (in speech), discuss. **2.** Suffixed form **ser-mon-.* SERMON, from Latin *sermō* (stem *sermōn-*), speech, discourse. **3.** Perhaps suffixed form **ser-ā-.* SEAR[2], (SERRIED), from Latin *sera,* a lock, bolt, bar (? < "that which aligns"). **4.** Suffixed zero-grade form **sr̥-ti-.* SORCERER, SORT; ASSORT, CONSORT, SORTILEGE, from Latin *sors* (stem *sort-*), lot, fortune (probably from the lining up of lots before drawing). **5.** Suffixed o-grade form **sor-mo-.* HORMOGONIUM, from Greek *hormos,* chain, necklace. [Pokorny 4. *ser-* 911.]

seuə-[1]**.** An important derivative is *son.*

seuə-[1]**.** To give birth. Suffixed zero-grade form in derivative noun **su(ə)-nu-,* son. SON, from Old English *sunu,* son, from Germanic **sunuz.* [Pokorny 2. *seu-* 913.] See also **sū-**.

seuə-[2]**.** Important derivatives are *soup, sup*[2]*, sop, sip, suck, soak, suction,* and *succulent.*

seuə-[2]**.** To take liquid.
I. Suffixed zero-grade form **suə-yo-,* contracted to **sū-yo.* HYETAL; ISOHYET, from Greek *huetos,* rain, from *huein,* to rain.
II. Possible extended zero-grade form **sūb-.* **1.a.** SUP[1], from Old English *sūpan, sūpian,* to drink, sip; **b.** SOUP, (SUP[2]), from Old French *soup(e),* soup. Both **a** and **b** from Germanic **sūp-.* **2.a.** SOP, from Old English *sopp-* in *soppcuppe,* cup for dipping bread in; **b.** SIP, from Middle English *sippen,* to sip, from a source probably akin to Low German *sippen,* to sip, possibly from **seuə-**[2]. Both **a** and **b** from Germanic **supp-.*
III. Possible extended zero-grade form **sūg-.* **1.** SUCK, from Old English *sūcan,* to suck, from Germanic **sūk-.* **2.** SOAK, from Old English *socian,* to steep, from Germanic shortened form **sukōn.* **3.** SUCTION, SUCTORIAL, from Latin *sūgere,* to suck. **4.** Variant form **sūk-.* SUCCULENT, from Latin *sūcus, succus,* juice. [Pokorny 1. *seu-* 912.]

skand-. Important derivatives are *scan, scansion, ascend, descend, transcend, scandal,* and *scale*[2]*.*

skand-. Also **skend-.** To leap, climb. **1.** SCAN, SCANDENT, SCANSION, SCANSORIAL; ASCEND, (CONDESCEND), DESCEND, TRANSCEND, from Latin *scandere,* to climb. **2.** Suffixed form **skand-alo-.* SCANDAL, from Greek *skandalon,* a snare, trap, stumbling block. **3.** Suffixed form **skand-slā-.* ECHELON, ESCALADE, SCALE[2], from Latin *scālae,* steps, ladder.

skei-. Important derivatives are *shin*[1]*, science, conscious, nice, shit, schism, rescind, shed*[1]*, sheath, ski, esquire,* and *squire.*

skei-. To cut, split. Extension of **sek-.** **1.a.** SHIN[1], from Old English *scinu,* shin, shinbone (< "piece cut off"); **b.** CHINE, from Old French *eschine,* backbone, piece of meat with part of the backbone. Both **a** and **b** from Germanic suffixed form **ski-nō-.* **2.** SCIENCE, SCILICET, SCIOLISM; ADSCITITIOUS, CONSCIENCE, CONSCIOUS, NESCIENCE, (NICE), OMNISCIENT, PLEBISCITE, PRESCIENT, from Latin *scīre,* to know (< "to separate one thing from another," "discern.") **3.** Suffixed zero-grade form **skiy-enā.* SKEAN, from Old Irish *scīan,* knife. **4.** Extended root **skeid-.* **a.** *(i)* SHIT, from Old English **scītan,* to defecate; *(ii)* SKATE[3], from Old Norse *skīta,* to defecate; *(iii)* SHYSTER, from Old High German *skīzzan,* to defecate. *(i), (ii),* and *(iii)* all from Germanic **skītan,* to separate, defecate; **b.** suffixed zero-grade form **sk(h)id-yo-.* SCHISM, SCHIST, SCHIZO-, from Greek *skhizein,* to split; **c.** nasalized zero-grade form **ski-n-d-.* SCISSION; EXSCIND, PRESCIND, RESCIND, from Latin *scindere,* to split. **5.** Extended root **skeit-.* **a.** *(i)* SHED[1], from Old English *scēadan,* to separate; *(ii)* SHEATH, from Old English *scēath,* sheath (< "split stick"), perhaps from **skei-.** Both *(i)* and *(ii)* from Germanic **skaith-, *skaidan;* **b.** SKI, from Old Norse *skīdh,* log, stick, snowshoe, from Germanic **skīdam;* **c.** o-grade form **skoit-.* ÉCU, ESCUDO, ESCUTCHEON, ESQUIRE, SCUDO, SCUTUM, (SQUIRE), from Latin *scūtum,* shield (< "board"). **6.** Extended root **skeip-.* **a.** SHEAVE[2], from Middle English *sheve,* pulley (< "piece of wood with grooves"); **b.** SKIVE, from a Scandinavian source akin to Old Norse *skīfa,* to slice, split; **c.** SHIVER[2], from Middle English *shivere, scivre,* splinter, possibly from a Low German source akin to Middle Low German *schever,* splinter. **a, b,** and **c** all from Germanic **skif-.* [Pokorny *skei-* 919.]

skel-[1]**.** Important derivatives are *shell, shale, scale*[1]*, scalp, shield, skill, cutlass, shelf, half, scalpel,* and *sculpture.*

skel-[1]**.** Also **kel-.** To cut. **1.a.** SHELL, from Old English *scell, sciel,* shell; **b.** SCAGLIOLA, from Italian *scaglia,* chip. Both **a** and **b** from Germanic **skaljō,* piece cut off, shell, scale. **2.a.** SHALE, from Old English *sc(e)alu,* husk, shell; **b.** SCALE[1], from Old French *escale,* husk, shell. Both **a** and **b** from Germanic **skalō.* **3.a.** SCALL, from Old Norse *skalli,* bald head (< "closely shaved skull"); **b.** SCALP, from Middle English *scalp,* top of the head, from a source akin to Old Norse *skalpr,* sheath, shell. Both **a** and **b** from Germanic **skal-.* **4.** SCALE[3], SKOAL, from Old Norse *skāl,* bowl, drinking vessel (made from a shell), from Germanic **skēlō.* **5.** SHIELD, from Old English *scield,* shield (< "board"), from Germanic **skelduz.* **6.a.** SKILL, from Old Norse *skil,* reason, discernment, knowledge (< "incisiveness"); **b.** SHELDRAKE, from Middle English *scheld,* variegated, from a Low German source akin to Middle Dutch *schillen,* to diversify, with past participle *schillede,* separated, variegated. Both **a** and **b** from Germanic **skeli-.* **7.** SCHOOL[2], SHOAL[2], from Middle Low German *schōle,* troop, or Middle Dutch *scōle,* both from Germanic **skulō,* a division. **8.** Suffixed variant form **kel-tro-.* COULTER, CULTRATE, CUTLASS, from Latin *culter,* knife. **9.** Suffixed zero-grade form **skl̥-yo-.* SCALENE, from Greek *skallein,* to stir up, hoe (> *skalenos,* uneven). **10.** Extended root **skelp-.* **a.** SHELF, from Middle Low German *schelf,* shelf (< "split piece of wood"), from Germanic **skelf-;* **b.** HALF, from Old English *healf,* half, from Germanic **halbaz* (< variant root **kelp-*), divided possibly from **skel-**[1]; **c.** perhaps variant **skalp-.* SCALPEL, SCULPTURE, from Latin *scalpere,* to cut, scrape, with derivative *sculpere* (originally as the combining form of *scalpere*), to carve [Pokorny 1. *(s)kel-* 923.]

skel-[2]**.** An important derivative is *shall.*

skel-[2]**.** To be under an obligation. O-grade (perfect) form **skol-.* SHALL, from Old English *sceal* (used with the first and third person singular pronouns), shall, from Germanic **skal,* I owe, hence I ought. [Pokorny 2. *(s)kel-* 927.]

sker-[1]**.** Important derivatives are *shear, share*[1]*, shears, scabbard, score, shard, short, shirt, skirt, skirmish, screen, carnage, carnal, carnation, carnival, carrion, carnivorous, incarnate, curt, cortex, sharp, scrap*[1]*, scrape, scrub*[1]*, shrub*[1]*,* and *screw.*

sker-[1]**.** Also **ker-.** To cut.
I. Basic form **sker-, *ker-.* **1.a.** SHEAR, from Old English *scieran, sceran,* to cut; **b.** SHEER[1], from Low German *scheren,* to move to and fro, and Dutch *scheren,* to withdraw, depart. Both **a** and **b** from Germanic **skeran.* **2.a.** SHARE[2], from Old English *scēar,* plowshare; **b.** SHARE[1], from Old English *scearu, scaru,* portion, division (but recorded only in the sense of "fork of the body," "tonsure"). Both **a** and **b** from Germanic **skeraz.* **3.a.** SHEAR, from Old English *scēar,* scissors, from Germanic **skēr-ō-* and **sker-ez-;* **b.** compound **skēr-berg-,* "sword protector," scabbard (see **bhergh-**[1]). SCABBARD, from Old French *escauberc,* scabbard, possibly from a Germanic source akin to Old High German *scarberc,* scabbard. Both **a** and **b** from Germanic **skēr-.* **4.** SCORE, from Old Norse *skor,* notch, tally, twenty, from Germanic **skur-.* **5.** SCAR[2], SKERRY, from Old Norse *sker,* low reef (< "something cut off"), from Germanic suffixed form **skar-jam.* **6.** Suffixed o-grade extended form **skorp-o-.* SCARF[2], from Old Norse *skarfr,* diagonally-cut end of a board, from Germanic **skarfaz.* **7.** Suffixed o-grade extended form **skord-o-.* SHARD, from Old English *sceard,* a cut, notch, from Germanic **skardaz.* **8.** Extended form **skerd-* in suffixed zero-grade form **skr̥d-o-.* **a.** SHORT, from Old English *scort, sceort,* "cut," short; **b.** SHIRT, from Old English *scyrte,* skirt (< "cut piece"); **c.** SKIRT, from Old Norse *skyrta,* shirt. **a, b,** and **c** all from Germanic **skurtaz.* **9.a.** SKIRMISH, from Old French *eskermir,* to fight with a sword, fence, and Old Italian *scaramuccia,* skirmish, from a source akin to Old High German *skirmen,* to protect; **b.** SCREEN, from Middle Dutch *scherm,* shield. Both **a** and **b** from Germanic extended form **skerm-.* **10.** Variant form **kar-.* CARNAGE, CARNAL, CARNASSIAL, CARNATION, CARNIVAL, CARRION, CARUNCLE, CHARNEL, CRONE; CARNIVOROUS, INCARNATE, from Latin *carō* (stem *carn-*), flesh. **11.** Suffixed o-grade form **kor-yo.* CORIACEOUS, CORIUM, CUIRASS, CURRIER; EXCORIATE, from Latin *corium,* leather (originally "piece of hide"). **12.** Suffixed zero-grade form **kr̥-to-.* CURT, CURTAL, KIRTLE, from Latin *curtus,* short. **13.** Suffixed o-grade form **kor-mo-.* CORM, from Greek *kormos,* a trimmed tree trunk. **14.** Suffixed o-grade form **kor-i-.* COREOPSIS, from Greek *koris,* bedbug (< "cutter"). **15.** Suffixed zero-grade form. SHORE[1], from Old English *scora,* shore, from Germanic **skur-ō.*
II. Extended roots **skert-, *kert-.* **1.** Zero-grade form **kr̥t-* or o-grade form **kort-.* CORTEX; DECORTICATE, from Latin *cortex,* bark (< "that which can be cut off"). **2.** Suffixed form **kert-snā-.* CENACLE, from Latin *cēna,* meal (< "portion of food").
III. Extended root **skerp-.* SCURF, probably from a Scandinavian source akin to Old English *sceorf,* scab, scurf, from Germanic **skerf-.*
IV. Extended root **skerb(h)-, *skreb(h)-.* **1.a.** SHARP, from Old English *scearp,* slope; **b.** SCARP, from Italian *scarpa,* embankment, possibly from a Germanic source akin to Gothic *skarpō,* pointed object. Both **a** and **b** from Germanic **skarpaz,* cutting, sharp. **2.a.** SCRAP[1], from Old Norse *skrap,* "pieces," remains; **b.** SCRAPE, from Old Norse *skrapa,* to scratch. Both **a** and **b** from Germanic **skrap-.* **3.a.** SCRABBLE, from Middle Dutch *schrabben,* to scrape; **b.** SCRUB[1], from Middle Dutch *schrobben,* to scrape. Both **a** and **b** from Germanic **skrab-.* **4.** SHRUB[1], from Old English *scrybb,* shrub (< "rough plant"), from Germanic **skrub-.* **5.** SCROBICULATE, from Latin *scrobis,* trench, ditch. **6.** SCREW, SCROFULA, from Latin *scrōfa,* a sow (< "rooter, digger"). [Pokorny 4. *sker-,* Section I. 938.]

sker-[2]**.** Important derivatives are *shrink, ring*[1]*, ranch, range, rank*[1]*, rink, arrange, ridge, curb, curve, crest, crepe, crisp, circle, search,* and *crown.*

sker-[2]**.** Also **ker-.** To turn, bend. Presumed base of a number of distantly related derivatives. **1.** Extended form **(s)kreg-* in nasalized form **(s)kre-n-g-.* **a.** SHRINK, from Old English *scrincan,* to wither, shrivel up, from Germanic **skrink-;* **b.** variant **kre-n-g-.* *(i)* RUCK[2], from Old Norse *hrukka,* a crease, fold; *(ii)* FLOUNCE[1], from Old French *fronce,* pleat, from Frankish **hrunkjan,* to wrinkle. Both *(i)* and *(ii)* from Germanic **hrunk-.* **2.** Extended form **(s)kregh-* in nasalized form **skre-n-gh-.* **a.** RING[1], from Old English *hring,* a ring; **b.** RANCH, RANGE, RANK[1], RINK; ARRANGE, DERANGE, from Old French *renc, reng,* line, row; **c.** RINGHALS, from Middle Dutch *rinc* (combining form *ring-*), a ring. **a, b,** and **c** all from Germanic **hringaz,* something curved, circle. **3.** Extended form **kreuk-.* **a.** RIDGE, from Old English *hrycg,* spine, ridge; **b.** RUCKSACK, from Old High German *hrukki,* back. Both **a** and **b** from Germanic *hrugjaz.* **4.** Suffixed variant form **kurwo-.* CURB, CURVATURE, CURVE, CURVET, from Latin *curvus,* bent, curved. **5.** Suffixed extended form **kris-ni-.* CRINOLINE, from Latin *crīnis* (< **crisnis*), hair. **6.** Suffixed extended form **kris-tā-.* CREST, CRISTA, CRISTATE, from Latin *crista,* tuft, crest. **7.** Suffixed extended form **krip-so-.* CREPE, CRISP, CRISPATE, from Latin *crispus* (metathesized from **cripsus*), curly. **8.** Extended expressive form **krīss-.* CRISSUM, from Latin *crīsāre,* (of women) to wiggle the hips during copulation. **9.** Perhaps reduplicated form **ki-kr-o-.* (CIRCA), CIRCLE, (CIRCUM-), SEARCH; CRICOID, from Greek *krikos* (with metathesis), a ring. **10.** Suffixed o-grade form **kor-ōno-.* (CORONA), CROWN, from Greek *korōnos,* curved. **11.** Suffixed variant form **kur-to.* KURTOSIS, from Greek *kurtos,* bent. [Pokorny 3. *(s)ker-* 935.]

sker-[3]**.** A derivative is *dreck.*

sker-[3]**.** Excrement, dung. Extension of **sek-,** "to cut, separate," hence "to void excrement." **1.** Suffixed unextended form **sk-ōr/n-.* SCATO-, SCORIA, SKATOLE, from Greek *skōr* (genitive *skatos* < **sk-n̥t-*), dung. **2.** Extended form **skert-* in taboo metathesis **sterk-os-.* **a.** STERCORACEOUS, from

Latin *stercus,* dung; **b.** variant forms **(s)terg-, *(s)treg-.* DRECK, from Middle High German *drëc,* dung, from Germanic **threkka-.* [Pokorny *sk̑er-d-* 947, 8. *(s)ter-* 1031.]

(s)keu-. Important derivatives are *sky, meerschaum, scum, obscure, hide*[2], *cuticle, recoil, hose, hoard, hide*[1], and *hut.*

(s)keu-. To cover, conceal. Zero-grade form **(s)ku-.* Variant **(s)keuə-,* zero-grade form **(s)kuə-,* contracted to **(s)kū-.* **1.** Suffixed basic form. **a.** SKY, from Old Norse *ský,* cloud; **b.** SKEWBALD, from a Scandinavian source akin to Old Norse *ský,* cloud. Both **a** and **b** from Germanic **skeu-jam,* cloud ("cloud cover"). **2.** Zero-grade form **skū-.* **a.** suffixed form **skū-mo-.* *(i)* SKIM, from Old French *escume,* scum; *(ii)* MEERSCHAUM, from Old High German *scūm,* scum; *(iii)* SCUM, from Middle Dutch *schūm,* scum. *(i), (ii),* and *(iii)* all from Germanic **skūmaz,* foam, scum (< "that which covers the water"); **b.** suffixed form **skū-ro-.* OBSCURE; CHIAROSCURO, from Latin *obscūrus,* "covered," dark (*ob-,* away from; see **epi**). **3.** Zero-grade form **kū̆-.* **a.** suffixed form **kū-ti-.* HIDE[2], from Old English *hȳd,* skin, hide, from Germanic **hūdiz;* **b.** suffixed form **ku-ti-.* CUTANEOUS, CUTICLE, CUTIS; CUTIN, from Latin *cutis* skin; **c.** possibly suffixed form **kū-lo-.* CULET, CULOTTE; BASCULE, RECOIL, from Latin *cūlus,* the rump, backside; **d.** suffixed form **ku-to-.* -CYTE, CYTO-, from Greek *kutos,* a hollow, vessel. **4.** Extended zero-grade form **kus-.* **a.** *(i)* HOSE, from Old English *hosa, hose,* covering for the leg; *(ii)* LEDERHOSEN, from Old High German *hosa,* leg covering. Both *(i)* and *(ii)* from Germanic **husōn-;* **b.** suffixed form **kus-dho-* (or suffixed extended form **kudh-to-*). HOARD, from Old English *hord,* stock, store, treasure (< "thing hidden away"), from Germanic **huzdam;* **c.** KISHKE, from Russian *kishka,* gut (< "sheath"). **5.** Suffixed extended zero-grade form **kut-no-.* CUNNILINGUS, from Latin *cunnus,* vulva (< "sheath"). **6.** Extended root **keudh-.* **a.** HIDE[1], from Old English *hȳdan,* to hide, cover up, from Germanic suffixed lengthened zero-grade form **hūd-jan;* **b.** HUT, from French *hutte,* hut, from Germanic suffixed zero-grade form **hūd-jōn-;* **c.** HUDDLE, from Low German *hudeln,* to crowd together, probably from Germanic **hŭd-.* **7.** SHIELING, from a Scandinavian source akin to Old Norse *skāli,* hut, from Germanic suffixed o-grade form **skaw-ala-.* [Pokorny 2. *(s)keu-* 951.]

skeud-. Important derivatives are *shoot, shot*[1], *shut, shuttle, sheet*[1], and *scuttle*[1].

skeud-. To shoot, chase, throw. **1.** SHOOT, from Old English *scēotan,* to shoot, from Germanic **skeutan,* to shoot. **2.a.** SHOT[1], from Old English *sceot, scot,* shooting, a shot; **b.** SCHUSS, from Old High German *scuz,* shooting, a shot; **c.** SCOT, (SCOT AND LOT), from Old Norse *skot* and Old French *escot,* contribution, tax (< "money thrown down"); **d.** WAINSCOT, from Middle Dutch *sc(h)ot,* crossbar, wooden partition. **a, b, c,** and **d** all from Germanic **skutaz,* shooting, shot. **3.** SHUT, from Old English *scyttan,* to shut (by pushing a crossbar), probably from Germanic **skutjan.* **4.** SHUTTLE, from Old English *scytel,* a dart, missile, from Germanic **skutilaz.* **5.a.** SHEET[2], from Old English *scēata,* corner of a sail; **b.** SHEET[1], from Old English *scēte,* piece of cloth. Both **a** and **b** from Germanic **skautjōn-.* **6.a.** SCOUT[2], from a Scandinavian source akin to Old Norse *skūta,* mockery (< "shooting of words"); **b.** SHOUT, from Old Norse *skūta,* a taunt. Both **a** and **b** from Germanic **skut-.* [Pokorny 2. *(s)keud-* 956.]

skrībh-. Important derivatives are *scribble, scribe, script, Scripture, ascribe, circumscribe, conscript, describe, inscribe, manuscript, postscript, prescribe, subscribe,* and *transcribe.*

skrībh-. To cut, separate, sift. Extension of **sker-**[1]. **1.** SCRIBBLE, SCRIBE, SCRIPT, SCRIPTORIUM, SCRIPTURE, SERIF, SHRIVE; ASCRIBE, CIRCUMSCRIBE, CONSCRIPT, DESCRIBE, FESTSCHRIFT, INSCRIBE, MANUSCRIPT, POSTSCRIPT, PRESCRIBE, PROSCRIBE, RESCRIPT, SUBSCRIBE, SUPERSCRIBE, TRANSCRIBE, from Latin *scrībere,* to scratch, incise, write. **2.** SCARIFY[1], from Greek *skariphos,* scratching, sketch, pencil. [Pokorny 4. *sker-,* Section II. 945.]

slēb-. An important derivative is *sleep.*

slēb-. To be weak, sleep. Possibly related to **slēg-** through a hypothetical base **slē-* (< **sleə-*). SLEEP, from Old English *slǣpan,* to sleep, and *slǣp,* sleep, from Germanic **slēpan, *slēpaz.* [In Pokorny 1. *leb-* 655.]

slēg-. Important derivatives are *slack*[1], *lax, relax,* and *languish.*

slēg-. To be slack, be languid. Possibly related to **slēb-** through a hypothetical base **slē-* (< **sleə-*). Zero-grade form **slag-,* becoming **slag-.* **1.** SLACK[1], from Old English *slæc,* "loose," indolent, careless, from Germanic **slak-.* **2.** Suffixed form **lag-so-.* LAX; RELAX, from Latin *laxus,* loose, slack. **3.** Suffixed nasalized form **la-n-g-u-.* LANGUISH, from Latin *languēre,* to be languid. **4.** Compound **lag-ous-,* "with drooping ears" (**ous-,* ear; see **ous-**). LAGOMORPH, from Greek *lagōs, lagos,* hare. **5.** Suffixed form **lag-no-.* ALGOLAGNIA, from Greek *lagnos,* lustful, lascivious. **6.** Basic form **slēg-.* CATALECTIC, from Greek *lēgein,* to leave off. [Pokorny *(s)lēg-* 959.]

sleubh-. Important derivatives are *sleeve, lubricate, cowslip, slop*[1], and *sloop.*

sleubh-. To slide, slip.
I. Basic form **sleubh-.* **1.** SLEEVE, from Old English *slēf, slīf, slīef,* sleeve (into which the arm slips), from Germanic **sleub-.* **2.** SLOVEN, from Middle Low German *slôven,* to put on clothes carelessly, from Germanic **slaubjan.* **3.** Suffixed form **sleubh-ro-.* LUBRICATE, LUBRICITY, LUBRICIOUS, from Latin *lūbricus,* slippery.
II. 1. a. SLIP[3]; COWSLIP, OXLIP, from Old English *slypa, slyppe, slipa,* slime, slimy substance; **b.** SLOP[1], from Old English **sloppe,* dung; **c.** SLOP[2], from Old English *(ofer)slop,* surplice. **a, b,** and **c** all from Germanic **slup-.* **2.** SLOOP, from Middle Dutch *slūpen,* to glide. Both **1** and **2** from variant Germanic root form **sleup-.* [Pokorny *sleub(h)-* 963.]

slī-. Derivatives are *sloe* and *livid.*

slī-. Bluish. Contracted from **sliə-.* **1.** O-grade form **sloi-.* SLOE, from Old English *slāh, slā,* sloe (< "bluish fruit"), from Germanic **slaihwōn.* **2.** Suffixed form **slī-wo-.* LIVID, from Latin *līvēre,* to be bluish. **3.** Suffixed form **slī-wā-.* SLIVOVITZ, from Serbo-Croatian *šljiva,* plum [Pokorny *(s)lī-* 965.]

smei-. Important derivatives are *smirk, smile, marvel, miracle, mirage, mirror,* and *admire.*

smei-. To laugh, smile. **1.** SMIRK, from Old English *smercian,* to smile (with *-k-* formative), from Germanic reshaped forms **smer-, *smar-.* **2.** SMILE, from Middle English *smilen,* to smile, from a Scandinavian source probably akin to Swedish *smila,* to smile, from Germanic extended form **smīl-.* **3.** Suffixed form **smei-ro-.* MARVEL, MIRACLE, MIRAGE, MIRROR; ADMIRE, from Latin *mīrus,* wonderful. **4.** Prefixed zero-grade form **ko(m)-smi-,* smiling with (**ko-, *kom-,* together; see **kom**). COMITY, from Latin *cōmis* (< *cosmis*), courteous. [Pokorny 1. *(s)mei-* 967.]

(s)mer-[1]**.** Important derivatives are *mourn, memorable, mermorandum, memory, commemorate,* and *remember.*

(s)mer-[1]**.** To remember. **1.** Suffixed zero-grade form **mr̥-no-.* MOURN, from Old English *murnan,* to mourn, from Germanic **murnan,* to remember sorrowfully. **2.** Reduplicated form **me-mor-.* **a.** MIMIR, from Old Norse *Mimir,* a giant who guards the well of wisdom, from Germanic **mi-mer-;* **b.** MEMORABLE, (MEMORANDUM), MEMORY; COMMEMORATE, REMEMBER, from Latin *memor,* mindful. [Pokorny *(s)mer-* 969.]

(s)mer-[2]**.** Important derivatives are *merit* and *emeritus.*

(s)mer-[2]**.** To get a share of something. **1.** Suffixed (stative) form **mer-ē-.* MERETRICIOUS, MERIT; EMERITUS, TURMERIC, from Latin *merēre, merērī,* to receive a share, deserve, serve. **2.** Suffixed form **mer-o-.* -MERE, MERISTEM, MERO-, -MEROUS; (ALLOMERISM), (DIMER), (ISOMER), (MONOMER), (TRIMER), from Greek *meros* (feminine *meris*), a part, division. [In Pokorny *(s)mer-* 969.]

snā-. Derivatives are *natant* and *natation.*

snā-. To swim. Contracted from **snaə-.* **1.** Extended form **snāgh-.* NEKTON, from Greek *nēkhein,* to swim. **2.** Suffixed zero-grade form **(s)nə-to-.* NATANT, NATATION, NATATORIA[illegible] PERNATANT, from Latin *natāre,* [illegible] SONESE, from Greek *nēsos,* islan[illegible] some to this root (but more likely obs[illegible] *snā-* 971.] See **(s)nāu-.**

(s)nāu-. Important derivatives are *nouris*[illegible] *nutrient,* and *nutrition.*

(s)nāu-. To swim, flow, let flow, whence suck[illegible] Contracted from **snaəu-;* extension of **snā-. 1.** Suffixed basic form **nāw-yo-.* NAIAD, from Greek *Naias,* fountain nymph, probably from *naein,* to flow. **2.** Variant root form **(s)neu(ə)-.* NEUSTON, from Greek *nein,* to swim. **3.** Zero-grade form **(s)nū-* (< **snuə-*) in suffixed form **nū-trī* (with feminine agent suffix). NOURISH, NURSE, NURTURE, NUTRIENT, NUTRIMENT, NUTRITION, NUTRITIOUS, NUTRITIVE, from Latin *nūtrīx,* nurse, and *nūtrīre,* to suckle, nourish. [In Pokorny *snā-* 971.]

(s)nē-. An important derivative is *needle.*

(s)nē-. Also **nē-.** To spin, sew. Contracted from **(s)neə-.* **1.** Suffixed form **nē-tlā.* NEEDLE, from Old English *nǣdl,* needle, from Germanic **nēthlō.* **2.** Suffixed form **snē-mn̥.* NEMATO-; AXONEME, CHROMONEMA, PROTONEMA, SYNAPTINEMAL COMPLEX, TREPONEMA, from Greek *nēma,* thread. **3.** Suffixed o-grade form **snō-tā-.* SNOOD, from Old English *snōd,* headband, from Germanic **snōdō.* [Pokorny *(s)nē-* 973.]

(s)neəu-. Important derivatives are *neuron* and *nerve.*

(s)neəu-. Tendon, sinew. Extension of **(s)nē-.** Suffixed form **(s)neəw-r̥-,* with further suffixes. **a.** **neu-r-o-.* NEURO-, NEURON; APONEUROSIS, from Greek *neuron,* sinew; **b.** metathesized form **nerwo-.* NERVE; ENERVATE, from Latin *nervus,* sinew. [Pokorny *snēu-* 977.]

so-. Important derivatives are *the*[1] and *she.*

so-. This, that (nominative). For other cases see **to-. 1.** THE[1], from Late Old English *the,* masculine demonstrative pronoun, replacing *se* (with *th-* from oblique forms; see **to-**). **2.** HOI POLLOI, from Greek *ho,* the. **3.** Feminine form **syā.* SHE, from Old English *sēo, sīe,* she, from Germanic **sjō.* **4.** Compound variant form **sei-ke* (**-ke,* "that"; see **ko-**). SIC[1], from Latin *sīc,* thus, so, in that manner. [Pokorny *so(s), sā, sī* 978.]

sol-. Important derivatives are *solid, consolidate, catholic, solicitous, solemn, salute, safe, salvage, salvo,* and *save*[1].

sol-. Also **sole-.** Whole.
I. Basic form **sol-.* **1.** Suffixed form **sol-ido-.* SOLID; CONSOLIDATE, from Latin *solidus,* solid. **2.** Suffixed form **sol-wo-.* HOLO-; CATHOLIC, from Greek *holos,* whole. **3.** Dialectal geminated form **soll-o-.* **a.** SOLICITOUS, from Latin *sollus,* whole, entire, unbroken; **b.** SOLEMN, from Latin *sollemnis* (second element obscure), celebrated at fixed dates (said of religious rites), established, religious, solemn.
II. Variant form **solə-.* **1.** Suffixed zero-grade form *sl̥ə-u-* giving **sal-u-.* SALUBRIOUS, SALUTARY, SALUTE, from Latin *salūs,* health, a whole or sound condition. **2.** Suffixed zero-grade form **sl̥ə-wo-* giving **sala-wo-.* SAFE, SAGE[2], SALVAGE, SALVO, SAVE[1], SAVE[2], from Latin *salvus,* whole, safe, healthy, uninjured. [Pokorny *solo-* 979.]

spē-. Important derivatives are *speed, despair,* and *prosper.*

spē-. To thrive, prosper. Contracted from **speə-.* **1.** Suffixed o-grade form **spō-ti-.* SPEED, from Old English *spēd,* success, from Germanic **spōdiz.* **2.** Suffixed form **spē-s-.* DESPAIR, ESPERANCE, from Latin *spērāre,* to hope, denominative of *spēs* (plural *spērēs*), hope. **3.** Suffixed zero-grade form **spə-ro-.* PROSPER, from Latin *prosperus,* favorable, prosperous (traditionally regarded as from *prō spērē,* according to one's hope; *pro-,* according to; see **per**[1]). [Pokorny 3. *sp(h)ēi-* 983.]

spek-. Important derivatives are *spy, espionage, specimen, spectacle, spectrum, speculate, aspect, circumspect, conspicuous, despise, expect, inspect, perspective, prospect, respect, respite, suspect, species,*

…, and *telescope.*

… SPY, from Old … AGE, from Old … rivative **speh-* … manic **spehōn.* … MEN, SPECIOUS, … PECULUM; AS- … SPISE, EXPECT, … PERSPECTIVE, … ECT, SUSPECT, … look at. **3.** … *-ēs,* a seeing, … (see **gherə-**) Latin *haruspex,* diviner; **b.** (see **awi-**) Latin *auspex,* augur. Both **a** and **b** from Latin *-spex* (< **-spek-*), "he who sees." **5.** Suffixed form **spek-ā-.* DESPICABLE, from Latin (denominative) *dēspicārī,* to despise, look down on (*dē-,* down; see **de-**). **6.** Suffixed metathetical form **skep-yo-.* SKEPTIC, from Greek *skeptesthai,* to examine, consider.
II. Extended o-grade form **spoko-.* SCOPE, -SCOPE, -SCOPY; BISHOP, EPISCOPAL, HOROSCOPE, TELESCOPE, from metathesized Greek *skopos,* one who watches, also object of attention, goal, and its denominative *skopein* (< **skop-eyo-*), to see. [Pokorny *spek̂-* 984.]

(s)pen-. Important derivatives are *spider, spin, spindle, pansy, pendant*[1], *pension*[1], *pensive, poise*[1], *append, appendix, compensate, depend, dispense, expend, penthouse, perpendicular, suspend, span*[1], *pound*[1], *ponder,* and *spontaneous.*

(s)pen-. To draw, stretch, spin.
I. Basic form **spen-.* **1.** Suffixed form **spen-wo-.* **a.** SPIDER, SPIN, from Old English *spinnan,* to spin, and *spīthra,* spider, contracted from Germanic derivative **spin-thrōn-,* "the spinner"; **b.** SPINDLE, from Old English *spinel,* spindle, from Germanic derivative **spin-ilōn-.* Both **a** and **b** from Germanic **spinnan,* to spin. **2.** Extended form **pend-.* PAINTER[2], (PANSY), PENCHANT, PENDANT[1], PENDENTIVE, PENDULOUS, PENSILE, PENSION[1], PENSIVE, PESO, POISE[1]; ANTEPENDIUM, APPEND, (APPENDIX), AVOIRDUPOIS, COMPENDIUM, COMPENSATE, DEPEND, DISPENSE, EXPEND, IMPEND, (PENTHOUSE), PERPEND, PERPENDICULAR, PREPENSE, PROPEND, SUSPEND, VILIPEND, from Latin *pendēre,* to hang (intransitive), and *pendere,* to cause to hang, weigh, with its frequentative *pēnsāre,* to weigh, consider. **3.** Perhaps suffixed form **pen-ya-.* -PENIA, from Greek *penia,* lack, poverty (< "a strain, exhaustion"). **4.** GEOPONIC, LITHOPONE, from Greek *ponos,* toil, and *ponein,* to toil, o-grade derivatives of *penesthai,* to toil.
II. O-grade forms **spon-, *pon-.* **1.a.** SPAN[2], from Middle Dutch *spannen,* to bind; **b.** SPANNER, from Old High German *spannan,* to stretch. Both **a** and **b** from Germanic **spannan.* **2.** SPAN[1], from Old English *span(n),* distance, from Germanic **spanno-.* **3.** SPANGLE, from Middle Dutch *spange,* clasp, from Germanic **spangō,* perhaps from **(s)pen-.** **4.** Suffixed and extended form **pond-o-.* POUND[1], from Latin *pondō,* by weight. **5.** Suffixed and extended form **pond-es-.* PONDER, PONDEROUS; EQUIPONDERATE, PREPONDERATE, from Latin *pondus* (stem *ponder-*), weight, and its denominative *ponderāre,* to weigh, ponder. **6.** Suffixed o-grade form **spon-t-.* SPONTANEOUS, from Latin *sponte,* of one's own accord, spontaneously, possibly from **(s)pen-,** but more likely to a homophonous Germanic verb **spanan,* to entice. [Pokorny *(s)pen-(d)-* 988.]

spend-. Important derivatives are *sponsor, spouse,* and *respond.*

spend-. To make an offering, perform a rite, hence to engage oneself by a ritual act. O-grade from **spond-.* **1.** Suffixed form **spond-eyo-.* SPONSOR, SPOUSE; DESPOND, ESPOUSE, RESPOND, from Latin *spondēre,* to make a solemn promise, pledge, betroth. **2.** Suffixed form **spond-ā.* SPONDEE, from Greek *spondē,* libation, offering. [Pokorny *spend-* 989.]

sper-. Important derivatives are *sprawl, sprout, spurt, spread, Diaspora, sperm*[1], *spore, sporadic,* and *spray*[1].

sper-. To strew.
I. Zero-grade form **spr-.* **1.** SPRAWL, from Old English *sprēawlian,* to sprawl, from Germanic **spr-.* **2.** Extended form **spreud-.* **a.** SPROUT, from Old English *sprūtan,* to sprout; **b.** SPRITZ, SPRITZER, from Middle High German *sprützen,* to spurt, spray; **c.** SPRIT, from Old English *sprēot,* pole (< "sprout, stem"); **d.** BOWSPRIT, from Middle Low German *bōchsprēt,* bowsprit. **a, b, c,** and **d** all from Germanic **sprūt-.* **3.** Extended form **spreit-.* SPRAY[2], SPREAD, from Old English *-sprǣdan,* to spread, from Germanic **spraidjan.*
II. Basic form **sper-.* **1.** Suffixed form **sper-yo-.* DIASPORA, from Greek *speirein,* to scatter, with derivative *spora,* a scattering, sowing (see **III. 1.**). **2.** Suffixed form **sper-mn̥.* SPERM[1], from Greek *sperma,* sperm, seed (< "that which is scattered").
III. O-grade form **spor-.* **1.** Suffixed form **spor-ā-.* SPORE, SPORO-, from Greek *spora,* a sowing, seed. **2.** Suffixed form **spor-n̥d-.* SPORADIC, from Greek *sporas* (stem *sporad-*), scattered, dispersed.
IV. Extended Germanic root **sprē(w)-.* SPRAY[1], from Middle Dutch *spraeien, sprayen,* to sprinkle, from Germanic **sprēwjan.* [Pokorny 2. *(s)p(h)er-* 993.]

sperə-. Important derivatives are *spur, spurn,* and *spoor.*

sperə-. Ankle. Zero-grade form **spr̥(ə)-.* **1.** SPUR, from Old English *spura, spora,* spur, from Germanic suffixed form **spur-ōn-.* **2.** Nasalized form **spr̥-n-ə-.* SPURN, from Old English *spurnan, spornan,* to kick, strike against, from Germanic **spurnōn.* **3.** SPOOR, from Middle Dutch *spor, spoor,* track of an animal, from Germanic suffixed form **spur-am.* [Pokorny 1. *sp(h)er-* 992.]

sreu-. Important derivatives are *stream, diarrhea, hemorrhoid,* and *rhythm.*

sreu-. To flow. **1.** Suffixed o-grade form **srou-mo-.* **a.** STREAM, from Old English *strēam,* stream; **b.** MAELSTROM, from Middle Dutch *stroom,* stream. Both **a** and **b** from Germanic **straumaz,* stream. **2.** Basic form **sreu-.* **a.** RHEO-, -RRHEA; CATARRH, DIARRHEA, HEMORRHOID, RHYOLITE, from Greek *rhein,* to flow, with o-grade *rhoos,* flowing, a flowing; **b.** suffixed form **sreu-mn̥.* RHEUM, from Greek *rheuma,* stream, humor of the body. **3.** Suffixed zero-grade form **sru-dhmo-.* RHYTHM, from Greek *rhuthmos,* measure, recurring motion, rhythm. **4.** Zero-grade extended form **srug-.* SASTRUGA, from Russian *struga,* deep place, perhaps from **sreu-.** [Pokorny *sreu-* 1003.]

stā-. Important derivatives are *steed, stud*[2], *stool, stage, stance, stanza, stay*[1], *arrest, circumstance, constant, contrast, cost, distant, instant, obstacle, obstetric, rest*[2], *substance, stand, understand, standard, stem*[1], *station, static, destine, obstinate, state, statue, statute, institute, prostitute, substitute, superstition, establish, stable*[1], *assist, exist, insist, resist, ecstasy, system, post*[1], *store, steer*[1], and *steer*[2].

stā-. To stand; with derivatives meaning "place or thing that is standing." Contracted from **staə-.*
I. Basic form **stā-.* **1.** Extended form **stādh-.* **a.** STEED, from Old English *stēda,* stallion, studhorse (< "place for breeding horses"), from Germanic **stōd-jōn-;* **b.** STUD[2], from Old English *stōd,* establishment for breeding horses, from Germanic **stōdō.* **2.** Suffixed form **stā-lo-.* **a.** STOOL, from Old English *stōl,* stool; **b.** (see **pel-**[2]) Germanic compound **faldistōlaz.* Both **a** and **b** from Germanic **stōlaz.* **3.** ESTANCIA, STAGE, STANCE, STANCH[1], STANCHION, (STANZA), STATOR, STAY[1], STET; ARREST, CIRCUMSTANCE, CONSTANT, CONTRAST, (COST), DISTANT, EXTANT, INSTANT, OBSTACLE, OBSTETRIC, (OUST), REST[2], RESTIVE, SUBSTANCE, from Latin *stāre,* to stand. **4.** Suffixed form **stā-men-.* ETAMINE, STAMEN, STAMMEL, from Latin *stāmen,* thread of the warp (a technical term). **5.** Suffixed form **stā-mon-.* PENSTEMON, from Greek *stēmōn,* thread. **6.** Suffixed form **stā-ro-.* STARETS, from Old Church Slavonic *starŭ,* old ("long-standing").
II. Zero-grade form **stə-* (before consonants). **1.** Nasalized extended form **stə-n-t-.* **a.** STAND, from Old English *standan,* to stand; **b.** UNDERSTAND, from Old English *understandan,* to know, stand under (*under-,* under-; see **n̥dher**); **c.** STANDARD, from Frankish **standan,* to stand; **d.** STOUND, from Old English *stund,* a fixed time, while, from secondary zero-grade form in Germanic **stund-ō.* **a, b, c,** and **d** all from Germanic **standan.* **2.** Suffixed form **stə-tyo-.* STITHY, from Old Norse *stedhi,* anvil, from Germanic **stathjōn-.* **3.** Suffixed form **stə-tlo-.* STADDLE, STARLING[2], from Old English *stathol,* foundation, from Germanic **stathlaz.* **4.** Suffixed form **stə-mno-.* STEM[1], from Old English *stefn,* stem, tree trunk, from Germanic **stamniz.* **5.** Suffixed form **stə-ti-.* **a.** *(i)* STEAD, from Old English *stede,* place; *(ii)* STADHOLDER, from Dutch *stad,* place; *(iii)* SHTETL, from Old High German *stat,* place. *(i), (ii),* and *(iii)* all from Germanic **stadiz;* **b.** STAT[2], from Latin *statim,* at once; **c.** STATION, from Latin *statiō,* a standing still; **d.** ARMISTICE, SOLSTICE, from Latin *-stitium,* a stoppage; **e.** STASIS, from Greek *stasis* (see **III. 1. b.**), a standing, a standstill. **6.** Suffixed form **stə-to-.* **a.** BESTEAD, from Old Norse *stadhr,* place, from Germanic **stadaz,* placed; **b.** -STAT, STATIC, STATICE, STATO-; ASTASIA, (ASTATINE), from Greek *statos,* placed, standing. **7.** Suffixed form **stə-no-.* **a.** DESTINE, from Latin *dēstināre,* to make firm, establish (*dē-,* thoroughly; see **de-**); **b.** OBSTINATE, from Latin *obstināre,* to set one's mind on, persist (*ob-,* on; see **epi**). **8.** Suffixed form **stə-tu-.* STATE, STATISTICS, (STATUE), STATURE, STATUS, STATUTE; CONSTITUTE, DESTITUTE, INSTITUTE, PROSTITUTE, RESTITUTE, SUBSTITUTE, SUPERSTITION, from Latin *status,* manner, position, condition, attitude, with derivatives *statūra,* height, stature, *statuere,* to set up, erect, cause to stand, and *superstes* (< **-stə-t-*), witness ("who stands beyond"). **9.** Suffixed form **stə-dhlo-.* STABLE[2]; CONSTABLE, from Latin *stabulum,* "standing place," stable. **10.** Suffixed form **stə-dhli-.* ESTABLISH, STABLE[1], from Latin *stabilis,* standing firm. **11.** Suffixed form **stə-tā.* -STAT; ENSTATITE, from Greek *-statēs,* one that causes to stand, a standing.
III. Zero-grade form **st-, *st(ə)-* (before vowels). **1.** Reduplicated form **si-st(ə)-.* **a.** ASSIST, CONSIST, DESIST, EXIST, INSIST, INTERSTICE, PERSIST, RESIST, SUBSIST, from Latin *sistere,* to set, place, stop, stand; **b.** APOSTASY, CATASTASIS, DIASTASIS, ECSTASY, EPISTASIS, EPISTEMOLOGY, HYPOSTASIS, ICONOSTASIS, ISOSTASY, METASTASIS, PROSTATE, SYSTEM, from Greek *histanai* (aorist *stanai*), to set, place, with *stasis* (**stə-ti-*), a standing (see **II. 5. e.**); **c.** HISTO-; HISTIOCYTE, from Greek *histos,* web, tissue (< "that which is set up"). **2.** Compound form **tri-st-i-,* "third person standing by" (see **trei-**). **3.** Compound form **por-st-i-,* "that which stands before" (**por-,* before, forth; see **per**[1]). POST[1], from Latin *postis,* post. **4.** Suffixed form **st-o-* in compound **upo-st-o-,* "one who stands under" (see **upo**).
IV. Extended root **stāu-* (< **staəu-*), becoming **stau-* before consonants, **stāw-* before vowels; basic meaning "stout-standing, strong." **1.** Suffixed extended form **stāw-ā.* STOW, from Old English *stōw,* place, from Germanic **stōwō.* **2.** Probable o-grade suffixed extended form **stōw-yā.* STOA, STOIC, from Greek *stoa,* porch. **3.** Suffixed extended form **stau-ro-.* **a.** *(i)* STORE; INSTAURATION, from Latin *īnstaurāre,* to restore, set upright again (*in-,* on; see **en**); *(ii)* RESTORE, from Latin *restaurāre,* to restore, rebuild (*re-,* anew, again; see **re-**); **b.** STAUROLITE, from Greek *stauros,* cross, post, stake. **4.** Variant **tau-ro-,* bull (see **tauro-**).
V. Zero-grade extended root **stū-* (< **stuə-*). Suffixed form **stū-lo-.* STYLITE; AMPHISTYLAR, ASTYLAR, EPISTYLE, HYPOSTYLE, PERISTYLE, PROSTYLE, STYLOBATE, from Greek *stulos,* pillar.
VI. Secondary full-grade form **steuə-.* Suffixed form **steuə-ro-.* THERAVADA, from Sanskrit *sthavira-,* thick, stout, old.
VII. Variant zero-grade extended root **stu-.* Suffixed form **stu-t-.* STUD[1], from Old English *stuthu, studu,* post, prop.
VIII. Secondary full-grade form **steu-.* **1.** Suffixed form **steu-rā.* STARBOARD, from Old English *stēor-,* a steering, from Germanic **steurō,* "a steering." **2.a.** STEER[1], from Old English *stīeran, stēran,* to steer; **b.** STERN[2], from Middle English *sterne,* stern of a boat, possibly from a source akin to Old Norse *stjōrn,* a rudder, a steering, derivative of *stȳra,* to steer. Both **a** and **b** from Germanic denominative **steurjan.* **3.** Suffixed form **steu-ro-,* a larger domestic animal. STEER[2], from Old English *stēor,* steer, from Germanic **steuraz,* ox. **4.** STIRK, from Old English *stīrc, stierc,* calf, from Germanic diminutive **steur-ika-,* probably from **stā-.** [Pokorny *stā-* 1004.]

(s)teg-. Important derivatives are *thatch, deck*[2], *deck*[1], *thug, tile, detect,* and *protect.*

(s)teg-. To cover.
I. O-grade form **tog-.* **1.a.** THATCH, from Old English *theccan,* to cover; **b.** DECK[2], from Middle Dutch *decken,* to cover; **c.** DECKLE, from Old High German *decchen,* to cover. **a, b,** and **c** all from Germanic **thakjan.* **2.a.** THATCH, from Old English *thæc,* thatch; **b.** DECK[1], from Middle Dutch *dec, decke,* roof, covering. Both **a** and **b** from Germanic **thakam.* **3.** Suffixed form **tog-ā-,* covering. TOGA, from Latin *toga,* toga. **4.** THUG, from Sanskrit *sthagayati,* he covers, possibly from **(s)teg-.**

II. Basic form *steg-. STEGODON, from Greek *stegein,* to cover.
III. Basic form *teg-. **1.** TECTRIX, TECTUM, TEGMEN, TEGMENTUM, TEGULAR, TEGUMENT, TILE, TUILLE; DETECT, INTEGUMENT, OBTECT, PROTECT, from Latin *tegere,* to cover, and *tēgula,* tile (with lengthened-grade root). **2.** TAJ, from Persian *tāj,* crown. [Pokorny 1. *(s)teg-* 1013.]

stegh-. Important derivatives are *sting* and *stag.*

stegh-. To stick, prick; pointed. **1.** Perhaps nasalized form *stengh-. STING, from Old English *stingan,* to sting, from Germanic *stingan. **2.** O-grade form *stogh-. **a.** STAG, from Old English *stagga,* stag, from Germanic *stag-; **b.** STOCHASTIC, from Greek *stokhos,* pointed stake or pillar (used as a target for archers), goal. [Pokorny *stegh-* 1014.]

stei-. Important derivatives are *stone, tungsten,* and *stein.*

stei-. Stone. Possibly contracted from *staəi-. **1.** Suffixed o-grade form *stoi-no-. **a.** STONE, from Old English *stān;* **b.** STEENBOK, from Middle Dutch *steen,* stone; **c.** TUNGSTEN, from Old Norse *steinn,* stone; **d.** STEIN, from Old High German *stein,* stone. **a, b, c,** and **d** all from Germanic *stainaz. **2.** Possibly suffixed form *stāy-r̥ (earlier *staəi-r̥). STEARIC, STEARIN, STEATITE, STEATO-; STEAPSIN, from Greek *stear,* solid fat, suet. [Pokorny *stāi-* 1010.]

steig-. Important derivatives are *stitch, stick, etiquette, ticket, distinguish, instinct, stigma, tiger, instigate,* and *steak.*

steig-. To stick; pointed. Partly blended with **stegh-.**
I. Zero-grade form *stig-. **1.** STICKLEBACK, from Old English *sticel,* a prick, sting, from Germanic suffixed form *stik-ilaz. **2.** Suffixed form *stig-i-. STITCH, from Old English *stice,* a sting, prick, from Germanic *stikiz. **3.** STICK, from Old English *sticca,* stick, from Germanic expressive form *stikkōn-. **4.** (ETIQUETTE), TICKET, from Old French *estiquier,* to stick, from Germanic stative *stikkēn, "to be stuck." **5.** SNICKERSNEE, from Middle Dutch *steken,* to stick, stab, from Germanic blended variant *stekan. **6.** Nasalized form *sti-n-g-. DISTINGUISH, EXTINGUISH, INSTINCT, from Latin *stinguere,* to quench, perhaps originally to prick, and its apparent derivative *distinguere,* to separate (phonological and semantic transitions obscure). **7.** Suffixed form *stig-yo-. STIGMA; ASTIGMATISM, from Greek *stizein,* to prick, tattoo. **8.** Suffixed reduced form *tig-ro-. TIGER, from Greek *tigris,* tiger (from its stripes), from the same Iranian source as Old Persian *tigra-,* sharp, pointed, and Avestan *tighri-,* arrow.
II. Basic form *steig-. INSTIGATE, from Latin *īnstīgāre,* to urge, from *-stīgāre,* to spur on, prod.
III. Suffixed o-grade form *stoig-ā-. STEAK, from Old Norse *steik,* roast, steak, and *steikja,* to roast (on a spit), from Germanic *staikō. [Pokorny *steig-* 1016.]

steigh-. Important derivatives are *stirrup, acrostic* and *stair.*

steigh-. To stride, step, rise.
I. Basic form *steigh-. STY[2]; STIRRUP, from Old English *stīgan,* to go up, rise, from Germanic *stīgan.
II. Zero-grade form *stigh-. **1.** STILE[1], from Old English *stigel,* series of steps, from Germanic *stigila-. **2.** Suffixed form *stigh-to-. STICKLE, from Old English *stiht(i)an,* to settle, arrange, from Germanic *stihtan, "to place on a step or base." **3.** Suffixed form *stigh-o-. STICH; ACROSTIC, CADASTRE, DISTICH, HEMISTICH, PENTASTICH, STICHOMETRY, STICHOMYTHIA, from Greek *stikhos,* row, line, line of verse.
III. O-grade form *stoigh-. **1.** Suffixed form *stoigh-ri-. STAIR, from Old English *stǣger,* stair, step, from Germanic *staigrī. **2.** STOICHIOMETRY, from Greek *stoikheion,* shadow line, element. [Pokorny *steigh-* 1017.]

stel-. Important derivatives are *still[1], apostle, epistle, stall[1], installment[1], stallion, pedestal, install, gestalt, stole[1], stalk[1], stilt,* and *stout.*

stel-. To put, stand; with derivatives referring to a standing object or place.
I. Basic form *stel-. **1.** Suffixed form *stel-ni-. STILL[1], from Old English *stille,* quiet, fixed, from Germanic *stilli-. **2.** Suffixed form *stel-yo-. APOSTLE, DIASTOLE, EPISTLE, PERISTALSIS, SYSTALTIC, from Greek *stellein,* to put in order, prepare, send, make compact (with o-grade and zero-grade forms *stol-* and *stal-*).
II. O-grade form *stol-. **1.** Suffixed form *stol-no-. **a.** STALL[1]; FORESTALL, from Old English *steall,* standing place, stable; **b.** STALE[1]; INSTALLMENT[1], from Old French *estal,* place; **c.** STALLION, from Anglo-Norman *estaloun,* stallion; **d.** PEDESTAL, from Old Italian *stallo,* stall; **e.** INSTALL, from Medieval Latin *stallum,* stall; **f.** GESTALT, from Old High German *stellen,* to set, place, from Germanic denominative *stalljan. **a, b, c, d, e,** and **f** all from Germanic *stalla-. **2.** Suffixed form *stol-ōn-. STOLON, from Latin *stolō,* branch, shoot. **3.** Suffixed form *stol-ido-. STOLID, from Latin *stolidus,* "firm-standing," stupid. **4.** Suffixed form *stol-ā-. **a.** STALK[1], from Old English *stalu,* upright piece, stalk, from Germanic *stalō-; **b.** STOLE[1], from Greek *stolē,* garment, array, equipment.
III. Zero-grade form *stl̥-. **1.** Suffixed form *stl̥-to-. STULTIFY, from Latin *stultus,* foolish (< "unmovable, uneducated"). **2.** Suffixed zero-grade form *stl̥-no-. STULL, (STOLLEN), from Old High German *stollo,* post, support, from Germanic *stullōn-. **3.** Suffixed zero-grade form *stal-nā-. STELE, from Greek *stēlē,* pillar.
IV. Extended form *steld-. **a.** STILT, from Middle English *stilte,* crutch, stilt, from a source akin to Low German and Flemish *stilte,* stick, from Germanic *stiltjōn-; **b.** zero-grade form *stl̥d-. STOUT, from Old French *estout,* stout, from Germanic *stult-, "walking on stilts," strutting. [Pokorny 3. *stel-* 1019.]

(s)tenə-. Important derivatives are *thunder, Thursday, tornado, astonish, detonate,* and *stun.*

(s)tenə-. To thunder. **1.** Zero-grade form *stn̥ə-. **a.** THUNDER; THURSDAY, from Old English *thunor,* thunder, Thor; **b.** BLUNDERBUSS, DUNDERHEAD, from Middle Dutch *doner, donder,* thunder. **c.** THOR, from Old Norse *Thōrr* (older form *Thunarr*), "thunder," thunder god. **a, b,** and **c** all from Germanic *thunaraz. **2.** O-grade form *tonə-. TORNADO; ASTONISH, DETONATE, STUN, from Latin *tonāre,* to thunder. [Pokorny 1. *(s)ten-* 1021.]

ster-[1]. Important derivatives are *stare, stark, starch, stern[1], stereo-, stork, strut, start, startle, starve, torpedo,* and *torpor.*

ster-[1]. Stiff.
I. O-grade form *stor-. **1.** Suffixed form *stor-ē-. STARE, from Old English *starian,* to stare, from Germanic *staren. **2.** Extended form *stor-g-. **a.** STARK, from Old English *stearc,* hard, severe, from Germanic *starkaz; **b.** STARCH, from Old English *stercan,* to stiffen, from Germanic denominative *starkjan.
II. Full-grade form *ster-. **1.** STERN[1], from Old English *stierne, styrne,* firm, from Germanic *sternjaz. **2.** Suffixed form *ster-ewo-. STERE, STEREO-; CHOLESTEROL, from Greek *stereos,* solid. **3.** Lengthened-grade form *stēr-. STERIGMA, from Greek *stērizein,* to support.
III. Zero-grade form *str̥-. **1.** Extended form *str̥g-. STORK, from Old English *storc,* stork (probably from the stiff movements of the bird), from Germanic *sturkaz. **2.** STRUT, from Old English *strūtian,* to stand out stiffly, from Germanic *strūt-.
IV. Extended form *sterd-. **1.** REDSTART, from Old English *steort,* tail, from Germanic *stertaz. **2.a.** START, from Old English *styrtan,* to leap up (< "move briskly, move stiffly"); **b.** STARTLE, from Old English *steartlian,* to kick, struggle. Both **a** and **b** from Germanic *stert-.
V. Extended form *sterbh-. STARVE, from Old English *steorfan,* to die (< "become rigid"), from Germanic *sterban.
VI. Extended form *(s)terp- in suffixed (stative) zero-grade form *tr̥p-ē-. TORPEDO, TORPID, TORPOR, from Latin *torpēre,* to be stiff. [Pokorny 1. *(s)ter-* 1022.]

ster-[2]. Important derivatives are *structure, construct, destroy, instruct, obstruct, industry, strew, straw, street,* and *stratagem.*

ster-[2]. Also **sterə-.** To spread.
I. Extended form *streu-. **1.** STRAIN[2], from Old English *strēon,* something gained, offspring, from Germanic suffixed form *streu-nam. **2.** STRUCTURE; CONSTRUCT, DESTROY, INSTRUCT, OBSTRUCT, SUBSTRUCTION, from Latin *struere,* to pile up, construct. **3.** Zero-grade form *stru-. INDUSTRY, from Latin *industrius,* diligent, from Old Latin *indostruus* (*endo-,* within; see **en**). **4.** BREMSSTRAHLUNG, from Old High German *strāla,* arrow, lightning bolt, from Germanic *strēlō.
II. O-grade extended form *strou-. **1.** Suffixed form *strou-eyo-. **a.** STREW, from Old English *strē(o)wian,* to strew; **b.** STREUSEL, from Old High German *strouwen, strowwen,* to sprinkle, strew. Both **a** and **b** from Germanic *strawjan. **2.** Suffixed form *strow-o. STRAW, from Old English *strēaw,* straw, from Germanic *strawam, "that which is scattered."
III. O-grade extended form *stroi-. PERESTROIKA, from Old Russian *stroĭ,* order.
IV. Basic forms *ster-, *sterə-. **1.** Nasalized form *ster-n-ə-. STRATUS, STREET; CONSTERNATE, PROSTRATE, SUBSTRATUM, from Latin *sternere* (past participle *strātus* from zero-grade *strə-to-), to stretch, extend. **2.** Suffixed form *ster-no-. STERNUM, from Greek *sternon,* breast, breastbone.
V. Zero-grade form *str̥-, *str̥ə-. **1.** Suffixed form *str̥-to-. STRATAGEM; STRATOCRACY, from Greek *stratos,* multitude, army, expedition. **2.** Suffixed form *str̥ə-to-. STRATH, from Old Irish *srath,* a wide river valley, from Celtic *s(t)rato-. **3.** Suffixed extended form *str̥ə-mn̥. STROMA; (STROMATOLITE), from Greek *strōma,* mattress, bed. [Pokorny 5. *ster-* 1029.]

ster-[3]. Important derivatives are *star, stellar, constellation, aster, asterisk, asteroid,* and *disaster.*

ster-[3]. Star. **1.** Suffixed form *ster-s-. STAR, from Old English *steorra,* star, from Germanic *sterzōn-. **2.** Suffixed form *stēr-lā-. STELLAR, STELLATE; CONSTELLATION, from Latin *stēlla,* star. **3.** Oldest root form *əster-. ASTER, ASTERIATED, ASTERISK, ASTERISM, ASTEROID, ASTRAL, ASTRO-; ASTRAPHOBIA, DISASTER, from Greek *astēr,* star, with its derivative *astron,* star, and possible compound *astrapē, asteropē,* lightning, twinkling (< "looking like a star"; *ōps,* stem *op-,* eye, appearance; see **okʷ-**). **4.** ESTHER, from Persian *sitareh,* star, from Iranian stem *stăr-. [Pokorny 2. *ster-* 1027.]

streb(h)-. Important derivatives are *strop, strophe, apostrophe[1], catastrophe,* and *stroboscope.*

streb(h)-. To wind, turn. **1.** STREPTO-, STROP, STROPHE, STROPHOID, STROPHULUS; ANASTROPHE, APOSTROPHE[1], BOUSTROPHEDON, CATASTROPHE, DIASTROPHISM, from Greek *strephein,* to wind, turn, twist, with o-grade derivatives *strophē,* a turning, and *strophion,* headband. **2.** Unaspirated o-grade form *strob-. STROBILUS; STROBOSCOPE, from Greek *strobos,* a whirling, whirlwind. **3.** Unaspirated zero-grade form *str̥b-. STRABISMUS, STRABOTOMY, from Greek *strabos,* squinting. [Pokorny *strebh-* 1025.]

streig-. Important derivatives are *strike, streak, stroke[1], strain[1], strict, stringent, constrain, prestige,* and *restrict.*

streig-. To stroke, rub, press.
I. Basic form *streig-. **1.a.** STRIKE, from Old English *strīcan,* to stroke; **b.** TRICOT, from Old French *estriquier,* to strike. Both **a** and **b** from Germanic *strīkan. **2.** STRICKLE, from Old English *stricel,* implement for leveling grain, from Germanic diminutive *strik-ila-. **3.** STREAK, from Old English *strica,* stroke, line, from Germanic *strikōn-.
II. O-grade form *stroig-. STROKE[1], from Old English *strāc,* stroke, from Germanic *straik-.
III. Zero-grade form *strig-. **1.** Suffixed form *strig-ā-. STRIGOSE, from Latin *striga,* row of grain, furrow drawn lengthwise over the field. **2.** Suffixed form *strig-yā-. STRIA, from Latin *stria,* furrow, channel. **3.** Nasalized form *stri-n-g-. STRAIN[1], STRAIT, STRICT, STRINGENDO, STRINGENT; ASTRINGENT, CONSTRAIN, DISTRAIN, PRESTIGE, RESTRICT, from Latin *stringere,* to draw tight, press together. **4.** STRIGIL, from Latin *strigilis,* strigil, possibly akin to *stringere.* [Pokorny 1. *streig-* 1036; 4. *ster-* 1028.]

su-. A derivative is *swastika.*

su-. Well, good. **1.** SWASTIKA, from Sanskrit *svasti,* well-being, good luck, from *su-,* well- (see **es-**). **2.** Compound *su-gʷiə-es-, "having good life" (see **gʷei-**). [Pokorny *su-* 1037.]

sū-. Important derivatives are *swine, hog, socket, sow[2],* and *hyena.*

sū-. Pig. Contracted from *suə-; probably a derivative of **seuə-[1].** **1.** Suffixed form *suə-īno-. **a.** SWINE, from Old English *swīn,* swine; **b.** KEELSON, from Old Norse *svīn,* swine. Both **a** and **b** from Germanic *swīnam. **2.** Suffixed form *su-kā. **a.** HOG, from Old English *hogg,* hog, from British *hukk-; **b.** SOCKET, from Anglo-Norman *soc,* plowshare, perhaps from **sū-.** Both **a** and **b** from Celtic expressive form *sukko-, swine, snout of a swine, plowshare; **c.** SOW[2], from Old English *sugu,* sow, from Germanic *sugō. **3.** Basic form *sū-. SOW[2], from Old English *sū,* from Germanic *sū-. **4.** SOIL[2], from Latin *sūs,* pig. **5.** HYENA; HYOSCINE, from Greek *hus,* swine. [Pokorny *sū̆-s* 1038.]

swād-. Important derivatives are *sweet, dissuade, persuade, suave,* and *hedonism.*

swād-. Sweet, pleasant. **1.** SWEET, from Old English *swēte,* sweet, from Germanic *swōtja-. **2.** Suffixed form *swād-ē-. SUASION; (ASSUASIVE), DISSUADE, PERSUADE, from Latin *suādēre,* to advise, urge (< "recommend as good"). **3.** Suffixed form *swād-w-i-. SOAVE, SUAVE; ASSUAGE, from Latin *suāvis,* delightful. **4.** Suffixed form *swād-es-. AEDES, from Greek *ēdos,* pleasure. **5.** Suffixed form *swād-onā. HEDONIC, HEDONISM, from Greek *hēdonē,* pleasure. [Pokorny *su̯ād-* 1039.]

s(w)e-. Important derivatives are *self, gossip, bustle[1], suicide, secede, seclude, secret, secure, sedition, seduce, segregate, select, separate, sure, sober, sole[2], solitary, solitude, solo, sullen, desolate, soliloquy, custom, ethic, ethnic, idiom, idiot,* and *idiosyncrasy.*

s(w)e-. Pronoun of the third person and reflexive (referring back to the subject of the sentence); further appearing in various forms referring to the social group as an entity, "(we our-)selves." **1.** Suffixed extended form *sel-bho-. SELF, from Old English *self, sylf,* self, same, from Germanic *selbaz, self. **2.** Suffixed form *s(w)e-bh(o)-. SIB; GOSSIP, from Old English *sibb,* relative, from Germanic *sibja-, "one's own," blood relation, relative. **3.** Suffixed form *se-ge. BUSTLE[1], from Old Norse *-sk,* reflexive suffix, as in *būask,* to make oneself ready, from *sik,* oneself (reflexive pronoun), from Germanic *sik, self. **4.** Suffixed form *swoi-no-. SWAIN; (BOATSWAIN), from Old Norse *sveinn,* herdsman, boy, from Germanic *swainaz, "one's own (man)," attendant, servant. **5.** Suffixed form *s(u)w-o-, one's own. **a.** SUICIDE, from Latin *suī* (genitive), of oneself; **b.** SWAMI, from Sanskrit *svāmin,* "one's own master," owner, prince, from *sva-* (< *swo-), one's own. **6.** Extended form *sed. SECEDE, SECERN, SECLUDE, SECRET, SECURE, SEDITION, SEDUCE, SEDULOUS, SEGREGATE, SELECT, SEPARATE, (SURE), from Latin *sēd, sē, sē-,* without, apart (< "on one's own"); **c.** SOBER, from Latin compound *sōbrius,* not drunk (*ēbrius,* drunk; see **egʷh-**). **7.** Possibly suffixed lengthened o-grade form *sō-lo. SOLE[2], SOLITARY, SOLITUDE, SOLO, SULLEN; DESOLATE, SOLILOQUY, SOLIPSISM, from Latin *sōlus,* by oneself alone. **8.** Extended root *swĕdh-, "that which is one's own," peculiarity, custom. **a.** SODALITY, from Latin *sodālis,* companion (< "one's own," "relative"); **b.** suffixed form *swēdh-sko-. (CONSUETUDE), CUSTOM, DESUETUDE, MANSUETUDE, MASTIFF, from Latin *suēscere,* to accustom, get accustomed; **c.** ETHIC, ETHOS; CACOETHES, from Greek *ēthos,* custom, disposition, trait; **d.** suffixed form *swedh-no-. ETHNIC, ETHNO-, from Greek *ethnos,* band of people living together, nation, people (< "people of one's own kind"). **9.** Suffixed extended form *swet-aro-. HETAERA, from Greek *hetairos,* comrade, companion, earlier *hetaros.* **10.** Suffixed extended form *swed-yo-. IDIO-, IDIOM, IDIOT; (IDIOPATHY), (IDIOSYNCRASY), from Greek *idios,* personal, private ("particular to oneself"). **11.** Suffixed form *swei-no-. SINN FEIN, from Old Irish *fēin,* self. **12.** Suffixed (ablatival) form *swe-tos, from oneself. KHEDIVE, from Old Iranian *khvadāta-,* lord, by haplology from compound form *khvatō-dāta-, created from oneself (*dāta-,* created; see **dhē-**). [Pokorny *se-* 882.]

sweid-. An important derivative is *sweat.*

sweid-. Sweat; to sweat.
I. O-grade form *swoid-. **1.** SWEAT, from Old English *swǣtan,* to sweat, from Germanic *swaitaz, sweat, with its denominative *swaitjan, to sweat. **2.** Suffixed form *swoid-os-. SUDORIFIC; SUDORIFEROUS, from Latin *sūdor,* sweat. **3.** O-grade form *swoid-ā-. SUDATORIUM, SUINT; EXUDE, TRANSUDE, from Latin *sūdāre,* to sweat.
II. Suffixed zero-grade form *swid-r-os-. HIDROSIS, from Greek *hidrōs,* sweat. [Pokorny 2. *su̯eid-* 1043.]

s(w)eks. Important derivatives are *six, semester, sestet, sextant,* and *hexa-.*

s(w)eks. Six.
I. Form *seks. **1.** SIX; SIXTEEN, SIXTY, from Old English *s(i)ex, six,* with derivatives *sixtig,* sixty, and *sixtȳne,* sixteen (*-tȳne,* ten; see **dekm̥**), from Germanic *seks. **2.** SENARY, SEX-; SEICENTO, SEMESTER, from Latin *sex,* six. **3.** Suffixed form *seks-to-. SESTET, SESTINA, SEXT, SEXTANT, SEXTILE; SEXTODECIMO, from Latin *sextus,* sixth.
II. Form *sweks. HEXA-, HEXAD, from Greek *hex,* six. [Pokorny *su̯eḱs* 1044.]

swel-. Important derivatives are *swill* and *swallow[1].*

swel-. To eat, drink. **1.** SWILL, from Old English *swilian,* to wash out, gargle, from Germanic *swil-, perhaps from **swel-.** **2.** Extended form *swelk-. SWALLOW[1]; GROUNDSEL[1], from Old English *swelgan,* to swallow, from Germanic *swelgan, *swelhan. **3.** MANTICORE, from Greek *mantikhōras,* manticore, probably from Iranian *khvāra-, eating. [Pokorny 1. *su̯el(k)-* 1045.]

swen-. Important derivatives are *swan, sonic, sonnet, sound[1], unison, sonata, sonorous, consonant, dissonant,* and *resound.*

swen-. To sound. **1.** Suffixed o-grade form *swon-o-. **a.** SWAN, from Old English *swan,* swan, from Germanic *swanaz, *swanōn-, "singer"; **b.** SONE, SONIC, SONNET, SOUND[1]; UNISON, from Latin *sonus,* a sound. **2.** Form *swen-ā-. SONANT, SONATA, SONOROUS; ASSONANCE, CONSONANT, DISSONANT, RESOUND, from Latin *sonāre,* to sound. [Pokorny *su̯en-* 1046.]

swep-. Important derivatives are *insomnia* and *hypnosis.*

swep-. To sleep. **1.** Suffixed form *swep-os-. SOPOR; (SOPORIFIC), from Latin *sopor,* a deep sleep. **2.** Suffixed form *swep-no-. SOMNI-, SOMNOLENT; INSOMNIA, from Latin *somnus,* sleep. **3.** Suffixed zero-grade form *sup-no-. HYPNO-, (HYPNOSIS), HYPNOTIC, from Greek *hupnos,* sleep. [Pokorny 1. *su̯ep-* 1048.]

swer-. Important derivatives are *swear* and *answer.*

swer-. To speak, talk. O-grade form *swor-. **a.** SWEAR, from Old English *swerian,* to swear, proclaim, from Germanic *swarjan; **b.** ANSWER, from Old English *andswaru,* answer, from Germanic *and-swarō, "a swearing against," "rebuttal" (*andi-, against; see **ant-**). [Pokorny 1. *su̯er-* 1049.]

swesor-. Important derivatives are *sister, cousin,* and *sorority.*

swesor-. Sister. **1.** Zero-grade form *swesr-. **a.** SISTER, from Old English *sweostor,* sister, and Old Norse *systir,* sister, both from Germanic *swestr-; **b.** suffixed form *swesr-īno-. COUSIN, from Latin *sobrinus,* maternal cousin. **2.** SORORAL, SORORITY, from Latin *soror,* sister. [Pokorny *su̯esor-* 1051.]

swo-. Important derivatives are *so[1]* and *such.*

swo-. Pronominal stem; so. Derivative of **s(w)e-.** **1.a.** SO[1], from Old English *swā,* so; **b.** SUCH, from Old English *swylc,* such, from Germanic compound *swa-līk-, "so like," of the same kind (*līk-, same; see **līk-**). **2.** Adverbial form *swai. NISI, QUASI, from Latin *sī,* if, in *nisi,* unless (*nī,* not; see **ne-** + *sī,* if), *quasi* (*quam,* as; see **kʷo-** + *sī,* if). [In Pokorny 2. *seu-* 882.]

syū-. Important derivatives are *sew, seam, suture, couture,* and *hymen.*

syū-. To bind, sew.
I. Basic form *syū-. SEW, from Old English *seowian, siowan,* to sew, from Germanic *siwjan.
II. Variant form *sū-. **1.** SEAM, from Old English *sēam,* seam, from Germanic *saumaz. **2.** SUTURE; COUTURE, from Latin *suere* (past participle *sūtus*), to sew. **3.** Suffixed form *sū-dhlā-. SUBULATE, from Latin *sūbula,* awl (< "sewing instrument"). **4.** Suffixed form *sū-tro-. SUTRA; KAMASUTRA, from Sanskrit *sūtram,* thread, string.
III. Suffixed shortened form *syu-men-. HYMEN, from Greek *humēn,* thin skin, membrane. [Pokorny *si̯ū-* 915.]

tag-. Important derivatives are *tact, tangent, tangible, taste, tax, attain, contact, intact, entire, integer,* and *contaminate.*

tag-. To touch, handle. **1.** Nasalized form *ta-n-g-. TACT, TANGENT, TANGIBLE, TASTE, TAX; ATTAIN, CONTACT, INTACT, TACTORECEPTOR, TANGORECEPTOR, from Latin *tangere,* to touch, with derivatives *taxāre,* to touch, assess (possibly a frequentative of *tangere,* but probably influenced by Greek *tassein, taxai,* to arrange, assess), and *tāctus,* touch. **2.** Compound form *n̥-tag-ro-, "untouched, intact" (*n̥-, negative prefix; see **ne**). ENTIRE, INTEGER, INTEGRATE, INTEGRITY, from Latin *integer,* intact, whole, complete, perfect, honest. **3.** Suffixed form *tag-smen-. CONTAMINATE, from Latin *contāmināre,* to corrupt by mixing or contact (< *con-tāmen-, "bringing into contact with"; *con-, com-,* with; see **kom**). [Pokorny *tag-* 1054.]

tauro-. Important derivatives are *Taurus, toreador,* and *torero.*

tauro-. Bull. Derivative of **stā-,** but an independent word in Indo-European. **1.** TAURINE[1], TAURUS, TOREADOR, TORERO; BITTERN[1], from Latin *taurus,* bull. **2.** TAURINE[2]; TAUROCHOLIC ACID, from Greek *tauros,* bull. [In Pokorny *tēu-* 1083.]

tegu-. An important derivative is *thick.*

tegu-. Thick. THICK, from Old English *thicce,* thick, from Germanic *thiku-. [Pokorny *tegu-* 1057.]

tek-. A derivative is *thane.*

tek-. To beget, give birth to. **1.** Suffixed form *tek-no-, child. THANE, from Old English *thegn,* freeman, nobleman, military vassal, warrior, from Germanic *thegnaz, boy, man, servant, warrior. **2.** Suffixed o-grade form *tok-o-. OXYTOCIC, POLYTOCOUS, TOCOLOGY, from Greek *tokos,* birth. [Pokorny 1. *tek-* 1057.]

teks-. Important derivatives are *text, tissue, context, pretext, subtle, architect, technical,* and *technology.*

teks-. To weave; also to fabricate, especially with an ax; also to make wicker or wattle fabric for (mud-covered) house walls. **1.** TEXT, TISSUE; CONTEXT, PRETEXT, from Latin *texere,* to weave, fabricate. **2.** Suffixed form *teks-lā. **a.** TILLER[2], TOIL[2], from Latin *tēla,* web, net, warp of a fabric, also weaver's beam (to which the warp threads are tied); **b.** SUBTLE, from Latin *subtīlis,* thin, fine, precise, subtle (< *sub-tēla, "thread passing under the warp," the finest thread; *sub,* under; see **upo**). **3.** Suffixed form *teks-ōn, weaver, maker of wattle for house walls, builder (possibly contaminated with *teks-tōr, builder). TECTONIC; ARCHITECT, from Greek *tektōn,* carpenter, builder. **4.** Suffixed form *teks-nā-, craft (of weaving or fabricating). TECHNICAL, (POLYTECHNIC), TECHNOLOGY, from Greek *tekhnē,* art, craft, skill. **5.a.** DACHSHUND, from Old High German *dahs,* badger; **b.** DASSIE, from Middle Dutch *das,* badger. Both **a** and **b** from Germanic *thahsu-, badger, possibly from **teks-** ("the animal that builds," referring to its burrowing skill) but more likely borrowed from the same pre-Indo-European source as the Celtic totemic name *Tazgo-,* Gaelic *Tadhg,* originally "badger." [Pokorny *tek̑t-* 1058.]

telə-. Important derivatives are *toll[1], philately, tolerate, retaliate, talent, tantalize, Atlantic, Atlas, collate, elate, legislator, relate, superlative, translate,* and *extol.*

telə-. To lift, support, weigh; with derivatives referring to measured weights and thence to money and payment. **1.** Suffixed form *telə-mon-. TELAMON, from Greek *telamōn,* supporter, bearer. **2.** Suffixed form *tel(ə)-es-. **a.** TOLL[1]; PHILATELY, from Greek *telos,* tax, charge; **b.** TOLERATE, from Latin *tolerāre,* to bear, endure. **3.** Suffixed zero-grade form *tl̥ə-i-. TALION; RETALIATE, from Latin *tāliō,* reciprocal punishment in kind, possibly "something paid out," from *tali- (influenced by *tālis,* such). **4.** Suffixed variant zero-grade form *tala-nt-. TALENT, from Greek *talanton,* balance, weight, any of several specific weights of gold or silver, hence the sum of money represented by such a weight. **5.** Perhaps (but unlikely) intensive reduplicated form *tantal-. (TANTALIZE), TANTALUS, from Greek *Tantalos,* name of a legendary king, "the sufferer." **6.** Perhaps (but unlikely) zero-grade form **tl̥ə-.* ATLANTIC, ATLAS, from Greek *Atlas* (stem *Atlant-*), name of the Titan supporting the world. **7.** Suffixed zero-grade form **tl̥ə-to-.* ABLATION, COLLATE, DILATORY, ELATE, ILLATION, LEGISLATOR, OBLATE[1], PRELATE, PROLATE, RELATE, SUBLATE, SUPERLATIVE, TRANSLATE, from Latin *lātus,* "carried, borne," used as the suppletive past participle of *ferre,* to bear (see **bher-**[1]), with its compounds. **8.** Suffixed zero-grade form **tl̥ə-ā-.* TOLA, from Sanskrit *tulā,* scales, balance, weight. **9.** Nasalized zero-grade form **tl̥-n-ə-.* EXTOL, from Latin *tollere,* to lift. [Pokorny 1. *tel-* 1060.]

tem-. Important derivatives are *tome, anatomy, atom, diatom, epitome, temple*[1], and *contemplate.*

tem-. Also **temə-.** To cut.
I. Form **temə-.* Nasalized form **t(e)m-n-ə-.* TMESIS, TOME, (-TOME), -TOMY; ANATOMY, ATOM, DIATOM, DICHOTOMY, ENTOMO-, EPITOME, from Greek *temnein,* to cut, with o-grade forms *tomos,* cutting, a cut, section, volume, and *tomē,* a cutting.
II. Form **tem-.* **1.** Suffixed form **tem-lo-.* TEMPLE[1], TEMPLE[3]; CONTEMPLATE, from Latin *templum,* temple, shrine, open place for observation (augury term < "place reserved or cut out"), small piece of timber. **2.** Extended root **tem-d-* becoming **tend-* in o-grade suffixed (iterative) form **tond-eyo-.* TONSORIAL, TONSURE, from Latin *tondēre,* to shear, shave. [Pokorny 1. *tem-, tend-* 1062.]

ten-. Important derivatives are *tend*[1], *tendon, tense*[1], *tent*[1], *attend, contend, extend, intend, pretend, hypotenuse, sitar, tenacious, tenant, tenement, tenor, tenure, contain, continue, detain, entertain, lieutenant, maintain, obtain, pertain, retain, sustain, thin, tenuous, tender*[1], and *tone.*

ten-. To stretch.
I. Derivatives with the basic meaning. **1.** Suffixed form **ten-do-.* **a.** TEND[1], TENDER[2], TENSE[1], TENT[1]; ATTEND, CONTEND, DETENT, DISTEND, EXTEND, INTEND, OSTENSIBLE, PRETEND, SUBTEND, from Latin *tendere,* to stretch, extend; **b.** PORTEND, from Latin *portendere,* "to stretch out before" (*por-* , variant of *pro-,* before; see **per**[1]), a technical term in augury, "to indicate, presage, foretell." **2.** Suffixed form **ten-yo-.* TENESMUS; ANATASE, BRONCHIECTASIS, CATATONIA, EPITASIS, HYPOTENUSE, PERITONEUM, PROTASIS, SYNTONIC, TELANGIECTASIA, from Greek *teinein,* to stretch, with o-grade form *ton-* and zero-grade noun *tasis* (< **tn̥-ti-*), a stretching, tension, intensity. **3.** Reduplicated zero-grade form **te-tan-o-.* TETANUS, from Greek *tetanos,* stiff, rigid. **4.** Suffixed full-grade form **ten-tro-.* **a.** TANTRA, from Sanskrit *tantram,* loom; **b.** SITAR, from Persian *tār,* string. **5.** Basic form (with stative suffix) **ten-ē-.* TENABLE, TENACIOUS, TENACULUM, TENANT, TENEMENT, TENET, TENON, TENOR, TENURE, TENUTO; ABSTAIN, CONTAIN, (CONTINUE), DETAIN, ENTERTAIN, LIEUTENANT, MAINTAIN, OBTAIN, PERTAIN, PERTINACIOUS, RETAIN, (RETINACULUM), SUSTAIN, from Latin *tenēre,* to hold, keep, maintain (< "to cause to endure or continue, hold on to").
II. Derivatives meaning "stretched," hence "thin." **1.** Suffixed zero-grade form **tn̥-u-.* THIN, from Old English *thynne,* thin, from Germanic **thunniz,* from **thunw-.* **2.** Suffixed full-grade form **ten-u-.* TENUOUS; ATTENUATE, EXTENUATE, from Latin *tenuis,* thin, rare, fine. **3.** Suffixed full-grade form **ten-ero-.* TENDER[1], (TENDRIL), from Latin *tener,* tender, delicate.
III. Derivatives meaning "something stretched or capable of being stretched, a string." **1.** Suffixed form **ten-ōn-.* TENDON, TENO-, from Greek *tenōn,* tendon. **2.** Suffixed o-grade form **ton-o-.* TONE; (BARITONE), TONOPLAST, from Greek *tonos,* string, hence sound, pitch. **3.** Suffixed zero-grade form **tn̥-ya-.* TAENIA; POLYTENE, from Greek *tainia,* band, ribbon. [Pokorny 1. *ten-* 1065.]

terə-[1]**.** Important derivatives are *trite, detriment, thrash, thresh, threshold, turn, contour, return, drill*[1], *throw, thread, trauma,* and *truant.*

terə-[1]**.** To rub, turn; with some derivatives referring to twisting, boring, drilling, and piercing; and others referring to the rubbing of cereal grain to remove the husks, and thence to the process of threshing either by the trampling of oxen or by flailing with flails. Variant **trē-,* contracted from **treə-.*
I. Full-grade form **ter(ə)-.* **1.a.** TRITE, TRITURATE; ATTRITION, CONTRITE, DETRIMENT, from Latin *terere* (past participle *trītus*), to rub away, thresh, tread, wear out; **b.** TEREDO, from Greek *terēdōn,* a kind of biting worm. **2.** Suffixed form **ter-et-.* TERETE, from Latin *teres* (stem *teret-*), rounded, smooth. **3.** Suffixed form **ter-sko-.* **a.** (THRASH), THRESH, from Old English *therscan,* to thresh; **b.** THRESHOLD, from Old English *therscold, threscold,* sill of a door (over which one treads; second element obscure). Both **a** and **b** from Germanic **therskan, *threskan,* to thresh, tread.
II. O-grade form **tor(ə)-.* **1.** TOREUTICS, from Greek *toreus,* a boring tool. **2.** Suffixed form **tor(ə)-mo-,* hole. DERMA[2], from Old High German *darm,* gut, from Germanic **tharma-.* **3.** Suffixed form **tor(ə)-no-.* TURN; (ATTORN), CONTOUR, (DETOUR), (RETURN), from Greek *tornos,* tool for drawing a circle, circle, lathe.
III. Zero-grade form **tr-.* DRILL[1], from Middle Dutch *drillen,* to drill, from Germanic **thr-.*
IV. Variant form **trē-* (< **treə-*). **1.** THROW, from Old English *thrāwan,* to turn, twist, from Germanic **thrēw-.* **2.** Suffixed form **trē-tu-.* THREAD, from Old English *thrǣd,* thread, from Germanic **thrēdu-,* twisted yarn. **3.** Suffixed form **trē-mn̥* (< **treə-* or **trə-*). MONOTREME, TREMATODE, from Greek *trēma,* perforation. **4.** Suffixed form **trē-ti-* (< **treə-* or **trə-*). ATRESIA, from Greek *trēsis,* perforation.
V. Extended form **trī-* (< **triə-*). **1.** Probably suffixed form **trī-ōn-.* SEPTENTRION, from Latin *triō,* plow ox. **2.** Suffixed form **trī-dhlo-.* TRIBULATION, from Latin *trībulum,* a threshing sledge.
VI. Various extended forms **1.** Forms **trō-, *trau-.* TRAUMA, from Greek *trauma,* hurt, wound. **2.** Form **trīb-.* DIATRIBE, TRIBOELECTRICITY, TRIBOLOGY, TRYPSIN, from Greek *tribein,* to rub, thresh, pound, wear out. **3.** Form **trōg-, *trag-.* **a.** TROGON, TROUT, from Greek *trōgein,* to gnaw; **b.** DREDGE[2], from Greek *tragēma,* sweetmeat. **4.** Form **trup-.* TREPAN[1]; TRYPANOSOME, from Greek *trupē,* hole. **5.** Possible form **trūg-.* TRUANT, from Old French *truant,* beggar. [Pokorny 3. *ter-* 1071.]

terə-[2]**.** Important derivatives are *thrill, nostril, thorough, through, trans-, transient, trench,* and *trunk.*

terə-[2]**.** To cross over, pass through, overcome. Variant **trā-,* contracted from **traə-.*
I. Zero-grade form **tr̥(ə)-.* **1.** THRILL; NOSTRIL, from Old English *thyr(e)l, thӯrel,* a hole (< "a boring through"), from Germanic suffixed form **thur-ila-.* **2.** Suffixed form **tr̥ə-kʷe.* THOROUGH, THROUGH, from Old English *thurh, thuruh,* through, from Germanic **thurh.* **3.** (see **nek-**[1]) Greek *nek-tar,* overcoming death. **4.** Zero-grade form **tr̥ə-* and full-grade form **ter(ə)-.* AVATAR, from Sanskrit *tirati, tarati,* he crosses over.
II. Variant form **trā-* (< **traə-*). **1.** TRANS-, TRANSIENT, (TRANSOM), from Latin *trāns,* across, over, beyond, through (perhaps originally the present participle of a verb **trāre,* to cross over). **2.** Suffixed form **trā-yo-.* CARAVANSARY, from Persian *sarāy,* inn, from Middle Persian *srāyīdhan,* to protect, from Iranian *thrāya-,* to protect.
III. Possible extended form **tru-.* **1.** Suffixed form **tru-k-.* TRUCULENT, from Latin *trux* (stem *truc-*), savage, fierce, grim (< "overcoming," "powerful," "penetrating"). **2.** Suffixed nasalized form **tru-n-k-o-.* TRENCH, TRUNCATE, TRUNK, from Latin *truncus,* deprived of branches or limbs, mutilated, hence trunk (? < "overcome, maimed"). [Pokorny 5. *ter-* 1075.]

terkʷ-. Important derivatives are *queer, thwart, torch, torment, torque*[1], *tortuous, distort, extort, nasturtium,* and *retort*[1].

terkʷ-. To twist. Extension of **terə-**[1]. **1.** Possible variant form **t(w)erk-.* **a.** QUEER, from Middle Low German *dwer,* oblique; **b.** THWART, from Old Norse *thverr,* transverse. Both **a** and **b** from Germanic **thwerh-,* twisted, oblique. **2.** Suffixed (causative) o-grade form **torkʷ-eyo-.* TORCH, TORMENT, TORQUE[1], TORQUE[2], TORSADE, TORT, TORTUOUS, TRUSS; CONTORT, DISTORT, EXTORT, NASTURTIUM, RETORT[1], TORTICOLLIS, from Latin *torquēre,* to twist. [Pokorny *terk-* 1077.]

ters-. Important derivatives are *thirst, terrace, terrain, terrier, territory, inter, mediterranean, subterranean, toast*[1], *torrent,* and *torrid.*

ters-. To dry. **1.** Suffixed zero-grade form **tr̥s-.* **a.** THIRST, from Old English *thurst,* dryness, thirst, from Germanic suffixed form **thurs-tu-;* **b.** CUSK, from Old Norse *thorskr,* cod (< "dried fish"). Both **a** and **b** from Germanic **thurs-.* **2.** Suffixed basic form **ters-ā-.* TERRACE, (TERRAIN), TERRAN, RENE, TERRESTRIAL, TERRIER, TERRITORY, TUREEN; MITORY, INTER, MEDITERRANEAN, PARTERRE, SUBTE RANEAN, TERRAQUEOUS, TERREPLEIN, TERRE-VERTE TERRICOLOUS, TERRIGENOUS, TURMERIC, VERDITER, from Latin *terra,* "dry land," earth. **3.** Suffixed o-grade form **tors-eyo-.* TOAST[1], TORRENT, TORRID, from Latin *torrēre,* to dry, parch, burn. **4.** Suffixed zero-grade form **tr̥s-o-.* TARSUS, from Greek *tarsos,* frame of wickerwork (originally for drying cheese), hence a flat surface, sole of the foot, ankle. [Pokorny *ters-* 1078.]

teuə-. Important derivatives are *thigh, thousand, thimble, thumb, tumor, truffle, tuber, butter,* and *tomb.*

teuə-. Also **teu-.** To swell. **1.** Extended form **teuk-.* THIGH, from Old English *thēoh,* thigh, from Germanic **theuham,* "the swollen or fat part of the leg," thigh. **2.** Extended form **tūs-.* THOUSAND, from Old English *thūsend,* thousand, from Germanic compound **thūs-hundi-,* "swollen hundred," thousand (**hundi-,* hundred; see **dekm̥**). **3.** Probably suffixed zero-grade form **tu-l-.* **a.** THOLE PIN, from Old English *thol(l),* oar pin, oarlock (< "a swelling"), from Germanic **thul-;* **b.** TYLECTOMY, TYLOSIS[1], from Greek *tulos,* callus, lump. **4.** Extended zero-grade form **tūm-.* **a.** THIMBLE, THUMB, from Old English *thūma,* thumb (< "the thick finger"), from Germanic **thūmōn-;* **b.** suffixed (stative) form **tum-ē-.* TUMESCENT, TUMID, TUMOR; DETUMESCENCE, INTUMESCE, TUMEFACIENT, (TUMEFY), from Latin *tumēre,* to swell, be swollen, be proud; **c.** suffixed form **tum-olo-.* TUMULUS, from Latin *tumulus,* raised heap of earth, mound. **5.** Extended zero-grade form **tūbh-.* TRUFFLE, TUBER; PROTUBERATE, from Latin *tūber,* lump, swelling. **6.** Suffixed zero-grade form **tū-ro-* (< **tuə-ro-*). **a.** BUTTER, TYROSINE, TYROTHRICIN, from Greek *turos,* cheese (< "a swelling," "coagulating"); **b.** OBTURATE, from Latin *-tūrāre,* to stop up, possibly from **tūros,* swollen, coagulated, stopped up. **7.** Suffixed variant form **twō-ro-.* SORITES, SORUS, from Greek *sōros,* heap, pile. **8.** Suffixed variant form **twō-mn̥.* SOMA, SOMATO-, -SOME[3]; PROSOMA, from Greek *sōma,* body (< "a swelling," "stocky form"). **9.** Suffixed zero-grade form **twə-wo-.* CREOSOTE, SOTERIOLOGY, from Greek *sōzein,* to save, rescue, derivative of *saos, sōs,* safe, healthy (< "swollen," "strong"). **10.** Perhaps nasalized extended form **tu-m-b(h)-* (or extended zero-grade form **tum-*). TOMB, from Greek *tumbos,* barrow, tomb. [Pokorny *tēu-* 1080.]

teutā-. Important derivatives are *Dutch, Teuton,* and *total.*

teutā-. Tribe. **1.a.** DUTCH, from Middle Dutch *duutsch,* German, of the Germans or Teutons; **b.** PLATTDEUTSCH, from Old High German *diutisc,* of the people. Both **a** and **b** from Germanic **theudiskaz,* of the people, derivative of **theudā-,* people. **2.** Suffixed form **teut-onōs,* "they of the tribe." TEUTON, from Latin *Teutonī,* the Teutons, borrowed via Celtic from Germanic tribal name **theudanōz.* **3.** TOTAL, TUTTI; FACTOTUM, TEETOTUM, from Latin *tōtus,* all, whole, possibly from *teutā-* (? < "of the whole tribe"). [In Pokorny *tēu-* 1080.]

tkei-. Important derivatives are *home, hamlet, haunt, hangar,* and *situate.*

tkei-. To settle, dwell, be home. **1.** Suffixed o-grade form **(t)koi-mo-.* **a.** HOME, from Old English *hām,* home; **b.** NIFLHEIM, from Old Norse *heimr,* home; **c.** HAIMISH, from Old High German *heim,* home; **d.** HAME, from Middle Dutch *hame,* hame (< "covering"); **e.** HAMLET, from Old French *ham,* village, home; **f.** HAUNT, from Old French *hanter,* to frequent, haunt, from Germanic **haimatjan,* to go or bring home; **g.** HANGAR, from Old French *hangard,* shelter, possibly from Germanic **haimgardaz* (**gardaz,* enclosure; see **gher-**[1]). **a, b, c, d, e, f,** and **g** all from Germanic **haimaz,* home. **2.** Zero-grade form **tki-.* **a.** AMPHICTYONY, from Greek *ktizein,* to found, settle, from metathesized *kti-;* **b.** SITUATE, SITUS, from Latin *situs,* location, from suffixed form **si-tu-* from *si-,* probably from **tki-.* [Pokorny 1. *k̑ei-* 539, *k̑tei-* 626.]

to-. Important derivatives are *the*[1], *decoy, though, these, this, than, then, there, they, their, them, that, those, thus,* and *tandem.*

to-. Demonstrative pronoun. For the nominative singular see **so-.** **1.a.** THE[2]; NATHELESS, from Old

…umental case), by the; **b.** DE… …de, the. Both **a** and **b** from …UGH, from Middle English …andinavian source akin to …m Germanic **thauh,* "for …HIS, (THOSE), from Old English …from Germanic **thasi-.* **4.** THAN, … Old English *thanne, thænne, thenne,* …hen, from Germanic **thana-.* **5.** THENCE, …om Old English *thanon,* thence, from Germanic **thanana-.* **6.** THERE, from Old English *thǣr, thēr,* there, from Germanic **thēr.* **7.** THITHER, from Old English *thæder, thider,* thither, from Germanic **thathro.* **8.** THEY, from Old Norse *their,* they, from Germanic nominative plural **thai.* **9.** THEIR, from Old Norse *their(r)a,* theirs, from Germanic genitive plural **thaira.* **10.** THEM, from Old Norse *theim* and Old English *thǣm,* them, from Germanic dative plural **thaimiz.* **11.** Extended neuter form **tod-.* THAT, from Old English *thæt,* that, from Germanic **that.* **12.** THUS, from Old English *thus,* thus, from Germanic **thus-.* **13.** Adverbial (originally accusative) form **tam.* TANDEM, TANTAMOUNT, from Latin *tandem,* at last, so much, and *tantus,* so much. **14.** Suffixed reduced form **t-āli-.* TALES, from Latin *tālis,* such. **15.** TAUTO-, from Greek *to,* the. [Pokorny 1. *to-* 1086.]

tolk^{w}-. Important derivatives are *loquacious, circumlocution, colloquium, elocution, soliloquy,* and *ventriloquism.*

tolk^{w}-. To speak. Metathesized form **tlok^{w}-.* LOCUTION, LOQUACIOUS; ALLOCUTION, CIRCUMLOCUTION, COLLOQUIUM, (COLLOQUY), ELOCUTION, GRANDILOQUENCE, INTERLOCUTION, MAGNILOQUENT, OBLOQUY, SOLILOQUY, VENTRILOQUISM, from Latin *loquī,* to speak. [Pokorny *tolk$^{u̯}$-* 1088.]

tong-. Important derivatives are *thank, think,* and *thought.*

tong-. To think, feel. **1.** THANK, from Old English *thanc,* thought, good will, and *thancian,* to thank, from Germanic **thankaz,* thought, gratitude, and **thankōn,* to think of, thank. **2.** BETHINK, THINK, from Old English *(bi)thencan,* to think, from Germanic **(bi-)thankjan.* **3.** THOUGHT, from Old English *(ge)thōht,* thought, from Germanic **(ga)thanht-* (**ga-,* collective prefix; see **kom**). **4.** METHINKS, from Old English *thyncan,* (third person singular present indicative *thyncth*), to seem, from Germanic **thunkjan.* [Pokorny 1. *tong-* 1088.]

treb-. Derivatives are *thorp* and *trave.*

treb-. Dwelling. **1.** Zero-grade form **tr̥b-.* THORP, from Old English *thorp,* village, hamlet, from Germanic **thurp-.* **2.** TRABEATED, TRABECULA, TRAVE; ARCHITRAVE, from Latin *trabs,* beam, timber. [Pokorny *treb-* 1090.]

trei-. Important derivatives are *three, thrice, thirteen, thirty, trio, third, tertiary, triple, testament, testimony, attest, contest, detest, protest, testify, sitar,* and *trinity.*

trei-. Three.

I. Nominative plural form **treyes.* **1.a.** THREE, THRICE; THIRTEEN, THIRTY, from Old English *thrīe, thrēo, thrī,* three, with its derivatives *thrīga, thrīwa,* thrice, *thrītig,* thirty, and *thrēotīne,* thirteen (*-tīne,* ten; see **dekm̥**); **b.** TRILLIUM, from Old Swedish *thrīr,* three. Both **a** and **b** from Germanic **thrijiz,* **2.** TREY; TRAMMEL, TRECENTO, TREPHINE, TRIUMVIR, TROCAR, from Latin *trēs,* three. **3.** TRISKAIDEKAPHOBIA, from Greek *treis, tris,* three.

II. Zero-grade form **tri-.* **1.** Suffixed form **tri-tyo-.* **a.** *(i)* THIRD, from Old English *thrid(d)a, thirdda,* third; *(ii)* RIDING[2], from Old Norse *thridhi,* third. Both *(i)* and *(ii)* from Germanic **thridjaz,* third; **b.** TERCEL, TERCET, TERTIAN, TERTIARY, TIERCE; SESTERCE, from Latin *tertius* (neuter *tertium*), third. **2.** Combining form **tri-.* **a.** TRI-, TRIBE, TRIO, TRIPLE, from Latin *tri-,* three; **b.** TRI-; TRICLINIUM, TRICROTIC, TRIDACTYL, TRIGLYPH, TRITONE, from Greek *tri-,* three; **c.** TRIMURTI, from Sanskrit *tri-,* three. **3.** TRIAD, from Greek *trias,* the number three. **4.** TRICHOTOMY, from Greek *trikha,* in three parts. **5.** TRIERARCH, from Greek compound *triērēs,* galley with three banks of oars, trireme (*-ērēs,* oar; see **erə-**). **6.** Suffixed form **tri-to-.* TRITIUM; TRITANOPIA, from Greek *tritos,* third. **7.** Compound form **tri-pl-,* "threefold" (**-pl-* < combining form **-plo-;* see **pel-[2]**). TRIPLOBLASTIC, from Greek *triploos,* triple. **8.** Compound form **tri-plek-,* "threefold" (**-plek-,* -fold; see **plek-**). TRIPLEX, from Latin *triplex,* triple. **9.** Compound form **tri-st-i-,* "third person standing by" (see **stā-**). TESTAMENT, (TESTIMONY); ATTEST, CONTEST, DETEST, OBTEST, PROTEST, TESTIFY, from Latin *testis,* a witness. **10.** SITAR, from Persian *si,* three.

III. Extended zero-grade form **tris,* "thrice." **1.** TERN[2]; TERPOLYMER, from Latin *ter,* thrice. **2.** TRISOCTAHEDRON, from Greek *tris,* thrice. **3.** Suffixed form **tris-no-.* TRINE, (TRINITY), from Latin *trīnī,* three each.

IV. Suffixed o-grade form **troy-o-.* TROIKA, from Russian *troje,* group of three. [Pokorny *trei-* 1090.]

trep-. Important derivatives are *trope, contrive, retrieve, trophy, tropic,* and *entropy.*

trep-. To turn. **1.** -TROPOUS; APOTROPAIC, (ATROPOS), TREPONEMA, from Greek *trepein,* to turn, with o-grade *tropos,* turning. **2.** O-grade form **trop-.* **a.** suffixed form **trop-o-.* TROPE, (TROUBADOUR), (TROVER); CONTRIVE, (RETRIEVE), from Greek *tropos,* a turn, way, manner; **b.** suffixed form **trop-ā-.* TROPHY, TROPIC, TROPO-; ENTROPY, from Greek *tropē,* a turning, change. [Pokorny 2. *trep-* 1094.]

treud-. Important derivatives are *threat, thrust, intrude,* and *protrude.*

treud-. To squeeze. **1.** Suffixed o-grade form **troud-o-.* THREAT, from Old English *thrēat,* oppression, use of force, from Germanic **thrautam.* **2.** Variant form **trūd-.* THRUST, from Old Norse *thrȳsta,* to squeeze, compress, from Germanic **thrūstjan.* **3.** ABSTRUSE, EXTRUDE, INTRUDE, OBTRUDE, PROTRUDE, from Latin *trūdere,* to thrust, push. [Pokorny *tr-eu-d* 1095.]

tu-. Important derivatives are *thee, thou[1], thine,* and *thy.*

tu-. Second person singular pronoun; you, thou. **1.** Lengthened form **tū* (accusative **te, *tege*). (THEE), THOU[1], from Old English *thū* (accusative *thec, thē*), thou, from Germanic **thū* (accusative **theke*). **2.** Suffixed extended form **t(w)ei-no-.* THINE, THY, from Old English *thīn,* thine, from Germanic **thīnaz.* [Pokorny *tu-* 1097.]

ud-. Important derivatives are *out, utmost, carouse, outlaw, utter[1], utter[2], but, about, ersatz,* and *hubris.*

ud-. Also **ūd-.** Up, out. **1.a.** OUT; UTMOST, from Old English *ūt,* out; **b.** CAROUSE; AUSLANDER, from Old High German *ūz,* out; **c.** OUTLAW, from Old Norse *ūt,* out; **d.** UITLANDER, from Middle Dutch *ute, uut,* out; **e.** UTTER[1], from Middle Low German *ūt,* out; **f.** UTTER[2], from Old English *ūtera,* outer, from Germanic suffixed (comparative) form **ūt-era-;* **g.** BUT; ABOUT, from Old English *būtan, būte,* outside (adverb), from Germanic compound **bi-ūtana,* "at the outside" (**bi-,* by, at; see **ambhi**). **a, b, c, d, e, f,** and **g** all from Germanic **ūt-,* out. **2.** Extended form **uds.* **a.** ERSATZ, from Old High German *irsezzan,* to replace, from *ir-,* out; **b.** ORT, from Middle Dutch *oor,* out; **c.** (see **dail-**) Germanic **uzdailjam,* "a portioning out," judgment; **d.** URSPRACHE, from Old High German *ur-,* out of, original. **a, b, c,** and **d** all from Germanic **uz, *uz-,* out. **3.** Suffixed (comparative) form **ud-tero-.* HYSTERESIS, HYSTERON PROTERON, from Greek *husteros,* later, second, after. **4.** HUBRIS, from Greek compound *hubris,* violence, outrage, insolence (*hri-,* perhaps "heavy," "violent"; see **g^{w}erə-[1]**), from *hu-.* **5.** VIGORISH, from Russian *vy-,* out. [Pokorny *ŭd-* 1103.]

uper. Important derivatives are *over, sovereign, super-, superior, supreme, sirloin, superb, sum, summit, soprano, somersault,* and *hyper-.*

uper. Over. **1.** Extended form **uperi.* **a.** OVER, from Old English *ofer,* over; **b.** ORLOP, from Middle Low German *over,* over. Both **a** and **b** from Germanic **uberi.* **2.** Variant form **(s)uper.* **a.** SOUBRETTE, SOVEREIGN, SUPER-, SUPERABLE, SUPERIOR, SUPREME, (SUPREMO), SUR-; SIRLOIN, from Latin *super, super-,* above, over; **b.** suffixed form **(s)uper-no-.* SUPERNAL, from Latin *supernus,* above, upper, top; **c.** suffixed form **super-bhw-o-,* "being above" (**bhw-o-,* being; see **bheuə-**). SUPERB, from Latin *superbus,* superior, excellent, arrogant; **d.** suffixed (superlative) reduced form **sup-mo-.* SUM, SUMMIT, from Latin *summus,* highest, topmost; **e.** suffixed form **super-o-.* (SOPRANINO), SOPRANO, SUPRA-; SOMERSAULT, from Latin *suprā* (feminine ablative singular), above, beyond. **3.** Basic form **uper.* HYPER-, from Greek *huper,* over. [Pokorny *uper* 1105.]

upo. Important derivatives are *up, uproar, open, above, often, eaves, eavesdrop, sub-, supine[1], supple, hypo-, valet, vassal,* and *opal.*

upo. Under, up from under, over. **1.a.** UP, from Old English *up, uppe,* up; **b.** UP-, from Old English *ūp-, upp-,* up; **c.** UPROAR, from Middle Low German *up,* up; **d.** AUFKLÄRUNG, from Old High German *ūf,* up. **a, b, c,** and **d** all from Germanic **upp-,* up. **2.** OPEN, from Old English *open,* open, from Germanic **upanaz,* "put or set up," open. **3.** ABOVE, from Old English *būfan,* above, over, from Germanic compound **bi-ufana,* "on, above" (**bi-,* by, at; see **ambhi**). **4.** Possibly suffixed form **up-t-.* OFT, OFTEN, from Old English *oft,* often, from Germanic **ufta,* frequently. **5.** Extended form **upes-.* **a.** EAVES, from Old English *efes,* eaves; **b.** EAVESDROP, from Old English *yfesdrype,* water from the eaves, from Germanic **obisdrup-,* dripping water from the eaves (**drup-,* to drip, from **dhrub-;* see **dhreu-**). Both **a** and **b** from Germanic **ubaswō, *ubizwō,* vestibule, porch, eaves (< "that which is above or in front"). **6.** Variant form **(s)up-.* **a.** SOUTANE, SUB-, from Latin *sub,* under; **b.** SUPINE, from Latin *supīnus,* lying on the back (< "thrown backward or under"); **c.** suffixed form **sup-ter.* SUBTERFUGE, from Latin *subter,* secretly; **d.** (see **plāk-[1]**) Latin *supplex,* suppliant, from *sub,* under. **7.** Basic form **upo.* HYPO-, from Greek *hupo,* under. **8.** Suffixed variant form **ups-o-.* HYPSO-, from Greek *hupsos,* height, top. **9.** Basic form **upo-.* (see **reidh-**) Latin *verēdus,* post horse, from Celtic **wo-,* under. **10.** Probably compound **upo-st-o-.* (VALET), (VARLET), VASSAL, from Vulgar Latin **vassus,* vassal, from Celtic **wasso-,* "one who stands under," servant, young man (**sto-,* standing; see **stā-**). **11.** OPAL, UPANISHAD, from Sanskrit *upa,* near to, under (in *upaniṣad,* Upanishad). [Pokorny *upo* 1106.]

wal-. Important derivatives are *valence, valiant, valid, valor, value, avail, convalesce, equivalent, invalid[1], prevail,* and *wield.*

wal-. To be strong. **1.** Suffixed (stative) form **wal-ē-.* VALE[2], VALENCE, VALETUDINARIAN, VALIANT, VALID, VALOR, VALUE; AMBIVALENCE, AVAIL, CONVALESCE, COUNTERVAIL, EQUIVALENT, (INVALID[1]), INVALID[2], PREVAIL, (VALEDICTION), from Latin *valēre,* to be strong. **2.** Extended o-grade form **wold(h)-.* **a.** WIELD, from Old English *wealdan,* to rule, and *wieldan,* to govern, from Germanic **waldan,* to rule; **b.** (see **koro-**) Germanic **harja-waldaz,* "army commander," from **wald-,* power, rule. **3.** Suffixed extended o-grade form **wold-ti-.* OBLAST, from Old Church Slavonic *vlastĭ,* rule. [Pokorny *u̯al-* 1111.]

we-. An important derivative is *we.*

we-. We. For oblique cases of the pronoun see **nes-[2]**. Suffixed variant form **wey-es.* WE, from Old English *wē, we,* we, from Germanic **wīz.* [Pokorny *u̯ĕ-* 1114.]

wē-. Important derivatives are *weather, wind[1], window, vent, ventilate, wing,* and *nirvana.*

wē-. To blow. Contracted from **weə-;* oldest basic form **əwē-* (< **əweə-*). **1.** Suffixed irregular shortened form **we-dhro-.* WEATHER, from Old English *weder,* weather, storm, wind, from Germanic **wedram* wind, weather. **2.** Suffixed (participial) form **wē-nt-o-,* blowing. **a.** *(i)* WIND[1], from Old English *wind,* wind; *(ii)* WINDOW, from Old Norse *vindr,* wind. Both *(i)* and *(ii)* from Germanic **windaz;* **b.** VENT[1], VENTAIL, VENTILATE, from Latin *ventus,* wind. **3.** WING, from Middle English *wenge,* wing, from a Scandinavian source akin to Old Norse *vængr,* wing, from suffixed Germanic form **wē-ingjaz.* **4.** Basic form **wē-.* NIRVANA, from Sanskrit *vāti* (stem **vā-*), it blows. [Pokorny 10. *au̯(ē)-* 81.]

webh-. Important derivatives are *weave, web, weevil, wafer, waffle[1], wave,* and *wobble.*

webh-. To weave, also to move quickly. **1.** WEAVE, WOOF[1], from Old English *wefan,* to weave, from Germanic **weban.* **2.** WEFT, from Old English *wefta, weft,* cross thread, from Germanic **wefta-.* **3.** Suffixed o-grade form **wobh-yo-.* WEB, WEBSTER, from Old English *web(b),* web, from Germanic **wabjam,* fabric, web. **4.** WEEVIL, from Old English *wifel,* weevil (< "that which moves briskly"), from suffixed Germanic form **webila-.* **5.a.** *(i)* GOFFER, from

Old French *gaufre,* honeycomb, waffle; *(ii)* WAFER, from Old North French *waufre,* wafer. Both *(i)* and *(ii)* from a source akin to Middle Low German *wāfel,* honeycomb; **b.** WAFFLE[1], from Middle Dutch *wāfel,* waffle. Both **a** and **b** from suffixed Germanic form **wabila-,* web, honeycomb. **6.a.** WAVE, from Old English *wafian,* to move (the hand) up and down; **b.** WAVER, from Middle English *waveren,* to waver; **c.** WOBBLE, from Low German *wabbeln,* to move from side to side, sway. **a, b,** and **c** all from Germanic **wab-,* to move back and forth as in weaving, possibly from **webh-. 7.** Suffixed zero-grade form **ubh-ā-.* HYPHA, from Greek *huphē,* web. [Pokorny *u̯ebh-* 1114.]

wed-[1]. Important derivatives are *water, wet, wash, winter, hydrant, hydro-, undulate, abound, inundate, redundant, surround, otter, Hydra, whiskey,* and *vodka.*

wed-[1]. Water; wet. **1.** Suffixed o-grade form **wod-ōr.* **a.** WATER, from Old English *wæter,* water; **b.** KIRSCHWASSER, from Old High German *wassar,* water. Both **a** and **b** from Germanic **watar.* **2.** Suffixed lengthened-grade form **wēd-o-.* WET, from Old English *wǣt, wēt,* wet, from Germanic **wēd-.* **3.** O-grade form **wod-.* WASH, from Old English *wæscan, wacsan,* to wash, from Germanic suffixed form **wat-skan,* to wash. **4.** Nasalized form **we-n-d-.* WINTER, from Old English *winter,* winter, from Germanic **wintruz,* winter, "wet season." **5.** Suffixed zero-grade form **ud-ōr.* (HYDRANT), HYDRO-, (HYDROUS), UTRICLE; ANHYDROUS, CLEPSYDRA, DROPSY, HYDATHODE, HYDATID, from Greek *hudōr,* water. **6.** Suffixed nasalized zero-grade form **u-n-d-ā-.* UNDINE, UNDULATE; ABOUND, INUNDATE, (REDOUND), REDUNDANT, SURROUND, from Latin *unda,* wave. **7.** Suffixed zero-grade form **ud-ro-, *ud-rā-,* water animal. **a.** OTTER, from Old English *otor,* otter, from Germanic **otraz,* otter; **b.** NUTRIA, from Latin *lutra,* otter (with obscure *l-*); **c.** HYDRUS, from Greek *hudros,* a water snake; **d.** HYDRA, from Greek *hudra,* a water serpent, Hydra. **8.** Suffixed zero-grade form **ud-skio-.* USQUEBAUGH, (WHISKEY), from Old Irish *uisce,* water. **9.** Suffixed o-grade form **wod-ā-.* VODKA, from Russian *voda,* water. [Pokorny 9. *au̯(e)-* 78.]

wed-[2]. Important derivatives are *ode, comedy, melody, parody, rhapsody,* and *tragedy.*

wed-[2]. To speak. **1.** Oldest root form **əwed-* becoming **awed-* in possible reduplicated form **awe-ud-,* dissimilated to **aweid-,* with suffixed o-grade form **awoid-o-* (but more likely a separate root **əweid-* becoming Greek **aweid-,* to sing). ODE; COMEDY, EPODE, HYMNODY, MELODY, MONODY, PARODY, RHAPSODY, TRAGEDY, from Greek *aeidein* (Attic *aidein*), to sing, and *aoidē* (Attic *ōidē*), song, ode, with *aoidos* (Attic *ōidos*), a singer, singing. **2.** THERAVADA, from Sanskrit *vādaḥ,* sound, statement. [Pokorny 6. *au-* 76.]

weg-. Important derivatives are *wake[1], waken, watch, bivouac, wait, vegetable, vigor, vigil, vigilante, reveille,* and *velocity.*

weg-. To be strong, be lively. **1.** Suffixed o-grade form **wog-ē-.* WAKE[1], from Old English *wacan,* to wake up, arise, and *wacian,* to be awake, from Germanic **wakēn.* **2.** Suffixed o-grade form **wog-no-.* WAKEN, from Old English *wæcnan, wæcnian,* to awake, from Germanic **waknan.* **3.** WATCH, from Old English *wæccan,* to be awake, from Germanic **wakjan.* **4.** Suffixed form **weg-yo-.* (WICCA), (WICKED), WITCH; (BEWITCH), from Old English *wicca,* sorcerer, wizard (feminine *wicce,* witch), from Germanic **wikkjaz,* necromancer (< "one who wakes the dead"). **5.** BIVOUAC, from Old High German *wahta,* watch, vigil, from Germanic **wahtwō.* **6.a.** WAIT, from Old North French *waitier,* to watch; **b.** WAFT, from Middle Dutch and Middle Low German *wachten,* to watch, guard. Both **a** and **b** from Germanic **waht-.* **7.** Suffixed (causative) o-grade form **wog-eyo-.* VEGETABLE, from Latin *vegēre,* to be lively. **8.** Suffixed (stative) form **weg-ē-.* VIGOR, from Latin *vigēre,* to be lively. **9.** Suffixed form **weg-(e)li-.* VEDETTE, VIGIL, (VIGILANT), VIGILANTE; REVEILLE, SURVEILLANT, from Latin *vigil,* watchful, awake. **10.** Suffixed form **weg-slo-.* VELOCITY, from Latin *vēlōx,* fast, "lively." [Pokorny *u̯eĝ-* 1117.]

wegh-. Important derivatives are *weigh[1], wee, weight, way, always, away, wagon, wag[1], vogue, earwig, wiggle, vector, vehicle, convection, via, voyage, convey, deviate, devious, envoy[1], obvious, previous, trivial, vex,* and *convex.*

wegh-. To go, transport in a vehicle. **1.** WEIGH[1], from Old English *wegan,* to carry, balance in a scale, from Germanic **wegan.* **2.** WEE, from Old English *wǣg(e),* weight, unit of weight, from Germanic lengthened-grade form **wēgō.* **3.** Suffixed form **wegh-ti-.* WEIGHT, from Old English *wiht, gewiht,* weight, from Germanic **wihti-.* **4.a.** WAY; ALWAYS, AWAY, from Old English *weg,* way; **b.** NORWEGIAN, from Old Norse *vegr,* way. Both **a** and **b** from Germanic **wegaz,* course of travel, way. **5.** Suffixed o-grade form **wogh-no-.* **a.** WAIN, from Old English *wæ(g)n,* wagon; **b.** WAGON, from Middle Dutch *wagen,* wagon. Both **a** and **b** from Germanic **wagnaz.* **6.** Suffixed o-grade form **wogh-lo-.* **a.** WALLEYED, from Old Norse *vagl,* chicken roost, perch, beam, eye disease, from Germanic **waglaz;* **b.** OCHLOCRACY, OCHLOPHOBIA, from Greek *okhlos,* populace, mob (< "moving mass"). **7.** Distantly related to this root are: **a.** *(i)* WAG[1], from Middle English *waggen,* to wag, possibly from **wegh-;** *(ii)* GRAYWACKE, from Old High German *waggo, wacko,* boulder rolling on a riverbed. Both *(i)* and *(ii)* from Germanic **wag-,* "to move about"; **b.** VOGUE, from Old French *voguer,* to row, sail, from Old Low German **wogōn,* to rock, sway, from Germanic **wēga-,* water in motion; **c.** *(i)* EARWIG, from Old English *wicga,* insect (< "thing that moves quickly"); *(ii)* WIGGLE, from Middle Dutch and Middle Low German *wiggelen,* to move back and forth, wag. Both *(i)* and *(ii)* from Germanic **wig-.* **8.** Basic form **wegh-.* VECTOR, VEHEMENT, VEHICLE; ADVECTION, CONVECTION, EVECTION, INVEIGH, from Latin *vehere* (past participle *vectus*), to carry. **9.** Suffixed basic form **wegh-yā.* FOY, VIA, VOYAGE; CONVEY, DEVIATE, DEVIOUS, (ENVOI), ENVOY[1], OBVIOUS, PERVIOUS, PREVIOUS, (TRIVIAL), TRIVIUM, (VIADUCT), from Latin *via,* way, road. **10.** Suffixed form **wegh-s-.* VEX, from Latin *vexāre,* to agitate (< "to set in motion"). **11.** Probably suffixed form **wegh-so-.* CONVEX, from Latin *convexus,* "carried or drawn together (to a point)," convex (*com-,* together; see **kom**). [Pokorny *u̯eĝh-* 1118.]

wei-. Important derivatives are *wire, ferrule, vise, viticulture,* and *iris.*

wei-. Also **weiə-.** To turn, twist; with derivatives referring to suppleness or binding.
I. Form **wei-.* **1.a.** WIRE, from Old English *wīr,* wire; **b.** GARLAND, from Old French *garlande,* wreath, from Frankish **wiara, *weara,* wire. Both **a** and **b** from Germanic suffixed form **wī-ra-, *wēra-.* **2.** SEAWARE, from Old English *wār,* seaweed, from suffixed Germanic form **wai-ra-,* probably from **wei-. 3.** Suffixed zero-grade form **wi-ria-.* FERRULE, from Latin *viriae,* bracelets (of Celtic origin). **4.** Suffixed form **wei-ti-.* WITHY, from Old English *wīthig,* willow, withy, from Germanic **wīth-,* willow. **5.** Suffixed zero-grade form **wi-t-.* WITHE, from Old English *withthe,* supple twig, from Germanic **withjōn-.*
II. Form **weiə-,* zero-grade **wī-* (< **wiə-*). **1.** Suffixed form **wī-ti-.* VISE; VITICULTURE, from Latin *vītis,* vine. **2.** Suffixed form **wī-tā-* becoming **wittā.* VITTA, from Latin *vitta,* headband. **3.** Suffixed form **wī-men-.* MIMBRES, from Latin *vīmen,* withy, wicker. **4.** Probably suffixed form **wī-ri-.* (IRIDACEOUS), IRIDO-, IRIS, IRIS; (IRIDIUM), (IRITIS), from Greek *iris,* rainbow, and *Iris,* rainbow goddess. **5.** Perhaps suffixed form **wī-n-.* INION; EXINE, INOSITOL, INOTROPIC, from Greek *is* (genitive *inos*), sinew. [Pokorny 1. *u̯ei-* 1120.]

weid-. Important derivatives are *guide, wise[1], wisdom, guise, idol, kaleidscope, Hades, wit[1], unwitting, view, visa, vision, advice, clairvoyance, envy, evident, interview, provide, review, supervise, survey, idea, history, story[1],* and *penguin.*

weid-. To see.
I. Full-grade form **weid-.* **1.a.** TWIT, from Old English *wītan,* to reproach; **b.** GUIDE, from Old Provençal *guidar,* to guide; **c.** GUY[1], from Old French *guier,* to guide; **d.** WITE, from Old English *wīte,* fine, penalty, from Germanic derivative noun **wīti-.* **a, b, c,** and **d** all from Germanic **wītan,* to look after, guard, ascribe to, reproach. **2.** Suffixed form **weid-to-.* **a.** WISE[1], from Old English *wīs,* wise; **b.** WISDOM, from Old English *wīsdōm,* learning, wisdom (*-dōm,* abstract suffix; see **dhē-**); **c.** WISEACRE, from Old High German *wīssago,* seer, prophet; **d.** *(i)* WISE[2], from Old English *wīse, wīs,* manner; *(ii)* GUISE, from Old French *guise,* manner. Both *(i)* and *(ii)* from Germanic **wīssōn-,* appearance, manner. **a, b, c,** and **d** all from Germanic **wīs* **3.** Suffixed form **weid-es-.* EIDETIC, EIDOLON, IDO IDYLL, -OID; IDOCRASE, KALEIDOSCOPE, from Greek *eidos,* form, shape.
II. Zero-grade form **wid-.* **1.a.** WIT[1], from Old English *wit, witt,* knowledge, intelligence; **b.** WITENAGEMOT, from Old English *wita,* wise man, councilor. Both **a** and **b** from Germanic **wit-.* **2.** WIT[2]; UNWITTING, from Old English *witan,* to know, from Germanic **witan.* **3.** Suffixed form **wid-to-.* IWIS, from Old English *gewis, gewiss,* certain, sure, from Germanic **wissaz,* known. **4.** Form **wid-ē-* (with participial form **weid-to-*). VIDE, VIEW, VISA, VISAGE, VISION, VISTA, VOYEUR; ADVICE, (ADVISE), BELVEDERE, BLACK-A-VISED, CLAIRVOYANT, ENVY, EVIDENT, INTERVIEW, PREVISE, PROVIDE, REVIEW, SUPERVISE, SURVEY, from Latin *vidēre,* to see, look. **5.** Suffixed form **wid-es-ya.* IDEA, IDEO-, from Greek *idea,* appearance, form, idea. **6.** Suffixed form **wid-tor-.* HISTORY, (STORY[1]); POLYHISTOR, from Greek *histōr,* wise, learned, learned man. **7.** HADAL, HADES, from Greek *Haidēs* (also *Aidēs*), the underworld, perhaps "the invisible" and from **wid-.* **8.** Suffixed nasalized form **wi-n-d-o-.* **a.** COLCANNON, from Old Irish *find,* white (< "clearly visible"); **b.** PENGUIN, from Welsh *gwyn, gwynn,* white. **9.** (see **deru-**) Celtic compound **dru-wid-,* "strong seer" (**dru-,* strong).
III. Suffixed o-grade form **woid-o-.* VEDA; RIG-VEDA, from Sanskrit *vedaḥ,* knowledge. [Pokorny 2. *u̯(e)di-* 1125.]

weiə-. Important derivatives are *vim, violate,* and *violent.*

weiə-. Vital force. Related to **wī-ro-.** Zero-grade form **wī-* (< **wiə-*). VIM, VIOLATE, VIOLENT, from Latin *vīs,* force, with irregular derivatives *violāre,* to treat with force, and *violentus,* vehement. [In Pokorny 3. *u̯ei-* 1123.]

weik-[1]. Important derivatives are *village, villain, vicinity, diocese, ecology, economy,* and *parish.*

weik-[1]. Clan (social unit above the household). **1.** Suffixed form **weik-slā.* VILLA, VILLAGE, VILLAIN, VILLANELLE, (VILLEIN); (BIDONVILLE), from Latin *vīlla,* country house, farm. **2.** Suffixed o-grade form **woik-o-.* **a.** (VICINAGE), VICINITY; (BAILIWICK), from Latin *vīcus,* quarter or district of a town, neighborhood; **b.** ANDROECIUM, AUTOECIOUS, DIOCESE, DIOECIOUS, DIOICOUS, ECESIS, ECOLOGY, ECONOMY, ECUMENICAL, HETEROECIOUS, MONOECIOUS, PARISH, from Greek *oikos,* house, and its derivatives *oikia,* a dwelling, and *oikēsis,* dwelling, administration. **3.** Zero-grade form **wik-.* VAISYA, from Sanskrit *viśaḥ,* dwelling, house. [Pokorny *u̯eik̑-* 1131.]

weik-[2]. Important derivatives are *wicker, wicket, weak, week, vicar,* and *vicarious.*

weik-[2]. Also **weig-.** To bend, wind.
I. Form **weig-.* **1.a.** WYCH ELM, from Old English *wice,* wych elm (having pliant branches); **b.** WICKER, from Middle English *wiker,* wicker, from a Scandinavian source akin to Swedish *viker,* willow twig, wand; **c.** WICKET, from Old North French *wiket,* wicket (< "door that turns"), from a Scandinavian source probably akin to Old Norse *vikja,* to bend, turn. **a, b,** and **c** all from Germanic **wik-.* **2.a.** WEAK, from Old Norse *veikr,* pliant; **b.** WEAKFISH, from Middle Dutch *weec,* weak, soft. Both **a** and **b** from Germanic **waikwaz.* **3.** WEEK, from Old English *wicu, wice,* week, from Germanic **wikōn-,* "a turning," series.
II. Form **weik-.* Zero-grade form **wik-.* **a.** VICAR, (VICARIOUS), VICE-; VICISSITUDE, from Latin **vix* (genitive *vicis*), turn, situation, change; **b.** VETCH, from Latin *vicia,* vetch (< "twining plant"). [Pokorny 4. *u̯eik-* 1130.]

weik-[3]. Important derivatives are *vanquish, victor, convince,* and *evict.*

weik-[3]. To fight, conquer. **1.** WIGHT[2], from Old Norse *vīgr,* able in battle, from Germanic **wīk-.* **2.** Nasalized zero-grade form **wi-n-k-.* VANQUISH, VICTOR, VINCIBLE; CONVINCE, EVICT, from Latin *vincere,* to conquer. **3.** Zero-grade form **wik-.* ORDOVICIAN, from Celtic *Ordovices* (**ordo-wik-*), "those who fight with hammers" (**ordo-,* hammer). [Pokorny 2. *u̯eik-* 1128.]

weip-. Important derivatives are *waive, wipe, whip,* and *vibrate.*

…te, tremble ecstatically. **1.** … WAIF[1], WAIF[2], (WAIVE), …man *waif,* ownerless prop-… source probably akin to …ng thing, flag, from Germanic …ant form **weib-*. **a.** WIPE, from Old …pian, to wipe; **b.** GUIPURE, from Old … *guiper,* to cover with silk; **c.** WHIP, from …iddle English *wippen,* to whip. **a, b,** and **c** all from Germanic **wīpjan,* to move back and forth. **3.** Perhaps suffixed nasalized zero-grade form **wi-m-p-ila-*. **a.** WIMPLE, from Old English *wimpel,* covering for the neck (< "something that winds around"); **b.** (GIMP[1]), GUIMPE, from Old High German *wimpal,* guimpe; **c.** WIMBLE, from Middle Dutch *wimmel,* auger (< "that which turns in boring"), perhaps from **weip-.** **4.** Suffixed zero-grade variant form **wib-ro-*. VIBRATE, from Latin *vibrāre,* to vibrate. [Pokorny *u̯eip-* 1131.]

wekti-. Important derivatives are *wight[1], aught[2], naught,* and *not.*

wekti-. Thing, creature. **a.** WIGHT[1]; (AUGHT[2]), NAUGHT, (NOT), from Old English *wiht,* person, thing; **b.** NIX[2], from Old High German *wiht,* thing, being. Both **a** and **b** from Germanic **wihti-*. [Pokorny *u̯ek-ti-* 1136.]

wekʷ-. Important derivatives are *vocal, voice, vowel, equivocal, vocation, vouch, advocate, avocation, evoke, invoke, provoke, revoke,* and *epic.*

wekʷ-. To speak. **1.** O-grade form **wōkʷ-*. **a.** VOCAL, VOICE, VOWEL; EQUIVOCAL, UNIVOCAL, from Latin *vōx* (stem *vōc-*), voice; **b.** CALLIOPE, from Greek *ops,* voice. **2.** Suffixed o-grade form **wokʷ-ā-*. VOCABLE, VOCATION, VOUCH; ADVOCATE, AVOCATION, CONVOKE, EVOKE, INVOKE, PROVOKE, REVOKE, from Latin *vocāre,* to call. **3.** Suffixed form **wekʷ-es-*. EPIC, EPOS; EPOPEE, ORTHOEPY, from Greek *epos,* song, word. [Pokorny *u̯ekᵘ̯-* 1135.]

wel-[1]. Important derivatives are *well[2], wealth, will[1], will[2], gallop, gallant, volition, voluntary, benevolent, malevolent,* and *voluptuous.*

wel-[1]. To wish, will. **1.** WELL[2], from Old English *wel,* well (< "according to one's wish"), from Germanic **wel-*. **2.** WEAL[1], WEALTH, from Old English *wela, weola,* well-being, riches, from Germanic **welōn-*. **3.** WILL[1], from Old English *willa,* desire, will power, from Germanic **wiljōn-*. **4.** WILL[2]; NILL, from Old English *willan,* to desire, from Germanic **wil(l)jan*. **5.** (see **gʷā-**) Germanic compound **wil-kumōn-*. **6.** O-grade form **wol-*. **a.** GALLOP, from Old French *galoper,* to gallop; **b.** WALLOP, from Old North French **waloper,* to gallop; **c.** GALLANT, from Old French *galer,* to rejoice, from Frankish Latin **walāre,* to take it easy, from Frankish **wala,* good, well. **a, b,** and **c** all from Germanic **wal-*. **7.** Basic form **wel-*. VELLEITY, VOLITION, VOLUNTARY; BENEVOLENT, MALEVOLENCE, from Latin *velle* (present stem *vol-*), to wish, will. **8.** Suffixed form **wel-up-*. VOLUPTUARY, VOLUPTUOUS, from Latin *voluptās,* pleasure. [Pokorny 2. *u̯el-* 1137.]

wel-[2]. Important derivatives are *waltz, willow, walk, well[1], wallow, vault[1], vault[2], volume, evolve, involve, revolve, vulva, valve, valley,* and *helix.*

wel-[2]. To turn, roll; with derivatives referring to curved, enclosing objects. **1.a.** WALTZ, from Old High German *walzan,* to roll, waltz; **b.** WELTER, from Middle Low German or Middle Dutch *welteren,* to roll. Both **a** and **b** from Germanic **walt-*. **2.** WHELK[1], from Old English *weoluc, weoloc,* mollusk (having a spiral shell), whelk, from Germanic **weluka-*. **3.** WILLOW, from Old English *welig,* willow (with flexible twigs), from Germanic **wel-,* perhaps from **wel-[2].** **4.** WALK, from Old English *wealcan,* to roll, toss, and *wealcian,* to muffle up, from Germanic **welk-,* perhaps from **wel-[2].** **5.** O-grade form **wol-*. **a.** WELL[1], from Old English *wiella, wælla, welle,* a well (< "rolling or bubbling water," "spring"); **b.** GABERDINE, from Old High German *wallōn,* to roam; **c.** WALLET, possibly from Old North French **walet,* roll, knapsack. **a, b,** and **c** all from Germanic **wall-*. **6.** Perhaps suffixed o-grade form **wol-ā-*. **a.** WALE, from Old English *walu,* streak on the skin, weal, welt; **b.** (see **wrād-**) Old High German **wurzwalu,* rootstock, from **-walu,* a roll, round stem. Both **a** and **b** from Germanic **walō*. **7.** Extended form **welw-*. **a.** WALLOW, from Old English *wealwian,* to roll (in mud), from Germanic **walwōn;* **b.** VAULT[1], VAULT[2], (VOLT[2]), VOLUBLE, VOLUME, VOLUTE, VOLUTIN, VOLVOX, VOUSSOIR; CIRCUMVOLVE, CONVOLVE, DEVOLVE, EVOLVE, INVOLVE, REVOLVE, from Latin *volvere,* to roll; **c.** suffixed o-grade form **wolw-ā-*. VOLVA, VULVA, from Latin *vulva, volva,* covering, womb; **d.** suffixed zero-grade form **wl̥w-ā-*. VALVE, from Latin *valva,* leaf of a door (< "that which turns"); **e.** Suffixed zero-grade form **wl̥u-ti-*. ALYCE CLOVER, from Greek *halusis,* chain; **f.** suffixed form **welu-tro-*. ELYTRON, from Greek *elutron,* sheath, cover. **8.** Suffixed form *wel-n-*. ILEUS; NEURILEMMA, from Greek *eilein* (< **welnein*), to turn, squeeze. **9.** Perhaps variant **wall-*. VAIL[1], VALE[1], VALLEY, from Latin *vallēs, vallis,* valley (< "that which is surrounded by hills"). **10.** Possibly suffixed form **wel-enā*. ELECAMPANE, INULIN, from Greek *helenion,* elecampane, from the Greek name *Helenē* (earliest form *Welenā*), Helen. **11.** Suffixed form **wel-ik-*. HELIX, from Greek *helix,* spiral object. **12.** Suffixed form **wel-mi-nth-*. HELMINTH; ANTHELMINTIC, PLATYHELMINTH, from Greek *helmis, helmins* (stem *helminth-*), parasitic worm. [Pokorny 7. *u̯el-* 1140.]

welə-. An important derivative is *vulnerable.*

welə-. To strike, wound. **1.** Suffixed o-grade form **wol(ə)-o-*. **a.** VALHALLA, from Old Norse *Valhöll,* Valhalla; **b.** VALKYRIE, from Old Norse *Valkyrja,* "chooser of the slain," name of one of the twelve war goddesses (*-kyrja,* chooser; see **geus-**). Both **a** and **b** from Old Norse *valr,* the slain in battle, from Germanic **walaz.* **2.** Suffixed basic form **welə-nes-*. VULNERABLE, from Latin *vulnus* (stem *vulner-*), a wound. **3.** Suffixed zero-grade form **wlə-to-*. BERDACHE, from Old Iranian **varta-* (Avestan *varəta-*), seized, prisoner. [In Pokorny 8. *u̯el-* 1144.]

wemə-. Important derivatives are *vomit* and *emetic.*

wemə-. To vomit. **1.** WAMBLE, from Middle English *wam(e)len,* to feel nausea, stagger, from a Scandinavian source probably akin to Old Norse *vamla,* qualm, and Danish *vamle,* to become sick, from Germanic **wam-*. **2.** NUX VOMICA, VOMIT, from Latin *vomere,* to vomit. **3.** EMESIS, EMETIC, from Greek *emein,* to vomit. [Pokorny *u̯em-* 1146.]

wen-[1]. Important derivatives are *win, winsome, wont, wean[1], wish, venerate, venereal, Venus, venom, venial,* and *venison.*

wen-[1]. To desire, strive for. **1.** Suffixed form **wen-w-*. WIN, from Old English *winnan,* to win, from Germanic **winn(w)an,* to seek to gain. **2.** Suffixed zero-grade form **wn̥-yā*. WYNN, WINSOME, from Old English *wynn, wen,* pleasure, joy, from Germanic **wunjō*. **3.** Suffixed (stative) zero-grade form **wn̥-ē-,* to be contented. WON[1], (WONT), from Old English *wunian,* to become accustomed to, dwell, from Germanic **wunēn*. **4.** Suffixed (causative) o-grade form **won-eyo-*. WEAN, from Old English *wenian,* to accustom, train, wean, from Germanic **wanjan*. **5.** WEEN, from Old English *wēnan,* to expect, imagine, think, from Germanic denominative **wēnjan,* to hope, from **wēniz,* hope. **6.** Suffixed zero-grade form **wn̥-sko-*. WISH, from Old English *wȳscan,* to desire, wish, from Germanic **wunsk-*. **7.** Perhaps o-grade **won-*. **a.** VANIR, from Old Norse *Vanir,* the Vanir; **b.** VANADIUM, from Old Norse *Vanadīs,* name of the goddess Freya. Both **a** and **b** from Germanic **wana-*. **8.** Suffixed form **wen-es-*. **a.** VENERATE, VENEREAL, VENERY[1], VENUS, from Latin *venus,* love; **b.** suffixed form **wen-es-no-*. VENOM, from Latin *venēnum,* love potion, poison. **9.** Possibly suffixed form **wen-eto-,* "beloved." WEND, from Old High German *Winid,* Wend, from Germanic **Weneda-,* a Slavic people. **10.** Suffixed form **wen-yā*. VENIAL, from Latin *venia,* favor, forgiveness. **11.** Lengthened-grade form **wēn-ā-*. VENATIC, VENERY[2], VENISON, from Latin *vēnārī,* to hunt. **12.** Suffixed basic form **wen-o-*. WANDEROO, from Sanskrit *vanam,* forest. **13.** Possibly zero-grade suffixed form **wn̥-ig-*. BANYAN, from Sanskrit *vaṇik, vāṇijaḥ,* merchant (? < "seeking to gain"). [Pokorny 1. *u̯en-* 1146.]

wen-[2]. An important derivative is *wound[1].*

wen-[2]. To beat, wound. **1.** Suffixed zero-grade form **wn̥-to-*. WOUND[1], from Old English *wund,* a wound, from Germanic **wundaz*. **2.** Suffixed o-grade form **won-yo-*. WEN[1], from Old English *wen(n), wæn(n),* wen, from Germanic **wanja-,* a swelling. [In Pokorny 1. *u̯ā-* 1108.]

wep-. An important derivative is *evil.*

wep-. Bad, evil. From earlier **əwep-*. Suffixed zero-grade form **up-elo-*. EVIL, from Old English *yfel,* evil, from Germanic **ubilaz,* evil.

wer-[1]. Important derivatives are *artery, aerial, air, aria, malaria,* and *aura.*

wer-[1]. To raise, lift, hold suspended. Earlier form **əwer-*. **1.** Basic form **awer-*. AORTA, ARSIS, ARTERIO-, ARTERIOLE, ARTERY, from Greek *aeirein,* to raise, and *artēria,* windpipe, artery. **2.** (Obscure basic form **āwer-*). AERIAL, AERO-, AIR, ARIA; MALARIA, from Greek *aēr,* air, possibly referred to this root. **3.** Zero-grade form **aur-*. AURA, from Greek *aura,* breath, vapor (related to Greek *aēr,* air). [Pokorny 1. *u̯er-* 1151.]

wer-[2]. Important derivatives are *inward, worth[1], stalwart, weird, versatile, verse[1], version, versus, vertebra, vertex, adverse, anniversary, avert, controversy, convert, divert, invert, pervert, prose, universe, wreath, writhe, wrath, worry, wring, wrong, wrench, wrinkle, converge, wry, wriggle, wrist, wrestle, briar[1], warp, reverberate, wrap, rhapsody, worm,* and *vermin.*

wer-[2]. Conventional base of various Indo-European roots; to turn, bend.

I. Root **wert-,* to turn, wind. **1.a.** *(i)* -WARD, from Old English *-weard,* toward (< "turned toward"); *(ii)* INWARD, from Old English *inweard,* inward, from Germanic **inwarth,* inward (**in,* in; see **en**). Both *(i)* and *(ii)* from Germanic variant **warth;* **b.** WORTH[1]; STALWART, from Old English *weorth,* worth, valuable, and derivative noun *weorth, wierth,* value, from Germanic derivative **werthaz,* "toward, opposite," hence "equivalent, worth," perhaps from **wer-[2].** Both **a** and **b** from Germanic **werth-*. **2.** WORTH[2], from Old English *weorthan,* to befall, from Germanic **werthan,* to become (< "to turn into"). **3.** Zero-grade form **wr̥t-*. WEIRD, from Old English *wyrd,* fate, destiny (< "that which befalls one"), from Germanic **wurthi-*. **4.** VERSATILE, VERSE[1], VERSION, VERSUS, VERTEBRA, VERTEX, VERTIGO, VORTEX; ADVERSE, ANNIVERSARY, AVERT, BOULEVERSEMENT, CONTROVERSY, CONVERSE[1], CONVERT, DEXTRORSE, DIVERT, EVERT, EXTRORSE, (EXTROVERSION), EXTROVERT, INTRORSE, INTROVERT, INVERT, MALVERSATION, OBVERT, PERVERT, PROSE, RETRORSE, REVERT, SINISTRORSE, SUBVERT, TERGIVERSATE, TRANSVERSE, UNIVERSE, from Latin *vertere,* to turn, with its frequentative *versāre,* to turn, and passive *versārī,* to stay, behave (< "to move around a place, frequent"). **5.** VERST, from Russian *versta,* line, from Balto-Slavic **wirstā-,* a turn, bend.

II. Root **wreit-,* to turn. **a.** WREATH, from Old English *writha,* band (< "that which is wound around"); **b.** WRITHE, from Old English *wrīthan,* to twist, torture; **c.** WRATH, WROTH, from Old English *wrāth,* angry (< "tormented, twisted"). **a, b,** and **c** all from Germanic **wrīth-, *wraith-*.

III. Root **wergh-,* to turn. **1.** WORRY, from Old English *wyrgan,* to strangle, from Germanic **wurgjan.* **2.** Nasalized variant **wrengh-*. **a.** WRING, from Old English *wringan,* to twist, from Germanic **wreng-;* **b.** *(i)* WRONG, from Middle English *wrong,* wrong, from a Scandinavian source akin to Old Norse **vrangr, rangr,* curved, crooked, wrong; *(ii)* WRANGLE, from Middle English *wranglen,* to wrangle, from a Low German source akin to *wrangeln,* to wrestle. Both *(i)* and *(ii)* from Germanic **wrang-*.

IV. Root **werg-,* to turn. **1.** Nasalized variant form **wreng-*. **a.** WRENCH, from Old English *wrencan,* to twist; **b.** WRINKLE, from Old English *gewrinclian,* to wind (*ge-,* collective prefix; see **kom**). Both **a** and **b** from Germanic **wrankjan.* **2.** VERGE[2]; CONVERGE, DIVERGE, from Latin *vergere,* to turn, tend toward.

V. Root **wreik-,* to turn. **1.a.** WRY, from Old English *wrīgian,* to turn, bend, go; **b.** WRIGGLE, from Middle Low German *wriggeln,* to wriggle. Both **a** and **b** from Germanic **wrīg-*. **2.a.** WRIST, from Old English *wrist,* wrist; **b.** GAITER, from Old French *guietre,* gaiter, from Frankish **wrist-*. Both **a** and **b** from Germanic **wristiz,* from **wrihst-*. **3.** WREST, WRESTLE, from Old English *wrǣstan,* to twist, from secondary Germanic derivative **wraistjan.* **4.** Possibly o-grade form **wroik-*. BRIAR[1], (BRUSQUE), from Late Latin *brūcus,* heather, from Gaulish **brūko-*.

VI. RIBALD, from Old French *riber,* to be wanton, from Germanic root **wrib-*.

VII. Root **werb-,* also **werbh-,* to turn, bend. **1.** WARP, from Old English *weorpan,* to throw away,

from Germanic *werp-, *warp-, "to fling by turning the arm." 2. REVERBERATE, from Latin verber, whip, rod. 3. VERBENA, (VERVAIN), from Latin verbēna, sacred foliage. 4. Zero-grade form *wr̥b-. RHABDOMANCY, RHABDOVIRUS, from Greek rhabdos, rod. 5. Nasalized variant form *wrembh-. RHOMBUS, from Greek rhombos, magic wheel, rhombus.
VIII. Root *werp-, to turn, wind. 1. Metathesized form *wrep-. WRAP, from Middle English wrappen, to wrap, from a source akin to Danish dialectal vravle, to wind, from Germanic *wrap-. 2. Zero-grade form *wr̥p-. RAPHE, RHAPHIDE; RHAPSODY, STAPHYLORRHAPHY, TENORRHAPHY, from Greek rhaptein, to sew.
IX. Root *wr̥mi-, worm; rhyme word to k^{w}r̥mi-. 1. WORM, from Old English wyrm, worm, from Germanic *wurmiz. 2. VERMEIL, VERMI-, VERMICELLI, VERMICULAR, VERMIN, from Latin vermis, worm. [Pokorny 3. u̯er- 1152.]

wer-^{3}. Important derivatives are wary, aware, ward, lord, steward, warden, award, reward, wardrobe, guard, panorama, and revere^{1}.

wer-^{3}. To perceive, watch out for.
I. O-grade form *wor-. 1. Suffixed form *wor-o-. a. WARY, from Old English wær, watchful; b. AWARE, from Old English gewær, aware (ge-, collective and intensive prefix; see kom); c. WARE^{2}, from Old English warian, to beware. a, b, and c all from Germanic *waraz. 2. Suffixed form wor-to-. a. (i) WARD; LORD, STEWARD, from Old English weard, a watching, keeper; (ii) WARDER^{2}, from Old English weardian, to ward, guard; b. WARDEN; AWARD, REWARD, WARDROBE, from Old North French warder, to guard; c. GUARD, from Old French guarder, to guard; d. REARWARD^{2}, from Anglo-Norman warde, guard. a, b, c, and d all from Germanic *wardaz, guard, and *wardōn, to guard. 3. WARE^{1}, from Old English waru, goods, protection, guard, from Germanic *warō. 4. Suffixed form *wor-wo-. ARCTURUS, PYLORUS, from Greek ouros, a guard. 5. Probably variant *(s)wor-, *s(w)or-. EPHOR, PANORAMA, from Greek horan, to see.
II. Suffixed (stative) form *wer-ē-. REVERE^{1}, from Latin verērī, to respect, feel awe for. [Pokorny 8. u̯er- 1164.]

wer-^{4}. Important derivatives are weir, aperture, overt, overture, cover, warn, warrant, warranty, garage, garret, garrison, warren, garment, and garnish.

wer-^{4}. To cover.
I. Basic form *wer-. 1. WEIR, from Old English wer, dam, fish trap, from Germanic *wer-jōn-. 2. Compound form *ap-wer-yo- (*ap-, off, away; see apo-). APERIENT, APÉRITIF, APERTURE; OVERT, OVERTURE, PERT, from Latin aperīre, to open, uncover. 3. Compound form *op-wer-yo- (*op-, over; see epi). COVER, OPERCULUM, from Latin operīre, to cover. 4. Suffixed form *wer-tro-. AMBARELLA, from Sanskrit vātaḥ, enclosure, from lengthened-grade derivative *vārt(r)a-.
II. O-grade form *wor-. 1. WARN, from Old English *war(e)nian, to take heed, warn, from Germanic *war-nōn. 2.a. (i) GUARANTY, from Old French garant, warrant, authorization; (ii) WARRANT, (WARRANTEE), WARRANTY, from Old North French warant, warrant, and warantir, to guarantee; b. GARAGE, from Old French garer, to guard, protect; c. GARRET, GARRISON, from Old French g(u)arir, to defend, protect; d. WARREN, from Old North French warenne, enclosure, game preserve; e. GARMENT, GARNISH, from Old French g(u)arnir, to equip. a, b, c, d, and e all from Germanic *war-. 3. Suffixed form *wor-o-. BARBICAN, from Old Iranian compound *pari-vāraka-, protective (*pari-, around; see per^{1}). [Pokorny 5. u̯er- 1160.]

wer-^{5}. Important derivatives are word, verb, verve, adverb, proverb, and irony.

wer-^{5}. Also werə-. To speak. Variant *wrē-, contracted from *wreə-. 1. Suffixed zero-grade form *wr̥-dho-. WORD, from Old English word, word, from Germanic *wurdam. 2. Suffixed form *wer-dho-. VERB, VERVE; ADVERB, PROVERB, from Latin verbum, word. 3. Suffixed form *wer-yo-. IRONY, from Greek eirein, to say, speak. 4. Variant form *wrē- in suffixed form *wrē-tor-. RHETOR, from Greek rhētōr, public speaker. [Pokorny 6. u̯er- 1162.]

wē-r-. An important derivative is urine.

wē-r-. Contracted from *weə-r-. Water, liquid, milk. Related to euə-dh-r̥. Suffixed zero-grade form *ūr-īnā-. URINE, from Latin ūrīna, urine. [In Pokorny 9. au̯(e)- 78.]

werg-. Important derivatives are work, boulevard, allergy, dramaturge, energy, liturgy, metallurgy, surgery, wrought, wright, organ, and orgy.

werg-. To do.
I. Suffixed form *werg-o-. 1.a. WORK, from Old English weorc, werc, work; b. (BOULEVARD), BULWARK, from Old High German werc, work. Both a and b from Germanic *werkam, work. 2. ERG, -URGY; ADRENERGIC, ALLERGY, ARGON, CHOLINERGIC, DEMIURGE, DRAMATURGE, ENDERGONIC, ENDOERGIC, ENERGY, ERGOGRAPH, ERGOMETER, ERGONOMICS, EXERGONIC, EXERGUE, EXOERGIC, GEORGIC, LITURGY, METALLURGY, SURGERY, (SYNERGID), SYNERGISM, THAUMATURGE, from Greek ergon, work, action.
II. Zero-grade form *wr̥g-. 1. Suffixed forms *wr̥g-yo-, *wr̥g-to-. a. WROUGHT, from Old English wyrcan, to work; b. IRK, from Old Norse yrkja, to work. Both a and b from Germanic *wurkjan, to work, participle *wurhta-. 2. Suffixed form *wr̥g-t-. WRIGHT, from Old English wryhta, maker, wright, from Germanic *wurhtjō-.
III. O-grade form *worg-. a. ORGAN, ORGANON, from Greek organon (with suffix -ano-), tool; b. ORGY, from Greek orgia, secret rites, worship (< "service"). [Pokorny 2. u̯erĝ- 1168.]

wēro-. Important derivatives are warlock, verity, very, verdict, verify, severe, and persevere.

wēro-. True. 1. WARLOCK, from Old English wǣr, faith, pledge, from Germanic *wēra-. 2. VERACIOUS, VERISM, VERITY, VERY; AVER, VERDICT, VERIDICAL, VERIFY, VERISIMILAR, VOIR DIRE, from Latin vērus, true. 3. SEVERE; ASSEVERATE, PERSEVERE, from Latin sevērus, grave, serious; regarded by some as a compound of se-, sed, without (see s(w)e-), and vērus, true, but the semantic difficulties make this explanation improbable. 4. Normal grade *wero-, from *werə-o-. GALORE, from Old Irish roar, enough, from *ro-wero-, sufficiency (*ro-, intensive prefix, from *pro-; see per^{1}). [Pokorny 11. u̯er- 1165.]

wers-. Important derivatives are war, guerrilla, worse, worst, and liverwurst.

wers-. To confuse, mix up. Compare ers-.
I. Suffixed basic form. 1.a. WAR, from Old North French werre, war; b. GUERRILLA, from Spanish guerra, war. Both a and b from Germanic *werra-, from *werz-a-. 2. WORSE, from Old English wyrsa, worse, from Germanic comparative *wers-izōn-. 3. WORST, from Old English wyrsta, worst, from Germanic superlative *wers-istaz.
II. Suffixed zero-grade form *wr̥s-ti-. WURST; (LIVERWURST), from Old High German wurst, sausage (< "mixture"), from Germanic *wursti-. [Pokorny u̯ers- 1169.]

wes-^{1}. Important derivatives are was, were, and astute.

wes-^{1}. To stay, dwell, pass the night, with derivatives meaning "to be." 1. O-grade form *wos-. WAS, from Old English wæs, was, from Germanic *was-. 2. Lengthened-grade form *wēs-. WERE, from Old English wǣre (subjunctive), wǣron (plural), were, from Germanic *wēz-. 3. WASSAIL, from Old Norse vesa, vera, to be, from Germanic *wesan. 4. Perhaps suffixed form *wes-tā-. VESTA, from Latin Vesta, household goddess. 5. Possibly suffixed variant form *was-tu-. ASTUTE, from Latin astus, skill, craft (practiced in a town), from Greek astu, town (< "place where one dwells"). 6. Suffixed form *wes-eno-. DIVAN, from Old Persian vahanam, house. [Pokorny 1. u̯es- 1170.]

wes-^{2}. Important derivatives are wear, vest, invest, and travesty.

wes-^{2}. To clothe. Extension of eu-^{1}. 1. Suffixed o-grade form *wos-eyo-. WEAR, from Old English werian, to wear, carry, from Germanic *wazjan. 2. Suffixed form *wes-ti-. VEST; DEVEST, INVEST, REVET, TRAVESTY, from Latin vestis, garment. 3. Suffixed form *wes-nu-. HIMATION, from Greek hennunai, to clothe, with nominal derivative heima, hima (< *wes-mn̥), garment. [Pokorny 5. u̯es- 1172.]

wes-^{3}. Important derivatives are vend and bazaar.

wes-^{3}. To buy. 1. Suffixed form *wes-no-. VENAL, VEND, from Latin vēnum, sale. 2. Suffixed o-grade form *wos-no-. DUOPSONY, from Greek ōneisthai, to buy. 3. Suffixed form *wes-ā-. BAZAAR, from Persian bāzār, from Old Iranian *vahā-carana-, "sale-traffic." [Pokorny 8. u̯es- 1173.]

wes-pero-. Important derivatives are west, western, Visigoth, and vesper.

wes-pero-. Evening, night.
I. Reduced form *wes-. 1. Suffixed form *wes-to-. a. WEST, from Old English west, west; b. WESTERN, from Old English westerne, western; c. WESTERLY, from Old English westra, more westerly. a, b, and c all from Germanic *west-. 2. VISIGOTH, from Late Latin Visigothī, "West Goths" (Gothī, the Goths), from Germanic *wis-, possibly from wes-pero-.
II. Basic form *wespero-. 1. VESPER, VESPERTILIONID, from Latin vesper, evening. 2. HESPERIAN, from Greek hesperos, evening. [Pokorny u̯esperos 1173.]

wesr̥. An important derivative is vernal.

wesr̥. Spring. VERNAL; PRIMAVERA^{1}, from Latin vēr, spring (phonologically irregular). [Pokorny u̯es-r̥ 1174.]

wet-^{1}. Important derivatives are Wednesday, fan^{1}, and atmosphere.

wet-^{1}. To blow, inspire, spiritually arouse. Related to wē-. 1. Lengthened-grade form *wōt-. a. WODEN, from Old English Wōden, Woden; b. WEDNESDAY, from Old English Wōdnesdæg, "Woden's day"; c. ODIN, from Old Norse Ōdhinn, Odin; d. WOTAN, from Old High German Wuotan. a, b, c, and d all from Germanic suffixed form *wōd-eno-, *wōd-ono-, "raging," "mad," "inspired," hence "spirit," name of the chief Teutonic god *Wōd-enaz; e. WOOD^{2}, from Old English wōd, mad, insane, from Germanic *wōdaz. 2. Lengthened variant form *wāt-. VATIC, from Latin vātēs, prophet, poet. 3. Variant form *wat-. WEDELN, from Old High German wedil, fan, from Germanic suffixed form *wath-ila-. 4. Suffixed variant form *wat-no-. FAN^{1}, VAN^{3}, from Latin vannus, a winnowing fan. 5. Oldest basic form *əwet- becoming *awet- in suffixed form *awet-mo-. ATMOSPHERE, from Greek atmos (< *aetmos), breath, vapor. [Pokorny u̯āt- 1113.]

wet-^{2}. Important derivatives are wether, veteran, inveterate, veterinary, and veal.

wet-^{2}. Year. 1. Suffixed form *wet-ru-. WETHER, from Old English wether, wether, from Germanic *wethruz, perhaps "yearling." 2. Suffixed form *wet-es-. a. VETERAN; INVETERATE, from Latin vetus, old (< "having many years"); b. VETERINARY, from Latin veterīnus, of beasts of burden, of cattle (perhaps chiefly old cattle); c. ETESIAN, from Greek etos, year. 3. Suffixed form *wet-olo-. VEAL, VITELLUS, from Latin vitulus, calf, yearling. [Pokorny u̯et- 1175.]

wi-. Important derivatives are wide and with.

wi-. Apart, in half. 1. Suffixed form *wi-itos. WIDE, from Old English wīd, wide (< "far apart"), from Germanic *wīdaz. 2. Suffixed (comparative) form *wi-tero-. a. WITH, WITHERS, from Old English wither, against, with its derivative with, with, against; b. GUERDON; WIDDERSHINS, from Old High German widar, against. Both a and b from Germanic *withrō, against. [Pokorny 1. u̯ī- 1175.]

wīkm̥tī. A derivative is vigesimal.

wīkm̥tī. Twenty. Compound of wi-, in half, hence two, and *(d)km̥t-ī (nominative dual), decade, reduced zero-grade form of dekm̥. 1. VICENARY, VIGESIMAL, from Latin vīgintī, twenty. 2. ICOSAHEDRON, from Greek eikosi, twenty. 3. PACHISI, from Sanskrit viṁśatiḥ, twenty. [Pokorny u̯ī-km̥t-ī 1177.]

wī-ro-. Important derivatives are werewolf, world, virile, virtue, and virtuoso.

wī-ro-. Man. Derivative of weiə-. 1.a. WEREWOLF, WERGELD, from Old English wer, man; b. (i) WORLD, from Old English weorold, world; (ii) WELTANSCHAUUNG, from Old High German weralt, world. Both (i) and (ii) from Germanic compound *wer-ald-, "life or age of man" (*-ald-, see al-^{2}); c. LOUP-GAROU, from Old French garoul, werewolf, from Frankish *wer-wulf, "man-wolf" (*wulf, wolf; see **wl̥kʷo-**). Both **a** and **b** from Germanic *weraz, from shortened form *wiraz. **2.** VIRAGO, VIRILE, VIRTUE, (VIRTUOSA), (VIRTUOSO); DECEMVIR, DUUMVIR, TRIUMVIR, from Latin *vir,* man. **3.** CURIA, from Latin *cūria,* curia, court, possibly from **wī-ro-,** if regarded as from *co-vir, "men together" (*co-, together; see **kom**). [Pokorny u̯īro- s 1177.]

wl̥kʷo-. An important derivative is *wolf.*

wl̥kʷo-. Wolf. **1.a.** WOLF, from Old English *wulf,* wolf; **b.** AARDWOLF, from Middle Dutch *wolf, wulf,* wolf; **c.** WOLFRAM, from Old High German *wolf,* wolf; **d.** (see **wī-ro-**) Frankish *wulf, wolf. **a, b, c,** and **d** all from Germanic *wulfaz. **2.** Taboo variant *lupo-. LOBO, (LUPINE[1]), LUPINE[2], LUPUS; LOUP-GAROU, from Latin *lupus,* wolf. **3.** Taboo variant *lukʷo-. **a.** LYCANTHROPE, LYCOPODIUM, from Greek *lukos,* wolf; **b.** suffixed form *lukʷ-ya. LYTTA; ALYSSUM, from Greek *lussa,* martial rage, madness, rabies ("wolf-ness"). [Pokorny u̯l̥kᵘos 1178.]

wl̥p-ē-. A derivative is *vulpine.*

wl̥p-ē-. Fox. **1.** VULPINE, from Latin *vulpēs,* fox. **2.** Taboo variant *əlōpēk-. ALOPECIA, from Greek *alōpēx,* fox. [Pokorny u̯l̥p-, lup- 1179.]

wōs. An important derivative is *rendezvous.*

wōs. You (plural). RENDEZVOUS, from Latin *vōs,* you. [In Pokorny 1. i̯u- 513.]

wrād-. Important derivatives are *root[1], wort, radical, radish, eradiate, ramify,* and *licorice.*

wrād-. Branch, root.
I. Basic form *wrād-. ROOT[1]; RUTABAGA, from Old Norse *rōt,* root, from Germanic *wrōt-.
II. Zero-grade form *wr̥əd-. **1.a.** WORT[1], from Old English *wyrt,* plant, herb; **b.** GEWÜRZTRAMINER, from Old High German *wurz,* plant, root; **c.** MANGEL-WURZEL, from German *Wurzel,* root (< *wurzwala, rootstock; *-wala, a roll, round stem; see **wel-[2]**). **a, b,** and **c** all from Germanic *wurtiz. **2.** Suffixed form *wr̥əd-yā-. WORT[2], from Old English *wyrt,* brewer's wort, from Germanic *wurtjō-. **3.** RADICAL, RADICLE, RADISH, RADIX; DERACINATE, ERADICATE, from Latin *rādīx,* root. **4.** Suffixed form *wrəd-mo-. RAMOSE, RAMUS; RAMIFY, from Latin *rāmus,* branch. **5.** Perhaps suffixed reduced form *wr̥(ə)d-ya. RHIZO-, RHIZOME; COLEORHIZA, LICORICE, MYCORRHIZA, from Greek *rhiza,* root. [Pokorny u̯(e)rād- 1167.]

yē-. Important derivatives are *jet[2], object, adjacent, adjective, conjecture, ease, eject, inject, object, project, reject, subject, catheter,* and *enema.*

yē-. To throw. Contracted from *yeə-. **1.** Extended zero-grade forms *yak-yo- and *yak-ē- (stative). GIST, (GITE), JACTITATION, JESS, JET[2], JOIST; ABJECT, ADJACENT, ADJECTIVE, AMICE, CONJECTURE, DEJECT, (EASE), EJACULATE, EJECT, INJECT, INTERJECT, OBJECT, PARGET, PROJECT, REJECT, SUBJACENT, SUBJECT, SUPERJACENT, TRAJECT, from Latin *iacere,* to throw, lay, and *iacēre,* to lie down (< "to be thrown") and *iaculum,* dart. **2.** Basic form *yē- and zero-grade form *yə-. CATHETER, DIESIS, ENEMA, PARESIS, SYNESIS, from Greek *hienai,* to send, throw. [Pokorny i̯ē- 502.]

yeg-. An important derivative is *icicle.*

yeg-. Ice. ICICLE, from Old English *gicel,* icicle, ice, from Germanic *jakilaz, *jekilaz. [Pokorny i̯eg- 503.]

yek-. Important derivatives are *jewel, jocular, joke, juggle,* and *jeopardy.*

yek-. To speak. Suffixed o-grade form *yok-o-. JEWEL, JOCOSE, JOCULAR, JOKE, JUGGLE, (JUGGLER); JEOPARDY, from Latin *iocus,* joke. [Pokorny i̯ek- 503.]

yĕkʷr̥. An important derivative is *hepatitis.*

yĕkʷr̥. Liver. **1.** HEPATIC, HEPATO-; HEPARIN, (HEPATITIS), from Greek *hēpar,* liver. **2.** GIZZARD, from Persian *jigar,* liver. [Pokorny i̯ekᵘ-r̥t 504.]

yēr-. Important derivatives are *year, hour,* and *horoscope.*

yēr-. Year, season. **1.** Suffixed basic form *yēr-o-. YEAR, from Old English *gēar,* year, from Germanic *jēram. **2.** Suffixed o-grade form *yōr-ā-. HOUR; HOROLOGE, HOROLOGY, HOROSCOPE, from Greek *hōra,* season. [In Pokorny 1. *ei-* 293.]

yes-. Important derivatives are *yeast* and *eczema.*

yes-. To boil, foam, bubble. **1.** YEAST, from Old English *gist,* yeast, from Germanic *jest-. **2.** KIESELGUHR, from Old High German *jësan,* to ferment, and *jerian,* to cause to ferment, from Germanic *jes-. **3.** ECZEMA, ZEOLITE, from Greek *zeein, zein,* to boil. [Pokorny i̯es- 506.]

yeu-. Important derivatives are *youth, young, junior, juvenile,* and *rejuvenate.*

yeu-. Vital force, youthful vigor. Earliest form *əyeu-; variant of **aiw-.** Suffixed zero-grade form *yuwen- (< *yu-əen-), "possessing youthful vigor," young. **1.** Further suffixed form *yuwn̥-ti-. YOUTH, from Old English *geoguth,* youth, from Germanic *jugunthi-, *jugunthā-. **2.** Further suffixed form *yuwn̥-ko-. **a.** *(i)* YOUNG, from Old English *geong,* young; *(ii)* JUNKER, from Old High German *junc,* young; *(iii)* YOUNKER, from Middle Dutch *jonc,* young. *(i), (ii),* and *(iii)* all from Germanic *jungaz from *juwungaz; **b.** GALLOWGLASS, from Old Irish *ōac,* from Celtic *yowanko-. **3.** JUNIOR, JUVENILE; REJUVENATE, from Latin *iuvenis,* young. [Pokorny 3. i̯eu- 510.]

yeug-. Important derivatives are *yoke, jugular, subjugate, joust, adjust, juxtapose, join, junction, juncture, junta, conjugal, injunction,* and *yoga.*

yeug-. To join.
I. Zero-grade form *yug-. **1.** Suffixed form *yug-o-. **a.** YOKE, from Old English *geoc,* yoke, from Germanic *yukam; **b.** JUGATE, JUGULAR, JUGUM; CONJUGATE, SUBJUGATE, from Latin *iugum,* yoke; **c.** ZYGO- ZYGOMA, ZYGOTE, -ZYGOUS; (AZYGOUS), SYZYGY, from Greek *zugon,* yoke, and *zugoun,* to join; **d.** YUGA, from Sanskrit *yugam,* yoke. **2.** Suffixed (superlative) form *yug-istos. JOUST; ADJUST, JUXTAPOSE, (JUXTAPOSITION), from Latin *iuxtā,* close by, from *iugistā (viā), "on a nearby (road). **3.** Nasalized form *yu-n-g-. JOIN, JUNCTION, JUNCTURE, JUNTA; ADJOIN, CONJOIN, (CONJUGAL), (CONJUNCT), ENJOIN, INJUNCTION, SUBJOIN, from Latin *iungere,* to join.
II. Suffixed form *yeug-mn̥. ZEUGMA, from Greek *zeugma,* a bond.
III. Suffixed o-grade form *youg-o-. YOGA, from Sanskrit *yogaḥ,* union. [Pokorny 2. i̯eu- 508.]

yewes-. Important derivatives are *jurist, jury[1], conjure, injury, perjure, judge, prejudice,* and *just[1].*

yewes-. Law. **1.** JURAL, JURIST, JURY[1]; ABJURE, ADJURE, CONJURE, INJURY, JURIDICAL, JURISCONSULT, JURISDICTION, JURISPRUDENCE, (NONJUROR), OBJURGATE, PERJURE, from Latin *iūs* (stem *iūr-*), law, and its derivative *iūrāre,* "to pronounce a ritual formula," swear. **2.** Compound form *yewes-dik-, "one who shows or pronounces the law." (see **deik-**) Latin *iūdex,* judge. **3.** Suffixed from *yewes-to-. JUST[1], from Latin *iūstus,* just. [Pokorny i̯eu̯os 512.]

yewo-. A derivative is *zein.*

yewo-. Grain. Suffixed form *yew-ya. ZEIN, from Greek *zeia,* one-seeded wheat. [Pokorny i̯eu̯o- 512.]

yu-. Important derivatives are *ye[2]* and *you.*

yu-. You. Second person (plural) pronoun. YE[2], YOU, from Old English *gē* and *ēow,* you, from Germanic *jūz (nominative) and *iwwiz (oblique). [Pokorny 1. i̯u- 513.]

PICTURE CREDITS

The editorial and production staff wishes to thank the many individuals, organizations, and agencies that have contributed to the art program of the Dictionary.

Credits on the following pages are arranged alphabetically by boldface entry word. In cases where two or more illustrations complement an entry, the sources are separated by slashes and follow the order of the illustrations. Locator maps were rendered by Francis & Shaw, Inc., and by Publication Services, Inc.

The following abbreviations are used throughout: AA/ Animals Animals; BA/Bettmann Archive, Inc.; CC/Chris Costello; CDB/Cecile Duray-Bito; EPJCo./E.P. Jones Company; ES/Evelyn Shafer, New York; GEP/Gail Piazza; GHP/Grant Heilman Photography, Inc.; GP/Globe Photos, Inc.; HAR/H. Armstrong Roberts; HPS/Historical Pictures Service, Chicago; KAMD/*Knight's American Mechanical Dictionary*; LC/Laurel Cook; LOC/Library of Congress; LW/Lightwave; MMA/Metropolitan Museum of Art; NASA/National Aeronautics and Space Administration; NGA/ National Gallery of Art, Smithsonian Institution, Washington, D.C.; NMAI/National Museum of the American Indian, Smithsonian Institution; NY Zoological Society/New York Zoological Society; PC/The Picture Cube; PI/Positive Images; PR/Photo Researchers, Inc.; San Diego Zoo/Zoological Society of San Diego; SB/Stock, Boston; SLAM/The Saint Louis Art Museum; TG/Tech-Graphics (Susan Coons); TSW/Tony Stone Worldwide; USDA/ United States Department of Agriculture; WCFTR/Wisconsin Center for Film and Theater Research; WWP/AP-Wide World Photos.

aardwolf PR - Des Bartlett & Armand Denis **abacus** BA **Kareem Abdul-Jabbar** Courtesy of Kareem Abdul-Jabbar **abelmosk** CC **Aberdeen Angus** GHP **abracadabra** TG **abscissa** TG **absinthe** CC **abstract expressionism** SLAM, Museum Purchase **Abu Simbel** Russell A. Thompson **acanthus** CC **acciaccatura** TG **accordion** SB - Jean-Claude Lejeune **ace** LW - Oscar Palmquist **acerose** CC **achene** GEP **Achilles** BA **acid rain** GHP - Runk & Schoenberger **aconite** CC **acorn** LC **acorn squash** CC **acrobat** WWP **acropolis** BA **actinia** PR - Omikron **actinoid** PR - Jack Dermid **action painting** The Museum of Modern Art, New York, Gift of Mr. and Mrs. Ronald Lauder in honor of Eliza Parkinson Cobb **acupuncture** PR - Richard Hutchings **Abigail Adams** LOC **John Adams** LOC **John Quincy Adams** LOC **addax** San Diego Zoo - Ron Garrison **adder's tongue-fern** CC **Adélie penguin** Comstock - Russ Kinne **adjacent angle** TG **admiral** GHP - Runk & Schoenberger **adobe** Eric Kroll **adrenal gland** CDB **adz** Courtesy of The Oriental Institute of The University of Chicago/CC **aerenchyma** CDB **aerialist** HAR **aerial ladder** GP - George Nelson **aerie** PR - Karl H. Maslowski **aerosol bomb** TG **Afghan hound** LW - © 1988 Oscar Palmquist **A-frame** HAR **African violet** LC **Afro** PC - Sarah Putnam **agaric** LC **agave** CC **James Agee** BA **agitator** CC **agouti** San Diego Zoo - Ron Garrison **Agrippina the Younger** Anderson - Art Resource, New York **aigrette** BA **aiguille** HAR **aileron** LC **airbrush** LW - Steve Young **Airedale** LW - Oscar Palmquist **air rifle** LW - Oscar Palmquist **Akbar the Great** SLAM, Gift of J. Lionberger Davis **Akhenaton** BA **albatross** PR - George Holton/PR - Karl W. Kenyon **albino** PR - Richard Finke **alcazar** SB - Peter Menzel **Louisa May Alcott** Chicago Historical Society, neg. no. ICHi-09394 **alembic** CC **Alexander the Great** HPS **alfalfa** LC **Alfonso XIII** LOC **alga** PR - Hugh Spencer **Muhammad Ali** GP - Camera Press **alimentary canal** LC **Gracie Allen** BA **Woody Allen** WWP **alligator** HAR **allium** CC **allspice** CDB **alluvial fan** GHP **almond** LC **alpaca** PR - Andrew Rakoczy **alpenhorn** WWP **altar** PC - Franz Kraus **altazimuth** BA **alternate angle** TG **althorn** American Music Conference **amanita** GEP **amaryllis** W. Atlee Burpee & Company, Warminster, Pennsylvania **Amazon** BA **American Falls** PR - Vivienne della Grotta **ammonite** PR - Bucky & W.S. Reeves **amoeba** GHP - Runk & Schoenberger **amphibian** GP - Jim Thompson **amphipod** CDB **amphitheater** BA **amphora** MMA, Rogers Fund, 1917 **amulet** NMAI/Jewish Museum - Art Resource, New York **Roald Amundsen** BA **amusement park** PC - Emilio A. Mercado **anaconda** PR - Dade W. Thornton **anchor** LC **Marian Anderson** LOC **andiron** Courtesy, Museum of Fine Arts, Boston **anemone** GEP/PR - Jack Dermid **aneroid barometer** TG **angel** © The Frick Collection, New York **Angel Fall** WWP **angelfish** © 1991 Judith Winters **angiogram** © 1986 Martin M. Rotker, Deltona, Florida **angle**[2] LC **Angora goat** GHP **anhinga** AA - M. Krishnan **ani** PR - Stephen Krasemann **Anne of Cleves** LOC **annual ring** GHP - Runk & Schoenberger **annular eclipse** NASA **Annunciation** NGA, Samuel H. Kress Collection **anorak** SB - Ellis Herwig **ansate cross** BA **ant** LC **anta** CC **anteater** NY Zoological Society **antefix** GEP **anthemion** Alinari - Art Resource, New York **anther** LC **Susan B. Anthony** National Portrait Gallery, Smithsonian Institution, Washington, D.C. **anthurium** LC **antibody** LC **anticipation** TG **anticline** GEP **antimissile missile** PR - Omikron **antler** GEP **Anubis** MMA, Museum Excavations, 1928–1929 and Rogers Fund, 1930 (30.3.31) **anvil** HAR **ao dai** WWP **aorta** LC **aperture** TG **aphid** CDB **Aphrodite** LOC **apiarist** GHP **Apis** Alinari - Art Resource, New York **apogee** TG **Apollo** BA **Apostle** BA **appaloosa** *Appaloosa Journal*/Crown Center Farms, Columbia, Missouri **apparatus** GHP - Grant Heilman **appliqué** SB - Tom Cheek **apricot** LC **apron** SB - Arthur Grace **apse** LC **aquarium** GHP - Barry L. Runk **Aquarius** TG **aqueduct** HAR **Corazón Aquino** WWP **arabesque** Boston Ballet - John Burke/Walters Art Gallery, Baltimore, Maryland **Arabian horse** EPJCo. **Yasir Arafat** WWP **arbor**[1] SB - Dorothy Monnelly **arcade** SB - Fred Bodin **arch**[1] HAR/PC - Stanley Rowin/HPS **archaeopteryx** TG **archangel** MMA, Robert Lehman Collection, 1975 (1975.1.74) **archery** GP - Newton Nelson **architrave** LC **arctic fox** AA - Irene Vandermolen **arena** PC - Frank Siteman **argosy** PR - B.A. Lang, Sr. **argyle** GEP **Aries** TG **armadillo** PR - Keith Gunnar **armet** Courtesy, Museum of Fine Arts, Boston, Gift of Mrs. W. Scott Fitz and Mr. Edward J. Holmes **armillary sphere** BA **armoire** MMA, Fletcher Fund, 1959 (59.108) **armor** MMA, Rogers Fund, 1904 (04.4.2)/MMA, Rogers Fund and Pratt Gift, 1933 (33.164 a-x) **Louis Armstrong** WCFTR **Neil Armstrong** WWP **arrowhead** GHP/GEP **Artemis** LOC **artesian well** GEP **Chester A. Arthur** LOC **artichoke** LC **art nouveau** MMA, Sansbury Mills Fund, 1980 (1980.299) **ascender** CC **ascidium** CDB **ash**[2] CC **asparagus** LC **aspergillum** Comstock - Russ Kinne **ass**[1] PR - Tom McHugh **assassin bug** CDB **assembly line** PC - Steven Lewis **Assumption** BA **Fred Astaire** BA **astigmatism** CDB **astragal** CC **astrolabe** Courtesy of The Oriental Institute of The University of Chicago **astronaut** NASA **asymptote** TG **atamasco lily** GEP **atelier** Image Photos - Clemens Kalischer **Athena** BA **Atlas** WWP **atlatl** NMAI **atmosphere** TG **atoll** LC **atom bomb** LC **atrium** PC - Betty Barry **attaché case** EPJCo. **John James Audubon** PR **auger** GEP **auk** PR - Gösta Håkansson Visby **auscultation** © 1990 Walter Silver, Boston, Massachusetts **automated teller machine** PC - Therese Frare **aviator glasses** LW - Oscar Palmquist **avocado** LC **avocet** AA - Leonard Lee Rue III **awl** NMAI **awning** HAR **ax** CC **axle** KAMD **azalea** GEP **azimuthal equidistant projection** © 1986 by the American Congress on Surveying and Mapping

babirusa NY Zoological Society **baboon** SB - Ira Kirschenbaum **babushka** EPJCo. **Johann Sebastian Bach** LOC **bacillus** CDB **backboard** PI - Jerry Howard **backgammon** The Pierpont Morgan Library, New York (M.763, f.241v-242) **backhand** WWP **backhoe** Caterpillar Inc. **backpack** WWP **backsaw** LC **bacterium** LC **Robert Baden-Powell** LOC **Joan Baez** WWP **bagpipe** GP - A.G. Hutchinson **balalaika** MMA, Gift of Mr. Ustin Smolensky, 1948 (48.146) **balance** Yale University Medical Library **balance beam** SB - Cary Wolinsky **balcony** SB - Ira Kirschenbaum **bald eagle** AA - Irene Vandermolen **James Baldwin** National Portrait Gallery, Smithsonian Institution, Washington, D.C.; © of 1955 negative, Estate of Carl Van Vechten; © of 1983 photogravure, Eakins Press Foundation **ballast** BA **ball cock** TG **ballet** Comstock - Billy Brown Photography **balloon** PC - Stanley Rowin **balsam fir** GEP **baluchithere** TG **balustrade** Image Photos - Clemens Kalischer **Honoré de Balzac** The Granger Collection, New York **bamboo** SB - Mike Mazzaschi **banana** PC - Foto du Monde **bandoleer** PC - George N. Peet **band shell** HAR **banjo** SB - Jean-Claude Lejeune **banquette** The Cleveland Museum of Art, John L. Severance Fund (54.385) **banyan** CDB **baobab** CC **baptistery** Italian Government Travel Office/Courtesy, Museum of Fine Arts, Boston, Sarah F. Gorham & Alice H. Goddard Fund **barb**[1] BA **barbell** BA **bard**[2] Anderson - Art Resource, New York **Brigitte Bardot** WWP **barge** PR - Ray Ellis **bargeboard** The Preservation Society of Newport County **Barlow knife** PI - Jerry Howard **Christiaan Barnard** BA **barometer** GHP **baroque** Image Photos - Clemens Kalischer **barouche** From the collections of Henry Ford Museum & Greenfield Village, neg. no. B5240 **barracuda** PR - Ron Church **bartizan** Russell A. Thompson **Clara Barton** LOC **Mikhail Baryshnikov** GP **bascule** British Tourist Authority, New York **basenji** ES **Count Basie** GP - Dmitri Kasterine **basilica** CC **basketball** PC - Sarah Putnam **basket star** PR - C. Ray **bass clef** TG **bat**[2] PR - S. Bisserot **bathyscaph** Office of Information, Dept. of the Navy, Washington, D.C./Office of Information, Dept. of the Navy, Washington, D.C. **battering ram** HPS **bay window** PI - Jerry Howard **bazaar** Image Photos - Clemens Kalischer **beagle** ES **beak** CDB **beaker** Image Photos - Clemens Kalischer **bearskin** PC - Cynthia W. Sterling **Beatrix** BA **Simone de Beauvoir** PR - Gisele Freund **beaver**[1] PR - Ed Cesar **Thomas à Becket** Walters Art Gallery, Baltimore, Maryland **Bedlington terrier** EPJCo. **bedstead** The Connecticut Historical Society, Hartford, Connecticut **beefeater** British Tourist Authority, New York **beefsteak fungus** CDB **beehive** PI - Martin Miller **Ludwig van Beethoven** LOC **belaying pin** GEP **belemnite** GHP - Runk & Schoenberger **belfry** Russell A. Thompson **Belgian sheep dog** PR - Mary Eleanor Browning **Alexander Graham Bell** HPS **Bellerophon** Culver Pictures Inc. **bellows** CC **benchmark** GHP **bench-press** PC - Sarah Putnam **bend**[2] GEP **bend sinister** GEP **David Ben Gurion** BA **benzene ring** TG **beret** SB - Owen Franken **Bernese mountain dog** ES **Sarah Bernhardt** LOC **Leonard Bernstein** GP **Bessemer converter** BA **Mary McLeod Bethune** HPS **betony** CC **bevel gear** LC **bias-ply tire** GEP **biceps** LC **bicuspid** GEP **bicycle** SB - Owen Franken **bighorn** AA - Leonard Lee Rue III **billboard**[1] Eric Kroll **billy club** PR - Fred Lombardi **binocular** SB - Gale Zucker **biplane** WWP **birch** CC **bird** CDB **bird of paradise** LC **bireme** GEP **biretta** SB - Donald Dietz **bisector** TG **bishop** GEP **Otto von Bismarck** WWP **bison** AA - C.W. Perkins **bit**[2] GEP **bittern**[1] PR - Karl H. Maslowski **black bear** AA - Leonard Lee Rue III **blackberry** LC **blackboard** PC - Andrew Brilliant **black-eyed Susan** LC **blackjack** PC - Spencer Grant **black letter** CC **blacksmith** SB - Jean-Claude Lejeune **black widow** PR - Bucky Reeves **William Blake** BA **blanket** EPJCo. **blast furnace** TG **blastoff** NASA **bleeding heart** LC **blimp** Goodyear News Bureau **blinders** PC - Judith Sedwick **blindfold** PI - Patricia J. Bruno **block and tackle** GEP **blockhouse** LOC **bloodhound** ES **bloodroot** PR - J.M. Conrader **bloomer**[2] LOC **blowgun** NMAI - Frank G. Speck **blowhole** SB - W.B. Finch **bluebell** CC **blueberry** GEP **blue grouse** PR - Allan D. Cruickshank **blue whale** CC **blunderbuss** LC **boa constrictor** PR - Dade W. Thornton **boar** PR - Leonard Lee Rue III **boardwalk** Russell A. Thompson **boat** TG **boatbill** PR - Arthur W. Ambler **bobwhite** PR - Nell Bolen **bodkin** Mystic Seaport Museum, Inc. All rights reserved./Mystic Seaport Museum, Inc. All rights reserved. **body bunker** SB - John Coletti **body language** Palmer/Brilliant, Boston, Massachusetts **Humphrey Bogart** WWP **Bohr theory** TG **boiler** TG **bolero** SB - Peter Menzel **Anne Boleyn** National Portrait Gallery, London **Simón Bolívar** LOC **bollard** SB - Joseph Schuyler **boll weevil** CDB **bongo**[1] NY Zoological Society **bongo**[2] PC - Frank Siteman **bonnet** PC - David S. Strickler **bonsai** GHP - Runk & Schoenberger **bontebok** PR - Arthur W. Ambler **booby**[1] SB - Ira Kirschenbaum **boojum tree** PR - Jen & Des Bartlett **Daniel Boone** National Portrait Gallery, Smithsonian Institution, Washington, D.C. **Boötes** TG **John Wilkes Booth** LOC **borage** GEP **Lizzie Borden** The Granger Collection, New York **Cesare Borgia** Anderson - Art Resource, New York **borzoi** © 1991 Judith Winters **boss**[2] CC **Boston fern** PI - Jerry Howard **Boston rocker** Courtesy, Museum of Fine Arts, Boston **boutonniere** Palmer/Brilliant, Boston, Massachusetts **bouzouki** PI - Martin Miller **bowie knife** CC **bowling alley** HAR **boxer**[3] ES **boxing**[2] SB - Peter Southwick **box kite** GEP **box turtle** GHP **brace** CC **bracken** PR - Omikron

Mathew Brady LOC **Brahman** AA - R.F. Head **Johannes Brahms** BA **Braille** TG/EPJCo. **brain** LC **brake**[1] TG **brass knuckles** PI - Jerry Howard **brazier**[2] KAMD **Brazil nut** CDB **break dancing** SB - David Powers **breastplate** BA **breeches buoy** HPS **Leonid Brezhnev** WWP **bridge**[1] SB - Jeff Albertson/ Cunard Line Ltd. **bridle** EPJCo. **bristlecone pine** CDB **Brittany spaniel** PR - Leonard Lee Rue III **broccoli** CC **Brontë** National Portrait Gallery, London **brontosaur** CC **brooch** PI - Patricia J. Bruno **Gwendolyn Brooks** BA **brougham** From the collections of Henry Ford Museum & Greenfield Village, neg. no. A2081 **brown recluse spider** CDB **brown thrasher** PR - Allan D. Cruickshank **Pieter Brueghel the Elder** BA **Brussels sprouts** CC **James Buchanan** LOC **buckboard** Carriage Association of America, New Jersey **bucksaw** KAMD **Buddha**[1] PC - Bruce Rosenblum **buffing wheel** PI - Jerry Howard **bulb** GEP **bull**[1] GHP/AA- - Leonard Lee Rue III **bullboat** LOC **bulldog** HAR **bulldozer** GHP **bullet train** SB - J.R. Holland **bull terrier** PR - Mary Eleanor Browning **bumblebee** LC **Bunsen burner** SB - Jeffrey Dunn **Luis Buñuel** BA **buoy** United States Coast Guard Headquarters **Luther Burbank** LOC **burdock** GEP **burette** LC **Martha Jane Burk** LOC **burnoose** SB - Frank Siteman **George Burns** WWP **burrow** LC **burying beetle** CDB **Barbara Bush** The White House - David Valdez **George Bush** The White House - David Valdez **bust**[1] Alinari - Art Resource, New York **bustard** PR - Mark Boulton **butte** PC - Mike Rizza **butterfly valve** GEP **butternut** GEP **butt hinge** GEP **butt joint** TG **buzzard** PR - Allan D. Cruickshank **Richard E. Byrd** BA

cab[1] HAR **cabin** HAR **cable car** SB - Judy Canty **Mother Cabrini** LOC **cabriole** SLAM, Museum Purchase **cachepot** Cooper-Hewitt National Museum of Design, Smithsonian Institution - Art Resource, New York **cacomistle** PR - Jen & Des Bartlett **caddis fly** CDB **caduceus** LC **cairn** Comstock - Richard Harrington **calash** Shelburne Museum, Shelburne, Vermont **calceolaria** LC **caldron** NAMA, Gift of Mr. and Mrs. Milton McGreevy through the Westport Fund (F70-15/8) **calico** LW - Oscar Palmquist **caliper** GEP **Maria Callas** HPS **calligraphy** WWP **calliope** BA **calpac** American Museum of Natural History, Courtesy Department of Library Services, neg. no. 260455 **calumet** Peabody Museum, Harvard University - © 1987 Hillel Burger **Calvary cross** GEP **John Calvin** LOC **came**[1] PI - Martin Miller **camel** PR - George Holton **cameo** Walters Art Gallery, Baltimore, Maryland **camera** TG **camouflage** SB - Peter Menzel **campanile** Italian Government Travel Office, New York **Albert Camus** WWP **Canada goose** GHP - Hal Harrison **canal** HPS **Cancer** TG **candelabrum** SLAM, Gift of Virgil A. Lewis **cane** Mystic Seaport Museum, Inc. All rights reserved. **Canis Major** TG **Canis Minor** TG **canoe** SB - Fredrik Bodin **canopy** MMA/PC - Bruce Rosenblum **cantaloupe** CC **cantilever** TG **canvasback** AA - Leonard Lee Rue III **Capricorn** TG **capstone** BA **capsule** PC - Stanley Rowin **capuchin** PR - Robert C. Hermes **carabiner** LC **caravan** EPJCo. **caravel** Culver Pictures Inc. **carboy** GEP **carburetor** TG **cardinal** PR - Karl H. Maslowski **cardioid** TG **carpus** LC **carrack** Mystic Seaport Museum, Inc. All rights reserved. **carrel** © 1983 Walter Silver, Boston, Massachusetts **carriage** EPJCo. **carrick bend** TG **Johnny Carson** BA **Kit Carson** Courtesy, Colorado Historical Society **Jimmy Carter** The White House **Rosalynn Carter** Courtesy, Jimmy Carter Library **cartouche** Leo de Wys, Inc. - Gunter Reitz **Enrico Caruso** LOC **George Washington Carver** HPS **caryatid** Greek National Tourist Organization - Cyril Morris **cascade** Allen Moore **case**[2] SB - Christopher S. Johnson **cashew** LC **Mary Cassatt** National Portrait Gallery, Smithsonian Institution, Washington, D.C. **casserole** Phototake - Yoav Levy **cassowary** PR - Len Rue, Jr. **castanets** GEP **caster** Yale University Art Gallery, The Mabel Brady Garvan Collection - Joseph Szaszfai **castle** EPJCo. **Fidel Castro** GP **catafalque** SB - Deborah Kahn **catamaran** WWP **catapult** BA **cataract** EPJCo. **catboat** Mystic Seaport Museum, Inc. All rights reserved. **catcher** SB - Peter Southwick **catenary** TG **caterpillar** CDB **catfish** GHP - Runk & Schoenberger **cathedral** EPJCo. **Catherine de Médicis** Giraudon - Art Resource, New York **Catherine of Aragon** National Portrait Gallery, London **cathode-ray tube** TG **CAT scan** PR - James A. Prince **CAT scanner** WWP **cattle guard** Comstock - Russ Kinne **causeway** GHP - William Felger **C clef** TG **cecropia moth** CDB **cedar of Lebanon** CC **cedar waxwing** PR - Karl H. Maslowski **celestial sphere** TG **cell** LC **cellarette** Collection of the Museum of Early Southern Decorative Arts, Winston-Salem, North Carolina **cello**[1] Jeroboam, Inc. - Kent Reno **Celtic cross** Comstock - Russ Kinne **cement mixer** PC - Frank Siteman **cenotaph** SB - Mike Mazzaschi **censer** BA **centaur** BA **centipede** PI - Martin Miller **centrifuge** GHP - Runk & Schoenberger **Cerberus** Courtesy, Museum of Fine Arts, Boston, Gift of Mr. and Mrs. Cornelius C. Vermeule III **cerebellum** LC **Ceres** *Museum of Antiquity* by L.W. Yaggy and T.L. Haines, Standard Publishing House, © 1882 **cesta** Florida Dept. of Commerce, Division of Tourism **Cetus** TG **Paul Cézanne** Giraudon - Art Resource, New York **chafing dish** Courtesy, Museum of Fine Arts, Boston, Gift of Leverett, Muriel, and Richard Saltonstall **Marc Chagall** WWP **chain** GEP **chainlink fence** LW - © 1988 Jeff Thiebauth **chain mail** BA **chain saw** SB - Peter Menzel **chair lift** PI - Jerry Howard **chalice** Marburg - Art Resource, New York **chameleon** PR - George Porter **chamois** PR - Toni Angermayer **Chan Chan** EPJCo. **chandelier** MMA, American Wing Restricted Building Fund, 1968 (68.143.5) **chanterelle** CDB **chapel** WWP **Charlie Chaplin** WCFTR **chariot** MMA, Rogers Fund, 1903 (03.23.1) **Charles** British Information Services, New York **chase**[1] BA **chasuble** PR - Ray Ellis **chateau** Swiss National Tourist Office **chatelaine** MMA, Gift of Miss Sarah Lazarus in memory of Moses Lazarus, 1890 (90.22.7 ab) **Cesar Chavez** SB - Jon Chase **cheetah** AA - Leonard Lee Rue III **cherimoya** CDB **cherry** LC **cherry picker** PC - E. Williamson **cherub** BA **chess**[1] SB - Eric Neurath **chestnut** LC **cheval glass** MMA, Gift of Ginsburg and Levy, Inc., in memory of John Ginsburg and Isaac Levy, 1969 (69.183) **chevron** PR - Bettye Lane **Chiang Kai-shek** BA **Chichén Itzá** © 1984 Walter Silver, Boston, Massachusetts **chignon** Palmer/Brilliant, Boston, Massachusetts **Chihuahua**[2] EPJCo. **child restraint** PC - David S. Strickler **chimney sweep** PI - Martin Miller **chinchilla** PR - Russ Kinne **Chincoteague pony** AA - Robert Redden **chin-up** SB - Thomas Cheek **chipmunk** AA - Irene Vandermolen **Chippendale** Sotheby Parke Bernet **Chi-Rho** GEP **chisel** LC **chiton** HPS **chock** PI - Martin Miller **choir** Comstock - Sven Martson **choker** LW - Oscar Palmquist **Frédéric Chopin** WWP **chopine** MMA, Purchase, Irene Lewisohn Bequest, 1973 (1973.114.4ab) **chopstick** PR - Susan Woog-Wagner **chow**[1] ES **Agatha Christie** WWP **chromosome** GHP - Runk & Schoenberger **chrysanthemum** CC **church** GHP **Winston S. Churchill** BA **churn** New York Public Library **Churrigueresque** Comstock - Stuart Cohen **chute** San Francisco Maritime National Historic Park, Oliver Collection, Courtesy of the Bancroft Library **ciborium** Courtesy, Museum of Fine Arts, Boston, Theodora Wilbour Fund, in memory of Charlotte B. Wilbour **cinquefoil** CC **circle** LC **circuit** GEP **circular saw** SB - Donald C. Dietz **cirrocumulus** GHP - Grant Heilman **cirrus** GHP **cithara** MMA, Gift of Mr. and Mrs. Leon Pomerance, 1953 **cittern** MMA, The Crosby Brown Collection of Musical Instruments, 1889 **civet** San Diego Zoo **clamp** CC **clarinet** Comstock - Russ Kinne **William Clark** Independence National Historical Park **clavichord** Courtesy, Museum of Fine Arts, Boston, Gift of William Lindsey as a memorial to his daughter, Mrs. Leslie Lindsey Mason **clavicle** LC **claymore** MMA, Gift of Mrs. Alexander McMillan Welch, in memory of Alexander McMillan Welch, 1945 (45.160.2) **clean room** PR - Spencer Grant **cleats** PR - Tim Davis **Cleopatra** The Granger Collection, New York **clerestory** CC **clerical collar** SB - John Maher **Grover Cleveland** LOC **clevis** KAMD **cliff dweller** EPJCo. **clinch** LW - Oscar Palmquist **clipper** Peabody Museum of Salem, Massachusetts **clitellum** GEP **cloche** BA **clock**[1] Collection of the J. Paul Getty Museum, Malibu, California **cloisonné** Freer Gallery of Art, Smithsonian Institution, Washington, D.C.; accession no. 61.12, Chinese incense burner: Ming dynasty, 16th century; cloisonné, 5½" × 7½" **cloister** Palmer/Brilliant, Boston, Massachusetts **cloud chamber** TG **clove hitch** TG **cloverleaf** HPS **clown** PR - Susan McCartney **Clumber spaniel** ES **clutch bag** PI - Patricia J. Bruno **Clydesdale** AA - Robert L. Miller **coati** NY Zoological Society **coat of arms** BA **cobblestone** LW - © 1988 Jeff Thiebauth **cobra** AA - M. Krishnan **coccyx** LC **Jacqueline Cochran** WWP **cockatoo** BA **cock-of-the-rock** NY Zoological Society **cockpit** PR - Jeannine Niepce-Rapho **cockroach** LC **codpiece** Alinari - Art Resource, New York **William F. Cody** National Portrait Gallery, Smithsonian Institution, Washington, D.C. **coelacanth** GEP **coffee** LC **cog railway** Image Photos - Clemens Kalischer **coliseum** SB - Elizabeth Hamlin **collage** Photograph © The Solomon R. Guggenheim Foundation, New York - Gift, Katherine S. Dreier Estate from Marcel Duchamp (FN 53.1348) - Robert E. Mates **collie** Mrs. Kathy Peters - Gulie Krook **colonnade** Marburg - Art Resource, New York **Colorado potato beetle** CDB **color guard** SB - Lionel J-M Delevingne **colossus** Comstock - Richard Harrington **columbarium** Jeroboam, Inc. - Werner Hiebel **columbine** LC **Christopher Columbus** LOC **column** LC **combine** HPS **comet** Lick Observatory Photograph **comma** GHP - Runk & Schoenberger **command module** NASA **commode** MMA, Fletcher Fund, 1928 (28.154) **compact disk** LW - Oscar Palmquist **compass** LW - Oscar Palmquist **compass plant** GEP **complementary angles** LC **compote** SLAM, Bequest of Mrs. Christine Graham Long **compound eye** PR - Dr. Jeremy Burgess, Science Photo Library **computer** EPJCo. **concave** LC **concession** LW - S.E. Byrne **conch** PC - Frank Siteman **concourse** PR - David M. Grossman **condor** USDA **condyle** LC **cone** TG/Phototake - CNRI **Conestoga wagon** Shelburne Museum, Shelburne, Vermont **confessional** EPJCo. **confetti** PR - Bill Aron **Confucius** WWP **conga drums** LW - Oscar Palmquist **Congo eel** CDB **conic section** LC **Jimmy Connors** WWP **console**[2] CC **console table** Spencer Museum of Art, Lawrence, Kansas, The Williams Bridges Thayer Memorial (28.2053) **contact lens** LW - Oscar Palmquist **continental code** TG **continental shelf** GEP **contortionist** SB - Michael Grecco **convection** TG **convertible** WWP **convex** LC **conveyer** Jeroboam, Inc. - Olof Källström **Calvin Coolidge** LOC **Grace Coolidge** LOC **coop** Ewing Galloway **coot** TSW - Leonard Lee Rue III **cop**[2] LW - S.E. Byrne **coping saw** PC - Frank Siteman **John Singleton Copley** LOC **copperhead** PR - Karl H. Maslowski **coral** GHP - Runk & Schoenberger **coral snake** PR - Jack Dermid **corbel** Comstock - Stuart Cohen **corbie-step** Netherlands Board of Tourism, New York **core** LC **Corinth Canal** Greek National Tourist Organization, New York **Corinthian order** LC **cork oak** CC **cormorant** PR - Arthur W. Ambler **cornet** From the collections of Henry Ford Museum & Greenfield Village **cornrow** PI - Jerry Howard **cornucopia** MMA, Rogers Fund, 1916 (16.112) **Corona Borealis** TG **coronation** BA **corral** GHP - Grant Heilman **corsage** Palmer/Brilliant, Boston, Massachusetts **corset** PC - R.P. Kingston Collection **cortege** John. F. Kennedy Library, Boston, Massachusetts **Hernando Cortés** American Museum of Natural History, Courtesy Department Library Services, neg. no. 286846 **Corvus** TG **corymb** GEP **cosecant** TG **cosine** TG **costume** PI - Jerry Howard **cotangent** TG **cottonwood** CC **cotyledon** CDB **countersink** CC **Gustave Courbet** International Museum of Photography at George Eastman House, neg. no. 17527 **course** SB - Dean Abramson **Jacques Cousteau** GP - Jerry Watson **covalent bond** TG **coveralls** PC - Lauren Lantos **covered bridge** LOC **covered wagon** Carriage Association of America, New Jersey **cowcatcher** HPS **cowl** HPS **cowrie** GEP **coxswain** SB - Arthur Grace **crab**[1] GHP - Runk & Schoenberger **cradle** Courtesy, Museum of Fine Arts, Boston/PI - Jerry Howard **cradleboard** NMAI **crag** PC - Read D. Brugger **crampon** LC **crane** AA - Miriam Austerman/PC - David S. Strickler **crater** NASA **cravat** LW - S.E. Byrne **creamcups** CC **creamer** MMA, Edgar J. Kaufmann Charitable Foundation, 1969 (69.128.1,2) **credenza** LW - Aldo Mastrocola **creel** PC - Jeffrey Dunn **crenate** CC **crescent** LC **crew**[1] PC - Rick Friedman **cribbage** SB - Tom Cheek **crinkleroot** GEP **criosphinx** CC **crochet** CC **Davy Crockett** LOC **crocodile** NY Zoological Society **croissant** PC - Sarah Putnam **Oliver Cromwell** LOC **crop-dusting** PR - Joe Munroe **crosier** Museum of Fine Arts, Houston, Museum purchase, Laurence H. Farrot Bequest Fund **crossbow** HPS **cross-country skiing** PR - Keith Gunnar **crosse** Comstock - Sven Martson **crown** Giraudon - Art Resource, New York **crow's-nest** BA **Crucifixion** LOC **cruet** MMA, Gift of Audrey Love in memory of C. Ruxton Love, Jr., 1978 (1978.524.1a-e) **crust** LC **crutch** LC **crystal** Waterford Glass, Inc. **ctenophore** CDB **cube** TG **cubicle** PI - Patricia J. Bruno **cubism** MMA, The Alfred Stieglitz Collection, 1949 (49.70.34) **cuckoo clock** EPJCo. **cue ball** PI - Patricia J. Bruno **culverin** MMA, Gift of William H. Riggs, 1913 (14.25.1814) **Culver's root** GEP **culvert** LW - Oscar Palmquist **cummerbund** LW - S.E. Byrne **cumulonimbus** GHP **cumulus** SB - J.R. Holland **cuneiform** Comstock - Georg Gerster **Cupid** HPS **cupola** SB - Peter Southwick **curb cut** SB - Cary Wolinsky **curette** GEP **Marie Curie** BA **Pierre Curie** The Granger Collection, New York **currycomb** LW - Oscar Palmquist **George Armstrong Custer** LOC **cutaway** SB - Jeff Albertson **cutlass** National Museum of American History, Smithsonian Institution, Washington, D.C. **cuttlefish** CDB **Cybele** Alinari - Art Resource, New York **cycloid** TG **cyclotron** TG **cylinder** TG **cymbal** Jeroboam, Inc. - Philip Jon Bailey **cypress** CC

dachshund PR - Ylla **Dada** The Museum of Modern Art, New York, The Sidney and Harriet Janis Collection **daffodil** LC **dagger** MMA, Harris Brisbane Dick Fund, 1954 (54.3.4ab) **Salvador Dali** BA **Dalmatian** ES **dalmatic** MMA, Rogers Fund, 1954 (54.176.1) **dam**[1] WWP **Father Damien** WWP **dandelion** CDB **Dandie Dinmont** ES **Daphne** Alinari - Art Resource, New York **dapple-gray** PR **daredevil** BA **Darius I** Courtesy of The Oriental Institute of The University of Chicago **Clarence Darrow** BA **Charles Darwin** HPS **datura** CC **Bette Davis** WWP **davit** SB - Fredrik D. Bodin **Moshe Dayan** GP - Yvonne Plaut **day lily** CDB **D-day** BA **dead bolt** LW - Oscar Palmquist **James Dean** WWP **death cup** CDB **death mask** MMA, Gift of Mrs. Robert W. de Forest, 1903 (03.13) **Claude Debussy** HPS **decoy** PC - Edward Bishop **deer** AA - Len Rue, Jr. **deer fly** CC **Charles de Gaulle** HPS **Olivia de Havilland** WWP **dehumidify** TG **Eugène Delacroix** International Museum of Photography at George Eastman House, neg. no. 17527 **delft** Jewish Museum - Art Resource, New York **dells** PR - Myron Wood **delphinium** CDB **Delphinus** TG **demijohn** Jeffrey Dunn **demitasse** PI - Jerry Howard **demoiselle crane** AA - Irene Vandermolen **demolition** WWP **Deng Xiaoping** WWP **dentate** CC **dentin** LC **den.ist** Comstock - Stuart Cohen **Denver boot** SB - Peter Southwick **deodar** CDB **depot** California State Railroad Museum **derailleur** TG **derby** SB - Jeff Albertson **derrick** GHP - Alan Pitcairn **dervish** Turkish Culture and Information Office, New York **descender** CC **desert**[1] GHP - Alan Pitcairn **design** Palmer/Brilliant, Boston, Massachusetts **Hernando de Soto** BA **destroying angel** CDB **detector** SB - Peter Vandermark **devilwood** CC **Thomas Dewey** WWP **dhow** Mystic Seaport Museum, Inc. All rights reserved. **diagonal** LC **diamond** LW - Oscar Palmquist **Diamond Head** Hawaii Visitors Bureau - Peter French **Diana** Courtesy, Museum of Fine Arts, Boston **Diana** British Information Service, New York **Diane de Poitiers** HPS **diaphragm** LC **diatom** CDB **dibble** CC **Charles Dickens** BA **Emily Dickinson** HPS **Babe Didrikson** WWP **diesel engine** TG **differential windlass** LC **dig** Comstock - Georg Gerster **digestive system** LC **dihedral angle** TG **dik-dik** AA - D. Fawcett **dill** GEP **Joe DiMaggio** BA **dinghy** PC - William A. Todd, Jr. **dingo** PR - Des Bartlett **Dionysus** MMA, Purchase, Joseph Pulitzer Bequest, 1955 (55.1.5) **diorama** Museum of Science, Boston, Massachusetts **dirndl** Austrian National Tourist Office **dirt bike** GP - Mark Stoddard **disc brake** TG **disc jockey** PR - Spencer Grant **discus** SB - Barbara Alper **dish antenna** National Center for Atmospheric Research, National Science Foundation **disk harrow** Navistar **dislocate** Martin M. Rotker, Deltona, Florida/Martin M. Rotker, Deltona, Florida **Walt Disney** WWP **Benjamin Disraeli** BA **distaff** BA **distillation** LC **distillation column** TG **distortion** Jeroboam, Inc. - Michael Rothstein **diver** EPJCo. **divi-divi** CC **divining rod** BA **DNA** LC **Doberman pinscher** ES **dobsonfly** CDB **dock**[1] SB - Peter Vandermark **dodecagon** LC **dodecahedron** TG **Charles Dodgson** HPS **dodo** TG **dogsled** SB - Tim Carlson **dogtooth** CC **dogwood** GEP **doily** PI - Patricia J. Bruno **dollhouse** Deborah Buckley **dolphin** EPJCo. **dome** Italian Government Travel Office/Comstock - Stuart Cohen **domino**[1] LW - Oscar Palmquist **Fats Domino** GP - Camera Press **donkey** PI - Jerry Howard **donor** PR - Christopher Morrow **doornail** Image Photos - Clemens Kalischer **Dorado** TG **Doric order** LC **dormer** HPS **dory**[1] Mystic Seaport Museum, Inc. All rights reserved. **double bass** Jeroboam, Inc. - Emilio A. Mercado **double-decker** TSW - Michael Bertan **double dutch** SB - Gale Zucker **doublet** Yale Center for British Art, Paul Mellon Collection **Frederick Douglass** Sophia Smith Collection, Smith College **dovetail** TG **downspout** LW - Oscar Palmquist **dracaena** LC **Draco**[2] TG **draft** AA - Harry Cutting/ PI - Jerry Howard **dragonfly** CDB **dragon tree** CC **Sir Francis Drake** LOC **drawknife** GEP **dreadnought** GHP - Alan Pitcairn **dredge**[1] KAMD **dreidel** PI - Martin Miller **drill**[1] LW - Oscar Palmquist **drill press** LW - Oscar Palmquist **drinking fountain** SB - Jean-Claude Lejeune **dromedary** NY Zoological Society **drop leaf** From the collections of Henry Ford Museum & Greenfield Village, neg. no. B25492 **drought** USDA - John White **dry dock** WWP **Madame du Barry** LOC **W.E.B. Du Bois** BA **duck**[1] AA - Len Rue, Jr. **ducking stool** HPS **dulcimer** From the collections of Henry Ford Museum & Greenfield Village, neg. no. 33.402.1 **Daphne du Maurier** WWP **dumbwaiter** BA **dummy** PC - Steve Takatsuno **dump truck** Marilyn Root **Isadora Duncan** BA **dune buggy** SB - Virginia L. Blaisdell **dunk shot** PR - Jim Zerschling **Jimmy Durante** WWP **Albrecht Dürer** BA **dust storm** WWP **Dutchman's breeches** LC **Dutch oven** PI - Karen Bussolini **"Papa Doc" Duvalier** BA **Mary Dyer** Margaret Anne Miles **dynamo** TG

ear LC **Amelia Earhart** WWP **earmuff** Palmer/Brilliant, Boston, Massachusetts **Wyatt Earp** Kansas State Historical Society **earring** PC - Janice Fullman **earthquake** BA **earthworm** AA - Leonard Lee Rue III **earwig** CDB **easel** SB - Barbara Alper **Easter egg** Virginia Museum of Fine Arts, Richmond, Virginia, Bequest from the Estate of Lillian Thomas Pratt **Easter Island** Comstock - Richard Harrington **Easter lily** CC **George Eastman** WWP **eaves** PI - Martin Miller **ecce homo** LOC **eccentric** TG **echeveria** CC **echidna** NY Zoological Society **Mary Baker Eddy** LOC **edelweiss** LC **Gertrude Ederle** BA **Thomas Edison** Snark - Art Resource, New York **Edward VII** LOC **Edward VIII** GP - Camera Press **eel** CDB **egg**[1] GHP - Runk & Schoenberger **egg-and-dart** CC **eggplant** CC **Alexandre Eiffel** BA **Albert Einstein** HPS **Dwight D. Eisenhower** Dwight D. Eisenhower Library - U.S. Navy **Mamie Eisenhower** Dwight D. Eisenhower Library **eland** San Diego Zoo **elbow** GEP **Eleanor of Aquitaine** Walters Art Gallery, Baltimore, Maryland **electric guitar** Comstock - Russ Kinne **electrocardiogram** Martin M. Rotker, Deltona, Florida **electrocardiograph** SB - Paul Fortin **electromagnetic spectrum** TG **electrostatic generator** GHP **elephant** AA - Leonard Lee Rue III/AA - Irene Vandermolen **elevated railway** WWP **George Eliot** Sophia Smith Collection, Smith College **Elizabeth I** The Toledo Museum of Art, Gift of Edward Drummond Libbey **Elizabeth II** GP - Antony Armstrong Jones **Duke Ellington** BA **ellipse** TG **ellipsoid** TG **emblem** WWP **embroidery** LW - Oscar Palmquist **Empire** © The Frick Collection, New York/ From the collections of Henry Ford Museum & Greenfield Village, neg. no. B49284 **enamel** Art Resource, New York/LC **encaustic** Virginia Museum of Fine Arts, The Adolph D. and Wilkins C. Williams Fund **enceinte** PR - Omikron **endive** CC **endocrine gland** LC **endpin** PI - Martin Miller **Friedrich Engels** BA **English saddle** GEP

English setter TSW - Leonard Lee Rue III **engraving** PR - Fritz Henle **entablature** CC **eohippus** LC **epaulet** Culver Pictures Inc. **epergne** Courtesy, Museum of Fine Arts, Boston **epicycloid** TG **epiglottis** LC **Jacob Epstein** WWP **equator** LC **equestrian** PR - Richard Dibon-Smith **Erasmus** LOC **Erlenmeyer flask** EPJCo. **Max Ernst** BA **eruption** EPJCo. **Julius Erving** Philadelphia 76ers Basketball Club, Inc. **Leo Esaki** WWP **escalator** SB - Peter Menzel/TG **escapement** CC **escritoire** Courtesy, Museum of Fine Arts, Boston, Forsyth Wicks Collection **escutcheon** GEP **Esther** BA **étagère** Courtesy, Museum of Fine Arts, Boston, H.E. Bolles Fund **eucalyptus** LC **Eugénie** LOC **Europa** Anderson - Art Resource, New York **Everglades** BA **Chris Evert** WWP **ewer** MMA, Rogers Fund, 1944 (44.15) **exosphere** TG **expansion bolt** LC **explode** WWP **exposure meter** PI - Jerry Howard **expressionism** NGA, Rosenwald Collection **exterior angle** TG **extinguisher** PI - Jerry Howard **extravehicular activity** NASA - Lyndon B. Johnson Space Center **eye** LC **eye chart** HPS **eyelet** SB - T.A. Rothschild **eyeshade** WWP **eyespot** WWP **eyestalk** PR - Jen & Des Bartlett

facemask PC - Rick Friedman/Comstock - Sven Martson **Fahd ibn Abdel Aziz al-Saud** BA **fairlead** KAMD **fairwater** Department of Defense, U.S. Navy **fairy shrimp** CDB **falchion** MMA, Gift of Mrs. K.H. Schmidt, 1937 (37.186.1) **fallow deer** PR - Leonard Lee Rue III **fan [1]** SB - Joseph P. Schuyler/© 1989 Denver Art Museum **fang** PR - Leonard Lee Rue III **fantail** Comstock - Russ Kinne **farkleberry** GEP **Fannie Farmer** BA **Eileen Farrell** BA **farthingale** MMA, Irene Lewisohn Bequest, 1962 **fasces** GEP **fastback** LW - Oscar Palmquist **faucet** GEP **William Faulkner** WWP **fault** GHP - William Felger/LC **Faust** BA **feather** CDB **feather duster** LW - Oscar Palmquist **featherstitch** GEP **Federal** Courtesy, Winterthur Museum **fedora** The Granger Collection, New York **feedbag** EPJCo. **felucca** PR - Chester Higgins, Jr. **femur** LC **fencing** WWP **fender** SB - Akos Szilvasi **fennel** CC **fermata** TG **ferret [1]** WWP - National Geographic Society **Ferris wheel** Chicago Historical Society, neg. no. ICHi-02442 **ferrule** LC **ferryboat** Wolfgang Kaehler Photography **fess [1]** GEP **festoon** LC **fetlock** GEP **fez** Comstock - Russ Kinne **fiberscope** GHP - Barry L. Runk **fibula** LC/Walters Art Gallery, Baltimore, Maryland **fid** Mystic Seaport Museum, Inc. All rights reserved. **fiddlehead** PR - Hugh Spencer **fiddler crab** GHP - Runk & Schoenberger **Arthur Fiedler** WWP **field hockey** SB - Jean-Claude Lejeune **W.C. Fields** WWP **fig [1]** CDB **figurehead** SB - Jeff Albertson **figure skating** WWP **file [2]** LC **filigree** LW - Oscar Palmquist **Millard Fillmore** LOC **fin [1]** GHP - Runk & Schoenberger **fingerprint** EPJCo. **Vigdís Finnbogadóttir** WWP **fire ant** CDB **fire pink** CC **fire tower** SB - Bohdan Hrynewych **fireworks** PC - Michael F. Kullen **firkin** Hancock Shaker Village, Pittsfield, Massachusetts - Paul Rocheleau **fish** CDB **fisherman's knot** TG **fish ladder** PR - H.B. Carr **Ella Fitzgerald** BA **F. Scott Fitzgerald** BA **fjord** Russell A. Thompson **flag [1]** GHP **flagellum** CDB **flagon** Yale University Art Gallery, Gift of Mr. Donald R. Hyde **flagstick** GHP - Grant Heilman **flail** MMA, Museum Excavations, 1906–1907, Rogers Fund, 1907 (07.227.15) **flake [2]** American Museum of Natural History, Courtesy Department Library Services, neg. no. 22144 - N.G. Buxton **flambé** SB - David Krathwohl **flamenco** PC - Jeffrey Dunn **flamingo** CC **flange** CC **flask** Museum of Fine Arts, Houston, Museum purchase with funds provided by Dr. and Mrs. John R. Kelsey, Jr. **flatboat** LOC **flatworm** CDB **Gustave Flaubert** BA **flax** CC **flèche** Art Resource, New York **fleur-de-lis** SCALA - Art Resource, New York **flight deck** Official U.S. Navy Photo **flintlock** MMA, Gift of Wilfred Wood, 1956 (42.22) **flipper** Comstock - Russ Kinne **floe** PR - George Holton **floppy disk** PI - Jerry Howard **flotilla** Official U.S. Navy Photograph - PHz Robert D. Bunge **fluke [2]** CDB **fluorescent lamp** LC **flute** PI - Jerry Howard **fluting** SB - Frank Wing **fly agaric** GEP **flycatcher** PR - Peter & Stephen Maslowski **flying bridge** SB - Dean Abramson **flying buttress** PR - Omikron **flying squirrel** Leonard Rue Enterprises - Leonard Lee Rue III **foal** PI - Jerry Howard **foil [3]** PC - Jeffrey Dunn **folding door** GEP **folium** TG **folk dance** PI - Jerry Howard **Henry Fonda** GP **fondue** SB - Owen Franken **font [1]** Comstock - Russ Kinne **food processor** PI - Jerry Howard **fool's cap** GEP **football** GP - Joseph G. Constantino **footbridge** Comstock - Michael S. Thompson **footpath** Comstock - Stuart Cohen **footrope** PC - Jonathan Goell **Forbidden City** Wolfgang Kaehler Photography **forceps** LC **Betty Ford** WWP **Gerald Ford** LOC **forehand** Frank Siteman **foreshorten** Alinari - Art Resource, New York **forget-me-not** LC **forklift** EPJCo. **fossil** PR - Tom McHugh/GHP - Runk & Schoenberger **Stephen Foster** National Portrait Gallery, Smithsonian Institution, Washington, D.C. - Art Resource, New York **Foucault pendulum** PR - J.J. Barton **foundry** TSW - David S. Strickler **fountain** Image Photos - Clemens Kalischer **four-poster** Image Photos - Clemens Kalischer **foxglove** LC **fracture** LC **Jean Fragonard** HPS **Francis I** Cincinnati Art Museum, Bequest of Mary M. Emery, © Forth 1/82 (1927.384) **Francis Ferdinand** BA **Francisco Franco** BA **Benjamin Franklin** National Portrait Gallery, Smithsonian Institution, Washington, D.C., Gift of the Morris and Gwendolyn Cafritz Foundation **Franklin stove** CC **freesia** LC **free-weight** PC - Lora E. Askinazi **French curve** GEP **French door** Palmer/Brilliant, Boston, Massachusetts **French horn** PR - John Bova **French knot** GEP **fret [3]** LC **Sigmund Freud** HPS **Frey** *Encyclopedia of Source Illustrations, vol. II* **Freya** *Encyclopedia of Source Illustrations, vol. II* **frieze [1]** CC **frigate** PC - Jaye R. Phillips/WWP **Frigg** *Encyclopedia of Source Illustrations, vol. II* **fringe** PI - Karen Bussolini **frog** BA **frustum** LC **f-stop** TG **Carlos Fuentes** GP - Reg Gray **Mount Fuji** EPJCo. **funicular** BA **funnel** PI - Martin Miller **fur seal** PR - Jen & Des Bartlett **fuse [2]** LC **futon** LW - Oscar Palmquist **futurism** The Museum of Modern Art, New York, Acquired through the Lillie P. Bliss Bequest

gable roof BA **gaff [1]** LC **Yuri Gagarin** LOC **Thomas Gainsborough** HPS **gaiter** LW - Oscar Palmquist **galaxy** Lick Observatory Photograph/Lick Observatory Photograph **John Kenneth Galbraith** © Jim Kalett **Galileo** LOC **gambrel roof** USDA **gamelan** Wolfgang Kaehler Photography **gamopetalous** GEP **Indira Gandhi** BA **Mahatma Gandhi** WWP **Ganymede** Courtesy, Museum of Fine Arts, Boston, Gift of Charles C. Perkins **Greta Garbo** Archive Photos **Federico García Lorca** GP **gardenia** LC **James A. Garfield** LOC **gargoyle** SB - Barbara Alper **Giuseppe Garibaldi** New York Public Library **Judy Garland** WWP **garlic** CC **gas mask** SB - Lionel Delevingne **gas turbine** TG **gate [1]** HAR **gatehouse** EPJCo. **gaucho** Comstock - Stuart Cohen **gauntlet [1]** BA **gaur** NY Zoological Society **gavel** EPJCo. **gazebo** LOC **gecko** GHP - Hal Harrison **Lou Gehrig** WWP **Geiger tube** TG **Gemini** TG **gemsbok** SB - Ira Kirschenbaum **generator** SB - Daniel Brody **Genghis Khan** The Granger Collection, New York **geode** GHP **geodesic dome** Jeroboam, Inc. - Ilka Hartman **Saint George** Yale University Art Gallery, Purchased by the University, from James Jackson Jarves **George III** LOC **geranium** LC **German shepherd** ES **Geronimo** National Portrait Gallery, Smithsonian Institution, Washington, D.C. **gerrymander** New York Public Library, Special Collections **George and Ira Gershwin** WWP **geta** LW - Oscar Palmquist **geyser** Russell A. Thompson **ghat** PR - Arvind Garg **giant sequoia** GHP **gibbon** PR - Arthur W. Ambler **Gibson girl** BA **Gila monster** AA - Miriam Austerman **gill [1]** CDB **gimbal** TG **gimlet** LC **gingko** CC **Giotto** LOC **giraffe** AA - Leonard Lee Rue III **girandole** Photograph © 1991, The Art Institute of Chicago. All rights reserved. Gift of the Antiquarian Society, Jesse Spalding Landon Fund (1952.169) **glacier** WWP **gladiator** BA **glass blowing** EPJCo. **glean** The Museum of Fine Arts, Springfield, Massachusetts, the James Philip Gray Collection (39.04) **John Glenn** NASA **globe** Ewing Galloway **glockenspiel** PC - Carol Palmer **glove** LC **glowworm** CDB **glyph** LOC/LOC **gnu** PR - Clem Haagner **goalkeeper** PC - J.D. Sloan **goatee** Frank Siteman **goat's rue** CC **goblet** Jewish Museum - Art Resource, New York **Jean Luc Godard** BA **goggles** SB - Jonathan Rawle **golden club** CC **golden eagle** United States Dept. of the Interior - Karl H. Maslowski **golf** HAR **gondola** HAR/PC - Franz Kraus **gonfalon** SB - Mike Mazzaschi **goose** SB - Lionel J-M Delevingne **gooseberry** LC **goose step** Comstock - Robert Houser **Mikhail Gorbachev** BA **gorge** WWP **Gorgon** BA **gorilla** PR - Arthur W. Ambler **goshawk** PR - G. Ronald Austing **Gothic** SB - Owen Franken **gouge** LC **gourd** PI - Martin Miller **Francisco Goya** LOC **graben** GEP **Graces** HPS **graffito** EPJCo. **graft [1]** LC **grain elevator** GHP **granary** EPJCo. **Grand Canal** HPS **Grand Canyon** EPJCo. **grandfather clock** SLAM, Museum Purchase **grand piano** BA **Ulysses S. Grant** LOC **grape** LC **grapeshot** KAMD **grapnel** LC **grappling iron** PC - Jeffrey Dunn **grasshopper** LC **grater** LW - Oscar Palmquist **gray wolf** AA - Pat Crowe **grease gun** PI - Jerry Howard **great auk** PR **great seal** The White House **Great Wall of China** WWP **El Greco** Brown Brothers **Greek cross** GEP **greenhouse** SB - Eric Neurath **greenhouse effect** TG **greyhound** BA **griffin** The Nelson-Atkins Museum of Art, Kansas City, Missouri, Nelson Fund 47-47 **D.W. Griffith** WWP **grille** BA/PI - Jerry Howard **grindstone** LW - Oscar Palmquist **grizzly bear** LOC **groin** CDB **grotesque** Alinari - Art Resource, New York **grove** USDA - Soil Conservation Service **Grus** TG **guava** CC **gudgeon [2]** KAMD **gueridon** White House Historical Association **Guernsey [2]** GHP **guide dog** PC - Spencer Grant **guilloche** CC **guimpe** HPS **guinea fowl** PR - R. Van Nostrand **guitar** SB - Elizabeth Crews **gull [1]** PR - Alvin E. Staffan **gullwing** © 1991 Judith Winters **gully [1]** USDA - Tim McCabe **Johann Gutenberg** LOC **Nell Gwyn** HPS **gypsy moth** BA **gyroscope** GHP - Runk & Schoenberger

hackamore From *Horses and Tack* by M.E. Ensminger. © 1991 by M.E. Ensminger. Reprinted by permission of Houghton Mifflin Company. **hacksaw** PC - Frank Siteman **Hadrian** Giraudon - Art Resource, New York **hadrosaur** TG **haku** Comstock - Richard Harrington **halberd** MMA, Bashford Dean Memorial Collection, Purchase, Funds from various donors, 1929 (29.156.33)/MMA, Gift of Mary Alice Dyckman Dean, in memory of Alexander McMillan Welch, 1949 (49.120.12) **Edmund Halley** LOC **Halley's comet** WWP **halo** LOC **halter [1]** GHP **hamadryas** PR - Toni Angermayer **hame** KAMD **hammer** CC **hammock [1]** PI - Jerry Howard **Hammurabi** The Nelson-Atkins Museum of Art, Kansas City, Missouri, Nelson Fund 49-15 **Hampshire** Ewing Galloway **handcuff** EPJCo. **George Frederick Handel** LOC **handlebar mustache** BA **hand organ** SB - Peter Menzel **hand press** LOC **hang glider** WWP **hansom** Shelburne Museum, Shelburne, Vermont - Ken Burris **hardhat** LW - Aldo Mastrocola **Florence Harding** LOC **Warren G. Harding** LOC **hardy [2]** GEP **hare** AA - Robert Maier **harmonica** LW - Oscar Palmquist **harness** AA - Harry Cutting **harp** Lyon & Healy Harps, Inc., Chicago, Illinois/GEP **harpoon** NMAI, Gift of Glenbow Foundation, Calgary, Canada **harpsichord** HPS **harquebus** MMA, Gift of William H. Riggs, 1913 (14.25.1374) **Benjamin Harrison [2]** LOC **George Harrison** BA **William Henry Harrison** LOC **hartebeest** San Diego Zoo - Ron Garrison **hatch [2]** PR - Hal Harrison **hatchet** National Museum of American History, Smithsonian Institution, Washington, D.C. **Hatshepsut** MMA, Museum Excavations 1926–1928, Rogers Fund, 1931 (31.3.163) **hauberk** HPS **havelock** GEP **Nathaniel Hawthorne** LOC **Rutherford B. Hayes** LOC **haystack** EPJCo. **headdress** SB - Ira Kirschenbaum/SB - John Running **headphone** PC - Frank Siteman **headset** PI - Jerry Howard **headstand** SB - Elizabeth Hamlin **headstone** SB - Jeff Albertson **hearing aid** PR - Van Bucher **heart** LC **hearth** SB - Fredrik Bodin **hedgehog** PR - Eric Hosking **Jascha Heifetz** WWP **Heimlich maneuver** LC **helicopter** Comstock - Russ Kinne **Helios** BA **helix** TG **hellebore** CC **helmet** PC - Paul Nurnberg/SLAM, Museum Purchase **Ernest Hemingway** GP - Hy Simon **hemlock** CC **hemostat** LC **Jimi Hendrix** BA **Henry VIII** LOC **Hercules** Courtesy, Museum of Fine Arts, Boston, Perkins Collection/TG **Woody Herman** BA **hermit crab** PR - Jen & Des Bartlett **heron** PR - Allan D. Cruickshank **heterocercal** CDB **hex sign** GHP **Thor Heyerdahl** GP **hibiscus** CC **Wild Bill Hickok** BA **hieroglyphic** Marburg - Art Resource, New York **highboy** MMA, Purchase, Joseph Pulitzer Bequest, 1940 (40.37.1) **highchair** PI - Jerry Howard **high-hat cymbals** LW - Oscar Palmquist **high jump** SB - Barbara Alper **high relief** Courtesy, Museum of Fine Arts, Boston **hinge** GEP **Hirohito** BA **hitch** TG **Alfred Hitchcock** BA **Adolf Hitler** HPS **hive** Palmer/Brilliant, Boston, Massachusetts **hockey stick** Jeroboam, Inc. - Hap Stewart **hoe** LC **hogan** SB - Ira Kirschenbaum **holly** LC **Oliver Wendell Holmes** Sophia Smith Collection, Smith College **Holstein [2]** GHP **holster** © 1991 Judith Winters **Holy Ark** Jewish Museum - Art Resource, New York **Homburg** BA **Winslow Homer** BA **homocercal** CDB **homolosine projection** TG **honeycomb** AA - Stephen Dalton **hood [1]** Comstock - Sven Martson **hoof** GEP **hookah** The Pierpont Morgan Library, New York (M.1035.11) **hoop** PI - Martin Miller **hoopoe** NY Zoological Society **hoop skirt** Museum of the City of New York, Gift of the daughters of Edward and Alice Hendricks Brandon (34.348.2) **Herbert Hoover** LOC **Lou Hoover** LOC **Bob Hope** BA **hoplite** BA **hopper** LW - Oscar Palmquist **hornbill** PR - Jen & Des Bartlett **Lena Horne** WWP **Vladimir Horowitz** Archive Photos **horse** Frank Siteman/PC - Rick Friedman **horse chestnut** LC **horseshoe crab** GHP - Runk & Schoenberger **horst** GEP **Horus** Courtesy of The Oriental Institute of The University of Chicago **hot cross bun** PI - Patricia J. Bruno **hot dog** PR - Bill Bachman **Harry Houdini** LOC **hound's-tongue** CDB **houndstooth check** LW - Oscar Palmquist **hourglass** EPJCo. **housefly** CDB **Sam Houston** International Museum of Photography at George Eastman House, neg. no. 25540 **howdah** LOC **huarache** PI - Jerry Howard **hubcap** PI - Jerry Howard **Henry Hudson** WWP **Langston Hughes** National Portrait Gallery, Smithsonian Institution, Washington, D.C., © 1981 Center for Creative Photography, Arizona Board of Regents **huipil** NMAI **hula** GP - Ric Robinson **hull** TG **humerus** CC **hummingbird** AA - Len Rue, Jr. **hurdle** WWP **hurdy-gurdy** Courtesy, Museum of Fine Arts, Boston, Mary Smith Fund **hurricane lamp** EPJCo. **Hussein** BA **Aldous Huxley** WWP **hydra** PR - Omikron **hydrant** LW - © 1989 Aldo Mastrocola **hydroelectric** TG **Hydrus** TG **hyena** NY Zoological Society **hyoid bone** LC **hyperbola** LC **hyperboloid** TG **hyperopia** CDB **hypocycloid** TG **hypodermic syringe** EPJCo. **hypotenuse** LC **hyrax** PR - Jen & Des Bartlett

ibex AA - Irene Vandermolen **ibis** AA - C.C. Lockwood **Henrik Ibsen** HPS **iceboat** HAR **ice-cream chair** LW - Oscar Palmquist **ice hockey** SB - Frank Siteman **ichthyosaur** TG **icicle** GHP **icon** Alinari - Art Resource, New York **icosahedron** TG **idle wheel** GEP **Ignatius of Loyola** BA **iguana** AA - Len Rue, Jr. **iguanodon** TG **ikebana** © 1991 Judith Winters **ileum** CC **illumination** MMA, The Cloisters Collection, 1954 (54.1.2) **imbricate** SB - Owen Franken **impala** AA - Len Rue, Jr. **impatiens** CC **imperial** Culver Pictures Inc. **implosion** PC - George Mars Cassidy **impressionism** © The Frick Collection, New York **inauguration** WWP **Incan** PR - Michael Hayman **incandescent lamp** LC **incubator** Peter Arnold, Inc. - SIU **incuse** SB - James R. Holland **Indian club** LW - Oscar Palmquist **Indian tobacco** CDB **Indra** BA **Indus [2]** TG **infanta** Marburg - Art Resource, New York **inflatable** PR - Herman Emmet **inflorescence** GEP **William Inge** WWP **Jean Auguste Dominique Ingres** HPS **inhaler** LW - Oscar Palmquist **initial** BA **inkstand** Society of Inkwell Collectors, Minneapolis, Minnesota **inky cap** GEP **inlay** Deborah Buckley **Innocent III** BA **Ismet Inönü** WWP **inro** Cummer Gallery of Art, Jacksonville, Florida **instrument** Palmer/Brilliant, Boston, Massachusetts **instrument panel** PC - Frank Siteman **intaglio** Walters Art Gallery, Baltimore, Maryland **intarsia** SEF - Art Resource, New York **intercept** TG **internal-combustion engine** LC **interrupter** LW - © 1989 Aldo Mastrocola **intestine** LC **inverness** The Granger Collection, New York **involute** TG **io moth** AA - Stan Schroeder **Eugène Ionesco** BA - John Foraste **Ionic order** LC **iris** LC **Irish moss** GEP **Irish setter** ES **Irish wolfhound** ES **ironwork** SB - Mike Mazzaschi **irrigate** USDA - Soil Conservation Service **Washington Irving** National Portrait Gallery, Smithsonian Institution, Washington, D.C. **Isabella I** The Granger Collection, New York **Christopher Isherwood** BA **Isis [1]** HPS **issuant** GEP **Ivan the Great** HPS **Ivan the Terrible** HPS **ivory** MMA, The Michael C. Rockefeller Memorial Collection, Gift of Nelson A. Rockefeller, 1972 (1978.412.323) **ivy** PI - Jerry Howard **izar** SB - Owen Franken

jack PI - Jerry Howard **jackal** AA - Leonard Lee Rue III **jackhammer** Eric Kroll **Andrew Jackson** LOC **Jesse Jackson** BA **jaguar** San Diego Zoo **Jahangir** Freer Gallery of Art, Smithsonian Institution, Washington, D.C.; accession no. 42.16A, Indian painting: Mogul, 17th century, school of Jahangir; color and gold, $9^{13}/_{16}'' \times 7^{3}/_{16}''$ **jai alai** BA **jalousie** LW - © 1989 S.E. Byrne **Japanese beetle** CDB **jasmine** CC **javelin** SB - Jean-Claude Lejeune **J-bar** EPJCo. **Thomas Jefferson** LOC **jejunum** CC **jellyfish** GHP - Runk & Schoenberger **jellyroll** PI - Patricia J. Bruno **Jersey** LW - © 1989 Feza D. Oktay **Jerusalem artichoke** CC **Jesus** PR - Omikron **jet [2]** PR - Blair Seitz **jet engine** CC **jetpack** NASA **jib [1]** TG **jigsaw** PC - Jeffrey Dunn **jimsonweed** CC **jinriksha** Hong Kong Tourist Association **Joan of Arc** Giraudon - Art Resource, New York **jockey** WWP **jodhpurs** Palmer/Brilliant, Boston, Massachusetts **Andrew Johnson** National Portrait Gallery, Smithsonian Institution, Washington, D.C. **Lady Bird Johnson** GP **Lyndon B. Johnson** BA **John the Baptist** MMA, Fletcher Fund, 1936 (36.14a-c) **joist** LC **Jolly Roger** LC **jonquil** LC **Chief Joseph** National Anthropological Archives at the National Museum of Natural History, Smithsonian Institution, Washington, D.C. **Joshua tree** LC **James Joyce** The Granger Collection, New York **Juan Carlos** GP - Richard Open **judo** HPS **juggle** LW - © 1989 S.E. Byrne **jukebox** HAR **jump ball** PR - J.P. Defail-Rapho **jumping jack** Museum of the City of New York, Gift of Dewitt Clinton Cohen (35.248.14) **Carl Jung** Mary Evans Picture Library - Photo Researchers, Inc. **juniper** CC **junk [2]** HPS **Jupiter** NASA **Justinian I** BA

kachina PC - Jon Goell **kaffiyeh** PC - Jeffrey Dunn **kalimba** LW - Oscar Palmquist **Kamehameha I** National Portrait Gallery, Smithsonian Institution, Washington, D.C., Gift of the Bernice Pauahi Bishop Museum **kangaroo** San Diego Zoo **kangaroo rat** PR - Woodrow Goodpaster **Konstantinos Karamanlis** BA **karate** SB - James R. Holland **Boris Karloff** WWP/WWP **katydid** PR - John R. Clawson **Kenneth Kaunda** WWP **kayak** SB - Peter Menzel **kazoo** GEP **Buster Keaton** WCFTR **Helen Keller** The Schlesinger Library, Radcliffe College **kelp** LC **kendo** WWP **Jacqueline Kennedy** BA **John F. Kennedy** GP **kepi** Jeroboam, Inc. - Jeffrey Blankfort **Kerry blue terrier** ES **kestrel** National Agricultural Library, Forest Service Photo Collections **kettledrum** Comstock - Russ Kinne **keystone** CDB **Ruholla Khomeini** BA **Nikita Khrushchev** United Nations **kickboxing** PC - Lauren Lantos **Søren Kierkegaard** BA **Mount Kilimanjaro** PR - Lynn McLaren **killdeer** Leonard Rue Enterprises - Leonard Lee Rue III **kiln** SB - J. Berndt **kilt** LW - Oscar Palmquist **kimono** WWP **king** GEP **Billie Jean King** BA **Martin Luther King, Jr.** BA **king post** TG **kinkajou** NY Zoological Society **kiosk** SB - Owen Franken **Henry Kissinger** GP - Jeff Taylor **kite** PI - Martin Miller **kiwi** PR - R. Van Nostrand/CC **Paul Klee** BA **Klein bottle** LC **kneehole** Yale University Art Gallery, The Mabel Brady Garvan Collection **knight** GEP **knit** LC **knocker** Image Photos - Clemens Kalischer **knot [1]** TG/PC - Frank Siteman **John Knox** BA **koala** HAR **kohl** GP - Camera Press **kookaburra** AA - Ann Sanfedele **koto** Jeroboam, Inc. - Mitchell Payne **Kublai Khan** LOC **kudzu** USDA **Kufic** LOC **kumquat** LC **kylix** Courtesy, Museum of Fine Arts, Boston, William E. Nickerson Fund

laboratory PR - Kenneth Murray **labyrinth** Comstock - Georg Gerster **lace** LW - Oscar Palmquist **lacrosse** SB - Bruce M. Wellman

ladder-back Yale University Art Gallery, The Mabel Brady Garvan Collection **ladies' tresses** CC **ladybug** CDB **Marquis de Lafayette** National Portrait Gallery, Smithsonian Institution, Washington, D.C. **lag screw** CC **lamb** PR - Arthur W. Ambler **lammergeier** PR - Karl H. Maslowski **lamprey** PR - Karl H. Maslowski/CDB **lampworking** PR - Joseph Nettis **lancet** LC **lancet window** CC **landau** Shelburne Museum, Shelburne, Vermont - Ken Burris **Lillie Langtry** WCFTR **lantern wheel** GEP **Laocoon** Anderson - Art Resource, New York **lap joint** TG **large intestine** LC **largemouth bass** PR - Treat Davidson **lark** [1] PR - G. Ronald Austing **La Salle** LOC **Lascaux** PR - J.J. Languepin **laser** LC **lasso** TSW - Dom Franco **last** [3] Palmer/Brilliant, Boston, Massachusetts **lateen** CC **lathe** SB - Peter Vandermark **Latin cross** GEP **lattice** Image Photos - Clemens Kalischer **launch pad** NASA **laurels** LOC **lava** PR - Keith Gunnar **laver** [1] MMA, The Cloisters Collection (47.101.56 a,b) **Antoine Lavoisier** MMA, Purchase, Mr. and Mrs. Charles Wrightsman Gift, 1977 (1977.10) **lawn mower** PI - Martin Miller **T.E. Lawrence** GP **layback** PR - Gerard Vandystadt **lazy Susan** PI - Jerry Howard **lazy tongs** LC **leaf** LC **leaf spring** CC **lean** [1] Comstock - Stuart Cohen **least flycatcher** PR - Allan D. Cruickshank **leatherback** HPS **lectern** Image Photos - Clemens Kalischer **Leda** MMA, Wildenstein Fund, 1970 (1970.140) **lederhosen** Austrian National Tourist Office - Leo-Heinz Hajek **Le Duc Tho** BA **Robert E. Lee** LOC **leeboard** CC **leg-of-mutton** HPS **leg warmer** LW - Oscar Palmquist **lemming** PR - Tom McHugh **lemur** AA - George Roos **Vladimir Lenin** WWP **John Lennon** GP - Tom Hanley **lens** LC **Leo** TG **Leonardo da Vinci** BA **leopard** AA - Leonard Lee Rue III **leopard moth** PR - Lynwood M. Chace **lesser celandine** CC **levee** [1] LOC **level** LC **lever** LC **Meriwether Lewis** Independence National Historical Park **Libra** TG **lichen** PR - Jack Dermid **lierne** CC **lifeboat** LC **life jacket** SB - George Bellerose **life preserver** Culver Pictures Inc. **ligature** TG **lighthouse** GHP - Hal Harrison **lightning** AA - Michael Fredericks, Jr. **Liliuokalani** National Portrait Gallery, Smithsonian Institution, Washington, D.C., Gift of the Bernice Pauahi Bishop Museum **lily** LC **lily pad** PI - Jerry Howard **limousine** BA **limpet** GEP **Abraham Lincoln** LOC **Mary Todd Lincoln** LOC **Charles Lindbergh** LOC **linden** CC **linstock** MMA, Gift of William H. Riggs, 1913 (14.25.285) **lion** AA - Len Rue, Jr. **lionfish** PI - Martin Miller **Franz Liszt** HPS **litchi** LC **litter** AA - Terence A. Gili **live oak** CC **liver** [1] LC **llama** HPS **loblolly pine** CC **lobster** GHP - Runk & Schoenberger **lobster pot** Frank Siteman **lock** [1] LC/Ewing Galloway **John Locke** BA **locket** Comstock - Christine Rose/Comstock - Christine Rose **locomotive** PE - William A. Todd, Jr. **locust** GP - Anthony Bannister/LC **loganberry** LC **loggia** HPS **Lombardy poplar** CC **Henry Wadsworth Longfellow** National Portrait Gallery, Smithsonian Institution, Washington, D.C. **longhorn** PR - Clint Grant **long jump** Jeroboam, Inc. - Cheryl A. Traendly **loom** [2] Comstock - Stuart Cohen **loon** [1] Cornell Laboratory of Ornithology - Grimes **loosestrife** CC **loquat** CC **lorgnette** BA **lotus** PI - Jerry Howard **lotus position** SB - Jean-Claude Lejeune **Louis XIV** Giraudon - Art Resource, New York **loupe** LW - Oscar Palmquist **louver** LW - Oscar Palmquist **loving cup** Museum of the City of New York, Gift of Charles M. Eckman **Juliette Low** BA **lowboy** From the collections of Henry Ford Museum & Greenfield Village, neg. no. A3837 **low relief** The Nelson-Atkins Museum of Art, Kansas City, Missouri, Nelson Fund **Clare Boothe Luce** WWP **Henry Luce** WWP **luna moth** CDB **lune** TG **lungi** SB - Ira Kirschenbaum **luster** The Currier Gallery of Art, Manchester, New Hampshire, The Murray Collection of Glass (1974.45.1-.2) **lute** [1] Courtesy, Museum of Fine Arts, Boston, Leslie Lindsey Mason Fund **Martin Luther** Alinari - Art Resource, New York **lynx** AA - Leonard Lee Rue III **Lyra** TG **lyre** Courtesy, Museum of Fine Arts, Boston, William Francis Warden Fund (62.362) **lyrebird** PR - R.T. Littlejohns

Douglas MacArthur HPS **mace** [1] MMA, Rogers Fund, 1904 (04.3.59) **Niccolò Machiavelli** BA **machicolation** CC **Machu Picchu** SB - Ira Kirschenbaum **mackerel** CC **mackinaw** SB - Bohdan Hrynewych **Dolley Madison** LOC **James Madison** LOC **Madonna** NGA, Widener Collection **madroña** CC **Magen David** SB - Richard Sobol **magic square** TG **magnetic field** GHP - Runk & Schoenberger **magnetic resonance imaging** PR - Spencer Grant **magpie** PR - Allan D. Cruickshank **maidenhair fern** CDB **mainspring** LC **Madame de Maintenon** BA **maintop** SB - Frances M. Cox **majolica** SLAM, Museum Purchase **major scale** TG **malamute** ES **Malcolm X** BA **mall** [1] Martha Phelps/Jim Craig **mallard** PR - Gordon S. Smith **mallet** LC **Maltese cross** GEP **mammoth** TG **Manchester terrier** ES **manchineel** GEP **mandala** Los Angeles County Museum of Art, From the Nasli and Alice Heeramaneck Collection, Museum Associates Purchase **mandarin collar** CC **mandarin duck** AA - Leonard Lee Rue IV **Nelson Mandela** GP - Jan Kopec **mandolin** Courtesy, Museum of Fine Arts, Boston, Leslie Lindsey Mason Collection **Edouard Manet** International Museum of Photography at George Eastman House, neg. no. 4003 **mangle** [2] KAMD **manhole** SB - Rudolph Robinson **mannequin** PI - Jerry Howard **manometer** TG **mansard** LW - © 1990 S.E. Byrne **mantel** SB - Peter Southwick **mantle** LC **manual alphabet** TG **Manx cat** Ms. Meryl Parkton, Seattle, Washington **Mao Zedong** WWP **maple** CDB **marabou** PR - Arthur W. Ambler **maraca** LW - © 1990 S.E. Byrne **Jean Paul Marat** Giraudon - Art Resource, New York **Marcel Marceau** WCFTR **Margrethe II** GP - Camera Press **mariachi** SB - Jean-Claude Lejeune **Marie Antoinette** Walters Art Gallery, Baltimore, Maryland **Marie de Médicis** LOC **marigold** LC **marina** EPJCo. **marionette** Cooper-Hewitt National Museum of Design, Smithsonian Institution - Art Resource, New York **markhor** San Diego Zoo - Ron Garrison **marmot** Comstock - Phyllis Greenberg **marquee** PI - Martin Miller **marquetry** Peter Vandermark **Mars** NASA **martlet** GEP **Marx Brothers** WCFTR **Mary Queen of Scots** MMA, Gift of J. Pierpont Morgan, 1917 (17.190.2) **mask** Cincinnati Art Museum, Gift of Dr. and Mrs. W.W. Seely **mast** [1] Courtesy of the Society for the Preservation of New England Antiquities, Boston, Massachusetts - N.L. Stebbins **mastaba** LC **mastiff** ES **matilija poppy** CC **Henri Matisse** WWP **Matterhorn** Swiss National Tourist Office **mattock** LC **matzo** PC - Jeffrey Dunn **Somerset Maugham** WWP **mausoleum** SB - Ira Kirschenbaum **Maximilian** LOC **Mayan** PC - Cynthia W. Sterling **May apple** CC **Maypole** BA **Willie Mays** WWP **mazer** Wadsworth Atheneum, Hartford, Connecticut, J. Pierpont Morgan Collection **Paul McCartney** WWP **William McKinley** LOC **Margaret Mead** WWP **meadowlark** PR - Allan D. Cruickshank **meander** GHP **measure** TG **Mecca** GP - Camera Press **medal** SB - James R. Holland **medevac** PR - Spencer Grant **Lorenzo de Medici** NGA, Samuel H. Kress Collection **medlar** LC **meerschaum** Frank Siteman **megakaryocyte** PR - Biophoto Assoc. **megaphone** SB - Arthur Grace **meiosis** CDB **Golda Meir** GP **melon** LC **Herman Melville** BA **memorial** PC - Dennis MacDonald **menhir** Comstock - Georg Gerster **meniscus** LC **menorah** Peter Vandermark **Mercury** Courtesy of The Bostonian Society and Old State House/NASA **merganser** TSW - Leonard Lee Rue III **meridian** TG **merlon** CC **mermaid** EPJCo. **mesa** SB - Ira Kirschenbaum **metacarpus** LC **metamorphosis** LC **metaphase** CDB **metatarsus** LC **metate** NMAI - Edward H. Davis **meter** [3] SB - Frank Siteman **metronome** LW - © 1990 S.E. Byrne **mews** Marilyn Root **Michelangelo** BA **microbus** © 1991 Judith Winters **micrometer** [1] GHP - Runk & Schoenberger **microphone** PI - Martin Miller **microreader** Comstock - Russ Kinne **microscope** AA - George F. Godfrey **mihrab** Leo de Wys, Inc. - Alon Reininger **milestone** PI - Jerry Howard **milkweed** PI - Martin Miller **Edna Saint Vincent Millay** WWP **Glenn Miller** WWP **millinery** Palmer/Brilliant, Boston, Massachusetts **millipede** CDB **minaret** GP - Richard Harrington **Minerva** BA **miniature** The Nelson-Atkins Museum of Art, Kansas City, Missouri, Gift of Mr. and Mrs. John W. Starr through the Starr Foundation **miniature golf** PI - Jerry Howard **minor scale** TG **Minotaur** Anderson - Art Resource, New York **minuteman** SB - Lionel J-M Delevingne **mirror** SLAM, Gift of the Decorative Arts Society of City Art Museum **misericord** Marburg - Art Resource, New York **mission** Russell A. Thompson **mistletoe** LC **miter** PC - Michael F. Kullen **miter joint** TG **mitosis** CDB **François Mitterrand** WWP **mobcap** Collection of The J.B. Speed Art Museum, Louisville, Kentucky **mobile** Photograph © The Solomon R. Guggenheim Foundation, New York, Collection Mary Reynolds, Gift of her brother (FN54.1388) - Robert E. Mates **Möbius strip** LC **moccasin** NMAI **model** BA **modular** Image Photos - Clemens Kalischer **mola** [1] LW - Jim Cronk **molar** [2] LC **mold** [1] © 1991 Judith Winters **moldboard** USDA - Soil Conservation Service **moloch** CC **monarch butterfly** AA - Stan Schroeder **Thelonious Monk** WWP **monkey** NY Zoological Society **monkey bars** Jeroboam, Inc. - Suzanne Arms **monkey wrench** CC **monocle** Ewing Galloway **monolith** PR - David Moore **James Monroe** LOC **monstrance** Courtesy of the Hispanic Society of America, New York City **monteith** Courtesy, Museum of Fine Arts, Boston **Montezuma II** LOC **monument** HPS **moon** Lick Observatory Photographs **moonscape** NASA **Moorish** SB - Owen Franken **moose** PR - Leonard Lee Rue III **moped** Palmer/Brilliant, Boston, Massachusetts **moray** © 1991 Sea World, Inc. **Sir Thomas More** © The Frick Collection, New York **morel** CDB **Morgan** American Morgan Horse Association, Inc. **morion** BA **Samuel F.B. Morse** LOC **Morse code** TG **mortar** NMAI **mortarboard** PC - Kindra Clineff **mosaic** The Nelson-Atkins Museum of Art, Kansas City, Missouri, Nelson Fund **Grandma Moses** GP **mosque** GP - Photo Trends **mosquito** CDB **motorboat** EPJCo. **motorcycle** EPJCo. **motor scooter** Wolfgang Kaehler Photography **mountain ash** CDB **mountaineer** PR - Keith Gunnar **mountain laurel** LC **Louis Mountbatten** BA **mouth** LC **mouth-to-mouth resuscitation** CC **Wolfgang Amadeus Mozart** GP **muff** [2] Culver Pictures Inc. **muffler** LC **mule** [1] PR - Joe Munroe **mummer** Palmer/Brilliant, Boston, Massachusetts **Edvard Munch** The Art Museum, Princeton University, Gift of James R. Epstein **mural** BA **Musca** TG **musk ox** AA - Leonard Lee Rue III **Benito Mussolini** BA **mute** Peter Vandermark **myopia** CDB

nail CC **Napoleon I** NGA, Samuel H. Kress Collection **narwhal** PR - Richard Ellis **Gamal Abdel Nasser** WWP **nasturtium** LC **nativity** NGA, Samuel H. Kress Collection **nautilus** GHP - Runk & Schoenberger **nave** [1] CC **nebula** Lick Observatory Photograph **neck** Wyoming Travel Commission **neckerchief** Jeroboam, Inc. - Laimute Druskis **needle** LC **needlepoint** Allen Moore **Nefertiti** Art Resource, New York **nene** AA - Irene Vandermolen **neoclassicism** HPS **Neptune** [1] BA/NASA **nerd** Random House, Inc. From *If I Ran the Zoo* by Dr. Seuss. Copyright © 1950 by Theodor S. Geisel. Copyright renewed 1977 by Theodor S. Geisel and Audrey S. Geisel. Reprinted by permission. **Nero** Worcester Art Museum, Worcester, Massachusetts **nest** PR - Hal H. Harrison/AA - Leonard Lee Rue III/Museum of Art, Rhode Island School of Design, Gift of Mrs. Harold Brown **netsuke** MMA, Rogers Fund, 1913 (13.67.52) **neuron** LC **neuropteran** PR - Robert C. Hermes **newel** TG/Allen Moore **Newfoundland** [2] ES **newsstand** PR - Esaias Baitel **newt** PR - Treat Davidson **Isaac Newton** HPS **Niagara Falls** [1] HAR **niche** LOC **Nicholas II** WWP **Friedrich Nietzsche** HPS **Florence Nightingale** National Portrait Gallery, London **Vaslav Nijinsky** WCFTR **Nike** MMA, Rogers Fund, 1907 **nimbostratus** SB - George W. Gardner **nine-banded armadillo** PR - Jen & Des Bartlett **Pat Nixon** LOC **Richard M. Nixon** GP - Larry Stevens **No** [1] Japan National Tourist Organization **Noah** The Pierpont Morgan Library, New York (PML 17593, July 1488, f.34r) **Alfred Nobel** BA **Norfolk Island pine** Comstock - Richard Harrington **noria** KAMD **normal distribution** TG **Norway maple** CC **Norway spruce** CDB **Norwegian elkhound** ES **nose** LC **Nostradamus** HPS **Rudolf Nureyev** © 1986 Martha Swope, New York City **nut** LC **nutcracker** Peter Vandermark **nuthatch** AA - Leonard Lee Rue III **nutmeg** LC

oasis PR - E.A. Weber **obelisk** Margaret Anne Miles **oboe** Comstock - Russ Kinne **observatory** GHP - Runk & Schoenberger **obtuse angle** LC **ocarina** PI - Martin Miller **ocelot** NY Zoological Society **Sandra Day O'Connor** WWP **ocotillo** PR - Art Bilsten **octagon** LC **octahedron** TG **Octans** TG **octopus** GHP - Runk & Schoenberger **odalisque** Giraudon - Art Resource, New York **Oedipus** Alinari - Art Resource, New York **ogee** CC **oil well** Russell A. Thompson **okapi** PR - Frank Stevens **Georgia O'Keeffe** WWP **okra** LC **Old English sheepdog** AA - Terence A. Gili **olecranon** CDB **olive** LC **Laurence Olivier** The Granger Collection, New York **olla** Museum of Fine Arts, Houston, Gift of Miss Ima Hogg **omasum** CDB **Eugene O'Neill** WWP **onion** LC **open-hearth** TG **operating room** PR - Pamela Parlapiano **Ophiuchus** TG **ophthalmoscope** PC - Richard Wood **opium poppy** CC **opossum** GHP - Runk & Schoenberger **optic nerve** LC **orach** *Field Guide to Wildflowers* by Roger Tory Peterson and Margaret McKenny. © 1968 by Roger Tory Peterson and Margaret McKenny. Reprinted by permission of Houghton Mifflin Company. All rights reserved. **orangutan** AA - Miriam Austerman **orb** Marburg - Art Resource, New York **orbicular** CC **organ** Comstock - Russ Kinne **organ-pipe cactus** GHP - John Colwell **oriel** SB - Ellis Herwig **Orion** TG **José Orozco** WWP **orrery** The Granger Collection, New York **José Ortega y Gasset** WWP **George Orwell** WWP **Osiris** HPS **osprey** PR - Jen & Des Bartlett **ostrich** AA - Stewart D. Halperin **ostrich fern** CC **otter** San Diego Zoo **ottoman** High Museum of Art, Atlanta, Georgia, Virginia Carroll Crawford Collection (1981.1000.42) **outboard motor** Jeroboam, Inc. - Laimute Druskis **outcrop** PI - Jerry Howard **outhouse** EPJCo. **outrigger** Wolfgang Kaehler Photography **ovenbird** PR - Allan D. Cruickshank **overalls** SB - Jeffry W. Myers **overpass** HPS **Jesse Owens** BA **owl** PR - Karl H. Maslowski **ox** PR - Tom McHugh **oystercatcher** AA - Irene Vandermolen **Seiji Ozawa** BA

pacemaker SB - Harry Wilks **pad** [1] PC - Martha Stewart **paddle** [1] LC **paddle wheel** Jeroboam, Inc. - Cheryl A. Traendly **paddy** BA **padlock** GEP **pagoda** SCALA - Art Resource, New York **Mohammed Reza Pahlavi** WWP **painted lady** CDB **painter** [1] SB - Jon Chase **paisley** Allen Moore **palapa** Comstock - Richard Harrington **pale** [1] GEP **palette** PR - David M. Grossman **Palladian** [2] SEF - Art Resource, New York **pallbearer** PR - Spencer Grant **pallet** [1] PC - Spencer Grant **palmate** CC **Olaf Palme** WWP **palmette** Alinari - Art Resource, New York **palmistry** LOC **Pan** © 1898 *Bulfinch's Age of Fable or Beauties of Mythology* **Panama hat** PC - Ken Robert Buck **pancreas** LC **panda** GP - Popperfoto **Pangaea** TG **panpipe** GEP **Pantheon** Alinari - Art Resource, New York **pantry** SB - Peter Menzel **papaya** CC **papillote** CC **parabola** LC **paraboloid** TG **parachute** GHP **parallax** CC **paramecium** CDB **paramedic** PC - Spencer Grant **parapet** Palmer/Brilliant, Boston, Massachusetts **parasol** GP - Alex Waskinski **parbuckle** CC **parfleche** NMAI **parget** BA **paring knife** PI - Martin Miller **parka** PI - Jerry Howard **Rosa Parks** BA **parquetry** Comstock - Russ Kinne **Catherine Parr** National Portrait Gallery, London **Maxfield Parrish** WWP **parrot** AA - Pat Crowe **parsnip** CC **parterre** BA **Parthenon** Marburg - Art Resource, New York **partisan** [2] MMA, Gift of William H. Riggs, 1913 (14.25.454) **Blaise Pascal** Giraudon - Art Resource, New York **passant** GEP **passionflower** LC **Louis Pasteur** HPS **pasture** PI - Jerry Howard **patchwork** SB - Peter Southwick **patella** LC **patriarchal cross** GEP **Linus Pauling** Archive Photos **Luciano Pavarotti** GP - Jane Bown **pavis** MMA, Rogers Fund, 1923 (23.42.2) **Anna Pavlova** BA **Pavo** TG **pawl** LC **pawn** [2] GEP **pea** LC **peach** [1] LC **peacock** PR - Arthur W. Ambler **pear** LC **pearl** [1] Comstock - Christine Rose **Robert E. Peary** National Portrait Gallery, Smithsonian Institution, Washington, D.C. **peavey** GEP **peccary** PR - Leonard Lee Rue III **pectoral** BA **pedicab** PR - Bernard Pierre Wolfe **Pegasus** National Museum of American History, Smithsonian Institution, Washington, D.C., National Numismatics Collection/TG **I.M. Pei** Pei Cobb Freed & Partners - Evelyn Hofer **Pelé** BA **pelican** AA - Irene Vandermolen **peltate** CC **pelvis** LC **pendentive** CDB **pendulum** GEP **William Penn** The Historical Society of Pennsylvania **pennywhistle** PI - Jerry Howard **pentagon** LC/WWP **pepper** LC **pepper mill** LW - Jim Cronk **peppermint** CDB **Père David's deer** San Diego Zoo **peregrine falcon** PR - G. Ronald Austing **pergola** LW - Oscar Palmquist **Pericles** Alinari - Art Resource, New York **periodical cicada** PR - Alvin E. Staffan **peristyle** CC **periwinkle** [2] CC **Frances Perkins** HPS **Persian cat** PR - Ylla **persimmon** LC **peruke** Worcester Art Museum, Worcester, Massachusetts **pestle** BA **Peter the Great** The Granger Collection, New York **Roger Tory Peterson** Fred Collins Photographic Studio, Stamford, Connecticut **Francesco Petrarch** Alinari - Art Resource, New York **petri dish** PC - Tom McHugh **petroglyph** GHP - Alan Pitcairn **petunia** LC **pew** EPJCo. **peyote** GEP **phaeton** Shelburne Museum, Shelburne, Vermont - Ken Burris **phalanx** LC **Pharaoh** Alinari - Art Resource, New York **pheasant** AA - Robert Maier **Prince Philip** GP - John Lawrence **phlox** GEP **phoebe** PR - Allan D. Cruickshank **phoenix** BA **phonograph** From the collections of Henry Ford Museum & Greenfield Village, neg. no. B67930 **photoelectric cell** TG **phrenology** BA **phylactery** LOC **Edith Piaf** BA **piano** [1] Steinway & Sons, New York **Pablo Picasso** BA **pickax** GEP **picket fence** PI - Jerry Howard **Mary Pickford** GP **pickup truck** BA **pier** GHP - Runk & Schoenberger/PI - Jerry Howard **Franklin Pierce** LOC **pietà** LOC **pigmy hippopotamus** PR - Arthur W. Ambler **pike** [2] PR - Tom McHugh **pilaster** PC - Jeffrey Dunn **pileated woodpecker** AA - Irene Vandermolen **pilgrim** LOC **pillory** EPJCo. **pilothouse** PI - Jerry Howard **piñata** PI - Jerry Howard **pince-nez** BA **pine** [1] CC **pineapple** LC **pinking shears** PI - Patricia J. Bruno **pinnace** Peabody Museum of Salem, Massachusetts - Mark Sexton **pinnacle** Comstock - Stuart Cohen **pintail** AA - Leonard Lee Rue III **pinto** Comstock - Russ Kinne **piolet** PR - Rapho Agence **pipeline** GHP **pipkin** Museum of the City of New York, Gift of Mrs. Thomas K. Gale - John Parnell **piranha** PR - John H. Gerard **Pisces** TG **Piscis Austrinus** TG **pistachio** LC **pistil** LC **piston** LC **pitcher** [2] Museum of the City of New York, Bequest of Emily Frances Whitney Biggs **pitcher plant** CC **pith helmet** PI - Martin Miller **pitsaw** Shelburne Museum, Shelburne, Vermont **pit stop** PC - Martha Stewart **Francisco Pizarro** The Granger Collection, New York **placard** PR - Barbara Rios **place kick** PI - Jerry Howard **plaid** LW - © 1990 S.E. Byrne **plait** LW - © 1991 S.E. Byrne **plan** *Encyclopedia of Source Illustrations, vol II* **plane** [2] PC - Frank Siteman **planetary nebula** Lick Observatory Photograph **plastron** Comstock - M. Stuckey **platform** PR - Margot Granitsas **Sylvia Plath** Sophia Smith Collection, Smith College **Plato** BA **platypus** CDB **player piano** Marilyn Root **Pleiades** Lick Observatory Photograph **plexor** PI - Jerry Howard **pliers** CC **plinth** PC - Jeffrey Dunn **plover** AA - M. Krishnan **plow** GHP/USDA - John McConnell **plum** [1] LC **plunger** GEP **plus fours** PR **Pymouth Rock** GHP - John Colwell **Pocahontas** LOC **pocketknife** LW - © 1990 S.E. Byrne **podium** PI - Jerry Howard **pogo stick** Peter Vandermark **pointer** PR - Stan Wayman **pointillism** Giraudon - Art Resource, New York **poison ivy** LC **Sidney Poitier** BA **Poland China** GHP - John Colwell **polar bear** Leonard Rue Enterprises - Leonard Lee Rue III **pole vault** SB - George Bellerose **James K. Polk** LOC **polo** SB - Pamela Schuyler **Polyphemus** Courtesy, Museum of Fine Arts, Boston, Gift in honor of Edward W. Forbes from his friends (63.120) **polyphemus moth** CDB **pomegranate** LC **Pomeranian** AA - Paula Wright **Madame de Pompadour** Portland Art Museum, Portland, Oregon **Pony Express** American Antiquarian Society, Worcester, Massachusetts **pop art** The Museum of Modern Art, New York, Philip Johnson Fund. **poppy** CC **porcelain** National Museum of American History, Smithsonian Institution, Washington, D.C., Gift of Dr. and Mrs. Martin Wynyard **porcupine** PR - Des Bartlett **porcupine fish** PR - Omikron **porringer** Museum of the City of New York, Gift of Mrs. L.A. di Zerega - John Parnell **portcullis** CC **portico** PI - Jerry Howard **Portuguese man-of-war** GHP - Runk & Schoenberger **postimpressionism** Baltimore Museum of Art, The

Cone Collection formed by Dr. Claribel Cone and Miss Etta Cone of Baltimore, Maryland **potato** LC **potbelly stove** EPJCo. **potter's wheel** PR - Fritz Henle **powder horn** MMA, Gift of Mrs. J.H. Grenvelle, 1940 (40.105) **power shovel** PI - Jerry Howard **prairie dog** AA - Harry Engels **prayer rug** SLAM, Gift of James F. Ballard **prayer wheel** Collection of The Newark Museum, Purchase 1971, C. Suydam Cutting Endowment Fund - Bob Hanson **praying mantis** CDB **precipice** PI - Karen Bussolini **pre-Columbian** MMA, The Michael C. Rockefeller Memorial Collection, Bequest of Nelson A. Rockefeller, 1979 (1979.206.497) **prefab** PI - Jerry Howard **prehensile** AA - Leonard Lee Rue III **Pre-Raphaelite** The Art Museum, Princeton University, Museum Purchase, Surdna Fund **present arms** Official U.S. Navy Photograph - PHC Kirby Harrison **Elvis Presley** GP - Rangefinders **pretzel** LC **Leontyne Price** BA **pricket** MMA, The Cloisters Collection (55.40.1) **prickly pear** GEP **prie-dieu** Lloyd's Woodworking, Inc. **printed circuit** PR - Robert A. Isaacs **proboscis** AA - Leonard Lee Rue III **profile** NGA **Prohibition** LOC **prominence** PR - Science Source **promontory** GHP - Alan Pitcairn **pronghorn** AA - Tom Edwards **propeller** National Center for Atmospheric Research, National Science Foundation **prophase** CDB **prop root** LC **Proserpina** Alinari - Art Resource, New York **prospector** SB - Peter Southwick **prosthesis** BA **protozoan** GHP - Runk & Schoenberger **protractor** TG **prow** PI - Jerry Howard **Psyche** © The Frick Collection, New York **ptarmigan** AA - Charles G. Summers, Jr. **pterodactyl** TG **pterygoid** LC **Ptolemaic system** HPS **pueblo** SB - Peter Menzel **puffball** CDB **puffin** AA - Leonard Lee Rue III **pug**[1] PR - Mary Eleanor Browning **Joseph Pulitzer** Brown Brothers **pulpit** Jeroboam, Inc. - Frank Siteman **pump**[1] GEP **pumpkinseed** PR - Treat Davidson **punt**[1] Mystic Seaport Museum, Inc. All rights reserved. **punty** PR - Paolo Koch **pupa** CC **pupil**[2] TG **puppet** PC - Eric Roth **Puppis** TG **Purple Heart** Official U.S. Navy Photograph **pushup** PC - Spencer Grant **pussy willow** LC **putting green** PI - Martin Miller **Pygmy** AA - Miriam Austerman **pylon** CC **pyramid** SB - Peter Menzel **pyrrhuloxia** PR - Robert H. Wright **python** PR - Dade W. Thornton **pyx** MMA, The Cloisters Collection (54.117.3a,b)

quadriga Wadsworth Atheneum, Hartford, Connecticut, Bequest of Mrs. Gurdon Trumbull **quagga** TG **quail**[1] TSW - Len Rue, Jr. **quarrel**[2] GEP **quarry**[2] GHP - Isaac Geib **quarter horse** AA - George F. Godfrey **quatrefoil** PC - William A. Todd, Jr. **queen** GEP **Queen Anne** Museum of Fine Arts, Houston, The Bayou Bend Collection, Gift of Miss Ima Hogg **Queen Anne's lace** LC **quetzal** PR - Robert Hermes **quilt** © 1991 Judith Winters **quilting** Eric Kroll **quince** LC **Josiah Quincy** National Portrait Gallery, Smithsonian Institution, Washington, D.C., Gift of Mr. and Mrs. Paul Mellon **quipu** American Museum of Natural History, Courtesy Department of Library Services, neg. no. 321934 - Rota **quiver**[2] NMAI **quoin** CC

Ra[1] Leo de Wys, Inc. - Gunter Reitz **rabbit** GHP **François Rabelais** BA **raccoon** American Museum of Natural History, Courtesy Department Library Services, neg. no. 336665 - Jim Coxe **Sergei Rachmaninoff** BA **racket**[1] LC **radial symmetry** GHP - Runk & Schoenberger **radiograph** GHP - Runk & Schoenberger **radiometer** Peter Vandermark **radio telescope** National Radio Astronomy Observatory, operated by Associated University, Inc., under cooperative agreement with the National Science Foundation **radish** LC **radius** LC **radula** PR - David M. Phillips **rafflesia** CDB **raft**[1] LW - Jim Cronk **rainbow trout** GHP **rake**[1] CC **Sir Walter Raleigh** BA **Rameses II** The Granger Collection, New York **ramp**[1] SB - George W. Gardner **rampant** BA **ramrod** GEP **ranch house** Marilyn Root **Jeannette Rankin** Sophia Smith Collection, Smith College **rappel** EPJCo. **rasp** CC **Rasputin** BA **ratchet** LC **ratel** PR - Mark Boulton **rattlesnake** GHP - Hal Harrison **ray**[2] © 1991 by Sea World, Inc. **Nancy Reagan** GP - Lord Snowdon **Ronald Reagan** SB - Peter Southwick **reamer** CC/© 1991 Judith Winters **reap** PR - Arthur Tress **receptacle** LC **recliner** PI - Martin Miller **recorder** SB - Jean-Claude Lejeune **recycle** PI - Jerry Howard **Red Cloud** Smithsonian Institution National Anthropological Archives, Bureau of American Ethnology Collection **Red Cross** LW - © 1990 Feza D. Oktay **red fox** PR - Leonard Lee Rue III **redingote** New York Public Library, Special Collections **redshouldered hawk** PR - Austing & Koehler **red squirrel** PR - Leonard Lee Rue III **red-tailed hawk** National Agricultural Library, Forest Service Photo Collection **reed** EPJCo. **reel**[1] PR - Jan Halaska **referee** PC - Henry Horenstein **refracting telescope** LC **register** EPJCo./EPJCo. **reindeer** NY Zoological Society **relay race** PR - Kenneth Murray **relief** Courtesy of The Oriental Institute of The University of Chicago/Virginia Museum of Fine Arts, Richmond, Purchase, The Williams Fund, 1960/MMA, Fletcher Fund, 1936 (36.11.1) **reliquary** SLAM, Museum Purchase **Rembrandt** BA **Frederic Remington** Courtesy of the R.W. Norton Art Gallery, Shreveport, Louisiana **remora** BA **reniform** CC **repoussé** The Nelson-Atkins Museum of Art, Kansas City, Missouri, Nelson Fund **réseau** Denver Art Museum - Otto Nelson **respirator** Phototake - Yoav Levy **respiratory system** LC **rest**[3] TG **retaining wall** PI - Jerry Howard **reticulum** CDB **retinoscope** LW - Oscar Palmquist **retort**[2] LC **retriever** PC - Frank Siteman **revetment** GHP - Alan Pitcairn **revolver** LW - © 1990 Oscar Palmquist **revolving door** PC - Sarah Putnam **rhea** PR - Leonard Lee Rue III **rhesus monkey** AA - M. Krishnan **rhinoceros** PC - Lynn McLaren **Rhodesian ridgeback** ES **rhododendron** LC **rhombus** LC **rhubarb** CC **rib** LC **ribbing** CC **ribbon snake** PI - Jerry Howard **Richard the Lion-Hearted** PR - Fritz Henle **Richard III** National Portrait Gallery, London **Duc de Richelieu** BA **Sally Ride** BA **riding habit** Marilyn Root **rifle**[1] LW - © 1990 Oscar Palmquist **rig** PC - D.D. Morrison **rigging** GP - Camera Press **right angle** LC **ring-billed gull** PR - A.A. Francesconi **Charles Ringling** HPS **ring-necked pheasant** Comstock - Phyllis Greenberg **rink** EPJCo. **ripple**[2] KAMD **RNA** LC **roadblock** PI - Jerry Howard **roadrunner** PR - Allan D. Cruickshank **robe** NMAI **Paul Robeson** HPS **Robespierre** Giraudon - Art Resource, New York **robin** Peter Arnold, Inc. - Stephen J. Krasemann **Jackie Robinson** BA **Sugar Ray Robinson** BA **robot** SB - Phyllis Graber Jensen **rocking chair** LW - © 1990 Oscar Palmquist **rocking horse** BA **Norman Rockwell** SB - James R. Holland **rococo** MMA, Rogers Fund, 1927 (27.184.2-3) **rodeo** GHP **Auguste Rodin** Sophia Smith Collection, Smith College **Ginger Rogers** WCFTR **rolamite** TG **roller coaster** PC - Stanley Rowin **roller skate** LW - © 1990 Oscar Palmquist **rolling mill** TG **rolling pin** SB - Joseph Schuyler **Romanesque** Comstock - Stuart Cohen **romanticism** Giraudon - Art Resource, New York **rook**[2] LC **Edith Roosevelt** BA **Eleanor Roosevelt** National Portrait Gallery, Smithsonian Institution, Washington, D.C., Bequest of Phyllis Fenner **Franklin D. Roosevelt** HPS **Theodore Roosevelt** HPS **rooster** GHP - John Colwell **rorqual** CDB **rosary** PC - William A. Todd, Jr. **rose**[1] Massachusetts Historical Society **rosemary** CDB **Rosetta stone** BA **rose window** BA **rottweiler** ES **rotunda** BA **roulette** Ewing Galloway **rowel** CC **row house** Ewing Galloway **rudder** TG **ruddy duck** PR - Len Rue, Jr. **ruffed lemur** PR - Tom McHugh **Rugby**[2] SB - Michael Grecco **Rugby shirt** LW - Oscar Palmquist **rumen** CDB **runcible spoon** CC **runner** PC - Jaye R. Phillips **running board** BA **runway** SB - Arthur Grace **Mount Rushmore** GHP **rusine antler** PR - Irene Vandermolen **Lillian Russell** International Museum of Photography at George Eastman House, neg. no. 41919 **rutabaga** GEP **Babe Ruth** BA

saber-toothed tiger TG **Sabine's gull** PR - Eric Hosking **sabot** BA **Sacajawea** North Dakota Tourism Promotion, Bismarck, North Dakota **sacred ibis** PR - Clem Haagner **sacrum** LC **Anwar el-Sadat** BA **safe-deposit box** Ewing Galloway **safety net** PR - Tom Hollyman **Sagittarius** TG **saguaro** AA - Leonard Lee Rue III **saiga** PR - Tom McHugh **Saint Andrew's cross** GEP **Saint Bernard** ES **Andrei Sakharov** BA **salamander** GHP - Hal Harrison **Antonio de Oliveira Salazar** WWP **J.D. Salinger** WWP **sallet** SLAM, Museum Purchase **Salome** Marburg - Art Resource, New York **saltbox** LC **saltcellar** © The Frick Collection, New York **saltire** GEP **saluki** PR - Jeanne White **salver** Yale University Art Gallery, The Mabel Brady Garvan Collection **samara** CDB **Sam Browne belt** Comstock - Russ Kinne **samisen** BA **samovar** BA **Samoyed** AA - Paula Wright **sampan** SB - Ira Kirschenbaum **George Sand** LOC **Carl Sandburg** GP - Nat Dallinger **sandcastle** PC - Emilio A. Mercado **sand dollar** GHP - Runk & Schoenberger **sand painting** NMAI **sandwich board** PC - Gary Goodman **Margaret Sanger** BA **sansevieria** LC **Antonio López de Santa Anna** Courtesy of The New-York Historical Society, New York City **Santa Claus** Courtesy of The New-York Historical Society, New York City **sapsucker** PR - G. Ronald Austing **sarcophagus** Museum of Art, Rhode Island School of Design, Museum Appropriation **sari** HAR **sarong** TSW - Donald Smetzer **Jean Paul Sartre** PR - D. Berretty-Rapho **satellite** NASA **Saturn** NASA - Jet Propulsion Laboratory Photo **Satyr** BA **sauceboat** Yale University Art Gallery, The Mabel Brady Garvan Collection **Abdul Aziz ibn Saud** BA **sauropod** TG **sausage tree** CC **Savonarola** SEF - Art Resource, New York **saw**[1] GEP **sawfish** PR - Karl H. Maslowski **sawfly** CDB **sawhorse** CC **saxophone** PC - J.D. Sloan **scabbard** LW - © Oscar Palmquist **scaffold** GHP **scale**[3] Palmer/Brilliant, Boston, Massachusetts **scallop** PR - Jack Dermid/National Museum of American History, Smithsonian Institution, Washington, D.C. **scalpel** EPJCo. **scapula** LC **scarab** MMA, Rogers Fund, 1935 (35.2.1)/MMA, Rogers Fund, 1935 (35.2.1) **scarecrow** EPJCo. **scarf**[2] GEP **scarlet tanager** PR - Karl H. & Stephen Maslowski **scepter** Chicago Historical Society **schipperke** ES **Helmut Schmidt** WWP **schnauzer** PR - Mary Eleanor Browning **schooner** SB - Fredrik D. Bodin **Franz Schubert** PR **Charles Schulz** GP - Jane Bown **scimitar** National Museum of American History, Smithsonian Institution, Washington, D.C. **scissors** LC **scolex** CDB **scoliosis** Peter Arnold, Inc. - Dr. Freiburger **sconce**[2] SLAM, Museum Purchase **scoreboard** PC - Henry Horenstein **scorpion** CDB **Scorpius** TG **scotch**[2] LW - Oscar Palmquist **Dred Scott** Missouri Historical Society, neg. no. 001-007694 **screech owl** AA - Tom Edwards **screen** Giraudon - Art Resource, New York **screw** CC **scrimshaw** Mystic Seaport Museum, Inc. All rights reserved. **script** The Art Museum, Princeton University, Gift of John B. Elliott **scriptorium** BA **scroll** SB - Virginia Blaisdell **scuba diver** HAR **scuffle**[2] CC **sculptor** SB - Bohdan Hrynewych **scuttle**[2] Allen Moore **scythe** GHP **sea fan** HAR **sea horse** CDB **seal**[1] MMA, Bequest of A.T. Clearwater, 1933 (33.120.375)/PI - Karen Bussolini **Sealyham terrier** American Sealyham Terrier Club **Elizabeth Seaman** Courtesy of The New-York Historical Society, New York City **seaplane** HAR **sea turtle** © 1991 Sea World, Inc. **sea wall** PC - David Witbeck **secant** TG **secretary** The Connecticut Historical Society, Hartford, Connecticut **secretary bird** PR - Jen & Des Bartlett **Seder** Palmer/Brilliant, Boston, Massachusetts **Andrés Segovia** GP - Richard Open **seismograph** Comstock - Russ Kinne **self-heal** *Field Guide to the Wildflowers* by Roger Tory Peterson and Margaret McKenny. © 1968 by Roger Tory Peterson and Margaret McKenny. Reprinted by permission of Houghton Mifflin Company. All rights reserved. **self-portrait** WWP **David O. Selznick** WWP **semidome** LC **sennit** KAMD **sentry box** HAR **sepal** LC **Sequoya** LOC **serape** PR - Carl Frank **seriema** PR - Arthur W. Ambler **serif** CC **serpent** Cincinnati Art Museum, Gift of William H. Doane (1914.228)/Walters Art Gallery, Baltimore, Maryland **serval** PR - Mark Boulton **serve** PI - Martin Miller **service** PI - Jerry Howard **sesame** CDB/LW - © 1990 S.E. Byrne **sessile** CC **Elizabeth Seton** Mount St. Vincent-on-Hudson, Sisters of Charity Center, Bronx, New York **settee** The Baltimore Museum of Art, Gift of Lydia Howard de Roth and Nancy H. De Ford Venable, in memory of their mother, Lydia Howard De Ford; and Purchase Fund **settle** The Connecticut Historical Society, Hartford, Connecticut **Sèvres** Henry E. Huntington Library and Art Gallery **sexpartite** CDB **sextant** LC **Anne Sexton** WWP **Jane Seymour** The Granger Collection, New York **shackle** GEP **shadoof** KAMD **shadowgraph** PI - Martin Miller **shagbark** GHP **shaggymane** CDB **William Shakespeare** The Folger Shakespeare Library, Washington, D.C. **shallop** Peabody Museum of Salem, Massachusetts - Mark Sexton **shallot** CC **Harlow Shapley** WWP **sharpie** Mystic Seaport Museum, Inc. All rights reserved. **sharp-shinned hawk** PR - G. Ronald Austing **sharp-tailed grouse** PR - Harry Engels **George Bernard Shaw** WCFTR **shay** From the collections of Henry Ford Museum & Greenfield Village, neg. no. A2811 **shear** LC **sheath** NMAI **shed**[2] PI - Karen Bussolini **sheepshank** TG **sheet bend** TG **sheldrake** PR - Arthur W. Ambler **Mary Wollstonecraft Shelley** National Portrait Gallery, London **Percy Bysshe Shelley** National Portrait Gallery, London **Alan Shepard** BA **Sheraton** From the collections of Henry Ford Museum & Greenfield Village, neg. no. B36333 **William Tecumseh Sherman** LOC **Shetland pony** EPJCo. **Shetland sheepdog** ES **shield** The Granger Collection, New York **shillelagh** American Museum of Natural History, Courtesy Department Library Services, neg. no. 410658 **shinleaf** CDB **Shiva** The Nelson-Atkins Museum of Art, Kansas City, Missouri, Nelson Fund **shock absorber** TG **shoemaker** EPJCo. **shoofly** PI - Martin Miller **shoot-the-chute** SB - Mike Mazzaschi **shore crab** *Field Guide to Southeastern and Caribbean Seashores* by Eugene H. Kaplan. © 1988 by Eugene H. Kaplan. Reprinted by permission of Houghton Mifflin Company. All rights reserved. **short-tailed shrew** NY Zoological Society **shoulder holster** Comstock - Russ Kinne **shovel** CC **shrike** PR - G. Ronald Austing **shrimp** GHP - Runk & Schoenberger **shrine** SB - Judy Canty **Shropshire**[2] Marilyn Root **shuffleboard** Jeroboam, Inc. - Laimute Druskis **shutter** LW - © 1990 S.E. Byrne **shuttlecock** CC **Siamese cat** PR - Ylla **sickle** CC **sickle cell** LC **sideboard** Courtesy of the Rhode Island Historical Society **sidecar** Allen Moore **side chair** Johns Hopkins University, The Halstead Collection (L.23.013.023) **sieve** PC - Frank Siteman **signet ring** Deborah Buckley **signpost** Comstock - Georg Gerster **sika** PR - Leonard Lee Rue IV **silhouette** From *Silhouettes: A Pictorial Archive of Varied Illustrations.* Dover Publications, Inc. **silk-cotton tree** LC **silk-screen** SB - Gregg Mancuso **Beverly Sills** GP - Reg Wilson **silo** SB - Daniel Brody **silverfish** CC **Neil Simon** WWP **O.J. Simpson** WWP **Sinai Peninsula** NASA **Francis Albert Sinatra** Burson-Marsteller, Los Angeles, California **sine** TG **sine curve** TG **Isaac Bashevis Singer** WWP **sinusoidal projection** © 1986 by the American Congress on Surveying and Mapping **siphon** LC **David Siqueiros** WWP **sisal** Comstock - Georg Gerster **sistrum** MMA, Purchase, 1955, Joseph Pulitzer Bequest (55.137.1) **sitar** PC - Mikki Ansin Ehrenfeld **Sitting Bull** NMAI **skateboard** EPJCo. **skeleton** LC **skewback** CC **ski** SB - Dean Abramson **ski boot** LW - © 1990 S.E. Byrne **skiff** Mystic Seaport Museum, Inc. All rights reserved. **skimmer** AA - Irene Vandermolen **skink** GHP - Hal Harrison **Skinner box** PC - Ken Robert Buck **ski pole** CC **skull** LC **skull and crossbones** Margaret Anne Miles **skunk** AA - Leonard Lee Rue III **skydive** GP - Dan Hightower **skyline** Australian Overseas Information Service, New York **skyscraper** TSW - Michael Bertan **skywalk** PI - Martin Miller **slalom** PC - Phaneuf/Gurdziel **slash** Yale Center for British Art, Paul Mellon Collection **sled** © 1991 W. Hal Stewart **sledge** EPJCo. **sledgehammer** CC **sleeping bag** PR - Ulrike Welsch **sleigh** EPJCo. **slide** PI - Jerry Howard **slingshot** CC **slipknot** TG **sloop** Courtesy of the Commonwealth of Massachusetts, Metropolitan District Commission **sloth** PR - Jen & Des Bartlett **slug**[2] American Museum of Natural History, Courtesy Department Library Services, neg. no. 127917 **sluice** SB - Lionel J-M Delevingne **smack**[3] Mystic Seaport Museum, Inc. All rights reserved. **small intestine** LC **Joseph Smith** The National Portrait Gallery, Smithsonian Institution, Washington, D.C., Gift of the Reorganized Church of Jesus Christ of Latter-Day Saints, Independence, Missouri **Kate Smith** GP - Roy Pinney **Margaret Chase Smith** GP **smock** PC - Bob Kramer **smokestack** EPJCo. **snaffle** GEP **snail** GP **snake** LC **snake charmer** EPJCo. **snapdragon** LC **snifter** Marilyn Root **snorkel** Comstock - Russ Kinne **snowboard** Comstock - David Lokey **snow goose** PR - Allan D. Cruickshank **snowmobile** SB - Owen Franken **snowshoe** The Brooklyn Museum, Nathan Sturges Jarvis Collection **snuffers** Museum of the City of New York, Gift of Miss Mary Thurston Cockcroft (37.217.2) **soccer** GP **socket wrench** PI - Jerry Howard **Socrates** HPS **sofa** SLAM, Museum Purchase, Funds donated by the Friends of the Saint Louis Art Museum, The Sycamore Tree Trust and Decorative Arts Society funds, donated in memory of Mrs. Arthur B. Shepley, Jr. **soft-shelled turtle** PR - Alvin E. Staffan **solar cell** LC **solar house** PR - Robert Perron **solar panel** NASA **solleret** MMA, Rogers Fund, 1904 (04.3.295) **Solomon's seal** LC **sombrero** SB - Jean-Claude Lejeune **Sophocles** Alinari - Art Resource, New York **sorrel**[1] *Field Guide to the Wildflowers* by Roger Tory Peterson and Margaret McKenny. © 1968 by Roger Tory Peterson and Margaret McKenny. Reprinted by permission of Houghton Mifflin Company. All rights reserved. **souk** Leo de Wys, Inc. - Alon Reininger **sousaphone** Brent Jones, Chicago, Illinois **soybean** LC **Wole Soyinka** GP - Horst Tappe **space shuttle** NASA **spadix** CC **Spanish moss** Ewing Galloway **spanker** TG **spark plug** LC **sparrow hawk** GHP - Hal Harrison **spathe** CC **spear**[1] National Museum of American History, Smithsonian Institution, Washington, D.C. **spearmint** *Field Guide to the Wildflowers* by Roger Tory Peterson and Margaret McKenny. © 1968 by Roger Tory Peterson and Margaret McKenny. Reprinted by permission of Houghton Mifflin Company. All rights reserved. **spectacled** San Diego Zoo **spectroscope** TG **speed bump** PI - Jerry Howard **sphinx** MMA, Hewitt Fund, 1911, Rogers Fund, 1921, Munsey Fund, 1936, 1938, and Anonymous gift, 1951 (11.185) **sphygmomanometer** PC - Kindra Clineff **Steven Spielberg** GP - Richard Open **spinal column** LC **spinet** Courtesy Essex Institute, Salem, Massachusetts **spinnaker** PR - Fritz Henle **spinning wheel** PC - Edward Bishop **spiny-headed worm** CDB **spiral** EPJCo. **spirillum** GHP - Runk & Schoenberger **spittlebug** CDB **splice** TG **splint** PR - Peter G. Aitken **split rail** PI - Jerry Howard **Benjamin Spock** SB - Lionel J-M Delevingne **sponge** GHP - Runk & Schoenberger **spool** SB - James Dwyer **spoonbill** GHP **sporran** GP - Bassano **spotlight** PI - Jerry Howard **spotter** PC - Steve Takatsuno **spread eagle** Shelburne Museum, Shelburne, Vermont **spring** TG **springbok** AA - Leonard Lee Rue III **springer spaniel** GHP - John Colwell **sprinkler** PI - Jerry Howard **spruce**[1] USDA **spur** Worcester Art Museum, Worcester, Massachusetts **square knot** TG **squash**[1] LC **squeegee** PI - Jerry Howard **squid** GHP - Runk & Schoenberger **squinch**[1] CDB **squirrel** Allen Moore **stadium** LW - © Oscar Palmquist **Madame de Staël** Giraudon - Art Resource, New York **staff**[1] Arthur M. Sackler Museum, Gift of Frederick M. Watkins **stagecoach** From the collections of Henry Ford Museum & Greenfield Village, neg. no. A2768 **stained glass** PR - Jim Goodwin **stalactite and stalagmite** GHP - Runk & Schoenberger **Joseph Stalin** WWP **stall**[1] PI - Jerry Howard **stamen** LC **standard** Courtesy of The Bostonian Society and Old State House - Richard Merrill **Elizabeth Cady Stanton** Sophia Smith Collection, Smith College **starfish** GHP - Runk & Schoenberger **star-nosed mole** PR - Roy Pinney **Belle Starr** Oklahoma Historical Society **Ringo Starr** EPJCo. **starting block** SB - Barbara Alper **steamboat** LOC **steam engine** TG **steamroller** SB - Owen Franken **steel band** Comstock - Russ Kinne **steelyard** GEP **steeple** GHP - Alan Pitcairn **stein** Peter Vandermark **John Steinbeck** GP **Gloria Steinem** BA **stele** The Brooklyn Museum, Gift of Mr. and Mrs. Carl L. Selden through The Roebling Society (69.34) **stencil** PI - Jerry Howard **stentor** CC **Isaac Stern** WWP **stethoscope** SB - David Powers **stevedore** SB - Michael Dwyer **stickleback** PR - Laurence Perkins **still life** The Brooklyn Museum, Bequest of Mrs. W. Sterling Peters (50.143.1) **stilt** GP **stinkbug** CDB **stirrup** GEP **stocks** The Pierpont Morgan Library, New York (M.763, f.134v detail) **stole**[1] Jeroboam, Inc. - Bob Clay **stomach** LC **stomacher** SLAM, Gift of Edward Mallinckrodt/Walters Art Gallery, Baltimore, Maryland **stoneware** From the collections of Henry Ford Museum & Greenfield Village, neg. no. B16963 **stonework** EPJCo. **stopwatch** Peter Vandermark **stork** SB - Ira Kirschenbaum **storksbill** *Field Guide to Medicinal Plants of Eastern* *and Central North America* by Steven Foster and James A. Duke. Illustrations © 1990 by Jim Rose. Reprinted by permission of Houghton Mifflin Company. All rights reserved. **stovepipe** Culver Pictures Inc. **Harriet Beecher Stowe** Sophia Smith Collection, Smith College **straight razor** Peter Vandermark **strainer** Museum of the Historical Society of Delaware, Bequest of Miss Henrietta Jane Bedford (1827.10) **stratosphere** TG **Johann Strauss the Younger** BA **streetcar** LW - © 1990 S.E. Byrne **strigil** Alinari - Art Resource, New York **stroller** PI - Jerry Howard **strut** Alinari - Art Resource, New York **Gilbert Stuart** BA **J.E.B. Stuart** LOC **sturgeon** PR - Tom McHugh **Peter Stuyvesant** Courtesy of The New-York Historical Society, New York City **William Stryon** WWP **submersible** Woods Hole Oceanographic Institution - Rod Catanach **subway** GP - Camera Press **suffragist** BA **Sugarloaf Mountain** PR - George Holton **sugar maple** CC **Suleiman I** Turkish Culture and Information Office **sulky**[2] EPJCo. **sumac** CDB **sumo** Japan National Tourist Organization **sunburst** SB - Mike Mazzaschi **sundew** LC **sundial** Ewing Galloway **sunflower** PI - Jerry Howard **Sun Yat-sen** BA **surcoat** The Pierpont Morgan Library (M.52, f.558v) **surfboard** SB - T.D. Lovering **surfcasting** EPJCo. **surplice** Comstock - Russ Kinne **Mary Surratt** BA **surrealism** The Museum of Modern Art, New York, Purchase **surrey** National Museum of American History, Smithsonian Institution, Washington, D.C. **surveyor's level** GHP - John Colwell **suspender** PC - Thomas Craig **suspension** TG **suspension bridge** SB - Peter Menzel **Joan Sutherland** GP - Vivienne **swage** Courtesy, Old Salem Restoration, Winston-Salem, North Carolina, neg.no. S-799/Courtesy, Old Salem Restoration, Winston-Salem, North Carolina, neg. no. S-1465 **swallowtail** GHP - Runk & Schoenberger **swan** USDA - Soil Conservation Service **swastika** BA **swift** PR - G. Ronald Austing/Shelburne Museum, Shelburne, Vermont **Jonathan Swift** National Portrait Gallery, London **swimmeret** CDB **swing** © 1991 Judith Winters **sword** BA **sycamore** CC **symbiosis** Leonard Rue Enterprises - Leonard Lee Rue III **synagogue** LW - © 1990 S.E. Byrne **synapse** CC **syncline** GEP **syncopation** TG **John Millington Synge** The Granger Collection, New York **synthesizer** SB - Judy Gelles **syringe** PR - Leonard Lee Rue III **Henrietta Szold** WWP

tabard BA **table tennis** PI - Patricia J. Bruno **taboret** Giraudon - Art Resource, New York **tachina fly** PR - Richard Parker **tackle** LW - Oscar Palmquist **taco** Palmer/Brilliant, Boston, Massachusetts **tadpole** CDB **Helen Taft** GP **William Howard Taft** LOC **Takkakaw** PR - Charlie Ott **talaria** Alinari - Art Resource, New York **talisman** Bowdoin College Museum of Art, Florence C. Quinby in Memory of Henry Cole Quinby **tallith** BA **talon** CC **tamarind** LC **tambourine** PI - Martin Miller **tam-o'-shanter** © 1991 Judith Winters **tangent** TG **tank** EPJCo./Department of Defense **tankard** Museum of Fine Arts, Houston, The Bayou Bend Collection, Gift of Miss Ima Hogg **tapa** Denver Art Museum - Otto Nelson **tapeworm** CDB **tapir** PR - Jen & Des Bartlett **tarantula** AA - Karen Tweedy-Holmes **targe** MMA, Gift of William H. Riggs, 1913 (14.25.742) **target** LW - Oscar Palmquist **tarot** Marilyn Root **tarragon** CC **tarsal** LC **tartan**[1] EPJCo. **tassel** PR - Steve Kagan **tatami** Japan National Tourist Organization **tattoo**[2] GP **tau cross** GEP **Taurus** TG **Zachary Taylor** LOC **Peter Ilich Tchaikovsky** BA **tea caddy** Henry E. Huntington Library and Art Gallery **teasel** CC **teem**[2] EPJCo. **telecamera** Brent Jones, Chicago, Illinois **telephone booth** Image Photos - Clemens Kalischer **telescope** LC **telophase** CDB **template** LW - S.E. Byrne **temple**[1] SB - Ira Kirschenbaum **Ten Commandments** LOC **Tennessee walking horse** *Voice* magazine, Lewisburg, Tennessee **tennis** PC - Jaye R. Phillips **tent**[1] GEP **tepee** American Museum of Natural History, Courtesy Department Library Services, neg. no. 317248 - Rodman Wanamaker **Mother Teresa** GP - Camera Press **Valentina Tereshkova** GP - Camera Press **termitarium** PR - Bill Bachman **terrace** Comstock - Georg Gerster **terrapin** PR - Jack Dermid **tesseract** TG **test tube** PI - Jerry Howard **testudo** TG **tetrahedron** TG **thalamus** LC **Thanksgiving cactus** LC **U Thant** BA **thatch** Image Photos - Clemens Kalischer **Margaret Thatcher** GP - Norman Parkinson **Theodora** Marburg - Art Resource, New York **theorbo** Giraudon - Art Resource, New York **thermograph** PI - Jerry Howard **thermometer** LC **thermosphere** TG **Theseus** MMA, Bequest of John Cadwalader, 1914 (14.58.131) **thimble** LW - Oscar Palmquist **thistle** CC **Thomson's gazelle** SB - Ira Kirschenbaum **Thor** *Encyclopedia of Source Illustrations, vol. II* **thoroughbred** PR - Josephus Daniels **Jim Thorpe** BA **Thoth** Cincinnati Art Museum, John J. Emery Fund **three-decker** SEF - Art Resource, New York **throne** EPJCo. **thunderbird** NMAI **thyme** CC **thyroid gland** CC **thyrsus** CC **Tiananmen Square** PR - M.B. Duda **tiara** Valentine Museum, Richmond, Virginia **tibia** LC **tide**[1] SB - Fredrik D. Bodin/SB - Fredrik D. Bodin **Tiffany glass** William Doyle Galleries, New York **tiger** AA - Irene Vandermolen **tiger beetle** CDB **tightrope** BA **tile** LOC/Cooper-Hewitt National Museum of Design, Smithsonian Institution - Art Resource, New York/Cooper-Hewitt National Museum of Design, Smithsonian Institution - Art Resource, New York **tiller**[2] TG **tinamou** NY Zoological Society **tippet** Courtesy, Museum of Fine Arts, Boston, Gift of Amelia Peabody and William S. Eaton **tit**[1] PR - Stephen Dalton **Titian** Marburg - Art Resource, New York **Tito** BA **toad** GHP - Hal Harrison **toboggan** LC **toby** Shelburne Museum, Shelburne, Vermont **toggle bolt** CC **tokamak** TG **tokonoma** Japan National Tourist Organization **tollbooth**[1] PI - Jerry Howard **Leo Tolstoy** BA **tomahawk** NMAI **tom-tom** EPJCo. **Susumu Tonegawa** BA **tongs** Henry E. Huntington Library and Art Gallery **tooth** LC **top hat** SB - Owen Franken **topiary** BA **Torah** Jewish Museum - Art Resource, New York **torchère** Collection of Cranbrook Academy of Art Museum (1972.23) **torii** Leo de Wys, Inc. - Leo de Wys **tornado** PR - Max & Kit Hunn **torque**[2] Walters Art Gallery, Baltimore, Maryland **tortoise** TSW - Irene Vandermolen **Arturo Toscanini** BA **totem pole** AA - Leonard Lee Rue III **totipalmate** CDB **toucan** PR - Arthur W. Ambler **François Dominique Toussaint L'Ouverture** HPS **tower** PR - Jane Latta **towhee** PR - Karl H. Maslowski **tracery** Marburg - Art Resource, New York **tracheid** CDB **track and field** PC - Mac Donald/BA **tractor** SB - Cary Wolinsky **tractor-trailer** LW - Oscar Palmquist **Spencer Tracy** BA **tragopan** PR - Arthur W. Ambler **transept** LC **transformer** TG **transit** SB - Spencer Grant **transom** © 1981 Walter Silver, Boston, Massachusetts **trap**[1] GEP **trapeze artist** EPJCo. **trapezoid** LC **travois** LOC **trawler** Mystic Seaport Museum, Inc. All rights reserved. **treadmill** SB - Ellis Herwig **treble clef** TG **tree frog** GHP - Hal Harrison **trefoil** Photograph © 1991, The Art Institute of Chicago. All rights reserved. Gift of the Antiquarian Society (1948.107) - Terry Schank **trellis** LW - Oscar Palmquist **trephine** LC **triangle** LC/Comstock - Russ Kinne **triceps** LC **triceratops** LC **tricorn** SB - Charles Gatewood **trident** Alinari - Art Resource, New York **trifoliate** CC **triforium** CC **trilithon** SB - Spencer Grant **trilobite** CC **Trimurti** *Encyclopedia of Source Illustrations, vol. II* **Trinity** The Pierpont Morgan Library, New York **triplane** BA **tripod** SLAM, Gift of J. Lionberger Davis **triptych** MMA, Gift of J. Pierpont Morgan, 1917 (17.190.211) **triskelion** Alinari - Art Resource, New York **Triton** Courtesy, Museum of Fine Arts, Boston, Edwin E. Jack Fund **Trojan horse** BA **trombone** PI - Jerry Howard **trophy** SB - Phyllis Graber Jensen **tropic** LC **troposphere** TG **Leon Trotsky** BA **trough** SB - Elizabeth Hamlin **trowel** CC **Pierre Trudeau** GP - Hy Simon **Bess Truman** Courtesy the Harry S. Truman Library - Hessler Studio of Washington, D.C. **Harry S. Truman** Courtesy the Harry S. Truman Library - U.S. Army Photo **trumpet** PC - Dan Walsh **trundle bed** BA **truss bridge** LW - © 1990 Aldo Mastrocola **Sojourner Truth** National Portrait Gallery, Smithsonian Institution, Washington, D.C. **try square** LW - Aldo Mastrocola **tsetse fly** CDB **T-square** GEP **tuba** Jeroboam, Inc. - Frank Siteman **tube pan** LW - © 1990 Aldo Mastrocola **tuberose**[1] CC **Harriet Tubman** LOC **tugboat** BA **tulip** LC **tulip tree** CC **tumbler** Yale University Art Gallery, The Mabel Brady Garvan Collection, Gift of Francis P. Garvan **tuning fork** LW - Oscar Palmquist **turban** SB - Rick Smolan **tureen** Courtesy, Museum of Fine Arts, Boston, Bequest of Forsyth Wickes, Forsyth Wickes Collection **turnbuckle** CC **turnip** LC **turtle**[1] GHP - Hal Harrison **tusk** AA - Leonard Lee Rue III **Tutankhamen** MMA - Harry Burton **tutu** SB - Jean-Claude Lejeune **Desmond Tutu** GP - Godfrey Argent **tweezers** GEP **twinflower** LC **twinleaf** LC **John Tyler** In the Collection of The Corcoran Gallery of Art, Museum Purchase **tympanum** Comstock - Stuart Cohen **type** TG **Tyr** *Encyclopedia of Source Illustrations, vol. II* **tyrannosaur** LC **Tzu Hsi** BA

U-bolt LC **Galina Ulanova** BA **ulna** LC **ultrasonograph** National Institutes of Health, Bethesda, Maryland **umbrella** PI - Martin Miller **umbrella bird** NY Zoological Society **Uncle Sam** LOC **underhand** PI - Jerry Howard **unicorn** Courtesy, Winterthur Museum **unicorn plant** CC **unicycle** Aristide Abrahams, Redford, Michigan **Union Jack** EPJCo. **unitard** © 1991 Judith Winters **universal joint** LC **John Updike** BA **upland sandpiper** PR - Hugh M. Halliday **upright piano** PI - Martin Miller **uraeus** Wolfgang Kaehler Photography **Urania** Alinari - Art Resource, New York **Urban II** The Granger Collection, New York **urn** SLAM, Museum Purchase **Ursa Major** TG **Ursa Minor** TG **utensil** GEP **Maurice Utrillo** The Granger Collection, New York

valance © 1991 Judith Winters **Rudolf Valentino** WCFTR **Valhalla** Icelandic Manuscript Institute, Reykjavick, Iceland **Valkyrie** *Encyclopedia of Source Illustrations, vol. II* **valve** LC **vambrace** MMA, John Stoneacre Ellis and Augustus van Horne Ellis, 1896 (96.5.85) **vampire bat** CDB **Martin Van Buren** LOC **Van de Graaff generator** TG **Sir Anthony Vandyke** BA **vane** CDB **Vincent van Gogh** NGA **vanilla** CC **vanishing point** GHP **vase** SLAM, Bequest of Samuel C. Davis **vat** SB - Mike Mazzaschi **Sarah Vaughan** Archive Photos **vault**[1] CC **VDT** SB - Tim Barnwell **vector product** TG **veil** SB - Peter Menzel **velocipede** Smithsonian Institution, Washington, D.C., Cycle Collection **vender** SB - David Carmack **Venus** Alinari - Art Resource, New York **Venus's flower basket** CDB **Venus's-flytrap** LC **Giuseppe Verdi** Art Resource, New York **verdin** PR - Allan D. Cruickshank **vermiform appendix** LC **vernier caliper** GHP - Runk & Schoenberger **veronica**[2] NGA, Samuel H. Kress Collection **Giovanni da Verrazano** LOC **vervet** PR - Leonard Lee Rue III **vesper sparrow** PR - Allan D. Cruickshank **Amerigo Vespucci** SCALA - Art Resource, New York **vest** LW - © 1990 S.E. Byrne **vetch** *Field Guide to the Wildflowers* by Roger Tory Peterson and Margaret McKenny. © 1968 by Roger Tory Peterson and Margaret McKenny. Reprinted by permission of Houghton Mifflin Company. All rights reserved. **viaduct** LOC **victoria** Shelburne Museum, Shelburne, Vermont - Ken Burris **Victoria**[1] BA **Victoria Falls** PR - Frederick Ayer III **vicuña** San Diego Zoo **video game** PI - Jerry Howard **Élisabeth Vigée-Lebrun** Kimbell Art Museum, Fort Worth, Texas **Pancho Villa** Brown Brothers **vina** MMA, Gift of Alice E. Getty, 1946 **vinegarroon** CDB **viola da gamba** Courtesy, Museum of Fine Arts, Boston, William Lindsey Fund **violet** *Field Guide to the Wildflowers* by Roger Tory Peterson and Margaret McKenny. © 1968 by Roger Tory Peterson and Margaret McKenny. Reprinted by permission of Houghton Mifflin Company. All rights reserved. **violin** SB - Gale Zucker **viper** NY Zoological Society **vireo** PR - Steve Maslowski **virginal**[2] Cincinnati Art Museum, Gift of William H. Doane **Virgo** TG **vise** PC - Jeffrey Dunn **Vishnu** SLAM, Museum Purchase **Visitation** BA **visor** Comstock - Georg Gerster/LC **vitrine** LW - Oscar Palmquist **Volans** TG **volcano** LC **volleyball** PC - Ellis Herwig **voltaic pile** KAMD **Voltaire** NGA, Widener Collection **volva** CDB **voting machine** BA **votive** Courtesy, Museum of Fine Arts, Boston, H.L. Pierce Fund (04.6) **V sign** GP **Vulcan** *Encyclopedia of Source Illustrations, vol. II* **vulture** AA - Leonard Lee Rue III

waders Ewing Galloway **Richard Wagner** HPS **waistcoat** Photograph © 1991, The Art Institute of Chicago. All rights reserved. Gift of Mrs. Guy Antrobus through the Antiquarian Society of The Art Institute of Chicago (1924.1223). **wake**[2] Official U.S. Navy Photograph - PH2 Robert D. Bunge **Alice Walker** WWP **walkie-talkie** SB - Rhoda Sidney **walking stick** PI - Jerry Howard **wallaby** NY Zoological Society **walnut** CC **wampum** NMAI **wapiti** USDA - Chester F. Fry **warbler** Cornell Laboratory of Ornithology - Wilson Bloomer **war bonnet** American Museum of Natural History, Courtesy Department Library Services, neg. no. 324440 **Andy Warhol** GP - Deborah K. O'Brien **warming pan** Courtesy, Winterthur Museum **wart hog** PR - Tomas D.W. Friedman **washboard** Allen Moore **Booker T. Washington** National Portrait Gallery, Smithsonian Institution, Washington, D.C., Transfer from the National Gallery of Art **George Washington** National Portrait Gallery, Smithsonian Institution, Washington, D.C., Gift of Andrew W. Mellon, 1942 **Martha Washington** National Portrait Gallery, Smithsonian Institution, Washington, D.C. **washstand** Courtesy Essex Institute, Salem, Massachusetts **wasp** CDB **wasp waist** LOC **watchtower** SB - Jerry Berndt **water lily** PI - Jerry Howard **water line** Culver Pictures Inc. **water polo** SB - Ellis Herwig **water spaniel** ES **water tower** Ewing Galloway **water wheel** USDA **Watson-Crick model** LW - Oscar Palmquist **wattle** GHP **Evelyn Waugh** GP - Yevonde **John Wayne** BA **weasel** AA - Irene Vandermolen **weathercock** Courtesy Essex Institute, Salem, Massachusetts **weathering** EPJCo. **weathervane** EPJCo. **weave** SB - Charles Kennard/GEP **Daniel Webster** LOC **wedge** LW - © 1990 Aldo Mastrocola **weeping willow** LC **weevil** CDB **Weimaraner** ES **Orson Welles** GP - Camera Press **Duke of Wellington** National Portrait Gallery, London **Welsh corgi** AA - Jayne Langdon **Welsh terrier** EPJCo. **Mae West** BA **Western Wall** PC - Stanley Rowin **West Highland white terrier** ES **wet suit** PC - Herb Snitzer **Phillis Wheatley** National Portrait Gallery, Smithsonian Institution, Washington, D.C. **Wheatstone bridge** TG **wheelbarrow** LW - © 1990 Aldo Mastrocola **wheelchair** PC - Spencer Grant **wheelie** PC - Sarah Putnam **whelk**[1] LC **whippet** ES **whisk** Fowler Museum of Cultural History, University of California, Los Angeles, Gift of the Wellcome Trust **whisker** TSW - Peter Pearson **white admiral** CDB **white clover** GEP **White House** USDA/The White House - Mary Anne Fackelman **white pine** CC **white snakeroot** CC **whitewall tire** GP **Eli Whitney** BA **whooping crane** Peter Arnold, Inc. - Steven C. Kaufman **whorl** CC **wicker** LOC **wicket** PI - Jerry Howard **wickiup** NMAI **widow's walk** Allen Moore **Elie Wiesel** SB - Owen Franken **wigwam** NMAI **Oscar Wilde** BA **wild ginger** CC **wild turkey** PR - Jeanne White **Tennessee Williams** GP **willowware** Spencer Museum of Art, The University of Kansas, William Bridges Thayer Memorial **Edith Wilson** LOC **Ellen Wilson** LOC **Woodrow Wilson** HPS **wimple** Museum of Fine Arts, Houston, Edith A. and Percy S. Straus Collection **winch** PI - Jerry Howard **windbreak** USDA **windmill** BA/USDA **Duchess of Windsor** GP - Cecil Beaton **Windsor chair** Northampton Historical Society **windsurfing** SB - Peter Menzel **wine cooler** EPJCo. **winepress** Palmer/Brilliant, Boston, Massachusetts **wing chair** Art Resource, New York **wire fox terrier** EPJCo. **wishbone** EPJCo. **wisteria** LC **wolf** NY Zoological Society **wolverine** BA **wombat** NY Zoological Society **woodchuck** EPJCo. **Victoria Woodhull** Sophia Smith Collection, Smith College **woodpecker** PR - Leonard Lee Rue III **wood tick** CDB **woofer** GHP - Barry L. Runk **Virginia Woolf** BA **woolly bear** GHP **worktable** Valentine Museum, Richmond, Virginia **worm fence** Ewing Galloway **worm gear** LC **wren** Cornell Laboratory of Ornithology - O.S. Pettingill **Christopher Wren** National Portrait Gallery, London **wrench** LC **wrestling** Lou Jones Studio **Frank Lloyd Wright** BA **Wright Brothers** HPS/HPS **wristwatch** Culver Pictures Inc. **wrought iron** EPJCo. **Wyandotte**[2] USDA **Andrew Wyeth** BA

Xerxes I Courtesy of The Oriental Institute of The University of Chicago **x-ray** BA **xylem** CDB **xylophone** Comstock - Russ Kinne

yam CC **yang** LC **yarmulke** PR - Minoru Aoki **yashmak** Turkish Culture and Information Office **William Butler Yeats** BA **yellow jacket** CDB **yew** LC **yin** LC **yoke** CC **Yorkshire terrier** AA - Paula Wright **Andrew Young** BA **Brigham Young** Brigham Young University Photoarchives **yucca** SB - Eric Neurath **yurt** PR - Paolo Koch

Emiliano Zapata BA **zareba** Comstock - Georg Gerster **zebra** AA - Leonard Lee Rue III **zeppelin** BA **Zeus** Marburg - Art Resource, New York **Zhou Enlai** BA **zinnia** LC **zither** Smithsonian Institution, Washington, D.C., Division of Musical Instruments **zizith** Marilyn Root **zodiac** BA **Émile Zola** BA **zone** LC **zucchini** LC **Ulrich Zwingli** LOC **zygodactyl** CDB

Dnieper-Donet male From *In Search of the Indo-Europeans* by J.P. Mallory. Reprinted by permission of Thames and Hudson, Ltd., London **Dnieper-Donet female** From *In Search of the Indo-Europeans* by J.P. Mallory. Reprinted by permission of Thames and Hudson, Ltd., London **hillfort at Vučedol** From *The Journal of Indo-European Studies*. After Schmidt, 1945. **clay wagon** Magyar Nemzeti Múzeum, Budapest, Hungary **Kernosovka stele** From *In Search of the Indo-Europeans* by J.P. Mallory. Reprinted by permission of Thames and Hudson, Ltd., London

ABCDEFGHIJKL-RMV-998765432

THE INDO-EUROPEAN FAMILY OF LANGUAGES

The Indo-European family of languages, of which English is one member, are all descended from the prehistoric Proto-Indo-European language, which was spoken in an as yet unidentified area between eastern Europe and the Aral Sea around the fifth millennium B.C. This chart displays the genetic relationships among the principal languages of the Indo-European family and loosely suggests their geographic

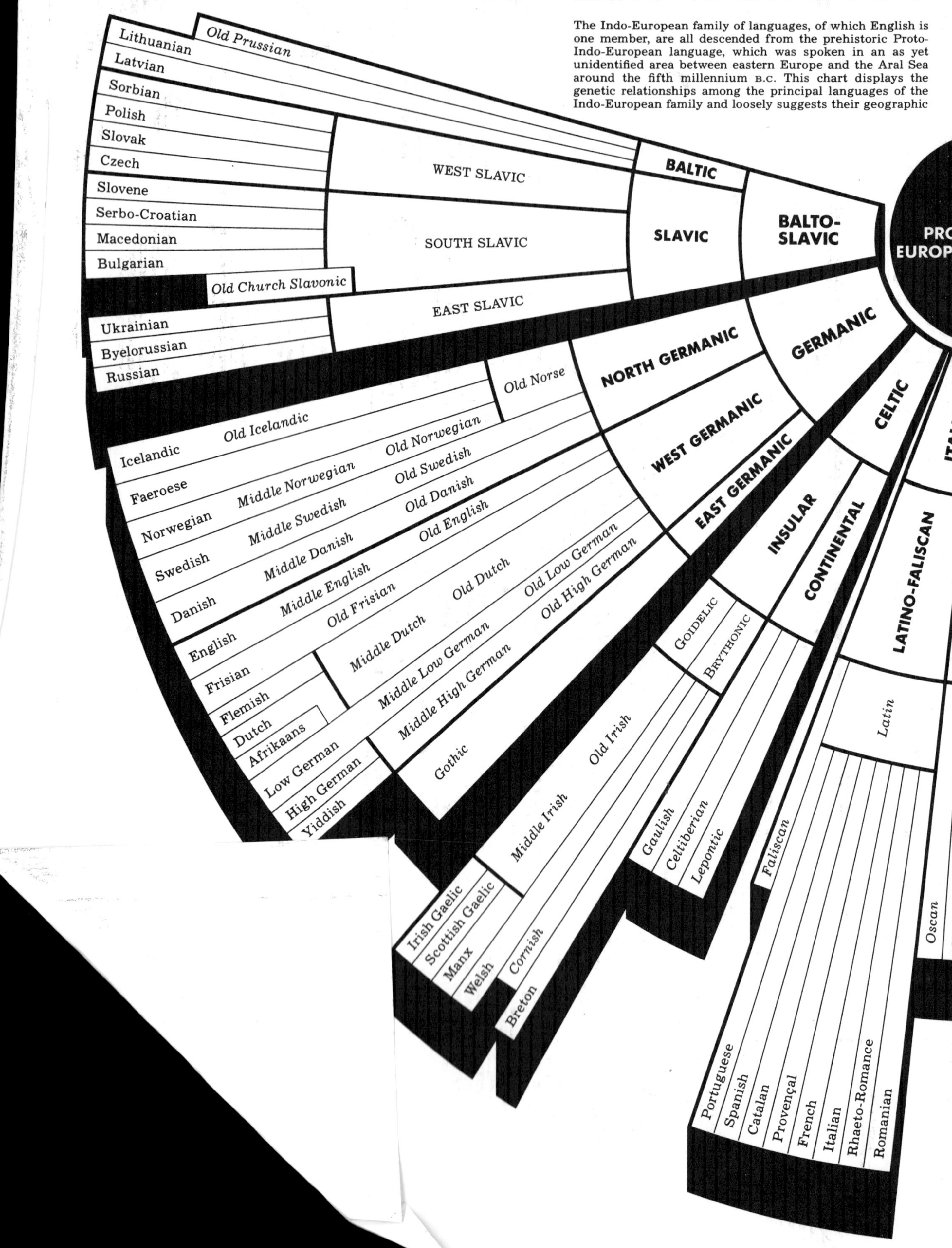